Dictionary of American Regional English

Dictionary of American Regional English

Volume II D-H

Frederic G. Cassidy
Chief Editor

Joan Houston Hall
Associate Editor

The Belknap Press of Harvard University Press
Cambridge, Massachusetts, and London, England
1991

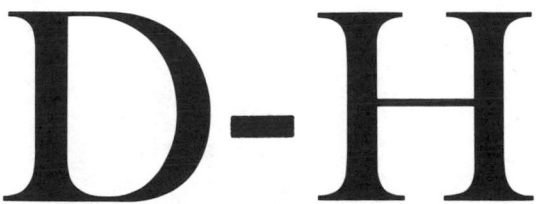

D-H

Printed in the United States of America
10 9 8 7 6 5 4 3 2 1

This book is printed on acid-free paper, and its binding materials have been chosen for strength and durability.

Design by Marianne Perlak

Library of Congress Cataloging in Publication Data
(Revised for vol. 2)

Dictionary of American regional English.

Vol. 2: Joan Houston Hall, associate.
1. English language—Dialects—United States—Dictionaries. 2. English language—United States—Dictionaries. 3. Americanisms—Dictionaries.
I. Cassidy, Frederic Gomes, 1907– II. Hall, Joan Houston.
PE2843.D52 1985 427′.973 84-29025
ISBN 0-674-20511-1 (v. 1 : alk. paper)
ISBN 0-674-20512-X (v. 2)

DARE Staff, Volume II

CHIEF EDITOR
Frederic G. Cassidy

ASSOCIATE EDITOR
Joan Houston Hall

SENIOR EDITOR, PRODUCTION
Luanne von Schneidemesser

SENIOR EDITOR, EDITORIAL COMPUTING
Craig M. Carver

SENIOR SCIENCE EDITOR
Sheila Y. Kolstad

ADJUNCT EDITOR
Audrey R. Duckert

CONSULTING EDITOR
John C. McGalliard

EDITORIAL STAFF
George H. Goebel
Edward C. Hill
Matt Hogan
Jean Howell Patau
Beth Lee Simon
Leonard Zwilling

CONTRIBUTING EDITORS
Martha Bateson (1981–85)
John F. Clark (1978–81)
Jennifer K. Ellsworth (1976–81)
Jeffrey A. Hirshberg (1977–83)
David L. Vander Meulen (1981–83)
Margaret Waterman (1973–80)

BIBLIOGRAPHERS
Goldye Mohr
Leonard Zwilling

COMPUTING STAFF
Jean W. Anderson
Thomas K. Johnson

PRODUCTION STAFF
Catherine R. Attig
Diane L. Balmer
Elizabeth Blake
Elizabeth R. Gardner
Stephen M. Kratky
Joseph D. Marek

OFFICE MANAGERS
Karen J. Krause
Carol H. Wilson

EDITORIAL/RESEARCH ASSISTANTS
Roland L. Berns
Gerald Esch
Nicholas Goetzfridt
Wilson B. Lindauer
John M. Heasley
Mary Zegers

Contents

Preface

Readers of Volume II of *DARE* are reminded that the front matter to Volume I contains explanatory materials essential for making full use of all volumes of the Dictionary. The Introduction explains the background of the project as well as the principles and methods used in writing the entries. "The *DARE* Map and Regional Labels" provides the rationale for the population-adjusted maps used in *DARE,* and defines the terms used in regional labels. "Language Changes Especially Common in American Folk Speech" explains some of the major linguistic processes affecting pronunciation, word formation, and grammatical constructions. The Guide to Pronunciation gives both an overview of the history of American English and a relatively detailed description of regional and social variation in pronunciation. In the Dictionary text, references to "Intro Language Changes" and to "Pronc Intro" refer respectively to the last two essays.

The front matter to Volume I also includes the text of the *DARE* questionnaire and a complete list of informants. In the Dictionary text, the questions asked by the *DARE* fieldworkers are often cited in abbreviated form; the full form of each question may be seen in the introductory matter. Similarly, the *DARE* informants are referred to by state codes and informant numbers in the text; but in the List of Informants the specifics of age, sex, race, level of education, community type, and community name are given in full.

It should be noted that the complete *DARE* survey involved 1,002 questionnaires, each administered in a single community, each community being represented on the *DARE* map by a single dot. In many communities, however, more than one informant was used to complete a single questionnaire. This was done because many people could not give the amount of time necessary to answer the complete set of questions. In Alabama, for instance, informants AL 1-5 are all listed as being from Jasper. This does not mean that there were five questionnaires from Jasper, but that five individuals contributed to one questionnaire, each answering specific sections. In all, 2,777 informants contributed to the 1,002 questionnaires.

Because each response was coded for the informant offering it, any word may be traced back to the individual who used it. (All the questions, and every response to each question, will be presented as the *Data Summary* in the final volume of *DARE.*) Whenever a *DARE* quotation includes the percentage of informants from a specified social group (age, sex, race, education level, community type) who use a given term, that figure is compared to the statistics for the pool of informants who answered that question, not to those for the informant pool as a whole.

In the text of the Dictionary, maps represent communities rather than informants. That is, each spot on the map shows the place in the United States where a particular term was offered. (The final volume of *DARE* will include maps that show distributions by social categories as well.) In most cases, the regional distributions shown on the maps correspond to those suggested by the other quotations in the entry. However, the maps represent only the fieldwork evidence, which was collected between 1965 and 1970; in assigning regional labels, all the quotations are considered, with their additional evidence as to regions of use.

In the illustrative quotations following the definitions in *DARE* entries, boldface dates refer to either the date of composition or the date of publication of a work (see Volume I, xxi). If a short-title is followed by the phrase "as of 1830" (or any other date), it means that the author purports to represent the speech of that date. Because such use is not verifiable, however, the quotation is entered chronologically by date of publication. Some "as of" dates are no doubt accurate in suggesting that the word or phrase being quoted was already in use before the date of publication, but DARE lacks the evidence to vouch for that. An "as of" date does at least alert the reader to the author's suggestion.

Acknowledgments

Major funding for the second volume of *DARE* was provided by the National Endowment for the Humanities, the Andrew W. Mellon Foundation, the National Science Foundation, and an anonymous private donor. Without their generous and continuing support, a work of this scope would have been impossible. Substantial financial assistance has also come from the University of Wisconsin Graduate School, and a large donation of computer equipment was made by IBM Corporation through its Project Trochos. Additional gifts have been received from the New York Times Foundation, the Quaker Oats Foundation, the Alexander Company, and a number of individuals.

By unfortunate oversight, two names were omitted from the acknowledgments in Volume I of people who had helped in the early years of *DARE*. Let us now warmly thank Professor Wolfgang Viereck, of Otto Friedrich Universität in Bamberg, Germany, who wrote in our support at a critical time when *DARE* was threatened with loss of funding, adding his voice to those of other foreign scholars as to the international value of the project. Also to be thanked is Helen Northup, who contributed a great part of the two-way file of common and scientific names of plants and animals.

Volume II has benefited greatly from the data collected by Lee A. Pederson and his staff of the *Linguistic Atlas of the Gulf States (LAGS)* and from Pederson's personal generosity in answering specific questions and sending us both published and prepublication materials. With the exception of those sections of Volume II that were already in an advanced state when Pederson's data became available, *DARE* makes frequent use of *LAGS* materials.

DARE gratefully acknowledges continuing help from staff of the G. & C. Merriam Company, who have been generous in furnishing quotations from the Merriam-Webster files. At the University of Wisconsin-Madison, librarians at the interlibrary loan desk have been particularly resourceful in locating elusive materials. Thanks are also due to Russell Tabbert for his continued generosity in sharing new material from his own dictionary of Alaskan English, in progress. Finally, we express our appreciation to Harvard University Press for taking on a project of this size, and in particular to former Editor in Chief Maud Wilcox for her unwavering encouragement over many years.

List of Abbreviations

Note: Periods are used for abbreviations in short-titles, but are generally omitted elsewhere.

a	ante (before); auxiliary informant
abbr(s)	abbreviated, abbreviation(s)
absol	absolute(ly)
abstr	abstract
acad	academy
acc	accusative
accd	according to
acct	account
ADD	*American Dialect Dictionary*
addit	additional
adj(s)	adjectival, adjective(s)
adv(s)	adverb(s), adverbial
advent	adventure(s)
advt	advertisement(s), advertiser
Afr	African
Afro-Amer	Afro-American
ag	agricultural, agriculture
agric	agriculturalist
AHD	*American Heritage Dictionary*
alt(s)	alternation(s), alternative
alter(s)	alteration(s)
Amer	America(n), Americana
AmFr	American French
AmInd	American Indian (language)
AmSp	*American Speech*
AmSpan	American Spanish (language)
AND	*Australian National Dictionary*
anon	anonymous
AN&Q	*American Notes & Queries*
anthol	anthology
anthro	anthropological, anthropology
antiq	antiquarian, antiquity
aphet	aphetic
apoc	apocopated, apocopation
app	appendix
appar	apparent(ly)
approx	approximate(ly)
Apr	April
arch	archaic
archeol	archeological, archeology
art	article
assim	assimilated, assimilation
assoc	associate, association
asst	assistant
astron	astronomical, astronomy
Atl	Atlantic
attrib	attribution, attributive
Aug	August
Austr	Australia(n)
autobiog	autobiographical, autobiography
aux	auxiliary
BBC	British Broadcasting Corporation
bd	board

betw	between
bib	bibliographical, bibliography
biog	biographical, biography
biol	biological, biology
bot	botanical
Brit	Britain, Britannica, British
bur	bureau
c	central; circa (about); copyright
Can	Canadian
CanEngl	Canadian English (language)
CanFr	Canadian French (language)
cap	capital
capt	captain
CB	citizens band
cent(s)	central; century (-ies)
Cent D	*Century Dictionary*
cf	confer (compare)
ch	chapter; church
chem	chemical, chemistry
Chr	Christian
chron	chronicle(s)
co	company; county
cogn	cognate
col	colonel
coll	collected, collection(s), collective; college
colloq	colloquial
comb(s)	combination(s), combine(s)
comm(s)	commission(ers); committee(s); community (-ies)
comp	compiler, compiled, composition
compar	comparative
concr	concrete(ly)
Cong	Congress
conj	conjunction
conjug	conjugation
cons	consonant
conserv	conservancy, conservation
constr(s)	construct(ed), construction(s); construed
contemp	contemporary
contr	contracted, contraction
contrib	contribution(s)
conv	conversation(al)
coop	cooperative
Corn	Cornish, Cornwall
corr(s)	correct, corrected, correction(s)
correl	correlated, correlation, correlative
corresp	correspondence
cpd	compound, compounded, compounding
crit	critical
cyclop	cyclopedia
d	died
DA	*Dictionary of Americanisms*

DAE	*Dictionary of American English*
Dan	Danish
DARE	*Dictionary of American Regional English*
DAS	*Dictionary of American Slang*
dat	dative
DBE	*Dictionary of Bahamian English*
DCan	*Dictionary of Canadianisms*
Dec	December
def art	definite article
defin	defining, definition, definitive
Delmarva	DE, eMD, eVA
dem	demonstrative
dept	department
deriv	derivation, derived, derivative
derog	derogatory
descr	description, descriptive
dial(s)	dialect(s), dialectal
dicc	diccionario
dict	dictionary
dimin(s)	diminutive(s)
diss	dissertation(s)
dissim	dissimilated, dissimilation
distrib	distribute(d), distribution, distributive
div	division
DJE	*Dictionary of Jamaican English*
DN	*Dialect Notes*
DNE	*Dictionary of Newfoundland English*
doc	document(ary)
DOST	*Dictionary of the Older Scottish Tongue*
Dr	Doctor
DS	Data Summary
DSL	*Dictionary of the Scottish Language*
DSNA	Dictionary Society of North America
Du	Dutch

e	east(ern)
ed	edition, editor, editorial
EDD	*English Dialect Dictionary*
EDG	*English Dialect Grammar*
educ	educated, education(al)
ellip	ellipsis, elliptical(ly)
EModE	Early Modern English
encycl	encyclopedia
engin	engineering
Engl	England, English
entomol	entomologica, entomological, entomology (-ist)
epenth	epenthesis, epenthetic
Episc	Episcopal
equiv	equivalence, equivalent
erron	erroneous(ly)
esp	especially
est	established
et al	et alii (and others)
etc	et cetera (and so forth)
etym(s)	etymological, etymology (-ies)
euphem(s)	euphemism(s), euphemistic(ally)
eve	evening
evid	evident(ly)
ex(x)	example(s)
exag	exaggerated
exc	except
exclam	exclamation, exclamatory
excr	excrescent
exped	expedition(s)
exper	experiment(al)
expl(s)	explain(ed), explanation(s)
explor	exploration(s)
expr(s)	expression(s)
ext	extended, extension
eye-dial	eye-dialect

f, ff	and following
famil	familiar(izing)
Feb	February
fem	feminine
fig	figurative, figure
Fin	Finnish
folk-etym	folk-etymological, folk-etymology
folkl	folklore
foll	follow(s), followed, following
Fr	French
Franco-Amer	Franco-American
FrCan	French Canadian (people)
freq	frequent(ly)
Fri	Friday
Fris	Frisian
ft	foot (measures); fort
funct	function(al)
fut	future
F&W	*Funk and Wagnalls Standard Dictionary*
FW	fieldworker

Gael	Gaelic
gaz	gazette(er)
gen	general(ly); genitive
geneal	genealogical, genealogy
genl	general
geog	geography
geogr	geographer, geographic(al)
geol	geological, geology
Ger	German
Gk	Greek
gloss	glossary
Gmc	Germanic
gov	governor
govt	government
gram	grammar, grammatical
gs	grade school
gt	great

Haw	Hawaiian
hdbk	handbook
Heb	Hebrew
herb	herbaceous
hist	historic, historical(ly), history
horticult	horticultural(ist), horticulture
hon	honorable
hs	high school
Hung	Hungarian
hydrog	hydrographical, hydrography

ibid	ibidem (in the same place)
ie	id est (that is)
illit	illiterate
illustr	illustrate(d), illustration
imit	imitation, imitative
imper	imperative(ly)
imperf	imperfect(ly)
impers	impersonal(ly)
in	inch
inc	incorporated
incl	include(d), including, inclusive
indef	indefinite(ly)
indic	indicative(ly)
inf(s)	informant(s)
infin	infinitive(ly)
infl	influence(d)
info	information
infreq	infrequent(ly)
init	initial(ly)
inst	institute, institution

interp	interpretation, interpreter
interrog	interrogative(ly)
intj	interjection
intr	intransitive(ly)
intro	introduced, introducing, introduction
Ir	Irish
irreg	irregular(ly)
is	island(s)
Ital	Italian
iter	iteration, iterative
Jan	January
jct	junction
joc	jocular(ly)
jrl(s)	journal(s)
l, ll	lake; line(s)
lab	laboratory
LaFr	Louisiana French
LAGS	*Linguistic Atlas of the Gulf States*
LAMSAS	*Linguistic Atlas of the Middle and South Atlantic States*
LANCS	*Linguistic Atlas of the North Central States*
LANE	*Linguistic Atlas of New England*
lang(s)	language(s)
Lat	Latin
LAUM	*Linguistic Atlas of the Upper Midwest*
LGer	Low German
lib	library
ling	linguistic(s)
lit	literature; literary
Luth(s)	Lutheran(s)
m	meter(s); monsieur
mag	magazine
malaprop	malapropism
Mar	March
masc	masculine
math	mathematical, mathematics
ME	Middle English (in etymologies; elsewhere = Maine)
med	medic(in)al, medicine
MED	*Middle English Dictionary*
mem(s)	memorial(s)
metall	metallurgical, metallurgy
metaph	metaphor, metaphorical(ly)
metath	metathesis, metathetic(ally)
Mex	Mexican, Mexico
MexSpan	Mexican Spanish
mfg(r)(s)	manufacture, manufacturer(s), manufacturing
mid	middle
mid-aged	middle-aged (of Infs: 40-59)
midl	midland
midwest	midwestern
misc	miscellaneous, miscellany
mispronc	mispronunciation
Missip	Mississippi
MJLF	*Midwestern Journal of Language and Folklore*
MLG	Middle Low German
MLJ	*Modern Language Journal*
MLN	*Modern Language Notes*
mod	modern
ModE	Modern English
Mon	Monday
monogr	monograph(s)
ms(s)	manuscript(s)
mt(s)	mountain(s)
mth(s)	monthly, month(s)
MW	midwest

n	noun; north(ern)
NADS	*Newsletter of the American Dialect Society*
N Amer	North America(n)
narr(s)	narrative(s)
nat	natural
natl	national
naut	nautical
NB	New Brunswick
nd	no date
ne	northeast
NEast	northeast
neg	negative
NEng	New England
neut	neuter
newsl	newsletter
newsp	newspaper(s)
Nfld	Newfoundland
no	number
nom	nominative
non-std	nonstandard
Norw	Norwegian
Nov	November
np	no page
N&Q	*Notes & Queries*
ns	new series
nth(n)	north(ern)
nw	northwest
NYC	New York City
NYT	*New York Times*
obj	objective
obs	obsolete
occas	occasional(ly)
Oct	October
OE	Old English
OED	*Oxford English Dictionary*
OEDS	*Oxford English Dictionary Supplement* (4 vols)
OF	Old French
old-fash	old-fashioned
ON	Old Norse
orig	origin, original(ly)
ornith	ornithological, ornithologist, ornithology
Oxfd	Oxford
p, pp	post (after); page(s)
PADS	*Publication of the American Dialect Society*
PaGer	Pennsylvania German
pejor	pejorative
perf	perfect
perh	perhaps
pers	person
pert	pertaining
petrol	petroleum
philol	philological, philology
philos	philosopher, philosophical, philosophy
phon	phonetic
phr(r)	phrase(s)
phys	physical
pl	plate; plural
PMLA	*Publications of the Modern Language Association of America*
poet	poetical
Pol	Polish
pop	popular(ly)
Port	Portuguese
poss	possessive; possible
ppl	participial
pple	participle

prec	preceded, preceding
pred	predicate, predication, predicative(ly)
pref	prefix(ation)
prehist	prehistoric, prehistory
prelim	preliminary
prep(s)	preposition(s)
pres	present
pret	preterite
prob	probable, probably
proc	proceedings
progr	progressive
pron	pronoun
pronc	pronounced, pronunciation
pronc-sp	pronunciation-spelling
Prot	Protestant
prov	proverb(ial); provincial
psych	psychological, psychology
pt	part; port
pub	public; publication(s), published, publisher, publishing
punct	punctuation
QR	questionnaire
qrly	quarterly
qu, qq	question(s)
quot(s)	quotation(s)
r	recto; river
rec	record(s)
recoll	recollections
redund	redundant
redup	reduplicated, reduplication, reduplicative
ref(s)	refer, reference(s)
refl	reflexive
reg	register; regular(ly)
rel	related, relation, relative
relig	religion, religious
repet	repetition, repetitive
repr	representative(s); represented, represent(s), representing; reprint(ed)
rept	report(s)
resp(s)	response(s)
rev	review
revol	revolution(ary)
rr	railroad(s)
Russ	Russian
s	south(ern)
Sat	Saturday
Scan	Scandinavian
sci	science(s)
Scotl	Scotland
Scots	Scottish
se	southeast
sec(s)	section(s)
secy	secretary
Sept	September
ser	series
serv	service
sess	session
sg	singular
sig	signature
SND	*Scottish National Dictionary*
soc	society (-ies)
sociol	sociological, sociology
sp(p)	spelling(s); species
Span	Spanish
SpanAm	Spanish American (people)
spec	specific(ally)
sp-pronc	spelling-pronunciation

st	saint; street
sta	station
statist	statistical(ly)
std	standard, standardized
StdE	Standard English
sth(n)	south(ern)
subj	subject
subjunc	subjunctive
subseq	subsequent(ly)
subsp(p)	subspecies
suff	suffix(ation)
sugg	suggest(ed), suggestion
Sun	Sunday
superl	superlative
suppl	supplement(ary)
surv	survey
sw	southwest
Sw	Swedish
syll	syllable
syn	synonym(ous)
tech	technical, technological, technology
terr	territory (-ies)
Thu	Thursday
topog	topographic(al), topography
tr	transitive
trans	transaction(s)
transcr	transcribe, transcription
transf	transfer(red)
transl	translate(d), translation, translator
treas	treasury
Tue	Tuesday
ult	ultimate(ly)
uncert	uncertain
uncom	uncommon
uncult	uncultivated
univ	university
unpub	unpublished
unstr	unstressed
US(A)	United States (of America)
usu	usual(ly)
v	verb; verso
var(r)	variant(s), various, varying; variety
vbl	verbal
vd	various dates
vet	veterinarian, veterinary
viz	videlicet (namely)
vocab(s)	vocabulary (-ies)
vol(s)	volume(s)
w	west(ern); weekly
W2	*Webster's New International Dictionary,* 2nd ed
W3	*Webster's Third New International Dictionary*
wd	word
Wed	Wednesday
WELS	*Wisconsin English Language Survey*
wildfl	wildflower
wks	works
WNID	*Webster's New International Dictionary*
wrn	western
yd	yard
yr(s)	year(s)
zool	zoological, zoology

State Abbreviations

AK	Alaska
AL	Alabama
AR	Arkansas
AZ	Arizona
CA	California
CO	Colorado
CT	Connecticut
DC	Washington, DC
DE	Delaware
FL	Florida
GA	Georgia
HI	Hawaii
IA	Iowa
ID	Idaho
IL	Illinois
IN	Indiana
KS	Kansas
KY	Kentucky
LA	Louisiana
MA	Massachusetts
MD	Maryland
ME	Maine
MI	Michigan
MN	Minnesota
MO	Missouri
MS	Mississippi
MT	Montana
NC	North Carolina
ND	North Dakota
NE	Nebraska
NH	New Hampshire
NJ	New Jersey
NM	New Mexico
NV	Nevada
NY	New York
OH	Ohio
OK	Oklahoma
OR	Oregon
PA	Pennsylvania
RI	Rhode Island
SC	South Carolina
SD	South Dakota
TN	Tennessee
TX	Texas
UT	Utah
VA	Virginia
VT	Vermont
WA	Washington
WI	Wisconsin
WV	West Virginia
WY	Wyoming

Signs and Symbols

~	is used to avoid repetition of a previously spelled-out word or phrase
‡	is used to indicate a word or sense of uncertain genuineness
*	is used to indicate unattested or hypothetical forms
+	is used for "and"
→	is used with dates to indicate first or last attestation
<	is used for "derived from"
>	is used for "from which is derived"
=	is used for "equals"

D

d. n *euphem*
The devil.
1965 *DARE* (Qu. NN24, *Humorous substitutes for stronger exclamations: "Why the son of a ______!"*) Inf **FL**18, S.O.B., he's a d. (devil).

d. adj [Abbr for *damned*] *euphem*
1968 *DARE* (Qu. NN17, *Something that keeps on annoying you . . . "That ______ fly won't go away."*) Inf **KS**16, D.

da n See **dah** n

da aux v See **duh** v

daa'ky See **dakky**

daa'tuh See **daughter**

dab v [*dab* to strike lightly and quickly] **West**
To throw (a looped rope) so that it fastens on to something.
1928 (1964) Santee *Cowboy* 252 **SW,** Joe dabbed his rope on the steer an' turned him end from end. **1956** Moody *Home Ranch* 42 **CO** (as of 1911), I been keepin' an eye on that sorrel gelding yonder, and aim to dab my rope on him if I can. **1976** Maclean *River Runs Through* 128 **wMT** (as of 1919), Even when he was sitting in the ranger station he would whirl little loops and "dab" them over a chair. **1978** Doig *This House* 149 **MT** (as of c1950), McGrath grabbed a lariat from his pickup, heaved onto the herder's surprised nag, and joggled away in pursuit. *Dabbed it on him first throw, too,* he blared to us at the next mealtime.

dab n^1 [**dab** v] **West**
A toss or throw of a looped rope so that it fastens to something.
1928 (1964) Santee *Cowboy* 250 **SW,** I made a lucky dab an' caught him [=a steer] goin' off the hill.

dab n^2 Also *pee-dab* [Cf *OED dab-stone* (at *dab* sb. 11) and **dib** n^1 **1, dob** n^2, **dub** n^2]
A small marble.
1968–70 *DARE* (Qu. EE6b, *Small marbles or marbles in general*) Inf **VA**5, Dabs; **TN**44, Pee-dabs; (Qu. EE6c, *Cheap marbles*) Infs **VA**5, 18, Dabs.

dab-ass n [From the way the bird walks, bobbing its rump]
=spotted sandpiper.
1945 McAtee *Nomina Abitera* 34, Spotted Sandpiper *(Actitis macularia)* . . Dab-ass, Great Smoky Mountains, Tennessee.

dabber See **dauber**

dabble v, hence vbl n *dabbling* Also with *out* [Engl dial]
To wash or rinse quickly.
1938 Stuart *Dark Hills* 330 **neKY,** Get to the dabbling-pan, you boys, and wipe the wrinkles out'n your faces. **1939** in 1944 *ADD* 152 **eWV,** I want to dabble & go to bed. **1950** Stuart *Hie Hunters* 24 **eKY,** I'll be in as soon as I do some dabblin'. **1953** Randolph–Wilson *Down in Holler* 238 **Ozarks,** *Dabblin' pan.* . . A wash basin. **1954** *Harder Coll.* **cwTN,** Dabble ye hands 'fore ye eat. **1970** *Thompson Coll.* **AL** (as of 1920s), I'll be ready to go soon as ever I get these few little pieces dabbled out.

dabbler n Also *mud dabbler* [See quot 1896]
=mummichog.
1896 U.S. Natl. Museum *Bulletin* 47.640, *Fundulus heteroclitus.* . . *Mud Dabbler.* . . [The fish is] everywhere very common in brackish waters, often burying itself in the mud in shallow lagoons. **1908** NJ State Museum *Annual Rept. for 1907* 155, Killifish. . . Called "dabbler" and "bull-head."

dabchick n Also *dobchick, dopchick* [*OED* a1575 for another bird of the same genus] Cf **didapper**
=pied-billed grebe.
1731 (1754) Catesby *Nat. Hist. Carolina* 1.91, *The Pied-Bill Dopchick.* . . These Birds frequent fresh water-Ponds in many of the inhabited parts of *Carolina.* **1839** MA Zool. & Bot. Surv. *Fishes Reptiles* 377, The *Pied-Billed Grebe,* or *Dobchick, Podiceps Carolinensis.* . . dive with great quickness, and use their wings under water. **1917** (1923) *Birds Amer.* 1.7, Pied-Billed Grebe—*Podilymbus podiceps.* . . Other Names.—Hell-diver; . . Dabchick; . . Thick-billed Grebe. **1925** (1928) Forbush *Birds MA* 1.11, *Podilymbus podiceps* . . Pied-billed Grebe. Other names: Dabchick; . . Little Diver. **1936** Roberts *MN Birds* 1.158, Pied-Billed Grebe: *Podilymbus podiceps podiceps* . . Dab-chick. **1957** Pough *Audubon W. Bird Guide* 291, Dabchick. *See* Pied-billed grebe.

dabster n *old-fash*
An expert; a quick, skillful, and enthusiastic worker.
a1824 (1937) Guild *Jrl.* 298 **VT,** So for the first time I attempted Ivory painting and went so much beyond my expectations that I thought I soon would be a dabster. **1884** Baldwin *Yankee School-Teacher* 21 **NY,** I let her putter round pretty much as she pleases. She's a dabster at piecin' quilts though! I do b'lieve she ruther do that than t'eat when hungry. **1889** *AN&Q* 3.255/2 **NJ,** Two of the most expressive words among Jerseyisms are 'dabster' and 'gawk.' 'Dabster' is a proficient person. **1909** *DN* 3.410 **nME,** *Dabster.* . . An adept. A versatile person. **1932** *DN* 6.283 **swCT,** *Dabster.* A person who gets things done; he is quick to see something and go at it. "He's a dabster to work." **1940** Weygandt *Down Jersey* 155 **sNJ,** This man was a dabster at felling trees. **1959** *VT Hist.* new ser 27.132, *Dabster.* . . A good worker; also a person who does odd jobs. Occasional. Orleans. **1968** Adams *Western Words* 88, *Dabster hand*—A cowboy expert at his work; used in eastern Washington. **1968** *DARE* (Qu. KK5, *A very skilled or expert person—for example, at woodworking: "He's a ______."*) Inf **NY**42, Dabster—old-fashioned.

dace n
Any of numerous freshwater fishes of the family Cyprinidae, but esp of the genera *Clinostomus, Phoxinus, Rhinichthys,* and *Semotilus.* **chiefly NEng** See Map For other names of var of these fishes see **chubsucker 2, fallfish, golden shiner, horned dace 2, leatherback, longnose dace, mud dace, potbelly, rainbow chub, redbelly dace, red dace, redfin dace, redside dace, rockfish, shiner, slicker, speckled dace, spring dace, striped dace**

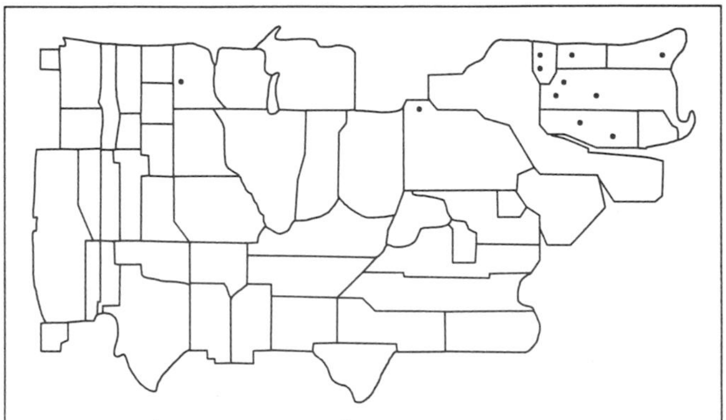
•dace (Qq. P3, P1, P7)

1654 (1974) Johnson *Wonder-Working* 79 **neMA,** *Salmon* and *Daice* cannot come up by reason of the Rocky falles. **1709** (1967) Lawson *New Voyage* 163 **Mid Atl,** Dace are the same as yours too. **1884** Goode *Fisheries U.S.* 1.616, The species of this family [Cyprinidae] known as "Minnows" . . and "Dace" literally swarm in all of the fresh waters of the United States. **1933** John G. Shedd Aquarium *Guide* 50, There are a hundred or more species of Cyprinidae, known variously as Dace, Minnows, Chubs, and Shiners, that are found in the Mississippi Valley and Great Lake region. **1939** Natl. Geogr. Soc. *Fishes* 267, But such fish as the cyprinids (minnows and dace), centrarchids (basses and sunfish), the ling, sculpins, trout, and whitefish, are found on both sides of the Divide. **1965–70** *DARE* (Qu. P3) Infs **CT**13, **ME**8, **MA**26, 47, 68, **NH**5, **VT**10, 12, Dace; (Qu. P7) Infs **ME**8, **MN**42, **VT**12, Dace; (Qu. P1) Infs **CT**14, **PA**234, Dace.

dad n[1]

=**daddy** n **3.**

c1960 *Wilson Coll.* **csKY,** *Dad*. . . Affectionate or joking name for husband. **1965–68** *DARE* (Qu. AA23, *Joking names that a woman may use to refer to her husband: "It's time to go and get supper for my ________.")* Infs **MD**35, **OK**7, Dad.

dad n[2] **esp Sth, S Midl** See Map Cf **dag, dog** n[1] **B7, fetched =dod.**

1834 Caruthers *Kentuckian* 1.216 **KY,** I'll be dad shamed if it ain't all cowardice. **1844** *S. Lit. Messenger* 10.47/1 **GA,** I'll be dad seized if I don't fling a handful o' fingers right in his face. **1845** Thompson *Pineville* 65 **GA,** I hope I may never see chinkapin time agin, dadfetch me! *Ibid,* Dadfetch . . if I don't bet my best dominecker. *Ibid* 114, Dadfetch your everlastin' picter! *Ibid* 182, I'll tetch 'em together quicker'n lightnin'—If I don't now, dad burn me! **1859** Taliaferro *Fisher's R.* 201 **nwNC** (as of 1820s), I'll be dadsamped ef one good butt ain't wuth two knocks. **1866** Smith *Bill Arp* 47 **GA,** I'll be dad-swamp'd if the commissary didn't keep his flour in 'em. **1869** *Overland Mth.* 3.130/2 **TX,** Dad-snatched if you can. **a1883** (1911) Bagby *VA Gentleman* 56, I'll be dad-shim'd if that off mule has been shod yit. **1884** Murfree *TN Mts.* 141 **eTN,** No man ez treats his wife like that dad-burned scoundrel Ike Peel do oughter be let live. **1884** Twain *Huck. Finn* 391 **MO,** Dey's de dadblamedest creturs to 'sturb a body. **1890** *Century Illustr. Mag.* 41.249 **IN,** You're two of the confoundest, dad-blastedest old eejits that ever was! **1901** Harben *Westerfelt* 195 **nGA,** Don't act so dadratted foolish. **1905** *DN* 3.76 **nwAR,** *Dad blame, dad blast, dad burn, dad dim, dad gone, dad gum*. . . Substitutes for 'God damn.' **1906** *DN* 3.133 **nwAR,** *Dad gast.* **1908** *DN* 3.304 **eAL, wGA,** *Dad-blame(d).* **1912** *DN* 3.575 **wIN,** *Dod* (or *dad*) *blast it.* **1912** Raine *Brand Blotters* 62 **West,** Dad gum it, I was aimin' to do that assessment work and couldn't jest lay my hands on the time. **1923** *DN* 5.205 **swMO,** *Dad blame,* interjection or expletive. Also *Dad burn, Dad blast, Dad damn, Dad durn, Dad gone, Dad swizzle.* **1941** Stuart *Men of Mts.* 53 **neKY,** Dad-durned my pictures if he hoes two rows of corn to my one. **1944** Clark *Pills* 156 **AL,** There was a sentiment that "a dad-blamed hog and a dad-gummed cow were the most aggravating things that ever made tracks on a piece of cotton land." **1959** *VT Hist.* new ser 27.132, *Dad burn it.* **1965–70** *DARE* (Qu. NN8b, . . *Expressions of annoyance: "This jar won't come open, ________ it.")* 21 Infs, **chiefly Sth, S Midl,** Dad-burn; 13 Infs, **scattered Sth, S Midl,** Dad-gum; **AL**12, **NC**82, **SC**24, **VA**15, Dad-blame; **MA**40, **SC**45, Dad-blast; **CA**158, **WA**3, Dad-bust; **MI**67, **MN**16, Dad-rat; **OK**27, Dad-gone; **NM**6, Dad-gum thing; (Qu. NN25b, *Weakened substitutes for 'damn' or 'damned': "Well, I'll be ________!")* 31 Infs, **chiefly Sth, S Midl,** Dad-gummed; **GA**77, **PA**209, **TX**81, Dad-blame(d); **AR**51, **GA**19, 31, **NC**72, **PA**223, Dad-burned; **AL**22, Dad-burn it; **CA**120, Dad-blasted; (Qu. NN9a, *Exclamations showing great annoyance: "________. The electric power is off again.")* 13 Infs, **scattered,** Dad-rat it; **AR**51, 52, **CA**158, **KY**70, 83, **NM**6, **WV**3, Dad-burn (it); **SC**11, **VA**11, 15, Dad-blame it; **CA**80, Dad-blast it; **TX**97, Dad-bop it; **VA**15, Dad-durn it; **MS**52, Dad-gum it; **GA**28, Dad-jim it; **TX**92, Dad-nab it; **LA**17, I'll be dad-gummed; **AL**3, Dad-blame juice is off; (Qu. LL37, . . *"I could have wrung her neck, I was so ________ mad.")* Infs **AR**6, 22, **VA**15, 42, Dad-blame(d); **MA**54, Dad-blasted; **AR**16, 51, **LA**2, 17, Dad-burned; **LA**8, Dad-goned; **AL**5, **TX**92, 98, Dad-gum(med); (Qu. LL36, . . *"Poor fellow. I think it's a ________ shame.")* Inf **TX**97, Dad-blasted; (Qu. HH31, *Somebody who is not from your community)* Inf **LA**17, Dad-gum foreigner. [Further exx in *DS,* sec NN; all exx are mapped.]

daddock n [Engl dial; *OED* a1624 →] **chiefly NEng** *old-fash* Cf *DS* KK7

Rotten wood; a rotten log.

1845 Judd *Margaret* 215 **MA,** The great red daddocks lay in the green pastures where they had lain year after year, crumbling away, and sending forth innumerable forms of vegetable life. **1848** Bartlett *Americanisms* 108, *Daddocks.* The heart or body of a tree thoroughly rotten. **1872** Schele de Vere *Americanisms* 461, *Daddock* . . is quite common in the rural districts of the New England States, and not unfrequent in the West, where the great trunks of fallen trees, slowly rotting away and turning into mould, are thus called. **1947** *Jrl. Amer. Folkl.* 60.157 **NEng,** Daddocks, the heart or body of a tree thoroughly rotten.

daddy n

1 One's father; hence n *daddy-in-law, grand-daddy.* **widespread, but somewhat more freq Sth, S Midl** See Map

1884 Smith *Bill Arp's Scrap Book* 79 **GA,** Talk to him and if possible persuade him not to whip his daddy. Tell him that it is wrong and unfilial. **1899** (1912) Green *VA Folk-Speech* 141, *Daddy*. . . A father; papa. Grand-daddy. **1932** (1974) Caldwell *Tobacco Road* 9 **GA,** You're Pearl's daddy, and you ought to make her behave. **1932** Stribling *Store* 488 **AL,** I had a little lawsuit with your daddy-in-law, Milt. [**1955** Williams *Cat Tin Roof* 7 **MS,** I sometimes suspect that Big Daddy [=her father-in-law] harbors a little unconscious "lech" fo' me.] **1957** *Sat. Eve. Post Letters* **csPA,** We nearly misjudged a new friend here when he spoke of his "daddy." Back home [=**seMA**], no boy or girl over six would use such a babyish term. . . But here it's always "daddy," no matter what your age. **1961** Hall *String Too Short* 13 **NH,** When my daddy died, the house was white. **1965–70** *DARE* (Qu. Z1, *What words do people around here use for 'father' within the family?)* 480 Infs, **widespread, but somewhat more freq Sth, S Midl,** Daddy; (Qu. Z10, *If a child looks very much like his father)* Infs **KY**66, **MS**6, **NC**3, Is his daddy made (*or* all) over; **MS**90, **GA**28, Is very much (*or* just) like his daddy; **IN**19, His daddy over again; **MO**9, Looks just like daddy; (Qu. Z7, *Nicknames and affectionate words for any other relatives)* Inf **OK**18, Daddy-in-law; (Qu. Z11a, . . *A child whose parents were not married)* Inf **NC**49, One that ain't got his own daddy; (Qu. Z11b, . . *A child of unwed parents)* Inf **MO**20, They don't know who the daddy is; (Qu. HH22c, . . *"He's mean enough to ________.")* Inf **TX**40, Steal from his daddy. **1965–70** *DARE* Tape **AL**31, My son's daddy-in-law owns it today; **CA**198, Daddy was

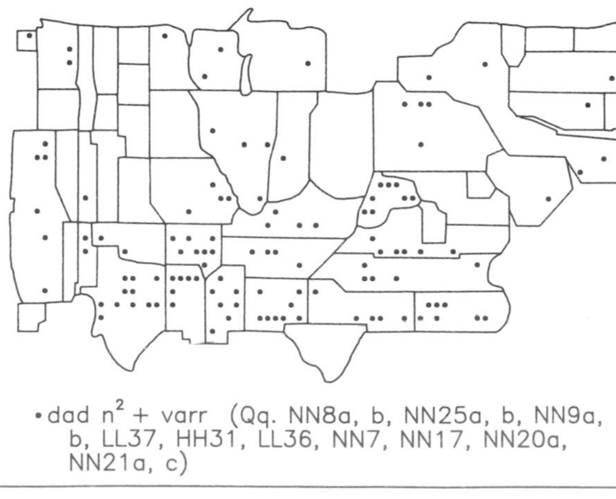

•dad n[2] + varr (Qq. NN8a, b, NN25a, b, NN9a, b, LL37, HH31, LL36, NN7, NN17, NN20a, NN21a, c)

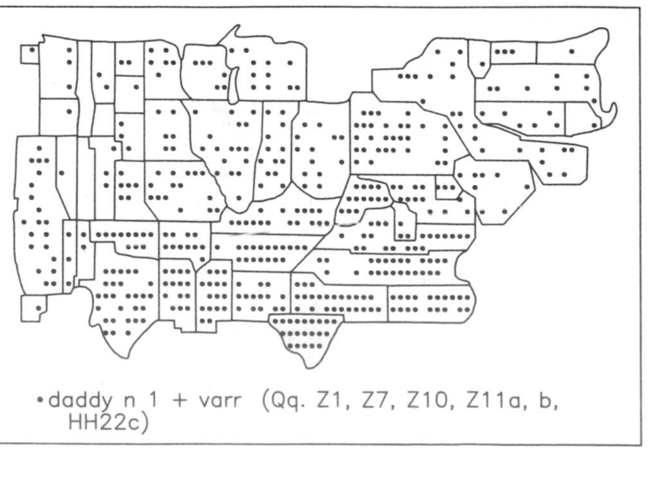

•daddy n 1 + varr (Qq. Z1, Z7, Z10, Z11a, b, HH22c)

born in Quincy; **FL**22, I said, "Daddy, what d' you do with your false teeth?"; **FL**24, My daddy . . and one of my brothers learned it; **FL**29, When I was born . . my daddy said if I was a boy he would hoist one lantern to the top of the flag pole. **1968** *DARE* FW Addit **New Orleans LA,** Daddy = father, generic term. **1969** *DARE* FW Addit **ceIL,** His daddy-in-law. **1970** Tarpley *Blinky* 215 **neTX,** *Daddy* and *papa* claim almost equal overall popularity as terms of affection for father, but distribution reveals that the use of *daddy* drops in age groups over 50 and in the lower educational categories. . . Another interesting result is that *daddy* is twice as popular among women than [sic] men. **1976** Ryland *Richmond Co. VA* 370, Daddy—used more often than "Father."

2 also *daddy-grand, ~-paw:* One's grandfather; an older man—sometimes used as a title. Cf **big daddy**

1883 (1971) Harris *Nights with Remus* 236 **GA,** To all appearances Daddy Jack had taken no interest in Uncle Remus's story . . and yet . . the old African began to twist and fidget in his chair. **1893** Shands *MS Speech* 26, *Daddy.* . . In Mississippi this word is used principally by negroes, and is frequently applied to old negroes without any idea of paternity. *Daddy* Jack would ordinarily mean an older negro than *Uncle* Jack. **1965–70** *DARE* (Qu. Z3, . . *Words . . for 'grandfather'*) Infs **GA**84, **LA**6, **PA**74, **TN**46, **VA**90, Daddy; **GA**84, **VA**5, Daddy plus first name; **AR**11, Daddy plus last name; **FL**18, **VA**41, Daddy plus name; **VA**90, Daddy-grand; **NC**31, Daddy-paw; **KY**74, Old daddy.

3 also *daddy-o:* A husband; a sweetheart. Cf **dad** n[1]

1909 Bradford *I'm Crazy 'Bout Your Lovin'* 2, [Song:] I've got a lovin daddy / Who cert'nly can love sweet. **1913** *San Francisco Examiner* (CA) 15 Apr 11 *(Zwilling Coll.),* [In the cartoon "Silk Hat Harry's Divorce Suit":] Here comes my daddy now. . . Oh pop oh pop oh pop. [*DARE* Ed: Cabaret singer to two men as they enter] **1923** in 1983 Taft *Blues Lyric Poetry* 66 [Black], Tell me pretty daddy : what's the matter now / Are you trying to quit me : and you don't know how. **1926** Van Vechten *Nigger Heaven* 285 [Black], *Daddy:* husband or lover. **1931** *AmSp* 7.28 [Black], *Daddy.* . . Husband or lover. **1962** *AmSp* 37.35, *Daddy* has a history beginning much earlier than 1935 as a term meaning simply 'lover' in Negro songs and blues. **1966–70** *DARE* (Qu. AA23, *Joking names that a woman may use to refer to her husband: "It's time to go and get supper for my ______."*) Infs **CA**9, 196, **FL**28, **LA**8, **MN**15, **NJ**67, **NY**205, **OK**31, **TX**37, **VA**90, Daddy; **ID**5, Daddy-o, sweet daddy; **IL**26, Big daddy; (Qu. AA3, *Nicknames or affectionate names for a sweetheart*) Inf **SC**69, Daddy; **NJ**67, My daddy. **1970** Tarpley *Blinky* 219 **neTX,** *How does the wife refer to her husband?* . . *Daddy* is an appelation [sic] with concentration among the least educated, outside the city, and in the age groups over 60.

4 =daddy longlegs 1.

1899 Bergen *Animal Lore* 58, Children say . . , "Daddy, daddy-long-legs, tell me which way you are going or I'll pull your legs off." The daddy stops, and . . points in the direction in which he is supposed to be going.

5 freq attrib: A male animal kept for breeding purposes. **chiefly Sth, S Midl** *euphem* Cf **father n B2, gentleman 2**

c1960 *Wilson Coll.* **csKY,** *Daddy.* . . Euphemism for stallion. **1966–70** *DARE* (Qu. K22, *Words used for a bull*) Infs **FL**12, **GA**80, **NC**44, Daddy (cow); **MO**5, Daddy of the herd; (Qu. K23, *Words used by women or in mixed company for a bull*) Infs **CO**4, **IL**19, **KY**6, **PA**191, **VA**46, Daddy cow; (Qu. K52, *A male pig kept for breeding is a ______*) Infs **MD**20, **VA**46, Daddy hog. **1970** Tarpley *Blinky* 166 **neTX,** *Male cow (euphemism).* . . Daddy cow. **1983** *MJLF* 9.1.37 **ceKY,** *Daddy cow* . . a euphemism for bull.

6 also *dad;* in var phrr used to warn a woman that her slip is showing: See quots. Cf **cotton 4, father n B5**

1950 *WELS* 1 Inf, **swWI,** Dad loves you more than mother. **1966–70** *DARE* (Qu. W24a) Inf **MO**6, Daddy likes your dress; **IL**113, **MO**4, Daddy loves you best; **OH**6, Do you love your daddy; **IA**30, You like your dad better'n you do your mother; **PA**115, You like your daddy best; **WI**66, Your dad likes you better than your mother; **IN**3, Your daddy likes you better than your mother; **GA**19, **MI**104, **MO**34, **TN**23, Your daddy loves you; **OK**18, Your daddy loves you best; **AR**27, Your daddy loves you better; **TN**3, **VA**26, Your daddy loves you better than your mother; **TN**13, Your daddy loves you the best; **IL**63, Your daddy loves you best; **NY**165, Your daddy's thinking of you.

daddy v

1 To father (a child), often out of wedlock.

1916 *DN* 4.283 **sAppalachians,** One may hear "Who daddied that kid?" for "Who is the father of that kid?" **1930** [see **2** below]. **1952** Brown *NC Folkl.* 1.532, *Daddy.* . . To beget a child. "He's daddied more children than he can feed."—West. **c1960** *Wilson Coll.* **csKY,** *Daddy.* . . To father a family. **1971** Dwyer *Dict. for Yankees* 25 **Sth, S Midl,** *Daddy*—To beget, usually illegitimately, i.e., "Who daddied that child?"

2 To acknowledge or identify the paternity of (a child).

1930 Shoemaker *1300 Words* 16 **cPA Mts** (as of c1900), *Daddy*—To father or acknowledge a child born out of wedlock. **1939** Aurand *Quaint Idioms* 23 [PaGer], Wonder who will *Daddy* this last child (father a child born out of wedlock; evidently not the first one thus born). **1952** [see **dummern**].

3 in phr *daddy oneself:* To resemble one's father (so as to leave no doubt of his paternity). [Cf Scots and nEngl dial *father* to indicate one's paternity by resemblance]

1916 *DN* 4.283 **sAppalachians,** One may hear . . "That kid daddies itself (resembles its father)."

4 To raise or act as parent to (a child).

1957 *Sat. Eve. Post Letters* **csPA,** I've heard [the expression] several times . . "to daddy"—a neighbor lady said she daddied her nephews because they were orphans.

daddy biglegs See **daddy longlegs 1**

daddy britches n

Prob **=Dutchman's breeches 1.**

1968 *DARE* (Qu. S26e) Inf **MD**24, Daddy-britches—grow in rock crevices; pink, blue, or white; shaped something like a person; bloom early in April.

daddy bug n

=daddy longlegs 1.

1859 *S. Lit. Messenger* 29.416/1, There were . . long-legged daddy-bugs striding over the ground.

daddy cow See **daddy n 5**

daddy-grand See **daddy n 2**

daddy hog See **daddy n 5**

daddy-in-law See **daddy n 1**

daddy longlegs n

1 also *daddy biglegs, ~ longleg:* An arachnid of the order Opiliones. Also called **daddy 4, daddy bug, father longlegs, granddaddy 2, ~ graybeard 1, ~ longlegs 1, ~ spider, grandfather, harvestman 1, longlegs, longlegged spider, moskeet spider, pointer, shepherd spider**

1870 *Amer. Naturalist* 3.46 **IL,** Several insects are described . . also part of a Cockroach, and a Harvest-man or Daddy-long-legs, allied to, but lower than the spiders. **1899** Bergen *Animal Lore* 38, Wish on a daddy-long-legs for good luck. **1910** Hart *Vigilante Girl* 326 **nCA,** Spanning some deep ravine with a straddling walk like that of a spider or a "daddy long-legs." **1930** Shoemaker *1300 Words* 19 **cPA Mts** (as of c1900), *Daddy long legs*—A large harmless insect of the spider family. **c1960** *Wilson Coll.* **csKY,** *Daddy-longlegs* . . a harvestman (*Phalangium opilio* [sic]); usually called granddaddy. **1965–70** *DARE* (Qu. R28) 408 Infs, **widespread,** Daddy longlegs; **PA**3, Daddy longleg; **NY**10, Daddy longlegs, daddy biglegs [Inf queries latter term]. **1980** Milne–Milne *Audubon Field Guide Insects* 919, Although daddy-long-legs resemble spiders, they are not.

2 =praying mantis.

1949 *PADS* 11.5 **wTX** (as of c1920), Daddy Long-Legs, devil's horse. . . The praying mantis. **1954** *Harder Coll.* **cwTN,** *Daddy long legs,* praying mantis.

3 =crane fly. [*OED* a1814 →]

1966–68 *DARE* (Qu. R15b) Inf **AK**9, Daddy longlegs—here a six-leg insect that eats spiders; **ME**8, Daddy longlegs—looks like a large mosquito but doesn't bite; **MI**36, Daddy longlegs.

4 A **grasshopper 1** of the family Acrididae.

1968 *DARE* (Qu. R6) Infs **NJ**35, **PA**128, Daddy longlegs.

5 =black-necked stilt. [See quot 1946]

1923 U.S. Dept. Ag. *Misc. Circular* 13.48, *Black-necked Stilt. . . Vernacular Names. . . In local use.* . . Daddy-long-legs (Wash.) **1925** (1928) Forbush *Birds MA* 1.384, "Daddy-long-legs". . . Despite its apparently unnecessarily long legs, it is a graceful and handsome bird. **1946** Hausman *Eastern Birds* 294, *Black-necked Stilt. . . Other Names* . . Daddy Long-legs. . . Very long slim pinkish or reddish legs. **1955** Forbush–May *Birds* 209, The Black-necked Stilt . . is also called . . 'Daddy-long-legs' in some localities.

6 =**long-billed curlew.**

1953 Jewett *Birds WA* 256, Northern Long-billed Curlew. *Numenius americanus parvus*. . . Other names: . . Daddy-long-legs.

daddynut n Also *daddynut tree*

A **linden.**

1893 *Jrl. Amer. Folkl.* 6.139, Tilia sp., daddy-nuts. Madison, Wis. **1930** Sievers *Amer. Med. Plants* 6, *Tilia americana*. . . Common names.—Basswood, . . daddynut tree. . . The roundish, grayish-green fruit is dry and woody and contains one or two seeds. **1960** Vines *Trees SW* 733, Daddynuts.

daddy-o See **daddy n 3**

daddy oneself See **daddy v 3**

daddy-paw See **daddy n 2**

daddy sculpin n

A **sculpin** (here: *Myoxocephalus scorpius*).

1882 U.S. Natl. Museum *Bulletin* 16.703, *Daddy Sculpin*. . . New York to Greenland, common; one of the largest sculpins. **1884** Goode *Fisheries U.S.* 1.258, On our Atlantic coast are found several species of this family [=Cottidae], generally known by the name "Sculpin," and also by such titles as . . "Daddy Sculpin." **1933** John G. Shedd Aquarium *Guide* 131, *Daddy Sculpin*. One of the largest of the sculpins, this fish is fairly common along the New England coast. **1960** Amer. Fisheries Soc. *List Fishes* 67, Sculpin, Daddy—see short-horn sculpin [=*Myoxocephalus scorpius*].

dade See **dead** adj

dad gum (it) See **gum** v^2

daeown See **down A**

daffadowndilly n

1 also *daffydowndilly*: =**daffodil 1.** [*OED* 1573 →]

1859 Elwyn *Glossary* 37, *Daff-a-down-dillies*. This word, that has sunk, in the progress of what is called refinement, to a vulgarism, was used by Spenser, in his "Shepherd's Calendar." **1873** *Harper's New Mth. Mag.* 46.752/1 **FL,** But outside meadows have daffadowndillies,/ And all the lake margin is white with lilies. **1904** *Harper's Mth. Mag.* 108.596/1 **NEng,** I wish I could see the daffodils,—only I should insist upon calling them daffy-downdillies, as I did when I was little. **1951** Teale *North with Spring* 218 **NC,** An American plant hunter. . . may return with juglans, kinnikinnic, . . missey-moosey, daffydowndilly, . . or robin-runs-away. **1964** *New Yorker* 20 June 11/1 **NYC,** Mr. V. likewise supports Isobel Robins, who imparts a fine daffadowndilly quality to whatever she sings.

2 as *daffydowndilly*: A **trillium** (here: *Trillium erectum*). Cf **daffodil 2**

1894 *Jrl. Amer. Folkl.* 7.102, *Trillium erectum*, . . daffy-down-dilly, . . Bradford, Vt. **1930** Sievers *Amer. Med. Plants* 48, *Purple Trillium*. . . *Other common names*. . . Daffydowndilly. **1971** Krochmal *Appalachia Med. Plants* 256, *Trillium erectum*. . . *Common Names* . . Daffydown-dilly.

daffodil n

1 Std: a plant of the genus *Narcissus*. Also called **butter-and-eggs 2, buttercup 4, Easter flower 2**

2 A **trillium.** Cf **daffadowndilly 2**

1969 *DARE* (Qu. S2) Inf **NC**64, Daffodils.

daffodil lily n

An **atamasco (lily) 1** (here: *Zephyranthes atamasco*).

1900 Lyons *Plant Names* 402, Southeastern U.S. Atamasco Lily, Daffodil Lily [etc].

daffydowndilly See **daffadowndilly**

dafter See **daughter**

dag n Cf **dad** n^2, **dod**

=**dog** n^1 **B7.**

1897 *KS Univ. Qrly.* (ser B) 6.86 **neKS,** *Dag on:* dog on. A mild oath. **1906** *DN* 3.117 **sIN,** *Dag gone*. . . A mild oath. "Dag gone it." **1908** *DN* 3.304 **eAL, wGA,** *Dag bust it*. . . An expletive. **1937** in 1972 Hall *Sayings Old Smoky* 54 **eTN, wNC,** You mighty dag-gone right I would! . . Well, I'll be dag-gone. **1965–70** *DARE* (Qu. NN8b, . . *Expressions of annoyance: "This jar won't come open, ______ it."*) 20 Infs, **scattered,** Dag-gone; **CA**211, **IN**40, 76, **TN**54, Dag-nab; (Qu. NN25b, *Weakened substitutes for 'damn' or 'damned': "Well, I'll be ______!"*) Infs **DE**1, **FL**48, **KY**65, **MD**20, 37, **MO**6, **NC**7, 26, **SC**26, 40, Dag-gone(d); **SC**31, Dag-gummed; **MI**46, Dag-nabbed; (Qu. GG21b, *If you don't care what a person does, you might say, "Go ahead—I don't give a ______."*) Inf **IL**45, Dag-gone, dag-gum; (Qu. NN8a, . . *"Oh ______. I've lost my glasses again."*) Inf **AR**41, Dag-gum; (Qu. NN9a, *Exclamations showing great annoyance: "______. The electric power is off again."*) Inf **DC**11, Dag; **PA**66, Dag-nab it; **IA**41, Dag-wam it; (Qu. NN9b, . . *"He's run off with my hammer again, ______!"*) Infs **MD**5, **NC**82, **VA**2, Dag-gone it (*or* boy); **MI**103, Dag-nab it; (Qu. NN17, *Something that keeps on annoying you . . "That ______ fly won't go away."*) Inf **NC**26, Dag-gone; **PA**242, Dag-rabbit; (Qu. NN20a, *Exclamations caused by sudden pain—a blow on the thumb*) Inf **IL**45, Dag-gum it; (Qu. NN25a, *Weakened substitutes for 'damn' or 'damned': "______ it all!"*) Infs **IA**5, **NY**42, **WI**34, Dag-nab; **MD**16, 20, Dag-gone; **IL**45, Dag-gum; **KY**60, Dag-take; (Qu. LL37, *To make a statement as strong as you can: "I could have wrung her neck, I was so ______ mad."*) Infs **AL**30, **LA**17, **MS**64, **NC**61, **SC**8, **TN**24, Dag-gummed; **TX**53, Dag-gum; **PA**242, Dag-nabbit.

dag v, hence ppl adj *dagged* [**dag** n]

=**dog** v **6.**

1965–70 *DARE* (Qu. NN8b, *Other expressions of annoyance: "This jar won't come open, ______ it."*) Infs **MD**5, **TN**54, Dag; (Qu. NN25a, *Weakened substitutes for 'damn' or 'damned': "______ it all!"*) Infs **NC**61, **OH**103, Dag; (Qu. NN25b, *Weakened substitutes for 'damn' or 'damned': "Well, I'll be ______!"*) Infs **MD**5, **NC**61, Dagged.

dagger n Also *dagger flower, ~ plant, ~ weed*

Any of var **yuccas: see quots.**

1876 Hobbs *Bot. Hdbk.* 30, Dagger flower, plant, . . Yucca gloriosa. **1900** Lyons *Plant Names* 401, *Y. aloifolia*. . . Dagger-plant. **1941** Writers' Program *Guide UT* 300, The soil is pink sand, supporting white sage, "dagger weed," rabbit brush, and cacti. **1949** Moldenke *Amer. Wild Flowers* 369, The common broad-leaved . . *dagger, Y. macrocarpa*, . . is often cultivated. **1959** Carleton *Index Herb. Plants* 35, *Dagger-plant:* . . Yucca (v). **1960** Vines *Trees SW* 52, *Yucca carnerosana*. . . Other vernacular names are Giant Dagger and Palma Samandoca. **1979** Little *Checklist U.S. Trees* 296, *Yucca carnerosana*. . . Giant-dagger. **1982** Perry–Hay *Field Guide Plants* 78, Spanish bayonet; dagger plant. . . *Leaves* . . strap-shaped with very sharp points.

dagger cockleburr n

A **cockleburr 1.**

1898 *Jrl. Amer. Folkl.* 11.230, *Xanthium spinosum*. . . Chinese thistle, dagger cocklebur. **1912** Blatchley *IN Weed Book* 151, *Xanthium spinosum* . . Spiny Cocklebur. Dagger Cocklebur. Burweed.

dagger fern n [From the shape]

Either of two **sword ferns: Christmas fern** or *Polystichum munitum*.

1938 (1958) Sharples *AK Wild Flowers* 108, *P[olystichum] munitum*. "Dagger Fern." . . Southeastern Alaska. **1938** Small *Ferns SE States* 296, *P[olystichum] acrostichoides* . . (Christmas-fern. Dagger-fern.) **1959** Anderson *Flora AK* 14, *P[olystichum] munitum* . . Dagger-fern.

dagger-fiber See **dagger string**

dagger flower n [From the pinnate leaves]

1 =**tahoka daisy.**

1936 Whitehouse *TX Flowers* 165, Tansy Aster. Dagger-Flower *(Machaeranthera tanacetifolia)*. **1949** Moldenke *Amer. Wild Flowers* 210, A relative of the aster tribe is the showy *daggerflower, Machaeranthera tanacetifolia*, of dry soil from South Dakota and Montana to Texas and California.

2 See **dagger.**

dagger grass n

=**lechuguilla.**

1951 *PADS* 15.29 **TX,** *Agave lecheguilla*. . . Dagger grass.

dagger plant See **dagger**

daggers' points, at adj phr Also *at dagger's point(s)*

At odds or in disagreement (with someone); at the point of fighting, hostile.

1859 in 1953 Lincoln *Coll. Wks.* 3.452 **sIL,** Now that all these conflicting elements should be brought, while at dagger's points, with one another, to support him, is a feat that is worthy for you to note and consider. **1965–69** *DARE* (Qu. II11b, *If two people can't bear each other at all, you'd say, "Those two are ______."*) Infs **AR**41, **GA**67,

NC52, **TX**18, **VA**26, At daggers' points (with each other); **FL**6, At dagger's point; **KY**6, Daggers' points; (Qu. KK68, *When people don't think alike about something: "We agree on most things, but on politics we're ______."*) Infs **GA**15, **NY**194, **OK**48, **PA**175, **TX**65, At daggers' points.

dagger string n Also *dagger-fiber* **[dagger]**

See quots.

1891 *Century Dict.* 7026, *Y[ucca] filamentosa, Y. aloifolia,* and *Y. gloriosa. . .* furnish a harsh, brittle, but very strong fiber, called *dagger-fiber,* used for packing and as a rude cordage. **1900** Lyons *Plant Names* 401, *Yucca. . . Leaves* of several species yield a fiber called dagger-fiber. **1967** *DARE* Tape **TX**24, [Inf:] They'd tie it in bundles. . . course those days they tied it with dagger string. [FW:] Now dagger string is stripped off of—? [Inf:] These Spanish daggers. You see you can take and roast that just a little bit and it's pliable.

dagger weed n

1 See **dagger.**

2 Prob a **dagger cockleburr.**

1970 *DARE* (Qu. S15) Inf **SC**70, Daggerweed.

daggle v

1 To drag (something) in the mud, to dirty; hence ppl adj *daggled.* [*OED* 1530 →]

1899 (1912) Green *VA Folk-Speech* 141, *Daggle. . .* To trail in the dirt; to trail through mud and water, as a garment. **1955** Adams *Grandfather* 110 **NY** (as of 1830s), Her husband appeared with the usual daggled smears on the white surface and the usual demand for fresh apparel.

2 with *down:* See quot.

1913 *DN* 4.43 **appar Chicago IL,** *Daggle down. . .* To hang down or trail so as to draggle, of a skirt. "That will be daggling down behind." Said to occur also in N[ew] E[ngland]. Perhaps from *dangle* and *draggle.*

daggled See **daggle 1**

daggle down See **daggle 2**

daggly adj [Engl dial; cf **daggle 1**] *arch*

1899 (1912) Green *VA Folk-Speech* 141, *Daggly. . .* Wet.

dago n

A low-lying meadow.

1955 *AmSp* 30.54 **neFL,** *Dago* . . a kind of grassy marsh or marshy prairie. **1971** Wood *Vocab. Change* 147 **wTN, eOK,** A low grassland . . dago. **1981** Pederson *LAGS Basic Materials (Low-lying grassland)* 1 inf, **cGA,** Dago.

dago bomb n

A kind of firework; see quots.

1960 Wentworth–Flexner *Slang* 138, *Dago bomb. . .* A white spherical firecracker. *Child use c1935.* **1966–69** *DARE* (Qu. FF14, . . *Kinds of firecrackers*) Inf **IL**98, Dago bombs; **GA**13, Dago bombs—flies into the air and blows up; **LA**46, Dago bombs—cardboard tube shoots a powerful charge into the air; (Qu. FF28, . . *Other kinds of fireworks*) Inf **LA**14, Dago bombs—cardboard tube that shoots a delayed charge into the air.

dago gull n

=**herring gull.**

1921 LA Dept. of Conserv. *Bulletin* 10.135, On the Mississippi at New Orleans this bird [=*Larus argentatus*] is known sometimes as "Dago gull."

dago red n Also *dago wine* [*dago* an Italian or Spaniard] **chiefly Nth and West** See Map

Cheap red wine.

1906 Aitken–Hilton *Hist. Earthquake* 120 **cwCA,** On the heights the houses were hung with blankets saturated in casks of wine (real "Dago red") and many were saved. **1919** Kyne *Capt. Scraggs* 171 **CA,** A lunch with a small bottle o' Dago Red thrown in. **1927** *DN* 5.443 [Underworld jargon], *Dago red. . .* Cheap wine. **1930** Irwin *Amer. Tramp* 220, They . . deprived themselves of their daily bread / When they blew the coin for dago red. **1965–70** *DARE* (Qu. DD27, . . *Nicknames . . for wine*) 104 Infs, **chiefly Nth and West,** Dago red; **LA**15, **VT**16, Dago wine; (Qu. DD28b, . . *Fermented drinks . . made at home*) Infs **CT**42, **LA**3, **MN**1, **PA**94, 167, 185, **WI**19, Dago red; **PA**227, Dago red wine; **MA**123, Dago wine; (Qu. DD21b, . . *Bad liquor*) Inf **CA**87, Dago red. **1966** Dos Passos *Best Times* 83 **NYC,** As we poured down the dago red he would become mischievous. **1976** *Capital Times* (Madison WI) 29 Dec 4 **csWI,** When all of our parents were making wine, everybody in Madison called it Dago Red. And nobody ever said anything about that.

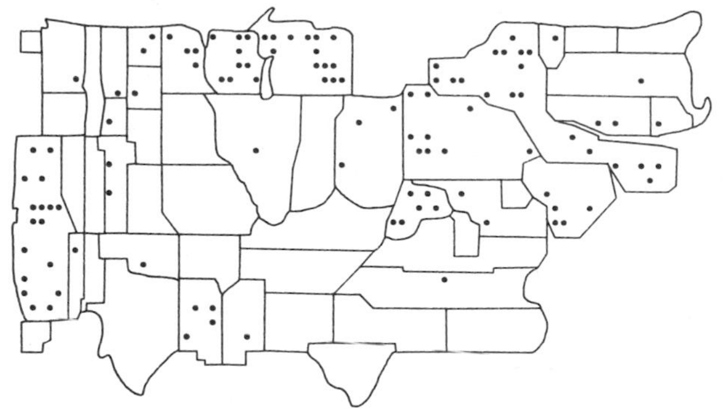

•dago red + varr (Qq. DD27, DD28b, DD21b)

dagwood n, also cap [See **bumstead**] **scattered, but esp MN, IA, CO** See Map Cf **grinder 3, hoagie**

A large sandwich, layered with various ingredients; occas a **submarine sandwich.**

1960 Wentworth–Flexner *Slang* 138, *Dagwood. . .* A gigantic sandwich. **1965–70** *DARE* (Qu. H42, *The kind [of sandwich] in a much larger, longer bun, that's a meal in itself*) 46 Infs, **scattered, but esp MN, IA, CO,** Dagwood (sandwich); **MN**37, Dagwood—piled high sandwich; **CA**54, Dagwoods—not long but high; **LA**31, Dagwood sandwich—they use french bread for this; **GA**17, Dagwood special—that's what they call all double and triple sandwiches; (Qu. H6) Inf **MO**34, Dagwood sandwich. **1976** *Yankee* Oct 154, The large Dagwood-like sandwich beloved by Americans was first called "The Grinder." **1978** *New Yorker* 15 May 157/1, At Shorehaven's Quelle Crêpe, "for a few dollars you could have a glass of wine and a crêpe with fromage . . et oeufs et jambon et asperges, like a francophile's Dagwood sandwich." **1986** Pederson *LAGS Concordance* **Gulf Region** *(Hero sandwich)* 11 infs, Dagwood (sandwich); 1 inf, Dagwood—stacked up; 1 inf, Dagwood—sandwich, different from poor boy, hero. **1988** *DARE* File, In Philadelphia in the 1950s, when I was a child, I often observed my dad make a late evening or midnight snack that he called a "dagwood sandwich." Between mayonnaise besmeared slices of white, rye, or pumpernickel bread, he would stack leaves of iceberg lettuce and thin slices of lunchmeats, cheeses, onion, and tomato, in that order.

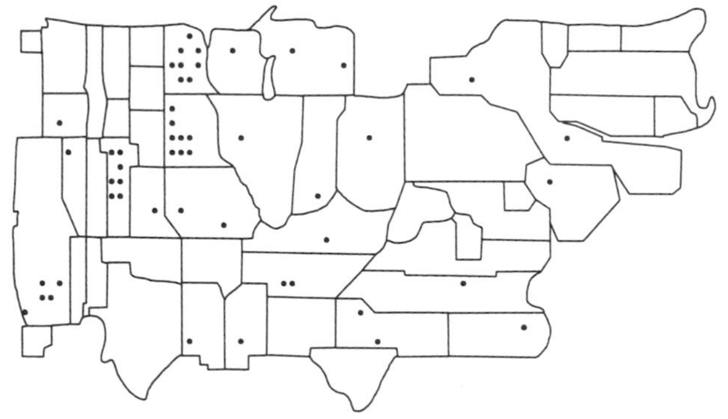

•dagwood + varr (Qq. H42, H6)

dah n |dɑ, dæ| Also sp *da* [Prob Ewe *da* mother] *Gullah*

See quot 1949.

1949 Turner *Africanisms* 191 **eGA, seSC,** West African Words in Gullah . . [da ('dada)] 'mother, nurse, an elderly woman.' **1950** *PADS* 14.25 **SC,** *Dah* [dɑ]. . . A Negro nurse. Charleston and coastal S.C. **1951** *AmSp* 26.14 **SC,** *Da* is the usual Charleston name for a child's Negro nurse. **1966** *DARE* FW Addit **SC** (as of c1945), [dæ], a *real* old time nurse or a live-in maid. Everybody called her this. She was like a part of the family.

dahlia n Usu |ˈdæljə|; also |ˈdæliə, ˈdeljə, ˈdæli|

Std senses, var forms.

1950 *WELS Suppl.* 3 Infs, **WI,** ['deljə]; 1 Inf, **csWI,** ['dæliə], ['dæljə], ['deljə]. **1969** *DARE* (Qu. S26e) Inf **KY**28, Dahlias ['dæliz].

dahoon n Also *dahoon holly* Cf **small-leaf dahoon**

A **yaupon** (here: *Ilex cassine*).

1731 (1754) Catesby *Nat. Hist. Carolina* 1.31, *The Dahoon Holly. This* Holly usually grows erect, sixteen Feet high. . . This is a very uncommon Plant in *Carolina.* **1884** Sargent *Forests of N. Amer.* 35, *Dahoon. Dahoon Holly.* Southern Virginia, southward near the coast to Mosquito inlet and Tampa bay, Florida, west along the Gulf coast to the prairie region of western Louisiana. **1938** Van Dersal *Native Woody Plants* 143, *Ilex cassine. . . Dahoon holly. . .* A large shrub to small tree or rarely a large tree. **1976** Bailey–Bailey *Hortus Third* 590, *Dahoon, cassina, cassine, cassena, yaupon.* Evergreen, puberulent tree, to about 40 ft.

daid See **dead** adj

daikon n [Japanese]

A large Japanese radish *(Raphanus sativus longipinnatus).*

1967 *DARE* (Qu. I3, . . *Large yellowish root vegetable, similar to a turnip*), Inf **HI**1, Daikon. **1972** Carr *Da Kine Talk* 91 **HI,** Indispensable items on the Japanese menu [in Hawaiian restaurants include] . . *daikon,* an edible root similar to a radish or turnip. **1975** Shurtleff–Aoyagi *Book Tofu* 1.320, *Daikon:* Literally "great root," this giant Japanese white radish is often as thick as a man's arm and 18 to 24 inches long. **1979** *DARE* File (as of c1970), Southern California supermarkets had many more fresh vegetables than I had seen in northern California stores, including the mild-flavored chayote and the radish-like daikon.

dainjus See **dangerous** adj

dainty cups n

A **lady's slipper** (here: *Cypripedium acaule*).

1959 Carleton *Index Herb. Plants* 35, *Dainty cups:* Cypripedium acaule.

dairter See **daughter**

dairy n

1 A building or room in which milk is stored and processed; by ext, any of various storage places for keeping food cool; see quot 1986. [*OED* c1290 →] **chiefly Atlantic** See Map Cf **dairy house, milk house, spring house**

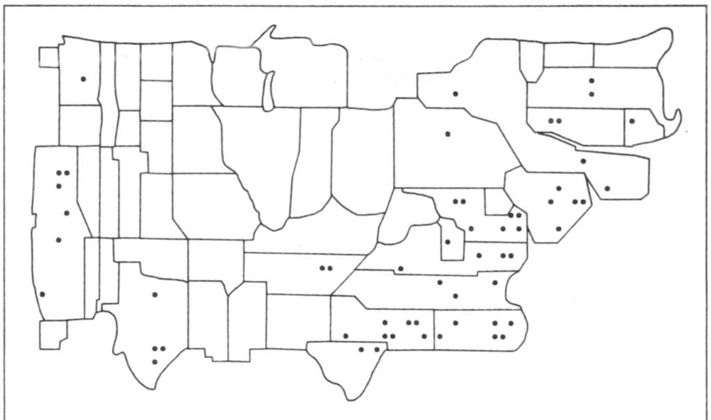

•dairy 1 (Qq. M18, M19)

1650 (1965) Bradstreet *Tenth Muse* 58 **MA,** The cleanly huswives Dary, now's ith' prime. **1864** Nichols *40 Yrs.* 1.22 **NEng,** Here were the farm buildings. . . a wash-house, dairy, wood-house, . . and hog-house. **1939** *LANE* Map 107, 1 inf, **cVT,** *Dairy*—a room, rarely a whole building. **1965–70** *DARE* (Qu. M18, *The separate building where milk is kept cool*) 57 Infs, **chiefly Atlantic,** Dairy; (Qu. M19, *A place for keeping carrots, turnips, potatoes, and so on over the winter*) Inf **TN**7, Dairy. **1976** Garber *Mountain-ese* 20 **Appalachians,** *Dairy. . .* milk cooling house—Put the milk in the dairy so it won't clabber afore supper. **1986** Pederson *LAGS Concordance (Dairy)* **Gulf Region,** [48 infs, 17 in **TN,** indicate that a *dairy* is a storage place; 26 specify that it is for milk or other dairy products; 7 mention other types of food. 14 infs, 12 in **eTN,** say that a *dairy* is in, or partly in, the ground. Some typical descriptions and comments are: "house built over stream, kept milk cool"; "processes milk, room in old houses"; "little storage house for milk, other food"; "put milk in postholes dug in the ground"; "place to keep milk and butter, a box on crosswalk between kitchen and house"; "walk-in cellar dug in side of hill"; "concrete floor cellar for canned goods."]

2a Dairy products. Cf **bakery 2**

1882 *Narragansett Hist. Reg.* 1.226 **RI,** Farmers used to sell their dairy in the Boston market.

b Esp: foods containing or compatible with milk according to Jewish dietary law. [Translation of Yiddish *milkhiks* n < *milkhik* adj]

1970 Feinsilver *Yiddish* 303, "Dairy" for "dairy products." . . "We're having dairy for supper." . . This is so common a usage that French's mustard ran an ad in a Jewish monthly in 1963 advocating that its product be used for "any meat sandwich," adding: "Great with dairy, too." **1982** Rosten *Hooray for Yiddish* 96 **NY,** Isadore Steinman. . . from Far Rockaway. . . Lifelong vegetarian. Ate mostly dairy. **1988** *Smithsonian* May 74 **NYC,** You know how kosher food is classified? There's meat and dairy, right?

dairy house n **esp Sth, S Midl**

=**dairy 1.**

1857 *Porter's Spirit of Times* 289/2, Any gentleman who has a spring . . such as supplies an ordinary dairy-house. **1874** U.S. Dept. Ag. *Rept. of Secy. for 1873* 248 **wNY,** He has adopted the plan of cooling his milk as soon as it comes from the cow to a temperature of 50° to 52°, . . then carrying [it] to his dairy-house, made of concrete with double walls, between which is an interval of 8 inches in depth. Into this house he admits air only at night, and here he is able to keep his milk two days before skimming. **1965–70** *DARE* (Qu. M18, *The separate building where milk is kept cool*) 28 Infs, **esp Sth, S Midl,** Dairy house. **1986** Pederson *LAGS Concordance (Dairy)* 1 inf, **neTN,** Dairy house—hole in ground, covered with stone; 1 inf, **ceTN,** Dairy house—near a stream; 1 inf, **ceMS,** Dairy house—for milk and butter.

dairy-pink n

=**cowherb.**

1933 Small *Manual SE Flora* 505, *V[accaria] Vaccaria. . . Cow-herb. Dairy-pink. . .* It is said to be a favorite food of cattle.

daisy n

1 Std: the English daisy *(Bellis perennis).*

2 Any of numerous other, somewhat similar, composite plants, as:

a An **oxeye** (here: *Chrysanthemum leucanthemum*).

1784 in 1785 Amer. Acad. Arts & Sci. *Memoirs* 1.483 **neMA,** *Chrysanthemum. . . White Weed. Goldens. Daisie. . .* The young leaves may be eaten as sallad. **1837** Darlington *Flora Cestrica* 490, *C[hrysanthemum] leucanthemum. . . Vulgo.* Daisy. . . This . . has become a serious nuisance in many neighborhoods. **1896** Freeman *Madelon* 324 **eMA,** This Dorothy . . could no more develop into aught towards which she herself inclined not than a daisy plant out in the field could grow a clover blossom. **1944** *Sat. Review* 23 Sept 27/2, Has pulling the petals of a daisy, one by one, to find out what kind of husband you are going to have gone out of fashion? **1959** Carleton *Index Herb. Plants* 35, *Daisy* . . Chrysanthemum leucanthemum in the United States. **1967–69** *DARE* (Qu. S21) Infs **CT**23, **NC**67, **PA**176, **RI**1, **TN**22, Daisies. [*DARE* Ed: Some Infs may be referring to other senses.] **1976** Bailey–Bailey *Hortus Third* 1242, Daisy: *Bellis, Chrysanthemum frutescens, C. Leucanthemum.*

b =**fleabane** (here: *Erigeron* spp). **esp West**

1828 Rafinesque *Med. Flora* 1.162, *Erigeron philadelphicum. . . Vulgar Names* . . Daisy. *Ibid* 164, A multitude of vulgar names are applied to these plants. . . Daisy alludes to the flowers which are similar to those of the true Daisy or *Bellis perennis.* **1843** Torrey *Flora NY* 2.1.355, *Erigeron annuum. . .* Sweet Scabious. Daisy, etc. . . *Erigeron strigosum. . .* Fleabane. Daisy. **1896** *Jrl. Amer. Folkl.* 9.192, *Erigeron Philadelphicus,* . . daisy, Sulphur Grove, Ohio; Burnside, No. [sic] Dak. *Erigeron pumilus,* . . daisy, Burnside, So. Dakota. **1901** Lounsberry *S. Wild Flowers* 513, *E[rigeron] vernus* . . bears . . many flower heads. They look much like little daisies, and are often so called. **1937** U.S. Forest Serv. *Range Plant Hdbk.* W67, *Erigeron* spp. . . Plants of this genus are commonly known as fleabanes, daisies, and erigerons. . . In the West, daisy is almost universally used for species of *Erigeron.* **1967** *DARE* Wildfl QR (Craighead) Pl.21.3 Infs **CA**24, **CO**15, Showy daisy; Pl.21.4 Inf **CO**15, Cutleaf daisy. **1973** Hitchcock–Cronquist *Flora Pacific NW* 512, *Erigeron* L. Daisy; Fleabane; Erigeron.

c An aster (*Aster* spp).

1896 *Jrl. Amer. Folkl.* 9.191, *Aster* (native species), daisies, Sulphur Grove, Ohio. **1898** *Ibid* 11.229, *Aster* (sp.), purple daisies, Monroe, Wis. **1900** Lyons *Plant Names* 51, *Aster*. . . Local names in America are Frost-flower, Good-bye-summer, Daisy (Ohio). **1937** U.S. Forest Serv. *Range Plant Hdbk.* W67, Daisy . . is popularly and rather loosely applied . . to asters (*Aster* spp.)

d =**western daisy.**

1933 Small *Manual SE Flora* 1362, *A. integrifolium*. . . *Daisy*. . . Various provinces N of Coastal Plain, Ala. to Tex., Ark. and Ky. **1940** Gates *Flora KS* 242, Astranthium integrifolium. . . Daisy. . . Moist ground. **1946** Reeves–Bain *Flora TX* 254, Astranthium. . . Daisy.

e A **black-eyed Susan 2.**

1965–70 *DARE* (Qu. S7) 10 Infs, **chiefly S Midl, Sth,** Daisy (or daisies). **1968** *DARE* Wildfl QR Pl.255 Inf **MN**37, Daisy.

f A **tidytips** (here: *Layia glandulosa*).

1966 Barnes–Jensen *Dict. UT Slang* 11, *Daisy*. . . A local name given Tidy Tips *(Layia glandulosa)*.

g A plant of the genus *Townsendia*. Cf **Easter daisy, ground daisy**

1973 Hitchcock–Cronquist *Flora Pacific NW* 554, *Townsendia*. . . Daisy.

3 A **spring beauty** (here: *Claytonia virginica*).

1940 Clute *Amer. Plant Names* 143, *C[laytonia] Virginica*. . . Daisy.

‡**4** See quot. [Prob *daisy* a humdinger]

1968 *DARE* (Qu. X20, . . *A black eye*) Inf **NY**80, Daisy.

5 See **daisy ham.**

daisy dwarf n

A **woolly daisy** (here: *Eriophyllum lanosum*).

1915 (1926) Armstrong–Thornber *Western Wild Flowers* 554, *Daisy Dwarf*. A quaint little desert plant, with thickish, pale gray-green leaves, covered with close white down, and pretty little flowers.

daisy fleabane n **chiefly eastern half US**

=**fleabane** (here: *Erigeron* spp).

1848 Gray *Manual of Botany* 206, *E[rigeron] annuum*. . . *Daisy Fleabane*. . . Fields and waste places, a very common weed. **1872** VT State Bd. Ag. *Report* 1.279, *E[rigeron] annuum,* and *E. strigosum, Daisy Fleabanes,* acrid plants, mingle their coarse stalks quite too freely with the hay from newly seeded land. **1916** Keeler *Early Wildflowers* 226, In the first place, the Daisy Fleabanes bloom in spring and early summer, not in autumn. **1931** Clute *Common Plants* 131, "Kiss-me-and-I'll-tell-you" replied an attractive native of the Southern States when asked the name of that plant which people of colder climes know as the daisy fleabane. **1953** Greene–Blomquist *Flowers South* 136, The daisy-fleabanes resemble on the one-hand [sic] daisies and on the other Asters. **1966** *DARE* (Qu. S26d) Inf **MI**31, Daisy fleabane. **1972** Brown *Wildflowers LA* 198, *Daisy Fleabane*. . . Ray flowers numerous, white to pink. Disk flowers yellow.

daisy ham n Also *daisy (roll)* [See quot 1977 *DARE* File] **chiefly NEng**

A pork shoulder butt which has been boned, cured, and rolled.

1959 Farmer *Cookbook* 183, *Daisy ham on a spit*. . . Select a long, narrow daisy ham. **1968** *Springfield Sunday Republican* (MA) 2 June 17, [Advt:] "Dubuque" lean mild *Daisies* small 2 to 3 lb. avg. **1977** *Athol Daily News* (MA) 10 Jan 10, [Advt:] Nepco tender lean daisy hams $1.29 lb. **1977** *DARE* File **Boston MA,** The term *daisy ham* was coined by an enterprising Armour salesman while observing an old meat cutter split and roll Boston butts in the old Faneuil Hall market about 60 years ago. The cross-sectional configuration of the roll looked to him very much like a daisy flower—hence the name was born. I believe only local processors use the term, in fact I'm sure of it. . . Daisy rolls and daisy hams are the same product. **1989** *DARE* File **cMA,** Daisy ham is still available in Amherst and Hadley, Massachusetts.

daitcher See **deutscher**

daitsch n [Var of *Deutsch* German; cf **Deutscher**]

1967–68 *DARE* (Qu. HH28, *Names and nicknames around here for people of foreign background*. . . *German*) Infs **MI**65, **NY**119, Daitsch [daɪč].

dake n [Prob var of **date**]

In marble play: see quot.

1958 *PADS* 29.32 **MO, WA,** *Dake*. . . A marble used as a stake in a game.

daked in adj phr [**dake**]

In marble play: see quot.

1958 *PADS* 29.32 **KY,** *Daked in*. . . Said of marbles placed within the ring.

da kine phr Also *da kind* **HI** Cf **honest kine**

See quot 1972.

1951 *AmSp* 26.26 **HI,** *Da kind* is a demonstrative-of-all-work. **1972** Carr *Da Kine Talk* 135 **HI,** *Kind, da kine* vs. *this kind of*—Used in innumerable ways, this is one of the most popular of all terms in Hawaii's nonstandard speech. It is a shibboleth—a phrase distinctive of Hawaii's local talk. The following examples show some of its patterns: *Substantive:* "Take da kine [Carr: broom] and sweep da floor." *Pronoun:* Q: "We goin' have one party. I like you come." A: "Where da kine [Carr: it] goin' be?" *Adjective:* Q: "You think Sam in love wid Alice?" A: "Man, he da kine [Carr: crazy] 'bout her!" *Suffix:* Q: "Oh, hey! We go show? Get da kine rock music!" A: "Oh, da rock-kine! I like!" **1981** *Pidgin To Da Max* np **HI,** [Cartoon dialogue:] " 'Ey Marie! Wheah da kine?" "Da kine?" "Yeah! You know, da kine!" "Oh. . . da kine! Try wait!" "T'anks eh, Marie!" "Bring 'em back when you pau [=done], yeah?" **1988** *DARE* File **csWI,** [Printed on a T-shirt in a sailboard shop:] *Da Kine / (Hawaii)*.

dakky v Also sp *daa'ky* [Pronc-sp for *darken*]

1909 *S. Atl. Qrly.* 8.43 **SC** [Gullah], Who dat dakky de hole? [=Who is that darkening (cutting off light from) the hole?] **1922** Gonzales *Black Border* 296 **sSC, GA coasts** [Gullah glossary], *Daa'ky*—darken, darkens, darkened, darkening.

Dakota potato n [From the edible tubers]

A **groundnut B1** (here: *Apios americana*).

1896 *Jrl. Amer. Folkl.* 9.185, *Apios tuberosa* . . Dakota-potato, Minn. **1900** Lyons *Plant Names* 39, *A. Apios*. . . Dakota Potato. . . Tubers edible. **1940** Brown *Amer. Cooks* 760 **SD,** Groundnuts, by the way, are called Dakota potatoes.

Dakota turnip n

=**Indian breadroot.**

1896 *Jrl. Amer. Folkl.* 9.186, *Psoralea esculenta*. . . Dakota turnip, Minn. **1910** Hodge *Hdbk. Amer. Indians* 2.760, *Tipsinah*—A name of "the wild prairie turnip used as food by the northwestern Indians". . . This plant is also known as the Dakota turnip.

dale See **dally** v

dalebuelta See **dally welter**

Dallas grass See **Dallis grass**

Dallas special n Cf *DS* F39

1949 *PADS* 11.5 **wTX** (as of c1920), *Dallas special*. . . A pocketknife with a blade longer than the legal limit. Common.

Dallis grass n Also folk-etym sp *Dallas grass* [See quot 1950]

A naturalized grass *(Paspalum dilatatum)* found chiefly in the South. Also called **bull grass 1, crowfoot 3, water grass**

1923 Amer. Joint Comm. Horticult. Nomenclature *Std. Plant Names* 358, *Paspalum dilatatum* . . Dallis Grass. **1943** *Democrat* 12 Aug. 4/4 *(DA)* **swAL,** Spend some time and gather Dallas grass seed to be planted in your pastures this fall. **1948** *Ponca City* (Okla.) *News* 4 July 16/4 *(DA)* **cnOK,** In the background is what is left of a field of clover and Dallis grass. **1950** Hitchcock–Chase *Manual Grasses* 615, Dallis grass was named for A.T. Dallis of La Grange, Ga., who grew it extensively. **1965–70** *DARE* (Qu. L9a, *Grass . . grown for hay*) Infs **AL**26, **GA**5, 9, 74, **MS**1, 4, **SC**63, Dallis grass; **GA**9, 74, **MS**1, **SC**63, Dallas grass; (Qu. S9, *Kinds of grass . . hard to get rid of*) Infs **AL**37, **AR**2, 49, 55, **CA**150, **TN**11, **TX**73, 91, Dallis grass. **1970** Correll *Plants TX* 161, *Paspalum dilatatum* . . Dallis grass.

dally n [Abbr for **dally welter 1**] **chiefly West**

A turn of rope made around a saddle horn or other object to act as a brake; hence attrib, using this method (rather than tying the rope to the saddle horn); also fig.

1915 (1922) Clark *Sun & Saddle* 78 **AZ,** This glory trail is rough,/ Yet even till the Judgment Morn / I'll keep this dally 'round the horn,/ For never any hero born / Could stop to holler: ' 'Nuff!' **1930** Raine–Barnes *Cattle* 313 **SW,** To avoid the strain the man using a reata never tied his rope to the saddle horn, but with about half its length in his left hand took a dozen turns or "dallies" . . around his saddle horn and then let it slowly slip as the strain came, thus easing the effect of the jerk. **1937** Coolidge *TX Cowboys* 57, One of them took a "dally" around the post and his new grass-rope popped like a pistol as it broke. **1937** *DN* 6.621 **swTX,** Cowpunchers are ordinarily either *tie-hard* or *dally men.* The "dally man" does not tie his rope to the pommel of the saddle, but very adeptly loops the rope or gives it a turn about the saddle horn. **1941** Writers' Program *Guide WY* 461, To 'take a dally' is to circle the rope around a post (snubbing post) or saddle horn in order to hold a roped animal. **1948** Baumann *Old Man Crow's Boy* 29, But the Old Man was a dally roper, and of course his boys were. **1953** *Western Folkl.* 12.185 **CA,** The Californian [used] a long rawhide *reata* made fast by means of dallies . . or turns. **1961** Adams *Old-Time Cowhand* 187, As a rule the cowman kept a dally on his temper. **1975** White *Git Along* 118 **AZ** (as of 1924), So Sandy Bob punched a hole in his rope,/ And he swang her straight and true,/ He lapped it on to the Devil's horns,/ An' he taken his dallies too.

dally v Also sp *dale* **chiefly West**

To make a **dally** n; to snub (a rope); also fig.

1921 *Outing* 77.246/3 **West,** When working with your rope loose (not tied to the saddle), the high horn is easier to "dally" on; that is to wind a few turns of the end after you have thrown. **1922** Rollins *Cowboy* 139, The user of that style needed more length in his rope than did the man who threw a "free" reata and thus, in other technical, interchangeable terms for this form of throw, "dallied," "daled," "vuelted," "felted," or "dale vuelted," his rope. **1940** Writers' Program *Guide NV* 77, In pursuit of his work a cowboy *dallies,* or holds an animal on the rope by wrapping it around the horn of the saddle counter clockwise. **1952** FWP *Guide SD* 84, *Dally:* to wind the rope around the saddle horn. **1968** Adams *Western Words* 88, *Dally your tongue*—A cowman's command to someone to stop talking.

dally boy, dally man, dally roper See **dally** n

dally welter n Also *dalebuelta, dally welta, ~ welte, dolly welter* [Span *dale vuelta* give it a turn] **West**

1 =**dally** n.

1908 (1966) Thorp *Songs Cowboys* 12, Whenever you start to tackle a steer / Never tie hard your maguey./ Put on your dalebueltas / 'Cordin' to California law. **1916** (1918) Lomax *Cowboy Songs* 382, Whenever you go to tie a snake [Footnote: Bad steer],/ Don't tie it to your tree;/ But take your dolly welters / 'Cordin' to California law. **1920** Hunter *Trail Drivers TX* 298, If a cowboy ropes a cow without hitching the rope to the saddle, "he takes a dolly welter." **1930** James *Lone Cowboy* 265, They had long rawhide ropes, made great big loops and instead of tying the other end, they take wraps, "dally welta," around the saddle horn. **1930** Knibbs *Songs Lost Frontier* 64 **West,** So long as your rope was stout enough and your terrapin shell stayed on,/ Dally-welte, or hard-and-fast, it was all the same to John. **1932** Bentley *Spanish Terms* 132, *Dale vuelta. . .* An expression often used by cowboys when ordering someone to wrap a lasso rope around the horn of a saddle, a post, or the like. From a command it has been adapted to a noun phrase in such an expression as 'he gave it a *dally welter.*'

2 See quot.

1939 Abbott-Smith *We Pointed Them* 45 **MT,** Davis was a dally welter, and he lost his rope. [Footnote to *dally welter:*] A roper who wraps the end of his rope around the saddle horn, Oregon style, instead of tying it fast the way the Texans do.

dam-buster n Also *Baptist dam-breaker* **esp Sth, S Midl**

A sudden heavy rain.

1962 Atwood *Vocab. TX* 38, *Torrential rain.* For an unusually heavy rain that does not last very long. . . A good many humorous phrases have a limited currency. . . Among these are . . *frog strangler, dam buster.* **1966–70** *DARE* (Qu. B25, . . *A very heavy rain*) Infs **AL**6, **GA**91, 92, **OH**45, **WV**1, 3, 4, 11, 14, Dam-buster; **SC**32, Baptist dam-breaker. **1986** Pederson *LAGS Concordance (Heavy rain)* 1 inf, **cGA,** Dam buster.

dame of honor n [Transl of Fr *dame d'honneur* literally "lady of honor" a lady-in-waiting]

A maid or matron of honor.

1966 *DARE* (Qu. AA17, *What other people . . do you usually have in a wedding party around here?*) Inf **NC**3, Maid of honor or dame of honor; **SC**11, Dame of honor—same as maid of honor, but older name for it. [Both Infs old]

damiana n [AmSpan]

1 A plant of the genus *Turnera,* esp *T. diffusa.*

1900 Lyons *Plant Names* 381, *Turnera* . . Damiana. **1942** Amer. Joint Comm. Horticult. Nomenclature *Std. Plant Names* 152/3, Damiana . . *Turnera diffusa.*

2 also *damianita, false damiana:* A low, spreading shrub *(Chrysactinia mexicana)* native to Texas.

1892 *DN* 1.247, *Damiána:* a small western Texas plant of the composite family, with yellow flowers, exhaling a strong aromatic odor. *Chrysactinia Mexicana* (Gray). Several plants bear the same name in Mexico. **1941** *Torreya* 41.53 **TX,** *Chrysactinia mexicana* . . Damiana. **1960** Vines *Trees SW* 1013, *Damianita—Chrysactinia mexicana* . . False Damiana. **1970** Correll *Plants TX* 1683, *Chrysactinia mexicana* . . Damianita.

damified ppl adj [Pronc-sp for *damnified* < *damnify* to cause injury, to damage; *OED* 1512 →; "Very common in 17th c.; now *rare*"]

Damaged.

1924 Raine *Land of Saddle-Bags* 101 **Appalachians,** His mill war consid'able damified (damaged). **1930** *VA Qrly. Rev.* 6.249 **S Midl,** The gentleman of the backwoods . . may testify . . that the roads are considerable damified by the floods.

damnation bow-wow(s) exclam, n

Damn! Hell.

1924 *DN* 5.265, *Damnation:* —, — *bow-wows.* **1967–68** *DARE* (Qu. CC9, . . *"That man is headed straight for ______."*) Inf **PA**49, Damnation bow-wows; (Qu. NN25a, *Weakened substitutes for 'damn'*) Inf **OH**28, Damnation bow-wow; (Qu. NN26b, *Weakened substitutes for 'hell'*) Inf **OH**74, Damnation bow-wow. [All Infs old]

damned sight See **sight**

damned Yankee See **damn Yankee**

damnly adv [Perh var of *damnably*]

Completely, quite.

1968 *DARE* (Qu. KK59, *To have a mistaken idea, or to be quite wrong about something: "If he thinks she'll help him, he's ______."*) Inf **NH**14, Damnly mistaken.

damn sight See **sight**

damn Yankee n Also *damned Yankee* **chiefly Sth**

A native of the northern US.

[**1812** *Niles' Natl. Reg.* 3.45/1, Take the middle of the road or I'll hew you down, you d'—d Yankee rascal.] **1833** in 1918 *MD Hist. Mag.* 13.361 **GA,** Their hatred of him [=Andrew Jackson] amounts to madness—it is only surpassed by their hatred of the d—d Yankees. **1862** in 1903 Norton *Army Letters* 79 **VA,** She wasn't going to have the d—d Yankees drink out of her well. **1904** *DN* 2.422 **nwAR,** *Yankee.* . . Northerner, whether from the east or west. 'He's a d—d yankee from Iowa.' **1909** Porter *Options* 95 **NYC,** You've had to go to work just as we 'damyankees,' as you call us, have always been doing. **1934** Carmer *Stars Fell on AL* 7, Y'all have to expect his sayin' things like that once in a while—till he gets used to us. He's a damn Yankee—and likely to tell the truth. **1966–70** *DARE* (Qu. HH28) Infs **AL**30, **AR**52, **LA**32, **TX**104, Damn Yankee; (Qu. HH30) Infs **AL**25, **NC**45, **TX**95, Damn Yankee; (Qu. HH31, *Somebody who is not from your community, and doesn't belong*) Inf **AL**10, Damn Yankee.

damp bug n Cf **water bug**

An unidentified insect.

c1955 in 1966 Goldstein-Byington *Two Penny Ballads* 143 **PA,** Damp bugs put into a "poke" around the neck will cure a cold and the sore throat.

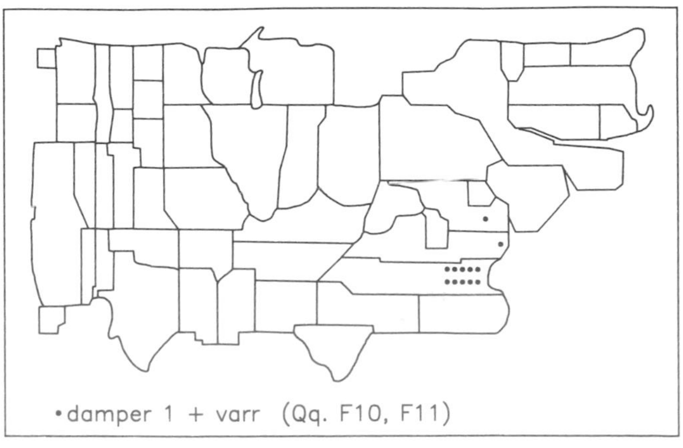

•damper 1 + varr (Qq. F10, F11)

damper n

1 =**cap** n[1] **2a. Mid Atl, esp eNC** See Map

1966–70 *DARE* (Qu. F10, *[On] . . wood-burning stoves—what do you call the round flat pieces that you take out to put in the wood?*) Infs **MD**44, **NC**8, 11, 14, 20, 25, 60, 76, 79, 82, **VA**47, Damper; **NC**1, Stove damper; (Qu. F11, *The thing you use to remove the lids . . from a wood-burning stove when it is hot*) Inf **NC**82, Damper handle; **NC**1, Damper hook; **MD**44, **NC**11, 76, 79, **VA**47, Damper lifter.

2 in phr *damper's down:* Used as a warning to a man that his trouser-fly is open.

1968 *DARE* (Qu. W24c) Inf **GA**17, Damper's down.

damper it v phr [Cf *put a damper on* to restrain]

1970 *DARE* (Qu. GG23c, . . *Other expressions [to tell someone to be patient]*) Inf **IL**116, Damper it—old-fashioned.

damper's down See **damper 2**

damsel bug n

An insect of the family Nabidae.

1905 Kellogg *Amer. Insects* 204, The damsel-bugs (Nabidae) are another small family of predaceous insects which usually lurk among flowers and foliage. **1926** Essig *Insects N. Amer.* 358, Nabidae.—Damsel Bugs. **1954** Borror–DeLong *Intro. Insects* 228, There are two common types of damsel bugs.

damselfly n [See quot 1949]

A slender **dragonfly** of the suborder Zygoptera. Cf **dancer 2, ruby spot, violet tail**

1905 Kellogg *Amer. Insects* 79, But of course all dragon-flies rest sometimes, and some of them, especially the damsel-flies, are at rest most of the time. **1940** Teale *Insects* 141, In addition to dragonflies, there are about seventy-five kinds of damsel-flies in the United States. **1949** Swain *Insect Guide* 65, Damselflies are weak flyers, delicately fashioned, with extremely slender abdomens; they hold their wings together over the back when at rest. **1964** Wigglesworth *Insects* 318, They [=dragonflies] either hold their wings extended laterally when at rest, as in the heavily built 'dragonflies' (Anisoptera), or fold them together above the back, as in the slender 'damsel-flies' (Zygoptera). **1967–70** *DARE* (Qu. R2) Inf **IL**119, Damselfly; **HI**14, Damselfly—like a miniature gray dragonfly; **PA**126, Damselfly is like it—she folds up her wings. **1980** Milne–Milne *Audubon Field Guide Insects* 382, Damselfly naiads, unlike dragonfly naiads, have external gills on the tip of the abdomen.

damsel plum n [Folk-etym for *damson plum*]

1967 *DARE* (Qu. I46) Inf **AL**34, Damsel ['dæmzəl] plums—big, purple.

dana clover n Also *dina clover* [Prob var of **ladino clover**]

Prob =**white Dutch clover.**

1968–70 *DARE* (Qu. L9b, *Hay from other kinds of plants*) Inf **NC**54, Dina clover; **VA**75, Dana clover—white blooms, very small plant.

dance n, v Usu |dæns|; also, **chiefly eNEng, eVA** |dans, dɑns|; for addit varr see quots Pronc-sp *daunce* Cf Pronc Intro 3.I.7

Std senses, var forms.

1831 in 1956 Eliason *Tarheel Talk* 309 **neNC,** *Dance*—daunce. **1902** *DN* 2.254 **eNEng,** It is well known that the long [æ] of such words as *path, . . dance,* etc. (as distinguished from the short [æ] in *pat, crack, passage,* etc.) has passed on to long [a] or even long [ɑ] . . in eastern New England as in southern England. But . . the conservative [æ], which still prevails, with but little variation, in most of America, is now crowding out the younger [a] or [ɑ] in New England. **1927** Shewmake *Engl. Pronc. VA* 22, There can be no doubt that the great majority of Virginians pronounce these words [=words like *path* and *dance*] with the sound that *a* has in *man,* but the pronunciation with the so-called broad . . *a* and also that which includes what is known as intermediate *a* are both heard at times. **1937** *AmSp* 12.284 **eVA,** The broad [ɑ] in *aunt, . . dance,* etc., persists in Eastern Virginia. *Ibid* **wVA,** The [æ] sound in *path, dance* . . is very high and tense and is often nasalized. **1942** *AmSp* 17.33 **seNY,** Dance . . [æ] 18 [infs] . . [a] 3 [infs]. **1942** Hall *Smoky Mt. Speech* 24 **eTN, wNC,** Dance . . ['dæ:ens]. **1961** Kurath–McDavid *Pronc. Engl.* 136, Words of the type of *calf, glass, dance,* in which the vowel is followed by a voiceless fricative or by /n/ plus a dental, have the vowel /æ/ of *bag* in all sections of the Eastern States, except that (1) in Eastern New England many speakers of all social levels use the /a/ of *car,* (2) some cultured urban speakers in other areas strive to adopt the /ɑ/ of *car,* and (3) some of the common folk (not the cultured) have a low-front [a] in such words along the coast of South Carolina and Georgia (from Charleston southward).

dance in the hog trough v phr Also *dance in the pig trough* [See quot 1977] **chiefly Midl**

Usu of a woman: to remain unmarried after a usu younger sibling is married; to be the last child in a family to remain unmarried; hence fig, to be abandoned—often used as a joc threat.

1936 *AmSp* 11.316 **Ozarks,** An unmarried girl whose younger sisters have married is said to be 'dancin' in a *pig trough.'* **1942** Warnick *Garrett Co. MD* 6 **nwMD** (as of 1900–18), When a younger sister or brother married before an older one, the latter was said to have to "dance in the hog trough." **1949** *NY Folkl. Qrly.* 5.300, She's left to dance in the hog trough. (Used to be said of a last unmarried daughter, according to Mrs. Frances Ramsay of Lake George.) [**1951** *PA Dutchman* 2.15.5/4 **sePA** (as of 1840s), My grandmother "hut im sei droke dunsa missa" (had to dance in the pig trough). In those days whenever a younger sister got married first, the elder one was said to have to dance in the pig trough.] **1956** McAtee *Some Dialect NC* 11, *Dance in the pig trough* . . be left in the lurch. "There I was dancin' in the pig trough." **c1960** *Wilson Coll.* **csKY,** *Dance in the hogtrough*—said about a girl whose younger sister gets married first. **1972** Cooper *NC Mt. Folkl.* 90, *Danced in the pig trough*—remained single after an older brother or sister had married. **1972** *KY Folkl. Rec.* 18.68, One or more students in each class have expressed familiarity with the expression, usually as *You'll have to dance in a pig trough* as a teasing and humorous remark to an unmarried girl who is approaching the age when she will be considered an "old maid." Some were specific in applying it to a girl whose younger sister seemed likely to marry first. Two students professed to use the expression themselves to tease a young male who was in danger of losing his girl friend to a rival. More often students have attributed the expression to older members of their families, especially grandparents. [**1977** *Western Folkl.* 36.169 **cnNE** (as of 1907), They made the older sister, which *I* was, and an older brother dance in the pig trough. Because we were older than the brother and sister getting married.] **1983** *MJLF* 9.1.47 **ceKY,** *Make her dance in the hog trough. . .* When a girl gets married before her older sister does, she is said to make her older sister "dance in the hog trough."

dancer n

1 pl; also *merry dancers:* The aurora borealis. [Scots dial]

1930 Shoemaker *1300 Words* 16 **cPA Mts** (as of c1900), *Dancers*—The Merry Dancers, or Northern Lights.

2 A **damselfly** of the genus *Argia.*

1980 Milne–Milne *Audubon Field Guide Insects* 386, *Short-stalked Damselflies*—"Dancers" (*Argia* spp.) *Ibid* 387, "Violet Dancer" *(Argia violacea)*. . . These striking damselflies are often seen flying in tandem over streams and ponds.

‡danchy n

1969 *DARE* (Qu. CC17, *Imaginary animals or monsters that people around here tell tales about*) Inf **TX**71, ['dænči], used to frighten children: "The danchy will get you."

dancing devil n **SW**

=**dust devil 1.**

1931 *AmSp* 6.389 **AZ,** To Arizonians the familiar whirlwinds of sand are "dancing devils." These whirlwinds are often fifty feet high, funnel shaped, and dance along on the little end. **1982** *TWA Ambassador* July 47, *Dust devil. . .* In the southwestern part of the United States, it is called a *dancing devil.*

dandelion n

1 Std: a plant of the genus *Taraxacum.* For other names see **arnica B2b, blow weed, butterflower 3, butterweed 7, carrot plant, china lettuce 2, coffee cup, dandy 2, down-head, fluff-weed 2, fortune-teller, granddaddy's whiskers, gray-haired grandmother, hawkbit 3, Irish daisy, lion's tooth, little captain, one o'clock, pissy-bed, puffball, puffweed, wine blossom, wine weed, yard flower**

2 Any of var plants which resemble the **dandelion 1,** as:

a =**false dandelion.**

1896 *Jrl. Amer. Folkl.* 9.193, *Troximon cuspidatum, . .* dandelion, Burnside, So. Dak.

b =**fall dandelion.**

1933 Small *Manual SE Flora* 1496, *Leontodon. . .* Dandelions.

dandelion bird n

A **goldfinch 1** (here: *Carduelis tristis*).

1956 MA Audubon Soc. *Bulletin* 40.254 **ME,** *Goldfinch. . .* Dandelion Bird. **1970** *DARE* (Qu. Q14, . . *Names . . for . . goldfinch*) Inf **VA**89, Wild canary, dandelion bird.

dander n [Etym uncert; freq connected with *dander* var of *dandruff*] Cf **dandruff**

Anger, temper.

1831 Finn *Amer. Comic Annual* 148 **VT,** A general roar of laughter brought Timmy on his legs. His dander was raised. **1839** Marryat *Diary* 1.198, "Rise my dandee [sic] up," from the human hair; and a nasty idea. **1844** Thompson *Major Jones's Courtship* 77 **GA,** I felt my dander risin when the imperent cus went and tuck a seat along side of Miss Mary. **1899** (1912) Green *VA Folk-Speech* 141, *Dander. . .* Anger; passion. "When his dander is up." **1905** *DN* 3.7 **cCT. 1907** *DN* 3.185 **NH. 1908** *DN* 3.304 **eAL, wGA. 1910** *DN* 3.440 **wNY. 1914** *DN* 4.71 **ME. 1942** Warnick *Garrett Co. MD* 7 **nwMD** (as of 1900–18), *Get one's dander up* . . become enraged. **1965–70** *DARE* (Qu. GG4, *Stirred up, angry: "When he saw them coming he got ———."*) 25 Infs, **scattered,** His dander up; (Qu. A21, *When someone is in too much of a hurry you might say, "Now just slow down! Don't ———."*) Inf **MN**33, Get your dander up; (Qu. GG23a, *If you speak sharply to somebody to make him be patient, you say, "Now just keep your ———."*) Infs **LA**35, **NE**11, **OH**57, **PA**175, **SD**8, **TX**91, Dander down; (Qu. GG23b, *If you speak sharply to somebody to make him be patient, you might say, "Hold ———."*) Inf **IN**35, Your dander down, don't get your dander up; (Qu. GG23c, . . *Other expressions to tell someone to be patient*) Infs **IL**4, 82, 136, **IN**35, **MN**33, 35, Don't get (*or* git) your dander up; (Qu. GG24, *Other words meaning to frighten: "Now don't let those fellows ——— you."*) Inf **WI**65, Get your dander up; (Qu. GG40, *Words or expressions meaning violently angry*) Inf **MN**33, Had his dander up; (Qu. II29b, . . *To explain the unpleasant effect that [a dislikable] person has on you: "He just ———."*) Infs **CA**53, **MO**7, **SD**3, **VA**101, Gets my dander up.

dandie-doe n Cf **dandle**

1966 *DARE* (Qu. EE31, *Playground equipment with a long board for two children to sit on and go up and down in turn*) Inf **AL**3, Dandie-doe [dændi do].

dandle n Also *dandle board, dandling board* [*dandle* to move (a child) up and down on the knee] **chiefly wRI**

=seesaw.

1933 *Hanley Disks* **Providence RI,** [Inf:] And of course the dandle, which I understand is known only in Rhode Island. . . [Hanley:] Did you always call it the dandle? [Inf:] Always. . . A saw horse in the middle and a long board and a child at each end. **1943** *LANE* Map 577 *(Seesaw)* 15 infs, **RI,** Dandle; 4 infs, **RI,** Dandle-board; 1 inf, **RI,** Dandling board. **1947** *Sun* (Baltimore MD) 20 Jan 1/2 *(Hench Coll.),* Children playing on a seesaw in the South . . a dandleboard in New England . . would be doing the same thing. **1969** *DARE* (Qu. EE31, *Playground equipment with a long board for two children to sit on and go up and down in turn*) Infs **RI**3, 6, 12, Dandle.

dandle v, hence vbl n *dandling* [**dandle** n]

To ride on a seesaw.

1931–33 *LANE Worksheets* **swRI,** We dandled through a fence or on a sawhorse; **cwRI,** I went dandling ['dændlɪŋ] when I was a young one.

dandle board See **dandle** n

dandling See **dandle** v

dandling board See **dandle** n

dandruff n

=dander.

1950 *WELS Suppl.* **csWI,** I've got my dandruff up! (Not used humorously). **1966–69** *DARE* (Qu. GG4, *Stirred up, angry: "When he saw them coming he got ———."*) Infs **GA**67, **KY**60, **MS**1, **NC**40, **NY**45, His dandruff up; (Qu. GG23c, *Any other expressions [to tell someone to be patient]*) Infs **KY**60, **TX**16, Don't get your dandruff up; (Qu. GG40, . . *Expressions meaning violently angry*) Inf **MS**21, He got up his dandruff.

‡dandual n

1970 *DARE* (Qu. H43, *Foods made from parts of the head and inner organs of an animal*) Inf **VA**46, Dandual ['dænduᵊl]—lights [=lungs], red pepper, salt, smoked [FW: *l* barely pronounced].

dandy adv

1952 Brown *NC Folkl.* 1.532 **c,eNC,** *Dandy. . .* Very. "She is feeling dandy fine today, thank you."

dandy n

1 A **bearberry 2** (here: *Arctostaphylos uva-ursi*).

1959 Carleton *Index Herb. Plants* 35, *Dandies:* Arctostaphyllos [sic] uva-ursi.

2 A **dandelion 1.**

1967–68 *DARE* (Qu. S11) Infs **AZ**2, **CA**41, Dandies.

dandyfunk n Also *dunde(r)funk, dundyfunk* [Orig naut]

A pudding usu made from crushed ship's biscuit, molasses, and grease.

1849 in 1988 *AmSp* 63.114, If mush runs low or dundyfunk, We eat our fill of cold salt junk. **1883** in 1959 *AmSp* 34.28, Dandy funk—A mess made of powdered biscuit, molasses, and slush. **1892** Duval *Young Explorers* 131 **swTX,** We sat down to a repast that would have tempted the appetite of an anchorite— . . fried bass and perch, flanked by platters of "dundefunk" highly seasoned with chili pepper. **1893** Barra *Tale of 2 Oceans* 76, Dandyfunk is a dish composed of navy biscuit soaked in water, mashed with a pestle, mixed with fat from the coppers in which the meat is boiled, sweetened with molasses and flavored with allspice, then put into a pan and baked in the oven. It isn't a very high-toned dish, but in the absence of something better it is very palatable to a sailor. **1900** *Boston Ev. Globe* 15 Oct. 7 *(DA),* Another institution dating from antiquity is 'cracker hash,' or 'hardtack hash.' . . The addition of molasses before baking makes 'dunderfunk' of this concoction, but molasses, . . is . . an expensive article of food,—hence dunderfunk is as rare as plum duff. **1927** *CA Hist. Soc. Qrly.* 6.207, By way of variety in our diet we had . . "dandy funk," a dish consisting of ship-biscuit and molasses, baked in the oven. **1939** (1962) Thompson *Body & Britches* 209 **NY,** Yankee ship's gone down the river,/ . . And what do you think they got for dinner?/ . . A dandy-funk and donkey's liver. **1941** *LANE* Map 292 *(Apple dumpling)* 1 inf, **ceMA,** [ˌdʌn'di fʌnt] [sic], fishermen's term for *pan dowdy.* **1945** Colcord *Sea Language* 63 **ME, Cape Cod, Long Island,** *Dandyfunk.* A sailor's term for a pudding made of cracker crumbs, slush and molasses.

danger adj, adv

Dangerous; dangerously.

1917 *DN* 4.410 **wNC,** *Danger. . .* Dangerous. "Thet's a powerful danger axe." **1940** *AmSp* 15.52 **S Midl,** Adjectives are formed from nouns: 'Hits a danger-long way.' 'A desert-lookin' hanted house.' **1943** Chase *Jack Tales* 64 **wNC,** Well, King, that sounds like the dangerest thing of all. **1949** Guthrie *Way West* 285, Which side is dangerest?

danger list, on the adj phr

1969 *DARE* (Qu. BB42, *If a person is very sick you say he's ———*) Infs **MA**38, 57, 69, On the danger list.

dangerous adj Usu |'denǰ(ə)rəs|; also |'denǰəs| Pronc-spp *dang'us, dainjus*

A Forms.

1891 *DN* 1.129 **cwNY,** |denǰəs| < *dangerous.* **1922** Gonzales *Black Border* 296 **sSC, GA coasts** [Gullah glossary], *Dainjus*—dangerous. **1927** Kennedy *Gritny* 226 **sLA** [Black], A cane-knife was such a dang'us-lookin' weepon.

B Sense.

Critically ill. [*OED* a1616 →; "now *dial.* and *U.S. colloq.*"]

1828 (1910) Ayer *Diary* 280 **MA,** Most of my friends thought me dangerous, and I did indeed think myself so. **1881** (1883) Cooke *Somebody's Neighbors* 348 **NEng,** Freedom's dreadful sick now: reelly [sic] he's dangerous. **1884** Hay *Bread-Winners* 253 **nOH,** He's dangerous; they don't think he'll live through the night. **1899** (1912) Green *VA Folk-Speech* 141, He is not *dangerous,* but very sick. **1905** *DN* 3.7 **cCT,** He's quite sick, but not dangerous. **1907** *DN* 3.211 **nwAR. c1960** *Wilson Coll.* **csKY. 1967–69** *DARE* (Qu. BB42, *If a person is very sick you say he's ———*) Infs **IL**30, **NJ**58, **TN**3, Dangerous.

dangerous adv Cf Intro "Language Changes" II.8

Dangerously.

1967 *DARE* (Qu. BB42, *If a person is very sick you say he's ———*) Inf **TN**12, Dangerous ill.

dangersome adj [*OED* 1567 →] *old-fash* Cf Intro "Language Changes" III.1

Dangerous.

1851 Hooper *Widow Rugby's Husband* 50 **AL,** It was dangersome for me to stay on the deck. **1885** Twain *Huck. Finn* 171 **MO,** He had ciphered out his idea about how to run in daylight without it being dangersome for Jim. **1891** Page *Elsket* 137 **VA** [Black], You mus'n' say you ain' do it, 'cuz dat's dangersomer 'n allowing you *is* do it. **1947** Ballowe *The Lawd* 67 **LA** [Black], "That Joomaker [=Jamaican] dangersome," Unc' Brutus said. "His *muti* too strong fer me."

dangleberry n

1 A **huckleberry 1** (here: *Gaylussacia frondosa*). Also called **blue dangler, blue huckleberry 2, blue tangle, tangleberry**

1848 Gray *Manual of Botany* 259, *G[aylussacia] frondosa*. . . Dangleberry. **1903** Small *Flora SE U.S.* 892, *Gaylussacia frondosa*. . . Dangleberry. **1941** *LANE* Map 274, 1 inf, **nwRI,** Dangleberry, hangs from the stalk like a cherry; 1 inf, **seRI,** Dangleberry, blue or black, grows in clusters on a high bush on swampy land; 1 inf, **swMA,** Dangleberries, grow in clusters, ripen late; 1 inf, **swMA,** Dangleberries. **1947** *Amer. Midland Naturalist* 38.54 **MD,** *Gaylussacia frondosa* (Dangleberry). Common (locally abundant) in pine-oak forest and upland oak forest. **1951** Hough *Singing in Morning* 95 **Martha's Vineyard MA,** The high-bush blueberry, often referred to as the dangleberry on the Vineyard because the berries dangle on long stems. **1969–70** *DARE* (Qu. I44, *What kinds of berries grow wild around here?*) Inf **CT**39, Dangleberries—blue, like huckleberries; on short bush; **MA**98, Dangleberries—blueberries with long stem; seedy; **RI**16, Dangleberries—light blue, seedy, hang down off long branches; grow in cut-down woods. **1974** (1977) Coon *Useful Plants* 135, *Gaylussacia frondosa*—Dangleberry.

2 A **deerberry a** (here: *Vaccinium stamineum*).

1833 Eaton *Botany* 380, *Vaccinium stamineum*, squaw whortleberry, deer berry, dangle berry. **1889** (1971) Farmer *Americanisms* 192/1, *Dangle Berry*.—A species of the blue whortleberry.

dangus n See **dingus**

dang'us adj See **dangerous** adj

Daniel n Usu |'dænjəl|; also |'dænəl, -ɪl, -ɛl| Pronc-spp *Dan'el, Dan(i)l*

Std sense, var forms.

1801 in 1956 Eliason *Tarheel Talk* 309 **ceNC,** *Daniel*—Danil. **1867** Twain *Jumping Frog* 14 **cCA,** Dan'l Webster was the name of the frog. **1892** *DN* 1.238 **cwMO,** *Daniel*. This name is pronounced in Kansas City both as [dænjɛl] and [dænl] [*DN* Ed: as in New England, where, however, a third pronunciation [dænɪl] or [-ɛl] is also known]. **1907** *DN* 3.185 **seNH,** *Dan'el*. . . Daniel. Universal. **1911** Wharton *Ethan Frome* 149 **wMA,** Dan'l Byrne's goin' over to the Flats to-day noon. **1934** *Hanley Disks* **csMA,** Inf, age 73, says her teacher used to be very strict about not saying ['dænəl]. **1938** Liebling *Back Where* 39 **seNY,** Old Dan'l Drew and the Peoples Line they bought out the opposition. **1940** *Time* 4 Mar 66/2, As rock-ribbed old Farmer Dawson says . . "If Dan'l Boone was livin' today, . . they'd make him get a non-resident huntin' license in every State." **1942** Hall *Smoky Mt. Speech* 66 **eTN, wNC,** Daniel [ˌdænəl] [sic]. **1959** *VT Hist.* new ser 27.132, *Daniel* ['dænəl] . . pronc. Common.

Daniel gull n

=**great black-backed gull.**

1917 *Wilson Bulletin* 29.2.75, *Larus marinus*. . . Daniel gull, Plymouth, Mass. **1956** MA Audubon Soc. *Bulletin* 40.22, *Great Black-Backed Gull*. . . Daniel Gull (Mass.)

daniel-line n [Folk-etym var of **dandelion**]

c1938 in 1970 Hyatt *Hoodoo* 2.1400 **seVA,** They only uses the red oak bark, cherry bark and the daniel-line [Hyatt: dandelion] flowers.

Danil See **Daniel**

Danish pastry n Also *Danish (roll)* **chiefly Nth, N Midl, West** See Map

A pastry or cake made with shortening and raised with yeast.

1934 (1943) *W2, Danish pastry*. **1950** Schulberg *Disenchanted* 44 **swCA,** The waitress . . brought him . . Danish pastry and coffee. **1965–70** *DARE* (Qu. H32, . . *Fancy rolls and pastries*) 75 Infs, **chiefly Nth, N Midl, West,** Danish pastry (*or* pastries); 35 Infs, **scattered Nth, N Midl, West,** Danish rolls; **CO**11, Danish pineapple rolls; (Qu. H28, *Different . . types of doughnuts [or other word]*) Inf **WA**13, Danish roll; (Qu. H29, *A round cake, cooked in deep fat, with jelly inside*) Infs **MI**1, Danish roll; **WI**20, Danish pastry; (Qu. H63, *Kinds of desserts*) Inf **LA**23, Danish pastry; (Qu. H65, *Foreign foods favored by people around here*) Inf **KY**5, Danish rolls; (Qu. HH30) Infs **CT**19, **MO**13, Danish pastry. **1977** *Capital Times* (Madison WI) 31 May advt suppl, We're very proud of the bakery products . . pies, cakes, Danish, you name it.

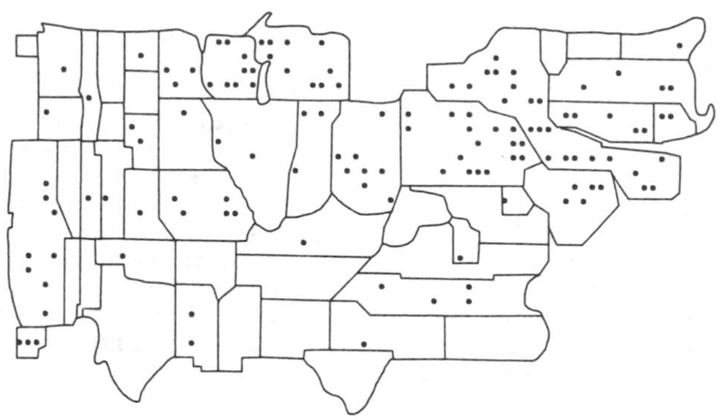

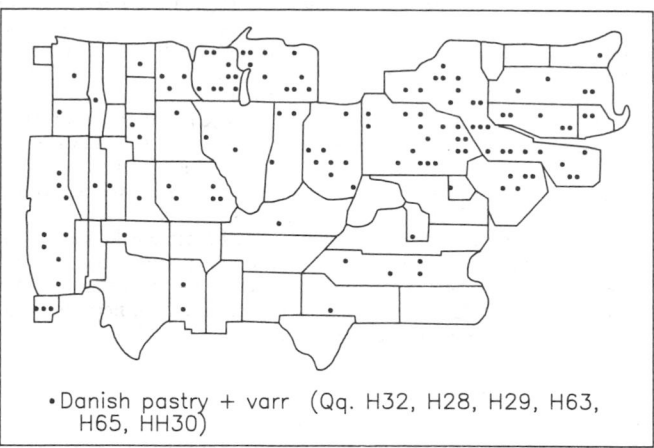

•Danish pastry + varr (Qq. H32, H28, H29, H63, H65, HH30)

dank v [Cf *OED dank* v. 1 "To wet, damp, moisten. . . *Obs.*"]

To apply, put on.

1939 *Esquire* 11.4.73/3 **neKY,** He danks big brushes of thick coal tar on the broken roof.

danke schoen exclam |'daŋkə šen, 'dæŋkɪ-|; for addit varr see quots Also *danke (sehr)* [Ger] **scattered, but esp N Cent, NEast** See Map

Thank you.

1956 *AmSp* 31.142, A sizable body of German words and idioms has entered the lingo of Army troops in Germany and Austria. . . *Danke schön* (Thanks; pronounced to rhyme with *fern*). **1963** Eddie Cano Quartet *Danke Schoen* (Phonodisc). **1965–70** *DARE* (Qu. II39, . . *Ways . . of saying 'Thank you'*) Infs **IN**35, **IL**4, 57, **MN**36, **OH**77, **PA**71, **WI**5, 51, 62, 71, Danke schoen; **MD**9, **MO**38, **OH**1, **WI**22, ['daŋkə šen]; **IL**61, ['dʌŋkə šen]; **IA**22, **NJ**36, ['dankə šen]; **GA**23, ['dæŋkɪˌšen]; **MD**30, ['dankə šən]; **MI**110, [dankə šun]; **MA**30, ['dankiˌšɝn]; **NJ**28, [dʌnkə še]; **NJ**43, ['dʌnkəˌšɪn]; **NY**105, [dʌŋkɚ šɝn]; **NY**114, ['dʌŋkə šiˀn]; **MA**6, Danke sehr [daŋkə sɚ]; **CA**1, Danke; **MI**123, [dɔnkə].

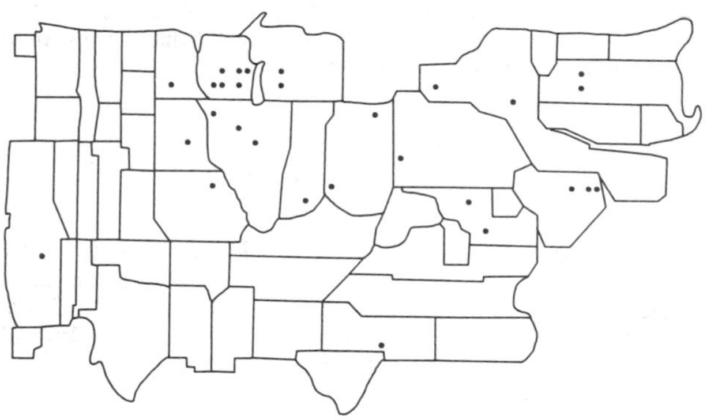

•danke schoen + varr (Qu. II39)

Dan'l See **Daniel**

dansy See **donsie**

d'ant v [By contr]

1952 Brown *NC Folkl.* 1.532, *D'ant* [dɔnt, dɔ̃(t)]. . . *Don't want*. "I d'ant a thing to eat."—Granville county.

Dan Tucker n [Prob from the song "Old Dan Tucker" by D.D. Emmett (1815–1904)] Cf **tucker**

1905 *DN* 3.76 **nwAR,** *Dan Tucker*. . . The name of a young people's dancing game, similar to the New England game of *'Tucker.'*

daoun See **down A**

daow adv Also *daowd, dow* [Varr of *no*] **chiefly NEng**

No—used to express emphatic denial.

1959 *VT Hist.* new ser 27.133, Dow [dou]. . . No. This and [do] are pronunciations of the word *no,* heard especially in rural areas. The sound has a nasal quality, and the whole word is pronounced quickly and sharply. It is a strong use of the word *no,* and it indicates conviction on the part of the speaker. **1975** Gould *ME Lingo* 69, *Daow!*—Impossible to toss this off unless to the manner born. It is the coastal Maine emphatic for *no!* **1977** *DARE* File **cnMA,** I've heard my brother (born 1924) deny a statement with a very emphatic *daow.* **1979** Lewis *How to Talk Yankee* [8] **nNEng,** *Daow.* . . Downeasters frequently use this expression instead of "No." (*Pronunciation Note:* it rhymes with the name of the late Chairman of the People's Republic of China.) **1980** *NADS Letters,* My father, who was born and bred in the Southern Tier of New York State and has spent a good portion of his life in the foothills of the Adirondacks (and, as far as I know, has never been to coastal Maine) has always used [do:] as an emphatic, often scoffing, negative. **1982** *DARE* File **coastal ME,** Daowd: means No, usually in answer to a question.

daown See **down A**

dap n, v

1958 McCulloch *Woods Words* 45 **Pacific NW,** *Dap.* . . A notch cut in a timber. . . To cut a notch in a timber so that another timber will fit into it.

dap adj Also, by reinterpretation as ppl adj, *dapped (down),* pronc-sp *dapt* *among Black speakers*

Dapper, well-dressed, good-looking.

1970 Major *Dict. Afro-Amer. Slang* 44, *Dap:* (1950's) dapper, dressed in style. **1970** *DARE* (Qu. W38, *When a man dresses himself up in his best clothes, you say he's* ______) Inf **FL**48, Dap. [Inf Black] **1971** Roberts *Third Ear* np [Black], *Dap, dapt* . . stylish; impeccably attired. **1972** Claerbaut *Black Jargon* 62, *Dapt* . . attractive; highly appealing. **1980** Folb *Runnin' Down* 111 **Los Angeles CA** [Black], There is even a larger vocabulary that refers to being well dressed *(tabbed, suited down, . . ragged out, . . dapped down, choked down).* Finally, there are expressions reserved for being extraordinarily well dressed *(clothed heavy, dapped to a tee, decked to death).*

dapa(s) See **dupa**

dapp v [PaGer *dappe* (Ger *tappen*)] Cf **doppich**

See quots.

1968 *Helen Adolf Festschrift* 35 **cePA,** The verb to *dapp* . . is used in the sense of 'to walk clumsily or awkwardly'; for example, "He dapped all over the place." **1987** *Jrl. Engl. Ling.* 20.169 **ePA,** *Dapp* 'to walk clumsily or awkwardly.' [11 of 100 infs indicated that they use this term; only one of them was under 45 years of age.]

dapp adj See **doppich**

dapped (down) See **dap** adj

dapper n Cf **didapper, dopper** n[1] **1**

1 =**bufflehead 2.**

1888 Trumbull *Names of Birds* 82, *Buffle-head* . . at Buzzard's Bay, Mass., *Dapper.* *Ibid* 110, *Ruddy duck* . . at Provincetown, Mass., . . Dapper. **1923** U.S. Dept. Ag. *Misc. Circular* 13.23, *Bufflehead (Charitonetta albeola).* . . *In local use* . . dapper (Mass.) **1925** (1928) Forbush *Birds MA* 1.252, *Charitonetta albeola* . . *Buffle-head.* . . Dapper. **1982** [see **2** below].

2 =**ruddy duck.**

1888 [see **1** above]. **1925** (1928) Forbush *Birds MA* 1.280, *Erismatura jamaicensis* . . *Ruddy Duck. Other names:* Butter-ball; . . Dapper; . . Spike-tail. **1982** Elman *Hunter's Field Guide* 192, *Ruddy Duck:* (*Oxyura jamaicensis,* also classified as *Erismatura jamaicensis* . .) *Common & Regional Names:* booby . . dapper, . . sinker. *Ibid* 211, *Bufflehead (Bucephala albeola)*—*Common & Regional Names:* butterball, . . dapper, . . woolhead.

dapper Dan n

=**fancy Dan 1.**

1967–70 *DARE* (Qu. AA6a, . . *A man who is fond of being with women and tries to attract their attention*) Infs **IL**10, **PA**245, Dapper Dan; (Qu. AA6b) Inf **SC**68, Dapper Dan; (Qu. W39, . . *Referring to a person's best clothes*) Inf **MA**7, Dapper Dan. **1986** Chapman *New Dict. Amer. Slang* 96, *Dapper* (or *fancy*) *Dan* . . An ostentatiously well-groomed man, usu one not inured to hard work.

dappich See **doppich**

dappledy See **dapply**

dapple-pod n

A **milk vetch** (here: *Astragalus lentiginosus*).

1941 Jaeger *Wildflowers* 122 **Desert SW,** *Dapple-pod. Astragalus lentiginosus Fremontii.* . . The mottled, papery, bladder-like pod is probably the most characteristic feature of this plant.

dapply adj Also *dappledy* [Varr of *dapple(d)*]

1966–68 *DARE* (Qu. K37, *What do you call a horse of mixed colors?*) Infs **MD**38, **MN**23, **NY**75, Dapply gray; **AR**21, Dappledy.

dapt See **dap** adj

dar See **dare** v **A1**

dare v

A Forms. Note: The non-standard forms treated here occur almost exclusively in auxiliary uses (but cf **A2** below, quot 1975). In std literary use *dare* is regular (past, past pple *dared*) when used transitively and usu when used with an infin with *to;* when used as an auxiliary it may occur with a bare infin and be followed by a subject pronoun or *not* to mark interrogation or negation, and show the following irregular forms: pres 3rd sg *dare (How dare he come? He dare not come),* archaic 2nd sg *darst;* past *durst.* Modern colloquial usage tends to avoid all irregular forms and constructions.

1 pronc-sp *dar.*

1851 Hooper *Widow Rugby's Husband* 128 **AL,** Who dars to call me *hit*? **1893** Shands *MS Speech* 26, *Dar* (da). Negro for *dare.*

2 pres, past, past pple: usu *dare(s), dared, dared* respectively; also *da(r)st, dares't*—sometimes used with hypothetical force. Note: The evidence is not sufficient to determine whether all users of this form use it in all these cases. [These forms prob represent primarily the archaic past *durst* infl by the vowel of pres *dare;* back-formation from the negative *da(r)snt* (**A3** below), following the analogy of *durst/dursn't,* and the archaic 2nd sg *darst* may also have played a role. For the tendency to confuse past and pres in this verb, see *OED dare* v.[1] 1. c. 5.]

1867 Lowell *Biglow* xxvii **'Upcountry' MA,** He [=the Yankee] says *darst.* **1877** *Harper's New Mth. Mag.* 54.299/1 **CT,** Stumped it all the way in the dark, did she? . . There ain't another gal in Pasco darst to ha' done it. **1893** *DN* 1.277 **wCT,** Dare—[past, past pple:] darst (negative in pres. *dassent* [pron. [dæsn̩t]]). **1899** Garland *Boy Life* 145 **nwIA** (as of c1870s), "You dassent fight." . . "We'll show you in about a minute whether we dast or not." **1909** *DN* 3.410 **cnME,** *Darst, v. i.* Dares or durst. **1910** *DN* 3.453 **VT,** *Dăst.* . . For dare, used like "dasn't" in all persons and numbers, altho it is usually preceded by the auxiliary "had." "You dasn't jump off that beam." "I had dast." Used much less frequently than dasn't and mostly by school-children in my neighborhood. **1936** *AmSp* 11.348 **eTX,** The form *dast* is often heard for *dares:* 'I wonder if he dast.' The negative is *dasn't.* (The author has never heard the form *darst.*) . . Preterit indicative. . . *Dast* (negative, *dasn't*). **1942** *Esquire* 18.1.50/3 **neKY,** All married where I darst set my feet on their ground. . . Seven marriages now and six I can visit. **1947** Guthrie *Big Sky* 78 **West,** Then we pole her along, close as we dast, and tie up. **1956** Moody *Home Ranch* 74 **CO** (as of 1911), Don't reckon we dast venture into them mountains till it's over. **1975** Gould *ME Lingo* 69, *Darst, durst, dasst*—Dared in the sense of challenged: "He darst me to hit him, so I did." Also in the sense of being rash: "Never darst talk back to the cap'n." **1982** [see **B** below].

3 as infin: usu *dare;* also *da(r)st, darse, das(s).* [Back-formation from **A2** above; the forms *darse, das(s)* have evid lost the final *-t* by assim to the following *to.*]

1890 *DN* 1.73 **NEng,** "You don't darse to" and "You don't darst" = you dare not. **1892** *DN* 1.210 **NEng,** *Dass* [dæs]. . . "I don't quite dass." **1892** *KS Univ. Qrly.* 1.96 **KS,** He don't dast to do it. **1892** [see **A4a** below]. **1899** Chesnutt *Conjure Woman* 100 **csNC** [Black], Solomon didn' das' ter let on 'bout w'at he 'spicioned. **1908** Lincoln *Cy Whittaker* 43 **MA,** He didn't dast to rub one shoe against t'other, it sounded up so. **1916** *DN* 4.273 **NE,** I wanted to do it but I didn't dast. **1933** Rawlings *South Moon* 78 **nFL,** Marthy don't dast leave the house. *Ibid* 318, He wouldn't dast show no money at the store, no-ways. **1942** McAtee *Dial. Grant Co. IN* 22 (as of 1890s), *Dass* . . dare; not an exclusive substitute, but familiar in such phrases as: "I dassn't", or

"Don't you dass to do it". **1948** Hurston *Seraph* 31 **wFL** (as of c1920), Git! And don't you dast to foot this place again. **1953** Atwood *Survey of Verb Forms* 33, Some four or five Eastern informants substitute *don't* (or *wouldn't*) *das(t) to go* /dont dæs tə go/ in this phrase [="You (dare not) go"]. **1963** Owens *Look to River* 58 **TX,** Jed wouldn't dast touch it, would you, Jed? **1974** Fink *Mountain Speech* 6 **wNC, eTN,** They don't dast go.

4 Neg forms:

a pres exc 3rd sg: usu *dare not;* also *daren't, durn't;* infreq *dursent, durstn't, ders(e)n't, daredn't.* [Contractions of *dare not, durst not, dared not;* for the use of past for pres see etym at **A2** above.]

1843 (1916) Hall *New Purchase* 355 **IN,** I daren't give you leave—I mustn't *see* you go. **1871** Eggleston *Hoosier Schoolmaster* 16 **IN,** You durn't do it. **1892** Eggleston *Hoosier Schoolmaster* 41 **IN,** [Footnote:] *Durn't, daren't, dasent, dursent,* and *don't dast* are forms of this variable negative heard in the folk-speech of various parts of the country. The tenses of this verb seem to have got hopelessly mixed long ago, even in literary use, and the speech of the people reflects the historic confusion. **1943** [see **B** below]. **1946** [see **A4c** below]. **1953** Atwood *Survey of Verb Forms* 33, *Daren't* [in the context "You (dare not) go"] /dɛrənt/ or /dærənt/ is uncommon in the East, appearing in the speech of less than 35 informants... *Durstn't* /dɜsənt/ is even more rare, there being but seven widely scattered occurrences... *Daredn't* /dærdənt/ appears four times. **1973** *PADS* 60.77 **seNC,** *Dare not...* Among our informants, only one used a contraction, *daren't.* **1986** Pederson *LAGS Concordance* **Gulf Region** *(You dare not)* 16 infs, Daren't; 1 inf, Durstn't.

b pres 3rd sg: usu *dares not;* also *dast.* [Prob by phonetic simplification of *dassn't* in dialects lacking the positive form *dast;* see **A2** above, quot 1910, **A4c** below, quot c1960]

1894 Riley *Armazindy* 4 **IN,** Plenty of *in*-vites to go,/ But das't leave the house, you know—/ 'Less'n *Sund'ys* sometimes. **1976** Garber *Mountain-ese* 20 **Appalachians,** He da'st play in the snow, lessen he might ketch his death uv dampness.

c pres, past: usu *dare(s) not, dared not* respectively; also *dar(e)sn't, darshin, das(s)n't, das(s)ent, dazzent.* Note: See note at **A2** above. Cf **daresome 1**

1795 Dearborn *Columbian Grammar* 135, Dazzent for Dare not. **1815** Humphreys *Yankey in England* 104, *Dasent,* dare not. **1836** (1955) *Crockett Almanacks* 54 **wTN,** He dassent so much as look over his shoulder; he was stuck in the mud like a Mississippi sawyer. **1843** (1916) Hall *New Purchase* 355 **IN,** He killed four or five of us; while we daresn't quit ranks and kill him. **1848** Lowell *Biglow* 143 **'Upcountry' MA,** Darsn't, used indiscriminately, either in singular or plural number, for *dare not, dares not,* and *dared not.* **1884** Twain *Huck. Finn* 401 **MO,** She was afraid to go to bed, but she dasn't set up. **1890** *DN* 1.73 **NEng,** Darsn't [dasnt]: dare(s) not. "I, you, he, we, they darsn't." .. Also pronounced [dæsnt]. **1892** [see **A4a** above]. **1893** Shands *MS Speech* 26, *Dassent* [dæsn̩t]. Negro for *dare not.* **1907** *DN* 3.185 **NH,** *Dassent...* Dare not. Conjugated: I dassent, you dassent, he dassent, we dassent, you dassent, they dassent. "I dassent tackle it." **1908** *DN* 3.304 **eAL, wGA,** *Da(r)sen't...* Dare not. (Originally third person *daresn't.*) "I dassen't touch it." **1909** *DN* 3.410 **cnME,** *Daresent... Dassent.* .. Dare not. **1910** *DN* 3.453, **seVT,** *Dasn't* [dæzn̩t] or [dæsn̩t]... Common... Same form used for all persons and numbers. **1910** *DN* 3.440 **cwNY,** I'll bet you dassent do it. **1913** *DN* 4.10 **MN,** *Dasn't...* Dare(s) not. **a1942** in 1944 *ADD* **cWV,** *Dassn't...* ['dɑršin] 'You darshin' to do this.' Older generation. Distinct *r.* **1942** Warnick *Garrett Co. MD* 6 **nwMD** (as of 1900–18), She dass'nt do it. **1946** *AmSp* 21.97 **sIL,** The word *das'n't* is used here .. although *daren't* is sometimes heard here also. **1953** Atwood *Survey of Verb Forms* 33, The negative form is recorded in the context "You (dare not) go." Most cultured informants lack a negative contraction of this verb, and about half the noncultured in s. N. Eng. fail to give such a form... The form *dasn't* /dæsənt/ is more common than any other .. in N. Eng.; and in N.Y... it is almost the only such form in use... *Daresn't* /dærsənt/ or /dersənt/ occurs about as often as *dasn't* in w. N. Eng.; in the Midland .. it is clearly the dominant form... *Darsn't* /dɑ(r)sənt/ is found in a scattered way in most parts of the East, but it also shows concentration in certain well-marked areas... In all the forms mentioned so far /z/ occasionally occurs instead of /s/. **c1960** *Wilson Coll.* **csKY,** *Dass...* Dare. The negative *dassn't* is common. **1963** Owens *Look to River* 118 **TX,** We dassent let 'em catch us running off. **1965–70** *DARE* (Qu. JJ47, *If there is something you can't do .. "Doctor's orders—I ________ eat any.";* total Infs questioned, 75) Infs **NM**12, **UT**3, Daresn't; **GA**15, **MS**14, Dassn't. **1967** *DARE* Tape **PA**6, We darsn't [dɑrsənt] let them lie in the sun too long. **1968** *DARE* FW Addit **neNY,** He goes everywhere up here but down there he dasn't [dæsn̩t]. **1982** *Barrick Coll.* **csPA,** *Daresn't—dare not* "Daresn't I go?"

B Sense.

To be allowed. [By identification with PaGer *daerfe* (Ger *dürfen,* 1st and 3rd sg *darf*), presumably originating in neg or interrog contexts where *dare* and *may* would be equally appropriate (see quot 1943)] **PaGer area**

1901 *DN* 2.138 **cePA,** "Dare I go with you?" = May I go? **1907** *German Amer. Annals* 9.373 **sePA,** Dare I be excused early to-day? **1922** *DN* 5.194, The use of *dare* for *may* .. certainly came from the so-called Pennsylvania Dutch. **1935** *AmSp* 10.17 **sePA,** Mom, dare I go to the store with Henry? **1939** Aurand *Quaint Idioms* 23 [PaGer], Mom says *I dassent* (dare not) go out to play. **[1943** *LANE* Map 696, The work sheets called for *you dassn't go* and synonymous expressions... The field workers recorded the expression (1) in the neutral meaning 'you are afraid to go', but (2) more often as a challenge or taunt .. ; or (3) as a prohibition from parent to child in the sense of 'don't you dare!' or 'you may not'. *Dassn't, darsn't, dersn't* usually have meanings (2) or (3).] **1982** *Barrick Coll.* **csPA,** *Dare—may* "Dare I go?" ["]Dares't [sic] I go?"

dare n [**dare** v **B**]

Permission.

1907 *German Amer. Annals* 9.373 **sePA,** May I have the dare to go?

dare-base n Also *dare-bas(e)t, ~-goal, tree dare-base*

Any of several varr of **prisoner's base,** a children's outdoor game, in which one team challenges the other to come into its territory and touch a goal; the goal in such a game.

1895 *DN* 1.398, *King...* A common game among boys is known variously as king and .. *dare bast* [der best]. **1899** Garland *Boy Life* 25 **nwIA** (as of 1860), The boys always went early, in order to have an hour at "dog and deer," or "dare-goal," or "pom-pom pullaway." *Ibid* 28, The small boys had little recreation beyond occasional games of "hi spy" or "dare-gool." **1905** *DN* 3.77 **nwAR,** *Dare-base(t)...* Prisoner's base. **1914** *DN* 4.105 **KS,** *Dare base...* A boy's running game. **1932** Randolph *Ozark Mt. Folks* 46, We played marbles an' blackman an' dare-base an' two-eyed-cat an' townball an' pig-in-a-hole. **1949** Webber *Backwoods Teacher* 48 **Ozarks,** Brother Helms was the leading spirit in a game of "darebase." He galloped madly and daringly from one base to the next when the chance offered, and cheered the others on occasion or "tagged out" venturesome spirits who tried to slip up behind him. **1964** Wallace *Frontier Life* 41 **swOK** (as of c1900), We all .. continued our games of Dare-base, Hop-scotch, Black-man, and a few of the kissing games. **1965–70** *DARE* (Qu. EE33, *Other outdoor games .. that children play now, or that were played in your childhood*) 15 Infs, **esp NCent, CA,** Dare-base; **WA**16, Dare-goal; **CA**136, Tree dare-base—everyone had own tree as base—"it" tries to catch anyone who dares to leave base; (Qu. EE16) Inf **IL**5, Dare-base—a base, two teams and they come up and dare the others to catch them—then they run back to their base; the other team tries to catch them or capture the other base; (Qu. EE27, *Games played on the ice*) Inf **KS**15, Dare-base. **1969** *DARE* Tape **CA**172, When the tide was out there was a pretty wide expanse of sand there that was just swell for playing certain games. Several of the favorites were dare-base, black man, three deep; and there were others too; **OH**87, Dare-base... You have a base and a man that's "it" and then people try to sneak up and touch the base or get on the base or take something off of the base. **1971** Lewis *Nothing Shadow* 101 **csSD,** With sticks, stones, piles of brush, and scratched lines on the ground we made houses, bases for dare base and baseball. **1986** Pederson *LAGS Concordance (Goal)* 1 inf, **cwFL,** Dare base—in hide-and-go-seek; 1 inf, **cTX,** Dare base—name of game; 1 inf, **neAR,** Dare base—played with sticks, like basketball.

dared See **dare** v **A2**

daredn't See **dare** v **A4a**

dare goal See **dare base**

daren't See **dare** v **A4a**

dares See **dare** v **A2**

daresn't See **dare** v **A4c**

daresome adj

1 Afraid.

1938 Rawlings *Yearling* 26 **nFL,** "I'll swear," Penny said, "I'm daresome to break the news to your Ma." *Ibid* 169, But I'm daresome to leave you, boy. Suppose you was to git lost, or snake-bit, too? **1953** Atwood *Survey of Verb Forms* 33, Four N.C. informants have . . *daresome* . . /jur dærsəm tə go/ [in the context "you (dare not) go"]. **1969** *DARE* FW Addit **Louisa KY,** "I'm daresome to do it"—when you're afraid to do something. **1986** Pederson *LAGS Concordance,* 1 inf, **nwFL,** Daresome—afraid? 1 inf, **cAL,** Kind of daresome.

2 Not afraid. Note: These examples perh represent a misunderstanding of **1** above.

1933 Rawlings *South Moon* 318 **FL,** He charged his rations as long as he was daresome to do so. **1938** Rawlings *Yearling* 229 **nFL,** He cuts as far back as he's daresome to do.

dares't See **dare** v **A2**

dare up to v phr

To confront.

1986 *New Yorker* 17 Nov 50/3 **MS** [Black], Roosevelt startled her by interrupting in a most impertinent tone. "Is that what he says? Let him dare up to me with it then."

dark adj

Severe.

1926 Roberts *Time of Man* 19 **cKY,** There was a dark quarrel and Ellen was shaken and slapped. **1967** *DARE* Tape **MA**28, His eyes were all [pause] not red red . . they looked like he had a dark cold.

dark n [Cf **darky**]

A Black person.

1862 *N.Y. Tribune* 4 March *(DA),* They [slaves] were assisted by two venerable old darks who were sitting cross-legged on the floor, and furnished music by clapping their hands, and singing a hymn. **1864** in 1912 Thornton *Amer. Gloss.* 1.229, He immediately dispatched a "dark" to get [the book]. **1903** in 1919 Hale *Letters* 384, Two darks are lying on their back on the sunny curbstone.

dark cloud See **cloud** n[1]

darkey, darkie See **darky**

dark-eyed Susan n

=**black-eyed Susan 2.**

1966–69 *DARE* (Qu. S7) Infs **MI**104, **NY**28, 99, **PA**111, **WA**3, Dark-eyed Susan. **1966** *DARE* Tape **ME**2, [FW:] Do you know of any wild flowers that grow around here? . . [Inf:] Dark-eyed Susan . . they're a stalk with a yellow all out and a black center.

darkey-head See **darky-head**

dark-faced adj

Of tobacco: darkened by decay.

1967 Key *Tobacco Vocab.* **TN,** Rot: black-faced/dark-faced—refers to color.

dark-fired adj Cf **fire-cure**

1940 *AmSp* 15.134 **KY,** *Fire-cured* or *dark-fired.* Type of [tobacco] leaf cured by smoke and heat from smoldering open fires.

dark frost n Also *dark-of-the-moon frost* Cf **black frost 1**

1966–68 *DARE* (Qu. B29, *A frost that does not kill plants is a* ______) Inf **MS**2, Dark frost; (Qu. B30, *A frost that kills plants is a* ______) Inf **NJ**17, Dark frost; **IL**19, Dark-of-the-moon frost—because it frosts when the moon isn't out or [it's] on the wane.

dark-hole n

An unlighted storage space in a house.

1903 *DN* 2.296 **Cape Cod MA** (as of a1857), *Dark-hole*. . . A dark closet or corner under the stairs or around the chimney. **1941** *LANE* Map 345 *(Attic)* 1 inf, **Cape Cod MA,** *Dark hole,* term used as a boy. [Inf old]

darkhouse n

1981 *Verbatim Letters* **swMI,** We . . wonder if anyone . . knows the term "darkhouse" as it is used near Three Rivers, Michigan. It apparently refers to shacks put on iced-over lakes and rivers and used as shelters for spear fishers. It is not the same as the ice shack used for line fishing; dark houses apparently do not have windows.

dark moon n [*OED* (at *dark* a. 1. c) 1653] Cf **dark of the moon**

See quot 1859.

1859 (1968) Bartlett *Americanisms* 114, *Dark moon.* The interval between the old moon and the new moon. *Western.* I always alter my colts and plant my 'taters during the dark moon.—Letter from a Western Farmer. **1984** Wilder *You All Spoken Here* 62 **Sth.**

dark of the moon n [*OED* (at *dark* sb. 1) 1651 →] Cf **dark moon**

The period of the waning moon, esp the last quarter; but see also quot 1949.

1871 Eggleston *Hoosier Schoolmaster* 87 **IN,** That's ile from a black dog. Ef it's rendered right, it'll knock the hind sights off any rheumatiz you ever see. But it must be rendered in the dark of the moon. **1899** (1912) Green *VA Folk-Speech* 142, *Dark of the moon:* nights when the moon does not shine, between the last of the last quarter and the new moon. **1949** Webber *Backwoods Teacher* 191 **Ozarks,** "The dark of the moon," i.e., the latter half of its period, when it is growing fuller, and when the uninitiated would expect it to be called "the light of the moon." **1958** Williams *Orpheus Descending* 160 **Sth,** I have a feeling we'll come together some night. . . In the dark of the moon, beside a broken fence rail in some big rolling meadow. **1966–67** *DARE* (Qu. L26) Inf **OK**43, Plant corn in the dark of the moon; (Qu. BB51b) Inf **NE**11, Plant a potato in the dark of the moon. **1966** *DARE* Tape **MI**21, In the dark of the moon, that's when you get your most whitefish; in the light of the moon they can see the net. **1972** *Foxfire Book* 221 **nGA,** Take taters. On th' dark of th' moon or th' old of th' moon—that's th' last quarter, . . they make less vine; and on the light of th' moon they makes more vine and less tater. **1977** *Old Farmer's Almanac* 92 **NEng,** Flowers and vegetables which bear crops below the ground should be planted during the *Dark* of the moon; that is, from the day after it is full to the day before it is new again. **1978** *Blair & Ketchum's Country Jrl.* Sept 40 **VT,** The homely root [=the potato] was said to be . . poisonous because of its botanical connection with nightshade, and should be planted only in the dark of the moon. **1984** Wilder *You All Spoken Here* 61 **Sth,** Dark of the moon, waste of the moon, down side of the moon, shrink of the moon: When the moon is waning, or decreasing. This is the time to plant root crops such as potatoes, turnips, rutabagas. **1986** Pederson *LAGS Concordance,* 1 inf, **wTN,** Plant your potatoes [on the] dark of the moon; 1 inf, **cTX,** The stuff you plant that produces under the ground makes better when you plant it on the dark of the moon.

dark-of-the-moon frost See **dark frost**

dark petrel n

=**sooty shearwater.**

1962 Imhof *AL Birds* 68, *Sooty Shearwater—Puffinus griseus.* . . Other Names: Albatross, Black Hag, Dark Petrel.

dark tobacco n Cf **black tobacco**

1 See quot.

1944 *PADS* 2.64 **sVA,** *Black-tobacco, dark-tobacco.* . . A variety of tobacco grown especially in western Kentucky.

2 See quots.

1944 *PADS* 2.64 **sVA,** *Black tobacco, dark tobacco* . . A shade of color of the cured leaf affecting the price on the market. . . This kind of tobacco has a stronger, more marked flavor which was preferred in certain foreign countries. [**1967** *DARE* (Qu. DD1, . . *Different forms . . [of] chewing tobacco*) Inf **OH**16, Dark fine cut tobacco.] [**1970** *DARE* Tape **KY**75, The dark type—what we call air-cured . . That's more or less a chewin' tobacco; **KY**93, [Inf:] One thing a little different between the dark and the burley. We have to fire dark. [FW:] What do they make out of a dark tobacco? [Inf:] They makes cigars, smokin' tobacco and chewin' tobacco.]

darktown n, usu attrib

A Black neighborhood or town—used esp in titles.

1884 in 1947 *AmSp* 22.202, [Currier and Ives print, title:] The Darktown Fire Brigade—Saved! **1906** Lib. of Congress *Catalog of Copyright Entries* 4 Oct 235/1, *Darktown (The) guards;* march, [by] Louis D. Surette, arr. by R. E. Hildreth. **1919** *Chicago Defender* (Natl. ed.) (IL) 12 Apr 9/2 **neIL,** [Advt:] S. H. Dudley offers his Darktown Frolics Co. A musical comedy. . . Jazz band and chorus. **1937** *Writer* 50.239, Here is a Negro-American vocabulary of nearly a hundred words and phrases picked up in the Cleveland, Ohio, dark-town bright spots. **1948** *Dly. Ardmoreite* (Ardmore Okla.) 1 April 14/6 *(DA),* A play 'The Darktown 13 Club' has been combined with a pic supper for presentation at 7:30 Friday evening at Lone Grove. **1951** Burton *Blue Book* 161 **seMI** (as of 1917) [Black], Shelton Brooks . . completed this amazing cycle of hits with another million-copy seller, *At the Darktown Strutters' Ball.*

dark white paint n

1966 *DARE* (Qu. HH14, *Ways of teasing a beginner or inexperienced person . . : "Go get me ______."*) Inf **ME**22, A can of dark white paint.

darky n Also sp *darkey*

1 A Black person—formerly often considered neutral or affectionate; now usu considered offensive.

1829 *N.Y. Morning Courier* 15 June 1/6 *(DA),* The Negroes keep their jubilee; While Cuffee, with protruding lip, *Bravuras* to the darky's skip. **1855** Douglass *My Bondage* 72 **eMD,** The old man always seemed pleased when he saw a troop of darkey little urchins. **1856** Moore *Songs & Ballads* 100 (as of 1775), The women ran, the darkeys too;/ And all the bells, they tollèd. **1899** Chesnutt *Conjure Woman* 15 **csNC** [Black], All de darkies fum Rockfish ter Beaver Crick wuz feared er her. **1899** (1912) Green *VA Folk-Speech* 142, Darkey. . . A negro. **1930** Shoemaker *1300 Words* 16 **cPA Mts** (as of c1900), *Darky*—A colored person. **1937** *Natl. Geogr. Mag.* 71.271 **MS,** "Sadaday" night is traditional "darkey night" up-State. Then whites stay off the streets and the black families in pre-Sunday best emerge from "catfish rows" and hold orderly carnival. **1938** Faulkner *Unvanquished* 126, "One of you darkies that can handle two span come here," the lieutenant said. **1941** *LANE* Map 452B, *Darky* is described as the usual or most common neutral term by [6 infs]; as rare by [3 infs]; as an old-fashioned term or as one formerly more common than today by [4 infs]; as a 'familiar' term by [1 inf]; as a polite or friendly term by [9 infs]; and as the term by which negroes refer to themselves by [2 infs]. **c1960** *Wilson Coll.* **csKY,** *Darky.* . . Negro; not often heard now. **1962** Atwood *Vocab. TX* 73, Darky . . is said by some to be polite, and is probably intended to give no offense. **1965–70** *DARE* (Qu. HH28, *Names and nicknames around here for people of foreign background*) 56 Infs, **scattered** Darky; **CT**37, Darky people. **1966–68** *DARE* Tape **AL**43, What we couldn't use we'd give to the darkies; **SC**31, Course we had darkies to do the cookin'; **SC**47, He had two yokes of oxen, he put four to a big cart and that darky sit back there on back of that cart; **SC**57A, Some of de . . ol' darkies aroun' here, colored people, used to make 'em. **1973** Allen *LAUM* 1.347 (as of c1950), Of the various terms recorded [for *Negro*] the only one which—while still suggesting the invidious presence of social distance—may be considered as also connoting some affection and friendly acceptance is *darky.* It is found in all five states [MN, IA, ND, SD, NE]. **1976** Brown *Gloss. Faulkner* 68 **MS,** *Darky* . . : Negro—an indulgent and affectionate term, not a contemptuous one.

2 A dark-colored marble.

c1970 Wiersma *Marbles Terms* **swMI,** *Darkies*—description of marble color, lustre. "Got some darkies?"

darky-head n Also sp *darkey-head* Cf **niggerhead**

A **black-eyed Susan 2** (here: either *Rudbeckia hirta* or *R. triloba*).

1897 IN Dept. Geol. & Nat. Resources *Rept. for 1896* 695, *R. triloba.* . . Darkey-head. . . One of the most showy of our common Compositae. **1912** Blatchley *IN Weed Book* 171, *Rudbeckia hirta.* . . Darkey-head. . . Disk globose, its flowers brownish-purple. **1914** Georgia *Manual Weeds* 462, *Black-eyed Susan. . . Other English names:* . . Darkey-head. **1935** (1943) Muenscher *Weeds* 512, *Rudbeckia hirta* L. Black-eyed Susan, Darky-head.

darlen n [By metath from *darnel*]

1899 (1912) Green *VA Folk-Speech* 142, Darlen. . . Darnel; cheat; a deleterious grass that grows in wheat.

Darling Nellie Gray n [After the ballad *Darling Nelly Gray* by B.R. Hanby, 1833–67]

1968 *DARE* (Qu. EE1, *What games do children play around here, in which they form a ring, and either sing or recite a rhyme?*) Inf **OH**82, Darling Nellie Gray—it's like a square dance; (Qu. FF5a, *Names for different steps and figures in dancing—in past years*) Inf **NY**69, Darling Nellie Gray [FW: heard].

darnation n, adj, adv, intj [*darn* euphem for *damn*] Cf **tarnation**

Used as a euphem for damnation, damn(ed).

1798 *Aurora Genl. Advt.* (Philadelphia PA) 14 Aug, It seems as if the Irish are actually as incorrigible in that way as the *darnation Bostonians!* **1828** *N.Y. Mirror* 2 Aug 26/3 *(DA),* 'New-Yark,' said he—and Jonathan was a frequent visiter here to sell his onions and wooden dishes—'would be a darnation fine place, if they ever got it done.' **1845** Thompson *Pineville* 90 **GA,** "Darnation!" petulantly exclaimed Mr. Van Scoik. **1855** Woodworth *Forest Rose* 14, Darnation take the garlic, I say. **1902** (1904) Rowe *Maid of Bar Harbor* 182 **ME,** Try it yerself, 'f ye think it's fun gettin' ducked in a darnation old dye-pot. **1905** *DN* 3.7 **cCT,** *Darnation* . . "I had a darnation good time." Rare. **1907** *DN* 3.185 **seNH,** *Darnation.* . . Softened form of damnation. "Darnation! Why couldn't he stay away?" . . Exceedingly, very. "I'm darnation tired, I know that." **1969** *DARE* (Qu. NN25a, *Weakened substitutes for 'damn' or 'damned'*) Inf **NY**132, Darnation.

darner See **darning needle 1**

darnful adj [*OED dernful* "Mournful, dreary. *Obs.*"]

Gloomy.

1916 *DN* 4.313 **Sth** [Dialect of folk songs], *Darnful.* . . Doleful? "She pitched him in that darnful well." **1944** *PADS* 2.18 **sAppalachians,** *Darnful.* . . Gloomy, mournful, lugubrious.

darnic(k) See **dornick**

darning needle n Cf **devil's darning needle**

1 also *darn needle, darner:* A **dragonfly,** often of the superfamily Aeshnoidea. [See quots 1895, 1933, 1967] **chiefly NEast, Inland Nth, West** See Map

1889 *Century Dict.* 1457, *Darning-needle,* the dragon-fly; the devil's darning-needle. **1895** Comstock-Comstock *Manual Insects* 90, Family *Libellulidae* . . *The Dragon-flies.* Darning-needles, Devil's-needles . . and Dragon-flies are some of the names given to those insects which dart back and forth over streams and wet places. . . But for all their terrible names Dragon-flies are entirely innocent of any harm to mankind. They neither sew up people's ears, as northern children think; nor bring dead snakes to life, as colored people in the South believe; but they are very fierce enemies to their insect kindred. Their long, narrow, closely netted wings are strong, carrying them swiftly; and their jaws are powerful. **1933** Bryan *Hawaiian Nature* 174, The two largest species of our dragonflies are called "darners," because they fly back and forth over the same area as a needle travels when darning socks. **1940** Teale *Insects* 147, When the dragonfly is hunting . . , it is darting at top speed through the air. . . A fly buzzes near you. The "darning needle" shoots past and the fly is gone. **1949** *AmSp* 24.108 **neGA,** Darning needle; devil's darning needle . . Dragonfly. **1950** *WELS Suppl.* 5 Infs, **WI,** Darning needle(s). **1954** Borror-DeLong *Intro. Insects* 113, *Family Petaluridae*—Gray Darners. . . *Family Aeshnidae*—Common Darners. **1961** *AmSp* 36.31 **neOH,** The fact that *(devil's) darning needle* is commonest among the oldest informants suggests that the native expression is dying out in Cleveland. **1964** *Hand Coll.* **OH,** A large dragonfly known as the darning needle will sew up your tongue. **1965–70** *DARE* (Qu. R2) 200 Infs, **chiefly NEast, Inland Nth, West,** Darning needle; **NY**73, 220, Darn needle; **OR**3, Old lady's darning needle. **1967** *DARE* File **seRI,** *Darning needle,* Dragonfly—it would sew up your mouth if you told a lie. **1980** Milne-Milne *Audubon Field Guide Insects* 364, *Darners (Family Aeschnidae).* . . are among the largest and fastest-flying North American dragonflies. . . "Darning Needle" *(Anax junius).*

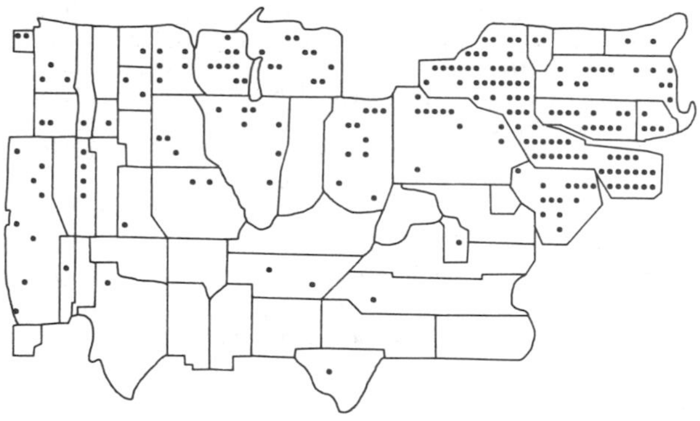

•darning needle 1 + varr (Qu. R2)

2 also *darn needle:* **=walkingstick.**

1965–70 *DARE* (Qu. R9a) 13 Infs, 11 **Missip-Ohio Valleys,** Darning needle; **CA**40, Darning needle—no wings, prominent eyes; **MD**22, Darn needle.

3 =beggar ticks 1.

1968–69 *DARE* (Qu. S14) Inf **GA**70, Spanish needles—two kinds: long and short; long ones called darning needles; **MD**32, Darning needles; Spanish needles [is the] proper name; **WV**8, Darning needle—black, half-inch, three prongs.

4 =needlegrass.

1967–68 *DARE* (Qu. S15) Inf **IL**6, Darning needles—black, long; **MN**42, Darning needle—long, sticking.

darning-needle cactus n
A **prickly pear** (here: *Opuntia ramosissima*).
1941 Jaeger *Wildflowers* 158 **Desert SW,** *Darning-needle cactus. . . Opuntia ramosissima.* . . The handsome fruits are . . covered with tawny, stout spines. . . The very slender, woody joints are usually marked with . . figures, from the center of which spring the long, solitary, yellow-sheathed spines. **1985** Dodge *Flowers SW Deserts* 65, Darning-Needle Cactus. . . *Opuntia ramosissima.*

darn needle See **darning needle 1, 2**

darn sight, darned sight See **sight**

darse See **dare** v **A3**

darshin See **dare** v **A4c**

darsn't See **dare** v **A4c**

darst See **dare** v **A2, 3**

dart n
1966–69 *DARE* (Qu. BB3a, *What do you call a pain that strikes you suddenly in the neck?*) Infs **MA**38, **WA**18, Dart.

darter n
1 Std: any of var fish of the genera *Ammocrypta, Etheostoma,* and *Percina.* See also **johnny darter, logperch, mud darter, rainbow darter, river darter, sand darter, snubnose darter, yellowbelly**
2 also *black(-bellied) darter:* =**anhinga.**
1814 Wilson *Amer. Ornith.* 9.82 **GA,** Female black-bellied darter. **1917** (1923) *Birds Amer.* 1.93, *Anhinga anhinga* . . Darter; American Darter; Black Darter; Black-bellied Darter. **1946** Hausman *Eastern Birds* 93, *Anhinga anhinga* . . Darter, Black Darter.
3 =**blue darter 2.**
1966–70 *DARE* (Qu. Q4, . . *Kinds of hawks*) Infs **NC**10, **VA**70, Darter.
4 See **daughter.**

dart hawk n Also *darting hawk*
=**blue darter 2.**
1966 *DARE* (Qu. Q4) Inf **NC**13, Dart hawk; **OK**1, Darting hawk.

das See **dare** v **A3**

dasent See **dare** v **A4c**

dash n [*OED dash* sb.[1] 13; cf Intro "Language Changes" III.4]
The dasher of a churn.
1858 (1867) Flint *Milch Cows* 226 **MA,** The most common form of the churn in small dairies is the upright or dash-churn. **1896** VT State Bd. Ag. *Rept. for 1895* 124 **VT,** I note the dash-churn [and] the primitive cheese-press. **1944** Adams *Western Words* 35, *Churn-dash calf*—One . . which has not the full benefit of the mother's milk. **1969** *DARE* Tape **IN**82, [FW:] Do these quilts have different patterns? [Inf:] Yes, they do. . . Churn dash, I believe, is one of 'em; **KY**17, My uncle, he saw that. He said he was ridin' across the mountain one night and said that churn with a dash in it was right in front a' him. Said it just went fer a long ways right in front a' him.

dash away v phr [Std in literary use, but rare in colloq speech; cf *DJE dash* vb 1 "In common use in Jamaica where *throw, fling,* and other words would be preferred elsewhere"] *Gullah* Cf *DBE*
To throw (something) away; also fig.
1909 *S. Atl. Qrly.* 8.41 **sSC coast** [Gullah], "Eh! eh! Ef'n yo' don' lak de tas'e er yo' bittle, dash um 'way an' be done!" [=Eh! eh! If you don't like the taste of your food, throw it away and be done!] *Ibid,* "Me use' fuh drunk; but me dash um 'way; me sobah now." [=I used to drink; but I gave it up; I'm sober now.]

dashboard n
1 in phr *have one's tail over the dashboard* and varr: See **tail.**
2 pl: One's feet.
1915 *DN* 4.244 **MT,** *Dashboards* . . Feet. "Clean your dashboards."
3 Among loggers: a farmer working as a logger. Cf **dashboard overalls**
1958 McCulloch *Woods Words* 45 **Pacific NW,** *Dashboards*—Farmers who work part time in the woods; from the bib overalls which they wear instead of ordinary pants worn by loggers.

dashboard overalls n pl Also *dashboard running jeans esp freq among loggers*
Bib overalls.
1942 Berrey–Van den Bark *Amer. Slang* 512.12 [In logging], Dashboard running jeans, *bibbed overalls.* **1950** *Western Folkl.* 9.381 **neCA** [Lumberjack language], *Dashboard overalls.* Bib overalls. **1967** *DARE* (Qu. W9, *Work garment, usually of blue cloth, covering the legs and sometimes the chest*) Inf **CO**47, Dashboard overalls—the dashboard is the bib part. **1969** Sorden *Lumberjack Lingo* 32 **NEng, Gt Lakes,** *Dash board overalls*—Bib overalls.

dasheen n [Perh Fr *de Chine* (imported) from China] **esp Sth**
=**taro.**
1910 U.S. Bur. Plant Industry *Bulletin* 164.27, It is not always easy to distinguish between the dasheens and the taros, for some of the dasheens have a tendency to throw sprouts from the tips of the tubers. **1933** Bryan *Hawaiian Nature* 82, Chief among the food plants of the Hawaiians, both ancient and modern, is the taro, called dasheen in the southern United States . . and known to science as *Colocasia antiquorum.* **1933** Small *Manual SE Flora* 248, A variety of *Colocasia antiquorum*—(Dasheen, Taro)—is cultivated for its edible tubers in Florida. **1941** O'Donnell *Great Big Doorstep* 99 **sLA,** They waded through the hairy ferns and waving dasheens as though under water. **1965** Neal *Gardens HI* 159, A few forms from Japan . . resemble dasheen [*C. esculenta* . .], a crop of the southern United States. **1982** Perry–Hay *Field Guide Plants* 98, *Colocasia esculenta (C. antiquorum esculenta . .)*—Taro; dasheen; elephant's ear.

dasher n
1968 *DARE* (Qu. Y11, *Other words for a very hard blow: "You should have seen Bill go down. Joe really hit him a ______."*) Infs **GA**17, Dasher.

dasn't See **dare** v **A4c**

dass See **dare** v **A3**

dassent, dassn't See **dare** v **A4c**

dast See **dare** v **A2, 3, 4b**

date n Cf **date up**
In marble play: a type of marble; a marble put up as a stake.
1942 Berrey–Van den Bark *Amer. Slang* 665.3, *Marbles put in the ring as a stake.* . . dates. *Ibid* 665.6, I got my dates, *I have won the same number of marbles as I had "dated up."* **1953** Goodwin *It's Good* 198 **sIL,** Spud and Cecil kept their prize aggies in a cigar box. The cheaper pee wees, dates, and ordinary glassies were kept in two large coal buckets. **c1970** Wiersma *Marbles Terms* **neIL** (as of 1928), Marbles that each person contributed to the pot were called dates. The way they played in Chicago in 1928 was to draw a huge circle with a small square in the middle. Then each player put his date into this square and everyone took turns from outside the big circle and tried to hit the dates out of the square. The dates were small and the shooting marbles were larger.

dated up See **date up**

date fish n
Either of two mollusks: a piddock (here: *Zirphaea crispata*) or the chubby mya *(Platyodon cancellatus).*
1838 *Knickerbocker* 11.446, What though its [=plum-pudding's] specific gravity was not much less than that of our twenty-four pound shot . . and each separate raisin therein embedded, bearing much resemblance to the date-fish in his rock? **1884** Goode *Fisheries U.S.* 1.707, Some cousins (*Zirphæa crispata, Platydon* [sic] *cancellatus,* etc.) are esteemed delicacies on the coast of California under the name of "Date-fish." **1884** U.S. Natl. Museum *Bulletin* 27.263, *Platydon cancellatus* . . Date Fish. . . *Zirphaea crispata* . . Date Fish. Northwest coast of America to California, Puget Sound, Vancouver Island, San Diego, and San Pedro.

date plum n
=**persimmon.**
1785 Marshall *Arbustrum* 40, *Diospyros.* The Date Plum, or Persimmon Tree. **1847** Darlington *Ag. Botany* 105, *Virginian Diospyros.* . . Persimmon. Date Plum. **1897** Sudworth *Arborescent Flora* 321, *Diospyros virginiana* . . Persimmon. . . Date Plum (N.J., Tenn.) **1974** (1977) Coon *Useful Plants* 129, *Diospyros virginiana*—Persimmon; . . date plum. **1976** Bailey–Bailey *Hortus Third* 389, *Diospyros* . . Persimmon. . . *[D.] virginiana* . . Date Plum.

dater See **daughter**

date up v phr, hence ppl adj *dated (up),* n *date-up(s)* Cf **date**
In marble play: see quot.
1942 Berrey–Van den Bark *Amer. Slang* 665.3, *Marbles put in the ring as a stake. . .* date-up, date-ups. *Ibid* 665.4, Ante up, date up, *to put marbles in the ring as a stake;* date one up, -two up &c. *to "date" a designated number of marbles. Ibid* 665.5, Dated (up) . . *having marbles in the ring.*

datil n Also *datil yucca, datila* [Span *dátil* date] **Desert SW**
=**banana yucca;** also its fruit.
1882 *Atlantic Mth.* 50.549/2 **nAZ,** The somewhat sweet fruit of the datila, or Spanish bayonet, is rendered sweeter by a like process. **1911** *Century Dict. Suppl., Datil. . . Yucca baccata.* **1913** Wooton *Trees NM* 33, *The Datil (Yucca baccata)* is a species . . almost stemless. **1940** Writers' Program *Guide NM* 359, *Dátil* . . was named by the early Spaniards for a fruit resembling dates found in the mountains. **1960** Vines *Trees SW* 52, Datil Yucca. *Yucca baccata. Ibid* 53, Vernacular names are Banana Yucca, Blue Yucca, Dátil [etc]. **1967** Dodge *Roadside Wildflowers* 2, *Datil Yucca. . .* is widespread throughout the Southwest at elevations from 3,000 to 8,000 feet.

datter v [Cf *EDD dather* v. 2 "To maze, bewilder"; *ditter* "To confuse, bewilder"]
1952 Brown *NC Folkl.* 1.532, *Datter. . .* To confuse, embarrass.—West.

datter n See **daughter**

daub-duck n Cf **dapper 2**
=**ruddy duck.**
1888 Trumbull *Names of Birds* 111, Since finishing the list of names heard by myself in more northern localities, Mr. Henry. P. Ives [sic], of Salem, Mass., a gentleman who is well acquainted with this species, tells me of hearing it commonly called the *Daub-duck* at Rangely Lake, Me. **1917** (1923) *Birds Amer.* 1.152, *Ruddy Duck—Erismatura jamaicensis* . . Other Names.—Dumpling Duck; Daub Duck; . . Stiff-tailed Widgeon. **1925** (1928) Forbush *Birds MA* 1.280, *Erismatura jamaicensis* . . *Ruddy Duck.*—Other names: Butter-ball; . . Daub Duck; . . Spike-tail.

daube n |dob| [Fr] **LA**
A type of stew; see quots; hence *daube glacée* a jellied meat dish.
1932 (1946) Hibben *Amer. Regional Cookery* 103 **New Orleans LA,** *Daube.* **1939** *AmSp* 14.256 **LA,** *Daube.* This French word, a back-formation from *dauber,* 'to stew,' is extremely well known in Louisiana, where it . . appears in such recipes as . . 'goose daube,' and 'turkey daube.' **1941** Writers' Program *Guide LA* 688, *Daube*—Pot roast. **1964** Amer. Heritage *Cookbook* 496, *Daube Glacé* [sic]—This Creole recipe is based, in part, on one found in *La Cuisine Creole,* thought to have been written by Lafcadio Hearn. **1968** *DARE* (Qu. H45, *Dishes made with meat, fish, or poultry that everybody around here would know, but that people in other places might not*) Inf **LA**23, Daube [doʊb]—veal in red gravy; daube glacée [ˌglɑˈseɪ]—veal in brown gravy with gelatin. **1983** *Reinecke Coll.* 4 **LA,** *Daube*—[do:b] pot roast of braised veal or beef, cooked with onions and other vegetables, esp. carrots, over slow fire in dutch oven. Has a thick brown roux sauce. Often had green olives added at last minute. Italian restaurants make a "daube" with typical Italian red tomato sauce, served over spaghetti. The native dish served over rice. Also "daube glacée["] [glɑˈse], jellied beef loaf—delicacy.

dauber n Also sp *dabber, dobber* [Abbrs for **dirt dauber, mud dauber**]
=**mud dauber.**
1859 Gosse *Letters from AL* 238, I watched with much interest the proceedings of a Dauber in building her mud-cells; it is a pretty species *(Pelopoeus flavipes).* **1872** Schele de Vere *Americanisms* 391, *Yellow-jacket* is the familiar and descriptive name of a small hornet (Pelopsus) and of the Sand-wasp (Ammophila), one of whose cousins is familiarly known by the name of *Dauber,* from the manner in which he builds his nest, literally daubing it all over, so as to make it waterproof and quite a strong structure. **1908** *DN* 3.308 **eAL, wGA,** *Dirt-dobber. . .* Also called simply *dobber.* **1965–70** *DARE* (Qu. R20) 20 Infs, 14 **N Cent, Appalachians,** Dauber; **OK**58, Dabber. [All Infs old]

daubler n [Frequentative var of *dauber*]
=**mud dauber.**
1969 *DARE* (Qu. R20) Inf **PA**184, Daubler [ˈdɔbələ]; nest narrow at the top, forms a bulb one inch long and dark colored.

dauby adj [*OED dauby* a. 2 *"dial."*]
1982 *Barrick Coll.* **csPA,** *Dauby*—messed up, sticky. "Let me wipe your fingers. They got all dauby."

daughter n Pronc-spp *daa'tuh, dafter, dairter, darter, dat(t)er, dorter*
Std sense, var forms.
1808 in 1930 *AmSp* 5.293 [Black], He wife die, two tree year ago, and he darter all marry. **1813** (1927) Gerry *Diary* 158 **OH,** Take care of my darter. **1837** (1955) *Crockett Almanacks* 85 **wTN,** My sons were all absent, but my wife and two darters at home. **1837** Sherwood *Gaz. GA* 69, *Dairter.* **1843** (1916) Hall *New Purchase* 258 **IN,** Why if I didn't sentimentally allow you was the two old folkses, and them two likely young gals, your two oldenmost daters. **1894** *Century Illustr. Mag.* 48.873, Major Vaughan, the New Hampshire colonial magistrate who says "haith," also writes "menester," "heither" for hither, . . and "dafter" for daughter. **1922** Gonzales *Black Border* 296 **sSC, GA coasts** [Gullah glossary], *Daa'tuh*—daughter, daughters. **1930** Shoemaker *1300 Words* 19 **cPA Mts** (as of c1900), *Darter.* **1939** Aurand *Quaint Idioms* 23 [PaGer], My *datter* (daughter) was always such a good girl. **1940** *AmSp* 15.48 **sAppalachian Mts and Ozarks,** The tendency is to supply [r] after [ɒ] or [ɔ] when the following syllable contains [ɚ]: warter, darter . . orter. **1961** *Mt. Life* 37.1.6 **sAppalachians,** Frequently *r* is inserted in other words: *bursh, pursh, . . dorter* (but also *datter*).

daunce See **dance**

daunc(e)y, dauns(e)y See **donsie**

dauncy-giddy See **donsie 2c**

dautie n [Scots, nEngl dial]
1930 Shoemaker *1300 Words* 19 **cPA Mts** (as of c1900), *Dautie*—A favorite child, or darling.

dav, daven See **davenport**

davenette n Also *davenet, davinette, davenant* [Trademark; see quot 1951] **chiefly S Midl** See Map
A usu small couch.
1951 U.S. Patent Office *Official Gaz.* 645.27/1, *Davenette. . .* For Upholstered Davenport Bed. [Applicant] claims use since Oct. 19, 1949. **c1960** *Wilson Coll.* **csKY,** Davinette . . A small davenport; a very modern word. **1965–70** *DARE* (Qu. E7, *The piece of upholstered furniture that you can stretch out on to rest*) Infs **IL**107, **LA**9, **MO**19, 36, 37, **TN**49, **UT**3, 4, Davenette; **AR**47, **MO**4, 16, 38, **VA**2, **WV**2, [ˈdævəˌnɛt]; **AR**56, [dɛvənɛt]; **TN**13, [ˈdævɪˌnæd]; **KY**85, Davenant—shorter [than a couch]; **MO**9, [dɛvɪˈnænə]; (Qu. E9, *A piece of upholstered furniture that seats three people*) Infs **AR**17, **MO**16, 21, 36, Davenette; **KY**26, **MO**38, [ˈdævɪˌnɛt]; **UT**4, [dævɛˈnɛt]; **IL**117, [ˌdɛvəˈnɛt]; **KY**89, Davenant = davenport; **KY**44, [ˌdævɪˈnɛnt]; **MO**9, [ˈdævɪˌnæn]. **1966** *DARE* Tape **AL**4, [FW:] What did you call the big thing that you sat down on, maybe three or four could sit on? [Inf:] Lounge, a davenette. **1983** *MJLF* 9.1.37 **ceKY,** *Davenet* . . a short davenport. **1986** Pederson *LAGS Concordance (Sofa)* 52 infs, **chiefly inland Gulf Region,** Davenette(s).

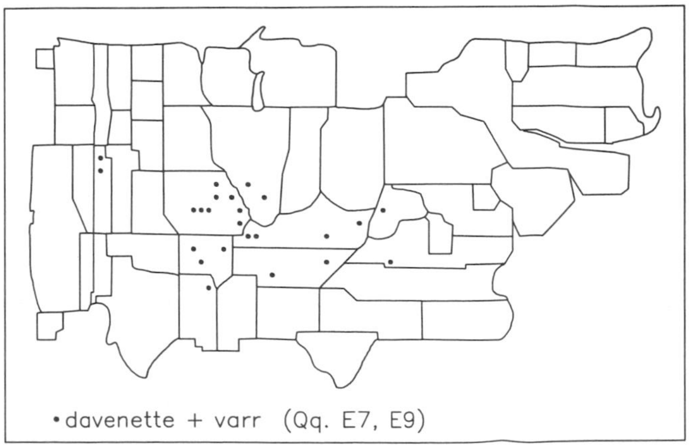

daveno n [Trademark *Daven-o;* see quot 1971] **chiefly NW**
=**davenport.**
c1955 Reed–Person *Ling. Atlas Pacific NW,* 4 infs, Daveno. **1966** *Port Townsend Leader* (WA) 1 Dec 8/2, [Advt:] *Good Bed Daveno,* $50. **1966–69** *DARE* (Qu. E7, *The piece of upholstered furniture that you can*

stretch out on to rest) Infs **IN**76, **WA**30, Daveno [used in conv]; **NC**82, ['dævɪ,no]; **WA**1, 31, ['dævɛ,no]; **WA**11, Daveno; **WA**13, Daveno—can be made into a bed; (Qu. E9, *A piece of upholstered furniture that seats three people)* Inf **CA**15, [dæ'vinouz]—modern word for davenport—advertising; **WA**1, Daveno. **1968** *ID Free Press* (Nampa) 21 Feb sec A 3/8, Used Furniture: 2 nice davenos. **1968** *ID Daily Statesman* (Boise) 25 Feb sec D 6, 2 pc. davenport and daveno set. **1968** *Recorder-Herald* (Salmon ID) 25 Jan 8/5, Used Daveno and Chair—$25.00. **[1971** U.S. Patent Office *Official Gaz.* 889.TM 148/1, *Daven-o...* For upholstered Davenport Beds... First use in or about January 1921.] **1977** *DARE* File **nCA** (as of c1950), My mother talked about sitting on the "daveno"; I thought it sounded funny, since everyone else called it a "davenport."

davenport n Abbrs *dav(en)* **widespread, but less freq Sth, S Midl, N Atl** See Map

Also in combs: An upholstered couch or sofa, sometimes convertible to a bed.

1902 *Sears Cat.* (ed. 112) 621 *(DA),* This Davenport Bed Couch is 6 feet long and 21 inches wide, with the added feature of one wing or side forming a divan back. **1903** *DN* 2.350 **NEast,** *Davenport...* A kind of settle. **1927** (1970) Sears *Catalogue* 867, *The Davenport...* Entire width, 72½ in. Size of seat 60 x 22 in. Height of back, 21 in. Deep padded and very comfortable. *Ibid* 870, *Bed davenport...* The bed opens out to long bed style, giving a generous sleeping surface... Outside length, 89 in. Entire height, 32½ in... *Stationary davenport...* Each of the three loose cushions contains 36 fine wire springs. *Ibid* 871, *The davenport bed...* Opens out to a three-quarter size bed. **1941** *LANE* Map 326 *(Sofa), Davenport* is commonly defined as a long, unholstered or 'overstuffed' sofa, often as a modern term for *sofa* or *lounge.* [*Davenport* was resp of 28 infs.] **1956** *PADS* 25.9 **WA,** Davenport 76 [infs], couch 11, lounge 8, sofa 3, divan 1, daveno 1. **1962** Atwood *Vocab. TX* 112, For a good many years, *davenport* was the favorite term in the catalogues, and no doubt in the stores, for the piece with arms and a back—*couch* for the flat type with an elevation at the head. *Ibid* 45, *Sofa...* In Texas the predominant words are *couch* (37 [% of approx 270 infs]), *sofa* (30), *divan* (27), and *davenport* (23). **1965-70** *DARE* (Qu. E9, *A piece of upholstered furniture that seats three people)* 281 Infs, **widespread, but less freq Sth, S Midl, N Atl,** Davenport; (Qu. E7, *The piece of upholstered furniture that you can stretch out on to rest)* 251 Infs, **widespread, but less freq Sth, S Midl, N Atl,** Davenport; **NY**135, Davenport lounge; **CA**79, Bed-davenport; **GA**72, Daven; **MI**1, Dav. **1966** *Ellsworth Amer.* (ME) 29 June 7/3, For Sale... davenports. **1968** *Blackfoot News* (ID) 23 Jan 7/6, Must Sell! Oxblood davenport, $30. **1968** *Milan Std.* (MN) 11 July 5/1, Auction!.. Davenport and Chairs. **1971** Bright *Word Geog. CA & NV* 144, There were 10 responses describing the davenport as having leather upholstery and wooden arms; the majority of these responses were from San Francisco. Of 25 responses describing it as having upholstered arms and back, the majority came from Los Angeles. **1977** [see **daveno**]. **1986** Pederson *LAGS Concordance (Sofa)* 167 infs, **Gulf Region,** Davenport(s).

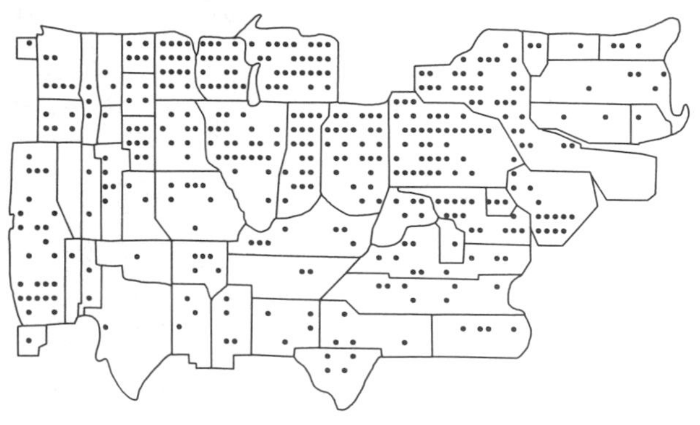

•davenport + varr (Qq. E9, E7)

David's harp n

A musical instrument, perh a variety of **dulcimer.**

1930 Shoemaker *1300 Words* 17 **cPA Mts** (as of c1900), *David's harp*—A mountaineer's musical instrument like a cruit [*DARE* Ed: = crwth].

davinette See **davenette**

daw n [Var of **taw**]

1968 *DARE* (Qu. EE6a, .. *Different kinds of marbles—the big one that's used to knock others out of the ring)* Inf **PA**115, Daw.

dawbug See **dorbug**

dawg See **dog** n[1]

dawn-darkle n

Appar the darkness just before sunrise.

1931 *AmSp* 6.270 **KY,** A large class of compounds is formed by combining two words, usually of the same part of speech, to express similar or related ideas .. dawn-darkle.

day See **duh** v

day and time n **chiefly Sth, S Midl**

A period of time; an era.

1887 (1967) Harris *Free Joe* 104 **GA,** Some sez he likes Babe, an' some sez he likes Susan's fried chicken. Now, in my day and time [*DARE* Ed: Speaker is interrupted]. **1913** Kephart *Highlanders* 285 **wNC, eTN,** Pleonasms are abundant... "In this day and time." **1952** Brown *NC Folkl.* 1.532, *Day and time, in this...* Now, at this time.—Caldwell county. **1966-69** *DARE* Tape **GA**1, This day and time there's very little saw timber in the—'round in this part anyway. Biggest thing now is pulpwood; **KY**24, We didn't .. have any florists back in that day and time; **VA**27, In place of steel, wasn't any steel at that day and time .. steel-bolsters like they use this day and time. **1986** Pederson *LAGS Concordance* **Gulf Region,** 11 infs, This (*or* that) day and time; 1 inf, *Molasses* was plural in her day and time.

day-bust n

Daybreak.

1941 J. Street *Father's House* 158 **seMS** *(ADD),* It was comin' day-bust, so I went and did my chores. **1971** Dwyer *Dict. for Yankees* 25 **Sth, S Midl,** *Day bust*—Dawn.

day chub n

=**cutlips minnow.**

1884 Goode *Fisheries U.S.* 1.618, The "Cut-lips," [=*Exoglossum maxillingua*], "Day Chub," or "Nigger Chub" .. [is] found in abundance only in the basin of the Susquehanna.

day clean n [Prob transl of a West African expression; cf quot 1949 and Fr Creole *ju netye* literally *jour nettoyé* day cleaned] **chiefly SC** *chiefly Gullah* Cf *DJE, DBE*

Daybreak, full day.

1867 Allen *Slave Songs* xxxiii, He was so black that "you can't sh'um [=see him] 'fo' day-clean." **1908** *S. Atl. Qrly.* 7.333 **SC** [Gullah], Me yiz yerry um buffo' day-clean soon er mo'nin'. [=I heard them before day-clean early in the morning.] **1922** Gonzales *Black Border* 27 **sSC, GA coasts** [Gullah], 'E tell'um .. 'e crap [=crop] ent stan' so berry good, 'cause nigguh' seem lukkuh [=like] dem ent lub fuh wu'k 'fo' day clean een de mawnin', en' dem .. wan' knock-off soon ez daa'k come. **[1928** Peterkin *Scarlet Sister Mary* 197 **SC** [Gullah], Keepsie got up before day was clean and did all his tasks before breakfast.] **1930** Stoney-Shelby *Black Genesis* 47 **seSC** [Gullah], 'Fore day-clean (dawn) in de mornin' o' de next day de creeter 'gin to come. **1949** Turner *Africanisms* 232 [Gullah], [de klin] 'dawn,' i.e., 'day clean,' being a translation of the Wolof expression [bər bu sɛt] 'dawn,' lit. 'the day clean.' **1950** *PADS* 14.25 **SC,** *Day-clean...* Broad daylight, sunrise, as opposed to daybreak, dawn. **1971** Cunningham *Syntactic Analysis Gullah* 52, I cough until dayclean. **1979** *DARE* File **SC** [Black], *Dayclean,* daylight. Current in Columbia SC, as "Its getting dayclean now."

day-dawzzle n

Appar the brightness of full daylight.

1931 *AmSp* 6.270 **KY,** A large class of compounds is formed by combining two words, usually of the same part of speech, to express similar or related ideas .. day-dawzzle.

day-day intj, n [Perh from Port pidgin, see quot 1950] *chiefly among Black speakers* Cf *DJE*

Goodbye; a gesture of farewell.

1901 Hobart *John Henry* 11 **NYC,** The four-flush call-down makes you back-pedal so hard that you grab for your hat, and you find yourself saying day-day long before Papa drops in. **1936** *Jrl. Amer. Folkl.* 49.234, [From "Turkey in the Straw," as of c1840] Crack my whip and the leader [of the team] sprung / I says "day-day" to the wagon tongue. **1950** *PADS* 14.25 **SC,** *Day-day...* A childish or lightly affectionate goodbye. Portuguese *adeos,* universally used on the west coast of Africa, God be with you! . . To shake *day-day,* is to wave the hand in farewell. **1966** *DARE* (Qu. II5b, *When you don't want to have anything to do with a certain person because you don't like him, you might say, "I'd certainly like to give him the ______.")* Inf **DC3**, Day-day (waving the hand).

day down n Cf **daylight down**

Sunset; late afternoon.

1895 *DN* 1.386 **VA coast,** *Day-down:* sunset. **1939** FWP *Guide NC* 98 **NC,** Late afternoon is "The pink of the evenin' " or "daydown." **1961** *Mt. Life* Fall 31 **Appalachians,** Mama found me there toward daydown, and made me come to the house and put on my good suit. **1972** Cooper *NC Mt. Folkl.* 90, *Day down*—late afternoon. **1982** Heat Moon *Blue Highways* 59 **NC,** The sun was just gone, the time Carolinians call "day down."

day fish n

A **smelt.**

1968 *DARE* (Qu. P2) Inf **CA**105, Smelt: a day fish or surf fish; (Qu. P7) Inf **CA**105, Smelt (day fish or surf fish).

dayflower n

Std: a plant of the genus *Commelina.* Also called **dewflower 1, wandering Jew, widow's tears**

day gown n

1969 *DARE* (Qu. W16a, *The full-length garment that a woman wears under her dress)* Inf **GA**77, Day gown—worn under the dress (old-fash).

day-herd n **West**

In a roundup, cattle separated from the main herd and held together; hence phr *stand day-herd* =**day-herd** v. Cf **cut n 3**

1884 Aldridge *Ranch Notes* 89 **eKS,** In the meantime two other round-ups have been proceeding, and our 'cuts' from them are brought along and all thrown together, forming the nucleus of what we call our 'day-herd.' **1929** Dobie *Vaquero* 16 **TX,** Mr. Driscoll . . put me in charge of holding the cattle during the day. Of course it has always been the boy's job to stand dayherd. **1966** *DARE* Tape **NM**14, Cattle that we were holding was put in what we called a day-herd. And that day-herd was kept by different men, men appointed each day to go with the day-herd, and that was what we held at night; **SD**8, Then [they would] cut out the four-year-old steers that they were gonna ship. . . They'd hold them in what they called the day-herd. They'd night herd them too. . . Herd 'em night and day, and every day they'd cut . . the beef out of this gathering, this roundup, and throw them into this day-herd; **OK**30 [see **day-herd** v].

day-herd v **West**

To stand guard over cattle during the day, esp the cattle of a **day-herd** n; hence n *day-herder.*

1902 *Out West Mag.* Oct 446, Step by step he had worked his way up the cowboy's painful promotion. He had been night-wrangler, horse-wrangler, day-herder, boy-rider, water mason, full hand, bronco buster, outside man. **1936** McCarthy *Lang. Mosshorn* np **West,** *Day-herd.* . . To guard the cattle while they graze and drink during the daytime. **1966** *DARE* Tape **OK**30, They'd have one man to day-herd the cattle. When they'd get the cattle, they'd have to drive their day-herd, their cut, to the next roundup place.

day-hunting owl See **day owl 2**

day-labor v

To work (on a farm) for fixed wages (rather than share-cropping).

1941 Perry *Hold Autumn* 15 **TX,** Just for a year, anyhow, I'd like to day-labor that little place, and know eatin was took care of for a few months.

daylight n

1 in phrr *beat* (or *scare*) *the daylights out of one* and varr: To beat (or scare) one severely. [Prob from *daylights* eyes, vital organs, but now usu used without precise reference]

[**1884** Nye *Baled Hay* 79 **Rocky Mts,** The driver bangs the mule that is ostensibly pulling his daylights out, humping up like an angle worm, without pulling a pound.] **1907** *DN* 3.186 **seNH,** *Daylights.* . . Eyes. Used in the v. phr. to knock one's daylights out. . . Cf N. W. Ark *lights.* **1921** *DN* 5.116 **KY,** *Daylights* . . eyes. "I'll beat the daylights out of you!" **1929** Ellis *Ordinary Woman* 61 **CO** (as of early 1900s), It is discovered and cut down by Henry, who declares he 'will thump the living daylights out of the next varmint that makes a swing.' **1944** *PADS* 2.26 **cwNC, cwOH,** *Daylights.* . . The eyes. "I'll beat the daylights out of him." (In some parts of VA: the lungs.) **1945** *Harder Coll.* **cwTN,** [Letter:] I thought sure she was going to faint. Liked to have scarred [sic] the daylights out of me. **1955** *AmSp* 30.234 **cIN** (as of 1890s), *Daylights. Knock the daylights out of* was part of a common threat and meant about the same as *knock the stuffin'* out of. In other words, we had no idea that *daylights* means eyes, as the dictionaries tell us. The word occurred nowhere else in our speech. **1955** Yerby *Treasure* 48 **SC** (as of 1845), Didn't mean to hit him. . . Meant to throw [=shoot in a duel] close to him and scare the living daylights out of him. **1956** McAtee *Some Dialect NC* 11, In the expression, "beat the daylights out of him," it manifestly did not refer to the eyes, the whole saying meaning to thrash comprehensively, give a good beating. **1965–70** *DARE* (Qu. Y15, *To beat somebody thoroughly: "John really ______ that fellow!")* Infs **KY**79, **MS**6, **OH**53, **WI**50, Beat the daylights out of; **NY**175, Beat the livin' daylights out of; **PA**164, Beat the daylight out of; (Qu. GG13a, *When something keeps bothering a person and makes him nervous, he may say, "It ______ me.")* Inf **WI**47, Irritates the living daylights out of; (Qu. GG24, *Other words meaning to frighten: "Now don't let those fellows ______ you.")* Inf **NY**202, Scare the daylights out of. **1966** Barnes–Jensen *Dict. UT Slang* 11, *Daylights.* . . the breath or the ability to see. To "beat the daylights out of one" is to give him a sound thrashing, even to leaving him unconscious. **1976** Lynn–Vecsey *Loretta Lynn* 107 **eKY,** He still rides in the rodeos around home—he even rides the bulls, which scares the daylights out of me.

2 =**windowpane.**

1884 Goode *Fisheries U.S.* 1.177, The Spotted Turbot . . in New Jersey is called Window-pane, or Daylight, because it is so thin that when held to the light the sun can be seen through its translucent flesh. **1889** *Century Dict.* 1466, *Daylight.* . . A name of the American spotted turbot, *Lophopsetta maculata,* a fish so thin as to be almost transparent, whence the name. Also called *window-pane.* **1895** *Std. Dict. Engl. Lang.* (Funk) 470/3, *Daylight.* . . [Local, U.S.] The sand-flounder or windowpane . . : named from its translucency.

3 in phr *show daylight:* Of a rider: to allow one's seat to leave the saddle. Cf **daylighting**

1929 *AmSp* 5.64 **NE,** One who "sits it" or rides "straight," sits uprightly and solidly in the saddle, shifting his balance with every change in the horse's position, is called . . a "top rider;" he doesn't "show daylight," space between his body and the saddle. **1939** (1973) FWP *Guide MT* 415, *Show daylight*—In bronc busting, to let light show between man and saddle; a usual preliminary to being "piled."

daylight down n *old-fash* Cf **day down**

The end of daylight; the beginning of darkness after sunset.

1769 (1903) Patten *Diary* 234 **NH,** I went to Lieut Moors Mill and got above a bushell of corn ground and we took notice of a blazeing star in the west about an hour high at daylight down. **1838** (1843) Haliburton *Clockmaker* (2d ser) 272, The last time I came by here, it was a bit arter daylight down, rainin' cats and dogs, and dark as Egypt. **1858** *N.Y. Tribune* 9 Oct. 3/3 *(DA),* It was e'en as much as I could do to git 'em into the wagons agin, and as it was, it was daylight-down before we got ten [sic] Crawford's. **1899** (1912) Green *VA Folk-Speech* 143, *Daylight-down.* . . When dark comes after sunset. "I expect him back by daylight-down."

daylighting vbl n Cf **daylight 3**

1936 McCarthy *Lang. Mosshorn* np **West,** *Daylightin'.* The term is used when a bronc bucks its rider out of the saddle so that one can see between the rider's seat and the saddle. Showin' daylight.

daylight in the swamp exclam

Among loggers: used as a wake-up call.

1944 Nute *Lake Superior* 209, The loudest . . voice was chosen to waken the men at dawn with . . "Daylight in the Swamp!" **1958** McCulloch *Woods Words* 45 **Pacific NW.** [**1966** *DARE* (Qu. A1, . . *Time in the early morning before the sun comes into sight)* Inf **ND**3, Daylight in the swamp.] **1967** Cerello *Dakota Co. MN* 53, Daylight in the swamp, boys! It's an old lumberjack saying how the cook would holler each morning to get the jacks to breakfast. **1969** Sorden *Lumberjack Lingo* 32 **NEng, Gt Lakes.** **1977** *Yankee* Nov 57 **ME,** Roll out, you tigers. It's daylight in the swamp!

daylight owl See **day owl 1**

daylight robber n Cf **cheater 2**

1956 Sorden–Ebert *Logger's Words* 11 **Gt Lakes,** Daylight-robber. . . log-scaler.

day lily n

1 Std: a plant of the genus *Hemerocallis.* For other names of var spp see **backhouse lily, corn lily 3d, ditch lily, Eve's thread 2, fire lily 1, homestead lily, lemon lily, orange lily, tiger lily, yellow lily**

2 A plant of the genus *Hosta.*

1889 *Century Dict.* 2412, *Funkia*. . . A genus of liliaceous plants. . . known as *day-* or *plantain-lilies.* **1902** Earle *Old Time Gardens* 70, At Napanock, . . New York. . . there were always the yellow Day Lilies somewhere in the flower beds, and the white and blue Day Lilies, the common Funkias. **1976** Bailey-Bailey *Hortus Third* 569, *Hosta*. . . *Plantain lily, daylily.*

‡day marble n

1968 *DARE* (Qu. EE6c, *Cheap marbles*) Inf **MD**26, Day marbles.

day mosquito n

1967 *DARE* (Qu. R15a, . . *Names . . for mosquitoes*) Inf **HI**4, Day mosquito (striped).

day owl n

1 also *daylight owl:* =**hawk owl 1.** [See quot 1872]

[**1844** Giraud *Birds Long Is.* 22, *Genus Surnia*. . . Day Owl.] **1872** Coues *Key to N. Amer. Birds* 205, *Hawk Owl. Day Owl*. . . It is the most diurnal bird of the family. **1898** (1900) Davie *Nests N. Amer. Birds* 245, *Hawk Owl*. . . A bird hawk-like in appearance, but nevertheless a true owl, and being the least nocturnal of its tribe, it is called Day Owl. **1936** Roberts *MN Birds* 1.614, *Súrnia úlula cáparoch*. . . Day Owl. **1946** Hausman *Eastern Birds* 357, *American Hawk Owl*. . . *Other Names* . . Daylight Owl. **1955** Forbush-May *Birds* 270, Day Owl. . . A conspicuous bird because of . . its habits of hunting in daylight.

2 also *day-hunting owl:* =**short-eared owl.**

1951 *AmSp* 26.278, *Day owl*. . . The short-eared owl (Pa.) **1967** *DARE* (Qu. Q2, *Other kinds of owls*) Inf **HI**14, Day-hunting owl.

day-port n Cf **davenport**

1968 *DARE* (Qu. E7, *The piece of upholstered furniture that you can stretch out on to rest*) Inf **NC**50, Day-port—some people call it this.

Dayton wagon n **esp MD, DE**

A type of horse-drawn wagon.

1887 *City of Balt. Half Century's Progress* 59 *(DA),* Two new engines had been built and placed in service, also one hose carriage, one Dayton wagon for the telegraph, one Concord wagon for chief engineer. **1968** *DARE* (Qu. N41a, . . *Kinds of horse-drawn vehicles*) Inf **DE**3, Dayton wagon—was covered carriage with four wheels; **MD**20, 29, Dayton wagon. [All Infs old]

‡day tripper n

1967 *DARE* (Qu. HH37, *An immoral woman*) Inf **WA**22, Day tripper.

dazzent See **dare** v **A4c**

d.d. n [Abbr for *drunk driving*]

=**d.w.i.**

1965-66 *DARE* (Qu. N13, *If someone has been drinking and then drives a car, he may be arrested for*) Infs **FL**27, **OK**11, D.d.

d.d.t.'s n pl [Joc var of *d.t.'s* delirium tremens]

1968-70 *DARE* (Qu. DD22, . . *Expressions meaning delirium tremens*) Infs **IA**47, **MD**42, **NY**241, D.D.T.'s.

de def art See **the**

de v See **duh** v

de prep See **duh** prep

deacon n

1 also attrib; also sp *deakin:* A very young calf, esp one that is runty or dies; the skin of such a calf. **chiefly Nth** Cf **bob veal**

1873 *Chicago Tribune* (IL) 2 Jan 6/2, Hides. . . Green butchers . . green salted . . dry kip . . dry calf . . deacons. 50-65¢. **1898** Westcott *Harum* 147 **cNY,** Jim brought three or four veals into town one spring to sell. . . 'I guess you got a "deakin" in that lot,' he [=Dick] says. . . 'You didn't never kill that calf. . . That calf died, that's what that calf done.' **1923** *DN* 5.234 **swWI,** *Deacon*. . . A calf of veal age; the hide or skin of such a calf. "That hide ain't worth much; it's only a deacon." *Deacon veal* is an equivalent of bob-veal. **1925** Arnold *Hides* 320 **NEng,** *Deacons* are skins of animals born alive which weigh, usually, below 5 or six pounds [green] . . and 2½ or 3 pounds [dry]. **1932** *Atlantic Mth.* 150.36/1 **NY,** I remember selling the hide of a farm-slaughtered cow for forty-three cents a pound, and deacon (newborn calf) skins for five dollars. **1949** *McDavid Coll.* **cwNY,** Deacon—a young calf killed for its hide. **1965-70** *DARE* (Qu. K20, *A calf that is sold for meat*) Infs **IN**69, **NY**187, Deacon; **MI**47, Deacon ['dikn̩] a very young calf ten days or younger, sold for meat and also sold to people that raises veal cattle; **MI**91, Deacon—a day-old calf. **1968** Adams *Western Words* 89, *Deacon*—A cowboy's name for a runty calf.

2 See quot.

1964 Hargreaves-Foehl *Story of Logging* 59 **MI,** *Deacon*—The shanty boy who could sing ballads or recite verses—play the harmonica, "squeeze box," fiddle, guitar, dulcimer, jewsharp—or tell a good yarn. He usually performed for the men in the bunkhouse on Saturday night—sitting or standing on the "deacon's bench" while entertaining.

deacon v

1 often with *off:* To read (a hymn) one or two lines at a time in order to lead a congregation in singing. **chiefly NEng** *old-fash*

[**1823** *MA Spy & Worcester Advt.* (Worcester MA) 8 Oct [2]/3 **cMA,** Some fifty years ago. . . it was the province of one of the Deacons, after the Psalm had been read from the pulpit, to repeat it line by line.] **1831** *Daily Eve. Transcript* (Boston MA) 27 Aug 2/1, In the olden times, . . it was a custom in many parts of New-England to sing the psalms and hymns by "deaconing" them, as it was called, that was, by the deacon's reading each line previous to its being sung. **1867** *Atlantic Mth.* 19.25 **ceMA,** A deacon he, you saw it in each limb,/ And well he knew to deacon-off a hymn. **1942** (1965) Parrish *Slave Songs* 68 **GA coast,** The deacon "deacons" a song when he reads it two lines at a time for the benefit of any in the congregation who have not a hymn book or who cannot read. The custom of "lining out" and then singing a hymn was copied from the whites.

2 To make (something) appear better than it is, esp to arrange (produce) with the best on top; to acquire by sharp practice; hence ppl adj *deaconed,* vbl n *deaconing.* **chiefly NEng**

1855 *Harper's New Mth. Mag.* 11.857/2, The practice of "topping off" a barrel of apples with the best is known by the name of "deaconing." *Ibid* 857 **ME,** A farmer down East . . sold a barrel of apples to his minister. . . The barrel . . was found to contain a very inferior quality. . . The minister . . made complaint to the farmer, who very coolly made answer: "Why parson, I rather guess you must have opened the barrel at the wrong end!" The only change it was known to produce . . was to make him careful afterward to "deacon" both ends. **1867** Lowell *Biglow* lxi **'Upcountry' MA,** To *deacon* berries is to put the largest atop. **1870** Alcott *Little Women* 1.168 **MA,** The blanc-mange was lumpy, and the strawberries not as ripe as they looked, having been skilfully "deaconed." **c1870** in 1950 *AmSp* 25.173 **CT, MA,** *To 'deacon' apples* is, in barrelling them for sale, to put the best on top. Danvers, Mass. The originator . . was Dea. (Lewis?) Norton, of Goshen, Conn. *To 'deacon' land* is to extend one's fence so as to include a portion of the highway. . . The originator . . was Dea. D . . n, of Middle-Haddam. **1904** *DN* 2.424 **Cape Cod MA** (as of a1857), *Deacon*. . . To put the best in sight, as to 'deacon a barrel of apples.' **1913** *DN* 4.54 **seNH,** *Deacon*. . . To arrange (fruit, vegetables, berries or the like) so that the best appear at the top; as, *deaconing* apples. **1922** Brown *Old Crow* 47 **NEng,** The old-fashioned men at Wake Hill used to read their Bible Sunday . . and go out early Monday morning to carry the apples to market all deaconed on top. **1975** Gould *ME Lingo* 70, *Deacon* . . to arrange apples in the top of a box or barrel so the customer presumes the same quality runs to the bottom. Thus, to put on a good front, perhaps with a mild effort at cheating, but at least giving an impression without backing it up: "He deaconed his barn by painting the side towards the ro'd."

3 To slaughter (a very young calf). [**deacon n 1**]

1839 MA Ag. Surv. *Rept. for 1838* 2.53 **wMA,** Most of them were killed at four days old. Throughout the county of Berkshire this mode of dealing with the calves is termed "deaconing" them. **1859** (1968) Bartlett *Americanisms* 115 **CT,** *To deacon a calf* is to knock it in the head as soon as it is born. **1925** Arnold *Hides* 321, [Footnote:] "To deacon" was to play a shabby trick—Thence, as one of several strained metaphors, to kill a calf while still very young. **1946** *McDavid Coll.* **cnNY,** To deacon calves is to butcher calves.

deaconed, deaconing See **deacon** v 2

deacon seat n Also *deacon's seat, ~ bench*

1 also *deacon's pew, ~ row:* A front row seat in church orig reserved for deacons.

1667 in 1883 Dorchester MA *Town Rec.* 146, [Men] to take Care about ordering the worke about the gallery and likwise a Table before the Deacons seate. **1857** *Atlantic Mth.* 1.96/1 **CT,** This important functionary was accustomed . . to take his place in the deacons' seat. **1965–70** *DARE* (Qu. CC5, . . *Seats in a church, especially near the front*) Infs **CA**7, **MA**7, **OH**95, Deacon's row; **CT**37, **MA**5, Deacons' pews; **KY**36, **WI**64, Deacon's bench(es); **SC**10, Deacon seat; **MO**29, Deacons' seats; **LA**6, Deacon's seat—front row on one side, the left, deacons' wives on the right.

2 Among loggers: a bench or settee, usu rough-hewn from a log and placed along the end of a row of bunks, often facing a fireplace. [See quot 1975] **chiefly Nth, esp ME** Cf *DCan*

1851 (1856) Springer *Forest Life* 71 **ME,** Directly over the foot-pole . . and in front of the fire is the deacon seat. . . The seat . . is . . a plank hewn from the trunk of a Spruce-tree some four inches thick by twelve inches wide, the length generally corresponding with the width of the bed. **1868** *Harper's New Mth. Mag.* 36.412/2 **MN,** At the foot of the bed . . was a long, flat beam, called the "Deacon's Seat." This Deacon's Seat is one of the representative places in a lumberman's camp. **1904** Day *Kin o' Ktaadn* 105 **ME,** The long "deacon-seats" stretch away into the shadows and the men sit in rows. **1907** *DN* 3.242 **eME,** *Deacon seat.* **1914** *DN* 4.71 **ME, nNH,** *Deacon-seat.* . . Long bench in lumber-camps. **1966** *DARE* FW Addit **nME,** *Deacon's bench*—the bench between bunks and against the wall in a lumber bunkhouse. **1968** *DARE* Tape **WI**59, He said, "Sonny, you and I are going to have a little visit tonight." I said, "Fine;" and so we sat down where no one could hear us on what they call the deacon seat in the bunkhouse. **1975** Gould *ME Lingo* 70, *Deacon-seat*—Because the deacons usually sat down front in church, the *deacon-seat* became the bench nearest the fire in a lumber camp.

deacon seater n [deacon seat]

1975 Gould *ME Lingo* 70, Sitting on it in the evening led to yarnin', and many a whopper took shape on the deacon-seat. A good tall story is a *deacon-seater.*

deacon's pew, deacon's row See **deacon seat 1**

deacon's seat See **deacon seat**

deacon veal See **deacon n 1**

dead adj Usu |dɛd|; also **chiefly Sth** *esp among Black speakers* |deɪd|; occas |dɛəd| Pronc-spp *dade, daid*

A Forms. [Proncs of the type [ded] are found in some Scots and Engl dial.]

1891 Page *Elsket* 123 **VA** [Black], Dee's mos' all daid b'fo' dis, suh? **1899** (1912) Green *VA Folk-Speech* 141, *Dade.* . . For *dead.* **1905** Culbertson *Banjo Talks* 21 **Sth,** Doan' weep w'en I is daid an' gone. **1909** *S. Atl. Qrly.* 8.40 **sSC coast** [Gullah], In Hartford Connecticut, 1776, *dead* was written *dayed;* the *Gullah* negro speaks it *daid,* today. **1929** Sale *Tree Named John* 34 **MS** [Black], Brer Fox daid! U-r-r my Lawd, Brer Fox daid! **1931** *AmSp* 6.167 **seVA,** In the records of several negroes and one white boy, *dead* is practically [deɪd]. **1934** Carmer *Stars Fell on AL* 208, Wasn't hardly a time when ole Man Smith wasn't daid to the worl'. **1941** *AmSp* 16.5 **eTX** [Black], *Dead, head* are both [dɛ:d], [hɛ:d], and [deɪd], [heɪd]. **1942** Hall *Smoky Mt. Speech* 20 **eTN,** Isolated examples of the same tendency [of [ɛ] to move toward [e]] are: *bed* [bɛ̝:ɪd], *dead* [dɛ̝əd], . . *death* ['dɛjəθ]. **c1960** *Wilson Coll.* **csKY,** *Dead* [ded]. Rare, usually humorous.

B Senses.

1 Unconscious, senseless. [Engl dial] **Sth, S Midl** *old-fash*

1887 *Scribner's Mag.* 2.482 **AR,** She war layin' on a log dead's a hammer. [Author's note:] They have a peculiar use of the word "dead" for "senseless." "He knocked him dead," they will say, or "She was plum' dead for an hour." **1903** *DN* 2.311 **seMO,** *Dead.* . . Unconscious. 'He was thrown from his horse and was dead for a few minutes, but he got up and rode home.' **1908** *DN* 3.304 **eAL, wGA,** *Dead.* . . Unconscious, senseless. "He was knocked dead for a few minutes." **1933** Rawlings *South Moon* 316 **FL,** My spells is comin' frequent. I were dead most all yistiddy evenin'. **1939** McGuire *FL Cracker Dial.* 173, I drank it and I was dead for a week. **1983** *MJLF* 9.39 **ceKY,** *Fall dead* [3 infs] . . to faint.

2 in var emphatic compar phrr:

a *dead as a doornail.* [*OED* c1350 →]

1825 Neal *Brother Jonathan* 3.277 **NEng,** If I didn't shoot him dead, you know; dead, as a door nail; ugh! it was all over with me. **1907** *DN* 3.186 **seNH,** *Dead as a door-nail.* **1908** *DN* 3.304 **eAL, wGA. 1910** *DN* 3.440 **cwNY. 1927** *AmSp* 2.352 **WV,** *Dead as a doornail* . . without any sign of life. "He looked to be dead as a doornail." **1969** *DARE* FW Addit **neKY, ceCT,** Dead as a door-nail.

b *dead as four-o'clock* and varr: See **four-o'clock 5.**

c *dead as a mackerel* (or *herring, pelcher, smelt*).

1838 (1843) Haliburton *Clockmaker* (2d ser) 130 **NEng,** Three Kentuckians were killed as dead as herrins. **1852** (1854) Kennedy *Horse-Shoe Robinson* 210 **VA,** The fellow was as dead as a pickled herring. **1853** Hammett *Stray Yankee in TX* 275, There . . lay a poor 'possum, . . to all appearance as dead as a mackerel. **1854** Riley *Puddleford People* 103 **West,** 'If it had'nt been for our party,' exclaimed Wiggins, in a loud voice, 'that great American eagle that has flew'd so long . . would now be as dead as a smelt, lying on his back, a-groaning for help.' **1927** *AmSp* 3.136 **eME,** "Pelcher" of "deader than a pelcher," still common on the Maine coast, appears in the *English Dialect Dictionary* as "pilchard, pilcher," "killed as dead as a salt pilcher." **1954** TN Folk Lore Soc. *Bulletin* 20.36 **eTN,** As dead as a mackerel. **1969** *DARE* FW Addit **ceNC,** Dead as a mackerel.

d in var other phrr: See quots. Addit exx in 1958 Taylor–Whiting *Dict. Amer. Proverbs*

1843 (1916) Hall *New Purchase* 385 **IN,** I'll . . kill you dead as chopped sassudge [=sausage]. **1899** (1912) Green *VA Folk-Speech* 26, Dead as a hammer; as a hatchet. **1906** *DN* 3.133 **nwAR,** *Dead as a door-post.* **1907** *DN* 3.186 **seNH,** *Dead as Hannah Emerson.* **1908** *DN* 3.304 **eAL, wGA,** *Dead as Hector.* . . Entirely dead. Very common. **1914** *DN* 4.71 **ME, nNH,** *Dead as hay,* or *deader'n' hay.* . . Lifeless; lacking energy. *Dead as Billy-be-damned.* . . Very dead. **1951** *PADS* 15.53 **ceIN,** *Dead as a nit.* . . Motionlessly dead. **1968–69** *DARE* FW Addit **swCA, ceCT,** Dead as a nit.

3 in var phrr; Fig: fishy; hidden; causing doubt or suspicion. **Sth, S Midl** Cf **dead cat on the line**

1965–70 *DARE* (Qu. V1, *When you suspect that somebody is trying to deceive you, or that something is going on behind your back you say, "There's ———."*) Infs **AL**10, **NC**36, **TN**24, **TX**26, Something dead up the creek; **SC**34, Something dead up the branch; **GA**77, **LA**13, **NC**33, Dead cat (up the branch); **LA**13, Dead duck up the stream; **AL**6, Something fishy about that; [something] dead up the creek; **NC**36, Dead rat; **LA**2, **TN**24, Dead nigger in the woodpile; **IL**114, Dead nigger somewhere.

4 In marble play, of a player or a taw: temporarily out of the game. Cf **deadline, fat adj**[2]

1890 *DN* 1.64 **KY,** *Dead-line:* a line . . beyond which every player must "plump" . . or he is *dead;* that is, out of the game for that time. **1908** *DN* 3.304 **eAL, wGA,** If one's taw falls short of this line on the first shot, he is *dead,* and must drop out of the game. **1922** *DN* 5.186, *Dead.* . . Out of play:—of a taw after another taw has hit it. **1955** *PADS* 23.15 **cwAL, cwTN,** *Dead.* . . Of a marble or taw that through some specific occurrence is deprived of play during a particular game. . . Of a marble or taw when it fails to clear the ring in which targets are placed. . . The taw must remain in the ring until one of the marbles is knocked out, in which case the taw is "dead" and is out of play for that particular game. **c1970** Wiersma *Marbles Terms* **Chicago IL** (as of 1955–62), Dead—any marble that rolled off of the . . carpet onto the linoleum was considered dead. The player who owned it was out of the game.

dead v

1 =**deaden 1.**

1638 in 1894 Watertown MA *Records* 1.5, Ordered yt whosoever shall dead any Trees up ye Commons . . shall pay for every Tree so killed. **1797** Imlay *Western Terr.* 477 **cwNY,** He continues cutting timber for fence rails, and deading trees on such land as he intends to prepare for cultivation during the ensuing season. **1856** in 1956 Eliason *Tarheel Talk* 268 **NC,** Deded ground. **1858** *Ibid,* Since the weather has opend I have stoped deading. **1899** (1912) Green *VA Folk-Speech* 143, *Dead.* . . A tree was deaded by cutting off the bark all around it. **1946** *PADS* 6.11 **VA, NC,** *Dead.* . . To chop the bark around the circumference of a tree to cause it to die. A tree so treated is deaded. Pamlico. Common.

2 To die; rarely, to cause to die; also used as past and past pple. **SC, GA coasts** *Gullah*

1888 Jones *Negro Myths* 43 **GA coast** [Gullah], You guine dead a po man. [=You'll die a poor man.] **1892** (1893) Botume *First Days* 119 **seSC** (as of c1864), You'na said you wanted to dead wid your own people. **1909** *S. Atl. Qrly.* 8.47 **sSC coast** [Gullah], De Lo'd gwine daid me ef me go. . . Me yent er-gwine. **1922** Gonzales *Black Border* 247 sSC, GA coasts [Gullah], Ef de 'ooman had'uh dead een de fall w'en de crop done lay by, I wouln' uh min' summuch, but 'e gone en' leddown en dead een June. [=If the woman had died in the fall when the crops were laid by, I wouldn't have minded so much, but she lay down and died in June.] *Ibid* 273, "When did his wife die?" I asked. "'E dead een Fibbywerry, suh." [=She died in February, sir.] **1928** Peterkin *Scarlet Sister Mary* 123 **SC** [Gullah], Sometimes, it [=a charm] works backwards as well as forwards, you might be de one to dead. **1930** Stoney-Shelby *Black Genesis* 108 **seSC** [Gullah], Br' Rabbit hair riz up. If Br' Wolf put fire in dat hollow he is goin' to dead *dead.*

dead n [Cf *EDD dead* sb.[2]]

Death.

1838 (1852) Gilman *S. Matron* 185 **eSC** [Gullah], "Ki!" said Jim, in a tone a little over a whisper, and snapping his fingers, "dead an't gwying for catch Maus Dick yet!"

dead as four-o'clock See **four-o'clock 5**

dead-ax wagon n Also *dead-ex wagon* [*dead* inert + **ax** n, **ex** n[1]]

A horse-drawn wagon with no springs, usu used for heavy loads.

1939 FWP *Guide MT* 249 (as of 1894), A "dead ax" wagon was sent 10 miles to borrow a small portable Mason and Hamlin organ. [**1948** Rittenhouse *Amer. Horse-Drawn Vehicles* 95, As the term indicates, dead axle drays had no springs, which could not be used when extremely heavy loads were hauled. These powerful drays were the mainstay of industry in the days before the truck.] **1967** *DARE* (Qu. N41b, *Horse-drawn vehicles to carry heavy loads*) Inf **OR**3, Dead-ex wagon—no springs; (Qu. N41c, . . *Light loads*) Inf **NV**2, Light, dead-ax wagon—no springs, i.e., dead axle. **1978** Doig *This House* 39 **MT** (as of c1920), The [sheep-shearing] crew had a dead-ax wagon to haul its outfit in.

deadbeat v [*deadbeat* a worthless person, idler, sponge] **esp Sth, S Midl**

To waste time, idle about; to take advantage of, impose (on); hence vbl n *deadbeating.*

1881 Stoddard *Esau Hardery* 177, He's dead beated on you. **1888** in 1971 Farmer *Americanisms* 194, No party [=person] can dead-beat his way on me these hard times. **1965-70** *DARE* (Qu. A9, . . *Wasting time by not working on the job*) Infs **AL**52, **GA**1, 9, **SC**3, 32, **TN**44, Deadbeating; (Qu. Y27, *To go about aimlessly, with nothing to do: "He's always ______ around the drugstore."*) Inf **TN**13, Deadbeating; (Qu. BB27, *When somebody pretends to be sick [often to get out of doing something] you'd say he's ______*) Infs **GA**9, 77, Deadbeating; (Qu. II33, *To get an advantage over somebody by tricky means: "I don't trust him, he's always trying to ______."*) Inf **GA**86, Deadbeat somebody; **NJ**33, Deadbeat you; (Qu. JJ26, *If somebody has been doing poor work or not enough, the boss might say, "If he wants to keep his job he'd better ______."*) Infs **KY**41, **SC**32, Stop (*or* quit) deadbeating. **1988** Lincoln *Avenue* 80 **wNC** (as of c1940) [Black], Trouble was that when it came time to pay Coley, he'd already spent the money. But Coley thought he was trying to deadbeat him just because Queenie was his sister.

dead bird See **death bird 2**

deadborn adj [*OED* "now chiefly *dial.*"]

Stillborn.

1940 (1941) Bell *Swamp Water* 139 **Okefenokee GA,** If she don't care nothing about you, your poor heart's busted and you wish you had been dead-born.

dead cactus n

A **prickly pear** (here: *Opuntia stanlyi* var *parishii*).

1941 Jaeger *Wildflowers* 159, Dead Cactus . . *Opuntia Parishii.*

dead cart See **dead wagon**

dead cat on the line n [Prob orig in ref to a catfish on a fishing line] **Sth, S Midl** See Map *esp common among Black speakers*

Something causing suspicion, mistrust, or concern; something immoral.

1965-70 *DARE* (Qu. V1, *When you suspect that somebody is trying to deceive you, or that something is going on behind your back you say, "There's ______."*) 20 Infs, **Sth, S Midl,** Dead cat on the line; **SC**10, Dead cat on the line behind me; [**GA**77, **NC**33, Dead cat up the branch]. [14 of 21 Infs Black] **1977** *DARE* File **sVA** [Black], "Dead cat on the line" is one of a store of expressions my mother had. I am sure that "cat" meant just that, a household pet. "Line" I am less sure of. We lived near a power line; so, as a child, I just assumed that she meant that. I now realize that she probably learned that expression as a young girl and that it could very well have been a railroad line. One thing is sure. The expression meant a stench in the air that no amount of cover up can conceal. **1980** *Ibid* **sLA,** I am originally from Louisiana, and the phrase "there's a dead cat on the line" is one that I have heard used . . by the black people. The area is about thirty miles due north of Baton Rouge, and is a back-water. It was somewhat common to hear about five years ago, but had passed out of usage except by the older people by about a year ago. . . When the phrase was used, it was to connote the feeling that there was something wrong at someone's house. It came from the saying "there is a dead catfish on the trot-line." What the translation is, is that someone has found a dead fish on another person's trot-line; therefore that person has not been out recently to run the line and check for fish. . . There must be something wrong over there. . . Something unusual has happened or is happening. **1981** *Ibid* **TN** [Black], [The phrase *dead cat on the line* has] nothing to do with a catfish, left too long on the fish line. 'Tis a female who must be having an affair because there's no movement during intercourse. **1982** *Smithsonian Letters* **neVA,** "Dead cat on the line" [is] an expression I had not heard since my youth in 1936. In our home in Loudoun County, Va. my father had an old 78 rpm record . . featuring sermons by a black minister named Reverend Gates. On one side . . was "You Midnight Ramblers" and on the other side "Dead Cat on the Line." . . [Story of the phone company not being able to get a message through; man sent to investigate reported that a cat had climbed up the telegraph [sic] pole and died on the line.] "If a child don't favor his father in some way, there's a dead cat on the line!"

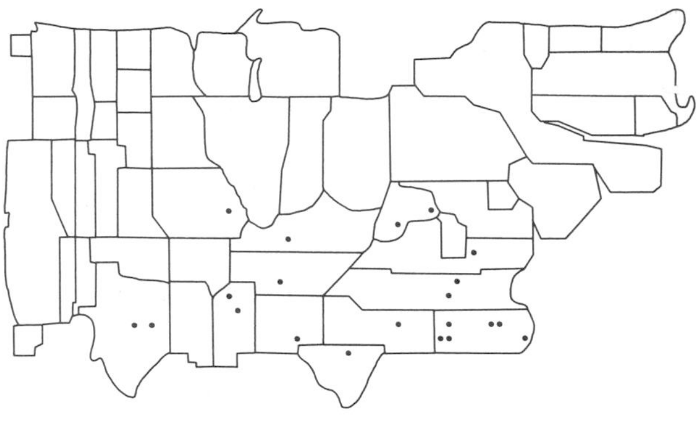

•dead cat on the line + var (Qu. V1)

dead devils n pl

See quots.

1968 *Foxfire* Fall-Winter 100 **nGA** [Stilling terms], *Dead devils*—tiny beads in the proof vial which indicate that the whiskey has been proofed sufficiently. Stop adding water or backings at the moment shaking the proof vial produces dead devils. **1969** *DARE* Tape **GA**72, If it's too high proof, the beads will be very coarse or very large and as you bring the alcoholic content of it down . . the beads will get finer and when they get very fine, it's dead. And when these very fine beads and these little fine specks come up, we call them dead devils, and when that happens you have killed it.

dead dog v phr

Lie down and remain still!—used as a command to a dog.

1965-70 *DARE* (Qu. J9a, *To tell a dog to lie down on the ground and keep still*) 12 Infs, **scattered Nth, N Midl,** Dead dog. **1986** *DARE* File **nwMA,** A 73-year-old woman was heard training her dog. One of the commands it knows is "Dead dog!"

deaden v

1 To kill (a tree) by cutting through its bark in a ring about its circumference; to clear (land) using this method; hence n *deadener,* vbl n *deadening,* ppl adj *deadened.* Cf **dead v 1**

1775 Adair *Amer. Indians* 405, They [=Indians] deadened the trees by cutting through the bark. **1843** (1916) Hall *New Purchase* 51 **IN,** The only field in sight was a few yards of "clearing," stuck with trunks of "deadened" trees. **1855** Sargent *Hist. Exped. Du Quesne* 84 **PA,** A good woodsman will soon deaden a number of acres, which by the next seed-time will be ready for cultivation. **1880** Burnett *Recollections* 14 **MO** (as of 1820s), The large trees [were] belted around with the axe, by cutting through the sap of the trees, which process was called "deadening." The trees belted would soon die. **1899** (1912) Green *VA Folk-Speech* 143, *Deaden*. . . To kill trees by belting. **1948** *Times-Picayune* (New Orleans LA) 24 Oct 6/4 **seLA,** These trees have been deadened. . . This is the first step in the logging of cypress. 'Deadeners' go into the section after it has been surveyed for cutting. **1954** *Harder Coll.* **cwTN,** *Deaden* . . To cut the bark from around trees so they will die; to girdle trees to clear land. **c1960** *Wilson Coll.* **csKY,** *Deaden*. . . To chop around a tree trunk to cause the tree to die. **1967** *DARE* FW Addits **AR, LA, OK, TX,** *Deaden*—to cut a ring around the bark of a tree near the ground to kill it. Chemical poisons are sometimes injected into the cuts. **1981** Hardeman *Shucks* 55, They continued the clearing of new ground annually until all the area ultimately intended for farming land had its trees deadened or removed.

2 To kill (someone).

1974 (1975) Shaw *All God's Dangers* 29 **AL** [Black], He flew in a passion over that book business and throwed that pistol on old Uncle Henry and deadened him right there.

deadened See **deaden 1**

deadener n

1 See **deaden 1.**

2 In logging: see quot.

1905 U.S. Forest Serv. *Bulletin* 61.34 [Logging terms], *Deadener*. . . A heavy log or timber, with spikes set in the butt end, so fastened in a log slide that the logs passing under it come in contact with the spikes and have their speed retarded. (Gen.)

3 See quot.

1927 *AmSp* 2.352 **WV,** *Deadener* . . an enormous meal eaten after having been deprived of food for some time. "He certainly ate a deadener for dinner."

4 in phr *to get the deadener on one:* See quot. Cf **deadwood**

1927 *AmSp* 2.352 **WV,** *Deadener on one, to get the* . . to obtain the proof against any one. "He has gotten the deadener on the other side in that law suit."

deadening n Pronc-spp *dead(e)nin'* **[deaden 1]**

1 Land cleared by girdling trees; see quot 1906. **chiefly S Midl**

1785 in 1940 *AmSp* 15.170 **VA,** 1000 Acres commonly called the poplar level and Including a pawpaw deadening. **1858** *Ibid* **VA,** To a pine sapling and fallen down white oak at the lower end of the Addair deadening. **1864** Gilmore *Down in TN* 100, A poor white man, however, who could be trusted, had a small "dead'nin' " about a mile away. **1903** *DN* 2.311 **seMO. 1906** *DN* 3.133 **nwAR,** *Deadening*. . . A clearing in the woods made by girdling the trees, which die, but remain standing for years, while the ground produces cotton, corn, etc. "Did you see the picture of a deadening in the Arkansas House at the World's Fair?" **1911** *DN* 3.538 **eKY. 1917** *DN* 4.410 **NC, KY. 1939** *Hall Coll.* **eTN, wNC. 1949** Guthrie *Way West* 52 **MO,** Land that won't grow a tree won't grow nothin'. Thing to do is to make deadenin's, like always, and cut your trees and plant among the stumps. **1953** Randolph *Down in Holler* 238 **Ozarks,** *Deadenin'*. . . An area in which the trees have been killed by girdling or collaring, but remain standing. When the trees are felled and cleared away, the *deadenin'* becomes a *clearin'*. **1960** Hall *Smoky Mt. Folks* 57 **eTN, wNC. c1960** *Wilson Coll.* **csKY. 1967** *DARE* FW Addit **ceLA,** *Deadening* . . an area where the trees have been deadened—such an area may be called a deadening even after it has been cleared. Common.

2 See **deaden 1.**

dead-ex wagon See **dead-ax wagon**

deadeye n

c1970 Wiersma *Marbles Terms* **NY** (as of 1960), Dead eye—a pure black marble.

dead fishing See **dead line fishing**

dead for sleep adj phr

1957 *Hall Coll.* **NC,** *Dead for sleep* . . deadly in need of sleep.

dead furrow n Cf **doubler 2**

See quot 1917.

1838 MA Ag. Surv. *Rept. for 1837* 1.68, It [=the side hill plough] saves considerable time in turning at the corner of a field, and it avoids a dead furrow in the center. **1873** IL Dept. Ag. *Trans.* 10.94, The land between the rows should be plowed toward the trees, so as to have the "dead furrow" in the center, to allow the water to pass off freely. **1896** *DN* 1.420 **NJ,** When a field is ploughed in strips or sections to avoid "dead furrows," each strip is called a *land.* **1917** *DN* 4.390 **neOH, IL, NY, NEng,** *Dead-furrow*. . . The double furrow or ditch left between two lands in plowing. **1927** *AmSp* 2.352 **WV,** *Dead furrow* . . a double furrow left in the ditch between the lands after plowing the field. "The dead furrow will serve to drain the fields."

deadhead n

1 One who receives goods or services without paying; hence attrib, non-paying.

1841 *Spirit of Times* 23 Jan. 564/1 *(DA),* The house on Tuesday was filled as far as $300 could fill, barring 'the dead heads.' **1892** *Congressional Record* 31 May 23.8.385/1 **WA,** The free-delivery service is burdened by the collection and delivery of thousands of tons of dead-head matter under the "penalty-postage system." **1899** (1912) Green *VA Folk-Speech* 143, *Deadhead*. . . One who is allowed to ride in a public conveyance, to attend a theatre or other public place of amusement without payment. **1905** *DN* 3.7 **cCT,** *Dead-head*. . . A person travelling, or receiving admission to games, theatres, etc., without charge. **1907** *DN* 3.211 **nwAR. 1927** *DN* 5.444 [Underworld jargon], *Dead head*. . . Specif., one who steals a ride on a train. **1931** *Writer's Digest* 11.41, *Deadhead* . . employee riding over the road on company pass and on company business. **1938** Hertzler *Horse & Buggy Dr.* 107 **KS,** The country doctor cannot bluntly refuse a call just because the patient is a confirmed and joyous deadhead. **1948** *Time* 23 Aug 63/3, Rickenbacker thinks he knows what is wrong with the industry: too many carriers, too low fares, too many deadhead services (e.g. free meals). **1962** [see **deadhead** v 3]. **1965–70** *DARE* (Qu. U17, . . *A person who doesn't pay his bills*) Infs **KY**24, **PA**44, Deadhead.

2 By ext: a lazy, worthless person or animal; an idler or loafer—used as a generalized term of disparagement. **esp Nth, N Midl**

1932 *RR Mag.* Oct 367, *Deadhead* . . fireman's derisive term for brakeman. **c1940** Eliason *Word Lists FL* 7 **wFL,** *Deadhead*. . . An old ox. . . "Your log team is all deadheads; I'll bet every ox in it is fifteen years old." **1965–70** *DARE* (Qu. A18, . . *Expressions . . about a very slow person: "What's keeping him? He certainly is _____."*) Infs **CA**153, **NH**14, (A) deadhead; (Qu. Y28, *A person who loiters about with nothing to do*) Infs **KY**24, **MD**24, Deadhead; (Qu. HH15, *A very inexperienced person*) Inf **NY**24, A deadhead [Inf queries]; (Qu. HH16, *Uncomplimentary words with no definite meaning—just used when you want to show that you don't think much of a person: "Don't invite him. He's a _____."*) Infs **MI**65, **MN**2, **NY**92, **OH**49, **PA**180, **WA**13, Deadhead; (Qu. HH20a, *An idle worthless person: "He's a _____."*) Inf **PA**151, Deadhead; (Qu. HH40, *Uncomplimentary words for an old man*) Inf **NY**217, Deadhead; (Qu. II18, *Someone who joins himself on to you and your group without being asked and won't leave*) Inf **DC**11, Deadhead. **1969** *DARE* Tape **CA**147, We used to call them [=volunteers who fought forest fires] deadheads. They wouldn't work anyway. They'd just go for the meals; **IL**98, [FW:] Were you active in things in high school too? [Inf:] Believe it or not, I was a deadhead in high school.

3 A railroad car or engine being pulled empty.

1938 Beebe *High Iron* 220, *Deadhead:* . . Empty [railroad] passenger car. **1943** *AmSp* 18.164 [Railroad jargon], *Deadhead*. . . Empty passenger car. **1945** Hubbard *Railroad Ave.* 339, *Deadhead*. . . A locomotive being hauled "dead" on a train.

4 also *deadhead log:* See quot 1896.

1896 *DN* 1.415 **wFL,** *Dead-head:* a log so soaked with water that it will not float. . . "He raised seven deadheads and held them up with live logs." **1902** White *Blazed Trail* 380 **ceMI,** He was enabled to catch the slanting end of a "dead head" log whose lower end was jammed in the crib. The dead head was slippery, the current strong. **1920** *DN* 5.81 **NW,** *Deadhead.* A log or loose pile, one end of which is waterlogged. Dangerous to small boats. **1938** FWP *Guide MN* 458, Old, nearly submerged floating logs, called deadheads, remnants of lumbering days, are frequent in the water [of Lake St. Croix]. **1957** McMeekin *Old KY Country* 83, Dead heads, water-soaked logs hard to see because they floated just under the surface. **1966** *DARE* (Qu. KK56, *Wood that is heavy from being in water a long time*) Inf **WA**6, Deadheads.

5 See quot. Cf *DS* C25

1984 *MJLF* 10.149 **neWI,** *Dead head.* A large rock just below the surface, struck when plowing.

deadhead v

1 To obtain goods, service, transportation, admission, etc, without paying; to sponge; to allow (someone) to do the same. **[deadhead n 1]**

1855 *Chi. W. Times* 6 Sep. 1/3 *(DA),* The 'fast boys' of Chicago prefer to be members of the police force, by virtue of which they 'dead head' at all the unlicensed taverns. **1858** *Olympia* (Wash.) *Pioneer* 27 Aug. (Th.) *(DA),* The conductor concluded that it was the intention of the trio to dead-head one party through. **1907** Stewart *Partners* 263 **TN,** She could 'a' dead-headed her way into a show without half trying. **1951** *AmSp* 26.308 **seWI** [Truckers' terms] *Deadheading, pres. part. . .* said of a driver who rides with another on a return trip. **1985** *DARE* File **wNC** (as of c1920), A railway trainman explained his presence in a passenger coach by saying, "I'm not on duty; I'm deadheading back to the division point"; **sCA,** My uncle, who worked for TWA, used to deadhead between Kansas City and Los Angeles several times a year on vacation trips.

2 See quot. [**deadhead n 3**]

1951 *AmSp* 26.308 **seWI** [Truckers' terms], *Deadheading, pres. part.* Driving a return trip without a load. **1969** *AmSp* 44.203 [Truck drivers' jargon], *Deadhead*—Run empty.

3 To convey (freight) without charge.

1962 *AmSp* 37.285, Trucking firms label as *deadhead freight* any shipment on which charges are waived. For example, shipments of clothing and supplies to schools for underprivileged children can be *deadheaded* by arrangement with the trucking firms.

4 See quot; hence vbl n *deadheading.* Cf **deadhead n 4**

1958 McCulloch *Woods Words* 45 **Pacific NW,** *Deadhead. . .* To salvage sunken logs lost in rivers or lakes after a drive; or those that sink to the bottom of a log pond. **1969** Sorden *Lumberjack Lingo* 33 **NEng, Gt Lakes,** *Deadheading*—Salvaging sunken logs.

5 See quot. Cf **dead horse 3.**

1958 McCulloch *Woods Words* 45 **Pacific NW,** Deadhead. . . To work at a useless job.

deadhead adv

Of a person or freight: without payment; of a railroad car or engine: without crew or load.

1873 Twain–Warner *Gilded Age* 275, Senators and Representatives . . always traveled 'dead-head' both ways. **1888** *Portland Transcript* 14 Mar. (Farmer *Americanisms*), [Those letters] which had to do with the stage business and went dead-head. **1945** *Greeley* (Colo.) *D. Tribune* 9 Aug. 1/6 *(DA),* The engine and caboose running deadhead to Dawson, were overturned by the impact. **1968** Adams *Western Words* 90, *Deadhead. . .* Freight that was shipped without charge was said to *go deadhead.*

deadheading See **deadhead v 4**

deadhead log See **deadhead n 4**

dead horse n [Cf *OED horse* sb. 18]

1 A debt (for wages paid in advance) which must be worked off.

1832 Wines *In the Navy* I.73 *(DAE),* Unfortunately, most of us had not 'worked out our dead horses.' *Ibid (DAE), Dead horses* are debts due to the purser on account of advances of pay. **1930** Shoemaker *1300 Words* 16 **cPA Mts** (as of c1900), *Dead horse*—Doing work that has been paid for in advance.

2 A debt of any kind.

1854 Shillaber *Life Partington* 291 **NH,** Working out a debt is often called "working a dead horse." **1945** Colcord *Sea Language* 63 **ME, Cape Cod, Long Island,** Dead horse. . . In shore speech, it means the paying off of any sort of debt. "We've at last got rid of the dead horse on the club-house."

3 Work that "doesn't pay" but must be done.

1969 Sorden *Lumberjack Lingo* 33 **NEng, Gt Lakes,** *Dead horse*—A sort of useless job. River pigs [=those who drive logs down a river] considered stream clearing dead horse work.

dead in the shell adj phr

1914 *DN* 4.105 **KS,** *Dead in the shell. . .* Utterly worn out. "If I have to go without sleep, I'll be just dead in the shell."

dead-level best n

The best of one's abilities; utmost.

1956 Gipson *Old Yeller* 27 **TX,** Right after me came Little Arliss, naked and running as fast as he could, doing his deal-level [sic] best to get close enough to hit me with the big rock he was packing. **1963** Edwards *Gravel* 69 **eTN** (as of 1920s), She did her dead-level best to unseat the rider, and he did his best to keep his seat. **1976** Garber *Mountain-ese* 21 **Appalachians,** *Dead-level-best. . .* Utmost—I did my dead level best to git here on time but I jist couldn't make it.

dead lice are falling off, like adv phr For varr see quots **chiefly S Midl, Sth**

Of a person's manner of action: slowly, lethargically.

[**1912** Green *VA Folk-Speech* 34, Lice are said to leave the body of a dying person.] **c1960** *Wilson Coll.* **csKY,** *Act like the dead lice are dropping off (one). . .* Be inactive, slow, poky. **1965–70** *DARE* (Qu. A18, . . *Expressions . . about a very slow person*) Inf **AR**56, Drag around like dead lice was dropping off of him; **CO**2, Like the dead lice is a-falling off him; **TN**66, Moves like dead lice are falling off of him; (Qu. A20, . . *Telling somebody to hurry: You might say, "______!"*) Inf **GA**17, Don't act like dead lice is falling off you; (Qu. Y21, *To move about slowly and without energy*) Infs **AR**56, **MS**37, Walk (*or* creep) around like dead lice was (*or* were) falling off him; **MO**37, **SC**19, Moving (*or* move) like the dead lice dropping (*or* is a-falling) off of you; **AL**3, **SC**55, Moves like the dead lice was (*or* are) dropping off (of) him; **GA**77, **KY**74, Move (*or* mosey along) like dead lice; **TX**32, Get around like dead lice was falling off of them.

dead-limb bird n

=wood pewee.

1927 Forbush *Birds MA* 2.347, *Myiochanes virens . .* Dead-limb Bird. **1955** Forbush–May *Birds* 319, *Eastern Wood Pewee—Myiochanes virens . .* Dead-limb Bird.

deadline n **Sth, S Midl** Cf **dead** adj **B4**

In marble play: **=taw line.**

1890 *DN* 1.64 **KY,** *Dead-line:* a line drawn a few inches from a ring of marbles on the "taw" side, beyond which every player must "plump" in coming from "taw," or he is *dead.* **1893** Shands *MS Speech* 26, *Dead-line. . .* A word used by boys in playing the game of marbles called ring-men. It is a line drawn two or three feet from the ring, between the ring and *taws.* **1908** *DN* 3.304 **eAL, wGA,** *Dead-line. . .* In the game of marbles, a line drawn near the ring. If one's taw falls short of this line on the first shot, he is *dead,* and must drop out of the game. **1955** *PADS* 23.15 **cwTN,** *Deadline. . .* The line behind which [a] player must not allow his shooter to touch the ground on the first shot; if the marble does touch the ground behind this line, the taw is out of play or is *dead.* **1966–69** *DARE* (Qu. EE8, *The line toward which the players roll their marbles before beginning a game, to determine the order of shooting*) Infs **KY**29, **MO**2, **WV**3, Deadline. **1971** Wood *Vocab. Change* 39 **Sth,** [*Marbles. . .* If the game requires its players to shoot from a line drawn on the ground, the prevalent name of that line is *taw.*] *Ibid* 368, Additional volunteered words: *deadline, shooting line.*

dead line fishing n Also *dead fishing*

Bottom fishing.

1967–69 *DARE* (Qu. P17, . . *Fish[ing] by lowering a line and sinker close to the bottom of the water*) Infs **OH**42, **PA**29, Dead fishing; **KY**53, Dead line fishing; **IA**29, Dead line fishing—settles on the bottom.

dead loads n pl Cf **dead oodles**

A great quantity.

1869 Twain *Innocents* 616, Oh, certainly; the old man's got dead loads of books. **1897** *KS Univ. Qrly.* (ser B) 6.86 **neKS,** *Dead:* a general intensive, as dead loads, dead game, etc. **1901** Harben *Westerfelt* 6 **nGA,** She's been off to Cartersville, you know, an' has come back with dead loads o' finery. **1901** *DN* 2.138 **NY,** It was dead-loads of fun. **1906** *DN* 3.133 **nwAR,** He's got dead loads of money. **1908** *DN* 3.304 **eAL, wGA,** (Dead)loads. . . A great quantity.

deadly nightshade n

Std: the black nightshade *(Solanum nigrum).* Also called **duscle, poisonberry, poisonweed, popolo, stubbleberry, trompillo, wild potato**

deadman n[1] [ME *deedman*]

1 In logging, mining, and similar activities: a heavy, solid object of wood, concrete, or the like, usu buried in the ground and used to anchor a cable, guy wire, or hawser.

1867 Hosmer *Trip to States by Way Yellowstone & Mo.* 61 *(DA),* The mate and four men went ashore and made a 'dead man.' **1905** U.S. Forest Serv. *Bulletin* 61.34 **Nth, Pacific,** *Deadman. . .* A fallen tree on the shore, or a timber to which the hawser of a boom is attached. **1920** *DN* 5.81 **NW,** *Deadman.* A pole used to fasten guy wires to. Logging. **1929** *AmSp* 4.372 [Mining terms], *Kingpin*—The same as deadman. It is a heavy object which is buried and by means of a cable is connected with trolley or machine wires to keep them from sagging. **1948** *Sat. Eve. Post* 4 Dec 66/3 **CA,** A gasoline motor began to clatter out there, cables running from the corners of the barge to deadmen anchored in the canyon rock, grew taut, and the whole equipment began to lurch toward the bank. **1958** McCulloch *Woods Words* 46 **Pacific NW,** *Deadman*—A sunken weight or a log, used to anchor a cable. **1966** *Daily Oklahoman* (Oklahoma City OK) 11 Dec mag sec 11/2 [Oil field jargon], A "deadman" is . . a cement block or any kind of weight used to hold down wires or lines extending from the derrick. **1974** *DARE* File **seCA,** Dead man. A block of wood buried in sand for leverage in pulling out a stuck truck or car. **1980** *DARE* File **AK,** Short logs, called "dead men," were buried next to the tents to hold the tent ropes in sandy soil, where tent pegs would not hold.

2 A similar device used to brace a fence post.

1928 *AmSp* 4.127 **NE,** Because of the sand, the "sandhiller" uses "dead men," buried pieces of wood or iron fastened to the wire fence to hold it down. **1949** *PADS* 11.5 **wTX** (as of c1920), *Dead man*. . . A brace for the corner post of a fence. Common. **1954** *Harder Coll.* **cwTN,** *Deadman*. . . A piece of wood used to brace the corner of a fence. **1957** *Sat. Eve. Post Letters* **eNM,** "Dead man" for the post buried in the ground to keep the upright fence post from leaning. **1961** Adams *Old-Time Cowhand* 205, Posts at corners were usually larger and were braced with "dead men." These were made by twistin' several strands of barbed wire into a cable and fastenin' it to the top of the post, the other end bein' fastened 'round a large rock which was buried deep into the ground. **1968** Kellner *Aunt Serena* 104 **IN,** Fence posts set then would come up, even with a deadman (buried brace) between them.

3 See quot.

1970 *DARE* File **cwTN,** Dead men. Names for concrete balks built across campus drives and such to prevent cars from going too fast.

4 See **deadman still.**

5 See **dead man's throttle.**

dead man n[2] Also *dead men's fingers* [From their being thought poisonous]

The gills of a crab.

1899 (1912) Green *VA Folk-Speech* 143, *Dead-men*. . . Some inside part (lungs?) of a crab, not to be eaten, "as they will kill you." *Ibid* 144, *Dead men's fingers*. . . A part of a crab held to be unfit for food. **1946** *PADS* 6.11 **swVA, eNC,** *Dead men*. . . The parallel layers of the insides of a crab. **1950** *PADS* 14.25 **SC,** *Dead man*. . . The lungs or gills of a crab, not edible. Usually in the plural; supposed by Negroes to be very poisonous. **1955** *Hand Coll.* **cnOH,** Never eat the "dead man" of a crab, it will kill you. **1968** *DARE* Tape **LA22,** That's not good to eat with the crab. You got to clean the dead man out. **1984** *DARE* File **Chesapeake Bay** [Watermen's vocab], Dead men (gills).

deadman choppers See **deadman teeth**

deadman's bryony n

=**greenbrier.**

1933 Small *Manual SE Flora* 309, *Dead-man's bryonys.*—The more common species are well known for their carrion-scented flowers.

dead man's button See **dead man's throttle**

dead man's ear n

Among loggers: see quot.

1966 *DARE* Tape **MI10,** Pointing to . . stewed, dried apples a lumberjack might ask if somebody would hand them the dead man's ears.

dead-man's-fingers n

1 A fungus of the genus *Xylaria,* esp *X. polymorpha.*

1949 Palmer *Nat. Hist.* 55, *Dead Man's Finger. Xylaria* sp. . . is highly variable in size, color, and form. **1966** *DARE* (Qu. S19, *Mushrooms that grow out like brackets from the sides of trees*) Inf **NC24,** Dead man's fingers—a bad-smelling mushroom that's about the shape of a finger, red in color. **1972** Miller *Mushrooms* 222, *Xylosphaera polymorpha*. . . "Dead Man's Fingers". . . Club-shaped, cylindrical to finger-like, dull black. **1981** Lincoff *Audubon Field Guide Mushrooms* 376, *Dead Man's Fingers*. . . Usually in clusters, on rotting deciduous wood, at bases of stumps, especially maple and beech. **1987** McKnight-McKnight *Mushrooms* 30, *Dead-Man's Fingers. Xylaria polymorpha*. . . Usually club-shaped (fingerlike), but often flattened, fanlike. Surface white to grayish and fleshy at first, becoming dark brown to black with a white interior.

2 also *dead-men's-fingers:* A sponge *(Chalina arbuscula).*

1879 Hyatt *Commercial Sponges* 12 **NEast,** *Chalinula oculata* . . [is] one of the commonest sponges on our coast. . . The fishermen call it by the horrible name of "Dead-man's-fingers." It is of a brownish or dark pinkish color, grows in a bushy form with round stick-like or palmate branches having finger-like extensions, and is abundant in places where there is a strong tide-way. **1935** Pratt *Manual Invertebrate Animals* 90, *C[halina] arbuscula*. . . Dead men's fingers. Body a cluster of branches, . . of delicate texture and white or grass in color: North Carolina to Cape Cod.

3 A **fringed orchid** (here: *Habenaria psycodes* var *grandiflora*). [Cf *OED dead man's finger* (at *dead man*) "A local name for various species of *Orchis*"]

1940 Clute *Amer. Plant Names* 48, *H. fimbriata*. . . Dead man's fingers. **1959** Carleton *Index Herb. Plants* 35, *Dead-man's-fingers:* Habenaria fimbriata.

dead man's pedal See **dead man's throttle**

dead man's pinch n [*EDD dead-man's pinches* (at *dead-man*)]

1953 *PADS* 19.10 **sAppalachians,** *Dead man's pinch*. . . Used to explain a black and blue spot on one's skin that one cannot account for.

dead man's stew n Cf **graveyard stew**

1977 *DARE* File **csWI,** Dead man's stew, graveyard stew, milk toast.

dead man's throttle n Also *dead man, dead man's button, ~ pedal*

In railroading: see quots.

1943 *AmSp* 18.164 [Railroad jargon], *Dead man's throttle.* Throttle requiring pressure to prevent power shut-off. **1945** Hubbard *Railroad Ave.* 339, *Dead man's throttle*—Throttle that requires pressure of operator's hand or foot to prevent power shut-off and application of brakes. An engine so equipped would stop instantly if the operator fell dead. Also called *dead man's button.* **1968** *AmSp* 43.286 [Railroad jargon], *Dead-man's pedal.* On road diesels, a pedal on the floor under the brake valve that has to be kept depressed whenever the engine is in motion. If the engineer should become ill, faint, or die (as has happened), the theory is that his foot will not hold the pedal down. When released, the brakes will apply automatically, and the diesel will shut down to an idle. **1969** *AmSp* 44.255 [Railroading jargon], *Dead man*—Control pedal on the floor of a locomotive, in front of the engineer's seat, that is depressed by the engineer during normal operation of the locomotive and, if released, causes the train to go into emergency automatically.

deadman still n Also *deadman* [From its resemblance to a coffin] Cf **hog B10a**

In moonshining: a low, flat still.

1969 [see **hog B10a**]. **1972** *Foxfire Book* 323 **GA,** The dead man still . . is a purely modern variety with a tremendous yield. The beer, rather than being made in separate boxes, *can* be made right in the still. *Ibid* Plate 279, These diagrams illustrate perhaps the simplest still of them all—the "dead man" or "flat." . . the still itself—a rectangular box.

dead man's wagon See **dead wagon**

deadman teeth n pl Also *deadman choppers*

1966–70 *DARE* (Qu. X13b, *Joking names for false teeth*) Inf **NC88,** Deadman choppers; **SC10,** Deadman teeth. [Both Infs Black]

deadmen's bells n

A **beardtongue** (here: *Penstemon digitalis*).

1897 *Jrl. Amer. Folkl.* 10.52, *Penstemon Digitalis* . . dead men's bells, [From growing on graves.] West.

deadmen's bones n [Cf *EDD dead-man's bones* (at *dead-man*) *"Stellaria holostea"*]

=**butter-and-eggs 1.**

1892 *Jrl. Amer. Folkl.* 5.101, *Linaria vulgaris* . . dead men's bones. Troy, N.Y. **1900** Lyons *Plant Names* 226, *L[inaria] Linaria* . . Deadmen's-bones. **1949** Moldenke *Amer. Wild Flowers* 272, The common name of *butter-and-eggs* for this plant seems appropriate because of the colors of the corolla, but the names *eggs-and-bacon, . . deadmens-bones,* . . and *rabbitflower* are a bit more obscure in their application.

dead men's fingers n

1 See **dead man** n[2].

2 See **dead-man's-fingers.**

dead nettle n

1 A plant of the genus *Lamium.* Also called **archangel 3, henbit 1, monkey-flower, rabbit meat, snowflake, white alexander** [*OED* 1398 →]

1830 Rafinesque *Med. Flora* 235, *Lamium* . . Deadnettle. **1840** MA Zool. & Bot. Surv. *Herb. Plants & Quadrupeds* 178, *Lamium amplexicaule.* L. Dead Nettle. Hen-bit. **1932** Rydberg *Flora Prairies* 687, *Lamium* . . Dead Nettle. **1944** AL Geol. Surv. *Bulletin* 53.195, *Lamium* . . (The Dead-nettles.). **1946** Reeves-Bain *Flora TX* 159, *Lamium* . . Dead Nettle. **1946** Tatnall *Flora DE* 221, *Lamium* . . Dead Nettle.

2 A **hemp nettle** (here: *Galeopsis tetrahit*).

1784 in 1785 Amer. Acad. Arts & Sci. *Memoirs* 1.461 **MA,** *Galeopsis* . . Allheal. Hempleaved Dead-Nettle. Blossoms purple. By the roadside. Gloucester. August. **1900** Lyons *Plant Names* 167, *G[aleopsis] Tetrahit* . . Hemp Deadnettle.

3 A **hedgenettle** (here: *Stachys palustris*).

1900 Lyons *Plant Names* 356, *S[tachys] palustris*. . . Dead-nettle. **1914** Georgia *Manual Weeds* 357, Dead Nettle. . . A coarse weed. . . Because of its prickly hairiness and unpleasant taste cattle refuse to eat the plant either green or cured in hay. **1974** (1977) Coon *Useful Plants* 163, *Stachys palustris* . . Dead-nettle . . has thousands of years of rated values behind it, but modern medicine finds little value in any use made of it.

4 =**angelica 1a.**

1876 Hobbs *Bot. Hdbk.* 30, Dead nettle, Angelica, Angelica atropurpurea. **1971** Krochmal *Appalachia Med. Plants* 46, *Angelica atropurpurea. . . Common Names:* . . dead nettle.

dead'nin' See **deadening**

dead oodles n Also *dead oodlins, ~ oogens* Cf *DS* U38a, LL8a, LL9a

A great quantity.

1869 *Overland Mth.* 3.131, A Texan never has a great quantity of any thing, but he has "scads" of it or "oodles" or "dead oodles," or "scadoodles," or "swads." **1883** Sweet-Knox *Mexican Mustang* 100 **TX,** When I kem here in '46 thar was dead-oodles of game all around here,—bar, and deer, and wild turkey, and all kinds of varmints. **1905** *DN* 3.63 **NE,** *Oceans, oodles, oogens,* or *dead oogens*. . . Large quantities. **1912** *DN* 3.574 **wIN,** *Dead oodlins*. . . Quantities, especially great quantities. "Why, there are dead oodlins of them on our trees." **1942** Berrey-Van den Bark *Amer. Slang* 20.3, *Large amount; many*. . . dead loads, ~ oodles, ~ oodlins, ~ oogens &c.

dead soldier n

1 See quot. Cf **deadman** n[1] **1**

1968-74 *DARE* File **nWI,** *Dead soldier*—A concrete or cement block buried to hold a pole steady; **nwWI** (as of c1910), *Dead soldier*—A block of concrete buried in the ground and used to support a pole (e.g. for a clothesline).

2 See quot.

1968 *DARE* (Qu. U29, . . *Worthless money*) Inf **WI**64, Dead soldiers.

dead wagon n Also *dead cart, dead man's wagon*

A vehicle used chiefly for transporting the dead, but sometimes also as an ambulance.

1894 *Outing* 14.7/1, Dead wagons, hospital ambulances and sanitary corps vehicles were the most prominent objects in the streets. **1939** FWP *Guide TN* 211, Then came the yellow fever epidemics of 1867, 1873, and 1878. . . As deaths mounted, the streets were deserted except for the dead wagons. **1943** *AmSp* 18.153, *Dead wagon* in upper South Carolina does not mean 'ambulance.' It usually means 'hearse' or . . a light truck in which bodies are carried to an undertaker's. . . (Professor George L. Trager says that in the New York area *dead wagon* is the common term for 'hearse.') . . In rural areas or small towns the same vehicle may serve both as ambulance and as hearse. Under either circumstance it would be natural to say that 'Grandpa went to the hospital in the dead wagon.' **1951** Johnson *Resp. to PADS 20* **DE,** Dead wagon comes for the body; the hearse takes it to the cemetery. **1954** *Harder Coll.* **cwTN,** Dead man's wagon: Hearse. **1965-70** *DARE* (Qu. N1, . . *An ambulance*) 81 Infs, **scattered,** Dead wagon; (Qu. N2, *The car used to carry a dead body for burial*) 64 Infs, **scattered,** Dead wagon; **ME**19, Dead cart; **AR**15, Dead man's wagon. **1977** *DARE* File **csWI** (as of c1950), We used to have lots of funerals, for dogs, cats, chickens, you name it. And I remember when the dead wagon came [for a horse or cow]; **CA** (as of 1930) Dead wagon? That's what we used to call it [=a hearse] too.

deadwood n Also rarely *deady* [See quot 1867; origin sugg in quot 1977 is erron since the term was in use before Hickok's death in 1876.] **chiefly S Midl, West**

Advantage, control, esp incriminating evidence—used in phrr *have* (or *have got*) *the deadwood on one.*

1851 in 1922 Clappe *Shirley Letters* 84 **CA,** If they ask a man an embarrassing question, or in any way have placed him in an equivocal position they will triumphantly declare that they have "got the deadwood on him." **1867** Richardson *Beyond the Mississippi* 134 **KS,** Another and more significant barbarism is 'the deadwood,'—from the game of 'ten-pins,' in which a fallen pin sometimes lies in front of the standing ones so that the first ball striking it will sweep the alley. 'I have the dead wood on him,' was used familiarly, meaning: 'I have him in my power.' **1895** *DN* 1.386 **West,** *Dead wood:* in phrase "to have the dead wood on anything" = to have control, or a firm hold, of it. **1905** *DN* 3.77 **nwAR,** *Deadwood, deady*. . . Advantage, control. 'I've got the (deadwood, deady) on you.' **1908** *DN* 3.304 **eAL, wGA,** *Deadwood*. . . Advantage. "I've got the deadwood on him now." **1916** *DN* 4.324 **KS,** *Have the dead wood on*. . . To have one in a position where he cannot, or prudently may not, help himself,—esp. with reference to information or knowledge possessed by the active agent. "He would have denied his part, but we had the dead wood on him." Phila[delphia]. General southeast. **1954** *Hall Coll.* **eTN,** *He had the deadwood on him.* He had the advantage over him; he had the upper hand. **1966** *DARE* (Qu. DD36; total Infs questioned, 75) Inf **NM**11, Don't deal with him unless you have an ace in the hole—you want to have the deadwood on him. **1977** Watts *Dict. Old West* 111, *Deadwood*—To have the advantage over someone, to have the drop on them. A term thought to have been derived from the shooting of Wild Bill Hickok in the back of the head by Jack McCall in Deadwood, South Dakota.

deadwood day n

1964 Smith *PA Germans* 119, *The First of August*—This date has been referred to as *Deadwood Day* by a number of informants in widely separated sections of the [Shenandoah] Valley. One said, "My dad always cut brush on August first because he claimed it wouldn't grow again." An informant born in 1870 recalled, " . . a day when we all had to go out, the girls and all, and hoe to grub out the brush and weeds along the fences. We were told that if we did it on that special day the weeds wouldn't grow up anymore." Others have reported that July 30th was the date for killing brush in their neighborhoods. All those holding such a belief were dialect-speakers of Pennsylvania German heritage.

deady See **deadwood**

deaf adj Usu |dɛf|; less commonly |dif| (the std pronc in EModE); also **chiefly Mid Atl** |dɪ(ə)f|; occas |deɪf, dɛɪf|; infreq |dæf, dɛθ| Pronc-spp *deef(e); eye-dial def(f)*

A Forms.

1789 Webster *Dissertations Engl. Lang.* 128, *Deaf* is generally pronounced *deef.* It is the universal practice in the eastern states; and it is general in the middle and southern; tho some have adopted the English pronunciation, *def.* The latter is evidently a corruption. **1836** [see **B1e** below]. **1840** (1847) Longstreet *GA Scenes* 30, Old Kit's both blind and *deef,* I'll be dod drot if he eint. **1858** *Knickerbocker* 52.428 **NEast,** *He* might have been as 'deefe' as a post, it seems to us without greatly affecting his preaching. **1899** (1912) Green *VA Folk-Speech* 144, *Deef.* **1903** *DN* 2.292 **Cape Cod MA** (as of a1857), Vowels were pronounced long in . . *itch (eetch), deaf.* **1906** *DN* 3.117 **sIN,** *Deaf*. . . Regularly pronounced [dif]. **1907** *DN* 3.186 **seNH,** *Deef.* **1908** *DN* 3.304 **eAL, wGA,** *Deef*. . . Still common. **1910** *DN* 3.440 **cwNY,** *Deef.* **1935** *AmSp* 10.292 **Upstate NY,** *Deaf* appears 33 times with [i] and 171 times with [ɛ]; . . the old form [dif] is dying out except in remote districts. **1946** *AmSp* 21.97 **sIL,** *Deef.* **c1960** *Wilson Coll.* **csKY,** *Deaf* [dif]—still common. **1961** Kurath-McDavid *Pronc. Engl.* 131, *Deaf*. . . Three different vowel phonemes occur in this word: the /ɛ/ of *left,* the /i/ of *leaf,* and the /ɪ/ of *stiff.* /ɛ/ is current throughout the Eastern States. . . The vowel /ɪ/ . . is widely current in folk speech, and to some extent in the speech of the middle class, in a well-defined area extending from the lower Potomac southward to the valley of the Neuse in North Carolina. . . A fair number of relics of /ɪ/ survive also on Delmarva and in South Carolina; scattered instances are found in western Pennsylvania and the South Midland, and even in New Jersey. Outside the /ɪ/ area . . *deaf* has predominantly the vowel /i/ . . in the folk speech of the Eastern States, except for the urbanized areas. . . In common speech its currency is more or less restricted to New England, central Pennsylvania, and the South Midland; even here it is yielding ground to /ɛ/. **1965-70** *DARE* (Qu. X19a) 748 Infs, **widespread,** (Partly *or* slightly, etc) deaf [dɛf]; 143 Infs, **widespread,** (Kinda *or* partially, etc) deef [dif]; **NJ**69, **NC**61, **TN**50, **SC**19, **VA**73, [dɪf]; **TX**1, [dɪəf]; **VA**39, [dɪɛf]; **IN**3, [deɪf]; **IN**27, [deəf]; **OK**47, **WA**3, 9, 11, [dɛɪf]; **NJ**7, [dæf]; **PA**94, [dɛθ] [Of all

Infs responding to this question, 28% were grade school educ or less; of those giving *deef* [dif] as a response, 38% were grade school educ or less]; (Qu. X19b) 633 Infs, **widespread,** (Stone) deaf; 332 Infs, **widespread,** Deaf (as a doornail, post, etc); 65 Infs, **scattered,** Deef [dif] [usu in compar phr]; **NC**61, 76, **VA**46, [dɪf]; **VA**39, [dɪɛf]. **1976** Allen *LAUM* 3.270 (as of c1950), Of the three pronunciations of *deaf* found in the eastern states, with the /ɛ/ of *left,* the /i/ of *leaf,* and the /ɪ/ of *lift,* only the first is general in the U[pper] M[idwest] and the third occurs as a single instance.

B Senses.

1 in var compar phrr indicating extreme deafness: See below. Cf **adder 3a**

a *deaf as a doornail* (or *doorbell, doorknob*). [*OED* a1400–50 →]

1950 *WELS* 8 Infs, **WI,** Deaf as a doornail; 1 Inf, **ceWI,** Deaf as a doorknob. **1965–70** *DARE* (Qu. X19b, . . *If a person's hearing is very bad*) 120 Infs, **widespread,** Deaf as a doornail; 27 Infs, **esp Sth, Midl,** Deaf as a doorknob; **GA**82, **LA**35, Deaf as a doorbell; **MN**39, **NY**7, 14, **WA**28, Deafer than a doornail; **WA**22, Deafer than a doorknob.

b *deaf as a post* (or *doorpost, fence post, mill post*). [*OED deaf* a. 1. d 1551 →]

1822 Watterston *L—Family* 52 **DC,** But, would you believe it, this poor walking ghost,/ Desires us to think him as deaf as a post? **1869** Barnum *Struggles* 122 **NYC,** To assist me properly you must seem to be as deaf as a post; wear a serious countenance; answer no questions; pay no attention to any one. **1908** *DN* 3.304 **eAL, wGA,** *Deaf as a (door) post.* **1942** McAtee *Dial. Grant Co. IN* 22 (as of 1890s), *Deef as a post.* **1965–70** *DARE* (Qu. X19b) 111 Infs, **widespread,** Deaf as a post; **AL**30, **MA**5, **NC**52, **SC**4, 24, **TX**33, Deaf as a doorpost; **AR**3, **MI**123, **VA**31, Deaf as a fence post; **GA**72, Deaf as a mill post.

c *deaf as a haddock.* [*EDD* (at *deaf*) 1746 →] **chiefly NEng, esp ME, MA**

[**1806** (1970) *Spirit of Pub. Jrls.* (Baltimore) 115, She, like a haddock, grew deaf.] **1865** Derby *Squibob* 32 **VA,** The simile . . 'deaf as a haddock,' had its rise from that circumstance [in an apocryphal anecdote about General Braddock]. **1943** *LANE* Map 502, 3 infs, **swME, eMA,** Deaf as a haddock. [**1966** *AmSp* 41.295 **Nfld,** *Deaf as a haddock.*] **1966–69** *DARE* (Qu. X19b, . . *If a person's hearing is very bad*) Infs **ME**5, 22, **MA**73, Deaf as a haddock; **ME**15, Deafer than a haddock.

d *deaf as a stone.* **chiefly Nth** [Prob from *stone deaf, OED stone* sb. 19 1837 →]

1943 *LANE* Map 502, 1 inf, **cCT,** *Deaf as . . a stone.* **1950** *WELS* 2 Infs, **WI,** Deaf as a stone. **1965–70** *DARE* (Qu. X19b) 14 Infs, **chiefly Nth,** Deaf as a stone.

e in var other phrr: See quots. Cf *DS* X19b

1836 (1838) Haliburton *Clockmaker* (1st ser) 258 **NEng,** I reckon you are as deff as a shad. **1899** (1912) Green *VA Folk-Speech* 26, Deaf as a beagle. **1950** *WELS* 1 Inf, **cnWI,** Deaf as a dormouse; 1 Inf, **ceWI,** Deaf as a mute; 1 Inf, **seWI,** Deaf as a log; 1 Inf, **ceWI,** Deaf as a mule. **1965–70** *DARE* (Qu. X19b) 9 Infs, **scattered,** Deaf as a bat; 9 Infs, **scattered,** Deaf as a stone wall. [See *DS* for further varr.]

2 also *deafy;* Of a nut: having a missing or shriveled kernel.

1943 in 1944 *ADD* **sPA,** *Deafy* . . containing a dried-up kernel or no kernel;—said of a (hickory) nut. . . ['difi]. **1981** in 1982 *Barrick Coll.* **csPA,** *Deaf* . . [dif]; . . *empty, hollow.* "I thought maybe the acorns would be deef; all the strength went to grow new leaves."

deaf v *old-fash*

To deafen, make deaf.

1897 Johnston *Old Times GA* 149 (as of 1830s), Been a fox, they'd a been have [sic] a dozen hounds in less than a hour, and enough hurraing and yelping and blowing of horns to deaf a body's ears.

deaf adder n

1 A **hognose snake** (here: *Heterodon platyrhinos*).

1842 DeKay *Zool. NY* 3.52, It is also called *Deaf Adder, Spreading Adder, Hog-nose* and *Buckwheat-nose.* **1860** Bartlett *Americanisms* 35, *Blauser.* . . The name given by the Dutch settlers to the hog-nosed snake. . . The other popular names in New York are Deaf-Adder and Buckwheat-nosed Adder.

2 =**copperhead snake 1.**

1872 Schele de Vere *Americanisms* 387, The *Copperhead* . . is known as . . Deaf Adder, even as Dumb Rattlesnake, because it does not give the warning before it strikes.

deaf duck n

1 =**ruddy duck.**

1888 Trumbull *Names of Birds* 111, The "punters" of St. Clair Flats, refer to the species *[Erismatura rubida]* still as . . *Deaf-Duck.* **1917** (1923) *Birds Amer.* 1.152, *Ruddy Duck—Erismatura jamaicensis* . . Deaf Duck. **1982** Elman *Hunter's Field Guide* 192, *Ruddy Duck:* (*Oxyura jamaicensis,* also classified as *Erismatura jamaicensis rubida*) Common & Regional Names: . . deaf duck.

2 A **scoter.**

1982 Elman *Hunter's Field Guide* 237, *American Scoter. . . Common & Regional Names* . . deaf duck. *Ibid* 240, *Surf Scoter.* . . Deaf duck. *Ibid* 250, *White-winged Scoter.* . . Deaf duck.

deaf ears n [*EDD* 1851 →]

See quot.

1896 *Daily News Cook Book* 503 **neIL,** Baked Beef Heart—See that the butcher removes the gristle and the "deaf ears," as the tough, red lobe at the top is called.

deaf pew n

1970 *DARE* (Qu. CC5, *Names for seats in a church, especially near the front*) Inf **MA**100, Deaf pew.

deafy See **deaf** adj **B2**

deakin See **deacon** n **1**

deal See **devil**

‡deal around v phr

To shop around.

1968 *DARE* Tape **KS**14, If you deal around a little you can do better in one place than another.

dealish See **devil** n

dear adj

1 See quot.

1930 *AmSp* 5.419 **sNH,** *Dear:* high-priced or extravagant. "Maggie is a dear cook."

2 Keen, ardent.

1955 FWP *Guide DE* 500, I always was a dear lover of scrapple.

dear n Pronc-sp *deah*

Used as a term of address.

1975 Gould *ME Lingo* 71, *Dear.* Dropped by newer generations. This was a word old-timers used in talking to one another, and it had none of the sweeter meanings. It was hardly more than a substitute for "you-there!" or "old chap." Presumably it began as a whimsical salutation, and survived without any meaning of endearment. . . "Do you want the high test [gasoline], dear?" **1979** Lewis *How to Talk Yankee* [8] **nNEng,** Don't be alarmed if you hear a couple of rough, tough clam diggers address each other as "De-ah." It's an old custom and indicates not a whit of effeminacy. The greeting crosses all lines of sex and age, and even total strangers may talk to each other thus. **1986** *DARE* File **cwMA,** [Heard from a shopkeeper:] Thank you, dear; enjoy your scallops.

dear intj Also freq *oh dear, (oh) dear me;* infreq *oh my dear, deary me* [Perh ellip for *dear God* or *dear Lord; OED* 1694 →] **chiefly Nth, N Midl, esp NEast** See Map

Used as an expression of surprise, annoyance, etc.

1848 Bartlett *Americanisms* 109, *Dear me,* or *deary me.* An exclamation of surprise, used in the same sense as "Oh dear!" **1872** Schele de Vere *Americanisms* 596, *Dear me,* also, is a purely English phrase. **1903** *DN* 2.296 **Cape Cod MA** (as of a1857), *Deary me! O deary me!* . . Addressed to babies. **1914** *DN* 4.71 **ME, nNH,** *Dear me suz.* Common exclamation with women. **1924** *DN* 5.266, Exclamations in American English. . . *dear:* (oh) —, . . (oh) — me (all disap[pointment], vex[ation]). **1943** *LANE* Map 600 **NEng,** The map shows a great variety of expressions used as exclamations of impatience, irritation, sudden anger and the like . . *pshaw, dear, the devil.* . . Most of these expressions are often preceded by *oh,* some of them nearly always. **1965–70** *DARE* (Qu. NN8a, . . *"Oh ______. I've lost my glasses again."*) 17 Infs, **chiefly NEast,** Dear; (Qu. NN9a, . . *"______. The electric power is off again."*) 10 Infs, **chiefly NEast,** Oh dear; **OH**27, Dear; **NJ**61, Dear, dear, dear; (Qu. NN7, *Exclamations of surprise*) Infs **IA**11, **NY**1, Oh dear (, dear, dear); (Qu. NN8b) Inf **CA**30, Oh dear; (Qu. NN9b) Inf **CA**30, Oh dear; (Qu. NN20b) Inf **OH**8, Oh dear; (Qu. NN21a) Infs **KS**2, 18, **NY**108, Oh dear; **NH**5, Oh dear, I've done it now; (Qu. NN21b) Inf **VA**29, Oh dear; (Qu. NN21c) Infs **CT**39, **MI**46, **NH**5, **NJ**47, **OH**41,

OR4, Oh dear; **CT**16, Oh dear me; **NM**9, **OH**8, Oo dear (, oo dear); (Qu. NN26a, *Weakened substitutes for "hell": "Oh ______."*) Infs **MD**49, **NY**219, Dear; (Qu. NN27b) Inf **ME**19, Oh dear; (Qu. NN32) Inf **NY**211, Oh my dear.

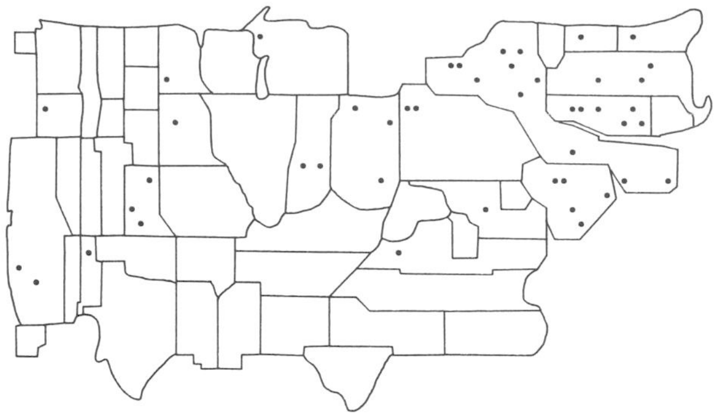

•dear intj + varr (Qq. NN8a, b, NN9a, b, NN7, NN20b, NN21a, b, c, NN26a, NN27b, NN32)

dearborn n, also attrib [Prob from Gen. Henry *Dearborn* (1751–1829); see quot 1818] **formerly widespread, now chiefly sePA, nMD, DE** Cf **Jersey wagon**

Orig a light horse-drawn wagon or carriage, often with curtained or slatted sides; now also a horse-drawn wagon in general.

1818 Hall *Travels* 187 **wNY,** Perhaps the change from a dusty jolting stage to an open easy waggon, or Dearborn, as they are called in this State disposed us to regard the landscape with more than usual complacency. [Footnote:] The body and carriage resemble a small waggon . . on wooden springs. Sometimes there are two seats, one behind the other. They obtained the name of Dearborn, from the General's taking the field in one. **1846** Cooper *Redskins* 1.227 **NY,** The well-known vehicle, called a dearborn, with its four light wheels and mere shell of a box, is in such general use as to have superseded almost every other species of conveyance. **1881** *Harper's New Mth. Mag.* 181/2 **DE,** The country people . . bring their produce to town in carts, dearborns, and market wagons. **1941** *AmSp* 16.183 **SW** (as of 1830s–50s), *Dearborn.* Four wheeled wagon with curtained sides. '. . nearly a hundred wagons beside a dozen dearborns.' **1955** *DE Folkl. Bulletin* 1.20, A horse gyp[sy] . . was one of a small group of men in the late nineteenth century who went downstate from Wilmington with a string of horses to trade or sell. They had a dearborn in which they slept at night. **1961** Eggenhofer *Wagons* 130, Both Dearborns and Jerseys were used well into the twentieth century; I have talked to old-timers who remember seeing them or even riding in them but cannot recall much about their construction or exact appearance. **1965–70** *DARE* (Qu. N41b, *Horse-drawn vehicles to carry heavy loads*) Inf **PA**27, Dearborn—called a Dearborn no matter if it was one of their wagons or not; **PA**34, Dearborn—a term which was adopted for all kinds of wagon whether made there or not; (Qu. N41c, . . *Light loads*) Inf **DE**1, ['dɝbən]; **DE**3, ['dɪrbən]; **DE**4, ['dɪrbərn]; **MD**34, ['dɪrbərn]—one horse; open body with rigging around, little slat sides. **1977** *DARE* File **sePA,** My uncle in Delaware County had a "dearborn" *not* dearborn wagon; it was a kind of pickup truck, with a team of two horses, Jess and Bess.

dear Dora n [Folk-etym; cf **deer darrow**]

A deodar *(Cedrus deodara).*

1968 *DARE* (Qu. T5, . . *Evergreens, other than pine*) Inf **NC**52, Dear Dora.

dear me See **dear** intj

deary me See **dear** intj

deastrict See **district**

death n Usu |dɛθ|; also **chiefly Sth** *among Black speakers* |dɛf| Pronc-spp *deat', def(f)* Cf Pronc Intro 3.I.17

Std senses, var forms.

1891 Harris *Balaam* 139 **cGA** [Black], My Marster en my young mistiss would'a sot dar en bodaciously starve deyse'f ter deff. **1899** Chesnutt *Conjure Woman* 153 **NC** [Black], He sweat so ha'd dat de stable boy got mos' skeered ter def. **1901** *DN* 2.181 **KY** [Black], *Death*—deff. **1928** Peterkin *Scarlet Sister Mary* 39 **SC** [Gullah], Budda would choke July to deat'. **1941** *AmSp* 16.13 **eTX** [Black], [θ] > [f] in *both, breath,* . . and sometimes in *death,* [bof], [brɛf], etc. **1942** [see **dead** adj **A**].

death adder n

A **hognose snake** (here: *Heterodon nasicus*).

1974 Shaw–Campbell *Snakes West* 69, *The Western Hognose Snake.* . . will hiss or blow loudly and strike out savagely toward the attacker. Again and again it will repeat this action in an altogether convincing performance that has earned it the names "puff adder," "death adder". . . If the attacker persists undeterred, . . the hognose snake shifts to "scene two". . . It turns over on its back and lies perfectly still, mouth gaping, to all appearances lifeless.

death alder n

A **spindle tree** (here: *Euonymus europaeus*).

1940 Clute *Amer. Plant Names* 258, *Euonymus Europaeus.* . . Death alder.

death angel n Also *angel of death*

A **death cap,** usu **destroying angel.**

1950 *WELS (A large round, mushroom, often bright colored)* 1 Inf, **cWI,** Death angel—white, poisonous. **1967–70** *DARE* (Qu. I38) Inf **TN**11, Death angel; (Qu. S18) Inf **VA**82, Angel of death (poisonous). **1985** Ammirati et al. *Poisonous Mushrooms* 85, *Amanita bisporigera.* . . Angel of death. *Ibid* 90, *Amanita verna.* . . Angel of death. *Ibid* 91, *Amanita virosa.* . . Angel of death. **1987** McKnight–McKnight *Mushrooms* 239, Other deadly poisonous species . . are found in N. America: . . Two-spored Death Angel *(A. bisporigera)* . . and . . Slender Death Angel *(A. tenuifolia).*

death baby n

=**stinkhorn** (*Phallus* spp).

1892 *Jrl. Amer. Folkl.* 5.105, *Phallus* sp., death-baby. Salem, Mass. . . Name given from the fancy that they foretell death in the family near whose house they spring up. I have known of intelligent people rushing out in terror and beating down a colony of these as soon as they appeared in the yard.

death ball n Cf *DS* E20

1979 *DARE* File **swMI,** Death balls, the balls of dust under furniture, were thought to be harbingers of a death in the family. [Speaker of Dutch descent]

death bell n **S Midl**

A ringing in the ears thought to foretell death.

1899 (1912) Green *VA Folk-Speech* 144, *Death-bell.* **1932** *Jrl. Amer. Folkl.* 45.15 **Ozarks,** A ringing in one's ears is known as the "death bells," and is supposed to foretell the death of an intimate friend or relative. **1949** Webber *Backwoods Teacher* 162 **Ozarks,** Presently someone mentioned the "death bells" which Uncle Johnny had heard the last new moon and we were off again on premonitions and "signs". **1976** Garber *Mountain-ese* 21 **Appalachians,** Death-bell . . omen—There's goin' to be a death soon cause I hyerd a deathbell in my err.

death bird n

1 The smooth-billed ani *(Crotophaga ani).*

1925 Bailey *Birds FL* 78, *Crotophaga ani* (Black parrot, Death-bird, Jew-bird).

2 also *bird of death, dead bird:* A vulture.

1967–70 *DARE* (Qu. Q13, . . *The vulture*) Inf **TN**53, Dead bird; **WA**28, Death bird; **MA**2, Bird of death.

death bones n

A rattling sound thought to foretell someone's death.

1932 *Jrl. Amer. Folkl.* 45.15 **Ozarks,** Many hillfolk claim to hear . . the "death bones" shortly before someone dies. An old woman once said to me: "I heerd Lucy's death bones a rattlin' this mornin', so I reckon she'll be dead afore night."

death camas n Also sp *death camass* **West**

A plant of the genus *Zigadenus.* Also called **camas 2, crow poison 2, lobelia, poison camas, poison sego, poison soaproot, soap plant, white camas.** For other names of var spp see **alkali grass 3, cockscomb 3, Easter candle, fly poison 2, hog potato 1, meadow death, merry hearts, mystery grass, Osceola's plume, poison grass, poison hyacinth, prairie onion, St. Agnes' feather, sand-corn, soap root, star lily, wand lily, water lily, wild hyacinth**

1889 *Century Dict.* 775, *Death camass,* the poisonous root of *Zigadenus venenosus,* of the same region [=West]. **1897** Parsons *Wild*

Flowers CA 6, *Z. venenosus*. . . The bulb is poisonous, and our Northern Indians call it "death camass." **1937** U.S. Forest Serv. *Range Plant Hdbk.* W209, *Zygadenus* [sic] spp. . . These plants are most commonly called deathcamases, to distinguish them from the somewhat similar, edible camases (*Quamasia* spp . .) with which they are often confused. **1951** Writers' Program *Oregon* 21, Death camas and yarrow, false solomon's seal and vervain, went into the pharmacopoeia of the tribes. **1966** *DARE* Wildfl QR (St. John) Inf **OR**12, Death camas. **1967** *DARE* (Qu. S26d) Inf **WY**5, Death camas. **1976** Bruce *How to Grow Wildflowers* 171, We find, for example, "Fly Poison" applied to two different plants, "Crow Poison" to another, and the grim epithet "Death Camass" to yet another. No doubt these names derive either from old-time pharmaceutical uses or from instances of livestock poisoning. **1984** Doig *English Creek* 68 **nMT,** The blossoms were deathcamas, and the mounds were the dead ewes.

death cap n

A poisonous mushroom of the genus *Amanita.* For other names of var spp see **death angel, destroying angel, fly agaric, fool's mushroom, grisette**

1972 Miller *Mushrooms* 28, *Amanita phalloides* . . "Death cap". **1981** Lincoff *Audubon Field Guide Mushrooms* 543, The Death Cap has been mistaken for edible mushrooms to which it bears little resemblance. **1987** McKnight–McKnight *Mushrooms* 215, *Deathcaps.* . . Genus *Amanita.*

death cup n

1 A **death cap** (here: *Amanita phalloides*).

1902 McIlvaine–Macadam *1000 Amer. Fungi* 622, We . . shall consider the poisons of the Amanita muscaria . . and the A. phalloides or "death cup." **1943** Fernald–Kinsey *Edible Wild Plants E. N. Amer.* 377, Our deadliest species, the *Death-Cup* or *Deadly Amanita, Amanita phalloides* . . has . . a cup at base when young and at least ruptured portions of it may usually be found on old specimens. **1985** Ammirati et al. *Poisonous Mushrooms* 88, *Amanita phalloides*. . . Death cup. . . Universal veil leaving a prominent white cuplike volva around the stalk base. . . This species is terrestrial, growing solitary to gregarious in humus.

2 The cuplike volva at the stalk base of some spp of *Amanita.*

1942 Hylander *Plant Life* 60, Amanitas have the swollen bag at the base (volva) which is often referred to as a "death cup" and used as a means of identifying this dangerous plant.

death damps n Also called **death sweat**

Perspiration that may appear at the time of one's death.

1849 in 1922 Melville *Works* 4.382, Death-damps chilled my brow. **1875** (1876) Twain *Tom Sawyer* 40, And then he would die—out in the cold world, with no friendly hand to wipe the death-damps from his brow.

death glow n

1976 De Vries *I Hear Amer.* 103 **IA,** Then there was a sudden revival of energy accompanied by a return of color to his cheeks, a definite brightening of the eye. But Mrs. Sigafoos dashed the hopes briefly roused by that turn for the better. "It's the death glow," she said, using the famous old wives' term for the flush that often precedes departure.

death-of-man n [See quots]

=**spotted cowbane.**

1828 Rafinesque *Med. Flora* 1.107, *Cicuta maculata*. . . *Vulgar Names* . . Death of man. . . One of the poisonous hemlocks. *Ibid* 1.110, The Indians when tired of life, are said to poison themselves with the roots of this plant. **1876** Hobbs *Bot. Hdbk.* 30, Death of man, Poison hemlock, Cicuta maculata. **1911** *Century Dict. Suppl., Death-of-man*. . . The American water-hemlock or spotted cowbane, . . so called from the poisonous properties of its root. **1931** Clute *Common Plants* 134, The water hemlock *(Cicuta maculata)* is death-of-man. This . . species is poisonous enough to deserve its name.

death owl n **chiefly SE**

=**screech owl.**

1946 Hausman *Eastern Birds* 352, *Otus asio naevius*. . . *Other Names* . . Death Owl. . . *Otus asio asio*. . . Death Owl. . . *Otus asio floridanus*. . . Death Owl. **1950** *PADS* 14.25 **SC,** *Death owl*. . . The screech owl. **1955** *Oriole* 20.8 **GA,** *Screech Owl*. . . *Death Owl* (owls in general are popularly regarded as birds of ill omen). **1962** Imhof *AL Birds* 306, Death Owl. . . The call . . is a quivering, mourning whistle that can be easily imitated. **1966–67** *DARE* (Qu. Q1, . . *Owl that makes a shrill, trembling cry*) Infs **LA**8, **SC**26, Death owl. **1969** Longstreet *Birds FL* 76, Screech Owl. Other names: . . Death Owl.

death rain n Also *death shower* [Folk-etym; see quot 1949] *among Black speakers*

A heavy rain, downpour.

1949 Turner *Africanisms* 192 [Gullah], ['dɛt ren] 'a heavy rain'—W[olof], [dɛt] 'a heavy rain that lasts several consecutive days.' **1968** *DARE* (Qu. B24, . . *A sudden, very heavy rain*) Inf **GA**45, Death rain—that's an old saying. [Inf Black] **c1970** Pederson *Dial. Surv. Rural GA* **seGA,** 1 inf, [dɛθ] rain (sug); [1 inf, [dɛ˞t] rain (sug)]; 1 inf, Death shower. [All Infs Black]

death scroll n

See quot.

1941 Writers' Program *Guide SC* 308, Until recent years, the 'Death Scroll' notified Dorchester folk of a funeral, as was done elsewhere in many places of the State. In ornate Spencerian chirography the facts were inscribed on a sheet of note paper ornamented with streamers of black ribbon, and the notice was sent through the community.

death's-head bat n [From the markings]

The spotted bat *(Euderma maculatum).*

1980 Whitaker *Audubon Field Guide Mammals* 327, *Spotted Bat*. . . Black above with *three large white spots on back* (one on each shoulder and at base of tail). . . Southern California and s Nevada through sw Colorado, Arizona, w New Mexico. . . It is called the Death's Head Bat because of its striking coloration.

death stick n *joc*

=**cancer stick.**

1969 *DARE* (Qu. DD6b, *Nicknames for cigarettes*) Inf **TX**68, Death stick.

death sweat n

=**death damps.**

1908 *DN* 3.285 **eAL, wGA,** *Death sweat*. . . Perspiration on a person just before dissolution.

death tick n Also *death watcher*

A deathwatch beetle (family Anobiidae); the sound made by such a beetle.

1853 in 1924 Melville *Works* 13.156 **MA,** I might as well have asked him if he had heard the death-tick. **1947** (1964) Randolph *Ozark Superstitions* 302, The famous death watch or death tick, a sharp snapping noise sometimes heard in log houses at night, is supposed to mean a death in the building within a few days. This noise . . is said to be produced by a beetle with a singular gift of divination. **1957** *Hand Coll.* **UT,** Beetles who make clicking noises when calling their mates are called "death watchers."

death warrant n

1983 *MJLF* 9.37 **ceKY,** *Death warrant*. . . a death omen.

deathwatch n

A wake.

1968–70 *DARE* (Qu. BB60, *When friends and relatives gather together at the place where the body is, usually the night before the funeral*) Infs **CA**80, **TX**103, Deathwatch.

death watcher See **death tick**

deathweed n

A **marsh elder** (here: *Iva axillaris*).

1935 (1943) Muenscher *Weeds* 505, *Iva axillaris*. . . Deathweed. . . Common in alkaline or saline soils.

debble, debil See **devil n A**

‡deceaseful card n

1967 *DARE* FW Addit **swAR,** Deceaseful cards—sympathy cards; they are read at Negro funerals here [=Magnolia AR].

deceive one's looks v phr

To belie one's appearance.

1903 *DN* 2.311 **seMO,** *Deceive one's looks*. . . To be better (or worse) than one appears. Often used by horse-traders in speaking of broken-down steeds. **1907** *DN* 3.230 **nwAR,** *Deceive one's looks.* . . To be better (or worse) than one appears. **1942** McAtee *Dial. Grant Co. IN* 22 (as of 1890s), *Deceive one's looks* . . to be different from what one appears; used of animals also. "Her heft's all below the middle so she deceives her looks". **c1960** *Wilson Coll.* **csKY,** *Deceive one's looks* . . To be quite different, usually better, than one appears.

deck n

1 In logging: a stack or pile of logs. **Nth**

1913 *DN* 4.2 **ME,** *Deck*. . . A pile of logs. **1966–70** *DARE* Tape **MI**11, They discontinued the use of hemlock and the stores of hemlock—the decks of hemlock that were in the yard—were then hauled down to the mills; **MI**20, They decked the logs on top of that bar, that had quite a high bank, and then when they couldn't log anymore, then they'd start the mill and break one of those decks and let the logs roll into the pond; **MI**56, That's all you had to do was turn that jammer around and deck here, pile 'em [=logs] all up in decks. **1969** Sorden *Lumberjack Lingo* 33 **NEng, Gt Lakes,** *Deck*—A pile of logs in the woods, at a landing, or at a mill. **1984** *MJLF* 10.149 **neWI,** *Deck.* Logs piled on skids, the deck. On the Thorpe farm, logs stacked at the mill, ready for sawing. Piling them thusly is decking them.

2 See quot.

1965–70 *DARE* (Qu. D40, . . *The upper balcony of a theater*) Infs **LA**11, **MA**29, Upper deck; **VT**16, Top deck.

3 See quot. [Abbr for *deck shoe*]

1970 *DARE* File **sLA** [Black], Decks = sneakers, tennis shoes.

4 pl; also in phr *deck of overalls:* (A pair of) overalls. [Prob from *deck* adorn, but cf *ducks* trousers made of *duck* a plain, tightly woven cloth]

1970 *DARE* (Qu. W10, *Work trousers made of rough cloth, usually blue*) Inf **TN**50, Decks. [Inf Black] **1988** Lincoln *Avenue* 143 **wNC** (as of c1940) [Black], He sat there propped against the tree in the warm sun . . wearing only his long white drawers and a faded deck of blue denim overalls.

deck v Also with *up* **chiefly Nth**

In logging: to stack (logs); hence ppl adj *decked,* vbl n *decking.*

1901 *Munsey's Mag.* 25.392/1 [sic *DA*—quot not found], Other men pile—technically 'deck'—them [=logs] exactly as in the woods. **1905** U.S. Forest Serv. *Bulletin* 61.35, *Deck up, to.* To pile logs upon a skidway. (Gen[eral].) **1948** *Times-Picayune* (New Orleans LA) 24 Oct mag sec 7/1 **LA,** Logs are "decked" in neat piles, first out along one side of the track, then back down the other side. **1958** McCulloch *Woods Words* 46 **Pacific NW,** *Deck*. . . To pile up logs; from which applied to the building up of almost any kind of stack. **1966–70** *DARE* Tape **MI**20, In the winter they'd cut the logs and deck them near the stream or haul them to the mill and deck them on the bank of the pond; **MI**56, [Inf:] I also decked out here at Loran at Quayville's mill. [FW:] What does that mean, "decking"? [Inf:] Piling the logs up on a pile; **WI**59, They would get their logs into the landings where they were decked up in piles. **1969** Sorden *Lumberjack Lingo* 33 **NEng, Gt Lakes,** *Deck up*—To pile up logs at a landing. **1972** *Yesterday* Mar–Apr 25, Decked logs were then loaded on sleighs. **1975** Gould *ME Lingo* 71, *Deck*—Besides the nautical meaning, this word applies to piling pulpwood. After being *yarded* from the woods, it is *decked* along the road for later *hauling* to the mill. **1984** [see **deck n 1**].

decker See **dicker v**

deck sheaf n [*deck* < Ger *decken* to cover] **PA**

=**cap** n[1] **1.**

1967 *DARE* Tape **PA**61, [FW:] What did you call the thing you put on top to keep the weather off it, on top of the shocks? [Inf:] Well, we put a sheaf on. [FW:] What did you call it? . . [Inf:] Deck sheaf. A cover. A cover sheaf, to make the water shed it. **1968** *DARE* (Qu. L31, . . *The top bundle of a shock*) Inf **PA**158, Deck sheave [dɪk šiv].

declare v Pronc-spp *clah, clar(e), declah, declar, declor* Note: Although this usage is known throughout the US as indicated by the responses to *DARE* Qu. NN32, which "cues" the Infs with analogous forms and with the pronoun "I," the responses to Qu. NN7, which does not cue a specific type of response, suggest that this usage is esp frequent **Sth, S Midl.**

Usu in phr *I declare* and varr: To swear, exclaim—used as a mere assertion or an exclam of surprise.

1849 Longfellow *Kavanagh* 176 **NEng,** Well, I declare! if it is not Mr. Kavanagh! **1884** *Anglia* 7.256 **SE,** I 'clar to gracious or goodnis! . . I 'clar! **1894** Twain *Pudd'nhead Wilson* 97 **MO,** "You's a-jokin', ain't you?" "'Clah to goodness I ain't." **1906** *DN* 3.133 **nwAR,** *Declare*. . . In the exclamation, "I'll declare." **1908** (1911) Gale *Friendship Village* 49 **WI,** I declare, I feel something like I ain't felt since I don't know when! **1922** (1926) Kephart *Highlanders* 386 **sAppalachians,** I went down into the valley, wunst, and I declar I nigh sultered [=sweltered, suffocated]! **1924** (1946) Greer-Petrie *Angeline Gits an Eyeful* 15 **csKY,** I declor . . I wouldn't swop places with her. **1926** Ferber *Show Boat* 114 **Sth** (as of late 1870s), "I declare to goodness I hoped it wouldn't be." . . She spoke with a Southern drawl. Her I was Ah. Ah declah to goodness—or approximately that. **c1937** in 1977 *Amer. Slave Suppl. 1* 1.397 **AL,** I 'clare fo' goodness, dey would grow nearly as big as a gallon bucket. **1965–70** *DARE* (Qu. NN32, *Exclamations like 'I swear' or 'I vow': "I ________.'*) 391 Infs, **widespread,** Declare; 77 Infs, **scattered, but chiefly east of Missip R,** Do declare; **LA**14, **MA**5, **NC**88, **NY**241, Declare to goodness; (Qu. NN7, *Exclamations of surprise: "They're getting married next week? Well, ________.'*) 109 Infs, **chiefly Sth, S Midl,** I declare; **IL**126, **KY**42, 91, **MS**73, **MO**15, **NC**82, I'll declare; **FL**52, **OH**41, **SC**34, 54, I do declare; **KY**53, Do declare. **1966–67** *DARE* Tapes **FL**46, **TX**4, I declare!

declare before the Lord v phr Also *declare to the Lord* (or *to God*) *esp freq among Black speakers*

=**declare.**

1922 Gonzales *Black Border* 293 **sSC, GA coasts** [Gullah glossary], *'Cla' to Gawd*—declare to God—a mild oath. **1960** (1962) Lee *Mockingbird* 56, **AL,** I declare to the Lord you're gettin' more like a girl every day! **1970** *DARE* (Qu. NN32, *Exclamations like 'I swear' or 'I vow': "I ________.'*) Infs **FL**48, **NC**84, 'Clare fo' de Lord; **NC**88, Declare before the Lord; (Qu. NN7, *Exclamations of surprise*) Inf **SC**69, I 'clare fo' de Lawd. [All Infs Black]

declor See **declare**

decomboblate See **discombobulate**

decorate the mahogany v phr

To put money on a table; hence to pay out money or to gamble.

1912 *NY Eve. Jrl.* (NY) 6 Jul 8 *(Zwilling Coll.),* [Cartoon:] You haven't paid the fine yet. Come back and decorate the mahogany. **1922** *WI News* (Milwaukee) 10 Oct 14 *(Zwilling Coll.),* [Cartoon:] Why I'd just say to England—"Here old fellow—decorate the mahogany a bit"—they should pay up now. **1950** *Western Folkl.* 9.117 **nwOR,** *Decorate the mahogany.* To gamble.

decorate the pot v phr *joc*

1967 *DARE* FW Addit **neOR,** *Decorate the pot.* In playing cards, to put money in the pot.

Decoration Day plant n Also *Decoration Day flower*

A peony (*Paeonia* spp).

[**1944** Howard *Walkin' Preacher* 29 **Ozarks,** What did it profit the man? An extra bunch of peonies laid on his plot on Decoration Day.] **1965–70** *DARE* (Qu. S11) Infs **AL**11, **IA**36, **IL**77, 110, **MA**18, **NY**49, **PA**1, **WV**14, Decoration Day plant; **IL**37, Decoration Day flowers.

decorator crab n

A spider crab *(Stenocionops furcata).*

1981 Meinkoth *Audubon Field Guide Seashore* 660, This (*Stenocianops* [sic] *furcata*) is the largest decorator crab of our southeastern coast. Its tendency is to decorate itself not so much with growing plants and animals as with bits of algae, turtle grass blades, and other objects which it jams among its hooked hairs.

decoy brand n

See quot 1968.

1961 Adams *Old-Time Cowhand* 170. **1968** Adams *Western Words* 91, *Decoy brand*—A small brand placed on an animal's belly or other out-of-the-way place; used by some ranchers to trap rustlers. Choice animals would be otherwise unbranded to tempt the thieves, but the ruse was rarely successful since the rustlers were suspicious and as smart as the ranchers.

decoy herd n

=**anchor cattle.**

1961 Adams *Old-Time Cowhand* 249, This [=a cut] was usually started with a "decoy herd," or "anchor cattle," a few cows used in startin' a cut of cattle. **1968** Adams *Western Words* 91, *Decoy herd*—A small herd of cattle used in snaring wilder animals or in starting a cut of cattle on roundup.

de-de phr Also sp *dere-dey* [Prob redup of *de* var of **there,** but cf **duh** v and *DJE de*[3]*, di-de*] *Gullah*

Is there.

1867 Allen *Slave Songs* xxvi **SC coast** [Gullah], "Ain't you know say cotton de-de?" In the last sentence "de-de" (accent on first syllable) means "is there;"—the first *de,* a corruption of *does* for *is* . . the other is a very common form for *dere,* there. **1892** (1969) Christensen *Afro-Amer. Folk Lore* 46, How Br'er Alligator, you tink I gwine le' you starve when dat nice piece light'ood dere dey?

dediviled adj [Var of *bedeviled*]
1903 *DN* 2.296 **Cape Cod MA** (as of a1857), *Dediviled*. . . Possessed.

dee adv See **deh** adv

dee' n See **deer**

deece v
1909 *DN* 3.419 **Cape Cod MA** (as of a1857), *Deece*. . . To run fast. Used among boys.

'deed and 'deed, 'deed and double See **indeed and double**

dee-dee n
A **chickadee** n[1] **1** (here: *Sitta carolinensis*).
1959 *AmSp* 34.74, I have perhaps been led to the writing of this article by my familiarity with one part of the field, the imitative names of birds, . . *dee-dee* (Carolina chickadee).

deedie n [Cf **biddy** n[3]] **Sth, S Midl** *old-fash*
A young chicken.
1885 Murfree *Prophet of Smoky Mts.* 275 **TN,** I jes' tole him 't war ez safe ez a unhatched deedie in a aig. **1886** Amer. Philol. Assoc. *Trans.* 17.45, Common Southern expressions—many of them vulgarisms—that have not, so far as I know, either old English or provincial English authority. . . *deedies* (young fowls). **1887** *Harper's New Mth. Mag.* Dec 67/2 **Smoky Mts,** They disputed about the best methods of tending the newly hatched deedies, that had chipped the shell so late in the fall as to be embarrassed by the frosts and the coming cold weather. **c1902** Clapin *New Dict. Amer.* 155, *Deedies.* In the South, a common name for chickens or young fowls.

deef(e) See **deaf** adj

deemer n [Var of *dime* + *-er*]
A dime; one who tips a dime; a dime tip.
1927 *AmSp* 2.390 [Argot of the vagabond], A dime is a *deemer.* **1935** *Amer. Mercury* 35.229 [Carnival jargon], Deemer: a dime. **1939** *AmSp* 14.239 **Los Angeles CA,** Deemer. One who tips a dime; a dime tip [in hotels]. **1950** *WELS (Nicknames for $.10)* 1 Inf, **csWI,** Deemer.

deep dish n
1 A serving bowl or covered baking dish; food prepared or served in such a dish.
1950 *WELS* 1 Inf, **seWI,** Deep dish—a dish in which the food is put on the table. **1965–70** *DARE* (Qu. G6, *Other dishes that you might have on the table for a big dinner or special occasion*) Infs **OH**18, 36, 66, Deep dish; **PA**234, Deep dish—bowl but bigger than a bowl. **1968** Kellner *Aunt Serena* 127 **cIN** (as of 1910), Women went by, too, in buggies loaded with cakes and pies and puddings, jams and pickles . . hams, chickens and Deep Dishes for the threshing dinner at noon.
2 See quot.
1950 *WELS* 1 Inf, **seWI,** Deep dish—a deep metal container used to boil food; old-fashioned.

deep-dish pie n Also *deep pie* Cf **apple pandowdy**
A fruit pie, usu with no bottom crust, baked in a deep pan or casserole.
1906 Gregory *Woman's Cookbook* 205, *Deep apple or plum pie.* Line a deep pie plate with pastry, place a layer of apples over this, and sprinkle brown sugar. Then another layer of apple [etc]. **1924** Allen *Modern Cookbook* 647, *Deep-dish fruit pies*—Fill a baking dish or shallow casserole with any desired fruit . . add sugar . . more fruit . . water. . . Cover with plain pie crust. **1939** Wolcott *Yankee Cook Book* 224 **NEng,** Deep Blueberry Pie . . 4 cups blueberries [etc]. . . Makes 1 deep dish (9-inch) pie. **1941** *LANE* Map 292 *(Apple Dumpling)* 1 inf, **csCT,** *Deep dish apple pie,* with a pie crust on top (recent term); 1 inf, **neRI,** Deep apple pie . . may have a thin pie crust instead [of biscuit dough]; 1 inf, **ceMA,** *Deep dish apple pie,* with a top crust and a bottom crust; 1 inf, **cME,** *Deep dish apple pie = pork apple pie,* containing pork and molasses. **1950** *PADS* 14.25, *Deep pie*. . . Same as pot pie. [*Ibid* 54, *Pot pie*. . . A fruit pie baked in a large, deep pan (formerly a pot) with wheat flour dumplings mixed in with the fruit.] **1965** *PADS* 43.24 **seMA,** Deep-dish apple pie [3 infs]. **1965–70** *DARE* (Qu. H63, *Kinds of desserts*) Infs **IL**113, **KY**8, **TN**61, Deep-dish pies; **AZ**16, Deep-dish pies—peach or apple with butter and sugar crust; **FL**8, Dewbies—a deep-dish pie with berries.

deep-dish supper n
=**covered-dish meal.**
1970 *DARE* (Qu. H70, *When people bring baked dishes, salads, and so forth to a meeting-place and share them together, that's a* ______) Inf **VA**108, Deep-dish supper.

deep pie See **deep-dish pie**

deep-root n
A **marsh elder** (here: *Iva axillaris*).
1973 Hitchcock-Cronquist *Flora Pacific NW* 533, Per[ennial] from deep-seated creeping roots. . . Deep-root. . . I[va] axillaris.

deep sea red rock cod n
A channel rockfish (here: *Sebastolobus alascanus*).
1953 Roedel *Common Fishes CA* 136, *Channel Rockfish*. . . *Unauthorized Names* . . deep sea red rock cod.

deep sea turkey n *joc* Cf **Cape Cod turkey**
1921 *DN* 5.111 **CA,** *Deep-sea turkey*. . . Salmon. From fact of salmon being served as holiday fare. Navy, and army.

deepwater adj **esp coastal ME**
Offshore, oceangoing.
1908 in 1962 *AmSp* 37.251 **coastal ME,** He [=a sailor] was a proper old deep-water feller. **1942** ME Univ. *Studies* 56.17, Deep-water also meant offshore, as a deep-water voyage, *i.e.,* to foreign ports, or a deep-water sailor, *i.e.,* one who sailed on square-rigged vessels. **1945** Saxon *Gumbo Ya-Ya* 372 **LA,** The types of ships docking at New Orleans have various names. A ship that crosses the sea is a *deep-water ship,* a coastwise vessel, a *shallow-water ship.* **1945** Colcord *Sea Language* 65 **ME, Cape Cod, Long Island,** *Deepwater.* When pronounced with the accent on the first syllable, this is an adjective, a deépwater voyage.

deep-water Baptist n **chiefly Sth, S Midl** See Map *somewhat old-fash* Also called **ducking Baptist, dunking ~, forty-gallon ~, wet-wash ~** Cf **dipper 8**
A member of a Baptist church that practices baptism by total immersion.
1949 *Hench Coll.* **cnVA,** If I weren't a deep-water Baptist, I believe I'd join your church. **1965–70** *DARE* (Qu. CC4, . . *Nicknames . . for various religions or religious groups*) 21 Infs, **scattered Sth, S Midl,** Deep-water Baptists. [18 of 21 Infs old]

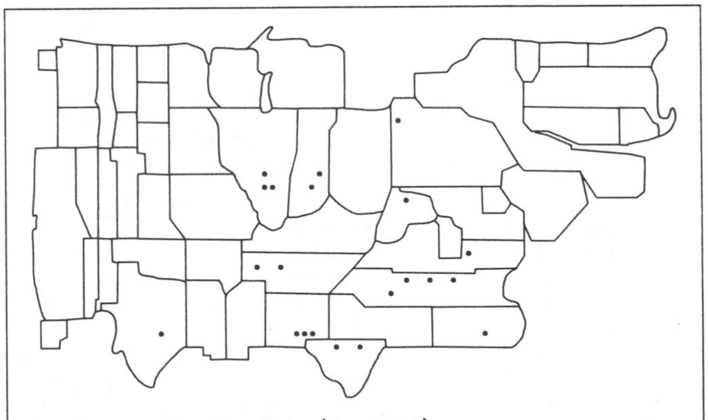
•deep-water Baptist (Qu. CC4)

deepwater cisco n Also *deepwater chub* [See quot 1947] Cf **shallowwater cisco**
A **cisco** (here: *Coregonus johannae*).
1947 Hubbs-Lagler *Fishes Gt. Lakes* 43, *Deepwater chub*—*Leucichthys johannae*. . . Deeper waters of lakes Michigan . . and Huron. **1957** Blair et al. *Vertebrates U.S.* 69, *Coregonus johannae*. . . Deepwater chub. **1983** Becker *Fishes WI* 333, *C[oregonus] johannae* (deepwater cisco) . . and *C. hoyi* (bloater)—are restricted to the Great Lakes basin. *Ibid* 367, *Deepwater Cisco*. . . Other common names: the chub, deepwater chub.

deepwater trout n

A **weakfish** (here: *Cynoscion regalis*).

1887 Goode *Amer. Fishes* 116, The . . Deep-water Trout, of Charleston, . . is without much question identical with the Northern Squeteague.

deep yellow adj Cf **high yellow**

Of a Black person: light-skinned.

1974 (1975) Shaw *All God's Dangers* 8 **AL** [Black], She was a deep yaller woman—her mother was a half-white woman.

deer n Pronc-spp *dee', dur*

A Pronc varr.

1908 *S. Atl. Qrly.* 7.342 **sSC coast** [Gullah], [A] hunter . . asked an old negro whom he met in the woods, if a certain clump of trees . . was a good deer-stand. . . "Me yent kin say, mossa," replied the old man, "W'en oona duh de-dey, de dee' no de-dey; w'en oona yent dey, de dee' duh de-dey!" [=I can't say, sir. . . When you are there, the deer are not there; when you are not there, the deer are there!] **1938** Matschat *Suwannee R.* 130 **GA,** At last the god tuk matters in his own hands an' made her into a dur.

B Gram form.

Pl usu *deer;* also double pl *deers.*

1915 in 1944 *ADD* 462 **wTX,** Deers. **1940** (1941) Bell *Swamp Water* 148 **Okefenokee GA,** I'd see him . . setting on that rail fence we built to keep the deers out. **1966–68** *DARE* Tape **IN**30, Deers; **LA**7, That is to scare the deers off; **SC**3, Wasn't any deers around here.

C Sense.

A children's hiding game.

1968 *DARE* Tape **PA**125, We had one gang playing around nights—around the alleys—what we called deer. It was nothing more than hide-and-seek. When you called, showing where you were, we said "deer."

deer and dog(s) n Cf **dog and deer, hunter and the deer** **=fox and hounds 1.**

1967 *DARE* (Qu. EE33, . . *Outdoor games*) Inf **TX**37, Deer and dog—team tried to catch one person; **LA**2, Deer and dogs—one kid ran, the others would follow him barking.

deer-and-hunter See **hunter-and-the-deer**

deer apple n

A desert plant *(Maxicmowiczia sonorae)* with a turniplike root.

1957 Jaeger *N. Amer. Deserts* 262, *Sonoran Deer Apple. . . Maxicmowiczia sonorae.* . . Fruit is a round red berry.

deer base See **dare base**

deerberry n

Any of var plants, as:

a A **blueberry 1,** esp *Vaccinium stamineum* which is also called **buckberry 1, dangleberry 2, highbush huckleberry 2, pigberry, squawberry, squaw huckleberry, squaw whortleberry**

1814 Pursh *Flora Americae* 1.285 *Vaccinium. . . stamineum.* . . In the mountains they are known by the name of *Deer-berries.* **1848** Gray *Manual of Botany* 260, *V. stamineum.* . . Deerberry. **1910** Graves *Flowering Plants* 313 **CT,** Buckberry. Deerberry. Squaw Huckleberry. . . A desirable shrub for planting in shaded situations. **1931** Harned *Wild Flowers Alleghanies* 375, *Deerberry.* . . One of our commonest mountain shrubs. **1976** Bailey–Bailey *Hortus Third* 1142, [*Vaccinium*] *caesium.* . . Deerberry, squaw h[uckleberry]. . . [*Vaccinium*] *stamineum.* . . Deerberry, squaw h[uckleberry]. **1981** Howell *Surv. Folklife* 68, *Vaccinium stamineum* Deerberry; squaw huckleberry —Fruit inedible raw but can be made into pies with heavy sweetening.

b A **wintergreen** (here: *Gaultheria procumbens*).

1828 Rafinesque *Med. Flora* 202, *Gautiera* [sic] *repens. . . Vulgar Names*—Partridge-berry, Grouse-berry, Deerberry. *Ibid* 204, The berries. . . are eaten greedily by Game and birds, Deer, Rabbits, Partridges, Grouse, &c. **1866** Lindley & Moore *Treas. Bot.* 522 *(DAE),* The berries [of *Gaultheria*] are known by various names, as Partridge-berry, Chequer-berry, Deer-berry, Tea-berry, Box-berry, and afford winter food to partridges, deer, and other animals. **1911** Henkel *Amer. Med. Leaves* 19, *Wintergreen. . . Other common names.* . . Deerberry, groundberry, hillberry, ivyberry. **1930** U.S. Dept. Ag. *Misc. Pub.* 77.63. **1971** Krochmal *Appalachia Med. Plants* 128, Deerberry. . . is primarily a source of true wintergreen oil.

c A **partridgeberry** (here: *Mitchella repens*).

c1873 in 1976 Miller *Shaker Herbs* 239, *Mitchella repens.* . . Deer Berry. One Berry. Checkerberry. **1900** Lyons *Plant Names* 250. **1911** Henkel *Amer. Med. Leaves* 34, *Squaw Vine. . . Other common names.* . . Deerberry. **1971** Krochmal *Appalachia Med. Plants* 176, Deerberry. . . has been described as astringent, diuretic, and toxic.

d A **holly 1** (here: *Ilex vomitoria*).

1920 *Torreya* 20.22, *Ilex vomitoria.* . . Deerberry, Texas.

e A **snowberry.**

1937 *Torreya* 37.100, *Symphoricarpos* sp. . . Deerberry, Missouri.

f A **false lily of the valley** (here: *Maianthemum dilatatum*).

1959 Anderson *Flora AK* 155, *Maianthemum dilitatum* [sic]. . . Deerberry. **1973** Hitchcock–Cronquist *Flora Pacific NW* 692, Deerberry. . . Attractive in the wild but apt to prove a nasty pest in the native garden.

g A **buffalo berry.**

1967 *DARE* (Qu. I44) Inf **NE**5, Deerberry—same as buffalo berry.

deer brier n Also sp *deer briar*

A **buckbrush 3c** (here: *Ceanothus fendleri*).

1937 U.S. Forest Serv. *Range Plant Hdbk.* B42, Fendler ceanothus, also known as . . deerbriar . . , is a low, loosely branched, usually deciduous shrub. **1973** Stephens *Woody Plants* 370, *Ceanothus fendleri.* . . Snow brush, deer brush, deer brier. . . In some areas of the southwest, this is an important part of the forage of deer.

deer broke adj

Of hunting dogs: trained not to follow deer.

1940 Weygandt *Down Jersey* 288 **sNJ,** They are all "deer broke," trained only to follow foxes.

deer brush n

1 Any of several western spp of **ceanothus,** but esp *Ceanothus integerrimus* which is also called **blueblossom, bluebrush, California lilac, mountain birch, mountain lilac, soap bush, sweet birch, white blossom, whitebrush, white tea-tree.**

1882 *Century Illustr. Mag.* 24.227/2, Up through the forest region, to a height of about nine thousand feet above sea-level, there are . . five or six species of ceanothus, called deer-brush or California lilac. **1911** Jepson *Flora CA* 253, *C. integerrimus Deer-brush.* . . Favors good soils. **1926** *Torreya* 26.6, *Ceanothus velutinus.* . . Deer-brush, Placerville, Calif. **1931** U.S. Dept. Ag. *Misc. Pub.* 101.105, *Ceanothus integerrimus.* . . Other local names include . . deer brush. *Ibid* 109, *C. fendleri* . . , known also as buckbrush and deer brush, occurs from South Dakota to western Texas and Arizona. **1938** Van Dersal *Native Woody Plants* 86, *Ceanothus crassifolius.* . . Deer brush. . . Fair browse for mule deer. *Ibid* 88, *Ceanothus integerrimus.* . . Deer brush. . . Of outstanding importance for mule deer; porcupine. The most important browse species for stock in California. **1969** *DARE* (Qu. S26e) Inf **CA**140, Deer brush.

2 **=mountain mahogany.**

1931 U.S. Dept. Ag. *Misc. Pub.* 101.43, *Mountain-mahoganies (Cercocarpus spp.)* . . Numerous other . . local names for these shrubs include . . deer brush, hard-tack [etc]. **1937** U.S. Forest Serv. *Range Plant Hdbk.* B49, *Cercocarpus* spp. . . Many other names, such as . . deerbrush, . . are applied to these shrubs in various localities. *Ibid* B51, *Cercocarpus.* . . is a good winter game browse, ranking as an outstanding winter forage for deer.

3 A **bitterbrush 1** (here: *Purshia tridentata*).

1927 U.S. Dept. Ag. *Misc. Pub.* 52, Bitterbrush *(Purshia tridentata)* is one of the most widely distributed western shrubs. . . This species . . is frequently called buckbrush; other English names often applied to it are antelope-brush . . deer brush, and quinine brush. **1937** U.S. Forest Serv. *Range Plant Hdbk.* B116, Bitterbrush [=*Purshia tridentata,* syn. *Kunzia tridentata*] is one of the most important browse plants on western ranges. . . Other common names often applied to this plant are antelope-brush, quinine-brush, black sage and deer-brush.

deer cabbage n

1 A plant *(Fauria crista-galli)* of bogs and wet meadows, native from the Pacific Northwest to Alaska.

1938 (1958) Sharples *AK Wild Flowers* 92, *N[ephropyllidium] Crista-gallii* [sic]. "Deer Cabbage." . . Leaves large, heavy and round, on stout stalks. **1959** Anderson *Flora AK* 397, Deer Cabbage. . . Rootstock thick and scaly. **1973** *Southeastern Log* (Ketchikan AK) Aug 5/2, Admiralty Island, AK, During summer months deer climb to the alpine regions on Admiralty's mountains and feed primarily on tender grasses, sedges and forbs such as deer cabbage. **1987** Hughes–Blackwell *Wildflowers SE AK* 50, Deer Cabbage *(Fauria crista-galli)*. . . Flowering stem is up to 12″ high and leafless. . . bottom leaves have long petioles.

2 A **lupine** (here: *Lupinus diffusus*).

1961 *W3, Deer cabbage* . . a blue-flowered . . evergreen lupine *(Lupinus diffusus)* of the southern U.S.

deer clover n **West**

=**deervetch.**

1911 Jepson *Flora CA* 232, *L[otus] glaber*. . . Esteemed as a bee-plant in the southern part of the State and also called Deer-clover. **1911** CA Ag. Exper. Sta. Berkeley *Bulletin* 217.997, *Lotus glaber*. . . Deer Clover. . . A very erratic honey producer. **1937** U.S. Forest Serv. *Range Plant Hdbk.* W110, Deervetches are known by a variety of local names including deerclover. **1967** Dodge *Roadside Wildflowers* 29 **TX,** Also known as deer clover and red-and-yellow pea, this low-growing plant is grazed by deer and cattle. . . *Lotus wrightii.*

deer darrow n [Folk-etym; cf **dear Dora**]

A deodar *(Cedrus deodara).*

1967 *DARE* (Qu. T5, . . *Evergreens, other than pine*) Inf **SC**41, Deer darrow—similar to fir; not local, but introduced to Greenville.

deer-eye daisy n

A **black-eyed Susan 2** (here: *Rudbeckia fulgida*).

1975 Hamel–Chiltoskey *Cherokee Plants* 30, Coneflower, black-eyed susan, deer-eye daisy. . . *Rudbeckia fulgida.*

deer fear See **deer fright**

deer fern n

A rather coarse fern *(Blechnum spicant).*

1938 (1958) Sharples *AK Wild Flowers* 80, *L[omaria] Spicant.* "Deer Fern." **1959** Anderson *Flora AK* 9, *B[lechnum] spicant* . . Deer-fern. **1959** Munz–Keck *CA Flora* 44, *Blechnum* . . Deer Fern. **1961** Thomas *Flora Santa Cruz* 59, *Blechnum spicant* . . Deer Fern. **1976** Bailey–Bailey *Hortus Third* 166, *Blechnum spicant* . . Deer fern.

deer fever n Cf **deer fright**

=**buck fever 1.**

1965–70 *DARE* (Qu. P36, *When a hunter sees a deer or other game animal and gets so excited he can't shoot, he has* ———) 24 Infs, **scattered NEast, Sth,** Deer fever.

deer flower n

=**meadow beauty** (here: *Rhexia* spp).

1953 Greene–Blomquist *Flowers South* 79, Meadow-Beauties, Deer-Flowers *(Rhexia).* About 13 species . . occur in the southern states.

deerfly n

1 Any of var flies of the family Tabanidae, esp of the genus *Chrysops.* Also called **buck fly 1, flag fly** Cf **buzzer 3**

1853 (1857) Benwell *Englishman's Travels* 127 **FL,** Dusky-looking deer-flies constantly alighted on our faces and hands, and made us jump with the severity of their bites. **1937** U.S. Pub. Health Serv. *Pub. Health Rept.* 52.103, This name [=*tularæmia*] was given to the disease by the writer in 1920 after establishing the identity of the California rodent disease and "deer-fly fever" in man. **1954** Borror–DeLong *Intro. Insects* 610, These tabanids *[Chrysops]* are called deer flies; they are usually encountered near marshes or streams and frequently buzz around one's head or get in his hair. **1965–70** *DARE* (Qu. R12) 253 Infs, **widespread exc Cent,** Deerfly; (Qu. R11) Infs **CA**165, **NY**52, 183, **OH**72, **WA**12, Deerfly.

2 The buck moth *(Hemileuca maia).*

1873 MO State Entomol. *Annual Rept.* 127, It is because it is seen flying in the fall when the deer run that it has been commonly dubbed Buck Moth or Deer Fly.

3 also *deer tick (fly):* A ticklike fly of the family Hippoboscidae, esp *Lipoptena depressa.*

1911 *Century Dict. Suppl., Deer-fly* . . . An American hippoboscid fly, *Lipoptena depressa,* which occurs on *Cervus virginianus:* also called *deer-tick.* **1926** Essig *Insects N. Amer.* 619, Two species of *deer tick flies (Lipoptena depressa; L. subulata)* occur upon deer in California. **1988** *DARE* File **ceTX,** A woman about 50 who hauls cattle told me about—*deer ticks* ("shaped like a large tear-drop" the woman said).

deer-foot n [Prob from the shape of the leaf]

1 =**water shield.**

1900 Lyons *Plant Names* 68, *B[rasenia] purpurea*. . . Deer-foot.

2 =**vanilla leaf.**

1915 (1926) Armstrong–Thornber *Western Wild Flowers* 156, *Achlys triphylla*. . . has . . only one large leaf, with . . three, oddly-shaped leaflets. . . It is also called . . Deer-foot. **1949** Moldenke *Amer. Wild Flowers* 21, On the Pacific Coast . . is found the . . deerfoot. . . Settlers on the Humboldt Coast prize the plant's delicate fragrance and hang bunches of the leaves in their houses. **1973** Hitchcock–Cronquist *Flora Pacific NW* 142, Deerfoot. . . Deep wood to open parks, often near streams.

deer fright n Also *deer fear* Cf **deer fever**

=**buck fever 1.**

1951 Johnson *Resp. to PADS 20* **DE,** *(When a hunter sees a deer and gets so excited he can't shoot, he has* ———*)* Deer fright. **1965–70** *DARE* (Qu. P36, *When a hunter sees a deer or other game animal and gets so excited he can't shoot, he has* ———) 13 Infs, **scattered,** Deer fright; **IL**138, **MA**125, Deer fear.

deer grass n

1 =**meadow beauty.**

1785 *Narr. John Narrant* 17 *(DA),* I . . saw at some distance bunches of grass, called deer-grass. **1822** Eaton *Botany* 426, *Rhexia*. . . *virginica* (meadow beauty, deer grass.) **1840** MA Zool. & Bot. Surv. *Herb. Plants & Quadrupeds* 51, Deer Grass, Meadow Beauty. . . Has no important properties, but great beauty, and is well deserving cultivation. **1901** Lounsberry *S. Wild Flowers* 358, The truly common species, distributed well over the country, is *Rhexia Virginiana* [sic], meadow-beauty, or quite as frequently called, deer grass. **1939** FWP *Guide KY* 18, The iron weed and meadow beauty (deer grass), grace the open woodlands or low meadows. **1969** *DARE* (QR, near Qu. T16) Inf **NC**76, Deer grass. **1974** (1977) Coon *Useful Plants* 186, *Rhexia virginica*—Meadow beauty, deer-grass . . [is] an especial treat for the deer, from which fact comes the name.

2 A **squawgrass** (here: *Xerophyllum tenax*).

1898 *Jrl. Amer. Folkl.* 11.282, *Xerophyllum tenax,* . . deer grass . . Cal.

3 A **wild indigo** (here: *Baptisia lanceolata*).

1901 *Torreya* 1.116 **GA,** *Baptisia lanceolata*. . . Deer-grass.

4 A **muhly grass** (here: *Muhlenbergia rigens*). **SW**

1911 *Century Dict. Suppl., Deer-grass*. . . A bunch-grass, *Epicampes rigens,* found in the southwestern United States: it is of some forage value. . . In Wyoming and Montana, the sheep's fescue, *Festuca ovina.* **1937** U.S. Forest Serv. *Range Plant Hdbk.* G87, Spike muhly, a tufted perennial grass, . . also known as . . deergrass . . , occurs in southwestern Colorado, Arizona, New Mexico, and Mexico. **1950** Hitchcock–Chase *Manual Grasses* 410, *Muhlenbergia rigens*. . . Deergrass. . . Dry or open ground, hillsides, gullies, and open forest, southern California. Used by Indians in basket making. **1970** Correll *Plants TX* 232.

5 A **fescue** (here: *Festuca ovina*).

1911 [see **deer grass 4**].

deer head n

A large fungus, perh a **puffball.**

1970 *DARE* (Qu. S18) Inf **IL**110, Deer head.

deerhead orchid n

=**fairy slipper.**

1934 Haskin *Wild Flowers Pacific Coast* 65, *Deer-Head Orchid.* . . *Cytherea bulbosa*. . . I showed it to some of my friends, and was informed that it was the "deer-head orchid."

deer hominy n

A **meadow beauty** (here: *Rhexia alifanus*).

1927 Boston Soc. Nat. Hist. *Proc.* 379 **Okefenokee GA,** 'I'll tell yer one thing, though, a Deer is a fool about [very fond of]. . . deer hominy' *(Rhexia Alifanus).*

deerhorn n

1 A **farewell-to-spring** (here: *Clarkia pulchella*). **chiefly Pacific NW**

1956 St. John *Flora SE WA* 272, *Clarkia pulchella* . . Deer Horn. **1963** Craighead *Rocky Mt. Wildflowers* 120, *Clarkia pulchella* . . Deer-horn. **1966** *DARE* Wildfl QR (St. John) Inf **WA**10, Deerhorn—*Clarkia pulchella.* **1973** Hitchcock–Cronquist *Flora Pacific NW* 305, *Clarkia* . . deer horn . . *C. pulchella.*

2 See **deerhorn cactus 1.**

deerhorn cactus n

1 also *deerhorn:* A **prickly pear** (here: *Opuntia acanthocarpa, O. echinocarpa,* or *O. versicolor*). Cf **buckhorn cholla, staghorn ~**

1941 Jaeger *Wildflowers* 158, *Deer-horn Cactus. . . Opuntia acanthocarpa. . .* A much-branched, long-stemmed cane-cactus. **1949** Curtin *By the Prophet* 59, *Opuntia versicolor. . .* Common name: Deerhorn cactus. *Ibid* 60, The fruit on both Deerhorn and Pencil cholla is always green. **1951** Corle *Gila* 348, A host of others [=cacti] that seem endless—the old man, the rainbow . . the deerhorn. **1957** Jaeger *N. Amer. Deserts* 141, Deer-horn cactus *(Opuntia echinocarpa)* . . and the Mohave niggerhead . . are found most frequently on the well-drained slopes.

2 =night-blooming cereus.

1960 Vines *Trees SW* 768, *Deerhorn Cactus. Peniocereus greggii.* . . Cactus erect or sprawling, slender-stemmed, few-branched, 1–3 (rarely to 6) ft. **1974** (1977) Coon *Useful Plants* 85, Deerhorn cactus. . . is found among the Creosote bushes from western Texas west and south to Mexico. **1985** Dodge *Flowers SW Deserts* 16.

deer hunter n

=Canada jay.

1937 *Scientific Mth.* 45.239 **CA,** Of particular interest to northern residents is a rather distant cousin of the bluejay—the *Canada Jay. . .* Moose-bird, meat-bird, camp-robber, deer-hunter (California). **1953** Jewett *Birds WA* 453, *Oregon Gray Jay, Perisoreus canadensis obscurus. . .* Other names . . Deer Hunter. *Ibid* 457, Deer hunters hate the bird, which, they say, will penetrate the toughest covering to get at the deer meat beneath. The jay strips off the fat first, and then attacks the flesh.

deer laurel n

A **rosebay** (here: *Rhododendron maximum*).

1940 Clute *Amer. Plant Names* 43, *R. Maximum. Great Laurel.* Deer laurel.

deer marsh grass n

A **cattail 1** (here: *Typha latifolia*).

1951 *PADS* 15.27 **TX,** *Typha latifolia* L.—Deer marsh grass, from young shoots said to have been eaten by deer, as they still are by cattle.

deer meat n

Venison.

1930 *VA Qrly. Rev.* 6.241 **Ozarks,** They'd cooked up 'most ever'thing —deer meat, fried ham, sausage, turkey and chickens and all sorts of gyarden stuff and pies and cakes. **1979** Lewis *How to Talk Yankee* [9] **nNEng,** Deermeat, not "venison," is the preferred local term. **1987** *DARE* File **ME** (as of 1980), The word venison was rarely heard in Maine. Deermeat was universally used and in the south-central apple growing country "orchard beef" was standard.

deer moss n

1 =Spanish moss.

1951 *PADS* 15.28 **TX,** *Dendropogon usneoides. . .* Deer moss. . . Deer use it in times of food scarcity.

2 A **reindeer moss.**

1959 Martin *Gunbarrel* 159 **WY,** From a distance the clumps of deer moss that dotted the meadow looked like whitewashed stones.

deer mouse n

=white-footed mouse.

1841 Catlin *Letters Indians* 1.194 **MO,** One of the spectators saw this strange animal catching and devouring a small "deer mouse," of which little and very destructive animals their lodges contained many. **1917** *DN* 4.431 **LA, NEng,** *Deer mouse.* The white-footed mouse (Peromuscus [sic] leucopus). **1935** Pratt *Manual Vertebrate Animals* 295, *Peromyscus* . . deer mice. **1952** Burt *Field Guide Mammals* 103, Deer Mouse. *Peromyscus maniculatus.* **1967** *Living Museum* 124 **sIL,** Meadow mice occur in the drier, upland grasslands while deer mice are in nearly every wooded area.

deer nut n

=jojoba.

1974 (1977) Coon *Useful Plants* 138, *Simmondsia chinensis*—Jajoba [sic], deer nut, goat nut. . . At one time, the bitter nuts were prepared as a coffee substitute.

deer oak n

An evergreen shrub *(Quercus sadleriana).*

1910 Jepson *Silva CA* 220, The acorns are eaten by deer and by bear, whence the folk names "Deer Oak" and "Bear Oak." **1931** U.S. Dept. Ag. *Misc. Pub.* 101.24, *Sadler oak (Q. sadleriana). . .* is a poor to fair browse, and, as the local names "deer oak" and "bear oak" intimate, its sweet and edible acorns are much relished, not only by wild life, but domestic livestock as well. **1959** Munz–Keck *CA Flora* 906, *Q[uercus] Sadleriana* . . Deer Oak. **1976** Bailey–Bailey *Hortus Third* 935, *Quercus Sadlerana* [sic] . . Deer oak.

deer owl n **GA, FL**

The barred owl.

1913 *Auk* 30.495 **Okefenokee GA,** The 'Deer Owl,' exhibit considerable curiosity; they responded frequently to poor imitations of their cry. **1927** Boston Soc. Nat. Hist. *Proc.* 38.379 **Okefenokee GA,** The local name of 'Deer Owl' is applied to the Florida Barred Owl . . , 'because when it hollers, it's feed-time fer the Deer.' **1938** Matschat *Suwannee R.* 53 **GA,** He had given the deep, booming hoot of the deer owl—a distress signal of the swampers when far from home. **1951** *AmSp* 26.278 **FL, GA,** Locally in Georgia and Florida, the barred owl is called *deer owl,* because hunters believe that its hooting coincides with the feeding time of deer. **1955** *Oriole* 20.8 **GA,** *Barred Owl.—Coo-coo . . ; Deer Owl.*

deer pea n

1 also *deer-pea vetch:* A blue-flowered **vetch** (here: *Vicia ludoviciana*).

1933 Small *Manual SE Flora* 741, *V[icia] ludoviciana. . .* Deer-pea. **1970** Correll *Plants TX* 874, Deer pea vetch. . . Widespread in e. half of Tex.

2 =deervetch.

1937 U.S. Forest Serv. *Range Plant Hdbk.* W110, Deervetches are known by a variety of local names including . . deerpea.

3 A leguminous, yellow-flowered plant *(Vigna luteola).* Also called **wild cowpea**

1972 Brown *Wildflowers LA* 94, Deer Pea, Wild Cowpea *(Vigna luteola). . .* Important deer browse. . . Also Texas and Mississippi. April to June.

deer-pea vetch See **deer pea 1**

deer-plum n

=gopher apple.

1938 Van Dersal *Native Woody Plants* 98, *Chrysobalanus oblongifolius. . . Deer-plum. . .* A small shrub. . . *Observations:* Gophers, turtles, and other short-legged animals. **1966** Grimm *Recognizing Native Shrubs* 144, *Deer-plum. . .* Coastal plain; South Carolina south to Florida, west to Mississippi.

deer-scared adj Cf **deer fever**

Afflicted with **buck fever 1.**

1966–70 *DARE* (Qu. P36, *When a hunter sees a deer or other game animal and gets so excited he can't shoot, he . . ———*) Infs **IA**36, **MS**47, **SC**66, **VA**73, [Is] deer-scared. [3 of 4 Infs Black]

deer's-ears n

=green gentian.

1949 Moldenke *Amer. Wild Flowers* 230, The *deersears, Frasera speciosa,* is a conspicuous large-leaved plant, . . growing . . from South Dakota to Oregon, thence southward to New Mexico and California. **1959** Carleton *Index Herb. Plants* 36, *Deer's Ears:* Frasera carolinense. **1970** Correll *Plants TX* 1209, *Deer's-Ears. . . Frasera speciosa. . .* A good browse that is much eaten by deer.

deertoe n Cf **elktoe, fawnfoot**

A **freshwater clam** (here: *Truncilla truncata*).

1982 U.S. Fish & Wildlife Serv. *Fresh-Water Mussels,* [Wall chart:] *Deertoe. . .* Shell color highly variable, usually with interrupted rays of green or brown, chevron-like markings; subtriangular, sharply pointed postbasally.

deer-tongue n Also *deer's tongue*

1 =vanilla plant. SE

1861 Wood *Class-Book* 413, *Deer's-tongue. . .* The fleshy leaves exhale a rich fragrance . . even for years after they are dry, and are therefore by the southern planters largely mixed with their cured tobacco, to impart its fragrance to that nauseous weed. **1883** *Century Illustr. Mag.* 26.383/2, A kind of fishing called "bobbing" is done among the lily pads, deer-tongue, and other aquatic plants. **1901** Lounsberry *S. Wild Flowers* 501, Hound's or Deer's Tongue. . . Although again and again assured of its likeness by the natives, it was rather a strain on my imagination to see that . . its thick leaves resembled the tongue of either a deer or a hound. **1927** Boston Soc. Nat. Hist. *Proc.* 38.214 **Okefenokee GA,** *Trilisa odoratissima* 'Dog-tongue'; 'deer-tongue'; 'vanilla'. **1939** FWP *Guide FL* 359, Along the St. Johns River the deer's tongue, a fragrant shrub, grows wild in the woods; its leaf is used in the preparation of smoking and chewing tobaccos. **1960** Williams *Walk Egypt* 296 **GA,** Deer's-tongue leaves hung from the rafters together with strings of pepper, onions, and thyme. **1967–68** *DARE* (Qu. S26c) Inf **GA**25, Deer-tongue; (Qu. S26e) Inf **SC**31, Deer-tongue. **1975** Duncan–Foote *Wildflowers SE* 198, Deer-tongue. . . Tons of leaves are collected from the wild each year and sold for flavoring smoking tobacco. **1980** *Verbatim Letters* **neFL** (as of c1938), Deer-tongue was also (I was told then) used . . as a source of an artificial vanilla-type flavoring. . . The dried herb was sent (we were told) to North Carolina to be mixed with tobacco in the production of cheap cigarettes.

2 =dogtooth violet.

1894 *Jrl. Amer. Folkl.* 7.101, *Erythronium albidum, . . Erythronium Americanum, . .* Deer's tongue. Anderson, Indiana. **1911** *Century Dict.,* Deer's-tongue. . . The white adder's-tongue, *Erythronium albidum.* **1936** Winter *Plants NE* 12, E[rythronium] americanum. . . Also called . . Deer's-tongue. **1949** Peattie *Cascades* 252, The white avalanche lily, Erythronium montanum, is sometimes called deertongue, adder's-tongue, and dogtooth violet. **1966–70** *DARE* (Qu. S1) Infs **KY**11, **MO**20, Deer-tongue; (Qu. S3) Inf **AR**41, Deer-tongue; (Qu. S11) Infs **IL**25, **KY**83, Deer-tongue; (Qu. S26c) Inf **IN**32, Deer-tongue.

3 A **green gentian** (here: *Frasera speciosa*). **Pacific NW**

1915 (1926) Armstrong–Thornber *Western Wild Flowers* 368, Deer's Tongue. . . A handsome plant, . . from two to six feet tall, with . . pale green leaves, in whorls of four and six, the lower ones sometimes a foot long. **1963** Craighead *Rocky Mt. Wildflowers* 144, Green Gentian. . . Other names: Deertongue [etc]. . . It is reported that Indians ate the fleshy root of this plant. **1966** Barnes–Jensen *Dict. UT Slang* 12, *Deer's tongue* . . a local name for the American Columbo (*Frasera* speciosa), which stands up like a leafy post in the mountains. **1966–67** *DARE* (Qu. I28b, *Kinds of greens that are cooked*) Inf **MT**5, Deer-tongues; (Qu. S11) Infs **ID**5, **WA**6, Deer-tongue.

deer-tongue grass n

A **panic grass** (here: *Panicum clandestinum*).

1894 *Jrl. Amer. Folkl.* 7.104, *Panicum clandestinum* . . deer-tongue-grass, West Va. **1910** Graves *Flowering Plants* 55 **CT,** Corn Grass. Deer-tongue Grass. Common. . . June–July. **1952** Strausbaugh–Core *Flora WV* 88, *P. clandestinum. . . Deertongue grass. . .* May be of value in reclaiming strip-mine spoil banks.

deer-tongue laurel n Also *deer-tongued laurel*

A **rosebay** (here: *Rhododendron maximum*).

1891 Ryan *Pagan* 23 **Allegheny Mts,** The deer-tongued laurel raises grotesque antlers above the azalias. **1897** Sudworth *Arborescent Flora* 315, *Rhododendrum maximum. . . Common Names* [include]. . . Deertongue laurel. **1908** Britton *N. Amer. Trees* 752, *Great Laurel* . . is also called . . Deer tongue laurel. **1936** Weygandt *Blue Hills* 38 **PA,** The humbler laurel is of those of our mid-June. Laurels are they both in our native speech, "laurel" the sun-seeking shrub, and "deer tongue laurel" its kin that loves the hemlock shade. **1950** Peattie *Nat. Hist. Trees* 517, *Rhododendron maximum. . .* Deer-tongue, or Great Laurel. Rose Bay.

deervetch n

A plant of the genus *Lotus.* Also called **bastard indigo 2, bird's-foot trefoil, deer clover, deer pea 2, deerweed 1, trefoil.** For other names of var spp see **compass plant 3, desert rock-pea, red-and-yellow pea, Spanish clover, witch's teeth**

1937 U.S. Forest Serv. *Range Plant Hdbk.* W110, The deervetches (*Lotus* spp.) . . are distributed throughout the West . . , but are largely natives of California, where 29 species occur. **1951** Martin *Amer. Wildlife & Plants* 404, The deervetches are . . small clover-like plants . . relished by wildlife. **1967** Dodge *Roadside Wildflowers* 29, *Deervetch* . . is grazed by deer and cattle. **1973** Hitchcock–Cronquist *Flora Pacific NW* 264.

deer vine n

=twinflower.

1893 *Bot. Gaz.* 19.430 **ME,** *Linnaea borealis* . . deer vine. **1900** Lyons *Plant Names* 227, *L[innaea] borealis* . . Deer-vine. **1959** Carleton *Index Herb. Plants* 36.

deerweed n

1 A **deervetch,** esp *Lotus scoparius* which is also called **buck-brush 3b, deer clover, tanglefoot, wild alfalfa, wild broom. West**

1897 Parsons *Wild Flowers CA* 152, *Hosackia glabra* [now *Lotus scoparius*]. . . Among the mountaineers it is known as "deer-weed" and "buck-brush," as both deer and stock are said to feed upon it and flourish, when pasturage is scarce, though they rarely touch it when other food is plenty. **1911** Jepson *Flora CA* 232, *L[otus] glaber. . .* Deer-weed. . . Esteemed as a bee-plant in the southern part of the State. **1937** U.S. Forest Serv. *Range Plant Hdbk.* W110, Deervetches are known by a variety of local names including deerclover, deerpea, and deerweed. **1941** Jaeger *Wildflowers* 99, Broom Deer-weed. *Lotus scoparius. Ibid* 102, Pygmy Deer-weed. *Lotus Haydonii. . .* Pale-leaved Deer-weed. *Lotus leucophyllus.* **1947** *Chr. Sci. Monitor* (Boston MA) 15 Jan 8/1, They graze their way up our stony mountain, sample all the bunch-grass, clovers, and deer-weed in Sky Valley. **1961** Thomas *Flora Santa Cruz* 210 **CA,** *L. scoparius. . .* Deerweed. A common plant of chaparral and dry open hills.

2 A **meadow beauty** (here: *Rhexia alifanus*).

1927 Boston Soc. Nat. Hist. *Proc.* 38.213 **Okefenokee GA,** *Rhexia Alifanus* 'Deer-weed'; 'deer hominy'.

3 A **bugbane 1** (here: *Cimicifuga racemosa*).

1959 Carleton *Index Herb. Plants* 36, *Deer-weed:* Cimicifuga racemosa.

deerwood n

A **hop hornbeam 1** (here: *Ostrya virginiana*).

1897 IN Dept. Geol. & Nat. Resources *Rept. for 1896* 615, *Ostrya. . . virginiana. . .* Deer Wood. Dry woods and sides of ravines; frequent. **1933** Small *Manual SE Flora* 416. **1960** Vines *Trees SW* 145, *Ostrya virginiana* . . Vernacular names are Ironwood, Leverwood, Deerwood, Hardhock, and Indian-cedar.

deeryard n **Nth**

A place in the woods where deer herd during the winter.

1849 Lanman *Letters Alleghany Mts.* 58, I discovered a large spot of bare earth, which I took to be a deer yard, and directly across the middle of it the fresh tracks of a large wolf. **1948** *Chicago Tribune* (IL) 29 Sept sec 3 3/3, We have visited deer yards in winter to see how tough it is for animals to find enough browse in overcrowded areas. **1966–67** *DARE* Tape **MI**2, I went back up in the deer yard; **MI**32, When you track coyotes, you track 'em in the deeryards, 'cause they are on the outskirts of the deeryard looking for the weak deer [in the woods]; **MI**42, Deer yard. **1977** *UpCountry* Dec 12 **VT,** Deer are the most vulnerable . . when the depth [of snow] reaches a certain point—they are confined to the beaten trails of their so-called "deer yards."

deesh See **dish** n

deestric(k), deestrict See **district**

deewee See **d.w.i.**

def adj See **deaf** adj

def n See **death**

defected adj [Prob for *defective*]

1967 *DARE* FW Addit **NJ**18, *Defected,* retarded, not normal. "He's a little bit defected."

Defenders' Day n **MD**

A day (September 12) commemorating the Battle of Baltimore in the War of 1812.

1940 Writers' Program *Guide MD* 196, Annual events [in Baltimore]: . . Old Defenders' Day (fireworks at Fort McHenry) Sept. 12. **1968** *DARE* (Qu. FF16, . . *Local contests or celebrations*) Inf **MD**8, Defenders' Day—September 12, a mock re-creation of the War of 1812 Battle of Baltimore, when the Star-Spangled Banner was written at Fort McHenry; **MD**49, Defenders' Day—early September, celebrates the Battle of Baltimore, Battle of North Point, when the British were beaten back at Fort McHenry.

defewgelty See **diffucalty**

deff adj See **deaf** adj

deff n See **death**

deft See **delft**

degati owl n [See quot]

=**barn owl 1.**

1949 Turner *Africanisms* 232 **seSC** [Gullah], [dɛgɑti ɒʊl] 'the barn owl,' [dɛgɑti] being a Wolof expression meaning 'listen to it again.' It is used among the Wolof in reference to the owl whose cry or hoot is frequently heard near their homes.

degore See **delore**

degree n [Cf *OED degree* sb. 4. c *"Obs."*]

A type or breed.

1962 Steinbeck *Travels* 9, A dog, particularly an exotic like Charley, is a bond between strangers. Many conversations en route began with "What degree of a dog is that?"

deh v See **duh** v

deh adv Also sp *dee;* redup *dey-dey* [Varr of **there;** cf *DJE de[1]*] *Gullah* Cf **de-de**

There.

1867 Allen *Slave Songs* 23 **SC coast** [Gullah], I wonder where [=whether] my mudder deh (there)... I wonder if my maussa deh... O de Lord he plant his garden deh. **1883** (1971) Harris *Nights with Remus* 144 **GA** [Black], 'E hop 'roun' dey-dey, un 'e do light da' broom-grass. **1887** (1967) Harris *Free Joe* 83 **nwGA,** Dee ain' no finer w'ite man dan him. No, suh; dee ain'.

dehorn v [Transf from *dehorn* to remove an animal's horns, to remove the dangerous component]

1 In logging: see quot 1905.

1905 U.S. Forest Serv. *Bulletin* 61.35, *Dehorn...* To saw off the ends of logs bearing the owner's mark and put on a new mark. (Kentucky.) **1958** McCulloch *Woods Words* 46, **Pacific NW,** *Dehorn...* To saw the brand off the end of a log so it can be stolen in greater safety.

2 See quot.

1942 Berrey–Van den Bark *Amer. Slang* 108.7, Cook alky, dehorn, naturalize, *to reclaim denatured alcohol.*

3 See quot.

1958 McCulloch *Woods Words* 46 **Pacific NW,** *Dehorn...* To water down alcohol, particularly if it is bad.

dehorn n

1 See quots. [Prob orig applied to denatured alcohol supposedly rendered fit for human consumption; cf **dehorn** v **2**]

1926 *Amer. Mercury* Apr xxx/2 **nwOR,** *Dehorn* means.. bootleg booze and its users. **1930** Williams *Logger-Talk* 22 **Pacific NW,** *Dehorn:* Cooked denatured alcohol. **1951** Morgan *Skid Road* 229 **Seattle WA,** The drunks were staged on denatured alcohol—"dehorn" to the initiated. **1968** Adams *Western Words* 91, *Dehorn...* A logger's word for any kind of drinking liquor.

2 also *dehorner:* One who drinks **dehorn** n **1;** a drunkard.

1926 [see **1** above]. **1942** Berrey–Van den Bark *Amer. Slang* 97.9, *Drunkard...* Dehorn. **1953** Shulman *Many Loves* 215 **MN,** The Jolity Theater.. on Minneapolis's skidrow.. is patronized largely by vagrants, winos, dehorns, grifters. **1958** McCulloch *Woods Words* 46 **Pacific NW,** *Dehorners*—Thirsty guys who would drink canned heat or anything else that smelled like alcohol. **1968** Adams *Western Words* 91, *Dehorn...* A hard drinker, especially one inclined to fight when drunk.

dehorned adj

Denied or deprived of position or authority.

1945 Hubbard *Railroad Ave.* 340, *Dehorned*—Demoted or discharged. **1971** Rice *Dehorned Bishop* 41 **ID,** [State Conferences were created by the Congregational churches of each state or area... [T]he man who directed the activities of a Conference was usually named Superintendent.] *Ibid* 42, The function of this man is to serve the churches of his state or area... He works always under the direction of his State Board... Perhaps "Dehorned Bishop" was not a bad name for us.

dehorny n

=**muley.**

1970 *DARE* (Qu. K13, *A cow that has had her horns cut off*) Inf **VA**38, Dehorny.

dehydrated water n

An imaginary substance used as the basis of a practical joke.

1970 *DARE* (Qu. HH14, *Ways of teasing a beginner or inexperienced person—for example, by sending him for a 'left-handed monkey wrench': "Go get me ______."*) Inf **CA**213, Dehydrated water.

deichsel n [Ger] **Ger settlement areas**

A wagon tongue.

[**1951** Danner *PA Dutch Dict.* 151, tongue [wagon]—deixel.] **1968** *DARE* (Qu. L45), Inf **PA**158, Tongue or deichsel ['daɪkˌsəl]. **1973** Allen *LAUM* 1.213 **NE** (as of c1950), *Tongue* (of a wagon)... *Deichsel..* used by an inf. of German parentage.

deil See **devil** n

deil's spoons See **devil's spoons**

deki v [Abbr for **co-dack,** which has varr |kə'dɪki| and |kə'dɛk|]

Come!—used to call sheep.

1970 *DARE* (Qu. K85, *The call to sheep to come in from the pasture*) Inf **NY**230, ['dɛki 'dɛki 'dɛki].

Delaware n [Perh because containers were used for trucking Delaware grapes]

1968 *DARE* (Qu. F17, *What peaches come in*) Inf **WV**8, Delaware—long, slim bushel [=basket] like an orange crate. They used to use Delawares rather than peach baskets because they could be packed into a truck better.

Delaware Moor n Cf **brass ankle**

1982 Heat Moon *Blue Highways* 376 **sNJ,** In Cumberland County we have a settlement of people called 'tri-bloods,' people that trace their history—or legend—back to a Moorish—Algerian specifically—princess who came ashore after a shipwreck in the first years of the nation. The Indians took her in, and, from the subsequent mixing of blood—later with a small infusion from the Negro—there developed a group composed of three races. The 'Delaware Moors,' they're called. A similar branch is the Carolina Yellowhammers.

delft n Also *deft, delf, delft ware, delph* [*Delft* town in Netherlands]

Dishware; spec glazed earthenware made in Delft, Netherlands.

1754 *SC Gaz.* (Charleston) 21–28 May 1/3 **SC,** China and delft ware, &c. to be sold, wholesale or retale [sic], by the subscriber, at very reasonable rates. **1766** in 1912 Augusta Co. VA *Chronicles* 1.132, Two delph plates attached, also 5 delph bowls. **1847** (1962) Robb *Squatter Life* 38 **IL,** The children.. sat listlessly upon the door sill, playing with bits of broken delf. **1880** Howells *Undiscovered Country* 261 **MA,** All that was colonial was to his purpose, from tall standing clocks to the coarsest cracked blue delft. **1891** *Scribner's Mag.* 10.347 **PA,** The Pilgrims could have brought few pieces of Delft-ware to New England on the Mayflower. **1944** *PADS* 2.19 **sAppalachians,** Iron and deft. Pots, pans, and dishes. **1973** Allen *LAUM* 1.195 **seNE** (as of c1950), *China...* One Nebraska inf. of New York and Indiana ancestry uses *delft.*

delge See **dulge**

Delhi belly n |'dɛli ˌbɛli| [From the high incidence of dysentery during World War II among American troops in the *Delhi,* India, area] Cf *DS* BB19

Dysentery; upset stomach and diarrhea.

1944 *Newsweek* 28 Feb 76/1, Joe was off again.. to be the first to hit the heat and filth of India... He got "Delhi belly" (a form of dysentery). **1948** *AmSp* 23.226, *Delhi Belly.* Dysentery, a common affliction in India. G.I.'s always considered dysentery especially characteristic of the Delhi area. This catchy term was very popular. **1972** *Des Moines Register* (IA) 18 June sec 1 1/8, *Montezuma's Revenge..* also known as.. Delhi Belly... In simple terms it is the traveler's upset stomach! Three government doctors warn about the use of a widely recommended remedy. **1978** *Capital Times* (Madison WI) 7 Apr 31/1, The malady has various names around the world and is also called Delhi Belly or simply travelers' diarrhea.

delicate adj **esp Sth, S Midl**

Of a person: finicky or picky in his eating habits; having a small appetite.

1965–70 *DARE* (Qu. H12, *If somebody eating a meal takes little bits of food and leaves most of it on his plate, you say he ______*) Infs **AR**17, **CO**20, **IN**30, **KY**22, 74, **MS**34, **SC**26, 29, **UT**6, **VA**39, [Is a] delicate eater, **RI**16, **TX**42, Is delicate, **ME**19, Kinda delicate; (Qu. H10, *If somebody never eats very much food, you say he's a ______;* total Infs questioned, 75) Infs **AR**17, 35, **FL**1, **MS**34, **NM**9, Delicate eater.

delicun squinton n

1946 *PADS* 6.11 **ceNC,** *Delicun squinton* ['dɛləkn̩ ˌskwɪntn̩]: Whisky. "Delicun squinton makes you speak the truth and gives you everlasting remembrance." Occasional among drinkers.

delirium tremors n Also *delirium trembles, delirious tremors* [Folk-etyms]

Delirium tremens.

1968–70 *DARE* (Qu. DD22) Inf **IA**22, Delirious tremors; **NC**52, Delirium trembles; **PA**243, Delirium tremors.

Del Mar pine n

=**Torrey pine.**

1897 Sudworth *Arborescent Flora* 19, *Pinus torreyana. . . Common Names. . .* Del Mar Pine (Cal.). **1979** Little *Checklist U.S. Trees* 199, *Torrey pine. . . Other common names*—Del Mar pine. . . Very rare and local on coast of s. Calif.

‡delore adj Also *degore* [Varr of *galore*] Cf **aglore**

Used postpositively: Plentiful, abundant.

1965–70 *DARE* (Qu. LL9b, . . *All you need or more . . :"She's got clothes ________."*) Inf **MS**56, Degore; **WA**24, Delore; **MO**23, Delore —in place of galore sometimes.

delove v [Perh infl by *beloved*]

To love (someone).

1959 Lomax *Rainbow Sign* 81 **AL** [Black], If she's old enough and got sense enough to delove this man; if she want him for a husband, how come you don't want her to marry him? *He* delove *her;* he say he do.

delph See **delft**

delphinium n

Std: a plant of the genus *Delphinium.* Also called **larkspur.** For other names of var spp see **cow poison, poisonweed, rabbitface, staggerweed**

delta potato n Also *delta duck potato* [From the edible tubers] **Gulf States**

An **arrowhead 1.**

1921 LA Dept. of Conserv. *Bulletin* 10.57 **LA,** The food of the pintail is . . vegetable matter, especially . . the seed and tubers of the delta potato and other arrowheads. *Ibid* 58, The redhead . . eats less of the . . delta potato . . than are taken by the canvasback. **1924** Howell *Birds AL* 58, The canvas-back feeds extensively . . on the tubers of the delta potato *(Sagittaria platyphylla).* **1932** Howell *FL Bird Life* 147, Examination of many stomachs [of canvasback ducks] in the Biological Survey shows that a variety of other vegetable food is taken, including the tubers of the delta duck potato *(Sagittaria platyphylla).*

delta whitefish n

A **cisco** (here: *Coregonus nasus*).

1902 Jordan–Evermann *Amer. Fishes* 121, *Broad Whitefish. . .* This species, known also as . . Delta whitefish, . . has been observed in . . Alaska.

democrat n

1 =**spruce grouse.**

1955 MA Audubon Soc. *Bulletin* 39.442, *Spruce Grouse. . .* Democrat . . (Maine).

2 A **sculpin** (here: *Myoxocephalus* spp).

1985 Rattray *Advent. Dimon* 48 **Long Is. NY,** Throwing away the sea robins and bottlefish and once in a while what they called a Democrat, a horned sculpin, ugly critter would give you blood poisoning with his prickers if you weren't careful.

3 See **democrat bug.**

4 See **democrat wagon.**

‡democrat bread n

1984 *DARE* File **ceMA,** A friend brought me half a loaf of what she calls Democrat bread. . . The loaf is rye and is made in a large round and very flat loaf.

democrat bug n Also *democrat* **Upper Missip Valley, Cent**

=**box-elder bug.**

1943 KS State Bd. Ag. *Report* 62.255.163, The "boxelder bug" . . is also known as "democrat bug" and "populist bug" in Kansas. **1968** *DARE* (Qu. R30, . . *Kinds of beetles*) Inf **IA**27, Box-elder bug or democrat bug. **1980** *Des Moines Register* (IA) 26 Oct 1 **swIA, ecMO,** The worst thing about being a Democrat around here this time of year is that the box elder bugs come out. Someone . . at some point in the past started calling those little insects "Democrat bugs." And that's what nearly everyone down here in the corner counties call them today. . . An Iowa State grad . . was familiar with the name. "I grew up in east-central Missouri, and people around there do call the box-elders Democrats," he said. **1980–81** *DARE* File **nwKS** (as of c1960), All my friends and I called them democrat bugs, but I was later told they were box elder bugs. *Ibid* **swIA, cKS,** We have been having an infestation of box elder bugs. Some people have been referring to them as *democrats.* My wife, who is from Chase, in central Kansas, calls them that, but I always thought it was a family joke in her staunchly Republican family. *Ibid* **cNE** (as of 1930s and 1940s), We called them both Boxelder Bugs and Democrats in central Nebraska, with the emphasis on Democrats. *Ibid* **swWI,** In Benton, Lafayette County, Wisconsin, "Democrat" . . is universally used as an alternative name for . . a box elder bug. . . Democrats are generally treated by school children much the way ladybugs are. . . It might be that people in this rock-ribbed Republican area . . call the insect a Democrat because it was viewed as a pesky outsider that seemed to serve no useful purpose and just got in the way. . . This special use of the word "Democrat" is known by every adult and child in Benton . . , and it's been used there for over 75 years. **1986** *WI Alumnus Letters* **csWI,** When I was a child growing up in Lyon County, Kansas, we always referred to those [=box elder] bugs as democrats. The old farmers in the region informed me that this was because the box elder bugs became prominent . . during the years of the F.D. Roosevelt administration. *Ibid,* In Marquette, McPherson County, Kansas, . . these *democrats* were familiar on chilly days in early spring, clustering on the warm sheltered south wall of the brick schoolhouse.

democrat hound n

1975 Gould *ME Lingo* 71, *Democrat hound*—An otherwise intelligent animal who takes up the wrong scent, as when a rabbit hound chases a fox. The term originated before Maine was a two-party state.

Democratic, go v phr

See quot.

1893 *KS Univ. Qrly.* 1.139 **eTN** [Black], *Gone Democratic:* failed, gone against one, as 'The game went Democratic,' i.e. the other side won; or 'Things have been going Democratic all day.'

democratic wagon See **democrat wagon**

democrat pasture n

1968 Adams *Western Words* 91, *Democrat pasture*—A pasture formed by closing a gap across a rimrock or a canyon.

democrat sleigh n [Cf **democrat wagon**] *old-fash* Cf *DS* N40a, b, c

=**pung.**

1976 *WI Then & Now* Dec 2, [Caption:] Bundled against the cold, a family posed for a picture sitting in a pung, or democrat, sleigh on bob runners at the turn of the century. *Ibid* 3, The democrat sleigh, used by farmers and mail carriers, was a later version of the pung.

democrat wagon n Also *democrat, democratic wagon, democrat's* ~ [Perh because it was relatively inexpensive and within the means of many people] **chiefly Nth** See Map on p. 38

A light, horse-drawn wagon with two or more seats.

1871 *Harper's New Mth. Mag.* 43.382/2, There were two teams running a race, and presently a white horse and green-bodied democrat wagon hove in sight. **1893** Frederic *Copperhead* 147 **nNY,** M'rye had set [the clock] going again on the seat of the democrat wagon. **1907** *DN* 3.186 **seNH,** *Democrat. . .* A high light wagon with several seats and without a top. **a1910** (1924) Twain *Autobiog.* 2.106 **csNY,** A democrat wagon stood outside the main gate with my trunk in it. **1911** *Century Dict.* 1527, *Democrat. . .* A light wagon without a top, containing several seats, and usually drawn by two horses. Originally called *democratic wagon.* [*Century* Ed: Western and Middle U.S.] **1945** Partridge *January Thaw* 62 **CT,** The democrat wagon creaked and rattled as it went slowly along the dirt road. **1950** *WELS (Horse-drawn vehicles)* 3 Infs, **WI,** Democrat wagon; 1 Inf, Democrat. **1965–70** *DARE* (Qu. N41a, . . *Horse-drawn vehicle . . to carry people*) 22 Infs, **chiefly Nth,** Democrat (wagon); **WI**5, Democrat's wagon; (Qu. N41b, . . *To carry heavy loads*) Infs **MA**42, **VT**4, Democrat wagon; (Qu. N41c, . . *To carry light loads*) 62 Infs, **chiefly Nth,** Democrat (wagon). **1966** *DARE* FW Addit **MA**6, *Democrat wagon*—light farm or ranch wagon having two or more seats, sometimes removable, usually drawn by two horses.

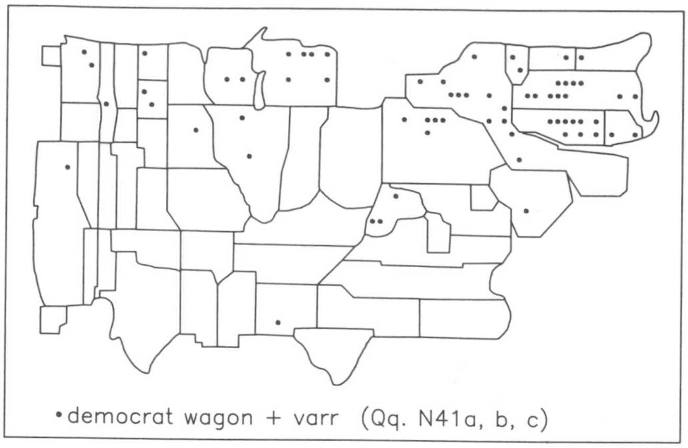

demoiselle n

1 A fish of the family Pomacentridae. Also called **rock pilot.** For other names of var genera or spp see **blue perch 4, dovetail fish, garibaldi, gregory, kelp perch, kupipi, maomao, night sergeant, reef-fish, sergeant major**

1882 U.S. Natl. Museum *Bulletin* 16.609, *Pomacentridae*. . . Demoiselles. **1898** U.S. Natl. Museum *Bulletin* 47.1543, *The Demoiselles*. . . Fishes . . feeding on small marine animals and plants in the coral reefs. . . The coloration is usually brilliant, sometimes changing much with age. **1933** John G. Shedd Aquarium *Guide* 137, The demoiselles . . are sprightly little fishes . . , most of them too small to be of any value as food.

2 =**Louisiana heron.**

1903 Coues *Key to N. Amer. Birds* 2.878 **LA,** *H[ydranassa] tricolor ruficollis* . . Louisiana Egret. Demoiselle. **1946** Hausman *Eastern Birds* 105, *Louisiana Heron*. . . Its names Demoiselle and Lady-of-the-Waters suggest that it is considered the most graceful of all the heron tribe. **1955** Forbush–May *Birds* 32, *Louisiana Heron*. . . In compliment to its slender and graceful beauty, it has been called 'the demoiselle of the marshes.'

3 A **dragonfly.** Cf **damselfly**

1966 *DARE* (Qu. R2) Inf **FL**27, Damoselle [sic].

demry n

1950 *PADS* 14.26 **SC,** *Demry*. . . A baked sweet potato. Gullah.

den n

1 also *den room:* A living room, sitting room. **chiefly Sth, S Midl** See Map

1944 *McDavid Coll.* **GA,** *Den room* = sitting room. "New term." **1965–70** *DARE* (Qu. D16, . . *Parts added onto the main part of a house*) 24 Infs, **chiefly Sth, S Midl,** Den; (Qu. D13, *The room where you entertain company*) 20 Infs, **chiefly Sth, S Midl,** Den [Of all Infs responding to these questions, 71% were old; of those giving this response, 47% were old.]; (Qu. D14, *The room where members of the family spend most of their time together when they are at home;* total Infs questioned, 75) 10 Infs, **MS, GA, FL, NM, OK,** Den.

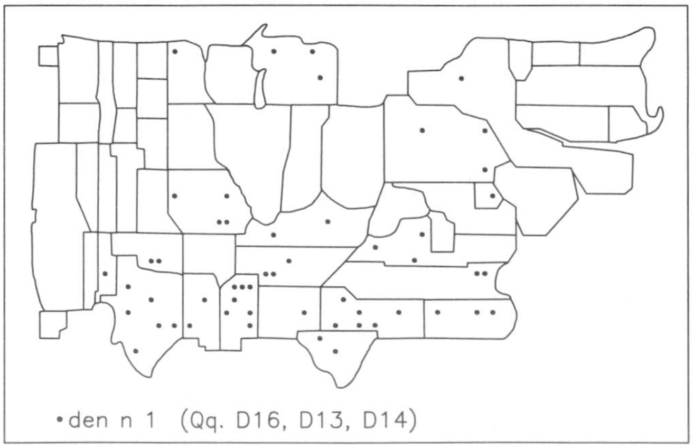

2 In the children's tag game **every man in his own den:** the designated base of each player.

1883 [see **every man in his own den**]. **1891** [see **every man in his own den**]. **1975** [see **every man in his own den**]. **1965–70** *DARE* (Qu. EE14, . . *The place where the player who is 'it' has to wait and count while the others hide*) Infs **CT**6, 16, **KY**23, **NJ**3, **NY**209, **NC**88, Den.

3 See **every man in his own den.**

den v Usu with *up,* infreq with *out* **esp Sth, S Midl**

To hibernate, go into a den for winter; to stay indoors; to hide out.

1843 *Amer. Pioneer* 2.171 **OH,** In that climate (Canada) the bears usually den up in the winter, and lie in something of a torpid state. **1894** *Home Missionary* 66.463 **AZ,** Our people [=Congregational Church members] . . are inclined to "den up" in the hot weather, as certain animals . . do in the cold season. **1908** *S. Atl. Qrly.* 7.344 **sSC coast** [Gullah], The bats den in the barn, the rats den under the hay-rick. **1914** *DN* 4.71 **ME, nNH,** *Den up*. . . To retire, or hibernate. **1922** Gonzales *Black Border* 297 **sSC, GA coasts** [Gullah glossary], *Den* . . to den, stay in a den. **1923** *DN* 5.205 **swMO,** *Den*. . . To hibernate, to remain indoors during bad weather. "We-all denned up when the storm come on." **1927** *AmSp* 2.352 **WV,** *Denned* . . to seek winter quarters. "The groundhogs denned there last year." **1951** Porter *Ragged Roads* 53 **wOK** (as of 1890s), This old house we air passin', well, nobody lives in 'er 'cept bats an' owls an' ghosts, an' too, they's an old man that dens up there in the old basement. **1954** *Harder Coll.* **cwTN,** *Den out*. . . Hole up, hide. "He denned out up there in that cave and the revenuers never did find him." **1958** Humphrey *Home from the Hill* 78 **TX,** Then it was the dead of winter. . . The squirrels denned up, the birds withdrew into the thickets, the ducks migrated on south. **c1960** *Wilson Coll.* **csKY,** *Den up*. . . Common for hibernate. **1966** *DARE* Tape **MI**2, They [=bears] get fattened up enough so they can den up . . in the fall. **1986** Pederson *LAGS Concordance,* 1 inf, **cnAR,** [Skunks] will den up under the house.

den adv See **then**

denature v [Cf **nature B**]

To castrate (an animal).

1968 *DARE* (Qu. K70, *Words . . for castrating an animal*) Inf **CA**105, Denature.

Dennis n [See quot 1951] *old-fash*

In phr *his name is Dennis:* See quots 1951, 1977.

[**c1880** in 1951 *AmSp* 26.288, We respectfully ask a trial order. . . We will treat you well, and if our relations are not pleasant as well as profitable to you, will willingly take a back seat labelled "Dennis."] **1893** *KS Univ. Qrly.* 1.138 **KS,** Dennis: failure, as 'His name is Dennis.' [**1898** Smith *Caleb West* 336 **NEast,** Within thirty seconds of the time the ominous words fell from the general's lips, the single word "Dennis," the universal sobriquet for a discharged man our working world over, was in every man's mouth.] **1951** *AmSp* 26.288, [Comment of M.M. Mathews to quot 1880:] There is not much doubt but that this use of *Dennis* is in allusion to an expression which may still be used, 'His name is Dennis.' In the early part of the past century, whalers applied the name Dennis to a whale so stricken with a harpoon that he spouted blood, or appeared to do so. Among the whalers the expression 'his name is Dennis' meant he is done for, he has had it. Many years ago I heard this expression, but it may now have died out altogether. **1977** *DARE* File (as of c1915), My father used the expression *his name is Dennis,* meaning "his name is mud."

Dennis the Menace n [From the comic strip by Hank Ketcham, first issued 1951]

A children's hiding game; see quot.

1977 *NY Times* (NY) 6 July 29 **NYC,** "Dennis the Menace," John Tricoche of South Brooklyn was explaining with patience, is a very simple game, sort of "like hide-and-seek backwards." "You get a bunch of guys . . and one of them is it. He's the Dennis. But he doesn't hide his eyes and count like you would. He hides, and all the other guys look for him, O.K.? Then when one finds him he's not caught, the two guys hide together."

den room See **den n 1**

dent See **dent corn**

‡**dental box** n *joc*

1969 *DARE* (Qu. X9, . . *A person's mouth*) Inf **GA**77, Dental box.

dentals n pl *joc*
Teeth; false teeth.
1942 Berrey-Van den Bark *Amer. Slang* 121.74, *Teeth* . . Dentals. **1966-68** *DARE* (Qu. X13b, . . *False teeth*) Infs **MD**31, **SC**7, Dentals.

dent corn n Also *dent, denter corn, dent maize* [From the indentation that develops in the maturing kernel] Cf **flint corn**
An **Indian corn** (here: *Zea mays* var *indentata*).
1854 MI State Ag. Soc. *Trans. for 1853* 5.125, The land . . was planted . . with the "Indian Yellow Dent." **1872** VT State Bd. Ag. *Report* 1.53, We cannot grow the Baldwin . . with more success than we could grow the dent, or the horse-tooth corn of the south and west. **1935** Sandoz *Jules* 390 **wNE** (as of 1880-1930), On the Flats . . [were] long cribs with the gold of yellow dent corn showing between slats. **1966-69** *DARE* (Qu. I34, *If you don't have sweet corn, you can always eat young* ______) Infs **CT**17, **GA**8, **MA**42, **NH**5, Dent corn; **AK**8, Yellow denter corn. **1970** *DARE* Tape **MA**117A, That was Indian corn, not dent corn that you used. **1976** Bailey-Bailey *Hortus Third* 1182, *Zea (mays indentata)* . . Dent Corn, Dent Maize.

dented adj
Of **dent corn:** mature.
1971 [see **dent, in**].

denter corn See **dent corn**

denticul, dentikul See **identical**

dent, in adj phr
Of **dent corn:** mature.
1971 WI Statist. Reporting Serv. *Report* 13 Sept. 1, Nearly two-thirds of the State's corn is in dent, still behind last year when three-fourths was dented.

dent maize See **dent corn**

de-nut v **chiefly Nth, N Midl** Cf **nut** v
To castrate; hence ppl adj *de-nutted.*
1950 *WELS (Words for castrating an animal)* 1 Inf, **ceWI,** De-nut. **1965-70** *DARE* (Qu. K70), 18 Infs, **chiefly Nth, N Midl,** De-nut; (Qu. K58, *A castrated pig*) Infs **MI**120, **MN**2, **PA**232, De-nutted (pig). **1973** Allen *LAUM* 1.251 **cwSD, ceMN** (as of c1950), *Castrate*. . . de-nut.

Denver See **Denver omelet**

Denver mud n [*Denver,* Colorado] **chiefly West**
A patent medicine used as a poultice.
1965-70 *DARE* (Qu. BB50a, . . *Remedies . . for a cough*) Infs **MT**2, **WY**4, Denver mud; **ID**5, **OR**10, Denver mud—patent medicine; (Qu. BB50b, . . *For chest colds*) Inf **IA**30, Denver mud poultice—a boughten mud, put between cloth; (Qu. BB50c, . . *For infections*) Infs **CA**154, **IA**41, **ID**5, **OR**10, **WY**4, Denver mud.

Denver omelet n Also *Denver* Cf **western sandwich**
An omelet containing ham, onions, and freq green pepper; hence n *Denver sandwich* such an omelet served between slices of bread.
1925 Lewis *Arrowsmith* 258 **Upper MW,** You might bring me a Denver sandwich from the Sunset Trail Lunch. **1932** (1946) Hibben *Amer. Regional Cookery* 193, *Denver Sandwich*. . . Fry . . chopped ham with the onion. . . Add slightly beaten eggs, parsley; . . Mix together and let brown lightly. . . Pile between slices of hot buttered toast. **1940** Brown *Amer. Cooks* 69, *Denver Sandwich*. . . This solid snack was born in covered wagon days, when eggs had to be hauled in over long, hot trails. They got so high in flavor that the kindest thing to do was smother them in onions. . . Early cowboys called the great-granddaddy of the Denver Sandwich "Ham Toast." **1967** *DARE* FW Addit **cnNY,** A western omelet or sandwich (egg, ham, pepper, onion) is called a Denver sandwich or omelet in the west. **1985** *DARE* File **Denver CO,** The chef at the Brown Palace Hotel . . says that out here a "Denver" is an omelet made with ham, green peppers and onions. A "Western" is a sandwich: it has the same ingredients as the "Denver," but is prepared in such a way that it can be eaten between two pieces of toast. . . They don't seem to use the "Denver" term back east.

depahter n [Pronc-sp for *departure*]
1927 Kennedy *Gritny* 227 **sLA** [Black], So da's how come she make de jew'lry take a depahter.

deparch v [Back-formation from *departure*]
1891 Johnston *Primes & Neighbors* 131 **GA,** Both you men has be'n a-co'tin' close and heavy, a'most amejiant [=immediately] when their wife deparched from the famblies in their charges.

depression n attrib
Associated with hardship, poverty.
1967 *DARE* (Qu. P35a, . . *Deer shot illegally*) Inf **MN**2, Depression meat—in early 1930s. **1987** *DARE* File **Detroit MI** (as of 1930s), *Depression eggs* was the name for pullets' eggs, because of their smaller size.

der See **duh** v

derby n
1 also attrib: See quot.
1933 *AmSp* 8.1.48 **Ozarks,** *Derby*. . . A young foxhound. A *derby dog* is a male under seventeen months old, while a *derby gyp* is a bitch of the same age.
2 See quot.
1983 *MJLF* 9.1.37 **ceKY,** *Derby* . . a group or pack of fox hounds.

dere adv See **there** adv

dere adj See **their**

dere dey See **de-de**

dern v, intj See **durn** v, intj

dern n See **durn** n

derrick n Also *hay derrick* **chiefly Rocky Mts**
An apparatus of ropes and pulleys rigged to a crossbeam which pivots usu at the top of a stout pole, used for hoisting bundles of hay; see quot 1985.
1931 *AmSp* 7.121 **eID,** A *hay derrick* is an implement for stacking hay. **1967** *DARE* (Qu. L16, *Machines used . . in handling hay*) Inf **WY**1, Derricks—slings were laid on the hay rack before loading. Thus, a rack full of hay could be stacked in two bunches [Drawing in QR shows a system of ropes and pulleys on a pivoting bar attached to the top of a tall pole.]; **WY**4, Stacker—also called a derrick—not used anymore. **1968** Adams *Western Words* 91, *Derrick*—A wooden crane used on ranches to stack hay. **1985** Attebery *ID Folklife* 3 **sID, wWY, UT, nwAZ,** Hay derricks of the alfalfa-growing districts of the Great Basin and upper Snake River Valley . . use the Jackson fork . . to carry the hay from load to stack. This fork grasps a sixth to an eighth of a wagonload at a time. It is carried from load to stack by a cable which travels over pulleys at appropriate points on the derrick and is pulled by a single horse, a team, or a tractor. When the hay has been raised to a point above . . the stack, . . the fork is tripped and the hay falls on the stack.

derrick v
1930 Shoemaker *1300 Words* 17 **cPA Mts** (as of c1900), *Derrick*—To execute or suicide by hanging.

Derryfield beef n [See quot] *joc* Cf **Albany beef, Cape Cod turkey**
Eels.
1939 Wolcott *Yankee Cook Book* 45, **NH,** Hauls of a hundred or more [eels] at night were not uncommon at the time of year when they returned. At Amoskeag they were taken in such numbers that they became known as "Derryfield Beef" after the old name for Manchester, N.H.

ders(e)n't See **dare** v **A4a**

des See **just**

dese See **these**

Deseret weed n
A **licorice** (here: *Glycyrrhiza lepidota*).
1924 *Amer. Botanist* 30.33, *Glycerrhiza* [sic] *lepidota* is said to be called "Deseret weed" very commonly in Utah.

desert almond n Also *desert range almond*
An intricately branched white-flowered shrub *(Prunus fasciculata).* Also called **desert peach-brush, wild almond, wild peach**
1913 *Agric. Research Jrnl.* Nov. *(DA),* [These] small downy fruits with thin dry flesh have won for them the local names 'wild almond' in the Great Basin region, wild peach or desert almond for another form in the Mohave Desert. **1925** Jepson *Manual Plants CA* 507, *P[runus] fasciculata* . . Desert Almond. **1941** Jaeger *Wildflowers* 92, Desert Range Almond, . . *Prunus fasciculata.* **1960** Vines *Trees SW* 395, In some

areas it [=*Prunus fasciculata*] is locally known as Desert Almond. **1981** Benson–Darrow *Trees SW Deserts* 278, *Prunus fasciculata* . . Desert Almond.

desert apricot n

A white-flowered shrub *(Prunus fremontii)* which somewhat resembles the cultivated apricot.

1925 Jepson *Manual Plants CA* 507, *P[runus] fremontii* . . Desert Apricot. **1941** Jaeger *Wildflowers* 92, Desert Apricot. *Prunus eriogyna.* **1981** Benson–Darrow *Trees SW Deserts* 278, *Prunus Fremontii* . . Desert Apricot.

desert ash n

=**velvet ash.**

1931 U.S. Dept. Ag. *Misc. Pub.* 101.137, *Leatherleaf ash* or desert ash. . . [has] some utility as winter, late fall, and early spring browse. **1938** Van Dersal *Native Woody Plants* 133, The desert ash . . is of some value as . . browse for stock. **1960** Vines *Trees SW* 863, Other names [for *Fraxinus velutina*] are . . Desert Ash . . and Fresno. **1979** Little *Checklist U.S. Trees* 137, *Velvet ash. . . Other common names* . . desert ash. . . *Range*—Trans-Pecos Tex., N. Mex., Ariz., extreme sw Utah, s. Nev., and s. Calif.

desert beauty n

An **indigo bush** (here: either *Dalea formosa* or *D. fremontii*).

1931 U.S. Dept. Ag. *Misc. Pub.* 101.85, *Desertbeauty* (*P. johnsoni* and *P. amoena* . .) is the common name of two very handsome, closely related bushes of the southern Great Basin region and Southwest. **1967** Dodge *Roadside Wildflowers* 30, *Desert Beauty. . .* Especially attractive when in blossom, . . the flowers are small but so colorful that they attract attention of the passer-by. . . *Dalea formosa.*

desert blite n

A **seepweed** (here: *Suaeda torreyana*).

1960 Vines *Trees SW* 246, Vernacular names for Torrey Seepweed [=*Suaeda torreyana*] are Desert Blite and Sea Blite.

desert bloom n

A **groundsel** (here: *Baccharis sarothroides*).

1960 Vines *Trees SW* 972, It [=*Baccharis sarothroides*] is also known under the vernacular names of Greasewood, Desert-bloom, . . and Groundsel.

desert broom n

1 A **groundsel tree** (here: *Baccharis wrightii*).

1941 *Torreya* 41.53, *Baccharis wrightii. . .* Desert broom, Arizona.

2 Spanish broom *(Spartium junceum).*

1951 Corle *Gila* 348 **AZ,** Other trees and shrubs common in the Gila basin are the yucca, hackberry, sycamore, . . desert broom, burro weed, and brittle brush.

desert calico n

A **gilia** (here: *Langloisia matthewsii*).

1941 Jaeger *Wildflowers* 192, Desert Calico. *Gilia Matthewsii* [=*Langloisia matthewsii*].

desert canary n Also *desert canary bird* [In joc allusion to its loud bray] **West** Cf **Arizona nightingale**

A burro.

1936 Adams *Cowboy Lingo* 202 **West,** Mules were called 'hard tails' or 'knob heads,' and burros 'desert canaries.' **1949** Emrich *Wild West Custom* 190, Jokingly referred to as the 'desert canary' . . the little burro was, nevertheless, the forerunner of all transportation on the desert and in the high mountain gulches. **1968** Adams *Western Words* 92, *Desert canary*—A westerner's name for a burro. **1971** Bright *Word Geog. CA & NV* 113, Desert canary (bird). [These responses were given by 4 informants as names for a burro or small donkey.]

desert candle n

1 A **yucca.**

1942 Hylander *Plant Life* 563, Desert Candles *(Yucca Whipplei). . .* forms . . rosettes of . . leaves, from the midst of which rises the stout flowering stalk. . . A hillside covered with these Yuccas looks like an area dotted with tall graceful candles. **1959** Carleton *Index Herb. Plants* 36, *Desert candle:* Eremurus (v); Yucca (v).

2 A plant of the genus *Eremurus.*

1959 [see 1 above]. **1976** Bailey–Bailey *Hortus Third* 434, *Eremurus. . .* Desert Candle, King's Spear.

3 A **sotol** (here: *Dasylirion texanum*).

1961 Wills–Irwin *Flowers TX* 96, *Dasylirion texanum. . .* Sotol or Desert-candle grows mostly in dry rocky mesas and hillsides.

4 A **wild cabbage** (here: *Caulanthus inflatus*).

1959 Munz–Keck *CA Flora* 223, *C[aulanthus] inflatus. . . Desert Candle. . .* Common on open flats and among brush. **1967** *DARE* (Qu. S26e) Inf **CA**2, Squaw cabbage or desert candles.

desert catalpa n

=**desert willow.**

1933 Jaeger *CA Deserts* 188, In the late spring and summer days the desert catalpa or so-called desert willow *(Chilopsis linearis)* cheers the wayfarer with its pendant green leaves and its wealth of gay, pink, tubular flowers. **1951** *PADS* 15.41 **TX,** *Chilopsis linearis* . . desert catalpa. **1979** Little *Checklist U.S. Trees* 88, *Chilopsis linearis* . . desert-willow. . . Other common names—desert-catalpa. **1985** Dodge *Flowers SW Deserts* 49, Desert-Catalpa. . . *Chilopsis linearis.*

desert chicory n [See quot 1985]

A plant of the genus *Rafinesquia,* usu *R. neomexicana,* native chiefly to the Southwest.

1941 Jaeger *Wildflowers* 310 **Desert SW,** *R[afinesquia] neo-mexicana,* called desert chicory, is . . also common on our deserts. **1960** Abrams *Flora Pacific States* 4.575, *Rafinesquia neo-mexicana. . .* Desert Chicory. . . Mesas and canyons, usually in the shade of shrubs. **1985** Dodge *Flowers SW Deserts* 20, *Desert-Chicory. . . Rafinesquia neomexicana. . . Rafinesquia californica. . .* The name . . is applied because of the superficial resemblance to the more robust blue flowered . . *cichorium intybus.*

desert chipmunk See **antelope chipmunk**

desert Christmas cactus n

A **prickly pear** (here: *Opuntia leptocaulis*).

1940 Benson *Cacti AZ* 29, *Opuntia leptocaulis* . . Desert Christmas Cactus. **1970** Correll *Plants TX* 1091, *Opuntia leptocaulis* . . Desert Christmas Cactus.

desert cooler n

A device for cooling by water evaporation; see quots.

1970 *DARE* (Qu. D10a) Inf **CA**207, Desert coolers—wet gunny sacks packed over items. **1976** *DARE* File **cAZ,** *Desert cooler* = an air conditioner using evaporating water as cooling agent.

desert daisy n

A **desert star** (here: *Monoptilon bellioides*).

1971 Dodge *100 Desert Wildflowers* 82, Also known as "desert daisy" . . Desertstar grows principally in southern Arizona and southern California.

desert dandelion n

A plant of the genus *Malacothrix.* For other names of var spp see **dwarf dandelion 2, snake's-head, yellow saucers**

1915 (1926) Armstrong–Thornber *Western Wild Flowers* 574, *Desert Dandelion. Malacothrix Fendleri. . .* An attractive little desert plant . . with . . pretty, very pale yellow flowers . . like a delicate sort of Dandelion. **1942** Hylander *Plant Life* 498, The Desert Dandelion *(Malacothrix)* has a . . basal tuft of leaves, woolly and pinnately divided. **1968** *DARE* (Qu. S11) Inf **CA**60, (Wild) desert dandelion. **1971** Dodge *100 Desert Wildflowers* 98, There are many species of malacothryx [sic]. . . Some are locally "desert dandelion." **1974** Munz *Flora S. CA* 208, *M. glabrata. . .* Desert-Dandelion.

desert fir n

=**pygmy cedar.**

1941 Jaeger *Wildflowers* 303, Desert-fir. *Peucephyllum Schottii.*

desert fivespot n Also *five-spot* [See quot 1957]

A malvaceous plant *(Eremalche rotundifolia)* with dark-spotted, purplish flowers. Also called **Chinese lantern 2, lantern flower**

1941 Jaeger *Wildflowers* 142, *Desert Five-spot. . .* Rose-purple with spots of carmine. **1957** Jaeger *N. Amer. Deserts* 278, *Five-spot. . .* A handsome annual with globe-like, pinkish-lilac flowers, each of the five petals conspicuously spotted with darker violet-pink. **1959** Munz–Keck *CA Flora* 122, *Desert Fivespot. . .* Mojave and Colo. deserts, Ariz., Nev.

desert fox n Also *desert kit fox* Cf **desert gray fox**

=**kit fox.**

1928 Anthony *N. Amer. Mammals* 141, Desert Kit Fox. —*Vulpes macrotis arsipus*. . Desert Fox. —*Vulpes macrotis neomexicana.* **1935** Pratt *Manual Vertebrate Animals* 269, *V[ulpes] macrotis* . . desert fox. **1957** Blair et al. *Vertebrates U.S.* 746, *Vulpes macrotis* . . Desert kit fox. **1968** *DARE* (Qu. P32) Inf **CA**62, Desert fox. **1982** Elman *Hunter's Field Guide* 353, The southwestern part of the range is shared with the kit fox, or desert fox *(Vulpes macrotis),* smallest and fastest of the American foxes.

desert glaze See **desert varnish**

desert gloss See **desert varnish**

desert gold See **desert sunflower**

desert grape n

A **grape** (here: *Vitis girdiana*) native to California.

1925 Jepson *Manual Plants CA* 625, *V[itis] girdiana. . . Desert Grape.* Stems 5 to 20 ft. long. **1938** Van Dersal *Native Woody Plants* 337, Grape, . . Desert *(Vitis girdiana).* **1942** Hylander *Plant Life* 370, The Desert Grape is a smaller vine of southern California, producing smaller and blacker berries. **1951** Abrams *Flora Pacific States* 3.82, Desert Grape. . . Stream banks . . ; Santa Barbara and Inyo Counties, California, southward to northern Lower California on both the desert and coastal slopes.

desert gray fox n

=**gray fox.**

1917 *Mammals of Amer.* 80 *(DA),* Desert Gray Fox.—*Urocyon cinereoargenteus texensis* Mearns. Paler than the Eastern Gray Fox; ears longer; tail longer. Texas.

desert hawk n Also *desert sparrow hawk*

A **sparrow hawk** (here: *Falco sparverius*).

1917 (1923) *Birds Amer.* 2.91, The Desert Sparrow Hawk *(Falco sparverius phalæna)* is larger than the stock form, with longer tail. **1923** Dawson *Birds CA* 4.1636, Desert sparrow hawk. **1961** Ligon *NM Birds* 83, *Falco sparverius. . .* The southwestern form is referred to . . as the Desert Sparrow Hawk. **1967** *DARE* (Qu. Q4) Inf **CA**1, Desert hawk.

desert holly n

1 A low composite plant *(Perezia nana)* with hollylike leaves.

1915 (1926) Armstrong-Thornber *Western Wild Flowers* 536, *Desert Holly. Perezia nana. . .* An odd little desert plant, only two or three inches high, with . . dull bluish-green leaves, with prickly edges, like holly leaves but not so stiff. **1936** Whitehouse *TX Flowers* 191, Closely kin to the nodding thistle is the desert holly *(Perezia nana).* **1970** Correll *Plants TX* 1721, *Desert Holly. . .* Ariz., N.M., Tex. . . Not often collected because rarely found in flower in spite of its abundance.

2 A **saltbush** (here: *Atriplex hymenelytra*).

1915 *Nature & Sci.* 173, The desert holly *(Atriplex hymenelytra)* . . is an attractive shrub with the leaves toothed as the true holly but silvery white in color. **1923** in 1925 Jepson *Manual Plants CA* 327, *A[triplex] hymenelytra. . .* Desert Holly. **1941** Jaeger *Wildflowers* 54 **Desert SW,** *Desert Holly. . .* The silvery leaves make it a desirable Christmas decoration and much of it is sold for that purpose. **1967** *DARE* (Qu. S26e) Infs **CA**4, 9, Desert holly. **1981** Benson-Darrow *Trees SW Deserts* 169, *Desert Holly. . .* California . . ; southern Nevada . . ; southwestern Utah; Arizona. . . This saltbush is well known to desert travellers as desert holly.

desert hollyhock n

A **globe mallow 1:** usu *Sphaeralcea ambigua,* but also *S. emoryi.*

1942 Hylander *Plant Life* 664, Desert Hollyhock. Sphaeralcea ambigua. **1949** Curtin *By the Prophet* 80, *Sphaeralcea emoryi* var. *variabilis. . .* Common name: Desert Hollyhock. **1959** Munz-Keck *CA Flora* 119, *S[phaeralcea] ambigua. . .* Desert-Hollyhock.

desert honeysuckle n

=**chuparosa 2.**

1945 Benson-Darrow *Manual SW Trees* 298, Anisacanthus is one of the better browse plants of the desert. Sometimes it is called desert honeysuckle. **1960** Vines *Trees SW* 932, *Anisacanthus thurberi* . . It is also known under the vernacular names of Desert-honeysuckle . . and Chuparosa. **1976** Bailey-Bailey *Hortus Third* 79, *Anisacanthus Thurberi* . . Desert Honeysuckle. **1981** Benson-Darrow *Trees SW Deserts* 216, Sometimes this species [=*Anisacanthus Thurberi*] is called desert honeysuckle.

desert hyacinth n

A **blue dicks** (here: *Brodiaea pulchella*).

1941 Jaeger *Wildflowers* 13, Desert Hyacinth. *Brodiaea capitata pauciflora* [=*Brodiaea pulchella*].

desert inky cap n

Either of two mushrooms similar to the **inky cap:** *Montagnites arenarius* or *Podaxis pistillaris.*

1981 Lincoff *Audubon Field Guide Mushrooms* 814, *Desert Inky Cap. Podaxis pistillaris. . .* This is a characteristic desert mushroom. **1987** McKnight-McKnight *Mushrooms* 280, *Desert Inky Cap. Montagnites arenarius. . .* On sandy soil in arid, desert shrub communities, sand dunes, roadsides or hillsides, Mexico to Texas and California, north to Oregon, southern Idaho, and Utah. . . Frequently confused with a sand-dune *Coprinus* (inky cap), to which it is closely related.

desert ironwood n

A small, broad-crowned tree *(Olneya tesota)* of the southwestern US deserts. Also called **ironwood, tesota**

1938 Van Dersal *Native Woody Plants* 175, *Olneya tesota* . . Desert ironwood. **1981** Benson-Darrow *Trees SW Deserts* 255, *Olneya* Desert Ironwood.

desert kit fox See **desert fox**

desert lavender n

An aromatic plant, usu *Hyptis emoryi* but also *H. alata.* The former is also called **bee sage 1, mountain sage**

1938 Van Dersal *Native Woody Plants* 142, *Hyptis emoryi. . . Desert lavender. . .* Much visited by hummingbirds. **1957** Jaeger *N. Amer. Deserts* 290, *Desert Lavender. . .* A fragrant shrub much visited by bees. **1965** Teale *Wandering Through Winter* 22 **CA,** During these winter days the insects were obtaining most of their nectar from the small flowers of the desert lavender. **1970** Correll *Plants TX* 1354, *Hyptis alata. . .* Desert Lavender. **1981** Benson-Darrow *Trees SW Deserts* 211, Desert Lavender, *Hyptis Emoryi. . .* The tall, lavender-scented shrubs are restricted to . . the desert foothills.

desert lily n

A white-flowered liliaceous plant *(Hesperocallis undulata)* native to southern California and southwestern Arizona. Also called **ajo**

1915 (1926) Armstrong-Thornber *Western Wild Flowers* 30, *Desert Lily. Hesperocallis undulata. . .* This is . . much like an Easter Lily. **1917** Saunders *W. Flower Guide* 4 *(DA),* The deep-seated bulbs of the Desert Lily used to form an item of importance in the diet of the Desert Indians. **1946** *Desert Mag.* March 30/1 *(DA),* In the Cronise area . . a fairly mild and moist winter already has assured that locality of its usual fine display of desert lilies. **1967-68** *DARE* (Qu. S26a) Inf **CA**94, Desert lily; (Qu. S26e) Inf **CA**4, Desert lily. **1976** Bailey-Bailey *Hortus Third* 558.

desert mahogany n

A **mountain mahogany** (here: *Cercocarpus ledifolius*).

1925 Jepson *Manual Plants CA* 502, *C. ledifolius. . . Desert Mahogany. . .* Arid slopes of ranges in and bordering the deserts or arid interior. **1937** U.S. Forest Serv. *Range Plant Hdbk.* B50, Curlleaf mountain-mahogany, also known as . . desert mahogany, is usually a shrub from 3 to 15 feet high. **1942** Hylander *Plant Life* 304, Most widely distributed is Desert Mahogany with narrow entire leaves and small flowers with long silky tails to the fruits.

desert mallow n

Any of var **globe mallows 1,** but esp *Sphaeralcea ambigua.*

1941 Jaeger *Wildflowers* 142 **Desert SW,** *Desert Mallow. Sphaeralcea ambigua. . .* A somewhat shrubby perennial, so handsome when in flower that many desert folk think it the climax of floral beauty. **1951** Abrams *Flora Pacific States* 3.87, *Sphaeralcea Orcuttii. . .* Orcutt's Desert-mallow. . . *Sphaeralcea Coulteri. . .* Coulter's Desert-mallow. . . *Sphaeralcea Emoryi. . .* Emory's Desert-mallow [etc]. **1969** *DARE* (Qu. S26a) Inf **AZ**15, Desert mallow. **1971** Dodge *100 Desert Wildflowers* 42, Desert-mallows flaunt their graceful, blossom-covered stems along roadsides or on the banks of sandy washes. **1974** Munz *Flora S. CA* 572, *Desert-Mallow. . .* Throughout the Calif. deserts; to Utah, Son[ora], L. Calif.

desert marigold n

A plant of the genus *Baileya* native to dry regions of the western US. Also called **wild marigold, woolly marigold.** For other names of var spp see **gold dollars, laxflower, paper daisy**

1933 *Torreya* 33.61 **Desert SW,** *Desert Marigold (Baileya multiradiata)* . . basal tufts of hoary silver foliage and . . flowers of deepest golden yellow. **1957** Jaeger *N. Amer. Deserts* 274, *Desert Marigold*. . . Found from deserts of western Texas to . . Utah and California. **1959** Munz-Keck *CA Flora* 1132, *Baileya* . . Desert-Marigold. **1976** Bailey-Bailey *Hortus Third* 134, *Baileya* . . Desert Marigold. **1985** Dodge *Flowers SW Deserts* 90, *Desert Marigold*. Desert-Marigold. . . In California, Desert baileya or "marigold" is cultivated for the flower trade.

desert olive n [In ref to its being of the family Oleaceae, which includes olives]

Any of var **forestieras;** see quots.

1945 Benson-Darrow *Manual SW Trees* 262, *Forestiera phillyreoides* . . Desert Olive. *Ibid* 263, *Forestiera neo-mexicana* . . Desert Olive. **1960** Vines *Trees SW* 851, It [=*Forestiera pubescens*] is also known as Desert Olive. **1970** Correll *Plants TX* 1199, *Forestiera angustifolia* . . Desert olive. **1981** Benson-Darrow *Trees SW Deserts* 184, *Forestiera Shrevei* . . Desert Olive.

desert paintbrush n

An **Indian paintbrush** (here: *Castilleja angustifolia*).

1941 Jaeger *Wildflowers* 239, *Desert Paintbrush. Castilleja angustifolia*. . . A flash of brilliant red . . generally calls our attention to this handsome paintbrush. **1967** *DARE* (Qu. S26a) Inf **CA**1, Desert paintbrush.

desert parsley n

=biscuit root 1.

1961 Peck *Manual OR* 571, *L. Howellii*. . . Howell's Desert Parsley. *Ibid* 572, *L. Gormanii*. . . Gorman's Desert Parsley. . . *L. Piperi*. . . Piper's Desert Parsley [etc]. **1963** Craighead *Rocky Mt. Wildflowers* 127, *Lomatium ambiguum*. . . Desert Parsley. *Ibid* 128, Desert-Parsley. *Lomatium dissectum*. **1967** *DARE* Wildfl QR (Craighead) Pl. 13.5, Inf **CA**24, Desert parsley. **1973** Hitchcock-Cronquist *Flora Pacific NW* 327, *Lomatium*. . . Biscuit-root; Desert-parsley; Lomatium.

desert pavement n **SW** Cf **desert varnish**

A ground surface of firmly bedded, tightly packed stones.

[**1901** Van Dyke *Desert* 39 **AZ,** Beyond Yuma on the Colorado there are thousands of acres of mosaic pavement. . . so hard that a horse's hoof will make no impression upon it.] **1939** Pickwell *Deserts* 39, **CA,** [Caption:] *A Wind-Made Desert Pavement in the Mohave*. *Ibid* 41, With the wind's help, this same gravel is bedded down in places with rain into interesting and strikingly level desert "pavements."

desert peach n

A thorny pink- or red-flowered shrub *(Prunus andersonii)*. Also called **Nevada wild almond, wild peach**

1925 Jepson *Manual Plants CA* 507, *P[runus] andersonii* . . Desert Peach. **1967** *DARE* (Qu. S26e) Inf **CA4,** Desert peach. **1976** Bailey-Bailey *Hortus Third* 918, *Prunus . . andersonii* . . Desert peach. **1981** Benson-Darrow *Trees SW Deserts* 278.

desert peach-brush n

=desert almond.

1960 Vines *Trees SW* 395, Desert Peach-Brush—*Prunus fasciculata*.

desert pink n

A **wire lettuce** (here: *Stephanomeria wrightii*).

1915 (1926) Armstrong-Thornber *Western Wild Flowers* 570 **nwAZ,** *Desert Pink. Ptiloria Wrightii*. . . Pale green foliage and . . flowers, three-quarters of an inch long, giving the effect of tiny, pale pink carnations. This grows at the Grand Canyon.

desert plume n

A **prince's plume** (here: *Standleya pinnata*).

1941 Jaeger *Wildflowers* 74 **Desert SW,** *Desert Plume*. . . Why Dr. C. Hart Merriam referred to this as a "miserable crucifer" is hard to conjecture, for it is one of the handsomest of plants. **1959** Carleton *Index Herb. Plants* 36, *Desert plume:* Standleya pinnata. **1967** Dodge *Roadside Wildflowers* 13 **SW,** The showy, almost gaudy spike of the . . desert plume, seems out of place on dry mesas or hot canyon walls.

desert polish See **desert varnish**

desert primrose n

An evening primrose such as *Oenothera caespitosa*.

1941 Jaeger *Wildflowers* 172, Large Yellow Desert Primrose. *Oenothera primiveris*. *Ibid* 173, Large White Desert Primrose. *Oenothera caespitosa marginata*. **1956** St. John *Flora SE WA* 279, *Oenothera caespitosa* Nutt., var. *marginata*. . . Desert Primrose. **1966** *Silver City Daily Press* (NM) 21 Mar 1/4, The California deserts welcomed the new season with carpets of desert primrose and sand verbena bursting into bloom. **1967** *DARE* (Qu. S2) Inf **CA**9, Desert primrose; (Qu. S26e) Inf **CA**4, Desert primrose.

desert quail n

=Gambel's quail.

1878 Campion *Frontier* 251 **Rocky Mts,** On going to the water-holes in the morning we see flocks of the pied or desert quail coming to the puddles. **1918** Grinnell *Game Birds CA* 540, Throughout its range the Desert Quail is a close associate of the mesquite or "quail brush," the latter being a species of *Atriplex*. **1961** Ligon *NM Birds* 97, Gambel's Quail—*Lophortyx gambelii* . . Although often referred to as the "Desert Quail," it is not, as above indicated, confined to the desert. **1968** *DARE* (Qu. Q7) Inf **CA**95, Desert quail. **1982** Elman *Hunter's Field Guide* 99, Desert quail [*Callipepla gambelii*] run hard and flush wild, yet some hunters use pointing dogs.

desert range almond See **desert almond**

desert rat n **West**

One who lives in the desert; a prospector in the desert.

1907 *Putnam's Mag.* July 482/2 **cNV,** This [is] the camp that had . . lured . . desert rats, dusty prospectors, mysteriously called as by some scent to this new ground of gold. **1914** *DN* 4.163 **NW,** *Desert rat*. . . A roving prospector for gold. *Southwest*. "Near the poison springs we came upon a desert rat, whose bleaching bones witnessed his lust for gold." **1931** *AmSp* 7.120 **eID,** A settler living on land *reclaimed* by irrigation, who is especially susceptible to the charms of the desert, is a *desert rat* or a *sage rat*. **1942** *CA Folkl. Qrly.* 1.274 **CA, NV, AZ,** *Desert rat*. . . A roving prospector or resident on arid land. **1968** Adams *Western Words* 92, *Desert rat*—A veteran prospector of the desert country, usually one without a mine or any other property.

desert rattler n

Prob the western **diamondback rattlesnake** *(Crotalus atrox)*.

1967 *DARE* (Qu. P25) Inf **TX**5, Desert rattler.

desert rind See **desert varnish**

desert rock-pea n

A **deervetch** (here: *Lotus rigidus*).

1941 Jaeger *Wildflowers* 102 **Desert SW,** *Desert Rock-Pea. Lotus rigidus*. . . A showy, somewhat woody species.

desert rock-squirrel n

A **ground squirrel** n **b** (here: *Spermophilus variegatus*).

1968 *DARE* (Qu. P27) Inf **CA**95, Desert rock-squirrel.

desert-rue n

=turpentine bloom.

1931 U.S. Dept. Ag. *Misc. Pub.* 101.91, *Desert-Rues (Thamnosma spp.)* . . Desert-rue is represented by two glandular, strong-smelling shrubs or undershrubs of the Southwest, unpalatable to grazing animals. **1960** Vines *Trees SW* 593, *Texas Desert-Rue. Thamnosma texana*. . . Tufted plant . . attaining a height of 8-16 in. . . Strong-scented foliage.

desert sage n

Any of several **sages;** see quots.

1931 U.S. Dept. Ag. *Misc. Pub.* 101.141, *Desert sage (S. carnosa . .)* is much the most widely distributed of all the shrubby western sages and is often common and abundant. **1968** *DARE* (Qu. S26e, *Other wildflowers not yet mentioned*) Inf **CA**91, Desert sage. **1976** Bailey-Bailey *Hortus Third* 999, *[Salvia] eremostachya*. . . *Desert s[age]*. Much-branched shrub, 2-2½ ft. **1981** Benson-Darrow *Trees SW Deserts* 207, *Salvia Dorrii*. . . Purple Sage, Desert Sage.

desert sagebrush n Also *desert sage*

=bud sagebrush.

1931 U.S. Dept. Ag. *Misc. Pub.* 101.172, *Bud sagebrush* . . is . . variously known as . . desert sage(brush).

desert saltbush n **AZ**

A **saltbush** (here: *Atriplex polycarpa*).

1936 in 1941 *Torreya* 41.47 **AZ,** *Atriplex polycarpa*. . . Desert saltbush. **1945** Benson-Darrow *Manual SW Trees* 125, *Desert Saltbush*. . . is an abundant plant, and it is valuable as forage for livestock. **1949** Curtin *By the Prophet* 67 **csAZ,** "The ancients," when starving, roasted and ground the collected seeds of desert saltbush to make *pinole.* **1981** Benson-Darrow *Trees SW Deserts* 170, *Desert Saltbush. . .* in southern Arizona . . occurs in pure stands or with mesquite or creosote bush.

desert savior n

A **live-forever** (here: *Dudleya lanceolata*).

1925 Jepson *Manual Plants CA* 453, *C[otyledon] lanceolata. . . Desert Savior.* Plants 8 to 15 in. high.

desert snapdragon n [From its resemblance to a snapdragon]

A desert plant of the genus *Mohavea.* For other names of *M. confertiflora* see **ghost flower 3, Mojave flower**

1949 Moldenke *Amer. Wild Flowers* 276, On rocky slopes in the Colorado and Mojave deserts of southern California and adjacent Nevada and Arizona one may, on occasion, find the showy *desertsnapdragons, Mohavea,* usually in sand and on talus slopes. **1951** Abrams *Flora Pacific States* 3.788, *Mohavea breviflora. . .* Golden Desert Snapdragon.

desert sparrow hawk See **desert hawk**

desert spoon n [From the spoon-like leaf bases]

A **sotol** (here: *Dasylirion wheeleri*); the leaf bases of such a plant.

1945 Benson-Darrow *Manual SW Trees* 77, *Dasylirion Wheeleri. . . Sotol; Desert Spoon.* Recognized by the forward-directed prickles on the leaf margins. **1968** *DARE* (Qu. S26e) Inf **MN**13, Desert spoon. **1971** Dodge *100 Desert Wildflowers* 13, *Sotol. . .* The stiff leaf bases, when pulled from the cluster, form the "desert spoons" sold in some curio stores. **1981** Benson-Darrow *Trees SW Deserts* 62, In recent years the sotol has become known as "desert spoon."

desert star n

A plant of the genus *Monoptilon.* For other names of *M. bellioides* see **desert daisy, rock daisy**

1915 (1926) Armstrong-Thornber *Western Wild Flowers* 548, *Desert Star. Erimiastrum bellidoides* [sic]. . . A charming little desert plant . . ornamented with many pretty little flowers. **1925** Jepson *Manual Plants CA* 1044, *M. bellioides. . . Desert Star. . .* Desert flats and mesas. **1941** Jaeger *Wildflowers* 270, *Mohave Desert-star. . .* A gay little annual, which clings close to the desert sands. **1959** Munz-Keck *CA Flora* 1192, *Monoptilon. . . Desert Star. . .* Two spp., of deserts of the sw. U.S. and n. Mex. **1980** Hogan *Quartzsite* 205 **AZ,** He found a stony slope covered with desert stars, little daisies smaller than a dime.

desert straw n

A **wire lettuce** (here: *Stephanomeria pauciflora*).

1941 Jaeger *Wildflowers* 310, Desert-straw. *Stephanomeria pauciflora . .* When growing in the shelter of shrubs it sends up a long stem, then branches to form a compact, rounded mass superficially resembling, when dry, a tuft of hay or straw.

desert sunflower n Also *desert gold, ~ sunshine*

A composite plant *(Geraea canescens)* native to the Southwest.

1923 Davidson-Moxley *Flora S. CA* 407, *G[erea] canescens. . .* Sandy soil of . . the Colorado and Mohave Deserts. . . *Desert Sunflower.* **1941** Jaeger *Wildflowers* 286 **Desert SW,** *Desert Sunflower. . .* This magnificent, sweet-scented species gives us the finest show of massed yellow on the desert. **1960** Abrams *Flora Pacific States* 4.125, *Geraea canescens. . .* Desert Sunflower. **1976** Bailey-Bailey *Hortus Third* 504, *Desert sunflower. . .* Utah, s. Calif., Ariz., n. Mex. **1985** Dodge *Flowers SW Deserts* 88, *Desertgold.* Desert-Sunshine, Desert Sunflower. . . *Geraea canescens. . .* Desertgold often forms . . gardens of luxuriant bloom along roadsides and in sandy basins early in the spring.

desert sweet n [See quot 1976]

=**fernbush 2.**

1925 Jepson *Manual Plants CA* 480, *Desert-sweet. . .* Herbage very fragrant. **1941** Jaeger *Wildflowers* 93, *Desert Sweet. . .* Stout, erect, branching shrub. . . Eastern slopes of the Panamint Mts., north to Ore., east to Wyo. **1961** Peck *Manual OR* 422. **1967** Dodge *Roadside Wildflowers* 20, Its [=*Chamaebatiaria millefolium's*] fragrant flowers lead to the appellation desertsweet.

desert swift n

A **chimney swift.**

1968 *DARE* (Qu. P32) Inf **CA**95, Desert swift; (Qu. Q3) Inf **CA**62, Desert swift.

desert tea n

=**Mormon tea.**

1970 Kirk *Wild Edible Plants W. U.S.* 21, *Ephedra* species. . . Desert Tea. . . All of the species make good tea, although some are better than others. . . To bring out the full flavor, a teaspoon of sugar per cup should be added along with some lemon juice or strawberry jam.

desert terrapin See **desert turtle**

desert thorn n

A **wolfberry** (here: *Lycium* spp).

1925 Jepson *Manual Plants CA* 889, *Lycium. . . Desert Thorn.* Shrubs, ours rough-spiny. **1931** U.S. Dept. Ag. *Misc. Pub.* 101.142, *Wolfberries* (*Lycium* spp.) . . are common and characteristic and a wealth of vernacular names has been bestowed upon them, including . . desert thorn. **1938** Van Dersal *Native Woody Plants* 161, *Cooper desert-thorn. . .* Stout, spiny and densely branched. **1960** Vines *Trees SW* 911, Other vernacular names for the plant are Anderson Desert-thorn and Squawberry. *Ibid* 916, *Lycium torreyi. . .* is also known by the vernacular names of Desert-thorn, Rabbit-thorn [etc]. **1970** Kirk *Wild Edible Plants W. U.S.* 238, *Lycium pallidum* and related species. . . Desert Thorn. . . These shrubby, spiny, plants may grow either spreading or erect. **1985** Dodge *Flowers SW Deserts* 110, Desert-Thorn. . . *Thorny shrubs, stiff and brushy, up to 6 feet. . .* Widely distributed throughout the desert.

desert thrush n Cf **cactus thrush**

Prob a **thrasher** (here: *Toxostoma* spp).

1967 *DARE* (Qu. Q14) Inf **CA**9, Desert thrush.

desert tortoise See **desert turtle**

desert trumpet n [See quot 1917]

A **buckwheat 2** (here: *Eriogonum inflatum*). Also called **bladderstem, bottle plant, Indian pipe weed, pickles**

1917 Saunders *W. Flower Guide* 42, The inflated stalks, swelling upward gradually like a musical horn, explain the popular designation Desert Trumpet. **1923** in 1925 Jepson *Manual Plants CA* 307, *Desert Trumpet. . .* Colorado and Mohave deserts, n. to the San Carlos Range; e. to Utah and N. Mex. **1937** U.S. Forest Serv. *Range Plant Hdbk.* W69, Desert-trumpet *(E[riogonum] inflatum),* sometimes called Indianpipe weed, is another interesting annual, which ranges from Colorado and New Mexico to California. **1949** Moldenke *Amer. Wild Flowers* 73, An unusual species called *deserttrumpet . .* has curiously inflated stems. **1957** Jaeger *N. Amer. Deserts* 264, *Desert Trumpet. . .* The young stems taste like sheep sorrel.

desert turtle n Also *desert tortoise, ~ terrapin* **SW, esp sCA**

A western **gopher** **n**[1] **1a** (here: *Gopherus agassizii*).

1933 Harrington *Gypsum Cave NV* 10, The desert tortoise was fairly abundant. **1965-70** *DARE* (Qu. P24) 13 Infs, **chiefly sCA,** Desert turtle; **CA**9, 87, 114, 117, **TX**5, Desert tortoise; **CA**2, 12, Desert terrapin.

desert varnish n Also *desert glaze, ~ gloss, ~ polish, ~ rind* **SW** Cf **desert pavement**

A polished, often discolored surface formed on exposed rock by the action of wind and water; hence adj *desert varnished.*

1903 Geikie *Geology* 436, On the sandy plains of Wyoming, Utah . . surfaces even of such hard materials as Chalcedony are etched into furrows and wrinkles, acquiring at the same time a peculiar and characteristic glaze ('desert polish'). **1904** U.S. Geol. Surv. *Monographs* 47.547 **West,** In arid regions the hardened film has frequently been smoothed by the wind-blown sand, so as to present a polished surface. Such polished hardened films are known as "desert varnish." **1925** Bryan *Papago Country* 85 **AZ,** Many of the granite boulders have a brown or blackish color from the so-called 'desert varnish.' **1961** Douglas *My Wilderness* 68 **UT,** Water seeped from the rock wall in weeping fashion. It had dripped for centuries down the face of the sandstone, leaving behind a coloring that varies from yellow to deep brown and is referred to as "desert varnish." **1965** Teale *Wandering Through Winter* 43 **Mojave Desert,** For the thin, glossy coating of its [=the stone's] exterior was desert varnish. This is sometimes called desert gloss or desert glaze or desert rind. **1967** *DARE* Tape **CA**4, Desert varnish is formed on the upper surface of the pieces of gravel, and the gravel is packed in in a peculiar way because of the wind on the desert that blows all of the sand and the light soil out, and the rocks settle down into a very solid type of pavement that is dark colored because of the varnish on the upper surface of the gravel. **1975** Zwinger *Run River* 243 **UT,** The bottom half [of the cliff] is heavily darkened with desert varnish, but the top, more protected, is fresher in color. **1988** *Wilderness* 52.182.1 **UT,** [Photo caption:] Yucca against a backdrop of desert varnish. Hackberry Canyon W[ilderness] S[tudy] A[rea], Utah. *Ibid* 49, [Photo caption:] Lichen on desert-varnished Navajo sandstone.

desert verbena n Also *desert verbenia*

A vervain, prob *Verbena gooddingii.*

1967–68 *DARE* (Qu. 26a) Inf **CA**91, Desert verbena; (Qu. 26e) Inf **CA**9, Desert verbenia.

desert wild plum n

Perh =**desert peach.**

1968 *DARE* (Qu. I46) Inf **CA**36, Desert wild plum.

desert willow n

A shrubby tree *(Chilopsis linearis)* native to the southwestern United States. Also called **desert catalpa, flowering willow 1, mimbre, willow-leaf catalpa**

1884 Sargent *Forests of N. Amer.* 116, *Chilopsis saligna* . . Desert Willow. **1936** Whitehouse *TX Flowers* 138, *Desert Willow (Chilopsis linearis)* . . is a common shrub along water courses from West Texas to Southern California. **1941** Jaeger *Wildflowers* 245, Desert Willow. . . *Chilopsis linearis.* **1946** *So. Sierran* Dec. 2/3 *(DA),* The desert willow . . is noticeable for its flower. **1970** Correll *Plants TX* 1444, *Chilopsis* . . Desert Willow. **1979** Little *Checklist U.S. Trees* 88, *Chilopsis* . . desert-willow. **1985** Dodge *Flowers SW Deserts* 49, *Chilopsis linearis.* . . Although a close relative of the catalpa, the willowlike foliage of the small tree has given it the name desertwillow.

desert yaupon n

An intricately-branched, somewhat spiny, red-fruited shrub *(Schaefferia cuneifolia)* native to Texas.

1938 Van Dersal *Native Woody Plants* 258, *Schaefferia cuneifolia. . . Desert yaupon.* . . A small, densely-branched, spinose shrub. **1960** Vines *Trees SW* 666, *Desert-yaupon. . . Range.* Western and southwestern Texas. **1970** Correll *Plants TX* 1000, *Desert yaupon.* . . Shrub mostly 1–2 m. high.

desireful adj [*OED* 1520 →] *arch*

Filled with desire or longing.

1969 *DARE* (Qu. GG17, . . *Words for longing* . . *"She was really ______ [to see him].")* Inf **GA**77, Desireful.

desk together v phr

1952 Brown *NC Folkl.* 1.532, *Desk together (with).* . . To sit at the same desk with another.—Central and east. Obsolescent.

Des Moines plunger n

A **redfin** (here: *Moxostoma macrolepidotum*).

1983 Becker *Fishes WI* 665, Shorthead Redhorse—*Moxostoma macrolepidotum* . . Other common names: . . Des Moines plunger.

Des Moines squash n

An acorn squash *(Cucurbita pepo).*

1967 *DARE* (Qu. I23, . . *Kinds of squash*) Inf **MA**13, Des Moines—somewhat oval-shaped, green, size of small melon; **MA**72, Des Moines squash—I don't know if it's grown around here. **1987** *DARE* File **wMA** (as of c1955), *Acorn squash* is now the common term for what I heard called *Des Moines squash.*

despair n [See quot 1976]

See quots.

1940 Faulkner *Hamlet* 332 **MS,** He ain't no more despair than to buy one of them things. [**1976** Brown *Gloss. Faulkner* 70, *Despair.* . . My colleague, Mrs. Tyus Butler, tells me that about 1920 she had an old Negro nurse who had been brought up near Griffin, Ga. . . who frequently said of someone: "He ain't got no more to spare than to" do something foolish. The word to be understood after *more* was something like *sense, gumption,* or *brains.* I feel certain this is the expression intended here [i.e., in quot 1940], and that *to spare* was mistaken for despair somewhere along the line of transmission.]

despise v **Sth, S Midl** *somewhat old-fash* Cf **admire B1**

Usu foll by infin: To dislike very much.

1902 *DN* 2.232 **sIL,** *Despise* ([dispaɪz] with strong accent on first syllable). . . To hate; detest; dislike. **1903** *DN* 2.311 **seMO,** *Despise.* . . Dislike. 'I despise to go out nights.' **1907** *DN* 3.230 **nwAR,** *Despise.* . . To dislike. **1908** *DN* 3.304 **eAL, wGA,** *Despise.* . . To dislike. "I despise to sweep." **1942** Hall *Smoky Mt. Speech* 53 **eTN, wNC,** 'I despise to see a fence growed up like that,' . . 'I despise such as that.' **1960** Williams *Walk Egypt* 286 **GA,** Sho despise to leave you, Miss Toy, but I 'bliged to go.

despite conj [*despite* prep]

Although.

1984 Burns *Cold Sassy* 14 **nGA** (as of 1906), Despite she had wanted a nice funeral, I knew she wouldn't expect a boy to walk around with a long face the rest of his life.

despizable adj

1975 Gould *ME Lingo* 72, *Despizable*—Pronounced des-spize-a'bl, it is the Maine improvement on despicable, but with a stronger meaning.

dest n [Pronc-sp for *desk*] **esp Sth, S Midl** Cf **-es suff[1] 1a**

1949 Webber *Backwoods Teacher* 137 **Ozarks,** She' cry an' bag [=beg] 'em to be good but they got up on the destes [Webber: desks] an' walked up an' down the rows alaughin' at her. **c1970** Pederson *Dial. Surv. Rural GA, (Children used to sit on benches at school, but now they sit at ______)* 5 infs, **seGA,** [dɛst]; 2 infs, **seGA,** [dɛstɪz]; 1 inf, **seGA,** [dɛstɨs]; 2 infs, **seGA,** [dɛsts]. **1984** Burns *Cold Sassy* 143 **nGA** (as of 1906), Pretty soon he come back to the ho-tel dest.

de-stone v

=**de-nut.**

1969 *DARE* (Qu. K70, *Words* . . *for castrating an animal*) Inf **NY**142, De-stone ['di ston].

destroy v intr

1919 *DN* 5.33 **seKY,** *Destroy.* . . To become, or get destroyed. "If hit don't stop rainin', them taters 'll destroy."

destroying angel n

Any of several **death caps,** but esp *Amanita virosa.*

1942 Hylander *Plant Life* 60, The Destroying Angel is also poisonous; in appearance it is a tall, ghostly white mushroom sometimes tinted with gray or brown, common to woods and thickets. **1949** Palmer *Nat. Hist.* 62, Destroying Angel—*Amanita verna.* **1972** Miller *Mushrooms* 27, *Amanita virosa* . . "Destroying Angel". **1981** Lincoff *Audubon Field Guide Mushrooms* 551, Several amanitas are called destroying angels: *A[manita] verna* has smooth stalk. *A. bisporigera,* a smaller, slender-stalked summer mushroom, has 2-spored basidia. . . *A. ocreata,* found in the Southwest . . , has center of cap becoming buff with age. . . All are deadly. **1985** Ammirati et al. *Poisonous Mushrooms* 85, *Amanita bisporigera.* . . Destroying angel. *Ibid* 88, *Amanita phalloides.* . . Destroying angel. *Ibid* 90, *Amanita verna.* . . Destroying angel. *Ibid* 91, *Amanita virosa.* . . Destroying angel. **1987** McKnight–McKnight *Mushrooms* 239, Other deadly poisonous species of . . deathcaps . . are found in N. America: Destroying Angel *(A[manita] virosa . .).*

destructful adj

Destructive.

1967 Cerello *Dakota Co. MN* 88, Our silo was blown down by a very destructful windie. **1968–70** *DARE* Tape **NJ**47, They're terribly destructful; **MA**74, I guess maybe girls ain't as destructful.

destructious adj Also sp *destructuous* **S Midl** *old-fash*

Destructive.

1927 *DN* 5.469 **sAppalachians,** *Destructious.* . . Prone to destroy. "Bears are destructious. They kill hogs." **1934** (1970) Wilson *Backwoods Amer.* 70 **Ozarks,** The commoner of the backwoods . . may testify that b'ar is destructious. **1942** Thomas *Blue Ridge Country* 289 **sAppalachians,** "Dynamite is powerful destructuous!" one tells the other. *Ibid* 313, "If all this had been on top of the earth," my mountaineer guide declared, "destructuous man would have laid it waste long ago." **1985** *NYT Mag.* 13 Jan 9 **sAppalachians,** Unruly boys were *contrarious,* occasionally *destructious.*

deuce, the n Pronc-sp *douse* [*OED deuce* sb.[2] b[1] 1694 →; prob ult from Ger *Daus*] *euphem*

In var collocations where *the devil* could be used, spec:

a in var phrr referring to serious trouble: See quots.

1824 Irving *Tales of a Traveller* 1.68 **NY,** The landlord was followed by the landlady, who was followed by the simpering chambermaids, . . all in a terrible hurry to see what the deuce was to pay in the chamber of the bold Dragoon. **1859** Shillaber *Knitting-Work* 309 **MA,** You'll find the deuce and all to pay. **1887** in 1950 *AmSp* 25.36 **New Orleans LA,** The new rules played the deuce with McDonough. **1913** *NY Eve. Jrl.* (NY) 21 Jan 10 *(Zwilling Coll.),* [In the cartoon "Daffydils":] They elected a committee to give the cop the deuce. **1931–33** *LANE Worksheets* **swCT,** Deuce [dus] . . Euphemism for the devil. I've got the deuce . . for saying stoop. **1968** *DARE* (Qu. II27, *If somebody gives you a very sharp scolding*) Inf **DE**3, He gave me the deuce.

b esp in phrr *(what) the deuce:* Used as a mild imprecation or exclam of surprise, anger, etc. **chiefly Nth**

1872 Schele de Vere *Americanisms* 595, *Darn, durn,* and *dang,* all but thinly disguised *damns,* appear far more vulgar than the open oath. . . The devil is in like manner concealed behind the *deuce.* **1916** *DN* 4.343 **MD,** *Douse.* = deuce. "What in the douse you doin' there." Southeast. Kan. **1927** *AmSp* 2.353 **WV,** The douse take it! **1943** *LANE* Map 600 **scattered NEng,** The map shows . . expressions used as exclamations of impatience, irritation, sudden anger and the like. . . *The deuce.* **1950** *WELS (Exclamations of annoyance or disgust: "Oh ______!")* 1 Inf, **csWI,** The deuce. **1954** *Harder Coll.* **cwTN,** *Douse*—Mild expletive for *deuce.* "Oh, the douse." **1965–70** *DARE* (Qu. NN26c, *Weakened substitutes for 'hell': "What the ______!"*) 20 Infs, **chiefly Nth,** Deuce; (Qu. NN9a, *Exclamations showing great annoyance*) Inf **GA**72, Oh the deuce.

c in compar phrr: See quots.

1941 *LANE* Map 474 **scattered NEng,** When a person runs very fast he is said to run like *a house afire. . . Like the deuce.* **1968** *DARE* (Qu. KK41, *Something that is very difficult to do: "I managed to get through, but it was ______."*) Inf **NC**82, Hard as the deuce; (Qu. LL11a, . . *"Good men are ______ these days."*) Inf **NC**82, Hard as the deuce to get.

d in other phrr: See quots.

1868 (1871) Alcott *Little Women* 1.314 **NEng,** I felt just ready to go to the deuce. **1901** *DN* 2.138 **NY,** *Deuce* . . In phrase 'to raise the deuce'; cf. raise Cain. **1966–70** *DARE* (Qu. GG22b, *When you have come to the end of your patience, you might say, "Well, that certainly ______."*) Inf **VA**42, Beats the deuce; (Qu. NN26b, *Weakened substitutes for 'hell': "Go to ______!"*) Infs **MI**28, **NY**226, The deuce.

Deutscher n Pronc-sp *Daitcher* [Ger] **Ger settlement areas** Cf **Dutcher, Irisher**

A person of German descent.

1950 *WELS (Nicknames for people of German background)* 2 Infs, **WI,** Deutscher. **1966–68** *DARE* (Qu. HH28) Inf **DC**1, Deutscher; **IA**17, Deutscher [doɪčɚ]; **IL**5, Daitchers [daɪčɚz]—used often by the townspeople; **WA**18, Daitcher ['daɪčɚ]; **NJ**12, **WI**62, Dutchers. **1988** *DARE* File **cnWI** (as of 1950s), I have heard [the term *Finlander*] around Tripoli, Tomahawk, and Rhinelander. The same area occas. says ['dɔɪčɚ] for a German.

devil n Pronc-spp **chiefly Sth** *representing Black speech, debble, debil; old-fash, deal, deil, divil, divle* Similarly, adj *dealish* [Proncs of the type [dɪvl̥] are widespread in Engl dial; those of the type [dil] are common in Scots, nEngl dial.]

A Forms.

1815 Humphreys *Yankey in England* 104, *Divil,* devil. **1876** in 1969 *PADS* 52.51 **seIL,** I have a deal of a time with my trial balance in book keeping. **1884** Lanier *Poems* 178 **AL** [Black], De Debble's comin' round dat bend. **1893** Shands *MS Speech* 26, *Debble. . .* Negro for *devil.* **1900** [see **devil's spoons**]. **1903** *DN* 2.296 **Cape Cod MA** (as of a1857), *Divle.* **1904** *DN* 2.424 **Cape Cod MA,** *Divil of a note.* **1905** Culbertson *Banjo Talks* 29 **SE** [Black], De debil lay low at de side er de paff. **1907** *DN* 3.206 **nwAR,** *Divil.* **1911** (1916) Porter *Harvester* 88 **IN,** "Dealish nice business!" he said. "I am here in the woods digging flower roots, while a gang of men in the city are searching for the girl I love." **1922** Gonzales *Black Border* 164 **sSC, GA coasts** [Gullah], Buckruh, de debble! *Ibid* 106, Dem good fuh nutt'n *debble'ub'uh* no'count boy. **1924** *DN* 5.283, Exclamations in American English. . . *Divil of Helle.* **1930** Shoemaker *1300 Words* 17 **cPA Mts** (as of c1900), *Deil*—The devil; "Deil's own buckie," one of the devil's kind. **1967** *DARE* (Qu. E22, *If a house is untidy . . "It looks like ______."*) Inf **CA**9, The divil. [Inf old]

B Senses.

1 possessive or attrib, denoting unpleasant or dangerous qualities: See below. Cf following entries in which *devil* or *devil's* is the first element.

a Of plants: poisonous, ill-smelling, very prickly, hard to get rid of, etc.

1731 [see **devil's-weed 1**]. **1830** [see **devil's root 1**]. **1894** [see **devil's pitchfork**]. **1930** [see **devil's head 1**]. **1974** [see **devil's spoons**].

b Of insects: ugly, having a severe sting, poisonous, etc.

1843 [see **devil's horse 1**]. **1911** [see **devil's riding horse 2**]. **1968** [see **devil ant**].

c Of land: barren, unproductive, unused.

1860 [see **devil's footstep**]. **1953** [see **devil's lane**]. **1968** [see **devil's half acre**].

d Of inanimate objects: unpleasant, abrasive, noisy.

1922 [see **devil's fiddle 1**]. **1968–70** [see **devil-on-a-sidewalk**].

2 in phrr *to beat* (or *whip*) *the devil round the bush* (or *stump*) and varr: To accomplish something by indirection or subterfuge; to be evasive or dilatory. **formerly more widespread, now chiefly Sth, S Midl**

1776 (1965) Carter *Diary* 2.1028 **VA,** It was only an artifice to whip the devil round the stump. **1786** in 1877 Belknap *Papers* 1.427 **VA,** You may save your feelings by applying to a different House from the one which offended you [for permission to use the General Court records]. This is not what the Virginians call *"whipping the devil round a stump,"* because in the eye of the law the present House is not the same as the last, though it may consist of the very same members. **1840** *Niles' Natl. Reg.* 22 Aug 388/2, The New York Commercial says: "There has been an attempt, as we are told, by the receiver general, to "whip the d—l round the stump," as the phrase is, in regard to the payment of duties under the sub-treasury law.["] **1863** Gilmore *S. Friends* 128 **ceNC,** The law requires a white man in that situation; and when I took charge of the plantation, the neighbors made a clamor about my having a black [as overseer]. . . I 'whipped the devil round the stump,' by hiring a white distiller, and *calling* him an 'overseer.' **1871** U.S. Congress *Congressional Globe* 16 Feb 1311/2 **VT,** This gentleman, who is familiar with all the ropes there [=in the U.S. Post Office], can show him how to "whip the devil round the stump," as the common phrase is. **1908** *DN* 3.289 **eAL, wGA,** *Beat the devil round a bush (stump). . .* To approach a subject in a round-about way, to do some reprehensible or evil thing under false appearances. **1914** *DN* 4.103 **KS,** *Beat the devil round the stump. . .* To accomplish one's purpose while saving one's conscience by indirection. "Calling these doings parties instead of dances is only beating the devil round the stump." **1922** *DN* 5.156 **AL,** *Beat the devil around a bush (stump).* **1924** *DN* 5.289, *Beat the devil around the stump. . .* To find a way of doing something you have promised not to do. **1948** Hurston *Seraph* 111 **wFL,** Why do we have to duck and dodge and whip the Devil around the stump and lay ourselves open to sorrow and trouble? **c1960** Wilson Coll. **csKY,** *Beat the devil round the stump. . .* Overcome someone by using his own tricks. **1965–70** *DARE* (Qu. A11, *When somebody takes too long about coming to a decision, . . "I wish he'd quit ______."*) Infs **AL**24, **NC**60, **OK**42, **TX**9, 37, Beating (*or* whipping) the devil around the stump; (Qu. JJ45, *When someone avoids giving a definite answer: "We tried to pin him down, but he just kept ______."*) Infs **AR**52, **TN**13, Beating (*or* whipping) the devil around a bush; (Qu. KK52, *To do something in an indirect and complicated way: "I don't know why he had to go ______ to do that."*) Infs **GA**31, **LA**14, **VA**25, Beating (*or* whip) the devil around the bush (*or* stump).

3 in phr *like the devil beating tanbark* and varr: Very fast, vigorously, severely—used as an intensifier of an action; see quots. Cf **hell n 5**

1851 (1969) Burke *Polly Peablossom* 153 **MS,** I'll larrup you worse nor the devil beatin' tan-bark! **1898** (1970) Hamblen *Genl. Manager* 129 **IL,** On this afternoon Dinny saw "some felly comin' like the divil batin' tan-bark." **1935** Davis *Honey* 13 **OR,** He was writing like the devil beating tanbark. **1951** Teale *North with Spring* 110 **cwLA,** "When I've got her [=a boat] wide open," he declared, "she goes like the devil beating tanbark."

4 in phrr *the devil is beating* (or *whipping*) *his wife:* It's raining (or snowing)—used esp when the precipitation occurs while the sun is shining. **chiefly Sth, S Midl**

[**1899** (1912) Green *VA Folk-Speech* 30, If it rains while the sun is shining out it is a sign that the devil is whipping his wife.] [**1919** *DN* 5.36 **NC,** *Devil a-whuppin' his wife.* A sign that it is raining, and the rain drops are the tears falling from the eyes of the devil's wife!] [**1924** *DN* 5.287 **Cape Cod MA,** When the sun comes forth during a summer shower, the devil is said to be fighting with his wife.] **1930** *DN* 6.80 **cSC,** *Devil is beating his wife* . . It is raining while the sun is shining. [**c1938** in 1970 Hyatt *Hoodoo* 2.1107 **cSC,** (What did they say about . . that dust that runs around in the road, those whirlwinds? What did they call those?) Dose ole *root doctahs* used tuh say it wus *de devil whippin' his wife.*] **1941** *Hall Coll.* **wNC,** *The devil's whuppin' his wife.* It is snowing. Raining? I heard it but twice. An 18-year old boy of Allens Creek . . explaining jocularly the cause of snow to a small boy said, "The devil's whuppin' his wife and all her feathers are comin' out." **1952** Brown *NC Folkl.* 1.393, The devil is whipping his wife. If the sun shines when it is raining, the Devil is beating his wife. **c1960** *Wilson Coll.* **csKY,** *Devil is* *beating his wife.* [Said] when rain and sunshine come together. **1967–68** *DARE* (Qu. B24) Inf **PA**66, The devil's beating his wife; (Qu. B25) Inf **TX**33, The devil's beatin' his wife. **1985** *DARE* File **AL,** *(Joking names for a very heavy rain)* The devil's beating his wife.

5 in var phrr suggesting a very untidy or messy house or room, spec:

a *the devil had an auction* and varr.

1950 *WELS (If a house is untidy and everything is upset)* 1 Inf, **csWI,** The devil has had an auction. **1967–69** *DARE* (Qu. E22, *If a house is untidy . . "It looks like ______ ."*) Infs **MA**83, **RI**3, The devil had an auction and hasn't taken (*or* forgot to take) his goods away; **MA**5, The devil's auction.

b *the devil had a fit in here.*

1966–69 *DARE* (Qu. E22, *If a house is untidy . . "It looks like ______ ."*) Infs **GA**46, 79, **NC**10, The devil had a fit in here (*or* in it).

c in other phrr: See quots.

1950 *WELS (If a house is untidy and everything is upset)* 1 Inf, **cwWI,** The devil shit aflyin'. **1967–70** *DARE* (Qu. E22, *If a house is untidy . . "It looks like ______ ."*) Inf **NC**88, The devil's been in here; **TX**104, The devil before day; **VT**8, The devil has stirred it up with a pitchfork.

6 in phr *the devil broke his apron string:* See quot.

1939 *Hall Coll.* **wNC,** *The devil broke his apron string around here.* This is said to be an old saying about a very rocky road. "Just like an old granny woman carryin' apples in her apron and her apron-string a-breakin."

7 in phr *the devil got it:* See quot.

1966 *DARE* (Qu. EE38b, *If the game of tick-tack-toe . . comes out so that neither X nor O wins*) Inf **GA**6, The devil got it.

devil v

1 rarely with *up:* To tease, annoy, harass. **chiefly Sth, Midl**

1819 in 1823 Faux *Memorable Days* 216 **IN,** Go . . tell our great father, the President, how we are deviled and cheated. **1883** Sweet–Knox *Mexican Mustang* 47 **TX,** They devilled the poor fellow almost to death. **1895** *DN* 1.371 **eTN,** *Deviling:* bothering. "Johnny, quit deviling the cat." **1902** *DN* 2.232 **sIL,** *Devil. . .* To annoy by jests and raillery; to tease; to annoy by persistently urging a cause. **1903** *DN* 2.311 **seMO. 1905** *DN* 3.77 **nwAR. 1906** *DN* 3.117 **sIN. 1939** *Hall Coll.* **eTN, wNC. 1940** McCullers *Lonely Hunter* 50 **GA,** Sometimes it was fun to devil Portia. **1944** *Chicago Tribune* (IL) 6 Aug sec 7 1/6 **Ozarks,** Aunt Lizzie knew every flower and plant, the smelly Indian turnip which young fellas used to carry to "devil" each other. **1954** *Harder Coll.* **cwTN. c1960** *Wilson Coll.* **csKY. 1965–70** *DARE* (Qu. GG3, *To tease: "See those big boys trying to ______ [that little one]."*) 28 Infs, **chiefly Sth, Midl,** Devil; **SC**44, Devil up; (Qu. Y6, . . *To put pressure on somebody . . : "He's a whole week late. I'm going to ______ ."*) Inf **NJ**56, Devil him to death; (Qu. Y7, *When one person never misses a chance to be mean to another or to annoy another: "I don't know why she keeps ______ me all the time!"*) Infs **IL**21, **PA**243, Deviling; (Qu. GG32a, *To habitually play tricks or jokes on people: "He's always ______ ."*) Inf **CO**4, Devilin' somebody; **KY**53, Deviling. **1967–68** *DARE* Tape **PA**70, One of the things that he had against his son was that he was always deviling him about being in the British army; **TX**3, He fell in love with me right then and devil the life out of me for a year or two and I finally married him.

‡**2** To bewitch, hex.

1970 *DARE* (Qu. CC14, *Words . . where one person supposedly casts a spell over another*) Inf **MA**123, Devil.

‡**devil and pitchforks, rain the** v phr

1966 *DARE* (Qu. B26, *When it's raining very heavily, you say, "It's raining ______ ."*) Inf **FL**35, The devil and pitchforks.

devil and Tom Walker, the n Also *the devil and Jack Walker,* euphem *the dickens and Tom Walker,* pronc-sp *dickunce* ~ **chiefly NEng, S Midl**

The Devil—freq used as an exclam or as an intensive.

1824 Irving *Tales of a Traveller* 2.278 **MA,** Such was the end of Tom Walker and his ill-gotten wealth. Let all griping money-brokers lay this story to heart. . . In fact, the story has resolved itself into a proverb, and is the origin of that popular saying, so prevalent throughout New England, of "The Devil and Tom Walker." **1908** *S. Atl. Qrly.* 7.343 **seSC** [Gullah], *Wey de debble an' Jack Walkeh dishyuh saddle lib?* asked Davy in despair. [=Where the devil and Jack Walker does this saddle live [i.e., belong]?] **1908** *DN* 3.304 **eAL, wGA,** *Dickunce and Tom Walker, the,* interj. phr. Very common. **1914** *DN* 4.71 **ME, nNH,** *Devil and Tom Walker. . .* "He wukked like the Devil an' Tom Walker." **1929** *AmSp* 5.130 **ME,** The devil and Tom Walker. **1936** *WV Review* Aug 346, Some of our expressions do smack of a desire to be humorous. . . Gol blame, The devil and Tom Walker. **1942** *AmSp* 17.130 **IN,** *Devil and Tom Walker.* 'I'll do it in spite of the devil and Tom Walker.' **1946** *PADS* 6.36 **VA,** The *dickens* and Tom Walker! (Exclamation of amazement at something told.) Salem. Reported, 1940. **1954** *Harder Coll.* **cwTN,** Dickens. Mild substitute for devil. Also in "the dickens and Tom Walker." **1958** Stuart *Plowshare* 145 **KY,** What in the devil and Tom Walker's got into you here lately? **1967** *DARE* (Qu. NN8a, *Exclamations of annoyance or disgust: "Oh ______ , I've lost my glasses again."*) Inf **TN**1, The devil and Tom Walker! **1969** Gordone *No Place* 12 **NY** [Black], Cora: Lawd! What in the devil an' Tom Walker you Nigros talkin 'bout now? **1972** Hall *Sayings Old Smoky* 56 **eTN, wNC,** As bad as the devil and Tom Walker.

devil ant n [**devil n B1b**]

A large stinging black ant.

1968 *DARE* (Qu. R17) Inf **IN**19, Devil ant.

devil around v phr [**devil v 1**]

See quots.

1902 *DN* 2.232 **sIL,** *Devil around. . .* 1. To seek mischief. 2. To try to annoy. 3. To lead a loose life. **1906** *DN* 3.117 **sIN,** *Devil around. . .* To see[k] mischief. "They were devilin' around all night."

devil backbone See **devil's backbone**

devilbit See **devil's bit c**

devil burr n [**devil n B1a**]

=**burr grass.**

1912 Baker *Book of Grasses* 83, *Devil-burs. . . Cenchrus carolinianus. . .* 6–20 round, spiny burs . . ; burs more or less downy, sometimes reddish; spines very rigid at maturity.

devil cactus See **devil's tongue**

devil chaser n Cf **nigger chaser**

A kind of firecracker.

1967–70 *DARE* (Qu. FF14, . . *Kinds of firecrackers*) Infs **DC**12, **VA**44, Devil-chasers; (Qu. FF28, . . *Kinds of fireworks*) Inf **TX**5, Devil-chasers.

devil clapper n Cf **devil's fiddle 1**

A type of noisemaker; see quot.

1979 *PA Folklife* 29.29/1 **PA,** Another callithumpian apparatus, the devil-clapper, has an obvious relationship with the rattletrap, being essentially the same object with the ratchet wheel being revolved against the pawl rather than the opposite, which is the case with the smaller noisemaker. . . Standing fifty inches high, this device is placed against the door of the newly wed couple during a callithumpian serenade and the handle is turned to produce a raucous rumpus.

devil-club See **devil's club 2**

devil crab n

A **king crab** (here: *Lopholithodes* spp).

1970 *DARE* (Qu. P1) Inf **AK**1, Devil crab: same as spider crab and king crab; (Qu. P18) Inf **AK**9, Devil crab—king crab.

devil-dancer n Also *devil dervish*

A small whirlwind; a gust of wind, esp on water.

1925 *Hand Coll.* **neOH,** I was walking through a grove of trees on the campus with this fellow, when he suddenly swerved to one side to avoid being caught in a "devil dancer." . . He was quite sure that to be caught in such a thing would bring bad luck. **1958** *Hand Coll.,* In Idaho a small whirlwind is called a "Devil Dancer." **1967** *DARE* (Qu. O12, *A disturbance caused by wind which seems to run and spread quickly along the surface of water*) Inf **IL**9, Devil dervish. **1970** *NC Folkl.* 18.55, When whirligusts, called devil dancers and little whirlwinds, are seen along roads, it is a sure sign of rain.

devil-diver n

1 Any of var grebes such as Holboell's **grebe, horned grebe,** or **pied-billed grebe.**

1876 *Forest & Stream* 7.276/3 **CT,** *Podiceps.* All varieties. Devil diver. **1917** (1923) *Birds Amer.* 1.5, *Horned Grebe—Colymbus auritus . .* Devil-diver. *Ibid* 1.7, *Pied-Billed Grebe—Podilymbus podiceps . .* Devil-diver. **1946** Hausman *Eastern Birds* 67, *Horned Grebe—Colymbus auritus . .* Devil-Diver. *Ibid* 68, *Pied-Billed Grebe—Podilymbus podiceps podiceps . .* Devil-Diver. **1951** Pough *Audubon*

Water Bird 326, Devil diver. . . Grebes. **1953** Jewett *Birds WA* 55, *Horned Grebe. Colymbus auritus* . . Devil-diver. **1955** MA Audubon Soc. *Bulletin* 39.309, *Holboell's Grebe*. . . Devil-diver (Maine. A tribute to its uncanny diving ability.). *Ibid* 310, *Horned Grebe.* Devil-diver (New England). . . *Pied-Billed Grebe*. . . Devil-diver (Maine). **1966–70** *DARE* (Qu. Q5) Infs **CT**10, **ME**20, Devil-diver; (Qu. Q9) Infs **IL**7, **WV**8, Devil-diver.

2 =**bufflehead 2.**

1955 MA Audubon Soc. *Bulletin* 39.316, *Buffle-Head*. . . Devil Diver (Maine). **1959** *Names* 7.111, Apparently it has been tempting to the folk to substitute "devil" for "hell" in the names of such birds; thus we have as devil-divers, the: . . common guillemot and bufflehead (Me.).

3 A **loon** (here: *Gavia immer*).

1955 MA Audubon Soc. *Bulletin* 39.309, *Common Loon*. . . Devil-diver (Maine).

4 See quot.

1956 MA Audubon Soc. *Bulletin* 40.80, *Black Guillemot*. . . Devil-diver, . . (Maine. With unusual, perhaps supernatural, diving ability.)

devil dog n

1 pl; also *devil horns:* A **unicorn plant.**

1967 *DARE* (Qu. S15, . . *Weed seeds that cling to clothing*) Inf **TX**28, Devil dogs. **1967** *DARE* Tape **TX**28, Devil dogs—a bush, it's much like an okra bush. The fruit of it, that's what it is, I guess, it's the fruit, looks much like an okra pod, except that when it dries it splits and the ends become like horns. Also called devil horns—has black seeds inside brown pod.

2 =**hellbender 1.**

1979 Behler–King *Audubon Field Guide Reptiles* 270, Commonly called Allegheny Alligator or Devil Dog. . . Hellbenders.

devil-downhead n [From their habit of going headfirst down a tree trunk] Cf **devil-downhill**

1 =**white-breasted nuthatch.**

1917 (1923) *Birds Amer.* 3.200, *White-Breasted Nuthatch—Sitta carolinensis carolinensis* . . Other Names. . . Devil Downhead. **1917** *Wilson Bulletin* 29.2.84, *Sitta carolinensis.*—Devil downhead. **1946** Hausman *Eastern Birds* 433, *Sitta carolinensis* . . Devil Downhead. **1956** MA Audubon Soc. *Bulletin* 40.127, *White-Breasted Nuthatch.* Devil-down-head (Mass. In clambering about trees, it seems as much at home head-downward as in any other position.)

2 =**red-breasted nuthatch.**

1955 Forbush–May *Birds* 354, *Red-Breasted Nuthatch—Sitta canadensis* . . Devil-down-head.

devil-downhill n Cf **devil-downhead**

A nuthatch (*Sitta* spp).

1969 *DARE* (Qu. Q23) Inf **PA**223, Devil-downhill.

devil-fire See **devil's lantern**

devilfish n

1 also *devil ray:* A large ray, usu *Manta birostris.* Also called **manta, sea devil**

1709 (1967) Lawson *New Voyage* 154, **NC, SC,** The Divel-Fish [sic] lies at some of our Inlets, and . . is shap'd like a Scate, or Stingray; only he has on his Head a Pair of very thick strong Horns, and is of monstrous Size, and Strength. **1884** Goode *Fisheries U.S.* 1.666, The Devil-fish, *Manta birostris* . . is especially abundant on the coast of South Carolina, where its pursuit is a favorite amusement among the planters. **1933** LA Dept. of Conserv. *Fishes* 240, Mantas, also known under the names of Blanket Fish, Sea Devils, Devilfish, and Sea Bats, are in reality gigantic members of the Ray family. **1935** Caine *Game Fish* 152, The devil ray [=*Manta birostris*] is variously known as devilfish, sea devil, giant ray and manta. **1939** Natl. Geogr. Soc. *Fishes* 169, I shall . . confine myself to the experience of our party in hunting and capturing a devilfish [=*Manta birostris*]. **1960** Amer. Fisheries Soc. *List Fishes* 56, Devil-fish, . . see ray, devil.

2 =**gray whale.**

1860 *Merc. Marine Mag.* VII.213 *(DA),* They [=California gray whales] have a variety of names among whalemen, as . . 'Hard-head,' 'Devil-fish.' **1888** *Amer. Naturalist* 22.511 **CA,** Of all the known species of whales, this is the most cunning, courageous and vicious. . . Few whalemen would court an encounter with it, and it early received the name of the Devil Fish. **1946** Dufresne *AK's Animals* 186, The Gray Whale, sometimes called . . Devilfish, is noted among whalers for the frenzied rushes it makes when harpooned, and for the mother's fierce guardianship of her young.

3 =**goosefish.**

1889 *Century Dict., Devil-fish*. . . The popular name of a large pediculate fish, *Lophius piscatorius.* **1889** (1971) Farmer *Americanisms* 199, *Devil-fish.*—A popular name for the *American angler* a fish of hideous appearance.

4 An octopus.

1933 John G. Shedd Aquarium *Guide* 205, This is the *Octopus,* or *Devil Fish (Octopus americanus).* **1933** LA Dept. of Conserv. *Fishes* 240, Although the name Devilfish is applied to the Manta, that term is more generally used to designate a completely different animal, the Octopus. **c1940** Eliason *Word Lists FL* 7, *Devilfish* [dɪvɪlfɪʃ] [sic]: An octopus.

devil fly n [**devil** n **B1b**]

1 Perh a tabanid.

1970 *DARE* (Qu. R9a) Inf **OK**58, Devil fly.

2 A **dragonfly.**

1970 *DARE* (Qu. R2) Inf **TN**65, Devil fly.

devil-grass See **devil's-grass**

devil greenbrier n [**devil** n **B1a**]

A **greenbrier** (here: *Smilax hispida*).

1960 Vines *Trees SW* 74, *Smilax hispida*. . . Vernacular names are Hagbrier, Devil Greenbrier [etc].

devil-head cactus See **devil's-head 2**

devil hog n

1954 *Sportsman* 2.4.62, The second [kind of wild boar] are the "Rooshans" or devil-hogs of western North Carolina—Tennessee.

devil horns See **devil dog 1**

devil horse See **devil's horse**

devil-in-the-bush n

1 also *devil-in-a-bush:* =**fennel flower.** [Engl dial]

1847 Wood *Class-Book* 149, *N[igella] damascena*. . . A hardy annual . . to which have been applied the gentle names of "ragged lady," "devil in a bush," &c. **1876** Hobbs *Bot. Hdbk.* 31, Devil in a bush, Fennel flower, Nigella Damascena. **1891** *Jrl. Amer. Folkl.* 4.148, When children, we knew Nigella damascena . . [as] Devil in the Bush. **1892** *Jrl. Amer. Folkl.* 5.91, *Nigella Damascena*. . . Devil-in-a-bush. Northern Ohio. **1940** Clute *Amer. Plant Names* 4, *Fennel Flower*. . . Devil-in-the-bush. **1959** Carleton *Index Herb. Plants* 36, *Devil-in-a-bush:* Saponaria officinalis . . ; Nigella damascena.

2 =**bouncing Bet 1.**

1959 [see **devil-in-the-bush 1**].

3 Prob =**fire-on-the-mountain.**

1975 Thomas *Hear the Lambs* 26 **nwAL,** Dat big red bloom by de chimley, it's a devil-in-de-bush, and some calls it de fire flower.

4 A **wild carrot.**

1901 *Plant World* 4.144, In Barren county [KY] I heard several local names of plants that were new to me . . devil-in-the-bush (wild carrot).

devil-in-the-ribbon-box n

A children's game; see quot.

1966 *DARE* Tape **NC**22, [In devil-in-the-ribbon-box] we always had a devil and . . a storekeeper. . . Each person had to be named a color of ribbon. And the devil would come up and knock on the storekeeper's back and say "I want to buy some ribbon," and he'd say "Well what color?" and when he named a color that you had, why that person had to run just hard as he could to keep the devil from catching him. And if he caught him then he had to go stay with him. And when he caught all of 'em why of course they'd have to start all over again.

devilish adj **chiefly Sth, S Midl** See Map on p. 48

Pesky, annoying, teasing.

1915 *DN* 4.182 **swVA,** *Devilish*. . . Given to jesting or twitting. **1965–70** *DARE* (Qu. NN17, *Something that keeps on annoying you* . . : *"That* ______ *fly won't go away."*) 28 Infs, **chiefly Sth, S Midl,** Devilish; (Qu. K50) Inf **AL**11, Devilish mule; (Qu. Z16, *A small child who is rough, misbehaves*) Inf **DC**8, Devilish; (Qu. GG32a, *To habitually play tricks or jokes on people: "He's always* ______*."*) Inf **MS**63, Being devilish; (Qu. GG32b) Inf **FL**14, Devilish; (Qu. LL26b) Inf **IN**55, Devilish; (Qu. KK37, . . *A very sly person: "He's* ______*."*) Inf **OK**58, Devilish.

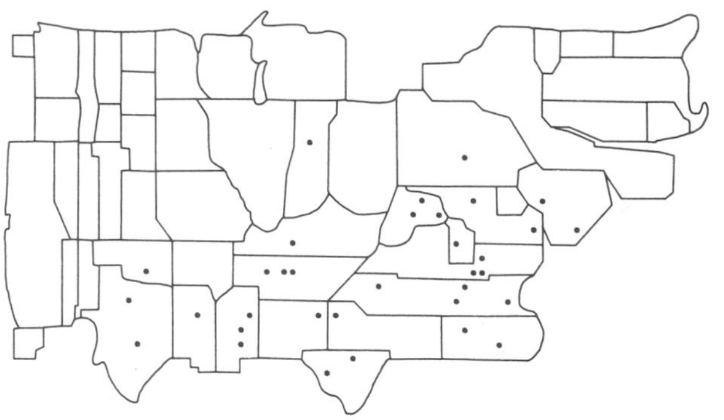

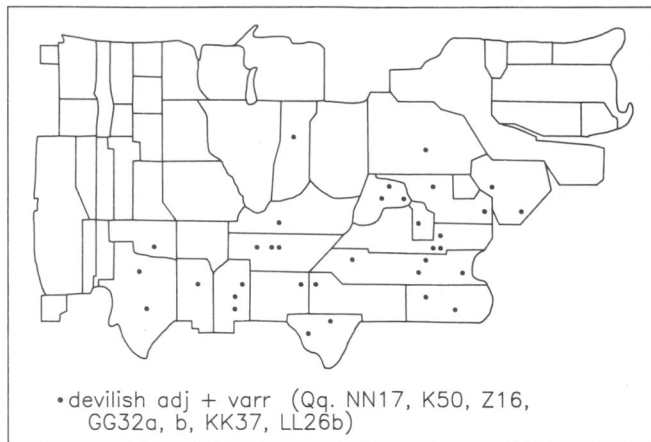

•devilish adj + varr (Qq. NN17, K50, Z16, GG32a, b, KK37, LL26b)

devilish adv

Very, extremely.

1968–70 *DARE* (Qu. GG40, . . *Violently angry*) Inf **PA**245, Devilish mad; (Qu. LL37, . . *"I could have wrung her neck, I was so ——— mad."*) Infs **MD**14, 20, Devilish.

devil lily n

A datura (here: *Datura arborea*). Cf **angel's-trumpet 1**

1930 Degener *Ferns of HI* 261, *Floripondio*. . . Locally it is known by the less correct names of angel's trumpet, devil lily, and *Datura arborea* L.

devilment n Pronc-spp *devilmaint, devilmaynt* **chiefly Sth, S Midl** Cf **devil** v **1, deviltry**

Mischief; teasing; frolicking.

1844 Thompson *Major Jones's Courtship* 146 **GA,** I jest want to tell a instance of the devilment he kicks up sometimes. **1899** (1912) Green *VA Folk-Speech* 145, *Devilment*. . . Roguery; mischief; trickery. **1902** *DN* 2.232 **sIL,** *Devilment* (last syllable pronounced *maynt*). . . Sportiveness or frolicsomeness, as:—'He is full of devilmaynt.' 2. Fun:—as 'He did it jes for devilmaynt.' 3. Malicious propensity. **1903** *DN* 2.311 **seMO,** *Devilment*. . . Mischief. **1905** *DN* 3.77 **nwAR,** *Devilment*. . . Teasing. **1911** Shute *Plupy* 64 **seNH** (as of 1860s), The amount of devilment those three boys can crowd into a half holiday beats all. **1915** *DN* 4.182 **swVA,** *Devilment*. . . Roguish fun. **1917** *DN* 4.410 **wNC,** *Devilmaint*. . . Variant of *devilment*. **1930** Faulkner *As I Lay Dying* 18 **MS,** Not that Jewel, the one she labored so hard to bear . . and him flinging into tantrums or sulking spells, inventing devilment to devil her. **1954** *Harder Coll.* **cwTN,** *Devilment*. **c1960** *Wilson Coll.* **csKY,** *Devilment*. **1965–70** *DARE* (Qu. GG32a, *To habitually play tricks or jokes on people: "He's always ———."*) Infs **AL**6, **IL**11, **MS**21, 49, 56, 60, 71, **NC**69, **SC**54, **TN**23, 65, Up to some (*or* his) devilment; **AL**20, In some devilment; (Qu. V1, *When you suspect that somebody is trying to deceive you . . you say, "There's ———."*) Inf **GA**72, He is up to some kind of devilment; (Qu. JJ19, *If somebody has dishonest intentions, or is up to no good, you might say*) Inf **TN**65, I think he's up to some devilment; (Qu. JJ35b) Inf **MO**20, For the devilment of it. **1968** *DARE* Tape **IN**17, The devilment in you.

devilment v Pronc-sp *devilmint*

To tease.

1919 *DN* 5.39 **TN,** *Devilmint*. . . "That boy keeps on devilmintin'."

devil-on-a-sidewalk n Also *devils-on-the-walk*

1968–70 *DARE* (Qu. FF14, . . *Kinds of firecrackers*) Inf **KY**84, Devil-on-a-sidewalk—roll with foot, they'd sparkle and crackle; (Qu. FF28, . . *Kinds of fireworks*) Inf **NY**111, Devils-on-the-walk.

devil ray See **devilfish 1**

devil's-apple n [**devil** n **B1a**]

1 A **jimson weed** (here: *Datura stramonium*) or its seed pod.

1793 *Columbian Centinel* (Boston MA) 26 Oct 3/2, Several children have very much injured themselves, by eating the seeds of Stramonium, or Thorn-Apple, commonly called Devil's Apple. **1876** Hobbs *Bot. Hdbk.* 31, Devil's apple, Datura Stramonium. **1897** Parsons *Wild Flowers CA* 96, *Jimson-weed*. . . is also called "mad-apple," . . and "Devil's apple." **1912** Blatchley *IN Weed Book* 128, Devil's Apple. . . Capsule dry, egg-shaped, about 2 inches long, densely prickly, the lower prickles shorter. **1931** Clute *Common Plants* 84, The prickly seed-pods of the jimson-weed *(Datura stramonium)* are also called devil's apples. **1959** Carleton *Index Herb. Plants* 36, *Devil's-apple:* Datura stramonium; Mandragora officinarum; Podophyllum peltatum.

2 A **mayapple** (here: *Podophyllum peltatum*). [See quot 1931]

1900 Lyons *Plant Names* 296, *P. peltatum*. . . Hog Apple, Devil's Apple, Indian Apple. . . *Fruit* edible. **1910** Graves *Flowering Plants* 194 **CT,** May Apple. . . Devil's Apple. . . The fruit is edible and harmless but disagreeable to many persons. **1931** Clute *Common Plants* 84, The devil's apple is often reputed to be the plant which we call the mandrake *(Podophyllum peltatum)*. . . Our plant, though quite harmless, happens to resemble the poisonous mandrake of Europe *(Mandragora)* and thus unjustly bears the disparaging name. **1971** Krochmal *Appalachia Med. Plants* 198.

devil's-apron n

A kelp of the genus *Laminaria*.

1858 Holmes *Autocrat* 190, I don't want my wreck to be washed up on one of the beaches in company with devil's-aprons, bladder-weeds, dead horse-shoes, and bleached crab-shells. **1901** Arnold *Sea-Beach* 70, They [=*Laminaria*] are commonly known as . . devil's-aprons . . sea-furbelows, and so on. **1977** *Yankee* Jan 112 **coastal ME,** The long-tailed kelp that washes up with the tide is a Devil's apron.

devil's backbone n Also *devil backbone*

=**jewbush.**

1955 *S. Folkl. Qrly.* 19.234, Both the devil and an angel acquired a namesake in the same plant . . Pedalanthus [sic] . . commonly called *Devil's Backbone* . . , perhaps from the jointed, angular, and branching stem. **1969** *SC Market Bulletin* 24 July 4/4, Devil Backbone, rooted, $1. **1976** Bailey–Bailey *Hortus Third* 832, *Pedilanthus*. . . *tithymaloides*. . . Devil's-backbone. **1982** Perry–Hay *Field Guide Plants* 70, Devil's backbone. . . flowers mainly in summer, but intermittently throughout the year.

devil's beggarticks n [**devil** n **B1a**]

=**beggar ticks 1.**

1948 Stevens *KS Wild Flowers* 384, *Bidens frondosa*—Devil's Beggarticks. **1968** Barkley *Plants KS* 355, *Bidens frondosa* . . Devil's Beggarticks. **1970** U.S. Ag. Research Serv. *Selected Weeds* 378, *Bidens frondosa*—Devils beggarticks.

devil's bit n [*OED* c1450 → in sense *Succisa pratensis* (see **d** below)]

Any of var plants with roots that appear to have been bitten off, as:

a also *devil's-bite:* =**blazing star 3,** esp *Liatris scariosa* or *L. spicata*.

1736 in 1894 *Documents Colonial & Post-Revol. Hist. NJ* 11.446 **NY,** To Drink give a Decoction of Devil's bitt or Robbins Plantain. **1778** Carver *Travels N. Amer.* 514, *Devil's Bit* is another wild plant, which grows in the fields, and receives its name from a print that seems to be made by teeth in the roots. **1784** in 1785 Amer. Acad. Arts & Sci. *Memoirs* 1.477 **Atlantic,** *Serratula*. . . *Devil's Bit.* The root appears as if bitten off. *Ibid* 478, *Staehelina*. . . *Prickly Devil's-Bit.* Blossoms purple. On *Winter-Hill* in Charlestown. July–August. **1830** Rafinesque *Med. Flora* 2.237, *Liatris*. . . Many vulgar names . . *Devilsbite, Rattlesnake master,* . . *Rough root,* &c. All have a tuberous medical root. **1876** Hobbs *Bot. Hdbk.* 31, Devil's bit, False unicorn, Helonias dioica. Devil's bit, Button snake root, Liatris spicata. **1894** *Jrl. Amer. Folkl.* 7.92, *Liatris scariosa* . . Devil's bite, Concord, Mass. **1901** Lounsberry *S. Wild Flowers* 501, Devil's-bite. **1910** Graves *Flowering Plants* 377 **CT,** Devil's Bit. **1931** Clute *Common Plants* 82, There are, for instance, the various devil's bits and devil's bites, *Chamaelirium luteum* and *Liatris scariosa* especially . . have rootstocks or other parts that end as if bitten off, and the explanation is that they were once so powerful in relieving the ills of distressed humanity, that the devil bit off the medicinal end for spite. . . The original devil's bit seems to have been . . *Scabiosa succisa*. . . Our own *Aletris farinosa* is one of the few devil's bits still used in medicine. **1974** (1977) Coon *Useful Plants* 113, *Liatris spicata* . . Devil's bit. . . A lovely wild plant of wet places.

b =**blazing star 2.**

1830 Rafinesque *Med. Flora* 2.182, *Abalon albiflorum*. . . *Devil's Bit*. . . Carver relates an Indian story about being once a cure for all disorders, the devil bit off part of the root to lessen its value, whence the name. **1843** Torrey *Flora NY* 2.318, *Helonias dioica*. . . Devil's-bit. Unicorn-plant. . . Meadows, and moist woods. . . The root is a popular tonic and anthelmintic. **1876** [see **a** above]. **1894** *Harper's New Mth. Mag.* 88.561/1, The little wild flower known as the devil's-bit *(Chamaelirium luteum),* whose long white tapering spire of feathery bloom may often be seen rising above the sedges in the swamp. **1931** [see **a** above]. **1952** Strausbaugh-Core *Flora WV* 224, *Devil's bit. Blazing star...* Moist meadows and thickets, local, but probably in every county. **1959** Carleton *Index Herb. Plants* 36, *Devil's bit:* Chamaelirium luteum; Tolpis barbata (Crepis barbata); Succisa pratensis (Scabiosa succisa). **1964** Batson *Wild Flowers SC* 126, *C. luteum..* Devil's-bit, Fairy Wand. **1976** Bruce *How to Grow Wildflowers* 172, *Chamaelirium luteum..* hardly lives up to some of the dramatic common names applied to it—Devil's Bit, Blazing Star, Fairy Wand, Rattlesnake Root.

c also *devilbit, devil's-bite:* **=Indian poke.**

1830 Rafinesque *Med. Flora* 2.273, *Veratrum viride... Indianpoke, Earthgall, Devilbit...* Poisonous active plant. **1876** Hobbs *Bot. Hdbk.* 31, Devil's bite, American hellebore, Veratrum viride. **1900** Lyons *Plant Names* 389, *V. viride...* Devil's-bite, Duck-retter, Earth-gall. **1930** Sievers *Amer. Med. Plants* 6, *American False-hellebore... Other common names...* Devil's-bite. **1971** Krochmal *Appalachia Med. Plants* 262, Devil's-bite... is very poisonous.

d An introduced plant *(Succisa pratensis)* with composite-like flower heads. Also called **devil's-root 2**

1847 Wood *Class-Book* 310, *S. succisa. Devil's-bit...* The stem is about 1f high. Corolla violet. **1900** Lyons *Plant Names* 336, *S. succisa...* Devil's-bit. **1931** [see **a** above]. **1950** Gray-Fernald *Manual of Botany* 1347, *Succisa... Devil's-bit...* From the praemorse [sic] rootstock, once supposed to have been bitten off by Satan. **1959** [see **b** above].

e A **colicroot 2** (here: *Aletris farinosa*).

1828 Rafinesque *Med. Flora* 1.37, *Aletris farinosa... Vulgar Names*—Star-Grass,.. Star-root, Devil's-bit. **1872** Schele de Vere *Americanisms* 406, A medicinal plant (Aletris farinosa),.. under the name of *Devil's Bit,* is highly esteemed in the West for its virtues. **1900** Lyons *Plant Names* 21, *A. farinosa...* Devil's-bit... *Rhizome* bitter, tonic, stomachic. **1931** [see **a** above]. **1971** Krochmal *Appalachia Med. Plants* 40, Devil's bit... The rhizomes and roots are reported to have therapeutic use as a diuretic tonic and sedative.

f An **ironweed** (here: *Vernonia noveboracensis*).

1937 *Torreya* 37.101, *Vernonia noveboracensis...* Devil's bit, Charleston, W. Va.

devil's-bite See **devil's bit a, c**

devil's-bones n

A **wild yam** (here: *Dioscorea villosa*).

1876 Hobbs *Bot. Hdbk.* 31, Devil's bones, Wild yam root, Dioscorea villosa. **1892** (1974) Millspaugh *Amer. Med. Plants* 697, Wild Yam... Com[mon] Names... Devil's Bones. **1930** Sievers *Amer. Med. Plants* 63, *Wild Yam... Other common names...* [are] colicroot, rheumatismroot, devil's-bones. **1951** Teale *North with Spring* 218 **NC,** He may bring home Aaron's-rod, Noah's ark, Jacob's ladder, or Devil's bones. **1971** Krochmal *Appalachia Med. Plants* 110, Devil's bones... This herb is used as an expectorant, emetic, antispasmodic, and diaphoretic.

devil's bootjacks See **bootjack 1**

devil's boots n

A **pitcher plant.**

1933 Small *Manual SE Flora* 581, S. purpurea... Devil's-boots. **1959** Carleton *Index Herb. Plants* 36, *Devil's Boots:* Sarracenia (v).

devil's bopeep n

1941 *LANE* Map 400, 1 inf, **ceMA,** The devil's bopeep. Name applied to a harum-scarum, i.e. a wild young girl.

devil's bouquet n [**devil** n **B1a**] **TX**

A musky-odored, red-flowered plant *(Nyctaginia capitata).* Also called **musk flower, sand verbena, skunk flower, stink verbena**

1936 Whitehouse *TX Flowers* 20, Devil's Bouquet.. is also called skunk flower because of its heavy, disagreeable odor. **1951** *PADS* 15.31 **TX,** *Nyctaginia capitata..* Devil's bouquet. **1961** Wills-Irwin *Flowers TX* 107, Flowering from April until fall, especially after wet periods, the Devil's-bouquet.. is an arresting plant.

devil's bread n

1 A bracket fungus.

1907 *St. Nicholas* July 846/1, "Shelves," often called "devil's bread".. grow on woodland stumps and trees and logs.

2 A toadstool.

1968 *DARE* (Qu. I38) Inf **NJ**17, Devil's bread.

devil's buckwheat n

A **galinsoga** (here: *Galinsoga parviflora*).

1940 Clute *Amer. Plant Names* 259, *Galinsoga parviflora.* Devil's buckwheat.

devil's cabbage n [**devil** n **B1a**]

A henbane (here: *Hyoxyamus niger*).

1937 *Torreya* 37.100, *Hyoscyamus* [sic] *niger..* devil's-cabbage .. Maryland, near Harper's Ferry.

devil's cactus See **devil's-tongue**

devil's cane n [**devil** n **B1b**]

=walkingstick.

1969 *DARE* (Qu. R9a, *An insect from two to four inches long that lives in bushes and looks like a dead twig*) Inf **MO**19, Devil's cane.

devil's cholla See **devil's tongue**

devil's cigar n

An urn fungus (here: *Urnula geaster*).

1987 McKnight-McKnight *Mushrooms* 36, Devil's Cigar... Upon opening its [sic] splits about halfway down or farther into 3-6 broad rays that resemble the rays on earthstars.

devil's-claw n [**devil** n **B1a**; *EDD* (at *devil* sb. 2) in sense **3** below] Also *devil's-claws*

1 A **cat's-claw** (here: *Acacia greggii*).

1897 Sudworth *Arborescent Flora* 250, *Acacia Greggii...* Devil's Claws (Nev.). **1903** Small *Flora SE U.S.* 578, *Acacia Greggii...* A shrub or small tree, commonly armed with short curved prickle-like spines... *Devil's Claws.* **1931** U.S. Dept. Ag. *Misc. Pub.* 101.71, *Catclaw...,* also called.. devil's claw,.. varies in size and form from a very prickly bush to a tall shrub or small tree. **1951** *PADS* 15.33 **TX,** *Acacia greggii...* Devil's-claw. **1979** Little *Checklist U.S. Trees* 37, Devils-claw... Range—S.,c., and Trans-Pecos Tex., w. to s. N. Mex., Ariz., extreme sw. Utah, s. Nev., and se. Calif.

2 **=unicorn plant.**

1900 Lyons *Plant Names* 240, *M. Louisiana...* Devil's-claw. **1912** Lumholtz *New Trails* 353, The pods of the *martynia* (devil's claw), split in two, furnish the black part of the texture. **1940** Gates *Flora KS* 189, Devil's Claw... Frequent in west two-thirds. **1949** Moldenke *Amer. Wild Flowers* 287, These plants [=*Proboscidea*] are often called *devils-claws* by cattlemen because the clawlike seeds sometimes get into the nostrils of cattle or sheep and may by infection cause the death of the animal. **1967** Dodge *Roadside Wildflowers* 68, *Devilsclaw..* is noticeable because of the strange fruit pods, which are shaped like a pair of tongs... Stockmen consider the plant a range pest because the horned pods become entangled in the fleece of sheep and on the hooves of horses and cattle. **1967-69** *DARE* (Qu. S14) Inf **TX**78, Devil's-claw; (Qu. S15) Infs **KS**1, 19, **TX**42, Devil's-claws; (Qu. S21) Inf **KS**15, Devil's-claws. **1968** *DARE* FW Addit **CO**7, Devil's-claw—when dried, [they] catch [in] the sheep['s wool].

3 A **buttercup 1** (here: *Ranunculus arvensis*).

1900 Lyons *Plant Names* 316, *R. arvensis...* Devil's-claws. **1931** Clute *Common Plants* 85, Of the plants known as hell-weeds or hell-roots, we may mention.. the buttercup *(Ranunculus arvensis)* also known as devil's claw. **1959** Carleton *Index Herb. Plants* 36, *Devil's claws:..* Ranunculus arvensis.

4 A spiny vine *(Pisonia aculeata).* Also called **old hook, pull-and-hold-back**

1933 Small *Manual SE Flora* 489, *P. aculeata...* Woody vine with branching thorns... *Devil's-claws.* **1960** Vines *Trees SW* 252, *Devils-claw Pisonia...* Usually along old resaca beds in.. Texas. **1971** Craighead *Trees S. FL* 200, Devil's claw, *Pisonia aculeata.*

devil's clothesline n [**devil** n **B1a**]

=greenbrier.

1913 *Torreya* 13.229, *Smilax* spp... Devil's clothes-line is the apt vernacular in parts of Maryland.

devil's club n [**devil** n **B1a**]

1 =**Hercules'-club 1.**

1860 in 1942 *Torreya* 42.163, *Aralia spinosa* L.—Devil's-club, Cambria County, Pa., R.M.S. Jackson (The Mountain, 1860, p. 237). **1931** Clute *Common Plants* 83, Another thorny species is the devil's walking-stick or devil's club *(Aralia spinosa).*

2 also *devil-club:* A large spiny shrub *(Oplopanax horridum)* native chiefly to the Northwest and Alaska.

1885 *Century Illustr. Mag.* 29.836/2 **WA,** A noticeable plant, called the devil's club from the brier-like character of its stem. **1935** Davis *Honey* 100 **OR,** Flem Simmons' land-holding was a half-mile-square homestead claim astraddle of a creek bottom full of devil's-club stalks and skunk cabbage and wild-currant bushes and alder saplings. **1944** *New Yorker* 7 Oct 38/3 **OR,** It is a jungle, a trackless forest of Douglas fir with a ground of devil clubs, chinquapin, and other brush. **1949** Peattie *Cascades* 138 **Pacific NW,** You may be scratched by the pestiferous devil's-club. **1950** FWP *Guide ID* 60, Devil's club. **1951** Writers' Program *Oregon* 20, Devil's club. **1966–68** *DARE* (Qu. S17) Inf **WA**1, Devil-clubs; (Qu. T16) Inf **AK**1, Devil's club. **1977** Churchill *Don't Call* 140 **nwOR** (as of c1918), Any logger who worked on the rigging and spent his days surrounded by devil's-club and nettles among other things wasn't about to go home and have nettles for supper.

devil scratcher n

A **hellgrammite 1.**

1953 Randolph *Down in Holler* 239 **Ozarks,** *Devil scratcher*. . . Hellgrammite, larva of the dobson fly *(Corydalus cornutus).*

devil's darning needle n [*EDD* (at *devil* sb. 1, 2) in senses **1, 5** below]

1 also *devil's darn needle, devil's needle:* A **dragonfly. [devil n B1b;** see also quots 1899, 1949] **scattered, but chiefly Nth** See Map Cf **darning needle 1**

1809 Irving *Knickerb.* VI.iv *(DAE), They . .* bore as a standard three Devil's darning needles, *volant,* in a flame coloured field. **1838** MA Zool. & Bot. Surv. *Repts. Zool.* 72, Dr. Green informs us that a species of dragon-fly or devil's-needle *(Libellula)* also destroys them [=rosebugs]. **a1862** (1864) Thoreau *ME Woods* 237, On Moosehead I had seen a large devil's-needle half a mile from the shore. **1899** Bergen *Animal Lore* 90, The devil's darning-needle will sew together the fingers or toes of a person who goes to sleep within its reach. *Dubuque Co., Iowa. . .* The devil's darning-needle is said to sew up the mouths of scolding women, saucy children, and profane men. *Kansas. . .* The devil's darning-needle will sting you to death. *Oneida, Ill. . .* The devil's darning-needle is . . in Eastern Iowa said sometimes to enter the ears and penetrate the brain of a person. *Dubuque Co., Iowa.* **1899** (1912) Green *VA Folk-Speech* 146, Devil's darning needle. . . Mosquito-hawk. Dragon-fly. **1907** *DN* 3.211 **nwAR, cCT,** *Devil's darning-needle.* **1910** *DN* 3.440 **cwNY,** *Devil's darning needle.* **1949** Swain *Insect Guide* 67, Large dragonflies, generally known as . . "devil's darning needles" because it was once popularly believed that they sewed up the ears of truant schoolboys. **1965–70** *DARE* (Qu. R2) 61 Infs, **scattered, but chiefly Nth,** Devil's darning needle; **CT**23, **ID**5, **PA**1, Devil's needle; **NY**75, 219, Devil's darn needle.

2 also *devil's darn needle, devil's needle:* =**walkingstick. [devil n B1b]**

1942 Warnick *Garrett Co. MD* 6 **nwMD** (as of 1900–18), *Devil's darn-needle . .* the insect known as walking-stick. **1950** *WELS Suppl.* **cwWI,** Devil's darning needle—used for dragon fly and walking stick. He sews liar's lips together in our valley. **1965–70** *DARE* (Qu. R9a) 19 Infs, **chiefly Midl,** Devil's darning needle; **MO**2, 37, Devil's needles.

3 =**praying mantis.**

1941 Writers' Program *Guide AR* 100, If the "devil's darning needle" (praying mantis) is not poisonous, "who in tarnation's going to let himself get bit just to make sure?" **1958** *PADS* 29.9 **cnTN,** The devil's darning needle is not the same thing at all [as the dragon fly]. It is the praying mantis. **1968** *AmSp* 43.52, [Of 1,518 infs, mostly students at Kansas State University, shown pictures of the two insects, 13 gave *devil's darning needle* as a name for the praying mantis and 11 gave it as a name for the dragonfly.] **1983** *MJLF* 9.1.37 **ceKY, TN,** *Devil's darning needle . .* a praying mantis.

4 A **virgin's bower** (here: *Clematis virginiana*).

1892 *Jrl. Amer. Folkl.* 5.91, *Clematis Virginiana. . .* Devil's darning needle. So. Vt. **1900** Lyons *Plant Names* 107. **1964** Batson *Wild Flowers SC* 46, *Devil's Darning Needle: C. virginiana. . .* A perennial climbing vine forming a heavy, leafy top or bower. **1970** Correll *Plants TX* 651, *Devil's darning-needle. . .* Achenes brown or rufescent, . . the styles 1–3 cm. long.

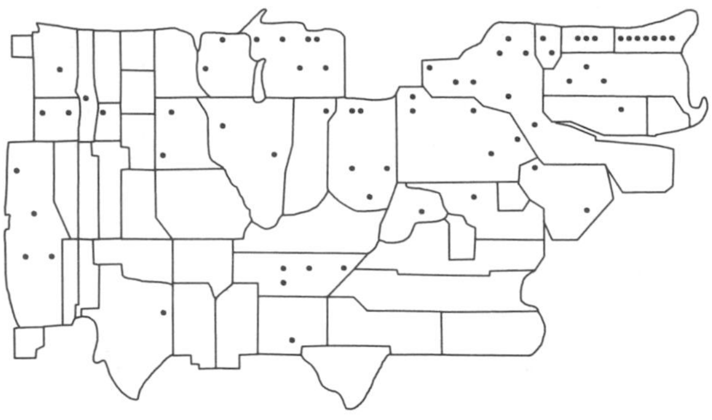

•devil's darning needle 1 + varr (Qu. R2)

5 =**Venus's-comb.**

1889 *Century Dict.* 1579, *Devil's darning-needle. . .* The Venus's-comb, *Scandix Pecten* [sic], from the long tapering beaks of the fruit. **1900** Lyons *Plant Names* 336, *S[candix] Pecten-Veneris. . .* Devil's-darningneedle. **1959** Carleton *Index Herb. Plants* 37, *Devil's-darning-needle:* Scandix pecten [sic].

6 =**needlegrass** (here: *Stipa* spp).

1891 *AN&Q* 6.162/2, The grass called *Stipa spartea,* or feather-grass, is known in Montana as the *devil's darning-needle.* It is a great pest for its sharp awns and seeds bury themselves deeply in the sides of cattle and horses. . . This plant grows as far East as Illinois and Michigan. **1932** Rydberg *Flora Prairies* 84, *Stipa* L. Spear Grass, . . Devil's Darning-needles. **1933** Small *Manual SE Flora* 97, *Stipa. . .* Articulation oblique, leaving a bearded sharp-pointed callus at the base of the floret. . . *Devils' darning-needles.* **1935** Sandoz *Jules* 196 **wNE** (as of 1880–1930), From a gray walking skirt she made him a pair of pants and a cap, consoling herself with the thought that it was too heavy here anyway, would only collect devil's darning needles and beggar-lice. **1967** *DARE* (Qu. S15) Inf **OR**5, Devil's darning needle—long needle, inch or so, gets into clothing, hard to push them through.

7 also *devil's needle:* =**beggar ticks 1.**

1950 *WELS Suppl.,* 1 Inf, **WI,** Devil's darning needle—a "stick-tight." **1965–70** *DARE* (Qu. S14) Infs **LA**6, **NJ**31, **PA**49, Devil('s) needles; **CA**7, **IL**11, Devil's darning needle(s); (Qu. S15) Infs **NC**87, **NJ**24, Devil's needle.

8 A **cockleburr.**

1966 *DARE* (Qu. S13) Inf **WA**8, Devil's darning needle.

devil's darn needle See **devil's darning needle 1, 2**

devil's dragon n

A **dragonfly.**

1954 *Harder Coll.* **cwTN,** Horse doctor. . . A fly, same as devil's dragon.

devil's dust n Cf **devil's snuffbox 1**

Prob a **puffball** or its spores.

1967 *DARE* (Qu. S18, *A kind of mushroom that grows like a globe . . sometimes gets as big as a man's head*) Inf **LA**6, Devil's dust.

devil's ear n

A **jack-in-the-pulpit** (here: *Arisaema triphyllum*).

1845 Judd *Margaret* 25, It was a wake-robin, commonly known as dragon-root, devil's ear, or Indian turnip. **1890** *AN&Q* 5.243, The plant wake-robin is called Devil's ear. **1900** Lyons *Plant Names* 45, *A[risaema] triphyllum. . .* Jack-in-the-pulpit, Wake-robin, . . Devil's-ear. **1930** Sievers *Amer. Med. Plants* 37, Jack-in-the-pulpit. . . Other common names [are] . . devil's-ear [etc].

devil's elbow n [From the crooked branches]

A **forestiera,** either **swamp privet** or *Forestiera pubescens.*

1960 Vines *Trees SW* 850, *Forestiera pubescens. . .* Also known under the vernacular names of Devil's-elbow [etc]. **1961** Wills–Irwin *Flowers TX* 170, Spring-herald, or Devil's-elbow, *Forestiera acuminata . .* is a native shrub of this [=olive] family.

devil's fiddle n

1 A homemade noisemaker, esp one made with a waxed or rosined string and a tin can; see quots. **[devil n B1d] chiefly NEng** Cf **dumb bull 1**

1906 Lovett *Old Boston Boys* 18, The American boy is nothing if not inventive, and anything that can be produced which will make a noise is dear to his heart. One of the earliest of such inventions which I recall was named the "locust," a harmless production, and one that no doubt paved the way for the later abomination known as the "Devil's fiddle." **1907** *DN* 3.186 **seNH,** *Devil's fiddle*. . . An unmusical instrument made by passing a waxed end through the bottom of a tin can. **1909** *DN* 3.410 **nME,** *Devil's fiddle* . . A resined string attached to a window on the outside and sounded as a Hallowe'en trick. **1922** Gonzales *Black Border* 35 **sSC, GA coasts** [Gullah], The little "Devil's Fiddles" which boys construct of empty tin cans and rosined string emit unchristian squeaks when played upon with smooth hardwood sticks. **1933** *Hanley Disks* **neMA,** *Devil's fiddle.* Some of them will get the tin can and . . what they call a waxed end. They put a hole in the bottom of the tin can . . and I believe they put rosin on. . . a string. That's what they call a devil's fiddle. **1941** *LANE* Map 409 1 inf, **seCT,** Devil's fiddle, a weighted plank run through a drygoods box [at a serenade].

2 =cicada. [Cf **devil n B1b** and quot 1906 at **1** above]

1967 *DARE* (Qu. R7) Inf **MI**67, A cicada, sometimes called a "devil's fiddle."

devil's-fig n [**devil n B1a**]

A **prickly poppy** (here: *Argemone mexicana*).

1876 Hobbs *Bot. Hdbk.* 31, Devil's fig, Prickly poppy, Argemone Mexicana. **1911** *Century Dict.* 3082, *Infernal fig, Argemone Mexicana*. . . Also called *devil's-fig.* **1931** Clute *Common Plants* 84, The plant we call the prickly poppy . . is the species often known as devil's fig. **1936** Whitehouse *TX Flowers* 34, Mexican Poppy . . extending into Southwest Texas. . . is also called . . devil's fig. **1970** Correll *Plants TX* 664, Devil's fig. . . In waste places, fields and along roadsides in s.-cen. Tex.

devil's-fingers n

Perh a **cholla.**

1940 Writers' Program *Guide TX* 641, In this section grow many weird varieties of cactus. Spanish dagger, . . devil's fingers, ocotillo, and various kinds of yuccas.

devil's fit n Cf **cat fit**

1983 *MJLF* 9.34 **ceKY,** *Cat fit* (see . . devil's fit, duck fit) . . : a severe fit (tantrum).

devil's-flax n

=butter-and-eggs 1.

1900 Lyons *Plant Names* 226, *L[inaria] Linaria* . . Devil's Flax.

devil's-flower n

=red campion.

1940 Clute *Amer. Plant Names* 63, *L[ychnis] dioica*. . . Devil's-flower. **1959** Carleton *Index Herb. Plants* 37, *Devil's-flower*: Lychnis dioica.

devil's foot n [From its resemblance to a cloven hoof]

=beggar ticks 1.

1967 *DARE* (Qu. S14) Inf **MI**53, Devil's foot.

devil's footstep n [**devil n B1c**]

A spot of barren ground; a gall.

1860 Holmes *Professor* 164 **MA,** There were two things, when I was a boy, that diabolised my imagination. . . The first was a series of marks called the "Devil's footsteps." These were patches of sand in the pastures where no grass grew . . but all was bare and blasted.

devil's footstool n **chiefly Sth, S Midl**

A large mushroom, perh a **puffball.**

1950 *WELS (A large round mushroom, often bright colored)* 1 Inf, **csWI,** Devil's footstool. **1965–70** *DARE* (Qu. S18) 16 Infs, **chiefly Sth, S Midl,** Devil's footstool. [6 Infs Black]

devil's fritters n

Appar **=tick trefoil.**

1969 *DARE* (Qu. S15, . . *Weed seeds that cling to clothing*) Infs **KY**47, Devil's fritters.

devil's-grandmother n

An elephant's foot (here: *Elephantopus tomentosus*). Also called **tobacco weed**

1894 *Jrl. Amer. Folkl.* 7.92, *Elephantus* [sic] *tomentosus* . . tobacco weed, Devil's grandmother, W. Va. **1931** Clute *Common Plants* 83, But how the elephant's foot . . deserves the name of devil's grandmother is hard to conjecture. **1970** Correll *Plants TX* 1538, Devil's-grandmother. Perennial herb . . with a persistent basal rosette . . s.e. U.S.

devil's-grass n Also *devil-grass* [**devil n B1a**]

1 =quack grass.

1872 VT State Bd. Ag. *Report* 1.289, *Triticum repens*. . . Its various English names, *Couch*, . . *Witch* and *Devil Grass,* attest how widespread it is becoming. **1895** U.S. Dept. Ag. *Farmers' Bulletin* 28.24, Devil's grass . . Agropyron repens. **1898** *Jrl. Amer. Folkl.* 11.282 **ME,** *Agropyron repens* . . devil's grass. **1912** Baker *Book of Grasses* 238, Couch-grass . . Devil-grass . . *Agropyron repens.* **1930** Sievers *Amer. Med. Plants* 49, *Quack Grass—Agropyron repens*—Other common names.—Dog grass, . . devil's grass. **1965–70** *DARE* (Qu. S8) Infs **CA**1, 7, 12, **IL**26, Devil-grass; **OR**13, Devil-grass—not here; **NC**31, Devil's-grass; (Qu. S9) Inf **CA**24, Devil-grass—a wide leaf, has deep-seated roots—a wider leaf than crab [grass].

2 =gum succory.

1894 *Bot. Gaz.* 19.431, *Chondrilla juncea* . . Devil's grass. (West Va.). **1900** Lyons *Plant Names* 94. **1959** Carleton *Index Herb. Plants* 37.

3 Bermuda grass.

1965–70 *DARE* (Qu. S8) Inf **CA**41, Devil's-grass (Bermuda, alternate term); **CA**207, Bermuda grass—devil-grass; **OK**18, Bermuda grass or devil-grass (same); (Qu. S9) Inf **CA**185, Devil-grass. **1970** U.S. Ag. Research Serv. *Selected Weeds* 54, *Cynodon dactylon* . . Bermudagrass, Devilgrass. **1974** Munz *Flora S. CA* 959, *Cynodon dactylon* . . *Bermudagrass*. . . Also, but incorrectly, called Devil's Grass.

devil's-grip n [**devil n B1a**]

A **carpetweed 1** (here: *Mollugo verticillata*).

1896 *Bot. Gaz.* 22.483, *Mollugo verticillata,* L., devil's grip, No. Berwick, Me.

devil's-guts n Also *devil's-gut* [**devil n B1a**]

1 =dodder. [*OED* 1670 →]

1830 Rafinesque *Med. Flora* 214, *Cuscuta americana*. . . *Dodder, Devil's gut.* **1876** Hobbs *Bot. Hdbk.* 31, Devil's gut, Dodder, Cuscuta Americana. **1900** Lyons *Plant Names* 126, *Cuscuta*. . . Names applied to the various species are . . Devil's-guts, . . Strangle-weed. **1914** Georgia *Manual Weeds* 324, *Cuscuta Epithymum*. . . Devil's Gut. **1931** Clute *Common Plants* 85, Of the plants known as hell-weeds or hell-roots, we may mention . . the flax dodder *(Cuscuta epilinum),* which also bears the inelegant name of devil's guts.

2 A **horsetail 1** (here: *Equisetum arvense*).

1891 *Jrl. Amer. Folkl.* 4.149, Equisetum arvense was called *Devil's Guts,* that is, the *fertile* stems, the name coming, I think, from Connecticut. **1950** Gray–Fernald *Manual of Botany* 4, *E[quisetum] arvense*. . . *Devil's-guts.*

3 Corn spurrey.

1896 *Jrl. Amer. Folkl.* 9.182, *Spergula arvensis,* . . devil's guts, Paris, M[ain]e. **1935** (1943) Muenscher *Weeds* 234, Spurry [sic], Devils-gut. . . Annual; reproducing by seeds. **1940** Clute *Amer. Plant Names* 273, *Spergula arvensis.* Devil's gut, wild flax.

4 A **buttercup 1** (here: *Ranunculus repens*). [*OED* 1879]

1900 Lyons *Plant Names* 316, *R. repens*. . . Creeping Buttercup, . . Devil's-guts.

5 Perh **ditch grass.**

1909 *DN* 3.414 **nME,** *Nigger's hair, n.* A kind of wild grass growing in swampy places. The same as *devil's guts.*

devil's-hair n

1 A **virgin's bower** (here: *Clematis virginiana*).

1893 *Jrl. Amer. Folkl.* 6.136, *Clematis Virginiana,* devil's hair, Va. **1900** Lyons *Plant Names* 107. **1910** Graves *Flowering Plants* 190 **CT,** *Clematis virginiana*. . . Devil's Hair. . . The leaves and flowers are medicinal.

2 =dodder; see quots.

1914 Georgia *Manual Weeds* 324, *Cuscuta Epithymum*. . . Devil's Hair. . . The seedling looks like a bit of yellowish red hair. **1935** (1943) Muenscher *Weeds* 372, *Cuscuta Epilinum*. . . Devils-hair. . . Parasitic, mostly on flax. **1967** Dodge *Roadside Wildflowers* 56, *Devil's Hair*. . . Masses of straw-colored growth covering plants along roadsides. . . *Cuscuta campestris.*

devil's half acre n Cf **hell's half acre**

1 also *devil's homestead:* A rough or unworkable piece of land. [**devil n B1c**]

1968 *DARE* (Qu. L6a, *What do you call a piece of land under cultivation—less than an acre?*) Inf **NJ**50, Devil's half acre—a rough section of land. **1969** *DARE* Tape **CA**154, [FW:] I don't like all . . the lava rocks, where it's just completely black. [Inf:] Oh. Devil's homestead. . . That's pretty wild.

2 A part of town notorious for lawless behavior.

1959 McAtee *Oddments* 10 **cNC**, *Devil's Half-acre*—Area between Hillsboro Street and Airport Road, once used by bootleggers. **1972** *NYT Article Letters* **ME**, My town in Maine has "The Devil's Half-Acre[""]—now shortened to "The Acre"—, so named because the residents of that little area fought so consistently in years past. **1975** Gould *ME Lingo* 72, *Devil's Half Acre*—That part of old Bangor where choppers and river drivers disported. The vicinity of lower Exchange Street, now re-urbanized.

devil's hawk n [**devil** n **B1b**]

A **grasshopper 1.**

1968 *DARE* (Qu. R9a) Inf **SC**57, Devil's hawk—if he spits in your eye, you'll go blind.

devil's hawkweed n [**devil** n **B1a**]

=**orange hawkweed.**

1948 Wherry *Wild Flower Guide* 173, *Devil's Hawkweed (Hieracium aurantiacum)*. . . A bad weed in the northern parts of our area [="Northeastern and Midland United States"].

devil's-head n [**devil** n **B1a**] **TX**

1 A **pincushion cactus** (here: *Mammillaria wrightii*).

1930 TX Folkl. Soc. *Pub.* 8.42, *Mammillaria wrightii*. . . Devil's-head. **1967** *DARE* (Qu. I46) Inf **TX**6, Devil's-heads.

2 also *devil('s)-head cactus:* A **barrel cactus,** either *Echinocactus horizonthalonius* or *E. texensis.*

1961 Wills–Irwin *Flowers TX* 161, *Devil's-head. Echinocactus texensis. Ibid* 162, Like most Texas cacti, Devil's-head blooms in late spring. **1969** *DARE* (Qu. S26e) Inf **TX**71, Devil-head cactus bloom. **1970** Correll *Plants TX* 1104, *Echinocactus horizonthalonius*. . . Devil's head. . . *Echinocactus texensis*. . . Devil's head. **1985** Dodge *Flowers SW Deserts* 96, Devils-Head Cactus. . . *Echinocactus horizonthalonius.*

devil's-head-in-a-bush n [Cf **devil-in-the-bush** and *OED devil* sb. 24]

=**flower-of-an-hour.**

1892 *Jrl. Amer. Folkl.* 5.93, *Hibiscus trionum*. . . Devil's-head-in-a-bush. N.H. **1940** Clute *Amer. Plant Names* 45, *Flower-of-an-hour*. . . Devil's-head-in-a-bush. **1959** Carleton *Index Herb. Plants* 37, *Devil's-head-in-a-bush:* Hibi[s]cus trionum.

devil shoestring See **devil's shoestring 1**

devil's homestead See **devil's half acre 1**

devil's hopvine n [**devil** n **B1a**; see quot 1931]

A **greenbrier** (here: *Smilax rotundifolia*).

1931 Clute *Common Plants* 83, Thorny species seem naturally to merit being named for the devil. On this account, the thorny *Smilax rotundifolia* is commonly known as the devil's hop-vine. **1960** Vines *Trees SW* 75, *Smilax rotundifolia*. . . Vernacular names for the plant are Biscuit-leaves, . . Devil's-hop-vine, . . and Sow-brier.

devil's-horn See **devil's-horns**

devil's hornet n [**devil** n **B1b**]

A **dragonfly.**

1967 *DARE* (Qu. R2) Inf **IA**1, Devil's hornet.

devil's-horns n Also *devil's-horn*

1 =**unicorn plant.** [See quot 1931]

1931 Clute *Common Plants* 83, The unicorn plant *(Martynia Louisiana),* whose fruits end in two curved hooks, is the devils' horns. **1949** Moldenke *Amer. Wild Flowers* 287, The *devilshorn, P. althaefolia* . . is a much lower and smaller plant with small, deeply lobed leaves. **1951** *PADS* 15.41 **TX**, *Martynia* spp.—Devil's . . horns. **1967–69** *DARE* (Qu. S14) Infs **AZ**2, **CA**150, **NY**24, Devil's-horn(s).

2 A **beggar ticks 1.** [**devil** n **B1a**; see quot]

1950 *WELS (Small flat seeds with two prongs that cling to clothing)* 1 Inf, **cwWI**, Devil's-horns.

devil's horse n Also *devil horse* [**devil** n **B1b**; cf *EDD devil's coach-horse, ~ racehorse* (at *devil* sb. 1) a rove beetle *(Ocypus olens)*]

1 also *devil's mare, ~ rear horse, ~ riding ~, ~ ridy ~:* =**praying mantis. chiefly Sth, S Midl, TX** See Map

1843 (1924) Oliver *8 Months* 71 **IL**, Anything very singular in nature is ascribed to the devil, as "devil's oven," "devil's lettuce," "devil's mare," (the last a singularly shaped insect). **1869** MO State Entomol. *Annual Rept.* 169, The Rear-horse, *alias* Camel-cricket, *alias* Devil's Riding Horse—*Mantis Carolina,* Linn. (Orthoptera Mantidae.) **1883** Sweet–Knox *Mexican Mustang* 629 **TX**, Another of the most peculiar and interesting insects in Texas is called the "devil's horse." **1899** Bergen *Animal Lore* 63 **TX**, Devil's riding horse, praying prophet, praying mantis, *Phasmomantis carolina.* **1907** *DN* 3.230 **nwAR, seMO,** *Devil's-horse*. . . The praying mantis. **1908** *DN* 3.304 **eAL, wGA,** *Devil's horse*. . . Sometimes called *devil's ridin(g) horse.* **1931** Read *LA French* 25, *Cheval Diable*. . . Praying Mantid . . other English names for this insect are "Soothsayer," "Mule Killer," "Devil Horse," and "Devil's Rear Horse." **1965–70** *DARE* (Qu. R9b) 77 Infs, **chiefly Sth, S Midl, TX,** Devil('s) horse; **KY**75, **NC**6, 21, **VA**43, 46, 75, 105, Devil('s) riding horse; **TX**40, Devil's ridy horse.

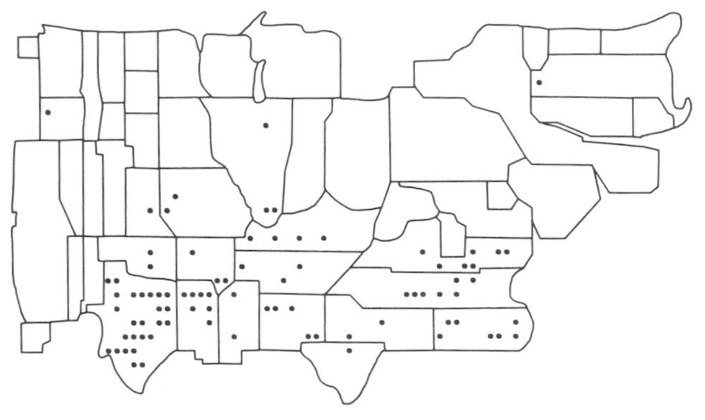

•devil's horse 1 + varr (Qu. R9b)

2 A **crawfish B1.**

1843 *Amer. Pioneer* 2.233 **New Orleans LA**, Very large black grasshoppers, called cheval du diable, or devil's horses, burrow in all the ground. They are, I believe, the same thing as craw-fish, or the shrimps which they use for food. They [=devil's horses] come up any where and every where in the night in the streets, making little chimneys of mud to mark their whereabouts.

3 A **grasshopper 1.**

1937 *Nature* (London) 140.264/1 **FL**, Less graceful but fascinating are the devils-horses, a showy grasshopper commonly six inches long which travels over the land by the million devouring vegetation as it goes. **1966–68** *DARE* (Qu. R6, . . *Grasshoppers*) Inf **AR**23, Devil's horses; **LA**44, Devil horse. **1967** LeCompte *Word Atlas* 198 **ceLA**, *Big black grasshoppers with red wings . . cheval carosse* [10 of 21 infs] . . devil's horse [1 inf]. . . The head of this grasshopper is said to resemble that of a horse. **1983** *Reinecke Coll.* 4 **LA**, *Devil horse* . . a very large black and red grasshopper. La. French "cheval diable."

4 also *devil's mare, ~ race horse, ~ riding ~, ~ ridy ~, stick devil horse:* =**walkingstick. chiefly Sth, S Midl** See Map

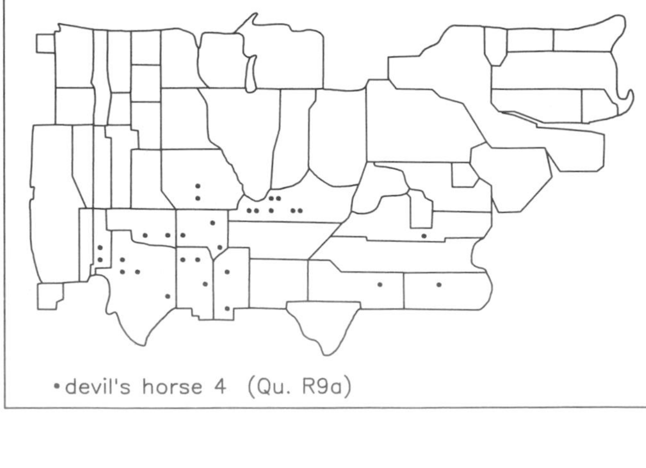

•devil's horse 4 (Qu. R9a)

1965–70 *DARE* (Qu. R9a) 13 Infs, **chiefly Sth, S Midl,** Devil's horse; **KY**11, 68, 76, 80, **VA**38, Devil's riding horse; **AR**28, **GA**6, **LA**6, **MS**1, 73, **MO**39, **OK**52, Devil horse; **NM**3, **TX**66, Devil's race horse; **KY**9, Devil's ridy horse; **TX**59, Stick devil horses; **AR**5, Devil's mare.

5 also *devil's riding horse*: A **dragonfly.**

1950 *WELS Suppl.* 1 Inf, **WI,** Devil horse—a dragonfly. **1966** *DARE* (Qu. R2, . . *Dragonfly*) Infs **AL**6, **MS**16, Devil('s) horse; **NC**16, Devil's riding horse.

‡devil's horse fly n **[devil n B1b]**
=devil's horse 1.

1969 *DARE* (Qu. R9b) Inf **GA**77, Devil's horse fly.

devil's ironweed n **[devil n B1a]**
A **wild lettuce** (here: *Lactuca canadensis*).

1894 *Jrl. Amer. Folkl.* 7.92, *Lactuca Canadensis* . . Devil's iron-weed, . . West Va. **1898** *Ibid* 11.230 *Lactuca Canadensis* . . devil's iron-weed, Kansas. **1940** Clute *Amer. Plant Names* 70, *L. Canadensis*. . . Devil's ironweed. **1959** Carleton *Index Herb. Plants* 37, *Devil's-iron-weed:* Lactuca canadensis.

devil's kindling wood n
See quot.

1988 *DARE* File **cnMA** (as of c1930), His grandmother . . didn't like for him to drink soft drinks or soda of any kind for fear it would get him started on the road to hard drinks. "The devil's kindling wood" was what she called soda of any kind.

devil's knitting-needles n
A **needlegrass** (here: *Stipa spartea*).

1889 Vasey *Ag. Grasses* 42, *Stipa spartea* is called . . devil's knitting-needles, from the long, stiff, twisted awns inclosing [sic] the seeds.

devil's lane n [Cf **devil n B1c**]
A narrow strip of land between parallel fences, resulting from the inability of neighbors to agree to build a common fence; also fig.

1872 Eggleston *End of the World* 27 **IN,** She had managed at one time or another to embroil him with almost all the neighbors, and his refusal to join fences had resulted in that crooked arrangement known as a "devil's lane" on three sides of his farm. **1888** *Century Illustr. Mag.* 36.82/2 **IL,** Where two of their fields joined without an intervening road they had not been able even to build a line fence together; but each man laid up a rail fence on the very edge of his own land, and the salient angles of the two hostile fences stood so near together that a half-grown pig could not have passed between. This is what is called, in the phrase of the country, a "devil's lane," because it is a monument of bad neighborhood. **1935** Sandoz *Jules* 92 **wNE** (as of 1880–1930), Once [in a debate] there was a test of authority, the Bible versus the dictionary, and the end was a devil's lane between two erstwhile good neighbors. **1944** Howard *Walkin' Preacher* 103 **MO,** "Well, who owns that narrow strip of ground between their fences?" I asked. "Oh," laughed Clark, "that's jist the devil's lane." . . "Andrews and Harmon each moved their fences back four feet from the surveyed line and that's called a devil's lane." **1953** Randolph–Wilson *Down in Holler* 239 **Ozarks,** When two farmers whose fields adjoin cannot agree to maintain a common fence, each man builds a fence on his own land. The space between the parallel fences, often only two or three feet, is called the *devil's lane.*

devil's lantern n Also *devil-fire* Cf **frog lantern 1, Jacob's lantern**
=will-o'-the-wisp.

1875 (1876) Twain *Tom Sawyer* 88 **MO,** "Look! See there!" whispered Tom. "What is it?" "It's devil-fire. O, Tom, this is awful." **1969** *DARE* (Qu. CC16) Inf **GA**72, Devil's lantern.

devil's lettuce n
A **fiddleneck 1** (here: *Amsinckia tessalata*).

1951 Martin *Amer. Wildlife & Plants* 414, Fireweed fiddleneck *(A. intermedia)* . . and devilslettuce *(A. tessalata)* are among the most common species . . used by wildlife.

devil's lice n **[devil n B1a]** Cf **beggar's lice 2**
A **tick trefoil.**

1966 *DARE* (Qu. S15) Inf **NC**14, Devil's lice—small, flat seeds.

devil's lily n **[devil n B1a]** Cf **devil's ear**
A **jack-in-the-pulpit.**

1966 *DARE* (Qu. S1) Inf **WA**15, Devil's lily.

devil's mantis n **[devil n B1b]** Cf **devil's horse 1**
=praying mantis.

1967 *DARE* (Qu. R9a) Inf **WA**28, Devil's mantis.

devil's mare See **devil's horse 1, 4**

devil's music box n

1949 Webber *Backwoods Teacher* 107, The better-thought-of folks did not hold with "round dancing" or "fiddle dancing." The fiddle was still, to many, "the devil's music box."

devil's needle See **devil's darning needle 1, 2, 7**

devil's night n
=cabbage night.

1983 *McDavid Coll.* **seMI,** Devil's night—night of October 30th, the night before Halloween when kids vandalize. **1984** *DARE* File, On October 31, I heard on a nationwide news program reports of numerous fires set in (usually) uninhabited buildings and garages by celebrants of "devil's night," the night before Halloween. **1985** *Capital Times* (Madison WI) 1 Nov 40/3 **seMI,** Officials in Detroit, meanwhile, were busy Thursday trying to assess damage from a wave of arson that sweeps the city every Halloween and the night before, called Devil's Night.

devil's nit fly n **[devil n B1b]**
Perh a botfly.

1969 *DARE* (Qu. R12) Inf **GA**77, Devil's nit fly, around cows—get through the hide.

devil's nose n
A toadstool.

1966 *DARE* (Qu. I38) Inf **FL**15, Devil's nose.

devil snuff See **devil's snuff**

devil's off-horse n

1940 Smiley *Gloss. New Paltz* **seNY,** "Contrary as the Devil's off-horse." Sanford Cross referring to a former employee.

devil's off-ox n
=Adam's off-ox 1.

1969 *DARE* (Qu. II26, . . *"I wouldn't know him from ________.")* Inf **KY**6, The devil's off-ox.

devils on horseback n Cf **angels on horseback 1**

1980 *Hand Coll.* **sCA,** "Devils on Horseback" are chicken livers wrapped in bacon.

devil's pack-peddler n

1939 *AmSp* 14.90 **eTN,** Devil's pack peddler. A gossiper. 'She's a devil's pack peddler.'

devil's paintbrush n **[devil n B1a]**

1 A **hawkweed,** esp *Hieracium aurantiacum.* **chiefly NEast**

1895 U.S. Dept. Ag. *Farmers' Bulletin* 28.25, Devil's paint brush. . . Hieracium praealtum. . . Meadows; pastures. **1898** *Jrl. Amer. Folkl.* 11.230, *Hieracium prooeltum* [sic] . . devil's paint-brush. **1900** *Plant World* 3.132, *Hieracium aurantiacum.* . . Most commonly it went by the name of Devil's Paint Brush—a name . . which well embodies the popular feeling towards the obnoxious plants. **1928** Chapman *Happy Mt.* 311 **seTN,** Devil's-paint-brush—the orange hawkweed; of the chicory family (Hieracium aurantiacum). **1948** Peattie *Berkshires* 55 **wMA,** I would . . find drifts of the devil's-paintbrush or tawny hawkweed, Hieracium aurantiacum. Nature seems to be excited about the neglected field, and the devil's-paintbrush proceeds to paint it with big bright orange-red blobs. **1965–70** *DARE* (Qu. S21) Infs **ME**3, 12, **MI**15, **MA**68, **NY**34, 115, 217, 222, **PA**234, Devil's paintbrush; (Qu. S26a) Infs **ME**8, **MI**26, **MA**49, **NY**6, 191, 199, **PA**191, Devil's paintbrush; (Qu. S26c) Infs **NY**211, **PA**225, Devil's paintbrush; (Qu. S26d) 12 Infs, **NEast,** Devil's paintbrush; (Qu. S26e) Infs **MA**25, 42, **NY**79, 227, Devil's paintbrush. **1966** *Monadnock Regionaire* (Bellows Falls VT) Summer 38/1 **swNH,** The hawkweeds, including the scarlet and orange Devil's Paintbrush, stipple the landscape canvas with bold, colorful splashes. **1966** *DARE* Wildfl QR Pl.223B Infs **NH**4, **WI**35, Devil's paintbrush.

2 =Indian paintbrush (here: *Castilleja* spp).

1959 Carleton *Index Herb. Plants* 37, *Devil's paintbrush:* Castilleja (v); Hieracium aurantiacum. **1970** *DARE* (Qu. S26e) Inf **CA**181, Devil's paintbrush.

3 =mullein.

1966–69 *DARE* (Qu. S20) Infs **CT**9, **ME**7, 12, **MI**15, **MN**14, **MA**29, **NY**220, **PA**200, Devil's paintbrush.

devil's pictures n pl Pronc-sp *deil's pictures* Also *devil's pasteboards* [Cf *OED devil's books* 1729 →]
Playing cards.
1930 Shoemaker *1300 Words* 19 **cPA Mts** (as of c1900), *Deil's pictures*—playing cards. **1986** *DARE* File **csWI** (as of 1930–50), *Devil's pasteboards*—heard occasionally for playing cards.

devil's pin n [**devil n B1a**]
A **beggar ticks 1.**
1967 *DARE* (Qu. S15) Inf **SC**32, Devil's pin—in bunches; appear after a yellow (?) flower about ½ as big as a dime; pins about 1″ long.

devil's pincushion n [**devil n B1a**]
1 A **barrel cactus** (here: *Echinocactus polycephalus*).
1901 James *Indian Basketry* 85, A stout, horny cactus spine from the devil's pincushion (Echinocactus polycephalus), set in a head of hard pitch, furnished the needle. **1982** *Smithsonian Letters* **TX,** Devil's pincushion—cactus plant.
2 =**prickly pear.**
1933 Small *Manual SE Flora* 899, *Opuntia*. . . Devil's pincushions.
3 A **burdock 1.**
1968 *DARE* (Qu. S13, . . *A common wild bush with bunches of round, prickly seeds . . [that] stick to your clothing*) Inf **GA**25, Devil's pincushion.

devil's-pitchfork(s) n [**devil n B1a**]
=**beggar ticks 1.**
1894 *Jrl. Amer. Folkl.* 7.91 **WV,** *Bidens frondosa*. . . Devil's pitchfork. **1950** *WELS Suppl.* 1 Inf, **cnWI,** Devil's pitchfork. **1965–70** *DARE* (Qu. S14) 12 Infs, **Nth,** Devil's pitchforks.

devil's-plague n [**devil n B1a;** see quot 1894]
A **wild carrot** (here: *Daucus carota*).
1894 *Jrl. Amer. Folkl.* 7.89, *Daucus carota*. . . Devil's plague, West Va. [Footnote:] The farmer . . finds the species a pestilent weed. **1914** Georgia *Manual Weeds* 307, *Daucus Carota*. . . Devil's Plague. **1933** Small *Manual SE Flora* 967, Wild-carrot. Queen Anne's lace. Devil's plague. **1950** Gray–Fernald *Manual of Botany* 1105, *Devil's-plague*. . . Dry fields and waste places, a pernicious weed.

devil's pocketbook n
1901 Arnold *Sea-Beach* 12, The so-called "Devil's pocket-books" are the egg-cases of the skate.

devil spoons See **devil's spoons**

devil's potato n
A white-flowered vine *(Echites umbellata),* native to Florida, which has a tuberlike root. Also called **rubber vine**
1933 Small *Manual SE Flora* 1063, *Devil's-potato*. . . This vine, particularly in the pinelands, is often very vigorous. **1949** Moldenke *Amer. Wild Flowers* 163, The devilspotato . . often grows in great profusion in the Florida pinelands. . . Its roots are tuberous and the trumpet-shaped blossoms . . are white. **1953** Greene–Blomquist *Flowers South* 102, *Devil's-Potato*. . . A vigorous vine, its stems and branches often intricately intertwined.

devil's puffball n [**devil n B1a**]
A **puffball.**
1967–70 *DARE* (Qu. S18) Infs **KY**77, **SC**41, Devil's puffball.

devil's race horse See **devil's horse 4**

devil's-rattlebox n [**devil n B1a**]
=**bladder campion.**
1896 *Jrl. Amer. Folkl.* 9.182, *Silene Cucubalus* . . devil's rattle-box, Stockbridge, Mass. **1959** Carleton *Index Herb. Plants* 37, *Devil's rattle-box:* Silene latifolia (A. [sic] inflata).

devil's rear horse See **devil's horse 1**

devil's riding horse n [**devil n B1b**]
1 See **devil's horse 1, 4, 5.**
2 An **assassin bug** (here: *Arilus cristatus*).
1891 *Century Dict.* 6891, *Wheel-bug*. . . *Prionidus cristatus*. . . Also called *devil's-riding-horse.* **1901** Howard *Insect Book* 295, It [=*Arilus cristatus*] is popularly known as the "wheel bug" and sometimes by the negroes as the "devil's riding horse."

devil's ridy horse See **devil's horse 1, 4**

devil's right bower n [*right bower* the jack of trump in the game of **euchre n 1**]
A wild hog.
1942 Kennedy *Palmetto Country* 237 **FL** (as of 1870s), As cattle king Hendry has written, "The razorback, or long-nosed wind-splitter, or Devil's right bower, as you choose to call him, rustles the marshes for wampee, a root similar to the arrow." **1953** Johnston *Legendary Mizners* 269 **FL** (as of 1925), Wild hogs. . . have been running wild since the old Spanish days. . . According to Marjorie Kinnan Rawlings, they know how to line up in football formation and crash through the doors of a granary. They are locally called "wind splitters" and "the Devil's right bowers," because of their speed and savageness.

devil's-root n [**devil n B1a**]
1 =**blazing star 2.** *obs*
1830 Rafinesque *Med. Flora* 2.182, *Blazing Star, . . Devil's Root*. . . Root large tuberous, nauseous, pungent bitter.
2 A **devil's bit** (here: *Succisa pratensis*).
1876 Hobbs *Bot. Hdbk.* 31, Devil's root, Wood scabious, Scabiosa succissa. **1900** Lyons *Plant Names* 336, *S. succisa*. . . Devil's-root.
3 A **broomrape 1** (here: *Orobanche minor*).
1900 Lyons *Plant Names* 268, *O. minor*. . . Devil's-root. **1914** Georgia *Manual Weeds* 389, *Clover Broom-rape*. . . *Other English names:* . . Devil's Root. **1970** *DARE* (Qu. S26d) Inf **SC**67, Devil's-root.

devil's seat n
1977 *Hand Coll.* **neOH,** A broad bridge on the nose is called the devil's seat.

devil's shoelace n
1 See **devil's shoestring 3.**
2 A brown seaweed *(Chorda filum).* [See quot 1949]
1942 Hylander *Plant Life* 42, Devil's Shoelace . . is another common brown seaweed often found growing with Rockweeds about low tide mark. **1949** Palmer *Nat. Hist.* 43, *Devil's Shoelace*. . . Fronds rope-like, slender, less than 1 in. in diameter but frequently over 12 ft. long and reported to 40 ft.

devil's shoestring n Also *devil's shoestrings* [In ref to the var stringlike processes of the plants, some of which can tangle the feet or otherwise hinder movement]
1 also *devil shoestring:* =**goat's rue** or its roots. **chiefly Sth, SMidl**
1830 Rafinesque *Med. Flora* 2.267, *Tephrosia*. . . *Devil's shoestrings*. . . *Roots matted very tough.* **1884** Smith *Bill Arp's Scrap Book* 73 **GA,** Then there's some flowers that he wears in his button-hole called the devil's shoestring and the devil in the bush. **1931** Clute *Common Plants* 84, The name of devil's shoestrings is applied to the strong slender roots of *Tephrosia Virginiana* which often bother the plowman when breaking new ground. **1933** Small *Manual SE Flora* 706, *Cracca virginiana* . . Devil's shoestrings. **1938** Stuart *Dark Hills* 89 **KY,** The devil shoestring vines ran over the loamy overflowed land. **c1938** in 1970 Hyatt *Hoodoo* 1.432 **cAR,** Dat devil-shoestring [Hyatt: goat's-rue—*Tephrosia virginiana*]—well, if anyone *hurt* chew, why yo' jis' git it an' jis' wear it in yore purse or pocketbook. **1941** *Natl. Geogr. Mag.* 79.291, In Oklahoma cypress swamps devil's-shoestring, or goat's rue, is used [to paralyze fish]. **1946** Reeves–Bain *Flora TX* 182, *Tephrosia* . . Devil's Shoestring. **1948** Wherry *Wild Flower Guide* 83, *Devils-shoestring Tephrosia virginiana*. . . The common name refers to the long, tough, stringy roots. **1966–69** *DARE* (Qu. S2) Inf **NC**49, Devil's shoestring; (Qu. S9) Inf **SC**31, Devil's shoestring; (Qu. S21) Infs **KY**83, **NC**14, Devil('s) shoestring; (Qu. S26b) Inf **NC**49, Devil's shoestring; (Qu. S26e) Inf **VA**69, Devil's shoestring. **1970** Correll *Plants TX* 833, *Tephrosia virginiana* . . Devil's shoestring.
2 =**hobblebush. chiefly NC**
1860 Curtis *Cat. Plants NC* 91, Hobble-Bush. . . *V. lantanoides*. . . The branches spread upon the ground . . form well secured loops for tripping the feet of . . wayfarers; a habit . . revenged . . by the unlucky, in the names . . *American Way-fairer's [sic] Tree* and the *Devil's Shoestrings.* **1901** Lounsberry *S. Wild Flowers* 478 **NC,** Its branches sprawl often, or lie over on the ground forming great loops which root readily from their ends. By this means it trips up many that seek to pass through its meshes, and the natives have therefore deemed "Devil's shoestrings" a not inappropriate designation. **1976** Bailey–Bailey *Hortus Third* 1243.

3 also *devil's shoelaces:* =**trumpet creeper.**

1901 Lounsberry *S. Wild Flowers* 472, The southern natives have no such poetical idea of it [=*Campsis radicans*]: they call it devil's shoe-strings because its interlaced growth hinders their progress. **1940** Steyermark *Flora MO* 490, In parts of Missouri it [=*Campsis radicans*] has spread into old fields, pastures, and bottom lands so profusely that its many interlacing stems make walking difficult. For this reason it has been called "Devil's Shoe-strings" or "Devil's Shoe-laces." **1946** *McDavid Coll.* **cSC,** *Devil's shoestring*—a type of itch producing plant, similar to poison oak/ivy. **1960** Vines *Trees SW* 925, Some of its [=*Bignonia radicans'*] vernacular names are Trumpet-vine, . . Devil's-shoestring . . and Cow-itch.

4 =**sand vine.**

1931 Clute *Common Plants* 84, A kind of milkweed with climbing stems, *Gonolobus laevis,* is less appropriately called by the same name [=*devil's shoestrings*]. **1959** Carleton *Index Herb. Plants* 37, Devil's shoestrings: *Gonolobus lævis.*

5 A **false indigo 1** (here: *Amorpha canescens*).

1930 OK Univ. Biol. Surv. *Pub.* 2.1.65, *Amorpha canescens. . .* Lead-plant. Devil's Shoe-string.

6 A **vetch** (here: *Vicia caroliniana*).

1933 Small *Manual SE Flora* 740, *V[icia] caroliniana. . . Devil's-shoe-string. . .* Ga. to Kan., Minn., Ont., & W N.Y.

7 =**bindweed 1.**

1951 *PADS* 15.38 **TX,** Wild morning-glories; . . devil's shoe strings.

8 A **coralberry 1** (here: *Symphoricarpos orbiculatus*).

1951 *PADS* 15.19, *Symphoricarpos orbiculatus. . .* Devil's shoe-strings, North Carolina.

9 A **yucca** (here: *Yucca filamentosa*).

1943 Weslager *DE Forgotten Folk* 162, Devil's Shoe String (Silk Grass)[,] *Yucca filamentosa. . .* Used to tie up meat while it is being smoked. **c1960** *Wilson Coll.* **csKY,** The common yucca (Yucca filamentosa) . . called elsewhere . . devil's shoestring.

10 =**bear grass 1b.**

1970 Correll *Plants TX* 403, *Nolina lindheimeriana* . . Devil's-shoe-string.

11 A **tick trefoil** (here: *Desmodium perplexum*).

1975 Hamel-Chiltoskey *Cherokee Plants* 59, Devil's shoe string—*Desmodium perplexum.*

12 See quot.

1901 *Plant World* 4.144 **KY,** In Barren County I heard several local names of plants that were new to me: . . devil's shoe-strings *(Pachysandra).*

13 A **skeletonweed** (here: *Lygodesmia juncea*).

1935 (1943) Muenscher *Weeds* 510, *Lygodesmia juncea. . .* Devils shoestring. Perennial; reproducing by seeds and roots. Meadows, fields and waste places; mostly in light dry soils.

14 Prob the root of a **sumac;** see quot.

c1938 in 1970 Hyatt *Hoodoo* 2.1102 **cSC,** [In a magical procedure to cause constipation:] Den yo' . . take some of dat same *shoemaker* root —some people call it de devil's-shoestring. [Hyatt: Shoe-make = the smooth sumac *Rhus glabra.*]

15 A **plantain** (here: *Plantago major*).

1973 *Foxfire 2* 85 **nGA,** Broadleaf plantain *(Plantago major)* . . devil's shoestring.

devil's snuff n Also *devil snuff* **[devil n B1a]**

A **puffball** or its powdery spores.

c1938 in 1970 Hyatt *Hoodoo* 2.1794 **Memphis TN,** Now, fo' luck, tuh he'p yo'self through things, yo' go out in de woods an' git de stuff dey call *devil snuff* [Hyatt: powder from the devil's snuffbox]. **1955** *DE Folkl. Bulletin* 1.17/2, The puffball was locally called Devil's Snuff and thought of as something unhealthful. **1966–69** *DARE* (Qu. S18, *A kind of mushroom*) Infs **GA**7, 89, **SC**40, Devil's snuff; **SC**31, Devil's snuff—dust comes out when dry. **1967** *DARE* (Qu. S18) Inf **SC**41, Devil's puffball, devil's snuffbox—contains devil's snuff. **1968** Haun *Hawk's Done Gone* 233 **eTN,** Said she died from a big boil that . . wouldn't ever stop bleeding—no matter how much spiderweb and devil's snuff they dusted on it.

devil's-snuffbox n **[devil n B1a]**

1 =**puffball.** [Engl dial] **chiefly Sth, S Midl** See Map

1884 Smith *Bill Arp's Scrap Book* 73 **GA,** And one day he showed me the . . devil's snuff box which explodes when you mash it, and one ounce of the stuff inside will kill a sound mule before he can lay down. **1899** *Jrl. Amer. Folkl.* 12.269, A toadstool is called the Devil's snuffbox, and the Devil's imps come at midnight to get the snuff. **1902** McIlvaine-Macadam *1000 Amer. Fungi* 589, *Lycoperdon. . .* The filaments. . . bear the spores—the dust which puffs out in such quantity and gives the common name to the plant . . —The Devil's Snuff-box. **1902** (1974) Chestnut *Plants Indians* 300 **CA,** The common puffball, or devil's snuffbox, . . was observed growing very plentifully on the ground after a prolonged rain storm in May, 1898. **1906** *DN* 3.133 **nwAR,** *Devil's snuff-box. . .* A puff-ball. **1908** *DN* 3.304 **eAL, wGA,** *Devil's snuff box. . .* A puff ball. **1940** (1978) Still *River of Earth* 29 **KY,** "I heered tell mushrooms is good eating," I said, stepping carefully among them. "I'd like to try a mess cooked in grease." "They ain't nothing but devil's snuff-boxes," Oates said, drawing his lips down sourly. "They're poison as rattlesnake spit." **1947** (1964) Randolph *Ozark Superstitions* 101, Best of all [to stop bleeding] is the dry dust from the fungi called puffballs, especially the big yellow kind known as the Devil's snuffbox. **1949** *AmSp* 24.108 **cGA,** *Devil's Snuffbox. . .* A kind of inedible mushroom that scatters powdery spores when crushed. **1954** *Harder Coll.* **cwTN,** Devil's snuffbox: A large globe-shaped mushroom. **1965–70** *DARE* (Qu. S18) 28 Infs, **Sth, S Midl,** Devil's-snuffbox(es); (Qu. I38) Inf **NC**87, Devil's-snuffbox. **1972** *DARE* File **csKY,** [For] nose-bleed put up the nose some spores of the devil's snuffbox fungus.

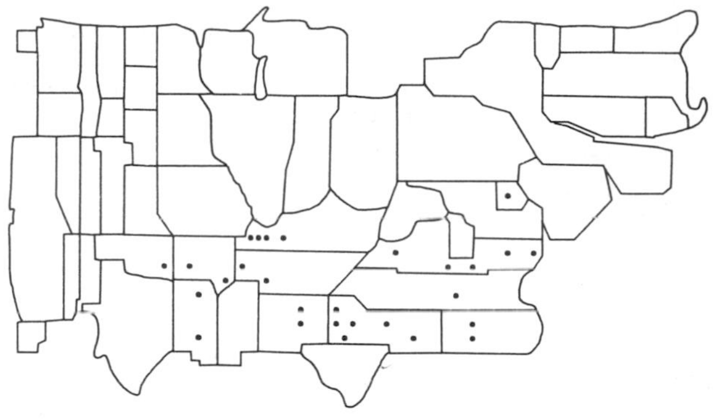

•devil's-snuffbox I (Qq. S18, I38)

2 Corn smut.

1892 *Jrl. Amer. Folkl.* 5.105, *Ustilago Maydis* (the smut of Indian corn), Devil's snuff-box. Chestertown, Md.

devil's spoons n Also *deil's spoons, devil spoons* **[devil n B1a;** see quots 1931, 1974; *SND deil's spoons* 1808 →**]**

A water plantain (here: either *Alisma plantago-aquatica* or *A. subcordatum*).

1900 Lyons *Plant Names* 22, *A[lisma] Plantago-Aquatica. . .* Deil's-spoons. **1931** Clute *Common Plants* 85, The devil's spoons are the oblong leaves of the harmless water plantain *(Alisma plantago-aquatica).* **1936** Winter *Plants NE* 6, *A[lisma] subcordatum. . .* Called also . . Devil's-spoons. **1959** Carleton *Index Herb. Plants* 36, *Deil's spoons:* Alisma plantago-aquatica. **1974** (1977) Coon *Useful Plants* 51, *Alisma plantago-aquatica* . . devil-spoons. . . Here the words "mad" or "devil" indicate a poisonous nature, which some books say it has when uncooked.

devil's stick See **devil's walkingstick 4**

devil's strip n Also *devil strip* [Prob from its being a sort of no-man's-land between public and private property; cf **devil's lane**] **chiefly neOH**

The strip of grass and trees between sidewalk and curb.

1957 *AmSp* 32.239 **neOH,** It [=a car] went out of control and jumped the curb, traveling partly on the road and partly on the devil strip. . . [The term] is known throughout the Youngstown, Ohio, area. **1964** *AmSp* 39.293 **neOH,** The Akron term [for the strip of grass or weeds between the sidewalk and the curb] is *Devil strip* or *Devil's strip.* There are a few, however, who think it vulgar or profane (although they recognize it), and to them it is the *berm.* **1966** *DARE* (Qu. N44) Inf **SC**2, Devil strip. [FW: She [=the Inf] never used it; heard it in Hartsville about 30 miles away. It's supposed to keep the devil out of your house.] **1966** *DARE* File **neOH,** The "parking" or the "boulevard" is known as the "devil's strip" from Cleveland to Youngstown. **1968** *DARE* FW Addit

csOH, *Devil strip.* The strip of grass and trees between the sidewalk and the curb. **1980** *Today Show Letters* **neOH,** The area between the sidewalk and the street usually called the tree lawn is called the "devil strip" in Akron. The reason for this designation was explained to me as a child. . . At some time a battle between a property owner and the city ensued over who should take care of the tree lawn area. (The home-owner's lot stops at the sidewalk and the tree lawn area is city property.) It went to court and the judge ruling in frustration said: "If it's not the city's upkeep and not the owner's upkeep then it must belong to the devil"— hence "devil strip." **1982** *Smithsonian Letters* **neOH,** One term that was common parlance in Akron appears to be a relatively narrow usage: What do you call the narrow strip of grass between the sidewalk and the street? We grew up calling it the 'devil strip', and all our friends and neighbors used the same term.

devil's tar n

Oil.

1949 *AmSp* 24.34 **OK, TX** [Language of the oil fields], *Black gold, crude, crude oil, Devil's tar* . . are synonyms [for oil]. **1958** *AmSp* 33.304 **csKY** (as of 1818), In 1818 David Beatty, drilling for salt water in Wayne County, Kentucky, struck oil instead. . . Beatty and his neighbors immediately dubbed the noxious liquid *devil's tar.*

devil's tether n [*EDD* (at *devil* sb. 2)]

=**black bindweed.**

1900 Lyons *Plant Names* 300, *P[olygonum] Convolvulus.* . . Devil's-tether. **1931** Clute *Common Plants* 83, The devil's tether *(Polygonum convolvulus)* . . is otherwise known as climbing buckwheat. So weak and slender a vine is much too weak to bind the devil and, if used as a tether, it is small wonder that he is so often found at large.

devil's thistle n [**devil n B1a**]

=**tick trefoil.**

1898 *Jrl. Amer. Folkl.* 11.225 **ME,** *Desmodium Canadensis* . . devil's thistle.

devil's thorn n [**devil n B1a**]

Appar =**beggar ticks 1.**

1967 *DARE* (Qu. S14, *Other prickly seeds, small and flat, with two prongs at one end, that cling to clothing*) Infs **CA**7, **NY**28, Devil's thorn(s).

devil's thorn-needle n [**devil n B1b**]

A **walkingstick.**

1969 *DARE* (Qu. R9a, *An insect from two to four inches long that lives in bushes and looks like a dead twig*) Inf **KY**47, Devil's thorn-needle.

devil's thread n

1 A **virgin's bower** (here: *Clematis virginiana*). Cf **devil's-hair 1**

1940 Clute *Amer. Plant Names* 2, *Clematis virginiana.* . . Devil's thread.

2 A **yucca** (here: *Yucca gloriosa*). [Cf **bear's thread**]

1978 in 1982 *Barrick Coll.* **csPA,** *Devil's thread*—Yucca gloriosa.

devil's tick n [**devil n B1a**]

A **stickseed.**

1969 *DARE* (Qu. S15) Inf **IL**44, Devil's ticks—little tiny round balls, early in summer—end of June, early July; almost impossible to get out of clothes or animal's hair.

devil-sticks intj

1903 *DN* 2.296 **Cape Cod MA** (as of a1857), *Divle-sticks.* . . Exclamation of contempt, evidently a corruption for *fiddle-sticks.*

devil's tobacco n [**devil n B1a**]

1 A **bearberry 2** (here: *Arctostaphylos uva-ursi*).

1951 *PADS* 15.18, *Arctostaphylos uva-ursi.* . . Devil's tobacco.

2 A **skunk cabbage** (here: *Symplocarpus foetidus*).

1967 Borland *Hill Country* 156 **cwCT,** Looking up botanical information about skunk cabbage, I found that among other common names for the plant is . . devil's tobacco. . . Devil's tobacco is also the colloquial name for two other wholly unrelated plants, false hellebore and giant mullein. **1970** *Living Museum* 31.180, Known by such descriptive epithets as swamp cabbage, parson-in-a-pillory, polecatweed, and devil's tobacco, the skunk cabbage, a relative of jack-in-the-pulpit, ushers in the growing season.

3 A **mullein** (here: *Verbascum thapsus*).

1967 [see **2** above].

4 A **false hellebore 1.**

1967 [see **2** above].

devil's-tongue n Also *devil('s) cactus, devil's cholla* [**devil n B1a**]

=**prickly pear.**

1892 *Jrl. Amer. Folkl.* 5.96, *Opuntia Rafinesque,* or *O. vulgaris.* Devil's tongue. N. Ohio. **1900** Lyons *Plant Names* 266, *Opuntia opuntia* . . Devil's-tongue. **1903** *Condor* 5.132, The nest was . . woven among the branches of the "cholla" or "devil cactus" so common in Southern California. **1931** Clute *Common Plants* 82, The devil's tongue . . is the prickly pear *(Opuntia)* whose flat spiny joints are sufficiently devilish to justify the name. **1933** Small *Manual SE Flora* 899, *Opuntia* . . Devil's-tongues. **1940** Benson *Cacti AZ* 44, *Stanly cholla* or *devil cholla.* . . Spines . . ½ to 2 inches long, . . fruit markedly spiny. **1941** *Torreya* 41.50, *Opuntia* spp. . . Cholla . . A cholla in southern California is called "devil cactus". **1949** Moldenke *Amer. Wild Flowers* 102, The *western pricklypear* or *devilstongue, O[puntia] humifusa,* . . has . . many, small, brownish bristles, which when they penetrate the skin are very painful. **1959** Munz-Keck *CA Flora* 313, *O[puntia] parishii* . . Devil's Cactus.

devil stool n [**devil n B1a**]

A toadstool.

1967 *DARE* (Qu. I38) Inf **TX**42, Devil stools.

devil's-tooth n [**devil n B1a**]

=**beggar ticks 1.**

1967 *DARE* (Qu. S14, *Other prickly seeds, small and flat, with two prongs at one end, that cling to clothing*) Inf **PA**26, Devil's-tooth.

devil's tremors n

1969 *DARE* (Qu. DD22, . . *Delirium tremens*) Inf **VT**12, Devil's tremors.

devil strip See **devil's strip**

devil's trumpet n [**devil n B1a**] Cf **angel's-trumpet 1**

A **jimson weed,** usu *Datura stramonium* but also *D. meteloides.*

1889 (1971) Farmer *Americanisms* 20, *Datura stramonium.* . . is also called the *devil's trumpet.* **1900** Lyons *Plant Names* 132, *D. Stramonium.* . . Devil's-trumpet. **1930** Sievers *Amer. Med. Plants* 38, *Jimson Weed.* . . *Other common names.* . . Devil's-trumpet. **1951** *PADS* 15.39 **TX,** *Datura meteloides.* . . Devil's trumpet. **1974** (1977) Coon *Useful Plants* 249, Devil's trumpet. . . A very widely spread, ill-scented weed.

devil's umbrella n [**devil n B1a**]

A fungus with an umbrella-shaped cap.

1892 *Jrl. Amer. Folkl.* 5.105, *Hymenomycetes* (any umbrella-shaped species), devil's umbrellas. Baltimore, Md. **1977** *DARE* (Qq. I37, 38) Inf **PA**77, Devil's umbrella.

devil's urn n

An urn fungus (here: *Urnula craterium*).

1981 Lincoff *Audubon Field Guide Mushrooms* 342, *Devil's Urn.* . . This is one of the first mushrooms to appear in spring in the East. **1987** McKnight-McKnight *Mushrooms* 36, *Devil's Urn.* . . Medium-sized, *brownish black to gray, goblet-shaped cup* with a *thin margin.* . . Midwest to Southeast. . . Inedible.

devil's vine See **devil vine**

devil's walkingstick n

1 =**tree of heaven.**

1900 Lyons *Plant Names* 20, A[ilanthus] glandulosa. . . Devil's-walkingstick. **1911** *Century Dict. Suppl., Devil's-walking-stick.* . . The ailantus [sic] tree, *Ailanthus glandulosa.* **1960** Vines *Trees SW* 600, Tree-of-heaven. . . Vernacular names for the tree are . . False Varnish-tree, and Devil's Walkingstick.

2 =**Hercules'-club 1.**

1910 Graves *Flowering Plants* 296 **CT,** *Aralia spinosa.* . . Devil's Walking-stick. **1926** *Torreya* 26.6, *Aralia spinosa.* . . Devil's walking-stick, Sapelo I[slan]d, Ga. **1942** Tehon *Fieldbook IL Shrubs* 211, The Devil's-Walkingstick . . is a large, erect shrub . . with . . many strong, straight, or curved spines, which are located mostly at the nodes. **1960** Vines *Trees SW* 792, *Devil's Walkingstick.* . . It is reported that the bark, roots, and berries are occasionally used in medicine. **1972** in 1983 Johnson *I Declare* 115 **nnFL,** Common in our woods and hedgerows is the *Aralia spinosa* . . , but if you ever grab one to save yourself from stumbling you'll never forget to call it "devil's walkingstick." **1974** Morton *Folk Remedies* 29 **SC,** *Devil's Walking Stick*. . . Many erect, straight, unbranched, spiny stems.

3 =**ginseng B1.**

1937 *Hall Coll.* **eTN,** Ginseng. . . Another common name is Devil's Walkingstick.

4 also *devil's stick:* A **walkingstick. [devil n B1b]**

1954 *PADS* 21.25 **SC,** *Devil's walking stick*. . . A stick insect, the *diapheromera femorata.* **1965–70** *DARE* (Qu. R9a, *An insect from two to four inches long that lives in bushes and looks like a dead twig*) 44 Infs, **scattered, but esp freq Midl,** Devil's walkingstick; **IL**138, Devil's stick.

devil's wand n **[devil n B1a]**

=**sugarstick.**

1934 Haskin *Wild Flowers Pacific Coast* 245, One of the most showy of the saprophytes found growing in our deep forests is the striped . . devil's wand. . . [which] resembles nothing so much as a brightly striped stick of candy.

devil's watermelon n **[devil n B1a]**

A **cockleburr 1.**

1967 *DARE* (Qu. S13, *There's a common wild bush with bunches of round, prickly seeds; when they get dry they stick to your clothing*) Inf **NE**3, Devil's watermelon.

devil's-weed n Also *devil-weed* **[devil n B1a]**

1 Appar =**scarlet pimpernel.**

1731 J. Seccomb *Father Abbey's Will* x *(DA),* Some Devil's Weed, And Burdock Seed, To season well your Porridge. **1877** VT State Bd. Ag. *Report* 4.138, The pimpernel . . in some States grows in old fields, and among grain, where I have heard it called "devil weed."

2 Any of several composite plants, as:

a A **wild lettuce** (here: *Lactuca canadensis*).

1894 *Jrl. Amer. Folkl.* 7.92, *Lactuca Canadensis* . . Devil's weed, West Va. **1911** *Century Dict. Suppl., Devil's-weed.* **1940** Clute *Amer. Plant Names* 70, *L. Canadensis*. . . Devil's-weed. **1959** Carleton *Index Herb. Plants* 37, *Devil's-weed:* Lactuca canadensis.

b An aster (here: either *Aster lateriflorus* or *A. spinosus*).

1894 *Jrl. Amer. Folkl.* 7.91, *Aster diffusus* . . devil-weed . . West Va. **1960** Vines *Trees SW* 1012, *Devil-weed Aster. Aster spinosus*. . . The species name, *spinosus,* refers to the soft spines.

c A **hawkweed** (here: *Hieracium* spp).

1895 U.S. Dept. Ag. *Farmers' Bulletin* 28.25, Devil's weed . . Hieracium præaltum. **1914** Georgia *Manual Weeds* 554, *Hieracium aurantiacum*. . . Devil's Weed. **1966–68** *DARE* (Qu. S21) Inf **NY**88, Devil-weed—a little weed that spreads by seeds—has a little yellow flower; **NC**6, Devil-weed; **PA**200, Pest weed—other name is devil-weed; **VA**15, Devil-weed.

d A **marsh elder** (here: *Iva axillaris*).

1935 (1943) Muenscher *Weeds* 505, *Iva axillaris*. . . Devils-weed.

3 =**bagpod.**

1901 *Torreya* 1.116 **GA,** *Glottidium vesicarium*. . . Devil-weed. Sumter.

4 A **heliotrope 1** (here: *Heliotropium curassavicum*).

1935 (1943) Muenscher *Weeds* 382, *Heliotropium curassavicum*. . . Devil-weed. . . Widespread from Delaware southward and westward to the Pacific Coast.

5 A **pennycress** (here: *Thlaspi arvense*).

1937 U.S. Forest Serv. *Range Plant Hdbk.* W187, Field pennycress . . known locally as devilweed . . formerly was a popular substitute for mustard.

6 A **wild carrot** (here: *Daucus carota*).

1951 Voss–Eifert *IL Wild Flowers* 167, Wild carrot . . is a pest when it gets into crop fields, and is then vigorously called devil's weed by farmers who find it difficult to eradicate.

devil's wood n

1911 (1913) Johnson *Highways Gt. Lakes* 264 **neWI,** You'll strike lots of Catholic lumber-jacks who won't have anything to do with cutting a popple tree. . . There's a tradition that the cross on which Christ was crucified was of popple, and they say the wood is cursed on that account. They call it the 'devil's wood,' . . and tell you to notice that the leaves never stand still whether the wind blows or not.

devil to pay and no pitch hot See **hell to pay and no pitch hot**

deviltry n Pronc-sp *diviltry* **chiefly Nth**

=**devilment.**

1788 *Thomas' MA Spy or Worcester Gaz.* (MA) 28 Aug 1/3, His shoes . . were made of the leather of hypocrisy, tanned with the bark of presumption, and curried in the shop of deviltry. **1828** Cooper *Prairie* 2.3, The imps [=Indians] will lie for hours . . brooding their deviltries. **1899** (1912) Green *VA Folk-Speech* 146, *Deviltry*. . . Diabolical action; malicious mischief. **1904** *DN* 2.425 **Cape Cod MA** (as of a1857), *Diviltry*. . . Mischief. **1965–70** *DARE* (Qu. GG32a, *To habitually play tricks or jokes on people: "He's always ______."*) 13 Infs, **chiefly Nth,** Up to some deviltry. **1968** *DARE* Tape **MI**96, You didn't have to worry about who people were around you at that time. Very seldom, you found anything that was too much outa the way. Accidents yes, but not real deviltry like you're having later here.

devil up See **devil** v **1**

devil vine n Also *devil's vine*

A plant of the family Convolvulaceae; see quots.

1914 Georgia *Manual Weeds* 323, *Convolvulus sepium*. . . Devil's Vine. . . The trailing or twining stems are three to ten feet or more in length. **1931** Clute *Common Plants* 86, The hedge bindweed *(Convolvulus sepium),* otherwise the devil's vine. **1951** *PADS* 15.38 **TX,** *Cuscutaceae*. . . Devil vine.

devil-weed See **devil's-weed**

devilwood n **[devil n B1a;** see quot 1832]

An evergreen tree *(Osmanthus americanus)* native to the southeastern US. Also called **wild olive**

1832 Browne *Sylva* 225, The wood . . when perfectly dry is excessively hard and very difficult to cut and split: hence is derived the name of Devil Wood. **1884** Sargent *Forests of N. Amer.* 113, *Devil Wood*. . . Wood heavy, very hard and strong, close-grained, unwedgeable, difficult to work. **1901** Lounsberry *S. Wild Flowers* 423, *Devil-wood*. . . has brought upon itself its rather forcible common name through the difficulty which is found in splitting its wood. **1938** Van Dersal *Native Woody Plants* 175, *Devilwood*. . . Usually a large shrub to small tree or rarely a large tree. **1960** Vines *Trees SW* 859. **1976** Bailey–Bailey *Hortus Third* 802, *Devilwood*. . . N.C. to Fla. and Miss.

devise v [*OED devise* v. 13 →c1570] *relic*

1952 Brown *NC Folkl.* 1.533, *Devise*. . . To tell, to narrate.

dew n Usu |du|; also **Sth, S Midl, occas NEng** |dju|; also **Sth** *esp freq among Black speakers* |ju| Pronc-spp, *doo, jew* **Cf due** and Pronc Intro 3.I.10

Std senses, var forms.

1888 Jones *Negro Myths* 41 **GA coast** [Gullah], Buh Rooster blan wake Buh Elephant duh mornin, so eh kin hunt eh bittle befo de jew dry. **1893** Shands *MS Speech* 40, *Jew* [ju]. Negro for *dew.* **1899** (1912) Green *VA Folk-Speech* 244, *Jew*. . . For *dew,* and *due.* **1905** Culbertson *Banjo Talks* 138 **SE** [Black], Befo' de jew 'gins fallin'. **1922** (1926) Kephart *Highlanders* 353 **sAppalachians,** Some words that most Americans mispronounce are always sounded correctly in the southern highlands, as dew and new (never doo, noo). **1927** Shewmake *Engl. Pronc. VA* 27, *Dew* . . diu. **1930** Stoney–Shelby *Black Genesis* 90 **seSC** [Black], Meet me in dis same place soon as de jew dry up offn de grass nex' Saturday. **1934** (1970) Wilson *Backwoods Amer.* 69 **Ozarks,** The southern mountaineer can consistently be depended upon to say *dew* and not *doo.* **1939** *LANE* Maps 242, 274, [Scattered instances of [du(w)], [dɪu], and [dju] occur]. **1941** O'Donnell *Great Big Doorstep* 11 **sLA,** A bole [=bold] bumble-bee roaming o'er the lea / Met a sweet clover blossom wet with jew. **1941** *AmSp* 16.7 **eTX** [Black], [ju] . . [is the vowel in] *dew, due.*

dew v See **do** v **A1**

dewater berry n

A **cloudberry** (here: *Rubus chamaemorus*).

1942 *Torreya* 42.160, *Rubus chamaemorus*. . . Dewater berry.

dew-bell n

A **mariposa lily** (here: *Calochortus albus*).

1891 Victor *Atlantis Arisen* 226 **NW,** Bending over springs may be found the lady's-ear-drop (Delphinium nudicaule), red; and the dainty dew-bell (Cyclobothra alba).

dewberry n Pronc-sp *jewberry* **chiefly Sth, Midl** See Map

1 Any of var more or less trailing plants of the genus *Rubus;* see quot 1976. Also called **running blackberry**

1709 (1967) Lawson *New Voyage* 105 **NC, SC,** Our Dew-Berries are very good. But the Black-Berries are bitterish, and not so palatable, as in England. **1785** Marshall *Arbustrum* 137, *Rubus hispidus.* American Dewberry Bush. **1899** Garland *Boy Life* 123 **nwIA,** All things not positively poisonous were eaten [by parties of boys on horseback], or at least tasted. The roots of ferns, black haws, . . clams, dewberries, May-apples—anything at all that happened to be in season or handy. **1912** Cobb *Back Home* 20, In the dewberry patch . . down by the creek the meadow larks strutted in buff and yellow. **1945** Saxon *Gumbo Ya-Ya* 29 **LA,** Cries of 'Jewberry, Lady! Nice jewberries!' may be heard. **1950** *WELS* 9 Infs, **WI,** Dewberries. **c1960** *Wilson Coll.* **csKY,** *Dewberry. . .* A trailing species of blackberry, with very luscious fruit; never as common as the tall species *(Rubus flugellaris).* **1965–70** *DARE* (Qu. I44) 289 Infs, **chiefly Sth, Midl,** Dewberries; **FL**33, **LA**33, **MS**63, **OH**38, **SC**32, Jewberries; (Qu. I46) Infs **GA**9, 28, Dewberries; (Qu. I53) Inf **WA**13, Dewberries; (Qu. H63) Infs **LA**19, **TX**62, Dewberry cobbler; (Qu. H66a) Inf **TX**85, Dewberry sauce; (Qu. DD28b) Infs **NC**54, **VA**43, Dewberry wine. **1976** Bailey–Bailey *Hortus Third* 376, *Dewberry.* Trailing blackberries of the genus *Rubus* are frequently called dewberries. . . They are characterized by canes that trail on the ground and in cultivation are not self-supporting but must be tied to poles or a trellis, and whose fruit clusters ripen earlier and are smaller or more open than those of the erect blackberry types. Dewberries belong to such species as *Rubus flagellaris, R. macropetalus, R. mirus, R. ursinus,* and *R. vitifolius.* **1979** *Greenfield Recorder* (MA) 22 Sept sec A 4/2, So many of those old graveyards have weeds, short sparse grass, maybe some checkerberries and dew berries.

2 =**lowbush blueberry.**

1976 in 1982 *Barrick Coll.* **csPA,** *Dewberries*—low-bush huckleberries that mature earlier and have a mushier flesh than others; so named from frosty appearance.

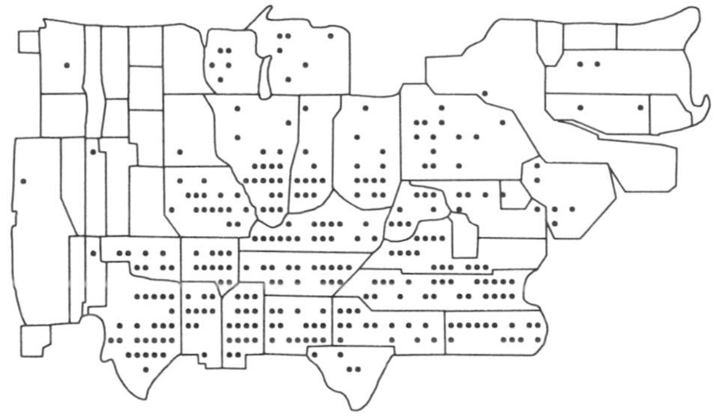

•dewberry + varr (Qq. I44, H63, H66a, I46, I53, DD28b

dew boil See **dew sore**

dewby n [Var of **dewberry**]

A **dewberry** cobbler.

1966 *DARE* (Qu. H63, . . *Desserts especially favored . . around here*) Inf **FL**8, Dewbies ['dubiz]—a deep dish pie with berries (special black [berries]). **1966** *DARE* Tape **FL**41, I have a patch of brierberries, you call 'em dewberries. . . You boil your berries. Some people like to leave the berries in but I takes my berries out; I strain it and just use the juice. Then you can make your cake dewby or . . plain bread dewby. . . You make it up like you're gonna make up biscuits, you see, jus' roll 'em in that juice. . . And sometimes you have whipped cream on it.

dew catcher See **dew web**

dewclaws n Pronc-sp *jew claw* [Transf from *dewclaw* a vestigial digit in some mammals]

1 See quot.

1909 *DN* 3.410 **ME,** *Dew claws* . . The new growth of claws of an animal which is supposed to shed its claws periodically. They are supposed to be particularly sharp. The term is used figuratively with reference to persons, as, "That hill is so steep you have to stick your dew claws in to get up."

2 Fig in var phrr referring to people: see quots.

1892 *KS Univ. Qrly.* 1.96 **KS,** *Dew-claws:* Hands and knees (?) as in, Get down on your d. = apply yourself intensely. **1909** [see **1** above]. **1933** Rawlings *South Moon* 81 **nFL,** Don't you go to rarin' back on your dew-claws! **c1935** *McDavid Coll.* **neGA,** Jew claws—'haunches.' **1944** *PADS* 2.18 **sAppalachians,** *Dew-claws. . .* Claws, feet. "Jud rared [=reared] back on his *dew-claws* and struck at Lonzo." **1961** Adams *Old-Time Cowhand* 87 **West,** One of 'em started searchin' for the money, and he went clear down the line, friskin' ever' man from forelock to dew-claws without findin' anything but small change.

dew cloud n

1970 *DARE* (Qu. B11, . . *Kinds of clouds*) Inf **VA**77, Dew cloud—a low cloud.

dew crack See **dew sore**

dewdad See **doodad**

dew down v phr [Alter, by hypercorrection, of *jew down* to haggle a seller for a lower price; cf pronc-sp *jew* at **dew** n]

1965–70 *DARE* (Qu. U12, *If you were buying something and you argued with the person selling it till you made him lower the price, you might say, "I ______ ."*) Inf **LA**25, Dewed him down ['dud ɪm daʊn]. [Inf:] How would you write that? *d-u-e-d?* **MS**59, Dewed him down.

dewdrop n [See quot 1948]

A perennial plant *(Dalibarda repens)* with violetlike leaves and white flowers. Also called **robin-run-away, spice root, star violet**

1893 *Jrl. Amer. Folkl.* 6.141, *Dalibarda repens,* dew drop. N.Y. **1933** Small *Manual SE Flora* 619, *Dewdrops. Star-violet. . .* Woods, often in acid soil, . . N.C. to Minn. and N.B. **1948** Wherry *Wild Flower Guide* 80, *Dalibarda repens. . .* An alternative name, *Dewdrop,* refers to the pearly buds. **1949** Moldenke *Amer. Wild Flowers* 123, A great favorite in the Northeast is the delicate *dewdrop.*

dewflap See **dewlap** n

dewflower n

1 A **dayflower.**

1903 Small *Flora SE U.S.* 241, *Commelina* . . Dew-flowers. **1932** Rydberg *Flora Prairies* 200, *Commelina* . . Dew-flower.

2 A **beardtongue** (here: *Penstemon cobaea*).

1959 Carleton *Index Herb. Plants* 37, Dew-flower: *Penstemon cobaea.*

dew-hoof n Pronc-sp *jew-huff* [Blend of *dewclaw* + *hoof;* cf prones at **dew** n, **hoof**]

The false hoof, dewclaw.

1906 Casey *Parson's Boys* 135 **sIL** (as of c1860), The dogs were close on it [=a deer], . . barkin' an' snappin', while Leetle Britches [=a hound] was trying to grab it by the jew-huff.

dew itch See **dew poison**

dewlap n, also attrib Also infreq *dewflap, dewlip* [*dewlap* the pendulous skin under the neck of a bovine animal; *OED* c1420 →] **chiefly West**

A strip of skin in the dewlap of a cow cut to hang free as an identifying mark.

1887 *Scribner's Mag.* 2.508/2 **West,** *Dewlap,* a cut in the lower part of the neck. **1908** *DN* 3.304 **eAL, wGA,** *Dewflap. . .* A mark of identification or ownership on cattle, made by cutting a strip of skin on the lower part of the neck just above the breast, so as to allow it to hang loose like a flap. Compare *dewlap.* **1920** Hunter *Trail Drivers TX* 298 **wTX,** A jud [sic] handled "dewlap" is a cut in the fleshy part of the throat, also used sometimes as a mark of distinction. **1940** (1942) Clark *Ox-Bow* 119 **NV** (as of 1885), We all know Drew's dewlap mark. **1961** Adams *Old-Time Cowhand* 264 **West,** The "dewlap" is made on the underside of the neck or brisket [of a cow] by pinchin' up a quantity of skin and cuttin' it all, but not entirely off. When healed it leaves a hangin' flap of skin. Some were slashed up and called "dewlaps up," others slashed down and called "dewlaps down." **1965–70** *DARE* (Qu. K18, . . *Mark . . to identify a cow*) Infs **AR**4, **CA**131, 136, **CO**4, **ID**3, **LA**2, **NM**13, **NV**8, **WA**3, Dewlap; **CA**31, Dewlip [FW: Inf a little unsure].

dewlap v

To cut a **dewlap** n; also fig.

1958 *AmSp* 33.269 **eWA,** *Dewlap.* To cut a strip of the dewlap and allow it to hang down, either to prevent fence-crawling or as a mark of identification. A hole may by pierced in the dewlap and a wire hook inserted, for the same purpose. Both practices are illegal. **1967** *DARE* (Qu. K18) Inf **SC**43, Dewlap them. **1971** Adams *Cowman* 70, You're wastin' a lot of good time dewlappin' yourself with that dull razor. That roan out in the corral will buck them whiskers off.

dewlip See **dewlap** n

dew pizen See **dew poison**

dew plant n

=**sundew,** esp *Drosera rotundifolia.*

1900 Lyons *Plant Names* 140, *D. rotundifolia. . .* Dew-plant. **1910** Graves *Flowering Plants* 213 **CT,** *Drosera rotundifolia. . .* Dew-plant. . . *Drosera longifolia. . .* Dew-plant. **1933** Small *Manual SE Flora* 579, *D. rotundifolia. . .* Dew-plant. Roundleaf sundew. **1959** Munz-Keck *CA Flora* 138, *Drosera* L. *Sundew.* Dew Plant.

dew poison n Also *dew itch, ~ poisoning* Pronc-sp *dew pizen* **chiefly S Midl, esp sAppalachians** Cf **dew sore**

Any of various rashes or infections of the feet or legs, believed to be caused by dew; the presumed agent causing such rashes or infections; rarely, a foot disease of cattle.

1912 Cobb *Back Home* 110 **KY,** He couldn't even go barefooted in summer, because if he did his legs would be broken out all over with dew poison. **1922** (1926) Kephart *Highlanders* 303 **sAppalachians,** "Dew pizen," presumably the poison of some weed, which, dissolved in dew, enters the blood through a scratch or abrasion. As a woman described it, "Dew pizen comes like a risin', and laws-a-marcy how it does hurt! . . My leg swelled up black to clar above the knee. . . I lay on a pallet on the floor for over a month. . . I've seed persons jest a lot o' sores all over, as big as my hand, from dew pizen." **1946** *PADS* 6.11 **eNC,** *Dew poison. . .* Sores on the feet, usually between the toes; caused by parasitic mites. Among bare-footed boys. . . Common. **1954** *PADS* 21.25 **SC,** *Dew poison* [dɪu, dʒu-] . . Ringworm on the feet, especially on the toes; athlete's foot; an infection caused by hookworm. Upcountry. In the Pee Dee this is called *foot itch.* **1960** Hall *Smoky Mt. Folks* 50 **eTN, wNC,** St. John weeds wet with dew . . will cause "sores and risin's" ("dew poisoning") on the skin. **c1960** *Wilson Coll.* **csKY,** *Dew poison. . .* Ringworm on the feet. Some cases may be hookworm. Also called ground-itch (eetch) or toe-itch. **1966-70** *DARE* (Qu. BB25, . . *Common skin diseases*) Inf **SC**32, Dew itch; **KY**34, Dew poison; **SC**3, Dew poisoning; (Qu. K28, . . *Diseases that cows have*) Inf **KY**86, Dew poison—same as foot or hoof rot. **c1974** Jones *Ozark Hill Boy* 10 **AR** (as of c1920), We went barefooted all summer and our stumped toes were too sore to bear shoes until almost Christmas. . . We always expected to have cold frost-bitten toes, blistered with dew poison before the first snow fell.

dew sore n Also *dew boil, ~ crack* Cf **dew poison**

A sore or rash on the feet or legs attributed to dew.

1884 Baldwin *Yankee School-Teacher* 92 **VA** [Black], It's so cur'us . . that the wet grass should make dew-boils on bare feet. **1958** *KY Folkl. Rec.* 4.101 **csKY,** My earliest memory of folk medicine begins with a wool string which was saturated with grease and tied around my toe for "dew crack." **1981** Mebane *Mary* 19 **cnNC,** My legs already had two of the biggest dew sores in the crowd [of children]. . . (Dew sores were tiny scratches or insect bites that were aggravated if early-morning dew got into them. The dew would keep any sore fresh and could make a new one out of the tiniest scratch.) **1981** *DARE* File **ceKY** (as of c1930), From the old notion that dew and night air can be poisonous (actually caused by walking barefoot on sawgrass or otherwise cutting the legs and starting an infection). . . "The jewelweed was good to cure dew sores."

dew tell See **do tell**

dew web n Also *dew catcher*

A spider web in the grass upon which dew has fallen.

c1950 *Atlas Checklists* **swWI,** *Dew web,* spider web outdoors. **1968-69** *DARE* (Qu. R29b, *What the spider spins—if it is outdoors*) Inf **CT**6, Dew web—on the grass in the morning; **GA**72, Dew catchers—in fall.

dew worm n [Prob from CanEngl (*DCan* 1889 →), ult from OE (*OED* c1000 →)] **chiefly Gt Lakes** See Map

=**earthworm.**

1943 *LANE* Map 236 **csVT,** Dew worm found in the morning. **1950** *WELS (Common worm used for bait)* 1 Inf, **cnWI,** Dew worm. **1951** *AmSp* 26.255, The evidence for Upstate [NY] borrowings from Canada is much easier to assay. . . New York State occurrences of. . *dew worm* . . are found predominantly in communities near the border, where it is reasonable to suspect Canadian influence. **1965-70** *DARE* (Qu. P5, . . *The common worm used as bait*) 11 Infs, **scattered Gt Lakes,** Dew worm; (Qu. P6, *Other kinds of worms also used as bait*) 13 Infs, **scattered Gt Lakes,** Dew worm. **1973** Allen *LAUM* 1.326 (as of c1950), *Earthworm. . . Dew worm,* not reported in New England or along the Atlantic coast, is considered an innovation by two of the three Duluth infs. using it. *Ibid,* In the data from 1,045 mail respondents[:] *Dew worm* . . turns up not only in Minnesota near the Canadian border . . but also six times in Iowa in both Northern and Midland speech territory. **1982** Sternberg *Fishing* 56, Sometimes called the *dew* or *rain worm,* the native nightcrawler appears on roads and sidewalks after spring rains. Average length is 6 to 7 inches, but some are 10 inches or longer. Its color varies from brownish-pink to purplish-red.

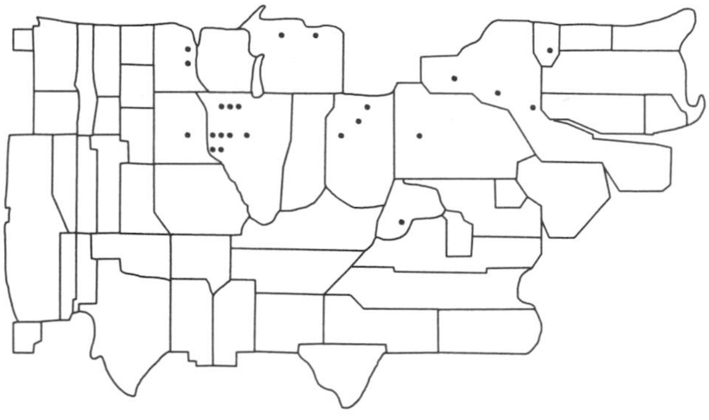

•dew worm (Qq. P5, P6)

dey pron[1] See **they**

dey pron[2] See **there**

dey adj See **their**

dey-dey See **deh**

d.g. road n [Abbr for *decomposed granite*]

1968 *DARE* (Qu. N27a, . . *Kinds of unpaved roads*) Inf **CA**80, Decomposed granite or d.g. road; **CA**86, Decomposed granite—the first covering, not dusty or slippery, a d.g. road.

diabetes weed n

A **crownbeard** (here: *Verbesina helianthoides*).

1940 Clute *Amer. Plant Names* 233, *Verbesina helianthoides* . . diabetes weed.

diacumbelicum n [Fanciful pseudo-Lat formation] Cf *DS* BB19

1908 *DN* 3.304 **eAL, wGA,** *Diacumbelicum. . .* Bowel trouble, diarrhoea. Facetious.

diagnus adv Cf *DS* MM16

Diagonally.

1970 Tarpley *Blinky* 272 **neTX,** *To go from one corner of a field to another is to walk* ______. [Among the "other responses":] Go diagnus.

diamond n Usu |ˈdaɪ(ə)mənd|; also **esp S Midl** |ˈdaɪmən(t), -mɪnt| Pronc-spp *di(a)ment, diamont, dimind, dimunt*

A Forms.

1843 (1916) Hall *New Purchase* 114 **IN,** Rite hand corner, grazin the dimind! **1902** *DN* 2.232 **sIL,** *Diamond-plow* ([daɪmən] or [daɪmənt]). **1903** *DN* 2.311 **seMO,** *Diamond. . .* Pronounced diament. 'You had better use the diment-plow.' **1906** *DN* 3.117 **sIN,** *Diamont.* Pronunciation of *diamond.* **1907** *DN* 3.221 **nwAR,** *Diamond. . .* Pronounced [daɪmənt]. **1923** (1946) Greer-Petrie *Angeline Doin' Society* 19 **csKY,** She had dimunts on her fingers. **1944** *PADS* 2.18 **sAppalachians,** *Diamont* [ˈdaɪmənt]. *Ibid* 28 **eKY, wNC,** *Diamond* [ˈdɑɪmənt]. **c1960** *Wilson Coll.* **csKY,** *Diamond* is /ˈdaɪmənd/ to the younger generation but /ˈdaɪmənt/ to the older ones. **1967** *DARE* (Qu. L18) Inf **MO**8, Diamond [ˈdɑɪmɪnt] plow. **1967** *DARE* FW Addit **cwAR,** [ˈdaɪmənts].

B Senses.

1 A town square; see quot 1977. [See quot 1984] **PA**

1829 Royall *Pennsylvania* 2.55 *(DAE),* In all the towns of Pennsylvania, of any size, the public buildings and offices are built on squares, in the centre of their towns. . . These squares are uniformly called 'The Diamond.' **1877** in 1977 *Geogr. Rev.* 67.140 **csPA,** [Caption:] The Diamond looking east showing the proposed New Fountain & Soldiers Monument. **1888** Gossler *Turnpike-Road* 30 **PA,** Like all interior towns in Pennsylvania, the public buildings—the Court-house and the market-house—stood in the "Diamond," an open space in the centre of the town. **1977** *Geogr. Rev.* 67.136 **cs, sePA,** The diamond, as it is called locally, is an open space consisting of the right-angle intersection of two streets at or near the most functionally central point of a town, along with rectangular corners cut out from the four adjoining blocks. In its fully developed form it is square in shape, but frequently the diamond is elongated. **1981** *NADS Letters,* "Diamond" instead of "square" or "common" . . is a term which seems to have followed the Irish and Irish-Scots to the western Pennsylvania or "tri-state" area. . . I understand that it is much in use in northern Ireland. Pittsburgh, of course, has its "diamond"—the square around the old city market. It is, in reality, a square—but it has always been called "the diamond", and the street leading from it is Diamond Street. **1984** *AmSp* 59.320, *Diamond. . .* Town square—A feature typical only of Ulster and Pennsylvania. . . It occurs in the Plantation towns [=those settled by English people] of the west of Ulster. . . It is therefore fairly certain to be of English rather than Scottish origin, although its ultimate source has not been traced. . . It was undoubtedly taken to Pennsylvania by the Scotch-Irish.

2 In marble play: a type of "ring" into which marbles are shot.

1934 *Hanley Disks* **seCT,** If we got in to the diamond we had a chance to clean the diamond.

3 See **diamond hitch.**

4 See **diamondback rattlesnake.**

diamondback n

1 See **diamondback rattlesnake.**

2 See **diamondback terrapin.**

diamond-backed in combs See **diamondback** entries

diamondback moccasin See **diamondback water snake**

diamondback rattlesnake n Also *diamond (rattler), diamond (rattle)snake, diamondback (rattler), diamond-backed rattlesnake*

A **rattlesnake** (here: *Crotalus adamanteus, C. atrox, C. ruber,* or *C. scutulatus*) with diamond-shaped markings on the back. For other names of var spp see **black-diamond rattler, coontail rattler, Mojave rattlesnake, spitting rattlesnake, Texas rattlesnake**

1861 *New Amer. Cyclop.* 23.773/1 **S Atl,** The diamond or water rattlesnake . . dark brown or dusky above, with a series of large rhomboidal spots continuous from head to tail. **1873** Beadle *Undeveloped West* 231 **KS,** One farmer told us of a diamond snake biting his horse so badly that the animal fell dead. **1894** Cable *J. March* xxvii *(DAE),* Di'mon'-back rattlesnake hisself cayn't no mo' scare me 'n if I was a hawg. **1894** U.S. Natl. Museum *Proc.* 17.335, In the interior of Florida the diamond-backed rattlesnake is scarce, but not so along the coast and on some of the Florida keys. **1908** Ditmars *Reptile Book* 449 **SC,** The flattened trails of the big Diamond-backs across the dry, sandy roads . . were as straight as the course of a wheel. **1952** Ditmars *N. Amer. Snakes* 246, The Florida Diamond-back Rattler and the Western Diamond-back are the giants of the genus. *Ibid* 247, Western Diamond Rattlesnake, *Crotalus atrox atrox.* *Ibid* 248, Red Diamond Rattlesnake, *Crotalus ruber.* *Ibid* 249, Mohave Diamond Rattlesnake, *Crotalus scutellatus. . .* Compared with the powdery-gray Western Diamond-back, . . the Mohave Diamond Rattler is a clearly definable snake. **1965-70** *DARE* (Qu. P25) 45 Infs, **scattered,** Diamondback; 30 Infs, **scattered,** Diamondback rattler; **CA**130, **MO**27, **NV**8, **NY**93, **ND**1, **TX**52, Diamondback rattlesnake; **CA**114, **CA**141, **GA**18, **NM**13, **OK**52, **SC**63, **TX**14, Diamond rattler; **OK**18, Diamond rattlesnake; **VA**1, Diamond. **1974** Shaw-Campbell *Snakes West* 219, The western diamondback is characterized by an easily identifiable tail. . . The term "western" is applied to distinguish this snake from the even larger "eastern" diamondback rattlesnake . . found in the Southeast. *Ibid* 220, Except for its redness the red diamond rattlesnake . . looks very much like the western diamondback. *Ibid* 229, Frequently the Mojave rattlesnake . . is called "diamondback," "desert diamond," or "Mojave diamond" rattlesnake.

diamondback terrapin n Also *diamondback (turtle), diamond-backed turkle* [See quot 1972] **chiefly C and S Atl**

A turtle *(Malaclemys terrapin)* with markings on each large scute, flecked or spotted legs and head, found in brackish water.

1877 Bartlett *Americanisms* 699, *Terrapin, (Palustris),* A name given to a species of tide-water tortoise, common in Connecticut and the Atlantic States south of New York, and considered an article of luxury. . . The most celebrated is the *diamond-back.* **1887** *Lippincott's* Sept 456 **MA,** Baltimore. . . the home of the soft-shell crab, the diamond-back terrapin, and the canvas-back duck. **1894** U.S. Natl. Museum *Proc.* 17.319 **FL,** *Malaclemys centrata. . .* The valued diamond-back terrapin is caught in the salt marshes along the east coast. **1906** Gregory *Woman's Cookbook* 86 **MD,** The kind [of terrapin] most in demand is the "diamond-back," or salt-water terrapin, and is never found far from the seacoast. Rarely does their length exceed ten inches, and their weight about eight pounds. *Ibid* 87, *Diamond-Back or Salt-Water Terrapin.* The diamond-back turtle is highly prized for food. **1933** John G. Shedd Aquarium *Guide* 194, Perhaps the most valuable of all the turtles is the *Diamondback Terrapin . .* of our southeastern salt marshes. **1952** Carr *Turtles* 167, Diamondback terrapins are pre-eminently inhabitants of tidal shore waters. . . Although they are able to tolerate fresh water for indefinite periods, I know of no record of the natural occurrence of a diamondback in completely fresh water. **1965-70** *DARE* (Qu. P14) Inf **MD**45, Diamondback terrapin; (Qu. P24, . . *Kinds of turtles*) 12 Infs, **chiefly C and S Atl,** Diamondback; 10 Infs, **chiefly Mid Atl, DE, MD,** Diamondback terrapin; **LA**37, **NC**1, **TX**14, 17, Diamondback turtle; **VA**55, Diamondbacked turkle; (Qu. P29) Inf **FL**24, Diamondback terrapin—good eating. **1972** Ernst-Barbour *Turtles* 107, The scutes are not periodically shed; rather, the layers of new growth push up the older layers so as to give a pyramidal appearance to each scute—hence the name diamondback.

diamondback water snake n Also *diamond-backed water snake, diamond(back) moccasin, diamond water snake*

A water snake *(Natrix rhombifera)* with rhomboid dark spots on the back.

1892 IN Dept. Geol. & Nat. Resources *Rept. for 1891* 509, *Natrix rhombifera. Diamond Water-snake. . .* On the middle of the back there is a series of about 50 squarish brown blotches. **1908** Biol. Soc. DC *Proc.* 21.75 **TX,** *Tropidonotus rhombifer. . . Diamond Water Snake.* This handsomely marked water snake is common in tanks and lagoons. **1928** Baylor Univ. Museum *Contrib.* 16.17 **TX,** *Natrix rhombifera. . .* I have frequently heard this species spoken of as the *Diamond Moccasin* or *Diamond-back Moccasion* [sic]. **1930** *Copeia* 2.35 **OK,** Diamond-back water-snake. Common. Especially found in the Verdigris River bottom lands, ponds, and streams. **1949** Dickinson *Lizards & Snakes WI* 48, *Diamond-back Water Snake. . .* Walworth County. **1958** Conant *Reptiles & Amphibians* 115, *Diamond-backed Water Snake. . .* The light areas on the back may be vaguely diamond-shaped, but the pattern is best described as consisting of dark brown chainlike markings on a ground color of lighter brown or dirty yellow.

diamond cactus n

A **prickly pear** (here: *Opuntia ramosissima*).

1941 Jaeger *Wildflowers* 158, Diamond Cactus . . *Opuntia ramosissima.* **1985** Dodge *Flowers SW Deserts* 65, Diamond Cactus. . . *Opuntia ramosissima.*

diamond cracker n Also *diamond pusher* [Abbr for **black diamond 1**]

Among railroad workers: the fireman on a coal-burning locomotive.

[**1900** in 1953 Botkin-Harlow *Treas. Railroad Folkl.* 314, [The] 'tallow pot' was cracking diamonds in the tank. . . this was translated to mean that. . . the fireman was breaking coal.] **1930** *RR Man's Mag.* June 470/1, *Diamond cracker*—Fireman. **1945** Hubbard *Railroad Ave.* 340, *Diamond cracker* or *diamond pusher*—Locomotive fireman.

diamond cross n

See quot.

1956 Moody *Home Ranch* 229 **CO** (as of 1911), "Reckon you could hold a course to ride diamond crosses?" "I could try," I shouted, "but I don't know what they are." "Light down!" he told me, then took a stick and drew a long straight line in the sand. "That's the wind." Then he drew three or four diamonds straddling it, with their points meeting along the line. "Them's diamonds. You ride this zigzag; I'll ride this one! Keep the wind blowin' your horses' [sic] mane acrost his right ear till you think you've gone a quarter mile, then turn him so's to bring it acrost his left! Go a quarter mile and stand still till I meet you!"

diamond flounder n Also *diamond turbot* [See quot 1933]

A **flounder** n **B** (here: *Hypsopsetta guttulata*) of the California coast.

1882 U.S. Natl. Museum *Bulletin* 16.830, *H[ypsopsetta] guttulata. . . Diamond Flounder. . .* Brown, with numerous pale-bluish blotches in life. **1884** Goode *Fisheries U.S.* 1.185, South of Point Concepcion [in s. Calif.] the name Diamond Flounder is in use. . . As a food-fish it ranks high. **1933** John G. Shedd Aquarium *Guide* 70, The Diamond Flounder *[Hypsopsetta guttulata]* receives its name from the shape of the body. **1953** Roedel *Common Fishes CA* 67, Diamond Turbot—*Hypsopsetta guttulata.* **1973** Knight *Cook's Fish Guide* 381, Flounder . . diamond—Turbot, Diamond.

diamond fold n

1947 (1964) Randolph *Ozark Superstitions* 69, Mrs. May Kennedy McCord, of Springfield, Missouri, says that the old women she knew as a girl were very careful never to make what is called a "diamond fold" in ironing table linen or bed sheets—anything folded "diamond-shaped" is likely to bring bad luck on the entire household.

diamond hitch n Also *diamond* **West**

A diamond-shaped knot used to fasten a pack on an animal.

1869 *New No. West* (Deer Lodge, Mont.) 8 Oct. 2/3 *(DA),* We took certain comprehensive and exhaustive lessons in that packing mystery known as the 'diamond hitch.' **1882** Baillie-Grohman *Camps* 45 **West,** You have at last managed the famous "diamond" or "Kit Carson" hitch to the lash rope. **1904** White *Mountains* 50 **SW,** The Diamond is good because it holds firmly, is a great flattener, and is especially adapted to the securing of square boxes. **1947** *Trail & Timberline* May 77/1 *(DA),* The single diamond is the simplest and most practical tie for this type of load. **1958** McCulloch *Woods Words* 47, *Diamond hitch*—One of the famous hitches used in loading packhorses. It requires expert workmanship and is the mark of a top-notch man at his trade. In sarcasm, the term is used to describe the mess which a green man makes of tieing up a bedroll. **1968** Adams *Western Words* 92, *Diamond hitch*—In packing, a common method of roping a pack on a pack animal; when completed, the rope is interlaced on top of the pack in the figure of a diamond. An ordinary knot is "tied," but a diamond hitch is always "throwed," because a rope of 40 or 50 feet long is thrown back and forth across the animal as the hitch is made.

diamond-leaf oak n [See quot 1962]

=**laurel oak.**

1960 Vines *Trees SW* 181, The lumbering possibilities of Diamond-leaf Oak *[Quercus obtusa]* are minor. **1962** Harrar-Harrar *Guide S. Trees* 224, Diamondleaf oak. . . According to Ashe the leaves of this species [=*Quercus obtusifolia*] tend to taper from the middle toward both apex and base, to form a diamondlike figure. **1979** Little *Checklist U.S. Trees* 234, *Quercus laurifolia* . . laurel oak . . Other common names— . . diamond-leaf oak, . . obtusa oak.

diamond-leaf willow n Cf **diamond willow**

The planeleaf willow *(Salix planifolia).*

1972 Viereck-Little *AK Trees* 118, Diamondleaf Willow (*Salix planifolia* . . ssp *pulchra*) . . *Leaves* elliptic to oblanceolate, pointed at both ends and often diamond-shaped. **1979** Little *Checklist U.S. Trees* 265, *Salix planifolia* . . diamondleaf willow, an erect much branched shrub, rarely a tree 15 ft . . tall in Alaska.

diamond moccasin See **diamondback water snake**

diamond pack n

A pack on which the **diamond hitch** has been used.

1936 Barnard *Rider* 25 **SW,** A diamond pack which held my bedding and supplies was put on him.

diamond plow n **esp Midl**

See quot 1872.

1872 (1876) Knight *Amer. Mech. Dict.* 698, *Diamond-plow.* A small plow having a mold-board and share of a diamond shape; that is, rhomboidal. One side of the rhomb runs level on the ground, another forms the breast, and the other two are the marginal lines of the backward extension of the mold-board. **1902** *DN* 2.232 **sIL,** *Diamond-plow* [daɪmən] or [daɪmənt]. . . The one-horse turning plow, for cultivating crops, being diamond shaped. **1903** *DN* 2.311 **seMO,** You had better use the diment-plow. **1906** *DN* 3.117 **sIN,** *Diamond.* Applies to a plow of a certain make. **1907** *DN* 3.222 **nwAR.** **1967-70** *DARE* (Qu. L18, *Kinds of plows*) Inf **MO**3, Used to use diamond plows (called such because they were shaped like a diamond—the moldboard); **MO**8, Diamond plow ['dɑɪmɪnt]; (Qu. L25) Inf **KY**84, Diamond plow—not a brand name, used for 'barring off,' shaped like a small breaking plow.

diamond pusher See **diamond cracker**

diamond rattler, diamond rattlesnake, diamond snake See **diamondback rattlesnake**

diamond turbot See **diamond flounder**

diamond water snake See **diamondback water snake**

diamond willow n [See quot 1972]

Any of var willows, but esp the Bebb willow *(Salix bebbiana);* see quot 1972.

1884 Sargent *Forests of N. Amer.* 170, *Salix cordata* . . Diamond willow. **1935** Sandoz *Jules* 20 **wNE,** When his fire of diamond willow crackled, he skinned a grouse, and fried it. **1939** FWP *Guide AK* 244, The Indians of this vicinity are noted for . . their carving of the diamond willow; the contrast of the white outer wood with the red inner heart produces an unusual effect. **1961** Douglas *My Wilderness* 120 **neMN,** We used for fuel some dry pussy willow that is locally called diamond willow. It is a reddish wood with diamond-shaped knots—a hard, hard wood that the northerners like to whittle. **1967-68** *DARE* (Qu. T15, . . *Kinds of swamp trees*) Infs **MN**16, **NE**1, Diamond willow. **1972** Viereck-Little *AK Trees* 116, Bebb willow is the most important producer of "diamond willow." This term applies to several species with diamond-shaped patterns on their trunks. . . Diamond willow is carved into canes, lamp posts, furniture and candleholders. . . The depressions or "diamonds" are caused by one or more fungi which attack the willow at the junction of a branch with the main trunk. . . In addition to the Bebb, the following also form "diamonds" although usually to a lesser degree: Park willow, feltleaf willow, littletree willow, and Scouler willow. **1979** Little *Checklist U.S. Trees* 260, *Salix bebbiana* . . Bebb willow . . Other common names—beak willow . . diamond willow.

diamont See **diamond**

diangling adv

See quots.

1914 *DN* 4.105 **KS,** *Diangling.* . . Contamination of *diagonal* and *angle.* "He went diangling across the block." **1923** *DN* 5.205 **swMO,** *Dianglin'.* . . Diagonally.

‡**diaper dragon** n *joc*

1969 *DARE* (Qu. R25, . . *A head louse, or body louse*) Inf **PA**223, Diaper dragons.

diarrhea n Usu |ˌdaɪəˈriə|; also |ˌdaɪ(ə)ˈri|; for addit varr see quots Pronc-sp *diarrhee*

Std sense, var forms.

1891 *DN* 1.157 **cNY,** [daɪəri] < *diarrhoea.* **1907** *DN* 3.186 **seNH,** *Diarrhee.* **1909** *DN* 3.420 **Cape Cod MA** (as of a1857), *Diarrhee.* **1942** Hall *Smoky Mt. Speech* 76 **eTN, wNC,** Diarrhea [ˌdaɪɚˈri·]. **1966** *Wilson Coll.* **csKY,** *Diarrhea* /ˈdaɪəˈriər/. **1966-68** *DARE* (Qu. BB19, . . *Looseness of the bowels*) Inf **PA**104, [diəˈri]; **SC**27, The [ˈdaɪrɪ]—negro; **SD**3, [ˈdaɪrin]; **WI**49, [daɪəˈri].

diasticutis n Also *diasticurious* [Pseudo-Latin formation prob based on *ass* buttocks] *joc*

The buttocks.

1937 (1977) Hurston *Their Eyes* 53 **FL,** Set you down on yo' royal diasticutis. **1966** *DARE* (Qu. X35, *Joking words for the part of the body that you sit on*) Inf **MA**6, Diasticurious [daɪjæstəˈkjuriəs].

dib n[1]

1 See quot. [Prob from *EDD dib* sb.[3] 2, 3 a sheep's knucklebone or pebble used in the game of *dibs*]

1973 Ferretti *Marble Book* 43 **NYC,** *Dibs.* Clay marbles, clayeys.

2 pl; also *dibbies:* A claim; rights; right of priority—often used as exclam. [Perh var of **dubs** exclam infl by **1** above]

1930 *DN* 6.80 **cSC,** *Dibs.* . . "I've got dibs on that" means "I speak for that; it is mine." Common. **1950** *WELS (Calls used in playing marbles. . . To get the right to do something:)* 2 Infs, **WI,** Dibs. **1956** *AmSp* 31.36 **ceMA,** 'I've got dibs on that,' meaning 'That's mine.' **1958** *PADS* 29.32 **WI,** *Dibs.* . . Evidently the same as *dubs;* it gives the right to divide the marbles or to take all the marbles. . . A phon. variant of *dubs* or perhaps from "divide" or "division." **1968-69** *DARE* (Qu. V5b, *If you take something that nobody seems to own, you might say, "Before anybody else gets it, I'm going to ______ this."*) Infs **IL**97, **WI**57, Get dibs on; **KS**10, Put my dibbies on. **1969** *DARE* File **WI,** "You better put your dibs on that" (i.e., put your name on a list to ensure getting a book when it arrives). **c1970** Wiersma *Marbles Terms* **swMI** (as of 1929-32), *Dibs* . . shouted out to signify first shot at the marble. . . "I shoot first 'cause I got first dibs." **1979** McPhee *Giving Good Weight* 168 **NJ,** Tom Cabot says he thinks he'll go through the Big Rapid with John Kauffman. He has the dibs, and rightly so. **1980** *NADS Letters* **NV,** The north and the cow counties get first dibs on that money. **1980** *Capital Times* (Madison WI) 10 Dec 66/4, I don't think any one organization should have 'dibbies' on the dates. **1988** *WI State Jrl.* (Madison) 31 Mar sec 3 1/1, [Headline:] Zoo wants dibs on Alaskan bears [Text:] The Vilas Park Zoo has asked for "first option" on one of two orphaned polar bear cubs.

dib n² Also *dibby, dip* **sAppalachians** Cf **biddy** n³
See quots.
1946 *PADS* 6.11 **swVA, eNC, wSC,** *Dib; dibby* . . A small chicken. . . Occasional. **1952** Brown *NC Folkl.* 1.533, *Dib* . . A little chicken. Piedmont. *Ibid, Dip*. . . A chicken. **1974** Betts-Walser *NC Folkl.* 7, Dibby: a young chicken (Cherryville).

dibbies See **dib** n¹ **2**

dibble n Also redup *dibble-dabble* Cf **dibs and dabs**
A small amount.
1966-67 *DARE* (Qu. LL6b, *A small, indefinite amount*) Inf **MI**9, Dibble; (Qu. LL7, *In small amounts, by small degrees: "She didn't get the money all at once. They sent it to her ______."*) Inf **NY**7, In dibble-dabbles; **WA**28, By dibbles and dabs.

dibble-dabble n
1 A game played in water; see quots. Also called **dribble-stick**
1950 *WELS (Games played in or on the water)* 1 Inf, **cWI,** Dibble-dabble—stick is hidden in water and players duck to find it. One finding it ducks to hide it again. **1950** *WELS Suppl.,* Dibble dabble—A swimming game: a group of players line up along a pier; one person swims off carrying a chip of wood which he releases whenever he feels like it (he may dive and let go, splash and let go, etc). As soon as a player on the pier sees the chip reappear, he dives in (several or all may do so at once) and tries to be the first to recover it. Whoever grabs the chip first cries "dibble dabble," and so earns the right to be the next to carry the chip. **1968** *DARE* (Qu. EE28, *Games played in the water*) Inf **WI**18, Dibble-dabble.
2 See **dibble.**

dibby See **dib**

dib-dabs See **dibs and dabs**

dibs See **dib** n¹ **2**

dibs and dabs n pl Also *dib-dabs* Cf **dibble, dribs and drabs** n pl
Small, often insignificant amounts.
1960 Williams *Walk Egypt* 34 **GA,** During the hot weather grinding [of corn] fell away to nothing but dibs and dabs. **1965-67** *DARE* (Qu. H67, *Food that was not finished at one meal*) Inf **IA**9, Dib-dabs—not enough for even one person; (Qu. LL7, *In small amounts, by small degrees: "She didn't get the money all at once. They sent it to her ______."*) Inf **NJ**16, In dib-dabs; **CA**15, **HI**1, **NY**22, 60, (By, in) dibs and dabs.

dichtie See **dicty** n

dicies n pl, but sg in constr
A marble game; see quot.
1973 Ferretti *Marble Book* 127 **CT,** *Dicies*. . . A marble was flattened on opposite sides . . so that a die could sit flatly on top. . . They [=shooters] shot at the stationary marble in the hope of jarring it with sufficient force to knock the die off. If successful they were awarded the number of marbles indicated by the fallen die.

dickcissel n [From the call]
The black-throated bunting *(Spiza americana).* Also called **harvest bird, Judas bird, little field lark, little meadowlark, May bird**
1874 Coues *Birds NW* 166, In Illinois, Mr. Ridgway tells me, it is called . . "Dicksissel [sic]," . . in allusion to its song. **1887** Ridgway *N. Amer. Birds* 452, Dickcissel, . . dark grey, becoming whitish on belly and lower tail-coverts. **1917** (1923) *Birds Amer.* 3.75, Dickcissel—*Spiza americana.* **1945** McAtee *John and Joe* 12 *(DA),* Was it change in conditions that impelled the dickcissel practically to desert the eastern part of its range? **1961** *New Scientist & Sci. Jrl.* 6 July 16/2, Nesting success of redwing blackbirds, dickcissels and other ground-nesting birds was very low on treated areas in Louisiana and Texas.

dicked ppl adj¹ [Perh var of Scots *dicht* (var of *dight*) ppl adj, dressed, adorned or *decked;* cf **dicty** adj, **dike** v]
1894 *DN* 1.330 **NJ,** *Dicked:* arrayed. Possible corruption of "decked." Not very common.

dicked ppl adj²
1969 *DARE* (Qu. NN25b, *Weakened substitutes for 'damn' or 'damned': "Well, I'll be ______!"*) Inf **IN**83, Dicked.

dickens and Tom Walker, the See **devil and Tom Walker, the**

dicker v, hence vbl n *dickering* Pronc-sp *decker* [Prob from *dicker* a unit of ten hides or other items of commerce; cf **dicker** n **2**]
1 To negotiate a trade or sale; to bargain, haggle; hence n *dickerer.* **chiefly Nth, N Midl** See Map
1802 *Port Folio* (Oldschool) 2.268/1 **CT,** In the gibberish of Connecticut horse jockies . . *Dickering* signifies all that *honest* conversation, preliminary to the sale of a horse, where the parties very laudably strive in a sort of gladiatorial combat of lying, cheating, and overreaching. **1848** Cooper *Oak-Openings* 1.32 **MI,** The white men who penetrated to those semi-wilds, were always ready to "dicker" and to "swap," and to "trade" rifles and matches, and whatever else they might happen to possess. **1902** McFaul *Ike Glidden* viii.62 *(DA),* Dunno as you would call 'em horse trades, b'cause some of the dickerers round here don't trade fair. **1905** *DN* 3.8 **cCT,** *Dicker.* **1921** Mulford *Bar-20 Three* 54 *(DAE)* **West,** Give him a chance to dicker over a herd an' he's happy for a week or more. **1923** *DN* [see **dicker** n **1**]. **1927** *AmSp* 2.352 **WV,** *Decker with one* . . to trade with a person. "We deckered horses last week." **c1960** *Wilson Coll.* **csKY,** *Dicker,* to bargain. **1965-70** *DARE* (Qu. U12, *If you were buying something and you argued with the person selling it till you made him lower the price, you might say, "I ______."*) 39 Infs, **chiefly Nth, N Midl,** Dickered (with him); **PA**135, Dickered him down; **CT**11, Dickering; **PA**3, Was dickering with him; **CT**1, **MO**12, (Had to) dicker. **1977** *Capital Times* (Madison WI) 2 Aug 4/1, Roosmalen gave the envelope containing the money to the man who went into the store ostensibly to dicker with the manager, he told police.

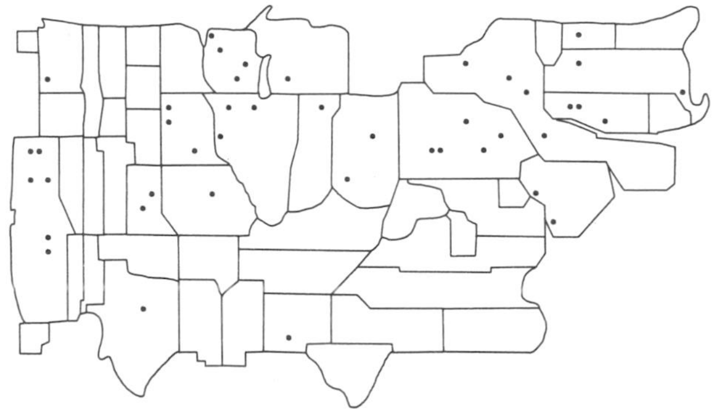

•dicker v 1 + varr (Qu. U12)

2 To argue. [Prob infl by *bicker*]
1966-70 *DARE* (Qu. KK13, . . *Arguing: "They stood there for an hour ______."*) Infs **FL**33, **IL**64, **MI**67, 119, Dickering.

dicker n
1 also attrib: A trade, bargain, deal; the action of trading by bargaining. **chiefly Nth, N Midl**
1818 Fessenden *Ladies Monitor* 171 **VT,** [In a list of provincialisms to be avoided:] *Dicker* for deal. **1831** *Boston Transcript* 22 Dec. 1/1 *(DA),* His 'dicker' was begun, And by aid of solemn face, He closed a bargain soon. **1863** Gilmore *S. Friends* 64 **NC,** And when I git 'bout a hun'red [Negroes] together, take 'em ter Orleans, and auction 'em. Thar's no fuss and dicker 'bout thet, ye knows. **1887** *Chicago Tribune* (IL) 5 May 2/3, A compromise was effected, he was reinstated, and the Pittsburg club got him, but had to release Milt Scott to Baltimore to complete the dicker. **1907** *DN* 3.211 **nwAR,** *Dicker, n.* Barter. **1907** Lincoln *Cape Cod* 51, He bought the last bed of Beriah Burgess, up at East Harniss, and had quite a dicker getting it. **1923** Adams *Pioneer Hist. Ingham Co.* 367 **MI,** The few citizens dealt with each other by making exchanges, one thing for another. Father said they would speak of it [=the exchange procedure] as "dicker." **1923** *DN* 5.205 **swMO,** *Dicker,* v. or n. Trade, exchange, 'swap.' **1925** *New Yorker* 11 July 11/1, They drove around to a [picture] framer's and made a dicker for an old frame, getting a bargain for one cut down. **1940** Writers' Program *Guide OH* 77, Silo filling, quilting parties and dicker days for swapping stock, still linger. **1942** Whipple *Joshua* 149 **UT,** He had just yesterday wound up a shrewd

dicker with Lars Hansen . . trading . . his oldest steers . . for the finest span of matched mules he had ever seen in his life! **1955** Warren *Angels* 51 **KY** (as of c1850), "Yeah, you niggers," Mr. Marmaduke yelled. . . "I aim to sell all of you, ever one—ever last one, you hear!—vendue or dicker—vendue or dicker—cry-off or *jew*-down—ever last one."

2 The goods taken in a trade.

1823 Cooper *Pioneers* 1.195 **NY,** 'I am told you have sold your betterments to a new settler. . . Was it cash or dicker?' . . 'Why, part cash and part dicker.' **1880** *Harper's New Mth. Mag.* 60.907/2 **West,** An old watch and shot-gun . . That he had taken as "dicker" on accounts.

3 See quot 1908.

1904 (1972) Harben *Georgians* 108, They soon had half a dozen cabins built accordin' to the latest dicker up North. **1908** *DN* 3.304 **eAL, wGA,** *Dicker.* . . Plan, fashion. "They got it up accordin' to the latest dicker." Rare.

dicker around v phr [**dicker** v]

To waste time in indecision.

1967 *DARE* (Qu. A11, *When somebody takes too long about coming to a decision . . "I wish he'd quit ______."*) Inf **TX**33, Dickering around.

dickerer, dickering See **dicker** v

dickety-boo n

1954 *PADS* 21.25 **cSC,** *Dickety-boo.* . . A ghost or "hant"; a bugaboo.

dickey n[1] Also sp *dicky* [Perh imit; cf quot 1888]

=ruddy duck.

1888 Trumbull *Names of Birds* 113, One Wilmington [NC] ducker told me of hearing the Ruddy called *Dickey* by certain South Carolina gunners,—"Don't you know," said he, "how, when they start, they go *dickey-dickey-dickey,* patting the water with their wings and feet?" **1917** (1923) *Birds Amer.* 1.152, Ruddy Duck—*Erismatura jamaicensis* . . Other Names. . . Dickey. **1944** Hausman *Amer. Birds* 511, Dickey—see Duck, Ruddy. **1950** *PADS* 14.26 **SC,** *Dicky.* . . The ruddy duck.

dickey n[2] Also sp *dickie*

1 A kind of sleigh or sled; see quots. [*OED dicky* sb. 9. b "A seat at the back of a carriage for servants, etc."; cf quot 1925] **chiefly NY, PA**

[**1925** *DN* 5.329 **Nfld,** Dickey seat. The small rear seat of a sleigh.] **1949** Kurath *Word Geog.* fig 80 **cnPA,** Bob sled . . dickie [4 infs]. **1965–70** *DARE* (Qu. N40b, *Different kinds of sleighs for carrying people*) Inf **NY**117, Dickey—two section sleigh; **NY**224, Dickies—two sleighs, one behind the other, for pleasure rides; **PA**193, [dɪgiz]; **PA**218, Dickies; (Qu. N40c, . . *For carrying other things*) Inf **NY**148, Dickey; Dickey double-cutter. **1986** *WI Alumnus Letters* **csWI,** My grandfather had a two-section sleigh called a *dickey.* These were quite common. . . The two-section sleigh simply had the front seats and rear seats on their own set of runners with the two connected by poles connected by a swivel.

2 A denim jacket; see quot. [Perh a trade name, but cf *EDD dicky* sb.[2] 3 "A short upper garment or over-jacket worn by working-men"] **NY** Cf *DNE* (at *dicky*)

[**1925** *DN* 5.329 **Nfld,** *Dickey.* . . A long outer jacket.] **1968–70** *DARE* (Qu. W4, . . *Men's coats or jackets for work and outdoor wear*) Inf **NY**69, Dickey—Made of blue denim . . hung loose . . had cuff buttons . . just came to waist; **NY**73, Dickey—made of denim, blue or blue and white striped jacket; **NY**233, Dickey—dungaree jacket. [All Infs old]

dickey-dooed up See **dickey up**

dickey pen n Cf **Dixie** n[1]

A children's game; see quot.

1940 Kennedy–Harlow *Schoolmaster* 226 **IN** (as of 1870s), It was during the seventies that the girls began to take part on the school grounds in such games as Dickey Pen—a simple but highly popular romp in which all the players but one gathered in a small pen made of plank or poles lying on the ground—it need be only a few inches high—while the catcher remained outside. Some of those inside would challenge him by escaping from the pen and running for it, perhaps around the schoolhouse. When he went in pursuit, everybody got out of the pen, though the timid ones didn't stray far. The first one he caught must take his place.

dickey up v phr, hence ppl adj *dickied up* Also ppl adj *dickey-dooed up* **sNEng** Cf **dicty** adj, **dike** v

To dress up in fine clothes; to make pretty or fancy.

1969–70 *DARE* (Qu. W30, . . *"I think I'll put on a few flowers to ______ it [=a hat] up."*) Infs **CT**36, **RI**15, Dickey; (Qu. W37, *When a woman puts on her good clothes . . she's ______*) Inf **RI**1, Dickey-dooed up; **RI**15, Dickied up. (Qu. W38, . . *A man dresses himself up in his best clothes . . he's ______*) Inf **MA**57, Dickied up. [3 of 4 Infs old]

dickie n[1]

=haddock.

1884 Goode *Fisheries U.S.* 1.224 **CT,** The haddock is often called "Dickie" by Connecticut fishermen. **1911** U.S. Bur. Census *Fisheries 1908* 310/2, *Haddock.* . . A food fish found in the Atlantic north of the Delaware capes; called "dickie" in some localities.

dickie n[2] See **dickey** n[2]

dickied up See **dickey up**

Dickie's land See **Dixie** n[1]

Dickinson's horse n Also *Dickinson's mare* Cf **devil's horse**

A **dragonfly.**

1899 Bergen *Animal Lore* 63, Dickinson's horse or Dickinson's mare, dragon-fly. . . Dubuque Co[unty], Iowa.

Dick-married-a-widow n [Echoic]

=chuck-will's-widow.

1955 *Oriole* 20.1.9 **GA,** *Chuck-wills-widow.*—All names are sonic unless otherwise explained. . . *Dick-married-a-widow.*

dick-nailer n [*dick* + *nailer* something superior of its kind]

Something or someone superior or extraordinary; hence adj *dick-nailing* extraordinary, amazing.

1892 in 1950 *PADS* 13.9 **AL,** Squire Rogers jumped on him with a ring-tail, dick-nailing reply. **1892** *KS Univ. Qrly.* 1.96 *Dick-nailer:* anything quite satisfactory, as in, He (it) is a dick-nailer. **1966** *DARE* (Qu. LL5, *Something impressively big: "That cabbage is really a ______."*) Inf **SD**8, Dick-nailer.

Dick's hatband n Cf *EDD*

1 in var compar phrr such as *as tight* (or *odd,* etc) *as Dick's hatband:* Very tight (or odd, etc). [*OED hatband* 1. b 1796 →; *EDD dick* sb.[1]]

1891 *AN&Q* 7.117/2, "As queer as Dick's hatband," or as crooked, etc. When a boy I often heard the addition, "It went around sixteen times and then wouldn't tie." **1892** *KS Univ. Qrly.* 1.96 *Dick's hatband,* in the phrase, As contrary as Dick's hatband. **1893** *Ibid* 1.138, *Dick's hatband,* in as *odd* as Dick's hat-band. **1909** *DN* 3.382 **eAL, wGA,** *Tight as Dick's hatband.* . . Very tight. *Ibid* 414 **nME,** *Odd as Dick's hat band.* . . Used to describe a person who is peculiar. **1939** *AmSp* 14.266 **IN,** As tight as Dick's hatband. **1968–70** *DARE* (Qu. U33, . . *Nicknames for a stingy person*) Inf **DC**11, Tight as Dick's hatband; (Qu. U41b, *Somebody who . . is very poor: "He's poor as ______."*) Inf **TX**74, Dick's hatband; (Qu. HH4, *Someone who has odd or peculiar ideas or notions*) Infs **NY**43, **PA**118, Odd as Dick's hatband.

2 A person or thing one does not know and cannot identify. Cf **Adam's hat(band)**

1968 *DARE* (Qu. II26, . . *"I wouldn't know him from ______."*) Inf **MD**49, Dick's hatband.

Dick Smith n Also *Dick Smither*

A lone drinker, a drink taken alone; one who does not buy drinks for others, or who depends on others to buy them; hence a stingy or solitary person; also v phr *Dick Smith it* to drink alone, to 'sponge' on others.

1876 *Congressional Record* 29 June 4260/2 **MI,** Provide that out of that fund this House may receive that pittance which shall enable it to supply the necessary wants of its members, without . . playing "Dick Smith" on the Senate. **1930** Williams *Logger-Talk* 22, *Dick Smith:* A drink of liquor taken privately; suggested by the famous Dick Smith who was given to such a sneaking practice to avoid buying a round. **1942** Berrey–Van den Bark *Amer. Slang* 102.16, *Private or surreptitious drink.* Dick Smith, lonesome, quiet one, sneaker. *Ibid* 670.1, Dick Smith, *a quiet, self-centered* [baseball] *player.* **1959** Tallman *Dict. Amer. Folkl.* 92, *"Dick Smith"*—A term the lumberjacks of the Michigan peninsula used for a man who bought himself a drink alone, a rare situation. When such an occasion arose, six "honest" jacks would toss him over the bar. **1966** *DARE* Tape **MI**10, And once you got out and bellied up to the bar—a tight spender among you immediately got the name of Dick Smith, who was supposed to be a character with short arms and deep pockets. **1966–69** *DARE* (Qu. U33, . . *A stingy person*) Inf **NY**133, A Dick Smith spends his money by himself; (Qu. DD12, . . *A person who drinks steadily or a great deal*) Inf **MI**24, If he drinks alone he's a Dick Smither. **1979** *San Francisco Examiner* (CA) 1 Apr 13, They've [=recent dictionaries] forgotten Dick Smith, whose name became a verb for the solitary drinker and/or sponger. Will "munch-out" take the place of "Dick Smithing it?"

dick-tee See **dicty** n

dickty See **dicty** adj, n

dickunce and Tom Walker, the See **devil and Tom Walker, the**

dicky See **dickey** n[1]

dicky breakfast n

1952 Brown *NC Folkl.* 1.533, *Dicky breakfast*. . . A breakfast fashionably late. Central and east.

dictee See **dicty** n

dicty adj Usu |'dɪkti|; also |'daɪkti| Also sp *dickty* [Perh from Scots *dicht* (see **dicked** ppl adj[1])] *chiefly among Black speakers* Cf **dike** v Cf *DBE*

Stylish, high-class; snobbish, haughty, conceited.

1926 (1949) Handy *Treas. Blues* 22, Gay cattin' 'roun' with dicty cats. *Ibid* 33, Dicty, uppish and conceited. **1926** Van Vechten *Nigger Heaven* 12 **NYC,** Winter Palace? She inquired. . . Naw, he retorted. Too many ofays and jig-chasers. Bowie Wilcot's is dicty. *Ibid* 285, *Dicty:* swell, in the slang sense of the word. **1930** *AmSp* 6.158 **NYC,** *Language of the Speakeasy*. . . *Dicty* is used to describe a high class person—a good sport. **1942** Hurston *Dust Tracks* 225 **FL** [Black], The performance [=loud-talking] . . would get better with the "dickty" negro as the butt of all the quips. **1946** (1972) Mezzrow–Wolfe *Really Blues* 72, In this dicty corral I learned that the great American public likes nothing better than to be roped in, and the tighter you squeeze 'em the more you please 'em. **1950** *PADS* 14.26 **SC,** *Dicty*. . . Proud, haughty. Urban Negroes apply this term to bright mulattoes who try to pass for white. **1968–70** *DARE* (Qu. W38, *When a man dresses himself up in his best clothes, you say he's* ______) Inf **DC**4, ['dɪkti]; **OK**54, Dicty; (Qu. HH11b, *Someone who is too particular or fussy . . a woman*) Inf **OK**58, ['dɪkti]; (Qu. HH35, *A woman who puts on a lot of airs: 'She's too* ______ *for me*) Inf **NY**235 ['daikti]. [All Infs Black] **1978** *New Yorker* 7 Aug 20/2 **NYC** [Black], When my family got a little dicty, we moved from One Hundred and Twenty-second up to Sugar Hill—our family was always on the rise.

dicty n Also sp *dichtie, dick-tee, dickty, dictee* [**dicty** adj] *among Black speakers*

A stuck-up, highfalutin person.

1928 McKay *Home to Harlem* 164 **NYC** [Black], The educated "dicktees" . . were often subjects for raw and funny sallies. He had once heard Miss Curdy putting them in their place. **1944** Smith *Strange Fruit* 177 **GA** [Black], Hardly any of them dichties ever noticed her or remembered her, or bothered to speak to her even at church cept Miss Nonnie and Miz Lowe. **1970** Major *Dict. Afro-Amer. Slang* 46, *Dicty (Dickty, Dictee):* a high-class or snobbish-acting person.

didapper n Also *didapper duck, didapple, diedapper, di(e)dipper, didopper, dip diver, dive dapper, ~ dipper, ~ dopper* Cf **dapper**

1 =pied-billed grebe. chiefly Sth, S Midl See Map

1616 Smith *N. Eng.* 16 *(DA),* Turkies, Diue-doppers, and many other sorts, whose names I knowe not. **a1782** (1788) Jefferson *Notes VA* 77, Besides these [birds], we have. . . [the] Didapper, or Dopchick. **1843** (1973) Porter *Big Bear AR* 41 **KY,** I aimed a sockdollager at him . . he can dodge like a diedapper. **a1883** (1911) Bagby *VA Gentleman* 126, 'Taint a duck either, it's a didapper. **c1960** *Wilson Coll.* **csKY,** Diedapper (or diedipper or divedapper): . . pied-billed grebe. **1965–70** *DARE* (Qu. Q9) 70 Infs, **Sth, S Midl,** Didapper; 34 Infs, **Sth, S Midl,** Didipper; **FL**7, 32, **TN**24, Didapple; **GA**3, **MS**6, Didopper; **VA**22, Dive dapper; (Qu. Q5) 10 Infs, **Sth, S Midl,** Didapper; **GA**76, Didapper duck; **FL**16, **TN**24, Didapple; (Qu. Q10) Inf **GA**1, Didapper; **AL**17, **FL**32, Didapple; **MS**73, Didipper. [Note: Some of these Infs may refer instead to **didapper 2** or **3**.] **1967** LeCompte *Word Atlas* 206 **seLA,** The ducklike bird that is able to dive below the water and remain submerged for long periods . . dive dipper [1 inf] . . dip diver [1 inf].

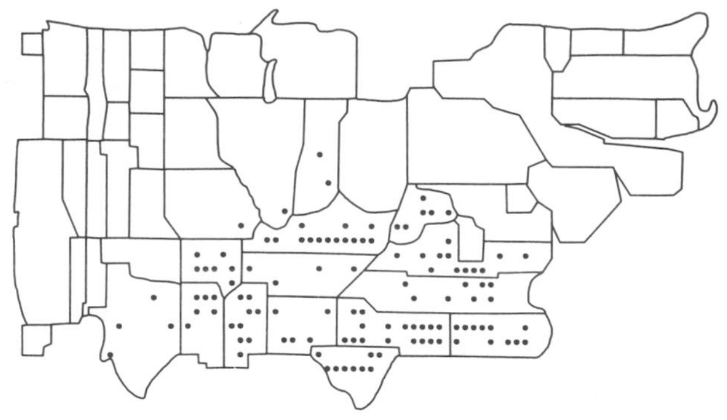

•didapper 1 + varr (Qq. Q9, Q5, Q10)

2 =bufflehead 2.

1844 DeKay *Zool. NY* 2.329, *The Buffle-headed Duck. Fuligula albeola*. . . The little duck is known under the various popular names of *Little Dipper, Diedapper* [etc]. **1888** Trumbull *Names of Birds* 82, The Buffle-head is the. . . *Die-dipper*. **1910** Eaton *Birds NY* 1.212, The Bufflehead, . . Diedapper, and Dipper, as this bird is called, is a fairly common transient visitant throughout the State. **1923** U.S. Dept. Ag. *Misc. Circular* 13.23, *Bufflehead*. . . *Vernacular Names*. . . *In local use*. . . Didapper (Miss.)

3 =hooded merganser.

1923 U.S. Dept. Ag. *Misc. Circular* 13.6, *Hooded Merganser*. . . *Vernacular Names*. . . *In local use*. . . Didapper (La.)

4 =Virginia rail.

1923 U.S. Dept. Ag. *Misc. Circular* 13.42, *Virginia Rail*. . . *Vernacular Names*. . . *In local use*. . . Didapper (Ark.)

diddie wa diddie See **diddy-wah-diddy**

diddle v

1 To walk unsteadily. [*OED* 1632]

1908 *DN* 3.304 **eAL, wGA,** *Diddle* . . To toddle.

2 To shake, jiggle; to dandle (a child). [*OED* 1786; this sense appears to be most common in Scots dial.]

1933 Miller *Lamb in His Bosom* 118 **GA,** Margot would humor Maggie's every whim and diddle Kissie on her knees while Cean stirred about cooking. **1942** Whipple *Joshua* 374 **UT,** Kissy began to whimper and diddle up and down with the burning of the sand through her thin moccasins.

3 To copulate; to copulate with (someone); hence vbl n *diddling;* n *diddler.* [Although this sense is attested later than the following ones, it is likely that they derive from it.] **esp Sth, S Midl**

1908 *DN* 3.304 **eAL, wGA,** *Diddle*. . . To copulate. **1930** Shoemaker *1300 Words* 18 **cPA Mts** (as of c1900), *Dark diddler*—A married man with a secret mistress. **1940** Faulkner *Hamlet* 165 **MS,** Just out of curiosity to find out for certain just which of them was and wasn't diddling her? **1944** *PADS* 2.42 **sVA,** *Diddle (with)*. . . To copulate. **1950** in 1977 Randolph *Pissing in the Snow* 182 **Ozarks,** The country girl says, "Have *you* ever been diddled?" The town girl says of course she has. **1950** *PADS* 13.17 **cTX,** *Diddle*. . . To copulate. **1954** *Harder Coll.* **cwTN,** *Diddle*. . . To play amorously, have intercourse with. Usually *diddle with.* "He diddled her. He diddled with her." **c1960** *Wilson Coll.* **csKY,** *Diddle*. . . To copulate, esp. illegally. **1968** *DARE* FW Addit **cnNY,** *Diddle*—to have intercourse. **1969** Kantor *MO Bittersweet* 127, 'Well, right in there is where Mark Twain and Becky Thatcher hid out. And, you know—' then he would bend close as in utmost confidence, and speak in a stage whisper. 'Folks say they was in there a-*diddling.*' **1970** *DARE* FW Addit **cwPA,** *Diddlin'*—puttin' out (as in "she puts out"). **1986** Hendrickson *Amer. Talk* 162, In Pennsylvania German. . . *Diddling* is sexual intercourse.

4a To cheat, swindle; hence vbl n *diddling* cheating. [*OED* 1806 →]

1846 Corcoran *Pickings* 171 **LA,** [Chapter title:] The Danger of Diddling a Barber. **1950** *PADS* 14.26 **SC,** *Diddle*. . . To cheat, overreach, swindle. **1959** Faulkner *Mansion* 59 **MS,** Montgomery Ward had more simple sense and judgment . . than to actively believe that ten thousand Lawyer Stevenses and Hub Hamptons, let alone jest one each of them, could a diddled Flem Snopes. **1968** *DARE* (Qu. LL22, *Less than you should get: "They'll try to give you ______ every time."*) Inf **NY**80, A diddlin'; (Qu. LL23, *Cheated, treated dishonestly: "These apples are wormy, I think you got ______."*) Inf **NY**42, Diddled. **1978** *NYT Book Rev.* 25 June 32/5, Today's super criminal is a smart technician who knows how to diddle the computer.

b Esp in marble play: see quot. [*EDD diddle* v.^{3} 5]

1955 *PADS* 23.16, *Diddle* . . To move the taw or shooter forward unfairly.

5 also with *around;* also *dittle, diddle-daddle, ~-diddle:* To waste time, dawdle; to fiddle (with). [*OED* 1826–29]

1899 (1912) Green *VA Folk-Speech* 146, *Diddle-daddle*. . . To dawdle about. "You go diddle-daddling about all day and do nothing." **1908** *DN* 3.304 **eAL, wGA,** *Diddle*. . . Dawdle. **1918** *Capital Times* (Madison WI) 30 May 6, [In cartoon "Indoor Sports":] Hello Wesley. I see you're diddling around the old boat again. **1950** *PADS* 13.17 **cTX,** *Diddle with* . . means to fool with. "I wouldn't diddle with that if I was you." **1950** *WELS (Wasting time by doing unimportant or useless things)* 4 Infs, **WI,** Diddling (around). **1957** Battaglia *Resp. to PADS 20* **eMD,** *Wasting time by doing useless or unimportant things,* Dittling around. **c1960** *Wilson Coll.* **csKY,** *Diddle* . . to fool around, doing nothing. **1965–70** *DARE* (Qu. A9, . . *Wasting time by not working on the job*) Infs **NE**8, **TN**52, Diddling; (Qu. A10, . . *"What are you doing?"* . . *"Nothing in particular—I'm just ______."*) Inf **SC**29, Diddling; **MI**98, **MA**1, 74, Diddling around; **NJ**31, Diddle-diddling; (Qu. A11, *When somebody takes too long about coming to a decision, you might say, "I wish he'd quit ______."*) Inf **WI**71, Diddling; **KY**41, **PA**220, Diddling around; (Qu. KK31, . . *"He doesn't have anything to do, so he's just ______."*) Inf **GA**15, Diddling; (Qu. KK60, . . *"I'd just as soon go with you this afternoon—I'm ______ anyway."*) Inf **KY**41, Diddling around.

diddle n^1 [**diddle v 2**]

A quick jumping or bouncing movement.

1840 (1847) Longstreet *GA Scenes* 16, Always giving two or three pretty little perchbite diddles, as she rose from a coupee: Nancy Ware was her very self.

diddle n^2 [*EDD diddle* sb.^{6} "Ducklings. . . A call for young ducks"] **chiefly sAppalachians** Cf **dib** n^2

A duckling or baby chick—also used as a call to such an animal.

1899 (1912) Green *VA Folk-Speech* 146, *Diddles*. . . Young ducks. *Diddle,* a word to call ducks. **1949** Arnow *Hunter's Horn* 5 **seKY,** They's a old hen . . she hid her nest out an has hatched eleven diddles right here, nearly September. **1968** *DARE* (QR p76) Inf **NJ**16, To call a duck—*diddle, diddle, diddle.* **1968** *DARE* FW Addit **swVA,** Diddle—baby chicks hatched by settin' hen. Used by "children of the holler"; also used by adults. **1970** *DARE* Tape **VA**43, My mother had some little diddles, that's young ducks. **1976** Garber *Mountain-ese* 22 **sAppalachians,** *Diddle* . . baby duck or chick. The mother hen has twelve diddles. **1982** Ginns *Snowbird Gravy* 189 **nwNC,** The rats got in Mother's chickens, and then I had to go out and get the rats out. . . They's arter them diddles, Mother's diddles, what was hatched out.

diddle around, diddle-daddle See **diddle v 5**

diddledee n [Etym uncert, but see quot 1916] **esp seMA** Cf *DS* T6

A pine needle.

1889 *Jrl. Amer. Folkl.* 2.64 **seMA,** *Diddledees*. . . At Hyannis . . it was the universal name for the fallen pine-needles that carpet the ground in the woods. **1916** Macy-Hussey *Nantucket Scrap Basket* 160, "Diddledees"—a curious old word used for pine-needles. This has always been something of a puzzle, but the Century again helps us out: "Diddledees—a shrub in the Falkland Islands and other Antarctic regions used for fuel." As pine-needles have been used as "kindlings" by the Nantucket people for generations past, may it not be that the word was brought from the Antarctic by the whalers? **1941** *Nature Mag.* 34.139/2, We find on Cape Cod the puzzling alias [for pine needles], diddledees.

diddle-diddle, diddle with See **diddle** v^2 **1**

diddling vbl n^1 See **diddle** v^2 **3**

diddling vbl n^2 [Perh var of *doodling*]

1967 *DARE* (Qu. JJ11, . . *Handwriting that's hard to read: "I can't make anything out of his ______."*) Inf **SC**45, Diddling.

diddling stick n

=**tip-up.**

1972 *DARE* File **WI,** A tip-up, used by Southern Wisconsin ice fishermen, is called by them a diddling stick.

diddly (bop) See **diddly squat**

diddly-damn n Also adj *diddly-damned*

See quots.

1968 *DARE* (Qu. NN17, *Something that keeps on annoying you* . . : *"That ______ fly won't go away."*) Inf **PA**93, Diddly-damned. **c1970** *Halpert Coll.* 16 **wKY, nwTN,** Not worth a diddly damn.

diddly squat n Also *diddly bop, ~ poop, ~ shit;* abbr *diddly*

=**doodl(e)y squat.**

1964 *AmSp* 39.117, Campus slang. . . *Bull-* and *diddly-shit* become *bull* and *diddly.* **1974** Cahn *Self Defense* 105, Now this is a beautiful, and no doubt, very useful ladder, but let me tell you: it isn't worth diddly-bop when getting puppies out of outhouses. **1977** *Capital Times* (Madison WI) 30 Apr 1/5, "You know how the bank said they were going to help everybody?" he added. "Well, they didn't say diddly poop to the zipper lady, the rock shop or the barber shop." **1981** *DARE* File **Milwaukee WI,** This hand [of cards] isn't worth diddly-squat. **1982** *Smithsonian Letters* **cOH,** A charming word I never heard before . . is: "diddlysquat"—something of not much account, as in "It isn't worth a diddlysquat." **1985** *Amer. Scholar* 54.439, About many things Mark Twain did not know diddly, but about lectures in churches he was brilliant.

diddy n Cf **dib** n^2

=**biddy** n^3.

1952 Brown *NC Folkl.* 1.533, *Diddy*. . . A little chicken.

diddy-wah-diddy n Also *doo-wah-diddy* Also sp *diddie wa diddie old-fash*

Used as a substitute for a word or name one does not want to use; hence as the name of an imaginary place, often conceived of as fabulous and far-off.

1929 in 1983 Taft *Blues Lyric Poetry* 30 [Black], Then I got: put out of church Because I talk: about diddie wa diddie too much. **1942** *Amer. Mercury* 55.223.91 **Harlem NYC** [Black], I'd walk clear to Diddy-Wah-Diddy to get a chance to speak to a pretty lil' ground-angel like that. *Ibid* 94, Diddy-wah-diddy—a far place, a measure of distance. (2) another suburb of Hell, built since way before Hell wasn't no bigger than Baltimore. The folks in Hell go there for a big time. **1960** Williams *Walk Egypt* 114 **GA,** It [=a radio program called Ozark Jubilee] was as real to him as Diddy-Wah-Diddy was to a Negro child, Diddy-Wah-Diddy where the roofs were made of pancakes and roast ducks flew by with knives and forks in their backs, quacking, "Sweet, sweet, come eat." **1981** *NADS Letters,* Southern Illinois (white) has *Doo-Wah-Diddy* as a similar imaginary place. . . It is often used as a thingamabob word for a place; it occurs in teasing answers to questions about location and so on. No longer current. *Ibid,* In my Mississippi childhood there was a song on the Grand Ole Opry (then strictly white) with the lines: "It ain't a town and it ain't a city,/ It's just a little place called Doo-Wah-Diddy." This, like Diddy-Wah-Diddy, seems to have been a Land of Cockaigne, especially of sexual license. **1988** *DARE* File **csWI,** Phil Harris popularized a song called "That's What I Like About the South" [*DARE* Ed: Words and music by Andy Razaf, c1944] that had these lines: "Let me tell ya' 'bout a place called Doo-Wah-Diddy / It ain't a town and it ain't a city / But it's awful nice and it's awful pretty / and that's what I like about the South."

didipper See **didapper**

dido n [Etym unknown]

1 usu pl; also *kedidoes* (cf **ker-**): A caper, prank, shenanigan; a fit of anger; an unexpected outburst—usu in phrr *cut (up) didoes* and varr. **widespread, but esp NEng, Sth, S Midl** Cf **dingdo**

1807 (1930) Shaw *Narr. Well-Digger* 181 **KY,** There commenced a roaring frolic with a set of . . jovial fellows . . amongst whom was a jolly Irishman, who cut as many didos as I could for the life of me. **1835** Thompson *Advent. Peacock* 170, Must all the world know all the didos we cut up in the [Masonic] lodge-room? **1836** (1838) Haliburton *Clockmaker* (1st ser) 143 **NEng,** I met a man this mornin, . . a real conceited lookin critter . . all shines and didos. **1872** Schele de Vere *Americanisms* 324, The rowdy . . is very fond of designating his peculiar proceedings as *cutting up* something. . . He *cuts capers,* he *cuts up shines,* he even *cuts didoes,* as if he would imitate famous Queen Dido in her cunning device by which she received her magnificent "hide" of land. Such at least is Professor Mahn's interpretation of an expression which so far has baffled all research. **1905** *DN* 3.7 **cCT,** *Cut didoes. . .* To be frolicksome. **1908** *DN* 3.303 **eAL, wGA,** *Cut (up) didoes. . .* To cut capers, to act smart. **1914** *DN* 4.75 **ME, nNH,** *Kedidoes. . .* Tricks, pranks, "cuttings-up." *Ibid* 70, *Cut didoes,* or *dingdoes. . .* To put on airs and graces. **1921** *DN* 5.116 **KY,** *Didoes, to cut,* to "act smart," "show off." **1923** *DN* 5.205 **swMO,** *Dido. . .* Prank, caper. "Bill's a-cuttin didoes like a young-un." **1929** *AmSp* 5.121 **ME,** A mischievous child was said to "cut up didoes." **1944** *PADS* 2.28 **Sth,** *Dido, to cut a. . .* To have a fit of anger or drunkenness, or to show any uncommon behavior. "Your pa'll cut a dido when he finds out about this." (Also: *to cut up didoes*) **1945** *PADS* 3.10 **cwNY,** *Dido, to cut a . .* Used in my family. It was not always accompanied by *cut:* "I'll have none of your didoes." **1945** Colcord *Sea Language* 66 **ME, Cape Cod, Long Island,** *Dido, to cut a.* Now completely a shore phrase; said to come from H.M.S. *Dido,* a very fast ship, whose commander used to sail her in circles around other vessels of his squadron to show off her fleetness. **1950** *WELS Suppl.* **cwWI,** That cow is cutting up didoes again. Said of animals or humans both. Old-fashioned. **1968** *DARE* FW Addit **csDE,** The fish started making didos. **1986** *NADS Letters* **cnTX,** A fish thrashing at the end of a line cuts didoes. A car skidding erratically cuts a dido. Children playing acrobatically cut didoes. When I shoot at a woodcock just as it cuts a dido in the air, I nearly always miss it.

2 Something fancy or frivolous.

1909 Wason *Happy Hawkins* 30, I bought a silver trimmed bridle an' some Mexican didoes. **1955** Adams *Grandfather* 107 **NY** (as of 1830s), When I wore *my* new collar to the First Church social, the excitement was intense. The report of the newfangled dido had preceded me. **1968** *DARE* (Qu. JJ12, *Little flourishes . . on . . handwriting or . . signature to make it look fancy*) Inf **WI**30, Didoes, **CA**96, Fancy didos.

3 See quots. [Punning reapplications of phr *cut a dido.* The artifice described in quot 1965 is that attributed in Roman legend to Queen Dido of Carthage, and prob reflects the often suggested origin of the phr in her name.]

1936 Lutes *Country Kitchen* 38 **sMI** (as of 1880s), Roll this [biscuit dough] out to three-fourths of an inch in thickness, cut a dido in the centre,—you know, a big S with eyelet holes slashed alongside,—and lay the crust over the apples, pinching it to the edge. **1965** Needham–Mussey *Country Things* 71 **seVT,** People used to wonder how he got rawhide of any length out of a small chuck skin. What he done was perfectly simple: he cut what they called a dido. He just went round and round, and cut a spiral as long as he wanted. **1986** Hendrickson *Amer. Talk* 50 **NEng,** A dido is the slash made in a pie crust to let out steam.

didopper See **didapper**

did she cackle n

A children's game.

1905 *DN* 3.72 **nwAR,** *Cackle,* v. intr. Used in the name of the game, 'Did she cackle?' Common.

didy n [By ext from *didy* baby's diaper]

1950 *WELS Suppl.* **cwWI,** *Didy*—Used of any white cloth square of flour sacking (in the time before head scarves were fashionable). "Annie, I'm going to strain the milk; where is the didy?" and "She's over there with the didy on her head."

did you ever exclam *somewhat old-fash*

Used as an exclamation of surprise.

1908 *DN* 3.305 **eAL, wGA,** *Did you ever,* interj. phr. Common among the women. **1913** Wharton *Custom of Country* 3 **NYC,** "Did you *ever,* Mrs. Heeny?" Mrs. Spragg murmured with deprecating pride. **1942** McAtee *Dial. Grant Co. IN* 22 (as of 1890s), *"Did you ever?" . .* exclamation of surprise or incredulity over actions or happenings. **1942** Warnick *Garrett Co. MD* 6 **nwMD** (as of 1900–18), *Did you ever . .* an exclamation of surprise or disappointment. **1965–70** *DARE* (Qu. NN7, *Exclamations of surprise . . "Well, ______."*) Infs **MA**5, **NJ**57, **VA**21, Did you ever. [All Infs old] **1968** *DARE* File **cnMA,** "Did you ever!" is one of the phrases I associate with middle-aged and old ladies. It was usually preceded by *well.* Someone seeing her grandchild take her first steps might exclaim, "Well, did you ever!"

did you ever see a lassie n Also *ever see a lassie, have you ever seen a lady*

A children's game; see quot 1909

1909 (1923) Bancroft *Games* 261, *Did you ever see a lassie? . .* A game for very little children. . . All of the players but one form a circle, clasping hands. They circle around, singing the first two lines of the verse. While they are doing this, the odd player stands in the center and illustrates some movement which he chooses for the others to imitate. During the last two lines of the verse the players stand in place, drop hands, and imitate the movements of the center player. . . When a boy is in the center, the word "lassie" should be changed to "laddie." **1965–70** *DARE* (Qu. EE1, . . *Games . . in which they [=children] form a ring, and either sing or recite a rhyme*) Infs **CA**118, 133, **NJ**13, Did you ever see a lassie; **PA**181, Ever see a lassie; (Qu. EE33, *Other outdoor games*) Inf **CA**142, Have you ever seen a lady.

did you ever see the ghost n

1905 *DN* 3.77 **nwAR,** *Did you ever see the ghost? . .* A children's game.

die v

To cause to die.

1941 Perry *Hold Autumn* 110 **TX,** He began planting [corn] there in a little patch which Ruston said had got in the habit of "dying" cotton. On land such as that, cotton just dies in patches for no apparent reason except that the land has been enfeebled by the gluttonous roots of twenty consecutive cotton crops.

diedapper, diedipper See **didapper**

die, dog, or eat the hatchet v phr Cf **eat, pig, or die**

=**root, hog, or die.**

1903 (1965) Adams *Log Cowboy* 36 **West,** I never questioned that man's advice; it was 'die dog or eat the hatchet' with me. **1929** in 1956 Wolfe *Letters* 177 **NC,** We are cutting out big chunks [of a manuscript], and my heart bleeds to see it go, but it's die dog or eat the hatchet.

dientical adj [Metath]

1893 Shands *MS Speech* 26, *Dientical* [daiˈɛntəkl̩]. Very frequently used by negroes and illiterate whites for *identical.*

die out v phr Also *die off*

Of a person: to die.

1887 *Scribner's Mag.* 2.474/2 **AR** [Black], Whut er sight er turbbel [sic] she done hab; fust de cap'n, an' now de onlies' chile she got dyin' off. **1913** *DN* 4.58 **TN,** *Die out. . .* To die: noted at Elkmont. "My old woman died out last Monday." **1937** *Hall Coll.* **eTN, wNC,** Old Bill Oliver, he died out.

die-up n Also *die-out* **SW**

See quot 1961.

1902 (1944) Biggers *From Cattle Range* 52 **wTX,** The first big die-up occurred . . in that portion of Western Texas [in 1844]. **1929** Dobie *Vaquero* ix **swTX,** This trail of mine will lead into immense boneyards that marked the drifts and die-ups of the open range. *Ibid* 24, In the disastrous "die-up" of 1872–1873, for instance, Jim Miller's outfit . . skinned 4000 dead cattle. **1961** Adams *Old-Time Cowhand* 160 **West,** The wholesale death of cattle as a result of blizzards, and sometimes droughts, over a wide range of territory was called a "die-up." **1971** Green *Village Horse Doctor* 166 **cwTX** (as of 1940s), I don't believe that I can be worried about him because you told me that when there was a 'die-out' here, there was always enough left to restock the country.

diff n [Perh var of Scots *dowf* a dull blow; cf *SND dowf* II. n. 2] Cf **biff** n[1], **dift**

A blow or stroke.

1877 Burdette *Rise & Fall* 208 **seIA,** The dog, looking up, misunderstood the motion and thought his master was going to hit him a diff with that hat. **1891** Harris *Balaam* 32 **cGA,** He got a big scyar [=scar] on de side er his neck now whar somebody hit 'im a diff. **1897** *KS Univ. Qrly.* (ser B) 6.52 **KS,** *Diff:* [a blow; as, Hit him a] diff.

diffabitterance n Also sp *diffabitterence* Also *dif of bitterness* **chiefly S Midl**

1921 *DN* 5.119 **KY,** *Dif of bitterness,* bit of difference. **1923** *DN* 5.245 **KS,** *Diffabitterence.* Transposition of *bit of difference,* used by boys as far back as 1883. **1942** McAtee *Dial. Grant Co. IN* 22 (as of 1890s), *Diffabitterence.* **1956** McAtee *Some Dialect NC* 12, *Diffabitterance.* **c1960** *Wilson Coll.* **csKY,** *Diffabitterance. . .* A humorous transposition of *bit of difference,* usually said to indicate one's utter lack of interest in what is being discussed.

differ n Pronc-sp *diffuh* [Abbr for *difference,* infl by *differ* v] **chiefly Sth, S Midl**

Difference; difference of opinion, argument, quarrel.

1873 in 1894 Lowell *Letters* 2.94 **NEng,** So far as I understood your "differ" with your electors I thought you were right. **1884** Murfree *TN Mts.* 141, He'll see a mighty differ nex' time I gits my chance. **1886** Amer. Philol. Assoc. *Trans.* 17.45 **Sth,** *Differ* (difference). **1909** *S. Atl. Qrly.* 8.50 **SC** [Gullah], In ordinary parlance, *a quarrel, or violent "falling out"* is not *to differ,* but *a differ: "Wut bin de diffuh? Dey yent bin no diffuh?"* **1922** (1926) Kephart *Highlanders* 357 **sAppalachians,** Hit don't make no differ. **1927** *AmSp* 3.9 **Ozarks,** Some of the best Ozark nouns are really converted verbs, as in . . *Wal, I reckon hit don't make no differ.* **1950** *PADS* 14.26 **SC,** *Differ*. . . 1. A quarrel. "What's the differ?" "Ain't no differ. We jus' arguin'." 2. Difference. "I don't allow no rabbit huntin' on my land." "I'm huntin' pattidges." "No differ what, rabbits or pattidges."

differ v **[differ n] Sth, S Midl**

To matter, to make a difference.

1893 Shands *MS Speech* 26, *Differs not* . . Sometimes used by illiterate whites for *matters not;* as "It differs not whether it be true or not." **1917** *DN* 4.410 **wNC,** *Differ*. . . To make a difference. "It didn't differ what that cow way [=weighed]." **1939** *Hall Coll.* **eTN, wNC,** "It might differ a little." "It don't differ a damn with me." Very common. **1966** *DARE* (Qu. KK54b, *Just about equal, very close: "It doesn't matter to me—it's ______."*; total Infs questioned, 75) Inf **FL**28, It doesn't differ. **1976** Garber *Mountain-ese* 23 **sAppalachians,** It don't differ whether you win or lose, it's how you play the game.

diffucalty n |dɪˈfjukəlti, -gəlti| Also sp *defewgelty, diffugalty* [Varr of *difficulty*] *joc*

1958 *Sat. Eve. Post Letters* **sIN** (as of 1910–20), Defewgelty (difficulty; "in a fix") (hard "g.") **c1960** *DARE* File **WI,** Yes, *there's* the diffucalty [dɪˈfjukəlti]! **1978** *DARE* File **sIN** (as of 1920), That's the diffugalty [dɪˈfjugəlti]! [=That's the trouble!]

diffuh See **differ** n

dift v Cf **diff**

To hit, strike.

1927 *DN* 5.474 **Ozarks,** *Dift*. . . To strike. "You-all orter a seed me dift him one side o' th' head." **1944** *ADD* 162 **Ozarks,** Somebody must of difted him with a axe handle.

dig v[1] Usu |dɪg|; also |dig| Past, past pple usu *dug;* also *digged, dugged* [*digged,* though now replaced by *dug* in StdE, is the older form; see *OED*]

A Forms.

1911 (1916) Porter *Harvester* 40 **IN,** He had digged several wagon loads of sassafras. **1934** *AmSp* 9.210 **Sth,** A great many words having standard [ɪ] before [g] . . change [ɪ] to [i]. . . *Big,* . . *dig.* **1934** *WV Review* Dec 77, Among these [=words found in central or southern West Virginia] are . . *digged.* **1966** *DARE* Tape **ME**22, I never dugged 'em [=worms] to sell.

B Senses.

1 To study. Cf **dig** n, **digger** n **2**

1827 *Harvard Reg.* Dec. 303 *(DA),* Here the sunken eye and sallow countenance bespoke the man who dug sixteen hours 'per diem.' **1907** *DN* 3.211 **nwAR, cCT,** *Dig*. . . To study. . . *Digging*. . . Studying hard. **1915** *DN* 4.233 **neOH** [College slang], *Dig*. . . To study. "I'm going to dig some German." **1963** *Freedomways* 3.57 **Harlem NYC,** *Dug:* studied.

2 To use snuff, to **dip** v **1;** hence vbl n *digging* taking snuff. *arch* Cf *DS* DD3b, **digger 1**

1860 (1934) Cowell *Cowells in Amer.* 66, With them [=certain tobacconists on Broadway] and their customers the practice is called 'digging' instead of 'dipping'. . . The quantity [of snuff] used by each 'digger' varies from one quarter of a pound to a pound per week [in New York]. **1877** Bartlett *Americanisms* 176, To dig is used among the lower classes at the South for the act of *dipping* or rubbing snuff. A friend informs me that *to dig* is more common than *to dip* snuff. **1887** *Chicago Tribune* (IL) 2 Apr 5/6 **DC,** Neither mind, health, self-respect, love for her husband, children or friends, can give her sufficient resolution to abstain from "digging" or "dipping," as snuff-chewing is called.

3 To cheat.

1914 *DN* 4.163 **OR,** *Dig*. . . To cheat. **1967** *DARE* FW Addit **cnLA,** *Dig*—to cheat. "I think he's a-diggin' you."

4 To make a cutting remark; to jab at verbally, insult. [*dig* a critical or insulting remark, *OED* 1840 →]

1950 *WELS (When one person never misses a chance to be mean to another: "I don't know why he keeps ______ me all the time!")* 1 Inf, **cwWI,** Digging. **1965–70** *DARE* (Qu. Y3, *To say uncomplimentary things about somebody*) Infs **CA**134, **MI**116, **WI**33, **WV**12, Dig; **LA**17, Dig 'em out; **OH**87, Dig at.

5 To bother, irritate (one).

1967–69 *DARE* (Qu. GG13a, *When something keeps bothering a person and makes him nervous, he might say, "It ______ me."*) Infs **MD**24, **SC**40, Digs; (Qu. II29b, . . *To explain the unpleasant effect that person [=someone who is disliked] has on you: "He just ______."*) Inf **PA**206, Digs me.

6 also *dig out, dig it* (or *them*) *up:* To run, dash away, depart rapidly.

a1855 Kelley *Humors* 384 *(DA),* Mad and furious, the young chaps made a general onslaught on the people present, who 'dug out' very quick, leaving the bacchanalians to their glory. **1884** (1958) Twain *Huck. Finn* 180 **MO,** I was about to dig out from there in a hurry. **1906** *DN* 3.133 **nwAR,** He'd just better dig and never come back. **1910** *DN* 3.440 **cwNY,** I guess I better be digging out for home. **1910** McCutcheon *Rose* 334 **NY,** If it wasn't for you, Davy, I'd cut it in a minute and dig for the wooly West. **1912** *DN* 3.574 **wIN,** *Dig out*. . . To go at once and in a hurry. "Well, if you are going, you had better dig out." **1912** Green *VA Folk-Speech* 147, *Dig*. . . To push forward; run fast: "He went digging down the road as hard as he could." *Dig out*. . . To run away. **1917** *DN* 4.391 **neOH,** "He dug out of there as fast as he could." "You dig out o' here." **1923** *DN* 5.205 **swMO,** *Dig out.* **1965–70** *DARE* (Qu. Y18, *To leave in a hurry: "Before they find this out, we'd better ______!"*) Infs **IL**114, **NJ**21, Dig out; (Qu. Y19, *To begin to go away from a place: "It's about time for me to ______."*) Inf **OH**28, Dig out; (Qu. Y20, *To run fast: "You should have seen him ______!"*) Inf **AL**34, Dig it up; **TX**32, Digging 'em up. **1986** *DARE* File **csWI** (as of 1940s), They just dug out and left the house in a mess and breakfast dishes still on the table. The sheriff wasn't far behind.

dig v[2]

1 To understand. [Etym sugg in 1977 questionable] *esp freq among Black speakers* Note: This sense seems to have been adopted by jazz musicians, then popularized by jazz fans.

1936 *NY World-Telegram* (NY) 6 Oct 16/1 **Harlem NYC** [Black musicians' lingo], "You dig?" is a short cut for "You understand?" **1941** *Life* 15 Dec 89, *Dig Me?*—understand me? **1946** (1972) Mezzrow-Wolfe *Really Blues* 332, *Dig:* Understand, appreciate, listen to, follow, grasp, get. **1950** *WELS (Ways of saying "Do you understand?")* 1 Inf, **csWI,** Dig me? **1954** Armstrong *Satchmo* 61 **LA** [Black], Before we could dig what was going on, these tough guys started shooting. **1958** *PADS* 30.45 [Language of jazz musicians], *Dig*. . . To understand and agree with: not limited to music alone. (Perhaps fr. a sense of "getting to the bottom" of things.) Comm[on], older ["roughly before 1943–44"], basic. **1965** Little *Autobiog. Malcolm X* 108 [Black], I want to get sent down South. Organize them nigger soldiers, you dig? **1965–70** *DARE* (Qu. NN5, *Other ways of saying 'Do you understand?': "You take hold of it this way, ______?"*) 13 Infs, **scattered,** Dig me? 3 Infs, (Do) you dig me? 8 Infs, (Do) you dig? 6 Infs, Dig? 5 Infs, (You) dig it? 3 Infs, Can (*or* do) you dig it? (Qu. X18, . . *When one person doesn't quite hear what another person said, what does he say?*) Inf **SC**64, I didn't dig you; (Qu. JJ16, *When there was something you didn't understand, then suddenly you do understand it, you might say, "Oh, now I ______."*) Infs **GA**80, 93, **IN**58, **NY**211, 238, **NC**37, 88, **OR**1, **PA**236, Dig (it *or* you); (Qu. JJ17, *When you know that somebody has been trying to deceive you, you might say, "He's not fooling me one bit, I'm ______ [him]."*) Infs **CO**29, **MD**41, [I] dig. [22 of 45 total Infs Black] **1977** Smitherman *Talkin* 45 [Black], Some further examples of Black English loan-translations from African languages are: . . *dig,* to understand or appreciate, from Wolof *dega,* literally "to understand." *Ibid* 69, "Slang," such as *cool, dig, jazz, jive, uptight.* Initially these latter terms moved out of the black community via white musicians and others of the artsy Hip Set.

2 also with *on:* To appreciate; to see or hear with understanding or agreement; to experience; to like, admire. *chiefly among young and mid-aged speakers; esp freq among Black speakers; esp freq in urban comms*

1935 *Hot News* 1.6.20/2, But if you listen enough, and dig him [=Freddy Jenkins, trumpet player in Duke Ellington's band] enough, you will realize that that much maligned riff is the high-spot of the record. **1944** Zolotow *Never Whistle* 52 **NY,** When they [=musicians] see a pretty girl they shout, "Dig the chick." **1946** (1972) Mezzrow-Wolfe *Really Blues* 76, Detroit was one place in particular I wanted to dig. **1947** DeToledano *Frontiers* x **NYC,** I recognize it when I see it, the same as I dig good Jazz when I hear it. **1965–70** *DARE* (Qu. AA10, *A very special liking that a boy may have for a girl . . "He ——— her."*) 31 Infs, **scattered, but esp freq Nth, N Midl,** Digs; **NY**250, They dig each other; (Qu. AA1, *When a man goes to see a girl often and seems to want to marry her, he's ——— her*) Inf **PA**79, Digging her—new term; (Qu. AA7a, . . *Words . . for a woman who is very fond of men and is always trying to know more—if she's nice about it*) Inf **DC**11, Men really dig her; (Qu. II11a, *If two people don't get along together, you'd say, "They don't ———."*) Infs **NY**211, **OH**103, Dig each other; (Qu. II29a, *An unexplainable dislike . . : "I just can't ——— him."*) Infs **FL**48, **LA**16, **MI**118, **NC**84, **NJ**54, **NY**238, **TN**50, **WA**18, Dig; (Qu. KK35) Inf **NY**238, I dig you; (Qu. NN2, *Exclamation of very strong agreement: Somebody says, "I think Smith is absolutely right," and you reply, "———."*) Inf **NY**250, I dig it; (Qu. NN3, *Words and expressions meaning 'don't you agree?': "She's a nice-looking woman, ———?" or "We ought to come back here again, ———?"*) Inf **IN**58, Dig?; Do you dig?; **NY**250, Dig it?; **SC**67, You dig? [Of 43 total Infs, 31 were young or mid-aged, 15 Black, 17 comm type 1 or 2.] **1968** *New Yorker* 30 Nov 55/1 **NYC,** I really dig Central Park, and I think it's a shame the way it's dirty. **1970** *DARE* Tape **NC**89 [Black], An' then I don't dig on some of the things they have to do to join. I think it's childish and stupid.

3 in phr *dig you later:* Used as a salutation in parting.

1940 in 1983 Taft *Blues Lyric Poetry* 23/2, Going to tell you baby: like the farmer told his potato / I'm going to plant you now woman: but I will dig you later. **1970** *DARE* (Qu. NN11, *Informal ways of saying 'goodbye' to people you know quite well*) Inf **PA**247, Dig you later. [Inf Black] **1970** Major *Dict. Afro-Amer. Slang* 46, *Dig you later:* (1930's and after) an expression of farewell; it was shortened to "later."

dig n [dig v[1] **B1**]

=**digger 2.**

1851 Hall *College Words* 99 **MA,** *Dig.* A diligent student; one who learns his lessons by hard and long continued exertion. **1942** [See **digger 2**]. **1968–69** *DARE* (Qu. JJ9, *Somebody who studies too hard or all the time*) Infs **IN**38, **TX**65, Dig.

digdee owl n Cf **death owl**

Prob =**screech owl.**

1919 *Jrl. Amer. Folkl.* 32.382 **VA,** If a digdee owl whoop on a tree near a house or on a chimney, it is a sign of death in the neighborhood or in the house.

digged See **dig** v[1]

digger n

1 One who uses snuff. [**dig** v[1] **B2**] *arch* Cf *DS* DD3a

1860 (1934) Cowell *Cowells in Amer.* 66 **NY,** The practice [of snuff-chewing] is called 'digging' instead of 'dipping' and those slaves to it are called 'diggers.'

2 See quot 1942. Cf **dig** n

1901 *DN* 2.135 **MA,** *Digger*. . . A grind. Wellesley [College]; cf plug, plugger. **1942** Berrey–Van den Bark *Amer. Slang* 412.2, *Diligent or hard-working person. . . Esp. a serious student. . .* Bone, dig, digger. *Ibid* 825.10, *Diligent student. . .* Dig, digger. **1950** *WELS (Somebody who studies hard all the time)* 3 Infs, **WI,** A digger. **1967–69** *DARE* (Qu. HH27a, *A very able and energetic person who gets things done*) Inf **NH**17, Driver, digger; (Qu. JJ9, *Somebody who studies too hard or all the time*) Inf **OH**11, Digger.

3 A jail. *joc* Cf **jigger**

1969 *DARE* (Qu. V11, . . *A county or city jail*) Inf **IN**75, Digger.

4 also *digger squirrel:* Any of several **ground squirrels n b** (here: *Spermophilus* spp).

1928 Anthony *N. Amer. Mammals* 193, *Otospermophilus grammurus. . .* Digger. *Ibid* 201, *Citellus columbianus. . .* Digger. . . A terrestrial, burrowing Squirrel. **1951** Martin *Amer. Wildlife & Plants* 247, *California Ground Squirrel. Citellus beecheyi. . .* is known locally as . . digger squirrel. **1966–69** *DARE* (Qu. P27) Infs **CA**101, 136, 160, **OR**3, **WA**1, Digger squirrel; **OR**5, Gray digger.

5 An armadillo (here: *Dasypus novemcinctus*).

1982 Heat Moon *Blue Highways* 142 **TX,** The conquistadors named the armadillo ("little armored one") but Texans call them "diggers" because of the animal's penchant for scratching up larvae and worms, especially from soft soil of new graves.

6 See **digger wasp.**

digger pine n [Because its nuts were eaten by the *Digger* Indians]

A pine *(Pinus sabiniana)* native to California. Also called **bull pine 1a, gray pine b, nut pine, squaw pine**

1884 Sargent *Forests of N. Amer.* 195, *Pinus Sabiniana. . . Digger Pine, Bull Pine. . .* The large edible nuts furnish the Indians an important article of food. **1928** Ritchie *Forty-Niners* 21 **CA,** In place of the tilled lands are thickets of manzanita, . . here and there a melancholy Digger pine gray as death. **1948** *Pacific Discovery* Nov–Dec 15/2 **CA,** The Digger pine, so unimposing, so seemingly worn and frayed by the winds and paled by the sun, produces in great numbers enormous cones, heavy, hooked, and filled with "nuts." **1965–70** *DARE* (Qu. T17, . . *Kinds of pine trees*) Infs **CA**20, 22, 97, 105, 137, 141, 150, 161, 204, Digger pine; (Qu. I43, . . *Nuts [that] grow wild*) Inf **CA**136, Digger pine. **1979** Little *Checklist U.S. Trees* 198, *Digger pine. . .* Foothills and mts. from n. Calif. s. in Coast Ranges and Sierra Nev. to s. Calif.

digger squirrel See **digger 4**

digger wasp n Also *digger* Cf **ground hornet**

A wasp, esp one of the families Pompilidae, Scoliidae, or Sphecidae, which digs its nest in the ground.

1882 (1903) Treat *Injurious Insects* 198, A very large digger wasp . . provides its nest with the Cicada. **1901** Howard *Insect Book* 22, *Life History of a Digger Wasp. . .* This large and ferocious wasp . . is very abundant . . , digging great burrows. **1940** Teale *Insects* 126, The great steel-blue diggers will send out a steady stream of dirt and sand as they work. **1961** Douglas *My Wilderness* 138 **sFL,** And there on the mound by the ranger station are hundreds of wasps that dig their holes in the ground. These are the digger wasps that are unique to this area and to portions of the Atlantic Coast. In places the ground was honeycombed with their holes. The holes—fairly shallow—are nests where the female lays her eggs. **1980** Milne–Milne *Audubon Field Guide Insects* 845, *Great Golden Digger Wasp (Sphex ichneumoneus). . .* These wasps sometimes construct tunnels between flagstones in a garden path or terrace.

digging adj *obs*

Remarkable, unusual; dear, expensive.

1820 Mead *Travels N. Amer.* 62 **MD,** I have often been amused with the manners and language of the lower class of people in the South. In Georgia anything a little uncommon is said to be "too digging." **1837** Sherwood *Gaz. GA* 69, *Digging,* dear or costly—*i.e.* a mighty digging price. **1872** (1973) Thompson *Major Jones's Courtship* 239 **GA,** Don't you think that's a little too digin, Mrs. Rogers, to make me pay sixteen dollars for a basket what aint no bigger than my fist.

digging vbl n See **dig** v[1] **B2**

diggings n pl, but sg or pl in constr [Transf from *diggings* a mine] **scattered, but esp freq Sth, S Midl**

A place, locality; premises.

1834 Simms *G. Rivers* 70 *(DA)* **GA,** He's been at this business in these diggings now about three years. **1846** (1968) Browne *Etchings Whaling* 59 **ME,** If whales live on small fish, they'd drive a smashin' business up the Kennebeck. I never see none up thar'. If I was a whale, I'd try them diggins. **1848** (1855) Ruxton *Life Far West* 194 **West,** No name, however, was better known . . than that of Kit Carson, "raised" in Boonlick county, of Missouri State, and a credit to the diggins that gave him birth. **c1885** in 1981 Woodward *Mary Chesnut's Civil War* 112 (as of 1861), One of these men told me he had seen a Yankee prisoner who asked him what sort of a diggins Richmond was for trade. **1899** (1912) Green *VA Folk-Speech* 147, *Diggings. . .* Neighbourhood. "In the diggings." **1908** *DN* 3.305 **eAL, wGA,** *Diggin(g)s. . .* Neighborhood, region. **1915** *DN* 4.225 **wTX,** *Diggings. . .* A certain vicinity, or even a certain home. **1944** *PADS* 2.42 **NC, VA, SC,** *Diggin's. . .* Deprecative designation of a locality. **1945** *New Engl. Homestead* 22 Sept 18/2, They came forth with a crop such as never was before in these particular diggings. **c1960** *Wilson Coll.* **csKY,** *Diggings.* Also *diggins.* Place, locality. Usually deprecatory, somewhat like sticks, neck of the woods. **1966** *DARE* Tape **MI**10, I was trying to find out more about my home diggings. **1967–69** *DARE* (Qu. Y19, *To begin to go away from a place: "It's about time for me to ———."*) Inf **KY**5, Leave these diggings; (Qu. MM22, *If you are talking to a friend who lives in another place and you want to inquire about his neighborhood, you might ask, "How are things ———?"*) Inf **AR**55, Down in your diggings.

dight See **dite**

dig it up See **dig** v[1] **B6**

dig on See **dig** v² **2**

dig out See **dig** v¹ **B6**

dig-out n

1938 FWP *Guide MN* 338 **nwMN,** Because wells in this area are not adequate to water the stock, the farmers have dug large open-pits 6 to 15 feet deep, 20 to 60 feet wide, and 50 to 100 feet long; the clay subsoil in these "dig-outs" holds the rainwater and keeps it comparatively clear.

digsies exclam Cf **dib** n¹ **2, halvsies**

1957 *Sat. Eve. Post Letters* **swMA** (as of 1920s), If two boys both saw a valuable item on the ground, but one picked it up first, the second could claim part ownership by saying "halfsies" or "digsies".

dig them up See **dig** v¹ **B6**

dig you later See **dig** v² **3**

dike v Usu with *out* or *up* Also *bedike* [Prob var of *dight* (cf *OED dight* v. 8, *EDD dight* v. 4) infl by *deck;* it is not clear whether this reflects the Engl dial survival or the 19th cent revival of *dight* past pple as a poetic synonym for *decked.*] Cf **dicty** adj **chiefly Sth, S Midl** See Map

To dress up in one's best clothes; to dress elaborately or ostentatiously; hence ppl adjs *diked out, ~ up.*

1851 Hall *College Words* 100, At the University of Virginia, one who is dressed with more than ordinary elegance is said to be *diked out.* **1895** *DN* 1.387 **SC,** *Diked out:* dressed up. *Ibid* **TX,** *Dike:* to prepare to go out. **1899** (1912) Green *VA Folk-Speech* 147, *Dike. . .* To dress fine. "You are diked up to-day." **1901** *DN* 2.139 **cVA,** *Dike up. . .* Dress up. **1906** *DN* 3.133 **nwAR,** *Dike out. . .* To dress up. "She was all diked out for the party." **1908** *DN* 3.305 **eAL, wGA,** *Dike. . .* To dress oneself so as to make a display, to dress well. "He diked himself in his Sunday-go-to-meetin clothes." Probably from *deck* with influence of *dight. Diked up (or out). . .* "He was all diked up in his best clothes." **1915** [see **dike** n²]. **1915** *DN* 4.225 **wTX,** *Dike. . .* To dress elaborately. **1927** *AmSp* 2.352 **WV,** He was all diked out for the party. **1933** Miller *Lamb in His Bosom* 344 **GA,** Tell Ma that I have got her a vermillion-dyed merino dress picked out and linnen cloathes aplenty to dike herself out in. **1942** Perry *Texas* 39, When the now-sanitary tramp was diked out in this finery, the boys took him to town and bought him a turkey dinner. **1942** (1971) Campbell *Cloud-Walking* 10 **seKY** (as of 1936–41), Ain't you got new shoes to dike out in? **1946** *PADS* 5.19 **VA,** *Dike up. . .* Get dressed up; fairly common. **1955** in 1958 Brewer *Dog Ghosts* 38 **TX** [Black], Dey was all diked up in dey bes' duds. **c1960** *Wilson Coll.* **csKY,** *Diked out.* Dressed up, sometimes obviously so; probably *dight.* **1964** *Mt. Life* Spring 54 **sAppalachians,** *Bediked* (over dressed). **1965–70** *DARE* (Qu. W38, *When a man dresses . . up . . , he's ______*) 66 Infs, **chiefly Sth, S Midl,** (All) diked out (*or* up); (Qu. W37, *When a woman puts on her good clothes and tries to look her best, you say she's ______*) 23 Infs, **chiefly Sth, S Midl,** (All) diked out (*or* up); **GA**17, Diking up; **NC**16, All diked up in her Sunday-go-to-meetin' clothes; **OH**63, Diked out like Mrs. Astor's plush horse; (Qu. W30, *When a woman adds decorations to . . something . . "I'll put on a few flowers to ______ it up."*) Infs **FL**15, **NC**50, Dike; (Qu. W40, . . *A woman who overdresses*) Inf **NC**11, All diked out; (Qu. HH35, *A woman who puts on a lot of airs: "She's too ______ for me."*) Inf **MA**5, Diked out—clothes.

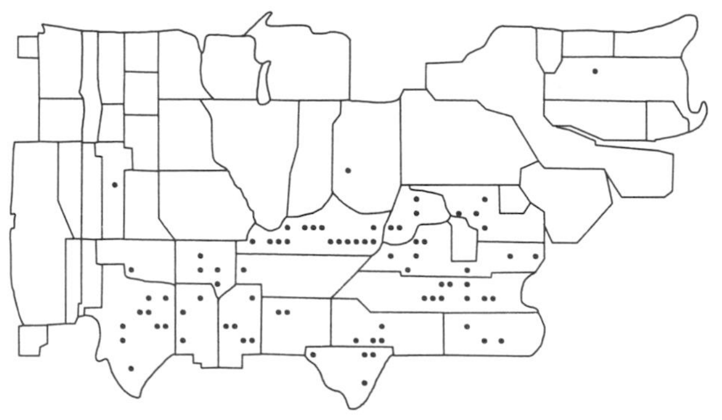

•dike v + varr (Qq. W38, W37, W30, W40, HH35)

dike n¹ [*OED dike* sb. 2 "A low wall . . of turf or stone. . . Now the regular sense in Scotland"; c1425 →]

An earthen bank.

1892 *DN* 1.210 **seMA,** *Dike:* bank of earth, without reference to water; *e.g.* bank of a terrace. **1899** (1912) Green *VA Folk-Speech* 147, *Dike. . .* A low wall of turf; a ditch-bank.

dike n² [**dike** v] *old-fash*

See quots.

1872 Schele de Vere *Americanisms* 597, *Dike,* denoting a man in full dress, or merely the dress, is a peculiar American cant term, as yet unexplained. To be *out on a dike* is said of persons, mainly young men, who are dressed more carefully than usual, in order to pay visits or to attend a party. It is not unlikely that the term is merely a corruption of the obsolete *dight,* which meant *decked out,* and is in this sense used by many old English writers. **1895** *DN* 1.382 **NJ,** *Dike . . :* "on a dike" = showing one's finery in public. **1908** *DN* 3.305 **eAL, wGA,** *Dike. . .* A display of dress. "He's on a big dike to-day." **1915** *DN* 4.182 **swVA,** *Dike, n.* and *v.* Display in dress.

dike-bread n [Perh for **dight-bread* 'made bread' (as opposed to **hard bread**); cf *OED dight* v. 14. b "To prepare, make ready (food, a meal)"]

1915 *DN* 4.240 **eMA,** *Dike-bread. . .* Bread made, on fishing vessels, with fermented dough.

dike climber See **dike jumper**

diked out, diked up See **dike** v

dike jumper n Also *dike climber joc*

A person of Netherlands ancestry.

1966–68 *DARE* (Qu. CC4, . . *Nicknames . . for various . . religious groups*) Inf **IL**27, Dike climber—Dutch Reformed (in Morrison); (Qu. HH28, . . *Nicknames . . for people of foreign background: . . Hollanders*) Inf **SD**3, Dike jumper.

dike out, dike up See **dike** v

dikey adj [**dike** v]

1966 *PADS* 46.25 **cnAR,** *Dikey. . .* Ultra-fashionable.—"He was a dikey kind of feller."

dilapidated adj Usu |də'læpə,detəd, dɪ-, -pɪ-|; also |-,tetəd, -,letəd|; for addit varr see quot Pronc-spp *dilaberdated, dilapilated, dilapitated*

Std senses, var forms.

1966–70 *DARE* (Qu. D21) Infs **ME**20, **PA**146, Dilapitated; **PA**142, Dilapitated [dɨ'læbɨ,dedɨd]; **PA**235, [də'lɪprietɪd]; (Qu. KK20a) Inf **IN**73, Dilapilated [də'læpə,letəd]; (Qu. KK20b) Inf **CA**209, [dɪ'læpəletɪd]; (Qu. KK23) Inf **OK**27, [dɪ'læpɪledɛd]; (Qu. KK70) Inf **TX**62, Dilaberdated.

dilatory adj Pronc-spp *dilitary, dilleterry, dillyterry* **S Midl**

Std sense, var forms.

1913 Kephart *Highlanders* 287 **sAppalachians,** She's so dilitary! **1923** (1946) Greer–Petrie *Angeline Doin' Society* 18 **csKY,** I'm sorry Betty's so dillyterry. **1931** *PMLA* 46.1304 **sAppalachians,** That gal of Zeke's is shorely dilitary. **1976** Garber *Mountain-ese* 22 **Appalachians,** He's so dilleterry he won't never git his homework done. **1978** Massey *Bittersweet Country* 206 **Ozarks,** He's the most dilitary I've seen.

dildally See **dilldally**

‡**dildow** n [Etym uncert, but cf *EDD dilly* sb.¹ 2 "A light wagon"]

1968 *DARE* (Qq. N41a,c, . . *Horse-drawn vehicles*) Inf **NJ**18, Dildow—A flat, uncovered wagon, has movable (sliding) seats in slots. Like a topless hack. Sides about a foot high. The seats were boards. They rested in a slot along the sides and could be slid back or front. You could move them back and carry people—or slide them out and carry a load.

dill n¹

1 A **button snakeroot 2.**

1959 Carleton *Index Herb. Plants* 37, *Dill:* Anethum graveolens; Eryngium (v).

2 A **biscuit root 1** (here: *Lomatium dissectum*).

1967 *DARE* Wildfl QR (Craighead) Pl.13.5 Inf **CO**15, Dill.

dill n[2], v [Pronc-sp for *deal*] Cf Pronc Intro 3.I.3.c

1982 McCool *Sam McCool's Pittsburghese* 9 **PA,** Dill: deal, as with cards, not pickles, unless it's a good dill of them. "I know a good dill when I seen one."

dilla n [Abbr for *armadillo*]

1982 Heat Moon *Blue Highways* 143 **TX,** In spite of both the belief that armadillos feed on corpses and the animal's susceptibility to leprosy, poor whites ate them with greens and cornbread during the Depression . . ; even now, poor blacks, calling them just "dillas," barbeque the soft meat.

dillberry n [*EDD dilberries* 1879] Also called **dingbat 6, dingleberry 3**

See quots.

1950 *PADS* 14.26 **SC,** *Dillberries. . .* The small lumps of excrement clinging to wool on the hindquarters of sheep at certain seasons. **c1960** *Wilson Coll.* **csKY,** *Dillberries. . .* Wool matted with mud or fecal matter, often found on sheep. Gipson's word is *dingleberries. . . dingleberries* is used in NC.

dilldally v Also sp *dildally* [Var of *dillydally*]

1908 *DN* 3.305 **eAL, wGA,** *Dil-dally. . .* To dilly-dally. **1968** *DARE* (Qu. A11, *When somebody takes too long about coming to a decision, you might say, "I wish he'd quit ______."*) Inf **IN**48, Dilldallying.

diller n [Var of *dilly*]

Something remarkable of its kind; see quot.

1968 *DARE* (Qu. LL5, *Something impressively big: "That cabbage is a ______."*) Inf **MN**16, Diller.

dillweed n Also *dilweed, dillidillweed, dilly, dillydil(l)weed*

A **dog fennel 1** (here: *Anthemis cotula*).

1828 Rafinesque *Med. Flora* 44, *Anthemis cotula. . . Vulgar Namer* [sic]—May-weed, . . Dilly, Dilweed, Fieldweed, &c. **1876** Hobbs *Bot. Hdbk.* 31, Dillydilweed, May weed, Anthemis cotula. **1900** Lyons *Plant Names* 37, *A. Cotula. . .* Dillweed, Dillidillweed. **1914** Georgia *Manual Weeds* 488, *Mayweed. . . Other English names: . .* Dillweed. . . No grazing animal will eat it because of its rank odor and acrid juices. **1940** Clute *Amer. Plant Names* 74, *A. cotula. . .* Dill-weed. *Ibid* 251, *Anthemis cotula.* Dillydill weed. **1959** Carleton *Index Herb. Plants* 37, *Dill-weed:* Anthemis cotula.

dilly bean n [*dill* an herb]

See quot 1968.

1968 *DARE* (Qu. H56, . . *Kinds of pickles*) Inf **UT**8, Dilly beans—made from tender young green beans with a solution of vinegar, alum, dill and red peppers. **1989** *Yankee* Aug 32 **ME,** You can buy just about anything . . from fresh organic fruits . . to . . dilly beans.

dilly bread n [*dill* an herb]

See quots.

1968 *DARE* FW Addit **neWI,** I saw "dilly bread" at the bakery. It is flavored with dill seed. **1968** *DARE* (Qu. H18, . . *Kinds of bread*) Inf **IN**37, Dilly bread—made with minced onion, dill seed, and cottage cheese; **KS**20, Dilly bread—has onion and dill in it; **MI**95, Dilly bread—with dill seed.

dillydil(l)weed, dilweed See **dillweed**

dime-a-dip dinner n Also *dime-a-dip, ten-cents-a-dip* Cf **jitney** n

A fundraising meal at which participants pay ten cents (or another specified amount) per portion of food.

1967 *DARE* (Qu. FF1, . . *A 'social'*) Inf **NV**1, Ten-cents-a-dip—the Mormon sale; food costs ten cents a piece. **1968** *Needles Desert Star* (CA) 7 Mar 3/4, The Latter Day Saints Church will hold a Dime-A-Dip dinner Thursday. **1968** *Mendocino Beacon* (CA) 30 Aug 4/5, A "Dime a Dip" dinner is scheduled for Sunday at the I.O.O.F. hall. . . Sponsor of the always popular event is Bethel 184, International Order of Job's Daughters. **1987** *NADS Letters* **CA, NV,** My first personal memory of the use of the term "dime-a-dip" is about 1961–62. . . I seem to recall that "dime-a-dip" could be used independently . . as in "We're going to have a dime-a-dip two weeks from now." . . Around 1961, the local congregation of my church in Anaheim [CA] . . was building a new chapel and they held "dime-a-dip" dinners to raise money to help pay for it. . . All of the people I talked to who had heard about this term are Mormons . . The term must not be generally known to all Mormons because the ones I asked about it, from Washington, Utah, and Idaho, had never heard of it. . . A friend from Fresno, California . . said she went to one somewhere around 1978–1980. . . Another friend said they had them in Concord, California . . and that he went to one maybe five years ago. It was a fund raiser for sending out a missionary for the Mormon Church. Another friend said they had them in Alamo, Nevada . . back in the late 1950s. It was a fund raiser in the Mormon Church. . . The food for the dime-a-dip dinner was provided by the members of the congregation. Every family brought something: a main course, salad, vegetable, dessert, etc. Then we would all serve ourselves buffet style and pay a dime (or more in later times) for each "dip" or portion of food that we took.

dime jig n

1969 *DARE* (Qu. FF5a, *Names for different steps and figures in dancing—in the past*) Inf **CA**166, Dime jig.

diment See **diamond**

dime, off the adj phr Also *off the nickel* **chiefly CA**

Active—usu in phr *get off the dime* to hurry, get going.

1927 *AmSp* 2.276 **CA** [Stanford Univ expressions], Get off the dime—start. **1938** *AmSp* 13.156 **swCA,** Get off the dime. To quit loafing. **1942** Berrey–Van den Bark *Amer. Slang* 58.4, *Leave; depart* . . get off the dime *or* nickel. *Ibid* 245.10, *Get busy; set to work energetically* . . get off the dime *or nickel.* **1967–69** *DARE* (Qu. A19, *Other ways of saying "I'll have to hurry."*) Inf **CA**15, Get off the dime; (Qu. A20, *Joking ways of telling somebody to hurry*) Infs **CA**125, 145, Get off the dime; (Qu. KK29, *To start working very hard: "He was slow at first but now he's really ______."*) Inf **CA**107, Off the dime. **1977–89** *DARE* File **cwCA,** Hurry up! If you don't get off the dime we'll never get there in time; **sCA,** I know and have used the phrase "get off the dime" from time out of mind, meaning "get busy," "get moving," "start doing something"; **seWI,** A friend of mine in Racine often urged people to "get off the dime" when he wanted them to get going or to get moving. I used the expression myself at the time (=late 1940s, early 1950s), and I still hear it occasionally.

dime on the counter phr

1967 *DARE* (Qu. W24c, *Sayings to warn a man that his trouser-fly is open*) Inf **CA**9, Dime on the counter—when unbuttoned.

Dimery n

=**Croatan.**

1950 *PADS* 14.26 **SC,** *Dimery. . .* A Croatan.

dimind See **diamond**

‡dimmy n

1968 *DARE* (Qu. C25, . . *Stone . . about . . [the] size of a person's head . . smooth and hard*) Inf **NY**80, Dimmy ['dɪmɪ].

dimunt See **diamond A**

din See **do** v **A5**

dina clover See **dana clover**

dinapaddy n

1967 *DARE* (Qu. R5, *A big brown beetle that comes out in large numbers in spring and early summer, and flies with a buzzing sound*) Inf **CA**12, Dinapaddy ['dɪnə,pædi]—in palm trees.

dinch n Also *dincher*

See quots.

1927 *DN* 5.444 [Underworld jargon], *Dinch. . .* The butt of a cigar or cigarette. **1942** Berrey–Van den Bark *Amer. Slang* 476.2, Tramp and Criminal [jargon]. . . *Cigarette or cigar stub.* Dinch, dincher, dobe. **1967** *DARE* (Qu. DD6b, *Nicknames for cigarettes*) Inf **NY**34, Dincher.

dindle n [Cf *EDD dindle* sb. sow-thistle, hawkweed, dandelion]

A **wild carrot** (here: *Daucus carota*).

1940 Clute *Amer. Plant Names* 257, *Daucus carota. . .* dindle.

‡dine v

1914 *DN* 4.71 **NH,** *Dine. . .* Go to bed.

dinero n

1 Money. [Span] **SW**

1856 *Butte Record* (Oroville, Calif.) 29 Aug. 2/6 *(DA),* They pungled [*DARE* Ed: =paid] the dinero, and observed that, as it was cheap, they had a mind to play the 'balance of the day out.' **1907** White *AZ Nights* 142, "Here's your dinero," says I, dumpin' the four big sacks on the ground. **1909** *DN* 3.395 **neOK,** *Dinero, the* or *el. . .* Money. **1940** Fergusson *Our Southwest* 339 **SW,** Then while you wrangle your dudes, I'll see what I can round up for the baile at night. Got enough dinero?

1965–70 *DARE* (Qu. U19a, . . *Money in general: "He's certainly got the ______."*) Infs **CA**107, 145, 181, **TX**4, 5, 28, Dinero.

2 A cook on a ranch or trail drive. [Appar in punning ref to *dine* or *dinner*]

1920 Hunter *Trail Drivers TX* 299, Naturally, the cook has many names applied to him. He is called a "sheffi," "dough roller," "dinero," "coocy" and "biscuit shooter."

ding v[1] [*OED ding* v.[1] 2 "To beat, knock, strike. . . (Now *dial.*, chiefly *Sc.* or *north.*)"]

1 To strike; to throw, fling. Cf **ding** n

1688 in 1960 Taylor *Poems* 47 **MA,** Hells Nymps with spite their Dog's sticks thereat ding / To Dash the Grafft off. **1859** Matsell *Vocabulum* 26, *Ding.* To throw away; to strike. **1967** *DARE* (Qu. C24b, *"The dog wouldn't go away so he took a stone/rock and [make gesture] ______ [it at it.]"*) Inf **OR**15, Ding?

2 To make a small dent or nick in (a vehicle); hence ppl adj *dinged up.* [Prob transf from **1** above, but cf **dinge** n[2], v] Cf **ding** n

1980 *Capital Times* (Madison WI) 31 Oct 1/3 **csWI,** If you see a lot of buses that are dinged up and not working properly, it's because we're trying to get the new ones out on the street. **1988** *DARE* File **sCA** (as of 1960s), I am familiar with the use of the verb *ding* from my father, a car dealer, who grew up and lived his adult life in Southern California. "Watch out or you'll ding that fender." To ding a car was to damage it in a slight but costly way—with small dents or nicks. **1988** *Capital Times* (Madison WI) 20 Apr 38, [*Crankshaft* cartoon:] The trickiest part of my [school bus] route is backing into the Keestermans' driveway to turn around! *Scrunge! Crunch! Smash!!* Oh, Oh! I think I dinged the Keestermans' mailbox again!

3 also with *at;* Fig: to din (something) into (someone), reiterate tiresomely; to nag, pester. [Cf *OED ding* v.[2] "To speak with wearying reiteration"; 1582 →; *EDD ding* v. 13]

1899 (1912) Green *VA Folk-Speech* 147, *Ding. . .* To keep repeating; impress by reiteration. "You have been dinging at that all day." . . "I cannot ding it into him." I cannot make him understand. **1914** *DN* 4.71 **ME, nNH,** *Ding at. . .* To worry, pester, tease. "He's allus dingin' at me." **1935** Davis *Honey* 78 **OR,** They had expected the interview to come out something like that, but they had consented to it to make old Geary shut up dinging about it. **1967** *DARE* Tape **OR**6, This is the thing I keep dinging at them. **1977** *Yankee* Jan 112 **csME,** *Dinging* is another word for nagging. . . Dora . . was discomboobleated and she took to dinging on how little they had and how would they ever make it through the winter.

4 By ext: to beg; hence v phr *put the ding on* beg from. Cf **dinger** n[2]

1929 *AmSp* 4.339 [Vocab of bums], *Ding*—To beg. **1970** *Thompson Coll.* **GA,** An old tramp who put the ding on me.

ding v[2] *euphem*

Also in combs: To damn, confound; hence adj, adv *ding(ed)* damned. Note: In combs *ding* is perh felt as a noun by some speakers.

1834 *S. Lit. Messenger* 1.159/2 **VA,** By jingo, Jack, clap on your hat; ding it, do as I do! **1844** *Ibid* 10.44/2 **GA,** I'll be ding'd if I don't offer myself, if I can't git a smarter man to offer. **1845** Thompson *Pineville* 47 **cGA,** It was ding hot, too, down thar in the lane. **1859** Taliaferro *Fisher's R.* 39 **nwNC** (as of 1820s), Git out'n here, you dinged old sloomy Yahoo! *Ibid* 104, Ding such big quality words. **1872** (1973) Thompson *Major Jones's Courtship* 254, "Ding'd if I don't see who it is," ses Bill; "I aint afraid of no ghost." **1885** Twain *Huck. Finn* 113 **MO,** Well, now, I be ding-busted! **1895** *DN* 1.396 **seNY,** *Dingswizzled* [dɪŋswɪzəld]: expression of surprise, consternation, etc. A person who is at a loss how to act says, "I'll be dingswizzled." **1903** McFaul *Ike Glidden* 109 *(DAE),* He was counted a dinged good ol' hoss then. **1911** *DN* 3.542 **NE,** *Dingblastit* . . expressing annoyance or exasperation. "Dingblastit, he didn't come." Compare also *dingblast.* "Dingblast this machine, any-way." **1924** *DN* 5.266, Exclamations in American English. . . *Ding:* . . — it, — the luck, I'll be —ed, gol — it, gosh — it, gol (gosh) — it to blazes, goll (gosh) — the luck, — bust it, I'll be —-busted. *Ibid* 285 **seNE,** *Bat:* ding — it. **1965–70** *DARE* (Qu. LL37, . . *"I could have wrung her neck, I was so ______ mad."*) Inf **FL**2, Ding busted; (Qu. NN8a, *Exclamations of annoyance or disgust*) Inf **CA**8, Ding bust it; (Qu. NN8b, . . *"This jar won't come open, ______ it."*) Infs **IN**5, **MI**67, Ding; **CA**2, Ding bust; (Qu. NN9a, *Exclamations showing great annoyance*) Inf **IL**28, Ding blast it; **NY**14, Ding bust it all; (Qu. NN9b, . . *"He's run off with my hammer again, ______!"*) Infs **AR**16, **NC**14, Ding bust him (*or* it); (Qu. NN17, *Something that keeps on annoying you . . : "That ______ fly won't go away."*) Infs **MO**12, **NC**51, **PA**215, Ding (busted *or* dang); **CA**97, Dinged; (Qu. NN25, *Weakened substitutes for 'damn' or 'damned'*) Infs **DC**3, **IN**5, 13, **NJ**18, 39, **PA**3, **TX**88, **WV**7, Ding-bust; **CA**97, 107, **IL**98, **MI**18, 46, **SC**9, 21, Ding; **SC**26, God ding; (Qu. NN25b, . . *"Well, I'll be ______!"*) Infs **NC**51, **NJ**22, Ding; **OH**15, **VT**7, Ding busted; **VA**54, **WI**34, Ding donged; **AK**8, Ding dung daddy; **CA**107, **IA**5, **IL**98, **SC**9, **WI**34, Dinged. **1966** *DARE* Tape **MI**17, It wouldn't do a ding busted thing.

ding n [**ding** v[1] **2**] Cf **dinge** n[2]

A dent, nick, or scratch.

1968–70 *DARE* FW Addit **neNJ,** Seen on a West Orange supermarket bulletin board: Surf board for sale. No dings. *Ibid,* **cnIN,** *Ding*—Dent or scratch in car. *Ibid,* **CA**191, *Dings*—In surfing lingo means "dents in your board." Inf, who had surfed for more than thirty years, said term was long-established and current. **1986** *DARE* File **sCA,** My husband always parks our car in the most deserted part of a parking lot to avoid getting dings in the paint. He also worries lest our small son put a ding in the furniture or paneling with his toy hammer.

ding adj, adv See **ding** v[2]

ding-a-ling n Also called **dingbat** n **4**

A person with strange or unconventional behavior; an eccentric; one who is crazy or mentally abnormal.

1944 *AmSp* 19.104 [Vocab of sailors], A man who acts up partly through liquor and partly through something defective in his parents is . . a *squirrel,* or some kind of *ding-a-ling.* **1955** *Western Folkl.* 14.135 **cwCA** [San Quentin Prison slang], *Ding-a-ling.* One who is mentally unbalanced. **1965–70** *DARE* (Qu. HH3, *A dull and stupid person*) Infs **MN**33, **NH**17, Ding-a-ling; (Qu. HH6, *Someone who is out of his mind*) Inf **NE**11, Ding-a-ling; (Qu. HH9, *A very silly or light-headed person*) Infs **CA**169, **MI**108, Ding-a-ling; (Qu. HH38, *A womanish man*) Inf **HI**13, Ding-a-ling. **1967** *New Yorker* 27 May 33, Always wearing black tights under her dress and other kinds of kinky gear. . . This kid is a dangerous ding-a-ling. **1971** *Time* 12 Apr 42, So we decided to frustrate the prosecution attempts to select a good jury and try to keep every ding-a-ling we could find, to get the worst possible jury [for the Manson trial].

dingar See **dinger** n[2]

dingass See **dingus**

dingbat n [Etym uncert]

1 Something thrown or fired with force.

1877 Bartlett *Americanisms* 177, *Dingbat.* A bat of wood that may be thrown (dinged); a piece of money; a cannon-ball; a bullet. **1895** *DN* 1.387 **eME,** *Ding-bat. . .* Flying missile. Penobscot river (noted as common among boys and river drivers).

2 also *dingbatler:* A piece of wood (prob used to paddle a child); a paddling, reprimand, punishment. Cf **battle** n[1]

1877 [see **1** above]. **1895** *DN* 1.387 **CT, ME, NH, VT,** *Ding-bat. . .* Blow or slap on the buttocks. . . (Also in form *dingbatlers.*) **1950** *WELS Suppl.* **seWI** (as of c1900), *Dingbats*—Always plural for this informant. Always a pair of *dingbats.* Naughty children got them in their Christmas stockings. Associated unpleasantly in Inf's mind with paddles and paddling. **1966** *DARE* File **csWI,** "I'll put the dingbats on you!" Mother's semi-threatening saying to children to make them obey. **1969** *DARE* (Qu. II27, . . *A very sharp scolding*) Inf **MI**106, I got the dingbats for that.

3 also *dingbattus:* Something whose name is not known or readily remembered; a thingamajig, a what-you-may-call-it; see quot 1965–70. *usu joc* Cf **dingus** n[1] **1**

1905 *DN* 3.66 **NE,** Indefinite expression applied to something, the name of which is not readily recalled. . . *Dingus,* . . *dingbat.* **1931** *AmSp* 6.257 **KS, NE,** To avoid searching out *le mot propre,* Americans . . like to make use of some whimsical indefinite substitute. . . Dingbat[,] dingbattus. **1931** Thurber *Owl in Attic* 78 **cOH,** It [=the owl] is sitting on a strange and almost indescribable sort of iron dingbat. **1946** [see **fimdiddle**]. **1958** (1972) Funk *Horsefeathers* 38, *Dingbat. . .* we Americans use it, as we do its derivative, *dingus,* as a momentary name of anything of which the proper name is out of mind or unknown. **1965–70** *DARE* (Qu. NN12b, *Things that people say to put a child off when he asks, "What are you making?"*) Infs **AL**41, 43, **IN**31, **ME**12, **MA**58, **NY**57, 102, A dingbat.

4 =ding-a-ling. [Prob from the *Dingbats* a comic strip family created in 1910 by George Harriman]

1915 *DN* 4.203, *Dingbat,* a fool. "The boss called Ralph a dingbat because he made fun of him." **1950** *WELS (Someone who is a little odd or peculiar)* 1 Inf, **seWI,** Dingbat. **1967** *DARE* (Qu. HH5, *Someone who is queer but harmless*) Inf **NE**11, A dingbat. **1968** *AmSp* 43.286 [Railroad vocab], *Dingbat.* A pompous, bumbling incompetent serving in a position of authority. **1969** Kantor *MO Bittersweet* 14, I'm a marvelous driver, but all the other drivers drive like dingbats. **1979** *Capital Times* (Madison WI) 28 Apr 15/5, Then Jean Stapleton, the venerable "dingbat" Edith, announced she planned to leave [the TV program "All in the Family"] after this season, leaving only Archie.

5 A vagabond, hobo; a bum.

1927 *AmSp* 2.386 [Vagabond argot], There are many names which vags use for one another. *Dingbat* is evidently a combination of *ding* and *batter,* both meaning "to beg." **1927** *DN* 5.444 [Underworld jargon], *Ding-bat. . .* A bum of the lowest order. **1934** Lomax–Lomax *Amer. Ballads* 124 **SW,** The lingering sunset across the plain / . . shone on a passing train close by,/ Where a dingbat sat on a rotten tie.

6 =dillberry.

1895 *DN* 1.387 **VT,** *Ding-bat. . .* Balls of dung on buttocks of sheep or cattle.

7 In var other senses: see quots.

1895 *DN* 1.387 **ME,** *Ding-bat. . .* Squabble of words or pushing. *Ibid,* **GA,** *Ding-bat. . .* Affectionate embrace of mothers hugging and kissing their children. . . "Ma just can't help it, she has got to put the ding-bats right on." *Ibid, Ding-bat. . .* Term of admiration. "They are regular ding-bats" (speaking of girls). **1944** *AmSp* 19.104 [Vocab of sailors], A woman who is neither your sister nor your mother is a *dingbat.*

ding bat v See **ding** v^2

dingbatler See **dingbat 2**

dingbatting n

1969 *DARE* FW Addit **ceNC,** Dingbatting—fishing term. Net fishing where fisher-men scare the fish into the net by splashing water.

dingbattus See **dingbat 3**

dingbatty adj [**dingbat 4**]

1911 *DN* 3.542 **NE,** *Dingbatty. . .* Half crazy, imbecile. "That fellow is dingbatty."

ding blast, ding bust(ed) See **ding** v^2

dingclicker n

1914 *DN* 4.71 **ME, nNH,** *Dingclicker. . .* An unusually fine or pleasing person or thing.

ding dang See **ding** v^2

dingdie n Also sp *dingdhi*

=dingbat 3.

1975 Gould *ME Lingo* 73, *Dingdhi*—Spelling may vary; it is not often written but it is spoken frequently in Maine; *ding-die.* It means anything; a dingus, a doodad, a doohicky, a fid, a cover, a catch, a lever. "Heave me that dingdhi!" can mean a wrench, a carburetor, a coffee pot.

dingdo n [Var of **dido,** perh infl by **dingus** n^1 **1**]

=dido 1.

1900 Day *Up in ME* 25, Allus cuttin' ding-does up—a master curis pill! **1902** Day *Pine Tree Ballads* 244 **ME,** They [=vaulters in a circus] did those ding-does master fine some twenty years ago. **1914** *DN* 4.70 **ME, nNH,** *Cut didoes,* or *dingdoes. . .* To put on airs and graces.

dingdong n

1 See quots.

1942 Berrey–Van den Bark *Amer. Slang* 513, *Miscellaneous logging terms . .* ding-dong, *the dinner gong.* **1968** Adams *Western Words* 93, *Ding-dong*—In logging, the steel triangle struck to notify the loggers that a meal is ready.

2 The head.

1929 *Sat. Eve. Post* 17 Aug 11/3 **LA,** Efn Cap'm Sam ketch you rattin'—ay-iah! He sho rap on yo' ding-dong!

3 =ding-a-ling.

1968 *DARE* (Qu. HH3, *A dull and stupid person*) Inf **IA**32, Dingdong.

4 See quots. euphem

1944 *PADS* 2.29 **NC, VA,** *Ding-dong. . .* The penis. **1956** *KY Folkl. Rec.* 20 **wKY,** Ding-dong. Penis.

dingdong v [Transf from *dingdong* ringing sound of a bell repeatedly struck, prob infl by **ding** v^1 **3;** *OED* 1797 →]

=ding v^1 **3.**

1944 *PADS* 2.29 **eKY,** *Ding-dong. . .* To annoy. "He jist ding-dongs his pa till he gits whatever he wants out of him." . . Common. **c1960** *Wilson Coll.* **csKY,** *Ding-dong . .* To annoy by repeating a scolding or an order.

ding donged See **ding** v^2

dinge n^1 |dɪnǰ| Also *dingy* [Back-formation from *dingy* adj] *derog*

A dark-skinned person, usu a Black.

1848 *Ladies' Repository* 8.316/1 [Thieves' jargon], *Covess Dinge,* A negress, sometimes called Dinge Blowen. . . *Dinge Kinch,* A negro child. *Dinge,* A negro man. **1896** *DN* 1.415 **cNY,** *Dingy.* A negro. **1909** (1913) Porter *Roads of Destiny* 134, These dingies will cheat you out of the gold in your teeth if you don't understand their ways. **1926** Van Vechten *Nigger Heaven* 285, *Dinge:* Negro. **1929** *Sat. Eve. Post* 7 Dec 130/2, I found that no-good dinge who cooks for us sleeping off a jag on the back porch. **1930** Williams *Logger-Talk* 15 **NW,** *Dinge:* A negro. **1935** *AmSp* 10.14 [Gangster argot], *Dinge.* A smoke-colored negro or mulatto. **1942** Berrey–Van den Bark *Amer. Slang* 385.14, *Negro . .* darky, dinge, dingy. *Ibid* 207.2, Dinge in the stovewood, *a concealed motive or reason.* **1967** *DARE* (Qu. HH28, . . *People of foreign background: Negro*) Inf **MA**71, Dinge.

dinge n^2 |dɪnǰ| [Scots, Ir, nEngl dial] Cf **ding** n

A dent.

1978 *New Haven Reg.* (CT) 30 Nov 68/1 **Pittsburgh PA,** Only Pittsburgh drivers know that when the streets are "slippy" they're likely to put a "dinge" or two in car fenders. **1982** *Barrick Coll.* **csPA,** *Dinge* pron. dinj. *dent* (in a fender, etc.) **1986** *DARE* File **Pittsburgh PA,** I was brought up saying dinge [dɪnǰ] for a dent in a car, or any other metal object . . like a metal cabinet . . not for anything wooden.

dinge v [**dinge** n^2] Cf **ding** v^1 **2**

c1970 *DARE* File, Dinge—to make a shallow dent, "The car fender was only dinged after being hit by the bicycle."

dinged adj, adv See **ding** v^2

dinged up ppl adj See **ding** v^1 **2**

dinger n^1 [In ref to the ringing of a bell]

1 Something or someone remarkable or superior; a humdinger.

1809 *Amer. Mag. of Wonders* Nov 1, This land of our dads . . is a dinger at nailing the scads. **1909** *DN* 3.395 **nwAR,** *Dinger. . .* Anything particularly liked. "The lecture course this year is a dinger." "Yes, it's a humdinger." **1911** in 1983 Truman *Dear Bess* 32 **MO,** Mamma gave me her prescription for dipping chickens [in a preparation designed to kill parasites] and it's a dinger I tell you. **1913** *DN* 4.16 **NE,** *Dinger.* Something very splendid, or stylish. Used by Nebraska students. "Isn't that hat a dinger?" "That fellow's a dinger." "Say, kid, that suit's a dinger." **1916** *DN* 4.322 **KS,** *Dinger . . =humdinger.* **1939** Steinbeck *Grapes* 37 **OK,** See how good the corn come along until the dust got up. Been a dinger of a crop. **c1960** Bailey *Resp. to PADS 20* **KS,** "Dinger" was an often used word to mean "[someone] good at something." It was used in many ways, usually in a complimentary sense. **1965–70** *DARE* (Qu. B3, *If a day is very hot, you say it's [a]* ______) Inf **MO**4, Dinger; (Qu. KK45, . . *Narrow escape . . "He really had a* ______.*"*) Inf **NM**9, Dinger—a general term; (Qu. LL5, *Something impressively big: "That cabbage is really a* ______.*"*) Inf **WA**30, Dinger. [All Infs old]

2 In railroading: see quots 1940, 1945.

1929 *Bookman* 69.524 [Railroad lingo], Do you think the Dinger is goin' to put you in their class? **1932** *Santa Fe Employes' Mag.* Jan 34, A yardmaster is a *general;* an assistant yardmaster is a *dinger.* **1940** Cottrell *Railroader* 124, *Dinger*—Yardmaster or one of his assistants. **1945** Hubbard *Railroad Ave.* 340, *Dinger*—Conductor (man who rings the bell) [=signals the engineer to stop or start the train]. **1967** *DARE* Tape **ID**9, Many years ago there were two types of telephones that a yard master used—a regular Bell telephone and then they had a telephone that worked just between yard offices. . . it was the old hand crank type. . . and you get a hold of a little handle and you just crank like mad—and it goes dingly-ding-ding-ding-ding all over—and it's very common to call a yard master a dinger, for this reason. . . The term *dinger* is pretty much dying out right now, some of the older heads still use it.

dinger n² Also sp *dingar*
=dingbat 5.
1927 *AmSp* 3.141 **ME** [Vanishing expressions], A "dinger" or "dingar" meant a tramp or worthless person or rover.

dinge up v phr [Back-formation from *dingy* soiled, discolored] See quot 1953.
1953 Randolph *Down in Holler* 239 **Ozarks,** *Dinge* [dɪnǰ]. . . To become dingy or murky. "The river dinged up last night" means that the water is no longer clear. **1954** *Harder Coll.* **cwTN,** *Dinge up,* become muddy or unclear, as a creek after a rain.

dingfad n Cf **dingfod**
1901 *DN* 2.139 **cwNY,** Dingfad. . . A good time; "doin's."

dingfod n
=dingbat 3.
1909 *DN* 3.395 **nwAR,** *Dingfod.* . . Any article referred to without naming; "Thinguma dodger." **1968** *DARE* (Qu. NN12b, *Things that people say to put off a child when he asks, "What are you making?"*) Inf TN26, Dingfod-gonna-doodaddle, also dingfod off the doodaddle.

dingis See **dingus** n¹

dingle n¹ [Engl dial adopted as a literary word in the 17th cent] **Nth, esp MA** Cf *DS* C19
A small valley or dell.
1660 in 1898 Springfield MA *First Century* 1.288, [This] Land lyes betweene two dingles. **1669** in 1899 *Ibid* 2.103, The said white Oak Soe markt is between ye two first dingles beyond ye low lands. **1835** Hoffman *Winter in West* (NY) 1.55 **NY,** Winding now through a deep dingle, . . we crossed a small brook. **1888** Green *Springfield 1636–1886* 126 **MA,** About 1662, the old road along the brow of the hill . . through the pines to the dingle, was laid out. **1981** *DARE* File **swWI,** Up here in the Kickapoo river area we use *dingle* all the time—like "I'm gonna go up the dingle."

dingle n² [Etym uncert] **chiefly ME**
1 A windbreak or protective structure at the entrance to a building.
1889 *Century Dict., Dingle.* . . The protecting weather-shed built around the entrance to a house. [*Century* Ed: North. New Eng.] **1895** *DN* 1.387, *Dingle:* a storm-door, built by standing spruce or fir poles close together in front of the camp-door. M[ain]e. lumbermen.
2 A usu covered walkway, esp between the bunkhouse and the cookhouse of a logging camp. Cf **alley** n¹ **7**
1905 U.S. Forest Serv. *Bulletin* 61.35, *Dingle.* . . The roofed-over space between the kitchen and the sleeping quarters in a logging camp, commonly used as a storeroom. (N[orth] W[oods], L[ake] S[tates]) **1914** *DN* 4.71 **ME, nNH,** *Dingle.* . . Open space between cook-room and bar-room [=sleeping quarters] in lumber-camps. **1944** Nute *Lake Superior* 208, At the other end [of the bunkhouse] was the "dingle," or passageway into the kitchen. **1948** *WELS Suppl.* **cME,** *Wangan* and *tote-road* are familiar terms to any lumber camp, I believe, but I'm not so sure about *dingle,* which we used to designate the area, roofed but open on both sides, which connected the cook-shack with the bunk-house. **1966** *DARE* Tape **ME**1, [FW:] What's that dingle? [Inf:] That's where they built two camps about . . fifteen feet apart, then they cover that over, and they sat the grindstone in there, and they put the food in there, and they called that the dingle; **ME**26, If it ain't too many horses [in a logging camp], you just build one hovel. But if there are a number . . they build along this side . . and build along *this* side. . . Right in the middle here is the dingle. . . you walk right along up through and feed from both ways, and you get 'em all. [FW:] Is that dingle an open place, like? [Inf:] Yeah, it's open, it runs right through the middle them two hovels.
3 A storehouse or storage area, esp in a logging camp or a **camp** n **1.**
1907 *DN* 3.242 **eME,** *Dingle.* . . A lean-to attached to the cook's quarters in a logging camp. In it the provisions are stored. **1941** *LANE* Map 344 1 inf, **ceME,** *Dingle,* where food is stored in a lumber camp. *Ibid* Map 352 *(Ell)* 1 inf, **ceME,** Cf. [dɪŋgḷ], a rude shelter in a lumber camp. **1957** Beck *Folkl. ME* 229, The dingle, found in the larger camps, was the storehouse for food and miscellaneous gear. It, too, was built of logs and rather more sturdily than the other buildings to deter molasses-hungry bears and salt-starved hedge-hogs. **1975** Gould *ME Lingo* 73, *Dingle* is now used for any storage or utility shed at a woods *camp,* provided it is strategically near the kitchen, and it has also been used for a porch and a piazza on a woods camp or cottage. It can mean a pantry or closet space off a kitchen.

dingleberry n
1 A **mountain cranberry** (here: *Vaccinium erythrocarpum*).
1923 Amer. Joint Comm. Horticult. Nomenclature *Std. Plant Names* 519, *Vaccinium . . erythrocarpum . .* Dingleberry. **1940** Clute *Amer. Plant Names* 166, Dingleberry. *Vaccinium erythrocarpum.*
2 See quot. *euphem* Cf **dillberry**
1952 Brown *NC Folkl.* 1.533, Dingle-berry. . . A testicle.—Orange county.
3 See quot 1986. Cf **dillberry**
c1960 [see **dillberry**]. **1986** *DARE* File **nOH** (as of 1920s), Dingleberries—balls of excrement found on cattle. **1987** *DARE* File **csWI** (as of 1940s), Dingleberries we called 'em—used of sheep, not cows.

dinglebob n
1 =dingbat n **3.**
1923 *DN* 5.205 **swMO,** *Dinkus.* . . Thing. Also . . *Dinglebob.*
2 =jinglebob.
1969 *DARE* (Qu. K18, . . *Mark . . used . . to identify a cow*) Inf **TX**71, Dinglebob—ear is cut and hangs down.

dingle cart n [Cf *EDD dingle* v.³ "To vibrate, resound, tremble"] Cf *DS* N41c, **swing-dingle**
A light one-horse cart.
1911 Shute *Plupy* 361 **seNH** (as of 1860s), They would load up a dingle cart with furniture and drive Nellie up to the new house. . . Nellie was a fast trotter, the old dingle cart rattled tremendously.

dinglefuzzie n Cf **dingus** n¹
1975 Gould *ME Lingo* 73, *Dinglefuzzie.* . . a word for somebody whose name you can't come up with, like Whoozit or Whatsisname. "Dinglefuzzie stopped in while you were gone; he wouldn't tell me what he wanted."

dingle maul See **dingmaul**

dingle-toes See **ding-toed**

dingmaul n Also *dingle maul* [**ding** v¹ **1** + *maul* mallet]
A heavy mallet; hence, appar from its use in joc threats, an imaginary beast; see quots.
1914 *DN* 4.71 **ME, nNH,** *Dingmaul.* . . Mythical animal in lumber-camp. **1939** Tryon *Fearsome Critters* 15, *The Dingmaul*—Both varieties are cat-like, being long, slim, slick, sorry-looking gentlemen having wolf-like pelts. . . The tail is very long. . . the California variety carries a medium-sized, bony ball on the end. . . The cry of the Eastern species is a dreadful, horrendous wail, while the call of the Western variety . . resembles the toot of a logging donkey. **1975** Gould *ME Lingo* 73, *Dingle maul*—Also *dingmaul.* A wooden hammer or mallet for securing the *dogs* of a sawmill carriage into the logs. It appears in speech as a hypothetical weapon (much like a *sled-stake,* which see): "The news staggered him as if he'd been clipped with a dingmaul."

dingnation n [Minced form of *damnation;* cf **ding** v²] **esp GA** *euphem, old-fash*
Damnation, hell.
1845 Thompson *Pineville* 167 **GA,** Dadfetch your everlastin' picter [=picture] to dingnation! **1872** (1973) Thompson *Major Jones's Courtship* 189 **GA,** "April Fool, dingnation!" ses I. "Fun's fun; but I'm dad blamed if theres any fun in any sich doins." **1885** Twain *Huck. Finn* 106 **MO,** Who in the dingnation's agoin' to *pay* for it? **1887** (1967) Harris *Free Joe* 47 **nwGA,** I'll . . canter to town an' see what in the dingnation the matter is. **1908** *DN* 3.305 **eAL, wGA.**

ding-toed adj, adv Also *dink-toed* [Cf *EDD ding-dew* (at *ding* v. 11. (1)) "a splay-footed person"] **NEng**
Pigeon-toed; by ext: given to stumbling; hence n pl, but sg in constr, *ding-toes, dingle-toes* a person given to stumbling.
1907 *DN* 3.186 **seNH,** *Dingle-toes, ding-toes.* . . One who stumbles. *Ding-toed.* . . Given to stumbling. **1969** *DARE* FW Addit **cnVT,** Ding-toed. **1977** *DARE* File **cnMA** (as of c1915), I have known "ding-toed" all my life. It was more common than "pigeon-toed," I think. A mother might say to a small child, "Watch your feet! You don't want to grow up walking ding-toed." **1980** *DARE* File (as of 1953), *Ding-toed.* Reported as common by two Springfield, Massachusetts natives; also by native of Newport, Vermont, and *dink-toed* by native of Gardner, Massachusetts, who both said the term was more common than pigeon-toed.

dingus n[1] Also *dangus, dinkus;* also sp *dingass, dingis* [Du *dinges* thingamajig, what's his name < *ding* thing]

1 Something whose name is not known or readily remembered; a thingamajig. Cf **dingbat 3, doodinkus**

1876 *Pioche* (Nev.) *D. Jrnl.* 23 Sep. 3/1 *(DA),* The latest thing in the way of a soul-warmer that the youths of Pioche have got up is a dingis made thusly. **1882** Peck *Peck's Sunshine* 21, They pull out a dingus and three joints of fish-pole come out. **1887** *Amer. Field* 27.14/2 **nIL,** I have not tried the paper negative yet but expect to commence experimenting with it soon. No doubt it is the dingass of the future. **1915** Lewis *Trail of Hawk* 203 **seNY,** That dingus in front is a whirling motor. **1923** *DN* 5.205 **swMO,** *Dinkus*. . . Thing. **1930** [see **2** below]. **1933** Williamson *Woods Colt* 80 **Ozarks,** Aw, thar was a little safety catch somewhar, some kind of a little dingus you have to push. **1944** Holton *Yankees Were Like This* 81 **eMA,** There was a funny dingus called a telephone coming into use, but most of us knew about it only by hearsay. **1944** *PADS* 2.25 **cwNC,** *Dingus*. . . A small article. **1945** *PADS* 3.10 **CT,** *Dingus.* **1955** Adams *Grandfather* 199 **NY** (as of 1880s), At the top of the plant was a queer-looking, half-formed cluster of pale berries. "What kind of a dingus do you call that?" Reno asked. **c1960** *Wilson Coll.* **csKY,** *Dingus*. . . An object that is nameless or useless.

2 The penis. *euphem* Cf **dink** n[1] **1**

1930 Shoemaker *1300 Words* 17 **cPA Mts** (as of c1900), *Dangus*—The male genital organ; any dangling article like a purse. **1982** *Smithsonian Letters* **cnWV,** I have secretly recorded some of the unusual phrases . . in my mother's conversation. . . Dinkus = penis.

dingus n[2] See **dyngus**

dingy n See **dinge** n[1]

dingy adj |ˈdɪŋi| **chiefly CA, NW** Cf **ding-a-ling**

Foolish, silly, crazy.

1911 *DN* 3.550 **WY,** *Dingy,* [ŋ], foolish, not quite right in the head; about the same as "batty." "He's dingy." **1911** in 1983 Truman *Dear Bess* 94 **MO,** She's plumb dingy over those twins. *Ibid* 294, I guess they give us those things to do to keep us from going dingy. **1930** Williams *Logger-Talk* 22 **Pacific NW,** *Dingy:* Goofy. **1965–70** *DARE* (Qu. GG2, . . *Confused, mixed up*) Inf **CA**187, Dingy; (Qu. HH5, *Someone who is queer but harmless*) Inf **CA**169, Dingy; (Qu. HH9, *A very silly or light-headed person*) Infs **CA**107, 177, Dingy. **1975** *AmSp* 50.57 **AR,** *Dingy* /ˈdíŋɪ/. . . Silly, foolish. "Don't bring your dingy girlfriend."

dining day n **chiefly VA** *old-fash*

A dinner party.

1805 in 1888 Cutler *Life* 2.190 **DC,** If I had time I would give some history of a dining day, of the table and its furniture. **1827** (1935) Bolling *Diary* 43.248 **VA,** Rain . . disappointed us all of a visit to Ben Lomond, where the Dr. was to have had a "Dining Day". **1899** (1912) Green *VA Folk-Speech* 147, *Dining-day*. . . A dinner given to a large number of people was spoken of as a "dining-day." **1902** Eggleston *Dorothy South* 272 **VA** (as of a1860), We'll have a "dining day," as a dinner party is queerly called here in Virginia. **1976** Ryland *Richmond Co. VA* 370, *Dining-day*—family gathering at a homestead.

dining needle n [Var of **darning needle 1**]

A **dragonfly.**

c1970 *DARE* File **Long Is. NY,** *Dining needle*. . . Dragon fly; Darning needle also used. **1980** *NADS Letters* **sNY,** Here on Long Island I often encounter the term *dining needle* for *darning needle* ("dragon fly").

dining-room lumber n *joc* Cf **cordwood 2, lumber, timber**

See quots.

1950 *WELS Suppl.* **csWI,** Dining-room lumber—toothpicks. **1968–70** *DARE* (Qu. G11, . . *A toothpick*) Infs **NJ**21, 23, 56, **VA**69, **WV**16, Dining-room lumber.

dink n[1]

1 The penis. [Cf **dingus** n[1] **2;** perh infl by *dick*]

1942 McAtee *Dial. Grant Co. IN Suppl. 1* 4, *Dink* . . penis, especially the small one of a boy; "his little ———". **1968** *DARE* FW Addit **cnNY,** Dink—penis. **1984** Doig *English Creek* 171 **nMT,** As I remember it, I held myself in admirable rein until Ray came out with "turkey dink." *Ibid* 172, "Horse apple" was pretty far back down the scale from "turkey dink."

2 Used as a derog term for a person or animal.

1959 in 1965 *DARE* File **AR** [Unidentified newspaper], Dink—a horse trader. **1966–67** *DARE* (Qu. K46, . . *A horse or cow [that] is deformed;* total Infs questioned, 75) Inf **NM**13, A dink—a calf that is no good, an ill-shaped or small animal; (Qu. HH11a, *Someone who is too particular or fussy—if it's a man*) Inf **MA**1, Dink (homosexuality not implied). **1968** Adams *Western Words* 93, Dink—In rodeo, a roping or steer-wrestling horse that is poorly trained or does not perform well. **1988** *WI State Jrl.* (Madison) 5 Apr sec B 1/5, I've been asked to announce by the Dukakis campaign that my views aren't necessarily the views of the Dukakis campaign. . . Now that that's out of the way, isn't George Bush a dink?

3 A small marble, usu made of clay. [Cf *dinky* small, undersized]

1966 *DARE* Tape **NC**22, The little clay marbles . . are called dinks. . . Those dinks were jist about the size of your finger. **1969–70** *DARE* (Qu. EE6b, *Small marbles or marbles in general*) Inf **VA**69, Dinks; (Qu. EE6c, *Cheap marbles*) Inf **KY**5, Dinks—made of clay; **KY**89, Dinks.

dink n[2] See **dinky** n[2]

‡dinkeldorf n

1969 *DARE* FW Addit, *Dinkeldorf*. . . a silly person. Heard in Georgia (Athens). Said to have been used by a Philadelphia person.

dinkey See **dinky** n[1], n[2]

dinkey-donkey See **dinky** n[1] **1**

dink-toed See **ding-toed**

dinktum n[1]

=dingus n[1] **1.**

1911 *DN* 3.542 **NE,** Dinktum. . . Indefinite expression, like *thingumbob,* or *dingus.* "The man is not worth a pewter dinktum."

dinktum n[2] See **dinky** n[1] **4**

dinkus See **dingus** n[1]

dinky adj [Scots, nEngl dial *dink* neat, nice, finely dressed] *old-fash*

Neat, dainty, fine, slick.

1896 *DN* 1.415 **seNY,** "A dinky time," a nice time. **1905** *DN* 3.77 **nwAR,** *Dinky*. . . Right, satisfactory. 'It's just all dinky.' Common. **1908** *DN* 3.305 **eAL, wGA,** *Dinky*. . . Neat, trim. Common. **1913** in 1983 Truman *Dear Bess* 118 **MO,** There was once a Presbyterian one [=preacher] in Belton who was a quack doctor and a genuine dinky hoss trader. . . He could . . make a horse trader weep over his bargain. **1986** *NADS Letters* **MS** (as of 1930s), "She's a dinky little thing" = "She's a dainty child."

dinky n[1] Also sp *dinkie, dinkey* [*dinky* adj]

1 rarely *dinkey-donkey;* freq attrib: A small locomotive; a train pulled by such a locomotive; a small branch railway. *old-fash*

1874 *Kalama* (Wash.) *Beacon* 20 Jan. 4/2 *(DA),* The passenger train from Tacoma . . passed the Des Chuttes bridge . . an hour or two previous to the "dinkey." **1887** *Courier-Jrl.* (Louisville KY) 1 Feb 8/4, Wm Ragnall was fined $7.25 . . for jumping on a dinkey train while in motion. **1905** *DN* 3.77 **cwAR,** *Dinky*. . . Short branch railway. 'I come over on the dinky.' **1930** *DN* 6.87 **cWV,** *Dinky.* **1948** *Milwaukee Jrl.* (WI) 18 July 6/3, The huffing and puffing steam dinkeys . . still see service when traffic is heavy. **1965–70** *DARE* (Qu. N37, . . *A branch railroad that is not very important or gives poor service*) 67 Infs, **scattered,** Dinky (line, road, railroad, track, *or,* express). [Of all Infs responding to the question, 69% were old; of those giving this response, 90% were old.] **1966** *Good Old Days* Jan 34 **NC** (as of c1900), Rode a train about ten miles, then rode a dinkey up a big creek a long ways. A dinkey is a little log train. **1966** *DARE* Tape **DC**8, [FW:] Didn't you have any electric cars at one time? [Inf:] Oh yes, the Dinky line that used to go as far as the bridge on Carroll Avenue. **1968** Adams *Western Words* 93, *Dinkey*—A small logging locomotive. Also called *dinkey-donkey.* **1968** Haun *Hawk's Done Gone* 161 **eTN,** He sent them up there to unload some crossties out of a lot of things they called dinkies. **1969** *DARE* Tape **CA**143, We went out to the railroad tracks. . . we was always want to ride that little dinky-car. We wait for 'em to get off the work and we get a ride from, that quarter-mile from there to come in Folsom. **1986** *NADS Letters* **NJ,** The two-car train that connects Princeton proper with the main r[ail]r[oad] line at Princeton Junction is called the "dinkie" or "dinky," . . The local r.r. station is called the "dinky station." **1988** *WI State Jrl.* (Madison) 5 Dec sec C 1/1 **swWI,** Dad sent the fare (less than a dollar) and I boarded the dinky (a small locomotive with room behind it for several passengers) down to Ferryville.

2 **=ruddy duck.**

1888 Trumbull *Names of Birds* 113, Occasionally at Wilmington, same state [=NC], Dinkey ("Hard-head" being the common name). **1917** (1923) *Birds Amer.* 1.152, Ruddy Duck—*Erismatura jamaicensis*—Other Names.— . . dinky. **1944** Hausman *Amer. Birds* 510, Dinky—see Duck, Ruddy.

3 See quot.

1908 *DN* 3.305 **eAL, wGA,** *Dinky*. . . Sweetheart. Rare.

4 also *dinktum;* in phr *the very dinky:* The height of elegance, utility, or convenience.

1960 Carpenter *Tales Manchaca* 143 **cTX,** The new furnishings . . would be considered unsightly today, . . but we thought that they were the very dinktum. *Ibid* 106, I thought it was the very dinktum when I was able to board a Pullman in Manchaca and to arrive in Springfield, Missouri . . without . . changing trains. **1986** *NADS Letters* **cnTX,** If he misplaced his scissors and discovered that pruning shears did the job better, he might exclaim, "Boy howdy, I'll use pruning shears from here on. They're the very dinky!" I never recall hearing him apply the expression to anything except an artifact, but it is not limited to small gadgets; a lawn mower or a four-bottom plow might be considered the very dinky if it met some need extremely well.

dinky n[2] Also *dink, dinky-boat* Also sp *dinkey* [Prob var of *dinghy,* perh infl by *dinky* adj]

A small boat; see quots.

1849 *Pacific News* (S.F.) 27 Nov. 4/2 *(DA),* Picked up adrift in San Pablo bay a small copper Dinkey. **1913** *DN* 4.56 **Cape Cod MA,** *Dinky*. . . A small flat-bottomed boat, used as a tender and by children: noted at Provincetown. "You can't take the dory, but you can go out in the dinky." **1946** *PADS* 6.12 **eNC,** *Dinky* . . The small boat of a ship; perhaps from *dinghy.* Pamlico. Common among boatmen. **c1960** *Wilson Coll.* **csKY,** *Dinky boat* . . A small rowboat or fishing boat; also *joe boat,* a *john* or *johnny boat.* **1965–70** *DARE* (Qu. O1, . . *Small rowboat*) 24 Infs, **scattered,** *Dinky;* **IN**73, Dinky boat; (Qu. O2, . . *Old, clumsy boat*) Inf **NY**236, Dinky; **LA**20, Old dinky; (Qu. O9, . . *Kinds of sailboats*) Inf **KY**11, Dinkies. **1966** *DARE* Tape **FL**47, I've got a little skiff boat down there, a little dinky-boat it was. **1976** Warner *Beautiful Swimmers* 253 **eMD,** Not much more than eighteen feet in length, the dinkies had a single large sprit-sail and carried one hundred pound sandbags as movable ballast. **1987** *NADS Letters,* Dinky—Used along the New England coast for a small rowing boat to transport one or two of the crew to a sailboat or launch. . . It is sometimes referred to as a "dink".

‡dinky-flink n

1967 *DARE* (Qu. JJ12, *Little flourishes . . on . . handwriting*) Inf **NY**7, Dinky-flink.

dinnel n, v [Prob alter of *dinner;* cf **dinners**]

See quot 1954.

1954 *Harder Coll.* **cwTN,** *Dinnel* . . Milk from a woman's breast for the baby. . . To breastfeed a child. **1957** *AmSp* 32.158 **cwTN,** As recently as August, 1956, in Pope, Perry County, Tennessee, I heard *dinnel* ['dɪnəl] used as both a substantive and a verb. . . I took down two usages of the term: 'Give 'at young'un its dinnel,' and 'Better dinnel'im, he's a-gittin' cross as a bear.' . . I have heard the word all my life.

dinner n

1 The main meal of the day, spec:

a The midday meal.

1622 'Mourt' *Relation* 114 *(DAE)* **MA,** After dinner we tooke Boat for Nauset. **1834** (1898) Kemper *Jrl.* 397 **NY,** There was no drinking at table or sitting after dinner was over. Dinner at 1 & tea at 5. **1863** Dodge *Gala-Days* 114 **MA,** If it is nearer noon than morning, we call it dinner. If it is nearer night than noon, we call it supper, unless we have fashionable friends with us, and then we call it dinner, and the other thing lunch. **a1929** (1973) Faulkner *Flags* 168 **MS,** It had taken Belle some time to overcome Jefferson's prejudice against a formal meal between dinner and supper. **1965–70** *DARE* (Qu. H2, *The meal that people eat around the middle of the day*) 709 Infs, **widespread,** Dinner. **1968** Kellner *Aunt Serena* 82 **IN,** Only hicks had dinner at noon, and said things like, "I'll redd up the table." **1975** Gould *ME Lingo* 74, *Dinner*—Traditionally, the Maine *dinner* is served at noon. Lunch is reserved for a snack, a picnic, and a bedtime piece of pie. Supper, of course, comes at suppertime. What others call a lunch-box is still generally known in Maine as a *dinner*-pail or *dinner*-bucket. Workmen who do not come home at noon carry their *dinners.* There have been times that Mainers, invited to *dinner,* came at noon and astonished their *outlandish* hostesses. **1976** Garber *Mountain-ese* 22 **Appalachians,** *Dinner* . . noonday meal. **1978** Doig *This House* 175 **MT** (as of c1955), The vast midday meal—we called it dinner. **1984** *MJLF* 10.157 **cnWI,** *Supper.* The evening meal. Dinner is the noon meal. Lunch is a snack.

b The evening meal. **widespread, but less freq Lower Missip Valley, S Atl** See Map Cf **supper**

1898 Westcott *Harum* 36 **NY,** Will Mr. Carling go in to dinner to-night? **1898** (1908) Atherton *Californians* 183, Magdaléna sat amidst iridescent billows of ball-gowns, dinner-gowns, tea-gowns, négligés, demi-toilettes, [etc]. **1940** *DAE, Dinner hour*. . . The hour of dinner varies in different sections and among different classes of people. The dinner hour is usually in the evening among business, professional, and leisured classes. In rural communities and among many of the working people of the cities dinner is at noon, and to apply the term to the evening meal is felt to be an affectation. **1965–70** *DARE* (Qu. H3, *The meal that people eat at the end of the day*) 542 Infs, **widespread, but less freq Lower Missip Valley, S Atl,** Dinner.

2 See **dinner-time**

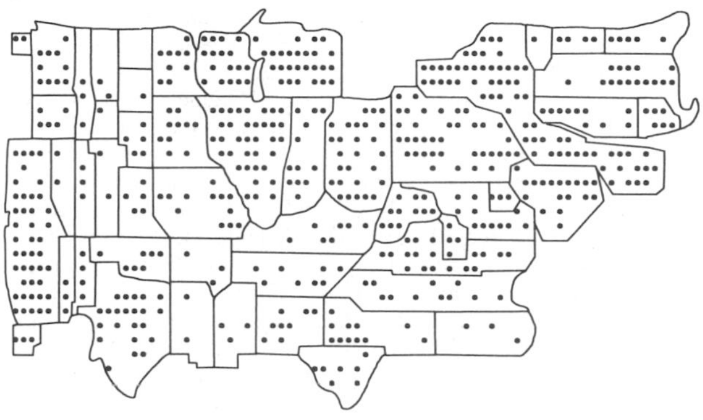

•dinner 1b (Qu. H3)

dinner bucket See **bucket 2e**

dinner buckets See **dinners**

dinner horn n Also called **Gabriel B**

A horn used to announce a meal to workers outdoors.

1838 (1852) Gilman *S. Matron* 51 **SC,** The business was scarcely settled, when the dinner-horn sounded. **1907** *DN* 3.186 **seNH,** *Dinner-horn*. . . Horn blown to announce that dinner is ready. "Haven't they blown the dinner-horn yet?" **1911** Clayson *Hist. Narr.* 37 **wWA** (as of 1868), The most inviting sound to them for several months at a time had been that of the "dinner horn," as its welcome sound echoed through the woods about noon. The "dinner horn" is a glorious old instrument. You can hear it farther than you can a heavy blast of dynamite, and it has charmed more hearts than a brass band ever did. **1946** *Reader's Digest* Jan 142/1 **ME,** My wife blew the dinner horn. **1949** Dean *Diamond Bess* 131 **TX** (as of c1860s), Tell Uncle Charles to blow the dinner horn for the negroes to come in from the fields. **1958** McCulloch *Woods Words* 47 **Pacific NW,** *Dinner horn*—A very long tin horn used in some of the earliest camps to announce grub on the table. **1969** Sorden *Lumberjack Lingo* 33 **NEng, Gt Lakes,** *Dinner horn*—A conical-shaped tin horn about three feet long used for calling lumberjacks to meals or, sometimes, for getting them up in the morning. **1982** *Barrick Coll.* **csPA,** *Dinner horn*—tin horn [used to call men in far fields].

dinner kettle n

1 A container in which to carry a meal, as to work or to school.

1907 *DN* 3.243 **eME,** *Dinner kettle*. . . Dinner pail. **1939** *LANE* Map 130 *(Dinner pail)* 4 infs, **ME,** Dinner kettle; [3 infs, **NB,** Dinner kettle].

2 A cooking vessel; see quots. **esp Inland Sth** Cf **wash kettle**

1939 Wolcott *Yankee Cook Book* 178, Maine apple pandowdy is something else again. "Try out 3 slices of home-raised salt fat pork in a dinner kettle." **c1960** *Wilson Coll.* **csKY,** *Dinner kettle*. . . The large iron kettle swung over the fireplace or set on the stove. **1970** *DARE* (Qu. F4, . . *The deep metal container used to boil foods*) Inf **KY**85, Dinner kettle—cast iron—old-fashioned. **1986** Pederson *LAGS Concordance* **inland Gulf Region, esp TN** *(Kettle)* 4 infs, Dinner kettle; 1 inf, Dinner kettle—black; 1 inf, Dinner kettle—small, on stove; 1 inf, Dinner kettle—large cooking vessel; 1 inf, Dinner kettle—to cook over fire, cast iron; 1 inf, Dinner kettle—cast iron, smaller than wash kettle; 1 inf, Dinner kettles—used to make hominy.

dinner on the ground(s) n [Prob orig *grounds* the open area around a building, and *ground* by folk-etym] **chiefly Sth, S Midl** See Map Cf **basket dinner**

An outdoor social gathering at which food is shared, usu in connection with a church meeting or **all-day singing;** the meal itself.

[**1909** *DN* 3.370 **eAL, wGA,** *Singing (all-day)* . . A gathering of singers to spend the day in practising. Dinner is served on the ground.] **1934** Carmer *Stars Fell on AL* 55 **AL,** I reckon y'all got a hankerin' to find out what's on th' inside o' them boxes. Well, it's time for dinner-on-the-grounds. *Ibid* 56, The informality of dinner-on-the-grounds had had its effect. . . the singers reached a greater volume than before. **1944** *PADS* 2.8 **AL,** *Dinner on the ground.* . . The co-operative picnic meal served at an all-day singing [*PADS* Ed: preaching or other meeting]. **1945** Wilson *Passing Institutions* 76 **csKY,** Be it said frankly, the dinner on the ground was the great thing; the sermon was only sauce to appetite. **1959** Sanders *Echoes* 11 **swAR,** They meet on the first Saturday in June for a grave-yard working and dinner on the ground. **1965–70** *DARE* (Qu. H70, *When people bring baked dishes, salads, and so forth to a meeting-place and share them together*) 19 Infs, **Sth, S Midl, esp KY,** Dinner on the ground; **SC**38, Dinner on the grounds. **1967** Green *Horse Tradin'* 41 **TX,** That weekend there was fall fair and Old Settlers reunion coming up. . . They were going to have a big program—speakin's, dinner on the grounds, games, something for everybody. **1967** *Jasper Free Enterprise* (TX) 3 Aug 5/4 **ceTX,** The Fifth Sunday Meeting is to be held at Bethel Chapel Baptist Church July 28, 29, and 30. There is to be a dinner-on-the-ground the 29 and 30. **1967** *DARE* Tape **TX**36, It's dinner on the table [=a picnic lunch at church] but we call it dinner on the ground. **1972** *Atlanta Letters* **cnGA,** Picnic—"Dinner on the ground." **1982** *Foxfire 7* 337 **nGA,** I remember once going to a singing convention over at Boiling Springs. . . When dinner came, why we had dinner on the *ground,* instead of putting the food on benches or tables. They always *said* "singing and dinner on the ground" but they generally put the dinner up on the table. That was the first and only time that I ever had dinner spread out on the ground like that.

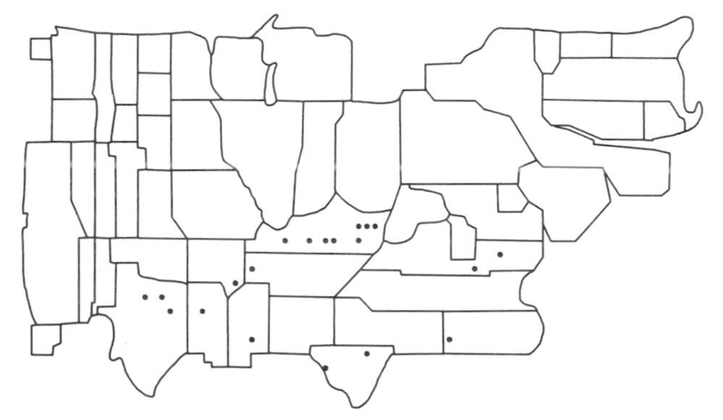

•dinner on the ground(s) (Qu. H70)

dinner out v phr

1914 *DN* 4.71 **ME, nNH,** *Dinner-out.* . . To take one's dinners at work in a mill, store, or in the woods.

dinner pail v phr [*dinner pail* a lunch container]

?To work at a job regularly.

1969 Gordone *No Place* 39 **NY** [Black], Givin' you a education or teachin' you to dinner-pail, didn't seem to me to be no way for you to grow up an' be respected like'a man.

dinner pot n **esp Sth, S Midl** Cf *put one's name in the pot* (at **pot**)

A large cooking-kettle.

1775 (1934) Fithian *Jrl.* 2.68 **NJ,** Tea. . . is boild in a common Dinner-Pot, of ten or fifteen Gallons, & from thence poured out in Tin Cups. **1887** (1967) Harris *Free Joe* 121 **GA,** He thes natchally dribbles at the mouth when he gits a whiff from the dinner-pot. **1891** (1905) Ryan *Told in Hills* 115 **nwMT,** This white man . . could give her [=a woman from KY] a floor of boards and a dinner-pot never empty. **1899** (1912) Green *VA Folk-Speech* 147, *Dinner-pot.* . . A large, iron pot holding about twenty gallons, in which dinner is cooked, ham and cabbage. Sometimes hung over the fire by pot hooks, sometimes standing on its three iron legs over the coals on the hearth. **1947** Bowles–Towle *New Engl. Cooking* 64, The banked coals . . held the great dinner pot. **1965–70** *DARE* (Qu. F4, . . *Deep metal container used to boil foods*) Infs **KY**48, **LA**2, **MD**12, **TX**91, Dinner pot.

dinners n pl Also *dinner buckets* *euphem, joc*

A woman's breasts.

1953 Randolph *Down in Holler* 120 **Ozarks,** The real old-time term for the female breasts is not bosom but *dinners.* . . A schoolmarm in southwest Missouri has truly enormous breasts, and is known as "Big Dinners" by almost everybody in town. **1965–67** *DARE* (Qu. X31, . . *A woman's breasts*) Infs **CO**20, **OK**28, Dinners; **OK**7, Dinner buckets.

dinnertime n Also *dinner*

Twelve o'clock p.m.; noon.

1902 *DN* 2.232 **sIL,** *Dinner-time.* . . Twelve o'clock. **1907** *DN* 3.222 **nwAR,** *Dinner-time.* . . Twelve o'clock. **1935** *AmSp* 10.167 **sePA,** Do you think he will be here this dinner (this noon)? **c1960** *Wilson Coll.* **csKY,** *Dinnertime.* . . Twelve o'clock noon; still common as a term. *Noon* sounds a little "furrin." **1977** *DARE* File **csWI,** [Radio announcer giving noon weather report:] At dinner-time we have 56°.

dinner tub n

A dinner bucket.

1909 *DN* 3.420 **Cape Cod MA** (as of a1857), Dinner tub. . . A small wooden sugar pail.

dint See **do** v **5**

dinwiddie n

Used as a derog term for a man.

1941 O'Donnell *Great Big Doorstep* 203 **sLA,** Philomene was a lovely girl and a perfect lady, and too good for any dinwiddie around here. *Ibid* 226, 'Papa—' 'He's a dinwiddie. Don't you never let him tangle you up tell [=till] he shows you the cash.'

dip v

1 rarely with *up:* To take (snuff), orig by using a **dipping stick 1** and applying the tobacco between the lip or cheek and gums; to use snuff in this manner; hence vbl n *dipping.* **chiefly Sth, S Midl** See Map Cf **dip** n[1] **2**

1830 Royall *Mrs. Royall's S. Tour* 1.138 **NC,** They [=women] do not snuff it up the nose, but take it into the mouth—they call it dipping. **1848** Bartlett *Americanisms* 116, *To dip snuff.* A mode of taking tobacco, practised by women in some parts of the United States, and particularly at the South, may be thus described: A little pine stick or bit of rattan about three inches long, split up like a brush at one end, is first wetted and then dipped into snuff; with this the teeth are rubbed. **1849** *Knickerbocker* 34.117 **GA,** The 'gude woman' sat in the corner 'rubbing snuff,' or 'dipping.' **1865** *Nation* 1.335/2 **NC,** The woman, going over to the mantel, took down a small circular tin box and began to dip snuff. **1908** *DN* 3.305 **eAL, wGA,** *Dip.* . . To use snuff. "She dips." **1941** Writers' Program *Guide AR* 297, Hill people consider dipping snuff, or putting it in the lower lip, an unclean habit, fit only for white trash and lowlanders. **1944** *PADS* 2.65 **S Midl,** *Dip.* . . To rub snuff on the gums. **1947** *Reader's Digest* Oct 35/1, They [=families living in log cabins] sprawled on the grass, old women dipping snuff, the men chewing midnight plug. **c1960** *Wilson Coll.* **csKY,** *Dip snuff.* . . To take snuff, either inside the lower lip or on a chewed blackgum or hickory-bark toothbrush. **1965–70** *DARE* (Qu. DD3b, *How do people take snuff around here?*) 21 Infs, **chiefly Sth, S Midl,** Dip (it *or* snuff); 6 Infs, **chiefly Sth,** Dip it with a black-gum stick chewed to a mop [and var phrr: see *DS*]; **GA**3, Dip in bottom lip or jaw; **NC**85, Pour it in box lid and dip it in mouth; **SC**24, Dipped it up on a brush, which is a stick; [**NM**6, Dip chicken bone in snuff; **CA**91, Chewed stick dipped in; **CA**145, Dip willow stick in loose snuff, put it under lower lip; **FL**39, Dipping in a stick]; (Qu. DD3a, . . *A person who uses snuff*) 10 Infs, **chiefly S Midl,** Dip(s) snuff; **AR**37, **GA**17, **NY**55, **OK**58, **SC**45, Dips; **CA**87, Dipping snuff; **MO**26, People that dip; (Qu. DD1, . . *Different forms* . . *[of] tobacco*) Inf **NM**6, Snuff—dipped. **1967** *DARE* Tape **TX**49, One thing about her, she would dip snuff. . . [FW:] How do you do that? [Inf:] Put it on your lip.

2 To collect (liquid crude turpentine from a **box** n **1** or a cup); hence vbl n *dipping* the operation of collecting turpentine; the turpentine collected at one time; n *dipper* one who collects turpentine; a tool used to collect turpentine. Cf **dip** n[1] **4, gather B1**

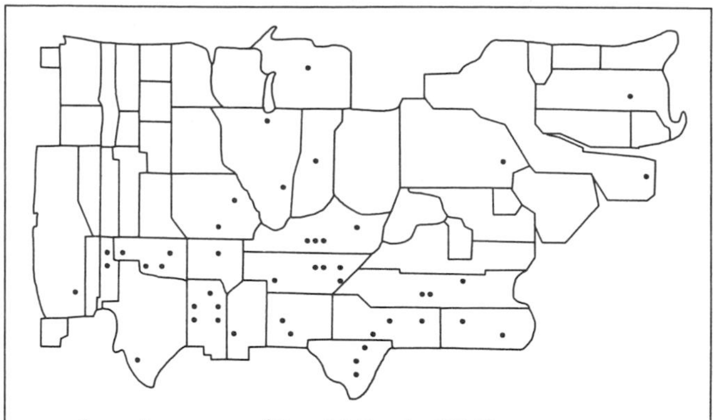

•dip v 1 + varr (Qq. DD3a, b, DD1)

1832 Browne *Sylva* 232 **C and S Atl,** The turpentine thus procured is the best, and is called *pure dipping.* **1859** Perry *Turpentine Farming* 66, A friend of mine has . . a set of boxes from which he dipped eighty-four barrels with five chippings. *Ibid,* Making a large dipping of turpentine appears to have been the point at which many have aimed. **1896** *Pop. Sci. Mth.* 48.470 **SE,** The resin which accumulates in the boxes is removed by a trowel-shaped dipper. The operation is known as "dipping." **1939** FWP *Guide FL* 378, When filled, cups are 'dipped' or emptied into metal buckets; these are emptied in turn into 50-gallon barrels, which are transported to the still. **1941** *AmSp* 16.237 **GA,** A paddle is used to get the gum out of the cups and the man who performs this work is referred to as a *dipper.* **1966** *DARE* Tape **FL**19, That's the only work they [=Black people] could get to make any money was the naval stores, was dippin' turpentine; **GA**7, Along when I was small, I knew a few people that could dip around . . nine or ten barrels in a day. . . Your first dipping used to be the raw gum full of leaves. . . It usually brings less price. . . If you wait long enough between dippings, you supposed to get about three standard barrels to a thousand. . . cups.

3 To fish with a dip net; hence vbl n *dipping.* Cf **dip** n¹ **10**

1954 *Harder Coll.* **cwTN,** *Dip.* . . To fish by use of a dip. **1965–70** *DARE* (Qu. P13, . . *Other ways of fishing* . . besides the ordinary hook and line) Infs **NY**177, **VA**32, Dipping; **MI**120, **NY**151, Smelt dipping; **MI**80, Dipping with a net; **MD**31, Dip—[use a] net on end of pole, dip up fish. **1966–70** *DARE* Tape **ME**17, They dip some smelts in the spring of the year up river here; **MI**32, And we have a walleye run, comes in the fall and we have smelt. They dip them with the dip nets; **MI**120, All ya do is jus' dip 'em [=smelt] up and throw 'em right in that tub; **NJ**67, Then you have the line in one hand and your net with the other, crab net . . a net basket and dip him up.

4 See quot. Cf **dip** n¹ **12**

1900 *DN* 2.32 **seNH** [College slang], *Dip.* . . To take hat off.

5 To intrude in someone's affairs; to eavesdrop on (someone).

1970 *DARE* (Qu. II22, *Expressions to tell somebody to keep to himself and mind his own business*) Inf **OH**103, Quit dipping; **WV**21, You're dipping. [Both Infs Black] **1984** *DARE* File **csPA,** Dip—eavesdrop on. Elem. school use, Chambersburg, Pa. "Don't dip me", Mar. 7, 1984.

‡6 To fry in deep fat.

1968 *DARE* Tape **MD**1, The oysters are all dipped over at Hasslingers.

dip n¹

1 A valley or ravine.

1927 Adams *Ranch on Beaver* 164 **West,** 'Come on, old scout,' urged the rider; 'the bugle calls to saddles. Can't you see the brakes of the river in the dip of the plain?' **1966–69** *DARE* (Qu. C19, . . *Low land running between hills*) Infs **FL**15, 35, **IN**62, Dip.

2 The amount of snuff that adheres to a brush or **dipping stick 1;** the action of taking a portion of snuff in this manner. **chiefly Sth, S Midl** Cf **dip** v **1**

1853 *Putnam's Mag.* 1.142 **sVA, NC,** She . . will hear ladies inviting ladies to "come over and take a dip." **1893** Shands *MS Speech* 26, *Dip* is also used for *dip of snuff,* the word *snuff* being generally omitted. **1908** *DN* 3.305 **eAL, wGA,** *Dip.* . . As much snuff as will adhere to a dampened wooden toothbrush. **1926** *DN* 5.399 **nwAR, swMO,** *Dip.* . . A mixture of powdered tobacco and molasses. It is taken on a chewed twig or *dip-stick,* like snuff. **1944** *PADS* 2.65 **S Midl,** *Dip.* . . The small amount of tobacco snuff into which a wooden "tooth-brush" is dipped before inserting brush and snuff into the mouth. **1954** *Harder Coll.* **cwTN.** **1967** *DARE* Tape **TX**49, The next thing she wanted was a dip of snuff. **1969** *DARE* (Qu. DD3a) Inf **GA**82, Dip of snuff.

3 =dipping stick 1.

1969 *DARE* (Qu. DD3b, *How do people take snuff around here?*) Inf **KY**39, Put on lower lip with a dip.

4 Liquid crude turpentine. **S Atl** Cf **dip** v **2**

1856 Olmsted *Journey Slave States* 343 **NC,** The flow of the first year . . is of higher value than the ordinary dip. **1859** Perry *Turpentine Farming* 123, There are but two natural qualities of turpentine, commonly known as hard and soft; the hard sticks on the face or scarred surface of the pine, and is called 'scrape,' but the soft runs in the box, and is called 'dip.' **1862** Gilmore *Among the Pines* 167 **SC,** I've four barr'ls of 'dip' and tu of 'hard.' **1896** *Pop. Sci. Mth.* Feb 473 **Sth,** The dip, or crude turpentine, is emptied. **1939** FWP *Guide FL* 378 **neFL,** From 8 to 10 50-gallon barrels of 'dip' [=turpentine sap] are emptied into the kettle, water added, and the cooking begins.

5 also *dipping, dippy:* A sweet sauce for pudding, ice cream, pie, cake, etc; by ext, cream. [Engl dial] **scattered, but esp N Cent** See Map Cf **dope** n **2**

1877 Bartlett *Americanisms* 178, *Dip.* Sauce for puddings. South-Western. **1893** Shands *MS Speech* 26, *Dip.* . . Illiterate white for sauce to be used with pudding. **1895** *DN* 1.382 **NJ,** *Dip:* pudding-sauce. **1905** *DN* 3.77 **nwAR,** *Dip.* . . Liquid sauce for pudding. 'I've got my pudding; where's the dip?' Common. **1911** *DN* 3.538 **eKY,** *Dip.* . . Cream, as used in coffee. **1927** *DN* 5.474 **Ozarks,** *Dip.* . . Sweetened cream, eaten with pie, apple dumpling, cobbler and the like. **1933** *AmSp* 8.1.26 **neTX,** Dip. Pudding Sauce. **1940–41** Cassidy *WI Atlas* **swWI,** Dippy: Pudding sauce. [85-year-old Inf] **1944** *PADS* 2.42 **cwNC,** *Dip.* . . Sweetened cream to put on pie. **1950** *WELS (The sweet liquid poured over pudding or ice cream)* 2 Infs, **wWI,** Dip. **1951** West *Witch Diggers* 25 **IN,** Uncle Wes lingered over his second helping of peach cobbler and dip. **c1960** *Wilson Coll.* **csKY,** *Dip.* . . A sauce for cake or fried pies. **1965–70** *DARE* (Qu. H66a, *The sweet liquid that you pour over a pudding*) 44 Infs, **chiefly N Cent,** Dip; **MO**8, Pudding dip; **MO**15, Sweet dip; (Qu. H66b, *The sweet liquid that you pour over ice cream*) 34 Infs, **chiefly N Cent,** Dip; **ND**2, Dipping; (Qu. H21, . . *The sweet stuff that's poured over [pancakes]*) Inf **SC**56, Dip; (Qu. H63, *Kinds of desserts*) Inf **IL**103, Cake with lemon dip. **1968** *DARE* Tape **SC**56, People use syrup . . and butter instead of the dip . . on waffles now. **1973** Allen *LAUM* 1.294 (as of c1950), *Sauce* (sweet liquid poured over pudding). . . *Dip* . . reveals a strong Midland orientation by its concentration in southern Iowa and Nebraska. An occasional inf. restricts this word to mean only sauce for ice cream.

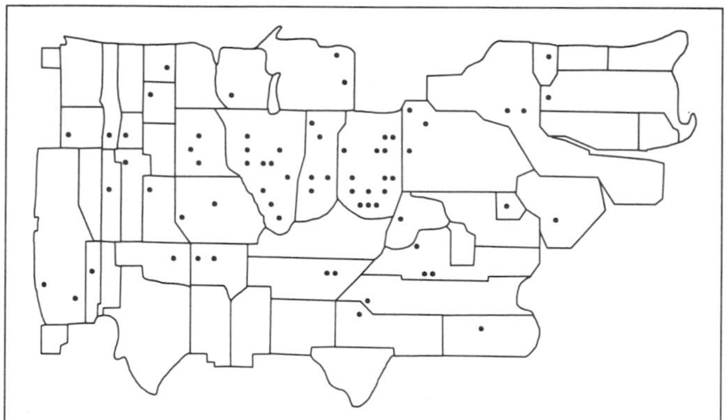

•dip n¹ 5 + varr (Qq. H66a, b, H21, H63)

6 also *dipping, dippy:* Gravy, meat drippings; infreq other flavored liquids in which food can be dipped. Cf **dope** n **1**

1846 Worcester *Universal Dict.* 205, *Dip.* . . Sauce made of fat pork for fish. *U.S.* **1894** Robley *Hist. Bourbon Co.* 26 **KS,** Some "rashers" are cut from the "flitch" of bacon and the grease tried out; eggs are fried, and "dip" is made. **1896** *DN* 1.415 **nwMD,** *Dippy:* fried meat grease or gravy. **1950** *WELS* (Gravy) 1 Inf, **nwWI,** Dip. **1959** *VT Hist.* new ser 27.132, *Dip.* . . Milk gravy. Rare. **c1960** *Wilson Coll.* **csKY,** *Dip.* . . An old name for gravy. **1961** Sackett–Koch *KS Folkl.* 112, *Dip.* . . Gravy. "Give me some dip on my bread too." **1965–70** *DARE* (Qu. H37, . . *Gravy*) Infs **CA**165, **KY**25, **MD**28, **NY**210, **WA**11, 22, **WV**8, 13, Dip; **PA**63, 150, Dippy; **PA**203, Dipping. [9 of 11 Infs old] **1967** *DARE* FW Addit **sePA,** Dippy—Anything you can dip something in—gravy, coffee [etc]. **1982** *Barrick Coll.* **csPA,** *Dip, dippy—gravy,* especially red-eye gravy.

7 See **dip toast.**

8 usu in comb *salt dip;* also *dipper:* An open container from which salt may be dipped. **chiefly Inland Nth** See Map

1965–70 *DARE* (Qu. G3, *A container for salt that's put on the table—if it's open*) 37 Infs, **chiefly Inland Nth,** Salt dip; **IN**41, 82, **MI**1, **NY**9, 12, 69, **PA**186, **WA**8, Dip; **IN**74, **PA**176, Salt dipper; (Qu. G6) Inf **AL**46, Salt dips.

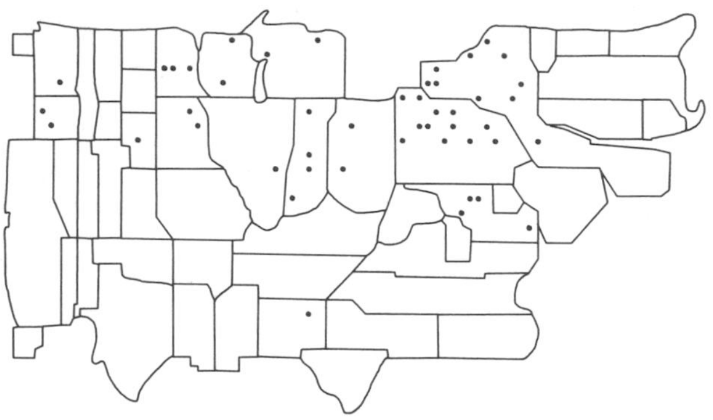

•dip n[1] 8 + varr (Qq. G3, G6)

9 A ladle. [Abbr for *dipper*] Cf **dip cup**

1966 *DARE* (Qu. F28, *The utensil with a small cup on a long handle, used to take water or milk out of a pail*) Inf **ME**11, Dip.

10 A dip net. Cf **dip** v 3

1954 *Harder Coll.* **cwTN,** *Dip*. . . A net used to catch fish, usually of cloth.

11 A hard blow; a jolt.

1897 *KS Univ. Qrly.* (ser B) 6.52 **KS,** *Dip:* a blow; as, Hit him a dip. **1966–70** *DARE* (Qu. Y1, . . *"He slipped on the steps and took quite a ______."*) Infs **MS**10, **TN**48, Dip. [Both Infs old]

12 See quots. [Because one tips or *dips* one's hat in greeting; cf **dip** v 4]

1912 *DN* 3.567 **MA, cNY,** *Dip*. . . Derby or stiff hat. **1913** *DN* 4.4 **ME,** *Dip*. . . A hat. **1970** Major *Dict. Afro-Amer. Slang* 46, *Dip:* a hat.

13 A pickpocket.

1859 Matsell *Vocabulum* 26, *Dip*. . . A pickpocket. **1900** Willard *Tramping* 393. **1926** Black *You Can't Win* 35 **MO,** No Missouri dip would take his roll, extract two fifty-dollar bills, and put the rest back in his pocket. **1927** *DN* 5.444 [Underworld jargon]. **1946** Dadswell *Hey There Sucker* 37, I have been told that Barnum sold the "dip privilege" for $5,000 a season. . . When a person's pocket was picked—a dip is a pickpocket—he would complain to police. The police would go . . for help to round up the culprit. An office stooge, in turn, would . . tip off the "dip" so he could "scram". **1967** *DARE* (Qu. V6, . . *A thief*) Inf **TX**9, Dip—pickpocket, learned this in Chicago.

dip n[2] See **dib**

dip cup n

1970 *DARE* (Qu. F28, *The utensil with a small cup on a long handle, used to take water or milk out of a pail*) Inf **TX**94, Dip cup.

dip diver See **didapper**

diphole n

1966–68 *DARE* (Qu. N30, . . *A sudden short dip in the road*) Inf **ME**9, Diphole; **VT**4, Dipholes—old term, used for hole filled with snow then crossed with a sleigh. **1967** *DARE* Tape **VT**1, [FW:] Someone was telling me about a very difficult thing, when the roads would get bad—a deep depression in the road, like this, where if you were driving with a sleigh, and the horse and the sleigh got down in it, it could snap the shafts. Did you ever run across a thing like that? [Inf:] Oh yes, when the snow was deep. . . What did we call those?—Dipholes.

‡diphtherobia n

1911 *DN* 3.542 **NE,** *Diphtherobia*. . . Apparently a blend of *diphtheria* and *hydrophobia.* "I fear Johnny has the diphtherobia." Use serious, not facetious. Rare.

dip in honey See **honey** n 4

dip nose n

A nose having a bend in the bridge.

1965–70 *DARE* (Qu. X15, . . *Kinds of noses*) Infs **NC**72, **OK**11, **PA**53, **WV**7, 8, 10, 14, 18, Dip nose.

dipped toast See **dip toast**

dip pen n Also *dipper, dipping pen*

A writing pen that must be dipped in ink.

1945 (1946) Macdonald *Egg & I* 114, An ink bottle and a dip pen. **1965–70** *DARE* (Qu. JJ10a, . . *Kinds of pens*) 82 Infs, **scattered,** Dip pens; **MS**6, Dipper; **CA**59, Dipping pen. **1968** Kellner *Aunt Serena* 46 **cIN** (as of c1920), My Grandmother opened the box and took out a sheet of paper and an envelope. She then assembled a stamp, a dip-pen, a bottle of ink, a penwiper, and a blotter. *Ibid* 96 **cIN,** We used dip-pens, which scratched loudly in the troubled silence. **1968** *DARE* FW Addit **VA**12, Dip pen is a writing pen with bone or wooden handle.

dipper n

1 =**hooded merganser.**

1737 (1911) Brickell *Nat. Hist. NC* 209, The *Dipper,* or *Fisher;* these are small Birds about the bigness of a *Teal.* **1876** *Forest & Stream* 7.212/3 **MA,** *Bucephala albeola.* Dipper or dopper. [*DARE* Ed: This term comes from a "list of Gunner's Names for Birds and Wild Fowl obtained in Plymouth Bay, Mass."] **1955** MA Audubon Soc. *Bulletin* 39.378, *Hooded Merganser*. . . Dipper (Mass. That is, diver).

2 also *dipper duck:* =**bufflehead 2.**

1832 Williamson *Hist. ME* 1.142, There [are] . . 5. *the river Coot, or ash coloured Duck;* 6. *the Dipper.* **1917** (1923) *Birds Amer.* 1.140, *Buffle-head—Charitonetta albeola* . . Dipper; Dipper Duck. **1917** *Wilson Bulletin* 29.2.77, *Charitonetta albeola*. . . dipper duck, Montauk, Long Island. **1955** *Oriole* 20.4, *Bufflehead*. . . *Dipper, Dipper Duck* (as an habitual diver). **1982** Elman *Hunter's Field Guide* 211, *Bufflehead (Bucephala albeola)* Common & Regional Names: . . dipper duck.

3 Any of var grebes, as:

a also *dipper duck:* =**pied-billed grebe.**

1844 DeKay *Zool. NY* 2.277, *The Dipper.—Hydroka carolinensis*. . . The *Dipper,* or *Pied Dobchick,* is common in the ponds and lakes of this State. **1903** Dawson *Birds OH* 2.631, *Pied-Billed Grebe* . . *Podilymbus podiceps* . . Dipper. **1925** (1928) Forbush *Birds MA* 1.11, *Podilymbus podiceps* . . *Pied-billed Grebe.—Other names:* . . Dipper . . Little Diver. **1936** Roberts *MN Birds* 1.158, Dipper *[Podilymbus podiceps].* **1940** Todd *Birds W. PA* 706, Dipper, *see* Grebe, . . Pied-billed. **1965–70** *DARE* (Qu. Q5) Infs **MD**18, 29, 45, **MA**58, **NY**207, **PA**115, 121, 188, Dipper (duck); **VA**47, Little dipper; (Qu. Q9) Infs **MD**25, 29, **NC**21, 27, **OH**79, **PA**1, Dipper; **MA**42, **NJ**1, 8, 28, **PA**104, **RI**4, 6, Dipper duck; (Qu. Q10) Inf **NY**207, Dipper duck. [Note: Some of these Infs may refer instead to other senses of **dipper.**]

b also *dipper duck:* =**horned grebe.**

1844 DeKay *Zool. NY* 2.274, *The Horned Grebe.—Podiceps cornutus*. . . This little aquatic bird, which is known under the various names of *Dipper,* . . and *Hell-diver.* **1890** Warren *Birds PA* 3, *Colymbus auritus* . . Horned Grebe; Dipper Duck. **1917** (1923) *Birds Amer.* 1.5, *Horned Grebe Colymbus auritus* . . Dipper. **1940** Todd *Birds W. PA* 37, Every gunner is familiar with the "Dipper," that elusive water bird which appears when the ducks arrive. **1946** Hausman *Eastern Birds* 67, *Horned Grebe Colymbus auritus* . . Dipper.

c =**red-necked grebe.**

1951 Pough *Audubon Water Bird* 326, Dipper. *See* Grebes. **1955** MA Audubon Soc. *Bulletin* 39.309, *Holboell's Grebe*. . . Dipper (Maine. That is, diver; early use, Albin, 1738).

4 also *dipper bird:* =**water ouzel.**

1848 in 1850 Cooper *Rural Hours* 10 **NY,** The Dipper, or ousel . . is still more at home in the water than the loon. **1878** U.S. Natl. Museum *Proc.* 1.397 **CA,** *Cinclus mexicanus* . . *American Water Ouzel; Dipper.* This bird is in summer abundant in the clear streams of Calaveras Co. **1917** (1923) *Birds Amer.* 3.172, *Dipper—Cinclus mexicanus unicolor* . . Other Names. . . American Dipper. **1941** Writers' Program *Guide UT* 27, Probably the most winning songster of all, a resident of canyons where swift water flows, is the water ouzel or dipper bird, which ranges throughout the Rocky Mountains. **1944** Hausman *Amer. Birds* 62, The Dipper, commonly called the Ouzel or Water Ouzel, is one of our most remarkable birds. **1961** Douglas *My Wilderness* 25 **CO,** Then another friend appeared, the American dipper or water ouzel. **1961** Ligon *NM Birds* 216, All the while the crossing was being prepared an alarmed Dipper kept flying back and forth over the stream. **1969** *DARE* (QR p119) Inf **CA**115, Dipper or water ouzel.

5 also *broadbill dipper, dipper duck:* **=ruddy duck.**

1888 Trumbull *Names of Birds* 110, *Ruddy Duck [Erismatura jamaicensis]* at Bath, Me., and Newport, R.I., *Broad-bill . . ;* at Fairhaven, Mass., *Broad-bill Dipper . . ; . .* at Provincetown, Mass., *Dipper, Dopper,* and *Dapper.* **1918** Grinnell *Game Birds CA* 205, *Ruddy Duck . .* Dipper Duck. **1925** (1928) Forbush *Birds MA* 1.280, *Ruddy Duck. Other names . .* broad-bill; . . broad-bill dipper. . . Bill broad, deep at base. **1938** Oberholser *Bird Life LA* 140, *Ruddy Duck—Erismatura jamaicensis. . .* Probably no duck has so many different names as this well-known bird. Some of those commonly heard are 'butterball', 'dipper', . . and 'Johnny bull'. **1982** Elman *Hunter's Field Guide* 192, Ruddy Duck: . . Common & Regional Names: booby . . dipper duck, . . sinker.

6 One who uses or dips snuff. **chiefly Sth, S Midl** See Map Cf **dip** v **1**

1852 *Knickerbocker* 40.93 **TX,** Fancy yourself . . married to a *'Dipper!'* **1897** *Boston Herald* 26 Sep. 25/4 *(DA),* The dipper . . would a-dipping go. **1908** *DN* 3.305 **eAL, wGA,** *Dipper. . .* One who uses snuff. **1944** Clark *Pills* 149 **Sth,** Among the hosts of "dippers" there was a curious folk legend about judging the quality of snuff from the outside of the bottle. **1965–70** *DARE* (Qu. DD3a, . . *A person who uses snuff*) 306 Infs, **chiefly Sth, S Midl,** (Snuff) dipper.

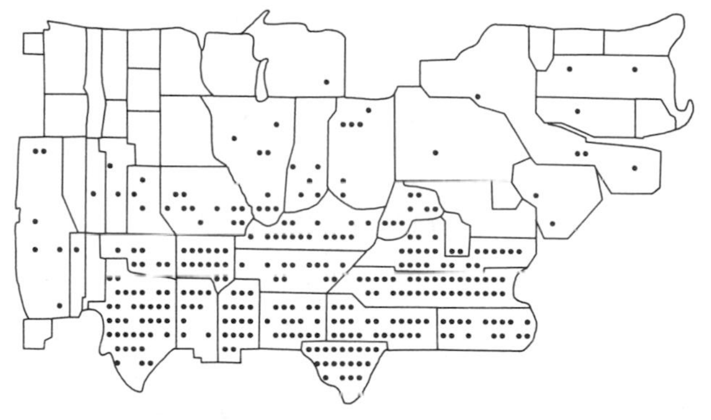

•dipper 6 + var (Qu. DD3a)

7 **=dipping stick 1.**

1967 *DARE* (Qu. DD3b, *How do people take snuff around here?*) Inf SC5, Rub it on the gums with a dipper.

8 One who practices baptism by immersion. Cf **Dunker**

1845 *Knickerbocker* 25.123 **GA,** And how the long-lunged dippers take / The lead of old Geneva. **1859** *Harper's New Mth. Mag.* 19.859/1 **WV,** You rascally 'Dipper,' I'll learn you not to interrupt my preaching! **1969** *DARE* (Qu. CC4, . . *Nicknames . . for various . . religious groups*) Inf **GA**89, Dippers—Baptists.

9 See **dip pen.**

10 See **dip** n^{1} **8.**

11 See **dip** v **2.**

‡**12** A tornado.

1968 *DARE* (Qu. B16, *A destructive wind that comes with a funnel-shaped cloud*) Inf **MD**40, Dipper.

dipper bird See **dipper 4**

dipper clam n Cf **dish shell**

A **surf clam** (here: *Spisula solidissima*).

1889 *Century Dict.* 1634, [The] *dipper clam. . .* attains a large size, is of a subtriangular form, and its valves are sometimes used as dippers or suggest such use. **1986** *NADS Letters, Dipper clam*—[term] still in use in New Bedford, Massachusetts.

dipper duck See **dipper 2, 3a, b, 5**

dipper gourd n

=bottle gourd.

1880 Allan-Olney *New Virginians* I.199 *(DA),* A bucket of spring-water with a dipper-gourd in it. **1897** Stuart *Simpkinsville* 146, Th' ain't nothin' too low down an' common for 'em to mix with . . f'om a punkin even down to a dipper-gourd. **1944** Duncan *Mentor Graham* 113 **IL,** Snow was melted in it, and the children drank from a common dipper-gourd. **1974** Morton *Folk Remedies* 162 **SC,** *Gourd. . .* Includes the various forms called "dipper gourd," "bottle gourd," etc. **1976** Bailey–Bailey *Hortus Third* 633, *Lagenaria. . . siceraria. . .* Includes the *Dipper . .* and *Trumpet Gourds.*

dipping vbl n See **dip** v **1, 2, 3**

dipping n See **dip** n^{1} **4, 5, 6**

dipping pen See **dip pen**

dipping stick n

1 also *dip stick:* A stick chewed or frayed at the end used to dip snuff. **chiefly Sth, S Midl** Cf **dip** v **1, snuff stick**

1868 *Putnam's Mag.* 2.53 **LA,** An officer . . rode up to a house at the fork of the roads, and inquired of the lean, scrawny woman who appeared at the door, vigorously plying the "dipping-stick," whether she had recently seen any cavalry. **1946** *Atlanta Journal Mag.* 3 March 9/1 *(DA),* A woman might ask for a little grain or smidgin of snuff to go on her dip-stick. **1954** *Harder Coll.* **cwTN,** *Dip-stick. . .* A stick used in taking snuff.

2 A divining rod. [Because it is supposed to 'dip' as it passes over a vein of water or mineral] Cf *DS* CC13a

1940 Stong *Hawkeyes* 261 **IA,** If elder is not better than willow for a "dipping stick" at least it is just as good.

dippity-do See **dipsy doodle**

dippy adj

Of a person: foolish, simple-minded; infatuated; peculiar.

1911 *DN* 3.542 **NE,** *Dippy. . .* Foolish, idiotic. . . "He was dippy about her." **1912** *DN* 3.574 **wIN,** *Dippy. . .* 1. Mildly insane. 2. Deeply in love. **1913** *DN* 4.10 **MN,** *Dippy. . .* Foolish, crazy. **1914** *DN* 4.105 **KS,** *Dippy. . .* Mentally unbalanced. "Ain't people that set the styles dippy?" **1915** *DN* 4.214, *Dippy,* shallowminded. "Smith is dippy over that girl." **1919** *DN* 5.71 **CA, NM,** *Dippy,* foolish, simple. "You are perfectly dippy about algebra." **1919** in 1983 Truman *Dear Bess* 290 **MO,** Some of 'em [=regular officers in the U.S. Army] are nuts on horse feed and some are dippy on how to take care of harness. **c1960** *Wilson Coll.* **csKY,** *Dippy. . .* Not bright, either naturally or "play-like." **1965–70** *DARE* (Qu. W41, . . *Someone whose clothes never look right or who always dresses carelessly*) Inf **WA**22, Pretty dippy; (Qu. HH5, *Someone who is queer but harmless*) Inf **PA**76, Dippy; (Qu. HH6, *Someone who is out of his mind*) Inf **MA**89, Dippy; (Qu. HH9, *A very silly or light-headed person*) Inf **MA**24, Dippy. [3 of 4 Infs young] **1967** *DARE* FW Addit **ceWA,** Dippy. Used to describe someone you don't like. (Said by a high school student.) **1977** *DARE* File, [Said by a teenager on a television program:] Oh, don't worry about what Dad thinks or says—he's just dippy.

dippy n See **dip** n^{1} **5, 6**

dippy bread See **dip toast**

dip-sop n [**dip** n^{1} **5, 6 + sop**]

A sweet sauce; gravy.

1967–68 *DARE* (Qu. H37, . . *Gravy*) Infs **CO**11, **MD**30, Dip-sop. **1978** *DARE* File **neOH** (as of 1940s), A woman who ran a boarding house in Hiram hastily apologized when she asked her boarders if they'd like more dip-sop for their pudding. "We used to say *dip-sop* at home when I was a child," she apologized, "but I didn't mean to say it here!"

dip stick See **dipping stick 1**

dipsy n [*OED dips(e)y, dipsie,* varr of *deep sea,* used esp in combs *dipsey lead, ~ line* "sounding lead, ~ line"; perh infl by *dip* v] **PA**

A fishing sinker or similar contrivance.

1848 Bartlett *Americanisms* 396 **PA,** Dipsy. A term applied in some parts of Pennsylvania to the float of a fishing-line. [*DARE* Ed: Bartlett changed "float" to "sinker" in the 3d (1860) ed.] **1872** Schele de Vere *Americanisms* 339, The *dipsy, . .* the sinker of a fishing-line, is only known in Pennsylvania; the name, of course, arises from the *dip* the little weight takes as soon as it touches the water. **c1875** in 1966 *PADS* 46.22, *Dipsy* an apparatus for catching fish, composed of a piece of whalebone, bent to an almost right angle, to the ends of which hooks are attached. This is sunk to the bottom by a sinker of lead. [*DARE* Ed: This is from Schele de Vere's own annotated copy of his 1872 *Americanisms.*] **1966** *DARE* (Qu. P17, *What do you call it around here when the people fish by lowering a line and sinker close to the bottom of the water?*) Inf **PA**1, Dipsy fishing—the sinker is called a dipsy.

dipsy doodle n Also *dippity-do, dipty-dip*

1 **=thank-you-ma'am.**

1946 *AmSp* 21.209, I have heard it [=a dip in the road] called a *dipsydoodle*—though where I couldn't say, except that it was in this country. **1969** *DARE* (Qu. N30, *What do you call a sudden short dip in the road?*) Inf **CA**111, Dippity-do; **PA**40, Dipty-dip. **1987** Childress *Out of the Ozarks* 157, Ozark highways are narrow and two-laned, dipping deep into swales like asphalt roller coasters, zooming up over the hills. . . These dipsy-doodle rides are high points when they [=young boys] visit me from California.

2 also *doodle:* **=woodcock** (here: *Philohela minor*).

1955 *Oriole* 20.7, American Woodcock.—*Dipsydoodle, Doodle* (doodle is a fanciful appellation of rather wide distribution; "dipsy" may have allusion to the bird's erratic flight).

3 The common **loon** *(Gavia stellata).*

1956 *AmSp* 31.187, *Dipsydoodle* is a facetious name for a diving bird (the common loon, Wis.)

dip-tail diver n Also *dip-tail*

=ruddy duck.

1888 Trumbull *Names of Birds* 112, At St. Augustine, Fla., Dip-Tail Diver *[Erismatura jamaicensis].* **1917** (1923) *Birds Amer.* 1.152, Ruddy Duck—*Erismatura jamaicensis* . . Dip-tail. **1944** Hausman *Amer. Birds* 511, Dip-tail—see Duck, Ruddy. **1954** Sprunt *FL Bird Life* 85, Ruddy Duck: *[Oxyura jamaicensis]* . . Local Names: . . Dip-tail Diver. **1982** Elman *Hunter's Field Guide* 192, Ruddy Duck: (*Oxyura jamaicensis,* also classified as *Erismatura jamaicensis rubida*) Common & Regional Names: . . dip-tail.

dip toast n Also *dipped toast, dippy bread, dip* arch

Toast or bread soaked in milk or other liquid.

[**1818** Palmer *Jrl.* 241, One or two dishes are peculiar to New England and always on the table, toast dipped in cream and *pumpkin pie.*] **1855** Thomson *Doesticks* 204 **NY,** Rest of bill of fare consists of salt ham, red flannel sausages, hash with hairs in it, dip toast made with sour milk, burned biscuit, etc. **1869** Hale *Ingham Papers* 17 **CT,** Good soul, she even made dip-toast for our suppers, and had hot apples waiting for us between the andirons. **1930s** in 1944 *ADD* 164/1 **eWV,** *Dip*. . . Bread & milk. **1939** Aurand *Quaint Idioms* 23 [PaGer], Give me some *dippy* (gravy, dressing)! I like *dippy bread.* **1976** Flexner *America Talking* 65, Early Americans. . . usually ate it [=toast] as *dipped toast* or *dip toast,* with milk or melted butter poured over it, which was commonly being called *milk toast* by the 1820s. **1977** *DARE* File **cnMA,** My grandmother used to serve *dipped toast* usually called wet toast for breakfast. It was well-browned toast dipped quickly in hot water, stacked up, and covered. It was served at the table, eaten with a fork. Toast with a cream sauce (a supper dish) was *creamed toast;* with hot milk and butter poured over it, it was *milk toast* (for people who were "ailing").

diptree n [Pronc-sp for *diphtheria*]

1970 *NC Folkl.* 18.19, For diphtheria ("diptree"), use vinegar and kerosene mixed, or a poultice of salt.

dipty-dip See **dipsy-doodle**

dip up See **dip** v **1**

directly adv, conj Usu |də'rɛk(t)li|; also **chiefly Sth, S Midl** |'drɛkli, t(ə)'rɛkli| and occas |'drækli| Pronc-spp *drackly, dreckly, ter(r)eckly, therreckly, threckly, toreckly, torectly, turrecly, rectly*

A Forms.

1851 [see **C** below]. **1874** (1895) Eggleston *Circuit Rider* 144 **sOH** (as of early 1800s), Her son Jake would be in thireckly, and she 'lowed he wouldn't turn nobody out in sech a night. **1887** (1967) Harris *Free Joe* 135 **GA,** She'll wake up therreckly. **1893** Shands *MS Speech* 62, *Terreckly* [tərɛkli]. Negro for *directly.* **1899** [see **B1** below]. **1902** *DN* 2.232 **sIL,** *Directly* (sometimes pronounced [dər'ɛkli]). **1909** *DN* 3.380 **eAL, wGA,** *Tereckly*. . . Directly, presently, soon. **1915** *DN* 4.182 **swVA,** *Dreckly.* Short for *directly.* **1927** *AmSp* 2.353 **WV,** Your girls came dreckly home. **1930** *DN* 6.80 **cSC,** *Directly.* Always pronounced [tərɛkli]. **1934** Carmer *Stars Fell on AL* 36, "Be there toreckly," he called. **1944** [see **B2** below]. **1954** Roberts *I Bought Dog* 6 **seKY,** He climbed down inside and rectly the giants called again, "Open the big gate!" **1954** [see **B2** below]. **1956** [see **B2** below]. **c1970** *Halpert Coll.* **wKY,** Directly . . Pronounced d'reckly. **1978** [see **B2** below].

B As adv.

1 Immediately, without delay. **chiefly Sth, S Midl** See Map

1899 (1912) Green *VA Folk-Speech* 453, *Torectly*. . . A form of *directly.* Directly; straight away; at once. "He'll come torectly." Toreckly. **1902** *DN* 2.232 **sIL,** 'When he saw that Jim was in the house, he come away directly.' This . . use would indicate precipitate haste. **1965–70** *DARE* (Qu. A13, *When something needs to be done immediately, you might say, "I'll do it _______!"*) 40 Infs, **chiefly Sth, S Midl,** Directly; **NC**11, Now directly; (Qu. A14, *Referring to a very short period of time*) Inf **ME**5, I'll be with you directly; (Qu. A23, *To do something at the very first try: "He got the right answer _______."*) Inf **MD**19, Directly; (Qu. B5, *When the weather looks as if it will become bad, you say it's _______*) Inf **MO**38, Going to be doing something here directly.

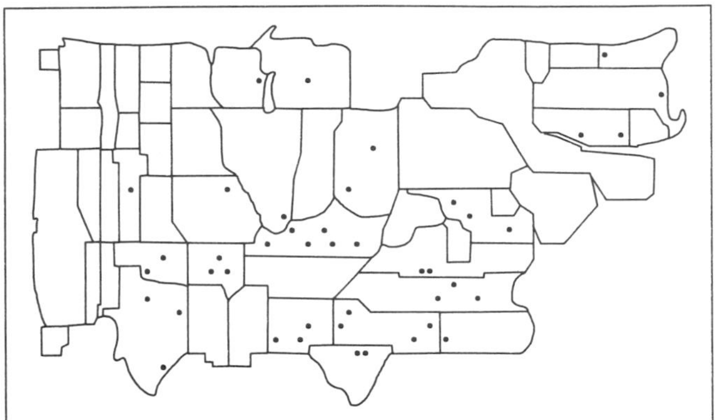

•directly B1 + varr (Qq. A13, A14, A23, B5)

2 Soon, after a while.

1942 McAtee *Dial. Grant Co. IN* 23 (as of 1890s), *Dreckly* . . directly, but it meant not at once but pretty soon, at the convenience of the speaker. **1942** Warnick *Garrett Co. MD* 6 **nwMD** (as of 1900–18), I'll do that dreckly—as soon as I finish sewing this button on. **1944** *PADS* 2.8 **Sth,** *Directly* [dɪ'rɛklɪ, 'drɛklɪ, 'trɛklɪ]. . . Presently, in a little while. Over wide areas of the South. **1954** *Harder Coll.* **cwTN,** Directly . . not immediately but later: "Le' me 'lone. I'll do it now drackly." **1956** McAtee *Some Dialect NC* 13, *Dreckly:* . . i.e., directly, meaning soon or at a convenient time, but not immediately. **1966** *DARE* FW Addit **cwNC,** Don't bother me now, I'll do it directly. **1978** *DARE* File **SC, GA coasts** [Gullah], Dem duh gwine on en turrecly dem come tuh one big ole briar patch. **1983** *MJLF* 9.1.37 **ceKY,** *Directly* . . after a short while.

3 Quickly.

1924 Raine *Land of Saddle-Bags* 105 **Appalachians,** Children grow up directly.

C As conj.

As soon as.

1851 Burke *Polly Peablossom* 72 **MS,** Torectly I spy the heatherns they commence takin' on. **1966** *DARE* FW Addit **nwNC,** I'll be there directly I get this done.

dirk n Also *dirk-knife* Usu |dɝk|; rarely |dɝč, dɝθ| [Scots *dowrk, durk* dagger; *DOST* 1567 →] **chiefly Sth, S Midl** Cf **dog knife**

A dagger, knife; a large pocket knife.

1820 *Niles' Natl. Reg.* 18.386/1 **ceMO,** The ladies, as well as the gentlemen . . wear dirks by their sides. **1835** Hoffman *Winter in West* (NY) 1.212 **NY,** I . . gave the game the *coup de grace* with a dirk-knife which I had about me. **1843** (1916) Hall *New Purchase* 161 **IN,** Tom [kept] talking and laughing away, like a fellow whittling poplar with a dirk-knife. **1880** Cable *Grandissimes* 228 **LA,** There was a dirk in her bosom. **1912** *DN* 3.574 **wIN,** *Dirk*. . . The blade used in cutting corn by hand. **1930** Knibbs *Songs Lost Frontier* [30] **West,** Wide strewn his leathern pack; Gay gauds and satin bands; A dirk upstandin' in his back, And dead leaves in his hands. **1965–68** *DARE* (Qu. F39, *A large pocket knife with blades that fold in and out*) Inf **AL**11, Dirk; **AL**34, Dirk—larger than a barlow knife; **FL**17, Dirk—long single blade; **GA**4, Dirk [dɝč]; **DC**7, Dirk-knife—big-bladed folding knife. **1965** *DARE* FW Addit **OK,** *Dirk*—a dagger or knife, here pronounced [dɝθ].

dirn See **durn** v, intj

dirt n

1 in phr *cut dirt:* To depart hastily, to run away fast. *arch* Cf *DS* Y19, 20

1829 in 1897 Barrère–Leland *Slang* 1.273 [Black], He jump up fo' sartin—he *cut dirt* and run. *Negro Song of* 1829. **1867** Lowell *Biglow* 66 **'Upcountry' MA,** Why, two-thirds o' the Rebbles 'ould cut dirt,/ Ef they once thought thet Guv'ment meant to hurt. **1872** Schele de Vere *Americanisms* 222, The slang phrase to *cut dirt,* vulgar but very suggestive as to the effect of the rapid motion of a horse on a muddy road, must be traced back to this fondness for the popular animal, and fast driving. "Now, I say, old *hoss,* if you don't hurry up and *cut dirt* like streak-lightnin', this child goes arter you, and you look out for a windin' sheet, you hear?" (*Border Adventures,* p. 231.)

2 in phr *meaner than* (or *mean as*) *dirt:* Very mean, unkind. **chiefly Nth, scattered West** See Map *old-fash* Cf **cat shit, dog** n[1] **B17d**

1851 (1852) Stowe *Uncle Tom's Cabin* 1.144 **KY,** Jest like as not, he'll take 'em all away. I know thar ways—mean as dirt, they is! **1878** Shillaber *Ike Partington* 213 **NH,** "He's going to shoot him!" said one of the boys. . . "Because of that time on the grass," said another. "It's mean as dirt," said a third. **1924** *DN* 5.291, *Meaner than dirt.* **1965–70** *DARE* (Qu. HH22b, *Talking about a very mean person, you might say, "He's meaner than _______.")* 77 Infs, **chiefly Nth, scattered West,** Dirt; **PA**175, Mean as dirt. [Of all Infs responding to the question, 64% were old; of those giving these responses, 83% were old.]

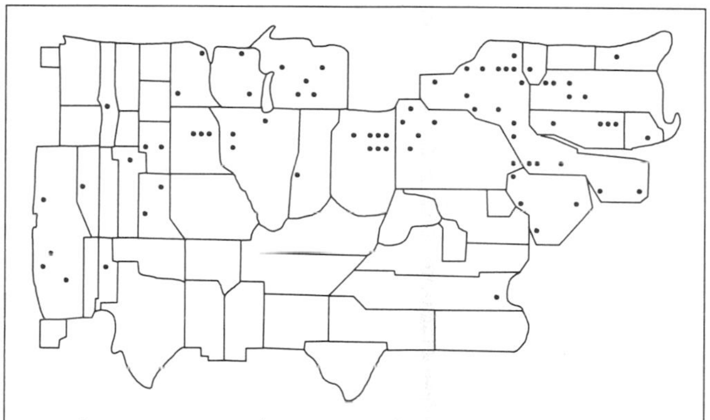

3 in phr *eat dirt:* To retract, to make a humiliating confession. [Cf proverb "Every man must eat a peck (*or* pound) of dirt before he dies," i.e., Everyone must at some time admit error and suffer the consequences.]

1885 *Mag. Amer. Hist.* 13.199/2, "To eat dirt" is to retract or "eat humble pie." **c1902** Clapin *New Dict. Amer.* 172, *Eat dirt.* To retract, to be penitent, the Yankee equiv of "to eat one's words." **1947** Willingham *End as Man* 200 **GA,** I ate dirt and apologized to that bastard. *Ibid* 201, I'll never forget how he made me eat dirt. **1975** *AmSp* 50.58 **AR** (as of c1970), *Eat dirt. . .* Retract one's words, having been shown they are wrong.

4 in phr *do dirt:* See quot.

1893 Owen *Voodoo Tales* 274 **MO,** Ef I tek ter doin' dirt, den Ise willin' ter be jacky-me-lantuhn [=**jack-o'-lantern,** sometimes supposed to be a wandering, homeless ghost]—an' sarve me right, too! [Footnote:] To do dirt, to act immorally.

5 in phr *do one dirt,* also rarely *do one dirty:* To deceive, mistreat, or harm one, esp underhandedly or by secret means. Cf **do** v **D2**

1897 *KS Univ. Qrly.* (ser B) 6.87, *Do dirt:* to treat meanly.—General. **1902** *DN* 2.233 **sIL,** *Do one dirt. . .* To injure by mischief or rascally tricks. **1903** *DN* 2.311 **seMO,** *Do one dirt. . .* To injure by secret means. To backbite. 'You ought to know me better than to think I would do you dirt.' **1905** *DN* 3.61 **NE,** Smith did him dirt in the election. **1906** *DN* 3.117 **sIN,** He done me dirt. *Ibid* 134 **nwAR,** *Do dirty. . .* To injure by secret means. "I never dreamed he'd do me dirty in that fashion." **1908** *DN* 3.306 **eAL, wGA,** *Do one dirt.* **1914** *DN* 4.105 **KS,** *Do (one) dirt. . .* To injure (one) in a contemptible way, especially betrayal. **1916** *DN* 4.274 **MA, NE, IL, PA,** Wouldn't I be likely to help him after he done me dirt like that? **1923** *DN* 5.205 **swMO,** He'll do you dirt. **1924** *DN* 5.289, *Do somebody dirt.* **1947** *Reader's Digest* 51.306 155/2 **DC,** People had been doing her dirt for 40 years. **1966** Barnes–Jensen *Dict. UT Slang* 12, He did her dirt by telling about her baby.

6 in phr *atop of dirt:* Alive.

1921 Haswell *Daughter Ozarks* 176 (as of 1880s), This time the big sheriff rode at her side, on his way to carry out his oath to "git" the other two who had attacked Haberton, "efsobe they was a'top of dirt!"

7 See quot.

1968 *DARE* (Qu. HH18, *Very insignificant or low-grade people*) Inf **PA**76, Dirts [laughter]; **PA**94, Dirts. [Both Infs college students]

8 attrib: See quot.

1956 McAtee *Some Dialect NC* 12, *Dirt dish:. .* pottery dish.

dirt v

1 often with *up:* To plow so that soil is thrown up against the plants; to throw soil around the base of; hence vbl n *dirting.* **chiefly Sth** Cf **bar off**

1850 in 1969 Turner *Cotton Planter's Manual* 36 **MS,** I can dirt easily four acres per horse. **1893** Shands *MS Speech* 26, *Dirt up. . .* In the cultivation of cotton this phrase is used as the exact opposite of *bar off.* When the intervening space between the rows is so plowed as to throw the dirt up to the cotton-plant, the cotton is said to be *dirted up.* **1944** Clark *Pills* 287 **Sth,** A middle-aged farmer flaunted himself in the face of progress and used a scraper to prepare cotton for chopping, and a twister for "dirting" corn. **1966** *DARE* Tape **GA**1, Get back then with a ruler plow and a sweep with a fender on your plowstock to keep from covering up that little plant. That's called dirting, putting dirt back to your cotton. **1967** *DARE* FW Addit **cnLA,** Dirt it up—to plow so as to throw dirt toward the rows, to cover seed or cover shallow roots. **1986** *State Jrl.-Reg.* (Springfield IL) 12 May 5, A few days later [=after "barring off" the corn field] we turned the cultivator discs around and "dirted" the corn, moving the soil toward and into the row, covering as many weeds as possible without covering the corn, and making a ridge.

2 To soil or dirty.

1940 (1978) Still *River of Earth* 129 **KY,** Lives in a house size of a hilltop, and never dirts his hands.

dirt box n

1983 *Reinecke Coll.* 4 **LA,** *Dirt Box. . .* [dɜɪt bɑks] garbage can (recorded in Kenner) rare. La. F. "boîte d'ordure".

dirt cellar n Also *earth cellar* **chiefly NEng, NY** Cf **ground cellar**

An unfinished basement or other underground space.

1931–33 *LANE Worksheets* **wCT,** Dirt cellar—An unfinished basement used for storage. **1965–70** *DARE* (Qu. D22, *Underground place to go in case of a violent windstorm*) Inf **NY**72, Dirt cellar—old-fashioned—they run right in the bank; (Qu. M19, *A place for keeping carrots, turnips, potatoes . . over the winter*) Infs **MA**75, **NY**80, 211, **OH**10, Dirt cellar; **CT**6, Earth cellar—part of the cellar not cemented over.

dirt dauber n Also *dirt dobber*

1 =**mud dauber.** [See quots] **chiefly Sth, S Midl** See Map on p. 82 and Map Section See also *DARE* 1.xxix

1855 *Home Friend* new ser 3.457 **AL,** The little boys informed me that these were the nests of the Dirt-daubers; and on taking down one of the shapeless lumps which had been fixed on the wall right over my bed's head, and carefully opening it, I found within it many long-oval cells, lined with a thin coat of brittle shelly substance. These were arranged side by side in two rows, each containing the slough of a perfected insect. **1908** *DN* 3.308 **eAL, wGA,** *Dirt-dobber.* **1912** Green *VA Folk-Speech* 148, *Dirt-dobber. . . Dirt-dauber.* The mud-wasp, or mason. **1915** *DN* 4.182 **swVA,** *Dirt-dobber.* **1933** Rawlings *South Moon* 287 **FL,** "Them hateful dirt-daubers!" She dug at one with a stick. "I'll kill him if I kin rout him." She knocked the wasp to the floor, where the child crushed it. **1950** *PADS* 14.26 **SC,** *Dirtdobber* ['dɜɪt͵dɑbə], *-dauber. . .* A mud-dauber wasp. **1965–70** *DARE* (Qu. R20, *Wasps that build their nests of mud*) 270 Infs, **chiefly Sth, S Midl,** Dirt dauber; (Qu. E22, *If a house is untidy . . you might say . . "It looks like_______.")* Inf **TX**11, A dirt dauber's nest—said of a camp. **1970** Anderson *TX Folk Med.* 44, Mix up honey and dirt dauber's nests and apply to the bite.

2 Among loggers and railroad workers: see quots. Also called **dirt hider**

1931 *AmSp* 7.53 [Lumberjack lingo], "Dirt dobbers" build the grades for the new railroads. **1977** Adams *Lang. Railroader* 45, *Dirt dauber:* A road grader.

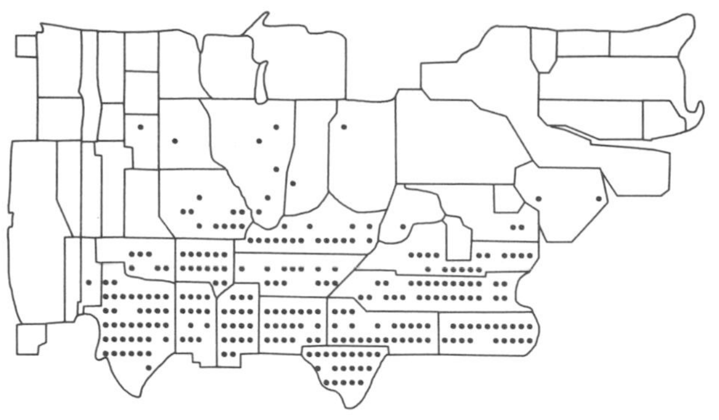

•dirt dauber 1 + var (Qq. R20, E22)

dirt-dog poor See **dog poor**

dirt-eater n

1 =**clay-eater 1. chiefly Sth** *usu derog* Cf *DJE, DBE dirt-eating*

1840 Hoffman *Greyslaer* 2.223 **NY,** Even Bettys, little fastidious as he was, recoiled from the fare which these "Dirt Eaters," as the Indians called them, placed before him. **1851** Hooper *Widow Rugby's Husband* 123 **AL,** "Is it a *rail* woman in thar?" asked a skeptical dirteater. **1871** Eggleston *Hoosier Schoolmaster* 71 **sIN,** Shall I not say that these bands of desperadoes still found among the "poor whitey," "dirt-eater" class are the outcroppings of the bad blood sent from England in convict-ships? **1908** *DN* 3.305 **eAL, wGA,** *Dirt-eater*. . . Clay-eater. The latter term is rarely used. **1913** Cole *Whig Party* 189 **AL** (as of c1851), The disunion men . . tried to discredit the Union movement in the eyes of Democrats by applying to it such epithets as "Federalists", "Feds", "Submissionists" . . "Dirt-eaters". **1941** Cummings *Amer. & Food* 87, Distinguished from other southerners by hookworm disease were dirt-eaters scattered in sand barrens and pine woods from South Carolina to Mississippi.

2 One who rides behind a herd of animals. Cf **eat drag dust, trailer**

1937 Sandoz *Slogum* 32 **NE,** A lone rider pointed the lean, horn-weary herd, two shambled along each side, and the trailer, the dirt eater, limbered up the drags with voice and knot-ended rope.

dirt farmer n

1 A person who actually farms the land; a countrified person; also n *dirt farming* the operating of a farm.

1920 *Boston Ev. Transcript* 2 Oct. IV. 1/1 *(DA)*, So Aggie . . goes on its way, doing its multiple duty of making dirt-farming a fine art; . . and of making the rural community and home a more livable town and place. **1924** H. Croy *R.F.D. No. 3* 148 *(DA)*, I'm going to put up the finest cattle barn in the state—that is, belonging to a real dirt farmer, not to one of them city dudes. **1932** Stong *State Fair* 248 **IA,** Occasionally a "dirt farmer" recognized the animal [=a prizewinning boar] and yelled his congratulations to Abel over the noise of the motors. **c1960** *Wilson Coll.* **csKY,** *Dirt Farmer*. . . An actual farmer and not merely a man who owns a farm. **1965–70** *DARE* (Qu. HH1, . . *A rustic or countrified person*) Infs **CA**169, **IA**11, **NC**1, **PA**138, Dirt farmer. **1966** *DARE* FW Addit **MS,** *Dirt farmer* . . the small farmer who spends all his energy in trying to ferret a living for himself and his family from the soil. **1977** *Capital Times* (Madison WI) 17 Dec 10/1, Her parents were poor dirt farmers. She picked crops along with seven other children in the family.

2 See quot.

1968 *DARE* FW Addit **neOH,** *Dirt farmer*, as opposed to a truck farmer or dairy farmer, grows root vegetables—especially a potato farmer with over two hundred acres of potatoes.

dirt frog n [Perh in contrast to *water frog*]

A toad.

1970 *DARE* (Qu. P23) Inf **VA**55, Dirt frog.

dirt hider n

Among loggers and railroad workers: =**dirt dauber 2.**

1930 Williams *Logger-Talk* 17 **Pacific NW,** *Dirt-hider:* A road grader. **1958** McCulloch *Woods Words* 47 **Pacific NW. 1969** Sorden *Lumberjack Lingo* 34 **NEng, Gt Lakes. 1977** Adams *Lang. Railroader* 45.

dirties n pl

In var combs: Diarrhea.

1966–69 *DARE* (Qu. BB19, . . *Looseness of the bowels*) Infs **SC**3, **TX**18, 43, 74, **UT**7, Thin dirties; **KS**2, Green-apple dirties; **GA**77, The shin dirties.

dirting See **dirt** v **1**

dirt, meaner than See **dirt** n **2**

dirt one's back See **dirty one's shirt**

dirt pea n

In marble play: see quot.

1970 *DARE* Tape **VA**38, We had a little small marble . . what we used to call dirt peas when I was a boy.

dirt pool n

A children's game; see quot.

1975 Ferretti *Gt. Amer. Book Sidewalk Games* 153, A shooter's game, on the other hand, is *Spanish Pool*, also called *Dirt Pool* and *Wishing Well*. This game requires an intricate ring made up of concentric circles. . . It is kind of a game of dirt darts played with marbles.

dirt spider n

An unidentified spider.

1968 *DARE* (Qu. R28) Inf **VA**2, Dirt spider—great big ole black spider.

dirt storm n

A dust storm.

1967 *DARE* (Qu. B18, . . *Any special kinds of wind*) Inf **CO**17, Dirt storm.

dirt tank n **TX**

See quots.

1962 Atwood *Vocab. TX* 42, *Artificial pool of water*. A body of water impounded for the watering of livestock and for other purposes is known throughout most of the state as a *tank*. . . This sort of pool is occasionally referred to as . . a *dirt tank*. **1967** *DARE* (Qu. C4b) Inf **TX**22, Dirt tank—formed by dam across a river, a small reservoir.

dirt up See **dirt** v **1**

dirtworm n

=**earthworm.**

1968 *DARE* (Qu. P5) Inf **NY**40, Dirtworm.

dirty adj

Of a place: having natural barriers which impede travel.

1969 *DARE* (Qu. C28, *A place where underbrush, weeds, vines, and small trees grow together so that it's nearly impossible to get through*) Inf **IL**81, Dirty timber—so thick you couldn't run a dog through. **1975** Gould *ME Lingo* 74, *Dirty water*—Long before ecologists brought us a new vocabulary, *dirty water* was the Maine term for any stretch of sea with shoals, ledges, and rocks that called for close attention to charts and a keen lookout. Most yachtsmen consider a good part of Casco Bay *dirty water* in the sense that it challenges their sailing skill and lends charm to their outing.

dirty v Also *dirty up*

To clutter or mess up (a place).

1965–70 *DARE* (Qu. Y37, *To make a place untidy or disorderly: "I wish they wouldn't ——— the room up so."*) 27 Infs, **scattered, but esp Sth, S Midl, West,** Dirty (up).

dirty bird See **dirty sparrow**

dirty dishrag n Cf **dirty spoon**

1969 *DARE* (Qu. D39, . . *A small eating place where the food is not especially good*) Inf **GA**84, Dirty dishrag.

dirty dozens See **dozen** n **B1**

dirty hearts n pl, but sg in constr Also *dirty English hearts* *esp freq among Black speakers*

Any of var card games; see quots.

1965–70 *DARE* (Qu. DD35, . . *Favorite card games*) 12 Infs, **scattered, but esp Sth, S Midl,** Dirty hearts. [9 of 12 Infs Black] **1974** Matthews-Amdur *My Race* 2 **NYC** [Black], "Dirty Hearts" was an offshoot of regular Hearts except that the first person to get twenty-six points in the game had to pay a penalty. Usually the penalty was drinking a pint of water. **1982** *Contract Bridge Letters* **Detroit MI,** Dirty Hearts. . . It is the ordinary game of Hearts, usu played by 3 people . . it is designed as a cutthroat game—each one for him/herself. Thus, in our area, it has acquired the colloquial nickname of Dirty Hearts. *Ibid* **MO,** Dirty English Hearts. . . I learned the game from a Michigan native. The play is the same as in regular hearts with the following point counts: Spade Q = 13; Heart A = 5; all other hearts = 1; Diamond J = -10. *Ibid* **CO,** I have played dirty hearts. . . The cards are shuffled and placed face down in the center of the table. . . A player draws a card. If he draws a heart, every other player gets to ask him a question.

dirty Irish trick See **Irish trick**

dirty one's shirt v phr Also *dirt one's back*
To throw someone; to be thrown; see quots.
1959 *VT Hist.* new ser 27.133, *Dirt one's back.* . . To throw one on one's back in wrestling: to defeat one. Occasional. **1961** Adams *Old-Time Cowhand* 297, There're a heap of slang terms for bein' throwed from a hoss, such as he . . "dirtied his shirt."

dirty rice n **sLA** [From its brown color]
A rice dish similar to **jambalaya;** see quots.
1965–70 *DARE* (Qu. H45, *Dishes made with meat, fish, or poultry that everybody around here would know but that people in other places might not*) Infs **LA**16, 31, 40, Dirty rice. **1967** LeCompte *Word Atlas* 211 **seLA,** A creole dish made of rice and some other important ingredients such as shrimp, oysters, or sausage: dirty rice. . . The response "dirty rice," though sometimes used for this concept, more often refers to the Creole rice dressing. **1972** Hewitt *NYT Heritage Cookbook* 249, One of the most interesting dishes in Louisiana cuisine bears the abrupt name of Dirty Rice. This is really a jambalaya made with chicken gizzards and livers and, when well made, it is delicious. **1978** *New Yorker* 17 Apr 114 **seLA,** The dirty rice—a sort of rice dressing made with chicken liver and chicken gizzard and onion and bell pepper and celery and garlic and spices and oil—was staggering.

dirty sparrow n Also *dirty bird, dirty urchin sparrow*
Prob =**English sparrow.**
1966–69 *DARE* (Qu. Q21) Inf **CO**22, Dirty urchin sparrow; (Qu. Q22) Infs **IA**3, **MN**7, Dirty sparrow; **IN**14, Dirty bird.

dirty spoon n **esp Nth, N Midl**
=**greasy spoon.**
1965–70 *DARE* (Qu. D39, . . *A small eating place where the food is not especially good*) 16 Infs, **scattered, but esp Nth, N Midl,** Dirty spoon.

dirty thirties n pl
The 1930s, when heavy dust storms were frequent in the western plains of the US.
1967 *DARE* (Qu. B18, . . *Special kinds of wind*) Inf **CO**17, Dirt storms, in the dirty thirties. **1986** *DARE* File **neSD,** My father-in-law to this day refers to the 1930's as the "dirty thirties." He was referring not only to the hard times of the depression years but especially to the fact that because that period was so windy dirt was constantly being blown through the air and everything was, therefore, covered with it.

dirty up See **dirty** v

dirty urchin sparrow See **dirty sparrow**

dirty work at the crossroads n **esp Gt Lakes**
Suspicious or concealed activity; see quot.
1965–70 *DARE* (Qu. V1, *When you suspect that . . something is going on behind your back, you say, "There's ______.")* 13 Infs, **esp Gt Lakes,** Dirty work at the crossroads.

dis See **this**

disabled adj Cf **disenabled**
Unable (to do something) because of illness or incapacity.
1968 *DARE* Tape **VA**2, My father was disabled to work in the mines and he was retired. **1974** (1975) Shaw *All God's Dangers* 69 **AL** [Black], Sweet . . told me to tell you that she is sick and disabled to come.

‡disabundance v
=**disfurnish 1.**
1942 (1971) Campbell *Cloud-Walking* 16 **seKY,** Now Sary, she never done this on purpose to disabundance you.

disappoint v, n, ppl adj Usu |ˌdɪsəˈpɔɪnt|; also |-paɪnt, -pəɪnt, -pɝnt| Pronc-spp *disappernt, disap(p)int* Cf Pronc Intro 3.I.11
A Pronc forms.
1843 (1916) Hall *New Purchase* 116 **IN,** You shan't be disapinted. **1908** *DN* 3.305 **eAL, wGA,** *Disappint* . . To disappoint. **1922** Gonzales *Black Border* 297 **sSC, GA coasts** [Gullah glossary], *Disapp'int*—(n. and v.) disappoint. **1940** *AmSp* 15.374 **NYC,** In the speech of certain less-educated New Yorkers. . . a variety of [ɔɪ] is found which. . . I shall indicate by the transcription [əɪ]. . . This group includes . . *disappoint.* **1942** Hall *Smoky Mt. Speech* 46 **eTN, wNC,** A high-school girl . . reports that her grandmother employs . . [ˌdɪsəˈpaɪnt] for *disappoint.* **1943** *New Yorker* 17 Apr 21/1, Why not have the general in the pickcha [=movie] give him a medal? In that way he could still be a private and his fans wouldn't be so disappernted.
B As verb.
To reject in love or marriage. *esp freq among Black speakers*
1857 *Putnam's Mag.* Sept 87 **CT,** Everybody knew why . . she was still "Miss" Eunice: she had been disapp'inted. **1967–70** *DARE* (Qu. AA11, *If a man asks a girl to marry him and she refuses, you'd say she ______*) Infs **FL**51, **MO**8, **TX**26, Disappointed him; (Qu. AA12, *If a man loses interest in a girl and stops seeing her, you'd say he ______*) Infs **CT**12, **FL**48, **LA**28, Disappointed her. [4 of 6 Infs Black]
C As ppl adj.
Disappointed.
1928 Peterkin *Scarlet Sister Mary* 245 **SC coast** [Gullah], If dat is what Seraphine craves, I hope e won' be disappoint.
D As noun.
Disappointment.
1922 Gonzales *Black Border* 297 **sSC, GA coasts** [Gullah glossary], *Disapp'int*—(n. and v.) disappoint, disappoints, disappointed, disappointing, disappointment, disappointments. **1930** Stoney–Shelby *Black Genesis* 181 **seSC** [Gullah], He been so sad till at last when he git home he most dead wid disapp'int.

‡disband v, n
1970 *Thompson Coll.* **cAL** (as of 1930s) [Black], *Disband.* . . To discard (a playing card). Also, a discarded playing card.

disbehave v [Engl dial; cf *EDD*]
1952 Brown *NC Folkl.* 1.533, *Disbehave.* . . To misbehave.—Central.

discaboobulation See **discombobulation**

discerning of day n Cf *DS* A2
1952 Brown *NC Folkl.* 1.533, *Discerning of day.* . . Daybreak; the first appearance of day.—West.

discharge v, n [*OED discharge* v. 1676 →, sb. 1727 →] **chiefly Nth** See Map
To suppurate; suppuration.
1965–70 *DARE* (Qu. BB36, *When there's an open sore and this yellowish stuff is coming out of it, you say it's ______*) 23 Infs, **chiefly Nth,** Discharging; (Qu. BB37, *When yellowish stuff comes out of a person's ear, he has a ______*) 13 Infs, **chiefly Nth,** Discharge; **IN**30, **MO**38, Ear discharge; **LA**31, Discharge in his ear; **NY**205, 107, Discharging (ear); **MI**96, Ear's discharging; (Qu. BB35, *The yellowish stuff that comes out of a boil when the head breaks*) Inf **GA**77, Poison discharge.

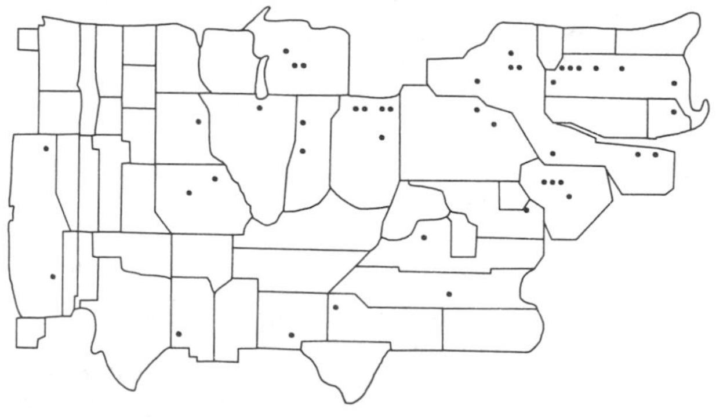

•discharge + varr (Qq. BB36, BB37, BB35)

discipline n, v Usu |ˈdɪsəplɪn, -ən|; also **chiefly S Midl** |ˌdɪˈsɪplɪn, -ən|

Std senses, var form.

1906 *DN* 3.133 **nwAR,** *Discipline*. . . This word has its principal stress on the second syllable. **1908** Lincoln *Cy Whittaker* 43 **Cape Cod MA,** We need dis*cip*line. **1942** Hall *Smoky Mt. Speech* 66 **eTN, wNC,** *Discipline* [dɪˈsɪplən] (once). **1958** *Sat. Eve. Post Letters* **swIN,** Expressions Used By My Grandfather . . dis-cip′-line. **c1960** *Wilson Coll.* **csKY,** *Discipline*, /dɪˈsɪplɪn/ quite common; I have heard it several times since the Job Corps came into being. **1967** *DARE* FW Addit **AL**20, *Discipline* pronc [dɪˈsɪplɪn].

discombobolation See **discombobulation**

discombobulate v Also *decomboblate, discombobble, discombooberate, discombooble, discomboobelate, discombulate, discumboberate* For addit varr, see quots [A pseudo-Lat concoction of *dis-* as in *disturbance* + *-com/-con/-cum* with + *bob* perh abbr for *bobbery* confusion + *-erate/-ulate* verbal suffixes] **chiefly Nth, N Midl** *joc* Cf **conbobberated**

To disarrange, put out of order; to confuse, perplex, disconcert; hence ppl adjs *discombobulated* and varr.

1834 *Sun* (NY NY) 21 Mar 2/3 **seNY,** I'll tell you what, if you'll just throw down them are clubs—and come out, one to time, may be some on you don't git *discombobracated.* **1840** Hoffman *Greyslaer* 2.27 **KY,** Let me tell you now that this discovery discomboberated me considerably. **1916** *DN* 4.322 **KS,** *Discumboberate*. . . To disconcert. "When I learned that I had to sing first, I was completely discumboberated." [*DN* Ed: In N. Eng. *discumbobulate* . . ; Medina Co., Ohio, in the nineties, *discombobelate.*] **1943** *AmSp* 18.141, *Discombooberated* is a variant of the *discombobolated, discomboberated,* etc., once current in slang usage. **1965–70** *DARE* (Qu. Y38, *Mixed together, confused*) Inf **PA**119, Discombobbled; (Qu. GG2, . . *Confused, mixed up*) Infs **CA**4, **DC**3, **GA**15, **IL**50, **ME**15, **NJ**48, **NY**25, **WI**47, Discombobulated; **WA**11, 28, Discombooberated; **IL**17, **MI**3, Discomboomerated; **WA**16, Disconbobberated; **AK**5, Discomboobelated; **CA**142, Discombooberated; (Qu. GG7, . . *Annoyed or upset*) Inf **CT**42, Discombobulated; **WA**16, Discomboobelated; **MA**58, Discombulated; (Qu. GG9, *To suddenly embarrass somebody and throw him off balance*) Inf **IL**96, Discomboberate; **NJ**58, Discombobulate; **WA**16, Discombobelate; (Qu. GG15, *Talking about a person who became over-excited and lost control*) Inf **CA**66, Got discomboobled; (Qu. KK19, . . *A machine or appliance . . temporarily out of order*) Inf **NY**42, Discombobulated; (Qu. KK20b, *Something that looks as if it might collapse any minute*) Inf **WA**16, Discombooberated; (Qu. KK22, . . *Completely shattered: "The jug fell out of the window and was ________."*) Inf **NY**109, Decomboblated. **1977** *Yankee* Jan 112 **csME,** Dora . . was discomboobleated and she took to dinging on about how little they had.

discombobulation n Also sp *discaboobulation, discombobolation* *joc* Cf **conbobberation**

Disarray, discomposure; a state of upset, perplexity.

1839 *Spirit of Times* 16 Mar 24/2 *(OEDS),* Finally, Richmond was obliged to trundle him, neck and heels, to the earth, to the utter discombobulation of his wig. **1911** *DN* 3.542 **NE,** *Discombobolation*. . . Discomfiture, state of being upset, or much shaken. "That will cause much discombobolation," "His discombobolation was complete." **1926** in 1963 Frost *Letters Untermeyer* 178 **NEng,** I put my own discombobulation first to lead up unnoticably [sic] to yours. **1986** *DARE* File **csWI** (as of c1920), *Discaboobulation* is my variant. I didn't hear the *-bob-* form as a kid; it sounds almost bookish to me now.

discombooberate, discombooble, discomboobelate, discombulate See **discombobulate**

discomfit v Usu |dɪsˈkʌmfɪt|; also |dɪskəmˈfɪt| Also sp *disconfit* **chiefly sAppalachians**

To inconvenience, bother.

1913 Kephart *Highlanders* 294 **sAppalachians,** To disfurnish or dis*confit* means to incommode: "I hope it has not disconfit you very bad." **1942** Hall *Smoky Mt. Speech* 55 **eTN, wNC,** *Discomfit* [ˌdɪskəmˈfɪt]. **1960s** *Hall Coll.* **wNC,** I wouldn't want to discomfit you. **1974** Fink *Mountain Speech* 6 **wNC, eTN,** *Discomfit*. . . to inconvenience. "Ef it don't discomfit ye none." **1976** Garber *Mountain-ese* 22 **sAppalachians,** *Discomfit* . . inconvenience—We hope our stayin' overnight won't discomfit you any.

‡discomgollifusticated ppl adj [Pseudo-Lat humorous formation]

1916 *DN* 4.274 **NE,** *Discomgollifusticated*. . . I heard the president of the University of Oregon use the word *discomgollifusticated.* It means, I think, discomforted [sic] or embarrassed.

disconfit See **discomfit**

discumboberate See **discombobulate**

discumfuddled ppl adj Cf **discombobulate**

1911 *DN* 3.542 **NE,** *Discumfuddledest*. . . Intensive of *fuddled;* very much bewildered, or shaken.

‡discumgalligumfricated ppl adj [Pseudo-Lat humorous formation]

1916 *DN* 4.274 **NE,** *Discumgalligumfricated*. . . "I saw a new word in the Congressional Library which you will no doubt be glad to add to your list. The word is *discumgalligumfricated,* and it means as near as I can make out from the context 'very greatly astonished but pleased.' "

disease and cure n

A children's game; see quot.

1941 *Jrl. Amer. Folkl.* 54.69 **eTN,** In "Disease and Cure" two lines, one of boys and the other of girls, were formed facing each other. . . A boy, a self-elected leader, went down the boys' line, whispering to each a disease and a cure. The cure was applicable not to his own but to his partner's ailment. Meanwhile, an assistant, a girl, went down the girls' line doing the same thing. Then all was in readiness to begin. Each girl asked her partner in the opposite line to name his disease and, upon being told, stated the cure previously indicated. Then the roles of "doctor" and "patient" were reversed. . . The fun, of course, consisted in the mention of humorous afflictions and treatments, in the complete lack of connection between the two, and in the ridiculous situations which would thus occur.

disenabled ppl adj

See quots.

1974 *AmSp* 49.62 **swME** (as of c1900), *Disenabled*. . . Disabled. **1975** Gould *ME Lingo* 74, *Disenabled*—Variation for disabled, for emphasis.

disencourage v, hence ppl adjs *disencouraged, disencouraging* Eye-dial sp *disincurridge* [*OED* 1626 →] **chiefly S Midl**

To discourage.

1903 *DN* 2.311 **seMO,** *Disencouraged*. . . Discouraged. **1906** Johnson *Highways Missip. Valley* 255 **MS** [Black], Tell him he gettin' along as well as could be expect. Hit never do to disencourage a sick person. Dey die den anyway. **1917** *DN* 4.410 **wNC,** *Disencourage*. . . To discourage. **1923** (1946) Greer-Petrie *Angeline Steppin'* 31 **csKY,** I never like to dis-incurridge him. **1927** Kennedy *Gritny* 240 **sLA** [Black], It sho was disencouragin'. **1938** FWP *Ocean Highway* 189 **NC,** "Disremember"[1] and "disencourage" are frequently used. **1953** Randolph *Down in Holler* 239 **Ozarks,** *Disencourage*. . . To discourage.

disfurnish v [*OED* 1531 →]

1 To deprive, inconvenience. **S Midl, Sth**

1886 Amer. Philol. Assoc. *Trans.* 17.45, Common Southern expressions [include] *disfurnish* (deprive). **1917** *DN* 4.411 **wNC,** *Disfurnish*. . . To deprive (oneself). "Don't disfurnish yourself." **1919** *DN* 5.33 **VA, seKY,** *Disfurnish*. . . To inconvenience, or discommode. **1927** *DN* 5.469 **sAppalachians. 1933** Rawlings *South Moon* 152 **FL,** Ma wouldn't of wanted I should dis-furnish you-all. **1934** (1970) Wilson *Backwoods Amer.* 70 **Ozarks,** The commoner of the backwoods. . . may . . [say] *disfurnish* for inconvenience. **1946** *PADS* 6.12 **swVA, eNC. 1950** *PADS* 14.26 **SC,** *Disfurnish* [dɪsˈfʌːnɪš]. . . To deprive. "I'd like to get some of your seed corn, but I don't want you to disfurnish yourself." **1960** Williams *Walk Egypt* 28 **GA,** How come you up here anyways?—not that you is disfurnishing me. **1972** *Atlanta Letters* **cGA,** You offer your friend . . your only tube of hand cream and she replies: "Oh don't disfurnish yourself!" *Ibid* **cnGA,** Are you sure you can spare it? I don't want to disfurnish you.

2 See quot.

c1960 *Wilson Coll.* **csKY,** *Disfurnish*. . . To tear up, to disarrange. Rare.

disguised ppl adj [*OED* 1607–1884; *"arch. slang"*] Cf *DS* DD15

Intoxicated.

1888 Johnston *Mr. Absalom Billingslea* 185 **GA,** Mr. Kittrell became a little "disguised" at the infare [=a party after a wedding] from apple-jack.

disgust v [*OED "Obs."*] **S Midl** *relic*

To detest, be disgusted by.

1913 Kephart *Highlanders* 282 **sAppalachians,** I disgust bad liquor. **1940** *AmSp* 15.52 **sAppalachians, Ozarks,** I *disgust* hawg-mollies an' mounting [=mountain] oysters.

dish n Usu |dɪš|; also **chiefly Sth, S Midl** |diš| Cf Pronc Intro 3.I.5.a Pronc-sp *deesh*

A Form.

1893 Shands *MS Speech* 26, *Deesh* [diš]. Illiterate white and negro pronunciation of *dish.* **1894** Riley *Armazindy* 136 **IN** [Black], Ponchus calls a dish a *"deesh"—*/Yes, an' *he* calls fishes *"feesh"!* **1902** *DN* 2.232 **sIL,** *Dish.* Pronounced [diš], as if spelled deesh. **1923** (1946) Greer-Petrie *Angeline Steppin'* 30 **csKY,** Wash up all them thar deeshes. **1930** Woofter *Black Yeomanry* 50 **seSC** [Gullah], *Deesh* for dish. **1933** *AmSp* 8.1.32 **wTX,** The West Texan . . has also a tendency to front and raise vowels . . *deeshes,* dishes. **1941** *AmSp* 16.112 **VA,** [i] in *dish.* **c1960** *Wilson Coll.* **csKY,** *Dish* among old people is often /diš/.

B Sense.

The seat of a saddle; hence adj *dished* having a seat of a specified type.

1961 Adams *Old-Time Cowhand* 109, The [saddle] seat's often called the "dish," and accordin' to its depth is spoken of as bein' "shallow-dished" or "deep-dished."

dish pron See **this**

dish-calm adj, n

See quots.

1976 Ryland *Richmond Co. VA* 370, Dish-calm—perfectly calm. **1979** *Rappahannock Rec.* (Kilmarnock VA) 22 Nov 3/2 **ceVA,** Still heard is the expression "dish-ca'm" for "calm weather" with the old short a and omission of the letter l as in the days of Shakespeare.

dish closet See **closet 1**

dishcloth n

1 A **trillium** (here: *Trillium erectum*).

[**1892** *Jrl. Amer. Folkl.* 5.104, *Trillium erectum,* dish-cloth or stinking dish-cloth. Franklin Center, P[rovince] Q[uebec].] **1900** Lyons *Plant Names* 378, *T. erectum. . .* Dishcloth. **1930** Sievers *Amer. Med. Plants* 48, *Purple Trillium. . . Other common names. . .* Dishcloth. **1971** Krochmal *Appalachia Med. Plants* 256, Dishcloth. . . has . . a single brown or greenish purple ill-scented flower.

2 See **dishrag 2.**

dishcloth gourd See **dishrag gourd**

dishclout n [**clout** n[1] **1;** *OED* 1530 →]

A dishcloth.

1899 (1912) Green *VA Folk-Speech* 149, *Dish-clout. . .* A dish-cloth. **1968** *DARE* FW Addit **NY88,** Dishclout—cloth for washing dishes. Old-fashioned.

dished adj See **dish** n **B1**

dished face See **dish-face**

dished nose See **dish nose**

dish-face n Also *dished face* **chiefly Sth, S Midl**

A face which appears slightly concave.

1878 IL Dept. Ag. *Trans.* 14.210, The head was short and fine, with a dished face, and rather thin jowls. **1898** Lloyd *Country Life* 148 **AL,** If the horse has got a dish face . . , there aint no room in my lot. **1903** KS State Bd. Ag. *Biennial Rept. for 1901–1902* 13.52, The first question asked as a description of a hog was, "Has he a short nose and a dished face?" **1954** *Harder Coll.* **cwTN,** *Dish-face.* Of a person whose face seems to be in the shape of a dish. **1965–70** *DARE* (Qu. X29, . . *A person's face*) Infs **OK**11, 13, **TX**98, Dish-face.

dish-faced adj [*OED* 1737; cf *DSL*] **chiefly Sth, S Midl**

Having a slightly concave face.

1883 *Harper's New Mth. Mag.* 67.725/2 **KY,** [The horses] are of many sorts and sizes, "dish-faced" and Roman-nosed. **1902** Eggleston *Dorothy South* 273 **VA,** Mammy would drive them all out of the house . . and call them 'dishfaced devils.' **1906** *DN* 3.133 **nwAR,** *Dish-faced. . .* Having a concave face. **1912** *DN* 3.574 **wIN,** *Dish-faced. . .* Flat-faced or hollow-faced. Applied especially to a face that lacks individuality. "Who is that dish-faced son of a hickory standing over there on the bank?" **1965–70** *DARE* (Qu. X6, *If a person's lower jaw sticks out prominently, you say he's ______*) Infs **AR**23, **FL**15, 36, **NC**55, Dish-faced; **OK**18, Dish-faced—if the chin sticks out and the mouth comes in; (Qu. X29, . . *A person's face*) Infs **AR**23, **KY**85, Dish-faced.

dish-face nose See **dish nose**

dish gravy n

Meat drippings served as gravy.

1968–69 *DARE* (Qu. H37, . . *Gravy*) Inf **IL**49, Dish gravy—comes right off the roast, as opposed to the gravy you make in the kitchen; **NY**48, Dish gravy—drippings from the pan.

dish kettle n [sEngl dial; see *EDD*] **chiefly NEng, NY** *old-fash*

A large, heavy pot for cooking and other uses.

1747 in 1915 NH *Prov. & State Papers* 33.468, I also give him . . one Dish Cettel. **1775** in 1876 Essex Inst. *Coll.* 13.186 **Boston MA,** 1 Brass Kettle, 1 large & 1 small iron Pot, 1 Dish Kettle, 1 Stewpan. **1842** Kirkland *Forest Life* 2.171 **MI** [writer from **CT, NY**], But the dish-kettle is not yet at rest for the night. It has still, after another "sca-ouring" process, to cook the supper, wash the dishes, carry the pigs' mess up the hill, and come home to be cleaned again in order that the beans may be put to soak for to-morrow's porridge. **1844** (1940) Arnold *Diaries* 167 **sVT, sNH,** Went to Walpole with Mary Ann to select cook stove—one was 30 dols. with furniture. . . 1 spider—cast iron pot and dish kettle with ten covers. **1904** *DN* 2.396 **NY** [Lumbermen's language], *Dish-kettle. . .* A shallow iron kettle for cooking small vegetables. **1968** *DARE* (Qu. F4, . . *Deep metal container used to boil foods*) Inf **NY**72, Dish kettle ['dɪš kɪtəl]—that had a bail on it. They took a lid off the stove and set this in the hole. [Inf old]

dish nose n Also *dished nose, dish-face ~, dish-pan ~*

A flat or concave nose.

1950 *WELS (Noses according to their appearance)* 1 Inf, **cwWI,** Dish nose. **1966–68** *DARE* (Qu. X15, . . *Kinds of noses, according to shape or size*) Inf **MI**20, Dish-face nose; **MO**38, Dish-pan nose; **PA**126, Dished nose.

dishrag n

1 A cloth or towel for drying dishes. [Transf from *dishrag* cloth used to wash dishes] **chiefly Sth, Midl**

1965–70 *DARE* (Qu. G16, *What do you dry the dishes with?*) 31 Infs, **chiefly Sth, Midl,** Dishrag; (Qu. G17, *Other kinds of towels*) Infs **GA**62, **IL**99, **SC**46, Dishrag.

2 also *dishcloth;* Fig: a lackey; someone or something of little value—usu in phrr contrasting it to *tablecloth;* see quots.

1906 *DN* 3.160 **nwAR,** *Table-cloth and dish-rag. . .* First and second fiddle. In the expression, "If I can't be table-cloth, I'm not going to be dishrag," i.e., "I'm not going to play second fiddle." **1945** *Sat. Review* 27 Jan 15/1 **KY,** If I can't be tablecloth, I shore don't aim to be dishrag. **c1960** *Wilson Coll.* **csKY,** If I can't be tablecloth, I won't be dishrag—said by a girl who was second choice by some boy who tried to date her. **1965–70** *DARE* (Qu. II19, *When you think somebody has been put ahead of you or has been given something you deserved, you might say, "I'd rather quit than ______.*") Infs **MI**111, **NJ**18, Be a dishrag to his tablecloth; **IN**42, If I can't be tablecloth I won't be dishrag; **KY**50, If I can't be the tablecloth, I'm not going to be dishrag; (Qu. II34, *If you think somebody is trying to use you to his advantage: "I'm not going to be his ______.*") Infs **AZ**2, **MO**15, **VA**41, Dishrag; **VA**41, Dishcloth.

3 See **dishrag gourd.**

4 An unidentified plant.

1969 *DARE* (Qu. S26e) Inf **KY**28, Dishrag—big leaf, oval 1 foot across, grow high, no flower, leaf rumpled on the edge.

dishrag gourd n Also *dishrag, ~ plant, ~ squash, ~ vine, dishcloth gourd* [See quots] **chiefly S Midl**

=vegetable sponge.

1890 *Century Dict., Sponge-gourd. . .* The netted fiber from the interior of the fruit is used for washing and other purposes, hence called *vegetable sponge* or *dish-rag.* **1895** Gray-Bailey *Field Botany* 192, *L[uffa] cylindrica. . .* The interior portion becoming detached when dry and useful as a sponge; whence the names *Vegetable Sponge* and *Dishcloth Gourd.* **1904** *NY Tribune* (NY) 22 sec 2 May 10/2, A novel enterprise, that of raising dishrags, is being exploited by a number of Southern California horticulturists. **1908** *DN* 3.305 **eAL, wGA,** *Dish-rag. . .* The sponge gourd, the towel-gourd. **1912** Cobb *Back Home* 289 **KY,** The Major was . . a clubman by instinct, yet with no club except . . the screening of dishrag vines and balsam apples on Priest's front porch. **1960** Williams

Walk Egypt 259 **nGA,** Walk along the fence where dishrag gourds hung with heavy fruit. **1969** *DARE* (Qu. I23) Inf **KY**40, Dishrag squash. **1971** *DARE* File **csKY,** Dishrag gourd—Mrs. Burge [65 years old] still grows them, but they are unknown to younger urban Kentuckians. **1975** McDonough *Garden Sass* 214 **AR,** There was always the dishrag gourd. Aunt Alma explains how it got its name: "You can take 'em and peel off that outside, and they make good dishrags—almost like a sponge." **1978** *DARE* File **AL** (as of c1900), The dish rag plant . . resembled a cucumber vine. It produced only three or four fruits a year . . about five inches around and six to eight inches long. . . They were cut open lengthwise, the seed and pulp removed, then the skin scraped off, leaving a mat of white fiber . . [which was] used with white sand as a pot scrubber.

dish safe n [*dish* + **safe** n]

1967 *DARE* (Qu. E5, *A piece of furniture with a flat top for keeping tablecloths, dishes, and such*) Inf **LA**2, Dish safe.

dish shell n Cf **dipper clam**

A **surf clam** (here: *Spisula catilliformis*).

1911 Keep *West Coast Shells* 106, *Spisula catilliformis*, . . the Dish-shell. . . These great Dish-shells sometimes reach a length of over five inches, and can hardly be mistaken for any other species.

dish squash n

Perh a **pattypan squash.**

1968–70 *DARE* (Qu. I23) Inf **IN**3, Hollow dish squash; **IL**117, White dish squash—shaped like a dish.

dish supper n [Abbr for *covered dish supper*]

=**covered-dish meal.**

1966–68 *DARE* (Qu. H70) Infs **FL**15, **MD**19, Dish supper.

dish table n

1967 *DARE* (Qu. E5, *A piece of furniture with a flat top for keeping tablecloths, dishes, and such*) Inf **TX**37, Dish table.

dishwasher n

1 =**flicker** n² **1.** *obs*

1799 Barton *Fragments Nat. Hist. PA* 15, Picus auratus. . . This bird is known, in Maryland, by the name of Dish-Washer.

2 A **kingbird** (here: *Tyrannus tyrannus*).

1887 *Amer. Field* 27.9.200, When living in Texas I noticed a bird they call the . . "bird of paradise;" they are great bee catchers and the dish-washer, bee martin or king bird, are also very destructive on bees. **1917** *Wilson Bulletin* 29.2.83 **TX,** *Tyrannus tyrannus*. . . Dishwasher.

3 =**whirligig beetle.** [Perh from the whirling motion]

1940 Teale *Insects* 150, Elsewhere they [=whirligigs] have local names such as . . "dishwashers."

‡dishwashy adj Cf **dishwater**

Of coffee: weak, dilute.

1969 *DARE* (Qu. H74, . . *Coffee . . very weak*) Inf **IL**40, Dishwashy.

dishwater n Also called **branch water 2, ditchwater**

Fig: a very weak beverage, esp coffee.

c1960 *Wilson Coll.* **csKY,** *Dishwater*. . . Literally the water in which dishes are washed. By transfer it means something not very tasty, maybe weak, like coffee. **1965–70** *DARE* (Qu. H74b, . . *Coffee . . very weak*) 306 Infs, **widespread,** Dishwater; [18 Infs, **scattered,** (Weak as *or* like) dishwater]; **NC**88, Colored dishwater; **AR**35, Dishwater coffee; [(Qu. H72b, . . *Very weak tea;* total Infs questioned, 75) Inf **MS**23, Weak as dishwater]; (Qu. DD25, . . *Nicknames . . for beer*) Inf **DC**8, Dishwater.

dishwater diarrhea n **MA** *joc, old-fash*

An imaginary disease afflicting reluctant dishwashers.

1969 *DARE* (Qu. BB28, *Joking names . . for imaginary diseases*) Inf **MA**57, Dishwater diarrhea; **MA**38, Dishwater diarrhea—the disease you got when you didn't want to do the dishes; (Qu. BB19, *Joking names for looseness of the bowels*) Inf **MA**48, Dishwater diarrhea. [All Infs old] **1979** *DARE* File **cnMA** (as of 1920s), My mother, born 1889, used to say of a girl who got all the way up to the sink to wash dishes and then decided that she had to go to the bathroom, "I guess she's got dishwater diarrhea." **1986** *DARE* File **nwMA** (as of 1960s), Every night when it came time for me to wash the dishes I would suddenly decide that I needed to go to the bathroom. My mother would say, "Dishwater diarrhea again? You'll still have to do the dishes when you come down."

dish-wheeled adj [Transf from *dish-wheeled*, of a vehicle, having slightly concave wheels]

1968 Adams *Western Words* 94, *Dish-wheeled*—Knock-kneed; said of a man or an animal.

dish wiper n **chiefly NEng** See Map *somewhat old-fash*

A towel used to dry dishes.

1939 *LANE* Map 140 **throughout NEng,** The cloth with which dishes are wiped dry after washing. . . *Dish wiper*. **1950** *WELS (What do you dry the dishes with?)* 5 Infs, **WI,** Dish wiper. **1965–70** *DARE* (Qu. G16) 15 Infs, **chiefly NEng,** Dish wiper. [12 of 15 Infs old, 3 mid-aged] **1979** *DARE* File **cnMA** (as of c1915), We used both *dish wiper* and *dish towel*. I think *dish towel* was perhaps a little more "dressed up." You might say, "Get me a fresh dish wiper! This one is soaking wet."

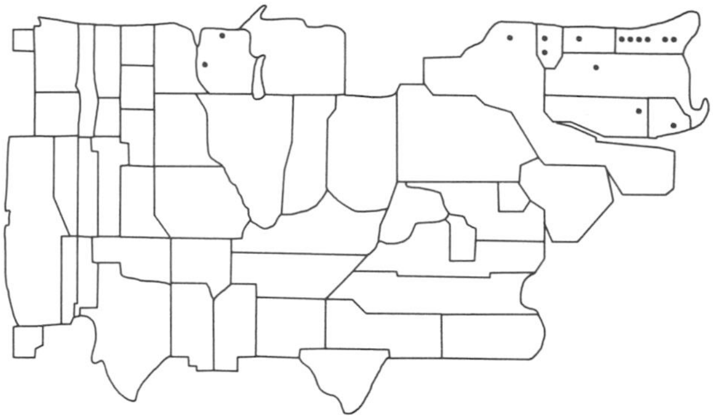

•dish wiper (Qu. G16)

dishybill(y) n [Pronc-sp for *dishabille;* cf *EDD dishabil, dishbill(e), deshabbily* (at *dishabille*)]

A state of disorder, dishevelment; hence adj *dishybilly* disheveled.

1920 *DN* 5.78 *Dishybilly*, déshabillé. "And there I was, all dishybilly, when the callers came." *Ibid, En dishybill*, or *dishybilly*, en déshabillé [sic]. "There we sat, en dishybilly."

disincurridge See **disencourage**

disinfect n Cf **fertilize**

Disinfectant.

1941 in 1944 *ADD* **eWV,** *Disinfect*. . . Disinfectant. **1971** *Foxfire* Winter 251 **nGA,** She said that she always washed her hands well with "disinfect."

dismals n pl

1 A melancholy mood, the blues—often in phr *weary dismals*. [*OED* 1762 →] **esp TN** *old-fash*

1777 in 1875 J. & A. Adams *Familiar Letters* 265 **eMA,** The spleen, the vapors, the dismals, the horrors seem to have seized our whole State. **1899** (1912) Green *VA Folk-Speech* 149, *Dismals*. . . Gloom; melancholy; dumps. **1939** FWP *Guide TN* 134, "I've got them weary dismals today," moans the hillman. **1952** Brown *NC Folkl.* 1.533, *Dismals*. . . The melancholies, low spirits. **1969** *DARE* (Qu. BB5, *A general feeling of discomfort or illness that isn't any one place in particular*) Infs **TN**31, 36, Weary dismals; (Qu. GG34a, *To feel depressed or in a gloomy mood*) Infs **TN**31, 34, 36, Weary dismals. [All Infs old] **1982** Heat Moon *Blue Highways* 35 **cTN,** It was cold and drizzling again. "Weather to give a man the weary dismals," Watts grumbled.

2 See quot.

1963 *DE Folkl. Bulletin* 1.40/2, Dressed in his dismals (work clothes).

disperlite adj [Pronc-sp for *dispolite*]

Impolite, rude.

1883 (1971) Harris *Nights with Remus* 263 **GA** [Black], Tooby sho', hit monst'us disperlite fer we-all fer to be gwine on dat a-way. [=To be sure, it is monstrously impolite for us to be behaving that way.]

disrecognize v

1 To recognize. [*dis-* prefix, perh for emphasis, + *recognize*]

1937 in 1958 Brewer *Dog Ghosts* 71 **TX** [Black], Seth gittin' olduh all de time, an' she don' wanna disrecognize de fac' dat his time ain't long on dis putty green carpeted soil.

2 To discount, ignore. [*dis-* prefix, do the opposite of, + *recognize*]

1974 (1975) Shaw *All God's Dangers* 55 **AL** [Black], He just disrecognized me, discounted me; wouldn't turn nothin over in my hands.

disrecollect v

=**disremember.**

1940 (1941) Bell *Swamp Water* 148 **Okefenokee GA,** I disrecollect how long that went on, but I know it were quite a spell. **1953** Randolph *Down in Holler* 239 **Ozarks,** *Disrecollect. . .* To forget, to fail to remember. **1954** *Harder Coll.* **cwTN,** Disrecollect, forget. Heard only once.

disregardless adj, adv [Redund; cf *irregardless*] **chiefly sAppalachians**

Regardless.

1917 in 1944 *ADD* **sWV,** *Disregardless.* Regardless. **1927** *Ibid, Disregardless. . .* Freq. **1974** Fink *Mountain Speech* 6 **wNC, eTN,** *Disregardless . .* regardless. **1976** Garber *Mountain-ese* 23 **sAppalachians,** I'm goin' to town disregardless uv whether it rains or snows.

disremember v [Prob orig Scots; *DOST* 1584 →] **scattered, but chiefly Sth, S Midl** See Map

Rarely with *of:* To be unable to remember; to forget; not to know.

1815 in 1910 Commons *Doc. Hist. Amer. Industrial Soc.* 4.25 **wPA,** I belonged to the society about fifteen months; as to the constitution I disremember, the rules I recollect. **1827** (1939) Sherwood *Gaz. GA* 69, *Disremember,* for forget, want of recollection. **1829** in 1956 Eliason *Tarheel Talk* 269 **NC,** I disremember the time. **1852** (1854) Kennedy *Horse-Shoe Robinson* xii **SC,** That mought be true, too; but my memory is treacherous—I disremember. **1885** Twain *Huck. Finn* 106 **eMO,** She started over . . in the house-ferry, to stay all night at her friend's house, Miss What-you-may-call-her, I disremember her name. **1887** (1967) Harris *Free Joe* 34 **GA,** I disremember of anybody name Davies. **1890** *DN* 1.58 **Sth,** *Disremember* is common in the South, though it is considered vulgar. **1893** Shands *MS Speech* 26, Disremember. . . It certainly is very largely used in Mississippi, and probably throughout the South, by the lower classes of both colors. **1895** *DN* 1.371 **eTN. 1899** (1912) Green *VA Folk-Speech* 149. **1902** *DN* 2.232 **sIL. 1903** *DN* 2.311 **seMO. 1905** *DN* 3.77 **nwAR. 1908** *DN* 3.305 **eAL, wGA. 1912** *DN* 3.574 **wIN. 1913** *DN* 4.47 **MS. 1915** *DN* 4.225 **wTX. 1929** Sale *Tree Named John* 103 **MS,** Ah disremembers jes zac'ly how hit come 'bout. **1933** Rawlings *South Moon* 28 **FL,** I dis-remember. I reckon some knows it and some don't. **1933** Williamson *Woods Colt* 116 **Ozarks,** "Well!" exclaims Windy, "whar the hell have you been to! I hain't seen hide nor ha'r of you since I disremember when." **c1937** in 1972 *Amer. Slave* 2.65 **SC,** Does I 'member much 'bout slavery times? Well, dere is no way for me to disremember, unless I die. **1950** *PADS* 14.26 **SC. c1960** *Wilson Coll.* **csKY,** *Disremember. . .* Negative of remember; most commonly it means "I just don't know." **1965–70** *DARE* (Qu. JJ30a, . . *Expressions for forgetting something: "I ______.")* 68 Infs, **scattered, but chiefly Sth, S Midl,** Disremember. **1966** *DARE* FW Addit **wNC,** I disremember where I put it. **1966** *PADS* 46.25 **cnAR. 1966–69** *DARE* Tape **AL**14A, I disremember how they did it, but I know they put this paint on this meat; **GA**23, You have to force it through so many layers, I disremember, fifty somethin' I believe it is; **KY**16A, One of 'em said, "What's your name?" or "Who are you"—I disremember which way he said it.

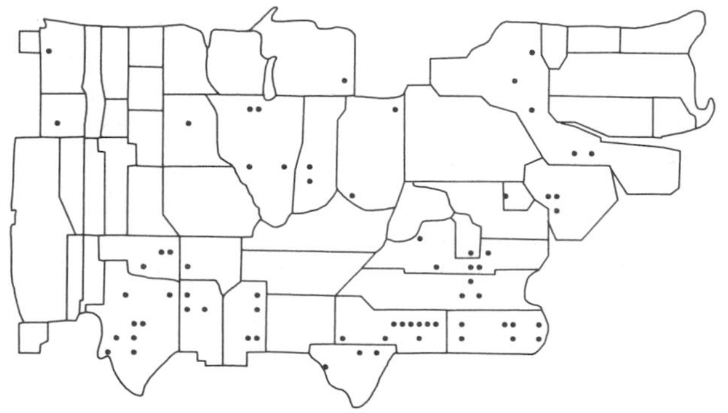

•disremember (Qu. JJ30a)

dist See **just**

distance n [*OED distance* sb. 11 c1384 →; "Now only in phr. *distance of time,* implying remoteness"]

An extent of time.

1939 *AmSp* 14.92 **eTN,** I've knowed him fur some distance.

distant n [Prob back-formation from *distance,* analyzed as pl *distants*]

A distance.

c1938 in 1970 Hyatt *Hoodoo* 1.81 **ceVA** [Black], After you git sich a distant . . from there . . don't choo look back. . . After you git sich a distant down the road . . you stop an' pick up nine pinches of dirt.

‡distant adj

Distantly related.

1969 *DARE* Tape **IL**39, My grandmother, she's distant to Stephen Foster.

‡distinct v [Prob by functional shift from *distinct* adj]

To distinguish.

1982 Ginns *Snowbird Gravy* 138 **nwNC,** When they're all running together on the scent of that fox, man, it's just one roar that's all. You can tell yours. You can distinct the mouth of each dog. They's just a little difference there.

distracted ppl adj

1 also pronc-sp *stracted:* See quots. *joc*

1908 *DN* 3.305 **eAL, wGA,** *Distracted meetin(g). . .* Protracted religious services. Facetious and usually abbreviated to 'stracted meetin'.' **1922** Gonzales *Black Border* 55 **sSC, GA coasts** [Gullah], At the tail of a "distracted meetin'" that had been running for several days . . they were in a state of exaltation. **1946** Driscoll *Country Jake* 176 **KS,** Farmers from far and near came to the Big Meetings, sometimes called Protracted Meetings, and, by the unsaved, Distracted Meetings, to see Mrs. Leonard glorify God with her circus stunt and hear her yell.

2 Of a gun: see quot.

1926 *AmSp* 1.413 **Okefenokee GA,** 'His gun must 'a' been "distracted,"[*] I remarked. 'I think Giles 'uz the one distracted. Must 'a' had buck ague.' [Footnote to first use of *distracted:*] A local expression applied to a gun that will not shoot straight.

distribute v Usu |dɪ'strɪbjət, -bjut|; also |'dɪstrə,bjut| and |,dɪs-trɪ'bjut|

Std senses, var forms.

1965 *DARE* FW Addit **MA**14, Distributed ['dɪstrə,bjutəd]. **1965** *DARE* File **csGA,** Distributed [,dɪstrɪ'bjutɪd]. *Ibid* **csWI,** Heard on WERN (Wisconsin Educational Radio Network) 27 March 1978, Distribute ['dɪstrə,bjut].

district n Pronc-spp *deastrict, deestric(k), deestrict* Cf Pronc Intro 3.I.5.a

Std senses, var forms.

1859 (1931) Tuttle *CA Diary* 15.70 **WI,** The country through which we passed is rather thinly settled being principally a mining deastrict. **1861** Holmes *Venner* 1.37 **MA,** He found himself the head of a large district, or, as it was called by the inhabitants, "deestric" school. **1871** Eggleston *Hoosier Schoolmaster* 35 **sIN,** He's the peartest *ole* man in this deestrick. **1871** (1882) Stowe *Fireside Stories* 10 **MA,** He'd been up to the deestrict o' Maine a-lumberin'. **1890** *DN* 1.17 **neOH,** The generation has passed away here that pronounced *hiah* for *Ohio,* and *deestrict* for *district.* **1907** *DN* 3.186 **seNH,** *Deestric . .* District. "School has always kept three terms a year in this deestric." This pronunciation of an older generation was very painful to youth trained by a correct school-ma'am. **1908** *DN* 3.304 **eAL, wGA,** *Deestric(t). . .* District. **1922** (1926) Kephart *Highlanders* 468 **ceKY,** She got, I reckon, about the toughest [school] deestric' in the ceounty. **1923** *DN* 5.205 **swMO,** *Deestrict.* **1939** *Sat. Review* 12 Aug 3 **sMI,** I . . taught a deestrick school. **1941** Stuart *Men of Mts.* 186 **neKY,** I come from the coal-mining deestrict. **1951** *PADS* 15.66 **wNH,** *Deestrict.* **1975** Gould *ME Lingo* 71, Deestrick—The way Mainers like to say district, but with special reference to the old-time local school districts.

district attorney n Cf **county attorney**

=**son-of-a-bitch stew.**

1944 Adams *Western Words* 50, *District attorney*—Another name for the *son-of-a-bitch stew.* When the law began its westward march and started to question and clamp down on the cowboy government of the happy, carefree days, the blame for this cramping of liberties was placed upon lawyers. This caused the riders of the range to feel somewhat resentful toward the law, and soon they began calling this dish *district attorney.*

‡distriminate v [Prob var of *discriminate*]

?To label unfavorably, make notorious.

1935 Hurston *Mules & Men* 162 **FL** [Black], You fool wid Aunt Hagar's chillun and they'll sho distriminate you and put yo' name in de streets.

disturbment n Pronc-sp *disturbmint* Cf Intro "Language Changes" III.1, **-ment**

A disturbance.

1916 in 1944 *ADD* **sAppalachians,** *Disturbment.* Also *-mint.* **c1938** in 1970 Hyatt *Hoodoo* 2.1157 **seLA,** Yo' kin throw that at a person. Dat's a *disturbment powder,* it makes yo' break up, an' tear down.

ditch n

1 =branch water 3. [Prob abbr for *ditch water*]

1966 *DARE* File **MT,** Drinkers say, "Give me bourbon and ditch" and "I'll take a shot and ditch." Heard all over Montana.

2 in phr *under ditch:* See **under ditch.**

ditch v

1 tr, intr: To leave or stay out of (school) without permission; to be truant. **esp c,sCA** See Map

c1939 in 1984 Lambert–Franks *Voices* 72 **OK,** Us kids would ditch school and go bum a ride off some truck driver and fool around out in the field all day long. **1942** Berrey–Van den Bark *Amer. Slang* 839.2, *Absent Oneself; "Cut" Class. . .* Ditch. *Ibid* 839.3, *Play Truant.* Ditch —, skip . . school. **c1950** *Atlas Checklists* **WV,** *Ditch school.* [Used by] Black male, 31 years old. Mostly Bluefield State College. **1960** *PADS* 34.44 **nCO,** Ditch school 'play hookey.' **1965–70** *DARE* (Qu. JJ6, *To stay away from school without an excuse*) Infs **CA**1, 14, 80, 96, 135, 177, 183, **OH**84, Ditch; **CA**59, 66, **CO**39, **IL**44, 59, Ditch school. [6 of 13 Infs young] **1967** *DARE* FW Addit **IL,** High School student says to *ditch* school is to stay away without an excuse. **1971** Bright *Word Geog. CA & NV* 200 **c, sCA,** He . . *skipped class . . ditched.* **1978** *DARE* File **sCA** (as of 1940–59), In Long Beach, California, we always spoke of *ditching school. Playing hookey* was our parents' and teachers' term. "I ditched school today. Did you ditch too?" someone might say. **1982** *Grit* (Williamsport PA) 4 July 17, He'll think back to the days when he wouldn't have minded "ditching school" and going fishing instead. **1984** *DARE* File **AZ,** The boys decided to ______ school one day: ditch. **1986** *Capital Times* (Madison WI) 27 Mar 14/5 **CO,** He is their high school's biggest jerk. He treats others shabbily, ditches and fails most of his classes, . . and bullies anyone who will tolerate it.

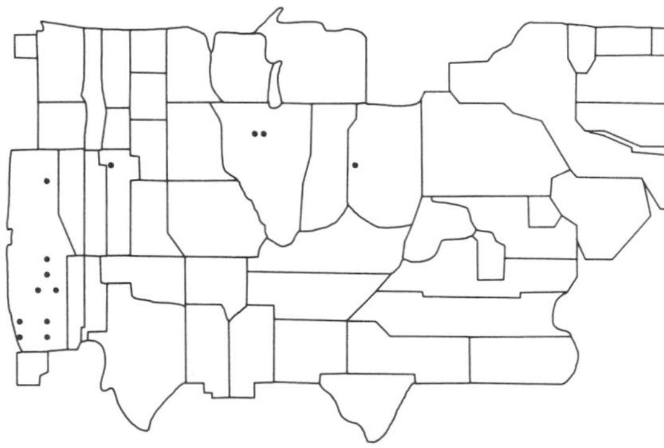

•ditch v 1 + var (Qu. JJ6)

2 See quot.

1967 *DARE* (Qu. Y18, *To leave in a hurry: " . . We'd better______.'*) Inf **CO**27, Ditch.

ditch blade n Also *ditch bank blade* **[blade 3]**

1967–68 *DARE* (Qu. L35, *Hand tools . . for cutting underbrush and digging out roots*) Infs **LA**7, 39, Ditch blade; **LA**15, **MS**21, Ditch bank blade. **1984** *DARE* File **csMS,** If you ask for a ditch bank blade, you get the same instrument [as a Kaiser blade or a brier blade]. You know what it is—simply a blade on the end of a handle you cut briers and stuff with.

ditch bluet n [From its similarity to **bluet 2**]

A swamp plant *(Hydrolea ovata).*

1951 *PADS* 15.38 **TX,** *Nama ovatum. . .* Ditch, pond, or prickly, bluet.

ditch boss See **ditch rider.**

ditchbug n

=crawfish B1.

1968 *DARE* (Qu. P19, . . *Freshwater crayfish*) Inf **LA**20, Ditchbugs.

ditchburr n Also sp *ditchbur*

=cockleburr 1.

1900 Lyons *Plant Names* 398, *X[anthium] strumarium . .* Ditch-bur.

ditch-edge child n Cf *DS* Z11

A child born out of wedlock.

1950 *PADS* 14.26 **SC,** *Ditch-edge chillun. . .* Illegitimate children. Cf. *long-a-de-paat* [=path] *chillun.* **1958** Humphrey *Home from the Hill* 66 **TX,** His qualities would have been recognized had he been the ditch-edge child of some share-cropping sandhill tacky.

ditch eel n

1 =congo snake 1. [See quot 1958]

1909 Biol. Soc. DC *Proc.* 22.132 **NC,** *Amphiuma means. Ditch Eel. . .* Of the two forms of the ditch eel I have had numbers of specimens and have never seen any intergrades. **1958** Conant *Reptiles & Amphibians* 205, *Amphiuma means. . .* This is the . . "ditch eel" of fishermen and country folk. . . Habitats include ditches, sloughs, pools, ponds, rice fields, swamps, streams, etc.

2 A **siren** (here: *Siren intermedia* or *S. lacertina*).

1928 Baylor Univ. Museum *Contrib.* 16.9, Great Siren. . . *Ditch Eel.* On account of its being frequently found in drainage ditches, this name has been applied to the Siren in many parts of the South. **1958** Conant *Reptiles & Amphibians* 205, "Congo (conger) eel," "lamper eel," or "ditch eel". . . are often applied to both species of *Siren.*

ditch 'em n

A team game similar to **run sheep run.**

1966–68 *DARE* (Qu. EE12, *Games in which one captain hides his team and the other team tries to find it*) Inf **FL**10, Ditch 'em—played at night; **MI**89, Ditch 'em—capture as many as possible.

ditch fish n

The swampfish *(Chologaster cornuta).*

1909 Biol. Soc. DC *Proc.* 22.130 **NC,** Among the fishes, . . ditch fishes *(Chologaster cornutus)* were abundant both in the lake and in the pools of water.

ditch frog n

Perh a chorus frog (*Pseudacris* spp).

1966 *Carteret Co. News-Times* (Morehead City & Beaufort NC) 16 Aug 8/5 **cOH,** The party of tourists he was with heard ditch frogs giving a concert.

ditch, give one the v phr [Prob *ditch* n < *ditch* to dismiss, abandon]

=bounce, give one the.

1969 *DARE* (Qu. II5b, *When you don't want to have anything to do with a certain person because you don't like him*) Inf **CA**169, Give him the ditch.

ditch grass n

1 A **cordgrass** (here: *Spartina alterniflora*). *obs*

1824 Bigelow *Florula Bostoniensis* 24, *Spartina glabra . .* Ditch grass.

2 A water plant *(Ruppia maritima).* Also called **duck grass 3, nigger wool, Peter grass, puldoo grass, redhead grass, sea grass, tassel grass, widgeon grass, zhebes**

1843 Torrey *Flora NY* 2.252, *Ruppia maritima . .* Ditch-grass. **1848** Gray *Manual of Botany* 454, *Ruppia . .* Ditch-grass. **1900** Lyons *Plant Names* 328, *R[uppia] maritima . .* Ditch-grass. **1959** Munz–Keck *CA Flora* 1319, *Ruppia . .* Ditch-Grass. **1967** *DARE* (Qu. S9) Inf **LA**6, Ditch grass.

ditch lily n

A **day lily 1** (here: *Hemerocallis fulva*).

1966 *DARE* Wildfl QR Pl.12 Inf **NC**36, Ditch lily.

ditch line n **chiefly sAppalachians**

A ditch by the side of a graded road.

1965–70 *DARE* (Qu. N24) Infs **KY**33, 42, 47, **NC**35, 55, **TN**14, Ditch line. **1971** Wood *Vocab. Change* 371 **GA,** [Footnote 88:] Volunteered [as a word for a ditch by the side of a graded road] . . Ditchline. [1 inf]

ditch moss n

An aquatic plant (*Elodea* spp) with elongated, moss-like stems. Also called **water thyme, waterweed**

1836 in 1840 Phelps *Lectures on Botany* (App.) 146, *Uldora* [sic] *canadensis*. . . Still waters, Ditch moss. Can. to Virg. **1840** MA Zool. & Bot. Surv. *Herb. Plants & Quadrupeds* 190, Ditch Moss. In waters, submerged, and stem much-divided. **1911** *Century Dict. Suppl., Ditch-moss*. . . The water-weed or water-thyme, *Philotria Canadensis*. **1931** Clute *Common Plants* 57, The harmless little ditchmoss *(Elodea canadensis)* . . moved to Europe some time ago and began to fill up the slow-moving streams. **1973** Hitchcock-Cronquist *Flora Pacific NW* 559, *Elodea*. . . Waterweed; Ditchmoss.

ditch pike n

=**redfin pickerel.**

1906 NJ State Museum *Annual Rept. for 1905* 175, *Esox americanus* . . Pike. . . Ditch Pike. . . Banded Pickerel.

ditch rider n Also *ditch boss, ~ walker* **West**

A person in charge of an irrigation system, keeping the canals in repair and allotting water to the users.

1902 Newell *Irrigation* 107 **SW,** The person charged with the management of the canal . . is usually known as the "watermaster" or "ditch-rider." . . It is his business to see that all stockholders or owners receive a fair amount of water. **1939** FWP *Guide MT* 414, *Ditch rider*—Irrigation patrolman who turns water into laterals and watches for breaks in ditch banks. **1940** (1966) Writers' Program *Guide AZ* 77, It is the duty of ditch bosses, or water distributors, to measure the allotment of each water user. **1940** Fergusson *Our Southwest* 251 **NM** (as of 1670s), Every man owed so many days' ditch work under the elected *mayordomo,* ditch boss, who also doled out the water so the man living up the stream did not rob his down-stream neighbor. **1941** Writers' Program *Guide WY* 289, Farmers in gum boots and 'ditch riders' on horseback, with glistening shovel blades above their heads, are familiar figures in the beet and hayfields in early summer. The ditch rider's duty is to be alert for leaks in the central canals and to watch for 'water hogs.' **1950** *AmSp* 25.164 **eCO,** The 'ditch boss' or the 'ditch rider' . . usually 'rides the ditch' on horseback though he may sometimes 'walk ditch.' **1956** *Seattle Daily Times* (WA) 5 Aug mag sec 10, [Caption:] Mrs. George Brown, one of three women ditch-riders in the Okanogan Irrigation District, checked a water-level scale at a canal gate. **1966–70** *DARE* Tape **NM**6, All the money that people pay in is used to pay for the maintenance of the ditch and for a ditch walker who periodically goes up and down the ditch and cleans out the trash; **TX**5, The farmer must wait and the ditch rider will tell him what hour to open his gate and get the water. . . He's a patrolman that is in charge of a certain area of ditches and he is in a government pick-up with a radio and he has direct contact with the office where the dispatcher holds forth.

ditch runner n Cf **ditch rider**

1967 *DARE* (Qu. N33, *A man whose job is to take care of roads in a certain locality*) Inf **OR**1, Ditch runner.

ditch stonecrop n [From its similarity to plants of the genus *Sedum*]

A weedy perennial plant *(Penthorum sedoides)* with scattered leaves and yellowish-green flowers.

1848 Gray *Manual of Botany* 147, *Ditch Stone-crop*. . . *P[enthorum] sedoides*. . . Ditches by road-sides and wet places everywhere. **1890** *Century Dict.* 4381, *P. sedoides* is the ditch-stonecrop of America. **1930** OK Univ. Biol. Surv. *Pub.* 2.64, *Penthorum sedoides* L. Ditch Stone-crop. **1947** *Amer. Midland Naturalist* 38.44 **MD,** (Ditch-stonecrop). Rare in margins of swamps on flood plain. **1970** Correll *Plants TX* 718, *Ditch-stonecrop*. . . Wet ground, usually along and on edge of water in streams.

ditch-stretcher See **stretcher**

ditch walker See **ditch rider**

ditch washer n

=**gully washer.**

1965–69 *DARE* (Qu. B25, . . *A very heavy rain*) Infs **IL**27, **MO**19, Ditch washer; (Qu. B27, *A sudden rush of water coming from heavy rain*) Infs **AL**14, **MS**60, **NY**80, Ditch washer.

ditchwater n

=**dishwater.**

1965–70 *DARE* (Qu. H74b, . . *Coffee* . . *very weak*) Infs **NY**21, 34, **OH**98, Ditchwater. [All Infs old]

ditch willow n

Perh a **sandbar willow.**

1966 *DARE* (Qu. T15) Inf **SD**8, Ditch willow.

ditchy adj [*OED* 1786 →]

Rough, uneven; having ditches or furrows.

1970 *DARE* (Qu. N27b, *When unpaved roads get very rough, you call them* ———) Inf **NJ**67, Ditchy. **1976** *DARE* File **nwMO,** The land lays good: it's fairly level, kind of rolling, but not too ditchy or hilly.

dite n Also sp *dight* [Scots and nEngl dial, pronc-spp for *doit;* cf Pronc Intro 3.I.11, *SND doit* n.[1] 2, *EDD doit* sb.[1] 2] **NEng**

A very small amount.

1890 *DN* 1.18 **seNH,** *Dight* [daɪt]: small portion, dab; as 'a little dight of butter.' **1907** *DN* 3.243 **eME,** *Dite*. . . A very small amount. **1909** *DN* 3.410 **nME,** *Dite*. . . Doit. **1914** *DN* 4.71 **ME, nNH,** *Dite*. . . A mite, a small amount. "A leetle dite." **1929** *AmSp* 5.123 **ME,** They asked for "just a dight" more of something at the table, meaning a little. **1966–69** *DARE* (Qu. LL6b, *A small indefinite amount—for example, of butter*) Inf **CT**12, Dite [daɪt]—also salt, etc; (Qu. LL6c, . . *Of cinnamon*) Inf **MA**58, Dite—a New Hampshire term; **CT**12, Dite. [Both Infs old] **1966** *DARE* FW Addit **ME**13, A dite [dɑɪt] of salt. **1971** *Today Show Letters* **swME,** "Move over a dight." "Put in just a dight more." **1975** Gould *ME Lingo* 74, Men adjusting a timber will say, "Shove it my way a dite!" A *dite* more of smashed potatoes at supper will be just a touch. Smidgen, dab, pinch, whisker, and words of that category are usually interchangeable with *dite*. **1977** *Greenfield Recorder* (MA) 10 Dec 8, "Dite" meant just a little bit, sometimes spelled "dight".

dits(e)y See **ditzy 2**

dittany n Pronc-sp *ditney*

A small, fragrant plant *(Cunila origanoides)* of the mint family. Also called **frostweed 5, high pennyroyal, stone mint, sweet horsemint, wild basil**

1676 Glover *Acc. Va.* in *Phil. Trans.* XI.629 *(DA),* Here is also an herb which some call *Dittany,* others *Pepper-wort;* it is not *Dittany of Candia,* nor *English Dittander*. **1738** Byrd *Dividing Line* (1901) 213 *(DA),* Dittany . . is a Sure Defense against [horseflies]. **1814** Pursh *Flora Americae* 2.406, The whole herb has an aromatic scent, and is used as tea in severe colds and other complaints, under the name of *Dittany*. **1910** Shreve *MD Plant Life* 477, *Cunila origanoides*. . . Dittany, Stone Mint. **1937** (1963) Hyatt *Kiverlid* 80 **sAppalachians,** I ain't no fool about sassafac . . I'd ruther have ditney tea. **1940** Richter *Trees* 56 **OH** (as of early 1800s), The dying fire flickered on the clumps of herbs. . . There were boneset for fever and dittany for supper tea and pennyroyal to purify the blood. **1947** *Amer. Midland Naturalist* 38.56 **MD,** (Dittany). Rare in pine-oak forest; one station in upland oak forest. **1974** (1977) Coon *Useful Plants* 156, Dittany. . . One reputation is that it will kill rattlesnakes when held to their noses, but how one would do that, this author does not know.

dittent See **do** v **A5**

dittle See **diddle** v[2] **1**

ditto n

Tick-tack-toe; see quot.

1965–70 *DARE* (Qu. EE38a, *A game played with pencil and paper where the players try to get three X's or three O's in a row*) Infs **AR**52, **FL**8, **IL**76, Ditto.

ditty n

1 See quot.

1906 *DN* 3.133 **nwAR,** *Ditty*. . . Social function. Common among students.

2 See quot 1968. [From *ditty bag* or *ditty box* a container for holding miscellaneous personal effects]

1961 Adams *Old-Time Cowhand* 102, Under his head for a pillow was his war-sack, which held all the useless ditties and do-funnies that he'd gathered in his years of followin' the wagon. **1968** Adams *Western Words* 95, *Ditty*—A cowboy's name for a new tool or contrivance, or for practically anything unfamiliar to him.

‡**ditty** adj

1967 *DARE* (Qu. KK41, *Something that is very difficult to do. "I managed to get through it, but it was ______."*) Inf **TX**32, Ditty; a job; brain teaser. [*DARE* Ed: This may instead be a noun.]

ditzy adj

1 Admirable, fine; hence n *ditz* a beauty, humdinger.

1975 *DARE* File (as of c1920), *Ditz, ditzy* ['dɪts(i)]—Common among boys in Akron, Ohio, e.g. "Look at my new knife." "Gee, that's a ditz!" Or, "That's ditzy!" **1986** *DARE* File **neOH**, I vaguely recall the word *ditzy*—It was used to describe anything first class. . . a number of friends and relatives . . agree with my recollection. I lived in Akron all of my early years and so did most of my family and friends.

2 also sp *dits(e)y:* Scatterbrained, irresponsible; hence n *ditz* a silly, scatterbrained person. **esp NYC**

1976 *New Yorker* 6 Dec 182 **NYC,** He thinks women who want equality are ditsey little twitches—ruthless, no-souled monsters who take men's jobs away from them. **1980** *NY Times* (NY) 17 Nov sec C 15/6, Tracy's philandering father, her ditsy mother and her sly Uncle Willie are played in varying degrees of blandness [in the stage play "Philadelphia Story"]. **1986** *NADS Letters, Ditzy* is "camp" for disorganized, scatterbrained. *Ibid* **NY,** Regarding *ditz,* it seems that the word has been used in the New York area for at least the last twenty years to mean 'a scatterbrain.' A ditzy person is confused, dis-oriented and not entirely in control of the situation at hand. One of my co-workers offers the folk etymology that *ditz* is derived from *dizzy.* **1986** *Wall St. Jrl.* (NY NY) 23 Oct 30/1, His parents . . are ditzes—L.A. rich who are prisoners of their money, their shrinks, their own dim brains.

div See **dive**

dive v

Std senses, var gram forms.

1 past: usu *dove* or *dived;* occas **Sth, S Midl, nNEng,** *old-fash, div;* also *among Black speakers* uninflected *dive;* rarely *diven, doved, duv.* [*OED "U.S.* and *Eng. dial. dove. . .* The modern dial. pa[st] t[ense] *dove* is app[arently] a new formation after *drive, drove,* or *weave, wove."*]

1837 (1955) *Crockett Almanacks* 81 **TN,** I div right into the Waybosh river. **1903** [see **2** below]. **1907** *DN* 3.243 **eME,** *Div. . .* Preterite of dive. "He div right into my woodshed." **1909** *DN* 3.410 **nME,** *Div. . .* The past tense of *dive.* **1923** *DN* 5.205 **swMO,** *Div. . .* Dived. **1943** *LANE* Map 580, The recorded [past] forms of the verb */dive/* are, in the order of frequency: *dove, dived, div* and *duv* [one instance in **nME**]. . . *Div* is used naturally by some informants in northern New England and remembered as an 'old' form by many others. **1953** Atwood *Survey of Verb Forms* 9, *Dive . .* preterite. . . *Dived* /daivd/ is uncommon throughout N. Eng., N.Y., n. Pa., and e. N.J. . . In a belt in n.c. and e. Pa. and along the upper Ohio, *dived* and *dove* /dov/ occur about equally, the former being more common among older informants. Elsewhere in the M[iddle] A[tlantic] S[tates] and the S[outh] A[tlantic] S[tates] to and including N.C., *dived* heavily predominates on all levels, being limited only by *div* (see below). In the northeastern area . . *dove* is almost universal. . . There is not the slightest doubt that the area of *dove* is extending itself to the south and west. South of the Peedee in S.C. *dove* is also fairly common, and it has some currency in coastal Ga. In these areas it is quite frequent in urban and cultured speech, somewhat less so in rustic speech. The form *div* /dɪv/ shows the typical distribution of an archaism, being most common in n.e. N. Eng. and the coastal and mountain areas of the South and the South Midland. . . There are five occurrences of *duv* /dʌv/, concentrated in s. N.J. near the mouth of the Delaware. A few Negro informants use the uninflected *dive.* **1954** *Harder Coll.* **cwTN,** *Div* [past]. I have never heard *dove* in the area. **1962** Atwood *Vocab. TX* 75, *Dived. . .* Div [as past tense] . . is only a remnant and is confined to the least-educated informants. [6 of 94 infs said *div.*] **1965–70** *DARE* (Qu. OO25b, *Talking about diving: "Only yesterday the children ______ [there]."*) 559 Infs, **widespread, but less freq S Midl,** Dove; 448 Infs, **widespread, but less freq Nth, N Midl,** Dived; **AR**47, **GA**19, 44, 86, **MD**46, **MS**1, 57, 69, **MO**34, **NM**11, **OK**42, **TX**36, Div [12 of 12 Infs saying *div* were old or mid-aged, 8 of 12 gs educ or less.]; **FL**48, **SC**10, 26, **VA**39, 71, Dive [5 of 5 Infs saying *dive* were Black.]; **PA**190, Doved; **OK**1, Diven. **1975** Allen *LAUM* 2.12 (as of c1950), The U[pper] M[idwest] incidence of the two preterit forms of *dive* strongly intimates that analogical English dialectal *dove* is becoming more widely accepted in preference to the historical *dived.*

2 past pple: usu *dived;* also freq *dove;* occas **Sth, S Midl,** *old-fash, div, diven;* also occas *esp among Black speakers* uninflected *dive;* rarely *doved, doven, duv.*

1890 *DN* 1.71 **LA,** *Div, dove:* dived (pret. and p.p.). **1892** *KS Univ. Qrly.* 1.96, *Diven,* past participle of *dive.* **1903** *DN* 2.293 **Cape Cod MA** (as of a1857), The same form for the past and past participle. . . *Dive—dove,* or *duv.* **1952** Brown *NC Folkl.* 1.533, *Div* [dɪv]. . . The past tense and past participle of *dive.*—General. Illiterate. **1965–70** *DARE* (Qu. OO25a, *Talking about diving: "The water is deep enough—the children have often ______ [there]."*) 581 Infs, **widespread, but less freq Nth, N Midl,** Dived; 436 Infs, **widespread, but less freq S Midl,** Dove; **AR**47, **GA**3, 19, **MD**46, **MS**1, 57, 69, **MO**9, 34, **NM**11, **OK**1, 42, 52, **TX**36, Div [10 of 14 Infs saying *div* were old, 12 of 14 gs educ or less.]; **FL**48, **MO**16, 36, **SC**10, 26, **VA**39, 71, Dive [5 of 7 Infs saying *dive* were Black.]; **MS**16, **NC**1, **VA**69, Diven; **MS**44, Doved; **CA**166, Doven.

dive and six n

1966 *DARE* (Qu. FF5a, . . *Steps and figures in dancing—in the past*) Infs **ME**1, Dive and six. [**1986** *NADS Letters* **Upstate NY,** Part of the [square-dance] call went something like "Duck and dive, six in line / Hurry up, you're way behind / No, you're not, you're just in time / Duck and dive, six in line."]

dive bomber n *joc*

1965–70 *DARE* (Qu. R15a, . . *Nicknames . . for mosquitoes*) Infs **HI**14, **MD**9, **MN**7, **NY**6, **SC**69, **WY**1, Dive bomber; (Qu. R15b, . . *An extra-big mosquito*) Infs **CA**87, **GA**72, **HI**14, **NH**18, **NY**183, **OH**20, **PA**68, Dive bomber.

dived See **dive** v **1, 2**

dive dapper, dive dipper, dive dopper See **didapper**

dive hole n

1968 *DARE* (Qu. N30, . . *A sudden short dip in a road*) Inf **VT**7, Dive hole.

diven See **dive**

diver n Also *diver duck* Cf **dipper**

Any of various water birds, such as the **ruddy duck, mergansers, grebes,** the **loon,** or a **bittern;** see quots.

1698 (1848) Thomas *Hist. & Geog. Acct.* 13, There are an Infinite Number of Sea and Land Fowl, of most sorts. *viz. . .* Geese, Divers, Brands [sic], Snipe. **1743** (1754) Catesby *Nat. Hist. Carolina* 2 [app] xxxvi, European Water-Fowls, which I have observed to be also Inhabitants of America, [include the following] . . The grey Plover. Elk or Wild Swan. Divers. Sea-Gulls. **1813** Wilson *Amer. Ornith.* 8.126, The Smew, or White Nun, . . is another of those Mergansers commonly known in this country by the appellation of Fishermen, Fisher Ducks, or Divers. **1857** Hammond *Wild N. Scenes* 142, We passed through these [ponds], in which there were several loons, or great northern divers, quietly floating. **1917** (1923) *Birds Amer.* 1.152, Ruddy Duck—*Erismatura jamaicensis . .* Diver. **1954** Sprunt *FL Bird Life* 4, Horned Grebe: *Colymbus auritus . .* Local Names: Diver; . . Diver Duck. **1965–70** *DARE* (Qu. Q5, . . *Kinds of wild ducks*) Infs **OH**20, **SC**67, 69, Diver; (Qu. Q8, *A water bird that makes a booming sound before rain*) Inf **DE**3, Diver; (Qu. Q9, *The bird that looks like a small, dull-colored duck*) Infs **DE**4, **MO**38, **OH**20, **SC**4, Diver; **DE**4, Diver duck.

‡**dividance** n

1968 *DARE* (Qu. N17, . . *The separating area in the middle of a four-lane road*) Inf **NC**50, Dividance [dɪ'vɑ•dɪns]; (Qu. N44, . . *The strip of grass and trees between the sidewalk and the curb*) Inf **NC**50, Dividance—what I would call it.

divide n **chiefly West**

1 A mountain range, ridge, or section of high ground which separates two watersheds.

1810 Pike *Expeditions* 136 **seKS, neOK,** Struck and passed the divide between the *Grand* river and the Verdegris river. **1842** in 1940 *AmSp* 15.172 **VA,** On the divide, between Leatherwood and Pinch Gut. **1861** U.S. Army Corps Topog. Engineers *Rept. Colorado R.* 3.44 **SW,** Basin-shaped depressions on this mesa contain fresh-water Tertiary strata, both east and west of the great "divide" [=Continental Divide]. **1932** *DN* 6.228 **West,** *Divide.* This word is heard all over the West, though not much in the country nearer the Mississippi, where the thing itself is not common. It is not a very early word; Bradbury (1809) says "what is called a dividing ridge." In the mid-century one is likely to see the word with quotation marks, as though it were an unfamiliar Westernism. In the last half of the century, The Grand Divide or The Great Divide was a name for the Rockies. **1949** *Sierra Club* (So. Calif. Chap.) Sched. 130, 31 *(DA),* The trail leads up Millard Canyon, past Dawn Gold Mine. . . to the Millard Canyon–Bear Canyon Divide. **1966** *DARE* (Qu. C15) Inf **ID**1, Divide—where water flows in opposite directions.

2 often cap; also *great divide;* Fig: the boundary between life and death. *old-fash* Cf *DS* BB56

1872 Tice *Over Plains* 214 **CO,** There is no lack of them [= tales] . . of these [= hunters] who long since 'have gone over the Divide.' **1912** Raine *Brand Blotters* 284 **AZ,** Since you've taken his place it will be you that crosses the divide, Mr. Sheriff. **1915** (1916) Young *Hard Knocks* 242, I am still residing in Portland, Oregon, . . where I hope to remain until I cross the Great Divide. **1942** Dale *Cow Country* 63, The little mound . . marked the last resting place of a cow hand who in the line of duty had crossed the Great Divide "to that new range which never fails." **1961** Adams *Old-Time Cowhand* 11, By the time modern ranchin', with its flivvers and helicopters, had caught up with 'im [=the cowboy], he'd passed over the Great Divide, or was too old to care.

3 A mountain pass. Cf **gap** n[1] **1, notch**

1965–70 *DARE* (Qu. C15, *A place in mountains or high hills where you can get through without climbing over the top*) Infs **CA**136, 137, **OH**49, **OK**21, Divide; (Qu. C19, . . *Low land running between hills*) Inf **CA**136, Divide. **1966** Barnes–Jensen *Dict. UT Slang* 12, Divide: n. a crossing over a mountain between two watersheds. It is always lower than the peaks on each side of it, hence is often used for sheep or cattle trails from one range to another.

divide the blankets v phr [In ref to a Cherokee wedding ceremony in which a couple carries two "united blankets" to their new cabin]

To become divorced.

1975 McDonough *Garden Sass* 194 **AR,** When he asked Blanket [=a Cherokee] if he had not been married the answer was, "Yes, once, but my wife was a singing bird and we divided the blankets." This unusual expression, indicating divorce, was made clear as Washburn learned of the Indian wedding ceremony.

divil See **devil** n

diviltry See **deviltry**

diving beetle n [See quot 1889] Cf **water tiger**

An aquatic beetle of the family Dytiscidae.

1889 *Century Dict.* 1707, *Diving-beetle.* . . A popular name for various aquatic beetles of the family *Dytiscidæ.* They swim freely in the water, and may often be seen diving rapidly to the bottom, whence their name. **1905** Kellogg *Amer. Insects* 255, Predaceous beetles of very different habitat are the . . diving-beetles. **1928** Metcalf–Flint *Destructive & Useful Insects* 198, Predaceous diving beetles. **1954** Borror–DeLong *Intro. Insects* 337, Predaceous Diving Beetles. . . are usually very common in ponds and quiet streams. **1969** *DARE* (Qu. R30) Inf **CA**114, Diving beetle.

divinity n Also *divinity fudge* [Prob with ref to its "divine" flavor] **esp west of Appalachians** See Map

Homemade candy made by pouring hot sugar syrup into beaten egg whites.

1913 E. H. Glover *'Dame Curtsey's' Book of Candy Making* 34 *(DA),* Divinity Fudge. Three and one-half cups of granulated sugar, one-half cup of 90 per cent corn syrup, two-thirds cup of water [etc.]. **1950** Bissell *Stretch on River* 42 **eMO,** We sat down in a booth. The whole place smelled of divinity fudge. **1953** *New Yorker* 5 Dec 49/1 **MS,** They spent all their time at the post office sending him things to eat. Divinity travels perfectly, if you ever need to know. **c1960** *Wilson Coll.* **csKY,** *Divinity Fudge.* . . A type of home-made candy. **1965–70** *DARE* (Qu. H80, *Kinds of candy . . made at home*) 357 Infs, **esp west of Appalachians,** Divinity; 15 Infs, **scattered,** Divinity fudge; (Qu. H82b, *Kinds of cheap candy that used to be sold years ago*) Infs **IL**82, **PA**9, **TN**35, **WV**17, Divinity. **1978** *UpCountry* Mar 16 **Cape Cod MA,** Maple Divinity. . . Boil a pint of maple syrup. . . Beat the white of two eggs until they are very stiff, then very slowly pour the syrup into the egg whites . . until you begin to get that lovely, fluffy yet slightly grainy "divinity" consistency. **1986** *DARE* File **neMA** (as of 1960s), Each year at Christmas, my great aunt would give my father a box of her home-made divinity fudge.

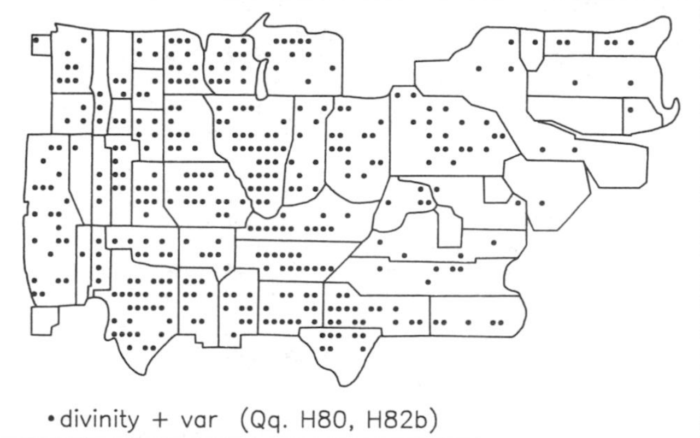

•divinity + var (Qq. H80, H82b)

divle See **devil** n

divvy v Often with *up;* rarely with *in, over* [Prob from *divide*] **widespread, but chiefly Nth, N Midl, Pacific** See Map

To divide or distribute (something of value) among two or more persons; to divide or share in profits or indebtedness.

1877 in 1940 *America's Lost Plays* 4.203 **NYC,** We divvy a cool $20,000. **1880** Hayes *New CO* 156 **CO,** The two men . . were "divvying up" the spoils in the middle of the road. **1890** *Congressional Record* 19 May 4933/2 **NC,** My Republican brethren, do you really mean to "divvy?" **1899** Tarkington *Gentleman* 206 **IN,** He'll divvy up, when he gets it. He'll stand by you, old man. **1920** Lewis *Main Street* 320 **MN,** Sure, you socialists are great on divvying up other folks' money. **c1960** *Wilson Coll.* **csKY,** *Divvy, divvy up.* . . To give each one his fair share or just dues. **1963** Burroughs *Head-First* 105 **CO,** We did "divvy up" with whatever youngster or youngsters we happened to be associating with at the moment. **1965–70** *DARE* (Qu. II8, *When one person wants to share or divide something with another person, he might say, "Let's ______ [on that].'*') 180 Infs, **chiefly Nth, N Midl, scattered elsewhere,** Divvy up; 37 Infs, **esp Nth, N Midl,** Divvy; **CA**107, **IL**34, **OK**9, **PA**167, **SC**59, **TN**31, Divvy it (*or* that) up; (Qu. II9, *If several people have to contribute in order to pay for something, you say, "Let's all ______.'*') 23 Infs, **chiefly Nth, N Midl,** Divvy up; **IA**27, **MD**39, **NY**224, **RI**6, Divvy in; **MT**1, **PA**190, **TN**12, Divvy; **CA**44, **GA**73, Divvy it (up); **MA**77, **MN**21, Divvy up on it (*or* the cost); (Qu. U18, *If you force somebody to pay money that he owes you, . . you might say, "I finally made him ______.'*') 30 Infs, **esp Nth, N Midl,** Divvy up; **IN**65, Divvy over.

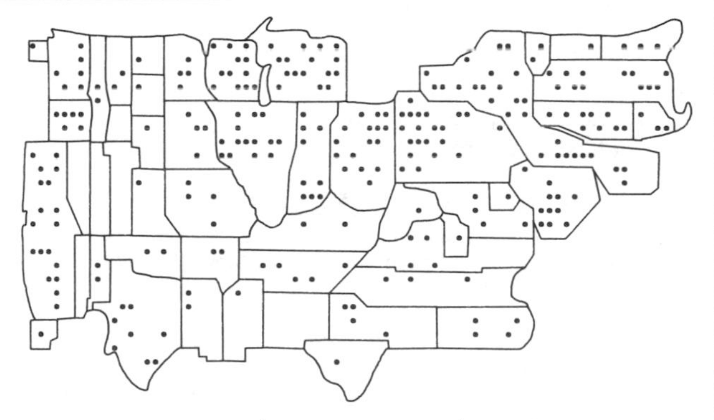

•divvy v + varr (Qq. II8, II9, U18)

divvy n Also sp *divy* [**divvy** v]

1 A division, share.

1872 in 1952 *AmSp* 27.77, Orville Grant, the President's brother proposed to Jussen, the collector of Internal Reveue [sic] of a Chicago district to go snacks [=share] on a fraudulent "divy" with the runner of a distillery there. **1872** Burnham *Memoirs U.S. Secret Service* 170, Disbrowe wrote to Tom that he wanted $3,000 in the "stuff" at once, of this 50 cent issue; and if he would bring it out himself, he agreed to make a fair "divvy" of the funds then in his hands. **1884** Hay *Bread-Winners* 150 **OH,** "You surely do not intend—" "To strike Saul for a divvy?" **1903** *McClure's Mag.* July 249/2 **ePA,** Once, for a joke, a party of boodlers counted out the "divvy" of their graft in unison with the ancient chime of Independence Hall. **1970** *DARE* (Qu. U15, *When you're buying something, if the seller puts in a little extra to make you feel that you're getting a good bargain*) Inf **IL**117, Extra divvy.

2 in phr *go divvies:* =**divvy** v.

1966–69 *DARE* (Qu. II8, *When a person wants to share or divide something with another person, he might say, "Let's ______ [on that].'*') Infs **CT**23, **MI**13, **NJ**30, Go divvies; **MN**2, Go halves or divvies.

divvy intj
1967 *DARE* (Qu. EE20, *When two boys are fighting, and the one who is losing wants to stop, he calls out, "———."*) Inf **CA**9, Divvy!

divvy in, divvy over, divvy up See **divvy** v

divy See **divvy** n

Dixie n[1] Also *Dixie's land, Dickie's* ~ Cf **dickey pen**
A children's game similar to **pom-pom-pullaway;** part of the verse recited by the players.
1872 in 1945 *AmSp* 20.238 **NY,** During any time within the last eighty years the term "Dixie's Land" has been in use with the New York boys while engaged in the game of "tag." **1895** *DN* 1.398 **eNY,** A common game among boys is known variously as *king . . pom-pom-pull-away . . dixie . . blackman.* **1901** *DN* 2.139 **cwNY,** *Dickie's land. . .* A game much like mossy except that the person who is *it* does not call for the others to cross. . . Cf Dixie . . of which this may be a corruption; or the reverse may be true, the word going back to Dick (=Old Hick . .). Note rime: "I'm on Dickie's land,/ Dickie don't know it,/ He's got a sore toe / An' he can't go it." This is sung by the players in leading out. In the South the verses begin, "I'm on Dixie's land."

Dixie n[2], also attrib Also *Dixie land* [Transf from *Dixie* the southern US]
The southern part of the Mormon settlement area, esp southern Utah.
1873 Beadle *Undeveloped West* 661, All that part of Mormondom south of the rim of the Great Basin is called Dixie, and extends some distance into Arizona. **1894** *Irrigation Age* Jan 38/1 **UT,** The famous 'Dixie Land,' comprising the counties of Millard, Washington and Beaver, is known as the land of the grape. **1942** Stegner *Mormon Country* 345, Utah's Dixie . . [has] a climate that grows figs, grapes, peaches, apricots, walnuts, almonds, cotton. **1965** Rice *Ambassador* 66 **sUT,** The St. George area is justly called "Utah's Dixie". The grapes raised there have an especially fine flavor. Dixie wine made from them is famous for its "kick". . . It seems to the uninitiated to be . . quite "tame", but woe be to him who underestimates its power!

Dixie bacon n [*Dixie* the South] *joc* Cf **Arkansas chicken**
1931–33 *LANE Worksheets* **swCT,** *Dixie bacon. . .* Hog jowls.

Dixie blackb(r)ush See **blackbrush 2**

Dixie boy (plow) n Also *boy Dixie, Dixie plow,* ~ *stock* [Prob orig a trade name] **S Atl** *old-fash*
A **turnplow,** usu with a wooden beam, used to turn and **break** v **B1** land.
1965–70 *DARE* (Qu. L18, *Kinds of plows*) Infs **SC**7, 9, Dixie plow; **SC**32, Dixie plow—a make of a turnplow, had a wooden beam, whereas later turnplows had a steel beam where you connect the singletree; **SC**57, Dixie plow or dixie boy—a turnplow used to throw up a bed or break land up; **SC**26, 30, Dixie boy—to open furrow; **SC**47, Dixie boy—breaks up land, one-horse cultivator; **SC**43, Dixie boy plow—a kind of turnplow; **FL**6, Dixie plow—one horse; **GA**19, 22, Dixie (boy); **FL**7, Boy Dixie—brand; **VA**38, Boy Dixies ['dɪksɪz]—old-fashioned, a wood beam plow, hand made in local blacksmith shops; **VA**77, Boy Dixie—wooden stock, old-fashioned brandname; **NC**68, Boy Dixie—horse drawn, has a beam of wood with an iron foot with a wing on it which throws dirt; **GA**87, One-horse boy Dixie—used for turning land and breaking, old-fashioned; **FL**34, Dixie stock. **1966** *DARE* Tape **SC**17, [Inf:] You take . . a Dixie plow . . you cover up so much. [FW:] What's a . . Dixie plow? [Inf:] That's a turnplow. [FW:] Oh, that . . something that throws up a big bed. [Inf:] Yeah.

Dixie butterpea n Also *Dixie speckled butter* Cf **butter bean 1**
A small-podded bush bean.
1970 *DARE* File **TN,** Dixie butterpea: a small lima-type bean seen at a seed store in Jackson, TN. **1976** *Wanigan Catalog* 8, *Dixie Speckled Butter.* **1988** Whealy *Garden Seed Inventory* (2d ed.) 65 **chiefly Sth, s Midl,** *Lima Bush Beans—Phaseolus lunatus. . . Dixie Butterpea Speckled* (Butterpea Speckled) . . brownish-red seeds speckled with darker-brown. . . Good in drought areas, Southern adapted. . . *(27 [varieties available] in 1981 . . 21 [varieties available] in 1987). Ibid, Dixie Butterpea White* (Butterpea White) . . White baby lima . . white seed. . . *(23 [varieties available] in 1981 . . 19 [varieties available] in 1987)*

Dixie punch See **Dixie wine**

Dixie's land See **Dixie**

Dixie speckled butter See **Dixie butterpea**

Dixie stock See **Dixie (boy) plow**

Dixie wine n Also *Dixie punch* [*Dixie* southern Utah where cotton & grapes were grown by early Mormon settlers]
See quot 1873.
1873 Beadle *Undeveloped West* 660 **swUT,** "Dixie wine," as the Mormons call it, is rather strong and pungent; it is simply fermented grape juice, and is quite inferior to other "native wines." **1968** *DARE* (Qu. DD27, . . *Nicknames . . for wine*) Inf **UT**10, Dixie punch.

‡diz v [Prob back-formation from *dizzy*]
1914 *DN* 4.105 **KS,** *Diz. . .* To make dizzy; daze. "When the block fell on his head, it dizzed him."

‡dizable adj [Perh var of *drizzle* + *-able*]
?Threatening to drizzle.
1948 *McDavid Coll.* **cNY,** Dizable [dɪzəbl̩]—'cloudy'. 82 year old, male informant—no formal schooling.

dizzies n pl
A spell of dizziness.
1943 *Sat. Eve. Post* 22 May 93/1 ?**AR, MO,** They asked did I like the Air Fo'ce, and I can't climb a tree, even, without the dizzies.

dizzy adj
1 also *dizzy-headed;* Esp of a woman: silly, foolish. [*OED* c825 →, "Now only *dial.*"] *usu derog*
1878 Beadle *Western Wilds* xxxv [*sic OEDS*-quot not found], Dance houses and saloons multiplied and 'dizzy doves' gave an air of abandon to the streets. **1886** in 1950 *AmSp* 25.38 **New Orleans LA,** The keeper of a sporting mansion [=brothel]. . . a dizzy dusky damsel. **1888** in 1971 Farmer *Americanisms* 205 **TX,** There seems little likelihood of any professional beauties or maidens, commonly called dizzy blondes, attempting the hardships of a stage life this winter. **1937** (1959) Weidman *I Can Get It* 9 **NYC,** Lugging half the sample line . . so some dizzy broad . . can make one more selection before her train leaves. **1965–70** *DARE* (Qu. HH9, *A very silly or light-headed person*) 81 Infs, **widespread, but esp Nth, N Midl,** Dizzy; **MN**6, **OR**10, **WA**28, Dizzy blonde (*or* dame, dolt); **SC**21, Dizzy in the head; **VA**29, Dizzy-headed.
‡2 Damned, confounded.
1970 *DARE* (Qu. NN17, *Something that keeps on annoying you—for example, a fly that keeps buzzing around you: "That ——— fly won't go away."*) Inf **DC**13, Dizzy.

do v
A Pronc varr.
1 *do:* usu |du|; also |diu, dju| (cf Pronc Intro 3.I.10). Eye-dial or pronc-spp spp *dew, doo, du* Cf **dew, due A**
1739 in 1969 *AmSp* 44.304 **GA,** *Dooin* 'doing.' **1815** Humphreys *Yankey in England* 104, *Du,* do. **1857** *Putnam's Mag.* Sept 347/2 **CT,** Dew tell! *Ibid* 353/2, There! you see parson I doo swear dreadful. **1867** Lowell *Biglow* 166 **'Upcountry' MA,** The pinch comes in decidin' wut to *du.* **1893** *DN* 1.277 **wCT,** *Do* (pron. [diu]). **1915** (1916) Johnson *Highways New Engl.* 188 **Cape Cod MA,** I asked the fellers once, 'What d'you dew with them old things?' **1930** *AmSp* 5.342 **ceVA,** [ɪju] in *due, new;* [u] in *do. Ibid* 345 **cGA,** [ɪu] in *new, due, do. Ibid* 348 **ceMA, CT, ME,** [u] in *due, new, do. Ibid* 350 **cIL,** [ɪu] appears in *do. Ibid* **swTX,** The vowel in *do* and *move* approaches [iu]. **1931** *AmSp* 6.165 **ceVA,** [u] is characterized by unusual tenseness and it is somewhat fronted. The vowel is often prolonged until it is difficult to tell whether [u] has become [ju] or [ɪu]. *Due* is rarely distinguished from *do. Ibid* 399 **seME,** *Do* and *due* are homonyms [du]. **1936** *AmSp* 11.29 **eTX,** *Due* and *do* are always distinguished in East Texas speech. *Due* is [dɪu] . . and *do* is [du]. **1952** *AmSp* 27.188 **WA,** *Dew, do* are frequently pronounced . . [diuw], sometimes with a centralized vowel, but are also commonly heard as . . [duw].
2 *don't:* usu |dont|; also |dõ|. Pronc-sp *don', doan', non't*
1899 Chesnutt *Conjure Woman* 12 **csNC** [Black], Ef you en young miss dere doan' min. **1915** *DN* 4.186 **swVA,** *Non't.* Variant contraction of *do not.* **1922** Gonzales *Black Border* 297 **sSC, GA coasts** [Gullah glossary], *Don'*—don't, doesn't. **1952** Brown *NC Folkl.* 1.534, *Don't* [dõ] *pronc. Don't.*—General. Illiterate.
3 *does:* usu |dʌz|; also **chiefly NEast,** *old-fash* |duz, dʊz|. Pronc-spp *doos, dooz, duse*
1815 Humphreys *Yankey in England* 104, *Duse,* does. **1847** Hurd *Grammatical Corrector* 80, Does . . [Hurd: Incorrectly pronounced]

dooz. **1848** Lowell *Biglow* 144 **'Upcountry' MA,** Doos, *does.* **1872** Schele de Vere *Americanisms* 599, *Don't . .* is still objectionable slang when connected with the third person, thus changing *does* into do. "He don't tell the truth." As the New Englander invariably says *doos* for *does,* he is not so likely to commit this blunder. **1885** Howells *Rise Lapham* 50 **VT,** "Your mother does." He said *doos,* of course. **1896** *DN* 1.415 **wCT, wMA, NYC, NJ,** *Do, does,* pron. [duz]. **1910** *DN* 3.440 **cwNY,** *Does.* Often pronounced either [dʊz] or [duz]. **1914** *DN* 4.71 **ME, nNH,** *Doos* [duz]. Does. **1927** Adams *Congaree* 19 **cSC** [Black], You can do anything ef you doos it in de name of God. **1943** *LANE* Map 686 **nNEng,** *I Do; He Does. . .* Pronunciations of the type of [dʊz] are described as older or old-fashioned though still in use. **1944** [see **B2** below].

4 *doesn't:* usu |'dʌzn̩t|; also occas |'dʌdn̩(t)| (cf Pronc Intro 3.I.17). Pronc-spp *dudn'(t)*

1949 *PADS* 11.6 **wTX** (as of c1920), *Dudn't* ['dʌdn̩t]. . . Doesn't. Frequent. **1967** *DARE* Tape **AR**47, It's just people that doesn't ['dʌdn̩] know. **1981** *PADS* 67.49 **Mesabi Iron Range MN,** For one informant . . /z/ regularly assimilates to /d/ in *doesn't.* **1984** Burns *Cold Sassy* 104 **nGA** (as of 1906), You need to understand that in Cold Sassy . . [w]e . . say . . *dudn'* for doesn't.

5 *didn't:* usu |'dɪdn̩t|; also |dɪnt, 'dɪdn̩, 'dɪtn̩t, 'dɪʔn̩, 'dɪdɛnt|. Pronc-spp *di(d)n, dint, dittent*

1843 (1916) Hall *New Purchase* 149 **IN,** I dad, if I din't ketch myself a crying like a child. **1902** *DN* 2.232 **sIL,** *Didn* for didn't. **1934** in 1944 *ADD* **cwNY,** |dɪnt|. **1942** Hall *Smoky Mt. Speech* 88 **eTN, wNC,** There is frequent omission of [d] before [n] in *couldn't* and *didn't:* [kʊnt], [dɪnt]. *Ibid* 90, Final [t] may disappear after . . [n], as in . . couldn't, didn't . . ['kʊdn], etc. *Ibid* 101, 'It didn't run': [hɪt 'dɪdn 'rʌn]. **1942** *New Yorker* 11 July 18/1 **sCA,** The old man din like the idear. **1945** O'Hara *Pipe Night* 33 **PA,** So I din go the Hays office. **1949** in 1986 *DARE* File **MI,** [dɪdɛnt]. **1950** Bissell *Stretch on River* 92, I tole her to shove it ifn she din' like it. **c1960** *Wilson Coll.* **csKY,** Didn't /'dɪtn̩t/. Common. **1968** *DARE* FW Addit **cs, seMD,** ['dɪʔn̩]—glottal stop frequently accompanies dental and often substitutes for it. . . Heard all over eastern shore of Maryland and Smith Island. **1982** McCool *Sam McCool's Pittsburghese* 10 **PA,** Dittent: did not, as in "I dittent do my homework, did you?"

B Gram forms.

1 infin: Usu *do;* also **chiefly Sth,** *esp among Black speakers* esp with compound tense, *done.*

1907 *DN* 3.243 **eME,** *Done. . .* To do (after a compound tense). "I shouldn't have let him done it." Common. **1928** Peterkin *Scarlet Sister Mary* 84 **seSC** [Gullah], I come mighty nigh marryin him . . , but I'm glad now I didn' done it. **1930** Faulkner *As I Lay Dying* 128 **MS,** I'd have had better sense than to done what I just done. **1930** Stoney–Shelby *Black Genesis* 10 **seSC** [Gullah], Br' Dog see he chance. "Why I can't done dat for a task, for help you out?" **1945** FWP *Lay My Burden Down* 99 **MS** [Black], Old Doctor just started to done farming on it when I was took away. **1966** *DARE* Tape **GA**4 [Black], I didn't done too much with the fifth school [=grade].

2 pres (exc 3rd pers sg): usu *do,* neg *don't;* also **chiefly Sth,** *old-fash, does,* neg *doesn't.*

1823 in 1944 *ADD* 169, I doesn't. J.F. Cooper. **1843** (1916) Hall *New Purchase* 121 **IN,** I doesn't know a single letter in the A B C's. **1893** Shands *MS Speech* 27, *Does. . .* Used by negroes for *do;* as, "I does; they does." **1913** Johnson *Highways St. Lawrence to VA* 259 **nwMD,** I don't like the way people does you. **1928** Peterkin *Scarlet Sister Mary* 24 **seSC** [Gullah], Does you tink dey fits me, Budda? Does you like em, Auntie? **1943** *LANE* Map 686, 1 inf, **seNH,** I [du˗z], *you ~, we ~,* older. **1944** *PADS* 2.33 **NC,** *Does* [duz]. . . Present tense of *do* ((generally singular but may be plural)). Negroes in most of the South. **1966–68** *DARE* Tapes **GA**3, 30, A lot of people does; **IL**29, We got some that does that; **NC**9, **PA**14, **SC**16, Some people does; **TN**13, The mountain people mostly does it.

3 pres 3rd pers sg: usu *does;* also **chiefly Sth, S Midl, esp Mid and S Atl** *now esp among Black speakers, do.* [*OED* "The form *he do* is now s.w. [Engl] dial."; 1547 →]

1884 Murfree *TN Mts.* 250 [White], It do beat all that I can't remember them Jeemes boys' horses! **1899** Chesnutt *Conjure Woman* 55 **ceNC** [Black], Hit tuk longer dem days ter saw a log 'en [=than] it do now. **1934** Carmer *Stars Fell on AL* 191 [Black], Anythin' the Lord do is right. **1943** Smiley *Gloss. New Paltz* **seNY** [White], He goes fishing every evening, he do. **1953** Atwood *Survey of Verb Forms* 27, The third person singular of *do* is recorded in the three contexts "He (does) it all the time," "(Does) he do that sort of thing?," and "He (does)" (emphatic). . . In the Piedmont and Tidewater areas of Va., part of e.N.C., S.C., and Ga. the uninflected form *do* /du/ occurs fairly commonly in all of these contexts. . . A large majority of the users fall into Type I [=old, with little educ]. **1965–70** *DARE* (Qu. K7, *What sickness can a cow get in her udder—for example, if she's left unmilked too long*) Inf **GA**52, Her bag do gets hard; (Qu. NN20b) Inf **IN**45, Oh that do smart; (Qu. OO38a, *About shoes fitting just right*) Inf **GA**44, Hit sho' do fit you good—Negro, means "it's becoming to you." **1966** *DARE* Tape **AL**24, I don' know what kin' of a work she do; **GA**9, Sometime we have a mild winter, that it doesn't take quite as much feed as it do others; **MS**61, And then when it do that, you let your shoes come out . . one quarter of an inch . . beyond the hoof; **SC**3, I would say my thirteen [dollars] went about as far . . as their eighty do now; **SC**17, It do now. Used to, our best cropping was our first tobacco. [2 of 3 Infs Black] **1967** *DARE* FW Addit **seAR** [Black], He kinda wants it, Tommy Cox do. **1977** Smitherman *Talkin* 8 [Black], Contemporary Black English structures like *My momma do that all the time.*

4 neg constr; pres 3rd pers sg: usu *doesn't;* also *esp among speakers with little formal educ, don't.*

1670 in 1902 RI Hist. Soc. *Coll.* 10.102, Evidence of. . . River being more than 11 Miles Long but how Much More dont say. **1774** (1900) Fithian *Jrl.* 202 **nVA,** A Sunday in Virginia dont seem to wear the same Dress as our Sundays to the Northward. **1862** in 1903 Norton *Army Letters* 120 **VA,** It don't take ten thousand acres here to support one family. **1953** Atwood *Survey of Verb Forms* 28, In N.Eng. *he don't* /dont/ is used by about two fifths of the cultured informants (mostly in the older group) and by more than five sixths of the other types. . . In the M[iddle] A[tlantic] S[tates] . . [o]f the cultured informants, nearly three fourths use *he don't. . .* Cultured informants who use only *doesn't* are mostly to be found in or near New York City or Philadelphia. In the S[outh] A[tlantic] S[tates], also, *don't* is universal in Types I [=old, with little educ] and II [=mid-aged, with approx hs educ]. About half of the cultured informants use *don't,* occasionally alongside *doesn't.* **1965–70** *DARE* (Qu. H69, *When food is hard on your stomach, . . it______*) 125 Infs, **scattered,** Don't (set well, agree with me,etc) [Of all Infs responding to the question, 27% were gs educ or less; of those giving these responses, 51% were gs educ or less.]; (Qu. KK26, . . *"It ______ me."*) 14 Infs, **scattered,** Don't make much difference (and varr); (Qu. GG21a) 12 Infs, **scattered,** It don't make any difference to me (and varr); (Qu. II11a, . . *He ______*) Inf **CT**39, Don't chew his food; (Qu. H12, . . *He ______*) Infs **IL**69, 83, **LA**6, 9, **OH**89, **SC**9, 32, **TN**5, Don't eat much (*or* well, good, enough); **PA**203, Don't clean his plate; **DE**3, Don't know what he wants; **OH**76, Don't get invited back; **IL**40, Don't enjoy his food; **MO**16, He don't like it; (Qu. K9, *If one quarter of a cow's udder does not give milk, . . she's ______*) Infs **MN**17, **VA**40, Don't give milk in more than (*or* out of about) three (tits); **SC**57, She don't give no milk; (Qu. K42) Inf **TN**62, He don't ride. [Addit exx throughout *DS*]

5 past: usu *did;* also *esp among speakers with little formal educ, done;* infreq *doed, doned.*

1739 in 1969 *AmSp* 44.304 **GA,** A bullet which *done* no execution. **1830** *MA Spy & Worcester Co. Advt.* (Worcester MA) 28 July 4, *Southerner. I done* it for the sake of information—that's all. **1847** in 1870 Drake *Pioneer Life* 63 **KY,** The weavil . . "done" great injury to that grain. **1873** Twain–Warner *Gilded Age* 307 **DC,** I think it done him good. **1884** *Anglia* 7.252 **Sth,** *Pres.* do—*Past.* done, doed. **1893** *DN* 1.277 **wCT,** Do . . [past and past pple] done. **1910** *DN* 3.440 **cwNY,** *Done, pret.* of *do.* **1943** McAtee *Dial. Grant Co. IN Suppl. 2* 7 (as of 1890s), *Done,* v., past tense of do; did little used. **1953** Atwood *Survey of Verb Forms* 9, In N. Eng., only, the preterite is recorded in the context "He (did) it last night." *Did* is universal among cultured informants. Among the other types the form *done* /dʌn/ predominates rather strongly except in Mass. and R.I., where the two forms are about equally divided. *Done* is about as common among the more modern informants as among the more old-fashioned. **1965–70** *DARE* (Qu. OO33b, . . *"This morning as usual we ______ [the chores]."*) 709 Infs, **widespread,** Did; 220 Infs, **widespread,** Done; **AR**56, **WI**42, Done up; [Of all Infs responding to the question, 43% were comm type 5, 72% were old, 38% were gs educ or less; of those giving the response *done,* 55% were comm type 5, 80% were old, 59% were gs educ or less.]; (Qu. OO35a, . . *"Last year we fertilized the garden, and the plants really ______."*) Infs **GA**17, **KY**44, **PA**176, **TN**1, Done (real) good; **CA**77, **CO**3, **IN**52, **NY**72, Done better (*or* great, well); (Qu. KK63, . . *"It will never last—He just ______."*) Infs **MD**19, **MA**45, **NY**200, **OH**16, **TX**19, Done a bum (*or* hell of a, poor, slaphappy, slipshod) job; **LA**37, **NY**70, Done it halfway (*or* roughly); **AL**50, Halfway done it; (Qu. II28) Inf **TN**1, Regardless of what he done, I'd never like him; (Qu.

OO12b, . . *"It was a big black dog that ——— him."*) Inf **CA**105, Done the biting. [Addit exx in *DS*] **1965–70** *DARE* Tape **AR**43, She says, "You done good;" **FL**24, We done fairly good that day; **FL**37, I don't know how he done it, but he said he did; **IA**8, That's what he done; **LA**2, I done good; **ME**26, The way they done that; **MI**125, We done our own swamping; **OH**22, They done that; **OK**24, You done it all; **WA**24, Them days he done everything in blacksmith shop. **1974** Cohen *Ramapo Mt. People* 149 **neNJ,** What he doed was stamp his foot and the snake laid right down and curled up. **1987** *DARE* File **nwMS,** Here are words . . that I collected in interviews with Black people in Marks . . back in the sixties: Doned [dʌnt]—did. [hɪi dʌnt ðæt] he did that.

6 past pple and ppl adj: usu *done;* also **esp Sth, S Midl** *did.*

1853 Simms *Sword & Distaff* 289 **SC,** Kaint be did, McKewn, even if I was willing. **1944** *PADS* 2.8 **Sth,** *Did:* p.p. of *do.* Slightly less frequent than *done.* "It's already did." Over much of the South. Negro. **1949** in 1986 *DARE* File **MI,** [Radio:] When we have did the things we ought not to have done. **1965–70** *DARE* (Qu. OO33a, . . *"Seven days a week, chores have to be ———."*) 875 Infs, **widespread,** Done; 40 Infs, **scattered, but somewhat more freq Sth, S Midl,** Did [21 Infs responding *did* were gs educ or less]; (Qu. W29, . . *Expressions . . for things that are sewn carelessly? "They're ———."*) Inf **NY**249, Badly did; (Qu. KK41, . . *"I managed to get through with it, but it was ———."*) Inf **MS**45, A job to get it did; (Qu. KK43, *When the hardest part of a task is finished*) Inf **LA**6, Worst part of it's did; **MS**61, Have did the hardest part; (Qu. LL18, . . *"She hasn't ——— all day."*) Infs **GA**7, **LA**7, **MA**33, **MS**47, 60, **OH**48, **PA**230, **VA**46, Did anything (*or* nothing, a thing); (Qu. OO35b, . . *"That land is poor—nothing has ever ——— there."*) Inf **PA**66, Did good; (Qu. OO42, *About stealing money: "He says it's the first time he has ever ———."*) Inf **LA**18, Did it. **1966–69** *DARE* Tape **CA**151, They might have did; **OK**19, I haven't never did that.

C Syntax.

1 used periphrastically:

a with infin to form positive, unemphatic periphrastic tense. [*OED do* v. 25. a c893 →; "dying out in normal prose in 18th c.; but still retained in s.w. [Engl] dialects."] Note: Only examples which appear from context to be unemphatic are included here; since emphasis is marked by stress, it is possible that some of these represent std emphatic use.

1965–68 *DARE* (Qu. AA12, *If a man loses interest in a girl and stops seeing her, you'd say he ———.*) Inf **MO**1, Did jilt her; (Qu. GG22b, *When you have come to the end of your patience, . . "Well, that certainly ———."*) Inf **DE**1, Beats everything I ever did hear; (Qu. OO2b, . . *"I don't feel right—I think I ——— too much."*) Inf **OK**48, Did eat; (Qu. OO25b, . . *"Only yesterday the children ——— [there]."*) Inf **LA**12, Did jump; (Qu. OO37a, . . *"The first time my wool socks were washed they ———."*) Inf **MO**4, Did shrink. **1966** *DARE* Tape **NC**9, Some people does use a fork.

b with *you* and verb to form emphatic imperative. [*OED do* v. B. 30. a. "In the Imperative *positive,* adding force to entreaty, exhortation, or command (this usually with the pronoun inserted as 'do you go at once!')."] *arch*

1871 Eggleston *Hoosier Schoolmaster* 165 **IN,** Now, Shocky, do you run ahead. **1871** (1892) Johnston *Dukesborough Tales* 70 **GA,** Well, never do you mind.

c with *don't:* and verb to form negative imperative. [Perh by analogy, according to the pattern *come: don't come:: do come: do don't come*] **chiefly S Atl** *esp freq among Black speakers; old-fash*

1837 Sherwood *Gaz. GA* 69, *Provincialisms. . . Do don't,* do not. **1838** (1852) Gilman *S. Matron* 32 **SC,** *"Do, if you please, don't* give up teaching us! We will *behave."* **1859** (1968) Bartlett *Americanisms* 123, *Do don't,* for *do not* or *don't,* is a common expression in Georgia and South Carolina, and not by any means confined to the uneducated classes. **1867** Allen *Slave Songs* xxxiv **seSC,** I bring dis same chile to school, sir: *do* don't let 'em stay arter school done. **1884** *Anglia* 7.257 **Sth,** *Interjections. . .* Do please don't! **1892** (1969) Christensen *Afro-Amer. Folk Lore* 33, Do don't le' go if you kin possuble hol' on a leetle longer. **1910** *DN* 3.458 **FL, GA,** *Du don't. . .* Please don't. **1928** Peterkin *Scarlet Sister Mary* 259 **seSC** [Gullah], *Fool* is a awful sinful word. Honey, do don' say em no more.

2 By ext from std use in imper:

a in phr *do pray:* Please, I entreat you! [Cf *OED pray* v. 8. d 15 . . →]

1912 Green *VA Folk-Speech* 152, *Do pray.* Exclamation of disapproval. "Do pray don't talk like that." **1940** Harris *Folk Plays* 46 **NC,** *Cynthy.* I forgot about them two open graves. . . *Liza (shivering).* Hush, do pray! *Ibid* 58, *Cynthy.* It won't be in no two-horse wagon when I go. It'll be in the—*(With evident relish.)* hearse. *Liza (shuddering).* Cynthy! Do, pray!

b used to add force to direct address. [Cf *OED do* v. B. 32 "*Do,* the imperative, was used absolutely, as a word of encouragement or incitement." 1440–1610] **chiefly S Atl** *esp freq among Black (esp Gullah) speakers*

1927 Adams *Congaree* 67 **cSC** [Black], *Voice:* Great God! You reckon all dat true, Tad? *Tad:* I ain' know, but it sound like de truth. . . *Voice:* My God! *Another Voice:* Do Jesus! *Ibid* 87, He [=a talking crow] look up in de old lady face an' say: "Go down below!" An' she said, "Do Bubber, I jest come here on a visit. Dis ain't my church." **1928** Peterkin *Scarlet Sister Mary* 279 **seSC** [Gullah], "Do, Auntie!" Mary laughed. "Now how could dat be?" *Ibid* 311, "Dat is too much," Unex protested when Mary filled the [baby] bottle almost full. . . Mary laughed. "Do, fo Gawd's sake, Unex. Emma'll know when e belly gits full." **1930** Stoney–Shelby *Black Genesis* 72 **seSC,** Do, Br' Guinea-fowl, I'd be too scared to try to tek care o' you' property. **1940** Harris *Folk Plays* 66 **eNC,** I ain't ready to be parted right and left. Take pity sakes! Do Jesus! **1948** Hurston *Seraph* 28 **wFL** [Black], "Oh, do, Jesus!" Maria Henson panted. "Look like she's took worse than usual." *Ibid* 29, "Git that spoon in her mouth before she bites her tongue! Do, my Maker!" *Ibid* 227, "Do, Jesus!" and Arvay moved herself a little. "Oh, my Maker! Do, Father!" **1966–67** *DARE* (Qu. NN6a, *Exclamations of joy*) Inf **SC**40, Do Lordy-Mamma!; (Qu. NN7, *Exclamations of surprise*) Inf **SC**26, Do Jesus; (Qu. NN21c, *Exclamations caused by sudden pain—a twisted ankle*) Inf **SC**26, Do, Lord. [Both Infs Black]

3 used prec its subject (or, rarely, with omission of subject) and without *if* to express conditional meaning. Cf **be** v **B5c(1)** Note: This archaic construction survives in mod stdE with the forms *had, should,* and *were.*

1938 Rawlings *Yearling* 102 **nFL,** "Do you ever ask your Ma into leavin' you have sich as that [=If you ever talk your mother into letting you have something like that]," Penny told him, "you belong to git one [=a bear cub] young enough to train easy." **1939** Rawlings in *Sat. Eve. Post* 25 Nov 60/3 **nFL,** Who be I to tell you a man that has his freedom is the man don't particular want it? And the man drove with a short rein, do he be a man, is the one just ain't going to be drove? **1949** Webber *Backwoods Teacher* 73, You tell them kids at school do they pick on these younguns I'll waylay 'em an' have it out of their hides. **1955** Roberts *S. from Hell-fer-Sartin* 134 **seKY,** And so that night that man he was sleepin' next to the door, and he heared somethin' comin' down through there, said, "Let me in or I'll knock this door down." . . It kept right on, "Don't let me in I'll knock this door down." . . "Don't let me in I'll knock this door down." **1958** Latham *Meskin Hound* 35 **cTX,** Do Jess Pickett come home unexpected . . Sugar'll likely leave faster'n I did! **1967** Williams *Greenbones* 6 **GA** (as of c1910), Did you stick leaves through de hoss's harness, de bugs'd keep off.

4 used conjunctionally: Or else, otherwise. [Engl dial (cf *EDD do* v. II. 3); prob orig abbr for *do you* (=*if you do*) etc following negative statements or commands]

1935 Hurston *Mules & Men* 233 **FL** [Black], Dat's a thing dat's got to be handled just so, do it'll kill you. **1937** (1977) Hurston *Their Eyes* 53 **csFL** [Black], Don't you change too many words wid me dis mawnin', Janie, do Ah'll take and change ends wid yuh! *Ibid* 100, You got to have a subjick tuh talk from, do yuh can't talk. *Ibid* 193, Yuh can't live on de muck 'thout yuh take uh bath every day—Do dat muck'll itch yuh lak ants. *Ibid* 209, Ah never dreamt so many different kins uh black folks could colleck in one place. Did Ah never woulda come. **1948** Hurston *Seraph* 29 **wFL** [Black], Git this spoon betwixt her teeth do she's liable to bite her tongue off. **1986** *DARE* File **eNC** (as of c1915–30), I remember hearing White people, speakers with moderate education, saying things like "Shut the door tight, do it'll blow open before morning," and "Leave the note in the middle of the table, do she won't see it."

5 *done:* used as perfect aux in past, present, and future perfect. [Perh **do** v **B5**] **chiefly Sth, S Midl** Note: In contexts where either a perfect or the simple past tense is possible, some quots may illustrate the adverbial use of *done* rather than its use as the perfect aux; cf **done** adv.

1827 (1939) Sherwood *Gaz. GA* 139, *Done said it,* for has said it. *Done did it,* for has performed, or done it. **1872** Schele de Vere *Americanisms* 598, But the main peculiarity of the word [=*do*] is its constant addition to every other verb used in the past tense, not only by the negroes of the South universally, but also by all but the best-educated whites. . . "He done gone long ago." . . 'He done come down early.' **1884** *Anglia* 7.249 **Sth,** The Negro perfect is most commonly formed by the auxiliary *done* (from *do*) inserted between the pronoun and the past participle; I *done* gone, he *done* gimme sump'n, &c. *Have* is also used, though in pure Negro, not so prevailingly as *done.* **1887** *Scribner's Mag.* 2.475/1 **AR,** She done hilt [=held] Bulah en her arms ever sence she dressed of her. **1888** Jones *Negro Myths* 2 **GA coast,** Wen eh tink Buh Alligatur done gone tersleep. **1906** *DN* 3.117 **sIN,** "I done gone to dinner." . . "I done gone went to town." **1937** *Hall Coll.* **eTN,** I already done seed three [=trout]. **1942** Faulkner *Go Down* 28 **MS,** I either got to give a nigger away, or risk buying one that you done already admitted you cant keep at home. **1953** Brewer *Word Brazos* 4 **eTX** [Black], Bless de Lawd! Mah prayers done been answered. **1954** *Harder Coll.* **cwTN,** "I done done it." Also "I done went and done it." **1963** Wright *Lawd Today* 15 **Chicago IL** [Black], You just done made up your mind that you ain't going to be no good to me. **1965–70** *DARE* (Qu. K3a, *When a cow stops giving milk, you say she* ———) Inf **SC**52, Done dried up; (Qu. K11, *When a cow has a calf, you say she* ———) Inf **SC**30, Done freshened; (Qu. N8, . . *"He* ——— *me how to drive."*) Inf **TX**16, Done taught; (Qu. U39, . . *"During the depression he* ———.*"*) Inf **TX**106, Done went broke; (Qu. X55b, . . *Breaking wind*) Inf **LA**8, He done fizzled; (Qu. AA13, *When two people who . . were engaged, stop going together . . ,"I guess they* ———.*"*) Inf **LA**8, Done quit; **SC**26, Done bust up; (Qu. AA15b, . . *Getting married . . "He* ———.*"*) Inf **VA**35, Done gone and broke his neck; (Qu. AA27, . . *Menstruation*) Inf **TN**46, Dam done broke; (Qu. BB54, . . *"He's* ———.*"*) Inf **SC**10, He done give up; **KY**19, They done give him up; (Qu. DD11, . . *"I hear he* ———.*"*) Inf **LA**6, Done quit; (Qu. DD15) Inf **VA**24, Done got out; (Qu. GG22a) Inf **LA**37, You done got me riled up; (Qu. II22) Inf **LA**3, Better look out now, you done gone fur enough; (Qu. JJ30a, . . *"I* ———.*"*) Infs **CA**21, **PA**230, Done forgot (it); (Qu. JJ30b, . . *"It* ———.*"*) Inf **MO**8, Done messed my head up; (Qu. KK43, . . *"We* ———.*"*) Inf **SC**26, Done done the worst part; (Qu. OO45a, . . *"He thought nobody was looking but I* ——— *[him hide it]."*) Inf **OK**52, Done seen. **1966–70** *DARE* Tape **GA**1, That scent [of a skunk] done gone all in their nose and they couldn't do any tracking; **LA**12, Just done got too old to get 'bout on my own; **SC**15, After he done shot the gator; **SC**17, You done got your color and all, all you're doing is drying your [tobacco] stem out; **SC**26, But I done come this far and I ain't 'bout to turn back; **VA**38, After the moon maybe done fulled. **1977** Smitherman *Talkin* 24, When used in combination with another verb, *done* usually indicates only recently completed action. . . It is correct Black English to say *I done finish my work today,* but it is *not* correct . . to say *I done finish my work yesterday.* *Ibid* 25, Here's how Black English speakers render this future perfect. . . *I be done finish before anyone arrive.* **1980** Folb *Runnin' Down* 22 **Los Angeles CA** [Black], I done had bad luck *all* my life in d' family way.

6 *done and:* followed by past ppl or adj in a perfect v phr emphasizing completion of an action or achievement of a state. **esp S Midl** Cf *gone and* (as in *Now you've gone and said it*)

1918 *DN* 5.20 **cNC,** *Done and gone.* "He has done and gone." **1946** *PADS* 6.12 **swVA, eNC,** *Done and.* . . Already. "He's done and done it." . . Common among uneducated. **1955** Roberts *S. from Hell-fer-Sartin* 100 **seKY,** When he got 'em rolled out in the river they wa'n't no coming back because they's done and dead. **1968** *DARE* Tape **AR**43, [Immediately after singing a song, Inf said:] I've done and sang. **1976** Garber *Mountain-ese* 23 **sAppalachians,** Charlie needed some help but he's done 'n did it all hisself.

7 used in place of aux *be.* [Perh influenced by Gullah **duh** v] Cf **be** v **B3d,** and *DJE do* v[2] 1

1949 Turner *Africanisms* 279 **seSC** [Gullah], I don't afraid. [=I wasn't afraid.] **1966** *DARE* Tape **SC**10 [Gullah], I didn't ['dɪdn̩] use to it. [=I wasn't used to it.]

D Senses.

1 To cheat, swindle, take advantage of (someone). [*OED do* v. B. 11. f 1641 →]

1894 *Century Illustr. Mag.* 47.706/2 **NYC,** He is hated by all the beggars above him, and they "do" him every chance they get. **1909** *DN* 3.395 **nwAR,** *Do.* . . To swindle. "What's Henry doing now?" "Everyone he can." **1958** *VT Hist.* new ser 26.272, Mean enough to do his own granny. **1965–70** *DARE* (Qu. HH22c, *Talking about a very mean person, . . "He's mean enough to* ———.*"*) Inf **DC**1, Do anybody; (Qu. II33, *To get an advantage over somebody by tricky means: "I don't trust him, he's always trying to* ———.*"*) Infs **PA**97, **VA**26, Do you; **PA**55, **SC**39, Do somebody (*or* the other fellow). **1980** Folb *Runnin' Down* 67 **Los Angeles CA** [Black], Ain't but two kinda people in d' world here—dem dat do you and dem dat don't.

2 To treat, behave toward (someone)—freq in phr *do one that way* and varr, indicating unfair or harmful treatment. **Sth, S Midl**

1891 (1900) French *Otto* 163 **AR,** She do dem chil'en good as a mudder. **1907** Wright *Shepherd* 285 **Ozarks,** Bring your logs over to Fall Creek when you get ready to build, Lou; we'll sure do you right. **1910** *DN* 3.456 **seKY,** *Do.* . . To treat badly, "It wasn't fair for you to do me like that." **1928** Peterkin *Scarlet Sister Mary* 93 **seSC,** Mary wept quietly for she could think of no words to tell July how hurt she was, how utterly grieved at the way he was doing her now. *Ibid* 300 [Gullah], You must be forgot how July done me, Auntie; how July suffered me. **1940** Stuart *Trees of Heaven* 143 **neKY,** The land will do Subrinea like it has done Ma. It will break Subrinea. **1944** *PADS* 2.8 **Sth,** *Do.* . . To treat; ill-treat, but without general slang notion of cheating. . . "I think it's awful for you to do me that way." . . General, up to high popular use. **1954** *Harder Coll.* **cwTN,** Don't do me that way again. **1960** Lee *Mockingbird* 211 **sAL,** That old Mr. Gilmer doin' him thataway, talking so hateful to him. **1966–68** *DARE* Tape **AL**14, Mother would do her children the same way; **IN**21, Fever don't do me that way; **IN**36, He [=a fish] done him [=a fisherman] that way I don't know how many times; **TX**35, I think that fellow was real mean to do the old colored fellow thataway.

3 To provide for a household; to do chores.

1938 Rawlings *Yearling* 176 **nFL,** With only Penny to do, we ain't got the rations plentiful like you Folks. **1956** McAtee *Some Dialect NC* 12, *Do.* . . Perform housework. "She helped me to do." *Now Colloq.*

4 in var euphem phrr referring to defecation or urination; see quots. Cf **do** n[1] **4**

1899 (1912) Green *VA Folk-Speech* 245, Do a *job,* to go to stool. **1938** Goldberg *Wonder* 108, The child . . never defecates or urinates; he . . does his 'duty'. **1942** Berrey–Van den Bark *Amer. Slang* 124.4, *Defecate* . . do one's business. **1942** McAtee *Dial. Grant Co. IN Suppl. 1* 4, *Do a job, do one's business* . . defecate. **1954** *Harder Coll.* **cwTN,** *Do (one's) do* . . evacuate one's bowels. **1960** Carpenter *Tales Manchaca* 170 **cTX** (as of 1915), Tommie was forced to "do his business" where he lay. . . The orderlies scurried to hang sheets dipped in disinfectant in front of the doors.

5 in phr *do one for a joke:* To play a joke on one.

1958 Blasingame *Dakota Cowboy* 146, It was well to be alert if you did Bill for a joke, for the one he would return was certain to be plenty miserable.

do n[1]

1 See quot. [*OED do* sb.[1] 1 →1708]

1872 Schele de Vere *Americanisms* 598, *Do,* as a noun, flourishes in America as well as in England, and even enjoys a far more extended usefulness here. "There is a *do* for you," means, there is noise and confusion enough for you.

2 A party or social affair. Cf **doing 2**

1952 *Holiday* Jan 42/1 **seFL,** I go to the Washington's Birthday dinner dance and a few of the main *do's* just to put in an appearance. **1967–69** *DARE* (Qu. DD34, *A party at which there is considerable drinking*) Inf MI67, Do; (Qu. FF9, *A Christmas gathering . . "Are you going to the* ———*?"*) Inf **MI**67, Do; **IN**54, Big do. **1968** Kellner *Aunt Serena* 100 **cIN** (as of c1920), They had a big Do at the church Sunday, two gospel singers and a temperance preacher. **1971** Roberts *Third Ear* np [Black], *Do* . . a party or social affair; e.g. Are you going to the do tonight?

3 See quot 1977. *among Black speakers* Cf **conk** n[3] **1, process**

1971 Roberts *Third Ear* np [Black], *Do* . . slick, processed hair. **1972** Claerbaut *Black Jargon* 62, *Do.* . . a processed hairstyle. See also *mop, process.* **1977** Smitherman *Talkin* 65 [Black], A *do,* also called *process,* is a Black Semantic term referring to the black male's artificially straightened hair, once praised but now damned. . . They used the method of straightening with a basic mixture of lye and hair grease.

4 also *doos, dooze;* hypocoristic *do(o)-do(o), doody:* Excrement, also fig. [**do** v **D4;** *doody* may be infl by *duty* in phr *do one's duty*]

1938 Daniels *Southerner* 5, The leaves of the magnolia made excellent sandals to protect bare feet from the ubiquitous unpleasantness of chicken doos. **1970** [see **doo-doo** v]. **1983** *Lutz Coll.* **NJ,** As a child I never heard the expression "BM" for fecal matter; though mother was a trained nurse and dad a scientist, the family's word was *dooze.* I rather think it was mother's word, from her Philadelphia-English background. **1983** Heath *Ways with Words* 163 **sNC,** Here Danny [=a child] . . used a taboo word, *do-do.* . . he had been playing outside . . and a bird had flown over, leaving droppings on his jacket. **1986** Chapman *New Dict.*

Amer. Slang 106/1, *Do. . .* Excrement, feces: *I stepped in doggy-do. Ibid* 109/2, *Doo-doo. . .* Excrement. **1986** *DARE* File **cwCA, nUT, ceWI,** As children, we called dog excrement *dog do.* **1988** *Capital Times* (Madison WI) 7 Nov 12/3, [Mike Royko column:] Read my lips. I will bet you $5,000 that George Bush is feeding us a line of doo-doo, to use one of his favorite macho words. *Ibid* 12/5, Read my lips: That is deep doo-doo you are talking.

5 in phr *do one's do:*

a To do all that can possibly be done or that could be expected; to fulfill an intended purpose. [*OED* (at *do* sb.[1] 2) 1650 →; "now *rare* or *arch.*"] **chiefly Sth, S Midl**

1917 *DN* 4.411 **wNC,** *Do (one's) do. . .* "The fall of the year is when sweet-potatoes does their do." **1927** *AmSp* 2.352 **WV,** *Do one's do . .* to have done all that one can. "He did his do before the harvest was gathered." Or, "The crops will have to do their do before frost comes." **1942** Berrey–Van den Bark *Amer. Slang* 243.5, *Do what one has to do. . .* Do one's do. **1954** *Harder Coll.* **cwTN,** *Do (one's) do . .* do the best one can. **1966–68** *DARE* (Qu. X47, . . *Ways . . of saying, "I'm very tired, at the end of my strength."*) Inf **TX**36, About done my do; (Qu. KK20a, *Something that looks as if it might collapse any minute: "That old shed is certainly _______."*) Inf **MS**71, Done its do; (Qu. KK20b, . . *"Our old washing machine is _______."*) Infs **FL**6, 35, **KY**33, **SC**39, **VA**5, (Has) done its do.

b See **do v D4.**

do' n[2] See **door**

do' adv, conj See **though**

do about v phr

=**do around;** see quot 1908.

1908 *DN* 3.305 **eAL, wGA,** *Do about. . .* To bestir one-self, get busy, hurry. "Do about, boys, and let's get this job done." **1956** McAtee *Some Dialect NC* 12, *Do about. . .* Engage in earnestly; keep busy. **c1960** *Wilson Coll.* **csKY,** *Do about. . .* Keep busy. **1965** Will *Okeechobee Boats* 47 **FL,** He begun to do about and promote his new town of La Belle. *Ibid* 54, Back in them days when Hamilton Disston was doing about in Kissimmee, bringin' in settlers and making business for the steamboats, there was blamed little happenin' here.

do a flip-flop See **flip-flop 3**

doah See **door**

do a hook See **hook, shoot a**

doaley See **doley**

doamajig See **doojigger**

doan' See **do v A2**

do around v phr Also *do round* **Sth, S Midl**

To busy oneself; to bustle about; see quots 1905, 1936.

1905 *DN* 3.77 **nwAR,** *Do around. . .* To do something, be occupied with work of some kind. 'They're kinder doin' around over there.' **1936** *AmSp* 11.368 **nLA,** *Do around.* To have a good time; to mingle with others; to go from place to place. **1937** (1977) Hurston *Their Eyes* 72 **csFL** [Black], Tell yo' womenfolks tuh do 'round 'bout some pies and cakes and sweet p'tater pone. **1942** Hurston *Dust Tracks* 130 **nFL** [Black], Den I has to scuffle up dem stairs and do round, cause effen I didn't, dis here place would be like a hawg-pen. **1949** Guthrie *Way West* 325 **MO,** "I'm not tired. We'll need more water." "You will be if you do around all day." **1968** *DARE* (Qu. A19, . . *Ways of saying "I'll have to hurry"*) Inf **GA**30, I've got to do around there. **1970** *DARE* Tape **NC**86, He still comes afternoons and does aroun'.

do a thing to, not to v phr Also *not to do a thing with*

To punish severely—used ironically in threats.

1914 *DN* 4.105 **KS,** *Do a thing to. . .* Used ironically with a negative to denote decisively defeating or demolishing. "The Aggies won't do a thing to the Tigers." **1923** *DN* 5.205 **swMO,** *Do a thing. . .* Ordinarily used in the negative and meaning severe punishment. "Don't call me a liar er I won't do a thing to you." **1942** McAtee *Dial. Grant Co. IN* 23 (as of 1890s), *Do a thing to . .* in negative espressions meant do a plenty to, punish severely, injure: "Lemme ketch you at that agin and I won't _______ you". **1956** McAtee *Some Dialect NC* 12. **c1960** *Wilson Coll.* **csKY,** *Do a thing. . .* Understatement for *do a-plenty:* "If you don't let me alone, I won't do a thing with you."

doaty See **doty**

dob n[1] [Cf **gob** n[1] **2,** *EDD dob* sb.[1] "A small piece of anything; a lump, 'dollop' "]

1967 *DARE* (Qu. LL8a, *A large amount or number: more than enough—for example, of time: "He's got _______ of time."*) Inf **NY**24, Dobs ['dɑbz].

dob n[2] Also *dob-taw* [*EDD dob-taw* (at *dob* v.[1] 2 "To throw stones, &c., at a mark") "A large marble, a 'lobber' "] Cf **dab** n[2], **dobber** n[2], **dobe 5, dub** n[2]

A playing marble; see quots.

[**1899** in 1955 *PADS* 23.16 **cEngland,** As boys we used to play a game of marbles here known as 'dob in the ring,' which consisted of starting from a certain point known as 'taw' and endeavouring to knock out with a big 'dob' as many marbles as possible.] **1955** *PADS* 23.16 **cwTN,** *Dob. . .* Also dobber. A large marble. *Ibid, Dob-taw. . .* A large marble. **1967** *DARE* (Qu. EE6c, *Cheap marbles*) Inf **OR**3, Mud dobs—baked mud marbles.

dob n[3] See **dod n 1**

dob v[1] See **dub** v[2]

doba See **dobe**

dobabe, dobaby See **dough baby**

dobb See **dub** v[2]

dobber n[1] [Prob *EDD dobber* sb. 3 "The float of an angler's fishing line"; but cf Du *dobber* < dobberen to bob up and down]

1 also *dobbler:* A float on a fishing line; a bobber. **chiefly NY, NJ** *arch*

1809 W. Irving *Knickerb.* II.v. (1849) 113 *(OED),* He floated on the waves . . like an angler's dobber. **1844** *Knickerbocker* 23.72 **NY,** Sit all on a rock watching your float, or cork, or *dobber,* as the Dutch boys call it, dance merrily over the waves. **1872** Schele de Vere *Americanisms* 339, The *dobber,* . . the float of the [fishing] line, is peculiar to New York. **1889** Mellick *Story Old Farm* 5 **NJ,** Again we are boys, with cork dobbers, buckshot sinkers and hickory poles, angling in the pond above for the slippery catfish. **1889** (1971) Farmer *Americanisms* 205, *Dobbler.*—The float attached to a fishing-line. New York. **1984** Wilder *You All Spoken Here* 196 **Sth,** Dobber: A float on a fishing line. **1986** *DARE* File **NY** (as of 1950s-60s), At home, around Catskill, we always went fishing with a worm and a dobber.

2 Transf: see quot.

1970 *DARE* (Qu. H27, . . *Joking names for doughnuts*) Inf **CA**205, Dobbers.

dobber n[2] [*EDD dobber* sb. 2 "A large, heavy taw or marble"] Cf **dob** n[2]

1934 (1947) O'Hara *Appointment* 186, There was marbles, and there was a game of marbles called Dobbers, played with marbles the size of lemons. You played it in the gutter on the way home from school, throwing your Dobber at the other fellow's and he would throw his at yours. **1955** [see **dob** n[2]]. **1967–70** *DARE* (Qu. EE6c, *Cheap marbles*) Inf **OR**3, Mud dobbers—baked mud marbles; (Qu. EE6d, *Special marbles*) Inf **PA**245, Dobbers—steel, 2½" in diameter, thrown at marbles.

dobber n[3] See **dauber**

dobbey, dobbie See **dobe**

dobbich See **doppich**

dobbin in the ring See **dob in the ring**

dobble v [Var of *dabble*] Cf **dabble** v

1899 (1912) Green *VA Folk-Speech* 150, *Dobble. . .* Dabble. "To dobble in the mud," as children.

dobbler See **dobber** n[1] **1**

dobby See **dobe**

dobbyhorse n [*EDD dobby-horse* 2 "*pl.* The wooden horses or roundabouts at fairs," 1879 →; cf *hobbyhorse*]

1969 *DARE* File **RI,** A homemade merry-go-round used in Bristol fifty years ago was called a dobbyhorse.

dobchick See **dabchick**

dobe n, also attrib Also sp *dobie, doby;* pronc-spp *doba, dobbey, dobbie, dobby* [Aphet forms of **adobe**] **chiefly West, esp SW**

1 =**adobe 1;** see quot 1971.

1834 in 1934 Frear *Lowell & Abigail* 95 **MA,** Saturday, have laid dobes all day—some three or four tiers all round the house. **1838** in 1936 Hulbert *Marcus Whitman* 6.294 **OR,** There being no stone near I had walled the cellar with dobies the same as the walls of the house. **1838** Parker *Jrl. Rocky Mts.* 347, The buildings [in Honolulu] generally are in the native style, thatched; many are built with *doba* walls after the spanish manner. **1842** J. Williams *Tour to Oregon* (1921) 84 (*OEDS* at *dobie*), Some of them build their houses with what they call 'dobbeys', made of mud, in the shape of brick. **1845** in 1928 Clyman *James Clyman Amer. Frontiersman* 168 **nCA, sOR,** A strong doba or mud walled fort. **1854** in 1940 MT Hist. Soc. *Contrib.* 10.2, Men commenced Dobbie making. **1872** Twain *Roughing It* 44 **csNE,** The station buildings were long, low huts, made of sun-dried, mud-colored bricks, laid up without mortar (*adobes,* the Spaniards call these bricks, and Americans shorten it to *'dobies*). **1885** *Outing* 7.52/1, Half sand and the other half 'doby' mud. **1935** Sandoz *Jules* 55 **wNE** (as of 1880–1930), Jules looked back to Fort Robinson . . a tiny smudge of log and dobe buildings along the foot of the far bluffs. **1966–68** *DARE* Tape **NM**8, In a brick-making frame there are three holes to put the dobies in. . . They would empty it on the ground and make long layers of dobies; **UT**8, This house is built of dobe; **TX**24, Dobe house; **TX**71, It's just an old dobe building. **1971** Bright *Word Geog. CA & NV* 149 **s,cCA, s,cNV,** *Adobes* /earth blocks used in building; mixed with straw?/ . . *(a)dobe bricks . . dobe* 16% [of 300 informants]. *Ibid* 150, Sun-dried clay for building . . *dobe* 34% [of 300 informants].

2 =adobe 2.

1865 in 1930 *Annals WY* 7.380, Julesburg. . . This magnificent city has one log house and two "dobies." **1879** *Chicago Tribune* (IL) 7 Mar 9/6 **KS,** Though you may curl your lip at the humble squatter's "dobby,"—to-morrow you may be forced to regard with more respectful consideration this little mud hut as the birthplace of a leader of men. **1892** *DN* 1.243 **TX,** The forms *doby, dobies* are found in the Galveston *News,* April 19, 1892 with the meaning of *adobe* house(s). **1940** Fergusson *Our Southwest* 353, Then follow the caprock till you pass a couple of Texas gates and one cattle-guard. There's a doby there. **1981** *KS Qrly.* 13.2.66, *Dobe/adobe . .* building made of local adobe bricks.

3 =adobe 4. SW, Pacific See Map

1893 *Outing* July 309/1 **CA,** "Don't hurry, young man; it's raining, and you can't ride your horse in the doby." . . The road here was of a sandy nature, and was excellent for a few miles; then came a miserable stretch of "doby" into the town of Marysville. **1965–70** *DARE* (Qu. C31, . . *Heavy, sticky soil*) 16 Infs, **SW, Pacific,** Dobe; **OR**5, Dobe land. **1967–69** *DARE* Tape **CA**136, It's just solid cinder, and then all around it will be dobe land and kind of a glacier rocks around water rolled rocks or glacier; **TX**5, Clay land, or dobe land, as we call it.

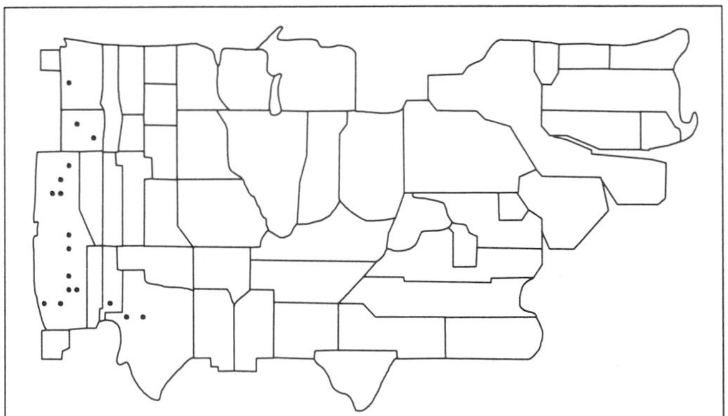

•dobe 3 + var (Qu. C31)

4 freq *dob(i)e dollar:* A Mexican silver dollar or peso. Cf **adobe dollar**

1906 Adams *Cattle Brands* 154 *(DA),* Uncle Sam's strong-box yielded up over a thousand dobes. **1910** *Sat. Eve. Post* 8 Oct 4/3, They said I had to pay five hundred dobie dollars before I went ahead with the work. **1940** Writers' Program *Guide AZ* 438, Two cowpunchers, embarking on careers in crime, placed dynamite on the messenger's strongbox and weighted it down with sacks of 'dobe dollars (Mexican pesos) which they found in the express car. **1940** Writers' Program *Guide NM* 112, *'Dobe Dollars* Mexican dollars *(pesos).* **1965** *DARE* FW Addit **NM**12, 'Dobe dollars—Mexican dollars. **1968** Adams *Western Words* 4, *Adobe.* . . The Mexican silver dollar is sometimes spoken of as a *'dobe* because the cowman holds it to be of little value. **1977** Watts *Dict. Old West* 4, *Adobe.* . . Anything inferior: a Mexican dollar was called a *'dobe dollar, 'dobie dollar* or simply a *'dobie.*

5 A marble made from baked clay. **West, esp CA** Cf **agate 3, dob** n^2, **dough baby, doggie 1**

1921 *DN* 5.109 **CA,** *Dobie, doby.* . . Clay marble. Originally probably a construction of 'an adobe' or 'the adobe.' **1932** Bentley *Spanish Terms* 87 **SW,** Marbles made of clay and painted various colors are known among American boys as *dobies.* **1965–70** *DARE* (Qu. EE6c, *Cheap marbles*) Infs **CA**9, 15, 102, 158, 165, 169, **TX**5, **UT**3, Dobies; **CA**166, Dobies—from adobe clay; **MT**3, Dobies—baked clay; **UT**7, Dobbies; (Qu. EE6d, *Special marbles*) Inf **NV**3, Dobies—adobe clay. **1969** O'Connor *Horse & Buggy West* 84 **cAZ,** Ordinary players like me used cheap marbles of baked clay with glazed surfaces. Those we called "dobies," probably because they were of clay—"adobe." **1971** Bright *Word Geog. CA & NV* 205, *Marbles . . dobies* 18% [of 300 informants] S[cattered].

6 =dogie 1; transf: a small child.

1897 Hough *Cowboy* 137 **West,** A "dogy" or "dobe" yearling (a scrubby calf that has not wintered well). **1922** Rollins *Cowboy* 217 **West,** This . . provoked much discussion of stock that "had not wintered well," and of . . "dobes," these last being calves . . that were still scrubby and anaemic. **1950** *PADS* 14.75 **FL,** *Dobie, dogie.* . . A motherless calf. **1970** *DARE* (Qu. Z12, *A small child*) Inf **TX**98, Dobe [dobi].

7 See quots.

1942 Berrey–Van den Bark *Amer. Slang* 111.10, *Cigar or cigarette stub.* . . Dobe. **1968** *DARE* (Qu. DD6a, . . *Nicknames for cigars*) Inf **MD**31, Dobe ['dobi].

dobe blasting n Also *dobie shooting* **[dobe 3]**

See quot 1940–41.

1940–41 Cassidy *WI Atlas* **neWI,** *Dobe blasting,* according to a sixty-year-old man in the quarry business, is blasting a rock or chunk of stone by placing dynamite sticks on top and covering them with mud or "doby" instead of drilling a hole to put the dynamite in. **1964** Will *Hist. Okeechobee* 285 **FL,** After he had used enormous quantities of dynamite in "dobie shooting," and without even trying to drill, Barr had to give up the [dredging] job.

dobe dollar See **dobe 4**

dobiddie See **doobob**

dobie See **dobe**

dobie dollar See **dobe 4**

dobie shooting See **dobe blasting**

dobinnie See **doobob**

dob in the ring n Also *dobbin in the ring* [Cf **dob** n^2, *EDD dab at the hole* "A game of marbles"] Cf **dog in the ring**

A marble game; see quots 1899 and 1968.

[**1899** [see **dob** n^2].] **1955** *PADS* 23.16 **cwTN,** *Dob in the ring.* . . A marble game. **1965–70** *DARE* (Qu. EE7, . . *Marble games*) 10 Infs, **scattered,** Dob in the ring. **1968** *DARE* Tape **IA**37, The game "dobbin'-in-the-ring" has four or five players . . up to a dozen. You draw a circle about a foot acrost, . . stand back around ten feet. You couldn't shoot for it, you had to toss em. If your marble went out of the ring . . you dropped out. . . The last player won all the marbles.

dobob, dobobbis, dobobble, dobobbus, dobobby See **doobob**

‡dob o' goody n

1967 *DARE* (Qu. AA3, . . *Affectionate names for a sweetheart*) Inf **OR**15, Dob o' goody.

do brown See **do up brown**

dobsonfly n Also *dobson*

A large insect *(Corydalus cornutus)* or its larva, the **hellgrammite 1.**

1884 Kingsley *Std. Nat. Hist.* 2.156 **Pacific,** They [=*Corydalus cornutus*] are called by fishermen "crawlers," "dobsons," and sometimes "hellgrammites." **1917** Kephart *Camping & Woodcraft* 2.411, One of the best natural baits for bass, when the water is clear, is that fierce-looking creature called hellgrammite, dobson, or grampus. **1931–33** *LANE Worksheets* **ncCT,** Dobson . . Hellgramite. **1966–68** *DARE* (Qu. R4, *A large winged insect that hatches in summer in great numbers around lakes or rivers, crowds around lights, lives only a day or so, and is good fish bait*) Infs **OH**82, **PA**1, Dobsonfly; (Qu. P13, . . *Other ways of* *fishing . . besides the ordinary hook and line*) Inf **NY**71, Dobson—kind of nymph. **1968** *DARE* FW Addit **neNY,** Dobson = larva or nymph found under rocks, used for fish bait, especially for bass. **1982** Sternberg *Fishing* 85, Adult dobsonflies are large; some types have a wingspread exceeding 5 inches. Their bodies may be black, brown or orange, and their wings are transparent. Lights often draw them far from water.

dob-taw See **dob** n[2]

doby n See **dobe**

doby adj [**dobe 3**]

1896 *DN* 1.415 **cnTX,** *Doby:* sticky (of mud). "The Ft. Worth streets are doby."

doc n [Abbr for *doctor*]

1 A dentist. **chiefly PA, NY** See Map Note: In ref to a physician, the term *doc* is widespread.

1965–70 *DARE* (Qu. BB52, . . *Joking words . . for a dentist*) 17 Infs, **chiefly wPA, seNY,** Doc.

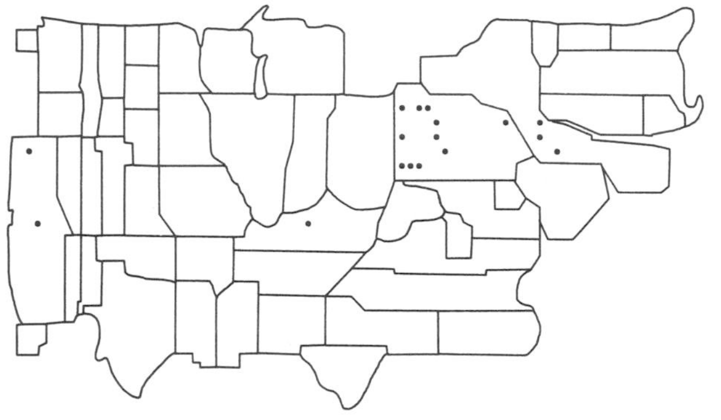

•doc 1 (Qu. BB52)

2 An athletic coach—usu used as a title or nickname. *old-fash*

1909 in 1914 *DN* 4.119, [Univ of Nebraska yearbook caption:] 'Doc' Clapp tries to run a shenanigan on the Athletic Board. **1915** *DN* 4.236 **neOH,** *Doc* . . 'professor of physical training.' **1918** *DN* 5.24 **NW,** *Doc*. . . The physical director. Used very much like Prex. "I told doc." "The new doc." "Doc X." General in school communities. **1942** Berrey–Van den Bark *Amer. Slang* 826.5, Athletic coach. . . doc.

3 Used as a nickname or in direct address: see quots.

1940 Faulkner *Hamlet* 310 **MS,** Jody Varner came through the group, shouldering himself to the front of it. "Watch yourself, doc," a voice said from the rear. But it was already too late. The nearest animal rose on its hind legs . . and struck twice with its forefeet at Varner's face. **c1960** *Wilson Coll.* **csKY,** *Doc*. . . A common nickname, especially for some self-important person. **1960** Wentworth–Flexner *Slang, Doc 2.* An unknown fellow or guy; used in direct address. **1970** *DARE* (Qu. NN10a, *Expressions . . used when you meet somebody you know quite well*) Inf **DC**13, "What's up, doc?"—a man's expression. **1976** Brown *Gloss. Faulkner* 72, *Doc* . . abbreviation of *doctor,* familiar but implying some position of authority or dignity in the person addressed. A voice from the crowd can call Jody Varner this at Frenchman's Bend, but Jody would never address, say, Mink Snopes in this way.

docious adj, adv [Prob from *docity* by analogy with *audacious/audacity* etc] Cf **docity**

Docile, quiet, civil; quietly, submissively.

1853 Hammett *Stray Yankee in TX* 120 **TN,** I stood it all quite docious, tell the doctor talked of trying arsenic, and then I kicked. *Ibid* 123, I can hardly keep my tongue docious now to talk about it. **1858** Hammett *Piney Woods Tavern* 43 **TX,** We walked out quiet and docious, give a darkey a quarter to show us home, and marvelled off with our tails atween our legs. **1859** (1968) Bartlett *Americanisms* 123, *Docious.* A corruption of *docile,* as "a docious young man," "a docious horse."

docity n [Prob var, by syncope, of *docility; OED* 1682 →; "dial.,"] *old-fash* Cf **docious**

Ability to comprehend; tractability.

1816 Pickering *Vocab.* 81, *Docity,* (pronounced *dosity.*) A low word, used in some parts of the United States, to signify *quick comprehension.* It is used only in conversation, and generally with a negative, thus: He has no *docity.* **1836** (1838) Haliburton *Clockmaker* (1st ser) 243 **NEng,** She's all docity jist now, keep her so. **1872** Schele de Vere *Americanisms* 597, *Docious* and *docity* . . are substitutes for docile and docility, in daily use in the South; the latter generally qualified by a negative, as, he has no docity, in which sense it is not unknown in England also. **1955** Adams *Grandfather* 89 **NY** (as of 1830s), I could readily see that commerce was a matter on which the lady had no docity, and she frankly sought to enlist my services.

dock n[1] Cf **burdock 1, cuckold dock, dove dock, prairie dock, round dock, succory dock, velvet dock**

Std: a plant of the genus *Rumex.* Also called **sorrel, Indian tobacco.** For other names of var spp see **bitter dock, canaigre, curled dock, garden patience, horse dock, little vinegar plant, poison dock, red sorrel, sand dock, sheep sorrel, sorrel dock, sour dock, sour grass, sour greens, spinach dock, spring dock, white dock, wild begonia, wild hydrangea, wild sorrel, wood sorrel**

dock n[2] [*EDD dock* sb.[2] 3 "The solid . . part of an animal's tail. . . The nether end of the human body; of a felled tree"]

1 See quot.

1930 Shoemaker *1300 Words* 19 **cPA Mts** (as of c1900), *Dock*—The butt end of a felled tree; generally discarded.

2 also *dock(ed) horse, docked-tail, docktail (horse):* A bobtailed horse. **chiefly Nth, Midl, West** See Map

1965–70 *DARE* (Qu. K41, *A horse with its tail cut short*) 58 Infs, **scattered, but chiefly Nth, N Midl,** Dock; 37 Infs, **scattered, but chiefly Inland Nth, N Midl, West, TN,** Docktail; 33 Infs, **scattered, but chiefly Nth, N Midl,** Docked (horse); **CT**2, **PA**6, Dock horse; **CA**23, 97, Docked-tail; **LA**29, Docktail horse.

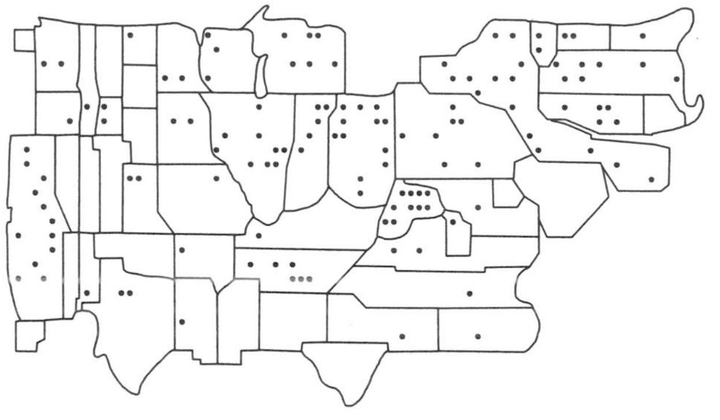

•dock n[2] 2 + varr (Qu. K41)

‡docked ppl adj [Prob from **dike** v]

Dressed up.

1968 *DARE* (Qu. W38, *When a man dresses himself up in his best clothes, you say he's* ______) Inf **VA**2, Docked.

docked horse, docked-tail, dock horse See **dock** n[2] **2**

dockmackie n Also sp *dockmakie*

A **viburnum** (here: *Viburnum acerifolium*). Also called **arrow-wood a, flowering maple 1, maple-leaved viburnum, possum haw, squashberry**

1822 Eaton *Botany* 510, Indians in that vicinity [=Columbia County NY] considered the external application of the leaves of the dockmackie as a sovereign remedy in every kind of inflammatory tumour. **1857** Gray *Manual of Botany* 168, *Maple-leaved Arrow-wood, Dock-mackie*. . . Rocky woods, common. May, June. **1901** Lounsberry *S. Wild Flowers* 479, Dockmakie . . makes quite a gay flutter of bloom with its many small perfect flowers. **1942** Van Dersal *Ornamental Amer. Shrubs* 111 *(DA),* Other names for it are dockmackie, arrowwood, squashberry and possumhaw. **1967** Borland *Hill Country* 160 **nwCT,** I do know that one of our native viburnums is known as dockmackie. **1976** Bruce *How to Grow Wildflowers* 132, Very different from the foregoing (and belonging to a different section of the genus) is Dock-mackie or Maple-leaved Viburnum, *V. acerifolium.*

dock on the rock See **duck on a rock**

dock swallow n

=**barn swallow 1.**

1968 *DARE* (Qu. Q20, . . *Kinds of swallows*) Inf **MI80**, Dock swallow —old-fashioned—same as barn [swallow].

docktail (horse) See **dock** n^2 **2**

doctor n

1 Orig among sailors, also among loggers: a cook.

1821 *MA Spy* (Worcester MA) 1 Aug 4/4 **PA**, The cook, at sea, is generally called doctor. **1859** (1968) Bartlett *Americanisms* 124, *Doctor.* The cook on board a ship; so called by seamen. **1895** *Std. Dict. Engl. Lang.* (Funk) 539/2, Doctor. . . The cook in a logging-camp. **1910** White *Rules of Game* 70 **WA**, "Where's the drive, doctor?" asked the lumberman. "This is the jam camp," replied the cook. **1916** Macy-Hussey *Nantucket Scrap Basket* 129, "Doctor, the"—the name by which the cook is always known at sea.

2 A practitioner of voodoo. Cf **hoodoo n 1b**

1931 *Jrl. Amer. Folkl.* 44.320, As in formal medicine, some of the doctors are general practitioners, and some are specialists. For instance, Dr. Grant makes court cases his specialty, while Dr Barnes specializes in restoring broken relations. **c1938** in 1970 Hyatt *Hoodoo* 1.54 **seMD**, There wus a lady, her husband left her, she wanted to bring him back. So she got ready an' she went to this *doctor.* So she ast [=asked] 'er, she said, "Could joo get my husband back?" She told 'er "Yes." **1946** Roberts *Lake Pontchartrain* 193 **LA**, An oddity was the rise to chief eminence of a voodoo queen who tolerated none but the most servile *mamalois*, and the relegating of the *papalois* to the lesser status of "doctors." **1970** Hyatt *Hoodoo* 1.165, Where to begin is the problem because *doctors* are many-sided persons—healer, witch doctor, ghost layer, seer, fortune-teller . . and just about anything wanted.

3 One who sells liquor. [In ref to medicinal uses of alcohol]

c1960 *Wilson Coll.* **csKY**, *Doctor Block.* . . Nickname for a bootlegging joint, at the Block House. Some drinker would complain of not feeling good and then add, "I guess I'll have to see Dr. Block." **1969** *DARE* (Qu. DD32, *A person who sells illegal liquor*) Inf **GA72**, Doctor. **1979** Lewis *How to Talk Yankee* [15], *Green Front* or *Doctor Green's.* State liquor store, so called because of the color of the exterior in former days. Also "state store" or "package store."

4 See **doctorfish.**

5 also *doctor's fly:* =**dragonfly.** Cf **snake doctor**

1965-70 *DARE* (Qu. R2) Inf **PA247**, Doctor; **AR42**, Doctor's fly.

doctor v

1 To receive medical treatment; to take medicine; hence vbl n *doctoring* medical treatment. **chiefly Sth, S Midl, NEng**

1854 Stephens *High Life in NY* 175, I raly feel as if I must doctor a leetle. **1880** *Harper's New Mth. Mag.* 687/1 **NEng**, Joe Adams's wife . . is a sister to her, and she's forever a-doctorin'. **1899** (1912) Green *VA Folk-Speech* 150, *Doctor.* . . To receive medical treatment; to take medicine. **1911** Wharton *Ethan Frome* 193 **MA**, Not as she's ever given up doctoring, and she's had sick spells right along. **1927** *AmSp* 2.352 **WV**, Mother has doctored with all of 'em, and is going to try the yarb doctor next. **1929** *AmSp* 5.17 **Ozarks**, *Doctor.* . . This word is used in a peculiar passive sense; it does not mean to treat, but rather to be treated; it is not the physician who *doctors,* but the patient. "I ben a-doctorin' 'ith ol' Doc Mollynix, but 'pears like he don't do me no good." **1954** *Harder Coll.* **cwTN**, [She's] doctored with all of 'em. **1975** Gould *ME Lingo* 74, *Doctor.* . . "He had it bad enough to doctor for it." **1976** Garber *Mountain-ese* 23 **sAppalachians**, I've been doctorin' fer a cold almost all winter. **1982** *DARE* File **NH**, They also say . . "I've been doctoring with him for 12 years," or "I've never doctored with her."

2 also with *up:* To treat (a person or ailment); to apply a medicinal remedy. **chiefly S Midl**

1937 *Hall Coll.* **eTN**, For fever [we] generally had a doctor. [But mostly] people doctored their own selfs. **1954** *Harder Coll.* **cwTN**, "I doctored him up with white linament." "She doctored up some 'n kep a-goin'." . . "Gi'me a box o' snuff 'n' I kin doctor up bettern a doctor." **1966-68** *DARE* Tape **FL36**, He [=a veterinarian] come and doctored him; **UT8**, They didn't know how to doctor for it [=a disease]. **1968** Haun *Hawk's Done Gone* 116 **eTN**, While he talked she watched the blood gush out of his upper lip. She got some devil's snuff and some spider web to doctor it. **1976** Wolfram-Christian *Appalachian Speech* 97, If I taken the cold, they just doctored it themselves the way they thought it sposeta been doctored.

3 with *on:* To treat with voodoo medicine.

c1938 in 1970 Hyatt *Hoodoo* 1.428 **seGA** [Black], Well, yo' pound dat [=skin of a chicken gizzard] up an' if yo' were *doctorin* on anybody dat had any kinda *poison* in 'em, yo' jes' pound it up an' put it in his medicine. *Ibid* 2.1190 **seGA**, Yo' take an' put him in dat room—yo' *doctoring* a man, yo' see, an' he's in dat condition.

4 To castrate or spay an animal. **NEast** *euphem*

1939 *LANE* Map 210 5 Infs, **wVT, seMA, wCT**, The map shows the verbs *castrate, sterilize, . . doctor,* applied to the castrating of male domestic animals. **1966-69** *DARE* (Qq. J3a,b, *To make a female dog* [or *cat*] *so that she can't breed, she must be* ______) Inf **MA40**, Doctored; (Qu. K70, *Words . . for castrating an animal*) Infs **ME12**, **NY68**, Doctor.

5 See quot.

1968 Adams *Western Words* 95, *Doctor.* To cut the knee tendon of a wild longhorn so that he can walk but cannot run.

doctor balsam n

1969 Sorden *Lumberjack Lingo* 34 **NEng, Gt Lakes**, *Doctor balsam*—The balsam pitch lumberjacks often used as a medicine for colds and sore throats or as a salve on cuts or cracks.

doctor bird n Cf **doctor Jesus**

Prob =**pileated woodpecker.**

1968 *DARE* Tape **GA25**, Then we have another bird here [=Okefenokee swamp] known as the doctor bird. He's the one with the real big bill.

doctorfish n Also *doctor*

A **surgeonfish** (here: *Acanthurus chirurgus*).

1883 *Nat. Museum Bul.* No. 27, 364 [sic *DAE*—quot not found], A fish of the genus *Anarrhichthys,* called the 'doctor-fish,' is only eaten by the medicine men [of the Mokah Indians]. **1884** Goode *Fisheries U.S.* 1.279, On the coast of Florida . . occur two species of this family, *Acanthurus coerulens* and *A. nigricans,* generally known as "Doctor-fish" or "Surgeon-fish." **1889** *Century Dict.* 1715, *Doctor-fish.* . . A fish of the genus *Acanthurus:* so called from the sharp and glassy, lancet-like, movable spines with which it is armed on each side of the tail. . . Also called *doctor, surgeon, surgeon-fish, barber-fish.* **1933** John G. Shedd Aquarium *Guide* 125, *Acanthurus hepatus.* . . Doctorfish. . . It is common on the south Atlantic coast as far north as the Carolinas.

doctor gate n

1968 Adams *Western Words* 95, *Doctor gate*—A gate in a corral, usually in a lane down which animals are driven and then "dodged" (separated) by swinging the gate back and forth to shunt them into various classifying pens.

Doctor Green's medicine n Also *Doctor Greenwade's medicine* Cf **peach tree tea**

See quots.

1905 *DN* 3.77 **nwAR**, *Doctor Green's medicine.* . . Punishment with a green stick. 'If you don't dry up, I'll give you a dose of Doctor Green's medicine.' **1986** *DARE* File **wNC** (as of c1918), I knew the term *Doctor Greenwade's medicine,* referring to the use of a slender limb of a tree to strike or whip a child as punishment.

doctor gum n [From its medicinal use; see quot 1884]

A **poisonwood** (here: *Metopium toxiferum*).

1884 Sargent *Forests of N. Amer.* 54, *Doctor Gum.* . . A resinous gum, emetic, purgative, and diuretic, is obtained from incisions made in the bark of this species [=*Metopium toxiferum*]. **1897** Sudworth *Arborescent Flora* 274, *Poisonwood. . . Common Names.* . . Doctor Gum. **1908** Britton *N. Amer. Trees* 612, *Poisonwood.* . . is also locally known as Doctor-gum and Coral sumac. **1933** Small *Manual SE Flora* 808, *M. toxiferum.* . . *Doctor-gum.* . . The sap is a powerful skin-poison.

doctoring See **doctor v 1**

Doctor Jesus n

=**pileated woodpecker.**

1950 *PADS* 14.43 **ceSC**, *Lawd-Gawd.* . . The pileated woodpecker. . . This bird is also known among the Negroes of the *Peedee* as *Doctor Jesus.*

Doctor Jesus, ready for adj phr

Fatally ill.

1966 *DARE* (Qu. BB54, *When a sick person is past hope of recovery, you'd say he's* . . ______) Inf **SC27**, Ready for Doctor Jesus.

doctor lady See **doctor woman**

doctor medicine n **sAppalachians**
See quots.
1917 *DN* 4.411 **wNC,** *Doctor medicine.* Differentiated from home remedies. **1927** *AmSp* 2.352 **WV,** If there had not been so much doctor medicine given to that baby, it would still be alive. **1952** Brown *NC Folkl.* 1.533 **wNC,** *Doctor-medicine.* . . Medicine prescribed or given by a doctor. **1976** Garber *Mountain-ese* 23 **sAppalachians,** I've been takin' doctor medicine since my herbs didn't help much.

doctor's club n Cf **Hercules' club 2**
A **prickly ash** (here: *Zanthoxylum coriaceum*).
1908 Britton *N. Amer. Trees* 571, *Doctor's Club—Xanthoxylum coriaceum.* . . is a spiny shrub or small tree growing in southern peninsular Florida and the adjacent Keys.

doctor's crop n
1981 *McDavid Coll.* **cnOK** (as of c1960), Bob Van Riper heard "doctor's crop" as meaning a "top crop" of cotton.

doctor's fly See **doctor n 5**

doctor shop n Cf *DJE, DBE*
A pharmacy or herb doctor's shop.
1923 Parsons *Folk-lore Sea Islands* 198 **csSC** [Gullah], A . . caul might be secured from "de docter shop."

doctor snake n
A **green snake** (here: *Opheodrys aestivus*).
1966 *DARE* (Qu. P25, . . *Kinds of snakes . . around here*) Inf **SC**26, Green snake = doctor snake.

doctors' row n
1968 *DARE* (Qu. II24, . . *Nicknames for the part of a town where the well-off people live*) Infs **PA**114, **UT**11, Doctors' row.

doctor stuff n *arch* Cf **doctor medicine**
Medicine.
1831 in 1948 Weingarten *Suppl. Notes* 26, The Huntonites were all sick, and they must take some doctor stuff. **1843** (1916) Hall *New Purchase* 68 **IN,** Here we kept "the doctor stuff," and also the skeleton of Red Fire, an Indian chief. **1889** Murfree *Despot* 223 **eTN,** The rest of 'em in the Cove had better not git sick soon; no mo' doctor-stuff whar that kem from.

Doctor Tinker's weed n
A **horse gentian** (here: *Triosteum perfoliatum*).
1892 (1974) Millspaugh *Amer. Med. Plants* 74, *Triosteum perfoliatum.* . . Com. Names. . . Dr. Tinker's Weed.

doctor up See **doctor v 2**

Doctor Walker n
Appar an edible green such as a plantain (*Plantago* spp).
1937 (1963) Hyatt *Kiverlid* 79 **KY,** Shad sot out with me yisterday to pick what all we could find. We picked wild mustard, . . polk, blue thistle, Doctor Walker, . . an' dandelion an' butter-weed . . I think maybe some creeces, too.

doctor woman n Also *doctor lady*
1 A woman skilled at voodoo, conjuration, or herbal medicine. [Cf **doctor n 2**]
c1938 in 1970 Hyatt *Hoodoo* 1.778 **New Orleans LA,** When you go there . . you say you want to see the *Doctor Lady.* When you get inside, this white girl will come to you and ask you if you want to see Madam Helen. . . Well, Madam Helen, she'll tell the girl to bring you in. . . She'll be in the room where the altar and all this mess be all round her. **1943** Weslager *DE Forgotten Folk* 166, Old Mary Morgan who used to live in Cheswold was a doctor woman. She's dead now. She could make a boil go away by powwowing over it. She would take a table fork and wave it over the boil, all the time powwowing so no one could understand. A few days later the boil would go away by itself.
2 A midwife. **Sth, S Midl** Cf **granny woman**
1966–68 *DARE* (Qu. AA30, *An older woman who comes in . . to help when a baby is going to be born*) Infs **NC**49, **SC**26, Doctor woman. **1972** Cooper *NC Mt. Folkl.* 91, *Doctor-woman*—a midwife or female herb doctor. **1986** Pederson *LAGS Concordance (Midwife)* 1 inf, **neLA,** Doctor woman. **1987** *DARE* File **nwMS,** Here are words . . that I collected in interviews with Black people in Marks . . back in the sixties: doctor lady—a midwife.

Doc Yak n [From the comic strip "Old Doc Yak" (syndicated 1912–1919, 1930–1935) by Sidney Smith]
1967–69 *DARE* (Qu. BB53a, . . *Joking names . . for a doctor*) Inf **TX**31, Doc Yak; (Qu. BB53b, . . *A doctor who is not very capable or doesn't have a very good reputation*) Inf **MI**110, Old Doc Yak.

dod n [Euphem for *God*] Cf **dad** n^2, **dag** n, **dog** n^1 **B7**
1 also *dob:* in var euphem v phrr: See quots.
1825 Neal *Brother Jonathan* 1.104 **CT,** Dod burn *his* hide! **1835** Longstreet *Ga. Scenes* 29 *(DAE),* His back's mighty bad off; but dod drot my soul if he's put it to daddy as bad as he thinks he has. **1842** *Amer. Pioneer* 1.347 **seOH,** "Dod rot'em," said the old hunter, "I would not let them have a bushel." **1866** Smith *Bill Arp* 49 **GA,** Confound 'em, dod rot 'em; I begin to believe our old devil is dead. **1869** Browne *Adventures* 40 **MO,** "Now git, dodrot ye!" was the climax of these uncontrollable bursts of wretchedness. *Ibid* 50 **MO,** He . . yelled at the mules with ungovernable fury, "You git, dodburn you!" **1883** Twain *Life on Missip.* (Boston) 226 **MO,** "Dod dern" was the nearest he ventured to the luxury of swearing. **1907** *DN* 3.243 **eME,** *Dod gum.* . . Mild form of *God damn.* **1908** *DN* 3.305 **eAL, wGA,** *Dob darn.* . . Mild imprecation. **1915** *DN* 4.182 **swVA,** *Dod drot.* . . A mild oath. **1941** Fisher *Illusion* 98 **ID,** But I can't shoot, Eilley, Dodgast it, I ain't never fired a gun in all my born days. **1942** (1960) Robertson *Red Hills* 52 **SC,** Why not tell it? Dod blast it, they've separated. **1967–68** *DARE* (Qu. NN8b, . . *Expressions of annoyance: "This jar won't come open, _______ it'"*) Inf **AR**47, Dod durn; (Qu. NN25a, *Weakened substitutes for 'damn' or 'damned': "_______ it all!"*) Inf **DE**3, Dod blame.
2 in var euphem passive and ppl adj phrr: See quots.
1835 Longstreet *Ga. Scenes* 231 *(DAE),* I'll be dod blamed if I do. *Ibid,* I'll be dod durned if Broadcloth don't give some of you the dry gripes if you stand too close thare. **1851** (1969) Burke *Polly Peablossom* 33 **GA,** Dod-drapped ef I don't bet four hundred and fifty-one dollars. **1853** Hammett *Stray Yankee in TX* 116, The Northern man will be *"gaul darned,"* and the Southron *"dod derned."* **1889** (1971) Farmer *Americanisms* 206, *Dodfetched.* . . *Dodrotted.* **1890** Harte *Waif* 92, That's your blamed dod-gasted luck, eh! *Ibid* 155, Mind that you ain't such a fool agin to let 'em make you tote their dod-blasted tools fur them! **1893** Frederic *Copperhead* 138 **nNY,** They ain't such dod-rotted cowards as you be! **1919** Kyne *Capt. Scraggs* 9 **CA,** The skipper didn't leave that dod-gasted whistle alone. **1967** *DARE* (Qu. NN25b, *Weakened substitutes for 'damn' or 'damned': "Well, I'll be _______."*) Inf **AR**47, Dod-darned.

dodab See **doodad 2**

dodabbus, dodack, dodad, dodaddle, dodaddy See **doodad 1**

dodder n
Std: a plant of the genus *Cuscuta.* Also called **angels' hair, beggarweed 2, choke 'em, coral vine 2, corn silk 2, devil's guts 1, goldthread 2, hairweed, hairy-bind, hell-bind, hellweed 1, love-in-a-tangle, love vine, robber vine, strangle vine, strangle-weed, tangle-gut, witches' shoelaces**

doddle v [Prob var of *dodder* to shake, move unsteadily; perh infl by *toddle*]
1 To shake or nod (as the head).
1938 Stuart in 1944 *ADD* **neKY,** Patting old Rodger's head as he doddles it up and down and tries to shake off the bridle. **1940** Stuart *Trees of Heaven* 216 **neKY,** Anse doddles his head as the lightning flashes. **1952** Giles *40 Acres* 202 **KY,** He swings his arms high and his head doddles on his neck.
2 To toddle; to saunter.
1899 (1912) Green *VA Folk-Speech* 150, *Doddle.* . . To toddle. **1940** (1978) Still *River of Earth* 138 **KY,** There I was, coming off the bench, me thinking you were abed, and beholt! You come doddling along the ridge.
3 See quot.
1975 Gould *ME Lingo* 75, *Doddle*—Probably from dawdle; but Mainers use it for stagger and reel. Also to fiddle around, tinker, . . and make waste motions.

doddly adj Also sp *doddley* **[doddle] S Midl**
See quots.
1953 Randolph *Down in Holler* 240 **Ozarks,** *Doddly.* . . Nervous, shaky, unsteady. "I'm so doddly this mornin', I couldn't pour cider out of a boot." **1954** *Harder Coll.* **cwTN,** *Doddly.* . . Tottering, old, and not very well. **c1960** *Wilson Coll.* **csKY,** *Doddly.* . . Shaky, unsteady. **1983** *MJLF* 9.37 **ceKY,** *Doddley* . . shakey, unsteady.

dodelheimer n Also *dodenheimer, dudelheimer, dudenheimer* [Cf **doodle** n[1] **6**]

=**doohickey 1.**

1931 *AmSp* 6.258 **KS, NE,** Indefinite names. . . Thingum . . thing-em-bob . . dudelheimer—dudenheimer. **1942** Berrey-Van den Bark *Amer. Slang* 75.4, *Contrivance; indefinite object; "gadget."* . . dodel-heimer, dodenheimer.

dodge v [*OED* 1680 →]

1 To avoid; to shun or evade. **chiefly Sth** See Map Note: The earlier sense "to evade (responsibility, commitment, etc) by pretext and subtlety" (*OED* 1573 →), is widespread.

1954 *Harder Coll.* **cwTN,** Let's dodge 'is town. **1965–70** *DARE* (Qu. Y51, . . *'To avoid' things or people—for example: "He's not your kind —you'd better _____ him."*) 12 Infs, **chiefly Sth,** Dodge; (Qu. AA12, *If a man loses interest in a girl and stops seeing her*) Inf **SC**3, Staying shy of her, dodging her; (Qu. II5b, *When you don't want to have anything to do with a certain person*) Inf **GA**30, I'd like to dodge him; (Qu. JJ6, *To stay away from school without an excuse*) Inf **MS**61, Dodge school. **1968** *DARE* Tape **GA**30, After he [=a bear cub] gets two years old she [=its mother] dodges 'im, gets away from 'im, leaves 'im.

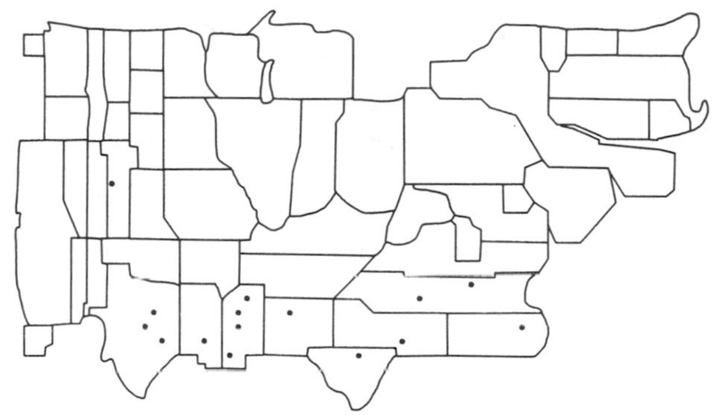

•dodge 1 + varr (Qq. Y51, AA12, II5b, JJ6)

2 also with *out:* =**cut** v **5.**

1920 Hunter *Trail Drivers TX* 297 (as of c1880), When fences became more common the calves were cut out through a cutting chute or "dodged out" so they could be counted. **1942** *AmSp* 17.74 **NE,** Calves that have been cut from a herd and counted are dodged out. **1968** [see **doctor gate**].

dodge around v phr

Of the wind: to suddenly change direction.

1970 *DARE* (Qu. B15, *When the wind suddenly begins to blow in a different direction, you say it _____*) Inf **TX**96, Dodged around.

dodge-ass n

=**spotted sandpiper.**

1945 McAtee *Nomina Abitera* 34, Spotted Sandpiper *(Actitis macularia)*—All of the names here . . have references to the constant tail-bobbing. . . dodge-ass, Portsmouth Island, North Carolina.

dodge bread n [**dodger** n[1] **1**]

=**corn dodger 1.**

1966 Dakin *Dial. Vocab. Ohio R. Valley* 2.316 **KY,** *Corn (bread) dodger* (occasionally *dodge bread* in Kentucky).

dodge, give one the v phr Cf **dodge 1**

To shun or avoid someone.

1967 *DARE* (Qu. II6, *If you meet somebody who used to be a friend, and he pretends not to know you: "When I met him on the street he _____."*) Inf **SC**39, Gave me the dodge.

dodge-post fence n

1968 Adams *Western Words* 95, *Dodge-post fence*—A wire fence built with posts set 6 feet apart, alternating first on one side of the wire and then the other.

dodger n[1] [Prob Scots *dadge* a **bannock,** perh infl by Scots *dodge* 'A pretty large cut of any kind of food' *(DSL)* or *dodgel* 'A large piece or lump' *(DSL)*]

1 also *dodger bread, ~ cake:* =**corn dodger 1. Sth, S Midl**

1831 Peck *Guide for Emigrants* 152 **KY, TN,** *Dodgers,* are masses [of cornmeal] like small loaves of bread, prepared in a similar manner [i.e., with water or milk], and baked in the spider or skillet. **1832** Trollope *Domestic Manners* (NY) 66 **OH,** They all console themselves . . by taking more tea, coffee, hot cake and custard, hoe cake, johnny cake, waffle cake, and dodger cake. **1851** (1852) Stowe *Uncle Tom's Cabin* 1.39 **KY,** Her corn-cake, in all its varieties of hoe-cake, dodgers, muffins, and other varieties . . ., was a sublime mystery to all less practised compounders. **1894** *Harper's New Mth. Mag.* 89.628/1 **WV,** His wife makes it into big rocklike 'dodgers' or pone-cakes with salt and water and 'no rising.' **1903** *DN* 2.311 **seMO,** *Dodger.* . . A loaf of corn bread, baked in a skillet. **1907** *DN* 3.230 **nwAR, seMO,** *Dodger.* **1908** *DN* 3.305 **eAL, wGA,** *Dodger.* **1940** Richter *Trees* 80 **OH** (as of c1800), She took down a gut of bear's oil to fry some dodgers for supper. **1949** Kurath *Word Geog.* fig 118 **WV, n,wVA, wNC,** *(Corn) Dodger* . . *Dodger,* a cake. **c1960** *Wilson Coll.* **csKY,** *Dodger.* . . Small loaf of cornbread made with hands; corn-dodger. **1965–70** *DARE* (Qu. H14, *Bread that's made with cornmeal*) Infs **KY**5, **SC**7, **TX**102, Dodgers; (Qu. H25, . . *Fried cornmeal*) Inf **TN**31, Dodger bread.

2 =**corn dodger 2. chiefly Mid Atl**

1860 Hundley *Social Relations S. States* 86 **KY,** Almost always the cook would make with water and corn-meal and a little salt, dough-balls, throw them into the pot, and boil them thoroughly with the rest [i.e., the vegetables and bacon]. These were called dodgers, from the motion giving [sic for *given*] them by the boiling water in the pot. **1949** Kurath *Word Geog.* fig 118 **DE, eMD, csVA, eNC, eSC,** *Dodger,* a dumpling. **1966** Dakin *Dial. Vocab. Ohio R. Valley* 2.318 **KY,** *Dodger* is also sometimes used in Kentucky as a name for a dumpling cooked with vegetables but this usage from the Carolina and Georgia coast is apparently not common.

‡3 See quot.

1966 *DARE* (Qu. H27, . . *Joking names for doughnuts*) Inf **MT**4, Dodgers.

dodger n[2]

1 See quot.

1968 *DARE* (Qu. R30, *What other kinds of beetles are known around here—for example, because of their odor or color or something else?*) Inf **LA**15, Dodger—a black beetle; when you touch him he changes ends and goes in the other direction. It sucks tender stalks.

2 A cottontail (here: *Sylvilagus floridanus*).

1966 *DARE* (Qu. P30, *Do you have wild rabbits around here? What kinds?*) Inf **MS**6, Cottontails, dodger, hillbillies, sailor [are the] same.

dodge time n

See quots.

1933 *AmSp* 8.1.48 **Ozarks,** *Dodge times.* . . Spare times, odd moments. *I jest work at this hyar basket-makin' in dodge times.* **1954** *Harder Coll.* **cwTN,** *Dodge times.* . . Spare moments.

dodiddie See **doobiddie**

dodinkus See **doodinkus**

dodo n[1] [*dodo* a large flightless bird now extinct, ult from Port *doudo* simpleton, fool]

1 A dull, stupid person; a queer, awkward, or disagreeable person. **chiefly Nth, N Midl** *esp among young speakers*

1924 in 1963 Fitzgerald *Letters* 164 **MN,** Tom Boyd wrote me that Bridges had been a dodo about some Y.M.C.A. man. **1930** *AmSp* 5.238 **NY** [College slang], *Dodo:* an unintelligent person, especially a student. **1965–70** *DARE* (Qu. HH3, *A dull and stupid person*) 14 Infs, **chiefly Nth, N Midl,** Dodo; **AR**18, **MI**120, **NM**9, (Old) dumb dodo; (Qu. HH5, *Someone who is queer but harmless*) Inf **CT**8, Dodo; (Qu. HH13, . . *A person [who] is not very alert or not aware of things*) Infs **NY**239, 249, **OH**99, **OR**15, (Dumb) dodo; (Qu. HH16, *Uncomplimentary words . . to show that you don't think much of a person: "Don't invite him. He's a _____."*) Infs **IL**25, 73, 136, **MI**120, Dodo; (Qu. HH21, *A very awkward, clumsy person*) Inf **NY**241, Dodo; (Qu. HH40, *Uncomplimentary words for an old man*) Infs **ME**16, **OR**15, Dodo. [11 of 25 Infs young]

2 In marble play: see quot.

c1970 Wiersma *Marbles Terms* **ceMI,** Dodo—any middle-sized marble. *Ibid,* Do-do. . . Large marble mainly used for shooting, worth about 5 regular marbles. . . Name for biggest, most valuable marble.

Ibid **neNJ,** Do-do . . type of small marble . . ["]all he's got is do-dos["] (used derogatorily). *Ibid* **neNJ,** Do-do. . . A large marble.

do-do n² See **do** n¹ **4**

dodo, go v phr Also *(make) dodo* [Fr *faire (un) dodo* (in baby talk) to take a nap, go to sleep < *dormir* to sleep] **esp LA**

To go to sleep, take a nap; also imper: Go to sleep!

[**1931** Read *LA French* 38, *Fais-dodo*. . . A country dance; from the *fais dodo,* "go to sleep," of children's speech.] **1968** *DARE* (Qu. X40, . . *Ways . . of saying, "I'm going to bed"?*) Inf **LA**23, To go dodo ['doʊ ˌdoʊ]—used especially for children; **LA**35, A small child will say "I want to go dodo [ˌdo 'do]" = I want to go to bed. **1969** Cagnon *Franco-Amer. Terms* 223 **neRI,** *Dodo* . . [dodo] Sleep, nap. . . "Go make dodo now." "You made (a) nice dodo." "Dodo!" = Go to sleep! **1983** *Reinecke Coll.* 4 **LA,** *Dodo*. . . ['doˌdo] child's word. . . "Make dodo" to sleep, from "Faire dodo." Still common.

do don't See **do** v **C1c**

dodunk n [Perh alter of **dodo** n¹ **1**]

See quot 1895.

1895 *DN* 1.387 **VT,** *Dodunk:* a stupid, simple person. **1915** *DN* 4.203. **1959** *VT Hist.* new ser 27.133, *Dodunk*. . . Someone not very bright. Occasional.

dody See **doty**

doe n

1 A ewe or female sheep; rarely, a female goat.

1939 *LANE* Map 201 **swCT, seMA, scattered ME,** The map shows the terms *ewe,* . . and *doe,* denoting the mature female sheep. . . 1 inf, **seMA,** 'A doe is older than a ewe.' [**ceMA,** The informant's wife, a native of Newfoundland, uses *doe.*] **1965–70** *DARE* (Qu. K62, . . *A female sheep*) 14 Infs, **scattered,** Doe; (Qu. K67b, . . *A female goat;* total Infs questioned, 75) Inf **OK**49, Doe. [All Infs male and old] **1966** Dakin *Dial. Vocab. Ohio R. Valley* 2.239 **swIN,** [One informant] says a *male sheep* is a *stag.* The same speaker says *doe* for a female sheep in contrast to the usual *ewe.*

2 A woman (in contrast to a man); also transf: a woman's toilet. Addit exx at **buck** n¹ **2h**

1909 Ware *Passing Engl.* 52/1, *Buck or a doe (Anglo-Amer.).* A man or woman. **1967** *DARE* (Qu. M21b, *Joking names for an outside toilet building*) Inf **CO**38, Does and bucks—two separate buildings.

doe bird See **doughbird**

doe cat n Cf **doe deer**

1914 *DN* 4.151 **csME,** *Doe cat*. . . A she cat. Evidently a woodman's term.

doed See **do** v **B5**

doe deer n Cf **doe 1, doe cat**

A female deer, doe.

1938 Rawlings *Yearling* 150 **nFL,** He shot a doe-deer and used the liver to draw out the pizen [=poison]. **1966–68** *DARE* (Qu. P34, . . *A female deer;* total Infs questioned, 75) Inf **FL**16, Doe-deer; (Qu. P35a, *Names . . for any deer shot illegally*) Inf **LA**10, Doe-deer; **VA**27, Doe-deer, fawn—killed unlegal [sic].

doflicker, doflickety, doflickus, doflicky, doflinkie, doflinkus, doflop(pie), dofloppus See **dooflicker**

do for v phr [*OED* 1523 →]

To take care of; to support, earn the living for.

1887 Freeman *Humble Romance* 264 **MA,** Let me come home an' cook fur you, an' do fur you agin. **c1960** *Wilson Coll.* **csKY,** *Do*. . . Work for, support. "He won't do for his family." **1963** Owens *Look to River* 41 **TX,** I don't mind doing for old John. *Ibid* 148, How many days and weeks and months ahead, doing for the Cap'n? **1966** *DARE* Tape **AL**14, [My brother] was so near my age, we just grew up together, we'd do for one another. **1983** De Vries *Slouching* 50 **ND,** Ma Pettigrew fended for herself in a stubbornly executed solitude unrelieved save for one surviving child, a strapping state trooper named Oswald who "did" for her with faithful daily calls.

dofotchet n

=**doohickey 1.**

1976 Garber *Mountain-ese* 23 **sAppalachians,** Lem bought a new do-fotchet fer his car but it didn't save any gas.

dofunny See **doofunny**

dog n¹ Usu |dɔ(ə)g|; also **chiefly Nth, N Midl** |dɒg, dɑg|; also **chiefly NEng, S Midl** |dɒɔg, dɔog, dɔʊg|; infreq |dɔrg, dʊəg|; rarely |daʊg| Pronc-spp *dawg, dorg* Cf Pronc Intro 3.I.6.b

A Forms.

1867 Harris *Sut Lovingood Yarns* 215 **TN,** I hearn his collar-buttons snap, an' he went outen that shut [=shirt] like a dorg outen a badger-barril. **1890** *DN* 1.67 **KY,** *Dog* [dɔəg]. *Ibid* 72 **LA,** *Dog, hog, log* (with the vowel ɔ). A frequent pronunciation of these words. **1901** *DN* 2.181 **neKY** [Black], *Dogs*—dawgs. **1903** *DN* 2.292 **Cape Cod MA** (as of a1857), Before final *d, g, o* was long [ɔ] in *dog, hog, . . log.* **1917** *DN* 4.391 **neOH,** *Dog* [dɔg, dɑg]. . . A native of R.I. always used *dɔg* on ordinary occasions but in a specialized playful sense he would say, "Ah, you little dɑg!" (to child). **1933** *AmSp* 8.4.60 **Delmarva,** [ɔ] rather than [ɑ] or [ɒ] occurs in *dog, log, long*. . . Often [ɔ] is intensified and becomes very similar to the characteristic [ɔ⊥] of New York City speech. The sound approaches [oə]. **1934** (1943) *W2* xlix, An overlong and closely rounded ô [=ɔ] in *dog* is sometimes ridiculed by the spelling *"dawg"* but such a pronunciation is rare in educated speech. **1939** *AmSp* 14.126 **neTN,** [doʊg]. **1939** *LANE* Map 211, *Dog* [**chiefly MA, NH, VT, ME,** [dɒɔg, dɔog]; **widespread NEng, exc eMA, eCT, RI,** [dɔ(ə)g]; **widespread NEng, exc wMA, wCT,** [dɒ(ə)g]; **chiefly wNEng,** [dɑg]; 1 inf, **swCT,** [dɔrg], low-class pron[unciation]]. **1942** Hall *Smoky Mt. Speech* 32 **eTN, wNC,** Before [g], [k]: August ['ɔo gəst], dog, fog, frog, hog. **1961** Kurath–McDavid *Pronc. Engl.* Map 24, Diaphones of /ɔ~ɒ/ in *dog* [**chiefly NEast** [ɒ·~ɒ·ə]; **widespread Atlantic** [ɔ·~ɔ·ə]; **chiefly NEng, Mid Atl, WV** [ɒɔ~ɔ·ɔ~ɔo]; **chiefly wNEng** [ɑ·~ɑ·]]. **1964** O'Hare *Ling. Geog. E. MT* 207, The vowel nucleus of 'dog.' [5 infs [ɒə]; 3 infs [ɒr]; 2 infs [ɒ]; 1 inf [ɒʊ]; 1 inf [ɔu]]. **1964** *AmSp* 39.297 **ceNY,** Here in Albany, a part of the dialect pattern is a change of [ɔ] to something closely approximating [ʊə]. Thus *Albany* is ['ʊəˌbənɪ], *dog* is [dʊəg], and *call* is [kʊəl]. **1966** *DARE* FW Addit **cwNC,** *Dog* pronounced [daʊg]. **1973** Gawthrop *Dial. Calumet* 48 **nwIN,** /ɔ/. This vowel occurs in the speech of all informants . . before a voiced stop: log, bawd, dog. **1976** Allen *LAUM* 3.23 (as of c1950), The Vowel in *law, dog, strawberries*. . . The fully rounded [ɔ], which dominates western New England, northern New York, southeastern Pennsylvania, and western Maryland, expectedly dominates the U[pper] M[idwest] as well. . . The weakly rounded low-back [ɒ], which is common in central New York and in much of Pennsylvania, consistently appears also in both Northern and Midland speech areas of the UM. . . The fact that both vowels often appear in the same locality reflects the intermingling of settlers with antecedents in distinct [ɔ] and [ɒ] areas in the East. *Ibid* 24 Fig 8 **chiefly IA, NE, sSD,** [ɒɔ] in dog.

B Senses.

1 An animal that resembles a dog, spec:

a =**prairie dog.** [From its bark]

1805 *Balance & Columbian Repository* (Albany NY) 17 Sept 304 **LA,** How Mr. Lewis . . came to call the *ground-fox squirrel* a dog, it is indeed difficult to imagine. **1872** Tice *Over Plains* 82 **WY,** Hundreds of the dogs, big and little, can be seen running for dear life to their holes. **1928** Anthony *N. Amer. Mammals* 223, Today the West is changing; . . and the snake feed on the young "Dogs" [=*Cynomys* spp] when they are lucky enough to catch one. **1935** Sandoz *Jules* 21 **wNE** (as of c1900), They plodded their ponies . . to a wide prairie-dog town, thousands of little crater-like holes, with the derisive dogs bobbing out of sight with a flirt of the stubby tails. *Ibid* 59, Jules . . gathered up his gun and crutch, and went out to the dog town west of the tree patch for a rabbit for breakfast.

b A coyote.

1959 Robertson *Ram* 185 **ID** (as of c1875), Dog Valley was so named because of the coyotes which abounded there.

2 In logging: the hook or tooth-like device on any of several tools for gripping logs or lumber, spec:

a A metal hook with one sharp end for gripping logs and a hook or eye at the other end to which a rope, etc, is attached.

1678 in 1904 New Castle DE Court *Records* 1.361, 2 doggs to draw Timber. **1883** *Harper's New Mth. Mag.* Jan 206/1 **wCA,** Near the lower end of the log an iron hook, called a 'dog,' is driven in, where the drag-chain is attached. **1893** *Atlantic Mth.* Feb 195/2 **wWA,** The "dogs"—half-hooks of steel—were driven deeply into the back of the log that was to be jerked out of its bed into the roadway. **1905** U.S. Forest Serv. *Bulletin* 61.35 [Logging terms], *Dog*. . . A short, heavy piece of steel, bent and pointed at one end and with an eye or ring at the other. It is used for many purposes in logging, and is sometimes so shaped that a blow directly against the line of draft will loosen it. **1950** *Western Folkl.*

9.121 **nwOR** [Sawmill workers' speech], *Dog*. . . A straight-shanked, right-angle, wedge-shaped hook attached to a rope or cable. **1958** McCulloch *Woods Words* 48 **Pacific NW,** *Dog*. . . A short metal stake sharp on one end, with an eye on the other. Driven into a log it gave a hold to tie to another log. Used frequently in tieing logs together for hauling down a fore-and-aft road. Still used in booming logs. **1969** Sorden *Lumberjack Lingo* 34 **NEng, Gt Lakes,** *Dogs*—Skidding tongs.

b The hinged hook on a peavey or cant hook.

1966 *DARE* Tape **ME**1, [Inf:] They had a dog hooked to that [=a peavey], and a pick in it, and that pick you'd drive right in the log anywhere and hang on, or that dog would start to turn logs rolling. [FW:] What was that dog like? [Inf:] That dog was a crook like this. . . Just like a fishhook; **ME**19, The cant dog . . had a dog on it so they could roll 'em [=logs]; **ME**26, Some people call 'em peavies. Some people call 'em cant dogs. It's got a pick on it, got a bigger band, got a dog on it to roll anything, hook on 'n roll; **NH**14, [A cant dog had] a pick and a dog on it . . a floating hook where you catch into the log. **1975** Gould *ME Lingo* 75, *Dog*—The sharp hinged hook on a canthook or peavey which bites into a log.

c See quot 1968.

1828 Webster *Amer. Dict.* np, *Dog*. . . An iron used by sawyers to fasten a log of timber in a saw-pit. **1950** *Western Folkl.* 9.121 **nwOR** [Sawmill workers' speech], *Dog* . . a hook-shaped adjustable instrument attached to a lever fastened on the head block of a log carriage; it holds the log on the carriage and prevents it from turning. **1968** Adams *Western Words* 95, *Dog*—In logging, a large spiked steel arm that holds the log in position while being sawed. **1969** Sorden *Lumberjack Lingo* 34 **NEng, Gt Lakes,** *Dog*. . . A device for holding a log in place when sawing into lumber. **1975** Gould *ME Lingo* 75.

d See quot.

1969 Sorden *Lumberjack Lingo* 34 **NEng, Gt Lakes,** *Dog*. . . A device attached to the runner of a sleigh that digs into the ground and prevents the sleigh from sliding backward when going uphill when the team is rested.

3 =andiron. [*OED* 1596 →] **scattered, but less freq NE, Upper MW, NW** See Map Cf **dog iron 1**

1641 in 1850 CT (Colony) *Pub. Rec.* 1.444, A fire pan & doggs & some other old iron. **1719** in 1888 Sewall *Letter-Book* 2.106 **MA,** A Brass Hearth for a Chamber, with Dogs, Shovel, Tongs and Fender of the newest Fashion. **1767** in 1886 Brooks *Quaint Adverts.* 13 **eMA,** One Pair of Brass Doggs, cast solid, very heavy and large. **1867** Lowell *Biglow* xlii, *Dogs* for *andirons* is still current in New England. **1949** Kurath *Word Geog.* 51, The andirons in the fireplace are generally known as *fire dogs, dogs,* or *dog irons* in the greater part of the South, the South Midland, and in southwestern Pennsylvania. **1965** Carmony *Speech Terre Haute* 16 **cwIN,** *Andirons*. . . The oldest informant . . gave the South Midland and Southern *dogs*. **1965-70** *DARE* (Qu. D32, *The metal stands in a fireplace that the logs are laid on*) 32 Infs, **scattered, but less freq NE, Upper MW, NW,** Dogs. **1966** Dakin *Dial. Vocab. Ohio R. Valley* 2.36, *Fire dogs* does not appear in the Bluegrass and is rare north of the [Ohio] river, but the simplex *dogs* is scattered from the upper Ohio to the Mississippi—occurring most frequently . . in Ohio. **1967** LeCompte *Word Atlas* 128 **sLA,** Irons to hold logs for burning in fireplace . . dogs. [1 inf] **1967** Faries *Word Geog. MO* 72, *Andirons*. . . *Dogs* is used by seven informants, mostly in the area south of the Missouri River.

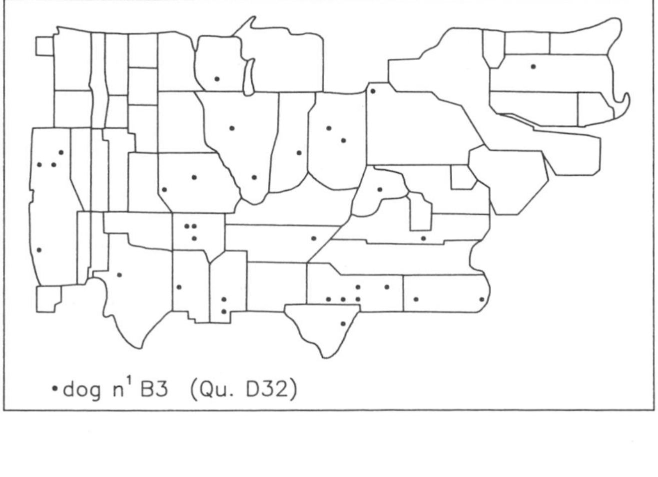

•dog n[1] B3 (Qu. D32)

4 Style; pretentiousness, affected display.

1871 [see **5a** below]. **1889** W.D. Howells *Hazard of Fortunes* I.267 *(OEDS),* He's made the thing awfully *chic;* it's jimminy; there's lots of dog about it. **1900** *DN* 2.32 **cnOH** [College slang], *Dog*. . . Style; good clothes. **1902** (1903) Lorimer *Letters* 233 **neIL,** [He] handed me his new card four times and explained that it was the rawest sort of dog to carry a brace of names in your card holster. **1923** *Nation* 22 Aug 188/2 **IL,** Youthful and masculine is Chicago—generous, impulsive, and somewhat skeptical of "dog." **1950** in 1966 Stevens *Letters* 670 **cCT,** Sweeney is completely without side or dog.

5 in phrr *put on (the) dog:*

a occas *put on the dogs, throw* (or *kill*) *the dog:* To dress stylishly; to be ostentatious or make a display of stylishness; to affect an air of importance. **scattered, but less freq S Atl** See Map

1871 Bagg *4 Yrs. at Yale* 44 **CT,** *Dog,* style, splurge. To *put on dog,* is to make a flashy display, to cut a swell. **1897** Lewis *Wolfville* 126 **SW,** The Dallas sharp, puttin' on a heap of hawtoor an' dog, walks over to the tavern ag'in. **1915** *DN* 4.233 **neOH,** *Put on the dog,* to dress with elaborate care. **1934** Farrell *Young Manhood* 282 **Chicago IL,** They were all trying to put on the dog, show they were lace-curtain Irish, and lived in steam-heat. **1950** *WELS (People who show off or make a big display: "When they give a party, they really ______")* 31 Infs, **WI,** Put on the dog; 1 Inf, **cnWI,** Throw the dog; 1 Inf, **cWI,** Kill the dog. **1965-70** *DARE* (Qu. W37, *When a woman puts on her good clothes and tries to look her best, you say she's ______.*) 38 Infs, **scattered,** Putting on the dog; **CT**1, Put on the dog; **CA**196, Putting on dog; **AL**30, Putting on the big dog; **CT**23, **DE**2, Putting on the dogs; [**SC**70, Got her dogs on (laughter)]; (Qu. W38, *When a man dresses himself up in his best clothes, you say he's ______.*) 18 Infs, **scattered,** Putting on the dog; **CA**196, Puttin' on dog; (Qu. W40, . . *A woman who overdresses or who spends too much on clothes*) 9 Infs, (She's) putting on the dog (too much); **CA**36, **CT**40, **IL**60, **MO**35, **OH**87, Puts on the dog; **MD**21, **MN**33, Tries (*or* trying) to put on the dog; **AL**26, Putting on the dogs; (Qu. GG19a, *When you can see from the way a person acts that he's feeling important or independent: "He surely is ______ these days."*) 13 Infs, **esp Nth, N Midl,** Putting on the dog; **DE**1, Putting on the dogs; (Qu. HH35, *A woman who puts on a lot of airs*) 13 Infs, **scattered,** Putting (*or* puts) on the dog; (Qu. Y22, *To move around in a way to make people take notice of you: "Look at him ______."*) 8 Infs, Put (*or* putting) on the dog; (Qu. W36, . . *A woman who uses a lot of cosmetics*) Infs **NY**24, 75, **WI**32, (Sure) putting on the dog; (Qu. W39, . . *A person's best clothes*) Infs **IN**65, **UT**7, Putting on the dog; (Qu. AA8, *When people make too much of a show of affection in a public place*) Inf **NY**10, Putting on the dog; (Qu. HH2, . . *A citified person*) Inf **MO**36, Putting on the dog; (Qu. HH17, *A person who tries to appear important, or who tries to lay down the law in his community*) Inf **NY**88, Puttin' on the dog. **1967** *DARE* Tape **IA**8, You had to put on just a little bit of dog; it didn't look right just smoking old Bull Durham.

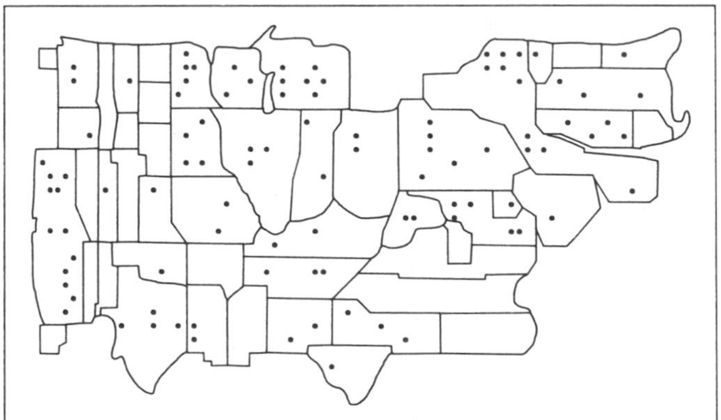

•dog n[1] B5a + varr (Qq. W37, W38, W40, GG19a, HH35, W36, W39, Y22, AA8, HH2, HH17)

b To do something energetically or vigorously; see quot.

1966-68 *DARE* (Qu. FF18, . . *A noisy or boisterous celebration or party: "They certainly ______ last night."*) Infs **NC**33, **SC**3, **VA**26, Put on the dog; (Qu. KK29, *To start working very hard: "He was slow at first but now he's really ______."*) Inf **MD**36, Putting on the dog.

6 A foot or shoe.

1913 *NY Eve. Jrl.* (NY) 7 July Home ed 13 *(Zwilling Coll.)*, [In cartoon panel:] They pay $15,000 for a player from a hick league and me only getting $70 a day waitin for my sore dog to heal up? **1914** *Ibid* 26 Oct 12 *(Zwilling Coll.)*, [In the cartoon "Indoor Sports: Watching the office tightwad buy a shine":] He's been working on those old dogs for an hour now. **1919** Lardner *Real Dope* 126 **neIL,** We was on the march and by the time night come around my dogs fret me so bad I couldn't think of nothing else. **1926** Van Vechten *Nigger Heaven* 285, *Dogs:* feet. **1939** Steinbeck *Grapes* 65 **OK,** We ain't gonna walk no eight miles . . tonight. My dogs is burned up. **1965** *AmSp* 40.254, *Bum dogs.* Ailing or weak feet. **1965–70** *DARE* (Qu. X38, . . *Unusually big or clumsy feet*) 10 Infs, **scattered,** (Big) dogs; **FL**48, Bad dogs; (QR, near Qu. BB2) Inf **CA**15, *Bum dogs*—Feet. Used to be lots more people with bum dogs.

7 in var euphem exclams, esp *dog bite (it), ~ take (it)* and varr: See quots. [Euphem for *God*] **chiefly Sth, S Midl** Cf **dod, dog** v **6**

1902 *DN* 2.233 **sIL,** *Dogtake*. . . An emphatic expletive. **1906** *DN* 3.117 **sIN,** *Dog take*. . . A mild oath. **1907** *DN* 3.222 **nwAR,** *Dogtake.* **1908** *DN* 3.306 **eAL, wGA,** *Dog take it.* **1924** *DN* 5.259, Dog:—blame it,—blast it. **1938** Rawlings *Yearling* 334 **nFL,** Dog take it, time was I didn't have to stop. **1965–70** *DARE* (Qu. NN8a, *Exclamations of annoyance or disgust: "Oh ———. I've lost my glasses again."*) Infs **LA**45, **NY**250, Dog; **VA**71, Dog bite it; (Qu. NN9a, *Exclamations showing great annoyance: "———. The electric power is off again."*) Inf **FL**52, Dog; **WA**16, Dog-garn it; (Qu. NN9b, *Exclamations showing great annoyance: "He's run off with my hammer again, ———!"*) Inf **MS**6, **VA**71, Dog bite him (*or* it); **KY**24, **MD**30, Dog take; **VA**39, Dog foot it; (Qu. NN20b, *Exclamations caused by sudden pain—a slight burn*) Inf **GA**72, Dog bite it; (Qu. NN25a, *Weakened substitutes for 'damn' or 'damned': "——— it all!"*) Inf **NC**7, Dog bite; **OK**27, Dog blast; **NY**1, Dog damn; **VA**39, Dog foot. **1970** Tarpley *Blinky* 298 **neTX,** Mild expressions of disgust . . dog take it. **1978** *DARE* File **cSC,** *Dog bite it*—a softening of "damn it." Often used in such expressions as "Dog bite her hide." But sometimes used alone also.

8 Used in nicknames for small or out-of-the-way places; see quots. *derog* Cf **Dog Town**

1935 *AmSp* 10.80 **seMO,** *'Possum Hollow* . . is one of the most popular expressions used to relegate a settlement to the 'backwoods of nowhere.' I have also heard *Dog-Trot Hollow* . . used in much the same sense. **1950** *WELS (Nicknames for nearby cities, villages, or districts)* 1 Inf, **swWI,** Dogpatch. **1968–69** *DARE* (Qu. C33, . . *An out-of-the-way place, or a very unimportant place*) Inf **NY**52, Dogtail Corners; (Qu. C34, *Nicknames for nearby settlements, villages, or districts*) Inf **MO**39, Dog Holler; **VA**13, Dog Ridge—where everyone kept from one to six dogs; **MO**16, **NY**198, Dogpatch; **IL**117, Dog Walk; (Qu. C35, *Nicknames for the different parts of your town or city*) Infs **NC**13, 83, Dog Corner; **OH**45, Dog-ham.

9 in phr *never say dog* and var: Not to say the least thing.

1821–22 in 1956 Eliason *Tarheel Talk* 269 **NC,** At 8 the ladies retired & said not *dog.* **1895** *DN* 1.376 **eTN,** Where's that boy? He went off and never said dog. **1942** *AmSp* 17.170 **sIL** [College slang], I never said dog to them about it.

10 A sausage or frankfurter; a hot dog. Cf **doggie 2**

1900 *DN* 2.32 **MA** [College slang], *Dog*. . . Sausage. **1916** *DN* 4.322 **KS,** *Dog*. . . Sausage. Not local. **1948** Cain *Moth* 50 **Baltimore MD,** It had a big icebox. . . And today, with the brother away and a lot of dogs, butter, ground meat, pop and stuff on hand, there was plenty to spoil if we didn't get the ice there quick. **c1960** *Wilson Coll.* **csKY,** *Dog*. . . A very modern name for a sausage, especially one served in a bun. Also for the kind of meat found in a hot dog, whether in small or larger forms. **1968–69** *DARE* (Qu. H40, *A small sausage that is put into a long roll*) Infs **CA**77, **NY**57, **PA**115, **RI**3, Dog.

11 See quot.

1973 *DARE* File **cTX** (as of 1870s), Dog. . . A biscuit made from scraps of dough left by a circular biscuit cutter, perquisite of Negro cook. . . This was never served in the (White) family dining room; it remained the rather unaccountably cherished property of the cook. . . I was occasionally punished for . . trying to steal this "dog" from the . . stove.

12 An inexperienced person, novice; see quots.

1934 *AmSp* 9.288 **sePA** [Black college slang], *Dog* (also *canine, hound, pup,* and *puppy*). The usual and commonly applied term for a freshman. **1970** *DARE* (Qu. HH15, *A very inexperienced person*) Inf **VA**41, Dog. [Inf Black]

13 An inferior animal. Cf **dog feed** and *DS* K15,44

1919 *Boston American* (MA) 17 Nov 11 *(Zwilling Coll.)* [In cartoon "Indoor Sports: Trying to work as the office plungers exchange stories of big wagers on the merry-go-round":] Well, I got that dog in the fifth at 20 to 1. I couldn't miss him—he stuck out a mile. **1935** *AmSp* 10.270 [Language of the livestock mart], *Dogs.* Low grade animals, canners. **1940** Writers' Program *Guide NV* 77, *Dogs* are poor weak calves, while rawhides are weak cows. **1950** *WELS (A pig that is poor or no good)* 1 Inf, **seWI,** Dog. **1951** *PADS* 16.24 [Racetrack argot], *Dog*. . . A cheap horse.

14 A lackey, stooge. Cf **dog robber 1**

1968–70 *DARE* (Qu. II34, *If you think somebody is trying to use you to his advantage: "I'm not going to be his ———."*) Infs **MD**24, **MO**39, **PA**242, **VA**38, Dog.

15 Sexual desire, lust. Cf **doggish 1**

1965 Brown *Manchild* 371 **NY** [Black], I'm talking about that old light-skin heifer that's always comin' around here to see your daddy. . . One day, you'll probably understand. . . when the dog in you starts comin' out. **1970** *DARE* (Qu. AA6b, . . *A man who is fond of being with women and tries to attract their attention—if he's rude or not respectful*) Inf **FL**48, Full of dog. [Inf Black]

16 in phr *your dog is going to get out:* See quot.

1967 *DARE* (Qu. W24c, *Sayings to warn a man that his trouser-fly is open*) Infs **OR**10, 14, (Your) dog is gonna get out.

17 used emphatically in various compar phrr: See below.

a in phrr *eat like a dog* and varr: To eat noisily and greedily. **chiefly Sth, S Midl**

1965–70 *DARE* (Qu. H11a, *If somebody eats rapidly and noisily, you say he ———*) Infs **GA**4, 10, **KY**25, **MS**65, 79, **MO**5, **OH**44, **SC**22, **TN**52, **WV**17, Eats (just) like a dog; (Qu. H11b, *If he makes a noise with his food, he ———*) Inf **KY**28, Laps it up like a dog.

b in phr *poor as a dog:* Very poor. Cf **dog poor**

1968–70 *DARE* (Qu. U41b, . . *"He's poor as ———."*) Infs **IL**99, **LA**37, **VA**18, 35, **WV**20, A dog.

c in phr *tired as a dog:* Exhausted. Note: The usage *dog tired* is not regional.

1965–70 *DARE* (Qu. X47, . . *Ways . . of saying "I'm very tired, at the end of my strength"*) Infs **IN**80, **OR**3, **SC**26, 29, 64, Tired as a dog.

d in phrr *meaner than a (mad) dog* and varr: Very mean, unkind. **chiefly Sth, S Midl** Cf **cat shit, dirt** n **2, dog-mean**

1965–70 *DARE* (Qu. HH22b, *Talking about a very mean person, you might say, "He's meaner than ———."*) 12 Infs, **esp Sth, S Midl,** A dog; 10 Infs, **esp Sth, S Midl,** A mad dog; **MS**1, **WV**16, 18, 21, A yard dog; **DE**1, Mean as a dog; (Qu. HH22a, *A mean or disagreeable person;* total Infs questioned, 75) Inf **MS**49, Mean as a yard dog.

e in phr *sweat like a dog:* To sweat profusely.

1965–70 *DARE* (Qu. X56b, . . *Sweating very heavily*) Infs **CA**36, 162, **GA**82, **IA**27, 32, **TN**65, **TX**27, **WY**2, Sweat like a dog; **NY**237, **PA**227, **WI**62, Sweating like a dog.

f in phr *sick as a dog:* Very ill.

1909 *DN* 3.403 **nwAR,** I ate something last night that didn't agree with me and I was as sick as a dog for awhile. **1951** *PADS* 15.67 **NH,** *Sick as a dog*. . . Very sick. **1965–70** *DARE* (Qu. X52, . . *A person . . who had been sick was looking ———*) Inf **NH**13, Sick as a dog; (Qu. BB38, *When a person doesn't look healthy, or looks as if he hadn't been well for some time, you'd say, "He looks ———."*) Inf **MI**118, Sicker than a dog; (Qu. BB41, *Not seriously ill, but sick enough to be in bed*) Inf **RI**6, Sick as a dog; (Qu. BB42, *If a person is very sick you say he's ———*) Infs **CA**118, **MO**39, **NH**2, **NY**130, Sick as (*or* sicker than) a dog.

g in phrr *mad as a dog* and varr: Very angry.

1965–70 *DARE* (Qu. GG40, . . *Violently angry*) Infs **CA**166, **FL**33, **KY**94, **LA**8, 35, **RI**13, **SC**65, Mad as a (mad) dog; [**MD**31, Like a mad dog;] **IL**17, Mad as a red-assed dog.

h in phr *drunk as a dog:* =**dog drunk.**

1966–70 *DARE* (Qu. DD15, *A person who is thoroughly drunk*) Infs **AL**10, **GA**72, **SC**34, **TX**100, Drunk as a dog.

i in phr *vomit like a dog:* See quot. Cf *sick as a dog* at **B17f** above

1966–67 *DARE* (Qu. BB18, *To vomit a great deal at once*) Infs **AR**18, **TX**37, (Vomited) like a dog; **TX**13, Vomit like a sick dog.

18a attrib or possessive: Inferior; base.

1889 [see **dog stud**]. **1899** [see **dog trick**]. **1954** [see **dog doctor**]. **1958** [see **dog Latin**]. **1967–68** [see **dog salmon**].

b Spec, of plants: having a strong odor; considered unattractive, undesirable or unfit for human consumption. [Cf *OED dog* sb. 18. d]

1832 [see **dogberry b**]. **1931** [see **dog camomile**]. **1931** [see **dogweed 2**]. **1937** [see **dog currant**]. **1963** *AmSp* 38.35, *Unattractive and worthless plants.*—The viability of *dog* . . is perhaps best illustrated . . in the names of plants usually thought of as obscure, unattractive, or worthless. . . [C]anine terms . . may vary in meaning from mild pejoratives . . to much harsher extremes. **1968** [see **dogwood 6**].

19 attrib; Of a dog or fox: male. Cf **boar**

1769 (1925) Washington *Diaries* 1.314, Started and killed a Dog fox, after havg [sic] him on foot three hours. **1902** *DN* 2.233 **sIL,** *Dog-fox.* . . The male fox. **1907** *DN* 3.220 **sIL, nwAR,** *Dog fox.* . . Male fox. **1938** Rawlings *Yearling* 189 **nFL,** One was a dog-fox, and one a vixen. **1942** *AmSp* 17.238 **NE,** A breeder of dogs will speak of a litter of pups as being so many *dog pups* (the males) and so many bitches (the females). . . The use seems to cease after the pups reach maturity. **1966** *DARE* Tape **DC**9, Don't say dog—that's a dirty word. They're hounds . . they're dog-hounds and bitch-hounds . . but they're hounds; **SC**19, I kept that one dog pup and the bitch.

20 Fig: the largest or most difficult part of a job; see quot.

1958 *Sat. Eve. Post Letters* **swIN,** If you can get over the dog, you can get over the tail. **1967–68** *DARE* (Qu. KK43, *When the hardest part of a task is finished: "We've still a long way to go, but at least we ________ ."*) Inf **IL**11, We're over the dog, we'll get over the tail too; [**PA**150, I got over the head, I can get over the dog's tail].

21 See **dog salmon.**

dog n[2] See **dogs**

dog v

1 To chase (usu an animal) with a dog; to hunt with a dog; hence vbl n *dogging.*

1690 in 1882 Sheldon *Doc. Hist. Suffield* 111 **cnCT,** If any man taking Swine doing him damage . . shall either by dogging ym, or any other cruell usage, maime, or kill their neighbors swine, they shall not only loose all their owne damage; but pay double to the owner. **1886** *Harper's New Mth. Mag.* 73.323/2 **IA,** He threatened to mash B into the earth if he ever dogged his hogs again. **1899** (1912) Green *VA Folk-Speech* 150, *Dog.* . . To chase cattle with dogs. **1906** *DN* 3.133 **nwAR,** *Dog.* . . To chase away by using a dog. "We could dog the hogs off in the daytime." **1910** *DN* 3.453 **seVT,** *Dog.* . . To drive cattle with a dog. "He dogged the cattle out of the mowin'." **1966** *DARE* FW Addit **NM**12, *To dog 'em* is to sic the dogs on—generally on an animal. **1967–68** *DARE* (Qu. P35b, *Illegal methods of shooting deer*) Inf **PA**166, Dogging them; **NC**48, Dogging deer. **1967–69** *DARE* Tape **OR**18, You have to dog the hell out of them [=sheep] to get them to move; **PA**185, Just start and dog them [=wild turkeys] real careful. . . I've walked up within ten yards of them before I've flushed them. **1983** Montell *Don't Go Up* 41 **csKY, cnTN,** We turn the cows out in the woods and we dog them up when it's time to milk them, and their bowels act while the dogs are running them. So we don't have this stuff to clean out!

2 with *around:* To follow assiduously.

c1938 in 1970 Hyatt *Hoodoo* 2.1834 **neSC,** (All you have to do is to find one of his foot tracks and put that peg right down into it?) Yes suh, but now it mustn't be a day old or somepin lak dat. See, it's whut dey call *doggin'* a person. Dey'll *dog* behin'. **1946** (1972) Mezzrow-Wolfe *Really Blues* 332, *Dog around:* Follow. **1966–69** *DARE* (Qu. Y7, . . *"I don't know why she keeps ________ me all the time."*) Inf **RI**15, Dogging my footsteps; (Qu. Y8, *To keep after a person . . to get him to do things;* total Infs questioned, 75) Inf **AR**40, Dogging his tracks.

3 also with *at* or *around:* To nag, pester, harass; to mistreat, upset, discomfit.

1896 Harris *Sister Jane* 102 **GA,** Don't cry, sis. . . The folks in the house'll . . think I'm doggin' at you. **c1960** *Wilson Coll.* **csKY,** *Dog at.* . . To provoke, annoy, nag, vex. **1962** Fox *Southern Fried* 18 **SC,** He was jealous of Wilma and kept dogging her. He never gave her a moment's peace. *Ibid* 129, They dogging me. They stand there watching me. I can't work with them bastards watching me. **1965–70** *DARE* (Qu. Y7, *When one person never misses a chance to be mean to another or to annoy another: "I don't know why she keeps ________ me all the time!"*) Infs **MD**14, **PA**29, **SC**2, **WA**13, Dogging; **GA**9, Dogging at; (Qu. Y6, . . *To put pressure on somebody to do something he ought to have done but hasn't: "He's a whole week late. I'm going to ________ ."*) Inf **OR**4, Dog him; (Qu. CC12b) Inf **CO**42, Dogged; (Qu. GG6, *Talking about a person's feelings being hurt: "When she said she couldn't go with him, he was quite ________ ."*) Inf **DC**12, Dogged; (Qu. GG13a, *When something keeps bothering a person and makes him nervous, he may say, "It ________ me."*) Inf **PA**91, Dogs; (Qu. II19, *When you think somebody has been put ahead of you or has been given something you deserved, you might say, "I'd rather quit than ________ ."*) Inf **VA**38, Be dogged around.

4 In lumbering and logging: to secure or pin as with a **dog** n[1] **B2.** [*OED* 1591 →]

1879 *Lumberman's Gaz.* 15 Oct 4/1, We can dog directly into the hardest knot in the heaviest timber and hold the log perfectly safe and true. **1886** *Encycl. Brit.* (9th ed) 21.345/2, When the log reached the carriage it was dogged . . by the simple movement of a lever. **1950** *Western Folkl.* 9.121 **nwOR** [Sawmill workers' speech], *Dog, To.* To fasten securely. **1975** Gould *ME Lingo* 75, *Dog*—The sharp hinged hook on a canthook or peavey which bites into a log. . . To *dog* a thing is to get a good grip on it and to be in control of it.

5 To stop (a locomotive).

1958 McCulloch *Woods Words* 48 **Pacific NW,** *Dog 'er*—An order to stop. **1962** *AmSp* 37.132 **nCA,** *Dog 'er.* . . To put chalks [*DARE* Ed: chocks] under the wheels to stop a locomotive.

6 To damn; hence ppl adj *dogged* (pronc-sp *dog*), damned, darned. [Euphem] **chiefly Sth, S Midl** See Map Cf **black-dogged, dog** n[1] **B7**

1843 (1916) Hall *New Purchase* 145 **IN,** I'll be dogg'd if thare warn't a wild cat jist about to spring. **1857** IL State Ag. Soc. *Trans.* 2.232 **wVA,** I *did* want it, but I'll be dogged if I could use it. **1875** (1876) Twain *Tom Sawyer* 209 **MO,** 'Tain't a dream! Somehow I most wish it was. Dog'd if I don't, Huck. **1906** *DN* 3.134 **nwAR,** *Dogged.* . . In the exclamation, "I'll be dogged." **1908** *DN* 3.289 **eAL, wGA,** I'll be dogged if I do it. **1914** *DN* 4.159 **VA,** Ah'll be dogged! **1933** Rawlings *South Moon* 17 **FL,** Looks jest like feather-stitchin', . . dogged if it don't. **1939** *Hall Coll.* **eTN,** *Dogged.* . . Euphemism for darned, damned. "I'll be dogged if I know." (This saying is extremely common.) **1941** O'Donnell *Great Big Doorstep* 2 **sLA,** Topal loaded [her slingshot] again, and shot. 'God dog it to hell!' she whispered. *Ibid* 46, He don't care if Arthur swallows the god-dog [pool] ball. **1943** Writers' Program NC *Bundle of Troubles* 33, That-air needle look jes like the Whang Doodle's tongue; dog ef it don't. **1943** *Sat. Eve. Post* 13 Feb 68 **MS,** I be dog if I'm going to set here by myself. **1954** *Harder Coll.* **cwTN,** Dog if I know. **1965–70** *DARE* (Qu. NN25b, . . *"Well, I'll be ________ !"*) 13 Infs, **chiefly Sth, S Midl,** Dog; 10 Infs, **chiefly Sth, S Midl,** Dogged; **VA**39, Dogged my foot [FW: heard in conv]; (Qu. NN7, *Exclamations of surprise: "They're getting married next week? Well, ________ ."*) Infs **MS**8, 73, **OH**28, **SC**26, 34, 39, 40, 44, 45, **TN**54, I'll be dog; **GA**1, **MO**16, **SC**32, I'll be dogged; **AR**55, I be dog; **KY**85, Be dogged; (Qu. NN8a, *Exclamations of annoyance or disgust: "Oh ________ . I've lost my glasses again."*) Infs **LA**45, **NY**250, Dog; (Qu. NN9a, *Exclamations showing great annoyance: "________ . The electric power is off again."*) Infs **VA**5, **SC**3, (Well) I'll be dogged; **FL**52, Dog; **SC**34, Well I'll be dog; (Qu. NN17, *Something that keeps on annoying you . . "That ________ fly won't go away."*) Infs **SC**3, **VA**69, Dogged; (Qu. NN25a, *Weakened substitutes for 'damn' or 'damned': "________ it all!"*) Inf **NY**250, Dog it all; (Qu. NN32, *Exclamations like 'I swear' or 'I vow': "I ________ ."*) Infs **AR**41, **KY**65, **MS**73, **TN**14, Be dogged.

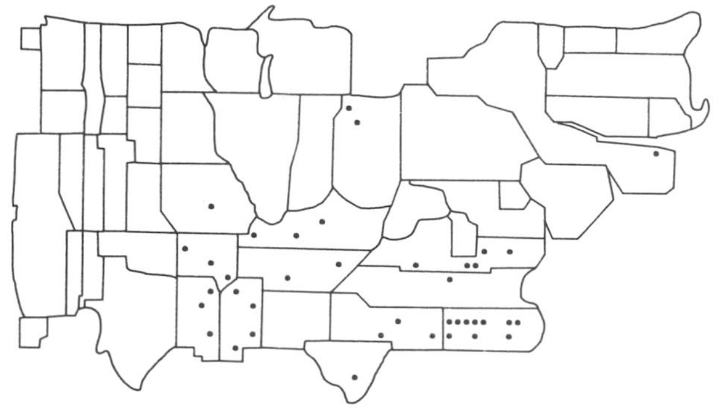

•dog v 6 + varr (Qq. NN25a, b, NN7, NN8a, NN9a, NN17, NN32)

7 with *up:* In marble play: see quots; hence vbl n *dogging up.*

1922 *DN* 5.186 **KY,** *Dog up. . .* To shoot a taw not at the ring but away from it or nearer to it. "Dogging up" is sometimes advantageous in manouvering [sic] for position. **1955** *PADS* 23.16, *Dog up. . .* To roll a marble to a more advantageous position, either nearer or sometimes farther away from the target.

8 usu with *it,* occas with *off, around:* To shirk or not do one's best, especially on the job; to waste time, to loaf; to malinger. **chiefly Nth, N Midl, West**

1910 *NY Eve. Jrl.* (NY) 25 Mar 20 *(Zwilling Coll.),* He [=Stanley Ketchel] says that Papke couldn't beat him in Pittsburg, and that Papke was dogging it at the end. **1920** *Collier's* 15 May 62/3 *(DA),* I'm afraid if Roberts gets hurt, early, bein' green, he'll play safe and be satisfied to stall the rest of it and dog it. **1930** Williams *Logger-Talk* 22 **Pacific NW,** *Dog it:* Work half-heartedly. **1948** *Sat. Eve. Post* 7 Aug 31/1 **MN,** They might not be all-city, but they'll play for me, not dog it! **1950** *WELS (Wasting time by loafing on the job)* 2 Infs, **WI,** Dogging it; *(When someone is pretending to be sick)* 1 Inf, **cwWI,** Dogging it; [1 Inf, **cWI,** Got the dog]. **1958** McCulloch *Woods Words* 48 **Pacific NW,** *Dog it*—To lay down on the job. **1965–70** *DARE* (Qu. A9, . . *Wasting time by not working on the job)* Infs **CA**107, **LA**15, **MI**105, **MN**2, **PA**176, Dogging (it); **MO**27, Dogging off; (Qu. Y21, *To move about slowly and without energy)* Inf **OH**47, Dogging; (Qu. BB27, *When somebody pretends to be sick [often to get out of doing something] you'd say he's* ______) Infs **AK**1, **IL**97, **NJ**54, **OH**47, **OR**14, 15, **PA**199, **RI**6, Dogging (it); **IL**25, Dogging off; (Qu. JJ26, *If somebody has been doing poor work or not enough, the boss might say, "If he wants to keep his job he'd better* ______.") Inf **CA**119, Quit dogging it. **1975** *AmSp* 50.58 **AR** (as of c1970), *Dog around. . .* Neglect or take academic responsibilities lightly.

9 See quot.

1938 *AmSp* 13.5 **seAR,** *Dog. . .* To tell a lie. "I'm not dogging."

10 To cheat (someone).

1967 *DARE* (Qu. LL22, *Less than you should get)* Inf **KY**34, They dogged me out of that.

11 with *it:* See quot. Cf **dog** n[1] **B4, 5a, dogged out**

1938 *AmSp* 13.152 **sIN** [Black], *Dog it.* To show off to advantage. A smartly dressed person struts along, and an admiring observer ejaculates, 'Aw, dog it now.'

12 See quot 1974. Cf **bulldog** v[2]

1954 *Courier-Jrl.* (Louisville KY) 25 Apr mag sec 7/1 **eKY,** They are "dogging" . . booze from the charred-oak barrels in which it was once stored for aging at distilleries. **1974** Maurer-Pearl *KY Moonshine* 114, *Bulldog. . .* To heat used barrels by setting them against a large oil drum in which a fire is built in order to sweat out the whiskey that has soaked into the barrel staves. In some areas a slower process involves setting closed barrels in hot sunlight. . . Also "to dog," "to sweat."

13 To serve in a menial capacity; to "fetch and carry."

1968 Haun *Hawk's Done Gone* 51 **eTN,** Me and Amy got to rest from being bossed about and dogging for him.

14 in phr *dog the watches;* In sailing: to split a night watch into two shifts in order to change the rotation of workers. Cf **dogwatch**

1957 Beck *Folkl. ME* 171, To alleviate monotony, every so often the watches would be "dogged" or split.

dog ppl adj See **dog** v **6**

dogadget See **doogadget**

dog-ail n

Distemper.

1931–33 *LANE Worksheets* **seMA,** Quinine pills and whisky are given to a dog for dog-ail.

dog alley n [Cf **alley** n[1] **7**]

=dogtrot.

1974 Fink *Mountain Speech* 6 **wNC, eTN,** *Dog trot* or *dog alley* . . open but covered runway between the two parts of a log cabin.

dogan n Also *dugan* [Perh from the Irish surname *Dogan,* but cf Scots *dugon,* used as a term of contempt for a poor, weak, or worthless person *(DSL, SND, EDD); DCan dogan* 1854 →] **nMI, nMN** *somewhat derog*

A Roman Catholic.

1966–67 *DARE* (Qu. CC4, . . *Nicknames . . for various religions or religious groups)* Inf **MI**3, Dogans ['dogənz]—for Catholics, the Orangeman's (those in this community) uncomplimentary name for a Catholic; Orangemen here on a certain holiday (July 12?) would parade with tin pans, noisemakers of all sorts, in front of Catholic churches and homes of known Catholics and give them a kind of Bronx-cheer serenade; **MI**16, Dogans—for Catholics; **MN**3, Dugans ['dugənz]—Catholics.

dog and bone n

A children's game; see quot.

1969–70 *DARE* (Qu. EE3, *Games in which you hide an object and then look for it)* Inf **NY**186, Dog and bone; (Qu. EE33) Inf **TX**88, Dog and bone—bone is put under chair that blindfolded player sits in; if you are heard getting it, you sit in the chair.

dog and deer n Cf **deer and dog(s), fox and geese 2**

A children's chase game played in the snow.

1899 Garland *Boy Life* 26 **nwIA,** "Dog and deer," or "fox and geese," could be played only when the snow was new-fallen and undisturbed, which was seldom, for the wind . . stripped the ground bare in one place, to build some fantastic structure in another, . . and the games of loops and circles were over. **1969** *DARE* (Qu. EE26, . . *Games . . children play in the snow)* Inf **MI**92, Dog and deer—two circular tracks made for deer to run on, dogs could jump from one [track] to another but not the deer.

dogan-headed adj [Perh **dogan**]

1927 *AmSp* 3.141 **coastal ME,** Whence comes "dogan-headed" for full, dense, unless it is a corruption of "doughhead"?

dog ant n

A large black stinging ant.

1966 *DARE* (Qu. R17) Inf **FL**20, Dog ants.

dog apple n

1 A **pawpaw** (here: *Asimina* spp).

1933 Small *Manual SE Flora* 530, Pityothamnus [=Asimina] . . Dog-apples. **1953** Greene-Blomquist *Flowers South* 36, Dog-Apples *(Asimina).* **1966** Grimm *Recognizing Native Shrubs* 111, This [=*Asimina speciosa*] and the preceding species [=*Asimina angustifolia*] are often called . . Dog-apple.

2 **=persimmon.**

1984 Wilder *You All Spoken Here* 177 **Sth,** Ozark dates, dog apples: Persimmons.

dog around See **dog** v **3, 8**

dog at See **dog** v **3**

dog bait See **dog's bait**

dog balls n

A sea squirt *(Molgula manhattensis).*

1954 McAtee *Suppl. to Nomina Abitera* **NJ,** Sea-squirt *(Molgula manhattensis)* Dog-balls.

dog banana See **banana B1**

dogbane n [See quot 1840 at **a**]

Any of var plants of the family Apocynaceae as:

a also *dog's-bane:* A plant of the genus *Apocynum.* Also called **Indian hemp.** For other names of var spp see **spreading dogbane**

1784 in 1785 Amer. Acad. Arts & Sci. *Memoirs* 1.423 **NEng,** Dogsbane. *Umbrella weed.* Blossoms white, striped with red. Borders of wood land. July. **1820** in 1832 MA Hist. Soc. *Coll.* 2d ser 9.146, *Apocynum androsaemifolium,* . . Dog-bane. **1840** MA Zool. & Bot. Surv. *Herb. Plants & Quadrupeds* 146, *Apocynum. . .* Dog's Bane. . . From its supposed offensiveness to that animal. **c1873** in 1976 Miller *Shaker Herbs* 137, *Bitterroot. Apocynum androsaemifolium. . .* Dogsbone [sic]. . . Dogbane. **1886** *Harper's New Mth. Mag.* Dec 102/1, The sprightly trap of the genista is an innocent affair compared to that of the dog-bane . . another very common and pretty plant. **1931** Harned *Wild Flowers Alleghanies* 389, The Dogbane is a near relative of the Milkweed, and contains a gluey, milky juice. **1966** *DARE* Wildfl QR Pl. 170a Infs **MN**14, **WA**10, Dogbane. **1968** McPhee *Pine Barrens* 129 **cNJ,** Someone asked him, pointing to a small plant with greenish-white leaves. "Dogbane," he said. "Why 'dogbane' no one knows. I never saw a dog pay any attention to it." **1970** *DARE* (Qu. S26a) Inf **MA**78, Dogbane.

b usu *climbing dogbane:* **=star jasmine.**

1936 IL Nat. Hist. Surv. *Wildflowers* 239, *Trachelospermum difforme. . .* The Climbing Dogbane is found in Illinois only in the southernmost counties. **1938** Rawlings *Yearling* 103 **nFL,** A patch of hammock joined the pines. Dogbane grew thickly here, lifting its yellow bells. **1946** Reeves-Bain *Flora TX* 127, Climbing Dogbane... Flowers pale or greenish yellow; corolla-tube about 5 mm. long, the spreading or recurved lobes somewhat shorter. **1960** Vines *Trees SW* 878, *Trachelospermum difforme...* Also known under vernacular names of Dogbane [etc]. **1970** Correll *Plants TX* 1215, Climbing dogbane.

c as *Texas dogbane:* A **blue star 1** (here: *Amsonia ciliata* var *texana*).

1936 Whitehouse *TX Flowers* 99, *Texas Dogbane. Blue-Star (Amsonia texana)..* is perennial, growing in low clumps on limestone hillsides of Texas. **1951** *PADS* 15.38 **TX,** *Amsonia texana...* Texas dogbane.

dog bed n

1966-67 *DARE* (Qu. W4, .. *Men's coats or jackets for work and outdoor wear*) Infs **NC**30, 41, Dog bed.

dogberry n [Cf **dog** n[1] **B18b**]

Any of var plants or their berries as:

a also *dogberry tree:* A **red osier dogwood** (here: *Cornus stolonifera*).

1784 in 1785 Amer. Acad. Arts & Sci. *Memoirs* 1.412 **MA,** *Cornus... Cornel. Dogberry.* The stem is quadrangular... Blossoms white. In woodland. May-June. **1900** Lyons *Plant Names* 118, *C[ornus] stolonifera...* Dogberry tree. **1940** Clute *Amer. Plant Names* 98, *C. stolonifera. Red Osier...* Dogberry tree.

b The berry of **poison sumac.**

1832 Williamson *Hist. ME* 1.117, Its berries [i.e. those of the poison ash or sumac].. have been called "dogberries."

c also *dogberry tree:* A **chokeberry 1** (here: *Aronia arbutifolia*).

1892 *Jrl. Amer. Folkl.* 5.95, *Pyrus arbutifolia,* dog-berry. N.E. **1901** Lounsberry *S. Wild Flowers* 248, *A. arbutifolia,* red chokeberry or dogberry tree,.. bears fruit which when ripe is a bright red. **1940** Clute *Amer. Plant Names* 10, *P. arbutifolia. Chokeberry...* Dog-berry. **1960** Vines *Trees SW* 413, Chokeberry—Also known under the vernacular names of Choke-pear and Dogberry.

d A **bead lily,** usu *Clintonia borealis,* but also *C. umbellata.*

1894 *Jrl. Amer. Folkl.* 7.101, *Clintonia borealis,..* dogberry, Bath, M[ain]e. **1940** Clute *Amer. Plant Names* 11, *C. borealis...* Dogberry. *Ibid* 256, *Clintonia umbellata.* Dog-berry. **1959** Carleton *Index Herb. Plants* 38, *Dog-berry:* Clintonia borealis.

e A **gooseberry 1** (here: *Ribes cynosbati*).

1900 Lyons *Plant Names* 321, *R. Cynosbati...* Dogberry. *Fruit* esculent. **1903** Small *Flora SE U.S.* 511, A straggling shrub, 1-2 m. tall, with spine-armed and often prickly stems... *Dogberry.* **1940** Richter *Trees* 33 **sOH** (as of c1800), Down in Pennsylvania the whites were thick as dogberries and the few Indians left knew their place. Away back here the whites were scarce as birds' teeth and the Indians plenty as dogberries. **1966** Grimm *Recognizing Native Shrubs* 116, *Prickly Gooseberry...* Also called Pasture Gooseberry and Dogberry. **1967-70** *DARE* (Qu. I44) Inf **MA**122, Dogberries; (Qu. S26a) Inf **LA**7, Dogberry; (Qu. T16) Inf **WI**22, Dogberry bush. **1976** Bailey-Bailey *Hortus Third* 969.

f Any of var spp of **mountain ash:** see quots.

1900 Lyons *Plant Names* 351, *S[orbus] Americana...* Dogberry. **1938** (1958) Sharples *AK Wild Flowers* 140, "Mountain Ash," "Dogberry." .. *S[orbus] sitchensis.* **1950** Gray-Fernald *Manual of Botany* 760, *P. americana...* Dogberry... *P. decora...* Dogberry. **1971** Krochmal *Appalachia Med. Plants* 238, *Sorbus americana... Common Names:..* dogberry... Large, dense, showy clusters of bright red berries.. appear in late fall.

g =**hobblebush.**

1900 *Plant World* 3.133, *Dogberry,* for *Viburnum lantanoides,* Mich. **1940** Clute *Amer. Plant Names* 56, *V. alnifolium. Hobble-bush...* Dogberry. **1976** Bailey-Bailey *Hortus Third* 1153, *Hobblebush,.. dogberry,.. witch-hopple...* Late spring... Zone 4.

h A **winterberry** (here: *Ilex verticillata*).

1916 *Torreya* 16.238, *Ilex verticillata...* Dog Berry,.. Matinicus Id., Me. **1940** Clute *Amer. Plant Names* 127, *I. verticillata...* Dog-berry. **1952** Taylor *Plants Colonial Days* 96, Winterberry is a deciduous shrub of the holly family... Other common names include.. dogberry.

i A **mountain holly** (here: *Nemopanthus mucronatus*).

1929 *Torreya* 29.150, *Nemopanthus mucronata...* Dogberry. **1940** Clute *Amer. Plant Names* 264, *Nemopanthes* [sic] *mucronata* [sic]. Cat-berry, dog-berry, brick timber.

j A perennial plant *(Comandra lividum)* native to the Pacific Northwest and Alaska.

1966 Heller *Wild Flowers AK* 97, *Northern Comandra, Dogberry...* Fruit an orange or red, round to oblong berry, edible but not tasty.

dogberry tree See **dogberry a, c**

dog-bit See **-bit** suff

dog bite (it) See **dog** n[1] **B7**

dog bit 'em phr Cf **him** pron **B3,** *DS* AA20, 28

1941 *McDavid Coll.* **nwSC,** "Dog bit 'em"—of an unmarried, pregnant woman.

dog boat n [**dog** n[1] **B2**]

In logging: see quots.

1905 U.S. Forest Serv. *Bulletin* 61.35 **Pacific NW,** *Dog boat... See* Rigging sled [=a sled used to haul hooks and blocks on a skid road]. **1958** McCulloch *Woods Words* 48 **Pacific NW,** *Dog boat*—See pig. [*Ibid* 134, *Pig*—A hollowed log which was used on fore-and-aft roads to take the dogs and other tools back to the woods or yarder donkey [=engine].]

dog-bodied adv phr *euphem* Cf **dog** v **6**

Damned, darned.

1942 (1971) Campbell *Cloud-Walking* 60 **seKY,** He said he never thought even a breath about mountain folks being so dog-bodied foolish that they would work and slave to raise a house for brought-on learning.

dog boist See **boist**

dog bones n pl *joc*

1966 *DARE* (Qu. X13b, .. *False teeth*) Inf **GA**9, Dog bones [laughter].

dog box n **AK** Cf **dog coop**

See quot 1972.

1972 Attla *Everything I Know about.. Sled Dogs* 176 (Tabbert *Alaskan Engl.*), *Dog box:* A large plywood box divided into individual compartments which is mounted on a truck and used to transport a dog team. **1976** Vaudrin *Racing Alaskan Sled Dogs* 85 (Tabbert *Alaskan Engl.*), The initial $10,000 is for dogs, sleds, houses, chains, collars, harnesses, towlines, dog pans and a pickup or some other vehicle with a dog box built onto it to haul them around in.

dogbread n Also *dog corn bread* **Sth, S Midl** Cf **ashdog, hush puppy 1**

A type of cornmeal bread baked in cakes or **pones.**

c1945 *McDavid Coll.* **SC,** There are a few examples.. of corn pone being called *dog bread.* **1961** Folk *Word Atlas N. LA* Map 1104, Bread made of corn meal.. dog bread. **1966** Dakin *Dial. Vocab. Ohio R. Valley* 2.315 **KY,** Corn bread... *Dog corn bread.* **1967** Faries *Word Geog. MO* 100, A griddle cake made of corn meal with or without an admixture of flour.. *corn dodger,* and *dog bread.* **1968** *DARE* (Qu. H14, *Bread that's made with cornmeal*) Inf **TX**51, Dog bread—cold water, cooked in pones.

dog brier n

A **greenbrier** (here: *Smilax rotundifolia*).

1897 *Jrl. Amer. Folkl.* 10.145, *Smilax rotundifolia..* dog brier, Mass.

dog burr n Also sp *dog bur*

=**hound's-tongue 1.**

1894 *Jrl. Amer. Folkl.* 7.95 **WV,** *Cynoglossum,* sp.,.. dog-bur. **1898** *Ibid* 11.275 **KS,** *Cynoglossum officinale..* dog-burr. **1912** Blatchley *IN Weed Book* 114, *Cynoglossum officinale..* Hound's-tongue, Dog Bur. **1940** Clute *Amer. Plant Names* 66, *C[ynoglossum] officinale...* dogbur. **1963** Craighead *Rocky Mt. Wildflowers* 155, *Houndstongue—Cynoglossum officinale..* Other names:.. Dogbur, Woolmat.

dog bush n

1966 *DARE* (Qu. S11, .. *Other names.. for.. dogtooth violet*) Inf **SC**10, Bear bush, dog bush—violet flowers, springtime—varicolored leaves.

dog button n [See quot 1951]

The seed of the nux vomica plant; also the plant *(Strychnos nux-vomica)* itself.

1857 Hammond *Wild N. Scenes* 77 **NY,** A dose of 'dog buttons,' or a taste of strychnine, administered with a tempting bit of cold steak,.. might have aided the operation. **1882** Peck *Peck's Sunshine* 80

WI, Six promising pups that had been presented to us . . had gone the way of all dog flesh, with the distemper and dog buttons. **1900** Lyons *Plant Names* 358, *S[trychnos] Nux-vomica* . . Dog-buttons. **1951** *PADS* 15.53 **cnIN,** *Dog button*. . . Nux vomica, the seed from which strychnine is obtained; used to poison dogs. . . The term is in colloquial use.

dog camomile n Also *dog's camomile* [See quot 1931; cf **dog** n[1] **B18b**]

=**dog fennel 1.**

1900 Lyons *Plant Names* 37, *A[nthemis] Cotula*. . . Dog's Camomile. **1931** Harned *Wild Flowers Alleghanies* 591, *Dog's Camomile*. . . The odor of the foliage is strong and unpleasant and its acrid taste is well known to all those who have been required to drink . . "Camomile Tea." **1936** Whitehouse *TX Flowers* 185, *Dog's Camomile* . . is a strong-scented herb widely scattered in America. **1936** Winter *Plants NE* 160, Dog or Fetid Camomile. . . A common weed in the U.S.

dogcart n [Because it orig had a compartment for carrying dogs; *OED* 1803 →] *old-fash*

A small, two-wheeled carriage drawn by one horse and having back-to-back seats.

1859 Vielé *Following* 40 **nwVT,** He had a dog-cart, horses, guns. **1893** *Scribner's Mag.* Jan 26/2 **NYC,** This was before the days of dog-carts. **1893** (1896) Post *Harvard Stories* 4 **ceMA,** One day Jack was out in his dog-cart, . . and met Varnum walking. **1940** Faulkner *Hamlet* 107 **MS,** She had the first and only perambulator the countryside had ever seen, a clumsy expensive thing almost as large as a dog-cart. **1968** *DARE* (Qu. N41a, . . *Horse-drawn vehicles . . to carry people*) Inf **NY**103, Dog cart; **WI**19, Dog cart—for two people. [Both Infs old] **1976** Brown *Gloss. Faulkner* 72, *Dog-cart* . . : a light, two-wheeled carriage with back-to-back seats (and originally a compartment for carrying hunting dogs). **1979** *UpCountry* July 13 (as of c1900), My own grandfather in rural Virginia, took his entire family back and forth by rockaway and dog cart each autumn between somnolent Radford and bustling Roanoke, a distance of some 40 miles.

dogcatcher n

1 also *dogcatcher crew, dogchaser;* In railroading: see quots. Cf **dog law**

1931 *Writer's Digest* 11.41 [Railroad terms], *Dog Catchers*—A crew sent to relieve a crew that has become outlawed. **1940** Cottrell *Railroader* 124, *Dog chaser*—A relief crew sent out to bring in a train which cannot be legally moved by its own crew. **1945** Hubbard *Railroad Ave.* 340, *Dogcatchers*—Crew sent out to relieve another that has been *outlawed*—that is, overtaken on the road by the sixteen-hour law, which is variously known as *dog law, hog law,* and *pure-food law.* **1976** Gould *Blackie's RR Hdbk.* 6, *Crew (sent to relieve a crew account of Federal Law):* Dog Catcher Crew.

2 See quot. *joc*

1969 *DARE* (Qu. V10c, . . *A constable*) Inf **MA**26, Dogcatcher.

dog chain n [**dog** n[1] **B2a**]

In logging: see quot.

1959 *AmSp* 34.77 **nCA,** *Dog chain*. . . A chain used to hold the logs together in the log pond, or boom.

dog chaser See **dog catcher 1**

dog-cheap adj [*OED* 1526 →; *"arch."*] Cf **dog n[1] B18a**

1859 Elwyn *Glossary* 40 **NEng,** *Dog cheap,* for *extremely cheap,* we have preserved from our North Country ancestors [of England]. **1908** *DN* 3.305 **eAL, wGA,** *Dog cheap*. . . Very cheap.

dog cherry n Also *dog hackberry* [Cf **dog** n[1] **B18b**]

A **hackberry** (here: *Celtis occidentalis*).

1908 Britton *N. Amer. Trees* 354, It [=*Celtis occidentalis*] is also known as . . Dog-cherry. *Ibid* 355, *Dog Hackberry*. . . is known to occur from New York to Illinois and South Dakota, southward to Pennsylvania and Missouri.

dog chimney n [Var (prob folk-etym) of *(wattle and) daub chimney;* cf **cat n 4**]

1954 *Harder Coll.* **cwTN,** *Daubed chimley*. A chimney made of sticks and mud. Also *dog chimney.*

dog coop n Cf **dog box**

A small enclosure or cage for a dog; a dog house.

1970 *DARE* (Qu. M22, . . *Kinds of buildings . . on farms*) Inf **NY**233, Dog coop. **1984** *McDavid Coll.* **csOK,** Dog coop—cage on a pickup truck, to take dogs on hunts. Informant: retired farmer, 72 years old, 6th grade educ. **1988** *DARE* File **ceWI,** We're going to tear down the old dog coop [=a large outdoor pen] and build a new one.

dog corn bread See **dogbread**

dog currant n

A **currant B1** (here: *Ribes hudsonianum* var *petiolare*).

1937 U.S. Forest Serv. *Range Plant Hdbk.* B132, The berries of this species . . , because of their peculiar, musky odor, are rarely used by man. This perhaps partly explains why western black currant is sometimes known as dog currant.

dog daisy n

1 =**dog fennel 1.** [*EDD* 1887, 1891]

1900 Lyons *Plant Names* 37, *A[nthemis] Cotula*. . . Dog . . Daisy. **1931** Harned *Wild Flowers Alleghanies* 591, *Anthemis Cotula*. . . Various appellations have been generously assigned to this common plant, such as "Dog Daisy." **1940** Clute *Amer. Plant Names* 74, *A. cotula*. . . Dog-daisy. **1959** Carleton *Index Herb. Plants* 38, *Dog-daisy:* Anthemis cotula.

2 An **oxeye** (here: *Chrysanthemum leucanthemum*). [*EDD* 1888 →]

1889 *Century Dict.* 1444, *Oxeye daisy*. . . Also called . . *dog-daisy.* **1900** Lyons *Plant Names* 98, *C. Leucanthemum*. . . Dog-daisy. **1940** Clute *Amer. Plant Names* 79, *Ox-eye Daisy*. . . Dog-daisy. **1959** Carleton *Index Herb. Plants* 38, *Dog-daisy:* Anthemis cotula; Chrysanthemum (v).

3 A **yarrow** (here: *Achillea millefolium*).

1900 Lyons *Plant Names* 12, *A[chillea] Millefolium*. . . Dog-daisy. **1911** Henkel *Amer. Med. Leaves* 39, *Yarrow*. . . *Other common names*. . . Dog daisy. **1971** Krochmal *Appalachia Med. Plants* 30, *Achillea millefolium*. . . *Common Names*. . . Dog daisy. **1974** (1977) Coon *Useful Plants* 100, Dog daisy. . . has feathery, fern-like leaves and quite beautiful heads of white to pink blooms.

dog dandelion n

=**fall dandelion.**

1900 Lyons *Plant Names* 219, *L[eontodon] autumnalis*. . . Dog Dandelion.

dog dare See **double-dog dare**

dog-day cicada n Also *dog-day harvest fly, ~ locust, ~ musician, ~ singer* [From its being heard esp in late summer]

A **cicada.**

1854 Emmons *Agriculture NY* 5.152, *Cicada canicularis,* Dogday Harvestfly. **1855** Amer. Inst. NYC *Annual Rept. for 1854* 216, The seventeen year and the dog-day cicada are . . familiarly known to us as locusts. **a1862** (1864) Thoreau *ME Woods* 236, I heard the dog-day locust here. . . The area for locusts must be small in the Maine woods. **1909** Hertwig *Manual Zool.* (transl. Kingsley) 489, The . . *C[icada] tibicen,* or dog-day harvest fly, . . [is] noticeable from . . [its] shrill notes. **1932** *DN* 6.283 **swCT,** *Dog day singers.* Locusts. They come about the time dog days begin. **1942** Berrey-Van den Bark *Amer. Slang* 120.52, Dog-day musician, *a locust.* **1962** *AmSp* 37.197, *Dog-Day Cicada.* One of an American genus commonly heard in late summer. **1970** *Living Museum* 32.212 **IL,** The larger [i.e. than the periodical cicadas] dog-day cicadas are black with green markings and have a life-cycle extending over two to five years.

dog days, in adv phr

For a very long time.

1969-70 *DARE* (Qu. A16, *A very long period of time: "I haven't seen him ______."*) Infs **NC**78, **VA**69, In dog days.

dog derby n **AK**

A dogsled race.

1935 *Alaska Sportsman* Jan 20 (Tabbert *Alaskan Engl.*), Fairbanks' annual dog derby, an eighty-mile non-stop dog team race from Fairbanks to Salchaket and return to Fairbanks will be held March 10, 1935. **1945** *Anchorage Daily Times* (AK) Mar 23 (Tabbert *Alaskan Engl.*), The greatest event of the Galena social season, the "Dog Derby," took place last Sunday and Monday. **1966** Huntington *On Edge of Nowhere* 127 **AK,** Around this time, 1938 and 1939, the people got all interested in dogsled racing again. It had been a big thing around Nome during gold rush days . . but when the gold played out, so did the dog derbies.

dog doctor n [**dog** n^1 **B18a;** cf *horse doctor* an incompetent doctor]

See quots.

1954 *Harder Coll.* **cwTN,** *Dog doctor:* A physician who is not very capable. **1970** *DARE* (Qu. BB53b, . . *A doctor who is not very capable or doesn't have a very good reputation*) Inf **SC**70, Dog doctor.

dog driver n

1 =**dog musher.** [*DCan* 1857 →] **AK**

1915 Stuck *10000 Miles* 401 **AK,** There is a great deal of cruelty and brutality amongst dog drivers in Alaska. **1943** *Alaska Sportsman* Apr 11 (Tabbert *Alaskan Engl.*), Dog drivers with more than two or three dogs have to be especially careful to harness their teams so that dogs with clashing temperaments are kept apart. **1976** [see **dog punch**].

2 In logging: see quot. [**dog** n^1 **B2a**] Cf **dog tripper**

1958 McCulloch *Woods Words* 48 **Pacific NW,** *Dog driver*—The man who drove dogs into logs so they could be hauled back into deep water when recovering stranded logs on the rear of a drive.

dog driving n **AK**

=**dog mushing.**

1862 in 1942 James *First Scientific Explor.* 94 **AK,** Here is a pleasure which you unfortunate outsiders can never even form an idea of [—] Dog driving! **1938** Wickersham *Old Yukon* 133 **AK,** "Mushon" . . is the dog-driver's rendering of the French-Canadian driver's command of "marche on,"—to go—hence, also the Alaskan verb "to mush," meaning to travel, in dog driving.

dog drunk adj phr **chiefly Sth, S Midl** See Map Cf **dog** n^1 **B17h, hog drunk**

Very drunk.

1859 Taliaferro *Fisher's R.* 94 **nwNC** (as of 1820s), He . . hated a "feller what would git down dog drunk under yer foot on the yeth." **1942** Berrey-Van den Bark *Amer. Slang* 106.7, *Drunk.* . . Dog drunk. **1954** *Harder Coll.* **cwTN,** Dog drunk: Intoxicated. **1965-70** *DARE* (Qu. DD15, *A person who is thoroughly drunk*) 29 Infs, **chiefly Sth, S Midl,** Dog drunk [15 of 29 Infs were gs educ; 15 were comm type 5.]; [**AL**10, **GA**72, **SC**34, **TX**100, Drunk as a dog]. **1976** Lynn-Vecsey *Loretta Lynn* 31 **eKY,** One time me and Marie were supposed to be cleaning the kitchen but we got into some home-brewed beer my brother left around. We got dog drunk before we remembered we were supposed to be cleaning up.

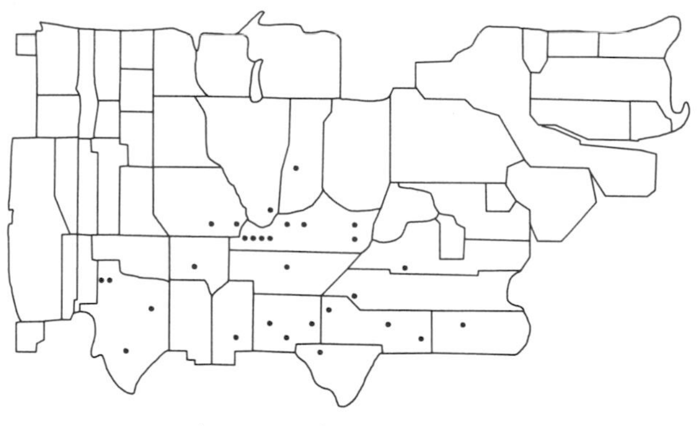
•dog drunk (Qu. DD15)

dog-ear tear n Also *dog ear* Cf **calf tail**

1965-70 *DARE* (Qu. W27, . . *A three-cornered tear in a piece of clothing from catching it on something sharp*) Infs **AZ**16, **CA**161, **IL**77, 83, 84, **NE**3, **NY**165, **PA**7, **TN**36, Dog-ear tear; **TX**51, Dog-ear tear—heard [FW sugg]; **KY**5, **WV**16, Dog ear.

‡dog-eat-cat adj

Ruthlessly competitive, "dog-eat-dog."

1966 *DARE* FW Addit **seWA,** *Dog-eat-cat*—used by a gas station attendant to describe a competitive situation.

dogee See **dogie**

dog elder n

=**highbush cranberry.**

1931 Clute *Common Plants* 94, Among species certainly named for the dog are the dog-rose *(Rosa canina)* . . the dog-elder (*Viburnum Americanum* [sic]), and the dog-laurel (*Leocothoe Catesbaei* [sic]). The last three mentioned are mis-applications . . for they are neither tansy, elder, nor laurel.

dogey See **dogie**

dog eye n

1 See quot.

1944 *AmSp* 19.106 [Vocab of sailors], The reproachful or supplicatory stare is the *dog-eye* or the *moose-eye* ('And here is this big Korean dog-eyeing me all the time'). **1986** *NADS Letters* **AR,** [A *dog eye* is a] strong, direct stare[.] No blink refex [sic][.] "Don't dog eye my biscuit—you can not have it."

2 also *dog's-eye:* In marble play: see quot. Cf **cat's-eye 1**

c1970 Wiersma *Marbles Terms, Dog-eye* or *dog's-eye.* . . (1) An otherwise consistently colored marble with a single scratch or crack (2) esp. in plural, the type of game played using such marbles. *Ibid, Dog-eyes.* . . Multi-colored marbles.

dog-eye v

1944 [see **dog eye** n **1**]. **1986** [see **dog eye** n **1**].

dogface n Also *dog-face butterfly, dog's-head* [See quot 1902]

Either of two similar butterflies: *Colias eurydice* or *C. caesonia.* Also called **flying pansy**

1902 Holland *Butterfly Book* 288, The dark outer borders [of the wings] . . [are] disposed upon the lighter ground color so as to present the appearance of a rude outline of the head of a dog, whence these butterflies [=*Meganostoma eurydice* and *M. caesonia*] have sometimes been called the "dog-face butterflies." **1911** *Century Dict. Suppl., Dog's-head.* . . An American pierid butterfly, *Zerene caesonia,* occurring abundantly in the southern United States. . . The outline of the yellow of the fore wings suggests the head of a dog. **1926** Essig *Insects N. Amer.* 637, *The flying pansy* or *California dog-face, Zerene eurydice* . . has a wing expanse of 25-50 mm. **1980** Milne-Milne *Audubon Field Guide Insects* 726, This [=California dog face *(Colias eurydice)*] is the state butterfly of California, . . The larger Southern Dog Face *(C. caesonia), . . has yellow wings.*

dog-faced adj

Contemptible.

1962 Fox *Southern Fried* 149 **SC,** I came right back at him and called him a dog-faced liar.

dog-faced rattlesnake See **dog-headed rattlesnake**

dogfall v **West** Cf **dogfall** n **2**

Among cowboys: see quot 1941.

1941 Writers' Program *Guide WY* 461, *Dog-fall.* . . To throw a steer with feet under him. **1968** Adams *Western Words* 95.

dogfall n

1 See quots 1909, 1933. **chiefly S Midl**

1898 Lloyd *Country Life* 84 **AL,** So we called it a dog fall as to the first round and quit. **1909** *DN* 3.395 **nwAR,** *Dog-fall.* . . A fall in wrestling in which neither party has the advantage. **1933** *AmSp* 8.1.48 **Ozarks,** *Dog fall.* . . A tie, a draw. The term is commonly used with reference to fights or wrestling matches. **1954** *Harder Coll.* **cwTN. c1960** *Wilson Coll.* **csKY.**

2 Among cowboys: a throw in which the steer falls with all four legs under him; a steer that falls in this way. **West** Cf **bulldog** v^1, **dogfall** v

1936 McCarthy *Lang. Mosshorn* np **West** [Rodeo term], *Dogfall.* A steer of this type invariably falls on all four legs straight down. Cowhorn steers generally fall on their side. The dogfall animal must be let up and the cowboy again tries to roll the steer over. **1970** *DARE* File **West** [Unidentified newspaper clipping, headed "Parade Kicks off 41st Fiesta De Los Vaqueros"], The curse of the bull doggers is a dog fall. A steer must fall with all four legs parallel with the ground before the timer blows the whistle. When the critter falls with his legs under him the steer wrestler must spend valuable seconds getting him laid out flat.

dog feed n Also *dog meat* Cf **crowbait**

1966-70 *DARE* (Qu. K44, *A bony or poor-looking horse*) Infs **CA**210, **PA**23, Dog feed; **FL**12, Dog meat.

dog fennel n

1 also *dog-fennel daisy, dog's fennel:* A strong-scented camomile *(Anthemis cotula).* [*OED* 1523 →] **chiefly S Midl, Sth** Also called **chiggerweed 1, dillweed, dog camomile, dog daisy 1,**

goose grass 1h, hog fennel 1, horse daisy 2, jayweed, Johnny-Appleseed's-weed, madder, manzanillo, mayweed, oxeye camomile, pathweed, pigsty daisy, piss-the-bed, poison daisy, stinking camomile, stinking daisy, stinking mayweed, stinkweed

1797 Imlay *Western Terr.* 263 **nwFL,** The wild or dog's fennel affords a ready and proper material for it [=silkworm cocoon]. **1828** Rafinesque *Med. Flora* 1.44, *Vulgar Names*—May-Weed, Dog's Fennel [etc]. **1867** Beecher *Norwood* 61 **NEng,** A little girl . . held out her little hands full of dog-fennel to him. **1885** *Bot. Gaz.* 10.214, In this article is mention of the distribution by the same party of seeds of dog-fennel or May-weed, under a belief in its antimalarial virtues. **1899** Tarkington *Gentleman* 196 **IN,** [The dog's] surprised head [was] rakishly garnished with a hasty wreath of dog-fennel daisies. **1940** Faulkner *Hamlet* 30 **MS,** What dust the three horses raised blew lightly aside on the faint breeze, among the dogfennel and bitterweed just beginning to bloom in the roadside ditches. **1960** Hall *Smoky Mt. Folks* 51 **wNC, eTN,** She depended on . . dog fennel for "rheumatiz." **1965–70** *DARE* (Qu. S6) Infs **GA**5, **MO**8, 13, Dog fennel; (Qu. S11) Inf **AR**28, Dog fennel; (Qu. S17) Infs **AR**24, **KY**9, 48, **TN**13, Dog fennel; (Qu. S20) Inf **MO**34, Dog fennel; (Qu. S21) 84 Infs, **chiefly Sth, S Midl,** Dog fennel; **FL**16, Dog fennels; (Qu. S22) Inf **MO**15, Dog fennel; (Qu. S26a) Infs **DC**5, **KS**1, **KY**40, Dog fennel; (Qu. S26d) Infs **MD**15, 20, Dog fennel; (Qu. S26e) Infs **CA**105, 200, **MO**39, **VA**24, Dog fennel. [*DARE* Ed: Some of these Infs may refer instead to other senses of **dog fennel.**]

2 usu *yellow dog-fennel:* A **sneezeweed** (here: usu *Helenium amarum,* but also *H. autumnale*).

1866 Smith *Bill Arp* 35 **GA,** Flowers have bloomed sweetly, . . dog fennel has yallered the ground. **1898** *Jrl. Amer. Folkl.* 11.229, *Helenium tenuifolium,* . . yellow-dog-fennel. **1935** (1943) Muenscher *Weeds* 495, *Helenium tenuifolium*. . . Bitterweed, Fennel, Yellow dog fennel, Sneeze-weed. **1940** Steyermark *Flora MO* 541, *Yellow Dog Fennel*. . . Fields and waste ground. . . Stock avoid eating it. **1959** Carleton *Index Herb. Plants* 38, *Dog-fennel:* Anthemis cotula; Aster ericoides; Helenium autumnalis [sic]. **1974** Morton *Folk Remedies* 71 **SC,** *Yellow Dog-fennel*. . . *Helenium amarum . . (Helenium tenuifolium . .).* Some people break off below leaves, boil the entire top and drink "tea" for fever.

3 also *dog's fennel:* An aster (here: *Aster ericoides*).

1900 Lyons *Plant Names* 52, *A[ster] ericoides*. . . White Heath-aster, . . Dog-fennel. **1940** Clute *Amer. Plant Names* 76, *White Heath-aster*. . . Dog's fennel. **1959** [see **dog fennel 2**].

4 A **boneset 1** (here: either *Eupatorium capillifolium* or *E. compositifolium*). **chiefly S Midl, Sth**

1901 *Torreya* 1.117 **GA,** *Eupatorium compositifolium*. . . Dog-fennel. . . This and *Anthemis Cotula,* the dog-fennel of north Georgia, are not usually found in the same vicinity, hence there is little if any confusion of names. **1946** Tatnall *Flora DE* 252, *E. capillifolium*. . . *Dog Fennel*. . . Frequent. **1953** Greene–Blomquist *Flowers South* 130, *Dog-Fennel (Eupatorium capillifolium)*. . . Although classed as a "weed," it is one of the picturesque plants of autumn. **1964** Batson *Wild Flowers SC* 110, *Dog-fennel: Eupatorium compositifolium*. . . Summer and fall. North Carolina to Florida. **1970** Correll *Plants TX* 1553, *Eupatorium capillifolium*. . . Dog-fennel. . . Corolla white.

5 also *yellow dog-fennel:* A **fetid marigold** (here: *Dyssodia papposa*).

1912 Blatchley *IN Weed Book* 161, *Bœbera papposa*. . . Yellow Dog-fennel. . . The odor . . is . . disgusting. **1914** Georgia *Manual Weeds* 485, *Dyssodia papposa*. . . Yellow Dog-fennel. . . A vile weed. **1931** U.S. Dept. Ag. *Misc. Pub.* 101.166, *Prairie dogweed . . ,* also called dog fennel or fetid-marigold, . . is . . fair horse feed in parts of northern New Mexico.

6 =**robin's plantain.**

1966 *DARE* FW Addit **KY**17, Dog fennel—robin's plantain *(Erigeron pulchellus).*

dogfight n

1 A fistfight, brawl.

1879 (1880) Twain *Tramp Abroad* 626 **MO,** The daily journals of Hamburg, Frankfort [etc]. . . contain no "editorials" whatever; . . no information about prize fights or other dog fights. **1923** Cook *50 Yrs.* 115 **TX,** Fistfights . . were called "dog fights" by the cowboys. Fighting "dog style" was of such rare occurrence among cowboys that . . I never saw one instance in which men threw down all weapons and engaged in a slugging match. **1968–70** *DARE* (Qu. Y12b, *A real fight in which blows are struck*) Infs **KY**94, **NC**86, **VA**31, Dogfight; (Qu. Y13, *A fist fight with several people in it*) Inf **IL**76, Dogfight. **1968** Adams *Western Words* 96, *Dog fight*—A cowboy's name for a fist fight. The early cowman felt that such fights were beneath his dignity. As one said "If the Lord had intended me to fight like a dog, He'd a-give me longer teeth and claws."

2 A coarse, vulgar event. Cf **catfight**

c1970 *Halpert Coll.* **wKY,** I wouldn't be seen with him at a dogfight. **1975** Gould *ME Lingo* 75, *Dog fight*. . . The Maine mind was able . . to imagine the *dog fight* to be a gauge of sartorial judgment, as if one should choose the clothing he wears to a *dog fight* just as much as he chooses the outfit he will wear to a wedding. This unlikely juxtaposition of unsimilar situations is used often in Maine speech, in this fashion: "What did you think of Rob's red necktie?" "That god-awful thing! I wouldn't wear it to a dog fight." **1979** *DARE* File **MA,** Awful looking pants! I wouldn't have worn them to a dogfight.

dog finger n **Sth**

The index or the middle finger; see quots.

1926 (1968) Puckett *S. Negro* 46 **Sth,** Some Negroes have a peculiar belief about the so-called "dog-finger." This finger is the first, or middle finger (opinions differ) of the right hand (one conjurer claims it is the index finger, while another informant says the second finger of the left hand). **c1938** in 1970 Hyatt *Hoodoo* 1.609 **neSC,** Yo' git de lengt' of dat lef' han' fingah—dat *dog fingah*. . . The fingah off her lef' han'—de *dog fingah.* **1952** Brown *NC Folkl.* 1.533, *Dog finger*. . . The index finger. **1972** Jones–Hawes *Step it Down* 12 **eGA** [Black], Tom Thumb, dog finger, middle finger. . . Your dog finger, that's your bad-luck finger. . . causes bad luck to people. . . If an old man or old lady point their dog finger at you, you know you're going to have bad luck.

dogfish n

1 Any of var sharks of the families Carcharhinidae, Scyliorhinidae, or Squalidae, but esp *Mustelus* spp and *Squalus acanthias.* For other names see **dog shark, grayfish, houndfish 2, sand shark, skittle-dog**

1674 in 1889 Gt. Brit. Pub. Rec. Office *Calendar State Papers Colonial Amer.* 581, On the sea coasts, whales, grampus, seals, sharks, herringhogs, porpoise, dogfish, sturgeons. **1709** (1967) Lawson *New Voyage* 158 **NC,** The Dog-fish are a small sort of the Shark Kind; and are caught with Hook and Line. **1814** Bentley *Diary* IV.297 *(DAE),* The dog fish have been up to the mills in great numbers. **1856** *Porter's Spirit of Times* 20 Sept 43/2, Fishermen in our waters are often annoyed by the water-terrapin, the gar, . . and the dogfish. **1880** *Harper's New Mth. Mag.* Aug 340/2 **ME,** Everywhere there was the most execrable character of the dogfish. **1889** Munroe *Dorymates* 39 *(DAE),* Dog-fish, sharks, and other hungry sea pirates were breakfasting off the newly arrived strangers. **1928** Pan-Pacific Research Inst. *Jrl.* 3.3.11, *Squalidae.* The dogfishes. **1960** Amer. Fisheries Soc. *List Fishes* 7, Chain dogfish . . *Scyliorhinus retifer*. . . Smooth dogfish . . *Mustelus canis. Ibid* 8, Spiny dogfish . . *Squalus acanthias.* **1965–70** *DARE* (Qu. P2) Inf **VA**46, Dogfish (young shark); **VA**55, Dogfish—sharklike; (Qu. P4) 15 Infs, **chiefly Atlantic, Pacific,** Dogfish; (Qu. P14) Inf **VA**55, Dogfish. **1975** Gould *ME Lingo* 75, The *dogfish* is a small shark that feeds on edible fish and is the bane of the handliner. About the time a haddock should be taken, the *dogfish* moves in and spoils everything.

2 =**bowfin. chiefly Upper Missip Valley, Gt Lakes** See Map

1842 DeKay *Zool. NY* 4.270, Under the head of *A. calva,* Dr. Kirtland states that "the *Dog-fish* is found in Lake Erie, where it is frequently called *'The Lake Lawyer.'*" **1882** U.S. Natl. Museum *Bulletin* 16.94, *A. calva*. . . *Mud-fish; Dog-fish*. . . A voracious fish of remarkable tenacity of life. **1905** U.S. Bur. Fisheries *Rept. for 1904* 591, The male dog-fish *(Amia calva)* also cuts off the young shoots when building its nest. **1908** Forbes–Richardson *Fishes of IL* 39, The usual local name of this species [=*Amia calva*] is "dogfish" in the Great Lake [sic] region and the upper Mississippi Valley. **1956** Harlan–Speaker *IA Fish* 51, The dogfish is primarily carnivorous, feeding largely on fishes of all kinds . . , frogs, crayfish, large insects and their larvae, leeches, and other aquatic life. **1965–70** *DARE* (Qu. P3) 45 Infs, **chiefly Upper Missip Valley, Gt Lakes,** Dogfish. **1973** *DARE* File, In the Upper Midwest the bowfin is called dogfish. **1983** Becker *Fishes WI* 251, *Bowfin*. . . Other common names: dogfish, mudfish [etc].

3 =**burbot.**

1842 DeKay *Zool. NY* 4.285, *The Spotted Burbot. Lota maculosa* . . is known under the various local names of *La Loche, Methy, Dog-fish* and *Eel-pout.* **1884** Goode *Fisheries U.S.* 1.236, The Burbot is known . . as the Dogfish in Lake Erie. **1983** Becker *Fishes WI* 747, *Burbot*. . . Other common names: . . dogfish (Minnesota).

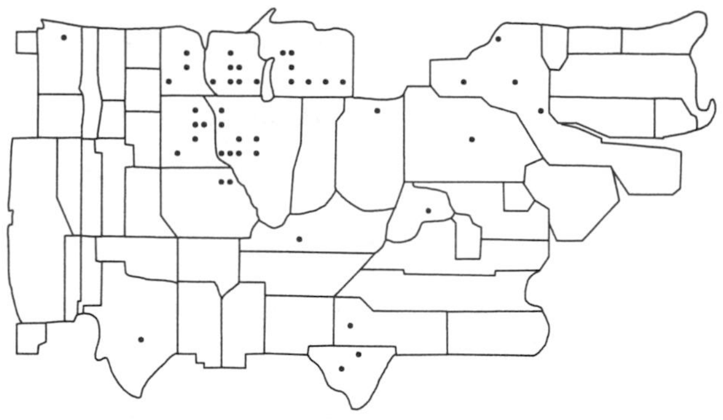

•dogfish 2 (Qu. P3)

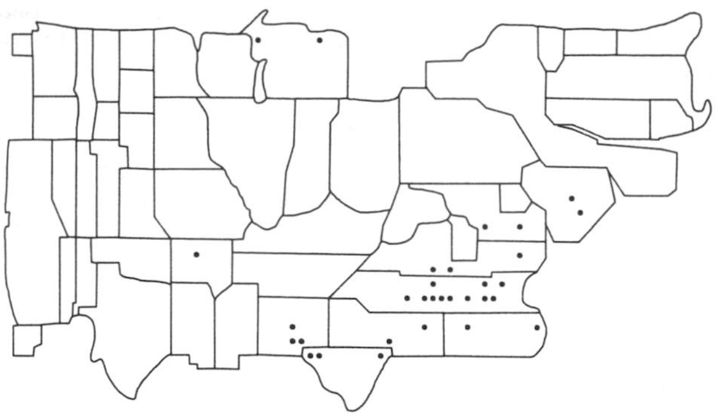

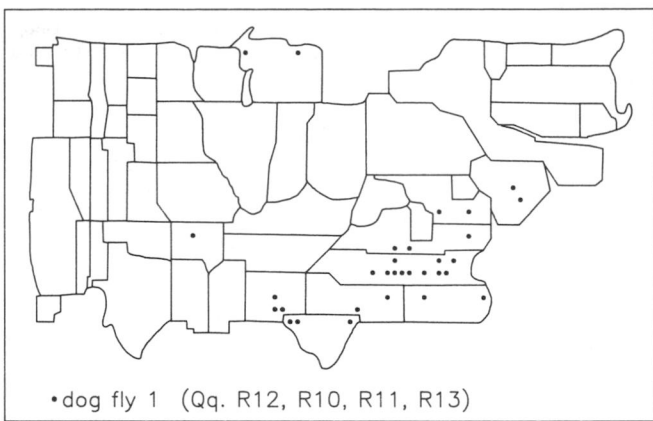

•dog fly 1 (Qq. R12, R10, R11, R13)

4 A **mudminnow** (here: *Umbra limi*).

1882 U.S. Natl. Museum *Bulletin* 16.350, *U[mbra] limi*. . . Mud Minnow; Dog-fish. **1896** *Ibid* 47.623, *Dogfish*. . . Coloration dull olive green, mottled with darker and with about 14 narrow, pale, transverse bars. [**1908** Forbes–Richardson *Fishes of IL* 203, Mud-minnows . . are frequently mistaken by fishermen for the young of the dogfish, from which, however, they are very readily distinguished by the short dorsal fin.] **1966** *DARE* (Qu. P7) Inf **MI**20, Dogfish. **1983** Becker *Fishes WI* 387, *Central Mudminnow*. . . Other common names: . . dogfish. *Ibid* 390, The central mudminnow is used extensively as a bait minnow in Wisconsin and other states where it is plentiful.

5 also *electric dogfish:* A **stargazer** (here: *Astroscopus* spp).

1882 U.S. Natl. Museum *Proc.* 5.289, *Atroscopus anoplus*. . . *Dog-fish; Electric Dog-fish*. . . The fishermen at Galveston ascribe to it electric powers in life. **1911** *Century Dict. Suppl., Dogfish*. . . *Electric dogfish*, any fish of the genus *Astroscopus*.

6 =blackfish 3.

1889 *Century Dict.* 1719/2, *Dogfish*. . . A name of the *Dallia pectoralis*. . . Also called *blackfish*. [**1933** John G. Shedd Aquarium *Guide* 56, *Alaskan Blackfish*. . . The natives use it for food for themselves and their dogs.]

7 A **killifish:** either the **mummichog** or *Fundulus diaphanus*.

1906 NJ State Museum *Annual Rept. for 1905* 188, *Fundulus heteroclitus macrolepidotus*. . . Dog Fish. . . Mummichog. *Ibid* 193, *Fundulus diaphanus*. . . Killie Fish. Dog Fish.

8 A **toadfish** (here: *Opsanus tau*).

1931 *Copeia* 2.50 **TX,** *Opsanus tau*. . . A local name seems to be "dogfish," because "it sort of barks."

9 =northern pike.

1967 *DARE* (Qu. P1) Inf **IL**9, Dogfish—pike.

10 A **mudpuppy** (here: *Necturus maculosus*).

1889 *Century Dict.* 1719/2, *Dogfish*. . . A name of the menobranchus or mud-puppy, *Necturus maculatus,* a batrachian reptile.

dog fishing n

1967 *DARE* (Qu. P17, . . *Fish[ing] by lowering a line and sinker close to the bottom of the water*) Inf **ID**5, Dog fishing.

dog fit n Cf **cat fit, duck fit**

An emotional outburst, usu of anger.

c1960 *Wilson Coll.* **csKY,** *Dog fit*. . . A nervous outburst. **1967** *DARE* (Qu. KK11, *To make great objections or a big fuss about something: "When we asked him to do that, he ______."*) Inf **TX**36, Had dog fits. **1984** Wilder *You All Spoken Here* 206 **Sth,** Havin' a dog fit: A conniption fit; upset and agitated.

dog fly n

1 A fly such as those of the families Muscidae and Tabanidae; see quots. **chiefly C and S Atl, AL** See Map

1965–70 *DARE* (Qu. R12) 26 Infs, **chiefly C and S Atl, AL,** Dog fly; **FL**22, Dog fly—comes in September, leaves with frost, bites; **GA**3, Dog fly—looks like a housefly, but bites; (Qu. R10) Inf **FL**17, Dog fly; (Qu. R11) Infs **FL**17, **NC**80, Dog fly; (Qu. R13), Inf **AR**23, Dog fly. **1969** *DARE* File **neNC,** Dog fly—small fly similar to a housefly, which bites.

2 =cicada. Cf **dog-day cicada**

1966 *DARE* (Qu. R12) Inf **MI**2, Dog fly or July fly.

dogfoot n [Prob from the shape of the flower panicles]
=orchard grass.

1915 *DN* 4.182 **VA,** *Dog-foot*. . . Orchard grass. **1967** *DARE* (Qu. L9a) Inf **TN**7, Dogfoot.

dogged See **dog** v **6**

dogged out adj phr Also *dogged up* Cf **dike** v, **dog** n[1] **B4, 5a, dog** v **11**

Dressed up.

1934 Farrell *Young Manhood* 120 **Chicago IL,** He was thin and sallow, and dogged out in classy clothes. **1968–70** *DARE* (Qu. W37, *When a woman puts on her good clothes and tries to look her best, you say she's ______*) Inf **WV**2, All dogged out; (Qu. W38, *When a man dresses himself up in his best clothes, you say he's ______*) Infs **OK**57, **WI**21, Dogged up (*or* out). **1968** *DARE* FW Addit **csLA,** All dogged out = dressed in your best clothes. This is common, not limited to teenage usage.

dogger n

1 In logging:

a See quots. [**dog** n[1] **B2a**]

1905 U.S. Forest Serv. *Bulletin* 61.35 **Sth, Pacific NW,** *Dogger*. . . One who attaches the dogs or hooks to a log before it is steam skidded [=moved with a steam engine]. **1958** McCulloch *Woods Words* 48 **Pacific NW,** *Dogger*—a. The man who drove in the dog for the dog tripper to knock out. The name was also applied to the man who drove dogs into logs to make up a turn ready to be hauled down the skidway by animals. b. The man who pried dogs out of logs when they came to the landing in animal skidding days. **1959** *AmSp* 34.77 **nCA,** *Dogger*. . . The person who pries the dogs . . out of the logs.

b In logging: see quot 1969. [**dog** n[1] **B2c**]

1950 *Western Folkl.* 9.121 **nwOR** [Sawmill workers' speech], *Dogger*. One who rides the carriage and operates the dogs. **1969** Sorden *Lumberjack Lingo* 34 **NEng, Gt Lakes,** *Dogger*—One who rides the head rig carriage in a sawmill and sets the dogs into the wood to hold the logs in place while being sawed. Same as carriage rider.

2 One who wrestles or throws a steer to the ground; a bulldogger; the horse used in bulldogging. **West** Cf *bulldogger* at **bulldog** v[1], **dogging n**

1947 *Reader's Digest* Oct 113/2 **West,** It took Rambo three years to train his two horses—a roper and a dogger. **1965** [see **bulldog** v[1]]. **1968** Adams *Western Words* 96, *Dogger*—One who bulldogs.

doggery n **chiefly Sth, S Midl** Cf **dog hole 1, grocery 1**

A saloon, groggery, "dive."

1821 in 1830 Royall *Letters AL* 145, A Doggery is a place where spirituous liquors are sold. **1856** Cartwright *Autobiog.* 376 **IL,** There was a general rally from . . the loose-footed, doggery-haunting, dissipated renegades of the towns. **1859** (1942) Patterson *Travel Diary* 185 **VA,** There are gaming tents, restaurants, stores, little doggeries where poor whiskey is retailed at "10 cents a nip". **1866** Smith *Bill Arp* 136 **GA,** About twice in a while I go to the doggery and git *blue*. **1867** Harris *Sut Lovingood Yarns* 230 **TN,** I'd foun a doggery in full milk, an' hated pow'ful bad tu leave that settilment. **1899** (1912) Green *VA Folk-Speech* 150, *Doggery*. . . A mean grog-shop. **1903** *DN* 2.311 **seMO,** *Doggery*. . . A saloon or dram shop. **1912** Lewis *Apaches of NY* 13 **NYC,** Tricker stopped for a moment in a little doggery from which came the tump-tump of a piano and the scuffle of a dance. **1953** Randolph

Down in Holler 240 **Ozarks,** *Doggery.* . . A saloon, a dramshop, a *grocery.* "That fool boy orter be a-workin' instead of hangin' around them doggeries."

doggie n

1 In marble play: =**dobe 5.** Cf **doogie**

1895 *DN* 1.387, *Doggies:* the commonest kind of marbles, generally colored brown. **1955** *PADS* 23.16, *Doggie.* . . Very cheap clay marbles.

2 =**dog** n[1] **B10. esp PA**

1900 *DN* 2.32 [College slang], *Doggie.* . . A sausage. **1965–70** *DARE* (Qu. H40, *A small sausage that is put into a long roll or bun to make a sandwich*) Infs **MD**28, **NJ**53, **PA**22, 41, 136, 143, Doggie; (Qu. FF2, . . *Kinds of parties*) Inf **PA**242, Doggie roast—campfire and kids singing, party at night.

3 See quot. Cf **dog nut**

1967 *DARE* (Qu. H30, *An oblong cake, cooked in deep fat*) Inf **NJ**3, Doggie.

4 in phr *doggie, doggie, where's your bone* and varr: See quot. Cf **button 2a**

1967–70 *DARE* (Qu. EE3, *Games in which you hide an object and then look for it*) Inf **MA**8, Doggie, doggie, who's got your bone; **MI**123, Doggie, doggie, your bone is gone; **NY**28, Doggie, doggie, where's your bone; **NY**161, Doggie, doggie, wish a bone.

5 in phr *my doggie won't bite you* and varr: See quot.

1983 *DARE* File *(What games do children play around here, in which they form a ring, and either sing or recite a rhyme?)* 2 Infs, **UT,** My (little) doggie won't bite you; 1 Inf, **WY,** I've gotta little doggie.

doggies, by exclam Also *by dogies* Cf **dog** n[1] **B7, dog** v **6,** and *DS* NN6–9

1956 Moody *Home Ranch* 20 **CO** (as of 1911), "Fifty miles, huhh!" he snorted, "By dogies." **c1970** *Halpert Coll.* **wKY, wTN,** By doggies = a mild oath.

dogging vbl n See **dog** v **1**

dogging n Cf **bulldog** v[1]

Throwing a calf or steer to the ground by twisting its neck.

1967 *DARE* Tape **TX**25, In some . . professional rodeos they have a steer tyin' or steer ropin', where it's just like in the steer doggin', only they come from behind the barrier like they're ropin' calves and one man ropes the head and the other one ropes the heels of the steer.

dogging up See **dog** v **7**

doggins n [**dog** v **12**] Cf **bulldog** v[2]

1949 *AmSp* 24.9 [Argot of the moonshiner], *Doggins.* . . Liquor obtained from used barrels by the process of sweating.

doggish adj

1 also *doggy:* Lecherous; brutish. [*OED* →1610; *"Obs."*] Cf **dog** n[1] **B15**

1965 Brown *Manchild* 370 **NY** [Black], That old nogood damn doggish husband of mine had to go and get himself in jail, just for bein' so goddamn doggish. *Ibid* 371, I remembered Mama telling me, "Boy, don't be so doggish," when I would bring home one girl one day and another girl the next. **1970** *DARE* (Qu. AA6b, . . *A man who is fond of being with women and tries to attract their attention—if he's rude or not respectful*) Inf **FL**48, Doggy, full of dog. [Inf Black]

2 Greedy, stingy.

1968 *DARE* (Qu. U36b, . . *A person who saves in a mean way or is greedy in money matters: "She certainly is ______."*) Infs **MS**60, **OK**54, Doggish. [Both Infs Black]

doggity adj

1954 *Harder Coll.* **cwTN,** *Doggity.* . . Hateful, stubborn, mean. "He's just doggity."

doggone my cat(s) See **dog my cats**

dog grass n

1 =**quack grass. chiefly NEast, esp RI**

c1873 in 1976 Miller *Shaker Herbs* 167 **NY, PA,** Dog Grass—*Agropyron repens.* **1876** Hobbs *Bot. Hdbk.* 44, Dog grass, Couch grass. **1910** Graves *Flowering Plants* 79 **CT,** *Agropyron repens* . . Dog Grass. **1930** Sievers *Amer. Med. Plants* 49, *Quack Grass—Agropyron repens* . . Dog grass. **1968–69** *DARE* (Qu. S8) Infs **RI**5, 10, 12, 15, Dog grass; (Qu. S9) Infs **MA**40, **RI**4, Dog grass; (Qu. L8) Inf **LA**31, Dog grass hay. **1974** (1977) Coon *Useful Plants* 145, *Agropyron repens* . . dog-grass.

2 A **goosegrass 2b** (here: *Eleusine indica*).

1903 Small *Flora SE U.S.* 138, *Eleusine Indica* . . Dog Grass.

doggy adj

1 Stylish, fashionable. [**dog** n[1] **B4;** orig coll slang] *old-fash*

1897 *Bookman* 5.448/2, Twenty years ago the college man had a most picturesque and variegated vocabulary . . [including] such words as "banger," "snab," . . "doggy," "mucker." **1915** *DN* 4.233 **neOH** [College slang], *Doggy.* . . Dressy; neat; handsome. **1925** *Lit. Digest* 14 Mar 65/1 **RI** [Brown University students' speech], "Doggy" [is] being well-dressed somewhat consciously and slightly conspicuously. **1945** Webster *Town Meeting* 180 **NEng,** It was no doggy place with tables.

2 See **doggish 1.**

3 Listless, lacking in energy. Cf **dog** v **8**

1930 Williams *Logger-Talk* 22 **Pacific NW,** *Doggy:* Indolent. **1950** *WELS (Feeling lifeless or without energy)* 3 Infs, **WI,** Doggy. **1966–70** *DARE* (Qu. BB39, *On a day when you don't feel just right, though not actually sick, you might say, "I'll be all right tomorrow—I'm just feeling ______ today."*) Inf **LA**2, Doggy; (Qu. KK30, *Feeling slowed up or without energy: "I certainly feel ______."*) Infs **IL**66, 78, **MI**9, 55, 119, Doggy.

dog hackberry See **dog cherry**

dog hair n

1 A **spikerush** (here: *Eleocharis tenuis*). Cf **hairgrass 2**

1952 Strausbaugh–Core *Flora WV* 160, *E[leocharis] tenuis* . . Dog-hair. **1970** *DARE* (Qu. S9) Inf **CA**195, Dog hair.

‡**2** See quot.

1945 Beck *Jersey Genesis* 199 **cNJ,** The waste [from cedar logs], curled up shavings the boys call dog-hair, that goes to the poultry people and nurseries and kennels.

dog-hair v, hence ppl adj *dog-haired* [Cf simile "thick as dog hair"]

See quots.

1953 Randolph *Down in Holler* 240 **Ozarks,** *Dog-hair.* . . To grow slender, by reason of too much crowding. A farmer said, "I'm afeared them oats is goin' to dog-hair on me. We done planted 'em too thick." **1958** McCulloch *Woods Words* 48 **Pacific NW,** *Dog-haired*—[Said of:] A dense stand of saplings or other second growth usually too young to log.

doghair grass n Cf **dog grass 1, hairgrass 1**

1983 *MJLF* 9.1.37 **ceKY,** *Doghair grass* . . a type of lawn grass.

dog hammer See **dog knocker**

dog head n

In moonshining: see quots.

1972 *Foxfire Book* 316 **nGA,** *Dog heads*—when the beer is almost ready to run, it will boil up of its own accord in huge, convulsive bubbles which follow each other one at a time. **1974** Maurer–Pearl *KY Moonshine* 117, *Dog head.* . . A large viscous bubble that forms in the still just before the cap is sealed.

dog-headed rattlesnake n Also *dog-faced rattlesnake*

A **rattlesnake** (here: *Crotalus molossus*).

1928 Baylor Univ. Museum *Contrib.* 16.19, On account of its head being unusually large as compared to the girth of its body, the Black-tailed Rattlesnake is sometimes called *Dog-headed Rattlesnake.* It inhabits only a limited area of western Texas. **1974** Shaw–Campbell *Snakes West* 227, For reasons hard to guess at, this two-and-a-quarter- to four-and-a-quarter-foot serpent [=*Crotalus molossus*] is sometimes called the dog-faced rattlesnake.

dog hobble n [See quot 1901 at **1**]

1 A **fetterbush 3** (here: *Leucothoe editorum*). **chiefly sAppalachians** Also called **dog laurel, hemlock 3, ivy, poison hemlock, switch-ivy**

1901 Lounsberry *S. Wild Flowers* 389, *Dog Hobble.* . . *Leucothoë Catesbaei.* . . The shrub's interwoven, thick growth makes it at times impossible for a dog to pass through. **1911** *Century Dict. Suppl., Dog-hobble.* . . One of the calfkills, *Leucothoë Catesbaei:* so called because its dense growth arrests dogs in the hunt. **1922** *Outing* Apr 292/3 **wNC,** I found it to be a small creek . . running under laurel and dog-hobble, spraying itself through windfalls, running around slippery logs. **1938** *Hall Coll.* **eTN,** Dog hobble, between a vine and a bush; hemlock; long, slim dark-colored bush, stays green all the time like a la'rel. **1939**

Ibid **wNC,** Pretty soon I found where the bear had went through the laurel and dog hobble in the direction of the other fork of the creek, 'cross the Woolly Head Ridge. **1961** Douglas *My Wilderness* 175 **wNC,** The dog-hobble shrub has whitish flowers that grow like chandeliers. **1964** Campbell *Great Smoky Wildflowers* 44, Dog hobble is restricted to the Southern Appalachians. . . In pre-park days, when bear hunting was practiced, the heavy bears could escape pursuing dogs by forcing their way through dense thickets of these shrubs, whereas the dogs became "hobbled" by the tangled growth. **1966–67** *DARE* (Qu. T5) Inf **TN**14, Dog hobble; (Qu. T16) Inf **NC**36, Dog hobble.

2 =hobblebush.

1940 Clute *Amer. Plant Names* 275, *Viburnum alnifolium*. . . Dog-hobble.

doghole n

1 =doggery. *obs*

1818 Fearon *Sketches* 194 **wPA,** "The Fountain Inn" is a miserable log-house, or what you would call a dog-hole: it was crowded with emigrants. **1859** (1968) Bartlett *Americanisms* 181, *Groggery*. A place where spirituous liquors are sold and drank; a grogshop. In the West, often called a Doggery or Dog-hole, and in New York a Rum-hole.

2 A small, shallow bay, used for loading lumber. **nCA, sOR coasts**

1919 Kyne *Capt. Scraggs* 187 **CA,** And there's a dog-hole down on the Gold Coast where I intended to land this cargo. **1949** Powers *Redwood Country* 79 **sOR, nCA,** He could put his ship into one of the 'dog-holes' of the coast in the blackest midnight. **1958** McCulloch *Woods Words* 48 **Pacific NW,** *Dog hole*—A small shallow bay or bight on the Mendocino coast where small lumber schooners could find enough shelter to take on a cargo.

3 A small mine, esp a coal mine.

1943 Korson *Coal Dust* 4 **Bituminous coal-mining areas,** Some farmers . . operated small mines variously called "country banks," "wagon mines," "dog holes," "gopher holes," or "father-and-son" mines. **1966** *DARE* Tape **OK**52, Years ago I had a few little dogholes myself, but . . there's always water aroun' kept me drownded out from some ol' mine . . that done give up. **1969** *DARE* FW Addit **CA**114, *Dogholes* [Gold] mines dug into the side of a hill, look like prairie-dog holes. **1973** *PADS* 59.34 **Bituminous coal-mining areas,** *Doghole mine* [*PADS* Ed: from the appearance of the entrance to such a *mine,* no bigger than a hole a dog might dig] . . a very small *mine* operated by a few men, usually taking coal which lies very near the surface. **1976** Lynn–Vecsey *Loretta Lynn* 139 **eKY,** This mine was what they call a drift mine— . . a tunnel straight back into the mountain. But it was one of those dog-holes, a cheap, nonunion mine.

4 In mining: see quots.

1960 Climax Molybdenum Co. *Manual* 46, *Doghole*—Any small opening driven in rock. **1973** *PADS* 59.29 **TN,** *Breakthrough* . . a small opening made through a *pillar,* now at legally predetermined distances, to permit air to pass freely from one *room* to another. . . [Also called] monkey hole, . . doghole (small).

dog hook n [**dog** n[1] **B2a**]

1 In logging: see quot. Cf **dog warp**

1905 U.S. Forest Serv. *Bulletin* 61.35 **Nth,** *Dog hook*. . . The strong hook on the end of a dogwarp.

2 In logging: see quots.

1905 U.S. Forest Serv. *Bulletin* 61.35 **Pacific NW,** *Dog hook*. . . A hook on the end of a haul-up chain of a size to permit its being hooked into a link of the chain when the latter is looped around a log or other object. **1958** McCulloch *Woods Words* 48 **Pacific NW,** *Dog hook*—A short coupling chain with hooks, used to tie logs together when skidding with animals. **1969** Sorden *Lumberjack Lingo* 34 **NEng, Gt Lakes,** *Dog hook*—Hook coupled with a short chain and used to bind logs together in horse skidding.

doghouse n

1 A **caboose** n[1] **2;** occas, the cupola on it; see quot 1977.

1898 (1970) Hamblen *Genl. Manager* 43 **IL,** You go back in the doghouse, an' don't you see nothin' that's goin' on; only git up in the cupalo an' watch out . . that yer train don't break in two. **1916** *DN* 4.356, *Dog-house*. A freight caboose. **1922** *DN* 5.181 **NW,** *Dog-house*. . . The cupola on a caboose. Railroad usage. **1932** *RR Mag.* Oct 367, *Dog house*—Caboose. **1937** *AmSp* 12.154 *Dog house*. Caboose. **1946** in 1953 Botkin–Harlow *Treas. Railroad Folkl.* 350, If you ever have occasion to locate the caboose on a freight train . . don't ask the ORC (conductor) to show you the way to the . . dog-house. . . Ask for the *caboose* . . for that's exactly what railroad men call the little red car that rides the rear end of every freight train. **1950** *WELS (The last car on a freight train)* 2 Infs, **WI,** Doghouse. **1977** Adams *Lang. Railroader* 46, *Doghouse:* A caboose. The cupola of a caboose. In logging railroading, a cabin placed on the tender of the locomotive for the conductor's use.

2 See quot.

1936 Adams *Cowboy Lingo* 14, The 'bunk-house' was equally well known as the 'dog-house,' 'dice-house,' 'dump,' 'shack,' or 'dive.'

3 Among oil field and farm workers: a shed or shelter in the field often used for changing clothes and eating; a toolshed; see quots.

1918 *DN* 5.24 **NW,** *Doghouse man*. . . The man who sews sacks under a weather shelter on a combine. Farmers. **1966** *Daily Oklahoman* (Oklahoma City OK) 11 Dec mag sec 11/2, There's nothing wrong with being in the "doghouse" at a well. It's a toolhouse located near the derrick. **1966–67** *DARE* Tape **OK**29, Doghouse. . . Ordinarily, it's the place where the crews change clothes and where you keep all your records; **TX**19, Out away from the [oil] rig there they've got what they call a doghouse, which is a place for the crew to change clothes, and if they get time, to eat. . . They also have a doghouse out in a producer, when the area's in production, like that where I work, my headquarters out there, called a doghouse. 'Course that one's kind of deluxe; we've got telephones in there. **1968** *DARE* (Qu. M22, . . *Kinds of buildings . . on farms*) Inf **CA**36, Doghouse—the shed used to sit in on the oil fields or citrus areas. [19 other Infs gave *doghouse* in its standard sense.] **1969** *DARE* File **CO,** Doghouse—a warming hut where lunches and extra gear are stored in oil fields.

4 A dormer; hence *doghouse window* the window in a dormer or a gable.

1923 Nutting *MA Beautiful* 26, The Cape Cod house is further characterized in its best form by three minute windows on each end in the gable, one on each side under the eaves lighting the long closets in the otherwise useless space divided off from the attic room, and the third at the point of the gable, ventilating the dead air space over the attic room. These little windows, invariably with four lights of glass, are sometimes called "dog house windows." **1941** Writers' Program *Guide SC* 279, The roofs are punctured with 'dog houses,' or typical Low Country dormers. **1954** *Harder Coll.* **cwTN,** Doghouse. . . A dormer. **1986** *WI Alumnus Letters* **seWI,** "Dog-house window" was the term we have heard to describe small, gable-roofed dormers. . . Context: "They live in a little house with 'them' dog-house windows in the roof."

5 A cupola or ventilating structure on the roof of a barn. Cf **cupola B1**

1966–70 *DARE* (Qu. M2, . . *The small wooden construction on top of a barn with slats for ventilation*) Infs **AL**38, 43, **AR**15, **KY**75, Doghouse.

6 A protective structure around the entrance to a building or a root cellar.

1883 Peck *Bad Boy* 163 [sic *DAE*—quot not found], It was cold out there in the storm door dog house. **1969** *DARE* (Qu. D12, *The part that's put on in winter around an outside door to give extra protection from the cold*) Inf **CA**153, Doghouses—on a potato cellar.

7 See quot. *joc*

1937 *Writer* 50.239 **neOH** [Black], *Dog house*—a good old southern name for a jail. **1965–70** *DARE* (Qu. V11, . . *A county or city jail*) 10 Infs, **scattered,** Doghouse.

8 in phr *in the doghouse:* In disfavor or disgrace, usu temporarily; out of luck.

1932 *Editor* 6 Feb 110/2 *(OEDS), Dog-house:* in disfavor. 'My moll caught me tryin' to make that twist, so I'm in the dog-house now.' **1949** Webber *Backwoods Teacher* 59, No one asked the teacher to play. The teacher was in the doghouse. **1967** *DARE* FW Addit **LA**14, *In the doghouse* has a more specific meaning than "in disfavor"; it means that a man's wife has "cut off his source of supply." **1968** *DARE* (Qu. CC12b, . . *If a person has a lot of bad luck, you might say, "He's been ———."*) Inf **OH**70, In the doghouse.

doghouse stirrup n **West** *old-fash*

See quot 1944.

1944 Adams *Western Words* 51, *Dog-house stirrups*—A slang name for old, wide, wooden stirrups of the early range. It was claimed that they had enough lumber in them to build a dog-house. **1927** (1944) Russell *Trails Plowed Under* 117 **MT,** He's sittin' in an old-fashioned low-horn saddle with 'doghouse' stirrups.

doghouse window See **doghouse 4**

dogie n Also sp *dogee, dogey, dogy, doughgie* [Orig uncertain; perh from *doggie;* perh infl by **dobe 6**] **West**

1 also *dogie calf:* A young often runty calf, usu one that has no mother.

1888 *Century Illustr. Mag.* 14.837/1 **West,** A bunch of steers had been seen traveling over the scoria buttes to the head of Elk Creek; they were mostly Texan *doughgies,* — a name I [=Theodore Roosevelt] have never seen written; it applies to young immigrant cattle, — but there were some of the Hash-Knife four-year-olds among them. **1892** *Outing* Feb 358/2 **KS,** I remember noticing in a herd of cattle south of Dodge City a queer, pot-bellied little dogy (a calf prematurely weaned by the death of its mother and developed into a runt). **1896** *DN* 1.415 **nwTX,** *Dogy:* a motherless calf, a poor worthless one. "A dogy is a sorry yearling." **1907** White *AZ Nights* 84, "Maybe it's a 'dogie,' " says Larry Eagen — we calls calves whose mothers have died "dogies." **1911** *DN* 3.550 **WY,** *Dogies,* calves. **1915** *DN* 4.225 **wTX,** *Dogy*. . . A motherless range-calf. The term was invented by a Texas ranchman. **1920** Hunter *Trail Drivers TX* 130 (as of c1880), Baylor . . would give him a dogie calf that had got into the herd several days before and we did not want it. **1921** *DN* 5.109 **AZ, CA,** *Dogee, dogie*. . . ['dogi] A young calf. **1934** *AmSp* 9.114, *Dogie* comes from the Texas cattle ranges where it is pronounced to rime with *bogey.* It has no relation to *dog* but denotes an animal of stunted growth or a motherless calf, or the cattle of other persons. **1947** *Trail Riders Bul.* Feb. 20/1 *(DA),* 'That's jest the idea,' comes back Sluefoot, with a grin on his puss like a li'l dogey what's foun' a new ma. **1950** *PADS* 14.75, *Dobie, dogie.*

2 also *dogie lamb:* See quots.

1921 *DN* 5.109 **AZ, CA,** *Dogee, dogie* . . a young lamb. **1968** Adams *Western Words* 96, *Dogie lamb* — An orphan lamb.

dogie calf See **dogie 1**

dogie lamb See **dogie 2**

dogieman n [**dogie**]

1944 Adams *Western Words* 52, *Dogieman* — A small rancher or nester who gets his cattle from outside farm districts.

dogies, by See **doggies, by**

dog in the manger n [By ext of orig sense (*OED* 1564 →), a person who selfishly withholds from others things that he does not want or cannot use himself, in allusion to the fable of the dog who would not let the ox or horse eat the hay, even though he could not eat it himself]

A surly person; see quots.

1968–69 *DARE* (Qu. GG35b, *Of a person who acts annoyed or disappointed you might say, "Because she couldn't go, she's been ______ all day."*) Inf **MA**58, Dog in the manger; bellyaching, bitchin'; (Qu. GG39, *Somebody who seems to be looking for reasons to be angry: "He's a ______."*) Inf **OH**49, Dog in the manger. [Both Infs old] **1986** *DARE* File **sCA,** My husband uses the phrase *dog in the manger* for someone who is being surly or contrary.

dog in the ring n [Prob folk-etym for **dob in the ring**]

In marble play: see quot.

1970 *DARE* (Qu. EE7, . . *Kinds of marble games*) Inf **MI**118, Dog in the ring — played in a circle, you keep what you shoot out.

dog iron n Pronc-sp *dog arn*

1 =andiron. [Perh blend of **andiron + dog** n[1] **B3**] **chiefly Sth, S Midl** See Map

1790 *Penna. Packet* 1 March 3/3 *(DAE),* William Robinson. . . hath for Sale. . . Iron Castings, consisting of, tea kettles, bake pans, spiders, skillets, dog irons, & flat irons. **1846** (1973) Porter *Quarter Race* 17 **KY,** His likeness had been moulded on dog-irons to frighten the children from going too near the fire. **1867** Harris *Sut Lovingood Yarns* 92 **TN,** Clapshaw's ole mam wer es deaf es a dogiron. **1884** Twain *Huck. Finn* 153 **MO,** They had big brass dog-irons that could hold up a saw-log. **1915** *DN* 4.182 **swVA,** *Dog-arns*. . . Fire irons. **1923** *DN* 5.205 **swMO,** *Dog iron*. . . Andiron. **1933** *AmSp* 8.1.48 **Ozarks,** *Dog irons*. . . Rude andirons, made by the country blacksmiths. **1949** Kurath *Word Geog.* 51, *Andirons*. . . *Dog irons* predominates from the lower James River (the Norfolk area) to the lower Neuse in North Carolina and in the South Midland. **1958** *PADS* 29.9 **TN,** *Dog irons.* **c1960** *Wilson Coll.* **csKY,** *Dogirons.* **1965–70** *DARE* (Qu. D32, *The metal stands in a fireplace that the logs are laid on*) 106 Infs, **chiefly Sth, S Midl,** Dog irons. **1966** *DARE* Tape **AL**14, We had things you call dog irons. They hold the wood in place in the fire till they [=logs] burn and fall in two. **1976** Garber *Mountain-ese* 23 **sAppalachians,** She polished her brass dog-arns.

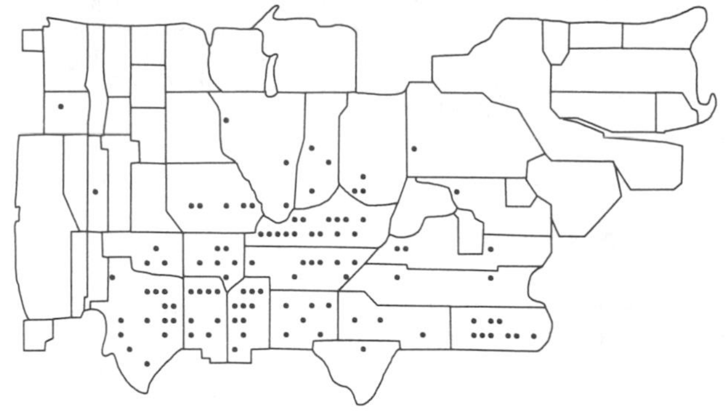

•dog iron 1 (Qu. D32)

2 In logging: see quot 1958. [**dog** n[1] **B2**]

1958 McCulloch *Woods Words* 48 **Pacific NW,** *Dog iron* — a. A piece of iron rod with a right angle turned at each end and sharpened. These pointed ends were driven into one edge of a block being sawed off a log and then into the log itself, to steady the block when sawing. b. Also used to mean any of the various kinds of dogs. **1969** Sorden *Lumberjack Lingo* 34 **NEng, Gt Lakes,** *Dog irons* — Used by the bull cook to hold logs in place while sawing wood for the cookstove.

dog is going to get out, your See **dog** n[1] **B16**

dog it See **dog** v **8, 11**

dog killer n

1 Inferior or adulterated liquor.

1968 *DARE* (Qu. DD21b, . . *Bad liquor*) Inf **WI**26, Dog killer.

‡**2** See quot.

1966 *DARE* (Qu. HH43b, *The assistant to the top person in charge of a group of workmen*) Inf **FL**4, Dog killer.

dog knife n *old-fash* Cf *DS* F39

Appar a small knife or pocketknife.

a1883 (1911) Bagby *VA Gentleman* 49, Split his thumb open slicing "hoss-cakes" with a dog-knife sharpened, contrary to orders, on the grindstone. **1883** in 1983 Zeigler *Lexicon Middle GA* 84, It might be an hour befor [sic] he got to a hardwar-store [sic] and found a dog-knife for his little boy. **1897** (1952) McGill *Narrative* 12 **ceSC,** He [=a pre-school boy] is interesting to the members of the household, as he plays and romps about in their sight, with his stick horse, made streaked and spotted by his dog knife or a one-bladed seven pence one.

dog knocker n Also *dog hammer* [**dog** n[1] **B2**]

In logging: see quots.

1958 McCulloch *Woods Words* 48 **Pacific NW,** *Dog knocker* — A light maul used to knock dogs out of logs. **1969** Sorden *Lumberjack Lingo* 34 **NEng, Gt Lakes,** *Dog knocker* or *Dog hammer* — A small sledge used to knock chain hook dogs from logs.

dog knot n Cf **cat's ass 1**

In logging: see quot.

1958 McCulloch *Woods Words* 48 **Pacific NW,** *Dog knot* — A knot pulled tight in a line or cable.

dog Latin n

=hog Latin 2; see quot 1958.

1908 *DN* 3.305 **eAL, wGA,** *Dog-Latin*. . . A kind of language made up of transposed syllables, initial letters, etc., used by children. **1958** (1972) Funk *Horsefeathers* 35 **OH,** *Dog Latin* — Properly, this is just very bad Latin, a mongrel Latin — whence the name — composed of a mixture of Latin and English. But in my own childhood (in Ohio), what we called *dog Latin* was a gibberish of decapitated English words, the initial letters transposed to the rear, plus "ay"; as, "Ohnny-jay ust-may o-gay ome-hay." **1986** *NADS Letters* **sMS, seTX,** As children (forty to fifty years ago) we said "dog latin," never "pig latin." **1986** *DSNA Letters* **sLA, AL** (as of c1920), "Dog latin." As a child . . "dog latin" (the phrase we used) and "pig latin" were used interchangeably and meant then what "pig latin" as far as I know means today. . . I believe I heard "dog-latin" *before* "pig-latin"—possibly from my own older sisters & brother.

dog laurel n

=**dog hobble 1.**

1860 Curtis *Cat. Plants NC* 96, Dog laurel (*Leucothoe Catesbaei,* Gray.)—Found only in the mountains, where it is also called *Hemlock,* growing on the cool margins of streams. **1931** Clute *Common Plants* 94, Among species certainly named for the dog are . . the dog-laurel *(Leocothoe catesbaei).* **1966** *DARE* Wildfl. QR Pl. 156a Inf **SC**41, Dog laurel.

dog law n

In railroading: a law prohibiting a train crew from working longer than sixteen continuous hours.

1945 [see **dogcatcher 1**].

dogleg n Also *dog-leg tobacco* [From the shape, resembling a dog's hind leg] **esp S Midl** Cf *DS* DD1

Poor quality tobacco, sold in twists.

1858 *Nat. Intelligencer* 10 July 3/3 *(DAE),* A large quantity of 'dog-leg' tobacco and red pepper is then thrown into the tub. **1863** Gilmore *S. Friends* 48 **eNC,** The other [half of the store] was densely crowded with logwood, "dog-leg," . . and cistern water. **1885** Twain *Huck. Finn* 70 **MO,** I had my pipe en a plug er dog-leg, en some matches in my cap. **1891** Ryan *Pagan* 25 **Alleghany Mts,** Then the black-and-tan man treated himself to a fresh chew of "dog-leg." **c1960** *Wilson Coll.* **csKY,** *Dog-leg. . .* Twist tobacco, because of its shape, also cheap tobacco.

dogleg ash n

The Gregg ash *(Fraxinus greggii).*

1979 Little *Checklist U.S. Trees* 136, *Fraxinus greggii. . . Other common names . .* dogleg ash.

dog-leg tobacco See **dogleg**

dog lichen n

A common lichen *(Peltigera canina)* with fruiting bodies that resemble dogs' teeth.

[**1861** H. Macmillan *Footnotes fr. Nat.* 105 *(OED),* The common *dog-lichen *(Peltidea canina)* . . was formerly employed . . as a cure for hydrophobia (hence its specific name).] **1975** Zwinger *Run River* 25 **UT,** This is my idea of the forest primeval: filled with deadfall, very still, ground soft and cushioned, a windrow of porcupine needles, big circles of dog lichen, trees festooned with old man's beard.

dog lily n

A **spatterdock** (here: *Nuphar luteum*).

1832 Williamson *Hist. ME* 1.126, Of the lily tribe, we have several species. [Footnote:] Such as the yellow water-lily, or dog-lily, or beaver-root. **1892** *Jrl. Amer. Folkl.* 5.91, *Nuphar advena. . .* Dog-lily. New England. **1940** Clute *Amer. Plant Names* 119, *N. advena. . .* Dog-lily. **1959** Carleton *Index Herb. Plants* 38, *Dog-lily:* Nymphozanthus advena. **1969** *DARE* (Qu. S26b, *Wildflowers that grow in water or wet places*) Inf **RI**4, Dog lily—comes up like pond lily, small & bunchy, don't flower out like a pond lily.

dog lizard n

An earless lizard *(Holbrookia texana).*

1928 Baylor Univ. Museum *Contrib.* 16.11, *Holbrookia texana. . .* In middle and western Texas, where this species is very common, it is . . known as the . . *Dog Lizard.* The last mentioned name has been given to it on account of the way it has of carrying its tail curled after the manner of a puppy dog above its back.

dog loop n **West** Cf **blocker** n[1]

A small loop in a lariat, most often used to rope calves.

1945 Thorp *Pardner* 243 **SW,** Two men on horseback would ride through the cattle in the corral, and with little dog loops (small-size loops in their ropes) would catch and drag the calves up to the fire for the branding. **1961** Adams *Old-Time Cowhand* 233, The "small loop man" throwed a little loop often called a "dog loop," and they were usually experts at ketchin' calves.

dog-mean adj Cf **dog** n[1] **B17d, hog B2**

Ill-tempered, malicious; hence *dog-meanness* ill will, spite, malice.

1914 Furman *Sight* 70 **KY,** I just slid right down thar on my unworthy knees . . and with bitter tears beseeched of her to forgive and forgit my hard-heartedness and stone-blindness and dog-meanness. **c1970** *Halpert Coll.* **wKY, wTN,** *Dog-mean* describes a person or animal of extremely bad temper and premeditated malice. "He's just pure dog-mean!"

dog meat See **dog feed**

dog mint n

A **wild basil** (here: *Satureja vulgaris*).

1830 Rafinesque *Med. Flora* 2.211, *Clinopodium. . .* Dogmint. **1876** Hobbs *Bot. Hdbk.* 32, Dog mint, Field thyme, Clinopodium vulgare. **1900** Lyons *Plant Names* 108, *C. vulgare. . .* Dog-mint. **1950** Gray–Fernald *Manual of Botany* 1241, Dogmint. . . Corolla with slender tube, lilac-pink to whitish. **1961** Smith *MI Wildflowers* 327, *Dogmint. Satureja vulgaris. . .* In open woods or thickets, along roads and in rocky or alluvial soil. **1976** Bailey–Bailey *Hortus Third* 287.

dog mire n Cf **dog weather**

1970 *DARE* (Qu. B25, . . *A very heavy rain . . "It's a regular ______.")* Inf **VA**74, Dog mire—leaves puddles.

dog moccasin n **AK**

A leather footcovering for a sled dog.

1902 Cantwell *Rept. U.S. Revenue Steamer Nunivak* 161 (Tabbert *Alaskan Engl.*) **AK,** Dog moccasins, made of dressed moose hide and fitted with thongs for lashing them on above the first joint of the leg, are in common use throughout the country, and no prospector who has the proper care of his team at heart should ever start on a journey without a full supply of these articles. **1915** Stuck *10000 Miles* 8 **AK,** When the dog comes out of water into snow again the snow collects and freezes between the toes, and if not removed will soon cause a sore and lameness. Then a dog moccasin must be put on and the foot continually nursed and doctored. **1951** Schwalbe *Dayspring* 35 **AK,** This was done during the winter when it was necessary to go provided with all of the trappings for sled travel. There must be a good team of dogs, and fish for dog feed and dog moccasins to prevent bleeding feet on rough trails.

dog mouth n Cf **dog's mouth**

=**butter-and-eggs 1.**

1968 *DARE* (Qu. S11, . . *Wild snapdragon*) Inf **PA**111, Dog mouth.

dog musher n **[musher] AK** Cf **dog driver** Cf *DCan*

The driver of a dog team.

1907 Jack London *White Fang* 215 *(DA),* Dog-mushers' cries were heard. . . They saw, up the trail, two men running with sled and dogs. **a1922** (1953) Brooks *Blazing* 406 **AK,** Many long journeys have been made over well-beaten trails by good "dog mushers" where a day's average travel was 25 miles. **1943** *AK Sportsman* Apr 11 (Tabbert *Alaskan Engl.*), A good dog musher is able to judge with some accuracy the abilities of each dog in his team. **1976** [see **dog mushing**]. **1976** [see **dog punch**].

dog mushing n **AK** Cf **dog driving**

Traveling by dogsled; driving a team of sled dogs for travel or as a sport.

1936 *AK Sportsman* Mar 14 (Tabbert *Alaskan Engl.*) **AK,** Although the term "dog mushing" is a familiar expression to Alaskans today, it cannot be said that this means of travel was important to the original citizens of our northernmost territory. **1953** *Jessen's Weekly* Dec 14 (Tabbert *Alaskan Engl.*), Dog mushing is king of Alaskan winter sports. **1955** *AK Sportsman* Jan 37 **AK,** Dog mushing can be funny, as well as fun. **1976** *Fairbanks Daily News–Miner* (AK) 6 Nov sec B 16, The best way to get into dog mushing is to hang around dog mushers. That's the advice of . . a North Pole veterinarian who has been mushing dogs for a year.

dog my cats intj Also *dog my hide* (or *skin, time*), *doggone* (or *dog on*) *my cat(s)* [Cf **dog** v **6**] **chiefly Sth, S Midl** *euphem*

Used as an expression of surprise, amazement, annoyance, etc; see quots.

1853 Hammett *Stray Yankee in TX* 18 **TX,** *Dog* on my cat! ef thar hain't been *bar* about, ye can take my hat! **1871** Hay *Pike Co. Ballads* 22 **cwIL,** Now dog my cats ef I kin see / . . What you've got to do with the question / Ef Tim shill go or stay. [**1883** (1971) Harris *Nights with Remus* 9, **cnGA,** Brer Fox he say ter hisse'f dat he be dog his cats ef he don't slorate [=destroy, get the better of] ole Brer Rabbit ef it take 'im a mont'.] **1884** Twain *Huck. Finn* 9 **MO,** Say—who is you? Whar is you? Dog my cats ef I didn' hear sumf'n. **1890** *DN* 1.67 **KY,** Dog-gone my cats. **1899** Harte *Poet. Wks.* 184 **CA,** Dog my skin, ef thar was one in eight. **1905** *DN* 3.77 **nwAR,** *Dog my cats.* **1908** *DN* 3.305 **eAL, wGA,** *Dog(-gone) my cats.* **1919** Kyne *Capt. Scraggs* 210 **CA,** McGuffey, your argument does you a heap of credit. It's—it's—dog my cats, McGuffey, it's masterly. **1922** *DN* 5.183 **GA,** *Dog my cats.* **1928** McKay *Home to Harlem* 24 **NYC** [Black], Dog mah cats! You done tasted the real life a'ready? **1941** Stuart *Men of Mts.* 27 **neKY,** Dog my hide if it ain't old Dusty Boone. **1941** *Sat. Eve. Post* 13 Sept 49 **SC,** "Well, dog my time!" he cried in glee. **1951** *PADS* 15.69 **nLA,** *Dog my cats.* **1954** *Hall Coll.* **cwTN,** *Dog my cats.*

dognap n, v

A brief or light sleep, a catnap; to catnap.

1835 Hoffman *Winter in West* (NY) 1.77 **NY,** The tired domestic . . was catching a dog nap before the stage-coach should drive to the door. **1860** in 1881 Phillips *Speeches* 295 **eMA,** They [=the Democratic Party] remind one of that sleepy crier of a New Hampshire court, who was ever dreaming, in his dog-naps, that the voice of judge or lawyer was a noisy interruption, and always woke shouting, "Silence!" **1908** *DN* 3.305 **eAL, wGA,** *Dog-nap. . .* A slight or troubled sleep. *Cat-nap* is more common in this sense. **1970** *DARE* (Qu. X41, *When you're going to sleep for a very short while, you might say, "I'm just going to ——."*) Inf **PA**244, Dognap.

dog nettle n

1 A **hemp nettle** (here: *Galeopsis tetrahit*).

1900 Lyons *Plant Names* 167, *G[aleopsis] Tetrahit* . . Dog Nettle. **1935** (1943) Muenscher *Weeds* 391, *Galeopsis Tetrahit* . . Hemp nettle, Dog nettle. **1959** [see **2** below].

2 =**dead nettle 1.**

1900 Lyons *Plant Names* 214, *L[amium] purpureum* . . Dog Nettle. **1959** Carleton *Index Herb. Plants* 38, Dog-Nettle: *Galeopsis ladanum; Lamium* (v).

3 A **burning nettle.**

1950 Gray-Fernald *Manual of Botany* 558, *U[rtica] urens* . . Dog-Nettle. **1970** Correll *Plants TX* 502, *Urtica urens* . . Burning Nettle, Dog Nettle.

dog nut n *joc*

1967 *DARE* (Qu. H27, . . *Joking names for doughnuts*) Inf **OR**1, Dog nuts.

dog off See **dog** v **8**

dog officer n Cf **dog warden**

A dogcatcher.

1969 *Cape Cod Std.-Times* (Hyannis MA) 22 Jan 1, Patterson explained how the old pound is a nuisance to neighbors and that it is so small it forces the dog officer to violate state regulations at times by having too many dogs in one stall. **1978** *UpCountry* Oct 4 **Cape Cod MA,** Dog officer Judy Stetson, who patrols the Wellfleet dog front, received 47 complaints [of barking dogs] through the middle of July. . . Judy notes, ". . . Tied dogs bark."

dog on a stick n [**dog** n[1] **B10**]

A cooked frankfurter sold on a stick.

1966 *AmSp* 41.280 **Pacific** [Carnie talk], *Dog, . . dog on a stick. . .* A frankfurter. **1978** *DARE* File **nNJ, WI,** I enjoy taking my kids to county fairs, but I detest the food: cotton candy, dogs on sticks, and greasy french fries never fail to make me sick to my stomach.

dog on my cats See **dog my cats**

dog-on-the-shore n

1975 Gould *ME Lingo* 217, *Pothellion.* An old coastal term for a kind of fish hash, sometimes called dog-on-the-shore.

dog-on-wood n Cf **wood tag,** *DS* EE33

A game of tag; see quot 1987.

1890 Howells *Boy's Town* 84 **OH** (as of c1850), With the races came the other plays which involved running, like dog-on-wood. **1987** *NADS Letters* **SC,** I played "dog on wood" as a child in Aiken County, South Carolina, in the early 1950's. . . a player was "safe" from being tagged as long as he touched a tree. Players had to move from one tree to another when he who was "it" called "dog on wood." Only one player could touch one tree to be safe from tagging, so if the trees were few enough, . . and the players more than a few, pandemonium reigned when "dog on wood" was called and players tried to avoid being tagged as they ran to an available tree.

dogood See **doogood**

dog owl n [**dog** n[1] **B1a**]

=**burrowing owl.**

1935 Sandoz *Jules* 371 **wNE,** (as of 1880–1930), Now and then . . a dog owl hooted.

dog park n Also *dog-walking area* **NYC** Cf **parking strip**

See quots.

1964 *AmSp* 39.293 **NYC,** That strip of grass and weeds between the sidewalk and the curb. . . I did have an aunt in uptown New York City who called it the *dog park,* but I have no way of knowing whether this was her own poetic invention. **1968** *DARE* (Qu. N44, *In a town, the strip of grass and trees between the sidewalk and the curb*) Inf **NY**43, Dog-walking area.

dog pecker n [*pecker* penis]

A mushroom of the genus *Morchella.*

1973 Kluger *Wild Flavor* 54 **sIN,** Another variety of morel . . has a tiny cone of a head . . atop a long white stem. . . The stem may be twice as long as the cap of the morel. Local country people call this variety of morel by the homely and descriptive name "dog pecker." It is edible, but thin-fleshed.

dog-pecker gnat n [Perh < **dog pecker**]

An unidentified gnat.

1985 Doxey *Cousins Kudzu* 242 **GA,** Go up'n down the road a piece and there's red-eyed flies and dog-pecker gnats thick as fleas. Skeeters, too, big' uns.

dogpelter n [By analogy with *dogcatcher*] **chiefly S Midl** *derog*

See quot 1903.

1859 Taliaferro *Fisher's R.* 232 **nwNC** (as of 1820s), Sich a onhuman man can't git my vote fur dog-pelter. **1902** *DN* 2.233 **sIL,** *Dog-pelter. . .* A term of contempt. **1903** *DN* 2.311 **seMO,** *Dogpelter. . .* An imaginary official. Used in contempt. 'I wouldn [sic] vote for him for dogpelter.' **1944** *PADS* 2.25 **cwNC, cwOH,** *Dog-pelter. . .* A term of contempt; an officer of extremest inconsequence. My father used to say: "I wouldn't vote for a Democrat for a dog-pelter." **c1960** *Wilson Coll.* **csKY,** *Dog pelter. . .* An imaginary worthless official; a fling at some self-important officer.

‡dog pile n

A type of horseplay; see quot.

1962 Bailey *Jayhawker* 94 **KS,** If we [=news carriers] staged a fight on the post-office lawn next door, or a dog-pile, the postmaster would come out to protect his tender grass. *Ibid* 96, The only time he [=the carriers' boss] hears us is when we have raised the din past human levels, and into the realm of wild animals. Let's go boys. Dog-pile, dog-pile, dog-pile! . . Running the gantlet required space, because the victim had to have a running, sporting chance. . . The fast trip down the tunnel of swinging love pats always damaged the lawn where the victim had dug into the sod for a quick take-off.

dog plum n

A **bead lily** (here: *Clintonia umbellata*).

1940 Clute *Amer. Plant Names* 11, *C[lintonia] umbellata. . .* Dog-plum. **1959** Carleton *Index Herb. Plants* 38, Dog-Plum: *Clintonia umbellata.*

dog poor adj phr Also *dirt-dog poor* Cf **dog** n[1] **B17b**

Very poor.

1895 in 1950 *PADS* 13.6 **AL,** The Lucases were big rich, whilst the Simkinses were *dog poor.* **1954** *Harder Coll.* **cwTN,** *Dog poor.* Very poor. **1960** Williams *Walk Egypt* 93 **GA,** He was dirt-dog poor. **1984** Wilder *You All Spoken Here* 127 **Sth,** Dirt-dog poor: On the rim edge of poverty.

dog pot n **AK**

A large cooking-vessel, often half of a large (e.g., fifty gallon) drum, used for cooking dog food; the dog food cooked in such a vessel.

1915 Stuck *10000 Miles* 42 **AK,** The dog pot, filled with snow, into which the fish are cut up, is put upon the outdoor fire as soon as man-supper begins cooking in the tent. **1973** *AK Mag.* Apr 38, Your trapline also feeds your dogs. Meat of marten, mink, wolverine, wolf and fox boiled with whale blubber, makes a good base for a dogpot. **1974** in 1981 Tabbert *Alaskan Engl.,* A "dog pot" is a pot in which dog food is cooked. Many are made from the bottom half of a 50 gallon fuel drum.

Scraps, dry fish, corn meal or rolled oats may be cooked together in this pot over an open fire out-of-doors. While in the village it is felt that dogs keep up their strength and work better when given a hot meal each day. On the trail they may only get dry fish. **1977** McPhee *Coming Country* 419 **AK,** The butchery, merely a roof on poles, is also his fish cache, and the shelter for his dog pot—half a fifty-five-gallon drum that sits like a caldron above a fire and is a pot-au-feu for huskies.

dog punch v phr **esp AK** Cf **dog driver, dog musher**

To drive a team of sled dogs; hence n *dog puncher.*

1901 White *Jrl. Yukon River Exped.* Mar 28 (Tabbert *Alaskan Engl.*), Bishop Rowe arrived today from Circle, dog punching all alone. **1926** Willoughby *The Trail Eater* 61 (Tabbert *Alaskan Engl.*) **AK,** Slim will take out the champion team, and I've already sent up the Yukon for Jake Minto and Harry Dunn, both A-1 dog-punchers. **1928** Collins *Dog-Puncher* 32 (Tabbert *Alaskan Engl.*) **AK** (as of 1896–97), Early this winter, when I was in Circle City, I made up my mind I would become a freighter, or what was called locally a "dog-puncher." **1955** *AK Sportsman* Jan 13, At times dog men have been called dog punchers, but the term has not caught on. **1976** Vaudrin *Racing Alaskan Sled Dogs* 11 (Tabbert *Alaskan Engl.*) **AK,** "Mush" has been used for at least 150 years, but the phrase "dog musher" is quite recent. Up until the first part of the 20th century a dog musher was known as a "dog driver" or a "dog puncher." **1986** *WI State Jrl.* (Madison) 8 Jan 1/4 **neMN,** John Beargrease was a Chippewa dog-puncher who carried the U.S. mail to remote, snowbound outposts along the North Shore between 1887 and 1900.

dog ribs n Also *dog's rib* Cf **ribgrass, ribwort**

=**buckhorn plantain.**

1900 Lyons *Plant Names* 294, *P[lantago] lanceolata* . . dog's rib. **1940** Clute *Amer. Plant Names* 110; *P[lantago] lanceolata*. . . dog-ribs. **1963** *AmSp* 38.32, Dog-Ribs. Narrow-leaved plantain.

dog rob v phr [Back-formation from **dog robber**]

To act as a **dog robber 1.**

1969 *DARE* FW Addit **MA**68, Dog robber = an enlisted man who works for a commissioned officer. You might say, "He's dog robbin' for Capt. so-and-so."

dog robber n [Orig military slang; see quot 1984]

1 An officer's orderly or servant; a handy-man at a camp; a subservient person.

1868 *Harper's New Mth. Mag.* 36.300/2 **KS,** "Dog-robber" was the name by which the soldier designated the cooks and detailed soldiers who were the occupants of the second table of an officers' mess. **1889** *Century Illustr. Mag.* 37.901/1 **AZ,** On the following morning I was awakened by the lieutenant's dog-rubber [sic], and got up to array myself in my field costume. [Footnote to *dog-rubber:*] Soldier detailed as officer's servant. **1914** *DN* 4.105 **KS,** *Dog-robber*. . . A menial servant of army officers;—used by soldiers returned from the Philippines. **1921** *DN* 5.111 **CA,** *Dog-robber*. . . Valet to an officer. **1929** Parker *Old Army* 17 **OK,** They persecute and call "dog robber" any soldier who acts as an officer's servant. **1929** (1951) Faulkner *Sartoris* 63 **MS,** One day de Captain's dog-robber foun' whar he kep' dese here unloaded passes and he tuck a han'ful of 'um. **1930** *DN* 6.87 **neWV,** *Dog robber,* an odd-jobber about camp. **1940** *AmSp* 15.213 [C.C.C. slang], A 'dog-robber' is the officers' orderly, the fellow who fixes the officers' mess and tidies their quarters. **1969** *DARE* (Qu. II34, *If you think somebody is trying to use you to his advantage: "I'm not going to be his ______."*) Inf **MA**61, Dog robber—army expression; (Qu. JJ3b, *When a school child makes a special effort to 'get in good' with the teacher in hopes of getting a better grade: "She's an awful ______."*) Inf **IN**58, Dog robber. **1984** Smith *SW Vocab.* 122, *Dog robber:* A striker, an enlisted soldier acting as a personal servant or attendant to a commissioned officer. In today's egalitarian army such service would be unthinkable, and any assigned duty resembling servitude would be subject for investigation. In the old army such service was much sought after. The job brought extra pay, extra rations, and release from tedious soldierly duties. The popular version of the term's origin is that since the dog-robber ate his meals not in the company mess but in his employer's kitchen, he was robbing the officer's dog of its food.

2 Among loggers: see quot.

1958 McCulloch *Woods Words* 48 **Pacific NW,** *Dog-robber*—A camp cook who uses up the scraps too closely in feeding the loggers, has nothing left to feed the dog.

dog run n **chiefly S Midl, occas Sth**

=**dogtrot.**

1904 *New Engl. Mag.* 30.41/2 **eKY,** Frequently, when the house is enlarged, instead of the second room being joined to the first, it is built at a distance of twelve feet and the roof extended to the first cabin. Thus a third open room or court is formed. This is called the "dog run," but in reality is the family sitting room. **1938** Nixon *40 Acres* facing p. 15, [Caption of photograph:] The dog-run serves as a porch in the cabin of a Georgia tenant farmer. **1943** *Sat. Eve. Post* 15 May 58 **sFL,** His house was of that homestead variety seemingly sired by a mansion and foaled by a cabin, with a dog run through the middle. **1956** Gipson *Old Yeller* 9 **TX,** The dog run was an open roofed-over space between the two rooms of our log cabin. It was a good place . . to sleep when the night breezes weren't strong enough to push through the cracks between the cabin logs. **1966** *DARE* (Qu. D23, *A house that is divided in two through the middle*) Inf **NC**16, Dog run or dogtrot on old country houses—an open space through the middle with rooms built on each side.

dogs n Also rarely *dog* [From **dos gris**] Cf **dogy** n[2]

The **greater scaup** and the **lesser scaup.**

1911 *Forest & Stream* 77.173, *Marila affinis*. . . Grayback or collectively Dogs (contraction of the French name [=dos gris]). **1917** *DN* 4.427 **LA,** *Lesser scaup*. . . "Dogs": used of this scaup when in a flock. **1921** LA Dept. of Conserv. *Bulletin* 10.59 **LA,** The lesser scaup. . . in south Louisiana . . goes almost invariably under the name of "dos gris" . . , sometimes abbreviated familiarly to "dog". **1923** U.S. Dept. Ag. *Misc. Circular* 13.19, *Scaup Ducks . . In local use.*— . . dosgris (. . sometimes corrupted to dogs). (Ala., Miss., La.) **1962** Imhof *AL Birds* 149, *Greater Scaup—Aythya marila* . . Dogs.

dog's age n Also *dog's years* **chiefly Nth** See Map *somewhat old-fash*

A long time—usu in phrr *in* (or *for*) *a dog's age.*

1836 *Knickerbocker* 7.17 **seNY,** That blamed line gale has kept me in bilboes such a dog's age. **1909** *DN* 3.410 **nME,** *Dog's age*. . . A long time. "I haven't seen you in a dog's age." **1916** Wilson *Somewhere* 175 **WA,** Booming pained surmises through the house as to what fearful state it would get to be in if she didn't fight it to a clean finish once in a dog's age. **1922** *DN* 5.161 **AR, MO, ME,** I haven't seen you in a dog's age. **1927** *AmSp* 2.352 **WV,** I haven't seen you for a dog's age. **1931–33** *LANE Worksheets* **cMA,** I don't suppose you'd hear it here once in a dog's age. **1950** *WELS (A very long period of time: I haven't seen him ______)* 7 Infs, **WI,** In a dog's age; 3 Infs, **WI,** For a dog's age. **1965–70** *DARE* (Qu. A16, *A very long period of time: "I haven't seen him ______."*) 40 Infs, **chiefly Nth,** In a dog's age; **ME**1, **NY**88, **PA**88, **WI**10, For a dog's age; **NY**34, In dog's years [40 of 45 Infs old]; (Qu. A15, *Something that happens only occasionally: "He comes around ______."*) Infs **MI**9, **NY**123, 230, **RI**1, **VT**2, Once in a dog's age.

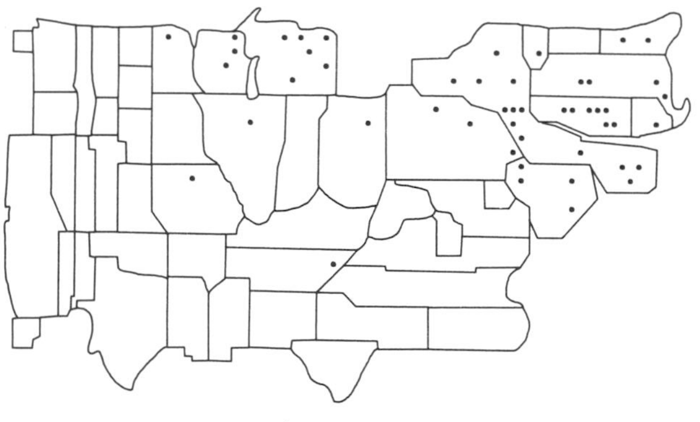

•dog's age + varr (Qq. A16, A15)

dog salmon n Also *dog* [Cf **dog** n[1] **B18a**] **NW, AK** Cf **dog-tooth salmon**

A **salmon,** esp the **chum salmon.**

1869 *Amer. Naturalist* 3.127 **MT,** *Dog salmon (Salmo canis . .).* Below the forks of the Spokan, the Indians were catching myriads of this salmon. **1920** *DN* 5.81 **NW,** *Dogs.* Dog salmon. **1967–68** *DARE* (Qu. P1) Inf **AK**1, Dog salmon; (Qu. P3) Inf **AK**9, Dog salmon—not especially good; (Qu. P14) Inf **WA**20, Dog salmon—same as coho. **1972** Sparano *Outdoors Encycl.* 353, The dog salmon *[Oncorhynchus keta]* closely resembles the chinook salmon. **1975** *AK Mag.* Apr 37, There was even a fish buyer . . paying $1.25 per dog salmon. "When I buy 'em, I call 'em dogs. When I sell 'em, I call 'em chums," he chuckled.

dog-salmon aristocracy n [By analogy with **codfish aristocracy**]

1951 Morgan *Skid Road* 84 **Seattle WA** (as of 1880s), They joined the ranks of the unemployed and listened to the oratory of Populists like Mary Kenworthy, who was belaboring the Business Man's backers with such salty epithets as "our dog-salmon aristocracy."

dogs and fox See **fox and hounds 1**

dog's-ass fly n Also *dog's-rear-end fly*

Appar a **black fly.**

1969 *DARE* (Qu. R12, *What other kinds of flies are common around here—for example, those that fly around animals?*) Inf **MA**15, Called in Maine a black fly; dog's-ass fly [and] dog's-rear-end fly [are the] same; come in spring—little, black.

dog's back leg See **dog's hind leg**

dog's bait n Also *dog bait* **[bait n 1d] Sth, S Midl**

A large or excessive amount (usu of food).

1933 *AmSp* 8.1.48 **Ozarks,** *Dog's bait*. . . An excessive amount of anything. *I done stood for a lot o' this hyar foolishment, but enough's enough, an' too much is a dawg's bait.* **1935** *Atlantic Mth.* 156.44/2 **eGA,** I eat a dog's bait of 'em. **1964** Wallace *Frontier Life* 98 **OK** (as of 1893-1906), Other expressions were . . "dog's bait" for huge amount of food, [etc]. **1965-70** *DARE* (Qu. LL4, *Very large: "He took a ______ helping of potatoes."*) Infs **MS**56, **NC**69, 88, **TX**36, 37, 98, Dog's bait; **SC**19, Dog bait.

dog's ballocks n Cf **dogstone**

A **lady's slipper** (here: *Cypripedium acaule*).

1945 McAtee *Nomina Abitera* 10, The showy ladies-slipper *(Cypripedium acaule)* . . is in New England called . . dog's ballocks.

dog'sbane See **dogbane a**

dog's body n [*OED* 1858 →] Cf **dog-on-the-shore**

1945 Colcord *Sea Language* 67 **ME, Cape Cod, Long Island,** *Dog's-body.* A sea dish of peas boiled in a cloth like pudding.

dog's camomile See **dog camomile**

dog's dick n [*dick* penis]

=**golden club 1.**

1945 McAtee *Nomina Abitera* 8, Golden Club *(Orontium aquaticum)* —Dog's dick.

dog's dinner n [See quot 1963]

=**beach heather.**

1896 *Jrl. Amer. Folkl.* 9.182 **MA,** *Hudsonia tomentosa,* . . *dog's dinner.* **1898** *Ibid* 11.223 **MA,** *Hudsonia ericoides,* . . dog's dinner. **1900** Lyons *Plant Names* 194, *H[udsonia] tomentosa* . . Dog's-dinner. **1940** Clute *Amer. Plant Names* 134, *H[udsonia] tomentosa.* . . dog's dinner. **1963** *AmSp* 38.36, *Dog's dinner*. . . The synonym *poverty grass* explains *dinner.*

dog's egg n *joc* Cf **hen's tooth 1,** *DS* HH14

1973 *Patrick Coll.* **cAL,** Dog's eggs—something nonexistent. "Hard to find as dog's eggs."

dog's eye See **dog eye 2**

dog's fennel See **dog fennel 1, 3**

dog's-foot See **dog-toes**

dog's foot, the intj Also *a dog's foot* **esp Sth** Cf **foot** intj

See quot 1908.

1838 Kettell *Yankee Notions* 145, "A dog's foot!" exclaimed Aunt Judy. **1908** *DN* 3.306 **eAL, wGA,** *Dog's foot, the*. . . Used as an expression of disgust or contempt. **1941** *Sat. Eve. Post* 22 Mar 122 **NC,** He could sleep right there in the grove on the wagon seat, if it wasn't convenient—"The dog's foot! We got beds." **1952** Brown *NC Folkl.* 1.533, *Dog's foot, the*. . . A mild exclamation.—General.

dog's hair n

An alga of the genus *Cladophora.*

1933 Bryan *Hawaiian Nature* 110, The most conspicuous of the marine species are sea lettuce *(Ulva),* "dog's hair" *(Cladophora),* and *limu eleele (Enteromorpha).*

dog shark n Also *dog sherk*

A **dogfish 1** of the families Carcharinidae and Squalidae.

1882 U.S. Natl. Museum *Bulletin* 16.19, *M[ustelus] hinnulus* . . Dog Shark. *Ibid* 16.20, *T[riacis] semifasciatus* . . Dog Shark. **1884** Goode *Fisheries U.S.* 1.676, *Mustelae californicus* . . Dog Shark. San Francisco and southward. **1906** NJ State Museum *Annual Rept. for 1905* 60, *Cyanis canis* . . Dog Shark. Dog Sherk. *Ibid* 66, Family *Squalidae*—The Dog Sharks. **1935** Caine *Game Fish* 156, *Sand Shark—Squalus acanthias*—Known variously as the dogfish, dogshark . . is probably the most numerous of the entire shark family. **1968** *DARE* (Qu. P4) Inf **NJ**16, Dog shark.

dog's head See **dog face**

dog's hind leg n Also *dog's back leg*

In phrr *crooked as a dog's hind* (or *back*) *leg* and varr: very crooked, bent; devious, deceptive, fraudulent.

1840 Haliburton *Clockmaker* (3d ser) 49 **NEng,** He ain't worth powder and shot, and dat is de fack, for he is more crookeder in his ways nor a dog's hind leg. **1903** *DN* 2.310 **seMO,** *Crooked as a dog's hind leg*. . . Very crooked. **1944** *PADS* 2.22 **sAppalachians,** It's as crooked as a dog's hind legs. **1946** *CA Folkl. Qrly.* 5.335, As crooked as a dog's back leg. **1967-70** *DARE* (Qu. V1, *When you suspect that somebody is trying to deceive you, or that something is going on behind your back, you say*) Inf **AZ**1, Crooked as a dog's hind leg; (Qu. V2a, *What do you call a deceiving person, or somebody that you can't trust?*) Infs **AK**9, **IL**114, Crooked as a dog's hind leg.

dogshore n

Fig: see quot.

1975 Gould *ME Lingo* 75, *Dog shore*—The props and blocking that hold a boat upright on the ways while it is being built are called *shores.* These are knocked away to let the finished vessel slide into the water. The last prop to be knocked away, giving the vessel her freedom, is the *dog shore.* Because there is some danger in knocking away the *dog shore,* a nimble and alert man does it. So, a man fit for *dog shoring* will have more than ordinary ability. The main prop or crux of an argument or discussion may be its *dog shore.*

dog's mess n [**mess** n]

=**dog's bait.**

1968 *DARE* (Qu. LL4, *Very large: "He took a ______ helping of potatoes."*) Inf **DE**1, Had a dog's mess on his plate.

dog's mouth n Cf **dog mouth**

A snapdragon (*Antirrhinum* spp, esp *A. maius*).

1876 Hobbs *Bot. Hdbk.* 32, Dog's mouth, Snapdragon, *Antirrhinum majus.* **1900** Lyons *Plant Names* 39, *A[ntirrhinum] majus* . . Dog's-mouth. **1959** Carleton *Index Herb. Plants* 38, Dog's Mouth: Antirrhinum (v).

dog snapper n Cf *DJE dog-teeth snapper*

Either of two **snappers:** usu *Lutjanus jocu,* but also **schoolmaster.**

1775 (1962) Romans *Nat. Hist. FL* lii, The fish. . . most commonly caught are such as seamen know by the following names, viz . . *red, grey and black snappers, dog snappers,* . . *mangrove snappers.* **1898** U.S. Natl. Museum *Bulletin* 47.1257, *Neomænis jocu*. . . *Dog Snapper*. . . This species is about equally abundant with *N. apodus* about Florida Keys. **1911** *Century Dict. Suppl., Dog-snapper*. . . A fish, *Lutjanus jocu,* known from the Florida Keys to Brazil. **1935** Caine *Game Fish* 123, *Schoolmaster*. . . *Synonyms* . . Dog Snapper. *Ibid* 127, *Lutjanus jocu*. . . The dog snapper is. . . a hard and vigorous fighter. **1946** LaMonte *N. Amer. Game Fishes* 59, *Schoolmaster—Lutianus apodus* . . —Names: Caji, . . Dog Snapper. **1973** Knight *Cook's Fish Guide* 391, Snapper . . Dog (some say poisonous, some say good).

dog soldier n [Transf from *dog soldier* an American Indian who is an outcast or runaway from his tribe and who bands together with other such Indians; see *DA*]

See quot.

1952 Dobie *Mustangs* 252 **KS,** Roan stallions were more numerous [than black stallions], but most of them were without mares, hundreds roaming about alone or by twos and threes. The local name for these outcasts was "dog soldiers."

dog's rear-end fly See **dog's-ass fly**

dog's rib See **dog ribs**

dogstail grass n

1 also *dogtail:* A grass of the genus *Cynosurus.* [See quot 1840]

1790 in 1793 Amer. Philos. Soc. *Trans.* 3.161 **sePA,** *Triandria. . . Digynia. . .* Cynosurus, Dog's tail-grass. [**1840** MA Zool. & Bot. Surv. *Herb. Plants & Quadrupeds* 242, *Cynosurus.*—Named from the Greek for *dog's tail,* from the form of the spike of flowers.] **1850** U.S. Patent Office *Annual Rept. for 1849: Ag.* 156 **MS,** Dogs-tail grass . . grows with great vigor. **1950** Hitchcock–Chase *Manual Grasses* 183, *Cynosurus . .* Dogtail . . *Cynosurus cristatus . .* Crested dogtail. **1952** Strausbaugh–Core *Flora WV* 130, *C[ynosurus] cristatus . .* crested dogtail. **1961** Peck *Manual OR* 104, *C[ynosurus] cristatus . .* Crested Dog's-tail Grass.

2 also *dogtail grass:* A **goose grass 2b** (here: *Eleusine indica*).

1822 Eaton *Botany* 270, *Eleusine. . . indica . .* dog-tail grass. **1848** Gray *Manual of Botany* 588, *E[leusine] Indica . . (Dog's-tail or Wire Grass.)* **1894** *Jrl. Amer. Folkl.* 7.104, *Eleusine Indica, . .* dog's tail-grass, wire-grass. West Va. **1911** *Century Dict.* 2603/2, *Dog's-tail grass. . . Eleusine Indica.*

dog's tail, not by a adv phr

Not at all; not by a long shot.

1967 *DARE* (Qu. KK55a, *To deny something very firmly: "No, not by a ______."*) Inf **WY3**, Dog's tail.

dog's toes See **dog toes**

dogstone n [*OED dogstones* "transl. med. L. *Testiculus canis . .* from the shape of the tubers."] Cf **dog's ballocks**

Appar an orchid, prob *Orchis rotundifolia.*

1957 Beck *Folkl. ME* 44, Dogstone, "which is found in salt marshes" is used to make love potions.

dog's tongue n Also *dog tongue*

1 =**vanilla plant.** [From the shape of the leaf]

1900 Lyons *Plant Names* 378, Dog's-tongue. . . *Leaves* have an agreeable vanilla-like odor. **1927** Boston Soc. Nat. Hist. *Proc.* 214 **Okefenokee GA,** *Trilisa odoratissima* 'Dog-tongue'; 'deer-tongue'; 'vanilla.' **1930** Sievers *Amer. Med. Plants* 20, *Trilisa odoratissima. . .* Dog's-tongue. **1971** Krochmal *Appalachia Med. Plants* 254, Dogtongue. . . is used as a blend with tobacco, and . . has been used to flavor medicinal compounds.

2 A violet (here: *Viola septemloba*).

1974 Morton *Folk Remedies* 140, Young sassafras leaves are cooked with . . "dog's tongue" *(V. septemloba . .)* to make soup.

3 A **wild buckwheat** (here: *Eriogonum tomentosum*). **chiefly SE**

1901 *Torreya* 1.116 **GA,** *Eriogonum tomentosum. . .* Dog-tongue. Bulloch. **1933** Small *Manual SE Flora* 445, Dog-tongue. . . Dry pinelands and sandhills, Coastal Plain, Fla. to Ala. and S.C. **1953** Greene–Blomquist *Flowers South* 27, *Dog-Tongue . . Eriogonum tomentosum. . .* This dog-tongue is distinguished by its whorled leaves which are green above and white-wooly beneath. **1975** Duncan–Foote *Wildflowers SE* 26, Dog-tongue; Wild-buckwheat. . . Basal leaves prominent, . . sometimes dying with age or because of drought.

4 =**pickerelweed.**

1933 Small *Manual SE Flora* 266, *Pontederia. . .* Pickerel-weeds. Dog-tongues.

dog's tooth See **dogtooth 1**

dog's-tooth violet See **dogtooth violet**

dog stud n [**dog** n[1] **B18a** + *stud* a male animal used for breeding] *old-fash, derog*

See quots.

1899 (1912) Green *VA Folk-Speech* 151, *Dog-stud. . .* The husband of a woman who had no children was called a *dog-stud.* **1952** Brown *NC Folkl.* 1.533, *Dog-stud. . .* A childless husband.—Chapel Hill.

dog's years See **dog's age**

dog tag n [Transf from *dog tag* an animal license or military identification tag]

A receipt; a label attached to raw materials to give credit to the appropriate producer.

1967 Key *Tobacco Vocab.* 75 **TN,** *Dog tag. . .* Receipt for a crop of tobacco. **1969** *DARE* Tape **KY39**, You see these coal loaders they had their tag on this car, their number . . They weighed this coal, and . . every night they put every man's weigh tag number . . and his name here, y'see. That's the way the coal miners got their pay. They got paid the number of ton that they loaded, y'see. That's the way they done, had everybody's tag, dog tag we call 'em.

dogtail n

1 See **dogstail grass 1.**

2 pl: A **knotweed** (here: *Polygonum aviculare*).

1897 *Jrl. Amer. Folkl.* 10.54, *Polygonum aviculare . .* dog-tails, St. Joseph, Mo.

3 A **dragonfly** of the genus *Tetragoneuria.* [Perh from its manner of moving its tail from side to side] Also called **wag**

1929 Needham–Heywood *Hdbk. Dragonflies* 178, *Tetragoneuria . .* Dog-tails. . . These dragonflies. . . are pugnacious and often pursue larger species about as a kingbird harasses a crow.

dog-tail railroad n Cf *DS* N37

1888 J. Kirkland *McVeys* 204 *(DA),* It's a 'dog-tail railroad,' as they say around here. A line that starts from a place of no consequence and runs nowhere.

dog take (it) See **dog** n[1] **B7**

dog the watches See **dog** v **14**

dog thistle n

=**Canada thistle.**

1900 Lyons *Plant Names* 81, *C. arvensis. . .* Dog-Thistle.

dog tick n

1 A wood tick *(Dermacentor variabilis).* [See quot 1926] **chiefly Sth, S Midl** See Map

1926 Essig *Insects N. Amer.* 21, The American dog or wood tick, *Dermacentor electus,* is the commonest tick in the Eastern part of the United States, but also occurs along the Pacific Coast in California and Oregon with the Rocky Mountain Region apparently free. . . The dog is the common host . . although they also infest cattle, horses, deer, rabbits, squirrel, racoon, opossum, coyote, badger, skunk, and sometimes humans. **1954** Borror–DeLong *Intro. Insects* 791, The American dog tick, *Dermacentor variabilis . .* (Ixodidæ). **1965–70** *DARE* (Qu. R23a) 20 Infs, **chiefly Sth, S Midl,** Dog ticks; **AR55**, **KY76**, 84, 86, **LA18**, **OK23**, **TN26**, Dog ticks—fat (*or* full, swollen) ones; **LA14**, 15, Dog ticks—same as deer ticks; **KS5**, **VA15**, Dog ticks—same as wood ticks; **DE4**, Dog ticks—they stay on a dog long enough to swell up; **LA12**, Dog ticks—swollen ticks named according to what they're on; **OK18**, Dog ticks—usually bother dogs; not many here; **TN26**, Dog ticks—they blow up like a big balloon. **1988** *DARE* File **NEast,** A man from upstate New York . . mentioned *red ticks* and *dog ticks* as being present in the Northeast.

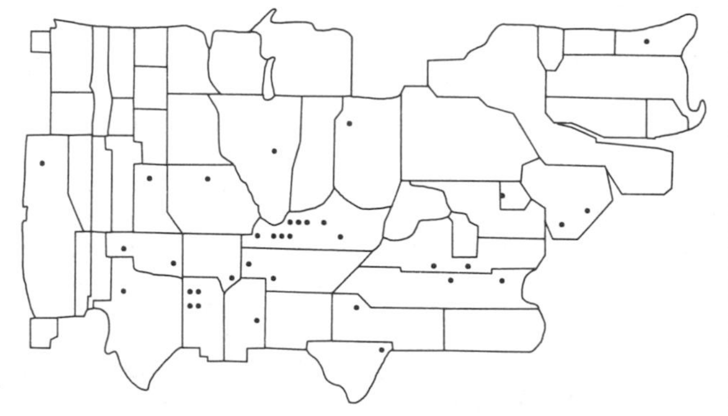

•dog tick 1 (Qu. R23a)

2 An unidentified plant; see quot.

1940 (1978) Still *River of Earth* 18 **KY,** You ought to plant a leetle dogtick around. Hit's the best mole-bane I ever heered tell of. *Ibid* 232, Father's cheeks grew ashen. He looked blue-pale and wizened, like a last year's dogtick stalk.

3 A **burdock 1.**

1968 *DARE* (Qu. S13, *There's a common wild bush with bunches of round, prickly seeds; when they get dry they stick to your clothing—what are these called around here?*) Inf **MD29**, Dog tick; (Qu. S15, *Do you have any other weed seeds that cling to clothing?*) Inf **VA24**, Leather root = dog tick = beggar lice.

dog-toes n Also *dog's-toes, ~foot* [Prob from the shape of the flower head] **chiefly Nth**

A **pussytoes,** usu *Antennaria plantaginifolia.*

1886 *Century Illustr. Mag.* Sept 787/1, First it [=an Iowa prairie] is white with 'dog-toes.' **1892** *Jrl. Amer. Folkl.* 5.98, *Antennaria plantaginifolia,* . . dog toes. N.H. **1894** *Ibid* 7.91, *Antennaria plantaginifolia,* . . dog-toes, Concord, Mass. **1896** *Ibid* 9.191, Dogs' toes (staminate flowers), Auburndale, Mass. **1898** *Ibid* 11.229, Dog's foot, Andover, Mass. **1940** Clute *Amer. Plant Names* 74. **1959** Carleton *Index Herb. Plants* 38.

dog tongue See **dog's tongue**

dog-tongue blossom n

Purple loosestrife *(Lythrum salicaria).*

1966 *DARE* Wildfl. QR Pl. 143b Inf **NC**28, Dog-tongue blossom.

dog-tongue wampee n Cf **wampee**

1 A **pickerelweed** (here: *Pontederia cordata*).

1913 *Torreya* 13.229, *Pontederia cordata.* . . Dog-tongue wampee, Santee Club, S.C.

2 An **arrowhead 1** (here: *Sagittaria falcata*).

1916 *Torreya* 16.236, *Sagittaria falcata.* . . Dog-tongue wampee, Cat I[slan]d, S.C.

dogtooth n

1 also *dog's tooth:* See quots. [*OED* 1382 →]

1906 *DN* 3.134 **nwAR,** *Dog-tooth.* . . A human tooth resembling a canine tooth, though not necessarily the tooth situated between the incisor and bicuspid teeth. "You mustn't lose that tooth; some dog may find it, and then you'll have a dogtooth." (Addressed to a boy or girl when a milktooth is removed.) **1966–70** *DARE* (Qu. X12, . . *Large front teeth that stick out of the mouth*) Infs **CO**20, **MT**3, Dog teeth; **NC**36, Buck teeth (front), dog teeth (on sides); **AL**3, Dog's teeth; (Qu. X13a, . . *Joking names . . for teeth*) Inf **KY**81, Dog teeth (eye teeth); **TX**92, Dog teeth.

2 A **cottonwood 1.** [Perh in ref to the toothed leaves]

1966 *DARE* (Qu. T13) Inf **ME**8, Dogtooth.

dog-toothed violet See **dogtooth violet**

dogtooth grass n

A **panic grass** (here: *Panicum repens*).

1942 *Torreya* 42.157, *Panicum repens* L.—Dogtooth grass, . . Louisiana. **1947** *Jrl. Wildlife Management* 2.51 **LA,** When early spring floods deeply inundate the flats and interior marshes, geese feed on rhizomes of dog-tooth grass *(Panicum repens).*

dogtooth salmon n

=chum salmon.

1857 Swan *NW Coast* 140 **WA,** There are several varieties of fall salmon, the most plentiful of which is the hawk-nosed, or hook-billed, or dog-tooth salmon (for it has all those names).

dogtooth violet n Also *dogtooth, dog's-tooth (violet), dog-toothed violet*

A plant of the genus *Erythronium.* Also called **Adam-and-Eve 3, adder's tongue 1, avalanche lily, chamise lily 1, Easter bell 1, fawn lily, glacier lily, hound's-tooth violet, lilian, lillette, rattlesnake violet, scrofula root, snakeroot, starstrikers, trout flower, trout lily.** For other names of var spp see **adder's violet 2, amber bell 2, brandywine lily, cornflower 3, curly lily, deer tongue 2, Easter lily 1, fishhook 2, grandmammy's nightcap, jonquil, lamb's tongue, March lily, roosters, serpent's tongue, snakeleaf, snow lily, spring lily, tulip, yellow bells, yellow lily, yellow snowdrop**

1804 (1905) Lewis *Orig. Jrls. Lewis & Clark Exped.* 6.172 **MA,** The dogs tooth violet, and may apple appeared above ground. **1822** Eaton *Botany* 276, Dog-tooth violet, adder's tongue. . . Leaves oblong-ovate, glabrous, spotted. **1882** *Century Illustr. Mag.* 24.153/2, Mr. Robinson recommends a score or more of American plants as. . . American cowslip, . . dog's-tooth violet, and a few others. **1901** Stillman *Autobiography* 1.44 **NY,** I knew every sunny spot where came . . the little white violets, their yellow sisters, then the "dogtooth violet." **1949** Peattie *Cascades* 252, The white avalanche lily . . is sometimes called . . dogtooth violet. **1965–70** *DARE* (Qu. S11) 136 Infs, **chiefly Nth, Midl,** Dogtooth violet; **MN**14, Dog's-tooth; (Qu. S3) 32 Infs, **chiefly Nth,** Dogtooth violet; **MI**100, **PA**128, Dogtooth; **PA**70, **VT**10, Dog's-tooth violet; **WA**6, Dog-toothed violet; (Qu. S26a, *What other wildflowers do you have around here, not yet mentioned? Roadside flowers*) Inf **MT**3, Dogtooth violet; (Qu. S26c, *Wildflowers that grow in woods*) Infs **IL**29, **SC**2, Dogtooth violet; **PA**70, Dog's-tooth violet; (Qu. S26e, *Other wildflowers not yet mentioned*) Inf **CA**204, Easter lilies or dogtooth violet. **1966–67** *DARE* Wildfl QR Pl.15a Infs **MI**57, **NC**28, **SC**41, **WA**15, 30, Dogtooth violet. **1976** Bailey–Bailey *Hortus Third* 446, *Erythronium.* . . Dog-tooth violet.

Dog Town n **chiefly Nth, Midl, West** Cf **dog** n[1] **B1a, 8**

A small, out-of-the-way place; a poor or depressed section of a town; hence *Dog Towner* one who resides in such a place or section.

1838 Kettell *Yankee Notions* 174, The territory in the neighborhood of Dogtown is remarkable for its fertility, bating that part of it which is covered with rocks, the salt meadow, the pine woods, the clay-ponds and the swamps. *Ibid* 175, The Dogtowners are remarkably industrious, for they get a living, although constantly grumbling of hard times. **1889** Nelson *50 Yrs.* 146 **West** (as of 1855), A small town named Dog Town had sprung up in our absence, about three miles from the fort. It consisted of two stores, a few dwelling-houses, and four whiskey saloons. **1941** *LANE* Map 450 **neMA,** Dog-towner, one who lives in Byfield, the western part of Newbury, or by extension in any primitive community. **1950** *WELS (An out-of-the-way place or an unimportant village)* 1 Inf, **WI,** Dog town; *(Nicknames for nearby cities, villages, or districts)* 2 Infs, **WI,** Dog town. **1965–70** *DARE* (Qu. C34, *Nicknames for nearby settlements, villages, or districts*) 11 Infs, **Nth, Midl,** Dog Town; (Qu. C33, . . *An out-of-the-way place, or a very unimportant place*) Infs **CA**204, **MA**5, **NY**88, Dog Town; (Qu. C35, *Nicknames for the different parts of your town or city*) Infs **DE**1, **IA**8, **ND**1, **TN**37, **UT**8, Dog Town; (Qu. II25, . . *The part of a town where the poorer people, special groups, or foreign groups live*) Infs **DE**1, **MD**39, **MA**5, **ND**1, **NY**234, **TN**30, Dog Town.

dogtown grass n [**dog** n[1] **B1a**]

A **needlegrass** (here: *Aristida longiseta*).

1913 (1979) Barnes *Western Grazing* 43, Owing to the presence in many portions of both these desert regions of a grass known as needle or dogtown grass (Aristida) and porcupine grass (Stipa spp.), the sharp awns of each of which work into the wool and finally into the very skin of the animals, sheep cannot be successfully grazed in these lower desert ranges. **1937** U.S. Forest Serv. *Range Plant Hdbk.* G20, Red three-awn, also known as dogtown grass, . . is an aggressive invader of . . soils recently disturbed by burrowing animals. **1968** Barkley *Plants KS* 38, Aristida longiseta. . . Dogtown Grass. . . Dry or sandy plains and foothills.

dog tracks n pl Cf **chicken tracks**

=chicken scratch 1.

1968–69 *DARE* (Qu. JJ11, . . *Handwriting that's hard to read*) Infs **KY**5, **MA**48, Dog tracks.

dog-treat v

To treat badly.

1942 (1971) Campbell *Cloud-Walking* 50 **seKY,** It would have made the whole settlement mad, being dog-treated when they stopped in to see a sick person.

dog tree n *obs*

A **flowering dogwood** (here: *Cornus florida*).

1828 Rafinesque *Med. Flora* 1.131, *Cornus florida.* . . *Vulgar Names* —Dogwood, Dogtree, Boxtree.

dog trick n [*OED* c1540 →, "? *Obs.*"]

1899 (1912) Green *VA Folk-Speech* 151, *Dog-trick.* . . A currish or mean trick; an ill-natured practical joke.

dog tripper n [**dog** n[1] **B2**]

In logging: **=dogger 1.**

1958 McCulloch *Woods Words* 48 **Pacific NW,** *Dog tripper*—The man who knocked dogs out of logs on the landings or on the river. When a log grounded on a shoal or bank a dog was driven in it, and a team was hitched to the chain attached to the dog. When the log was horsed into water deep enough to float it, the dog tripper knocked the dog loose and the teamster headed back for shore.

dogtrot n, also attrib [So called because a dog could trot through] **chiefly Sth, S Midl** Cf **alley** n[1] **7, breezeway, dog run, turkey trot**

A covered, open passageway between two sections of a house or cabin.

1901 *Amer. Jrl. Sociol.* 7.1.11 **eKY,** It consists, sometimes, of two rooms under one roof, with an open space between, called a "dog-trot." **1912** in 1955 *KY Folkl. Rec.* 1.107 **eKY,** It was a log house, built Virginia style, with a wide, covered porch through the center separating the two sides. This *dog-trot* was a cool place in warm weather, a cool place to churn, and wash, a place to visit, and sew, or even take a nap. **1924** Mackaye *Fine-Pretty* xi **eKY,** Next door, in the dog-trot, are the looms and spinning-wheels. **1937** *Natl. Geogr. Mag.* 71.290 **MS,** The dogtrot house is . . characteristic of Mississippi. . . In its primitive form this dwelling has two rooms with a floorless and doorless passage between, and a roof over all. . . It emerges now in more elaborate homes with additional rooms on each square side, and the dogtrot is a hallway. **1949** *AmSp* 24.108 **neSC,** *Dog-trot house.* . . House built in two pens under one roof, with the central hallway open at both ends. **1960** (1962) Lee *Mockingbird* 103 **AL,** Mrs. Dubose lived alone except for a Negro girl . . in a house with steep front steps and a dog-trot hall. **1962** Faulkner *Reivers* 167 **MS,** It was a dog-trot house, paintless but quite sound and quite neat among locust and chinaberry trees. **1966** *PADS* 46.25 **cnAR. 1966–70** *DARE* (Qu. D11, *When you go into a house, the part just beyond the front door is the* ______) Inf **AR**52, Dogtrot—an open hall, leading directly from the front door to the back without doors; (Qu. D16, . . *Parts added on to the main part of a house*) Inf **MS**36, Dogtrot—this is an open place between an old part and the new part; **NC**55, Dogtrot—between two buildings; **TX**11; Dogtrot; (Qu. D23, *A house that is divided in two through the middle*) Inf **LA**14, Dogtrot house—this is an old-fashioned single-family house with open hallway down the middle; **NC**16, Dogtrot. **1966–67** *DARE* FW Addit **swAR,** Dogtrot—an open hallway through a house with entrances to rooms on right and left; it led directly from the front porch to the back porch; **KY**84, Dogtrot or turkeytrot—the space between two sections of a house; function: to catch a breeze; **seWA,** Dogtrot—a breezeway, a covered area between two buildings or two parts of a building.

dog turd n *joc*

1967–69 *DARE* (Qu. DD6a, . . *Cigars*) Infs **MN**35, **OR**1, Dog turd [laughter]; (Qu. DD7, . . *Cigars . . according to size, shape, or the way they're made*) Inf **PA**214, Dog turds—very big ones.

dog up See **dog** v 7

dog violet n

A violet (*Viola conspersa*). Also called **meadow violet, tufted violet**

1937 *Torreya* 37.64 **NY,** Only a few herbs were seen in flower namely: Bloodroot, Fawn Lily, . . Wake Robin, . . Dog Violet and Pale Violet. **1950** Stevens *ND Plants* 209, *Viola conspersa* . . Dog Violet. **1961** Smith *MI Wildflowers* 235, American Dog Violet—*Viola conspersa.* **1976** Bailey-Bailey *Hortus Third* 1158, *V[iola] conspersa* . . American dog violet.

dog wagon n

1 A small, usu short-order restaurant in a converted vehicle (as a bus or railway car) or a building made to resemble such a vehicle; a diner. [In ref to the sale of hot dogs]

1900 *DN* 2.32 **MA** [College slang], *Dog-wagon.* . . Night lunch wagon. **1937** Thurber *Let Your Mind Alone* 112, "I wish you wouldn't call them *dog*-wagons," she said. . . "That's what they are," he said. "Dog-wagons." She waited a few seconds. "*Decent* people call them *diners,*" she told him. **1950** *WELS (Nicknames . . for a small eating place)* 1 Inf, **ceWI,** Dog wagon. **1968** *DARE* (Qu. D39, . . *A small eating place where the food is not especially good*) Inf **WI**5, Dog wagon.

2 See quot.

1966–69 *DARE* (Qu. N3, *The car or wagon that takes arrested people to the police station or to jail*) Infs **AL**14, 34, 56, **CA**87, **KY**47, Dog wagon.

3 See quot. Cf **dogcart**

1968 *DARE* File **sRI,** *Dog wagon*—a two-wheeled wagon drawn by one horse with two or three people on the seat facing the front and two or three passengers on another seat facing the rear. Used in the first decades of this century.

dog walk n

=dogtrot.

1966 Dakin *Dial. Vocab. Ohio R. Valley* 2.56, Several field records from Kentucky . . and one from Gallatin County, Illinois, have entries which would seem to refer to the open hall between two parts of a house. *Dog walk, dog trot, hall, passage, breezeway* each appear one time. **1969** *DARE* (Qu. D16, . . *Parts added on to the main part of a house*) Inf **KY**5, Dog walk—between lean-to and main house.

dog-walking area See **dog park**

dog warden n Cf **dog officer**

An official in charge of a dog pound; a dog catcher.

1967 *Chagrin Valley Herald* (Chagrin Falls OH) 21 Sept sec A 2/1, A dog warden will be hired. **1969** *Cape Cod Std.-Times* (Hyannis MA) 22 Jan 1, Town Dog Warden Fred Patterson appeared before the Finance Committee to justify his request for a helper.

dog warp n, v **[dog n[1] B2a]** Cf **dog hook 1**

In logging: a rope with a hook on the end; to use such a rope.

1905 U.S. Forest Serv. *Bulletin* 61.35 **Nth,** *Dogwarp.* . . A rope with a strong hook on the end, which is used in breaking dangerous jams on falls and rapids and in moving logs from other difficult positions. **1905** Wiggin *Rose o' the River* 16 **ME,** I must be down to the bridge 'fore they start dog-warpin' the side jam. *Ibid* 44, They'd get horses an' dog-warp it off, log by log.

dogwatch n [By ext from nautical use; see quot 1945]

The evening hours.

1945 Colcord *Sea Language* 67 **ME, Cape Cod, Long Island,** *Dog-watch.* The period from 4 to 8 p.m., which is divided into two watches in order that periods of night duty may alternate daily. . . In newspaper slang, the dogwatch covers the evening hours when the paper is being made up. **1975** Gould *ME Lingo* 76, *Dog watch*—Properly, *dogwatch.* The four-hour watch aboard ship became two watches of two hours each between 4:00 and 8:00 P.M.—the first and second *dogwatches.* Now and then Mainers toss off *dogwatch* for suppertime or the cocktail hour.

‡dog weather n [Perh from *dog days*]

Dry weather.

1970 *DARE* (Qu. B28, *When there is no rain for a long time*) Inf **TN**56, That's dog weather.

dog wedge n Cf **dog n[1] B2c**

In logging: see quot 1905.

1905 U.S. Forest Serv. *Bulletin* 61.35 **Nth,** *Dog wedge.* An iron wedge with a ring in the butt, which is driven into the end of a log and a chain hitched in the ring for skidding the log by horsepower; also used in gathering up logs on a drive by running a rope through the rings and pulling a number of logs at a time through marshes or partially submerged meadows to the channel. **1969** *DARE* Tape **KY**39, Back years ago they'd use what's called a dog wedge [in hauling logs]; drive a half a wedge with a ring in it. Drive it in that log, and hook in that ring. Pulled 'em that way.

dogweed n

1 A **crownbeard** (here: *Verbesina encelioides*).

1898 *Jrl. Amer. Folkl.* 11.230 **KS,** *Verbesina encelioides* . . dog weed.

2=fetid marigold. [See quot 1931; cf **dog n[1] B18b]**

1931 U.S. Dept. Ag. *Misc. Pub.* 101.165, Dogweeds, often called fetid-marigolds, . . have, especially when bruised, a strong pungent odor, pleasant in some species and disagreeable in others. **1948** Stevens *KS Wild Flowers* 393, *Dogweed.* . . may cause dermatitis in susceptible persons. **1954** *Harder Coll.* **cwTN,** Dogweed. **1960** Vines *Trees SW* 1014, Prickly-leaf Dogweed. *Dyssodia acerosa.* **1967** *DARE* (Qu. S21) Infs **AL**27, **LA**2, Dogweed. **1976** Bailey-Bailey *Hortus Third* 405.

3 A **trillium** (here: prob *Trillium erectum*). [Prob from the odor] Cf **dogwood 11, wet-dog trillium**

1967 *DARE* (Qu. S2, . . *The flower that comes up in the woods early in spring, with three white petals that turn pink as the flower grows older*) Inf **IL**19, Dogweed.

dog willow n

Perh a **sandbar willow.**

1973 Eby *That Disgraceful* 201 **csWI,** Somewhere in that amorphous waste of marsh and hummock, hidden by dog willow and sedgy aquatic growth, Black Hawk was believed to be hiding.

dog-winter bird See **dogwood-winter bird**

dog with two tails, proud as a adj phr

Very proud or pleased with oneself.

1899 (1912) Green *VA Folk-Speech* 37, Proud as a dog with two tails. **1909** *DN* 3.360 **eAL, wGA,** *Proud as a dog with two tails.* . . Very proud. **1912** *DN* 3.586 **wIN. 1983** *Lutz Coll.* **NJ** (as of 1940s).

dog won't hunt, that phr Also *that cock won't fight*
That won't succeed.
1933 Williamson *Woods Colt* 148 **Ozarks,** That feller is jest naturally a fool for the lack of sense, a-tryin' to mix whiskey an' lyin'. He ort t' of knowed that dog won't hunt! **1984** Wilder *You All Spoken Here* 57 **Sth,** That dog won't hunt, that cock won't fight: The hell you say; it ain't practical; my hind foot; you're trying to sell me a bill of goods; I won't buy that excuse; that won't wash.

dogwood n
1 also *dogwood tree:* A plant of the genus *Cornus.* [*OED* 1617 →] For other names of var spp see **bunchberry 1, flowering dogwood, green alder 2, green osier, kinnikinnick, miner's dogwood, mountain dogwood, pagoda dogwood, pigeonberry, purple dogwood, red brush, red osier dogwood, red willow, rose willow, squash willow, swamp dogwood, swamp sassafras, umbrella tree**
1671 in 1897 SC Hist. Soc. *Coll.* 5.333, This Land bears very good . . Poplar, Beach, Elme, Laurell, Bay, Sassaphrage, dogwood, Black Wallnutt. **1709** (1967) Lawson *New Voyage* 240 **NC,** Others name them by the Trees that blossom; especially, the Dogwood-Tree. **1785** Marshall *Arbustrum* 35, Cornus candidissima. *Swamp American Dogwood. . .* The flowers are produced at the extremity of the branches, in clusters, and are succeeded by whitish succulent berries. **1807** in 1857 *S. Lit. Messenger* 24.309/1 **VA,** The Dog-wood and the Peach flaunted their gaudy blossoms to the sun. **1881** Tourgée *Royal Gentleman & Zouri* 452, The poor-white woman . . bowed by the rocky seat under the newly-leaved dogwood trees. **1914** in 1925 Bryan–Bryan *Memoirs* 417 **NC,** The red berries and bronze leaves of the dogwood . . lent their beauty to our path. **1938** Rawlings *Yearling* 394 **nFL,** The dogwood had not finished blooming. **1938** Van Dersal *Native Woody Plants* 107, *Dogwoods.* The species are often difficult to separate, the characters used to distinguish them often being very minor. **1965–70** *DARE* (Qu. T16, *What kinds of trees are 'special' around here?*) 249 Infs, **widespread but chiefly Appalachians, C and S Atl,** Dogwood tree; **MO**4, **PA**105, **SC**53, **WA**28, Pink dogwood; **MO**15, **PA**105, 111, **SC**53, White dogwood tree; **MI**36, **MO**15, **PA**111, Red dogwood tree; **MI**36, Silver dogwood; **NJ**69, Wild dogwood; (Qu. S26e) 21 Infs, **chiefly Sth, S Midl,** Dogwood; (Qu. S26c) 20 Infs, **chiefly Sth, Midl,** Dogwood; (Qu. S26a) Infs **MO**39, **WV**17, Dogwood; (Qu. S26b) Infs **MS**8, **OK**32, Dogwood; (Qu. S26d) Infs **MS**47, **NC**12, Dogwood; (Qu. T15, *What kinds of swamp trees do you have?*) Infs **DE**1, **FL**20, **KY**9, **LA**20, **ME**8, **NC**49, **NJ**17, Dogwood. [*DARE* Ed: Some of these Infs may refer instead to other senses of **dogwood.**]

2 **=striped maple.**
1838 (1969) Torrey–Gray *Flora N. Amer.* 1.246, *A[cer] Pennsylvanicum. . .* Striped Maple. Moose-wood. Dog-wood.

3 **=poison sumac. chiefly Nth**
1847 Wood *Class-Book* 203, *R[hus] venenata. . . Poison Sumac. Dogwood. . .* The whole plant is very poisonous to the taste or touch, and even taints the air to some distance around with its pernicious effluvium. **1850** *New Engl. Farmer* 2.60 **NEng,** The Dogwood. . . is not to be confounded with the Poison Sumac, usually called Dogwood. **1872** Schele de Vere *Americanisms* 423, A strange confusion of names has thrown two trees, entirely different in family and features, into the same class. . . *Dogwood* is the name given to the *Cornel-tree* (Cornus florida), and to the *Poison Sumac* (Rhus venenata). . . The latter, an inmate of swamps, and well known by the beauty of its semi-tropical foliage, hides a violent poison in its leaves, and even affects susceptible persons who approach it too nearly. **1897** Sudworth *Arborescent Flora* 276, *Rhus vernix. . . Common Names. . .* Dogwood (Vt., Mass., R.I., Wis., Mich., Iowa, Nebr., Minn., La.) **1907** *DN* 3.186 **seNH,** *Dogwood. . .* A poisonous tree (Rhus vernix). **1931** Otis *MI Trees* 275, *Poison Sumac,* also known as *Dogwood . . ,* is an upright shrub or small tree, sometimes 15–20 feet in height. **1967–70** *DARE* (Qu. S17) Infs **MA**42, 74, 100, **NY**200, **RI**15, Dogwood; **MA**40, Wild dogwood tree; (Qu. T13, *What other names do you have around here for these trees: . . sumac?*) Inf **NE**11, Shoemake—dogwood is the same. **1983** *Lutz Coll.,* When I was a little girl, about 1912 to 1920, I heard my friends here in Ramsey [NJ] refer to sumac bushes or trees as *dogwood.* My father, who was a scientist, set me right.

4 **=hobblebush.**
1896 *Jrl. Amer. Folkl.* 9.190, *Viburnum lantanoides* [sic] . . . Dogwood . . Bath, M[ain]e. **1900** Lyons *Plant Names* 391, *V. alnifolium. . .* Dogwood. **1940** Clute *Amer. Plant Names* 56, *Hobble-bush. . .* Dog-wood.

5 A **serviceberry** (here: *Amelanchier canadensis*).
1896 *Jrl. Amer. Folkl.* 9.186, *Amelanchier Canadensis. . .* Dogwood, . . West.

6 also *dogwood sage:* **=sage.** [See quots]
1931 *AmSp* 7.120 **eID,** *Dogwood* is a nickname given because of the odor of the sagebrush when wet, which resembles that of a dog's wet coat of fur. **1966** *DARE* (Qu. S21, . . *Weeds . . that are a trouble in gardens and fields*) Inf **ND**1, Dogwood sage. **1968** Adams *Western Words* 96, *Dogwood.* A cowboy's name for sagebrush because its odor when wet is like wet dog's fur.

7 A **burning bush 1.**
1931 Clute *Common Plants* 92, The original . . dog-wood was probably the Old World *Euonymus Europaeus,* but the name has been passed on to our native *Euonymus atropurpureus* and related species.

8 **=pin cherry.**
1931 Clute *Common Plants* 93, Other species . . often called dogwoods are the bird cherry *(Prunus Pennsylvanica)* [etc].

9 A buckthorn (*Rhamnus* spp).
1931 Clute *Common Plants* 93, Other species besides the cornels that are often called dog-woods are . . the buck-thorn *(Rhamnus frangula).* **1940** Clute *Amer. Plant Names* 131, *R. alnifolia. . .* Dogwood.

10 A **bittersweet** (here: *Solanum dulcamara*).
1931 Clute *Common Plants* 93, Other species . . often called dogwoods are . . the bittersweet *(Solanum dulcamara)* [etc].

11 A **trillium.**
1966–70 *DARE* (Qu. S2) Infs **DC**13, **OK**52, UT7, Dogwood.

12 An anemone (here: *Anemone patens*).
1968–69 *DARE* (Qu. S3) Infs **NY**205, **WI**72, Dogwood.

dogwood bitters n
A tonic or remedy.
1843 (1916) Hall *New Purchase* 267 **IN,** Mr. James Jimmey will take strange students (students not belonging to Woodville) to board, at one dollar a week, and find every thing, washing included, and will black their shoes three times a week to boot, and—*give them their dog-wood and cherry-bitters every morning into the bargain!* **1966** *DARE* (Qu. BB50d, *Favorite spring tonics around here*) Inf **AR**39, Dogwood bitters.

dogwood rain n Cf **dogwood winter**
1899 Bergen *Animal Lore* 108 **MD,** There is a rain at the time of the dogwood *(Cornus florida)* blooming, hence called "dogwood rain."

dogwood sage See **dogwood 6**

dogwood toothbrush n *old-fash*
1954 *PADS* 21.25 **SC,** *Dogwood toothbrush. . .* A device made by bending a green dogwood twig back and forth at one place until the fibers are thoroughly loosened. Then the twig is broken at this place, presenting two ends which are suitable for brushing the teeth. Soot from the open chimney was formerly used as an abrasive. . . Cf. *DA, blackgum toothbrush,* which is also heard in South Carolina.

dogwood tree See **dogwood 1**

dogwood winter n [Ref to the time of year, usu April and May, when dogwoods bloom] **chiefly S Midl** Cf **blackberry winter, dogwood rain**
A period of cold weather in the spring.
1904 (1913) Johnson *Highways South* 162 **KY,** I reckon this must be the dogwood winter. We always have a cold spell when the dogwood is in blossom, and that's what we call it. **1907** *Jrl. Amer. Folkl.* 20.236 **NC,** In May, when the dogwood tree is in bloom. . . there is cold, disagreeable, cloudy weather and often a touch of frost. Down our way it never fails, and we call it *dogwood winter.* **1940** (1978) Still *River of Earth* 127 **KY,** "Even come spring," Grandma said, "we've got a passel of chills to endure: dogwood winter, redbud, service, foxgrape, blackberry. . . There must be seven winters, by count. A chilly snap for every time of bloom." **1944** *PADS* 2.42 **wNC. 1949** Hornsby *Lonesome Valley* 53 *(Hench Coll.)* **swVA, nwNC,** The weather turned cold. Uncle Lihugh said it was blackberry winter, but Aunt Rhody argued that it was dogwood winter. **1952** Brown *NC Folkl.* 1.533. **1953** Randolph *Down in Holler* 240 **Ozarks,** Dogwood winter. . . A cold spell in spring while the dogwood is blooming. . . Isabel France (*Arkansas Gazette,* April 11, 1948) says that "*dogwood winter* is a few hours flashback to winter while the mountain dogwood trees are in full blossom." **c1900** *Wilson Coll.* **csKY.**

dogwood-winter bird n Also *dog-winter bird* **[dogwood winter]** **=scarlet tanager.**

1951 *AmSp* 26.277 **eKY,** In the eastern Kentucky mountains, an unseasonable cold spell occurs often enough at the time when the flowering dogwood is blooming to have received the name *dogwood winter.* The scarlet tanager, migrating and thus being seen most frequently at about the same period, is accordingly termed dogwood-winter bird. **1962** *AmSp* 37.196, *Dog-Winter Bird.* The tanager.

dogy n[1] See **dogie**

dogy n[2] [See quot 1951] Cf **dogs** **=ring-necked duck.**

1911 *Forest & Stream* 77.173, *Marila collaris...* Dogy, eastern shore of Virginia. **1951** *AmSp* 26.94 **VA,** The name *dos gris* (gray-back) for the ring-necked duck (La.) was transformed to *dogy* when transplanted to the eastern shore of Virginia. **1982** Elman *Hunter's Field Guide* 202, *Ring-necked Duck (Aythya collaris)—Common & Regional Names:* .. dogy.

Doherty wagon See **Dougherty wagon**

dohickus, dohinkie, dohinkus See **doohickey 1**

do how See **do what**

dohunkus, dohunky See **doohickey 1**

doily n Pronc-sp *dolly* Cf Pronc Intro 3.II.15

A Form.

1983 *MJLF* 9.38 **ceKY,** *Dollies* .. doilies.

B Senses.

1 A cloth napkin. [*OED* 1711 →] **S Atl** *old-fash*

1905 in 1961 Pringle *Woman Rice Planter* 197 **SC,** You fill a basket, put a dainty doily over it, and despatch your inevitable small boy to your neighbor. **1918** *DN* 5.18 **NC,** *Doily,* doily or napkin. **1938** *AmSp* 13.17 **GA,** *Doily...* 'I can never like anybody any more after he calls a *napkin* a *doily.*' **1966–67** *DARE* FW Addit **SC,** Doily—old name for napkin of cloth; **SC**19, Doily—napkin; **SC,** Doily—older name for a napkin made of cloth, frequently had some sort of design, usually a flower and in the same color as the napkin; it was used at supper, folded in a triangle and had doily rings to hold them; a napkin is larger, used at dinner and folded in a square. **1979** *DARE* File **NC** (as of 1915–40), Doily—a napkin, usually made of cloth.

2 See quot. *joc*

1966 *DARE* (Qu. X1a, .. *False hair, worn by men*) Inf **SD**2, Doily.

doin See **during**

doing n, usu pl but sometimes sg in constr Pronc-spp *doin's*

1 often in combs: Food or drink; a prepared dish. **chiefly Sth, S Midl** Cf **chicken fixings 1, common doings, fixing n 2, 3**

1839 *Daily Picayune* (New Orleans LA) 25 Jan 2/2 **MS,** [He] recommends the printers in that county to set up a shop for retailing the extra "white-eye" [=alcoholic beverages] and "flour doins" sent them for publishing marriage notices. **1847** (1962) Robb *Squatter Life* 65 **MO,** I walked out upon the steam boat 'guard' to cool off from the effects of considerable liquor doin's, participated in during the day. **1859** *Knickerbocker* 53.317 **AR,** Tell *Sal* to knock over a chicken or two, and get out some flour, and have some flour-doin's and chicken-fixin's for the stranger. *Ibid* 318 **AR,** Instead of 'store-tea,' they only had 'saxifax tea-doin's,[sic] without milk. **1887** *Century Illustr. Mag.* 34.881/2 **GA** [Black], I sot up mighty nigh twel day tryin' ter make some 'lasses candy fer ter put in dar wid de yuther doin's. **1908** *DN* 3.306 **eAL, wGA,** *Doing(s)...* Prepared dishes, especially fancy dishes. **1932** (1974) Caldwell *Tobacco Road* 44 **GA,** His doings is good enough for me.

2 also double pl *doinses* (cf **-es 2**): A social gathering or activity; a party or celebration. **chiefly NEng, Sth, S Midl**

1892 *DN* 1.229 **KY,** *Doin's* .. entertainment. "What kind o' doins are you goin' to have at your house?" [*DN* Ed: Vulgar in Michigan.] **1905** *DN* 3.77 **nwAR,** *Doin's...* Entertainment. 'Goin' to the doin's at the school-house tonight?' **1907** Wright *Shepherd* 26 **Ozarks,** Uncle Ike .. did it much better when he said .. the night of the "Doin's" at the Cove School, "Ba thundas!" **1910** *DN* 3.440 **cwNY,** There was great doin's at the Grange last night. **1914** *DN* 4.105 **KS,** *Doin'ses.* .. Doings. **1914** *DN* 4.71 **ME, nNH,** *Doin's...* Any form of activity. **1923** *DN* 5.205 **swMO,** *Doin'ses...* Doings, any form of social gathering. "We-all aim on havin' some doin'ses at our house this evenin'." **1931** Hannum *Thursday April* 83 **wNC,** He was much in demand at a doin's as the best dancer in the hollow. **1931–33** *LANE Worksheets* **cRI,** The teacher was going to have some sort of a doing [duɪn]. **1934** Carmer *Stars Fell on AL* 86, Suppose we walk over to the doin's together. **1941** *LANE* Map 414 **scattered NEng,** The map shows general terms for a social gathering or party, usually private: .. *(big) doings, goings-on.* **1967–70** *DARE* (Qu. DD34, *A party at which there is considerable drinking*) Inf **IL**135, Doin's ['duɪnz]; (Qu. FF9, *A Christmas gathering, at church or at someone's home, where there are songs and presents: "Are you going to the ______?"*) Inf **MD**23, Doings ['duɨnz]; **MO**38, Christmas doings ['duɪŋz]; **NY**92, Christmas doings—at school. **1968–70** *DARE* Tape **CA**196, They'd always have the Christmas tree doings at the schoolhouse; **IN**12, In the fall, they have .. a big Indian doings, and they come from all over the United States there. And they have dances and parades and, oh, everything; **KS**18, We always have a big doin's Decoration Day.

3 See quot 1909. **NEng** *old-fash*

1861 in 1961 *VT Hist.* 29.67 **neVT,** I and Gelia scattered the buckets this morning on the crust. It was fine doing. **1872** Schele de Vere *Americanisms* 597, *Doin',* instead of *doing,* is universal in most of the New England States to denote the state of the roads. **1907** *DN* 3.243 **eME,** *Doing...* Condition of the roads. "It's good doing now." **1909** *DN* 3.410 **nME,** *Doing...* The condition of the roads for sleighing or sledding.

4 in phr *great doin's:* Used as an exclamation of surprise, annoyance, etc.

1969 *DARE* (Qu. NN29a, *Exclamations beginning with 'great': "Great ______!"*) Inf **CA**137, Doin's.

do-it fluid n *joc*

1968 *DARE* (Qu. DD21a, *General words .. for any kind of liquor*) Inf **PA**66, Do-it fluid ['duɪt 'fluɪt]. [Inf Black] **1980** Folb *Runnin' Down* 235 **Los Angeles CA** [Black], *Do-it fluid*—Liquor.

do Jesus See **do v C1d**

dojigger, dojiggie, dojiggum, dojiggus, dojiggy, dojimmie, dojinnie, dojisser, dojohn(nie) See **doojigger**

doldern intj Also *doldurned, doldum* [Varr of *gol-durn* (at **durn**)] *euphem* Cf *DS* NN25

See quots.

1902 *DN* 2.233 **sIL,** *Doldern... Doldum...* An emphatic expletive. **1907** *DN* 3.222 **nwAR, sIL,** *Doldern...* An emphatic expletive. **1959** *VT Hist.* new ser 27.138, *Dol durned!...* Occasional.

dole v [From *dole* distribute evenly]

To deal (playing cards).

1903 *DN* 2.296 **Cape Cod MA** (as of a1857), *Dole, v. tr.* To deal. **1927** *AmSp* 2.352 **WV,** *Dole the cards* .. to deal the cards. "The players doled the cards slowly." **1986** *NADS Letters* **ceTX** (as of c1950), With reference to *dole* for *deal* in cards. "Dole 'em out," was used in the '40s and '50s in this area.

Dole's beard n Also *Mr. Dole* [See quot 1965] **HI** **=Spanish moss.**

1929 Neal *Honolulu Gardens* 61, Spanish moss, .. "Mr. Dole" *(Tillandsia usneoides).* **1965** Neal *Gardens HI* 170, In Hawaii, it [=*Tillandsia usneoides*] .. is known as hinahina, or as "Mr. Dole" because its slender, gray, flexible, hanging stems and leaves resemble the beard of the "grand old man of Hawaii." **1967** *DARE* Tape **HI**2, There's the Spanish moss of the Southern states, which here locally is called Dole's beard, after .. Sanford Dole .. who had a beautiful, long, full gray beard, which looks exactly like Spanish moss hanging from a tree... Dole's beard is a great favorite of the Hawaiian families, and they always have a ring of wire with this hanging down in their garden.

dolesome adj [*OED* 1533 →] Cf *DS* GG34a

Depressed, melancholy, doleful; hence adv *dolesomely* in a doleful manner, and n *dolesomeness* gloominess, dejection.

1899 (1912) Green *VA Folk-Speech* 151, *Dolesome...* Doleful; gloomy; sorrowful; dismal. *Dolesomely...* In a dolesome manner. *Dolesomeness...* Gloom; dismalness. **1940** (1978) Still *River of Earth* 34 **KY,** "How's Ma getting along?" Mother asked. "I've been dolesome, hearing no word." **1984** Wilder *You All Spoken Here* 207 **Sth,** *Dolesome:* Sad; worried.

do-less adj Rarely sp *doo-less, dulless* [Scots (*DSL* 1788 →); *do* + *-less,* but in some cases infl by *dowless* feeble, weak] **chiefly S Midl**

Lacking energy, inactive, lethargic; lazy, shiftless; hence n *do-less* a lazy or shiftless person.

1859 (1968) Bartlett *Americanisms* 125, *Doless.* Inefficient. "He's a doless sort of a fellow." **1889** *Century Illustr. Mag.* 37.407/1 **nVA,** He's a do-less kind of a devil, Sprouse is, but he's some punkins with the gang. **1890** *DN* 1.61 **swOH,** *Do-less* or *doo-less:* do-nothing, good for nothing. Common. **1892** *DN* 1.234 **KY,** *Do-less.* **1930** Shoemaker *1300 Words* 18 **cPA Mts** (as of c1900), *Dulless*—Stupid, worthless, insipid. **1944** *PADS* 2.26 **cwOH, wNC,** *Do-less. . .* Shiftless. **1946** *PADS* 6.12 **wVA,** *Do-less. . .* Lazy. **1953** Randolph-Wilson *Down in Holler* 240 **Ozarks,** *Doless. . .* Inactive, slothful, lazy. **1958** *PADS* 29.9 **cnTN,** *Do-less:* Lazy. **1965-70** *DARE* (Qu. BB5, *A general feeling of discomfort or illness that isn't any one place in particular*) Inf **TN**3, Do-less; (Qu. BB39, . . *When you don't feel just right, though not actually sick . . "I'll be all right tomorrow—I'm just feeling ______ today."*) Infs **MI**114, **OH**93, **OK**7, **VA**11, **WV**4, 16, Do-less; (Qu. BB41, *Not seriously ill, but sick enough to be in bed: "He's been ______ for a week."*) Inf **IN**76, Do-less; (Qu. HH9, *A very silly or light-headed person*) Inf **IL**46, Do-less—a laxidaisical [sic] person who does nothing; (Qu. HH18, *Very insignificant or low-grade people*) Inf **MO**15, Do-less people; (Qu. HH20a, *An idle, worthless person: "He's a ______."*) Infs **IN**76, **KY**26, **OH**45, Do-less; (Qu. KK30, *Feeling slowed up or without energy: "I certainly feel ______."*) Infs **IA**9, **KY**26, **VA**21, Do-less.

doley n Also sp *doaley*

Prob =**Indian breadroot.**

1914 *DN* 4.105 **KS,** *Doley. . .* An edible root, usually egg-shaped, milky white, tender, and sweet. It is not cultivated but found wild on the prairies. Also *doaley.*

do-little n [*OED* →1586]

1 also *do-littler:* An idler. Cf **do-less, do-nothing 1**

1859 (1968) Bartlett *Americanisms* 125, *Dolittle.* A drone; an idle person. **1915** *DN* 4.209, *Do-little . .* an idle person. **1968** *DARE* (Qu. Y28, *A person who loiters about with nothing to do*) Inf **PA**90, Do-little; (Qu. HH20a, *An idle, worthless person: "He's a ______."*) Inf **FL**20, Do-littler.

2 See quot.

1966 *DARE* (Qu. C33, . . *An out-of-the-way place, or a very unimportant place*) Inf **FL**7, A do-little.

do-little adj

=**do-less.**

1983 *MJLF* 9.37 **ceKY,** *Do little . .* shiftless.

doll n [*OED doll* sb.[2] "The palm of the hand" c1460-1565 "*Obs;*" *EDD doll* sb.[3] "The hand, chiefly used of a child's hand" 1790-1891]

A paw.

1943 Chase *Jack Tales* 79 **wNC,** I done told you [=a cat] not to sop your doll in there. **1974** Betts-Walser *NC Folkl.* 19, A black cat slid up beside Jack while he was eating supper, put out its paw ("doll") for some food and said, "Sop doll."

dollar n

A Gram form.

Used as pl: dollars. Cf Intro "Language Changes" II.7

1941 Stuart *Men of Mts.* 307 **neKY,** I made one-hundred and seven dollar out'n my timber-cuttin job. **1969** *DARE* (Qu. U8a) Inf **NC**76, It cost ten dollar.

B Senses.

1 See quot.

1966 *Wilson Coll.* **csKY,** *Dollar. . .* Doily—crocheted and put on furniture. "We called 'em dollars."

2 One's last dollar, "bottom dollar." Cf **dollar dog**

1966-68 *DARE* (Qu. JJ20, *If you felt very sure about something, and wanted to show it: "I'm so sure, I'd ______ it."*) Infs **OH**38, **TX**5, Bet my dollar on; (Qu. KK55b, *To deny something very firmly: "Would you work for him?" "Not on your ______."*) Infs **CO**39, **NY**39, Dollar; (Qu. NN32, *Exclamations like 'I swear' or 'I vow': "I ______."*) Inf **MI**18, Bet my dollar.

dollar and dime store See **dollar store**

dollar bug n

=**whirligig beetle.**

1899 Bergen *Animal Lore* 12, *Gyrinidae* are called . . "dollar bugs," because it is said that if you catch one in the hand you'll find a dollar in it. . . *Eastern Massachusetts.*

dollar cactus n Cf **dollar-joint prickly pear**

A **prickly pear** (here: *Opuntia violacea* var *santa-rita*).

1976 Bailey-Bailey *Hortus Third* 795, *[Opuntia] violacea. . .* Var. *santa-rita. . . Dollar cactus.* Joints orbicular, to 8 in. long.

dollardee n [Etym unknown]

=**bluegill 1.**

1876 in 1877 NY Acad. Sci. *Annals Lyceum Nat. Hist.* 10.375 **seKY,** We heard several peculiar vernacular names for fishes on the Rock Castle and Cumberland, some of which may be worth recording: Dollardee. Helioperca pallida. **1882** U.S. Natl. Museum *Bulletin* 16.479, *L[epomis] pallidus . .* Blue Sunfish; . . Dollardee. **1887** Goode *Amer. Fishes* 67, The Blue Sun-fish, *Lepomis pallidus,* is also known as the "Blue Bream" . . and in Kentucky sometimes as the "Dollardee." **1935** Caine *Game Fish* 11, Bluegill—*Lepomis pallidus*— . . Dolladee [sic]. **1983** Becker *Fishes WI* 844, *Bluegill. . .* Other common names: . . dollardee.

‡dollar dog n Cf **dollar B2**

Something of great value; see quot.

1968 *DARE* (Qu. KK62, *When you want to make it clear that you will not do something: "I wouldn't do that for ______."*) Inf **KS**19, A dollar dog.

dollarfish n [From the roundish shape]

1 A **butterfish 1** (here: *Poronotus triacanthus*).

1884 Goode *Fisheries U.S.* 1.333, The "Butter-fish" of Massachusetts and New York, sometimes known . . in Maine as the "Dollar-fish" . . is common between Cape Cod and Cape Henry. **1896** U.S. Natl. Museum *Bulletin* 47.967, *Rhombus triacanthus . .* (Dollar-fish; Harvest-fish; Butter-fish). **1939** Natl. Geogr. Soc. *Fishes* 68, *Poronotus triacanthus* has several names, being known as dollarfish in Maine, as butterfish in Massachusetts and Norfolk . . and pumpkinseed in Connecticut.

2 A **moonfish** (here: *Vomer setapinnis*).

1889 *Century Dict., Dollar-fish. . .* A carangoid fish, *Vomer setipinnis:* so named from the roundness and silvery color of the young. Also called *moonfish.*

3 =**lookdown.**

1906 NJ State Museum *Annual Rept. for 1905* 260, *Selene vomer. . .* Dollar Fish. . . Body very closely compressed, much elevated, and profile very oblique, or nearly vertical with an abrupt occipital angle. **1908** NJ State Museum *Annual Rept. for 1907* 167, *Selene vomer. . .* Dollar Fish. . . The record . . was based on an example seen on the beach at Cape May.

4 A sand dollar.

1911 *Century Dict. Suppl., Dollar-fish. . .* A flat, disk-shaped echinoderm, *Echinarachnius parma,* found along the Atlantic coast. Also known as *cake-urchin* and *sanddollar.*

5 =**hardtail 1.**

1935 Caine *Game Fish* 48, *Blue Runner—Caranx crysos— . . Synonyms:* Cojinua. . . Dollarfish, Hardtail.

dollar grass n

=**pennywort.**

1972 Brown *Wildflowers LA* 125, Pennyworts, Dollar-grass—*Hydrocotyle umbellata . . Hydrocotyle verticillata.*

‡dollar house n

1967 *DARE* (Qu. M21b, . . *An outside toilet building*) Inf **MO**11, The dollar house—named because years ago it took about a dollar's worth of lumber to build it.

dollar-joint prickly pear n Cf **dollar cactus**

A **prickly pear** (here: *Opuntia chlorotica*).

1942 Amer. Joint Comm. Horticult. Nomenclature *Std. Plant Names* 76, *[Opuntia] chlorotica.* Dollarjoint P[ricklypear]. **1960** Vines *Trees SW* 775, *Dollar-joint Prickly Pear. . . Joints.* Broadly obovate or oval, flat, 6-10 in. long, 5-8 in. broad.

dollarleaf n

1 A **false wintergreen 1** (here: *Pyrola rotundifolia*). [See quot 1911]

1876 Hobbs *Bot. Hdbk.* 32, Dollar leaf, Round leaved pyrola, Pyrola rotundifolia. **1900** Lyons *Plant Names* 312, *P. rotundifolia. . .* Dollar-leaf. **1911** *Century Dict. Suppl., Dollar-leaf. . .* The round-leaved wintergreen, *Pyrola rotundifolia:* so called from the shape and size of the leaf. **1940** Clute *Amer. Plant Names* 43, *Shin-leaf.* False wintergreen, . . dollar-leaf.

2 A **tick trefoil** (here: *Desmodium rotundifolium*). [See quot 1901]

1901 *Torreya* 1.116 **GA,** *Meibomia Michauxii*. . . Dollar-leaf. . . From the size and shape of its leaves or leaflets. **1940** Clute *Amer. Plant Names* 18, *Desmodium. . . Michauxii. Tick Trefoil.* Dollar-leaf. **1959** Carleton *Index Herb. Plants* 38, *Dollar-leaf:* Desmodium michauxi.

3 See **dollar weed 1.**

dollar off v phr

1949 *PADS* 11.20 **CO,** *Dollar off*. . . To buy cattle in the field instead of taking them in and weighing them, to sell by so many dollars a head instead of so much a pound.

dollar orchid n [See quot 1950]

A **tree orchid** (here: *Epidendrum boothianum*).

1950 Correll *Native Orchids* 287, *Epidendrum Boothianum. . . Common Names:* Dollar-orchid. *Ibid* 289, It is an attractive little plant with rather showy flowers, and the peculiar flat round pseudobulbs have given rise to its common name, Dollar-orchid. **1971** Craighead *Trees S. FL* 200, Dollar orchid, *Epidendrum boothianum.* **1976** Bailey–Bailey *Hortus Third* 426, *[Epidendrum] Botthianum. . . Dollar orchid. . .* Petals yellow, spotted with dark brown to magenta-purple. . . S. Fla.

dollar plant n

1 See **dollarweed 1.**

2 A **pennywort.**

1968 *DARE* Tape **GA**30, It's pennywort—dollar plant, lot a' people call it, just has a little small, round—'bout the size of a dollar, the leaf is.

dollar spot n

A grass fungus *(Sclerotinia homeocarpa);* a small patch of brown grass caused by the fungus.

1926 *Bull. U.S. Golf Assoc. Green Section* May 129 *(OEDS),* Small [brown-] patch is generally limited to about the size of a silver dollar, from which it has been commonly referred to as 'dollar spot'. **1935** *Gardeners' Chron.* 23 Feb. 129/1 *(OEDS),* Investigation of diseases of turf of lawns and greens has been prosecuted in the U.S.A. for many years, and the commonest diseases and causal organisms are well known, viz. Brown-patch, . . and Dollarspot, due to an unnamed species of Rhizoctonia. **1966** *Citrus Co. Chron.* (Inverness FL) 31 Mar [np], Your grass may develop the disease called dollarspot. . . As implied, the fungus kills grass in patches the size of a silver dollar. . . To cure a mild case of dollarspot, give the grass a generous shot of nitrate of soda.

dollars to doughnuts n Also *dollars to a doughnut, ~ to buttons, ~ to cobwebs*

A virtual certainty, something assured; something valuable wagered against something insignificant in a "safe" bet.

1884 (1890) Peck *Peck's Boss Book* 130 **seWI,** It is dollars to buttons that . . she will be blown through the roof. **1890** *Texas Siftings* 8 Nov. 6/3 *(OEDS),* It is dollars to a doughnut . . That some one will start a fire. **1904** *Boston Herald* 8 Aug. 6 *(OEDS),* It is dollars to cobwebs that every such person will be disappointed. **1904** *Utica Observer* (NY) 29 June 6/6 **NYC,** They talk of fire drills; . . it is dollars to doughnuts that not an excursion boat in New York harbor ever had one. **1932** *Atlantic Mth.* 149.390/2, It is dollars to doughnuts not a soul will see him. **1959** *VT Hist.* new ser 27.133, *Dollars to doughnuts. . .* Usually with *bet.* Common. **1968** *DARE* (Qu. JJ20, *If you felt very sure about something, and wanted to show it: "I'm so sure, I'd ——— it."*) Infs **NY**93, **WI**34, Bet (you) dollars to doughnuts.

dollar store n Also *dollar and dime store* [By analogy with *dime store*]

A variety store that sells inexpensive items, sometimes used as a front for illegal activities.

1872 Crapsey *Nether Side N.Y.* 72 *(DA),* Gift jewelry, prize candy, 'Milton gold,' gift concerts, dollar stores, . . and circular swindles of every description, have been only a few of his devices for wheedling people of their money. **1892** Quinn *Fools of Fortune* 402 *(DA),* Another professional sport . . figured prominently before the public at that time as proprietor of two 'dollar stores,' with back-room attachments where 'bunks' and 'top and bottom' were played. **1967–68** *DARE* (Qu. U43, . . *The kind of store where most articles cost [or used to cost] only five or ten cents*) Infs **LA**6, **MO**5, 35, **NC**50, Dollar store; **MN**12, Dollar and dime store—new term.

dollar sunfish n

A **sunfish** *(Lepomis marginatus).*

1955 Carr–Goin *Guide Reptiles* 92, *Lepomis marginatus* . . Dollar Sunfish. **1960** Amer. Fisheries Soc. *List Fishes* 27, Dollar sunfish . . *Lepomis marginatus.* **1968** *FL Wildlife* July 13 **FL,** Dollar sunfish, a small bream . . found statewide.

dollar weed n

1 also *dollarleaf, dollar plant:* A **snoutbean,** usu *Rhynchosia reniformis.* **chiefly SE** [See quot 1901]

1869 Porcher *Resources* 226 **Sth,** *Dollar-plant,* (*Rhyncosia* [sic] *tomentosa?*). . . This plant, receiving its name probably from the shape of the leaf, is reputed, in the neighborhood of Aiken, S. C., and elsewhere, to be a valuable agent in arresting troublesome diarrhoea. **1901** *Torreya* 1.116 **GA,** *Dolicholus simplicifolius*. . . Dollar-weed. . . From the size and shape of its leaves or leaflets. **1919** *Jrl. Amer. Folkl.* 32.392 **csNC,** For "de snake-bit," dollar-weed is a remedy. **1933** Small *Manual SE Flora* 715, *Rhynchosia simplicifolia* . . (Dollar-weed.) **1964** Batson *Wild Flowers SC* 68, Dollar Weed. . . Leaves about the size and shape of silver dollar and very prominently netted veined. **1970** Correll *Plants TX* 885, *Rhynchosia reniformis. . . Dollar-leaf*. . . Leaflets 25–54 mm., reniform or orbicular. **1975** Duncan–Foote *Wildflowers SE* 86, Dollar-weed—*Rhynchosia reniformis.*

2 **=moneywort.**

1966 *DARE* (Qu. S21, . . *Weeds . . that are a trouble in gardens and fields*) Inf **GA**11, Dollar weed—same as money vine.

3 Alkali mallow *(Sida hederacea).*

1970 Correll *Plants TX* 1051, *Sida hederacea* . . Dollar weed.

doll baby n

1 A doll. **esp Sth, S Midl**

1853 (1854) Baldwin *Flush Times* 292 **AL,** The little girls, who had been petted by their fathers and mothers like doll-babies. **1897** Stuart *Simpkinsville* 59 **AR,** Every word she'd say would sound clair an' fine same ez ef a doll-baby was to commence to talk by machinery. **1908** *DN* 3.306 **cAL, wGA,** *Doll-baby*. . . A doll. **c1938** in 1970 Hyatt *Hoodoo* 2.1133 **seGA,** He makes whut dey call a *doll baby,* de image of a man—wit his name on it. **1939** Rollins *Gone Haywire* 259 *(DA),* Tumblin' K don't want to hurt any man; but, if all you folks is plum' starvin' for excitement an'll be responsible, th' brute's your doll baby. **c1960** *Wilson Coll.* **csKY,** *Doll-baby*. . . A doll. **1968–70** *DARE* (Qu. W36, . . *A woman who uses a lot of cosmetics*) Inf **MD**29, Painted doll baby; (Qu. EE33) Inf **DC**12, Cutting out doll babies.

2 An attractive young woman; a sweetheart.

1908 *DN* 3.306 **eAL, wGA,** *Doll-baby*. . . A sweetheart. **1910** *NY Eve. Jrl.* (NY) 20 Aug 6 *(Zwilling Coll.), [In the cartoon "Wanted A Skirt":] I have been looking for a doll baby for the past two weeks but what I met were all bush leaguers.* **1919** *WI News* (Milwaukee) 1 Dec 9 *(Zwilling Coll.),* [In cartoon:] What is your present address Miss Dollbaby. **1966–69** *DARE* (Qu. AA3, . . *Affectionate names for a sweetheart*) Infs **CA**36, **DC**8, **IL**102, **IN**3, **MS**1, **NC**82, **PA**177, **WI**71, Doll baby.

3 A small wooden device used in making a **mecate;** see quot 1936. **West**

1930 Raine–Barnes *Cattle* 314 **West,** The little wooden spinners were called "doll babies" and were whittled out of pieces of hardwood. **1936** Adams *Cowboy Lingo* 63, The little wooden pegs used in making horsehair ropes were called 'doll babies.'

4 See quot. Cf **doll buggy,** *DS* N41a–c

1968 Adams *Western Words* 97, *Doll baby*—A two-wheeled cart used for short-distance hauling. **1977** Dunlop *Wheels West* 171, Some vehicles used on the ranch were unsuitable for trail drives. The "doll baby" was a two-wheeled cart used for hauling small loads around the outbuildings.

doll buggy n Cf **doll baby 4**

In logging: **=dolly 2.**

1931 *AmSp* 7.53 **Sth, SW** [Lumberjack lingo], "Doll buggies" are small two-wheeled carts used to haul big "timbers" short distances in order to save loading them on a wagon.

dollhouse n *joc* Cf **dollar house**

1969 *DARE* (Qu. M21b, . . *An outside toilet building*) Inf **GA**77, Little Mary dollhouse; **OH**88, Dollhouse.

doll rags n pl **chiefly Sth, S Midl**

1 Bits, pieces.

1845 Hooper *Advent. Simon Suggs* 14 **ceAL,** He pitched dollars with Bob Smith himself, and could "beat him into doll-rags" whenever it came to a measurement. **1851** Hooper *Widow Rugby's Husband* 131 **AL,** I'd kick the old rascal into doll-rags. **1905** *DN* 3.77 **nwAR,** *Doll-rags*. . . Small pieces; 'He was torn into doll-rags.' **1908** *DN* 3.306 **eAL, wGA,** *Doll-rags*. . . Small pieces, bits.

2 Clothes, personal belongings.

1905 *DN* 3.77 **nwAR,** *Doll-rags*. . . Belongings. 'You'd better pack your doll-rags and git out.' Common. **1908** *DN* 3.306 **eAL, wGA,** *Doll-rags*. . . Belongings, clothes. **1955** Stong *Blizzard* 46 **IA,** "You've *got* to get my suitcase, Dude." . . "You look good to me, and what else matters? Better you should wear a wrinkled dress than I should freeze my-ears-off looking for your doll-rags."

doll's daisy n

A tall plant *(Boltonia diffusa)* with small asterlike flowers.

1933 Small *Manual SE Flora* 1363, *B[oltonia] diffusa*. . . *Doll's-daisy*. . . Coastal Plain and adj. provinces, Fla. to Tex., Ill., and S.C. **1971** Craighead *Trees S. FL* 200, Doll's daisy, *Boltonia diffusa*.

doll's-eyes n Also *china-doll's eyes* [See quots]

=**white baneberry** or its fruits.

1931 Harned *Wild Flowers Alleghanies* 171, *White Baneberry*. . . Fruit a white, ovate berry with a very conspicuous, purple-black eye. . . A common name for the berries . . is doll's eyes. **1949** Moldenke *Amer. Wild Flowers* 9, *White baneberry*. . . The poisonous berries are . . shiny white, often with a dark purple spot at the apex, resembling the china eyes placed in children's dolls and giving rise to the popular name of *dollseyes* used for this plant in New England. **1961** Douglas *My Wilderness* 280 **cnME,** And near the water's edge I found the white baneberry in fruit—known in Maine as doll's-eyes because its white, rounded berry has a dark spot in its center. **1966** *DARE* Wildfl QR Pl. 63b Inf **NH**4, China-doll's eyes. **1968** *Foxfire* Summer 47, Another sang-sign plant [=a plant indicating the presence of ginseng] . . is the white baneberry (Actaea), the "doll's-eyes" of the mountain healers. **1976** Bailey–Bailey *Hortus Third* 23, Doll's-eyes. **1984** *DARE* File **cwMA,** *Doll's eyes* is a common term for white baneberry here, at least where the baneberry is.

dolly n

1 =**doll baby** n 2.

1967–68 *DARE* (Qu. AA3, . . *A sweetheart*) Infs **CA**21, **CT**11, **MO**26, **NY**83, **WI**56, Dolly.

2 In logging: see quot 1958. Cf **doll buggy**

1958 McCulloch *Woods Words* 49 **Pacific NW,** *Dolly*—A two-wheeled log cart. **1969** Sorden *Lumberjack Lingo* 35 **NEng, Gt Lakes,** *Dolly*—A two-wheel cart for hauling lumber. Same as buggy, lumber buggy.

3 In railroading: see quots.

1932 *RR Mag.* Oct 367, *Dolly*—Switch stand. **1938** Beebe *High Iron* 220 [Railroad terms], *Dolly:* Switch stand. **1976** Gould *Blackie's RR Hdbk.* 12, *Dolly:* Switch Stand.

4 See **Dolly Varden 1.**

5 See **doily** n

dolly flapper n [**dolly** n 3]

In railroading: see quots.

1932 *RR Mag.* Oct 367, *Dolly flapper*—Switch tender. **1938** Beebe *High Iron* 220 [Railroad terms], *Dolly flapper:* Switch tender. **1976** Gould *Blackie's RR Hdbk.* 1, *Switch Tender:* Dolly Flapper—Cinder Cruncher.

dolly-flower n

A **kittentails** (here: *Synthyris reniformis*).

1934 Haskin *Wild Flowers Pacific Coast* 323, *Grouse Flower. Synthyris rotundifolia*. . . Children sometimes call them blue-bells. . . They are also called dolly-flowers.

dolly in the blanket n

A children's game: =**roly poly.**

1916 *DN* 4.343 **cnMD,** *Dolly in the blanket.* =roly poly.

dolly-over-teakettles adv phr

=**ass-over-teakettle 1.**

1982 *Ft. Myers News–Press* (FL) 24 Jan sec A 6, I backed into a carton of motor oil parked on the floor, and why I did not go dolly-over-tea-kettles was due to good foot work and grabbing onto something that did not move.

dolly up v phr [*doll up* to dress up, to make more attractive]

To make more attractive by adding decorative details; to clean up or put in order.

1968–69 *DARE* (Qu. E21, *Talking about a room that needs to be put in order, you might say, "I'm just going to* _____ *this room."*) Inf **VA**8, Dolly up; (Qu. W30, . . *To make something more attractive—for example, a hat . . "It's too plain—I think I'll put on a few flowers to* _____ *it up."*) Infs **IL**39, **NJ**11, Dolly.

Dolly Varden n [In ref to *Dolly Varden,* brightly dressed character in Dickens' *Barnaby Rudge*]

1 also *Dolly, Dolly Varden trout:* A spotted trout *(Salvelinus malma).* **chiefly NW, AK** Also called **Arctic trout, bull trout, goldenfin, lake trout, malma, Oregon char, red-spotted trout, salmon trout**

1876 *Yreka* (Calif.) *Union* 3 June *(DA),* The first spotted trout were caught in McCloud river by white men—Messrs. Josiah Edson of Shasta Valley and Geo. Campbell of Soda Springs, and were given the name of Dolly Vardens by Elda McCloud, a niece of Mr. Campbell. **1879** Williams *Pacific Tourist* 310/1 *(DA),* The Dolly Varden species, with bright red dots on the side, weigh from one pound to twelve pounds. **1946** Dufresne *AK's Animals* 234, In southeastern Alaska the . . Dolly Varden spends a large part of its adult life in or near salt water. . . For several weeks of each spring and early summer the "Dollies" may move in and out of the river-mouths with the tides. **1965–70** *DARE* (Qu. P1) Infs **ID**3, **NM**6, **OR**3, 13, **WA**31, Dolly Varden (trout); **AK**1, Dolly Varden—a char; **AK**9, Dolly Varden—has round dots, similar to rainbow trout; **MT**4, Bull trout—Dolly Varden; **WY**1, German brown—sometimes locally called Dolly Varden. **1968** *Hungry Horse News* (Columbia Falls MT) 20 Dec 23/1, *Dolly Varden* weighing 15½ and 8½ pounds were caught . . in Flathead River.

2 A calico horse.

1907 Cook *Border & Buffalo* 343, Well, Sam, if we don't get him back when we go out after the Quohada again we will get you a Dolly-Varden horse like that buzzard-headed pinto of Cook's that went off with him.

3 A **goat's rue** (here: *Tephrosia virginiana*).

1933 Small *Manual SE Flora* 706, *C[racca] virginiana*. . . Devil's shoe-strings. Dolly-Varden. **1953** Greene–Blomquist *Flowers South* 58, *Dolly-Varden (Tephrosia virginiana)*. . . The pea-like flowers are medium-sized with a pale-yellow standard and pink or purplish wings and keel.

4 A **crappie.**

1947 Dalrymple *Panfish* 84, Here, my friend, are the various names by which you would address . . the Crappie . . : Dolly Varden, Goggle-Eye [etc]. **1949** Caine *N. Amer. Sport Fish* 32, The white and black crappies' combined nicknames mount into the following total of fifty-seven . . *Colloquial Names*. . . Croppie, Dolly Varden [etc].

5 The calico crab *(Hepatus epheliticus).*

1961 *W3, Dolly varden crab*. . . Calico crab. **1981** Meinkoth *Audubon Field Guide Seashore* 637, *Calico Crab.* "Dolly Varden." *(Hepatus epheliticus)*. . . Dull . . with *many large, round or irregular, light red spots* with dark borders.

6 A calico cat.

1969 *DARE* (Qu. J5, *A cat with fur of mixed colors*) Inf **MA**68, Calico, Dolly Varden.

7 In railroading: see quots.

1916 *DN* 4.356, *Dolly Varden.* The buffer on a locomotive tender of the old link and pin coupling type.

8 as *Dolly Varden cake:* A cake with easily distinguishable layers.

1890 James *Mother James' Cooking* 303, *Dolly Varden Cake*. . . Bake one-half of this [batter] in two pans; to the remainder of this add . . molasses, . . raisins, . . currants, . . citron . . , . . cinnamon, cloves and nutmeg. Bake in two pans and put in sheets alternately with a little jelly or white of an egg beaten to a froth. **1968** Kellner *Aunt Serena* 200 **cIN** (as of c1920), We never had Dolly Varden cake any more because Ella said . . she didn't have time to make it.

dolly welter See **dally welter**

dololly See **doololly 1**

do Lord n Cf **Lord God**

=**pileated woodpecker.**

1945 McAtee *Nomina Abitera* 46, The most godified of our birds . . It is none other than the pileated woodpecker *[Ceophus pileatus]* . . Do Lord (South Carolina).

do Lord intj See **do** v **C2a, b**

dolphin n

1 A fish of the genus *Coryphaena.* [*OED dolphin* sb. 2 1578–1628 →] Also called **dorado, mahimahi**

1862 Acad. Nat. Sci. Philadelphia *Proc. for 1861* 34, *Coryphaena Lesuerii* . . "Dolphin." **1887** Goode *Amer. Fishes* 235, The name Dolphin is unfortunately applied [to the *Coryphaenidæ*], this being the peculiar property of a group of small cetaceans. **1933** LA Dept. of Conserv. *Fishes* 275, Dolphins [=*Coryphaenidæ*] are fishes of extraordinary interest. . . The term Dolphin is to be correctly applied only to a group of small sea mammals, the porpoises of the genus *Delphinus,* but, though erroneous, it has now become general and permanent usage to call these beautiful fishes by this name. **1946** LaMonte *N. Amer. Game Fishes* 42, Dolphin—*Coryphaena hippurus.* **1960** Gosline–Brock *Hawaiian Fishes* 181, The mainland name for the mahimahi [=*Coryphaena hippurus*] is dolphin, which by derivation and by usage refers properly to a porpoise. **1965–70** *DARE* (Qu. P2, *Saltwater fish . . good to eat*) Infs **FL**4, **HI**4, **LA**26, **NC**60, 82, **VA**41, Dolphin; (Qu. P4, *Saltwater fish . . not good to eat*) Inf **DE**4, Dolphin; (Qu. P14, *If commercial fishing . . what do the fishermen go out after?*) Inf **SC**66, Dolphin. **1972** Sparano *Outdoors Encycl.* 378, The dolphin [=*Coryphaena hippurus*]. . . The head is extremely blunt, being almost vertical in large specimens (called bulls [as in bull dolphin], though they may be either male or female). **1975** Evanoff *Catch More Fish* 214, The dolphin (*Coryphaena hippurus*) is also called the dorado and mahimahi. . . Dolphin are found in most of the warmer waters of the world.

2 In logging: see quots. [Transf from *dolphin* a post, piling, or structure of pilings used for moving boats]

1905 U.S. Forest Serv. *Bulletin* 61.35 **Pacific NW,** *Dolphin.* . . A cluster of piles to which a boom is secured. **1958** McCulloch *Woods Words* 49 **Pacific NW,** *Dolphin*—Several piles driven in a bunch to form booming grounds for logs, or to make docks.

dolphin fly n

=**bean aphid.**

1889 *Century Dict.* 1726/2, *Dolphin-fly.* . . An insect of the aphis tribe, *Aphis fabae,* which destroys the leaves of bean-crops.

dolt n [*OED* 1543 →] **chiefly Nth, N Midl** See Map Cf **doltish**

A dull, stupid person.

1806 (1970) Webster *Compendious Dict.* 92, *Dolt* . . a heavy stupid person, blockhead[,] dunce. **1965–70** *DARE* (Qu. HH3, *A dull and stupid person*) 88 Infs, **chiefly Nth, N Midl,** Dolt; (Qu. HH21, *A very awkward, clumsy person*) 11 Infs, **chiefly Inland Nth,** Dolt; (Qu. GG41, *To lose patience easily: "You never did see such a ______ person."*) Inf **WI**29, Dolt; (Qu. HH5, *Someone who is queer but harmless*) Infs **IL**47, **OH**47, **WI**71, Dolt; (Qu. HH9, *A very silly or light-headed person*) Inf **WA**28, Dizzy dolt; (Qu. HH16, *Uncomplimentary words . . just used when you want to show that you don't think much of a person: "Don't invite him. He's a ______."*) Infs **NM**12, **WI**9, Dolt; (Qu. HH20a, *An idle, worthless person: "He's a ______."*) Inf **NM**12, Dolt; (Qu. HH40, *Uncomplimentary words for an old man*) Inf **NY**102, Dolt.

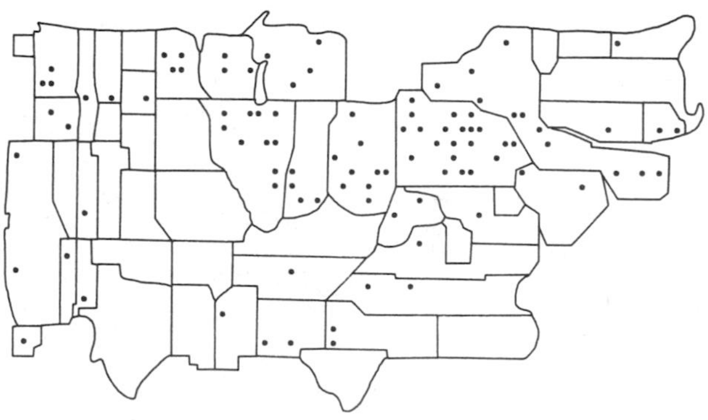

•dolt + var (Qq. HH3, HH21, GG41, HH5, HH9, HH16, HH20a, HH40)

doltage n [Var of *dotage,* infl by **dolt**]

1908 *DN* 3.306 **eAL, wGA,** *Doltage.* . . Dotage. Not common.

doltish adj [*OED* 1543 →]

Dull, stupid; like a **dolt.**

1806 (1970) Webster *Compendious Dict.* 92, *Doltish* . . stupid, blockish, dull, heavy, mean. **1851** (1976) Melville *Moby-Dick* 164 **eMA,** A doltish stare. **1967** *DARE* (Qu. HH21, *A very awkward, clumsy person*) Inf **OR**6, Doltish.

dom n [Abbr]

=**dominicker** n **1.**

1937 *Hall Coll.* **eTN,** I thought you-all 'ud kill them doms (chickens). **1967** *Ibid* **eTN, wNC,** *Dominecker.* . . When used of chickens sometimes shortened to 'doms' [dɑmz], [dɒmz].

domajig(ger), domajiggus, domawadja See **doojigger**

dom cop See **dummkopf**

dome n

1 A rounded mountaintop—used chiefly in place names.

1833 (1841) Catlin *Letters Indians* 1.78 **MT,** "The Grand Dome". . . is, perhaps, one of the most grand and beautiful scenes of the kind to be met with in this country. **1864** *Alta California* (S.F.) 16 Jan. 1/4 *(DA),* On the road to Castle Dome, we had passed some fine specimens of that gigantic species of cactus known as the *petahaya.* **1890** Townsend *U.S. Index* 138 *(OED),* Carter Dome, New Hampshire; The Dome, State of New York. **1932** *DN* 6.229 **West,** *Dome.* Found in place-names of mountains that look like domes, as Dome and Half Dome in the Yosemite, or Lone Dome in Utah. **1943** Peattie *Great Smokies* 40, Dome may describe a shape, but often indicates a barren rock summit. **1946** Sierra Club *Bulletin* Dec 9 **cCA** (as of 1884), We . . then built a fire on the highest point in view of the whole valley, to let people know that Half Dome had been conquered! **1968–70** *DARE* (Qu. C17, . . *A small, rounded hill*) Inf **CA**41, Dome—on the desert; **CA**117, **PA**245, **WI**75, Dome. **1986** *DARE* File **nwMA,** There is a beautiful view of The Dome (a small symmetrically rounded mountain), across the valley from the Mt. Prospect lookout.

2 also in combs *chrome dome, double ~, ivory ~:* A person's head. *joc*

[**1891** Farmer–Henley *Slang* 2.305, *Dome* . . (common).—The head.] **1918** Sandburg *Cornhuskers* 60 **neIL,** Your bony head . . / Those grappling hooks . . /The dome and the wings of you. **1923** Paine *Comrades* 160, He got tired of trying to shove the book stuff into ivory domes like yours, and thought he'd rather risk getting drowned for a change. **1943** (1945) Smith *Life Putty Knife* 153, That great thinker among modern men, Arthur Brisbane . . was known among fellow newspapermen as Old Double Dome. **1965–70** *DARE* (Qu. X28, *Joking words . . for a person's head*) 43 Infs, **scattered,** Dome; **IL**97, Chrome dome—for a bald head; **AR**40, Ivory dome; [Of all Infs responding to this question, 53% were female, 47% male; of those giving this response, 37% were female, 63% male.]; (Qu. HH9, *A very silly or light-headed person*) Inf **OR**3, Not much in the dome. **1972** Claerbaut *Black Jargon* 63, *Dome* . . a person's head: *Got hit on the dome.*

3 =**cupola B1.** Cf **dome-roof barn**

1967–68 *DARE* (Qu. M2, . . *The small wooden construction on top of a barn with slats for ventilation*) Infs **AL**33, **PA**127, Dome.

dome barn See **dome-roof barn**

domenecker See **dominicker n 1**

dome-roof barn n Also *dome barn* [Cf **dome 3**]

Prob a barn with a dome-shaped roof, or a barn with a **dome 3.**

1967–70 *DARE* (Qu. M1, . . *Kinds of barns . . according to their use or the way they are built*) Infs **MI**40, **PA**234, Dome-roof barn; **WA**27, Dome barn—dome-topped.

domestic n

1 also attrib: Plainwoven cotton cloth. **chiefly Sth, S Midl**

1817 in 1924 Amer. Hist. Assoc. *Annual Rept. for 1919* **ceMO,** The Domesticks I expected, have Not arrived they are uncommonly difficult to obtain. **1869** Twain *Innocents* 286, Then you stretch a great sheet of "cotton domestic" from the point where the joists join the hill-side down over the joists to the ground. **1883** U.S. Bur. Indian Affairs *Rept. for 1883* 193, Supplying . . a flannel skirt or goods to make the same, . . calico and domestic. **1903** *DN* 2.311 **seMO,** *Domestic* or *bleached domestic.* . . Cotton cloth. **1908** *DN* 3.306 **eAL, wGA,** *Domestic.* . . A coarse white cotton cloth, bleached or unbleached. Not used in the plural form except for grades or rolls of the goods. A merchant speaks of getting in his *domestics,* but he sells five yards of *domestic.* **1948** *Sat. Eve. Post* 21

Aug 47/1 **csTX,** The girls are taught Mexican national dances—not in their ordinary clothes, mind you, but in gay and flashing little costumes made from old sugar sacks or unbleached domestic. **1952** Giles *40 Acres* 134 **KY,** Forty years ago the huckster made his weekly trip around the ridge in a covered wagon, peddling such things as country people buy. . . Thread, needles, pins, unbleached domestic, and cotton batting. **1966** *DARE* (Qu. F19, *A cloth container for grain*) Inf **MS**1, Brown domestic sack; (Qu. G17, . . *Kinds of towels*) Inf **MS**72, Domestic cloth.

2 See quot. [*OED domestic* sb. 2. b 1719 →; *"Obs rare"*]

1909 *DN* 3.395 **nwAR,** *Domestics*. . . Domestic animals.

domicils n pl

1899 (1912) Green *VA Folk-Speech* 151, *Domicils*. . . Household furniture.

domiewadjie See **doojigger**

dominacker See **dominicker** n

domine See **dominie**

domineck(er) See **dominicker** n

domineckered woodpecker n [Var of **dominicker** n + *-ed*] =**flicker** n[2] **1.**

1969 *DARE* (Qu. Q17, . . *Kinds of woodpeckers*) Inf **KY**5, Domineckered woodpecker—flicker; has a speckled breast.

dominecker gnat See **dominicker** n **6**

domineck(er) hawk See **dominicker** n **4**

dominica, dominick See **dominicker** n **1**

dominick chicken See **dominicker** n **3**

dominicker n Also *dominecker* [From *Dominique, Dominica* island in the West Indies]

1 freq attrib; also *dominica, dominiquer, dommernecker, dominick, domineck,* for addit varr see quots: A Dominique fowl; also any chicken with barred or mottled plumage, such as Plymouth Rock. **scattered, but chiefly S Midl** Also called **dom, dommer**

1806 (1905) Lewis *Orig. Jrls. Lewis & Clark Exped.* 4.128 **VA,** This mixture gives it very much the appearance of that kind of dunghill fowl which the hen-wives of our country call *dommanicker.* **1843** W.T.Thompson *Chron. Pineville* 65 *(DAE)* **GA,** 'Dadfetcht,' said he, 'if I don't bet my best dominecker,' (Sam *fit* chickens occasionally). **1881** *Reinbeck* (Ia.) *Times* 15 Sept. 4/1 *(DAE),* Ain't nothin' fallen, as I know of, nor set neither—only the old dominiker hin. **1899** (1912) Green *VA Folk-Speech, Dominica* . . A large white fowl covered with black spots; a *dominica* hen. **1902** Wister *Virginian* 71, "He was a right elegant Dominicker," he continued. **1906** *DN* 3.134 **nwAR,** *Dominecker*. . . A Dominique cock or hen. "Go kill that old Domenecker." **1907** *DN* 3.243 **eME,** *Dominec*. . . Dominique fowl. Probably associated in folk-etymology with *neck.* **1908** *DN* 3.306 **eAL, wGA,** *Domineck(er)*. . . A breed of chickens having a mottled coloration. Also used attributively. "Catch that ole dominecker hen." *Dominique* is not used. **1917** *DN* 4.411 **wNC,** *Dominecker chicken*. . . A large white fowl, black spotted. Also La., Ill., S. Car., Kan., Ky. **1919** *DN* 5.33 **KY,** *Dominacker.* **1925** Benefield *Chicken-Wagon Family* 19 *(DAE),* And what would you teach her—how to smoke a pipe, how to trade a tin pan for a Dominick setting hen? **1942** McAtee *Dial. Grant Co. IN* 23 (as of 1890s), *Dominick, dominicker* . . a speckled hen. **1954** *Harder Coll.* **cwTN,** *Dommernecker:* A breed of chickens. **c1960** *Wilson Coll.* **csKY,** *Dominicker* /-ˌnɛkɚ/: A Plymouth Rock chicken, black and white speckled. **1966** *Ibid, Dominicker.* /ˈdɑmɪˌnɛkɚ/ Our old dominicker rooster. **1967** *Hall Coll.* **eTN,** *Dominecker chicken*. . . They were bred up to about forty years ago. They was a grayish chicken. **1968–69** *DARE* (Qu. K76, . . *Other kinds of poultry*) Inf **NJ**56, Dominick; **WV**7, Dominicks (chickens). **1984** Ehle *Last One Home* 160 **NC** (as of c1910), And he said he was marrying a bride from a poor family and didn't have more than her clothes and a flock of dominiquers.

2 as *dommernecker;* Fig: a coward.

1987 [see **dominicker** v].

3 in comb *dominick chicken:* See quot.

1923 *DN* 5.240 **swWI,** *Dominick chicken*. . . Any grouse killed and served out of season. "He must be livin' on Dominick chicken."

4 also *domineck(er) hawk:* =**red-shouldered hawk.**

1953 *AmSp* 28.276, A related christening is that of *dominicker* for the red-shouldered hawk in Georgia. **1955** *Oriole* 20.1.5 **GA,** *Red-shouldered hawk*. . . *Dominicker* (from a fancied resemblance in color pattern to that of the breed of poultry of that name). **1966–70** *DARE* (Qu. Q4, . . *Kinds of hawks*) Inf **GA**9, [ˈdɑmənɛkə] hawk; **KY**5, **VA**38, Dominecker hawk; **OK**18, Domineck hawk.

5 =**downy woodpecker.**

1953 *AmSp* 28.276, When even the little downy woodpecker in the neighborhood of Golden Pond, Kentucky, is called *dominecker,* the allusion is to its speckled plumage, suggesting that of a race of chickens.

6 also *dominecker gnat:* A **punkie.**

1917 *DN* 4.411 **wNC,** *Dominecker gnat.* A punkie. **1967** *Hall Coll.* **wNC, eTN,** *Dominecker*. . . Used especially of a kind of gnats with speckled wings. **1967** *DARE* (Qu. R11, *A very tiny fly that you can hardly see, but that stings*) Inf **TN**13, [ˈdɑmɪnɪkɚz]—very small.

7 A person of mixed racial heritage, usu of Black, Indian, and White ancestry. **FL** Cf **brass ankle**

1939 FWP *Guide FL* 445, In adjacent back country [between Ponce de Leon and Chipley] live 'Dominickers,' part Negro and part white, whose history goes back to the early 1860's. . . The name originated, it is said, when a white in suing for divorce described his wife as 'black and white, like an old Dominicker chicken.' **1963** Berry *Almost White* 27, People similar to Tennessee's Melungeons, . . and New York's Jackson Whites are by no means a rarity. Pennsylvania has its . . Pools, . . Florida its Dominickers, and Alabama its Creoles and Cajuns.

dominicker v Also with *out* Pronc-sp *dommernecker*

To show cowardice or lack of perseverance.

1954 *Harder Coll.* **cwTN,** *Dommernecker* . . To avoid or evade. **1987** *DARE* File **cwTN** (as of 1930–40), We would say, "He dommerneckered out," meaning that he was a coward or failed to complete something we believed he (or she) should have done. As a noun it meant "a coward." I suspect that it had something to do with our present meaning of "to chicken out." The dominicker rooster would always run, or so we thought, whenever another type of rooster challenged him.

dominicker sky n Also *dominicker clouds, dominick sky* [**dominicker** n **1**] Cf **mackerel sky**

A sky with mottled clouds reminiscent of the plumage of a **dominicker** n **1;** the clouds themselves.

1956 *Hand Coll.* **OH,** Dominicker sky,/ Storm close by. This is a speckled sky. **1969** *DARE* (Qu. B11, . . *Kinds of clouds that come often around here*) Inf **KY**5, Dominicker [ˈdɑməˌnɪkɚ] clouds; **KY**49, Dominick sky—speckled, dark and light.

dominie n Also sp *domine* [Du *dominee* clergyman, minister] **chiefly in Du settlement areas, esp NY** *somewhat old-fash*

Orig a pastor of the Dutch Reformed Church; later a minister of any Protestant church.

1669 N.Y. State Col. Hist. XII.466 *(DA),* I perceiue the Little Domine hath played ye Trumpeter to this disorder. **1701** Wolley *2 Yrs. Jrl.* 82 **seNY,** Two other Ministers or *Domines* as they were called there . . one a *Lutheran* . . the other a *Calvinist.* **1824** Irving *Tales of a Traveller* 2.364 **NY,** There are two family oracles, one or other of which Dutch housewives consult . . the dominie and the doctor. **c1860** in 1960 Dickinson *Complete Poems* 150, [Poem 318:] Till when they reached the other side, a Dominie in Gray—Put gently up the evening Bars—And led the flock away. **1872** Schele de Vere *Americanisms* 464, *Dominies*—with a long *o,* not *dŏminies,* as in Scotland, for schoolmasters—is a title still used for their ministers by the so-called Dutch Reformed Church in portions of New York and New Jersey. **1894** *DN* 1.330 **NJ,** *Dŏminies.* **1913** *DN* 4.54 **sNY,** *Dominie* [ˈdomɪnɪ]. . . Clergyman; minister: in general use in the Catskills. "I told the Dominie about it." **1941** *LANE* Map 439 *(The Reverend Mr. Simpson),* [Six infs responded *dominie* (all with prons of the type [ˈdo(U)mɛnɪ, -mənɪ]). Five were from southwest New England, close to the New York border; the sixth, from Boston, remarked that it was "common in the country." Two used it as a title; five as a common noun. Two indicated that it was obsolete.] **1948** Manfred *Chokecherry* 15 **nwIA,** Why couldn't y'u . . ha' become a domeny like young Bud Hillich? **1967–69** *DARE* (Qu. CC10, . . *An unprofessional, part-time lay preacher*) Infs **NY**35, 42, 43, 48, 53, 209, Dominie. [5 of 6 Infs in NYC; all Infs old] **1982** Wiersma *Style* 19 **nwIA** [In a Dutch community], It is style in all Reformed churches / for the janitor to put a glass of water / inside the pulpit in case the dominie gets thirsty. **1986** *DARE* File **Holland MI,** I grew up hearing "dominie" [ˈdomɨni] in the '50s and '60s, but I know of few people who use it today except for special effect (though it's still widely recognized). But Grandma Shirley says that the "older generation" at the nursing home still will say things like "The dominie was here today." *Ibid* **Grand Rapids MI,** *Dominie* . . is still used by a handful of chauvinists like myself, seriously, and by a few more oldsters facetiously, to annoy preachers... It's usually pronounced ['domɨni], but I've heard ['domɨne], especially among older immigrants... It's probably more often a common noun, but it's used as a term of direct address.

dominiker, dominiquer See **dominicker n 1**

domino v [See quot 1987] **TX**

To give birth.

1967 *DARE* (Qu. AA28, . . *Joking or sly expressions . . women use to say that another is going to have a baby . . "She('s) ———."*) Inf **TX5**, Getting ready to domino. **1984** Weaver *TX Crude* 110, *To domino.* To give birth, to bear a child. "How's the wife?" "Oh, she's fixin' to domino here about March or April." **1987** *NADS Letters* **ceTX,** You will hear from Texans by the score about *domino* as an old euphemism for "giving birth." To say "She's about to domino," or "She just dominoed" means that the long process (the long game) is about over or has ended, as in the game, "to domino" is to end it. I have lived here 57 years, and I can remember the expression as almost the norm rather than a sometime thing, in Houston especially.

dominoes n pl [From the resemblance to the dots on dominoes] =**dot n 3.**

1967 *DARE* (Qu. H82a, *Cheap candies sold especially for schoolchildren around here*) Inf **CO5**, Dominoes—the name for the paper with sugar dots.

domino man n Also *domion*

1945 Saxon *Gumbo Ya-Ya* 78 **LA** (as of c1925), The Domino Man appeared in the Gentilly section of New Orleans... A creature wearing a white robe and hood... would drop from trees, chase little girls, gesticulating wildly, then vanish... Apparently his only desire was to frighten the children. **1968** *DARE* (Qu. CC17, *Imaginary animals or monsters that people . . tell tales about—especially to tease greenhorns*) Inf **LA37**, Domion ['dɔm'jɔ̃]—it's like a ghost, a man walking around catching people; (Qu. EE41, *A hobgoblin that is used to threaten children and make them behave*) Inf **LA37**, Domion ['dom,jɔ̃].

dommanicker See **dominicker n 1**

dommer n [Telescoped form of **dominicker**] =**dominicker n 1.**

1919 *DN* 5.33 **KY,** *Dominacker...* A species of chicken (Dominique, or Domenico?). Also *dominecker.* Sometimes clipped to *dommer.* **1935** *Atlantic Mth.* July 44/2 **nAL,** I took a red flint rock about the size of a Dommer hen egg from my pocket and throwed it at the bunch of squibs. **1938** *Hall Coll.* **eTN,** Dommer ['dɑmɚ], spotted Plymouth Rock [chicken]. **1940** (1978) Still *River of Earth* 84 **KY,** Look at that old dommer hen planting three grains of wheat. *Ibid* 170, We raised thirty-six dommers. They scarcely pecked at the bran we threw out.

dommer hen See **dommer**

dommernecker n See **dominicker n 1, 2**

dommernecker v See **dominicker v**

don' See **do v A2**

donagher See **donicker n**[1]

donation party n Also *donation day* *old-fash*

1 also *donation, donation bee, ~ supper, ~ visit:* An occasion at which members of a church give gifts to the minister. **scattered, but esp NEast** **Cf pounding**

1839 *Chicago Daily Amer.* (IL) 17 Dec 2/3, Our worthy and talented fellow citizen, the Rev. Mr. Hinton of the Baptist Church, has a *donation party* at his residence, on Thursday evening next. **1845** Judd *Margaret* 290 **NEng,** One day there was a donation party at our house. The ladies of the town brought their wheels and spun quantities of flax, which they gave to my mother; and the young men made an ox-sled, which, with a yoke of oxen, they presented to Pa [a clergyman]. **1849** Brown *America* 23, They [=Methodist ministers] have also the benefit of a *"donation."* Invitations are given to all the members and their friends to attend this party, and each guest takes something with him . . which may be useful to the preacher and his family. **1858** *Salem Advocate* (IL) 14 Apr 3/1, A donation supper will be given for the benefit of Rev. Wm. Finley, Pastor of the Cumberland Presbyterian Church, on Thursday evening. *Ibid* 26 May 3/2, Donation Suppers seem to have been "all the go," during the past winter. **1860** *Ladies' Repository* 20.386/2 [sic *DA*—quot not found], It was at last settled . . that they would make Mrs. Brainard, the minister's widow, a genuine old-fashioned donation visit. **1865** *Atlantic Mth.* 15.449 **CT,** No man in the parish brought a heavier turkey to the parson's larder on donation-days. **1880** *Scribner's Mth.* 20.545/2 **NY,** A hundred dollars per annum, a bar'l of apples a month, a pair of fowls monthly, donation-bee once a winter, with two demi-johns of cider! **1905** *DN* 3.8 **cCT,** *Donation party...* A party of friends to present a gift to a country minister. **1910** *DN* 3.440 **cwNY,** *Donation...* A party at the house of a country pastor, at which the members of the congretation make contributions of money, less often of food or clothing. **1917** Garland *Son Middle Border* 182 **neIA,** Occasionally . . these audacious young people would turn a church social or donation party into a dance, much to the scandal of the deacons. **c1960** *Wilson Coll.* **csKY,** *Donation party...* A shower given for a preacher by his parishioners. **1969** *DARE* Tape **NY139**, They'd all come to the church and give these donation parties, and a lot of the stuff that was donated [to the minister in lieu of salary] was just stuff that a lot of people couldn't use themselves. **1975** McDonough *Garden Sass* 140 **AR,** Another church activity that most older people remember was the custom of "poundings" or "donation parties." This was a type of housewarming held when a new minister and his family came to the community.

2 An occasion at which contributions are collected for some charitable purpose. Cf *DS* L5

1897 *Chicago Rec.* (IL) 3 Mar 5/1, St. Luke's hospital "Donation day" occurred yesterday. The women of the auxiliary committee solicited contributions of linen, food and clothing for the poor patients. **1940** Writers' Program *Guide TX* 390 **neTX,** In this agricultural region "donation parties" are given when misfortune overtakes a neighbor; a house may be rebuilt, crops worked out, or the larder restocked.

donation supper See **donation party 1**

donation visit See **donation party 1**

donc(e)y See **donsie**

done adj See **done in**

done adv [Prob **do v C5**] **Sth, S Midl** Note: The following senses are not always clearly distinguishable, and some quots may instead be instances of **do v C5.**

Used to emphasize the attainment of a state or completion of action, spec:

a with a perfect tense.

1892 Smith *Farm & Fireside* 235 **GA** (*PADS* 13.5), I say, Gim, is you done gone clean dead? **1905** *DN* 3.77 **nwAR,** 'He's done did it.' 'They've done done it.' **1908** *DN* 3.306 **eAL, wGA,** *Done...* This is commonly used as an expletive auxiliary, adding the force of completed action to the main verb. "He's done gone and done it." **1914** *DN* 4.163 **TX,** "He's done delivered the mail." . . "He's done did the same thing over again." **1923** *DN* 5.205 **swMO,** "He's done got well." "I've done been over thar." "He's done done his do." **1930** Faulkner *As I Lay Dying* 144 **MS,** Then she begun to sing again . . like she had done give up folks and all their foolishness and had done went on ahead of them, marching up the sky, singing. **1935** Hurston *Mules & Men* 234 **FL** [Black], He want me . . , but dat 'oman he got she got roots buried and he can't git shet of her—do we would of done been married. **1937** (1977) Hurston *Their Eyes* 32, Marse Robert's son had done been kilt at Chickamauga. **1942** Faulkner *Go Down* 49 **MS,** It would be like I had done said. *Ibid* 76, He had done spent the money. **1944** *PADS* 2.8 **Sth** [Black], *Done...* "I's done seen him." . . "It's done did." **1968–69** *DARE* (Qu. CC12b, . . *If a person has a lot of bad luck*) Inf **RI4**, He's done had it; (Qu. OO37b, . . *About clothes shrinking: . . "They've ———."*) Inf **VA9**, Done shrunk too much and got too little. **1970** *DARE* Tape **VA43**, You just don't have time enough for to grow a crop of tobacco like it oughta be growed... First thing you know it's done slipped up past the time to get a plant bed, and you don't know whether the weather's going to be favorable or not.

b with an adj or ppl adj: Already, completely.

1903 *DN* 2.312 **seMO,** 'Done' is prefixed to a verb only when action is completed... 'The bread is done burnt up.' **1904** *DN* 2.418 **nwAR,** *Done...* 'Yes, it is done gone.' **1922** Gonzales *Black Border* 297 **sSC, GA coasts** [Gullah glossary], *Done...* already. **1928** Peterkin *Scarlet Sister Mary* 208 **seSC** [Gullah], Ma is done too old to be all de time gwine round a-catchin chillen for people. **1937** (1977) Hurston *Their Eyes* 30 **FL** [Gullah], Ah ain't gittin' ole, honey. Ah'm *done* ole. **1949** Turner *Africanisms* 283 **seSC** [Gullah], And when time crop done plant and cotton come up, . . you ain't had to pick no grass from the cotton hill then. [=And at the time when the crop was planted and the cotton came up, you didn't have to pick grass from the cotton hill then.] **1953** *Hall Coll.* **wNC,** We'd go out an holler for [sic] and see if we could hear 'em coming in anywhere—it was done dark then. **1965** *DARE* (Qu.

X47, . . *"I'm very tired, at the end of my strength."*) Inf **OK**13, Done run down. **1966** *DARE* Tape **SC**9 [Black], That [=a harrow] is to mash up those sod fine. When you get that done mash [=mashed] up, then you're fixing to plant your rice.

done v *Gullah* Cf **do** v **C5, done** adv

To finish or complete; to stop.

1838 (1852) Gilman *S. Matron* 94 **eSC** [Gullah], Dat one screech-owl been screech on de oak by Dinah house *tree* night last week. When he didn't done screech, Plato took one lightwood torch, and light 'em, and fling 'em into de tree, and den he gone. **1922** Gonzales *Black Border* 297 **sSC, GA coasts** [Gullah glossary], *Done*. . . finish, finished, as: "W'en you gwine done da' t'ing?"—when are you going to finish that thing? "Uh done'um," . . —I have done or finished it. **1971** Cunningham *Syntactic Analysis Gullah* 69, C[reole:] That beans was hard to done. E[nglish:] Those beans were hard to cook (until done). *Ibid* 70, C[reole:] I don't done till six o'clock. E[nglish:] I don't finish (working) until six o'clock.

done- prefix

In combs: Used to make adjs indicating that something has been finished; see quots.

1908 *S. Atl. Qrly.* 7.344 **sSC coast** [Gullah], A *done-tass niggah,* [is] used either to mean a worn-out negro laborer, too weak, too old to work any more, or lightly, to signify the laughing darkey, his day's work done, and his hoe canted over his shoulder. **1928** Peterkin *Scarlet Sister Mary* 167 **SC** [Gullah], When he had finished, he smiled a one-sided smile and said very kindly, "Now, Si May-e, I'm a done-talk man. I hope I ain' wasted my breath."

Don Eagle n [*Don Eagle* pseudonym of Carl Donald Bell, a professional wrestler of Indian heritage] Cf **Iroquois, Mohawk**

See quot 1978.

1967–70 *DARE* (Qu. X5, . . *Different kinds of men's haircuts*) Inf **OH**97, Don Eagle—strip down middle, named after a wrestler; **PA**24, Don Eagle [FW illustr: a head shaved on the sides with a strip of hair down the middle]. **1978** *DARE* File **csOH** (as of 1950s), Don Eagle—a haircut for males with a single bushy strip of hair down the center of the head, coming to a point at both ends. The rest of the head is shaved.

done and See **do** v **C6**

doned See **do** v **B5**

done for adj phr See **done in**

donegan n[1] See **donicker** n[1]

donegan n[2]

1 See quot.

1945 Hubbard *Railroad Ave.* 340, *Donegan*—Old car, with wheels removed, used as residence or office. Originated about 1900, when a Jersey Central carpenter and two foremen, all named Donegan, occupied three shacks in the same vicinity. People were directed to the Donegans so often that the shacks themselves came to be known by that name. The name stuck, even after the men had passed on and the shacks had been replaced by converted old cars.

2 See **donicker** n[2].

donegar See **donicker** n[1]

done in adj phr Also *done, done for,* ~ *out* **chiefly Nth, Midl** See Map Cf **done up 1**

Tired, exhausted.

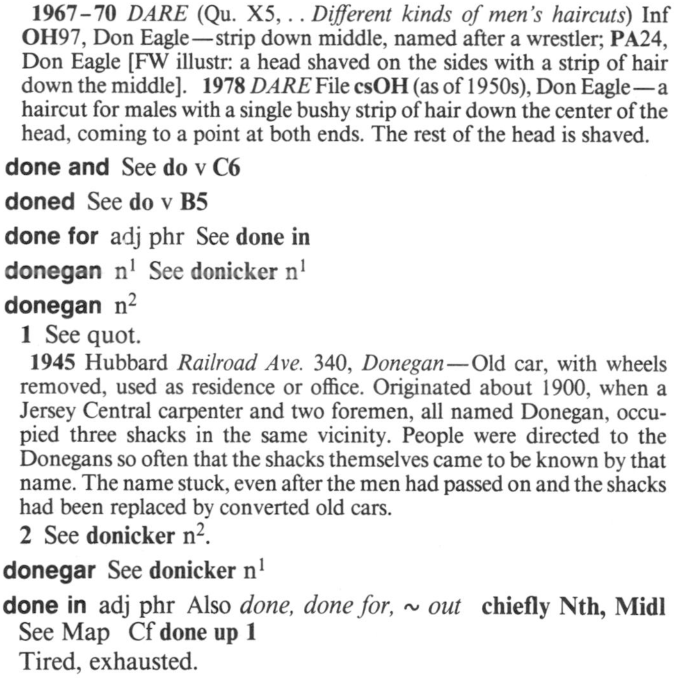

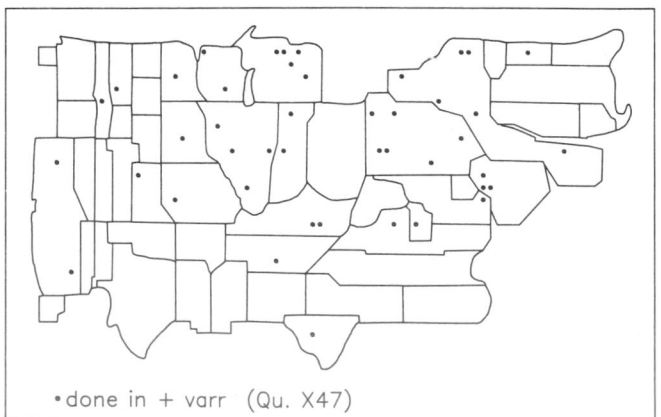

•done in + varr (Qu. X47)

1944 *PADS* 2.55 **nwMO,** *Done in*. . . Very sick [*PADS* Ed: exhausted?]. Caldwell Co. Uneducated. Common. **1965–70** *DARE* (Qu. X47, . . *Ways . . of saying, "I'm very tired, at the end of my strength."*) 32 Infs, **chiefly Nth, Midl,** (All) done in; **ID**5, **MI**20, **MT**1, **NJ**48, **NY**20, 103, **TN**34, Done out; **MI**20, 67, **MO**6, **NJ**69, Done; **IL**19, **MI**2, **NY**29, (About) done for; **KY**24, All done. **1968** Kellner *Aunt Serena* 145 **cIN** (as of c1910), If they felt exhausted, they were done in, give out, wore to a frazzle, or weak as water. **1985** Ladwig *How to Talk Dirty* 25 **Ozarks,** I'm about done in from it. **1986** *WI Alumnus Letters* **Ozarks,** I worked until I'm just done out.

done up adj phr

1 **=done in.** [*OED* 1803 →]

1835 Hoffman *Winter in West* (NY) 2.187 **NY,** John seemed to have retired [=gone to bed], completely done up. **1899** (1912) Green *VA Folk-Speech* 151, *Done-up*. . . Thoroughly fatigued; tired out. **1950** *WELS Suppl.* 1 Inf, **csWI,** *Done up*—Tired, exhausted. "Three times up the stairs already. I'm almost done up." **c1960** *Wilson Coll.* **csKY,** *Done up*. . . Very tired, worn out. **1966–68** *DARE* (Qu. X47, . . *Ways . . of saying, "I'm very tired, at the end of my strength."*) Infs **CA**36, **IL**5, 50, **MA**5, **NE**8, **OH**77, **SC**4, **TX**9, Done up.

2 Ill: anywhere from slightly to seriously ill.

1848 (1934) Boynton *Jrl.* 43.369 **VT,** I caught cold last night, and am nearly "done up" to day. **1931–33** *LANE Worksheets* **nwCT,** *Done up*. . . Ill to the point of death. "To be done up means there isn't much help for him." **1968** *DARE* (Qu. BB5, *A general feeling of discomfort or illness that isn't any one place in particular*) Inf **CT**16, Feeling done up.

3 Pregnant. Cf **knocked up**

1941 *LANE* Map 392 *(Pregnant),* Jocular, crude and vulgar synonyms of *pregnant* as used by men. . . 1 inf, **sRI,** Done up.

4 Dilapidated; not functioning.

1968–69 *DARE* (Qu. KK20a, *Something that looks as if it might collapse any minute: "That old shed is certainly ______."*) Inf **IL**72, Done up; (Qu. KK20b, . . *"Our old washing machine is ______."*) Inf **SC**59, About done up.

5 See quot.

1967 *DARE* (Qu. DD15, . . *Thoroughly drunk*) Inf **IL**5, Done up.

6 See **do up 5.**

doney n[1] [Prob abbr for *donick* (at **dornick 1**)] **chiefly CO**

1 A rounded stone; see quots. Cf **gooney 4**

1949 *PADS* 11.20 **CO,** *Doney*. . . A roundish stone peculiarly suited for throwing purposes; a small rock often used with a sling; goodsized rocks about three inches in diameter, too big for sling shot; a rock of any size. **1967–68** *DARE* (Qu. C22, *A piece of stone too big for one person to move easily*) Inf **PA**119, Doney ['doni]; (Qu. C25, . . *Stone[s] . . about . . [the] size of a person's head . . smooth and hard*) Inf **CO**11, Doney—any color. **1975** *DARE* File **cnCO,** *Doney,* used in the phrase "chunking doneys," = throwing rocks. Said by the Informant to have been his childhood usage in Hygiene, Colorado. He is now approx. 50 years of age. **1981** *Ibid* **wCO** (as of c1930), A doney is a large stone, but of throwable size.

2 In marble play: see quot.

1949 *PADS* 11.20 **CO,** *Doney*. . . A non-gate [sic; prob for "non-agate"] marble used as a target, but not to shoot with; a shooter marble; any kind of marble.

doney n[2] Also *doney-girl* Also sp *dony* [Prob var of Brit slang *doña* a woman, sweetheart (*OED* 1873 →)] **chiefly sAppalachians**

A sweetheart, girlfriend.

1908 *DN* 3.306 **eAL, wGA,** *Dony*. . . Girl, sweetheart. "My dony don' wear no drawers,"—a line from a popular negro song. **1917** *DN* 4.411 **wNC,** *Doney* ['doni]. . . Sweetheart. Also *doney gal.* **1921** *DN* 5.116 **eKY,** In the hills, *dona* means *sweetheart,* usually coupled with "gal," as in "dony-gal." **1937** (1963) Hyatt *Kiverlid* 14 **KY,** Jed's a-claimin' you fer his doney-girl. **1941** *LANE* Map 400, The map shows the terms *sweetheart, . . doxy, dony* and *flame, . .* denoting the girl whom a young man is 'courting' or 'keeping company with.' . . 1 inf, **cCT,** *Dony,* still used; 1 inf, **cCT,** *Dony,* common. **1946** *PADS* 5.20 **VA,** *Doney:* Girl friend; not common. **1952** Brown *NC Folkl.* 1.534 **wNC,** *Doney (gal)* ['donɪ gjæəl]. . . A female sweetheart. **1976** Garber *Mountain-ese* 23 **sAppalachians,** *Doney-gal* . . sweetheart.

dong n [Perh with ref to the clapper of a bell]

The penis.

1930 *AmSp* 5.390 **coastal NEng,** *Dong*. . . The male organ. **1939** Steinbeck *Grapes* 245 **OK,** Tell 'em ya dong's growed sence you los' your eye. **1985** Irving *Cider House* 491 **eME,** "I guess what's the matter with Homer is that he's a man," Melony observed. "I only ever met one who didn't let his dong run his life"—she meant Dr. Larch—"and he was an ether addict."

donic See **dornick**

donicker n Also *donegan, donigan;* for addit varr see quots [*EDD dunnekin* "A privy; an open cesspool"]

1 A toilet or privy; a toilet room.

1926 Finerty *Criminalese* 17, *Donigan*—The toilet room. **1930** Irwin *Amer. Tramp* 64, *Donegan.*—A toilet or wash-room. **1931** *AmSp* 6.330 [Carnival cant], *Donnicker*. . . A toilet or water-closet. **1938** *AmSp* 13.156 **sCA,** *Doniker.* A wash-room. **1942** Berrey-Van den Bark *Amer. Slang* 84.11, *Toilet*. . . Donagher, donegan, donegar, doniker. **1945** O'Hara *Pipe Night* 185 **NYC,** But when you finally want to leave and you ask what's the bruise, your man is in the donnicker or making a phone call. **1953** *AmSp* 28.115 [Carnie talk], *Donniker*. . . Toilet. **1955** *PADS* 24.120 **neIL,** I'm going to tear this thing [=a package of pornographic photographs] up and put it down the donicker. **1966** *DARE* (Qu. F37, . . *An indoor toilet*) Inf **GA**13, Donicker—indoor or out. **1973** Allen *LAUM* 1.181, A supplementary study by a graduate student reveals that 31% out of 37 interviewed residents of Stillwater, Minnesota, are familiar also with the term *donnicker,* which apparently has escaped its earlier context of carnival and underworld slang.

2 In railroading: see quots. [Prob from the resemblance of the brakeman's hut on a railroad car to a privy; cf **shack**]

1932 *RR Mag.* Oct 367, *Donicker*—Freight brakeman. **1942** Berrey-Van den Bark *Amer. Slang* 771.16 [Railroad terms], *Brakeman*. . . Donegan, donicker, donniker. **1946** in 1953 Botkin-Harlow *Treas. Railroad Folkl.* 351, As long as railroad books are written and railroad vocabularies are compiled, we may expect to hear brakemen called *block-heads, donickers, ground-hogs, shacks, snakes*. . . but in print only.

donk n [Etym unknown]

1929 *AmSp* 5.17 **Ozarks,** *Donk*. . . Alcohol. "Them touristers they puts this hyar donk inter their sody-pop constant."

donkey n

1 freq attrib: A donkey engine; see quot 1958. **chiefly Nth, esp Pacific NW**

1904 *DN* 2.379 [Oil-field jargon], *Donkey*. . . A variety of small steam-pump used on the pipe-line. **1905** U.S. Forest Serv. *Bulletin* 61.35 **Pacific NW,** *Donkey sled.* The heavy sled-like frame upon which a donkey engine is fastened. **1920** *DN* 5.81 **nwWA,** *Donkey sled.* Log platform upon which the engine is mounted. **1923** *DN* 5.243 **LA,** *Donkey boiler.* In logging, a small independent boiler, used to get up steam quickly on a boat. **1958** McCulloch *Woods Words* 49 **Pacific NW,** *Donkey*. . . An endless variety of steam, gas, diesel, or electric power plants, plus drums to hold wire rope; all used to haul logs from the woods, to load at landings, move equipment, rig up trees, and in the old days, to lower cars down inclines. . . Donkey was a term originally applied to a little steam engine of less than one horse power. Dolbeer adapted a ship's capstan for his logging rig, and it is possible that he also brought along the usual seafaring term for the engine itself. . . *Donkey driver*. . . *Donkey float*. . . *Donkey mover*. . . *Donkey puncher*. . . *Donkey sled* [etc]. **1967-70** *DARE* Tape **CA**100, I went to work in the logging woods . . bucked water for the logging donkeys. . . We carried water for the donkeys, or the engines, we called 'em donkey engines or little side spoolers; **OR**6, My husband's a logger and he logged; he run donkeys. . . A donkey is a big machine that brings logs in out of the woods. . . He started back in the days when they had steam donkeys, and now they use all diesel donkeys; **VA**79, They start pullin' it [=a fish net] in with a donkey engine—that's a small, approximately five- to seven-horsepower engine mounted in a boat they call a donkey boat; **WA**24, Now they've done away with that steam altogether. They use diesel donkeys now. **1982** *Smithsonian Letters,* I was raised in the lower Columbia river logging country . . (early 1900s). . . The logs were pulled to the railroad track by a large steam engine with drums wound with cable which were known as "donkeys." They were mounted on a large sled made out of 2 logs about 4 feet in diameter and 50 feet long . . The donkeys were powerful enough to move themselves over most any terrain.

2 In railroading: a member or foreman of a section gang.

1932 *RR Mag.* Oct 367, *Donkeys*—Section men. **1940** *RR Mag.* April 42, *Donkeys*—Derisive term for section men.

3 An outdoor children's game played with a ball; see quots.

1967 *DARE* FW Addit **NYC** (as of 1950s), Donkey—game with small or large ball, played against a wall. Line of people, one behind another. Leader throws ball against wall and must jump over it on first bounce, second person on second bounce, etc. Last person catches ball and goes to front becoming leader. If someone misses the ball, he gets a "d." Next miss he gets an "o." When someone gets d-o-n-k-e-y, he leans against the wall, facing it, and others throw the ball at his rear end. **1968** *DARE* (Qu. EE33, . . *Outdoor games*) Inf **PA**126, Donkey—throw ball up to wall and try to jump it when it comes down.

donkey ball n Also *donkey baseball, ~ basketball, ~ softball*

A ball game, usu a form of baseball or basketball, in which the players ride donkeys.

1966 *Carteret Co. News-Times* (Morehead City & Beaufort NC) 16 Aug 2/1, Fun and thrills promise to be offered those attending the donkey baseball game to be played at the Beaufort baseball park Thursday night. *Ibid, Donkey Ball Game*. . . Rules:—All players except pitcher and catcher ride donkeys. When the batter gets a hit he must mount his donkey and ride around the bases in proper order—if he can. There are no strike-outs or walks. Fielders must ride to within a step of the ball before dismounting and must remount before throwing the ball. Soft-ball is used. Nine players on each team. Game plays 5 to 7 innings. **1967** *Hollister Eve. Free Lance* (CA) 27 Nov 4/6, Hollister High School's annual Donkey Basketball Game will be played Thursday night at the gym. . . Five men on each team will ride donkeys wearing rubber shoes to protect the floor's surface. **1967** *Star Leader* (Clinton MD) 26 July 2/1, On Monday evening . . the Allentown Recreation Council will present its annual Donkey Baseball Game. **1967** *DARE* Tape **AZ**2, What we call donkey softball. And a player must be aboard the back of a donkey when he makes a run, retrieves a ball, or anything. **1968** *Cape May Co. Gaz.* (Cape May Court House NJ) 11 July sec D 3/3, Donkey Ball . . played from the backs of trained donkeys, is reputed to be wilder than a rodeo and funnier than a circus.

donkey barbecue n

1967 *DARE* (Qu. II27, *If somebody gives you a very sharp scolding, you might say, "I certainly got a ______ for that."*) Inf **TX**11, Oil patch men say they're going to a donkey barbecue.

donkey baseball, donkey basketball See **donkey ball**

donkey dust n [Euphem; cf *bullshit*] *joc*

Nonsense, baloney.

1969 *DARE* (Qu. NN13, *When you think that the thing somebody has just said is silly or untrue: "Oh, that's a lot of ______."*) Inf **MA**56, Donkey dust.

donkey's breakfast n

Esp among sailors and loggers: a mattress filled with straw or, less freq, corn shucks.

1937 FWP *Guide MA* 331, A ship bunk's mattress was a 'donkey's breakfast.' **1940** White *Wild Geese* 17 **WA** (as of 1890s), Nice to get a mattress for the bunk, if they had any at the store. If not, John could get a donkey's breakfast from the stable boss and fix things up. **1945** Colcord *Sea Language* 67 **ME, Cape Cod, Long Island,** *Donkey's breakfast.* A straw mattress in a sailor's bunk. The term is used jokingly and disparagingly alongshore. **1968** Adams *Western Words* 97, *Donkey's breakfast*—A logger's name for a straw bed. **1975** Gould *ME Lingo* 76, *Donkey's breakfast*—A sailor's mattress, from the hay or corn shucks in the tick. A less than comfortable bed.

donkey softball See **donkey ball**

donnick See **dornick**

donnicker n[1] See **dornick 1**

donnicker n[2] See **donicker**

donnock See **dornick**

donnybrook n Also abbr *donny* [*Donnybrook* a suburb of Dublin, Ireland, whose annual fair was famous for its brawls; *OEDS* 1852 →] **chiefly Nth, N Midl** See Map

A fight or brawl; a quarrel; a noisy, disorderly scene or gathering.

1915 *Lit. Digest* 50.863/2, A campaign which the New York *World* called a "Donnybrook." **1964** *Word Study* Feb 1, The lexicographical donnybrook provoked by *Webster's Third New International Dictionary* (1961) in the journalistic world . . can now be surveyed conveniently in the Sledd and Ebbitt casebook. **1965-70** *DARE* (Qu. Y13, *A fist fight with several people in it*) 26 Infs, **chiefly Nth, N Midl,** Donnybrook; **FL**5,

Donny; (Qu. Y12a, *A fight between two people, mostly with words*) Inf **NE**11, Donnybrook; (Qu. Y12b, *A real fight in which blows are struck*) Infs **CA**107, 120, **IL**64, **IN**45, **ME**13, **PA**18, 227, **WI**64, Donnybrook; (Qu. FF18, . . *A noisy or boisterous celebration or party: "They certainly ______ last night."*) Inf **CT**19, Had a donnybrook; (Qu. KK15, *A disagreement or quarrel: "They had ______ about where the fence was to be."*) Inf **CA**3, Donnybrook. **1968** *DARE* Tape **NY**105, There was lots of hard cider and lots of whiskey floating around. Well, there was always a lot of animosity between the town boys in the village and the farmer boys, so, when they went to these paring bees, as a rule, they wound up in a good donnybrook. They had a good fight.

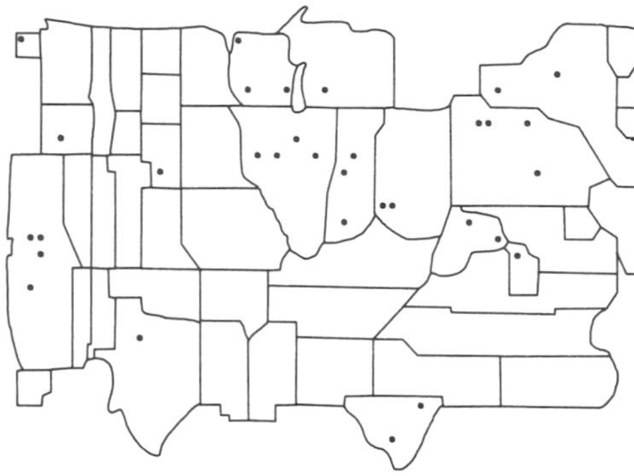

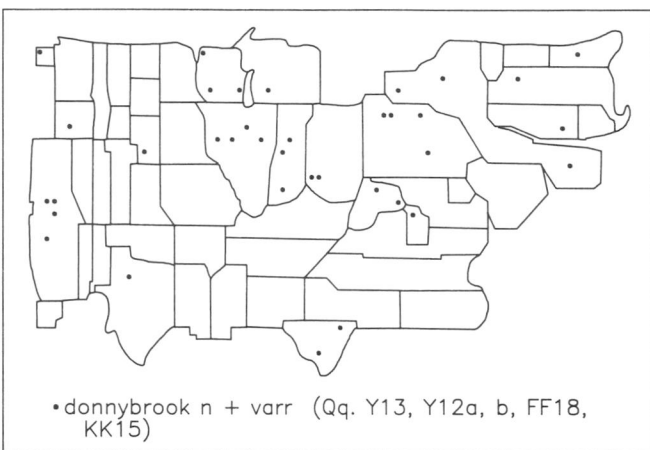

•donnybrook n + varr (Qq. Y13, Y12a, b, FF18, KK15)

‡donnybrook v

To hit or strike (someone).

1970 *DARE* (Qu. Y14a, *To hit somebody hard with the fist*) Inf **NY**232, Donnybrook.

donoch, donock See **dornick**

do-not n [Alter of *doughnut*] *joc* Cf **dog nut**

1965 *DARE* (Qu. H27, . . *Joking names for doughnuts*) Inf **MS**25, Do-not ['du ˌnaət].

do-nothing adj

=do-less.

1832 Irving *Alhambra* 2.10 **NY,** The invalids, old women, and other curious do-nothing folk. **1890** in 1950 *PADS* 13.6 **GA,** She knows what care is and work is, and one of these do-nothing women can't stand it. **1983** *MJLF* 9.37 **ceKY,** *Do nothing* . . shiftless.

do-nothing n [*OED* 1579 →]

1 =do-less. Cf do-little n 1

1869 Stowe *Oldtown Folks* 29 **MA,** Every New England village, if you only think of it, must have its do-nothing as regularly as it has its school-house. **1899** (1912) Green *VA Folk-Speech* 151, *Donothing*. . . One who does nothing; an idler. **1915** *DN* 4.209, *Do-little, -nothing,* an idle person. **1965–70** *DARE* (Qu. A9, . . *Wasting time by not working on the job*) Inf **DC**12, Part-timers, do-nothings; (Qu. HH18, *Very insignificant or low-grade people*) Inf **NJ**2, Do-nothings; (Qu. HH19, . . *A tramp*) Inf **KS**7, Do-nothing; (Qu. HH20a, *An idle, worthless person: "He's a ______."*) Infs **GA**74, **IL**37, **KY**85, **OR**1, **PA**245, **VA**31, Do-nothing.

2 =bull-grinder.

1980 *Foxfire 6* 162 **nGA,** *Bull Grinder*. . . I've heard them called do nothings and smoke grinders. . . It's a little toy that's good for absolutely nothing except for passifying [sic] oneself with something to do other than twiddling his thumbs.

donsie adj Also sp *dansy, daunc(e)y, dauns(e)y, donc(e)y, donsy, douncy* [Scots, nEngl dial *donsie;* prob from Scots Gael *donas* evil, harm, per with infl from obs *daunch* fastidious, squeamish, *dunce,* and other words]

1 Fastidious; lacking appetite; squeamish; also fig.

1805 in 1912 Thornton *Amer. Gloss.* 2.261 **sePA,** Citizen Lafferty must have a "doncy" opinion of the cause, when he is afraid to bet even. **1846** Farnham *Life in Prairie Land* 39 **IN,** I shall give her enough to eat and wear, and I don't calculate she'll be very *daunsey* if she gets that. **1913** Kephart *Highlanders* 289 **sAppalachians,** A remarkable word, common in the Smokies, is dauncy, defined for me as "mincy about eating," which is to say fastidious, over-nice. **1926** *DN* 5.399 **Ozarks,** *Dauncy*. . . Lacking appetite, manifesting a dyspeptic fastidiousness about food. "My ol' woman's got so dauncy like, we-all caint git her t' eat nothin' sca'cely." **1927** *AmSp* 2.352 **WV,** *Dauncy*. . . Fastidious. "She is so dauncy about her work that no one can please her." **1938** *Hall Coll.* **eTN,** Dauncy about eatin', [is used of one who] don't feel good, don't feel like eatin'. **1942** (1971) Campbell *Cloud-Walking* 248 **seKY,** She never had no fever but just turned dauncy about victuals. **1944** *PADS* 2.25 **NC,** *Dauncy*. . . Squeamish, fastidious. **1952** Brown *NC Folkl.* 1.532 **wNC,** *Dauncy* ['dɔnsɪ]: . . Particular. **1953** Randolph–Wilson *Down in Holler* 238 **Ozarks,** *Dauncy* ['dɔnsɪ]. . . Lacking appetite, fastidious about food. **1980** *DARE* File **AR, wKY, wTN, eTX,** Douncy = selective.

2 Sickly, unwell, spec:

a Having a general feeling of unwellness; indisposed, "under the weather." **esp N Midl** See Map

1874 (1895) Eggleston *Circuit Rider* 61 **sIN,** "Sick, Mort? Goin' to have a chill? . . You look powerful dauncy," said the old man. **1891** *PMLA* 6.169 **WV,** *I feel rather dauncy,* meaning *I feel rather poorly.* **1897** *KS Univ. Qrly.* (ser B) 6.52 **PA,** *Dauncy:* indisposed. **1905** *DN* 3.77 **nwAR,** *Doncy*. . . Indisposed. 'I'm feeling a little doncy this morning.' Used of animals also. Not common. **1912** Cobb *Back Home* 148 **wKY,** He looks sort of dauncy and low in his mind. **1912** *DN* 3.574 **wIN,** *Dauncey.* **1916** *DN* 4.273 **NE, KY, TN, MO,** *Dauncy.* **1923** *DN* 5.205 **swMO,** *Dauncy.* **1927** *AmSp* 2.352 **WV,** *Dauncy.* **1944** *PADS* 2.25 **OH,** *Dauncy*. . . Qualmish, slightly unwell. **1952** Brown *NC Folkl.* 1.532 **c,eNC,** *Dauncy*. . . Sick, sickly. **1954** *DE Folkl. Bulletin* 1.16/1, Dauncy ("I'm not really sick, just kind of dauncy.") **1965–70** *DARE* (Qu. BB39, *On a day when you don't feel just right, though not actually sick, you might say, "I'll be all right tomorrow—I'm just feeling ______ today."*) Infs **IL**96, 113, **IN**3, 28, 38, 45, **KY**24, **MD**23, 24, **MS**33, **OH**61, 78, **VA**18, Donsie; (Qu. BB5, *A general feeling of discomfort or illness that isn't any one place in particular*) Infs **IL**96, **OH**50, 78, Donsie; **MD**24, Feel donsie; (Qu. BB38, *When a person doesn't look healthy, or looks as if he hadn't been well for some time, you'd say, "He looks ______."*) Infs **IN**3, **OH**78, **VA**18, 33, Donsie; (Qu. BB41, *Not seriously ill, but sick enough to be in bed: "He's been ______ for a week."*) Inf **PA**126, Donsie; (Qu. KK30, *Feeling slowed up or without energy: "I certainly feel ______."*) Inf **KY**25, Donsie. [All Infs old] **1983** *Barrick Coll.* **csPA,** *Donsy*—sickly, in bad shape. "He's lookin' pretty donsy."

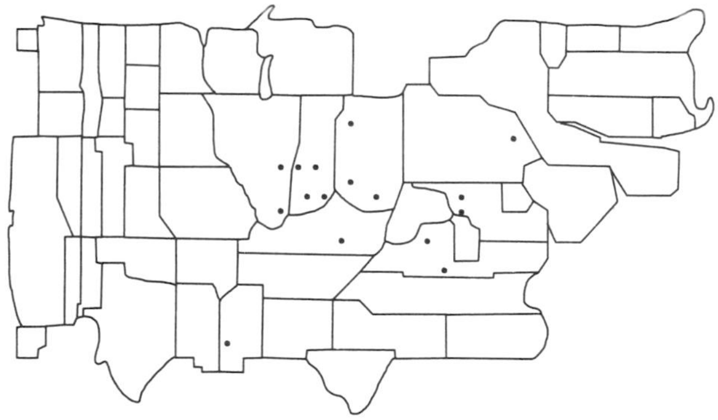

•donsie 2a + var (Qq. BB39, BB5, BB38, BB41, KK30)

b Frail; weak.

1872 Schele de Vere *Americanisms* 462, *Dansy* is used, in Pennsylvania, of persons who are failing from old age. **1883** Amer. Philol. Assoc. *Trans.* 14.47, *Dansy* . . is still used also in Virginia . . where it applies, I believe, only to a feeling of physical dulness or weariness or weakness. **1891** Ryan *Pagan* 82 **swPA,** He ain't one o' yer skim-milk, dauncy ones. He's as stout as a young bull. **1913** (1980) Hardy *OH Schoolmistress* 100 (as of c1850), *Doncy* meant something very like softly sentimental or weak; it was sometimes used to mean tired and feeble—with perhaps a sprinkle of laziness. To be called *doncy* was very uncomplimentary. **1933** *AmSp* 8.25 **WV, KY,** In central and southern West Virginia and Kentucky *dauncy* is used for infirm or feeble. One hears *Ol' man Brown's gettin' dauncy, in fact he's gettin' so feeble he can't get 'round much.*

c rarely *dauncy-giddy:* Dizzy; light-headed.

1917 *DN* 4.410 **KY,** *Dauncy*. . . dizzy. **1930** Shoemaker *1300 Words* 16 **cPA Mts** (as of c1900), *Donsie*—Light headed, not feeling up to the mark; giddy. **1931** *AmSp* 6.230 **neOR,** To feel 'dauncy' is to feel dizzy. **1944** *PADS* 2.55 **MO,** *Dauncy*. . . Dizzy, sickly. **1953** Randolph-Wilson *Down in Holler* 238 **Ozarks,** *Dauncy*. . . Dizzy; a *dauncy spell* is a brief period of dizziness. **1954** *Harder Coll.* **cwTN,** *Dauncy-giddy:* sick. **1973** *DARE* File **swPA,** Dauncy. . . Light-headed . . Ligonier Valley PA, 1973 and before. **a1975** Lunsford *It Used to Be* 178 **sAppalachians,** [To be] "Doncey" is to be kind of giddy. **1985** *DARE* File **WV,** Dauncy: In West Virginia it means dizzy.

d Nauseated, bilious.

1951 West *Witch Diggers* 36 **IN,** All that rich food made me kind of dauncy. **1967-69** *DARE* (Qu. H69, *When food is hard on your stomach, you say that it* _____) Inf **TN**5, Makes you feel a little donsie; (Qu. BB16b, *If something a person ate didn't agree with him, he might just feel a bit* _____) Infs **IN**76, **TN**3, Donsie. **1968** Kellner *Aunt Serena* 6 **cIN** (as of c1920), When my Grandmother called me to supper, I feebly called back that I didn't want any. This had the effect of bringing the whole family upstairs in alarm, for my appetite was all but legendary. . . "Do you feel dauncy?". . . " . . maybe a little,". . . "Probably been at the pickles again." *Ibid* 145, Those nauseated were bilious or dauncy.

e Moody, melancholy, depressed.

1853 in 1912 Thornton *Amer. Gloss.* 2.262, [She brought some letters] to my room, to keep me from feeling "donsy." **1921** *DN* 5.113 **CA,** *Daunsy*. . . Downcast, moody. Middlewest original turning up in California. **1968** Adams *Western Words* 89, *Daunsy*—A cowman's word for moody or downcast. **1984** Wilder *You All Spoken Here* 207 **Sth,** Dauncy, daunsy: Moody; depressed.

3 Ill-tempered, testy; saucy.

1909 *DN* 3.410 **nME,** *Doncy*. . . saucy, restive, testy. **1945** *AmSp* 20.151 **cwIN,** I have often heard the word *dauncy* applied to a child after he gets up cross and tired from an afternoon nap. **1952** Brown *NC Folkl.* 1.532 **c,eNC,** *Dauncy*. . . Bad tempered.

4 Stupid; confused, dazed; intoxicated.

1937 *Hall Coll.* **eTN, wNC,** *Doncy*. . . 1. "kind of dazed-like; off your mind a bit." 2. "intoxicated a little." 3. used of "a dumb child." **1952** Brown *NC Folkl.* 1.532, *Dauncy* ['dɔnsɪ]: . . Mentally unstable. **1953** Randolph-Wilson *Down in Holler* 238 **Ozarks,** *Dauncy*. . . Stupid or confused.

don't See **do** v **B4, C1c**

‡don't-and-do ship n

1945 Saxon *Gumbo Ya-Ya* 372 **LA** [New Orleans Black longshoremen's language], A *don't-and-do ship* sailing in *Suicide Alley* is the worst sort of ship to be on because that is a merchantman sailing in a war zone.

don't-care-ish adj Also *don't-care-ified* Cf **-ified**

Lazy; indifferent.

1927 Kennedy *Gritny* 142 **sLA** [Black], She bin too good a ooman to leave dem don'-care-ified niggers lay 'uh away, yonder in potter's fiel'. **1959** Lomax *Rainbow Sign* 58 **AL** [Black], There was some folks that didn't have nothin, nothin at all. Some of them were just *don't-care-ish.* They'd plant stuff and wouldn't work it, wouldn't plow it. Or just half plow it. *Ibid* 64, Old Rafe is just a don't-carish [sic] man. His favorite songs are about don't-carish people like Railroad Bill.

don't peek n

=Mexican sweat.

1987 *DARE* File **OK,** I have actually seen the card game of Mexican sweat played by a father and his two small sons. The game is also known as "Don't peek."

don'ts n pl

1967-70 *DARE* (Qu. GG34a, *To feel depressed or in a gloomy mood: "He has the* _____ *today."*) Infs **AR**52, **TX**42, 95, Don'ts.

dony(-girl) See **doney** n[2]

doo v See **do** v **A1**

doo n[1] See **dew**

doo adj, n[2] See **due**

dooamajig See **doojigger**

doobob n Also *doobab, doobiddie, doobinnie, doobobbis;* for addit varr see quots

=doohickey 1.

1911 *DN* 3.543 **NE,** *Doobobbus, doobobbis*. . . Vague designation used when the exact word is not recalled, or is purposely avoided. "Hasn't she a cute doobobbus on her head?" "Did you find that doobobbis I wanted?" **1931** *AmSp* 6.257 **KS, NE,** Indefinite names. . . "Thingum" . . "thing-em-bob" . . doobob, doobobble, dobobbus, doobiddie, doobinnie . . doodibbie, doodiddie. **1942** Berrey-Van den Bark *Amer. Slang* 75.4, *Contrivance; indefinite object; "gadget."* . . dobiddie, dobinnie, dobob, dobobbis, dobobble, dobobbus, dobobby . . dodibbie, dodiddie . . doobab.

doochy n

=doohickey 1.

1905 *DN* 3.77 **nwAR,** *Doochy*. . . What-do-you-call-it? 'Bring me that doochy.' Rare.

doodad n Also *dewdad, doodab(bus), doodack, doodaddle, dudad;* for addit varr see quots

1 =doohickey 1.

1905 *DN* 3.66 **eNE,** Indefinite expression applied to something, the name of which is not readily recalled. . . *Doodad, doodaddle.* **1908** McGaffey *Sorrows* 187 **NYC,** This machine [=automobile] has got a dudedad on it that prevents it from going more than ten. **1911** *DN* 3.543 **NE,** *Doodabbus.* **1912** *DN* 3.574 **wIN,** *Do-dad.* **1921** *DN* 5.120 **CT, IL,** *Dewdad*. . . Gimcrack; any old thing. "Let's take the dewdad a moment." **1927** *AmSp* 2.352 **WV,** *Doodad.* **1931** *AmSp* 6.258 **KS, NE,** Indefinite names. . . "Thingum" . . "thing-em-bob" . . doodad, doodaddle, doodaddy. **1942** Berrey-Van den Bark *Amer. Slang* 75.4, *Contrivance; indefinite object; "gadget."* . . dodabbus, do-dad, dodad, dodaddle, dodaddy, . . doodad. **1966-70** *DARE* (Qu. NN12b, *Things that people say to put off a child when he asks, "What are you making?"*) Infs **CA**158, **IA**5, **IN**61, **PA**242, **WA**3, **WI**44, Doodad; **VT**16, Doodacks.

2 Something small or fancy usu added for decoration.

1914 *DN* 4.71 **ME, nNH,** *Doodab,* or *doodad*. . . Any small, fancy, fussy thing. "Her bunnet was all hung raound with little doodabs." **1929** Ellis *Ordinary Woman* 275 **CO,** I will make some of those little piecrust dodads. *Ibid* 279 **CO,** See, I've brought you some of those little nut dodads. **1940** (1978) Still *River of Earth* 39 **KY,** Little dodacks here and there. 'Pon my word and honor, you can't stretch your arms withouten knocking flower pots over. **1942** Perry *Texas* 159, On the marble floors beneath its stately dome are many impressive, inlaid doodads. **1944** *PADS* 2.29 **KY, SC,** *Dudab, dudad*. . . A frill; a fussy ornament; a "monkey-shine." "What's that little dudab for?" "What's that little dudab that hangs down at the back of the mouth?" **1965-70** *DARE* (Qu. JJ12, *Little flourishes that some people put on their handwriting or signature to make it look fancy*) 16 Infs, **scattered,** Doodads; **IL**50, Doodad; **CA**138, Do-dabs; **IN**28, **KY**65, Doodaddles; (Qu. E6, *A small shelf hanging on the wall with small decorative articles on it*) 9 Infs, **scattered,** Doodad (shelf); (Qu. W39, . . *A person's best clothes*) Inf **PA**167, Doodads—for accessories. **1968** Kellner *Aunt Serena* 13 **cIN** (as of c1920), Aunt Serena, who had no use for fancy doodads, would have sent him on his way in two shakes of a sheep's tail.

3 See quot.

1967 *DARE* (Qu. W39, . . *A person's best clothes*) Inf **DC**1, Doodads.

4 Nonsense, silly talk.

1935 Davis *Honey* 258 **sOR,** Why don't you explain to these people how it happened, in place of all this doodaddle about witnesses?

doodaddle v **[doodad 2]**

1969 *DARE* (Qu. W30, *When a woman adds decorations to make something more attractive—for example, a hat, she might say, "It's too plain—I think I'll put on a few flowers to* _____ *it up."*) Inf **NC**61, Doodaddle it.

doodibbie, do(o)diddie See **doobob**

doodinkus n Also *dodinkus, do(o)dingle, dooginkus, dudinkus* **chiefly KS, NE**

=doohickey 1.

1911 *DN* 3.543 **NE,** *Doodinkus.* **1914** *DN* 4.105 **KS,** *Dinkus*. . . Thing; jigger. Also *dodinkus, dudinkus.* "This little dudinkus belongs to an automobile." **1923** *DN* 5.205 **swMO,** *Doodinkus.* **1931** *AmSp* 6.258 **KS, NE,** Indefinite names. . . "Thingum" . . "thing-em-bob" . . doodingle, doodinkus . . dooginkus. **1942** Berrey-Van den Bark *Amer. Slang* 75.4, *Contrivance; indefinite object; "gadget."* . . dodingle, dodinkus.

doodle n[1] [Etym unknown; prob by convergence of several words, with echoic and frequentative elements. For some possible connections, see etyms at the individual senses.]

1 also *doodlebug:* A small pile of hay, haycock; a small bundle of hay or sometimes grain; by ext, a pile of anything. [Prob euphem for **cock** n[2] (cf **2** below); perh suggested by *cock-a-doodle-doo,* but cf *SND doddle* n. 2 "The male genitals"] **chiefly IN, OH, PA** See Map

1899 Garland *Boy Life* 107 **nwIA** (as of c1870s), At this time he was too small to have a set task, and was put to look for berries and tumble down the "doodles." **1907** *German Amer. Annals* 9.374 **sePA,** Throw the windrows up into doodles. **1916** *DN* 4.337 **PA, neOH, NE,** *Doodle. . .* A small pile of hay; haycock. "A storm was coming; so we put the hay in doodles as fast as we could." **1928** *AmSp* 4.132 **cnNE,** A "doodle," "noodle," or "shock" is a small hay stack made by gathering the hay and piling it by hand. **1938** Stuart *Dark Hills* 33 **KY,** He tore down a doodle of Mr. Wheeler's cane hay by running and tumbling over it. *Ibid* 177 **neTN,** Each boy . . stacked the hay in what Anthony called "doodles." **1940** Stuart *Trees of Heaven* 125 **neKY,** He walks up to the stack of [dead] crows. "Gentlemen," he says, "the biggest doodle of crows I ever saw in one doodle." **1949** Kurath *Word Geog.* 35 **wPA,** Among the local words we may mention *doodle* . . for the haycock, which we encounter from the crest of the Alleghenies to the Ohio state line and again in a well-defined area on the lower course of the Kanawha in West Virginia. **1954** *Harder Coll.* **cwTN,** *Doodle. . .* A pile of manure usually, or a pile of anything. **1961** *AmSp* 36.268 **CO,** *(Hay) doodle* even shows signs of geographical division in its variable meaning. In northwestern Colorado the *doodle* is smaller than the 'usual' hay *stack,* but is offered as a synonym. Southern Colorado informants use *doodle* as a synonym for *hay shock.* **1965–70** *DARE* (Qu. L12, . . *Small piles of hay standing in the field*) 31 Infs, **chiefly IN, OH, wPA,** Doodles; 14 Infs, **chiefly IN, OH, wPA,** Hay doodles; (Qu. L30a, *When grain is cut it is [or used to be] tied up in* ______) Inf **OH**90, Doodles; (Qu. L30b, *Then these sheaves . . are set together in piles called* ______) Inf **OH**87, Doodles. **1966** *DARE* File **WV,** *Hay doodle*—A small size mound or stack of hay. In the hilly country, these doodles were dragged in by looping a rope around them and pulled by a horse. **1973** Allen *LAUM* 1.185 (as of c1950), *Haycock. . .* The West Midland euphemism, *doodle,* weakly survives in southwestern U[pper] M[idwest]. *Ibid* 186, *Doodlebug* [for *haycock,* was reported] once in North Dakota from a farmer born in Minnesota.

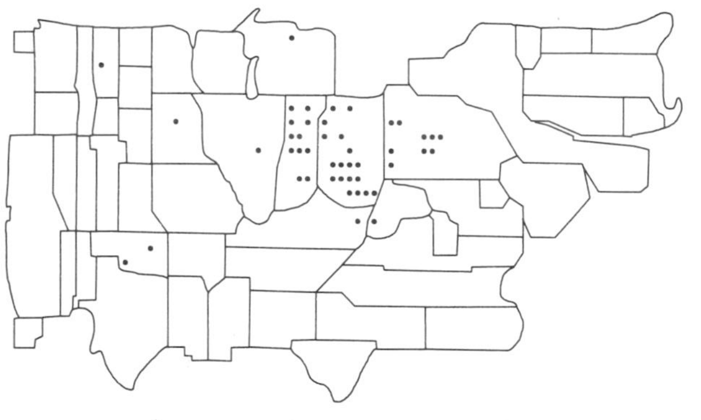

•doodle n[1] 1 + var (Qq. L12, L30a, b)

2 See quot. [See **1** above]

1912 Green *VA Folk-Speech* 151, *Doodle. . .* Male member.

3 See quot. [Prob from resemblance to **1** above]

1953 Randolph–Wilson *Down in Holler* 240 **Ozarks,** A boil or carbuncle is sometimes called a *doodle.*

4 See quot. [Prob from the resemblance to **1** above]

1953 Randolph–Wilson *Down in Holler* 240 **Ozarks,** *Doodle. . .* Occasionally the term means a small knoll or hill.

5 Something that is remarkable or exceptionally good; someone who is extraordinary or pleasing. [Cf *SND doddle* n. 3 "A small lump of home-made toffee. . . Hence used of something easy or attractive . . or of 'money easily obtained'."]

1913 *DN* 4.16 **NE,** *Doodle.* Fine, splendid, pleasing. Used by Nebraska students. "That hat is just a doodle." "Isn't that book a doodle?" "He's a doodle." **1970** *DARE* (Qu. FF17, . . *A very good or enjoyable time: "We all had a* ______ *last night."*) Inf **FL**51, Wingding doodle. **1978** *DARE* File **sOH** (as of 1940s), *Doodle,* something extraordinary or remarkable. "That's a real doodle."

6 also *doodlebum, doodlefadgit, doodleflicker, doodleflickus, doodlegadget:* =**doohickey 1.**

1931 *AmSp* 6.258 **KS, NE,** Indefinite names. . . "Thingum" . . "thing-em-bob" . . doodle, doodlefadgit. **1942** Berrey–Van den Bark *Amer. Slang* 75.4, *Contrivance; indefinite object; "gadget." . .* doodle, doodlefadgit,—flicker,—flickus,—bum,—gadget.

7 A frill, adornment, embellishment.

1941 *AN&Q* 1.39/1 **NEng,** Its name "doodle" suggests a "little or nothing of importance" cake which was given a hasty dusting of decorative sugar and cinnamon, spice, or cocoa powder to dress it up. **1966–68** *DARE* (Qu. JJ12, *Little flourishes that some people put on their handwriting or signature to make it look fancy*) Infs **MI**32, **MO**21, **NY**7, **OH**21, **PA**163, **UT**6, Doodles.

8 In marble play: see quot.

1968 *DARE* (Qu. EE6c, *Cheap marbles*) Inf **VA**24, Clay doodles.

doodle n[2] See **doodlebug 1, 6b**

doodle n[3] See **dipsydoodle 2**

doodle n[4] [Var of **diddle** n[2]]

1953 *PADS* 19.10 **nwNC,** *Doodle* . . Chick.

doodle v[1]

1 To stack or pile (a harvested crop); hence vbl n *doodling.* [**doodle** n[1] **1**]

1899 Garland *Boy Life* 109 **nwIA** (as of c1870s), He kept his feet stoutly braced to the trip-lever until a big roll of gathered hay bulged beneath him, then, with a mighty pull, raised the teeth and dropped his load at the "win'row." Three times round the piece, and the "doodling" began. **1941** in 1944 *ADD* **neKY,** We were doodlin' the hay up—'stackin' ' I guess you say. **1944** *AmSp* 19.206 **IN,** My barber—who is also a farmer—recently heard a neighbor say that he had been *'doodlin'* beans [*AmSp* Ed: soy beans].'

2 To idle about, dawdle. [Infl by *dawdle*]

1965–70 *DARE* (Qu. A10, . . *Doing little unimportant things: Somebody asks, "What are you doing?" and you answer, "Nothing in particular—I'm just* ______*."*) 15 Infs, **scattered,** Doodling (around); (Qu. A9, . . *Wasting time by not working on the job*) Infs **PA**146, **TN**52, Doodling; (Qu. KK31, *To go about aimlessly looking for distraction: "He doesn't have anything to do, so he's just* ______ *around."*) Inf **GA**73, Doodling.

3 To decorate.

1941 *AN&Q* 1.39/1 **NEng,** The cake was baked in drops or leaves, but was always "doodled up" with a surface decoration.

doodle v[2] Cf **crawfish v 2, doodlebug 1**

1950 *PADS* 14.26 **SC,** *Doodle, doodle bug. . .* The larval ant lion. . . The backward, crablike movement of the insect gives rise to the verb to *doodle,* to back out of an agreement. *Ibid* 27, *Doodle. . .* To back off from a position, to back out of an agreement. "I don't crawfish, and neither do I doodle."

doodlebug n

1 also *doodle, doodle ant, doodle-doodle-do bug:* A larva of the ant lion. **Sth, S Midl** Also called **dooly(-bug)**

a1883 (1911) Bagby *VA Gentleman* 48, [A true Virginian must] call doodle-bugs out of their holes. **1909** *DN* 3.395 **nwAR,** *Doodle bug. . .* A yellow beetle that lives in the ground and shows its presence by the hole it makes. It is caught by children who put a straw in the hole and call *'doodle bug.'* It is not supposed to grasp the straw unless called. **1917** *DN* 4.411 **wNC, LA, SC, KY,** *Doodle-bug.* **1946** *PADS* 6.12 **VA, eNC,** *Doodle-ant. . .* A small fuzzy-looking insect that burrows in soft dry earth. It is supposed to come to the surface when entreated with the words, "Doodle-ant, doodle-ant, house is afire," repeated several times. ((In s. Va. and c. N. C.: *doodle bug. Myrmeleonia.*)) **1950** *PADS* 14.26 **SC,** *Doodle, doodle bug. . .* The larval ant lion. Children are wont to shout over the conical pit of the ant lion: "Doodle, doodle, house afire." When he cautiously appears, they order him back with "Hack, doodle, hack!" **1958** *PADS* 29.9 **seTN,** *Doodle bug.* **c1960** *Wilson Coll.* **csKY,** *Doodle-bug.* **1967** *DARE* FW Addit **nwAR,** *Doodlebug*—Lives in dry, dusty places, makes hollowed cones to trap insects in. Kids say, "Doodle bug, Doodlebug, come get your corn. House on fire, children cryin." The doodlebug goes to working in the sand and the kids catch him. **1968**

DARE (Qu. R30, . . *Other kinds of beetles*) Inf **CA**87, Doodle or doodle-doodle-do bug—you can get it to come out if you say "doodle-doodle-do" to it; gray-colored bug, a sand burrower; **VA**15, Doodlebug. **1984** Welty *One Writer's Beginnings* 13 **MS,** She invited me to catch her doodlebugs; under the trees in her backyard were dozens of their holes.

2 A larva of the tiger beetle (*Cicindela* spp).

1949 Swain *Insect Guide* 115, *Tiger Beetles—Family Cicindelidae. . .* The larvae, locally called "doodlebugs," looking as though their powerfully jawed heads were on upside down, lie in wait for their insect prey.

3 A **sow bug.**

1887 *Harper's New Mth. Mag.* 75.276/1 **seLA,** She wondered how the nice, fat little round "doodles" were getting on in their tin can under the house. **1942** (1960) Robertson *Red Hills* 214 **SC,** While Mary talked to the Indian, her brother searched the satchel and found cat bones, snake bones, doodle bugs, red flannel, and many other kinds of conjure things. **1968** *DARE* (Qu. R27) Inf **LA**33, Doodlebug—a little bug that rolls into a ball. **1968** *DARE* FW Addit **New Orleans LA,** *Doodlebug, roly poly*—Alternate terms for the little bugs with lots of legs that roll up into a ball.

4 A **dung beetle.**

1969 *DARE* FW Addit **neNC,** *Doodlebug*—Bugs which roll up manure into big piles are called doodlebugs and turd rollers. **1970** *DARE* (Qu. R30, . . *Other kinds of beetles*) Inf **SC**67, Doodlebug—digs in ground, cats' waste, looks something like June bug, not as long, green and red, also called tumblebug; **NC**85, Doodlebug—larger than June bug, fat body, blue with blue wings. **1976** Garber *Mountain-ese* 24 **sAppalachians,** *Doodle-bug* . . dung beetle—You can call a doodlebug outta his hole by hummin' to it.

5 Any device reputed to detect underground oil, ore, or water; hence n *doodlebugger* one who uses such a device; n *doodlebuggery* the use of such a device. Cf *DS* CC13a

1924 Henderson *Keys to Crookdom* 157, One old fraud who was tried in the Federal court had a "chemical battery" or "doodlebug" oil location [sic], which he said would spot oil-producing ground at once. **1941** Vestal *Short Grass Country* 289 **Plains States, SW,** Many of these tales have to do with finding oil with doodlebugs. The term "doodlebug" is commonly applied to any gadget, from a hazel switch to elaborate machinery mounted on trucks—any device in which men have faith. . . In some cases the doodlebug was simply a divining rod like that used by water-witches. **1944** *CA Folkl. Qrly.* 3.53 **eTX,** There is certainly no justification of or scientific approach to the practice of doodlebuggery; it falls into the limbo of superstition and is in some ways a modern survival of the black arts. [Footnote:] Doodle Bug . . any bogus mechanical instrument . . employed to divine the location of oil. The term is also widely used . . with reference to . . locating mineral deposits. *Ibid* 55, In east Texas near the town of Linden a doodlebugger had located an oil field "that would make Spindle Top look like a rainbow on a slush pit." **1945** Saxon *Gumbo Ya-Ya* 547 **LA,** With the discovery of oil in North Louisiana, divining rods of all sorts made their appearance. Some are of metal and others merely branches from trees. A divining rod which is capable of finding underground oil deposits is generally known as a 'doodle bug.' This term is likewise used for the true appliances used by geologists. **1948** *Chi. Tribune* 5 April 1.13/4 *(DA),* A new device in prospecting . . was a 'doodlebug' which seemed to employ radar in locating likely ground. **1965** Teale *Wandering Through Winter* 185 **AR,** Nor has any greater success been chalked up by an infinite variety of doodlebugs, homemade divining instruments. **1978** *DARE* File, I knew the word *doodlebug* when I was growing up in Southern California in the 1950s. It was a homemade device, usually a forked branch, for detecting subsurface water.

6 A small sometimes modified or homemade vehicle or vehicle system used in place of the standard larger apparatus, as:

a In railroading: a self-propelled railcar.

1940 *RR Mag.* April 42, *Dingdong*—Gas or gas-electric coach, usually used on small roads or branch lines not important enough to support train service. . . Sometimes called *doodlebug.* Another meaning for *doodlebug* is rail-motor car used by section foreman, line-men, etc. **1947** Beebe *Mixed Train* 331 **AZ,** If you have missed the early morning doodlebug of the Tucson, Cornelia and Gila Bend in the Arizona Desert, you can ride the parlor on the daily freight later on, about noon. *Ibid* 355/2, *Doodlebug:* Gasoline rail car either for passenger service or transportation of section gangs.

b also *doodle:* A small local train. **chiefly Gulf States, Cent, N Midl** See Map Cf **dinky** n^1 **1**

1942 (1960) Robertson *Red Hills* 85 **SC,** We would travel to our grandfather's house by the Southern Railroad from Calhoun to Easley, where we would change to the Pickens Doodle. Always on the Doodle we would tell Mr. Partridge, the conductor: "We are going to our grandfather's, so will you please let us off at the house?" **1965–70** *DARE* (Qu. N37, . . *A branch railroad that is not very important or gives poor service*) 21 Infs, **esp Gulf States, Cent, N Midl,** Doodlebug; **MS**88, **NY**220, **PA**182, **TX**3, **UT**9, Doodlebug [FW sugg]; **AR**52, **LA**14, (A) doodle; **AL**2, Yankee doodle; **GA**11, Doodlebug—Savannah to Atlanta; **OK**28, Doodlebug—a motor car that pulled one passenger car; **SC**42, Pickens doodle; (Qu. N35) Inf **MS**47, Doodlebug; **OK**31, Doodlebug—used to be a crazy-looking passenger train, three to four cars, thirty or forty years ago; (Qu. N36, . . *A slow train or one that stops at every station;* total Infs questioned, 75) Inf **FL**22, Doodlebug.

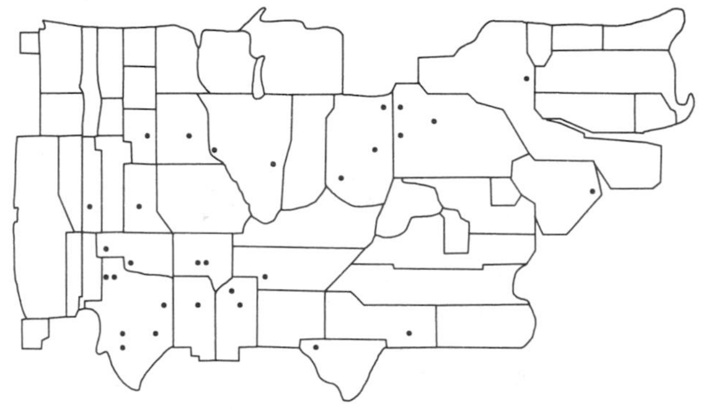

•doodlebug 6b (Qq. N37, N35, N36)

c A small or makeshift tractor or towing device, esp one made from an old car.

1967 *DARE* Tape **TX**8, You come out in the field with a combine with a doodlebug or [with] a rice cart behind a tractor an' auger the rice from the hopper on the combine to the rice cart. **1967–68** *DARE* FW Addit **Upstate NY,** Doodlebug—automobile made over into a tractor. This was reported from several places in Upstate New York; **NY**93, Doodlebug—an old car converted to a tractor; **cnNY,** *Doodlebug*—A car with a winch to hook to a tree to pull a car out of snow or mud. Four-wheel drive and low gears. **1968** *DARE* (QR, near Qu. L18) Inf **NY**96, Doodlebug—a car used as a tractor [FW photo: an old (c1930s) automobile stripped to bare essentials, with wooden flatbed, and chains on the rear tires]; (Qu. N5, *Nicknames for an automobile, especially an old or broken-down car*) Inf **NJ**6, Old doodlebugs. **1969** *AmSp* 44.203 [Trucker jargon], *Doodlebug*—Small tractor used to pull two-axle dollies in the warehouse.

d See quot.

1988 *DARE* File, An Amherst, Massachusetts woman with cerebral palsy uses a golf cart for mobility and calls it her doodlebug.

e attrib: See quot. Cf **doodlebug 5**

1969 *DARE* Tape **CA**128, So they dredge [the creeks, in placer mining]. . . They come in with what they call a doodlebug dredge . . a small dredge. Then they used a crane, or a clam shell . . ahead of it.

7 See **doodle** n^1 **1.**

doodlebum See **doodle** n^1 **6**

doodle-doodle-do bug See **doodlebug** n **1**

doodledy shit n [Prob var of **doodl(e)y squat**]

=**doodl(e)y squat.**

1965 *DARE* FW Addit **OK,** *Doodledy shit* ['dudḷdi 'šɪt]—nothing at all. "He didn't have doodledy shit to show that he really owned the car." Heard in conversation.

doodlefadgit, doodleflicker, doodleflickus, doodlegadget See **doodle** n^1 **6**

doodlegee n

The fruit of a **nannyberry.**

1903 *DN* 2.351 **seNY,** *Doodlegee* [dudəlǰi]. . . The tree and fruit of the sheepberry or nannyberry.

doodler n

1 One who dawdles; an idler. [**doodle** v^{1} **2**]

1968–69 *DARE* (Qu. A18, . . *A very slow person: "What's keeping him? He certainly is ______!"*) Inf **NY**80, A doodler; (Qu. HH20a, *An idle, worthless person: "He's a ______."*) Inf **IL**97, Doodler.

2 =**doodle** n^{1} **6.**

1970 *DARE* (Qu. NN12b, *Things that people say to put off a child when he asks, "What are you making?"*) Inf **PA**245, A doodler—probably not common.

3 Among tobacco workers: see quot.

1967 Key *Tobacco Vocab.* **KY, MD, NC, TN,** *Pinhooker* . . one who practices pinhooking. [Also called:] *Speculator, . . doodler, yellow hammer.* [*Ibid, Pinhook*. . . To speculate in tobacco by buying from the farmer and reselling at auction on low profit margins. These transactions often take place just outside a warehouse, and the pinhooker will attach his sales tag to a lot of tobacco waiting to be received by the warehouse workers.]

4 See quot.

1947 *McDavid Coll.* **GA,** Doodlers—older hens.

doodler's damn n Cf **fiddler's damn**

Something completely worthless; a tinker's damn.

1966 *DARE* (Qu. KK17, . . *'Worthless' "It isn't worth ______."*; total Infs questioned, 75) Inf **OK**27, Doodler's damn.

doodlesniptious adj

1919 *DN* 5.73 **NM,** *Doodlesniptious,* snippy, haughty. "You need not be so doodlesniptious about your hat, I don't like it."

‡doodle soup n Cf **rivel soup**

1969 *DARE* (Qu. H36, *Kinds of soup*) Inf **CA**136, Doodle soup—chunks of dough cooked in milk.

doodle wagon n

1968 *DARE* (Qu. U6, *Someone who sells vegetables or other articles from a wagon or truck, going from house to house*) Inf **MO**9, Well, we don't have that here, but they call that the doodle wagon across the river [in nwTN].

doodl(e)y squat n Also *doodle(ly) squat, doodlum ~, squat doodle* [See quot 1946; cf *do one's do* (at **do** v **D4**)] **chiefly Sth, SMidl** *euphem*

The slightest thing; something of absolutely no value.

1934 Hurston *Jonah's Gourd Vine* 217 **cFL** [Black], She ain't never had nothin'—not eben doodly-squat, and when she gits uh chance tuh git holt uh sumpin de ole buzzard is gone on uh rampage. **1946** (1972) Mezzrow-Wolfe *Really Blues* 92, I had made up my mind in advance that these cats [=musicians] weren't from doodlely-squat. *Ibid* 332, [Glossary:] *Doodlely-squat:* nothing, no more than the product of a child who squats to do his duty. **1966–70** *DARE* (Qu. HH20c, *Of an idle, worthless person you might say, "He isn't worth ______."*) Inf **VA**42, Doodly squat; (Qu. JJ15b, . . *A person who seems to you very stupid: "He doesn't know ______."*) Inf **VA**93, Doodly squat; **MS**52, Doodly squat, squat doodle; **AR**13, Doodle squat; (Qu. LL16, *The most basic thing, the simplest thing: "He doesn't know ______ thing about plumbing."*; total Infs questioned, 75) Inf **MS**73, Doodlum squat. **1973** Vonnegut *Breakfast* 12, Most other countries didn't have doodley-squat. Many of them weren't even inhabitable anymore. **1976** Garber *Mountain-ese* 24 **sAppalachians,** *Doodly-squat* . . worthless thing—He bought a new car but it haint worth doodley-squat. **1977** Dillard *Lexicon* 154 [Black], Doodley squat—"nothing." **1978** *DARE* File **cSC** [Black], *Doodley squat*—A euphemism for shit. "He isn't worth doodley squat." "She never said doodley squat to me, now she's pretending to be my friend." **1982** *Smithsonian Letters* **neVA,** "The whole thing was not worth doodley-squat!" . . doodley-squat—nothing, insignificance. **1983** *DARE* File **AL** (as of 1940s), In phrase indicating ignorance: "He don't know doodlum squat about that."

doo-doo n See **do** n^{1} **4**

doo-doo v Also *doody* Cf **do** n^{1} **4**

1970 *Thompson Coll.* **AL** (as of c1920), Doo-doo, doody . . excrement, to defecate.

‡doody n^{1} [Hypocoristic] Cf **boody 2**

1966 *DARE* (Qu. X35, . . *The part of the body that you sit on—for example, "He slipped and came down hard on his ______."*) Inf [illegible], Doody [dudɪ].

doody n^{2} See **do** n^{1} **4**

doofis See **doofus**

dooflicker n Also *doflick(et)y, dooflinkie, dooflop;* for addit varr see quots

=**doohickey 1.**

1905 *DN* 3.66 **eNE,** Indefinite expression applied to something, the name of which is not readily recalled. . . *Dooflinkus, dooflicker.* **1912** *DN* 3.575 **wIN,** *Do-flicker.* . . Any little mechanical contrivance that the speaker cannot readily name. "Here! Try to tighten it up with this do-flicker." **1914** *DN* 4.71 **ME, nNH,** *Dooflicker. Ibid* 105 **KS,** *Doflickety.* . . Any small article. Also *duflickety.* **1931** *AmSp* 6.258 **KS, NE,** Indefinite names. . . Thingum . . thing-em-bob . . dooflicker, dooflickus, dooflinkie, dooflinkus, dooflop, doofloppie, doofloppus. **1942** Berrey-Van den Bark *Amer. Slang* 75.4, *Contrivance; indefinite object; "gadget."* . . doflicker, doflickety, doflickus, doflicky, doflinkie, doflinkus, doflop, dofloppie, dofloppus. **1942** Warnick *Garrett Co. MD* 6 **nwMD** (as of 1900–18), *Dooflicker, doofunny* . . an object the speaker cannot readily name.

dooflunky n Cf **dooflicker**

1989 *DARE* File **sAL,** Dooflunky—an impersonal reference to someone whose name is either not recalled or not provided. "I saw dooflunky downtown today." Current in southern half of Alabama. Unknown in South Carolina apparently.

doofunny n Also *dofunny, doojumfunny, dufunny*

=**doohickey 1.**

1897 *KS Univ. Qrly.* (ser B) 6.52, *Doofunny:* A thing not easily described, or thus mentioned to save description. **1902** *DN* 2.233 **sIL,** *Dofunny.* **1905** *DN* 3.66 **eNE,** Indefinite expression applied to something, the name of which is not readily recalled. . . *Doo-funny, doojumfunny. Ibid* 77 **nwAR,** *Do-funny.* **1908** *DN* 3.306 **eAL, wGA,** *Doofunny.* **1912** *DN* 3.575 **wIN,** *Do-funny.* **1914** *DN* 4.105 **KS,** *Dofunny.* . . Also *dufunny.* **1915** *Amer. Mag.* Dec 87/2 **CA,** Winifred (from whom a do-funny [for Christmas]) . . card followed by another do-funny. **1916** *DN* 4.340 **se,neOH,** *Dofunny.* **1931** *AmSp* 6.258 **KS, NE,** Indefinite names. . . Thingum . . thing-em-bob . . doofunny . . doojumfunny. **1931** *Harper's Mth. Mag.* Dec 78 **NY,** Many and marvelous . . were the gadgets and do-funnies offered in the accessory stores. **1942** [see **dooflicker**]. **c1960** *Wilson Coll.* **csKY,** *Dofunny.* . . A name for something that is not known by name. **1967** *DARE* (Qu. NN12b, *Things that people say to put off a child when he asks, "What are you making?"*) Inf **IA**5, Doofunny. **1982** *Barrick Coll.* **csPA,** *Do-funny—thingamajig; whatchmacallit.* All three are common.

doofus n Also *doofis, doofus-bowangus*

An awkward, stupid, or foolish person; hence broadly, a fellow, guy.

1970 *DARE* (Qu. HH21, *A very awkward, clumsy person*) Inf **NY**241, Doofus ['dufəs]. **1975** *AmSp* 50.58 **AR** (as of c1970), *Doofus* ['dufəs]. . . Person of little or no judgment or common sense: "Don't bother to see Dean Fairchild; he'll do his best to make you feel like a doofus." **1986** *Capital Times* (Madison WI) 5 July 11, [In the comic strip "Bloom County":] The secret of the universe . . is "with knowledge ye shall be free"! The secret is . . "with ice cream ye shall be a pig." What *isn't* a secret . . is that Mr. Spock is a *doofus*! **1988** *DARE* File **MA,** A *doofus* is a man whose name is not known to the speaker—a *guy, joker, jasper.* It's used mainly by males, and is not usually complimentary. *Ibid* **NYC** (as of 1955), Doofus—one of the more common words used by kids (in the Bronx, at least) for a jerk or a fool. There was also a fuller form doofus-bowangus. *Ibid* **ceWI** (as of 1950s), As a boy growing up around adults who used German words, I heard "doofus" ['dufəs] a lot. A person would say "you doofus" to mean something like "you dumbass." It wasn't a harsh thing to say to someone; it was pretty playful. **1988** *WI State Jrl.* (Madison) 18 Dec comics sec, [In the comic strip "Shoe":] It's not bad enough that I'm stuck here in a huge line at the airline ticket counter. . . No, I have to be in front of this self-important doofis with his portable phone.

doogadget n Also sp *dogadget*

=**doohickey 1.**

1931 *AmSp* 6.258 **KS, NE,** Indefinite names. . . Thingum . . thing-em-bob . . doogadget. **1942** Berrey-Van den Bark *Amer. Slang* 75.4, *Contrivance; indefinite object; "gadget."* . . dogadget.

doogaloo n Also sp *dougaloo* **Sth**

In logging and mining: see quot.

1973 *PADS* 59.34 **AL,** *Doogaloo, dougaloo.* . . =*scrip.* [*Ibid* 50, *Scrip* . . tokens, bills, or other markers given to [coal mine] workers in place of money payment, which were good for full value at a company store but were discontinued [sic] as much as ten percent in other places.] **1977** *Foxfire 4* 311 **nGA,** Since they were only paid every thirty days, [logging camp] employees would make their purchases with what they called "doogaloo"—credit vouchers against their forthcoming paychecks. **1984** Wilder *You All Spoken Here* 196 **Sth,** Doogaloo: Credit vouchers against upcoming pay in the Champion Fibre lumbering operations in old days in western North Carolina.

doogie n [Cf *EDD doogs* the number of marbles one has risked in a game (*"Obs."*)] Cf **doggie 1**

A playing marble.

1958 *PADS* 29.32 **MO,** *Doogies*. . . A general term for marbles. **1965–70** *DARE* (Qu. EE6b, *Small marbles or marbles in general*) Inf **AR**47, Doogie; **OK**42, 48, 52, Doogies; (Qu. EE6c, *Cheap marbles*) Infs **NJ**6, **NY**211, 219, **WI**50, Doogies; **TX**104, Doogie; (Qu. EE7, . . *Marble games*) Inf **OK**42, Doogie game—just playing marbles. **1966** *DARE* Tape **OK**42, Playin' marbles, playin' doogies . . do you wanta play some doogies?

dooginkus See **doodinkus**

doogler n

A **stonecat** (here: *Noturus flavus*).

1983 Becker *Fishes WI* 725, *Stonecat. Noturus flavus*. . . Other common names: . . doogler.

doogood n Also sp *dogood*

1 See quot.

1887 Kirkland *Zury* 537 **IL,** *Do-good*. . . An expedient. A makeshift.

2 =**doohickey 1.**

1911 *DN* 3.543 **NE,** *Doogood*. **1931** *AmSp* 6.258 **KS, NE,** Indefinite names. . . Thingum . . thing-em-bob . . doogood. **1942** Berrey–Van den Bark *Amer. Slang* 75.4, *Contrivance; indefinite object; "gadget."* . . dogood.

doohickey n Also *do-hicky, doohickus, doohinkie, doohinkus, doohunkie;* for addit varr see quots

1 Something whose name is unknown or forgotten; a gadget.

1914 *Our Navy* (U.S.) Nov. 12 *(OEDS)*, We were compelled to christen articles beyond our ken with such names as 'dohickeys', 'gadgets' and 'gilguy'. **1931** *AmSp* 6.258 **KS, NE,** Indefinite names. . . Thingum . . thing-em-bob . . doohickie, doohickus, doohinkie, doohinkus, doohunkie, doohunkus. **1942** Berrey–Van den Bark *Amer. Slang* 75.4, *Contrivance; indefinite object; "gadget."* . . dohickie, dohicky, dohickus, dohinkie, dohinkus, dohunkus, dohunky. **1944** *PADS* 2.55 **MO, VA, NC, SC,** *Do-hicky* ['du,hɪkɪ]. . . A term used as the substitute for the name of something. "What is that do-hicky you are making?" **1945** *PADS* 3.10 **wNY,** *Do-hicky*. **1954** *Harder Coll.* **cwTN,** *Do-hickey*. **1958** Blasingame *Dakota Cowboy* 247, See this little do-hickey? It's called a can opener. **c1960** *Wilson Coll.* **csKY,** *Dohickey* (or *doohickey*). **1967–68** *DARE* (Qu. NN12b, *Things that people say to put off a child when he asks, "What are you making?"*) Infs **CT**16, **IL**9, Doohickey. **1982** *Barrick Coll.* **csPA,** *Do-hicky*—thingamajig.

2 Something small or fancy added for decoration.

1966 *DARE* (Qu. JJ12, *Little flourishes that some people put on their handwriting or signature to make it look fancy*) Inf **SC**11, Doohickeys [laughter].

3 A pimple or skin blemish. [Infl by **hickey** n² **a**]

1966–68 *DARE* (Qu. X39, *A mark on the skin where somebody has sucked it hard and brought the blood to the surface*) Inf **CA**93, Doohicky; (Qu. X59, . . *Small infected pimples that form usually on the face*) Inf MA6, Doohickies.

doojigger n Also *dooamajig, doojiebob, doojig(gie), doojohn, doomawadja;* for addit varr see quots Cf **-ma-** infix

=**doohickey 1.**

1905 *DN* 3.66 **eNE,** Indefinite expression applied to something, the name of which is not readily recalled. . . *Doojohn, doojohnny*. **1931** *AmSp* 6.258 **KS, NE,** Indefinite names. . . Thingum . . thing-em-bob . . doojiebob, doojohn, doojohnie, doojigger, doojiggie, doojiggum, doojiggus, doojinnie . . doomiejig, doomawadja, doomiewadjie. **1942** Berrey–Van den Bark *Amer. Slang* 75.4, *Contrivance; indefinite object; "gadget."* . . doamajig, . . dojigger, dojiggie, dojiggy, dojiggum, dojiggus, dojimmie, dojinnie, dojisser, dojohn, dojohnnie, . . domajig, domajigger, domajiggus, domawadja, . . domiewadjie; dooamajig. **1966** Barnes–Jensen *Dict. UT Slang* 13, *Doo-jigger* . . something the name of which is out of mind. **1967–68** *DARE* (Qu. JJ10b, *Parts of an ink pen*) Inf **MA**8, Doojiggy; (Qu. NN12b, *Things that people say to put off a child when he asks, "What are you making?"*) Inf **OH**71, Doojig. **1969** *DARE* FW Addit **neNC,** It's got two little doojiggers on the top.

doojumfunny See **doofunny**

doo-less See **do-less** adj

dooley n [Perh from surname *Dooley*]

1 A sweet potato. **chiefly Sth**

1908 *DN* 3.306 **eAL, wGA,** *Dooley(-yam)*. . . A favorite variety of the yam sweet potato. **1967** *DARE* (Qu. I9, . . *Potatoes*) Inf **AL**30, Doolies ['duliz]; **TX**6, Doolies ['duliz]—sweet potatoes.

2 An outdoor toilet. [See quot 1971] *joc*

1968 *DARE* (Qu. M21b, . . *An outside toilet building*) Infs **WI**65, 72, Dooley ['duli]. **1971** *Today Show Letters* **TX** (as of c1933), "Dooley" for privy. . . Seems that a certain man named "Dooley" was commissioned to built [sic] these edifices in public places during the Roosevelt administration . . and they became known by his name, a tribute to his superior craftsmanship. **[1973** Allen *LAUM* 1.181 **Ontario Canada,** *Privy* [1 inf] dooley.] **1979** *Yankee* May 26, [Advt:] Doggie Dooley® works like a miniature septic tank. . . Simply install heavy plastic rust-proof Doggie Dooley® anywhere in ground.

doololly n Also sp *dololly*

1 =**doohickey 1.**

1931 *AmSp* 6.258 **KS, NE,** Indefinite names. . . Thingum . . thing-em-bob . . doololly. **1952** Brown *NC Folkl.* 1.534, *Do-lolly*. . . A generalized term applied to some object not named, perhaps because the name is not known or cannot be recalled, or because the speaker holds the object in contempt. **1968** *DARE* (Qu. NN12b, *Things that people say to put off a child when he asks, "What are you making?"*) Inf **LA**17, Doololly.

2 Money.

1969 *DARE* (Qu. U19a, . . *Money in general: "He's certainly got the ———."*) Inf **GA**74, Doololly ['du,lɔli].

dooly(-bug) n

=**doodlebug 1.**

1899 Bergen *Animal Lore* 62, Doodle-bug or doodle. . . Dooly-bug or dooly, ant-lion. *Indiana and Southern States.*

doomawadja, doomiejig, doomiewadjie See **doojigger**

do one dirt(y) See **dirt** n 5

do one for a joke See **do** v D5

do one like that See **do** v D2

do one's do See **do** n¹ 5

do one that way See **do** v D2

doop pot n [Cf Du *doop* dipping, and *dopen* to dip]

1983 *Lutz Coll.* **seNY** (as of 1900), *A doop pot* (*doop* rhymes with English *soup*) was an iron or tin pot to carry coals from a neighbor's house to relight one's own fire.

doopy adj [Cf *EDD doobie* (at *dobby* sb.¹) "A fool, simpleton, stupid fellow"]

Silly, simple-minded.

1968 *DARE* (Qu. HH9, *A very silly or light-headed person*) Inf **VA**25, Doopy [dupi], simple.

door n Usu |dɔr, dor|; also **chiefly NEast** |dɔə|; **chiefly Sth** |do(ə)| Pronc-spp *do', doah*

A Forms.

1875 *Scribner's Mth.* 10.239 **Sth** [Black], Th'u' de cracks dat's in de do'. **1887** Page *In Ole VA* 223 **VA** [Black], Whyn't you go 'long 'way from dat do'? **1893** Shands *MS Speech* 26, *Do* [do]. Negro for *though* and for *door*. **1901** *DN* 2.181 **KY** [Black], *Door*—doah. **1913** Kephart *Highlanders* 281 **sAppalachians,** In some mountain districts we hear do' (door), flo', mo', . . but such skipping of the *r* is common only where lowland influence has crept in. **1934** Carmer *Stars Fell on AL* 180 **AL** [Black], She burst into de do'. **1937** *AmSp* 12.286 **wVA,** *Poor* and *your* have the vowel [ɔ] of *floor* and *door*. **1942** *AmSp* 17.39 **seNY,** [All of the 104 infs used the vowel [ɔ] in *door*.] **1961** Kurath–McDavid *Pronc. Engl.* 120, In the South—from the Potomac to Georgia—*four, door,* etc., are usually pronounced as . . /foə̧, doə̧/, especially by cultured speakers. . . In eastern North Carolina, where postvocalic /r/ is often retained, such pronunciations as . . /for ~ foə̧, dor ~ doə̧/, are not uncommon. The South Midland regularly has /for, dor/, pronounced as [fo·ɚ ~ foɚ] . . the [o] being close and usually long. This pronunciation occurs as far north as the southwestern corner of Pennsylvania. In New England and Upstate New York the vowel in *four, door,* etc. is usually rather short and not infrequently lowered. **1973** *PADS* 60.57 **seNC,** *Door.* . . Two only [of 12 infs in Carteret Co.] had the general Southern /ə/; all others had /r/ [in *door*].

B Senses.

1 in phr *behind the door when (something) was passed out* and varr: Not endowed with (something).

1853 Haliburton *Sam Slick's Wise Saws* 2.273 **CT,** She warn't behind the door when beauty was given out. **1860** Haliburton *Season-Ticket* 11 **MI,** Well, for all that, they *did* stare, . . for it ain't often they saw such a gall as Miss Jemima, I can tell you, though the Irish galls warn't behind the door neither when beauty was given out, that's a fact. **1899** (1912) Green *VA Folk-Speech* 47, You were behind the door when beauty was given out. You were not behind the door when noses were given out. **1939** *AmSp* 14.262 **swIN,** One who is not over-intelligent . . 'was behind the door when the brains were passed out.' **1953** Randolph–Wilson *Down in Holler* 192 **Ozarks,** A gentleman in Washington County, Arkansas, was known for his invincible stupidity; it was said that "poor Charley was behind the door when the brains was passed out." **1953** *New Yorker* 5 Dec 56/1 **MS,** When the brains were being handed around, my son Daniel was standing behind the door. **1967** *DARE* (Qu. HH13, . . *A person [who] is not very alert or not aware of things "He's certainly_______."*) Inf **IL**20, He was behind the door when the brains were passed out; (Qu. II21, *When somebody behaves unpleasantly or without manners: "The way he behaves, you'd think he was _______."*) Inf **WA**28, Behind the door when the brains were passed out. **c1970** *Halpert Coll.* **wKY,** He wasn't behind the door when the feet were handed out. **1984** Burns *Cold Sassy* 26 **nGA** (as of 1906), Aunt Loma was behind the door when they passed out the tact.

2 in phr *behind the door:* Old-fashioned, out of step with the times.

1913 Johnson *Highways St. Lawrence to VA* 196, As she got older she wa'n't up-to-date enough. She was like a minister—he gits behind the door a little, and they want some one younger.

3 with *the;* also *back door:* A rejection, dismissal—used in phrr *give one* (or *get*) *the door.* [Var of *show one the door*] **esp Atlantic** Cf **mitten, give one the**

1941 *LANE* Map 406 *(She gave him the mitten)* 1 inf, **seVT,** He got the door; [1 inf, **swNH,** She showed him the door]. **1965–70** *DARE* (Qu. II5b, *When you don't want to have anything to do with a certain person because you don't like him, you might say, "I'd certainly like to give him the _______."*) 20 Infs, **esp Atlantic,** Door; **VA**2, Door to the road; **NJ**36, Back door; [**MA**6, Back-door chute; **NJ**1, Back-door treatment;] (Qu. AA11, *If a man asks a girl to marry him and she refuses, you'd say she _______*) Infs **DC**6, **MA**42, Gave him the door.

4 In var phrr indicating mistrust: see quot. Cf **behind a dime**

1966–70 *DARE* (Qu. V2b, *About a deceiving person, or somebody that you can't trust, you might say: "I wouldn't trust him _______."*) Infs **NC**85, **TX**103, Behind the door; **IN**32, **MD**6, Behind a closed (*or* screen) door; **WI**52, From here to the door; **NC**9, From the front door to the back door; **MA**44, **SC**26, Out (*or* outside) the door; **TX**103, With the door shut.

doorbell night n Cf **gate night**

=cabbage night.

1904 *DN* 2.396 **neOH,** *Door-bell night.* . . The night but one before Hallowe'en (Oct. 29), when door-bells are rung by prankish children.

doorbug See **dorbug**

door-buster n [Cf *gate-crasher* one who attends or participates without invitation]

1970 *DARE* (Qu. II18, *Someone who joins himself on to you and your group without being asked and won't leave*) Inf **WV**21, Door-buster. [Inf Black]

door-face See **doughface**

door, give one the See **door B3**

door grass n

=knotgrass (here: *Polygonum aviculare*).

1892 *Jrl. Amer. Folkl.* 5.102, *Polygonum aviculare* . . door-grass. So. Ind. **1900** Lyons *Plant Names* 300, *P[olygonum] aviculare* . . Door-grass.

‡doorkeeper n

1966 *DARE* (Qu. HH26, *A person who is always ready to stir up trouble*) Inf **SC**10, Doorkeeper—he keeps his door open all the time for make trouble.

doorknob n *joc*

1 See quot.

1965–70 *DARE* (Qu. H27, . . *Joking names for doughnuts*) Infs **GA**92, **MD**24A, **MS**46, 60, **TX**85, **WI**13, Doorknob.

2 See quot.

1967–68 *DARE* (Qu. X28, *Joking words . . for a person's head*) Infs **AR**55, **IA**30, Doorknob.

3 See quot.

1968 *DARE* (Qu. X31, . . *A woman's breasts*) Infs **NY**45, **WV**2, Doorknobs.

4 =buffalo n 4.

1976 Warner *Beautiful Swimmers* 139, Bad weather brings out the worst in crabs under confinement. They tangle together in large masses, lopping off limbs and killing the weak among them. There will be more "doorknobs," as buffaloes are called today, and you can almost count on the crabs as a barometer. **1984** *DARE* File **Chesapeake Bay** [Watermen's vocab], Buffalo crab, doorknob.

doormat n

=hogchoker.

1984 *DARE* File **Chesapeake Bay** [Watermen's vocab], Flounder, floormat, doormat, hogchoker.

door neighbor n [*OED* 1562–1711]

See quot 1899.

1899 (1912) Green *VA Folk-Speech* 151, *Door-neighbours.* . . People living next door to each other; "next-door-neighbours." **1952** Giles *40 Acres* 55 **KY,** Frony didn't come to see me for three days after we moved to the ridge, and she was practically a "door neighbor" too. *Ibid* 57, Frony was almost, but not quite, a "door neighbor." A door neighbor, of course, lives right next.

door potato n

=Madeira vine.

1953 Randolph *Down in Holler* 240 **Ozarks,** *Door 'tater.* . . The so-called Madeira vine *(Boussingaultia gracilis),* which has buds or fruit like tiny potatoes. This plant is grown in dooryards for shade and ornament, and is sometimes called *mignonette.*

door rock See **door stone**

door scraper n

1909 *DN* 3.410 **ME,** *Door scraper.* . . A strip of iron fastened to a doorstep and used to clean the mud from boots.

‡door shopper n

1966 *DARE* (Qu. U6, *Someone who sells vegetables or other articles from a wagon or truck, going from house to house*) Inf **SC**11, Door shopper—the name when they used to have them here.

door shutter n [Redund] Cf Intro "Language Changes" I.4

1903 *DN* 2.312 **seMO,** *Door-shutter.* . . Door. 'The door-shutter is offen its hinges.'

doorstep child n Also *doorstep baby* Cf **yard child**

A child of unwed parents.

1949 *AmSp* 24.108 **cwSC,** *Doorstep child.* . . Bastard. **1960** *PADS* 34.52 **CO,** The Denver and Georgetown *doorstep child* 'bastard' seems to be an apt urban euphemism. **1967** *DARE* (Qu. Z11b, . . *A child of unwed parents*) Inf **TX**3, Doorstep baby. **1969** *DARE* Tape **PA**215, Her dad was the doorstep baby. His mother had left him at the County Home, the poorhouse. They even left babies there then.

doorstep, sweep one's own v phr Also *clean one's own dooryard*

To mind one's own business.

1967–68 *DARE* (Qu. II22, *Expressions to tell somebody to keep to himself and mind his own business*) Infs **MI**68, **NJ**18, Sweep (off) your own doorstep; **WI**52, Clean your own dooryard.

doorstone n Also *door rock* [Scots, nEngl dial] **chiefly NEng**

A large, flat stone used as a doorstep or threshold.

1764 in 1889 NH Hist. Soc. *Coll.* 9.170 **csNH,** Helped split a large door stone. **1863** (1889) Whitney *Faith Gartney* 196 **eMA,** Glory went away, and sat down on the door-stone. **1877** Bartlett *Americanisms* 187,

Door-Rock. The door stone or step. Western. **1893** Owen *Voodoo Tales* 209 **MO,** The aunties searched under every doorstone for "tricks," but, it is needless to say, found none. **1945** Partridge *January Thaw* 29 **CT,** I know the title as well as I know my own doorstone. **1965** Needham–Mussey *Country Things* 50 **sVT,** John Gale himself had a quarry for nothing but doorstones and bridges. **1975** Gould *ME Lingo* 76, *Doorstone*—The granite, etc., block doorstep at the front entrance of an old-time Maine home, especially along the coast. **1980** *Greenfield Recorder* (MA) 8 Nov np, Many hours were spent [in gathering stones for a stone wall] before there was any granite cut for hearth stones and door stones. They used to call them "door rocks" and that's what they were, a carefully selected field rock, as flat and smooth as was to be found.

door stool n

1926 *AmSp* 2.79 **ME,** Practically all doorways are built with a threshold that may trip the unwary visitor accustomed to continuous floors between rooms. This is always called a "door-stool."

door stoop n **[stoop]**

A small porch.

1941 *LANE* Map 351 *(Porch)* 1 inf, **neMA,** Door stoop. **1967** Fetterman *Stinking Creek* 63 **seKY,** A mother nursing a baby can send [=spit] a stream of the brown fluid [=tobacco juice] . . out through an open door six feet away without getting a drop on her, the baby, or the doorstoop. **1969** *DARE* (Qu. D17, . . *The platform, sometimes with a roof, that's built on the front or the side of a house*) Inf **MO**32, Door stoop—just covers the door, not large.

doorstop n Cf **footstool 3**

Fig: a stooge, dupe

1966 *DARE* (Qu. II34, *If you think somebody is trying to use you to his advantage: "I'm not going to be his ______."*) Inf **MI**18, Doorstop.

door stretcher See **stretcher**

doorweed n Cf **door grass**

=knotweed.

1843 Torrey *Flora NY* 2.152, *Polygonum aviculare* . . Door-weed. **1876** Hobbs *Bot. Hdbk.* 32, Door weed, . . Polygonum persicaria. Polygonum hydropiper. **1903** Small *Flora SE U.S.* 374, *Polygonum* . . Doorweed. **1912** Blatchley *IN Weed Book* 67. **1937** U.S. Forest Serv. *Range Plant Hdbk.* W154, Knotweeds [=*Polygonum* spp], also known as doorweeds, compose a fairly large and widely distributed genus. **1971** Krochmal *Appalachia Med. Plants* 204. **1973** Hitchcock–Cronquist *Flora Pacific NW* 85, *Polygonum* . . Doorweed . . *P. aviculare* . . doorweed.

dooryard n **chiefly NEng, NY**

The grounds closely surrounding a house or, less freq, a farm building.

c1764 in 1850 Woolsey *Hist. Discourse* 54 **CT,** The Freshmen . . are forbidden to wear their hats . . in the front door-yard of the President's or Professor's house. **1835** in 1940 VT Hist. Soc. *Proc.* 8.114 **swNH,** Agreed to pay . . 14 cts. per running cord for chopping and splitting fine the east pile of wood in the door yard. **1856** in 1862 Colt *Went to KS* 22 **NY,** Found the snow very deep . . obliging us to drive through people's door-yards. **1865–66** (1959) Whitman *Drum-Taps & Sequel* 2.3 **NY,** When lilacs last in the door-yard bloom'd,/ And the great star early droop'd in the western sky in the night,/ I mourn'd. **1899** (1912) Green *VA Folk-Speech* 152, *Dooryard*. . . A yard about a door. **1939** *LANE* Map 115 *(Picket Fence)* 3 infs, **wVT,** Door yard fence. **1967–69** *DARE* Tape **MA**6, Just a good-sized dooryard to my father's store from that gate; **NY**209, Why the dooryard is this here whole business around your house, it's your lawn. **1968–69** *DARE* (Qu. M14, *The open area around or next to the barn*) Inf **NY**122, Dooryard; (Qu. V2b, *About a deceiving person, or somebody that you can't trust* . . *"I wouldn't trust him ______."*) Inf **VT**3, Across my own dooryard; (Qu. II22) Inf **WI**52, Clean your own dooryard; (QR p92) Inf **IL**41, [In conv:] For backyard, my grandmother used to tell me to go play in the [doʊ] yard; (QR p93) Inf **NY**213, Dooryard—yard around the house. **1969** *DARE* FW Addit **ceCT,** The dooryard—the grounds right around the house; **swMA,** Dooryard—front yard, the yard between the door and the street, "Could set in our dooryard"; **seNY,** Dooryard—yard around the house.

dooryard call n Also *dooryard visit* **NEng**

See quots.

1959 *VT Hist.* new ser 27.133, *Dooryard call*. . . A neighborly visit carried on outside the house. Occasional. **1968** *DARE* (Qu. II14, . . *A short visit*) Inf **NH**14, A dooryard call. **1975** Gould *ME Lingo* 77, *Dooryard visit*—Or dooryard call. Although still used with automobiles, this meant a buggy visit when the occupants didn't descend to come into the house. It was a neighborly call, in passing.

dooryard, clean one's own See **doorstep, sweep one's own**

dooryard knotweed n

A **knotweed** (here: *Polygonum aviculare*).

1953 Nelson *Plants Rocky Mt. Park* 60, Dooryard knotweed, *Polygonum aviculare.*

dooryard plantain n Also *dooryard weed*

A **plantain** (here: *Plantago major*).

1900 Lyons *Plant Names* 294, *P[lantago] major*. . . Door-yard Plantain. **1912** Blatchley *IN Weed Book* 136, *Plantago major*. . . Common Dooryard Plantain. . . Very common in dooryards, along walks and roadsides and in enriched cultivated fields. **1914** Georgia *Manual Weeds* 391, Dooryard Plantain. . . A very persistent intruder in yards and lawns, no doubt because of the long vitality of its seeds. **1936** Winter *Plants NE* 109, Common or Dooryard Plantain. . . Throughout the state, especially in the east.

dooryard visit See **dooryard call**

dooryard weed See **dooryard plantain**

doos v See **do v A3**

doos n See **do n[1] 4**

doosenwhacker See **doowhacker**

do-over n

In children's games: a round of a game that must or may be repeated; the right to make a second try.

1968 *DARE* (Qu. EE38b, *If the game of tick-tack-toe* . . *comes out so that neither X nor O wins, you call that ______*) Inf **NY**64, A do-over—something that has to be done over because the outcome is unclear. **1975** Ferretti *Gt. Amer. Book Sidewalk Games* 101, [In a strict game of jacks] there are no re-throws or do-overs.

doo-wah-diddy See **diddy-wah-diddy**

doowhacker n Also *doosenwhacker, doowhopper, doowitchet;* for addit varr see quots

=doohickey 1.

1931 *AmSp* 6.258 **KS, NE,** Indefinite names. . . Thingum . . thing-em-bob . . doosenwhacker, doowhacker, doowhackie, doowhopper . . dudenwhacker. **1942** Berrey–Van den Bark *Amer. Slang* 75.4, *Contrivance; indefinite object; "gadget."* . . dowhacker, dowhackie, dowhacky, dowhackus, dowhopper. **1969** *DARE* (Qu. NN12b, *Things that people say to put off a child when he asks, "What are you making?"*) Inf **GA**89, Doowitchet [du'wɪčɪt].

dooz See **do v A3**

doozanberry n Also *doozandazzy* Cf **doohickey 1**

1916 *DN* 4.274 **KS, MA, NE,** *Doozanberry, Mr., Mrs.,* or *Miss.* In occasional use for some one whose name is not known. "There goes that Miss Doozanberry he took to the dance the other night." *Ibid* **NE,** *Doozandazzy*. . . Something the name of which is not readily recalled. "Hand me that doozandazzy."

dooze See **do n[1] 4**

doozer n

1 See quot.

1893 Shands *MS Speech* 71, *Doozer*. . . The hole made in a top by the spindle of another top. In the game of "pecking tops," it is the ambition of every boy to put the biggest *doozers* in the tops of his fellows.

2 See **doozy.**

doozy n Also *doozer, dozy* *esp freq among young and mid-aged speakers*

Something remarkable or outstanding of its kind, a humdinger; a person remarkable for a particular attribute or feature.

1916 *DN* 4.274 **eOH,** *Dozy*. . . Term of praise. "Isn't that fish a dozy?" **1965–70** *DARE* (Qu. LL5, *Something impressively big: "That cabbage is really a ______."*) 32 Infs, **scattered,** Doozy; **CA**15, **NY**109, **WA**22, Doozer; (Qu. B25, . . *A very heavy rain* . . *"It's a regular ______."*) Infs **MI**68, **PA**244, Doozy; (Qu. X20, . . *A black eye*) Infs **NC**37, **VA**5, Doozy; (Qu. X60, . . *A lump that comes up on your head when you get a sharp blow or knock*) Inf **GA**17, Doozy; (Qu. Y4, . . *A very uncomplimentary remark*) Infs **MN**28, **PA**134, Doozy; (Qu. Y11, . . *A very hard* *blow: "You should have seen Bill go down. Joe really hit him a ——."*) Infs **AK**8, **CA**80, **MO**25, **NY**151, **PA**237, **VA**2, Doozy; (Qu. HH9, *A very silly or light-headed person*) Inf **MA**1, A real doozy; (Qu. KK27, *A very lively, active old person: "For his age, he's ——."*) Inf **AR**31, He's a doozy; (Qu. KK41, *Something that is very difficult to do: "I managed to get through with it, but it was ——."*) Infs **IL**30, **NJ**7, **PA**135, A doozy. [Of 50 total Infs, 11 were young, 15 mid-aged, 24 old.]

doozy adj

1911 *DN* 3.543 **NE,** *Doozy*. . . "Sporty," or "flossy."

‡dopa n

1968 *DARE* (Qu. X38, . . *Unusually big or clumsy feet*) Inf **PA**162, Dopa ['dopə].

dopchick See **dabchick**

dope n [Du *doop* sauce]

1 also *doup:* Gravy. *old-fash*

1807 Irving *Salmagundi* 1.200 **NY,** Philo Dripping-pan was remarkable for his predilection to eating, and his love of what the learned dutch call *doup.* **1809** Irving *Hist. NY* 3.3.149 **NY,** The tea table was crowned with a huge earthen dish, well stored with slices of fat pork, fried brown, cut up into mouthfuls, and swimming in doup or gravy. **1904** White *Mountains* 189 **swCA,** The batter is . . poured into the piping hot greased pan, "flipped" when brown on one side, and eaten with larrupy-dope or brown gravy. **1923** *DN* 5.205 **swMO,** *Dope*. . . Meat gravy. **1938** *AmSp* 13.237 **KY,** He [=the great grandfather of the contributor] did not find the breakfast very appetizing, but his hospitable host encouraged him to get his share of the food. 'Don't be *squeamish,* stranger, don't be squeamish! *Wallop your dodger in the dope.*' The dodger was corn dodger and the dope was sowbelly gravy. **1950** *WELS (Gravy)* 1 Inf **cwWI,** Dope. **1968** *DARE* (Qu. H37, . . *Gravy*) Inf **IN**19, Dope. [Inf old]

2 A dessert topping, usu for pudding or ice cream; rarely, an ice cream sundae. **chiefly OH** See Map *old-fash*

1929 in 1960 Wentworth–Flexner *Slang* 156, "All dopes [*DAS:* sauce put over ice cream] 5 cents extra." Sign in ice cream fountain. **1949** *PADS* 11.6 **cOH,** *Dope*. . . A sundae. **c1960** *Wilson Coll.* **csKY,** *Dope*. . . Sweet sauce to pour over cakes or puddings. **1965–70** *DARE* (Qu. H66b, *The sweet liquid that you pour over ice cream*) 18 Infs, **chiefly OH,** Dope; (Qu. H66a, *The sweet liquid that you pour over a pudding*) Infs **IL**61, **OH**24, Dope. [18 of 19 total Infs old]

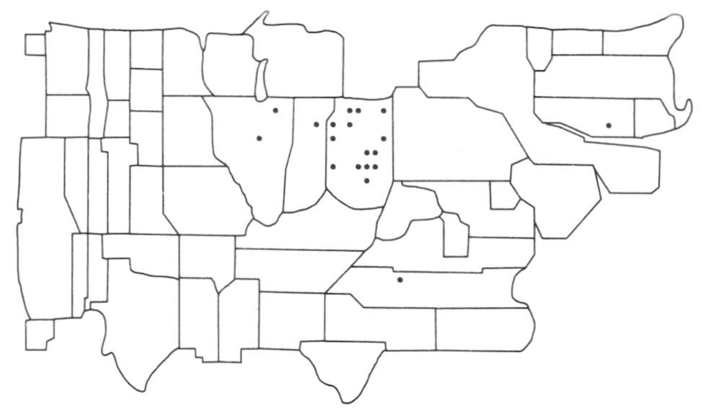

•dope n 2 (Qq. H66a, b)

3 Any medicine, vaccine, anesthetic, or stimulant; see quots. [Prob by ext from *dope* opium]

1902 *DN* 2.233 **sIL,** *Dope*. . . Facetiously for medicine. **1915** Poole *Harbor* 60 **NYC,** Joe's father vaccinated about a score of children that week. The "dope" he used was mailed to him by a drug firm in Chicago. **1930** Faulkner *As I Lay Dying* 191 **MS,** "Is it medicine you want?" "That's it," she said. . . I thought maybe her ma or somebody had sent her in for some of this female dope and she was ashamed to ask for it. **1946** *AmSp* 21.32 **ceTX** [College slang], *Dope*. . . Coffee. **1960** Hall *Smoky Mt. Folks* 52 **eTN, wNC,** For times when a mild anesthetic was desired, they recommended "strong, hot, creamy coffee for dope." **1961** Adams *Old-Time Cowhand* 259, They [="doctors" or "medicine men"] jumped 'bout nimble as a flea with their daubs and pot of tar, or other disinfectin' dope to smear the wounds of the operation. **1966–69** *DARE* Tape **CA**156, He [=a veterinarian] shoots her [=a cow with milk fever] full of dope; **MS**61, When you bore that hole in there [=in a horse's hoof], it don't go up any further. You put a dope in there an' pack it. . . It's iodine an' . . hot tar; **MA**28, [FW:] What do you call dope? [Inf:] Well this is it, it ranges from . . all kinds of hallucination drugs to Robitussin . . nasal spray. **1967** *DARE* FW Addit **LA**11, *Dope*—A laxative or Bayer's [=aspirin] etc. "My cold is worser, I must take some dope."

4 A carbonated beverage, usu one flavored with cola. [Prob from **3** above, in allusion to the supposed "tonic" effects of some early soft drinks; cf **tonic**] **chiefly S Atl, esp SC** See Map Cf **coca-cola, cold drink**

1915 *Printer's Ink* 23 Sept 46/2, Finally there is the problem with which we are immediately concerned, the propensity of a large proportion of those who regularly drink Coca-Cola to call for their favorite drink as "dope" or "coke" or "koke." **1918** *DN* 5.18 **NC,** *Dope,* coco-cola. Slang. **1929** Wolfe *Look Homeward* 271 **NC,** Drink Coca Cola. They say he stole the formula from old mountain woman. $50,000,000 now. Rats in the vats. Dope at Wood's better. Too weak here. *Ibid* 474, Make it a dope. **1931** Caldwell *Amer. Earth* 20 **GA,** Everybody likes Coca-Cola. There is nothing better to drink on a hot day, if the dopes are nice and cool. **1933** Rawlings *South Moon* 230 **nFL,** "You want a dope?" She nodded. He . . fished in his pocket for a dime for the two bottles of Coca Cola. **1942** Berrey–Van den Bark *Amer. Slang* 821.2, *Soda Fountain.* Dope shop. **1963** *AmSp* 38.154 **GA, SC, NC, VA,** Drugstores or soda shops are likely to be called *dope shops* by native speakers. *Ibid,* There is . . a distinct possibility that the slang term *coke* (cocaine) became fused at this time [c1910] with the abbreviated copyrighted trade name *Coke* (Coca-Cola), and this fusion led to the application of *dope* to Coca-Cola in the Southeast. Thereafter, of course, *dope* came to mean any cola or carbonated beverage. **1965–70** *DARE* (Qu. H78, *Ordinary soft drinks, usually carbonated*) 25 Infs, **chiefly SC, sAppalachians,** Dope; **SC**43, Cold dope; **GA**17, 19, **NC**55, Dopes. **1966–68** *DARE* FW Addit **SC,** *Dope* is any brand of soft drink, according to some. Others say dope is a Coke only; **NC,** Dope—soda pop; **nGA** (as of c1930), Dope and cherry [=a cherry coke]. **1983** *MJLF* 9.1.38 **ceKY,** *Dope* . . soft drinks.

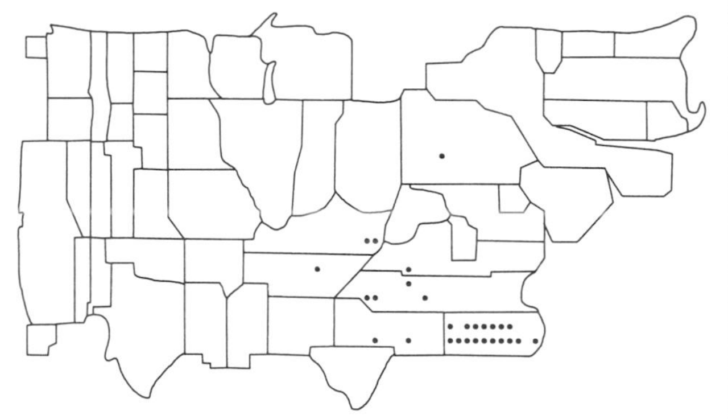

•dope n 4 + varr (Qu. H78)

5 Any of various sticky or thick, semi-liquid substances or mixtures; see quots.

1893 *KS Univ. Qrly.* 1.138 **KS,** *Dope:* paste. **1901** Ade *40 Modern Fables* 188 **IN,** Give me some perfumed Dope that will restore a Peaches and Cream Complexion. **1902** *DN* 2.233 **sIL,** *Dope*. . . Any kind of lubricator, emulsion, or salve. **1905** *DN* 3.100 **nwAR,** *(Wagon-) dope*. . . Axle-grease. **1923** *DN* 5.205 **swMO,** *Dope*. . . Axle grease. **1935** *AmSp* 10.76 **nwWY,** *Dope.* A mixture of sawdust and kerosene used in building fires. **1939** in 1953 Botkin–Harlow *Treas. Railroad Folkl.* 329, One of the least desirable jobs about the freight yard is that of the "dope pullers" who extract "dope" (woolen waste soaked with grease, which is packed inside the journal boxes to lubricate the wheels). **1940** Faulkner *Hamlet* 311 **MS,** They looked at his ear. "Happen to any man careless around a horse. Put a little axle-dope on it and you wont notice it tomorrow though." **1947** Dalrymple *Panfish* 161 (*DA,* at *fly dope*), Take this little bottle of fly dope, which is really only a mixture of paraffin dissolved in energine, and waterproof your fly with it. **1967–68** *DARE* (Qu. Y40b, . . *Sticky stuff: "I've got to wash my hands. They're all covered with ——."*) Inf **MO**4, Dope; (Qu. KK38, *To put preparations on the hair to hold it close to the head and make it shiny: "I wish he wouldn't —— his hair down so!"*) Inf **CO**47, Put so much dope on; **LA**20, Put that dope in his hair; **NY**73, Put dope on.

6 A pesticide, herbicide, or insect repellent. Cf **dope n 3**

1897 *Outing* 30.377/1, One thing must not be forgotten, which is the "fly dope," or preventive against the attacks of insects. **1903** White *Forest* 109 **MI,** Next in order come the various "dopes." . . From the stickiest, blackest pastes to the silkiest, suavest oils they range. **1948** *Chicago Tribune* (IL) 11 July 7/1, New mosquito dopes are being tested by fishermen. . . Most of these new dopes (developed as a result of war discoveries) are sure to repel denizens of the skeeter and black fly world. **1965–67** *DARE* FW Addit **ME,** Fly dope—anything put on skin, clothing, etc. to keep insects away—used throughout Maine; **neNY,** Fly dope—anti-fly oil; various brand names, always local products; **cnNY,** Fly dope—any spray or smelly stuff to keep off flies. **1967–69** *DARE* Tape **IA**12, He's got an acre up there that he put some kind a dope on an' got rid of the weeds; **IL**78, After they [=farm laborers] quit at six o'clock in the afternoon, why, if we needed to put out another tank of dope, why they was always willing to do it; **IN**45, Now there's a . . type that you can pour in the top of the [tobacco] plant and let it go all the way around the plant to the . . ground, and it lodges above each leaf, see, and that's where the sucker would come out. Now you can use that type of dope or . . there's another type that you can have sprayed on commercially.

7 See quot. [Cf *dope* information]

1906 *DN* 3.134 **nwAR,** *Dope*. . . Cajolery; optimistic talk; humbug. "He's just givin' you dope." "He gave him some dope about the investment."

8 Stuff; something referred to unspecifically.

1909 *DN* 3.395 **nwAR,** *Dope*. . . Not only any kind of drug but nearly anything else. "Swell dope is anything and everything mental, oratorical, musical, artistic, or gastronomic that the speaker approves of." **1915** *DN* 4.225 **wTX,** *Dope*. . . Contemptuous name for any article, as "Don't buy any of the dope he's selling."

9 In railroading: see quots. [Ext of *dope* information]

1930 *RR Man's Mag.* June 470, *Dope*—Orders; official instructions. **1938** Beebe *High Iron* 220 [Railroad terms], *Dope:* Official orders or instructions; company business. **1976** Gould *Blackie's RR Hdbk.* 7, *The Dope:* Official orders and instructions.

10 See **dope stick.**

dope v

1 To lubricate; to smear or daub (with a greasy or viscous liquid); hence n *doper* [**dope n 5**]

1868 *Putnam's Mag.* 2.363/2 **eCA,** With their snow-shoes thoroughly "doped," the crowd resort to some suitable place for the contest, which begins with a grand dash, all participating. **1902** *DN* 2.233 **sIL,** *Dope*. . . To smear, or lubricate. . . To put salve on a wound. **1906** *DN* 3.117 **sIN,** *Dope*. . . To use a liquid for almost any purpose, as to oil a wagon. . . "He doped the wagon wheels." **1907** *DN* 3.222 **nwAR, sIL,** *Dope*. . . To smear or lubricate. **1935** Davis *Honey* 12 **OR,** The supper was all everyday victuals. . . There was . . a salad of lettuce whittled into shoestrings, wilted in hot water, and doped with vinegar and bacon grease. **1950** *WELS* 1 Inf, **ceWI,** I wish he wouldn't dope his hair so! **1968** *AmSp* 43.286 [Railroad vocab], *Doper.* One who packs and lubricates car journal boxes. **1970** *DARE* Tape **CA**196, My dad used to make skis . . plane 'em out, then soak 'em in hot water, put 'em in the bender. Then they'd all get together and dope 'em . . put tar and pitch on 'em so they'd slide on the snow.

2 To treat (a person, animal, or disease) with medicine; to take a medicine or drug; hence v phr *dope up on* to dose oneself with; vbl n *doping.* [**dope n 3**] Cf **doctor v 1, 2**

1891 Farmer–Henley *Slang* 2.309, *Dope*. . . (American).—To drug with tobacco. Also *doping* = the practice. **1902** *DN* 2.233 **sIL,** *Dope*. . . With reflexive pronoun, as 'to dope yersef,' to take medicine in excessive quantities. **1906** *DN* 3.117 **sIN,** *Dope*. . . To take medicine. . . "He's dopin' for the chills." *Ibid* 134 **nwAR,** *Dope*. . . To dose, take medicine. "I just doped up on quinine." **1906** in 1942 Asher–Heal *Send No Money* 95, You would like to know just where you are at before you "dope" that kind of stock with a strange mixture. **1923** *DN* 5.205 **swMO,** *Dope*. . . To take medicine. "Dope yourse'f 'ith quinine." **1931** *K.C. Times* 16 Sep. *(DA),* Chief Getzem of Ore worked late Saturday evening doping his hens with louse powder. **1988** *DARE* File **csWI** (as of 1940s), Dope your cold with VapoRub.

3 To drink to excess; hence ppl adj *doped* drunk. Cf **dopey 3**

1965–66 *DARE* (Qu. DD11, *When somebody gives up drinking: "I hear he ______."*) Inf **GA**1, Quit doping; (Qu. DD15, *A person who is thoroughly drunk*) Inf **OK**1, Doped, half-doped.

4 See quot.

1902 *DN* 2.233 **sIL,** *Dope*. . . Rarely, to dump.

5 usu with *out:* To predict the winner of a contest on the basis of previous performance; to figure out, discover, usu by means of concentrated thought; hence vbl n *doping.* **chiefly Nth**

1902 (1906) Porter *4 Million* 163 **NYC,** All the same, I believe it was the hand of Fate that doped out the way for me to find her. **1914** Davis *With the Allies* 10 **NYC,** We would study the morning papers and . . from them try to dope out the winners. **1916** *Amer. Mag.* May 26/1, The system of "doping" is based entirely upon [baseball players'] averages and comparisons. **1922** *DN* 5.141 **sePA,** *Dope out*. . . To master a lesson or assignment by concentrated mental effort. "I doped that all out myself! Nancy didn't help me a bit." **1922** *Short Stories* Feb. 102/2 *(OEDS),* 'How'd you dope it out, Kid?' asked one. 'Tell us how you could do such good detective work.' **1926** Black *You Can't Win* 367 **cwCA,** I had all the criminal lawyers in San Francisco doped out like race horses by this time, and my choice was Sam Newburgh. **1968–69** *DARE* (Qu. JJ36, *To work out a plan, especially a secret plan: "Mary knows more about that, you and she can ______ together."*) Infs **NY**54, **RI**1, **WI**30, Dope it out.

6 with *off:* To be inattentive to one's business; to "goof off."

1963 Burroughs *Head-First* 85 **CO,** [Of a small boy who has failed to evoke the Devil by the use of profanity:] At last, having decided that either the Devil was doping off or that I had been misinformed, I gave it up. **1967** *DARE* (Qu. A11, *When somebody takes too long about coming to a decision, you might say, "I wish he'd quit ______."*) Inf **NC**46, Doping off.

doped ppl adj See **dope v 3**

doped up ppl adj phr Cf *souped up*

1967 *DARE* (Qu. N6, *An old car that has been fixed up to make it go fast or make a lot of noise*) Inf **SC**55, Doped up.

dope off See **dope v 6**

dope out See **dope v 5**

doper n

1 One who smokes (cigarettes) excessively. [Transf from *doper* one who uses narcotics] Cf **dope stick**

1968 *DARE* (Qu. DD9a, . . *A person who smokes a great deal? "He's a ______."*) Inf **IN**18, Cigarette doper.

2 See **dope v 1.**

dope stick n Also *dope* [*dope* a narcotic drug] Cf **doper**

A cigarette.

1904 *NY Eve. Jrl.* (NY) 1 Jul (10 o'clock ed) 10 *(Zwilling Coll.),* [In column "The Old Sport On Fitz":] The old sport took another drag on the dope stick and faded away in the darkness. **1968–69** *DARE* (Qu. DD6b, . . *Cigarettes*) Infs **IN**35, **MD**36, **RI**17, Dope stick; **PA**164, Dope.

dopey adj Also sp *dopy*

1 Listless, sluggish; slightly ill, under the weather. **chiefly Nth, N Midl**

1896 *Sun* (N.Y.) Dec. *(OEDS),* A man who acts as if under the influence of the poppy drug is said to be dopy. **1900** Ade *More Fables* 179 **Chicago IL,** A Young Man with Hair who played the 'Cello. He was so wrapped up in his Art that he acted Dopey most of the time. **1965–70** *DARE* (Qu. BB5, *A general feeling of discomfort or illness that isn't any one place in particular*) Infs **MA**51, **NY**8, Dopey; **MN**37, Dopey feeling; **MN**15, Feel dopey; (Qu. BB13, . . *Chills and fever*) Inf **MN**10, Dopey; (Qu. BB39, *On a day when you don't feel just right, though not actually sick, you might say, "I'll be all right tomorrow—I'm just feeling ______ today."*) Infs **CA**134, **IN**28, **NY**52, **OH**2, **WI**76, Dopey; (Qu. BB41, *Not seriously ill, but sick enough to be in bed: "He's been ______ for a week."*) Inf **NY**27, Dopey; (Qu. GG34a, . . *Depressed or in a gloomy mood*) Inf **NY**232, Dopey; (Qu. KK30, *Feeling slowed up or without energy: "I certainly feel ______."*) Infs **IN**80, **MD**17, **MN**10, **MO**12, **NY**2, **WA**9, 16, Dopey.

2 Dull-witted, stupid. **scattered, but chiefly Nth, N Midl** See Map on p. 142

1896 *Cin. Enquirer* 2 Aug. 2/1 *(DA),* There is an impression of truth to the rather 'dopy' proposition that makes it worthy of newspaper space. **1948** *Sat. Eve. Post* 14 Aug 80/4 **sCA,** If he wasn't so dopey he could've got the whole hundred dollars out of Mr. McCallum. **1965–70** *DARE* (Qu. HH13, . . *Not very alert or not aware of things: "He's certainly ______."*) 37 Infs, **chiefly Nth, N Midl,** Dopey; (Qu. HH3, *A dull and stupid person*) Infs **CT**30, **MN**3, **MO**10, **NJ**10, **NV**4, **NY**22, **PA**122, Dopey; (Qu. HH5, *Someone who is queer but harmless*) Inf **NY**22, Dopey.

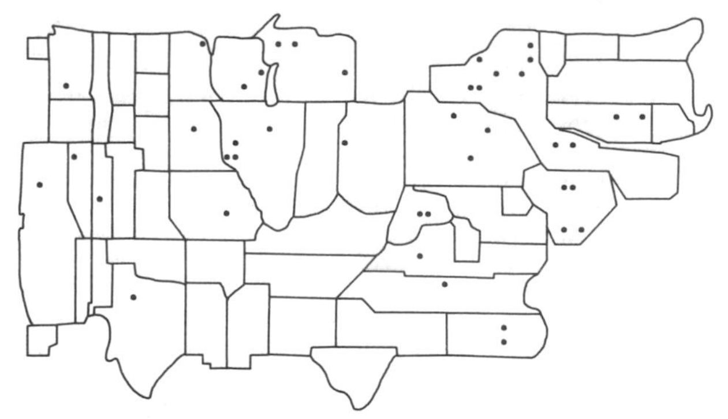

•dopey 2 (Qq. HH13, HH3, HH5)

3 Drunk, inebriated. Cf **dope v 3**

1967–68 *DARE* (Qu. DD13, *When a drinker is just beginning to show the effects of the liquor, you say he's* _____) Inf **MI**44A, 47, Getting dopey; (Qu. DD14, *When a person is partly drunk, "He's* _____.*"*) Inf **IL**29, Dopey.

doping vbl n

1 The act of bewitching or casting a spell on.

1966 *DARE* (Qu. CC14, *Words or expressions used here, where one person supposedly casts a spell over another*) Inf **SC**10, A doping.

2 See **dope v 5.**

doppel n Also *dopper* [Cf Ger *Tölpel*] **PaGer area** Cf **doppich, doppes(s)**

A clumsy, awkward person.

1914 *DN* 4.158 **PA,** *Dopper*. . . A clumsy person. **1978** *DARE* File **sePA,** He's such a doppel [=an awkward person].

dopper n[1] [Obs *dop* to dive]

1 =**bufflehead 2.**

1852 in 1876 *Forest & Stream* 9 Nov 212/3 **MA,** List of Gunner's Names for Birds and Wild Fowl obtained in Plymouth Bay, Mass.: . . *Bucephala albeola*. Dipper or dopper. **1917** (1923) *Birds Amer.* 1.140, *Buffle-head—Charitonetta albeola* . . Dopper. **1944** Hausman *Amer. Birds* 511/1, Dopper—see Buffle-head; see also Duck, Ruddy.

2 =**ruddy duck.**

1888 Trumbull *Names of Birds* 110, Ruddy Duck. . . At Provincetown, Mass., . . Dopper. **1917** (1923) *Birds Amer.* 1.152, *Ruddy Duck—Erismatura jamaicensis*. . . Dopper. **1925** (1928) Forbush *Birds MA* 1.280, *Erismatura jamaicensis* . . Ruddy Duck. . . Dopper. **1944** [see **1** above].

dopper n[2] See **doppel**

doppes(s) n [Perh var of Yiddish *tipesh* a fool]

See quots.

1968 Rosten *Yiddish* 100 **NYC** [Jewish], *Doppess*—Pronounced dop-*pess,* to rhyme with "mop-less." Not Hebrew but Ameridish: a local coinage of the garment center in New York. Useless but commiserating bystander; ineffectual observer who is of little help. . . *Doppess* . . a character type known in all cultures: the useless observer who, in a crisis, does nothing more than offer obligatory sympathy. **1971** *AmSp* 46.300 **Los Angeles CA** [Yiddish words in English], Doppes . . blockhead, slob.

doppich adj Also *dappi, dappich, dobbich, dop(p)lich, doppick, doppling, doppy* [Cf Ger *täppisch*] **chiefly PaGer area** Cf **doppel**

Clumsy, awkward.

1914 *DN* 4.158 **PA,** *Dopper*. . . A clumsy person. (From *doppick* ? adj.) **1939** Aurand *Quaint Idioms* 12 [PaGer], You are so darn *dobbich* (or "doplich;" awkward). Du bisht so dobbich. **1948** Mencken *Amer. Lang. Suppl. 2* 202 **PA,** *Doppich*. Awkward. **1967–70** *DARE* (Qu. J2) Inf **PA**9, Dopplich [dɑplɪk] = clumsy; (Qu. HH21, *A very awkward, clumsy person*) Inf **IL**46, FW: I mentioned that my Pennsylvania Dutch grandmother used to say I was *dopplich* (uncoordinated); the informant and his wife both said they knew the word as *doppling* ['dɑplɪŋ]; to the wife it also meant just uncoordinated, but to the informant it connotes simple-minded, even senile; **IN**68, [dɑpəg]; **PA**11, Dopplich [dɑplɪk]; **PA**42, 138, Doppy ['dɑpi]; **PA**202, Doppich ['dɑpɪk]—German word; **PA**242, Dappich ['dæpik]—Pennsylvania Dutch. **1967** *DARE* FW Addit **PA,** *Doppich,* ['dɑpɪš], [dɑpɪk], and *dopplich,* meaning clumsy, are used interchangeably in the "Dutch area" of Pennsylvania. **1968** *Helen Adolf Festschrift* 35 **cePA,** The adjective *dappi* (Pennsylvania German *dappe*) meaning 'clumsy,' is . . used occasionally; for example, "Don't be so dappi on your feet." **1985** *DARE* File **ceOH,** Doppy—this, with a short o, is applied to anyone who is clumsy or awkward in the manner of an adolescent boy. . . "You are the doppiest person I've ever seen."

do pray See **do v C1e**

do pray tell See **do tell**

dopy See **dopey**

dorado n Also *dourade* [Span "gilded"]

=**dolphin 1.**

1896 U.S. Natl. Museum *Bulletin* 47.952, *Coryphaena hippurus* . . (Common Dolphin; Dorado; dourade.) **1946** LaMonte *N. Amer. Game Fishes* 42, *Dolphin—Coryphaena hippurus*. . . Names: Dorado. **1947** Caine *Salt Water* 18, It [=*Coryphaena hippurus*] is also known as dorado, dourade, and, in Hawaii, as mahimahi. **1960** Amer. Fisheries Soc. *List Fishes* 56, Dorado—see dolphin [=*Coryphaena* spp].

do-rag n [**do** n[1] **3**] *among Black speakers* Cf **conk** n[3] **1, head rag, stocking cap**

See quot 1977.

1970 *Current Slang* 5.2.7 [Black], *Do-rag*. . . A silk scarf used to protect a "do". **1971** Roberts *Third Ear* np [Black], *Do rag* . . a rag or handkerchief worn on the head to protect one's "do" (processed hair). **1972** Claerbaut *Black Jargon* 63, *Do-rag* . . a head scarf often worn over a processed hairdo. **1977** Smitherman *Talkin* 65 [Black], Brothers, like Sisters, had to avoid water to keep their do's [=artificially straightened hair] from going back, and they wore a scarf or *stocking cap* . . to keep the waves in place during sleep. The scarf was called a *do-rag*.

do-ray-me See **do-re-mi**

dorbug n Also sp *doorbug;* pronc-sp **chiefly NEng** *dawbug* [*OED dor, dorr* a700 →, applied alone or in combs to various large buzzing insects]

A **June beetle.**

1812 *Thomas' MA Spy or Worcester Gaz.* (MA) 1 July 4/1, At gentle hour of evening grey,/ A Daw bug o'er thy neck I'd creep. [Footnote:] *Better known by this name to the good people of New England than to* Linnaeus *or* Buffon. **1833** Greene *Life Dr. Dodimus* 1.86 **NEng,** It's a dorbug! **1837** *Harvardiana* 361 iii (1912 Thornton *Amer. Gloss.*), Sonnet to a dawbug. **1837** *S. Lit. Messenger* 3.500, An enormous door-bug or hedge chafer . . bounced . . into the room. **1843** *Lowell Offering* 3.183, I helped the daw-bug dig his hole,/ And burrowed for the poor blind mole. **1882** (1903) Treat *Injurious Insects* 73, Comparatively few are aware that the frequent White Grub and the familiar May-bug, or June-bug, or Dor-bug, are different forms of the same insect. **1949** Guthrie *Way West* 61 **MO,** Damn the dor-bugs. Damn distance. Damn gullies, streams, trees. Keep going. Three cheers for Oregon. **1975** *DARE* File **cnMA** (as of c1915), We called them June bugs or *dawbugs*—with good Massachusetts pronunciation.

doré See **dory** n[1] **1**

‡**do-reenus** n [Perh var of **do-re-mi 2**]

1967 *DARE* (Qu. U19a, . . *Money in general: "He's certainly got the* _____.*"*) Inf **TX**12, Do-reenus [do'rinəs].

do-re-mi n Also sp *do-ray-me* [The first three notes of the major scale]

1 A method of sight-singing using seven syllables (instead of four) to denote the tones of a scale. Cf **buckwheat note, fasola**

1933 Jackson *White Spirituals* 317, [Heading:] Fasola Offspring, The Dorayme Folk. *Ibid* 319, He saw clearly that rural America was not going to allow anyone to take away its beloved patent notes, and that if the do-re-mi manner were to gain ground, it would have to do so while holding to the shape-note benefits.

2 Money. [Punning extension of *dough* money] **chiefly Inland Nth, N Midl**

1933 *Sat. Review (DAS),* Get the rubber band off the do-re-mi. **1948** Manfred *Chokecherry* 105 **nwIA,** "Kaes ain't paid me for my last work there." "Well, get after him. He's got the do-re-mi." **1954** *Harder Coll.* **cwTN,** *Do-ray-me.* Money. **c1960** *Wilson Coll.* **csKY,** *Do-ray-me*. . . Humorous name for money. **1965–70** *DARE* (Qu. U19a, . . *Money in general: "He's certainly got the* _____.*"*) 28 Infs, chiefly Inland Nth, N Midl, Do-re-mi; NY70, Do-re-mi-fa-sol-la-ti-do; (Qu. U37, . . *Somebody who has plenty of money*) Inf **NY**233, In the do-re-mi.

dorey See **dory** n^{2}

dorg See **dog** n

do-right boy n Also *do-right* **TX** *joc*

A policeman, spec a highway patrol officer.

1967–70 *DARE* (Qu. N4, *A police vehicle with a red, blue, or yellow flashing light on top*) Inf **TX**72, The do-right boys [FW: that is, the police in the car]; (Qu. V9, . . *Nicknames . . for a policeman*) Inf **TX**37, His name is Wright and they call him 'do-right'; **TX**89, The do-right boys [FW: this refers to the highway patrol].

dormant window n [*OED dormant* a. A. 5 1651–1823] *arch*

1823 Cooper *Pioneers* 1.136 **NY,** The dormant windows in the roof, the paint, the window-shutters, and cheerful fire that shone through the open door, gave it [=the inn] an air of comfort. **1899** (1912) Green *VA Folk-Speech* 152, *Dormant window*. . . Window in a slanting roof.

dormer n

1 A meat and rice dish; see quots.

1896 *Daily News Cook Book* 234 **cWI,** *Dormers*—One pound of cold boiled mutton . . , one cup of boiled rice, . . salt, . . pepper, one egg and a little water . . chip the meat fine, add the rice and seasoning, roll into sausages, cover with egg and bread crumbs, fry in hot lard a nice brown. **1963** Adamson *Household Hints* 199 **NEng** (as of late 1800s), *Dormers*—Chop ½ lb. of cold lamb, 2 oz. of beef suet, and 3 oz. of boiled rice. Pepper and salt to taste. Roll into sausage shapes, dip them into a beaten egg, roll them in bread crumbs, and fry.

‡2 A **cupola B1.**

1968–69 *DARE* (Qu. M2, . . *The small wooden construction on top of a barn with slats for ventilation*) Inf **CA**105, Dormer; **GA**80, Dormer—a little house-like thing on top of the roof.

dormeur n [Fr "sleeper, sluggard"] **esp LA**

1 **=tripletail.**

1898 U.S. Natl. Museum *Bulletin* 47.1235, *Lobotes surinamensis* . . Dormeur. **1933** LA Dept. of Conserv. *Fishes* 206, The Tripletail, *Lobotes surinamensis* . . elsewhere . . has been called Flasher, Dormeur, . . and Black Grunt.

2 **=dowitcher.**

1911 *Forest & Stream* 77.174 **LA,** *Macrorhamphus griseus scolopaceus.* Dormeur. **1916** *Times-Picayune* (New Orleans LA) 2 Apr 5/8, *Long-billed dowitcher*. . . While possessing a very long bill like a snipe, this bird is easily distinguished by its reddish-brown plumage sprinkled with black. In winter, when here in great numbers, the "Dormeur" as it is known in the lowlands, is gray above and white below. **1923** U.S. Dept. Ag. *Misc. Circular* 13.51, *Dowitcher (Limnodromus griseus)*. . . *In local use* . . dormeur . . (La.) **1962** Imhof *AL Birds* 251, *Short-billed Dowitcher—Limnodromus griseus*. . . Other Names: . . Dormeur.

dormidera n [Span "soporiferous, narcotic"]

1 **=California poppy.**

1897 Parsons *Wild Flowers CA* 114, "California poppy," . . "dormidera." **1898** *Out West Mag.* Dec 49, The Dormidera, or wild "poppy" of California. **1911** Jepson *Flora CA* 176, *E[scholtzia] californica*. . . On account of its gorgeous beauty it has been favored with an exceptional number of . . names . . such as . . "Dormidera." **1915** (1926) Armstrong-Thornber *Western Wild Flowers* 164, It [=California poppy] is the State flower of California and has many . . names, such as . . Domidera [sic].

2 A garden poppy (*Papaver* spp).

1914 Saunders *With Flowers in CA* 191, A bed of poppies—*dormideras* . . —were wide awake in the sun.

dornel feather n

=dragonfly.

1949 *AmSp* 24.108 **ceSC,** *Dornel feathers*. . . Dragonflies.

dornful adv [Perh blend of *doleful* + *mournful,* but cf *OED dernful* "*Obs*. . . Mournful, dreary."]

Mournful.

1937 in 1977 *Amer. Slave Suppl. 1* 1.41 **AL,** One ob de songs dey usta to sing at de funerals wuz: 'Hark! from de tune ob dornful sorrow.'

dornick n Also sp *darnic(k), dornic,* pronc-spp *donic, donnick(er), donoch, don(n)ock* [Ir *dornōg* a small stone]

1 A stone or rock, spec:

a A stone small enough to be thrown. **formerly more widespread; now esp N Cent, PA** See Map Cf **doney** n^{1} **1**

1840 *Daily Pennant* (St. Louis MO) 18 June 2/4, That ar man he tooks up a dornick and made a heap of cavortins. **1853** Hammett *Stray Yankee in TX* 117, In Arkansas, however the term *donoch* usurps the place of either rock or stone. **1859** (1968) Bartlett *Americanisms* 127, *Donock.* A stone; a term almost peculiar to Arkansas, though used more or less throughout the South. **1869** Twain *Innocents* 385 **West,** I have found him [=a fellow passenger from the Far West] breaking a stone in two, and labeling half of it "Chunk busted from the pulpit of Demosthenes," and the other half "Darnick from the Tomb of Abelard and Heloise." **1897** [see **b** below]. **1906** *DN* 3.117 **sIN,** *Donnick*. . . A pebble; brickbat. **1913** (1980) Hardy *OH Schoolmistress* 101 (as of c1850), *Donnick* was used as the name of a small cobblestone that one might pick up on the road or in the field. . . I am told that a similar word, *darnic,* with the same meaning was used further west. **1923** *DN* 5.205 **swMO,** *Darnick*. . . Stone. **1927** *AmSp* 2.276 **CA,** *Dornick*—Stone. *Ibid* 353 **WV,** *Dornick* . . a stone. "They threw dornicks at us." **1951** West *Witch Diggers* 35 **IN,** Christie got out a big iron spoon and hacked away at the banana ice-cream, now frozen harder than a donnicker. **1953** *AmSp* 28.248 **csPA,** *Dornick, darnick*. . . A stone, not too big to throw. Popular speech. 'He threw a dornick through Paley Weaverling's window.' **1953** Randolph *Down in Holler* 240 **Ozarks,** *Donnick*. . . A stone, usually one small enough to be thrown or used as a weapon. **1965–70** *DARE* (Qu. C24a, *A small piece of stone that you could easily throw*) Infs **CA**36, **IA**8, **IN**30, 58, 71, **MI**91, **OH**15, **PA**67, 188, Dornick; (Qu. C25, . . *Kinds of stone . . about so big [Show size of a person's head], smooth and hard*) Infs **IL**126, **MI**112, **NY**146, **OH**61, 66, **PA**74, Dornick.

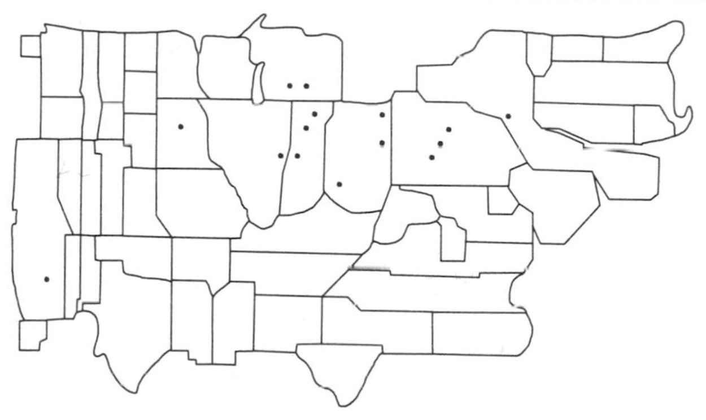

•dornick 1a (Qq. C24a, C25)

b By ext: a game played with such a rock; **=duck on a rock.**

1897 *KS Univ. Qrly.* (ser B) 6.52 **KS, NY, MI,** *Dornics* or *Donics:* a game with small stones, also the stones themselves; . . equivalent to 'duck-off', 'duck-on-a-rock.'

c A large boulder or slab.

1894 *DN* 1.341 **wCT,** *Donnock* [dɑnək]: a large stone or boulder imbedded in the ground, but not a "tight stone" or ledge. **1944** *Life* 22 May 110 **KY, WV,** [Caption:] *"Dornick" gravestone* of Cal McCoy, killed by Hatfields at the time of the "house-burning scrape." Dornicks are natural slabs of stone which are set up without aid of a professional stonecutter. **1967–69** *DARE* (Qu. C22, *A piece of stone too big for one person to move easily*) Infs **IA**8, **IN**22, **MA**42, **OR**14, **WI**19, Dornick.

‡2 See quot.

1903 *DN* 2.312 **seMO,** *Donnick* or *dornick*. . . A small mound or tussock.

do round See **do around**

dort v [Scots; cf *EDD, SND*] Cf **dorts**

1940 *AmSp* 15.46 **sAppalachians, Ozarks,** *Dort,* to skulk [sic for *sulk*].

dorter See **daughter**

dorts n pl [Scots] Cf **dort**

Ill humor, sulks.

1928 Chapman *Happy Mt.* 291 **seTN,** Micajah was smit with the dorts and answered him: "No! Hit's more 'n likely there ain't nothing in it I don't know already."

dory n^{1} [Fr *doré* gilded]

1 also *doré:* **=walleye.**

1877 U.S. Natl. Museum *Bulletin* 10.46, *Stizostethium (sic) vitreum* . . Wall-eyed Pike . . "Dory" . . Doré. **1902** Jordan–Evermann *Amer. Fishes* 361, In different parts of its range it is known by different names. Among the Great Lakes it is called the wall-eyed pike . . doré or dory . . and pickerel. **1933** LA Dept. of Conserv. *Fishes* 367, A member of the True Perch Family . . , the Walleye [=*Stizostedion vitreum*], like so many of our fishes, has come to bear a variety of often meaningless, common names. They are: Walleye, . . Dory, . . and River Trout. **1949** Caine *N. Amer. Sport Fish* 115, In this country, most of its names inaccurately align it [=walleye] with the pike family. . . The most common are: Blue Pike—Dore—Dory— . . Yellow Pikeperch. **1974** WI Univ. *Fish Lake MI* 26, *Walleye—Stizostedion vitreum*. . . common names: walleye pike, . . doré.

2 =sauger.

1983 Becker *Fishes WI* 880, *Sauger*— . . Other common names: eastern sauger . . dory, . . pickering, jackfish, jack salmon.

3 =round pompano.

1906 NJ State Museum *Annual Rept. for 1905* 262, *Trachinotus falcatus* . . Spinous Dory. Round Pampano.

dory n[2] Also sp *dorey* [Perh Miskito *dôri, dûri* dugout] **chiefly NAtl** See Map

A flat-bottomed boat with wide flaring sides, noted for its stability in the seas.

1709 (1967) Lawson *New Voyage* 20, The *French* were very officious in assisting with their small Dories, to pass over these Waters. **1832** *Boston Eve. Transcript* (MA) 10 May 2/1, Witelham, one of the crew of the sch[oone]r Hero, . . left that vessel, as usual, with fishermen, in a small "dorey" to fish on Wednesday afternoon last. **1851** (1857) Hawthorne *Twice-Told* 2.91 **MA,** I launched my dory, my little flat bottomed skiff. **1882** Godfrey *Is. Nantucket* 147, The fishermen put off from the shore in little boats called dories,—mere egg-shells, but probably as safe surf boats as any in the world. **1904** Day *Kin o' Ktaadn* 150 **ME,** Sh'd say by the gait it's Jim Clintock in his dory. **1911** (1912) Lincoln *Cap'n Warren* 231 **seMA,** No Corot paintin's nor five thousand dollar tintypes of dory codders. **1965–70** *DARE* (Qu. O1, . . *A small rowboat, not big enough to hold more than two people*) 15 Infs, **chiefly N Atl,** Dory; (Qu. O10, . . *Other kinds of boats*) 9 Infs, **chiefly N Atl,** Dories; (Qu. O2, . . *An old, clumsy boat*) Inf **CA**3, Dory. **1966** *DARE* Tape **ME**17, They're in a dory and use an outboard and tow 'em [=nets] out. . . A dory is flat-bottomed but she is long and deep-sided; **NH**19, Another type of boat used a lot is a dory, . . a fishing dory . . it's high and . . kind of narrow . . but they're very stable. They usually seat about eight people. . . I think they're [made of] oak but I'm not sure. They're a hard wood.

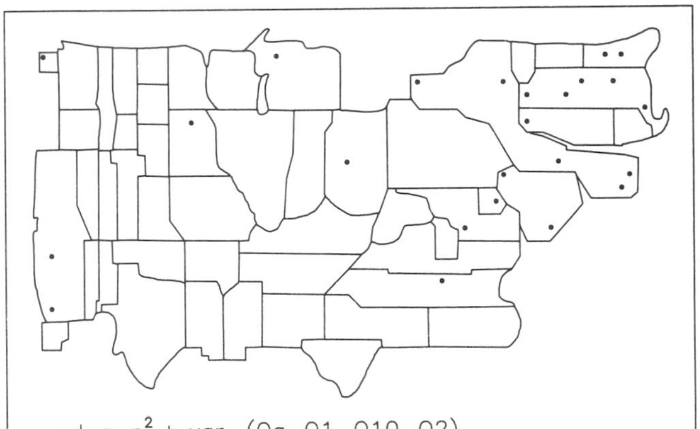

•dory n² + var (Qq. O1, O10, O2)

dorymate n [**dory** n[2]]

A close friend or companion; see quots.

1889 Munroe *Dorymates* 25 *(DA)*, He delighted in being called his father's 'dorymate.' **1975** Gould *ME Lingo* 77, *Dorymate*—In the old days of handlining, two men would fish from each dory, and there was an essential quality of compatibility. Being *dorymates* implied something more than simple friendship, because one not only had to get along with and put up with his *dorymate*, but depend on him often for survival. "Closer than *dorymates*" is a relationship of the strongest kind.

dose n, v Usu |do(ʊ)s|; also **chiefly Sth, S Midl** |dost|; rarely |dosɛt| Pronc-spp *dost(e), doset*

A Forms.

1886 Amer. Philol. Assoc. *Trans.* 17.43 **eTN,** I tuck me a four finger dost ove bumble-bee whiskey. **1887** (1967) Harris *Free Joe* 180 **GA,** If you like sech folks it's a thousand pities you've come here, for you'll git a doste of 'em. **1902** *DN* 2.233 **sIL,** *Dose.* Pronounced [dost] with excrescent t. **1903** *DN* 2.312 **swMO,** *Doste,* n. Dose. **1907** *DN* 3.230 **nwAR, seMO,** *Doste,* n. Dose. **1908** *DN* 3.306 **eAL, wGA,** *Dost,* n. and v. Dose. . . The plural is *dostes.* **1916** *DN* 4.314, **sAppalachians** [Folksong terms], A doste of old morphine. *Ibid* 411 **wNC,** *Doset* [dosɛt]. . . Dose. Also Ill. [*DARE* Ed: Perh in ref to pronc in quot 1902 above], Ky. **c1938** in 1970 Hyatt *Hoodoo* 1.205 **seNC** [Black], The doctor kept dostin' her with medicine an' she didn't get any better. **1952** Giles *40 Acres* 104, Hit like to of gagged me! I'd ruther of took a dost of salts. **1954** *Harder Coll.* **cwTN,** *Dose.* Dost [dost] 'at mule good. **1968** *DARE* Tape **GA**30, Drop a few drops of turpentine right in the castor oil an' then drink it—it makes a pretty bad dost.

B As noun.

1 in phr *go through like a dose of salts:* To do or accomplish something quickly. [In allusion to the cathartic properties of Epsom (and other similar) salts]

1837 (1955) *Crockett Almanacks* 81 **TN,** I'll go through the Mexicans like a dose of salts. **1889** Munroe *Golden Days* 124 **CA,** He'd gone through the pockets like a dose of salts. **1969** *DARE* (Qu. A22, . . *'To start working hard': "She had only ten minutes to clean the room, but she* ______ *[and had it done in no time]."*) Inf **MO**27, Went through like a dose of salts.

2 An attack of venereal disease, usu gonorrhea.

1914 *DN* 4.105 **KS,** *Dose.* . . Venereal disease. **1923** *DN* 5.205 **swMO,** *Dose.* . . Venereal affliction. "Bill got hisse'f a dose." **1942** McAtee *Dial. Grant Co. IN Suppl. 1* 4, *Dose* . . attack of venereal disease, usually the clap or gonorrhea. **1972** (1974) Wilson *Playboy's Words* 92, *Dose*—Venereal disease, usually gonorrhea, as in "He came down with a dose."

dosey See **dozy**

dos gris n |ˌdo'gri, 'doˌgri| [LaFr "gray back"] **chiefly LA =scaup.**

1839 Audubon *Synopsis Birds* 286, Fuligula Ferina. . . Red-headed Duck.—Dos-gris. . . Male . . back and scapulars pale greyish-white, being minutely traversed by dark brownish-grey lines. . . Abundant on the Chesapeake, New York Bay, Ohio, and Mississippi, with their tributaries. None seen westward of the Mississippi. **1897** *Auk* 14.286 **LA,** *American Scaup Duck.*—Most commonly known as *Dos gris.* **1916** *Times-Picayune* (New Orleans LA) 26 Mar 2/5, *American scaup* (Marila marila). Dos-Gris de Mer. . . *Lesser scaup* (Marila affinis). Dos-gris. **1955** Lowery *LA Birds* 175, The "salt-and-pepper" color of the back . . gives the scaups [=greater scaup *(Aythya marila)*] their common name of *dos-gris*. . . It [=lesser scaup *(Aythya affinis)*] goes mainly by two names, "blue-bill" or *dos-gris.* **1962** Imhof *AL Birds* 149, *Greater Scaup—Aythya marila* . . Dos-gris. **1966** LA Wild Life Comm. *Hunting Fishing Regulations 1967–68* 2, *Bonus Ducks:* Additional to above limits. Scaup (bluebill, dos gris). **1968** *DARE* (Qu. Q5) Infs **LA**31, [ˌdoʊ'gri]; **LA**37, ['doˌgri]. **1968** *DARE* FW Addit **seLA,** *Dos gris* [ˌdo'gri] the lesser scaup. **1983** *Reinecke Coll.* 4 **LA,** *Dos-gris*—['doˌgri] scaup duck; males have light gray plumage on back. Elsewhere, "blue-bill." *General.*

dosh n [Perh var of *dash* a gift, tip] *arch* Cf *DS* U19a

Money.

1890 *AN&Q* 6.45/2 **MA,** Thirty or forty years ago *dosh* was not uncommon as a slang name for money. I have not heard it for many years. **1902** Day *Pine Tree Ballads* 21 **ME,** Cheerful crab was that old Posh,/—Warn't afflicted much with dosh,/—Fact, he worked round sawin' wood,/ Earnin' what few cents he could.

dosh v See **douse** v

do-something n Cf **doohickey 1**

1968 *DARE* (Qu. NN12b, *Things that people say to put off a child when he asks, "What are you making?"*) Inf **LA**20, A little do-something.

dos reales n [Span; see quot 1932 and cf *two bits* twenty-five cents] Cf *DS* U23

See quot 1909.

1909 *DN* 3.393 **OK, nwAR,** *Dos reales.* . . Twenty-five-cent-piece. [**1932** Bentley *Spanish Terms* 193, *Real.* . . A monetary denomination; a coin; a bit. . . It is possible . . that the common use of *dos reales, seis* *reales, ocho reales* by the Spanish-speaking element along the border has increased the use of the English "two bits," "four bits," and "six bits" in the same region.]

doss over v phr Cf *doss* to sleep, bed down

1977 *Yankee* Jan 113 **ceME,** And to reaffirm your welcome somebody will stand in the door and holler after you, "Doss over more often!"—which in native tongue means come again.

dost(e) See **dose** n, v

do-stick n

A music conductor's baton.

1978 Massey *Bittersweet Country* 362 **Ozarks,** Mr. Dennis always carried a baton, a Do-stick. He kept time and he was very, very strict on time. That was one of the greatest things he taught because, if you lost time in music, you'd lost it all.

dot n

1 A small amount, a dab or pinch (of something).

1966–70 *DARE* (Qu. LL6b, *A small, indefinite amount—for example, of butter: "I'll put in just a ______ of butter."*) Infs **IA**31, **KY**25, **MA**127, **NC**36, 82, **OR**1, **PA**230, **WA**6, Dot; (Qu. LL6c, .. *"It still needs just a______of cinnamon."*) Inf **IN**32, Dot.

2 pl; also *dot game, dots and dashes* (or *squares*), *join-the-dots:* A pencil-and-paper game; see quot 1968.

1965–70 *DARE* (Qu. EE39, .. *Games played on paper by two people*) 71 Infs, **widespread,** Dots; **DC**2, Dots—A square of dots, each person had a turn, join two dots; object to make a complete square and initial it. Most initialed squares at end, won. On completing a square, one had another turn; **IL**80, Dots—dots across and down in grid, each player makes squares, one line at a time, puts his initial in. The one with the most boxes at the end wins; **SC**24, Dots—one tries to connect the dots to form squares without setting up boxes for the opponent; 9 Infs, **scattered,** Dot game; **IA**32, Dot game—you make rows of dots, one dot right under the other. Then you connect the dots with lines, each player drawing one line at a time. If you draw the last line of the box you put your initial in the box and get to draw another line; **PA**167, Dots and dashes; **ME**9, Dots and squares; **PA**165, Join-the-dots. [Of all Infs responding to this question, 7% were Black; of those giving these responses, 22% were Black]. **1968** *DARE* FW Addit **swLA,** *Dots*—Game played on paper by two or more people. A grid of dots is made; each player draws one line in turn and places his initials in any square he can complete with his line. The player with the most initialed squares wins.

3 pl: Small round hard candies, usu attached in rows to waxed paper. Cf **dominoes**

1967–70 *DARE* (Qu. H82a, *Cheap candies*) Infs **MN**1, **NJ**30, Dots; **NY**81, Dots—small round sugar candies on paper; **NY**240, Dots—bits of colored sugar on paper strips; **NY**36, 65, Dots on (a piece of) paper.

dot adj [Perh abbr for *dotty,* but cf **doty 2**]

1952 Brown *NC Folkl.* 1.534, *Dot.* . . Crazy.

dot and carry one n, also attrib Cf **ride and tie**

See quots.

1946 Mora *Trail Dust* 211 **West,** One . . would . . ride the horse a certain prearranged distance, . . dismount, tie the horse . . , and proceed on foot. The other . . walking till he came to the tied horse. . . He would pass his companion and ride on to another chosen spot where he would dismount, tie, and continue on foot. Well, in this dot-and-carry-one manner they'd continue till they reached their destination. **1958** McCulloch *Woods Words* 50 **Pacific NW,** *Dot and carry one*—A one-legged man.

dote v

1 Usu of wood: to rot or decay; hence ppl adj *doted* decayed, partially rotten. **chiefly Sth, S Midl, NEng** Cf **doty 1**

1859 (1968) Bartlett *Americanisms* 127, *Doted.* Changed, or half rotten; as "doted wood." West and South. **1865** Crockett *Life* 148 **TN,** The big tree . . was nothing but a shell on the outside, and all doted in the middle. **1884** Amer. Philol. Assoc. *Trans.* 14.47, *Doted,* 'decayed inside,' of a tree. It is quite common in South Carolina and other Southern States. A correspondent in Ohio "has heard it, but not often." **1917** *DN* 4.411 **wNC,** *Doted.* **1929** *AmSp* 4.356 **MA, ME,** *Dote*—The verb "dote" is used for wood becoming spongy or punkey. . . We have heard it at Bridgewater, Massachusetts, and Mt. Desert, Maine. This summer we asked a Maine man if white birch made good stove wood. "Yes, if it doesn't dote," he said. "Skag every stick of it once or twice with your axe, to let in the air, and put it under cover, or you will find it doted in the spring. White birch always gets doted if it ain't clifted." **1968** *DARE* (Qu. KK7, *When wood—for example, a tree stump—is starting to decay inside, you'd say, "It's ______ inside."*) Inf **MD**30, Doted.

2 To anticipate.

1927 *DN* 5.474 **Ozarks,** *Dote.* . . To anticipate with pleasure. "I shore caint miss th' singin' convention now—I jes' been a-dotin' on hit all winter." **1937** in 1958 Brewer *Dog Ghosts* 97 **TX** [Black], He kin allus dote on gittin' 'bout twenny dolluhs for de night, an' dis heah mo'n de school teachuh mecks in a couple of weeks. **1954** *Harder Coll.* **cwTN,** *Dote*—anticipate: Desire something that is good.

dote n

Decay or rot in wood; wood that is partially rotted.

1872 (1876) Knight *Amer. Mech. Dict.* 1.564/1, *Clear-stuff;* Boards free from knots, wane, wind-shakes, ring-hearts, dote, sap. **1905** U.S. Forest Serv. *Bulletin* 61.35 [Logging terms], *Dote.* . . The general term used by lumbermen to denote decay or rot in timber. **1917** *DN* 4.411 **wNC, KY,** *Dote* [dot]. . . Wood partly decayed by a fungus. **1969** Sorden *Lumberjack Lingo* 35 **NEng, Gt Lakes,** *Dote*—Decay or rot in timber.

doted ppl adj

1 =**doty 2.**

1914 *DN* 4.105 **KS,** *Doted.* . . Affected by dotage.

2 See **dote** v **1.**

do tell exclam Also *do pray tell* Eye-dial spp *dew tell, du* ~ **formerly NEng, now more widespread** Cf *do pray* at **do** v **C2a**

Really!—used as an exclam of surprise.

1815 Humphreys *Yankey in England* 104, *Du pry tel* (exclamation probably from) do pray tell. **1848** Bartlett *Americanisms* 119, *Do tell!* A vulgar exclamation common in New England, and synonymous with really! indeed! is it possible! **1848** in 1935 *AmSp* 10.42 **Cape Cod MA,** *Du tell.* **1857** *Putnam's Mag.* 10.347/2 **CT,** 'Dew tell!' sez I. **1895** Brown *Meadow-Grass* 132 **NEng,** Do tell! **1905** *DN* 3.8 **cCT.** **1907** *DN* 3.186 **seNH.** **1936** *WV Review* Aug 346, The short expletives that can be shot out for any reason, or for no particular reason, are numerous. . . In this category [is] . . Do tell. **1951** *PADS* 15.67 **NH,** *Tell!, Do.* . . "You don't say!" **1965–70** *DARE* (Qu. NN7, *Exclamations of surprise*) 66 Infs, **scattered,** Do tell.

dotey See **doty**

dot eye n Also *dot-eyed bean*

A cultivated bush bean with a single dot of color on each side of the hilum. Also called **molasses face, yellow eye, yellow-eyed china**

1966 *DARE* (Qu. I20, . . *Kinds of beans*) Inf **ME**20, Dot-eyed beans. **1978** *Wanigan Catalog* 8, Dot Eye is a white, size 4 plump seed having a single dot of color on each side of the hilum.

dot game, dots and dashes, dots and squares See **dot 2**

dotted black snake n

A **king snake 1** (here: *Lampropeltis getulus holbrooki*).

1928 Baylor Univ. Museum *Contrib.* 16.16, In the eastern half of Texas, this species [=*Lampropeltis getulus holbrooki*] is variously known as. . . Dotted Black Snake.

dotterel n

=**killdeer.**

1881 *Forest & Stream* 17.226 **IA,** Kill-deer . . , called here "dotterel," are abundant summer residents. **1917** *Wilson Bulletin* 29.2.80, *Oxyechus vociferus.*—Dotterel, Iowa. **1923** U.S. Dept. Ag. *Misc. Circular* 13.69, *Killdeer. . . Vernacular Names. . . In local use.* . . Dotterel (Iowa). **1932** Bennitt *Check-list* 28 **MO,** *Killdeer.* . . Dotterel.

dot, to the adv phr Also *to a dot;* for addit varr see quots

Precisely, completely, perfectly.

1839 *Spirit of Times* 9 Nov 428/3 **wNY,** There were a large number of horses in attendance . . and amongst them were some who had the "go along" in them to a "dot." **1854** (1923) Holmes *Tempest & Sunshine* 215 **MA,** That was one of Tempest's capers to a dot. **1880** *Harper's New Mth. Mag.* 61.509/1 **NEng,** The careful housewife . . knew how to regulate the laying of the cloth, and the lifting of the cover of the boiling pot, to the dot of an i. **1902** *Harper's Mth. Mag.* 104.431/1 **CA,** Wells-Fargo, you've got him down to a dot. **1965–70** *DARE* (Qu. KK50, *When something is planned out carefully, down to the last detail: "He had it all worked out ______."*) Infs **AR**56, **CA**202, 206, **CO**29, **NY**127, **NC**15, 17, **ND**1, **OH**38, To the (last) dot; **AL**3, **AZ**15, **FL**10, 15,

NC11, WV16, 18, WI61, To the dot on the (last) *i;* FL2, NC7, Down to the (last) dot; FL6, To the last little dot; NY43, Right to the dot; GA12, Down to the dot on the last *i.*

‡dot weed n

1966 *DARE* (Qu. S21, . . *Weeds . . in gardens and fields*) Inf **NC**10, Dot weed—kind of like a dandelion.

doty adj Also sp *doaty, dotey;* pronc-sp *dody*

1 Of wood: rotting, spongy, soft; waterlogged; also fig. **[dote v1] chiefly Sth, S Midl** See Map Cf **dozy**

1883 *Philad. Telegraph* XL. No. 44.8 *(OED),* A log may be doty in places, and even hollow, and yet have . . good timber in it. **1903** *DN* 2.312 **seMO,** *Doty.* **1905** U.S. Forest Serv. *Bulletin* 61.35 [Logging terms], *Doty. . .* Decayed. **1906** *DN* 3.117 **sIN,** *Doty.* **1908** *DN* 3.306 **eAL, wGA,** *Doty.* **1916** *DN* 4.302 **csLA, KS, VA,** *Doty.* **1917** *DN* 4.411 **wNC,** *Dotey.* **1927** *AmSp* 2.352 **WV,** *Doaty . .* half-rotten. "The wood is doaty." **1944** *PADS* 2.26 **cwOH, cwNC,** *Doty.* **1953** *PADS* 19.10 **sAppalachians,** *Doty timber. . .* Use[d] figuratively to indicate that one has some bad traits. "Dan is jest doty timber. He'll never amount to nothing." **1954** *Harder Coll.* **cwTN,** *Doty.* **c1960** [see **2** below]. **1965–70** *DARE* (Qu. KK7, *When wood—for example, a tree stump—is starting to decay inside, you'd say, "It's ______ inside."*) 32 Infs, **chiefly Sth, S Midl,** Doty; (Qu. KK56, *Wood that is heavy from being in water a long time: It's ______.*) Infs **LA**8, **MO**21, Doty. **1968** Haun *Hawk's Done Gone* 221 **TN,** He liked to set in the hollow of it [=an oak] and come out smelling of the doty wood.

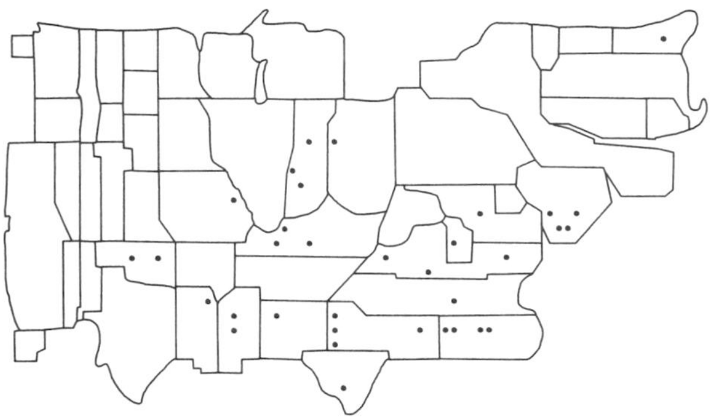

•doty 1 (Qq. KK7, KK56)

2 Senile, weak-minded.

1940 Harris *Folk Plays* 31 **NC,** You are just a silly, dotey, spoiled, old young'un that we been . . tryin' to keep from makin' a fool of hisself. **1944** *PADS* 2.26 **cwOH, cwNC,** *Doty. . .* Applied to . . persons [sic] whose mind is "tetched." **c1960** *Wilson Coll.* **csKY,** *Doty. . .* Rotting or rotten wood; by transference [applied to] somebody who is becoming old and declining in strength and in mental power. **1969–70** *DARE* (Qu. X48b, . . *If a person is not so young any more, you might say, "He's ______."*) Inf **KY**60, Getting doty; (Qu. HH9, *A very silly or light-headed person*) Inf **VA**69, Dody; (Qu. HH40, *Uncomplimentary words for an old man*) Inf **IL**30, Doty. **1974** Fink *Mountain Speech* 7 **wNC, eTN,** *Dotey . .* aged or senile. "He's got plumb dotey." **1986** *Barrick Coll.* **csPA,** *Doty*—senile; febbleminded [sic]—"Do you think he's gittin' doty?"

double n

1 also pl: See quot 1925. **VA**

1851 *S. Lit. Messenger* 17.46/2 **VA,** The stranger who has been left alone in the doubles of the mountains of Western Virginia, has a fair chance of passing the night without supper or bed. **1925** Campbell et al. *Valley Coal Fields VA* 267, At the Ceres-Burke Garden road . . a distinct faulted syncline comes in, which splits Brushy Mountain into two distinct ridges. The place where the ridge splits is locally called the "Doubles." **1928** in 1940 *AmSp* 15.173 **VA,** The ore was mined high up in the double of the mountain.

2 A ride (by a second person) on a bicycle. Cf **double-head 2**

1981 *DARE* File **csWI,** "Give me a double!" is said to a person on a bicycle, meaning *let me ride double,* or *give me a ride.*

3 A pair of teamed draft animals.

1966 *DARE* (Qu. K26, *If six oxen are hitched together two and two, you have three ______.*) Infs **MT**1, **ND**1, Doubles.

4 See **double sawbuck.**

5 See **double house 2.**

6 pl: See **double crabs.**

double v

1 occas with *over;* In railroading: see quots. Cf **double the hill**

1916 *DN* 4.356 [Railroad terms], *Double over. . .* To divide a train in sections and haul one after the other. **1932** *RR Mag.* Oct 367, *Double*—In going up a hill, to cut the train in half and take each section up separately. **1961** Labbe–Goe *Railroads* 257 **Pacific NW** [Gloss.], *Double:* As to "double a train." A railroad term used to describe the operation whereby a train was separated and taken up a grade a section at a time. **1969** *AmSp* 44.256 [Railroad terms], *Double*—Divide a train into two sections that are then separately hauled over a steep grade.

2 also with *out:* See quots; hence vbl n *doubling out.*

1969 *AmSp* 44.248 [Railroad terms], ICC regulations guarantee eight hours of rest between marking up and going on duty for a second assignment. Going back to work before eight hours of rest is termed *doubling* out. *Ibid* 256, *Double out*—Work a second job on the Extra Board or Road Board with less than eight hours rest. **1970** *Current Slang* 5.1.6 [Railroad jargon], *Double. . .* To work two consecutive shifts. **1978** Kalibabky *Hawdaw* 1.[5] **neMN** [Iron mining], Double out: Working two shifts in a row. "I'm doublin' out tonight. Dey got lotsa guys callin' in sick."

3 In railroading: see quot.

1970 *Current Slang* 5.1.6 [Railroad jargon], *Double. . .* To couple a line of cars on one track to a line of cars on another track.—Pull the cars from Track 9 and double to Track 10.

4 also with *back;* In moonshining:

a To strengthen (whiskey) by redistillation or by the use of a **thump barrel;** to redistill; of whiskey: to become stronger; hence vbl n *doubling* redistillation. **sAppalachians** Cf **double and twist 1, doubler 5, doublings a**

c1960 *Hall Coll.* **wNC, eTN,** *Double back. . .* To redistill (a process in mountain moonshining). **1969** *DARE* Tape **GA**72, If you're making pure corn whiskey, you run what you call the singlings first. . . You pour these singlings up and that is what you call the doubling; when it comes out condensed . . then it is hot shots or high shots; That thump barrel sets between your condenser and your still; it doubles the whiskey. You put backings or beer in this barrel and it butts against the strength of your beer in your still. . . It speeded up the process; instead of having your doubled [sic], it doubled in this barrel and was whiskey when it come out at the condenser or your worm, either one. **1972** *Foxfire Book* 323 **nGA,** Perhaps the most revolutionary addition was the thump barrel. Steam bubbling up through the fresh beer in this barrel was automatically doubled thus removing forever the necessity of saving the singlings and running them through again to double their strength. **1974** Dabney *Mountain Spirits* 14 **sAppalachians,** Mr. Young explained how he and his associates made corn whiskey in the old way, singling and doubling with a copper pot still. **1974** Maurer–Pearl *KY Moonshine* 8, Now we must do what the moonshiner calls *doubling;* that is, we must redistill the result of our first endeavor.

b See quot.

1974 Maurer–Pearl *KY Moonshine* 117, *Double* or *double back. . .* To remash at the same place, in the same vats, using the slops from the preceding distillation as a part of the mash. "We doubled back and made a good run." Also "to mash back."

5 See **double up 1.**

double action goes over exclam

In marble play: see quots.

1942 Berrey–Van den Bark *Amer. Slang* 665.6, Double action goes over!, *said if two marbles are hit at the same time, to require the player to take the play over.* **1955** *PADS* 23.16 **cwTN,** *Double action goes over:* interj. (Perh. fr. billiards). A call that nullifies an opponent's hitting two marbles at once.

double A-harrow n [A-harrow]

See quots.

c1960 *Wilson Coll.* **csKY,** *Double-A harrow:* A big home-made harrow. Mrs. Tarter says she often rode on one to add weight. **1970** *DARE* (Qu. L20, *The implement used in a field after it's been plowed to break up the lumps*) Inf **KY**84, Double A-harrow—teeth staggered, old-fashioned.

double and twist v phr [From an operation in thread manufacture in which fibers are combined and twisted together; cf *OED* double v. 7]

1 In moonshining: to redistill (liquor); hence ppl adj phrr *double(d) and twisted* redistilled; also n *double and twist* fig, a strong drink. [Joc extension of **double v 4a**] **sAppalachians**

1834 Caruthers *Kentuckian* 1.63 **KY,** Only a small breeze or so; a few tumblers of punch, made of that doubled and twisted Irish whiskey... It was as strong as *pison* [=poison]. **1932** *Durant Daily Democrat* (OK) 12 Nov 4/6 **GA,** "It [=corn whiskey] is then run through the still a second time, the 'double-running,' which in mountain jargon, is 'double and twisted.' " This . . drives out of the distillation most of the impurities. This "double and twisted" whiskey then is placed in plain earthen jugs. **c1960** *Wilson Coll.* **csKY,** *Double(d) and twisted*... Very strong, whether a string or a drink. Some of the sulphur water at Red Boiling Springs, Tennessee, is called Double-and-twist. **1967** *Hall Coll.* **eTN,** *Double and twist*... 'To double back' liquor being distilled, i.e. to redistill the first-run whiskey (singlings). 'Twist' may possibly refer to condensation of the steam in the worm, or, tautologically, to the doubling back process (or there may perhaps be an allusion to twisting tobacco). "The old people they used to double and twist it." **1969** *DARE* Tape **GA**72, If you save these high-shot backings, pour back in your thump barrel, or if you're making the old-fashioned doubled an twisted corn liquor, which is double-stilled whiskey, the alcoholic content of these high-shot backings will up the produce, the production of your next still-full. **1972** *Foxfire Book* 317 **nGA,** In the old stills, all the singlings were saved and then run through at the same time thus doubling their strength. Whiskey made in this fashion was called doubled and twisted. *Ibid* 323, It was called "doubled and twisted" whiskey, the first because it was double strength, and the second, because it twisted slightly as it came out of the worm.

2 ppl adj phr *double and twisted:* See quot.

1929 *AmSp* 5.124 **ME,** A spinster might be a "double and twisted old maid."

double apartment See **double house 2**

‡double arithmetic n *old-fash*

1970 *DARE* FW Addit **ceMA** (as of c1910), The children felt proud when they got to double 'rithmetic—multiplication by two numbers.

double back v phr

1 To plant the same crop two years in succession. Cf **double-crop**

1967 *DARE* Tape **TX**8, My farm . . it's just adapted to rice... I've doubled back 'n planted two years in succession and made successful crops.

2 See **double v 4.**

double-back-action adj **chiefly Sth, S Midl** *old-fash*

Superior; powerful; newfangled.

1848 *New Negro Forget-me-not Songster* 39 *(DA),* I pick upon de Banjo string, Wid de double back action spring. **1862** Newell *Orpheus C. Kerr* 1.316 **DC,** In about three minutes there was a double back-action machine [=a fire engine] standing in that chap's front entry, with three-inch streams [of water] out of all the back windows. **1872** Eggleston *End of the World* 111 **IN,** She's told pay-tent [=patent] double-back-action lies that worked both ways. **c1960** *Wilson Coll.* **csKY,** *Double-back action*... A humorous way of saying something is strong. Pre-Hollywood exaggeration.

double balsam fir n Also *double (fir) balsam, double needle* [Perh in ref to the density of the foliage] Cf **single balsam**

Either of two similar trees: **Fraser fir** or a **balsam fir** (here: *Abies balsamea*).

1814 Pursh *Flora Americae* 2.639 **ePA,** *Pinus* . . *Fraser*... This species, known among the inhabitants by the name of *Double-balsam fir.* **1847** Wood *Class-Book* 516, *A[bies] Fraseri* . . Double Balsam Fir. **1897** Sudworth *Arborescent Flora* 50, *Abies fraseri* . . Double Fir Balsam (Tenn.) **1967–68** *DARE* (Qu. T5, . . *Evergreens*) Inf **WI**50, Double needle; (Qu. T16, *What kinds of trees are 'special' around here?*) Inf **NY**1, Double balsam. **1986** *DARE* File **cnWI,** People always say that they want a double balsam for a Christmas tree. The double balsam refers to balsams that grow in optimal conditions; in full sun. The needles grow all the way around the branch. You can have double and single balsam all on the same tree. If it's a tall, mature tree, the top will be double because it gets the sun and the lower branches will have needles growing on two sides of the twig, giving it a flat look.

double bar n **esp C Atl**

=doubletree 1.

1966–70 *DARE* (Qu. L47, *The two movable bars behind a team of horses* . . *fastened to a longer piece*) Infs **DC**5, 8, **FL**36, **PA**207, **VA**77, 105, 111, 75, **CA**138, **DE**5, Double bar.

double barn n Cf **double house 2**

See quot 1968.

1968 *DARE* (Qu. M1, . . *Special kinds of barns* . . *according to their use or the way they are built*) Inf **PA**127, Double barn—two side-by-side. **1976** Wells *Barns U.S.A.* [5] (prob as of 19th cent), There were advertisements in the papers such as the following: "For Sale, Plantation . . Two story, four-room dwelling, double barn, outside kitchen and milk house."

double-barrel n Also *double-barrel road* [In allusion to a double-barreled gun] **eMA** Cf **double-barreled bridge**

A four-lane highway with a median strip.

1967–69 *DARE* (Qu. N16a, . . *A highway with two lanes on each side and a separation down the middle*) Inf **MA**55, Double-barrel road; **MA**72, Double-barrel. **1969** *Cape Cod Std.-Times* (Hyannis MA) 4 Nov 4, Eastham, Wellfleet and Truro boards of selectmen are against the double barrel as it is presently planned because it would take too much taxable land... A double-barrel all the way from the Canal through to Provincetown has been a long time dream.

double-barrel(ed) adj **West**

Of a saddle: **=double-rigged.**

1922 Rollins *Cowboy* 123 **West,** The saddle of two cinches was designated . . popularly . . as . . "double-barrelled." **1933** White *Dog Days* 197 **CA,** The stock saddle, then, was the choice... One broad cinch or two narrower ones?—"center fire" or "double barrel"?

double-barreled bridge n Cf **double-barrel**

1953 Van Wagenen *Golden Age* 150 **ceNY** (as of c1855), It may be taken as a perfect representative of its type, the so-called "double-barreled" bridge, which has two driveways separated from each other by a center timber truss.

double-barrel road See **double-barrel**

double barrels n pl Cf **long handles**

1969 *DARE* (Qu. W14, . . *Underwear*... *Men's—long*) Inf **TX**72, Double barrels.

double belly-buster n [**belly-buster 1**]

A **belly-buster 1** in which two persons coast downhill on the same sled.

1950 *WELS Suppl.* **WI,** Double belly-buster—two people run and fall on a sled.

double bit n Also *double bitter*

Among loggers: a double-bitted ax.

1958 McCulloch *Woods Words* 50 **Pacific NW,** *Double-bit*—An ax with two cutting edges, used throughout the West Coast woods. **1966** *DARE* Tape **ME**26, The double bitter was quite the ax [for logging] then.

double-bitting n Cf **double-jack v**

1967 *DARE* FW Addit **neOR,** Double-bitting—one man working on hammer, one man on spike. Heard in conversation.

double-black-dog dare See **double dog dare**

double bladderpod n

A plant of the genus *Physaria.* Also called **bladderpod 5, twinpod**

1949 Moldenke *Amer. Wild Flowers* 41, Other interesting groups of crucifers are the *bladderpods (Lesquerella)* and *double bladderpods (Physaria).* **1950** Stevens *ND Plants* 160, *Physaria brassicoides* . . Double Bladderpod. **1956** St. John *Flora SE WA* 175, *Physaria.* Double Bladder Pod. **1973** Hitchcock–Cronquist *Flora Pacific NW* 174, *Physaria* . . Double Bladderpod.

double block n [**block n 2b**]

A duplex.

1968–70 *DARE* (Qu. D23, *A house that is divided in two through the middle so that two families can live in it*) Inf **MD**21, Double block; **PA**245, Double block—two houses side by side, only a wall between.

double bobsled n Also *double bob*

=double-runner b.

1907 *DN* 3.243 **eME,** *Double bobsled*... Two connected stout sleds used to haul wood and other loads. **1969** *DARE* (Qu. N40a, . . *Sleighs* . . *for hauling loads*) Inf **MA**30, Double bobs.

double-box n Cf **double wagon**

1968 *DARE* Tape **MI96**, A high wagon, a double-box we called it, and then there'd be a seat on top of that.

‡double-breasted house n

Prob a duplex or a **double house 1.**

1887 in 1950 *AmSp* 25.32 **New Orleans LA,** Dere hall is at 275 Dauphine Street in a double-breasted house.

double buggy n

A horse-drawn vehicle with two passenger seats, one behind the other.

1844 *Mass. Statutes* lxxv *(DA),* [Toll on] double buggy drawn by one horse, 15 cents. **1898** Page *Red Rock* 225, Dr. Still . . drove over to Birdwood the very next evening in a double buggy. **1967–69** *DARE* (Qu. N41a, . . *Horse-drawn vehicles . . to carry people*) Inf **IN69**, Single buggy, double buggy; **MI56**, Double buggy—has two seats, I understand they even have three-seaters on Mackinac Island; **MI66**, Double buggy.

double-bunk sleigh See **double sleigh**

double cabin n Also *double log, ~ log(ged) cabin, ~ log house* **chiefly Sth, S Midl** *old-fash*

A **double pen(ned)** dwelling.

1834 *Knickerbocker* 3.32 **wTN,** I pursued my way, until, . . immediately on the road, appeared a large rude double logged cabin, with a Buck's Horn nailed over the door. **1837** (1848) Peck *New Guide* 124, A double cabin consists of two such buildings [=standard log cabins], with a space of ten or twelve feet between, over which the roof extends. **1843** (1969) Lewis *Odd Leaves* 147 **LA,** The house consisted of a double log cabin, of small dimensions, a passage, the full depth of the house, running between the "pens." **1852** Regan *Emigrant's Guide* 245 **nwIL,** Old Abe's dwelling was what is called a double log-house, consisting of an apartment at each end, with a wide entrance in front, sufficient to run a wagon into. On each side of this *shed* were the smaller entrance-doors of each apartment, right and left. **1853** Hammett *Stray Yankee in TX* 345, A double log-cabin . . consists usually of two large rooms, separated by a wide hall, which . . being generally open at both ends, is not used in inclement days. **1873** Beadle *Undeveloped West* 405 **ceOK,** The residence of a "White Cherokee," the usual double log with porch between. **1908** *DN* 3.306 **eAL, wGA,** *Double-cabin.* . . A cabin of two log rooms with an open hall between, and all covered under one roof. **1931** Willison *Here They Dug* 17 **cCO,** Already thirty or more log houses are built or building to either side of the . . double cabin. **1940** Wilson *Wabash* 102 **cnIN** (as of 1837), Nor was Ma-con-a-quah allowed to remain because of her double log house, the center of a farm as large and prosperous as any white man's.

double carry n [*double* + folk-etym for *Kerria*]

An ornamental plant (here: *Kerria plenifolia*).

1970 *DARE* (Qu. S26e) Inf **VA43**, Double carry. **1970** *DARE* FW Addit **VA,** "Double carry" is a yellow blooming bush. The flowers look like tall marigolds. It blooms late in April and has heavy foliage.

double cat's-eye n Also *double cat-eye* [**cat's-eye 1**]

See quots.

1968 *DARE* Tape **IA27A**, [FW:] Now that one you called a double cat-eye . . describe that one for me. [Inf:] Well, it's just the same of [sic] the cat-eye only [it] has two colors in it. [FW:] Yeah, the top part of the eye is made of one color, and the bottom of another. **c1970** Wiersma *Marbles Terms* **cwMI,** *Double cat's-eye* . . a glass marble containing two opaque bands of color. Used in southwest Grand Rapids in the late 1950's and early 1960's.

double-cinch adj **West**

Of a saddle: =**double-rigged;** also n *double-cinch* a saddle having two cinches.

1907 White *AZ Nights* 245, They were good men, addicted to the grass-rope, the double cinch, and the ox-bow stirrup. **1953** *Western Folkl.* 12.185, The former [=the Texas cowboy] employed a double-cinch, square-skirted saddle, the latter [=the California cowboy] a single "center-fire" cinch and round skirts. **1966** *DARE* FW Addit **neWA,** Montana cowboys used two cinches on saddles, thus a "double-cinch."

double-claw n [From the pod, often two-clawed when ripe]

A **unicorn plant** (*Proboscidea* spp).

1830 Rafinesque *Med. Flora* 2.241, *Martynia proboscidea.* . . *Double claw.* On the Mississippi. Fruits make good pickles when young. **1876** Hobbs *Bot. Hdbk.* 32, Double claw, Martynia, Martynia proboscidea. **1900** Lyons *Plant Names* 240, *M. louisiana.* . . Double-claw. **1949** Moldenke *Amer. Wild Flowers* 287, The *doubleclaw, P. arenaria,* has its blossoms copper-colored outside.

double-clutch adj Also *double-clutching* [*double clutch* to shift gears by changing first to neutral, then to the desired (usu lower) gear, disengaging the clutch each time]

Of or relating to a truck driver; hence n *double-clutcher* a heavy boot worn by truck drivers.

1950 *Western Folkl.* 9.381 **nCA** [Loggers' jargon], *Double-clutch hat.* A cap with a visor, usually worn by truck drivers. **1968** *DARE* (Qu. W11, *Men's low, rough work-shoes*) Inf **CA106**, Double-clutchers, double-clutching boot—because they had to double-clutch the logging trucks. **1971** Tak *Truck Talk* 48, *Double-clutchin' boots:* a trucker's boots; so named because of the technique of double-clutching. . . *double-clutchin' man:* a trucker.

double cousin n

1 See quot 1954; similarly, n *double niece.*

1953 Randolph *Down in Holler* 241 **Ozarks,** *Double cousins.* . . When two brothers marry two sisters, the children are known as *double cousins.* Such relationships are very common in the Ozarks, and are considered somehow significant. In referring to each other these people seldom say simply, "He's my cousin," but rather, "We're double cousins." . . The Eureka Springs, Ark., *Times-Echo* (January 27, 1949) prints a picture of a girl described as "a double niece of Rev. and Mrs. Herman Williams," but this usage is not common. **1954** *Harder Coll.* **cwTN,** Double cousins. . . The children of brothers who have married sisters, or of a brother and sister married to a brother and sister. "Them kids's double cousins; they turned plum alike; they favor one 'nother too." **1967** *DARE* (Qu. Z7, . . *Words for any other relatives*) Inf **NJ1**, Double cousin. **1968** *DARE* FW Addit **GA44**, We're double first cousins. **1970** *DARE* Tape **AR56**, That's how come me and Oscar Brummage to be double cousins.

‡2 pl: A children's game; see quot.

1968 *DARE* (Qu. EE2, *Games that have one extra player—when a signal is given, the players change places, and the extra one tries to get a place*) Inf **CA59**, Double cousins—partners stand one behind the other, and chase to an area and back for the empty spot.

double crabs n pl Also *doubles* Cf **doubler 4**

A pair of mating crabs.

1817 Acad. Nat. Sci. Philadelphia *Jrl.* 1.5.9, In this state [=soft shell] the crab is incapable of any defense against its enemies; the male usually retires to a secluded situation for security, but the adult female is protected by a male, whose shell is hard, they are then called *double crabs.* **1984** [see **doubler 4**].

double-crested cormorant n

Std: a large cormorant *(Phalacrocorax auritus)* distinguished by tufts of feathers on each side of the head. Also called **bull goose 1, crowduck 1, gannet 6, Irish goose, lawyer, nigger goose, sea crow, sea goose, shag, shape, sharke, Taunton turkey, water buzzard, water turkey**

double-crop v Cf **double back 1**

To plant (farmland) twice in one season; similarly, *triple-crop.*

1970 *DARE* Tape **CA175**, It got to the point where the ground was being double-, almost triple-cropped, each year.

double-cut v

1 See quot.

1947 Steed *KY Tobacco Patch* 81, We double-cut the field, which is nothing more than traversing the area up and down, and then across and back, with the cutting harrow.

2 See quot.

1958 McCulloch *Woods Words* 51 **Pacific NW,** *Double cut*—To cut a new path through wood when sawing, instead of following the previous cut.

doubled and twisted See **double and twisted**

double dare, double-darse dare, double-D dare See **double-dog dare**

double-deck(er) barn n Also *double-story barn* Cf **forebay**

A barn with a second story usu for storing feed.

1965–68 *DARE* (Qu. M1, . . *Special kinds of barns . . according to their use or the way they are built*) Inf **AR52**, Double-decker barn—with a hay loft; **MD**32, Double-decker barn—cattle below, grain and hay storage above, you can drive into upper floor, sloping driveway leads up; **PA**127, Double-decker barn—two barn floors; **OK**11, Double-deck barn; **LA**18, Double-story barn—had place upstairs for storing hay.

double-dog dare v phr Also *dog dare, double-black-dog dare, double-dare, ~-darse dare, ~-D dare, ~-nigger dare, ~-niggle dare* **chiefly Sth, S Midl** Note: The formulaic phrr build both on alliteration and (usu euphemistic) intensifiers. Cf **dog** n[1] **B7,** v **6**

To challenge defiantly; hence vbl n *double darse-daring;* n *double-dog dare* challenge.

1892 *DN* 1.229 **KY,** *Dare* [dæə]. Children in quarrelling say, "I dare you," "I dog dare you," "I black dog dare you," "I double dog dare you," "I double black dog dare you." [*DN:* In Michigan *dare* and *double dare.*] **1905** *DN* 3.76 **nwAR,** *Dare, dog-dare, double-dog-dare. . .* To challenge. Children say, . . 'I dog-dare you.' . . Common. **1908** *DN* 3.305 **eAL, wGA,** *Dog-dare, double-dog-dare. . .* To challenge defiantly. **1940** (1978) Still *River of Earth* 228 **KY,** "I be not to go." "I double-niggle dare you." I shook my head, and walked on. **1941** *Sat. Eve. Post* 6 Dec 112/4 **MS,** I'll just double-dog dare you to run your dog against mine. **1954** Forbes *Rainbow* 223 **NH,** He is definitely working right under the Sheriff's nose with the obvious intent of what children would call "double darse-daring him." **1955** *Time* 1 Aug 14/2 **csMS,** I double-dog dare the Supreme Court . . to tell us we have violated a law. **c1960** *Wilson Coll.* **csKY,** *Double-dog dare. . .* A heavy dare, usually accompanied by an insulting rhyme: "Whoever takes a double-dog dare / Will steal a dog (or pig) and eat its hair." **1968** *DARE* FW Addit **csNC,** I double-D dare you to skin the cat. **1969** *DARE* (Qu. Y5, . . *To urge somebody to do something he shouldn't: "Johnny wouldn't have tried that if the other boys hadn't ______."*) Inf **IL**96, Double-dog dared, double-nigger dared.

double dome See **dome** n **3**

double duck n Cf **duck on a rock**

See quots.

1967 *DARE* (Qu. EE18, *Games in which the players set up a stone, a tin can, or something similar, and then try to knock it down*) Inf **PA**11, Double duck—put pennies on rock and try to knock off with stone, keep pennies. **1967** *DARE* FW Addit **sePA,** Double duck—a game in which pennies placed on a stone are knocked off with a stone thrown by a player, who may keep as many as he knocks off.

double Dutch n

1 See **Dutch** n **2**

2 also *double Irish, ~ orange:* Any of var jump-rope games in which two ropes are used; hence v phr *double Dutch;* adv phr *double Dutch.* **chiefly Nth, N Midl**

1904 *DN* 2.396 **NYC,** *Double-Dutch. . .* A little girls' game of skipping two ropes at a time. **1953** Brewster *Amer. Nonsinging Games* 119 **IN,** Jumping the Rope. . . Occasionally two ropes are used, each of the turners holding an end in each hand. Both ropes may be turned inward or outward, or one may be turned in one direction and the second in the other. The first form is known as "Double Dutch," the second as "Double Irish." **1966–68** *DARE* Tape **IN**1, Double Dutch is when two people are holding a rope in their left hand and the same two people are holding one in their right. They're long ropes, they're not the individual ropes. And they turn in opposite directions so that the person who jumps in has to get in between both ropes at the same time; **MD**8, [FW:] What do you call the jump rope game that you play with two ropes? [Inf:] Double Dutch. . . We used to play that; **PA**49, Double Dutch. That's where you have two ropes going. **1967** *DARE* FW Addit **NYC,** When jumping ropes simultaneously you call it *double Dutch* if the ropes turn in, *double orange* when the ropes turn out. **1968** *DARE* (Qu. EE33, . . *Outdoor games . . that children play*) Inf **MD**2, Double Dutch —jump rope game, very fast jumping with two ropes; (Qu. HH30, *Things that are nicknamed for different nationalities*) Inf **DC**11, Double Dutch—a jumping rope game played with two ropes; **MD**9, Double Dutch—girls' jump rope game, played with two ropes turned in opposite directions. **1983** *Milwaukee Jrl.* (WI) 9 Jan mag sec 11/2, But inside Jamie there is still a 10-year-old who grew too tall too fast and stumbled over double dutch—the twin jump rope game of her peers. . . "It seemed like every girl around could jump double dutch, except me." . . "I still can't double dutch." **1985** *Yankee* June 56 **cCT,** Inside the twirling Double Dutch ropes, this state's cleverest jumping kids simultaneously cartwheel, dance, play ball, even jump a third rope—without missing a beat. **1988** *NY Times* (NY) 16 July 33, [Caption:] A Double Dutch team going through its routine at Hoffman Park in Queens.

double dwelling See **double house 2**

double eagle See **eagle 3**

double-ender n

1 See quot 1975. **chiefly N Atl**

1864 U.S. Congress *Congressional Globe* 38th Cong 1st Sess 24 Feb 786/1 [Navy language], The side-wheel gunboats known as "double enders." **1882** *Harper's New Mth. Mag.* 64.554/1 **cnMI,** The surface of the lake is flecked with the . . overgrown, and stanch double-enders known as Mackinac boats. **1905** *Eve. Post* (NY NY) 30 Aug 2/5 **NYC,** If she wasn't a double-ender the Manhattan [=a ferry boat] would do very well for a yacht. **1968–69** *DARE* (Qu. O9, *What kinds of sailboats are used around here?*) Inf **RI**4, Dory double-ender—a fisherman's row boat; (Qu. O10, *What other kinds of boats are used around here?*) Inf **CA**65, Double-ender—a clipper bow and a fish tail rear; [they] have jig poles on top. **1975** Gould *ME Lingo* 77, *Double-ender*—Any boat with bow and stern alike. **1985** Rattray *Advent. Dimon* 101 **Long Is. NY** (as of c1890), I got aboard the railroad ferry Southampton, . . a double-ender with a pilot house at either end and a rudder for each one.

2 In railroading: see quot.

1977 Adams *Lang. Railroader* 47, *Double-ender:* A locomotive built to run either direction. It has twin boilers with a central cab and firebox and a trucklike cylinder and driving-wheel assembly beneath each barrel.

‡double evener n [**evener 1**]

=doubletree.

c1950 *Atlas Checklists* **ceWI,** Double evener—bar for two horses. Female informant, white, 66 years old.

double-ex See **ex** n[2]

double-eyes n pl *joc*

Eyeglasses (or perh a nickname for the person wearing them).

1966–69 *DARE* (Qu. X23, . . *Eyeglasses*) Infs **NC**45, 61, Double-eyes.

double fir balsam See **double balsam fir**

double-fire adj [By analogy with **center fire**] **West**

Of a saddle: **=double-rigged;** also n *double-fire* a saddle having two cinches.

1922 Rollins *Cowboy* 123 **West,** The saddle of two cinches was designated . . popularly . . as "double fire," "rim fire," or "double-barrelled". **1961** Adams *Old-Time Cowhand* 111 **West,** A two-cinched saddle's knowed as a "double-barreled," "double-fire," or "double-rigged" saddle.

double fist n

See quots.

1954 *PADS* 21.25 **SC,** *Double fist. . .* The size of the fists together. Used only as an expression of size: "As big as your double fist." **1954** *Harder Coll.* **cwTN,** *Double fist. . .* A measure of quantity: the size of two fists placed together. **1956** McAtee *Some Dialect NC* 13, *Double-fist:* . . the two fists together; "as big as your double-fist."

double-fisted adj

Strong, husky, large; two-fisted.

1853 in 1912 Thornton *Amer. Gloss.* 1.448 **WA,** A big double-fisted *Hoosier,* with a pair of yellow whiskers, gray eyes, and long flowing soap-locks. **1877** Bartlett *Americanisms* 532 **WY,** I'm your rip-roaring raccoon of the mountains, . . your goul-darned [sic] and double-fisted son of an ingine. **1954** *Harder Coll.* **cwTN,** *Double-fisted. . .* Of a man: large. **c1960** *Wilson Coll.* **csKY,** *Double fisted. . .* Very strong.

double-foot n [By analogy with *single-foot*]

1915 *DN* 4.182 **swVA,** *Double-foot. . .* A gait of a riding horse.

double-foot plow See **foot** n **C3**

double guts n *joc*

1969 *DARE* (Qu. X53a, . . *An oversize stomach*) Inf **IL**96, Double guts.

double hand's length exclam

In marble play: see quot.

1934 *AmSp* 9.75 **csND,** *Double hand's length.* This cry permits a player to move his shooter two hand's lengths nearer to the marbles before shooting.

double harness n

Used in var fig phrr referring to marriage.

1838 *Lexington Observer & Rep.* 2 June (*DA,* at *harness*), We soon hitch'd traces to trot in double harness. **1966–69** *DARE* (Qu. AA15a, *What joking ways do you have around here of saying that people got married? "They ________."*) Inf **MS**16, Jumped in double harness and trotted through life; **WA**6, Went into double harness; (Qu. AA15b, *What joking ways do you have around here of saying that a man is getting married? "He ________."*) Infs **AK**1, Decided to run in double harness; **CA**154, Got in double harness; **TX**65, Took on a double harness.

double-head v

1 Of a train: to run with two or more engines; to power a train with two or more engines; hence vbl n *double-heading* running a train in such a way. [Back-formation from **doubleheader 1**]

1904 *Delineator* Sept 374/1, A heavy freight train had double-headed up the mountain from the west, and at the summit . . the leading engine had been cut off to run down ahead of the train. **1947** Beebe *Mixed Train* 195 **NV,** When more than a dozen cars of freight are to be hauled over the 2.5-percent grade on this stretch the train is double headed. *Ibid* 355, *Double-head:* To power a train with two locomotives. **1962** *AmSp* 37.131 **nwCA** [Logging railroad jargon], *Battery, double headin'*. . . Two or more engines that are spaced for safety and power along a train on a long haul from the woods. **1968** *AmSp* 43.286 [Railroad vocab], *Double-heading.* The use of two locomotives to haul one train.

2 See quot. Cf **double** n **2**

1968 *DARE* FW Addit **cSC,** To give someone a ride on one's bicycle: "Double-head me to the corner."

double-head(ed) adj Cf **four-headed, two-headed** *among Black speakers*

Extraordinarily learned, esp in hoodoo practice.

c1937 in 1970 Yetman *Voices* 257 **GA,** [Ex-slave speaking:] He was what we called a "double-headed nigger"—he could read and write, and he knowed so much. **c1938** in 1970 Hyatt *Hoodoo* 1.280 **ceVA,** A white fellow came to me and asked me to go with him down to one of these *double-head doctors*. . . We goes down and she [=the *double-head doctor*] fixed him. She told his fortune and told him what to do and stopped him from going to court.

double-headed hammer n

A nonexistent item used as the basis of a practical joke.

1967–70 *DARE* (Qu. HH14, *Ways of teasing a beginner or inexperienced person—for example, by sending him for a 'left-handed monkey wrench': "Go get me ________."*) Infs **DC**1, **IL**113, **IN**30, **NJ**22, **NY**123, 149, 200, 241, **TN**62, **VA**69, Double-headed hammer.

doubleheader n

1 In railroading: a usu heavy train pulled by two engines; the engines themselves. Cf **double-head 1**

1878 Pinkerton *Strikers* 216 **PA,** "Double-headers," or freight trains composed of a larger number of cars than the single train, and drawn by two engines, which economized labor. **1891** *Denver D. News* 20 Dec. *(DA),* A double-header drawing twenty cars of Durango coal from the Porter Mine, will leave Rico at 7 o'clock tomorrow morning. **1903** Brady *Bishop* 94 **CO,** The expresses required double-headers to draw them up the heavy grades. **1925** in 1953 Botkin–Harlow *Treas. Railroad Folkl.* 120, I took two miles of material loaded on a train with a double header to push it up ahead of the engines, so it could be unloaded close to the end of the last rail laid in the track. **1977** Adams *Lang. Railroader* 48, *Doubleheader:* A train hauled by two engines, especially in mountains and during heavy snows.

2 In logging: see quot 1905.

1905 U.S. Forest Serv. *Bulletin* 61.35 **NW, Gt Lakes,** *Double header.* A place from which it is possible to haul a full load of logs to the landing, and where partial loads are topped out or finished to the full hauling capacity of teams. **1969** *DARE* Tape **NY**219, The fellows there that loaded logs would load ya', and you'd go to the doubleheaders or to the landin' and dump your load.

3 A large cloud appearing before a rain storm; a thunderhead; sometimes, a thunderstorm.

1951 Hough *Singing in Morning* 85 **Martha's Vineyard MA,** They [=thunderstorms] came up at the end of a summer day, with doubleheaders looming larger and larger in the sky. **1969–70** *DARE* (Qu. B9, . . *The big clouds that roll up high before a rainstorm*) Inf **MA**55, Doubleheader clouds; **VA**47, Doubleheaders. **1979** *DARE* File **cMA** (as of c1915), We used to have severe thunderstorms when I was a child, doubleheaders we called the worst ones which usually came late in the afternoon.

4 See quot.

1968–69 *DARE* (Qu. BB33b, . . *A swelling under the skin . . very big or serious*) Infs **NC**61, **VA**26, Carbuncle, doubleheader.

5 Two ounces or shots of liquor.

1968 *DARE* (Qu. DD18, *A drink of liquor, or the amount of liquor taken in one swallow: "He took a good ________."*) Inf **IA**22, Doubleheader—two shots.

double-heading See **double-head 1**

double house n

1 A house with rooms on either side of an entrance hall; see also quot 1923.

1707 *Boston News-Letter* (MA) 17 Mar 2/2, Several other parcels of Land . . Having thereon a good double House, 4 Rooms on a Floor fit for an Ordinary. **1837** (1928) Cooper *Gleanings France* 109 **DC,** The building she inhabited was one of the ordinary American double-houses, as they are called, with a passage through the centre, the stairs in the passage, and a short corridor, to communicate with the bed-rooms, above. **1923** Nutting *MA Beautiful* 22 **seMA,** The stranger at Cape Cod is often puzzled by the term "double house." In the Cape Cod significance this phrase refers to a house with a chimney in the middle and a room on both sides. . . Of course, the term "double house" used elsewhere of a dwelling for two families, confuses the stranger. **1941** Writers' Program *Guide SC* 138 **Charleston SC,** The double house, symmetrical and almost square, had its entrance fronting the street. Its center hall plan provided kitchen and servants' quarters in the basement; parlors, dining room, and library or office on the first floor; and large drawing room and bed chambers on the second floor. **1944** Barbour *Vanishing Eden* 35 **FL,** It is a queer old structure, really a double house.

2 also *double, ~ apartment, ~ dwelling, ~ shot-gun house, ~ side-by-side, ~ tenement:* A house or residential building in which two families live in adjoining sections separated by a common wall; a duplex; occas, a two-story two-family dwelling. **scattered, but chiefly NEast, N Midl** See Map Cf **double tenant**

1923 [see **1** above]. **1965–70** *DARE* (Qu. D23, *A house that is divided in two through the middle so that two families can live in it*) 172 Infs, **scattered, but chiefly NEast, N Midl,** Double (house); **PA**245, Double house—for two families, each on separate stories; **ME**15, **MO**27, **NJ**1, **VA**72, Double tenement; **GA**8, Double apartment; **MS**1, Double apartment, duplex; **PA**70, Double dwelling; **CA**23, Double shot-gun house—two doors, two apartments; **NY**199, Double side-by-side. **1971** *Today Show Letters* **seLA,** A duplex in Detroit is two houses side by side—this structure in New Orleans is called a double.

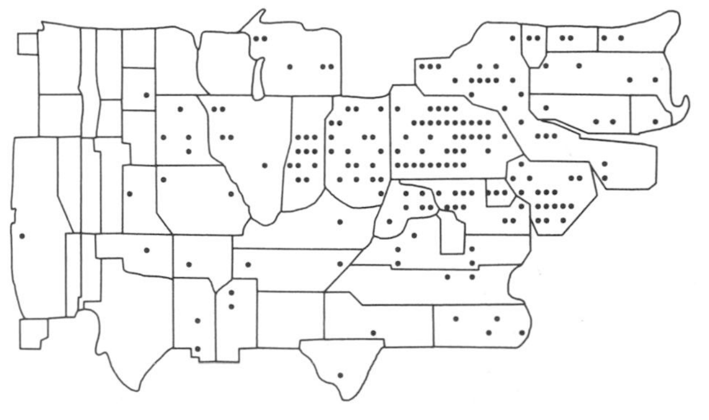

•double house 2 + varr (Qu. D23)

double Irish See **double Dutch 2**

double jack n [*jack* abbr for *jackhammer* a hand-held rock drill] **chiefly West**

In mining: a heavy sledge hammer.

1949 Emrich *Wild West Custom* 251 **West,** The hardrock men, who worked with steel and drill, singlejack and doublejack—the heavy hammers . . were the recognized lords of the shift. **1960** Climax Molybdenum Co. *Manual* 46 [Gloss.], *Double-jack*—Sledge hammer. **1966** *DARE* Tape **NM**15, [Inf:] It was mined during the old days . . the old hand drillers, they used to drill the rock . . by hand steel; a single jack. [FW:] What's a single jack? [Inf:] It's a hammer that you handle with one hand. . . A double jack is one that you handle with both hands.

double-jack v, hence vbl n *double-jacking* **chiefly West** Cf **double bitting**

In mining or oil drilling: to work in a team, one person holding a drill and the other(s) hitting it with a **double jack** n; also n *double-jacker* one who works in this way.

1926 *AmSp* 2.87 **CA** [Mining jargon], The old *hardrock* miners (now nearly extinct) were either *single jackers* or *double jackers.* The first held his own *steel* in one hand and hammered with the other. In double jacking, one man held the *jack* while the other hammered. **1949** Emrich *Wild West Custom* 206 **West,** Pat Harrington, doublejacking at the Little Earl Mine near Tin Cup, joshed his partner, who was holding the drill. **1968** Adams *Western Words* 98, *Double-jacker*—In mining, one who uses both hands on a large hammer and strikes the jack or wedge used to separate rocks for blasting. **1969** *DARE* FW Addit **CA**114 [Oil field vocabulary], *Double-jack*—One man holds the drill while two others are hitting it alternately with sledge hammers. **1976** Maclean *River Runs Through* 134 **wMT** (as of 1919), When you are blasting, naturally you first make a hole in the rock for your powder. Nowadays it is done with a pneumatic drill; then it was done by hand and a jackhammer. If you worked in a team of two it was called "double jacking."

double-jointed adj Pronc-sp *double-jinted*

1 See quots 1912, c1960. [*EDD double jointed* "extra strong"] **S Midl, Sth**

1887 (1967) Harris *Free Joe* 103 **nGA,** Don't set her atter me, Abe—don't. . . she'll be a-yerkin' me aroun' thereckly like I wuz a rag-baby. I'm a-gittin' too ole fer ter be romped aroun' by a great big double-j'inted gal like Babe. **1908** *DN* 3.306 **eAL, wGA,** *Double-jointed.* . . very large and strong: often pronounced [ǰaɪntəd]. **1912** Green *VA Folk-Speech* 152, *Double-jointed.* . . A person particularly large and strong is said to be "double-jointed." **1946** *PADS* 6.12 **eNC** (as of 1900–10), *Double-jointed.* . . Big, strong, muscular. . . Occasional. **c1960** *Wilson Coll.* **csKY,** *Double-jointed.* . . Big, strong, well-muscled, but not necessarily big in the joints.

2 See quots.

1947 *PADS* 8.18 **ceIA,** *Double-jointed:* Lacking in co-ordination; awkward. **1968** *DARE* (Qu. HH21, *A very awkward, clumsy person*) Inf **GA**53, Double-jointed.

double-jointed thistle tube n

A nonexistent item used as the basis of a practical joke.

1970 *DARE* (Qu. HH14, *Ways of teasing a beginner or inexperienced person—for example, by sending him for a 'left-handed monkey wrench': "Go get me ______.")* Inf **TN**65, Double-jointed thistle tube—done in the lab.

double log, double log(ged) cabin, double log house See **double cabin**

double-maw n Cf *DS* Z4

A grandmother.

1948 Hurston *Seraph* 247 **wFL** [Black], Poor Double-Maw! Poor Grandmaw! Dead and gone! Done left us here behind!

double-minded adj [*OED* 1552 →]

Undecided, "of two minds."

1946 McCullers *Member* 64 **AL,** About the promise for that evening she felt double-minded.

double-moldboard plow n Also sp *double mouldboard plow*

See quot 1872.

1858 (1867) Flint *Milch Cows* 194, The Michigan or double-mouldboard plough leaves the land light. **1872** (1876) Knight *Amer. Mech. Dict.* 1.727, *Double-moldboard Plow.* . . A plow having a moldboard on each side of the *sheth,* so as to throw the soil away right and left. It is used in hilling up crops, such as potatoes and cabbages. Not used for corn; the rows are too wide apart. **1907** (1910) Hunt *Forage Crops* 352, Or by means of a middle "buster," which is a double mold board plow. **1968** *DARE* (Qu. L18, *Kinds of plows*) Inf **AK**4, Double-moldboard plow—twelve inches and fourteen inches.

double needle See **double balsam fir**

double niece See **double cousin 1**

double-nigger dare, double-niggle dare See **double-dog dare**

double orange See **double Dutch 2**

double out See **double** v **2**

double pedro n Also *double pedie* **[pedro]**

=cinch n[1] **3.**

1899 (1900) Ade *Fables in Slang* 48 **IN,** While in Camp they played Double Pedie, smoked Corn-Cob Pipes, and cussed the Rations. **1913** *Official Rules of Card Games* 154, *Cinch.* High-Five (Double Pedro). . . Four players (partners, two against two). . . *Objects of the Game.*—To hold in hand Ace of trumps (high and low); and to take tricks in which J, 10, 2 and 5 of trumps and 5 of suit same color as trumps are played. **1932** [see **hollow jack**]. **1938** Asbury *Sucker's Progress* 323 **cwCA,** At first the Nevadans used the room principally as a place in which to play Cinch, a variation of All-Fours which was also known as Double Pedro or High Five, but after a few years it was devoted almost entirely to Poker. **1968** *DARE* (Qu. DD35, . . *Card games*) Inf **NV**9, Double pedro—throw all but major suit and ask for more (down to six), have to make the tricks you bid.

double-pen(ned) adj **[pen]** **chiefly Sth, S Midl** Cf **double cabin**

Of a log building: consisting of two essentially independent log structures connected by a roofed passageway.

1870 Sparks *Memories* 484 **cnGA,** Uncle Ned's tavern was one of those peculiar buildings . . designated, in some parts of Georgia at that time, as a two-storied house, with both stories on the ground; in other words, a double-penned cabin with passage between. **1941** Writers' Program *Guide AL* 346 **neAL,** The Happiness House "family" was first housed in a shack and a tent; later, with the help of neighbors, a "double-pen" log cabin was built. **1966** *DARE* (Qu. D23, *A house that is divided in two through the middle so that two families can live in it*) Inf **MS**1, Double pen [pɪn] house. **1966–69** *DARE* Tape **GA**5, Renfro lived in an old-time double-pen log house. There's a hall through it. . . Instead of glass or windows, there were board windows with shutters, no glass; **GA**50A, She lived in a double-pen log house. **1984** Joyner *Down by Riverside* 119 **SC coast** (as of a1866), [A] common folk house-type in the South was the double pen, in which a one-room cabin (or single pen) had another room added. **1987** *Hall Coll.* **ceTN,** In the time of my father and grandfather, they built double pen log cabins and double pen barns near where I live today. **1987** *NADS Letters* **nAL,** A double pen house is one that was started as a log cabin, and later had a room added, connected by a floored and covered breezeway. It's not the same as a shotgun house.

double plumbing n

1961 *Seattle Daily Times* (WA) 21 May 28, [Real estate question column:] Question: What is double plumbing . . ? Answer: This question comes to our attention quite often from persons arriving here from communities where the term "double plumbing" is not used. It refers to two bathrooms.

doublepod n

=star jasmine.

1960 Vines *Trees SW* 87, *Fruit.* Follicles 2, slender, elongate. . . Also known under vernacular names of . . Double-pod, and Southern Jasmine. . . *Trachelospermum difforme.*

doubler n

1 =double-runner; see also quot 1905. Cf *DS* N40a–b, EE24a

1877 [see **double-ripper**]. **1905** *Providence Jrnl.* 23 Feb. 1 *(DA),* The doubler comprised three clipper sleds, upon each of which a tall block was fastened, a board nailed to the blocks furnishing the seat.

2 See quot.

1917 *DN* 4.391 **neOH,** *Doubler* [dʌbl̩r̩]. . . The double ridge thrown up from the furrow on each side in beginning to plow a land.

3 See quot. Cf **doubletree 1, evener 1,** and *DS* L47

1939 *LANE* Map 173, *Evener*—When a vehicle is drawn by two horses, each hitched to its own whiffletree . . , the two whiffletrees are usually not fastened directly to the vehicle, but to the opposite ends of a cross bar which serves to equalize the pull of the two horses. . . In general, the following terms usually refer to the cross bar alone: *cross bar,* . . *doubler.* . . 1 inf, **ceMA,** *Doubler,* on a plow.

4 pl: A pair of mating crabs. **Chesapeake Bay** Cf **double crabs**

1905 U.S. Bur. Fisheries *Rept. for 1904* 405, During these times mated crabs, "doublers," as they are called by the fishermen, are found in considerable numbers. *Ibid* 427, Very often a male and female crab when mating are taken together on a trot line. . . The pair are called "doublers," or "channeler and his wife." **1942** Chesapeake Biol. Lab. *Pub.* 52.8 **Chesapeake Bay,** When the female becomes a peeler about to shed for the last time she is sought out by a male, who carries and protects her until she sheds. . . Such paired crabs are known as "doublers." **1976** Warner *Beautiful Swimmers* 29, The male grabs the female from above, makes sure that she is face forward, and carries her lightly underneath him with his walking legs for two or three days prior to her moult. Scientists call it cradle carrying, an accurate and felicitous phrase. To the watermen the two crabs are now doublers or a "buck and rider." **1984** *DARE* File **Chesapeake Bay** [Waterman's vocab], Doubler . . doubles . . double crabs.

5 In moonshining: see below. **[double v 4a]**

a A small still used for redistillation.

1963 Carson *Social Hist. Bourbon* 236, *Doubler*—A pot still used for redistilling singlings, or low wines.

b also *doubling barrel:* **=thump barrel.**

1962 Fox *Southern Fried* 153 **SC,** Well, I had to get kind of technical when I came to the doubler. This is a straight steam-rigged barrel with a drain valve. The doubler re-distills before you hit your condenser box. **1969** *DARE* Tape **GA**72, That is back in the days before the thump barrel was introduced in this country, and that thump barrel is also known as the doublin' barrel or the doubler. **1974** Maurer-Pearl *KY Moonshine* 117, *Doubler. . .* A processing keg, placed between the still and the flakestand, that redistills the liquor by using the heat of the vapor itself, thus eliminating the need to distill twice or use separate stills. "Listen to that old doubler chuckle." Also called "thumper," "thump-keg."

double rail n

A **king rail** (here: *Rallus elegans*).

1911 *Forest & Stream* 77.453 **NC,** King Rail.—Double Rail, New Bern.

double-reverse flow-check valve n

A non-existent item used as the basis of a practical joke.

1967 *DARE* (Qu. HH14, *Ways of teasing a beginner or inexperienced person—for example, by sending him for a 'left-handed monkey wrench': "Go get me ______."*) Inf **MA**1, Double-reverse flow-check valve—on cars.

double-rigged adj Also *double-rig* **West** Also called **double-barreled, double-cinch, double-fire** Cf **center fire**

Of a saddle: designed to take two cinches; hence n *double rig* a saddle so designed; such a design.

1887 *Scribner's Mag.* 2.509 **West,** *Rig, single-rig, double-rig* (in very general use throughout the Western States). **1913** (1979) Barnes *Western Grazing* 381, *Double Rig Saddle.*—A saddle with two cinches; a "rim fire" saddle. **1922** Rollins *Cowboy* 123 **West,** The saddle of two cinches was designated technically as "double-rigged" or "double rig". **1923** Cook *50 Yrs.* 113 **TX,** Double-rigged saddles, or those with both a front and back cinch, did not require this. **1929** *AmSp* 5.61 **NE,** A saddle is "double rigged" or has a "double rig," if it has two cinches. **1958** *AmSp* 33.269 **eWA,** *Double rig. . .* A saddle fastened to the horse by two bands. **1966** *DARE* (Qu. L42) Inf **NM**13, Double-rig saddle. **1977** Watts *Dict. Old West* 118, *Double rig*—A saddle with two cinch rings on either side—one below the front skirt of the saddle, the other below the cantle—thus enabling the rider to have two saddle girths.

double-ripper n Also *double-rip, ~-whipper* **chiefly swNEng =double-runner;** see also quot 1966-69.

1877 Bartlett *Americanisms* 188, *Double Ripper.* Two sleds from six to ten feet apart connected by a plank, upon which boys slide down hill. . . Also called a *Doubler.* **1912** *DN* 3.566 **CT,** Two sets of runners attached, for example, with reach and box; or merely two sleds joined together by a board in coasting. . . *double ripper.* **1943** *LANE* Map 573-574, [*Double ripper* (or *rip*) is the commonest term in Connecticut and western Massachusetts for a double sled, but is rare elsewhere. One inf, **csMA,** gives the variant *double whipper.*] **1949** [see **double-runner a**]. **1966-69** *DARE* (Qu. N40b, . . *Sleighs for carrying people*) Inf **MA**6, Traverse sled or double ripper—made like drag sled, used for people; not horse-drawn; (Qu. EE24a, *When there's snow, children go down the hill on a ______*) Inf **CT**12, Double ripper = two pig-stickers, side by side, with a board between; old-fashioned; **MA**21, Double rip or double ripper—two sleds hitched together with a long board; steerer on front sled, pusher on back sled. **1983** *Greenfield Recorder* (MA) 22 Jan 6, The boy's [sic] "double rippers" for pleasure sliding were called traverses also.

double run n Cf **double** v **4a**

1966 *DARE* (Qu. DD31, *Joking names for homemade hard liquor;* total Infs questioned, 75) Inf **FL**7, Double run.

double-runner n **chiefly eNEng** See Map Cf **double-ripper**

Two bobsleds joined in tandem by a board; spec:

a Tandem sleds used for coasting.

1883 *Harper's New Mth. Mag.* 68.146/1 **Boston MA,** The vehicle was a large two-handed boy's sled—not what you call a double-runner. **1905** *DN* 3.70 **seNH,** A coasting sled composed of two small bobs or pairs of runners connected lengthwise by a long seat or board. . . *double runner.* **1934** *Hanley Disks* **neMA,** I had a double-runner . . two sleds together. The first was on a swivel—the front one—and the back one was put on with hinges so it would rock up and down; and of course the board runs from the front to the back, and there would be side boards to rest your feet on. **1943** *LANE* Map 573-574, [*Double runner* is the commonest term in eastern New England for a double sled; the forms *double runner sled* and *double runner pung* are given by one inf each.] **1949** Kurath *Word Geog.* 59, A coasting sled consisting of two short sleds or *bobs* that are fastened together, tandem-fashion, with a heavy board. . . *Double runner* is current in the entire coastal area from Narragansett Bay to New Brunswick, including Worcester County in Massachusetts and all of New Hampshire except the northern third. *Double ripper,* occasionally shortened to *ripper* or *double rip,* is found in all of Connecticut and in western Massachusetts. **1962** Morison *One Boy's Boston* 34 **eMA,** Two boys' sleds connected by swivels with a long board made what was called a "double-runner". **1965** *PADS* 43.26 **seMA.** **1967-70** *DARE* (Qu. N40b) Inf **MA**68, Double-runner—kids would go down hills on them; (Qu. EE24a, . . *Children go down the hill on a ______*) Inf **MA**82, Double-runner—two sleds, one front, one back; **MA**100, Double-runner—child's bobsled. **1972** *PADS* 57.43 **Marietta OH** [Older native speakers], *Double runner.* This term from the coastal New England region was given by [an old Black woman with 7th grade educ], who accompanied it with a description, and [an old, well educ White woman of New England heritage].

b also *double-runner sleigh:* Tandem sleds or sleighs used for transporting loads or people.

1966-69 *DARE* (Qu. N40a, . . *Sleighs . . for hauling loads*) Infs **NY**5, **RI**8, Double-runner; **MA**15, Double-runner sleighs—in past; **MA**36, Double-runner—two-horse rig; same as bobsled; **MA**42, Double-runner—a light sleigh and a heavier one; for working around the farm and in the woods and like o' that; **NH**5, Double-runner—two short sleds hitched together; (Qu. N40b, . . *Sleighs for carrying people*) Infs **MA**47, 55, 68, **OH**42, Double-runner(s).

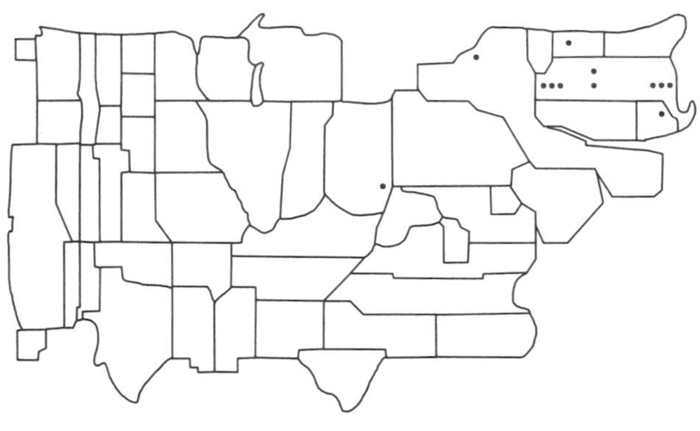

•double runner + var (Qq. N40a, b, EE24a)

doubles n pl Cf **doubles** exclam, **dubs 1**

In marble play: two marbles; a game played with two marbles in a ring.

1890 *DN* 1.24 **KY,** "Dubs" means "doubles" or two "men" (marbles). **1942** Berrey-Van den Bark *Amer. Slang* 665.2, Doubles, dubs, *two marbles.* **1955** *PADS* 23.16 **cwTN,** *Doubles. . .* Two marbles. **1967** *DARE* (Qu. EE7, . . *Marble games*) Inf **LA2**, Doubles—where you put up two in a ring playing for keeps. **c1970** Wiersma *Marbles Terms* **ceMI,** Doubles, dubs—two marbles.

doubles exclam

In marble play: see quot.

1963 *KY Folkl. Rec.* 9.3.62, *Demand for right to possess marbles when two (2) are knocked off the square or out of the ring:* Doubles.

double sawbuck n Also *double, ~ saw* **[sawbuck a ten-dollar bill] scattered, but chiefly Nth, N Midl** See Map

A twenty-dollar bill; rarely, twenty dollars in other denominations.

1850 *Knickerbocker* 36.297, Send me the two double 'saw-bucks'. **1948** *Time* 17 May 87/1, Any tout or hustler around the track can usually work Eddie for "a double sawbuck." **1950** *WELS (Names for twenty-dollar bill)* 10 infs, **WI,** Double sawbuck. **1951** in 1960 Wentworth-Flexner *Slang* 158, A terrible conspiracy which already has printed so many sheets of dollars, ten-spots and double-saws. **c1960** *Wilson Coll.* **csKY,** *Double sawbuck*. . . Joking name for a $20 bill. **1965-70** *DARE* (Qu. U28c, . . *A twenty-dollar bill*) 49 Infs, **scattered, but chiefly Nth, N Midl,** Double sawbuck; **IL**117, **MS**1, **NY**205, 209, **SC**55, Double saw. **1966** *AmSp* 41.280 [Carnie talk], *Double*. . . Twenty dollars. Not necessarily a twenty-dollar bill. Short for *double sawbuck*.

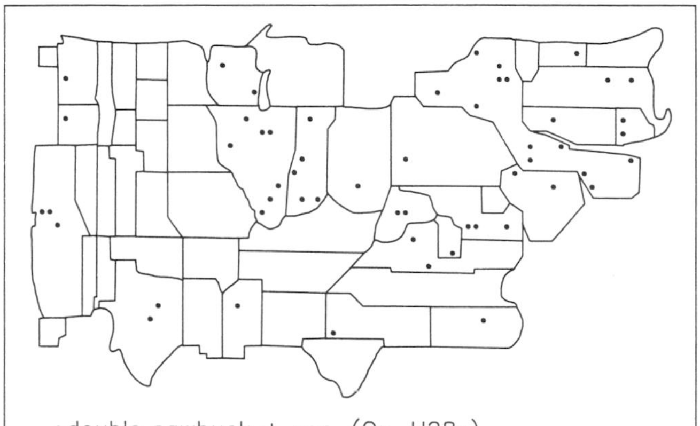
•double sawbuck + var (Qu. U28c)

double shot-gun house See **double house 2**

double shovel plow n Also *double shovel, double shoveled plow* **chiefly S Midl** See Map

A simple plow with two shares, used esp in cultivating growing crops.

1853 in 1854 PA State Ag. Soc. *Report* 1.180 **sePA,** There are . . the *Double Shovel Plow,* for dressing corn, and the *Horse Hay Fork,* for unloading hay. **1891** Garland *Main-Travelled Roads* 162 **SD,** Julia Peterson . . was toiling back and forth between the corn-rows, holding the handles of the double-shovel corn-plough. **c1960** *Wilson Coll.* **csKY,** *Double shovel*. . . A plow with two bull-tongue points, esp. designed, it seems, to bust the middles when corn is laid by. **1965-70** *DARE* (Qu. L18, *Kinds of plows*) 37 Infs, **chiefly S Midl,** Double shovel plow; **LA**8, Walking double shovel plow; (Qu. L25, *The implement used to clean out weeds and loosen the earth between rows of corn*) 22 Infs, **chiefly S Midl, esp KY,** Double shovel (plow); **OH**50, Double shoveled plow; (Qu. L20, *The implement used in a field after it's been plowed to break up the lumps*) Inf **MS**46, Double shovel. **1968-70** *DARE* Tape **OH**58, The double shovel [plow], they generally used that to plow corn. They'd have the two shovels so that one of 'em was behind the other; **KY**84, [FW:] What implements were used to cultivate it [=tobacco]? [Inf:] Usually a diamond sidin'-off plow or a double shovel, in those days; **VA**38, As the [tobacco] plant grows . . you'd maybe use a cultivator. Old people use what they call double shovel . . to cultivate and freshen that bed up and work fresh dirt back to it so you'd have a loose soil there next to your plant. **1976** Garber *Mountain-ese* 24 **Appalachians,** *Double-shovel* . . two-point plow—We allers lay off our garden with a bull tongue and cultivate it with a double-shovel.

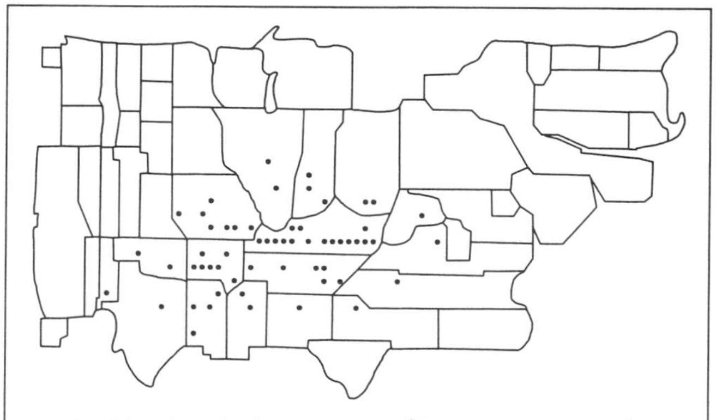
•double shovel plow + varr (Qq. L18, L25, L20)

double shuffle n

1 A kind of syncopated tap dance; the basic step in such a dance; hence v phr *double shuffle.* **chiefly Sth, S Midl, orig also NEng** Cf **double trouble**

1835 Longstreet *GA Scenes* 13, Jim Johnson kept up the double shuffle from the beginning to the end of the reel. **1869** Stowe *Oldtown Folks* 35 **ceMA,** He was equally prepared . . to raise a funeral psalm or whistle the time of a double-shuffle. **1896** Harris *Sister Jane* 24 **GA,** Why don't [William] . . drop his wing and cut the double-shuffle around her? I lay that would fetch her. **1940** Writers' Program *Guide TX* 114, Noah Smithwick described a wedding of 1828: "When young folks danced in those days, they danced. . . they 'shuffled' and 'double-shuffled,' 'wired' and 'cut the pigeon's wing.' " **1963** Pilgrim Soc. Plymouth MA *Notes* 13.7, [In earlier days] they danced [at the Tavern] four-handed reels, and some did the double shuffle or played games. **1965-69** *DARE* (Qu. FF5a, . . *Steps and figures in dancing—in past years*) Infs **DE**7, **FL**22, **IN**30, **KY**19, Double shuffle; **KY**5, Double shuffle—square dance step.

2 See quots. **West**

1937 *DN* 6.619 **swTX,** A good bronco can shift from one gait to the other quickly, and a sudden shift in bucking style is known as the *double shuffle.* **1942** Berrey-Van den Bark *Amer. Slang* 61.1, Double-shuffle, *a treacherous shifting at an unexpected moment, as by a pitching horse. Ibid* 922.1, *Bucking*. . . Double-shuffle, *a sudden treacherous shifting of gait.* **1956** Moody *Home Ranch* 51 **CO,** He [=a horse] didn't sunfish, and he didn't swap ends, but he did every double-shuffle, fence row, and zigzag in the book.

3 See quot.

1930 Shoemaker *1300 Words* 17 **cPA Mts** (as of c1900), *Double-shuffle*—A quick get-away or escape.

double side-by-side See **double house 2**

double sight n

1 Very clear vision.

1934 *Hanley Disks* **csME,** After my eye got well . . I had double sight. I could see a great deal farther.

‡**2** See quot.

1966 *DARE* (Qu. X23, . . *Joking words . . for eyeglasses*) Inf **SC**10, Double sight, windshields.

double-sighted adj

Clairvoyant.

1923 Parsons *Folk-lore Sea Islands* 198 **csSC** [Gullah], There is the familiar belief that a child born with a caul will see ghosts, is "double-sighted."

double singletree n Also *double swingletree* **[singletree] scattered, but esp C and S Atl** See Map

=doubletree 1.

1966-70 *DARE* (Qu. L47, *The two movable bars behind a team of horses . . fastened to a longer piece*) 14 Infs, Double singletree; **NJ**56,

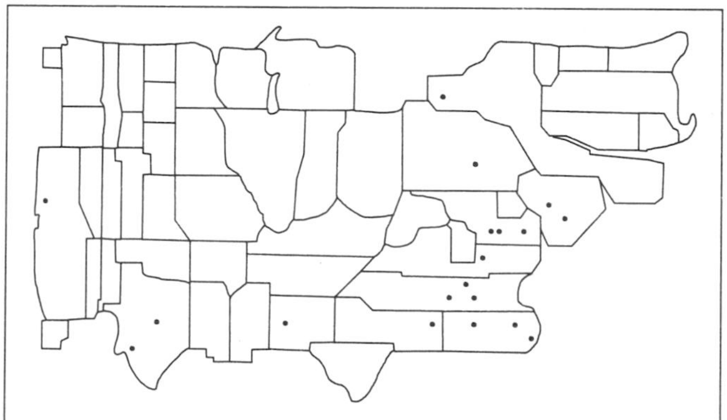
•double singletree + var (Qu. L47)

MD9, 15, NC3, 8, Double swingletree. **1972** *PADS* 58.16 **cwAL,** *Double-tree* (12 [infs]) and *double singletree* (1) are used for the two-horse rig.

double sled n **chiefly NEng** Cf **double-ripper, double sleigh**
=double-runner.

1931–33 *LANE Worksheets* **cCT,** *Double sled*—two sleds bolted together, same as *double ripper.* **1943** *LANE* Map 573–574 **seMA, csME,** Terms for 'double sleds', consisting of two sets of short runners joined by a reach or a plank . . [include] *double sled* [used by 2 infs in **seMA, csME**]. **1966** *DARE* (Qu. N40a, . . *Sleighs . . for hauling loads*) Inf **ME**5, Double sled—two sets of runners.

double sleigh n Also *double-bunk sleigh* Arch spp *double slay, ~ sley* Cf **double-runner b, double sled**
A sleigh drawn by two horses; two sleighs or sleds in tandem.

1737 (1899) Parkman *Diary* 10 **cMA,** Mary Tilestone took a ride with me in a double Slay. **1855** in 1946 Cook *Letters* 7 Mar 13 **neNY,** Your Pa says to Charley since we came home that they must rig out the double sley and all go. **1966–69** *DARE* (Qu. N40a, . . *Sleighs . . for hauling loads*) Inf **IL**48, Double sleigh—fixed sleigh on the rear axle; **NY**24, Double sleigh; **MN**15, Double-bunk sleigh—could be lengthened like a bobsled, a following portion; **MT**4, Double-bunk sleigh—for logs.

double span exclam
In marble play: a call which allows a player to shoot from a point two hand-lengths closer to the target.

1966 *DARE* Tape **NC**22, If you could call "double span" before the other people said "no spans," why you could get double.

double spruce n
1 A spruce: usu either **white spruce** or **black spruce 1,** but also **red spruce.**

1810 Michaux *Histoire des Arbres* 1.18, *Black* or *Double Spruce* . . dans les Etats du nord, [et] le District de Maine. **1897** Sudworth *Arborescent Flora* 34, *Picea mariana* . . Double Spruce (Me., Vt., Minn.) *Ibid* 37, *Picea canadensis* . . Double Spruce (Vt.) **1908** Britton *N. Amer. Trees* 55, *White Spruce—Picea canadensis*. . . Also called Single spruce, Cat spruce, Double spruce. *Ibid* 56, *Red Spruce—Picea rubens*. . . Variously called Black spruce, Double spruce, . . some of which perhaps are more appropriate to the Swamp spruce. **1927** Keeler *Our Native Trees* 472, In the early botanies the Black and the White Spruce were designated respectively as double and single spruce, for reasons which are not apparent, as the disposition of the leaves of each is the same. **1976** Bailey–Bailey *Hortus Third* 871, *[Picea] mariana* . . Double spruce.

2 **=Fraser fir.** Cf **double balsam fir**

1822 Eaton *Botany* 391, *Pinus fraseri* . . double spruce. **1897** Sudworth *Arborescent Flora* 50, *Abies fraseri* . . Double Spruce (N.C.) **1900** Lyons *Plant Names* 7, *A[bies] Fraseri* . . Double Spruce.

double stone wall n Also *double wall* **[stone wall]** Cf **balanced wall, face wall**
A **stone wall** in which the two faces are built separately and filled with smaller stones.

1932 *Hanley Disks* **cMA,** Double stone wall . . fill in the spaces between with small stones picked up in the fields . . Often built with a tilt, broader at bottom. **1933** *Ibid* **seCT,** Double wall's got two faces. It's faced . . on both sides, on the back side and the front side. **1989** *DARE* File **cMA,** Double wall.

double-story barn See **double-deck(er) barn**

double supper n

1968 *DARE* (Qu. EE1, . . *Games . . children play . . in which they form a ring, and either sing or recite a rhyme*) Inf **IN**16, Double supper; (Qu. EE33, . . *Outdoor games . . that children play*) Inf **IN**14, Double supper.

double swingletree See **double singletree**

double tansy n

1971 Krochmal *Appalachia Med. Plants* 246, *Tanacetum vulgare* . . double tansy.

double team n
1 A two-animal team; a vehicle drawn by such a team. **[team** a single draft animal]

1855 *NY Herald* (NY) 31 Dec 1/5 **NYC,** The city railroads were sadly incommoded. Double teams were employed to drag the cars, which even then progressed very slowly. **1856** Whitcher *Bedott Papers* 25 **cNY,** A mess o' men in a double team . . hysted us out. **1939** *LANE* Map 174 *(Team)* **scattered NEng,** [8 infs use the term *double team* to refer to "two horses and the vehicle to which they are hitched"; 4 infs use it to mean "two horses, usually harnessed together or hitched to a vehicle."]

2 A four-animal team. **[team** a pair of draft animals]

1966 *DARE* (Qu. L50, *What does the word 'team' mean on farms around here?;* total Infs questioned, 75) Inf **MS**72, Two or four horses or mules, four would be a double team.

double-team v
1 To use two teams of draft animals in hauling through difficult terrain. *old-fash*

1843 in 1939 OR Hist. Soc. *Hist. Qrly.* 40.235 **cTN,** We crawsed . . a smawl streem. Dubeld teamed & crawsed the hill. **1934** Vines *Green Thicket* 111 **cnAL,** The long string advanced a few miles . . going through mudholes well-nigh impassable. Often they had to double-team to help the weaker teams, poorer drivers, or heavier loads through. **1949** Guthrie *Way West* 215 **Oregon Trail** (as of 1847), It was push now, pull and push and strain at spokes, for some teams couldn't climb a rise alone. Push or double-team.

2 often with *on;* also *double teams, double-teen:* To bring extra force to bear on (someone or something); to gang up on. **chiefly Sth**

1860 U.S. Congress *Congressional Globe* 36th Cong 1st Sess 12 Jan 423/3 **IL,** I saw a disposition . . to "double teams" on me, as they did last year when a debate grew up, five or six on one. *Ibid* 424/2, In respect to the Senator's allusion to "double-teaming" upon him, . . I do not exactly agree with my friend from Mississippi. **1865** (1905) Chesnut *Diary from Dixie* 346 **SC,** Beauregard and Lee were expected, but Grant had double-teamed on Lee. **1904** (1905) Watson *Bethany* 197 **eGA** (as of 1860s), On the next day we double-teamed on one section of his army. **1922** Gonzales *Black Border* 69 **eSC,** Three or four yellow men double-team a black man and beat him up. He doesn't take them to court but waits his chance. **1935** Hurston *Mules & Men* 206 **FL,** Good Bread jumped up with her pocket knife out. "Who y'all tryin tuh double teen? Trying tuh run de hawg over de wrong one now." **1942** Hurston *Dust Tracks* 49 **FL** [Black], Mary Ann and I had started to fighting and I was doing fine until her older sister Janie and her brother Ed, who was about my size, had all doubleteened me. **1980** *AmSp* 55.202 **swMS,** I ain't scared of nothing, not with no gun. Like I got a dozen people off me one day. I was a boy, and they all kind of double-team(ed) me. . . You go out in the hills, all of them'll come at you.

3 also *double-team it;* Of two persons: to work together.

1884 Twain *Huck. Finn* 183 **Missip Valley,** "Old man," says the young one. "I reckon we might double-team it together; what do you think?" "I ain't undisposed." **1966** Barnes–Jensen *Dict. UT Slang* 13, *Double-team it* . . to act together in concert. "I liked him so we double teamed all winter on the trap line."

double-teams, double-teen See **double-team** v 2

double tenant n [Perh folk-etym for *double tenement* (at **double house 2**)] **chiefly Sth** *esp freq among Black speakers*
=double house 2.

1965–70 *DARE* (Qu. D23, *A house that is divided in two through the middle so that two families can live in it*) Infs **AL**14, 60, **AR**7, **GA**91, **KS**5, **MS**60, **NJ**1, **NY**213, **TN**52, Double tenant. [6 of 9 Infs Black]

double tenement See **double house 2**

double the hill v phr Cf **double** v **1**
Among loggers and railroad workers: see quot 1958; also fig: to die.

1945 Hubbard *Railroad Ave.* 330, His friends called to him in sad refrain./ He smiled and said, "I've broken the chain."/ Then, closing his eyes, he said no more./ He was "doubling the hill" to the further shore. **1958** McCulloch *Woods Words* 51 **Pacific NW,** *Double the hill*—To use two sets of power to get a load up a hill—as a cat pulling a truck up a steep pitch on a logging road. **1977** Adams *Lang. Railroader* 48, *Double the hill.*

double-tides adv Cf **double** v **2**
In phr *work double-tides:* To work unusually long or hard.

c1885 in 1981 Woodward *Mary Chesnut's Civil War* 594 **SC** (as of 1864), Sundays Bones [=the maid] and I do our own work, or Bones works double tides. Fortunately, she does not mind. **1943** Colcord *Sea Language* 68 **ME, Cape Cod, Long Island,** *Double-tides.* To work double-tides is to have a long-drawn-out spell of work, originally one that could not be completed in a single ebb-tide. "We worked double-tides hauling up the boats."

double-tooth n [From the two barbed awns; transl of *Bidens*]
A **beggar ticks 1** (here: *Bidens cernua*).
1900 Lyons *Plant Names* 63, *B[idens] cernua* . . Double-tooth. **1959** Carleton *Index Herb. Plants* 38, Double Tooth: *Bidens cernua.*

doubletree n [Appar by analogy with **singletree,** folk-etym for **swingletree**] **widespread exc NEast** See Map and Map Section Cf **evener 1**
On a horse-drawn vehicle: a pivoting bar whose center is attached directly or indirectly to the vehicle and whose ends are attached to **singletrees;** also, sometimes pl, the pair of **singletrees** or the apparatus as a whole. Note: A few *DARE* Infs appear to use **doubletree** in the sense of **singletree** or even to interchange their senses; this probably reflects confusion due to lack of familiarity with the implements or simply misunderstanding of the question.
1847 (1848) Webster *Amer. Dict.* 1034/3, A single-tree is fixed upon each end of the double-tree when two horses draw abreast. **1878** U.S. Bur. Indian Affairs *Report* 151 **WY,** A great many parts of the harnesses have been lost or destroyed, and the hard-wood double-trees and single-trees used up and devoted to other uses. **1886** *Congressional Record* 10 Mar 17.3.2273/2 **IL,** I will pull with the gentleman from Kansas and the gentleman from Michigan . . to keep up my end of the double-tree. **1902** *DN* 2.233 **sIL,** *Double-tree.* . . The draught bar of a two-horse vehicle or plow, to which the single-trees are attached. **1905** *DN* 3.78 **nwAR,** *Double-trees.* . . A pair of whiffle-trees. 'Her husband was thrown down among the tongue, double-trees, and the heels of the horses, and there hammered to death.' **1908** *DN* 3.306 **eAL, wGA,** *Double-tree.* . . A pair of whiffletrees for a two-horse wagon; also the beam to which the single-trees are attached. **1909** Wason *Happy Hawkins* 193, Now, me an' Ches was about as different as they ever get, most ways, an' yet we pulled a level double-tree out in the open. **1915** *DN* 4.182 **swVA. 1927** [see **evener 1**]. **1937** Sandoz *Slogum* 41 **NE,** A pair of doubletrees at a plough standing in the furrow. **1939** *LANE* Map 173 *(Evener),* The terms *doubletree* and *double whiffletree* denote (a) the two whiffletrees . . (b) the cross bar to which they are attached . . or (c) the assembly. [*Doubletree* is given by 20 infs scattered throughout New England.] **1965–70** *DARE* (Qu. L47, *The two movable bars behind a team of horses are fastened to a longer piece; this is a* ______) 581 Infs, **widespread, exc NEast,** Doubletree; (Qu. L46, *Behind each horse there's a movable bar*) 21 Infs, **scattered,** Doubletree [*DARE* Ed: 2 Infs corrected this resp to *singletree;* 8 specified that this was used with two horses; 3 indicated that this referred to the bar to which the singletrees were attached.]; **MI**83, Doubletree—two singletrees hooked together; **WA**8, Singletree and doubletrees; **WI**42, If there are two they're called doubletrees. **1983** *MJLF* 9.1.38 **ceKY** (as of 1956), *Doubletree* . . the crossbar to which the two singletrees are attached when using a team of horses.

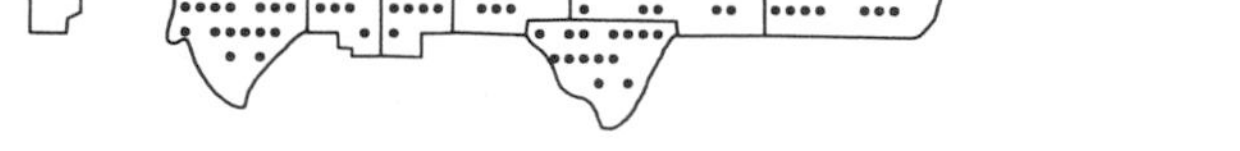

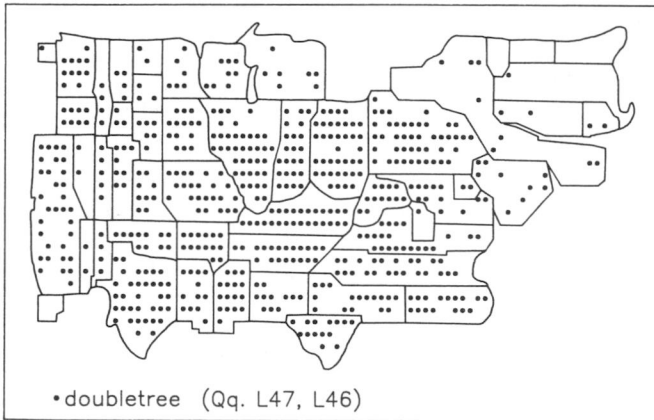

•doubletree (Qq. L47, L46)

doubletree up with v phr Cf **double harness**
Fig: to marry (someone).
1948 Manfred *Chokecherry* 27 **nwIA,** He's been junin' . . [y]er old gal friend. . . An' you'd better step fast if you still intend to doubletree up with her.

double-trouble n *old-fash* Cf **double shuffle 1**
A dance step; see quot 1813.
1809 Irving *Hist. NY* 2.105 **NY,** They . . did likewise introduce the far-famed step in dancing called "double trouble." **1813** Paulding *Scottish Fiddle* 209, This is a favourite step, and considered the test of good dancing among the farmers' sons and daughters. It was undoubtedly introduced into America by the natives of Africa. . . The dancing step, called "double trouble," from its being twice as much trouble to dance it, as to dance any other, . . consists in moving both feet without lifting them from the floor, in such a manner as to keep time to the music. **1899** (1912) Green *VA Folk-Speech* 152, *Double-trouble.* . . Double shuffle; kind of dance. **1903** *DN* 2.312 **seMO,** *Double-trouble.* . . A negro dancing step. **1907** *DN* 3.230 **nwAR,** *Double-trouble.*

‡double-trough n
A funnel.
1968 *DARE* (Qu. F9, *To get a liquid through a narrow opening—for example, the neck of a bottle—you'd pour it through a* ______) Inf **LA**43, ['dʌbl̩ˌtruθ] [FW: Inf's spelling *double-trough*].

double-u n Usu |'dʌbl̩ju, -jə|; also **chiefly Sth, S Midl** |'dʌbjə|; also |dʌb(z)| Pronc-spp *dub(s), dubya*
Std sense (the letter "w"), var forms.
1941 *AmSp* 16.14 **eTX** [Black], Hello. Is this 2384-W? . . ['hɛlo ɪ'zɪs tu θri et fo 'dʌbjə]. **1942** in 1944 *ADD* 175 **Sth,** *Double-U.* . . The letter *w.* . . |dʌbjə|. In deliberate speech. **1979** *DARE* File (as of c1930), One of my . . friends in college was from ['luəvl̩] she said, a place I finally identified as Louisville, Kentucky. . . My college nickname was MW, which she pronounced in an un-Yankee fashion—['ɛmˌdʌbjə]. **1984** Burns *Cold Sassy* 104 **nGA** (as of 1906), You need to understand that in Cold Sassy . . [w]e . . say *dubya* for the letter "W." **1989** *DARE* File **cwWA,** The current abbreviation for the University of Washington (Seattle) is *U-dubs* ['ju 'dʌbz]. It is also so pronounced by townspeople. *Ibid* **csWI,** The University of Wisconsin is sometimes called ['ju 'dʌb].

double up v phr
1 also *double:* To marry; to become engaged; to live together. Cf **double harness**
1817 *Niles' Weekly Reg.* 12.112/1 **Boston MA,** Jonathan Russell, (to use a yankee phrase) lately "doubled" with a Miss Smith. The approaching nuptials were thus announced in the *Boston Centinel.* **1894** *DN* 1.330 **NJ,** *Double up:* to marry. **1950** *AmSp* 25.32 **New Orleans LA,** Of an unmarried couple, to live together. [From *The Lantern*] Nov. 10, 1886, 2/1: 'Isaac Sontheiner and Grace Richards . . concluded, in the parlance of the fancy, to double-up.' **1969** *DARE* (Qu. AA15a, . . *Ways . . of saying that people got married: "They* ______.") Inf **MA**38, Doubled up.
2 See quot. **chiefly Midl, esp N Midl**
1965–70 *DARE* (Qu. Y32, *To squeeze yourself into a small space: "If you're going to fit in there you'll have to* ______.") 14 Infs, **chiefly N Midl,** Double up; **PA**70, Double up yourself.
‡3 See quot.
1968 *DARE* (Qu. II8, *When one person wants to share or divide something with another person, he might say, "Let's* ______ *[on that].")* Inf **MD**17, Share, double up.
4 To work quickly. [Perh from *on the double* quickly, or *double-time* to move or do something quickly]
1968 *DARE* (Qu. A22, . . *'To start working hard': "She had only ten minutes to clean the room, but she* ______ *[and had it done in no time]."*) Inf **NC**81, Double[d] up on it.

double wagon n Cf **double-box**
Any of var usu heavy wagons or carts drawn by draft animals.
1966–70 *DARE* (Qu. N41b, *Horse-drawn vehicles to carry heavy loads*) Infs **NJ**67, **VA**78, Double wagon—two horses; **NY**68, Double wagon—a big heavy wagon with four wheels; **NY**27, Double wagon; **SC**19, Double wagon—two wheeled timber cart with real high wheels for hauling logs; **VT**7, Double wagon—for logs, could put on [=install] hay racks [to use it as a hay wagon]; (Qu. N41c, *Horse-drawn vehicles to carry light loads*) Inf **LA**8, Double wagon—with two mules.

double wall See **double stone wall**

double whiffletree n Also *double whippletree, ~ whiffle, ~ whipple* [**whiffletree**] Cf **double singletree**
=**doubletree 1.**

1939 *LANE* Map 173 *(Evener),* The terms *doubletree* and *double whiffletree* denote (a) the two whiffletrees . . (b) the cross bar to which they are attached . . or (c) the assembly. [*Double whiffletree* (or *whippletree*) is given by 41 infs, chiefly on the eastern coast and in western Connecticut.] **1969** *DARE* (Qu. L47, *The two movable bars behind a team of horses are fastened to a longer piece; this is a ———*) Inf **NY**206, Double whipple, double whiffle; **NY**213, Double whippletree.

double-whipper See **double-ripper**

double-X n

1 See quot 1950. [**ex** n²]

1841 *Spirit of Times* 20 Mar 25/3 **NC,** Enclosed I transmit a "double X," turned out from one of the Currency Manufactories here. **1950** *WELS (A twenty-dollar bill)* 2 Infs, **WI,** Double-X. **1967–69** *DARE* (Qu. U28c) Infs **ID**5, **MA**58, Double-X.

2 Something of high quality, the best; hence adj phr *double-X* excellent, very good.

1951 *PADS* 16.24 [Racetrack argot], *Double-X. . . A best bet* [=the horse most likely to win]. **1968** *DARE* (Qu. KK1a, *Other words meaning very good—for example, food: "That pie was ———."*) Inf **CA**39, Double-X.

double yoke adv phr Cf **double harness**

In the state of matrimony.

1968 *DARE* (Qu. AA15a, . . *Joking ways . . of saying that people got married*) Inf **PA**118, Traveling double yoke.

doubling barrel See **doubler 5b**

doubling liquor See **doublings**

doubling out See **double** v **2**

doublings n pl, but sg in attrib use [**double** v **4a, b**] **chiefly S Midl** Cf **backings, singlings**

In moonshining:

a Redistilled liquor.

1867 U.S. Congress *Congressional Globe* 39th Cong 2d sess 21 Jan app 60/1 **KY,** The singling tub is placed aside and the doubling tub put to the outlet of the worm. *Ibid,* Backings are too valuable to be lost, and are placed back into the still, run through again and come out doublings or proof whiskey. **1884** Harris *Mingo* 102 **nGA,** Teague Poteet owned and managed two stills. He was looking after some "doublings" when the notes of the horn dropped down into the gorge. **1924** Raine *Land of Saddle-Bags* 131 **Appalachians,** After the "run" is finished, the still is emptied and the singlings poured in it to be distilled a second time into "doublings," which are thus freed from the rank oils and other impurities. **1934** (1970) Wilson *Backwoods Amer.* 165 **AR, MO,** The liquor of second distillation is called "doublings." If under-distilled, the doublings will be rank and weak; if over-distilled, almost pure alcohol. **1968** *Foxfire* Fall–Winter 55 **nGA,** When all the beer had been run through once, . . all the "singlins" [were] placed into the still at one time. . . The result was the "doublins," or good whiskey. **1974** Dabney *Mountain Spirits* xxi **sAppalachians,** Doubling Liquor: Whiskey run through a copper pot still twice, which produces a proof of well over 100. Sometimes known as high wines or "doubled and twisted whiskey." **1976** Garber *Mountain-ese* 24 **sAppalachians,** I'm savin' a jug uv doublin's jist special fer Christmas time.

b See quot.

1974 Maurer–Pearl *KY Moonshine* 117, *Doublings n. (plural only).* The complete cycle that is made by running fermented beer [*DARE* Ed: =**beer 1**] through a still, extracting the alcohol, and doubling or mashing back. "Yeah, we made ten doublings at that place."

doubs See **dubs** exclam **1**

doubt n [*OED doubt* sb. 2 "A matter or point in obscurity"; →1693]

A matter of doubt—used in phr *it is a doubt if.*

1914 *DN* 4.81 **ME, nNH,** *Think it's a doubt ef. . .* I think it doubtful if. **1979** *AmSp* 54.97 **seME** (as of 1899–1910), *Doubt. . .* "It's a doubt if you get wet today."

dougaloo See **doogaloo**

dough v

1952 Brown *NC Folkl.* 1.534, *Dough. . .* To feed dough to chickens. "Jane, go out and dough the biddies while I get supper."—Harnett county.

dough conj See **though**

dough baby n Also *dough babe, ~ bob;* also sp *dobabe, dobaby* [Perh folk-etym of **dobe** n **5;** cf **doughboy** n² **2**] **chiefly West** Also called **dough marble, doughy** Cf **crockery, dough roller 3**

A clay marble, esp an unglazed one.

1949 *PADS* 11.20 **CO,** *Dough baby. . .* A clay marble. **1958** *PADS* 29.32 **WA,** *Dough-babe. . .* A common clay marble. **1966–68** *DARE* (Qu. EE6b, *Small marbles or marbles in general*) Inf **CA**59, Dough babes—the little glazed clay ones; **WA**6, Dough babies; (Qu. EE6c, *Cheap marbles*) Infs **AZ**1, **OR**14, **WA**6, Dough babies; **WY**1, Dough babies—made out of pottery; **CA**2, Dough babies—made of adobe; **CA**59, **WA**13, Dough babes; **UT**4, Dough bob ['do,bɑb]. **1966–69** *DARE* Tape **CA**172, The dough babies were made of clay. They were the cheapest kind of marble; **WA**6, Dough babies were just clay without very much glaze on it. **1971** Bright *Word Geog. CA & NV* 116 **CA,** Marbles: . . dobabes/dobabies 13 [responses].

dough bait n Cf **doughball 2**

Fish bait made of dough.

1967 *DARE* Tape **LA**5, Plenty of 'em would call it a dough bait but it actually wasn't a dough bait—it was made out of cornmeal. Now you can make the dough bait the same way . . you just roll out dough like you gonna make biscuits. Roll it into little strings. . . Drop them strings in that boilin' water. **1970** *DARE* (Qu. P13, . . *Ways of fishing . . besides the ordinary hook and line*) Inf **TX**78, Dough bait.

dough baker See **dough beater**

doughball n

1 A cornmeal dumpling. Cf **doughboy** n¹ **1**

1835 (1836) Gilman *Life on the Lakes* 2.155 **Lake Superior,** The boiling mess was cooked and poured out into a deep tin pan; pork, fish, dough-balls, and no inconsiderable portion of the liquor, called by the men . . soup, all together. **1860** Harris *Louie's Last Term* 168 **cwNJ,** "Dough-balls" were her acknowledged passion. **1898** Smith *Caleb West* 56 **NYC,** Dinner was announced, and the Screamer's crew went below to more sizzle and doughballs. **1966** *DARE* (Qu. H24, . . *Boiled cornmeal*) Inf **AL**11, Doughball.

2 also *doughball bait:* A lump of flour, meal, or cereal mixed with water and used as fish bait; see quots 1920, c1960. **scattered, but less freq NEast, C and S Atl, Pacific** See Map Cf **dough bait**

1908 Forbes–Richardson *Fishes of IL* 183 **Missip-Ohio Valley,** The channel-cat is taken very frequently in bait nets . . baited usually with "dough-balls," made by mixing flour and water, allowing the paste to sour, and then baking it. **1943** McAtee *Dial. Grant Co. IN Suppl. 2* 8 (as of 1890s), *Dough-ball . .* a bait for the carp made of flour dough mixed with cotton so that it would last longer on a fish-hook; it would be scented or flavored according to the secret formula of each fisherman. **1948** *Pop. Mechanics* June 190/2, If you work carefully when baiting, the dough ball can be made to cover the hook entirely. . . This is the trick in taking the wary channel cat with dough-ball baits. **1954** *Harder Coll.* **cwTN,** *Dough ball*—Ball of dough used as fish bait. **c1960** *Wilson Coll.* **csKY,** *Dough ball. . .* A fish bait made by saturating cotton balls in dough and then baking the balls. Also called *dough-ball bait.* **1965–70** *DARE* (Qu. P13, . . *Ways of fishing . . besides the ordinary hook and line*) 25 Infs, **scattered, but less freq NEast, C and S Atl, Pacific,** Doughball; (Qu. P8, . . *'White bait';* total Infs questioned, 75) Infs

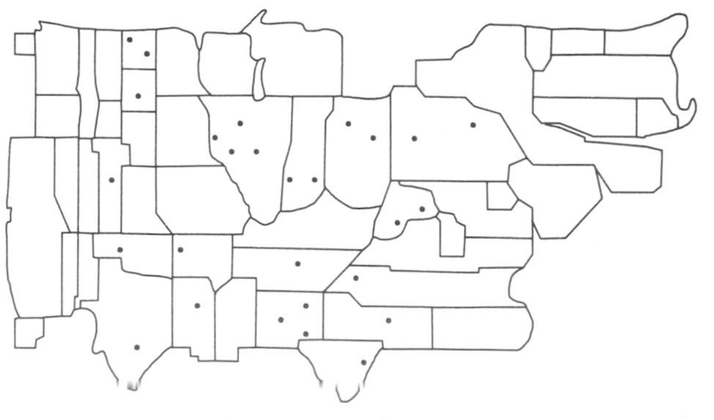

•doughball 2 (Qq. P13, P8)

AR41, GA1, OK3, Doughballs. **1968** *DARE* Tape **IN**36, He used Wheaties for a doughball—regular breakfast cereal. Just wet them a little bit, work 'em in your hand. Just make the finest doughball you ever seen. Put that on your hook and just let 'er out there.

3 A piece of dough cut from the center of a doughnut and deep fried. Cf **doughnette**

1967–69 *DARE* (Qu. H28, *Different shapes or types of doughnuts*) Infs **CA**22, Doughballs—the centers; **IL**91, Doughballs; **PA**167, Doughballs—the holes.

4 A marine alga (here: *Polysiphonia olneyi*). [See quot 1882]

1879 U.S. Natl. Museum *Bulletin* 14.266 **Long Is. NY,** *Polysiphonia olneyi*. . . Dough-balls. **1882** U.S. Bur. Fisheries *Rept. for 1879* 7.171, In its typical form *P[olysiphonia] Olneyi* forms dense soft tufts, sometimes called dough-balls by the sea-shore population. **1901** Arnold *Sea-Beach* 88, *P. Olneyi* (dough-balls). . . It is common in summer on stones and on eelgrass, at low-water mark, from Cape Cod to New York.

doughball bait See **doughball 2**

dough bat n

1906 Lovett *Old Boston Boys* 52, Do you remember . . apple "dough bats"? The exterior of these last was of a beautiful doughnut brown, and they contained in some part of their depths a trace more or less of apple sauce, like the ring in a cake.

dough beater n Also *dough baker* **sAppalachians** *joc*

A wife, woman.

1911 *DN* 3.538 **eKY,** *Dough-bēater*. . . Wife. **1940** (1978) Still *River of Earth* 215 **KY,** "A feller who's got a doughbeater promised is square in luck,". . . "Nothing sorry as a bachelor feller." **1941** Stuart *Men of Mts.* 288 **neKY,** I'd give everything that I won if I had a dough-beater pretty as Daisy who thought that much of me. **1941** Nixon *Possum Trot* 38 **neAL,** But that style of [horse and buggy] courting was one way to win a "dough-baker." **1967–69** *DARE* (Qu. AA22, *Joking names that a man may use to refer to his wife: "I have to go down and pick up my ———."*) Infs **KY**44, **TN**1, **VA**2, Dough beater.

dough-bellied See **doughbelly 4**

doughbelly n

1 A **stone roller** (here: *Campostoma anomalum*). [See quot 1983]

1896 U.S. Natl. Museum *Bulletin* 47.205, *Campostoma anomalum*. . . Dough-belly. **1908** Forbes–Richardson *Fishes of IL* 110, *Dough-belly*. . . Belly satiny whitish. **1933** John G. Shedd Aquarium *Guide* 49, *Doughbelly*. . . A little fish found in sandy or rocky creeks and small streams of the eastern United States. **1960** Amer. Fisheries Soc. *List Fishes* 56, Doughbelly—see stoneroller. **1983** Becker *Fishes WI* 476, *Central Stoneroller. Campostoma anomalum*. . . Doughbelly. . . Breeding males dark slate with white belly.

2 See quot. Cf **doughboy** n[1] **6**

1968 Adams *Western Words* 98, *Dough-belly*—A cowboy's name for the cook.

3 =**doughboy** n[1] **3.**

1968 *DARE* (Qu. H18, . . *Special kinds of bread*) Inf **IA**30, Doughbelly—fried hunks of bread dough.

4 A large stomach; a fat person; hence adj *dough-bellied* fat, flabby. **chiefly S Midl**

1936 *Esquire* Sept 32/1 **KY,** You're getting dough-bellied Fonse. You ain't doing enough running up and down the hills. **1965–70** *DARE* (Qu. X50, . . *A person who is very fat*) Inf **GA**84, Doughbelly; (Qu. X53a, . . *An oversize stomach*) Infs **AR**56, **IL**96, **OK**47, **SC**10, **TX**32, Doughbelly. **1980** *DARE* File **AR, wKY, wTN, eTX,** Doughbelly = fat stomach.

doughbird n Also *doe bird* [See quot 1955 at **1** below]

1 =**Eskimo curlew.**

1835 Audubon *Ornith. Biog.* 3.69 **MA,** The Esquimaux Curlew . . are met with on the high sandy hills near the sea-shore, where they feed on the grasshoppers and on several kinds of berries. On this food they become fat . . in consequence . . they have probably acquired the name of "Dough Bird," which they bear in that district. **1844** Giraud *Birds Long Is.* 274, *Numenius Borealis*—Esquimaux Curlew.—In the Eastern States it is called "Doe Bird." **1909** Field Museum Nat. Hist. *Zool. Ser.* 423 **IL, WI,** Eskimo Curlew.—*Local name:* Dough Bird. **1936** Roberts *MN Birds* 1.485, *Eskimo Curlew: Phaeopus borealis*— . . Doe-Bird, Dough-Bird. **1949** Harvard Univ. Museum Compar. Zool. *Bulletin* 102.206 **ME,** Loring, in his shooting journal, made a distinction between "Curlew," "Jack Curlew" [Hudsonian], and "Dough bird" [Eskimo Curlew]. **1955** MA Audubon Soc. *Bulletin* 39.446, *Eskimo Curlew*. Dough Bird (Maine, Mass., R.I. Misspelled also Doe Bird. They have "a much thicker layer of fat than is usually seen in other birds, hence their local name . . from the saying 'as fat as dough.' " MacKay, *Auk,* 1892.)

2 Either of two similar birds: the **marbled godwit** or the **Hudsonian godwit.**

1898 (1900) Davie *Nests N. Amer. Birds* 143, *Marbled Godwit*. . . The sportsmen call them "Dough" or "Doe" birds. **1917** (1923) *Birds Amer.* 1.24, *Hudsonian Godwit*. . . *Other Names*. . . Smaller Dough- or Doe-bird. *Ibid* 241, *Marbled Godwit*. . . *Other Names*. . . Dough- or Doe-bird. **1946** Hausman *Eastern Birds* 289, *Limosa fedoa*. . . Doebird. *Ibid* 290, *Limosa haemastica*. . . Small Doebird. **1956** MA Audubon Soc. *Bulletin* 40.20, *Marbled Godwit*. . . Dough Bird (Maine. Mass. See note on that name under Eskimo Curlew.) . . *Hudsonian Godwit*. . . Dough Bird (Maine.) . . Smaller Doughbird (Mass. See note under Eskimo Curlew, which it equalled or exceeded in size; "smaller" thus is in contrast with the Marbled Godwit.)

dough biscuit See **bread-dough biscuit**

dough bob See **dough baby**

dough box n

=**dough tray.**

1967 *DARE* FW Addit **cePA,** A place to let dough rise . . dough box. **1968** *Budget* (Sugarcreek OH) 25 July 14, [Auction ad:] *Antiques* . . dough box. **1988** *DARE* File **cwMA** (as of 1925), *Dough box* was known in rural areas.

dough boxer See **dough roller 1**

doughboy n[1]

1 A flour or cornmeal dumpling. Cf **doughball 1**

1753 *Boston Gaz. or Weekly Advt.* (MA) 20 Mar 2/2 **Boston MA,** They had breckfasted [aboard ship] and were preparing for Dinner, their Dough-boys being made and a Leg of Pork wash'd ready for the Pot. **c1770** in 1833 Boucher *Glossary* l **MD,** Broth . . with . . dough-boys. [Footnote:] *Dough-boys;* hard, or Norfolk dumplings; not seldom also made of Indian meal. **1791** in 1843 *Amer. Pioneer* 2.153 **swOH,** I got a doughboy or water-dumpling, and proceeded. **1966** *DARE* Tape **FL**40, I like the stewed conchs with dumplin's, some people call 'em doughboys . . boiled dumplin'. **1969** *DARE* (Qu. H24, . . *Boiled cornmeal*) Inf **NC**72, Doughboy. **1975** Gould *ME Lingo* 77, *Doughboy*—Very old word asea and ashore for dumplings. **1980** *Yankee* Jan 166, Sea pies, or doughboys, were a flour dumpling made with pieces of porpoise meat and bones.

2 Any of var kinds of bread; see quots.

a1861 in 1913 Winthrop *Canoe & Saddle* 93 **cWA,** [Cakes of unleavened bread . . confected of flour and the saline juices of fire-ripened pork, and kneaded well with drops of the living stream. Baked then in frying-pan, they stood now, . . toasting crustily till crunching-time should come.] *Ibid* 95, We had all met . . to . . partake of toasted doughboys. **1965–68** *DARE* (Qu. H14, *Bread that's made with cornmeal*) Inf **AL**14, Corn pone, doughboys, hoe-cake, spoon bread—spoon bread is the only different one; **FL**17, Doughboys—goes with fish chowder; **PA**66, Doughboys—a biscuit; (Qu. H25, . . *Fried cornmeal*) Inf **FL**26, Doughboys; **GA**46, Doughboys—same as hush puppies.

3 A cake of deep fried bread dough; a doughnut. **chiefly NEng** Cf **doughbelly 3**

1887 Custer *Tenting* 516, A doughboy is a small round doughnut, served to sailors on shipboard, generally with hash. **1941** *LANE* Map 285 **csRI,** Cakes fried in deep fat. . . [doʊ bɔɪz], [fraɪd] ~, of doughnut dough. **1966–70** *DARE* (Qu. H18, . . *Special kinds of bread*) Inf **RI**5, Doughboys—fried; (Qu. H27, . . *Doughnuts*) Inf **CT**39, Doughboys—if it's bread dough; **ME**16, Doughnuts used to be called doughboys; **MA**98, **NY**49, Doughboys; (Qu. H28, *Different shapes or types of doughnuts*) Inf **WA**27, Doughboys—no hole; (Qu. H32, . . *Fancy rolls and pastries*) Inf **RI**1, Doughboys—raised bread cooked in deep fat. **1989** *DARE* File **RI** (as of p1950), Doughboy: fried dough covered in sugar.

4 See quot.

1950 *PADS* 14.27 **SC,** *Doughboy*. . . A conjuring puppet figure of biscuit dough, made to represent the object of one's resentment, baked, and stood so near the fire as to scorch and char to a cinder, or ruthlessly broken, thus supposedly inflicting severe pain and perhaps death on the victim of this sorcery. Cf. the ancient wax figure of witchcraft. The doughboy was sometimes broken to bits and fed to the chickens, thus insuring the humiliation and destruction of a rival in love., etc.

5 See quot. Cf *DS* X32

1950 *WELS (Uncomplimentary names for hands)* 1 Inf, **ceWI,** Doughboys.

6 Among loggers: see quot. Cf **doughbelly 2**

1969 Sorden *Lumberjack Lingo* 35 **NEng, Gt Lakes,** *Doughboys*—The camp cook and his helpers. Often referred to river drive cooks.

doughboy n[2] [Folk-etym for *adobe*]

1 =adobe 1a.

1856 in 1940 MT Hist. Soc. *Contrib.* 10.74 **MT,** The Carpenters at Work getting the Doughboy tools ready. *Ibid* 75, The men mixed their mud in preparation for making doughboys.

2 =dobe n **5.** Cf **dough baby**

1942 Berrey–Van den Bark *Amer. Slang* 665.2, Doughboy, muddie, *a clay marble.* **1955** *PADS* 23.16 **cwTN,** *Doughboy*. . . A marble made of clay. **1970** *DARE* (Qu. EE6a, . . *Marbles—the big one that's used to knock others out of the ring*) Inf **CA**209, Doughboy. **1971** Bright *Word Geog. CA & NV* 116 **cwCA,** Marbles: . . doughboys 2 [responses] . . "Baked clay."

dough bread n

=light bread.

1937 Sandoz *Slogum* 216 **NE** (as of c1915), And after lunches of dry fried sowbelly between dough-bread, Libby's cooking would toll a bull-whacker to a Sunday School picnic. **1941** *Sat. Eve. Post* 10 May 112/3 **KY,** Mother was putting dough bread and rashers on the table. **1968** *DARE* (Qu. H18, . . *Special kinds of bread*) Inf **VA**9, Dough bread—made at home.

doughdab n Cf **dough god**

1909 *DN* 3.411 **nME,** *Doughdabs*. . . Small flat cakes.

dough dish n **chiefly NEng** *old-fash*

=dough tray.

1845 *Lowell Offering* V.148 *(DA)* **MA,** Aunt Levi went up to get meal for the 'dough dish.' **1891** (1967) Freeman *New Engl. Nun* 190 *(DA),* Jane strode after her, the hens' dough-dish in her hand. **1939** Coffin *Capt. Abby* 121 **ME** (as of 1860s), I helped do the cooking for the cabin. . . And you couldn't have pried Abby Pennell away from the dough-dish with a cant-dog!

Dougherty wagon n Also sp *Doherty wagon;* also *Dougherty ambulance,* ~ *spring wagon* *old-fash* Cf **ambulance B1** and *DS* N41a

See quot 1961.

1901 *N. Amer. Rev.* 172.228, The Americans had thirteen four-mule army-wagons and one pack train of forty freight mules, besides two or three ambulances and a Dougherty wagon. **1943** Wood *W. Reed* 92 *(DA),* The doherty wagon, a primitive ancestor of the station wagon, with seats that could be converted into beds at night and canvas sides that rolled down, lurched and bounced behind its four-mule team. *Ibid,* The road had turned out to be so rough that any progress faster than a walk threatened to shake both the ambulance (as the doherty wagon was also called) and its occupants apart. **1961** Eggenhofer *Wagons* 122 (as of c1865), This Dougherty spring wagon, drawn by four mules, was open in front, where the driver sat underneath the canvas awning. Behind him there were two additional seats running crosswise; a door in the side gave access to them, in the manner of a coach. The open sides had roll-down curtains for protection against rain and snow, and there was a covered baggage rack in the rear. . . It was designed primarily for the accommodation of passengers. . . On an inspection trip to one of the important posts General Sherman and his staff rode in a "Dougherty Ambulance". . . Other, lesser visiting dignitaries . . were likewise regularly transported in Dougherty wagons. **1984** Smith *SW Vocab.* 123, *Dougherty wagon:* An army ambulance or passenger wagon used extensively throughout the Southwest in the period of Western migration. It was named for its inventor, whose last name, obviously, was Dougherty, but whose first name despite the most diligent and painstaking research remains a mystery.

doughey See **doughy**

doughface n Also, by folk-etym, *door-face* **chiefly Sth, S Midl**

A mask; a person wearing a mask; also fig.

1809 in 1853 U.S. Congress *Debates & Proc.* 10th Cong 2d sess 23 Feb 1509 **VA,** Yes, sir, said he [=John Randolph], it may bring us to fighting and to disgrace; it is something like dressing ourselves up in a dough-face and winding-sheet to frighten others. **1872** (1973) Thompson *Major Jones's Courtship* 40 **GA,** That chap with the fan had a dough face on, that looked as pitiful as if all his relations was ded. **1883** Twain *Life on Missip.* (Boston) 528 **MO,** I saw those giddy young ladies come tiptoeing into the room where Miss — sat reading at midnight by a lamp. The girl at the head of the file wore a shroud and a doughface; she crept behind the victim, touched her on the shoulder, and she looked up and screamed, and then fell into convulsions. **1883** Eggleston *Hoosier Schoolboy* 120 **sIN,** Two boys . . agreed to furnish dough-faces for them all. Nothing more ghastly than masks of dough can well be imagined. **1899** (1912) Green *VA Folk-Speech* 152, Dough-face. . . A mask made of thick paper moulded to form, and usually of hideous aspect. False-face. **1908** *DN* 3.306 **eAL, wGA,** *Dough-face*. . . A false-face or mask, especially a comical or ugly one; also a person wearing such a mask, especially in costume as a mummer (see *fantastic*). Originally *dough-face* was literally a face made of dough. **1939** Harris *Purslane* 149 **neNC,** There still were the serenaders to look forward to, and brave threats were made to jerk off the door-faces [Footnote: dough-faces] and see who the serenaders were. **1943** Powell *I Can Go Home* 70 **swGA** (as of late 19th cent), They would array themselves in grotesque garb, put on one of those comical papier-mâchè masks. Which are called "door-faces." **1950** *PADS* 14.27 **SC,** *Dough face*. . . A false face. *Dough* may have been used originally in forming these fantastic masks. **1966** Barnes–Jensen *Dict. UT Slang* 13, *Dough face*. . . Term used for actual face made of flour to scare Indians. (My grandfather used one in Eagle Valley, Nevada in early days.) **1966–70** *DARE* (Qu. W36, . . *A woman who uses a lot of cosmetics*) Inf **GA**1, Puts on a doughface; **GA**13, Doughface; (Qu. X29, . . *Uncomplimentary words for a person's face*) Inf **NC**86, **VA**39, Doughface.

dough-faced adj [Cf **doughface**]

1919 *DN* 5.72 **NM** [Student slang], *Dough-faced,* dull, shallow. "She is so dough-faced that I tire of her."

doughgie See **dogie**

dough god n Also *dough gob*

1 also *dough goddy:* A biscuit or similar type of bread or cake, usu cooked over an open fire. **chiefly West**

1899 *Mth. S. Dakotan* 1.176/1, When the noon hour came and the cattle were turned to their turnips and the hay boy flung himself on the canadensis carpet and ate his dinner of dough-god and bacon with hearty relish. **1913** *DN* 4.26 **West,** *Dough god*. . . Flour and water cooked in a frying-pan like biscuit. **1915** *DN* 4.244 **MT,** *Dough god*. . . Biscuit. "I don't care for dough gods." **1918** *DN* 5.24 **NW,** *Dough-gob, dough-god*. . . A loaf of baking powder bread baked in a pan by an open fire; not always "done." Woodsmen, prospectors, etc. **1920** *DN* 5.81 **nwWA,** *Dough god.* Camp bread. **1942** Whipple *Joshua* 38 **UT** (as of c1860), Abijah finished his steaming porridge, dipped his 'dough-god' in his salt-pork grease, and looked northward. **1964** Jackman–Long *OR Desert* 130, I was reduced to flour with no yeast. You'd be amazed how good dough gods taste if you have nothing else. **1966–68** *DARE* (Qu. H18, . . *Special kinds of bread*) Infs **CA**87, **WA**6, Dough gods; (Qu. H19, . . *A biscuit*) Inf **MT**5, Dough god—a baking powder biscuit; **SD**5, Called dough goddy ['doˌgadɪ] on the ranch; (Qu. H20b, . . *Pancakes*) Inf **CA**59, Hotcakes, griddle cakes, dough gods—a camp term, means anything soggy and baked or cooked in an easy way; **WA**8, Hotcakes, flapjacks, dough gods ['dogæds]—that's mountain vocabulary, around cattle camps, baked, cooked at open fire; (Qu. H25, . . *Fried cornmeal*) Inf **ID**4, Bannock, dough gods. **1973** Allen *LAUM* 1.277 **Upper MW** (as of c1950), Other kinds of bread made with flour. . . *Doughgods* is . . a western term echoing the early days of range-riding by cattlemen and cowpunchers. *Ibid* 278, Doughgods [response given by 11 informants]. *Ibid* 279 **neMN,** *Dough gods:* Biscuits dropped in Mulligan stew. **1977** Jones *OR Folkl.* 101/2, *Dough god:* campbread; also dough gob (1947).

2 =doughboy n[1] **3. Nth, esp NEng**

1941 *LANE* Map 285 **Martha's Vineyard MA, nME,** Cakes fried in deep fat. . . [doʊ gɒ˕ədz] = [fraɨd keɪks], of raised dough. . . ['doʊ˄ gɒ˕əd], no hole, spoon-dipped. **1947** Bowles–Towle *New Engl. Cooking* 206, *Maine Doughgods*—Some people call the small rounds of dough made by the center of the doughnut cutter "doughgods." Others make them as follows: . . Roll out this dough and cut in small squares. Fry like doughnuts. Serve with maple syrup. **1947** *Harper's Mag.* 195.81/2 **neNH,** He delighted in baking beans in the ground, fried excellent doughnuts and a somewhat similar product which he called "dough-gods." **1950** *WELS Suppl.* **ME,** Dough gods—fried yeast bread dough. **1966** *Good Old Days* Mar 38 **cMI,** How we used to beg to have Dough-Gods! (also variously known as Dough-Gobs and Dough-Boys. . .) When the dough was risen chunks of it were sliced off and fried in butter. **1966–67** *DARE* (Qu. H27, . . *Doughnuts*) Inf **MI**1, Dough god ['dogad, 'dogɑd], fried cake; **WA**30, Dough god; **WA**31, ['duˌgadz].

dough goddy See **dough god 1**

dough gut n **West** Cf **dough-gutted**

See quots.

1929 *AmSp* 4.331 **TX,** *Dogie* . . is applied to calves that have lost their mothers and are fed with the cattle. The sudden change in diet causes their bodies to swell. According to Mr. J.A. Lomax of Austin the cowboys gave the name *dough guts* to these calves, and the name was later shortened to *dogie.* **1936** *AmSp* 11.218 **WY** (as of 1880s), According to these old-timers [cowmen of the 1880s], The cowboys . . began to refer to her collection of orphan calves as *dough guts,* which by common usage eventually became *dogey,* or *dogie.* **1971** Adams *Cowman* 32, Here this one's singin' 'Git 'Long Little Doggie' like he's singin' about a pup instead of the dough-guts that's done so much to develop my cuss words.

dough-gutted adj

1939 McGuire *FL Cracker Dial.,* Dough gutted. . . Pot-bellied.

doughhead n

A foolish or stupid person; hence adj *dough-headed* foolish, stupid.

1838 Kettell *Yankee Notions* 124 **NEng,** Nonsense, Josh, you silly dough-head. **1854** (1923) Holmes *Tempest & Sunshine* 157 **KY,** When he saw that no one exclaimed or turned pale, . . he inwardly accused them all of being "doughheads," and wondered he had never before discovered how little they knew. **1903** *DN* 2.296 **Cape Cod MA** (as of a1857), *Dough-head.* . . A thick-headed person. **1905** *DN* 3.8 **cCT,** *Dough-head.* . . A fool. **1908** Porter *Gentle Grafter* 53 **SW,** Do you mean to tell me that them infernal clod-hopping, dough-headed, pup-faced, goose-brained, gate-stealing, rabbit-eared sons of horse thieves have soaked us for that much? **1966** Barnes–Jensen *Dict. UT Slang* 13, *Dough head* . . one very stupid. **1966–67** *DARE* (Qu. HH3, *A dull and stupid person*) Inf **WY**1, Doughhead; (Qu. HH9, *A very silly or light-headed person*) Inf **MI**26, Doughhead.

doughie See **doughy**

dough, in (the) adj phr **[dough stage]** Cf **milk, in the**

Of grain: in the stage of development just preceding full maturity.

1863 U.S. Dept. Ag. *Rept. of Secy. for 1862* 93 **IN,** The American farmer understands the different stages of maturity [of wheat] by the terms "in the milk," "in the dough," and ["]ripe." **1967** WI Statist. Reporting Serv. *Report* 29 Aug, Only in the main corn areas . . is corn . . perhaps 1/3 in dough. **1969** *DARE* (Qu. I33, . . *Ears of corn that are just right for eating*) Inf **IN**69, In the dough.

dough marble n

=**dough baby.**

1967 *DARE* (Qu. EE6c, *Cheap marbles*) Inf **TN**8, Dough marble.

doughnette n [Dimin of *doughnut*]

=**doughball 3.**

1967–68 *DARE* (Qu. H28, *Different shapes or types of doughnuts*) Inf **CA**6, Doughnette—in a ball; **NY**35, **WV**1, Doughnette; (Qu. H31, *Other foods made with dough and cooked in deep fat;* total Infs questioned, 75) Inf **DC**4, Doughnette—the hole that's cut out is fried, something new.

doughnut n

A coiffure in which the hair is braided or twisted into a doughnut shape; see quot 1979.

1967–69 *DARE* (Qu. X3, *When a woman puts her hair up on her head in a bunch, you call this a* ______) Inf **CA**166, Doughnut—rolls around the ears; **CO**47, **HI**9, **MA**8, Doughnut. **1979** *DARE* File **cMA,** *Doughnuts*—I don't know when it started. I knew it in the 1920s and 1930s, but it was certainly one of the ugliest hairdos women have ever invented. You had to have very long hair, which you made into two braids. These you twisted into "doughnuts" over your ears and pinned each one together tightly. You spoke of a girl's "wearing her hair in doughnuts."

doughnut hole n Also *doughnut center* **scattered, but less freq Sth, S Midl** See Map

A ball of dough, usually from the center of a doughnut, deep fried and sometimes sugared or frosted.

1965–70 *DARE* (Qu. H28, *Different shapes or types of doughnuts*) 69 Infs, **scattered, but less freq Sth, S Midl,** Doughnut hole; **CO**35, Doughnut center—balls of dough; (Qu. H27, . . *Joking names for doughnuts*) Inf **IA**32, Doughnut hole—used for the centers.

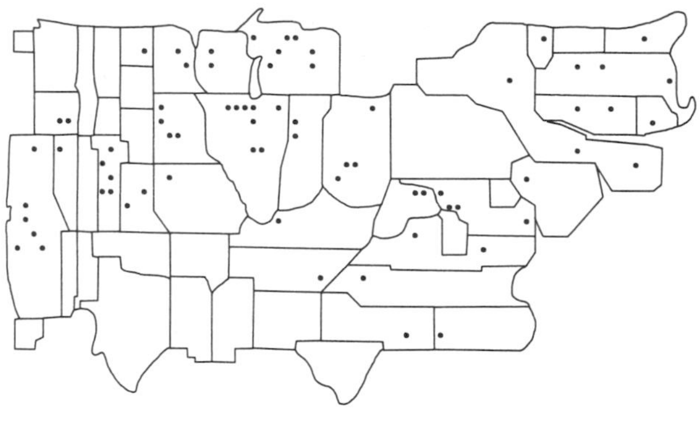

•doughnut hole + varr (Qq. H28, H27)

dough roller n

1 also *dough boxer,* ~ *pounder,* ~ *puncher:* A baker or cook.

1914 *DN* 4.150 [Navy slang], *Dough puncher.* . . Baker. **1920** Hunter *Trail Drivers TX* 299, The cook has many names applied to him. He is called . . "dough roller," . . and "biscuit shooter." **1946** *Western Folkl.* 5.383 [Navy slang], Humorous too are *tin bender, dough-puncher,* and *dynamo-buster* for the metalsmith, baker, and electrician. **1963** *AmSp* 38.271 **cKS** [American Indian student slang], Baker—*dough roller.* **1968** Adams *Western Words* 98, *Dough boxer. . . Dough puncher. . . Dough roller*—A cowboy's and logger's name for the cook. **1969** Sorden *Lumberjack Lingo* 35 **NEng, Gt Lakes,** *Dough boxer*—A cook. *Dough pounder*—A baker. *Dough roller*—A cook.

2 See quots.

1954 *PADS* 21.26 **SC,** *Dough roller.* . . A rolling pin. **1967** *DARE* FW Addit **seAR,** Dough roller—rolling pin.

3 See quot. Cf **dough baby.**

1968–69 *DARE* (Qu. EE6a, . . *Marbles—the big one that's used to knock others out of the ring*) Infs **GA**72, **NC**53, Dough rollers.

dough stage n Also *dough state* [From the internal dough-like consistency of the kernels] Cf **dough, in the**

Of grains: the stage of development preceding full maturity.

1858 *Texas Almanac 1859* 67 *(DA),* The usual harvesting season extends from the 1st to the last of May. The proper time is when the grain is in the transition from the 'dough' to a hard state. **1869** U.S. Dept. Ag. *Rept. of Secy. for 1868* 417, The results . . are corroborative of the theory, already well established, that wheat should be cut when the grain is in the *dough* state. **1945** *Democrat* 9 Aug. 2/5 *(DA)* **swAL,** Turn hogs on the field of corn when it has passed the dough stage. **1967** WI Statist. Reporting Serv. *Report* 29 Aug, Corn progresses slowly in the absence of warm nights. About ¼ of the state's grain corn acreage is now in dough stage or beyond. **1985** *NC Folkl. Jrl.* 33.29 **wNC** (as of c1912), We knew that if you waited until it was too ripe, the grain would shatter out of the heads during harvesting and be lost. For that reason, it was cut in what was called the "dough" stage, meaning that the inside of the grain was doughy in consistency.

‡dough table n

A table with a **dough tray.**

1950 Giles *Enduring Hills* 33 **KY,** Across from the stove was the dough table, which Grampa Dow had made. No one else had a dough table whose tray slid so smoothly in its groove; and Grampa had thought of the clever little shelf in the corner of the flour bin to hold the soda and salt.

dough tray n Also pronc-sp *doughtry* **scattered, but esp PA** Also called **dough box, dough dish**

A wooden trough or box for kneading and raising bread dough.

1846 (1973) Porter *Quarter Race* 89 *(DAE)* **TN,** I jist grabbed the dough-tray and split it plumb open over his head! **1880** *Harper's New Mth. Mag.* 61.927/2 **cnKY,** It [=a pig] could . . proceed to investigate the dough tray or pan of rusk, left to rise. **1891** Ryan *Pagan* 150 **swPA,**

"Did Mrs. Riker bring up the bread?" he asked, glancing into an empty dough-tray. **1930** Shoemaker *1300 Words* 19 **cPA Mts** (as of c1900), *Dough-tray*—A wooden trough for keeping dough; a kneading-box. **1967** *DARE* FW Addit **cePA,** Doughtry ['dɔtri]. A place to let dough rise; also . . ['dotri]; **cnCO,** In museum: *dough tray,* used to mix and raise dough in; knead dough on it. **1968–69** *DARE* (Qu. D9, *To prevent bread and cake from drying, you put them in a ______*) Inf **NJ**51, Dough tray—the real thing: a wooden trough with a top, bread was kept in it; [it was originally] used for mixing or for raising dough; **NJ**56, Dough tray—box 3½ feet long 20 inches wide, sloped down at bottom; for making dough, not storing bread. **1976** *PA Folklife* Spring 31/2, The doughtray is often listed [on salebills] as pronounced, *doughtry.* **1982** *Barrick Coll.* **csPA,** *Dough-tray*—wooden box used for mixing dough. *Dough-tray scraper*—metal utensil used for scraping dough from dough-tray.

dough up v phr [*dough* money]

To pay or make payment.

1968 *DARE* (Qu. U18, *If you force somebody to pay money that he owes you, but that he did not want to pay, you might say, "I finally made him ______."*) Infs **OH**41, 70, Dough up.

doughy n Also sp *doughey, doughie*

=**dough baby.**

1949 *PADS* 11.20 **CO,** *Doughey*. . . A clay marble. **1950** *WELS (Marbles: Cheap ones)* 1 Inf, **neWI,** Doughies. **1958** *PADS* 29.33 **WI,** *Doughy*. . . A cheap clay marble, usually painted red, blue, green, or brown. **1971** Bright *Word Geog. CA & NV* 116 **swCA,** Marbles: . . doughie . . "Larger, dough-colored."

Douglas fir n

Std: a tall evergreen conifer (*Pseudotsuga menziesii*). Also called **Columbian pine, Douglas spruce, Oregon pine, Puget Sound pine, red fir, red pine, spruce, yellow fir**

Douglas spruce n Also *Douglass spruce, Douglas tree*

=**Douglas fir.**

1853 in 1856 U.S. Congress *Serial Set* 793.2.79 **AZ,** *Douglass spruce,* which is also abundant upon the sides of the mountains, would afford a better material for railroad ties. **1897** Sudworth *Arborescent Flora* 47, *Pseudotsuga taxifolia* . . Douglas Spruce (Cal., Colo., Mont.). Douglas Fir (Utah, Oreg., Colo.). . . Douglas Tree. **1908** Britton *N. Amer. Trees* 70, The Douglas spruce [=*Pseudotsuga menziesii*], also called . . Douglas fir . . and Douglas tree, is the most abundant . . of western North America. **1958** McCulloch *Woods Words* 52 **Pacific NW,** *Douglas spruce*—Douglas fir. **1977** Hanify–Blencowe *Guide to Hoh* [10] **wWA,** *Douglas Fir:* . . "Douglas Spruce". **1979** Little *Checklist U.S. Trees* 218, *Pseudotsuga menziesii* . . *Douglas-fir* . . Other common names . . Douglas-spruce.

douncy See **donsie**

doup See **dope** n 1

do up v phr

1 To perform, complete (chores).

1818 (1920) Clark *Diary* 2319 **CT,** Washed my floor did up my house work did up a cap for Mrs Canfield. **1910** [see **4** below]. **1937** (1963) Hyatt *Kiverlid* 29 **KY,** Put down yer bread to bake and git yer work done up. **c1960** *Wilson Coll.* **csKY,** *Do up*. . . Clean things, esp. laundry, chores, etc. **1966–70** *DARE* (Qu. L4b, . . *The time early in the morning and at night when you have to feed livestock, clean stalls, and so on . . "I've got to go now, it's ______."*) Infs **AL**2, **IL**114, **MS**72, Time to do up the chores, (*or* the things, the work); (Qu. OO33b, *Talking about doing chores: "This morning as usual we ______ [the chores]."*) Infs **AR**56, **WI**42, Done up.

2a To clean or wash and make ready for use; esp, to launder.

1818 [see **1** above]. **1842** Buckingham *E. & W. States* 1.177 **ME,** The chambermaid, on our leaving the bedroom, accosted us by saying, "Shall I *do you up* while you are at breakfast?"—meaning to ask whether she should put the bedroom in order. **1876** Harte *Gabriel Conroy* 91 **CA,** I'll do up the dishes ef you'll excuse my kempany. **1886** (1961) Stockton *Casting Away* 65, Some . . pretty adornments of dress were borrowed from Emily . . and, after having been 'done up' and fluted . . were incorporated by Ruth into her costume. **1908** *DN* 3.306 **eAL, wGA,** *Do up*. . . To wash, starch, and iron (clothes). **1910** [see **4** below]. **1950** *WELS Suppl.,* 3 Infs, **sWI,** Do up—to iron. "Do up a shirt." "Do up curtains" = wash, starch, iron. Do up—used in "Do up clothes" = wash, starch and iron. "Do up the wash" sometimes means washing only. **c1960** [see **1** above].

b intr: To withstand laundering.

1988 *DARE* File **csWI** (as of c1940s), "Get sharkskin," said my grandmother, speaking of a rayon-and-cotton mixture of dress material, "them do up so nice."

3 To wear out, finish off; to overcome, beat, cheat.

1835 Hoffman *Winter in West* (NY) 2.187, John seemed to have retired, completely done up. **1887** *Amer. Field* 27.482/1, The officers of the club had allowed themselves to be "done up" by one of the club's debtors. **1893** *KS Univ. Qrly.* 1.138 **KS,** *Do up:* to overcome, as 'He did me up.' **1894** *Harper's New Mth. Mag.* 89.389/1 **cwCA,** Then they do up Buck. Shoot a hole through his spine. **1897** *KS Univ. Qrly.* (ser B) 6.52 **KS,** *Do up:* to beat; to cheat. **1907** *German Amer. Annals* 9.373 **sePA,** *Done up.* All gone; exhausted. "The apples are done up." **1967–68** *DARE* (Qu. GG22b, *When you have come to the end of your patience, you might say, "Well, that certainly ______."*) Inf **NV**4, Did it up; **NC**55, Done me up one; **TX**4, Does it up in a brown ball.

4 To preserve (fruit or vegetables). Cf **do ups**

1907 *German Amer. Annals* 9.373 **sePA,** *Do up.* Can; preserve. "I will do up the cherries to-day." . . fr. Pa. Ger. *uf doo;* Ger. *auf thun.* **1910** *DN* 3.440 **cwNY,** *Do up* . . (1) To can (fruit). "I must do up peaches to-day." (2) To wash (dishes). "I must do up the dishes now." (3) To accomplish a domestic task. "I must do up the washing this forenoon." **1948** *AN&Q* 8.90 **NJ,** "Put up" or "Do up." To me, canning peaches in jars has always been "putting up" peaches. That, at any rate, is North Carolina usage. In New Jersey, however, I find that the universal term is "do up." **1950** *WELS Suppl., Do up*—to can (fruit). **1978** *DARE* File **cMA** (as of c1915), You could "do up" peaches. That meant you "put them up," i.e., canned them.

5 To dress up; to put on makeup or cosmetics; hence ppl adj *done up.*

1916 *DN* 4.337 **PA,** *Do up*. . . To dress up. "She was done up for the party." **1969** *DARE* (Qu. W36, . . *About a woman who uses a lot of cosmetics*) Inf **KY**19, Really done up.

do up brown v phr Also rarely *do brown* [Cf **brown n 5**]

To do thoroughly or properly.

1840 *Daily Picayune* (New Orleans LA) 15 Aug 2/1 **New Orleans,** [It was] the most magnificent . . Flounder that we ever saw. . . We sent it to Hewlett's, where it was "done up brown." **1873** *Newton Kansan* (KS) 30 Jan 3/2, The play of Michael Erle or the Maniac Lover will be done up brown. Don't fail to go. **1905** *DN* 3.4 **cCT,** *Brown*. . . Completely. 'To do a thing up brown.' [**1907** *DN* 3.209 **cCT, nwAR,** *Brown*. . . Completely.] **1942** McAtee *Dial. Grant Co. IN* 23 (as of 1890s), *Do up brown* . . make a good job, in either a constructive, or destructive, sense. Slang. **1950** *PADS* 14.17 **SC,** *Brown*. . . Well, excellently, suitably. "Done up brown." Applies to all sorts of activities. **1950** *WELS (People who show off or make a big display: "When they give a party they ______.")* 2 Infs, **WI,** Do it up brown. **1968–69** *DARE* (Qu. FF18, . . *About a noisy or boisterous celebration or party: "They certainly ______ last night."*) Inf **IL**102, Did it up brown; **WI**44, Done themselves brown; (Qu. KK3a, . . *The perfect condition—for example, in cooking*) Inf **VT**16, Done up brown; (Qu. KK3b, *Something done perfectly—for example, a piece of work*) Inf **IL**76, He did it up brown; (Qu. KK9, *When someone undertakes something too big for him to handle: "This time you've ______."*) Inf **OH**80, Done it up brown.

doup-end n [Scots, Ir, nEngl dial *doup* bottom end (of an egg, candle, the human body, etc)]

The butt end.

1967 Williams *Greenbones* 26 **GA** (as of c1910), They ate the doup-end of the ham and the rest of the cornbread with fig preserves.

do up in shape v phr

=**do up brown.**

1965–67 *DARE* (Qu. KK3b, *Something done perfectly—for example, a piece of work*) Inf **OK**13, Done up in good shape; (Qu. KK4, *When things turn out just right, you might say, "Everything is ______ now."*) **MO**8, Done up in shape.

do-ups n pl [**do up 4**] *old-fash*

1895 *DN* 1.382 **NJ,** *Do-ups:* preserves.

dour adj [Scots] Note: In Scotland, usu |dur|; in US often |daʊr|

1 See quot.

1930 Shoemaker *1300 Words* 18 **cPA Mts** (as of c1900), *Dour*—Difficult, hard to manage.

2 See quot.

1952 Brown *NC Folkl.* 1.534 **wNC,** *Dour*. . . Dark.

3 Sullen, moody, melancholy.
1969 *DARE* (Qu. GG34b, *To feel depressed or in a gloomy mood: "She's feeling ______ today."*) Inf **CA**145, Dour.

dourade See **dorado**

dourie adj Also sp *doury* [Cf **dour 3,** *EDD doury* "dismal, gloomy" (at *dour* 2), and *EDD durried* "Confused, bewildered"]
1952 Brown *NC Folkl.* 1.534, *Dourie, doury:* . . Uneasy, worried.—West.

douse v Usu |daʊs|; also |daʊš, dɑš, doʊs| Also sp *dowse;* pronc-sp *dosh*
A Forms.
1965–70 *DARE* (Qu. Y436, . . *To put out a fire*) Infs **GA**73, **IL**5, [daʊš]; **KY**94, Douse, dosh; **NY**96, [doʊs]; **OK**15, [dɑš].
B Senses.
1 See quot. [*OED douse* v.² 1 →1662; "To plunge vigorously *in* water or the like"]
1930 *AmSp* 5.419 **csNH,** *Douse:* roll. "The boy was doused in the snow."
2 To extinguish (a lantern, cigarette, etc); by ext, to switch off (an electric light)—often in phr *douse the glim* and varr. [*OED* 1785 →; prob by ext from *douse* to throw water over (*OED* 1606 →)]
1824 Irving *Tales of a Traveller* 2.344 **NY,** "Dowse the light!" roared the hoarse voice from the water. **1899** (1912) Green *VA Folk-Speech* 152, *Douse.* . . To put out a light. **1916** Macy–Hussey *Nantucket Scrap Basket* 129 **seMA,** "Douse the Glim"—To put out the light; not local, but one of the slang nautical terms which still lingers. **1919** *DN* 5.37 **OK,** *Douse.* . . To put out. Thus in an early poem, or dance "call" common in the Oklahoma of earlier days:—Shorty, shed that old sombrero,/ Broncho, *douse* that cigarette./ Stop your cussin', Casimero,/ For the ladies now, all set. **1932** *RR Mag.* Oct 367, *Douse the glim*—To extinguish a lantern by a sudden upward movement. **1945** Colcord *Sea Language* 68 **ME, Cape Cod, Long Island,** To douse the glim is to put out a lamp or lantern. **1965–70** *DARE* (Qu. Y42, . . *Put* . . *out a lamp or light*) 59 Infs, **chiefly Nth, N Midl, West,** Douse; 21 Infs, **chiefly Nth, N Midl, West,** Douse the glim; **MO**26, **NY**213, 249, **WI**12, Douse the light (*or* a lamp); **NY**166, Douse the glimmer; **WA**17, Douse the gleam. **1966** Barnes–Jensen *Dict. UT Slang* 13, *Douse* . . put out (usually in connection with fire). Douse your cigarette. **1979** *DARE* File, My aunt's husband, born in southern New Hampshire c1875, frequently said, "Douse the glim" when he meant "turn off the electric light." He always said it as if it were a great joke, but it sounded countrified and old-fashioned even then (c1920).

douse n [Scots, Engl dial]
1899 (1912) Green *VA Folk-Speech* 152, *Douse.* . . A blow; a stroke; a blow in the face.

douser n [*douse* to drench]
1968 *DARE* (Qu. B25, . . *A very heavy rain*) Inf **MD**21, Douser.

douse, the See **deuce, the**

dout v Also with *out* [*do* + *out; OED* 1526 →] **chiefly UT, WY** Cf **douse v 2**
To extinguish or put out (a fire).
1936 *AmSp* 11.191 **swWY,** *To dout.* To put out. 'Dout the fire.' **1942** Whipple *Joshua* 39 **UT** (as of c1860), Dout the fires thoroughly and see that none of the children lag behind. **1965–68** *DARE* (Qu. Y43b, . . *To put out a fire*) Infs **UT**3, **WY**4, Dout; **UT**4, Dout the fire; **UT**9, Dout it out.

dout prep [Var of *without;* cf Pronc Intro 3.I.17] *chiefly among Black speakers*
1888 Jones *Negro Myths* 88 **SC, GA coasts** [Gullah], De shot drap offer um dout hot [=hurt] um. **1955** in 1958 Brewer *Dog Ghosts* 122 **TX** [Black], He c'd . . shoot de cigar smoke offen de top of a cigar bein' smoked by somebody way cross de street . . 'dout ebun techin' de cigar.

dout conj Also *douten* [Varr of *without;* cf Pronc Intro 3.I.17]
1908 *DN* 3.306 **eAL, wGA,** *Dout(en), conj.* Unless.

dout out See **dout v**

dove n Pronc-sp *dub* Cf Pronc Intro 3.I.17
Std sense, var form.
1853 Simms *Sword & Distaff* 116 **SC** [Black], So long as dere's 'coon and 'possum, . . pattridge and dub (dove) . . Tom will always hab 'nough somet'ing to cook! **1922** Gonzales *Black Border* 298 **GA, SC coasts** [Gullah glossary], *Dub*—dove, doves.

dove(d) See **dive v 1, 2**

dove dock n
=**coltsfoot 1.**
1900 Lyons *Plant Names* 381, *T[ussilago] farfara,* . . Dove-dock. **1914** Georgia *Manual Weeds* 280, Coltsfoot—*Tussilago farfara* . . Dove-dock. **1930** Sievers *Amer. Med. Plants* 24, Coltsfoot—*Tussilago farfara* . . Other common names.—Coughwort . . dove-dock, . . gowan. **1959** Carleton *Index Herb. Plants* 38, Dove-dock: *Tussilago farfara.*

dovefoot (geranium) See **dove's-foot geranium**

dove hawk n
=**goshawk 1.**
1917 (1923) *Birds Amer.* 2.68, *Astur atricapillus atricapillus.* . . *Other Names.* . . Dove Hawk. **1946** Goodrich *Birds in KS* 316, Colloquial Name. . . Hawk, dove. . . Common name, A.O.U. Check-List. . . Goshawk, eastern. **1955** Forbush–May *Birds* 100, *Eastern Goshawk.* . . Dove Hawk.

dovekie n [Scots dimin of *dove*]
A small auk *(Plautus alle).* Also called **ice-bird, little pigeon, noddy, pigeon diver, pineknot, rotch, seadove**
1858 Baird *Birds* 918, *Mergulus alle,* Linnaeus. The Little Auk; The Sea Dove; Dovekie. . . One of the most abundant of the sea birds of northern America and Europe, straying south in the winter occasionally to the coasts of the Middle States. **1872** Coues *Key to N. Amer. Birds* 343, *Sea Dove,* or *Dovekie.* Glossy blue-black, below from the breast . . white; scapulars white-striped; secondaries white-tipped; white speck over eye; bill black, short, obtuse, turgid. . . N. Atlantic, abundant, S. in winter to New Jersey. . . *[Mergulus] alle.* **1917** (1923) *Birds Amer.* 1.31, The little dovekies *[Alle alle]* or "Sea Doves" . . in the winter come down the coast where less ice abounds. **1956** MA Audubon Soc. *Bulletin* 40.80, *Dovekie.* That name (Maine, Mass. Little dove, from its small size.)

doven See **dive 2**

dove-on-the-mountain n
=**fringed polygala.**
1957 *AmSp* 32.80, To the various recorded popular names for *Polygala paucifiora* . . I should like to add *dove-on-the-mountain.* The name was given to the flower presumably because of the blossom. This is a New Hampshire usage which goes back to the nineteenth century. I learned it when I was a boy in New Hampshire.

dove plum n [See quot 1962]
=**pigeon plum.**
1962 Harrar–Harrar *Guide S. Trees* 271 **sFL,** *Doveplum.* . . The fruit of this species is much sought after by doves of the region; hence the name *doveplum.* **1971** Craighead *Trees S. FL* 200, Dove plum . ., *Coccoloba diversifolia.* **1979** Little *Checklist U.S. Trees* 93, *Pigeon-plum.* . . *Other common names*—doveplum.

Dover sole n
=**slippery sole.**
1953 Roedel *Common Fishes CA* 64, *Dover Sole. Microstomus pacificus.* . . Alaska to northern Baja California. . . Dover sole are found in deeper water than most of our flatfishes, frequent muddy bottoms and feed on invertebrates. They reach at least 15 years of age. **1973** Knight *Cook's Fish Guide* 381/1, Flounder . . slippery see Sole, Dover.

dove's-foot geranium n Also *dovefoot (geranium), dove's foot* [From the shape of the leaf]
A **cranesbill 1,** usu *Geranium maculatum* or *G. molle.*
1876 Hobbs *Bot. Hdbk.* 32, Doves' foot, Cranesbill, Geranium sylvaticum. **1900** Lyons *Plant Names* 172, *G. maculatum.* . . Dove-foot. **1910** Graves *Flowering Plants* 262 **CT,** *Geranium molle.* . . Dove's-foot Geranium or Cranesbill. **1933** Small *Manual SE Flora* 744, *G. molle.* . . Dove's-foot. **1959** Carleton *Index Herb. Plants* 39, *Dove's foot:* Geranium (v). **1973** Hitchcock–Cronquist *Flora Pacific NW* 280, Dovefoot g[eranium]. . . *G. molle.* **1974** (1977) Coon *Useful Plants* 144, *Geranium maculatum.* . . Dove's foot.

dovetail fish n
=**demoiselle 1.**
1898 U.S. Natl. Museum *Bulletin* 47.1563, *Abudefduf taurus* . . *Dovetail Fish.* **1911** *Century Dict. Suppl., Dovetail-fish.* . . A fish, *Abudefdul* [sic] *taurus,* of the family *Pomacentridae.*

dovetail flycatcher n

Perh a scissor-tailed flycatcher *(Muscivora forficata).*

1966 *DARE* (Qu. Q20, . . *Kinds of swallows and birds like them . . around here*) Inf **FL**29, Dovetail flycatcher.

doveweed n [Because the seeds are eaten by doves]

1 Any of several plants of the genus *Croton:* see quots.

1913 *Torreya* 13.232, *Croton punctatus.* . . Dove-weed, St. Vincent I[slan]d, Fla. Doves *(Zenaidura macroura)* are fond of the seeds. **1942** *Torreya* 42.162, *Croton capitatus.* . . Bighead doveweed, Oklahoma. . . *Croton texensis.* . . Texas doveweed. **1967** Dodge *Roadside Wildflowers* 40 **SW,** Plants of this genus *[Croton],* of which there are 30 species in the United States, are known as doveweeds because their seeds are relished by three species of native doves. **1967** *DARE* (Qu. S21) Inf **TX**13, Doveweed.

2 =turkey mullein.

1935 (1943) Muenscher *Weeds* 319, *Eremocarpus setigerus.* . . Doveweed. . . Pacific Coast states. Native. July-August. **1941** Jaeger *Wildflowers* 130 **Desert SW,** *Turkey Mullein, Dove Weed.* . . Shallow-rooted, silver-green annual. **1959** Munz-Keck *CA Flora* 162, *Dove Weed.* . . *E. setigerus.* . . Seeds much eaten by doves and quail. **1973** Hitchcock-Cronquist *Flora Pacific NW* 284, Doveweed; Turkey-mullein.

dow See **daow**

dowd n [*OED* c1330–1814; perh a recent back-formation from *dowdy* of dress: lacking taste, shabby]

A person who dresses shabbily or unstylishly; a dowdy person.

1930 Shoemaker *1300 Words* 17 **cPA Mts** (as of c1900), *Dowd*—A slatternly woman. **1967** *DARE* (Qu. W41, . . *Someone whose clothes never look right or who always dresses carelessly*) Inf **MI**68, Dowd.

dowdy n Cf **apple pandowdy**

=pandowdy.

1936 Lutes *Country Kitchen* 37 **sMI,** Apple Dowdy is not a dumpling, a pudding, or a pie—deep-dish or otherwise. It is just a dowdy—sort of common, homely . . but it has character.

dowdy v

1989 *WI State Jrl.* (Madison) 9 Aug sec D 1/2, As for pandowdies, some cookbooks would have you believe they are just double-crusted apple pies. Not so. When the pie is partially baked, you "dowdy" the crust into the fruit by chopping it with a knife, then add more liquid and continue baking. . . Whether they are slumped or buckled or dowdied, these old-fashioned fruit desserts . . are nearly foolproof.

dowhacker, dowhackie, dowhackus, dowhacky See **doowhacker**

do what interrog exclam Also *do how,* ~ *which* **chiefly SE** Cf **do v C2**

What did you say?

1918 *DN* 5.20 **NC,** *Do which,* what did you say? Used in asking for the repetition of a question. **1926** *AmSp* 1.408 **Okefenokee GA,** The good friends who used to question me with a delightful 'Do how?' have transformed it into a prosaic 'What?' **1952** Brown *NC Folkl.* 1.533, *Do how (what).* . . Used in asking one to repeat what he said = "What did you say?" **1968–70** *DARE* (Qu. X18, . . *When one person doesn't quite hear what another person said, what does he say?*) Infs **GA**59, **SC**64, Do what?; **SC**58, Do how?; **TX**106, Do which? **1974** (1975) Shaw *All God's Dangers* 49 **AL** [Black], "Son, Jim Flint's cows is just ruinin my bottom of corn. . . " I said, "Do what, Papa?" He said, "Yeah, just ruinin it." **1976** Wolfram-Christian *Appalachian Speech* 173, FW: Did they use whiskey alot? Inf: Do which? **1986** Pederson *LAGS Concordance* **Gulf Region** *(What's that?)* 3 infs, Do how?; 1 inf, Do how? [means] do what? **1988** *Ms.* Dec 20/1 **TX,** Esther Ann said, "Honey, I cain't [color your hair silver]." I said, "Esther Ann, how come?" She said, "Dear, you're sprang [=spring]." I said, "Do what?" She said, "You're sprang. You can't have a winter color like silver next to your face."

dowhopper See **doowhacker**

dowich(es) See **dowitcher**

dowitch n [AmInd; see quot 1931 at **dowitcher**]

1 =pectoral sandpiper.

1888 Trumbull *Names of Birds* 176, At Essex, Conn., and mouth of Connecticut River, *Dowitch [Pisobia maculata].* **1923** U.S. Dept. Ag. *Misc. Circular* 13.54, *Pectoral Sandpiper (Pisobia maculata).* . . In local use.—Brownback, . . dowitch . . (Conn.) **1925** (1928) Forbush *Birds MA* 1.406, *Pisobia maculata* . . Pectoral Sandpiper. Other names: . . Dowitch . . Creaker.

2 See **dowitcher.**

dowitcher n Also *dowich(es), dowitch(ee), dowits* [Iroquoian; see quot 1931]

Either of two similar shorebirds: the short-billed *Limnodromus griseus* or the long-billed *L. scolopaceus.* For other names of both species see **brownback 1, dormeur 2, driver 10, fool plover, German snipe, grayback 1c, gray snipe 1, jack snipe, jackson snipe, kelp plover, longbill, longbilled plover, quail snipe, red-bellied snipe, redbreast, red-breasted snipe, robin snipe, sea pigeon, sea quail, sleeper.** For addit name of *L. griseus* see **brown snipe 1;** for other names of *L. scolopaceus* see **whitetail dowitcher**

1841 *Spirit of Times* 9 Jan. 529/3 *(DA),* [The music would] rise and rise . . like the mellow attenuated trill of the soaring dowitcher. **1844** DeKay *Zool. NY* 2.255, The *Dowitchee [Limnodromus griseus]* . . or *Brown-back,* arrives on the coast of New-York towards the latter part of April. **1844** Giraud *Birds Long Is.* 264 **seNY,** Our gunners, as if fearful that nothing would be left to connect the past with the present generation, cling to the old provincial names for birds, recognising this species *[Limnodromus griseus]* by the singular and unmeaning name of "Dowitcher." **1876** *Forest & Stream* 7.68/3 **NJ,** *Scolopax noveboracensis.* Dowitch. *Ibid* 149/2 **Long Is. NY,** The dowits are next in increasing size, and take their name from their call or whistle. In familiar parlance about here, people call them "dowiches." **1888** Trumbull *Names of Birds* 160, At Stratford, Conn., and Seaford (Hempstead), L.I., *Dowitcher [Limnodromus griseus];* on Long Island at Shinnecock Bay, Moriches, and Bellport, and at Barnegat, N.J., *Dowitch.* . . These names Dowitch and Dowitcher meant originally that this was the Dutch, or German, snipe *(Duitsch, Deutscher).* **1923** U.S. Dept. Ag. *Misc. Circular* 13.51, *Dowitcher (Limnodromus griseus).* . . In local use:—Brownback . . ; dowitcher (also spelled dowitchee, dowiches, and dowits; all these terms are traceable to duitsch or deutscher, meaning that this is the Dutch or German snipe. . .) (Conn., N.Y., Va., introduced westwardly in Mo., Ark., Tex., Idaho, and Wash.) **1925** (1928) Forbush *Birds MA* 1.396, *Limnodromus griseus griseus* . . Dowitcher. *Ibid* 398, *Limnodromus griseus scolopaceus* . . Long-billed Dowitcher. **1931** Read *LA French* 6, The book name of this species of snipe [=*Limnodromus griseus*] is now *Dowitcher,* a word of Iroquois origin—compare Cayuga and Mohawk *tawis,* Onondaga *tawish,* "snipe." **1940** White *Wild Geese* 367 **OR** (as of 1890s), She came upon a small pool of water that had not drained, and around it and in it stalked a half-dozen long-legged dowitchers. **1955** MA Audubon Soc. *Bulletin* 39.20, *Dowitcher.* . . Brownback Dowich (Mass . .); Dowitch (Mass.); Dowitcher (Conn.)

down adv, prep, adj, n[1], v Usu |daʊn|; also |dæʊn, dɑʊn, dʌʊn|; for addit varr see quots at **A** Pronc-spp *da(e)own, daoun* Cf Pronc Intro 3.II.14

A Forms.

1858 (1892) Holmes *One Hoss Shay* 15 **eMA,** It should be so built that it *couldn'* break daown! **1861** Holmes *Venner* 2.298 **wMA,** If they break daown, as all of 'em are liable to do at any time. **1916** *DN* 4.344 **VA, KY, GA, NC, SC, FL, VT, NY, PA,** *Down* [daʊn]. **1926** *AmSp* 2.83 **ME,** He ken knock a haouse daoun! **1927** Shewmake *Engl. Pronc. VA* 41, *Down. Daeown* is heard in the speech of many whose language habits are, in the main, good; and it is general among the illiterate. **1931** *AmSp* 6.400 **ceME,** The first element in the diphthong [aʊ] is noticeably tense and fronted. . . [dæʊn]. **1933** *AmSp* 8.4.54 **csVA,** The general American [ɑʊ] appears invariably as [aʊ]. In this too, the speech is intermediate between the Tidewater and the Valley. In the Tidewater, [æʊ] and [ɜʊ] are heard, while the Valley usually has [ɑʊ]. Examples of the singer's characteristic diphthong are *down* [daʊn], *pound* [paʊn]. **1939** *AmSp* 14.125 **neTN,** [ðə ren kem dæʊn ɪn tɑrənts]. **1941** *AmSp* 16.7 **eTX** [Black], [aʊ]—In Negro speech this diphthong is not often flattened to [æʊ] as in 'hill type' speech, but retains its standard form, with lengthening of the first element. . . Examples: . . *down, found.* **1942** Hall *Smoky Mt. Speech* 45 **eTN, wNC,** The following words almost always have [æʊ] rather than [aʊ]: About, . . brown, . . down. . . There are, however, occasional instances of a lower and more retracted vowel in the first element, as in . . '. . . when the dogs quieted down [dɑːʊn].' **1942** *AmSp* 17.150 **seNY,** Down . . [æʊ] 43 [informants] . . [aʊ] 70 [informants] . . [ɑʊ] 19 [informants]. **1943** *LANE* Map 720, [The diphthong in *down* occurs most often as [æʊ, aʊ, ɑʊ, ao, ɑo]. Occasional instances of [æo, ɛʊ, au, ɐʊ, ɐu, ɑɔ] were also recorded.] **1976** Allen *LAUM* 3.25 (as of c1950), The vowel in *house, out, down, mountain*. . . As in the North and North Midland areas of the eastern states, the dominant variety is a diphthong with an onset ranging from [a] to [ɑ], that is, from low-front to low-central. *Ibid* 26/1 **wNE, seSD, sMN,** [æʊ, a˄ʊ] . . down. *Ibid* 26/2 **csMN, seIA,** [ɜʊ, əʊ] . . down. *Ibid* **eIA, seNE, cSD, nMN,** [aʊ, a·ʊ] . . down.

B As adv.

1 Used variously to indicate direction toward or away from a center, to a lower elevation, downstream, etc; see quots. **esp NEng** Cf **down east** adv phr

1926 *AmSp* 2.81 **ME,** One always goes "up to Boston," quite as one returns down to Maine. Hence one lives "down in Maine." **1943** *LANE* Map 720 *(Up in Boston),* On the eastern seaboard, from Narragansett Bay to New Brunswick, . . *down* means 'away from Boston' or 'down toward the sea'. . . On Long Island Sound . . *down* means 'downstream' (south). . . New York City is *down* from any point in Connecticut. . . On Narragansett Bay . . *down* means 'toward the sea'. . . In New Hampshire . . and in Vermont east of the Green Mountains, the course of the Merrimack river and of the Connecticut River determines the use of *up* and *down*. . . In western Vermont and in central and western Massachusetts the regional orientation is very complicated and varied. **1950** *WELS Suppl.* **neWI,** *Down the county, down north.* These are used interchangeably in Door County. The open sea [=Lake Michigan] is to the north. To go down the county is to go down north. The movement is from the source at the south end to the open water at the north end. Only foreigners with no feeling for water argue: "You can't go down north." [**1958** *AmSp* 33.74, In the Yukon and the Northwest Territories, particularly in the valley of the Mackenzie River, *down north* is a natural manner of expression, in accord with the direction of river flow.] **1960** *Eaton Coll.* **FL,** On the St. Johns River . . , northward flowing, where the boatman cruises down north and up south. **c1965** *DARE* File **MA,** I had a letter from a man down at Colby College (in Waterville, Maine). The people down there seem to be quite interested in her. **1967** *DARE* FW Addit **neNY,** *Down north, up south.* Any point south of Chateaugay is above Chateaugay, any point north of Chateaugay is below it, because of its peculiar location on a mountain above the Canadian plateau. For instance, one goes down to Montreal and up to New York. **1969** *DARE* FW Addit **seKY,** People in Pineville say "down to Barbourville" because the elevation is lower and despite the fact the direction is north. **1982** *Barrick Coll.* **csPA,** *Down*—easterly or southerly direction; associated with direction of flowing streams in the area. **1983** Beyle *How Talk Cape Cod* 34, You can often tell just who is native to the place and who's not by their sense of direction. For instance, you go "down" to Provincetown here, not "up"—even though you'll be traveling north for the most part.

2 also *real down:* Very, extremely. [Cf *EDD down adv.* 10 "Used as an intensive;" possibly a minced form for *damn*] Cf **hard down** adv phr

1893 Shands *MS Speech* 52, *Real down*. . . Used by cultivated whites to mean *exceedingly* or *extremely*. A thing that is extremely nice is said to be *real down* nice. **1952** Brown *NC Folkl.* 1.534, *Down*. . . Very, exceedingly. "He's a down good hoehand."—Central and east. **1968** *DARE* (Qu. JJ21, *If you want to be very positive: Somebody asks you "Are you really going to do that?" And you answer, "You ______."*) Inf **PA**114, You're down right.

3 Through.

1970 *DARE* Tape **VA**112, He'll do that same thing all the whole summer down.

C As prep.

To, towards; in. [Cf **B1** above] Cf **down cellar, down city, down home, down the country**

1916 *DN* 4.343 **NC,** *Down Bingham.* To the South: among negroes. "When are you going down Bingham?" **1938** FWP *Guide NH* 119, Some unusual New Hampshire expressions are . . 'down Maine.' **1943** *LANE* Map 720 *(Up in Boston)* 2 infs, **ce, neMA,** Down Maine; 1 inf, **ceMA,** Down Portland; 1 inf, **ceMA,** Go down Portland; 1 inf, **csMA,** Going down Boston.

D As adj.

1 Melancholy, depressed; depressing. **scattered, but chiefly Nth, N Midl** See Map *esp among speakers with coll educ* Cf **down-and-out 3, down under** adj phr **1** Note: The phr *get one down* is widespread and is not included here.

a1862 (1865) Thoreau *Cape Cod* 240, The Captain is rather down about it, but I tell him to cheer up. **1942** Berrey–Van den Bark *Amer. Slang* 283.7, *Dejected; sad; blue* . . down. **1961** Salinger *Franny* 132 **NYC,** And there was old Dick. So down, so *blue,* so full of important news that couldn't wait till this afternoon. **1965–70** *DARE* (Qu. GG34b, *To feel depressed or in a gloomy mood: "She's feeling ______ today."*) 70 Infs, **scattered, but chiefly Nth, N Midl,** Down [Of all Infs responding to the question, 11% were young, 33% coll educ; of those giving this response, 21% were young, 51% coll educ.]; (Qu. GG6, . . *"When she said she couldn't go with thim, he was quite ______."*) Inf **IN**73, Down; (Qu. GG27b, . . *"Don't ______."*) Infs **NY**81, **IL**5, Be (so) down; Infs **IN**75, **OK**58, Get down (so); (Qu. GG34a, *To feel depressed*) Infs **OH**89, **CA**187, He's down; **CO**13, Is really down; (Qu. GG35a, *To sulk or pout*) Inf **OK**58, Get down; (Qu. GG35b, . . *"Because she couldn't go, she's been ______ all day."*) Infs **CA**187, **PA**165, **WA**20, **WI**72, Down. **1972** *New Yorker* 5 Aug 21 **NYC,** "A beautiful picture." "It's too down. I don't like down movies. I like up movies." **1978** *New Yorker* 20 Mar 90, Primarily, a down week with a couple of lighter spots, specifically, the lunches with two of our [Harvard Law School] professors.

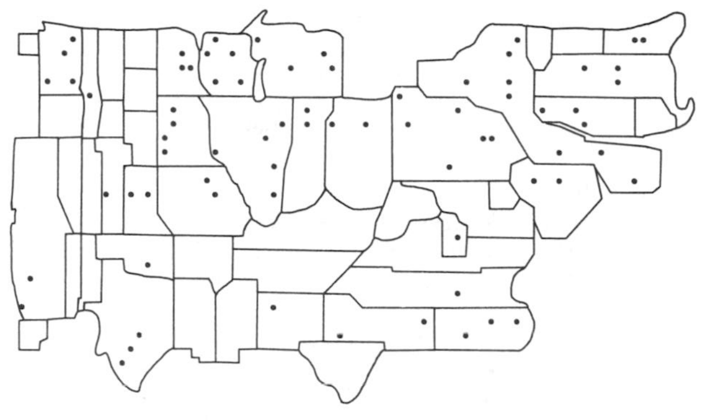

•down adj D1 + varr (Qq. GG34b, GG6, GG27b, GG34a, GG35a, b)

2 Downed; fallen. **chiefly Midl, West** Note: the predicate adj use of *down* is std.

1881 Stoddard *Esau Hardery* 263, There was plenty of old "down timber" to be cut up, and cleared away. **1899** Garland *Boy Life* 220 **nwIA** (as of c1870s), The horses walked astride one row [of corn]—bending it beneath the axle; this was called the "down row," and was invariably set aside as "the boys' row." *Ibid* 222, The "down" ears [of corn] were often covered with frost or dirt and sometimes with ice. **1928** *Sat. Eve. Post* 10 Mar 28/2, His rifle was reclining against a down log ten feet away. **1935** Sandoz *Jules* 106 **wNE,** The twenty-second of September brought three days of rain, to spoil the winter range, any down hay, and the cow chips. **1940** Stuart *Trees of Heaven* 151 **neKY,** [In a description of land to be sold:] Leaving said Callihan's line and re-crossing said road . . to old down black oak . . thence . . to a stake by a down beech. **1958** McCulloch *Woods Words* **Pacific NW,** *Down timber*—a. Felled timber. b. Trees knocked over in a windstorm. **1968** *DARE* FW Addit **cnMD,** *Down wood,* Fallen wood, lying on the ground in woods. **1974** Fink *Mountain Speech* 7 **wNC, eTN,** *Down* . . fallen. "A heap of down timber." **1976** Garber *Mountain-ese* 24 **sAppalachians,** *Down-stock* . . fallen crop—We sawed some uv the down-stock uv trees fer winter firewood.

3 Placed or situated on the ground; growing close to the ground.

1939 *Hall Coll.* **wNC,** *Down laurel,* "Laurel on a mountain, right down on the ground, like a jungle and you can't get through it hardly. . . Well sir, it was just so rough he [=a bear] couldn't run. Hit was down-laurel and he couldn't do nothin' but jump up an down." . . "So I was climbin' up through the down-laurel. . . And hit was so rough down-laurel that I couldn't see without gettin' up within strikin' distance." **1966** *DARE* FW Addit **OK**52, *Down log,* The solid log laid on the ground in alternate sections of a split-rail fence to keep rails off the ground.

4 Of an animal: unable to stand because of illness or exhaustion. Cf **downer**

1956 Moody *Home Ranch* 222 **CO** (as of 1911), If he didn't break a leg in a prairie-dog hole, or stumble over a down animal and fall on me. **1968** Adams *Western Words* 99, *Down steer*—An animal off its feet in a loaded stockcar.

5 in phrr *down in one's* (or *the*) *back* (or *legs, arms,* etc): Ailing, unwell, in pain (in a specific part of the body). **chiefly S Midl**

1907 Wright *Shepherd* 17 **Ozarks,** Pap he's down in th' back now, an' ain't right peart. **1927** *AmSp* 2.353 **WV,** *Down in yer back* . . one who is crippled by a weak back. "Grandfather has been down in his back all week." **1954** *Harder Coll.* **cwTN,** *Down in* (his) *back* (legs, arms, kidneys, etc.) Weak (in some part of the body). **c1960** *Wilson Coll.* **csKY,** *Down in the back*—Suffering from lumbago or any other back trouble. **1970** *Thompson Coll.* **cnAL** (as of c1950), *Down in the parts.* Ailing in one's genito-urinary system. **1978** Massey *Bittersweet Country* 206 **Ozarks,** *Down in the back* (ailing): My father has been down in his back all week.

6 See quot. Cf **down-and-out 2**

1965–68 *DARE* (Qu. DD15, . . *Thoroughly drunk*) Infs **DE**7, **LA**2, **MS**59, **TX**12, 26, Down.

7 See quots. **among Black speakers**

1968 *New Yorker* 18 May 48/3 **NYC** [Black], I developed a secret desire to see what everybody was enjoying so much. I wanted to be one of the crowd, to be hip, down, part of the image. **1970** *Current Slang* 5.2.7 [Black], *Down.* . . Aware; cool; hip. **1972** Claerbaut *Black Jargon* 63, *Down* . . appealing; socially attractive: *He's real down.* **1977** Smitherman *Talkin* 72 [Black], Church folk refer to . . religious ecstasy as *gittin happy.* On Friday . . (pay day), secular folk look forward to *gittin high.* Musicians and dancers hope to achieve a spirit-catharsis by *gittin down.* **1980** Folb *Runnin' Down* 235 **Los Angeles CA** [Black], *Down* . . Prepared, ready. . . Knowledgeable.

E As noun.

1 in phr *have a down on:* To dislike.

1969 *DARE* Tape **PA**181, When we finally did arrive . . we were just completely dead, and . . maybe that's one reason we had sort of a down on the city.

2 pl; also *downers:* A depressed or melancholy state of mind, the blues.

1967–70 *DARE* (Qu. GG34a, *To feel depressed or in a gloomy mood: "He has the ______ today."*) Inf **GA**91, **OH**8, Downs; **CA**169, Downers.

F As verb. [Cf *OED down* adv. VI "With ellipsis of a verb: so that *down* itself functions for the verbal phrase."]

1 See quot. [Abbr for *come down*]

1914 *DN* 4.105 **KS,** *Down.* . . Used without a verb. He down with his fist and jarred the table.

2 To plant (a crop).

1936 *AmSp* 11.275 **eTN,** To *down potatoes.* To plant potatoes. 'We downed potatoes today.'

3 To insult, verbally demean (someone); to slander.

1954 *Harder Coll.* **cwTN,** *Down*—Defame, insult. "Don't down me no more." **1968–70** *DARE* (Qu. Y3, *To say uncomplimentary things about somebody*) Infs **NY**59, **OH**93, Down. **1969** *DARE* FW Addit **ceNC,** "I don't want to down him," i.e., say things against him.

4 To draw or pull (something) down. **esp SC**

1966–70 *DARE* (Qu. E13, . . *To pull the shades . . down: "When the sun is too bright, you go to the window and ______."*) Infs **SC**9, 26, 43, 62, 69, Down the shade(s) [3 of 5 Infs Black].

down n² [From similarity to *down* feathers]

Also *goose down:* See quots. **chiefly Sth, S Midl** See Map Cf **feather n B4**

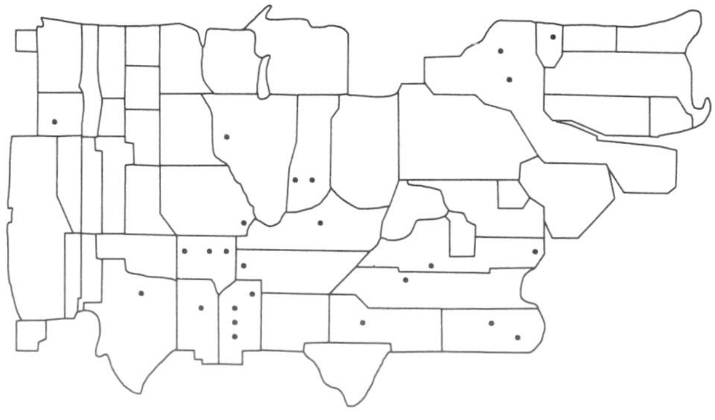

•down n² + var (Qu. E20)

1965–70 *DARE* (Qu. E20, *Soft rolls of dust that collect on the floor under beds or other furniture*) 24 Infs, **chiefly Sth, S Midl,** Down; **OR**1, Goose down. **1970** *DARE* FW Addit **cwTN** [Black], Down [dɒn] = lint on clothing.

down n³ [Var of *dung*] *euphem* Cf *hen flint* (at **flint**)

1906 *DN* 3.119 **sIN,** *Hen-down.* . . Fowl fæces or castings. "There's hen-down all over the gears (*i.e.* harness)." **1967** *DARE* (Qu. P24, . . *Kinds of turtles*) Inf **SC**43, Cow-down [=**cow-dung cooter**]—smells awful.

down-along adv phr [Cf **along** adv **1** and *EDD downalong* "downwards, down the street or road, some little distance"] See quots.

1848 in 1935 *AmSp* 10.40 **Nantucket MA,** *Down-a-long.* On change, or in some resort near the wharves. **1913** *DN* 4.56 **Cape Cod MA,** *Down-along.* . . Toward the western end of the town (there is no difference in level): noted at Provincetown. "Going down-along to the wharf?" "No. Going up-along to the Mays." **1916** Macy–Hussey *Nantucket Scrap Basket* 129, "Down Along"—Many Nantucketers, when asked as to where they are bound, reply "Oh, jest down along." . . The North Shorer, the Upper Maine Streeter, or the Chicken Hiller means . . that he is going down town. The Newtowner . . also uses it to express a port in the opposite direction, as when he heads for home. The Under-the-Banker also uses it to indicate both up town and down town. **1944** *AN&Q* 3.188/2 **neMA,** In Newburyport, Massachusetts, uptown is "up-along" and downtown is "down-along."

down-and-out adj [By ext from *down-and-out* totally incapacitated, financially ruined]

1 rarely *out-and-down:* Mildly or indefinitely ill; "under the weather." **chiefly Sth, Midl** See Map

1965–70 *DARE* (Qu. BB39, . . *When you don't feel just right, though not actually sick*) 32 Infs, **chiefly Sth, Midl,** Down-and-out; **MS**71, All down-and-out; (Qu. KK30, *Feeling slowed up or without energy*) 24 Infs, **chiefly Sth, Midl,** Down-and-out; **TX**32, Out-and-down; (Qu. X52, . . *You'd say that a person . . who had been sick was looking ______*) Infs **GA**17, **IN**75, Down-and-out; (Qu. BB5, *A general feeling of discomfort or illness*) Infs **AL**20, **GA**74, **IL**135, **MA**69, **NC**13, **TX**65, *Down-and-out;* **OR**13, Down-and-out feeling; **CT**16, **SC**58, Feel(ing) down-and-out; (Qu. **BB**28, *Joking names . . for imaginary diseases*) Inf **AL**20, Down-and-out; (Qu. BB38, *When a person doesn't look healthy*) Infs **NJ**35, **PA**142, **TX**103, Down-and-out; (Qu. BB41, *Not seriously ill, but sick enough to be in bed*) Infs **MN**15, **NJ**58, 67, **SC**58, Down-and-out.

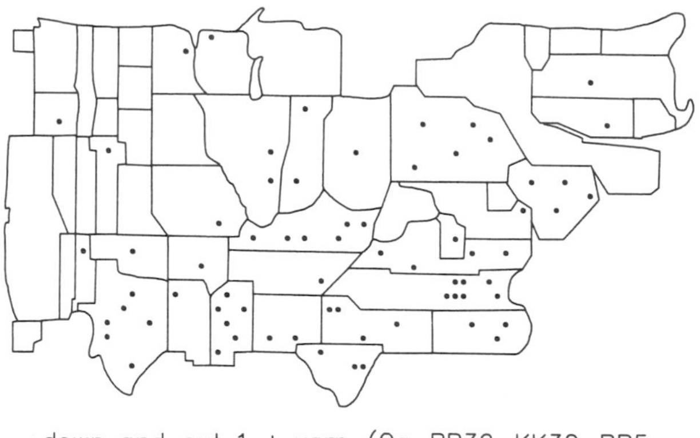

•down-and-out 1 + varr (Qq. BB39, KK30, BB5, X52, BB28, BB38, BB41)

2 =**down adj D6.**

1967–70 *DARE* (Qu. DD15, . . *Thoroughly drunk*) Infs **AL**28, **CA**105, **CO**4, **CT**17, **NY**232, **PA**148, **TX**38, **WA**25, **WI**26, Down and out. [All Infs old]

3 =**down adj D1. scattered, but esp Sth, S Midl** See Map

1965–70 *DARE* (Qu. GG34b, . . *Depressed or in a gloomy mood*) 53 Infs, **scattered, but esp Sth, S Midl,** Down-and-out; (Qu. GG27b, *To get somebody out of an unhappy mood. . . "Don't ______."*) Inf **GA**77, Be so down-and-out; (Qu. GG34a) Inf **LA**17, He's down-and-out; (Qu. GG35b, . . *"Because she couldn't go, she's been ______ all day."*) Inf **MS**49, Down-and-out.

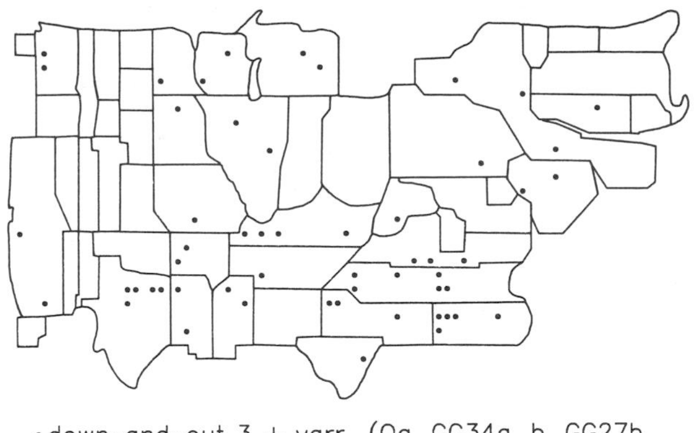

•down-and-out 3 + varr (Qq. GG34a, b, GG27b, GG35b)

down-and-outer n

See quot.

1975 Ferretti *Gt. Amer. Book Sidewalk Games* 84 **NYC,** [In the game "errors"] The player tries to foil the opposing fielder by putting backspin on the spaldeen, by skidding grounders close to the concrete, by throwing curve balls and sliders (we used to call them "down-and-outers").

down-and-out fight n

1968 *DARE* (Qu. Y12b, *A real fight in which blows are struck*) Inf **NY**48, A down-and-out fight.

down-and-out shower n Cf **burnout shower**

A social gathering to which people come to give gifts to someone who has suffered a misfortune.

1967 *DARE* (Qu. FF3, . . *'Showers' or 'gift parties'*) Inf **NE**11, Down-and-out shower—for someone who has had a fire or something.

down-at-the-heel(s) adj Also *down-to-the-heel(s)* [Transf from *down-at-the-heel* shabby or destitute] Cf **run down at the heels**

Unwell; lethargic; depressed or melancholy.

1871 Jones *Life Batkins* 197 **MA,** Aunt Dolly was in dreadful low spirits about my going to Boston; to tell the truth, I did feel a little down at the heel too. **1927** *AmSp* 2.353 **WV,** *Down at the heel* . . in poor condition physically. "I have felt down at the heel all spring." **1966–69** *DARE* (Qu. GG34b, *To feel depressed or in a gloomy mood: "She's feeling ——— today."*) Inf **MA**35, Down-to-the-heel; (Qu. KK30, *Feeling slowed up or without energy: "I certainly feel ———."*) Inf **ME**22, Down-to-the-heels; **NE**3, Down-at-the-heel. **1973** Allen *LAUM* 1.362 **seSD** (as of c1950), *Tired.* . . down at the heels [1 inf].

down basement See **down cellar**

down beam See **down light**

downbeat, on the adj phr [Cf *downbeat* gloomy, pessimistic]

1968 *DARE* (Qu. BB41, *Not seriously ill, but sick enough to be in bed: "He's been ——— for a week."*) Inf **VA**11, On the downbeat.

down-bed n

=**made-down bed.**

1967–70 *DARE* (Qu. E18, *A temporary or emergency bed made up on the floor*) Infs **KY**85, **LA**2, **NC**55, Down-bed.

down below adv phr

1a To or in a region which is lower in elevation or towards the south; hence n *down below* such a region.

1943 Weslager *DE Forgotten Folk* 170, A down below man [inhabitant of Sussex County] used to tell us to cut the end off a black cat's tail and rub the grease from it on the shingles. **1959** *VT Hist.* new ser 27.133 **ceVT,** Down below. . . To Massachusetts. Occasional. **1967** *DARE* FW Addit, *Down below* or *inside* (used less frequently)—When people of the Mojave Desert east of San Bernardino go to San Bernardino or Los Angeles, or so it seems anywhere west to southwest of the San Berdino [sic] Mountains, they are going "down below". **1969** *DARE* Tape **CA**145, My dad's dad was a guide before nineteen hundred to rich people, would come up [to northern California] from down below [=San Francisco]; **CA**137, From then on I worked steady until I went into the service. Then when I come back I went down below [=to San Francisco Bay area] and went to work in a gas company down there. **1988** [see **down the line**].

b spec: To or in the contiguous states of the US; hence n *down below* the contiguous states. **AK**

1898 Henderson *Rainbow's End AK* 90, "Win" was taking it "down below," the Alaskan expression for into the States. **1902** McKee *Land of Nome* 149 **AK,** It was near this same island that the *Lane,* our transport of last year, struck a reef on her way "down below" (Nome lingo for Washington, Oregon, or California) a month later. **1938** *AK Sportsman* Sept 7 (Tabbert *Alaskan Engl.*), Alaska people . . have looked with askance [sic] at the reports of millions poured into various communities "down below" to further develop already over-developed areas. **1944** *AK Sportsman* July 23 (Tabbert *Alaskan Engl.*), Frank Blasher . . is now "down below" in California. **1968** *DARE* (QR p151) Inf **AK**9, Turnover = "riffraff from the States"—people who can't "make it" down below and come up to Alaska and probably don't stay. **1968** *DARE* (Qu. HH31, *Somebody who is not from your community, and doesn't belong*) Inf **AK**5, From down below.

2 To hell; hence n *down below* hell. *euphem; esp freq among younger speakers* Cf **downstairs, down under n 1**

c1960 *Wilson Coll.* **csKY,** *Down Below*—euphemism for *hell.* **1965–70** *DARE* (Qu. CC9, . . *Hell: "That man is headed straight for ———."*) 55 Infs, **widespread,** Down below [Of all Infs responding to the question, 10% were young; of those giving this response, 22% were young.]; (Qu. NN26a, *Weakened substitutes for 'hell': "Oh ———!"*) Inf **FL**28, Down below; (Qu. NN26b, *Weakened substitutes for 'hell': "Go to ———!"*) Infs **CA**120, **ID**5, **NY**122, Down below. **1967** *DARE* (Qu. NN26b, *Weakened substitutes for 'hell': "Go to ———!"*) Inf **NJ**2, Go down below.

downburst n [Prob blend of *downpour* + *cloudburst*]

A heavy rain.

1967 *DARE* (Qu. B25, . . *A very heavy rain*) Inf **NY**11, Downburst. **1978** *DARE* File **csWI,** A weather report given September 12 on TV Channel 3 (WISC, a CBS affiliate station) identified a very hard shower as a *downburst,* using the word twice.

down by the head adj phr

1916 Macy–Hussey *Nantucket Scrap Basket* 130, A vessel loaded heavily forward, so as to put her bow too deep in the water, is said to be "down by the head" and the expression is sometimes applied to a person bowed by age or infirmity.

down cellar adv phr Also *down basement* [Cf *EDD down house* downstairs] **chiefly Nth, N Midl, esp NEast** See Map Cf **up attic**

a In or to a cellar or basement.

1845 (1876) Cooper *Chainbearer* 343 **cNY,** "He's up-stairs"—cried one—"he must be down cellar," said another. **1871** (1882) Stowe *Fireside Stories* 72 **MA,** Now she'd go singin' down cellar. **1895** Brown *Meadow-Grass* 163 **NEng,** They're down cellar under the arch. **1900** Day *Up in ME* 3, He'd . . trot down cellar. **1906** *Pocumtuc Housewife* 47 **nwMA,** Put it in the soap-grease barrel down cellar. **1946** Gould *Yankee Storekeeper* 27 **NEng,** Two were shaking dice down cellar. **1965–70** *DARE* (Qu. D19, *Referring to the part of the house below the ground floor, you might say, "I'm going ———."*) 200 Infs, **chiefly Nth, N Midl, esp NEast,** Down cellar; **IL**23, **MI**61, **MA**48, **OH**81, Down basement. **1965–69** *DARE* Tape **MA**92, I . . kept some old wasted strands that was half dried up and so forth down cellar or somewhere; **MA**30, I says to my wife . . , "We'd better get down cellar" [during a hurricane].

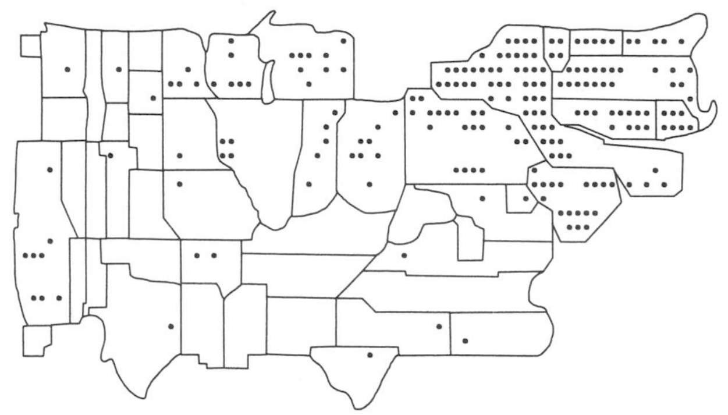

•down cellar + var (Qu. D19)

b Used in joc evasive expressions; see quots.

1969 *DARE* Tape **NY**209, "Going down cellar to tie the dog loose?" That was an old expression that they used. People come in and say, "Well, where's your wife?" or "Where's your husband?" "Oh, they're down cellar tyin' the dog loose." But when they didn't have a dog a-tall. **1988** *DARE* File **seWI,** It was the mother who usually said, "There's more down cellar in a tea cup." Everyone would smile, knowing she meant *no more available. All gone. . .* It was sort of a smart but funny remark and I don't believe I've heard it since.

down city adv Cf **downstreet**

1962 *AmSp* 37.158 **ceNY,** Instead of referring to the central business district as *downtown,* after any form of the verb *to go,* they [=old inhabitants of Troy, New York] say *down city.* Many who use *down city* also employ the New England term *downstreet,* but with a clear distinction in meaning. One goes *down city* only if he is going to the business center; if he is going no farther than the nearest grocery store or shopping center, his destination is *downstreet.*

downcome n [Metath of *comedown*]

1894 *DN* 1.330 **NJ,** *Downcome:* a fall or attendant disaster. Used with reference to politics.

down country adv phr Cf **down** adv **B1, down the country, up country**

Toward or in lower land; also n *down country,* a low-lying region, esp the eastern seaboard.

1823 Cooper *Pioneers* 1.60 **cNY,** To them, the road, that made the most rapid approaches to the condition of the old, or, as they expressed it, the *down* countries [=preRevolutionary settlements along the Hudson and Mohawk Rivers and near Long Island Sound], was the most pleasant. **a1870** Chipman *Notes on Bartlett* 129 *(DA), Down-Country.* Used in the interior to denote on or toward the seaboard; occasionally, the seaboard, or the land nearer a river's mouth. **1895** *DN* 1.382 **NJ,** *Down country:* New York City and vicinity (Sussex Co.) **1931** Hannum *Thursday April* 18 **wNC,** His movements carried a directness and sureness which bespoke the tempering of down-country training.

downdrain See **downpipe**

down East n

The northeastern part of the United States, spec:

a New England, esp the northeastern areas. Cf **down Easter 1a**

a1828 (1887) Bernard *Retrospections* 240, He [=a Connecticut farmer] had lately quitted "Down East," and was coming South to "explore" a brother, hid away somewhere among the niggers in Virginny. **1840** (1847) Longstreet *GA Scenes* 56, Mrs. Stallings and Mrs. Durham stepped simultaneously into the store of Zephaniah Atwater, from "down east." **1893** Owen *Voodoo Tales* 58, The speechless amazement of that good ecclesiastic from "Down East." **1905** *DN* 3.8 **cCT,** *Down East. . .* The country districts of New England to the north and east. **1948** Rowe *Maritime Hist.* 207, A word about this phrase "down east." It is as pure American as apple pie. Beyond the confines of New England the benighted user of the phrase has reference to New England. He is wrong. In Connecticut . . the thumb will be jerked over the left shoulder toward Massachusetts. In Boston it means Maine. But in Maine it is always a bit farther off. If you are in Casco Bay, Penobscot Bay is down east and Eastport and the maritime provinces are away down east.

b Maine and the Canadian maritime provinces. **chiefly NEng** Cf **down Easter 1b**

1825 Neal *Brother Jonathan* 1.28, A little boy, from 'down east,' whom she was teaching, all one summer, to ride on a cane. **1839** *Boston Eve. Transcript* (MA) 26 Feb 1/2, As I am always called Squire Smith round in these parts, I want you to direct it to John Smith, Esquire, Swithville [sic], Down East, and it will come to me straight as a hair. **1850** *New Engl. Farmer* 2.10 **Boston,** This was in the cold region of Down East. **1907** *DN* 3.186 **seNH,** *Down East. . .* Maine. "He comes from down East." **1945** Colcord *Sea Language* 68 **ME, Cape Cod, Long Island,** *Down East.* A general term for Maine and the Maritime Provinces of Canada. People from these parts "go up" to Boston, and return "down home." **1948** [see **a** above]. **1957** Beck *Folkl. ME* 154, The term ["Down East"] is ubiquitous in Maine. Moreover, it has no location. No matter where one goes along the coast inquiring for "Down East" the reply is always, "It's further down." When one reaches Eastport the answer is, "I don't know." **1966** *Ellsworth Amer.* (ME) 29 June 1/4, The annual Downeast Festival will be held in Ellsworth on Saturday and Sunday Aug. 6 and 7. **1966–69** *DARE* FW Addit **ME**14, "Down East"—used to refer to Canadian provinces east of Maine: New Brunswick and Nova Scotia; **MA**68, "Down East" = Nova Scotia, Prince Edward Island, Maine. **1975** Gould *ME Lingo* 78, *Down East*—Coastal Maine and the Maritime Provinces, in relation to Boston. . . But the usual explanation, always offered inquiring tourists, is that one sailed down-wind from Boston to Maine, and then beat back up-wind on the return.

c Eastern Massachusetts, esp the metropolitan Boston area. **wMA**

1969 *DARE* FW Addit **MA**42, Down east = southeastern Massachusetts. **1969** *DARE* Tape **MA**30, She was born down towards Boston. . . When I say down East I mean . . say somewhere around Concord and Boston. I ain't no down East Mainer.

down East adv phr

1 In, into, or toward New England.

1829 *MA Spy & Worcester Co. Advt.* (Worcester MA) 25 Nov [1]/4 **cMA,** "Where the deuce is Dennis [=a port city]?" "Oh, down east." **1835** *Knickerbocker* 5.206, She was built in conformity to that convenient system of naval architecture prevalent 'down east.' **1850** *Knickerbocker* 35.550, At a revival-meeting, not long ago, in a town 'down east,' one of the clergymen present read a passage from the Bible. **1906** *DN* 3.134 **nwAR,** *Down East. . .* In New England.

2 In, into, or toward Maine. **chiefly NEng**

1833 in 1834 Smith *Letters Jack Downing* 139 **ME,** To my old friend, the editor of the Portland Courier, away down east in the state of Maine. **1861** Holmes *Venner* 1.28 **NEng,** There are three towns [=Newburyport, Portsmouth, and Portland] lying in a line with each other, as you go "down East," each of them with a *Port* in its name. **1886** Hutchinson *Diary* 2.438, He went by steamer from Boston down east to the Penobscot river. **1904** *DN* 2.425 **Cape Cod MA** (as of a1857), *Down East. . .* In the state of Maine. **1966** *DARE* (Qu. KK62, *When you want to make it clear that you will not do something: "I wouldn't do that for _______.")* Inf **ME**16, A farm down East. **1979** *UpCountry* Sept 14 **MA,** Usually when my husband and I go cruising out from our home port of Scituate, we sail Down East or out around Cape Cod and the islands.

3 In or to the east.

1966 *Carteret Co. News–Times* (Morehead City & Beaufort NC) 16 Aug 2/6, Electric service down east will be interrupted. **1968** *DARE* FW Addit **Brooklyn NYC,** Going down East = going to Long Island.

down Easter n [**down East n**]

1 A person from the northeastern United States, spec:

a A New Englander. Cf **down East n a**

a1828 (1887) Bernard *Retrospections* 37, This curious class of mammalia [=New Englander], the "Down-Easter" as it is often called, is divisible into three species—the swapper, the jobber, and the pedler. **1858** Hammett *Piney Woods Tavern* 122, There was an old, long-legged down-easter aboard. **1881** Buel *Border Outlaws* 167 **MO,** A Mr. Taylor, of Boston, who had the unmistakable appearance of a "down easter," was persecuted. **1905** *DN* 3.8 **cCT,** *Down Easter. . .* A New Englander. **1906** *DN* 3.134 **nwAR,** *Downeaster. . .* A New Englander. "He's a down-easter; he says, 'you hadn't oughter.' " **1945** *Reader's Digest* July 25/1, A down-Easter sat beside me on the grass where I was untangling my fish line.

b A resident of Maine or the Canadian maritime provinces. **chiefly NEng** Cf **down East n b**

1833 Neal *Down-Easters* 1.91 **NEng,** The down-easter stood leaning over the table with his knife and fork in the air. **1904** *DN* 2.425 **Cape Cod MA** (as of a1857), *Downeaster. . .* A person from Maine. **1907** *DN* 3.186 **seNH,** *Downeaster. . .* A person from Maine. *Ibid* 243 **eME,** *Downeaster. . .* A person from the easternmost part of Maine or from New Brunswick. **1945** Colcord *Sea Language* 68 **coastal NEng,** A "down-easter" may be either a person or a vessel hailing from that region [=Maine and the Canadian maritime provinces].

2 A full-rigged sailing ship built in Maine; see quots.

1835 Ingraham *South-West* 1.161, There were . . miserable-looking sloops and schooners, compared to which, our 'down easters' are packet ships. **1935** Chapelle *Hist. Sailing Ships* 287, Though not as heavily sparred and canvassed as the clippers, the down-easters nevertheless had enough sail area to drive them at great speed. *Ibid* 288, The failure of the down-easters to survive was due to the operating cost of the ship-rig, a handicap that led to the almost total disappearance of the brig and barque. **1948** Rowe *Maritime Hist.* 208, In the maritime world of two generations ago "down-easter" was a term of fixed and no uncertain meaning. It conveyed a picture par excellence of a full-rigged wooden ship or a bark with her canvas spread in the wind, designed, built and launched in a shipyard on the coast of Maine, and more often than not commanded by a Maine captain. **1975** Gould *ME Lingo* 79, The *Down-easter* followed the *clipper,* and added a good quarter century to the era of sail. . . essentially the *clipper* was designed for the Gold Rush trade, and her lines and rigging were altered to make the Down-easter, which carried the heavier burdens of California wheat to Europe.

3 Someone who lives east of the speaker's town of residence. Cf **down East** adv phr **3**

1966 *DARE* (Qu. C34, . . *Nearby settlements, villages, or districts*) Inf **NC**11, Down Easter—any one who lives east of Beaufort [the Inf's town]; (Qu. HH1, . . *A rustic or countrified person*) Inf **NC**11, Down Easter—of people from east of Beaufort.

downer n **esp West** Cf **down D4**

A sick, exhausted, or injured animal, esp one not able to stand up.

1913 (1979) Barnes *Western Grazing* 381, *Downers.*—Cattle and other stock which have been down in the cars during shipment and arrive at the stockyards bruised, dirty and unfit for sale as beef. **1935** *AmSp* 10.270 **NE** [Language of the livestock mart], *Downer.* An animal that cannot stand on its feet. A weak or crippled animal. **1950** *WELS Suppl.* **neWI,** Your downer in livestock may have been so called because [it was] likely to go down which is nearly curtains for animals, which will try to stand if possible. *Ibid* **seWI,** Downers—rejected cattle at stock yards. **1968** Adams *Western Words* 99, *Downer*—A cow which, after a drought or a hard winter, is weak from undernourishment; every time she attempts to move faster than a walk she falls and has to be tailed up again.

downers See **down** n[1] **E2**

downface v [Perh by metath from *face down* to confront, dispute]

1899 (1912) Green *VA Folk-Speech* 153, *Down-face.* . . To contradict flatly. "She down-faced him that she didn't say it."

downfall n

1 A heavy rain. [Perh blend of *downpour* + *rainfall*] **chiefly NEast, Gt Lakes**

1939 *LANE* Map 93, The map shows the terms used of a brief but heavy rainfall: . . *rain storm, downfall, pour.* . . 1 inf, **sRI,** Downfall of rain. **1967–70** *DARE* (Qu. B24, . . *A sudden, very heavy rain*) Infs **MI**81, **MA**15, **NY**210, **OH**7, **PA**156, **SC**69, Downfall; (Qu. B25, . . *Joking names . . for a very heavy rain . . "It's a regular ________."*) Infs **MI**118, **NY**11, **RI**3, Downfall.

2 See **downpipe.**

3 A deadfall.

1957 *Eaton Coll.* **Washington Island WI,** Downfall . . naturally fallen tree.

down-go n

1 in adj phr *on the down-go:* Declining in health; declining, getting worse. **sAppalachians** Cf **down-gone**

1917 *DN* 4.411 **KY, wNC,** *Down-go.* . . Decline in health. "I love strong coffee, but when I get on the down-go I caint hardly come it." **1922** (1926) Kephart *Highlanders* 368 **sAppalachians,** If declining in health, he is on the down-go. **1931** Hannum *Thursday April* 228 **wNC,** Hit's jest scandulous the way them women of Penlin's let things peeter out. Hain't a thing about the house but what's on the down-go. **1952** Brown *NC Folkl.* 1.534, *Down-go.* . . Economic descent; in a worse condition —age, health. "That family is surely on the down-go." **1974** Fink *Mountain Speech* 7 **wNC, eTN,** *Down-go* . . declining health. *"He's been on the down-go fer sometime."* **1976** Garber *Mountain-ese* 24 **Appalachians,** *Down-go* . . wane, decline—Business has been on the downgo ever since the first uv the year.

2 A descent, downhill course.

1966 *PADS* 46.25 **cnAR,** *Down go.* . . A watercourse on a steep slope. —"That gully's where the water has a down go at it." **1984** Burns *Cold Sassy* 177 **nGA** (as of 1906), We felt mighty fancy on the down-go to Cold Sassy, and we made mighty good time.

downgone adj [**down-go 1**]

In poor condition, shabby, run-down.

1928 Chapman *Happy Mt.* 52 **seTN,** Uncle Shannon just stood shaking both fists . . and looking the picture of a down-gone Santa Claus that hadn't been washed since last Christmas.

downgutter See **downpipe**

down-head n

A **dandelion** (here: *Taraxacum officinale*).

1973 *Foxfire 2* 88 **nGA,** *Taraxacum officinale* . . down-head.

downhill haul n

Among loggers: see quot 1958.

1958 McCulloch *Woods Words* 52 **Pacific NW,** *Downhill haul*—a. An easy job. b. A smooth running show. **1969** Sorden *Lumberjack Lingo* 35 **NEng, Gt Lakes,** *Downhill haul*—Any woods job which is easy going.

down-hill-of-life n

=moneywort.

1894 *Jrl. Amer. Folkl.* 7.94, *Lysimachia nummularia.* . . down-hill-of-life Lincolnton, N.C. **1931** Clute *Common Plants* 134. **1959** Carleton *Index Herb. Plants* 39.

down home n

One's native region; the language of one's native region.

1931 *AmSp* 7.120 **eID,** *Down home* is Utah. **1977** Smitherman *Talkin* 258 [Black], *Down home,* any place south of the Mason-Dixon line; conceptually, suggests place of psychological peace and nitty-gritty blackness; *down home* began to be particularly longed for after the vast urban migration of blacks to the "promised lands" of Northern Black Bottoms. **1987** *DARE* File, In the summer of 1971 I heard two Black university students use the phrase "to talk down home" to mean to speak Black English. One was from North Carolina and the other was from Ohio.

down-home adj

From or characteristic of one's native region; by ext, simple, unpretentious.

1958 Holmes *Horn* 85 **NYC,** Maybe later pick up gigs with a downhome band. [*DARE* Ed: Speaker is native of the South.] **1967** *AmSp* 42.238, This usage [of *home boy* and *home girl* for people who come from the same hometown as the speaker] seems to have none of the connotations of *down home,* such as rusticity and naiveté, or simple tastes and simple goodness. **1970** Major *Dict. Afro-Amer. Slang* 48, *Down home:* (1950's) [of] an honest, unpretentious life style or personality; in jazz, an earthy way of playing. **1976** *NY Times* (NY) 4 June sec A 3/2, He is cheerful and chatty, full of stories of his photographic experiences around the world, . . all told in the soft down-home accent of his native Nebraska. **1979** *Capital Times* (Madison WI) 7 Sept 41, [Caption:] Down home hospitality colors couple's world. **1982** *New Yorker* 31 May 70/3 **neFL,** "We don't mind if you refer to Crescent City . . as 'the sticks' or 'red-neck country,' " the brochure . . for the Catfish Festival says. "We're a down-home community." **1984** *Ibid* 9 Apr 122/3, "Mayor," his political memoir, . . continues . . to enhance the bank account of the hundred-and-ten-thousand-dollar-a-year Mayor, who, nonetheless, thanks to his down-home style (New York version), is still viewed by many . . as representing the city's jus' folks. **1987** *DARE* File **WI,** An advertisement heard on the radio during a Milwaukee Brewers baseball game included the following lines: What'll you have?/ Down-home flavor / What'll you have?/ True-blue flavor / . . Pabst Blue Ribbon beer.

down-home adv

In, to, or at one's home or native region; in the manner of one's native region.

1924 (1946) Greer–Petrie *Angeline Gits an Eyeful* 1 **csKY,** Down home, when a passle of able-bodied men and wimmen have a getherin', they all jine in and skear up somethin' to do that's been a-needin' gittin' done. **1969** *DARE* (Qu. MM22, *If you are talking to a friend who lives in another place and you want to inquire about his neighborhood, you might ask, "How are things ________?"*) Inf **MA**56, Down home. **1969** *DARE* Tape **IL**88, My brother and sister lived down home until their deaths. **1972** Claerbaut *Black Jargon* 63, *Down home* . . the South: *We're goin' down home next week.*

down-homer n Cf **home boy**

See quots.

1938 *Hench Coll.* **VA** (as of c1900), The North Carolinians who came to Richmond to take city jobs and become city boys were called by Richmond people "down homer" because they kept saying "Well, down home, they do it this way," or "Down home we don't treat people that way." **1957** Battaglia *Resp. to PADS 20* **eMD** *(A city person's names and nicknames for a country person)* Down-homer.

down in a well See **down the well** adj phr

down in one's back See **down** adj **D5**

down in one's boots adj phr Also *down in the boots*

1 See quot.

1968 Adams *Western Words* 99, *Down in his boots*—Frightened; cowardly, said of a person, in cowboy parlance, "as yeller as mustard without the bite."

2 See quot. Cf **down at the heel(s)**

1969 *DARE* (Qu. GG34b, *To feel depressed or in a gloomy mood: "She's feeling _____ today."*) Inf **RI4**, Down in the boots.

down in the back See **down** adj **D5**

down in the boots See **down in one's boots**

down in the bushes adj phr

1913 *DN* 4.26 **OR,** *Down in the bushes*. . . Sick, in hard luck, etc. Used in the mountains of Oregon. "Bill is feeling a little down in the bushes to-day."

down in the kinks adj phr Also *down in the cans* Cf **down at the heel(s)**

Unwell, lacking energy; depressed or melancholy.

1966–70 *DARE* (Qu. BB39, *On a day when you don't feel just right, though not actually sick . . "I'll be all right tomorrow—I'm just feeling _____ today."*) Inf **NC83**, Down in the kinks; (Qu. GG34b, *To feel depressed or in a gloomy mood: "She's feeling _____ today."*) Inf **SD5**, Down in the cans.

down in the middles adj phr [Cf *middle* the mid-part of the human body] Cf *DS* BB5 and **down at the heel(s)**

See quots.

1940 *AmSp* 15.447 **TN,** *Down in the middles.* Ill or in poor health. 'I'm down in the middles.' **c1970** *Halpert Coll.* **wKY,** To be *down in the middles* = to be ill or in poor health.

down in the weather adj phr [Prob blend of *down in the dumps* (or **kinks,** mouth, etc) + *under the weather*]

1968 *DARE* (Qu. BB39, *On a day when you don't feel just right, though not actually sick . . "I'll be all right tomorrow—I'm just feeling _____ today."*) Inf **PA94**, Down in the weather.

down light n Also *down beam*

The dim light of a car's headlight.

1966–68 *DARE* (Qu. N10, . . *The bright and dim lights on a car*) Infs **NC50**, **UT4**, Down lights; **WA3**, Up beam and down beam; [**NY103**, Lights up and down].

down one's parts adv phr

In one's neighborhood.

1906 *DN* 3.134 **nwAR,** *Down our parts*. . . In our neighborhood. **c1960** *Wilson Coll.* **csKY,** *Down our parts* . . In our neighborhood or section. **1968–69** *DARE* (Qu. MM22, *If you are talking to a friend who lives in another place and you want to inquire about his neighborhood, you might ask, "How are things _____?"*) Infs **NY201**, **OH70**, **VT12**, Down your parts.

downpipe n Also *downdrain, ~fall, ~gutter, ~pour*

A downspout.

c1960 *Wilson Coll.* **csKY,** *Down pipe*. . . The pipe or gutter that takes the water from the eaves to the cistern or the ground. **1965–70** *DARE* (Qu. D29, *The pipe that takes the collected rain-water down to the ground or to a storage tank*) 30 Infs, **scattered,** Downpipe; **LA31**, **NC23**, **NH10**, Downdrain; **VA26**, Downfall; **LA11**, Downgutter; **KS5**, Downpour. [Of all Infs responding to the question, 70% were old; of those giving these responses, 93% were old.]

down-setting n [Scots; cf *SND doonset, down-,* n.3 "A scolding; a crushing rebuke" 1824–1868]

1930 Shoemaker *1300 Words* 16 **cPA Mts** (as of c1900), *Down-setting*—An abusive attack, a humiliation.

down sick adj phr

Very ill, bedridden.

1745 in 1912 Essex Inst. *Coll.* 48.299 **neMA,** Returned very ill—Expecting to be Down sick but Grew a Little Better. **1817** Brown *Western Gaz.* 354 **cNY,** If you feel indisposed, wait not till you are *down sick,* but take medicine without delay. **1833** (1930) Phelps *Diary* 216 **IL,** I done the housework until I got down sick. **1914** *DN* 4.77 **nNH, ME,** [As definition of *in one's naked bed*] Down sick. **c1960** *Wilson Coll.* **csKY,** Get down sick. **1969** *DARE* (Qu. BB42, *If a person is very sick you say he's _____*) Inf **PA216**, Really down sick. **1984** Wilder *You All Spoken Here* 203 **Sth,** He's down sick with the low blood.

downside bottom upwards adj phr, adv phr Cf *DS* MM3

c1970 *Halpert Coll.* 18 **wKY, nwTN,** Downside bottom upwards = upside down.

downside of the moon n Cf **dark of the moon**

1984 Wilder *You All Spoken Here* 61 **Sth,** Down Side of the Moon, Shrink of the Moon: When the Moon is waning, or decreasing.

downsies exclam

In marble play: see quot 1955.

1942 Berrey–Van den Bark *Amer. Slang* 665.6, Downsies!, knuckles down!, knucks!, *said to a [marble] player who has lifted his hand off the ground to shoot.* **1955** *PADS* 23.16 **cwAL,** *Downsies*. . . A call demanding that the shooter keep his knuckles on the ground when shooting.

down-spirited adj Pronc-sp *down sperited* Cf **down in the kinks**

Dispirited.

1902 (1904) Rowe *Maid of Bar Harbor* 141 **ME,** You've no idea how good company kind o' chirks a body up when they get spleeny and down sperited. **1970** *DARE* (Qu. BB39, *On a day when you don't feel just right, though not actually sick . . "I'll be all right tomorrow—I'm just feeling _____ today."*) Inf **MO22**, Down-spirited.

downspout n **esp S Midl**

A heavy rain, a downpour.

c1960 *Wilson Coll.* **csKY,** *Downspout*. . . A sudden, heavy shower, a downpour. **1967–69** *DARE* (Qu. B24, . . *A sudden, very heavy rain*) Infs **KS16**, **TN30**, Downspout; (Qu. B25, . . *Joking names . . for a very heavy rain . . "It's a regular _____."*) Inf **TX43**, Downspout; (Qu. B27, *A sudden rush of water coming from heavy rain*) Inf **TX38**, Downspout.

downstair adv [Var of *downstairs*] Cf **down cellar, upstair**

1966 *DARE* (Qu. D19, *Referring to the part of the house below the ground floor . . "I'm going _____."*) Inf **MA6**, Downstair. **1975** Gould *ME Lingo* 305, *Upstair*—Not so much in southern Maine, but in Aroostook *upstair* is heard for *upstairs:* "Now, you children get right *upstair* to bed!" The same is true of *downstair.* Back of this there seems to be a concept that *upstair* and *downstair* are places, rather than directions.

downstairs n *euphem* Cf **down below** adj **2**

1967–70 *DARE* (Qu. CC9, *Other words . . for hell: "That man is headed straight for _____."*) Infs **MI67**, **NJ69**, **TX32**, Downstairs.

down steps adv phr

Downstairs.

1968 *DARE* (Qu. D19, *Referring to the part of the house below the ground floor . . "I'm going _____."*) Inf **OH81**, Down steps.

downstreet adv **chiefly NEng, Upstate NY** See Map Cf **down city**

Down the street; to or into the main or business section of a town; downtown.

1831 (1927) Rodman *Diary* 89 **seMA,** Walked down street with Sister P[hoebe]. **1851** (1852) Stowe *Uncle Tom's Cabin* 2.140 **sLA,** I believe I'll go down street, a few moments, and hear the news, to-night. **1863** (1889) Whitney *Faith Gartney* 57 **MA,** A second charge of Miss Melindy's . . was dashing in that direction again, to "look down street after Care'*line*." **1877** Wright *Big Bonanza* 365 **NV,** I was told down

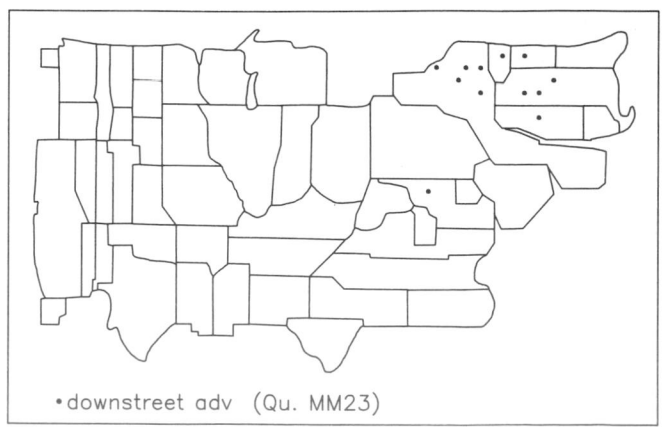

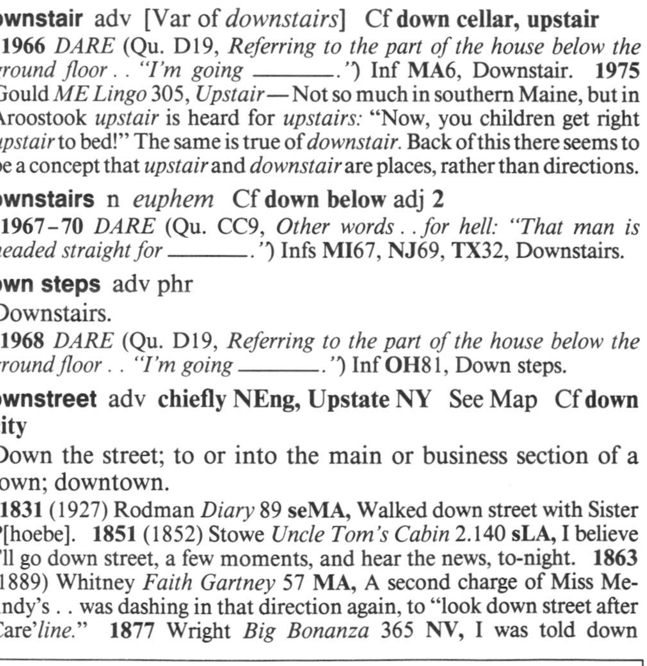
•downstreet adv (Qu. MM23)

street . . that there was a regular row in one of the shebangs up this way. **1900** Dix *Deacon Bradbury* 171 **VT,** I must be gittin' down street. **1911** Wharton *Ethan Frome* 110 **MA,** Eady and his assistant were both "down street." **1914** Steele *Storm* 283 **seMA,** "Everybody down-street!" I bellowed again, and fought my way in that direction. **1934** *Hanley Disks* **swNH,** It makes me homesick to go downstreet and see that Cheshire House gone. **1943** *LANE* Map 720, 1 inf, **RI,** *Downstreet* [*DARE* Ed: Ref is to location, not direction]; 1 inf, **cVT,** *Go downstreet,* into the village. **1962** [see **down city**]. **1965–70** *DARE* (Qu. MM23) 12 Infs, **chiefly NEng, Upstate NY,** Downstreet. **1967** *DARE* FW Addit **cnNY,** *Downstreet,* downtown; **neNY,** *Downstreet*—Used for in town, in the center of town. **1973** *DARE* File **swPA,** Down to the main street. . . "We're going down street."

down street n

1959 *VT Hist.* new ser 27.133 **cwVT,** *Down street*. . . (With emphasis on the word *down*) . . Of no one's concern.

down the country adv phr

In or into a rural area.

1967 Green *Horse Tradin'* 209 **TX,** I told him I guessed I'd better take them [=mules] on with me—that I believed they would be a little higher down the country. **1967** *DARE* (Qu. N7) Inf **HI**6, Took a ride down the country. [Inf from Honolulu] **1970** *DARE* FW Addit **VA**51, "Down the country" meaning south [i.e., in a southern direction down the Chesapeake peninsula of Virginia]. **1972** Carr *Da Kine Talk* 129 **HI,** "We goin' down da country" is heard in Honolulu to announce weekend excursions to rural Oahu.

down the country, give one v phr Also *give one down country,* ~ *down the road,* ~ *down the river, run one down the country* **chiefly Sth, S Midl** [Prob **down the country** in ref to banishment, but sometimes reanalysed as v + n phr]

To scold, reprimand, give a tongue lashing to; to insult, speak badly of.

1896 *DN* 1.415 **AL, NC, TX,** *Down the country:* to give down the country = to upbraid, call to account, "rake over the coals." **1909** *DN* 3.397 **nwAR,** *Give down the country*. . . To call to account. "Professor Campbell gave us down the country for not turning in the themes on time." **1936** Morehouse *Rain on Just* 150 **NC,** Dolly had given Bilow down the road for chasing after her so. **1939** *AmSp* 14.267 **swIN,** One sometimes finds it necessary to . . 'give someone "down the country." ' **1940** Rawlings *When Whippoorwill* 196 **FL,** The Klan talks some o' givin' him down the country for it. **1944** *PADS* 2.7 **AL, NC, SC, VA,** *Country, to give down the*. . . To "lecture" someone thoroughly. . . Colloquial, jocular. **1946** *PADS* 6.12 **seNC,** *Down-the-country:* . . A severe tongue lashing, usually when the victim is absent. "She gave him down the country." . . Occasional. **1956** McAtee *Some Dialect NC* 13, *Down the country:* . . Blame, criticism. "They're allus givin me down the country." **1966–69** *DARE* (Qu. Y3, *To say uncomplimentary things about somebody*) Infs **KY**11, 45, 68, Give him down the road; **MS**10, Run him down the country; **OK**20, Sure give him down country; (Qu. Y4, . . *A very uncomplimentary remark*) Infs **NC**6, **TX**36, Give him down the country; **KY**11, Down the road—giving him down the road; (Qu. JJ22, *To express your opinion—for example, at a public meeting: "I went to the meeting, and ———."*) Inf **SC**21, Gave 'em down the river. **1966** *DARE* Tape **SC**21, He failed me in English, and I give him down the road. **1976** Garber *Mountain-ese* 34 **Appalachians,** Bett will shore give him down the road when she hears about this. **1984** Burns *Cold Sassy* 222 **nGA** (as of 1906), Loma stormed into the store and gave her daddy down the country, blessing him out right in front of Papa, Uncle Camp, me, and two customers.

‡down-the-cricker n [*down-the-creek,* suggesting rural simplicity + *-er* nominalizing suff; cf **creek** n[1] **A**]

1968 *DARE* (Qu. H49, *Dishes made by boiling potatoes with other foods*) Inf **DE**4, Down-the-cricker—salted pork is fried, with potatoes and onions, salt and pepper. It is steamed done and you have it with tomato sauce. This is only a local dish.

down the hill adv phr

1977 Jones *OR Folkl.* 19, Some traditional folk speech you might hear from fishermen off the Oregon Coast are the phrases *down the hill* to indicate heading south from port and *up the hill* to indicate going north along the coastline.

down the hill exclam

Among loggers: see quots.

1958 McCulloch *Woods Words* 52 **Pacific NW,** Down the hill. . . A timber faller's warning when a tree is about to fall. **1969** Sorden *Lumberjack Lingo* 35 **NEng, Gt Lakes,** *Down the hill*—A cry to let other workers know a tree was falling. Same as tim-ber.

down the line adv phr

See quot.

1988 *DARE* File **nwMI,** "Down below" or "down the line": a reference often heard in the 1950's and 1960's which meant [to] the big cities south of the U.P., namely Milwaukee, Chicago, Green Bay, or Detroit. Thus: "He went down the line." It also meant where mail order houses were, and it was common to hear this: "I sent off down the line for it."

down the river n

The poker game, seven-card stud.

c1939 in 1984 Lambert–Franks *Voices* 167 **OK,** We . . gambled away our money at night; poker, faro, red-eye, coon-can, down the river, [etc]. **1952** Culbertson *Card Games* 87, *Seven-Card Stud*—This game is also called Down the River, Seven-Toed Pete, Peek Poker, and by other names. **1968** *DARE* (Qu. DD35, *What are the favorite card games that people play around here?*) Infs **CA**59, **LA**37, 45, Down the river. **1974** Gibson *Hoyle* 229, *Seven-Card Stud:* This spells action from the start, as indicated by its nickname, "down the river."

down-the-road n Cf etym note at **down the country, give one**

1966 *DARE* (Qu. V11, . . *A county or city jail*) Inf **MI**24, Down-the-road.

down the street adv phr

=**downstreet** adv.

1923 *DN* 5.243 **LA,** *Down the street*. . . Down town.

down the well adj phr Also *down in a well*

Suffering from misfortune, down-and-out; depressed or melancholy.

1939 in 1954 Porter *103 Lyrics* 27, [Lyrics to "Friendship":] If you're ever up a tree,/ Phone to me./ If you're ever down a well,/ Ring my bell. **1966** *DARE* (Qu. CC12b, . . *If a person has a lot of bad luck . . "He's been ———."*) Inf **NC**22, Down the well; (Qu. GG34b, *To feel depressed or in a gloomy mood: "She's feeling ——— today."*) Inf **MS**49, Down in a well.

down-the-well n

In marble play: see quot.

1967 *DARE* (Qu. EE7, . . *Kinds of marble games*) Inf **TX**33, Down-the-well—knock opponent into a hole.

down to the ground adv phr Also *down to the bottom*

See quot 1902.

c1902 Clapin *New Dict. Amer.* 166, *Down to the ground.* Entirely, completely. "That suits me down to the ground." **c1960** *Wilson Coll.* **csKY,** *Down to the ground*. . . Completely. "He's a gentleman [down] to the ground." **1969–70** *DARE* (Qu. KK50, *When something is planned out carefully, down to the last detail: "He had it all worked out ———."*) Inf **KY**47, Down to the bottom; **TN**52, Down to the ground.

down-to-the-heel(s) See **down-at-the-heel(s)**

down to the last (nail) hole See **hole** n **10b**

down under adj phr

1 =**down** adj **D1.**

1950 *WELS (Only a little bit sick . . "I'm ———.")* 1 Inf, **cwWI,** Kinda down under. **1967–70** *DARE* (Qu. GG34b, *To feel depressed or in a gloomy mood: "She's feeling ——— today."*) Inf **MA**81, Down under; (Qu. BB39, *On a day when you don't feel just right, though not actually sick, you might say, "I'll be all right tomorrow—I'm just feeling ——— today."*) Inf **HI**9, Down under.

2 =**down sick.**

1968 *DARE* (Qu. BB43, *A person who has to stay in bed all the time: "For two years now he's been ———."*) Inf **MO**36, Down under.

down under n

1 See quot. **chiefly NEast** Cf **down below** n **2**

1965–70 *DARE* (Qu. CC9, . . *Hell: "That man is headed straight for ———."*) 13 Infs, **chiefly NEast,** Down under.

2 See quot.

1969 *DARE* (Qu. II25, . . *The part of a town where the poorer people, special groups, or foreign groups live*) Inf **MA**24, Down under.

downward plum n

=**saffron plum.**

1884 Sargent *Forests of N. Amer.* 103, *Ants' Wood. Downward Plum. . .* A small tree, rarely exceeding 4 meters in height. **1897** Sudworth *Arborescent Flora* 320, *Bumelia angustifolia. . . Common Names. . .* Downward Plum (Fla.) **1933** Small *Manual SE Flora* 1033, *Downward-plum . .* is used for cabinet-work. **1960** Vines *Trees SW* 835, Some of the vernacular names are . . Antwood, Downward-plum [etc]. **1979** Little *Checklist U.S. Trees* 65, *Bumelia celastrina. . . Saffron-plum. . .* Downward-plum.

down-weed n [*down* fluff]

=cotton rose 2.

1940 Clute *Amer. Plant Names* 83, *Gifola germanica. . .* Down-weed. **1959** Carleton *Index Herb. Plants* 39, *Down-weed:* Filago germanica.

down-yonders n Cf **go-yonders**

c1966 *Wilson Coll.* **csKY,** *Down yonders. . .* Nervous impatience. "He's acting like he had a spell of the down yonders." Used by black speakers.

downy woodpecker n

Std: a woodpecker *(Dryobates pubescens).* Also called **checker-backer, chib-chab, dominicker n 5, driller, little guinea woodpecker, little speckled woodpecker, little spotted woodpecker, peckerwood, sapsucker, Tommy woodpecker**

dowse See **douse** v

dowsel n [Var of **dowser 2**]

1970 *DARE* (Qu. CC13a, . . *A forked stick that's used to show where there's water underground*) Inf **OH**93, Dowsel [ˈdaʊzəl].

dowser n Usu |ˈdaʊzə(r), ˈdaʊs-|; occas |ˈdozər|

1 One who uses a divining rod. **scattered, but chiefly NEast** See Map

1939 (1962) Thompson *Body & Britches* 22 **NY,** The Mineral-Rod. This valuable apparatus is a fork of witch-hazel, such as our *dowsers* upstate use in finding water-wells. **1951** Roberts *Henry Gross* 7 **ME,** My primary reason for writing this book was to place on record the peculiar facts in the case of Henry Gross, so that they might readily be consulted by amateur and professional dowsers. **c1960** *Wilson Coll.* **csKY,** *Dowser. . .* A water-witch. **1965–70** *DARE* (Qu. CC13b, . . *The person who knows how to use a forked stick to find water*) 89 Infs, **scattered, but chiefly NEast,** (Water) dowser; **CT**3, [ˈdozɚ]. **1968** Adams *Western Words* 99, *Dowser*—In mining, one who searches for subterranean supplies of water, ore, etc., with the aid of a *divining rod.* **1979** *Yankee* Sept 37 **neVT,** By now I have become aware that dowsers, or many of them, not only diagnose illnesses but have been credited with paranormal healing.

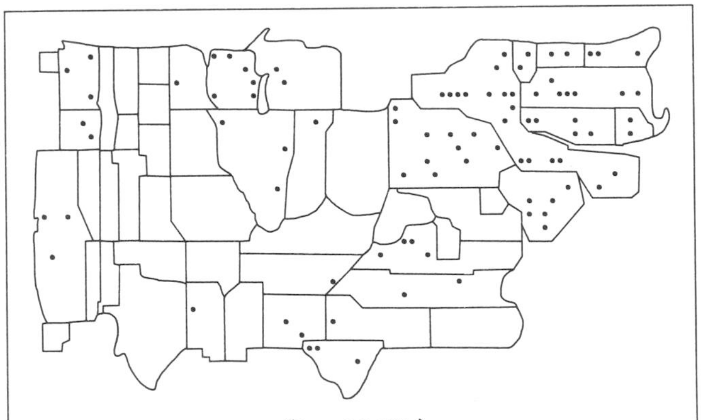

•dowser 1 + varr (Qu. CC13b)

2 also *dowser stick:* **=dowsing rod. chiefly Nth**

1965–70 *DARE* (Qu. CC13a, . . *A forked stick that's used to show where there's water underground*) 18 Infs, **chiefly Nth,** (Water) dowser; **RI**4, Dowser stick.

dowsing rod n Also *dowsing fork, ~ stick, ~ switch, ~ twig* [*OED* (at *dowse*) 1691 →] **chiefly Nth, esp NEast** See Map

A stick or rod used to divine underground water, minerals, etc.

c1960 *Wilson Coll.* **csKY,** *Dowsing rod* or *switch* used by a *dowser.* **1965–70** *DARE* (Qu. CC13a, . . *A forked stick that's used to show where there's water underground*) 32 Infs, **chiefly Nth, esp NEast,** Dowsing rod; 9 Infs, **chiefly Nth,** Dowsing stick; **NY**111, **MA**6, Dowsing (fork). **1967** Williams *Greenbones* 240 **GA** (as of c1910), But he had turned in Nin's hand like a dowsing-twig. **1979** *UpCountry* July 17/2 **cVT,** It took only a little checking to disclose that Henry and his dowsing stick had located water for various farmers and homeowners. **1983** *MJLF* 9.38 **ceKY,** *Dowsing stick . .* a dowsing rod.

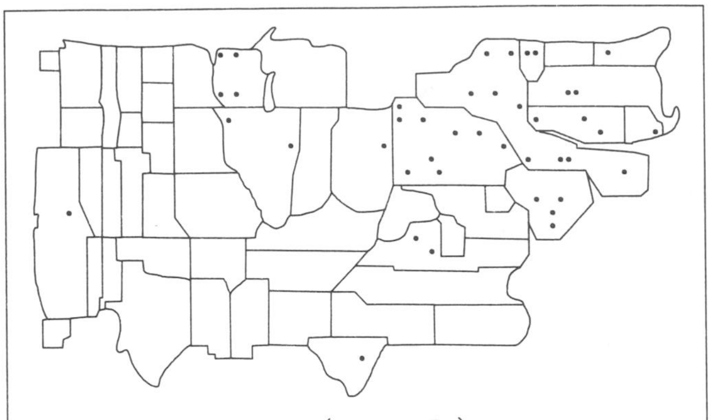

•dowsing rod + varr (Qu. CC13a)

dow stick n [Prob assim from *dowse stick*]

=dowsing rod.

1969 *DARE* (Qu. CC13a, . . *A forked stick that's used to show where there's water underground*) Inf **NJ**58, Dow [ˈdaʊ] stick.

dowty n

An unidentified fish; see quot.

1968 *DARE* (Qu. P4, *Saltwater fish that are not good to eat*) Inf **MD**42, *Dowty* [ˈdaʊti˙]—something like a catfish, large mouth.

‡doxology n

1970 *DARE* (Qu. JJ13, . . *Joking words . . for a name signed to a paper . . "I'll put my ______ on that."*) Inf **PA**242, Doxology.

doxy n [*OED* c1530 →]

1 An immoral woman, trollop.

1806 (1970) Webster *Compendious Dict.* 94, *Doxy . .* a soldier's trull, loose wench. **1942** Berrey–Van den Bark *Amer. Slang* 439.1, *Woman of easy morals. . .* Doxy. **1967** *DARE* (Qu. HH37, *An immoral woman*) Inf **NE**9, Doxy.

2 A slovenly woman.

1896 *DN* 1.415 **seNH,** *Doxy:* awkward, slatternly woman. **1915** *DN* 4.202, *Doxy,* slovenly woman. "I can't blame Stewart for trying to get a divorce from his doxy."

3 A sweetheart, lover.

1837 (1955) *Crockett Almanacks* 91 **wTN,** I determined to make a call on my doxy. On arriving . . what should I see but my little gal sitting in the lap of a tarnal pedlar. **1941** *LANE* Map 400 *(His Sweetheart),* 1 inf, **cCT,** *Doxy, dony,* still used. . . 1 inf, **seNH,** *Doxy,* old-fashioned.

doze n [**doze** v[1]]

Decay in wood.

1975 Gould *ME Lingo* 80, *Doze*—A word peculiar to Maine for a certain kind of rot in wood, usually firewood. The fiber changes color, becomes not quite punky, but the stick doesn't disintegrate, so that an unprincipled farmer may sell *dozey* wood, and the customer won't know it until he tries to get heat out of it. Beech and gray birch are most susceptible to *doze,* and of the softwoods hemlock is often infected. Carpenters often use *doze,* perhaps not with accuracy, for rot that appears in construction timbers, both in buildings and in boats.

doze v[1], hence ppl adj *dozed* **chiefly NEng** *somewhat old-fash*

=dote v 1.

1705 in 1960 Taylor *Poems* **MA,** All Light delights. Yet Dozde [sic] wood light is cold. **1872** Schele de Vere *Americanisms* 464, *Dozy* and *dozed* are said in Pennsylvania of timber beginning to decay and unfit for use, while the decay is yet hardly perceptible, but the timber already brittle. **1892** *DN* 1.210 **seMA,** *Doze:* to decay. **1907** *DN* 3.243 **eME,** *Doze. . .* To decay; to soften. Used of wood. "That wood was cut last summer; so it ain't dozed any." **1913** *DN* 4.4 **ME,** *Doze. . .* To become dozey.

doze v[2], hence vbl n *dozing* Also with *out* [Abbr for *bulldoze*]

To clear (land), clear out (obstructions) with a bulldozer.

1967–69 *DARE* (Qu. L36, . . *[To] dig out roots and underbrush to make a new field*) Infs **CO**38, Have a cat doze out the trees; **LA**14, Dozing—using a bulldozer to clear land; **MO**3, Dozing it out; **MO**20, We had this field dozed for cultivation.

dozed See **doze** v[1]

dozen n Infreq *dozent*

A Form.

1905 *DN* 3.57 **eNE,** *Dozen(t)* . . sometimes heard.

B Senses.

1 usu pl; usu with *the;* often in comb *dirty dozens* (hence, *clean dozens*): Insulting language, often directed against one's opponent's mother; a ritualized exchange of such insults, often in verse form; hence phr *play the dozens* to engage in an exchange of insults; phrr *put one in the dozen(s), shoot dozens at one, read one the dozens,* etc, to insult, curse one. [Origin unknown; see conjectures in quots 1960, 1977] *among Black speakers; esp urban* Cf **signify**

1919 *Current Opinion* 67.165/1 **Sth,** The chorus runs like this: . . Oh, the old dirty dozen,/ The old dirty dozen;/ Brothers and cousins,/ Livin' like a hive of bees./ . . / There wasn't a good one in the bunch. **1930** in 1983 Taft *Blues Lyric Poetry* 196 **Chicago IL** [Black], [Song title:] New Dirty Dozens. . . [Lyrics:] Come all you folks : and start to walk / I'm fixing to start : my dozen talk. **1931** Bradford *John Henry* 213 **cMS** [Black], Maybe de happy dust cross me up and de preacher put me in de dozens. **1937** (1977) Hurston *Their Eyes* 123 **csFL** [Black], Y'all really playin' de dozens tuhnight. **1941** Percy *Lanterns* 301 **nwMS** [Black], "Then some fool nigger puts you in the dozen." . . "What's putting you in the dozen?" "That's sho nuff bad talk. . . That's talkin' about your mommer." **1944** *PADS* 2.33 **NC** [Black], *Dozens, to shoot.* . . To curse. "Don't come shooting no dozens at me." **1960** (1961) Oliver *Blues Fell* 128, 'Putting in the Dozens' developed as a folk game in the late nineteenth century. A number of persons would gather and endeavour to exceed each other in the insults that they invented with a view to goading someone present to eventual wrath. In the process many obscene and scandalous inferences as to the ancestry of the individuals concerned would be made. *Ibid* 130, Intentionally evil, it [=the dozens] takes its name from the dice throw of twelve, the worst in crap-shooting. But though the 'Dirty Dozens' is in part improvised, it is somewhat on the fringes of the blues. **1969** Brown *Die Nigger Die* 27 **LA** [Black], The real aim of the Dozens was to get a dude so mad that he'd cry or get mad enough to fight. . . Signifying is more humane. Instead of coming down on somebody's mother, you come down on them. **1970** Major *Dict. Afro-Amer. Slang* 46, *Dirty Dozens:* a very elaborate game traditionally played by black boys, in which the participants insult each other's relatives, especially their mothers. The object of the game is to test emotional strength. The first person to give in to anger is the loser. **1977** Smitherman *Talkin* 132, In its indigenous folk style, the Dozens consists of set responses in versified form, usually rhymed couplets. Some refer to various sexual acts committed with "yo momma"—the mother of whoever is being addressed. The term "Dozens" probably comes from the fact that the original verses involved twelve sex acts, each stated in such a way as to rhyme with the numbers 1 to 12. **1980** Folb *Runnin' Down* 235 **Los Angeles CA** [Black], *Dozens, the*—Ritualized or spontaneous insults directed most often at another's mother (the *dirty dozens*) or an opponent (the *clean dozens* . .) **1987** Rose *I Remember Jazz* xi, A Lonnie Johnson, reading somebody the "dirty dozens," has the effect of suggesting an entirely new art form.

2 A shock of grain made up of twelve sheaves or bundles. Cf **dozen** v

1968 *DARE* (Qu. L30b, . . *Sheaves . . are set together in piles called* ———.) Inf **WV**3, Dozens—12 bundles.

dozen v Cf **dozen** n **B2**

To make shocks of grain containing twelve sheaves each.

1927 *AmSp* 2.353 **WV,** *Dozen* . . to gether [sic] the bound sheaves by dozens. "The boys have dozened all the wheat on that side of the hill." **1966** *DARE* FW Addit **NC**33, To dozen—to tie shocks up, twelve to a bundle.

dozens See **dozen** n **B1**

dozent See **dozen** n

doze out See **doze** v[2]

dozer n [Abbrs for *bulldozer*]

1942 *Infantry Jrnl.* (U.S.) Oct. 51 *(OEDS),* The blade of the dozer is not much good. **1958** McCulloch *Woods Words* 52 **Pacific NW,** *Dozer*—Short for bulldozer. **1968** *DARE* (Qu. L36, . . *[To] dig out roots and underbrush to make a new field*) Inf **MD**22, Now they use dozers. **1968–70** *DARE* Tape **CA**147, [FW:] How long would it take you to dig under like that? [Inf:] Oh, just a matter of minutes . . with a dozer; **CA**201, No dozers, none of that stuff; **IN**42, He wouldn't bring the dozer out here; **KY**39, In the later years you use a dozer, a cat, a bulldozer.

dozing See **doze** v[2]

dozy adj Also sp *dosey, dozey* [**doze** v[1]] **chiefly NEast, esp ME** =**doty 1.**

1872 [see **doze** v[1]]. **1887** (1956) Kirkland *Zury* 537 **cIL,** *Dozy.* . . Disintegrated, useless, tending to decay. **1892** *DN* 1.210 **seMA,** *Dozy:* decaying. "A dozy post." **1905** U.S. Forest Serv. *Bulletin* 61.35 [Logging terms], *Doty.* . . Decayed. . . Syn[onym]: dozy. **1913** *DN* 4.4 **ME,** *Dozey.* . . Partly decomposed, of wood poorly seasoned. "That wood is too dozey to burn well." **1917** *DN* 4.411 **ME,** *Dosey.* **1924** *DN* 5.295 **csNH,** *Dozy.* . . Soft, punky:—applied to wood. **1940** *Harper's Mag.* 182.107/2 **ME,** Wood that hasn't properly seasoned is dozy. **1946** *McDavid Coll.* **NY,** A dozy piece of timber. **1959** *VT Hist.* new ser 27.134 **c,cnVT,** *Dozey.* . . Decayed; rotten, as of wood. Rare. **1966–69** *DARE* (Qu. KK7, *When wood—for example, a tree stump—is starting to decay inside, you'd say, "It's* ——— *inside."*) Infs **CT**9, **ME**1, 5, 11, 19, 22, **NY**209, **WI**59, Dozy. **1984** *MJLF* 10.149 **cnWI,** *Dozy.*

dozy n See **doozy**

drab n[1] *derog*

1 A slovenly, untidy woman. [*OED* c1515 →] Cf **drag n 13b**

1899 (1977) Norris *McTeague* 22 **San Francisco CA,** What a stupid drab was this Maria! **1967–68** *DARE* (Qu. HH36, *A careless, slovenly woman: "She's just an old* ———*."*) Infs **GA**67, **LA**14, Drab. [Both Infs coll educ]

2 Used as a disparaging epithet.

1968 *DARE* (Qu. HH12, *A person who is always finding fault about unimportant things*) Inf **CA**81, A drab; (Qu. HH13, . . *A person [who] is not very alert or not aware of things: "He's certainly* ———*."*) Inf **CA**94, A drab.

drab adj Also *drabby*

Unwell, under the weather.

1968–70 *DARE* (Qu. BB39, *On a day when you don't feel just right, though not actually sick, you might say, "I'll be all right tomorrow—I'm just feeling* ——— *today."*) Inf **PA**247, Drab; **MD**23, Drabby.

drab n[2] [From **dribs and drabs** n pl]

A small amount.

1967–68 *DARE* (Qu. LL7, *In small amounts, by small degrees: "She didn't get the money all at once, they sent it to her* ———*."*) Infs **AL**27, **MD**25, **PA**94, **TX**29, In drabs.

drabbed up ppl adj phr

1977 Miles *Ozark Dict.* 2, *Drabbed up*—Gray looking, overcast. "The sky's drabbed up today."

drabble v[1] [*OED* a1400–50 →; *EDD*] *old-fash*

To get (oneself or one's clothing) muddy or wet; hence ppl adj *drabbled.*

1848 Bartlett *Americanisms* 121, *To drabble.* To draggle; to make dirty by drawing in dirt and water; to wet and befoul; as, to drabble a gown or cloak. A word common in New England. **1912** Green *VA Folk-Speech* 153, *Drabble.* . . To draggle; make dirty, as by dragging in the mud and water: wet and befoul. **1949** *AmSp* 24.108 **cnGA,** *Drabbled,* adj. Water-soaked. 'Like a drabbled rat.' **1950** Moore *Candlemas Bay* 188 **ME,** It [=the wind] knocked Clay down and rolled him over in a puddle. Everybody came back with drabbled clothes and had to change. Clay had to be washed and dressed from the skin out.

drabble v[2] [Var of **grabble v 1**]

1953 *PADS* 19.10 **sAppalachians,** *Drabble.* . . To dig up. "I must go to the garden and drabble some potatoes."

drabbled See **drabble** v[1]

drabbletail See **draggletail 2**

drabby See **drab** adj

drackly See **directly**

dradful See **dreadful**

draft n[1] Usu |dræft|; also |drɔf, drɔθ|; also, prob based on sp *draught,* |drɔt|; for addit proncs see quot 1965–70 at **A** Also sp *draught;* pronc-sp *draff*

A Forms.

1908 *DN* 3.306 **eAL, wGA,** *Draff*. . . Draft. "Draff horses." **1949** Webber *Backwoods Teacher* 93, Hit beats anything you can buy at the store—that there Black Draught [Webber: rhymes with "caught" at Big Piney] an' stuff. **1965–70** *DARE* (Qu. BB22, . . *Home remedies . . for constipation*) 25 Infs, **chiefly Sth, S Midl,** Black draught [drɔ(ʊ)t]; **KY**34, **MS**60, **NC**45, **NJ**67, **TN**14, **SC**58, Black [drɔ(ə)θ]; **AL**33, **AR**27, **NC**50, **TX**92, 86, Black [drɔf]; **AL**19, 34, **KY**84, **NC**22, **SC**27, Black [dræ(ɪ)f]; **MO**12, **NC**88, **VA**69, Black [drɒt]; **FL**51, **SC**67, Black [drɒf]; **KY**11, **TX**42, **VA**13, Black [dræ(ʊ)t]; **FL**49, Black [drɒ]; **IL**96, Black [draʊf]; **KY**74, Black [dræʊθ]; **MO**39, Black [draf]; **NC**83, Black [drɔə]; **SC**70, Black [draʊ]; **TN**62, Black [draʊt]; **TX**71, Black [draʊt]; (Qu. DD18, *A drink of liquor, or the amount of liquor taken in one swallow: "He took a good ______."*) Infs **MA**4, **NY**202, Draft [dræft].

B Senses.

1 A small stream; a tributary. [Cf *OED draught* sb. 23 "A current, stream, flow"; 1601 →] **chiefly Appalachians**

1731 in 1924 *MD Hist. Mag.* 19.192 **csPA,** I have now ten thousand Acres of Warrant located on the Creeks called Conawago Codoras & their Draughts on Susquehanna. **1736** in 1940 *AmSp* 15.173 **VA,** By the head of a Draft that runs into James River. **1760** in 1912 Augusta Co. VA *Chronicles* 3.364, 510 acres on head of east fork of Cook's Creek and a draft of Smith's Creek. **1788** in 1940 *AmSp* 15.173 **VA,** To a spruce Pine and a Lynn standing on the South West branch of Mill Run a Draft of Pattisons Creek. **1805** (1808) Gass *Jrl.* 144 **PA,** Captain Clarke and his party returned, having found a tolerable good road, except where some draughts crossed it. **1913** Kephart *Highlanders* 220 **sAppalachians,** After close study of mountain speech I have failed to discern that the word draft is understood, except in parts of the Virginia and Kentucky mountains, where it means a brook. **1944** *PADS* 2.19 **sAppalachians,** *Draft*. . . A brook or small stream.

2 By ext: a narrow valley, gully, ravine. **chiefly Appalachians** Cf **draw n 2** Note: The 1655 quot assigned to this sense in *DA* appears rather to belong to the sense "surveyed tract" (*DAE draught* n. 4).

1806 (1808) Gass *Jrl.* 333 **PA,** We proceeded over some very steep tops of the mountains, and deep snow; but the snow was not so deep in the drafts between them. **1894** *Harper's New Mth. Mag.* 89.883/1 **c,sAppalachians,** Now you . . climb up and down a never-ending succession of ridges and "drafts," as the ravines are called. **1912** Green *VA Folk-Speech* 153, *Draft*. . . Drift. A gully worn in the ground by water, between hills and used as a road. "Watson's Draft." **1930** Shoemaker *1300 Words* 17 **cPA Mts** (as of c1900), *Draft*—A glen or hollow in the mountains. **1968** *DARE* (Qu. C29, *A good-sized stretch of level land with practically no trees*) Inf **WV**1, Draft—a very narrow valley.

3 A home remedy for fever and colds that is applied to the feet. [Because it is supposed to "draw out" the fever] **chiefly NEast**

1817 in 1918 IN Hist. Soc. *Pub.* 6.2.326 **NY,** We had one onion on board. I applied that to his feet as a draft. **1955** *NY Folkl. Qrly.* 11.286 **NY,** To draw out colds, put "drafts" on the feet. "Drafts" can be made of pounded burdock leaves tied to feet with cloths. **1966** *DARE* (Qu. BB50a, . . *Remedies . . for a cough*) Inf **ME**4, A draft—if they had a fever with a cold, they put pork rind on the feet, or hot salt or mustard, to draw the fever. **1975** Gould *ME Lingo* 95, *Fish draft*. . . A home remedy guaranteed to break up a high fever. The patient is warmly wrapped in bed with his feet sticking out at the foot. Then a salt fish is bandaged to the flat of each of his feet, and these are supposed to "draw out" his fever.

4 A pattern used in weaving; see quot 1941. [*OED* 1822 →] **chiefly S Midl**

1932 Randolph *Ozark Mt. Folks* 107, The loom used in making these pieces had six treadles, and the weaver worked from a complicated pattern or "draft" marked on paper. **1937** (1963) Hyatt *Kiverlid* 23 **KY,** The old weaver untied a yellowed "poke". . . "What pattern air you set on usin' fer your kiverlid, Marthy Lou?" She carefully smoothed the time yellowed drafts over her lap, some of them drafts of old patterns from across the sea. **1941** Writers' Program *Guide WV* 151, The weaver of the coverlet follows a pattern or 'draft' marked on strips of paper; some of these are very old and extremely difficult to decipher. **1941** Writers' Program *Guide IN* 128, The actual weaving [of coverlets] was done from homemade 'drafts' composed of lines, spaces, and numbers, which guided the weavers as they passed the wool through their looms. **1937** McMeekin *Old KY Country* 156, "Drafts?" Why, her grannie had a "chist" brimmed with them patterns. . . They are strips of tow linen, patched and backed with yellowed paper. . . Here are the directions for threading and setting up the looms. **1960** Hall *Smoky Mt. Folks* 48 **eTN, wNC,** Most of the elderly women liked to speak of their weaving. . . "My coverlid (bedspread) designs were the Irish Chain, the Double Rose and the Fan." Coverlids were made according to a "draft" or pattern.

5 pl: The game of checkers; hence n *draftman* a piece used in the game. [The std Brit name for this game; *OED draught* sb. 22 c1400 →]

1844 Thompson *Major Jones's Courtship* 146 **GA,** Mary and me was playin a game of drafts, and I was jest about to pen her with three kings, when one of the checks happened to drap off the board. **1887** (1967) Harris *Free Joe* 22 **GA,** Playing chess or draughts under the China-trees that shaded the sidewalks. **1908** *DN* 3.307 **eAL, wGA,** *Draf(t)-man*. . . One of the pieces used in the game of checkers or drafts. *Ibid, Draf(t)s*. . . Checkers: rarely called by the regular name.

draft n[2] See **drought A6**

draftman See **draft** n[1] **B5**

drag n

1 A harrow, esp a simple wooden one; see quots. **chiefly Inland Nth, Midl** See Map Cf **A-drag, drag harrow, drag v B1**

1655 in 1916 MA (Colony) Probate Court (Essex Co.) *Records* 1.203 **neMA,** One dragge, 10d.; one paire of old bootes. **a1817** (1821) Dwight *Travels* 2.465 **NEng,** The instrument, employed for this purpose, is a large and strong harrow; here called *a drag,* with very stout iron teeth; resembling in its form the capital letter A. It is drawn over the surface, a sufficient number of times to make it mellow, and afterwards to cover the seed. **1880** *Harper's New Mth. Mag.* 62.160/2 **nNY,** "You have a drag?" "Yes, wid five teeth in it." **1930** Shoemaker *1300 Words* 16 **cPA Mts** (as of c1900), *Drag*—A wooden harrow. **1939** *LANE* Map 167 *(Harrow)* 20 infs, **chiefly wNEng,** Drag. [4 infs indicated that the term was old-fashioned or obsolete.] **1948** Davis *Word Atlas Gt. Lakes* 157 **MI, nIL, IN, OH,** Drag. **c1960** *Wilson Coll.* **csKY,** *Drag*. . . A series of logs or planks, fastened together to make a crusher of clods. **1965–70** *DARE* (Qu. L20, *The implement used in a field after it's been plowed to break up the lumps*) 151 Infs, **chiefly Inland Nth, Midl,** Drag; 19 Infs, **chiefly MI,** Spiketooth (*or* springtooth, etc) drag; **PA**129, **WI**6, Drags; (Qu. L23, . . *Machinery . . used . . in putting in . . seed*) Inf **KY**46, Disk harrow and drag; (Qu. L35, *Hand tools used for cutting underbrush and digging out roots*) Inf **CO**12, Drag—[made of] two railroad irons; sage raked into windrows and burned. **1967–68** *DARE* Tape **OH**58, Used to, they had drags, they'd make 'em out of wooden beams and bolt 'em together like steps and they'd drag them over it and break the clods up; **TX**8, Then they come behind and usually harrow it in lightly with a harrow or . . drag . . just to cover it. **1973** Allen *LAUM* 1.217 **MN, eND, eSD, eNE, nIA** (as of c1950), For breaking up clods of earth after plowing three different types of implements are typically employed. The oldest, once made entirely of wood, consists of pegs or spikes set in horizontal bars. . . [It] is generally known as a *drag,* although outside the Northern speech zone it is more likely to be called a *harrow.* **1984** *MJLF* 10.149 **cnWI,** Drag. A harrow used for leveling out plowed and disked fields preparatory to planting.

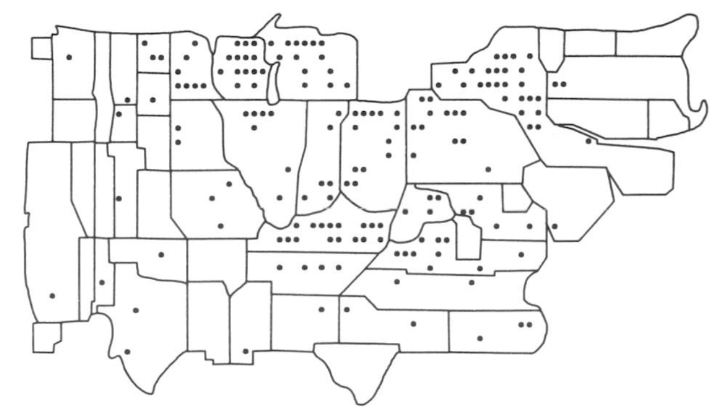

•drag n 1 + varr (Qq. L20, L23, L35)

2 also *dragger, drogue, droog, drug:* A sledge for hauling heavy loads. [*OED drag* sb. 1. c 1576 →; cf *OED drogue* and *drug* sb.[2]] **formerly chiefly eNEng, now widespread** Cf **drag sled, stone drag**

1731 *Weekly Journal* 18 Oct. *(DAE),* A stick of timber which he was drawing to his house with a Dragg. **1803** in 1888 Cutler *Life* 2.125 **eMA,** Could you not . . haul the rocks, with the cart or drag, off the plow land in the farm. **1884** *Century Illustr. Mag.* 27.446/2, Two skids fastened together made a "drag," or "sledge," to which was hitched a single ox or horse, for drawing burdens over the grass or ground in summer. This sledge was used on the northern frontier, in Pennsylvania, and in Carolina, and with it the Maryland and Virginia planter sometimes dragged his tobacco hogsheads to the place of shipment. **1909** *DN* 3.411 **nME,** *Drag. . .* Same as *stone boat.* **1939** *LANE* Map 168 **throughout eNEng,** A flat sledge-like vehicle on which heavy stones are transported from a field, usually drawn by horses or oxen, now sometimes by a tractor: . . *(stone) drag (droog, drogue, drug).* **1949** Kurath *Word Geog.* 58, The wheelless horse-drawn vehicle made of heavy planks, which is used for dragging stones from the fields, is known as a *stone sled* or *drag sled* in the Midland and as a *stone boat* in the North, except for the coastal area of New England, which has *drag* or *stone drag.* **1965–70** *DARE* (Qu. L57, *A low wooden platform used for bringing stones or heavy things out of the fields*) 150 Infs, **widespread,** Drag; **SC**26, Dragger; (Qu. L13, . . *Wagon used for carrying hay*) Inf **MA**47, Drag or boat; (Qu. N40a, . . *Sleighs . . for hauling loads*) Infs **MA**47, **NC**50, **RI**17, Drag; (Qu. N41b, *Horse-drawn vehicles to carry heavy loads*) Inf **CT**5, Drag = stoneboat; **FL**48, **IA**32, Drag; **MA**36, Sleds, scoot, drag; (Qu. N40c, . . *To carry light loads*) Inf **FL**48, Sleds or drags.

3 The group of slow-moving animals at the rear of a herd; a slow-moving member of a herd; also fig. **West** Cf **drag driver**

1907 White *AZ Nights* 106, As my horse was somewhat winded, I joined the "drag" at the rear. Here by course of natural sifting soon accumulated all the lazy, gentle, and sickly cows, and the small calves. The difficulty now was to prevent them from lagging and dropping out. **1914** *DN* 4.165 **AZ,** *Drag. . .* Lazy or sickly cattle at the rear of a herd. **1920** Hunter *Trail Drivers TX* 49 (as of 1867), We put them [=cattle] back on the trail and by the time the drags got near the river the leaders were climbing the east bank. **1929** Dobie *Vaquero* 190 **TX,** Now, in any and every herd on earth, whether of men, goats, cattle, or horses, there are always some drags. The draggiest drag of our herd was an old gray mare; she was always behind and always seemed to be asleep. **1936** McCarthy *Lang. Mosshorn* **West** [Range terms], *Drags. . .* Cattle which fall behind the rest of the bunch. **1952** FWP *Guide SD* 85, *A drag:* an individual sheep too weak to keep up with the bunch. *The drag:* the rear end of a moving band of sheep. **1966** [see **drag driver**].

4 See **drag driver.**

5 In railroading: a freight train, usu a slow one; any slow train.

1927 *AmSp* 2.388 [Vagabond argot], A freight is called a *drag. Disedrag* (merchandise), *silk-drag, coal-drag, fruit-drag* and *slow drag* result from this word. **1932** *RR Mag.* Oct 367, *Drag*—Heavy train of dead freight; any kind of slow freight train. **1939** FWP *ID Lore* 245, *The drag*—train with dead freight. **1965–70** *DARE* (Qu. N36, . . *A slow train or one that stops at every station;* total Infs questioned, 75) Inf **MS**59, Slow drag; (Qu. N37, . . *A branch railroad that is not very important or gives poor service*) Infs **AL**2, **KS**18, **NC**72, **VA**70, Slow drag. **1967** Williams *Greenbones* 139 **GA** (as of c1910), Nin slept restlessly, pillowed on an arm, under the trains, the fast drags and the double-headers spewing their sparks down. **1967** *DARE* Tape **ID**6, So here I am on a freight drag going west. A drag, by the way, is just an ordinary old slow train, nothing important about it. **1968** *AmSp* 43.286 [Railroad vocab], *Drag.* A slow freight usually composed of empty cars, or a heavy tonnage train which cannot speed along the division; a long, slow, heavy train.

6 In gathering shellfish: a pass made by a trawl over a fishing ground. Cf **drag fishing**

1955 *AmSp* 30.75 **cwTN** [Musseling terms], *Drag. . .* A movement across the mussel beds. **1966** *DARE* Tape **NC**12, We get up about 4 o'clock in the morning. . . We make about two, what we call twilight drags [for shrimp]. We pull until almost sun-up within the first drag and then the next drag and the sun's up about an hour high.

7 Influence, "pull." Cf **clout** n[1] **3**

1896 (1898) Ade *Artie* 105 **Chicago IL,** He knows I've got a drag in the precinct, and he says if I'll jump in and do what I can for him he'll see that I got a good job. *Ibid* 160, If you've got any drag with him I wish you'd go and get him in the house before he breaks his neck. **1918** in 1983 Truman *Dear Bess* 248 **MO,** I have made Masons out of both Colonel Klemm and Colonel Danford since we've been here, so I guess maybe that helps my *drag* [influence] somewhat, although it's not supposed to. **1925** (1958) Hemingway *In Our Time* 167 **nIL,** We had a big drag with the waiter because my old man drank whisky and it cost five francs, and that meant a good tip. **1928** *AmSp* 3.219 **KS** [College slang], *Drag. . .* Influence, pull. "She must have a drag with Agnes, to get away with that stuff." Agnes is the name of the Dean of Women. **1948** Manfred *Chokecherry* 234 **nwIA,** Yes, sometimes Esther complains I got too much drag with the boy. She thinks I favor him. Spoil him.

8 A share, percentage of earnings; a loan.

1907 London *Road* 202 **CA,** I had a sneaking idea that [the brakeman] got a "drag" out of the constable fees. **1927** *DN* 5.444 [Underworld jargon], *Drag. . .* A loan. **1980** Banks *First-Person America* 106 **VT** (as of c1939), Right now all I do is run a poker game and sell a little beer. No money in beer, but the game pays me pretty good. I get a drag on every pot, sure, and I win plenty of pots myself.

9 Among coal miners: scrip; a token or wage advance for purchasing goods from a company store. Cf **clacker 1**

1943 Korson *Coal Dust* 73, The same colloquial terms were used for scrip and store orders, such as "stickers," "clackers," "flickers," and "drag." **1973** *PADS* 59.34 [Bituminous coal mining vocab], *Drag . . = scrip.*

10 A dancing party; a dance step.

1923 in 1960 Wentworth–Flexner *Slang* 160, "Shoeshiner's Drag," title of song. **1927** *AmSp* 3.131 [College slang], A party is referred to as: . . "a drag." **1942** Berrey–Van den Bark *Amer. Slang* 366.3, *Dance . .* drag . . varsity drag, *a college dance.* **1952** Ulanov *Hist. Jazz* 115, The cotillion orchestra and polite quartet that accompanied high society drags. *Ibid* 220 **NYC** (as of 1929), The records they made ('Harlem Fuss' and 'Minor Drag') caused quite a stir. **1965–70** *DARE* (Qu. FF4, . . *Kinds of dancing parties*) Infs **CA**197, **CO**31, **NC**30, **NY**123, **TX**9, Drags; **MN**2, Drag—used when Inf was young; (Qu. FF5a, . . *Different steps and figures in dancing—in past years*) Inf **PA**247, Slow drag; **LA**8, Slow drag dance; **WA**30, Varsity drag; (Qu. FF5b, *More recent dance steps*) Infs **FL**51, **LA**8, Slow drag; **OR**4, Drag. [10 of 11 Infs old or mid-aged; 10 of 11 Infs hs or coll educ]

11 See quot.

1966–68 *DARE* (Qu. DD18, *A drink of liquor, or the amount of liquor taken in one swallow: "He took a good _______."*) Infs **NC**30, **VA**12, Drag; (Qu. DD30, . . *A place where liquor is [or was] sold and consumed illegally*) Inf **PA**165, Drag joint—now used even if the liquor is sold legally.

12 A cigarette. [By ext from *drag* an inhalation or puff of cigarette smoke]

1942 *Amer. Mercury* 55.223.96 **Harlem NYC** [Black], *Reefer*—marijuana cigaret, also a *drag.* **1956** Longstreet *Real Jazz* 128, Sit around with a glass in your hand and a drag smoking on your lip, and just listen. **1966–70** *DARE* (Qu. DD6b, *Nicknames for cigarettes*) Infs **FL**52, **MS**8, **SC**2, **VA**26, Drag.

13 A person held in low esteem, spec:

a A boring, dull, or stupid person. *esp freq among Blacks and among young and mid-aged speakers*

1942 Berrey–Van den Bark *Amer. Slang* 406.1, *Gloomy or irritable person; pessimist. . .* Drag, drip. **1949** *NYT Mag.* 6 Mar 33/1, A youth who used such a dated expression would be strictly a "drag." **1964** *AmSp* 39.189 [College slang], *Party pooper, wet blanket, drag, . .* 'one who puts a damper on a party.' **1965–70** *DARE* (Qu. HH16, *Uncomplimentary words with no definite meaning—just used when you want to show that you don't think much of a person: "Don't invite him. He's a _______."*) 44 Infs, **widespread,** Drag; (Qu. HH3, *A dull and stupid person*) 10 Infs, **scattered,** Drag; (Qu. HH12, *A person who is always finding fault about unimportant things*) Inf **VA**71, Drag; (Qu. HH13, *Expressions meaning that a person is not very alert or not aware of things: "He's certainly _______."*) Inf **WI**34, Drag; (Qu. HH19, . . *A tramp*) Inf **SC**65, Drag; (Qu. HH20a, *An idle, worthless person: "He's a _______."*) Infs **SC**68, **TX**35, **VA**2, **WI**67, Drag; (Qu. II7, *Somebody who doesn't seem to 'fit in' or to get along very well, you might say about him, "He's kind of a _______."*) Inf **MS**88, Drag. [46 of 60 Infs young or mid-aged, 19 Black] **1970** Major *Dict. Afro-Amer. Slang* 48, *Drag. . .* (1940's) a bore, a dull person.

b An unkempt woman; a woman of low morals. Cf **draggletail** *derog*

1968–70 *DARE* (Qu. W41, . . *Someone whose clothes never look right or who always dresses carelessly*) Inf **MO**23, She's a drag; (Qu. AA7b, . . *A woman who is very fond of men and is always trying to know more—if she's not respectable about it*) Inf **WA**3, A drag; (Qu. HH34, *General words . . for a woman, not necessarily uncomplimentary*) Inf **OH**42, Drag; (Qu. HH36, *A careless, slovenly woman: "She's just an old _______."*) Infs **RI**15, **WI**71, Drag; (Qu. HH37, *An immoral woman*) Inf **SC**65, Public drag.

c also *dragger:* A pest, tagalong, hanger-on.

1966–70 *DARE* (Qu. Y9, *Somebody who always follows along behind others: "His little brother is an awful ______."*) Infs **FL**2, **GA**89, **IA**17, **IL**57, **MO**16, **NC**35, **NY**34, **TX**5, 86, **WA**26, Drag; (Qu. II18, *Someone who joins himself on to you and your group without being asked and won't leave*) Infs **OK**55, **SC**65, **TX**19, Drag; **NY**9, Dragger—he's dragging on you.

14 A boring social event or situation. *esp freq among Black speakers and among young and mid-aged speakers*

1954 Armstrong *Satchmo* 126 **LA** [Black], Life can be such a drag one minute and a solid sender the next. **1955** *AmSp* 30.303 [College slang], *Drag*. . . Something dull. 'This class is a drag.' **1965–70** *DARE* (Qu. FF19, *Words used about a very dull or unenjoyable time: "The party was ______."*) 90 Infs, **widespread,** Drag; **TN**46, A slow drag. [Of all Infs responding to the question, 11% were young, 25% mid-aged, 76% hs or coll educ, 6% Black; of those giving these responses, 41% were young, 32% mid-aged, 91% hs or coll educ, 19% Black.]

15 A ritualized insult expressed in verse.

1988 [see **drag** v **B2**].

16 A period or "spell" of sickness; hence phrr *on the drag(s), on a drag* in a decline, unwell.

c1938 in 1970 Hyatt *Hoodoo* 2.1071 **seLA,** Well, if a person wanta see yo' *drag*—dat's whut yo' call "yo' put 'em on a *drag.*" **1966–70** *DARE* (Qu. Y21, *To move about slowly and without energy*) Inf **GA**72, [To be] on the drag; (Qu. BB39, *On a day when you don't feel just right, though not actually sick . . "I'll be all right tomorrow—I'm just feeling ______ today."*) Infs **AR**21, **VA**42, On the drag(s); (Qu. BB45, *The time that an illness lasts . . "He's been having a long ______ of stomach trouble."*) Inf **MO**36, Drag.

17 See quot. Cf **dragsaw**

1984 *MJLF* 10.149 **ME, cnWI,** *Drag.* A log of wood cut for firewood.

‡18 See quot.

1967 *DARE* (Qu. JJ12, *Little flourishes that some people put on their handwriting or signature to make it look fancy*) Inf **TX**26, Drags.

drag v

A Gram forms.

1 past: usu *dragged;* also freq *drug;* occas *drag;* rarely *drugged.*

1890 *DN* 1.61 **OH, IN,** *Drag* . . pret. *drug* (instead of *dragged*). *Ibid* 67 **KY,** *Drug* . . for *dragged.* "He drug him out of the house." [*DN:* Also reported by Professor Pearce from Louisiana as pret. and p.p.] **1894** *DN* 1.330 **NJ,** *Drugged:* pret. of *drag.* **1908** *DN* 3.307 **eAL, wGA,** *Drug, pret.* of *drag. Very common.* **1916** *DN* 4.274 **IL, KS, MA, NE, NC, PA, TN,** *Drug.* Frequent pret. of *drag.* **1916** Howells *Leatherwood God* 79 **OH,** [He] drug her up from the floor. **1932** Randolph *Ozark Mt. Folks* 60, He floundered round an' drug in half th' school 'fore he was done. **1940** Stuart *Trees of Heaven* 108 **KY,** I walked up the road the way he drug wood to the house. **1953** Atwood *Survey of Verb Forms* 9, The preterite is recorded in the context "(dragged) a log." *Dragged* /drægd/ predominates among cultured informants everywhere, but it predominates among the other types only in N.Y, n. Pa., e. Va., S.C., and Ga. Elsewhere in these types it is more or less narrowly limited by the competing form *drug* /drʌg/. *Drug* occurs in the middle Hudson Valley, throughout N.J., in all of Pa. except the northernmost portion, in W. Va., and in almost all parts of the S.A.S. [=South Atlantic States] to and including N.C. **1965–70** *DARE* (Qu. OO46a, *Talking about dragging something heavy: "We hitched the log on and ______ it out [of the woods]."*) 462 Infs, **widespread exc NEng,** Drug; 450 Infs, **widespread,** Dragged; **IA**36, **IL**27, **MO**8, 13, **SC**9, 26, **VA**26, 27, 49, 77, Drag; (Qu. W41, . . *Expressions . . for someone whose clothes never look right or who always dresses carelessly*) Inf **MS**37, Looks like something the cat drug in. **1966–68** *DARE* Tape **GA**30, Finally got my leg out of his [=an alligator's] mouth and drug him on out; **IL**23, She drug me down and had me join the church; **IN**18, [The dredge boat] drug up and down the river, pulling up snags and one thing or other; **OK**18, They drug a chain behind it; **VA**27, Drug the logs for miles. **1975** Allen *LAUM* 2.79 **ceIA** (as of c1950), *Drag. Drug* is the past tense for [one] inf[ormant].

2 past pple: usu *dragged;* also freq *drug;* occas *drag, drugged.*

1901 Harben *Westerfelt* 171 **nGA,** Will you git down, or do you want to be drug off like a saddle? **1913** Kephart *Highlanders* 37 **sAppalachians,** Sometimes no harrow was used at all, the plowed ground being "drug" with a big evergreen bough. **1915** *DN* 4.182 **swVA,** *Drug, pret.* and *part.* Dragged. **1933** Miller *Lamb in His Bosom* 112 **GA,** She could not die in peace for fear that her boys and grandboys would be drug off to war. **1944** *PADS* 2.8 **VA, NC, AL,** *Drug:* pret, and p. p. of *drag.* **1965–70** *DARE* (Qu. OO46b, *Talking about dragging something heavy: "Half a mile or so we must have ______ [it]!"*) 483 Infs, **widespread exc NEng,** Drug; 427 Infs, **widespread,** Dragged; **SC**26, **TN**36, **VA**27, 49, Drag; **SC**12, 43, Drugged; (Qu. V8b, *Of a person who has been given a paper ordering him into court you might say: "He was ______ into court."*) 37 Infs, **scattered,** Dragged; 24 Infs, **scattered,** Drug. **1966–70** *DARE* Tape **GA**1, It was drug in; **VA**52, I couldn't 've drug it out to the porch. **1975** Allen *LAUM* 2.79 **seSD** (as of c1950), *Drag. Drug* is . . the participle for [one] inf[ormant]. **1982** *Barrick Coll.* **csPA,** *Drug*—p.t. and p.p. of *drag.*

B Senses.

1 To cultivate or treat with a harrow; hence v phr *drag in* to bury (seed) with a harrow. Cf **drag n 1**

1828 Webster *Amer. Dict., Drag,* . . To break land by drawing a drag or harrow over it; to harrow; *a common use of this word in New England.* **1839** MA Ag. Surv. *Rept. for 1838* 31, After sowing, the ground was dragged (harrowed) every day for five or six days. **1899** (1912) Green *VA Folk-Speech* 153, *Drag.* . . To break the clods by hauling an iron-toothed drag over the ploughed ground. **1950** *WELS Suppl., Drag*—used generally here for harrow. "I ain't dragged the corn land yet." **1954** *Harder Coll.* **cwTN,** *Drag.* . . To crush lumps or clods with a drag. "You drag ground with a drag." **1966–69** *DARE* (Qu. L22, *When talking about a crop he intends to plant . . a farmer might say*) Inf **CA**57, Broadcast and drag them in—old-fashioned method for grain; **MI**23, Drag in [oats]—because they'd seed broadcast and drag in the seeds; **MI**107, Wheat would also be dragged. **1976** Garber *Mountain-ese* 25 **Appalachians,** We drug the field with a drag-harrow.

2 To tease, bait; hence vbl n *dragging* teasing, spec "playing the dozens" (see **dozen B1**). **chiefly S Midl**

1887 *Scribner's Mag.* 2.478 **AR,** Wal, I didn't aim ter drag ye, Jeff, but—law me! **1908** *DN* 3.307 **eAL, wGA,** *Dragging.* . . Impertinence, fooling. "I don't perpose to take no draggin'." **1915** *DN* 4.182 **swVA,** *Drag.* . . To tease; twit. **1916** *DN* 4.344 **NC,** *Drag.* . . To rally; joke. Perhaps from *rag.* "The boys have been dragging John about being tin-canned." **1950** *PADS* 14.27 **SC,** *Drag.* . . To rally, to tease. **1988** Lincoln *Avenue* 29 **wNC** (as of c1940) [Black], In the early days of his listening . . the doctor's sensibilities were particularly oppressed by a popular but unusually vicious bit of doggerel called a "drag." Dragging was a variation of the dozens, and it usually required a vulgarity so gross that when it was addressed to all the members of the group, those who claimed exemption from its allegations would hasten to give up their anonymity, yelling out, "Hold on! I caught that drag!" But in catching the drag, they inadvertently admitted being vulnerable to its claims.

3 To cause (someone) to suffer ill health or misfortune.

c1938 in 1970 Hyatt *Hoodoo* 1.808 **New Orleans LA,** They writes . . the name of you on that candle. . . And as this candle burns down, well, it's burning your name. They calls it *to drag you*—you'll suffer with headaches and all that stuff. *Ibid* 813 **swAL,** And jest burn dat can'le out until hit down to dat oil . . and dat will make . . whomsoever dat chew hate . . jes' git down in hard luck. . . See, dat's what chew call putting a person [Hyatt: off] dey feet . . *draggin' em, making 'em drag.*

4 also with *it* or *up:* To hurry; to move or leave quickly. [Cf *drag* to race] Cf **haul ass 1**

1944 Adams *Western Words* 53, *Drag it*—To leave. Usually used with reference to going under compulsion. **1966–69** *DARE* (Qu. A21, *When someone is in too much of a hurry you might say, "Now just slow down! Don't ______."*) Inf **MA**6, Drag; (Qu. Y18, *To leave in a hurry: "Before they find this out, we'd better ______!"*) Inf **NY**92, Drag; **CA**87, Drag out of here; (Qu. Y20, *To run fast: "You should have seen him ______!"*) Inf **TX**37, Drag up. [All Infs old or mid-aged; all Infs comm type 4 or 5]

5 often with *around:* To waste time, loaf; to go about aimlessly or without purpose, gad about. **chiefly Sth, S Midl**

1939 Writers' Program *Guide KY* 271, The farmer tells his wife, "Court day hain't no fit'n time f'r women folk to be draggin' roun' town nohow." **1965–70** *DARE* (Qu. KK31, *To go about aimlessly looking for distraction: "He doesn't have anything to do, so he's just ______ around."*) Infs **AL**22, **GA**77, **IL**14, **KY**21, **LA**2, **MO**30, **NJ**30, **SC**40, Dragging; (Qu. A9, . . *Wasting time by not working on the job*) Inf **GA**7, Dragging around; (Qu. A10, . . *Doing little unimportant things: Somebody asks, "What are you doing?" and you answer, "Nothing in particular—I'm just ______."*) Inf **FL**7, Dragging; (Qu. A11, *When somebody takes too long about coming to a decision, you might say, "I wish he'd quit ______."*) Infs **GA**7, **LA**15, Dragging (around); (Qu. Y22, *To* *move around in a way to make people take notice of you: "Look at him ———."*) Inf **DC**13, Dragging; (Qu. Y27, *To go about aimlessly, with nothing to do: "He's always ——— around the drugstore."*) Infs **GA**7, NC49, Dragging; (Qu. Y29a, *To 'go out' a great deal, not to stay at home much: "She's always ———."*) Inf **GA**72, Dragging around; (Qu. Y29b, . . *About a man who doesn't stay home much: "He's always ———."*) Inf **LA**15, Dragging around.

6 in var phrr: Used to warn a woman that her slip is showing. Cf **cotton 4**

1950 *WELS (Expressions or sly words of warning for a woman's slip showing)* 2 Infs, **eWI,** Your anchor is dragging. **1968** *DARE* FW Addit, You're dragging in the transom = your slip is showing. Heard on television program "Truth or Consequences." **1968–69** *DARE* (Qu. W24a, . . *Expressions . . to warn a woman slyly that her slip is showing*) Inf **CA**80, Dragging your transom; **KS**12, You're dragging; **MI**102, You're dragging anchor; [**MI**106, Your underwear is dragging].

drag a lot of water v phr Cf **drag water aft, draw water 1**

To be a person of consequence or importance.

1957 Beck *Folkl. ME* 167, An important person "drags a lot of water."

drag around See **drag** v **B5**

drag ass v phr Also *drag one's ass, drag (one's) freight*

=haul ass 1.

1958 McCulloch *Woods Words* 52 **Pacific NW,** *Drag freight*—To pull out, quit camp, hunt for greener pastures. **1962** Steinbeck *Travels* 100, I wouldn't want to get you in trouble with your boss. Think I ought to drag ass now? **1967** *DARE* (Qu. A20, *Joking ways of telling somebody to hurry: You might say, "———!"*) Inf **NY**23, Drag your ass; (Qu. Y18 . . *To leave in a hurry: "Before they find this out, we'd better ———!"*) Inf **OR**6, Drag our freight.

drag-ass adj Also *drag(gy)-assed*

1 Slow, late; lacking energy. Cf **dragged out**

c1960 *Wilson Coll.* **csKY,** *Draggy*. . . Slow, tardy, aimless. Also *draggy-assed.* **1968** *DARE* (Qu. X47, . . *Ways . . of saying, "I'm very tired, at the end of my strength"*) Inf **WI**33, Dog tired, drag-ass, dragged out.

2 Bedraggled.

1984 Wilder *You All Spoken Here* 204 **Sth,** Draggly; Bedraggled; drag-assed.

drag-daddy n [**drag** n **6**]

1968 *DARE* (Qu. P13, . . *Ways of fishing . . besides the ordinary hook and line . . [special kinds of bait, hooks, lures, nets, traps, spears, etc.]*) Inf **VA**32, Dragnet, seine or drag-daddy.

drag day n Cf **drag up 2, draw day**

Among loggers: see quot 1938.

1938 (1939) Holbrook *Holy Mackinaw* 260, *Drag day.* That day of the month when a man can draw his wages in advance of the day they are due. **1958** McCulloch *Woods Words* 52 **Pacific NW,** *Drag day*—A day on which a logger could draw money against his next pay day.

drag driver n Also *drag, drag man, ~ rider* [**drag** n **3**] **West** Cf **tail rider**

A cowhand who rides at the rear of a herd.

1888 *Century Illustr. Mag.* 35.862/1 **wND, wSD,** The rest are in the rear to act as "drag-drivers" and hurry up the phalanx of reluctant weaklings. **1923** Cook *50 Yrs.* 123 **TX,** He did his work well as a "drag driver." **1939** Rollins *Gone Haywire* 166 **MT** (as of 1886), Behind the drag rode still another puncher, the so-called drag man or tail rider. It was his duty, by much riding to and fro, by occasional blows with the hondo of his lariat, and by continuous blasphemy, to prevent lazy and malingering beasts from quitting the procession. **1966** *DARE* Tape **NM**14, The drag drivers are the ones in the back [of a herd of cattle]. And the drag driver is the most important man of the business because for any weak, poor or cripples, they always fell to the back. . . That was the drag of the herd. **1968** Adams *Western Words* 100, *Drag rider*—A cowboy whose duty it is to follow the drags. . . This is the most disagreeable job in cattle driving because the man has to ride in the dust kicked up by the entire herd and contend with the weak and lazy critters until his patience is sorely tried. **1981** *KS Qrly.* 13.2.66, *Drag* . . rider at the end of a column or herd of cattle being driven.

drag-'em-out See **drag out** n

drag fishing vbl n

A method of fishing; see quot.

1966–70 *DARE* (Qu. P15, . . *Fishing that's done from a slowly moving boat*) Infs **KY**93, **MS**16, **MO**18, 32, Drag fishing; **LA**8, Drag fishing—with an artificial bait; same as trolling; (Qu. P17, . . *Fish[ing] by lowering a line and sinker close to the bottom of the water*) Infs **NJ**13, **NY**185, **PA**10, Drag fishing.

drag freight See **drag ass** v phr

dragged out ppl adj phr Also *dragged, drag out, drug(ged) out* Cf **draggy 2**

Tired, exhausted; weak, sickly.

1831 in 1834 Smith *Life Jack Downing* 126 **ME,** The poor Huntonites seemed to be a most dragged out. **1866** in 1894 Lowell *Letters* 1.374 **eMA,** I needed some more pungent food in my rather dragged-out condition. **1924** Raine *Land of Saddle-Bags* 207 **Appalachians,** I'm pint-blank drug out, but I shan't keer nary grain if Sally Ann's baby lives. **1931** *AmSp* 7.93 **eKY,** *Drug-out,* exhausted. "She wuz plum drug-out 'gin she got there with that young 'un on her hip." **1933** Smiley *Gloss. New Paltz* **seNY,** At the end of the season the employees are all tired and *drug out.* **1938** Steinbeck *Long Valley* 136 **cwCA,** I'm kind of dragged out. **1950** *WELS (Feeling lifeless or without energy)* 2 Infs, **ceWI,** Dragged out. **1952** Brown *NC Folkl.* 1.535, *Drug-out*. . . Tired out. "I'm allus so drug-out when dinner is over, I can't hardly git out of my cheer." **1955** *AmSp* 30.303 [College slang], *Dragged*. . . Tired. **1965–70** *DARE* (Qu. KK30, *Feeling slowed up or without energy: "I certainly feel ———."*) 62 Infs, **scattered,** (All) dragged out; **MA**122, **RI**15, Dragged; **NJ**39, All drug out; **MI**75, Drugged out; **SC**26, Drag out [Of all Infs responding to the question, 37% were young or mid-aged; of those giving these responses, 60% were young or mid-aged.]; (Qu. X47, . . *Ways . . of saying, "I'm very tired, at the end of my strength"*) Infs **GA**23, **WI**33, (About) dragged out; (Qu. BB38, *When a person doesn't look healthy, or looks as if he hadn't been well for some time, you'd say, "He looks ———."*) Infs **CO**14, **MN**15, **PA**79, (All) dragged out; **NJ**39, All drug out; (Qu. BB39, *On a day when you don't feel just right, though not actually sick, you might say, "I'll be all right tomorrow —I'm just feeling ——— today."*) Inf **MN**33, Dragged out; **NJ**39, Drug out.

dragger See **drag** n **2, 13c**

dragging See **drag** v **B2**

dragging shoe n Cf **dragon B4**

Prob **=brogan 1.**

1970 *DARE* (Qu. W11, *Men's low, rough work shoes*) Inf **SC**70, Dragging shoes—some low, some come to the ankle.

draggle v

=drabble v[1].

1899 (1912) Green *VA Folk-Speech* 153, *Draggle*. . . To drag or draw along on damp ground or mud, or on wet grass; to drabble.

draggletail n

1 An unkempt person, esp a woman or child.

1899 (1912) Green *VA Folk-Speech* 153, *Draggletail*. . . An untidy woman. **1930** Shoemaker *1300 Words* 16 **cPA Mts** (as of c1900), *Draggle-tail*—A ragged, unkempt child.

2 also *drabbletail:* **=drag** n **13b.**

1899 (1912) Green *VA Folk-Speech* 153, *Drabbletail*. . . A slattern. **1942** Berrey–Van den Bark *Amer. Slang* 439.2, *Woman of easy morals*. . . *Slut*. . . Draggletail. **1942** Faulkner *Go Down* 360 **MS,** Even a Delta peckerwood would look after even a draggle-tail better than that.

draggletailed adj [**draggletail 1, 2**]

Untidy; slatternly.

1899 (1912) Green *VA Folk-Speech* 153, *Draggletailed*. . . Untidy; bedraggled. **1942** Faulkner *Go Down* 360 **MS,** You sound almost like a Northerner even, not like the draggle-tailed women of these Delta peckerwoods. Yet you meet a man on the street. . . And a month later you go off with him and live with him until he got a child on you.

draggly adj

Untidy, bedraggled.

1870 in 1941 Raymond *Bark Shanty Times* 26 **ceMI,** The man with the shawl was seen in town today and looking not very scrumpshous—sort of dragely [sic]. **1899** (1912) Green *VA Folk-Speech* 153, *Draggly*. . . Bedraggled. "She came through the tall grass with her coats all draggly." **1984** Wilder *You All Spoken Here* 204 **Sth,** *Draggly:* Bedraggled; drag-assed; drearisome.

draggy adj

1 Slow, late; aimless, shiftless.

1927 *DN* 5.474 **Ozarks,** *Draggy*. . . Slow, late. "Th' job's all right, but the pay's a leetle draggy a-gittin' hyar, mostly." **1952** Dorson *Bloodstoppers* 34 **nMI,** The LeVakes were all a shiftless, draggy lot. **c1960** *Wilson Coll.* **csKY,** *Draggy*. . . Slow, tardy, aimless. **1968–70** *DARE* (Qu. A18, . . *A very slow person: "What's keeping him? He certainly is ______!"*) Infs **GA**17, **NC**53, 67, **OH**44, **TX**96, **VA**13, Draggy. **1972** Jones–Hawes *Step it Down* 5 **eGA** [Black], You sing some of those hymns, old draggy songs, you likely to go off to sleep with the baby.

2 Lacking energy, weak, unwell. **chiefly Midl, S Atl** See Map Cf **dragged out**

1954 *Harder Coll.* **cwTN,** *Draggy:* Poorly, tired. "I'm sort o' draggy today. Had the old rheumatiz all night." **1965–70** *DARE* (Qu. KK30, *Feeling slowed up or without energy: "I certainly feel ______."*) 46 Infs, **scattered, but esp Midl, S Atl,** Draggy; (Qu. BB39, *On a day when you don't feel just right, though not actually sick, you might say, "I'll be all right tomorrow—I'm just feeling ______ today."*) 24 Infs, **esp Midl,** Draggy; **OK**50, Kind of draggy and low; (Qu. X48b, . . *If a person is not so young any more, you might say, "He's ______."*) Inf **GA**44, Draggy; (Qu. Y21, *To move about slowly and without energy*) Inf **MO**25, Draggy; (Qu. BB5, *A general feeling of discomfort or illness that isn't any one place in particular*) Inf **VA**13, Feel draggy; (Qu. BB38, *When a person doesn't look healthy, or looks as if he hadn't been well for some time, you'd say, "He looks ______."*) Inf **IL**130, Draggy.

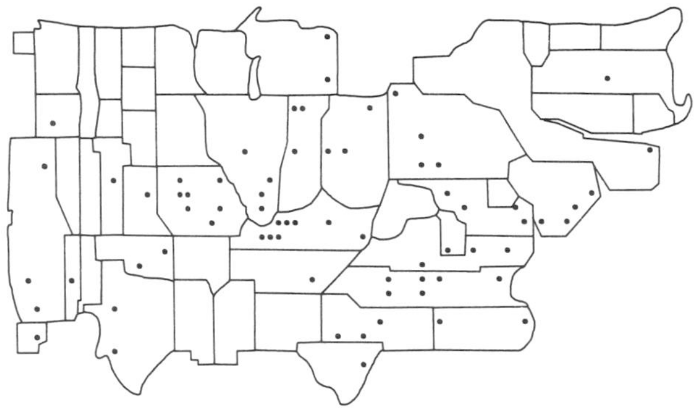

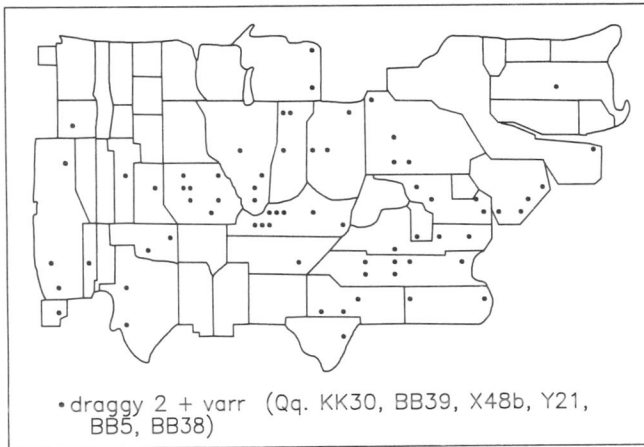

•draggy 2 + varr (Qq. KK30, BB39, X48b, Y21, BB5, BB38)

3 Boring, dull; unpleasant. Cf **drag n 14**

1967–68 *DARE* (Qu. FF19, . . *A very dull or unenjoyable time: "The party was ______."*) Infs **AR**55, **IL**4, **MD**38, **WA**22, Draggy.

draggy-assed See **drag-ass adj**

drag harrow n Also *harrow drag* **chiefly Sth, S Midl** See Map =**drag n 1.**

1788 (1925) Washington *Diaries* 3.325 **neVA,** The cross harrowing . . being in part done (for dispatch) with the large or drag harrow, it is not improbable but that the grass-seeds may be buried too deep. **1939** *LANE* Map 167, 1 inf, **cwMA,** The agricultural implement with which the ground is smoothed or the soil pulverized. . . [dræg hɛro]. **1948** Davis *Word Atlas Gt. Lakes* 157 **sOH,** Drag-harrow. **1965–70** *DARE* (Qu. L20, *The implement used in a field after it's been plowed to break up the lumps*) 31 Infs, **chiefly Sth, S Midl,** Drag harrow; **MO**5, Harrow drag.

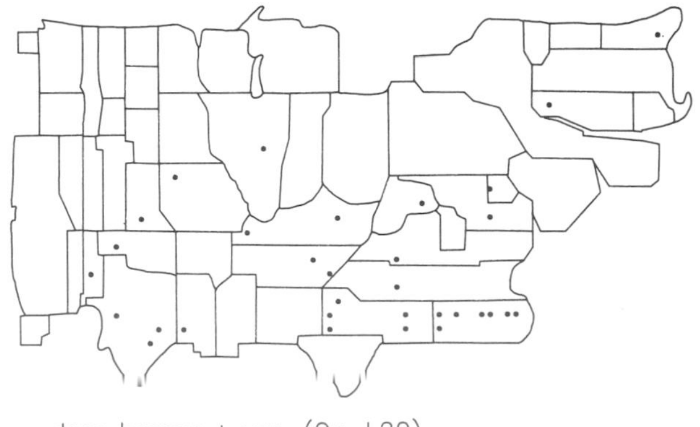

•drag harrow + var (Qu. L20)

drag her v phr Cf **drag ass** v phr

Among loggers: see quots.

1930 Williams *Logger-Talk* 22 **Pacific NW,** *Drag her:* Draw your time and leave camp. **1958** McCulloch *Woods Words* 52 **Pacific NW,** *Drag 'er*—To quit the job. **1968** Adams *Western Words* 99, *Drag her*—A logger's expression meaning *to quit a job and go on one's way.* **1969** Sorden *Lumberjack Lingo* 36 **NEng, Gt Lakes,** *Drag 'er*—To quit.

drag in See **drag v B1**

drag it See **drag v B4**

dragline n

1 See quot.

1969 *DARE* (Qu. L49, *Leathers or ropes, fastened to the collar, that a horse or mule pulls by*) Inf **MO**20, Draglines.

2 In marble play: =**lag line.**

1968 *DARE* (Qu. EE8, *The line toward which the players roll their marbles before beginning a game, to determine the order of shooting*) Inf **WV**1, Dragline.

drag man See **drag driver**

drago n

=**sangre de draco.**

1886 Havard *Flora W. & S. TX for 1885* 513, *Mozinna spathulata*. . . Drago. . . The stems, . . as well as the roots, . . are employed . . as a remedy to cleanse the teeth and harden the gums. [**1942** Santamaría *Dicc. Americanismos* 582, *Drago*. . . En el norte de Méjico y en Tejas, planta euforbiácea *(Jatropha spatulata)*.] **1960** Vines *Trees SW* 626, *Jatropha dioica* . . is known under many vernacular names . . including . . Drago. **1967** *DARE* Tape **TX**29, There's another plant that makes an excellent toothbrush. . . Drago [drægo] it's called.

drag oil n

A nonexistent item used as the basis of a practical joke.

1970 *DARE* (Qu. HH14, *Ways of teasing a beginner or inexperienced person—for example, by sending him for a 'left-handed monkey wrench': "Go get me ______."*) Inf **KY**78, Drag oil.

dragon n Also *dragoon*

A Form.

c1938 in 1970 Hyatt *Hoodoo* 2.1051 **csNC,** Yo' heah 'em talk of dis heah dragoon's [Hyatt: dragon's] blood. Git dat *dragoon's powder* an' put it in wit it. **1983** [see **B1** below].

B Senses.

1 freq *old dragon:* Satan, the devil. [*OED* 1340–1707] **esp Sth, S Midl**

1858 Hammett *Piney Woods Tavern* 279 **ceTX,** Heah's Santanner [=Santayana] right across the San Jacinto, a raisin' the old dragon, and whose [=who's] to help? **1966–70** *DARE* (Qu. CC8, *Other names for the devil*) Infs **AR**21, **GA**77, **TN**53, **VA**46, (Old) dragon. **1983** *MJLF* 9.38 **ceKY,** *Dragoon* . . the devil.

2 A larva of the **dobsonfly.**

1901 Howard *Insect Book* 212, The names in use in Rhode Island alone for this insect . . are: Dobsons, . . dragon and hell-diver. **1905** Kellogg *Amer. Insects* 226, Names . . applied to the larva: . . dragon.

3 A large lobster; see quot.

1979 McPhee *Giving Good Weight* 216, He looks at a crate of lobsters. They are dragons—up into their salad years—and three of them fill the crate, their heads seeming to rest on claws the size of pillows. "People think they're dragons because they look like dragons, but they're called that because they are caught in dragnets."

4 See quot. [Perh erron for *draggin'* < **dragging shoe**]

1950 *PADS* 14.27 **SC,** *Dragons*. . . Old shoes. Possibly from such shoes being worn through at the toe, and thus gaping like a *dragon.*

dragon arum n **chiefly NEast**

A **jack-in-the-pulpit,** usu **green dragon.**

1837 Darlington *Flora Cestrica* 529, *Dragon Arum*. . . *Berries* in an ovoid cluster round the base of the spadix, smooth, reddish-orange when mature. **1848** in 1850 Cooper *Rural Hours* 90 **cNY,** We landed and gathered the singular flower of the dragon arum, or Indian turnip, as the country folk call it. **1857** Gray *Manual of Botany* 426, *Arisaema*. . . Dragon-Arum. **1891** Jesup *Plants Hanover NH* 47, A[risaema] Dracontium. . . (Dragon Arum.) **1910** Graves *Flowering Plants* 109 **CT,** *Arisaema*. . . Dragon Arum. Indian Turnip. **1951** Voss-Eifert *IL Wild Flowers* 71, Dragon arum grows from a solid corm which is set not very deeply in the ground.

dragon-bushes n

=butter-and-eggs 1.

1959 Carleton *Index Herb. Plants* 39, *Dragon-bushes:* Linaria vulgaris.

dragonclaw n

=pinedrops. *obs*

1830 Rafinesque *Med. Flora* 2.68, *Pterospora andromedea*. . . Scaly Dragonclaw. . . Root . . full of irregular curved fleshy tubercules, resembling the claws of animals.

drag one's ass See **drag ass v phr**

drag one's foot v phr

See quot 1976.

1942 Faulkner *Go Down* 11 **MS,** She had never looked at him and she wasn't talking to him and he knew it, although he was prepared and balanced to drag his foot when Uncle Buck did. "Welcome to Warwick." He and Uncle Buck dragged their foot. **1962** Faulkner *Reivers* 100 **MS,** "Lucius," Boon said. "Make your manners to Miss Reba," he told me. I did so, the way I always did: that I reckon Grandfather's mother taught him and Grandmother taught Father and Mother taught us: what Ned called "drug my foot." **1976** Brown *Gloss. Faulkner* 74, *Drag one's foot* . . to make a deep, formal bow. One begins standing upright, with the feet equally advanced; then, as one bows at the waist, the right foot is dragged back about 18″ or so.

drag one's freight See **drag ass v phr**

drag one's navel in the sand v phr

1929 *AmSp* 5.76 **NE,** A fast running horse or man is "draggin' 'is navel in the sand."

dragonfly n

Std: an insect of the order Odonata. For other names see **airplane 1, arrow hawk, bee-butcher, blue dragon, bluetail fly 2, bottle fly 2, chookabama, damsel fly, darner, darning needle 1, demoiselle 3, devil fly 2, devil's darning needle 1, devil's hornet, devil's horse 5, dining needle, doctor 5, dornel feather, ear cutter, ear needle, ear sewer 1, eye stitcher, fish feeder, flying adder, four-eyes, gallinipper 1d, gauze hawk, glassmaker, globe-skimmer, gnatcatcher 2, green jacket, hawk n 2, helicopter 1, horse doctor, horsefly 2, horse stinger, jarfly, kingfisher fly, long-ass butterfly, measuring stick, mosquito, mosquito catcher, mosquito fly, mosquito hawk, mule killer, needle, old ladies' darning needle, perch bug, pinao, sewer, sewin' bug, sewing needle, shake-fly, skeeter, skeeter hawk, skimmer, snake charmer, snake doctor, snake eater, snake feeder, snake fly, snake guarder, snake heeder, snake servant, snake waiter, snyder, Spanish needle, spindle, stinger, stitcher, tombo, water beater, water dipper, water fly, water mosquito, water skipper, witch doctor**

dragonhead n

1 also *dragon's head:* A plant of the genus *Dracocephalum.* Also called **false dragonhead 2**

1784 in 1785 Amer. Acad. Arts & Sci. *Memoirs* 1.463 **MA,** *Dracocephalum*. . . *Dragon's Head*. . . By stone walls in *Dedham.* July. **1822** Eaton *Botany* 269, *Dracocephalum* . . *virginianum* . . dragon-head. **1876** Hobbs *Bot. Hdbk.* 32, Dragon head, Dracocephalum Virginianum. **1900** Lyons *Plant Names* 140, Dragon-head. **1931** Clute *Common Plants* 86, There are two dragon-heads (*Dracocephalum parviflorum* and *Prunella vulgaris*). **1976** Bailey-Bailey *Hortus Third* 398, *Dracocephalum L.* Dragonhead.

2 =false dragonhead 1.

1837 Darlington *Flora Cestrica* 603, *P[hysostegia] virginiana,* Benth. . . *Virginian Physostegia. Vulgo*—Dragon-head. **1949** Leopold *Sand Co. Almanac* 52 **cWI,** The Eleocharis sod, greener than ever, is now spangled with blue mimulus, pink dragon-head, and the milk-white blooms of Sagittaria. **1961** Wills-Irwin *Flowers TX* 194, *P[hysostegia] virginiana* . . , variously known as . . Dragon-head, . . is a perennial.

3 A **self-heal** (here: *Prunella vulgaris*).

1894 *Jrl. Amer. Folkl.* 7.96, *Brunella* [sic] *vulgaris*. . . Dragon-head, Deer Lodge, Mont. **1931** [see **1** above]. **1971** Krochmal *Appalachia Med. Plants* 208, *Prunella vulgaris*. . . *Common Names:* . . dragonhead.

4 =green dragon.

1946 Reeves-Bain *Flora TX* 33, *A[risaema] dracontium*. . . Dragon Head. . . Spadix long-exserted, with a slender whip-like tip.

dragonroot n

1 =jack-in-the-pulpit.

1784 in 1785 Amer. Acad. Arts & Sci. *Memoirs* 1.487 **MA,** *Arum*. . . Cuckowpint. Dragon-root. Wake-Robin. **1828** Rafinesque *Med. Flora* 66, *Arum triphyllum*. . . *Vulgar Names* . . Dragon Root. [*Ibid* 67, The vulgar names are common to all the North American species, which have similar roots.] **1891** *Jrl. Amer. Folkl.* 4.140, Arisaema triphyllum was always *Dragon Root,* or *Lady in a Chaise.* **1910** Graves *Flowering Plants* 110 **CT,** *Arisaema Dracontium*. . . Green Dragon. Dragon Root. **1933** Small *Manual SE Flora* 247, *Dragon-root*. . . Rich woods and bottoms. **1968** *DARE* (Qu. S26b, *Wildflowers that grow in water or wet places*) Inf **PA**99, Dragonroot. **1971** Krochmal *Appalachia Med. Plants* 62, *Arisaema triphyllum*. . . *Common Names:* . . dragon root. **1974** (1977) Coon *Useful Plants* 65, Dragon root. Similar to Jack-in-the-pulpit, but without the pulpit.

2 =pinedrops. *obs*

1830 Rafinesque *Med. Flora* 2.68, *Pterospora andromedea*. . . *Names*. . . *Vulgar.* Dragon root.

dragon's-claw n Also *dragon's-claws* [See quot 1911]

A **coralroot 1,** usu *Corallorhiza odontorhiza.*

1833 Eaton *Botany* 106, *Corallorhiza* . . *odontorhiza*. . . Dragon's claw. **1847** Wood *Class-Book* 531, *C. odontorhiza*. . . Dragon's-claw. Coral-root. **1876** Hobbs *Bot. Hdbk.* 32, Dragons' claw, Crawley root, Corallorhiza odontorhiza. **1911** *Century Dict. Suppl., Dragon's-claw*. . . The coralroot, *Corallorhiza odontorhiza* or *C. multiflora:* so called from the claw-like form of the root. **1950** Correll *Native Orchids* 330, *Corallorhiza odontorhiza*. . . Numerous small knobs projecting from the coralloid rhizome. . . Dragon's-claw. **1971** Krochmal *Appalachia Med. Plants* 104, *Coralorhiza*. . . *Common Names:* . . dragon's claws.

dragon's eye n

1 An introduced tree *(Euphorbia longan)* or its edible fruit. **HI**

1889 *Century Dict.* 1757, *Dragon's-eye*. . . The fruit of *Archontobroma Longana* of China, much resembling the litchi, but smaller. Also *longan.* **1929** Neal *Honolulu Gardens* 191, A close relative of the litchi is the longan. . . Its fruits, called "dragon's eyes," . . are served in Chinese restaurants. **1965** Neal *Gardens HI* 534, *Dragons eye. Euphorbia longan*. . . The longan, a tree about 30 feet high, from China, is cultivated for its edible fruit. . . Small, yellowish-white, brownish-woolly flowers . . are borne at branch tips and leaf bases.

2 An unidentified flower.

1972 *DARE* File **HI,** *Dragon's eye,* a red flower similar to a calla lily.

3 In marble play: see quot.

1962 *PADS* 37.1 **cKS,** *Dragon's eye.* A Chinese spinner, according to some informants; according to others, a cat's eye in which the design has opened out more than in a Chinese spinner but still not completely.

dragon's head See **dragonhead 1**

dragon's-mouth n

1 =swamp pink.

1892 *Jrl. Amer. Folkl.* 5.103 **MA,** *Arethusa Bulbosa,* dragon's mouth. **1900** Lyons *Plant Names* 44, *A[rethusa] bulbosa* . . Dragon's-mouth. **1931** Clute *Common Plants* 86, There are . . two dragon's mouths (*Arethusa bulbosa* and *Antirrhinum majus*).

2 A snapdragon (here: *Antirrhinum majus*).

1900 Lyons *Plant Names* 39, *A[ntirrhinum] majus*. . . Dragon's-mouth. **1931** [see **1** above].

3 =butter-and-eggs 1.

1967-69 *DARE* (Qu. S11) Infs **CA**157, **MI**69, Dragon's-mouth—wild snapdragon.

dragon spider n

An unidentified spider.

1970 *DARE* (Qu. R28 . . *Kinds of spiders* . . *around here*) Inf **FL**48, Dragon spider.

dragon's tail n
=**green dragon.**
1931 Clute *Common Plants* 86, A dragon's tail *(Arisaema dracontium).* **1959** Carleton *Index Herb. Plants* 39, *Dragon's tail:* Arisaema dracontium.

dragon's teeth n
=**coral tree.**
1933 Small *Manual SE Flora* 715, *Erythrina*. . . Coral-beans. . . Dragon's-teeth. **1960** Vines *Trees SW* 561, *Erythrina crista-galli*. . . Some of the vernacular names in use are . . Crybaby-tree, Dragon's Teeth [etc].

dragon's-tongue n
=**spotted wintergreen.**
1900 Lyons *Plant Names* 96, *C[himaphila] maculata*. . . Dragon's-tongue. **1931** Clute *Common Plants* 86, There are two dragon-heads . . and a dragon's tongue *(Chimaphila maculata).* **1971** Krochmal *Appalachia Med. Plants* 88, *Chimaphila maculata*. . . *Common Names:* Spotted wintergreen, dragon's tongue.

drag, on the (or a) See **drag** n **16**

dragon tooth n
A **dogtooth violet.**
1968 *DARE* (Qu. S11) Inf **NJ**39, Dragon tooth—dogtooth violet.

dragon turnip n [See quot 1930]
=**jack-in-the-pulpit,** usu *Arisaema triphyllum.*
1828 Rafinesque *Med. Flora* 1.66, *Arum triphyllum*. . . *Vulgar Names* . . Dragon Turnip. [*Ibid* 1.67, The vulgar names are common to all the North American species, which have similar roots.] **c1873** in 1976 Miller *Shaker Herbs* 188, *Indian Turnip*. . . Dragon Turnip. **1930** Sievers *Amer. Med. Plants* 37, Dragon-turnip. . . The underground portion . . is shaped like a turnip. **1971** Krochmal *Appalachia Med. Plants* 62, *Arisaema triphyllum*. . . *Common Names:* . . dragon turnip.

dragoon See **dragon**

drag out n [Abbr for *knock-down, drag-out*] Also *drag-'em-out*
A fight, brawl; one who brawls.
1859 (1968) Bartlett *Americanisms* 130 **Sth,** "He's a rael stormer, ring clipper, snow belcher, and drag out."—*Southern Sketches.* **1870** *Nation* 10.411/2 **NYC,** We have been forcibly struck with the number of encounters, . . knock-downs, drag-outs . . in which the Representative of the Fifth Massachusetts District has been engaged. **1968–69** *DARE* (Qu. Y13, *A fist fight with several people in it*) Infs **IN**9, 79, Drag out; **IL**39, Drag-'em-out.

drag out adj phr See **dragged out**

drag pan See **drag scoop**

drag plow n Cf **drag** n **1**
1968–69 *DARE* (Qu. L18, *Kinds of plows*) Infs **CT**2, **PA**191, Drag plow.

drag rake n
1965 *DARE* (Qu. L16, *Machines used around here in handling hay*) Inf **FL**22, Drag rake—eight point, pulled with a tractor.

drag rider See **drag driver**

drag road n
Esp among loggers: see quots.
1932 *DN* 6.222 **West,** In the woods they [=settlers] called a wood road a *tote-road,* a *hay-road,* or a *dragroad,* according to its use. **1969** Sorden *Lumberjack Lingo* 36 **NEng, Gt Lakes,** *Drag road*—A long skid road from woods to skidway. Same as dray road, runway, gutter road, travois road.

dragsaw n **chiefly Nth, N Midl**
Esp in logging: a powered crosscut saw set to cut on the draw stroke.
1868 IA State Ag. Soc. *Rept. for 1867* 220, Drag-saw, for cutting logs into fire-wood. **1872** (1876) Knight *Amer. Mech. Dict.* 1.737, *Drag-saw.* A cross-cut sawing-machine in which the effective stroke is on the pull motion, not the thrust. **1909** *DN* 3.411 **nME,** *Drag saw*. . . A saw similar to a cross-cut saw fastened at one end and run by machinery. It is used to cut large wood. **1920** *DN* 5.81 **nwWA,** [Advt:] To sell or will trade my drag saw. **1945** (1946) Macdonald *Egg & I* 60 **WA,** The dragsaw barked and smoked. **1958** McCulloch *Woods Words* 52 **Pacific NW,** *Drag saw*—A crosscut saw powered by a small and often cranky gas engine; the ancestor of the modern power saw. One of the early well known makes was the Vaughn. Steam and air were used to power some of the early drag saws, but were not as widely used as the gas type. **1967** *AmSp* 42.294 **IN** [Limestone industry terms], *Dragsaw.* The crosscut reciprocating saw, a large horizontal saw that trims slabs before they go to gang-saws or before planing. **1969** Sorden *Lumberjack Lingo* 36 **NEng, Gt Lakes,** *Drag saw*—Any crosscut saw, portable or stationary, powered by a small gasoline engine. Some early models were powered by steam in Wisconsin. **1984** *MJLF* 10.149 **ME, cnWI,** *Drag saw.* A crosscut saw, often powered by a gas engine, used to saw large logs into firewood.

dragsaw man n [**drag saw**]
Among loggers: see quot.
1958 McCulloch *Woods Words* 52 **Pacific NW,** *Drag saw man*—A wood buck, the man who kept the camp in firewood.

drag scoop n Also *drag pan*
See quot 1969.
1969 *DARE* FW Addit **MA**40, Drag scoop—more or less the same shape as a shovel only larger. On the front was an open lip. On the sides were two handles. When you lifted up on the handles it nosed the lip into the ground. It was pulled by a horse and was the way cellars for houses were dug. **1970** *DARE* (Qu. L41, *A device for moving dirt*) Inf **VA**43, Drag pan.

drag sled n
1 =**drag** n **2.**
1949 [see **drag** n 2]. **1966–70** *DARE* (Qu. L57, *A low wooden platform used for bringing stones or heavy things out of the fields*) Infs **MD**31, **NJ**50, **PA**43, 92, 153, 163, 211, Drag sled. [6 of 7 Infs gs educ or less; 6 Infs old, 1 mid-aged]
2 also *drag sleigh:* A snow sled with runners used to haul loads.
1966–70 *DARE* (Qu. N40a, . . *Sleighs* . . *for hauling loads*) Inf **IL**119, Drag sled; **NY**117, Drag sleigh; (Qu. N40c, . . *Sleighs for carrying other things*) Inf **IL**83, Drag sleigh; **MA**6, Drag sled—for hauling lumber. **1967** *DARE* Tape **MA**5C, [FW:] When a tree has been chopped down, and you've taken the limbs off. . . how do you get it into the mill to get it sawed? [Inf:] They have what they call drag sleds, that's a long sled, 'bout eight foot long with wooden shoes on it, generally four by four wooden shoes, and just two beams, and drawn by horses, but now they use tractors. . . If they [=logs] were big enough so y'couldn't lift 'em, you roll 'em onto the drag. **1969** Sorden *Lumberjack Lingo* 36 **NEng, Gt Lakes,** *Drag sled*—A two-runner sled used to haul logs out of the woods. Same as dray, bob, crotch, drag sled, lizard, scoot, skidding sled, sloop, yarding sled.

drags, on the See **drag** n **16**

drag the rag v phr
=**drag** v **B4.**
1969 *DARE* (Qu. A20, *Joking ways of telling somebody to hurry: You might say, "______!"*) Inf **MA**46, Drag the rag.

drag up v phr
1 To raise or bring up (a child), usu with little attention to manners or civility. [*EDD drag up* (at *drag* v. II. 5) "to bring up children badly"] Cf **jerk up**
1966–70 *DARE* (Qu. Z17, *To take care of or bring up a child: "All her children were ______ [on the farm]."*) Inf **NY**206, Dragged up; **GA**57, Born and drug up; **PA**244, Drug up; (Qu. II21, *When somebody behaves unpleasantly or without manners: "The way he behaves, you'd think he was ______."*) Infs **NY**46, 64, **PA**245, Dragged up; **MN**2, Dragged up by your feet; **NJ**19, Dragged up in a stable; **NJ**18, **NY**83, **SC**19, Drug up; **AZ**15, Drug up in a barn. [All Infs old or mid-aged]
2 See quots. Cf **drag day**
1941 Writers' Program *Guide OK* 122, In general use in the oil-field world are the following expressions: . . Drag-up—To draw one's pay and quit. **1973** *DARE* File **nwCO,** *Drag up.* To draw pay in full, as in quitting, in oilfields.
3 See **drag** v **B4.**

drag water aft v phr Cf **drag a lot of water**
To have heavy hips or large buttocks.
1945 Colcord *Sea Language* 68 **ME, Cape Cod, Long Island,** *Drag water aft.* Same as broad in the *beam,* q.v. [*Ibid* 31, In coastal dialect, broad in the beam is a facetious description of a person with heavy hips or buttocks.]

drail n [From obs *drail* to drag or trail along] **NEng** *somewhat old-fash*

A fishhook with a weighted shank used for trolling; a line with such a hook.

1634 Wood *New Engl. Prospect* 35, These Macrills are taken with drailes which is a long small line, with a lead and hooke at the end of it. **1839** MA Zool. & Bot. Surv. *Fishes Reptiles* 58, [The bluefish] is caught from shore by throwing a drail—a hook fixed into a piece of bone or ivory, and sometimes pewter, something in the form of a fish. **1879** U.S. Natl. Museum *Bulletin* 14.101, Hooks... Jigs and drails... Bluefish-drail. Peculiar to Hyannis, Mass... When used, covered with an eel-skin. **1894** *Youth's Companion* 22 Nov 562/4 **MA,** Armed with weighted hooks called 'drails.' **1935** Lincoln *Cape Cod Yesterdays* 188, Why it is a "drail", we know not. It is, and on Cape Cod it has always been... It .. is made of some heavy metal, is bright and shiny and has the hook rigidly set in its after end... Pulled .. through the water, it looks like a rapidly swimming sand eel or "shiner" and the bluefish darts to snap at it.

drail v, hence vbl n *drailing* **[drail n] NEng** *somewhat old-fash*

To fish with a **drail** n.

1636 (1863) MA Hist. Soc. *Coll.* 4th ser 6.570 **ME,** Richard Fox-will .. spake with a boate of ours (draylinge for mackrell). **1873** U.S. Bur. Fisheries *Rept. for 1871–72* 1.248 **MA,** The usual method of taking them with the line is by drailing or trolling. **1879** U.S. Natl. Museum *Bulletin* 14.96, Trolling tackle: .. Drailing-tackle... Surf-tackle for throwing and hauling: .. Tide-drailing tackle. **1884** Goode *Fisheries U.S.* 1.300, Capt. James Turner, of Isle au Haut, Maine, .. assures us that as late as 1815 the fishermen drailed for mackerel. **1934** *Hanley Disks* **Martha's Vineyard MA,** They used to call it drailing for bluefish.

drain v, n[1] Usu |dren|; also **chiefly Sth, S Midl, occas NEng** |drin| Pronc-spp *drean, dreen*

A Forms.

1 Pronc varr. For addit quots see **B** and **C** below

1719 [see **C2** below]. **1795** Dearborn *Columbian Grammar* 135, *List of Improprieties...* Dreen for Drain. **1853** Simms *Sword & Distaff* 531 **SC,** To pay for it in money, won't drean your pocket. **1888** *Jrl. Amer. Folkl.* 1.78 **ME,** Dreen for drain was formerly common in Maine and Massachusetts. **1890** *DN* 1.72 **LA,** *Dreen:* drain *(n., v.)* **1897** *KS Univ. Qrly.* (ser B) 6.52 **KS,** *Drean,* v. and s.: drain. **1903** *DN* 2.296 **Cape Cod MA** (as of a1857), *Drain...* Pronounced *drean.* **1908** *DN* 3.307 **eAL, wGA,** *Dreen.* **1909** *DN* 3.411 **nME,** *Drain...* Pronounced *dreen.* **1910** *DN* 3.440 **wNY,** *Dreen.* **1911** *DN* 3.543 **NE,** *Dreen...* Frequent pronunciation of *drain.* **1912** *DN* 3.575 **wIN,** *Dreen.* **1926** *DN* 5.386 **ME,** *Drain* (dreen). **1928** Peterkin *Scarlet Sister Mary* 293 **SC** [Gullah], I could look at you same as a stranger an' not a water wouldn' drean out my eye. **1930** *AmSp* 6.98 **cNY,** We'll let the cups dreen. **1944** *PADS* 2.55 **MO,** Did you dreen the pipes? **1954** *PADS* 21.17 **SC,** The dialectal pronunciation of *drain* as *dreen* is widespread and common throughout the northwestern half of South Carolina. **1961** Kurath–McDavid *Pronc. Engl.* 150, *Drain* with the vowel /i/ of *bean* is nearly universal in the folk speech of the South and the South Midland, rather common in the New England settlement area (except for Massachusetts and parts of New York State), but decidedly infrequent in Pennsylvania (except for the northern counties) and no longer current in the cities of the North and North Midland. **1966–68** *DARE* (Qu. C1) Infs **DE4, GA65,** Dreen; (Qu. F6) Inf **SC9,** Dreen; (Qu. G15) Inf **MS72,** Dreen; (Qu. H72) Inf **AR53,** Dreen; (Qu. N24) Inf **MD20,** Side [drin]; (Qu. BB36) Infs **SC24,** 27, Dreening. **1968** *DARE* Tape **IN41,** With new ways of dreening, clearing, there's been a lot of ground cleared. **1975** Gould *ME Lingo* 80, The kitchen sink *dreens* into the cesspool.

2 Gram forms.

Past and past pple: usu *drained;* pronc-spp *dreen(ed), drint.*

1927 Adams *Congaree* 84 **cSC** [Black], He got that glass and dreen it. **1962** *Mt. Life* 38.1.16 **sAppalachians,** Verbs which retain either the strong preterites of Middle English or variant preterites of the English dialects... *Present*—dreen[,] *Past*—dreened[,] drint[,] *Past Participle*—dreened[,] drint. **1975** Gould *ME Lingo* 80, Coffee is *dreened* to the last drop.

B As verb.

1 See **C5** below.

2 with *out:* See quot.

1884 *Anglia* 7.263 [Black], To dreen outer or outen = to escape, get away.

‡3 To rinse.

1940–41 Cassidy *WI Atlas* **nwWI,** Drain the dishes. [FW questioned inf to verify meaning.] **1966–69** *DARE* (Qu. G15, *When you pour hot water on the dishes to get the soap off, you ______ them.*) Inf **CA115,** Drain.

C As noun.

1 A ditch for draining off water. **scattered, but esp Mid and C Atl** See Map Cf **drain ditch**

1640 in 1897 CT Hist. Soc. *Coll.* 6.28, Their shalbee A drey[ne] .. made in the Litle meaddow in thee low valley. **1693** *Boston Rec.* 215 *(DAE),* Such as were annoyance .. should remove viz. Stillers to such places where there feces may be carried into some Common Shoar or Drein. **1766** in 1940 *AmSp* 15.173 **VA,** Praying that an Act of Assembly may pass to empower him to cut a Drain or Ditch from his Land .. to the Head of Malchapongo Creek. **1795** in 1916 *New Engl. Hist. & Geneal. Reg.* 70.17 **MA,** I dug a dreen between my house & barn. **1899** (1912) Green *VA Folk-Speech* 154, *Drean...* A small ditch. **c1960** *Wilson Coll.* **csKY,** *Drain* /drin/: Roadside ditch. Common pron[unciation]. **1965–70** *DARE* (Qu. N24, *A ditch along the side of a graded road*) 35 Infs, **scattered, but esp Mid and C Atl,** Drain; **MD20, VA59,** Side drain.

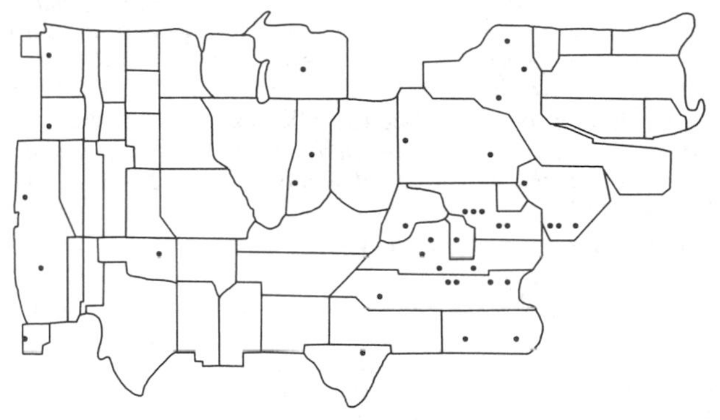
•drain v, n[1] C1 + var (Qu. N24)

2 A small stream or tributary; a spring. **scattered, but esp Mid and S Atl**

1719 in 1940 *AmSp* 15.173 **VA,** Down the sd. Meadow side to the great drean thereof then down the said drean to the River. **1763** (1925) Washington *Diaries* 1.192 **VA,** There is a pretty considerable fall on the West side [of the swamp] through all the drains that make into Nansemond River. **1836** Irving *Astoria* 3.76 **WY,** About noon, the travellers reached the "drains" and brooks that formed the head waters of the river. **1858** Braman *Info. TX* 40, Old Caney, the most important stream .. is very little else, above tide-water, than a large prairie drain. **1899** (1912) Green *VA Folk-Speech* 154, *Drean...* A small stream of water. **1908** *DN* 3.293 **eAL, wGA,** *Branch...* A small stream, a brook... [Other terms are] *dreen, ditch* .. and *creek.* **1932** *DN* 6.229 **Sth,** *Drain...* The upper waters of a creek. **1939** *Hall Coll.* **eTN, wNC,** *Drain* (pronounced *dreen*)—A small spring where there's very little water, on a mountain side or in a little hollow; not the same as a swamp or marsh. [Moonshiners] set up their still on a little dreen .. because revenuers hunt up creeks and a dreen would be hard to find. The dreen is up so steep [moonshiners] could dam it up and pipe [the water] to a barrel. **1960** Hall *Smoky Mt. Folks* 57, *Drain* (nearly always pronounced *dreen*): a small spring with little water, on a mountain side or in a little hollow. **1968** *DARE* (Qu. C1, .. *A small stream of water not big enough to be a river*) Infs **DE4, GA65,** Dreen.

3 A gully or ravine.

1782 in 1940 *AmSp* 15.173 **VA,** From the top of the ridge each way made down small dreans. **1788** *Ibid,* The Junction of two drains or gullies. **1821** (1904) Austin *Jrl. TX* 293 **VA,** The Country from Corpus to this place is very handsome, rolling Prairies, intersected by dreans in most of which water was standing in holes. **1887** (1967) Harris *Free Joe* 104 **GA,** He's in the dreen now... He's a-ridin' a gray. **1893** Shands *MS Speech* 27, *Dreen* .. Negro for *drain,* meaning a ravine or ditch. **1915** Hall *Claib Jones* 7 **KY,** I traveled all that day in the woods, late in the evening I went up a drain, struck a fire and roasted my meat. **1966** *DARE* (Qu. C21, *A deep place cut in sloping ground by running water*) Inf **FL3,** Drain.

4 A saltwater channel. **Atlantic**

1929 *AmSp* 5.160 **Long Island NY,** *Drain,* a channel in the salt marches [sic]. Bulkhead Drain and Goose Island Drain are found on the [U.S. Geol. Surv.] Babylon Sheet. **1932** *DN* 6.229, *Drain. . .* on the [East] coast it may mean a channel in salt flats or salt marshes. **1966** *DARE* (Qu. C1, . . *A small stream of water not big enough to be a river*) Inf **FL**15, Tidal drain—"on sea coast." **1970** *DARE* **FW** Addit **VA**51, Taylor's gut—a low place where tidal water collects in high tide—drains in during high tide and out through a drain during low tide. Common usage. **1976** Warner *Beautiful Swimmers* 8 **Chesapeake Bay,** Down every tidal gut and through every big "thorofare" and little "swash" or "drain," as the breaks in the marsh are called, there comes an enormous and nourishing flow of silage.

5 also *drain tide:* An ebb tide; an ebb; hence v *drain;* of a tide: to ebb. **ME**

1888 *Jrl. Amer. Folkl.* 1.78 **ME,** *Dreen.*—On the island of Mount Desert, the ebb of the tide is spoken of as the *dreen;* the tide is said to *dreen* out, that is drain out. **1961** *AmSp* 36.306, On the coast of Maine . . lobstermen . . speak of *dreen tides.* **1966** *DARE* File **seME,** *Drain tide,* A very low tide (minus two feet). **1975** Gould *ME Lingo* 80, Clam diggers like a low dreen of tide.

6 A downspout; a rain gutter. Cf **eaves drain**

1965-70 *DARE* (Qu. D29, *The pipe that takes the collected rain-water down to the ground or to a storage tank*) 41 Infs, **scattered,** Drain; (Qu. D28, *What hangs below the edge of the roof to carry off rain-water?*) Infs **CA**105, 163, **CO**7, **MN**2, **MA**6, **NC**41, **NJ**67, 69, **PA**248, Drain(s).

7 A colander; drainer. See Intro "Language Changes" III.4

1966 *DARE* (Qu. F6, *The kitchen utensil with holes punched through the sides and bottom, to drain off liquids from foods*) Inf **WY**2, Drain; **SC**9, Dreen.

drain n[2] [Perh var of *grain*] **eSC**

One-eighth of a dollar, a bit.

1966 *DARE* (Qu. U23, *Other words for a 25-cent piece*) Inf **SC**10, Two drain; (Qu. U24, *Other words for a 50-cent piece*) Inf **SC**10, Four drain. **1980** *DARE* File **SC,** About *drain* . . a young black woman from Charleston . . says that . . when she started working in "The City" she heard "kids and middle-aged people" use it. . . My informant speculated that the kids had heard it on "the Islands". . . The most commonly used expression is "two drains," meaning 25¢.

drain cloth n Cf **drain B3**

1966 *DARE* (Qu. G13, *The cloth that you use to wash the dishes with;* total Infs questioned, 75) Inf **MS**46, Drain cloth.

drain ditch n Also *drainer ditch* **scattered, but less freq Nth, N Midl** See Map Cf **drain C1**

=**barrow ditch.**

1962 Fox *Southern Fried* 36 **SC,** They'd push one another back and forth until one would go skidding down into the drain ditch between the field and the highway. **1965-70** *DARE* (Qu. N24, *A ditch along the side of a graded road*) 43 Infs, **scattered, but less freq Nth, N Midl,** Drain ditch; **NC**85, Drainer ditch.

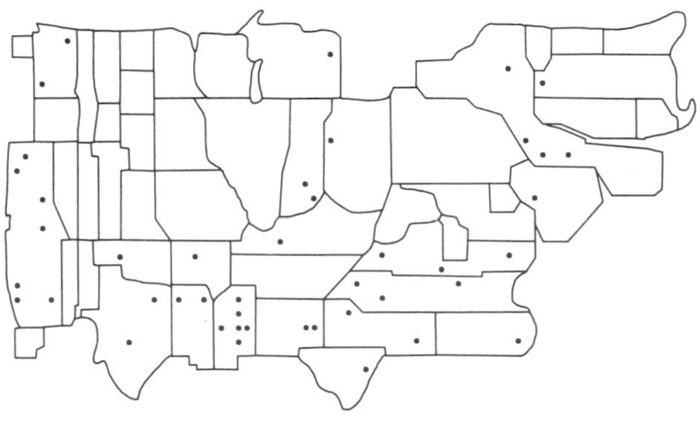

•drain ditch + var (Qu. N24)

drain, go down the v phr **chiefly Nth**

To fall in an endeavor, to lose one's money or wealth, to decline in value, become worthless.

1965-70 *DARE* (Qu. U39, *Somebody who has lost all his money: "During the depression he ——."*) Infs **MN**2, **NJ**67, **PA**237, **TX**83, Went down the drain; (Qu. U41a, *Somebody who has lost everything and is very poor: "He's ——."*) Inf **CA**107, Went down the drain; (Qu. KK10, . . *Something failing—for example, a plan: "He didn't work it out carefully enough, and his plan ——."*) Infs **NJ**44, **NY**46, 109, 241, **OH**21, **PA**8, 220, Went down the drain; (Qu. KK64, *Speaking of the part of a city that was once very fine, but isn't any more: "The neighborhood is sort of ——."*) Inf **MA**59, Gone down the drain.

drain out See **drain** v **B2**

drain tide See **drain** n[1] **C5**

drake n[1] See **drake fly**

drake n[2]

1 also *wild drake:* A **mallard.**

1888 Trumbull *Names of Birds* 15, Mallard *[Anas platyrhyncha]:* Green-Head: Wild Drake . . Common Wild Duck. **1923** U.S. Dept. Ag. *Misc. Circular* 13.8, Mallard *(Anas platyrhyncha). . . In local use.*—Black duck . . , wild drake (Md.) **1942** [see **drake tail**].

2 An **eider duck.**

1917 (1923) *Birds Amer.* 1.146, *Eider—Somateria dresseri. . .* Other Names.—American Eider; . . Drake. **1966** *DARE* (Qu. Q5) Inf **WA**18, Drakes.

3 pl; In marble play: see quot. [Cf *EDD drakes* sb. pl.[2] "The mark from which boys begin to 'taw' at marbles"]

1955 *PADS* 23.16 **cwTN,** *Drakes:* . . A term used in the game of *hundreds;* the line from which the marbles are rolled.

4 See quot. [Cf **duck n 5**]

1968 *DARE* (Qu. DD6b, *Nicknames for cigarettes*) Inf **VA**3, Duck, drake; (Qu. DD8, *The part left over when a cigar or cigarette is smoked*) Inf **VA**3, Butt, duck, drake.

drake fly n Also *drake*

A **mayfly,** such as *Ephemera simulans.*

1969 *DARE* (Qu. R4) Inf **TX**68, Drake fly. **1980** Milne-Milne *Audubon Field Guide Insects* 361, The Brown Drake *(E[phemera] simulans)* . . has translucent wings with dark mottling.

drake's eye n Also *duck's eye* Cf **goose eye**

In moonshining: a large **bead** n **3.**

1969 *DARE* Tape **GA**72, The bead or what we call the drake's eye . . which is the bubble, when you shake it—if the bead flies up there coarse it's high proof, if it's . . very fine, it's low proof. *Ibid,* You kin shake it lightly an' they'll pop up there big—we call em frog-eyes, an' duck's eyes, sometimes, an' drake's eyes.

drake tail n Also *drake's* (or *drakes'*) *tail, drake-tail curl*

A somewhat curled lock of hair.

1935 Sandoz *Jules* 10 **wNE,** His dark hair turning up in silky drakes' tails under the large belly-tan hat. **1937** Sandoz *Slogum* 133 **NE,** The mayor of Fairhope . . had a drake-tail curl on his forehead. **1938** Rawlings *Yearling* 24 **nFL,** [His hair] . . grew in tufts at the back. "Drakes' tails," his mother called them. **1942** McAtee *Dial. Grant Co. IN* 23 (as of 1890s), *Drakestail* . . a [sic] upturned lock of hair at the middle of the nape; the reference is to the recurved upper tail-coverts of the common drake or mallard. **c1960** *Wilson Coll.* **csKY,** *Drake* (or *drake's*) tail. . . A lock of unruly hair sticking up like a drake's tail.

dram n

1 A usu small amount or drink of liquor; hence *have one's drams up* to be drunk. **chiefly S Midl** See Map

1704 (1935) Knight *Jrl.* 3 **MA,** I . . gave him a Dram . . to bind the bargain. **1768** in 1976 Freneau *Poems* 14 **NJ,** *Rum ne'er shall meet my lips* (cry'd honest *Sam*)/ *In shape of toddy, punch, grog, sling, or dram.* **1842** (1930) Hitchcock *Jrl.* 139, Dying from liquor, he will want a dram when he awakes in the other world. **1887** (1967) Harris *Free Joe* 33 **GA,** Ef I fine a thrip in my britches-pocket for to buy me a dram. **1899** (1912) Green *VA Folk-Speech* 154, *Dram. . .* As much spirits as is drunk at once. As liquor was furnished to soldiers on service it was usually spoken of as *drams:* "a bottle of drams." **1935** Sheppard *Cabins* 302 **wNC,** Where did ye get it? I was aimin' to give you fellows a dram bye and bye. **1937** *Writer* 50.239 **neOH** [Black], "He had his drams up," meaning he was high as a Georgia pine. **1954** *Harder Coll.* **cwTN,** *Dram*—A drink of liquor, or the amount taken in one swallow; a big drink of liquid. *Tapering-off dram,* a nightcap. **c1960** *Wilson Coll.* **csKY,** *Dram* . . A good-sized drink, larger than a snort or a snifter. **1965-70** *DARE* (Qu. DD18, *A drink of liquor, or the amount of liquor taken in one swallow:*

"He took a good ______.") 34 Infs, **chiefly S Midl,** Dram; (Qu. DD13, *When a drinker is just beginning to show the effects of the liquor, you say he's ______*) Inf **TN**16, Had a dram; (Qu. DD19, *A little drink: "I'll just take ______."*; total Infs questioned, 75) Infs **FL**7, 22, **OK**42, Dram; (Qu. DD26b, *Other words for a beer glass;* total Infs questioned, 75) Inf **AR**31, Dram glass; (Qu. G2, . . *A glass that you drink water from*) Inf **VA**13, Dram glass—like a cocktail glass, but smaller. **1969** *DARE* Tape **GA**74, Sam would drop behind us . . to take a dram of liquor.

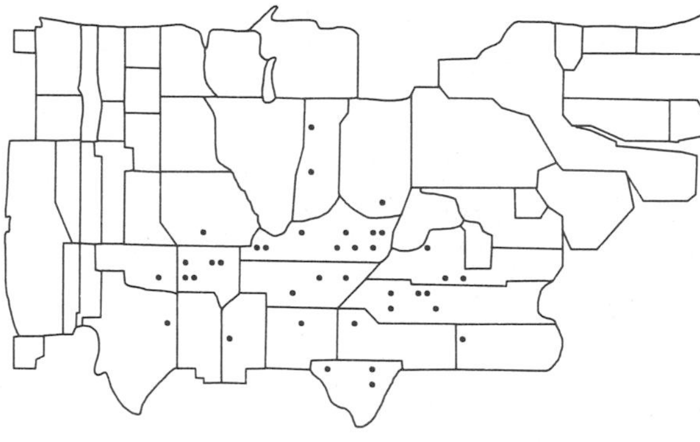

•dram n 1 + varr (Qq. DD18, G2, DD13, DD19, DD26b

2 By ext: whiskey.

1899 (1900) Harris *On the Wing* 172 **GA,** It's a little stronger'n water an' not quite as strong as dram. **1908** *DN* 3.307 **eAL, wGA,** *Dram*. . . Whisky. A general term not always limited to the sense 'a drink of whisky.' **1977** *AmSp* 52.115 **nGA,** Whiskey: . . *dram.*

dram v[1], hence vbl n *dramming* **[dram n] chiefly S Midl, esp sAppalachians**

To drink liquor; to give liquor to.

1771 in 1887 Franklin *Complete Wks.* 1.74, Whether they discover'd his dramming by his breath, or by his behaviour, . . he met with no success in any application. **1857** Goodrich *Recollections* 1.69 **NEng,** What I contend against is this dramming, dramming, dramming, at all hours of the day. **1883** (1971) Harris *Nights with Remus* 63 **GA** [Black], W'iles dey wuz drinkin' en drammin' en gwine on, w'at you 'speck Brer Rabbit doin'? **1899** (1912) Green *VA Folk-Speech* 154, *Dram*. . . To give a dram or drams to; ply with drink. **1924** Raine *Land of Saddle-Bags* 134 **Appalachians,** The habit of tippling or dramming is not uncommon. But the men that drink heavily do so only on great occasions which they "celebrate" by drinking steadily until completely intoxicated. **1927** *DN* 5.469 **Appalachians,** *Drammin'*, n. Drinking. **1942** (1971) Campbell *Cloud-Walking* 121 **seKY,** Neither one wouldn't stand for no drinking and dramming and going hog-wild with celebrating.

dram v[2] See **dream 1**

dram-drinker n **[dram** n; *OED* 1744 →**]** Cf **drammer**

A tippler.

1847 Melville *Typee* 210, He . . is a most inveterate dram-drinker. **1939** in 1972 Hall *Sayings Old Smoky* 63 **eTN,** A dram-drinker makes [=becomes] a drunkard. **1965–69** *DARE* (Qu. DD12, . . *A person who drinks steadily or a great deal*) Inf **IL**81, Dram-drinker—just drinks a little now and then, perhaps every hour, never can say he's drunk; **KY**6, Dram-drinker; **MS**59, Dram-drinker—doesn't get drunk but drinks all the time. **1976** Garber *Mountain-ese* 25 **Appalachians,** *Dram-drinker* . . light social drinker—Dwane ain't no drunk; he's jist sort of a dram-drinker.

dramed See **dream 1**

‡drammel v [Perh var of *EDD drumble* v.[1] "To be sluggish and slow in movement; . . to fumble"]

1970 *DARE* (Qu. DD13, *When a drinker is just beginning to show the effects of the liquor, you say he's ______*) Inf **VA**69, Drammeling ['dræmlɪn].

drammer n Also *dramster* **[dram n]** Cf **dram-drinker**

See quots.

1936 *AmSp* 11.315 **Ozarks,** *Drammer*. . . One who takes an occasional dram, not a steady drinker. **1949** Guthrie *Way West* 6 **MO,** His red-veined, popped eyes swam to them. You could tell Hitchcock was a good drammer from the looks of him. **1952** Brown *NC Folkl.* 1.534, *Dramster*. . . One who drinks—takes a dram.—General.

dramming See **dram** v[1]

drammy adj **[dram n]**

Drunk.

1883 (1971) Harris *Nights with Remus* 65 **GA** [Black], He tuck one tumbeler full, en 't wa'n't long 'fo' he tuck 'n'er'n, en w'en a man do dis a-way, . . he bleedz [=is obliged] ter git drammy.

dramp See **dream 1**

dramster See **drammer**

drank v See **drink v A1**

drank n See **drink n**

dranked, dranken See **drink v A3, 4**

drap See **drop A, B1, 2**

‡draperage n

1942 *McDavid Coll.* **cwNY,** Draperage = drapery. Informant was a 57 year old farmer with 8th grade education.

drapt See **drop B1, 2**

drar See **draw** v

drastic adj

Exciting; venturesome.

1900 in 1919 Hale *Letters* 363 **MA,** Well, the occasion was an interesting and drastic one. **1979** Lewis *How to Talk Yankee* [9] **nNEng,** *Drastic*. . . adventuresome. "I got to feeling drastic and took in the girly show at the carnival." "How was it?" "Not worth the money. They said if you really wanted to see something, it would be another five dollars on top of the three I paid to get in! I *wan't* about to go that." "Don't blame you a mite."

drat v, hence ppl adj *dratted Pronc-sp drot(ted), drattet* **[***OED* 1815 →**]** *esp among educ speakers and women; euphem* Cf **dod**

To curse, confound—used as a euphem for *damn.*

1834 Simms *Guy Rivers* 2.100 **GA,** 'Drot the man, . . says I, who hasn't the courage to get in a passion. **1851** Hooper *Widow Rugby's Husband* 95 **AL,** You're a drotted old hog. **1856** (1928) Twain *Advent. Snodgrass* 26 **IA,** Drat my buttons, if I wasn't astonished. **1895** *DN* 1.376 **TN,** Drat their hides! **1915** *DN* 4.182 **swVA,** *Drot.* **1917** *DN* 4.411 **wNC, KY,** *Drotted.* **1924** *DN* 5.266, *Drat:*—it,—the luck. **1944** *PADS* 2.29 **eKY,** *Drotted, dratted, drattet* [drɑtəd, drætəd, drætət]. . . Diminutive oath for "God rotted." **1950** *PADS* 14.26 **SC,** *Dratted, drotted:* Expletive expressing displeasure, disapproval. Applied to persons or things. **c1960** *Wilson Coll.* **csKY,** *Dratted*. . . A softened *damned.* **1965–70** *DARE* (Qu. NN8b, *Other expressions of annoyance: "This jar won't come open, ______ it."*) 32 Infs, **scattered,** Drat (it); (Qu. NN17, *Something that keeps on annoying you—for example, a fly that keeps buzzing around you: "That ______ fly won't go away."*) 22 Infs, **scattered,** Dratted; (Qu. NN25a, *Weakened substitutes for 'damn' or 'damned': "______ it all!"*) 21 Infs, **scattered,** Drat; (Qu. NN8a, *Exclamations of annoyance or disgust: "Oh ______. I've lost my glasses again."*) 16 Infs, **scattered,** Drat (it); (Qu. NN9b, *Exclamations showing great annoyance: "He's run off with my hammer again, ______!"*) 14 Infs, **scattered,** Drat (him, it, his hide); (Qu. NN9a, *"______. The electric power is off again."*) 9 Infs, **scattered,** Drat (it); (Qu. NN21c, *Exclamations caused by sudden pain —a twisted ankle:*) Inf **NE**9, Drat it. [48 of 84 Infs coll educ, 59 of 84 Infs female] **1976** Garber *Mountain-ese* 25 **Appalachians,** *Drat-it* . . expletive for damn—Drat it all, I drapped my gum and somebody stepped on it.

drat n [Perh var of Scots *drit(e), dret* dirt, excrement] **esp KY, TN**

In marble play: a marble made of baked clay and often painted; a game played with such marbles.

1890 *DN* 1.64 **KY,** *Drats* [dræts]: little brown marbles. "Let's play drats." **1955** *PADS* 23.16 **cwTN,** *Drat*. . . A small dirty-brown marble. **1957** *Sat. Eve. Post Letters* **wKY,** Those [marbles] made of painted baked clay were "coobies" or "drats" according to their size; no one was sure which were the bigger and which the smaller. **1970** *DARE* (Qu. EE6b, *Small marbles or marbles in general*) Infs **KY**80, 94, Drats; (Qu. EE6c, *Cheap marbles*) Inf **KY**80, Drats—made of mud or clay and painted; **KY**94, Drats. **c1970** Wiersma *Marbles Terms* **MI,** *Drat*—a small brown marble.

drathers See **druthers**

dratted, drattet See **drat** v

draught See **draft** n[1]

‡**drave** n [Prob var of *dray*]
1968 *DARE* (Qu. N11, *A very large truck used to haul freight, new cars, and other big loads*) Inf **IL**29, Draves [drevz].

drave v See **drive** v **A2**

draw v Pronc-spp *drar, dror*

A Pronc var.

1848 Lowell *Biglow* 144 **'Upcountry' MA,** Dror, *draw.* **1910** in 1944 *ADD,* Droring room. **1982** *AmSp* 57.192 **ceIL** (as of 1887), Intrusive /r/ occurs in . . *drar* ('draw').

B Gram forms.

1 past: usu *drew;* also **esp Sth, S Midl** (See Map) *chiefly among rural speakers, male speakers, and speakers with little formal educ, drawed;* occas *drawn;* infreq *draw;* rarely *drewed.* For addit quots see **C** below

1814 (1922) Tatum *Jrl.* 7.77 **NC,** [The Creek Indians were removed] in consequence of the War which they had commenced against that Government, which drawn on them a necessary scourge. **1823** in 1944 *ADD,* Drawed. **1836** in 1925 *Vineland Hist. Mag.* 10.48 **NY,** He . . drawed his chair close by the side of the President. **1843** (1916) Hall *New Purchase* 144 **IN,** She always shot the door at night, and a sort a draw'd the bedstid agin it. **1884** Lanier *Poems* 175 **GA,** Tennessy was . . / A-raisin' meat and corn, all which / Draw'd money to Atlanta. **1893** [see **B2** below]. **1903** *DN* 2.293 **Cape Cod MA** (as of a1857), There is a tendency to make strong verbs weak. Thus the following forms in *-ed* are in general use: *growed, . . drawed.* **1904** *DN* 2.418 **nwAR,** *Draw,* vb. tr. (with weak preterit). Even among students, the verb is often weak. 'I drawed that machine.' **1922** (1926) Kephart *Highlanders* 358 **sAppalachians,** In many cases a weak preterite supplants the proper strong one: . . drawed, growed, knowed. **1943** [see **B2** below]. **1953** Atwood *Survey of Verb Forms* 10, *Draw.* . . The preterite is recorded in the context "He (drew) it out." *Drew* /dru/ predominates in cultivated speech and in Type II speech in all areas. The weak form *drawed* /drɔd/ is very clearly rustic and rather rapidly receding. It is somewhat uncommon in e. N. Y. and N. J., being confined to less than one fourth of Type I; in n. and w. N. Y. and in Pa. a little less than half the informants of this type use it. To the southward it becomes more frequent, being used by nearly nine tenths of Type I informants in N. C. In Type II, *drawed* hardly occurs in e. N. Y. or N. J., and never reaches a frequency of more than one fourth in any area of the M[iddle] A[tlantic] S[tates] or the S[outh] A[tlantic] S[tates]. One Negro informant uses the uninflected *draw* /drɔ/. **c1960** [see **B2** below]. **1965–70** *DARE* (Qu. OO18b, *Talking about drawing a plan: "I know that man ______ [it].")* 906 Infs, **widespread,** Drew (up); 87 Infs, **esp Sth, S Midl,** Drawed (up) [Of all Infs responding to the question, 29% were comm type 5, 23% gs educ, 44% male; of those giving the response *drawed (up),* 53% were comm type 5, 55% gs educ, 59% male.]; **AR**27, **GA**23, **IL**9, 77, **TN**31, **TX**5, 12, 19, Drawn [Of 8 Infs, 6 were comm type 5, 2 comm type 4, 6 old, 2 mid-aged, 6 male.]; **SC**10, 26, Draw [Both Infs Black, gs educ or less]; **OR**6, Drewed [Inf gs educ]. **1965–67** *DARE* Tape **ME**26, The old fellow couldn't write too much, so he drawed the picture; **MS**1, They drawed straws to see which one was goin' git 'im; **OK**24, Drawed a draft right there at the depot and paid for it; **SD**5, The suction drawed the sand right through them flues. **1969** Emmons *Deep Rivers* 53 **eTX** [Black], He sent word and the law come out there and they drawed up the papers.

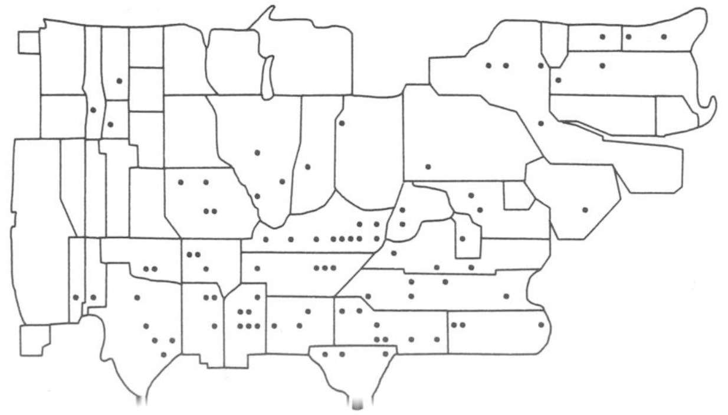

•drawed + var (at draw v B1) (Qu. OO18b)

2 past ppl: usu *drawn;* also **esp Sth, S Midl** (See Map) *chiefly among rural speakers and speakers with little formal educ, drawed;* also **esp Nth, West** (See Map) *chiefly among rural speakers, male speakers, and speakers with little formal educ, drew;* occas *draw.* See also quots at **C** below

1823 in 1944 *ADD,* Drawed. **1861** Holmes *Venner* 2.147 **wMA,** She's the beautifullest-shaped lady that ever had a shinin' silk gown drawed over her shoulders. **1893** *DN* 1.277 **wCT,** Draw—[preterit and past participle] drawed. **1940** Stuart *Trees of Heaven* 170 **neKY,** I've got a ar-tickle I had drawed up by Lawyer John Oscar Simmons. **1943** McAtee *Dial. Grant Co. IN Suppl. 2* 8 (as of 1890s), *Drawed* . . p. and pp. of drew. **c1960** *Wilson Coll.* **csKY,** *Draw*—drawed [preterit], drawed [past participle]. Almost universal. **1965–70** *DARE* (Qu. OO18a, *Talking about drawing a plan: "Last year the plan for the new school was ______ [up].")* 853 Infs, **widespread,** Drawn; 105 Infs, **scattered, but esp Sth, S Midl,** Drawed [Of all Infs responding to the question, 29% were comm type 5, 23% gs educ, 44% male; of those giving the response *drawed,* 53% were comm type 5, 51% gs educ, 57% male.]; 46 Infs, **scattered, but esp Nth, West,** Drew [Of those giving this response, 41% were comm type 5, 46% gs educ, 57% male.]; **SC**10, 26, Draw [Both Infs Black, gs educ or less]; (Qu. II11b) **TX**98, Have drawed the hatchet. **1967–69** *DARE* Tape **RI**5, The warp is drew in; **TX**39, Had drew [Inf corr to *drawn*].

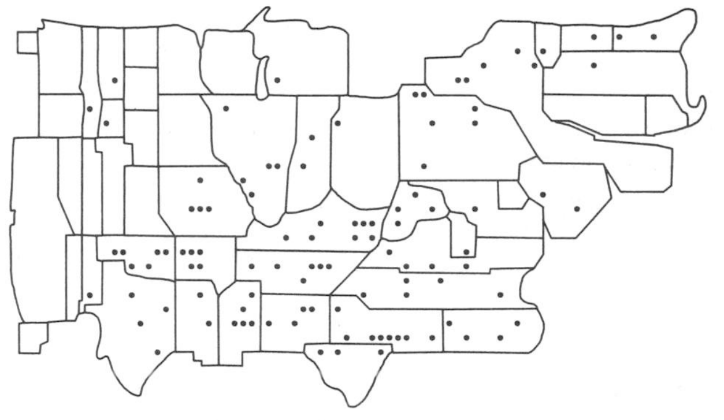

•drawed (at draw v B2) (Qu. OO18a)

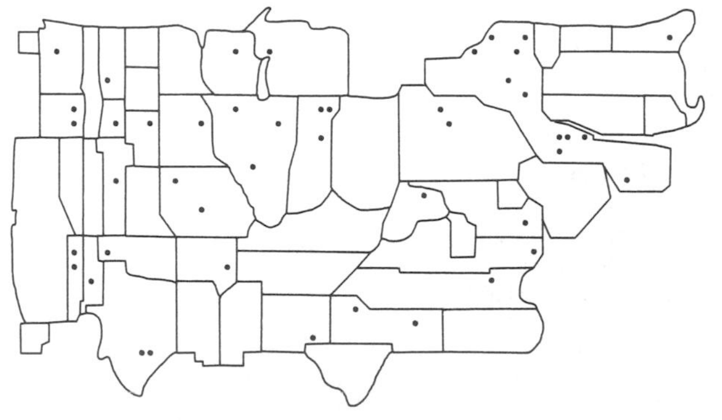

•drew + var (at draw v B2) (Qu. OO18a)

C Senses.

1 also with *in, off, out:* To drag, pull, haul; to carry. **chiefly Upstate NY, wNEng** See Map

1860 (1936) Hawley *Diary* 19.330 **WI,** He was . . away drawing bridge timber. **1917** Garland *Son Middle Border* 69 **WI,** Father was busy with his team drawing off wheat and hogs and hay. **1917** *DN* 4.391 **neOH, VT, NH, MA, NY,** *Draw* [drɔ]. . . The regular word for "haul on a vehicle", as, draw hay, oats, wood, etc. Also draw in, out. *Haul* is also common and superseding *draw.* "We're going to draw wheat today." "He's drawing in hay." "He's drawing out manure." **1931–33** *LANE*

Worksheets, 1 inf, **nwCT,** He's got four wagons he draws hay on; 1 inf, **cCT,** Vexation was term for a little hill because it was difficult to traverse or draw wood from that neighborhood; 1 inf, **swRI,** A sled is used for drawing wood. **1934** *Hanley Disks* **nwMA,** Get stuck in the mud and then you have to get drawed off—drawn out. **1949** Kurath *Word Geog.* 57, *Hauling* is generally known also in the North, but the regional expression *drawing* or *carting* comes more readily to the lips of the common folk in the countryside. The expression *drawing wood* is current (1) in all of New England (except only the southeastern sector extending from the New London area to the Plymouth area, Cape Cod, and the islands offshore), (2) in all of New York State except the Metropolitan area, and (3) in the northern counties of Pennsylvania. **1965–70** *DARE* (Qu. L54, *If someone was transporting firewood [or dirt] in a wagon, you'd say he was ______ firewood.*) 32 Infs, **chiefly Upstate NY, wNEng,** Drawing; **NY**224, Drawing in; (Qu. L11, *What do you do to hay in the field after it's cut?*) Inf **PA**103, Drawing it in; **NY**209, Git it dry and draw it in; (Qu. OO46a, *Talking about dragging something heavy: "We hitched the log on and ______ it out [of the woods]."*) Infs **MA**66, **NY**123, Drew; (Qu. OO46b, *Talking about dragging something heavy: "Half a mile or so we must have ______ [it]!"*) Inf **MA**66, Drew. **1966–68** *DARE* Tape **CT**4, It was difficult to traverse or draw wood from that neighborhood; **NH**5, We'd generally have the neighbors come with their horses and a dray, and draw in that loose corn; **VT**1A, It would be hard on the horses to draw a load . . through a long bridge; **MA**5C, They have a gang chopping logs all the time. . . They'll keep just a day or two ahead of the team that is drawing them in. **1967** *DARE* FW Addit **neNY,** To draw out of Albany, to haul out of Albany—to drive a truck from Albany. **1967** Borland *Hill Country* 272 **nwCT,** Talking with a townsman just the other day I heard him say, "We sent a truck out to draw a load of sand." I constantly hear the word "draw" in that meaning among farm folk, a meaning for which I instinctively would use either "haul" or "drag." But "draw" is one of the old words, deeply embedded in these New England hills and valleys. It goes back to the days of oxen. **1972** *NYT Article Letters* **cNY,** I recently heard a woman speak of "drawing the mail" as her husband was a rural carrier. **1973** Allen *LAUM* 1.216 (as of c1950), *Hauling,* the dominant form in the eastern states, has increased its dominance in the U[pper] M[idwest]. Northern *drawing* survives only as a relic with five speakers, one of them in Manitoba.

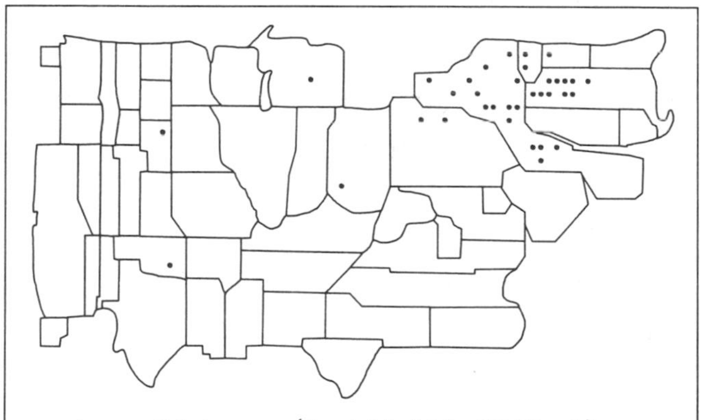

•draw v C1 + varr (Qq. L54, L11, OO46a, b)

2 with *up:* To move one's chair close to a table, fireplace, etc; to pull (one's seat) close. **chiefly Sth, S Midl**

1899 (1912) Green *VA Folk-Speech* 154, *Draw up. . .* To move one's seat up to a table to eat. "Draw up your chair and have some supper." **1930** *DN* 6.87 **cnWV,** *Draw up* . . an invitation involving some degree of cordiality, issued by a foreman to a newcomer in camp, a request to sit down to a meal; an injunction that needs no repetition. **1938** Rawlings *Yearling* 56 **nFL,** If I'd of knowed you was comin' . . I'd of cooked somethin' fitten. Well, draw up. **1946** McCullers *Member* 103 **AL,** Very well. Draw up that stool before the organ. **c1960** *Wilson Coll.* **csKY,** *Draw up a chair*—said to guest before fireplace or at table. **1967** *DARE* (Qu. II15, *When somebody is passing by and you want him or her to stop and talk a while, you might say, "______."*) Inf **TX**5, Draw up a chair.

3 with *up:* To shrink; to shrivel up, wither; hence ppl adj phrr *drawed up, drawn (up).* **chiefly Sth, S Midl** See Map

1944 *PADS* 2.8 **AL, NC, TX, TN, VA,** *Draw up. . .* To shrink. "When my blue dress was washed, it drew up dreadfully; now I can't wear it." **1946** McAtee *Dial. Grant Co. IN Suppl. 3* 4 (as of 1890s), *Draw up* . . shrink. **1965–70** *DARE* (Qu. OO37a, *Talking about clothes shrinking: "The first time my wool socks were washed they ______."*) 34 Infs, **chiefly Sth, S Midl,** Drew up; 33 Infs, **chiefly Sth, S Midl,** Drawed up; **SC**10, 26, Draw up; (Qu. OO37b, *Talking about clothes shrinking: "I can't get them on because they've ______ [too much]."*) 37 Infs, **chiefly Sth, S Midl,** Drawed up; 14 Infs, **chiefly Sth, S Midl,** Drawn up; **KY**24, **LA**3, **VA**4, 45, Drew up; **SC**26, Draw up; (Qu. LL3b, *Shrunk, dried up: "He's a little ______ old man."*) 9 Infs, **chiefly Sth, S Midl,** Drawed up; **DE**3, **FL**8, **VA**50, 92, 94, Drawn up; (Qu. LL3a, *Shrunk, dried up: "These apples are all ______."*) Infs **AL**51, **GA**77, **LA**11, **TN**1, Drawed up; **VA**39, Drawn; (Qu. H44, *Beef that has been dried to preserve it*) Inf **TX**85, Drawn beef. **1970** *Thompson Coll.* **cnAL** (as of 1920s), It drawed up sumpm awful. It's done drew up to whirr I cayn't even git close to hit. **1974** Fink *Mountain Speech* 7 **wNC, eTN,** *Draw up* . . shrink. *"My jacket drawed up 'till purt nigh couldn't get hit on."* **1976** Garber *Mountain-ese* 25 **Appalachians,** *Draw-up* . . shrink, decrease—You'd better buy yore overalls long; they'll draw up when they're washed. **1983** *MJLF* 9.1.38 **ceKY** (as of 1956), Drawed up . . shrunk.

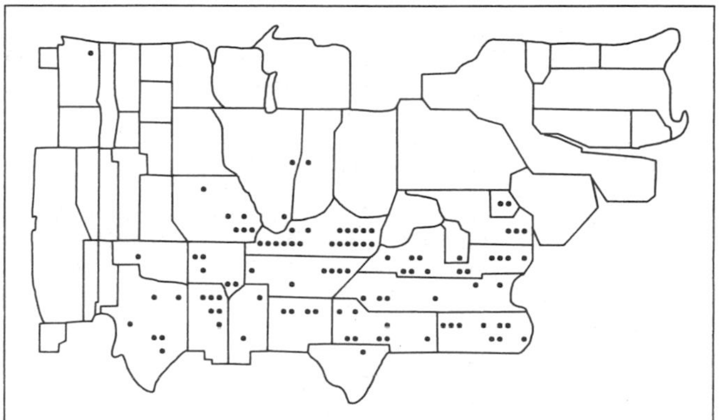

•draw v C3 + varr (Qq. OO37a, b, LL3a, b, H44)

4 usu with *up;* also with *in, together:* To squeeze or crowd together. **chiefly Sth, S Midl** See Map

1965–70 *DARE* (Qu. Y32, *To squeeze yourself into a small space: "If you're going to fit in there you'll have to ______."*) 87 Infs, **chiefly Sth, S Midl,** Draw up; **GA**44, **IL**96, **LA**31, **NJ**67, **NY**29, **TX**12, 42, Draw in; **IL**85, **NJ**19, **NY**209, Draw yourself together; **IL**83, **TN**33, **VA**74, Draw yourself up; **MO**19, **OK**28, Draw up a little; **AZ**1, Draw 'em; **TX**104, Draw it in; **MD**39, Draw up in a knot; **GA**77, Draw up tight; **NC**49, Draw yourself in; (Qu. Y52, *To move over—for example, on a long bench: "We have to make room for one more. Can you ______ [a little]?"*) Infs **GA**82, **KY**94, **NE**11, Draw up.

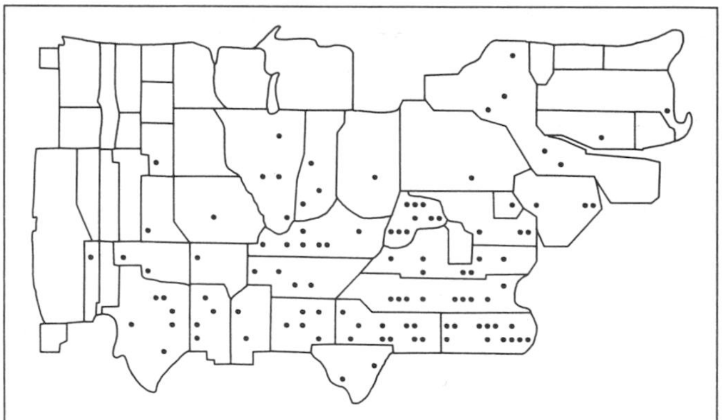

•draw v C4 + varr (Qq. Y32, Y52)

5 usu with *together, up:* To stitch, mend. **chiefly Inland Nth, N Midl**

1965–70 *DARE* (Qu. W28, *When a woman is in a hurry and has to sew up a torn place quickly, she might say, "I'll just ______."*) 18 Infs, **chiefly Inland Nth, N Midl,** Draw it together; **IN**30, **NJ**69, **SC**11, **MD**26, Draw it up a little bit; **SC**66, Draw it shut. **1968** *DARE* Tape **MD**19, [FW:] What else can you sew besides buttons? [Inf:] Oh, I draw some holes up, patch a little bit. But I'm no expert. [FW:] What about holes in socks? What do you do to that? [Inf:] Draw 'em up. Not much. Nothing.

6 with *in:* See quot 1917.

1899 Garland *Boy Life* 185 **nwIA** (as of c1870s), When the stacker wishes to "carry the stack up straight," he lays the sheaves [of grain] sidewise. When he wishes to "lay out" his bulge, he turns the long point of the "slanch" upward. When he wishes to "draw in," he reverses them, putting the point down and the slant upward,—"and always keep your middle full," Duncan reiterated to his son. "Pack your middle hard, especially when you come to draw in. Tramp it down well, and you won't have any wet grain." **1917** *DN* 4.391 **neOH, NEng, KY, KS,** *Draw in. . .* In loading or stacking hay or grain, to lay the outer tiers successively nearer the center, so as to contract the load or stack. Cf. *lay out.* "You are a little heavy on the off side; you'd better draw in that corner a little." "It is time to begin to draw in now."

7 To steep, brew (tea or coffee); to undergo steeping; hence vbl n *drawing* the beverage made at one time, the amount of tea or coffee needed to make a full pot. **scattered, but esp Sth, S Midl**

1856 Whitcher *Bedott Papers* 53 **cNY,** She sent to borrer somethin or other—a loaf o' bread—or a drawin' o' tea. **1883** *Harper's New Mth. Mag.* 66.829/2, To these . . is given the second drawing of the tea. **1911** (1916) Porter *Harvester* 341 **IN,** 'To draw the tea in.' . . That fool woman meant to set my grandmother's weddin' present . . on the stove to bile the tea in. **1941** *LANE* Map 310 *(Make some coffee)* 1 inf, **swMA,** Draw the coffee; 1 inf, **eLong Is. NY,** When I get my coffee drawed; [1 inf, **New Brunswick,** Draw some tea, a drawing of tea (a cup or portion of tea)]. **1966–70** *DARE* (Qu. H72, . . *Preparing tea: "Pour on the water and let it* ______ *."*) Infs **CA**15, **DE**2, **MD**21, **MS**79, **SC**4, 9, 11, 26, **TX**5, **VA**48, 74, 108, **WV**3, Draw; (Qu. H73, . . *Preparing coffee:* . . *"I think I'll go and* ______ *some coffee."*) Inf **SC**11, Draw.

8 in phr *draw the fire:* To remove the fire from under a pot or cooking vessel.

1938 Matschat *Suwannee R.* 133 **GA,** Slowly the contents of the kettle changed in color. . . When it showed glints of golden red . . , Cella called her father to draw the fire: the first pot was done. **1965** Needham–Mussey *Country Things* 116 **VT,** They told him to run out the batch that was in the still. . . He wasn't an expert, because he didn't draw the fire. The thing blew up.

9 See quot. [Cf **C3** above and *W3* [1]*draw* 4. b "to contract, pucker, wrinkle"]

1899 (1912) Green *VA Folk-Speech* 154, *Draw. . .* To injure paint by being near the fire. "Heat will draw the paint."

10 with *up:* See quot. Cf **draw** n **4, draw day**

1930 *DN* 6.87 **cnWV,** *Draw up. . .* To get money before pay day.

11 also in phr *draw one's rocking chair;* To live on welfare; hence vbl n *drawing.*

1967 Fetterman *Stinking Creek* 33 **seKY,** The words of Golden Slusher: "What don't work is drawin'." The majority are "drawin'." They draw welfare checks or commodities or both, and these are the basis of their economic security. **1969** *DARE* FW Addit **KY**17, "Drawing his rocking chair"—someone who's drawing welfare (most often), or a pension, or social security.

12 To summon (into court), subpoena. [Cf **draw** v **C1**]

1966–69 *DARE* (Qu. V8b, *Of a person who has been given a paper ordering him into court you might say: "He was* ______ *into court."*) Infs **AR**40, **CO**15, **IN**65, **PA**216, Drawn; **MA**15, Drawed.

13 In logging: see quots; hence vbl n *drawing.*

1958 McCulloch *Woods Words* 52 **Pacific NW,** *Draw. . .* To pull a falling tree away from the direction in which it leans by making side cuts and wedging. **1969** Sorden *Lumberjack Lingo* 36 **NEng, Gt Lakes,** *Drawing a tree*—Notching a tree to make it fall in a desired direction.

14 In tobacco farming: see quot 1970.

1966 *DARE* Tape **DC**5, More labor with 'bacco, than with any other crop we grow. When you go to plant, you draw 'em out of bed, plant by plant. You plant 'em one plant at a time. **1967** Key *Tobacco Vocab.* 170 **KY,** "You draw [the plants] off the bed;" **MD, TN,** Draw. **1970** *DARE* FW Addit **KY**80, *Draw plants to set*—to remove tobacco plants from the tobacco beds to set [=plant] in the field.

15 in phrr *draw (up) an idea* (or *a suspicion*): To suspect, conclude. **esp Ozarks**

1923 *DN* 5.206 **swMO,** *Draw an idea. . .* To suspect. "I draw a' idee he' harder up 'n he lets on t' be." **1923** (1946) Greer–Petrie *Angeline Doin' Society* 2 **csKY,** Somehow, he'd draw'd up the idy [=idea] the parson had stretched his blanket. **1949** Webber *Backwoods Teacher* 236 **Ozarks,** I reckon I better mosey along. Hi'll draw a suspicion I've been carried off. *Ibid* 237, From the first I had "drawed a suspicion" that a big part of Tibo's reason for telling his boys they couldn't be in the Christmas program was that they did not have proper clothes. **1953** Randolph–Wilson *Down in Holler* 241 **Ozarks,** *Draw an idea. . .* To perceive, to infer, perhaps sometimes to decide. "Soon as I laid eyes on that feller, I just drawed a idy he warn't up to no good." In an old song, "The State of Arkansas," are these lines: *He says you are a stranger,/ This idea I do draw,/ On yonder hill is my hotel,/ The best in Arkansas.*

16 in phr *draw a face:* To grimace. [Cf *draw* to pucker]

1932 Smiley *Gloss. New Paltz* **seNY,** "Drawed a face and said" means made a face and said.

17 in phr *draw a bite:* To prepare a meal.

1936 *AmSp* 11.315 **Ozarks,** *Draw a bite. . .* To prepare a meal. A woman tells us: 'Wal, I got t' git home an' draw a bite for the ol' man.' One of our neighbors was 'mad 'cause he didn't get th' bite drawed on him,' that is, he didn't get his dinner. **1954** *Harder Coll.* **cwTN,** *Draw a bite,* get something to eat.

draw n

1a A drawer. [Pronc-sp for *drawer*] **chiefly Nth, Sth** See Map

1692 in 1904 Manwaring *Digest CT Probate* 1.463, I giue to Elizabeth Thomson . . one table with a draue in it. **1748** in 1915 NH *Prov. & State Papers* 33.565, I give . . my Chist of draws to my dafter Lidea. **1829** in 1846 Mackenzie *Life Van Buren* 170 **NY,** My original copy [of a letter] . . got into that celebrated receptacle of Chancery papers, . . the draw or bushel basket, (I don't know which,) of his venerable predecessor. **1898** Westcott *Harum* 143 **cNY,** They're in the draw there. **1905** *DN* 3.61 **NE,** *Draw,* used occasionally for *drawer, n.* "Open that there draw in the desk." **1965–70** *DARE* (Qu. E4, *Section in a piece of furniture that you pull in and out*) 91 Infs, **chiefly Nth, Sth,** Draw; **WI**35, Dresser draw; (Qu. D9, *To prevent bread and cake from drying, you put them in a* ______) Infs **MI**104, **NY**186, (Bread) draw; (Qu. E3, *A piece of furniture in which you lay clothes flat:*) Infs **MI**66, **MT**5, Draw; **NC**17, **NY**75, 213, **VA**45, 74, Chest of draw(s); **NY**68, Bureau draw; (Qu. E5, *A piece of furniture with a flat top for keeping tablecloths, dishes, and such*) Inf **NY**88, Buffet draw; (Qu. Y38, *Mixed together, confused: "The things in the drawer are all* ______ *."*) Inf **NC**16, My draw is a hodge-podge.

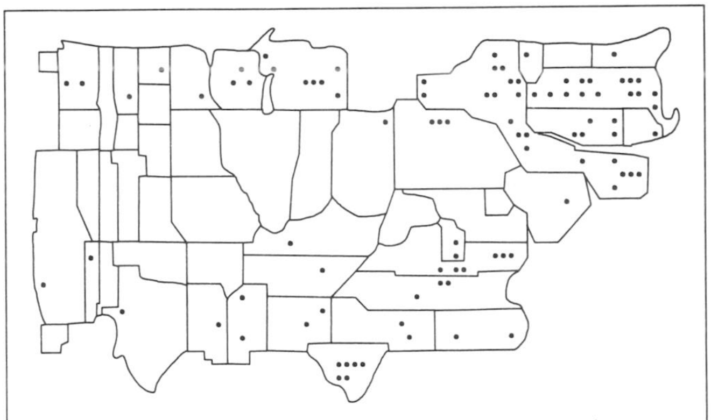

•draw n 1a + varr (Qq. E4, D9, E3, E5, Y38)

b pl: Drawers; pants or underwear. **esp S Midl**

1721 *Weekly Mercury* 21–28 Sept. 2/2 *(DAE),* He wears a yellow Thickset Coat, . . an Ozenbrig Shirt and Draws, and a Pair of white Yarn Stockings. **1966–70** *DARE* (Qu. W14, *Names for underwear*) Infs **FL**33, **MS**88, **NY**48, **NC**14, **VA**39, 42, 54, 78, **SC**40, (Long) draws.

2 Any of various types of valleys or low places, spec: see below. Note: It is sometimes difficult to distinguish among the following senses.

a A steep-sided gully or ravine; a stream-bed, often one that runs dry. **chiefly West** Cf **arroyo**

1897 Lummis *King of Broncos* 9 **NM,** The draw was no more than a smooth gully, its steep banks hedged with a tangle of scrub-oaks and piñons. **1933** *AmSp* 8.1.31 **nwTX,** *Draw.* A tributary cañon; a small dry streambed. **1950** *WELS Suppl.,* A wedge-shaped depression in the land—too steep to be called a valley. Quite narrow. A ravine. **1962** Atwood *Vocab. TX* 40, *Dry creek (bed). . .* In parts of West and Northwest Texas, *draw* is the most usual word. **1966–69** *DARE* Tape **SD**8,

You got a pretty good view of that rough country back there. There's all kinds o' canyons and draws and brush and timber; **TX**24, There's a waterhole there that in the three years that I was there, it went dry one time. Farther on down the draw, there's three more; **TX**70, If you'd come in to town [in a car], if you'd hit a draw, you know that's running, why you might have to wait there a half a day or a day before you could get through. **1967–68** *DARE* (Qu. C21, *A deep place cut in sloping ground by running water*) Infs **AK**7, **CA**62, **NE**11, **OR**10, **TX**28, Draw; **TX**2, Deep draw; (Qu. C1, . . *A small stream of water not big enough to be a river*) Inf **TX**43, Running draw; **TX**80, Draw—dry except during rain.

b also *drawer:* A gently sloping valley; a dell. **chiefly West of Missip R Cf dingle** n[1]

1895 *DN* 1.387 **MO, NE,** *Draw* . . : a broad ravine. **1905** *DN* 3.61 **NE,** *Draw,* occasionally *drawer* . . .Valley. "A draw runs through the farm." **1919** Cather *My Antonia* 19 **NE,** There in the sheltered draw-bottom the wind did not blow very hard. **1935** Cather *Gayheart* 216 **NE,** In the draws, between the low hills, thickets of wild plum bushes were black against the drifts. **1949** *PADS* 11.6 **wTX** (as of c1920), *Draw*. . . A gently sloping hollow. Common. **1952** FWP *Guide SD* 86, *Draw:* any swale or depression down which water drains or "draws." **1954** *Harder Coll.* **cwTN,** *Draw:* The upper end of a hollow. **c1960** *Wilson Coll.* **csKY,** *Draw*. . . A gently sloping hollow or valley, a natural drain or gully, not one washed out within the memory of people. **1965–70** *DARE* (Qu. C19, . . *Low land running between hills [With and without water]*) 24 Infs, **chiefly west of Missip R,** Draw; (Qu. C20, *What if it's broader or larger?;* total Infs questioned, 75) Inf **OK**25, Draw.

c A passageway through a mountainous area. Cf **gap** n[1] **1, notch**

1882 Baillie-Grohman *Camps* 340 **WY, Rocky Mts,** Among the rough and steep chains of mountain full of "draws," "pockets," and gulches, . . the search is anything but easy. **1939** *LANE* Map 36 *(Ravine, Notch)* 1 inf, **neNH,** Draw, a small 'cut' in the mountains; 1 inf, **neMA,** Draw. **1950** *WELS (A low place in mountains or high hills where you can get through without climbing over)* 4 Infs, **WI,** Draw. **1966–70** *DARE* (Qu. C15, *A place in mountains or high hills where you can get through without climbing over the top*) Infs **CO**7, 26, **IL**54, 126, **IN**49, **KY**5, **MO**20, **NM**6, Draw.

3 A small stream or stretch of still water. Cf **draft** n[1] **B1**

1944 *PADS* 2.55 **nwMO,** *Draw*. . . A small creek. . . Common. **1967–70** *DARE* (Qu. C1, . . *A small stream of water not big enough to be a river*) Infs **IL**23, **VA**5, Draw; **TX**68, Draw, Johnson's Draw, Killbear Draw; (Qu. C14, *A stretch of still water going off to the side from a river or lake*) Inf **MO**27, **TN**14, Draw.

4 The receipt of money; an amount paid or advanced to one. Cf **draw** v **C10**

1892 *Jrl. Amer. Folkl.* 5.236 **TN,** *Draw.*—In Tennessee, at a stated time in the year, the school-teachers assemble for *"the draw,"* the receiving of their salary, which is graduated to the number of scholars the teacher has. **1952** Giles *40 Acres* 161 **KY,** We thought it mighty fancy of them to spend their draw [=welfare payment] on boloney, bubble gum, and soda pop instead of good, solid food. **1958** McCulloch *Woods Words* 52 **Pacific NW,** *Draw*. . . An advance on pay. **1967** *DARE* FW Addit **NJ**18, "He'd let him have a draw" = he gave him credit. Heard in conversation.

5 See quot. [Abbr for *drawing*]

1917 *DN* 4.411 **wNC,** *Draw*. . . Drawing. "Are you making a draw of the fence."

6 See quot.

1943 Peattie *Great Smokies* 247, Streams and waterfalls cool the air in the mountains so that each night in the valleys there is a "draw"—a steady wind such as one feels when standing in the bow of a ship. It is the cool air flowing down to the lowlands to replace the heated columns rising above sun-baked cotton fields.

7 In phrr *slow* (or *quick*) *on the draw:* Slow (or quick) to understand or to act. [*draw* the removing of a revolver from its holster]

1966–70 *DARE* (Qu. A18, . . *About a very slow person: "What's keeping him? He certainly is ______!"*) Infs **CO**47, **TX**51, Slow on the draw; (Qu. HH13, . . *A person [who] is not very alert or not aware of things "He's certainly ______."*) Infs **AL**6, **MN**33, **TX**28, 80, 81, **VT**16, Slow on the draw; **NJ**43, **OH**37, Not very quick on the draw.

8 A draft of beer.

1988 *DARE* File **csWI** (as of 1955–60), A draw [drɔ] of beer at Wilma's tavern at Starvation Corners . . was a glass of draft beer; **csWI,** In a tavern, "Give me a draw" means give me a mug or glass full of beer.

draw a bite See **draw** v **C17**

draw a bucket of water n

A children's singing game; see quot 1937.

1883 Newell *Games & Songs* 90 **NY, MA,** *Draw a Bucket of Water.* Four girls cross hands, and pull in rhythmical movement against each other while singing, one pair changing the position of their hands from above to below that of the other pair at the words [in a sung verse], "Here we go under." **1937** (1947) Bancroft *Games* 345, *Draw a bucket of water*—This game is played in groups of four, generally by girls. Two players face each other, clasping hands at full arm's length. The other two face each other from the other directions, with their arms crossing those of the first couple at right angles. Bracing the feet, the couples sway backward and forward, singing the . . rhyme. . . As the last line is said, the players all raise their arms without unclasping the hands and place them around their companions, who stoop to step inside. They will then be standing in a circle with arms around each other's waists. The game finishes by dancing in this position around in a ring, repeating the verse once more. **1946** TN Folk Lore Soc. *Bulletin* Mar 20, Other singing games were "Green Gravel," "Draw a Bucket of Water," . . and such.

draw a face See **draw** v **C16**

‡drawback n Cf **fall-away** n

1968 *DARE* (Qu. CC7, . . *A person who goes to church very seldom or not at all*) Inf **MD**20, Drawback.

drawbar n

1 See quot 1899. **formerly NEng, now chiefly S Midl**

1670 in 1880 Groton MA *Early Rec.* 36, A sufficiẽt pair of draw barrs to [be] Kept and maintained at the end [of] Natha[niel] Lawrances feild [sic]. **1836** *S. Lit. Messenger* 2.162/2 **VA,** On every side I was met by gates, drawbars, and *gaps.* **1859** Taliaferro *Fisher's R.* 119 **nwNC** (as of 1820s), At last we cum chug up to a fence that had no draw-bars nur gate. **1899** (1912) Green *VA Folk-Speech* 154, *Draw-bar*. . . A bar or set of bars, in a fence, which can be drawn back or let down to allow passage, as along a road or path. **1902** *DN* 2.233 **sIL,** *Draw-bars*. . . Ordinary bars set in a fence for the retention of livestock. **1903** Stiles *4 Yrs.* 225 **VA,** There, right abreast of his wagon, was an enticing set of draw-bars. **1903** *DN* 2.312 **seMO,** *Draw-bars*. . . Bars. 'Let down the draw-bars so the cattle can go out.' **1907** *DN* 3.222 **nwAR, sIL,** *Draw-bars.* **1917** *DN* 4.411 **wNC,** *Draw bar*. . . A removable bar in a fence. **1937** (1963) Hyatt *Kiverlid* 30 **KY,** Watching Marthy Lou come down the path from the draw-bars with her piggin and pail brimming with foaming milk. **c1960** *Wilson Coll.* **csKY,** *Drawbars*. . . Poles or rails that can be drawn out of place to open a gap in a fence; also called a *slip gap.*

2 =evener 1. Cf **doubletree.**

1966–69 *DARE* (Qu. L47, *The two movable bars behind a team of horses are fastened to a longer piece; this is a ______*) Infs **ME**19, **MS**74, **MA**40, **NJ**44, **NY**62, Drawbar.

‡3 A crowbar.

1968 *DARE* (Qu. L39, *An iron bar with a bent end, used for pulling nails, opening boxes, and so on*) Inf **IN**27, Drawbar.

draw base See **draw gool**

draw bucket n

See quots.

1899 (1912) Green *VA Folk-Speech* 154, *Draw-bucket*. . . A bucket to draw water from a well. **1945** Colcord *Sea Language* 68 **ME, Cape Cod, Long Island,** *Draw-bucket.* A canvas bag about 2½ feet long, used to dip up water from over the side. Alongshore, since I was the bigness of a draw-bucket means since I was a small child.

draw day n [**draw** n **4**] Cf **drag day**

The day on which pay or rations are issued.

1868 *Harper's New Mth. Mag.* 36.794/2 **nwSC,** The first Monday of the month, generally known in the South as "sale day" on account of its customary public auction, acquired the additional title of "draw day," because it was used for the issue of rations. **1958** McCulloch *Woods Words* 52 **Pacific NW,** *Draw day*—Pay day. **1984** Wilder *You All Spoken Here* 74 **Sth,** Draw day: The weekly date to draw rations from the plantation commissary or the company store.

draw down fine See **draw fine**

drawed See **draw** v **B1, 2**

drawed over ppl adj phr

Stooped over.

1942 (1971) Campbell *Cloud-Walking* 84 **seKY,** Some folks were so drawed over with hoeing and grubbing and rheumatiz and raising up younguns that they couldn't do no good standing up. **1967–69** *DARE* (Qu. LL3b, *Shrunk, dried up: "He's a little ______ old man."*) Infs **KY**11, **TN**14, Drawed over.

drawed up See **draw** v **C3**

drawer See **draw** n **2b**

draw fine v phr Also *draw down fine*

To cut (something) close; to allow no leeway.

1923 *DN* 5.237 **swWI,** *Draw too fine, drawn* [sic] *down too fine. . .* To act conservatively. The figure is from drawing a bead in rifle shooting. "He didn't make much on that deal; he drew down too fine." **1968** *DARE* (Qu. KK45, . . *A narrow escape: "That time, he really had a ______."*) Inf **AK**5, He drew it fine.

draw fire v phr, hence vbl n *fire-drawing* Also *draw out fire*

=blow fire (out).

1968 *Foxfire* Mar 22 **neGA,** I can stop blood. I can draw out fire, and I can take off warts. *Ibid* 64, But if it's a pretty bad burn and I go to draw th'fire out of it, it hurts worse'n when it went in for a minute. . . But in maybe thirty minutes time it's quit hurtin' and you've forgot all about it. *Ibid* 70 **wNC,** About th'biggest point I get in that is t'add a little mystery t'th'party that don't believe maybe we'll say, in fire drawin'. **1972** *Foxfire Book* 367 **neGA,** To draw fire pass your hand over the exposed burn, open and palm down, in a direction away from you and away from the patient. . . Do this slowly *three* times, at the same time blowing gently on the burn. . . Simultaneously, and each of the three times you do the above, repeat the secret healing verse silently.

draw gool n Also *draw base* Cf **goal**

A children's game; see quots.

1957 *WELS Suppl.* **seWI** (as of c1890s), *Draw gool*—Sides chosen. Like "prisoner's gool" except captives from other side were absorbed by their captives [sic] instead of being placed in prison but subject to release by their side. Player leaving gool last could tag the other unless he got back home and touched his base. **1967** *DARE* (Qu. EE33, . . *Outdoor games . . that children play*) Inf **TN**1, Draw base—teams try to beat each other to the opposite base.

draw in See **draw** v **C1, 4, 6**

drawing See **draw** v **C7, 11, 13**

drawing spell n Cf *DS* BB6–7

1984 *Annals Internal Med.* 100.6.899 **cwAL,** I saw a patient said to be having a *drawing spell,* which was hyperventilation. A standard meaning of draw is to inhale. Patients with hyperventilation have trouble breathing in; they cannot draw in a satisfying deep breath. The condition is not simply a matter of excessive breathing, as the word hyperventilation indicates. A *drawing spell,* therefore, is a more accurate term than hyperventilation and is virtually specific in western Alabama of this diagnosis.

drawing spider n

Prob **=writing spider.**

1970 *DARE* (Qu. R28, . . *Different kinds of spiders*) Inf **VA**73, Drawing spider ['drɔɪn 'spadə]—A small brown spider. Its webs are called 'spit-webs' because the creature spits out the material.

draw in one's horse See **horse B13**

draw line n

In marble play: **=lag line.**

c1960 *Wilson Coll.* **csKY,** *Drawline. . .* Term in playing marbles. **1968–69** *DARE* (Qu. EE8, *The line toward which the players roll their marbles before beginning a game, to determine the order of shooting*) Infs **KY**11, **VA**1, Draw line.

draw lots of water See **draw water 1**

drawn v See **draw** v **B1**

drawn (up) See **draw** v **C3**

draw off See **draw** v **C1**

draw-off n [**draw** v **C1**]

A horse-pulling contest.

1981 *Greenfield Recorder* (MA) 5 Sept sec A 7, The horse-pulling contests were watched with keen interest, and I remember as a boy of 8 or 9, staying well after dark with my dad, watching the draw-off with some help from the headlights from the cars aimed at the pulling area.

draw one's checks v phr Cf **checks, cash in one's**

See quot.

1969 *DARE* (Qu. X48b, *Or if a person is not so young any more, you might say, "He's ______."*) Inf **IN**75, Drawin' his checks, over the hill.

draw out See **draw** v **C1**

draw out fire See **draw fire**

drawt See **drought A4**

drawth See **drought A3**

draw the fire See **draw** v **C8**

draw the frying pan See **frying pan 3**

draw the miller v phr

=drown the miller 2.

1940 *AmSp* 15.447 **eTN,** *Draw the miller.* To use too much milk in making biscuit. 'Tilda always draws the miller when she makes biscuit.' **c1970** *Halpert Coll.* **wKY,** To *draw the miller* = to use too much milk in making biscuit.

draw together See **draw** v **C4, 5**

draw up See **draw** v **C2, 3, 4, 5, 10**

draw water v phr

1 in phr *draw lots of water;* Fig: to be influential; to "carry a lot of weight"; hence *not to draw much water* to be inconsequential. [*draw* (a particular depth of) *water* of a ship: to have a draft of (a particular depth)]. Cf **drag a lot of water**

1916 Macy–Hussey *Nantucket Scrap Basket* 130, "Draw Lots of Water"—Influential, substantial, of some importance. **c1935** *Thompson Coll.* **cnAL,** Ol' man Chatman sure don't draw much water aroun' here since they caught him messin' up with that mill-town bat. **1967** *DARE* (Qu. HH9, *A very silly or light-headed person*) Inf **TX**5, Doesn't draw much water.

2 Of the sun shining through clouds: to display long vertical streaks of light. **esp ME**

1942 ME Univ. *Studies* 56.59 **ME,** When the sun behind a cloud showed rays of light it was said to be *drawing water.* **1950** *WELS Suppl.* **ME,** Sun *drawin' water*—sun giving illusion of vertical lines to and through the clouds. Sign of clear weather. **1966** *DARE* (Qu. B10, . . *Long trailing clouds high in the sky*) Inf **ME**5, Some clouds like streamers coming down were said to be "drawing water." **1979** *DARE* File **cnMA** (as of c1915), When you saw streams of light shining through thin clouds, you said to someone, "Oh look, the sun's drawing water!"

3 Of a tree: to lean toward water.

c1938 in 1970 Hyatt *Hoodoo* 1.57 **seNC,** Ve [=we] had a little tree up against de chimley *drawin water* [Hyatt: in folklore a tree leans toward water.]

draw well n [*OED* c1400 →]

See quot 1899.

1779 in 1906 *Documents Revol. Hist. NJ* 3.90, On said place is an orchard . . and a draw-well at the door. **1832** Kennedy *Swallow Barn* 1.296 **VA,** Amongst these relics of former habitation were the vestiges of a draw-well . . ; and the tall post, with the crotch in its upper extremity, still supported the long piece of timber that balanced the bucket, according to a device yet in use in many parts of the country. **1899** (1912) Green *VA Folk-Speech* 154, *Draw-well. . .* A deep well from which water is drawn by a sweep, a long pole and bucket.

drawy adj [*draw* to pucker, wrinkle]

Puckery.

1975 McDonough *Garden Sass* 237 **AR,** The important thing was to make sure that the fruit was fully ripe since it made the mouth "drawy" if it was picked before the first frost.

dray n

1 Any of various wheelless vehicles used for dragging heavy loads, esp: a **stoneboat,** a pair of runners supporting one end of a log, or a pair of poles on which a load can be placed. **chiefly Nth** Cf **crazy dray, drag** n **2, drag sled**

1902 White *Blazed Trail* 52 **MI,** A number of pines had been felled out on the ice, cut in logs, and left in expectation of ice thick enough to bear the travoy "dray." **1905** U.S. Forest Serv. *Bulletin* 61.30 **Nth,** *Dray. . .* A single sled used in dragging logs. One end of the log rests upon the sled. **1939** *LANE* Map 168 *(Stone Boat)* 7 infs, **eNEng,** (Stone) dray. **1942** ME Univ. *Studies* 57.132, *Dray.* Two large poles mounted on a set of wheels or on a sled at the front end, and at the rear end allowed to drag on the ground. **1943** *LANE* Map 573–574 *(Sled; Sleigh)* 1 inf, **swNH,** Dray, for hauling lumber. **1956** Sorden–Ebert *Logger's Words* 12 **Gt Lakes,** *Dray,* Two runners with a bunk in the center to haul logs out of the woods; a single sled used in dragging logs. One end of the log rests upon the sled, the other on the ground. Same as bob, crotch, drag-sled, lizard, scoot, skidding-sled, sloop, yarding-sled. **1958** McCulloch *Woods Words* 53 **Pacific NW,** *Dray*—A small sled or stone-boat used in logging with animals. Front ends of logs were placed on a bunk on the dray to keep them off the ground when being yarded to the landing. **1965** Needham–Mussey *Country Things* 88 **VT,** A dray is a short sled with a body pivoted on a pin, practically the same as a traverse sled with the back sled knocked out; it has the poles dragging out at the back. Drays was used in rough places, and generally loaded crossways with four-foot wood. A team of horses will draw more on a dray than on a sled, and it's much safer because it won't tip over so easy, and the horses don't get hurt so often. **1966–70** *DARE* (Qu. L57, *A low wooden platform used for bringing stones or heavy things out of the fields)* Infs **ME**12, 14, **MI**2, 8, 120, Dray; **ME**12, Stone dray; (Qu. N40a, . . *Different kinds of sleighs . . for hauling loads)* Infs **MN**15, **MA**122, **PA**34, **VT**4, Dray; **MI**27, Dray—just two runners over bob; **MI**56, Dray—one pair of runners and either a single bunk or a double bunk; **MN**5, Dray—a sleigh on runners for hauling freight; **MA**23, Dray—a short bob for drawing cordwood; everything sat on a slant; **NH**14, Sled and a dray—two-log frame in sled for pulp[wood]; **NY**68, Dray—the back end of the rack drags on the ground; **WI**18, Dray—way back; had wheels in summer, runners in winter; (Qu. N40c, . . *Sleighs for carrying other things)* Inf **NY**75, Dray—for hauling wood; it had a bob ahead and poles extending behind; sometimes had wooden runners like a log-boat.

2 also *dray wagon:* A wagon or cart for hauling loads. **widespread, but less freq S Midl, Cent**

1701 *Boston Rec.* 12 *(DAE),* Ordered, That henceforth no cart, Dray, Trucks or Sled drawn by either horse or horses, . . shall be suffered to pass through any of the streets. **1838** Gilman *S. Matron* 40 **SC,** "What is a dray?" "That thing, sir, with wheels, out by the potato-field." . . "That is a truck." "We call it a dray, sir," said I. **1901** Harrigan *Mulligans* 202 *(DAE),* Their massive trunks were heaped upon two large drays. **1903** *DN* 2.312 **seMO,** *Dray.* . . A wagon or cart used for hauling about town. Elsewhere a cart only. **1907** *DN* 3.230 **nwAR** *Dray.* **1965–70** *DARE* (Qu. N41b, *Horse-drawn vehicles to carry heavy loads)* 161 Infs, **widespread, but less freq S Midl, Cent,** Dray; **AR**47, 52, **MI**2, **NC**55, **NY**36, Dray wagon; **IN**56, Dray lines; (Qu. N41a, . . *Horse-drawn vehicles . . to carry people)* 15 Infs, **scattered,** Dray; (Qu. N41c, *Horse-drawn vehicles to carry light loads)* 15 Infs, **scattered,** Dray; **KY**86, **LA**12, **MS**16, **NY**2, **OH**39, **VA**30, Dray wagon; **OH**56, Light dray; (Qu. L13, *The kind of wagon used for carrying hay)* Infs **GA**45, **MD**38, (Hay) dray; (Qu. N11) Inf **MA**72, Dray—it was horse-drawn; **NC**13, Drays—pulled by a mule. **1966** *DARE* Tape **NH**5, We generally have the neighbors come with their horses and a dray, draw in that loose corn.

3 A motortruck.

1966–69 *DARE* (Qu. N11, *A very large truck used to haul freight, new cars, and other big loads)* Infs **CA**71, Dray [Inf was doubtful]; **IN**74, Dray; **WA**14, Dray [Inf corrected resp to *truck*].

4 See quot.

1966 *DARE* (Qu. O2, . . *An old, clumsy boat)* Inf **NH**10, Dray—flat-bottomed, for carrying loads.

dray v, hence vbl n *draying* Also *dray haul, dray in* **Nth**

To haul on a **dray.**

1872 *Newton Kansan* 29 Aug. 2/7 *(DA), (Advt.),* Draying . . attended to at all hours of the day. **1902** White *Blazed Trail* 49 **MI,** When you going to dray-haul that Norway across Pine Lake? **1905** U.S. Forest Serv. *Bulletin* 61.36 **Nth,** *Dray in.* To drag logs from the place where they are cut directly to the skidway or landing. **1967** *DARE* Tape **MN**4, Cuttin' it [=wood] and pilin' it by hand out in the woods, and then they'd dray it in. **1969** Sorden *Lumberjack Lingo* 36 **NEng, Gt Lakes,** *Dray in*—To skid a log. Same as drag in, skid.

dray dog n

1930 *DN* 6.87 **cnWV,** *Dray dog,* a helper to a hauler of tanbark, so named presumably because of the heaviness of the work.

dray haul, dray in, draying See **dray** v

dray road n

In logging: see quot 1905.

1905 U.S. Forest Serv. *Bulletin* 61.36 **Nth,** *Dray road.* A narrow road, cut wide enough to allow the passage of a team and dray. **1956** Sorden–Ebert *Logger's Words* 12 **Gt Lakes,** *Dray-road,* A long skid road to drag logs from woods to skidway. Same as drag-road, run-way.

dray wagon See **dray** n 2

dread v [*OED* c1250–1681]

To cause to fear; to frighten.

1933 *AmSp* 8.1.48 **Ozarks,** Doc he says I got t' go t' th' tooth-dentist, but it jest dreads me plumb t' death.

dread n

An attack of fear or anxiety.

1914 *DN* 4.71 **ME, nNH,** *Dread to me, it strikes a. . .* I fear it greatly. **1984** *Annals Internal Med.* 100.6.900 **cwAL,** They rarely, if ever, complain of depression. Their opening complaint, however, is often diagnostic: *I can't make myself go; I wake up in a dread; Seems like nothing don't satisfy me no more.*

dread colic n

1978 Massey *Bittersweet Country* 269 **Ozarks,** Common causes of death for adults were pneumonia, typhoid fever, and ruptured appendix, which the people called "dread colic."

dreadful adj, adv Pronc-spp *dradful, dreffle, dreffful,* **chiefly NEng** *dretful*

A Forms. Addit exx in **B** below

1845–47 in 1981 *AmSp* 56.155 **swIL,** It hangs on *dradful,* this hauling hay. **1848** [see **B** below]. **1871** [see **B** below]. **1874** (1895) Eggleston *Circuit Rider* 215 **NEng,** They was a dreffle craoud of folks to that meetin'. **1887** Freeman *Humble Romance* 255 **NEng,** Dretful. **1902** (1904) Rowe *Maid of Bar Harbor* 58 **ME,** Dretful. **1940** in 1944 *ADD* [Black], Dreffful. Maj. Hoople cartoon. **1941** *LANE* Map 426 1 inf, **cNH,** [dretfɫ]; 1 inf, **neME,** [dretfl]. **1959** Lomax *Rainbow Sign* 40 **AL** [Black], Sukie run onto that stump—a dreffful, dreffful fall—I hate to think about it now.

B As adverb.

Very, extremely. **chiefly NEng**

1704 (1825) Knight *Jrls.* 12 **MA,** I never see a woman on the Rode so Dreadful late. **1815** Humphreys *Yankey in England* 104, *Dreadful,* used often as, very, excessively; even as it regards beauty, goodness, &c. **1848** (1894) Lowell *Biglow* 44 **MA,** The parson was dreffle tickled with 'em. **1871** (1882) Stowe *Fireside Stories* 7 **MA,** He was a dreffle smart man, Cap'n Eb was. *Ibid* 54, Huldy was a dreffful chipper sort o' gal. **1892** *DN* 1.210 **MA,** Her [=a kitten's] mother was a dreadful good miser [=mouser]. **1894** *DN* 1.341 **wCT,** He's dretful farse [=fierce] to go fishin'. **1894** Twain *Pudd'nhead Wilson* 322, You are dreadful wet. **1907** *DN* 3.211 **nwAR,** *Dreadful.* . . Very. **1914** *DN* 4.71 **ME, nNH,** Them 'tarnal corns frets me suthin' dretful. **1916** *DN* 4.335 **Nantucket MA,** 'Twould muckle me dretful to go to bottom in an old tub like this. **c1960** *Wilson Coll.* **csKY,** *Dreadful.* . . An intensifier meaning very. **1985** *DARE* File **ME,** Dretful moderate: In Maine, someone slow of speech.

dreadless adv [*OED* → 1535, *"Obs."*]

1984 Wilder *You All Spoken Here* 170 **Sth,** *Dreadless:* Doubtless.

dreadnought n Also sp *dreadnaught, dreadnot* [*dread* v + *nought* nothing, and, by folk-etym, *not*]

1 =**fearnought. chiefly East** *old-fash*

1829 *VA Lit. Museum* 23, A dreadnought great coat, buttoned to the neck. **1852** *Knickerbocker* 39.203 **NYC,** The capacious pocket of our 'dread-naught!' **1876** *Wide Awake* 96 *(DAE)* **MA,** She put on the old waterproof dread-naught and her hood. **1958** (1972) Funk *Horsefeathers* 154, Sometimes the cloth is known as *fearnought* and the garments made from it are *dreadnoughts,* but the terms are often used interchangeably.

2 A fearless person.

1836 Irving *Astoria* 1.301, They proved to be three Kentucky hunters, of the true "dreadnought" stamp. **1942** Berrey–Van den Bark *Amer. Slang* 384.3, Dreadnaught . . *an aggressive woman. Ibid* 403.1, *Brave or plucky person . .* dread-not. **1970** Berlin *Best of Families* 30 **NY** (as of 1908), The older ladies who ringed the floor at dances and from under their parasols observed the beach were known as the dread-naughts. . . The young and even the younger middle-aged were afraid of their sharp eyes and their acid tongues. . . Self-appointed guardians of society must still exist though the young haven't even a name for them any more.

dream n

1950 *WELS Suppl.* **neWI,** Dreams—granules in the corners of eyes.

dream v

Std senses, var forms.

1 past: usu |drimd, drɛm(p)t| *dreamed, dreamt;* also *dre(a)mpt, dremt;* also **chiefly Sth, S Midl** *dre(a)mp;* rarely *dream, drem, dram(ed), dramp, drump.*

1893 *DN* 1.277 **wCT,** *Dream*—dreamt (pron. [drɛmpt]). **1894** Riley *Armazindy* 20 **IN,** I *dreamp'* about 'em. **1896** Harris *Sister Jane* 360 **GA** [Black], He say, 'I dunno how come. I speck I des up an' dremp it.' **1901** Harben *Westerfelt* 13 **nGA,** Some'n' you never dreamt could 'a' happened. **1908** *DN* 3.307 **eAL, wGA,** I dremp a dream last night. **1912** *DN* 3.575 **wIN,** *Dremp.* **1915** *DN* 4.182 **swVA,** *Dremp.* **1939** *Hall Coll.* **wNC,** His brother was telling me of a dream he dremp one time. **1946** *AmSp* 21.97, Some other forms from the dialect of Appalachia which are in more or less common use in Southern Illinois are as follows: . . *drempt,* dreamed. **1953** Atwood *Survey of Verb Forms* 10, The form *dreamed* /drimd/ is used by about one third of the informants in the East. . . The principal variant is *dreamt.* This nearly always shows the "intrusive" /p/, /drɛmpt/, and . . more often than not, loss of final /t/, /drɛmp/. . . Throughout N. Eng., N.Y., and N.J. there is nothing to indicate that *[dreamt]* is an archaic or receding form. . . Throughout the S[outh] A[tlantic] S[tates] *dreamt* is very clearly receding. . . Fifteen or 20 informants, nearly all in N.C. and S.C., use /drɪmp/ and /drɪmpt/ . . . Other forms that occur in isolation from once to three times each are *dream* /drim/, *dramp* /dræmp/, *drump* /drʌmp/, and *dramed* /dremd/. **1954** *Harder Coll.* **cwTN,** Dream . . past: dremp, occasionally dremt. **1965** *DARE* (Qu. OO31a, *To dream: "Last night I ______ I was going away.";* total Infs questioned, 75) 43 Infs, Dreamed; 20 Infs, Dreamt; **MS**69, **NM**7, Dreampt; **FL**19, **GA**3, Dremp. **1967** LeCompte *Word Atlas* 367, [In context "I dreamed all night"] Dreamed [7 infs] . . drempt [5] . . dream [4] . . dremp [2] . . dram [1] . . drem [1]. **1968** *PADS* 50.36 **swTN** [Black], For the past tense of *dream* nineteen of the twenty-two informants have /drimd/. Two of the ten type II informants . . have /drɪmpt/. . . [One] has /drim/. **1969** *DARE* Tape **KY**16A, He'd tell bad dreams he dreamp' every mornin', you know, he'd get up. And she'd say that's awful bad but it could be worse. **1975** Allen *LAUM* 2.13 (as of c1950), The eastern over-all 2:1 ratio between *dreamt* and *dreamed* . . persists in the U[pper] M[idwest] with no appreciable regional variation except that the frequency of *dreamt* is somewhat lower in Nebraska. *Ibid* 14, Minor variants are /drɛmt/ and, once, /drɪmp/. **1981** *PADS* 67.42 **cnMN,** Three-fourths of the Iron Range and other Minnesota informants alike use *dreamt* . . while *dreamed* is frequent for both groups. . . In *dreamt* Iron Range informants characteristically lack the intrusive /p/, whereas other Minnesota informants usually have it. One Iron Range informant of Cornish background . . has the form [drɛmp].

2 past ppl: usu *dreamed, dreamt;* also sp *dreampt, dremt;* also *dremp.*

1954 *Harder Coll.* **cwTN,** *Dream* . . past participle: dremp, occasionally dremt. **1965** *DARE* (Qu. OO31b, *To dream "I have ______ that same thing often.";* total Infs questioned, 75) 39 Infs, Dreamed; 18 Infs, Dreamt; **FL**19, **GA**1, 3, **OK**18, 41, Dremp; **NM**7, Dreampt.

dream about one's grandmother v phr Also *dream of one's great-grandmother*

To have a bad dream.

1942 McAtee *Dial. Grant Co. IN* 23 (as of 1890s), *Dream about your grandmother* . . "If you eat any more of that mince pie you'll ______", i.e., your sleep will be disturbed. **1978** *DARE* File **cnMA, swNH** (as of late 19th cent), "Mince pie at this time of night? Why, you'd dream of your great-grandmother!" Said to children who asked for indigestible food near bedtime.

dream boat n

A pedal-operated pleasure boat used on a small lake or pond.

1969 *DARE* FW Addit **cwGA,** Dream boats—pedal boats; frequent around here.

dream book n Cf **wish book**

Prob a mail-order catalog.

1968 *DARE* (Qu. BB51b, . . *'Magical' cures for corns or warts*) Inf **GA**44, I used to go to the dream book religiously.

dream cake n [Cf *SND dreaming-bread* (also *~-bit*) a wedding or christening cake; *EDD dream-bit* "a piece of wedding-cake to dream upon"]

1912 Green *VA Folk-Speech* 154, *Dream-cake.* . . A piece of the bride-cake put under the head at night to make one dream of his or her sweetheart.

dream-drunk adj

Extremely intoxicated.

c1940 *Hall Coll.* **wNC,** Dream-drunk. . . "That's when you're sotty drunk." "When you are so damn drunk you couldn't wake him up."

dream line n

1880 *Harper's New Mth. Mag.* 61.351/2, They represented that if a certain particularly salt strip in the centre [of a salt-fish], called the "dream line," were eaten before going to bed, the girl or the young man one was to marry would be indicated by appearing in a vision and handing him or her a glass of water.

dream off v phr

1942 McAtee *Dial. Grant Co. IN Suppl. 1* 4, *Dream off* . . have an emission of semen while asleep.

dream of one's great-grandmother See **dream about one's grandmother**

dreamp See **dream 1**

dreampt See **dream 1, 2**

drean See **drain** v, n[1]

dreap See **drip** v

drearisome adj Cf Intro "Language Changes" III.1

See quots.

1899 (1912) Green *VA Folk-Speech* 154, *Dearisome,* [sic] . . . Very dreary; gloomy; forlorn. **1984** Wilder *You All Spoken Here* 141 **Sth,** *Drearisome:* Gloomy; very dreary.

dreck n Pronc-sp *dreckt* [Yiddish *drek,* Ger *Dreck* excrement, filth, dregs] *urban, chiefly in Jewish and German settlement areas*

1 Excrement; filth.

1939 Aurand *Quaint Idioms* 12 [PaGer], "Hans," you'd better go to the store quick for some *Divel's dreck* (Devil's manure—because of its ugly, bitter taste—assafoetida). **1968** Rosten *Yiddish* 102, *Dreck.* . . 1. Excrement. 2. Trash, junk, garbage. 3. Cheap or worthless things. 4. Plays, movies or performances, in any of the arts, of grossly inferior quality. *Dreck* is forceful, but vulgar—like its English equivalent, "crap." **1968** *DARE* (Qu. L17, *Other names . . for manure used in the fields*) Inf **PA**158, Dreck—dirt. [Inf of PaGer heritage] **1971** *AmSp* 46.82 **Chicago IL,** [Words for] excrement and bowel movement: . . *dreck.*

2 By ext: Trash, junk; anything of inferior quality.

1939 *AmSp* 14.80 **Manhattan NYC,** A *dreck* is a dress which has been skimped in cutting, . . made of cheap, flimsy material, subject to fading [etc]. **1950** Bissell *Stretch on River* 222 **Upper Missip Valley,** And all the "beautiful dreck" of the big city. **1950** *WELS (Low-grade, or of poor quality: a piece of merchandise:)* 1 Inf, **seWI,** Dreckt—very common among Jewish people. **1968** Rosten [see **1** above]. **1971** Bright *Word Geog. CA & NV* 110, [drɛk] 1 response for 'junk'. Jewish informant. **1987** *Isthmus* (Madison WI) 5 June 33/1 **NY,** As it stands, the film is simply second-rate, drive-in dreck.

dreckich adj Also *drecky* **[dreck]**

Dirty; inferior, cheap.

1939 Aurand *Quaint Idioms* 13 [PaGer], I never saw such a *Dreckich* (dirty) child. **1969** *DARE* (Qu. KK6, *Something low-grade or of poor quality—for example, a piece of merchandise: "I wouldn't buy that, it's ______.")* Inf **NY**131, Drecky ['drɛkɪ]. [Inf of Jewish heritage]

dreckly See **directly**

dreckt See **dreck**

drecky See **dreckich**

dredge n[1], v Usu |drɛǰ|; also **chiefly N and Mid Atl, Delmarva** |drʌǰ| Pronc-spp *drudge, dreg*

Std sense, var forms.

1892 *DN* 1.210 **MA, DE,** *Drudge* . . to dredge. **1894** *DN* 1.330 **NJ,** *Dreg, drudge:* pronunciations for *dredge* among the oystermen. **1899** (1912) Green *VA Folk-Speech* 157, *Drudge.* . . A dredge. "They have been arrested for drudging oysters against the law." *Drudge.* . . To dredge; to catch oysters in deep water with a drudge—dredge. **1932** *Hanley Disks* **seCT,** We'd use [drʌǰɨz] with bags on 'em. . . On a good [oyster] bed you could haul those drudges as fast as four men could take care of the oysters. **1941** O'Donnell *Great Big Doorstep* 202 **sLA,** I coulda been a politician with the road paved in front of my house and drudge-boats named after my babies! **1945** Saxon *Gumbo Ya-Ya* 560

LA, Drudged—dredged. **1945** Colcord *Sea Language* 68 **ME, Cape Cod, Long Island,** *Dredge* (Pronounced drudge). To scrape up from the bottom, as shellfish. **1955** *AmSp* 30.75 **TN,** *Dredge* (also *drudge*). **1966–70** *DARE* Tape **NC**1, A [drʌǰ] for oysters; **VA**55, You ain't 'lowed to [drʌǰ] clams around here; **VA**112, That's them big heavy ones, big solid things, crab drudge, they're built the same way [as a crab scrape] only they're more heavier, an' they got long teeth on 'em. **1968** *DARE* (Qu. O9) Inf **MD**45, [drʌǰ] boats. **1976** Warner *Beautiful Swimmers* 54 **Chesapeake Bay,** Rough weather always made things slower. "Your drudge is like yerking on the bottom," he said. **1982** Heat Moon *Blue Highways* 391 **DE,** Scrape and pot for crabs in summer, drudge for oysters in winter.

dredge n² See **dredger 2**

dredge boat n [See quot]
=**shoveler.**
1956 *AmSp* 31.186 **LA,** Dredge boat . . *Bird* . . Shoveler. . . From its mud-digging proclivities.

dredge box n Also *dredging box;* pronc-sp *drudging* ~ Also called **dredger 1**
A small container with holes in the lid which is used to sprinkle flour (or some other powdered substance) over food.
1899 (1912) Green *VA Folk-Speech* 157, *Drudging-box.* . . Dredging-box. A small box, usually of tin with holes in the top, used to sprinkle flour on roasting meat, or a kneading-board. **1902** Sears *Catalogue* 593, *Dredge Boxes.* . . Size, 2¼ x 3½. Weight, each, 4 ounces.

dredger n
1 =**dredge box.**
1867 Hill *Homespun* 1.125 **NEng,** Spoons, and knives, and rolling-pins, and flour-dredgers. **1968** *DARE* FW Addit **CA**105, Flour dredger —used for shaking flour. It is *not* a flour sifter. [*DARE* Ed: FW's sketch shows small can approx 3″ high, 2″ in diameter, with handle and perforated lid.]
2 also *dredge:* A flour sifter. **NEng**
1939 *LANE* Map 134 **Boston MA,** [Flour sieve:] *Flour dredge,* with a crank. **1967–68** *DARE* (Qu. F8, *The kitchen utensil that you pass flour through*) Inf **CT**16, Sifter; some people call it a dredge; **MA**72, Dredger.

dredging box See **dredge box**

dreeft See **drift** v

dreeled-down adj [Prob *EDD drail* (pronc [dril, dreəl]) "To drag or trail along"]
See quot.
1950 Moore *Candlemas Bay* 170 **ME,** She wouldn't be bad if you took them sunbonnets off of her and them dreeled-down dresses, that without doubt was Candy's cast-offs.

dreen See **drain** v, n¹ **A1, 2**

dreened See **drain** v **A2**

dreep See **drip** v

dreet n [Norw *dritt* excrement] Cf **dreck**
Manure.
1950 *WELS (Names for barnyard fertilizer used in the fields)* 1 Inf, **swWI,** Dreet. [Inf of Norw parentage]

dreffle, dreful See **dreadful**

dreg See **dredge** n¹, v

dreidel n Also sp *dreydel* [Yiddish *dreidl* < Ger *drehen* to turn] *in Jewish communities*
A four-sided die, each side bearing a Hebrew letter, which spins like a top and is used as a toy, esp during the celebration of Hanukkah; also, a game played with the dreidel.
1967 *Canarsie Courier* (Brooklyn NY) 21 Dec 7/2, Chanukah bags with candies and dreidles [sic] will be distributed to the children. **1970** Feinsilver *Yiddish* 235, *Dreydel*—Little top used on Chanuka for a game of put-and-take. On each of the four sides of the top, there is a Hebrew letter which stands for one of the four words associated with the holiday: *Neys godol hayo shom.* **1979** *Capital Times* (Madison WI) 15 Dec 9/2, We play dreidel, which is a game with a top. . . There are four Hebrew letters on the dreidel.

drem See **dream 1**

dremp See **dream 1, 2**

drempt See **dream 1**

dremt See **dream 1, 2**

drench n
1 A drink, draft.
1942 (1960) Robertson *Red Hills* 73 **SC** [Black], When she finds she is not going to fall asleep at all, she just gets up and takes a drench of wine.
2 In tobacco growing: see quot. [By ext from *drench* a medicinal or poisonous draft] Cf **drench** v **2**
1966 *PADS* 45.11 **KY,** *Drench.* . . A water-borne chemical used to sterilize tobacco beds. . . "Vapam is a type of drench."

drench v
1 as vbl n *drenching:* Administering a drink (to a person). [By ext from *drench* to administer a dose of medicine to an animal]
1968 *DARE* FW Addit **neWV,** A drenching is pouring the tea down someone's throat.
2 In tobacco growing: see quot 1966. Cf **drench** n **2**
1966 *PADS* 45.11 **KY,** *Drench.* . . To sterilize by soaking chemicals into the soil of the tobacco bed. . . "I use a hand sprinkler to drench my beds." [**1967** Key *Tobacco Vocab.* **KY,** [Drenching] used to be done, but [is] hardly ever known now.]
‡**3** To rinse.
1973 Allen *LAUM* 1.202 **ND** (as of c1950), She *rinses* the dishes. . . One inf. . . responded with *drench,* a use perhaps reflecting a confusion with the phonological variant *rench.*
4 In marble play: see quot.
1950 *WELS Suppl.* **seWI,** *Drench*—to win over one's opponent. Used by kids in marble games.

drencher n Cf *goose-drencher* (at **goose-drownder**)
A downpour, cloudburst.
1950 *WELS (A heavy rain that keeps on falling)* 2 Infs, **csWI,** Drencher; *(A sudden, very heavy rain)* 1 Inf, **seWI,** Drencher. **1965–70** *DARE* (Qu. B24, . . *A sudden, very heavy rain*) Infs **ID**1, **IL**71, **KY**28, **NE**7, Drencher; (Qu. B25, . . *A very heavy rain*) Infs **CA**21, 117, **IL**124, **KY**66, **MI**118, **NH**16, **NY**198, **UT**5, **WI**10, Drencher. **1984** *DARE* File **UT,** *(Joking names for a very heavy rain: you might say, "It's a regular ———.")* Drencher.

drenching See **drench** v **1**

drench one's gizzard v phr Cf *DS* DD17
To drink liquor immoderately.
1930 *Outlook* 26 Mar 154.516/2 **VA,** Our more affluent citizens . . run up to New York to drench their gizzards. **1942** Berrey–Van den Bark *Amer. Slang* 102.22, *Drink liquor, esp. intemperately.* . . drench the gizzard.

dress v
1 To array, deck, arrange; spec:
a To set (a table).
1942 in 1944 *ADD* **WV,** Dress the table. **1966–69** *DARE* (Qu. G9, . . *"It's time to ———."*) Infs **IL**5, 91, **NC**14, Dress the table.
b To make (a bed).
1942 in 1944 *ADD* **WV,** 'Dress the bed.' Reported by 2 persons. **1943** *Times* (Pocahontas Co WV) 25 Feb 4/3 *(ADD),* A demonstration on how to care for a sick person . . [and how to] dress a bed.
c To prepare (a body) for burial.
1956 *Hall Coll.* **eTN,** Charlie shot Sam with a shot gun. I saw Sam layin' on the bed after they'd kindly dressed him.
d To harness (a horse).
1973 Allen *LAUM* 1.268 **SD,** [In context "I want to *harness* the horses"] 1 inf, Dress. [Labeled old-fashioned]
2 with *down;* also vbl n *dressing down:* To clean and salt fish for preserving. [By ext from *dress* to clean and prepare a food animal for cooking]
1861 *Harper's New Mth. Mag.* 22.460 **NEng,** The order was given . . to . . fall to splitting and salting [fish]. This operation, which is known as "dressing down," is performed on hogshead tubs or boards placed between two barrels. **1889** K. Munroe *Dorymates* 143 *(DAE),* Owing to the delay of the morning, the second catch had to be 'dressed down' by lantern-light.

3 also with *off:* To fertilize, apply manure to. Cf **dressing 5**

1795 in 1892 Washington *Writings* 13.112 **neVA,** Clover, when I can dress lots well, succeeds . . to my full expectation. **1804** Roberts *PA Farmer* 33, Manures cannot always be procured in sufficient quantities to dress all the land the farmer would wish. **a1817** (1821) Dwight *Travels* 2.343 **VT,** Lands, dressed with gypsum, have been equally favourable to wheat. **1968** *DARE* Tape **GA**39, The land has been turned well and worked, in order that the land can be dressed off good for seeding a good crop of okra.

4 To castrate (an animal); hence ppl adj *dressed* castrated. **PA, wMD** *euphem*

1930 Shoemaker *1300 Words* 17 **cPA Mts** (as of c1900), *Dressed*—A castrated animal, especially a dog. **1967–69** *DARE* (Qu. K70, *Words . . for castrating an animal*) Infs **MD**26, **PA**13, 153, 204, Dress; **PA**147, 198, Dressing; (Qu. K58, *A castrated pig is a* ______) Inf **MD**20, Dressed pig; (Qu. J3a, b) Infs **PA**72, 202, Dressed.

5 In **hoodoo A1a:** to sprinkle, smear, or otherwise treat (something) to give it magical power; to apply a magical preparation to; hence *dress up* to put a spell on (someone). Cf **dressing 6, feed** v

1931 *Jrl. Amer. Folkl.* 44.388 **New Orleans LA** [Black], I was sent out to buy a cheap suit of men's underclothes. This we turned wrongside out and dressed with the prepared graveyard dust. . . I had been sent to the prison with a "dressed" Bible. **c1938** in 1970 Hyatt *Hoodoo* 1.128 **cwFL,** Yo' rub dis ovah yore face. . . Ah have to *dress* yo' wit dis heah stuff to keep yo' from being scared. *Ibid* 1.371 **swAL,** He'd taken it [=a stocking] to someone and they had *dressed* it fo' him—that was to keep you down [=sick] in yo' laig and yo' feet. *Ibid* 1.711 **ceGA,** Yo' kin *dress* de house [to attract business], 'sposed tuh be wit rice. [*DARE* Ed: The rice is put in one's shoes for three days, then sprinkled on the floor.] **1939** FWP *These are Our Lives* 271 **NC,** 'Why, auntie,' I told her, 'you're tricked. Somebody has dressed you up.' The colored people say they've been 'dressed up' when they mean somebody has conjured them. **1967** *Psychosomatic Med.* 29.484/1 **Sth** [Black], One may have a root worker "dress" his hand so that merely touching the victim will bring on the hex. **1973** Walker *In Love* 69 [Black], I was to show Mrs. Kemhuff how to "dress" the candles in vinegar so they would be purified for her purpose [=to put a curse on another woman].

6 To address (a letter). [*OED dress* v. 16 *"Obs."* Perh simply aphet form of *address* rather than a relic]

1966–68 *DARE* (Qu. JJ14, . . *"I'll mail this letter as soon as I* ______ *it."*) Infs **AL**10, **PA**138, Dress.

7 To put shoes on (one's feet).

1968 *DARE* FW Addit **nNY,** Dress your feet. **1986** *DARE* File **cVT,** What is the distinction between clothing and footware [sic]? Some people around here will say—"dress your feet." . . There were clothing stores and stores that sold only boots and shoes.

dress n See **dressing 5**

dress around v phr [Calque; see quot 1907] **PaGer area** Cf **dress out**

To change one's clothes.

c1902 Clapin *New Dict. Amer.* 167, *Dress around.* In parts of Pennsylvania, to change outer garments. "I must dress around before I go to town." **1907** *German Amer. Annals* 9.374 **sePA,** *Dress around.*—Change clothes. "I must dress around before I go." . . fr. Pa. Ger. *rumshdripa;* Ger. *umziehen.* **1916** *DN* 4.337 **csPA,** *Dress around.* . . [Ger. *umkleiden.*] To change or adjust one's attire. "If you are going to town, you had better dress around first." **1939** Aurand *Quaint Idioms* 28 [PaGer], If I am going out this evening I must *dress around;* or *dress up!* **1987** *Jrl. Engl. Ling.* 20.2.169 **ePA,** Of the ten informants [of c105] using *dress around,* only one . . is not a Mennonite or Brethren.

dress down v See **dress v 2**

dress-down adj [By analogy with *dress-up*]

Informal.

1969 *DARE* (Qu. FF2, . . *Kinds of parties*) Inf **MI**93, Dress-down parties; (Qu. FF4, . . *Dancing parties*) Inf **NY**175, Dress-up; dress-down.

dressed See **dress v 4**

dressed egg n

A deviled egg.

1969 *DARE* FW Addit **KY**5, Dressed eggs. **1984** Wilder *You All Spoken Here* 90 **Sth,** *Dressed eggs:* Deviled eggs garnished with parsley.

dressed like a preacher See **dressed up like a preacher**

dressed out ppl adj phr

Well or fancily dressed; dressed up.

1967 *DARE* FW Addit **sePA,** You're all dressed out like Mrs. Astor's off-side horse. **1967–68** *DARE* (Qu. W37, *When a woman puts on her good clothes . . you say she's* ______) Inf **OH**16, Dressed out like a new saloon; (Qu. W38, *When a man dresses himself up in his best clothes, you say he's* ______) Infs **MO**17, **OH**4, (All) dressed out.

dressed up like a preacher adj phr Also *dressed like a preacher;* for addit varr see quots

Well dressed; spruced up.

1967–70 *DARE* (Qu. W38, *When a man dresses himself up in his best clothes, you say he's* ______) Infs **IA**12, **KY**8, **PA**57, **VA**35, Dressed (up) like a preacher; **MA**79, **NJ**3, (All) dressed (up) like a minister; **DE**2, Dressed up like a nigger preacher. **1975** Gould *ME Lingo* 80, *Dressed like a deacon*—All rigged out, all decked out, all duded up. . . The pious deacon has always been a low-comedy personality in Maine affairs.

dressed up like a sore thumb adj phr Also *dressed up like a sore finger* (or *leg, toe*) [Humorous ref to *dress* to bandage] *joc*

Overdressed, flashily dressed.

1919 *DN* 5.73 **NM,** There goes that girl all dressed up like a sore finger. **1951** *DE Folkl. Bulletin* 1.4/2, All dressed up like a sore thumb. **1951** Johnson *Resp. to PADS 20* **DE** *(When somebody dresses up in . . fine clothes)* Dressed up like a sore thumb. **1968** Adams *Western Words* 100, *Dressed up like a sore toe*—A cowboy's expression meaning *dressed in fancy togs.* **1968–69** *DARE* (Qu. W37, *When a woman puts on her good clothes and tries to look her best, you say she's* ______) Inf **GA**81, Dressed up like a sore thumb; **MI**78, All dressed up like a sore leg.

dresser n

A shelf, sideboard, set of shelves, or cupboard often placed in the kitchen and used as a work surface and a place to store dishes, utensils, etc. [*OED* c1420 →] **esp NEast** *old-fash*

1651 in 1880 Suffolk Co. MA *Deeds* 1.136, In the Larder, one square table bannisters dressers & shelvs round. **1710** in 1882 *Documents Colonial & Post-Revol. Hist. NJ* 4.13, A Pantry with dressers and shelves . . is under Lock & Key. **1775** (1934) Fithian *Jrl.* 2.116 **NJ,** Her Pewter on the Dresser glistened. **1868** Smith *Theatrical Management* 9 **NY,** Nicely-arranged "dressers" (shelves) for plates, platters, mugs, tea-cups and saucers. **1899** (1912) Green *VA Folk-Speech* 155. **1911** Wharton *Ethan Frome* 93 **MA,** She spread out the pieces of glass on the kitchen dresser. **1932** *Hanley Disks* **cMA,** But they used for their crockery what they used to call a dresser. . . It was space between . . two rooms . . and there was . . shelves on both sides and we called it the dresser. . . There was no doors, it was all open. **1941** *LANE* Map 339, *(Bureau)* 21 infs, **chiefly NH, ME,** Dresser. [Four infs say *dresser* is old-fashioned. Other comments: "For food, 'in the eating room' "; "an old term for the sideboard in the dining room"; "for dishes, in the dining room"; " 'a shelf to work on,' at the base of a wall cupboard"; "a broad shelf near the kitchen sink 'to put things on'."] **1968–70** *DARE* (Qu. E5, *A piece of furniture with a flat top for keeping tablecloths, dishes, and such*) Infs **CA**82, **MO**16, **NJ**64, **TN**60, **VA**22, Dresser.

dress horse n [Var of *clotheshorse*]

1968 *DARE* (Qu. W40, . . *A woman who overdresses or who spends too much on clothes*) Inf **GA**17, Dress horse.

dressified adj Cf **-ified**

Concerned about one's clothing; flashily dressed.

1943 Writers' Program NC *Bundle of Troubles* 26, He ain't got no use for that braggin', dressified dude nohow. [*Ibid* 27, [He was] dressed up fit to kill.] **1953** Randolph–Wilson *Down in Holler* 45 **Ozarks,** *Dressified* means particular about clothing.

dressing n

1 A sweet sauce used as a topping for desserts or pancakes. **chiefly Inland Nth, N Midl** See Map Cf **dressing gravy**

1931–33 *LANE Worksheets* **swRI,** Sweet dressing—a sweet sauce of any flavor, served with pudding. **1941** *LANE* Map 293 **scattered NEng,** [For 'a sweet sauce served with puddings' 7 infs offered the term *dressing.*] **1965–70** *DARE* (Qu. H66a, *The sweet liquid that you pour over a pudding*) 18 Infs, **chiefly Inland Nth, N Midl,** Dressing; **NJ**21, Cream dressing; **NE**8, Hard dressing; **MI**66, Pudding dressing; (Qu. H66b, *The sweet liquid that you pour over ice cream*) 14 Infs, **chiefly Inland Nth, N Midl,** Dressing(s); **PA**29, Fudge dressing; (Qu. H21) Inf **WA**27, Pancake dressing. [30 of 34 Infs old; one mid-aged Inf labels term *old-fash*] **1973** Allen *LAUM* 1.294 (as of c1950), *Dressing,* sporadic in New England, survives as a relic in the first settled parts of the U[pper] M[idwest].

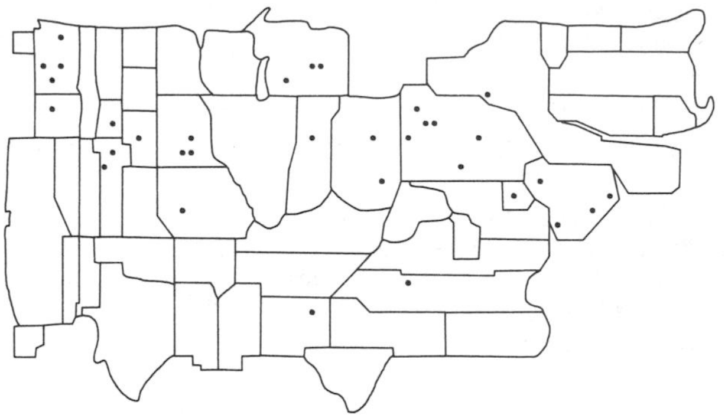

•dressing 1 + varr (Qq. H66a, b, H21)

2 Frosting.

c1960 *Wilson Coll.* **csKY,** *Dressing. . .* Covering for cake, icing. **1968** *DARE* (Qu. H64, *The sweet covering spread on top of a cake*) Inf **MO**10, Dressing.

3 See quot.

1897 *KS Univ. Qrly.* (ser B) 6.56 **KS,** *Dressing*—sugar and cream in coffee.

4 Gravy. **chiefly PA** See Map

1899 (1912) Green *VA Folk-Speech* 155, *Dressing . .* gravy. **1937** *AmSp* 12.204 **sePA,** [A Pennsylvania German] will very likely call *gravy* 'dressing.' **1967–69** *DARE* (Qu. H37) Infs **PA**9, 13, 22, 29, 40, 105, 136, 143, 146, 176, 200, **MD**28, Dressing.

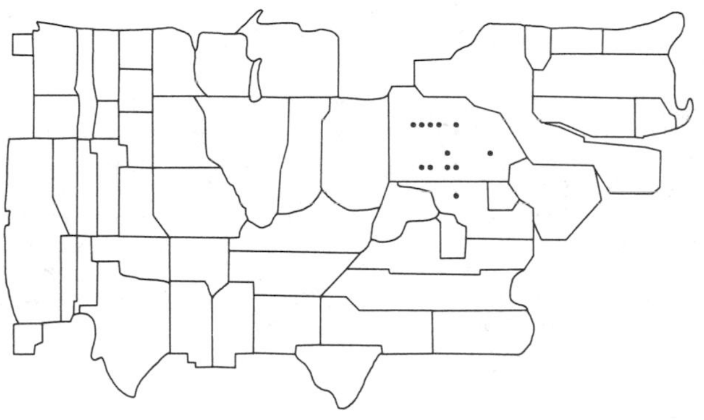

•dressing 4 (Qu. H37)

5 also *dress:* Manure used as fertilizer. **chiefly Nth, esp NEng** See Map *euphem* Cf **dress** v **3**

1872 VT State Bd. Ag. *Report* 1.71, Let the soil be stirred to the depth of a few inches several times during the summer, adding a dress of manure after each heavy crop. **1882** ME Bd. Ag. *Ag. ME* 26.50, The farmer finds that he can plant but little corn, because he has but little dressing. **1934** *Hanley Disks* **seMA,** Dressing. **1938** Damon *Grandma* 97 **CT** (as of late 1800s), The Cow . . did enrich our vegetation, though but willy-nilly; (in our circle men couldn't say "manure"; they looked embarrassed and said "dressing," at least before us [=children]). **1940** *Harper's Mag.* 182.107/2 **ME,** Manure is always dressing, never manure. I think . . that manure is considered a nasty word, not fit for polite company. The word dung is used some but not as much as dressing. **1950** *WELS (Barnyard fertilizer used in the fields)* 2 Infs, **cwWI,** Land (*or* top) dressing. **1965–70** *DARE* (Qu. L17, . . *Manure used in the fields*) 10 Infs, **NEng,** Dressing; **CT**2, **ME**12, **NH**3, **NY**96, **OH**87, **PA**178, **VT**2, **WA**20, Top dressing; **AL**11, **CA**101, **CT**6, **IL**59, **IN**8, **NY**200, 230, Meadow dressing; **NH**14, **RI**8, Cow dressing; **NH**14, Horse dressing; **WI**52, Soil dressing; **ME**5, Barn dressings. **1975** Gould *ME Lingo* 80, *Dressing*—Barn manure when applied to the land. Enrichment!

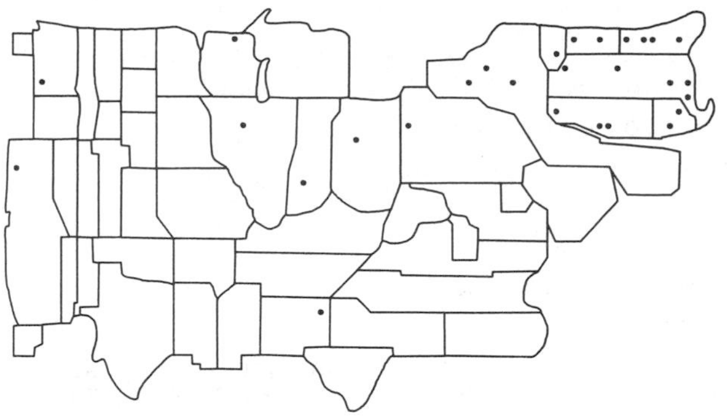

•dressing 5 + varr (Qu. L17)

6 In **hoodoo** n **1a:** something applied to an object to give it magical power. **[dress** v **5]**

c1938 in 1970 Hyatt *Hoodoo* 1.371 **swAL,** Yo'll find a . . spot on your floor that had a lot of new nails drove in de flo'. . . When you wash the house . . that will take the *dressing* off of those nails. . . That was to make yo' hold your head down and not look up to be happy when you were home.

dressing case n *old-fash*

A dressing table; dresser.

1834 *Amer. Railroad Jrl.* 3.726/1, Fine specimen of Portable Writing Desk and Dressing Case. **1885** Howells *Rise Lapham* 215 **NEng,** Irene pushed some of Penelope's things aside on the dressing-case, to rest her elbow. **1899** (1967) Chesnutt *Wife of Youth* 49, She went to the maple dressing-case, and opened one of the drawers. **1941** *LANE* Map 339 *(Bureau)* 1 inf, **cwMA,** Dressing case, with a mirror; 1 inf, **swCT,** Dressing case. **1964** Wallace *Frontier Life* 10 **OK** (as of 1893–1906), This room [=the "front room"] also contained the "dressing case" and "commode," with their marble tops.

dressing down See **dress** v **2**

dressing gravy n [*dressing* n attrib, something which enhances] Cf **dressing 1, gravy 1**

A sweet sauce poured over desserts.

1971 Wood *Vocab. Change* 45 **Sth,** A sweet liquid served with pudding is customarily called *sauce. . . Dressing gravy* is the second preference in Georgia, Alabama, Mississippi, Florida, and Louisiana.

dressing-out n Cf *blessing-out* (at **blessing)**

A severe reprimand; a dressing down.

1856 Whitcher *Bedott Papers* 331 **NY,** The Slaters was wonderful tickled to see the squire's wife git such a *dressin' out,* as they called it. **1969** *DARE* (Qu. II27, *If somebody gives you a very sharp scolding . . "I certainly got a ______ for that."*) Infs **GA**72, **NY**209, **VT**16, Dressing-out.

dressmake v [Back-formation from *dressmaker*]

To make dresses, be a seamstress.

1884 Jewett *Country Dr.* 6 **ME,** She might dressmake or do millinery work. **1891** (1967) Freeman *New Engl. Nun* 260, Lucy dress-makes, an' I hev to pick out all the bastin's. **1901** *DN* 2.139 **c,eNY,** *Dress-make. . .* To make dresses; act as a dressmaker.

dress off See **dress** v **3**

dress out v phr [Calque; see quot 1916] **PaGer area** Cf **dress around**

To undress.

c1902 Clapin *New Dict. Amer.* 167, *Dress out.* Often heard for undress, in Pennsylvania. **1916** *DN* 4.337 **csPA,** *Dress out. . .* [Ger. *auskleiden*] To undress. "Then I dressed out and went to bed."

dress-suitcase n

A clothes trunk or suitcase.

1965 Gould *You Should Start* 29 **ME,** No seafaring man ever took a trunk or a "dress-suitcase" aboard ship. . . in Maine you don't hear the term suitcase—it is dress-suitcase, in full.

dress-tail n

See quots.

1956 McAtee *Some Dialect NC* 13, *Dress-tail:*. . "I filled my dress-tail with apples and carried them home." This applies to the front, not the back, part of a dress, hence opposite to the usual meaning of "tail." c1960 *Wilson Coll.* csKY, *Dress-tail:* n. Dress.

dress up See **dress** v **5**

dress up drunk See **drunk** adv

dretful See **dreadful**

drew See **draw** v **B2**

drewed See **draw** v **B1**

dreydel See **dreidel**

drib n [Prob back-formation from *dribble, driblet;* also in Engl, Scots, Ir dial] **chiefly Midl** See Map Cf **dribs and drabs** n pl
A drop; a small quantity.
1862 in 1864 Raymond *Hist. Lincoln* 241, We are sending such regiments and dribs from here and Baltimore as we can spare to Harper's Ferry. **1908** *DN* 3.307 **eAL, wGA,** *Drib*. . . A driblet, a drop, a small quantity. "He paid him up in dribs." **c1960** *Wilson Coll.* **csKY,** *Drib*. . . A small amount. **1965–70** *DARE* (Qu. LL7, . . *"She didn't get the money all at once, they sent it to her _______."*) 13 Infs, **Midl,** In dribs; **CA**39, **IL**55, **KS**6, In (*or* by) little dribs; **KY**30, **PA**138, By (the) dribs; (Qu. LL6a, . . *"I'll take just a _______ of cream in my coffee."*) Inf **OR**1, Drib.

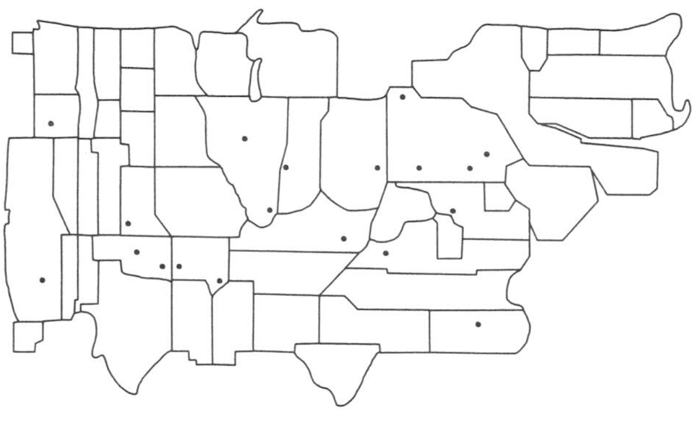

drib and drab adv phr Also *dribs and drabs*
Little by little.
1968 *DARE* (Qu. LL7, . . *"She didn't get the money all at once, they sent it to her _______."*) Inf **LA**45, Drib and drab; **PA**113, Dribs and drabs.

dribbies n pl Cf **jeberdees**
1968 *DARE* (Qu. W14, *Names for underwear*) Inf **MD**9, Dribbies—jockey shorts.

dribble v, hence vbl n *dribbling* [Engl dial] Cf **dribbles** exclam
In marble play: to cause a marble to move slowly, esp in short hops.
1899 (1912) Green *VA Folk-Speech* 155, *Dribble*. . . To move slowly; a boy *dribbles* by shooting his marble, rolling along the ground slowly towards its object. *Dribbling*. **1958** [see **dribbles** exclam].

dribble n [Perh var of *drivel*]
Nonsensical talk; chatter.
1942 Berrey–Van den Bark *Amer. Slang* 151.3, *Nonsensical talk* . . dribble. **1967** *DARE* File [Heard on television], Dribble talk—A kind of patter used by entertainers in which they never finish a sentence but go on into another and continue endlessly so.

dribble-drap n [Prob var of *dribbles and drabs* (at **dribs and drabs** n pl)]
A series of small amounts.
1966 *DARE* (Qu. LL7, . . *"She didn't get all the money at once, they gave it to her _______."*) Inf **GA**3, In dribble-drap.

dribbles n pl
1 also *dribbling shits:* Looseness of the bowels. Also called **drizzles**
1967–69 *DARE* (Qu. BB19) Infs **GA**72, **IL**7, (The) dribbles; **LA**14, The dribbling shits.
2 Incontinence.
1969 *DARE* (Qu. BB20) Inf **KY**11, The dribbles.

dribbles exclam [**dribble** v]
1958 *PADS* 29.33 **WI,** *Dribbles*. . . A call claiming the right to dribble one's marble.

dribbles and drab(ble)s See **dribs and drabs** n pl

dribble-stick n [Prob var of *dibble* to dip repeatedly] Also called **dibble-dabble 1**
A game played in water.
1967 *DARE* (Qu. EE28) Inf **TX**33, Dribble-stick—one [person] swims under water with the stick and lets it go any time. The rest, on the bank, jump in and get it. The one who does, gets to dribble it next.

dribbling n Cf **drib**
See quots.
1899 (1912) Green *VA Folk-Speech* 155, *Dribblings*. . . Drippings of any liquid. **1903** *DN* 2.296 **Cape Cod MA** (as of a1857), *Dribblings* [drɪblɪnz]. . . Dregs. **1970** *DARE* (Qu. LL7, . . *"She didn't get the money all at once, they sent it to her _______."*) Inf **VA**50, In dribblin's.

dribbling vbl n
1 See **dribble** v.
2 See quot.
1966 *DARE* (Qu. P17, *What do you call it . . when . . people fish by lowering a line and sinker close to the bottom of the water?*) Inf **FL**7, Dribbling.

dribbling shits See **dribbles** n pl **1**

drib-drabs See **dribs and drabs** n pl

dribe v See **drive** v

dribe n See **drive** n

dribs and drabs n pl Also *dribbles and drab(ble)s, drib-drabs, dribs and drabbles, drips and drabs* [Redup from **drib**] **chiefly Nth, N Midl, esp NEast** See Map Cf **dibs and dabs, drib, drib and drab**
Small amounts, usu distributed over a period of time.
1942 *New Yorker* 1 Aug 20/2, It comes in drips and drabs. **1942** *Sat. Eve. Post* 10 Jan 54/1 **NJ,** Cheap, inferior pencils . . steal [time] in dribs and drabs. **1957** Battaglia *Resp. to PADS 20* **eMD** (*"They sent it to her _______."*) In dribbles and drabs. **1960** Rockwell *Adventures* 431 **NY,** "Cut me a slice," he kept saying, "I don't want shavings. A *slice,* not dribs and drabs." **1965–70** *DARE* (Qu. LL7, . . *"She didn't get the money all at once, they sent it to her _______."*) 61 Infs, **chiefly Nth, N Midl, esp NEast,** By (*or* in) dribs and drabs; **GA**12, **NY**55, 130, **PA**82, By drips and drabs; **CT**42, In dribs and drabbles; **IL**50, **TX**18, By (*or* in) dribbles and drabs; **GA**11, **MD**2, By (*or* in) drib-drabs; **PA**50, In dribbles and drabbles.

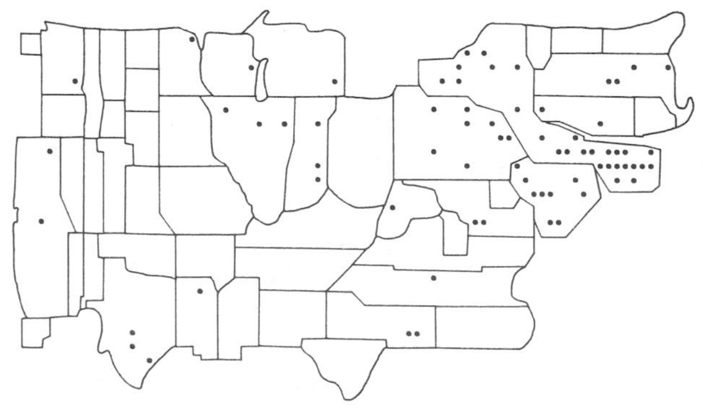

dribs and drabs adv phr See **drib and drab**

dribs-like adv [**drib**]
1908 *DN* 3.307 **eAL, wGA,** *Dribs-like, adv.* In small quantities. "His money come to him dribs-like."

driddle along v phr [*SND driddle* v. 2. (1) "To spill, dribble, trickle, drop in small quantities"]
To release in small bits; to string out.
1935 Davis *Honey* 102 **sOR,** He could take the measliest little episode . . and string it out and wool it around and supple it and driddle it along for hours.

driddle water n [Cf *SND driddle* v. 2. (2) "To urinate in small quantities"] Cf **horse piss**
1970 *DARE* (Qu. H74b, *Different words for coffee according to how it's made—very weak*) Inf **VA**42, Driddle water.

dried See **dry out**

dried-apple damn n Also *dried-apple durn,* ~ *cuss* Cf *DS* KK26
The smallest, most inconsequential thing.
1845 (1969) Hooper *Advent. Simon Suggs* 142 **AL,** I wouldn't care a dried-apple d—m for *'the boys'* to know it. **1859** Taliaferro *Fisher's R.* 117 **nwNC** (as of 1820s), But I helt a stiff upper lip; let on like I didn't care a dried-apple durn, and left. *Ibid* 204, But I was mad as flugence, and didn't care a dried-apple cuss whether I lived or died. **1908** *DN* 3.307 **eAL, wGA,** *Dried-apple dam(n).* . . Used to express the trifling or worthless nature of a thing. "It ain't wuff a dried-apple dam(n.)" **1940** *Hench Coll.* **cVA,** Gordon made a remark today I've heard him say often: "I don't give a dried apple damn whether he likes it or not."

drier See **drying cloth**

driffle v [Prob var of *dribble* or of *drivel* to trickle]
1906 *DN* 3.117 **sIN,** *Driffle, v.t.* To drip; cause to drop. "He driffles the molasses over the table."

drift n
1 See quot. [Scots and Engl dial *drift* a drove, herd, flock]
1952 Brown *NC Folkl.* 1.534 **c,eNC,** *Drift.* . . A great number.
2 also attrib: A persistent movement of a herd of cattle, esp in response to a storm; a herd that has thus strayed from its home range. **West** Cf **drift v B1, drift fence 1**
1907 White *AZ Nights* 112, There were present probably thirty men from the home ranches round about, and twenty representing owners at a distance, here to pick up the strays inevitable to the season's drift. **1920** Hunter *Trail Drivers TX* 213, When these 'drifts' take place every man . . is in front of the herd, holding them as much as possible. **1936** Adams *Cowboy Lingo* 73, Cattle will drift day and night in a blizzard until it is over. . . Such marching in wholesale numbers was called a 'drift.' *Ibid,* The single animal or a small bunch were referred to as 'strays,' but when a large number of brutes were 'bunched up' or 'banded up' and marched away from their home range, and so long as they stayed together, the group was said to be a 'drift.' **1941** Dobie *Longhorns* 119, In a way, drifts were more persistent than stampedes. A herd, more often than not in wet weather, might be impelled by something in cattle nature to drift—not running at all, but walking with solid determination. *Ibid* 196, In the spring of 1880 . . representatives from ranges in Nebraska, Colorado and even Wyoming . . , took part in the roundups . . in Texas in order to take their drift cattle back home. *Ibid* 200 (as of 1885), Probably not half of the original drift reached the home ranges. **1966** *DARE* Tape **NM**14, We would be fifteen or twenty days, workin' what we called the drift back onto their range where they come from. . . A drift wagon was just a reg'lar wagon composed of about half the amount of cowboys that usually worked with the summer wagons. Because it's only after these severe spells that the drift wagon would go out.
3 A mass of natural debris accumulated in a stream.
1804 (1904) Clark *Orig. Jrls. Lewis & Clark Exped.* 1.68, The Boat turned twice on the quick Sand & once on a raft of Drift. **1825** in 1940 *AmSp* 15.174 **VA,** Below the Old drift and on the west side of the Old River. **1856** Cartwright *Autobiog.* 329 **nIL, sWI,** I then pursued the creek . . in search of a drift or tree across the stream. **1858** Beckwourth *Life* 289, I came upon a gulch, or dry creek, in which was a drift pile composed of a large accumulation of dry wood. **1906** [see **drifting boat**]. **1939** *Hall Coll.* **wNC,** So I went on down and the bear was under a drift. They had came a waterspout in time and drifted in a whole lot . . of timber. . . I could hear the bear in the water under the logs a-splashin' the water. **1958** McCulloch *Woods Words* 53 **Pacific NW,** *Drift.* . . Flood trash and logs piled up on a river bar.
4 In turpentine production: a group of trees for which one worker is responsible. [Cf **1** above]
1935 Hurston *Mules & Men* 219 **FL,** He went out in uh drift uh woods. [Footnote: 10,000 "faces" in the turpentine woods, i.e. tree trunks that have been cut on one side to make the sap run from which turpentine is made.] *Ibid* 220, So de white man . . went back in de drift. **1948** Hurston *Seraph* 38 **FL,** He rode or walked through the "drifts" inspecting faces on the trees. . . Jim loved the silent chasms of the drifts. The growths, the birds and the sounds of the wind in the pines. . . The limit of a "drift," a territory of one chipper, is known as the "butting-line or block."
5 in v phr *put one on a drift:* See quot.
c1938 in 1970 Hyatt *Hoodoo* 1.844 **New Orleans LA,** [Inf:] To kill a person and *put 'em on a drift,* you know, have 'em sleepyfied? [Hyatt:] Yes, how would they do that? [Inf:] Well, you just takes a red candle . . [Hyatt: or] a black candle. And they burns that candle in ink for nine days, you'll just drift, just drift away, and you don't . . feel sick or nothing, only just drowsy and sleepy all the time.
6 The process of putting out and drawing in a fishing net. Cf **drift fishing**
1968 *DARE* (Qu. P13, . . *Other ways of fishing*) Inf **AK**1, We made three drifts this morning.

drift v Pronc-sp *dreeft*
A Form.
1931 *Scribner's Mag.* 89.453/2 **nFL,** "Won't they [=fishing nets] float, with all them big corks?" . . "Iffen they does float, they'll dreeft on beyant where we could ketch 'em at."
B Senses.
1 Of cattle: to move beyond the home range (usu as a group), esp during a storm; hence n *drifter.* **West** Cf **drift n 2**
1874 McCoy *Cattle Trade* 227, It was impossible to hold them in any given bounds. They were driven before the storm, or, in cattle man's parlance, "drifted" with the gale. **1941** Dobie *Longhorns* 188 **West,** His longhorns used to drift annually . . from sixty to seventy-five miles to the salt waters of Crooked Creek. After satisfying their spring craving for salt, they would generally return to the home range. **1943** Hamner *Short Grass* 57, The strays . . drifted before the wind, a pounding, maddened mass, with cowboys vainly trying to stem the motion. **1956** Moody *Home Ranch* 221 **CO** (as of 1911), A few were lying down, others stood humped with their tails to the storm, and some were drifting away down the wind. If the drifters weren't stopped before full dark came on, I knew they'd keep right on going all night. **1966** *DARE* Tape **OK**30, Cattle should not be allowed to drift in a storm.
2 To depart.
1930 *AmSp* 5.238 [Colgate University slang], Drift, brother, and close that door behind you. **1931** *AmSp* 6.204 **MO** [University slang], *Drift:* go away, get out. **1967** *DARE* (Qu. Y18, *To leave in a hurry: "Before they find this out, we'd better________!"*) Inf **KS**6, Drift. **1972** Claerbaut *Black Jargon* 63, *Drift* . . to leave; go away: *Got to drift out of this place.*
3 with *up:* To gather together; hence phr *it's drifting up rain* it's clouding up and threatening rain.
1954 *Harder Coll.* **cwTN,** *Drift up*—To gather in a crowd. "Whar's 'em folks driftin' up?" means 'Where are they gathering?' *Ibid,* It's a-driftin' up rain.
4 To dig a tunnel; to make by digging or tunneling; hence vbl n *drifting.* [*drift* a mine tunnel] **chiefly West**
1851 in 1922 Clappe *Shirley Letters* 82 **neCA,** I intend, some day, . . to bore you with profound remarks upon the claiming, drifting, sluicing, ditching, fluming, and coyoting politics of the "diggins." **1853** *Harper's New Mth. Mag.* 6.447 **nWI,** The shafting and drifting gets only the copper which is in the immediate course of those operations. **1870** Victor *River of West* 80 **WY** (as of 1830), A pit is dug. . . The men then drift from this under a bank of solid earth, and excavate a room . . in which the furs are deposited. **1870** in 1872 U.S. Treas. Dept. *Mines* 179 **OR,** They have sunk a shaft . . over 50 feet, and intend to go to a depth of 200, drifting east and west at 100 feet. **1969** *DARE* Tape **CA**128, When you get back into the ledge, why then you drift on that. . . They drift in on this quartz, drive their tunnel. **1976** Hobbs–Specht *Tisha* 93 **AK,** "When you mine coal you have to tunnel deep down into the ground." "They do that here too sometimes," Robert Merriweather said. "It's what they call drifting."
5 To drive (cattle, etc) slowly. **West**
1895 *Std. Dict. Engl. Lang.* (Funk), *Drift.* . . To drive cattle slowly, letting them feed as they go. **1903** (1965) Adams *Log Cowboy* 51, Throwing the two bunches together, we drifted them a free clip towards camp. **1920** Hunter *Trail Drivers TX* 50 (as of 1882), Here the manager met us . . , saying the country up to the South Platte was easy driving and

that they would drift the horses along with two outfits instead of four. **1940** Writers' Program *Guide NV* 77, Moving cattle from one range to another *throws* or *drifts* them. **1958** Latham *Meskin Hound* 128 **cTX,** The hog hunters drifted a bunch of hogs down the long twisting canyon that led toward the rock pens. **1967** *DARE* Tape **TX**24, [We] drift cattle and sheep.

drift boat n
A boat which moves slowly to facilitate **drift fishing.**
1975 Evanoff *Catch More Fish* 149, Party boat skippers do a lot of drifting with their boats and get a lot of fish for their customers. In fact, these head boats are called "drift boats" in Florida.

drift cat n
Perh a **channel catfish.**
1966 *DARE* (Qu. P1) Inf **MS**72, Drift cat.

drifter See **drift** v **B1**

drift fence n
1 A fence built to prevent cattle from straying from their home range. **[drift** v **B1]** **chiefly West**
1907 White *AZ Nights* 243, [Parallel fences . . offered a check to the cattle drifting toward the clutch of the renegades.] *Ibid* 244, He . . had followed the trail of a stampeded bunch . . to the cut drift fences. **1914** *DN* 4.163 **NW,** *Drift-fence*. . . On cattle ranges, a line of fence to keep cattle from straying. **1920** Hunter *Trail Drivers TX* 344 (as of c1885), About sixty miles south of the Palo Duro River I saw my first drift fence, which had been constructed to catch drifting cattle during blizzards. **1941** Dobie *Longhorns* 198 (as of 1884), The plains afforded no harbor or shelter. As endless strings of cattle going with the wind crowded up to the first drift fence, the leaders stopped, stiffened and went down, to be trampled on by followers until piles of the dead made overpasses. **1941** Writers' Program *Guide WY* 461, *Drift fence*—Fence separating different ranges. **1966-67** *DARE* (Qu. L65) Inf **CO**19, Drift fence—a fence that would guide the cattle toward a windbreak; **SD**5, Drift fence—a long straight fence with wings on the ends to turn cattle back on the range; **TX**37A, Drift fence—where cattle are likely to drift. **1966** *DARE* Tape **FL**35, Eventually they got to buildin' a drift fence. That may cover a area of a whole county, y' know.
2 A snow fence.
1969 *DARE* (Qu. L65) Inf **TX**71, Drift fence—of picket or wire, close together; to keep snow from drifting.

drift fishing n
1 also *drifting:* Fishing from a slowly moving boat (usu following the current rather than using a motor). **chiefly Mid Atl, Gulf States**
1965-70 *DARE* (Qu. P15) 16 Infs, **scattered Atlantic and Gulf States,** Drift fishing; **DE**3, **FL**51, **KY**84, **LA**22, **NJ**31, **NY**82, Drifting; **NH**4, **VA**75, Drifting—going with the current; **DE**4, Drift fishing—without power; trolling—under power; **NJ**22, Drift fishing—drift with the tide; **CA**65, Drifting—going under six knots; trolling—over six knots; **LA**15, Drifting—just let 'er float; **SC**40, Drifting . . throwing net and drifting with it; don't use a motor.
2 See quot. Cf **float fish**
1956 Harlan-Speaker *IA Fish* 206, Float or drift fishing involves the technique whereby your bait is kept continually moving. . . drift fishing does not use the bobber and the bait is allowed to roll along or tumble over the bottom of the stream.

drift fowl n Cf **raft duck**
1953 *AmSp* 28.277, Some of the older denominations of wild ducks contained this element [=*fowl*]: *flocking fowl . . ; troop fowl . . ,* and *drift fowl* (redhead, canvasback, and scaups, D.C.), all in allusion to the pronounced gregariousness of these birds.

drifting vbl n
1 See **drift** v **B4.**
2 See **drift fishing 1.**
3 See quot.
1970 *DARE* (Qu. P15) Inf **VA**47, Drifting—hand lining or using gill nets.

drifting boat n Cf **drift** n **3**
1906 Johnson *Highways Missip. Valley* 253 **Missip Valley,** Certain of these gasoline craft are floating sawmills and are known as "drifting boats." In every bend of the river is lodged an enormous "drift" of floodwood—"millions of cords,"—explained a Cairo man. "And some drifts are a mile across. Why, there's enough firewood in the drifts between here and Memphis to supply the whole United States for six months. The drifting boats made considerable money dragging logs out of the mass, sawing them into boards, and selling the boards at the small towns along."

drift net n
A gill net with floats on the top edge and weights on the bottom, which drifts with the tide or current.
1870 *Amer. Naturalist* 4.515 **MA,** Fishing with 'drift-nets' is practiced in the night. **1880** *Scribner's Mth.* 20.492/1, The ordinary gill or drift net used for shad fishing in the Hudson is from a half to three-quarters of a mile long, and thirty feet wide. **1939** Natl. Geogr. Soc. *Fishes* 289, Drift nets vary from 700 feet to 1800 feet in length and from 24 to 45 meshes in depth. **1966-68** *DARE* (Qu. P13, . . *Ways of fishing*) Infs **DE**4, **WA**20, Drift nets; **GA**5, Shad net or drift net—lead line on cork line strung between two boats to catch shad; **MD**34, Drift net—long, fine-mesh net; let it drift with the tide out of a boat, haul it in after several hours; **MD**45, Drift net—throw it out of a boat, let it drift, then pull it in; **NC**10, Drift nets—from a moving boat; **NJ**21, Drift net—net floats freely with tide, you follow along in your boat; the net has cork rings on top, weights on the bottom; used for sturgeon long ago, offshore for mackerel.

driftpin n
In mining and logging: see quot 1958.
1942 ME Univ. *Studies* 57.132 **nwME** [Lumbering], *Drift Pins.* Steel spikes usually about 1 inch in diameter and of variable lengths, used to fasten *crib* [=logs fitted together in rectangles or squares]. **1958** McCulloch *Woods Words* 53 **Pacific NW,** *Drift pin*—A pointed iron rod used like a very big spike to anchor a timber. **1966** *DARE* Tape **SD**4, [Aux Inf:] Lagging [=timbers used to prevent mine cave-ins] would stand in upright and would be spiked in there with drift pins. That's nothing but an enlarged spike. **1969** Sorden *Lumberjack Lingo* 37 **NEng, Gt Lakes,** *Drift pin*—A heavy pointed iron rod used to anchor timbers.

drift smoke n
1958 McCulloch *Woods Words* 53 **Pacific NW,** *Drift smoke*—A light smoke from a slow-burning fire, drifting from the point of origin, making the fire difficult to spot.

drift up See **drift** v **B3**

driftway n [*drift* the driving of cattle; cf **drift** v **B5]** **NEng, now esp RI** Cf **driveway 1**
Orig a road used for driving cattle to pasture or market; now usu a private road open to the public for access to the sea.
1638 in 1878 Boston Registry Dept. *Records* 3.4 **MA,** Tenn acres of woodland . . butting west upon the drift way. **1729** in 1886 Braintree MA *Records* 132 **MA,** Then voted, that the way . . be continued to be a drift way for the use of the Town. **1884** Hale *Christmas* 41 **RI,** All rode down the drift-way together to Rocky Point. "Drift-way," . . is . . a cross-road to the sea by which the sea-weed . . may be hauled up to their homes. **1899** Corey *Hist. Malden MA* 63, The drift-way on the westerly side, towards the North River, remains only in the form of ancient rights of way to the salt marshes. **1939** *LANE* Map 44, 8 infs, **RI,** [4 infs indicate that a driftway is a private road, one adding that it is open to the public if it leads to the seashore.] **1955** Taber *Stillmeadow Daybook* 147 **swCT,** George's cows stand in pleasant aimlessness in the driftway as we go by.

drigail n [See quot 1931]
Used as an exclam—see quot 1967.
[**1931** Read *LA French* 36, *Drigail*. . . Effects, belongings, furniture; everything that one owns. . . The word is pronounced as if written *drigaille*.] **1967** LeCompte *Word Atlas* 342 **seLA,** Expressions of mild disgust . . drigail [1 of 21 infs]. . . *Drigaille* is dialectal for "baggage."

driggle n [Prob Engl dial *driggle* to fall in drops, trickle]
A bit of leftover food.
1968 *DARE* (Qu. H71) Inf **OH**65, I like the driggles on a pot roast—the scraps and broth left over.

dri-ki See **dry-ki**

drill v[1] [*OED drill* v.[1] "*Obs.* (exc. *dial.*) . . 4. To draw or entice (a person) *in, into* a place"] *relic*
To lure, entice (to).
1926 *AmSp* 1.416 **seGA,** The Jackdaw, the Raccoon, an' the Bear will eat the aigs. They shore love a aig. They're drilled ter it. They go right ter the place.

drill v²

1 In railroading: see quot 1889.

1889 *Century Dict.* 1771, *Drill.* . . On American railroads, to shift (cars or locomotives) about, or run them back and forth, at a terminus or station, in order to get them into the desired position. **1947** *Sat. Eve. Post* 1 Feb 53/3, Sometime between six and six-thirty the two cars for 139 are 'drilled'—shifted by a switch engine to the platform where the Washington train to which they are attached is being made up.

2 To walk, go on foot. *esp among hoboes*

1893 in 1902 *Independent* 28/2, Professional H.B's [=hoboes]—Those that make a Profession of Begging and stealing and won't work, never did work. . . This class never walk, or 'drille' [sic] as they call it: they will wait at a water tank, or the end of a division . . sometimes a week to get a train. **1927** *AmSp* 2.385 [Argot of vagabonds], The word *drill,* a relic of the Civil War, is still in use; it means "to hike." **1927** *DN* 5.444 [Underworld jargon], *Drill.* . . To walk,—a most humiliating calamity to the brethren of the rails. This degrading method of locomotion is also known as *marching* and *dragging one's piles.* **1930** Irwin *Amer. Tramp, Drill* . . to walk. **1942** Berrey-Van den Bark *Amer. Slang* 63.3, *Walk* . . drill.

drill n

1 Any of several marine mollusks which bore holes through oyster shells.

1881 Ingersoll *Oyster-Industry* 244, *Drill.*—A small mollusk. **1884** Goode *Fisheries U.S.* 1.696, Under the name of 'Drill' is included a numerous class of univalve mollusks, which are . . armed with a tongue-ribbon so shaped and so well supplied with flinty teeth that by means of it they can file a round hole through an enemy's shell. **1886** *Scientific Amer. Suppl.* 22.8868/1, The little *littorinas,* the destructive "drill," which works its way into the shell of the young oysters. **1894** *DN* 1.333 **NJ,** *Snail bore:* a mollusk, also called "drill," "borer," etc. **1948** *AmSp* 23.297 **WA,** One of the oysterman's worst enemies in the Puget Sound region is the *drill,* a sort of whelk or snail that bores through the oyster's shell and sucks it empty.

2 See **drill crew.**

drill bug n [Because it pierces the skin]

A mosquito.

1967 *DARE* (Qu. R15a) Inf **IL**26, Drill bugs.

drill crew n Also *drill* [**drill** v² **1**]

In railroading: a switch engine crew or yard crew.

1898 (1970) Hamblen *Genl. Manager* 26, Simmons . . was the conductor of a "drill," a switch engine crew. **1932** *RR Mag.* Oct 367, *Drill crew*—Yard crew.

driller n

=**downy woodpecker.**

1917 (1923) *Birds Amer.* 2.141, *Downy Woodpecker. . . Other Names.* . . Black and White Driller.

drill face n

=**Wilson's snipe.**

1956 *AmSp* 31.184 **WI,** Drill face. Common Snipe. . . From its long bill.

drillmaster n Also *drill sergeant joc*

A dentist.

1950 *WELS* 1 Inf, **seWI,** Drillmaster. **1968-69** *DARE* (Qu. BB52) Inf NY226, Drillmaster; WI64, Drill sergeant.

drindl n [By metath from *dirndl*]

A dirndl skirt.

1980 *DARE* File **cwMA** (as of 1953), *Drindl*—(used by two speakers).

drindle v Also with *away, out* Pronc-spp *drin(n)le* [Perh var of *dwindle,* but cf Engl dial *drindle* to trickle, run slowly] **chiefly S Midl, esp sAppalachians** Cf **pindling**

To diminish, shrink; to waste away, die out; hence ppl adj *drinling* in failing health.

1894 in 1983 Zeigler *Lexicon Middle GA* 84 **cGA,** The most of 'em [=bees] 'll jes' give up, and not do one blessed thing, they'll drindle and they'll keep on a-drindlin' until they'll all perish out, jes' so. **1923** (1946) Greer-Petrie *Angeline Doin' Society* 19 **csKY,** She totes a pa'r of specks [=spectacles] fastened to the end of a dimunt [=diamond] stick, and when she looks at you thoo [=through] 'em, you kin jest feel yose'f *drindlin'* away. **1924** Raine *Land of Saddle-Bags* 14 **sAppalachians,** I hain't no right to complain. I've had my health for nigh onto sixty years, but now I'm foolish [Footnote: Frail] and kind o' drinlin'. But all I want in this world's a chance to git to a better. **1933** *AmSp* 8.2.30 **eKY,** He had one neighbor who was *contrarious* . . and *witchy* . . , and another who was *flighty and drinlin'* (fragile and failing). **1942** Thomas *Blue Ridge Country* 289 **nGA,** When a body's old and drinlin'. **1942** (1971) Campbell *Cloud-Walking* 215 **seKY,** Seemed like after Sabriny was gone that Viny just sorter give down and drinled away. **1944** *PADS* 2.19 **sAppalachians,** *Drinlin.* . . Puny, ailing. **1946** *AmSp* 21.271 **neKY,** *Drinnle.* . . To dwindle. . . 'The creeks has just kindly drinnled out.' **1949** Webber *Backwoods Teacher* 206 **Ozarks,** Once a . . settlement of Slocums lived up it [=Slocum Holler], but now they had "drindled away," the old ones dying off and the young ones getting fancy ideas and moving to town. **1952** Giles *40 Acres* 4, Here there is a pocket of pure Appalachianism and our older people still speak the tongue. . . A person in ill health is said to be "drinlin'." **1969** Emmons *Deep Rivers* 85 **eTX** [Black], Mollie Braddix of Franklin, after the death of her father, kept seeing him every night. She was "drindlin' away" until the family were concerned about her health. **1984** Wilder *You All Spoken Here* 201 **Sth,** *Drinlin':* Puny; pindly; frail; in old age and decay.

drindle n [Engl dial]

A small channel to carry off water.

1939 *LANE* Map 41, The smallest watercourses, usually dry during part of the year, are called *brooks, rivulets* . . , *drains* . . , *drindles* or *runs.* [1 inf, **neMA,** offers *drindle.*]

drindle away See **drindle** v

drindle out See **drindle** v

drink v

A Forms.

1 pres (exc 3rd pers sg): usu *drink;* occas *drank* (cf Pronc Intro 3.I.6.d).

1937 *Frontier & Midland* 18.15/2 **eKY,** I was drankin right peart. **1954** *Harder Coll.* **cwTN,** I love to drank mek [=milk].

2 pres 3rd pers sg: usu *drinks;* rarely *drink.*

1966 *DARE* Tape **SC**16, But that drink pretty good.

3 pret: usu *drank;* also freq *drunk;* occas *dranked, drink(ed);* rarely *dranken, drinken(ed), drunked.*

1772 in 1915 *New Engl. Hist. & Geneal. Reg.* 69.15 **MA,** Abel Chase Drunked a Quart of Molases at Once. **1778** in 1886 MA Hist. Soc. *Proc.* 2d ser 2.445, Arivd at King Henricks Fort drinkd some grog in his pallace. **1855** *Knickerbocker* 45.454, He never drinked a drop after she talked to him. **1884** Jewett *Mate of Daylight* 201 **ME,** They said he drunk the spring dry three times! **1884** *Anglia* 7.252 [Black], To the regular forms of the Irregular verbs as used by the whites, the Negro adds the following forms of his own. . . *Pres.* drink—*Past.* drinked, drink, drunked—*Pass.* [sic] *Part.* drinked. **1893** Shands *MS Speech* 27, Even . . educated people . . say: "I drunk". **1908** *DN* 3.307 **eAL, wGA,** *Drunk.* **1923** *DN* 5.206 **swMO,** *Drinked.* **1953** Atwood *Survey of Verb Forms* 10, The preterite *drank* . . very strongly predominates among all classes. . . The preterite *drunk* . . is rare throughout the entire Northern area. . . It is also rare in the South. . . In the Midland *drunk* is somewhat more frequent. . . The preterite *drinked* . . is considerably more frequent than *drunk* in N. Eng. . . Elsewhere in the East . . there are scattered occurrences of *drinked* in all major areas. . . [About 15 infs] use the uninflected preterite *drink.* . . [There are rare occurrences of *dranked, dranken, drinken, drinkened.*] **1954** *Harder Coll.* **cwTN,** I drunk my coffee. I dranked it all up. **1962** *Mt. Life* 38.1.17 **sAppalachians,** The past and past participle of . . drink [become] drinkened. **1965-70** *DARE* (Qu. OO3b, *Speaking about drinking coffee: "There's not a drop left—we ______ [it all].")* 903 Infs, **widespread,** Drank; 77 Infs, **scattered,** Drunk; **GA**88, **KY**40, 81, **LA**6, **MS**79, 85, **MO**8, 16, **OH**88, **SC**7, **TN**27, Dranked [5 of 11 Infs Black, 6 of 11 gs educ or less]; **AL**11, 14, **AR**47, **KY**57, **LA**6, **MS**60, **NY**70, 88, **TX**32, Drinked [5 of 9 Infs Black, 8 of 9 gs educ or less]; **AZ**8, **MS**16, 24, **OR**3, **SC**9, 26, **TN**1, Drink. **1967** *DARE* FW Addit **swAR,** He went on back to the hotel and drinken him some coffee. **1975** Allen *LAUM* 2.14 (as of c1950), As the preterite, *drank* consistently is predominant from the East through the North Central states to the western limits of the U[pper] M[idwest]. . . Analogical *drinked* . . is used by only two infs. . . *Drunk* is used by two.

4 past pple: usu *drunk, drank;* occas *drinked, dranked, drink;* rarely *dranken, drinken(ed), drunken, drunked.* Note: Although for years *drunk* was recognized as the std participial

form, *drank* has been accepted by many cultivated speakers. See 1953 *AmSp* 28.106–11 and 1957 *College English* 18.263–65.

1726 *New-Engl. Courant* (Boston MA) 19 Feb 1/2, The quantitys of *Wine* and *Brandy-Punch* drank . . by these Clubs, is incredible. **1810** (1912) Bell *Journey to OH* 5 **MA,** The deacon has drank. **1884** [see **A3** above]. **1893** Shands *MS Speech* 27, Even . . educated people . . say . . "I have drank." **1908** *DN* 3.307 **eAL, wGA,** *Drank, pp.* Drunk. "I have already drank." *Drunk* is avoided by the fastidious, apparently on account of the association with *drunk,* intoxicated. The regular pp. *drunk* is in common use in rural speech. It is also used as a preterite. **1914** *DN* 4.72 **ME, nNH,** *Drinked.* **1927** *AmSp* 3.3 **Ozarks,** *Past participle* . . drinked, drank, drunk. **1933** Miller *Lamb in His Bosom* 212 **GA,** He had drunken too much. **1953** Atwood *Survey of Verb Forms* 11, Among the very large number of informants who do not use the standard forms the prevalent practice is the leveling of preterite and past participle. Thus throughout N. Eng. the usual leveled form is *drank;* but here, and elsewhere, those who use *drunk* or *drinked* as preterite forms also use them as past participle forms. The archaic past participle *drunken* . . is used by 15 informants. . . Nine of these are cultured informants. [Other forms that occur rarely are *dranken, drinken,* and (once) *drink.*] **1953** *AmSp* 28.108, In New England, the very citadel of the prestige dialect, the leveled combination *drank–drank* was recorded for 16 out of 42 cultured [Linguistic Atlas] informants. . . Elsewhere in the Northern speech area the incidence of the participle *drank* is not so high. *Ibid* 110, In West Virginia 5 out of 6 cultured informants . . responded with . . *drank.* . . In the North Central states there is a fairly high incidence of the *drank–drank* combination. . . The prevailing usage in the South is clearly *drank-drunk.* **1962** *Mt. Life* Spring 17 **sAppalachians,** The past and past participle of [drink] become . . *drinkened.* **1965–70** *DARE* (Qu. OO3a, . . *"The coffee's all gone—we must have ______ [a lot].")* 543 Infs, **widespread,** Drank; 447 Infs, **widespread,** Drunk; 14 Infs, **scattered,** Drinked [11 of 14 Infs gs educ or less]; **AL**14, **KY**40, **LA**6, **MS**79, 85, **SC**7, **TN**27, **VA**35, Dranked [4 of 8 Infs Black]; **IA**12, **MS**57, **MO**9, **SC**9, **TN**1, Drink (it up) [4 of 5 gs educ or less, 5 of 5 old and comm type 5]; **AL**11, Drinken; **PA**186, Drunken; **VA**42, Drunked. **1973** *PADS* 60.65 **seNC,** Among our informants we found the following preterite-past participle combinations: *drank : drunk* (5 [of 12 infs]); *drank : drank* (3); and *drunk : drunk* (3). **1975** Allen *LAUM* 2.14 **Upper MW** (as of c1950), [As participle,] *drank* . . is preferred by Types I [=old, with little educ] and II [=mid-aged, with approx hs educ] but is even the usual form for nearly one-half of the cultured infs. as well.

B Senses.

1 To provide water or other drink for. *arch*

1860 *Baraboo Republic* (WI) 19 Apr [2/2] **csWI,** I think that Madison ought to be perfectly satisfied with our eating and drinking them to the tune of nearly a thousand dollars. **1893** *DN* 1.277 **wCT,** *Drink* . . used often causatively, = to water: "go drink them oxen".

2 To be potable; to taste (good, etc). Cf **eat** v **B3**

1917 *DN* 4.411 **wNC,** "Wonder if that water'd drink." "That drinks right." **1923** *DN* 5.206 **swMO,** I got a-holt o' some likker 't drinked right well. **1966** [see **A2** above].

3 in phr *drink oneself up:* See quot.

1987 Jones-Jackson *When Roots Die* 117 **sSC coast** [Gullah], "Now I want you, Ber Rabbit . . de bring a gator tail de me—from the water." Rabbit say, "I can bring that!" Rabbit drank up heself [Jones-Jackson: got up his nerve], and he gone down de the river.

drink n Pronc-sp *drank* Cf Pronc Intro 3.I.6.d

A Form.

1937 *Frontier & Midland* 18.15/1 **eKY,** I went outside with a couple o' fellers to take a drank.

B Sense.

A carbonated, non-alcoholic beverage. **chiefly Sth** See Map Cf **bottled drink, cold drink**

1965–70 *DARE* (Qu. H78, *Ordinary soft drinks, usually carbonated*) 23 Infs, **chiefly Sth,** Drink(s). **1967** *DARE* FW Addit **AR,** *Drink* or *cold drink* is a carbonated soft beverage. **1967** *News Reporter* (Whiteville NC) 7 Aug 2/7, A passenger in a passing vehicle hurled a drink bottle from the car.

drink adj

Drinking; used for drinking.

1948 *AmSp* 23.236 **sePA,** *Drink glasses,* instead of drinking glasses, like P[ennsylvania] G[erman] *Drinkglesser. Drink water,* instead of drinking water, like P. G. *Drinkwasser.* **1987** *Jrl. Engl. Ling.* 20.2.169 **ePA,**

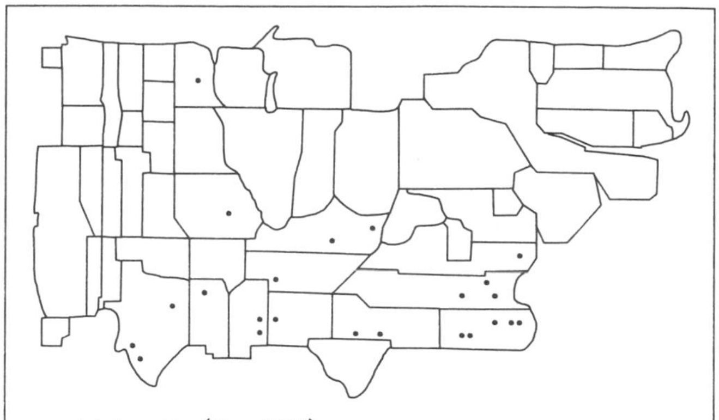

•drink n B (Qu. H78)

Drink glasses 'drinking glasses'. . . The only informant was a 20-year-old female Mennonite from Lancaster County.

drink a cherry soda (or a red soda water) See **drink muddy water**

drink at the branch v phr

1 See quot.

1905 *DN* 3.78 **nwAR,** *Drink at the branch.* . . In declining a drink a countryman sometimes says, 'No, thank you, I drank at the branch.'

2 See quot.

1984 Wilder *You All Spoken Here* 151 **Sth,** *I drank at the branch:* I'm ahead of you and your story.

drink box n [**drink n**] **chiefly Sth**

An ice chest in which bottled drinks are kept cold.

1967 *News Reporter* (Whiteville NC) 7 Aug 15/3, *For Sale:* One drink box. **1983** *Ledger-Star* (Norfolk VA) 5 Apr A4, Outside Williamston, . . [they] were lounging around the drink box at a store off U.S. Highway 64. **1983** *DARE* File **seVA,** The drink box was usually a box for all soft drinks (iced down) in a store. **1983** *NADS Letters* **ce, nwAL,** In Sylacauga . . I did get drinks out of a drink box in the small stores near my home. . . Many small stores in Alabama and throughout this area [Greenville, Laurens] still have drink boxes. Other[s] . . identified the experience of sticking a hand through the cold ice to pull out a co-cola or an RC. *Ibid* **cwAL** (as of 1950s), "Drink box" was definitely used quite frequently here in Tuscaloosa County during the Fifties. My uncle had a country store with a drink box and my father had one at his service station. We don't come across very many drink boxes anymore . . , but when we do, we still call 'em by their right name. *Ibid* **eGA,** Drink box: we have both heard this often: "Go back to the 'drink box' and help yourself," at filling stations and some small grocery stores.

drink coffee See **drink muddy water**

drinked, drinken(ed) See **drink** v **A3, 4**

drink from the same quill v phr Also *drink through the same quill*

To think or act alike; to get along well.

1967 *DARE* (Qu. II3, *Expressions to say that people are very friendly toward each other*) Inf **TN**15, They drink from the same quill; (Qu. II11a, *If two people don't get along well together, you'd say, "They don't ______."*) Inf **TN**15, Drink from the same quill. **1984** Wilder *You All Spoken Here* 4 **Sth,** *He and the devil drink through the same quill:* He's mean and sorry as the devil.

drinking adj

1903 *DN* 2.312 **seMO,** *Drinking.* . . Drunk. 'I suspect he is a little drinking.'

drink like a fish v phr [*OEDS* 1640 →] *esp among young and mid-aged speakers and among well educ speakers*

To drink alcohol habitually and excessively.

1849 Haliburton *Old Judge* II 151 (Taylor–Whiting *Dict. Amer. Proverbs* at *fish 12*), He drank like a fish. **1942** Berrey–Van den Bark *Amer. Slang* 102.22, *Drink liquor, esp. intemperately.* . . drink like a fish. **1956** McAtee *Some Dialect NC* 13, *Drink like a fish:* simile, that is all the time. **1965–70** *DARE* (Qu. DD12, . . *A person who drinks steadily or a great deal*) 22 Infs, **scattered,** Drinks like a fish; (Qu. DD17, . . *"He doesn't just drink, he ______."*) Infs **CA**191, **MA**123, **OH**90, **OK**48,

PA94, **VA**26, Drinks like a fish. [19 of 28 Infs young or mid-aged, 25 of 28 hs or coll educ] **1966** Barnes–Jensen *Dict. UT Slang* 14, *Drink like a fish* . . to imbibe liquor too freely practically all the time.

drink muddy water v phr Also *drink coffee, ~ a cherry soda, ~ a red soda water*

In var phrr used to indicate that a person is very thin or that a person is blocking one's vision: See quots.

1954 *PADS* 21.26 **SC,** *Drink muddy water:* . . *proverbial.* When one interferes with another's vision or stands in another's light, he is told that he has been *drinking muddy water.* If the intruder does not understand . . he is told that he has evidently been *drinking muddy water* since one cannot see through him. Darlington County. **1968–70** *DARE* (Qu. X49, *Expressions used about a person who is very thin*) Inf **PA**209, He must drink coffee so you can see him; **PA**237, Drinks muddy water so's you won't see through him; **TN**52, So thin you should drink muddy water to keep people from looking through you; **TX**98, You could drink a red soda water and look like a thermometer; **WI**47, So skinny she drinks a cherry soda and looks like a thermometer.

drink of black coffee n [In ref to the strong or bitter taste]

A severe reprimand.

1968 *DARE* (Qu. II27, *If somebody gives you a very sharp scolding, you might say, "I certainly got a ______ for that."*) Inf **PA**167, Drink of black coffee.

drink oneself up See **drink** v **B3**

drink one's milk from a saucer v phr

To indulge in malicious gossip, be catty.

1946 *PADS* 6.37 **VA,** She drinks her milk from a saucer too. (Said of a woman who makes "catty" remarks about someone, generally another woman.) Salem and Petersburg, Va.

drink out of a gourd v phr

To do the most rudimentary thing.

1967 *DARE* (Qu. JJ15a, . . *A person who seems* . . *very stupid: "He hasn't sense enough to ______."*) Inf **AL**27, Drink out of a gourd.

drink pudding n [Perh echoic]

A **bittern.**

1966 *DARE* (Qu. Q8, *A water bird that makes a booming sound before rain, and often stands with its beak pointed almost straight up*) Inf **ME**3, Crane or drink-puddin'.

drink some water and suck one's thumb v phr

1972 Cooper *NC Mt. Folkl.* 91, *Drink some water and suck our thumbs*—eat a scant meal.

drink through the same quill See **drink from the same quill**

drinkwater n Cf **jerkwater**

1970 *DARE* (Qu. N37, . . *A branch railroad that is not very important or gives poor service*) Inf **CA**210, Drinkwater.

drinky adj *arch* Cf **drinking** adj

Slightly drunk; tipsy.

1845 (1969) Hooper *Advent. Simon Suggs* 44 **AL,** But *then* he was "drinky and played careless". *Ibid* 166, When a little "drinky," he was wont to exhibit very fair horsemanship. **1859** *Harper's New Mth. Mag.* 19.572/2 **LA,** Being *considerable drinky* he . . concluded he could bluff. **1884** Harris *Mingo* 133 **GA,** "The boys wuz a little drinky," said Teague, apologetically.

drinle See **drindle** v

drinling See **drindle** v

drinnle See **drindle** v

drint v[1] See **drain** v **A2**

drint v[2], hence ppl adj *drinted* [*EDD drent* sb. "Also in form *drint*. . . A stain or mark left on badly-washed linen. . . 'If clothes are left wet . . , they will be covered with brown marks where the water has dried back; they are then said to have drinted, or to be covered with drint.' "]

1915 *DN* 4.242 **ceTN,** *Drint, v.i.* To fade. "The dress drinted a good deal." "The drinted spots were mostly on the under side."

drip v Pronc-spp *dreap, dreep*

A Forms.

1648 [see **dripping pan**]. **1929** in 1944 *ADD* **eWV,** 'Is it going to rain?' 'Well, it dreeped a few draps this mornin'.

B Senses.

1 To milk a cow; to empty a cow's udder; hence vbl n *dripping* the act of milking a cow or emptying the udder. [Engl dial] **Mid Atl** See Map Cf **drippings 4**

1970 *DARE* (Qu. K6, . . *Taking the last of the milk from the udder*) Infs **DC**5, **MD**13, **NC**37, **VA**10, 77, Dripping; **VA**57, Dripping; if you use an electric milker, you go back and drip 'em; (Qu. K8, *Joking terms for milking a cow.* . . *"Well, it's time to go out and ______."*) Infs **VA**40, 75, Drip the (*or* that) cow. [All Infs comm type 5]

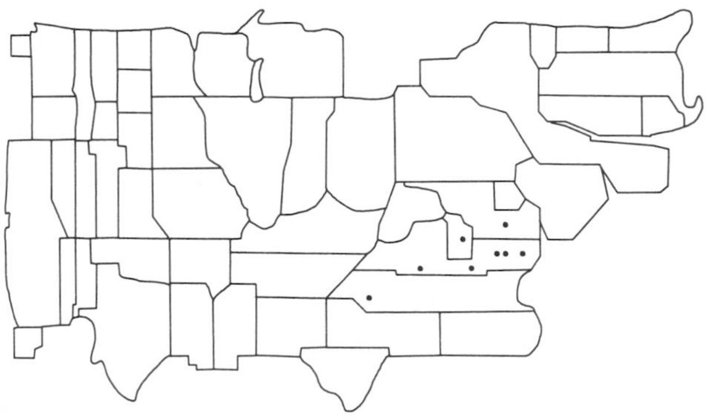

•drip v B1 + varr (Qq. K6, K8)

2 To brew (coffee) by letting boiling water seep slowly through finely ground coffee beans. **scattered, but esp LA** Note: As an adj (as in *drip coffee*), *drip* is widespread.

1885 Custer *Boots & Saddles* 15, And there the never absent 'eureka' coffee-pot was produced and most delicious coffee dripped. **1965–70** *DARE* (Qu. H73, . . *Preparing coffee* . . *"I think I'll go and ______ some coffee."*) 22 Infs, **scattered, but** 8 **LA,** Drip. **1973** Allen *LAUM* 1.296 (as of c1950), *Drip,* a singleton in St. Paul, refers to the special process of preparing coffee by allowing hot water to drip through the grounds. **1986** Pederson *LAGS Concordance,* [Of 20 infs using *drip* as a verb (as in "I drip my coffee"), 10 are from **LA,** 4 from **sMS.**]

drip n

1 See quot. **chiefly Nth** *somewhat old-fash* Cf **drib**

1965–70 *DARE* (Qu. LL6a, *A small, indefinite amount* . . *"I'll take just a ______ of cream in my coffee."*) Infs **CA**204, **CT**6, **MI**93, **MN**15, **PA**108, 167, 177, 234, 242, **WI**21, Drip; **VT**6, Drip or two. [10 of 11 Infs old, 7 of 11 coll educ]

2 The edge of a roof from which rain water falls; the ground area on which this water falls; perh also a gutter. [Cf *SND drap* n. 5 "The water which falls from the eaves of a house; hence 'the eaves of a house; the line of raindrops from the eaves'."] **chiefly S Midl**

1902 *DN* 2.233 **sIL,** *Drip.* . . In expression 'the *drip*' the eaves of a house. **1907** *DN* 3.222 **nwAR,** *Drip.* . . Eaves of a house. **1934** Vines *Green Thicket* 50 **cnAL,** In the fall the drip of the house was always filled with beech mast, acorns, and hickory nuts. **1966–68** *DARE* (Qu. D28) Inf **NC**55, The drip of the house is flat, and hangs over the gutter; (Qu. BB51b, . . *'Magical' cures for corns or warts*) Inf **NC**30, Bury a dishrag under the drip outside a house; **TN**16A, Tie a knot in a yarn-string for each wart, put it in the drip of the house; when it rots, the warts will be gone.

3 See quot.

1938 *AmSp* 13.5 **seAR,** *Drip.* . . Something easily accomplished. 'That course was just a drip for me.' Possibly a transfer from the use of this word for snow, a *soft* substance—one which is easily dissolved.

drip-drop n [Redup] Cf **drib, drip** n **1**

A small indefinite amount.

1970 *DARE* (Qu. LL6a, . . *"I'll take just a ______ of cream in my coffee."*) Inf **SC**69, Drip-drop or two.

‡drip-drop frying pan n

1968 *DARE* (Qu. F1) Inf **LA**17, Drip-drop frying pan—has little points inside the lid to let condensed water drip back onto the food.

drip drop the handkerchief n [Var of *drop the handkerchief*]

A children's game.

1957 *Sat. Eve. Post Letters,* When I was a child in Reading, Pennsylvania, we played singing games with these names: . . "Farmer in the Dell" . . "Drip Drop the Handkerchief."

dripping See **drip** v **B1**

dripping pan n Also called **baker-sheet, sheet pan**

A shallow rectangular metal pan used orig for roasting meat, now also freq for baking; also transf.

1640 in 1850 CT (Colony) *Pub. Rec.* 1.448, *An Inventory of the goods and Cattell of James Olmestead*. . . [includes] 1 dripping pan. **1648** in 1916 MA (Colony) Probate Court (Essex Co.) *Records* 1.93 **neMA,** A Box and a Dreaping Pan. **1759** *Newport Mercury* (RI) 26 June [4/3], To be Sold by Jacob Richardson. . . Iron-frying and Dripping Pans. **1834** *Life Andrew Jackson* 248, They say that your opposition is *personal and political,* 'cause it wont come intu, and be under, the direction of your *under,* or as some call it *drippin-pan* Cabinet! **1897** *Outing* 29.489/1 **MT,** The cooking utensils consisting of three dripping pans, one patented baker and one large coffee-pot. **1912** Green *VA Folk-Speech* 156, *Dripping-pan*. . . A pan put under meat roasting on a spit to catch the gravy, or *drippings.* **1926** *AmSp* 2.79 **TN,** She baked her biscuits in a dripping-pan. **1968** *DARE* FW Addit **cnVA,** Dripping pan—used for baking cakes, etc—13″ x 10″ x 2″. **1978** *DARE* File **MA** (as of c1920), Both my mother and grandmother used what they called dripping pans for baking rolls, biscuit, perhaps a large sheet cake. They were tin, shallow, rectangular, rather thin for roasting meat, I should think, which must have been their original use.

drippings n pl

1 Gravy made from the juice in the **dripping pan** when meat is roasted.

1916 *DN* 4.274 **LA, MA, NE, OH, PA,** *Drippings*. . . Gravy. "You have forgotten to bring in the drippings." **c1960** *Wilson Coll.* **csKY,** *Drippings*. . . Sometimes used for gravy. **1965–70** *DARE* (Qu. H37, . . *Gravy*) 43 Infs, **scattered,** Drippings.

2 Animal excrement; droppings.

1940 Stuart *Trees of Heaven* 248 **neKY,** I was lookin fer sheep drippins over the pasture field to see if any of my sheep has stummick worms. **1970** *DARE* (Qu. L17, . . *Manure used in the fields*) Inf **OK**53, Drippings, leavings.

3 See quot. [Perh **drip** n **2**]

1946 *PADS* 6.37 **swVA,** Under the drippings of the sanctuary. (Up close to the speaker; near the amen corner, etc.) Salem. Occasional among the *cognoscenti.*

4 The last drops of milk drawn from a cow. [Cf **drip** v **B1**]

1968 *DARE* (Qu. K6) Infs **NC**79, **VA**10, The drippings.

dripple n [Prob var of *dribble,* but cf *SND dripple* v. "To fall in small drops"] Cf *dribbles and drabbles* (at **dribs and drabs** n pl)

A small amount.

1968 *DARE* (Qu. LL7, . . *"She didn't get the money all at once, they sent it to her ______."*) Inf **PA**69, In dripples.

drip-primrose n

A primrose (here: *Primula mistassinica*).

1897 *Jrl. Amer. Folkl.* 10.50, *Primula Mistassinica,* . . drip-primrose.

drippy adj [Cf *EDD dreepy* "drooping, spiritless" (at *dreep* 4) and *OED dreep* "to lose courage, grow faint. . . *Obs.*"]

Lacking energy, spiritless, droopy.

1966–69 *DARE* (Qu. KK30, *Feeling slowed up or without energy: "I certainly feel ______."*) Infs **IN**57, **ME**11, Drippy.

driprock n **chiefly S Midl**

See quots.

1953 Randolph–Wilson *Down in Holler* 241 **Ozarks,** Driprock. . . Stone deposited by water, which forms stalactites and stalagmites in the Ozark caverns. **1954** *Harder Coll.* **cwTN,** *Drip-rock:* a rock that is formed from dripping of water. **1983** *MJLF* 9.1.38 **ceKY,** *Driprock* . . a dripstone, a stalactite or stalagmite.

drips and drabs See **dribs and drabs** n pl

drip torch n

In logging: see quot.

1960 *Seattle Daily Times* (WA) 30 Oct pictorial sec 10, [They] prepared drip torches, the tools used to set slash blazes. . . At a signal to begin the burn, the men lighted their torches, which drip fire when they are tipped up, and spread over the debris-strewn hill.

drisk n [Origin unknown; cf *EDD drisky* drizzly, from Cornwall] **NEng** *obs*

A drizzle, heavy mist.

1717 (1882) S. Sewall *Diary* 27 Apr 3.129 **MA,** My Calash defended me well from the Cold Drisk. **1851** (1949) Thoreau *Jrl.* 2.356 **eMA,** I sailed . . notwithstanding the drizzling rain, or "drisk," as Uncle Ned called it. **1857** (1864) Thoreau *ME Woods* 180, Again we mistook a little rocky islet seen through the "drisk," . . for the steamer.

driv See **drive** v **A2, 3**

drive v Pronc-sp *dribe* See Pronc Intro 3.I.17

A Forms.

1 pres 3rd pers sg: usu *drives;* occas *drive.*

1922 Gonzales *Black Border* 298 **sSC, GA coasts** [Gullah glossary], *Dribe*—drive, drives, drove, driven, driving. **1966** *DARE* (Qu. N12, . . *Somebody who drives carelessly or not well*) Inf **SC**26, He drive fool.

2 past: usu *drove;* also *driv;* occas *drave, drive, drived, driven(ed), droved, druv.*

1818 Fessenden *Ladies Monitor* 171 **VT,** Some provincial words and phrases . . *driv* for drove. **1845** Thompson *Pineville* 65 **cGA,** "And how fast they druv," observed one. **1884** *Anglia* 7.252 [Black], To the regular forms of the Irregular verbs as used by the whites, the Negro adds the following forms of his own. . . *Pres.* drive—*Past.* driv', druv', driven, drivened. **1890** *DN* 1.71 **LA,** *Driv.* **1893** Shands *MS Speech* 28, *Druv*. . . Negro for *drove* (verb). *Driv* . . is sometimes heard. . . Both *driv* and *druv* are common in Louisiana. **1902** *DN* 2.233 **sIL,** *Driv.* **1906** *DN* 3.134 **nwAR,** *Drove* . . [drʌv]. **1907** *DN* 3.186 **seNH,** *Driv. Ibid* 222 **nwAR,** *Driv.* **1912** *DN* 3.575 **wIN,** *Driv.* **1914** *DN* 4.72 **ME, nNH,** *Druv.* **1915** *DN* 4.182 **swVA,** *Druv.* **1923** *DN* 5.206 **swMO,** *Driv.* **1934** *Hanley Disks* **seMA,** I driv a pump there last fall. **1939** *Hall Coll.* **wNC, eTN,** Well, the drivers driv through, out to the Burnt Spruce Gap. **1954** *Harder Coll.* **cwTN,** *Drive* . . past: drove, droved (often), driv (occasional). **1965–70** *DARE* (Qu. OO40a, . . *"They borrowed our car last night and John ______."*) 974 Infs, **widespread,** Drove; **GA**23, 30, 40, **KY**94, **MD**20, **MS**69, Driv; **MD**43, **OH**60, **OK**57, **TN**11, **VA**22, 73, Driven; **KS**5, **NE**7, **NC**21, **SC**9, 26, Drive; **MD**20, **VA**22, Drived; (Qu. N7, . . *"We ______ to X last week."*) 764 Infs, **widespread,** Drove (over, down, up, *or* out); **VA**73, Drived; **SC**9, 26, Drive; **GA**30, **MD**20, Driv (down). **1968** *PADS* 50.36 **swTN** [Black], For the past tense of *drive* one of the seven type I [=old, with little educ] informants . . has /drovd/. **1972** Cooper *NC Mt. Folkl.* 91, *Drave*—drove. **1975** Allen *LAUM* 2.15 (as of c1950), *Drove* heavily dominates . . throughout the U[pper] M[idwest]. . . *Driv* . . turns up only twice. . . *Druv* . . is used by two UM Type 1 [=old, with little educ] speakers. . . *Drived* occurs once.

3 past pple: usu *driven;* freq *drove;* occas *driv, drive, droved, droven, druv.*

1676 in 1856 New Plymouth Colony *Records* 5.216 **MA,** Divers p[er]sons . . have, from time to time, drove into . . the lands att Pocassett. **1799** Williamson *Settlement Genesee* 16 **NY,** In the . . woods are abundance of deer; they may be easily drove into the bay. **1815** Humphreys *Yankey in England* 104, *Druv,* driven. **1864** (1868) Trowbridge *3 Scouts* 16 **TN,** The devils have stripped the house of everything to eat, and druv off the cattle. **1871** (1882) Stowe *Fireside Stories* 159 **MA,** He sees a woman in a cloak . . put into a kerridge, and driv off, atween three and four o'clock in the mornin'. **1890** *DN* 1.71 **LA,** *Druv.* **1914** *DN* 4.72 **ME, nNH,** *Druv.* **1915** *DN* 4.182 **swVA,** *Druv.* **1926** *AmSp* 1.417 **seGA,** These Alligators . . must 'a' driv all the fish out er this big lake. **1931–33** *LANE Worksheets* **csCT,** The hinges are two staples drove in; **ceMA,** I've been driv to death. **1940** Faulkner *Hamlet* 15 **MS,** Like he had druv up to the house. **1954** *Harder Coll.* **cwTN,** *Drive* . . past pple: drove, droved (often), driv (occasional). **1958** Hale *New Engl. Girlhood* 23 **MA,** But nowadays. . . I've been driven—"druv," as the old Yankees used to say—all summer. **1965–70** *DARE* (Qu. OO40b, . . *"That was the first time John had ever ______ [four car]."*) 778 Infs, **widespread,** Driven; 227 Infs, **widespread,** Drove; **GA**3, 30, 40, 72, **NY**183, **OK**52, Driv; **KY**6, **MS**1, **MO**21, **NY**209, Droven; **ID**3, **SC**9, 26, Drive; (Qu. OO27b) Inf **NY**4, I've drove horses. **1968** *DARE* Tape **NJ**21, He'd tell people how somebody'd drove up there and stold it. **1975** Allen *LAUM* 2.15 (as of c1950), *Driven* . . competes with analogical *drove* . . with the highest incidence of *drove* among Type 1 [=old, with little educ] infs.

B Senses.

1 To cause (a game animal) to run to a place where it can be killed; to pursue (a game animal); to hunt in this fashion. Cf **drive n 2**

1622 Mourt's Relation *Iournall Plimoth* 11 **MA,** [It was] onely a path made to driue Deere in. **1823** *MA Spy & Worcester Advt.* (Worcester MA) 10 Dec 3/3, Mr. Winslow in company with . . two of his neighbors, had been in the woods . . driving for deer or other game. **1838** (1852) Gilman *S. Matron* 210, The boys then commenced driving by whooping and riding about in the swamp, every now and then speaking to and encouraging the dogs. **1939** *Hall Coll.* **eTN, wNC,** Yeh, some'd go to the stands, you know, and generally two of us drove all the time. Just tuck two to lead the dogs, you know. **1966** *DARE* Tape **AR**15, You got to have a dog that what we call drives the fox . . a dog that just keeps drivin'; **SC**15, Do deer hunting with hound, driving, hound driving the deer and them sit on the blind. **1966–68** *DARE* (Qu. P39a, *When a hunter or a dog finds a game animal and makes it start running, you'd say he ——— it*) Inf **MO**25, He drove it; **OH**19, He drove it—like deer drives; **MI**32, Drives it out; **RI**6, **VA**8, **WI**78, Is driving.

2 To comb, scour (an area) in search of game or stray animals. **now esp Sth, S Midl**

1643 Williams *Key into Language* 141 **RI,** They pursue [deer] . . two or three hundred in a company . . when they drive the woods before them. **1646** in 1857 New Haven (Colony) *Records* 1.231 **CT,** It was propownded . . that bro: Cooper drive the necke . . whose cattle soeuer be fownd there. **1747** in 1906 *Colonial Rec. GA* 6.184, No Men or Horses . . were found capable of driving that Swamp and Places adjacent. **1853** Hammett *Stray Yankee in TX* 298 **seTX,** We must procure all the assistance that we can, and drive every thicket about here. **1869** *Overland Mth.* 3.126/2 **TX,** Sometimes, too, when they have made a march through a dense chaparral, they halt, go back, and 'drive' it, by riding systematically through it, in search of stragglers. **1921** *DN* 5.110 **CA,** *To drive the hill*. . . To go deer hunting. Sierra and Nevada Counties. **1939** *Hall Coll.* **wNC, eTN,** Our drivers driv the Easy Ridge and Pole Road . . and the standers stood on Bear Waller Ridge. **1959** Faulkner *Mansion* 31 **MS,** They came out with their . . bear and deer hounds and set the standers and drove the bottom where the bear had been seen but it was gone by then.

3 In logging: to float or direct (logs) downstream; to direct logs down (a river); hence vbl n *driving*. **chiefly Nth** See also **driving**

1846 (1864) Thoreau *ME Woods* 41, It was easy to see that driving logs must be an exciting as well as arduous and dangerous business. **1860** *Harper's New Mth. Mag.* 20.297/1 **ME,** When the ice clears out of the river all hands commence driving the logs down the stream. *Ibid* 448/2, How glad I am . . that you have obtained a substitute to 'drive' the river. **1864** *Mich. Gen. Statutes* (1882) I.1000 *(DA),* Such owner shall be liable to such corporation for the breaking of such jams, and the driving, booming, rafting of said logs, timber and lumber. **1902** White *Blazed Trail* 87 **MI,** Thorpe looked for some of Radway's crew 'driving' the logs down the current. **1944** Nute *Lake Superior* 211 **nWI, nMI** (as of c1900), Small camps often did their own "driving," however. **1947** *Sat. Eve. Post* 8 Mar 20/3 **WI,** He'd driven the Namakagon, the Totogatic, the Eau Claire and the main river before he'd gone to the Chippewa. **1958** McCulloch *Woods Words* 53 **Pacific NW,** *Drive*—To send logs down a river on the high water of fall rains (in the West) or on the spring freshet. **1966** *DARE* Tape **ME**19, There was a river driver—he'd drive 'em [=logs] down.

4 To throw.

1942 Berrey–Van den Bark *Amer. Slang* 66.3, *Throw; hurl*. . . drive. **1982** *DARE* File **swNH,** To drive a rock or something at someone (throw).

5 in phrr *let* (or *cut*) *drive:* To fire a gun, to throw something.

1893 *KS Univ. Qrly.* 1.139 **KS,** *Drive:* go, in 'I let drive with both barrels,' i.e. fired. **1919** *DN* 5.35 **KY,** Jep cut drive with a big rock an' scamped Dish. **1938** *Esquire* July 71 **neKY,** I took th' big ripe peach and I cut drive at that spider's eyes. **1939** *Hall Coll.* **eTN, wNC,** I cut drive at 'im. I was shootin' a thirty-thirty and I broke both of his underjaws, just snapped 'em in two. **1943** Chase *Jack Tales* 11 **wNC,** Jack he picked him out a rock and cut-drive at the giant in front—jumped him right in the back of the head. **1968** *DARE* (Qu. Y10, . . *"He picked up a stone and ———."*) Inf **VT**3, Let drive at him.

6 To hit.

1968 *DARE* (Qu. Y14a, *To hit somebody hard with the fist*) Inf **OH**47, Drive him.

7 See quot.

1944 *PADS* 2.42 **sVA,** *Drive at*. . . To do, to work at. Usually in questions. "Well, John, what are you going to drive at today?" . . Old people. Becoming rare.

8 in phrr *drive team* (or *truck,* etc): To guide work animals or operate work equipment (usu habitually or for a living).

1842 Kirkland *Forest Life* 1.115 **MI,** And when our friend Dan engaged to 'drive team' for Mr. Margold, he had no idea but that he was to be . . one of the party. **1862** Winthrop *John Brent* 280 **MO,** He ken drive team, an' do a little j'iner work, an' shoe a mule. **1907** [see **drive nails in a snowbank**]. **1913** London *Valley of Moon* 40 **CA,** I'll have to drive team to-morrow with 'em. **1959** Robertson *Ram* 124 **ID** (as of c1875), Father drove header-box. . . Obe drove derrick for the thresher. **1966–67** *DARE* Tape **MI**42, There was a German family up there . . and one a' the fellas, he drove team; **MI**2, After that I started drivin' truck.

9 See quot.

1927 *AmSp* 2.353 **WV,** *Drive* . . to take a female animal to be bred. "We will have to drive the spotted cow this morning."

drive n Pronc-sp *dribe*

1 A rounding up of livestock for a specific purpose, such as branding; the moving of lifestock overland, esp to a shipping point or marketplace. **chiefly West**

1846 Thorpe *Mysteries* 14 **LA,** In the excitement of the *drive,* horses fall, or run headlong over slow-footed cows. **1890** *Harper's New Mth. Mag.* 81.240/1 **TX,** [Cowboys] have little to do when not on the drive or in branding time. **1912** Raine *Brand Blotters* 121 **AZ,** [Melissy was] to make the drive herself in place of Antonio. There were fifteen hundred sheep in the bunch, and they must be taken care of at once by somebody. **1944** Adams *Western Words* 54, *Drive*—The moving of cattle on foot from one location to another.

2 A hunt in which animals are driven to a place where they may be killed; the place in which such a hunt is held or to which the animals are driven. Cf **driveway 2**

1833 *Sketches D. Crockett* 196, We were soon on foot, moving merrily forward to a small hurricane [=an area devastated by a hurricane], which had been agreed upon for a drive. **1835** Ingraham *South-West* 2.132, We . . proceeded . . toward the 'drive' . . as the hunting station is technically termed. *Ibid* 137, Our "driver," with the whole pack, had turned off into the "drive" some time before. **1856** *Knickerbocker* 48.356, Come up, my men, and get ready for a 'drive.' [Footnote:] This is the hunter's term for driving deer into a lake with hounds, and shooting them in the water. **1858** *Harper's New Mth. Mag.* 17.616/2, The [deer] hunters having finally reached the 'drive,' a consultation is held as to which *stands* are most available. **1890** *Opelousas* (La.) *Democrat* 29 March 4 *(DAE),* A California Rabbit Drive . . resulted in the death of 12,000 rabbits. **1922** Gonzales *Black Border* 298 **sSC, GA coasts** [Gullah glossary], *Dribe* . . a run, cover, or section of woods where certain game is found or hunted. **c1940** *Hall Coll.* **eTN, wNC,** *Drive*—The driving of animals by men and dogs in a hunt. **1967–70** *DARE* (Qu. P39a) Inf **OH**19, Deer drives; (Qu. FF16) Inf **MO**27, Fox drives; **TX**80, Rabbit drives.

3 A fence arranged to assist in directing the movement of animals.

1886 in 1909 Roe *Army Letters* 342 **MT,** At one corner of the corral was a small, funnel-shaped "drive," the outer opening of which was just large enough to squeeze a sheep through. **1890** *Opelousas* (La.) *Democrat* 29 March 4/7 *(DAE),* The rabbit scourge . . is now threatening parts of California. . . A drive has been made by stretching fine wire netting about three feet high and seven miles in length, A shaped.

‡**4** See quot.

1969 *DARE* (Qu. J2, . . *Joking or uncomplimentary words . . for dogs*) Inf **GA**74, He's an old drive.

5 A mass of logs to be floated downstream. **Nth, esp NEng**

1851 (1856) Springer *Forest Life* 41 **ME,** The butt log was so large that the stream did not float it in the spring, and when the drive was taken down we were obliged to leave it behind. **1889** (1971) Farmer *Americanisms* 215, *Drive*. . . In Maine and Canada a collection of logs brought together near a stream ready for floating. **1899** (1900) Van Dyke *Fisherman's Luck* 27 **NEast,** Every day the lumbermen sent a 'drive' of ten thousand spruce logs rushing down the flooded stream. **1909** *DN* 3.411 **nME. 1956** Sorden–Ebert *Logger's Words* 13 **Gt Lakes,** Drive, A body of logs or timbers in process of being floated from the forest to the mill or shipping point.

6 The process of floating logs downstream. **Nth, esp NEng, Gt Lakes**

1860 *Harper's New Mth. Mag.* 20.440/2 **ME,** The stream must be cleared of obstructions for the 'drive' in the spring. **1900** Bruncken *N. Amer. Forests* 84 **Gt Lakes,** There is usually a few days' interval between breaking camp and the beginning of the 'drive,'—the floating of the logs down the river. **1961** Holbrook *Yankee Loggers* 121 **NEng,** *Drive (The)*. . . The sending of logs down a river. The word dates from earliest days of logging in North America when this was the only way of moving the raw product to the sawmill over long distances. **1966–68** *DARE* Tape **WI**59, They would have a drive; **MI**47, A fellow that works on the drive; **ME**19, Roll 'em [=logs] down the river . . in a drive. **1968** *DARE* FW Addit **WI**59, *Drive*—The sending of the logs down the river in the springtime. Term used in the logging camps in and around Antigo, Wisconsin. **1969** Sorden *Lumberjack Lingo* 37 **NEng, Gt Lakes. 1975** Gould *ME Lingo* 81, *Drive* . . the whole business of bringing a harvest of lumber or pulpwood from the forest down a spring-swollen river to the mill.

7 See quot. Cf **driver 7**

1909 *DN* 3.411 **nME,** *Drive*. . . A row of trees partly cut and then driven down by a heavy tree felled against the end of the row.

8 A highway, road. **chiefly Sth, S Midl** *esp among Black speakers* Cf **driveway 3**

1965–70 *DARE* (Qu. N16a, . . *A highway with two lanes on each side and a separation down the middle*) 12 Infs, **chiefly Sth, S Midl,** Four-lane drive; **MS**72, 88, **MO**37, **SC**7, Two-lane drive; **MA**122, **MO**9, **NC**79, Two-way drive; **LA**7, **MS**60, Four-way drive; **IL**50, Divided drive; **NC**50, Four-way drive extry; (Qu. N20, . . *A circular arrangement . . where cars can go around till they come to the road they want*) Infs **GA**45, **MD**40, **VA**38, Circle drive; **OK**49, Cloverleaf drive. [9 of 23 Infs Black]

drive a beef off on foot See **drive home the beef**

drive a nail See **drive the nail**

drive barn n

1970 *DARE* FW Addit **nwPA,** The drive barn—a barn in town where everyone coming to town leaves horses.

drived See **drive** v **A2**

drive home the beef v phr Also *drive a beef off on foot* [See quot 1923]

To win the top prize.

1923 *DN* 5.237 **swWI,** *Beef, drive home the*. . . To win, or to gain, everything at stake. The figure is from the shooting match, in which one or more beeves were the prizes. The most expert shot won the four quarters and the hide, and therefore could drive his beef home. **1960** Hall *Smoky Mt. Folks* 17, "He . . was such a good shot that he was ruled out of most of the shooting matches. He driv many a beef off on foot." He was referring to the practice of awarding cows as prizes in these contests.

drive horse n Cf **lead horse**

1968 *DARE* (Qu. K32a, *With a team of horses, what do you call the horse on the driver's right hand?*) Inf **CT**6, The drive horse—the steadiest horse of the pair. You put a skittish horse near an old one.

drive-in n

A driveway.

1948 Manfred *Chokecherry* 11 **nwIA,** The graveled drive-in cut his feet.

driven See **drive** v **A2**

drive nails in a snowbank v phr Cf *DS* JJ15a

Fig: to perform the easiest task.

1907 White *AZ Nights* 62, I don't aim to run no home for incompetents. I had a son of a duke drivin' wagon for me; and he couldn't drive nails in a snow-bank.

drivened See **drive** v **A2**

drive one's ducks to a poor market v phr For varr see quots [*market* metaph ref to marriage; cf *EDD market* sb. 2. (4), (5) and *SND mercat* n. 4] **chiefly S Midl, Sth**

To marry unwisely; to move in the "wrong" social circle.

1933 Williamson *Woods Colt* 56 **Ozarks,** You're a-drivin' your ducks to a mighty pore puddle, if that's your idy of a gal. **1939** *AmSp* 14.263 **sIN,** 'She drove her ducks to a poor market,' said of a girl making a bad marriage. **1946** Stuart *Tales Plum Grove* 133 **seKY,** "He's driven his goose to a bad market," Pa said. **1951** Porter *Rugged Roads* 34 **OK,** Here was a woman whose poise, intelligence, and pleasant manner implied true greatness, but who after all, had perhaps driven her ducks to a poor market. **1966–70** *DARE* (Qu. AA15c, . . *Joking ways . . of saying that a woman is getting married*) Inf **KY**74, Taken her ducks to a poor market; **NC**36, She drove her ducks to a poor market; **TX**6, Drove her ducks to a hell of a bad market; **TX**42, Drove her ducks to a poor market—if he's not worth much; (Qu. AA15b, . . *A man is getting married*) Inf **NY**234, He drove his ducks to market [FW: laughter]. **1967** *DARE* FW Addit **sePA,** She drove her pigs to a poor market = she made a poor marriage. **c1970** *Halpert Coll.* **wKY, TN,** Driving her ducks to a poor (bad) market = marrying poorly. **1984** Wilder *You All Spoken Here* 150 **Sth,** *She drove her ducks to a bad market; drove her ducks to a poor puddle:* She fell in with the wrong crowd and went to the bad.

drive pigs See **call hogs**

driver n

1 One who herds cattle overland; one who rounds up cattle or horses. **chiefly West**

1884 *Harper's New Mth. Mag.* 70.107/2 **eVA,** [The horses] had grown exceedingly wild. . . The drivers were, however, familiar with the work before them. **1887** *Scribner's Mag.* 2.512/1 **TX,** I am not travelled enough to say what the mode is everywhere among the drivers of cattle. **1966** *DARE* Tape **NM**14, The flankers were behind the swing men and just in front of the drag driver.

2 An overseer of a group of workers (formerly, of slaves). **chiefly Sth**

1760 *South Carolina Gazette* 10 May (*AmSp* 27.283), Brought to the Work-house . . a new Negro Fellow, that can't tell his Master's Name, but by what I can learn, the Driver's name is *Mingo*. **1860** (1863) Olmsted *Journey* 47 **Sth,** There was also a driver of the hoe-gang who did not labor personally. **1886** Amer. Philol. Assoc. *Trans.* 17.34, [Among] words that were imported during or after the war from the South into Southern Ohio. . . *driver* (overseer) is beginning to be used even by intelligent people. **1887** *Century Illustr. Mag.* 35.109/2, An intelligent old Negro . . was a 'driver' in slave days and is still a 'driver'—not of mules, be it understood, but of men. . . On some plantations the title of foreman is coming into use, the negroes objecting to the old word. **1936** Smith–Sass *Carolina Rice* 64 **SC coast** (as of 1850s), Of the negroes on the plantation the most important was the Driver, who was a very high dignitary indeed. He bore when on duty his emblem of authority. This was a whip with a tapering hickory handle. **1942** Berrey–Van den Bark *Amer. Slang* 459.3, *Task master*. . . driver. **1966** *DARE* (Qu. HH43b, *The assistant to the top person in charge of a group of workmen*) Inf **SC**24, Driver [FW sugg]; **SC**26, Driver—occasional.

3 In hunting: one who drives game animals toward waiting shooters. **[drive v B1] chiefly Sth** Cf **stander**

1851 *S. Lit. Messenger* 17.45/2, Often the deer . . comes within range of the driver, and is laid low. *Ibid,* The driver has done his part—if the game is secure he shares the glory. **1858** *Harper's New Mth. Mag.* 17.616/2, The *driver,* accompanied by the pack, scours through the outside of the range, circling round until the dogs come upon the trail of the deer. **1939** *Hall Coll.* **wNC, eTN,** So our drivers driv the Easy Ridge . . and the standers stood on Bear Waller Ridge. **1959** *Washington Post & Times Herald* (DC) 4 Dec 13/6, The other half of the party—the "drivers" or "dogs"—make a big circle until they're a mile or two away and opposite the hunters. The drivers then whoop it up, . . as they head toward the hunters.

4 also *river driver:* One who guides logs down a river. **[drive v B3] chiefly Nth, esp NEng**

1846 (1864) Thoreau *ME Woods* 25, Just above McCauslin's, there is a rocky rapid . . and many "drivers" are there collected, who frequent his house for supplies. **1925** *AmSp* 1.135 **ME, MI, MN,** In the spring the logs are driven down the rivers to the mills by "river drivers." **1944** Nute *Lake Superior* 211, They would be turned over to professional "drivers," who did nothing but guide logs to market down the swollen streams of spring. **1966** *DARE* Tape **ME**19, River drivers' shoes . . had corks on 'em . . so you wouldn't roll on a log. **1975** Gould *ME Lingo* 81, The man who works on a *drive* is a river-driver.

5 Fig: a leg. [*driver* one of the driving wheels of a locomotive]

1977 Adams *Lang. Railroader* 49, *Driver:* . . A leg; the trainman sometimes calls his legs *drivers.*

6 A railroad engineer; an operator of a **donkey 1.**

1942 Berrey–Van den Bark *Amer. Slang* 771.18, *Railway employees*. . . Engineer. . . Casey Jones driver. **1958** McCulloch *Woods Words* 53 **Pacific NW,** *Driver*. . . An old term for a donkey puncher on a yarder. **1968** Adams *Western Words* 101, *Driver*—In logging, a railroad engineer.

7 A tree at the end of a row of notched trees which, when felled, knocks the others down in succession. Cf **drive n 7**

a1890 (1944) Robinson *Hist. Morrill* 106 **ME,** The choppers would notch in a large piece, then select a driver and cut onto the others so as to carry down the whole piece. . . He started his driver and took down the whole piece.

8 See quots.

1945 Colcord *Sea Language* 69 **ME, Cape Cod, Long Island,** *Driver, a*. . . A fast worker. **1979** Lewis *How to Talk Yankee* [10] **nNEng,** *Driver*. . . hard worker. "Bertha was the first in town to have her cannin' done." "*Ayuh,* ain't she a driver!"

9 See quot.

1966 *DARE* (Qu. K73, . . *The rump of a cooked chicken*) Inf **AR**40, The driver.

10 =dowitcher. [See quot 1956]

1876 *Forest & Stream* 7.212/3 **eMA** (as of 1852), *Macrorhamphus griseus.* Driver. *Ibid* 7.245/2 **eMA,** The "driver," (red-breast snipe) . . puzzled me. **1888** Trumbull *Names of Birds* 160, At North Plymouth, Mass., *Driver [Limnodromus griseus].* **1889** *Century Dict.* 1774/1, *Driver*. . . A bird, the dowitcher. **1923** U.S. Dept. Ag. *Misc. Circular* 13.51, *Dowitcher (Limnodromus griseus)*. . . In local use.—Brownback . . ; driver (Mass.) **1946** Hausman *Eastern Birds* 283, Eastern Dowitcher *Limnodromus griseus*. . . Other Names—Brown Snipe, . . Driver, German Snipe. **1956** MA Audubon Soc. *Bulletin* 39.20, *Dowitcher [Limnodromus griseus]*. . . Driver (Mass. This name may refer to some of the bird's calls resembling syllables used in driving horses.)

11 =red-backed sandpiper.

1956 MA Audubon Soc. *Bulletin* 39.19, *Red-backed Sandpiper [Pelidna alpina]*. . . Driver (Mass.)

drive shed n Cf **car shed**

1966 *DARE* (Qu. M22) Inf **MI**2, Drive shed—a large open building in which farm equipment is kept.

drive strip n Cf *DS* N44

1984 *DARE* File **UT,** In a town, the strip of grass and trees between the sidewalk and the curb: drive strip.

drive team See **drive v B8**

drive the nail v phr, hence vbl n Also *drive a nail, drive the center, ~ cross* *old-fash*

To hit the center of a target (orig a nailhead); by ext, to perform effectively, "hit the nail on the head."

1831 Audubon *Ornith. Biog.* 1.292, To *drive a nail* is a common feat, not more thought off [sic] by the Kentuckians than to cut off a wild turkey's head, at a distance of a hundred yards. *Ibid* 293, Those who drive the nail have a further trial amongst themselves, and the two best shots out of these generally settle the affair. . . This is technically termed *Driving the nail.* **1840** (1847) Longstreet *GA Scenes* 198, He was very confident of . . *driving the cross with her* [=a gun]. *Ibid* 208, The cross was driven three times . . and the bull's-eye was disfigured out of all shape. **1850** (1928) Loomis *Jrl. Birmingham* 4 July 72, We spent a short time in sellibrating the forth with a shootingmatch, in which I Baird came out best, the senter was drove however several times. **1869** Twain *Innocents* 84, They . . kept them [=prisoners] hopping about and dodging bullets for half an hour before they managed to drive the centre. **1923** *DN* 5.238 **swWI,** *Drive the nail*. . . To do a thing aptly, especially to speak aptly. A phrase from old-fashioned target shooting, in which the marksman often shot at—and hit the head of a nail, driving the shank into the board. . . "He got up and said only a few words, but he drove the nail." **1942** McAtee *Dial. Grant Co. IN* 24 (as of 1890s), *Drive the nail* . . to do a thing aptly, especially to speak to the point, equivalent to "hit the nail on the head". Actually to ——— in a shooting match meant to hit the nail in the center of the square bit of white paper that was used for a target.

drive truck See **drive v B8**

drive up v phr

To set or plant (a signpost or marker) in the ground.

1965 *DARE* Tape **KY**1, I went on out to where my [property] line was. I couldn't drive the sign up with this crippled hand. I asked another feller . . to drive it up and he did. **1984** Wilder *You All Spoken Here* 199 **Sth,** *Drive up a stob:* Plant a figurative marker to signify or symbolize a promise or achievement, as in memorializing one who stood up and was counted in a significant political contest.

driveway n

1 See quot. *arch* Cf **driftway.**

1891 Welch *Recoll. Buffalo* 64 **NY** (as of 1830s), From Virginia to Goodell, and what is now Edward Street, was then a driveway or cow-lane for the use of the owner of the adjoining property.

2 An area through which game animals are driven in a hunt. *arch*

1875 Temple–Sheldon *Hist. Northfield* 46 **MA,** They were wonderfully expert in killing game with arrows, and in capturing both larger and smaller sorts by means of drive-ways, and in rude traps and yank-ups. **1883** Zeigler–Grosscup *Heart of Alleghanies* 156 **eTN,** We four city boys were to occupy drive-ways, and watch for, halt, and slay every deer that passed.

3 A roadway. Cf **drive n 8**

1870 U.S. Congress *Congressional Globe* 41st Cong 2d Sess 2 Feb 42.2.966/3 **VT,** I doubt as to the policy of allowing this railroad to go along exactly in the track of where we propose to have a public driveway. **1904** Smith *Promoters* 263 *(DA),* There are no driveways in the world pleasanter to travel over than Nebraska roads. **1950** *PADS* 14.22 **SC,** *Cooter-backed*. . . Applied especially to dirt roads which are so constructed as to shed the rainfall and thus to prevent water from standing in the driveway and puddling the road. **1953** Van Wagenen *Golden Age* 150 **NY,** It may be taken as a perfect representative of its type, the so-called "double-barreled" bridge, which has two driveways separated from each other by a center timber truss.

4 A lane or passageway for the conveyance of hay, grain, etc into and through a barn.

1839 MA Ag. Surv. *Rept. for 1838* 80, The building should be so placed that . . the drive-way be into the end directly under the roof. **1868** U.S. Dept. Ag. *Rept. of Secy. for 1867* 242 **VT,** Where it is practicable, it is best to have the drive-way for drawing in hay, grain and corn fodder enter the gable end. **1917** *DN* 4.399 **nOH,** *Scaffold*. . . A loft for grain . . located over the driveway of a barn. **1949** *Pacific Spectator* Spring 226 **CT,** The upper floor, right on a level with the driveway, had a big haymow on the left. **1966** *DARE* (Qu. M4a) Inf **NM**3, Lanes or driveways—goes from one side of a barn to another. **1967** Sloane *Age of Barns* 43 **CT,** [Illustr caption:] A bridged driveway bay.

driving vbl n See **drive v B3**

driving vbl n attrib [**drive v B3**] **Nth**

In logging: used in or suitable for a **drive n 6.**

1877 *Scribner's Mth.* 15.149/2, Each man . . carries a "driving-pike" . . for the purpose of prying out the logs and releasing them from jams. **1908** White *Riverman* 11 **Nth,** Members of the driving crew leaped shouting from one log to another. **1914** *DN* 4.72 **ME, nNH,** *Drivin'-head*. . . Sufficient volume of water in river to drive logs. **1938** (1939) Holbrook *Holy Mackinaw* 260, *Driving pitch.* High water suitable for driving logs down a river. **1968** *DARE* Tape **NH**14, Wearing them driving shoes and standing on a log. **1969** Sorden *Lumberjack Lingo* 37 **NEng, Gt Lakes,** *Driving boots*—Pegged boots for riding logs on drives.

driving form n

The compact conformation necessary when a herd of cattle is driven overland.

1966 *DARE* Tape **NM**14, Then we would let 'em spread out . . and graze . . but keep everything headed in the right direction but not in the driving form, in the grazing form. Then along about ten or eleven o'clock we'd throw 'em back in the driving form and then generally walk for a couple o' miles.

driving spiles vbl n

1901 *DN* 2.139, *Driving spiles*. . . A game. Steuben Co., N.Y.

driving stick n

A goad.

1869 Fuller *Uncle John* 147 **NEng,** Ned Franklin said we ought to have a *flag.* So he took Jack's long driving-stick, and fastened the brightest shawl he could find to the end of it, and set it erect in the hinder part of the wagon. **1966** *DARE* (Qu. K27, . . *The sharp-pointed stick used to get oxen to move*) Inf **FL**7, Driving stick.

drizzle v Cf **drizzles**

See quot.

1978 Doig *This House* 200 **MT** (as of c1955), Without the fresh grass, the ewes' milk was weak and their lambs came down with diarrhea. . . "Damn-it-all-to-hell, these lambs are all gonna drizzle themselves to death if we don't do something."

drizzle-drazzle n Also *drizzle-drazzle rain* [Redup of *drizzle*] Cf **drizzle-fizzle**

A continuous, drizzling rain.

1855 *Golden Era* (S. F.) 7 Jan 2/4 *(DA),* The morning brought just what the old deacon wanted, a 'regular old-fashioned drizzle-drazzle.' **1923** *Star* (Kansas City MO) 23 Apr 22/2, The *"drizzle-drazzle"* is another kind of rain. . . It is neither a gully-washer nor a sod-soaker. It is more than a mist, and yet not a rain. **1939** *LANE* Map 95 1 inf, **cwCT,** *O Lord, send us rain, but don't go to overdoing things; don't send us a cloudburst—kind of a* [dɹɪzl dɹɒzl] *rain is what we want;* 1 inf, **nwCT,** 'A minister praying for rain asks for an easy [drɪzl drɔzl]'; 1 inf, **cCT,** A [drɪzl dræzl], 'not much more than heavy fog'. **1959** *VT Hist.* new ser 27.134 **neVT,** *Drizzle-drazzle*. . . A light rain; a slow, drizzling rain. . . Occasional. **1982** *Smithsonian Letters* **IA,** One of my uncles (Pella, Iowa) in his childhood ([approx] 90 yrs ago . .) recalled attending a prayer meeting to end the drought of all droughts, where the minister prayed for "not a great, big gully-buster, oh Lord; just a nice gentle little drizzle-drazzle." . . Drizzle-drazzle: gentle, sustained ground-penetrating rain slightly less than a drizzle and widespread. **1984** Wilder *You All Spoken Here* 140 **Sth,** *Sizzle sozzle, sizzly sozzly, drizzle drazzle.*

drizzle-fizzle n [Redup of *drizzle,* with added sense of *fizzle* a failure] Cf **drizzle-drazzle**

An insufficient rain shower.

1969 *DARE* (Qu. B23, . . *A light rain that doesn't last*) Inf **MO**19, We always called it just a drizzle-fizzle.

drizzle nose n

A runny nose.

1943 *Sun* (Baltimore MD) 27 Nov 7/4 *(Hench Coll.),* "Cat fever" a form of grippe accompanied by high temperatures, nausea and cold, but without the discomfort of the "drizzle nose," associated with regular grippe, appeared to be on the decline here [=Norfolk VA].

drizzle oak n Cf **droozly-make**

=Jerusalem oak.

1968 *DARE* (Qu. S21, . . *Weeds . . that are a trouble in gardens*) Inf **GA**35, Drizzle oak, same as Jerusalem oak.

‡drizzler n [Prob var of *dribbler*]

Something that quickly dwindles away, loses its power.

1912 Chadwick *Baseball Joe* 83 (*AmSp* 26.31), Only pounded out a little drizzler that Sam quickly gathered in and threw to first.

drizzles n pl Also *drizzlies, drizzlings, drizzling shits* Cf **drizzle**

=dribbles 1.

1966–69 *DARE* (Qu. BB19, . . *Looseness of the bowels*) Infs **OK**42, **TX**43, Drizzles; **CA**140, Thin drizzlings; **MN**15, The drizzling shits. **1978** Doig *This House* 162 **MT** (as of c1955), That . . lamb has the drizzles. **1986** Pederson *LAGS Concordance,* 1 inf, **neTX,** The drizzlies.

drizzling adj

Having little water, trickling.

1884 Baldwin *Yankee School-Teacher* 11 **VA,** Dis now am Flat Crick. An' mighty drizzlin' it looks now. We c'n step over 'thout de bridge, b't in de long season [=rainy period] in May, when de rain jess 'pears like t' pour, dar's no cross'n', even on de bridge—de waters done kiver it.

drizzling-drazzling See **drizzly-drazzly**

drizzlings, drizzling shits See **drizzles**

drizzly-drazzly adj Also *drizzling-drazzling* **[drizzle-drazzle]**

Drizzling, misty.

1939 *LANE* Map 95 1 inf, **cwNH,** A [drɪzlɪn dræzlɪn] rain, [term used] in telling a story; it's kind o' misty. **1968** *DARE* (Qu. B23, . . *A light rain that doesn't last*) Inf **MD**17A, A drizzly-drazzly rain.

droggy adj [Perh var of *draggy,* infl by *groggy*]

Mildly ill; "under the weather."

1967 *DARE* (Qu. BB5) Inf **MA**51, [drɒgi].

drogue See **drag** n 2

droll adj

1 Odd, queer, unusual. [Engl dial] **Sth, S Midl**

1899 (1912) Green *VA Folk-Speech* 156, *Droll. . .* Ludicrous; queer; laughable. **1909** *S Atl Qrly* 8.41 **soSC** [Gullah], *Droll* [is used] to mean *strange, savoring of roguery,* not merely humorous or funny. **1931** Hannum *Thursday April* 129 **wNC,** Merrily she turned to Square and Phoebe to explain. "Yore pap's plumb droll turned!" **1942** (1971) Campbell *Cloud-Walking* 8 **seKY,** He 'lowed Big Nelt was mighty quare-turned and droll-natured but a right accommodating man. **1970** *DARE* (Qu. W41, . . *Someone whose clothes never look right or who always dresses carelessly*) Inf **VA**90, Droll; **VA**35, Looks droll.

2 Uncanny, weird. Cf **droll** n

1934 Vines *Green Thicket* 311 **cnAL,** Going with the story was the saying that the place was so droll and so *hainted* with loneliness that any girl there alone for any length of time with the one she loved would lose her head. **1950** *PADS* 14.27 **SC,** *Droll. . .* Uncanny, terrifying; e.g., a reported case of a deceased uncle calling on the family in his grave clothes, was described as *droll.*

3 See quots.

1952 Brown *NC Folkl.* 1.534, *Droll. . .* Lifeless, not well. "I feel kinda droll today."—Granville county. Old people. **1984** Wilder *You All Spoken Here* 202 **Sth,** *Droll:* Unwell; lifeless.

droll n **[droll** adj **2]** Cf **boo-daddy**

See quot 1941.

1938 FWP *Ocean Highway* 204 **SC,** A wide variety of ghosts including . . boo-daddies, boo-hags, and drolls. **1941** Writers' Program *Guide SC* 287, Drolls are spirits of infants who died a painful death, and who can be heard crying in the swamps in the hour before 'fus' dawn'.

drone n, v Pronc-sp *droon*

A Form.

1954 *PADS* 21.17 **SC,** In the same neighborhood [=a section of the Dutch Fork lying between Wateree Creek and the town of Chapin] occur the pronunciations *boon, droon, groon, stoon,* etc. for *bone, drone, groan, stone,* etc. **c1960** [see **C** below].

B As noun.

A boring, dull, or stupid person.

1947 Berrey–Van den Bark *Amer. Slang Suppl.* 1.8, *Unpopular person; "drip."* . . drone. **1966–69** *DARE* (Qu. HH3, *A dull and stupid person*) Infs **ME**9, **WA**18, (Awful) drone; (Qu. HH16, *Uncomplimentary words with no definite meaning—just used when you want to show that you don't think much of a person: "Don't invite him. He's a ______."*) Inf **NJ**54, Drone.

C As verb.

With *around:* To move without energy, to go about in a sluggish or lazy manner. [*OED drone* v², 1509 →]

c1960 *Wilson Coll.* **csKY,** *Drooning around*—acting as if sick or lifeless or lazy. **1968** *DARE* (Qu. Y21, *To move about slowly and without energy*) Inf **WV**2, Drone around.

droodle v [Cf Scots *driddle* to dawdle; to idle away]

1970 *DARE* (Qu. KK31, *To go about aimlessly looking for distraction: "He doesn't have anything to do, so he's just ______ around."*) Inf **NY**237, Droodles.

droog See **drag** n 2

droon See **drone**

droop v Freq with *around* Cf **droopy 2**

To move without energy; to go about in a sluggish or lazy manner.

1967–70 *DARE* (Qu. Y21, *To move about slowly and without energy*) Infs **CO**27, **KY**63, 74, **NJ**27, **TN**65, Droop; **IN**3, **MO**29, Drooping (around); (Qu. BB41, *Not seriously ill, but sick enough to be in bed: "He's been ______ for a week."*) Infs **KY**34, **UT**4, Drooping around.

droop n

1 also *drooper:* A dull, ineffectual, or unpleasant person. Cf **droopy 3**

1932 Farrell *Young Lonigan* 181 **Chicago IL,** He was afraid that he might be acting like a droop. **1940** in 1942 *AmSp* 17.205, Don't be a droop. **1951** Hough *Singing in Morning* 70 **Martha's Vineyard MA,** What price society if it has nothing but droops in it. **1965–70** *DARE* (Qu. HH3, *A dull and stupid person*) Inf **PA**39, Droop; **AZ**3, **MS**60, Drooper; (Qu. HH16, *Uncomplimentary words with no definite meaning—just used when you want to show that you don't think much of a person: "Don't invite him. He's a ______."*) Infs **MI**4, **NY**22, 36, Droop; (Qu. II36a, *Somebody who talks back or gives rude answers: "Did you ever see such a ______?"*) Inf **WA**1, Droop.

2 also *droop neck:* A disease of chickens.

1950 Bissell *Stretch on River* 110, He ain't gonna be content with what he can make off a bunch of scabby old chickens with the droop and the pip and pneumonia. **1968** *DARE* (Qu. K78, *What diseases do chickens commonly get?*) Inf **AL**43, Droop neck.

3 pl: A feeling of melancholy, "the blues."

1966–70 *DARE* (Qu. GG34a, *To feel depressed or in a gloomy mood: "He has the ______ today."*) Infs **CA**123, **IL**116, **MS**45, **NY**228, Droops.

droop around See **droop** v

droop-down adj

Droopy.

1963 Owens *Look to River* 117 **TX**, He's pure bloodhound. You c'n tell by the droop-down ears.

drooped up ppl adj phr

1 Suffering from **droop** n **2.**

1952 Brown *NC Folkl.* 1.534, *Drooped up:* . . Sick. "The old hen is all drooped up."—Central and east.

2 =**droopy 1, 2.**

1972 Cooper *NC Mt. Folkl.* 91, *Drooped up*—disappointed in love; ill or indisposed.

drooper n

1 See **droop** n **1.**

2 See quot.

1968 *DARE* (Qu. O19, *Different kinds or degrees of wind that are important when you're in a boat*) Inf **NJ**21, Droopers—white storm clouds with a back wind; you head for shore when you see these; wind comes from the opposite direction suddenly.

droop horn n Also adj *droop-horned* Also called **chongo 2**

See quots.

1942 Berrey–Van den Bark *Amer. Slang* 916.2, Droop-horned cattle. **1956** Gipson *Old Yeller* 31 **TX**, The bull . . had one great horn set for hooking, while the other hung down past his jaw like a tallow candle that had drooped in the heat. He was what the Mexicans called a *chongo* or "droop horn." **1961** Adams *Old-Time Cowhand* 158, An animal with droopin' horns was called a "droop horn."

droop neck See **droop** n **2**

droopy adj

1 Melancholy, gloomy; dejected, sulky. Cf **droop** n **3**

1967–70 *DARE* (Qu. GG34b, *To feel depressed or in a gloomy mood: "She's feeling ______ today."*) Infs **KY**36, 74, **VA**15, Droopy; (Qu. GG35b, *Of a person who acts annoyed or disappointed you might say, "Because she couldn't go, she's been ______ all day."*) Inf **NE**8, Droopy.

2 Sick, ailing; weak, **puny.** Cf **droop** v

1956 McAtee *Some Dialect NC* 13, *Droopy:* . . Ailing, when speaking of chickens. **c1960** *Wilson Coll.* **csKY**, *Droopy*—ailing, puny, poorly. **1965–70** *DARE* (Qu. X52, . . *A person . . who had been sick was looking ______*) Infs **CO**22, **FL**2, **OK**28, Droopy; (Qu. BB5, *A general feeling of discomfort or illness that isn't any one place in particular*) Infs **AR**21, **MI**69, **MO**18, Droopy; **IN**69, Feel droopy; (Qu. BB16b, *If something a person ate didn't agree with him, he might just feel a bit ______*) Inf **MO**18, Droopy; (Qu. BB38, *When a person doesn't look healthy, or looks as if he hadn't been well for some time, you'd say, "He looks ______."*) Infs **AR**21, **MO**18, **OH**44, Droopy; (Qu. BB39, *On a day when you don't feel just right, though not actually sick, you might say, "I'll be all right tomorrow—I'm just feeling ______ today."*) Infs **CO**33, **IL**72, **LA**2, **NC**41, **NY**232, Droopy; **SC**10, Droopy down; (Qu. BB41, *Not seriously ill, but sick enough to be in bed: "He's been ______ for a week."*) Inf **GA**17, Droopy; (Qu. GG26, *A feeling of weakness from fear: "When she saw the dog coming at her she got ______."*) Inf **TN**26, Felt right droopy.

3 Dull, boring; unpleasant. Cf **droop** n **1**

1947 Berrey–Van den Bark *Amer. Slang Suppl.* 3.4, Unsatisfactory; displeasing. . . *spec.* drippy, droopy, drizzly, drooly . . , *descriptive of a "drip" or "jerk."* **1968–70** *DARE* (Qu. B2, *If the weather is very unpleasant, you say it's a ______ day*) Inf **NY**76, Droopy; (Qu. FF19, . . *A very dull or unenjoyable time: "The party was ______."*) Inf **OH**40, Droopy; (Qu. HH3, *A dull and stupid person*) Inf **OH**95, Droopy, a dud, dullard.

4 See quot.

1966 *DARE* (Qu. W41, . . *Expressions . . for someone whose clothes never look right or who always dresses carelessly*) Inf **GA**6, Droopy.

drooth See **drought A5**

droozly-make n [Var of *Jerusalem oak,* when pronc as |ǰəˈruzlɪm ˈeɪk| or var] Cf **drizzle oak**

=**Jerusalem oak.**

1952 Brown *NC Folkl.* 1.534, *Droozly-make.* . . Jerusalem oak—a kind of plant used to make medicinal syrup.

drop n, v Usu |drɑp|; also **chiefly Sth, S Midl** |dræp| Pronc-sp *drap*

A Pronc var. [Cf *OED drap* "Sc. dial. form of *drop sb.* and *v.*"] Cf **crop** n

1795 Dearborn *Columbian Grammar* 135, *List of Improprieties,* commonly called *Vulgarisms,* which should never be used in *Speaking, Reading, or Writing.* . . Drap for Drop. **1803** Davis *Travels* 387 **VA** [Black], This was a poor comfort without a little drap of whiskey now and dan. **1837** Sherwood *Gaz. GA* 69, *Drap,* for drop. **1851** Hooper *Widow Rugby's Husband* 131 **AL**, Let's drap funnin' and take a drink. **1890** *DN* 1.72 **LA**, *Drap:* drop, *n.* and *v.* [*DN* Ed: Not unknown in New England.] **1893** Shands *MS Speech* 27, Drap [dræp], Negro for *drop.* **1902** *DN* 2.233 **sIL**, *Drap* [dræp]. . . Drop. **1903** *DN* 2.312 **seMO**, *Drap.* **1906** *DN* 3.117 **sIN**, *Drap* [dræp]. *Ibid* 134 **nwAR**, *Drap.* **1907** *DN* 3.230 **nwAR, seMO**, *Drap.* **1908** *DN* 3.307 **eAL, wGA**, *Drap.* . . Drop. **1908** Fox *Lonesome Pine* 60 **KY**, I want you . . to drap yer guns. **1923** *DN* 5.206 **swMO**, *Drap.* **1934** Stribling *Unfinished Cathedral* 16 **AL**, I gwi' drap along up de street. **1940** *AmSp* 15.46 **sAppalachians, Ozarks**, *Drap.* **1950** *PADS* 14.27 **SC**, *Drap.* **1963** Watkins–Watkins *Yesterday Hills* 25 **cnGA**, Aw, Pa, I just drapped a few little old catterges [=cartridges] in the heater to hear them pop. **1969** *DARE* FW Addit **cs,ceNC**, Drop [dræp].

B Gram forms.

1 past: usu *dropped;* pronc-spp *drap(t).*

1887 [see **D3** below]. **1892** Smith *Day at Laguerre's* 181 **VA** [Black], I drap [=dropped] it in de snow-bank. **1922** Gonzales *Black Border* 298 **sSC, GA coasts** [Gullah glossary], *Drap* . . dropped. **1940** *Sat. Eve. Post* 24 Feb 25/1 **cTX** (as of c1890) [Black], I drap [=dropped] off. **1967** *DARE* FW Addit **LA**7, The grain [dræp] down there.

2 past pple: usu *dropped;* pronc-spp *drap(t).*

1899 Chesnutt *Conjure Woman* 155 **NC** [Black], She foun' dis yer little bag de sparrer had drap' in front her do'. **1908** *DN* 3.307 **eAL, wGA**, *Drap(t), pret.* and *pp.* of *drop.*

C As noun.

1 pl: Liquid medicine, esp of the kind measured in drops. **formerly widespread, now chiefly S Midl** *somewhat old-fash*

1723 *Amer. Weekly Mercury* 21 Mar 2/2 **Philadelphia PA**, The Spirit of Venice-Treacle, known by the name of Mary Banister's Drops; at Reasonable Rates. **1871** Harte *East West Poems* 117 **CA**, I am taking the drops, and am using the paste. **1908** *DN* 3.307 **eAL, wGA**, *Draps.* . . Liquid medicine to be given in doses of so many drops; hence, any liquid medicine. **1927** *DN* 5.474 **Ozarks**, *Draps.* . . Drops, liquid medicine. "My woman was ailin'-like, but Doc he gin her some powders an' draps." **1946** McAtee *Dial. Grant Co. IN Suppl. 3* 4 (as of 1890s), *Drops* . . liquid medicine, "You can stop the pills but keep on with the drops." **1953** Randolph–Wilson *Down in Holler* 241 **Ozarks**, *Drops.* . . Liquid medicine, especially medicine to be largely diluted with water. **1954** *Harder Coll.* **cwTN**, *Drops.* . . Any liquid medicine.

2 The lambs or number of lambs (born in a certain period). [*drop* to give birth to] Cf **drop band**

1931 *AmSp* 6.357 **Plains States**, The day's "drop" is brought together toward evening by "lambers" or "nurse maids." **1954** Jordan *Hell's Canyon* 67 **wID**, The lamb "drop" was heavier this spring.

3 An animal bred by accident; hence an illegitimate or abandoned child.

1944 *Collier's* 114.12 **Harlem NYC** [Black], A drop or rustle is a boy of completely undetermined parentage. . . He is the casual offspring of a man and a woman who have either taken up with each other for the duration of their mutual curiosity, which is frequently brief, or of parents who were conventionally wedded and thought no more about it. Harlem is thickly sown with drops or rustles whose home influence, lacking both home and influence, is discouragingly nil. **1966** *DARE* (Qu. K43) Inf **GA**9, Drop. **1970** Major *Dict. Afro-Amer. Slang* 48, *Drop:* an orphan, especially one whose parents are unknown.

4 also attrib: A piece of fruit that has fallen from a tree. [Engl dial]

1942 *Daily Progress* (Charlottesville VA) 20 Oct 2/1 *(Hench Coll.)* **cwVA**, The "drops" were mostly winesaps. . . All harvest hands began the task of gathering "drops" and other fruit remaining on the trees. **1944** in 1957 Old Farmer's Almanac *Sampler* 125 **NH,** Drop apples should be gotten out of the orchard as soon as possible. . . Best drops bring a fair price, but run no drops in with hand-picks. **1950** *WELS Suppl.* **swMN,** Drop-apples—used for wind-fall apples. **1983** *Barrick Coll.* **csPA,** *Drops*—fallen apples.

5 See **drop cake 2.**

6 Of nonliquid substances: a small amount. Cf **drip n 1**

1965–70 *DARE* (Qu. LL6b, *A small, indefinite amount—for example, of butter: "I'll put in just a ______ of butter."*) Infs **DE**7, **HI**13, **IL**63, **MA**2, **OH**16, 80, **VT**12, Drop; (Qu. LL6c, *A small, indefinite amount—for example, of cinnamon: "It still needs just a ______ of cinnamon."*) Infs **CT**39, **IN**78, **KS**16, **LA**23, **MA**2, **VA**11, Drop; **LA**23, Drop—we'd still say this and you don't drop cinnamon.

7 In marble play:

a usu pl but sometimes sg in constr: The action of dropping a marble from a height to hit an opponent's marbles; a game in which this action is used; marbles so dropped; hence exclams *drops, drop-ins*—calls claiming the privilege to use this action. Cf **bombsie(s), drop eye, dropsie 2**

1908 *DN* 3.307 **eAL, wGA,** *Drops*. . . In the game of marbles, the privilege of standing and dropping one's taw upon an opponent's taw when he has called and taken the privilege of *ups*. . . Sometimes called *draps.* **1966** *DARE* Tape **NC**22, Sometimes we would call "drop-ins," an' we would stand up an' hold [a marble] an' drop it down on the marble. **1969** *DARE* (Qu. EE7, . . *Marble games*) Inf **WI**77, Drops. **c1970** Wiersma *Marbles Terms,* Drop . . the action taken when two marbles are touching in certain game-situations where a player tries to hit an opponent's marble from a specified height: 'he gets a drop'. *Ibid,* Knee drops. When the player drops his marble from a kneeling position. "Try knee drops." *Ibid* **IL,** Drops—marbles which are dropped into the playing area. . . "That's a drops." *Ibid* **MI,** Drops . . a call made by the player which allows him to drop, rather than shoot his marble at the opponent's piece. *Ibid,* When marbles land next to each other your opponent calls "drops"; brings marble to chest and drops it at the other marble. "These marble[s] are too close, so I'm calling drops."

b See quot.

1955 *PADS* 23.16 **cwTN,** *Drop*. . . An expert marble player.

c See quot.

c1970 *Wiersma Marbles Terms* **MI,** Drop. . . The opening play of a marble game, used to determine the order of play. In "the drop" each player attempts to throw his marble and have it hit a designated spot. The player who comes the closest has the first turn, etc.

8 **=flag station.**

1983 *DARE* File **eNC** (as of 1912), As our train from Charlotte, North Carolina moved along near midnight, my mother asked how far we were from Wilmington, our destination. The conductor said "two drops"—meaning two flag stops, where the flag was lowered as a signal for the train to stop.

9 See **dropper 1.**

D As verb.

1 To put (seeds or seedlings) in place for planting; to plant (a crop); to act as a **dropper 2.** [*EDD drop* v. 15 "To plant potatoes; to sow seed at regular intervals. . . Hence . . *Dropper* . . a woman or child employed to drop seed . . into the holes made by the 'dibblers'."] **chiefly Sth, S Midl** See Map

1751 (1901) Hempstead *Diary* 569 **CT,** I was out to the Cornfield dropping Corn. **1837** (1930) Sewall *Diary* 181 **IL,** Commenced planting corn. . . Henry and Jane dropped, John Erskine covered with hoe, and I laid off with two horses. **1899** Garland *Boy Life* 76 **nwIA,** In those days the corn was still planted by hand and covered with a hoe. Lincoln . . was . . eager to drop corn. **1909** Porter *Girl Limberlost* 218 **cnIN,** I earned it myself, dropping corn. **1912** Green *VA Folk-Speech* 156, *Drop*. . . To *drop* corn at regular distances at planting. **1926** Roberts *Time of Man* 4 **cKY,** If you're a mind to drap [tobacco plants] you better be a-goen up there. **1944** *PADS* 2.66 **S Midl,** *Drop*. . . To distribute [tobacco] plants on the row in the proper places. **1947** Steed *KY Tobacco Patch* 81, Except as an experiment I wouldn't have dared to try such a plan of dropping seeds or plants without plowing if I were preparing the seedbed for a clean cultivated crop. **1965–70** *DARE* (Qu. L22, *When talking about a crop he intends to plant . . a farmer might say, "This year, I'm going to ______ a crop of oats / corn / cotton, etc."*) 36 Infs, **chiefly Sth, esp SC,** Drop corn (*or* cotton, peanuts, etc); (Qu. L23) Inf **AL**14, Dropped by hand. **1966** *DARE* Tape **FL**41, [FW:] How do you grow peanuts? [Inf:] You just drop them like you do corn or something like that, peanuts in the ground. **1967** Key *Tobacco Vocab.,* Before the mechanical transplanter . . one person went ahead and "dropped" a seedling at regular intervals along the row. Another person followed behind and "set" the seedling, making a hole with a peg and pushing the dirt up around it. **1981** *Broaddus Coll.* **ceKY.**

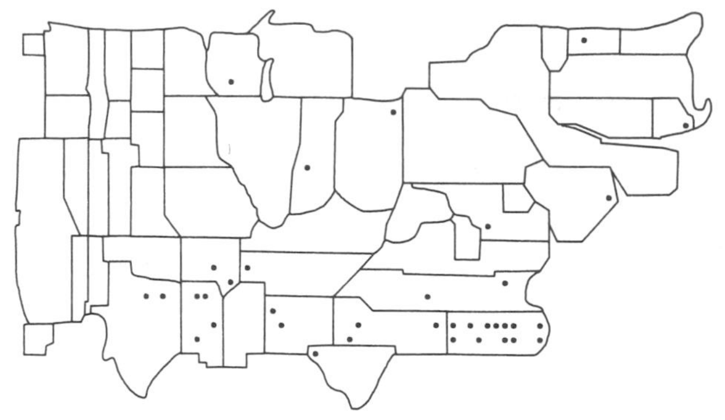

•drop D1 + varr (Qq. L22, L23)

2 Of a dog: to crouch down at a signal or at the sight of game. Cf **charge B2**

1844 Uncle Sam *Peculiarities* 2.220, I've a dog, . . a grand, clever, liver-coloured pointer, . . perfect, stand and back, drop to the hand, drop to game, fast, as a steamer. **1889** *Century Dict.* 1777, *To drop to shot,* to drop or charge at the discharge of the gun: said of a field-dog. *Ibid To drop to wing,* to drop or charge when the bird flushes [said of a field-dog]. **1968** *DARE* (Qu. J9a, *To tell a dog to lie down . . and keep still*) Infs **CT**9, **NY**92, Drop; (Qu. J9b, *To tell a dog to stand without moving*) Inf **CT**9, Drop.

3 To forget, lose from memory.

1887 (1967) Harris *Free Joe* 186 **cGA,** I 'lowed maybe you moughter hearn [=heard] the name named, an' then drapt it.

4 To rain lightly. [Engl and Scots dial]

1927 in 1944 *ADD* **sLA** [Black], Drappin' [Wentworth: = raining]. **1937** *AmSp* 12.231 **NJ,** Negroes use *drappin'* (dropping) in the sense 'raining' or 'rainy.' **1967–69** *DARE* (Qu. B21, *When fine drops of moisture are falling, you say it's doing what?*) Inf **NC**41, Dropping; **PA**40, Dropping a little.

5 in phr *drop to sleep:* To cause to go to sleep.

1956 *Hall Coll.* **wNC,** [Adult reminiscing:] Mommy, she give me a little old pet lamb. I'd drop it to sleep. . . I'd drop it to sleep and bed it down in the corner and hit'd lay there till next mornin'.

6 To exchange sight unseen—usu in phr *drop knives;* hence vbl n *dropping (knives).*

c1960 *Wilson Coll.* **csKY,** Drop knives: . . Exchange knives "sight unseen." **1967–70** *DARE* (Qu. U14, . . *Exchanging with somebody when neither one has seen what the other has*) Infs **AR**56, **IN**49, Drop knives; **AR**51, Dropping knives—I'll drop with you; **IN**43A, Drop the knife; **KY**18, Dropping knives; **IN**45A, Dropping.

7 To release.

1968 *DARE* (Qu. X55b, . . *Breaking wind from the bowels*) Inf **MD**9, Drop one; **WI**34, Dropped a few.

drop a stitch v phr [From *drop a stitch* in knitting with pun on *stitch* a sharp sudden local pain] **ME, MA**

To experience a sudden pain, usu in one's back.

1964 Gould *Parables of Peter* 166 **ME,** I have been having some trouble with my back lately since I put the cider down, and I did drop a stitch, so I figured the long ride had settled me in somehow and I had become a paralytic. **1966–70** *DARE* (Qu. BB3b, *A sudden pain that strikes you in the back*) Infs **ME**5, **MA**38, 69, Dropped a stitch (in his *or* my back); **MA**65, 72, 98, Drop a stitch (in back); **MA**40, Dropping a stitch; (Qu. BB3c, . . *In the side*) Inf **ME**10, Dropped a stitch. **1975** Gould *ME Lingo* 81, *Drop a stitch*—From knitting, where a dropped stitch leaves its own evidence; a *crick* or catch in the back or neck which is painful and annoying. "Henry dropped a stitch, and can't stand up." **1980** *DARE* File **cnMA** (as of c1915), When I use the phrase *drop a stitch* I'm talking about knitting (rather un-knitting). But I remember hearing it as a child. Two old codgers might meet downtown, one very stooped and leaning on his cane more than usual. And his friend might say, as he observed his hand pressed against his lower back, "Dropped a stitch in your back, did ye?" So far as I know *dropping stitches* is used only of back pain.

drop away See **drop out** v phr **1**

drop band n [*drop* to give birth to + **band** n²] **chiefly West** Cf **drop C2**

A flock of pregnant ewes and ewes with newborn lambs.

1931 *AmSp* 6.357 **Plains States,** The drop band herder . . must so maneuver his "lead" that the new mothers are always in the "tail" of the band, so that as they drop behind they will not be disturbed by the rest of the flock before they have become thoroughly habituated to family cares. **1939** FWP *Guide MT* 414, *Drop band*—Band of ewes being lambed in the spring. **1952** FWP *Guide SD* 85, *Drop bunch:* the ewes which have not lambed yet. **1954** Jordan *Hell's Canyon* 69 **wID,** The drop-band moved slowly up the ridges, and the herders and lambers moved with it.

drop biscuit n

1 =**drop cake 2.** *obs*

1839 Randolph *VA Housewife* 131, *To Make Drop Biscuit.* Beat eight eggs very light, add to them twelve ounces of flour, and one pound of sugar; when perfectly light, drop them on tin sheets, and bake them in a quick oven. **1853** Webster *Improved Housewife* 119 *(DA),* Virginia Drop Biscuit.

2 also *drop cake, dropped biscuit:* A quick bread made from a soft or sticky dough which is spooned onto a baking sheet or into muffin tins. Cf **beaten biscuit**

1936 Lutes *Country Kitchen* 203 **sMI** (?as of c1890), Another variation of the same [=baking-powder] biscuit dough is to make drop biscuits by adding about three tablespoonfuls of milk to the rule [=recipe], beating well, and dropping from a spoon into greased muffin tins. **1940** Brown *Amer. Cooks* 550 **NH,** *Exeter Rye Drop Cakes. . .* Have the iron gem pans, roll or cup shaped, very well buttered and very hot . . bake in hot oven. **1965–70** *DARE* (Qu. H19, *What do you mean by a biscuit? How are they made?*) 12 Infs, **scattered,** Drop biscuit(s); **MO**32, **SC**22, 56, Dropped biscuit(s). **1968** *DARE* Tape **SC**56, You can make drop biscuits. I do that sometimes. Have the dough soft, you know, . . take the spoon, drop 'em in the pan, bake 'em that way. **1987** *DARE* File **nwMA,** I make drop biscuits now for the same reason my mother made them when I was growing up. She worked full time and drop biscuits are the quickest and easiest kind to make. You don't roll out the dough, just spoon it onto a cookie sheet. There's no mess to clean up afterward either.

drop box n

1 also *drop in the box* (or *hole*), *drop (the) marble:* A marble game; see quots. Cf **dropsie 1**

1958 *PADS* 29.33 **WI,** *Drop-box. . .* A marble game in which marbles are dropped from chin height through a small hole in the top of a box (such as a cigar box). **1966–70** *DARE* (Qu. EE7, . . *Kinds of marble games*) Inf **IL**9, Drop box—drop the marbles into a box that has one hole drilled; first one to drop one in, wins; **MO**23, Drop in the box; [**ME**15, Drop in cigar box]; **NC**52, Drop the marble—try and drop marbles in a cigar box with holes in it; **WI**68A, Drop in the hole; **TX**104, Drop marble—dig a hole and drop em from [a] height. **c1970** Wiersma *Marbles Terms* **swMI** (as of 1940s), Drop in the Box—a marble game in which one player owns a box with a hole in it big enough for a marble's passage, and the others take turns dropping their marbles at the hole. If they miss, the box owner gets the marble; if they make it, he must give them five, or whatever amount is agreed upon. "Let's play Drop in the Box." **1976** *WI Acad. Rev.* Mar 10/2 (as of 1920s), *Drop Box,* a game of skill, relied on a steady hand. . . A drop box was a wooden cigar box with the top removed and a square or rectangular hole cut in the bottom. . . A drop-box owner would shout, "Drop box! Drop box!" to entice players. . . When a player agreed to try, the box was held bottom up between his feet and he tried to drop a marble through the hole.

2 By ext: the box used in such a game.

c1970 Wiersma *Marbles Terms* **MI,** Drop box . . is the name given to the box which the players carried their marbles in. In the top or cover of the box, there was a small hole just for dropping marbles in while playing the Drop Box Game or the Dropping Game. "I brought my drop-box; want to try a drop!?" **1976** *WI Acad. Rev.* June 20/3 (as of 1920s), We usually kept our major supply of marbles in our drop boxes; therefore, we put the drop holes on top of the cigar boxes so the marbles didn't leak out.

drop button n Cf *DS* HH5, 6

1950 *PADS* 14.27 **SC,** *Drop button. . .* A person mentally lacking, one who "ain't so right," "kind of cracky." . . A drop button is supposed to walk about looking around as if he had lost a button.

drop cake n

1 also *drop(ped) doughnut:* A small sweet cake usu fried in hot fat. **chiefly NEng**

1835 *Liberator* (Boston MA) 5 Dec 196/5, The travellers on whom I bestowed your *drop cakes* at midnight have leavened this loaf with a blessing. **1939** Wolcott *Yankee Cook Book* 363, *Drop Cakes.* A Yankee dish not unlike a fritter. **1940** Brown *Amer. Cooks* 550 **NH,** *Old Amherst Rye Drop Cakes* . . drop from spoon in hot fat. These are very good with maple syrup. **1941** *LANE* Map 284 *(Doughnut),* Lumps of sweetened dough dropped into deep fat from a spoon. . . 24 infs, **scattered,** *Drop cake(s);* 1 inf, **cNH,** *drop doughnut.* **1952** Dorson *Bloodstoppers* 100 **nMI,** A French cook was busily stirring a big batch of batter in the cookhouse. A jack standing by asked him what he was making. "I don' know," he said. "I drop pieces in de wataire. If they float dey're doughnuts. If dey sink dey're dropcakes." **1967–69** *DARE* (Qu. H28) Inf **WA**19, Drop doughnuts (just small pieces of dough); **WI**47, Drop doughnuts; **MA**57, Dropped doughnut.

2 also *drop, drop cookie:* A small sweet cake usually baked on a greased pan. Also called **drop biscuit 1**

1796 (1962) Simmons *Amer. Cookery* 38, A Butter Drop. **1896** (c1973) Farmer *Orig. Cook Book* 419, *Sponge Drop.* Drop Lady Finger mixture from tip of spoon on unbuttered paper. **1901** Kander *Settlement Cook Book* 372, *Chocolate Drop Cakes; Cocoanut Drop Cookies; Peanut Drop Cakes. . .* Makes twenty-four cookies. *Ibid* 368, Sponge Drops . . drop mixture from the tip of a spoon on ungreased tin sheet. . . Put together in pairs with jelly between. **1908** (1911) Gale *Friendship Village* 34 **WI,** "Well, a couple o' your cherry pies an' a batch o' your nice drop sponge cakes," she directed. **1940–41** Cassidy *WI Atlas* **csWI,** *Drop cake*—a sweetened wheat-flour muffin. **1956** Ker *Vocab. W. TX* 257, A variant of cooky is *drop cake* or *drop cookie.* **1965** *Settlement Cook Book* 154, *Drop cookies.* The dough for drop cookies is soft, and cannot be rolled or molded.

3 See **drop biscuit 2.**

drop cookie See **drop cake 2**

drop cord See **drop line**

drop-dead n Cf **coffin tack**

A cigarette.

1968 *DARE* (Qu. DD6b) Inf **LA**45, Drop-dead—a cigarette.

drop door n Cf **klop-door**

1970 *DARE* (Qu. D20, . . *A sloping outside cellar door*) Inf **IL**134, Drop door.

drop doughnut See **drop cake 1**

drop-down n

An incline, slope.

1950 *Hench Coll.* **cVA,** They're going to build a wall where the drop-down is.

drop edge of yonder n Cf **yonder** n **esp TN**

The brink of death.

1939 FWP *Guide TN* 134, Granny Tatum's standing on the drop-edge of Yonder, and we'll soon be laying her down in her silent grave. **c1970** *Halpert Coll.* **wKY, eTN,** To be on the drop edge of yonder = to be at the point of death. **1982** Heat Moon *Blue Highways* 33 **cTN,** "I got some bad ham meat one day," Miss Ginny said, "and took to vomitin'. All day, all night. Hangin' on the drop edge of yonder. I said to Thurmond, 'Thurmond, unless you want shut of me, call the doctor.' " **1984** Wilder *You All Spoken Here* 207 **Sth,** *Standin' on the drop edge of yonder:* About to peg out; about to hang it up.

drop egg See **dropped egg**

drop-eye n Cf **bombsie(s), drop C7a, dropsie 2, eye-drop a** [*EDD drop-eye* (at *drop* v. 12. (6))]

In marble play: see quots.

1966 *DARE* (Qu. EE7, . . *Kinds of marble games*) Inf **MT**3, Drop-eye (marble in ring—drop taw from above to try to knock others out of ring). **1966** *DARE* Tape **NM**6, When I was a youngster going to school . . we used to play . . Drop-eye. [There] was a very small ring with very few marbles in and a heavier marble used as the dropping object onto these and you usually stood up over them and dropped your larger marble onto the others and whatever marbles came out of the ring was yours. . . This ring was probably a foot . . 18 inches in diameter.

drop fishing n
Fishing with a **drop line.**
1970 *DARE* (Qu. P17, *What do you call it . . when the people fish by lowering a line and sinker close to the bottom of the water?*) Inf **NY**236, Drop fishing, deep fishing.

drop flower n [Perh from the drooping heads]
A **rattlesnake root,** usu *Prenanthes serpentaria.*
1861 Wood *Class-Book* 471, *Drop Flower.* . . Prenanthes L. **1892** (1974) Millspaugh *Amer. Med. Plants* 94, *Prenanthes serpentaria.* . . Drop Flower. **1914** Georgia *Manual Weeds* 553, Gall-of-the-Earth. *Prenanthes serpentaria. . . Other English names:* . . Drop Flower, Cankerweed.

dropgate n Also *drop gap*
A temporary passageway in a wire fence.
1914 *DN* 4.105 **KS,** *Dropgate.* . . A passageway made by holding down the wires of a fence. **1956** Ker *Vocab. W. TX* 90, Place to let cars or trains pass through a fence . . drop . . gap . . drop gap . . gate . . drop gate. **1968** Adams *Western Words* 101, *Drop gap*—In cattle raising, a place in a wire fence where nails rather than staples are driven into posts, from which the wires can be lifted and fastened down until they are passed over and then replaced on the nails.

drop-in n
1 See quot 1953; an uninvited guest.
1953 Randolph-Wilson *Down in Holler* 241 **Ozarks,** *Drop-in.* . . A casual visitor, a transient. The keeper of a village hotel told me that he had four regular lodgers and averaged about three *drop-ins* a day. **1968** *DARE* (Qu. II18, *Someone who joins himself on to you and your group without being asked and won't leave*) Inf **NJ**52, Drop-in, party-crasher.
2 See quots.
1967 *Herald* (Rock Hill SC) 25 Jan 5/5, Mrs. Thomas Howard and Miss Lucey Lowry were honored at a drop-in at the home of Mr. and Mrs. William W. Hall. **1969** *DARE* File **TN, OK,** Drop-in—a party at which guests may "drop in" and leave at any time within stated limits; [held] any time of year. "I went to five drop-ins yesterday." **1976** *6000 Words* 61, *Drop-in* . . an informal social gathering at which guests are invited to drop in.

drop-ins See **drop C7a**

drop in the box (or hole) See **drop box 1**

drop in the well n
A move or sequence in the knife-tossing game of **mumblety- peg.**
1909 *DN* 3.351 **eAL, wGA,** The following terms are used in the game: *turn-in, turn-out, drop in the well, shave the pate* [etc].

drop-jaw n
See quot 1965.
1901 U.S. Dept. Ag. *Yearbook for 1900* 233, The dumb form of rabies is very common, and many persons know it as "drop jaw" who have no idea of its true nature. **1911** *Century Dict. Suppl., Drop-jaw.* . . Paralytic rabies in the dog: so called from the half-open mouth. **1965** *Dorland's Med. Dict.* 768, *Drop jaw,* the paralytic stage of rabies in a dog, in which the jaw falls.

drop-jawed adj
1969 *DARE* FW Addit **KY**40, Drop-jawed—shocked, surprised.

drop knives See **drop D6**

droplet n Cf **eardrop 1**
A small earring that dangles below the ear.
1968 *DARE* (Qu. W34) Inf **MN**15, Droplets. **1986** *Washington Post* (DC) 21 Feb sec D 1 **TX,** Princess Di earrings. . . heart-shaped droplets dangling from gold and diamond bows. **1988** *NADS Letters* **csMI,** *Droplets*—several students in the class were familiar with the term, but with the restriction that the term meant only earrings that dangle. One student from Wisconsin agreed. All who knew the term heard it from their grandmother, i.e., the term, though known, seems to be fading. *Ibid* **ceTX,** About *droplets,* several of my senior students remembered hearing that term in East Texas and the Houston area.

drop light n
The low beam on a car's headlight.
1966–67 *DARE* (Qu. N10) Inf **MI**36, Drop light—the running light and the drop light; **PA**3, Drop lights.

drop line n Also *drop cord*
A weighted fishing line with numerous leaders, usu used without a pole.
1847 Lanman *Summer in Wilderness* 158 **MI,** I have paddled to where the water was fifty feet in depth, and with a drop-line have taken, in twenty minutes, more trout than I could eat in a fortnight. **1855** Hammett *Wonderful Advent.* 143, Whether the fish be taken by rod and reel, or by drop-line, by drag-net or cast-net, it is about the same thing. **1963** *Fisherman's Encycl.* 245, Drop lines equipped with leaders will catch fish in localities where lines not so equipped will not. **1965–70** *DARE* (Qu. P17) 22 Infs, **scattered,** Drop-line fishing; **AK**9, Drop-cord fishing; (Qu. P13, . . *Other ways of fishing*) Inf **NJ**27, Drop line—just a string, no rod; **NY**76, Drop line—hook and line; **TX**26, Drop line, but one end is tied to a rock and heaved into water; **WI**50, Drop line. **1966** *DARE* Tape **MI**27, Drop line—a line used in ice fishing. It goes to the bottom of the lake. **1988** *DARE* File **ceNY** (as of 1950-60), A drop line isn't a trot line or a set line, it's one you fish by hand—not with a pole necessarily, just over the side of the boat. It's a line with several short lines coming off it, with bait at the end of each.

drop marble See **drop box 1**

drop net n **esp NC**
A type of fishing net.
1966 *DARE* (Qu. P13, . . *Ways of fishing*) Infs **NC**8, 13, Drop net. **1969** *DARE* Tape **NC**65, Always fish pound nets or what we call the drop nets. . . Just one boat, two of us in her was always in the boat.

drop off v phr
1 To die. [*OED* 1699 →] **esp sAppalachians** *euphem* Cf **drop out** v phr **1**
1913 Kephart *Highlanders* 224 **sAppalachians,** Looks like he mought drap off, him bein' weak and right narvish and sick with a head-swimmin'. **1916** *DN* 4.322 **KS,** *Drop off.* . . To die. **1927** *AmSp* 2.353 **WV,** *Drop off* . . to die. "Mrs. James dropped off last night." **1943** *LANE* Map 521, Jocular and disrespectful synonyms of *died:* . . 1 inf, **cMA,** *Dropped off.* **1954** *Harder Coll.* **cwTN,** *Drop off*—to die.
2 To lose weight. Cf **fall off** v phr **1**
1969 *DARE* (Qu. X51, *To lose weight because of sickness*) Infs **NY**154, 224, **OH**88, Dropped off.
3 See quot.
1954 *Harder Coll.* **cwTN,** *Drop off*—To close a letter. "Well guess I had better drop off."

drop one's bait can v phr
=drop one's candy.
1893 Shands *MS Speech* 27, *Dropped his bait-can.* . . A negro expression meaning *made a mistake.* Its origin is evident, one of the most serious mistakes that an angler can make, is to drop his bait-can, especially if it fall into the water. Thus *dropped his bait-can* has acquired the general meaning of making any serious mistake.

drop one's candy v phr [See quot 1908] **esp Sth, S Midl**
To make a serious mistake; to lose out.
1908 *DN* 3.307 **eAL, wGA,** *Drop one's candy.* . . To make a big blunder, do something to cause the failure of a plan. Probably the phrase originated at the candy-pullings . . , which were often held out of doors; if one dropped his candy, he naturally lost it on account of the grit and dirt. **1939** *AmSp* 14.90 **TN,** *Dropped his candy.* Defeat or loss of prestige. 'Aleck Jones dropped his candy in the Sheriff's race.' **1968** *DARE* (Qu. AA15c, . . *Joking ways . . of saying that a woman is getting married*) Inf **GA**18, Dropping her candy. **c1970** *Halpert Coll.* **wKY.** **1975** Newell *If Nothin' Don't Happen* 168 **nwFL,** Whether he was just mad from the way Effie had left him, I'll never know. But I want to tell you he grabbed that little old gal and they went to cuttin' a flutter! When Effie seen *that,* it didn't take her long to figure that she'd done dropped her candy and she'd better be a-pickin' it up.

drop one's cookies See **cookie** n[1] **4**

drop one's oar v phr *euphem*
=drop out v phr **1.**
1943 *LANE* Map 521, Jocular and disrespectful synonyms for *died:* . . 1 inf, **nwCT,** Dropped his oar.

‡**drop one's tailfeathers** v phr
1966 *DARE* (Qu. GG30, *To suddenly break out laughing: "When he told her that, she just ________.")* Inf **GA**13, Dropped her tailfeathers.

drop one's watermelon v phr
=**drop one's candy.**
1884 *Anglia* 7.275 **Sth, S Midl** [Black], *To drap yo' water-million* = to make a mistake.

drop one's wing v phr [Cf *EDD to wing down to* to court, pay attention to]
To make affectionate advances; to flirt.
1887 (1967) Harris *Free Joe* 94 **nwGA** [Black], Dee wuz times, suh, w'en it seem like ter me dat Marse Fess Trunion wuz a- cuttin' he eye at Miss Lady, en den I 'low ter myse'f, 'Shoo, man! . . you nee'nter be a-drappin' yo' wing 'roun' Miss Lady, kaze she too high-strung fer dat.' **1896** Harris *Sister Jane* 24 **GA,** Why don't [William]—drop his wing and cut the double shuffle around her? I lay that would fetch her.

drop out v phr
1 also *drop away:* To die. *euphem* Cf **drop off 1**
1943 *LANE* Map 521 **CT, cMA, VT,** Jocular and disrespectful synonyms for *died:* . . 4 infs, *Dropped out;* 2 infs, *Dropped away.* **1966–69** *DARE* (Qu. BB56, *Joking expressions for dying: "He ________.")* Inf NY206, Dropped out; **NH**11, Dropped out quick. **1986** Pederson *LAGS Concordance,* 1 inf, **nMS,** Dropping out—dying.
2 To have a parting of the ways; see quot.
1968 *DARE* (Qu. AA13, *When two people who have been 'going steady' or were engaged, stop going together, you might say, "I guess they ________.")* Inf **NY**59, Dropped out.
3 Of the wind: to die down, diminish.
1966 *DARE* (Qu. B13, *When the wind begins to decrease, you say it's ________.*) Inf **ME**22, Diminishin', droppin' out.
4 See quot.
1966 *DARE* (Qu. II22, *Expressions to tell somebody to keep to himself and mind his own business*) Inf **FL**28, Knock it off, drop out.

dropout n
1 The game of musical chairs.
1968 *DARE* (Qu. EE2, *Games that have one extra player—when a signal is given, the players change places, and the extra one tries to get a place*) Inf **MO**35, Musical chairs, dropout.
2 A dull, boring person; an undesirable person. [Prob ext from *dropout* one who quits school before graduating]
1968 *DARE* (Qu. HH3, *A dull and stupid person*) Inf **MD**40, Fool, clown, dropout; (Qu. HH16, *Uncomplimentary words with no definite meaning—just used when you want to show that you don't think much of a person: "Don't invite him. He's a ________.")* Inf **CA**106, Fink, dropout; **MD**20, Dropout [FW: Inf understands this has nothing to do with dropping out of school].

dropped biscuit See **drop biscuit 2**

dropped doughnut See **drop cake 1**

dropped egg n Also *drop egg* [Prob from Scots dial; cf *SND drap* v. 5. (2) (b) 1824 →] **chiefly NEng** See Map *somewhat old-fash*
A poached egg.

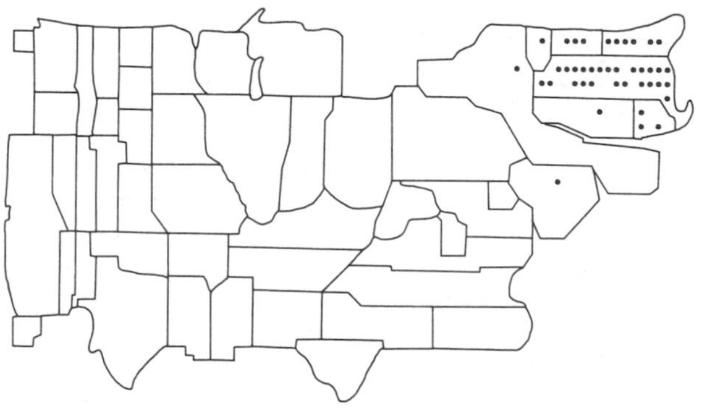

•dropped egg + varr (Qu. H35)

1884 *Harper's New Mth. Mag.* 69.306/1 **MA,** Martha was . . eating her toast and a dropped egg. **1896** (c1973) Farmer *Orig. Cook Book* 93, *Dropped Eggs* (Poached). **1933** *Hanley Disks* **neMA,** Dropped egg—take and put a pan of milk on the stove and boil and drop the egg in and let it cook. **1941** *LANE* Map 295 (Poached Eggs), **throughout NEng,** *Dropped eggs.* . . 1 inf, **ceVT,** Drop eggs. **1948** Peattie *Berkshires* 323 **wMA,** In Berkshire . . you could not get a poached egg, but you could get a "dropped" egg, which was the same thing. **1965** *PADS* 43.24 **seMA,** 6 [infs] poached eggs, 4 [infs] dropped eggs, 1 [inf] dropped egg on toast. **1965–70** *DARE* (Qu. H35, *When eggs are taken out of the shell and cooked in boiling water, you call them ________ eggs*) 40 Infs, **chiefly NEng,** Dropped; **NH**15, Dropped egg on toast. [33 of 41 Infs old] **1975** Gould *ME Lingo* 82, *Dropped egg*—Maine for poached egg, usually on toast. **1977** *Yankee* Jan 73 **Isleboro ME,** The people on Isleboro eat dropped eggs instead of poached.

dropped stitch n
1 A mentally defective person.
1845 Judd *Margaret* 207 **ME,** "She's a dropt stitch," said one woman, who had been busy during the proceedings footing a stocking.
2 Time lost from a planned schedule.
1868 Hale *If* 284, The meeting of Coram set us back that dropped-stitch in our night's journey.

dropper n
1 also *drop:* A bird dog of mixed breed. [**drop D2,** but perh infl by **drop C3**]
1889 *Century Dict.* 1778, *Dropper.* . . A dog which is a cross between a pointer and a setter. **1966–68** *DARE* (Qu. J1) Inf **GA**1, Drop—a mixed bird dog like a pointer-setter [mix]; **LA**15, Drop—they use this especially for a bird dog with impure blood; **OK**51, Dropper (for bird dogs—a cross between a setter and a pointer—a good dog). **1967** *DARE* File **csWI,** Dropper—a hound-dog mongrel. Term used by hunters in Madison, Wisconsin. **1981** Pederson *LAGS Basic Materials,* 1 inf, **neTX,** Drops, a drop—so called "because they got all kinds of different blood in 'em," term used esp. if he "shows a lot of bird dog."
2 A person or machine that places seeds or seedlings where they are to be planted. [**drop D1**]
1887 *Century Illustr. Mag.* 35.111/1 **sLA,** Big stout carts . . haul the resurrected canes to the field prepared for planting. Here a gang of women called "droppers" take up the canes by armfuls and drop them in heaps at intervals beside the furrows. **1899** Garland *Boy Life* 76 **nwIA,** It was the custom of the best farmers to wait and mark it [=the earth] the other way, just ahead of the droppers, in order that the grain should fall into moist earth. *Ibid* 78, And the skilful hoemen pressed the droppers hard. **1944** *PADS* 2.66 **S Midl,** *Dropper.* . . A person or a machine that drops or places plants at regular intervals. **1966** *PADS* 45.11 **cnKY,** *Dropper.* . . One who places [tobacco] seedlings on the ground at regular intervals in the field being planted by hand. . . "The dropper goes in front of you while you peg." **1967–70** *DARE* (Qu. L23, *What machinery is used . . in putting in the seed?*) Infs **CT**32, **MO**6, **TX**38, Dropper; **KY**43, **PA**235, Corn dropper. **1967** Key *Tobacco Vocab.* **CT, GA, MO, NC, PA,** Dropper.
3 A reaping machine that drops grain in bundles on the ground. Cf **drop reaper**
1872 (1876) Knight *Amer. Mech. Dict.* 1.754/2, *Dropper.* . . One form of a reaping machine in which the grain falls upon a slatted platform, which is *dropped* occasionally to deposit the gavel upon the ground. **1886** *Scientific Amer.* 55.373/3, It causes a Westerner to laugh to see small grain being cut with a 'dropper' or a self-raking reaper. **1970** *DARE* (Qu. L28, *Tools used in the past for cutting grain*) Inf **TN**62, Dropper.
4 also *dropper-fly:* In fly-fishing: a fly connected by a short leader above the main fly; also fig.
1879 *Scribner's Mth.* 19.19/1 **nMI,** If in fishing with a whip of three flies the angler hooks a fish on either of his droppers, the stretcher fly as it sails around beneath is pretty sure of enticing another. **1883** *Century Illustr. Mag.* 26.379/1 **KY,** The swirl of a bass was seen near the dropper fly. **1899** (1900) Van Dyke *Fisherman's Luck* 44 **PA,** He does not entangle the dropper-fly in the net and tear the tail-fly out of the fish's mouth. **1975** Gould *ME Lingo* 82, Sometimes trout will ignore the lead fly but hit the dropper. Accordingly, to have somebody "take your dropper" suggests you have been artful in your persuasion.

dropping (knives) See **drop D6**

dropping the broom See **drop the broom**

drop reaper n esp NEast
=**dropper 3.**

1966–70 *DARE* (Qu. L28) Inf **PA**103, Drop reaper—dropped it [=the grain] in a bunch (old-fashioned). Then [the grain was bound by] a reaper and binder; **NY**233, Drop reaper; (Qu. L29) Inf **NH**5, Drop reaper—dropped grain in bundles; **NY**96, Drop reaper—didn't bind it (old-fashioned); **NY**209, Drop reaper—cut it and left [it] in bunches. **1966** *DARE* Tape **NH**5, They had the old drop reaper that was pulled by two horses, and it pushed the grain off on a platform in a bundle.

drops See **drop C7a**

drop seat n [In ref to the buttoned flap that covers the buttocks] Cf *DS* W14

1958 McCulloch *Woods Words* 53 **Pacific NW,** *Drop seat*—Any long-handle union suit type of underwear.

dropseed n Also *dropseed grass*

1 =**muhly grass,** *Muhlenbergia schreberi.* [See quot 1889]

1822 Eaton *Botany* 358, *Muhlenbergia . . diffusa* (dropseed-grass). **1840** MA Zool. & Bot. Surv. *Herb. Plants & Quadrupeds* 247, *Muhlenbergia . . diffusa* . . found in this State; . . and called *Drop-seed Grass.* **1848** Gray *Manual of Botany* 579, *Muhlenbergia. . . Drop-seed Grass. . .* Chiefly perennials, . . with short narrow leaves. **1890** *Century Dict.* 3887, *Muehlenbergia. . .* On account of the early deciduous seed these grasses are called *dropseed,* especially *M. diffusa* (also called *nimble-will*). **1914** Georgia *Manual Weeds* 43, Mexican Drop-seed—*Muhlenbergia mexicana. Ibid* 44, Drop-seed Grass—*Muhlenbergia Schreberi.* **1930** OK Univ. Biol. Surv. *Pub.* 2.2.51, *Muhlenbergia arenicola. . .* Drop-seed Grass. . . *Muhlenbergia sobolifera. . .* Rock Dropseed. *Muhlenbergia sylvatica. . .* Woodland Dropseed. **1935** (1943) Muenscher *Weeds* 163, *Muhlenbergia mexicana . .* Mexican drop-seed. *Ibid* 164, *Muhlenbergia Schreberi . .* Drop-seed. **1950** Gray–Fernald *Manual of Botany* 169, *Muhlenbergia Schreberi . .* Drop-seed. **1959** Carleton *Index Herb. Plants* 39, Drop-seed: *Muehlenbergia* [sic] *diffusa.* **1973** Hitchcock–Cronquist *Flora Pacific NW* 650, *Rough-l[ea]v[e]d dropseed . . M[uhlenbergia] asperifolia.*

2 A perennial grass *(Brachyelytrum erectum)* native to most of the eastern half of the US *hist*

1822 Eaton *Botany* 358, *Muhlenbergia . . erecta* [=*Brachyelytrum erectum*] (woods dropseed-grass.) **1840** MA Zool. & Bot. Surv. *Herb. Plants & Quadrupeds* 247, *Muhlenbergia . . erecta . .* called *Drop-seed Grass.*

3 A grass of the genus *Sporobolus.* Also called **rush grass.** For other names of var spp see **bunchgrass 1, hairgrass dropseed, lightwood-knotgrass, sacaton, salt grass, smut grass, swamp grass, wiregrass**

1894 Coulter *Botany W. TX* 518, *Sporobolus . .* (Dropseed grass.) **1912** Wooton–Standley *Grasses NM* 82, *Sporobolus . .* Drop Seed Grasses. **1950** Hitchcock–Chase *Manual Grasses* 413, *Sporobolus . .* Dropseed. **1970** Correll *Plants TX* 217, *Sporobolus . .* Dropseed.

drop shed n esp Sth
A roofed structure with open sides, sometimes attached to a barn, used for storage or shelter.

1949 *AmSp* 24.108 **seSC,** *Drop shed. . .* A kind of lean-to, near the barn or away from it, used to shelter sheep, especially ewes in lambing time. **1967** *DARE* (Qu. D16) Inf **LA**2, Drop shed—an open area roofed to keep wood dry; (Qu. M1) **LA**7, Drop-shed barn—the kind with a staple top and drop sheds on it. **1986** Pederson *LAGS Concordance,* 1 inf, **ceAL,** Drop shed—a crude extension of the barn; 1 inf, **ceLA,** Drop shed.

dropsie n [Cf **drop C7a, -ie**]

1 also sp *dropsy:* In marble play: =**drop box 1.**

1970 *Thompson Coll.* **cnAL** (as of 1920s), *Dropsy*—A marble game in which the marks try to drop marbles through a hole in the top of a cigar box. **c1970** Wiersma *Marbles Terms* **swMI,** Dropsie—game in which each player tried to drop a set number of marbles through a hole in a shoe box top. The one who got the most through collected the marbles in the box. "I brought a shoe box so let's play dropsie."

2 pl: In marble play: =**bombsie(s).**

c1970 Wiersma *Marbles Terms* **MI,** A shot which consists of holding a marble at waist height and dropping it on the opponent's marble. "No dropsies this game!" *Ibid,* Dropsies—Same as bombsies, player holds marble over opponent's marble and "bombs" it. *Ibid,* Dropsies—Same as bombard or bombers. *Ibid, Knee dropsies . .* game where the player drops a marble from knee height in attempting to hit another marble. . . *Waist dropsies . .* game where the player drops a marble from waist height.

drops of gold n
A **fairy bell 2** (here: either *Disporum hookeri* or *D. trachycarpum*) or its berries.

1897 Parsons *Wild Flowers CA* 377, *Disporum Hookeri.* The common name, "drops of gold," applies to the berry. **1915** (1926) Armstrong–Thornber *Western Wild Flowers* 54, *Drops of Gold. Disporum trachycarpum. . .* The berry when unripe is orange color and suggested the name Drops of Gold, but becomes bright red when it matures in June.

drop spout n
A downspout.

1950 *WELS (The pipe that takes the water from these [=eaves troughs] to the ground or to the cistern)* 1 Inf, **cwWI,** Drop spout. **1966** *DARE* (Qu. D29) Inf **ND**3, Drop spout.

dropsy n[1] Usu with *the* [Punning allusion to *dropsy* edema] *joc*

1 Lethargy, laziness. **esp Sth, S Midl**

c1960 *Wilson Coll.* **csKY,** *Dropsy*—Humorous reference to a person's habit of dropping into a chair too often and too easily; hence must have dropsy. **1967** *DARE* Tape **TX**1, That's a saying, "He's got the dropsy." Every time he gets a chance, he'll drop down in a chair. **1967–69** *DARE* (Qu. BB28, . . *Imaginary diseases: "He must have the ______."*) Inf **AK**1, Dropsy (for a lazy person); **CA**21, Dropsy—he drops into the nearest chair; **MI**106, Dropsy [or] heart-failure; he's dropped down and doesn't have the heart to get up; **MO**39, **WV**8, Dropsy and heart trouble—that's when you drop down and ain't got the heart to get up; **LA**35, 40, **MO**8, Dropsy; (Qu. Y21) Inf **AL**34, Dropsy—he's got the natural dropsy. **1972** Hall *Sayings Old Smoky* 63 **eTN,** He's got the dropsy. Every time he gets near a chair he drops into it.

2 Clumsiness, a tendency to drop things.

1942 McAtee *Dial. Grant Co. IN* 24 (as of 1890s), *Dropsy, to have the, . .* a punning expression referring to a person's dropping almost everything; "I must ______ today, 'pears like I can't hang onto anything." **1956** McAtee *Some Dialect NC* 13, Dropsy, to have the . . a punning expression referring to a person's dropping almost everything, as on an "off day." **1968** *DARE* (Qu. HH21, *A very awkward, clumsy person*) Inf **NY**93, [You have] got the dropsy—when you break things. **1972** Hall *Sayings Old Smoky* 63 **wNC,** "Have you ever had the dropsy?" . . "Yeh, you just cain't hold onto somethin'; you drop it all the time." **1982** *Barrick Coll.* **csPA,** *Dropsy. . .* the habit of dropping things. Humorous, "oops, I must have dropsy."

dropsy n[2] See **dropsie 1**

dropsy plant n Also *dropsywort*
=**lemon balm.**

c1873 in 1976 Miller *Shaker Herbs* 131, Dropsy Plant. Useful in low fevers. **1876** Hobbs *Bot. Hdbk.* 32, Dropsy plant, Balm lemon, Melissa officinalis. **1940** Clute *Amer. Plant Names* 25, *M. officinalis.* . . Dropsy-wort. **1974** (1977) Coon *Useful Plants* 160, Dropsy plant . . was highly regarded for headaches and neuralgia.

dropsy weed n
=**Indian hemp.**

1971 Krochmal *Appalachia Med. Plants* 52, *Apocynum cannabinum. . .* Because of its use . . in treating dropsy, it has been called dropsy weed.

dropsywort See **dropsy plant**

drop the broom n Also *dropping the broom*
A dancing game in which partners are exchanged and the odd person out dances with a broom.

1966 *DARE* (QR, near Qu. EE2) Inf **MI**8, Drop the broom—dancing—one extra man; **NJ**22, Dropping the broom—a dance, you switch partners and odd man gets the broom.

drop-the-hat n
A children's game; see quot 1988.

1964 *Mt. Life* Summer 41 **sAppalachians,** In the winter we skated on the ice behind the school house and in the summer we played round-town, or long cat or short cat, or drop-the-hat or hot pepper. **1970** *DARE* (Qu. EE1) Inf **IL**135, Drop-the-hat. **1988** *NADS Letters* **NC,** My department head . . used the expression "drop the hat" for a game played in Chapel Hill in the 1930's and 1940's. His description is very like the game we call "drop the handkerchief" here in East Texas. The forming of a circle, with one member as "it" who drops whatever (hat or hankie) behind one member of the circle is the same. The person receiving the object must chase the person who dropped it around the circle fast enough to beat him to the place in the circle vacated by the former. If the person holding the object is too slow, then he must walk around the circle and drop the object as the new "it."

drop the marble See **drop box 1**

drop to sleep See **drop D5**

drop up v phr

In marble play: =**dog** v **7.**

1922 *DN* 5.186 **KY,** *Drop up* . . = dog up. **1955** *PADS* 23.16 **cwTN,** *Drop up.* Same as dog up.

drop weight n

1967 Lanham *Paste-Pot Man* 27 **TX** (as of c1900), They would stop their wagons or buggies on the street in front of the house, toss down a mound of iron with ringbolt and tether-rope called a throw-weight, or drop-weight, and stand by the picket fence.

dropworm n

1 A **bagworm** (here: *Thyridopteryx ephemeraeformis*).

1856 U.S. Patent Office *Annual Rept. for 1855: Ag.* 79, The "drop-worm" . . generally infests the arbor-vitae, larch, and hemlock-spruce. **1882** (1903) Treat *Injurious Insects* 180, It is from this habit of dropping upon persons, that they *[=Thyridopteryx ephemeræformis]* have been called "Drop-worms." **1889** [see **2** below].

2 The larva of any of var moths of the family Geometridae: see quot.

1889 *Century Dict.* 1778, *Drop-worm.* The larva of one of many insects. Specifically—*(a)* of any geometrid moth. Also called *span-worm, inch-worm, measuring-worm,* etc. *(b)* Of *Thyridopteryx ephemeræformis.* Also called *hang-worm* and *bag-worm.* **1899** (1912) Green *VA Folk-Speech* 239, *Inch-worm.* . . A drop worm or measuring-worm.

dropwort n

1 An **Indian physic** (here: *Gillenia trifoliata*).

1900 Lyons *Plant Names* 303, *[Gillenia] trifoliata.* . . Western Drop-wort.

2 =**cowbane 2.**

1933 Small *Manual SE Flora* 985, *Oxypolis.* . . Perennial herbs. . . Five species, North American. . . Dropworts.

dror See **draw** v

dross n **chiefly S Atl**

A mixture of wood chips and rosin, often used for kindling; see quots.

1938 FWP *U.S. One* 248 **GA,** The dross, chips of pine wood covered with inflammable rosin, is gathered and sold for kindling. **1949** *AmSp* 24.108 **seSC,** *Dross.* . . Waste pine gum, mixed with dead leaves, etc., collected from around the base of pine stumps. *Dross-stand,* . . vessel in which dross was burnt, indoors, for repelling mosquitoes. **1966** *DARE* Tape **FL**6, You let your rosin out . . and it's strained through this cotton batting to get out all the chips. . . They strain all these chips off with a big, old dipper. . . These chips are called dross. It's good kindling for fires. **1968** *DARE* (Qu. D34, . . *The small pieces of wood and other stuff that are used to start a fire*) Inf **GA**32, Dross [drɔs]—leftovers after rosin is cooked; used to start fire under a still. **1972** *DARE* File **nwFL,** Dross—small wood shavings off turpentine trees; what kindling is usually made of.

drot See **drat** v

drothers See **druthers**

drotted See **drat** v

drought n For pronc varr see **A** below [See *OED* for hist development of forms, and 1974 Orton-Wright *Word Geog. Engl.* for contemporary distribution of proncs]

A Forms.

1 |draʊθ|; pronc-spp *drouth, drowth.* [Scots and nEngl dial] **widespread** *somewhat old-fash*

1828 Webster *Amer. Dict.* np, *Drouth.* . . This is usually written *drought,* . . but improperly. The word generally used is now, as it was written by Bacon, *drouth* or *drowth;* its regular termination is *th.* **1834** (1925) Evans *Jrl.* 3.210 **IN,** Prairies with poor grazing for horses owing to the drouth. **1886** *S. Bivouac* 4.343 **sAppalachians,** Drouth . . (drought). **1961** Kurath–McDavid *Pronc. Engl.* 167, Except in western Pennsylvania, /drauθ/, riming with *mouth,* is nearly universal in folk speech and predominates decidedly in the speech of the middle group; in cultivated speech it occurs not infrequently by the side of /draut/ in the New England settlement area, but is rather rare elsewhere. **1965–70** *DARE* (Qu. B28) 354 Infs, **widespread,** Drouth; **GA**77, [dræθ]; [**GA**4, [draʊs]; **MO**3, A drouths]. [Of all Infs responding to the question, 30% were comm type 5, 70% old, 31% gs educ or less, 31% coll educ, 50% male; of those giving the response *drouth,* 41% were comm type 5, 81% old, 39% gs educ or less, 25% coll educ, 58% male.] **1968** *DARE* Tape **GA**31, Water maybe washes over them during flood periods and becomes dry during drouth [draʊθ] periods.

2 |draʊt|. **widespread**

1961 Kurath–McDavid *Pronc. Engl.* 167, *Drought.* . . /draut/, riming with *out,* is common only in cultivated speech, but has some currency among the middle class, especially in urbanized areas. **1965–70** *DARE* (Qu. B28) 275 Infs, **widespread,** Drought. [Of all Infs responding to the question, 6% were comm type 1, 30% comm type 5, 70% old, 31% coll educ, 50% female; of those giving this response, 15% were comm type 1, 17% comm type 5, 59% old, 47% coll educ, 61% female.]

3 |drɑθ, drɔθ|; pronc-sp *drawth.* **scattered, but less freq Sth, S Midl**

1939 *LANE* Map 97, [Eleven infs, **chiefly wNEng,** gave proncs of the type [drɔθ, drɑθ]; two infs, **eMA,** gave proncs of the type [drɔt].] **1961** Kurath–McDavid *Pronc. Engl.* 167, *Drought* rimes either with *out,* with *mouth,* with *tooth,* with *bought,* or with *moth.* Many, who normally use *dry spell,* know this expression only from print. . . The vowel /ɔ/ of *bought* (presumably a spelling pronunciation of an unfamiliar word) occurs in scattered instances in New England, New York State, and the German section of eastern Pennsylvania, rarely elsewhere. **1965–70** *DARE* (Qu. B28) 32 Infs, **scattered, but less freq Sth. S Midl,** Drawth. **1976** Allen *LAUM* 3.268 (as of c1950), *Drought.* . . Instances of the form with /ɔ/, all with final /θ/ except for two . . with final /t/, are sporadic in the U[pper] M[idwest], the greatest frequency being in Minnesota.

4 |drɑt, drɔt|; pronc-sp *drawt.* **chiefly Nth, N Midl** See Map

1939 [see **A3** above]. **1952** Brown *NC Folkl.* 1.534, *Drought* [drɔt]. . . *Drought.*—West. Rare. **1961** [see **A3** above]. **1965–70** *DARE* (Qu. B28) 28 Infs, **chiefly Inland Nth, N Midl,** Drawt. **1976** [see **A3** above].

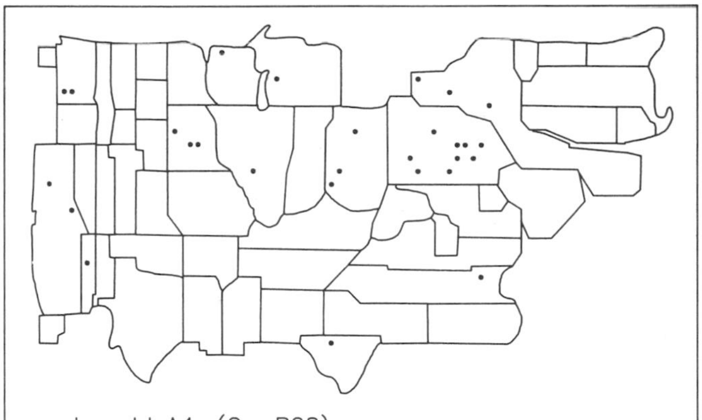

•drought A4 (Qu. B28)

5 |druθ|; pronc-sp *drooth.* [Scots, nIr dial] **esp wPA**

1961 Kurath–McDavid *Pronc. Engl.* 167, *Drought.* . . The vowel /au/ of *out* has nearly universal currency everywhere, except in western Pennsylvania, where the word is rather generally pronounced /druθ/, riming with *tooth.* This is one of the very few Scotticisms that have survived in any area in which the Ulster Scots were numerous among the early settlers. **1965–70** *DARE* (Qu. B28) Infs **MI**68, **NY**19, **PA**141, Drooth [druθ].

6 |draʊf(t), drɔf(t), dræft|; pronc-sp *draft.*

1939 *LANE* Map 97 *(Drought)* 1 inf, **neMA,** [dræ˙θ], [inf corrected to:] [dræ·ft]. **1965–70** *DARE* (Qu. B28) Inf **SC**42, [dræ˙ʊf]; **VA**47, [drəʊf]; **WI**47, [draʊft]; **PA**216, 233, [drɔft]; **VA**69, [drɒf]; (Qu. Q14) Inf **VA**47, [dræʊf] bird. **1970** Tarpley *Blinky* 60 **neTX,** *Long period of dry weather* . . [1 of 200 infs] draft.

7 |draʊ|.

1968–70 *DARE* (Qu. B28) Infs **FL**48, **IN**79, **NC**87, [draʊ]; **MD**41, [dræʊ].

B Sense.

See quot. [*OED drought* sb. 4 1393 →; "*arch.* and *dial.*"] Cf **droughty**

1899 (1912) Green *VA Folk-Speech* 156, *Drouth*. . . Thirst; want of drink.

drought bird n

=**yellow-billed cuckoo.**

1970 *DARE* (Qu. Q14) Inf **VA**47, Drought [dræuf] bird—yellow-billed cuckoo—heard in dry weather.

drought fly n

A **cicada.**

1969 *DARE* (Qu. R7, *Insects that sit in trees or bushes in hot weather and make a sharp, buzzing sound*) Inf **MO**20, [My] grandmother's term was drought flies ['drɒθ ˌflɑˑɪz].

droughty adj Pronc-sp *drouthy* [*OED* 1626 →] *old-fash*

Thirsty; dry, abstaining from alcoholic beverages.

1869 *Republican Journal* (Lawrence) 5 March *(DA)* **KS**, Strangers visiting the State for the first time can scarcely realize that this is *'drouthy Kansas.'* **1878** Beadle *Western Wilds* 432, 'Droughty Kansas' was a standing joke. **1899** (1912) Green *VA Folk-Speech* 157, *Drouthy*. . . Dry; thirsty, requiring drink; thirsty from heat or fever. **1920** Hunter *Trail Drivers TX* 444 (as of c1875), A man standing on the opposite side [of the street], without asking a word, but I think from Comb's drouthy look sized us up and said: "Go back two doors and go in a back room and you will find what you are looking for."

drounding See **drown 2**

d'rout See **without**

drouth See **drought A1**

drouthy See **droughty**

drove See **drive** v **A3**

droved See **drive** v **A2, 3**

droven See **drive** v **A3**

drown v

Std senses, var forms. Cf **goose-drownder**

1 infin, pres: usu *drown;* also *drownd.*

1891 in 1944 *ADD* 181 **cNY,** [draʊnd]. **1924** Lardner *How to Write* 196, He could drownd out the Subway. **1936** [see **2** below]. **1940** *AmSp* 15.48 **sAppalachians,** Excrescent [d] is also present in . . *drownd* (present) and *drownding.* **1967–68** *DARE* (Qu. Y43b, *Expressions meaning to put out a fire*) Inf **NY**68, Drownd it; **TX**26, Drownd out. **1982** *Barrick Coll.* **csPA,** *Drownd—drown* "He's gonna drownd in there."

2 pres pple, vbl n: usu *drowning;* also *drownding, drounding.*

1844 Thompson *Major Jones's Courtship* 45 **GA,** How upon yeath I ever got out without droundin I can't see. **1927** *DN* 5.470 **Appalachians,** *Drowning*—drownding. **1929** Sale *Tree Named John* 70 **MS,** You could swolly a hawg bladder ef h'it 'uz gwi [=going to] keep you f'um drowndin'. **1936** *AmSp* 11.239 **eTX,** *Drown, drowned, drowning:* [drɑ̃ʊ̃nd], ['drɑ̃ʊ̃ndɪd], [drɑ̃ʊ̃ndɪn]. **1940** [see **1** above]. **1966–68** *DARE* (Qu. P9, *When you're fishing but not catching any, you might say, "________."*) Infs **ND**1, **NJ**2, Drownding minnows (*or* bait); (Qu. X56b, . . *Sweating very heavily*) Inf **NJ**33, Drownding. **1966** *DARE* Tape **MS**68, And I liked to seen two drowndings.

3 past, past pple, ppl adj: usu *drowned;* also, *esp among speakers with little formal educ, drownded;* occas (past, past pple) *drown.*

1781 *PA Jrl. & Weekly Advt.* (Philadelphia) 16 May 1/2, He was *drownded* in the Delaware—This is so common, that I have known a gentleman reading it in a book to a company, though it was printed *drowned,* read *drownded.* **1843** (1916) Hall *New Purchase* 227, I was sentimentally afeer'd now he'd git drownded. **1899** (1912) Green *VA Folk-Speech* 157, Drownded. . . For *drowned.* **1903** *DN* 2.296 **Cape Cod MA** (as of a1857), *Drownded rat*. . . In expression 'wet as a drownded rat.' **1908** *DN* 3.307 **eAL, wGA,** *Drownded, pret.* and *pp.* of *drown.* Almost universally pronounced in two syllables. **1926** *DN* 5.383 **NEng,** *Drownded* for drowned. **1936** [see **2** above]. **1953** Atwood *Survey of Verb Forms* 12, *Drown*. . . The past participle is recorded in the context "He was (drowned)." The standard *drowned* /draund/ is almost universal in cultured speech everywhere. . . *Drownded* / draundəd/ is used by about one fourth of the N. Eng. informants, with the heaviest concentration in n. N. Eng. and in Conn. . . Elsewhere in the Eastern States *drownded* is distinctly a Type I [=Infs with poor educ] form, varying in frequency from one third (e. N.Y.) to nine tenths (N.C.). In Type II [=Infs with fair educ] *drownded* is used by less than one tenth in e. N.Y., by about one fourth in Pa., Va., and N.C., and by slightly less than half in W. Va. About two thirds of the Southern Negro informants use this form. **c1960** *Wilson Coll.* **csKY,** *Drownded* . . almost regular for past and past participle. **1965–70** *DARE* (Qu. OO26a, . . *"Several people have ________ [there]."*; not asked in early QRs) 785 Infs, **widespread,** Drowned; 165 Infs, **widespread,** (Got) drownded; **AL**20, 37, **GA**1, **KS**8, **NC**51, 52, 63, 77, **NH**17, **SC**26, Drown; (Qu. OO26b, . . *"A boy was ________ [there]."*; not asked in early QRs) 792 Infs, **widespread,** Drowned; 152 Infs, **widespread,** (Got) drownded; **AL**37, **MO**36, **NC**51, 63, **SC**26, Drown; (Qu. OO26c, . . *"Lots of people have been ________ here."*; total Infs questioned, 75) 56 Infs, Drowned; 20 Infs, Drownded [Of all Infs responding to Qq. OO26a, b, c, 29% were from comm type 5, 25% gs educ or less; of those giving the response *drownded* to one or more of these Qq., 43% were from comm type 5, 46% gs educ or less]; (Qu. OO26d, . . *"A child ________ here."*; total Infs questioned, 75) 59 Infs, Drowned; 17 Infs, Drownded; **GA**1, Drown; (Qu. P9, *When you're fishing but not catching any, you might say, "________."*) Inf **VA**70, Fish got drownded; **SC**32, Fish have all drowned. **1966–68** *DARE* Tape **CA**89, I think one of the Indian boys drownded in that pool; **GA**1, I carried 'em in, drownded 'em; **IL**2, Pour in water till the gopher'd be drownded out; **SC**15, He take you down the river and drownded you. **1976** Allen *LAUM* 3.16 (as of c1950), Regular *drowned* is the majority form for the past participle of *drown* in the speech of U[pper] M[idwest] infs., although it competes with *drownded* among the less educated. . . A variant *drown,* without the inflectional ending, is a rare minor form in Minnesota and Iowa.

drownd See **drown 1**

drownded See **drown 3**

drownding See **drown 2**

drowned land n

Inundated land, a marsh.

1752 in 1916 Mereness *Travels* 306 **NY,** [We] lodged at the canoeing place from said lake to the drowned land. **1781** in 1940 *AmSp* 15.174 **VA,** *Drowned Lands.* Bounded thence downward by the Drowned lands of the Mississippi to the Carolina line. **1836** Weston *Visit U.S.* 141 **NY,** The townships of Warwick and Goshen contain some large tracts of what are called drowned lands, on which some good flax is occasionally raised; but they are sometimes overflowed with water, and the crop entirely buried under the fresh alluvial soil. **1968** *DARE* (Qu. C7, . . *Land that usually has some standing water with trees or bushes growing in it*) Inf **MI**98, Drowned land.

drowning worms, drown minnows, drown the bait See **drown worms**

‡drown the duck n

A water game.

1967 *DARE* (Qu. EE28, *Games played in the water*) Inf **IA**3, Drown the duck.

drown the miller v phr [Scots and Engl dial]

1 To dilute liquor with too much water.

1899 (1912) Green *VA Folk-Speech* 157, *Drown the miller*. . . To pour two [sic] much water into the spirit when mixing grog. **1942** Berrey–Van den Bark *Amer. Slang* 795.2, Drown the miller, *to dilute liquor too much.* **1975** Gould *ME Lingo* 82, *Drown the miller*—Often *drownd:* "Don't *drownd* the miller!" It is almost always heard in this negative imperative, because it means to over-water the rum or whiskey, which is never taken to kindly.

2 To add excess liquid to dough. **esp S Midl** Cf **draw the miller**

1916 *DN* 4.322 **cKS,** *Drown the miller*. . . In breadmaking, to use too much water in proportion to flour. **1939** *AmSp* 14.265 **sIN,** A cook who uses a great deal of water in mixing her bread is 'drowning the miller.' **1944** *PADS* 2.58 **nwMO,** *Miller, to drown the*. . . "Better go to the mill, Jim. I drowned the miller this morning and need some flour." **1944** *ADD* **cWV, swIN, sTN,** *Drown the miller.* **1952** Brown *NC Folkl.* 1.444, Drown the miller. (Too much water [milk] in flour in making bread). **1953** Randolph–Wilson *Down in Holler* 205 **Ozarks,** When a woman runs out of flour before her dough is properly mixed, so that the *kneadin'* is too thin and there's no flour to thicken it, they say, "She has done *drownded the miller.*"

drown worms v phr, hence vbl n *drowning worms* For varr see quot 1966–69

To fish, esp unsuccessfully.

1966–69 *DARE* (Qu. P9, *When you're fishing but not catching any, you might say, "______."*) Inf **AL**53, Drowning worms [dræʊndɨn wɝmz]; **IL**74, I'm drowning worms [FW sugg]; **ND**1, I'm drownding minnows; **NJ**2, Drownding the bait. **1967** *DARE* File **nIL**, Drown a worm—to go fishing. **1982** *Grit* (Williamsport PA) 4 July 17, There's nothing like a relaxing Saturday afternoon of drowning some worms. Whenever Mrs. Baker hears her husband say that, she knows he's heading down to his favorite fishing spot.

drowsy adj [Perh infl by *lousy*]

1 Unwell, sick. **esp Gulf States, Ohio Valley** See Map

1965–70 *DARE* (Qu. BB5, *A general feeling of discomfort or illness that isn't any one place in particular*) Infs **LA**8, **MS**88, **OH**40, **TX**35, (I feel) drowsy; (Qu. BB16b, *If something a person ate didn't agree with him, he might just feel a bit ______*) Infs **MO**18, **OH**53, Drowsy; (Qu. BB39, *On a day when you don't feel just right, though not actually sick, you might say, "I'll be all right tomorrow—I'm just feeling ______ today."*) Infs **AR**55, **FL**14, 33, **GA**8, **KY**35, **LA**37, **OK**1, **TX**86, Drowsy.

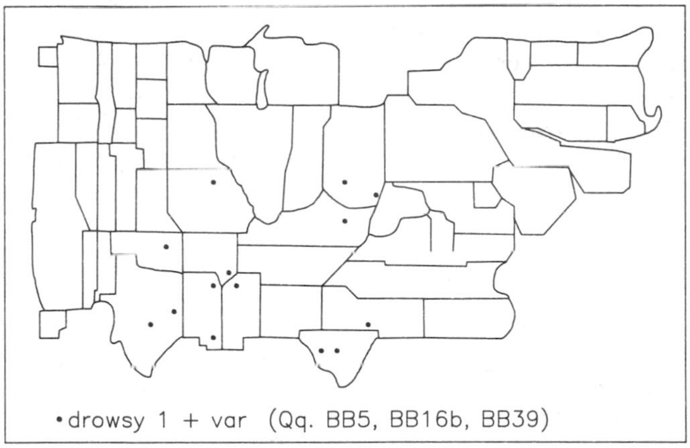

2 Of the weather: unpleasant.

1970 *DARE* (Qu. B2, *If the weather is very unpleasant, you say it's a ______ day.*) Inf **OH**91, Drowsy [FW: sic]; **VA**39, Miserable, drowsy.

drowth See **drought A1**

drozzle v

To dribble.

1909 *DN* 3.420 **Cape Cod MA** (as of a1857), *Drozzle.* "You've drozzled your milk all over your bib."

drubs exclam [Var of **dubs** exclam **2**] Cf **dib** n[1] **2**

1940 *Qrly. Jrl. Speech* 26.266 **nwVA**, What children in the North call "dibs on it," meaning *I claim a share,* Virginia children may call . . "drubs on it".

druce v [From *introduce;* cf Intro "Language Changes" I.7, 9]

1950 *PADS* 14.27 **SC**, *Druce.* . . To introduce. Gullah. "Ain't hunnah gwine to de chu'ch to druce yuh new bruddah?"

drudge See **dredge** n[1], v

drudging box See **dredge box**

drug v See **drag** v **A1, 2**

drug n[1], hence adj *druggy* [Var of *dreg* sediment, lees] **chiefly S Midl**

1892 *DN* 1.233 **KY**, *Druggy* [drʌgɪ]: dreggy. **1895** *DN* 1.371 **eTN**, The old woman has the rheumatiz; I reckon hit's the drugs of the fever. **1899** (1912) Green *VA Folk-Speech* 157, *Drugs.* . . Dregs; sediment in any liquid. **1902** *DN* 2.233 **sIL**, *Drugs.* **1906** *DN* 3.117 **sIN**, *Drugs.* . . Sediment, settlings, dregs. *Ibid* 134 **nwAR**, *Druggy.* . . Dreggy. "My! Isn't this water druggy." *Drugs.* . . Dregs. "You can see the drugs in the water from that well." **1916** *DN* 4.347 **TX, LA**, *Drugs.* . . Dregs. **1917** *DN* 4.411 **KY, wNC, NY, SC**, *Drugs.* . . Variant of *dregs.* **c1960** *Wilson Coll.* **csKY**, *Dregs* is often [drʌgz].

drug n[2] [Cf *OED drogue*]

1 See quot.

1905 Wasson *Green Shay* 83 **NEng**, Of course John Ed could n't make no fist of it towin' that much drug [Footnote: Drag] astern, and had to cut her adrift.

2 See **drag** n **2.**

‡**drug** n[3] [Abbr for *drugstore*]

1967 *DARE* FW Addit **LA**11, Drug—Get medicine at the drug.

drugged See **drag** v **A1, 2**

drugged out See **dragged out**

druggy adj[1]

1 Sleepy, groggy.

1950 Giles *Enduring Hills* 123 **KY**, "Have to git up early in the mornin'," he said, "an' ifen I stay up too late at night, I'm druggy the next day." **1968** *DARE* (Qu. X43b, *If you sleep later than usual one day on purpose, you'd say, "I ______."*) Inf **NC**49, Felt druggy.

2 Slightly inebriated.

1968 *DARE* (Qu. DD14, *When a person is partly drunk, "He's ______."*) Inf **GA**26, Druggy.

druggy adj[2] See **drug** n[1]

drug out See **dragged out**

drum n

1 also *drumfish:* Any of several fish of the family Sciaenidae. [See quots 1887, 1983] See also **black drum, croaker** n[1] **1a, freshwater drum, red drum, sea drum**

1650 in 1844 Force *Tracts* 3.11.11 **NC**, Sturgeon of ten feet, Drummes of sixe in length. **1737** (1911) Brickell *Nat. Hist. NC* 229, The *Drum-fish,* whereof there are two sorts, *viz.* the Red and the Black. **1790** *PA Packet & Daily Advt.* (Philadelphia) 3 Mar 3/2 **Savannah GA**, Maxwell, at one haul, took up as many bass, drum, trout, mullet, and whiting . . as filled a six oared boat. **1887** Goode *Amer. Fishes* 136, The name "Drum," as everyone knows, alludes to the loud drumming noise which is heard, especially in the breeding season, and is doubtless the signal by which the fish call to their mates. This habit of drumming is shared by many fishes of this family. **1933** LA Dept. of Conserv. *Fishes* 177, The Sea Drum or Black Drum . . Additional popular names . . Big Drum. **1948** *Chicago Tribune* (IL) 25 Jan sec 2 4/6 **seTX**, Then we caught good sized drums, silvery, husky fish that won't give up a fight. **1965–70** *DARE* (Qu. P1) 18 Infs, **Inland Sth, Cent,** Drum(s); (Qu. P2) 18 Infs, **Sth,** Drum(s); **MD**5, 40, **NC**49, **SC**66, Drumfish; (Qu. P3) 8 Infs, **chiefly Cent, Missip Valley,** Drum(s); **OK**42, Drumfish; (Qu. P4) Infs **MS**73, **TX**11, 53, Drum; (Qu. P14) Infs **KY**16, **MS**58, 60, **NC**27, 82, Drum. **1966** *DARE* Tape **FL**16, If you want to catch drum you have to go out into the mouth of the rivers that come in from the ocean. . . An' drum is a fish that you fish with crab. **1983** Becker *Fishes WI* 956, Most species of the drum family have a complicated swim bladder with special muscles and tendons that are capable of producing audible sounds when vibrated against the bladder.

2 A carpsucker (here: *Carpiodes cyprinus*).

1902 Jordan–Evermann *Amer. Fishes* 43, *Lake Carp.* . . By the fishermen of Lake Champlain this species is known as "buffalo," "carp sucker," or "drum." **1983** Becker *Fishes WI* 630, *Carpiodes cyprinus.* . . Other common names: . . lake carp, . . drum.

3 =**pompon.**

1935 Caine *Game Fish* 114, *Pompon. Anisotremus surinamensis.* . . Drum.

drumfish See **drum 1**

drumheads n

A **milkwort** (here: *Polygala cruciata*).

1900 Lyons *Plant Names* 299, *P. cruciata,* eastern U.S., . . Drumheads. **1933** Small *Manual SE Flora* 771, *P. cruciata.* . . Drum-heads. **1949** Moldenke *Amer. Wild Flowers* 52, Without the conspicuous basal rosettes of leaves . . is . . *drumheads.* **1975** Duncan–Foote *Wildflowers SE* 92, *Drum-heads.* . . *Polygala cruciata.* . . Wet places, pinelands, savannahs, bogs.

drumlin n [Etym uncert, but cf *drum* percussion instrument and Ger *trommeln* to beat a drum, make a loud noise]

A **shivaree.**

1968 *DARE* (Qu. AA18, . . *A noisy neighborhood celebration after a wedding, where the married couple is expected to give a treat*) Inf **PA**110,

"Shivaree" if older people did it, "drumlin" if young kids did it—throw change out.

drumly adj, adv [Scots and Engl dial] *rare*

Muddy; darkly, gloomily.

1928 Chapman *Happy Mt.* 231 **eTN,** And how weariness of the summer had eaten her down till her heart was drumly dark. **1952** Brown *NC Folkl.* 1.535, *Drumly.* . . Muddy.—West.

drummer n

1 Either of two **weakfish:** *Cynoscion nebulosus* or *C. regalis.*

1807 in 1846 MA Hist. Soc. *Coll.* 2d ser 3.57, The squittee, or drummer, is taken in the Sound, but principally in the harbours and lagunes, in summer. **1887** Goode *Amer. Fishes* 112, "In the days of my boyhood," said Capt. Atwood, when before the Rhode Island Legislature in 1871, "my neighbors often spoke of a fish called the 'drummer,' which is the same variety that you call the Squeteague." **1892** *Outing* Apr 54/1 **MA,** The squetauge or weak-fish [is] . . known about Cape Cod as the 'drummer,' 'silver fish,' and 'spotted boy.' **1935** Caine *Game Fish* 145, Weakfish—*Cynoscion regalis*—Spotted Weakfish—*Cynoscion nebulosus* . . Synonyms: Alligator Trout . . Drummer . . Winter Trout, Yellow-fin Trout. **1946** LaMonte *N. Amer. Game Fishes* 75, Weakfish. *Cynoscion regalis.* . . Names: Squeteague . . Drummer, Gray Squeteague. *Ibid,* Spotted Weakfish. *Cynoscion nebulosus.* . . Names: Spotted Squeteague . . (also any of the names used for Weakfish).

2 A **cabezon** (here: *Scorpaenichthys marmoratus*).

1884 Goode *Fisheries U.S.* 1.259, The Cottidae . . are represented on the Pacific coast by about eighteen separate species, known by such names as "Sculpin," "Drummer," "Salpa," [etc]. . . "Drummer" comes from the quivering noise made by many species when taken alive out of the water.

3 also *drummond:* **=freshwater drum.**

1968–69 *DARE* (Qu. P1) Inf **KY**56, Drummers; **OH**58, Drummonds.

4 also *drumming grouse, ~ partridge, ~ pheasant:* A **ruffed grouse.**

[1655 [see **groundhog 1**].] **1783** Latham *Genl. Synopsis Birds* 2.739 **PA, NY,** Ruffed Gr[ouse]. Tetrao umbellus. . . Size between a *Pheasant* and a *Partridge.* . . This species inhabits *Pensylvania* [sic], *New York.* . . They are called by some the *Drumming Partridge.* **1917** (1923) *Birds Amer.* 2.17, *Ruffed Grouse—Bonasa umbellus.* . . Other Names.—Grouse; . . Drumming Grouse; . . Drumming Pheasant; Mountain Pheasant. **1953** Jewett *Birds WA* 206, *Columbian Ruffed Grouse. Bonasa umbellus affinis* . . Other names: Drummer; Gray Ruffed Grouse. . . During the spring and summer, in ruffed grouse country, one is likely to hear peculiar muffled booming, the so-called drumming of this bird.

5 =bullfrog 1.

1969 *DARE* (Qu. P22, *Names or nicknames for a very large frog that makes a deep, loud sound*) Inf **KY**65, Drummer = bullfrog.

6 One who solicits trade; a traveling salesman. **widespread, but chiefly Sth, S Midl** See Map *somewhat old-fash*

1839 (1969) Briggs *Advent. Franco* 1.77 **NYC,** Mr. Lummucks . . was a drummer . . sent out to drum up customers for his employers. **1882** Sweet-Knox *Sketches TX Siftings* 12 *(DAE),* The drummer . . sleeping in a baggage car or the caboose of a freight train. **1903** (1965) Adams *Log Cowboy* 208 **West,** All of a sudden here comes this livery rig along with that drummer. **1906** *DN* 3.133 **nwAR,** *Doctor drummer.* . . A solicitor of practice for a physician. "The government is going to do away with the doctor drummers at Hot Springs." **1917** Mathewson *Sec. Base Sloan* 57 *(DAE),* June had the enormous sum of twenty cents, earned by carrying a drummer's sample cases from store to store for a period of well over an hour. **1942** Faulkner *Go Down* 96 **MS,** I want to know about that damn Saint Louis drummer. **1965–70** *DARE* (Qu. U7, *A man who goes from town to town selling things*) 213 Infs, **widespread, but chiefly Sth, S Midl,** Drummer; **AL**10, Door-to-door drummer; **GA**77, Road drummer [Of all Infs responding to the question, 66% were old; of those giving these responses, 78% were old.]; (Qu. U5, *Someone who sells small articles on a street corner*) Inf **NC**16, Drummer; (Qu. U6, *Someone who sells vegetables or other articles from a wagon or truck, going from house to house*) Inf **VA**63, Drummer. **1967–69** *DARE* Tape **KY**16A, Just as I got off of that horse some coffee drummer drove up there; **LA**12, He's . . a paint drummer. **1984** Burns *Cold Sassy* 72 **nGA** (as of 1906), There were . . usually four or five drummers who would set up their merchandise in a hotel room.

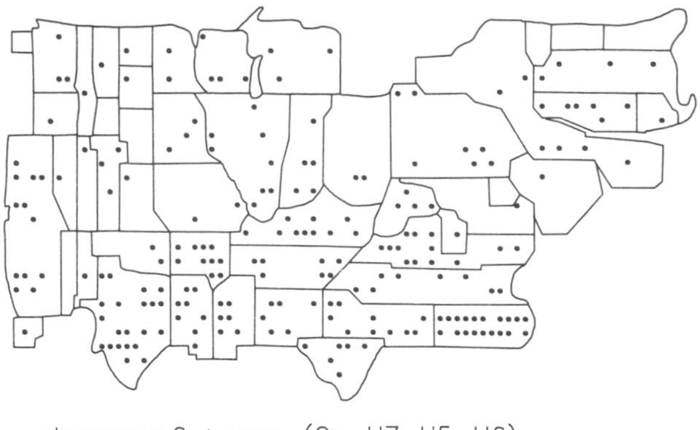

•drummer 6 + varr (Qq. U7, U5, U6)

drumming grouse (or partridge, pheasant) See **drummer 4**

drummond See **drummer 3**

drummy ground n

In mining; see quot.

1940 Writers' Program *Guide NV* 61, *Drummy ground* produces a hollow sound when struck and indicates loose rock, which must be removed or supported by timbering.

drump See **dream 1**

drumstick n

1 =stilt sandpiper.

1880 *Forest & Stream* 15.4/3, Long-legged sandpiper *(Micropalama himantopus)* . . drum-stick.

2 A **knapweed** (here: *Centaurea nigra*).

1900 Lyons *Plant Names* 89, *C. nigra.* . . Drumstick.

drunk adj [Cf *OED drunk* ppl. a. 2 "Of a thing: Drenched; saturated with as much moisture as it can take in or receive. *Obs.*" 1382–1697]

Of food, esp baked goods: overly moist, soggy; heavy, unrisen.

1944 *PADS* 2.42 **sVA, wNC,** *Drunk.* . . Said of cake, bread, potatoes, etc., which "fall" or become heavy when cooked. **1947** *AmSp* 22.73 **swGA,** "We'll have *drunk potatoes* because the fire has gone out." When the process of boiling is interrupted and resumed after cooling, the potatoes apparently soak up considerable quantities of moisture, a development which would account for the exclamation from a native Georgian in military service, "Drunk potatoes again!" **1952** Brown *NC Folkl.* 1.535, *Drunk.* . . Of a cake or lightbread: heavy, not risen.—General. Rare.

drunk adv Cf *DS* W37, 38 and **drunk and dressed up**

In phr *dress up drunk:* To dress in an excessive or ostentatious manner.

1859 (1968) Bartlett *Americanisms* 131, In the South, *to dress up drunk* . . to overdress, dress to excess. **1984** Wilder *You All Spoken Here* 52 **Sth,** To be dressed up drunk is to be dressed to excess.

drunk n

Drunkenness.

1931 Hannum *Thursday April* 101 **wNC,** Wal, when yo're a-makin' yore cider, bile some. Damn me efn hit don't make drunk come quick. **c1938** in 1970 Hyatt *Hoodoo* 1.13 **seGA** [Black], Well, dey 'rest [=arrested] her two-three time of drunk'.

drunk and dressed up ppl adj phr Cf **drunk** adv

1906 *DN* 3.134 **nwAR,** *Drunk and dressed up.* . . To feel stiff, showy, and uncomfortable when dressed in one's best. "I feel like I'm drunk and dressed up."

drunkard n

1 A fruit fly (Drosophilidae). **chiefly Mid Atl** See Map

1899 (1912) Green *VA Folk-Speech* 125, *Drunkards.* . . Small flies that fly about and light in sweetened liquors. **1952** Brown *NC Folkl.* 1.535, *Drunkard.* . . A small yellowish fly that sucks fermenting juices.—Central and east. **1963** TN Folk Lore Soc. *Bulletin* 29.4 **KY,** *Bugs.* . . This term includes . . drunkards . . (*Drosophila* Sp.) **1965–70** *DARE* (Qu. R13, *Flies that come to meat or fruit*) 13 Infs, **chiefly Mid Atl,** Drunkard; (Qu. R10, *Very small flies that don't sting, often seen hovering in large* *groups or bunches outdoors in summer*) Inf **NC**36, Drunkards. **1975** McDonough *Garden Sass* 245 **AR,** People of the Ozarks. . . call the little flies that buzz around their homemade wine "drunkards".

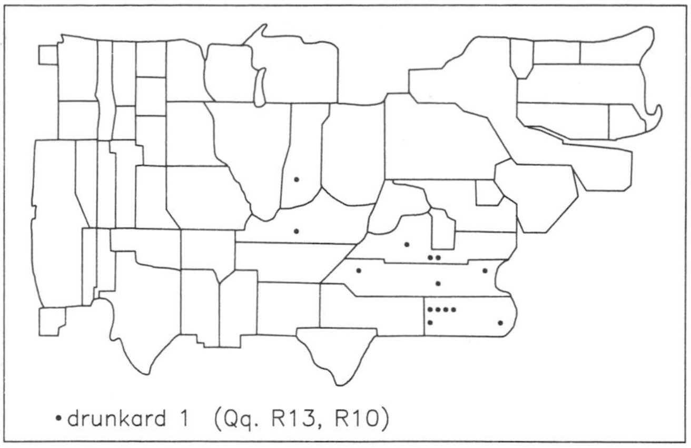

2 pl: A **wintergreen** (here: *Gaultheria procumbens*); also its leaves. [See quots 1890, 1892]

1890 *Jrl. Amer. Folkl.* 3.64 **MA,** *Drunkards.*—At Hyannis this is the name by which the young, tender leaves of the checkerberry are called. . . Perhaps the name was given . . on account of their use as a leading ingredient in the making of home-brewed beer. **1892** *Ibid* 5.100, *Gaultheria procumbens,* young plantlets; drunkards. Barnstable, Mass. . . Believed by children to intoxicate. **1911** Henkel *Amer. Med. Leaves* 19, *Wintergreen. . . Other common names. . .* Drunkards. **1930** Sievers *Amer. Med. Plants* 63, Drunkards. . . This small native plant frequents sandy soils in cool, damp woods. **1951** Hough *Singing in Morning* 241 **Martha's Vineyard MA,** Checkerberry or wintergreen. . . Next spring one will pick the delicately flushed new leaves and chew them for the same flavor; the old people had their name for these leaves too—the rather swashbuckling one of "drunkards." **1959** Carleton *Index Herb. Plants* 39, *Drunkards:* Caltha palustris; Gaultheria procumbens.

3 pl: A **marsh marigold** (here: *Caltha palustris*).

1900 Lyons *Plant Names* 76, *C[altha] palustris. . .* Drunkards. **1940** Clute *Amer. Plant Names* 254, *Caltha palustris. . .* Drunkards. **1959** [see **2** above].

4 In railroading: see quots.

1945 Hubbard *Railroad Ave.* 341, *Drunkard*—Late Saturday-night passenger train. **1977** Adams *Lang. Railroader* 50, *Drunkard:* A late Saturday night passenger train. The last commuting train from a city terminal.

drunk as a dog See **dog** n **B17h**

drunk as a fiddler's bitch See **fiddler's bitch**

drunked See **drink** v **A3, 4**

drunken See **drink** v **A4**

drunken monkey See **monkey** n

drupe n

=**staghorn sumac.**

1970 *NC Folkl.* 18.27, A poultice made from crushed berries of "drupe" or hoghorn [sic] sumac *(Rhus typhina)* and stewel [=stool] was good for cleaning out poisons.

druther adv [By metanalysis from *(woul)d rather;* cf Intro "Language Changes" I.2]

Preferably.

1887 (1967) Harris *Free Joe* 129 **nGA,** I'd a heap druther see you fillin' them slays . . than to see you a-whinin' 'roun' atter any chap on the top side er the yeth.

druthers n pl, but sg or pl in const Pronc-spp *drathers, drothers* **[druther]**

1 Preference, desires. *now esp among speakers with coll educ*

1895 *DN* 1.388 **Sth,** *Druthers:* choice, preference. **1896** Harte *Tales of Argonauts* xxviii, When you've lived as long as I have, stranger, you'll find that in this yer world a man don't always get his 'drathers.' **1923** *DN* 5.206 **swMO,** *Druthers. . .* (Rathers) Preference. "I caint he'p havin' m' druthers." **1937** in 1958 Brewer *Dog Ghosts* 80 **TX** [Black], Dey wanna git shed of dey earthly life an' mosey on into de Holy Lan'; dat is if'n dey kin hab dey d'rothers. **1944** *PADS* 2.55 **sMO, VA, NC,** *Druthers, to have* (one's) ['drʌðɚz]: *phr.* To have one's desires ((rathers)). **1965–70** *DARE* (Qu. JJ33, *When you can't choose, but have to take what you're given: "I'll take a cat, but if I had my ______ I'd take a dog."*) 143 Infs, **widespread,** Druthers; **CA**142, **GA**86, **IA**27, **KY**21, **MO**29, **OK**13, **TX**5, Drathers. [Of all Infs responding to the question, 63% were old, 35% were coll educ; of those giving this response, 50% were old, 51% were coll educ.] **1975** (1982) Ludlum *Road to Gandolfo* 105, But if I were you and had my druthers, I'd choose to fight the government treason charges rather than our investor.

2 See quot—perh used as an exclam.

1950 *WELS Suppl.* **cwWI,** For "dibs" or "druthers," children at school say, "I bonny that one."

druv See **drive** v **A2, 3**

dry adj

1 Plain, without accompaniments. **chiefly Sth** *esp among Black speakers* Cf **dry so** adj phr

1912 Green *VA Folk-Speech* 158, *Dry-bread. . .* Bread alone, usually corn-bread, without meat. **1927** Kennedy *Gritny* 15 **sLA** [Black], Ain' had a dry nickel to pay for 'um. **1968–70** *DARE* (Qu. KK61, *Food taken alone, with nothing added: "Would you like milk or lemon in your tea?" "No, thanks, I'll take it ______."*) Infs **GA**28, 61, **SC**66, Dry. [2 of 3 Infs Black]

2 See quot. [By ext from *dry* not giving milk]

1939 McGuire *FL Cracker Dial.* 174, *Dry. . .* Infertile (woman or female animal).

3 See quots.

1942 Warnick *Garrett Co. MD* 6 **nwMD** (as of 1900–1918), *Dry . .* offended or sullen—not having much to say. **c1960** *Wilson Coll.* **csKY,** *Dry. . .* Sullen, sour.

dry n

1 Thirst for liquor. [*OED dry* sb. 1. b *"Obs."* 1377–c1460] *hist*

1848 (1855) Ruxton *Life Far West* 66 **MO, Rocky Mts,** When every cent has disappeared from their pouches, the free trapper often makes away with rifle, traps, and animals, to gratify his "dry" (for your mountaineer is never "thirsty"). **1947** Guthrie *Big Sky* 133 **West** (as of 1830s), We had a awful dry. We was tryin' to scout up a drink.

2 Esp in mining: see quots. [Abbr for **dry room]**

1922 *DN* 5.181 **nID,** *Dry. . .* Quarters fitted with tubs, showers, etc., at the 'works' of a mine. "Why doesn't he go to a dry and clean up?" **1939** (1973) FWP *Guide MT* 414, *Dry, the. . .* Room where miners change clothing after work. **1980** *DARE* File **neMN,** Drys—the showers used in the mines. It goes back to the time when the work clothes were put in a basket and hoisted up to the ceiling to dry out. This was particularly common in the underground mines. The term has been generalized to include other showers at places of work such as railroad yards.

dry v

1 To diaper (a baby).

1969 *DARE* (Qu. Z13, *If a mother has to leave her baby for a little while, she might ask a neighbor, "While I'm gone, will you ______ the baby for me?"*) Inf **MO**15, Dry. [FW: The Inf explained that "dry" was an old term for "diaper" the baby and that was what they used to say.]

2 See **dry out.**

dry-acting adj

Having a dry or ironic sense of humor.

1935 Smiley *Gloss. New Paltz* **seNY,** "A dry-acting sort of fellow"—He has a dry sense of humor.

dry aim n [*dry* used only for practice]

1950 *WELS Suppl.* **csWI,** *Dry aim*—pointing a gun and taking a sight at a target without shooting. "I'll just take dry aim at does [but shoot at bucks]."

dry ass n

Among loggers: see quots.

1956 Sorden-Ebert *Logger's Words* 13 **Gt Lakes,** Dryass, A sack filled with hay for a teamster to set [sic] on when riding on snowy, frozen logs. **1958** McCulloch *Woods Words* 54 **Pacific NW,** *Dry ass*—A sack filled with straw or moss to make a seat cushion when sitting on some cold metal equipment.

dry blizzard n Also *dry storm* Cf **black blizzard, Mormon rainstorm**

A dust or sand storm.

1934 *Sun* (Baltimore MD) 15 May 12/1 *(Hench Coll.),* The recent "dry blizzard" was the first to visit the Eastern States. . . Such dry and windy weather must be expected occasionally. **1968** Adams *Western Words* 102, *Dry storm*—A cowboy's name for a sandstorm.

dry-bone n Also *dry-bone ore* [See quot 1918]

An ore of zinc: usu smithsonite, but also calamine.

1844 Lapham *Geogr. Descr. WI* 61, Mixed in with it in every proportion, and even sometimes getting the better of the galena, and shutting it out completely, occur both the carbonate and sulphuret of zinc; the one known to the miners by the name of "dry bone," the other "black Jack." **1918** Peele *Mining Engineers' Hdbk.* 101, "Dry-bone" is a local name in Mississippi Valley, the oxidation products suggesting old bones. **1968** Thrush *Dict. of Mining* 357/1, *Dry-bone ore.* A miner's term for an earthy, friable carbonate of zinc, smithsonite. Often frequently applied to the hydrated silicate, so-called calamine. Usually found associated in veins or beds in stratified calcareous rocks accompanying sulfides of zinc, iron, and lead.

dry-bone adj

1922 Gonzales *Black Border* 298 **sSC, GA coasts** [Gullah glossary], *Dry-bone*—dry-boned—thin, lean, often applied to dusky ladies who do not incline to *embonpoint.*

dry bridge n **esp NEng, VA**

A bridge that does not span water; an overpass.

1821 Stansbury *Pedestrian Tour* (1822) 63 *(DA),* A large dry-bridge leads the turnpike over a broad ravine. **1876** *Richmond Daily Dispatch* 4 Oct 3/1 *(Hench Coll.),* As the train approached the dry bridge . . a brakeman . . motioned them to sit down. **1945** *Hench Coll.* **cVA,** Negroes and many whites . . call the C&O bridge across the road a "dry bridge." **1966–70** *DARE* (Qu. N19, . . *A structure that carries a road above railroad tracks, or above another road or a deep gully*) Infs **CT**36, **MA**1, 5, 6, 30, 42, **VA**105, **VT**12, Dry bridge.

dry camp n, v phr **chiefly West** Cf **water camp**

A camp made where there is no water; to camp where there is no water.

1869 Browne *Adventures* 128 **AZ,** A few hours of night-travel brought us to the Pecacho, a little beyond which we made a dry camp till morning. **1886** in 1887 *Outing* 10.4/2 **seAZ,** We halted on an open space at the edge of a cañon, and went into dry camp. **1920** Hunter *Trail Drivers TX* 312 (as of c1880), The round up boss . . called for two or three men . . to . . make what is called a "dry camp." **1966** *DARE* Tape **NM**13, They had to camp where there's water or if the men had dry camped, they had to have enough water in the barrel for the meal. **1968** Adams *Western Words* 102, *Dry-camp*—To camp without water. **1981** *KS Qrly.* 13.2.66, *Dry camp* . . a buckaroo camp that has no fresh water supply.

dry cellar n

A root cellar.

1967–69 *DARE* (Qu. M19, *A place for keeping carrots, turnips, potatoes, and so on over the winter*) Infs **MD**3, **NY**109, 187, **PA**21, Dry cellar.

dry clean Methodist n [Joc ref to the method of baptism]

1970 *DARE* (Qu. CC4, . . *Nicknames . . for various religions or religious groups*) Inf **FL**51, Dry clean Methodist—baptize by sprinkling, not total immersion; **SC**69, Dry clean Methodist—baptizes by sprinkling; wet wash Baptist immerses.

dry closet n Also *dry toilet* Cf *DS* M21a-b

An outhouse.

1931–33 *LANE Worksheets* **cMA,** *Dry closet.* . . Outhouse. **1940** *Hench Coll.* **cVA,** Several of the members [of the school board] spoke of the great numbers of *dry closets* still in use. **1941** *LANE* Map 354 *(Privy)* 2 infs, **MA,** *Dry closet;* 1 inf, **swNH,** *Dry toilet.* **1945** *Richmond News Leader* 17 July 3/3 *(Hench Coll.),* [Caption:] There are 28 dry closets as pictured above. The refuse is removed every two weeks by the city.

dry cloth See **drying cloth**

dry clothes man n

A revenue officer.

1938 Stuart *Dark Hills* 135 **eKY,** He thought I was a "dry-clothes" man snooping around to see if he was selling licker.

dry drizzle n Also *dry rain* **chiefly Sth, S Midl**

A very light rain.

1923 *DN* 5.206 **swMO,** *Dry drizzle.* . . A light shower of rain. **1953** Randolph–Wilson *Down in Holler* 242 **Ozarks,** *Dry drizzle.* . . A sprinkle of rain, a light shower. **1954** *Harder Coll.* **cwTN,** *Dry drizzle.* . . A light rain. **1968–70** *DARE* (Qu. B23, . . *A light rain that doesn't last*) Inf **VA**47, Dry drizzle; **KS**16, Dry rain. **1979** *DARE* File **ceTX,** "Dry drizzle" . . apparently means mist. We had one on a day last week. My driveway stayed dry all day beneath the long branches of the big willow oak even though a mist kept the street wet. *That's* a dry drizzle. **1986** Pederson *LAGS Concordance,* 1 inf, **nwAL,** Dry drizzle—husband's expression, amuses her; 1 inf, **swAL,** Dry drizzle—very slow and light.

dry drought n Pronc-spp *dry drout(h)* [Redund; cf Intro "Language Changes" I.4] **chiefly GA, SC, Gulf States** *esp freq among Black speakers*

A protracted period of very dry weather.

1883 (1971) Harris *Nights with Remus* 243 **GA** [Black], De wedder got hot un den a long dry drouth sot in. **1884** Smith *Bill Arp's Scrap Book* 176 **GA,** Them snakes I've been a killin' brought all this dry drouth on my land and ruined my crop. **1888** Jones *Negro Myths* 7 **GA coast,** De dry drout come. Ebry ting stew up. Water scace. **1922** Gonzales *Black Border* 298 **sSC, GA coasts** [Gullah glossary], *Drought* . . "dry drought," protracted drought. **1930** Stoney–Shelby *Black Genesis* 147 **seSC,** De sun jus' shine an' shine in de sky, and de rain hol' back. . . 'Tis de drout'. De dry drout'. **1939** Griswold *Sea Is. Lady* 598 **sSC,** For a terrible "dry-drought" was parching all the sea-island fields. **1966** *DARE* (Qu. B28, *When there is no rain for a long time, that's a ______*) Inf **SC**26, Dry drought. [Inf Black] **1986** Pederson *LAGS Concordance,* 7 infs, **coastal Gulf Region,** Dry drought [4 infs Black].

dryer, dryer cloth (or dishrag, rag) See **drying cloth**

dry fence See **dry wall**

dry fish n **AK**

Fish cured by drying; see quot 1974.

1870 Dall *Alaska* 27, They are well roofed and are used only as storehouses for provisions, dry fish, and furs. **1940** Osgood *Ingalik Material Culture* 192 **AK,** To make dry fish the green (freshly caught) fish are first cut. **1957** Butler–Dale *Alaska* 139 (Tabbert *Alaskan Engl.*), The tired, hungry dogs are unharnessed and chained to their individual hitching posts before each is tossed its daily ration of dry fish. **1967** *AK Sportsman* June 28 (Tabbert *Alaskan Engl.*), One has his choice of roasted bear, moose and caribou meat, dry fish, moosehead soup. **1974** in 1981 Tabbert *Alaskan Engl.* 256, The cured fish are referred to as "dryfish", not dried fish. They are tied in "bundles" of about 40 salmon and stored in caches for winter use.

dry fly n

1 also *dry-weather fly* (or *bug*): A **cicada. chiefly Sth, S Midl** See Map

1897 Terhune *Old-field School* 3 *(DA),* A locust—'a dry-weather fly,' the people there-abouts called it—had perched on the sill on the sunniest window and sang shrilly. **1930** Dos Passos *42nd Parallel* 269 **nVA,** You'd ride slowly home hating . . the katydids and the dryflies jeering out of the sapling gums. **1954** *Harder Coll.* **cwTN,** *Dryfly.* . . An insect that makes a scraping sound. Cicada. **1956** *Jrl. Amer. Folkl.* 69.87 **TX,** In Texas . . the popular name of the cicada is "dry fly." **1965–70** *DARE* (Qu. R7, *Insects that sit in trees or bushes in hot weather*

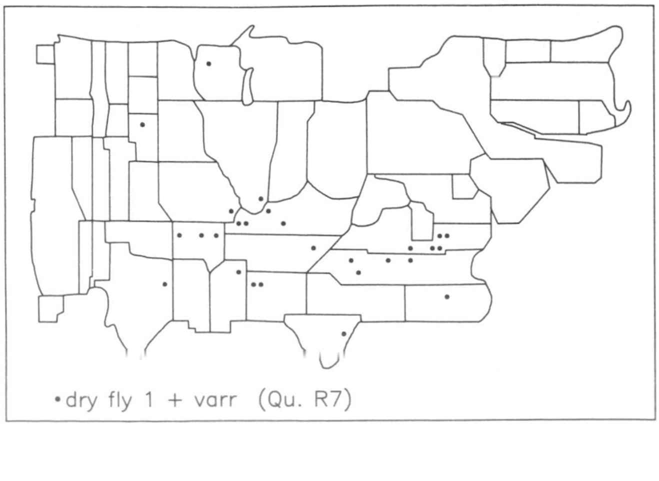

•dry fly 1 + varr (Qu. R7)

and make a sharp, buzzing sound) 24 Infs, **chiefly Sth, S Midl,** Dry fly; **AR**42, **KY**76, Dry-weather fly; **KY**86, Dry-weather bug. **1966** *PADS* 46.25 **cnAR,** *Dry fly*. . . A locust.—"I heard a dry fly today."

2 Perh a **June beetle.**

1967–69 *DARE* (Qu. R5, *A big brown beetle that comes out in large numbers in spring and early summer, and flies with a buzzing sound: [Note: some are green]*) Infs **IL**93, **NC**47, Dry fly.

dry frost n Cf **water frost**

A light frost.

1967–70 *DARE* (Qu. B29, *A frost that does not kill plants is a ______*) Infs **KY**44, 86, **TX**13, **VA**1, Dry frost.

‡**dry grin** v phr [**dry grin** n]

To smile in an embarrassed manner.

1942 *Sat. Eve. Post* 26 Dec 76/4 **LA,** Mandy, stop sitting up there dry-grinning like a possum.

dry grin n **chiefly Sth, S Midl** [*dry* not showing emotion or betraying hurt (cf *W3* [1]*dry* 10. a)]

An embarrassed or forced smile—usu in phr *the dry grins.*

1883 (1971) Harris *Nights with Remus* 263 **GA** [Black], He tuck'n kotch de dry grins terreckerly. But dey all howdied. *Ibid* 293, Brer Fox talk so close ter de fatal trufe, dat Brer Wolf got tooken wid de dry grins. **1884** *Anglia* 7.263 [Black], To have er spell er dry grins = to be greatly embarrassed. **1892** *DN* 1.230 **KY,** *Dry grins:* the smiles of one teased. **1893** Shands *MS Speech* 71. **1905** *DN* 3.78 **nwAR,** *Dry grins*. . . The smiles of one unable to parry a joke. **1908** *DN* 3.307 **eAL, wGA,** *Dry-grins*. . . A state of feeling in which one is so teased, embarrassed, or chagrined that he can do nothing but grin. "Look at John. He's got the dry-grins." **1915** *DN* 4.182 **swVA,** *Dry-grins, to have the*. . . Said of one sorely teased but striving to smile. **1956** McAtee *Some Dialect NC* 14, *Dry-grin.* **c1960** *Wilson Coll.* **csKY,** *Dry grin*. . . A forced or insincere grin. **1968** *Foxfire* Fall–Winter 25 **neGA, cwNC,** And another told of a friend he knew who, when caught in a white lie or a practical joke, would look sheepish and "take a bad case of the dry grins." **1972** *Atlanta Letters* **ceGA,** Have you ever had a case of the "Dry grins"? The victim is any person, child or adult, who is "found out" and whose only defense is to stand there, grinning foolishly, without mirth.

dry gulch v **chiefly West**

To ambush and kill (someone); to attack and beat or harm (someone).

1930 Raine–Barnes *Cattle* 51 **West,** Ben Turner, an ally of the Horrells, was dry-gulched. **1941** Writers' Program *Guide WY* 461, *Dry-gulch*. . . To kill a man in a gulch either by stringing him up to a tree or shooting him. **1945** Thorp *Pardner* 176 **SW,** Such an outfit needed fellows who were prepared to steal cattle, blot brands, dry-gulch enemies, and otherwise do the devil's business on the range. **1959** *Washington Post* (DC) 25 Dec sec A 13/1 *(Hench Coll.),* The frontier sheriff was leery of a narrow canyon because he was hemmed in by walls and could easily be "dry gulched" and shot by some outlaw. **1968** *Civil Liberties* 257.1/2 **NJ,** The police . . physically and verbally abused citizens, sometimes drygulching them late at night, beating them and leaving them lying on the streets.

dry-hide See **hide** n[2] **1**

dry hides on the bone v phr [Cf **hide** n[2] **1**]

1906 *DN* 3.134 **nwAR,** *Dry hides on the bone*. . . To keep and use an emaciated horse. "He's drying hides on the bone."

dry house n

A building for drying, and also for preserving and storing, agricultural produce.

1776 in 1926 Fries *Rec. Moravians* 3.1101 **NC,** The dry-house for flax caught fire. **1903** Eggleston *First of Hoosiers* 21 **seIN** (as of 1840s), He built a great stone "dry house," which I remember very well. . . Its upper story was for the storage of all farm produce that frost might injure. . . In the basement of his dry house he built long stone furnaces with big and little kettles . . [and] with broad areas left bare for the purpose of drying fruits upon them. Here every year . . the lard from some hundreds of hogs was rendered, . . the preserves were put up, the apples and peaches dried. **1966** *DARE* (Qu. M19, *A place for keeping carrots, turnips, potatoes, and so on over the winter*) Inf **AR**4, Dry house.

drying See **dry out**

drying cloth n Also *dry cloth, dry(ing) rag, dry(ing) towel* For addit varr see quots **chiefly Sth, S Midl** See Map

A towel for drying dishes.

1929 Dobie *Vaquero* 264, Sometimes he used it [=his bandana] as a cup towel, which he called a "drying rag." **1939** *LANE* Map 140 *(Dish towel)* 3 infs, **sVT, wMA,** Drying cloth; 1 inf, **sVT,** Drier. **1954** *Harder Coll.* **cwTN,** *Dry rag*—A cloth used to dry dishes. **c1960** *Wilson Coll.* **csKY,** *Drying cloth*. . . A cloth to dry dishes, after they have been rinsed. *Drying* (or *dry*) *rag*. . . A tea towel. **1965–70** *DARE* (Qu. G16, *What do you dry the dishes with?*) 26 Infs, **chiefly Sth, S Midl,** Drying cloth; 13 Infs, **chiefly Sth, S Midl,** Dry cloth; 13 Infs, **chiefly Sth, S Midl,** Drying rag; 13 Infs, **chiefly Sth, S Midl,** Drying towel; **LA**2, Dry rag; (Qu. G17) Inf **NJ**69, Dry towel. **1966** Dakin *Dial. Vocab. Ohio R. Valley* 2.126, *Drying towel* (scattered older speakers in Ohio, Illinois, and eastern Kentucky). . . The simplex *dryer* . . and *dryer dishrag* . . also appear. *Ibid* 127, *Drying* (sometimes simply *dry*) *rag* and *dry(ing) cloth* are the most common. . . Several speakers in northeastern and north-central Kentucky say *dryer rag* or (more rarely) *dryer cloth.* **1967** *PADS* 47.6 **Midl,** Drying cloth, ~ rag, ~ towel 'dish towel'. **1973** Allen *LAUM* 1.203 **Upper MW** (as of c1950), *Dish towel* (for drying dishes). . . drying cloth [4 infs], ~ rag [2 infs], ~ towel [3 infs].

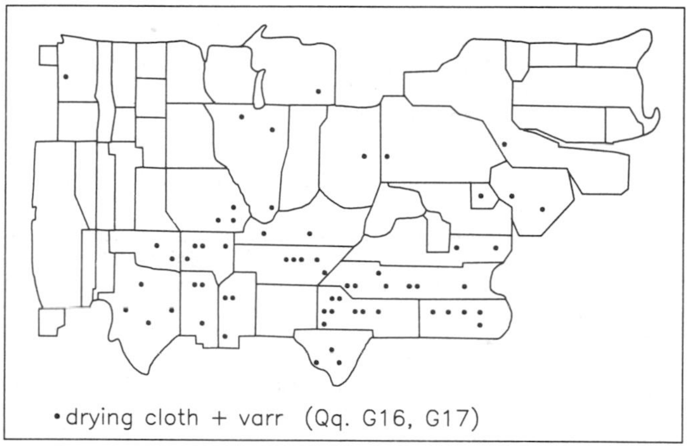

drying room See **dry room**

drying towel See **drying cloth**

dry-ki n |draɪ kaɪ| Also sp *dri-ki, dry-ky(e)* **chiefly Nth, esp ME**

Dead timber, esp that killed by flooding; dry branches; driftwood; land where such timber predominates.

1904 Day *Kin o' Ktaadn* 144 **ME,** With coffee hot and grub a lot / And dry-kye snappin' beneath the pot. **1905** U.S. Forest Serv. *Bulletin* 61.36 **Nth,** *Dry-ki*. . . Trees killed by flooding. **1914** *DN* 4.152 **ceME,** *Dry ky*. . . Dead timber about a lake or river the level of which has been raised by a dam. In general dead branches and underbrush suitable for fire wood. Wood useless for lumber. "I won't take any of the good wood; I was just picking up a little dry ky." Used widely in the woods. **1942** ME Univ. *Studies* 57.132, *Dri-ki.* Trees killed by being flooded with water above a dam. Also driftwood in a lake or river. **1955** *Moosehead Gazette* (Dexter, Maine) Feb 20/2 *(Hench Coll.),* Except for a few undersized speckled waifs [=fish] snagged in close to the dry-ki, we got nothing but another big dose of fresh air and exercise. **1964** Gould *Parables of Peter* 132 **ME,** There was a cove there that they made into, and you can still see blueberry dri-ki there, where they hung in. **1967** *DARE* FW Addit **nME,** Dry-kye ['draɪ kaɪ]—a burnt land, where new trees are coming up and old trees either are still standing or have fallen over. **1969** Sorden *Lumberjack Lingo* 37 **NEng, Gt Lakes,** *Dry-kye*—Driftwood and dead trees in the water along the edge of a pond or lake. Variously spelled. **1988** *DARE* File **ME** (as of 1980), The south end of Chesuncook Lake is always packed with dri-ki (driftwood).

dry-kill n [Perh folk-etym for **dry-ki**]

In logging; see quot.

1956 Sorden–Ebert *Logger's Words* 13 **Gt Lakes,** Dry-kill, Trees killed by flooding. Often found in areas flooded by beaver dams.

dry-ky(e) See **dry-ki**

dry-land cress n

A **winter cress** (here: *Barbarea verna*).

1973 *Foxfire 2* 78 **nGA,** *Barbarea verna* . . dry land cress. . . This cress grows to two feet high in damp ground, along streams, and in old fields.

dry-land daisy n

A **fleabane** (here: *Erigeron subtrinervis*).

1953 Nelson *Plants Rocky Mt. Park* 163, Dryland daisy . . *Erigeron subtrinervis.*

dry-land duck n

Perh =**Florida duck.**

1966 *DARE* (Qu. Q5, . . *Kinds of wild ducks*) Inf **FL**26, Dry-land duck.

drylander n **West**

1 One who farms without irrigation; a dry farmer.

1921 *Frontier* Feb 11 *(DA),* It is good house. He build summer kitchen. None of drylanders have summer kitchen. **1936** McCarthy *Lang. Mosshorn* np **West** [Range terms], *Drylander*. . . A homesteader or farmer dependent upon rain for a crop. **1943** Howard *Montana* 37, Neighbors helped themselves to the drylander's abandoned house. **1950** Williams *Rocky Mts.* 246 **CO,** There was a great fiction to the effect that the rain belt was moving to the east at a fine rate of speed, and that if the dry landers took homestead claims while the lands were still arid, they would be in on the ground floor when it started to rain on the prairies.

2 One who farms arid land by irrigating it.

1921 *DN* 5.113 **CA, CO,** *Dry-lander*. . . A farmer of irrigated land. Colorado original. Rare in California. **1968** Adams *Western Words* 102, *Dry-lander*—What the cowboy called a farmer of irrigated land.

dry-land fish n **chiefly KY, TN**

1 An edible mushroom, usu a morel (*Morchella* spp). Also called **woodfish**

1952 Giles *40 Acres* 93 **eKY,** We also have *dry land fish.* Mushrooms to you. But they are not the familiar mushroom of the city market. They are a big, oval, porous plant, brown on top and pearly pink beneath. Henry tells me their botanical name is the common morel. They spring up in shady, damp places in the woods, especially after a rain, and we gather them by the pecks. . . They do have a slight fishy taste. I think it is actually more a fish texture than a taste. **c1960** *Wilson Coll.* **csKY,** *Dry-land fish*. . . Fried mushrooms. **1967–69** *DARE* (Qu. I37, . . *[Mushrooms] which are safe to eat)* Inf **KY**21, Dry-land fish—an edible mushroom, tall and cone-shaped, 2–6″ high; **KY**22, Dry-land fish—a cone-shaped mushroom, eatable, a spring delicacy; **KY**37, Dry-land fish—umbrella-shaped, but honeycombed, shaped like Christmas tree bulb; **KY**34, 40, Dry-land fish. **1978** *NADS Letters* **GA,** "Dryland fish" is an expression used in North Georgia and they are just plain mushrooms. . . A Black told me years ago that "dey smells bad like a feesh when dey's rotten." **1981** *High Coll.* **ceKY** (as of c1930), There was mushrooms, the kind you could eat; we called them morels, or dry-land-fish. **1983** *MJLF* 9.38 (as of 1956), *Dry land fish* . . a variety of mushrooms. **1983** Montell *Don't Go Up* 178 **csKY, cnTN,** Times was hard during the Depression. I know one time we was hunting dryland fish. We called it that—some type of mushroom. Only come up in the spring of the year when peach and apple trees are in full bloom. They only stay up for a week or ten days. They were a specialty because it was something different from the beans and potatoes you was used to. **1986** Pederson *LAGS Concordance,* 5 infs, **TN,** Dry-land fish.

2 See quot.

1969 *DARE* (Qu. I23) Inf **KY**17, Dry-land fish—joking name for squash.

dry-land frog n Cf **highland frog, land frog**

A **toad.**

c1950 *Atlas Checklists* **WI,** Dryland frog—a toad. [2 infs] **1965–70** *DARE* (Qu. P23) Infs **AL**14, **DC**4, **IL**95, **VA**27, 75, 79, **WV**3, Dry-land frog.

dry-land moccasin n Cf **highland moccasin, water moccasin**

=**copperhead snake 1.**

1966–70 *DARE* (Qu. P25, *What kinds of snakes are found around here?*) Inf **KY**47, Dry-land moccasin—poisonous; **KY**84, Dry-land moccasin—a hill snake; **OK**23, Dry-land moccasin.

dry-land sled n Cf *DS* L57

1974 Fink *Mountain Speech* 7 **wNC, eTN,** *Dry land sled* . . sled to be used in fields or dirt roads.

dry-land turtle n Also *dry-land tarrypin, ~ terrapin, ~ tortoise* **chiefly Sth, S Midl, Cent, SW** See Map and Map Section

=**land turtle.**

1965–70 *DARE* (Qu. P24, *What kinds of turtles are found around here?*) 31 Infs, **chiefly Sth, S Midl, Cent, SW,** Dry-land (turtle); 9 Infs, **chiefly S Midl, SW,** Dry-land terrapin; **MS**58, Dry-land tarrypin; **IA**29, Dry-land tortoise; (Qu. P29) Infs **FL**13, 16, 27, 51, Dry-land turtle; [**KY**35, Dry-land booger].

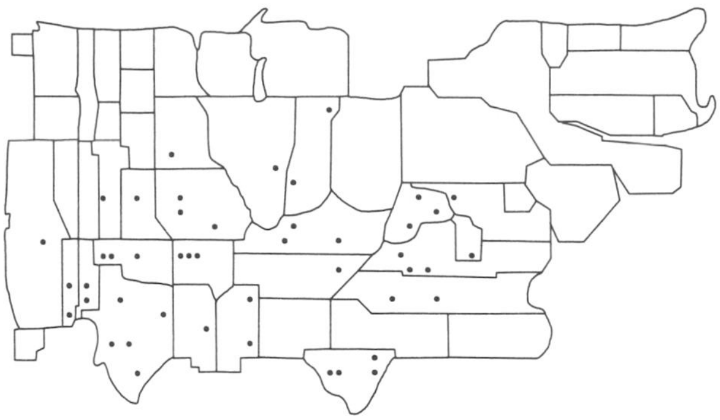

•dry-land turtle + varr (Qq. P24, P29)

dry long so adv phr See **dry so** adv phr

dry long so adj phr See **dry so** adj phr

dry month n

See quot 1953.

1852 in 1956 Eliason *Tarheel Talk* 148 **NC,** I have two [Irish laborers] at the Road . . who work well and by the dry month. **1953** Randolph–Wilson *Down in Holler* 242 **Ozarks,** *Dry month*. . . Four weeks of dry weather. A farm hand hired "by the dry month" gets his month's wages after he has worked twenty-four days; no pay for the days when it is too wet for work in the field.

dry moon n Cf **wet moon**

A quarter moon that appears tilted from the horizontal, believed to be an indicator of rain.

1944 *AmSp* 19.121 **neMA,** 'Dry moon' and 'wet moon,' designating the positions of the crescent in the sky, [are] regarded as a prognostic of the weather. . . If the saucer of the moon stands so that it will hold water, the water will not come down; but if it is so tipped as to let the water all spill out, then down comes the rain. **1964** De Vries *Reuben* 249 **CT,** There is a quarter moon—a dry moon we used to call it because it's tilted so that if you poured water into it the water would run out.

dry mouth n

See quot.

1971 Green *Village Horse Doctor* 20 **cwTX** (as of 1940s), When sheep affected by lechuguilla were brought in from the ridges and placed in corrals with feed and water, they refused to eat or drink and the symptoms were what was commonly referred to as "dry mouth."

dry off v phr

1 To cause (a cow or sheep) to stop giving milk; to stop producing milk. **chiefly NEast** See Map

1838 MA Ag. Surv. *Rept. for 1837* 1.39 **neMA,** They feed their cows well, and . . keep them in milk as long as they will pay well for their keeping, . . then they dry them off at once. **1864** Randall *Practical*

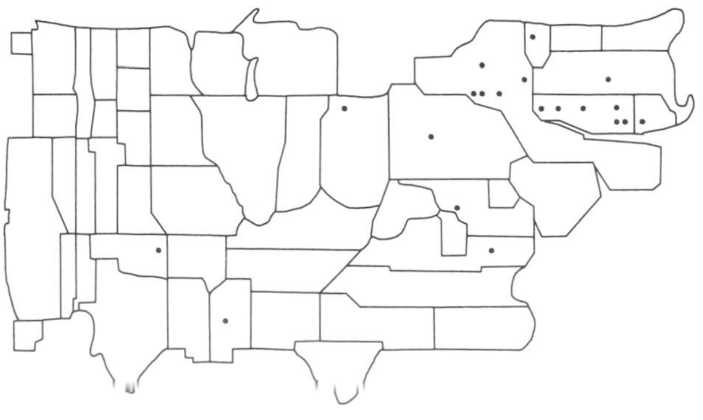

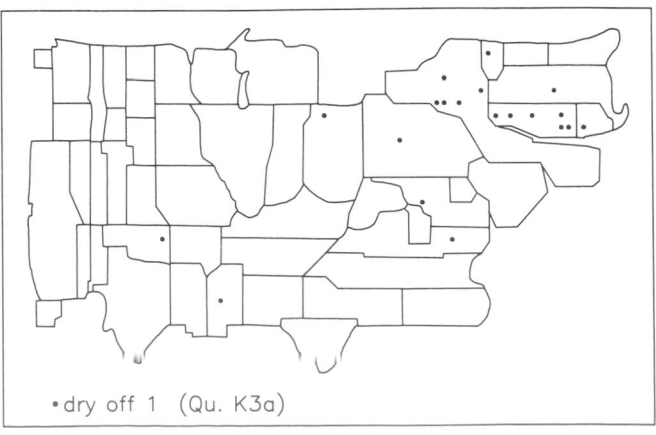

•dry off 1 (Qu. K3a)

Shepherd 158 **NY,** If it becomes necessary to dry off a ewe, even a young one not having much milk, she should . . be fed on dry feed. **1950** *WELS Suppl.,* Dry off—said of a cow which is such a good milker that she must be made to stop giving milk by leaving some unmilked each time until she ceases entirely, usually before calving or because of some udder trouble. **1950** *WELS (When a cow stops giving milk, you say she ——)* 1 Inf, **cwWI,** Dried off. **1965–70** *DARE* (Qu. K3a) 19 Infs, **chiefly NEast,** Dried off; **OH**27, Dries off.

2 Of rainy weather: to clear up. Cf *DS* B7

1915 (1916) Johnson *Highways New Engl.* 190, The next morning was dull and rainy, and though the hotel cook was very sure at breakfast time that the rain was "going to dry off" at once, the weather continued dubious until late in the afternoon.

dry out v phr Also *dry (up)* [Folk-etym for *try out* to render (fat)] To melt down (fat, lard, etc), to render; hence ppl adj *dried,* vbl n *drying.*

1851 in 1927 Jones *FL Plantation Rec.* 425, 1 [slave] drying up Lard. **1899** (1912) Green *VA Folk-Speech* 158, *Dry out. . .* The act of separating fat by heat. "We have been drying out lard all day." **1968** *DARE* Tape **GA**25, The bear, we'd kill a fat 'un, we'd dry the grease out of him, you know, just like we did the hogs' lard. **1970** *DARE* (Qu. B19) Inf **VA**69, Cracklin biscuit—dried hog fat, mashed and added to biscuit dough. You get cracklin when you dry the lard out of hog fat. The cracklin is the residue. It is brown and crisp from the drying process.

dry rag See **drying cloth**

dry rain See **dry drizzle**

dry roll v phr

In logging: see quot 1958.

1956 Sorden-Ebert *Logger's Words* 13 **Gt Lakes. 1958** McCulloch *Woods Words* 54 **Pacific NW,** *Dry roll*—To roll stranded logs into the water behind the drive.

dry room n Also *dry shack, drying room*

In logging and mining: see quots.

1958 McCulloch *Woods Words* 54 **Pacific NW,** *Dry room*—A shack where loggers can dry their wet clothes; often attached to, or part of the bath house in a camp. *Ibid, Dry shack*—A shanty used for drying clothes. *Ibid, Drying room*—Part of a bath house set aside for drying work clothes. Common in coastal camps. If a separate shanty, then known as the dry shack. **1960** Climax Molybdenum Co. *Manual* 47, *Dry room*—Locker or basket room in which employees change clothes, dry their damp clothes, shower, etc.

dry salt adj phr, also used absol [From *dry-salted* ppl adj < *dry salt* to cure by drying and salting] **chiefly Lower Missip Valley, TX**

Of pork: cured by drying and salting.

1961 Folk *Word Atlas N. LA* fig 1015, Home-cured bacon . . dry salt bacon. **1962** Atwood *Vocab. TX* 62, Sides of pork preserved in salt, usually at home. . . Term in occasional use in Texas . . *side bacon, dry salt (bacon).* **1966–67** *DARE* (Qu. H38, *Other words for bacon*) Infs **LA**11, **MS**23, Dry salt meat; **TX**26, Dry salt; **LA**14, Dry salt pork. **1967** Faries *Word Geog. MO* 103, Write-ins [for *salt pork*] are *bacon, salt side, dry salt,* and *fresh pork.* **1981** Pederson *LAGS Basic Materials* **Gulf Region,** [There are nine instances of *dry salt* recorded, with seven of *dry salt meat,* two of *dry salt bacon,* and one of *dry salt pork.* Stress patterns vary, with some infs suggesting the syntactic pattern *dry salt + meat* (or *bacon, pork*), and others suggesting the pattern *dry + salt meat* (or *bacon, pork*).]

dry shack See **dry room**

dry shave n Cf **dutch rub, noogie**

1968 *DARE* FW Addit **csOK,** *[To give one a] dry shave*—playfully to rub vigorously one's knuckles over the top of the head of someone else. Also called a "Dutch rub."

dry-smoke v

1912 Green *VA Folk-Speech* 158, *Dry-smoke. . .* Keeping an unlit pipe or cigar in the mouth.

dry so adv phr Also *dry long so* **chiefly Sth, S Midl**

1 Plainly, straightforwardly; without embellishment, as is, just so.

1898 Johnston *Pearce Amerson's Will* 151 **cGA,** I been a-hopin' they'd compermise it, which as for breakin' a will dry so, because it don't read accordin' to what people think they'd do if it was them and theirn, I can't but be ag'in' sech as that. **1899** (1912) Green *VA Folk-Speech* 158, *Dry so. . .* In that manner. "He said it just dry so." **1903** *DN* 2.312 **seMO,** *Dry so. . .* Plainly; just so. 'I told him dry so I didn believe him.' **1907** *DN* 3.230 **nwAR, seMO,** *Dry so. . .* Plainly, just so. "The first conscious thing you ever did was to smile—you cried just dry so." **1922** Gonzales *Black Border* 298 **sSC, GA coasts** [Gullah glossary], *Dry so*—just so. **1937** (1977) Hurston *Their Eyes* 71 **csFL** [Black], Y'all know we can't invite people to our town just dry long so. I god, naw. We got tuh feed 'em something.

2 For no reason.

1896 *DN* 1.415, *Dry so:* in S. C. in answer to a question. "Why did you do that?" "Oh, I don't know; dry so." **1972** *Atlanta Letters* **ceGA,** Dry 'long so (meaning for no reason).

dry so adj phr Also *dry long so* **chiefly Sth, S Midl**

=**dry** adj **1.**

1872 (1973) Thompson *Major Jones's Courtship* 111, The Stallinses bein Washingtonians [=temperance people], ther wasn't no wine, but the cake wasn't bad to take jest dry so. **1905** *DN* 3.78 **nwAR,** *Dry so. . .* As it is, with no liquid, in the original state. 'I take quinine just dry so.' **1908** *DN* 3.307 **eAL, wGA,** *Dry so. . .* Plainly, just so. "I always take my whisky dry so." **1967–68** *DARE* (Qu. KK61, *Food taken alone, with nothing added: "Would you like milk or lemon in your tea?" "No thanks, I'll take it ——."*) Infs **LA**17, **TX**37, Dry long so; **TX**11, Dry so. **1980** *Progressive* Nov 53, Drylongso. The word means ordinary in black English.

dry stone fence (or wall) See **dry wall**

dry storm See **dry blizzard**

dry strawberry n *obs*

=**dewdrop.**

1822 Eaton *Botany* 262 *(DAE), Dalibarda fragaroides . .* dry strawberry. **1832** MA Hist. Soc. *Coll.* 2d ser 9.149 **cwVT,** Dalibarda fragarioides, *(Michaux.)*—Spice-root, dry strawberry. **1869** Fuller *Uncle John* 79, The fruit is dry and hard, on which account it is sometimes called the 'Dry Strawberry.'

dry toilet See **dry closet**

dry towel See **drying cloth**

dry up See **dry out**

dry wall n Also *dry (wall) fence;* for addit varr see quots [*OEDS* 1778 →] **chiefly NEast, C Atl** See Map

A stone wall made without mortar.

1965–70 *DARE* (Qu. L60, *A fence made of stone or rock without mortar*) 53 Infs, **chiefly NEast, C Atl,** Dry wall; **MD**31, **MI**86, **NC**36, **NJ**56, **NY**230, **PA**235, **VA**38, Dry fence; **KS**17, **MD**31, **PA**3, 23, Dry wall fence; **CT**13, **HI**12, **MA**4, **WV**12, Dry laid (rock wall); **CT**2, **DC**2, **HI**2, Dry stone wall; **MD**32, **PA**163, Dry stone (fence); **TN**62, Dry masonry. **1971** *AmSp* 46.170 **Chicago IL,** 'Fence or wall made of loose rock or stone': . . *drywall fence* [1 inf].

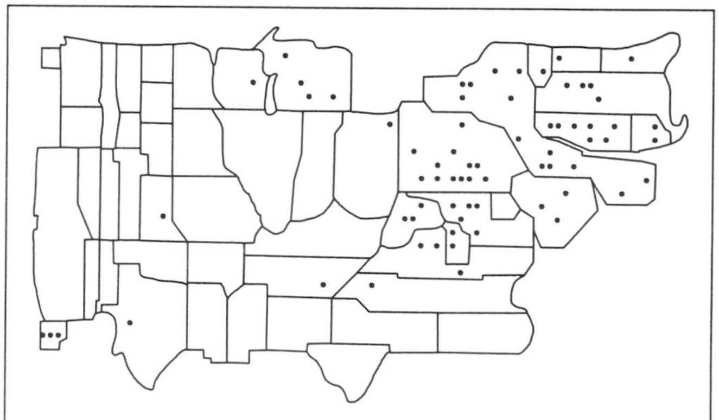

•dry wall + varr (Qu. L60)

dry-weather bug See **dry fly 1**

dry-weather Christian n

1968 *DARE* (Qu. CC7, *Words for a person who goes to church very seldom or not at all*) Inf **OH**40, Dry-weather Christian.

dry-weather fly See **dry fly 1**

dry-weather French See **frenching**

dry-weather shower n Also *dry-weather rain*
=**dry drizzle.**
1939 *Hench Coll.* **cVA,** H.P. Johnson told me of the local name for short, one or two minute rains in long hot and dry spells: dry-weather rain. **1967–69** *DARE* (Qu. B23, *Speaking of a light rain that doesn't last, you would say it's just a* ______) Infs **KY**31, 41, Dry-weather shower. **1984** Wilder *You All Spoken Here* 142 **Sth,** *Dry weather shower:* A shirt-sleeve rain; not enough rain to lay the dust; a smidgen; a mizzle.

dry whiskey n Also sp *dry whisky* [See quots 1886, 1911]
=**peyote.**
1886 Havard *Flora W. & S. TX for 1885* 521, It is principally as an intoxicant that the Peyote has become noted. . . If chewed it produces a sort of delirious exhilaration which has won for it the designation of "dry whisky." **1911** *Century Dict. Suppl., Mescal-buttons. . .* These buttons have narcotic properties and in Texas are sometimes called *dry whisky.* **1920** Saunders *Useful Wild Plants* 252, This is the so-called . . Dry Whisky, Peyote . . names given in common speech to a small cactus, *Lophophora Williamsii.* **1941** *Torreya* 41.50, *Lophophora williamsii. . .* Dry whiskey. **1965** Teale *Wandering Through Winter* 150 **TX,** All across Texas, a host of . . names have been bestowed on the wild plants. . . They run from . . dry whiskey . . to shame vine.

dry wilts n pl
See quot 1929.
1929 *AmSp* 5.17 **Ozarks,** *Dry wilts. . .* A condition of extreme decrepitude or desiccation. "Thet ol' feller's got th' dry wilts, an' he aint no call t' go a-sparkin' 'roun' them gals that-a-way." **1933** Williamson *Woods Colt* 82 **Ozarks,** When I come home I had the dry wilts so bad the old woman didn't know me.

du See **do** v **A1**

dual highway n Also *dual* **scattered, but chiefly Mid and C Atl** See Map Cf **dual lane highway**
A divided highway.
1965–70 *DARE* (Qu. N16a, . . *A highway with two lanes on each side and a separation down the middle*) 62 Infs, **scattered, but chiefly Mid and C Atl,** Dual (highway); (Qu. N17, . . *The separating area in the middle of a four-lane road*) Inf **MD**20, Drain—because water from the duals runs into it.

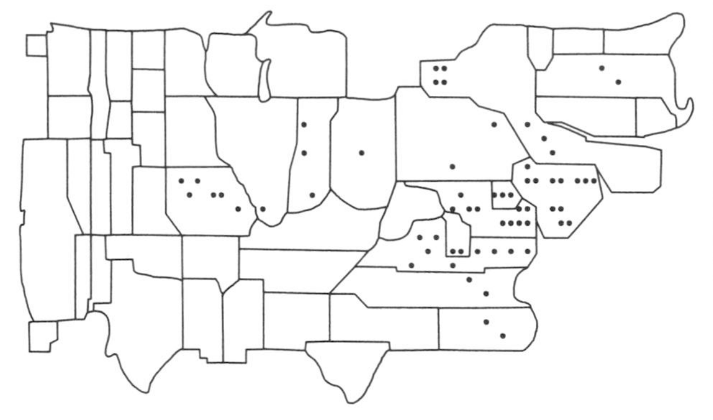

•dual highway + var (Qq. N16a, N17)

dual lane highway n Also *dual lane (road)* **chiefly Mid Atl, esp SC**
=**dual highway.**
1965–70 *DARE* (Qu. N16a) 12 Infs, **chiefly SC,** Dual lane; **IN**68, **MD**31, Dual lane highway; **SC**43, Dual lane road.

dub n[1] [Perh var of **dud** n **1**]
1 also *dubs, dubber:* An inexperienced, unskillful, or awkward person; a dull or stupid person.
1887 *Courier–Jrl.* (Louisville KY) 20 Jan 6/4, Dem dubs is goin' to git it in de neck in a minit. **1903** Willard *Rise of Ruderick* 71 **NYC,** He's an old dubs. He'd never 'a' caught me at all 'f I'd had any shoes. **1912** Wason *Friar Tuck* 106 **WY,** We kept this up until Horace lost patience an' called me a confounded dub. **1913** *DN* 4.10 **MN. 1915** *DN* 4.199 **NE. 1919** *DN* 5.66 **NM. 1941** *LANE* Map 465 *(Fool)* 2 infs, **seNH,** Dub. **1950** *WELS (A dull and stupid person)* 1 Inf, **ceWI,** Dub. **1950** Kimbrough *Innocents* 7 **IN** (as of c1910), I'd been a dub. That's what Charles Robbins was always saying to me, "You're such a dub." **1968–70** *DARE* (Qu. HH16, *Uncomplimentary words . . to show that you don't think much of a person*) Infs **NC**61, **OH**95, Dub; (Qu. HH40, *Uncomplimentary words for an old man*) Inf **NH**14, Dub. **1969** *DARE* FW Addit **ceNY,** Dubbers—"half-assed phonies." **1976** Hobbs-Specht *Tisha* 85 **AK,** You worm-eaten dub . . why you think she came over—ta spend the day with ya?
2 Something that fails; a flop, blunder.
1926 *AmSp* 1.632, *Dub.* A dub shot is made when the [golf] ball is not hit squarely and fails to go as planned. **1942** Berrey–Van den Bark *Amer. Slang* 656.1, *Billiards. . .* dub, *a bad shot. Ibid* 711.4, Dub, *a bungling stroke* [in golf]. **1955** *PADS* 23.17 **cwTN** [Marbles terms], *Dubs: . .* Blunders. **1960** *VT Hist.* new ser 28.208, [In a list of proverbs:] The greatest number of dubs are found under the best apple tree. **1965–70** *DARE* (Qu. FF15, *When a firecracker doesn't go off . . you call it a* ______) Infs **CA**97, **FL**51, **GA**44, **IA**34, **MI**81, **MA**48, **OK**48, **SC**67, **TN**53, Dub; (Qu. FF19, . . *A very dull or unenjoyable time: "The party was* ______.") Inf **AL**5, A dub.

dub n[2] [Prob *dib* pebble, knucklebone used in games, infl by **dubs** exclam]
=**dob** n[2].
1966 *DARE* (Qu. EE6b, *Small marbles or marbles in general*) Inf **MI**8, Megs; pee-wees; dubs. **c1970** Wiersma *Marbles Terms* **csIA** (as of c1935), *Dubs up*—In marble play: elevating the target marble with dirt to make it easier to hit.

dub n[3] [Abbr for *double*]
1 See quot.
1967 *DARE* (Qu. II1, . . *A close friend . . "He's my* ______.") Inf **AR**47, **TX**38, Dub, pal.
2 See **double-u.**

dub n[4] See **dove**

dub v[1]
1 See quot. [*OED dub* v.[1] 10 1711 →]
1899 (1912) Green *VA Folk-Speech* 158, *Dub. . .* To cut down with an adze. To work with an adze.
2 with *off:* To blunt, take the edge off. [*OED dub* v.[1] 11, *EDD dub* v.[4]]
1966 *DARE* Tape **ME**26, The other blade [of a double-bitted ax] was dubbed off thicker, a chopping blade is ground right out, thin. **1985** in 1986 *Barrick Coll.* **csPA,** *Dubbed off*—chipped or damaged along the edge. . . (auctioneer usage).

dub v[2] Also with *along, around, off* Also *dob(b), dubb* [Cf *EDD dub* v.[3] 4 "to walk heavily, with short steps"]
To move along slowly; to waste time, fool around, putter.
1900 Day *Up in ME* 101, We was dobbin' along with dumpy sails in a nigh-about dead calm. **1914** *DN* 4.71 **ME, nNH,** *Dobb,* or *dubb (along). . .* Move along, slowly. **1969** *DARE* (Qu. A10, . . *Doing little unimportant things . . " . . I'm just* ______.") Inf **OH**88, Dubbing; (Qu. JJ26, . . *The boss might say, "If he wants to keep his job he'd better* ______.") Inf **VT**16, Stop dubbing off; (Qu. KK31, *To go about aimlessly looking for distraction: . . "He's just* ______ *around."*) Inf **OH**88, Dubbing. **1979** Lewis *How to Talk Yankee* [10] **nNEng,** Pat likes to dub around in that canoe, but she still can't paddle a straight line. **1981** *Greenfield Recorder* (MA) 14 Nov sec A 4/1, "Oh," the neighbor replied, "just dubbin' around."

dubber See **dub** n[1] **1**

dubbins n [*EDD dubbings* (at *dubs*)]
A marble game.
1966 *DARE* (Qu. EE7) Inf **PA**1, Dubbins ['dʊbɪnz]—with a ring.

dubbs See **dubs** exclam **1**

duberous See **dubious A3**

dubersome See **dubious A4**

dubious adj
A Forms. [All these types are found in Engl dial; cf *EDD dubious, duberous, dubersome*]

1 pronc-spp *jubious, gubious*

1887 *Scribner's Mag.* 2.478/1 **AR,** I wisht you a seen 'im; fust he looked mighty gubious; then he begins ter laff. **1892** Harris *Uncle Remus & Friends* 105 **GA** [Black], Ole Brer Elephen flop his years en shake his snout like he sorter jubious.

2 pronc-spp *dubus, jub(o)us.* **Sth, S Midl**

1836 (1955) *Crockett Almanacks* 54 **wTN,** 'Twa'nt because he didn't love her, only 'twas a dubus thing to make the first attempt, and not know nothing about the way he would be received. **1845** [see **B2** below]. **1859** Taliaferro *Fisher's R.* 204 **nwNC** (as of 1820s), I felt mighty skittish and jubus uv Davis, fur he was allers a-swaggerin', and cavortin', and boastin' about, tellin' how many men he'd licked. **1883** (1971) Harris *Nights with Remus* 263 **GA** [Black], Brer Fox, he look sorter jub'ous, he did, des lak folks does w'en dey walks up in a crowd whar de yuthers [=the others (are)] all a-gigglin'. **1888** *Century Illustr. Mag.* 36.550/2 **GA,** He said nothin'; but he look like he were pestered and jubous in his mind. **1903** *DN* 2.312 **seMO,** I always was jubous about that man. **1936** *AmSp* 11.162 **eTX,** The pronunciation ['dʒubəs] for dubious is widespread in the speech of older or more ignorant people in rural districts. **1950** *PADS* 14.41 **SC,** ['dʒubəs]. **1952** Brown *NC Folkl.* 1.555, *Jubus.* **1966** *DARE* FW Addit **NC,** ['ǰubəs].

3 pronc-spp *dub(e)rous, juber(o)us, jub(b)ers.* **chiefly S Midl, also NEng, Sth**

1871 Eggleston *Hoosier Schoolmaster* 188 **sIN,** Things is awful juberous. **1895** *DN* 1.372 **eTN,** He was juberous about crossing the stream. **1899** (1912) Green *VA Folk-Speech* 158, *Duberous.* **1906** *DN* 3.120 **sIN,** I'm jubbers of that fellow. *Ibid* 143 **nwAR,** The fire broke out and things looked mighty juberous for a while. **1914** *DN* 4.72 **ME, nNH,** *Dubrous. Ibid* 109 **KS,** *Juberous.* **1917** *DN* 4.413 **wNC,** *Juberous.* **1923** *DN* 5.212 **swMO,** I'm juber'us 'bout a-gorn in thar. **1927** *AmSp* 3.140 **ME,** "Duberous" (dubious) . . [was] often heard. **1939** [see **B2** below]. **1944** *PADS* 2.29 **KY, NC,** ['dʒubɚəs]. **1950** *PADS* 14.41 **SC,** ['dʒubərəs]. **1966** *Wilson Coll.* **csKY,** I would be duberous about his fine promises. **1966** *DARE* (Qu. B5, *When the weather looks as if it will become bad, . . it's ———*) Inf **NM**11, Unsettled; it looks ['ǰubɚəs]. **1982** *Smithsonian Letters* **cnKY** (as of 1930s), If he were sizing up a man or an animal or a deal, he was likely to be "a little juberous," meaning doubtful.

4 as *dubersome, jubersome.* [Blend of *duberous, juberous* (see **A3** above) + *-some;* cf Intro "Language Changes" III.1]

1836 (1838) Haliburton *Clockmaker* (1st scr) 283 **NEng,** He made a considerable of a long pause, as if he was dubersome whether he ought to speak or not. **1848** Bartlett *Americanisms* 124, *Dubersome.* Doubtful. A vulgarism common in the interior of New England. **1875** Holland *Sevenoaks* 277 **NEng,** I should think she was gittin' oneasy, an' a little dubersome about my comin' to time. **1890** *DN* 1.67 **KY,** Jubersome. **1895** *DN* 1.382 **NJ,** *Dubersome* . . also in form *jubersome.* **1899** (1912) Green *VA Folk-Speech* 158, Dubersome. **1909** *DN* 3.395 **nwAR,** *Dubersome.* **1914** *DN* 4.109 **KS,** Jubersome.

B Senses.

1 Inclined to suspect. *obs*

1853 Simms *Sword & Distaff* 76 **SC,** Toby, I'm jubous, der's somet'ing wrong in dis bis'ness. . . He can't fool dis nigger. . . I'm jubous Bossick is yer in dese parts. **1856** Simms *Eutaw* 185 **Sth,** And what's the good of her, I wants to know—a mean, lazy, sleepy-head, and, I'm jubous, a runaway?

2 Hesitant, afraid.

1845 Thompson *Pineville* 174 **GA,** Well, I begun to feel sort o' jubous of 'em. **1939** *Hall Coll.* **wNC,** ['dʒub(ə)rəs]. *Ibid* **wNC,** You go around him [a bear]. I'm jubers ['dʒubərs] and I'll go below him. **1959** *Hall Coll.* **eTN,** [The Wolf Pit was] a place I was juberous ['dʒubərəs] to pass at night. **1972** Cooper *NC Mt. Folkl.* 93, *Jubus, juberous*—dubious, frightened.

Dublin n

An area inhabited by Irish immigrants or thought to resemble Ireland in some way.

1963 Pilgrim Soc. Plymouth MA *Notes* 13.7 (as of c1900), Over the frozen, springy land known as "Dublin," and out onto the frozen harbor. **1967–69** *DARE* (Qu. C34, *Nicknames for nearby . . districts*) Inf **NY**82, Dock is called Dublin, because of so many Irish there; (Qu. C35, *Nicknames for . . parts of your town*) Inf **CT**2, Dublin—lots of Irish there at one time; **MA**50, The Flats; Dublin; Swedeville; Skunk Hollow; **NJ**48, Dublin—where Irish lived (a short street); (Qu. II25, . . *Nicknames for the part of a town where . . foreign groups live*) Inf **IA**17, Dublin—downtown Dubuque—Irish.

dub off v phr[1] See **dub** v[1] **2**

dub off v phr[2] See **dub** v[2]

dubrous See **dubious A3**

dubs n pl [*EDD dubs* sb. pl. 1; cf **dubs** exclam, **dub** n[2]] Cf **fen** exclam

1 In marble play: two marbles, usu that have been knocked out of the ring at once.

1883 Newell *Games & Songs* 186, Under certain circumstances a boy who puts down a second marble is said to "dub" (double) a marble, or to play "dubs." **1890** *DN* 1.24 **KY,** "Dubs" means "doubles" or two "men" (marbles). **1899** [see **dubs** exclam **1**]. **1905** *DN* 3.78 **nwAR,** *Dubs*. . . Doubles. Term used in playing marbles. **1955** *PADS* 23.17 **KY,** *Dubs*. . . Two marbles. **1973** Ferretti *Marble Book* 43 **NYC,** *Dubs.* Hitting two or more marbles out of a ring with one shot.

2 A marble game; see quot. Cf **dubbins**

1973 Ferretti *Marble Book* 95, *Potsies*. . . It is also called *dubs* or *25-a-dub* or *100-a-dub.* Each player contributes a given number of marbles to the "pot," which is a large ring drawn on the ground. . . The object is to knock marbles out of the ring while keeping one's own shooter *inside.* If the shooter goes outside the next player plays. The first player to win enough marbles necessary for a majority is entitled to take all the rest of the marbles in the ring.

dubs exclam Also *dubsies* [*EDD dubs* sb. pl. 1; perh < *double;* cf **dib** n[1] **2**]

1 also *doubs, dubbs;* In marble play: used to lay claim to two or more marbles knocked out of the ring by the same shot.

1883 Foote *Led-Horse* 62 **CO,** 'What is it the boys say when they play marbles?—"Fend" something,' she asked, with fitful gayety. 'Fend dubs?' Hilgard suggested. **1890** Howells *Boy's Town* 82 **sOH** (as of 1840s), When another boy's toy drove one marble against another and knocked both out of the ring, he holloed "Fen doubs!" before the other fellow holloed "Doubs!" **1893** Shands *MS Speech* 71, *Dubs*. . . In playing marbles, the player who knocks out two marbles at one time cries *dubs,* in order to have the right of keeping both marbles out of the ring. The Century Dictionary says that *dubs* is a contraction of *doublets.* **1899** (1912) Green *VA Folk-Speech* 158, *Dubs*. . . Doublets at marbles. A player knocking two marbles out of the ring cries, "dubs," and thereby claims both. **1908** *DN* 3.308 **eAL, wGA,** *Dubs*. . . A term in marbles, used when two men are knocked out of the ring; doubles. **1917** *DN* 4.421, *Dubs*. . . *Marbles.* In La., counted as a foul unless the shooter calls "No dubs." **1934** *AmSp* 9.75 **ND,** *Dubbs.* A general cry, giving claim to all marbles. **1935** *AmSp* 10.159 **NE,** *Dubbs.* Not a 'general cry,' but a particular one which the player must utter in order to lay claim to two marbles knocked from the pot with a single shot. **1955** *PADS* 23.17 **cwTN,** *Dubs*. . . A call giving the player the right to take all marbles. **1958** *PADS* 29.33 **IN,** *Dubs*. . . A call claiming possession if two marbles were shot out of the ring. **1963** *KY Folkl. Rec.* 9.3.62 **KY,** Dubs [10 counties] . . dubsies [1 county]. **1966** *DARE* Tape **OK**42, [Inf:] If you knock more than two marbles out . . and a feller say, "venture dubs," . . before I shot, if I knock both of 'em out I'd have to put one of 'em back. [FW:] Is there something you'd say so that you could get 'em both? [Inf:] I'd say "dubs." But if you said "venture dubs" before I said "dubs," I'd have to put one of those marbles back. **1980** *DARE* File **KS** (as of 1890), If you said "dubs" before your opponent said "vent dubs," you could keep both marbles, not just one. **1983** *MJLF* 9.1.38 **ceKY,** *Dubs* . . the call which enables keeping both marbles knocked out.

2 also in comb *dubs I;* By ext: used to lay claim to some thing or privilege.

1892 *DN* 1.220 **MO,** *Dubs* means, not doublets, but that the player has blundered, and by crying "dubs" is entitled to play again. **1956** *AmSp* 31.36, *No divvies, no dubs, no dibs,* . . —these are almost self-explanatory expressions for 'You can have no part of what I have.' *Ibid* 38, The forms . . *pike I,* and *dubs I* argue that the *ie* of hosie was once *I. Whackie, dibsie,* and *dubsie* are parallel forms.

dubs n[1] See **dub** n[1] **1**

dubs n[2] See **double-u**

dubs I See **dubs** exclam **2**

dubsies See **dubs** exclam

dubstand n [*EDD dubstand* (at *dubs*) "a term used in the game of marbles"] Cf **dubs** n pl

In marble play: see quot.

1955 *PADS* 23.17 **cwTN,** *Dubstand. . .* In a game of keeps . . , a marble placed in the ring as a bet.

dubus See **dubious A2**

dubya See **double-u**

duc See **duck n 3**

duck n

1 The game **duck on a rock;** a stone used in the game.

1878 *Harper's New Mth. Mag.* 56.258/1 **NY,** Find a rock and a duck, also some smaller stones. . . We will make Reg duck and rock keeper. **1890** *DN* 1.77 **MA,** *Duck. . .* Always *duck* in Essex Co., Mass. . . *duck on the rock* in Jersey City, N.J. **1892** *DN* 1.215 **ceMA,** *Duck. . .* " 'To play duck' was the only phrase" in Boston. **1899** Champlin–Bostwick *Young Folks' Games* 273, *Duck,* or *Duck on the rock,* a game. **1909** (1923) Bancroft *Games* 81, Each player is provided with a stone, called a "duck," about the size of a baseball. A large rock or post is chosen as the duck rock. . . On this duck rock one player places his duck. **1950** *WELS (Games in which you set up a stone . . and try to knock it down)* 1 Inf, **seWI,** Duck. **1967** *DARE* (Qu. EE18) Inf **AZ**8, Duck.

2 In marble play: the target marbles in the ring.

1895 *DN* 1.388 **KY,** *Ducks:* marbles in the ring. **1922** *DN* 5.186 **KY,** *Duck. . .* The "stakes" in "keeps." **1937** (1947) Bancroft *Games* 161, The term *marbles* in these rules is used to denote the object marbles only, variously known as *mibs, miggs, . . ducks.* **1955** *PADS* 23.17 **cwTN.** *Ibid* 34 **seKY,** *Duck. . .* A stake in the game of keeps. **1963** *KY Folkl. Rec.* 9.61 **KY. c1970** Wiersma *Marbles Terms* **swMI,** *Duck*—A small marble placed in the ring. *Ibid* (as of 1920s), *Duck*—Small playing marble put in the ring. **1973** Ferretti *Marble Book* 43 **NYC,** *Ducks.* Object marbles, to be shot at.

3 also *duc:* A rock cairn used as a trail marker.

1921 Hall *Hdbk. Yosemite* 291, In meadows, stakes or ducs are sometimes set along the trail if the trail is not marked where it leaves the meadow. **1980** *DARE* File **ceCA,** In Yosemite National Park, ducks (small cairns made of three or four flat stones) are used to mark the trails.

4 An alcoholic beverage; hence vbl n phr *chasing the duck.*

1905 *DN* 3.5 **cCT,** *Chasing the duck. . .* Going after intoxicating liquors. **1972** Claerbaut *Black Jargon* 63, *Duck . .* wine.

5 A partly smoked cigarette; a cigarette butt. **chiefly SE** See Map Also called **drake** n[2] **4**

1908 *DN* 3.308 **eAL, wGA,** *Duck. . .* A cigarette stub. **1939** *AmSp* 14.26 **SC,** *Duck. . .* Partially consumed cigarette. *Ibid* 90 **cTN,** Give me your ducks. **c1940** *Hall Coll.* **eTN,** *Duck*—A cigarette butt. (I have heard it used only by young boys, but that is possibly because of a custom which prevails in the Smokies. If an older person is smoking a cigarette and young boys are around, he is likely to be asked by one for the 'duck'.) **1965–70** *DARE* (Qu. DD8, *The part left over when a cigar or cigarette is smoked*) 27 Infs, **chiefly SE,** Duck; (Qu. DD6b, *Nicknames for cigarettes*) Inf **GA**1, Duck—a cigarette which has been smoked some but is re-lit after going out; **VA**3, Duck; drake.

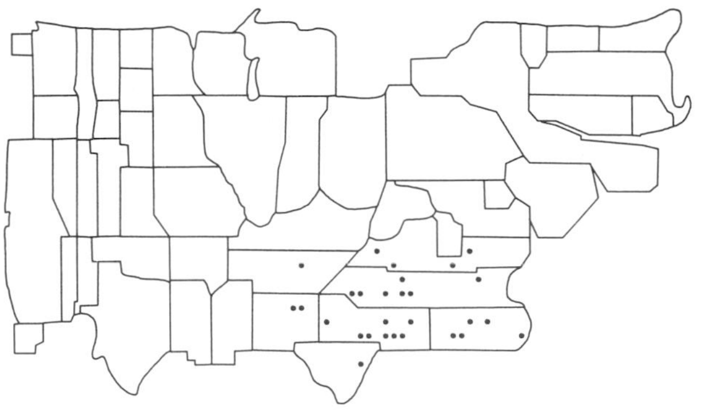

•duck n 5 (Qq. DD8, DD6b)

6 A score of zero. [Abbr for **duck egg**]

1900 *DN* 2.33 **MN,** *Duck. . .* Cipher in a game. **1942** Berrey–Van den Bark *Amer. Slang* 18.3, *Zero; Naught.* Duck.

7 See quots. [From its shape] Cf *DS* F38

1968 Adams *Western Words* 102, *Duck*—What the logger calls a bed urinal. **1986** Chapman *New Dict. Amer. Slang* 118, *Duck. . .* A hospital bedpan.

8 A kind of sailboat.

1970 *DARE* (Qu. O9, *What kinds of sailboats are used around here?*) Inf **MA**97, Turnabout—smallest single sail; duck—eighteen feet long; sailfish.

9 in phr *get one's ducks in line* (or *a row*): To get things organized; to make preparations.

1944 *Newsweek* 29 May [1], [Advt:] "Getting your ducks in a row" is a bit of business vernacular, as you know, which means organizing the situation so you can go through it efficiently. **1970** Brewer–Evans *Dict. Phrase & Fable* 348, *To get one's ducks in a row.* An American expression meaning to have one's arrangements completed, to have things organized or lined up; or, literally, to have one's skittles set up. In an American bowling alley the skittles, or pins, are called ducks. **1981** *Capital Times* (Madison WI) 2 Jan 4/3, Contrary to the impression in most news stories, the Kremlin is still getting its ducks in line. It isn't ready yet . . to invade [Poland].

duck v

1 To baptize by immersion; hence vbl n *ducking.* Cf **ducking Baptist**

1908 *DN* 3.308 **eAL, wGA,** *Duck. . .* To baptize by immersion. Facetious. *Ibid, Duckin(g). . .* Baptismal services. "Did you go to the ducking?"

2 To avoid (someone). **chiefly Nth, N Midl, esp NEast**

1896 (1898) Ade *Artie* 55 **IL,** He was with a lot o' them Prairie avenue boys, and purty soon he ducks 'em and comes over an' touches me for two cases. **1926** Black *You Can't Win* 80 **MI,** We'll get a passenger train out of Cheyenne, kid, if we can duck Jeff Carr. **1950** *WELS (You'd better _____ people like that)* 1 Inf, **ceWI,** Duck. **1965–70** *DARE* (Qu. Y51, . . *"He's not your kind—you'd better _____ him."*) 12 Infs, **chiefly NEast,** Duck; **NY**249, Duck that stud. [Of all Infs responding to the question, 48% were male; of those giving this response, 77% were male.]

3 To mark with a **duck n 3.**

1948 *So. Sierran* May 6/1 *(DA)* **CA,** The route was 'ducked' for future climbers.

duck acorn n [See quot 1933] **chiefly Sth**

=**water chinquapin;** also its fruit.

1900 Lyons *Plant Names* 258, *N[elumbo] lutea. . . Seeds,* Duck Acorn. **1910** Graves *Flowering Plants* 184 **CT,** Duck Acorn. Water Chinquapin. **1933** Small *Manual SE Flora* 540, Fruits acorn-like, imbedded in the top of the receptacle. . . *N. lutea. . . Duck-acorn.* **1945** Saxon *Gumbo Ya-Ya* 562 **LA,** Water chinquapins: seeds of the yellow lotus. (Also called duck acorns.) **1953** Greene–Blomquist *Flowers South* 38, *Duck-acorn . .* bears large, pale-yellow flowers of many petals.

duck and davy See **duck on davy**

duck-and-dip n Cf *DS* N30

A sudden short dip in the road; a **thank-you-ma'am.**

1944 *AmSp* 19.70 **neOH,** In Ashtabula County, Ohio . . thank-you-ma'ams are also called *ducks-and-dips.* **1945** *AmSp* 20.156 **SC, GA,** *Kiss-me* readily became *kiss-me-quick* by rhythmic analogy with such terms as *thank-you-ma'am, duck-and-dip,* and *hug-me-tight.*

duck and drake See **ducks and drakes 3**

duck and drakes with, play See **ducks and drakes 2**

‡duckatoon n [Prob pronc-sp of *ducatoon* an obsolete silver coin]

1952 Brown *NC Folkl.* 1.535 **wNC,** *Duckatoon. . .* Something of little value.

duckback adj Also *ducksback*

Water-repellent.

1939 *Hall Coll.* **wNC,** Well, I'd got a considerable lot of blood on my duck-back clothes. **1939** in 1978 Hall *Yarns Gt. Smokies* 40 **cwNC,** He went to the hardware and bought him a ducksback suit, bowie knife and a fly rod, and we went down to . . this creek, and commenced fishin'. [Footnote to *ducksback:*] I have seen the trade name something like "Duxbak," for water-proof hunting and fishing clothes in an outdoor magazine ad of about the 1890–1910 era.

duckberry vine n

A bittersweet.

1957 McMeekin *Old KY Country* 206 **KY,** It will have duckberry vines (bittersweet) and tall velvety false tobacco (mullein) and golden rod and Bouncing Bet.

duckbill n

1 A **lousewort,** usu *Pedicularis ornithorhyncha.*

1915 (1926) Armstrong–Thornber *Western Wild Flowers* 502, *Duckbill. Pedicularis ornithorhyncha. . .* The flowers . . are very eccentric in shape and the upper lip has a ludicrous resemblance to the head of a duck. **1932** Rydberg *Flora Prairies* 727, *Pedicularis. . .* Duck-bill. **1940** Clute *Amer. Plant Names* 266, *Pedicularis canadensis. . .* Duck-bill.

2 also attrib: A hand truck used in tobacco warehouses. **S Midl** Also called **spoonbill**

1940 *AmSp* 15.134 **KY,** *Duckbill or Spoonbill.* Small hand truck used to move baskets of tobacco around the warehouse floor. **1966** *PADS* 45.12 **KY,** Duckbill. . . A small hand truck used to move baskets to the floor of the warehouse. (Also *spoonbill*). . . "A duckbill looks like a duck's bill in front." **1967** Key *Tobacco Vocab.* **MD, MO, TN,** Duckbill; **MD,** Duckbill truck; **NC,** Duckbill—a type of equipment used to move tobacco around in the warehouse; **KY,** The ones that packs it usually puts it on the duckbills and trucks it over the scales.

duckbill cat n Also *duck-billed cat* [See quot 1933]

=**paddlefish.**

1882 U.S. Natl. Museum *Bulletin* 16.83, *P[olyodon] spathula. . .* Paddle-fish; Spoon-bill Cat; Duck-bill Cat. **1884** Goode *Fisheries U.S.* 1.660, The "Paddle-fish" or "Duck-billed Cat," *Polyodon spathula,* is one of the most characteristic fishes of the rivers of the Western and Southern States. **1908** Forbes–Richardson *Fishes of IL* 17, Various names . . have been applied to this fish, the commonest of which are . . duck-bill cat, and spade-fish. **1933** LA Dept. of Conserv. *Fishes* 374, Spoonbill, Duckbill Cat . . refer to the Paddlefish's . . long, thin, expanded, blade-like snout which . . appears to be a sensitive organ of touch possibly used in stirring up the mud and in seeking the minute animals upon which the Paddlefish feeds. **1983** Becker *Fishes WI* 233, *Paddlefish. . .* Other common names: . . duckbill cat. . . Long paddle-like snout.

duck-billed eel n

A deepwater eel.

1933 Bryan *Hawaiian Nature* 222, The "sorcerers" or "duck-billed eels" *(Nettastomidae)* lack pectoral fins and have the tail ending in a slender filament.

duck-billed gar See **duckbill gar**

duck-billed pike n Also *duck-billed pickerel*

1 =**chain pickerel.**

1927 Weed *Pike* 45, *Esox niger. . .* Duck-billed Pike; North Carolina. **1935** Caine *Game Fish* 22, *Pickerel—Esox reticulatus—* . . Duck-billed Pike. **1946** LaMonte *N. Amer. Game Fishes* 128, *Eastern Pickerel—Esox niger* . . Duck-billed Pike . . Chain Pike. **1973** Knight *Cook's Fish Guide* 386, Pickerel . . duckbilled—Chain.

2 =**northern pike 1.**

1927 Weed *Pike* 43, *Esox lucius. . .* Duck-billed Pickerel; Illinois–Wisconsin. Duck-billed Pike; Illinois–Wisconsin.

duckbill gar n Also *duckbill garfish, duck-billed gar, duck's-bill gar*

=**shortnose gar.**

1877 U.S. Natl. Museum *Bulletin* 9.43, *Duck-Bill Garfish, Lepisosteus platostomus.* **1877** Bartlett *Americanisms* 240, At least three species of this fish are found in our Western rivers: the *Duck's-bill Gar,* and the *Ohio,* or common *Gar.* **1908** Forbes–Richardson *Fishes of IL* 35, The short-nose gar *[Lepisosteus platostomus]* is generally common throughout the Mississippi Valley, being most abundant . . in the southern part of its range. . . It is locally known by Illinois River fishermen as the "duck-bill gar." **1933** LA Dept. of Conserv. *Fishes* 406, *The Short-Nosed Gar. . .* Known also under the names of Duck-billed and Short-billed Gar, this species ranges from the Great Lakes to the Gulf Coast. **1983** Becker *Fishes WI* 241, *Shortnose Gar—Lepisosteus platostomus* . . Other common names: broadnosed gar, . . duckbill gar, billy gar.

duck blood soup See **duck's blood soup**

duckboard n

1 A board or boardwalk laid on a loose, wet, or slippery surface usu for pedestrians.

1941 Writers' Program *Guide MI* 560 **nMI** (as of 1880s), 'Fighting Jim' Morrison was undisputed king of the duck-board sidewalks, and those who failed to give way when they met him simply 'weren't real bright.' **1962** Fox *Southern Fried* 119 **SC,** He loved that fountain and he knew every square inch of chrome and every square foot of duckboard that ran the length of the long counter. **1980** *DARE* File **Princeton NJ** (as of 1930s), When walks were muddy or snowy, planks were placed on them for pedestrians and were called "duck boards." **1980** *DARE* File **swMI,** When gravel trucks have to drive across loose sand they ride on duck-boards, which are slats of heavy lumber nailed across two long planks.

2 By ext: see quot.

1977 Adams *Lang. Railroader* 50, *Duckboard:* The platform running along the top of a boxcar.

duckboat n Also *ducking boat, duck punt,* ~ *scow,* ~ *skiff* **chiefly Inland Nth** See Map

Any of various low-lying shallow boats used by duck hunters.

1876 *Fur, Fin, & Feather* Sept. 89 *(DAE),* The interest of the party was . . given to the examination of a new duck boat. **1950** *WELS (A very small row-boat)* 5 Infs, **WI,** Duckboat; *(Other kinds of boats)* 4 Infs, **WI,** Duckboat. **1958** Humphrey *Home from the Hill* 46 **TX,** In the center of the room hung a two-man boat, a double-pointed duck punt. **1965–70** *DARE* (Qu. O1, . . *A small rowboat, not big enough to hold more than two people*) 18 Infs, **chiefly Inland Nth,** Duckboat; **NJ**17, Ducking boat; (Qu. O10, . . *Other kinds of boats*) Infs **IA**47, **MN**10, **PA**155, Duckboats; **CA**36, Duckboats—duck hunters use, also duck scow. **1972** Sparano *Outdoors Encycl.* 472, Many features to look for in a duckboat are present in this model: broad (42-inch) beam and built-in flotation for safety; strong aluminum keel and stems; double ends for slipping easily into cover. **1980** *DARE* File **seWI,** Duck skiff—a squarish flat-bottom boat for duck hunting. It lies quite low and looks about the same at both ends, except that the front is rounded up slightly.

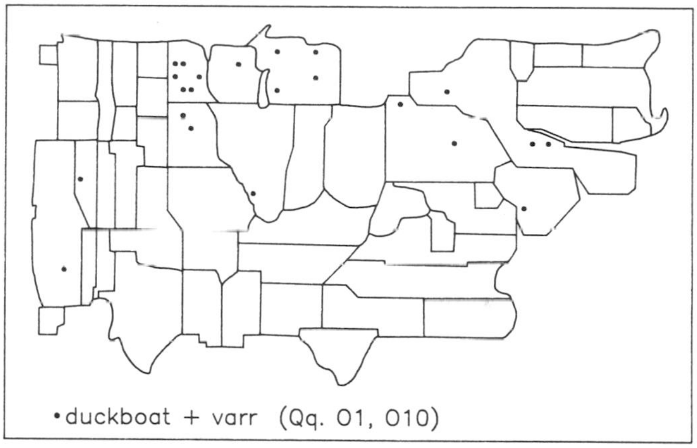

duck bubble n

1957 *Hand Coll.* **cnOH,** During a rain, if bubbles called "duck bubbles" appear on the water, the rain is not over with.

duck bumps n pl [From the resemblance to the skin of a plucked duck] **chiefly Nth** See Map

=**gooseflesh.**

1942 Berrey–Van den Bark *Amer. Slang* 935, Duck-bumps, *goose-pimples.* **1949** *PADS* 11.21 **CO.** **1965–70** *DARE* (Qu. X58, *When you*

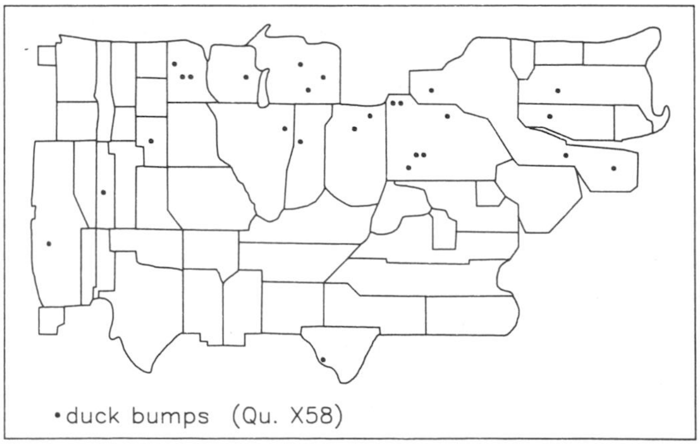

are cold, and little points of skin begin to come on your arms and legs, you have ——) 26 Infs, **chiefly Nth,** Duck bumps. [21 of 26 Infs female] **1973** Allen *LAUM* 1.405 (as of c1950), *Duck bumps* seems to be a facetious synonym used by persons who otherwise say *goose pimples* or *goose flesh.*

duck butter n

1 Smegma; semen. **chiefly S Midl** Cf **gnat butter, headcheese n 2**

1933 *AmSp* 8.1.48 **Ozarks,** *Duck butter*. . . Sperm, seminal fluid. **1944** *PADS* 2.19 **sAppalachians,** *Duck butter*. . . Smegma (In s. Va.: *gnat-bread.*) **1950** in 1977 Randolph *Pissing in the Snow* 221 **AR,** He smeared a handful of duckbutter right under the town girl's nose. **1954** *Harder Coll.* **cwTN,** *Duck butter*—Smegma. Taboo; common among school boys. **c1960** *Wilson Coll.* **csKY,** *Duck butter*. . . A cheese-like bacterial growth on the glans; also called *gnat bread;* technical name—*smegma.* **1981** *AmSp* 56.16 **Sth,** In my own native dialect (of the Gulf coastal plain of Texas) *duck butter* means 'smegma.' To make sure that definition was not merely private or local, I found several other users of the term in its preputial sense (all of my informants happen to come from Southern states, coastal or inland, including Oklahoma). **1981** [see **headcheese n 2**].

2 See quot.

1978 *AmSp* 53.214, *Goose butter*. . . and *duck butter* are used with the same meaning, namely, the yellowish matter or the dried, gritty residue of it in the eyes after sleep. I knew it as a child in the 1940s and 1950s in central Indiana (Danville).

duck by duck adv phr

One at a time; each one separately.

1942 Hurston *Dust Tracks* 243 **nFL,** I did not have to consider any racial group as a whole. God made them duck by duck and that was the only way I could see them.

duck celery n

=tape grass.

1951 *PADS* 15.27 **TX,** *Vallisneria americana* . . —Duck celery.

duck clam n

1 An **egg cockle** (here: *Laevicardium mortoni*).

1945 Beck *Jersey Genesis* 203 **NJ,** Broadbill used to feed on what we call duck clams, about as big as a grain of corn. **1949** Palmer *Nat. Hist.* 358, *Morton Cockle, Duck Clam*. . . Shallow waters (to 30 ft.) on sand flats. . . Common south of Cape Cod. [**1981** Meinkoth *Audubon Field Guide Seashore* 557, *Morton's Egg Cockle* . . is eaten by wild ducks.]

2 A thin-shelled clam of the genus *Anatina* or *Raeta.*

1974 Abbott *Seashells* 492, *Anatina anatina* . . Smooth Duck Clam. North Carolina to Florida and to Texas. . . *Raeta plicatella* . . Channeled Duck Clam. North Carolina to Florida, Texas. . . *Raeta undulata* . . Pacific Duck Clam. San Pedro, California, to Peru.

duck coffee n

1967 *DARE* (Qu. H74b, . . *Coffee* . . *very weak*) Inf **TX**4, Duck coffee.

duck-drencher, duck-drownder See **goose-drownder**

duck duck goose n Also *duck duck drake, ~ gray duck;* for addit varr see quots **chiefly Inland Nth** See Map

A children's game; see quot 1967.

1965–70 *DARE* (Qu. EE1, . . *Games* . . *children play* . . *in which they form a ring, and either sing or recite a rhyme*) 10 Infs, **chiefly Inland Nth,** Duck duck goose; **VA**78, Duck duck duck goose; **MN**34, Duck duck gray duck; **PA**194, Duck duck drake; [**MI**89, Dug dug goose]; (Qu. EE2, *Games that have one extra player—when a signal is given, the players change places, and the extra one tries to get a place*) Infs **IN**1, **NJ**13, Duck duck goose; **PA**229, Duck duck goose goose; **IA**7, Duck duck gray duck—played in a ring; (Qu. EE33, *Other outdoor games*) Inf **NY**186, Duck duck goose. **1967** *DARE* Tape **IN**1, Children are seated in a circle, one person is it and they go 'round and they tap people on the head lightly, sing "duck," as they sing sorta a lyrical way "duck" all the way around, until they decide they want to say "goose"—and whoever the goose is has to chase them and see who gets back to the empty space first. **1980** *DARE* File **swMI,** When there were enough kids around, such as at school or at birthday parties, we played duck duck goose. **1983** *DARE* File **MN,** *(What games do children play in which they form a ring, and either sing or recite a rhyme?)* Duck, duck, gray duck.

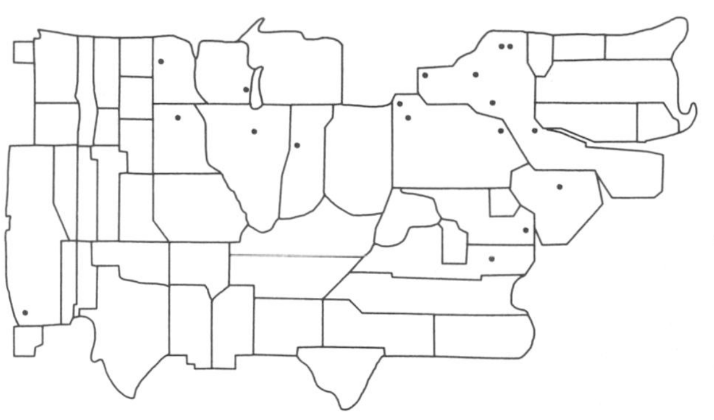

•duck duck goose + varr (Qq. EE1, EE2, EE33)

duckee See **dukie**

duck egg n [From the shape of the numeral 0] Also called **duck n B6**

A score or grade of zero.

1868 *N. Eng. Base-Ballist* 5 Nov. 54/2 *(DA),* In the 7th inning the Atlantics were neatly disposed of for a duck-egg. **1900** *DN* 2.15, In student language. . . the *goose-egg,* the *duck-egg* is a zero, whether got in recitation or in athletic games. *Ibid* 33 **MN, PA,** Duck-egg. . . Cipher in a game (cricket game). **1922** *DN* 5.161, *Duck-egg*. . . Cipher in game (cricket).

ducker n

1 A duck hunter.

1838 Audubon *Ornith. Biog.* 4.8, Old duckers recommend that the *nearest* duck should be in perfect relief above the sight. **1888** Trumbull *Names of Birds* 113, One Wilmington [North Carolina] ducker told me of hearing the Ruddy called *Dickey* by certain South Carolina gunners. **1903** *Sun* (NY NY) 8 Nov sec 3 6/1, The professional ducker goes about his work in an entirely different manner.

2 =duckboat.

1972 Sparano *Outdoors Encycl.* 473, This aluminum ducker for two hunters has a square transom suitable for an outboard, but the boat is easy to row.

duck eye n Cf **cat's-eye 1**

A kind of marble; see quot.

c1970 Wiersma *Marbles Terms* **swMI** (as of 1973), *Duck-eyes:* cat-eyes with colored specks throughout the normally clear part.

duck fit n **chiefly Sth, Midl** Cf **cat fit, chicken fit, dog fit**

An outburst of excitement or anger.

1896 *DN* 1.415 **New Orleans LA,** *Duck-fit* = *cat-fit* . . and *conniption-fit.* **1899** (1900) Harris *On the Wing* 195 (as of 1863), I [=Abraham Lincoln] said as much to Horace Greeley, and he and his friends had a good many duck-fits about it. **1905** *DN* 3.78 **nwAR,** *Duck-fit*. . . State of excitement. 'He went into a duck-fit.' Common. *Duck-fit backwards*. . . State of great excitement. 'He had a duck-fit backwards.' Rare. **1908** *DN* 3.308 **eAL, wGA,** *Duck-fit*. . . A fit of excitement, impatience, or uneasiness; a spell of 'jim-jams'; a tantrum. **1912** *DN* 3.567 **IL, MO, wPA.** *Ibid* 577 **wIN.** **1927** *AmSp* 2.353 **WV,** He took a duck-fit because I dropped the hammer on the ground. **1954** *Harder Coll.* **cwTN.** **1956** McAtee *Some Dialect NC* 14. **1965–69** *DARE* (Qu. KK11, *To make great objections or a big fuss about something: "When we asked him to do that, he ——."*) Infs **AL**3, **MS**56, Throwed a duck fit; **KY**60, Pitched a duck fit; **TN**30, Had conniption fits; raved and ranted; threw a duck fit. **1966** Barnes–Jensen *Dict. UT Slang* 14, He took a duck fit when I told him. **1976** Ryland *Richmond Co. VA* 370. **1983** *MJLF* 9.1.38 **ceKY.**

duckfoot n

1 See **duck's-foot.**

2 also *duck's-foot;* also attrib: See quots. **chiefly West**

1884 Knight *New Mech. Dict.* 280/1, *Duck's-foot Cultivator.* A cultivator with wide flanged shares, resembling the splayed foot of a duck. **1930** *AmSp* 6.11 **CO,** Various cultivator attachments have been devised, bearing such descriptive names as *spider, duck foot, irrigation shovel.* **1931** *Walters* (Okla.) *Herald* 20 Aug. 8/2 *(DA),* Preparing a firm seedbed on fallowed land by means of a duck-foot cultivator. **1939** FWP

Guide MT 61, Land is cultivated with . . the duck-foot cultivator, which turns up large clods. **1944** Walker *Winter Wheat* 97 **MT,** I took it with me down to the barn and climbed up in the seat of the duckfoot to read it. **1966–69** *DARE* (Qu. L18, . . *Kinds of plows*) Inf **MT**3, Disks; duckfoots; **OR**17, Mow board (turns ground over); gang disk; duckfoot (double plowshare without mow board to turn ground).

3 in comb *duckfoot drag:* See quot.

1969 *DARE* (Qu. L20, *The implement used in a field after it's been plowed to break up the lumps*) Inf **WI**77, Duckfoot drag—had teeth (five inches, very heavy) and four-foot frame; for soil not worked much before; used with oxen (or horses).

4 See quot; hence adj *duckfooted.*

1967–69 *DARE* (Qu. X37, . . *Words . . to describe people's legs if they're noticeably . . not right*) Inf **LA**23, Duckfeet—toes point out; **MA**1, Duckfoot—turned out; **DE**2, Duckfooted or wing-footed—feet point out; **MD**27, Duckfooted—toes point out; (Qu. X38, . . *Joking names for unusually big or clumsy feet*) Inf **IA**11, Flat-footed; duckfeet; **PA**227, Plowfeet; duckfeet.

duckfoot drag See **duckfoot 3**

duckfooted See **duckfoot 4**

duck, go milk a v phr Cf **duck's milk**

Mind your own business! Go away!—used in imper.

1968 *DARE* (Qu. NN26b, *Weakened substitutes for 'hell'*) Inf **MD**37, Go milk a duck. **c1970** *Halpert Coll.* 18 **wKY, nwTN,** Go milk a duck! = attend to your own business.

duck grass n

1 A **bluegrass 1** such as *Poa palustris.* Cf **fowl meadow grass**

1751 in 1934 Eliot *Field Husbandry* 61 **CT,** The other is *Fowl-Meadow,* sometimes called Duck-Grass, and sometimes *Swamp-wire-Grass.* **1805** Parkinson *Tour* 2.346 **NEng,** [Herd grass . . grows on swampy ground.] *Ibid* 354, It used to be called duck grass. **1875** *Fur, Fin & Feather* 118 *(DAE),* [Along the eastern coast] the duck-grass and wild celery abound. **1910** Graves *Flowering Plants* 73 **CT,** *Poa triflora. . .* Duck Grass. . . Moist meadows. . . A desirable grass for hay in wet ground.

2 Fennel-leaved **pondweed** *(Potamogeton pectinatus).*

1920 *Torreya* 20.18, *Potamogeton pectinatus. . .* Duck grass, Salt Lake Valley, Utah. **1959** Carleton *Index Herb. Plants* 39, *Duck-grass:* Potamogeton pectinatus.

3 =**ditch grass 2.**

1951 *PADS* 15.27 **TX,** *Ruppia maritima* . . Duck grass.

4 A **pipewort** (here: *Eriocaulon septangulare*).

1950 Gray-Fernald *Manual of Botany* 391, *E[riocaulon] septangulare. . . Duckgrass. . . Leaves* subulate, *fragile, pellucid. . .* Shallow ponds or streams and on sandy, gravelly or peaty shores.

duck hawk n [See quots 1812, 1844]

A medium-sized, bird-hunting falcon *(Falco peregrinus).* Also called **bullet hawk, chicken hawk 1, Dutch hawk, great-footed hawk, hen hawk, ledge hawk, peregrine falcon, pigeon hawk, rock eagle, vulture, wandering falcon**

1812 Wilson *Amer. Ornith.* 6.85 **sNJ,** Few gunners in that quarter are unacquainted with the *Duck Hawk,* as it often robs them of their wounded birds before they are able to reach them. **1844** DeKay *Zool. NY* 2.13, *The Duck Hawk. Falco Anatum. . .* Its usual food consists of birds, which are struck on the wing. **1848** in 1850 Cooper *Rural Hours* 410 **cNY,** The Duck-hawk, or Peregrine Falcon, is chiefly found on the coast. **1874** Coues *Birds NW* 341, *Falco Communis. . .* Peregrine Falcon; Duck Hawk. **1884** Roe *Nature's Serial Story* 131 **NY,** Our duck or great-footed hawk is almost identical with the . . peregrine falcon of Europe. . . It measures about forty-five inches in the stretch of its wings, and its prevailing color is of a dark blue. *Ibid* 132, In a few instances the duck-hawk has been known to nest in trees. **1917** (1923) Pearson *Birds Amer.* 2.88, The quick wing beats resembling the flight of a Pigeon . . readily identify the Duck Hawk in the field. **1940** in 1946 Stanwell-Fletcher *Driftwood* 247 **KY,** We've been watching a duck hawk . . feeding on a large freshly killed snowshoe rabbit out on the middle of the lake. **1966–70** *DARE* (Qu. Q4) 8 Infs, **scattered,** Duck hawk.

ducking n esp **TX**

1 often attrib: Duck, a hard, plain, usu cotton fabric.

1895 Remington *Pony Tracks* 241, The drinking . . helps to soften the asperities of a Dakota blizzard which is raging on the other side of the "ducking." **1904** *NY Times* (NY) 10 May 4, [Advt:] Splendid selection of duckings from which to make them [=awnings]. **1915** *DN* 4.226 **wTX,** *Duckin'. . .* Duck. "Give me some duckin' to make cotton sacks with." **1920** Hunter *Trail Drivers TX* 177 (as of c1880), The silver . . was placed in duckin' sacks, and was loaded on a pack horse or mule. **1966** *DARE* Tape **OK**43, They've got a seven-and-a-half or nine-foot duckin' sack . . [with] a strap; it's put over their shoulders, and they go down the row, pickin' this fleecy cotton. . . It's just a white, heavy sack. **1967** *DARE* (Qu. W4, . . *Names . . for men's coats . . for work and outdoor wear*) Inf **TX**1, Duckin' jacket—cowboys; brown; hung down loose. Now denim jacket—tight around waist; **TX**4, Ducking jacket—light tan, often with corduroy reinforcement on pockets and above front; **TX**13, Duckin' jacket—worn by cowboys; belt length; made of heavy canvas; blue, tan, or brown. [All Infs old] **1969** Green *Wild Cow Tales* 146 **TX** (as of 1930s), I ripped the sleeves out of a duckin' jacket.

2 pl; By ext: work clothes, esp overalls, made of this fabric.

1929 *AmSp* 5.17 **Ozarks,** *Duckins. . .* Everyday clothes, usually blue overalls, as distinguished from those reserved for Sunday or holiday wear. **1940** *AmSp* 15.447 **eTN,** *Duckings.* Overalls. 'The boys wear duckings in the 'bacco patch.' **1952** in 1958 Brewer *Dog Ghosts* 106 **TX** [Black], He wouldn't buy her onlies' brothuh Tom nothin' but duckins to w'ar. **1956** Ker *Vocab. W. TX* 189, The common term for the outer working garment is *overalls. . .* The old-fashioned *duckins* is reported eight times. *Duckins* are so called because they are made of duck cloth. **1960** Criswell *Resp. to PADS 20* **Ozarks,** *Duckings* [dʌkəns]—Blue jeans; named for the material; no longer common. **1962** Atwood *Vocab. TX* 51, *Working clothes. . . Duckins . . ,* which can apply to the pants, or the jacket, or both, is more or less limited to West Texas. **1963** Owens *Look to River* 11 **TX,** That'll get you some duckings and shoes from the catalogue. **1966–67** *DARE* (Qu. W9) Inf **OK**28, Duckins—a nickname for overalls; (Qu. W10, . . *Work trousers made of rough cloth, usually blue*) Inf **TX**3, Duckings—tan; **TX**43, Duckings. **1967** *PADS* 47.11 **SW.**

ducking vbl n See **duck** v **1**

ducking Baptist n [**duck** v **1**]

=**deep-water Baptist.**

1968 *DARE* (Qu. CC4, . . *Nicknames . . for . . religious groups*) Inf **NJ**8, Ducking Baptists.

ducking boat See **duckboat**

duckinmallard n [See quot 1888; cf *DJE dokantiil*]

=**mallard.**

1806 (1905) Lewis *Orig. Jrls. Lewis & Clark Exped.* 4.148 **OR,** The duckinmallard or common large duck w[h]ich resembles the domestic duck are the same here with those of the U'Sts. **1888** Trumbull *Names of Birds* 16, The species is several times referred to by Lewis and Clarke, 1814, as *Duckinmallard.* If this word occurred but once it might be considered a typographical error, but it certainly seems to have been so printed intentionally. Old writers commonly referred to this fowl as the "duck and mallard." . . The above queer name is therefore believed to have grown from this old custom. **1911** *Forest & Stream* 77.453 **NC,** I recently heard the name Duckinmallard used by an old resident of Bladen county in speaking of the varieties of ducks frequenting White Lake in winter. This, of course, applies to the mallard and is mentioned by Trumbull. **1923** U.S. Dept. Ag. *Misc. Circular* 13.8, Duckinmallard (N.Y., N.C., Fla., an old name, corruption of duck and mallard, probably obsolete now) [is a local name for the mallard, *Anas platyrhyncha*].

duck in the oven, have a See **oven**

duckity duck n

=**duck on a rock.**

1901 *DN* 2.139, *Duckity-duck. . .* The same as *duck on a rock. . .* Allentown, Pa.

duck knuckle adj phr Cf **fucky-knuckle, knuckle** v

1921 *DN* 5.109 **CA,** *Duck knuckle,* adj. ph. A manner of shooting a taw, in marbles, propelling from between the first and second joints of the index finger instead of with the thumb nail from the tip of the index finger. Common in other parts of United States.

duck-legged adj

Having short legs.

1809 Irving *Hist. NY* 2.78, Never did two valiant train band captains . . marshal their gallows-looking, duck-legged, heavy-heeled, sheep-stealing myrmidons with more glory and self-admiration. **1899** (1912) Green *VA Folk-Speech* 159, *Duck-legged. . .* Having short legs like a duck. **1936** U.S. Dept. Ag. *Yearbook* 187, Sometimes there is a shortening of the leg bones in cattle which gives them a squat appearance. In certain sections of the South, these animals have been called duck-legged cattle. **1967–68** *DARE* (Qu. X37, . . *Words . . to describe people's legs if they're noticeably . . not right*) Inf **LA**11, Duck-legged ['dʌk,lɛgd]—short legs with big foot on the end; (Qu. X50) Inf **MO**36, Duck-legged.

duck lettuce n

A **saltbush** (here: *Atriplex patula*).

1933 *Torreya* 33.83, *Atriplex hastata*. . . Duck lettuce, Bear River, Utah.

‡**duck light** n [Perh from *duck* to lower] Cf **drop light**

1967 *DARE* (Qu. N10, . . *Words . . for the bright and dim lights on a car*) Inf **NE**7, Duck lights.

duck louse n

A bedbug.

1968 *DARE* (Qu. R24, . . *Other names . . for a bedbug*) Inf **AK**9, Duck lice.

duck meat See **duck's-meat**

duck-milker n Cf **duck, go milk a; duck's milk**

See quot.

1967 Williams *Greenbones* 58 **GA** (as of c1910), And sitting there knitting, she would say, "Son, one day you'll become a doctor or a lawyer or a duck-milker. You'll be looked up to. You'll be respected."

duck millet n

=barnyard grass.

1933 *Torreya* 33.82, *Echinochloa crus-galli* . . Duck-millet, Mississippi Delta, La . . ; blue duck millet, wild duck millet.

duck moss n

Fennel-leaved **pondweed** *(Potamogeton pectinatus).*

1920 *Torreya* 20.18, *Potamogeton pectinatus*. . . Duck moss, . . Salt Lake Valley, Utah. **1959** Carleton *Index Herb. Plants* 39, *Duck-moss:* Potamogeton pectinatus.

duck nest See **duck's nest**

duck oak n

A **water oak** (here: *Quercus nigra*).

1884 Sargent *Forests of N. Amer.* 152, *Quercus aquatica*. . . Water Oak. Duck Oak. **1897** Sudworth *Arborescent Flora* 175, Common names [of the water-oak include] . . Duck Oak, Possum Oak, Punk Oak. **1933** Small *Manual SE Flora* 428, *Quercus nigra* . . Water-oak. . . Duck-oak. **1960** Vines *Trees SW* 181, Vernacular names [for *Quercus nigra*] are Bluejack Oak, Duck Oak, . . and Possum Oak.

duck oats n [Cf CanFr *folle avoine* wild oats, *Zizania aquatica*]

=wild rice.

1933 *Torreya* 33.82, *Zizania aquatica*. . . Duck oats.

duck off (the rock) See **duck on a rock**

duck on a June bug, like a See **June bug**

duck on a rock n Also *duck on (the) rock, ducky on a* (or *the*) *rock, duck the rock, duck off (the rock), dock on the rock, duke on a rock* [Engl dial *duck* a stone used in games] **chiefly Nth, N Midl, West** See Map *old-fash* Also called **duck n 1, duck on davy, ducks and drakes 3, duckstone** Cf **double duck**

A game in which each player throws a stone to try to knock another stone off a rock; see quots.

1878 *Harper's New Mth. Mag.* 56.258/1 **NY,** 'Duck on the rock' . . is far ahead of polo, pallone, lawn tenis [sic], or Aunt Sally. . . The first thing to do . . is to find a rock and a duck, also some smaller stones. . . put this largest stone on the grass—so; that is our rock; now this smaller pointed one on the top of it; that is our duck. You see, we are each to take a stone, stand off as far as you like, and aim at the duck. If you succeed in knocking it off, you must run and get your stone and be back at the home before the duck is placed in position. **1883** Newell *Games & Songs* 189, *Duck on a Rock*. . . The drake is a good-sized stone, which is placed on an elevated position, or boulder. . . The "ducks" are stones about the size of the fist. The object is to knock the drake off the rock. **1905** *DN* 3.70 **nwAR.** **1923** Acker *400 Games* 109, *Duck on a Rock*. . . Each player has a "duck"—a fair-sized stone. A large rock is chosen as the duck rock and a throwing line is marked off twenty feet from this rock. **1950** *WELS (Games in which you set up a stone . . and try to knock it down)* 12 Infs, Duck on a rock; 13 Infs, Duck on the rock; 1 Inf, Ducky on a rock; 2 Infs, Ducky on the rock; 1 Inf, Duck off the rock; 1 Inf, Duck off. **c1960** *Wilson Coll.* **csKY,** *Duck on the Rock*—common children's game. **1965–70** *DARE* (Qu. EE18, *Games in which the players set up a stone . . and then try to knock it down*) 152 Infs, **chiefly Nth, N Midl, West,** Duck on a rock; 21 Infs, **chiefly Nth,** Duck on the rock; **OR**6, **PA**234, Ducky on a rock; **IN**69, **NJ**2, **OH**98, Ducky on the rock; **UT**3, Duck on rock; **IL**35, **NY**68, Dock on the rock; **IN**58, Duke on a rock; **MA**100, Duck the rock. [Of all Infs responding to the question, 65% were old; of those giving these responses, 82% were old.] **1966** *DARE* File **neIL,** *Dock on the rock.* A children's game, reported by sixty-four-year-old woman. **1966** *DARE* Tape **MA**118, One of the main things was duck on the rock. . . We'd put one small rock on top of the big rock and then we had to stand back with rocks; we all took rocks about the same size, and we stood in a line and see if we could hit that one off the top.

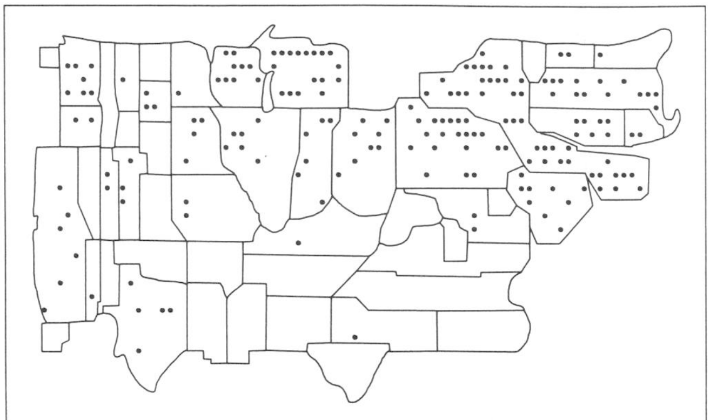

•duck on a rock + varr (Qu. EE18)

duck on davy n Also *duck and davy, duck on davies* **chiefly NJ, PA, IN**

=duck on a rock.

1890 *DN* 1.77 **PA,** *Duck on the rock* in Jersey City, N.J. . . ; *duck on Davy* in Philadelphia . . ; *duck and Davy* in western Pennsylvania. **1892** *DN* 1.215 **DC,** In Georgetown, D.C., *duck on davy.* **1940** Kennedy–Harlow *Schoolmaster* 227 **cIN** (as of c1870), Duck-on-Davy or Duck on a Rock, which many old-timers will remember, was becoming popular in my early boyhood. **1951** *PADS* 15.54 **neIN,** *Duck-on-davy*. . . Our name for the game usually called *duck-on-a-rock.* **1955** *AmSp* 30.233 **csIN,** *Duck-on-davy* was the name of a game. The 'davy' was a large rock on which was placed a smaller one—the 'duck,' which was the target of stones tossed by the players. **1965–70** *DARE* (Qu. EE18, *Games in which the players set up a stone . . and then try to knock it down*) Infs **NJ**18, 33, 48, 53, **PA**98, Duck on davy; **IN**30, Duck on davies.

duck on (the) rock See **duck on a rock**

duckpond lily n

Either the **banana waterlily** or *Nymphaea elegans.*

1951 *PADS* 15.32 **TX,** *Castalia elegans* . . and *C. mexicana* . . —Duckpond lily; Mexican water-lily.

duck potato n [See quot 1931]

1 =arrowhead 1.

1913 *Torreya* 13.227, *Sagittaria latifolia*. . . This is the famous . . duck potato of the Northwestern States. **1931** Clute *Common Plants* 22, The arrow arum was also known as wampee and the name is still applied to the starchy tubers of the arrow-leaf *(Sagittaria latifolia),* though they are now more frequently known as duck potatoes, in reference to the wild duck's fondness for them. **1946** Kopman *Wild Acres* 38 **LA,** The duck potato, tuberlike rootstock of a species of arrowhead, is a very important food for the delta expanses. **1948** *Chicago Daily Tribune* (IL) 17 Oct sec 2 4/2 **IL,** The Mississippi river bottoms have excellent stocks of natural food for ducks this year . . with long leaf, sago pondweek [sic] and duck potato making up the bulk of the waterfowl food supplies. **1951** *PADS* 15.27 **TX,** *Sagittaria* spp.—Indian potatoes, duck potatoes; tubers eaten by both red men and birds. **1976** Bruce *How to Grow Wildflowers* 278, *Sagittaria*—Arrowhead. . . Common names for various species include Swamp potato, Duck potato, and the Indian name "Wapato."

2 =water chinquapin. Cf **duck acorn, Indian potato**

1988 *DARE* File **wWI,** The duck hunters over by Ferryville call the seeds of the American lotus *duck potatoes.* They say that the ducks eat the seeds.

duck punt See **duckboat**

duckretter n [Etym unknown]

=**Indian poke.**

1828 Rafinesque *Med. Flora* 273, *Veratrum viride* . . Ich-weed, . . Dackretter [sic], Puppet root, &c. **1900** Lyons *Plant Names* 389, *Veratrum viride* . . Duck-retter. **1930** Sievers *Amer. Med. Plants* 6, *American False-Hellebore—Veratrum viride* . . Other common names. . . tickleweed, duckretter.

duck rice n

1 =**wild rice.** Cf **duck oats**

1951 *PADS* 15.27 **TX,** *Zizania aquatica* L.—Wild-rice; duck-rice.

2 =**barnyard grass.** Cf **duck millet**

1951 *PADS* 15.27 **TX,** *Echinochloa crusgalli* L.—Wild-rice; duck-rice.

duck-run See **goose-run**

ducks n[1]

1 A **spatterdock** (here: *Nuphar luteum*). [See quot]

1892 *Jrl. Amer. Folkl.* 5.91, *Nuphar advena,* . . ducks. Chestertown, M[arylan]d. . . Qu[er]y. *docks,* as in spatter-dock?

2 A **lady's slipper.** [See quot 1894]

1894 *Jrl. Amer. Folkl.* 7.100, *Cypripedium,* any sp[ecies], ducks, Wyoming Valley, Pa. . . When the flower is partly filled with sand and set afloat on water, it looks like a duck. **1949** Moldenke *Amer. Wild Flowers* 384, A smaller relative . . is *C. candidum,* the *small white ladyslipper,* sometimes called *ducks.* **1950** Correll *Native Orchids* 18, In some sections of Pennsylvania any species of lady's-slipper is called "ducks," in allusion to the appearance of the flowers when the lip is partly filled with sand and the flowers placed upon water. **1959** Carleton *Index Herb. Plants* 39, *Ducks:* Cypripedium [sic] hirsutum.

ducks exclam, n[2] [Perh var of **dubs** exclam, infl by **duck** n 2]

A call establishing claim to something; a claim to something.

1939 *AmSp* 14.26 **SC,** *Ducks* . . with verbal force. 1. Request for a portion of a cigarette, candy bar, etc., after the owner has had enough. 2. Request for the use of an article after the owner is through, as 'Ducks on your electric razor.' **1940** *Qrly. Jrl. Speech* 26.266 **nwVA,** What children in the North call "dibs on it," meaning *I claim a share,* Virginia children may call "ducks on it" (1893), perhaps from a boys' game called duckstones. **1942** Berrey–Van den Bark *Amer. Slang* 891.8, *Request for a partially smoked cigarette.* Butts on you, ducks, give me butts. **1956** *AmSp* 31.36, Still others said 'I have beans on your seat' or 'I have ducks on your pie.'

ducks and drakes n

1 See quot. [*OED* 1583 →] Cf **lame duck**

1966–69 *DARE* (Qu. EE30, *Throwing a flat stone over the surface of water so that it jumps several times*) Infs **WA**7, **NY**144, Ducks and drakes.

2 in phrr *make ducks and drakes of, play duck and drakes with:* To misuse, squander, make a mockery of. [*OED* c1600 →]

1835 Crockett *Account* 58 **TN,** Such cute teaching as makes them know how to make ducks and drakes of us out yonder, when they come among us. **1856** Durivage *3 Brides* 231 (Taylor–Whiting *Dict. Amer. Proverbs*), "Making ducks and drakes" of the pretty little fortune left him by his defunct sire. **1928** *AmSp* 4.123 **IN,** *More Animal Comparisons.* . . duckling stage. . . lame duck. . . to make ducks and drakes of. **1954** Forbes *Rainbow* 173 **NEng,** Or Jude . . playing ducks and drakes with the Seventh and Eighth Commandments.

3 also *duck and drake:* =**duck on a rock.** *old-fash*

1890 *DN* 1.21 **ME** (as of 1860), *Duck.* A game known some thirty years ago in Bath, Me., as *duck and drake* is, or was not long ago, called simply *duck* in Waterville, Me., and *duck on a rock* is used in Massachusetts. *Ibid* 77 **MA,** *Duck* . . known in Chicopee, Mass., as *duck on a rock* or *duck and drake.* **1901** *DN* 2.139 **cNY,** *Ducks and drakes.* . . A variant of duck and drake, duck on a rock, etc.

4 A matter of indifference.

1967 *DARE* (Qu. KK26, *Something that makes no difference . . : "He can think what he likes, it ______ me."*) Inf **ID**5, Is ducks and drakes with.

ducks and geese n

=**fox and geese 2.**

1967–70 *DARE* (Qu. EE26, . . *Games . . children play in the snow*) Inf **MI**117, Ducks and geese, same as fox and geese; **NY**24, Ducks and geese.

ducksback See **duckback**

duck's-bill gar See **duckbill gar**

duck's blood soup n Also *(duck) blood soup* **chiefly in Polish settlement areas** Cf **czarnina**

See quot 1950.

1941 Writers' Program *Guide WI* 484, After the church ceremony, the guests return to the bride's home to eat boiled chicken, roast pork, . . and, most indispensable of all, czarina, or blood soup. **1950** *WELS (Kinds of soup)* 1 Inf, **cwWI,** Sour soup; Polish soup; duck's blood soup—salt, duck, duck's blood, diced potato, and wine; *(Dishes made using vinegar)* 1 Inf, **cwWI,** Cold slaw, . . duck blood soup, . . pig's feet. **1968** *DARE* (Qu. H65, *Foreign foods favored . . around here*) Inf **MI**75, Duck's blood soup; **WI**47, Duck's blood soup (charnina [čɑr'ninə]).

duck scow See **duckboat**

duck's eye See **drake's eye**

duck's-foot n Also *duckfoot*

1 A **mayapple** (here: *Podophyllum peltatum*).

1830 Rafinesque *Med. Flora* 2.59, *Podophyllum montanum.* . . *Names.* . . *Vulgar.* Mandrake, Wild Lemon, Ducksfoot. . . Leaves peltate palmate. **1876** Hobbs *Bot. Hdbk.* 32, Duck's foot, American Mandrake, Podophyllum peltatum. **1900** Lyons *Plant Names* 296, *P. peltatum.* . . Duck's-foot. . . *Fruit* edible. **1940** Clute *Amer. Plant Names* 117, *May-apple.* . . Duck's foot. **1959** Carleton *Index Herb. Plants* 39, *Duck foot* . . Podophyllum peltatum. **1974** (1977) Coon *Useful Plants* 76, Duck's foot. . . The roots are the part used medicinally for its effect on the liver.

2 See **duckfoot 2.**

ducks in line (or a row), get one's See **duck** n **9**

duck skiff See **duckboat**

duck's-meal n

A **duckweed 1** (here: *Wolffia* spp).

1951 Martin *Amer. Wildlife & Plants* 448, Sometimes one finds mixtures of these two [=*Lemna minor* and *Spirodela polyrhiza*], together with the tiny, almost granular appearing ducksmeal *(Wolffia).*

duck's-meat n Also *duck meat* [From its being eaten by ducks]

=**duckweed 1.**

1766 (1942) Bartram *Diary of a Journey* 41 **FL,** Having most of its surface covered with duck-meat. **1824** Bigelow *Florula Bostoniensis* 2.5, *Duck meat* . . multiplies extensively in stagnant ponds and ditches, frequently giving a green appearance to their whole surface. **1843** Torrey *Flora NY* 2.245, *Lemna minor.* . . *Lesser Duckweed,* or *Duck-meat.* . . Stagnant waters, covering the surface with a green mantle. **1861** Wood *Class-Book* 670, *Lemnaceae.* Duckmeats. **1876** Hobbs *Bot. Hdbk.* 32, Ducks' meat, a floating aquatic plant, Lemna minor. **1900** Lyons *Plant Names* 218, *Lemna.* . . Duck's-meat. *Ibid* 397, *Wolffia.* . . Duckmeat. **1940** Clute *Amer. Plant Names* 151, *L[emna] trisulca.* . . Duck's meat. . . *S[pirodela] polyrhiza.* . . Duckmeat. **1959** Carleton *Index Herb. Plants* 39, *Duck meat:* Lemna (v); Spirodela polyrhiza.

duck's milk n Cf **duck, go milk a**

An imaginary substance used as the basis of practical jokes.

1967 *DARE* (Qu. HH14, *Ways of teasing a beginner or inexperienced person . . : "Go get me ______."*) Inf **CO**47, Quart of duck's milk.

duck's nest n Also *duck nest*

Fig: a shallow depression or small cavity—used in var usu technical senses; see quots.

1948 Mencken *Amer. Lang. Suppl. 2* 763 [Argot of oilfield workers], *Duck's nest.* The firebox of a boiler. **1969–70** *DARE* Tape **KY**13, It [=part of the apparatus that raised or lowered the millstones with respect to each other] had a, I called it a duck nest, it was a bearing down there; **KY**84, You have to also keep a clean fire [in a forge]. If you get clinkers, or cinders, in the bottom of your duck's nest, you have to remove them. **1973** *PADS* 59.35 [Bituminous coal mining vocab], *Duck's nest* . . in an *air shot* the enlarged area for the charge at the end of a drill hole. **1983** *MJLF* 9.1.38 **ceKY,** *Duck's nest* . . a chuck hole.

duck soup n **widespread, but less freq S Midl** See Map

An easy task; something or someone easy to handle.

1902 *Bulletin* (San Francisco CA) 5 July 5 *(Zwilling Coll.)*, [Drawing of a man juggling a number of objects at once, saying:] Duck soup. **1912** Lewis *Apaches of NY* 84 **NYC**, 'Them Gophers are as tough a bunch as ever comes down the pike.' 'Tough nothin'!' returned Slimmy: 'they'll be duck soup to Ike.' **1932** *AmSp* 7.331 **MD.** **1950** *WELS (Expressions about a person who does something very easily: "For him, that would be ———.")* 24 Infs, **WI**, Duck soup. **1965–70** *DARE* (Qu. KK42a) 116 Infs, **widespread, but less freq S Midl**, Duck soup. **1975** (1982) Ludlum *Road to Gandolfo* 108, A war was duck soup compared to 400 million hysterical Catholics. **1980** *New Yorker* 18 Feb 32 **wKY**, "Duck soup," says Grandmother. "Duck soup?" Sandra says. "What does that mean?" "It means something is real easy," says Grandmother. "Easy as pie."

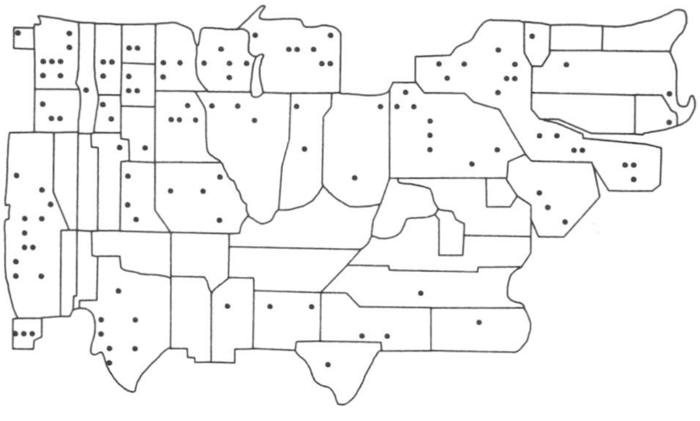

•duck soup (Qu. KK42a)

duck sparrowgrass n [Perh from the whorled, asparaguslike leaves] Cf **sparrowgrass**

A **hornwort 1** (here: *Ceratophyllum demersum*).

1951 *PADS* 15.31 **TX**, *Ceratophyllum demersum* L. . —Duck sparrow-grass (asparagus).

duckstone n, also pl

=**duck on a rock.**

1892 *DN* 1.213 **seMA**, *Duck. . . Duck-stone* was my name of the game. **1940** *Qrly. Jrl. Speech* 26.266 **nwVA**, Virginia children may call "ducks on it" . . , perhaps from a boys' game called duckstones.

ducktail n

1967 *DARE* (Qu. B10, . . *Long trailing clouds high in the sky*) Inf NY34, Ducktails—from Long Island duck shooting.

duck the rock See **duck on a rock**

Ducktown n Cf **frog n B4**

1970 *DARE* (Qu. C34, *Nicknames for nearby . . districts*) Inf **PA**245, Ducktown—down at the bottom of the valley; often gets flooded.

duck tracks n pl Cf **chicken tracks, hen tracks**

=**chicken scratch 1.**

1967–68 *DARE* (Qu. JJ11, *Joking names for handwriting that's hard to read: "I can't make anything out of his ———."*) Infs **IN**30, **NY**34, Duck tracks.

duckweed n

1 Std: a plant of the family Lemnaceae. Also called **duck's-meat, mallard weed.** For other names of *Lemna* see **frog buttons, mardling, toadspit, water lentil.** For other names of var spp of *Lemna* see **fairy paddle, frog spit 2, greed, ivy-leaved duckweed, star duckweed, windbags.** For other names of var spp of *Spirodela* see **minnow-fole, water flaxseed.** For other names of var spp of *Wolffiella* see **mud-midget.** For other names of *Wolffia* see **duck's-meal, watermeal**

2 A **purslane** (here: *Portulaca oleracea*).

1903 Small *Flora SE U.S.* 416, *Portulaca oleracea. . .* Pussley. Duckweed. **1914** Georgia *Manual Weeds* 152, *Purslane. . . Other English names: . .* Duckweed. **1933** Small *Manual SE Flora* 496, *Duckweed. . .* Hammocks, pinelands, cult. grounds, and waste-places.

3 A **smartweed** (here: *Polygonum longistylum*).

1951 *PADS* 15.30 **TX**, *Persicaria longistyla. . .* Duckweed. . . Wild birds like the flowers and seeds of the smartweed.

duck wheat n

A **buckwheat 1** (here: *Fagopyrum esculentum* or *F. tataricum*).

1911 *Century Dict. Suppl., Duckwheat. . .* A local name for *Fagopyrum Tataricum*, the Tartarian buckwheat or India wheat. **1940** Clute *Amer. Plant Names* 259, *Fagopyrum esculentum* . . duck-wheat. **1976** Bailey–Bailey *Hortus Third* 470, *F[agopyrum] tataricum. . .* India wheat. . . Has been known as *duckwheat.*

duckwing n

A domestic fowl with a distinctive dark-colored wing covert.

1871 Lewis *People's Poultry Book* 54 **NY**, The *pure* Duck-wing Game fowls are the Silver Grays—though there are Yellow or Birchen Duck-wings. *Ibid* 55, The plumage of the Duck-wing Bantams is precisely similar to that of the larger breed. **1969** *SC Market Bulletin* 9 Jan 2, Game bantams, black Old English and Modern Duckwings.

ducky n

1 also *ducky down, ~ drake:* =**duck on a rock** or a similar game. Cf **ducks and drakes 3**

1950 *WELS (Games in which you set up a stone, a tin can, or something similar, and try to knock it down)* 1 Inf, **cnWI**, Ducky. **1967–69** *DARE* (Qu. EE18) Inf **IA**11, Ducky or ducky down—set a three-cornered stick up on ice and throw clubs at it; **IL**26, Duck on a rock; ducky; shinny; **NY**213, Ducky drake—two rocks one atop the other; gotta get the top without hittin' the bottom.

2 See quot.

1968 *DARE* (Qu. F37, . . *An indoor toilet*) Inf **OH**72, Ducky.

ducky down (or drake) See **ducky 1**

ducky on a (or the) rock See **duck on a rock**

ducy n

1927 *DN* 5.474 **Ozarks**, *Ducy. . .* Penis. Pronounced so as to rhyme with Lucy. This word seems to be used mostly by the old women in the Ozarks.

dud n [Engl and Scots dial]

1 A dull, ineffective, or socially awkward person. **scattered, but less freq Sth** See Map Cf **dub** n[1] **1**

1870 *Putnam's Mag.* 5.142/2 **NEng**, Think! I think she is dressed like a dud. Can't say how she would look in the costume of the present century. **1950** *WELS (Names . . for a person you don't like to have around: "Oh, he's an awful ———.")* 1 Inf, **csWI**, Dud. **1965–70** *DARE* (Qu. HH16, *Uncomplimentary words with no definite meaning —just used when you want to show that you don't think much of a person: "Don't invite him. He's a ———."*) 48 Infs, **esp Inland Nth, N Midl, West**, Dud; (Qu. HH3, *A dull and stupid person*) 11 Infs, **scattered**, Dud; (Qu. U17, . . *A person who doesn't pay his bills*) Inf **MD**16, Dud; (Qu. W41, . . *Someone whose clothes never look right or who always dresses carelessly*) Inf **MA**5, Dud; **PA**26, A dud—i.e., like a nothing; (Qu. AA21, *Joking expressions . . about . . a husband who takes . . [orders] from . . [his wife]*) Inf **OH**25, He's a servant, a dud; (Qu. HH1, . . *A rustic or countrified person*) Inf **CA**56, A dud; (Qu. HH5, *Someone who is queer but harmless*) Inf **WI**70, Dud; (Qu. HH13, *Expressions meaning that a person is not very alert or not aware of things: "He's certainly ———."*) Infs **NY**75, 220, (Kind of a) dud; (Qu. HH20a, *An idle, worthless person: "He's a ———."*) Infs **MA**73, **NY**84, Dud; (Qu. HH15, *A very inexperienced person, one who is just learning how to do a*

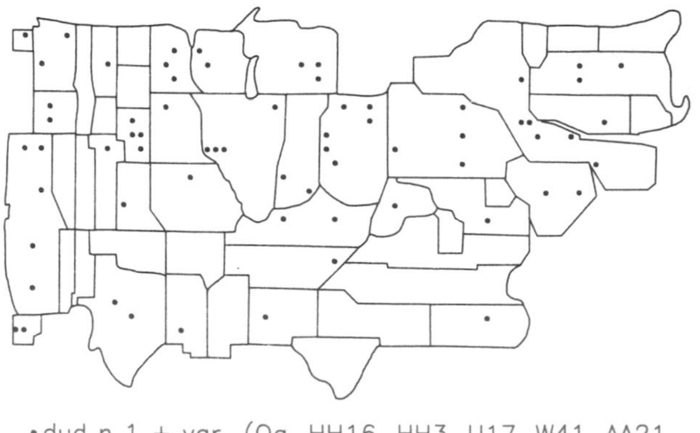

•dud n 1 + var (Qu. HH16, HH3, U17, W41, AA21, HH1, HH5, HH13, HH15, HH20a, II17)

new thing) Inf **MI**67, Dude, dud; (Qu. II7, *Somebody who doesn't seem to 'fit in' or get along very well, you might say about him, "He's kind of a ______.'*) Inf **MA**3, Dud.

2 A well-dressed person. [Perh var of *dude,* infl by *dud* article of clothing]

c1902 Clapin *New Dict. Amer.* 169, *Dud, Dude.* What we might call a very convenient tailor's block [=mannequin]. If not American by origin, it is certainly so by usage. **1950** *WELS (When a woman puts on her good clothes and tries to look her best, you say she's ______)* 1 Inf, **ceWI,** Dressed like a dud. **1968** *DARE* (Qu. W38, *When a man dresses himself up in his best clothes, you say he's ______*) Inf **PA**154, A dud.

dud v [*dud* an article of clothing]

1 also with *up, out:* To dress, get dressed; hence ppl adj *dudded.*

1942 Berrey–Van den Bark *Amer. Slang* 89.2, *Get dressed. . .* dud the body. *Ibid* 89.3, Dress up; primp. . . dud up, dude up. *Ibid* 89.5, Dressed. . . dudded (up). *Ibid* 89.6, Dressed up; primped. . . (all) dudded out *or* up. **1957** Battaglia *Resp. to PADS 20* **eMD** *(When somebody dresses up in a lot of fine clothes and tries to make a big showing, you might say he is ______)* Dudded out.

2 To undress (oneself).

1927 *AmSp* 2.353 **WV,** *Dud yourself. . . ,* to remove your clothes. "Let's see who can dud himself and be in the water first." **1975** Gainer *Witches* 9 **sAppalachians,** You got your clothes all wet; you'd better dud yourself before the fire.

dudab See **doodad 2**

dudad See **doodad**

dudded See **dud v 1**

dudder-grass n [Cf *OED dudder* v. *"Obs.* exc. *dial."* . . To shudder, shiver]

=maidenhair fern.

1900 Lyons *Plant Names* 15, *A[diantum] Capillus-Veneris. . .* Dudder-grass. **1938** Small *Ferns SE States* 121, Being an attractive fern, popular names are abundant. The more common are . . *Dudder-grass* [etc].

dude n [From *dude* a flashy dresser] *esp freq among Black speakers*

A fellow, guy.

1930 Williams *Logger-Talk* 23 **Pacific NW,** *Dude:* Used as a general term for a man as *fellow* is used; *that fellow, that dude,* are synonymous. **1966–70** *DARE* (Qu. GG14, . . *Someone who fusses or worries a lot)* Inf **PA**236, Dude—could mean other things like "nice guy"; (Qu. II10a, . . *What you'd say to a boy: "Say, ______, where's the post office?"*) Inf **CA**187, Dude; (Qu. II23) Inf **NC**37, Rich dudes; (Qu. II35) Inf **NY**238, You can't tell that dude nothing. [2 of 4 Infs Black] **1967–70** *DARE* Tape **TX**4, He was a traveling dude; **TN**46, This dude, this white guy, ya know, went and shot him; **VA**9, I seen that dude standin' in there, he's a great big ol' tall red headed dude. **1969–70** *DARE* FW Addit **ceNC,** The word *dude* is used often, it seems to me, in the same way I would use *guys,* as "You dudes get over here"; **TN**50, His woman had run out on him with another dude [FW: Among young Blacks, *dude* = "man"]. **1972** Claerbaut *Black Jargon* 63, *Dude* . . an ordinary fellow; a regular man or boy: *He's an all right dude.* **1974** *Harper's Mag.* Nov 89/2 **NYC** [Black], There was so many dudes in the 'A' pen once that I couldn't sit down. **1976** *NYT Mag.* 18 Apr 71/2 [Black], Black teen-agers—some of the roughest, most street-wise dudes you will ever meet—respond to that appeal.

dude v

To run a dude ranch.

1967 *DARE* Tape **WY**2, [My father] took more to guiding and duding than he did ranching.

dudedad See **doodad 1**

dudeen n Also *dudheen* [IrGael *dūidīn,* dimin of *dūd* pipe]

A short clay tobacco pipe.

1850 Garrard *Wah-to-yah* 176 **NM,** With a short "dudeen" in his mouth, he would sit cross-legged by the warm coals. **1853** *Harper's New Mth. Mag.* 7.318/1 **swCA** (as of 1848), A pipe (Carson's own particular "dudheen"), being put in requisition for the occasion, was duly filled with tobacco, lighted, and . . passed to the oldest man among our Indian guests. **1888** *Century Illustr. Mag.* 35.807/1, The representative Americans of the present day . . [are] the Micks and the Pats, the Hanses and the Wilhelms, redolent still of the dudeen and the sauerkraut barrel. **1912** E. V. Cooke *Baseballogy* 15 *(DAE),* An incense from the Cuban isle, A dudheen puffing, black and vile. **1950** *WELS (Nicknames for a tobacco pipe)* 1 Inf, **csWI,** Irish dudeen.

dudelheimer, dudenheimer See **dodelheimer**

dudelsack n Also *dudelsok* [PaGer *dudelsack*]

A bagpipe.

1930 Shoemaker *1300 Words* 16 **cPA Mts** (as of c1900), *Dudelsok*—Home made bagpipes, played by wandering pipers. **1947** Mitchell *Old PA Custom* 21, Every Saturday night mysterious music and rough folk laughter was heard issuing from the cavern as the young people tripped it to the strains of the dulcimer, the dudelsack, and the geik or fiddle.

dudenwhacker See **doowhacker**

‡dudes n pl [Var of *dud* an article of clothing]

1970 *DARE* (Qu. W39, *Joking ways of referring to a person's best clothes*) Inf **TN**65, Dudes.

dudheen See **dudeen**

dudie n [Dimin of *dude* n]

1889 Daly *Great Unknown* 12 *(DA),* You ought to have seen how miserable he looked. Poor little dudie! **1968** *DARE* (Qu. AA6a, . . *A man who is fond of being with women and tries to attract their attention —if he's nice about it*) Inf **NY**68, Kind of a dudie ['dudɪ].

‡dudied up adj phr [Prob var of *duded up;* but cf **dudie**]

1968 *DARE* (Qu. W38, *When a man dresses himself up in his best clothes, you say he's ______*) Inf **CA**87, All dudied ['dudid] up; he's a dude.

dudified See **-ified**

dudinkus See **doodinkus**

dudn'(t) See **do v A4**

du don't See **do v C1c**

dud out (or up) See **dud v 1**

dudy-over n

=Antony-over A.

1969 *DARE* (Qu. EE22, . . *The game in which they throw a ball over a building*) Inf **IN**76, Dudy-over.

due adj, n **chiefly Nth, N Midl, West** |du|; **chiefly Sth, S Midl** |dju, dɪu, ǰu| Pronc-spp *doo, jew, jue* Cf **dew** n and Pronc Intro 3.I.10

A Forms.

1861 Holmes *Venner* 2.299 **eMA,** Here is your accaount [sic], Miss Darley, and the balance doo you. **1893** Shands *MS Speech* 40, *Jew* is also used for *due* by negroes. **1899** (1912) Green *VA Folk-Speech* 244, *Jew. . .* For *dew,* and *due.* **1903** *DN* 2.312 **seMO,** *Due. . .* Pronounced jew [ǰiu]. **1913** Kephart *Highlanders* 278 **sAppalachians,** Most hillsmen say . . jue (due). **1922** Gonzales *Black Border* 308 **sSC, GA coasts** [Gullah glossary], *Jue*—due, dues. **1930** *AmSp* 5.341–55, [*Due* has the phone [u] in csME, cwNH, cnNY, seMA, cCT, NYC, sePA, ceMO; [ɪu] in ceIL, sePA, seSC, cSC, cGA, neTX; [ɪJu] in ceVA, cnTX; [iu] in neTX.] **1942** Hall *Smoky Mt. Speech* 38 **wNC, eTN,** *Due* . . is [dɪu] on many of the discs. It is almost always distinguished from *do,* which, however, may have a fronted vowel. **1943** *LANE* Map 563, Pronunciations of *dues* or *due* or both with a diphthong of the type of [ɪu] or [ɪU] are described as more natural by . . [1 inf.] and as older though still in use by . . [9 infs.]. Three informants . . characterize this diphthong as old-fashioned in *dues* but not in *due;* three others . . characterize it as old-fashioned in *due* but not in *dues.* **c1960** *Wilson Coll.* **csKY,** Dues /djuz/; /du/ heard rarely by very young people who have picked it up from visitors or their schools. **1961** Kurath–McDavid *Pronc. Engl.* 174, The alveolar consonants in *new, due, Tuesday,* etc., are followed either by the vowel /u/ of *two,* the sequence /ju/, or the back-gliding vowel /iu/. . . The dissemination of the variants is largely regional. The type of /nu, du, tuzde/ is current throughout the North and the North Midland. In Pennsylvania, northeastern West Virginia, New Jersey, and Metropolitan New York, /u/ is universal; in the New England settlement area it is the predominant pronunciation, but not the only one. The type of /nju, dju, tjuzde/ has general currency in the South and the South Midland. . . Here the sporadic [iu] phone may be a prosodic variant of the /ju/ sequence. In the North /ju/ is infrequent, though preferred by some cultured speakers, as in Metropolitan New York. The type of /niu, diu, tiuzde/, with back-gliding decrescendo vowel, is largely confined to New England and the Yankee settlements to the west. It is especially common in folk speech, but is also used by some cultured speakers in

New England (not in Upstate New York, it seems). . . Within the /ju/ area of the South and the South Midland, the sequences /dju, tju-/ are partly replaced by assibilated [džu, tšu-], phonemically /ǰu/ as in *June* and /ču-/ as in *chew.* This pronunciation is fairly common in folk speech, but is avoided by cultured speakers. **1973** Gawthrop *Dial. Calumet* 62 **nwIN,** Words such as *tube, dues,* and *new* are pronounced /tub/, /duz/, and /nu/. **1976** Allen *LAUM* 3.307 (as of c1950), In the U[pper] M[idwest] a full [dj] is recorded three times . . in northeastern Minnesota and once in South Dakota in the speech of an inf. . . who has a New England background. A diphthongal form, however, appears in the speech of 26 infs., most of whom are in the Midland speech territory of southern Iowa and Nebraska. Perhaps six of them retain the falling diphthong of New England. . . /du/All others.

B As adj.

Of a person: owing, obligated to give. [*OED* 1413 →; "Now *dial.* or *colloq.*"]

1893 Shands *MS Speech* 28, *Due me a compliment* [dju . .]. A phrase used quite frequently by illiterate whites for *owe me an apology;* as, "Mr. Smith, you are due me a compliment for the way you acted yesterday."

due in See **during**

dueno n [Span *dueño*] **SW**

An owner, proprietor.

1919 Chase *CA Desert* 320, While I drank my milk and talked with the dueño . . the phonograph was turned on for my pleasure. **1927** Beals *Brimstone & Chili* 306, The *duenõ* [sic] of this little business filled one of my pockets from a wooden measuring-scoop. **1930** Dobie *Coronado* 106 **swTX,** The white panther was the soul of the dead *dueño* of the treasure, there to watch it.

duenst See **during**

duff n

1 A flour pudding, usu with fruit, boiled in a bag. [Engl dial *duff* var of *dough*] **chiefly coastal NEng**

1816 in 1977 Hill *Voyages* 130 **ME,** For Sunday dinner we have "duff and molasses." Duff is a pudding made from flour and water, and I do not think there is anything added, for sometimes it is rather thick and heavy. . . Such is a sailor's mode of living. **1893** Barra *Tale of 2 Oceans* 30 **MA** (as of 1849), The duff is composed of flour, lard, raisins, saleratus and water, with eggs mixed in when they can be had. When well mixed it is put into a canvas bag, . . boiled two hours . . served with wine sauce when it can be had, or else with vinegar, butter, sugar and water boiled well together and thickened with flour and flavored with nutmeg. **1903** *DN* 2.295 **Cape Cod MA** (as of a1857). **1916** Macy-Hussey *Nantucket Scrap Basket* 158, *Duff*—Boiled in a cloth, was on the menu twice weekly. **1941** *LANE* Map 292, 7 Infs, **coastal NEng,** Apple duff. **1945** Colcord *Sea Language* 69 **ME, Cape Cod, Long Island,** *Duff.* A boiled or steamed pudding served on Sundays at sea. It is known by this name alongshore, and is not unknown to landspeople. **1947** Bowles-Towle *New Engl. Cooking* 177, Genuine duff is nothing more or less than gingerbread dough which is steamed instead of baked. **1950** *WELS (Kinds of pudding served in your neighborhood)* 1 Inf, **swWI,** Figgy duff. **1957** Beck *Folkl. ME* 194, A line in one sea song says that all the crew gets to eat "is a stinking little piece of beef and a damn small bag of duff." **1984** Smith *SW Vocab.* 125, *Duff:* A pudding, usually offered as plum-duff, or apple-duff.

2 By ext: any sweet food or dessert.

1899 (1912) Green *VA Folk-Speech* 159, *Duff.* . . Name given to all sorts of dessert. University word. **1914** *DN* 4.150 [Navy slang], *Duff.* . . Any sweet edible. **1942** Berrey-Van den Bark *Amer. Slang* 91.20, *Desserts; cakes; pastries; confections.* Duff, fancy fixin's. *Ibid* 91.34, *Sugar.* Dirt, duff.

3 A pancake. Cf *DS* H20b

1949 *McDavid Coll.* **cwNY,** *Duffs* [dʌfs]—pancakes. Male [inf], 77 years old, high school education.

4 The decaying vegetable matter, esp needles and cones, on a forest floor. [Scots dial] **NEast, Pacific NW**

1874 VT State Bd. Ag. *Report* 2.547, The opinions of men vary in regard to the desirableness of burning off the scurf, duff, or muck, of soft wood land. **1886** NY Forest Comm. *Annual Rept. for 1885* 1.102 **neNY,** A surveyor says: " . . Fires will be carelessly left by guides, or will be smouldering in the duff." [Footnote to *duff:*] Local term for the vegetable growth covering the forest ground of the Adirondacks. Under the spruce trees, the falling needles accumulate to considerable depth, forming the "spruce duff," a peculiar and interesting variety of forest humus. **1955** U.S. Arctic Info. Center *Gloss., Duff.* . . In botany, the needles, twigs, cones, and other organic debris, in various stages of decomposition, on top of the soil and humus. *Specif.,* the accumulation under coniferous trees growing in cool regions. Also called 'mull,' 'litter.' **1958** McCulloch *Woods Words* 54 **Pacific NW,** *Duff*—Moss, needles, and other litter on the top of the ground in the forest. **1959** *AmSp* 34.77 **nCA.** **1960** *Seattle Daily Times* (WA) 30 Oct pictorial sec 13 caption *(Perrin Coll.)* **NW,** The fire was described as a "cool" one, meaning that the surface litter (the slash) . . was dry enough to flare quickly and soon be reduced to ashes, while the underlying duff was deeply wet, preventing the development of "hot spots," which cook, harm the soil. **1970** Rogers *Grandma's Is.* 5 **seME** (as of 1924), It was terribly dry and the duff would burn and the fire run along the spruce roots and flame up in a new place. [Author's ms. note:] *Duff*—In our woods largely pine needles, dried, brown, crumbly, forming the surface of the ground.

5 The buttocks. [*EDD duff* sb.[1] 5] **chiefly Nth**

1950 *WELS (Joking words for the part of the body that you sit on)* 3 Infs, **WI,** Duff. **1952** *Time* 25 Aug 12/2 **CA,** We kidded him because we others were a bunch of lazy guys sitting around on our duffs and Stevenson was doing things. **1967-69** *DARE* (Qu. X35, *Joking words for the part of the body that you sit on)* Infs **CA**15, **WI**12, 47, 50, **WV**18, Duff. **1968** *Chatham Courier-Rough Notes* (NY) 20 June sec B 3, Hunters: Now is the time for you to get off your duff[.] You may not have another chance. **1979** *UpCountry* Feb 4 **cwMA,** She's writing Guinness to tell him to get his duff off the 24-foot chair in Iceland, currently listed as the champ. **1981** *Capital Times* (Madison WI) 5 Mar 17/1, We need to get off our duffs and exercise on a regular, organized basis.

6 Money. [Cf *dough* money]

1967 *DARE* (Qu. U19a, . . *Money in general)* Inf **HI**9C, Duff.

7 See **duffer.**

duff v Usu with *in* [Cf *EDD duff* v.[3] 2 "To dive, plunge"] **chiefly NEng**

To work or set to work energetically.

1913 *DN* 4.56 **Cape Cod MA,** *Duff.* . . To work energetically; usually with *in.* "I'm all beat out; I've been duffing in all the morning." **1943** *LANE* Map 567, These expressions were usually recorded in the sentence *You'd better pitch in* (i.e. start working), as spoken to a hired laborer who is idling when he should be at work. . . *Duff in,* heard in Boston [by inf from Bridgewater MA]. **1959** *VT Hist.* new ser 27.134, *Duff.* . . To get to work immediately.

duffer n Also *duff* [*OED duffer* sb.[2] 1 *"colloq."* 1842 →] **chiefly Nth, N Midl** See Map *somewhat old-fash*

An ineffectual, bumbling or stupid person, usu a man; a fellow, guy, codger—used with a wide range of connotations from derog to affectionate.

1901 *DN* 2.139 **cnNY,** *Duffer.* . . A boaster. **1902** *Harper's Mth. Mag.* 104.429/2, Duffers like us don't know what real thought *is.* **1904** Number 1500 *Life in Sing Sing* 247 **NY,** *Duffer.* A name applied in contempt. **1948** Manfred *Chokecherry* 197 **nwIA,** Finally one old duffer says, "Since nobody's claimin' it, an' there ain't no name on it . . , I'm takin' it as a sign." **1950** *WELS (Uncomplimentary words for an old man)* 2 Infs, **WI,** Duffer; 4 Infs, Old duffer; *(Affectionate names meaning a young child)* 1 Inf, Duffer. **1959** *VT Hist.* new ser 27.134, *Duffer.* . . A lazy person. Occasional. **1960** Wentworth-Flexner *Slang* 166, *Duffer.* . . A dull, stupid, or unrealistic person. *Obs.* **1965-70** *DARE* (Qu. HH40, *Uncomplimentary words for an old man)* 72 Infs, **chiefly**

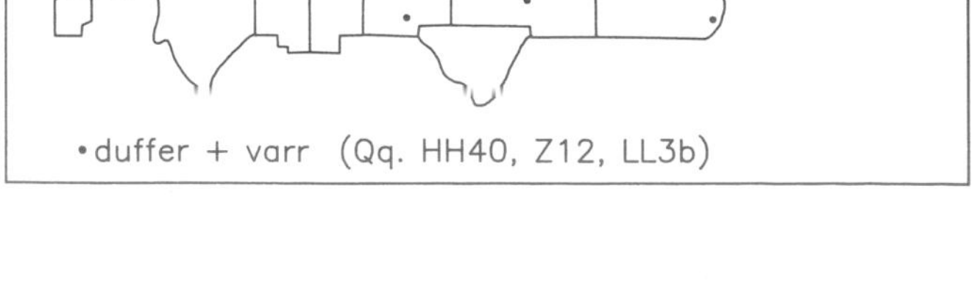

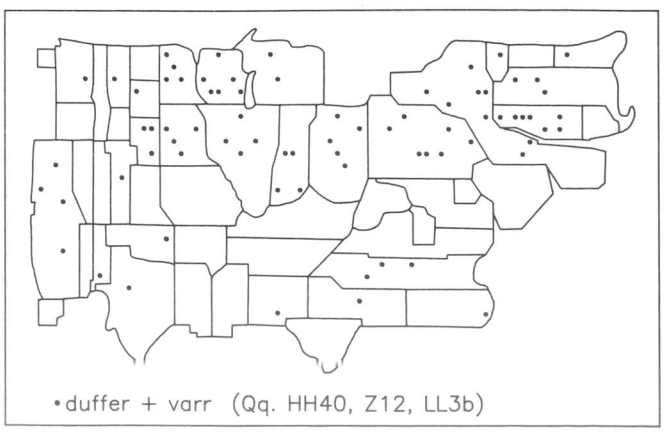

•duffer + varr (Qq. HH40, Z12, LL3b)

Nth, N Midl, Duffer; **CA**97, **MI**81, **MN**42, Old duffer; **OH**87, Old duff [Of all Infs responding to the question, 64% were old; of those giving these responses, 85% were old.]; (Qu. Z12, . . *Nicknames . . meaning 'a small child': "He's a healthy little ______.")* Inf **VT**16, Duffer, lad; (Qu. LL3b, . . *Shrunk, dried up: "He's a little ______.")* Inf **ME**19, Wizzled-up old duffer. **1975** Gould *ME Lingo* 83, *Duffer*—Another word for chap, party, character, fellow, and so on, but with kindly tone: "He's a pleasant old duffer."

duff in See **duff** v

duffing n [*EDD duff* v.^{3} 3, sb.^{4} 4]
1968 *DARE* (Qu. Y16, . . *A thorough beating: "He gave the bully an awful ______.")* Inf **PA**66, Duffing.

duffle n
A **mullein** (here: *Verbascum thapsus*).
1940 Clute *Amer. Plant Names* 274, *Verbascum thapsus* . . duffle. **1959** Carleton *Index Herb. Plants* 39, *Duffle:* Verbascum thapsus.

duffnut n [Sp pronc of *doughnut;* cf **duff** n **1**]
1950 *WELS (Joking names for doughnuts),* 1 Inf, **csWI,** Duffnuts. **1967** *DARE* (Qu. H27) Inf **TN**11, Duffnuts.

duffy adj [From **duff** n **1;** cf Scots dial *duffy* soft, spongelike]
Doughy.
1864 in 1926 Twain *Sketches* 137 **cwCA,** They will bake you up a couple . . burnt . . on one side, and flabby and "duffy" . . on the other.

duflickety See **dooflicker**

dufunny See **doofunny**

dug See **dig** v^{1}

dugan See **dogan**

dugan's dew n [Perh from *Dugan,* an Ir surname + *dew* alcoholic beverage] Cf **mountain dew**
1950 *WELS (Nicknames for whiskey)* 1 Inf, **csWI,** Dugan's dew.

dugged See **dig** v^{1}

dugout n
1 A primitive dwelling built wholly or partly underground. **chiefly OK, KS, NE** *hist*
1860 Young *Journal Disc.* 8.293 (1912 Thornton *Amer. Gloss.*), When you have built splendid habitations, be as willing to leave them as you would leave a dug-out. **1886** Ebbutt *Emigrant Life* 94 **KS,** Their dug-out was a wretched place to live in, as such places usually are. A hole is dug in the side of a hill, a few forked posts are put in the corners, poles are laid in the forks, brush and straw are put on the poles, the earth dug out of the hole is thrown over the straw as thick as will keep out rain, and with a door in front and a chimney cut in the bank, the house is ready for occupation. **1907** *DN* 3.230 **OK. 1920** Hunter *Trail Drivers TX* 393 (as of 1870s), The prairies near Abilene, Kansas, where we held our herds, were partly taken up by grangers who lived in dug-outs, a square hole in the ground or in the side of a bluff, with timbers placed across and covered with dirt. **1928** *AmSp* 4.128 **NE. 1937** Sandoz *Slogum* 42 **NE** (as of 1900–20), Behind them was nothing except a dug-out, little more than a mound the height of a new grave above a prairie that was so level a man could n't squat in privacy. **1956** Ker *Vocab. W. TX* 111, We was doin' good enough. They had two dug-outs ready for us when we got here in 1900. **1965–67** *DARE* Tape **AZ**7, One of my grandparents' families lived in what they called a dugout. They would find a hill, dig a hole out of it and frame the door part at the opening and . . dig back into the hill; **KS**6, My folks was very poor and they made a dugout to start with; **OK**1, I was born in what you call a dugout . . what they used to call an ol' cellar an' a place dug out an' covered over with poles an' dirt; **OK**39, [Inf:] Dug a hole in the ground—about three or four feet deep, and built up the ends with logs, picket fashion, and I had some lumber with me that I made sides above the . . ground where you cut the hole . . built lumber from there up, on the sides. [FW:] What did they call a house like that? [Inf:] Called 'em a shanty an' a dugout . . generally called 'em a dugout.
2 A rough cellar.
1915 *DN* 4.225 **wTX,** *Cellar.* . . Universal for *storm-house.* Sometimes also called *dug-out,* though the latter is usually one's permanent habitation. **1960** *PADS* 34.63 **CO,** *Older speech.* . . dugout [for] 'cellar'. **1965–70** *DARE* (Qu. D22, *Underground place to go to in case of a violent windstorm*) 22 Infs, **scattered,** Dugout; (Qu. M19, *A place for keeping . . [vegetables] over the winter*) 9 Infs, **scattered,** Dugout. [25 of 31 Infs old] **1968** *DARE* Tape **IN**23, They hid him for weeks an' weeks. They had a trap door, in their kitchen or someplace and there was a kind of a dugout underneath that floor . . and he lived down in there in the daytime.

dugway n **formerly widespread, now esp West**
A roadway dug into or through a steep hillside.
1718 in 1884 Lancaster MA *Early Rec.* 183, Neer where the path now goes to witt the parth called the dugway. **1819** Dana *Geog. Sketches* 43 **wPA,** The spacious dug ways by the side of, and around the adjoining hills, gave them the facility of speedily gaining their fort. **1829** in 1910 Buffalo Hist. Soc. *Pub.* 14.233 **NY,** The darkness concealed many of the terrors of the descent of the dangerous pass of the dug-way, into the gulf of the Irondequoit. **1889** *Manti* (Utah) *Home Sentinel* 20 Mar. 4/3 *(DA),* I was delighted to find the county road between those two cities at a place on the dug-way where some few years ago, my life was imperiled from a narrow ill constructed road. **1930** Raine-Barnes *Cattle* 88 **TX** (as of c1870), Huge "dugways" had to be graded down the steep banks to let cattle and wagons into and out of the stream. **1932** *DN* 6.229 **West,** *Dugway.* A dugway was originally a road along a slope, of which one side was dug out from the hill. In this sense it may still be heard in mountain country all over the West, chiefly in Utah, and parts of Colorado and Wyoming. **1941** Writers' Program *Guide UT* 270, The word "dugway" . . designate[s] a species of road which consisted essentially of a deep rut scraped into the face of a hill. A wagon with its upper wheels sunk to the hub in this rut, and with a spare team pulling uphill to keep it from tipping, could "go up, down, or around almost any hill with a pitch less than 90 degrees." **1966–69** *DARE* (Qu. C15, *A place in mountains or high hills where you can get through without climbing over the top*) Inf **NY**127, Dugway; (Qu. C35, *Nicknames for the different parts of your town*) Inf **NM**11, South Dugway. **1967** *DARE* Tape **WY**2, They'd do a little improvement on the pass road [in the mountains] each year—put in a few dugways so it wouldn't be so steep in places. **1975** Zwinger *Run River* 122 **UT,** Today, a dugway in the soft sand angles up out of the river, and a dust devil scurries a cloud of dust. **1980** *Greenfield Recorder* (MA) 18 Oct sec A 4, The road . . was called "The Dug Way," for that's what it was, a road dug out of the side hill to make a direct route down into the village and to the church. *Ibid,* They don't say "Dug Way" anymore, except a few old-timers.

dug worm n **esp NY**
An **earthworm.**
1968–69 *DARE* (Qu. P5, . . *The common worm used as bait*) Inf **NY**74, Night crawler—big ones; angleworm—same as dug worm (called this because people dig them); **NY**87, Night crawler, dug worm; (Qu. P6, . . *Other . . worms*) Inf **NY**177, Dug worms (small).

duh v |də, dɛ, de| Also sp *da(y), de(h), der* Cf *DJE* da$^{3, 4, 5}$, de$^{3, 4}$ *Gullah* Cf **de-de** Note: *duh* and varr are never inflected.
1a To be—usu equivalent to StdE present finite forms.
1888 Jones *Negro Myths* 72 **eGA,** De cunjur man . . tell um say him kin pint out way de Ring day. [=The conjure man told them he can point out where the ring is.] *Ibid* 73, Nobody kin fine out who duh de tief. [=No one can find out who is the thief.] Buh Fox, Buh Rabbit, an Buh Coon, dem day fas fren [=they are fast friends]. **1922** Gonzales *Black Border* 19 **sSC, GA coasts** [Gullah], Dem two twin duh my'own. [=Those two twins are my own.] *Ibid* 180, You know dat same Mistuh Middletun lib close Adam' Run deepo? Well, she duh my juntlemun now, en' me duh Mis' Middletun. [=You know that same Mister Middleton who lives near Adam's Run depot? Well, he is my gentleman now, and I am Mrs. Middleton.] **1949** Turner *Africanisms* 213, [sʌpm də kʌmɪn] 'Something is coming.' *Ibid* 262, [nɒʊ dat də sʌpm!] [=Now that is something!] **1971** Cunningham *Syntactic Analysis Gullah* 41, *Deh* (/dɛ/ or /de/) 'be'. . . C[reole:] John deh home, ma. E[nglish:] John is at home, ma'am. . . C[reole:] Anywhere you deh in there, I'll find you. E[nglish:] Anywhere you are in there, I'll find you. C[reole:] Mary deh church. E[nglish:] Mary is at church. **1987** Jones-Jackson *When Roots Die* 101 [Gullah], "That cow de yours?" *Yeah!* Man say, "Yeah, that cow de mine." *Ibid* 121, Ber Wolf say . . "Now all the time you kept coming . . you know you de eating the butter." *Ibid* 141, *De* appears most frequently in contemporary Gullah speech as a replacement for present-tense forms of English *be* verbs: *am, is, are.*
b without preceding subject: It is, it was.
1837 (1976) Simms *Martin Faber* 2.95 **SC,** No Jehu, Mossa,—da Tom. [=It is not Jehu, Master,—it's Tom.] **1922** Gonzales *Black Border* 105 **sSC, GA coasts** [Gullah], Great Gawd, duh *my'own! Duh my foot duh bu'n!* [=Great God, it's my own! It's my foot burning.] **1949** Turner *Africanisms* 213 [Gullah], [wɛn də deləɪt, ɒɪ mɛk mɪ lo kʌcɪ] 'When it is daylight, I make my low curtsy' . . [də gɒd wʌk] 'It is God's work.' . . [ən

də hɪm sew mi] 'And it was he who saved me' . . [ɒɪ no də ɒgəs] 'I know it was August.' **1987** Jones-Jackson *When Roots Die* 106 [Gullah], De mine! [=It's mine!]

2 with an unmarked verb: Used as a preverb usu to express progressive action, equivalent to the following in StdE:

a Present.

1867 Allen *Slave*

me, O Lord! Je-ri-cho da wor-ry me. **1922** Gonzales *Black Border* 48 **sSC, GA coasts** [Gullah], Go'way, Joe! You duh dream. **1928** Peterkin *Scarlet Sister Mary* 34 **SC** [Gullah], How-come you duh gaze at me so hard? **1949** Turner *Africanisms* 210 [Gullah], [Dɛm də cɑ əm] . . 'They are carrying them.' *Ibid* 213, [Dɛm dɛ də kəmplen] 'Those there are complaining.' . . [ɒɪ də (s)te dɛ] 'I am staying there.' *Ibid* 214, The uses of the Gullah *də* 'to be' are in many ways similar to those of the Ibo *de*$_1$, a verb of incomplete predication meaning 'to be.' **1971** Cunningham *Syntactic Analysis Gullah* 66, The present progressive aspect markers are *dE* [=[də]] and *ing. . . DE* always precedes the verb. . . The two aspect markers do not co-occur. . . C[reole:] I still dE look. . . E[nglish:] I am still looking. C[reole:] You dE yent. E[nglish:] You are kidding. . . C[reole:] My head dE hurt me. E[nglish:] My head is hurting me. **1987** Jones-Jackson *When Roots Die* 125 [Gullah], I de go store for get sugar for make pie. [=I am going to the store to get sugar to make a pie.] *Ibid* 141, English: . . She shells them. . . Gullah: . . She (e, he) de shell em.

b Past.

1888 [see **2d** below]. **1892** (1969) Christensen *Afro-Amer. Folk Lore* 8, Cooter da arnswer um from de odder side o' de pos'. **1908** *S. Atl. Qrly.* 7.341 **sSC coast** [Gullah], "You hailed them then?" "Me duh holleh." **1922** Gonzales *Black Border* 129 **sSC, GA coasts** [Gullah], Dem wing' duh sing sukkuh bee duh swawm, en' de mule' duh trot wid all fo' dem foot. [=The wings sang like bees swarming, and the mules trotted with all four feet.] **1949** Turner *Africanisms* 213 [Gullah], [Dɪ kɒtn də drɒp blɒsm] 'The cotton was dropping its blossom.' **1987** Jones-Jackson *When Roots Die* 125 [Gullah], So they de look, de look—and de look for Sister. . . By and by, spring de come.

c Future or conditional.

1922 Gonzales *Black Border* 263 **sSC, GA coasts** [Gullah], I mos' sho', rokkoon duh walk duh paat' dis berry night! [=I'm very sure, a raccoon will walk down the path this very night!] **1949** Turner *Africanisms* 213 [Gullah], [dɛn yu də brɒg] 'Then you will brag.' **1987** Jones-Jackson *When Roots Die* 141 [Gullah], The preverb *de,* in *I de shell em,* can often be heard and understood as *I shelled them,* as well as *I will shell them.* *Ibid* 69, He said, "Well you de come on and de go with me and you de see what I got [=have]." . . She . . said, "What for I ben go with you, you ain't know what fe do with me if you de get me!"

d Nonfinite verb phr.

1867 Allen *Slave Songs* 34 **eSC,** [Words to a song:] I yed-de de bell da ring. [=I heard the bells ringing.] **1888** Jones *Negro Myths* 41 **eGA,** Wen Buh Elephant done full, an der tan onder de tree duh flop eh yez, eh see Buh Rooster, dist es spry, duh walk bout an der swaller seed an grasshopper an wurrum. [=When Brother Elephant was full, and was standing under the tree flopping his ears, he saw Brother Rooster, just as spry, walking about and swallowing seeds and grasshoppers and worms.] **1922** Gonzales *Black Border* 20 **sSC, GA coasts** [Gullah], One time uh count fo' t'ous'n' head uh nigguh' duh hoe rice een de baa'nyaa'd fiel'. [=Once I counted four thousand negroes hoeing rice in the barnyard field.] *Ibid* [see **2b** above]. **1987** Jones-Jackson *When Roots Die* 125 [Gullah], She over the other side de stay with the grandma awhile. *Ibid* 126, He yeddy [=heard] somebody de sing and de sing.

duh prep Pronc-sp *de* *Gullah* Cf *DJE da*^{2}

1 At, in, by, to, toward.

1888 Jones *Negro Myths* 41 **eGA,** Buh Rooster blan wake [=was in the habit of waking] Buh Elephant duh mornin. *Ibid* 84, Bimeby eh gone duh garret, an eh see one do up day wuh bin lock. [=By and by he went to the garret, and he saw one door up there that was locked.] **1922** Gonzales *Black Border* 21 **sSC, GA coasts** [Gullah], Duh summuhtime 'e does dribe duh plantesshun now en' den. [=In the summertime he drives to the plantation now and then.] *Ibid* 105, You seddown duh fiah. [=You sat down by the fire.] *Ibid* 188, Uh nebbuh fuh gone to da' place no mo' duh night-time! [=I'll never go to that place any more at nighttime!] **1949** Turner *Africanisms* 210 [Gullah], [də], following a verb of direction, is best translated by 'toward,' 'to': [i rɒɪd də ǰɑksnbʌrə] 'He rides to (or toward) Jacksonboro.' **1987** Jones-Jackson *When Roots Die* 108 [Gullah], And he come out de his twelve disciple and ask them. *Ibid* 116, Bring anything white de me.

2 Used instead of *to* to mark the infinitive.

a In an adverbial purpose clause. Cf **for B2a**

1949 Turner *Africanisms* 210 [Gullah], In Gullah when [də] is used between two verbs, it means 'to,' 'in order to,' . . : [yu go də grɒɪn əm] 'You go to grind them'; . . [dɛm də cɑ əm də ǰi əm dɪ pipl] . . 'They are carrying them in order to give them to the people.'

b In other infinitival functions.

1949 Turner *Africanisms* 210 [Gullah], [dɑt mɛk dɛm də sew dɛ mʌnɪ] 'That causes them to save their money'; . . [pipl wɑt hɑw mɑn ən wɐif ən cɪlən də wʌk fə dɛm] ' . . people who have man and wife and children to work for them.' **1987** Jones-Jackson *When Roots Die* 106 [Gullah], And buzzard start de lie. Start de show em old man John farm. . . And e start de duck, and de monkey start de choke em.

duke n^1

1 A man of showy demeanor or appearance. [*OED* a1700 →]

1966–69 *DARE* (Qu. W38, *When a man dresses himself up in his best clothes, you say he's ______*) Inf **DC**4, Dude, duke; (Qu. HH2, . . *Nicknames for a citified person*) Inf **PA**230, Duke, sheik.

2 A bull. *euphem*

1914 *DN* 4.106 **KS,** *Duke. . .* A bull. **1944** Holton *Yankees Were Like This* 98 **Cape Cod MA** (as of c1890), On one of our visits, I learned soon after arrival that there was a duke in the barn. . . He was a very satisfactory animal indeed. . . This was the time I learned that nice little Victorians must never, never talk about bulls. **1965** *DARE* File, Duke, gentleman cow, bull. **1969** *DARE* (Qu. K23, *Words used by women or in mixed company for a bull*) Inf **MA**58, Duke. **1973** Allen *LAUM* 1.244 **MN** (as of 1950s), Duke [1 inf]; **SD,** Duke [1 inf, laughter].

duke v [Scots and nEngl dial var of *duck* to avoid, evade] *relic* Cf **jouk**

1927 *DN* 5.474 **Ozarks,** *Duke. . .* To duck, to dodge. "I seen a feller duke in behint th' barn."

duke n^2 See **dukie**

duked up adj phr Also *duked out* [Perh var of **dike** v, infl by *duded up* or **duke** n^1 **1**]

Of a man: dressed up.

1950 *WELS (When a man puts on his good clothes and tries to look his best, you say he's ______)* 2 Infs, **WI,** All duked up (*or* out). **1967–69** *DARE* (Qu. W38) Infs **NJ**16, **NY**65, **HI**6, (All) duked up; **NY**209, Duked out.

duke on a rock See **duck on a rock**

duke's mixture n [From a brand of pipe and cigarette tobacco]

1 A mixture or conglomeration of things; a state of confusion.

1914 *DN* 4.106 **KS,** *Duke's mixture. . .* Conglomerate; also, confusion. . . "When that sleeper went off the rails and turned over, we had a Duke's mixture." **1923** *DN* 5.206 **swMO,** *Duke's mixture. . .* A confused mass. **1954** *Harder Coll.* **cwTN,** *Duke's mixture. . .* Beans, potatoes, corn; all vegetables. **1958** McCulloch *Woods Words* 55 **Pacific NW,** *Duke's mixture . .* anything mixed up, any confused situation. **1973** *DARE* File **swPA** (as of 1920s), If you had three or four different foods on your dinner plate or if you mixed two things which were unheard of, that was called a duke's mixture. **1978** *DARE* File **cSC,** *Duke's mixture*—a phrase my mother used to describe a mixture of things on one's plate. **1988** *Ibid* **csWI** (as of early 1980s), If I put on clothes which my grandmother considered loud or ill-matched, she would pronounce my outfit a "duke's mixture." She also used the term to describe a meal which had been thrown together haphazardly (such as my father's hotdish, which was a dreadful jumble of macaroni and any leftovers he could find in the refrigerator).

2 A person or animal of mixed or indeterminate ancestry.

1961 *McDavid Coll.* **csOK,** Duke's mixture—mixed breed [of] dog. **1962** *Ibid* **cOK,** Duke's mixture—A person of mixed ethnic ancestry, "like most Americans." **1965–70** *DARE* (Qu. J1, *What do you call a dog of mixed breed?*) Infs **CA**107, **IA**8, **OK**1, 43, **WI**47, Duke's mixture; (Qu. J2, . . *Joking or uncomplimentary words . . for dogs*) 10 Infs, **scattered N Midl, Cent,** Duke's mixture; (Qu. K43, *A horse that was not intentionally bred, or bred by accident*) Inf **IL**36, Duke's mixture; (Qu. HH29a, *Names . . for people of mixed blood—part Indian*) Infs **MN**16, **NE**8, Duke's mixture. **1967** *DARE* FW Addit **swOR,** "Duke's mixture"—A man's pedigree: a little French, a little Irish, a little English, a lot of etc. **1971** Wood *Vocab. Change* 43 **AR,** A dog of mixed and uncertain breed. . . *Duke's mixture.* **c1974** Jones *Ozark Hill Boy* 9 **AR** (as of c1920), The favorite dogs included "Old head", a hound; . . and "Old Joe", a duke's mixture belonged to us.

3 An animal of mixed colors.

1965–70 *DARE* (Qu. J5, *A cat with fur of mixed colors*) Infs **IA**8, **MS**55, Duke's mixture; (Qu. K37, . . *A horse of mixed colors*) Inf **CA**195, Duke's mixture.

dukie n, also attrib Also *duckee, duke* Also sp *dukey* [Prob var of *EDD docky* "A slight meal, taken by farm labourers in the middle of the morning"]

A parcel of food; a lunch box; transf, a meal ticket.

1914 Jackson *Criminal Slang* 30, *Dukie*. . . A hand-out, or donation of cold victuals to a beggar. **1927** *DN* 5.454 [Underworld jargon], *Lump*. . . Food given to a tramp which is wrapped up in a paper parcel. Also *ball, poke-out, duckee,* etc. **1928** *AmSp* 3.253 [Carnival talk], *Dukie*—Meal ticket. **1950** in 1951 *AmSp* 26.76, A dukey run . . [is] what the 'Big One,' Ringling Brothers, folks call any between-shows jump of more than 250 miles, when no cook house is available and boxed lunches, or 'dukey boxes' are handed out for the trip. **1967** Cerello *Dakota Co. MN* 54, He pegged his duke and bought his lunch at noon. . . He often would bring us a dukie of fresh-caught fish. . . As children, our dukies were often partially frozen by the time we ended our long, cold walk to school. **1972** *DARE* File **neOH,** Dukey ['duki]—a lunch box; a steel mill term.

dulce n |'dulse, -ɪ| [Span *dulce* sweet] **chiefly West, esp SW**

1 also *dulcy:* A sweetmeat; candy.

1844 Kendall *Santa Fé Exped.* 2.347, At the termination of [the dance] . . the males are expected to treat their partners to refreshments in the way of dulces. **1890** *Outing* 16.355/1 **sCA,** He bought cakes and sticks of *dulce* for the solemn-eyed babies. **1892** *DN* 1.247 **TX,** *Dulce, -s,* sweets; all sorts of desserts, sweetmeats, and candies are called *dulces.* Mostly used in the plural. **1912** Lumholtz *New Trails* 176 **swAZ,** It [=honey] is often used instead of sugar, and a kind of *dulce* is made from it. **1940** Writers' Program *Guide TX* 340, Venders [sic] offer unusual wares, from a live *cabrito* (kid) to a penny's worth of bright *dulces* (candies or cakes). [**1964** *AmSp* 39.281 **nwCA** (as of 1880–1920) [Boontling], *Dulcy*. . . Candy.]

2 A sweetheart, girl friend.

1897 Hough *Story Cowboy* 212 **TX,** It [a letter] may be from his "girl," as he calls it (his *"dulce,"* it would be in the South). **1932** Coolidge *Fighting Men* 275 **AZ,** The next time I visit my *dulce,* I could show her this fine pistol. **1932** Bentley *Spanish Terms* 134, It is common in the Southwest to hear the sweetheart of a young man referred to as his *dulce* or his *dulce corazon* (literally sweet heart).

dulcimer n Also freq *dulcimore* [Transf from *dulcimer* a zither-like instrument played with small hammers (*OED* c1475 →)] **formerly Appalachians, now widely recognized**

A musical instrument having usu three or four strings stretched over a fretted soundbox and played with a plectrum or the fingers.

1917 Campbell–Sharp *Engl. Folk Songs* x, In Kentucky . . singers occasionally play an instrument called the dulcimer, a shallow, wooden box, with four sound-holes, in shape somewhat like a flat, elongated violin, over which are strung three (sometimes four) metal strings, the two (or three) lower of which are tonic-drones, the melody being played upon the remaining and uppermost string which is fretted. As the strings are plucked with the fingers and not struck with a hammer, the instrument would, I suppose, be more correctly called a psaltery. **1924** Raine *Land of Saddle-Bags* 88 **Appalachians,** At night the twanging of a banjo or the picking of a "dulcimore" comes cheerily out of the darkness. **1927** *DN* 5.470 **Appalachians,** Dulcimer—dulcimore. **1930** Shoemaker *1300 Words* 18 **cPA Mts** (as of c1900), *Dulcimore*—A popular musical instrument in the mountains, (Dulcimer.) **1931** Randolph *Ozarks* 176, The old-time singers tell me that the accompaniments were formerly played on the "dulcimore", a homemade instrument which has been replaced by "store-boughten" fiddles and guitars. The only dulcimer I have ever seen was a crude, short-necked affair with three wire strings. Holding the instrument against his thigh, the musician presses one string at a time with the fingers of his left hand, while a piece of leather in his right is swept slowly across all three strings. **1944** *PADS* 2.19 **sAppalachians,** *Dulcimore* ['dʌlsɪ,mor]. . . Variant of *dulcimer,* a native harp of the highlands. **1947** [see **dudelsack**]. **1952** Brown *NC Folkl.* 1.535, *Dulcimore* ['dʌlsɪ,mor]: . . Dulcimer.—West. **1975** *Foxfire 3* 188 **neGA,** I . . never saw nor heard of the dulcimer until the late 1940s. Some of the craftsmen of the Southern Highland Handicraft Guild began making them, using old ones for patterns. Their popularity has been growing ever since . . with the revival of the folk music and handicrafts.

dulcy See **dulce 1**

dulge v Also *delge*

To dig; to delve.

1949 Webber *Backwoods Teacher* 63 **Ozarks,** There were other interesting localisms such as "dulge" (rhymes with bulge) for dig. Perhaps it is a corruption of "delve," for some say "delge." But there seems to be in the word also the added sense of digging for the purpose of hunting or disclosing something. *Ibid* 109, For the outsider to "dulge" into such matter is useless. *Ibid* 171, 'Tis a possum that's been a diggin' an' dulgin' into Pa's grave.

dull adj

1 in phr *dull of hearing:* Hard of hearing, partially deaf. [Engl dial]

1899 (1912) Green *VA Folk-Speech* 159, *Dull*. . . "Dull of hearing," hard of hearing. **1969–70** *DARE* (Qu. X19a, *When a person's hearing is not very good, you say he's* ______) Infs **GA**77, **VA**53, Dull of hearing.

2 also absol; Of tobacco: of poor quality, low grade. Cf **bright** adj **1**

1850 U.S. Patent Office *Annual Rept. for 1849: Ag.* 322, There ought, if the quality of the crop will permit, to be four sorts of tobacco, *"Yellow," "Bright," "Dull,"* and *"Second." Ibid,* The next person . . strips off all the *bright* leaves, . . and throws the plant to the next, who takes off all the rest, being the *"dull."* [**1966** *DARE* Tape **DC**5, [FW:] What's dull tobacco? [Inf:] It [sic] the tip and the dark grade. . . [Aux Inf:] It's the worst grade of tobacco.] **1966** *PADS* 45.12 **cnKY,** *Dull-crop*. . . Leaves that are sick in body and dull in color. . . "Dull-crop may be caused by too much nitrogen in the soil." **1967** Key *Tobacco Vocab.* **TN,** Dull-crop. " . . that's when you don't make anything . . a bad crop: drowned out, not enough rain."

3 in var compar phrr: Extremely dull.

a *dull as a (grub) hoe.*

1803 in 1977 Whiting *Early Amer. Proverbs* 213, But now I am dull, as a hoe. **1849** Haliburton *Old Judge* 59/2 **MA,** Your story is like a broken needle, it has got no point; or like an axe without an edge, as dull as a hoe. **1929** *AmSp* 5.130 **ME,** The following comparisons were common: . . "dull as a hoe." **1946** *CA Folkl. Qrly.* 5.335, As dull as a grub hoe. **1956** McAtee *Some Dialect NC* 14, *Dull as a hoe.*

b *dull as a froe* (or *frow*). **chiefly Sth, S Midl**

1908 *DN* 3.308 **eAL, wGA,** *Dull as a frow*. . . Very dull: said of any cutting tool. The meaning of *frow* is almost entirely lost sight of, but the expression is a common one. "My old knife is as dull as a frow." **1912** Green *VA Folk-Speech* 27, Dull as a froe. **1946** *PADS* 6.37 **eNC,** Dull as a froe. (Very dull—a knife, an ax, a person's mind.) **1953** Randolph–Wilson *Down in Holler* 175 **Ozarks,** In the Ozarks one often hears *dull as a frow,* a reference to the tool used in riving out shingles and clapboards. **1967** *DARE* (Qu. FF19, . . *About a very dull or unenjoyable time: "The party was* ______.") Inf **TX**40, Dull as a frow. **1967** *Hall Coll.* **eTN,** That pocket knife is dull as a froe. A froe was kept dull so as not to splinter the logs in making shingles. **1986** *NADS Letters* **sIL,** Phrases . . which . . come from my [60-year-old] mother, a native of northern Pope County, Illinois. If an axe or knife gets dull, she still says "That old th*a*ng is dull as a froe." I didn't have any idea what a froe was until I was in college.

c *duller than a widow woman's ax.*

1953 Randolph–Wilson *Down in Holler* 175 **Ozarks,** *Duller than a widder-woman's ax* is common [in the Ozarks] also, and needs no explanation. An unsatisfactory knife is *so dull you could ride to mill on it.*

dull v^1

See quots.

1896 *DN* 1.415 **cNY,** *Dull:* to make a mistake. "That's where you dulled." **1914** *DN* 4.72 **ME, nNH,** *Dull*. . . To make a mistake, miscalculation, or stupid blunder. "When she married that 'ar Bud Hayes, she shore dulled."

dull n, v^2 [Cf *EDD dull* sb. "Irel. A horse-hair noose or snare for catching trout" < Ir Gael *dol, dul* a loop, snare]

A snare used in fishing; to fish using a snare; hence vbl n *dulling.*

1880 *Forest & Stream* 14.104/2 **VA,** I hope that the barbarous practice called "dulling" has gone out of fashion. **1889** *Century Dict.* 1795 **Sth,** *Dull*. . . A noose of string or wire used to snare fish; usually, a noose of bright copper wire attached by a short string to a stout pole. . . To fish with a dull: as to *dull* for trout. **1943** in 1944 *ADD* 184/2 **sePA,** Dullin' fish. **1968** *DARE* (Qu. P13, . . *Ways of fishing . . besides the ordinary* *hook and line*) Inf **VA27**, Dull fish—[you can use] a slip loop made of horse hair if you ain't ketched at it. [FW: It's illegal.]

dull as a froe (or frow) See **dull** adj **3b**

dull as a (grub) hoe See **dull** adj **3a**

duller than a widow woman's ax See **dull** adj **3c**

dulless See **do-less**

dulling See **dull** v[2]

dull of hearing See **dull** adj **1**

dulse n

An edible seaweed *(Rhodymenia palmata).*

1889 *Century Dict.* 1785, *Dulse*. . . A seaweed, *Rhodymenia palmata*. . . It is eaten in New England. **1975** Gould *ME Lingo* 83, *Dulse*—A coarse, reddish seaweed of the Maine and Maritime coasts which makes a snack or confection when dried. Some say it was named *dulcet* (sweet) by Champlain's sailors, but the word really comes from the Gaelic *duileasg*. *Dulse* is not to be confused with Irish moss (see *moss*). In eastern Maine, tourists will find *dulse* in the stores. Might like. **1988** *DARE* File **csWI** (as of c1950), Dulse—They used to have this for sale at a fish market in Madison.

dumb v, adj, intj Also *dumbed* Also sp *dum, dummed* [Euphems for *damn, damned*] **chiefly Nth**

1790 Tyler *Contrast* 31 **MA**, I must needs say her father is pretty dumb rich. **1845** Judd *Margaret* 134 **NEng**, He'll have to lose his oxen if it an't paid dum soon. **1893** Frederic *Copperhead* 154 **nNY**, "They take a dummed curious way of showin' it, then," commented Abner, roundly. **1898** Westcott *Harum* 106 **nNY**, He'll find he's bit off a dum sight more'n he c'n chaw. **1911** Quick *Yellowstone Nights* 104 **SD**, A feller makes a dumb fool of himself such times, neighbor. **1914** *DN* 4.72 **ME, nNH**, *Dum* . . Damn; damned. **1949** in 1986 *DARE* File **cwMI**, I was so dumb tired last night. **1966–70** *DARE* (Qu. LL37, *To make a statement as strong as you can: "I could have wrung her neck, I was so ______ mad."*) Inf **NY96**, Dumb; (Qu. NN17, . . *"That ______ fly won't go away."*) Infs **DC11, IA17, MI33, MN33, PA183, TX88**, Dumb; (Qu. NN25a, *Weakened substitutes for 'damn' or 'damned': "______ it all!"*) Infs **NM9**, NY96, **PA223**, Dumb; (Qu. NN25b, . . *"Well, I'll be ______!"*) Infs **MI103**, NY105, Dumbed; **NY96**, God-dumb. **1985** Rattray *Advent. Dimon* 165 **Long Is. NY**, I heard Sylvester grunt; he'd darted the lance: "There, dum ye."

dumb ague n Pronc-sp *dumb ager* Cf **ague B1**

=**dumb chill.**

1789 Amer. Philos. Soc. *Trans.* 3.iv **PA**, The lesser degree of it [=fever and ague] generally called *dumb ague*, is not rare in the most salubrious places during the months of September and October. **1839** *S. Lit. Messenger* 5.65/2, We'll all take a drop, to keep off the dumb ague. **1859** [see **dumb chill**]. **1870** Harte *Luck Roaring Camp* 148 **CA**, He himself had been troubled with a dumb "ager" since last conference. **1903** *DN* 2.312 **seMO**, *Dumb-ague* (ager). . . Ague and fever, not accompanied by shaking. **1906** *DN* 3.134 **nwAR**, *Dumb ague*. . . A chill not noticed till it is followed by fever. **1945** Pickard–Buley *Midwest Pioneer* 18 (as of a1850), There were different kinds of ague—dumb ague, shaking ague, chill fever—and variations. **1968** *DARE* (Qu. BB13, . . *Words . . for chills and fever*) Inf **CA87**, Malaria, dumb ague—mostly fevers, in Sacramento Valley specifically.

dumb as four-o'clock See **four-o'clock 6**

dumb bell See **dumb bull 1**

dumb bird n Also *dumb duck, dummy duck* [See quot 1955] Cf **dunbird**

=**ruddy duck.**

1895 *Std. Dict. Engl. Lang.* (Funk) 563/1, *Dumb-bird*. . . [Local, U.S.] The ruddy duck. **1917** (1923) *Birds Amer.* 1.152, *Ruddy Duck—Erismatura jamaicensis*. . . Other Names—Dumpling Duck . . Dumb-bird . . Stiff-tailed Widgeon. **1925** (1928) Forbush *Birds MA* 1.280, *Erismatura jamaicensis* . . Ruddy Duck.—Other names: Butter-ball . . Dumb Bird . . Spike-tail. **1951** Pough *Audubon Water Bird* 327, Dumb bird. *See* Ruddy duck. **1954** Sprunt *FL Bird Life* 85, *Ruddy Duck: Oxyura jamaicensis* . . Local Names: Spiketail . . Dumb Bird . . Hardhead. **1955** MA Audubon Soc. *Bulletin* 39.378, *Ruddy Duck*. . . Dumb Bird, Dumb Duck (Mass. As being generally silent.) **1982** Elman *Hunter's Field Guide* 192, *Ruddy Duck:* (*Oxyura jamaicensis*, also classified as *Erismatura jamaicensis rubida*)—Common & Regional Names: booby, . . dummy duck, . . sinker.

dumb bull n

1 also *dumb bell, dumb bow:* A noisemaker, esp one consisting of a resonating vessel with a taut covering through which a cord is pulled; see quot 1953. **esp S Midl** Cf **barker 2, bull-roarer 2, devil's fiddle 1, horse fiddle**

1843 *Knickerbocker* 21.46, Another instrument of peculiar construction, entitled 'dumb-bull,' . . is prepared . . to lend dignity to the music, and conceal all aberrations from harmony in its deep resounding bass. **1872** Eggleston *End of the World* 294 **IN**, Bob Short had a dumb-bull, a keg with a strip of raw-hide stretched across one end like a drum-head, while the other remained open. **1907** Cockrum *Pioneer IN* 488, Carrying with them three dumb-bulls, as many hickory rattles and many noisy things. **1923** *DN* 5.234 **swWI**, *Dumb bull* . . An instrument made of a tin pan, pail, etc., to the bottom of which is attached a rosined cord or rope. The dumb bull was much used at charivaris, or mock serenading parties for newly-married couples. **1953** Randolph–Wilson *Down in Holler* 242 **Ozarks**, Dumb bull. . . A section of hollow log with rawhide stretched over one end, like a drum. This rawhide is pierced by a leather thong smeared with resin. When the thong is pulled, a deep roaring sound is produced. Popular at shivarees and similar parties. **1961** *AmSp* 36.299 **ceIN**, *Dumb bull*. . . In Grant County a miniature of this device was made with a cord (rosined, not waxed) and a tin can. [**1966** *DARE* (Qu. CC17, *Imaginary animals or monsters that people around here tell tales about—especially to tease greenhorns*) Inf **GA8**, Dumb bull—makes a horrible fierce noise.] **1980** *Foxfire 6* 194 **nGA**, When you pull against the waxed part of the string it makes a sound just like a bull a'bellering. There ain't as many haint [=ghost] stories in the mountains as there used to be. That's because there ain't as many dumb bells being made! **1984** Gilmore *Ozark Baptizings* 174 **MO**, One time we made us a dumb-bow. Made it of old cans. Boy, you could hear it from here to Kansas. **1988** *NADS Letters* **nwSC** (as of 1940s), *Dumb-bull.* This apparatus . . made the sound of a wild animal. . . Yesterday I called Dad in SC to have him tell me how to make a *dumb-bull*. He gave me the following steps: 1. get a wooden nail keg, approx. 100 lb. 2. take out both ends of the keg. 3. around 1 end, attach a piece of heavy brown paper, something that won't tear easily. 4. tie the paper onto the end with heavy string or cord. 5. punch a small hole (just large enough to pass a cord or string through) into the middle of the paper. 6. run a string or cord (nylon, cloth, etc.) through the hole and attach 1 end of the cord to a nail or piece of wood, so that the cord is snug against the inside of the paper. 7. position the keg a reasonable distance (perhaps 100 yards) from the long end of the cord. 8. get a cake of bee's wax and rub onto the cord. the sound produced is like that of a wild animal. In the northwest corner of SC (specifically Laurens and Greenville counties), this apparatus was used at night to scare those whom you did not like, and could be used on any occasion.

2 =**bull-roarer 1.** Cf **wolf scarer**

1970 *Foxfire* Spring–Summer 10 **nGA**, You ever see'd a dumbull? Piece a'board about that long [*Foxfire* Ed: about six inches]—right thin—y'cut'em off sort'a in th'shape of a old fashioned coffin—diamond shaped. He'd made'im one . . , and I heered it, an' I thought it'uz somethin' in th'river at th'start. I thought it'uz a dog takin' a fit. . . It'd just goin' "Whoo, whoo, whoo!" **1980** *Foxfire 6* 194 **nGA**, He'd make what they called the "dumb bull." . . He'd take a plank and whittle it down thin . . and sharpen the edges in some way, and bore a hole in one end. You'd attach a string to it . . and whirl it around, and it'd make the awfulest racket you ever heard.

dumb cake n [Engl dial] Cf **dumb supper**

1899 (1912) Green *VA Folk-Speech* 159, *Dumb-cake*. . . A cake made in silence, on St. Mark's Eve, with numerous ceremonies, by girls, to discover their future husbands.

dumb chill n **chiefly Sth** Cf **dumb ague**

A usu mild chill, esp in conjunction with a malarial fever.

1859 (1968) Bartlett *Americanisms* 133, *Dumb chill*, or *Dumb Ague*. An expression common in malaria regions to denote that form of intermittent fever which has no well defined "chill." **1880** Cable *Grandissimes* 389 **LA**, "The country's chill day," said Doctor Keene; "dumb chill, hot fever." **1905** *DN* 3.78 **nwAR**, *Dumb chill*. . . An unnoticed or scarcely noticed malarial chill. 'I must have had a dumb chill because I have so much fever.' Universal. **1908** *DN* 3.308 **eAL, wGA**, *Dumb-chill*. . . Ague and fever without the violent rigor. "I had a dumb chill this morning." **c1938** in 1970 Hyatt *Hoodoo* 1.362 **swAL**, I was sitting to my machine sewing when I taken sick in this arm and in the spine of my back; felt just like a chill begin to run over me. And from there my heart begin to beat too fast and I thought once or twice that I might just had a *dumb chill* when it first struck me. **1944** *PADS* 2.8 **VA, NC, MS, AL,** *Dumb chill*. . . A chill acompanied by shaking. . . Lay use. Popular. **1945** *PADS* 3.10 **SC,** *Dumb chill*. . . A chill *un*accompanied by shaking. **1966–70** *DARE* (Qu. BB13, . . *Words . . for chills and fever*) Infs **AL**24, **MS**6, 10, 45, 73, **NC**40, **SC**27, **TN**43, **TX**12, Dumb chill(s). **1975** Thomas *Hear the Lambs* 161 **nwAL,** You may jist be havin' dumb chills. A heap o' folks thinks dey gon' die ever' time dey gits sick.

dumb coot n

The American **scoter** *(Melanitta americana).*

1955 MA Audubon Soc. *Bulletin* 39.377, *American Scoter*. . . Dumb Coot (Maine. It is no more silent than the other species.)

dumb devil n

=**dumb bull 1.**

1952 Brown *NC Folkl.* 1.535, *Dumb-devil*. . . "A bucket with a stretched sheep-skin rosin string."—Central and east.

dumb'd fish See **dumbfish**

dumb duck See **dumb bird**

dumbed See **dumb**

dumbfish n Also *dumb'd fish, dumfish* **NEng** *hist*

=**dunfish.**

1746 *Boston News-Letter* (MA) 2 Oct 2/2, Choice good Dum Fish to be Sold. **1762** *Ibid* 30 Dec 4/1, Choice Isle of Shoal Winter Dumb'd Fish, To be sold cheap for cash. **1792** Belknap *Hist. NH* 3.214, Large thick fish [=codfish], which after being properly salted and dried, is kept alternately above and under ground, till it becomes so mellow as to be denominated dumb fish. **1872** *Atlantic Mth.* Feb 29.166/2, Dunfish, in the old newspaper, were sometime called 'dumb'd fish.'

dumbfloundered adj [Var of *dumbfounded;* cf **founder** v]

1944 *ADD* 184, I'm dumbfloundered.

dumb foxglove n [*dumb,* perh with ref to the closed mouth of the flower]

A **closed gentian** (here: *Gentiana andrewsii*).

1940 Clute *Amer. Plant Names* 223, *Gentiana Andrewsii.* Dumb foxglove.

dumbguzzled adj Cf **dumfoozled**

1979 *DARE* File **VT,** Have you an explanation for "hornswoggled" or "dumbguzzled"? They are both words I have often heard an elderly Vermont cousin of mine use. "Dumbguzzled" appears to mean "astounded" or "dumbfounded."

dumbie See **dummy 3**

dumb mockingbird n Cf **French mockingbird 2**

=**loggerhead shrike.**

1911 *Forest & Stream* 77.174, *Lanius ludovicianus*. . . Dumb Mockingbird, Vinton, La. **1917** *DN* 4.423 **LA,** *Butcher bird*. . . Also called *dumb mockingbird.*

dumbo n [Prob infl by the title character in the animated cartoon *Dumbo* (1941)]

A dimwit; a mute or silent person.

1950 *WELS (A dull and stupid person)* 1 Inf, **cnWI,** Dumbo. **1967–70** *DARE* (Qu. HH3) Infs **NJ**64, **NY**190, **OH**47, 94, **WA**25, **WI**47, Dumbo; (Qu. HH24, *Somebody who doesn't talk very much, who keeps his thoughts to himself*) Inf **WA**16, Dumbo.

dumb palsy n Cf **dumb ague, dumb chill**

Paralysis of the speech organs.

1970 *NC Folkl.* 18.11, Properties of . . lily of the valley, in May, are noteworthy . . in restoring speech to those with dumb palsy, for gout, [etc].

dumb party See **dumb supper**

dumb rattlesnake n

=**copperhead snake 1.**

1872 Schele de Vere *Americanisms* 387, The *Copperhead*. . . is known as . . Dumb Rattlesnake, because it does not give the warning before it strikes.

dumb school See **dummy school**

dumb-skull n [Prob folk-etym for *numskull*]

1968–69 *DARE* (Qu. HH3, *A dull and stupid person*) Infs **GA**19, **RI**4, Dumb-skull.

dumb-sock n Also *dumb socks*

A person considered dull or stupid.

1932 Farrell *Young Lonigan* 276 **Chicago IL,** He's the biggest dumbsock I ever saw. **1935** *AmSp* 10.52 [Comic strip jargon], Epithets disparaging mentality: The dumb sok [sic]; You hammerheads. **1942** Berrey–Van den Bark *Amer. Slang* 433.3, *Stupid person*. . . Dumb smack *or* sock. **1950** *WELS (Uncomplimentary words with no definite meaning—just used when you want to say something unfavorable about a person)* 1 Inf, **ceWI,** Dumb sock. **1964** *PADS* 42.39 **Chicago IL,** *Dumb Swede* and *dumb-socks* were also applied to all Scandinavians.

dumb supper n [*dumb* mute, silent] Also *dumb party* Cf **dumb cake**

See quots.

1905 *DN* 3.78 **nwAR,** *Dumb supper*. . . The name of a young people's game. 'I wouldn't care to play dumb supper, it's too ghosty.' **1941** Writers' Program *Guide SC* 106 **wSC,** 'Dumb supper,' rarely found below the fall line, is prepared by young folk who wish to find out their future mates. Corn bread, with meal and salt in almost equal proportions, must be cooked and eaten in perfect silence. Then comes bedtime, and still no word has been spoken. If one speaks, the whole spell will be broken, but if not, the dreams that follow this salty repast will disclose the dreamer's future spouse, who will appear with a drink of water. **1955** *KY Folkl. Rec.* 1.75 **wKY,** "Dumb supper". . . A sumptious [sic] evening meal was prepared with every step being a backward step, every activity completed with the hands behind the back, and not a word spoken. **1970** *DARE* (Qu. FF12b, *What do you call the night of May first?*) Inf **VA**50, Dumb supper—single girls got together the evening of May day and ate supper without speaking. Each girl had an empty chair and place setting next to her. If all went right, she'd see her future husband sit next to her to join in the meal. **1980** *AR Gaz.* (Little Rock) 11 Mar Omnibus sec 1/2, Did you ever hear of a Dumb Supper? Well, my mother, when she was a young girl . . used to have these Dumb Parties as a May Day custom. . . Two young lassies would get together to prepare a meal, but neither could speak a word. Also, everything had to be done backwards, even to placing the chairs backwards at the table. Usually blankets were placed over the doors to shut out any light. . . Dinner ready, the two would sit down to eat their meal and any young fellers that came at that time . . would supposedly be their intended!

‡dumbwaiter n

A wheelbarrow.

1968 *DARE* (Qu. L41) Inf **LA**15, Dumbwaiter [laughter], occasional.

dumb watches n Also *dumb watch* Cf **clock dials**

A **pitcher plant** (here: *Sarracenia purpurea*).

1893 *Jrl. Amer. Folkl.* 6.137, *Sarracenia purpurea*. . . Dumb watches or watch. Cape May Co., N.J. **1910** Graves *Flowering Plants* 213 **CT,** *Sarracenia purpurea*. . . Dumb Watches. . . The root and leaves are medicinal. **1959** Carleton *Index Herb. Plants* 39, *Dumb Watches:* Sarracenia purpurea.

dumbwit n [Var of *dimwit*]

1970 *DARE* (Qu. HH3, *A dull and stupid person*) Inf **MI**123, Clod, dumbwit, dim-wit, dummy.

dumby adj

1884 *Anglia* 7.269 **Sth, S Midl** [Black], *To look mighty dumby* = to look 'glum'.

dumfish See **dumbfish**

dumfoozled adj [Perh blend of *dumbfounded* + **bumfoozle**]

1 also *dumflustered:* Confused; dumbfounded.

1845 Thompson *Pineville* 172 **GA,** If I hadn't a been completely dumfoozled, I'd never a killed Blaze [=his mule] like I did. **1888** Stockton *Dusantes* 70, Don't you see he's so dumflustered that he hardly knows who he is himself!

2 also *dumfuzzled:* See quot. *euphem*

1967–69 *DARE* (Qu. NN25b, *Weakened substitutes for 'damn' or 'damned': "Well, I'll be ——!"*) Inf **IL**11, Dumfoozled; **MO**19, Dumfuzzled [laughter].

dumifutchet n [Cf *doodlefadgit* at **doodle** n[1] **6**]

=**doohickey 1.**

1952 Brown *NC Folkl.* 1.535, *Dumifutchet* ['dʌmɪˌfʌtʃɪt]. . . A gadget; a term used humorously or because the speaker is unable to think of the name of some object.—West.

dumkopf See **dummkopf**

dummed See **dumb**

dummern n [Var of *womern* (at **woman**)]

A woman.

1913 Kephart *Highlanders* 279 **wNC,** The word woman has suffered some strange sea-changes. . . In Michell [sic] County, North Carolina, we hear the extraordinary forms ummern and dummern ("La, look at all the dummerunses a-comin'!") **1952** Brown *NC Folkl.* 1.401, His [? Hits] a poor dummern that can't daddy her youngun by hits favor.

dummkopf n Also *dumkopf, dom cop, dummkup* [Ger *Dummkopf,* Du *domkop*] **chiefly Nth**

A blockhead, a dumbhead.

1809 Irving *Hist. N. Y.* (1927) v.ii.252 *(DA),* We may picture to ourselves this mighty man of Rhodes like a second Ajax, strong in arms, great in the field, but in other respects (meaning no disparagement) as great a dom cop, as if he had been educated among that learned people of Thrace, who Aristotle most slanderously assures us, could not count beyond the number four. **1923** Watts *Luther Nichols* 15 **OH,** All I got to do is wait on dumkopfs! **1939** Aurand *Quaint Idioms* 13 [PaGer], You are such a *Dummkup* (dumb, idiotic); why don't you watch out where you're going? **1948** *AmSp* 23.108 **swIL,** Mildly derogatory terms are . . *dummkopf* (blockhead), and *lump* (a low fellow). **1967** *DARE* File **NYC,** *Dumkopf.* **1967–69** *DARE* (Qu. HH3, *A dull and stupid person*) Infs **CA**4, **MI**44, **NY**34, 87, Dummkopf; **MI**103, **PA**138, ['dʌm,kəp]; **CT**16, ['dʌm,kɑpt]; **MO**11, ['dʌm,kɒf]; **PA**199, ['dum,kɔf]; **OH**33, ['dʌm,kɑf]; **PA**151, ['dum,kɑp]; (Qu. X28, *Joking words . . for a person's head*) Inf **MI**75, ['dum,kʊf]; (Qu. HH16, *Uncomplimentary words with no definite meaning— . . to show that you don't think much of a person: "Don't invite him. He's a ________."*) Inf **NY**111, Dummkopf. **1988** *DARE* File **csWI** (as of c1950), *Dummkopf* was pronounced ['dʊm,kɔpf] by folks who knew no German themselves.

dummy n

1 also *dummy line:* A branch railway; a small train. **esp Sth** [*dummy* an early, relatively quiet locomotive; *DA* 1864 →; cf *EDD dummy* "A nickname for a tram, a colliery carriage"]

1894 Frederic *Marsena* 14 **nNY,** He . . excelled in convincing people that the portraits of themselves, which Marsena had sent down to him in the dummy to be dried and varnished, and which they hated . . were really . . works of art. **1905** *DN* 3.78 **nwAR,** *Dummy.* . . Short branch railway. 'To get to Searcy, go to Higginson and take the dummy.' Rare. **1908** *DN* 3.308 **eAL, wGA,** *Dummy.* . . A small-sized locomotive engine; also the train pulled by such an engine. "Are you going to Opelika on the dummy?" **1912** in 1983 Truman *Dear Bess* 98 **MO,** The dummy . . that brought me here was exactly on the tick [=on time] but it ran so fast I didn't get much sleep. **1937** in 1977 *Amer. Slave Suppl. 1* 1.127 **AL,** I does 'member de mule cars in Mobile, and how we had tuh pay 10 cents to go on de ox car out tuh de dummy line what run out to de Hill, an' den pay twenty-five cents when us got on de dummy. **1966–68** *DARE* (Qu. N37, *Joking names for a branch railroad that is not very important or gives poor service*) Infs **DE**4, **LA**26, 29, Dummy; **FL**29, **LA**29, Dummy line. **1968** *DARE* FW Addit **LA**40, *Dummies*—small trains through the logging country. Used to haul timber only. **1969** *AmSp* 44.256 [Railroading jargon], *Dummy*—Suburban train with conventional equipment.

2 also *dummy policeman:* See quot 1974.

1968 *DARE* (Qu. N20, *What do you call a circular arrangement on one level at a big intersection, where cars can go around till they come to the road they want?*) Inf **PA**163, A dummy. **1974** *DARE* File **MA,** Dummy. . . A small white concrete post or figure at the center of a rotary, sometimes with a sign for a head or a yellow light in its middle with or without a grassy pedestal. **1988** *Ibid* **csMA** (as of 1953), In Wilbraham it [=the post in a rotary] was locally called a dummy policeman.

3 also sp *dumbie:* See quots.

1966 *DARE* Tape **ME**22, [FW:] Any names for a lobster that's got only one claw . . ? [Inf:] Well, we call. . . one with no claws we call pistol. . . call 'em dummies too. Yeah, dummies. **1975** Gould *ME Lingo* 83, *Dumbie*—A lobster that has lost one or both claws, but the word isn't heard so much as *pistol.*

dummy duck See **dumb bird**

dummy game n

A tie game in tick-tack-toe.

1968 *DARE* (Qu. EE38b, *If the game of tick-tack-toe . . comes out so that neither X nor O wins, you call that ________*) Inf **MN**28, Dummy game; [**OH**44, Dummy won].

dummy line See **dummy 1**

dummy policeman See **dummy 2**

dummy school n Also *dumb school*

A children's game; see quot 1960.

1960 Korson *Black Rock* 331 **PA,** *Dummy school.* . . This game is usually played on steps. One girl has a small object . . which is hidden in one hand. She holds out both hands, and one girl after another is asked to guess which hand it is in. If you guess right, you are promoted and go up a step. Every time you guess right, you take one more step. The first girl to get to the top step wins the game. **1970** *DARE* (Qu. EE33, . . *Outdoor games . . that children play now, or that were played in your childhood*) Inf **PA**247, Dumb school.

dummy weed n

=**coltsfoot 1.**

1900 Lyons *Plant Names* 381, *T[ussilago] Farfara.* . . Dummy-weed. **1930** Sievers *Amer. Med. Plants* 24, *Coltsfoot. . . Other common names.* . . Dummyweed.

dump n[1] Also *dump up*

In marble play: a mound of earth on which a marble is placed; hence v *dump up* to put a marble on such a mound.

1958 *PADS* 29.33 **MO,** *Dump up.* . . To put a marble on a mound of earth. . . The mound itself, usually placed inside a *pink* [=a small circular ring used in the game of *pinks*]. *Ibid, Dump.* . . The same as *dump up, n.*

‡dump n[2]

One's head.

1968 *DARE* (Qu. X28, *Joking words . . for a person's head*) Inf **VA**24, Dump.

dump around v phr Cf **dumpy**

To feel unwell, to be "under the weather."

1970 *DARE* (Qu. BB41, *Not seriously ill, but sick enough to be in bed: "He's been ________ for a week."*) Inf **NY**232, Dumping around [laughter].

dump box n

1969 *DARE* (Qu. L57, *A low wooden platform used for bringing stones or heavy things out of the fields*) Inf **NY**164, Dump box—used to have them.

dump cake n Cf **dump salad**

See quots.

1965 *DARE* File **seME** (as of 1957), Dump cake—the recipe [in a local cookbook] began 'Dump . . ' all the ingredients into a bowl. **1980** *DARE* File **csWI** (as of late 1930s), I can't say that dump cake was ever popular but people sometimes made it. This was before we had cake mixes—and it was very easy. You put the dry ingredients in a cake pan, then added the liquid ingredients and stirred it all up and baked it. Result: a chocolate dump cake. **1984** *Ibid* **csMN,** [Radio:] Dump cake. . . Take one can pineapple, sliced; take one box cake mix; take one large bag miniature marshmallows. [Mix ingredients and bake.] **1984** *Capital Times* (Madison WI) 28 Mar 19/4 **csWI,** *Dump Cake.* . . Dump in undrained pineapple, filling corners. Dump in cherry pie filling. . . Sprinkle dry cake mix over fruit. . . Melt butter and dribble over top. . . Bake.

dumperling See **dumpling**

dumpey, dumpid See **dumpy**

dumping it off vbl n

Snoring.

1968 *DARE* (Qu. X45, . . *Joking expressions [for] . . snoring*) Inf **MD**6, Sawing wood, dumping it off.

dumping rake See **dump rake**

dumpish adj [*OED* 1545 →; *"Obs."*] Cf **dumpy**

Sluggish, without energy; inactive.

1903 *DN* 2.297 **Cape Cod MA** (as of a1857), *Dumpish.* . . Lifeless, of a cat that sleeps under the stove; she is said to be dumpish or to have the dumps. **1969** *DARE* (Qu. KK30, *Feeling slowed up or without energy: "I certainly feel ________."*) Inf **MA**41, Dumpish.

dumpling n Also *dumperling*

A Form.

1887 (1967) Harris *Free Joe* 128 **GA,** For a mess er turnip-greens an' dumperlin's that man 'u'd do murder. **1971** Dwyer *Dict. for Yankees* 25

Sth, S Midl, *Dumperling*. . . "I love chicken and dumperlings."

B Sense.

See quot.

1954 *Harder Coll.* **cwTN,** *Cow dumpling*—a dropping of cow manure. *Ibid, Horse dumpling*—A piece of horse manure.

dumpling cactus n [From the shape]

=peyote.

1976 Bailey-Bailey *Hortus Third* 686, *[Lophophora] Williamsii*. . . Peyote, dumpling cactus.

dumpling duck n [Perh from its plumpness]

=ruddy duck.

1888 Trumbull *Names of Birds* 113, *Ruddy Duck [Erismatura rubida]*. . . on the Savannah River (above Savannah), *Dumpling-Duck.* **1889** *Century Dict.* 1789 **GA,** *Dumpling-duck.* Same as *daub-duck* [=the ruddy duck]. **1917** (1923) *Birds Amer.* 1.152, *Ruddy Duck—Erismatura jamaicensis* . . Other Names.—Dumpling Duck . . Stiff-tailed Widgeon. **1944** Hausman *Amer. Birds* 511, Dumpling Duck—see Ruddy Duck. **1982** Elman *Hunter's Field Guide* 192, *Ruddy Duck:* (*Oxyura jamaicensis,* also classified as *Erismatura jamaicensis rubida*) Common & Regional Names: booby, . . dumpling duck, . . sinker.

dumpling mover n [Prob **dumpling B**] Cf *DS* B24, 25

1962 Atwood *Vocab. TX* 38, For an unusually heavy rain that does not last very long, . . [many other terms] occur only once each, but may not necessarily be original: . . *Duck drencher, dumplin mover.*

dump rake n Also *dumping rake* Cf **dump reaper**

A horse- or tractor-drawn hay rake with a mechanism for dumping the hay; hence v phr *dump rake* to rake (hay) with such a rake.

1950 *WELS (What do you do to hay in the field after it has been cut?)* 1 Inf, **cWI,** Dump rake it into windrows. **1966–70** *DARE* (Qu. L16, *Machines used around here in handling hay*) Infs **CA**208, **IN**59, **KY**75, **MI**83, 97, **MN**23, **MO**21, **NJ**16, **WI**17, Dump rake; **OK**52, Dumping rake. **1967** *DARE* Tape **MN**4, We cut our hay in the meadows, . . pull it out by hand and then stack it. . . A lot of that stuff we carried in, . . or we'd rake, pull it in with the old dump rakes. Lot of people used a single horse on the rakes but we pretty near always used a team. **1982** *Barrick Coll.* **csPA,** *Dump rake*—horse-drawn implement used in making hay.

dump reaper n

1968–69 *DARE* (Qu. L28, *Tools used in the past for cutting grain*) Inf **PA**120, Dump reaper—for buckwheat; **PA**201, Dump reaper.

dump road n

1923 *DN* 5.234 **swWI,** *Dump-road*. . . A road built by hauling in and dumping loose dirt.

dump salad n Cf **dump cake**

See quot.

1988 Tyler *Breathing Lessons* 84 **sePA,** "The dump salad is mine," Serena's neighbor said. . . "Dump salad?" "You take a packet of orange Jell-O powder, a can of crushed pineapple, a carton of Cool Whip. . ." Some woman . . said hello and the neighbor turned to greet her.

‡dump scoop n

1969 *DARE* (Qu. L41, *A device for moving dirt and other loads, with one wheel in front and handles to lift and push it behind*) Inf **NY**200, Dump scoop.

dumpsey See **dumpy**

dump up n, v See **dump n**[1]

dumpy adj Also *dumpsey, dumpid* Also sp *dumpey* [*OED* a1618 →] Cf **dump around, dumpish**

Unwell, "under the weather"; depressed, gloomy, sullen.

1862 *NY Daily Tribune* (NY) 12 Mar 4/6, We find that an English journal—the sweet, courteous, amiable, and good-natured *Saturday Review*—has dumpy misgivings upon the same point. **1908** *DN* 3.308 **eAL, wGA,** *Dumpy*. . . Grumpy, sullen. Common. **1916** *DN* 4.274 **seNE,** *Dumpsey*. . . Ailing somewhat. "That chicken is dumpsey." . . [*DN* Ed: In Kan., *dumpey, dumpid.*] **1938** Hertzler *Horse & Buggy Dr.* 3 **KS** (as of early 20th cent), The child is dumpy, listless and feverish. **1965–70** *DARE* (Qu. KK30, *Feeling slowed up or without energy: "I certainly feel ______."*) Infs **CA**61, **IA**36, **IL**11, **NC**40, **SD**5, **TN**46, **TX**10, **WI**77, **WV**3, Dumpy; (Qu. BB5, *A general feeling of discomfort or illness that isn't any one place in particular*) Infs **PA**237, **MN**37, Dumpy (feeling); (Qu. BB16b, *If something a person ate didn't agree with him, he might just feel a bit ______*) Inf **MI**78, Dumpy; (Qu. BB39, *On a day when you don't feel just right, though not actually sick, you might say, "I'll be all right tomorrow—I'm just feeling ______ today."*) Infs **CA**137, **IL**43, **MI**78, **MN**37, **OH**25, **WI**30, 64, (Kind of) dumpy; (Qu. GG34b, *To feel depressed or in a gloomy mood: "She's feeling ______ today."*) Inf **IN**10, Dumpy.

dumsquizzled adj

See quots.

1909 *DN* 3.420 **Cape Cod MA** (as of a1857), *Dum squizzled*. . . A mild oath to express surprise. "Well, I'll be dum squizzled." **1912** *DN* 3.575 **wIN,** *Dum-squizzled*. . . 1. Exhausted. 2. Puzzled.

dun v, hence ppl adj *dunned,* vbl n *dunning* [See quot 1889] **NEng** *arch* Cf **dunfish**

To cure (codfish).

1818 *Thomas' MA Spy or Worcester Gaz.* (MA) 23 Dec [4]/5, *Dun Fish.*—When cod-fish is dunned, it ought not to be boiled at all. **1828** Webster *Amer. Dict., Dunning*. . . The operation of curing codfish, in such a manner as to give it a particular color and quality. Fish for dunning are caught early in spring. . . split and slack-salted; then laid in a pile for two or three months, in a dark store, covered . . with salt-hay or eel-grass, and pressed. . . opened and piled again . . till July or August, when they are fit for use. **1873** Thaxter *Among Isles Shoals* 83 **seNH,** The process of dunning, which made the Shoals fish so famous a century ago, is almost a lost art, though the chief fisherman at Star still "duns" a few yearly. **1889** *Century Dict.* 1797 **NEng,** *Dun*. . . To cure, as cod, in such a manner as to impart a dun or brown color.

dun n

The subimago of a **mayfly** (Ephemeroptera).

1964 Wigglesworth *Insects* 306, May-flies. . . The insect that emerges from the full grown nymph has perfect wings, but these have a dull appearance and the power of flight is weak; it is called by anglers a 'dun' and by entomologists a 'subimago.' **1980** Milne-Milne *Audubon Field Guide Insects* 355, *Mayflies (Order Ephemeroptera)*. . . The last aquatic stage leaves the water, molts, and gains smoky wings. Called . . dun by fisherman [sic], it soon sheds another skin to become a clear-winged adult. **1982** Sternberg *Fishing* 83, *Mayfly Life Cycle*. . . A newly-emerged *subimago* or *dun* hardens its wings, then flies off to nearby vegatation. . . After a day or two, the dun molts into a mature insect. *Ibid* 84, Mayfly duns are winged, but still sexually immature. Most are dull-colored and have gray wings, though some species have mottled wings.

dunbird n Cf **dumb bird**

=ruddy duck.

1834 Nuttall *Manual Ornith.* 2.427, They [=ruddy ducks] are common in the market of Boston, generally known by the name of Dun-Birds, and their flesh is good and much esteemed as game. **1888** Trumbull *Names of Birds* 112, *Ruddy Duck [Erismatura jamaicensis]* . . Dun-Bird. **1917** (1923) *Birds Amer.* 1.152, *Ruddy Duck—Erismatura jamaicensis* . . Other Names.—Dumpling Duck . . Dun-bird . . Stiff-tailed Widgeon. **1944** Hausman *Amer. Birds* 512, Dun-bird—see Ruddy Duck.

Duncard See **Dunkard**

dunce cap n

Either of two related **mushrooms** with tall, conical caps: *Conocybe lactea* or *C. tenera.*

1981 Lincoff *Audubon Field Guide Mushrooms* 560, *White Dunce Cap. Conocybe lactea*. . . In lawn and grassy areas. *Ibid* 561, *Brown Dunce Cap. Conocybe tenera*. . . In lawns, grassy areas, and in rich soil.

dun codfish See **dunfish**

duncy adj

Stupid.

1907 *German Amer. Annals* 9.374 **sePA,** *Duncy*. . . Rather stupid. "He's a duncy fellow." **1916** *DN* 4.337 **NE,** *Duncy*. . . Stupid. "He can't ever learn anything, he's so duncy." **1937** (1963) Hyatt *Kiverlid* 84 **KY,** Naw, Shad, you'r duncy. **1968** *DARE* (Qu. HH13, *Expressions meaning that a person is not very alert or not aware of things "He's certainly ______."*) Inf **VA**25, Duncy.

dunde(r)funk See **dandyfunk**

dun diver n

1 **=ruddy duck.** Cf **dunbird**

1844 DeKay *Zool. NY* 2.327, *The Ruddy Duck [Erismatura jamaicensis]*. . . The *Dun-bird, Looby* or *Dun Diver,* is rather rare on the coast of this State. **1888** Trumbull *Names of Birds* 112, *Ruddy Duck [Erismatura jamaicensis]* . . Dun-Diver. **1917** (1923) *Birds Amer.* 1.152, *Ruddy Duck—Erismatura jamaicensis. . .* Other Names. . . Dun Diver. **1944** Hausman *Amer. Birds* 511, Dun Diver—see Ruddy Duck.

2 The common **merganser** *(Mergus americanus),* esp the female.

1844 DeKay *Zool. NY* 2.318, This large species [=*Mergus merganser*] is known on our coast under the names of *Sheldrake, Sawbill,* and *Dun Diver.* **1889** *Century Dict.* 1798, *Dun-diver. . .* The female merganser or goosander, *Mergus merganser:* so called from the dun or brown head. **1917** (1923) *Birds Amer.* 1.110, *Merganser—Mergus americanus. . .* Other Names.—American Goosander . . Dun Diver. **1923** U.S. Dept. Ag. *Misc. Circular* 13.5, American Merganser *(Mergus merganser . .) . . In local use. . .* Dun-diver (Long Id., N.Y.)

dundyfunk See **dandyfunk** n

dune broom n

A low, broomlike, much-branched shrub *(Parryella filifolia).*

1960 Vines *Trees SW* 564, *Dune Broom. . .* Sandy rolling hillsides at altitudes of 4,400–6,000 ft in New Mexico and northern Arizona.

dune grass n

A grass such as a **wild rye.**

1950 Hitchcock-Chase *Manual Grasses* 251, *Elymus mollis* . . American Dunegrass. **1968** *Cape May Co. Gaz.* (Cape May Court House NJ) 11 July Sec D 1/1, Among the many [participants in a costume parade] noted along the line of march were "Miss Mosquito," surrounded by dune grass.

dune willow n [See quots]

Any of three **willows:** Piper willow *(Salix piperi),* **heartleaf willow,** or blueleaf willow *(Salix glaucophylloides).*

1923 in 1925 Jepson *Manual Plants CA* 266, *S[alix] piperi. . . Dune Willow. . .* Sand dunes along the north coast. **1938** Van Dersal *Native Woody Plants* 361, Willow, Dune *(Salix piperi).* **1942** Tehon *Fieldbook IL Shrubs* 46, *Salix adenophylla. . . Dune Willow. . .* is a shrub of northern sandy regions. . . It was at one time an abundant shrub on the sandy shores of Lake Michigan north of Chicago. **1952** Gleason *New Britton & Brown* 2.12, *Salix glaucophylloides. . .* Dune Willow. . . Sandy shores, calcareous slopes, and sometimes swamps. **1959** Munz-Keck *CA Flora* 916, *S[alix] Piperi. . . Dune W[illow]. . .* Wet sandy places at mouth [sic] of streams, below 500 ft.

dunfish n Also *dun codfish* [**dun** v + *fish*] **NEng** *arch* Cf **dumbfish**

A salted and dried codfish.

1818 *Thomas' MA Spy or Worcester Gaz.* (MA) 23 Dec 4/5, *Dun Fish. . .* the dun or dried cod-fish ought not to be boiled. **1844** *Knickerbocker* 24.471, We unanimously agreed that there was nothing so delicious as the dun-codfish. **1873** Thaxter *Among Isles Shoals* 83 **seNH,** A real dunfish is handsome, cut in transparent strips, the color of brown sherry wine. **1889** *Century Dict.* 1798 **NEng,** *Dunfish. . .* Codfish cured by dunning. **a1909** (1937) King *When I Lived* 98 **neMA** (as of 19th cent), It must be a *dun* fish (whatever that may be) and the proper way to prepare it was to boil it encased in a cloth between two thin fishes.

dung adj, also used absol [Folk-etym for *dun*]

Of a horse: having a dun color.

1950 *WELS (Horse of a dirty white color)* 2 Infs, **ceWI,** Dung color. **1965–70** *DARE* (Qu. K38) Infs **AR**40, **FL**21, **PA**187, Dung; **VA**95, Dung horse; **NE**3, Dung colored; **ID**3, Muckledy-dung.

dungarees n pl **esp Atlantic** See Map

Blue jeans, overalls.

1945 Colcord *Sea Language* 70 **ME, Cape Cod, Long Island,** *Dungarees.* Working-clothes of blue jean. **1950** *WELS (A heavy outer work garment, usually blue, worn mostly by farmers)* 6 Infs, **WI,** Dungarees. **1965–70** *DARE* (Qu. W10, *Work trousers made of rough cloth, usually blue*) 239 Infs, **esp Atlantic,** Dungarees; **IN**13, Dungaree; **NY**65, Dungareens [FW: Inf not sure if she really says it with the "n"]; (Qu. W9, *A work garment, usually of blue cloth, covering the legs and sometimes the chest, worn by farmers*) Infs **MA**33, **MI**123, **NC**61, 79, **VT**16, Dungarees; **NC**79, Strap dungarees; **MI**81, Dungaree [FW: Inf used pl at Qu. W10].

dungavenhooter n Cf *DS* CC17

An imaginary animal.

1939 Tryon *Fearsome Critters* 17, Shaped a good deal like an alligator, but . . has no mouth. . . Concealing itself . . behind a whiffle bush, the

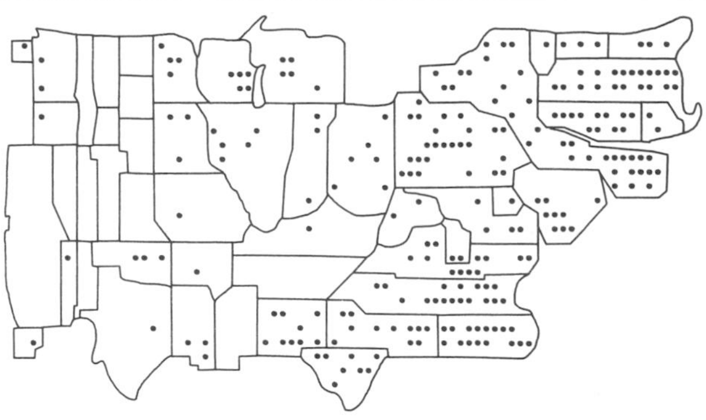

•dungarees + varr (Qq. W10, W9)

Dungavenhooter awaits the passing logger. On coming within reach of the dreadful tail, the victim is knocked senseless and then pounded steadily until he becomes entirely gaseous, whereat he is greedily inhaled through the wide nostrils.

dung beetle n

Std: any of var beetles of the families Geotrupidae and Scarabaeidae. Also called **cow-chip beetle, doodlebug 4**

dunger n [Perh var of *dunghill*]

1946 *PADS* 6.12 **swVA, eNC,** *Dunger* ['dʌŋgɚ -ə]. . . A cultivated area that was formerly the site of a dwelling, sometimes abounding in kitchen middens. Probably the same word as *dunghill. . .* Older persons.

dunghill n Also *dungil*

An animal, esp a chicken, that is not purebred.

1846 (1847) Porter *Quarter Race* 121 **OH,** Anybody that has seen a "quarter-horse" run by a "dunghill" *knows* how this was. **1874** VT State Bd. Ag. *Rept. for 1873–74* 2.398, This horse makes no claim to blood, but calls himself a cold-blooded sprout, or a dung hill. **1899** (1912) Green *VA Folk-Speech* 160, *Dungil. . .* Dunghill. **1939** FWP *Guide FL* 456 **ceFL,** Any mongrel [gamecock] is a 'dunghill.' **1949** *McDavid Coll.* **swNY,** Dunghills: scrub chickens.

dung hister n [*histe* var of *hoist* to lift] Cf *DS* HH1

1969 Sorden *Lumberjack Lingo* 38 **NEng, Gt Lakes,** *Dunghister*—A farmer. To call a lumberjack a farmer was an insult and meant a fight.

dung house n

1967–68 *DARE* (Qu. M21b, *Joking names for an outside toilet building*) Infs **AR**55, **MA**9, Dung house.

dung-hunter n

=**great black-backed gull.**

1945 McAtee *Nomina Abitera* 38, Great Black-Backed Gull *(Larus marinus)*—Dung-hunter, from its jaeger-like aggressions.

dungil See **dunghill**

dung out v phr

To remove dung from (a barn); also fig.

1929 *AmSp* 5.17 **Ozarks,** *Dung out. . .* To clean, to carry out rubbish. Used originally of barns or stables where the matter removed actually was dung, but now often used facetiously, as in the sentence: "I tol' th' ol' woman t' dung out th' shanty afore company run in onto us agin." **1933** Williamson *Woods Colt* 75 **Ozarks,** Fellers like that cain't never learn nothin'; there's no use for 'em to try; they ort to be turned out to graze, an' the barn dunged out. **1958** McCulloch *Woods Words* 55 **Pacific NW,** *Dung out*—To clean out a bunkhouse or other camp building or to dispose of trash. This is a hangover from the old days when stables were part of every logging camp. **1966–69** *DARE* (Qu. E21, *Talking about a room that needs to be put in order, you might say, "I'm just going to _____ this room."*) Inf **WA**31, Dung out; (Qu. KK49, *When you don't have the time or ambition to do something thoroughly: "I'm not going to give the place a real cleaning, I'll just _____."*) Inf **CA**145, Dung 'er out.

dunk n [Var of *dung*]

1969–70 *DARE* (Qu. L17, *Other names . . for manure used in the fields*) Infs **CT**32, **MS**81, Dunk, dung.

dunkadoo n [See quot 1814]

A **bittern** (here: *Botaurus lentiginosus*).

1814 Wilson *Amer. Ornith.* 8.35, [The] American Bittern, *Ardea Minor. . .* On the sea coast of New Jersey it is known by the name of *Dunkadoo,* a word probably imitative of its common note. **1889** *Century Dict.*1799, *Dunkadoo. . .* The American bittern, *Botaurus mugitans* or *lentiginosus.* [Local, New Eng.] **1932** Bennitt *Check-list* 15 **MO,** *American bittern. Botaurus lentiginosus . .* Stake-driver . . dunk-a-doo. **1946** Hausman *Eastern Birds* 110, American Bittern *Botaurus lentiginosus. . .* Other Names . . Dunkadoo, Brown Bittern. **1955** Forbush-May *Birds* 38, American Bittern—*Botaurus lentiginosus. . . Other names:* Stake-driver; . . Dunk-a-doo; . . Sun-gazer.

Dunkard n Also sp *Duncard* [Varr of **Dunker**] **chiefly N Midl** See Map

=Dunker.

1750 (1888) Walker *Jrl.* 40 **VA,** The Duncards are an odd set of people, who make it a matter of Religion not to Shave their Beards. **1831** Peck *Guide for Emigrants* 260 **seIL,** The *Dunkards. . .* are known by their long beards, by trine immersion, inoffensive manners, and refusal to bear arms. **1859** Taliaferro *Fisher's R.* 111 **nwNC** (as of 1857), As to a full-grown beard, except among the "Dunkards," it was "onhearn on." **1903** Waltz *Pa Gladden* 268, Melonie Hathaway chose to wear the white serge gown and dove-gray Dunkard bonnet in which her beauty was subdued to a positive loveliness. **1907** Twain *Chr. Sci.* 194, It is hair-splitting differences of opinion over disputed text-meanings that have divided into many sects a once united Church. . . Dunkards (4 bodies). **1954** *AmSp* 29.48 **ePA,** *Dunkard* is apparently a corruption of *Dunker.* Among the Pennsylvania Germans *Dunkard* is rather generally regarded as the 'English' equivalent of the dialect word. . . This term of derision was applied to the German Baptists, especially in the early history of this denomination in America, because of their practice of trine immersion. **1965–70** *DARE* (Qu. CC2, . . *Predominant religious denominations around here*) Infs **OH**72, **PA**1, 4, Dunkards; **IN**54, Dunkards—called that because of their practice of dunking three times in baptism; called Brethren now; **MD**30, Church of the Brethren or Dunkard; (Qu. CC3, . . *Religions . . a bit different from the common ones*) Infs **ID**5, **PA**63, 150, Dunkards; **VA**26, Dunkards ['dʌŋˌkɚts]; **IA**3, Brethren or Dunkard (Amish or Mennonite)—because of total immersion baptism; **MD**20, Dunkards—men wear beards; hold church service Sunday; attend Brethren Church; (Qu. CC4, . . *Nicknames . . for . . religious groups*) Infs **IN**22, **MD**18, **PA**243, Dunkards; **VA**27, Dunkards ['dʌŋˌkɚts]; **DE**3, Dunkards—for Amish; **DE**5, Dunkards—for Mennonites; **OH**93, Dunkards—a respectable nickname for Church of the Brethren; **PA**1, Plain folk (Amish, Mennonites, Dunkards, etc); **IA**3, Hook-and-eyers—for Old Order Amish and Dunkards—because they never use buttons. [19 of 20 Infs old] **1969–70** *DARE* Tape **CA**53, They'll see once in a while a stray Dunkard, you know, who was just kind of a holdover from the small line that used to be here; **OH**91, Our denomination is the Old German Baptist. . . We used to be called the Dunkard, but we aren't no more. I mean some people still call us the Dunkard.

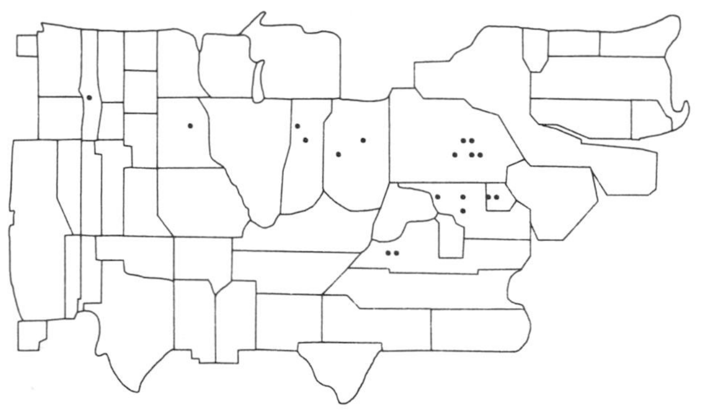

•Dunkard (Qq. CC2, CC3, CC4)

dunkel dun adj [Prob Ger *dunkel* dark, dim, murky] Cf **muckle dun**

1916 *DN* 4.274 **NE,** *Dunkel-dun. . .* An indefinite gray-brown: usually in disparagement. "The paper on the wall was an ugly dunkel-dun color." One contributor.

Dunker n Also *Dunker-Baptist, Tunker* [PaGer *dunke,* Ger *dunken, tunken* to dip] **chiefly N Midl, esp PA** Cf **brethren B**

A member of a religious group, esp one of the German-American denominations, that practices baptism by total immersion.

1744 in 1826 MA Hist. Soc. *Coll.* 2d ser 7.181, The Governor, the honourable the commissioners, and several other gentlemen, went to the Dunkers' nunnery. **1789** Morse *Amer. Geog.* 324 **PA,** They appear to be humble, well-meaning Christians, and have acquired the character of the *Harmless* Tunkers. **1826** Flint *Recollections* 40 **swOH,** The Tunkers, with their long and flowing beards, have brought up their teams with their fat mutton and fine flour. **1877** in 1917 Twain *Letters* 1.308 **cNY,** Aunty Cord is a violent Methodist and Lewis an implacable Dunker-Baptist. **1882** (1971) Gibbons *PA Dutch* 134, The Dunkers do not like to be called by this name; their chosen title is Brethren. **1940** *Sat. Eve. Post* 30 Mar 37/4 **PA,** 'Dunking' springs from the same German word ordinarily used to denote baptism by total immersion. Believers in this form of baptism split off from the main body of Mennonites and they have not held so strictly to ancient customs. . . What sticks is their nickname, the Tunkers, or Dunkards. **1945** *AmSp* 20.86 **ePA,** The former [=Amish dialect] is employed for all normal everyday conversation . . with other Amish and Plain sectarians (Mennonites, Dunkers, etc.) **1967–70** *DARE* (Qu. CC4, . . *Nicknames . . for . . religious groups*) Infs **ID**5, **IN**69, Dunkers; **IA**3, **MD**15, **MN**38, Dunkers—Baptist; **PA**243, Church of the Brethren: Dunkers, Dunkards; **VA**11, Dunkers—same as drunkers (near Pulaski).

dunking Baptist n

=deep-water Baptist.

1967 *DARE* (Qu. CC4, . . *Nicknames . . for various religions or religious groups*) Inf **OR**4, Dunking Baptists.

dunking stick n

1968–69 *DARE* (Qu. H27, . . *Joking names for doughnuts*) Inf **OH**88, Dunkin' stick; (Qu. H30, *An oblong cake, cooked in deep fat*) Inf **GA**81, Dunkin' stick—have seen this name in a doughnut shop; **OH**46, Dunking stick.

dunlin n Also *dunlick*

=red-backed sandpiper.

1834 Nuttall *Manual Ornith.* 2.106, The Dunlin, or Red-backed Sandpiper of the United States, according to the season of the year, is met with throughout the northern hemisphere. **1874** Coues *Birds NW* 489, *Tringa Alpina var. Americana . .* American Dunlin. . . The Dunlin has only been observed by Mr. Allen . . in the Missouri region, he finding it near Leavenworth. **1881** *Forest & Stream* 17.227/1 **NEng,** The red-backed sandpiper, . . better known here as "Dunlin," is a regular visitant, though not in large numbers. **1956** MA Audubon Soc. *Bulletin* 40.19, *Red-backed Sandpiper. . .* Dunlick (Mass. A variant of the next name.); Dunlin (Maine, Mass.) **1964** Phillips *Birds AZ* 35, The Dunlin is a middle-sized "peep" with a long and somewhat decurved bill.

dunned, dunning See **dun** v

dunt adj Also *dunty* [Engl dial] *relic*

1952 Brown *NC Folkl.* 1.535, *Dunty, dunt. . .* Stupid.

dupa n Also *dapa(s)* [Prob Pol *dupa* arse, but cf Ukrainian *dupa,* Serbo-Croatian *dupe*] Cf **bumba, doody** n[1]

The buttocks; also used as an affectionate term for a person.

1968–70 *DARE* (Qu. X35, . . *The part of the body that you sit on—for example, "He slipped and came down hard on his ______."*) Inf **MI**123, Dupa [dupə]—used by a few local persons; **PA**76, Dupa [dupə]; **PA**234, Dupa [dupa]. **1986–89** *DARE* File **neIL,** My father, whose parents were Czech, and my father-in-law, whose parents were Slovak, both use the term *dupa* ['dupə] to playfully refer to the buttocks, as in "Careful! You don't want to fall on your dupa!" Both grew up mostly in or near Chicago. My father-in-law says *dupa* is Polish. *Ibid* **ceWI,** My father, who grew up in Wisconsin with Polish as his first language, frequently used *dupa* in English contexts. As an excuse not to go in swimming with us he'd say "I don't want to get my dupa wet." *Ibid* **wMA,** *Dupa* is well known and widely used as a nursery term and a jocular vulgarism in the Connecticut Valley, especially among Polish people. A student says his mother has a bumper sticker that says "You Betcha Dupa I'm Polish." *Ibid* **Milwaukee WI,** The most common Polish word you'll hear in Milwaukee is "dupa" ['dupə]. It means something like "you little ass," but it's always meant affectionately. *Everyone,* everyone, in Milwaukee says this, everyone on the south side [=primarily working class] anyway. You hear "you dupa" [Inf laughs] every day. I say it all the time, especially to my sister's kids. Sometimes I say "dupa," sometimes "dapa" ['dɑpə]; people say both without noticing the difference. *Ibid* **ceWI,** Do you know "dapas" ['dʌpəs]? It means "little ass"—but it's not a bad thing to say. Someone who cares for you, your father for instance, who is pretending to be angry, might say "you little dapas."

duppy n [Bube (a Bantu language of West Afr) *dupe* ghost; *OED* 1774 →] Cf *DJE, DBE*

A ghost or familiar spirit.

1919 *Jrl. Amer. Folkl.* 32.398 **AL** [Black], From this list one conspicuous type of Negro tale has been omitted,—the ghost-story, the tale based on a belief about "hants" or "bugies" or "duppies." **1947** Ballowe *The Lawd* 6 **LA** [Black], "You saw the Duppy?" "Nossuh, Ah warn't bawn with no double caul, an' 'sides, when you looks at a Duppy, hit fades; but Ah seed his claws, whut de Obeah Man had tempered and sharpened." *Ibid* 84, Mathan asked him with great respect what a Duppy really was. "Depends upon where you find them. Some serve a master, some are mongrel trash, and some are on their own, free-lance hell-raisers."

dur See **deer**

Durand oak n

Std: a moderately sized oak *(Quercus durandii)* of the south-central US. Also called **basket oak 2, bastard oak 1, pin oak, scrub oak, shin oak, southern oak, white oak**

durango root n [From *Durango,* Mexico]

A plant *(Datisca glomerata)* native to southern California.

1911 Jepson *Flora CA* 269, *D[atisca] glomerata. . . Durango Root.* . . Dry stream beds of the Coast Ranges and Sierra Nevada to Southern California. **1923** Davidson–Moxley *Flora S. CA* 241, Durango Root. Common along mountain streams. **1964** Kingsbury *Poisonous Plants U.S.* 388, Two acres along a wet creek bottom had been fenced in. . . Much of the . . area was covered with durango root.

durfee grass n Also *durfa grass* [Etym unknown]

=quack grass.

c1873 in 1976 Miller *Shaker Herbs* 167, Durfa Grass. Useful in conditions in which it is desirable to promote or increase the flow of urine. **1895** U.S. Dept. Ag. *Farmers' Bulletin* 28.24, Durfee grass. Agropyron repens. **1898** *Jrl. Amer. Folkl.* 11.282, *Agropyrum* [sic] *repens* . . durfee grass. **1910** Graves *Flowering Plants* 79 **CT,** Durfee . . Grass. Common. Fields, cultivated ground and waste places. **1930** Sievers *Amer. Med. Plants* 49, *Quack Grass. . . Other common names. . .* Durfa grass, durfee grass.

durgen n [Cf *EDD durgin* "A big, ill-tempered person, a stupid fellow"; *EDD durgan* sb.[1] 1 "A short, undersized person or animal, a dwarf"]

1 An uncouth, clumsy person.

1926 *DN* 5.399 **Ozarks,** *Durgen. . .* An awkward, uncouth hillman, regarded as less polished and sophisticated than his neighbors. **1930** *VA Qrly. Rev.* 6.250 **S Midl,** Occasionally one runs upon . . such waning linguistic forms as durgen, a clumsy person. **1931** Randolph *Ozarks* 69, The danged ol' durgen—he should orter be bored fer th' simples!

2 See quot.

1894 *DN* 1.330 **NJ,** *Durgen:* old horse, worn out by use.

3 See quot.

1954 *Harder Coll.* **cwTN,** *Durgen. . .* A bull.

‡4 See quot.

1966 *DARE* (Qu. N41b, *Horse-drawn vehicles to carry heavy loads*) Inf **AL**2, Durgens—way back.

‡5 A childish fit of anger, a tantrum.

1979 *DARE* File **OR,** When a small child has a loud-screaming, foot-stomping, falling-down-kicking tantrum, it is referred to as "having a durgen". . . the g sound as in *give.*

durgen adj [**durgen n 1**]

Countrified, uncouth; awkward.

1936 *Jrl. Amer. Folkl.* 49.206 **Ozarks,** In recent years the younger hillfolk have come to regard the party-games as "durgen," a dialect word which means countrified or old-fashioned. **1936** *AmSp* 11.315 **Ozarks. 1953** Randolph–Wilson *Down in Holler* 242 **Ozarks,** Durgen ['dɝgen]. . . In McDonald County, Mo., I often heard it as an adjective; the social activities of a certain family were said to be "just plumb durgen."

durin' See **enduring** adj

during prep Pronc-spp *chiefly among Black speakers, doin, due in, dyoin', duenst*

Std sense, var forms.

1899 Chesnutt *Conjure Woman* 27 **csNC** [Black], He tuk good keer uv 'im dyoin' er de winter. **1927** Adams *Congaree* 22 **cSC** [Black], One er dem ole sister dead an' slipped into heaven duenst a big storm. **1937** (1977) Hurston *Their Eyes* 31 **FL** [Gullah], Ah was born back due in slavery. **1977** Smitherman *Talkin* 18, Doin the civil right crisis, we work hard.

durn v, intj Also sp *dern, dirn* [Varr of *darn*] **chiefly Sth, S Midl** See Map

Used as a euphem for *damn;* hence adj, adv *durn(ed).*

1830 *Western Mth. Rev.* 3.358 **Missip Valley,** He *derned,* and grunted, but could not move a muscle. **1835** Longstreet *GA Scenes* 18, Old Boler's . . broke a dish and two plates all to durn smashes! *Ibid* 66, I'd o' took it up myself, be durned if I wouldn't. **1853** Hammett *Stray Yankee in TX* 98 **TX,** These dern no-account pups arn't worth shucks. **1856** Derby *Phoenixiana* 49, Now, dern your skin, *can't* you be easy? **1856** Olmsted *Journey Slave States* 312, Seems to me them gol-durned lazy niggers aint a goin' to come over arter you now. **1873** Beadle *Undeveloped West* 369 **neOK,** Him and two other Cherokees . . scared some Eastern fellers dirned near to death. **1894** Twain *Pudd'nhead Wilson* 168, He wanted me to challenge that derned Italian savage. **1903** Freeman *Six Trees* 201 **seMA,** It's durned hard work, housecleanin'. **1932** (1974) Caldwell *Tobacco Road* 8 **GA,** I'm getting pretty durn tired of it by this time. **1940** Faulkner *Hamlet* 400 **MS,** Be durn if you dont look like you aint been to bed in a week. **1965–70** *DARE* (Qu. NN25b) 136 Infs, **chiefly Sth, S Midl,** Durned; **AL**33, **LA**17, **SC**44, (Gol) durn; **CA**97, Gol-durned; (Qu. NN25a) 92 Infs, **chiefly Sth, S Midl,** Durn; **IA**8, **NM**6, Gol-durn; **GA**54, Ding-durn; **NM**11, Durn my buttons; (Qu. NN8b) 48 Infs, **chiefly Sth, S Midl,** Durn; 9 Infs, **scattered,** Gol (*or* gosh, dod) durn; **GA**28, Durn the luck; **MO**15, Oh durn; (Qu. LL30) 34 Infs, **chiefly Sth, S Midl,** Durn near; (Qq. LL35–37) 22 Infs, **chiefly Sth, S Midl,** Durn(ed); **TX**39, God-durned; **TX**97, Gol-durn; (Qu. NN9b) 17 Infs, **chiefly Sth, S Midl,** Durn (him *or* it); **SC**2, 11, 65, Durn his hide (*or* soul); (Qu. NN9a) 15 Infs, **Sth, S Midl,** (Dad) durn (it); **KY**33, Oh durn; **SC**54, By durn; **LA**3, **VA**5, I('ll) be durned; (Qu. NN17) 18 Infs, **chiefly Sth, S Midl,** Durn(ed); (Qu. NN8a) 13 Infs, **Sth, S Midl,** (Gosh) durn (it); (Qu. JJ21) Infs **PA**215, **SC**11, Durn tootin'; **MI**75, **MO**16, **TN**65, **TX**43, (You're) durn right (I am); (Qu. NN1, 2) Infs **DE**1, **IL**97, **KY**10, **NY**42, **SC**11, 19, **TN**14, (Ya, yer, *or* you're) durn(ed) tootin'; **MD**32, **TX**35, (You're) durn right; (Qu. NN7) Infs **DE**1, **GA**83, **IL**126, **TX**39, 98, **UT**8, I'll be durned; **FL**4, **KY**6, **NC**33, **SC**65, Durned; (Qu. NN32) Infs **AL**3, **DE**1, **MD**42, **MS**1, **NC**37, (Swan and) be durned. [Further exx throughout *DS;* all exx are mapped.] **1967** *DARE* Tape **TX**1A, I had a wood stove 'n' you can make 'em pretty durn hot.

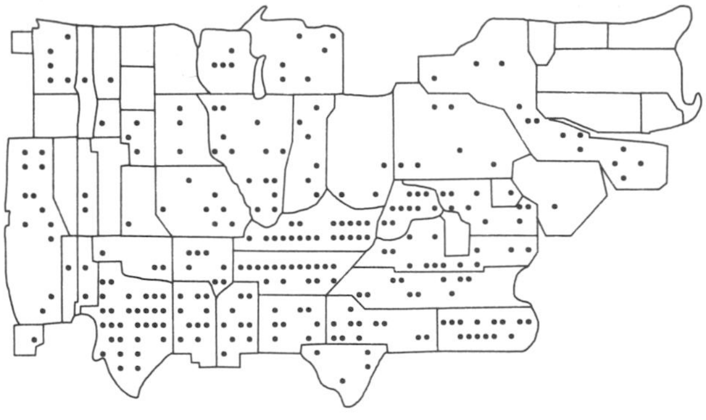

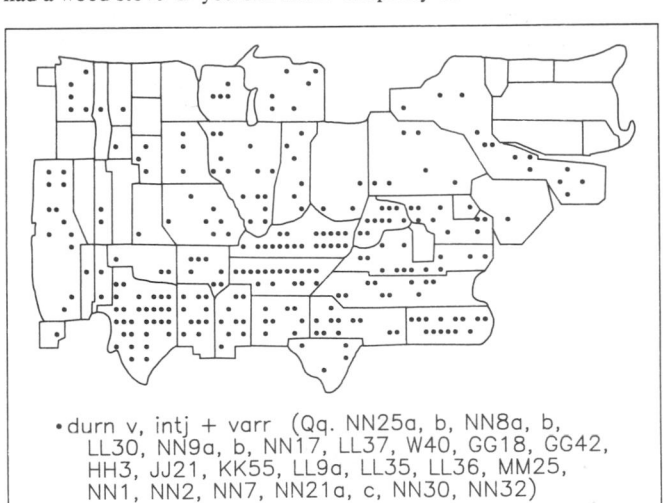

•durn v, intj + varr (Qq. NN25a, b, NN8a, b, LL30, NN9a, b, NN17, LL37, W40, GG18, GG42, HH3, JJ21, KK55, LL9a, LL35, LL36, MM25, NN1, NN2, NN7, NN21a, c, NN30, NN32)

durn n Also sp *dern*

Fig: something of very little value.

1853 *S. Lit. Messenger* 19.222/1 **KY,** Cave said he did not care a *dern* for the oysters. **1859** Taliaferro *Fisher's R.* 94 **cVA** (as of 1820s), He was raised in "Albermarle, Fudginny," and didn't care "a durn whether he b'longed to one of the fust famblys uv Fudginny ur not." **1875** (1876) Twain *Tom Sawyer* 65 **MO,** I wouldn't give a dern for spunk-water. **1946** McCullers *Member* 5 **AL,** I don't give a durn about it. **1967–70** *DARE* (Qu. GG21b, *If you don't care what a person does, you might say, "Go ahead—I don't give a ________.")* Infs **GA**28, **IL**78, 116, **KY**11,

SC44, 45, 58, TX95, Durn; (Qu. HH20c, *Of an idle, worthless person you might say, "He isn't worth ______.")* Inf **IL**78, A durn; (Qu. KK26) Inf **KY**16, I don't give a durn. **1969** *DARE* Tape **IL**78, You might not be worth a durn as a teacher.

durned See **durn** v, intj

durn sight See **sight**

durnt, durstn't See **dare** v **A4a**

duscle n

=deadly nightshade.

1900 Lyons *Plant Names* 349, *S[olanum] nigrum. . .* Duscle. **1911** *Century Dict. Suppl., Duscle. . .* [*Century* Ed: Appar. an artificial formation from *dusk.*] The black nightshade, *Solanum nigrum.* **1914** Georgia *Manual Weeds* 364, *Solanum nigrum. . . Names:* Deadly Nightshade, Duscle. **1940** Clute *Amer. Plant Names* 51.

dus' dark See **dusk dark**

duse See **do** v **A3**

dusk dark n Also *dust dark* Pronc-sp *dus' dark* [Cf *EDD dusk o' dark*] **chiefly Sth** See Map and Map Section Cf **dusky dark, dust** n², **dust dawn**

Dusk, twilight.

1933 Rawlings *South Moon* 208 **FL,** Zeke come thu the hammock 'bout a hour 'fore sun and goed back about dusk-dark. **1936** in 1977 *Amer. Slave Suppl. 1* 1.132 **AL,**'Long 'bout dusk dark when Ebenezer wuz ober at de court house. **1941** *Sat. Eve. Post* 213.45.112/3 **KY,** Nobody passed upcreek or down, nobody we glimpsed daybreak to dust dark. **1950** *PADS* 14.75 **cnFL,** *Dus'-dark. . .* Early sundown. Suwannee River area. **1954** *PADS* 21.26 **cSC,** *Dusk dark.* **1957** in 1958 Brewer *Dog Ghosts* 7 **TX** [Black], "Well de Lawd be praised," yell Unkuh Jonas; "Ah gonna do dat ver' thing rat tonight." So 'long 'bout dusk-dark dat same evenin' when Unkuh Jonah think dey ain't nobody much stirrin', he slips outen his cabin an' mecks his way down to the woods. **1957** Faulkner *Town* 34 **MS,** It was jest dust-dark and we had done et supper. **1965–70** *DARE* (Qu. A5, *The time right after the sun goes out of sight, before it becomes all dark*) 17 Infs, **chiefly Sth,** Dusk dark; TN26, 52, Dust dark; (Qu. A4, *The time of day when the sun goes out of sight*) Inf **GA**17, Dust dark. **c1974** Jones *Ozark Hill Boy* 25 **AR** (as of c1920), About dusk dark I began looking for a comfortable roadside place where I could lie down for the night. **1986** Pederson *LAGS Concordance* **Gulf Region,** 6 infs, Dusk dark; 1 inf, Dust dark.

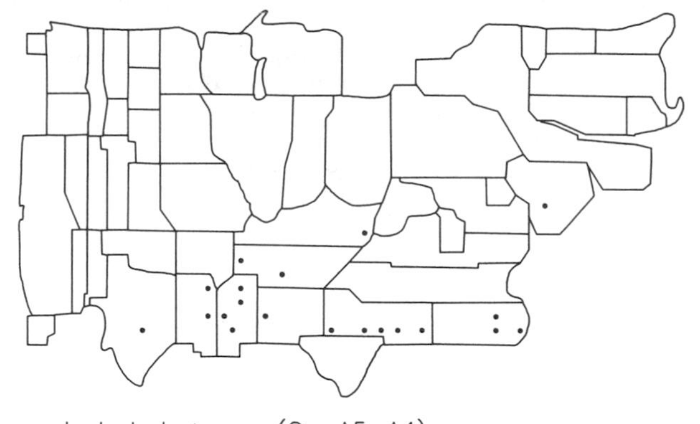

•dusk dark + var (Qq. A5, A4)

dusking n

Hunting at twilight or dusk.

1937 Pearson *Adventures* 120 **eNC,** I accompanied gunners who went "dusking" for black ducks in the woods on the Hatteras banks. **1985** Rattray *Advent. Dimon* 96 **Long Island NY,** They wandered back to the blinds smoking cheroots for the dusking. This was not as lively as the morning shooting.

dusky n

=dusk dark.

1954 Forbes *Rainbow* 312 **MA,** It was on to dusky when we came into the biggest of them. **1968** *DARE* (Qu. A5, *The time right after the sun goes out of sight, before it becomes all dark*) Inf **TN**24, Dusky—occasional. We laughed at people who said this.

dusky dark n Also *dusty dark* **chiefly S Midl** See Map and Map Section

=dusk dark.

1941 *Sat. Eve. Post* 213.45.36/2 **KY,** The wagon was unloaded by dusty dark. **1944** Howard *Walkin' Preacher* 97 **Ozarks,** Meet me at the big oak at dusky dark tonite. **1960** Hall *Smoky Mt. Folks* 66 **eTN,** Just about dusky dark it was snowing like water pourin' out of a bucket. **c1960** *Wilson Coll.* **csKY,** *Dusky dark. . .* Early twilight. **1965–70** *DARE* (Qu. A5, *The time right after the sun goes out of sight, before it becomes all dark*) Infs **AR**14, 53, 56, **GA**73, **KY**28, **OK**21, **TN**24, 41, 56, **VA**44, Dusky dark; **KY**31, **NC**53, 67, **TN**14, **VA**44, Dusty dark; (Qu. A4, *The time of day when the sun goes out of sight*) Infs **AL**52, **OK**21, Dusky dark; **TN**14, Dusty dark. **1971** *Foxfire* Spring–Summer 34 **nGA,** And I plowed—hit was a dusky dark when I got in. **1981** *AR Gaz.* (Little Rock) 16 Aug F1/5, "We don't let him stay too late," the son said. "If he hasn't come in by dusky dark . . [we] bring him in." **1983** *MJLF* 9.1.38 **ceKY,** *Dusty dark* . . dusk. **1986** Pederson *LAGS Concordance (Sunset)* 2 infs, **AL,** Dusky dark; 1 inf, **ceTN,** Dusky dark—after the sun is down, just before dark; *(The part of the day after supper)* 1 inf, **neMS,** Dusty dark.

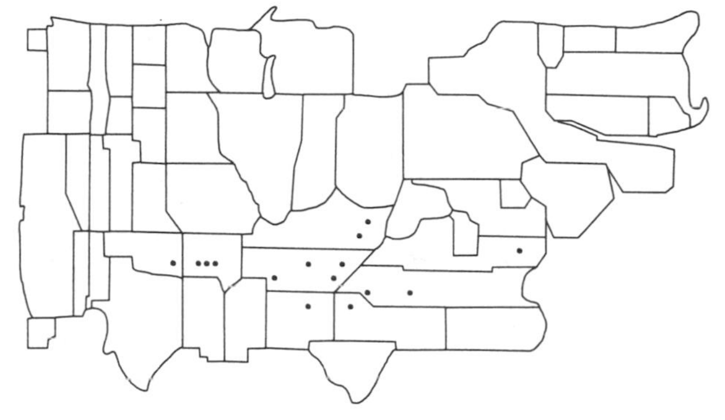

•dusky dark + var (Qq. A5, A4)

dusky duck n

1 A **black duck 1** (here: *Anas rubripes*).

1804 *Cabinet Nat. Hist.* 49 *(DA),* A New-York dusky Duck . . *Anas obscura Amer.* Sept. **1844** Giraud *Birds Long Is.* 301, When at Niagara, I was informed that on the 16th of October, 1840, eighty-three Dusky Ducks were killed by flying into the Falls. **1858** Baird *Birds* 775, *Anas Obscura* . . Dusky Duck. **1923** U.S. Dept. Ag. *Misc. Circular* 13.9, *Black Duck (Anas rubripes). . .* dusky duck. **1925** (1928) Forbush *Birds MA* 1.195, *Anas rubripes tristis* . . Black Duck.—*Other names:* Dusky Duck.

2 **=Florida duck.**

1944 Barbour *Vanishing Eden* 92, Moreover it was often possible to pick up a few gallinules and the native Florida dusky ducks. **1951** Pough *Audubon Water Bird* 326, Dusky duck. *See* Mottled duck *[Anas fulvigula].*

dusky flycatcher n

=phoebe.

1917 (1923) *Birds Amer.* 2.198, *Phoebe—Sayornis phoebe* . . Other Names.—Phoebe Bird; . . Dusky Flycatcher. **1946** Hausman *Eastern Birds* 401, *Eastern Phoebe Sayornis phoebe* . . Other Names—Bridge Bird, . . Dusky Flycatcher.

dusky grouse n

A chicken-sized, tree-perching bird *(Dendragapus obscurus)* of the western US. Also called **blue grouse 1, bull grouse, fool hen 3, hooter 1, pine grouse, pine hen, sooty grouse, wood grouse**

1828 Bonaparte *Amer. Ornith.* 3.34, The Dusky Grous [=*Tetrao obscurus*] is eminently distinguished from all other known species, by having the tail slightly rounded. **1917** (1923) *Birds Amer.* 2.13, The Dusky Grouse [=*Dendragapus obscurus*] is a western bird, the largest and finest of American wood Grouse. **1923** U.S. Dept. Ag. *Farmers' Bulletin* 1375.16 **ID,** *Open seasons:* . . Blue or dusky grouse. . . Sept. 15–Oct. 15. **1965** *Silver City Press Frontier* (NM) July Frontier Recreation ed [14] **swNM,** [Advt:] A variety of birds are found . . also ducks, dusky grouse.

dusky mallard n

1 A **black duck 1** (here: *Anas rubripes*).

1888 Trumbull *Names of Birds* 17, *Anas obscura* . . Dusky Mallard. **1917** (1923) *Birds Amer.* 1.116, *Black Duck—Anas rubripes* . . Other Names. . . Dusky Mallard; . . Spring Black Duck. **1923** U.S. Dept. Ag. *Misc. Circular* 13.9, *Black Duck (Anas rubripes)*. . . dusky mallard.

2 =**Florida duck.**

1932 Howell *FL Bird Life* 132, *Florida Duck: Anas fulvigula* . . Other Names: . . Dusky Mallard.

dust n[1]

1 Money. [*OED* 1607 →]

1843 (1916) Hall *New Purchase* 218 **IN,** So down with your dust. **1899** (1912) Green *VA Folk-Speech* 161, *Dust*. . . Money: "down with the dust." **1909** *DN* 3.395 **nwAR,** *Dust, the*. . . Money. **1937** *Writer* 50.239 **neOH,** *Dust*—means money. A gold rush term in current use. **1969** *DARE* FW Addit **NYC,** *Dust*—money. **1970** *DARE* (Qu. U19a, . . *Money in general: "He's certainly got the ______."*) Inf **CA**177, Dust. **1972** Claerbaut *Black Jargon* 63, *Dust* . . money. **1976** *DARE* File **seLA** [Black], I don't have any dust.

2 also *dusting:* A small amount (of a pulverized substance, esp flour or meal). **chiefly Sth, S Midl**

1899 (1912) Green *VA Folk-Speech* 161, *Dust*. . . A small quantity of any powdered substance. A beggar will often say: "I haven't a dust of meal in the house." **1922** (1926) Kephart *Highlanders* 33 **sAppalachians,** Marg . . offered to barter it for "a dustin' o' salt." **1926** Roberts *Time of Man* 88 **cKY,** There was not a dusten [sic] of meal in the house. **1931** *Jrl. Amer. Folkl.* 44.416 **Sth** [Black], *To Make a Tonic*. One quart of wine, three pinches of raw rice, three dusts of cinnamon (about one heaping teaspoon), [etc]. **1939** *AmSp* 14.90 **eTN,** I had to borrow a dust of meal to make pony bread for supper. **1939** *Hall Coll.* **eTN,** They had a muzzle-loading gun but not a dust of powder. **1952** Brown *NC Folkl.* 1.535, *Dust.* **c1960** *Wilson Coll.* **csKY,** *Dust.* **1968–70** *DARE* (Qu. V2b, . . *"I wouldn't trust him ______."*) Inf **NC**88, Behind a dust of flour; (Qu. LL6c, *A small, indefinite amount . . "It still needs just a ______ of cinnamon."*) Infs **MD**17, 28, **MN**19, **NC**55, **VA**69, Dust. [5 of 6 Infs comm type 5 and old, 2 Infs Black] **1969** *DARE* Tape **TN**34, One night they didn't have a dust of flour. They didn't have a thing to eat.

3 also *bumblebee dust:* Snuff; tobacco.

1940 *AmSp* 15.83 **nWV,** The parent was 'only using a little *bumble-bee dust.*' The procedure . . was the dabbing of a bit of snuff under the upper lip. Snuff is often spoken of simply as *dust.* **1984** Wilder *You All Spoken Here* 195, Dust an' paper: Makin's. [*Ibid* 194, Makin's: Cigarette papers and smoking tobacco for roll-your-own smoking.]

4 Manure. *euphem* Cf **heifer dust 2**

1942 Berrey–Van den Bark *Amer. Slang* 124.2, *Dung*. . . heifer dust. **1950** *WELS (Names for barnyard fertilizer used in the fields)* 2 Infs, **WI,** Heifer dust. **1966–69** *DARE* (Qu. L17, *Other names . . for manure used in the fields*) Inf **ID**3, Steer dust; **MA**58, Heifer dust.

5 as count noun: =**dust bunny.**

1969 *DARE* FW Addit **csPA,** Dust—A roll of dust under furniture; count noun; **HI,** *Dust bunnies,* also called *dusts,* which is pronounced both [dʌsts] and ['dʌstəz].

dust v Also with *off* Cf **dust it up**

To beat or whip—often in phr *dust one's jacket* and varr.

1807 *Eagle* (Staunton, Va.) 28 Aug. 4/2 *(OEDS),* Go in peace, or I will dust thy jacket with this horse-whip. **1885** Twain *Huck. Finn* 333 **MO,** So she took and dusted us both with the hickry. **1893** *KS Univ. Qrly.* 1.139 **KS,** *Dust:* to whip. **1905** *DN* 3.78 **nwAR,** *Dust one's linen*. . . To punish one. 'I'll dust your linen, if you don't quit that.' Common. **1906** *DN* 3.134 **nwAR,** *Dust one's linen (or coat).* **1950** *Time* 30 Jan 14/2, At Brownsville, Pa. . . 3,000 men of John Lewis' District 4 gathered the same day to rail at District Leader William Hynes, threatened to dump him in the Monongahela River and dusted one of his lieutenants with an old shoe for trying to talk them back to work. **1967–69** *DARE* (Qu. Y15, *To beat somebody thoroughly: "John really ______ that fellow!"*) Inf **NE**3, Dusted him off; **TX**68, Dusted. **1971** Roberts *Third Ear* [6/2] [Black], *Dust* . . to beat up; to completely defeat.

dust n[2] [Cf Intro "Language Changes" IV.4] Cf *dust dark* (at **dusk dark**) **esp Mid Atl**

Dusk.

1930 Shoemaker *1300 Words* 18 **cPA Mts** (as of c1900), *Dust*—The gloaming or dusk. **1967–70** *DARE* (Qu. A5, *The time right after the sun goes out of sight, before it becomes all dark*) Infs **KY**55, **MD**19, **NC**49, 79, **SC**42, 51, **VA**39, 42, Dust; [**NC**49, Dusty].

dust baby n

=**dust bunny.**

1968 *DARE* (Qu. E20) Inf **WI**5, Dust baby.

dustbird n

A **whippoorwill** (here: *Caprimulgus vociferus*).

1945 *AN&Q* 5.11, Despite the dominance of *whippoorwill,* there are a number of local names for the bird: . . "dustbird" (Mississippi, from being seen on country roads, probably in search of insects).

dust bunny n Cf **bunny tail, kitten**

A soft roll of dust, such as is found beneath beds or other pieces of furniture.

1965–70 *DARE* (Qu. E20) Infs **CO**28, **HI**8, **IL**97, 141, **IN**41, **KY**50A, **LA**23, **NJ**21, **OH**38, **UT**3, Dust bunnies. **1966** *Anniston Star* (AL) 19 Nov 2/1, Uncovering in the process the most horrendous collection of dust bunnies imaginable. **1969** *DARE* FW Addit **HI,** Dust bunnies. **1980** *New Yorker* 18 Feb 31 **KY,** Her grandmother always told her to dust under her bed, so the dust bunnies would not multiply and take over. **1984** Wilder *You All Spoken Here* 28 **Sth.**

dust dark See **dusk dark**

dust dawn n [By analogy with *dust dark* var of **dusk dark**]

Morning twilight.

1930 Faulkner *As I Lay Dying* 67 **MS,** It was long a-past midnight when we drove the last nail, and almost dust-dawn when I got back home. **1957** Faulkner *Town* 245 **MS,** How is Jefferson going to be steady blessed without me steady willing from dust-dawn to dust-dark, rain or snow or sun, to say much oblige?

dust devil n

1 also *dust whirl:* A small whirlwind which picks up sand and dust. [*OEDS* 1888 →; cf *OED devil* sb. 11 1835 →] **esp West**

1923 Sinclair *Parowan Bonanza* 19 **ceCA,** A dry lake lay baked yellow, hard as cement, with dust devils whirling dizzily down its bald length. **1942** Whipple *Joshua* 194 **UT,** The blue of the sky was washed white with brilliance, and dust-devils whirled in southward-sweeping clouds. **1966–70** *DARE* (Qu. B16, *A destructive wind that comes with a funnel-shaped cloud*) Infs **CA**4, 48, 62, **OR**1, Dust devil; (Qu. B18, . . *Special kinds of wind that you get around here*) Infs **CA**90, **IN**41, **MN**6, **NV**6, **SC**26, **TX**84, **WV**11, Dust devil. **1967** *DARE* FW Addit **swWA,** A dust devil—same as whirly wind. **1975** Zwinger *Run River* 122 **UT,** Today, a dugway in the soft sand angles up out of the river, and a dust devil scurries a cloud of dust. **1982** Heat Moon *Blue Highways* 156 **AZ, NM,** People of the Old Testament heard the voice of God in desert whirlwinds, but Southwestern Indians saw evil spirits in the spumes and sang aloud if one crossed their path; that's why, in New Mexico and Arizona today, the little thermals are "dust devils." **1982** *TWA Ambassador* July 47, *Dust devil*. . . It also is called a *dust whirl.*

2 =**dust bunny.** Cf **angel 3**

1967–69 *DARE* (Qu. E20) Infs **IL**97, **LA**14, **NY**23, Dust devils. **1984** Burns *Cold Sassy* 315 **nGA,** She didn't seem to care that there were dust devils under the beds.

dust dolly n

=**dust bunny.**

1968 *DARE* (Qu. E20) Inf **NJ**15, Dust dollies.

dusted adj

1 See quot.

1944 Adams *Western Words* 55, Dusted—Thrown from a horse.

2 Tired, exhausted. [Cf **dust** v]

1967 *DARE* (Qu. X47, . . *Ways . . of saying "I'm very tired, at the end of my strength"*) Inf **IL**2, Dusted.

duster n

1 A dust or sand storm.

1935 *Dly. Oklahoman* 7 April 1/4 *(heading) (DA),* New Duster May Blanket State Today. **1941** Daniels *Tar Heels* 188 **NC,** I had followed the progress of the big duster from its point of origin in northeastern New Mexico, on into the Ohio Valley, and had every reason to believe it would eventually reach Washington. **1944** *PADS* 2.55 **cnMO,** *Duster*. . . A sandstorm. **1948** *Dallas Morning News* (TX) 5 Dec Book Sec 4/1, Another series of "dusters" may be imminent. **1962** Atwood *Vocab. TX* 77, *Duster*. . . A heavy sandstorm. Recorded in the Panhandle. **1966** *DARE* (Qu. B18, . . *Special kinds of wind*) Inf **NM**1, Duster—a dust storm.

2 See quot.

1941 *LANE* Map 341 *(Bedspread)* 1 inf, **swNH,** Duster.

3 A (salt or pepper) shaker.

1953 Randolph-Wilson *Down in Holler* 242 **Ozarks,** *Duster*. . . A vessel with small openings in the top, for salt or pepper. In many parts of the Middle West they are called *shakers,* but the Ozarker speaks of *salt-dusters* and *pepper-dusters.* **1967** Cerello *Dakota Co. MN* 55, Dusters were always used in my day and many were of pretty colored glass. **1968-70** *DARE* (Qu. G4, *A container for salt that has a cover with holes in it)* Infs **KY**85, **MD**28, Salt dusters.

4 In railroading: see quot.

1977 Adams *Lang. Railroader* 51, *Duster:* A locomotive.

dust feather See **feather n B4**

dusting See **dust** n[1] **2**

dust it up v phr Cf **dust** v

1968 *DARE* (Qu. EE21b, *When boys were fighting very actively, you might say, "For a while those fellows really ______.")* Inf **WI**29, Dusted it up.

dust kitten (or kitty) See **kitten**

dust man n

=**dust bunny.**

1966-68 *DARE* (Qu. E20) Infs **IN**34, **MS**45, Little dust men.

dust mitten n

=**dust bunny.**

1966 *DARE* (Qu. E20) Inf **AL**1, Dust mittens.

dust mouse See **mouse**

dust off See **dust** v

dust-off, give one the v phr

See quots.

1942 Berrey-Van den Bark *Amer. Slang* 27.5, *Eliminate; discard; get rid of*. . . give the brush-off, -the dust-off. **1967** *DARE* (Qu. II5b, *When you don't want to have anything to do with a certain person . . "I'd certainly like to give him the ______.")* Inf **TX**43, Dust off. **1967** *DARE* FW Addit **ncNY,** Gave me the dust-off—the brush-off.

dust one's back v phr Cf **dusted 1**

1914 *DN* 4.72 **ME, nNH,** *Dust yer back*. . . Wrestle; throw a man. "Fer two cents I'll dust yer back!"

dust one's jacket See **dust** v

dust puppy n Cf *DS* E20

=**dust bunny.**

1950 *WELS (Soft rolls of dust that collect on the floor under beds or other furniture)* 1 Inf, **ceWI,** Dust puppies. **1979** Stegner *Recapitulation* 38 **UT,** The radiator puffed its warm breath against his legs, the dust puppies fluttered in its grill.

dust pussy See **pussy** n

dust settler n

A light rain.

1950 *PADS* 14.28 **wSC,** *Dust settler*. . . A light rain, sufficient only to settle the dust. **1950** *WELS (A light rain)* 1 Inf, **ceWI,** Dust settler. **c1960** *Wilson Coll.* **csKY,** *Dust-settler*. . . A light rain. **1969** *DARE* (Qu. B23, . . *A light rain that doesn't last)* Inf **VT**16, Dust settler; [**PA**157, Enough to settle the dust].

dust tiger n

=**dust bunny.**

1989 *DARE* File **OH,** Dust tigers—balls of dust under the bed.

dust web n

A dusty cobweb or other accumulation of dust.

1939 *LANE* Map 242 *(Spider Web)* 11 infs, **scattered NEng,** Dust web. **1948** Davis *Word Atlas Gt. Lakes* 266 **MI, IL, IN, OH,** *Dust web.* **1955** Potter *Dial. NW OH* 138, *Dust web.* **1966-70** *DARE* (Qu. E20, *Soft rolls of dust that collect on the floor under beds or other furniture)* Inf **NJ**9, Dust webs; (Qu. R29a, . . *The thing that a spider spins and lives in—If it is indoors)* Infs **KY**94, **MO**1, **NC**6, Dust web.

dust whirl See **dust devil 1**

dusty adj

1 in phrr *your brain is* (or *brains are*) *dusty:* See quot.

1966-68 *DARE* (Qu. NN18, *When somebody sneezes, what do people say to him?)* Inf **ID**1, Your brain is dusty; UT4, Your brains are dusty.

2 See quot. Cf **ashy 1**

1969-70 *DARE* (Qu. GG4, *Stirred up, angry: "When he saw them coming he got ______.")* Inf **NC**88, Dusty; (Qu. HH22b, . . *A very mean person)* Inf **IN**75, Dusty.

dusty dark See **dusky dark**

dusty maiden n

A **morning brides** (here: either *Chaenactis alpina* or *C. douglasii*).

1963 Craighead *Rocky Mt. Wildflowers* Pl. 24, *Dusty Maiden, Chaenactis alpina*. . . A dusty-looking plant with flesh-colored tubular flowers and much-dissected leaves. *Ibid* 200, *Morning-Brides. Chaenactis douglasii*. . . *Other names:* Dusty Maiden. . . A dusty-looking plant with 1 to several stems 4-18 in. tall, coming from a taproot.

dusty miller n [Scots, nEngl dial for the common auricula *Primula auricula*]

1 =**mullein pink.**

1900 Lyons *Plant Names* 231, *L[ychnis] coronaria* . . Dusty-miller. **1940** Clute *Amer. Plant Names* 166, Dusty miller. *Lychnis coronaria.* **1976** Bailey-Bailey *Hortus Third* 688, *Lychnis* . . *Coronaria* . . Mullein pink, Rose campion, Dusty-miller.

2 A **wormwood,** esp *Artemisia stelleriana.*

1910 Graves *Flowering Plants* 401 **CT,** *Artemisia Stelleriana* . . Dusty Miller. **1938** Damon *Grandma* 167 **CT** (as of late 1800s), A ruffle of leaves unrelated to the rest of the bouquet finished it off—dusty miller and southernwood were favorites. **1950** Gray-Fernald *Manual of Botany* 1522, *A[rtemisia] Stelleriana* . . Dusty Miller. **1976** Bailey-Bailey *Hortus Third* 112, *Artemisia* . . *Stellerana* [sic] . . Beach wormwood, Old-woman, Dusty-miller. **1976** Bruce *How to Grow Wildflowers* 217, Farther north it may be replaced by another, similar plant also called Dusty Miller, but perhaps more properly Beach Wormwood, *Artemisia stelleriana.*

3 Any of several **star thistles,** esp *Centaurea cineraria.*

1942 Hylander *Plant Life* 496, Dusty Miller [=*Centaurea cineraria*] is a low growing whitish woolly plant from the Mediterranean region, often used as a bedding plant in gardens; the prickly involucre is topped by purple flowers. **1961** Thomas *Flora Santa Cruz* 376 **cwCA,** *C[entaurea] cineraria* . . Dusty Miller. **1965** Neal *Gardens HI* 857, Dusty miller *(C. cineraria).* **1974** Munz *Flora S. CA* 134, *C[entaurea] cineraria* . . Dusty Miller. **1976** Bailey-Bailey *Hortus Third* 242, *Centaurea* . . *cineraria* . . Dusty-miller . . *[C.] gymnocarpa* . . Dusty-miller . . *[C.] ragusina* . . Dusty-miller. **1976** Bruce *How to Grow Wildflowers* 216, Another dune plant is very much worth growing—the well-known Dusty Miller. It is botanically a star-thistle, *Centaurea cineraria,* as its rose or mauve thistle flower heads attest.

4 Any of var garden flowers; see quots.

1876 Hobbs *Bot. Hdbk.* 33, Dusty miller, . . Cineraria maritima. . . Senecio cineraria. **1959** Carleton *Index Herb. Plants* 40, *Dusty Miller:* . . Primula auricula; . . *Stachys lanata.* **1976** Bailey-Bailey *Hortus Third* 1035, *Senecio* . . *Cineraria* . . Dusty-miller. *Ibid* 1038, *Senecio* . . *Vira-vira* . . Dusty-miller. **1976** Bruce *How to Grow Wildflowers* 217, There are several other exotic beach dwellers called Dusty Miller. I have grown a beautiful one known botanically as *Chrysanthemum* (or *Pyrethrum*) *ptarmicaefolium,* but it will not winter with me.

5 Any of var moths such as those of the family Arctiidae; see quots. [redund *dusty* + **miller;** see quot 1911]

1909 Porter *Girl Limberlost* 243 **nIN,** Small insects of night gathered, and at last a little dusty miller, but nothing came of any size. **1911** *Century Dict. Suppl.*, *Dusty-miller* . . Same as *miller, 3* [="A moth whose wings appear as if dusted over with flour or meal, like a miller's clothes"]. **1983** *Barrick Coll.* **csPA,** *Dusty miller*—moth . . common in 1940s. **1987** *NADS Letters* **cIL,** In my youth (1930s) the term "dusty miller" was widely used to describe . . moths that had large quantities of white wing scales. Usually they . . collected around lights after dark, crashing into the light bulb leaving wing scales behind. An aside: Often a man with the surname Miller had "Dusty" as a nickname. *Ibid* **csMN,** I used to hear my grandmother call a small white moth by that name [=dusty miller]. *Ibid* **ceTX,** *Dusty miller* is both a moth here and a plant that is basically grey but looks like it has been dusted with flour.

Dutch adj

1 German; hence n pl *Dutch* people of German or German-speaking birth or ancestry. [*OED Dutch* adj. 1 "*Obs.* exc as a historical archaism, and in some parts of U.S."] **scattered, but less freq Sth, NEast** Cf **Deutscher, Dutch n 1, Dutcher, Dutchman 1**

1742 in 1906 *Colonial Rec. GA* 6.45 **ceGA,** The Body of Dutch Servants . . [applied] to this Board that they might have Lands granted them. **1826** Flint *Recollections* 233 **seMO,** He must allow the honest Dutch, as they call themselves, to partake of the native beverage. **1863** U.S. Congress *Congressional Globe* 37th Cong 3d Sess 7 Feb 793/3 **MO,** A gentleman . . told me that he saw a squad of Dutch soldiers . . take possession of the polls. . . They were a crowd of Germans who could say nothing but "yaw." **1867** *Atlantic Mth.* 19.659/1 **MO,** Let us drink, . . in foaming lager, to the "Damned Dutch of St. Louis." **1906** *DN* 3.134 **nwAR,** *Dutch, adj.* German. The former word is usual among the uncouth. **1939** (1962) Thompson *Body & Britches* 149 **NY,** As a matter of fact, the Albany County "Dutch"—whether they came from Holland or from the Palatine, Germany—have their own stock of tall tales. **1964** *PADS* 42.38 **Chicago IL,** [2 of 31 infs offered *Dutch (bastard)* as a derogatory term for a German.] **1964** Smith *PA Germans* 6, There is a strong reluctance among some people who were "raised Dutch" to reveal it, particularly after they move into the towns and cities. . . There is a stigma associated with being "Dutch" and the younger people attempt to avoid ridicule. . . It is little wonder that people able to speak or understand the dialect avoid its use among non-dialect speaking peoples. **1965–70** *DARE* (Qu. HH28, *Names and nicknames for people of foreign background—German*) 47 Infs, **scattered, but less freq Sth, NEast,** Dutch [13 of these Infs also offered *Dutch* for "Hollander"; 98 Infs offered *Dutch* only in that sense.]; **CA**154, Big Dutch; **IA**3, Flat-footed Dutch—used of Germans in a heavily German area; **NJ**15, Dumb Dutch.

2 By ext: foreign, un-English, incomprehensible. Cf **Dutchman 2**

1885 *Century Illustr. Mag.* 29.827/2, In many parts of the United States, owing to a curious series of historical associations . . anything foreign and un-English is called "Dutch." **1982** *Barrick Coll.* **csPA,** Dutch—hard to understand. "Aw, you're Dutch."

3 Of the color of cooked food: dark.

1979 *DARE* File **neOH** (as of 1920s), Dutch brown = dark brown. Said of baked goods. "That pie is a real Dutch brown." Used originally in communities where Germans and Yankees came together. German cooks baked pastry longer, roasted meat longer.

Dutch n

1 The German language. [**Dutch** adj **1**]

1748 (1925) Washington *Diaries* 1.10 **VA,** They [=German immigrants] would never speak English but when spoken to they speak all Dutch. **1826** Flint *Recollections* 235 **seMO,** To reinstate himself . . , it was only necessary for him to . . give them a vehement discourse, as they phrased it, in the pure old Dutch, and give them a German hymn of his own manufacture. **1845** *S. Lit. Messenger* 11.754/1 **sePA** (as of 1834), He told us that he was a prodigy of erudition, that he spoke Latin and French as well as "Dutch." **1852** (1854) Kennedy *Horse-Shoe Robinson* 23 **SC,** So, said I, coming up boldly to him, 'Hans, wie gehet es.' . . That was all the Dutch I could speak. **1865** (1889) Whitney *Gayworthys* 116 **ceMA,** Mother hollered Dutch at him, but he did n't stop to listen. *Ibid* 115, **ceMA,** Emigrant ship Adelheid, from Hamburg. Hundred and seventy poor souls on board, screaming and praying in Dutch. **1906** *DN* 3.134 **nwAR,** *Dutch.* . . The German language. . . A German lesson. "I've got to get my Dutch before I can go with you."

2 also *double Dutch, high Dutch;* By ext: incomprehensible speech; a children's jargon made by systematically deforming English words. [*OED* 1789 →] Cf **Dutch** adj **2**

1899 (1912) Green *VA Folk-Speech* 161, *Dutch.* . . Any speech not understood is said to be "Dutch." "That's all Dutch to me." **1942** Berrey–Van den Bark *Amer. Slang* 172.1, Dutch, double Dutch . . *anything unintelligible, esp. speech. Ibid* 172.4, *Unintelligible; vague.* . . Double *or* high Dutch, Dutch. **1945** Colcord *Sea Language* 67 **ME, Cape Cod, Long Island,** *Double-Dutch.* Unintelligible language. **1966** *DARE* File **neMN** (as of 1946), *Double Dutch*—A children's language name in which "eese" was put before the vowel in each syllable of a word, e.g., *peese-a-peese-per* for "paper," *beese-ook* for "book." Played by teenagers. **1967–68** *DARE* (Qu. HH30, *Things that are nicknamed for different nationalities*) Inf **MD**37, Sounds like Dutch to me; **TN**15, That's all Dutch to me. [**1982** *Barrick Coll.* **csPA,** *Dutch*—hard to understand. "Aw, you're Dutch."]

3 pl: See **Dutch** adj **1.**

4 One's fighting spirit, dander—often in phr *get one's Dutch up.* **chiefly PA** Cf **African** n[1] **B1, Indian, Irish**

1893 Leland *Memoirs* 320 **sePA,** It woke Colonel John Forney up to the very highest pitch of his fighting "Injun," or, as they say in Pennsylvania, his "Dutch." **1945** Tryon *Poor Man* 32 **PA,** Hilda would have stopped me from doing anything rash, but my "Dutch was up," as our Pennsylvania neighbors used to say. **1968–70** *DARE* (Qu. GG4, *Stirred up, angry: "When he saw them coming he got ______.")* Inf **NJ**23, His Dutch up; (Qu. GG23c, . . *Expressions [to tell someone to be patient]*) Inf **PA**242, Don't get your Dutch up.

5 See **Dutch clover a.**

Dutch adv Also *Dutch treat* [*Dutch treat* n] Cf **arkansaw** adv

With each person paying his or her share—usu in phrr *go Dutch (treat).*

1914 Lewis *Our Mr. Wrenn* 63 **NY,** We'll go Dutch. **1965–70** *DARE* (Qu. HH30, *Things that are nicknamed for different nationalities*) 41 Infs, **scattered,** Go(ing) Dutch; (Qu. II8, *When one person wants to share or divide something with another person . . "Let's ______ [on that].")* 47 Infs, **scattered,** Go Dutch (treat); (Qu. II9, *If several people have to contribute in order to pay for something, you say, "Let's all ______.")* 57 Infs, **scattered,** Go Dutch (treat). [Of all Infs responding to Qq. HH30, II8, and II9, 54%, 53%, and 53% respectively were women; of those giving these responses, 71%, 70%, and 77% respectively were women.]

Dutch v

1 also *Dutch it:* To pay one's own share.

1965–70 *DARE* (Qu. HH30, *Things that are nicknamed for different nationalities*) Inf **FL**18, Dutch treat—each one pays, all Dutch it, all go Dutch; **FL**28, We'll Dutch it—each pays his own way; (Qu. II8, *When one person wants to share or divide something with another person, he might say, "Let's ______ [on that].")* Infs **AL**25, **IN**32, **MS**71, Dutch; **AL**27, **GA**89, **MA**123, Dutch it; (Qu. II9, *If several people have to contribute in order to pay for something, you say, "Let's all ______.")* Infs **AL**22, **FL**8, **GA**73, Dutch it; **MS**73, Dutch.

2 with *in:* See quot.

1985 Kidder *House* 265 **MA,** He makes patches that will become invisible under paint, and while at this chore Jim seems mildly entertained. "I have to Dutch these suckers in. That means to patch a hole. I think it comes from the old finger in the dike."

Dutch ball n

A bat and ball game; see quot 1950.

1950 *WELS Suppl.* **seWI,** Dutch ball—the batter faced the pitcher at right angles to the field. Batter batted, ran to base and back before the ball was returned to the pitcher. If made "out," he became the last fielder. **1969** *DARE* (Qu. HH30, *Things that are nicknamed for different nationalities*) Inf **IL**107, Dutch ball.

Dutch bath n

1953 *AmSp* 28.144, There are several colloquial or slang synonyms of *sponge bath.* . . *Bird bath, Dutch bath,* and *wipe-off* are baths requiring a minimum of water.

Dutch, beat the See **beat the Dutch**

Dutch bed n Cf **apple turnover**

1905 *DN* 3.78 **nwAR,** *Dutch bed.* . . A bed which has been disarranged, and (usually) the slats of which have been removed. Used by young women students of the state university.

Dutch beech n

A **cottonwood 1** (here: *Populus alba*).

1900 Lyons *Plant Names* 302, *P[opulus] alba.* . . Dutch beech. **1933** Small *Manual SE Flora* 411, *P. alba.* . . Dutch-beech.

Dutch boiled dinner n Cf **boiled dinner, New England boiled dinner**

1968 *DARE* (Qu. H49, *Dishes made by boiling potatoes with other foods*) Inf **OH**75, New England boiled dinner, Dutch boiled dinner—[the latter] has dumplings.

Dutch cabbage n

1 Boiled cabbage.

1969 *DARE* (Qu. H52, *Dishes made with fresh cabbage*) Inf **PA**200, Boiled cabbage, also called Dutch cabbage.

2 See quots.

1917 WI Farmers' Inst. *Women's Bulletin No. 10* 55, *Dutch Cabbage.* Chop a small cabbage with one small onion and . . pour over the fat from a small slice of fat salt pork... Add the pork, and into the frying pan pour sufficient vinegar to moisten... Add seasonings of salt and red pepper. Pour over the vinegar boiling hot and serve at once. **1969** *DARE* (Qu. H65, *Foreign foods favored by people around here*) Inf **MA**14, Mother made Dutch cabbage—cabbage chopped very fine, vinegar, sugar, salt, pepper added.

Dutch cake n Cf **apee**

Any of various sorts of cake.

1844 in 1959 *AmSp* 34.28, Dutch cake. **1860** G.T. Clark *MA. Diary* 1 *(DAE),* Ate some of Dutch cake for the first time. **1954** *AmSp* 29.46 **sePA,** The term *apee cake* is used to designate a breakfast cake,.. which becomes palatable only when dunked in coffee or milk... It is practically unknown in the western part of the PaG [=Pennsylvania German] speech island. In that area an 'apee cake' is called a 'Dutch cake.' **1967–70** *DARE* (Qu. H32,.. *Fancy rolls and pastries*) Inf **PA**41, Dutch cake—cinnamon, raised cake, sugar on top; (Qu. HH30, *Things that are nicknamed for different nationalities*) Inf **VA**74, Dutch cake. **1982** Weaver *Quaker Woman's Cookbook* 1, In the Middle Atlantic region, black cake was more commonly called Dutch cake and was sold either in large "wheels" or in small loaves, particularly at Christmas.

Dutch cap n **seMA** Cf *DS* L14

=barrack.

1939 *LANE* Map 104 **seMA,** Hay *stack; cock*... In southeastern Mass. the square or oblong stack may have a roof sliding on four corner posts, which is called a *Dutch cap* [by 3 infs] or a *hay cap.* These terms are presumably applied also to the stack together with the roof. **1949** Kurath *Word Geog.* 55, The Dutch settlement area.. has *barrack,* a term of Dutch origin. This type of stack has a square base and a roof that slides on four corner posts. Stacks of this construction can also be seen east of Narragansett Bay and are locally known as *Dutch caps* or *hay caps.* **1965** *PADS* 43.31 **seMA,** *Dutch caps*—for the sliding roofs sometimes put over hay stacks in the field—was given by one informant. **1967** *PADS* 47.7 **sNEng,** Dutch cap—'haystack.'

Dutch caseknife (bean) See **caseknife bean**

Dutch cheese n **chiefly Nth** See Map *somewhat old-fash* Cf **Irish cheese**

A cheese made of skimmed or partly skimmed milk, now esp cottage cheese.

1829 Royall *Pennsylvania* 1.171, While standing in the market, I saw a great curiosity, called Dutch cheese... It is made from curds of skimmed milk, and is not very tempting. **1855** (1888) Holmes *Homestead Hillside* 133 **NEng,** Sally had filled the pantry with cakes, pies, gingerbread, and dutch cheese. **1876** VT State Bd. Ag. *Rept. for 1875–76* 3.92, The milk has stood so long in hot weather as to separate from the whey and dry into "Dutch cheese." **1884** Barber *Diary* **cnMA,** She sent me sugar and others Dutch cheese. **1910** *DN* 3.440 **cwNY,** *Dutch cheese*... Cottage cheese; smear case; etc. **1949** Kurath *Word Geog.* 71, Maine and adjoining parts of New Hampshire have *curds, curd cheese.* In coastal New England.. *sour-milk cheese* predominates. The remaining greater part of New England, except for southwestern Connecticut, has *Dutch cheese*... *Dutch cheese,* named with reference to the Dutch in the Hudson Valley, has also become established in the New England settlements of New York State, Pennsylvania, and Ohio, and has spread to some extent into West Virginia from Marietta. **1965–70** *DARE* (Qu. H60, *The lumpy white cheese that is made from sour milk*) 50 Infs, **chiefly Nth,** Dutch cheese; (Qu. HH30, *Things that are nicknamed for different nationalities*) Infs **MN**30, **NY**12, 220, **WA**1, 3, 20, 25, Dutch cheese. **1966** Dakin *Dial. Vocab. Ohio R. Valley* 2.344, The New England name *Dutch cheese* predominates in the Marietta [Ohio] area, but appears only in rare scattered instances elsewhere. **1973** Allen *LAUM* 1.292 **scattered Upper MW** (as of c1950), *Cottage cheese*... It is remarkable that 32 of the 76 infs. familiar with *Dutch cheese* declare that for them it is old-fashioned; they no longer use it. Some infs. admit that they retain it for home use only.

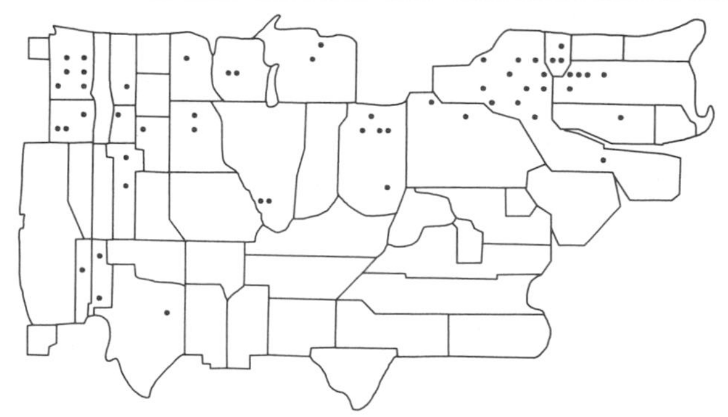

•Dutch cheese (Qq. H60, HH30)

Dutch clover n

Either of two naturalized legumes:

a also *Dutch:* **=white Dutch clover.**

1800 Tatham *Agric. & Commerce* 111 *(DAE),* The soil in which white (or what some in America call *Dutch,* possibly mistaking this for another species, and meaning thereby *German*) clover delights. **1858** (1867) Flint *Milch Cows* 170, White or Dutch Clover *(Trifolium repens).* **1889** Vasey *Ag. Grasses* 82, *Trifolium repens* (White Clover; Dutch Clover). **1889** *Century Dict.* 1805, *Dutch*... The common white clover, *Trifolium repens:* an abbreviation of *Dutch clover.* **1938** Madison *Wild Flowers OH* 70, *White or Dutch Clover*... Fragrant. May–Dec. Fields and waste places. **1968–70** *DARE* (Qu. L9b) Infs **NY**93, **VA**77, Dutch clover. **1973** Hitchcock–Cronquist *Flora Pacific NW* 276, Dutch c[lover]. *T[rifolium] repens.*

b Black medic *(Medicago lupulina).*

1833 Eaton *Botany* 221, *Medicago*... *lupulina* (hop medick, nonesuch, dutch clover.) **1876** Hobbs *Bot. Hdbk.* 33, Dutch clover, Medicago Lupulina.

Dutch courage n

Courage derived from intoxication; liquor; also fig.

1812 in 1853 U.S. Congress *Debates & Proc.* 24.1593 **VA,** The spirit of the people is not up to it [=war] at this time; if so there would be no necessity of those provocations to excite this false spirit—this kind of Dutch courage. **1835** Crockett *Account* 23, I met several gentlemen, and took some refreshment, not passing by a little Dutch courage. Of the latter there was plenty; and I observed the man of the house, when he asked me to drink,.. told me to help myself. **1852** Bristed *Upper Ten Thousand* 153 **NYC,** But then came reflection in the shape of a bottle of true Dutch courage—genuine Knickerbocker Madeira. **1945** Colcord *Sea Language* 70 **ME, Cape Cod, Long Island,** *Dutch courage.* Liquor; from the gin which sailors believed was always served out in the Dutch navy before a battle. **1957** Beck *Folkl. ME* 32, The idea of serpents and tritons and witches are [sic] a shade too real at this hour and this time even with the added Dutch courage of kill devil [=rum] and good company. **1967–68** *DARE* (Qu. HH30, *Things that are nicknamed for different nationalities*) Inf **IN**39, Dutch courage—comes out of a bottle; **NE**11, Dutch courage—when you don't have courage to do what you have to do so you get a couple of stiff drinks to help you.

Dutch crossing n Cf **Dutchman 4**

1917 *DN* 4.420 **sLA,** *Dutch crossing*... A crossing of a street in the middle of a block. [Obsolete.]

Dutch crow n [See quot 1956]

=fish crow 1.

1930 Shoemaker *1300 Words* 19 **cPA Mts** (as of c1900), *Dutch Crow*—The fish crow. **1956** *AmSp* 31.180, Two.. names refer to cries differing from those of a common relative as if the bird had a foreign accent: *Dutch crow* (fish crow, Pa.) and *Dutch whippoorwill* (chuck-will's-widow, S.C., Ala., Ky., Tenn.)

Dutch cuss n [See quots]

An **oxeye** (here: *Chrysanthemum leucanthemum*).

1896 *DN* 1.416 **neNJ,** I have always heard it [=*Dutch cuss*] used, among farming people, as the specific name of the common, or ox-eyed, daisy... [A]n aged.. lady.. gave me an account of the origin of this use. She.. remembered the coming one spring of many Dutch Reformed ministers... Their teams were hitched to the fences... In this place.. sprang up the daisies, which were before unknown, and.. the worst foe the farmers had to fight. **1941** *Torreya* 41.53, *Chrysanthemum leucanthemum*... Dutch-cuss (*i.e.,* curse), New Jersey.

Dutch doughnut n

1967 *DARE* (Qu. H28, *Different shapes or types of doughnuts*) Inf **OR**15, Dutch doughnut—center is translucent instead of a hole, old-fashioned.

Dutcher n [*OED* 1671 →] Cf **Deutscher** n[1]

A person of German descent.

1823 Cooper *Pioneers* 113, The Germans, or "High Dutchers," as they were called, to distinguish them from the original or Low Dutch colonists, were a very peculiar people. **1968** *DARE* (Qu. HH28, . . *People of foreign background—German*) Infs **NJ**12, **WI**62, Dutchers.

Dutch fox n
=**gray fox.**
1930 Shoemaker *1300 Words* 19 **cPA Mts** (as of c1900), *Dutch fox*—The grey fox, or colishay.

Dutch fried potatoes n pl
=**German fried potatoes.**
1967–70 *DARE* (Qu. H47, *Kinds of fried potatoes*) Infs **IL**63, **TX**81, Dutch fried; **PA**63, Dutch—panfried.

Dutch goose n
See quots.
1957 Showalter *Mennonite Cookbook* 75 **PA,** Roasted Pig's Stomach—*Dutch Goose.* **1970** *DARE* (Qu. H45, *Dishes made with meat, fish, or poultry*) Inf **PA**242, Dutch goose—hogmaw, stuffed pig stomach.

Dutch grass n
=**quack grass.**
1930 Sievers *Amer. Med. Plants* 49, *Quack Grass. Agropyron repens. . . Other common names. . .* Dutch grass.

Dutch hawk n
=**duck hawk.**
1951 *AmSp* 26.91, Among other instances [of folk-etymology] in bird names are: . . *Dutch hawk* (Mich.) for the duck hawk or peregrine falcon.

Dutch hill See **Dutch town**

Dutch honey n
1962 *McDavid Coll.* **cwOK,** Dutch honey—cream, brown sugar and white sugar cooked together, brought to boil.

Dutch hop n
See quot 1949.
1949 *PADS* 11.21 **CO,** *Dutch hop. . .* A barn dance; a rather important celebration as after a wedding. **1967** *DARE* (Qu. HH30, *Things that are nicknamed for different nationalities*) Inf **CO**3, Dutch hop—hop-dance.

Dutchified adj [*OED* (at *Dutchify*) 1680 →] *often derog* Cf **Dutchy**
Heavily influenced by German language or culture.
1774 (1961) Adams *Diary* 2.132 **MA,** I strolled, to the Moravian Evening Lecture where we heard soft, sweet Music and a dutchified english Prayer and Preachment. **1948** Weingarten *Suppl. Notes* 16, He said it was the *callathumpians,* (or some such *Dutchiffed* [sic] name,) who always went round New Year. **1971** *Today Show Letters* **sePA,** A delight of Reading area Dutchisms was the way a country or Dutchified person would give directions. **1986** *Amer. Tongues* (Video recording) **sePA,** They call me Dutchified. . . I wouldn't make fun of them because they talk the way they do. . . Why make fun of me because I sound Dutchified? You're dumb—just as soon as it's Dutchified or German, you're dumb.

Dutch in See **Dutch** v **2**

Dutch it See **Dutch** v **1**

Dutch kiss n
See quots.
1950 *WELS Suppl.* **cwWI,** Dutch kiss—the ordinary variety, but one takes hold of the ears of the kissee. Very satisfactory end of a row, since it is exclusively a female's and children's kiss, and the kisser can get one last bit of revenge with a sharp pinch of the lobe. **1950** *WELS* (*Things that are nicknamed for different nationalities*) 1 Inf, **cwWI,** Dutch kiss—hold nose and ear and kiss cheek. **c1960** *Wilson Coll.* **csKY,** Dutch kiss—a stolen kiss or one supposedly stolen. **1967–70** *DARE* (Qu. HH30) Inf **CA**15, Dutch kiss—butt of the head [Inf doubtful]; **IL**138, **NY**102, **PA**118, Dutch kiss.

Dutch leave n
Leave taken without permission or without saying anything.
1898 Harris *Tales Home Folks* 206 **GA,** You've gone and broke the rules and articles of war. . . You took Dutch leave. **1967–68** *DARE* (Qu. Y10, *To leave in a hurry: "Before they find this out, we'd better ______!"*) Inf **MI**68, Take Dutch leave; (Qu. HH30, *Things that are nicknamed for different nationalities*) Inf **NY**34, Dutch leave—to leave without saying anything; **NY**102, Dutch leave—AWOL.

Dutch letter See **letter**

Dutch loaf n
1968 *DARE* FW Addit **MD**18, Dutch loaf—a very large loaf of bread.

Dutch love, hotter than adj phr Also *hot as Dutch love* **Nth**
Usu of weather: very warm; also fig, of intimate relationships: passionate.
1950 *WELS* (*If a day is very hot, you say it's ______.*) 1 Inf, **cWI,** Hotter than Dutch love; 1 Inf, **nwWI,** Hotter than Dutch love in harvest. **1966–70** *DARE* (Qu. B3) Infs **MI**17, 22, **NY**34, **PA**102, **WI**23, 64, Hotter than Dutch love; (Qu. HH30, *Things that are nicknamed for different nationalities*) Inf **MI**44, The weather is hotter than Dutch love; **MI**103, A romance might be called "hotter than Dutch love"; **MN**28, Dutch love—passionate love, "hotter than Dutch love"—not used about weather; **NY**34, Hot as Dutch love; **NY**88, Dutch love—"hotter'n Dutch love" often used when somebody can't figure out what is going on at a neighbor's house, for a gathering that looks hotter'n Dutch love; **NY**123, Dutch love—of coffee, it's hotter than Dutch love; **PA**245, Hotter than Dutch love; **WI**65, Dutch love, hotter than Dutch love; [**CT**37, Dutch love—extra hot]. **1982** *Smithsonian Letters,* My Aunt, who would be about 100 yrs. now, and was descended on both sides from the early Dutch settlers, would say, when walking into a hot kitchen on a summer's day: "Whew, it's hotter'n Dutch love in here." **1988** *DARE* File **NY,** Hotter Than Dutch Love—An expression heard in the Mohawk Valley of New York.

Dutch lunch n Also *Dutch luncheon* **chiefly west of Appalachians** See Map
Usu either a lunch for which each individual pays separately or a simple informal lunch, often served buffet style and consisting of cold meat, cheese, beer, etc. Note: In the following quots it is not always possible to determine which sense is meant.
1904 *Columbus Post-Dispatch* 21 Aug [n.p.] *(DAE),* Dancing was enjoyed by all as was the Dutch lunch which was partaken of at intervals during the evening. **1948** *Dly. Ardmoreite* (Ardmore, Okla.) 12 May 2/5 *(DA),* Carter County Oil Men's association will stage a dutch lunch meeting at Lake Murray state park Thursday night. **1950** *WELS* (*Things that are nicknamed for different nationalities*) 1 Inf, **swWI,** Dutch lunch—crackers and cheese. **1965–70** *DARE* (Qu. HH30, *Things that are nicknamed for different nationalities*) 33 Infs, **chiefly west of Appalachians,** Dutch lunch; **AL**8, **AZ**10, **IL**68, **IN**30, **KS**8, 14, 16, **MA**53, **MN**42, **MS**71, **NE**9, **PA**104, **TN**43, **TX**53, Dutch lunch [*DARE* Ed: Infs indicated this is a lunch at which one pays for one's own meal.]; **MT**1, 2, 3, **SD**5, 8, Dutch lunch—sausage, cheese, (beer), etc; **ID**4, Dutch lunch—beer, cold cuts, etc; **NY**50, Dutch lunch—open sandwich and beer; **ND**1, Dutch lunch—the way Germans made lunch: sausage, cheese, beer; **ND**5, Dutch lunch—beer, sausage, cheese; **SD**2, Dutch lunch—bread, cheese, cold cuts; **TX**4, 28, 43, Dutch lunch—cold cuts, etc; **TX**11, Dutch lunch—sausage, etc; **TX**19, Dutch lunch—beer, cheese, and sausage; **CA**87, Dutch lunch—cheese, milk, etc; **IA**46, Dutch lunch—having a little bit of everything to eat for a meal; **MI**4, Dutch lunch—snack just set out in the kitchen; **MI**28, Dutch lunch—a quick, hurried-up lunch; **MN**35, Dutch lunch—help yourself; **IN**35, Dutch lunch—restaurant lunch; **IN**42, Dutch lunch—free lunch; **MS**6, 49, Dutch luncheon; [**PA**71, Dutch meal; **TN**1, Dutch picnic or dinner—"Dutch" anything means everybody pays for or brings their own; **VA**33, Dutch supper; **TN**53, Dutch plate].

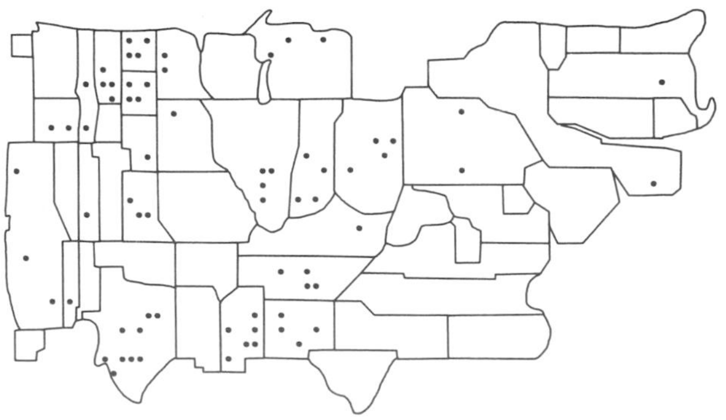
•Dutch lunch + var (Qu. HH30)

Dutchman n [**Dutch** adj **1**]

1 A person of German or German-speaking ancestry. **widespread exc Sth, S Midl** See Map *sometimes derog*

1778 *MD Jrl. & Baltimore Advt.* (MD) 24 Nov [4]/1 **cnMD,** This affidavit-man is a Dutchman, with whom I was obliged to converse by an interpreter. **1852** (1854) Kennedy *Horse-Shoe Robinson* 23 **SC,** I came to one of your pipe-smoking, gin-drinking Hessians, keeping sentry near the road . . —a fellow that had no more watch in him . . —as these Dutchmen hav'n't—than a duck on a rainy day. **1859** *Knickerbocker* 53.403 **NYC,** *The Glasspteen-man* [sic] is almost invariably a German, or, as the profane have it, a Dutchman. **1890** Howells *Boy's Town* 122 **OH,** There was a company of Germans, or Dutchmen, as the boys always called them. **1926** Stoke *Episodes* 188 **cKS** (as of 1870s), "All right, I trade," said the German, "he no look so goot, but he fine horse." . . "Why, you blamed Dutchman, this horse is blind," he exclaimed. **1929** Weygandt *Red Hills* x [PaGer], Our people, home-loving though they are as a race, have their restless elements, and "Dutchmen" with a wanderlust found their way to all corners of the states. **1963** Owens *Look to River* 41 **TX,** He's about the best old Dutchman I ever seen. **1964** *PADS* 42.36 **Chicago IL,** [7 of 31 infs offered *Dutchman* as a derogatory term for a German.] **1965–70** *DARE* (Qu. HH28, *Names and nicknames . . for people of foreign background . . German*) 172 Infs, **widespread exc Sth, S Midl,** Dutchman [*DARE* Ed: 10 of these Infs also offered *Dutchman* for "Hollander"; 33 Infs offered *Dutchman* only in that sense.]; **OK**18, Dutchman—including Hollands, Germans, and Bohemians; **IL**80, **NJ**43, Dumb Dutchman; **LA**46, Squarehead Dutchman. [Of all Infs responding to the question, 64% were old; of those giving these responses, 75% were old.]

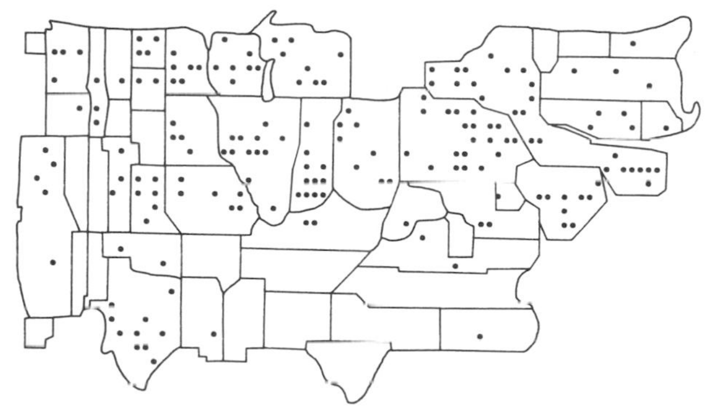

•Dutchman 1 + varr (Qu. HH28)

2 By ext: a foreigner, esp one who speaks English poorly; also used as a vague term of abuse.

1857 Borthwick *3 Yrs. CA* 329, Europeans . . save French, English, and "Eyetalians" are in California classed under the general denomination of Dutchmen, or more frequently "d—d Dutchmen," merely for the sake of euphony. **1894** *DN* 1.341 **wCT,** *Dutchman:* any foreigner who speaks English brokenly or not at all. (Going out of use.) **1898** Westcott *Harum* 253 **cNY,** The 'rig'nal Verjoos come an' settled here some time in the thirties, I reckon. He was some kind of a Dutchman, I guess [Westcott: "Dutchman" was Mr. Harum's generic name for all people native to the Continent of Europe]. **1909** *DN* 3.395 **nwAR,** *Dutchman. . .* Any foreigner who speaks English brokenly or not at all. **1910** Eggleston *Recollections* 3 **sIN,** To us in the West, at least, all foreigners whose mother tongue was other than English were "Dutchmen." **1912** *DN* 3.567 **cNY,** *Dutchman. . .* A person awkward in speech or action. "You're a little Dutchman;" to a child who does not talk plainly. **1915** *DN* 4.226 **wTX,** *Dutchman. . .* Contemptuous name applied to foreigners or to a native one dislikes. **1932** Smiley *Gloss. New Paltz* **seNY,** *Dutchman. . .* A general symbol of a foreigner. **1970** Tarpley *Blinky* 254 **neTX,** *Nicknames for Jewish People*—Dutchmans [offered by less than 7.5% of 200 infs].

3 in phr *I'm a Dutchman:* Used to express the improbability of a preceding statement.

1912 Green *VA Folk-Speech* 161, *Dutchman. . .* "If I do I'm a Dutchman." A mild oath. **1919** Kyne *Capt. Scraggs* 250 **CA,** If this ain't the best idea I ever heard of, I'm a Dutchman. **1952** *Western Folkl.* 11.30, *Well, I'm a Dutchman!* An exclamation of strong incredulity.

4 in phr *make a Dutchman:* To go at a diagonal; to jaywalk. Cf **Dutch crossing**

1970 *DARE* (Qu. MM16) Inf **PA**234, Cut acrosst, jaywalk, make a Dutchman.

5 See quot.

1968 *DARE* (Qu. N30, . . *A sudden short dip in a road*) Inf **MO**25, Dutchman.

Dutchman breeches See **Dutchman's breeches 1**

Dutchman, I'm a See **Dutchman 3**

Dutchman, make a See **Dutchman 4**

Dutchman pipe See **Dutchman's pipe**

Dutchman's anchor n

1945 Colcord *Sea Language* 70 **ME, Cape Cod, Long Island,** *Dutchman's anchor.* Something important that has been forgotten or left behind; from the old jest about a Dutch shipmaster who had forgotten to bring his anchor along, and so lost his ship.

Dutchman's breeches n

1 also *Dutchman breeches, Dutchman's britches, Dutchmen's breeches:* A **bleeding heart 1** (here: *Dicentra cucullaria*). [From the shape of the flower] **chiefly Nth, N Midl** See Map Also called **bachelor's breeches, boys-and-girls 1, boy and girl's pants, breeches flower, butterfly banner(s), colicweed 2a, daddy britches, eardrop 3, fly-flower 2, Indian boys and girls, kitten breeches, lady britches, leather breeches, little boy's breeches, man's breeches, monkshood, old man's britches, pantaloon flower, pearl harlequin, snowboys, soldier's cap, staggerweed, white hearts, yellow breeches**

1830 Rafinesque *Med. Flora* 2.216, *Fumaria cucullaria. . . Colic weed, Dutchman breeches. . .* The decoction purifies the blood. **1928** Aldrich *Lantern* 35 **NE,** She went into the timber to look for anemones and Dutchmen's breeches, for dog-toothed violets and the first signs of Mayflower buds. **1932** *Country Life* 62.67 **sAppalachians,** Most adored of its family by many of us, who so much love the woodland flowers, is Dutchman's-breeches, alias Whitehearts, alias Soldier's-cap, alias Eardrops. **1961** Douglas *My Wilderness* 166 **wNC,** The quaint Dutchman's-breeches was almost in bloom. **1965–70** *DARE* (Qu. S26c) 23 Infs, **chiefly Nth,** Dutchman's britches; **IL**37, **MN**11, 14, **MA**50, **NY**115, **PA**176, 231, Dutchman's breeches; (Qu. S26a) 9 Infs, **chiefly Nth,** Dutchman's britches; (Qu. S3) Infs **IA**12, **IN**76, Dutchman's britches; (Qu. S26b) Infs **IL**33, 135, Dutchman's britches; **IN**54, Dutchman's breeches; (Qu. S26d) Infs **MO**25, **NY**233, Dutchman's britches; (Qu. S26e) Infs **IL**7, **MA**6, **NY**232, **OH**21, 90, **WI**78, Dutchman's britches; **IL**135, **NY**21, Dutchman's breeches. **1976** Bailey–Bailey *Hortus Third* 380, *[Dicentra] cucullaria. . .* Dutchman's-breeches.

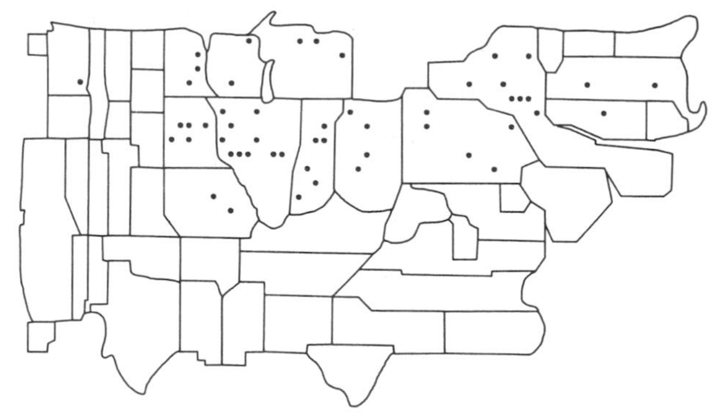

•Dutchman's breeches 1 + var (Qq. S26a, b, c, d, e, S3)

2 A **golden corydalis** (here: *Corydalis aurea*).

1915 (1926) Armstrong–Thornber *Western Wild Flowers* 172, *Golden Corydal* [sic]. . . In the West it is sometimes called Dutchman's Breeches and confused with that plant, but rather absurdly so, for the Dutchman could have only one leg!

3 =**turpentine bloom,** usu *Thamnosma texana.* [From the shape of the fruit] **esp TX**

1936 Whitehouse *TX Flowers* 35, The plant in Texas which is called Dutchman's breeches from the shape of the seed case is *Thamnosma texana.* **1939** Tharp *Vegetation TX* 59, Dutchman's Breeches *(Tham-*

nosma). **1960** Vines *Trees SW* 593, *Thamnosma texana*. . . is also known under the vernacular names of Turpentine Bloom, . . or Dutchman's Breeches, for the oddly shaped fruit. **1970** Correll *Plants TX* 908, *Thamnosma*. . . *Dutchman's Breeches*. . . Fruit . . in the shape of inflated "dutchman's breeches" with the legs projected upward.

4 See quot.

1911 *Century Dict. Suppl., Dutchman's-breeches*. . . The streaks of blue sky seen between the alto-stratus clouds after a storm begins to abate.

5 in phr *enough blue sky to make a pair of Dutchman's breeches* and varr: Clear sky, the promise of fair weather.

1945 Colcord *Sea Language* 70 **ME, Cape Cod, Long Island,** A small patch of blue sky at the end of a storm is spoken of as "enough to make a Dutchman a pair of breeches." **1950** *WELS Suppl.* **swWI,** "Blue to make a Dutchman's breeches." Heard in 1927–28 said by a lady born and grown up in Pennsylvania. *Ibid* **csWI,** There is enough blue sky to make a pair of Dutchman's breeches—clearing weather. *Ibid* **cwWI,** If you find a patch of blue big enough to make a Dutchman's breeches, it will clear up. **1968** *DARE* (Qu. B7, *When clouds begin to decrease, you say it's* ______) Inf **OH**63, Enough blue to make a Dutchman's breeches. [**1975** Gould *ME Lingo* 84, The first showing of blue sky when a storm clears. . . "There's enough blue sky to make a *Dutchman* a pair of *pants*."]

‡6 See quot.

1968 *DARE* (Qu. H28, *Different shapes or types of doughnuts*) Inf **VA**26, Dutchman's britches.

Dutchman's britches See **Dutchman's breeches 1**

Dutchman's horse n

1950 *WELS* (*A horse with his tail cut short is called a* ______) 1 Inf, **csWI,** Dutchman's horse.

Dutchman's measure n

=**lagniappe.**

1967 *DARE* (Qu. U15, *When you're buying something, if the seller puts in a little extra to make you feel that you're getting a good bargain, you call that* ______) Inf **TX**35, Dutchman's measure.

Dutchman's nose n

=**pope's nose.**

1968 *DARE* (Qu. K73, . . *The rump of a cooked chicken*) Inf **AL**43, Dutchman's nose.

Dutchman's pipe n [From the shape of the flower]

1 also *Dutchman pipe:* =**birthwort 1,** esp *Aristolochia durior.*

1845 (1849) Phelps *Lectures on Botany* 76/1, *Aristolochia sipho,* (Dutchman's pipe), . . A vine climbing over large trees. Flowers solitary, brown. **1861** Wood *Class-Book* 602, *A. Sipho*. . . *Dutchman's Pipe*. . . Flowers . . bent at nearly a right angle, in the form of a (siphon or) tobacco pipe. **1905** Valentine *H. Sandwith* 26 *(DAE),* The house had . . small hooded doorways, over which in summer-time Dutchman's pipe and pea-vines clambered. **1931** Harned *Wild Flowers Alleghanies* 148, Dutchman's Pipe. . . is said to closely resemble the old-fashioned Dutch pipe, with its greenish-yellow veiny tube and a flattened, 3-lobed purple-brown throat. **1949** Moldenke *Amer. Wild Flowers* 23, Best known is the dutchmanspipe. . . Blooming from May to June, it may be expected in rich woods from southern Pennsylvania to Minnesota, south to Kansas and Georgia. **1961** Douglas *My Wilderness* 172 **wNC,** They were intertwined with a vine called the *aristolochia,* or Dutchman's-pipe, whose stem was nearly two inches thick. **1968** *DARE* (Qu. S26c) Inf **PA**176, Dutchman pipe. **1971** Krochmal *Appalachia Med. Plants* 64, *Aristolochia serpentaria*. . . Dutchman's pipe. . . Brownish pipe-like flowers grow from base of the plant stem. **1976** Bailey–Bailey *Hortus Third* 108, *[Aristolochia] durior*. . . Dutchman's pipe.

2 =**Indian pipe.**

c1873 in 1976 Miller *Shaker Herbs* 173, Indian Pipe. . . Dutchman's Pipe. **1894** *Jrl. Amer. Folkl.* 7.93 **NJ,** *Monotropa uniflora*. . . Dutchman's pipe. **1900** Lyons *Plant Names* 252, *M[onotropa] uniflora*. . . Dutchman's-pipe. **1966** *DARE* (Qu. S26e) Inf **MA**6, Dutchman's pipe, pipe plant. **1966–67** *DARE* Wildfl QR Pl.152b Infs **AR**45, **WA**30, Dutchman's pipe.

3 A **virgin's bower** (here: *Clematis ochroleuca*). Cf **Indian pipe**

1966 *DARE* Wildfl QR Pl.74 Inf **CO**11, Granddaddy's pipe—Dutchman's pipe.

Dutchman's quail n

=**flicker** n² **1.**

1956 *AmSp* 31.181 **KY,** Most of the monickers . . are derisive . . , attaching the name of some race to a bird deemed inferior as food or game. . . Dutchman's quail. Yellow-shafted flicker.

Dutchman's razor n Cf **cut one's foot**

See quots.

1912 Green *VA Folk-Speech* 161, *Dutchman's razor*. . . When a person treads in dung he is said to cut his foot with a Dutchman's razor. **1950** *WELS Suppl.* **cwWI,** When barefooted children step in cow manure they say "I cut my foot on a Dutchman's razor." **1962** Bailey *Jayhawker* 65 **KS,** The clay pigeons they did not hit were smashed to bits when they struck the hard ground; a few landed in tufts of soft grass, or on a Dutchman's razor.

Dutch measles n

Prob German measles.

1950 *WELS (Common itching diseases)* 1 Inf, **seWI,** Dutch measles.

Dutchmen's breeches See **Dutchman's breeches 1**

‡Dutch mess n

1967 *DARE* (Qu. H50, *Dishes made with beans, peas, or corn*) Inf **MO**38, Dutch messes—any strange concoction of various foods mixed together.

Dutch milk n *joc*

Beer.

1905 *DN* 3.78 **nwAR,** *Dutch milk*. . . Beer. 'You can get Dutch milk by express.' **1967** *DARE* (Qu. DD25, . . *Nicknames . . for beer*) Inf **OR**15, Dutch milk.

Dutch morgan n [*EDD* (at *Dutch* adj. 1. (9))] Cf **Dutch cuss**

An **oxeye** (here: *Chrysanthemum leucanthemum*).

1900 Lyons *Plant Names* 99, *C. Leucanthemum*. . . Dutch morgan. **1940** Clute *Amer. Plant Names* 79, *Ox-eye Daisy*. . . Dutch morgan. **1959** Carleton *Index Herb. Plants* 40, *Dutch morgan:* Chrysanthemum leucanthemum.

Dutch myrtle n

=**sweet gale.**

1824 Bigelow *Florula Bostoniensis* 366, *Myrica Gale*. . . *Dutch Myrtle*. A branching shrub, about four or five feet in height. **1847** Wood *Class-Book* 500, *Dutch Myrtle*. . . Fruit and leaves, when crushed, with a pungent, spicy odor. **1876** Hobbs *Bot. Hdbk.* 73, Myrtle, Dutch, Meadow fern, Myrica gale. **1910** Graves *Flowering Plants* 143 **CT,** Dutch . . Myrtle. . . The leaves and buds are aromatic and medicinal. **1940** Clute *Amer. Plant Names* 159, *Sweet Gale*. . . Dutch myrtle. **1974** (1977) Coon *Useful Plants* 190, Dutch myrtle. . . is a low shrub growing on moist peaty soils.

Dutch nickel n

See quots.

1949 *PADS* 11.6 **wTX** (as of c1900), *Dutch nickel*. . . A hug. **c1960** *Wilson Coll.* **csKY,** *Dutch nickel*. . . A kiss, presumably stolen. Called also a *Yankee dime.* **1969** *DARE* (Qu. HH30, *Things that are nicknamed for different nationalities*) Inf **MO**32, Dutch nickel.

Dutch nightingale n *joc* Cf **Irish nightingale**

=**bullfrog 1.**

1942 Berrey–Van den Bark *Amer. Slang* 120.33, Dutch nightingale, *a bull frog.*

Dutch pike n *hist*

A **bullhead 1b.**

1856 *Spirit of Times* 20 Sept 43/2 **IL,** Kentucky counted up two catfish (dutch pike) one shiner, three half-grown minnows, a dogfish and one gar. **1857** *Porter's Spirit of Times* 3 Jan 286/1 **IL,** We [rea]ched it [Long Lake] in good season for fishing . . and our only reward was three or four bull-headed cats (dutch pike), and two or three shiners.

Dutch quarter n

1970 *DARE* (Qu. HH30, *Things that are nicknamed for different nationalities*) Inf **AR**56, Dutch quarter—kick another in the posterior.

Dutch rub n **chiefly N Midl** See Map Cf **dry shave**

The act of rubbing someone's scalp vigorously, usu with the knuckles, as a prank or punishment.

1938 Stuart *Dark Hills* 17 **KY,** He reached out with the handle part of his cane and hooked me around the neck. . . drew me over to him and gave me what he called the "dutch-rub". . . rubbing his fist over my head. **1963** Burroughs *Head-First* 98, Here I again took Delavan down and treated him to so thorough a "Dutch rub" (vigorously massaging your antagonist's scalp with the knuckles of your closed fist) . . that his eyes filled with tears. **1965–70** *DARE* (Qu. HH30, *Things that are nicknamed for different nationalities*) 34 Infs, **chiefly N Midl,** Dutch rub; **AR**56, Dutch rub—doubling the fist and rubbing the head of a child; **CA**32, Dutch rub—bare knuckle on head; **IL**113, Dutch rub—with whiskers; **IL**116, Dutch rub—vigorous knuckle rub on scalp; **IN**42, Dutch rub—where they rub your head; **PA**161, Dutch rub—rub head with knuckles; **SD**5, Dutch rub—rub with knuckles; **WV**4, Dutch rub—vigorous rub with the fist on the head. [28 of 42 Infs male]

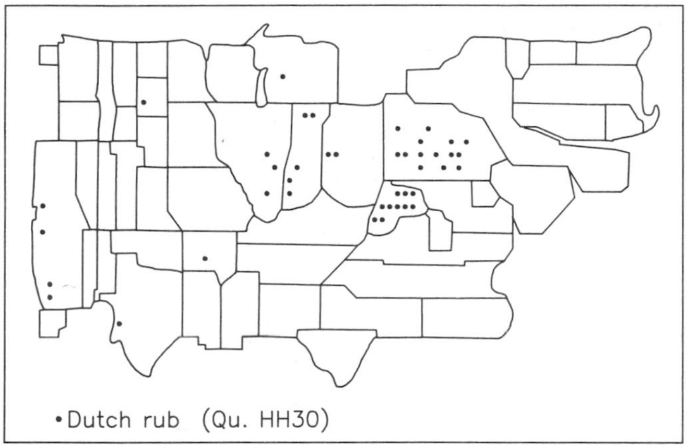

Dutch rush n
A **horsetail 1** (here: *Equisetum hyemale*).
1868 (1870) Gray *Field Botany* 359, *E[quisetum] hyemale,* Dutch Rushes. **1900** Lyons *Plant Names* 147, *E[quisetum] hyemale* . . Dutch Rush. **1918** Farrow *Dict. Military Terms, Gunbright,* Dutch rush *(Equisetum hyemale)* much used in scouring gun barrels. **1973** Hitchcock-Cronquist *Flora Pacific NW* 43, Dutch rush, . . *E[quisetum] hyemale.*

Dutch salad n
1960 Korson *Black Rock* 200 **PA,** "Dutch salad" . . is a regional adaptation of what residents of Allentown, Bethlehem, Reading, and Lancaster know as dandelion salad. It is made with young tender plants eaten in the early spring. . . a hot bacon dressing is used.

Dutch settlement See **Dutch town**

Dutch shelf n
1968 *DARE* (Qu. E6, *A small shelf hanging on the wall with small decorative articles on it*) Inf **NY**77, Knickknack shelf, Dutch shelf.

Dutch snipe n
=**dowitcher.** Note: This word may derive from misunderstanding of quot 1888.
[1888 [see **German snipe**].] **1916** *Times-Picayune* (New Orleans LA) 2 Apr mag sec 5/7 **LA,** *Dowitcher* (Macrorhamphus griseus). Dutch Snipe.

Dutch squeeze n Cf **Dutch kiss**
1968 *DARE* (Qu. HH30, *Things that are nicknamed for different nationalities*) Inf **MO**35, Dutch squeeze—a hug.

Dutch town n Also *Dutch hill, ~ settlement* **esp N Cent**
A section of a city populated primarily by persons of Dutch or German heritage.
1967–69 *DARE* (Qu. C34, *Nicknames for nearby settlements, villages, or districts*) Infs **KS**1, **OH**29, **IN**62, **NY**123, Dutch settlement (*or* town); **OH**59, 79, **MI**81, Dutch town (*or* hill); (Qu. II25, . . *Nicknames for the part of a town where the poorer people, special groups, or foreign groups live*) Infs **IA**9, **MI**51, 81, Dutch town.

Dutch treat See **Dutch** adv

Dutch wedding n
1936 *Jrl. Amer. Folkl.* 49.203 **Ozarks,** The game called "Dutch Wedding" begins in this wise: A girl sits down on the floor and chooses a male partner to sit beside her. Then he chooses another girl . . and so on until all the players are seated on the floor so as to form a circle. Then the first girl holds a dime between her lips, and passes it to her partner who must receive it with *his* lips. . . Then he passes it on to the next girl, and so forth. If the coin is dropped it must be returned to the original player, and started on its course anew.

Dutch wheelbarrow n
1890 *DN* 1.63 **KY,** A "Dutch wheelbarrow" is made by taking a boy by the ankles and holding his legs up in the air, and letting him walk on his hands.

Dutch whippoorwill n **chiefly Sth**
=**chuck-will's-widow.**
1932 Howell *FL Bird Life* 297, *Antrostomus carolinensis*. . . Dutch Whip-poor-will. [*Ibid* 298, The Chuck-will's-widow is. . . very frequently confused under the name of the latter species [=whippoorwill], and few people in the South realize that they are not the same.] **1950** *PADS* 14.28 **SC,** *Dutch whippoorwill*. . . The chuck-will's-widow. **1955** Forbush-May *Birds* 279, *Chuck-will's-widow*. . . *Other names:* Dutch . . Whip-poor-will. **1956** [see **Dutch crow**]. **1962** Imhof *AL Birds* 314, *Chuck-will's-widow*. . . *Other Names:* . . Dutch Whip-poor-will. **1963** TN Folk Lore Soc. *Bulletin* 29.4.82, The Chuckwill's-widow was a *Dutch Whippoorwill* to many people.

Dutch whistle n
Among loggers: see quot.
1950 *Western Folkl.* 9.117 **nwOR** [Logger speech], *Dutch whistle.* A piece of bark lying with the slippery side down; an unwary logger stepping on it may have his feet shoot out from under him with surprising suddenness.

Dutchy adj
1 Characteristically German or Dutch; hence adv *Dutchy. derog* Cf **Dutch** adj **1**
1862 in 1893 Gray *Letters* 495 **cNY,** I was . . copying out Grisebach's manuscripts for the printer (for the printer won't touch the Dutchy-looking thing). **1935** [see **get awake**]. **1947** *WELS Suppl.* 1 Inf, **csWI,** "She refers to her hair as 'they' and pronounces many words with a slight German accent"—referring to a woman who "talks Dutchy." **1973** *DARE* File **csWI,** They talk kind of Dutchy—"Dem," "Dese and dose," "Tunder and lightning." **1975** *Studies in Honor of Kasten* 29 **swIL,** *Dutchy* . . person or thing of German origin insufficiently Americanized (rustic, in poor taste, crude). Used especially by urban persons of German origin.
2 By ext: low-class, slovenly, dowdy.
1901 *DN* 2.139 **swME, eNY,** *Dutchy*. . . Slovenly; unkempt; the same as tacky. *Ibid* **wNY,** *Dutchy*. . . Loud, of ill-matched colors. **1941** *LANE* Map 466 *(Slovenly)* 1 inf, **csCT,** Dutchy. **1967–68** *DARE* (Qu. W41, . . *Someone whose clothes never look right or who always dresses carelessly*) Infs **CO**27, **IL**19, **IA**46, **WI**18, 50, (Looks) Dutchy. **1967** *DARE* FW Addit **sePA,** Anything looked down on is called *Dutchy* or *Dutch.* **1969** *DARE* FW Addit **cIA,** *Dutchy*—dowdy in dress, frumpy looking. **1989** *DARE* File **cIA** (as of 1960s), My mother, nostrils flaring slightly, would say that a person looked "Dutchy." By this she meant that the person's clothes were cheap-looking and worn without grace.

du tell See **do tell**

Dutton corn n
A var of **Indian corn.**
1838 Ellsworth *Valley Upper Wabash* 47, If you send to your son any grains, I wish half a bushel . . of 'Dutton corn.' **1856** U.S. Patent Office *Annual Rept. for 1855: Ag.* 166, *"Dutton Corn"* . . is cultivated in Massachusetts. It has a small yellow kernel and a large cob, weighing 830 grains. **1894** (1934) Robinson *Danvis Folks* 37 **VT,** I druther hev a peck o' Dutton corn, yis, er Tucket, than a bushel o' their hoss-tooth corn.

duv See **dive**

dwaddle v, hence vbl n *dwaddling* Also *dwiddle* [Perh blends of *dawdle* or **diddle** v **5** + *twiddle*]
To waste time.
1950 *WELS (Wasting time by doing unimportant or useless things)* 2 Infs, **WI,** Dwaddling. **1967–69** *DARE* (Qu. A9, . . *Wasting time by not working on the job*) Inf **IN**69, Dwaddling ['dwɑdləŋ]; (Qu. A11, *When somebody takes too long about coming to a decision, you might say, "I wish he'd quit ______."*) Inf **TX**10, Dwiddling.

dwale n
A **bittersweet** (here: *Solanum dulcamara*).

1900 Lyons *Plant Names* 349, *S[olanum] Dulcamara* . . Bittersweet . . Dwale. **1930** Sievers *Amer. Med. Plants* 11, *Bitter Nightshade — Solanum dulcamara* . . Other common names.—Bittersweet . . dwale, skawcoo.

dwarf alder n

1 A buckthorn (here: *Rhamnus alnifolia*).

1822 Eaton *Botany* 426, *Rhamnus franguloides,* dwarf alder . . Berries black. **1896** *Bot. Gaz.* 22.478, Rhamnus . . dwarf alder, West. **1911** *Century Dict. Suppl., Alder*[1] . . . *Dwarf alder.* (a) The alder-leafed buckthorn, *Rhamnus alnifolia.* (b) A shrub of the genus *Fothergilla,* of the southeastern United States.

2 =**witch alder.**

1900 Lyons *Plant Names* 163, *F[othergilla] Carolina* . . Eastern U.S., called . . Dwarf Alder. **1903** Small *Flora SE U.S.* 509, *Fothergilla* . . Dwarf Alder. **1908** Britton *N. Amer. Trees* 410, In addition to the arborescent genus that occurs in our area, the genus of shrubs, *Fothergilla,* known as Dwarf alder, which occurs only in eastern North America, from Virginia southward, is represented by three species. **1911** [see **1** above]. **1940** Clute *Amer. Plant Names* 147, *F[othergilla] Gardeni.* Witch Alder. Dwarf alder.

dwarf ash n

1 The single-leaf ash *(Fraxinus anomala).*

1897 Sudworth *Arborescent Flora* 325, *Fraxinus anomala* . . Dwarf Ash (Ariz., Utah). **1960** Vines *Trees SW* 862, *Fraxinus* . . *anomala* . . Vernacular names are Dwarf Ash and Fresno. **1979** Little *Checklist U.S. Trees* 134.

2 A **hop tree** (here: *Ptelea trifoliata*).

1946 *Nat. Hist.* 55.143/1, The pretty little tree or shrub known scientifically as *Ptelea trifoliata* has many peculiarities and many names. . . Some people think it resembles the ash and call it Dwarf or Wafer Ash. **1951** *PADS* 15.15, *Ptelea trifoliata.* . . Dwarf ash.

3 =**goutweed.**

1940 Clute *Amer. Plant Names* 100, *A[egopodium] podagraria.* . . Dwarf ash.

dwarf birch n

A shrubby birch, as **scrub birch, a swamp birch** (here: *Betula pumila*), or *Betula nana* which is also called **buckbrush 3n.**

1950 Stevens *ND Plants* 115, *Betula pumila,* var. *glandulifera.* . . *Dwarf Birch.* Small shrub, 1–2 m. high in thick clumps. **1966** Grimm *Recognizing Native Shrubs* 91, *Dwarf Birch. Betula glandulosa.* . . A leaf-losing shrub 1 to 6 feet high. **1972** Viereck–Little *AK Trees* 130, *Dwarf Arctic Birch* (*Betula nana* L.) Other names: dwarf birch, dwarf alpine birch. . . *Resin Birch* (*Betula glandulosa* Michx.) Other names: . . dwarf birch. **1976** Bailey–Bailey *Hortus Third* 160, *[Betula] glandulosa.* . . Dwarf birch. **1977** *New Yorker* 9 May 94/1 **AK,** The trails would go along, well cut and stamped out through moss campion, reindeer moss, sedge tussocks, crowberries, prostrate willows, dwarf birch, bog blueberries . . ; then, abruptly, and for no apparent reason, the trails would disappear.

dwarf chinquapin oak See **chinquapin oak**

dwarf cornel n

=**bunchberry 1.**

1848 Gray *Manual of Botany* 168, *C[ornus] Canadensis* . . Dwarf Cornel. **1900** Lyons *Plant Names* 118, *C[ornus] Canadensis* . . Dwarf Cornel. **1940** Clute *Amer. Plant Names* 97. **1950** Stevens *ND Plants* 220. **1967** *DARE* FW Addit **MA5**, Bunchberry is also called dwarf cornel. **1976** Bailey–Bailey *Hortus Third* 314, *Cornus canadensis* . . Bunchberry, Dwarf Cornel.

dwarf dandelion n

1 A plant of the genus *Krigia.* Also called **goatsbeard 3.** For other names of var spp see **false dandelion, goat dandelion 1, potato dandelion**

1889 *Century Dict.* 1451, Dwarf dandelion, of the United States, *Krigia Virginica.* **1895** Gray–Bailey *Field Botany* 256, *Krigia,* Dwarf Dandelion. **1930** OK Univ. Biol. Surv. *Pub.* 2.1.85, *Krigia dandelion.* . . Dwarf Dandelion. . . *Krigia occidentalis.* . . Western Dwarf Dandelion. . . *Krigia virginica.* . . Eastern Dwarf Dandelion. **1961** Smith *MI Wildflowers* 435, *Dwarf Dandelion.* . . Heads yellow, solitary at the end of the slender flowering stem. **1976** Bailey–Bailey *Hortus Third* 628, *Krigia.* . . Dwarf dandelion.

2 A **desert dandelion** (here: *Malacothrix californica*).

1949 Moldenke *Amer. Wild Flowers* 182, The *California dwarfdandelion* . . has . . heads . . canary-yellow in color.

dwarf elder n

A **sarsaparilla** (here: *Aralia hispida*).

1792 Belknap *Hist. NH* 3.187, A hint was taken to make use of elder, and especially the dwarf elder, as a means of preserving the seeding leaves of young esculent vegetables, and even the branches of trees, from being destroyed by insects. **c1873** in 1976 Miller *Shaker Herbs* 168, *Elder, dwarf. Aralia hispida*—Very valuable in dropsy, gravel, suppression of urine, and other urinary disorders. **1876** Hobbs *Bot. Hdbk.* 34, Elder, Dwarf, Aralia hispida. **1940** Clute *Amer. Plant Names* 96, *Bristly sarsaparilla.* . . Dwarf elder. **1950** Gray–Fernald *Manual of Botany* 1077, *Dwarf-elder.* . . Leaves twice pinnate; leaflets oblong-ovate, acute, cut-serrate.

dwarf huckleberry n

1 A **huckleberry 1** (here: *Gaylussacia dumosa*).

1848 Gray *Manual of Botany* 259, *G. dumosa.* . . *Dwarf huckleberry.* . . Sandy low soil. . . Fruit insipid. **1901** Mohr *Plant Life AL* 657, *Gaylussacia dumosa.* . . Dwarf Huckleberry. **1931** Harned *Wild Flowers Alleghanies* 374, *Dwarf or Bush Huckleberry.* . . Fruit black, without bloom, insipid. **1953** Greene–Blomquist *Flowers South* 92, Dwarf-huckleberry is a common low shrub of dry sandy soil of the Coastal Plain areas. **1964** Batson *Wild Flowers SC* 129, Plants less than 2 ft. tall, from long horizontal stems. . . Dwarf Huckleberry.

2 A **blueberry 1** (here: *Vaccinium caespitosum*).

1961 Peck *Manual OR* 596, *V. caespitosum.* . . *Dwarf Huckleberry.* . . In sphagnum bogs along the coast. **1973** Hitchcock–Cronquist *Flora Pacific NW* 350, Dwarf h[uckleberry]. . . *V. caespitosum.*

dwarf laurel n

1 A **sheep laurel** (here: *Kalmia angustifolia*).

1770 J.R. Forster tr. P. Kalm *Travels N. Amer.* II.215 *(DAE),* Dwarf laurel *(Kalmia angustifolia).* **1876** Hobbs *Bot. Hdbk.* 184, *Kalmia angustifolia* var. *ovata,* Dwarf laurel. **1911** *Century Dict. Suppl., Laurel* . . —*Dwarf laurel,* the sheep-laurel, *Kalmia angustifolia.*

2 A **sweet bay** (here: *Magnolia virginiana*).

1854 Simms *Woodcraft* 151 **SC,** A clump of bays, or dwarf laurel, interposed to receive him.

3 A **rhododendron** (here: *Rhododendron minus*).

1860 Curtis *Cat. Plants NC* 97, Dwarf Laurel. *(R[hododendron] punctatum.)* **1901** Lounsberry *S. Wild Flowers* 381, *Rhododendron punctatum,* . . dwarf laurel, dotted-leaved rhododendron, is the smallest of our evergreen species.

dwarf maple n

Std: a western **maple** (here: *Acer glabrum*). Also called **mountain maple, rock maple, Rocky Mountain maple, Sierra maple, soft maple**

dwarf myrtle n

A **wax myrtle** (here: *Myrica pusilla*).

1927 Boston Soc. Nat. Hist. *Proc.* 213, *Shrubs.* . . *Myrica pumila* [sic]. Dwarf myrtle.

dwarf palmetto n

1 A fan-leaved palm *(Sabal minor).* **chiefly SE** Also called **blue palmetto 2, bluestem 4, scrub palmetto, swamp palmetto**

1860 Curtis *Cat. Plants NC* 65, *Dwarf Palmetto.* . . This is but 3 or 4 feet high, never forming a trunk like the preceding. **1901** Mohr *Plant Life AL* 96, Dwarf or blue palmetto *(Sabal adansonii).* **1933** Small *Manual SE Flora* 240, *Dwarf-palmetto.* . . More frequently browsed by cattle than any other palm. **1964** Batson *Wild Flowers SC* 26, *Dwarf palmetto.* . . Low palm usually from underground stem but sometimes from low trunk. **1969** *DARE* File, Dwarf palmetto, plant common on Hatteras Island, N.C. **1976** Bailey–Bailey *Hortus Third* 991.

2 =**blue palmetto 1.**

1951 *PADS* 15.9, *Rhaphidophyllum hystrix.* . . Dwarf . . palmetto.

3 A **yucca** (here: *Yucca gloriosa*).

1900 Lyons *Plant Names* 401, *Y. gloriosa.* . . Dwarf Palmetto.

dwarf plum n

A **wild plum** (here: either *Prunus minutifolia* or *P. pumila*).

1951 *PADS* 15.33 **TX,** *Prunus minutifolia.* . . Dwarf . . plum. **1960** Vines *Trees SW* 390, *Prunus pumila.* . . Vernacular names are Dwarf Plum and Peach Plum.

dwarf Queen Anne's lace n

=**prairie lace.**

1936 Whitehouse *TX Flowers* 87, *Dwarf Queen Anne's Lace (Bifora americana)*. . . The umbrella-clusters of white flowers are very showy.

dwarf rhododendron n

A **rhododendron** (here: *Rhododendron minus*).

1961 Douglas *My Wilderness* 175 **wNC,** Higher up, dwarf or Carolina rhododendron shows rose-pink flowers along the trail. At times this low shrub grows so thick it crowds the trail. **1964** Campbell *Great Smoky Wildflowers* 48, The dwarf rhododendron *(R. minus)* . . is the only one of the three evergreen rhododendrons with short leaves (3 or 4 inches long).

dwarf Solomon's seal n Also *dwarf Solomon seal*

=**false lily of the valley.**

1822 Eaton *Botany* 248, *[Convallaria] bifolia* . . dwarf solomon seal. . . Flowers tetrandrous. **1840** MA Zool. & Bot. Surv. *Herb. Plants & Quadrupeds* 212, *C. bifolia*. . . Dwarf Solomon's Seal. . . Spreads over the woods on hills and valleys. **1931** Fassett *Spring Flora* 31 **WI,** *Dwarf Solomon's Seal. M[aianthemum] canadense*. . . Northern, south to Dane and Iowa Counties.

dwarf sumac n

Std: a common **sumac** *(Rhus copallina)* native to the eastern half of the US. Also called **mountain sumac, red sumac, shoemaker berry, smooth sumac, sourball bush, upland sumac, varnish sumac, winged sumac**

dwarf sunfish n

=**orangespotted sunfish.**

1956 Harlan–Speaker *IA Fish* 136, *Lepomis humilis*. . . Dwarf sunfish. . . Very few people actually fish for the orangespotted sunfish because of its small size. Many are taken, however, since they are everywhere in shallow water and have ravenous appetites. **1983** Becker *Fishes WI* 840, *Orangespotted Sunfish*. . . Other common names . . dwarf sunfish.

dwarf sunflower n

1 =**bitterweed** (here: *Hymenoxys* spp).

1959 Carleton *Index Herb. Plants* 40, *Dwarf sunflower:* Hymenoxys (v).

2 =**mule-ears.**

1961 Peck *Manual OR* 806. **1963** Craighead *Rocky Mt. Wildflowers* 235, Mule-ears *Wyethia amplexicaulis*. . . Other names: Smooth Dwarf Sunflower.

dwarf tiger lily n

=**blackberry lily.**

1892 *Jrl. Amer. Folkl.* 5.103, *Belamcanda Chinensis,* dwarf tiger-lily. Mansfield, O. **1940** Clute *Amer. Plant Names* 147, *Blackberry Lily*. . . Dwarf tiger-lily. **1959** Carleton *Index Herb. Plants* 40, *Dwarf-tiger-lily:* Belamcanda chinensis.

dwarf white morning-glory See **baby morning-glory**

d.w.i. n Usu |ˈdi ˈdʌbl̩ju ˈaɪ|; also |ˈdi wi| Pronc-sp *deewee* [Abbr for *driving while intoxicated*] **scattered, but chiefly Sth, S Midl, TX** See Map

1965–70 *DARE* (Qu. N13, *If someone has been drinking and then drives a car, he may be arrested for:*) 65 Infs, **scattered, but chiefly Sth, S Midl, TX,** D.w.i. [32 of 65 Infs young or mid-aged] **1970** *Time* 5 Jan 32/1 **AZ,** He persuaded municipal judges to order hundreds of local citizens convicted of D.W.I. (Driving While Intoxicated) to attend his four-week course or face the loss of their operator's license. *Ibid* 32/2, The D.W.I. offender is generally an individual under pressure, anxious about financial or domestic troubles. **1988** *NADS Letters* **csMI,** *D.w.i.—seems to be the common term in southern lower Michigan;* **Los Angeles CA,** *Deewee* (pronounced [ˈdi:wi]) seemed to be the most common abbreviation for "driving while intoxicated" or "D.W.I.," with *D.U.I.,* for "driving under the influence," running a close second.

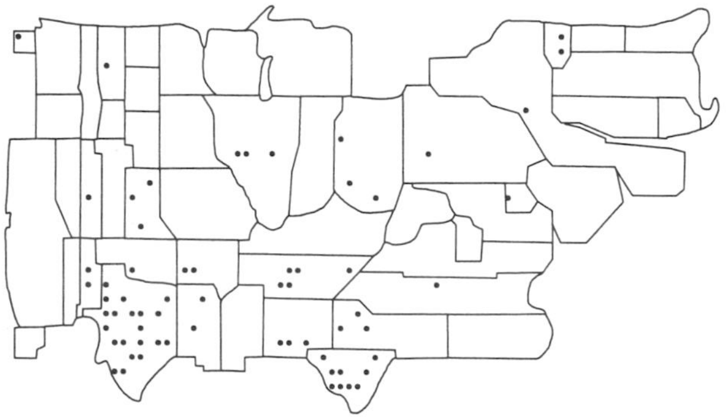

•d.w.i. (Qu. N13)

dwiddle See **dwaddle**

dwindle v Also with *out*

1914 *DN* 4.72 **ME, nNH,** *Dwindle (out)*. . . Spend. "She's allus dwindlin' out her pension."

dwindles n pl

A process of wasting away from illness or old age.

1936 Morehouse *Rain on Just* 21 **NC,** For time unbeknownst, she [=a very old woman] had been perishing of the dwindles. **1984** Wilder *You All Spoken Here* 207 **Sth,** Dwindles: A wasting away, as in "He's dying of the dwindles."

‡dworthy adj

1969 *DARE* (Qu. BB38, *When a person doesn't look healthy, or looks as if he hadn't been well for some time, you'd say, "He looks ________."*) Inf MO39, [ˈdworθi] [FW query].

dye bark n

=**elephant tree.**

1941 Jaeger *Wildflowers* 142 **Desert SW,** Elephant tree, torote, dye bark. . . The bark exudes a red sap which is used in dyeing.

dyebush See **dyeleaves 1**

dye flower n

A coreopsis (*Coreopsis* spp).

1894 *Jrl. Amer. Folkl.* 7.92, *Coreopsis,* sp., . . dye-flowers, Banner Elk, N.C. **1969** *DARE* (Qu. S26d) Inf **GA**70, Dye flowers are yellow.

dyeleaves n

1 also *dyebush:* =**sweetleaf.** [See quot 1960]

1894 *Jrl. Amer. Folkl.* 7.94, *Symplocos tinctoria,* . . dye-leaves, Banner Elk, N.C. **1940** Clute *Amer. Plant Names* 114, *Sweet-leaf*. . . Dye-leaves. **1950** Peattie *Nat. Hist. Trees* 552, At Saluda, North Carolina, a recipe is given for dyeing wool yellow with the leaves of Dyebush, as the native craftsmen prefer to call it. **1960** Vines *Trees SW* 840, A tincture, or dye, is made from the leaves and roots. . . Vernacular names are . . Dye-leaves, and Horse-sugar.

2 An **inkberry** (here: *Ilex glabra*).

1900 Lyons *Plant Names* 199, *I[lex] glabra*. . . Dye-leaves. **1960** Vines *Trees SW* 652, Inkberry Holly. . . Also known as Appalachian Tea, . . and Dye-leaves.

dyeroot n [From its use as a dye]

A **redroot** (here: *Lachnantes caroliniana*).

1933 Small *Manual SE Flora* 358, Herbs with colored rootstocks. . . *G. tinctoria*. . . Dye-root.

dyeroot puccoon n

A **puccoon** (here: *Lithospermum carolinense*) whose root is used as a source of dye.

1951 *PADS* 15.39 **TX,** *Lithospermum gmelinii*. . . Pineywood, or dye-root, puccoon.

dyer's oak n [See quot 1950]

A **black oak** (here: *Quercus velutina*).

1897 Sudworth *Arborescent Flora* 169, *Quercus velutina*. . . *Common Names*. . . Dyer's Oak (Tex.) **1908** Britton *N. Amer. Trees* 290, [Black oak] is also called Yellow oak, . . Dyer's oak, . . and Spotted Oak. **1950** Peattie *Nat. Hist. Trees* 225, Dyer's . . Oak. *Ibid* 226, In the old days, before the invention of aniline dyes, the intense yellow color this [=inner bark] produced was an important article of commerce, and native weavers may still use it in the Appalachian coves. **1960** Vines *Trees SW* 191, *Quercus velutina*. . . Vernacular names are Dyers Oak [etc] . . The inner bark yields . . a yellow dye for woolen goods.

dyer's weed n Also *dyeweed*

A **goldenrod 1:** usu *Solidago nemoralis,* but also *S. rugosa.*

1900 Lyons *Plant Names* 350, *S[olidago] nemoralis* . . Dyer's-weed. . . *S. rugosa* . . Dyer's-weed. **1914** Georgia *Manual Weeds* 423, *Gray Goldenrod*. . . Dyer's Weed. **1940** Clute *Amer. Plant Names* 88,

S. nemoralis. . . Dyer's-weed. . . *S. rugosa*. . . Dyer's-weed. *Ibid* 272, *Solidago nemoralis*. . . Dye-weed. *Ibid* 273, *Solidago rugosa*. Dye-weed. **1972** Courtenay-Zimmerman *Wild Flowers* 125, *Dyer's Weed, S. nemoralis*. . . Flowers cover upper ⅓ of plant.

dyestone n

See quot 1889.

1889 *Century Dict.* 1808, *Dyestone*. . . A red ferruginous limestone occurring in Tennessee, used occasionally in the place of a dye, although insoluble and not properly a dye. **1939** FWP *Guide TN* 8, There are four principal iron areas in the State: the eastern belt . . the "dyestone" or red iron district which forms a belt skirting the eastern bases of the Cumberland Plateau and Walden's Ridge; the Cumberland Plateau; and the western belt.

dyeweed See **dyer's weed**

dying adj, adv **esp Sth** Cf *crying shame*

Damned; extremely.

1966-70 *DARE* (Qu. LL36, *To make a statement much stronger: "Poor fellow. I think it's a ______ shame."*) Infs **MS**69, **NC**14, 38, 61, 82, **SC**32, 45, **VA**69, Dying; (Qu. LL37, *To make a statement as strong as you can: "I could have wrung her neck, I was so ______ mad."*) Inf **GA**77, Dying.

dynamite n Also *white dynamite* **chiefly Nth** Cf **white lightning**

Strong liquor, usu of poor quality; moonshine.

1950 *WELS (Names for any kind of bad liquor)* 2 Infs, **WI**, Dynamite. **1958** McCulloch *Woods Words* 56 **Pacific NW**, *Dynamite in a jug*—Aquavit, the very stout liquor preferred by Scandinavians. **1967-69** *DARE* (Qu. DD21a, *General words . . for any kind of liquor*) Inf **NY**27, Dynamite; (Qu. DD21b, *General words . . for bad liquor*) Infs **CA**125, **MN**38, Dynamite; (Qu. DD21c, . . *Whiskey, especially illegally made whiskey*) Infs **MA**35, **WI**26, Dynamite; (Qu. DD27, *Nicknames . . for wine*) Inf **MN**2, White dynamite; (Qu. DD28b, . . *Fermented drinks . . made at home*) Inf **MN**1, White dynamite. **1968** Adams *Western Words* 104, *Dynamite*—A cowboy's name for cheap whisky.

dyngus n Also sp *dingus* [Pol, Czech] **chiefly in Polish settlement areas**

A folk custom involving dousing and switching practiced on Easter Monday; the switch so used; see quots.

[**1938** FWP *Guide MN* 393, In Silver Lake [where Czechs settled in 1874] small boys still go from house to house early Easter Monday, in Czech called *Dyngus*, with whip and baskets to collect Easter eggs from the girls and threaten to switch those lying abed. The ancient significance of this as a fertility rite has apparently been forgotten.] **1970** *DARE* (Qu. FF16, . . *Local contests or celebrations*) Inf **MI**120, Dingus—old-fashioned Polish name. Same as *Switch day*. Grown-ups go around switching all the women. **1970** *DARE* FW Addit **cnMI**, *Dingus* ['dɪŋgus]. After Easter. A switch day, old Polish tradition. They'd go around, take a branch off a tree and they'd give each woman or girl a switchin', and then they'd treat 'em with eggs and give 'em a drink. **1979** *NADS Letters* **wNY**, An older Polish informant. . . said "We would go out into the woods and cut these little switches, you know, the little *dynguses*." Whether etymologically sound or not, many treat the item *dyngus* as "switch". . . In Dunkirk New York, through the Second World War, older men would actually go into the houses on [Easter] Monday, straight to the girls' bedrooms, whip back the covers, and water and switch the girls. . . The event is no longer observed locally. *Ibid*, The event is either *smigus, dyngus* (often spelled *dingus* in English), *smigus-dyngus* (never the other way around) or *lany Poniedziatek*. The last term means something like "dousing Monday."

dyoin' See **during**

dysentery root See **dysentery weed 2**

dysentery weed n

1 A **cudweed 1** (here: *Gnaphalium uliginosum*). [See quot c1873]

c1873 in 1976 Miller *Shaker Herbs* 207, *Gnaphalium uliginosum*. Dysentery Weed. . . Used in coughs, diarrhea, and obstructions. **1900** Lyons *Plant Names* 176, *G. uliginosum*. . . Dysentery-weed. **1911** *Century Dict. Suppl., Dysentery-weed*. . . The low cudweed or wartwort, *Gnaphalium uliginosum*.

2 also *dysentery root:* A **stickseed** (here: *Hackelia virginiana*). [See quot 1911]

1876 Hobbs *Bot. Hdbk.* 33, Dysentery root, . . Dysentery weed, Virginia mouse ear, Cynoglossum Morrisoni. **1911** *Century Dict. Suppl., Dysentery-root*. . . The stickseed or beggar's-lice, *Lappula Virginiana*, from the supposed medicinal properties of the root. Also called *dysentery-weed*. **1931** Clute *Common Plants* 123, Familiar examples are . . dysentery weed (*Lappula Virginica* [sic]), . . and belly-ache root *(Solidago bicolor)*. **1959** Carleton *Index Herb. Plants* 40, *Dysentery-root*. . . *Dysentery-weed:* Lappula virginiana.

dyspepsia coffee n [Perh thought to ease indigestion]

1940 Brown *Amer. Cooks* 231 **KS**, Kansan "dyspepsia coffee," made with one-half coffee and one-half corn meal moistened with molasses, put in a baking pan, and browned the same as coffee, for brewing later.

E

e pron See **he** pron

e intj |e| Also sp *ea, 'ey* **HI**

Hey!

1843 in 1934 Frear *Lowell & Abigail* 163 **HI,** Ea! . . Look at this! Lord Paulett has annulled the law against adultery. **1938** Reinecke *Hawaiian Loanwords* 9, *E*. . . An exclamation with the same force as English *hey!* **1968** *Jrl. Engl. Ling.* 2.80 **HI,** *E* [e:]. . . Hey! Say! Oh! **1981** *Pidgin To Da Max* **HI,** *'Ey!* (ay!) Hey! Hey you, wake up! This is an attention-getter.

ea See **ayuh**

eaceworm n |ˈis,wɜm, -,wɝm| Also sp *eas(s)worm, eesworm;* folk-etym spp *easterworm, eastworm* [ME *ees* bait; cf *EDD easse*] **chiefly sNEng, esp RI**

An **earthworm.**

1896 *DN* 1.416 **RI,** *Ees-worm.* **1914** *DN* 4.154 **NH,** *Eass-worm.* **1933** *AmSp* 8.4.14, *Easworm* [ˈis,wɜm] . . occurs as the usual term in northern Rhode Island (Providence and Kent counties) and in the Rhode Island settlements in the Berkshires. In Rhode Island, three of the better instructed, more urban informants offered the variants *eastworm, easterworm,* adding by way of explanation, "These worms come out when the east wind blows"; but the usual word is *easworm.* **1934** *Hanley Disks* **nwMA,** Eaceworm. **1967** Faries *Word Geog. MO* 135, *Missouri frequency of the dialect expressions used in the major speech areas of the eastern United States—North Expressions* . . eace worm—1 [of 700 infs]. **1969** *DARE* (Qu. P5) Inf **RI**6, Angleworm, garden worm, eastworm.

each See **itch**

each and every pron Also *all and each* (or *every*) [Cf *OED all* adj. 12. c] **S Midl**

Everybody, one and all; every one.

1794 (1914) Clark *Jrl.* 423 **VA,** The Comdr in Chief [Wayne] rejected all & every of his plans. **1843** (1916) Hall *New Purchase* 220 **IN,** The whole four panes [of glass] were all and each, and every . . cracked and broken. **1913** Kephart *Highlanders* 298 **sAppalachians,** Phil's Ann give it out to each and every that Walt and Layunie 'd orter wed. **1926** *DN* 5.399 **nwAR, swMO,** Mary she run right out an' tol' each an' ev'ry all 'bout it. **1928** Chapman *Happy Mt.* 86 **seTN,** Fayre Jones told each and every.

each, by the adv phr

Individually, singly.

1969 *DARE* (QR p52) Inf **IL**97, Buy them [=individually wrapped candies] by the each.

eaf See **eephing**

eager adv, v Usu |ˈigə(r), -gəl; also |ˈɪgər|

A Form.

1937 in 1944 *ADD* **VA,** /ɪgr̩/. Common.

B As adv.

Especially.

1942 (1971) Campbell *Cloud-Walking* 235 **seKY,** "Sary, I reckon I'll walk down the mountain to meet Squire." "That would be a good way to make him eager welcome," Sary told her.

C As verb.

‡To become animated.

1932 Faulkner *Light in August* 135 **MS,** The buggy jolted on, the stout, wellkept team eagering, homing, barning. **1976** Brown *Gloss. Faulkner* 76, *Eagering, homing, barning*. . . Horses normally perk up as they get close to home and their stalls at the end of a trip.

eager n See **ague**

eager-eye n [Alter of **eagle-eye 1**]

1943 *AmSp* 18.164, *Eager eye*. . . Locomotive engineer, who must be constantly on the lookout for signals and obstacles.

eagers n pl [From *eager* adj] *old-fash*

Feelings of desire, impatience, or anxiety.

1928 *AmSp* 3.219 [Kansas Univ slang], *Eagers*. . . Anxiety or haste. "Don't get the eagers now—just take things easy." **1944** Wellman *Bowl* 73 **KS,** Gawd, she looks good enough to give a man the eagers, sure! **1963** *AmSp* 38.175 [Kansas Univ slang], The word *eagers,* meaning 'anxiety or haste' in 1926, was completely unknown to students in 1962.

eagle n

1 also *eagle-hawk:* A **roughleg** (here: *Buteo regalis*).

1893 Fisher *Hawks & Owls U.S.* 92, When this hawk [=*Buteo regalis*] is hunting its flight appears labored and heavy, but when circling high in the air its flight is graceful and resembles closely that of the Golden Eagle. In fact, in parts of the West it is known by the name Eagle. **1953** Jewett *Birds WA* 174, *Ferruginous Hawk*. . . Other names: . . Eagle Hawk.

2 A silver dollar.

1950 *WELS (A silver dollar)* 1 Inf, **cnWI,** Eagle. **1966–70** *DARE* (Qu. U27) Infs **IN**3, **ME**13, **PA**245, **WI**18, Eagle; **MN**2, Eagle—in old days; **GA**44, Silver eagle; **IL**21, Spread eagle; **KY**21, American eagle; **SC**26, Eagle head.

3 A ten-dollar bill; hence n *double eagle* a twenty-dollar bill. [From *eagle* a ten-dollar gold piece]

1967–70 *DARE* (Qu. U28b, . . *Ten-dollar bill*) Infs **NJ**63, **NC**87, Eagle; (Qu. U28c, . . *Twenty-dollar bill*) Infs **NJ**63, **TN**1, Double eagle; [**IA**11, Eagle—a gold one, a twenty-dollar gold piece].

4 In allusive uses: see quots. Cf **squeeze the eagle**

1942 Berrey–Van den Bark *Amer. Slang* 553.9, The eagle's bowels move today . . *it is payday.* **1947** *AmSp* 22.55 [Military language], *Eagle's Day.* Pay day (the day on which the eagle screams). **1977** Smitherman *Talkin* 72 [Black], On Friday, *eagle-flyin* day (pay day), secular folk look forward to *gittin high.* **1978** *DARE* File **Akron OH** (as of c1920), When eagle shit [=on payday], I get thirty dollars; **San Francisco CA** (as of c1940), On Friday, eagle shit [=it's payday; used by dock workers]. **1979** Gillespie–Fraser *To Be Or Not To Bop* 281 [Black], Most bebop language came about because some guy said something and it stuck. . . When's the "eagle gonna" fly, the American eagle, meant payday.

eagle beak n

1 also *eagle's beak, eagle nose:* A hooked nose. **chiefly Nth, N Midl**

1907 White *AZ Nights* 169, His eyes blazing each side his big eagle nose. **1950** *WELS (Words for noses according to their appearance)* 4 Infs, **WI,** Eagle beak. **1965–70** *DARE* (Qu. X15) 25 Infs, **chiefly Nth, N Midl,** Eagle beak; **IL**2, Eagle's beak; **HI**9, **KY**45, **NY**84, **TX**65, Eagle nose; (Qu. X14) Infs **MD**9, **MN**2, **NY**6, **WI**12, Eagle beak.

2 also *eagle-eyes:* A lawyer.

1968 *DARE* (Qu. HH44) Inf **PA**108, Eagle-beak, eagle-eyes.

eagle bill n Also *eagle-billed tap(adero)* **West**

An ornamental **tapadero.**

1951 Grant *Cowboy Encycl.* 60, *Eagle-bills.* Cowboy term for tapaderos with extremely long points which hang well below the stirrups and resemble eagles' beaks. **1955** Harris *Look of Old West* 242, For fiesta or parade there were eagle-billed taps, with a snout like an eagle's in front and wide, down-sweeping wings that sometimes all but scraped the ground. *Ibid* 243, [Caption:] *Eagle-billed tapadero.* **1961** Adams *Old-Time Cowhand* 215 **West,** Ever' saddle was equipped with heavy bull-nosed tapaderos, never the long, fancy eagle bills of other sections.

eagle brant See **eagle-head goose**

eagle claws n

A **barrel cactus** (here: *Echinocactus horizonthalonius*).

1976 Bailey–Bailey *Hortus Third* 411, *[Echinocactus] horizonthalonius. . . Eagle-claws. . .* Spines straight or recurved, to 1½ in. long.

eagle-eye n

1 A locomotive engineer. Also called **eager-eye**

1916 *DN* 4.356 **East.** **1927** *DN* 5.445 **NC.** **1929** *Ruppenthal Coll.* **KS.** **1932** *RR Mag.* Oct 367, *Eagle-eye*—Locomotive engineer. **1958** McCulloch *Woods Words* 57 **Pacific NW.**

2 pl: See **eagle beak 2.**

eagle gull n

=**great black-backed gull.**

1955 *AmSp* 30.181, Of bird names given for size, consider . . *eagle gull* . . (greater black-backed gull, Maine).

eagle-hawk n

1 See **eagle 1.**

2 =**winklehawk.** [Prob by folk-etym]

1967 *DARE* (Qu. W27, . . *A three-cornered tear in a piece of clothing*) Inf **NJ**2, Eagle-hawk.

eagle head See **eagle 1**

eagle-head goose n Also *eagle brant, eagle head, eagle-headed brant*

=**blue goose 1.**

1931 Read *LA French* 52, The Blue Goose . . in English [is] called also . . *Eagle-headed* Brant. **1955** Lowery *LA Birds* 157, The adult Blue Goose, with its dark body and white head, is often called the "eagle-head goose." **1955** *AmSp* 30.180, *Eagle brant* (. . La.), *eagle-headed brant* (La.), and *eagle-head* (La., Texas), liken the white head of the blue goose to that of the so-called 'bald' eagle. **1982** Elman *Hunter's Field Guide* 292, Blue Goose. . . Common & Regional Names: . . eagle-headed brant.

eagle nose See **eagle beak 1**

eagle owl n [*OED* 1802 →]

Appar a large owl such as the **great horned owl.**

1950 *WELS (Other kinds of owls in your neighborhood)* 1 Inf, **seWI,** Eagle owl. **1955** *AmSp* 30.181, Of bird names given for size, consider . . *eagle owl* (horned owl, Ala., British Columbia; also in long-time British provincial use). **1955** U.S. Arctic Info. Center *Gloss.* **AK,** *Eagle-owl. . .* A large woodland bird, *Bubo bubo,* with soft, mottled, dark brown plumage, and two tufts of feathers or horns on the head.

eagle ray n [See quot 1933]

A stingray of the family Myliobatidae. See also **bat ray, cownose ray**

1884 Goode *Fisheries* 1.666, Of the Eagle Ray family, *Myliobatidæ,* . . all except the Bishop Ray straggle north to Southern New England in summer. . . The 'Eagle Ray,' . . *Mylobatis* [sic] *Fremenvillei,* does not attain a large size and is comparatively unusual in occurrence. **1933** John G. Shedd Aquarium *Guide* 25, The name eagle ray is suggested by the shape of the head. **1960** Amer. Fisheries Soc. *List Fishes* 9, Myliobatidae—eagle rays.

eagle rock n, v *esp freq among Black speakers* Cf **Easter rock**

A dance; to do the dance; also fig.

1929 in 1983 Taft *Blues Lyric Poetry* 186/2 **GA** [Black], Went to the door: and the door was locked / Think my baby: trying to eagle rock. **1930** in 1975 Albertson *Bessie Smith* 100 [Black], [Blues lyrics:] I want to be somebody's baby doll. . . He can be ugly, he can be black, so long as he can eagle rock and ball the jack. **1945** Saxon *Gumbo Ya-Ya* 491 **New Orleans LA** [Black], I was a mess. Had women shakin' down and doin' the Eagle Rock wid dollar bills in their hands. **1968** Stearns–Stearns *Jazz Dance* 26, The Eagle Rock was named after the Eagle Rock Baptist Church in Kansas City, according to Wilbur Steadman: "They were famous for dancing it during religious services in the years following the Civil War." The dance may well have been much older, but like the Buzzard Lope and a religious dance known as the Shout . . , it has the high arm gestures associated with evangelical dances and religious trance. . . The Eagle Rock spread north and south. . . White people seldom if ever danced the . . Eagle Rock.

eagle's beak See **eagle beak 1**

ear n[1] Usu |ir, iə, ɪr, ɪə|; freq **SC, GA** |er, eə|; freq **S Midl** |jiɚ, jɛɚ, jɚ, jæə|; for addit varr see **A** below Pronc-spp *yea(h), year(e), yer, yez, yur*

A Forms.

1853 Simms *Sword & Distaff* 116 **SC,** He will gib we de tail and yea's. **1883** Amer. Philol. Assoc. *Trans.* 14.56 **Sth,** *Year,* as a pronunciation of the word *ear.* I run the risk perhaps of being charged with maligning my people when I call this a Southernism; but while it is the universal pronunciation among the lower classes, it was not confined to them a few years ago. I recall two ladies of excellent family, both professors' wives, who regularly pronounced it *year,* or rather *yer.* **1888** Jones *Negro Myths* 41 **GA coast,** Buh Elephant . . der tan onder de tree duh flop eh yez. **1893** Shands *MS Speech* 69, *Year. . .* The common pronunciation of *ear* among the uneducated; also used to some extent by educated people. **1899** Chesnutt *Conjure Woman* 55 **csNC** [Black], De tree did n' hab no years. **1899** (1912) Green *VA Folk-Speech* 494, *Year. . .* Ear of corn. "Shall pay three barrels of *yeares.*" **1903** *DN* 2.337 **seMO,** *Year* (of corn). . . Ear. Curiously, this pronounciation [sic] does not apply to the ears of animals. [*DARE* Ed: questionable; see other quots.] **1906** *DN* 3.165 **nwAR,** *Year* [jæə and jir] . . "I'll cut your years off." "I grabbed the old sow by the years." **1909** *S. Atl. Qrly.* 8.44 **sSC coast** [Gullah], De buttah melt; eh ron een 'e yeye an' 'im yez [=The butter melted; it ran in his eyes and his ears]. **1922** Gonzales *Black Border* 52 **sSC, GA coasts** [Gullah], 'E cut 'e t'roat f'um yez to yez. [It [=a rifle ball] cut its [=a lion's] throat from ear to ear.] *Ibid* 340, [Glossary:] *Yez*—ear, ears (human or animal). **1926** *AmSp* 1.410 **seGA,** Didn't open 'is mouth, jest there with 'is yurs laid back. **1926** Roberts *Time of Man* 15 **KY,** Oh, Grannie, what makes your years so big? To hear you the better, my child. **1927** Shewmake *Engl. Pronc. VA* 32, Still other cases of vowel shifting sometimes occur in the pronunciation of such words as *ear, fear,* and *sincere,* in which the sound of *e* as in *meat* gives place to the sound of the same letter in *met.* **1929** Sale *Tree Named John* 109 **MS,** Brer Elefunt . . jes flop dem yeahs uv his'n. **1933** *AmSp* 8.1.31 **nTX,** He don't know no more than a mule-yeared rabbit about brandin'. **1933** Rawlings *South Moon* 80 **nFL,** They wouldn't hear a year o' corn to drop. **c1940** Eliason *Word Lists FL* 13 **wFL,** *Ear* [jɝ]. **1942** Hall *Smoky Mt. Speech* 94, Before a front vowel (or an original front vowel) [j] has developed as a palatal glide . . initially in *ear* [jiɚ], [jɝ] [jɛɚ] (beside [ɪɚ], [ɝ]). **1949** *AmSp* 24.108 **nGA,** *Earwigs* ['jɜɚˌwɪgz]. **1954** *Harder Coll.* **cwTN,** Earbob ['jɜrˌbɑb]. **c1960** *Wilson Coll.* **csKY,** Ear /jir/ rather often, or /jɛr/. **1961** Kurath–McDavid *Pronc. Engl.* 117, Three (or four) different vowel phonemes occur in *ear, beard,* etc.: high-front /i~ɪ/ [are widespread, but less freq Sth, S Midl], mid-front /e/ [in SC, GA], and mid-central /ɜ/ [in NC, VA, sWV, eMD]. . . Disyllabic *ear, beard* [ijə, bijəd] . . appear occasionally under heavy stress in Eastern New England and in other areas that lack post-vocalic /r/. **1966–68** *DARE* FW Addit **GA**19, Earmarked ['ɛɚˌmɑɚkt]; **GA**28, Ear [ɛɚ]; **swNC,** Ears [jɛɚz]. **1968** *DARE* Tape **GA**25, ['eɚˌeɪk]. **1976** Allen *LAUM* 3.30 (as of c1950), In *ear* and the other key words historic /i/ appears only along the range from [i] to [ɪ] in the U[pper] M[idwest].

B Sense.

In phr *(up) on one's ear* and varr: Angry; stirred up; embarrassed.

1871 in 1872 Schele de Vere *Americanisms* 479, To *get up on one's ear,* is regular slang, meaning, to rouse one's self to a great effort: "They called me bully boy, altho' I've seen nigh threescore years,/ And said that I was lightening, when I got up on my ear." **1890** *DN* 1.64 **KY,** *Ear.* "To spin round on one's ear" means *to get violently angry.* Slang. [*DN* Ed: Cf. *to get up on your ear* (New England), in a similar sense.] **1892** *DN* 1.215, *To go off on his ear* = to go away angry, and *to get on his ear* = to get angry . . perhaps universal in the United States. **1897** *KS Univ. Qrly.* (ser B) 6.52, *Ear:* as, He is on his ear (angry), or he walked off on his ear. **1909** *DN* 3.397 **nwAR,** *Get up on one's ear. . .* To get violently angry. **1922** *DN* 5.163 **AR, NE, NEng,** *Get up on your ear. . .* To get violently angry. "Now there ain't no use to get up on your ear about it." **1941** *LANE* Map 472 *(Angry)* 1 inf, **swCT,** He got up on his ear. **1967–69** *DARE* (Qu. GG4, *Stirred up, angry*) Inf **CO**7, Up on his ear; (Qu. GG7, . . *Annoyed or upset*) Inf **MI**81, On her ear; (Qu. GG9, *To sud-*

denly embarrass somebody) Inf **MN**15, Put him out on his ear; **IL**111, Set him on his ear; (Qu. GG11, *To be quite anxious about something . . "The letter hasn't come and he's ______ ."*) Inf **IN**30, On one ear; [**MO**3, Standing on his ears]. [All Infs old]

ear n² See **year**

ear v Usu with *down,* hence vbl n *earing down* **West**

To restrain a horse by grasping or twisting its ears; transf, to keep (someone) from moving; to pin down; see quots.

1929 *AmSp* 5.64 **NE,** Sometimes the "hazers" will "ear 'im" or "ear 'im down," twist the horse's ear to keep it from bucking while the rider is mounting. **1933** *AmSp* 8.1.28 **nwTX,** *Ear-down.* To hold a horse in subjection by grasping his ears and twisting; some cowboys catch an ear between their teeth. **1946** Mora *Trail Dust* 179 **SW,** To the reader who does not know what "earing down" means, let me clarify. In this operation, a twister reaches either over or under the horse's head for his off ear, and grabs it with his right hand, while he likewise fastens to the near one with his left. Then he holds down as tight as he can, crowding in and trying to make himself as unshakable a part of that horse's head as possible. **1958** Blasingame *Dakota Cowboy* 174, I . . always had to "ear him down" to mount. But twisting his ear generally kept his attention until I could mount. **1961** Adams *Old-Time Cowhand* 295, Others let the hazer "ear down" the bronc, distractin' the hoss's attention so the rider could mount. . . If the hoss was on his feet and bein' eared, the buster forked 'im as easy as he could. **1967** Green *Horse Tradin'* 98 **swTX,** Ear this horse down. **1967** *DARE* FW Addit **TX,** If I can ever get him eared down long enough to tape it.

ear banger n Cf **bang ears**

1957 Battaglia *Resp. to PADS 20* **eMD** *(When a student tries to be extra nice to the teacher in hopes of getting a better grade: "She's an awful ______ .")* Ear banger.

ear beater See **ear bender**

ear-beating n

A severe scolding, tongue-lashing.

1968 *DARE* (Qu. II27) Infs **PA**76, 93, 167, Ear-beating. [All Infs young, coll educ]

ear bender n Also *ear beater* [Cf *bend one's ear*]

An overly talkative person.

1936 Hargan *Gloss. Prison Lang. (Hench Coll.), Ear bender*—one who talks too much. **1945** *AmSp* 20.148 [Soldiers' slang], *Ear beater.* A person who doesn't give you a chance to get a word in edgeways. **1957** Battaglia *Resp. to PADS 20* **eMD** *(Someone who always talks a great deal)* Ear bender.

earbob n Also rarely *earbobber* [*bob* ornamental pendant] **chiefly Sth, S Midl** See Map

An earring.

1756 in 1898 Hamilton *Letters to Washington* 1.364, Neat Stone Ear-bobs set in Silver from 2/6 to 3/6—a pair. **1837** Irving *Rocky Mts.* 2.110, The old man welcomed them once more . . and his respectable squaw and hopeful son, cherishing grateful recollections of the hatchet and earbobs, joined in a chorus of friendly gratulation. **1903** *DN* 2.312 **seMO,** *Ear-bob.* **1906** *DN* 3.117 **sIN,** *Ear-bob. Ibid* 134 **nwAR,** *Ear-bob.* **1908** *DN* 3.308 **eAL, wGA,** *Ear-bob.* **1926** Roberts *Time of Man* 14 **cKY,** [She has got] her hoop earbobs on, maybe. **1942** Warnick *Garrett Co. MD* 6 **nwMD** (as of 1900–1918), *Ear-bob.* **1942** McAtee *Dial. Grant Co. IN* 24 (as of 1890s), *Ear-bob.* **1950** *WELS (Jewelry that a woman wears on her ears)* 4 Infs, **WI,** Earbobs. **1954** *Harder Coll.* **cwTN,** *Earbobs. . .* Jewelry that a woman wears on her ears. Also *earbobbers.* **1960** Williams *Walk Egypt* 253 **GA,** Daddy's gonna make us cherry-stone earbobs. **c1960** *Wilson Coll.* **csKY,** *Ear-bob. . .* Any ear ornament worn by a woman. **1965–70** *DARE* (Qu. W34) 155 Infs, **chiefly Sth, S Midl,** Earbob(s).

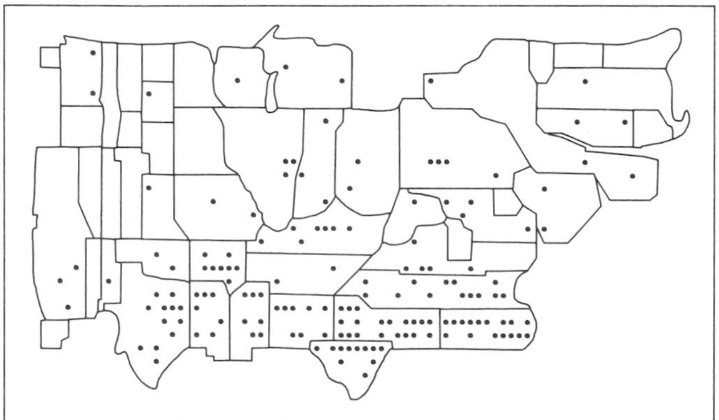

•earbob (Qu. W34)

ear brand n

A kind of **earmark** n.

1966–67 *DARE* (Qu. K18) Inf **AL**14, Ear brand; **OK**33, Ear brand—a tattoo in the ear, had by a lot of registered cattle.

ear bridle See **ear-head**

ear-burn n Cf **ear-beating**

A severe scolding.

1966 *DARE* (Qu. II27) Inf **MA**6, Ear-burn.

ear button n

1 =**ear tag.**

1967 *DARE* (Qu. K18, *What kind of mark is used . . to identify a cow?*) Inf **TN**1, Ear button—metal button clamped through ear.

2 An earring worn directly on the earlobe rather than dangling below it.

1970 *DARE* (Qu. W34, . . *Jewelry that a woman wears on her ears*) Inf **VA**69, Ear button.

earclamp See **earclip 1**

earclapper n [Perh from the children's game of naming body parts, saying "Eye winker, ear clapper, nose dropper," etc]

The ear.

1931–33 *LANE Worksheets* **cCT,** When they used to hit you on the side of the ears they'd say you got a sidewinder on the earclapper.

earclasp See **earclip 2**

earclip n

1 also *earclamp:* An **ear tag.**

1965–70 *DARE* (Qu. K18, *What kind of mark is used around here to identify a cow?*) 36 Infs, **chiefly east of Missip R,** Earclip; **KY**32, Earclamp.

2 also *earclasp:* An earring with a clip fastener.

1950 *WELS (Jewelry that a woman wears on her ears)* 1 Inf, **cwWI,** Earclips. **1965–70** *DARE* (Qu. W34) 10 Infs, **Sth, Midl, West,** Earclip(s); **FL**48, Earclip—clip-ons; **KY**22, Earclasps.

ear corn n **esp Upper MW** Cf **cob corn**

Corn left on the cob, not shelled; corn intended to be eaten from the cob.

1872 Eggleston *End of the World* 140 **IN,** Cynthy Ann . . speedily put a bushel of ear-corn in the great wash-boiler. **1967** *Rock Co. Leader* (Bassett NE) 14 Sept 7/5, For sale—Ear corn this fall. **1967–68** *DARE* (Qu. I33, *What do you call ears of corn that are just right for eating?*) Inf **IL**7, Ear corn; [**PA**150, Corn on the ear]. **1968** *Harmony News* (MN) 11 Jan 8/1, *Wanted to buy:* Ear corn and baled hay. **1973** Allen *LAUM* 1.312 (as of c1950), *Ear corn* and the nonce-variant *corn on the ear* are limited to Nebraska and, with one example each, to southwestern Minnesota and western Iowa, close to the Nebraska border. **1977** Churchill *Don't Call* 141 **nwOR** (as of c1918), We used to plant carrots, beets, tomatoes, spuds, lettuce, cabbage, and sometimes ear corn.

ear crop n

=**ear cut.**

1853 Hammett *Stray Yankee in TX* 42, In the agonies of death, lay a fine young heifer, bearing Joe's ear-crop and brand. **1966–70** *DARE* (Qu. K18, . . *Mark . . used around here to identify a cow*) Infs **AL**34, **KY**86, **SC**19, **TX**3, 4, 6, Ear crop. [All Infs old]

ear cut n Also *ear cutting* Also called **ear crop**

An **earmark** made by cutting away part of the ear of a cow or hog.

1952 *Argosy* (NY) June 100 **LA,** Ear-cuttings prove ownership, and honesty is strictly observed when the sorting-out is done. *Ibid,* He showed me some of the ear-cuts or brand marks. "Smooth crop on left, figure seven on right . . Bullet hole . . Splits . . Under bit and over bit . . Swallow forks." **1965–70** *DARE* (Qu. K18, . . *Mark . . used around here to identify a cow*) Infs **CA**90, **FL**15, **KY**29, **MS**39, **MO**34, **NC**85, **SC**57, Ear cut(s).

ear cutter n [From the belief that the insect will cut the ears of children who lie] Cf **ear sewer 1, sewer, sewing bug, sneeder**
A **dragonfly.**
1950 *WELS Suppl.* **WI,** Ear cutter—dragonfly. **1969** *DARE* (Qu. R2) Inf **NH**18, Ear cutter.

ear cutting See **ear cut**

eardangle n
=**eardrop 1.**
1968 *DARE* (Qu. W34, *Jewelry that a woman wears on her ears*) Inf **NJ**53, Eardangles.

ear down See **ear** v

eardrop n
1 An earring, usu one with a pendant. Cf **earbob, eardangle**
1859 (1968) Bartlett *Americanisms, Ear-bob.* An ear-drop. **1879** (1880) Twain *Tramp Abroad* 304, The smaller ones [=lakes] . . did not look like puddles, but like blue ear-drops which had fallen and lodged in slight depressions. **1903** *DN* 2.297 **Cape Cod MA** (as of a1857), *Ear-drop.* . . Earring. **1950** *WELS (Jewelry that a woman wears on her ears)* 5 Infs, **WI,** Eardrops. **1965–70** *DARE* (Qu. W34) 10 Infs, **chiefly Nth, Midl,** Eardrops. [All Infs old] **1966** *DARE* Tape **MS**75, Girl with the eardrops . . hanging down. **1988** *NADS Letters* **ceTX,** I remember . . *ear drops,* but I haven't heard the expression in years, not since the 1940's.
2 A fuchsia. [From the pendant flower] Cf **lady's eardrops**
1822 Eaton *Botany* 283, *Fuchsia.* . . Ear-drop. . . Flowers pendulous. **1876** Hobbs *Bot. Hdbk.* 33, Ear drop, Fuchsia Magellanica. **1959** Carleton *Index Herb. Plants* 40, *Eardrops:* Fuchsia (v).
3 also *eardrops:* A **bleeding heart 1,** usu either *Dicentra spectabilis* or *D. cucullaria.* [From the pendant flower] Cf **golden eardrops**
1861 Wood *Class-Book* 225, *Dicentra.* . . *Ear-drop.* **1886** in 1951 *PADS* 15.12, *Dicentra cucullaria* . . Eardrops, New Jersey. **1896** *Jrl. Amer. Folkl.* 9.181, *Dicentra spectabilis* . . ear-drops, Sulphur Grove, Ohio. **1910** Graves *Flowering Plants* 198 **CT,** *Dicentra Cucullaria.* . . White Eardrops or Hearts. . . Rocky woods in rich soil. **1932** *Country Life* 62.67 **NC,** Most adored of its family by many of us . . is Dutchman's-breeches, . . alias Eardrops.
4 also *eardrop vine:* The buckwheat vine *(Brunnichia cirrhosa).* [See quot 1960]
1933 Small *Manual SE Flora* 460, *B[runnichia] cirrhosa.* . . Eardrop. Buckwheat-vine. Buck-vine. **1946** Reeves–Bain *Flora TX* 116, *Brunnichia.* . . Eardrop Vine. **1960** Vines *Trees SW* 228, *Brunnichia cirrhosa.* . . The fruit somewhat resembles ear pendants and the vine is known as Eardrop-vine in some localities. **1970** Correll *Plants TX* 527, Eardrop vine.

eardrops See **eardrop 3**

earf See **earth**

earflop n
=**earbob.**
1966 *DARE* (Qu. W34, *Jewelry that a woman wears on her ears*) Inf **GA**3, Earflops.

‡earflopper n
=**earlapper 1.**
1966 *DARE* Tape **ME**19, They had caps, earfloppers on 'em.

ear fly n [Because it attacks horses' ears] **chiefly Midl** Cf **face fly, horsefly 1, nose fly**
A tabanid, esp a **deerfly 1.**
1806 (1965) Lewis–Clark *Hist. Lewis–Clark Exped.* 1019, Most of the insects common to . . the United States are seen in this country . . except one species of [the horse-fly], the gold-colored ear-fly. **1851** *S. Lit. Messenger* 17.374/2 **Plains States,** The triangular looking *earfly* is hatched on young pines. **1910** NJ State Museum *Annual Rept. for 1909* 738, These are moderate or large species, popularly known as "horse flies," but locally and referring to special types, also as "gad-flies," "deer-flies," "ear-flies," "golden-eyed flies," "strawberry flies," etc. **1966–70** *DARE* (Qu. R12, . . *Other kinds of flies*) Infs **AR**56, **DE**4, **KY**84, 86, **MA**58, Ear fly (*or* flies); **OK**23, Ear flies—bite horses' ears in spring and early summer.

ear-hack v [*hack* to cut] Cf **ear slit**
To cut an identifying mark in the ear of a calf or cow.
1935 Davis *Honey* 349 **OR,** Every calf has to be branded, ear-hacked, and the male ones have to be castrated.

ear-head n Also *ear bridle* **West**
See quot 1944.
1944 Adams *Western Words* 55, *Ear-head*—A headstall made in two pieces, with a loop for the right ear, one buckle on the left cheek, and no nose-band, throat-latch, or brow-band. The bit ties in with buckskin strings. **1961** Adams *Old-Time Cowhand* 116, "Ear bridle," or "ear-head."

earhoop n [*DA* →1845 *"obs."*]
A hoop-shaped earring.
1808 *Thomas' MA Spy or Worcester Gaz.* (MA) 18 May, A large assortment of Earhoops, of different sizes. **1845** Judd *Margaret* 64 **ME,** Many [ladies] wore ear-hoops of pinch-beck, as large as a dollar. **1950** *WELS (Jewelry that a woman wears on her ears)* 1 Inf, **swWI,** Ear-hoops. **1955** Adams *Grandfather* 176 **NY** (as of 1830s), He wore a coonskin cap, a gay linsey-woolsey jacket, morocco boots, and gold ear-hoops like a gyppo.

earing down See **ear** v

earjewel n [From the pendant flowers]
A **jewelweed** (here: *Impatiens biflora*).
1893 *Jrl. Amer. Folkl.* 6.139, *Impatiens fulva* . . ear-jewel, Ferrisburgh, Vt. **1959** Carleton *Index Herb. Plants* 40, *Ear Jewel:* Impatiens biflora.

earl n[1] Usu |ɝl, ɜl|; also |ɜɪl, əɪl| See Pronc Intro 3.II.12 Cf **early**
Std sense, var forms.
1937 *AmSp* 12.170 **NYC,** The pronunciation [əɪl] for *earl* is by no means limited to the East Side and the Bowery. A New Yorker might have this pronunciation in the *r-* words and consider the same sound in *oil, boil* a crude pronunciation, since he would have [ɔɪ] in these words. **1950** Hubbell *Pronc. NYC* 69, When /ə̃ɪ/ appears in their [=cultivated informants'] speech in *curl, earl, learn,* such words are not homonyms of *coil, oil,* and *loin* [in which they use /ɔ̃ɪ/]. . . When diphthongs distinct phonetically from [ə̃ɪ] are used . . [by uncultivated informants] their exact quality varies. . . *Coil-curl, oil-earl, loin-learn* are homonyms.

earl n[2] See **oil**

earl v [Echoic] Cf **ralph, urp**
To vomit; hence n *Earl,* used in var euphem phrr.
1986–87 *DARE* File **nIN,** If you had to throw up or vomit, we'd say you had to "earl." We also would say that "Earl's knocking at the door"; **AR,** We'd say "earl" for vomit. You know, because that's what it sounded like. We'd also say "going to see Earl."

earlapper n [*lap, lappet* a flap in a garment]
1 also *earlap(pet):* The earflap of a cap or hat. **NEast** Cf **earflopper**
1863 Taylor *Hanna Thurston* 79 **nPA,** Woodbury recognized, projecting between ear-lappets of fur, the curiously planted nose . . which belonged to the Rev. Mr. Waldo. **1907** *DN* 3.243 **eME,** Why don't you have earlappers put on your cap? **1915–23** in 1944 *ADD* **cNY,** Earlappers. Usual. Attached inside a winter cap, not a hat. **1937** Mitchell *Horse & Buggy* 72 **CT,** On May Day he changed his heavy winter hat with its earlaps for a large, broad-brimmed, farmer's straw hat. **1988** *DARE* File **csWI** (as of 1930s), *Earlaps* was the only term I heard.
2 An earmuff.
1904 Day *Kin o' Ktaadn* 89 **ME,** I've seen the time I wisht I hadn't left my ear-lappers out in my overco't pocket.

earlappet See **earlapper 1**

Earl of Hell n [Orig Scots; see *SND*]
The devil.
1939 (1962) Thompson *Body & Britches* 113 **NY,** The witch's master, the Earl of Hell, alias the devil, appears in plenty of Dutch folklore, especially such as is connected with place-names. *Ibid* 139, He was walking in a field of his father's when he suddenly met that Enemy of Mankind whom Bill's Scottish ancestors named respectfully the Earl of Hell. **1952** Brown *NC Folkl.* 1.402, As black as the Earl of Hell.

ear lug n [*lug* the flap of a cap or bonnet]
=**earlapper 1.**
1937 *AmSp* 12.102 **eNE,** The winter caps are equipped with *ear-lugs,* to be used in cold weather.

early adv, adj Pronc-spp *airly, arly, oily, uhlly, yearly, yuhlly* Similarly *'arliest* See Pronc Intro 3.I.1.f and 3.II.12 Cf **earl** n[1]
Std senses, var forms.

1837 Sherwood *Gaz. GA* 72, *Provincialisms. . . Yearly,* for early;—come right *yearly* . . for come soon or early. **1841** in 1927 *AmSp* 2.482 **nNY,** 'Arly, 'arliest. **1848** (1894) Lowell *Biglow* 46 **MA,** You've gut to git up airly / Ef you want to take in God. **1851** Burke *Polly Peablossom* 117 **KY,** Joe and I went up airly in the spring. **1872** Schele de Vere *Americanisms* 577, *Airly,* for early, is New England slang, though not unknown in Pennsylvania, and derived from its orthodox sound in the 17th century. **1906** *DN* 3.117 **sIN,** *Early. . .* Pronounced with *e* as in *hen,* not as in *her.* **1906** in 1960 *AmSp* 35.46 **IN,** *Airly.* **1907** *DN* 3.180 **seNH,** *Airly. . .* Early. Used by old people. "Got breakfast airly, aint yer?" **1922** Gonzales *Black Border* 336 **sSC, GA coasts** [Gullah glossary], *Uhlly, yuhlly*—early. **1930s** in 1944 *ADD* **NYC,** *Early. . .* Freq. sp. & heard as *oily.*

early boughten adj phr [*early* premature + *boughten*]
Green; inexperienced.

1968 Adams *Western Words* 104, *Early boughten*—A cowboy's term occasionally used for a greenhorn.

early candlelight n Also *early candlelighting* [**candlelight**] **chiefly S Midl**
Dusk.

1809 in 1929 Weems *Mason Locke Weems* 2.404 **eVA,** The Rev. Mason L. Weems, will deliver a discourse, this Evening . . at early candle light. **1854** Smith *'Way Down East* 37 **ME,** By early candle-light, the company began to drop in. **1859** (1968) Bartlett *Americanisms* 135, Used to denote the beginning of the evening; as, "The meeting will begin at early candle-light." **1890** Howells *Boy's Town* 231 **sOH,** There will be an auction this evening at early candle-light. **1903** *DN* 2.312 **seMO,** *Early candle-lighting. . .* Early in the evening. 'There will be preaching at early candle-lighting next Sunday.' (A common announcement.) **1904** *DN* 2.418 **nwAR,** *Early candle-light.* **1905** *DN* 3.8 **cCT,** *Early candle-light.* **1907** *DN* 3.230 **nwAR,** *Early candle-lighting.* **1923** *DN* 5.203 **swMO,** *Can'le light. . .* Dusk, twilight. Modified by 'early can'le light' or 'late can'le light.' **c1960** *Wilson Coll.* **csKY,** *Early candlelight. . .* Dusk. "We'll be there by early candlelight." **1966** *DARE* (Qu. A5) Inf **AR**38, Early candlelight. [FW: Inf has heard] **1968** *Filson Club Hist. Qrly.* 157 **KY,** We assembled at the church at early candle lighting.

earmark n Pronc-sp *yearmark* **formerly more widespread, now chiefly Sth, Midl, West** See Map Also called **ear brand, ~ crop, ~ cut, ~ notch, ~ slit** Cf **mark** n, v
An identifying mark cut or branded in the ear of a cow or other animal.

1637 in 1855 New Plymouth Colony *Records* 1.62 **MA,** It is also agreed by the bench that all that haue not brought in their eare marks of their cattle betwixt this and the next Court shalbe fyned in default thereof at the descretion of the bench. **1859** (1968) Bartlett *Americanisms, Earmark.* The mark made on a sheep's ear by its owner. **1907** White *AZ Nights* 78, In that manner he don't have to look at the brand, except to corroborate the ears; and, as the critter generally sticks his ears up inquirin'-like to anyone ridin' up, it's easy to know the brand without lookin' at it, merely from the ear-marks. **1923** *DN* 5.225 **swMO,** *Year-mark,* Earmark. **1929** *AmSp* 5.70 **NE,** Cattle are frequently given not only a "scorch" but a "mark," often called . . an "ear mark" or "ear splitting," if the ear is notched or the tip of it cut. **1929** *Sat. Eve. Post* 17 Aug 139/2 **Missip Valley,** These hogs run wild through the woods; the only attention they get is when they are caught, as tiny pigs, and marked with registered earmarks by the owners. . . If the earmarkings show the hogs to belong to some other farmer the dogs are whistled off and sent hunting another drove. **c1960** *Wilson Coll.* **csKY,** *Earmarks. . .* Slits, crops, etc., used in an animal's ear to denote ownership. **1965–70** *DARE* (Qu. K18, *What kind of mark is used around here to identify a cow?*) 135 Infs, **chiefly Sth, Midl, West,** Earmark.

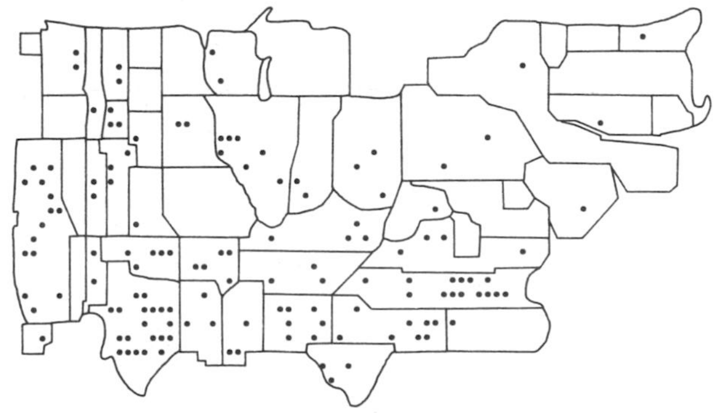

•earmark n (Qu. K18)

earmark v, hence vbl n *earmarking* [**earmark** n]
To cut an identifying mark on the ear of an animal; hence n *earmarker* a tool for doing this.

1639 in 1892 Dedham MA *Early Rec.* 52 **swMA,** It is ordered yt eury Swyne shalbe Earemrked. **1879** *Harper's New Mth. Mag.* 59.714/1 **sTX,** All the cattle are brought together, the calves ear-marked and branded. **1907** White *AZ Nights* 78, A sleeper is a calf that has been ear-marked, but not branded. Every owner has a certain brand, as you know, and then he crops and slits the ears in a certain way, too. **1927** (1970) Sears *Catalogue* 975, "Can't Root" Combined Hog Tamer and Ear Marker. **1966** *DARE* (Qu. K18, . . *To identify a cow*) Inf **FL**32, Used to earmark and brand; **NM**6, Earmarking—cut off or notch part of ear.

earmarker n
1 See **earmark** v.
2 =**ear tag.**

1968 *DARE* (Qu. K18, . . *To identify a cow*) Inf **MN**12, Earmarker—made of metal or plastic, pinched on the ear.

earmarking See **earmark** v

earn v Usu |ɝn, ɜn|; also |ɑrn| Pronc-spp *old-fash, airn, arn;* **chiefly S Midl** *old-fash, yarn, yearn* See Pronc Intro 3.I.1.f
Std senses, var forms.

1818 Fessenden *Ladies Monitor* 171 **NEng,** Some provincial words and phrases . . *Arn'd* for earned. **1841** (1952) Cooper *Deerslayer* 121 **nNY,** 'Twould n't be a bad title to begin with, and it has been fairly 'arned. **1887** Freeman *Humble Romance* 260 **MA,** You'll think I ain't airnin' my own vittles. **1894** Riley *Armazindy* 1 **IN,** She's airnt the good / Will o' all the neighborhood. **1899** (1912) Green *VA Folk-Speech, Arn. . .* "He can't arn his living." *Ibid, Yarn.* **1903** *DN* 2.337 **seMO,** *Yearn. . .* 'He doesn't yearn his salt.' **1911** *DN* 3.540 **eKY,** *Yearn.* **1917** *DN* 4.407 **wNC,** *Arn. . .* Also Ill., N.H. **1924** Raine *Land of Saddle-Bags* 105 **sAppalachians,** They take the "y" from "yeast," but add it to "earn." **1941** in 1942 McAtee *Dial. Grant Co. IN* 78, Earned (yurnt). **1959** *VT Hist.* new ser 27.134 **nwVT,** Earn [ɑrn] . . Rare. **1985** *DARE* File **sIN, KY** (as of c1910), He never [ɑ·rnd] a cent.

earnest adj, n Usu |ˈɝnəst, ˈɜ-, -nɪst|; for addit varr see quots Pronc-spp *arnest, airnest, yearnest* See Pronc Intro 3.I.1.f and 3.II.12
A Forms.

1836 (1955) *Crockett Almanacks* 55 **wTN,** He was so arnest, that he kept on preaching in the tree. **1841** (1952) Cooper *Deerslayer* 71 **nNY,** They are in ra'al 'arnest to smoke you out. **1844** Thompson *Major Jones's Courtship* 24 **GA,** They're shootin in good yearnest! **1887** Freeman *Humble Romance* 260 **MA,** I'm in airnest. **1894** *DN* 1.330 **swNJ,** *Earnest. . .* [ærnəst]. **1917** in 1944 *ADD* **sWV,** Airnest. **1920s** in 1944 *ADD* **cNY,** [ˈɝnɪst], not -[əst]. **1942** *AmSp* 17.151 **seNY,** Earnest. . . [ɝ] 13 [infs], [ɜ] 4 [infs], [ɜɪ] 1 [inf].

B As noun.
In marble play: a game in which winners keep the marbles. [From **in earnest**] Cf **keeps**

1955 *PADS* 23.17 **TN,** *Earnest. . .* A game in which the players keep the marbles they knock from the ring; a variant of *keeps.*

‡earnestly, in adj phr [By hypercorrection]
In earnest.

1959 Lomax *Rainbow Sign* 46 **AL** [Black], He knows when you're in earnestly about a thing and when you ain't.

ear needle n [Prob blend of **ear sewer 1** + **darning needle 1**]
A **dragonfly.**

c1955 Reed–Person *Ling. Atlas Pacific NW,* 1 inf, Ear needles.

ear notch n Cf **ear cut**
An **earmark** made by cutting a wedge from the ear of a cow.

1965–70 *DARE* (Qu. K18, . . *Mark . . used . . to identify a cow*) 13 Infs, **chiefly east of Missip R,** Ear notch(es); **KY**90, Ear notch—old-fashioned; **TN**14, Ear notch—old-fashioned . . Used when they used to put their cows all out on the mountain together.

ear of corn n

The egg capsule of the ten-ridged whelk *(Neptunea lyrata decemcostata).*

1901 Arnold *Sea-Beach* 12, Cylindrical piles of little capsules, sometimes called "ears of corn," hold the eggs of *Chrysodomus.* **[1981** Rehder *Audubon Field Guide Seashells* 551, The New England Neptune or Ten-ridged Whelk. . . lays its egg-capsule masses in the form of elevated, cylindrical towers.]

earp See **urp**

ear pulling vbl n

=ear weight contest.

1973 *Pioneer All-Alaska Weekly* (Fairbanks AK) 27 Jul 3/2, The Eskimos will have high kicks, ear pulling, . . the nulukatuk or blanket-toss and many others.

earrings n [Perh from the curved shape of the flower, which would allow it to be hooked over the ears]

A **grass pink 1** (here: *Calopogon barbatus*).

1938 Matschat *Suwannee R.* 221 **nFL, sGA,** She showed him a picture of the orchid in her hand. "This little one, which covers the low grounds along the riverbanks, is called earrings by the children; there are three or four different kinds blooming from winter to mid-summer—some of them are pink, and others are white tinged with purple." *Ibid* 291, [Glossary:] Earrings: *Limodorum graminifolium.*

ears, at adj phr Cf **ear** n[1] **B**

At odds; in disagreement.

1968 *DARE* Tape **MI**96, Buckley school and the music school are at ears all the time. Music wants to have the whole pie, and Buckley doesn't want them to infringe here.

ears back, get one's v phr

1968 *DARE* (Qu. DD13, *When a drinker is just beginning to show the effects of the liquor, you say he's ______*) Inf **PA**98, Getting his ears back.

ears chewed down, get one's See **ears knocked down, get one's**

earscrew n **chiefly Gulf States, Lower Missip Valley** See Map

An earring, esp one with a screw fastener.

1927 (1970) Sears *Catalogue* 733, Solid 18-karat white gold earscrews, for pierced ears. **c1960** *Wilson Coll.* **csKY,** *Ear screws. . .* Very modern type of ear bobs; older women had their ears punctured. **1965–70** *DARE* (Qu. W34, *Jewelry that a woman wears on her ears*) 35 Infs, **chiefly Gulf States, Lower Missip Valley,** Earscrews. [28 Infs old, none young] **1968** *DARE* FW Addit **TN**17A, Earscrews—Inf talking about earrings.

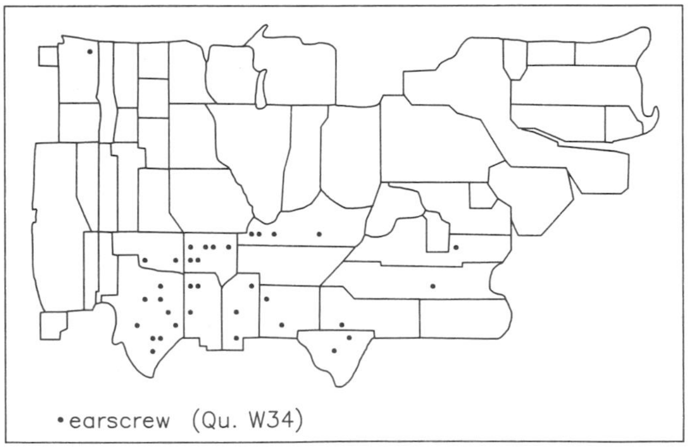

•earscrew (Qu. W34)

ear sewer n |ˈɪrˌsowər| [See quot 1949]

1 A **dragonfly.** See also **ear cutter, eye stitcher, sewer, sewing bug, sneeder**

[1949 (1972) Funk & Wagnalls *Dict. Folkl.* 324, Children are told that if they tell lies the (dragonfly) will sew up their mouths; it is even likely to sew up nose and ears and go right on through the head.] **1956** *PADS* 25.9 **WA,** Ear sewer. **1961** *AmSp* 36.31 **Cleveland OH,** *Ear-sewer* alternates with *(devil's) darning needle. . .* Both terms show a marked decline in use as cultivation of the informant rises. **1969** *DARE* (Qu. R2) Inf **NY**183, Ear sewer. **1971** Bright *Word Geog. CA & NV* 113, Earsewer . . 17 [infs] . . [chiefly] S.F. Bay Area. . . "He will sew your ears up, they used to tell us." **1971** Wood *Vocab. Change* 35 **Sth,** *Ear sewer* has a slight distribution east of the Mississippi.

2 =praying mantis.

1968 *AmSp* 43.52 **KS,** One student marked *ear-sewer* as 'a dragonfly' and 2 marked it as 'a praying mantis.'

earsipelus See **erysipelas**

ears knocked down, get one's v phr Also *get one's ears chewed down*

To receive a severe scolding.

1966–69 *DARE* (Qu. II27, *If somebody gives you a very sharp scolding, . . "I certainly got a ______ for that."*) Infs **ID**5, **SD**5, **TX**65, My ears knocked down; **GA**3, My ears chewed down. [3 of 4 Infs old]

ear slit n Also *ear split(ting)* **chiefly Sth, Midl** Cf **split**

An **earmark** made by a horizontal cut in the ear *(split)* or a cut on the underside of the ear *(slit)* of a cow or other animal.

1929 *AmSp* 5.70 **NE,** Cattle are frequently given not only a "scorch" but a "mark," often called . . an "ear mark" or "ear splitting," if the ear is notched or the tip of it cut. **1965–70** *DARE* (Qu. K18, . . *Mark . . used . . to identify a cow*) 15 Infs, **chiefly Sth, Midl,** Ear slit; **GA**87, **VA**46, Ear slit—old fashioned; **MD**24, Ear slit—a V cut in the ear to show one kind of vaccination, a plain slit for another; **NY**163, Used to use ear slits—two cuts on this part of the ear [*DARE* Ed: Illustr in QR indicates underside of ear.]; **GA**77, **SC**9, Ear split(s).

ears lowered, get one's v phr Also *get one's ears set back, ~ down, ~ out joc*

To get a haircut.

1950 *WELS (Joking names for getting your hair cut)* 11 Infs, **WI,** Get my ears lowered; 1 Inf, Get my ears set back; 1 Inf, Get my ears set down; 2 Infs, Get my ears set out. **1954** *Harder Coll.* **cwTN,** Get (one's) ears lowered . . get a haircut. **c1960** *Wilson Coll.* **csKY,** Get my ears lowered. . . Get a much-needed haircut; haircuts used to be very far apart. *Ibid,* Get my ears set down. **1960** *VT Hist.* new ser 28.128 **VT,** To get one's ears lowered. **1967–68** *DARE* (Qu. X5) Inf **AZ**1, Ears lowered; **TX**54, Got roached; ears lowered. **1978** Doig *This House* 77 **MT** (as of c1950), *Well, I gotta go in and get my ears lowered* was the standard excuse to come to town for a night of carousing.

ear split(ting) See **ear slit**

ear-string n [**string** tendon of an animal body; *OED* 1810] Cf **gizzard string, pop one's**

A supposed tendon or nerve of the ear; fig in phr *bust one's ear-string* to become disillusioned and deaf to another's speech.

1917 Torrence *Granny Maumee* 52 [Black], I done got my ear-string bus' now an' dem preachah wu'ds can't fool me no mo'.

eart' See **earth**

ear tag n Also *ear tab* **chiefly Nth, Midl** See Map Also called **ear button 1, ~ clip 1**

An identification marker, usu of metal, fastened to the ear of a cow or other animal; hence v *ear-tag* to identify with such a marker.

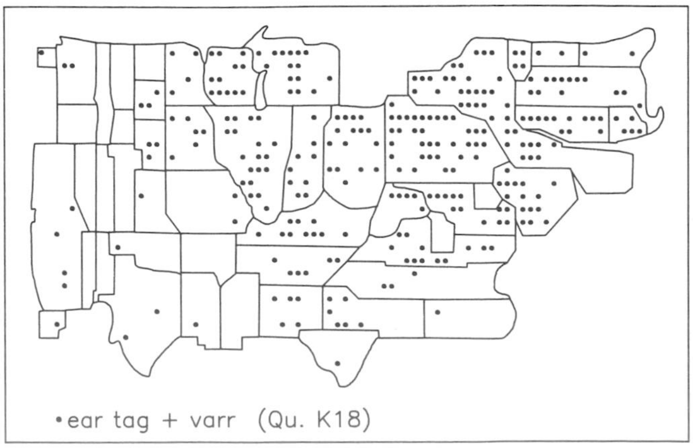

•ear tag + varr (Qu. K18)

1907 White *AZ Nights* 150, I remember a New England movement looking toward small brass tags to be hung from the ear. Inextinguishable laughter followed the spread of this doctrine through Arizona. Imagine a puncher descending to examine politely the ear-tags of wild cattle on the open range or in a round-up. **1950** *WELS (What kind of mark do you use to identify a cow?)* 19 Infs, **WI,** Ear tag(s). **1965–70** *DARE* (Qu. K18, . . *Mark . . used . . to identify a cow*) 284 Infs, **chiefly Nth, Midl,** Ear tag(s); **MI**83, **OH**78, Ear tab; **MI**38, Cows are probably ear-tagged.

ear tattoo See **tattoo**

earth n Pronc-spp *airth, 'arth* (see Pronc Intro 3.I.1.f), *uth;* **chiefly Sth, S Midl,** *old-fash, yairth, yarth, yearth, yeath, yeth, yuth; chiefly among Black speakers, earf, urf, yearf; Gullah, eart, ye't, yut* (see Pronc Intro 3.I.17)

Std senses, var forms.

1823 Cooper *Pioneers* 2.279 **cNY,** A man that's taking his last look at the 'arth. **1844** Thompson *Major Jones's Courtship* 27 **GA,** Wher upon yeath is you all gwine! *Ibid* 103, The yeath-quake has shuck all her sense out of her. *Ibid* 76, Whar upon yeth is Jarsey, anyhow. **1848** (1894) Lowell *Biglow* **'Upcountry' MA** [Glossary], Airth. **1859** (1968) Bartlett *Americanisms, Yeath. . .* among the illiterate at the South. **1871** Eggleston *Hoosier Schoolmaster* 12 **sIN,** Heaven and yarth can't make him let go. **1884** Lanier *Poems* 164 **GA,** What above / This yea'th can be your line? **1887** (1967) Harris *Free Joe* 128 **GA,** What upon the top side er the yeth ails you? **1891** Cooke *Huckleberries* 13 **CT,** There ain't no reason on airth why you should n't keep company with him, ef you like him. **1891** Page *Elsket* 123 **VA,** De Scripturs say you is to multiply an' replanish de uth. **1892** Eggleston *Hoosier Schoolmaster* 43 **sIN,** This prefixed *y* is a mark of a very illiterate or antique form of the dialect. I have known *piece yarthen* used for "a piece of earthen" (ware). . . "The earth" pronounced in a drawling way will produce *the yearth.* **1893** Shands *MS Speech, Yearth. . .* is certainly more common [than *yeath*] in Mississippi, although the other pronunciation is sometimes heard. **1901** *DN* 2.182 **neKY** [Black], *Earf.* **1903** *DN* 2.290 **Cape Cod MA** (as of a1857), *Airth.* **1905** Culbertson *Banjo Talks* 87 **Sth** [Black], W'at on yearf dis mean? **1908** *S. Atl. Qrly.* 7.335 **SC** [Gullah], Dish yut . . mash up wud pledgah an' pain. **1909** *DN* 3.390 **eAL, wGA,** *Yearth, yarth.* **1917** Torrence *Granny Maumee* 73 [Black], Does you know how you stan' 'pon top er dis yu'th? **1922** Gonzales *Black Border* 298 **sSC, GA coasts** [Gullah glossary], *Eart'*—earth, world, or soil, ground. *Ibid* 339, *Ye't, Yu't* earth. **1923** *DN* 5.200 **swMO,** *Airth.* **1928** *AmSp* 3.404 **Ozarks,** The word *earth* is usually sounded something like *airth,* but sometimes one hears an initial *y* sound—*yairth.* **1929** Sale *Tree Named John* 6 **MS** [Black], De Bible say "ez de moon wax strong in de heb'm, so will de young on de ye'th." *Ibid, passim.* **1940** Faulkner *Hamlet* 394 **MS,** "Wait," he said. "There air anger in the yearth. . . For what's rendered to the yearth, the yearth will keep until hit's ready to reveal hit." **1942** Hall *Smoky Mt. Speech* 42 **wNC, eTN,** Development of a glide . . before [ɝ] and variants thereof (original front vowels) occurs in . . *(the) earth* [ðɪ'jɝθ], [ðɪ'jɛθ], [jeθ]. **1949** Turner *Africanisms* 268 **eSC** [Gullah], [ʌtkwek]. . . [ʌt]. **1953** Brewer *Word Brazos* 10 **eTX** [Black], De pastuh of Mothuh Mt. Zion Chu'ch, say, "Gawd so lacked [=liked] de worl' in sich a way, dat he done sen' de onlies' son he got down to de urf so dat dem what b'lieve on 'im gonna be saved." **1959** *VT Hist.* new ser 27.134, *Earth* [ʌθ] . . Common in rural areas. **c1960** *Wilson Coll.* **csKY,** *Earth* [jɝθ] very rare among elderly. **1974** Fink *Mountain Speech* 30 **wNC, eTN,** *Yearth* . . earth.

earth cellar See **dirt cellar**

earth club n [*earth* soil + *club,* with ref to the blunt shape of its root]

=**squawroot.**

1876 Hobbs *Bot. Hdbk.* 33, Earth club . . Orobanche Americana. **1900** Lyons *Plant Names* 114. **1959** Carleton *Index Herb. Plants* 40, *Earth Club:* Conopholis americana.

earth crab n [See quot 1940]

A mole cricket *(Gryllotalpidae).*

1889 *Century Dict.* 1820, *Earth-crab. . .* An occasional name of the mole-cricket, *Gryllotalpa vulgaris.* **1940** Teale *Insects* 211, This cricket [=the mole cricket] is the largest of the family. Its hard, shell-like body has given it the nickname of "earth crab."

earthernware n [Var of *earthenware*]

1741 in 1906 *Colonial Rec. GA* 6.20, Andrew Duchee . . petitioned this Board that he might have leave to cut Ash Wood upon the said Island to burn Earthern Ware with. **1920s** in 1944 *ADD* **cNY,** ['ɝðṛnweṛ] earthernware. **c1935** *New Yorker* in 1944 *ADD,* [Advt:] Earthernware.

earth juice n *joc* Cf **Adam's Ale**

1939 *AmSp* 14.90 **TN,** *Earth juice.* Water. "I'll draw up a pail of cold earth juice."

earth mover n *joc* Cf **gully washer, trash mover**

1969 *DARE* (Qu. B25, . . *A very heavy rain*) Inf **GA**84, Earth mover—old-fashioned.

earth mulberry n

A **strawberry** (here: *Fragaria vesca*).

1963 Craighead *Rocky Mt. Wildflowers* 82, *Strawberry. Fragaria vesca. . . Other names:* Earth Mulberry.

earthquake n Also *bottled earthquake* *obs*

An alcoholic mixed drink.

1869 Twain *Innocents* 149, The uneducated foreigner could not even furnish a Santa Cruz Punch, an Eye-Opener, a Stone-Fence, or an Earthquake. **1891** Farmer–Henley *Slang* 3.251, *Earthquake.* Bottled earthquake . . (American).—Intoxicating drinks. **1897** Barrère–Leland *Slang* 1.323, [Quoting *Chicago Tribune,* nd:] *Bottled earthquakes* are just as bad as the other kind. Scratch a *bottled earthquake* and you'll find a cocktail.

earthquake weather n **CA**

Hot, humid, windless weather, sometimes thought to precede or forecast an earthquake.

1865 in 1926 Harte *Sketches* 29 **CA,** Yet it is a proof of the rarity of really pleasant weather in this climate, rather than of any logical acumen or scientific knowledge on the part of San Franciscans, that they invariably look with suspicion upon this atmospheric blandness, and . . call it "earthquake weather." **1939** *Newsweek* 6 Feb 23/3, Some seismic experts . . believe that "earthquake weather" is more than a feeling in the bones of weather-wise peasants. **1963** Didion *Run River* 119 **Sacramento CA,** The sky was overcast with the peculiar yellow haze Edith Knight called earthquake weather. **1967–69** *DARE* (Qu. B4, *A day when the air is very still, moist, and warm—it's ______*) Infs **CA**80, 113, Earthquake weather; **CA**15, Earthquake weather—old fashioned now; probably from days after quake of 1906. **1982** *Milwaukee Jrl.* (WI) 23 Sept 2/5 **sCA,** The belief in earthquake weather is "persistent and unshakeable". . . "The most common description of this phenomenon is an unusually warm and muggy day—with overcast skies and a still, breathless quality to the air." **1982** *Smithsonian Letters* **sCA,** Earthquake weather is very hot & at first dry, then in the afternoon or late morning it gets sultry or muggy. The air is . . so still it makes you think everything is still. . . It gives you . . the feeling that the air, trees, insects whatever, are themselves expecting something to happen. The use of the term earthquake weather is limited to the West Coast. . . I don't believe it's used north of San Francisco. **1989** *Capital Times* (Madison WI) 18 Oct 1/4 **San Francisco CA,** "People kept saying it was earthquake weather," . . He said earthquakes seem to occur more when the weather is particularly hot and humid, as it has been there for the last few days.

earthslide n

A landslide.

1942 *Sun* (Baltimore MD) 31 Dec 6/1 **VA,** [Headline:] Earthslide Derails Four Cars Of N. & W. . . [Text:] The avalanche of earth and rocks crashed against the express cars. **1967–68** *DARE* (Qu. C16, *When a mass of earth and rock comes loose from a high place and rushes down*) Infs **AR**47, **GA**19, **LA**18, **OH**51, **TN**7, Earthslide.

earth snake n

Std: a snake of the genus *Virginia.* Also called **gray snake, ground snake c, worm snake**

earth squirrel n

A **ground squirrel n b** (here: *Spermophilus* spp).

1857 Chandless *Visit to Salt Lake* 311 **sCA,** Little heaps of earth thrown out from the burrowings of the earth-squirrel, who generally sat on the top of the heap, sunning himself.

earthworm n **widespread exc Rocky Mts, Upper MW; esp freq Sth** See Map

Any of var annelid worms, esp of the family Lumbricidae. Also called **angledog, angler worm, angleworm, angling worm, bait n 3, baitworm, bloodworm 1, bluebait, crawler n[1] 1, creeper 6, dewworm, dirtworm, dug worm, eaceworm, eelworm, fish bait 1, fishing worm, fishworm, garden worm, ground bait, ground rattler 2, groundworm 1, gunter worm, land worm, manure worm, muck worm, mudworm, night crawler, night prowler, night**

walker, rainworm, red wiggler, redworm, ringler, sandworm, sea worm, shitworm, stretch worm, trinkle, wiggler, wiggleworm, worm, wriggler

1737 (1911) Brickell *Nat. Hist. NC* 159, The *Earth-worms,* whereof there are several sorts, and are the same here as with us in *Ireland.* **1832** Williamson *Hist. ME* 1.168, We have among us, in summer, a variety of native *Worms.* . . These are the *Grub;* the *Earthworm;* the *Brandling.* **1912** *DN* 3.566 **cNY,** *Angle-worm* . . Common word for *earth worm,* which is seldom used. **1933** *AmSp* 8.4.12 **sSC coast** [Gullah], [ʌtwʌrəm] is the term in common use by the Negroes on the islands in Charleston Co. **1949** Kurath *Word Geog.* 45, The Carolinas and Georgia are the only part of the Eastern States where *earthworm* . . is a folk word. Elsewhere it is a book word or a city word. *Earthworm* is used by the common people from the mouth of Chesapeake Bay southward. In North Carolina we find it along the shore and in the eastern part of the piedmont, in South Carolina in the Low Country and in the entire piedmont. It occurs also in Gullah. **1961** Folk *Word Atlas N. LA* Map 0914, Worm used for fish bait—earth worm[,] 50%[;] red worm[,] 13%[;] fish worm[,] 11%[;] others[,] 26%. **1961** *AmSp* 36.31 **neOH,** *Earthworm* . . becomes progressively more popular as the informants become younger and more cultivated. **1962** Atwood *Vocab. TX* 58, As in the coastal areas of the Carolinas, *earthworm* . . is the most usual word for the annelid used for fish bait. **1965–70** *DARE* (Qu. P5, . . *The common worm used as bait*) 296 Infs, **widespread exc Rocky Mts, Upper MW; esp freq Sth,** Earthworm. **1966** Dakin *Dial. Vocab. Ohio R. Valley* 2.394, *Earthworm* appears to have rare use as a true folk word in eastern and southern Kentucky and is fairly common in folk use in southern Illinois. This word is also attested a number of times in southwestern Ohio and once in the Whitewater Valley. In this section *earthworm* also appears to have currency as a folk term and could well have been established by the Quaker settlement from the eastern Carolinas. *Earthworm* appears scattered elsewhere, sometimes characterized by the informant as "a book word." **1967** Faries *Word Geog. MO* 111, *Earthworm* (53 occurrences), a folk word in the south and a book word in the north, is limited almost altogether to the area south of the Missouri River, especially to the Southeast Lowland. **1971** *AmSp* 46.180 **Chicago IL,** Potentially productive are words recurring in the speech of younger, well-educated members of the dominant (white) culture, such as *peach seed,* . . and *earthworm.* **1971** Wood *Vocab. Change* 36, *Red worm* is preferred in Tennessee and Arkansas; *earthworm* in Georgia (just one point more than *fish bait*), Alabama, Mississippi, Florida, Louisiana, and Oklahoma. **1973** Gawthrop *Dial. Calumet* 73 **nwIN,** *Worm used for bait in fishing:* earthworm 45, fishing worm 21, fishworm 21, [*DARE* Ed: 5 other terms totaling 67]. **1973** Allen *LAUM* 1.326 **Upper MW** (as of c1950), Literary *earthworm* appears as a relatively infrequent variant in all five states.

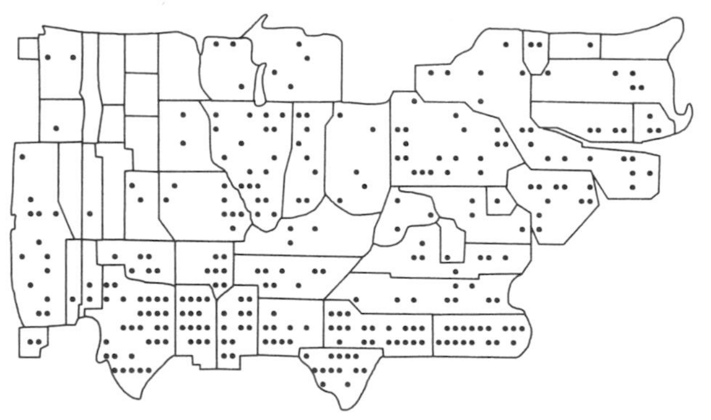

•earthworm (Qu. P5)

ear weight contest n **AK** Also called **ear pulling**

An orig Eskimo contest in which the participants walk as far as possible while carrying weights strung from loops around their ears.

1977 *Tundra Times* (Fairbanks AK) 3 Aug 6/1, Ear weight contest (walking as far as possible with 16 lbs.) **1977** *AK Advocate* (Anchorage) 4 Aug 12/2, Don Ahsoak of Barrow carried 17 pounds of weights attached to a string looped over his ear for more than 1,000 feet to win the ear weight contest.

earwig n

A centipede (Chilopoda)

1938 Brimley *Insects NC* 500, Centipedes. . . are locally called "earwigs" in North Carolina.

earworm See **corn earworm**

eas' See **east** n[2]

ease v

1 with *up* or *off;* rarely with *down:* Of the wind: to abate. **scattered, but esp Nth, N Midl**

1939 *LANE* Map 92, **ceMA, seNH, nwVT,** Easing up. **1950** *WELS* (*When the wind is decreasing*) 2 Infs, **WI,** Easing up. **1961** Folk *Word Atlas N. LA* Map 0106, The wind is ______[;] laying[,] 24%[;] easing up[,] 19%[;] not blowing so hard [,] 11% [;] others[,] 46%. **1962** Atwood *Vocab. TX* 39, When a strong wind begins to abate, it is said to be *laying* . . or occasionally . . *easing up.* **1965–70** *DARE* (Qu. B13, *When the wind begins to decrease, you say it's* ______) Infs **MA**1, **NH**14, **NY**8, 49, **OH**36, **TX**43, Easing off; **IL**98, **VT**16, **WV**3, 5, **WI**64, Easing up. **1966** Dakin *Dial. Vocab. Ohio R. Valley* 2.29, *Laying down* (2), *slackening* ~ (1), . . *easing* ~ (1) are also attested [in the Ohio R. Valley]. . . The two Darke County, Ohio, informants say only *easing up* and *slackening up. Easing up* also appears once each in Clermont County, Ohio; Clay County, Indiana . . ; and Monroe County, Illinois. . . Two Kentucky informants say *easing off.*

2 with *away, down, off, out,* or *over:* To back down, as from a position. [Perh by ext of naut sense of *ease* to steer less closely into the wind]

1916 Macy–Hussey *Nantucket Scrap Basket* 130 **Nantucket MA,** "Ease off"—To give way slowly, as in argument. **1945** Colcord *Sea Language, Ease off* or *away.* To steer less closely into the wind. . . Ashore, the phrase means to be less severe; moderate one's conduct. **1968** *DARE* (Qu. II31, *In an argument between two people, when one of them claims too much and the other shows him up: "He saw that he was wrong, so he started to* ______.") Infs **MD**12, **OH**72, Ease down (*or* out, over).

3 usu with *about, off, over,* etc: To move quietly or unobtrusively. **chiefly Sth, S Midl** See Map

1949 Guthrie *Way West* 22 **MO** (as of 1847), "Just easin home," the man answered. **1949** Hornsby *Lonesome Valley* 269 (*Hench Coll.*) **eKY,** There was no sound of anything but water, running down the branch, and wind, easing through the trees. **1955** Roberts *S. from Hell-fer-Sartin* 139 **seKY,** He [=a giant] eased around and told it to the king. And he [=the king] got a-holt of it and he eased around to the tailor and told him that if he would get rid of these giants . . he would give him his daughter. **1965–70** *DARE* (Qu. Y26b, *To walk very quietly: "The children filled their pockets and* ______ *out the back way."*) 21 Infs, **chiefly Sth, S Midl,** Eased; (Qu. Y26a, *To walk very quietly: "She came* ______ *to the baby's bed."*) Infs **FL**51, **KY**28, **MS**16, **TN**1, **TX**95, Easing around; **GA**72, **TX**86, Easing in (to the house); **FI**27, Eased along; (Qu. A21) Inf **UT**4, Ease off; (Qu. Y19) Inf **GA**67, Ease along; (Qu. Y21) Inf **TX**95, Ease about; (Qu. Y32) Infs **GA**72, **SC**64, Ease in (*or* up); (Qu. AA7a) Inf **PA**237, Trying to ease up on a man.

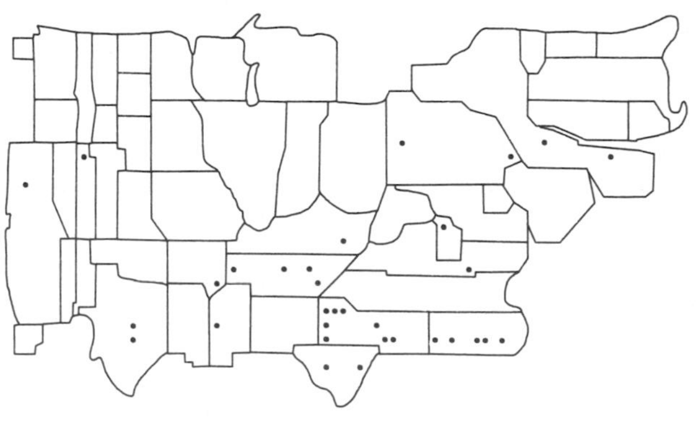

•ease 3 + varr (Qq. Y26a, b, A21, Y19, Y21, Y32, AA7a)

4 with *along* or *on:* To take one's leave, depart.

1959 *AmSp* 34.154 **FL,** With all plans made clear in typical Gator gab, it's time to hop out, hop off, or ease on (make a parting gesture). **1966** *DARE* (Qu. Y19, *To begin to go away from a place: "It's about time for me to* ______.") Inf **GA**7, Ease along.

5 tr; also with *on* or *up:* To treat gently or carefully.

1966–70 *DARE* (Qu. BB2, *If a person is careful not to put too much weight on his injured leg, you might say he was ——— that leg*) Infs **FL**2, **MD**28, **MO**4, **VA**106, Easing [All Infs old]; **NC**83, **PA**94, 130, Easing up (on).

ease about See **ease 3**

ease along See **ease 4**

ease away See **ease 2**

ease down See **ease 1, 2**

easement n Pronc-sp *asement* [*OED easement* sb. 2, "*Arch.* or *obs.*"]

Comfort, consolation, relief.

1823 Cooper *Pioneers* 1.191 **cNY**, The Sargeant read me the chapter about him, . . and a mighty asement it was, to listen to any thing from the book [=the Bible]. **1881** Twain *Prince & Pauper* 63, Give thy misgivings easement. **1914** Furman *Sight* 37 **KY**, I named it Evy, thinking to give her some easement or pleasure. **1938** Rawlings *Yearling* 391 **nFL**, "I'll git easement direckly." "You're likely ruptured." "Even so—Hit'll clare up."

ease off See **ease 1, 2, 3**

ease on See **ease 4, 5**

ease out See **ease 2**

ease over See **ease 2, 3**

ease up See **ease 1, 5**

easies exclam Cf **baby up**

In marble play: see quot 1955.

1942 Berrey–Van den Bark *Amer. Slang* 665.6, *Easies!*, a call for permission to shoot easy, or a partner's signal to shoot easy. **1955** *PADS* 23.17 **cTN**, *Easies*. . . A call that allows the player to shoot in an easy or slow fashion towards the target. **c1970** Wiersma *Marbles Terms* **swMI**.

easies n

A version of the game of jacks with easy rules.

1975 Ferretti *Gt. Amer. Book Sidewalk Games* 101, In "easies," a player can touch other jacks while picking up the one or ones she is after. . . "Easies" also permits the separation of "kissies."

easily See **easy** intj

easing-down ppl adj [Cf **ease 1**]

Gentle.

1979 *DARE* File **AR**, [1959 newspaper:] Then [late in March] came an easing down rain which drew the frost out of the ground.

easing powder n **sAppalachians** Cf **resting powder**

An analgesic.

1917 *DN* 4.411 **wNC**, *Easin'-powder*. . . An opiate. . . [also] *restin' powder*. **1922** (1926) Kephart *Highlanders* 298 **sAppalachians**, Cain't you-uns give her some easin'-powder for that hurtin' in her chist? **1974** Fink *Mountain Speech* 8 **wNC**, **eTN** (as of 1910–65), *Easing powders*. . . drug to ease pain. **1976** Garber *Mountain-ese* 26 **sAppalachians**, *Easing-powders* . . pain killers. I gotta go home and git some easin' powders fer my headache.

eassworm See **eaceworm**

East n[1]

Usu with *the:* The eastern part of the United States (relative to the speaker; see quot 1907). Cf **back East, down East**

1782 (1975) Freneau *Poems & Misc. Wks.* 277 **PA**, The *east* and the *south* losing communication, / The Yankies will die by the act of *Starvation*. **1869** Stowe *Oldtown Folks* iii **MA**, North, South, East and West have been largely populated from New England. **1885** *Century Illustr. Mag.* 30.55/1, This, indeed, is the feeling of most people in the East to-day regarding Indians. **1906** *DN* 3.134 **nwAR**, *East*. . . Northeast. "He's from the *East*—from Massachusetts." **1907** *Springfield Republican* 28 Feb. 7 *(DA)* **MA**, The East is a relative term as one traverses the American continent. Thus when the Californian newspapers report that settlers from the East are locating in Glynn county, the far easterner is surprised to read that the reference is to people coming from Dakota. **1944** Johnson *As Much* 277 **NE**, The people [of Nebraska] . . think of the East as though it were a remote province. **1969** *DARE* FW Addit, In California, or at least in Bakersfield, the East means anything east of Denver. They say that "in the East" means Missouri, Kansas, etc. I found this in almost everybody I talked to.

east n[2] |ist|; also **chiefly Sth, S Midl** *chiefly among Black speakers* |is| Pronc-sp *eas'* [Var of *yeast*] **widespread, but chiefly Sth, Midl** See Map *esp freq among speakers with gs educ or less*

Yeast.

1872 Schele de Vere *Americanisms* 439, Yeast, the initial letter . . [is] persistently dropped (east). **1891** *PMLA* 6.175 **TN**, *Yeast* is called *east*. **1892** *DN* 1.234 **KY**, *Yeast* [ist]. [*DN* Ed: So occasionally in Michigan]. **1893** *KS Univ. Qrly.* 1.96 **KS**, *East*. **1899** (1912) Green *VA Folk-Speech*, East. **1902** *DN* 2.233 **sIL**, *East*. **1906** *DN* 3.118 **sIN**, *East*. *Ibid* 134 **nwAR**, *East*. **1908** *DN* 3.308 **eAL, wGA**, *East* [ist]. **1912** *DN* 3.567 **cNY**, Yeast . . sometimes called *'east*. **1914** *DN* 4.106 **cKS**, *East*. **1916** *DN* 4.274 **NE**, *East* . . not very common (Also Mass., Ill., Pa., N. Car., Kan.). **1923** *DN* 5.206 **swMO**, East. **1924** Raine *Land of Saddle-Bags* 105 **sAppalachians**, They take "y" from "yeast," but add it to "earn." **1927** *AmSp* 2.353 **WV**, The east did not rise well. **1942** Hall *Smoky Mt. Speech* 87, *Yeast* loses its [j] ([ist]), by assimilation to the following vowel. **1946** *PADS* 6.12 **ceNC**, *East*. . . Common. **c1960** *Wilson Coll.* **csKY**, *East* is heard often, on all levels, for yeast. **1961** Kurath–McDavid *Pronc. Engl.* 174, Except for relics of /ist/ (chiefly in the folk speech of Eastern New England), /jist/ prevails on all social levels throughout the Northern area. . . In the Midland and the South, on the other hand, /ist/ is the most common pronunciation of *yeast*. **1965–70** *DARE* (Qu. H16) 161 Infs, **widespread, but chiefly Sth, Midl**, East; **MD**37, East powder; **MD**24, **NC**55, Hop (*or* potato) east; 16 Infs, **chiefly Sth, S Midl**, Eas' [is] [14 Infs Black]; (Qu. H17) 49 Infs, **chiefly Sth, Midl**, East [in var combs: see *DS*]; **MI**34, **VA**39, 48, Eas' cake(s); **KY**81, **VA**39, Cake (*or* dry, Fleischmann's) eas'; (Qu. H15) Infs **KY**52, **NJ**67, **VA**48, East bread (*or* biscuits, rolls); (Qu. H18) Inf **MS**46, East bread; (Qu. H19) Inf **KY**74, East biscuits; (Qu. H28) Inf **NC**55, East doughnut; (QR p42) Inf **AL**25, Roll is made with east [ist]. [Of all Infs responding to Qq. H16 and H17, 26% and 25% respectively were gs educ or less; of those giving these responses, 49% and 48% respectively were gs educ or less.] **1965** Carmony *Speech Terre Haute* 78 **cwIN**, The pronunciation of *Yeast* as /jist/ is regular in cultivated speech. . . /ist/ as in *east* is regular among the folk. **1966–68** *DARE* Tapes **IN**3, 16, East [for yeast]; **MI**22, Flour, sugar, dry east or cake east; **TX**32, I . . use buttermilk an' bakin' soda . . an' shortnin' an' sugar an' salt and a package of east; **WA**2, [FW:] What kind of bread did you make? [Inf:] I made eas' bread, just like we have today. We made our own east. **1967** *DARE* FW Addit **CO**4, Yeast [ist]; **MS**, [ist]. **1973** Allen *LAUM* 1.284 **Upper MW** (as of c1950), The "east" pronunciation [of *yeast*] is distinctly old-fashioned. . . Furthermore, it occurs largely in the eastern half of the UM and rarely in the more recently settled western portion. **1979** *Up-Country* Jan 38 **csME**, Mother always served " 'east bread," hot from the oven.

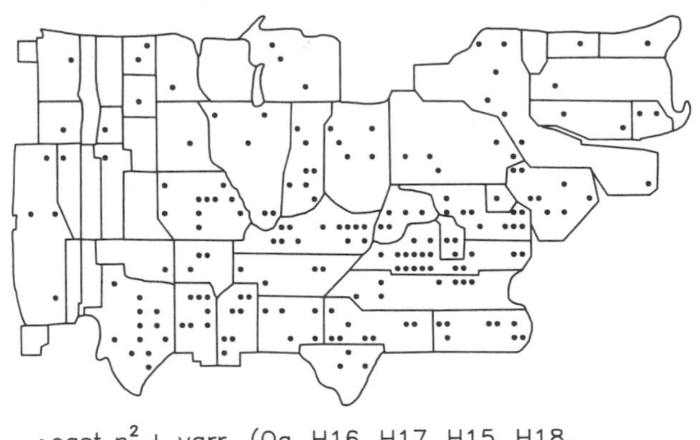

•east n[2] + varr (Qq. H16, H17, H15, H18, H19, H28)

east, about adj, adv phr [See quot 1889] *arch*

In proper form, acceptable; directly, completely.

1848 Bartlett *Americanisms* 375, *To walk into*. . . I did walk into the beef, and taters, and things, about east. *Ibid* 398, *About east*, is about right; in the proper manner. A common slang expression in New England. **1856** Whitcher *Bedott Papers* 303 **cNY**, If ther's any body that *won't* knuckle tew her, I tell ye they have to take it *about east*. **1857** *Knickerbocker* 49.37 **NYC**, Some men, after smashing Clausen as about east as you seem to have done it, wouldn't take the idea for much of a compliment. **1867** Lowell *Biglow* xvii **MA**, There was not a Yankee in his audience whose problem had not always been to find out what was *about east,* and to shape his course accordingly. **1889** (1971) Farmer *Americanisms* 4, Everybody and everything connected with the East, *i.e.,* his [=the frontiersman's] native land, is commendable. To his mind they cannot be surpassed—hence the things he would hold up to admiration he says are *about East, i.e.,* "about right."

east and west adv phr For varr see quots Cf **galley-west**

In every direction, every which way.

1942 Berrey–Van den Bark *Amer. Slang* 5.5, *Disorderly; in confusion* . . east, west and crooked. **1966–69** *DARE* (Qu. MM12a, . . *'In all directions' . . "He shot into a flock of birds and they went ______."*) Infs **NC**35, **OH**40, **SC**34, **VA**21, (Scattered) east and west; **KY**40, Eastwest, northwest, and crooked.

east'ard adv, n Also sp *easterd* [Var of *eastward*] **N Atl**

1783 in 1915 *New Engl. Hist. & Geneal. Reg.* 69.295 **MA,** Ellis Bartlett went off to the Easterd ye 17 Day. **1823** Cooper *Pioneers* 1.266 **cNY,** The wind was here at the south'ard and east'ard. **1903** *DN* 2.291 **Cape Cod MA** (as of 1850s), The *w*-sound frequently assimilated or disappeared after a consonant . . *eastard, westard.* **1916** Macy–Hussey *Nantucket Scrap Basket* 8 **Nantucket MA,** Replying that you are "bound to the south'ard" or to the "east'ard," as the case may be, you are urged to "heave to" or to "come alongside." **1945** Colcord *Sea Language* 71, *Eastward* (Pronounced east'ard). Towards the east.

easter n Cf **northeaster**

A strong east wind.

1967 *DARE* (Qu. B18, . . *Special kinds of wind*) Inf **IL**5, Easter.

Easter bell n [*Easter* the season when the flower blooms + *bell* from the shape]

1 =**dogtooth violet.**

1897 *KS Univ. Qrly.* (ser B) 6.52 **KS,** *Easter-bells:* Easter-lilies, March lilies, Granmammy's night-caps, Dog-tooth-violets; Kansas; Brandywine lily; Adder Tongue, (Ohio). (Erythronium albidum). **1915** (1926) Armstrong–Thornber *Western Wild Flowers* 28, *Erythronium grandiflorum.* . . Pushing their bright leaves right through the snow they gayly [sic] swing their golden censers in the face of winter. . . Easter Bells is a Utah name. **1937** FWP *Guide ID* 67, Horrendously named avalanche lily by some, lamb's tongue by others, Easter bells in Utah, dog-toothed violet in the east.

2 A **chickweed 1a** (here: *Stelleria holostea*).

1900 Lyons *Plant Names* 25, Greater stitchwort . . Easter-bell. **1910** Graves *Flowering Plants* 176 **CT,** *Stellaria Holostea.* . . All-bone. Easter Bell. Greater Stitchwort or Starwort. **1959** Carleton *Index Herb. Plants* 41, *Easter Bells:* Stellaria holostea (Alsine holostea).

Easter bread n Cf **pascha**

See quot 1968.

1968 *DARE* (Qu. H18, . . *Special kinds of bread*) Inf **PA**110, Easter bread—plait bread in ring for crown of thorns—birds in the thorns; a non-raised bread; it's a secret recipe, [I] will not tell [it]—[also called] Holy bread paska. **1972** *Complete World Cookery* 225 [Russian dishes], *Easter Bread* . . yeast . . sugar . . milk . . butter . . flour . . candied fruits . . egg yolks. . . Form [mixture] into plaited loaves.

Easter bush n [Perh from the time of bloom]

Forsythia.

1944 *PADS* 2.33 **wNC,** *Easter bush.* . . Forsythia.

Easter candle n

A **death camas** (here: *Zigadenus nuttallii*).

1951 *PADS* 15.28 **TX,** *Toxicoscordion nuttalli.* . . Easter candle; wild hyacinth; poison hyacinth.

Easter Christian n For varr see quots Cf **Christmas and Easter Christian**

A backslider; a person who attends church only on major holidays such as Easter or Christmas.

1950 *WELS* 2 Infs, **WI,** Easter (-Sunday) Christian. **1965–70** *DARE* (Qu. CC7, . . *A person who goes to church very seldom or not at all*) Infs **NY**30, **NC**13, **OH**87, **RI**10, Easter Christian; **IL**109, **MA**77, **PA**134, **WI**62, Easter-and-Christmas Christian (*or* attendant); **LA**14, Easter Sunday Methodist; **ME**11, Easter Worshipper; **OH**57, Easter Church-goer.

easterd See **east'ard**

Easter daisy n **West** Cf **ground daisy**

A low-growing plant of the genus *Townsendia*—usu *T. exscapa*—with daisylike flower heads.

1950 Stevens *ND Plants* 275, *Townsendia exscapa.* . . Easter Daisy. . . is the nearest to a true daisy which we have. **1953** Nelson *Plants Rocky Mt. Park* 158, Easter-daisy. . . [is] probably the earliest of all our flowers to bloom. It is found in late February in the foothills and . . in April around Estes Park. In May it is at the height of its bloom. **1973** Hitchcock–Cronquist *Flora Pacific NW* 555. **1975** Zwinger *Run River* 189 **UT,** Easter daisy *(Townsendia exscapa).* **1976** Bailey–Bailey *Hortus Third* 1118, *[Townsendia] exscapa. . . Easter daisy.* . . Ray fl[ower]s white or pinkish. Man. to N. Mex. . . *[Townsendia] Hookeri. . . Easter daisy.* . . Ray fls. white, pinkish underneath. S. B.C., Al[ber]ta, Sask., s. to Utah and Wyo. **1990** *Plants SW* (Catalog) 40, *Townsendia exemia. Easter Daisy.* . . A perfect choice for a wildflower bouquet.

Easter egg n, also attrib [*Easter egg* a brightly colored egg associated with the celebration of Easter] *joc*

A woman wearing too much makeup.

1967–68 *DARE* (Qu. W36, . . *A woman who uses a lot of cosmetics*) Inf **IL**29, They're Easter eggs; **TX**9, Easter-egg type. [Both Infs old]

Easter egg chicken n Also *Easter hen*

An orig South American var of the domestic chicken *(Gallus gallus)* which lays colored eggs.

1968 *DARE* (Qu. K76, *What other kinds of poultry are raised around here?*) Inf **PA**80, Easter hens—they lay different colored eggs. **1969** *SC Market Bulletin* 9 Jan 2, Easter egg chickens.

Easter fire n Also called **rabbit fire**

A bonfire: see quot.

1940 Writers' Program *Guide TX* 637 **cTX,** Another observance is that of "Easter fires" on the surrounding hills. For years beacons of blazing brush, lighted by local high school students, have thrown their flames skyward every Easter Eve.

Easter flower n

1 An anemone. [*OED* (at *pasque-flower*) 1597]

1863 Higginson *Outdoor Papers* 62 **MA,** Beautiful wood-anemones I found to be sure, trembling on their fragile stems, deserving all their pretty names,—Wind-flower, Easter-flower, Pasque-flower, and homoeopathic Pulsatilla. **1937** U.S. Forest Serv. *Range Plant Hdbk.* W159/2, Other appellations as April-fools, Easter-flower, . . wild crocus, and windflowers have variously designated this species. **1949** Moldenke *Amer. Wild Flowers* 5. **1968** *DARE* (Qu. S23) Inf **IA**18, Wind flowers, anemone, Easter flowers [are] all the same thing—lavender, shaped like little tulips; **WI**66, Pasqueflowers or Easter flowers.

2 A daffodil (*Narcissus* spp). **chiefly Midl**

1877 Bartlett *Americanisms* 446, Easter flower. *(Narcissus pseudo-narcissus).* **1892** *Jrl. Amer. Folkl.* 5.103 **cOH. 1894** *Jrl. Amer. Folkl.* 7.101 **cwNC. c1960** *Wilson Coll.* **csKY,** Easter flowers. . . Daffodils. Also called buttercups, cups and saucers, March flowers. **1969** *DARE* (Qu. 26a) Inf **KY**11, Easter flowers—golden yellow bell-like flower[s], blossom around Easter—daffodils. **1974** Peden *Speak to Earth* 226 **cIN,** Audrey Wilson was . . looking at a clump of pale-yellow jonquils, . . "I think Grandma Fannie must have planted these Easter flowers," she said.

3 A similar early-blooming flower such as **hepatica.** Cf **pass blummies**

1968–69 *DARE* (Qu. S26e, *Other wildflowers*) Inf **MI**96, Easter flower [and] hepatica [are the] same; (Qu. S26c, *Wildflowers that grow in woods*) Inf **MO**32, Little Easter flowers.

Easter hen See **Easter egg chicken**

Easter lily n

1 =**dogtooth violet. chiefly CA**

1897 *KS Univ. Qrly.* (ser B) 6.52 **KS,** Easter-lilies. . . Erythronium albidum. **1911** Jepson *Flora CA* 96, *E[rythronium] californicum.* . . Middletown and Healdsburg to Cloverdale (where it is very abundant and called "Easter Lily"). **1932** *Discovery* Aug 256/2 **CA,** The Easter lily, the Madonna lily, the royal lily, and the leopard or tiger lily of California were the members of this [=lily] family which were most frequently examined. **1934** Haskin *Wild Flowers Pacific Coast* 25, Giant dog-tooth violet. . . Other local names are spring lily, Easter lily [etc]. **1968–70** *DARE* (Qu. S11, *What other names do you have around here for . . dog-tooth violet?*) Infs **CA**99, 150, Easter lily; (Qu.

S26e, *Other wildflowers not yet mentioned*) Inf **CA**204, Easter lily or dog-tooth violet.

2 =**trillium. chiefly WA**

1967 *DARE* (Qu. S2, *What do you call the flower that comes up in the woods early in spring, with three white petals that turn pink as the flower grows older?*) Infs **IA**8, **WA**20, 24, 30, Easter lily; **WA**28, Wild Easter lily. **1967** *DARE* Wildfl QR Pl.23A Inf **WA**30, Easter lily.

3 =**zephyr lily,** esp *Zephyranthes atamasco.* **Sth**

1894 *Jrl. Amer. Folkl.* 7.101 **cGA,** *Zephyranthes Atamasco* . . Easter lily. **1900** Lyons *Plant Names* 402, Atamasco Lily . . Easter Lily. **1933** Small *Manual SE Flora* 320, *Atamasco. . . Easter-lily. . .* Colonies of this plant are so densely populated that year after year great quantities of the flowers are gathered about Easter time and sold especially in southern cities. *Ibid* 321, *A[tasmasco] treatiae. . .* Easter-lily. **1966–70** *DARE* (Qu. S11) Inf **MS**8, White [Iris]—Easter lily; (Qq. S26a, b, . . *Other wildflowers*) Inf **GA**20, Easter lily; (Qu. S26c, *Wildflowers that grow in woods*) Inf **KY**74, Wild Easter lilies—yellow; (Qu. S26d, *Wildfowers that grow in meadows*) Inf **MD**43, Marsh lily—come[s] up around Easter—also called Easter lily. [*DARE* Ed: Some of these Infs may refer instead to other senses of **Easter lily.**]

4 Any of several other usu cultivated flowers that bloom in early spring such as the Bermuda lily, the madonna lily, or the daffodil.

1877 Bartlett *Americanisms* 446, The Calla is frequently called Easter Lily. **1900** Lyons *Plant Names* 257, Daffodil . . Easter or Yellow Lily [etc]. **1927** (1930) *WNID, Easter lily* . . The Annunciation lily *(Lilium candidum). . .* A large-flowered and early forcing variety (var. *eximium*) of the common trumpet lily *(Lilium longiflorum)* . . obtained originally from Bermuda, whence it is also called *Bermuda lily.*

5 Transf: a person who attends church chiefly at Easter time. *joc* Cf **Easter Christian**

1967–68 *DARE* (Qu. CC7, *Words for a person who goes to church very seldom or not at all*) Inf **TX**5, Poinsettias, Easter lilies; **WI**52, Easter lily [laughter].

Easter mackerel n

The Pacific mackerel *(Scomber japonicus).* See also **tinker mackerel**

1884 Goode *Fisheries U.S.* 1.304 **Pacific Coast,** The Tinker Mackerel, *S[comber] pneumatophorus,* is known as 'Mackerel,' 'Easter Mackerel,' . . and 'Little Mackerel.'

eastern pickerel n

=**chain pickerel.**

1896 U.S. Natl. Museum *Bulletin* 47.627, *Lucius Reticulatur* . . Eastern Pickerel. **1946** LaMonte *N. Amer. Game Fishes* 128, *Eastern Pickerel. . . Esox niger.* **1968** *DARE* (Qu. P1) Inf **GA**25, Eastern pickerel.

Easter rock n Cf **eagle rock**

A church ceremony consisting of marching, singing, eating and drinking held from midnight till the Easter sunrise service; see quot.

1942 *Jrl. Amer. Folkl.* 55.212 **LA** [Black], An Easter rock is one of those pagan rites clothed in Christian symbolism. . . Its practice . . seems never to have been very widespread, being restricted today to that part of Louisiana lying in the lower Mississippi delta. . . The Easter rock itself does not begin until midnight. *Ibid* 215, [After an initial procession,] singing and marching give way to eating and drinking. . . At this stage of an Easter rock it begins to be evident that both the participants and the spectators are having rather free access to the ecclesiastical (and temporal) supply of angeliquor. With supper ended, rocking is started anew, and with much heightened spirit. *Ibid* 218, The name, as the first deacon . . explains it, is derived from the fact that "everything rocks." The sancts [=saints, church members] rock; the church (always a frame building) rocks; the earth rocks; and the sun rocks as it comes over the horizon.

Easter winter n Cf **blackberry winter**

1983 *MJLF* 9.38 **ceKY,** *Easter winter* . . a period of cold weather at Easter time.

easterworm See **eaceworm**

easting n **N Atl**

Movement to the east; orientation toward the east.

1827 Cooper *Red Rover* 2.9, If I am any judge of the weather, the wind will have more easting in it, than you may happen to find to your fancy. **1863** Dana *Manual Geol.* 539 **ME,** In Maine the courses [of the rock-groovings] have an unusual amount of easting. **1918** (1926) Hergesheimer *Java Head* 86 **MA,** Weeks of snow and hail and fog and gales; and not for anything can you keep an easting. **1945** Colcord *Sea Language* 71 **ME, Cape Cod, Long Island,** *Easting.* Progress to the eastward; the ship makes easting.

eastman n *among Black speakers; old-fash* Cf **east** n²

A man who lives on money earned by a woman.

1911 *Jrl. Amer. Folkl.* 24.354 **Sth** [Black], The "Eastman" is kept fat by the women among whom he is universally a favorite. **1925** Odum–Johnson *Negro Songs* 211 **Sth,** I got it writ on the tail o' my shirt, / I'm a natu'al-bohn Eastman, don't have to work. **1926** Van Vechten *Nigger Heaven* 285 **NYC** [Black], *Eastman:* a man who lives on women. **1977** Dillard *Lexicon* 87 [Black], The term *Eastman* is found in diverse sources, almost all of them older and rural.

east pasture n Cf **back forty, the**

A distant place.

1967 *DARE* FW Addit **sePA,** When one is speaking of something *far* away, one says, "It is in your east pasture."

east, west, and crooked; eastwest, northwest, and crooked See **east and west**

eastworm, easworm See **eaceworm**

easy adj

1 Free from pain or discomfort. [*OED easy* a. 3 →1809]

1969 *DARE* FW Addit **TN,** My brother was given drugs all night and they couldn't get him easy. *Ibid,* I took two aspirin but I couldn't get my head easy.

2 Of persons: credulous; easily prevailed upon.

1896 *DN* 1.416 **cNY, nOH, seMI,** *Easy:* easily hoodwinked . . "You are *easy.*" Also *easy fruit, dead easy.* **1905** *DN* 3.8 **cCT,** *Easy* . . Easily fooled. "Ain't he easy," easily prevailed upon. **1907** *DN* 3.212 **nwAR,** *Easy. . .* Easily deceived. **1965–70** *DARE* (Qu. U32) Infs **KY**94, **NJ**48, **PA**3, 94, (Too) easy.

3 prec infin: Likely, prone, inclined. **Sth, S Midl** Cf **awful 3, bad adj B4, hard adj 4**

c1937 in 1977 *Amer. Slave Suppl. 1* 1.465 **AL** [Black], It was cold that day so he thrust his hands and feet down into the shucks to get them warm. As they got warmer he got sleepy. "All niggers is easy to go to sleep" so when the master came to see where he was he found Frank asleep. **1959** Lomax *Rainbow Sign* 112 **AL** [Black], Women are just easy to touch, I reckon. They're more easy to feel anything than a man. **1965–70** *DARE* (Qu. GG8, *When a person is very easily offended: "Be careful what you say to him, he's ______."*) Inf **GA**6, Easy to be hurt; **GA**1, Easy to fly off the handle; **WV**4, Easy to take exception; **AR**47, **MO**8, **NC**49, **SC**7, **TN**62, **VA**42, Easy to get mad; (Qu. GG41, *To lose patience easily*) Inf **KY**17, Easy to get out of hand. **1966** Dakin *Dial. Vocab. Ohio R. Valley* 2.468 **eKY, sIN,** *Easy to get mad* is attested several times in the southern Mountains. This expression also appears in the Indiana hills and in the Pocket. **1980** *DARE* File **cwNY** [Black speaker orig from GA], I say to him, they's easy to have heart attacks, if they's overweight you know; **cTX,** [Nationally televised psychologist describing patients' reactions to a heat wave:] They fuss and fight more; they're easier to quarrel in the counseling room. **1982** *Capital Times* (Madison WI) 15 July 6/2 **OH,** The people who work out here are sensitive to Carol and how easy she is to get hurt.

4 Free, unrestrained, profuse.

1947 Ballowe *The Lawd* 228 **LA,** Until he could do better, the two shirts that he had must last. He was an easy sweater. When he . . worked himself into a frenzy of appeal . . preaching, his shirt was soaked. **1950** *WELS (What do you say about a cow that gives . . a lot of milk)* 1 Inf, **WI,** An easy milker; *(Someone who spends money very freely)* 1 Inf, A free and easy spender; 1 Inf, Easy with the dough; *(A generous person)* 1 Inf, Easy with the cash. **1966** *DARE* (Qu. U31, . . *A person who spends money very freely;* total Infs questioned, 75) Inf **MS**39, An easy spender.

5 Soft.

1959 *VT Hist.* new ser 27.134 **VT,** Easy butter. . . Soft butter. Occasional.

easy adv Note: *Easy* meaning "slowly, calmly" in such expressions as *take it easy* and *go easy* is widespread; see *DS* GG8, JJ23, KK25, 42b.

1 Softly, quietly, gently. [Cf *EDD easy* adv. 8] Cf **ease 3**

1873 Harte *Mrs. Skaggs* 147 **CA,** Culpepper says, I do not, quite cool-like and easy. **1890** *DN* 1.18 **NH,** *Easy:* gently, softly. "Talk easy . . walk easy." *Ibid* 78 **LA, nwOH.** **1892** *DN* 1.215 **NC, TN.** **1903** *DN* 2.312 **seMO,** *Easy*. . . Gently, "Speak easy to her." **1907** *DN* 3.230 **seMO, nwAR.** **1928** Peterkin *Scarlet Sister Mary* 117 **SC,** He began whispering to her so easy she could hardly make out what he said. **1968–70** *DARE* (Qu. Y26a, *To walk very quietly: "She came______ to the baby's bed"*) Infs **GA**30, **OH**53, **TN**27, (Very *or* walking) easy; (Qu. Y26b) Inf **TX**103, Slipped out easy; (Qu. Y21) Inf **NC**55, Creep easy; (Qu. B13) Infs **CA**210, **NH**14, Blowing easy (*or* easier); (Qu. B14) Inf **MA**1, Brisk and easy.

2 Used as a command to a cow; see quot. **chiefly Inland Nth, N Midl**

1965–70 *DARE* (Qu. K81, *To make a cow stand still—for example, when milking her—you say, "______."*) 20 Infs, Easy; **NY**212, Easy now.

easy intj Also *easily*

1972 Carr *Da Kine Talk* 129 **HI,** *Easy!* This local word of farewell may be accompanied by special gestures and facial expressions. . . "The phrase started as 'Easily, Bla!' [=easily, brother!] and was accompanied by . . blowing on the fingers and then polishing them on the lapel. . . The gesture became a waggle of the hand from the wrist, with the thumb and little finger extended. The meaning was expanded to include 'Don't worry about anything.' In saying goodbye, it implied 'Okay, everything will be all right. Take it easy!' "

easyfied ppl adj **[-ified]**

Easy.

1937 in 1977 *Amer. Slave Suppl. 1* 1.248 **AL,** Dat's right easyfied ter 'splain.

easy-go-lucky adj [Blend of *easygoing* + *happy-go-lucky*]

1967 *DARE* (Qu. KK46, . . *Taking things as they come and not worrying: "The whole family was sort of______."*) Infs **IL**14, **TX**29, Easy-go-lucky.

easy keep(er) n **[keep]**

An animal or person requiring little care.

1942 Warnick *Garrett Co. MD* 6 **nwMD** (as of 1900–1918), *Easy keeper* . . an animal requiring but little feed. **1943** *Chicago Sun* 7 Oct. 19 *(DA),* She describes herself as "easy keep." It's a term she picked up from a cowboy friend, and on the range it means a horse who feeds on almost anything and thrives on it. **1950** *WELS (If somebody always eats very little)* 2 Infs, **WI,** He is an easy keeper. **c1960** *Wilson Coll.* **csKY,** *Easy keeper*. . . An animal that does not require much care; transferred to person[s].

easy on (the) trigger adj phr

Quick-tempered, excitable.

1912 *DN* 3.575 **wIN,** *Easy on trigger*. . . Excitable or high-tempered. **1968** Adams *Western Words* 104, *Easy on the trigger*—A cowboy's expression meaning *excitable* or *quick to anger*.

easy rider n Also *rider orig among Black speakers*

1 A sexually satisfying lover.

1914 in 1949 Handy *Treas. Blues* 75, [Lyrics:] E'er since Miss Susan Johnson lost her Jockey, Lee, . . You can hear her moaning night and morn. Wonder where my Easy Riders [sic] gone. **1926** Faulkner *Soldiers' Pay* 198 **MS,** Oh, oh, I wonder where my easy rider's gone. **1927** in 1983 Taft *Blues Lyric Poetry* 6 [Black], Did you ever wake up: between midnight and day / And felt for your rider: she done eased away. *Ibid* 128, Now tell me: where my easy rider's gone / Now easy riding woman: always in the wrong. **1927** *Jrl. Abnormal Psych.* 22.16, "Easy rider." This apt expression is used to describe a man whose movements in coitus are easy and satisfying. . . "I wonder where my easy rider's gone," is a sort of by-word with Southern negroes. **1947** DeToledano *Frontiers* 37, "Rider," "easy rider," which term means both lover and (not either, or) procurer. . . Fidelity to his woman is expected of the easy rider. **1956** Longstreet *Real Jazz* 150, A lot of words that were once obscene are now part of jazz talk: *shortnin' bread, seafood, jelly-roll* and *easy rider*. *Ibid* 140, Easy rider struck this burg today / On a south-bound rattler / Side-door Pullman car. **1971** *Current Slang* 5.4.10 **VT** [College slang], *Easy rider*. . . Girl who "gives everything" on a first date.

2 By ext: a man who lives off women; a pimp.

1926 (1949) Handy *Treas. Blues* 61 **TN,** [In "The Memphis Blues":] Mister Crump don't 'low no easy riders here. **1970** *Current Slang* 3–4.43 **NM** [College slang], *Easyrider*. . . A man who lives off what his wife makes as a prostitute. **1972** (1974) Wilson *Playboy's Words* 96, *Easy rider*—A *pimp,* in Southern slang. . . The connotation behind the term is that pimps live off their *whores'* earnings.

3 Transf: a guitar.

1946 Blesh *Shining Trumpets* 128, In rural Negro parlance . . *easy rider* meant the guitar . . carried suspended by its cord. In the double meaning of Negro imagery, the femininely formed guitar . . typifies also a woman companion. In Negro 'city talk,' the term *easy rider* has come to mean either a sexually satisfying woman or a male lover who lives off a woman's earnings. **1958** Gammond *Decca Book* 24, For the blues singer, the most valuable instrument was the guitar, . . and, as his "easy rider," could be slung across his back when he wished to travel.

easy sign n Cf **easy** adv **1**

In railroading: see quot 1945.

1943 *AmSp* 18.165, *Easy Sign.* **1945** Hubbard *Railroad Ave.* 342, [Railroad lingo:] *Easy sign*—Signal indicating the train is to move slowly. **1977** Adams *Lang. Railroader* 53, *Easy sign.*

easy walker n **chiefly Gulf States, SC** Note: The trademark *Easy Walkers,* for shoes, was registered in 1958.

A rubber-soled canvas shoe; a sneaker.

1954 Armstrong *Satchmo* 47 **New Orleans LA,** The band's uniform consisted of long white pants . . , black easy-walkers, or sneakers as they are now called. . . To stand out as the leader of the band I wore cream colored pants, brown easy-walkers and a cream colored cap. **1956** Rayford *Whistlin' Woman* 95 **AL,** Albert Lamie was never neat. He was a fisherman. . . He wore easy walkers. **1966–67** *DARE* (Qu. W8, . . *Low canvas-top shoes with rubber soles*) Infs **AL**30, **GA**6, **MS**6, 72, **SC**11, 21, 55, Easy walkers; (Qu. W21, *Soft shoes that people wear only inside the house*) Inf **AR**55, Easy walkers. **1980** *DARE* File **AL,** *Easy walkers* is the only term I ever heard in the '30's for oxford lace-up canvas and rubber shoes. . . Later these were called tennis shoes.

eat v

A Forms.

1a pres (exc 3rd pers sg): usu *eat;* rarely *ate, et.*

1837 [see **B2** below]. **1938** Matschat *Suwannee R.* 70 **nFL, sGA,** Then the gators turned cannibals, an' et an' et till they could et no more. *Ibid* 111, Howdy, mens. Come an' et.

b pres 3rd pers sg: usu *eats;* rarely *ets.*

1938 Matschat *Suwannee R.* 69 **nFL, sGA,** A cannibal is any kind of animal that ets up hits own kind.

2 past: usu |et|; also: See below. Note: It is not always possible to determine pronunciations on the basis of spelling.

a |it|; pronc-sp *eat.* **chiefly Sth, S Midl** See Map *esp freq among speakers with little formal educ*

1774 (1957) Fithian *Jrl. & Letters* 73, I gathered and eat some Pisimmonds. **1818** Fessenden *Ladies Monitor* 171 **VT,** Some provincial words and phrases which ought to be avoided. . . *eat* for ate in the preterite. **1893** *DN* 1.277 **wCT,** Eat [as past tense]. **1905** *DN* 3.59 **eNE,** Yesterday when I *come* to the table and *eat* my supper, the talk *run* on the corn crop and all of us *give* our views. **1943** *LANE* Map 646 **scattered NEng,** Preterite . . of the verb *eat*. . . [it], [ijt]. **1953** Atwood *Survey of Verb Forms* 12, *Eat* [as past tense] . . covers a large area in c.Pa., part of e.W.Va., most of Va. except the Tidewater area, and nearly all of N.C. In this entire area the frequency of *eat* is very great, particularly as one moves southward. . . there is some evidence, particularly in the eastern mixed areas, that *eat* is the more rustic and [less] in favor [than *et*].

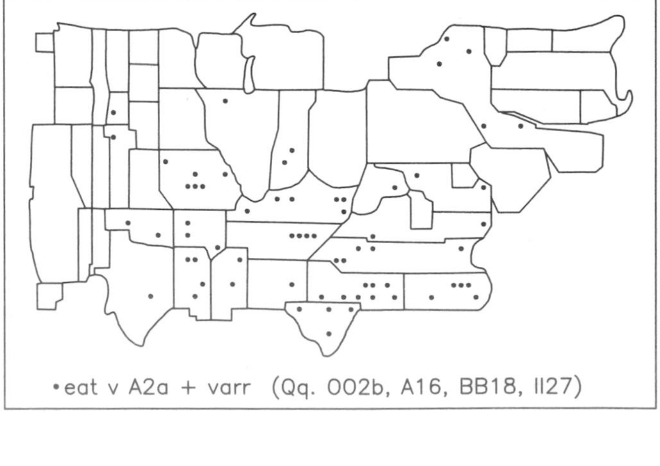

•eat v A2a + varr (Qq. 002b, A16, BB18, II27)

c1960 *Wilson Coll.* **csKY,** *Eat* [it] p[ast] . . of eat. **1965–70** *DARE* (Qu. OO2b, *Talking about eating: "I don't feel right—I think I ______ too much."*) 63 Infs, **chiefly Sth, S Midl,** Eat; **LA**2, Eat too big a bait of something or nother [Of all Infs responding to the question, 27% were gs educ or less; of those giving these responses, 68% were gs educ or less.]; (Qu. A16) Inf **OK**42, Since the hogs eat my little brother up; (Qu. BB18) Inf **NC**55, Puked up everything he eat; (Qu. II27) Inf **OK**6, He really eat my ass out; (QR, near Qu. LL27) Inf **MS**71, The boss eat him out. **1967–70** *DARE* Tapes **IN**23, 36, 51, **MI**115, **TX**24, 27, **VA**38, Eat [as past tense]. **1975** Allen *LAUM* 2.16 (as of c1950), One-fifth of the Type I infs. [=the oldest group, with no more than eighth-grade educ] use *eat* [as past tense], largely in the southeastern quadrant of the U[pper] M[idwest], that is, not in the most recently settled portions. **1976** Wolfram–Christian *Appalachian Speech* 183, They's the best stuff and you ever eat.

b |ɛt|; pronc-sp *et.* **scattered, but esp Sth, S Midl, N Atl** See Map *somewhat old-fash*

1827 (1939) Sherwood *Gaz. GA* 139, *Et,* for ate. **1892** *DN* 1.237 **wMO, MI.** **1903** *DN* 2.293 **Cape Cod MA** (as of a1857). **1907** *DN* 3.187 **seNH.** **1908** *DN* 3.308 **eAL, wGA,** *Eat* . . Pret. *et,* even among the best of families. . . *ate* . . has come in through the schools. **1910** *DN* 3.440 **wNY.** **1914** *DN* 4.72 **ME, NH.** **1923** *DN* 5.206 **swMO.** **1926** *DN* 5.399 **swMO, nwAR.** **1936** *AmSp* 11.14 **eTX,** *Ate* is frequently [ɛt] in East Texas among less literate speakers, as it is in many parts of the South. **1937** *AmSp* 12.322, Colleagues from Charleston, South Carolina assure me that the [ɛt] pronunciation is heard frequently among cultured people of that city, and I have had it reported also from Gates County, North Carolina. **1943** *LANE* Map 646 **throughout NEng,** The preterite . . of the verb *eat* . . [ɛt]. **1943** Faulkner *Hamlet* 53 **MS,** So I taken the plates back and we set against the fence and et. **1953** Atwood *Survey of Verb Forms* 12, The area of [past] *et* . . covers all of N.Eng. except Conn., and parts of N.Y. and n.Pa. *Et* is by no means confined to rustic usage; it is given by slightly over half the older informants . . but also by over one third of the younger. . . Five cultured informants in this area use *et.* . . More than 10 cultured informants along the seaboard use *et,* and none use *eat.* These facts would indicate that in the past *et* has enjoyed more favor than *eat,* and that it is still a preferred form—even a prestige form—among many of the older cultured people of the coastal area. **1965–70** *DARE* (Qu. OO2b) 67 Infs, **scattered, but esp Sth, S Midl, N Atl,** Et [ɛt] [Of all Infs responding to the question, 70% were old; of those giving this response, 88% were old.]; (Qu. II27) Inf **LA**8, He sho' et me up. **1966** *DARE* Tape **OK**30, The only kind of fruit you ever et [ɛt]. **1966–70** *DARE* FW Addit **SC,** The Inf never heard *ate* until she was in school in New Jersey. Proper people wouldn't think of [using] *ate.* They were "scandalized" when she came home using it instead of [ɛt]; **TX**89, Ate [ɛt]. **1975** Allen *LAUM* 2.17 (as of c1950), *Et* [as past tense] occurs with somewhat lower frequency [than *eat*], chiefly in southeastern Iowa and the eastern Dakotas. . . It apparently has lost the older prestige status reported by Atwood as persisting in much of New England, since it is the choice of no Type I infs. and of only three Type II's.

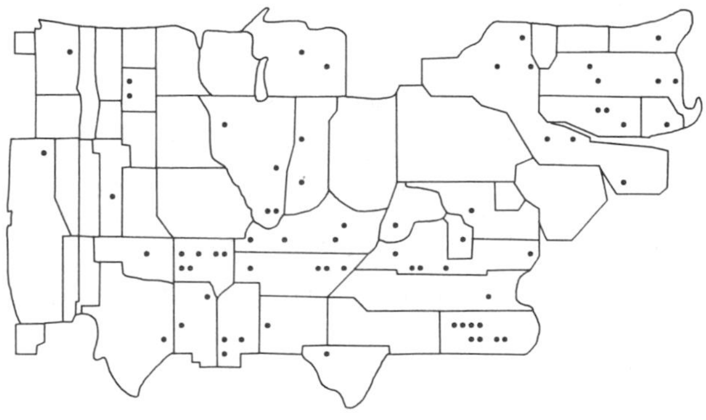

•eat v A2b + varr (Qq. OO2b, II27)

c |'ɛtn̩|; pronc-sp *eten.*

1967 *DARE* (Qu. OO2b) Inf **MO**5, Eten ['ɛtn̩].

3 past pple: usu |itn̩|; also: See below. Note: It is not always possible to determine pronunciations on the basis of spelling.

a |it|; pronc-sp *eat.* **chiefly Sth, S Midl** See Map *esp freq among speakers with little formal educ*

a1651 (1899) Bradford *Plimoth Plantation* 151, They would have eate it up. **1838** (1932) Chardon *Jrl.* 147 **PA,** The train came back Without Meat, the Wolves having eat it all. **1843** (1916) Hall *New Purchase* 119 **IN,** A switch tail . . kind a eat off by his other colt. **1844** in 1938 Tripp *Flukes* 102, The sad news has come that they have eat the cooper. **1844** Thompson *Major Jones's Courtship* 74 **GA,** I haint eat nothin but back-bone and turnips. **1893** *DN* 1.277 **wCT,** Eat [as past pple]. **1908** *DN* 3.308 **eAL, wGA,** [it] . . used in the [past pple]. **1927** *Ruppenthal Coll.* **KS,** We have eat a whole hog this winter already. **1934** *WV Review* Dec 79/3 **WV,** Quite often we hear *eat* in the past tense and the past participle. **1943** *LANE* Map 646 **scattered NEng,** The past participle of the verb *eat* . . [it, ijt]. **1945** in 1954 *Harder Coll.* **cwTN,** If he was the last man on earth I would not want him, for I have eat enough of the Doddo. **1953** Atwood *Survey of Verb Forms* 13, Where the preterite *eat* is used, the past participle is almost invariably leveled. . . The combination *et-eat* is extremely rare . . and is confined to Type I informants and Negroes, mostly in the Southern coastal areas. . . *Ate-eat* occurs only once in N.Eng., but it has some currency in the M[iddle] A[tlantic] S[tates], showing most frequency in w.Pa. **c1960** *Wilson Coll.* **csKY,** *Eat.* . . [past pple] of *eat.* **1965–70** *DARE* (Qu. OO2a) 81 Infs, **chiefly Sth, S Midl,** Eat [it] [Of all Infs responding to the question, 27% were gs educ or less; of those giving this response, 62% were gs educ or less.]; Inf **MO**39, Eat too much; (Qu. OO2b) Infs **IN**52, **SC**3, **TX**26, Have eat; (Qu. H12) Inf **KY**40, Hasn't eat any; (Qu. K14) Inf **KY**16, She's eat weeds [or] wild onions; (Qu. II27) Infs **AR**31, **GA**72, **LA**32, Eat out; (Qu. LL17) Inf **IN**35, All eat up. **1968** *DARE* Tapes **IN**23, 36, **VA**25, Eat [as past pple]. **1975** [see **3b** below]. **1976** Wolfram–Christian *Appalachian Speech* 183, I've eat it, I've eaten it twice.

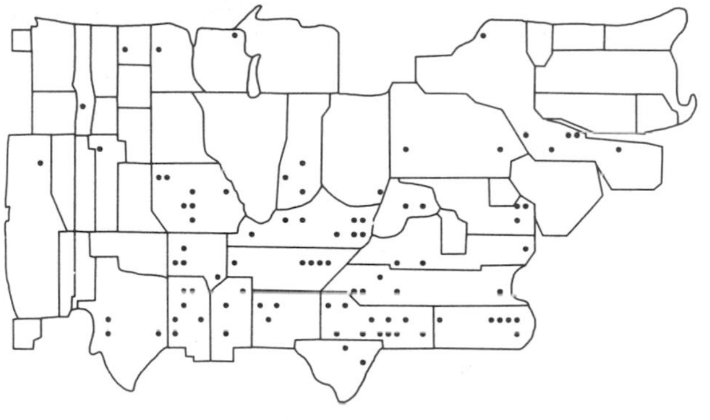

•eat v A3a + varr (Qq. OO2a, b, H12, K14, II27, LL17)

b |ɛt|; pronc-sp *et.* **scattered, but esp Sth, S Midl, N Atl** See Map on p. 264

1892 *DN* 1.237 **wMO, MI.** **1899** Catherwood *Queen of Swamp* 40 **OH** (as of 1850), Your sheer's [=share's] e't. **1903** *DN* 2.293 **Cape Cod MA** (as of a1857). **1907** *DN* 3.187 **seNH.** **1908** *DN* 3.309 **eAL, wGA.** **1908** (1911) Gale *Friendship Village* 37 **WI,** Bake it in my oven, so's we can hev it et hot. **1910** *DN* 3.440 **wNY.** **1914** *DN* 4.72 **ME, NH.** **1915** *DN* 4.226 **wTX.** **1923** *DN* 5.206 **swMO.** **1932** (1974) Caldwell *Tobacco Road* 18 **GA,** I ain't et nothing all winter but meal and fat-back, and I'm wanting turnips something powerful. **1936** *AmSp* 11.349 **eTX,** In addition to the regular forms, the present indicative, the preterit, and an analogical weak form are used for the past participle of strong verbs. . . [e.g.] *et.* **1938** Rawlings *Yearling* 77 **FL,** You better put a biscuit-two and some meat in your pocket. You ain't et. **1943** *LANE* Map 646 **throughout NEng,** The past participle of the verb *eat* . . [ɛt]. **1953** Atwood *Survey of Verb Forms* 13, Cultured informants in all areas who use [past] *et* invariably differentiate the preterite and the past participle. . . There are also from six to eight occurrences of each of these combinations [of past = past pple]: *eat-ate, eat-et,* and *ate-et.* **1954** *Harder Coll.* **cwTN,** Eat. . . Past pple: et, occas. **1965–70** *DARE* (Qu. OO2a) 69 Infs, **scattered, but esp Sth, S Midl, N Atl,** Et; (QR, near Qu. P3) **KS**6, I've heard of people that didn't eat carp, but I've et [ɛt] them; (Qu. LL17, . . *"The potatoes are ______."*) Inf **TN**23, Et up. **1975** Allen *LAUM* 2.17 **Upper MW** (as of c1950), Nor . . is there a marked regional pattern apparent in the distribution of . . *eat* and *et* [as past pples], unless it be that the latter is less likely in the more recently settled areas, and indeed, it occurs there only once in Nebraska and once in the Red River Valley of North Dakota.

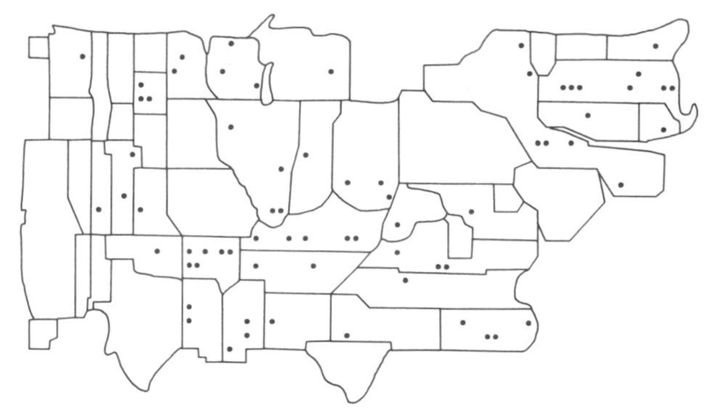

•eat v A3b + varr (Qq. 002a, LL17)

c |et|; pronc-sp *ate.* *esp freq among speakers with little formal educ*

1873 *Winfield Courier* (KS) 15 May 1.19.[2], The cake was the very best we have ate for a long time, and the donors have the thanks of the entire *Courier* force. **1905** *DN* 3.102 **nwAR,** Preterites occur in the speech of the uneducated or partly educated as perfect participles. Cf. . . came, ate, spoke. **1908** *DN* 3.308 **eAL, wGA,** [ɛt, it, itn, . . et] are used in the pp. **1927** *AmSp* 3.3 **swMO, nwAR,** Eat. . . Past Participle: et, eat, ate. **1930s** in 1944 *ADD* **nWV,** *Ate* . . Eaten. **1939** Rawlings in *Sat. Eve. Post* 25 Nov 7/1 **FL,** And seems like ary piece of rations I've ever ate has just wrapped itself around my middle and stayed there. **1943** *LANE* Map 646 **scattered NEng,** The past participle of the verb *eat* . . [et, eɪt]. **1953** Atwood *Survey of Verb Forms* 13, Among the leveled combinations, *ate-ate* is the least common, being used by only eight informants in N.Eng. and 12 in the S[outh] A[tlantic] S[tates]. In the M[iddle] A[tlantic] S[tates] these forms are a little more common, particularly in Pa. . . and W.Va. . . There are also from six to eight occurrences of each of these combinations: *eat-ate, eat-et,* and *ate-et.* **1965–70** *DARE* (Qu. OO2a, *Talking about eating: "He feels sick—he must have ______ something [that disagreed with him]."*) 187 Infs, **widespread,** Ate [et] [Of all Infs responding to the question, 24% were gs educ; of those giving this response, 37% were gs educ.]; (Qu. K14) Inf **MD**18, She's ate something. **1975** Allen *LAUM* 2.17 **Upper MW** (as of c1950), *Ate* itself is the main competitor [with *eaten*], with a conspicuously even geographical spread of its 1:4 frequency among Type I infs. [=old, with little educ] and 1:9 frequency among Type II's [=mid-aged, with approx hs educ].

d |etn̩|; pronc-sp *aten.*

1967 *DARE* (Qu. OO2a) Inf **IA**12, [eɪtɨn]; **TX**36, Aten. [Both Infs old, hs educ or less] **1978** *DARE* File **seWI,** The fish in Port Washington is O.K., but I've aten [etn̩] it just as good in other places. [Inf young, gs educ]

e |ɛtn̩|.

1896 *DN* 1.416 **cNY,** Eat: ppl. [etn̩] sometimes heard.

f *eated.*

1968 *DARE* (Qu. OO2a, *Talking about eating: "He feels sick—he must have ______ something [that disagreed with him]."*) Inf **MD**36, Eated.

B Senses.

1 To drink. *obs*

1818 in 1824 Knight *Letters* 107 **KY,** Some words are used, even by genteel people . . in a new sense; and . . pronounced very uncouthly, as:—to eat a liquid.

2 tr: To provide with food; to feed. **scattered, but esp Sth, S Midl** *old-fash*

1837 (1955) *Crockett Almanacks* 92 **TN,** 'Well, Capting, do you ate us, or do we ate ourselves?' 'Eat yourselves, to be sure.' **1846** Corcoran *Pickings* 47 **LA,** Squire, I was told you'd give us two dollars a day and *eat us.* **1864** (1868) Trowbridge *3 Scouts* 16 **TN,** I might hide ye; but I can't eat ye. **1913** Morley *Carolina Mts.* 180, The land is so good that two or three acres of it will "eat a family." **1928** Benét *John Brown* 367 **VA,** You ought to be et./ We'll eat you up to the house when it's mealin' time. **1938** FWP *Guide MS* 27, On the other hand, if he is working for wages and "eating himself," he can live a surprisingly long time on three soda crackers, a can of sardines, and a nickel's worth of cheese. **1939** Aurand *Quaint Idioms* 29 [PaGer], The fellow I work for pays me $2 *if I eat myself,* and $1 (per day) *if he eats me.* **1954** Forbes *Rainbow* 136 **NH** (as of c1850), Although Mr. Butters "slept" travelers he didn't "eat" them.

3 intr: To taste when eaten. **chiefly Sth, S Midl** Cf **drink** v **B2**

[**1744** in 1877 *PA Mag. Hist. & Biog.* 1.126 **VA** [Scottish native], Some fine Ice Cream, which, with the Strawberries and Milk, eat most Deliciously.] **1847** in 1942 *UT Hist. Qrly.* 10.163 **KY,** I shot hawks and crows and they ate well. **1895** *DN* 1.371 **neTN,** *Eats:* tastes. Of woodchuck: "It eats like bar (bear)." **1902** *DN* 2.233 **sIL. 1905** *DN* 3.78 **nwAR. 1907** *DN* 3.222 **nwAR, sIL. 1910** *DN* 3.440 **cwNY. 1917** *DN* 4.411 **wNC. 1927** *Ruppenthal Coll.* **KS,** It eats better than it looks—said of food that does not appear appetizing but proves to please the taste; canteloupes eat just as well as muskmelons. **1939** *Hall Coll.* **wNC,** Eat. . . Occasionally used by one old speaker in the sense "taste." . . "I'll guarantee you in the mornin' . . it'll eat just as good as it is now." **c1960** *Wilson Coll.* **csKY. 1966** *DARE* (Qu. LL35) Inf **SC**9, This cake eat good (*or* fine). **1966–70** *DARE* Tape **LA**8, On account of their flavor, I like the way they eat; **SC**15, Eat so good, I buy four; **VA**38, Maybe it didn't look so good, but it eat all right. **1982** Heat Moon *Blue Highways* 345 **ME,** A mack [=mackerel] looks better than it eats, unless you're a cat.

eat n Cf **eats**

A meal; a social gathering at which a meal is served.

1904 *Westm. Gaz.* 20 May 10/1 *(OEDS),* One Tennessee innkeeper described his establishments as . . 25 cents a sleep, 25 cents an eat. **1969–70** *DARE* (Qu. FF1) Inf **MA**58, Sugar eat; (QR, near Qu. FF17) Inf **NC**84, A good dinner party—a good eat.

eatables n pl *old-fash* Cf **eats**

Food.

1823 Cooper *Pioneers* 1.213 **cNY,** There's good eatables and drinkables enough in the house for a body's content. **1852** Watson *Nights Block-House* 48 **Ohio Valley,** The rangers . . sat upon the benches near the table, which was now clear of the eatables. **1893** Frederic *Copperhead* 184 **nNY,** Ni, with much deliberation, had filled both hands with selected eatables. **1942** Whipple *Joshua* 160 **UT** (as of c1860), You should have been in the house helpin' ready the eatables. **1950** *WELS (What general words do you have meaning "food"?)* 2 Infs, **WI,** Eatables. **1967** *DARE* Tape **MI**44, All our supplies, our eatables for practically the whole winter, were on these three boats. [Inf old]

eat acorns v phr [Perh ref to being reduced to eating only acorns; cf *DA come to acorns* to experience adversity, and **acorn calf**]

In the card game of **Florida flip:** see quot.

1935 Hurston *Mules & Men* 223 **FL** [Black], Heard somebody else in the game [=Florida flip] say, "Beggin' " and the dealer told him, "Eat acorns." [Footnote:] I give you one point.

eat another biscuit exclam

=**pigtail** exclam.

1966 *DARE* (Qu. EE23b, *In the game of andy-over . . if you fail to get the ball over the building and it rolls back, what do you call out?*) Inf **GA**3, Eat another biscuit.

eat a pumpkin through a knothole, be able to v phr For varr see quots Cf **pumpkin-eater**

To have buck teeth.

1950 *PADS* 14.78 **FL,** She could eat a pumpkin to the hollow through a crack in a board fence. Description of a buck-toothed girl. Suwannee River backwoods speech. **1966–70** *DARE* (Qu. X12) Inf **SD**8, Could eat an apple through a knothole; **TX**98, He could bite a punkin through a rail fence. **1978** *DARE* File **ID** (as of c1960), He could eat corn off a cob through a knothole. **1980** *Houston Chron.* (TX) 9 June sec 3, [She] says she heard a buck-toothed man [described as one] who "could eat corn-on-the-cob through a picket fence." **1985** *DARE* File **Terre Haute IN,** A person who has an overbite, buckteeth, "could eat corn through a picket fence."

eat at the same table See **eat out of the same dish**

eat away from (one) v phr

To deprive someone of food by eating his share.

1927 *Ruppenthal Coll.* **KS,** *Eat away from (one)*—To eat or devour with the effect that others have none or not enough to eat. "The big hogs always eat the corn away from the little pigs." "The chickens can eat faster and eat the feed away from the ducks." "There were several apples but the big greedy boy ate them all away from his brothers."

eat boiled crow See **eat crow**

eatch See **itch**

eat cheese v phr [Cf **cheese-eater**] *among Black speakers* Cf **cheese v 2**

To ingratiate oneself, apple-polish.

1970 *DARE* (Qu. JJ3a, *When a schoolchild makes a special effort to 'get in good' with the teacher . . "He's trying to ______ again."*) Inf **FL**52, Eat cheese; (Qu. JJ3b) Inf **VA**39, Eating cheese. [Both Infs Black] **1974** Matthews-Amdur *My Race* 153 **NYC** [Black], Then, in my sophomore year, I thought it might be a neat way of "eating cheese," or trying to get on the good side of Mrs. Jones as a teacher, so I joined the society.

eat crow v phr Also *eat boiled crow, eat dog, ~ turkey* Cf **dirt n 3, eat one's words 1**

To back down from an untenable position; to assume the responsibility for what one has said or done.

[**1851** *S.F. Picayune* 3 Dec. 1/6 *(DA),* The bet was made, the crow was caught and nicely roasted, but before serving it up, they contrived to season it with a good dose of Scotch snuff. Isaac sat down to the crow, he took a good bite, and began to chew away. 'Yes, I kin eat a crow! . . *I kin eat a crow, but I'll be darned if I hanker after it.*'] **1877** *N&Q* 5th ser 8.186/1 **wPA,** A newspaper editor, who is obliged by his "party" . . to advocate "principles" different from those which he supported a short time before, is said to "eat boiled crow." **1885** *Mag. Amer. Hist.* 13.199, "To eat crow" means to recant, or to humiliate oneself. **1912** Raine *Brand Blotters* 128 **AZ,** I suppose Norris has explained our mistake and eaten crow for all of us. **1928** *AmSp* 4.123 **IN,** To eat dog. **1950** *WELS (When somebody says something and then later has to admit that he was wrong: "I made him ______.")* 6 Infs, **WI,** Eat crow. **c1960** *Wilson Coll.* **csKY,** *Eat crow.* . . To eat one's words or "take something back." **1965-70** *DARE* (Qu. II31, *In an argument between two people, when one of them claims too much and the other shows him up: "He saw that he was wrong, so he started to ______."*) Infs **DC**8, **IN**5, 68, **MA**40, **OH**99, **SC**40, **TN**13, Eat crow; (Qu. JJ25, . . *"He thought he could take the place over, but I made him ______."*) Infs **MN**38, **MO**25, 29, **MA**79, **NE**11, **NY**64, **TX**81, Eat crow; **MO**2, Eat turkey; (Qu. JJ40 . . *"It was my fault and I'm willing to ______."*) Infs **GA**72, 73, **IN**30, **LA**32, **NC**33, **NJ**7, **SC**8, Eat crow.

eat dirt v phr

1 See **dirt 3.**

2 See **eat gravel.**

eat drag dust v phr [**drag n 3**]

See quot.

1944 Adams *Western Words* 56, *Eatin' drag dust*—Said of one riding in the drag dust of a trail herd; also used in the sense of being humiliated.

eat dried apples v phr For varr see quot 1965-70 [See quot 1976] **Nth, esp N Atl** Cf **Adam's fruit 2, eat pumpkin seeds**

To become pregnant; to show signs of pregnancy.

1965-70 *DARE* (Qu. AA28, . . *Joking or sly expressions . . women use to say that another is going to have a baby . . "She['s] ______."*) Infs **CT**27, 29, **IA**22, **ME**5, 16, **NY**92, 145, **VT**16, **WI**30, Been eating dried apple(s); **NJ**56, Been eating a lot of dried apples and drinking water; **NY**88, Been eating green apples; **CT**12, Eating dried apricots; **CT**6, Eating dried fruit; **SD**8, Eating for dried apples. **1975** Gould *ME Lingo* 305, One look at her, and you can see she's been eatin' dried apples. **1976** *Harper's Weekly* 26 Jan 19 **csOH,** A girl or woman who "has eaten dried apples" is pregnant. Dried apples put in water swell up a lot.

eated See **eat v A3f**

eater n

A fruit that is good to eat uncooked.

1926 Roberts *Time of Man* 358 **KY,** But the best peaches are the Mayflower, and that's a white cling, white meat and a good pie peach or eater. **1933** *AmSp* 8.4.80 **NE,** *Eaters* as applied to apples good to eat without cooking was used in a grocer's advertisement in a Lincoln paper recently.

‡eatereetis n

Perh a compulsion to eat; see quot.

1968 *DARE* (Qu. BB28, *Joking names that people make up for imaginary diseases*) Inf **IN**3, Eatereetis [ˌitəˈritɪs].

eat gravel v phr Also *eat dirt, ~ grass* [Cf *bite the dust*] **West**

To be thrown to the ground by a horse or steer.

1933 (1950) Allen *Cowboy Lore* 58 **SW,** *Eating gravel,* Being thrown from a bucking bronc or wild steer. **1936** Adams *Cowboy Lingo* 102, When the horse 'unloaded' his rider, . . the victim . . was 'eatin' dirt'. **1977** Watts *Dict. Old West* 124, *Eat gravel.* Also *eat grass.* To be thrown by a horse or cow; nice alternatives to *"bite the dust."*

‡eatified ppl adj [**-ified**] Cf **eatish**

1953 Randolph *Down in Holler* 45 **swMO,** Uncle Jack Short, of Galena, Missouri, once remarked, "I ain't been very eatified the last few days," meaning that his appetite was poor.

eating vbl n

Appetite.

1939 Aurand *Quaint Idioms* 29 [PaGer], *His eating went away* (as is said when one loses his appetite).

eating chill n

See quot 1979.

1954 *Harder Coll.* **cwTN,** *Eating chill,* chills and fever. **1979** *DARE* File **TN,** *Eating chill.* . . The chill occurs after a person has eaten too much: "He made a pig of hisself, and now he's got an old eating chill." Children were especially prone to such a sickness. As late as 1975, I heard the term in Tennessee.

eating iron n Also *eating tool* Cf **iron n**

An eating utensil.

1966 *DARE* (QR, near Qu. G1) Inf **OK**44, Knives, forks, etc, called "weapons" or "eating tools." **1968** Adams *Western Words* **SW,** *Eatin' irons*—What the cowboy calls the knives, forks, and spoons with which he eats.

eating joint n Also *eat(s) joint* **scattered, but esp Sth, S Midl, SW** See Map

A small, inferior restaurant.

1942 Berrey-Van den Bark *Amer. Slang* 814.1, *Restaurant.* . . Beanery . . eat joint . . eats joint. **1965-70** *DARE* (Qu. D39, . . *A small eating place where the food is not especially good*) 24 Infs, **scattered, but esp Sth, S Midl, SW,** Eating joint.

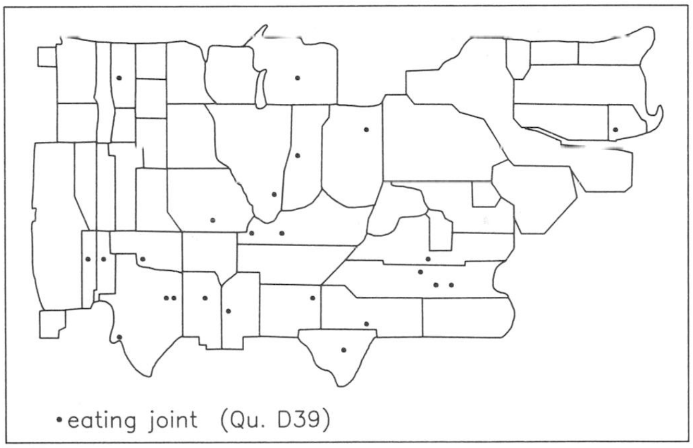

‡eating member n Cf **belly member**

1967 *DARE* (Qu. CC7, . . *A person who goes to church very seldom or not at all*) Inf **NE**11, Eating member—if they just show up for special occasions when there's a dinner.

‡eating poss n [*poss,* perh alter of *pasch* Passover, Easter; cf Scots *pace* Easter, Engl dial *pace-egg* Easter egg]

An Easter custom; see quot.

1968 *DARE* FW Addit **NY**73, Boys used to steal eggs at Eastertime and go out in the woods and boil them. They would eat as many as possible and call the custom "eatin' poss" [ˈitn̩ˈpɔs].

eatings n pl

=eats.

c1938 in 1970 Hyatt *Hoodoo* 1.78 **ceVA** [Black], You get that *black cat bone* and anything you want you get it. If you see somebody with *eatens* and you want it, you say, "Bring that tray to me," and that man will bring that tray right to you.

eating spaghetti See **eat spaghetti**

eating table n **chiefly sAppalachians**

A dining table; a dinner table.

1933 Miller *Lamb in His Bosom* 8 **GA,** The meal was spread on the eating-table. **1938** Stuart *Dark Hills* 383 **neKY,** I got upon the eatin' table at home and put a toe under each corner and my hands on the other corners and stretched. **1966–67** *DARE* Tape **AL4**, We called 'em a eatin' table; **KY2**, He made a table, a eatin' table. **1968** *DARE* (Qu. E5) Inf **NC50**, Eating table.

eating tobacco n

Chewing tobacco or snuff taken orally.

1940 Stong *Hawkeyes* 16 **IA**, Chewing tobacco (known by connoisseurs as eating tobacco). **1949** *Sat. Eve. Post* 2 Apr 79/3, If things are going well, he presents all hands with gifts of eating tobacco, apples [etc]. **1950** *Western Folkl.* 9.117 **nwOR** [Logger speech], *Eatin' tobacco.* Chewing tobacco. **1952** Callahan *Smoky Mt.* 14, Most of them [=frontiersmen] chewed tobacco—they often called it "eatin' terbaccer," supposedly because they swallowed some of the juice. **1960** Heimann *Tobacco* 109, Smoked leaf is used in "eatin' tobacco," that is, quid and snuff. (The latter is no longer sniffed but is held in the mouth without chewing.) *Ibid* 236, That year [=1890] saw the use of "eatin' tobacco" reach its per capita peak—nearly three pounds of plug, twist, or fine-cut being chewed for every man, woman and child. **1963** Haywood *Yankee Dict.* 53 **NEng**, *Eating tobacco*—Another name for a plug of chewing tobacco.

eating tool See **eating iron**

eat in the same plate See **eat out of the same dish**

eatish adj Cf **eatified**

1941 in 1944 *ADD* **eWV**, *Eatish*. . . Having an appetite; usu. in negative.

eat it v phr

=**eat one's hat.**

1966–68 *DARE* (Qu. JJ20, *If you felt very sure about something . . "I'm so sure, I'd ——— it."*) Infs **MN16**, **NE10**, **NC13**, **NY36**, Eat.

eat joint See **eating joint**

eat like a dog See **dog** n[1] **17a**

eatments n pl Cf **-ment** suff

Food.

1942 Berrey–Van den Bark *Amer. Slang* 91.1, Food . . eatments. **1950** *WELS (General words . . meaning "food")* 1 Inf, **WI**, Eatments.

eat oneself (done) v phr [Calque from PaGer; see quot 1968]

To finish one's food.

1939 Aurand *Quaint Idioms* 23 **sePA**, Fitzie, come in to eat; Ma and Pa are on the table and Johnny has *et himself already.* **1968** *Helen Adolf Festschrift* 39 **cePA**, The reflexive construction is used more frequently than in Standard American English; for example, "Eat yourself done" (Pennsylvania German *Ess dich satt*).

eat one's hat v phr Also *eat one's head*

Fig: to make a public admission of having been wrong—usu used in stating one's assurance of being right.

1903 *DN* 2.312 **seMO.** **1906** *DN* 3.118 **sIN.** **1908** *DN* 3.308 **eAL**, **wGA.** **1909** *DN* 3.395 **nwAR.** **1912** *DN* 3.575 **wIN**, *Eat one's head*. . . A mock serious vow. "If I'm not there on time, I'll eat my head." **1965–70** *DARE* (Qu. JJ20, . . *"I'm so sure, I'd ———."*) Infs **CA8**, **MD39**, **MS15**, **OR6**, Eat my hat; **NJ68**, Could eat my hat; (Qu. JJ25, . . *"He thought he could take the place over, but I made him ———."*) Inf **IL82**, Eat his hat; (Qu. NN32, *Exclamations like 'I swear' or 'I vow'*) Infs **MD28**, **WA3**, Eat my hat.

eat one's own words See **eat one's words 1**

eat one's white bread v phr

To be well off.

1929 Ellis *Ordinary Woman* 4 **MO**, She often used the Southern expression that, when one is doing well, 'he is eating his white bread now.' *Ibid* 9, With all the work and hardships, she was 'eating her white bread' then, although she did not know it. *Ibid* 244, I am getting tired of this little mining camp (had I only known it, I was eating my white bread then).

eat one's words v phr

1 also *eat one's own words:* To retract what one has said. Cf **eat crow**

1950 *WELS (When somebody says something and then later on has to admit that he was wrong: "I made him ———.")* 14 Infs, **WI**, Eat his (own) words. **1965–70** *DARE* (Qu. II31, *In an argument between two people, when one of them claims too much and the other shows him up: "He saw that he was wrong, so he started to ———."*) 34 Infs, **scattered**, Eat his (own) words; (Qu. JJ25, . . *"He thought he could take the place over, but I made him ———."*) Infs **IN61**, **MA9**, **NY46**, 109, **TX90**, Eat his words. **1969** *DARE* Tape **CA107**, I saw him about three years later . . and he said, "I'd like to eat my words." He was a nice guy . . after it all turned out.

2 To speak incoherently, mumble.

1968 *DARE* (Qu. X18, . . *When one person doesn't quite hear what another person said*) Inf **MI96**, Quit your eating your words.

eat-out n

See quots.

1947 *Jrl. Wildlife Management* 2.53 **LA**, **eTX coasts**, Blue and snow geese, . . feeding in the same area twice a day for several weeks, can produce radical changes in a marsh. Often the ground is completely denuded of vegetation . . and the soil may be broken to a depth of 5 to 8 inches. . . The damaged marsh resembles land destroyed by muskrats. Trappers . . term such destruction by geese or muskrats as an "eatout." The dead marsh that results and which persists until recovery is referred to as a "crevey" (French, *crevé*, dead or broken). **1979** Hallowell *People Bayou* 24 **sLA**, [Muskrat] populations sometimes shoot up to levels that put an unbearable strain on the vegetation, chewing it down to its foundations in the mud. Trappers call such a destructive orgy an "eat-out." Hunger follows, and then disease, and finally a slow, lingering death for thousands of animals.

eat out of the same dish v phr Also *eat at the same table*, *~ in the same plate*

To get along; to have a genial relationship.

1954 *Harder Coll.* **cwTN**, *Eat out of the same dish*. . . To live peaceably with (someone). "They been a-eatin' out of the same dish for 'bout two months now. Wonder how long it'll last?" **1968–70** *DARE* (Qu. II11a, *If two people don't get along well together, you'd say, "They don't ———."*) Inf **LA20**, Eat in the same plate; **PA245**, Eat at the same table.

eat peaches v phr

=**eat dried apples.**

1967 *DARE* (Qu. AA28, . . *Going to have a baby*) Inf **IL14**, Eating peaches.

eat peas out of a bottle v phr Cf **pour piss out of a boot**

1970 *DARE* (Qu. JJ15a, . . *"He hasn't sense enough to ———."*) Inf **MO29**, Eat peas out of a bottle.

eat, pig, or die v phr

=**root, hog, or die.**

1835 Crockett *Account* 90, Apples . . so sour, that when a pig sticks his tooth into 'em, he lays back his jaw, and hollers, you might hear him a mile: but it's 'eat, pig, or die'—for it's all he's got.

eat pumpkin seeds v phr Cf **swallow a pumpkin seed**

To swell with pregnancy.

1967–68 *DARE* (Qu. AA28, . . *Going to have a baby . . "She[ʼs] ———."*) Inf **PA167**, Eating pumpkin seeds; **MI47**, She musta been eating some pumpkin seeds, she's gonna bust pretty soon.

eat razor soup v phr

To say something sharp or impertinent.

1939 *AmSp* 14.262 **IN**, The wisecracker 'has been sleeping by a grindstone,' has been 'riding a grindstone,' or 'eating razor soup.' **1979** *DARE* File **swWI**, If we talked back the way some of my students do now, my father would say we were eating razor soup.

eats n pl Also *ets*

Food; groceries.

1900 in 1944 *ADD* **cNY**, *Ets*. . . Common. **1910** *Salt Lake Tribune* 27 Nov. 32/7 *(DA)* **UT**, The Chief made himself solid with the members because of the toothsome 'eats' he served. **1913** *DN* 4.10 **MN**, *Eats*. . . Food. "We had such good eats." **1946** *New Harmony* (Ind.) *Times* 15 Feb. 3/4 *(DA)*, Eats will be served and a club membership card is the only ticket required. **1965–70** *DARE* (Qu. H6, . . *Food in general*) 104 Infs, **scattered**, Eats; (Qu. U1b, . . *Buying groceries*) Infs **IL29**, **MI30**, After (*or* buying) eats; **NC41**, 82, To buy (*or* to look for) some eats. **1968–69** *DARE* Tape **IL77**, They have a big supper, chicken 'n' dumplin's, chicken 'n' dressing, 'n' all kinda eats; **LA25**, Somethin' goin' on, some eats or somethin'; **MO4**, I cook quite a lot like Germans—I like their eats; **VA9**, I'd give Momma the rest of it to get eats with.

eats joint See **eating joint**

eats, off one's See **feed, off (of) one's 1**

eat spaghetti v phr, hence vbl n *eating spaghetti*

To perform a trick with a yo-yo; see quots; also n *eat-the-macaroni.*

1967 Conroy *Stop-Time* 116 **FL,** The witty nonsense of Eating Spaghetti, the surprise of The Twirl, . . I could do them all, without false starts or sloppy endings. I could do every trick in the book. **1968** *DARE* Tape **LA**46, And the other one was called eat-the-macaroni. You'd take the yo-yo, you'd throw it down and let it stay down and you'd just take all the string and just pour it all in one bunch when the yo-yo is about a few inches from your hand and you'd just drop the whole thing and the yo-yo just winds it all up and you got the yo-yo back in your hand again. **1979** Zeiger *World on String* 74, So try eating *Spaghetti!* Throw a fast spinner. . . Continue to wrap the yo-yo string around these two fingers as if you were twirling spaghetti around a fork. When you almost run out of string, bring the whole wrapped wad to your mouth and pretend to eat it.

eat supper v phr Cf **build the fence**

Fig: to conceive a child.

1984 Wilder *You All Spoken Here* 98 **Sth,** They planted corn a-fore the fence was built: They had a baby in progress before they married. . . They ate supper before they said grace.

eat the grease v phr

1923 *DN* 5.239 **swWI,** *Eat the grease*. . . To eat the cream; to take the best of something. . . "I calculates t' eat the grease."

eat the greaser v phr [See quot 1923] **esp NY**

=**eat one's hat.**

1901 *DN* 2.141 **NY** [College words and phrases], *Greaser*. . . "I'll do it or eat the greaser." Probably obsolescent. **1923** *DN* 5.239 **swWI,** *Eat the greaser*. . . To eat the pork and rind used to grease a griddle. (Fig.). "If that ain't so, I'll eat the greaser." **1939** (1962) Thompson *Body & Britches* 499 **NY,** If that isn't so, I'll eat the greaser. (The salt pork used to grease the pancake-griddle.) **1968** *DARE* FW Addit **NY** 52, If such-and-such happens, I'll eat the greaser ['grisɚ].

eat-the-macaroni See **eat spaghetti**

eat-the-peg n

=**mumblety-peg.**

1967 *DARE* (Qu. EE5, *Games where you try to make a jackknife stick in the ground*) Inf **MA**8, Eat-the-peg.

eat turkey v phr

1 See **eat crow.**

2 To play second fiddle.

1966–70 *DARE* (Qu. II19, *When you think somebody has been put ahead of you or has been given something you deserved . . "I'd rather quit than ______.")* Inf **WA**9, Eat turkey.

eatup n Also *neatrup* [Algonquian *netop* close friend; *eatup* may be the result of metanalysis: *a netop* > *an etop*]

=**netop.**

1932 *DN* 6.283 **swCT,** *Eat ups* or *neatrups*. A sudden and violent affection between two persons. "They are great eatups (or neatrups)."

eat with one's toe in the fire v phr Also *eat with one's foot in the milk bucket*

See quots.

1980 *DARE* File **Ozarks** (as of c1920), "Miss Ida, I could eat this with my toe in the fire." One of our farm hands said this about my mother's fresh apple pie. **1989** *DARE* File **cAR,** My mother knows the expression "Eat with one foot in the milk bucket" to mean that something is so good you ignore the circumstances—although I don't know why it's a milk bucket.

‡**eave cat** n Cf **alley-cat** v, **cat** v **2, tomcat**

Fig: a man in pursuit of a sexual mate.

1940 Faulkner *Hamlet* 185 **MS,** That aint his way. No sir. This here man aint no trifling eave-cat.

eave drain See **eaves drain**

eavedrop See **eavesdrop**

eave pan n Cf **eaves trough**

1966 *DARE* (Qu. D28, *What hangs below the edge of the roof to carry off rain-water?*) Inf **FL**9, Eave pan.

eave pipe See **eaves pipe**

eaves drain n Also *eave drain*

=**eaves trough.**

1940–41 Cassidy *WI Atlas* **cwWI,** Eave drain . . eaves spout. **1966–69** *DARE* (Qu. D28, *What hangs below the edge of the roof to carry off rain-water?*) Inf **NH**14, Eave drain; (Qu. D29, *The pipe that takes the collected rain-water down to the ground*) Infs **VT**16, **WA**5, Eaves drain.

eaves draw n

=**eaves trough.**

1983 *DARE* File **MI,** *(What hangs below the edge of the roof to carry off rain-water?)* Eaves draw; *(The pipe that takes the water from these to the ground or to a storage tank)* Eaves draw.

eavesdrop v Usu |'ivz,drɑp|; also, by syncope, |'i(v),drɑp| Pronc-spp *eavedrop, e'edrop, e-drop*

Std sense, var forms.

1941 in 1944 *ADD* **eWV,** *E'edrop*. Rare. *Eavedrop* is usual. **c1960** *Wilson Coll.* **csKY,** *Eavesdrop* is usually |'iv,drɑp|. **1967** *DARE* (Qu. Y9, *Somebody who always follows along behind others: "His little brother is an awful ______."*) Inf **LA**6, [He was] e-dropping ['i,drɑpɪn]; that is what people do when they follow along in order to overhear. [Also] e-dropper.

eaves pipe n Also *eave pipe* **Nth**

A downspout.

1941 *LANE* Map 349 1 inf, **seCT,** Eaves pipes. **1950** *WELS,* 3 Infs, **WI,** Eave(s) pipe. **1967–69** *DARE* (Qu. D29, *The pipe that takes the collected rain-water down to the ground or to a storage tank*) Infs **MI**108, **NY**162, 200, **WA**24, Eave pipe.

eaves spout n Also *eave spout, eave(s) spouting* **chiefly Nth, N Midl** See Map Cf **spouting**

=**eaves trough.**

1846 in 1956 Eliason *Tarheel Talk* 270 **NC,** Put up smart [sic] of the eve spout. **1889** Cooke *Steadfast* 369 **CT,** A wild November storm . . shrieked and wailed in the eave-spout. **1949** Kurath *Word Geog.* 53, *Eaves spouts* is common in the Upper Connecticut Valley and to the east thereof, except for the coastal area; and relics of it are found in Rhode Island, on Cape Cod, and on Nantucket, all parts of Eastern New England. Whether the *eaves spouts* of the northern counties of Pennsylvania and the Western Reserve of Ohio is a direct descendant of this New England expression or, at least in part, a blend of the New England *eaves troughs* and the Pennsylvania *spouting, spouts* is an open question. **1950** *WELS (The pipe that takes the water . . to the ground or to the cistern)* 9 Infs, **WI,** Eave(s) spout. **1951** *AmSp* 26.256 **NY,** A clear example of the introduction of a lexical item from two different directions is *eaves spouts, rain spouts, spouts* . . which appears in two widely separated parts of the state: (1) the Champlain Valley and the Adirondacks, where it is most likely spread from Vermont; (2) the southwestern corner of the state, where it occurs as a variant of Midland *spouting* (perhaps blended with the common Northern term *eaves troughs*). **1965–70** *DARE* (Qu. D28, *What hangs below the edge of the roof to carry off rain-water?*) 34 Infs, **scattered Inland Nth, wNEng, N Midl,** Eave(s) spout; **OH**42, Eaves spouting; (Qu. D29, *The pipe that takes the collected rain-water down to the ground or to a storage tank*) 24 Infs, **scattered Inland Nth, wNEng,** Eave(s) spout; **OH**90, **PA**131, Eave(s) spouting. **1971** Wood *Vocab. Change* 48 **Sth,** *Eaves spouts, spouting,*

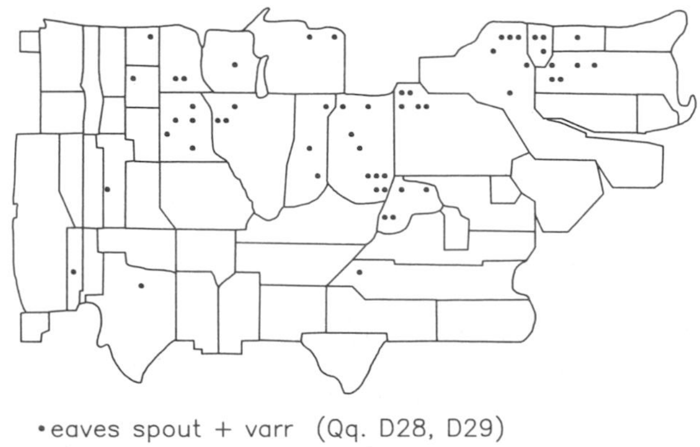

•eaves spout + varr (Qq. D28, D29)

and *spouts* have scattered occurrences and may be influenced by the commercial *down spouts.* **1973** Allen *LAUM* 1.177 (as of c1950), *Eaves spouts,* the regional designation in northern New England and northern Pennsylvania, is centered in southern Minnesota and northern Iowa.

eaves swallow See **eave swallow**

eaves trough n Also *eave trough, eave(s) troft, ~ troth* **chiefly Nth, N Midl, West** See Map Cf **trough**

The horizontal gutter which carries rainwater from the roof of a house; sometimes the downspout.

1851 MI State Ag. Soc. *Trans.* 3.185, Lightning rod, tin eave troughs, and a permanent cement cistern. **1893** Frederic *Copperhead* 63 **nNY,** An eaves-trough had fallen down. **1949** Kurath *Word Geog.* 53, *Eaves troughs* (sometimes *eaves troths*) is current in all of New England, except the coastal section from Cape Cod to Maine, and in the New England settlement area. Scattered instances of *eaves troughs* . . occur on Delaware Bay, Chesapeake Bay, the Carolina coast, and in western Virginia and North Carolina, mostly in the speech of older people. . . Moreover, *eaves troughs* is rather common in west-central West Virginia, especially in the Ohio Valley section of it. **c1960** *Wilson Coll.* **csKY,** *Eaves-troughs.* . . Gutters. **1961** *AmSp* 36.24 **neOH,** *Eaves troughs* and *eaves* . . trail far behind the commercial term [=*gutters*]. Their markedly greater use by Group A informants [all sixty-six years of age or older] suggests that both terms are on the way out. **1962** Atwood *Vocab. TX* 43, Neither the Northern *eaves troughs* (6 [infs]) nor the Midland *spouts* . . has established itself. **1965–70** *DARE* (Qu. D28, *What hangs below the edge of the roof to carry off rain-water?*) 53 Infs, **chiefly Nth, N Midl, West,** Eaves trough; 54 Infs, **chiefly Inland Nth, wN Midl,** Eave trough; 45 Infs, **chiefly Nth, esp Upstate NY,** Eave(s) troth; 20 Infs, **scattered,** Eave(s) troft(s); (Qu. D29, *The pipe that takes the collected rain-water down to the ground or storage tank*) Infs **MN**38, **MO**38, Eave trough; **NY**215, Eaves troth. **1968** *PADS* 49.16 **Upper MW,** Another reason for vocabulary change is the widespread use of commercial terms. . . examples are . . *gutters* for *eaves* (field informants, 9.6% [of 208 infs]; students, 1.0% [of 100 infs]), *eave(s) troughs* (field informants, 50%; students, 53%), *spouts* . . , and *spouting.* **1969** *Reminder* (Wilbraham MA) 23 Apr 16/2 **csMA,** [Advt:] Eavetroughs cleaned, oiled, and repaired. **1970** *AmSp* 45.65, In the Eastern States *eave-troughs* is confined to the New England settlement area. . . In England *eave-troughs* is largely confined to East Anglia, the obvious home of the New England term. **1971** Wood *Vocab. Change* 48 **Sth,** The first preference is *gutters.* . . *Eaves* is the second. . . *Eaves troughs* occurs everywhere [within the 8 states studied] but in Mississippi. **1973** Allen *LAUM* 1.177 (as of c1950), Western New England and New York state *eave(s) troughs* or *eavestroths* dominates the U[pper] M[idwest], although with lower frequency in the Midland areas of southern Iowa and Nebraska.

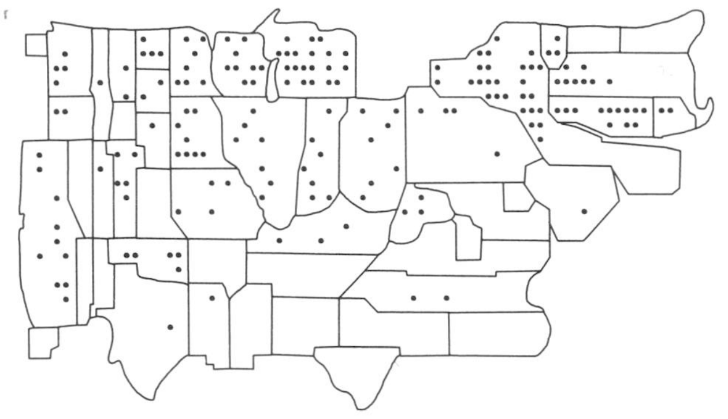

•eaves trough + varr (Qq. D28, D29)

eave swallow n Also *eaves swallow* **chiefly Nth**

1 =**cliff swallow.**

1874 Coues *Birds NW* 88, *Petrochelidon lunifrons.* . . Cliff swallow, eave swallow. **1898** (1900) Davie *Nests N. Amer. Birds* 410, Eave swallows. . . As the name implies, . . this bird fixes its queer bottle-shaped nest . . under shelter of eaves. **1917** (1923) *Birds Amer.* 3.85, The flocks of Bank, Barn, and Tree Swallows absorb these Eave Swallows, and together they work to clean the air of the island lakes of all the flies and mosquitoes. **1956** MA Audubon Soc. *Bulletin* 40.84, *Cliff Swallow.* Eaves Swallow. . . Its mud nests are often built under eaves. **1966–69** *DARE* (Qu. Q20, . . *Kinds of swallows and birds like them*) Infs **IL**32, **ME**6, 12, **MA**30, 42, 67, **NY**106, Eave swallow; **OH**70, Eaves swallow. [All Infs old] [*DARE* Ed: Some of these Infs may refer instead to sense **2** below.]

2 =**tree swallow.**

1917 (1923) *Birds Amer.* 3.88, *Tree Swallow.* . . *Other Names* . . White-bellied Swallow; Stump Swallow; Eave Swallow. **1946** Goodrich *Birds in KS* 319, Colloquial Name. . . Swallow, eave. . . Common name. . . Swallow, northern cliff. . . Swallow, tree.

eaves waterdrop n Cf **waterdrop**

A downspout.

1965 *DARE* (Qu. D29) Inf **MS**55, Eaves waterdrop.

eave troft, eave troth, eave trough See **eaves trough**

ebah, eb(b)er See **ever** adv

ebbery See **every** adj

ebbm, ebbn See **even**

‡ebb-tide butter n Cf **come B1**

Butter that does not **come** when being churned.

1923 Parsons *Folk-lore Sea Islands* 209 **sSC** [Gullah], A child from Paris Island said that her mother would sing as she churned, "Churn de butter wid de tide." If the butter did not churn, she would say, "Butter, why dontsher churn?" calling it ebb-tide butter.

eben See **even**

ebenezer n [Cf 1 Samuel 7:12]

1 in phr *set up one's ebenezer:* To firmly make up one's mind. [By ext from *to set up one's ebenezer* to acknowledge divine aid; *OEDS* 1693 →] **NEng** *old-fash*

c1840 Neal *Beedle's Sleigh Ride* 26 *(DA)* **ME,** I took a resolution, and stuck to it firm, for when I once set up my ebenezer I am just like a mountain. **1891** Cooke *Huckleberries* 65 **NEng,** When folks set up their Ebenezer as if 't was n't never goin' to come down for anybody, it don't very often get so much as joggled. **1903** Pidgin *Quincy Adams* 71 **seMA,** I sot up my Ebenezer, and I says, 'Silas Putnam, if you gives your property to any one you gives it to me.'

2 Anger, temper. *obs* Cf **African** n[1] **B1, Irish**

1836 *Pub. Ledger* (Philadelphia PA) 27 July 4/2, Says I, Deb, . . I'll send you enough wool to make a wig. That ris Deb's ebenezer. **1838** (1843) Haliburton *Clockmaker* (2d ser) 305 **NEng,** If you go for to raise your voice at him, . . his Ebenezer is up in a minit'. **1844** Stephens *High Life in NY* 1.50 **CT,** A gal kicks over the milk pail when she lets her ebenezer git up before a feller. *Ibid* 16, I felt my ebenezer a gitting up to hear her call her husband's own uncle and aunt sich stuck up names. **1849** Nason *Journal* 14 *(DA),* Our steward is under the constant necessity of a checkrein upon his ebenezer.

ebenin See **evening**

eber See **ever** adv

ebil See **evil** adj

eb'm, eb'n See **even** adj, adv, v

ebony n

1 also *son of ebony,* abbr *ebon:* A Black person. *arch*

1820 *Western Carolinian* 11 July *(DA),* Many of the free states . . find the ebon part of their citizens to be, at times, very troublesome. **1851** (1976) Melville *Moby-Dick* 292 **NEng,** The old black . . came shambling along from his galley . . this old Ebony floundered along. **1851** (1852) Stowe *Uncle Tom's Cabin* 1.70 **KY,** Black Sam, as he was commonly called, from his being about three shades blacker than any other son of ebony on the place. **1863** Gilmore *S. Friends* 69 **eNC,** The scented ebony roared. **1889** (1971) Farmer *Americanisms* 222, An *ebony* is a negro in common parlance. **1895** *Outing* 26.428/2 **eBlue Ridge Mts,** A little ebon, who had been watching from a gatepost, to set open the gates.

2 also *ebony tree:* =**Texas ebony. TX**

1900 Lyons *Plant Names* 294, *P[ithecellobium] flexicaule* . . Texas to California and Mexico, is called locally Ebony. **1922** Sargent *Manual Trees* 588, *Ebony.* . . *Wood* exceedingly heavy, hard, compact, close-grained, dark rich red-brown slightly tinged with purple. **1965** Teale *Wandering Through Winter* 130 **TX,** We came upon the largest ebony tree in Texas. . . Like the live oak, the ebony sheds its foliage a few leaves at a time. **1967** *DARE* (Qu. T5, . . *Kinds of evergreens*) Infs **TX**22, 28, 31, Ebony (tree); (Qu. T16, *What kinds of trees are 'special' around here?*) Infs **TX**26, 29, 31, Ebony.

ebry See **every** adj

echo(-over) n, exclam

=**Antony-over.**

1966–67 *DARE* (Qu. EE22, . . *The game in which they throw a ball over a building . . to a player on the other side*) Inf **DC**2, Echo-over; **DC**8, Echo; (Qu. EE23a, . . *What do you call out when you throw the ball?*) Inf **DC**2, 'Echo!' Other side would reply 'over;' **DC**8, Echo.

‡echo party n

A gathering to reminisce about a shared experience.

1968 *DARE* Tape **PA**135, Then [after returning from a trip to Hawaii] we had an echo party of it in St. Louis in the fall—showed our pictures and everything.

ecknowledge See **acknowledge**

eckrydock n [Pronc-sp for *aqueduct*]

1944 *AmSp* 19.71 **wOH,** Some thirty years ago, before the abandonment of the old Miami and Erie Canal connecting Cincinnati and Toledo, the term "eckrydock" was used by the men and boys . . who used to go swimming at a special point in the canal. . . "Eckrydock" was specialized in meaning and was applied only to aqueducts. . . The term was used generally in this region.

E Clampus Vitus n Also *E Clampsus Vitus* [On the pattern of *E pluribus unum,* perh comb of *eclampsia* sudden convulsions, with *St. Vitus's dance*] **CA** Cf **Clamper**

A mock fraternal organization popular in the 1850s and revived in the 1930s; see quots.

1849 MS [Huntington Library, Dane Family Collection], This Institution shall be called by and known as E clampus Vitus Lodge or Knights of Honor. **1852** Sacramento *Union* 28 Sept (1930 *CA Hist. Soc. Qrly.* 9.73), Although we are not prepared to say that [E Clampus Vitus] is precisely similar to those [associations] we have heretofore known, yet we can state . . that the term implied a degree of waggery to be practised by the knowing ones upon greenhorns; and that its existence was merely nominal—its meetings being held only when a victim presented himself for initiation, and consequent immolation. **1856** (1930) DeLong *Jrls.* 27 Apr **CA,** Helped organize the E Clampsus Vitus Order on the hill. **1904** Farish *Gold Hunters* 82 **CA,** About this time [=c1855] was established, at Downieville, the ancient and honorable order of "E Clampsus Vitus." The initiation fee of which was made always to suit the pecuniary circumstances of the proposed initiate; and usually expended in paying for beer. **1928** Ritchie *Forty-Niners* 247 **CA,** E Clampus Vitus was the noblest wheeze ever launched under guise of fraternal brotherhood. **1930** *CA Hist. Soc. Qrly.* 9.73 **CA,** The Ancient and Honorable Order of *E Clampus Vitus* (sometimes written "E Clampsus Vitus") was one of the most ludicrous sideshows of life in the mines of California. . . The chief aim of the Order was to procure liquid refreshment from its luckless initiates. **1969–70** *DARE* (Qu. FF22b) Inf **CA**114, The Inf belongs to E Clampus Vitus [which] has chapters all over California. . . [It is the] most unique and democratic organization of its kind—every member has a title, every member carries card number one, anybody [male] can belong . . there have never been minutes taken at a meeting because nobody's ever sober enough to take them; **CA**137, E Clampus Vitus was formed to help families of unfortunate miners—now is sort of a humorous fraternity; **CA**197, E Clampus Vitus.

-ed suff [The *-ed* of the regular past tense and of the past pple, although historically unrelated, are now phonologically identical and are thus conveniently treated together.]

Std senses, var applications.

1 added redundantly to the std past and past ppl of regular verbs. Cf **ailded, attackt** v, **belong A2, cease** v², **clifted, foal** v **A2, 3**

1689 in 1889 ME Hist. Soc. *Doc. Hist.* 4.463, The enemy Attacted mr ffoxwells Garison att Blwu pwinte. **1795** Dearborn *Columbian Grammar* 135, [List of improprieties:] Galded for Gall'd. **1815** Humphreys *Yankey in England* 108 **NEng,** *Stunded,* stunned. **1835** in 1926 *Missip. Valley Hist. Rev.* 12.553 **VA,** We . . encampted on a small branch of the Nemahow. **1891** *DN* 1.165 **cNY,** [ə'tæktɪd], "attacked." *Ibid* 166, [draʊndɪd] . . drowned, . . [foldɪd] . . foaled. **1899** (1912) Green *VA Folk-Speech* 466, The place is all underminded with rats. **1902** *DN* 2.248 **sIL,** The work ain't so hard when you get usted to it. **1903** *DN* 2.314 **seMO,** That horse is badly galded. *Ibid* 324, He pawnded his watch for the money. **1919** *DN* 5.36 **KY,** *Walded,* preterit of the verb *wall.* Other examples are *attacted, drownded.* **1924** Raine *Land of Saddle-Bags* 97 **sAppalachians,** He tosted us the hay. **1926** *DN* 5.395 **KS,** The following have been observed in speech and writing: drownded, . . attacted, . . equipted. . . Also misted (for missed). . . "Homer confinded himself to a very narrow idea" (a freshman's examination). **1938** Rawlings *Yearling* 89 **FL,** Nothin' ailded me but green brier-berries. **1942** Thomas *Blue Ridge Country* 54 **sAppalachians,** Swoonded dead away! **1943** in 1944 *ADD* **WV,** As a penality [sic], he was banded from all radio broadcasts for . . 12 months. **1953** Atwood *Survey of Verb Forms* 12, *Drownded* . . is used by about one fourth of the N. Eng. informants. . . Elsewhere in the Eastern States *drownded* . . [varies] in frequency from one third (e. N.Y.) to nine tenths (N.C.). . . About two thirds of the Southern Negro informants use this form. **1965–70** *DARE* (Qu. OO26a, . . *"Several people have ______ [there]."*) 181 Infs, **widespread,** Drownded; (Qu. OO26b, *"A boy was ______ [there]."*; not asked in early QRs) 151 Infs, **widespread,** Drownded; (Qu. OO26d, . . *"A child ______ here."*; total Infs questioned, 75) 17 Infs, Drownded. [Of all Infs responding to Qq. OO26a, b, 29% were from comm type 5, 26% had less than hs educ, and 41% were male; of those giving this response, 44% were from comm type 5, 46% had less than hs educ, and 50% were male.] **1979** *DARE* File **csWI,** I must have got sidetrackted ['saɪdtræktɪd] somewhere along the line.

2 added to the infin of irregular verbs to form past tense and past ppl forms. [Cf *EDG* §427, 428, 432, 433] **chiefly Sth, S Midl** *more freq among rural speakers, males, and speakers with less than hs educ* Cf **blow** v¹ **A2, cost A2**

1815 Humphreys *Yankey in England* 105 **NEng,** *Heerd,* heard. *Ibid* 106, *Know'd,* knew. **1893** Shands *MS Speech* 36, *Heeyrd* . . for *heard. Ibid* 42, *Knowed. Ibid* 55, *Seed.* **1924** Raine *Land of Saddle-Bags* 97 **sAppalachians,** They say *throwed, growed, knowed.* **1933** Rawlings *South Moon* 6 **FL,** No man kin say where they goed. *Ibid* 12, I seed deer! A hull mess o' deer! *Ibid* 100, You'd think he were a growed man. **1934** in 1983 Taft *Blues Lyric Poetry* 52/1 [Black], Now I knowed when I quit her: I was doing wrong. **1952** Brown *NC Folkl.* 1.535, Past tense and past participle of many strong or irregular verbs appear in N.C. folk speech as regular weak verbs . . *blowed . . catched . . costed . . growed . . hurted . . knowed . . seed.* **1953** Atwood *Survey of Verb Forms* 42 **Atlantic,** For most of the strong verbs examined in this survey, from a handful to a considerable number of informants give the weak forms (e.g., *rised, freezed, swimmed, teached*). **1965–70** *DARE* (Qu. OO2a, . . *"He . . must have ______ something."*) Inf **MD**36, Eated; (Qu. OO6a, . . *"The . . dough ______."*) 77 Infs, **scattered,** Rised; (Qu. OO6b, . . *"She put the dough in the oven too soon—before it had ______ enough."*) 26 Infs, **scattered,** Rised; (Qu. OO11a, . . *"Our cat ______ [them]."*) 16 Infs, **scattered,** Ketched; 10 Infs, **scattered,** Catched; (Qu. OO11b, . . *"That makes five she's ______ this week."*) 15 Infs, **scattered,** Ketched; **TX**29, Catched; (Qu. OO13a, . . *"He . . ______ his leg."*) Infs **IL**77, **MS**69, **NY**10, **TX**103, 106, Breaked; (Qu. OO13b, . . *"He has ______ [that leg]."*) Inf **IL**77, Breaked; (Qu. OO14a, . . *"The wind ______."*) 112 Infs, **chiefly Sth, S Midl,** Blowed; (Qu. OO14b, . . *"One of my apple trees was ______ [down]."*) 134 Infs, **chiefly Sth, S Midl,** Blowed; (Qu. OO15a, . . *"My ears nearly ______."*) Inf **IL**93, Freezed; (Qu. OO15b, . . *"He would have ______ [his ears]."*) Inf **MS**44, Freezed; (Qu. OO16a, . . *"You should have ______ [the hammer]."*) Inf **VA**53, Bringed; (Qu. OO16b, . . *"I also ______ [a saw]."*) Inf **VA**53, Bringed; (Qu. OO17a, . . *"Her son ______ home."*) Inf **KY**5, Comed; (Qu. OO17b, . . *"He . . should have ______."*) Infs **AL**3, **CA**134, **PA**161, **SC**11, Comed; (Qu. OO22a, . . *"I ______ [him well]."*) 74 Infs, **scattered, but most freq Sth, S Midl,** Knowed; (Qu. OO22b, . . *"I've ______ [him well]."*) 86 Infs, **scattered, but most freq Sth, S Midl,** Knowed; (Qu. OO23a, . . *"He ______."*) 129 Infs, **chiefly Sth, S Midl,** Growed; (Qu. OO23b, . . *"You wouldn't think a child could have ______ [so fast]."*) 146 Infs, **chiefly Sth, Midl,** Growed; (Qu. OO29a, . . *"We have always ______ [there]."*) 35 Infs, **chiefly Sth, S Midl,** Swimmed; (Qu. OO29b, . . *"We ______ [there too]."*) 34 Infs, **chiefly Sth, S Midl,** Swimmed; (Qu. OO30a, . . *"John . . was ______ [off]."*) 190 Infs, **widespread, but less freq Pacific, Gt Lakes, least freq OH, NYC,** Throwed; (Qu. OO30b, . . *"The same horse ______ [his brother]."*) 190 Infs, **widespread, but less freq Pacific, Gt Lakes, least freq OH, NYC,** Throwed; (Qu. OO37a, . . *"The first time my wool socks were washed they ______."*) 10 Infs, **esp Sth, S Midl,** Shrinked (up); (Qu. OO37b, . . *"They've ______."*) 9 Infs, esp Sth, S Midl, Shrinked; (Qu. OO39a, . . *"Has the meeting ______ [yet]?"*) Inf **KY**75A, Beginned; (Qu. OO39b, . . *"Yes, it ______ [an hour ago]."*) Inf **MO**16, Beginned; (Qu. OO45a, . . *"I ______ [him hide it]."*) 15 Infs, **Sth, S Midl,** Seed; (Qu. OO45b, . . *"I've ______ him hide things."*) 17 Infs, **chiefly Sth, S Midl,** Seed. [Of all the *DARE* Infs, 31% were from comm type 5, 27% had less than hs educ, and 50% were male; of those giving the responses noted here, 48% were from comm type 5, 52% had less than hs educ, and 61% were male.] **1975** Allen *LAUM* 2.10 (as of c1950), The incidence of *catched* as the preterit of *catch* is much less in the U[pper] M[idwest] than on the Atlantic Coast. *Ibid* 14, *Drinked* . . is used by only two infs. *Ibid* 15, *Drived* occurs once. *Ibid* 19, *Growed* . . has about one-fifth frequency in all states. *Ibid* 20, *Heared* . . turns up three times. *Ibid* 25, *Seed,* a South Midland variant [as past of *see*], occurs only in the speech of two . . infs. *Ibid* 26, A solitary instance of *shrinked.* *Ibid* 30, *Throwed* . . is . . strongest with . . [old] speakers in the UM.

3 added to the std past tense of irregular verbs to form past tenses and past pples. [Cf *EDG* §426] **scattered, but chiefly Sth, S Midl**

1953 Atwood *Survey of Verb Forms* 44 **Atlantic,** Loss of the preterite affix /-t, -d, -əd/ in weak verbs is as a rule not common in popular speech . . it is even added sometimes to strong verbs, as in *stoled, swoled, frozed, tored, tooked*. . . This type of form is not, however, very common. **1963** Owens *Look to River* 78 **TX,** Would they tell me you ain't stoled nothing? **1965–70** *DARE* (Qu. OO42a, . . *"He* . . ——— *[the money]."*) 88 Infs, **scattered, but most freq Sth, S Midl,** Stoled; (Qu. OO42b, . . *"He says it's the first time he has ever* ——— *[money]."*) 73 Infs, **scattered, but most freq Sth, S Midl,** Stoled [Of all Infs responding to Qq. OO42a, b, 29% were from comm type 5, 27% had less than hs educ, and 50% were male; of those responding *stoled,* 45% were from comm type 5, 56% had less than hs educ, and 60% were male.]; (Qu. V4, . . *"Somebody* ——— *my watch."*) 16 Infs, **chiefly Sth, S Midl,** Stoled; **NJ**2, Tooked; (Qu. OO3b, . . *"We* ——— *it all."*) 11 Infs, **esp Sth, S Midl,** Dranked; (Qu. C24b, . . *"He* ——— *[it at it]."*) Inf **OK**46, Threwed; (Qu. U11, . . *"I* ———*."*) Inf **MO**19, Stoled; (Qu. Y26b, . . *"The children* . . ——— *out the back way."*) Infs **TX**83, **WI**60, Stoled; (Qu. AA13, . . *"They* ———*."*) Inf **GA**15, Have broked off; (Qu. OO13a, . . *"He* ——— *his leg."*) Inf **KY**81, Broked; (Qu. OO15a, . . *"My ears nearly* ———*."*) Infs **NC**1, 49, 60, **TX**56, Frozed; (Qu. OO15b, . . *"He would have* ——— *[his ears]."*) Infs **KY**5, 37, **MD**43, **NC**60, **VA**38, **WI**47, Frozed; (Qu. OO18b, . . *"That man* ——— *[it]."*) Inf **OR**6, Drewed; (Qu. OO20b, . . *"Has the bell* ——— *[yet]?"*) Inf **MS**60, Ranged; (Qu. OO30b, . . *"The same horse* ——— *[his brother]."*) Inf **MO**39, Threwed; (Qu. OO37a, . . *"They* ———*."*) Infs **NC**50, **KY**81, Shranked (up); (Qu. OO41a, . . *"He* ——— *[too many chances]."*) Inf **MT**2, Tooked; (Qu. OO45a, . . *"I* ——— *[him hide it]."*) Infs **GA**84, **KY**11, 84, Sawed; (Qu. OO45b, . . *"I've* ——— *him."*) Inf **KY**84, Sawed.

4 added to the std past pple of an irregular verb or a non-std var of it to form past tenses and past pples. [Cf *EDG* §431]

1902 *DN* 2.239 **sIL,** He was mistakened. **1953** Atwood *Survey of Verb Forms* 11 **Atlantic,** Other [past tense—past participle] combinations . . are *drank—drinken, . . drinkened—drinken.* *Ibid* 22, Other forms that occur [as past tenses] . . are *swollened* . . , *swellened.* *Ibid* 24, There are 26 instances of the preterite *takened* . . , most of which are in Delmarva, the Tidewater area of Va., and the eastern half of N.C. . . Of those who use the preterite *takened,* two thirds level the preterite and the past participle. The forms *takened—taken* occur in six scattered instances. The following occur from once to five times each: . . *taken—takened, tuck—takened, toke—takened.* **1967–70** *DARE* (Qu. AA2) Inf **AR**51, Lot of 'em say "He takened her"; (Qu. AA15c) Inf **MD**41, Was takened in; (Qu. LL3a, . . *"These apples are all* ———*."*) Inf **IL**30, Shrunkened; (Qu. OO29b, . . *"We* ——— *[there too]."*) Inf **KY**94, Swummed; (Qu. OO41a, . . *"He* ——— *[too many chances]."*) Infs **AR**51, 55, **LA**2, **TN**26, Takened; (Qq. OO42a, b) Inf **TN**27, Takened.

5 omitted from past tense and past pple of regular verbs. **chiefly Sth, S Midl** *esp among rural Infs with less than hs educ* Cf Pronc Intro 3.I.22

1888 Jones *Negro Myths* 6 **GA coast,** An dat de way Buh Cooter fool [=fooled] Buh Deer an win [=won] de bet. **1905** *DN* 3.69 **nwAR,** I ask him yesterday about it. **1922** Gonzales *Black Border* 331 **sSC, GA coasts** [Gullah glossary], *Tackle*. . . tackled. **1953** Atwood *Survey of Verb Forms* 5 **Atlantic,** The leveled combination *ask : ask* [=infinitive : past] occurs in a very scattered way in Pa. and Md., and becomes fairly common in Va., where more than one fourth of the noncultured informants use it. It is also in use, though less commonly, in N.C. and S.C. *Ibid* 9, The uninflected *climb* /klaim/ is used by two Negro informants. **1965–70** *DARE* (Qu. OO9a, . . *"I've* ——— *him many times."*; total Infs questioned, 75) 14 Infs, Ask; (Qu. OO9b, . . *"I* ——— *him yesterday."*; total Infs questioned, 75) 14 Infs, Ask; (Qu. OO5a, . . *"Our house was* ——— *[with a stove]."*) Infs **GA**5, **MS**63, **MO**8, **SC**26, **TN**34, **WI**23, Heat; **MA**6, Stove heat; (Qu. OO5b, . . *"Years ago they* ——— *[the house] with a stove."*) Infs **MO**8, 39, **SC**26, **TN**34, Heat; **MS**69, Heated, heat; (Qu. OO10a, . . *"We often* ——— *[trees]."*) Infs **GA**1, **KY**34, **ME**6, 16, **SC**10, 26, Climb; (Qu. OO25a, . . *"The* . . *children have often* ——— *[there]."*) Infs **FL**48, **MO**16, 36, **SC**10, 26, **VA**39, 71, Dive; (Qu. OO25b, . . *"Only yesterday the children* ——— *[there]."*) Infs **FL**48, **NC**4, **SC**10, 26, **VA**39, 71, Dive; (Qu. OO26a, . . *"Several people have* ——— *[there]."*) Infs **AL**20, 37, **GA**1, **KS**8, **NC**51, 52, 63, 77, **NH**17, **SC**26, Drown; (Qu. OO26b, . . *"A boy was* ——— *[there]."*; not asked in early QRs) Infs **AL**37, **MO**36, **NC**51, 63, **SC**26, Drown; (Qu. OO26d, . . *"A child* ——— *here."*; total Infs questioned, 75) Inf **GA**1, Drown; (Qu. OO35a, . . *"Last year* . . *the plants really* ———*."*) Infs **AL**6, **FL**49, **LA**11, **MS**87, **NC**31, **SC**26, **TN**4, **VA**71, Thrive; (Qu. OO35b, . . *"Nothing has ever* ——— *there."*) Infs **AL**6, **FL**49, **OK**42, **SC**26, **VA**71, Thrive; (Qu. OO43a, . . *"She* . . ——— *[with me to stay]."*) Infs **LA**20, **SC**10, 26, Plead; **AL**25, **NY**166, **SC**26, Beg; (Qu. OO43b, . . *"I wouldn't have stayed if she hadn't* ——— *[so hard]."*) Infs **MD**26, **OH**16, **SC**10, 26, **VA**73, Plead; **MO**2, Ask; **SC**26, Beg; (Qu. OO46a, . . *"We* . . ——— *it out [of the woods]."*) Infs **IL**27, **IA**36, **MO**8, 13, **SC**9, 26, **VA**26, 27, 49, 77, Drag; (Qu. OO46b, . . *"We must have* ——— *[it]!"*) Infs **SC**26, **TN**36, **VA**27, 49, Drag. [Of all *DARE* Infs, 31% were from comm type 5 and 28% had less than hs educ; of those enumerated here (excluding Qq. OO9a, b), 50% were from comm type 5 and 37% had less than hs educ.]

6 added redundantly to adjs formed from nouns + *-ed.*

1968–69 *DARE* (Qu. X6, *If a person's lower jaw sticks out prominently*) Inf **NC**49, Long-chinneded; (Qu. X26a) Inf **AL**50, Cross-eyeded.

edads intj [Prob var of *egads*]

1924 *DN* 5.285 **seNE,** [Interjections:] *Edads.*

eddekashin See **educate**

edder See **other** pron

eddicated, eddication See **educate**

eddy n [*eddy* whirlpool]

1 also freq *eddy water,* infreq *eddy hole:* Still water usu along the side of a river. **scattered, but esp freq S Midl**

1938 in 1977 Randolph *Pissing in the Snow* 45 **Ozarks,** Nobody likes a woman that just lays there like a turd in a dead eddy. **1965–70** *DARE* (Qu. C14, *A stretch of still water going off to the side of a river or lake*) 18 Infs, **chiefly S Midl,** Eddy; **AR**17, 53, **SC**32, Eddy water; **GA**84, Eddy water—water that is barely moving in the river; **OK**21, Eddy hole; [**GA**77, Eddied water;] (Qu. O17, *When the water is very smooth and still, you call that a* ———) Infs **AL**32, **AR**31, 51, **GA**3, **KY**47, **MS**58, Eddy water; **AR**48, 51, Eddy; **OK**42, An eddy—the lake's quiet; (Qu. C4a, . . *A* . . *large body of fresh water*) Inf **MO**19, Eddy [FW: He remarks an eddy was not fresh water. Stagnant pool?]; (QR, near Qu. C4a) Inf **KY**18, Eddy—still water between shoals in the river. **1969** *DARE* Tape **KY**21, We would find an eddy somewhere to swim in, where the water was dead; **KY**16, [Inf:] They had a big eddy about a mile long down here . . a wide eddy. . . [FW:] What is an eddy? [Inf:] It's just still part of water. . . 'Tween the shoals. **1969** *DARE* FW Addit **KY**21, Inf's illustration shows an eddy as a stretch of still water off the side of a river. "When the river is flooded the current may force itself into an eddy and cause a whirlpool or boil"; **KY**28, Eddy water—the place in a stream or river where there is little or no current, especially along one side.

2 also *eddy water:* A pool or body of water left behind after a river has flooded and subsided.

1969 *DARE* (QR p15) Inf **KY**39, Eddy—water builds up and stands still in a place and the silt settles—result of tide or flood. **1969** *DARE* FW Addit **KY**46, Eddy water—water that remains standing after the river has flooded.

3 A roughened place on the water's surface. **chiefly Nth, N Midl**

1965–70 *DARE* (Qu. C3, *A place in a swift stream, where the surface of the water is broken*) 61 Infs, **chiefly Nth, N Midl,** Eddy; (Qu. O12, *A disturbance caused by wind which seems to run and spread swiftly along the surface of water*) Infs **CA**191, **CT**32, **MI**24, **NY**107, 133, **RI**1, Eddy; (Qu. O15, . . *Different kinds of waves*) Inf **IN**19, Eddies; **NY**47, **OH**78, Ripples, eddies.

eddycashun, eddycated, eddycation See **educate**

eddy hole See **eddy 1**

eddykatin' See **educate**

eddy-tide n Also *tide-eddy*

A whirlpool.

1966–70 *DARE* (Qu. C8, . . *A place in a stream where water flows round and round*) Inf **VA**47, Eddy-tide; **NC**25, Tide-eddy; (Qu. C3) Inf **MA**55, Whirlpool, eddy-tides, eddies.

eddy water See **eddy 1, 2**

edecation, edercate See **educate**

edge n, v Usu |ɛǰ|; also freq **chiefly Sth, Midl, eNEng** |e(ɪ)ǰ|; also |æǰ| Pronc-spp *a(d)ge, ai(d)ge, aje, eedge* See Pronc Intro 3.I.5.b

A Forms.

1847 Hurd *Grammatical Corrector* 81, *Edge. . . Incorrectly pronounced:* aje. **1867** Lowell *Biglow* 221 **'Upcountry' MA,** The eedge of a mow. **1891** *DN* 1.129 **cNY,** [eǰ] . . "edge." **1893** Shands *MS Speech* 16, *Adge* [eǰ]. Negro for *edge.* **1899** Garland *Boy Life* 307 **IA,** Let's kinder aige 'em along toward each other. **1900** Day *Up in ME* 52 **ME,** I never see'd a winter have a durnder, sharper aidge / Than in the year of Sixty-one, the year that I drove stage. **1902** *DN* 2.233 **sIL,** *Edge* . . [eǰ]. **1906** *DN* 3.134 **nwAR,** *Edge* . . [eɪǰ]. **1917** *DN* 4.407 **IL, KY, wNC, NEng, OH,** *Aidge.* **1918** *DN* 5.17 **eMA,** *Wedge. . .* Pronounced almost as in wage. *Edge* has a similar "a" sound. **1923** *DN* 5.200 **swMO,** *Aidge* n . . v . . "Aidge over so's I'll have more room." **1925** *DN* 5.360 **seGA,** De sky git kina white roun de aiges. **1929** Sale *Tree Named John* 8 **MS,** Ah wants you t' put a aige on a knife fer me. *Ibid* 65, De aige uv de watter. **1939** *LANE* Map 159 **nwMA,** *Whetstone,* to put an [ɛɪǰ] on a scythe. **1942** *AmSp* 17.31 **seNY,** Variations between [e] and [ɛ] include . . *edge* [e] 1, from Suffolk County, [ɛ] 189 [infs]. **1958** *PADS* 29.29 **OK,** *Ageing* . . A pron. variant of *edging.* **1970** [see **edge iron**]. **1975** Gould *ME Lingo* 33, *Aidge*—Edge. With a coastal accent, *aidges* are put on knives, appetites, curt remarks.

B As noun.

1 See **age 1.**

2 A mild state of intoxication—usu in phr *get an edge on* somewhat old-fash

1905 *DN* 3.8 **cCT,** *Edge. . .* "He's got an edge on." Slang for he is drunk. **1920** Fitzgerald *This Side of Paradise* 122 **NY,** We'll drink to Fred Sloane, who has a rare, distinguished edge. **1925** (1958) Hemingway *In Our Time* 60 **nMI,** "How do you feel?" . . "Swell. I've just got a good edge on." **1966–69** *DARE* (Qu. DD13, *When a drinker is just beginning to show the effects of the liquor*) Infs **FL**39, **NY**59, 177, Getting an edge on; **VT**4, **VA**33, Got an edge on. [All Infs old]

3 See quot.

1972 Claerbaut *Black Jargon* 63, *Edge* . . a knife or dagger, often employed as a weapon: *packin' an edge.*

C As verb.

1 usu with *on:* To provoke; to egg on.

1965–70 *DARE* (Qu. Y5, . . *To urge somebody to do something he shouldn't*) 25 Infs, **scattered,** Edged him on; **NH**16, Edged him; (QR, near Qu. Y5) Inf **ME**5, Edge him on. [FW: used conv; Inf then corrected this to *egg him on.*]

2 usu with *away, off,* or *out:* To back down; to avoid assuming responsibility. [By ext of *edge* to move by insensible degrees; perh infl by *hedge*] Cf **egg** v²

1966–69 *DARE* (Qu. JJ45, *When someone avoids giving a definite answer*) Inf **CT**5, Edging; **IL**29, **NH**14, **NY**120, **PA**118, **WA**12, **WI**34, Edging away (*or* off, out of it); (Qu. II31, . . *"He saw that he was wrong, so he started to ——."*) Infs **IA**30, **KS**5, **OH**8, **OR**6, Edge away (*or* off, out); (Qu. II32, *To manage some way to shift the responsibility*) Infs **MO**20, **NY**220, Edge out of it.

edge, at adj phr

At odds.

1970 *DARE* (Qu. KK68, . . *"We agree on most things, but . . we're ——."*) Inf **VA**103, At edge on others.

edge away See **edge C2**

edge iron n [Because placed at the edge or side of a fireplace] =**andiron.**

1970 *DARE* (Qu. D32) Inf **TX**94, Edge irons [æjaɚnz].

edgemcation See **edumacation**

edge of dark n Also *edge of dusk, ~ night, ~ the evening* **chiefly NEng, Mid Atl**

Early evening, twilight.

1758 in 1874 Essex Inst. *Coll.* 12.133 **MA,** Soaked with a heavy rain in ye edge of ye evening. **1809** (1918) Putnam *Diary* 6.18 **MA,** Took a walk in the edge of the evening to buy some oil at chases. **a1864** (1870) Hawthorne *Passages Engl. Note-Books* 1.8 **MA,** At about the edge of dusk the carriage drew up to the door to take us home. **1931–33** *LANE Worksheets* **cwMA,** Edge of the evening; **cwCT,** The edge of the evening is just about supper time. **1953** *PADS* 19.10 **wNC,** *Edge of dark. . .* Twilight. **1966–70** *DARE* (Qu. A5) Infs **ME**22, **VA**74, Edge of dark; **NC**25, On the edge of dusk; **MA**5, Edge of the evening. **1975** Gould *ME Lingo* 33, With a coastal accent . . seiners go for herring at the *aidge* of night or the *aidge* of dark. **1982** Heat Moon *Blue Highways* 437 **Chesapeake Bay,** Just before the edge of dark, the light would turn the working sails gold as angels' wings. **1983** *Lutz Coll.* **neNJ,** We came down the mountain at the edge of dark.

edge off See **edge C2**

edge of night (or the evening) See **edge of dark**

edge on See **edge C1**

edge out See **edge C2**

edger n

1 In marble play: see quot 1955.

1942 Berrey–Van den Bark *Amer. Slang* 665.3, Edger. **1955** *PADS* 23.17 **cTN,** *Edger. . .* A marble or taw that is near the edge of the ring or of the shooting line. **c1970** Wiersma *Marbles Terms,* 4 infs, **esp MI,** Edger. **1973** Ferretti *Marble Book* 43, *Edgers.* Marbles near the edge of the ring.

2 One who is not straightforward; a deceiver.

1969 *DARE* (Qu. V2a, . . *A deceiving person or somebody that you can't trust*) Inf **NY**219, An edger [eǰɚ]—edging around.

‡edge-up n Cf **lower-edge cut**

A haircut which neatens the lines without changing the style; a trim.

1970 *DARE* (Qu. X5) Inf **NC**86, Edge-up—razor line around the hairline to even it up without cutting off any of the top.

edgeways adv Also pronc-sp *ageways*

A Form.

1887 Eggleston *Graysons* 5 **IL,** You wouldn't let me get in a word ageways with him.

B Sense.

Fig: on edge.

1898 Westcott *Harum* 212 **nNY,** "I don't think I ever enjoyed a glass of wine so much, or," turning to Aunt Polly, "ever enjoyed a dinner so much," which statement completely mollified her feelings, which had been the least bit in the world "set edgeways."

edgewise adj Cf **edge, at**

At odds, antagonistic.

1914 *DN* 4.106 **KS,** *Edgewise. . .* At enmity. "The two feel edgewise toward each other." **1928** *Ruppenthal Coll.* **KS,** *To feel edgewise toward (a person)*—To feel somewhat unfriendly, as indignant, resentful, peeved. . . I felt edgewise toward him ever since he failed to help me in the county campaign.

edging n Pronc-sp *ageing* [Perh from **age 1**]

In marble play: see quot.

1958 *PADS* 29.33 **OK,** *Edging. . .* The *ante* in marble playing. *Ibid* 29, *Ageing. . .* A pron. variant of *edging.*

edgy adj

Of the weather: crisp, frosty.

1926 *AmSp* 2.80 **ME,** A favorite greeting on a frosty morning is, "It's sharp this mornin'," or perhaps, "It's kinder edgy."

edication See **educate**

Edisto cat n [*Edisto* River, South Carolina]

=**channel catfish.**

1855 Simms *Forayers* 275, The blue-cat of the Edisto is one of the nicest fish that swims. . . Take an Edisto cat in July if you can.

edoocation See **educate**

e-drop See **eavesdrop**

educate v, hence vbl n, ppl adj Usu |ˈɛǰuˌket, ˈɛdju-, ˈɛǰɪ-, ˈɛǰə-|; also |ˈɛdɪˌket| Pronc-sp *edercate* Similarly vbl n *eddykatin';* ppl adj *eddicated, eddycated;* n *eddication, eddycation, iddicasion;* for addit varr see quots Cf **edumacation**

A Forms.

1836 (1955) *Crockett Almanacks* 51 **wTN,** The schoolmaster . . had got his eddycation in some big city. **1836** (1838) Haliburton *Clockmaker* (1st ser) 42 **CT,** If they only have edication here, they might learn to do so too, but they don't know nothin'. **1843** (1916) Hall *New Purchase* 325 **IN,** People's eddekashin money *bought* that! **1844** Thompson *Major Jones's Courtship* 31 **GA,** Edecation is the most surprisinest thing in the world—specially female edecation. **1859** Elwyn *Glossary, Iddicasion,* for *education.* This Yorkshire method of pronouncing this word is not unfrequent in New England. **1861** Holmes *Venner* 1.163 **NEng,** Edoocation is the great business of the Institoot. **1867** Lowell *Biglow* 95 **'Upcountry' MA,** Ef eddykatin' done the thing, they'd be some skurcer here. **1867** Twain *Jumping Frog* 14, He ketched a frog one day, and took him home, and said he cal'k'lated to edercate him. . . all a frog wanted was education. **1871** Eggleston *Hoosier Schoolmaster* 40 **sIN,** Ef a gal had gone clean through all eddication, . . that would-n buy a feather-bed. **1901** *DN* 2.182 **KY** [Black speaker], *Educated* . . edyecate'. **1905** *DN* 3.57 **eNE,** Vowels in middle or final syllables are likely to be much slurred, or to be dropped . . *edication.* **1908** in 1953 Botkin–Harlow *Treas. Railroad Folkl.* 320, He'd more idjucation, had Flannigan. **1922** Gonzales *Black Border* 234 **sSC, GA coasts** [Gullah], You smaa't 'nuf fuh know w'en man got gun een 'e han', but yo' eddycashun cyan' specify w'en 'e come fuh tell w'en shell' cawn got pizen een um. **1926** Vollmer *Sun-Up* 13 **wNC,** Emmy's eddicated purty well. **1929** Sale *Tree Named John* 31 **MS,** Ah ain' eddycated en Ah cain' read ner write. . . Eddycation is all right fer some folks. . . W'en you eddycate him you jes done made a no'count, uppity, know-it-all. **1936** *AmSp* 11.311 **nNY,** *Educate* is normally ['ɛǰəket], but may occasionally be heard as ['ɛdjuket]. **1938** Stuart *Dark Hills* 182 **neKY,** This world don't need no eddicated people. **1942** *AmSp* 17.40 **seNY, NYC,** *Educated* /dju/ 1 [inf], /ǰu/ 17 [infs]. **1942** Hall *Smoky Mt. Speech* 96 **wNC, eTN,** [d] is combined with a following palatal glide [j] to form the voiced affricate [ǰ] in *dubious, education.* **1943** *LANE* Map 535, Pronunciations of the type of [ɛdɨkeɪʃən] are regarded as older though still in use by [34 infs in **sME, NH, sVT**]. **1966** *DARE* Tape **WA**17, He'd been educated ['ɛdɪˌketɪd] as a druggist.

B Senses.

Ppl adj *educated:*

a Fraudulent.

1949 *San Diego Union* (CA) 7 Nov sec B 1/3 **swCA,** This reporter bought an "educated" deck, complete with instructions. So skilfully is the marking done that the uninstructed would find it almost impossible to detect it. Yet to the professional the cards can be read as easily from their backs as from their faces. **1950** *Western Folkl.* 9.117 **nwOR** [Logger speech], *Educated stick.* Scaler's rule, or scale rod. [*DARE* Ed: Prob in ref to the idea that the scaler tries to cheat the piecework logger by underestimating the amount of timber cut.] **1951** *PADS* 16.26 [Racetrack argot], *Educated currency.* . . Bets which are placed on a horse as a result of supposedly authentic information.

b Sophisticated, worldly.

1968 Adams *Western Words* 105, *Educated thirst*—A cowboy's phrase describing a man who drinks champagne and fancy mixed drinks.

c In facetious and humorous combs: see quots.

1966–69 *DARE* (Qu. HH44, *Joking . . names for lawyers*) Inf **AL**30, Educated crook; (Qu. II35, *A person who . . seems to know everything*) Infs **PA**192, **TX**9, Educated fool; (QR p93) Inf **MA**6, Educated backhouse—a flush toilet.

edumacation n Also sp *edgemcation* [**-ma-** infix] *somewhat derisive*

Education.

1833 in 1962 Nathan *Dan Emmett* 68, In *Bone Squash* the colored dandy is represented by a swell called "Spruce Pink" . . and in *O Hush!* he becomes "Sambo Johnson," a "consumquencial darkey" who has made money in the lottery and therefore, so he figures, has acquired "edgemcation" (education). **1969** *DARE* (Qu. II21, *When somebody behaves unpleasantly or without manners*) Inf **NC**61, No edumacation [ˌɛdǰəmə'kešən]. **1977** Smitherman *Talkin* 88 [Black], Y'all know you got some radio directors with two years of edu-ma-cation.

edxactly See **exactly**

edyecate' See **educate**

edzackly See **exactly**

edzact v [*exact* precise] **sAppalachians, Ozarks**

1 To perfect, render exact.

1917 *DN* 4.411 **wNC,** *Edzact.* . . To make precisely right. "Let me study this over: then I can edzact it." **1953** Randolph *Down in Holler* 242 **Ozarks,** *Edzact.* . . To adjust precisely.

2 also with *out:* To figure out.

1928 Chapman *Happy Mt.* 126 **seTN,** She might maybe edzact what it was uneasied her. **1952** Brown *NC Folkl.* 1.536 **wNC,** *Edzact.* . . To reason out. "I'd better *edzact* that out for myself." **1953** Randolph *Down in Holler* 242 **Ozarks,** *Edzact.* . . sometimes to understand fully. One of my neighbors took a complicated machine apart, looked puzzled, and said, "I cain't *edzact* the damn' thing to suit me." **1972** Cooper *NC Mt. Folkl.* 91, *Edzact*—to reason out.

edzactly See **exactly**

edzact out See **edzact 2**

ee See **he** pron

ee-aw See **hee-haw**

eeben See **even**

eebie-jeebie See **heebie-jeebies 1**

eech See **itch**

eech out See **itch out**

eeder See **either**

eeder-so See **either E2**

eedge See **edge**

eedie-aidi-over n

1969 *DARE* (Qu. EE33) Inf **CA**142, ['iˌdi 'ɑiˌdi ovɚ]—a jump-rope game.

eediot See **idiot**

e'edrop See **eavesdrop**

eeduh See **either**

eeduhso See **either E2**

eeeeve See **iiwi**

ee-ell exclam

In **hide-and-seek A:** used as a call announcing the readiness of the hiders.

1966 *DARE* Tape **GA**13, He'd holler "Ready!" and they [=the players who were hiding] would holler "Ee-ell" ['iˌɛl], then the baseman would start running.

eegit See **idiot**

eegnunt See **ignorant**

eejit See **idiot**

eek See **ooch** n

eekal See **equal** n, v, adj

eel n

1 in phr *slick* (or *sleek*) *as an eel:* Deceptive, shrewd, elusive; slippery as an eel. **chiefly Sth, S Midl**

1906 *DN* 3.156 **nwAR,** *Slick as an eel* . . slippery as an eel. **1922** *DN* 5.175 **AR,** *Slick as an eel.* **1952** Brown *NC Folkl.* 1.402, As slick as an eel. . . As sleek as an eel. . . As slippery as an eel. **1965–69** *DARE* (Qu. KK37, . . *A very sly person*) Infs **DE**1, **KS**6, **MS**15, 30, **SC**40, 66, Slick as an eel.

2 An elusive, shrewd, or deceptive person; also as a nickname. *usu derog*

1838 (1843) Haliburton *Clockmaker* (2d ser) 264, People from every state in the Union . . have all nicknames. There's the hoosiers of Indiana, . . the wolverines of Michigan, the eels of New England, and the corn-crackers of Virginia. **1848** in 1961 *AmSp* 36.297, New-Yorkers are called *Eels.* **1933** *AmSp* 8.3.26 [Prison dictionary], *Eel.* . . "Whitey," who escaped three times from solitary confinement . . , was an acknowledged *eel.* **1935** *AmSp* 10.51 [In comic cartoons], Epithets of disparagement. . . The eel. **1956** *AmSp* 31.98 **sTX,** If the smuggler has any doubts about his operations, he will look for *eels,* or spies, in his *ring.* **1966–68** *DARE* (Qu. V2a, . . *A deceiving person*) Infs **AL**6, **CT**19, Slippery eel; (Qu. KK37, . . *A very sly person*) Inf **SC**5, Slippery eel.

3 also *silver eel:* A cutlassfish (here: *Trichiurus lepturus*).

1882 U.S. Natl. Museum *Proc.* 5.267 **seTX,** *Trichiurus lepturus. . . Silver Eel. . .* Rather common about Galveston. *Ibid* 592 **seSC,** *Silver-eel.* Very abundant in the Charleston Harbor, being brought in by every seine-boat. **1884** Goode *Fisheries U.S.* 1.335 **seGA,** *The Cutlass-Fish. . .* at Brunswick, Georgia, . . is known as the "Silver Eel." . . Its appearance is very remarkable on account of its long, compressed form and its glistening silvery color. **1955** Zim–Shoemaker *Fishes* 53, Several other elongate fishes, such as the Cutlass Fish . . are mistakenly called eels.

4 Any of var somewhat eel-shaped salamanders of the genera *Siren* and *Amphiuma.* See also **congo eel 2**

1928 Baylor Univ. Museum *Contrib.* 16.9, In many east Texas and Louisiana localities all so-called eels are amphibians, the true (fish) eels being known by other names. **1958** Conant *Reptiles & Amphibians* 202, Greater Siren. . . An "eel" with forelegs and external gills. *Ibid* 205, Amphiuma. . . An "eel" with 2 pairs of tiny, useless-looking legs. **1967** LeCompte *Word Atlas* 217 **seLA,** A snake like creature with four tiny legs / usually found in ditches after a heavy rain / . . an eel [4 of 21 infs]. **1969** *DARE* FW Addit **seGA,** Eel. . . Black lizard-like animal about 1 foot long, circular cross-section, external gills; killed by Inf.

eel v, hence vbl n *eeling* **chiefly Atl States**

To fish for eels.

1780 in 1882 *Narragansett Hist. Reg.* 1.104 **RI,** Made an eel spear. Went eeling. **1843** *Knickerbocker* 22.426 **NY,** No clammin', no eelin', and no pastur' to feed your cow onto. **1895** *Outing* 26.406/2 **eNEng,** It was only when he couldn't go eeling . . that we could secure his priceless services. **1915** (1916) Johnson *Highways New Engl.* 209 **Nantucket MA,** I've seen twenty-five men out here on the harbor eeling in winter. We jog for the eels through holes cut in the ice. **1933** *Hanley Disks* **seMA,** We used to do quite a lot of eeling. Oh, we've been eeling here for years. **1968** *DARE* (Qu. P13, . . *Other ways of fishing*) Inf **NJ**8, Eeling —string fishworms on thread, put on pole, pull up when [the eel] bites and drop in tub—also called bobbing for eels; **NC**82, They used to eel some.

eel-back flounder n Also *eel-back* [See quot 1884]

A **flounder** n **B** (here: *Liopsetta putnami*) of the New England coast. Also called **foolfish 2**

1884 Goode *Fisheries U.S.* 1.183, The Smooth Flounder, or Christmas Flounder, *Pleuronectes glaber,* . . may be distinguished . . by its smooth skin, which has given to the species, in some localities, the name "Eel-back." **1898** U.S. Natl. Museum *Bulletin* 47.2650, *Eel-back Flounder. . .* Length 10 inches. Atlantic coast of North America, from Cape Cod northward. . . Specimens are frequently found in the markets. **1911** *Century Dict. Suppl., Flounder. . . Eel-back flounder,* a species of flounder, *Liopsetta putnami,* found along the New England coast; the female is nearly scaleless.

eelbait n

=**eelworm.**

1949 *AmSp* 24.108 **GA,** *Eel-bait. . .* Long earthworms.

eel basin See **eel rack**

eel basket n **nwNJ** Cf **eelpot 1**

A usu wooden device placed within an **eel rack** and used for catching eels.

1967–68 *DARE* (Qu. P13, . . *Ways of fishing*) Inf **NJ**10, Eel basket; (Qu. P14) Inf **NJ**1, Eel basket under dam—not common ever. **1967** *DARE* Tape **NJ**2, We had eel baskets—a wooden eel trap.

eel bug n

=**whirligig beetle.**

1941 *Nature Mag.* 34.138, I will not try to explain the names lackey bug and eel bug, which are given to the whirligigs in Massachusetts and North Carolina, respectively.

eel car n [car n^2] Cf **fish car**

1913 *DN* 4.56 **eMA,** *Eel-car. . .* The large, heavy, cubical crates in which eels are confined under water after being taken from the eel-pots. They are kept there till prices rise. "Eel forty dollars a bar'l an' not one in my eel-cars!"

eel catfish n Also *eel cat* [See quot 1933 John G. Shedd Aquarium *Guide*]

A large unspotted yellowish catfish *(Ictalurus anguilla)* with a broad heavy head, found throughout much of the Mississippi River drainage. Also called **fulton cat 2, niggerlip ~, ponehead ~, willow ~**

1898 Jordan–Evermann *Fishes* 3.2789, The eel cat rarely attains a greater weight than 5 pounds. **1908** Forbes–Richardson *Fishes of IL* cxix, List of Illinois Food Fishes . . Second class . . Eel cat *(anguilla)* (rare). **1911** *Century Dict., Eel-cat. . .* One of the channel catfish, *Ictalurus anguilla.* **1933** LA Dept. of Conserv. *Fishes* 421, The Eel Cat . . was first discovered by Dr. Evermann in the Atchafalaya River, Louisiana in 1897. **1933** John G. Shedd Aquarium *Guide* 53, *Ictalurus anguilla. . .* It gets its name Eel Catfish from its color which is very much like that of the Common Eel. **1967** *DARE* Tape **LA**5, We have . . eel cats.

eel fly n **cnNY**

=**mayfly.**

1889 *Century Dict.,* Eel-fly. . . A shad-fly. [St. Lawrence River] **1960** Teale *Journey into Summer* 38, Along the St. Lawrence they [=mayflies] are known as eel flies. **1967–69** *DARE* (Qu. R4, *A large winged insect that hatches in summer in great numbers around lakes or rivers, crowds around lights, lives only a day or so, and is good fish bait*) Infs **NY**6, 122, Eel fly; **NY**97, Eel fly—they are so thick sometimes that the road gets greasy; (Qu. R2) Inf **NY**171, Eel fly; (QR p120) Inf **NY**10, Eel fly—long wings, long tail, eels et 'em.

eelgrass n Cf **green eelgrass**

1 A submerged marine plant *(Zostera marina)* with grasslike leaves, native to the coastal US. **chiefly NEng** Also called **barnacle grass, grass** n **2, grass wrack 1, sea oar, tiresome weed, turtle grass**

1790 Deane *New Engl. Farmer* 19/1, The farmer . . may cart into it [=a stockyard] . . marsh-mud, eel-grass, flats, or even sand and loam [for making manure]. **1840** MA Zool. & Bot. Surv. *Herb. Plants & Quadrupeds* 223, Grass Wrack. . . grows in the muddy waters of the sea-coast, sometimes called *Eel-grass.* **1864** Lowell *Fireside Travels* 45 **MA,** The kelp and eel-grass left by higher floods. **1891** *Century Dict., Zostera. . . Z. marina* is known in America as *eel-grass* and in England as *grass-wrack* [etc]. **1933** *Hanley Disks* **ceMA,** The eel grass is gone—it all disappeared and is now coming back. **1948** Pearson *Sea Flavor* 117 **NEng,** Eelgrass gets its name logically, for it waves like the bodies of eels. **1966** *DARE* Tape **ME**22, We call 'em giant crabs and eelgrass crabs. There's two different kinds that we get. **1973** Hitchcock–Cronquist *Flora Pacific NW* 567, Alas[ka] to s Cal, Atl coast; Europe; e[el-grass], grass-wrack. **1978** Whipple *Vintage Nantucket* 241 **MA,** Not far from the low-tide line the water turned darker; under it were acres of eelgrass, swinging slowly in the current.

2 =**tape grass.**

1843 Torrey *Flora NY* 2.265, *Valisneria spiralis* . . Tape-grass. Eel-grass. . . Slow-flowing rivers and shallow bays. . . It is generally believed that the roots of this plant are the favorite food of the Canvass-back Duck. **1910** Graves *Flowering Plants* 47 **CT,** Eel Grass. Wild Celery. Common in the waters of the Connecticut and Housatonic Rivers and their larger tributaries. **1940** Steyermark *Flora MO* 53, Eel-grass. . . A favorite food of wild ducks. **1952** Strausbaugh–Core *Flora WV* 64, Eelgrass. . . Leaves thin, ribbon-like, narrowly linear.

3 A **pondweed** (here: either *Potamogeton pectinatus* or *P. zosteriformis*).

1913 *Torreya* 13.226, *Potamogeton pectinatus. . .* Eel grass, Lake Surprise, Texas, Centre Moriches, L[ong] I[sland], Currituck Sound, N.C. **1950** Stevens *ND Plants* 49, *Potamogeton zosteriformis. . .* Eel-grass. . . A rather common and striking species because of the long, parallel-sided leaves and wide, flat stems.

eeling See **eel** v

eel out v phr

To evade a situation or responsibility; to worm out (of a situation).

1968 *DARE* (Qu. II32, *To manage some way to shift the responsibility: "He said it wasn't his fault and tried to ________.'*') Inf **OH**47, Eel out.

eelpot n

1 A trap-like box placed within an **eel rack** and used for catching eels. **Atlantic**

1631 in 1769 Hutchinson *Collection* 51 *(DAE)* **MA,** The yeele potts you sent for are made. **1643** in 1827 RI Hist. Soc. *Coll.* 1.105 [In Roger Williams's glossary of the language of American natives], Mihtúck quashep, An Eele-pot. **1869** *Amer. Naturalist* 3.19 **nCT,** There was one taken in the Farmington River, some six miles from this place, in an eel-pot. **1913** *DN* 4.56 **eMA,** *Eel-car* . . crate in which eels are confined after being taken from the eel-pots. **1966–68** *DARE* (Qu. P13, . . *Other ways of fishing*) Infs **CT**2, **NC**18, Eelpot; **NC**82, They used to eel some—used [an] eelpot.

‡**2** A Methodist. [Perh **eel** n **2** + **pot** one's head] *derog*

1968 *DARE* (Qu. CC4, . . *Nicknames . . for various religions*) Inf **NY**83, Eelpots—Methodists.

eelpout n

1 Any of var saltwater fish of the family Zoarcidae, but esp *Zoarces anguillaris,* an eel-like fish of the Atlantic coast which is also called **conger eel 2, congo ~ 1, lamper ~, ling, mother of eels, muttonfish, yowler.**

1772 in 1924 Phillips *Notes B. Romans* 124, Besides these there are three species of Eel Ponts [sic], but these are in every Sea or River on the Earth besides. **1842** DeKay *Zool. NY* 3.155, The *Thick-lipped Eel-pout* . . is caught on the coast, in company with the common cod. It . . affords a very savory food. **1889** *Century Dict.,* Eel-pout . . the conger-eel or lamper-eel, *Zoarces anguillaris,* of North America. **1906** NJ State Museum *Annual Rept. for 1905* 406, Eel Pout. Conger Eel Pout. . . It is usually recorded from our shore in cold weather.

2 =burbot. [*OED* 1740 →] **chiefly NEng, Gt Lakes**

1839 MA Zool. & Bot. Surv. *Fishes Reptiles* 135, *L[ota] compressa,* Le Sueur. *The Eel Pout* . . was sent me from Keene N.H. **1842** DeKay *Zool. NY* 4.285, *The Spotted Burbot. Lota maculosa* . . is known under the various local names of *La Loche, Methy, Dog-fish* and *Eel-pout.* **1884** Goode *Fisheries U.S.* 1.236, In Vermont it [=the Burbot] is called the "Eel-pout" . . by which name also it is known in Mohawk River, New York, . . in Massachusetts . . , in Connecticut . . , and in Bighorn River, Montana. **1908** Forbes–Richardson *Fishes of IL* 331, Burbot; ling; eel-pout. . . The range of this species is throughout New England and the Great Lakes region and northward to the Arctic zone. **1967** *DARE* (Qu. P3, *Freshwater fish that are not good to eat*) Inf **MN**5, Eelpout. **1968** *WI Conserv. Bulletin* May/June 14/3 **WI,** Did you know we have codfish right here in Wisconsin? Yes, it's the burbot, often called the lawyer or eelpout.

3 A sea lamprey *(Petromyzon marinus).* [Cf *OED eelpout* sb. 1 quot 1601] Cf **lamper eel**

1968 *DARE* (Qu. P3, *Freshwater fish that are not good to eat*) Inf **MN**21, Eelpout—an eel with a suction.

eel rack n Also *eel basin, ~ trap* **C and N Atl**

A structure for catching eels which diverts them into an enclosure.

1968–70 *DARE* (Qu. P13, . . *Other ways of fishing*) Infs **PA**83, 126, Eel rack; **NJ**6, Eel rack—V-shaped breakwater [which] forces eels into narrow traps; **PA**136, Eel racks were called fish pots; **CT**6, 14, **NJ**45, Eel trap; **PA**155, Fish walls—called eel trap; **NJ**3, Eel basins—V-shaped rock structures.

eel rut n

A small inlet partially drained at low tide.

1908 Wasson *Home from Sea* 93 **ME,** I can take and run this bo't chock up into an eel-rut betwixt them islants yonder. **1975** Gould *ME Lingo* 85, *Eel rut* A very small harbor or tidal inlet that *dreens* [i.e., drains] out at low tide. So called because an eel crossing mud leaves a small track that reminds one of the residual tiny channel in a cove that drains completely.

eelsnap n **[snap]**

A three-pronged **eelspear;** see quot.

1913 *DN* 4.56 **eMA,** *Eel-snap.* . . A spear for catching eels in channels and pools. The "snap" is a trident of which the middle prong is sharp and shorter than the other two. These two are broad and blunt, and so arranged as to snap apart to permit the eel to be impaled, and then to snap back and retain it on the middle prong.

eelspear n **chiefly NEng** Cf **eelsnap**

A barbed spear for catching eels.

1780 in 1882 *Narragansett Hist. Reg.* 1.104 **RI,** Made an eel spear. **1842** Hawes *Sporting Scenes* 1.212 **NY,** This was all heathen Greek to Jerry, whose learning did not extend much beyond a "scapnet," and an "eelspear." **1861** Holmes *Venner* 2.140 **wMA,** There wa'n't a pitchfork or an eel-spear or some sech weep'n within reach. **1910** *DN* 3.453 **seVT,** *Eel-spear.* . . A spear with two or more barbed prongs for catching eels. **1911** Shute *Plupy* 14 **seNH** (as of 1860s), He pictured himself lying dead in the river with the boats full of people with boat-hooks and eel spears. **1913** *DN* 4.56 **eMA.** **1933** *Hanley Disks* **neME,** An eel spear is made out of pronged barbs put on an ordinary clothes pole . . about ten feet long.

eel stifle n **[stifle** a stew] **eMA**

See quot 1952.

1832 in 1975 Jones *Amer. Food* 4 **Boston MA,** *Eel Stifle*—cut the eels into pieces about four inches long: take two onions . . a little mace . . a pint of good gravy, the same of Port wine . . Let all boil together. **1939** Wolcott *Yankee Cook Book* 44 **eMA,** *Martha's Vineyard eel stifle.* . . All good Island cooks know what Eel Stifle is, and very few visitors ever leave the Island without having a taste of this popular Vineyard dish. **1952** Tracy *Coast Cookery* 104 **MA,** *Eel stifle*—A scalloped dish made with eels, onions, potatoes, and salt pork. A favorite on Martha's Vineyard. **1978** *New Yorker* 6 Nov 129 **seMA,** Mrs. Combs has testified about traditional Indian dishes such as sheldrake stew, eel stifle, [and] a stew called potato bargain.

eel trap See **eel rack**

eel tricker n

=red-throated loon.

1956 *AmSp* 31.186 **NC,** Eel tricker . . Red-throated loon . . Presumably as an expert eel fisher.

eelworm n **chiefly Atl** Cf **eelbait**

=earthworm.

1896 *DN* 1.416 **CT,** *Eel-worm.* **1939** *LANE* Map 236 **cwCT,** There are lots of names for 'em but we call them eelworms; **csNH,** [ijlwɜ˞·mz]. **1941** *Nature Mag.* 34.137, Other names [for the earthworm] and localities provide: dew-worm (southern Vermont), eel-worm (western Connecticut), . . and rain-worm (Pennsylvania). **1949** Kurath *Word Geog.* Fig 140, Eelworm. [3 infs **ceNC,** 6 infs **sNJ,** 1 inf **NYC,** 1 inf **wCT**] **1965–68** *DARE* (Qu. P5, . . *The common worm used as bait*) Infs **FL**7, 18, 20, **NJ**16, 31, Eelworm. **1967** *PADS* 47.6 **ceGA, csSC,** Eel worm 'earthworm.' **1971** Wood *Vocab. Change* 36 **Sth,** Only scattered responses [are reported] for . . *eel worm.*

e'en n[1] See **even** n

een n[2], v See **end**

eenamost adv Also *eeny most, enymost* [Engl dial; *e'en* even + **amost**] **chiefly NEng** *old-fash* Cf **in about**

Almost; nearly.

1781 *Pennsylvania Jrnl.* (Philadelphia) 20 June *(OEDS),* I once heard a man say, another 'swore terribly; he swore *e'en amost like a wood pile'.* **1815** Humphreys *Yankey in England* 105 **NEng,** *E'en-a-most,* almost. **1834** Smith *Letters Jack Downing* 168 **ME,** He didn't make that treaty with the Cherokees; and it was made so long ago, he has enymost forgot it. **1887** (1967) Harris *Free Joe* 115 **GA,** They're gittin' so these days they'll whirl in an' do e'enamost any thing what you don't want 'em to do. **1894** Frederic *Marsena* 148 **nNY,** I could e'en a'most 'a' thought it was Alvy talkin. **1903** *DN* 2.297 **Cape Cod MA** (as of a1857), *Een amost.* . . Almost (old). **1911** *DN* 3.543 **NE,** *Eenamost.* . . Not common. **1946** *Jrl. Amer. Folkl.* 60.157 **NEng,** Eeny most . . almost.

eench See **inch**

eend See **end**

eenie-eenie-eye-back exclam

=pigtail exclam.

1983 *DARE* File **WY,** *(If you fail to get the ball over the building, what do you call out?)* Eenie-eenie-eye-back.

eenie-eenie-over n, exclam Also *eenie-eenie-eye-over, eenie-eyenie-over* Cf **anti-i-over**

=Antony-over.

1957 *Sat. Eve. Post Letters* **ceMI,** Just talked to a fellow . . raised in Muskegon, he played Andy Andy over as eenie-eenie-eye-over. **1967–70** *DARE* (Qu. EE23a) Inf **KS**4, Eenie-eenie-over [ˌɨni ɨni 'ovɚ]; **MI**123, Eenie-eyenie-over. **1980** *DARE* File **swMI** (as of 1950s), We used to call the game *eenie-eyenie-over;* **seIL** (as of 1930s), Eenie-eenie-over. **1983** *DARE* File **WY,** *(The game in which they throw a ball over a building . . to a player on the other side)* Eenie-eenie-eye-over; *(In this game, what do you call out when you throw the ball?)* Eenie-eenie-eye-over.

eenjinin' adj [Pronc-sp for *adjoining*]

1922 Gonzales *Black Border* 268 **sSC, GA coasts** [Gullah], Sambo Hawlback buy groun' eenjinin' de same lan'.

eenjurin' See **enduring** prep

eenjy See **enjoy**

eensy-weensy See **eentsy**

eent n, v[1] See **end**

een't v[2] See **ain't** v[1]

eentsy adj Also *eentsy-teen(t)sy, een(t)sy-ween(t)sy, eeny-teeny, ~-weeny* [Phonosymbolic]
Tiny.
1950 *WELS (A very small, indefinite amount: A child says, "Can I have a ——— bit of cake?")* 1 Inf, **WI,** Eensy-weensy. **1967–70** *DARE* (Qu. LL1, *Something very small: "I took only a ——— one."*) Infs **CA**80, **IL**4, Eentsy; **NY**146, **VA**21, Eentsy-teen(t)sy (bit); **CA**61, **NC**63, Eentsy-weentsy; **MI**93, Eeny-teeny; **VA**54, Eeny-weeny. **1979** *Comments on Etym.* 1 Oct 11, *Eentsy-weentsy* is a blend of *itsy-bitsy* and *teeny-weeny*. . . These blendings are . . a final stage in a series of developments concerning children's terms for 'tiny.'

een'-ways See **endways**

eeny See **any**

eeny most See **eenamost**

eeny-teeny, eeny-weeny See **eentsy**

eeolee n
=**wood thrush.**
1946 Hausman *Eastern Birds* 458, *Wood Thrush. . . Other Names* . . Eeolee. . . The song may be approximately imitated . . *Ah-o-lée.* **1956** MA Audubon Soc. *Bulletin* 40.128, *Wood Thrush. . .* Eeolee (Mass. Sonic).

eephing vbl n [Echoic] Cf **hoodling, whoop B**
Creating wordless vocal music made up of nonsense syllables and percussive sounds; also n *eaf* such music.
1971 in 1978 *I'm On My Journey Home* (Phonodisc) **wTN,** [My maternal uncle] called it hoodlin'; they call it eephin' now. He [=the uncle] got it from somebody at a dance up at Dyersburg, Tennessee. **1978** Wolfe *I'm On My Journey Home* 2/1, [Liner notes:] Eephing (or hoodling) is one of a number of vocal-percussive effects still found in the mid-South. . . [It can be] . . created by tickling . . [the] throat . . altering . . [the] mouth cavity. . . tapping the cheeks. . . Other forms of "mouth music" documented in the South include clicking the tongue, rapping the teeth . . blowing into cupped hands, and humming on and blowing into instruments both common (like the tissue covered comb) and uncommon (like a blown-up rubber glove). . . It has been reported in Arkansas, Kentucky, and Mississippi. . . Eephing has also been found among Afro-Americans. It is customarily performed informally in relaxed social situations. **1978** Dance *Shuckin' & Jivin'* 323 **VA** [Black], Have you ever heard this thing called "The Eaf"? Ee-poop-se-de-da-pa-de-da. . . Well, Bill Robinson [1878–1949, also known as "Mr. Bojangles"] and I used to go around and say that thing [=a long rhyme]. . . And then we start singing, "Ee-doop, se-da-da-pa-de-da-pa-pop!"

eepies See **apee**

e'er a See **ary**

eesworm See **eaceworm**

eetch n, v See **itch**

eetch-weed See **itchweed**

eetchy See **itchy**

eether See **either**

eevy-ivy-over n, exclam
=**Antony-over.**
1968–70 *DARE* (Qu. EE22, . . *The game in which they throw a ball over a building*) Inf **CA**80, Eevy-ivy-over; (Qu. EE23a, . . *What do you call out when you throw the ball?*) Infs **CA**80, **MI**117, Eevy-ivy-over.

eeyaw adj, adv Cf **weewaw**
1975 Gould *ME Lingo* 85, *Eeyaw* . . lopsided, askew, aslant. A sagging shed is eeyaw; poorly woven cloth goes eeyaw on the machine and makes the seamstress unhappy; a framed picture hanging askew is eeyaw.

eezimer n [Pronc-sp for *eczema*]
1954 *Harder Coll.* **cwTN,** *Eezimer* ['i,zɪmɚ]. . . A skin disease.

ef conj See **if** conj

effeminine adj [Blend of *effeminate* + *feminine*]
Effeminate.
1967–69 *DARE* (Qu. HH38, *A womanish man*) Infs **NY**141, 153, 174, **OR**10, Effeminine.

effen See **iffen**

effet n Also *evet* [sEngl dial; cf *EDD* (at *evet*)] **NEng** *old-fash*
An eft; a newt.
1891 Jesup *Plants Hanover NH* 61, *Diemyctylus viridescens. . .* Newt. Evet. Eft. Abundant. **1891** in 1895 IL State Lab. Nat. Hist. Urbana *Bulletin* 3.354, *Diemyctylus miniatus. . . Newt, Eft, Evet, Red Eft. . .* Length, including the tail, about three inches. **1927** *AmSp* 3.139 **ME coast,** The older people spoke of . . "effet" for eft. **1938** *AmSp* 13.43 **wVT,** My mother (from eastern Vermont) taught me to call them *lizards;* but the farm boys around my home . . called them *evets*—which . . would seem to be not a corruption of the literary monosyllable *eft* but more nearly a survival of the original from which *eft* was shortened.

efn See **iffen**

efsobe See **if so be**

efter See **after**

egert n [By metath from *egret*]
1968–69 *DARE* (Qu. Q7, . . *Other kinds of game birds*) Inf **WI**32, Egert ['ɛgɚt]—crane; has disappeared; (Qu. Q10, *Other water birds*) Inf **TX**62, Egert ['ɛgɚt].

egg n Usu |ɛg|; freq **chiefly Sth, S Midl, NEast** |e(ɪ)g|; occas **chiefly S Midl** |æg| Cf Pronc Intro 3.I.6.a Pronc-spp *agg, aig(g)*
A Forms.
1837 Sherwood *Gaz. GA* 69, *Provincialisms. . . Aig,* for egg. **1851** Burke *Polly Peablossom* 90 **SC,** Ben.—Got any eggs? C. (looking testy).—Aiggs? Aiggs be d———d. **1888** Jones *Negro Myths* 94 **GA coast,** Buh Rabbit an Buh Wolf gone long de ribber bank fuh hunt Cooter ägg. **1890** *DN* 1.6 **cNY,** [e] instead of [ɛ] in *egg.* **1892** *DN* 1.238 **wMO,** *Egg.* The natives seem to pronounce [eg]; [ɛg] prevails in . . Kansas City. . . In New England [eg] for [eɪg] is common. **1903** *DN* 2.292 **Cape Cod MA** (as of a1857), Vowels were pronounced long in . . *egg (aig). Ibid* 305 **seMO,** *Aig.* . . Almost universal in the South. **1905** *DN* 3.103 **nwAR,** [eg] and [æg]. **1908** *DN* 3.285 **eAL, wGA,** *Aig.* **1909** *DN* 3.411 **cnME,** *Egg. . .* Pronounced with long vowel. **1923** *DN* 5.200 **swMO,** *Aig,* or *agg. . .* Egg. **1933** *AmSp* 8.1.23 **n,cWV,** One hears . . *banes, aggs, brad* and similar words. **1934** *AmSp* 9.211 **Sth,** Some words with standard /ɛ/ before /g/ or /k/ change /ɛ/ to /eɪ/ or /e/. . . *Beg, egg, keg* [etc]. **1941** *AmSp* 16.5 **eTX** [Black], *Egg* is always /eːɪg/. **c1960** *Wilson Coll.* **csKY,** Egg. . . /eg/ often, or /æg/. **1961** Kurath–McDavid *Pronc. Engl.* 103, Before the voiced velar /g/ in *egg,* monophthongal [ɛ], often raised, predominates in western New England and New York State, is almost universal in the North Midland . . and of common occurrence in Maryland and Delaware. . . Upgliding [ɛᵻ ~ ɛɪ ~ eᵻ ~ eɪ], is widely used in most of the South and South Midland. It is also common in Eastern New England and occurs to some extent in the greater part of the New England settlements of Upstate New York and Pennsylvania. Such pronunciations of the vowel in *egg* are most frequent in folk speech and almost entirely avoided by cultured speakers. **1966** *DARE* FW Addit **swNC,** Egg. . . [æg]. **1968** *DARE* (Qu. AA21) Inf **IN**8, [ən eɪg]. **1976** Allen *LAUM* 3.271 (as of c1950), The pronunciation /eg/, often ridiculed by the spelling *aig,* is not without prestige in the U[pper] M[idwest], where it is heard from Type III [=mid-aged, with coll educ] speakers as well as those in Types I [=old, with little educ] and II [=mid-aged, with approx hs educ].
B Senses.
1 The yolk of an egg.
1954 *Harder Coll.* **cwTN,** The parts of a egg is a shell, lining, white, yolk, but I call it "the yellow" or egg.
2 A husband subject to his wife's domination.
1968 *DARE* (Qu. AA21, . . *Expressions . . about a wife who gives the orders and a husband who takes them from her*) Inf **IN**8, An egg; henpecked.
3 in var phrr denoting strong coffee: See quots. **scattered, but esp Nth, N Midl** See Map
1950 *WELS* 2 Infs, **WI,** Strong enough to (*or* Would) float an egg. **1965–70** *DARE* (Qu. H74a, . . *Coffee . . very strong*) 45 Infs, **scattered, but esp Nth, N Midl,** (Would) float an egg; **LA**28, Float a egg; **PA**52, So

strong you could float an egg on it; **PA**159, Egg would float; 15 Infs, **NEast, Gt Lakes,** (Strong enough to) hold up an egg; **NY**135, **PA**63, **WI**62, (Black enough to) hold an egg (up); **CA**157, Strong enough to hold an egg up; **CT**24, Could hold up an egg; **SC**34, Hold up a egg; **CT**26, **IN**12, 82, **ME**16, **OH**68, Strong enough to (*or* Coffee that will) bear up an egg; **OH**70, **VA**9, Strong enough to (*or* Would) carry an egg; **AL**21, Egg stands up in it; **VA**48, Strong enough to pop an egg.

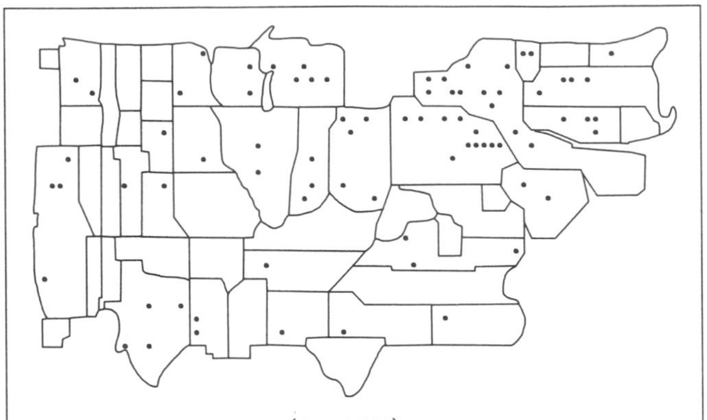

•egg n B3 + varr (Qu. H74)

egg v^1 Usu |ɛg|; freq **chiefly Sth, S Midl** |æg| (See Map); occas |eg| Pronc-spp *ag(g), aig* [Note that the pronc of **egg** n as [æg] and its pronc-sp *ag* indicate that the *ag(g)* forms given here are prob to be derived from *egg* v; however, it is possible that some of these forms are instead to be related to **hag** v^1 with loss of initial *h-;* cf *EDD hag(g)* v.^{1} 1.]

A Forms.

1890 *DN* 1.72 **LA,** *Agg on.* **1893** Shands *MS Speech* 16, Ag on. . . Negro and illiterate white for *egg on,* meaning to urge on, to incite. **1899** (1912) Green *VA Folk-Speech* 62, *Agg.* . . "They agged him on." **1902** *DN* 2.233 **sIL,** *Egg.* . . To incite. Pronounced [æg]. **1903** *DN* 2.304 **seMO,** *Agg on.* **1906** *DN* 3.118 **sIN,** *Agg on.* *Ibid* 124 **nwAR,** *Agg on.* . . Universal. **1908** *DN* 3.285 **eAL, wGA,** *Agg on.* **1917** *DN* 4.407 **wNC Mts,** Both sides agged it up. **1922** Gonzales *Black Border* 287 **sSC, GA coasts** [Gullah glossary], Him aig'um on. **1923** *DN* 5.200 **swMO,** *Agg on.* **1926** Vollmer *Sun-Up* 4 **wNC,** I sorter aigged it on. **1952** Brown *NC Folkl.* 1.513, *Agg on.* **c1960** *Wilson Coll.* **csKY,** *Egg.* . . Regularly /æg/. **1965–70** *DARE* (Qu. Y5, . . *To urge somebody to do something he shouldn't: "Johnny wouldn't have tried that if the other boys hadn't ______ ."*) 46 Infs, **chiefly Sth, S Midl,** Agged him (on); **AL**51, 56, **LA**18, **TN**42, Agged; **AR**51, **GA**77, Agged him up (to it); **GA**28, Agged it on.

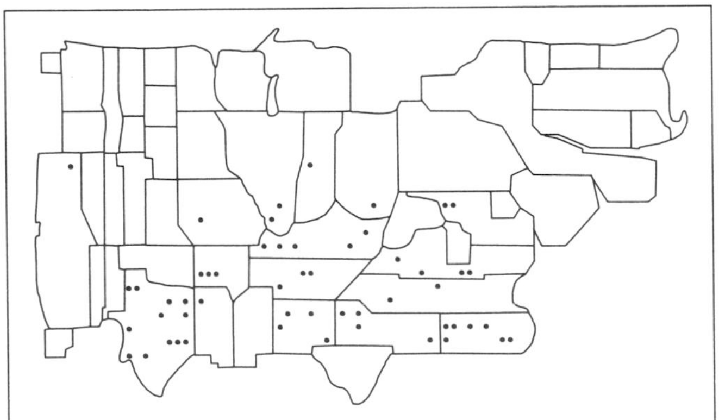

•egg v^1 A + varr (Qu. Y5)

B Sense.

To annoy, pester; to tease. [Engl dial; cf *EDD egg* v. 2]

1967–69 *DARE* (Qu. Y7, *When one person never misses a chance to be mean to another or to annoy another: "I don't know why she keeps ______ me all the time!"*) Infs **NY**29, **WI**52, Egging; **LA**25, Agging; (Qu. GG3, . . *"See those big boys trying to ______ [that little one]."*) Inf **IN**79, Egg.

egg v^2

To move delicately.

1887 *Scribner's Mag.* 2.512 **TX,** It is said that the audacious among "bullwhackers" dance from this elevation [i.e., in high-heeled boots], but only he can believe it who has seen them egging around in a doleful *bolero.* **1950** *WELS (To get out of an uncomfortable situation . . : "They thought they had him cornered, but he managed to ______ .")* 1 Inf, **cnWI,** Egg his way out.

eggabuster n [Prob from the shape and effect of the pill]

A laxative; see quot.

1964 Wallace *Frontier Life* 66 **OK** (as of 1893–1906), Groves Tasteless Chill Tonic . . was the administered cure-all during my first seven years, given with an occasional big, white pill called an "eggabuster," when a laxative was needed.

egg-and-butter money, egg-and-chicken money See **egg money**

egg-bag n

The uterus of a chicken or other fowl.

1942 McAtee *Dial. Grant Co. IN* 24 (as of 1890s), *Egg-bag* . . oviduct of a hen or other fowl. **c1960** *Wilson Coll.* **csKY,** *Egg-bag.* . . Uterus of chicken or other fowl. **1966** *DARE* (Qu. K78, *What diseases do chickens commonly get around here?*) Inf **MI**8, Egg-bag goes bad. **1966** *DARE* Tape **OK**19, [She] sees that all the lungs and the egg-bags and everything are put out of the turkeys and the chickens.

egg ball n **NYC** Cf **half-ball, spaldeen**

1975 Ferretti *Gt. Amer. Book Sidewalk Games* 190 **NYC,** [In stickball games] there does come a time when your spaldeen splits—a calamity, but not a dire one because then you can play *Egg Ball,* a Brooklyn game of chance rather than skill, featuring either no runs or floods of runs, all dependent upon the "egg", which is one half of a spaldeen. The ball is pitched and, when hit, flops about. No line drives are possible, and the egg barely makes it past the pitcher's mound, but it is a chore to catch the ball cleanly.

eggbeater n [Suggesting rotary motion like that of an *eggbeater*]

1 See quot.

1950 *Western Folkl.* 9.158 **nCA,** *Egg-beater.* A head-over-heels fall in skiing.

2 In jump rope: see quot.

1967 *DARE* Tape **IN**1, [Inf:] There are a lot of different forms to jump-roping. . . There's . . the eggbeater, [in] which the person crosses the rope over, an individual rope, and this is done singly. . . He crosses [a short rope] in his hands as he jumps, and do it very fast. . . It's a cross-over. [FW:] Like the pictures you see of boxers? [Inf:] Yes.

egg bonnet n [**bonnet B1d**]

=**water shield.**

1920 *Torreya* 20.21 *Brasenia schreberi.* . . Egg bonnet, purple bonnet, Reelfoot Lake, Tenn. **1959** Carleton *Index Herb. Plants* 41, *Egg-bonnet:* Branchenia [sic] schreberi.

egg bread n

1 Corn bread made with eggs. **chiefly Sth, S Midl, esp GA** See Map

1847 (1979) Rutledge *Carolina Housewife* 22 **SC,** Corn Egg Bread. . . One quart of milk . . three eggs . . butter, one pint of cornmeal. **1886** Smith *Hist. KY* 400, A most delicious egg-bread . . is made. The same cornmeal is the body; and to this is added buttermilk, soda, and salt, eggs, milk, and some lard. **1901** *DN* 2.136, *Batter-bread.* . . A preparation like hominy, eaten with butter, possibly like the *egg bread* of Tenn. **1903** *DN* 2.312 **seMO,** *Egg-bread.* . . Cornbread made with eggs. **1906** *DN* 3.135 **nwAR. 1908** *DN* 3.308 **eAL, wGA. 1941** Daniels *Tar Heels* 32 **NC,** It begins . . with a North Carolina breakfast of shad roe, broiled shad, egg bread, batter cakes, boiled eggs and coffee. **1949** [see **egg pone**]. **1958** *PADS* 29.9 **TN. c1960** *Wilson Coll.* **csKY. 1962** Atwood *Vocab. TX* 63, *Egg bread* . . a better variety of corn bread . . occasionally a synonym of *spoon bread.* *Ibid* 114, Since corn bread is not offered in stores, many people are no longer familiar with . . *egg bread.* **1965–70** *DARE* (Qu. H14, *Bread that's made with cornmeal*) 18 Infs, **Sth, S Midl, esp GA,** Egg bread; **NC**14, Soft egg bread; (Qu. H18) Infs **GA**1, 36, **NC**16, **PA**189, **TN**34, Egg bread. **1972** Hilliard *Hog Meat* 49, Corn dodgers, hoecake, corn muffins, and egg bread, were simply variations of corn bread.

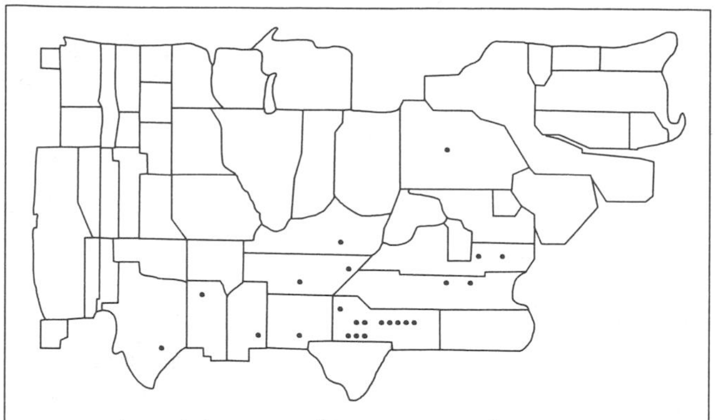

•egg bread 1 + var (Qq. H14, H18)

2 French toast.

1920s in 1944 *ADD* **cNY,** *Egg-bread. . .* French toast. Usual. **1930** *DN* 6.80 **cSC,** *Egg-bread. . .* French toast. The expression French toast is unknown. **1957** *Sat. Eve. Post Letters* **NE,** My mother, also a Nebraskan, often made our family a delicious breakfast dish, bread dipped in egg batter and browned in a skillet. I was about nine or ten when I learned that the French toast I had heard my classmates talk about was our good old egg bread.

egg butter n *old-fash*

A food spread made from molasses and eggs.

1885 *Buckeye Cookery* 250 *(DA)* **OH,** Egg Butter. Boil a pint of molasses slowly . . add three eggs well beaten. **1940** Brown *Amer. Cooks* 475 **MO,** Egg butter. . . Pure sorghum, often 'going to sugar,' was melted in the old black skillet and, when thinned and hot, she dumped in a bowl of beaten eggs, stirring vigorously; just a sprinkle of nutmeg added at the last. **1966** *Good Old Days* Feb 10 **OK,** Here is the recipe for Egg Butter: Heat one pint of Sorghum molasses to boiling. Watch carefully so that it does not boil over. Pour over 4 well-beaten eggs. Cook one minute, stirring constantly. Add a dash of nutmeg or cinnamon if desired. **1981** Stratton *Pioneer Women* 182 **KS** (as of late 1800s), Then [in winter] Mary felt that with some vegetables and a 'spread'—eggbutter, pumpkin, or apple butter—she could await with pleasure Brother Craft's visit.

egg cheese n [Engl dial; cf *EDD* (at *egg* sb. 1)]

1970 *DARE* (Qu. H60, *The lumpy white cheese that is made from sour milk*) Inf **PA**242, Egg cheese—egg and milk.

‡eggclair n [Pronc-sp, prob infl by folk-etym, for *eclair*]

1968 *DARE* (Qu. H32) Inf **NY**70, Eggclairs ['ɛg,klæɚz]—chocolate on top, custard inside.

egg cockle n Also *egg-shell cockle* [Prob from the thin, often white shell]

A mollusk of the genus *Laevicardium.* For other name of *L. mortoni* see **duck clam 1**

1952 Morris *Field Guide Shells* 42, *Laevicardium substriatum . .* Egg-shell Cockle. . . This is a little fellow, about an inch in length. . . The color is mottled yellowish brown, the interior yellow with purple spots and blotches. **1974** Abbott *Seashells* 485, *Laevicardium laevigatum . .* Common Egg Cockle. North Carolina to both sides of Florida. *Ibid* 486, *Laevicardium substriatum . .* Common Pacific Egg Cockle. Ventura County, California, to the Gulf of California. **1981** Meinkoth *Audubon Field Guide Seashore* 556, *Common Egg Cockle. . .* This cockle, capable of leaping by means of powerful thrusts of its long foot, was observed by one collector to escape by jumping out of a boat.

egg coffee n *old-fash* Cf **company coffee**

Boiled coffee to which an egg has been added.

[**1896** (c1973) Farmer *Orig. Cook Book* 42 **Boston MA,** Coffee made with an egg has a rich flavor which egg alone can give.] **1950** *WELS (Words for coffee according to the way it is made)* 3 Infs, **cWI,** Egg coffee. **1978** Crocker *Cookbook* 342, *Egg Coffee for a Crowd. . .* Heat 5 quarts water to boiling. Mix coffee, egg, and ¾ cup water: pour into boiling water. Heat to a rolling boil. . . Remove from heat; add ½ cup cold water to settle grounds.

egg cracking n

=egg picking.

1954 *PADS* 21.26 **cnSC,** *Egg cracking. . .* Same as *egg picking.* **1972** Jones-Hawes *Step it Down* xii **eGA** [Black], We would have egg crackings and taffy pullings.

egg cream n **chiefly NYC**

A soft drink made with seltzer water, chocolate syrup, and milk.

1964 (1968) Goldman *Boys & Girls* 62 **Chicago IL,** He spun into a candy store, ordered an egg cream and downed it in a swallow. **1966** *DARE* FW Addit **NYC,** Egg cream—a soda without the ice cream. The soda is made in the normal way, but the scoops of ice cream are not added. **1968** *DARE* Tape **NY**118, Egg creams were always big. . . First of all, there's no eggs and there's no cream in an egg cream whatsoever. It's like chocolate syrup, seltzer and milk, all mixed together, and it's really delicious. **1978** *DARE* File **csWI,** [In a conv with owner of Jewish delicatessen:] You can go anywhere in New York City, on Fifth Avenue or the Garment District, where there's a soda fountain, and get an egg cream. There's three categories of soda: for two cents plain, that's seltzer; chocolate phosphate, add chocolate; and egg cream, add milk. **1988** *DARE* File **NYC** (as of 1925), A common candy store or luncheonette treat of my childhood was the egg cream, which contained no eggs, but was a combination of chocolate syrup, milk, and seltzer.

egg custard (pie) n Also *egg pie* **chiefly Sth, S Midl, esp MS** See Map

A dessert made from eggs, flour, and milk, and usu served in the form of a pie.

1965 *Colonial Kitchens* 106 **GA,** *Egg custard.* 3 Eggs, 1 cup Sugar, (scant), Tbs. Butter, 2 Tbs. Milk, 1 Tbs. Flour. . . Cook on crust till firm. **1965–70** *DARE* (Qu. H63, . . *Desserts especially favored*) 11 Infs, **chiefly Sth, S Midl, esp MS,** Egg custard; **MS**79, Egg custard: 3 eggs, 1½ cups milk, ¾ cup of sugar, 2½ tablespoons of flour, 2 tablespoons of butter—makes one pie; **KY**84, 85, **PA**2, 213, **VA**39, Egg custard pie; **KY**63, **MS**60, Egg pie; **AL**34, Egg pie—yolks of three eggs are thickened with flour and used as filling, egg whites are beaten to form topping; **KY**22, Egg pie—custard; **LA**23, Egg custard with brandy. **1971** *Foxfire* Spring-Summer 95 **GA,** *Aunt Arie's recipe for egg custard* (cooked on a wood stove). Line a small pie pan with plain biscuit dough rolled thin. . . Mix up one egg . . , one cup of sweet milk, a handful of flour, a teaspoon of nutmeg, a half a teacup of sugar. Mix it all up well, pour it into the crust.

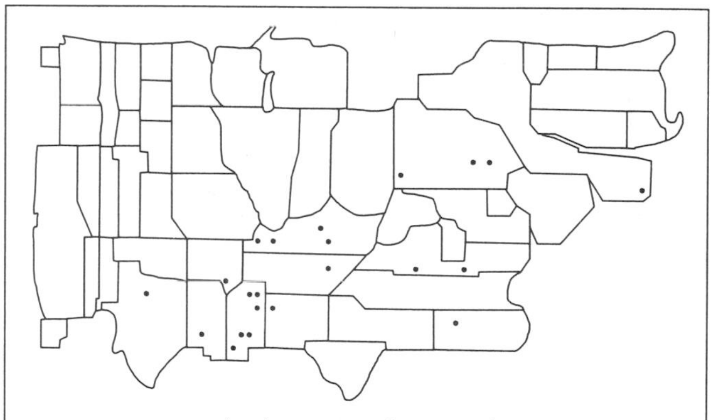

•egg custard (pie) + varr (Qu. H63)

egg drop n

=dropped egg.

1984–86 *DARE* File, *(When eggs are taken out of the shells and cooked in boiling water, you call them ______)* 1 inf, **VA,** Egg drop; 1 inf, **UT,** Poached egg drop.

egg dye n

A **tickseed** (here: *Coreopsis major*).

1941 Walker *Lookout* 52 **TN,** Starry coreopsis is one of the most abundant yellow flowers growing on . . the mountain. . . The mountain people know it by the name of "egg dye," because they use its green leaves for coloring eggs.

eggeater n

=opossum.

1968 *DARE* (Qu. P31) Inf **CT**2, Egg-eaters—opossum.

egger n

One who gathers seabirds' eggs to sell for food.

1834 Audubon *Ornith. Biog.* 2.370 **sFL,** Turtles . . deposit their eggs in the burning sand, and clouds of sea-fowl arrive every spring for the same purpose. These are followed by persons called "Eggers." **1918** Johnson *Highways FL* 188, Clouds of sea-fowl arrived every spring to make their nests on the isles. There came also at this season men commonly spoken of as eggers, who, when their cargoes were completed, sailed away to market their plunder.

egger worm See **fever-and-ague worm**

egget See **agate**

egg-eyed adj
Of persons: having very round eyes.
1966 *DARE* (Qu. X21c) Inf **FL**8, Egg-eyed.

egg flip(per) See **egg turner**

egg fighting See **egg picking**

egg gourd n
c1960 *Wilson Coll.* **csKY,** Egg gourd. . . A small gourd used as a nest egg.

egg house n
A hen house.
1818 in 1824 Knight *Letters* 90 **KY,** Some few of the plantation-seats, however, are of brick, and accommodated with ample out-buildings. The egg-houses, for the laying and incubation of fowls, are as capacious as cots [=cottages]. **1966** *DARE* (Qu. M17, *A building where chickens or hens are kept*) Inf **WA**5, Egg house.

eggies exclam [Var of **aikie(s)**]
In marble play: used as a call to claim an equal share.
1973 Ferretti *Marble Book* 43 **seNY,** *Eggies.* Short for "Can I borrow a few marbles?" as in "Eggies on the aggies?" **1979** *DARE* File **Queens NYC,** In South Ozone Park . . near JFK airport, eggies! . . for 'sharesies!'

egg kiss n
1969 *DARE* FW Addit **neKY,** Egg kisses—old-fashioned homemade candy.

egg lifter See **egg turner**

egg money n Also *butter-and-egg money, egg-and-butter ~, egg-and-chicken ~* Cf **butter money**
Money earned by a farmwife from the sale of eggs, butter, and chickens; extra spending money.
1896 Freeman *Madelon* 201 **MA,** Guess she's been saving her egg-and-butter money. **1935** *Amer. Mercury* Aug 410/2 **NC,** So that's how you spend my egg money. **1936** Lutes *Country Kitchen* 248 **MI,** [We used] the sprigged rose pattern that my mother had bought not so long ago with carefully hoarded egg money. **1942** Warnick *Garrett Co. MD* 4 **nwMD** (as of 1900–18), *Butter and egg money.* **1946** Stuart *Tales Plum Grove* 71 **KY,** Mom was helping him all she could with cream money and egg and chicken money. **1948** Jacobs *We Chose Country* 119 **WI,** There was plenty of egg money, so she could go shopping in town or choose her luxuries from the brilliant pages of the mail-order catalogues. **1963** Owens *Look to River* 27 **neTX,** Cannie brought out her egg money and bought powder for herself and pink soap for Sunday.

egg mushroom n
A chanterelle (here: *Cantharellus cibarius*).
1980 Marteka *Mushrooms* 83, *Golden Chanterelle. . . Common Names . .* egg mushroom. . . *Cap . .* egg-yolk yellow or paler.

egg picking vbl n Also *egg fighting, ~ pecking* [Cf Ger *Eierpicken*] Cf **bully** v², **pip** v
A game usu played at Easter time in which contestants strike eggs together to see whose egg will not be broken.
1840 (1847) Longstreet *GA Scenes* 7, Michael was employed in relieving Zeph's storehouse of its provisions; and, truly, its contents told well for Zeph's skill in egg-pecking. **1949** *Sun* (Baltimore MD) 17 Apr mag sec 9/1, "Egg picking," an Eastertide game that has been played by children in Baltimore for more than 200 years. Ours is one of the few American cities in which the old game survives. [**1949** (1972) Funk & Wagnalls *Dict. Folkl.* 341, In many parts of the world egg-tapping takes place, and the person whose egg cracks first is the loser. *Ibid* 335, The children's game of "nicking" Easter eggs is common in the world from Egypt to England, and is also fairly general in the United States, especially among Southern Negroes. Two children, each with an Easter egg in his hand, will knock the two eggs together; the one whose egg cracks the least under the treatment appropriates the other's eggs.] **1954** *PADS* 21.26 **SC,** *Egg picking. . .* A custom of the Easter season in the Dutch Fork. This is a contest in which two opponents each hold an egg and strike or pick them together until one egg is cracked. The holder of the cracked egg is the loser. . . It is known also in Wisconsin and probably in Pennsylvania and elsewhere where Germans have settled. [*PADS* Ed: Common in Frederick County, Maryland and no doubt elsewhere in northwestern Maryland where Palatinate Germans settled.] . . *egg pecking,* also current in S.C. **1964** Smith *PA Germans* 113 **wVA,** Egg Picking—A popular game among the young people was called "picking" eggs or egg "fighting." A person selected what he considered to be his strongest egg and challenged someone else to "pick" against him. The eggs were tapped against each other until one of the egg shells cracked, then the owner of the other egg claimed the cracked one as prize.

egg pie See **egg custard (pie)**

eggplant n
1968 *DARE* (Qu. HH28, *Names . . for people of foreign background: . . Negro*) Infs **NJ**18, 39, Eggplant.

egg pone n
Egg bread made in the oval form of a **pone.**
1898 Dunbar *Folks from Dixie* 39 **cnKY,** They all sat down to the evening meal, of crisp bacon, well-fried potatoes, egg-pone, and coffee. **1949** Kurath *Word Geog.* 68, A soft cake of corn meal and eggs, baked in a pan, is served in the Carolinas, in Virginia, and in southern Maryland. It is called . . *egg bread* in the Carolinas, and *egg bread* or *egg pone* in southern Maryland and the southern part of the Eastern shore of Maryland.

egg pop n **N Atl** *?obs*
A kind of eggnog sometimes strengthened with spirits and flavored with fruit.
1776 in 1859 NJ Hist. Soc. *Proc.* 1st ser 8.122 **MA,** Many Decanters of Wine suffered shipwreck . . nor was Egg Pop forgot among our Dainties. **1809** (1918) Putnam *Diary* 6.13 **MA,** He feasted his friends with flowing bowls of egg-pop. **1834** Davis *Letters Downing* 30 **NEng,** We had all been drinking putty considerable of switchel, and cider, and egg-pop, with a little New England in it. **1844** *Knickerbocker* 23.586 **MA,** In Boston we also have the perfume of lobsters and egg-pop blended with that of orange-peel and pine-apple. **1851** Hall *College Words* 205 **eMA,** [A mock honorary degree:] Gulielmus Emmons, Prænominatus Pickleïus, qui orator eloquentissimus nostræ ætatis; poma, nuces, *panem-zingiberis,* suas orationes, *'Egg-popque'* vendit, D.M. Med. Fac. honorarius. [=William Emmons, nicknamed Pickles, the most eloquent orator of our age, who sells apples, nuts, gingerbread, his own speeches, and egg-pop (is made) an honorary Doctor of Medicine of the Medical Faculty.] **1860** Holmes *Professor* 4 **MA,** The folks used to come down from the tents on 'Lection and Independence days with their pails to get water to make egg-pop with.

egg roast n
1906 *DN* 3.135 **nwAR,** *Egg roast. . .* A party or festival usually held during the Easter season. On such an occasion eggs are covered with mud and roasted in a fire.

eggs See **eggs in a basket 1**

eggs-and-bacon n
=butter-and-eggs 1.
1936 IL Nat. Hist. Surv. *Wildflowers* 301, *Linaria vulgaris. . .* Other names are Brideweed, Flaxweed, and Eggs and Bacon. **1949** Moldenke *Amer. Wild Flowers* 272, The common name of *butter-and-eggs* for this plant seems appropriate because of the colors of the corolla, but the names *eggs-and-bacon . .* and *rabbitflower* are a bit more obscure in their application.

eggshell n
1 See quot. [Prob from its appearance of fragility; cf *DA eggshell* canoe]
1968 *DARE* (Qu. N40b, . . *Sleighs for carrying people*) Inf **CT**9, Cutter—a one-horse sleigh; eggshell—[a] very fine cutter.
2 A **freshwater clam** (here: *Obovaria olivaria*).
1982 U.S. Fish & Wildlife Serv. *Fresh-Water Mussels,* [Wall chart:] Eggshell . . *Obovaria olivaria.*

egg-shell cockle See **egg cockle**

eggshell tea n

A folk remedy; see quots.

1947 (1964) Randolph *Ozark Superstitions* 98 **swMO,** A young girl near Forsyth . . used to take large quantities of tea made by boiling toasted egg shells in water, but I was unable to find out what was the matter with her, or what effect this "egg-shell tea" was expected to produce. **1953** *Jrl. Amer. Folkl.* 66.337 **Ozarks,** Eggshell tea is made by boiling toasted or charred eggshells in water.

eggs in the basket n

1 also *eggs:* A hand movement in the children's game of jacks; see quots 1937, 1978. [In ref to the jacks' being thought of as eggs, and the left hand as a basket]

1937 (1947) Bancroft *Games* 138, *Eggs in Basket.*—Scatter jacks, toss ball, pick up one jack, right hand only used, and *while ball bounces once,* transfer jack to the left hand, then catch ball with the right hand. When all jacks have been picked up and transferred to the left hand, the jacks are all put in the right hand and scattered again. **1953** Brewster *Amer. Nonsinging Games* 137 **AR,** Somewhat similar to this is the third movement, "Eggs," which consists of picking up a jack with the right hand and transferring it to the left before the ball bounces. **1966** *Good Old Days* Feb 7/1 **WI** (as of c1910), "Let's play Jacks, now!" First came Ones, then backwards, then pigs in the pen, eggs in the basket, ladies in the carriage, quick hoefly [sic]. **1967** *DARE* Tape **IN**1, There's eggs in the basket—where they don't let the ball bounce at all. . . The object is to get to ten. The first time you throw your jacks down, you pick them up one at a time, and if you can successfully complete that turn, you do it two at a time, and then three at a time, until you reach ten. And then there's also one that's done doing it backwards from ten down to one. **1978** *DARE* File **nCA** (as of 1950s), After progressing through the onesies, twosies, etc, through tensies, we'd go on to the harder moves, like "eggs in the basket." For that round we had to pick up the jacks and put them in the left hand before catching the ball with the right, instead of simply catching the ball with the jacks still in the right hand.

2 as *eggs in a basket* (or *bush*): **=jack-in-the-bush.**

1953 Brewster *Amer. Nonsinging Games* 9 **KY,** Jack in the Bush. . . Other names by which this game is known are Snake in the Grass, Eggs in a Bush, and Eggs in a Basket.

egg snake n

=king snake.

1709 (1967) Lawson *New Voyage* 139 **NC,** The Egg or Chicken-Snake is so call'd, because it is frequent about the Hen-Yard, and eats Eggs and Chickens. **1853** Baird & Girard *Cat. N. Amer. Reptiles* I.165 *(DA),* Egg Snake *(Ophibolus Sayi).* **1911** *Century Dict.* 5724, *Egg-snake,* one of the king-snakes, *Ophibolus sayi.*

egg spatula See **egg turner**

egg stove n

Appar a wood- or coal-burning stove with a rounded top.

1936 *Sun* (Baltimore MD) 25 Feb 10/7, *An Egg Stove* is a stove which is shaped more or less like an egg and is favored in the rural districts. It is usually equipped with foot rests. **1940** Mencken *Happy Days* 309 **OH** (as of c1890), I helped the younger Almroths (it was at their house that we stayed) to crack walnuts in the barn, to fetch up apples from the cellar, and to haul wood for the great egg-stoves that kept us warm. **1943** *Sun* (Baltimore MD) 23 Jan 4, [Caption:] In an effort to make the diminishing fuel-oil supply last through the heating period, two classes of St. Leo's parochial school take their places each day around an eggstove located in the basement of the parish church. Working on an alternating plan, the unused classrooms are closed and radiators turned off. **1951** Peirce *Fire on the Hearth* 244, Design for "Egg Stove" David Stuart, Phila., Pa., 1864. **1988** *NADS Letters* **cwNY,** An *egg stove* is a cast iron stove that sits on a fairly conventional arrangement to catch ashes as they fall through the grate. There was one at the . . Railroad Station at Angola, New York, during the 1940s. The employees did not like them because the domed top made it impossible to keep a pot of coffee going. The one I recall was about four or five feet high.

egg-sucker n

1 A worthless animal, esp a dog; by ext, a mean and worthless person. [Cf **suck-egg dog**] **Sth, S Midl** *derog*

1853 Simms *Sword & Distaff* 204 **SC,** They [=sheriffs] are blood-suckers, and egg-suckers, and throat-cutters. **1932** Faulkner *Light in August* 312 **MS,** Get them durn eggsuckers on back to town. **1954** *Harder Coll.* **cwTN,** *Egg-sucker.* A dog or mule that sucks eggs. **1962** Fox *Southern Fried* 41 **SC, GA** (as of 1940s), Sic 'em, hound. Get him, you flea-bitten egg-sucker. **1976** Garber *Mountain-ese* 26 **sAppalachians,** *Egg-sucker* . . sneak-thief. Jud ain't no good, he's allers been an egg-sucker. **1984** Burns *Cold Sassy* 13 **nGA** (as of 1906), "But first you gather the eggs like you been told to. You go'n let the rats get'm. Or that no-count egg-sucker dog of yours." I resented that. T.R. didn't suck eggs. But I said yes'm.

2 =black-billed cuckoo.

1956 MA Audubon Soc. *Bulletin* 40.80, *Black-billed Cuckoo. . .* Egg-sucker (Maine. apparently the cuckoos sometimes prey upon the eggs of other birds.)

egg-sucking ppl adj [Cf **egg-sucker 1**] *derog*

Disgusting, mean, contemptible.

1875 *Atlantic Mth.* 35.448/2 **Lower Missip Valley,** You dash-dashed aig-suckin', sheep-stealin', one-eyed son of a stuffed monkey! **1950** *PADS* 14.75 **FL,** *Egg-sucking dog. . .* A dog that robs the hen's nest; uncomplimentary epithet sometimes applied to human beings. **c1960** *Wilson Coll.* **csKY,** *Egg-sucking dog. . .* Also used to mean a sneak-thief. Sometimes suck-egg dog. **1985** Ladwig *How to Talk Dirty* 32 **Ozarks,** He's as ornery as an egg-suckin' hound.

egg turner n Also *egg flip(per), ~ lifter, ~ spatula* **chiefly Sth, S Midl** See Map Cf **cake turner, flipper** n[1] **2, turner**

A spatula.

c1960 *Wilson Coll.* **csKY,** *Egg-turner. . .* A spatula or pancake turner. **1965–70** *DARE* (Qu. F3, *When you're frying things—for example, eggs—you turn them over with a ______*) 67 Infs, **chiefly Sth, Midl,** Egg turner; **NC**43, **SC**19, Egg flipper; **GA**19, Egg flip; **SC**21, Egg lifter; **NC**84, Egg spatula.

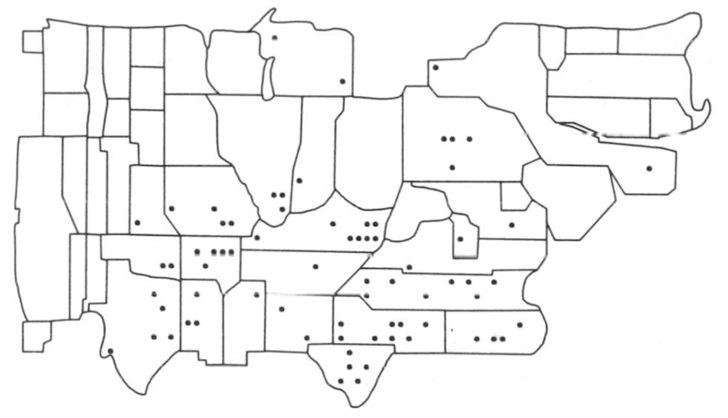

•egg turner + varr (Qu. F3)

egg-walker n Cf *DS* V9

A police officer.

1950 *WELS (Joking names for a policeman)* 1 Inf, **ceWI,** Egg-walker.

egg yellow n Pronc-sp *egg-yaller* Cf *DS* H34, **yellow**

Egg yolk.

1902 *DN* 2.233 **sIL,** *Egg-yaller. . .* The yolk of an egg; yolk is not used. **1907** *DN* 3.222 **nwAR,** *Egg-yaller.* **1954** Roberts *I Bought Dog* 22 **seKY,** Tom threw down his egg and a great river of egg yellow came around her.

egg-zactly See **exactly**

egret n

Std: any of var birds of the family Ardeidae such as the American egret *(Casmerodus albus),* the **cattle egret,** or the **snowy egret.** For other names of *c. albus* see **angel bird, crane 2, ghost bird 4, golden clipper, great white heron 2, long white, piglin, plume bird, white crane, white egret, white heron, white old-hand, white shitepoke**

egvice, egvise See **exwice**

Egypt n

1 The southern part of Illinois lying between the Ohio and Mississippi Rivers; hence n *Egyptian* a resident or native of this region; also adj *Egyptian* of or pertaining to this region. [In ref to Cairo, Illinois, and to the fertile alluvial land along the Ohio and Mississippi Rivers] **chiefly sIL**

1843 *Quincy* (Ill.) *Whig* 11 Jan. 2/6 *(DA)*, Here was something to stir up the bile of the 'gentleman from Egypt'! What! a 'nigger' in the Senate of Illinois! Monstrous! **1846** *Ibid* 12 Feb. 3/2 *(DA)*, Is an attack upon him [Stephen A. Douglas] indicative of an assault upon the Egyptian idol, whose shadow has been like that of a rock in the desert to many a renegade Whig. **1872** in 1954 *Names* 2.52 **sIL**, In the summer of 1824, there was not a bushel of corn to be had in central Illinois. My father settled that year in Springfield. We had to live there for a time on venison, blackberries and milk while the men were gone to Egypt to harvest and procure breadstuffs. **1889** (1971) Farmer *Americanisms* 223, *Egypt*. . . The inhabitants themselves derive it from the fertility of the land . . whilst enemies rather unkindly aver that the allusion is to the crass ignorance and mental darkness there prevalent. **1942** *AmSp* 17.169 **sIL**, "Egypt" as a nickname for this section . . has long been adopted by dwellers in the lower reaches of Illinois to indicate their particular part of the state. They call themselves "Egyptians," and so they are termed out-of-state as well. **1947** *Chicago Tribune* (IL) 14 June 10/7 **sIL**, If there is anything further you wish to know in connection with wit and humor, just ask one of us Egyptian agriculturists. **1966** *Champaign-Urbana Courier* (IL) 27 Dec 28/4, A college professor with whom we were invited to have luncheon turned out to be a native of Southern Illinois. . . It was good to have concurrence by a fellow Egyptian of the reports we make . . of the different living in the years of our farm boyhood.

2 A nickname for geographical areas or parts of towns. [From the agricultural, economic, or demographic characteristics of the regions]

1966-70 *DARE* (Qu. C34) Inf **CT**4, Egypt—1816, frost every month of the year; [one] man alone had corn [and] all went to him (the Pharaoh) for seed; **NC**15, Egypt—very dry and hot; **VA**59, Egypt—poor land; (Qu. C35) Inf **KY**53, The Egypt—the nigger end of town; **NC**62, Egypt—inaccessible area outside of town, good for hunting, very rocky.

3 An outdoor toilet. Cf *DS* M21a, b, **King Tut's tomb**

1984 Burns *Cold Sassy* 30 **nGA** (as of 1906), [Grandpa] said he didn't mind going to Egypt, which was what everybody in town called privies. *Ibid* 266, Before Grandpa knew what happened, he would decide one day that it shore would be nice not to have to go out to Egypt on a rainy night or a cold winter morning.

Egyptian n, adj See **Egypt 1**

Egyptian bean n

=**hyacinth bean.**

1868 (1870) Gray *Field Botany* 109, *D[olichos] lablab* . . Egyptian bean. **1900** Lyons *Plant Names* 212, *L[ablab] lablab* . . Egyptian Bean. **1933** Small *Manual SE Flora* 726, *D[olichos] lablab* . . Egyptian bean. **1976** Bailey-Bailey *Hortus Third* 394, *D[olichos] lablab* . . Egyptian bean.

Egyptian corn n

1 Appar a kind of popcorn (*Zea mays*, var *praecox*).

1849 Emmons *Agriculture NY* 2.265, *Canada pop-corn, Egyptian corn*. . . There are several varieties . . used only for popping.

2 also *gyp corn:* Sorghum or a var of sorghum.

1856 *Porter's Spirit of Times* 18 Oct 118.1, The *Western Farmers' Journal* speaks of the cultivation of the sugar millet in Warren Co., Ohio, which is used for fattening cattle. . . It is called there Egyptian Corn. **1911** Wright *Barbara Worth* 218 **CO**, By midsummer many acres of alfalfa, with Egyptian corn and other grains, showed broad fields of living green cut into the dull, dun plain. **1913** *Pacific Coast Avifauna* 9.70 **CA**, Farmers regard this bird with considerable disfavor . . because of its attacks upon ripening Kaffir, or Egyptian, corn. **1942** Amer. Joint Comm. Horticult. Nomenclature *Std. Plant Names* 102, White Durra. . . Egyptian Corn; Gyp Corn; Jerusalem Corn; Rice Corn; White Egyptian Corn; White Gyp. **1969** *DARE* (Qu. I34, *If you don't have sweet corn, you can always eat young* ______) Inf **CA**170, Gyp corn; (Qu. L34) Inf **CA**116, Egyptian corn—has like a little beehive with corn kernels in it. **1976** Bailey-Bailey *Hortus Third* 1240, Corn. . . Egyptian: *Sorghum vulgare*.

Egyptian grass n

1 =**crowfoot 3.**

1857 Gray *Manual of Botany* 554, *Dactyloctenium*. . . Egyptian Grass. **1901** Mohr *Plant Life AL* 376, *Dactyloctenium aegyptium*. . . Egyptian Grass. **1933** Small *Manual SE Flora* 118, *Egyptian-grass. . . Crowfoot-grass.* Waste-places, roadsides, and cult. grounds.

2 also *Egyptian millet, gyp grass:* =**Johnson grass.**

1900 Lyons *Plant Names* 352, *S[orghum] Halepense*. . . Egyptian Grass, Egyptian Millet. **1914** Georgia *Manual Weeds* 22, Johnson-Grass—*Sorghum halepense*. . . Egyptian-grass. **1933** Small *Manual SE Flora* 47, *H[olcus] halepensis*. . . Egyptian-millet. **1945** Wodehouse *Hayfever Plants* 58, Johnson grass *(Sorghum halepense . .)*, also called evergreen or Egyptian millet, is an erect perennial. **1935** (1943) Muenscher *Weeds* 157, *Holcus halepensis*. . . Egyptian-grass. **1968** *DARE* (Qu. L9a, . . *Kinds of grass . . grown for hay*) Inf **NC**54, Gyp [jɪp] grass [FW: used by Inf in conv]. **1976** Bailey-Bailey *Hortus Third* 1061, *Sorghum . . halepense*. . . Egyptian millet.

Egyptian onion n [*OEDS* 1880 →] Cf **top onion**

A cultivated onion (here: *Allium cepa*, Proliferum Group).

1950 *WELS (The kind of onions that last from year to year)* 1 Inf, **seWI**, Egyptian onions. **1968-69** *DARE* (Qu. I5, *The kind of onions that keep coming up without replanting year after year*) Infs **MA**58, **NJ**55, Egyptian onions; **CT**4, Egyptian or top onion. **1976** Bailey-Bailey *Hortus Third* 49.

eh pron See **he** pron

eh interrog exclam |e(ɪ), ɛ| **chiefly N Cent, NEast** See Map *often joc*

What did you say? Don't you agree?

1950 *WELS (Words and expressions meaning "Don't you agree?": "We ought to come back here again,* ______*?")* 3 Infs, **WI**, Eh? **1965-70** *DARE* (Qu. X18, . . *When one person doesn't quite hear what another person said, what does he say?*) 22 Infs, **chiefly N Cent, NEast**, Eh [e, eɪ, ɛ]; **IL**55, [e] [FW: rising tone]; **MI**33, [ɛ]—kids, acting funny; **MI**70, Eh?—definitely jokingly here; **TX**27, Eh?—old people; (Qu. NN3, *Words . . meaning "Don't you agree?"*) 9 Infs, **esp N Cent**, Eh. [**1983** Beyle *How Talk Cape Cod* 16, And, their [=Canadian tourists'] standard question seeking approval is the telltale "eh?" It translates roughly into "isn't that right?"]

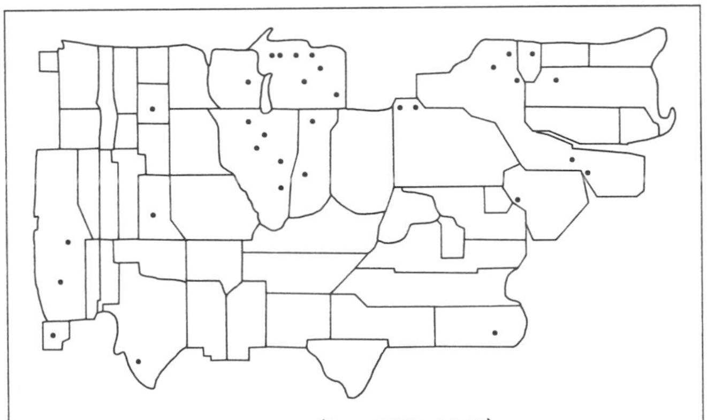

•eh interrog exclam (Qq. X18, NN3)

eha n, v, adj **HI**

See quots.

1938 Reinecke *Hawaiian Loanwords*, Eha ['e,hɑ]; n., v. 1. Pain. . . 2. To suffer; to be hurt. **1967** *DARE* (Qu. BB5, *A general feeling of discomfort*) Inf **HI**4, Eha—sore; eha ka body—sore in the body.

ehbody pron [Pronc-sp for *anybody;* cf ME *ei* any (at *OED any*)]

1914 *DN* 4.72 **ME, nNH**, *Ehbody.*

eh-eh intj *Gullah* Cf *DJE e-e*

Hey!—used variously, as to express surprise, diffidence, negation, or to call attention to something.

1883 (1971) Harris *Nights with Remus* 79 **GA** [Black], He beg en he beg Brer Tarrypin fer ter sell 'im dem quills; but Brer Tarrypin, he hol' on t' um tight, en say eh-eh! *Ibid* 242, "Eh-eh, honey!" replied Aunt Tempy, with a display of genuine bashfulness; "eh-eh, honey! I 'fraid you all 'll set up dar un laugh me outer de house." **1908** *S. Atl. Qrly.* 7.332 [Gullah], Eh! Eh! Hackless! wuh yuh try fuh do? [=Eh! Eh! Hercules! What are you trying to do?] **1922** Gonzales *Black Border* 163 **sSC, GA coasts** [Gullah], At last they were turned over to Mingo Brown, a pompous corporal, so puffed up with "a little brief authority" that most of the negroes grinned in his face, and some openly guffawed, "eh, eh, Buh Mingo swonguh fuh sowl!" [=Eh, eh, Brother Mingo is surely haughty!] *Ibid* 125, Eh, eh! Da' felluh pull *hebby!* [=The fellow pulls heavy, i.e., (mockingly) he's a weighty person.]

ehself See **'eself**

ehu n **HI**

1 A fish.

1967 *Honolulu Star-Bulletin* (HI) F1/4, Ehu—Red Snapper. Bake. Fry. Broil.

2 Transf: see quot.

1967 Reinecke-Tsuzaki *Hawaiian Loanwords* (as of 1938), *Ehu*. . . A type of Hawaiian with a reddish tinge in skin and hair, erroneously believed by some to be due to mixture a few centuries ago with European castaways. **1981** *Pidgin To Da Max* np **HI,** *Ehu*. . . Red-headed Hawaiian.

eider See **either**

eider duck n Also *eider, eiderdown duck* Cf **king eider**

A white-backed, black-bellied duck *(Somateria mollissima)* noted for its feathers. Also called **coot** n[1] **2c, Eskimo duck, mongrel, raft duck, shoal ~, squam ~**

1814 Wilson *Amer. Ornith.* 8.122, The native regions of the Eider Duck extend from 45° north to the highest latitudes yet discovered. **1844** Giraud *Birds Long Is.* 331, *Fuligula Mollissima* . . Eider Duck. **1946** Hausman *Eastern Birds* 163, *Somateria mollissima* . . Other Names . . Eider Duck. **1951** Pough *Audubon Water Bird* 108, *Eider—Somateria mollissima.* **1955** U.S. Arctic Info. Center *Gloss., Common eider.* A large sea duck, *Somateria mollissima,* divided into subspecies such as the northern or arctic eider, the American eider, and the Pacific eider. **1965-70** *DARE* (Qu. Q5) Infs **FL**17, **MA**5, 78, **NY**123, **PA**132, Eider duck; **VA**47, 79, Eider; **KS**8, Eiderdown duck.

eight n

One of the two lead horses in an **eight-up.**

1967 *DARE* Tape **NV**2, On the team there are pointers. Then the next is the six and the eights.

eight-day match n *old-fash*

A long-burning match.

1965 Needham-Mussey *Country Things* 10 **sVT,** By my time [=c1910] they had the old brimstone matches that they used to call eight-day matches because you'd strike one and have to wait eight days before the sulphur would burn off. **1967** *DARE* (Qu. F46, . . *The kind of matches you can strike anywhere*) Inf **NY**24, Eight-day matches; **NY**2, Eight-day matches—old-fashioned, stayed burning a long time, a lot of sulphur.

eight-dollar bill n *joc*

A nonexistent item used as the basis of a practical joke.

1970 *DARE* (Qu. HH14, *Ways of teasing a beginner or inexperienced person . . : "Go get me ______."*) Inf **VA**54, A eight-dollar bill.

eighteen-hundred-and-fast-asleep n [By analogy with **eighteen-hundred-and-froze-to-death** and similar forms]

See quot.

1914 *DN* 4.106 **KS,** It happened in eighteen hundred and fast asleep.

eighteen-hundred-and-froze-to-death n Also *eighteen-hundred-and-freeze-to-death* **NEng, esp ME** *hist*

The period of 1816-17; see quots.

1917 in 1947 Botkin *Treas. New Engl. Folkl.* 831, One of the worst years Maine ever experienced was 1817. An unusually cold winter was followed by a backward spring, and the weather continued to be so unseasonable that the crops were failures, and the year was long after familiarly known as eighteen hundred and freeze to death. **1966** *DARE* FW Addit **MA**5, My grandpa, born in 1818, heard about eighteen-hundred-and-froze-to-death from his father, who had suffered through that very cold period of 1816-17. **1966** *Ellsworth Amer.* (ME) 29 June 16/3, Summer never came at all in the discmal [sic] year of "eighteen-hundred-and-froze-to-death." The chilly spring of 1966 was nothing compared to that of 1816. The weather . . turned New England into a frigid disaster adea [sic]. **1979** *Scientific Amer.* June 176, In New England, Canada and western Europe the summer of 1816 was extraordinarily cold. . . In New England the loss of most of the staple crop of Indian corn and the great reduction of the hay crop caused so much hardship on isolated subsistence farms that the year became enshrined in folklore as "Eighteen Hundred and Froze to Death."

eighth month See **first month**

eight-hooter n [See quots] **esp NEast**

A barred owl.

1914 Eaton *Birds NY* 2.116, The commonest of its [=the barred owl's] performances has gained it the name of "eight hooter" among the north woods guides. **1944** Hausman *Amer. Birds* 232, Among country dwellers the Barred Owl is known . . more commonly as the Eight-Hooter from the number of notes in its commonest call. **1956** MA Audubon Soc. *Bulletin* 40.81, Barred Owl. . . Eight-hooter (Maine. The calls are often given in a series of four pairs.) **1966** Rodimer *Year Outdoors* 19 **NJ,** Many predators watched the winter world . . the mink, the hawks, and "the eight hooter," the barred owl.

eight-o'clock fever See **nine-o'clock blues**

eight-square adj, also used absol [*OED* 1538 →; "*Obs.* exc. *Naut.*"] *old-fash*

Octagonal; a rifle having an octagonal barrel.

1897 Lewis *Wolfville* 104 **AZ,** Cherokee . . sends out for Jack Moore's Winchester, which is an 'eight-squar',' latest model. **1907** White *AZ Nights* 4, He . . carried across his saddle a heavy "eight square" rifle. **1943** Chase *Jack Tales* 92 **wNC,** He gave Jack a drill shaved out of a stick. It was eight-square like a steel drill and about a foot long. **1955** *Hench Coll.* **csPA,** The 8 square school house . . is situated near Fishertown in East St. Clair township. It is without a doubt, the oddest shaped building for a schoolhouse and likely there is something in reference to plans made by Quakers who are largely the settlers in that vicinity. . . Mary has greatly criticized the name, 8 square as applying to the building having 8 corners, two sets of 4 corners.

eight-up n Also *eight-up team* **West**

A team of eight draft animals.

1921 Thorp *Songs Cowboys* 11 **NM,** But I've driv my eight-up to wagon / That were locked three in a row. **1951** Grant *Cowboy Encycl.* 61, *Eight-up.* A team of eight horses, mules, or oxen. **1967** *DARE* Tape **TX**26, We call 'em a six-up or eight-up, or whatever, how many of 'em you got . . an eight-up team.

eighty n Cf **forty** n **B1**

Eighty acres of land, half of a quarter section.

1842 Kirkland *Forest Life* 2.207 **MI,** Happy he whose far-reaching "eighties" enclose a sugar bush! **1872** *Amer. Naturalist* 6.77 **CO,** The whole surface of the plains is sere and brown save some "eighties" or larger tracts that are fenced. **1913** Porter *Laddie* 219 **cnIN,** Then I hurried . . across the west eighty to the woods. **1923** *DN* 5.234 **swWI,** *Eighty*. . . A tract of land containing eighty acres. The phrase "across an eighty" indicates therefore about a quarter of a mile. . . "How far is it over there?" "Oh, 'cross an eighty an' a forty." **1936** M. H. Bradley *Five-Minute Girl* v. 74 *(OEDS),* So his ax had set to work on the maples and hemlocks in his north eighty.

eighty-four n

A domino game utilizing two sets of dominoes, each containing forty-two pieces.

1966-69 *DARE* (Qu. DD37, . . *Table games played a lot by adults*) Inf **OK**25, Eighty-four—a domino game; **TX**53, Forty-two, eighty-four; [(Qu. FF2) Inf **TX**58, Forty-two and eighty-eight [*DARE* Ed: error for *eighty-four*?]—these are domino games. Eighty-eight: two sets of dominoes, six people].

ei nei intj [Haw *ei nei* or *eia nei* you there]

Say! You there!—used to get someone's attention.

1967 *DARE* (Qu. II15, *When somebody is passing by and you want him or her to stop and talk a while*) Inf **HI**6, Ei nei—[said when] beginning to address him. [FW: =Say!]

either adj, adv, pron, conj Usu |ˈiðə(r)|; also **esp urban areas of the NEast,** *esp among well educ speakers* |ˈaɪðə(r)| (often considered affected); occas **esp N Midl** |ˈɪðə(r)|; infreq **esp NEng,** *old-fash* |ˈɛðə(r)| Pronc-spp *eeder, eeduh, eether, eider, ether, ither, ithur, uther* Cf **teither**

A Forms.

1789 Webster *Dissertations Engl. Lang.* 114, The words *either, neither* . . are generally pronounced, by the eastern people, *ither, nither*. . . These are errors; all the standard authors agree to give *ei,* in these words, the sound of *ee.* **1823** Cooper *Pioneers* 1.13 **cNY,** A younger hand than 'ither your'n or mine. **1838** Cooper *Amer. Democrat* 119 **NY,** The polite pronunciation of "either" and "neither," is "i-ther" and "ni-ther," and not "eether" and "neether." **1843** (1916) Hall *New Purchase* 174 **IN,** No, worldlins, you couldn't, the most high larn'd ither, couldn't make any of them thare things. **1847** Hurd *Grammatical Corrector* 81, *Either. . . Incorrectly pronounced:* 'ithur [with *i* as in *pine*]. **1888** Jones *Negro Myths* 132 **seGA,** Fetch um er fat hog, but eh musnt be eider er sow-hog, neider er bo-hog, but eh mus be er fat hog. **1896** Harris *Sister Jane* 148 **GA,** I pulled right along wi'out lookin' uther to the right or uther to the left. **1906** *DN* 3.118 **sIN,** *Either. . .* Generally pronounced *ither.* "I won't go *ither.*" **1912** Green *VA Folk-Speech* 469, *Uther. . .* For *either.* **1922** Gonzales *Black Border* 239 **sSC, GA coasts** [Gullah], I mos' t'ink 'e bin eeduh de 'Postle Paul, elseso Pollido'. [=I mostly think he was either the Apostle Paul, or else Polydore.] **1927** *Ruppenthal Coll.* **KS,** Ether—variant of either, and pronounced to rime with nether. **1930** [see **E2** below]. **1931** *AmSp* 6.170 **ceVA,** *Either* is with one or two exceptions [iðə]. **1935** *AmSp* 10.292 **Upstate NY,** *Either* and *neither* are normally [iðr] and [niðr]. **1942** *AmSp* 17.31 **seNY,** Other variations include [i] 27 [infs], [aɪ] 10, in *either. Ibid* 151, [ɚ] 22, [ə] 15 [in final syllable]. **1943** *LANE* Map 610, Only the type of [iðr, iðə] is common. The type of [aɪðə, aɪðr] is natural to a small number of younger and educated informants; it is regarded as affected or amusing by several others, and as old-fashioned (perhaps rather unfamiliar or unusual) by some others, especially in Maine. The type [ɛðə] is used in conversation by [one inf each in Vermont and New Hampshire]; it was reported as an old-fashioned pronunciation by several others in N.H. and Me. **1943** in 1944 *ADD* **sPA,** *Either . .* [ɪðr]. There's no money in it ither. **1961** Kurath–McDavid *Pronc. Engl.* 149, *Either, neither. . .* The vowel [i] of *three* predominates decidedly on all social levels in all sections of the Eastern States (except parts of Pennsylvania, New Jersey, and Delmarva), and is almost the only pronunciation current in the North and the Lower South. The most frequent variant has the vowel [ɪ] of *pith,* which is rather common in parts of the North Midland. . . Though most frequent in folk speech, it is also used to some extent by the middle group. . . *Either* with the vowel [ai] of *five* is distinctly a sporadic feature of the cultivated speech of Metropolitan New York and Philadelphia. . . it is in all probability a recent adoption from British English. **1967** *DARE* FW Addits **TN**13, 14, *Either*—pronounced ['ɑɪðɚ] [almost] consistently by these Infs, yet they seem to feel it is "wrong." On her *[DARE]* tape recording, Inf **TN**13 pronounced it ['iðɚ]. **1976** Allen *LAUM* 3.248 (as of c1950), Almost unanimous is the U[pper] M[idwest] pronunciation of *either . .* with the vowel [i] of *see. . .* The minor variant with [ai], found in some eastern urban speech especially in New York City, is not characteristic of UM speech.

B As adj.

1 Any. Cf **D** below

1968 *DARE* FW Addit **MD,** "I didn't see either crab there"—said on Smith Island. **1976** Warner *Beautiful Swimmers* 164 **Eastern Shore MD,** Them chicken neckers, they's more of them now than either year. **1979** *Rappahannock Rec.* (Kilmarnock VA) 22 Nov 3/3 **ceVA,** On bad days he [=the Northern Neck native] is heard to complain that he hasn't caught "either" or "neither" oyster.

2 Every.

1937 *Hench Coll.* **eVA,** Either = every. . . widely heard on the Eastern Shore of Virginia, in the truck vegetables & berry district. a. Go out and bring in either sack you come to (= bring back every sack you come to). b. [To pickers going over a field a second time] Go out and pick up either one you find. c. Bring in either one as you come to it (said of bags of potatoes or other things laid in a row or rows[)].

C As adv.

Instead.

1916 *DN* 4.302 **cwVA,** *Either. . .* Instead. "You can have the cart *either.*" "You can do that *either.*" **1937** *AmSp* 12.287 **nwVA,** The vocabulary and idioms of the [Shenandoah] Valley have been influenced by the Pennsylvania Germans and by the mountain people. . . The Shenandoah German may say . . *either* for *instead.* **1940** *Qrly. Jrl. Speech* 26.264 **wVA,** "Either" may be used for *instead,* as "You can have this book either." **1967** *DARE* Tape **LA**11, This [=filé] flavors up the juices of the soup or you can use it in gravy either if you want to.

D As pron.

With ref to more than two persons or things: any. [*OED either* pron. 4. c 1616 →] Cf **B1** above

1781 *PA Jrl. & Weekly Advt.* (Philadelphia) 9 May 1/2, [In a list of Americanisms:] 'The United States, or *either* of them.' This is so far from being a mark of ignorance, that it is used by many of the most able and accurate speakers and writers, yet it is not English. **1793** in 1957 Old Farmer's Almanac *Sampler* 61 **NH,** Take bean-flower water, or elder-flower water, or May dew, gathered from corn, of either, the quantity of four spoonfuls, and add to it one spoonful of oil of tartar. **1970** *DARE* FW Addit **VA**51, I wouldn't marry either of the girls on the main. [FW: He meant "none of them"; occas [use] on mainland, common on seaside islands.]

E As conj.

1 in phr *or either(wise):* Or else. **chiefly Sth**

1898 Lloyd *Country Life* 15 **AL,** Everything had been moved out or moved in or either moved off. **c1938** in 1970 Hyatt *Hoodoo* 1.163 **neNC,** He'd always heard that you could draw a person if you was a witch and draw dey pitchure on a shingle, or eitherwise on a cake of bread. **1968** *DARE* FW Addit **GA**40, It's a cattle crossing or either a cattle gap. **1970** *Foxfire* Spring–Summer 26 **nGA,** Roll'em in flour . . an' fry'em; or either y'can take buttermilk'n'an'egg an' whip it t'gether. **1971** *Ibid,* Winter 249 **neGA,** Most all I can remember walked, or either there would be somebody go get them in a buggy. **1972** Jones–Hawes *Step it Down* 51 **eGA,** We'd do it in the yard or either in the house. **1976** Ryland *Richmond Co. VA* 374, Or either—"That cow is Black Angus or either Holstein, one." **1981** *DARE* File **Buffalo NY,** They'll just have to fix it, or either they'll have to give me my money back. **1987** *DARE* File (as of 1970), I heard *or either* frequently in Georgia: "It was this one or either that one."

2 also with *so:* Or; or else. *among Black speakers*

1922 Gonzales *Black Border* 263 **sSC, GA coasts** [Gullah], Ef my juntlemun kin git uh hawss, eeduhso uh oxin . . , I will mek she go 'long too. *Ibid* 139, You nebbuh buy uh candy, eeduhso uh sugar, fuh sweet'n dem mout'. **1927** Kennedy *Gritny* 59 **sLA** [Black], You ain' in no bar-room. Either yonder on de levee-front. *Ibid* 100, She come up at me full-fo'ce, like she wan' scratch my face, either butt me. **1930** Stoney–Shelby *Black Genesis* 6 **seSC,** Ebery time God' fork, eeder he spoon, lef' de plate, Br' Dog eye ketch it an' gone wid it right to he mout'. *Ibid* 41, How is a pusson like me goin' to fly high, eeder-so low?

eitherwise See **either E1**

eizenburg See **osnaburg**

ekal See **equal** n, v, adj

eke n [*SND eik* n.^{2} 3; cf *OED eke* sb.^{1} 1 "A piece added on.," "*Obs.* exc. *dial.*"]

1939 *AmSp* 14.89 **cTN,** *An eke.* Material added to a dress pattern to make the dress larger. "I'm putting an eke in my dress."

ekil, ekle See **equal** n, v, adj

eks See **ex** n^{1}

elastic (band) n Also *elastic rubber, rubber elastic* Aphet forms *lastic* and, by metath, *laskit* **chiefly Nth, N Midl, esp N Atl** See Map *somewhat old-fash* Cf **gum band**

A rubber band.

c1950 *Atlas Checklists* **cnMA,** Elastic—rubber band. **1965–70** *DARE* (Qu. F49) 117 Infs, **chiefly Nth, N Midl,** Elastic (band); **MA**5, 7, Rubber elastic; **MA**40, **VA**22, Lastic (band); **TN**27, Laskit bands. [Of all Infs responding to the question, 69% were old; of those giving these responses, 84% were old.] **1967** *DARE* FW Addit **neMA,** Elastic—used in Haverhill, Mass. for rubber band; **neND,** Elastic band [ˌlæstək 'bænd]—term for . . a rubber band. **1973** Allen *LAUM* 1.397 (as of c1950), *Elastic band* is used by four of the five Canadian infs. and persists with four Minnesotans and one North Dakotan. *Elastic, elastic rubber,* and *rubber elastic* are rare variants, all in Northern territory except for one

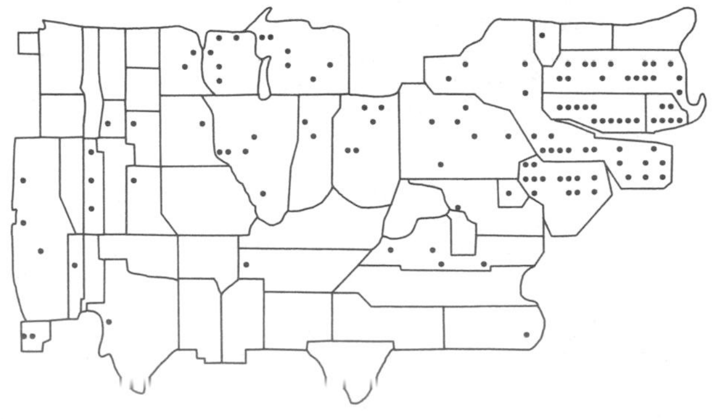

•elastic (band) + varr (Qu. F49)

instance of *elastic* in Nebraska. **1977–78** Foster *Lexical Variation* 67 **NJ,** *Elastic* or *elastic band* 'rubber band' is the form preferred by elderly informants, but it is less popular in the younger age groups.

elbedritsch n Usu |ˈɛlbəˌdrɪč, ˈælbə-| Also sp *elbedritsche,* dimin *elbedritschel;* occas *elfedritsch, -trich; elde(r)britsch; elpentrecher; albedritsch, -tritsch; albertwitsch;* for addit varr see quot 1967–70 [PaGer, from Ger *Elbe(n)tritsch;* see 1960 *Hessische Blätter für Volkskunde* 51/52 Textteil pp 170–217, esp 208–212; perh also infl by Scots *eldritch* weird, unnatural] **sePA** See Map Cf **snipe hunt**

An imaginary creature which, as a practical joke, a greenhorn is sent to hunt or capture.

1889 *AN&Q* 3.115/1 **PA,** Catching Elfetriches.—Among the "Pennsylvania Dutch" this expression would imply playing a trick upon a person, or making an April fool of him. The "elfetrich" is described as a small animal, like a rat or a squirrel, which can only be caught on a dark night, and in due time the hunter discovers that it is a humbug. **1935** *AmSp* 10.170 **PA,** Other German words used in English are . . *elbedritsch,* a mythological creature (to go *elbedritsch* hunting is equivalent to going snipe hunting in the Middle West—someone is left holding the bag). **1950** Klees *PA Dutch* 336, If a young man sufficiently guileless turns up, he'll be set to catching an *elbedritsche,* a mythical animal now extinct. . . The difficulties of catching an elbedritsche are dwelt upon in loving detail. Almost grudgingly the old men consent to the young man joining the hunt. The greenhorn is given a bag in which to catch one and taken far off . . and stationed behind a rock or tree while the old men separate—or so he is given to understand—to drive the elbedritsches toward him. There he is left literally holding the bag. **1953** *AmSp* 28.245 **sePA,** *To go elpentrecher hunting* . . denotes waiting, burlap bag in hand, to snare the shy and elusive elpentrecher, as time-consuming an occupation as snipe hunting in other parts of the Union. **1959** Tallman *Dict. Amer. Folkl.* 105, *Elbedritsche*—A mythological animal that young men of the Pennsylvania Dutch use as a device for fooling naive or guileless visitors. **1967–70** *DARE* (Qu. CC17, *Imaginary animals or monsters that people around here tell tales about—especially to tease greenhorns*) Infs **PA**22, 29, 36, 45, 54, Albedritsches; **PA**36, They would give them a stick and light; when they [i.e., albedritsches] ran to this light, they were to hit them with a huge stick; **PA**11, Albertwitsch [ˈælbɚtˌwɪč]; **PA**150, Eldebritsches [ˈɛldəˌbrɪčəs]; **PA**162, Elbedritschel [ˈɛlbəˌdrɪčəl]—little animal; must have a partner, give him a burlap bag—only found on the coldest night; **PA**243, Elfedritsches [ˈɛlfədrɪčəs]—small creatures, can be caught in a bag; initiate is left holding the bag in woods, waiting for elfedritsches; (Qu. EE33, *Other outdoor games*) Inf **PA**22, Albedritsch [ˈælbɪdrɪtč] hunts; (Qu. HH14, *Ways of teasing a beginner*) Inf **PA**11, Albetritsches [ˈælbɪˌtrɪčəz]; **PA**242, Elderbritsches—[we] left a novice standing holding bag expecting elderbritsches to run by. **1967** *DARE* Tape **PA**64, There's nothing like it. But they made him believe it. . . They gave him a big bag and he had to go out and hunt that albedritsch [ˈælbəˌdrɪč]. . . That's an old one. **1987** *Jrl. Engl. Ling.* 20.2.169 **ePA,** *Elbedritsch* 'a mythical creature often referred to as *snipe*'. . . Even though 49% of the [100] subjects acknowledged using *elbedritsch,* the large number of speakers who left the question blank demonstrates a growing unfamiliarity with the concept.

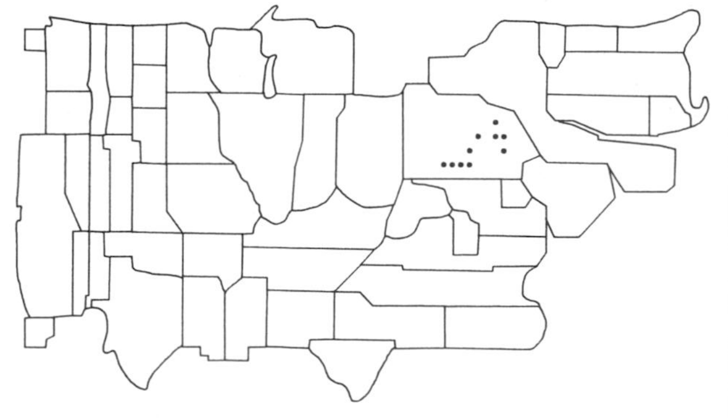

•elbedritsch + varr (Qq. CC17, EE33, HH14)

elbow bending n [**bend one's elbow**] *joc*

The act of drinking alcoholic beverages; also n *elbow bender* a habitual drinker.

1934 *Esquire* Apr 36/2, The gentlemanly art of refined elbow-bending. [**1939** *AmSp* 14.263 **IN,** His bibulous proclivities are sometimes euphemistically referred to by the remark 'Every time his elbow bends, his mouth flies open.'] **1957** *Playboy* May 14/3 **Chicago IL,** Time between ports for swimming, dancing and elbow bending. **1958** McCulloch *Woods Words* 57 **Pacific NW,** *Elbow bender*—A drinking man. **1968–69** *DARE* (Qu. DD12, . . *A person who drinks steadily or a great deal*) Inf **NY**42, Elbow bender; (Qu. DD37, . . *Table games played a lot by adults*) Inf **CA**114, Elbow bending [laughter; FW: i.e., drinking].

elbow brush See **elbow bush 1**

elbow bush n [Appar from the many-angled branches]

1 also *elbow brush:* =**buttonbush 1.**

1888 *Harper's New Mth. Mag.* Apr 743/2 **sLA,** Tufts of elbow-bushes, and broad reaches of saw-grass. **1913** *Torreya* 13.234, *Cephalanthus occidentalis*. . . Elbow brush, New Richmond, Mich. **1938** FWP *U.S. One* 252 **FL,** Here mistletoe is found clinging to the black gum, and palmettos grow in profusion. Prickly ash, elbow, and hurrah bushes are common. **1970** *DARE* FW Addit **KY**86, Elbow brush—low, tangled brush that grows along streams and ponds and in bottoms and marshes.

2 A **forestiera** (here: *Forestiera pubescens*).

1970 Correll *Plants TX* 1200, *Forestiera pubescens* . . Elbow-bush. . . Locally abundant in open pastures and brushy prairies where not too heavily browsed.

elbow cousin n Cf **shirttail relative**

1959 *VT Hist.* new ser 27.134, Elbow cousin. . . Distant cousin, not highly esteemed. Occasional.

elbow, go (all) around one's v phr Also *go (all) around one's elbow to get to one's thumb, go round one's fist ~, go around one's fingers ~, go all around one's thumb to get to one's elbow;* for addit varr see quots **chiefly SE, esp NC** See Map Cf **Robin Hood's barn, go all the way round**

To follow a roundabout course or course of action.

1914 *DN* 4.107 **KS,** *Go around one's fingers to get to* (or *at*) *his thumb*. . . To go circuitously. **1965–70** *DARE* (Qu. KK52, *To do something in an indirect and complicated way: "I don't know why he had to go ______ to do that."*) 21 Infs, **FL, GA, NC,** (All *or* all the way) (a)round his elbow to get to his thumb(s) [and var phrr: see *DS*]; 12 Infs, **chiefly SE, esp NC,** (All *or* all the way) (a)round his elbow; **NC**61, Round the devil's elbow; **GA**54, **SC**11, 44, 54, (A)round his elbow to get to his hand (*or* mouth, nose); **FL**19, By way of his elbow to his mouth; **AR**33, **FL**6, **MS**15, (All) around his thumb (to get to his elbow); **VA**54, Round his fist to get to his thumb; [**GA**45, All around the elephant's snout to get to his tail].

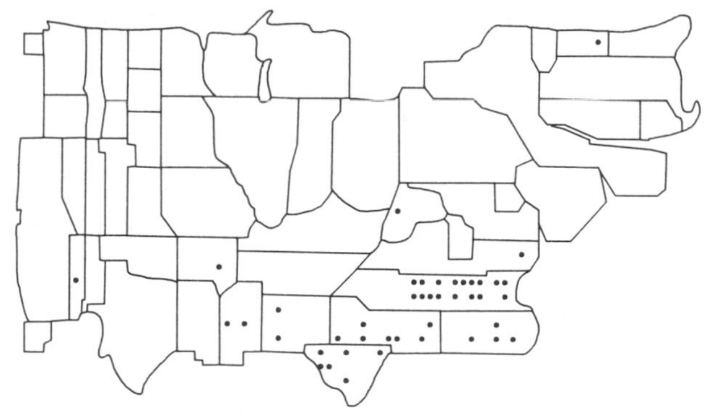

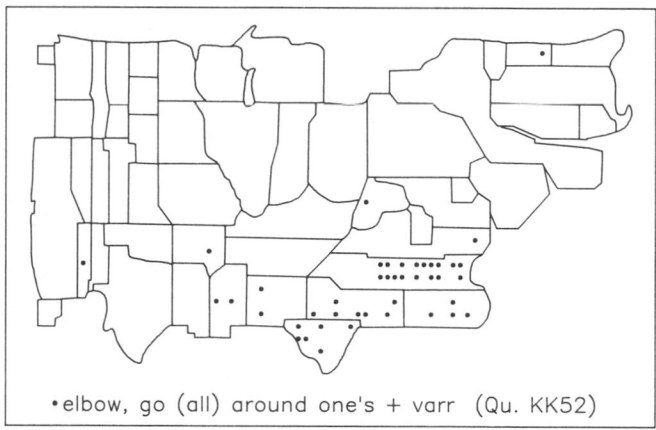

•elbow, go (all) around one's + varr (Qu. KK52)

elbow grease n [Ext of *elbow grease* expenditure of physical energy] *joc*

A nonexistent item used as the basis of a practical joke.

1966–67 *DARE* (Qu. HH14, *Ways of teasing a beginner or inexperienced person* . . *"Go get me ______."*) Infs **HI**1, **OK**31, **TX**32, (Some) elbow grease; **PA**24, **IL**50, A can (*or* pot) of elbow grease.

elbow walk n

1973 *DARE* File **Fairbanks AK,** Elbow walk—Ancient Eskimo game. Contestant in prone position propels self forward using only elbows and toes. No other part of the body can touch the ground. The contestant who goes farthest wins the game. Time is not an element.

‡el cabbagio n [Perh because the Cuban-like name ironically suggests high quality] *joc* Cf **el ropo**

A low-quality cigar.

1968 *DARE* (Qu. DD6a) Inf **CT**16, El cabbagio [kəbɑžo].

elcompenny See **elecampane**

eldebritsch See **elbedritsch**

elder n[1] *old-fash*

An udder.

1914 *DN* 4.106 **cKS,** *Elder*. . . Udder. **1967** *DARE* (Qu. K4, *The cow's udder*) Inf **PA**6, Elder. [Inf old]

elder n[2] [Abbr]

The elderberry.

1809 Rundell *Domestic Cookery* 179, Cut . . shoots of elder, which will look like bamboo. **1966** *DARE* (Qu. I46, . . *Fruits that grow wild*) Inf **AR**39, Mulberry; wild cherry or black cherry; elder.

elderblow n, often attrib Also *elderbloom* [*elder* + **blow** n[1], **bloom** n[1] **1**]

The blossom of an elder tree, often used to make tea or wine; occas the drink itself.

1832 L. M. Child *Frugal Housewife* 27 *(DA),* A poultice of elder-blow tea and biscuit is good as a preventative. **1845** Judd *Margaret* 274 **MA,** I wouldn't tech it sooner a cow'd eat elder blows. **1859** (1880) Darlington *Amer. Weeds* 162, An infusion of its flowers, Elderblow-tea, is a harmless and efficient diaphoretic. **1869** Stowe *Oldtown Folks* 103 **MA,** Elder-blow, catnip, hoarhound, hardhack, gentian, ginseng, and various other vegetable tribes, she knew well. **1899** Brown *Tiverton Tales* 205 **NEng,** The entire neighborhood knew that Mrs. Pitts . . was, at the moment, in a dark bedroom at home, helpless under elderblow. **1929** *AmSp* 4.387 **KS,** *Elderbloom* is a sparkling yellow wine made by fermenting elder blossoms in a mixture of water and sugar. **1934** Harwich Port Lib. Assoc. *From Cape Cod* 204, Elderblow wine . . a wine made from elder blossoms.

elderbritsch See **elbedritsch**

elder bug n

1967 *DARE* (Qu. R4, *A large winged insect that hatches in summer in great numbers around lakes or rivers, crowds around lights, lives only a day or so, and is good fish bait*) Inf **TN**13, Elder bug.

Eleanor n [Anna *Eleanor* Roosevelt (1884–1962), wife of President Franklin D. Roosevelt] Cf **F.D.R., federal building** and *DS* M21a, b

An outdoor toilet for women.

1973 Allen *LAUM* 1.180 **cwIA** (as of c1950), *Eleanor* and *Roosevelt* have political overtones, and both probably reflect Republican reaction to the project that also gave rise to the synonyms *WPA* and *WPA project.* [1 inf]

Eleanor club n [For Anna *Eleanor* Roosevelt wife of President Franklin D. Roosevelt] Cf **Elizabeth club**

A supposed but nonexistent organization of Southern Black women customarily employed as servants in White households.

1943 Odum *Race & Rumors* 87, Since there were no Eleanor Clubs in reality as a foundation for the great sweep of rumor [in 1942–43], it was clear that the basic complaint was one in which the main mode of domestic southern folkways of servant and mistress was being violated, both in the actual scarcity of help and in the revolutionary change in attitudes and status.

eleb'm See **eleven**

elecampane n Pronc-spp *allycumpain, elcompenny*

A large coarse composite plant *(Inula helenium).* Also called **horseweed 9, velvet dock, wild sunflower, yellow starwort**

1709 (1967) Lawson *New Voyage* 78 **NC,** The more Physical [herbs], are . . Elecampane, Comfrey, Nettle, the Seed from England, none Native. **1884** Twain *Huck. Finn* 334 **MO,** We like-to got a hornet's nest, but we didn't. . . Then we got allycumpain and rubbed on the places, and was pretty near all right again. **1966** *DARE* Wildfl QR Pl.250 Inf **MI**31, Elcompenny ['ɛlkəm,pɛnɪ]. **1968** *DARE* (Qu. S26b) Inf **PA**70, Elecampane.

elected ppl adj

1893 Shands *MS Speech, Elected.* . . Illiterate whites use this word to mean *to be provided with, to have a sufficient supply of.* They say: "I am *elected* as to corn"; i.e. "I am provided with corn"; "I have a sufficient supply of corn."

election cake n Also *election bun;* pronc-sp *'lection* ~ **NEng, esp MA** Cf **March meeting cake, town meeting ~**

A rich fruit cake or bun served on election day.

1831 (1940) Motte *Charleston to Harvard* 24 **Boston MA,** I got some very nice 'lection cake at Morse's house in Beacon street. **1860** Holmes *Professor* 38 **MA,** Recollects he had a glazed 'lection bun, and sat eating it and looking down on to the Common. **1878** *Harper's New Mth. Mag.* 57.581/1 **NEng,** Polly . . nussed him up with a mug o' flip and a lot o' 'lection cake. **1906** *Pocumtuc Housewife* 30 **MA,** Election Cake. **1932** (1946) Hibben *Amer. Regional Cookery* 25 **CT,** Hartford Election Cake. **1939** Wolcott *Yankee Cook Book* 252 **NEng,** *Connecticut Raised Loaf Cake* [Also called Election Cake, March Meeting Cake and Dough Cake]. . . March Meetin' or 'Lection Cakes were sold in the village stores all day at four pence a baker's dozen. *Ibid* 253, Election cake is said to have originated in Hartford, Conn., a century ago and was served to all who voted the straight ticket. **1941** *LANE* Map 283 **ceMA,** ['lɪkšn 'keɪks ə'lɛkšn ~], of flour and sweetened water, formerly served at town meetings. **1948** Coatsworth *South Shore* 64 **MA,** There are hot cross buns in the bakery window before good Friday, although they no longer display Election Cake or Town Meeting Cake, a sort of larger raisin bun once eaten for the noonday meal in the times when town meeting was an all-day affair.

election day n Pronc-sp *'lection day* [From the custom of inaugurating officers on the day on which they were elected] **MA, RI** *hist*

Inauguration day.

1860 Arnold *Hist. RI* 2.273, Instead of the first Wednesday in May, the third Wednesday in April [as of 1767] had become the period of decisive political struggle, while "election day," as it still continues from ancient habit to be called, ceased to be any thing more than the occasion for . . the inauguration of the new government at Newport. **1869** Stowe *Oldtown Folks* 337 **MA,** Election day, when the Governor took his seat with pomp and rejoicing, and all the housewives outdid themselves in election cake. **1887** *Narragansett Hist. Reg.* 5.343 **RI,** Election day, in Rhode Island . . the day called in other states Inauguration day.—'Lection day has been changed several times in the history of the state. **1902** Field *State of RI* 1.392, Newport . . was compelled to witness the loss of its cherished "election day" and the removal of its distinction as a state capital [in 1900]. **1947** *AN&Q* 7.61 **MA,** Amos Kendall, journalist and member of Andrew Jackson's famous "Kitchen Cabinet," described, in his *Autobiography* (Boston and New York, 1872), the festivities of "'Lection Day," or the day on which the Governor of Massachusetts was inaugurated. . . in the very early 1800's. . . The holiday, he said, came toward the end of May and farmers' boys used it for hunting or fishing. They would choose sides some days in advance, and would begin scouring the surrounding region for crows' nests. . . etc. An old crow . . brought as high as ten points, while a blackbird's egg scored as low as one. The side running up the larger score was, of course, the victor.

election pink n [From **election day**] **NEng**

A rhododendron: usu **pinxter flower,** but also *Rhododendron prinophyllum.*

1891 *Jrl. Amer. Folkl.* 4.148 **MA, NH,** Azalea nudiflora, [called] *Election Pink,* because in bloom at the old-time "election," when the governor took his seat in June. **1892** *Ibid* 5.100 **csNH,** *Rhododendron nudiflorum,* election pink. **1976** Bailey–Bailey *Hortus Third* 961, *[Rhododendron] periclymenoides. . . Pinxter flower, . . election pink. . . [R.] prinophyllum. . . Election pink.*

election posy n Cf **election pink**

An **Indian paintbrush** (here: *Castilleja coccinea*).

1892 *Jrl. Amer. Folkl.* 5.101 **csMA,** *Castilleia* [sic] *coccinea* . . election posies.

election sermon n **chiefly NEng** *hist*

A sermon preached on **election day.**

1644 in 1853 MA (Colony) *Rec. of Gov.* 2.71, The printer shall have leave to print the election sermon, wth Mr Mathers consent. **1723** *New-Engl. Courant* (Boston MA) 7–14 Jan 2/2 **MA,** The Rev. Mr. John Wise of Ipswich has been desir'd to preach the next Election Sermon. **1865** *Atlantic Mth.* 15.453 **CT,** In the spring of 1825 Mr. Johns was invited by Governor Wolcott to preach the Election Sermon before the Legislature convened at Hartford. **1878** Taylor *Between the Gates* 233, An old-time preacher's election sermon would pack such a day even-full of doctrine.

electorial adj [Substitution of *-ial* suff by analogy with *janitorial, preceptorial, professorial,* etc]
Electoral.
1906 *DN* 3.135 **nwAR,** *Electorial*. . . "This book shows the electorial vote for each year." Common. **1911** *DN* 3.549 **NE,** Analogical modification of suffix occurs frequently in . . *mischievious, grievious, blasphemious, electorial;* also (by students) *pastorial, Elizabethian.*

electric adj, n Usu |i'lɛktrɪk, ə-|; often |'lɛktrɪk| Pronc-sp *lectric;* similarly, *lectrical, lectricity*
A Forms.
1891 *DN* 1.127 **cNY,** [lɛktrɪk]. **1965–70** *DARE* (Qu. B22) 37 Infs, **scattered,** Lectric(al) storm (*or* shower); (Qu. L65) Infs **DC**5, **PA**226, 234, 242, Lectric fence; (Qu. N34) Infs **MA**40, **MO**6, **NJ**67, Lectric car(s); (Qu. HH14) Inf **MA**35, A bag of lectricity. **1966–70** *DARE* Tapes **AK**6, **IN**3, **MI**4, Lectricity; **CA**205, Lectrical storms.
B As noun.
Electricity. [Absol use of adj]
1941 in 1944 *ADD* **nWV,** *Electric*. . . "[Wasting] the electric." Other uses reported. Freq. in for-rent advts. **1942** Thomas *Blue Ridge Country* 263 **sAppalachians,** That unseen juice, or 'lectric. . . "I'd druther have 'lectric than a new cookstove . . ," any mountain woman will tell you. **1950** *WELS Suppl.* **cwWI,** "Electric" used for "electricity." "I started to iron, but surprise. The electric was off." **1950** Klees *PA Dutch* 282, Funny only in a mild way is the use of the adjective for the noun, as in . . "Did you have the electric put in the house?" **1955** Taber *Stillmeadow Daybook* 206 **swCT,** It is good to know our linesmen are ready. If the electric as we call it, goes off, they are there in no time at all. **1966–69** *DARE* Tape **FL**36, We didn't have no electric; **MO**16, We didn't have no lectric, we didn't have no runnin' water, no nothin'. **1968** *DARE* (Qu. F36) Inf **MD**44, [An] electric broom [is] like a carpet sweeper, but run by electric. **1971** *Today Show Letters* **KY, sIN** [Black], In 1932 they fetched in the lectric. . . I got to go to town to pay the lectric.

electrical shower n Also *electric shower*
An electrical storm.
1966 *DARE* (Qu. B22) Inf **SC**6, Lectrical shower. **1971** Wood *Vocab. Change* **FL, GA, LA, OK, TN,** Electric(al) shower [11 of 1000 infs].

electric bug See **electric light bug**

electric cloud n
A thunder cloud; an electrical storm.
1969 *DARE* (Qu. B22, *Rain accompanied by thunder and lightning*) Inf **GA**77, Electric cloud, storm cloud—old-fashioned. [FW: (This) *is* the same as a thunderstorm.]

electric dogfish See **dogfish 5**

electricity n
1 See **electric shock.**
2 An electric utility company.
1979 *New Yorker* 7 May 40/2 **NYC,** The man from the electricity came.

electricity bone n [Because the tingling felt when it is struck is like a mild electric shock]
=funny bone 1.
1966 *DARE* (Qu. X33, *The place in the elbow that gives you a strange feeling if you hit it against something*) Inf **FL**10, Electricity bone.

electric light bug n Also *electric bug* [See quots]
=giant water bug.
1901 Howard *Insect Book* 278, *Belostomatidae*. . . So attractive are electric lights to these great bugs that they. . . have in fact become known as "electric light bugs." **1905** U.S. Bur. Fisheries *Rept. for 1904* 583, Undoubtedly there must also be included among the enemies to the fish certain water bugs, such as *Belostoma* (commonly known as the "electric-light bug") and *Ranatra.* **1940** Mencken *Happy Days* 66, When arc-lights began to light the streets, along about 1885, they attracted so many beetles of gigantic size that their glare was actually obscured. These beetles at once acquired the name of electric-light bugs, and it was believed that the arc carbons produced them by a kind of spontaneous generation, and that their bite was as dangerous as that of a tarantula. **1942** McAtee *Dial. Grant Co. IN* 73 (as of 1890s), *Electric-light bug*. . . one of the giant water bugs (Belostomatidæ) that were attracted to arc-lights. **1943** KS State Bd. Ag. *Report* 62.255 177, The "giant water bugs or electric light bugs" are large, flat, brown bugs. . . often taken at electric lights during the summer. **1949** Swain *Insect Guide* 47, Electric Light Bug—*Lethocerus americanus*—Occurs throughout the United States and southern Canada. **1966–68** *DARE* (Qu. R4) Inf **FL**27, Water bugs, electric light bugs; (Qu. R5, *A big brown beetle that comes out in large numbers in spring and early summer, and flies with a buzzing sound*) Inf **FL**20, Electric bug; **NV**7, Electric light bugs—used to crowd around arc lights; (Qu. R30, . . *Other kinds of beetles*) Inf **AL**17, Lectric light bug. **1971** Kieran *Nat. Hist. NYC* 50, The giant water bugs are the only ones that commonly take to the air and, in that different medium, most persons who see them flying into the bright lights at night call them "electric-light bugs."

electric lightbulb plant n
=blue cohosh 1.
1964 Campbell *Great Smoky Wildflowers* 14, Blue cohosh. . . Other common names are electric light bulb plant and papoose-root.

electric light oil n Also *electric light trimmer* [Because electric lights require neither the oil nor the trimmer necessary for kerosene lamps] *old-fash*
A nonexistent item used as the basis of a practical joke.
1921 *DN* 5.94 **neOH** [Words used in practical jokes], *Electric-light oil.* **1969** *DARE* (Qu. HH14, *Ways of teasing a beginner . . "Go get me ———."*) Inf **IL**80A, Electric light trimmer—when coal oil lamps were widely used, electricity new.

electric light plant n
A **spider flower** (here: *Cleome spinosa*).
1940 Clute *Amer. Plant Names* 221, *Cleome spinosa.* Electric light plant.

electric owl n
Among railroad workers: a telegraph operator who works at night.
1943 *AmSp* 18.165, *Electric owl.* Night operator. **1945** Hubbard *Railroad Ave.* 342, Electric owl—night operator.

electric road n [Ellip]
An electric railroad.
1969 *DARE* Tape **MA**58, The electric road crossed the bridge there at Hillside.

electric shock n Also *electricity*
A children's game; see quot 1919.
1919 Elsom–Trilling *Social Games* 108, *Electric Shock* . . Those who participate form a circle, each player crossing his arms and joining hands around the circle. In the center stands the player who is to locate the "electric shock." The shock consists of a sudden little squeeze given by the thumb and forefinger to any adjacent player. This player in turn passes the "shock" to the next, and so on around the circle. **1968** *DARE* (Qu. EE3) Inf **PA**126, Electricity—try not to make a face.

electric shower See **electrical shower**

eleele adj |'ele'ele| **HI**
See quots.
1938 Reinecke *Hawaiian Loanwords, Eleele* ['ele'ele]. . . Dark; black. This word sometimes appears as a descriptive element in plant names. **1951** *AmSp* 26.22 **HI,** Other common Hawaiian words . . *eleele* (dark, black). **1972** Carr *Da Kine Talk* 86 **HI,** *Hawaiian Words Commonly Heard In Hawaii's English* . . *'Ele'ele.* Black, dark.

elegant bullsnake n
=glossy snake.
1974 Shaw–Campbell *Snakes West* 104, The glossy snake. . . is sometimes called the elegant bullsnake, for it can be confused at first glance with the gopher snake (also called bullsnake).

element n Pronc-spp *ellyment, yelement*
1 also pl: The sky; air; weather; rarely, water. [*OED element* sb. 10. a *"Obs."*] **chiefly Sth, S Midl** *esp freq among Black speakers*
1883 (1971) Harris *Nights with Remus* 34 **GA** [Black], Win', hit come up en blow, en fill de elements full er dust. **1884** *Anglia* 7.275, Up dar in de eleménts [third syllable stressed]. **1888** Jones *Negro Myths* 102 **GA coast,** Buh Rabbit . . nose duh twis from side ter side fuh ketch all de scent duh float een de element. **1908** *S. Atl. Qrly.* 7.346 **sSC coast** [Gullah], The use of the archaism, *element,* for the sky, the heavens, the ethereal air [is, perhaps, common to the negroes of the South, bar Louisiana]: *"Buh Tukrey Buzza'd duh sail 'roun een de element," . . "Yully een a mo'nin' de element 'tan' bright."* Occasionally, but only occasionally, will be heard the use of *element* to signify the

commonest fluid of earth: . . *"Dem drap t'rue intuh de element; dem scace is mek de sho'."* **1922** Gonzales *Black Border* 231 **sSC, GA coasts** [Gullah], We look high een de ellyment en' we see 'nuf buzzut flyin' high obuh de tree top. *Ibid* 51, 'E hawss jump' nine foot off de groun' een de ellyment. **1922** (1926) Kephart *Highlanders* 79 **sAppalachians,** I'll go see whut the el-e-ments looks like. **1930** Stoney–Shelby *Black Genesis* 48 **seSC,** He kin h'ist he tail high in de element like a flag, an' run 'bout. **1944** *PADS* 2.42 **sVA,** *Elements. . .* The sky, air, weather; generally in the plural. **1952** Brown *NC Folkl.* 1.536, *Element(s). . .* The sky, the weather. **c1960** *Wilson Coll.* **csKY,** *Elements. . .* The sky or weather.

2 Perh a natural propensity.

1886 Amer. Philol. Assoc. *Trans.* 17.45 **Sth,** Common Southern expressions. . . *element* . . "He's got sich er *element* in him."

Elenoise See **Illinois**

elepaio n |ˌɛlɪˈpaɪo| Also sp *elepio*

A flycatcher *(Chasiempis sandwichensis)* found on several of the Hawaiian islands.

1893 in 1972 Berger *Hawaiian Birdlife* 111, Perkins (1893) gave the following as told to him by a native woman in Kona: "Of all the birds the most celebrated in ancient times was the *Elepaio.*" **1930** Degener *Ferns of HI* 176, If the *elepio* . . were to settle on the log, this was considered an ill omen and work on it abandoned. **1967** *DARE* (Qu. Q17, . . *Kinds of woodpeckers*) Inf **HI**14, Elepaio [ˌɛlɪˈpaɪo]—performs somewhat as woodpeckers do in searching out insects in bark of trees.

elephant n

1 in phr *see the elephant:* To see what there is to see; to experience something to the end; to become jaded or disappointed. [Cf *OED lion* sb. 4] *old-fash*

[**1840** (1847) Longstreet *GA Scenes* 10, That's sufficient, as Tom Haynes said when he saw the elephant.] **1844** Kendall *Santa Fé Exped.* 1.108 **TX,** There is a cant expression, *"I've seen the elephant,"* in very common use in Texas. *Ibid* 110, When a man is disappointed in anything he undertakes, when he has seen enough, when he gets sick and tired of any job he may have set himself about, he has *"seen the elephant."* [**1851** (1865) Johnson *CA & OR* 324, If you think we have not shown you enough of the *elephant* . . please to mount him and take a view for yourself.] **1859** (1968) Bartlett *Americanisms* 136, To *see the elephant* is to gain experience of the world, generally at some cost to the investigator. **1872** Burnham *Memoirs U.S. Secret Service* 411, Many of them . . had "seen the elephant," and paid their hundreds of dollars, in advance . . to get their neat little box of dry sawdust, only, in return. **1902** (1906) Porter *4 Million* 86 **NYC,** He makes his rounds every evening; while you and I see the elephant once a week. **1907** *DN* 3.212 **nwAR, cCT,** *Elephant. . .* To see the elephant . . to view the sights in a city.

2 also *baby elephant:* A fat, awkward, or clumsy person. **scattered, but more freq Nth** *joc*

1914 *NY Eve. Jrl.* (NY) 28 Apr 14 *(Zwilling Coll.),* [In cartoon with caption "Listening to two fat dames talk about their shape":] We used to call her the baby elephant at school. **1942** Berrey–Van den Bark *Amer. Slang* 394.1, *Awkward or careless person* . . elephant. *Ibid* 429.1 *Corpulent person* . . elephant. **1966–70** *DARE* (Qu. X50, . . *A person who is very fat*) Infs **CA**113, **IL**2, **MA**75, 122, **NJ**25, **VA**18, **WA**3, **WI**43, Elephant; **AR**40, **MI**75, **MN**33, **NJ**21, Baby elephant; (Qu. HH21, *A very awkward, clumsy person*) Infs **OH**99, **WA**30, Elephant.

3 An excessive task or burden.

1966 *DARE* (Qu. KK9, *When someone undertakes something too big for him to handle: "This time you've ______."*) Inf **NC**4, Got an elephant on your hands.

4 See **white elephant.**

elephant bird n [See quot]

=winter wren.

1956 *AmSp* 31.183 **cNY,** American humor, noted for 'stretching' things, has not failed to exercise this proclivity in the folk nomenclature of birds. . . The greatest exaggeration of this sort is . . *elephant bird* for the four-inch winter wren; this name has been reported as in use among lumbermen of the Adirondack Mountains.

elephant car n

Among railroad workers: see quot 1945.

1945 Hubbard *Railroad Ave.* 342, *Elephant car*—Special car coupled behind locomotive to accommodate head brakeman. **1977** Adams *Lang. Railroader* 53.

elephant ear See **elephant's ear**

elephant-ear plant See **elephant's ear 2**

elephant flower n Also *elephant weed*

An **elephant's head** (here: *Pedicularis groenlandica*).

1937 U.S. Forest Serv. *Range Plant Hdbk.* W143, Elephantflower, elephant-trunk, elephant-weed. . . Most of the common names applied to this plant allude to the resemblance . . to the head of an elephant. **1963** Craighead *Rocky Mt. Wildflowers* 176, Elephant Flower. . . There is no other flower in the Rockies shaped like an elephant's head.

‡elephant grass n

1967 *DARE* (Qu. S26b, *Wildflowers that grow in water or wet places*) Inf **TN**13, Elephant grass.

elephant head See **elephant's head**

elephantitis n [For *elephantiasis;* cf **-itis**]

1967 *DARE* (Qu. X38, *Joking names for unusually big or clumsy feet*) Inf **WA**22, Elephantitis.

elephant-leaf tree n

A **magnolia** (here: prob *Magnolia fraseri*).

1968 *DARE* (Qu. T16, *What kinds of trees are 'special' around here?*) Inf **MO**35, Elephant-leaf tree—some call it the umbrella tree because they always look like an umbrella.

elephant's ear n Also *elephant ear* [Usu from the shape and size]

1 A plant of the genus *Begonia.*

1861 Wood *Class-Book* 366, Begoniads. . . Elephant's Ears. . . *Begonia discolor. . .* Many other species are found in conservatories—too many for our limits. **1895** Gray–Bailey *Field Botany* 193, *Begonia, Elephant's Ear. . .* There are very many species and hybrids. **1933** Small *Manual SE Flora* 918, *Elephant's-ears. Begonias.* Many species with showy leaves and highly colored wax-like flowers are widely cultivated. **1959** Carleton *Index Herb. Plants* 41, *Elephant Ear:* Begonia rex. **1976** Bailey–Bailey *Hortus Third* 143, *[Begonia] albo-coccinea. . . Elephant's-ear B.*

2 also *elephant('s)-ear plant:* Any of several large-leaved plants of the family Araceae, but esp the caladiums and taro (usu *Colocasia esculenta*): see quots.

1909 Doubleday *Amer. Flower Garden* 270, Certainly they [=cannas] shall not be placed in a circular bed, with or without "elephants' ears" that so frequently accompany them. *Ibid* 275, *Elephant's Ear. . .* Massive foliage heart-shaped, 2½ feet long. **1965** Neal *Gardens HI* 159, The name "elephants ear," given . . to taro, seems more suitable for large-leaved species of *Alocasia* and *Xanthosoma.* **1967** *DARE* (Qu. S26e) Inf **OR**4, Hawaiian primrose or elephant ear—because of [its] huge leaf. **1970** Anderson *TX Folk Med.* 87, Warts—Rub the warts with the juice of the elephant-ear plant. **1972** Brown *Wildflowers LA* 8, Elephant's-ear. . . Does not produce tubers, but ropelike stolons several feet long. A widespread introduction which has become a pest. **1976** Bailey–Bailey *Hortus Third* 1244, Elephant's-ear: *Caladium, Colocasia, Enterolobium cyclocarpum.* Elephant's-ear plant: *Alocasia, Colocasia.* **1979** *Burpee Seeds* 70, Elephant's Ear. . . Plants produce extremely large, broad, heart-shaped green leaves. **1982** Perry–Hay *Field Guide Plants* 98, *Colocasia esculenta. . .* Elephant's ear. . . *Leaves:* arise from base, large and shaped like the ears of an African elephant. *Ibid* 112, *Caladium bicolor.* Elephant's ear. . . *Leaves:* . . usually arrow-shaped or triangular.

3 A large ornamental shade tree *(Enterolobium cyclocarpum).* [See quot 1929]

1929 Neal *Honolulu Gardens* 122, *Elephant's ear. . .* Its large size and also the somewhat rough texture of the gray bark suggest an elephant. But the cause of the popular name is the dark-brown, shining pod, which is circular and flat. **1965** Neal *Gardens HI* 399, The elephants ear is a broad-canopied tree. **1976** Bailey–Bailey *Hortus Third* 425, *Elephant's-ear.* To 100 ft. or more, with broad spreading crown.

4 =velvetleaf.

1967–69 *DARE* (Qu. S21, . . *Other weeds* . . *that are a trouble in gardens and fields*) Inf **IL**7, Elephant's ears; **IL**44, Velvetweed, stinkweed, elephant's ears, buttonweed—all names for same plant—big leaves that look like elephant's ears and are velvety; small button-like seeds.

5 The rhubarb plant.

1968 *DARE* (Qu. I30) Inf **NY**79, Elephant ears.

6 pl: A **false morel** (here: *Gyromitra* spp) or a similar fungus; see quots.

1968–69 *DARE* (Qu. S19, *Mushrooms that grow out like brackets from the sides of trees*) Inf **CA**60, Elephant's ear—in Ohio; **IN**26, **IA**27, **MO**27, Elephant ears; **IL**110, Elephant ears or deerhead; **IA**29, Elephant ears or beefsteak—in clusters [and are] edible. **1985** Weber-Smith *Field Guide S. Mushrooms* 29, *Gyromitra fastigata. . . Elephant Ears. . .* Early reports on this species . . stated it was tender and well flavored; it was sold in markets in St. Louis around the turn of the century. **1985** Ammirati et al. *Poisonous Mushrooms* 122, *Gyromitra esculenta. . . Common names. . .* Elephant ears. . . The rounded shape and brain-like configuration of the cap, and the more or less cylindrical stalk with a single channel are good field characteristics.

7 An unidentified fish.

1968 *DARE* (Qu. P4, *Saltwater fish that are not good to eat*) Inf **NJ**50, Elephant's ears.

8 A **freshwater clam,** such as *Elliptio crassidens.*

1938 FWP *Guide IA* 327, The fisherman's haul usually contained a wide assortment of shells: the niggerhead, . . commanded the highest price; others, all salable, were the warty black, yellow back, mucket, washboard, pocketbook, pig toe, maple leaf, and elephant's ear. **1941** Writers' Program *Guide AR* 207 **neAR,** Dredging the White River and its tributaries for fresh-water mussles used for button making affords farmers a part-time occupation. . . Payment, made by the ton, varies according to the type of shell, "grandmaws," "pocketbooks," and "cucumbers" bringing less than "elephant ears" and "niggerheads." **1979** *WI Week-End* Apr 6, Meanwhile such shellfish as the elephant's ear . . go right on living . . in the quiet waterways of the Mississippi. **1982** U.S. Fish & Wildlife Serv. *Fresh-Water Mussels,* [Poster:] *Elephant Ear. . . Elliptio crassidens. . .* Shell brown or black, heavy, moderately compressed.

9 also *elephant track:* A round, swirled, sugar-glazed pastry.

1967–68 *DARE* (Qu. H32, . . *Fancy rolls and pastries*) Infs **CA**15, **KS**7, **WI**71, Elephant ears; **MN**42, Elephant track—big, thin, has a sugar coating. **1968** *DARE* FW Addit **swOH,** [In bakery:] Elephant ears—crisp Danish pastry. **1985** *Capital Times* (Madison WI) 18 July 23/1, Come one, come all, and sample the Brobdingnagian assortment of comestibles (food, that is) at the Dane County Fair. It's hard to go wrong with elephant ears and cotton candy. **1986** *DARE* File **IL, IN,** *Elephant Ears:* large oil-fried sheet of dough, usually sprinkled with confectioners sugar.

10 See quot.

1967 *DARE* FW Addit **swOR,** Elephant ears—maple bars.

11 A pickle.

1968 *DARE* (Qu. H56, . . *Different kinds of pickles*) Inf **MI**108, Elephant ears—from ripe cucumbers.

12 See quot.

1988 *DARE* File **csWI** (as of 1930s), Elephant ears were what we called big floppy leaves that were the only sign of life on old tulips that were not going to bloom. "No flowers, no buds, just elephant ears."

elephant's-ear plant See **elephant's ear 2**

elephant's head n Also *elephant head*

A western **lousewort,** esp *Pedicularis groenlandica* but also *P. attollens,* with flowers resembling miniature elephants' heads. The former is also called **butterfly tongue, elephant flower, elephant's trunk 2, fernleaf, Indian warrior, little elephants, pink ~;** the latter is also called **elephant snout**

1897 Parsons *Wild Flowers CA* 252, Elephants' Heads. *Pedicularis groenlandica. . .* Its tall pink spikes attract one . . by the wonderful resemblance of their blossoms to many small elephants' heads. **1915** (1926) Armstrong-Thornber *Western Wild Flowers* 504, Elephants' Heads. . . A handsome plant, with quaint flowers. **1940** Writers' Program *Guide NV* 161, Here [on Ruby Mt.] a trail starts zigzagging upward among increasingly beautiful beds of blue elephant's head. **1949** Peattie *Cascades* 256 **Pacific NW,** The elephant's head lousewort, Pedicularis surrecta, is sure to catch your eye. It grows in moist soil and boggy places and each of its red-purple blossoms is shaped just like an elephant's head—large ears, long trunk and all. **1959** Martin *Gunbarrel* 159 **WY,** Purple elephant-heads, and deep pink wild roses added to the color harmony. **1961** Douglas *My Wilderness* 20 **CO,** Elephant heads will not have passed entirely by mid-September. **1967** *DARE* Wildfl QR Inf **CO**7, Little elephant—Scrophulariaceae; Elephant head—same as little elephant: scrophulariaceae. **1973** Hitchcock-Cronquist *Flora Pacific NW* 432, Elephant's head. . . *P. groenlandica. . .* Little elephant's head. . . *P. attollens.*

elephant snout n Cf **elephant's trunk 2**

An **elephant's head** (here: *Pedicularis attollens*).

1925 Jepson *Manual Plants CA* 949, *P[edicularis] attollens. . . Elephant Snouts. . .* Upper lip . . produced into an abruptly and rather closely upturned slender proboscis. . . Sierra Nevada; White Mts., San Bernardino Mts.

elephant steps n

A children's game: =**giant steps.**

1950 *WELS (Games)* 1 Inf, **cwWI,** Red light, elephant steps.

elephant's trunk n

1 A **unicorn plant** (here: *Proboscidea louisianica*).

1884 Miller *Dict. Engl. Names of Plants* 217/2, *Martynia proboscidea.* Elephant's-trunk, Unicorn plant. **1911** *Century Dict. Suppl.* np, *Elephant's-trunk. . .* The unicorn-plant. **1974** (1977) Coon *Useful Plants* 186, Elephant's trunk. . . grows south from Delaware, and over into the Southwest, the pod-like fruit being boiled and eaten or used in pickling.

2 also *elephant trunk:* Any of several western **louseworts.** Cf **elephant's head**

1934 Haskin *Wild Flowers Pacific Coast* 331, *Pedicularis racemosa. . .* The name . . Elephant's trunk refers to the peculiar and uncommon shape of the flowers. . . *Pedicularis contorta* . . [is] also sometimes called elephant's trunk. **1937** U.S. Forest Serv. *Range Plant Hdbk.* W145, Elephant-trunk. . . Most of the common names applied to this plant allude to the resemblance of the reddish or purplish flowers to the head of an elephant, . . its prolonged and strongly curved beak being the trunk.

3 A treebine (here: *Cissus sicyoides*).

1911 *Century Dict. Suppl.* np, *Elephant's trunk. . .* The bastard bryony or china-root, *Cissus sicyoides.*

elephant teeth n pl *joc*

Buck teeth.

1969 *DARE* (Qu. X12) Inf **IL**60, Elephant teeth.

elephant track See **elephant's ear 9**

elephant tree n

A deciduous gray-barked shrub or small tree *(Bursera microphylla)* native to the Desert Southwest. Also called **dye bark, torote**

1925 Jepson *Manual Plants CA* 607, Elephant tree. Low round-headed tree with very thick stems and branches, 4 to 10 ft. high. **1941** Jaeger *Wildflowers* 142, Elephant tree, torote, dye bark. . . Common on the dry hillsides of Sonora, Baja Calif., and southern Ariz. A few elephant-tree colonies are known in California from the . . Colorado Desert. **1953** *AmSp* 28.101 **SW,** *Copal* (Mex. Sp. fr. Nahuatl *copalli*). *Torote* or elephant tree *(Bursera microphylla),* 1944 Benson & Darrow p. 216. Unidentified, 1938 Watson pp. 108, 111. **1965** Teale *Wandering Through Winter* 16, With silvery bark, contorted branches and swollen lower trunks, elephant trees . . lifted above a jumble of rocks. **1981** Benson-Darrow *Trees SW Deserts* 133, Its stout, sharply tapering trunk and branches have given rise to the name elephant tree.

elephant trunk See **elephant's trunk 2**

elephant tusks n [See quot]

A **unicorn plant** (here: *Proboscidea altheaefolia*).

1941 Jaeger *Wildflowers* 248, *Elephant-tusks. . .* The fruit is a woody pod, ending in two curved, prong-like appendages. **1985** Dodge *Flowers SW Deserts* 98, Elephant-Tusks. . . *Proboscidea parviflora . . Proboscidea altheaefolia.*

elephant walk n

=**wheelbarrow race.**

1966 *DARE* (Qu. EE33, *Other outdoor games*) Inf **NH**11, Elephant walk—one person wraps [his] legs around another's waist and bends over. Then they walk together.

elephant weed See **elephant flower**

elephant year n

1958 *Hench Coll.* **cVA** [Black], Elephant year—a bad-luck year (Negro folklore). . . Her cook, old Mathilda (of Charlottesville), in speaking about the fact that so-and-so's child was to be born . . lamented, "Oh, that's too bad. This is elephant year." No explanation was given or asked for.

elepio See **elepaio**

elevate v

To raise grain, hay, produce, etc into a storage area by means of an elevator.

1860 *Rep. Thos. S. Blackwell, Grand Trunk Railway* 9 *(DA),* The most complete appliances for storing, elevating, and transhipping produce has been provided. **1966** *DARE* Tape **ME9**, And they'll elevate 'em right outa the truck into another elevator which will take them somewhere into the potato house. **1968** *DARE* (Qu. L15, *When you are putting hay into a building for storage . . you are* ______) Infs **NY**107, **WI**63, Elevating it (in).

elevator apartment n **esp NYC** Cf **walk-up**

A dwelling in a building with an elevator.

1912 *NY Times* (NY) 21 July 6/6, [Advt:] High-class elevator apartment; electric light; parlor suite, three rooms. *Ibid* 1 Sept sec 9 1/6, [Advt:] Modern elevator apartment[,] 4 rooms, bath. **1958** Golden *For 2¢ Plain* 43 **NYC,** Thus did the Negro wind up with some of the most comfortable, steam-heated, elevator apartments in the big city, with a view of the Atlantic fleet lying at anchor, and the majestic Palisades. **1979** *DARE* File **NYC**, "I have an elevator apartment in Manhattan." "What's an elevator apartment?" "That's an apartment serviced by an elevator so you don't have to walk up and down stairs."

elevator ticket n

A nonexistent item used as the basis of a practical joke.

1968–70 *DARE* (Qu. HH14) Infs **PA**133, **TX**101, Elevator ticket(s); **TX**61, Sell someone elevator tickets.

eleven adj Usu |i'lɛvən, ə-|; also |'lɛvən, -n̩, -m̩|; occas **chiefly Sth, S Midl** |'lɛbən, -n̩, -m̩| Pronc-spp *(e)leb'm, eleving, lebem, leben, lebun*

Std sense, var forms.

1862 (1864) Browne *Artemus Ward Book* 170, Turned in at 15 minits parst eleving. **1889** *MLN* 4.208 **TN**, *'Leven. . .* Besides omitting the *e,* the *v* is sometimes changed to *b* by ignorant people, thus making the word become *'leben.* **1893** Shands *MS Speech, Lebenty-lebem. . .* Negro pronunciation for *eleventy-eleven.* **1899** (1912) Green *VA Folk-Speech* 259, *Leben. . .* For *eleven.* "He has been gone leben days." **1915** *DN* 4.184 **swVA,** *Leben.* Short for *eleven.* **1922** Gonzales *Black Border* 255 **sSC, GA coasts** [Gullah], A 'leben yeahs ole gal. **1927** Shewmake *Engl. Pronc. VA* 33, *Seven, eleven,* often become . . *seb'm, eleb'm* (or *leb'm*). **1936** *AmSp* 11.236 **eTX,** In . . *eleven* . . the [v] > [b] in careless or illiterate speech, the following vowel is elided, making the [n] syllabic, and then [n̩] > [m̩] by assimilation to [b]: ['lɛbm̩]. **1939** *LANE* Map 58, Forms of the type of [ilɛvən] presumably represent slow or careful pronunciations. In rapid utterance the first syllable and the vowel [ə] of the third syllable often disappear, in which case the final nasal may or may not be syllabic. **1942** Hall *Smoky Mt. Speech* 96 **wNC, eTN,** *Eleven* . . [(ə)'lɛbm̩] . . said to be fairly common, but not heard. **1953** Brewer *Word Brazos* 25 **eTX** [Black], 'Twas attuh de lebun o'clock servus. **c1960** *Wilson Coll.* **csKY,** Eleven. ['lɛvn̩] or ['lɛvm̩] or ['lɛbm̩] are all common. **1966** *DARE* Tape **FL**47, Eleven [ə'lɛbm̩]. **1976** Allen *LAUM* 3.318 (as of c1950), 10 informants, [əlɛbm̩]. An apparent geographic pattern with a concentration of the [bm] in eastern Nebraska is probably illusory. . . There is, however, some evidence for social differentiation, as in *seven, eleven,* and *seventy* 62% of the speakers with the [bm] cluster are in Type I [=old, with little educ] and only 38% in Type II [=mid-aged, with approx hs educ], with none at all in Type III [=mid-aged, with coll educ].

eleven-card n

A card game: =**cooncan.**

1935 Hurston *Mules & Men* 37 **FL,** The eleven-card layers [sic]. [Footnote:] Coon-can players. A two-handed card game popular among Southern Negroes.

eleven-fifteen n [Prob *eleven* number of cards usu dealt + *fifteen* number of cards dealt in three-pack canasta]

Canasta.

1969 *DARE* (Qu. DD35, . . *Favorite card games*) Inf **IL**40A, Canasta. Some call it eleven-fifteen.

eleventh month See **first month**

eleventy-eleven adj Also *eleventeen*

Many; an indefinitely large number.

1893 Shands *MS Speech, Lebenty-lebem. . .* Negro pronunciation for *eleventy-eleven,* an expression for an indefinitely great number. **1942** Berrey–Van den Bark *Amer. Slang* 18.6, *Indefinite number.* Eleventeen. **1985** *DARE* File **cwCA** (as of 1950s), When my grandfather (from Nebraska) used to tell stories, he would say there were ['lɛbm̩ti'lɛbm̩] horses, or giants, or whatever. We just knew that meant there were plenty.

eleven-up n

A children's game; see quot 1953.

1953 Brewster *Amer. Nonsinging Games* 179 **IN,** *Eleven Up. . .* Two to four players. . . make a stack of their hands. . . The bottom hand is pulled out and placed on top, and this is done eleven times. Then the hands are withdrawn one at a time from the top, and the owner of the bottom one is asked, "Will you take yes or no?" When he has made his choice, he is asked three questions. He must answer these with "yes" if he chose "yes," with "no" if he chose "no." The questions are made as humorous or embarrassing as possible. **1985** *NADS Letters, Eleven-up* —Still played in upper peninsula Michigan.

elever See **elleber**

eleving See **eleven**

elf See **elf owl 1**

elfedritsch, elfetrich See **elbedritsch**

elf-feather n

A **false lily of the valley** (here: *Maianthemum canadense*).

1949 Moldenke *Amer. Wild Flowers* 333, One of the precious joys of springtime . . is . . *elf-feather.*

elfin forest n [*elfin* diminutive, fairy-like] **Pacific**

A thicket.

1955 U.S. Arctic Info. Center *Gloss., Elfin forest.* Scrub forest. **1967** *DARE* (Qu. C28, *A place where underbrush, weeds, vines and small trees grow together so that it's nearly impossible to get through*) Inf **CA**4, Elfin forest. **1968** *DARE* Tape **CA**69, [Reading from a Sierra Club bulletin:] One of California's most attractive features is its elfin forest—dwarf trees and shrubs, all cut down.

elfin spur n

=**cranefly orchid.**

1933 Small *Manual SE Flora* 387, *Tipularia . . discolor. . .* Elfin-spur. **1950** Correll *Native Orchids* 277, Flowers . . producing a long slender spur at the base. . . Elfin-spur. **1976** Bailey–Bailey *Hortus Third* 1116.

elf owl n

1 also *elf:* A very small insectivorous owl *(Micropallas whitneyi)* native to the Desert Southwest.

1887 Ridgway *N. Amer. Birds* 267, Southwestern United States (southern Arizona and southeastern California . . *Elf Owl*). **1903** (1950) Austin *Land of Little Rain* 14 **Desert SW,** The chief witnesses of their presence near the spring are the elf owls. Those burrow-haunting, speckled fluffs of greediness begin a twilight flitting toward the spring, feeding as they go on grasshoppers, lizards, and small, swift creatures. **1928** Bailey *Birds NM* 326, Elf Owl. . . Major Bendire has found that the Elfs are attracted by a camp fire and its flying insects. **1945** *Natl. Geogr. Mag.* Apr 477 **swAZ,** No bigger than a sparrow, the *Elf Owl* snatches nectar-hunting insects as they are attracted to the yellow blossoms of a century plant. **1961** Douglas *My Wilderness* 98 **AZ,** Two elf owls (who average five inches in length) were calling—perhaps from the eaves of the old lodge, perhaps from a saguaro. **1968** *DARE* (Qu. Q2, *Other kinds of owls*) Inf **CA**78, Elf owl—the small desert owl—the size of a saltshaker.

2 =**burrowing owl.**

1968 *DARE* (Qu. Q2, *Other kinds of owls*) Inf **MN**38, Elf owl—[builds] a nest in the ground.

‡elf-toe n [From common picturing of elves as wearing long, pointed shoes]

A man's sharp-toed shoe.

1969 *DARE* (Qu. W42a) Inf **NY**205, Elf-toes.

elgible See **eligible**

eliber See **elleber**

eligible adj Usu |'ɛləǰəbəl|; for addit varr see quots Pronc-sp *elgible*

A Forms.

1934–44 in 1944 *ADD* **WV,** Elgible. **1942** Hall *Smoky Mt. Speech* 20 **wNC, eTN,** *Eligible* ['æljɪbəl] (once). **1988** *DARE* File **VT** (as of 1953), I heard *eligible* pronounced [ɛˈlɛjəbḷ] by a young woman speaking of eligible men.

B Sense.

Eager for marriage.

1966–68 *DARE* (Qu. AA4a, . . *A man who is very eager to get married*) Inf **VA**2, Eligible; (Qu. AA4b, . . *A woman*) Inf **PA**29, Eligible; **FL**8, She's eligible [laughter].

elimination n

=**bombardment 1.**

1969 *DARE* (Qu. EE33, . . *Other outdoor games*) Inf **IL**97, Elimination—also called bombardment.

Elizabeth club n [See quot 1985] Cf **Eleanor club**

See quots.

1960 Wentworth–Flexner *Slang* 172, *Elizabeth club*—An informal union or society of Negro household maids, cooks, and cleaning women. *It is doubtful if there has ever existed such an organization, but Southern housewives claim Elizabeth clubs meet on the members' afternoons off from work to exchange gossip about their employers, fix salary rates, and the like. Because Elizabeth is considered a typical name.* **1985** *DARE* File, [Letter from Stuart B. Flexner:] As far as I know, there is no specific person at all. . . *Elizabeth* was one of the most common black female given names . . from 1880 to 1920. Thus *Elizabeth* . . became a general word referring to almost any black woman. . . *Elizabeth Club* was just used to mean an informal club of black servants . . , most of whom had the same specific afternoon off each week and thus . . got together for a chat . . and probably devoted much of the conversation to . . working conditions, wages, the idiosyncrasies of their employers, etc.

elk n[1] See **elk tree**

elk n[2] See **yolk**

elk bark n

A **magnolia** (here: *Magnolia macrophylla*).

1830 Rafinesque *Med. Flora* 31, *Magnolia macrophylla*. . . Elk-bark. . . It was supposed that this tree was confined to a few districts of North Carolina, but it extends over the Allegheny and Cumberland mountains of Virginia, Kentucky, Tennessee, and Alabama. **1876** Hobbs *Bot. Hdbk.* 34, Elk bark, Magnolia, Magnolia macrophylla. **1911** *Century Dict.* 1879, Elk bark. **1960** Vines *Trees SW* 282, Vernacular names are . . Big-bloom Cucumber-tree, Silver-leaf, and Elk-bark.

elk-bird n

=**Canada jay.**

1917 *Wilson Bulletin* 29.2.82, I heard camp-bird, camp-robber, elk-bird, and tallow-bird in western Washington.

elk clover n

A **spikenard** (here: *Aralia californica*).

1925 Jepson *Manual Plants CA* 691, *A[ralia] californica*. . . *Elk clover*. . . Shaded cañons in moist spots and along living mountain streams.

elk-face n

1916 *DN* 4.322 **KS,** *Elk-face*. . . Physiognomy in which the cheek furrows run nearly parallel with the nose.

elk grass n [See quots 1963, 1976]

=**squaw grass.**

1925 Jepson *Manual Plants CA* 210, *X[erophyllum] tenax*. . . Elk Grass. Fire-Lily. **1949** Peattie *Cascades* 248 **Pacific NW,** It . . has the tongue-twisting name of Xerophyllum tenax. In days gone by the Indians used its tough leaves in making their baskets, which accounts for its common names of squaw grass and Indian basket-grass. It is so conspicuous and attractive that it has a number of other popular names, some of which are bear-grass, elk-grass, pine lily, and mountain lily. **1950** FWP *Guide ID* 71, Called variously soap grass, squaw grass, and elk grass, the gorgeous plant, more commonly known as bear grass, is a thorough rebuke to the unimaginativeness of the human mind. **1963** Craighead *Rocky Mt. Wildflowers* 31, *Beargrass*. . . *Other names* . . Bearlily, Elkgrass. [*Ibid* 32, The flowers, flowering stalks, and tender seed pods are avidly eaten by small rodents and game animals, especially elk.] **1976** Bruce *How to Grow Wildflowers* 173, There is a larger western species, *Xerophyllum tenax,* which is called Elkgrass, so grasslike are its leaves.

elkhorn n

1 =**vanilla leaf.**

1920 *DN* 5.81 **WA,** *Elkhorn*. . . Achlys leaves. **1941** *Torreya* 41.48 **WA,** Angel-leaves, elkhorn, smell-leaves.

2 A **club moss.** Cf **elk moss**

1958 McCulloch *Woods Words* 57 **Pacific NW,** *Elkhorn*—A low branchy moss-like plant found in the fir woods, sometimes used as Christmas greens.

3 A **farewell-to-spring** (here: *Clarkia pulchella*).

1973 Hitchcock–Cronquist *Flora Pacific NW* 305, Elkhorns c[larkia]. . . *C. pulchella.*

elkhorn cactus n [From the configuration of its branches] Cf **buckhorn cholla**

A **prickly pear.**

1940 Fergusson *Our Southwest* 95, The fuzzy nap on the elkhorn cactus turns out to be vicious spines.

elk moss n Cf **elkhorn 2**

A **club moss** (here: *Lycopodium clavatum*).

1961 Peck *Manual OR* 58, *L. clavatum*. . . *Ground- or Running-pine. Elk Moss*. . . Nearly cosmopolitan. **1973** Hitchcock–Cronquist *Flora Pacific NW* 40, Elk-moss; ground- or running-pine; stag's-horn moss.

elkslip n [Perh by analogy with **cowslip**]

A **marsh marigold** (here: *Caltha leptosepala*).

1898 *Jrl. Amer. Folkl.* 11.221, *Caltha leptosepala* . . elk slip, Union Pass, Wyo. . . Greedily eaten by elk. **1953** Nelson *Plants Rocky Mt. Park* 70, *White marsh-marigold* or *elkslip*. . . white inside, sometimes tinged with bluish outside. **1973** Hitchcock–Cronquist *Flora Pacific NW* 128.

elk thistle n [See quot 1963]

A western thistle *(Cirsium foliosum)*.

1936 McDougall–Baggley *Plants of Yellowstone* 136, *Elk thistle* . . has historical interest since . . it is said that when Truman Everts was lost in this region for more than a month in 1870, this plant . . served to keep him from starving. **1963** Craighead *Rocky Mt. Wildflowers* 206, Elk thistle is a favorite early summer food of elk and black and grizzly bears. **1973** Hitchcock–Cronquist *Flora Pacific NW* 505.

elktoe n [From its shape]

A **freshwater clam** (here: *Alasmidonta marginata*).

1979 *WI Week-End* Apr 6, Meanwhile such shellfish as . . elk toes . . go right on living . . in the quiet waterways of the Mississippi. **1982** U.S. Fish & Wildlife Serv. *Fresh-Water Mussels,* [Wall chart:] Elktoe . . *Alasmidonta marginata.*

elk tree n Also *elk (wood)* [See quot 1828 Rafinesque]

=**sourwood.**

1828 Rafinesque *Med. Flora* 41, *Andromeda arborea*. . . *Vulgar Names* . . Elk Tree, Elk Wood [etc]. [*Ibid* 42, The elk and deer eat those leaves, and even cattle like them.] **1828** (1934) Smith *Travels* 61, The banks [of the Missouri River], generally low, are timbered with ash, cottonwood, elk, sycamore, willow, and where the ground is sufficiently dry, some oak. **1876** Hobbs *Bot. Hdbk.* 34, Elk tree, Sorrel tree, Andromeda arborea. Elk wood. **1960** Vines *Trees SW* 812, Sour-wood was first cultivated in 1747. . . Vernacular names are Sorrel-tree, Sour-gum, Elk-tree, and Titi.

elk weed n [See quot 1963] **West**

=**green gentian,** usu *Frasera speciosa.*

1961 Douglas *My Wilderness* 17 **CO,** Green gentian or elk weed *(Swertia radicata)* with broad basal leaves every other year shows a stalk of creamy white flowers several feet high. **1963** Craighead *Rocky Mt. Wildflowers* 144, Green Gentian *Frasera speciosa*. . . Other names . . Elkweed. . . Elk and cattle . . eat it along with other spring plants. **1970** Correll *Plants TX* 1209, *Swertia*. . . Green Gentian. Elkweed. **1974** (1977) Coon *Useful Plants* 144, *Frasera speciosa*—Elkweed. . . In the higher elevations of the West, this perennial is noted for its greenish-purple spotted flowers.

elkwood n

1 Either the **mountain maple** or the **striped maple.**

1807 (1923) Pursh *Jrl. Bot. Excursion* 27 **nePA,** Acer montanum, very common throughout these woods, called Elkwood. **1834** *S. Lit. Messenger* 1.97/2 **sMD, nVA,** The underwood is mostly streaked maple or elkwood . . *Acer Striatum.* **1967** Borland *Hill Country* 160 **nwCT,** Elkwood is more generally known as mountain maple, but it shows that elk once were among the native animals even this far east.

2 A **magnolia,** esp *Magnolia tripetala.*

1814 Pursh *Flora Americae* 2.381, *Magnolia tripetala* . . is generally known by the name of *Umbrella-tree;* in the mountains they call it *Elk-wood.* **1830** Rafinesque *Med. Flora* 2.32, The genus *Magnolia* . . includes about ten American species. . . They are promiscuously called Laurels, Beaver-wood, Elk-wood, Sweet Bay [etc]. **1876** Hobbs *Bot. Hdbk.* 34, Elk wood, Magnolia, Magnolia macrophylla. **1880** *Harper's New Mth. Mag.* July 182/2 **neWV,** Vines and elk-wood cover both sides from the airy summits to the rushing brown water below. **1901** Mohr *Plant Life AL* 506, *Magnolia tripetala. . . Elkwood. Umbrella Tree.* . . Carolinian and Louisianian areas. Southeastern Pennsylvania, south along the mountains to Georgia and northeastern Mississippi. **1930** OK Univ. Biol. Surv. *Pub.* 2.62, *Magnolia acuminata.* . . Magnolia. Elk-wood. Cucumber Tree. **1960** Vines *Trees SW* 283, *Magnolia tripetala.* . . Also known under the names of Umbrella-tree, Cucumber-tree, and Elkwood. **1976** Bruce *How to Grow Wildflowers* 153, A widespread species in [sic] *M. tripetala,* called usually Umbrella Tree or Elkwood.

3 See **elk tree.**

ell n[1] Also sp *L* [Perh folk-etym, taking the building to be L-shaped; but cf *OED ell* sb.[2] "? var. of *ele,* aisle," suggesting Lat *ala* wing, as the ult source]

1 An extension, usu at right angles, to a house or other building. **widespread, but most freq NEast, least freq West**

1773 in 1887 Boston Registry Dept. *Records* 18.198, A Major part of the Selectmen of said Town . . [have] laid out and Established a New Street . . beginning at the North Easterly Corner of the Brick Tenement, (or Ell, so called) belonging to the Heirs of Mr. Meriam Tyler. **1883** *Harper's New Mth. Mag.* Feb 358/2 **MA,** An L of the house where she was born is still standing. **1892** Howells *Quality of Mercy* 368 **MA,** Matt could see a light in the ell-chamber. **1907** *DN* 3.187 **seNH,** *Ell-part.* . . "She's out in the ell-part." **1911** Wharton *Ethan Frome* 22 **wMA,** What is known in New England as the "L": that long deep-roofed adjunct usually built at right angles to the main house, and connecting it, by way of store-rooms and tool-house, with the wood-shed and cow-barn. **1926** *DN* 5.386 **ME,** *Ell-part.* **1941** *LANE* Map 352 **NEng,** The *ell* is commonly defined as a part or wing of a house, joined to the main structure either at an angle so as to form an L (whence the name) or as a straight continuation in the rear. It is described as "jutting out from the house" . . as built on at the gable or eaves . . as a "smaller part" or "lesser wing" of the house . . as a narrow rear extension used for storage . . as a small one-storied addition containing several rooms . . or as the entire back part of the house. **c1960** *Wilson Coll.* **csKY,** *Ell.* . . A part built on to a main house. Sometimes written *L.* **1965–70** *DARE* (Qu. D16) 195 Infs, **widespread, but most freq NEast, least freq West,** Ell; **MA**5, 68, 74, **MI**81, **SC**34, 51, Ell part. [Of all Infs responding to the question, 70% were old; of those giving these responses, 80% were old.] **1966** *Bar Harbor Times* (ME) 9 June 4/6, The building is a log cabin and very well built. . . If you don't feel like dancing, there's the ell, which houses the refreshment stands, benches and chairs and a fireplace. **1966–68** *DARE* Tape **AL**3, A five-room house with a what you call ell—it was in a L shape; **AL**4, When I came up we had a ell-type house, they called it. We had a kitchen, and the dining room was all together; and then we had the bedrooms: one for the boys and one for the girls and one for the dad and mother; **CT**3, They could still live in the ell of the house. **1973** Allen *LAUM* 1.179 (as of c1950), 1 inf, **swIA,** Ell—an attached shed.

2 also *kitchen ell;* By ext: a kitchen.

1941 *LANE* Map 352, *Ell* and *porch* are frequently used in a special sense. Since in most New England farm houses the kitchen . . is situated in the rear of the house, and often represents a later addition to the original building, the terms denoting such an addition have come to be used by a number of informants as more or less interchangeable equivalents of *kitchen.* Thus the *ell* is sometimes defined simply as a kitchen [by 6 infs] or as an open-air kitchen attached to the house [by 1 inf]. **1968** *DARE* (Qu. D16, . . *Parts added on to the main part of a house*) Infs **NJ**21, **WV**5, Kitchen ell; **CT**7, Kitchen ell—old farmhouses had woodsheds which were changed into kitchens; attached to house.

3 An L-shaped room.

1979 *Capital Times* (Madison WI) 27 Apr L/2, [Advt:] Excellent family kitchen, carpeted living room and dining "L." *Ibid,* Carpeted living room and formal dining "L."

4 An L-shaped tear in cloth.

1966–70 *DARE* (Qu. W27, *A three-cornered tear in a piece of clothing from catching it on something sharp*) Infs **AR**51, **LA**2, **NC**22, An ell; **MA**126, An ell tear.

ell n[2] Also sp *L* *euphem* Cf *DS* CC9

Hell.

1942 Berrey–Van den Bark *Amer. Slang* 330.3, *Hell.* Blazes, . . hot place, Jericho, L. **1950** *WELS (Weakened substitutes for 'hell': "What the ______.")* 3 Infs, **WI,** Ell.

ell and yard See **ellenyard**

elleber n Also sp *elever, eliber* [Alter of *hellebore*]

=**false hellebore 1.**

1894 *Jrl. Amer. Folkl.* 7.102, *Veratrum,* sp., branch eliber, Banner Elk, N.C. . . Equivalent to branch hellebore, *i.e.,* the hellebore which grows along the brooks or "branches." **1898** *Ibid* 11.282, *Veratrum viride* . . elever [Footnote: A corruption of hellebore], Bristol, Burlington, and Plymouth Co.'s, Conn. **1941** Writers' Program *Guide WV* 357, Along the course of Red Lick Run and in other moist spots grows the deep-rooted, spiral inflorescence of the bright green American hellebore, which the natives call "elleber". **1952** Strausbaugh–Core *Flora WV* 226, *V[eratrum] viride.* . . Called Elleber by mountain-folk, whence the names of topographical features such as Elleber Ridge and Elleber Run (Pocahontas County).

ellenyard n Also, by folk-etym, *ell and yard* [*ellen* var of *ell* measure of length; *OED ell-yard* (at *ell* sb.[1] 5)→c1450; cf *OED, SND ellwand*] **Sth, S Midl** Cf **hellinyear**

The belt in the constellation Orion.

1891 Harris *Balaam* 221 **GA,** The ell an' yard are a-makin' the'r disappearance. **1899** (1912) Green *VA Folk-Speech* 164, *Ellen-yard.* . . The yard-stick. The three stars in the belt of Orion. **1928** Chapman *Happy Mt.* 232 **seTN,** Up there now was the Hunter, chasing the Seven Sisters; and the Lost Ell 'n' Yard were hunting for the morning. **1952** Brown *NC Folkl.* 1.536 **c,eNC,** *Ell and yard.* . . The three stars in the belt of Orion. **c1960** *Wilson Coll.* **csKY,** *Ell and yard* or *Ellen Yard*—the three stars in Orion's girdle. This was common at Fidelity as far back as I can remember.

ell-over See **hail-over**

ellum See **elm**

ellwhop, ellwife, ellwop See **alewife**

ellyment See **element**

elm n Usu |ɛlm|; also **widespread but somewhat more freq Sth, S Midl** *esp freq among men and among rural Infs, somewhat old-fash* |'ɛləm|; occas |ɛəm|; for addit varr see quots Pronc-spp *el(l)um*

A Forms.

1858 (1892) Holmes *One Hoss Shay* 17 **NEng,** The hubs of logs from the "Settler's ellum,"—/ Last of its timber,—they couldn't sell em. **1891** *DN* 1.160 **cNY,** The introduction of a full vowel under the influence of *l* or *r* occurs occasionally. Examples . . [ɛləm] for *'elm.'* **1903** *DN* 2.312 **seMO,** *Elm.* . . Pronounced ellum. **1905** *DN* 3.58 **eNE,** *Slippery ellum.* **1906** *DN* 3.118 **sIN,** *Elm.* . . Regularly pronounced *ellum.* **1907** *DN* 3.187 **seNH,** *Ellum.* *Ibid* 243 **eME,** *Ellum.* **1908** *DN* 3.308 **eAL, wGA,** *Ellum* . . chiefly in *slippery ellum.* **1912** *DN* 3.590 **wIN,** *Slickery-ellum.* **1915** *DN* 4.178 **swVA,** Elum. **1916** *DN* 4.349, Narbeth, Pa., originally Elm, is said to have changed its name because of this pronunciation [=ɛləm]. . . Not confined to any section [of the country]. **1923** *DN* 5.206 **swMO,** *Ellum.* **1929** Sale *Tree Named John* 11 **MS,** Lawd, how tough a ellum is! **1931** *AmSp* 6.401 **coastal NEng,** After [ɛ], [l] may become the velar [ɫ], or it may vocalize, e.g., [ɛɫm] or [ɛəm] *elm.* **1936** *AmSp* 11.247 **eTX,** The usual pronunciations of . . *elm* . . are . . [ɛəm], [ɛlm] . . and . . ['ɛləm] . . in illiterate speech. **1941** *LANE* Map 243 **NEng,** Pronunciations of the type of [ɛləm] are regarded as older or old-fashioned though still in use by [29 infs]. **c1960** *Wilson Coll.* **csKY,** *Elm* is nearly always ['ɛləm]. **c1967** *Ibid,* Elm [ɛəm]. **1965–70** *DARE* (Qu. T11) 520 Infs, **widespread,** (American, Chinese, etc) elm; 166 Infs, **widespread but somewhat more freq Sth, S Midl,** (American, slippery, etc) Ellum ['ɛləm]; **AR**52, **DE**5, **LA**13, 28, **NY**73, 88, [ɛəm]; **LA**3, 10, [ɛɔm]; **GA**70, **KY**84, [ɛm]; **GA**76, [æm]; (Qu. R30) Inf **NV**5, Ellum beetle; (Qu. CC13a) Inf **KY**59, Ellum stick. [Of all Infs responding to Qu. T11, 38% were comm type 5, 70% old, 31% gs educ or less, 56% male; of those giving the response *ellum,* 55% were comm type 5, 83% old, 62% gs educ or less, 75% male.] **1966–67** *DARE* Tapes **MI**8, **TX**47, Elm ['ɛləm]. **1976** Allen *LAUM* 3.303 (as of c1950), *Elm* appears as [ɛləm] in the speech of four Dakotans.

B Sense.

Also *elm fork:* A saddle. **West**

1933 *AmSp* 8.1.29 **nwTX,** *Stay in your ellum. . .* The best saddles were made of elm wood. *Stay in the old ellum fork. . .* [These expressions] came into vigorous figurative use [as a shout of admonition or encouragement] in any sort of contest, argument, or rivalry. **1937** *DN* 6.618 **wTX,** The next problem is to saddle the pony, or, as the cowboy says, to put on the ellum (elm) and screw it down."

elm flour n *obs* Cf **slippery-elm poultice**

Prob the bark of the **slippery elm.**

1877 Still *Early Recoll.* 200, Poultice applied of yeast, charcoal, and elm-flour.

elm fork See **elm B**

elm peeler n

1 A runty variety of swine. *old-fash* Cf **hazel splitter 1**

1872 IL Dept. Ag. *Trans.* 9.204, Nearly all farmers strive to raise hogs of the best blood. The old fashioned "prairie rooter and elm peeler" are banished from the county. **1901** *Munsey's Mag.* 24.494/1 **ceKY** (as of c1870), In the vernacular of the South, they were razor backs; in that of the Ohio River country they were termed elm peelers. **1914** Whitson *Centennial Hist. Grant Co. IN* 1.91 **neIN,** The swine industry . . has grown from a few long nosed elmpeeler, acorn-gathering ancestors of a century ago when there were no white men in the woods of Grant county, to the sleek, blocky . . breeds of the present day.

2 See quot. Cf **barker 1**

1923 *DN* 5.234 **swWI,** *Elm-peeler. . .* A poor white who peels elm trees for slippery elm, which he sells. "He's no count—just an ellum-peeler."

elpentrecher See **elbedritsch**

el ropo n Also *el ropo stinkadoro* [Quasi-Span alter of **rope** by assoc with Cuban cigars] **chiefly Nth** *joc*

A cigar, esp a cheap or strong one.

c1960 *Wilson Coll.* **csKY,** *Rope. . .* Nickname for a strong cigar. Sometimes *El Ropo.* **1965–70** *DARE* (Qu. DD6a, . . *Nicknames for cigars*) 12 Infs, **chiefly Nth,** El ropo; **CA**46, El ropo stinkadoro; (Qu. DD7) Inf **OH**92, El ropo.

else adj, adv Usu |ɛls|; also |ɛlts|; occas |ɛlst| (cf **acrost, chance, once**) Pronc-spp *elst, e'se*

Std senses, var forms.

1824 in 1956 Eliason *Tarheel Talk* 310 **NC,** Elst. **1899** Chesnutt *Conjure Woman* 141 **NC,** But dis man say he want Becky, er e'se Kunnel Pen'leton could n' hab de race hoss. **1943** *LANE* Map 730 **seVT, cnME,** [ɛlts]. **1963** Edwards *Gravel* 23 **eTN** (as of 1920s), "Let's play something elst," said Hes finally. **1966** *DARE* Tape **FL**32, Just like you would anything elst [ɛlst].

elsehow conj *Gullah* Cf **elseso**

Or else.

1922 Gonzales *Black Border* 224 **sSC, GA coasts** [Gullah], Him is de class-leaduh een my chu'ch, en w'en eeduhso de preachuh on de sukkus, elsehow de locus preechuh, onable to fillfill de pulpit, den B'Cudjo does hol' saa'bis een de chu'ch. [=He is the class leader in my church, and when either the preacher is on the circuit or else the local preacher is unable to fill the pulpit, Brother Cudjo holds the service in the church.]

elseso conj [*else+so*] *Gullah* Cf **either E2, elsehow**

Or else.

1922 Gonzales *Black Border* 239 **sSC, GA coasts** [Gullah], I mos' t'ink 'e bin eeduh de 'Postle Paul, elseso Pollido. *Ibid* 299 [Gullah glossary], *Elseso*—else; unless; either [or].

elseways adv

Otherwise.

1955 Ritchie *Singing Family* 101 **seKY,** Sometimes my head hurts and it [=rubbing it] helps. . . And then it's something to do; I don't move around much elseways.

elst See **else**

el stinko n [Quasi-Span] *joc* Cf **el ropo**

1968–69 *DARE* (Qu. DD6a, . . *Nicknames for cigars*) Inf **PA**209, El stinko; (Qu. DD21b, . . *Words used . . for bad liquor*) Inf **IN**42, El stinko.

eltrot n Also *heltrot*

A **cow parsnip 1** (here: *Heracleum sphondylium*).

1950 Gray–Fernald *Manual of Botany* 1104, *H. Sphondylium* . . Eltrot or Heltrot.

elum See **elm**

elwife, elwop See **alewife**

em pron[1] See **him** pron

em pron[2] See **them**

emancipated ppl adj [Malaprop] See Intro "Language Changes" I.10

Emaciated.

1931–33 *LANE Worksheets* **neCT,** Emancipated [ə'mænsɨpetəd] . . emaciated. [FW says that this was the first, consciously elegant response.] **1967–68** *DARE* (Qu. X52, . . *A person [who had lost weight because of sickness] . . was looking* ______) Inf **IA**4, Emancipated [ɪ'mænsɪ,peɪtɨd]; **LA**40, Emancipated.

Emancipation (Proclamation) Day n *chiefly among Black speakers* Cf **juneteenth, nigger day**

An annual holiday, observed on different dates in different places, commemorating the emancipation of the slaves.

[**1868** Rose *Great Country* 151 **VA,** I was in Richmond on 3rd of April, the anniversary of its fall, which the darkies celebrated as the date of their emancipation.] **1875** *NY Herald* (NY) 13 Dec 2, A new song . . entitled *Emancipation Day.* **1905** *Hartford Courant* 3 Jan. 10 *(DA),* The 42nd anniversary of Emancipation Day was celebrated last evening by the colored people of this city. **1959** Tallman *Dict. Amer. Folkl.* 105, *Emancipation Proclamation Day, August 4,* In the spring of 1880 a group of Negroes from the South who sometimes called themselves the Exodusers founded a settlement in Kansas which they named Nicodemus. . . They built the typical sod houses of the area . . then determined upon a top holiday—August 4, when the whole community would celebrate the Emancipation Proclamation with a gala all-day picnic. **1966–70** *DARE* (Qu. FF16) Inf **AR**55, Niggers used to have Emancipation Day when they all wore yellow; **SC**26, Emancipation Day—January 1, [celebrated by a] parade, with singing [and a] march to the church for a program of speakers; **KY**87, Emancipation Proclamation Day—strictly Black, also called Homecoming: all Blacks of the town come back. [The] day is that one that they found out about the proclamation. [It is observed on] August 8 in Hickman, August 15 in Columbus [Kentucky].

embarcadero n Also *embarcadera* [Span] **chiefly CA**

A wharf, port, or landing place, esp one on a river serving an inland settlement.

1846 Sutter *MS Diary* (Soc. Calif. Pioneers Lib.) 13 Jan. *(DA)* **CA,** Rained, the launcheros did not come so the boat did not leave the embarcadero. **1868** (1871) Browne *Adventures* 57 **swAZ,** Six hundred tons of freight lay at the embarcadera awaiting transportation. **1890** *Outing* Nov 111/2 **CA,** In a slough one sometimes finds the decaying hulk of a schooner that once sailed to forgotten towns, and to deserted river landings, or "embarcaderos," as they were once called. **1910** Hart *Vigilante Girl* 121 **nCA,** "Here we are at the *embarcadero.*" All eyes were turned toward the landing-place. **1934** *CA Hist. Soc. Qrly.* 13.12 **CA** (as of 1849), A "city" had been surveyed at the embarcadero named "Sacramento." **1971** Bright *Word Geog. CA & NV* 102, Embarcadero . . wharf.

embarras n [Fr "obstacle"] *obs* Note: Fr *embarras* may be sg or pl; quots 1811 and 1814 suggest that some English speakers took it as **embarra* sg (by back-formation), or *embarras* sg. Quot 1867 is ambiguous in this respect.

A blockage in a watercourse caused by packed masses of driftwood.

1811 (1817) Bradbury *Travels* 32 **LA,** The navigation had been very difficult for some days, on account of the frequent occurrence of what is termed by the boatmen *embarras.* **1814** Brackenridge *Views of LA* 205, At the distance of every mile or two . . there are *embarras,* or rafts, formed by the collection of trees closely matted, and extending from twenty to thirty yards. *Ibid* 208, Passed an *embarras,* N.E. side, the most difficult since we started. **1867** Smyth *Sailor's Word Book* 276, *Embarras.* An American term for places where the navigation of rivers . . is rendered difficult by the accumulation of drift-wood. **1970** Detro *Generic Terms* 244 **LA,** The generic *embarras* . . was first recorded on the Broutin (1722) map of the Natchitoches area as *Embaras d'arbres.* D'Anville (1732) recorded the place name *Embarras de bois* at the head of the stream now called Bayou Lafourche. *Ibid* 245, *Embarras* was not recorded . . after 1850 and became obsolete.

embarrass v
Std senses, var forms.
1940 in 1944 *ADD* **AR,** *Embarrass* . . ['ɛm]-. **1942** Hall *Smoky Mt. Speech* 25 **wNC, eTN,** [ɑ] was observed [before *r*] . . in . . *embarrassed.*

‡embarrishment n [Pronc-sp for *embarrassment*]
1972 *Atlanta Letters* **cnGA,** Embarrishment.

‡ember stone n [Perh var of *emery stone*]
1968 *DARE* (Qu. L38, *What do you use . . to sharpen tools in the field?*) Inf **MD**15, Ember ['ɛmbə] stone—long rough stone, another name for sharpening stone. You polish blade back and forth.

embroidery n, v Usu |ɛm'brɔɪdəi, -dri, ɪm-|; also |ɪm'brɔdri| Pronc-spp *embr'idery, embroidry, imbrawdry*
A Forms.
1908 (1915) Calhoun *Miss Minerva* 34 **Sth,** She just wanted to know where her embroid'ry scissors was. **1916** *DN* 4.274 **NE,** *Embroidry.* **1917** in 1944 *ADD* **sWV,** *Embroidery* . . embr'idery. **1930s** *Ibid* **eWV,** *Embroidery* . . imbrawdry. **1954** *Harder Coll.* **cwTN,** *Embroidery* [ɪmbrɔdri].
B As noun.
=**ambrosia 2.** [Perh folk-etym]
1930 *DN* 6.80 **ceSC,** *Embroidery*. . . Ambrosia, the regular dessert after a Christmas dinner. General.
C As verb.
To embroider.
1916 *DN* 4.274 **NE,** *Embroidry, embroidery*. . . "I began to embroidery a towel for her." **1928** *Ruppenthal Coll.* **KS,** To embroidery . . to embroider. "She's going to embroidery that cap." **c1930** in 1944 *ADD* **cNY, eWV,** *Embroidery*. . . To embroider. **1954** *Harder Coll.* **cwTN,** *Embroidery* v. embroider.

emigrant car n Cf **zulu car**
A railroad boxcar used for transporting emigrants and their belongings to the western portions of the US.
1848 *Merchants' Mag.* 18.540 **nNY,** The property of the company consists of . . 20 eight-wheeled emigrant, 14 eight-wheeled baggage, and 4 eight-wheeled mail and baggage cars. **1902** Wilson *Spenders* 72 **West,** Oldaker found a man from New York on the train the other day, up in one of the emigrant cars. **1946** McWilliams *S. CA Country* 127 **swCA,** At one time as many as a hundred special emigrant cars were in use on the Southern Pacific line. **1959** Robertson *Ram* 11 **ID,** When my mother moved to Idaho, in 1888, a couple of emigrant cars were a feature of every train. The fare was low; the people brought most of their food and slept in their seats. **1966–67** *DARE* Tape **ID**4, They traveled then [=1903] in what they called emigrant cars on the Great Northern Railroad. . . They brought their farm stock, their farm machinery, and all their household goods [from Michigan to Idaho]; **NE**4, The railroad came to Valentine, Nebraska, . . and they came in an emigrant car. **1979** *DARE* File **swID,** [Letter:] Emigrant car. . . We were pleased and surprised when we moved from Nebr. to Idaho [in 1946] to find this service still available on the railroad. . . We put tractor, plow, car, and other machinery in one end plus the middle and tied everything down. . . Milt's Dad put in two heifers . . Milt fixed a pen for them and a place for himself to sleep. . . The bill is marked "Household goods and Emigrant. 2 heifers. Feed, water and rest in car. Man in charge."

emmet n [Engl dial] *old-fash*
An ant; also fig.
1904 *DN* 2.418 **nwAR,** *Emmet*. . . Industrious person. "He's an emmet." Rare. This word is never used in the sense of *"ant."* **1907** *DN* 3.187 **seNH,** *Emmet*. . . Small red ant. "Those nasty little red emmets have gotten into the buttery." **1926** *DN* 5.399 **Ozarks,** *Emmet*. . . A big black ant. . . I have never heard the word used in this figurative sense [in ref to quot 1904]. **1967** *DARE* (Qu. R18) Inf **MA**72, Emmets—small, red ants which live in the ground. They are grease-eating ants.

emmies n
1912 *DN* 3.575 **wIN,** *Emmies*. . . Molasses.

emmy See **immie**

emonization See **immunization**

empire See **umpire**

employ v Usu |ɛm'plɔɪ, ɪm-|; also |-'plɔɪ| Pronc-sp *emply* Similarly, *emplyer, emplyment*
Std senses, var forms.
1841 (1952) Cooper *Deerslayer* 260 **nNY,** No man here should harm him while empl'yed on such an arr'nd. *Ibid* 408, Tell your empl'yers. *Ibid* 454, Trapping, which is no empl'yment for a brave. **1867** Lowell *Biglow* xxiv **NEng,** For *joint, employ, royal* we have *jynt, emply, rȳle.* **1891** *DN* 1.153 **cNY,** The most characteristic [aɪ] of [Ithaca dialect] is that which, in common speech, is [ɔɪ] in many words. Examples are: *'boil'* (a sore), . . *'employment.'*

empt v [Engl dial] **chiefly NEng** *old-fash*
To empty.
1889 *AN&Q* 4.81/2 **NEng,** *Empt,* for empty (verb transitive), is a not infrequent rusticism in parts of New England. **1899** (1912) Green *VA Folk-Speech* 164, *Empt*. . . "Empt the water out of that pitcher." **1972** *NYT Article Letters* **ME,** You don't empty a pail, you empt' it. **1978** *DARE* File **csNH** (as of c1900), "Empt" for "empty" was used occasionally by my grandmother, to the great disgust of my aunt, who always corrected her. "I mustn't forget to empt the pan under the ice chest before I go to bed." **1979** *AmSp* 54.97 **ME** (as of c1900), *Empt vt* Empty.

emptins n pl, but sometimes sg in attrib use Usu |'ɛmptɪnz, -tənz|; occas |'ɛmptɪŋz|; for addit varr see quots Also sp *emptains, emptings, emptyin(g)s* [**empt** or *empty* v + *-in(g)s*] **chiefly NEng, Upstate NY** *old-fash*
1 A homemade leavening agent usu made from beer or boiled potatoes and often kept from one baking to the next; also fig.
1650 in 1903 *Essex Antiq.* 7.28 **MA,** Elizabeth Pinion . . having come into the house to borrow some emptings, Tobiah took her and threw her. **1867** Lowell *Biglow* xxiv **NEng,** I have never seen [in British literature] an instance of our New England word *emptins* in the same sense [leaven; yeast], nor can I divine its original. *Ibid* 11 **'Upcountry' MA,** A betch o' bread thet hain't riz once ain't goin' to rise agin,/ An' it's jest money throwed away to put the emptins in. **1889** *Jrl. Amer. Folkl.* 2.153 **eMA,** "To run like a boy after emptins," that is, to be in a great hurry. . . "Emptins," or emptyings, were the dregs of beer, out of which yeast was formerly made. **1891** *DN* 1.155 **cNY,** Contraction . . occurs in . . [ɛmptɪnz] < *emptyings* (yeast). **1894** *DN* 1.341 **wCT,** *Emptins:* yeast. **1903** *DN* 2.297 **Cape Cod MA** (as of a1857), *Emptyings* [ɛmptɪnz]. . . Sour dough, kept in an *emptins pot* and used to raise *emptins bread.* **1905** *DN* 3.8 **cCT,** *Emptyings*. . . Yeast. **1909** *DN* 3.416 **neME,** *Sour emptings bread. Ibid* 417, *Sweet emptings bread.* **1912** *DN* 3.567 **cNY,** *Emptins.* **1917** *DN* 4.391 **neOH,** *Emptyins, -ngs* [ɛmptiɪnz, -ɪŋz]. . . "I never heard *emptyings* applied to anything but salt-rising bread." . . Also Vt. **1931–33** *LANE Worksheets* **cVT,** Emptins [ɛmtɨnz]—a liquid substitute for yeast, made of boiled potatoes. **1941** *LANE* 2.290 **throughout NEng,** The term *emptins* (frequently recorded) or *emptin yeast* [1 inf] denotes a kind of liquid leaven formerly much used instead of yeast but now rare. It was often home-made [10 infs], and sometimes carried over from one batch of bread to the next. . . The term *emptins* or the preparation so called is regarded as older or old-fashioned though still in use by [16 infs]. The word is pronounced as *emptyings* only by [2 infs]. **1949** Brown *Amer. Cooks* 480 **MO,** The mush mixture, like homemade yeasts, was called variously "rising," "risin," or "lightnin' " according to local custom, and one old word, common in Missouri and the Midwest, was "emptyings." **1950** *WELS Suppl.* **ceWI,** Emptings—hop yeast, kept from one batch of yeast to make the next. **1967–69** *DARE* (Qu. H16, *What do people use to raise the bread before it's baked?*) Inf **CT**16, Emptins ['ɛmptənz]—old-fashioned; **NY**72, Emptins; **NY**209, Emptins ['ɛmptənz]; **NY**75, Milk emptins—old-fashioned. A starter that you keep over from one batch to another to start it a-raising; **NY**105, Emptings ['ɛmptɨŋz]—for salt-rising bread; (Qu. H17, . . *Different kinds*) Inf **MI**96, Emptings yeast—saved from one time to another; **NY**72, Emptins; (Qu. H18, . . *Special kinds of bread*) Inf **NY**5, Salt emptin bread; **NY**12, Salt emptins ['ɛmtənz] bread. [All Infs old] **1978** *Yankee* Oct 56, Dear Oracle: I've encountered an old recipe for 'Rich Plum Cake' that calls for a half-pint of "emptains," parenthetically identified as yeast. Just what are emptains?
2 Dregs—usu in phrr *run (to) emptins* to reach the dregs, become vapid.
1847 (1946) Hammond *Remembrance Amherst* 141 **MA,** A young lady . . and *gentleman* . . were *tête-à-tête* in one corner: and whatever their conversation may have been before I entered, it most plainly "ran emptins" afterward. **1848** *Knickerbocker* 31.88 **NY,** They "laughed consumedly" at the "empt'in's" of the joke. **1881** *Congressional Record* 15 Feb 1647/1 **NY,** Mr. Chairman, this bill is nearly played out and is running emptyings. **1894** *DN* 1.341 **wCT,** *Emptins*. . . *To run*

emptins is to show signs of not holding out well, as for instance a speech or an enterprise of any kind. Probably from analogy of a beer-barrel. **1898** Westcott *Harum* 282 **cNY,** Runs a good deal to emptins in his preachin' though, they say. **1909** in 1917 Twain *Letters* 2.487 **swCT,** Offers were made me for weekly literary contributions. . . I had known of no instance where a man had pumped himself out once a week and failed to run "emptyings" before the year was finished. **1917** *DN* 4.404 **neOH,** *Emptyings*. . . In the phrase *run emptins,* to talk nonsense.

empty n, adj, v Usu |'ɛm(p),ti|; also |ɪmpti| Pronc-sp *impty*

A Forms.

1915 *DN* 4.177 **swVA,** *E* and *i* standing before m or n in the same syllable . . are pronounced exactly alike, as i: impty (empty). **1937** *AmSp* 12.287 **nwVA,** Not infrequently found in the speech of uneducated [Shenandoah] Valley people: [ɛ] > [ɪ] in *kettle, get, . . empty.* **1940** *Sat. Eve. Post* 24 Feb 77/2 **TX,** You got, too, a impty belly.

B As noun.

Fig: a cloud; see quot. [Prob in ref to empty railroad freight cars]

1966–69 *DARE* (Qu. B7, *When clouds begin to decrease, you say . . ———*) Inf **MI**91, The empties are rolling back; (Qu. B8, *When clouds come and go all day*) Inf **NM**11, That's just the empties going back—clouds passing in one direction and then returning; **UT**5, Looks like the empties going back to Missouri.

C As adj.

Without money, broke. [*OED empty* a. and sb. 3. a →1724]

1970 *DARE* (Qu. U40, *Somebody who is temporarily out of money . . "At the moment he's ———."*) Inf **FL**51A, Empty. [Inf Black]

emptyin(g)s See **emptins**

en n, v See **end**

en conj See **and** conj

-en suff[1] Also sp *-'n* [Surviving prepositional inflection (from OE *-an,* ME *-en*) lost in mod StdE] Note: *OED* attests *abouten* 1301–1500, *withouten* →1600. *EDD* attests *abouten* 1853 →, *withouten* 1793 →, both from wide areas. The gaps in attestation suggest a relatively recent reintroduction of *-en,* perh by analogy with **outen** prep (cf **-en** suff[3]), but the wide geographical distribution of the Engl dial evidence argues for continuity from ME.

See quots.

1925 Glasgow *Barren Ground* 423 **VA,** I'se gwine out agin about'n sunup. **1941** Faulkner *Men Working* 199 **MS,** Never knowed a thing abouten it. **1979** *Antioch Rev.* 37.51 **MS,** Withouten you got injured so soon . . , you might could of been truly famous.

-en suff[2] [Surviving pl inflection (from OE *-an,* ME *-en* as in *oxen*) transf analogically to other nouns] Addit exx at **housen** n[1] **1**

See quots.

1823 Cooper *Pioneers* 2.108 **cNY,** Farms and housen. **1931** *N. Amer. Rev.* 231.433 **neNJ, seNY** (as of c1880), Within forty miles of New York City . . a race of mountaineers live in the hinterland of the Ramapos. They are known as the Jackson Whites. . . Several of the older Jackson Whites . . used *housen* as plural for *house* and *hosen* for *hose.* **1983** *DARE* File **seNY** (as of c1945), *Housen* as the plural of house.

-en suff[3] Also sp *-in, -'n* [Pronc-spp for contr of **on** of] Cf **because** conj, **offen, outen** prep, **outsiden**

See quots.

1871 (1892) Johnston *Dukesborough Tales* 59 **GA,** Ding my skin ef you sha'n't larn it, or I'll paddle you as long as thar's poplars to make paddles outen. **1903** *DN* 2.322 **seMO,** *Offen*. . . Off of. 'I can't make good corn offen that land.' **1908** *DN* 3.290 **eAL, wGA,** Because. Sometimes *kasin.* **1928** McKay *Home to Harlem* 33 **NYC** [Black], Git off'n her. 'Causen she's down. *Ibid* 66, You thinks I only hangs out with low-down trash becassin Ise in a place like this, eh? **1940** *AmSp* 15.52 **sAppalachians,** Dialectal *on* for *of* is contracted: off'n, out'n. **1953** Brewer *Word Brazos* 4 **eTX** [Black], Evuhbody wonder what de trouble be an' staa't lookin' outen de windows. **1954** *Harder Coll.* **cwTN,** He fell off'n the roof.

-en suff[4] See **-ing**

-en suff[5] [Verb-forming suffix orig added redundantly to existing verbs in ME, later used to derive verbs from adjs and still later from other parts of speech] Note: Sometimes the *-en* suff, when attached redundantly to verbs, appears in examples attested only in the pres pple (e.g., **assen around**), suggesting that it is perh instead *-en* (at **-ing**).

See quots.

1806 (1905) Clark *Orig. Jrls. Lewis & Clark Exped.* 5.72, The hole was enlargened. **1916** *DN* 4.338 **PA,** *Outen*. . . To extinguish. "Be sure to outen the light when you go to bed." Esp. Pa. Dutch. **1923** (1946) Greer-Petrie *Angeline Doin' Society* 22 **csKY,** So fur, they hadn't pearten'd up a bit. **1928** Chapman *Happy Mt.* 295 **seTN,** Offen your hand from me! **1939** Harris *Purslane* 279 **cNC,** Now le's find a empty bench on Capitol Square and quieten our stomachs. **1942** ME Univ. *Studies* 56.58, Changes in the wind are indicated in various ways. . . To *breeze* (or *breezen*) on . . mean to increase in velocity. **1953** Randolph-Wilson *Down in Holler* 45 **Ozarks,** There are some strange verbs ending in *n* or *en*. . . *Belongen* is a form of belong, as in . . "Them dogs belongen to Ab Landers." The old verb *enlargen* means to enlarge or expand; Wayman Hogue makes an Arkansas politician denounce his opponent who wants to "enlargen the free schools." **1966** *DARE* (Qu. A9, . . *Wasting time by not working on the job*) Inf **SC**19, Loafing and assening around. **1968** *DARE* Tape **NJ**10, In the wintertime you have to bedden 'em [=cows].

enceno See **encino**

encenilla See **encinilla**

enchilada n Usu |ɛnčɪ'lɑdə|; for varr see quots **orig SW, CA, but now widely recognized** See Map

Usu a tortilla wrapped around any of var fillings such as cheese, meat, beans, etc, and baked, usu in a sauce seasoned with chili peppers; for varied preparations see quots.

1887 Iglehart *Face to Face* 410 **TX,** They go to some stand . . and eat *enchiladas* and *tamales* and drink *pulque.* **1894** *DN* 1.324 **TX,** *Enchilada, -s:* a Mexican dish, the principal ingredient of which is *chile.* **1895** *Jrl. Amer. Folkl.* 8.62 **swTX,** *Enchiladas* are practically corn fritters allowed to simmer for a moment in chile sauce, and then served hot with a sprinkling of grated cheese and onion. **1910** Hart *Vigilante Girl* 221 **nCA,** Those are *enchiladas, . . tortillas* or pancakes with chile peppers rolled inside and cooked in milk. They are too fiery for any but Spanish tastes. **1940** Brown *Amer. Cooks* 119 **FL,** *Key West Crayfish Enchilada* —Steam the little lobsters [=Florida crayfish] . . and dice. . . Sauté . . onion . . garlic . . green pepper and sufficient tomato to make a sauce. . . add crayfish. . . Serve with rice. . . any American living along the border will agree . . that this is not an enchilada at all, because it isn't wrapped in a tortilla. It would . . make a good filling for . . real enchiladas, without the rice. **1949** *AmSp* 24.236 **AZ,** Mispronunciations . . [ɛnčɪlædə], *enchilada* . . a Mexican dish prepared more for *tourista* than for local consumption. **1954** Tolbert *Bigamy Jones* 127 **wTX** (as of 1870s) [Black], This was just barbecue and enshillolly day. **1965–70** *DARE* (Qu. H65, *Foreign foods favored . . around here*) 48 Infs, **chiefly SW,** Enchilada(s); **AR**52, [ɑnšɪ'lɑdəz]; **AR**55, [ˌænǰɪ'lɑdəz]; **LA**28, [ˌɪnčɪ'lɑdəz]; **OH**46, [ɛnčə'lɑdiz]; **OK**44, Mexican enchiladas; (Qu. H45, *Dishes . . that everyone around here would know, but that people in other places might not*) 17 Infs, **chiefly SW, esp sCA,** Enchilada(s); **CA**64, Chicken enchiladas; (Qu. H41) Inf **CA**15, Enchilada; (Qu. H50) Inf **CA**194, Enchiladas; (Qu. FF1) Inf **CA**65, Enchilada dinners. **1966** *Deming Graphic* (NM) 21 Mar 1/1, Members of the Deming High School Honor Society will conduct an enchilada supper Friday at the central cafeteria. **1967** *DARE* Tape **AZ**8, Enchiladas

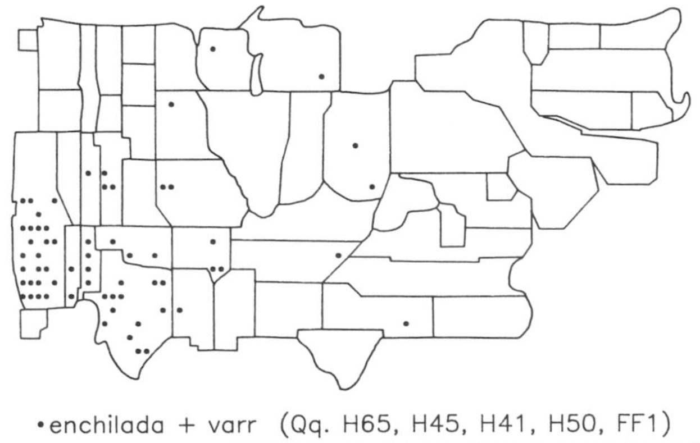

•enchilada + varr (Qq. H65, H45, H41, H50, FF1)

[ˌenčɪˈlɑdəz] is a combination dish of tortillas, beans, grated cheese, lettuce, hot sauce . . quite often a fried egg is added to the top; **TX**41, They sell . . mostly Spanish food, like tamales or tacos or enchiladas [ˌenčɪˈlɑdəz]. **1982** Lappé *Diet Small Planet* 256, *Enchilada Bake*. . . Onion . . garlic . . mushrooms . . green pepper . . can corn (optional) . . beans . . or 1 pound tofu . . chili powder . . red wine . . tortillas . . ricotta . . or cottage cheese and yogurt. **1989** *WI State Jrl.* (Madison) 6 Aug sec H 4/1, [Restaurant review:] The flour tortilla also helped push the chicken enchilada dinner . . beyond the ordinary. . . The sauce on top was . . a red chili base.

encina See **encino**

encinal n [Span "holm-oak grove"] **SW**

An oak grove or an area marked primarily by the growth of oaks.

1856 *Monterey* (Calif.) *Sentinel* 3 Feb. 1/3 *(DA)*, The site . . was covered with oaks, forming a beautiful park or *encinal*. **1933** *AmSp* 8.3.9 **SW**, This termination "al" (place where) is often used with words denoting a characteristic growth as *chapparral*, place of the brush . . *encinal*, place of the encinas oak. **1943** Dice *Biotic Provinces* 58 **seAZ, swNM**, The encinal belt covers most of the hills and the lower slopes of the mountains. This belt is dominated by oaks of several species.

encinilla n Also *encenilla* **TX**

A croton (here: *Croton corymbulosus* or *C. fruticulosus*).

1886 Havard *Flora W. & S. TX for 1885* 514, *Croton corymbulosus*. . . Encenilla; Chaparral Tea. . . Very common weed of valleys and prairies. . . It is much used by Mexicans, Indians and colored United States soldiers. The latter prefer it to coffee in the field. **1960** Vines *Trees SW* 615, *Croton fruticulosus* . . also has the vernacular names of Encinilla and Hierba Loca. **1970** Correll *Plants TX* 932, *Croton fruticulosus*. . . *Encinilla*. . . Frequent in brush on limestone uplands . . , infrequent on caliche cuestas.

encino n Also *encina, enceno* [Span *encina*] **esp CA**

Any of several evergreen oaks, esp **live oak.**

1884 Sargent *Forests of N. Amer.* 146, *Quercus agrifolia*. . . *Enceno. Coast Live Oak*. . . A large evergreen tree, 24 to 30 meters in height. **1897** Sudworth *Arborescent Flora* 165, *Quercus agrifolia*. . . Encina (Cal.) [**1914** Saunders *With Flowers in CA* 11, In the language of Spanish-Californians the valley oak, which is deciduous, is called *roble*, and the live oak, *encino* or *encina*.] **1938** Van Dersal *Native Woody Plants* 334 **CA**, Encina *(Quercus agrifolia)*. **1939** FWP *Guide CA* 239 **ceCA**, The name he selected from the numerous stands of encinas (evergreen oaks) that dotted the landscape. **1960** Vines *Trees SW* 168, *Quercus grisea*. . . Vernacular names are Shin Oak, Scrub Oak, Encina. *Ibid* 169, *Sandpaper Oak. Quercus pungens*. . . Also known as Scrub Oak and Encino. *Ibid* 194, *Quercus gravesii*. . . Vernacular names are Chisos Oak . . and Encina. **1970** Correll *Plants TX* 482, *Quercus virginiana*. . . Live oak, encino. **1970** *DARE* (Qu. T10, . . *Different kinds of oak trees*) Inf **CA**179, Encino oak. **1979** Little *Checklist U.S. Trees* 226, *Quercus agrifolia*. . . Encina. *Ibid* 231, *Quercus gambelii*. . . Encino. *Ibid* 243, *Quercus turbinella*. . . Encino. *Ibid* 244, *Quercus virginiana*. . . Encino.

end n, v

A Forms.

1 pronc-spp *een(d)*, rarely *eent*. **now chiefly Sth, S Midl**

1810 Lambert *Travels* 2.440 **SC**, In wheeling to the right, the right hand eend of the platoon stands fast, and the other eend comes round like a swingle tree. **1815** Humphreys *Yankey in England* 105 **NEng**, *Eend*, end. **1837** Sherwood *Gaz. GA* 69, *Provincialisms*. . . *Eend*, for end. **1867** Lowell *Biglow* xxxi **'Upcountry' MA**, *End*, which the Yankee more often makes *eend*. **1871** (1882) Stowe *Fireside Stories* 178 **MA**, I could tell ye a story now that'd jest make yer har stan' on eend. **1883** (1971) Harris *Nights with Remus* 244 **GA** [Black], Brer Rabbit, he tuck'n put all he fammerly in de behine een' er de waggin. **1893** Shands *MS Speech* 28, *Een*. . . Illiterate white for *end*. **1894** *DN* 1.330 **NJ**, *Fag eend:* the end piece of anything. **1899** Chesnutt *Conjure Woman* 148 **NC**, But to'ds de een' er de week he 'mence' ter git res'less ag'in. **1901** *Century Illustr. Mag.* 62.903/2 **AR**, Folks dat ain' know de business eend uv er mule f'om t'other. **1902** *DN* 2.249 **sIL**, *Yan*. . . Yon, as "Down to yon eend." **1911** *DN* 3.538 **eKY**, *End*. . . Pronounced *eend*. **1916** *DN* 4.283 **eTN**, But in eastern Tennessee one hears *eent* (end), while the usual pronunciation is *eend*. **1933** *AmSp* 8.1.24 **Appalachians**, Sometimes . . *end* is *eend*. **1966** *DARE* Tape **AL**1, End [iənd].

2 pronc-sp *ind*. Cf Pronc Intro 3.I.4

1821 Cooper *Spy* 2.29 **nNY**, To meet with sich an ind. **1841** (1952) Cooper *Deerslayer* 79 **nNY**, In at one ind, and out at the other. *Ibid* 96, That inds the matter. **1843** (1916) Hall *New Purchase* 135 **IN**, Like a powerful big prararee without any ind. **1907** *DN* 3.230 **nwAR**, *End* [Ind]. **1942** Hall *Smoky Mt. Speech* 19 **eNC, wTN.**

3 pronc-sp *en*. Cf Pronc Intro 3.I.22

1888 Jones *Negro Myths* 168 **seGA**, *En*, end. **1922** Gonzales *Black Border* 300 **sSC, GA coasts** [Gullah glossary], *En'*—end, ends.

B Sense.

See quot.

1903 *DN* 2.312 **seMO**, *End* (or *eend*) *of the road*. . . Turn of the road. 'Go to the forks of the road and take the right hand eend,' that is, turn to the right.

endboard n

1959 *VT Hist.* new ser 27.134 **VT**, Endboard. . . The heel or last slice on each end of a loaf of bread. Occasional.

endeavors, do one's v phr Also *do one's endeavor best* Pronc-spp *endivors, endeevior* *old-fash*

To exert oneself to the utmost.

1841 (1952) Cooper *Deerslayer* 307 **NY**, I'll do my endivors not to disgrace the people among whom I got my training. **1908** *DN* 3.308 **eAL, wGA**, [ɛndivɪor bɛst]. . . "I'll do my endeevior best to please you."

ender n

In jumping rope: the person who turns one of the rope ends.

1974 Skolnik *Jump Rope* 57, Remember that one end of the rope can be tied to a tree or pole when you can't round up another ender. *Ibid* 66, *Exams:* Another game which is fun for enders and is the jump-rope equivalent of Giant Steps. The teachers [Skolnik: *enders*] decide upon an exam to give the players. **1975** Ferretti *Gt. Amer. Book Sidewalk Games* 218 **NYC**, For those who are known as terrific jumpers, the Enders deliver "mustard and pepper," a speeded-up turning that tests jumping powers greatly.

end for end adv phr Also *end for about* [Orig naut use; see *OED end* sb. 19. a]

In inverted or reversed position; inside out.

1871 Lowell *Study Windows* 201 **MA**, Thoreau seems to have prized a lofty way of thinking (often we should be inclined to call it a remote one) not so much because it was good in itself as because he wished few to share it with him. . . He turns commonplaces end for end, and fancies it makes something new of them. **1912** Green *VA Folk-Speech* 165, *End for end*. . . When a body is changed about; "He changed the bench end for end." **1945** Colcord *Sea Language* 72 **ME, Cape Cod, Long Island,** *End for end*. The other way around. Its use seems largely confined to shipboard and alongshore. **1957** *DE Folkl. Bulletin* 1.28, End for about . . end for end. . . "Turn that piece end for about." **1967–69** *DARE* (Qu. Y15, *To beat somebody thoroughly*) Inf **WA**28, Knocked him end for end; (Qu. MM3, *When someone does something the wrong way round . . "This is the front, you've got the whole thing ______."*) Inf **NJ**35, End for end; **GA**77, Turn it end for end. **1967** *DARE* FW Addit **neNY**, Turned him end for end.

endgate n

1a The tailgate of a wagon.

1873 *Newton Kansan* 15 May 2/2 *(DA)*, An iron end gate rod was thrust easily into the excavation. **1911** Quick *Yellowstone Nights* 316 **WY**, The end-gates was jerked out. *Ibid* 165, Two boys . . tied to the feed-rack by Allen's hired man, and spanked with the end-gate of his wagon. **1935** Sandoz *Jules* 120 **wNE** (as of 1880–1930), They packed their bundles into their covered wagons, tied the milk cow to the endgate. **1940** Faulkner *Hamlet* 347 **MS**, Like a mad squirrel and scrabbling at the end-gate of the wagon. **1958** Blasingame *Dakota Cowboy* 168 **SD** (as of 1900–10), The whip lash caught me across the seat of my pants, and I thought it jerked my whole endgate off! **1963** Owens *Look to River* 83 **neTX**, Jed, squeezed in by the endgate, saw Luster with his back propped against the spring seat. **1969** *DARE* (QR p102) Inf **IN**58, Endgates—ends of a farm wagon.

b Fig: see quots.

1968 *DARE* (Qu. W24c, . . *To warn a man that his trouser-fly is open*) Inf **IL**54, Your endgate's open; (Qu. H71, . . *The last piece of food left on a plate*) Inf **MO**17, We call it the endgate; (Qu. GG22a, *When you have come to the end of your patience . . "Well that's the ______."*) Inf **IN**42, Endgate.

2 Among loggers: cheese. [See quot 1979] *joc*

1956 Sorden–Ebert *Logger's Words* 13 **Gt Lakes**, End-gate, Cheese. **1979** *DARE* File **Madison WI**, Cheese is binding. That's why the lumberjack called it "endgate," because it acted to block the digestive system.

ending See **inning**

endiron n Pronc-sp *eniron* [Folk-etym for **andiron**] Cf **edge iron**

1 =**andiron.**

1655 in 1916 MA (Colony) Probate Court (Essex Co.) *Records* 1.224, A p[air] of Endirons, firepan & toungs. **1899** (1912) Green *VA Folk-Speech* 165, *End-irons*. . . Short, thick, bars of iron used to hold the ends of the sticks in a wood-fire built on a hearth. **1965–70** *DARE* (Qu. D32) 14 Infs, **scattered,** ['ɛnd,aɪɚnz]. [12 Infs old] **1966** Dakin *Dial. Vocab. Ohio R. Valley* 2.34, North of the river, especially in Ohio, *andirons* clearly has a double status of an old common folk term and as a newer innovation from literary language. . . among the less educated and those who have learned it as a newer word but obviously are unfamiliar with the spelling of the literary form . . *endirons* (2 [of c200 infs]), *enirons* (2) . . are scattered. **c1970** Pederson *Dial. Surv. Rural GA* **seGA,** ['ɛnd,aɪənz].

2 One of a pair of movable iron plates on a cookstove which together control the width of the grate.

a1894 Brewer *Dict. Phrase & Fable* 269, *End-irons.* Two moveable iron checks or plates, still used in cooking-stoves to enlarge or contract the grate at pleasure. The term explains itself, but must not be mistaken for "dogs."

endive n

1 Std: a widely cultivated salad plant *(Cichorium endivia).* Also called **escarole**

2 also *wild endive:* =**chicory 1.**

1822 Eaton *Botany* 237, *Cichorium intibus* . . endive. **c1873** in 1976 Miller *Shaker Herbs* 153, Chicory—*Cichorium intybus* . . Endive. **1892** (1974) Millspaugh *Amer. Med. Plants* 93, *Cichorium intybus* . . Wild Endive. **1974** (1977) Coon *Useful Plants* 106, *Cichorium intybus* . . wild endive.

endivors See **endeavors, do one's**

end man n

1 Among railroad workers: see quots.

1932 *RR Mag.* Oct 367, *End Man*—Rear brakeman on freight train. **1938** Beebe *High Iron* 220 [Railroad terms], *End man:* Parlor brakeman on freight train.

‡2 A bull. *euphem*

1967 *DARE* (Qu. K23, *Words used by women or in mixed company for a bull*) Inf **PA**29, [We] used to call them the end man. [FW: no explanation]

endo v, n

See quots.

1938 *AmSp* 13.156 **sCA** [Airplane factory English], *Endo.* To heave, or pull an object. **1942** *AmSp* 17.281 **TX,** Collected . . while working in the Texas oil fields. . . *Endo.* Term of Spanish origin, meaning: (1) a chant while moving pipe by hand; (2) to place lines end to end. **1950** *Western Folkl.* 9.117 **nwOR** [Logger speech], *Endo.* To move an object in the direction parallel to its long axis. **1951** *PADS* 15.76 **TX,** [Oil field jargon], A very puzzling expression used by the pipeliners is a shouted command, "Endo!" meaning everybody shove. Equivalent to the sailor's *heave ho,* it is used to concert the action of the men when loading a heavy object. It is perhaps two words *End ho!* and is related to an obsolete-except-dialectal word *end* recorded in the . . *[OED],* meaning to *put into.* **1958** McCulloch *Woods Words* 58 **Pacific NW,** *Endo*—To move anything endways.

end of comeback n

=**end of nowhere.**

1966 *DARE* (Qu. C33, . . *An out-of-the-way place, or a very unimportant place*) Inf **GA**15, End of comeback.

end off v phr

To come to an end, terminate.

1934 (1970) Wilson *Backwoods Amer.* 126 **Ozarks,** The . . road ends off in Hanner's frog pond.

end of nowhere(s) n **appar Sth, Midl** *joc* Cf **backside of nowhere**

An out-of-the-way or unimportant place.

1965–70 *DARE* (Qu. C33) Infs **AL**27, **IL**27, **IN**30, **IA**17, 30, **NC**46, **SC**46, **VA**44, End of nowhere; **IL**3, Living end of nowheres; **IN**3, **LA**14, (On the) tail end of nowhere.

end of one's nose n Also *end of one's elbow* [Cf *under one's nose* in plain sight]

In phrr suggesting short-sightedness or distrust: see quots.

1952 Brown *NC Folkl.* 1.403, Can't see farther than the end of your nose. **1966–69** *DARE* (Qu. V2b,c, *About a deceiving person* . . *"I wouldn't trust him ______."*) Inf **LA**8, From here to the end of my nose; **MN**6, Any farther than the end of my nose; **MN**16, At the end of my nose; **MA**73, To the end of my nose; **AL**6, Till the end of your elbow. **c1970** *Halpert Coll.* **wKY,** Can't see over (beyond) the end of her nose . . can't foresee even the most obvious things.

end of one's row n [Cf std *end of one's rope*] **chiefly Sth, S Midl, exc Mid Atl** Cf **row's end**

The limit of one's patience or endurance.

1904 (1972) Harben *Georgians* 2, The old chap certainly is gittin' desperate. . . It's my opinion he's at the end o' his row. **1949** Faulkner *Knight's Gambit* 78 **MS,** This is the end of the row. . . I should have raised you better, but I didn't. **1965–70** *DARE* (Qu. GG22a, *When you have come to the end of your patience* . . *"Well that's the ______."*) Infs **AL**42, **AR**3, **IN**23, **KY**36, **LA**2, 12, **MO**25, **NY**75, **SC**11, **TX**13, 91, End of my (*or* the) row; (Qu. GG22b) Infs **MO**6, **TN**6, End of my (*or* your) row; [**WV**3, End of the bean row;] (Qu. X47, . . *"I'm very tired."*) Inf **KY**89, At the end of my row.

end-of-summer n [From the time at which it blooms] Cf **farewell-summer 1**

Prob an aster.

1969 *DARE* (Qu. S21, . . *Other weeds* . . *that are a trouble in gardens and fields*) Inf **KY**60, End-of-summer—white, daisy-like flower with yellow center.

end-of-the-garden pickle n Also *end-of-the-year pickle, end-of-the-season relish*

Pickled vegetables from the last harvest of a growing season.

1967–68 *DARE* (Qu. H56, . . *Different kinds of pickles*) Inf **IN**19, End-of-the-garden pickles—everything left at the end of the summer; **MD**17, End-of-the-garden pickles—lima beans, tomatoes, onions, peppers, cucumbers, pickled together; **PA**49, End-of-the-year pickle—put all leftover vegetables in vinegar. **1968** *DARE* Tape **WI**13, End-of-the-season relish—whatever was left in the line of tomatoes and whatever green tomatoes were left out on the vine—they'd take the whole thing and grind it up in a food grinder.

end on adv phr [Cf *EDD end* sb.[1] 1. (13)] *arch*

1899 (1912) Green *VA Folk-Speech* 165, *End-on.* . . In a great hurry. "He went at it end-on."

endourin See **enduring** prep

end over appetite adv phr Cf **ass-over-teakettle 1**

Head over heels.

1927 *Ruppenthal Coll.* **KS,** He went end over appetite when he was thrown from the bicycle. **1950** *WELS ("He knocked him ______.")* 1 Inf, **cwWI,** End over end; end over appetite.

end-over-end n

A tumble, somersault.

1970 *DARE* (Qu. Y1, . . *A person suddenly falling down: "He slipped on the steps and took quite a ______."*) Inf **CA**189, End-over-end; (Qu. EE9a, *The children's trick of turning over rapidly straight forward*) Inf **NY**234, Somersault; end-over-end.

endrig n [Scots; cf *SND en(d)rig(g)* at *en* I. 7]

1931–33 *LANE Worksheets* **swMA,** Endrigs [ɛndrɪgz]—Headland, unplowed space at the end of a field.

‡ends, at adj phr [Perh blend of *at odds* + *at opposite ends*]

At odds; in disagreement.

1970 *DARE* (Qu. KK68, . . *"We agree on most things, but on politics we're ______."*) Inf **CA**177, At ends.

end town n [Cf *DCan end of steel* a. *2, end-of-steel town*] *hist*

The settlement at the farthest extremity of a railroad under construction.

1870 Pine *Beyond the West* 179 **Cheyenne WY,** After "Hell," as the end town of the railroad was called, moved it on, was a very important question, whether to be or not to be—whether the place was truly anything or nothing. **1871** Richardson *Garnered Sheaves* 410 **WY,** Sheridan has the usual "hard" aspects of an "end town," tents, shanties, gambling places, bad liquor and all the other concomitants, of fighting and swearing. **1938** Asbury *Sucker's Progress* 339 **WY,** Cheyenne, probably the most notorious of the "end towns," was settled when the Union Pacific Railroad reached there in 1867.

end uppermost adv phr

?Topsy-turvy; upside down.

1887 (1967) Harris *Free Joe* 33 **GA,** The natchul world an' all the hummysp'eres 'll make the'r disappearance een'-uppermost.

endurable adj [Blend of *endure* + *durable*] **esp sAppalachians**

Durable, long-lasting, dependable; hence adv *endurably.*

1887 Amer. Philol. Assoc. *Trans.* 17.38 **TN,** *Endurable,* for "durable," may still be heard in some parts of Tennessee, and no doubt elsewhere (Ohio). I heard myself last summer a "foot-washing" Baptist preacher in Craddock's Great Smoky Mountains say, "Stone is the most *lastiest,* the most *endurablest* material there is"; and I heard a negro at Fisk University . . translate *perennius aere,* "more *endurable* than brass." **1924** Raine *Land of Saddle-Bags* 102 **sAppalachians,** Log houses are a heap *endurabler.* **1927** Boston Soc. Nat. Hist. *Proc.* 332 **seGA,** You kin go in the water er the dew with 'em, an' they won't never git hard. They're shore an endurable leather. They'll outlast two pair er shoes. **1927** *DN* 5.470 **sAppalachians,** Comparative in *-er: endurabler,* lasting longer. **1937** (1977) Hurston *Their Eyes* 171 **csFL** [Black], He got somethin' tuh put long side uh whut you got and dat make it more better. He's endurable. **1938** Stuart *Dark Hills* 141 **neKY,** Their dreams were being worked into steel and fashioned into short endurable things. *Ibid* 96, You can give me a body that is endurable in its season as this hill. *Ibid* 39, Some of those baskets were built so endurably that I saw one I sold years later. **1942** (1971) Campbell *Cloud-Walking* 71 **seKY,** Home made goods are a heap endurabler than brought-on goods.

enduring adj Also aphet *durin'* Pronc-spp *enduren, endurin* **chiefly Sth, S Midl**

Of a period of time: entire, whole, livelong—freq in phrr *the whole enduring day* (or *time* etc).

1891 (1967) Freeman *New Engl. Nun* 25 **MA,** It wa'n't ever quite so high-pitched as that Way girl's, mebbe; but she flats the whole durin' time. **1899** (1912) Green *VA Folk-Speech* 165, *Enduring. . .* The whole enduring day; all day long. **1908** *DN* 3.308 **eAL, wGA,** *Endurin(g)* . . lasting, continuing. "He slept the whole endurin time." **1914** *DN* 4.106 **KS,** *Enduring* . . long continuing. "I stood there the whole enduring time." **1915** *DN* 4.182 **swVA,** *Enduring. . .* Livelong. "He stayed the endurin' day." **1926** Roberts *Time of Man* 63 **cKY,** He might be somebody I'd know all my whole enduren life. **1927** *AmSp* 3.138 **eME,** A "cross-patch" was a child or person who cried "the whole enduring time." **1942** (1971) Campbell *Cloud-Walking* 4 **seKY,** I won't have to work and slave ever enduring minute to make things decent. **1950** *PADS* 14.28 **SC,** *Enduring. . .* Total, entire, whole. Only of time. "The enduring evening." Often with *whole:* "the whole enduring day." **1952** Brown *NC Folkl.* 1.536, *Enduring, (whole). . .* Entire, whole. "He loafed the whole enduring time he was supposed to work."—Granville county. **1960** Williams *Walk Egypt* 31 **GA,** They're up in them trees the whole enduring day. **1976** Ryland *Richmond Co. VA* 370, *Enduring*—"the whole enduring day."

enduring prep Also *enduring of,* rarely *endurance of* Pronc-spp *eenjurin', endourin, enduren, endurin, indurance* [*OED* "*Obs.*"] **Sth, S Midl**

During.

1857 *Porter's Spirit of Times* 26 Dec 259/3 **cGA,** Endourin the time that I have come to school to you, I have tried as hard as a boy ever did try. **1887** (1967) Harris *Free Joe* 190 **ceGA** [Black], Hit'll be de fus' time she y'ever sot foot in dish yer tavern less'n 'twuz indurance er de war. **1902** Eggleston *Dorothy South* 166 **VA,** It was "endurin of de feveh"—to use his own phrase by which he meant during the fever—that Dick's genius revealed itself. **1903** *DN* 2.312 **seMO,** *Enduring* or *endurin. . .* During. "I will be back some time enduring the week." **1908** *DN* 3.308 **eAL, wGA,** *Endurin(g).* **1917** *DN* 4.411 **wNC,** *Endurin'.* **1922** Gonzales *Black Border* 248 **sSC, GA coasts** [Gullah], Spile eb'ry Gawd' crop een de fiel' eenjurin' de week day. *Ibid* 207, Ole Maussuh' Clifton house wuh dem Nyankee bu'n down eenjurin' uh de wah. **1923** *DN* 5.206 **swMO,** *Endurin'.* **1926** Roberts *Time of Man* 238 **cKY,** Squire Sugan wants somebody enduren the set-out season. **1942** Rawlings *Cross Creek* 84 **FL,** En-durin' the time. **1950** *PADS* 14.28 **SC,** *Enduring of. . .* "He come in endurin' of the singing." **1953** Randolph *Down in Holler* 243 **Ozarks,** *Enduring. . .* This is still common in Stone County, Mo. "We had a hell of a time endurin' of the war." **1954** *Harder Coll.* **cwTN,** *Enduring* . . during. **c1960** *Wilson Coll.* **csKY.**

endways adv Also pronc-sp *een'-ways*

In the opposite direction; out of proper position or order.

c1871 Twain *Screamers* 31, He was all ready for the dog too, and knocked him endways with a rock when he came to tear him. **1887** (1967) Harris *Free Joe* 95 **nwGA,** Den de niggers, dee got slack, en eve'y thing 'gun ter go een'-ways. **1935** Davis *Honey* 66 **OR,** Let me alone, or I'll take this fence rail and knock you endways with it. **1968** *DARE* (Qu. H74a, . . *Coffee . . very strong*) Inf **MN**13A, Knock you endways; (Qu. MM13, *The table was nice and straight until he came along and knocked it* ______) Infs **IN**38, **WI**44, Endways.

energy n

Boldness, assertiveness.

1966–68 *DARE* (Qu. GG5, *When someone does something unexpectedly bold or forward . . "Well, she certainly has a lot of* ______*."*) Infs **MO**8, **NC**55, Energy; **SC**10, [ɪnǰɨdɨ]—[FW: perh =energy]; (Qu. GG37, *Somebody who is very brave or courageous: "He's got plenty of* ______*."*) Infs **GA**28, 44, **SC**10, Energy. [All Infs old]

enfair See **infare**

enfantigo See **impetigo**

enfare See **infare**

engagement child n Also *engagement baby* Cf *DS* Z11b

See quots.

1949 *AmSp* 24.108 **Charleston SC,** *Engagement child. . .* Bastard. **1949** Webber *Backwoods Teacher* 174 **Ozarks** *(Hench Coll.),* An engagement being in the final analysis almost as binding as a wedding, they thought no more of a girl's having her "engagement baby" a few months after her marriage than did the lusty Puritans of fabled morality.

engern See **onion**

engine n Usu |'ɛnǰɨn, -ǰən|; also freq |'ɪnǰɨn|; also *old-fash* |'ɛnǰaɪn, 'ɪn-| Pronc-spp *enjine, ingine, ingyne, injin(e)* Cf **Indian**

A Forms.

1823 Cooper *Pioneers* 1.266 **cNY,** He wanted to put out the Captain's fire with a gun-room ingyne. **1887** (1967) Harris *Free Joe* 115 **GA,** See the smoke er their ingines. **1890** *DN* 1.68 **KY,** *Ingine* [ɪnǰaɪn]. Negroes, for *engine.* **1891** *DN* 1.134 **cNY,** [ɪnǰən] . . "engine." **1891** Cooke *Huckleberries* 7, **CT,** Hoss got skeert by one o' them pesky ingines. **1892** *DN* 1.213 **eMA,** Ingine [ɪnǰaɪn]. . . This was the ordinary pronunciation till corrected in school. **1893** Shands *MS Speech* 39, *Injine* [ɪnǰaɪn]. This pronunciation of *engine,* although heard in other parts of the United States, is almost universal among negroes and illiterate whites of Mississippi. It is especially common also in Kentucky. **1903** *DN* 2.291 **Cape Cod MA** (as of c1857), *Injin = engine.* **1904** *DN* 2.425 **Cape Cod MA** (as of c1857), *Engine* [ɛnjaɪn]. **1905** *DN* 3.56 **eNE,** In many words, [ɛ] tends to become [ɪ]:—*kettle, engine, get.* **1906** *DN* 3.135 **nwAR,** *Engine* . . ['ɪnǰɪn]. **1922** Gonzales *Black Border* 42 **sSC, GA coasts** [Gullah], Two t'ing duh shine sukkuh injine headlight! [=Two things shining just like an engine's headlight!] **1926** *AmSp* 2.82 **ME,** A few still say "enjine." **1928** *Ruppenthal Coll.* **KS,** *Injine* . . engine. illit. pronunciation. **1959** *VT Hist.* new ser 27.134 **sVT,** Engine ['ɛnǰaɪn]. . . Rare.

‡B Sense.

A stooge. [Cf *OED engine* sb. 10 "*fig.* . . Of a person: An agent, instrument, tool. *Obs.*"]

1967 *DARE* (Qu. II34, *If you think somebody is trying to use you to his advantage: "I'm not going to be his* ______*."*) Inf **SC**65, Engine.

engineer n Usu |ˌɛnǰə'nir, -'niə|; also |ˌɪn-|; occas |'ɛn-| Pronc-sp *ingineer*

Std senses, var forms.

1867 Lowell *Biglow* 246 **'Upcountry' MA,** Is cute ez though an ingineer / Should claim th' old iron for his sheer. **1890** *DN* 1.68 **KY,** Ingineer [ɪnǰɪniə]. **c1960** *Wilson Coll.* **csKY,** *Recessive accent—Engineer.*

engineerman n [Redund] **Ozarks**

A locomotive engineer.

1903 *DN* 3.78 **nwAR,** *Engineer-man. . .* "Wouldn't you like to be an engineerman?" Not uncommon. **1936** *AmSp* 11.315 **Ozarks,** *Engineerman. . .* A locomotive engineer.

engine tamer n *joc*

Among railroad workers: see quot.

1977 Adams *Lang. Railroader* 55, *Engine tamer:* An engineer who breaks in a new locomotive.

England walnut See **English walnut**

English adj

1986 *WI State Jrl.* (Madison) 23 Nov 6/5 **csWI,** The youngsters . . look curiously at their "English" visitor. ("English" is a term the Amish use to describe their non-Amish neighbors.)

English n

1 A nonexistent object used as the basis of a practical joke. [*English* spinning motion put on a ball when hit or thrown] *joc* Cf *DS* HH14

1921 *DN* 5.94, *English.* Athletic coach sent boy to get English to put on the baseball.

2 A flourish in handwriting, a curlicue.

1967–70 *DARE* (Qu. JJ12, *Little flourishes that some people put on their handwriting or signature to make it look fancy*) Inf **MO**3, English; **DC**13, Put a little English on your writing—an old expression; **VA**109, She uses a lot of English in her handwriting; [**IL**45, English scroll].

3 A style of men's haircut; see quot 1957.

1957 *NYT Mag.* 2 June 26/2 **NYC,** Another hairdo, which originated in Britain, spread to the Continent and is now widely accepted here, is the *English*. . . Hair rides back from the temples, rests comfortably on top of the ears and keeps moving to the rear. Like Sir Laurence Olivier's. **1965–70** *DARE* (Qu. X5, . . *Different kinds of men's haircuts*) 14 Infs, **chiefly Midl, Sth,** English; [**LA**8, English front;] **SC**10, Short English, low English. [7 Infs Black]

English basement n

A basement that is usu largely at street level.

1861 *Vanity Fair* 9 Feb 62/1 **NYC,** Freestone front, all modern improvements, English basement, three stories and attic. **1884** *NY Herald* (NY) 27 Oct 2/1, A four story English basement brown stone house . . near Broadway. **1947** *Chicago Tribune* (IL) 26 Oct sec 5 4/4, Own your own apt. in unusually fine English bsmt. 4 apt. bldg.

English bean n **NEng** *?old-fash*

=**broad bean 1.**

1697 (1878) S. Sewall *Diary* 1.455 **MA,** Betty gets her Mother a Mess of English Beans. **1790** Deane *New Engl. Farmer* 19/2 **MA,** The English bean, to which the name windsor is applied. **1869** MO State Entomol. *Annual Rept.* 98, It attacks not only potato vines, but also honey locusts, and especially the English or Windsor bean. **1976** Bailey–Bailey *Hortus Third* 1155, *Vicia Faba* . . English bean.

English black duck See **English duck 3**

English bluegrass n

1 A **ryegrass** (here: *Lolium perenne*).

1894 *Jrl. Amer. Folkl.* 7.104 **WV,** *Lolium perenne* . . English bluegrass.

2 A **bluegrass 1** (here: *Poa compressa*). Also called **wire grass**

1889 Vasey *Ag. Grasses* 65, *Poa Compressa* (English Blue Grass; Wire Grass). This species has sometimes been confounded with the Kentucky blue grass. . . It thrives well on clay or hard, trodden, and poor soils. **1901** Mohr *Plant Life AL* 384, *Poa compressa*. . . English Blue Grass. . . Valuable pasture grass. **1968** *DARE* (Qu. S15, . . *Other weed seeds that cling to clothing*) Inf **IN**41, English bluegrass.

English boiled dinner n Cf **boiled dinner**

=**New England boiled dinner.**

1967–69 *DARE* (Qu. H49, *Dishes made by boiling potatoes with other foods*) Inf **NY**186, English boiled dinner; **MO**13, English boiled dinner —I see that on menus occasionally.

English broad bean See **broad bean 1**

English brown trout See **brown trout 1**

English bullseye n

A **black-eyed Susan 2** (here: *Rudbeckia hirta*).

1896 *Jrl. Amer. Folkl.* 9.193, *Rudbeckia hirta*. . . English bullseye, York County, Me. **1936** IL Nat. Hist. Surv. *Wildflowers* 364, *Rudbeckia hirta*. . . Other names are . . English Bull's Eye [etc].

English cockatoo n [Prob in ref to the bright red color of the male and its prominent crest]

=**cardinal 1.**

1957 *AmSp* 32.181 **PA,** English cockatoo. . . Cardinal.

English corn n **N Atl** *old-fash*

Wheat, or other small grain, in contradistinction to Indian corn or maize.

1629 (1792) MA Hist. Soc. *Coll.* 1st ser 1.118, They have tryed our English corne at New Plimmouth plantation. **1631** in 1834 NH Hist. Soc. *Coll.* 4.234, Both the English and Indian corne beeinge at tenne shillings a strike . . wee made laws to restraine the selling of corne to the Indians. **1780** (1925) MA Hist. Soc. *Coll.* 73.136 **Boston MA,** We have lately had fine rains, but they came too late for Hay, and a full Crop of English Corn. **1884** *Century Illustr. Mag.* 27.431/1 **NJ,** The device on the seal of East Jersey is wrought of "English Corn" and "Indian Corn,"—wheat and maize,—symbols of the soberer expectations at the period of the Scotch and Quaker migrations.

English cowslip n

=**marsh marigold.**

1876 Hobbs *Bot. Hdbk.* 68, *Caltha palustris* . . English cowslip. **1969** *DARE* (Qu. S22, . . *The bright yellow flowers that bloom in clusters in marshes in early springtime*) Inf **RI**10, English cowslip—a domestic variety.

English curlew n

=**bluestocking 2.**

1923 U.S. Dept. Ag. *Misc. Circular* 13.48 **MT,** Avocet *(Recurvirostra americana)* . . *Vernacular Names*. . . *In local use*. . . English-curlew.

English duck n **chiefly S Atl**

1 =**mallard.**

1838 in 1859 Gosse *Letters from AL* 158, Of these last *(Anas moschata)* there is always a troop of all ages and sizes; it is the only duck *patronised;* the "English duck," as our common species is called, being kept only as a curiosity. **1917** (1923) *Birds Amer.* 1.114, *Mallard. Anas platyrhynchos*. . . *Other Names.*—Common Wild Duck; Stock Duck; English Duck. **1936** Smith–Sass *Carolina Rice* 85 **SC,** The finest duck-shooting was of the Mallard or English duck, which in great quantities frequented during the day the marshes. **1957** *AmSp* 32.180 **NC, SC, GA, FL, AL,** *English duck* . . specifies the mallard, a well-known bird of the Old World, as also of the new. **1966–67** *DARE* (Qu. Q5, . . *Kinds of wild ducks*) Infs **GA**3, 12, 16, **SC**43, English duck.

2 =**pintail.**

1876 *Forest & Stream* 7.212/3 (as of 1852) **seMA,** *Dafila acuta*. . . English duck. . . An interesting "List of Gunner's Names," received from Mr. F.C. Browne. . . "was made . . at Clark's Island . . in the harbor of Plymouth, Mass., in 1852."

3 also *English black duck, English mallard:* =**black duck 1.** Cf **black English duck**

1911 *Forest & Stream* 77.453 **NC,** Blackduck.—English Duck, Cape Hatteras. **1923** U.S. Dept. Ag. *Misc. Circular* 13.9 **GA,** *Black Duck (Anas rubripes)* . . Vernacular Names. . . *In local use.*—English duck. **1955** *Oriole* 20.3, Black Duck . . English Duck. **1957** *AmSp* 32.180, Some of the names involved are, for the black duck, *black English duck* (S.C., Ga., Fl.), *English black duck* (La.), *English duck* (N.C., Ga.), and *English mallard* (Fla.)

4 =**Florida duck.**

1957 *AmSp* 32.180 **FL,** Mottled duck, *English duck.*

English flounder See **English sole**

English grass n **chiefly NEast**

Any of var hay or forage grasses (as timothy or some bluegrasses) orig introduced from England.

1665 in 1883 Dorchester MA *Town Rec.* 129, William Trescots request . . to haue some small parcell of Land . . for English grass about the Ox pen. **1771** in 1918 *MD Hist. Mag.* 13.265 **MD,** Severall small Boys & Girls Have been employed . . since the Receit of yr letters in Picking English grass & white Clover seed. **1874** VT State Bd. Ag. *Rept. for 1873–74* 2.203, The wild meadow grass begins to crowd out the English grass again. **1920** Howells *Vacation Kelwyns* 96 **NH, MA** (as of 1870s), I don't see . . how they s'pose I'm goin' to get that piece of English grass cut. **1943** Langdon *Everyday Things 1607–1776* 1.282 **PA, NJ, NY,** English forage plants were introduced into America as early as 1663 or 1665, probably by accident, in the fodder for cattle on shipboard. They were blue grass and white clover. These soon were known as "English grass."

English hay n Pronc-sp *Inglish hay* **NEast**
Hay from **English grass.**
1684 (1977) Mather *Essay Providences* 163 **MA,** Several Cocks of English-hay mowed near the house, were taken and hung upon Trees. **1730** *PA Gaz.* (Philadelphia) 29 Oct 4/1, A Plantation . . having near fifty Acres of very good intervale Meadows, which is most of it ploughable and brings extraordinary good English Hay. **1750** (1826) MA Hist. Soc. *Coll.* 1st ser 7.240 **MA,** English hay was then sold for £3 and £3–10, old tenor, per hundred. **1806** (1904) Roe *Diary* 29 **NY,** I have been to Judge Strongs & got a load of Inglish hay. **1853** (1864) Thoreau *ME Woods* 130, He cut seventy tons of English hay this year on this ground. **1907** *DN* 3.187 **seNH,** *English hay*. . . Hay, the seed for which was brought originally from England: "tame hay." **1969** *DARE* (Qu. L9a, *What kinds of grass are grown for hay*) Inf **MA**55, Around here there's salt hay—grows near salt water. English hay grows on higher land.

English herring n **Atlantic**
=**glut herring.**
1817 *NY Herald* (NY) 6 Aug 2/4 **ME,** Great numbers of Herrings, erroneously called English, have entered the principal rivers in the District of Maine, particularly the Sheepscot and Kennebec. **1839** MA Zool. & Bot. Surv. *Fishes Reptiles* 111, *The Common Herring*. . . This species . . is known in our market as the *"English herring."* **1884** Goode *Fisheries U.S.* 1.582 **Atlantic,** The *C. æstivalis* is the "Glut" Herring of the Albemarle and the Chesapeake, and the "English" Herring of the Ogeechee River.

English humbug See **humbug n 1**

‡**English kiss** n
1934 *Hanley Disks* **cMA,** But the results were the same [whether a girl or boy found the red ear at a husking bee], a good, generous English kiss.

English lark n
A starling *(Sturnus vulgaris).*
1957 *AmSp* 32.180 **DE,** *English lark* . . is a natural reference to a bird legitimately known as the English starling.

English mallard See **English duck 3**

English mockingbird n
1 =**mockingbird.** [See quot 1810]
1810 Wilson *Amer. Ornith.* 2.22, The first, or Brown Thrush, from its inferiority of song being called the French, and the other the English Mockingbird. A mode of expression probably originating in the prejudices of our forefathers; with whom every thing *French* was inferior to every thing *English.* **1883** Nuttall Ornith. Club *Bulletin* 8.74, *Mimus polyglottus*. . . We have . . *English Mockingbird* (to distinguish it from the "French" Mockingbirds of the Southern States—chiefly *Harporhynchus rufus*). **1957** *AmSp* 32.181 **PA,** English mockingbird. . . Mockingbird. **1966–69** *DARE* (Qu. Q14, . . *Other names . . around here for . . mockingbird*) Infs **DC**8, **KY**5, English mockingbird.
2 =**catbird 1.**
1957 *AmSp* 32.181 **IN, IL,** English mockingbird. . . Catbird.
3 =**orchard oriole.**
1957 *AmSp* 32.181 **NC,** English mockingbird. . . Orchard oriole.
4 =**loggerhead shrike.**
1957 *AmSp* 32.181 **GA,** English mockingbird. . . Southern shrike.

English monkey n [Prob humorous var of *Welsh rabbit*] *somewhat old-fash*
A simple cheese dish resembling Welsh rabbit.
1896 (c1973) Farmer *Orig. Cook Book* 469 **Boston MA,** *English Monkey.* [Recipe includes bread crumbs, milk, butter, cheese, egg]. . . Pour over toasted crackers. **1978** *DARE* File **cnMA,** English monkey was like Welsh rabbit, only it had tomatoes in it. It was the kind of thing my mother would serve at whist parties.

English nose n
See quots.
1967 *DARE* (Qu. X15, . . *Different kinds of noses*) Inf **MI**67, English nose—[one] with a high bridge; **NE**11, English nose. **1985** *DARE* File **csMI, csNM,** *English nose*—Synonymous with "eagle beak" in Union City, MI, and Las Cruces, NM.

English parrot n
=**evening grosbeak.**
1946 Hausman *Eastern Birds* 577, *Eastern Evening Grosbeak Hesperiphona vespertina* . . English Parrot. **1957** *AmSp* 32.181 **OR,** English parrot. . . Evening grosbeak.

English partridge n
=**Hungarian partridge 1.**
1927 Forbush *Birds MA* 2.12, *Perdix perdix* . . *European Partridge.* Other names: Hungarian partridge . . English partridge. **1982** Elman *Hunter's Field Guide* 43, *Hungarian Partridge (Perdix perdix)* Common & Regional Names: Hun, . . English partridge.

English pea n **esp Gulf States** See Map
=**garden pea**—often used to distinguish this vegetable from the **black-eyed pea.**
1634 (1865) *Relation MD* 21, We haue also English Peasen, & French-beanes. **1771** in 1789 Amer. Philos. Soc. *Trans.* 1.292 **C Atl,** Take any quantity of English pease intended for seed. **1930** Faulkner *As I Lay Dying* 212 **MS,** He looks back at us, his eyes and mouth three round holes in his face on which the freckles look like English peas on a plate. **1954** *PADS* 21.26 **SC,** *English peas*. . . Garden peas, cultivated for table use. Also called *sugar peas* . . *green peas, garden peas.* Not used in the singular. . . Not the variety of pea with edible pods. . . *English peas* are purveyed commercially and widely sold under the name *green peas.* All four of these terms are used generally in South Carolina, with the possible exception of *sugar peas.* **c1960** *Wilson Coll.* **csKY,** English peas. . . Garden peas as distinguished from field peas, cowpeas, stock peas, black-eyed peas. Sometimes called *sweet peas.* **1965–70** *DARE* (Qu. I20, *Other kinds of beans*) Infs **GA**85, **MS**25, **OK**27, **TN**24, 26, English peas; (Qu. I16, . . *Large flat beans*) Infs **TX**38, **VA**71, English peas; (Qu. I4) Inf **TX**77, English peas; (Qu. I14) Inf **GA**32, English peas; (Qu. I19) Inf **AL**6, English peas; (Qu. L34) Inf **MS**81, English peas; (Qu. H49) Inf **TN**24, Potatoes and English peas; (Qu. H50) Inf **GA**88, English pea salad; (QR p46) Inf **AL**14, English peas are just green peas to me. Down here peas are black-eyed peas. **1967** *Refugio Timely Remarks* (TX) 30 Mar 7/2, Refugio Public Schools Menus . . Baked chicken and dressing, English peas, cranberry sauce, hot rolls, milk. **1969** *DARE* FW Addit **GA**51, English peas—green peas. ("Peas" in this area often means "beans," e.g., black-eye peas.) **1986** Pederson *LAGS Concordance,* 85 infs, **Gulf Region,** English pea(s).

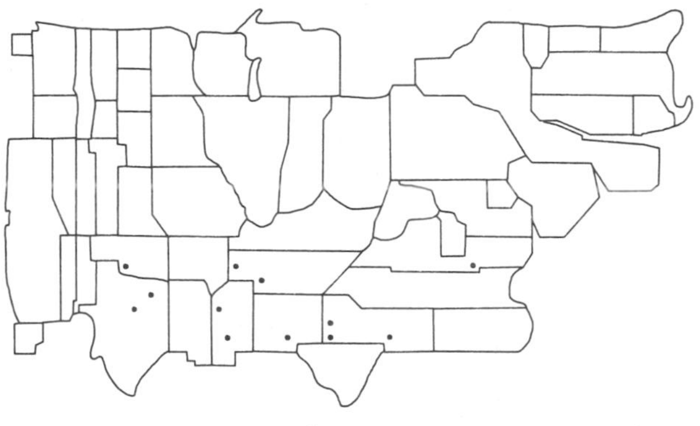

•English pea + varr (Qq. H49, H50, I4, I14, I16, I19, I20, L34)

English pheasant n [See quot 1898]
=**ring-necked pheasant.**
1898 (1900) Davie *Nests N. Amer. Birds* 179, It is generally called English Pheasant, for it is very common in England and throughout Europe in general. **1923** U.S. Dept. Ag. *Farmers' Bulletin* 1375.27 **NJ,** *Open season:* . . English or ring-necked pheasant cocks. . . Nov. 10–Dec.15. **1936** Roberts *MN Birds* 1.417, Ring-necked Pheasant. . . Other names: English Pheasant. **1963** Gromme *Birds WI* 216. **1968** *DARE* (Qu. Q7, . . *Other kinds of game birds*) Inf **WI**66, English pheasant.

English plantain n
=**buckhorn plantain.**
1843 Torrey *Flora NY* 2.15, *Plantago Lanceolata*. . . Rib-grass. English Plantain. . . Fields and upland meadows, very common. . . This plant is eaten by all kinds of stock. **1894** *Jrl. Amer. Folkl.* 7.96 **WV,** *Plantago lanceolata* . . buck-plantain, buck-horn plantain, ripple, ribwort, English plantain. **1950** Gray–Fernald *Manual of Botany* 1316, *Plantago lanceolata* . . English Plantain. **1967** *DARE* (Qu. S21, . . *Other weeds . . that are a trouble in gardens and fields*) Inf **OH**5, English plantain.

English plum pudding n Also *English pudding*

A pudding made with suet and dried fruits (sometimes plums), traditionally a holiday treat.

1896 (c1973) Farmer *Orig. Cook Book* 338 **Boston MA,** *English Plum Pudding.* [Recipe includes bread crumbs, milk, sugar, eggs, raisins, currants, figs, but no plums.] **1965** *Colonial Kitchens* 29 **GA,** *English Plum Pudding.* 4 tsp. Baking Powder, ½ tsp. Salt, 1 cup Bread Crumbs, 1 cup Suet (Shortening), 2 cups Rye or Graham Flour, 1 tsp. Cloves, 1 tsp. Cinnamon, 1 cup Seeded Raisins, 1 cup Chopped Apple, 1 cup Milk, 1 cup Molasses or Corn Syrup. Mix dry ingredients thoroughly, add suet and prepared fruit and mix well. Add gradually molasses and milk. Steam 2½ hours. Serve with hard sauce. **1965–68** *DARE* (Qu. H65, *Foreign foods*) Inf **FL**18, English plum pudding; **MO**25, English pudding.

English rail n

1 =**sora.**

1844 DeKay *Zool. NY* 2.262 **NY, NJ,** *The Sora Rail. Ortygometra carolina. . .* The *Sora* or *Soree, English Rail* or *Coot* of the Southern States, although numerous in . . New Jersey. . . It . . breeds in this state [=New York]. **1888** Trumbull *Names of Birds* 132.

2 =**purple gallinule.**

1923 U.S. Dept. Ag. *Misc. Circular* 44, *Purple Gallinule. . . Vernacular Names. . . In local use.*—Blue-Peter (Mo., La.); blue rail (La.); English rail (Tenn.) **1932** Bennitt *Check-list* 28 **MO,** *Purple gallinule. . .* Blue peter; blue rail; English rail. **1957** *AmSp* 32.181 **TN,** English rail. . . Purple gallinule.

English robin n

1 =**Baltimore oriole.**

1848 in 1850 Cooper *Rural Hours* 21 **nNY,** The early colonists gave to the gaudy oriole the name of "English robin," showing how fondly memory colored all they had left behind, since one bird is very plain in his plumage, the other remarkably brilliant. **1899** Bergen *Animal Lore* 61, English robin, for Baltimore oriole, *Icterus galbula. Bernardston, Mass.* **1917** (1923) *Birds Amer.* 2.258, *Baltimore Oriole. Icterus Galbula. . . Other names.*—Golden Robin; English Robin; Hang-bird [etc]. **1950** *WELS (Kinds of robins)* 2 Infs, **WI,** English robin. **1957** *AmSp* 32.181 **MA,** English robin. . . Baltimore oriole.

2 =**painted bunting.**

1917 *Wilson Bulletin* June 83, *Passerina ciris.*—English robin, Gloucester, N.C. **1957** *AmSp* 32.181 **NC,** English robin. . . Painted bunting.

3 =**scarlet tanager.**

1931–33 *LANE Worksheets* **sRI,** English robin—scarlet tanager. **1957** *AmSp* 32.181 **ME, MA, IA,** English robin. . . Scarlet tanager.

4 =**orchard oriole.**

1957 *AmSp* 32.181 **NC, IA,** English robin. . . Orchard oriole.

5 =**cedar waxwing.**

1957 *AmSp* 32.181 **NY,** English robin. . . Cedar waxwing.

6 =**rose-breasted grosbeak.**

1956 MA Audubon Soc. *Bulletin* 40.253 **CT,** *Rose-breasted Grosbeak.* English Robin. **1957** *AmSp* 32.181 **CT,** English robin. . . Rose-breasted grosbeak.

7 =**purple finch.**

1957 *AmSp* 32.181 **NY,** English robin. . . Purple finch.

English shoemake See **shoemake**

English snipe n

1 =**Wilson's snipe.** [See quot 1844]

1812 Wilson *Amer. Ornith.* 6.18 **PA, KY, Sth,** Snipe: *Scolopax gallinago. . .* is usually known by the name of the *English Snipe,* to distinguish it from the Woodcock. **1844** DeKay *Zool. NY* 2.256, *The Common American Snipe. Scolopax wilsoni. . .* The *Common Snipe,* or *English Snipe* as it is ignorantly called from its resemblance to the *S. gallinago* or *Common Snipe* of Europe. **1856** *Porter's Spirit of Times* 57/2 **NJ,** Of English snipe a few are on the meadows. **1883** *Century Illustr. Mag.* 26.923/1, Few of our birds are so poor in local names as this one, for it is almost everywhere known either as the "English" or the "jack" snipe. **1917** (1923) *Birds Amer.* 1.227, *Wilson's Snipe. . . Other Names.*—Common Snipe; English Snipe; American Snipe. **1953** Jewett *Birds WA* 253.

2 =**bluestocking 2.**

1957 *AmSp* 32.181 **OR,** English snipe. . . Avocet.

3 A **yellowlegs** (here: *Totanus melanoleucus*).

1957 *AmSp* 32.181 **IL,** English snipe. . . Greater yellowlegs.

English sole n Also *English flounder*

Any of three **soles** of the Pacific coast: esp *Parophrys vetulus,* but also *Psettichthys melanostictus* and **petrale sole.** For other names of *Parophrys vetulus* see **lemon sole**

1911 *Century Dict. Suppl., Sole*[2]. . . *English sole,* a name given in California to the flounder, *Eopsetta Jordani.* **1928** Pan-Pacific Research Inst. *Jrl.* 3.3.16/2 **OR, WA,** *Psettichthys melanostictus. . .* English sole. **1953** Roedel *Common Fishes CA* 62, *English Sole. Parophrys vetulus. . .* Used extensively in the fresh fish markets of California with most of the catch filleted. **1960** Amer. Fisheries Soc. *List Fishes* 47, English sole. P[acific]. *Parophrys vetulus. Ibid* 57, Flounder, . . English—see sole, English. *Ibid* 72, Sole, . . English . . see also sole, petrale. **1973** Knight *Cook's Fish Guide* 381/1, Flounder . . english see Sole, English.

English sparrow n

Std: an introduced sparrow *(Passer domesticus).* Also called **barn sparrow, bull ~, city ~, dirty ~, geedicker, grayback 1h, gray bird d, hoodlum 1, house sparrow, jickie bird, mobbing sparrow, spatzy, street sparrow, tramp**

English thistle n

A teasel (here: *Dipsachus sylvestris*).

1894 *Jrl. Amer. Folkl.* 7.90 **WV,** *Dipsachus sylvestris, . .* English thistle.

English walnut n Also *England walnut* [Because orig imported from England] **chiefly N and C Atl, CA** Cf **walnut**

An introduced walnut *(Juglans regia)* or its fruit.

1772 in 1919 *MD Hist. Mag.* 14.149 **MD,** It froze Here last Thursday night . . , it bit the Leaves of the English Walnut tree. **1790** Deane *New Engl. Farmer* 190/2, We have another sort, not indigenous, but the only one that is much cultivated in this country. It goes by the name of the English walnut. **1884** *Century Illustr. Mag.* 27.434/2, Neither Lane nor Wiggins . . succeeded in finding an important agricultural commodity suited to the New England sandy coasts and rocky hillsides; and this, . . in spite of the licorice, hemp, and indigo tried by [Eliot] . . and the English walnuts ingrafted by Judge Sewall. **1901** (1961) Greenough–Kittredge *Words* 340, In some parts of America the name *walnut* is given to the "shagbark," a kind of hickory nut, and the true walnut is known as the "English walnut." **1931–33** *LANE Worksheets* **seRI,** England walnuts . . English walnuts. **1941** *LANE* Map 277, Specific terms for particular kinds of walnuts and hickory nuts, incidentally offered by many informants, are here summarized: *English walnut* (Juglans regia). [60 infs, **throughout NEng**] *Ibid* 1 inf, **seMA,** *English walnut . .* so called to distinguish *walnut = hickory nut.* **1965–70** *DARE* (Qu. I43, *What kinds of nuts grow wild around here?*) 19 Infs, **chiefly C Atl, Upstate NY, CA,** English walnut(s); (Qu. I53, *Other fruits grown*) Inf **PA**92, English walnuts; (Qu. T16, *What kinds of trees are 'special' around here?*) 11 Infs, **chiefly sPA, wMD,** English walnut tree.

English woodpecker n

1 =**flicker** n[2] **1.** [See quot 1957]

1844 Giraud *Birds Long Is.* 181, *Golden-winged Woodpecker. . .* By some it is called "English Woodpecker." **1957** *AmSp* 32.180, *English woodpecker* (N.Y., Newfoundland) has been applied to the yellow-shafted flicker because of a fanciful resemblance of the bird to the European green woodpecker.

2 The pileated woodpecker.

1957 *AmSp* 32.181 **NJ,** English woodpecker. . . Pileated woodpecker.

eniron See **endiron 1**

enjine See **engine**

enjoy v Pronc-spp *eenjy, enj'y*

A Forms.

1841 (1952) Cooper *Deerslayer* 120 **nNY,** You've enj'yed yourself enough in that canoe. **1867** Lowell *Biglow* 22 **'Upcountry' MA,** Ye enjy the sense / O' lendin' lib'rally to the Lord. **1887** *Scribner's Mag.* 2.479/1 **AR,** How'd ye enj'y hevin' them two least ones tolled off by a gang er cotton-pickers? **1904** Day *Kin o' Ktaadn* 204 **ME,** Be your summer sojourners enj'yin themselves, Jairus? **1922** Gonzales *Black Border* 34 **sSC, GA coasts** [Gullah], Eenjy uh berry po' he'lt'.

B Senses.

1 tr: To make happy; to entertain. [*OED enjoy* v. 2. a →1610; *W2 "Obs."*] *relic*

1913 Kephart *Highlanders* 198 **sAppalachians,** "Well!" he exclaimed, "mebbe we-uns can find ye a pallet—I'll try to enjoy ye somehow."

Which, being interpreted, means, "I'll entertain you as best I can." **1926** *DN* 5.399 **Ozarks,** *Enjoy. . .* "We-all tried fer t' enjoy 'em, but they shore was th' sorriest compn'y I ever seen."

2 intr: To be happy; to enjoy oneself. [Prob infl by Yiddish syntax; see quots 1970, 1986] *esp in Jewish communities*

1958 Golden *For 2¢ Plain* 92 **NYC** (as of 1930s), When my mother served our meals . . she would always say, "Enjoy, enjoy." . . When the school had an outing and we all went off with our teachers, the last thing we heard as we went out of the door was "Enjoy, enjoy." . . The word enjoy was seldom used by itself. It was always repeated. **1970** Feinsilver *Yiddish* 306, "Enjoy" as an intransitive verb . . has become fairly common in recent years—largely encouraged . . by the usage of American Jews. "Enjoy yourself" was abbreviated to the simple "Enjoy" by the solicitous Jewish mother. Harry Golden . . made it popular around 1960 with his collection of reminiscences entitled *Enjoy, Enjoy!* . . In June 1966, over New York's radio station WQXR, Murray Shumach reported an interview with famed violinist Mischa Elman, quoting the musician's denial of being bitter: "I get a great kick out of life. I know how to enjoy." And several months later my local paper quoted . . a New Jersey sculptor . . : "Some people live to enjoy. I enjoy to live." **1978** *DARE* File **NYC,** [Advt accompanying kosher meal on a cross-country flight:] This *glatt kosher* meal has been prepared . . under . . strict rabbinical supervision. . . *Enjoy!* The crew of this flight . . wish you a hearty appetite, a pleasant flight and happy landing. **1986** Steinmetz *Yiddish & English* 71, *Enjoy* as an intransitive verb is an American Yiddishism derived from the hortative "Enjoy, Enjoy!"

‡enjoyous adj [Blend of *enjoyable* + *joyous*]
Enjoyable.

1968 *DARE* (Qu. FF17, . . *A very good or enjoyable time: "We all had a ——— last night."*) Inf **MO**34, Enjoyous time.

enjoy poor health v phr For varr see quots

1 To be ill. *somewhat old-fash*

1848 in 1935 *AmSp* 10.41 **Nantucket MA,** *I enjoy poor health.* Out of health. **1856** Whitcher *Bedott Papers* 143 **nNY, VT,** He enjoyed miserable health for a number o' year afore he died. **1905** *DN* 3.9 **cCT,** *Enjoy. . .* To experience, of health, as "he enjoyed good or bad health." [**1907** *DN* 3.212 **nwAR,** *Enjoy. . .* To experience. (Of the health.)] **1922** [see **enjoy A**]. **1926** *AmSp* 2.80 **ME,** Anyone having a persistent attack of poor health may be said to "enjoy" bad health, perhaps with more truth than poetry.

2 To malinger.

1966–68 *DARE* (Qu. BB27, *When somebody pretends to be sick*) Inf **ME**5, Some enjoy poor health; (Qu. BB28, . . *Imaginary diseases*) Infs **GA**12, **MI**78, **OH**63, **TX**18, He enjoys poor health.

enj'y See **enjoy**

enna See **ainna**

ennies See **anys**

ennominate v Cf **enduring** prep

1923 *DN* 5.206 **swMO,** *Ennominate. . .* To nominate.

enny, ennyhow, ennywhar See **any**

ennywheres See **anywheres**

enormous adv *old-fash*
Very, exceedingly.

1817 (1930) Sewall *Diary* 7 **ME,** Enormous cold morning, thermometer 25° below zero. **1931–33** *LANE Worksheets* **cwCT,** The sand wasp is an enormous big fellow. **1968** *DARE* (Qu. LL4, *Very large: "He took a ——— helping of potatoes."*) Inf **MD**20, Enormous big.

enough adj, adv, n Usu |i'nʌf, ə-|; freq aphet |nʌf|; rarely |i'nʌθ| Pronc-spp *enuff, enurf, ernuff* Also aphet *nough, nuf(f)*

A Forms.

1829 Tenney *Female Quixotism* 2.44 **Philadelphia PA** [Black], Love keep um warm nuff. **1834** *Life Andrew Jackson* 67 **TN,** The joke had gone far enuff. **1888** Jones *Negro Myths* 100 **seGA,** You hab sense nough aready. *Ibid* 122, Eh mek hole big nough, an den eh slip out. **1899** Chesnutt *Conjure Woman* 143 **NC** [Black], She'll see dat he gits ernuff ter eat. **1917** *DN* 4.411 **wNC,** *Enurf.* Variant of *enough.* **1922** Gonzales *Black Border* 209 **sSC, GA coasts** [Gullah], Ent you hab sense 'nuf mek yo' mannus w'en you see w'ite people? [=Haven't you sense enough to behave properly when you see white people?] **1936** *AmSp* 11.148 **eTX,** *Enough* . . pronounced [nʌf] . . in less literate speech. **1965–70** *DARE* (Qu. R15b) Inf **MS**70, Sho' nuff bad skeeter; (Qu. DD15) Inf **NM**3, Sure nuff drunk; (Qu. EE20) Infs **IL**55, **IN**39, 76, **NY**42, **OH**57, **PA**35, Nuff; (Qu. II11b) Inf **AR**47, Sure nuff at outs; (Qu. KK1a) Inf **MS**88, Sho' nuff good; (Qu. LL35) Infs **MS**88, **TN**46, Sho' nuff; (Qu. NN1) Infs **DE**1, **LA**17, **MO**30, Sho' (*or* sure) nuff; (Qu. NN2) Infs **FL**26, 52, **HI**1, **MO**30, **SC**8, **WA**9, Sure (*or* sho') nuff; (Qu. NN7) Infs **AR**51, **GA**84, **LA**3, **SC**67, **TN**26, 46, **TX**59, Sure (*or* sho') nuff. **1969** *DARE* FW Addit **cnCA,** Enough [i'nʌθ]. Inf said that his whole family has always used this pronunciation, [and that] he had to work very hard to acquire [the] proper pronunciation.

B As adv.
Sufficiently, considerably. *old-fash*

1856 Whitcher *Bedott Papers* 163 **nNY, VT,** It's enough ginteeler'n them flambergasted blue and yaller things. **1897** Stuart *Simpkinsville* 18 **AR,** You'd see one thet was enough pinker an' sweeter 'n the rest to make you climb for it. **1907** Freeman *By the Light* 32 **NEng,** I've seen folks enough worse than your mother git well.

C As adj.
Many.

1922 Gonzales *Black Border* 231 **sSC, GA coasts** [Gullah], We see 'nuf buzzut flyin' high obuh de tree top.

enough blue sky to make a pair of Dutchman's breeches See **Dutchman's breeches 5**

enough sight adv phr [*enough* adj + **sight**] **NEng** *old-fash*
Very much; a good deal.

1845 Judd *Margaret* 110 **NEng,** Their music is enough sight better than ours. **1887** Freeman *Humble Romance* 160 **MA,** If it's got to be done by anybody I'd enough sight rather 'twould be done by the town. **1891** (1967) Freeman *New Engl. Nun* 126, It was enough sight better than being cooped up in the shop. *Ibid* 407, They'd keep dusted 'nough sight cleaner. **1907** Lincoln *Cape Cod* 290 **eMA,** Van Senior took it enough sight more graceful than you'd expect, under the circumstances.

enough to dust a fiddle adj phr
See quot 1914.

1907 White *AZ Nights* 171, What's the matter with you and your old clothes? There ain't enough of them to dust a fiddle with anyway. *Ibid* 289, You ain't got clothes enough to dust a fiddle. **1914** *DN* 4.165 **AZ,** *Enough to dust a fiddle. . .* Used with negative to denote a very little. **1942** Perry *Texas* 134, Many splendid old Texasisms still prevail. Some Texans came here without enough clothes "to dust a fiddle."

enso See **inso**

ent v See **ain't** v[1]

ent interrog exclam See **enty**

'en't'e See **enty**

entertaining the general vbl n *euphem* Cf *DS* AA27
Menstruating.

1948 *Word* 4.183, Male personifications in American [as synonyms for menstruation] are limited: *little Willie* and *entertaining the general.*

enthralled ppl adj [Fig ext of *enthrall* to enslave] *old-fash*

1903 *DN* 2.312 **seMO,** *Enthralled. . .* Involved; indebted. 'He is enthralled so he can never pay out.'

enthusiasm n Usu |ɛn'θuziæzm̩|; also |ɛn'θɪu-, ɛn'θju-| Cf Pronc Intro 3.I.10
Std senses, var forms.

1927 Shewmake *Engl. Pronc. VA* 26, In the case of . . *enthusiasm* usage is by no means uniform. . . The *iu* pronunciation, which is . . hardly known to the average speaker and not at all used by him, must be classed as decidedly academic. Certainly it is so in Virginia, where not only the masses . . but even the majority of cultivated speakers employ the *oo* sound. **1936** *AmSp* 11.310 **Upstate NY,** *Blue, enthusiasm,* . . and *tune* occur a few times with [ɪu]. **1942** *AmSp* 17.40 **seNY,** Enthusiasm . . [u]—6 [infs] . . [ɪu]—0 . . [ju]—6. *Ibid* 41, Upstate speech uses [ɪu], [ɪʊ], [ju], and [jʊ] less frequently.

enti See **enty**

en' t'ing' See **and thing**

entire n [Absol use of *entire* whole, uncastrated; see *OED entire* adj. 4. b, sb. 3]

1930 Shoemaker *1300 Words* 20 **cPA Mts** (as of c1900), *Entire*—A stallion.

entire wheat bread n **NEng** *old-fash*
Whole wheat bread.
1941 *LANE* Map 281 **CT, RI, MA, VT,** 9 infs, Entire wheat (bread). *Ibid* **csCT,** Entire wheat bread, of wheat "ground but not bolted." **1978** *DARE* File **MA** (as of c1920), Entire wheat bread [was] common in Massachusetts when I was a child. I asked a baker once about the difference between graham bread, featured one day a week, and entire wheat, featured another. "The same, exactly the same," he said. "Some like one and some like the other."

entitle n Also *(en)titlement* **Sth** *esp freq among Black speakers; old-fash*
A name.
1883 (1971) Harris *Nights with Remus* 175 **GA** [Black], In dem days . . dey wuz a Witch-Rabbit, en dat wuz her entitlements—ole Aunt Mammy-Bammy Big-Money. **1893** Shands *MS Speech* 67, *What may be your entitlements?* Frequently used by illiterate whites for "what is your name?" **1901** Washington *Up from Slavery* 24 **Sth,** [After the Civil War] in many cases "John Hatcher" was changed to "John S. Lincoln" . . , the initial "S" standing for no name, it being simply a part of what the coloured man proudly called his "entitles." **1916** *Scribner's Mag.* 59.353/1 **VA** [Black], I ain't got no entitle 'scusin' [=except] Ommirandy. **c1937** in 1972 *Amer. Slave* 2.1.207 **SC** [Black], After freedom when us was told us had to have names, pappy say he love his old Marster Ben Clifton de best and him took that titlement, and I's been a Clifton ever since.

entitled ppl adj
1914 *DN* 4.106 **cKS,** *Entitled*. . . Obligated. "After he had done so much for us, we felt entitled to do this for him."

entitlement See **entitle**

‡entrailitis n [Folk-etym for *enteritis*]
1966 *DARE* (Qu. K78, . . *Diseases . . chickens commonly get*) Inf MA6, Entrailitis [ˌɛntrəˈlaɪtəs]—intestinal trouble.

entrails n pl Usu |ˈɛntrəlz|; also **chiefly Sth, Midl** |ˈɪntrəlz|; for addit varr see quots Pronc-sp *intrils* **scattered, but less freq Nth** See Map Cf **inwards**
Internal organs, guts.
1843 (1916) Hall *New Purchase* 277 **IN,** Sounds . . like the dying screech of that there animal out of whose intrils its strings is made. **1889** Twain *CT Yankee* 47, They would have dug his entrails out . . to get at that tale and squelch it. **1930s** in 1944 *ADD* **eWV,** *Entrails* |ˈɪntrəlz|. So pron[ounced] in butchering. **1935** *AmSp* 10.95 **GA,** *Entrails.* **1939** *LANE* Map 209 **ceMA,** [ɪnədz] = [ɛntreɪlz]; **csVT,** [ˈæ·nˌtɪɛ·lz]. **1942** Hall *Smoky Mt. Speech* 69 **wNC, eTN,** Entrails [ˈɪnˌtrəlz]. **1965–70** *DARE* (Qu. X8, . . *The organs inside the body*) 35 Infs, **chiefly Sth, Midl,** Entrails [ˈɪntrəlz]; 26 Infs, **chiefly Midl, West,** Entrails [ˈɛntrəlz]; **CA**157, **IL**97, **NY**197, [ˈɛnˌtre(ɪ)lz]; **CT**12, [ˈɪntrelz]; **KY**5, **VA**9, [ˈɛntrɔlz]; **VA**46, [ˈɪntrɔlz]; **MD**23, 35, [ˈɛntɚlz]; **KY**11, [ˈɛntrɪəlz]; **AL**3, [ˈɪntelz]; **NC**49, [ˈɪntəlz]; (Qu. H43, *Foods made from parts of the head and inner organs of an animal*) Inf **IL**124, Entrail [ˈɛntrel] sausage; (Qu. P13, . . *Other ways of fishing*) Inf **CO**20, Chicken entrails. **1967–70** *DARE* Tape **IN**51, You take the entrails [ˈɛntrəlz] out of him [=a cow]; **TX**40, They'd take the entrails [ˈɛntrəlz] [of a hog] out; **TX**94, We had . . our sausage stuffed in entrails [ˈɛntrəlz]; **TX**100, Entrails [ˈɛntrəlz] . . for catfish fishing. **1973** Allen *LAUM* 1.257 (as of c1950), For the edible internal organs of a pig or calf . . some volunteered what they thought to be roughly equivalent, such as *giblets* (of a fowl), *entrails*. . . The few instances are scattered, with no discernible correlations. **1978** *DARE* File **DE, MD, VA,** Entrails, hog intestines. **1983** *MJLF* 9.1.45 **ceKY,** *Interels* . . entrails.

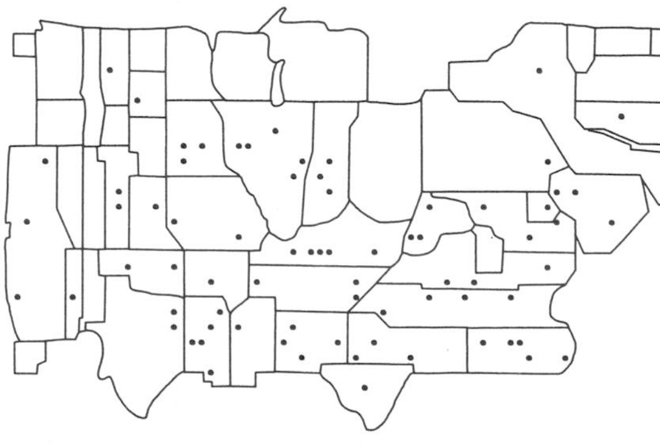

•entrails + varr (Qq. X8, H43, P13)

entry n
1 A place from which entry is made into a dwelling, as:
a also *entry shed:* A small enclosure at the entrance to a building affording protection from the weather.
1901 *DN* 2.139 **cNY,** *Entry*. . . A covered entrance from outside. **1967–69** *DARE* (Qu. D12, *The part that's put on in winter around an outside door to give extra protection from the cold*) Inf **CA**6, Entry; **MI**78, Storm door, entry; **MN**16, Entry—a box-like structure put on; **CT**29, **IN**76, **ME**5, Storm entry; **MN**2, Entry shed—in the past, not many used anymore. **1981** [see **entryway 2**].
b A passage or hallway open on both ends which divides a house in half.
1906 Johnson *Highways Missip. Valley* 86 **TN** [Black], The commonest type of negro home in the neighborhood was a long, single-story structure, with a kitchen at one end and sleeping apartments at the other, and an open passage-way between, known as "the entry." **1913** Kephart *Highlanders* 76 **sAppalachians,** A sagging clapboard roof covered its two rooms and the open space between them that we called our "entry." The State line between North Carolina and Tennessee ran through this uninclosed hallway.
c A porch or stoop.
1954 *Harder Coll.* **cwTN,** Entry, porch (of a house); formerly piazza. **c1960** *Wilson Coll.* **csKY,** *Entry*. . . Uncovered porch or portico. **1964** O'Hare *Ling. Geog. E. MT* 69, A raised platform at the front or back door of a house . . entry—without roof [1 occurrence on map]. **1966** *DARE* (Qu. D12) Inf **ME**23, Entry—some [call it a] portico. **1973** Allen *LAUM* 1.174 **csND** (as of c1950), For the open or partly enclosed structure attached to a house . . entry.
d See quot.
1968–69 *DARE* (Qu. D20, . . *A sloping outside cellar door*) Infs **IL**83, **MI**81, Entry.
2 also attrib; In coal mining: see quot 1973. Cf **back entry, entryway 3, panel entry, side entry**
1920 Fay *Gloss. Mining* 249/1, *Entry stumps.* Pillars of coal left in the mouths of abandoned rooms to support the road, entry, or gangway until the entry pillars are drawn. In Arkansas these pillars are called Entry stumps even when the rooms are first driven, before any pillars are pulled or the rooms abandoned. **1924** *Scribner's Mag.* 76.606/1 **PA,** Slipping into the rooms off the entries, lighting a burned body here and there . . they came to where tunnels diverged. **1929** *AmSp* 4.371 **Pittsburgh PA,** *Entry*. . . From this passage [=the main entry] entries are dug at intervals to work out sections of the coal. These entries, in other words, are off-shoots of the main passage. There are also off-shoots from these secondary entries. The latter off-shoots are called rooms. **1953** Goodwin *It's Good* 204 **sIL,** Dad had been quietly figuring how many entry feet he had cut [in a coal mine] that fortnight. **1967–69** *DARE* Tape **IA**8, You cut second growth white oak for entry props. Now entry prop was the big opening they made so's they could go in with their mules . . and haul the cars out . . generally you cut entry props 6 foot long; **KY**24, A large entry capable of taking in a pretty good-sized mule . . They had rooms turning off to the right and to the left. **1973** *PADS* 59.35 **AL, OH, PA, nWV,** An *entry* . . *cut* at a right angle to the *main entry* from which *rooms* are *necked off* and [which] serves as a *haulage road* to the main *haulage* system. *Ibid* **nWV, VA, eKY,** *Entry boss* . . = face boss.

entry pillar n [**entry 2** + **pillar**]
In coal mining: =**barrier.**
1920 [see **entry 2**]. **1973** *PADS* 59.35 **sIL, IN, wKY,** *Entry pillar* . . = barrier (pillar).

entry shed See **entry 1a**

entry stump n [**entry 2** + **stump**]
In coal mining: =**barrier.**
1920 [see **entry 2**]. **1973** *PADS* 59.35 **VA, eKY, TN,** *Entry stump* . . = barrier (pillar).

entryway n
1 The entrance hallway of a house. **chiefly Nth, West** See Map

1746 in 1915 NH *Prov. & State Papers* 33.391, It is also agreed by us that the Said Cellar great Doors and the yard the Entryway Stairs . . all be in Common. **1889** Cooke *Steadfast* 236 **CT,** His study door opened from the left hand of the little entry-way into which they stepped from without. **1950** *WELS (When you go into a house, the part between the front door and the rooms)* 5 Infs, **WI,** Entryway. **1965–70** *DARE* (Qu. D11) 44 Infs, **chiefly Nth, West,** Entryway. **1968** *DARE* FW Addit **PA**169, Entryway, part of a house.

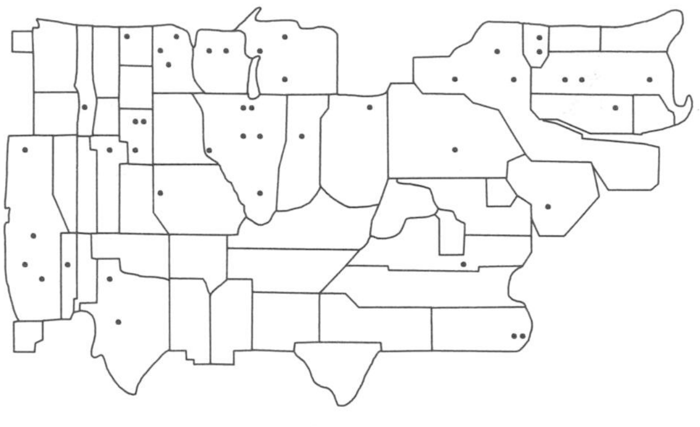

•entryway 1 (Qu. D11)

2 =entry 1a.

1966–69 *DARE* (Qu. D12, *The part that's put on in winter around an outside door to give extra protection from the cold*) Inf **IN**58, Storm door, entryway; **MT**2, Entryway; **VT**7, Storm shelter, entryway. **1969** *Cape Cod Std.-Times* (Hyannis MA) 22 Jan 29/2, [Advt:] On The Cove—Eastham. 3 bedroom, living room with fireplace, large kitchen, large enclosed porch, rear entryway. **1973** Allen *LAUM* 1.174 **neIA** (as of c1950), For the open or partly enclosed structure attached to a house . . entryway. [1 inf] **1981** *PADS* 67.20 **neMN,** The use of *entrance, entry(way), foyer, and vestabule* [sic] by Iron Range informants is interesting. Because of the long, severe winters of northern Minnesota, most porch-like structures—particularly on older houses—are completely closed. They more closely resemble small rooms or halls than they do open porches, and the vocabulary of the Iron Range reflects this common method of construction.

3 In coal mining: **=entry 2.**

1969 *DARE* Tape **KY**24, He pulled it on the entryway and they had rooms turning off.

enty interrog exclam Also sp *ent, 'en't'e, enti* [Prob *ain't* + *e* (at **he** pron)] **chiefly SC, GA coasts** *esp Gullah* Cf **ainna, ain't** v[2], **ain't it** interrog exclam[2], **inso, yent**

1 Isn't that true? Is that so? Really!—used as a tag question or exclam of surprise or affirmation.

1856 Simms *Eutaw* 210 [Black], "Benny fight for old maussa, enty?—" "Yes, Benny, you did, faithfully!" **1867** Allen *Slave Songs* xxvi **seSC,** *Enty* is a curious corruption, I suppose of *ain't he,* used like our "Is that so?" in reply to a statement that surprises one. "Robert, you have n't written that very well." "Enty, sir?" ["]John, it's going to rain today." "Enty, sir?" **1883** (1971) Harris *Nights with Remus* 136 **GA** [Black], "Enty!" assented Daddy Jack, admiringly. *Ibid* 202, B'er Rabbit say rice-bud yent kin fly in house wey de no win. Rice-bud say, 'Enty!' **1908** *S. Atl. Qrly.* 7.347, *Enty, now?,* ear-mark of the *Gullah* speaker, used as an intensive and affirmative exclamation or rejoinder, resolves itself into provincial English particles. A Warwickshire man says *yunt it* for *is it not,* and *yunt he,* by contraction . . from the older *be n't it,* and *be n't he* . . thus the familiar characteristic affirmative exclamation, *'en't'e, now? Enty?* as also the peasantrisms [sic], *ain't it, ain't he,* or *jest ain't he, now,* commonly elsewhere surviving. **1928** Peterkin *Scarlet Sister Mary* 137 **seSC** [Gullah], We may as well try to act mannersable, enty? **1942** Rawlings *Cross Creek* 85 **FL** [Gullah], "You trust me, enty?" and I said, "Yes." **1950** *PADS* 14.28 **SC,** *Enti* ['ɛntɪ]. . . "Is it not," "do we not," . . in repetition of a statement in the interrogative form for confirmation. **1960** Williams *Walk Egypt* 186 **GA** [Black], Dis the grindstone, enty, ma'm? **1966** *DARE* (Qu. NN3, *Words and expressions meaning 'Don't you agree?': "She's a nice-looking woman, ______?"*) Inf **SC**11, ['ɛnɨ]—Negroes only.

2 Isn't it true that ______?—used to introduce a yes-no question; see quots.

1853 Simms *Sword & Distaff* 204 **SC** [Black], "You have, heard, Tom, of such an animal as a Sheriff, or Sheriff's Deputy?" "Enty I know? He's a sort of warmint!" *Ibid* 235, Enty you see de hoss ready for you by de tree[?] **1888** Jones *Negro Myths* 156 **seGA,** Many time dem people wuh cant see sperit come pon top dem an dunno nuttne bout um. Enty wen you duh walk long de road der night you suttenly feel hot win bresh by you cheek? Enty you sometime smell dead man finger? *Ibid* 3, Enty you bin tell me you nebber meet up wid trouble? **1922** Gonzales *Black Border* 283 **sSC, GA coasts** [Gullah glossary], "Enty," "ent," "yent," sometimes "ain'," serve for isn't, aren't, didn't, don't, doesn't. "Ent you shum?" "enty you shum?" may mean didn't you see? or don't you see? him, her, it, or them. **1949** Turner *Africanisms* 221 [Gullah], The practice of repeating words and phrases throughout the sentence is general among both the Gullahs and the West Africans. . . [ɛnti, ɛnti rɛbl tɒɪm kʌmɪn bɑk? ɒl hu nɛwə šʌm—ɛnti də kʌmɪn bɑk?] "Is it not, is not rebel time (slavery) coming back? All who never saw it—is it not coming back?"

enuff, enurf See **enough**

envelope n

A matchbook.

1967 *DARE* (QR p36a) Inf **OR**4, Envelope—matchbook. **1967** *DARE* FW Addit **OR,** Envelope match[es]—book matches.

envious adj [*OED envious* a. 2 "Full of ill-will; malicious, spiteful. *Obs.* [exc dial]"]

Hostile.

[**1673** Penn *Chr. Quaker* iv.531 [sic *OED*—quot not found], Envious Displeasure against an Harmless Suffering People.] **1965** *DARE* (Qu. II11b, *If two people can't bear each other at all . . "Those two are ______."*) Inf **OK**13, Envious to each other.

envy-stripe n

Spite.

1927 Kennedy *Gritny* 119 **sLA** [Black], She knew somebody was burning a candle over her to keep bad luck in her way just for "envy-stripe."

enymost See **eenamost**

eow See **ewe** n

Ephraim n Also *Eph, Eph'm, Ephram* **West** *old-fash* Cf *DCan*

A grizzly bear—often used as a nickname.

1854 Reid *Hunter's Feast* 221 *(DA),* Thur I saddled my mar, an' then rid back to git my gun, an' perhaps, to give ole Eph'm a fresh taste o' lead. **1859** J. G. Wood *Nat. Hist.* 1.400 *(DA),* The Grizzly, or "Ephraim" as the creature is familiarly termed by the hunters. **1886** *Outing* 9.199/1 **Rocky Mts,** Thar, sure 'nuff, war Ephram, lookin' big ez a steer, rippin' up sods by the yard, an' chawin' fresh roots. *Ibid* 199/2, The bullet jest grazed the skin by Ephram's leg. **1889** Munroe *Golden Days* 152 **CA,** Old Eph's dead enough. **1908** (1924) Mulford *Orphan* 223 **SW,** "Reckon Ephraim mebby'll turn 'roun an' scratch hisself, if you hits 'im." "Won't that stop a b'ar?" he said.

epidoozick See **epizootic 2**

Episcopal adj, n Pronc-spp *Epistopal, 'Piscopal, 'Piskubble*

A Forms.

1916 *DN* 4.274 **NE,** *Epistopal.* Episcopal. Infrequent. **1922** Gonzales *Black Border* 319 **sSC, GA coasts** [Gullah glossary], *'Piskubble*—Episcopal, Episcopalian. **1954** in 1958 Brewer *Dog Ghosts* 83 **TX** [Black], He goes to de bigges' white 'Piscopal chu'ch in Eas' Texas.

B As noun. [Absol use of adj]

An Episcopalian.

1845 (1876) Cooper *Chainbearer* 134 **CT,** Your committee report that the Baptists, Universals and Episcopals ought to be dropped, and that the next vote, now to be taken. **1902** Wister *Virginian* 212, "At least two of Episcopals." "That's three. Then Methodists and Baptists, and ______." **1904** *DN* 2.418 **nwAR,** *Episcopal.* . . Churchman or churchwoman. . . "My mother was an Episcopal." **1908** *DN* 3.308 **eAL, wGA,** *Episcopal.* . . An Episcopalian. Common. **1970** *DARE* Tape **CA**185, Our social life was all there [=in church]. The Catholics did the same thing, the Episcopals did the same thing.

Episcopalian n, adj Pronc-spp *Episcolopian, Episcopolian, Episcopolopian, Pishopaligan* [Cf *SND Episcopaulian* 1828 →; *EDD Episcolaupian* 1889]

Std sense, var forms.

1906 *DN* 3.135 **nwAR,** *Episcolopian. . .* Episcopalian. **1920s** in 1944 *ADD* **cNY,** He's an [i'pɪskə'lopɪən]. **1936** Reese *Worleys* 37 **MD** (as of 1865) [Black], I's a Baptis' preachah, I is, an' dese heah is Pishopaligans. **1943** Lewis *Gideon Planish* 243 **Chicago IL,** "I guess we're supposed to be good Christians, aren't we?" "Sure-you-bet. Good Episcopolopians, anyway." **1954** *PADS* 21.27 **SC,** *Episcolopian. . .* Episcopalian. **1967–69** *DARE* (Qu. CC4, . . *Nicknames . . for various religions*) Infs **CT**35, **OH**20, Episcolopians; **OH**74, Episcopolians.

episoozick See **epizootic 2**

epistle n Cf **apostle, pestle**

Std senses, var forms.

1891 *PMLA* 6.166 **WV,** The *t* between *s* and *l* of words like *apostle, epistle,* etc., is sounded. **1922** Gonzales *Black Border* 319 **sSC, GA coasts** [Gullah glossary], *'Pistle*—Epistle, Epistles (Bible).

Epistopal See **Episcopal**

epitaph n Pronc-sp *epitap*

Std sense, var form.

1895 *DN* 1.375 **seKY, eTN, wNC,** *Epitap.*

epizeema n *joc* Note: Cf pronc of *eczema* as [ɪg'zimə].

1967 *DARE* (Qu. BB28, *Joking names . . for imaginary diseases*) Inf **PA**27, Epizeema [ɛpɪ'zimə].

epizootic n, freq pl Usu with *the* Std |ˌɛpɪzo'ɑtɪk|; but usu |ˌɛpɪ'zuṭɪk(s)|; also |-'zuti|; for addit varr see quot 1965–70 at **2** Also *epizooty*

1 also *hepizootic:* A disease of livestock, esp horses, usu of indeterminate nature.

1872 *Chicago Tribune* (IL) 31 Oct 1/3, After having thoroughly examined each horse they pronounced the malady to be the epizootic. **1887** (1967) Harris *Free Joe* 154 **ceGA,** And then, right on top of the whole caboodle, here comes the panic in the banks, and the epizooty 'mongst the cattle. **1908** *DN* 3.309 **eAL, wGA,** *Epizootics. . .* A disease among cattle. **1930** Shoemaker *1300 Words* 20 **cPA Mts** (as of c1900), *Epizooty*—A virulent disease once prevalent among horses. **1939** Aurand *Quaint Idioms* 24, You act as if you had the *epizooty* (a disease found among horses). **1950** *WELS (Diseases of horses)* 1 Inf, **seWI,** Epizootic. **1954** *PADS* 21.27 **SC,** *Epizootics* [ˌɛpɪ'zutɪks]: n. pl. Any disease of an animal, usually of a horse or mule, of indefinite nature. If an animal is "off his feed" or otherwise ailing from no known cause, it is said to have the epizootics. **1968** Adams *Western Words* 106, *Epizootic*—A cowboy's name for distemper or strangles, a catarrhal disease of horses. **1970** *DARE* (Qu. K47, . . *Diseases . . [of] horses or mules*) Inf **MA**75, Hepizootic [hɛpə'zudɪk], I think, years ago.

2 also *epidoozick, episoozick, epizootis, epizoozick, hepazootis:* A human illness or ailment; melancholy; an imaginary disease; also transf. Cf **cholera morbus**

c1883 Peck *Peck's Bad Boy & Pa* 20 **seWI,** It don't look reasonable that a man would catch epizootic and rheumatism just to fool his boy. **1908** *DN* 3.309 **eAL, wGA,** *Epizootics. . .* Among persons, "the blues," the mulligrubs. "He has a bad case of epizootics." **1930** *Atlantic Mth.* May 680/1 **ME,** Once when I was sick in bed with the epizootic, she come to me an' she says, "Be you prepared to die, Aunt Nebbie?" **1935** *AmSp* 10.170 **sePA,** There are *pow-wow* doctors, to whom one takes the baby sick with the *epizootic* to have it *pow-wowed.* **1950** *WELS (Imaginary diseases: "I guess he's got the ______.")* 1 Inf, **cwWI,** Epizootic. **1954** *PADS* 21.27 **SC,** *Epizootics. . .* The term is . . applied humorously to people. **1965–70** *DARE* (Qu. BB28, *Joking names . . for imaginary diseases: "He must have the ______.")* 81 Infs, **scattered,** Epizootic(s) [ˌɛpɪ'zuṭɪk(s), 'ɛpɪˌzuṭɪk(s), ɛpə-]; **AL**41, **AR**52, **IL**30, **IA**7, **KS**2, **TX**6, 62, Epizooty; **KS**5, **PA**209, Epizootis; **MO**15, [ˌɛpɪ'zuˑubɪks]; **NJ**22, [ɛpɪ'zɑtɪks]; **AL**27, [ɛpə'zotɪks]; **MS**59, [ˌɛpɪzu'ɑdɪk]; **NY**34, Epidoozick; **SC**58, Hepazootis ['hæpəˌzuṭəs]; **TX**104, Hepazootis ['hɛpəˌzudəs]; (Qu. BB5, *A general feeling of discomfort*) Inf **MI**55, Got the epizootic; (Qu. BB9, . . *Severe cough and difficult breathing*) Infs **IL**113, **IN**60, Epizootic; (Qu. BB13, . . *Chills and fever*) Inf **IL**126, Epizootics; (QR p191) Inf **IA**5A, I must have the epizootics [laughter]; (QR p207) Inf **OH**44, Epizootics—that's some kind of cold, not a bogus thing. **1967** *DARE* Tape **MI**55, There was a word that my mother used . . "epizootic" [ɛpɪ'zuṭɪk]—when somebody was, oh, not seriously ill but just out of sorts. **1978** *Blair & Ketchum's Country Jrl.* Sept 82 **NEng,** What in Tophet ails her [=a steam engine during an earthquake]? He was petrified with wonderment, but he managed to be helpful with suggestions of the epizoozick and the tickdoloroo. **1985** *DARE* File **cIA,** Whenever we would sneeze, my mother would say "You must be catching the episoozick."

epossom salts See **epsom salts**

eppes pron, n, adj, adv |'ɛpɪs| Also sp *eppis, eppus* [Cogn with Ger *etwas;* quots 1968, 1970, 1978, 1987 are clearly Yiddish; in the other quots *eppes* may stem independently from more than one Ger dialect: the Eastern Yiddish form is *epes;* in the Palatinate, Würtemburg, Switzerland *eppes* is the prevailing form; in Bavaria and Franconia it is *ebbes.*]

Something; the worst thing; a somebody; low class, lousy; something of, sort of; see quots.

1933 Ersine *Underworld Slang* 34, *Eppus. . .* The general implication is worthlessness. The word has a hundred uses, all carrying a feeling of scorn or contempt. "That's the eppus. He carries iron for an eppus outfit. Eppus on you!" **1966** *AmSp* 41.280 **Pacific** [Carnie talk], *Eppis. . .* Nothing. Usually accompanied by a shrug to indicate poor business. **1968** Rosten *Yiddish* 108, This delightful, resilient word has chameleon properties. . . "Eat eppes." (Eat something.) . . "That is eppes a beauty?" (. . "You call *that* a beauty . . ?" . .) "He thinks he's an eppes." (He thinks he's a somebody.) **1970** Feinsilver *Yiddish* 149, [*Eppes* . . [is] not only a noun, meaning "something," . . but it's an expressive particle as in *eppes a bekante*—something of an acquaintance.] *Ibid* 306, Eppis . . meaning "nothing" [in quot 1966] . . may be an ironic use of Yiddish *eppes . . ,* perhaps influenced too by the somewhat similar Pennsylvania German *ebbes.* **1978** *DARE* File **NYC,** "Eppes, nothing," is frequently said by one Jewish woman to indicate that something is inconsequential. **1987** *DARE* File **NYC,** Some uses of eppis as an English word: "He's eppis a doctor" meaning that he's a doctor but not as good a one as he, or others, might think. Along the same lines would be "He works for eppis a business" meaning that he works for a business but for not a very good one. "Do you think you're eppis a Diamond Jim Brady?" might be said to people who spend a lot of money as if they had plenty to burn but don't. "I have eppis a headache," that is, "I have a bit of a headache," and "So nu, tell me eppis," meaning "So tell me something already."

epsom salts n Also *epossom salts* *joc* Cf **iodine**

Among loggers: a camp doctor.

1931 *AmSp* 7.48 **Sth, SW** [Lumberjack lingo], Camp doctors are "Old Pills," . . or "Epossom Salts." **1968** Adams *Western Words* 106, *Epsom salts*—A logger's name for the camp doctor. **1969** Sorden *Lumberjack Lingo* 39 **NEng, Gt Lakes,** *Epsom salts*—A camp doctor.

equal n, v, adj Usu |'iˌkwəl|; also **chiefly Sth, S Midl** |'iˌkəl|; rarely |'ɪkḷ| Pronc-spp *e(e)kal, ekil, ekle*

Std senses, var forms.

1851 Hooper *Widow Rugby's Husband* 40 **AL,** Thar's nothin but deth can eekal him. **1867** Lowell *Biglow* 147 **'Upcountry' MA,** Jeff'son prob'ly meant wal with his "born free an' ekle." **1885** Murfree *Prophet of Smoky Mts.* 248 **eTN,** Pete air ekal ter that. **1903** *DN* 2.291 **Cape Cod MA** (as of 1840s), The *w*-sound frequently assimilated or disappeared after a consonant: *ekal* = *equal . . awkard* = *awkward.* **1929** Sale *Tree Named John* 88 **MS,** W'en Gawd made 'im, He jes made his ile de bes', so ez t' sorta ekil 'im up. **1931** *PMLA* 46.1317 **sAppalachians,** *Equal* becomes "ekal," *equality* becomes "ekality." **1942** Hall *Smoky Mt. Speech* 88 **wNC, eTN,** For *equal* and *equally,* the forms ['ikəl] and ['ikəli] are current, and there were single instances of *frequent* and *quadruple* without [w]. **1967** *DARE* (Qu. LL32, . . *One man's ability is not nearly as great as another man's: "John ______ Bill."*) Inf **TX**32, Can't [ɪkḷ] to.

equal adv

Equally.

1966 *DARE* (Qu. II9, *If several people have to contribute . . "Let's all ______."*) Inf **OK**18, Share equal in it.

equalizer n

1 =**evener 1.** [Because it equalizes the pull of the animals] *old-fash*

1872 (1876) Knight *Amer. Mech. Dict.* 1.807/2, *Equalizer.* An *evener* or whiffletree to whose ends the *swingle-trees* or *single-trees* of the individual horses are attached. **1927** Sears *Catalogue* 1002/3, *Three-Horse Wagon Equalizer. . .* Constructed so that each horse pulls an equal load. . . Main evener, 2x5x3 ft. 8 in. Singletrees 2x3x32 in. **1967** *DARE* (Qu. L47, *The two movable bars behind a team of horses are fastened to a long piece; this is a ______*) Inf **MA**72, Equalizer—heard, but not used. **1969** Sorden *Lumberjack Lingo* 39 **NEng, Gt Lakes,** *Equalizer*—A whiffletree carried high on the rumps of the horses and used when loading logs with a cable or chain. **1973** Allen *LAUM* 1.216 **cIA** (as of c1950), The device by which two—or more—horses are hitched to a buggy or wagon . . equalizer [1 inf]. [*Ibid* **sManitoba,** *Equalizer:* For more than two horses.]

2 A pistol. Cf **evener 2**

1931 Runyon *Guys* 89 **NYC,** He outs with the old equalizer and starts blasting away. **1936** Adams *Cowboy Lingo* 166, His personal weapons were spoken of as his . . 'equalizer'. **1951** Grant *Cowboy Encycl.* 61, *Equalizer.* Cowboy term for six-gun. It comes from the old western expression that "a Colt makes all men equal."

3 A severe winter.

1964 Jackman–Long *OR Desert* 42, But about once in ten years would come a winter that killed all the stock. That was called an "equalizer" and everyone started even again.

‡equinomiker n

An equal basis.

1975 Thomas *Hear the Lambs* 52 **nwAL,** "I bought me a new hat yesterday." She cast her eyes down toward her feet. "And new shoes too! . . I guess you wants yo' feets to be on a equinomiker wid yo' head."

equipment n

Std senses, var form.

1943 in 1944 *ADD* **neOH,** *Equipment.* . . |i'kwUpmənt|.

er- prep[1] See **of**

er- prep[2] See **a** prep[1] **5**

er v[1] See **have** v[1] **A1c**

er v[2] See **have** v[2]

er- Representing pronc of *a-, e-, o-* in unstressed syllables of such words as *about, ago, along, enough, innocent* **chiefly Sth** See quots.

1899 Chesnutt *Conjure Woman* 136 **NC,** I had a good marster befo' de wah, en I wa'n't sol' erway, en I wuz sot free. **1904** Day *Kin o' Ktaadn* 99 **ME,** It started innercent ernuff. **1905** Culbertson *Banjo Talks* 66 *(ADD)* **SE,** Yeard de chu'n a hour ergo. **1908** *S. Atl. Qrly.* 7.333 [Gullah], Do erbout; anseh de do'! **1909** *Ibid* 8.44, Erway. **1917** Torrence *Granny Maumee* 51 [Black], I got erbout—fifty er so. **1927** Boston Soc. Nat. Hist. *Proc.* 38.330 **seGA,** Referring to three young Fox Squirrels which they once had, Allen Chesser said: 'Now talkin' erbout eatin' grasshoppers, there's a thing that loved grasshoppers. . . Take 'im one er two, an' go erlong erbout 'is business.' **1941** Percy *Lanterns* 293 **MS,** Then *ernuther* cat come in.

-er Representing pronc of final unstressed syllables in such words as *meadow, piano, banana, idea* [Retroflexion of |ə|, perh by hypercorrection; cf Intro "Language Changes" IV.1b, c] **chiefly S Midl; also NEast**

1 in words spelled with *-o(w):* See quots.

1834 *Life Andrew Jackson* 208 **TN,** Who is us'd tu swaller what others prepare. **1851** Hooper *Widow Rugby's Husband* 45 **AL,** I seen the shadder of my face. **1857** *Putnam's Mag.* 10.348/2 **CT,** Red an' yeller. **1871** (1882) Stowe *Fireside Stories* 55 **MA,** It sort o' went thro' and thro' a feller! *Ibid* 56, Amaziah Pipperidge, a widder with snappin' black eyes. **1891** *DN* 1.164 **cNY,** Excrescent *r* is not infrequent. . . In unstressed syllables it occurs . . as final in [fɛlɚ, tælɚ, tə'bækɚ, wɪndɚ]. **1895** *DN* 1.374 **wNC, eTN, seKY,** *Shaller:* shallow. **1899** (1912) Green *VA Folk-Speech* 279, *Meller.* . . Mellow. **1915** *DN* 4.178 **swVA,** [o] in unaccented syllables at the end of words (with the spelling *-o* or *-ow*) becomes regularly *-er,* in which the *r* is always heard, even if it is indistinct: (po)tater . . , (to)baker . . , minner . . , feller . . , winder. **1942** Hall *Smoky Mt. Speech* 80 **wNC, eTN,** The sound [ɚ] . . is the prevailing one in most words spelled *-o, -ow.* It may be, and frequently is, modified to [ə]; and occasionally it is "corrected" to [o]. . . Banjo, mosquito [(mə)'skitɚ], negro ['nɪgɚ], piano [paɪ'ænɚ], potato, tobacco, tomato; fellow, follow, "holler" v . . , hollow n . . , meadow, mellow, pillow, shadow, shallow, tallow, wallow . . , widow, window, yellow. . . When *-r-* precedes *-ow* or *-o,* the treatment is not with [ɚ], but usually with [ə]. **1953** Randolph *Down in Holler* 28 **Ozarks,** Sometimes one hears *banjer* for banjo. **1961** Kurath–McDavid *Pronc. Engl.* 170, *Tomato* ending in constricted [ɚ] predominates in the folk speech of eastern and western North Carolina . . in the northern and western margins of South Carolina and in the hill country of Northern Georgia. Sporadic instances occur in the Valley of Virginia, in West Virginia, on Delmarva, and in western New York State. **1976** Wolfram–Christian *Appalachian Speech* 66, One of the characteristic aspects of the A[ppalachian] E[nglish] phonological system most noticeable to outsiders involves the alternation of final *ow* forms with *er* . . *holler* . . *tobaccer* . . *yeller* . . *potaters* . . *winders* . . *narrers*. . . The *er* alternation is observed only on items that have potential alternants as *ow.*

2 in words spelled with *-a(h):* See quots.

1837 Smith *Col. Crockett's Exploits* 87, Let us take an ideer. **1857** *Putnam's Mag.* 10.348/2 **CT,** The brightest . . bandanner you ever see. **1926** *DN* 5.385 **ME,** *-a* (final). Pronounced like -y or -er in such words as Amelia, America, Augusta, Canada, Ezra, Laura, Liza, Piazza, Veranda. Common. **1941** Stuart *Men of Mts.* 247 **neKY,** Train that goes to Atlanter, Georgia. **1942** Hall *Smoky Mt. Speech* 77 **wNC, eTN,** The tendency . . to develop [ə] into [ɚ] is manifest also in words spelled with *-a, -ah,* especially *Carolina* . . and *Hannah* (family and place-name): [kær'laɪnɚ], [kɚ'laɪnɚ] . . ['hænɚ]. These words also occur with [ə], but the forms with [ɚ] are by far the more common. Other instances . . are *Etta* (feminine given name) ['ɛtɚ], *lima* (beans) ['laɪmɚ], and *banana* [bə'nænɚ], ['nænɚ]. **1942** *AmSp* 17.154 **seNY,** In such words as *Asia, banana,* and *idea,* final [ə] frequently changes to [ɚ]. **1953** Randolph *Down in Holler* 28 **Ozarks,** A few old people shout *hallelujer* instead of hallelujah. **1967** *DARE* Tape **AL**15, Atlanta [æt'læntɚ].

-er compar suff

Std sense, var applications. Cf *EDG* §398

1 Suffixed to polysyllabic adjs and advs and disyllabics not ending in *-y, -ow, -le,* and *-er;* this contrasts with StdE where *-er* is usu restricted to monosyllabic adjs and advs and disyllabics in *-y, -ow, -le,* and *-er:*

a To adjs and advs normally compared with *more* in StdE.

1860 Holmes *Professor* 194 **NEng,** Seems to me he looks peakeder than ever. **1867** Lowell *Biglow* 18 **'Upcountry' MA,** A spotteder, ringstreakeder child the' warn't in Uncle Sam's / Holl farm. **1891** Page *Elsket* 137 **VA,** You mus'n' say you ain' do it, 'cuz dat's dangersomer 'n allowing you *is* do it. **1927** *DN* 5.470 **sAppalachians,** *Endurabler,* lasting longer. **1927** *AmSp* 3.8 **Ozarks,** In their comparisons . . the hillman is likely to overwork the *er* and *est* terminations. . . *Lucy is a lovin'er gal as Dolly, but Mary is th' lovin'est gal I ever seed.* **1936** *AmSp* 11.351 **eTX,** I don't know a trifliner cuss than old Wadell Smith. **1952** Brown *NC Folkl.* 1.537, *-er:* suffix. The comparative and superlative degrees of the adjective and adverb are generally formed by adding the suffixes *-er* and *-est* rather than by using the adverbs *more* and *most,* regardless of the length of the word. This principle is in conformity with early English. **1968** *DARE* Tape **NV**8, Things has got to be equaler.

b To adjs, including pples, not usually compared in StdE.

1915 *DN* 4.179 **swVA,** Present participles used attributively are compared as other adjectives: *a runnin'er horse.* **1940** *AmSp* 15.51 **sAppalachians,** Comparatives . . are formed by promiscuously suffixing an *-er* . . great-bigger . . fightin'er.

2 Suffixed to the positive form of those adjs and advs which in StdE undergo suppletion. Cf **bad** adj **A, far** adv, adj[1] **B**

1899 (1912) Green *VA Folk-Speech* 172, *Fer, ferrer, ferrest* . . For *far, farther, farthest.* **1908** *DN* 3.284 **eAL, wGA,** Badder . . farer. **1940** *AmSp* 15.52 **sAppalachians,** Abnormal comparisons abound: farer . . badder. **1952** Brown *NC Folkl.* 1.539, *Farrer, furrer* . . Farther, further. **c1960** *Wilson Coll.* **csKY,** *Farther.* . . [farr̩]. **1967** *DARE* (Qu. X52, . . *A person . . who had been sick was looking* ______) Inf **OH**12, Badder.

3 Suffixed to suppletive forms already showing the compar degree thus forming "double comparatives." Cf **-ed 1, -es** suff[1] **2, -est 3** Cf Intro "Language Changes" II.2

1908 *DN* 3.284 **eAL, wGA,** Betterer. **1930** *AmSp* 5.267 **Ozarks,** One of the Ozarker's commonest grammatical peculiarities [is] . . double comparatives or superlatives as *worser.* **1936** *AmSp* 11.351 **eTX,** *Worser.* **1940** *AmSp* 15.52 **sAppalachians,** Double comparatives . . are common: worser, more worser.

4 In constructions where *more* serves as an intensifier; cf StdE *much better.* [*OED more* C. 1. d "*Obs.* exc. *arch.*" c1205–1832]

1815 Humphreys *Yankey in England (ADD),* I cood form a more righter judgement of you. **1891** *PMLA* 6.170 **WV,** I noted *more pleasanter* on several occasions. **1909** *DN* 3.350 **eAL, wGA,** *More tireder.* . . "You'll be more tireder 'an what you are gin you git back." Also *more betterer, more prettier.* **1928** Peterkin *Scarlet Sister Mary* 150 **sSC** [Gullah], I can rest mo better to-night. **1930** *AmSp* 5.267 **Ozarks,** *More colder.* **1942** (1971) Campbell *Cloud-Walking* 86 **seKY,** It's spread out more wider in a nation of books. **1950** *PADS* 14.47 **SC,** *More.* . . Often used in double comparatives; "more sooner," "more better," "more older." **1967–70** *DARE* Tape **AZ**6, More better; **GA**93,

It's more hotter, warmer, there; **IL69**, They was fillin' that up with sand so to make it more stronger; **LA5**, They're more shorter, it seemed like. **1976** *DARE* File **Austin TX**, Many white middle-class r-ful students are familiar with and use [mo'bɛdə] for "better."

-er affix Usu suffixed, occas infixed, superfluously

1 added to nouns: See quots. [Perh from agentive *-er* suff] **chiefly Sth, S Midl**

1715 in 1940 *AmSp* 15.226 **NEng**, *Burglarer*, burglar. **1885** Twain *Huck. Finn* 18 **ceMO**, After supper she got out her book and learned me about Moses and the Bulrushers. **1899** (1912) Green *VA Folk-Speech* 188, *Furrer*. . . Fur of animals. *Ibid* 433, *Swinger*. . . Made by ropes overhead, and with a seat in which children swing backwards and forwards. **1906** *DN* 3.153 **nwAR**, *Residenter*. . . Resident. **1927** *DN* 5.475 **Ozarks**, [*Musicker*. . . A musician. . .] The term *musicianer* is also heard occasionally. **1931** *AmSp* 6.269 **KY**, Redundant or curiously assorted suffixes occur in the nouns poeter, loverer, musicianer. **1936** *AmSp* 11.275 **cTN**, *Handler*. Name. "What is your handler?" **1937** *Esquire* Apr 130/1 **swMO** *(ADD)*, He's never seen any [fine clothes], except on the touristers. **1942** Hall *Smoky Mt. Speech* 79 **wNC, eTN**, Two words have assumed the suffix *-er*, apparently by analogy with forms of similar type: *linguist* (?) becomes ['lɪnkəstɚ] "interpreter" . . and *resident* becomes *residenter* "old timer". . . *Wasp* frequently occurs as ['wɔ̜spɚ], ['wɔspɚ]. **1968** *DARE* (Qu. M16, . . *Small shelter for a hen*) Inf **GA68**, Cooper; (Qu. HH28) Inf **FL28**, Tourister.

2 added to verbs: See quots. [Perh from frequentative *-er;* see *OED -er* suffix[5]] Cf **conniver** v

1891 Harris *Balaam* 146 **cGA**, Me an' Wash done some mighty sly slippin' up en surrounderin'. **1902** *DN* 2.241 **sIL**, *Pelter*. . . To throw stones or other missiles at anything. **1905** Culbertson *Banjo Talks* 12 **SE**, Then we . . goes perawderin' [=parading] all in line. **1913** Kephart *Highlanders* 203 **sAppalachians**, Yea, la! I'm jist loaferin' about. **1942** Hall *Smoky Mt. Speech* 79 **wNC, eTN**, I'm just a-loaferin' around.

'er pron See **her**

ere adv

1 See **here A4.**

2 See **there.**

ere a See **ary**

erl See **oil**

erligion n [By metath of *religion*]

1898 Harris *Tales Home Folks* 414 **GA** [Black], Dey went on in dar mo' samer dan ef dey'd got erligion.

ermine owl n [See quot 1953]

=**snowy owl.**

1917 (1923) *Birds Amer.* 2.115, *Snowy Owl. Nyctea nyctea*. . . *Other Names*. . . Ermine Owl. **1946** Hausman *Eastern Birds* 520. **1953** Jewett *Birds WA* 356, Ermine Owl. . . Body pure white, sometimes almost unspotted, but usually marked more or less with transverse spots or bars of slaty brown.

ernuff See **enough**

ernurther See **another**

-eroo suff Also sp *-(a)roo* [Perh from **buckaroo**, erron analyzed as *buck* n + *-aroo*, perh infl by *kangaroo;* see 1942 *AmSp* 17.10–14] *joc*

Usu added to nouns as a somewhat vague intensifier suggesting qualities of exaggeration, flamboyance, or the like; see quots.

1919 *DN* 5.41 [Hobo Cant], *Jiggeroo*. . . *Cheese it:* a warning to be careful or escape. **1931** *AmSp* 7.45, [Walter Winchell] loves to . . [see] *terpsichorines* . . dance in *revusicals* which might even turn out *flop-eroos*. **1940** *AmSp* 15.221 **wTX**, He is pretty obviously "snoozemarooed" (drunk). **1941** *AmSp* 16.70, *Drunk* . . snoozamorooed. *Ibid* 158 **DC**, I got thousands of . . *gageroos* and they are all pretty good. But so decidedly English that they don't translate so spiffy. *Ibid* 306, Spanish . . has provided another suffix which is fast gaining in popularity: *-aroo*, from *buckaroo* "vaquero." Much of its success is undoubtedly due to the coincidental support of *kangaroo*, the image of the animal's antics contributing to the festive tone of all the *-aroo* words, and of words ending in the sound *-aree*, such as *charivari*. . . I have observed . . *ji-varoo, vibaroo* ("jivaroo on the vibaroo [Vibraphone] . . " . .); *wack-eroo* . . ; *kissamaroo* . . ; *babyroo*. **1942** *AmSp* 17.15, Four-fifths of the words (about forty) occur only once. One-fifth have from two to twelve quotations each: *swingaroo* . . , *buckaroo* . . (and two or three derivatives each); *flopperoo* . . , *smackeroo* . . ; *stinkeroo* . . ; *gaggeroo, jig-geroo*, . . and *snapperoo*. . . These figures point to (a) the great freedom with which *-eroo* combines with common words; and (b) the probable nonceness of most *-eroo* words. **1946** *AmSp* 21.230, A comedy was described as a *laugheroo*. . . I heard a newscaster call the Senate filibuster . . a *blabberoo*. **1965–70** *DARE* (Qu. AA9, . . *A loud or vigorous kiss*) 19 Infs, **scattered**, Smackeroo; **IL17, IN60**, Smoocheroo; (Qu. U20, . . *Dollars*) Infs **AK9, ID5, MO2, NY66, VA90**, Smackeroos; (Qu. U26, . . *Paper dollar*) Inf **MN28**, Smackeroo; (Qu. U28b, . . *Ten-dollar bill*) Inf **WI58**, Ten smackeroos; (Qu. FF19, . . *A dull or unenjoyable time*) Inf **SC21**, Stinkeroo. **1978** *AmSp* 53.51, The introduction of *-aroo* or *-eroo* . . is probably due to a twentieth-century conception of the cowboy. . . The suffix *-aroo* . . does generally appear to lend dramatic heightening to whatever it is attached to, as in *ace-eroo, buckeroo, danderoo, flopperoo, flunkeroo, jackeroo, punkaroo, smackeroo, sock-eroo*, and *switcheroo*. It may well have had the same function in the change of *buckayro*, with shift of stress, to *buckaroo*. **1984** Doig *English Creek* 47 **nMT**, He was a true grassaroo; knew how to graze sheep as if the grass was his own sustenance as well as theirs.

errand n Usu |'ɛɚənd|; for varr see quots Pronc-spp *arrand, arrant, arr'nd, errant*

A Forms.

1823 Cooper *Pioneers* 2.164 **cNY**, I've an arrand with you. **1837** Sherwood *Gaz. GA* 69, *Arrant*, for errand. **1841** (1952) Cooper *Deer-slayer* 91 **nNY**, I'll follow you . . on such an arr'nd, and will strive to do my duty. **1894** *DN* 1.330 **NJ**, *Errand* . . [ɛrənt]. [*DN* Ed: Known also in N.E.] **1895** Brown *Meadow-Grass* 117 **NH**, He went off on that fool's arrant arter elwives. **1903** *DN* 2.297 **Cape Cod MA** (as of 1850s), *Errand*. . . Pronounced *errant*. **1909** *DN* 3.395 **nwAR**, *Errant*. **1915–25** in 1944 *ADD* **cNY**, *Errand*. . . 'Go on an [ɚn(d)] for me.' 'Runnin [ɚnz].' Pron. like *urn, earn, earned*. **1927** *Ruppenthal Coll.* **KS**, Errant. . . errand. **1928** *AmSp* 3.404 **Ozarks**, *T* replaces the final *d* in words like *salad, ballad, killed, errand* . . so that these words are best rendered *salat, ballat, kilt, errant*. **1929** (1951) Faulkner *Sartoris* 107 **MS**, I reckon his paw sent him on a arr'nd. **1959** *VT Hist.* new ser 27.134 **VT**, Errand ['ɛrənt]. . . Occasional.

B Sense.

A message. [ME *erend* message, business; *OED errand* sb. 1 →1754] *arch*

1899 (1912) Green *VA Folk-Speech* 69, *Arrand*. . . Arrant. Old form of errand. Tidings. A message.

errest v [Pronc-sp for *arrest*]

1926 *AmSp* 2.81 **ME**, Short *e* is often substituted for short *a*. . . An officer "errests" a wrong-doer.

error n

A Forms.

1837 Sherwood *Gaz. GA* 69, *Erro*, error. **1899** Chesnutt *Conjure Woman* 179 **csNC** [Black], I tried ter l'arn him de arrer er [=of] his ways.

B Sense.

Cap: See quot. [Cf *OED error* sb. 3. b for similar personifications]

1968 *DARE* (Qu. CC8, *Other names for the devil*) Inf **GA18**, Error; the bad man; evil one.

error v [*error* n]

To err.

1953 Brewer *Word Brazos* 23 **eTX** [Black], Ken's wife Sadie know de pastuh done errored. **1967–68** *DARE* (Qu. JJ42, *To make an error in judgment and get something quite wrong: "He usually handles things well, but this time he certainly ______.")* Inf **AR55**, ['ɛrəd]; **MN15**, Errored. [Both Infs less than hs educ]

erster See **oyster**

erwten soup n |'ærtən sup, 'ɛrtən| [Du *erwtensoep*] **swMI** Also called **snert**

Pea soup.

1940 *AmSp* 15.82 **swMI, Cleveland OH**, These expressions . . seem to be common . . wherever Dutchmen reside [in the US]. *Ibid* 83, *Erwten soep* ['ɛrtən su:p] or *snert* [snɛ:rt]. Pea soup. **1964** (1971) *Eet Smakelijk* 513 **Holland MI**, *Erwtensoep*—Dutch Pea Soup—1 lb. peas[,] 1 medium pig hock or shoulder pork or metworst[,] 3 quarts water [etc]. [**1965** *Woman's Day Encycl. Cookery* 4.589, The Dutch are great soup eaters and often soup is the main dish of the meal. The famous Dutch pea soup is the best pea soup in the world. . . *Erweten soep* (Pea Soup).]

1969–70 *DARE* (Qu. H36, *Kinds of soup favored around here*) Inf **MI**102, Erwten ['ærtən] soup—Dutch pea soup; **MI**122, Erwten soup—Dutch name for pea soup.

erysipelas n Usu |ˌɛrɪ'sɪpələs, ˌɪr-, -ɪs|; also |ˌir-, ˌær-, ˌɑr-|; often, by syncope, |ˌɛr(ɪ)'sɪpləs, ˌɪr(ɪ)-, ɑr-| Pronc-spp *airesipelus, airosipelus, earsipilus*

A Forms.

1871 Eggleston *Hoosier Schoolmaster* 87 **IN,** And fer airesipelus, I don't know nothin' so good as the blood of a black hen. **1931–33** *LANE Worksheets* **ceMA,** Erysipelas [ɪrɪ'sɪpələs] . . disease. "My brother got the erysipelas loading stones onto a drag." **1936** *AmSp* 11.336 **eTX,** [ɪrɪ'sɪplɪs] . . [ɛr'sɪpləs] . . [ˌɪɚ'sɪpləs] . . [ˌɛrɪ'sɪpləs] . . [ˌɛr'sɪplɪs] . . [ˌɛː'sɪplɪs] . . [ˌɛrɪ'sɪplɪs]. **1942** Hall *Smoky Mt. Speech* 64 **wNC, eTN,** Erysipelas [ɑɚ'sɪplɪs] . . shows loss both after *r* and before *l*. **1966–70** *DARE* (Qu. BB25) Inf **MI**115, [ɪɚ'sɪpələs]; **OH**15, Earsipilus; (Qu. BB30) Inf **FL**8, [ærə'sɪpələs]; (Qu. BB49) Inf **IL**97, [ˌirə'sɪplɪs]; **IN**22, Airosipelus.

B Sense.

Something unimportant. *joc*

1928 *Ruppenthal Coll.* **KS,** It's erysipelas to me. **1967** *DARE* (Qu. KK26, *Something that makes no difference at all to you: "He can think what he likes, it ______ me."*) Inf **MO**7, Is erysipelas to.

-es suff[1] [The ME pl (<OE *-as*), 3rd sg pres (<OE *-es, -as*), and possessive (<Northumbrian *-es, -as*) all had a pronounced vowel before the *s*. In ModE, the vowel was subsequently lost in all three endings when not preceded by [s, z, š, ž, č, ǰ].]

1 also sp *-is;* plural-forming suff:

a for words ending in [-sp, -st, -sk]. [Engl dial; cf *EDG* §378] **chiefly sAppalachians, Ozarks**

1827 (1939) Sherwood *Gaz. GA* 139, *Textes,* for Texts. **1893** Shands *MS Speech* 28, *-es*. . . The plural form, ending in *es,* is given to nearly all words ending in *t,* by negroes; as *postes, ghostes, hostes.* **1895** *DN* 1.375 **seKY, eTN, wNC,** The most interesting thing . . is the use of a vowel in plurals and the third singular of verbs, giving such forms as *costes, vestes, postes, nestes*. . . No examples were sent of this usage except after *t.* **1902** *DN* 2.244 **sIL,** *Rusk*. . . The plural *ruskes,* pronounced in two syllables. Raised biscuit. **1908** *DN* 3.284 **eAL, wGA,** Abnormal plurals: . . nestes, postes, beastes. *Ibid* 310, *Fice, fist*. . . A small dog. . . Plural sometimes *fistes, faustes.* **1927** *DN* 5.470 **Appalachians,** Plurals in *-es* for *-s: beastes, frostes, ghostes, nestes, postes, waistes.* **1927** *AmSp* 3.10 **Ozarks,** A few nouns like *post, nest, beast* and *vest* take a superfluous vowel in the plural, reviving such ancient forms as *postes, nestes, beastes,* and *vestes.* **1942** Hall *Smoky Mt. Speech* 82 **wNC, eTN,** *-es* . . varies between [ə], [ɨ], [ɪ]. . . In the dialectal plurals and possessives of words like *nests, posts,* etc., the same vowels appear. . . *Nests* ['nɛstəs], ['nɛstəz], ['nɛstɪs], ['nɛstɪz]. . . *Posts* (like *nests*). . . *Fists* ['fɪstɪz]. . . *Wasps* ['wɔspəs]. **1967–69** *DARE* FW Addit **seTN,** [Heard in conv:] Nests ['nɛstɪz]; posts ['postɪz]; **GA**51, Desks ['dɛskɪz]. **c1970** Pederson *Dial. Surv. Rural GA* **seGA,** [Pronunciations of the type ['nɛstɪz] and ['fɪstɪz] occur frequently; those such as ['dɛskɪz] and ['wɑspɪz] are only occasional.] **1976** Wolfram–Christian *Appalachian Speech* 37, The [ɪz] plural may be added to items ending in *sp, st,* or *sk,* resulting in forms like *deskes* [dɛskɪz], *ghostes* [gostɪz], or *waspes* [waspɪz]. *Ibid* 38, "I really like *roastes* [rostɪz] or the steak." . . Because the addition of the [ɪz] plural following *sp, st,* or *sk* appears to be socially stigmatized, it is more characteristic of working class than middle class speakers.

b for words in which the consonant clusters have been reduced to [s]. [Engl dial; cf Jespersen *Mod. Engl. Gram.* 6.16.1.7] **Sth, S Midl**

1837 Sherwood *Gaz. GA* 69, *Babtises,* for Baptists. **1843** (1916) Hall *New Purchase* 147 **sIN,** History of the Baptisis and Methodisis. **1891** Page *Elsket* 145 **VA,** I fasten he wris'es wid he own gallowses. **1899** (1912) Green *VA Folk-Speech* 246, *Joices*. . . For *joists. Ibid* 266, *Locusses*. . . Locust trees. *Ibid* 94, *Breakfusses* . . breakfasts. *Ibid* 137, *Crusses* . . crusts. **1903** *DN* 2.319 **seMO,** His food was locusses and wild honey. **1905** Culbertson *Banjo Talks* 36 **SE** *(ADD),* Dey drinks de toas'es down. **1908** *DN* 3.284 **eAL, wGA,** Locusses. **1942** Hall *Smoky Mt. Speech* 82 **wNC, eTN,** *Joists* [ǰɔɪsəz]. . . *Locusts* (insects) ['lokəsəz]. **1967** *DARE* Tape **TN**15, It's the one I won two or three contes'es ['kɑntɛsəz] on. **c1970** Pederson *Dial. Surv. Rural GA* **seGA,** 2 infs, ['dɛsɨz]; 1 inf, ['wɔsɨz]. [All infs Black]

2 Plural-forming suff added to words already showing pl inflection thus forming "double plurals." [Engl dial; cf *EDG* §§383, 384] **chiefly Sth, S Midl** Cf **-ed 1, -er** compar suff **3, -est 3** Note: The pl nouns on which the "double plurals" are based may have been reanalyzed as singulars.

1653 *Order Book* (*ADD* at *folkses*) **VA,** There was a great many folkses in the house. **1843** (1916) Hall *New Purchase* 163 **IN,** Tongses. *Ibid* 258, The two old folkses. *Ibid* 264, Leather brichises. **1888** Jones *Negro Myths* 49 **GA coast,** Buh Rabbit an de tarruh beastises. **1893** Shands *MS Speech, Menses*. . . Sometimes used by illiterate whites for *men.* **1895** *DN* 1.375 **seKY, eTN, wNC,** *Currantses* (currants). **1899** Garland *Boy Life* 17 **nwIA,** Now I can spend my six centses. **1908** *DN* 3.284 **eAL, wGA,** Abnormal plurals: . . beasteses, galluses, . . tomatuses, . . mices, . . geeses. *Ibid* 345, *Lice*. . . The plural *lices* is fairly common among the illiterate. **1916** *DN* 4.275 **NE,** Gredientses. . . Ingredients. *Ibid* 347 **New Orleans LA,** Tawses [tɔzɛz]. . . Pl. of *taw,* a marble. **1917** Torrence *Granny Maumee* 52 [Black], I done give you de plankses in my flatfo'm an' I'm a-goin' to stan' on hit. *Ibid* 53, Dat money stays in de pu'se in de hip er my ol' jeanses. **1927** *AmSp* 3.10 **Ozarks,** The word *folk* is never heard in the Ozark country, but *folks* and *folkses* are both common, and seem to be used interchangeably. **1933** Rawlings *South Moon* 92 **FL,** Lant cried from his tree-crotch, "Hogses!" . . "Dog take them shoatses o' Posey's." **1935** (1944) Rawlings *Golden Apples* 265 **FL,** I got to git my feetses washed good. **1940** *Collier's* 2 Nov 42/3 **LA,** Efn you don't make no toby, you don't git no fo'-bitses; and efn you don't git no fo'-bitses, you don't eat. **1966** *DARE* (Qu. R17) Inf **GA**16, Black antses [æntzəz]. **1966–70** *DARE* Tape **SC**12, But they must not have been bulletses [sic], bulletses—I reckon they call 'em bullets because they's hard as a marble . . until after frost; **VA**55, You got a pound overboard with funnel into it, two bayses to it, then a hedgin' runnin' 'bout a hundred fathom 'round.

3 also sp *-us;* suff of 3rd sg pres tense of verbs:

a for words ending in [-st], [-sk], and occas [-ft]. **chiefly sAppalachians, Ozarks**

1895 [see **1a** above]. **1927** *DN* 5.470 **Appalachians,** Present tense with *-es* for *-s:* twistes. **1928** *AmSp* 3.407 **Ozarks,** A superfluous vowel is often used in plurals. . . The same thing occasionally marks some forms of certain verbs, and one often hears such sentences as *I allus stops an' restes of a ev'nin.* **1942** Hall *Smoky Mt. Speech* 82 **wNC, eTN,** The following verbal forms were pronounced with [ə] in the final syllable: *costs* ['kɔstəs], *tastes* ['teɪstəs], *interests* ['ɪntɚəstəz]. **1953** Atwood *Survey of Verb Forms* 28, *It costs*. . . A variation from the usual inflectional pattern . . is seen in the form *costes* [kɔstəz], which occurs occasionally in the Chesapeake Bay area, s. W. Va., N.C., S.C., and Ga. All together, 54 informants (51 of them in Type I [=old, with little educ]) use this form. **c1960** *Wilson Coll.* **csKY,** *-es* for *-s:* rustes, tastes, driftes, lastes, frostes, trustes, costes, roostes. **1977** Miles *Ozark Dict.* 2, It costus ten cents. **1985** Pederson *LAGS Material,* **neFL,** Askes [old Black inf]; **nwFL,** Diskes up land with it [=a plow] [old Black inf]; **cTN,** Diskes up the stalks [old White inf].

b for words in which the cons cluster has been reduced to [s].

1953 Atwood *Survey of Verb Forms* 28, A variation from the usual inflectional pattern . . is seen in the form *costes* [kɔstəz]. . . A similar form, *cosses* [kɔsəz], is used by nine additional Southern informants.

4 Possessive suff:

a added to sg nouns ending in [-st].

1909 *DN* 3.402 **nwAR,** We saw the wastes' (wasps) nestes on the bed postes at Mr. Westes. **1942** Hall *Smoky Mt. Speech* 82 **wNC, eTN,** *In Christ's time* [ɪn 'kraɪstɪs 'taɪm]. **1985** Pederson *LAGS Material,* **cnMS,** Christes birthday [old Black inf]; **ceAR,** Christes mother [old Black inf]; **cwAL,** Christes picture [old White inf].

b added to regular pl nouns ending in *-s;* this contrasts with StdE where the possessive of regular *-s* plurals is phonologically zero, represented in writing by an apostrophe only, e.g., *wasps'.* [Engl dial; cf *EDG* §391]

1845 Thompson *Pineville* 178 **GA,** Go on 'bout Gun Bustin gittin' into the waspses nest. **1985** *DARE* File **swMI,** We had a party at my folkses place.

-es suff[2] See **-est**

esac'ly See **exactly**

escalator n Usu |'ɛskəˌletə(r)|; occas |'ɛskju-| See Pronc Intro 3.I.23

Std sense, var form.

1940–41 in 1944 *ADD* **MA, NC,** Escalator ['ɛskɪuletr̩]. **1978–80** *DARE* File **csWI,** What we need around here is a good ['ɛskjuˌletɚ];

swMA (as of 1953), [Overheard on bus:] We thought maybe she was coming down on the ['ɛskju,letə].

escalin n Also sp *escalan* [Fr] **LA** *old-fash*
A bit; twelve and one-half cents.
1834 in 1941 *AmSp* 16.30 **LA,** Escalin, Schilling, 12½ cents, so in Louisiana genannt [=named]. **1883** Albany Inst. *Trans.* 10.336, The "shilling" of our own State [=New York] is the "levy" of Pennsylvania, the "bit" of San Francisco, the "ninepence" of old New England, and the "escalan" of New Orleans. **[1931** Read *LA French* 140, *Escalin* is rarely heard except from its occurrence in the phrase *six escalins,* "twenty-five cents" [sic].]

escape n, v Usu |ə'skeɪp|; also |ək-, ɛk-, ɪk-| Pronc-sp *excape*
Std senses, var forms.
1928 *AmSp* 3.406 **Ozarks,** In one case, at least, a medial *s* is replaced by *x*—the word *escape* is usually pronounced *excape.* **1937** in 1944 *ADD* **VA,** *Escape.* . . [ək'skeɪp]. Equally freq. in both parts of Va. **1939** *Ibid* **DE,** *Escape.* . . [ək'ske:p]. Freq. Also written *excape.* **1942** Hall *Smoky Mt. Speech* 54 **wNC, eTN,** *Escape* is often [ɛk'skeɪp], [ɪk'skeɪp], showing confusion with the *ex-* type or anticipation of the [k]. **1954** Roberts *I Bought Dog* 17 **KY,** I had a notion one day that I could ex-cape. **1967** *DARE* (Qu. II34, *If you think somebody is trying to use you to his advantage: "I'm not going to be his ——— ."*) Inf **OH33,** [ɛk'skep] goat. **1976** Garber *Mountain-ese* 27, *Excape.* . . It shore is hard to excape from a chain gang. **1978** Kalibabky *Hawdaw* 2 **neMN,** How Tark manages ta excape from gettin' squashed by dem big guys . . is beyond me.

escarole n **chiefly N and C Atl**
=endive 1.
1959 Farmer *Cookbook* 254, **Boston MA,** *Salad Greens.* . . *Romaine, Escarole, Watercress.* . . Separate leaf by leaf. Remove any hard or discolored part. Wash. **1965–70** *DARE* (Qu. I28a, . . *Kinds of* . . *'greens'*) 13 Infs, **chiefly N and C Atl,** Escarole; (Qu. I28b) Infs **CT39, NY39,** Escarole; (Qu. I4) Infs **CT29, WI58,** Escarole.

escavation n [Var of *excavation* by cons cluster reduction]
1970 *DARE* (Qu. C21) Inf **NY235,** Escavation.

escobita n [Span dimin of *escoba* broom] **chiefly CA**
An **owl's clover:** usu *Orthocarpus purpurascens,* but also *O. densiflorus.*
1897 Parsons *Wild Flowers CA* 228, *Pink Paint-brush. Escobita. Orthocarpus purpurascens.* . . The Spanish-Californians have a pretty name for these blossoms, calling them "escobitas," meaning "little whisk-brooms." **1911** Jepson *Flora CA* 385, *O[rthocarpus] densiflorus.* . . *Escobita.* . . Spike dense, 4 in. long or less. **1915** (1926) Armstrong–Thornber *Western Wild Flowers* 500, *Escobita, Owl's Clover. Orthocarpus densiflorus.* . . *O. purpurascens,* common in the Northwest and Southwest, is similar. **1937** U.S. Forest Serv. *Range Plant Hdbk.* W136, Purple owlclover *(O. purpurascens),* often called escobita, is another common West Coast species, which occurs in California and Oregon. **1961** Thomas *Flora Santa Cruz* 318 **cwCA,** Escobita. . . A common spring annual of grasslands, cultivated fields, and oak grasslands. San Francisco southward. **1976** Bailey–Bailey *Hortus Third* 802, *[Orthocarpus] purpurascens.* . . *Escobita.* Ann[ual], frequently much-branched. . . Calif., Ariz., adjacent Mex. **1985** Dodge *Flowers SW Deserts* 125, Escobita Owlclover. . . often grows . . mixed with goldpoppy, lupine, and other spring flowers.

escusada n [Span *excusado* washroom, toilet] **SW** *euphem*
Cf **excuse house**
A toilet.
1962 Atwood *Vocab. TX* 53, *Outdoor toilet.* . . a number of local, individualistic, and imaginative terms occur occasionally. [Footnote:] For example, . . *escusada* (two occurrences, both from Anglos). **1967** *DARE* (Qu. F37, . . *An indoor toilet*) Inf **CA31,** Escudo [sic]—if Spanish.

e'se See **else**

'ese'f See **'eself**

esel n [Ger *Esel* ass, donkey] **esp PA**
1967–68 *DARE* (Qu. K50, *Joking nicknames for mules*) Infs **NJ17, PA3,** 21, 141, Esel.

'eself pron Also sp *ehself, 'ese'f, esse'f* [**e** pron + *self*] *Gullah*
Cf **heself**
Himself, herself, itself.
1888 Jones *Negro Myths* 39 **GA coast,** Eh jaw duh run water, fuh eh tink ter ehself de Debble guine gem some nice brukwus. [=His jaw begins to run water because he thinks to himself the Devil is going to give him some nice breakfast.] **1899** Edwards *Defense* 216 **GA,** You sho' ain' gwine lef' dat po' littl' possum out hyah all by esse'f en de big swamp, ez yer? **1909** *S. Atl. Qrly.* 8.46 **SC coast,** Nobody knew how old ol' Mass' Pooshay was, 'cuz 'e tek mighty good cyeah er' esef. **1922** Gonzales *Black Border* 264 **sSC, GA coasts** [Gullah], Dis cow bin so hongry dat, w'en I git to weh de fench bruk down, 'e tek 'eself en' me en' all, en' gone een de fiel'.

Eskimo curlew n Also sp *Esquimaux curlew* [See quot 1955 U.S. Arctic Info. Center]
A **curlew 1:** usu *Numenius borealis,* but also *N. hudsonicus.* Also called **dough bird, fute, little curlew, prairie pigeon**
1813 Wilson *Ornithology* 7.22 *(DAE),* The Esquimaux Curlew . . is called by our gunners on the sea-coast, the Short-billed Curlew. **1833** Bonaparte *Amer. Ornith.* 4.118, Esquimaux Curlew. *Numenius Borealis.* **1839** MA Zool. & Bot. Surv. *Fishes Reptiles* 366, The *Esquimaux Curlew, Numenius Hudsonicus* . . are shot in Boston Harbor. *Ibid,* The *Small Esquimaux Curlew, Numenius borealis,* . . though sufficiently common here, . . is hardly ever seen in the southern states. **1840** MA Zool. & Bot. Surv. *Herb. Plants & Quadrupeds* 366, The Esquimaux Curlew, Numenius Hudsonicus, . . are shot in Boston Harbor. **1955** Forbush–May *Birds* 184, *Eskimo curlew—Phaeopus borealis.* . . *Other names:* Doe-bird, sometimes spelled Dough-bird; Prairie Pigeon. . . Now extinct or nearly so. The Eskimo Curlew formerly was one of the extremely abundant birds of America. . . It was rapidly and completely destroyed like the Passenger Pigeon for the price that it brought in the market. **1955** U.S. Arctic Info. Center *Gloss.* 28 **AK,** *Eskimo curlew.* A small nearctic bird, *Numenius borealis,* that formerly frequented the arctic coast from Coronation Gulf westward to Norton Sound, and migrated to southern South America in winter. Also called "doughbird."

Eskimo duck n
=eider duck.
1982 Elman *Hunter's Field Guide* 214, *American Eider (Somateria mollissima)* Common & Regional Names: . . Eskimo duck, . . pied wamp.

Eskimo goose n
1 A **brant 1** (here: *Branta bernicla nigricans*).
1953 Jewett *Birds WA* 106, *Black Brant.* . . Other names: . . Eskimo Goose.
2 =Canada goose.
1982 Elman *Hunter's Field Guide* 269, *Canada Goose.* . . *Common & Regional names* . . Eskimo goose.

Eskimo ice cream n **AK**
An Eskimo dish variously prepared with animal fat or tallow mixed with berries, snow and sometimes other ingredients, and whipped or kneaded to a thick consistency resembling ice cream.
1913 Hawkes *Inviting-in Feast* 9 **AK,** Eskimo "ice-cream"—a concoction of reindeer tallow, blueberries, and chunks of whitefish kneaded in the snow until it is frozen. **1933** Marshall *Arctic Village* 139 **AK,** One of the most luscious of all the Eskimo dishes is what they themselves jovially refer to as Eskimo ice cream, due to its resemblance to vanilla ice cream. It is made by extracting the marrow from caribou or sheep bones, mixing this with a great deal of fat and a few blueberries, melting them all together, removing the molten liquid from the fire and beating it much as you would whip cream, and finally allowing it to solidify into a beautiful, white substance, somewhat speckled by darker blotches. My estimate after eating some of this titbit is that it consists of about seventy per cent pure fat, ten per cent blueberries, ten per cent lean meat, and ten per cent animal hair. **1955** U.S. Arctic Info. Center *Gloss.* 28 **AK,** *Eskimo ice cream.* A beaten mixture of seal oil or caribou tallow, berries, and snow; substitutions are sometimes made for the basic ingredients. **1959** Hart *McKay's AK* 111, Feasting is an important part of these events, with muktuk to chew on, whale steaks, smoked fish, Eskimo ice cream. **1976** *Theata* 4.21 **AK,** For example, Natives use salmonberries to make aqutaq; aqutaq is a Native food that the whites call "Eskimo Ice Cream". It's made of tallow, Wesson oil, and water. These three items are mixed until they fluff up. Later you add the salmonberries and if you want, you can add other kinds of berries. Last of all the sugar is added, and that's what we call aqutaq.

Eskimo kiss n Also *Eskimo love* [See quot 1950]
An affectionate rubbing of noses.

[**1950** (1972) Funk & Wagnalls *Dict. Folkl.* 582/2, The "savage" kiss, also referred to as the olfactory or Malay kiss, or rubbing noses, is reported as common among the . . Eskimos. Descriptions are not in complete agreement though generally the kiss involves bringing the noses together and rubbing them.] [**1959** in 1965 Rowsome *Verse Burma-Shave* 117, Men / With Whiskers / 'Neath their noses / Oughta have to kiss / Like Eskimoses / Burma-Shave.] **1965–70** *DARE* (Qu. HH30, *Things that are nicknamed for different nationalities*) 54 Infs, **scattered,** Eskimo kiss [Of all Infs responding to the question, 13% were young, 27% mid-aged, 60% old; of those giving this response, 31% were young, 37% mid-aged, 31% old.]; **AK**8, Eskimo love.

Eskimo potato n **AK**

Any of three plants which produce edible corms, roots, or tubers: a **fritillary** (here: *Fritillaria camschatcensis*), a **spring beauty** (here: *Claytonia tuberosa*), or a **sweet vetch** (here: *Hedysarum alpinum*).

1937 Isobel Hutchinson *Stepping Stones from Alaska to Asia* 111 (Tabbert *Alaskan Engl.*), This time I worked through a ravine [on St. Paul Island] between huge, tumbled volcanic crags where tall ferns grew, and here and there were the stalks of the now withered Rice-root or "Eskimo potato" (*Fritillaria Camtschatcensis* [sic]), whose white tubers are said to form part of the food supply of both Eskimo and Aleut. Though I have heard several plants in this region called by the name of "Eskimo potato", I was assured in the Aleutians that the handsome dingy-flowered fritillaria is the true one. **1955** U.S. Arctic Info. Center *Gloss.* 28, **AK,** *Eskimo potato.* The edible root tubers of either of the two wild plants, the spring beauty, or wild sweet pea. **1966** Heller *Wild Flowers AK* 33, *Eskimo . . Potato. . . Hedysarum alpinum. . .* Root edible. *Ibid* 53, *Claytonia tuberosa. . . Eskimo Potato. . .* Perennial with underground corm about 1 inch in diameter, edible. **1977** McPhee *Coming Country* 32 **AK,** They eat what they call "white-man food," mainly from cans, but they also eat owl soup, sour dock, wild rhubarb, and the tuber *Hedysarum alpinum*—the Eskimo potato. **1977** Douglas Anderson et al. *Kuuvanmiit Subsistence. . .* (Kobuk River Valley) 148 (Tabbert *Alaskan Engl.*), One other important fall plant is Eskimo potato, which is dug up after the ground freezes in September.

Eskimo rhubarb n

A **knotweed** (here: *Polygonum alaskanum*). Also called **wild rhubarb**

1955 U.S. Arctic Info. Center *Gloss.* 28 **AK,** *Eskimo rhubarb.* A freely branching, edible, perennial herb, *Polygonum alaskanum,* with jointed reddish stems and attenuate leaves 2 to 8 inches long rising from coarse, fleshy roots; the flowers are large and feathery.

Eskimo yo-yo n **AK**

A toy consisting of two fur balls attached to leather strings; see quots.

1959 Hart *McKay's AK* 89, There are contests and exhibitions of all kinds: photography, auto ice-racing, the world's championship Eskimo yo-yo competitions. [*Ibid* 34, *Yo-Yo:* An Eskimo game played with two small fur balls, each attached to a leather string. The object of the game is to hold the leather strings in one hand and make the two balls on the other end revolve in opposite directions for a prolonged period of time. It requires a type of co-ordination like rubbing the head and patting the stomach at the same time.] **1960** *AK Sportsman* Jan 38/1, Recently they [=Eskimo women] began to produce the "Eskimo yo-yo," two small fur balls on sinew strings to be swung in fancy maneuvers, but an oldster Eskimo told me he had seen a yo-yo for the first time in 1953 when "all of a sudden they appeared." **1979** *DARE* File **CA,** When my father came back from a trip to Alaska, he brought me an Eskimo yo-yo. It has a very short handle with two strings attached, and a small fur ball at the end of each string. The object of the game (which looks deceptively simple) is to move the handle up and down so that one ball is kept circling clockwise while the other circles counterclockwise without hitting the first.

es macht mir nichts aus See **macht nichts**

espantoon n [Var of *espontoon* (from Fr *sponton, esponton*) orig used in Amer Engl for a half-pike carried by an infantry officer] **MD**

A policeman's club.

1931 *Sun* (Baltimore MD) 19 Jan 2/6 *(Hench Coll.),* In addition to pistols, espantoons, blackjacks, and a shotgun, the two large safes also yielded jewelry. **1936** (1947) Mencken *Amer. Lang.* 243, A policeman [in England] is a *bobby. . .* His club or espantoon is his *truncheon.* [*DARE* Ed: Author is native of Baltimore MD.] **1942** Footner *MD Main* 8, In Lexington . . the "poliss" swing their "espantoons." **1944** *AmSp* 19.19 **MD,** In Baltimore a synonym for *bludgeon* is *espantoon. . .* I pointed out . . the Fr. *esponton* 'demi-pique,' 'half-pike' (>Ital. *spuntone*). **1967** *DARE* File **Baltimore MD,** Espantoon—billy, billy club, nightstick. **1980** *Washington Post* (DC) 18 Oct sec A 20/3, In Baltimore, policemen don't hit people with their nightsticks, they hit them with their espantoons.

especially adv Usu |ɛ'spɛš(ə)li, ə-|; also |ɪk-| Pronc-spp *expecially, speshly, speshually* Cf **escape, essentially**

Std senses, var forms.

1887 (1967) Harris *Free Joe* 118 **GA,** Reason in all things, speshually when hit comes to gormandizin'. **1929** Sale *Tree Named John* 99 **MS,** Dat's a bad sign, spesh'ly in de daytime. **1942** Hall *Smoky Mt. Speech* 54 **ceTN,** [ɪk'spɛšəlɪ], *especially,* reported to be used in Jefferson Co., Tenn. **1953** Brewer *Word Brazos* 14 **eTX** [Black], Fin'ly, one night, though, Revun Randle, de pastuh, pray to de Lawd speshly for Pink. **1970** *DARE* Tape **GA**90, Especially [ɪk'spɛšli]. **1976** Garber *Mountain-ese* 27 **sAppalachians,** *Expecially. . .* especially.

esplanade n [Fr; in Texas, prob infl by Span *explanada* lawn]

The median, often grassed and landscaped, on a highway.

1967–70 *DARE* (Qu. N17, . . *The separating area in the middle of a four-lane road*) Infs **CT**29, **TX**12, 31, Esplanade; **CT**42, Esplanade—in the city [Bridgeport]; **TX**37, Esplanade ['ɛsplɪˌneɪd].

esquif n |ɛ'skif| [LaFr] **LA** Cf **skiff, creole skiff**

A small, flat-bottomed boat.

[**1931** Read *LA French* 135, French *esquif* . . and English *skiff* . . pronounced like *esquif* without the initial vowel—are other terms for a small boat.] **1956** Knipmeyer *Settlement Succession* 165 **LA,** Of all the folk boats in French Louisiana, none is more carefully distinguished than the *esquif* or "skiff." The essential features of this boat type are a flat bottom, pointed bow, and blunt stern. . . The distinguishing features are intangible. *Ibid* 166, The French *esquif* has come to have a restricted meaning, and in the region where the boat is used, *esquif* and "skiff" are synonymous and are not used in the general sense. *Ibid* 168, The Creole skiff characteristically occurs on small, interior water bodies, and attains its most typical development in the Atchafalaya Basin, where it is specifically *esquif.* The distinguishing features are a narrow beam, considerable sheer, and a high . . V-shaped stern.

Esquimaux curlew See **Eskimo curlew**

esse'f See **'eself**

essence n

1 A type of minstrel dance, popular from about 1850. *hist*

1930 Wittke *Tambo & Bones* 223 **NYC,** Dan Bryant's chief claim to fame rested upon his ability as a dancer of such favorites as "The Essence of Old Virginny," and "Shoo Fly." He had few rivals in "shaking up a grotesque essence." **1962** Nathan *Dan Emmett* 93, Another one [=minstrel dance], we are informed, included "the saltatorial efforts of genuine old negroes of both sexes," which Frank Brower is said to have introduced. Dances featuring such jumps and leaps were called "essences" from about the fifties on, of which the "Essence of Old Virginny" . . is the best known example. **1968** Stearns–Stearns *Jazz Dance* 50, The Essence was "based firmly on Negro source material," . . and a performance by Dan Bryant in 1858 is described as "a dance characteristic of the rude and untutored black of the old plantation." . . To illustrate the Essence, which he called "a combination of shuffles," James Barton did a series of walking steps . . progressing rapidly and intricately forward.

2 Any of various hoodoo preparations supposed to confer power over others; see quots. Cf *DJE balm oil, oil of —*

1931 *Jrl. Amer. Folkl.* 44.411 **LA** [Black], Essence of Van Van: Ten percent oil of Lemon Grass in alcohol. . . used for luck and power of all kinds. It is the most popular conjure drug in Louisiana. . . Fast Scrubbing Essence: A mixture of thirteen oils. It is burned with incense for . . business success. *Ibid* 412, Essence of Bend-over. Used to rule and have your own way. **1945** Saxon *Gumbo Ya-Ya* 543, *Other conjure paraphernalia*—Essence of Van Van, Oil of Lemon grass, in alcohol. . . the most popular conjure drug in Louisiana.

3 also *essence coffee:* A coffee substitute.

1954 in 1957 *DE Folkl. Bulletin* 1.27/1, Den after de pone crust was done, dey come essence. A box of essence we used to buy. Essence coffee. We put a teaspoonful of essence in thar [=a pot filled with pone crust and boiling water]. It looked like coffee. And then, so much water to the essence and made coffee. Had no (real) coffee.

4 Gravy. **esp MD, VA** *old-fash*

1957 Battaglia *Resp. to PADS 20* **eMD,** Gravy—essence (not thickened). **1968–70** *DARE* (Qu. H37, . . *Words . . for gravy*) Infs **MD**35, **NJ**56, **VA**66, 94, Essence. [All Infs old] **1969** *DARE* File **Brooklyn NYC,** Essence—meat juice; to make it gravy, flour must be added. [Used by Inf's aunt, who came from Virginia]

essence peddler n Also sp *essence pedlar* [Transf from *essence peddler* peddler of medicinal extracts] **Nth, esp NEng** *joc*

A **skunk** (here: *Mephitis mephitis*).

1849 in 1894 Lowell *Letters* 1.153 **MA,** A skunk was shot in our back-kitchen this morning. There were two of these "essence-peddlers," as the Yankees call them. **1872** Schele de Vere *Americanisms* 54, With biting irony the animal [=the skunk] is called by the Yankees an *essence pedlar.* **1890** Custer *Following* 200 **KS,** The doctor soon came hurrying back to say that the passage was disputed by a small but well-armed foe, and added that "as soon as that essence-peddler saw fit to move on, the major-general commanding would issue his order to march." **1899** Bergen *Animal Lore* 61 **NH,** Essence-peddler, skunk. **1923** *DN* 5.240 **swWI,** *Essence peddler. . .* A skunk. "He run across an essence peddler, and he's stayin' away." **1946** Peattie *Pacific Coast* 90 **Pacific NW,** Shunned because of their mephitic odor and potentiality for malicious mischief, these animals are called by a number of humorous nicknames—sachet pussy, perfume merchant, essence peddler, wood pussy—but a skunk by any other name. **1969** *DARE* (Qu. P26, . . *A skunk*) Inf **MA**55, Essence peddler. **1975** Gould *ME Lingo* 86, *Essence peddler*—A skunk.

essentially adv Cf **especially**

Std sense, var form.

1936 *AmSp* 11.311 **nNY,** A few words illustrate the intrusion of 'long *u*' in places where it does not historically belong. . . Other words hide a ghostly 'long *u*' in assimilated forms. Thus *tremendous. . .* I have also heard *stupendous* as [stʊ'pɛndʒəs] and *essentially* as [ɪ'sɛnʃʊəlɪ].

-est superl suff Also sp *-es, -ist* **chiefly Sth, S Midl** Cf **-er** compar suff

Std sense, var applications. Cf *EDG* §398

1 Suffixed to polysyllabic adjs and advs and disyllabics not ending in *-y, -ow, -le,* and *-er;* this contrasts with StdE where *est* is usu restricted to monosyllabic adjs and advs and disyllabics in *-y, -ow, -le,* and *-er:*

a To adjs and advs normally compared with *most* in StdE.

1663 in 1965 *AmSp* 40.237 **VA,** Comfortablest things. **1843** (1916) Hall *New Purchase* 176 **IN,** Johnny was jist the powerfullest smartest feller in the hole universal county, and could out sifer Jerry or other men all to smash. **1861** Holmes *Venner* 2.147 **wMA,** The beautifullest-shaped lady. **1885** Twain *Huck. Finn* 78 **MO,** Ignorantest. *Ibid* 81, Foolishest. *Ibid* 173, Blessedest. *Ibid* 286, Innocentest. **1891** Page *Elsket* 137 **VA,** I warn' git out, but I knew I cyarn do dat, 'cuz 'twuz de ambitiouses smellin' place I ever smelt in my life. *Ibid* 123, He's de wuthlisses one o' de whole gang. **1899** Chesnutt *Conjure Woman* 138 **NC,** De cutes', blackes', shiny-eyedes' little nigger you eber laid eyes on. **1903** *DN* 2.335 **seMO,** *Vigrous. . .* 'He keeps the vigrousest dog in town.' **1915** *DN* 4.179 **swVA,** *Grown upest, worn outest.* **1927** *AmSp* 3.8 **Ozarks,** *Beautifullest . . perfectest. Ibid* 9, *Growed-uppest.* **1927** *DN* 5.474, He's the fractiousest ol' feller I ever seed. **1936** *AmSp* 11.351 **eTX,** New Orleans is the wide-openest town I ever saw. **1952** Brown *NC Folkl.* 537, The comparative and superlative degrees of the adjective and the adverb are generally formed by adding the suffixes *-er* and *-est* rather than by using the adverbs *more* and *most,* regardless of the length of the word. **1960** Hall *Smoky Mt. Folks* 64 **wNC, eTN,** He was the crabbedest old feller ever I seed. . . Tom Barnes was the completest hunter I was ever acquainted with. **1967–70** *DARE* Tape **GA**92, She offered him the beautifullest woman in the world; **IA**8, They [=mules] can be the contrariest things that ever was. **1970** *DARE* (Qu. GG36b) Inf **KY**89, Hatefullest.

b To adjs, esp pples, not usually compared in StdE.

1857 *Putnam's Mag.* 10.350/2 **CT,** Them is the d-drowndedest sheep I ever see. **1915** *DN* 4.179 **swVA,** Present participles used attributively are compared as other adjectives: . . *singinest girl.* **1919** *DN* 5.32 **seKY,** *Bread-eatin'est. . .* A familiar example of the mountaineer's fondness for using the superlative suffix attached to the present participle. . . Sometimes this suffix is attached to a past participle. . . "That's the torn-downdest ole shack of a house aroun' here." **1926** Roberts *Time of Man* 148 **cKY,** Sweetheartenest man I ever see. **1927** *AmSp* 3.8 **Ozarks,** When present participles are used attributively, they are compared like any other adjectives. . . Superlatives of this type are very common—*fightin'est, dancin'est, shootin'est, . . tore-downdest,* and so on. **1936** in 1977 *Amer. Slave Suppl. 1* 1.275 **AL,** At . . Page's funeral they was the two outmourningest of everybody. **1936** *AmSp* 11.351 **eTX,** 'Old man McCullough is the out-whorinest old buzzard in this town,' 'He's the out-lyinest man in town.' **1940** *AmSp* 15.52 **sAppalachians, Ozarks,** Onliest, dancin'est, tore-downdest, beatin'est. **1976** Ryland *Richmond Co. VA* 370, -est—a superlative ("That's the barkin'est dog!")

2 Suffixed to the positive form of those adjs and advs which in StdE undergo suppletion. Cf **bad** adj **A, far** adv, adj[1] **C**

1867 Allen *Slave Songs* xxxiii **eSC** [Black], De boss he de baddest buckra ebber a-see. **1893** Shands *MS Speech* 73, *Goodest.* **1908** *DN* 3.284 **eAL, wGA,** Baddest . . farest. **1940** *AmSp* 15.52 **sAppalachians, Ozarks,** Farest, . . baddest. **1952** Brown *NC Folkl.* 1.539, *Farrest, furrest . .* Farthest, furthest. **1970** *DARE* (Qu. LL33, . . *New York or California—which is* ______?) Inf **DC**13, Farrest; (Qu. LL34, . . *This is . .* ______ *we can go*) Inf **MS**88, The farrest. **1971** *Foxfire* Spring–Summer 102 **nGA,** Thrash'em old peas out—have th'—goodest old time y'ever seen. **1976** Wolfram–Christian *Appalachian Speech* 101, The *baddest* dream.

3 Suffixed to suppletive forms already showing the superl degree thus forming "double superlatives." Cf **-ed 1, -es** suff[1] **2, -er** compar suff **3**

1871 (1882) Stowe *Fireside Stories* 71 **NEast,** Ef you jist give 'em the leastest sprig of any thing they make a great bush out of it. **1893** Shands *MS Speech* 73, *Mostest. . .* A double superlative form in very common use by the negroes. Analogous words are . . *bestest, worstest,* in none of which is the final *t* sounded. **1908** *DN* 3.284 **eAL, wGA,** Leastest, mostest. **1969** *DARE* Tape **GA**77, It would depend upon mostly what was needed to be done the worstest. **1976** Wolfram–Christian *Appalachian Speech* 101, The *mostest* people.

4 Suffixed to forms already showing the compar degree. *esp freq among Black speakers*

1867 Allen *Slave Songs* xxxiii **eSC** [Black], De morest part ob de mens dey git heaps o' clo'—more'n 'nuff; 'n I ain't git nuffin. **1922** Gonzales *Black Border* 314 **sSC, GA coasts** [Gullah glossary], *Mo'ris', mo'res'*—most. **1930** Stoney–Shelby *Black Genesis* 73 **seSC,** Dat back sure is de t'ing in dis worl' dat he needs de more-est. **1937** in 1972 *Amer. Slave* 2.46 **SC,** De worsest time of all fer us darkies wuz when de Ku Klux killed Dan Black.

5 In constructions where *most* serves as an intensifier. Cf StdE *very best*

1683 Penn *Letter to Free Soc. Traders* 6 **PA,** One of the *most wretchedst Spectacles in the World.* **1843** (1916) Hall *New Purchase* 395 **IN,** I tuk the most exactest aim. **1844** Thompson *Major Jones's Courtship* 31 **GA,** Most surprisinest thing in the world. **1916** *DN* 4.284 **sAppalachians,** That Boatright woman . . is the most knittin'est person I ever seen. **1930** *AmSp* 5.267 **Ozarks,** *Most best.* **1931** *AmSp* 7.93 **eKY,** *Law-abidin'. . .* "Bill was the most law-abidinest man o' these parts." **1934** *WV Review* Dec 79/3, On the upper Elk a year or so ago I heard a man say that an acquaintance of his was "the most bricketyest fellow" he knew. **1940** *AmSp* 15.52 **sAppalachians,** Most best.

6 Suffixed to nouns. Cf Jespersen *Mod. Engl. Gram.* 7.10.4.9

1857 (1928) Twain *Advent. Snodgrass* 44 **sOH,** Pooty soon there commenced the *eternalist, confoundest,* damnationist kickin in that basket. **1931** *AmSp* 6.268 **KY,** Dog-dayest. **1949** Guthrie *Way West* 285, "We need a rider at each side". . . "Which side is dangerest?" **1985** *Sunshine* (Madison WI) 28 May 9/4, [Advt:] *It's The Baconest* Hardee's gives you more of what you buy a Bacon Cheeseburger for—bacon.

estafiata n Also *estafiate* [MexSpan *estafiate*] **SW**

A **sagebrush** (*Artemisia* spp, esp *A. frigida*).

[**1913** Wooton *Trees NM* 145, The commoner herbaceous forms [of sagebrush], which are used extensively, go under the Spanish name of *Estafiata* among the Mexican herders.] **1931** U.S. Dept. Ag. *Misc. Pub.* 101.170, *Estafiata (A[rtemisia] frigida)* is undoubtedly the well-established vernacular name of this species in the Southwest, while pasture sagebrush is probably the name in most general use for the plant toward the North. **1947** Curtin *Healing Herbs* 82 **NM,** Although *estafiate* is the New Spanish term given rather loosely to several artemisias, the Artemisia Mexicana appears to be the most generally accepted recipient of the name. . . *Estafiate* is a mutilated survival of the speech of the ancient Aztecs, who called the same plant *yztauhiatl.* **1960** Vines *Trees SW*

967, *Artemisia frigida*. . . Other vernacular names in use are Estafiata [etc].

estero n [Span] **CA**

An estuary or inlet, esp when marshy.

[**1824** Poinsett *Notes on Mexico* 204, We passed the *Estero,* a large pond where our muleteers proposed to encamp last night.] **1856** in 1948 *Western Folkl.* 7.10 **sCA,** [Recording temperatures: 72°] in the water of the *Estero* of the town flat. . . This *estero* is shallow. **1913** in 1918 Grinnell *Game Birds CA* 410, There were eleven of the Lesser Yellow-legs present on our Estero, and they were to be found in varying numbers for about two weeks thereafter. **1927** Phillips *Hist. Santa Barbara* 1.29 **swCA,** Those days the estero, which is now only a swamp, was tidewater. **1929** Rogers *Prehist. Man* 368 **swCA,** In the estero grew a rank jungle of tules and rushes.

estimenia See **acetonemia**

estray(ed) adj, also used absol [*OED* 1581 → as a legal term; but perh infl by Span pronc *estray* for Engl *stray*] *old-fash*

Of an animal: strayed; also fig.

1858 Hammett *Piney Woods Tavern* 200, The captain deemed it safest to stop and pick up our two estrays. **1900** Graham *13 Stories* 141 **SW,** Me and my 'vaquerys' were around looking for an estray horse, just six of us. **1905** *DN* 3.78 **nwAR,** *Estrayed*. . . "Estrayed—A cow, from Minnow Creek. Black, unmarked."—Arkansas newspaper advertisement. Rare. **1922** Rollins *Cowboy* 245, All brute visitors from other ranges . . were technically termed "strays" or "estrays," though, in colloquial usage, these technical terms were usually reserved for the cattle. **1951** Grant *Cowboy Encycl.* 61, *Estrays.* Cattle which were recognized during a roundup as belonging on a distant range. These "visitors" were cut out and driven home.

estufa n [Span "stove, heated room"] **SW**

1 Among the Pueblo Indians: an assembly or council chamber, usu underground, containing a sacred fire. Cf **kiva**

1844 (1954) Gregg *Commerce* 189 **NM,** I have myself descended into the famous *estufas,* or subterranean vaults, of which there were several in the village [of Pecos]. **1872** U.S. Bur. Indian Affairs *Rept. for 1871* 382 **NM,** They kept burning upon the altars in the 'estufas' . . fire. **1875** *N. Amer. Rev.* 120.45 **SW,** Each building, if of any considerable size, is provided with one or more *estufas,* or subterranean chambers, . . where the men of the community meet for social, deliberative, and religious purposes. **1907** Hodge *Hdbk. Amer. Indians* 1.710 **SW,** *Kiva*. . . They were first described by the early Spanish explorers of the S.W., who designated them *estufas,* meaning 'hot rooms,' evidently mistaking their chief use as that of sweat-houses. **1927** Cather *Death Comes* 152 **NM,** And some place in there, you may be sure, they keep Popé's estufa, but no white man will ever see it. I mean the estufa where Popé sealed himself up for four years and never saw the light of day. **1944** (1967) McNichols *Crazy Weather* 71 **SW,** I went over housetops and through streets, through houses, through estufas where medicine men slept, leaving a yellow trail of meal behind me.

2 A stove; a room containing a stove. *old-fash*

1887 *Scribner's Mag.* 2.509/2 **Rocky Mts,** If the weather is cold, you will probably find him [=the cowboy] inside, hugging his *estufa* (Sp., stove). **1889** (1971) Farmer *Americanisms* 226, *Estufa.*—A stove. . . Part of the common speech of the Rocky Mountain States in which the Spanish element prevails. **1894** *DN* 1.324 **TX,** *Estufa:* a stove, for heating, not for cooking purposes. Also the room in which the stove is. **1950** Waters *Masked Gods* 56 **NM,** Cooking, not in the *brassero,* a brick oven suitable only for charcoal fuel, . . but outside, as did the Pueblos, in an adobe oven, the *estufa,* resembling in miniature the pueblo *kiva.*

et v See **eat** v **A1a, 2b, 3b**

et pron See **it**

etarnal, etarnel See **eternal**

etarnity See **eternity**

eten See **eat** v **A2c, 3d**

eternal adj Pronc-spp *atarnal, etarnal, etarnel, 'tarnal* Similarly, n *eternity;* pronc-spp *atarnity, etarnity, 'tarnity*

A Forms.

1815 Humphreys *Yankey in England* 103 **NEng,** Atarnal, eternal. *Atarnity,* eternity. **1823** Cooper *Pioneers* 2.283 **cNY,** Happy to the ind of etarnity. **1825** Neal *Brother Jonathan* 1.107 **CT,** What a 'tarnal shot he *is,* tho. **1839** *Knickerbocker* 13.445, Slam bang to etarnal smash! **1845** (1876) Cooper *Chainbearer* 106 **NY,** It would make etarnel peace atween us and our neighbor, for it had been etarnel war afore that. **1905** *DN* 3.56 **eNE,** Before *r,* especially among those of Irish descent, it sometimes becomes *a: marcy, sarpint, etarnal,* etc. **1937** in 1983 Beyle *How Talk Cape Cod* 16, What in 'tarnity's name . . was his helmsman trying to do? **c1960** [see **B** below].

B Sense.

Infernal, damned—usu used as an intensifier. *old-fash*

1825 [see **A** above]. **1836** (1838) Haliburton *Clockmaker* (1st ser) 44, Well, that's an etarnal pity, said the Clockmaker, for I should like to show you *Yankee Cyphering.* **1848** Lowell *Biglow* 1st ser 8 **NEng,** Guess you'd fancy / The etarnal bung wuz loose! **1853** Simms *Sword & Distaff* 298 **SC,** He told us all a-most etarnal lie, for he swore he couldn't find nothing. **c1960** *Wilson Coll.* **csKY,** Eternal ['tɑrnəl, ɪ'tɑrnəl]. . . Damned, or as near as the speaker dares to go.

eternity See **eternal A**

ether See **either**

Ethiopian n

1 also *son of Ethiopia:* A Black person. *old-fash*

1719 in 1888 Sewall *Letter-Book* 2.101 **MA,** The poorest Boys and Girls within this Province . . whether they be English, or Indians, or Ethiopians . . have the same right to Religion and Life, that the Richest Heirs have. **1853** Simms *Sword & Distaff* 171 **SC,** These sons of Ethiopia are all good men and true. *Ibid* 174, Appoint a couple of the Ethiopians, your Deputies for the occasion. **1907** London *Road* 2 **NV,** An irate Ethiopian [was] on the platform above trying to land him in the face with a number eleven. **1941** *LANE* Map 452A **cMA,** [iθɪjoʊpɪən], 'more genteel, I suppose'. **1966** Dakin *Dial. Vocab. Ohio R. Valley* 2.449, *African* and *Ethiopian* (several appearances in eastern Ohio and southern Kentucky) may be intended as neutral terms (that is = *Negro*). The informants' comments are rather ambiguous. **1970** *DARE* (Qu. HH28, . . *People of foreign background . . Negro*) Inf **PA**239, Nigger, Ethiopians, Afro-Americans. [Inf Black] **1976** Flexner *America Talking* 55, *Ethiopian* originally had an exotic connotation and was usually used in America to refer to a foreign, free, or educated Black, seldom being used to refer to a slave or a field hand. Thus the first minstrel troupe was billed as the *Ethiopian minstrelsy,* in 1843, . . with Americans calling minstrel shows *Ethiopian dramas* (1856) or *Ethiopian operas,* [and] collections of minstrel show jokes *Ethiopian joke books.*

2 in phr *Ethiopian in the fuel supply:* =**nigger in the woodpile.** Cf **African** n[1] **C2**

1969 *DARE* (Qu. V1, *When you suspect that somebody is trying to deceive you . . "There's ______."*) Inf **IL**81, Ethiopian in the fuel supply [laughter]; **NJ**56, Ethiopian in the fuel supply—[said by] W.C. Fields.

Ethiopian paradise n [Joc alter of **nigger heaven**] *old-fash*

See quots.

1900 *DN* 2.33 **wNY,** *Ethiopian paradise.* Top gallery in a theatre. **1976** Flexner *America Talking* 55, The upper balcony of a theater where Blacks were segregated [was called] Ethiopian paradise.

ethyl n [Trademark *Ethyl* a motor fuel additive, 1924 →] **chiefly west of Appalachians** See Map and Map Section Cf **high-test**

High-octane gasoline.

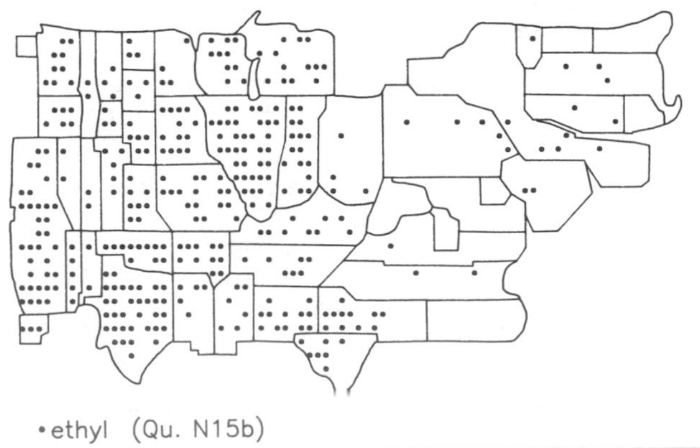

•ethyl (Qu. N15b)

[**1932** *Country Life* May 2, [Advt:] Announcing a new and higher standard for *Ethyl Gasoline* . . gasoline pumps throughout North America bearing the Ethyl emblem are being filled with an even better Ethyl.] **1948** *PADS* 9.25 **OK,** *Ethyl*. . . A short term for *tetraethyl lead*. . . Also used for *ethyl gasoline. Ibid, Ethyl gasoline*. . . A gasoline to which tetraethyl lead fluid has been added to meet the specifications set up by the Ethyl Corporation of America. **1965–70** *DARE* (Qu. N15b, *Gas stations . . usually have two kinds of gasoline: a more expensive kind that's called* ———) 344 Infs, **chiefly west of Appalachians,** Ethyl; [GA72, Miss Ethel].

étouffée n [Fr étouffer to smother] **chiefly LA**

A Cajun stew usu consisting of crawfish (sometimes chicken) and vegetables.

1968 *DARE* (Qu. H45, *Dishes made with meat, fish, or poultry*) Inf **LA**19, Chicken étouffée—chicken with rice and relish; **LA**20, Crawfish étouffee [ˌetu'fe]; **LA**23, Crawfish étouffée—shrimp creole with crawfish. **1968** *DARE* Tape **LA**17, [Chicken étouffée is] kind of a offshoot of crawfish étouffée ['etuˌfe], which is native to the state. . . They all seem to have bell pepper and celery and onions, chopped up, cooked with them, and you cut up a frying chicken. . . and you sautee that . . in a little butter, and you add your chopped bell pepper and celery and onions and let that sautee. . . You . . serve it over rice. **1976** *Capital Times* (Madison WI) 22 Sept 21/1 **csLA,** The non-athletic "croppos" [crapauds]—Cajun for frog—found themselves in batches of etouffee and jambalaya. **1979** Hallowell *People Bayou* 117 **sLA,** Boiled crawfish is . . thoroughly indigenous to the region. . . Other methods of preparation . . do exist. One of them is crawfish etouffée. I learned the recipe from . . a Cajun woman. . . She stood in her kitchen before a big bowl of pink, curled-up crawfish tails. Nearby was a smaller bowl full of greenish, semiliquid stuff. "That's the key to a good etouffée, right there in that bowl. That's the fat and that's what makes your roux take on a special taste." The fat, as she calls it, is actually the animal's liver and pancreas. **1985** *Austin Amer.-Statesman* (TX) 7 July sec B 1, A recipe for crawfish(dad) etouffee. . . You get three pounds of crawdad meat—that's the tails. . . Cook the veggies until they're soft. Then add the crawdad meat and stuff.

ets v See **eat v A2**

ets n pl See **eats**

euchre n Also sp *eucher, eucre, euker, uker* [Origin uncertain; see *DA euchre* n, note]

1 A card game, played usu by two to four persons with a deck from which all cards lower than seven have been removed, with the player who has determined the trump suit trying to take three of five tricks or else be "euchred," i.e., lose two points. **chiefly Nth, N Midl, esp N Cent** See Map Cf **buck euchre**

1841 *S. Lit. Messenger* 7.54/2 **sLA,** A month ere I embarked I lost at euker. **1855** (1929) DeLong *Jrls.* 8.341 **NY,** Playe[d] Euchre with John Atchison. **1858** Hammett *Piney Woods Tavern* 80, He and three others were a playin' uker. **1859** (1968) Bartlett *Americanisms, Eucre.* A sort of game played with cards, very much in vogue at the West. **1869** Twain *Innocents* 160, At night there were gaps in the eucher-parties which could not be satisfactorily filled. **1950** *WELS (Card games played a good deal in your neighborhood)* 10 Infs, **WI,** Euchre. **c1960** *Wilson Coll.* **csKY,** *Euchre*. . . A card game known to a small percentage, as playing cards was formerly regarded as very wicked. **1965–70** *DARE* (Qu. DD35, . . *Favorite card games*) 137 Infs, **chiefly Nth, N Midl, esp N Cent,** Euchre; (Qu. FF2, . . *Kinds of parties*) Infs **NJ**8, **OH**48, **PA**59, Euchre parties; (Qu. FF22a) Infs **IN**30, **WI**24, Euchre club. **1974** Gibson *Hoyle* 107, *Euchre:* Once the most popular "trump game" in America.

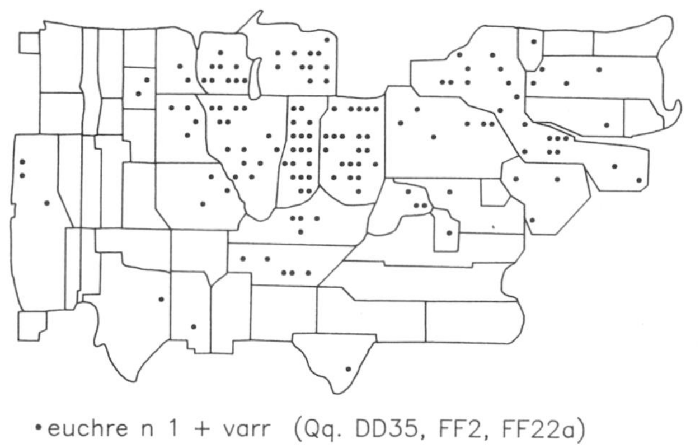

•euchre n 1 + varr (Qq. DD35, FF2, FF22a)

‡**2** Transf: a marble game.

1968 *DARE* Tape **TX**40, The big [marbles were used to] play euchre—we called it that in my day.

euchre v Also with *out* Pronc-spp *eucher, uker*

To defeat; to outwit; to cheat, trick.

1853 in 1951 *AmSp* 26.225 **sCA,** Watkins your a trump! and may you never get euchered. **1858** in 1930 Meine *Tall Tales* 254 **Missip Valley,** It's a figger of speech, and means going it alone and getting ukered. **1870** Harte *Luck Roaring Camp* 64 **CA,** Tennessee smiled, showed his white teeth, and saying, "Euchred, old man!" held out his hand. **1920** in 1946 *PADS* 6.12 **ceNC,** *Euchre out of*. . . To flimflam or trick. . . occasional. **1949** *Chi. Tribune* 15 Feb. 11/1 *(DA),* The belief that the British have euchred them out of the Marshall plan [has] . . given the inhabitants of this bomb battered island [Malta] a feeling of having been abandoned by Britain now that they are no longer needed in the war. **1950** *WELS* 1 Inf, **WI,** To be euchred—cornered; 1 Inf, He euchred (utterly defeated or bamboozled) them. **c1960** *Wilson Coll.* **csKY,** *Euchre*. . . To outsmart, outplay in cards or anywhere. **1966–67** *DARE* (Qu. II33, . . *"I don't trust him, he's always trying to* ———*."*) Infs **CO**29, **SD**8, Euchre me; (Qu. CC12b, . . *If a person has a lot of bad luck . . "He's been* ———*."*) Inf **CA**7, Euchred out.

eujifferous adj [Fanciful formation; cf **angeliferous, splendiferous**]

Grand, splendid.

1911 *DN* 3.543 **seNE,** *Eujifferous*. . . "I had a perfectly eujifferous time." **1942** Berrey–Van den Bark *Amer. Slang* 20.9, *Great; considerable in degree*. . . eujifferous, . . spanglorious. *Ibid* 29.4, *Excellent*. . . eujifferous.

euker See **euchre**

eulachon n |'juləkən| Also sp *eulikon, oulachan, ulken* [Chinook Jargon *ulâkân*] **Pacific NW**

A smeltlike food fish *(Thaleichthys pacificus)* of the Pacific coast. Also called **candlefish 1, Columbia River smelt, hooligan**

1806 (1808) Gass *Jrl.* 271, In the afternoon, some of the natives came to visit us, and brought some of the small fish, which they call Ulken. **1872** Schele de Vere *Americanisms* 386, *Oulachan* . . is the native name, often misrepresented as Hoolikan, and even Eulachon, of a small salmonoid fish of the Pacific coast. **1951** Writers' Program *Oregon* 26, In marked contrast to the gigantic salmon is the smelt or eulachon, called anchovy by Lewis and Clark, and also known as candlefish because their small dried bodies, rich in oil, were formerly utilized as torches. **1962** Salisbury *Quoth the Raven* 241 **seAK,** Besides salmon and the herring, there is a fish called the eulikon, or candle fish, about a foot long and on the herring order, which is finely flavored and is considered a great delicacy by the natives. **1968** *DARE* (Qu. P4, *Saltwater fish that are not good to eat*) Inf **AK**1, Eulachon ['juləkən]—also called "hooligan," a prime source of oil or grease among Indians; valued in interior; = "candlefish," can be burned like a candle.

eureka dumpling n

An apple dumpling.

1931–33 *LANE Worksheets* **seRI,** Eureka dumpling. . . Sweet dish made with biscuit crust and apples. **1987** *NADS Letters* **RI** (as of 1930s), I have heard *eureka dumpling* in my 1930s boyhood in Jamestown, R.I.—in Narragansett Bay. And I remember its yummy taste.

European (brown) trout See **brown trout 1**

European widgeon n

Std: a duck *(Anas penelope)* native to Eurasia, but sometimes found along the coasts of the US. Also called **gray duck h, ice duck, marsh widgeon, Norwegian widgeon, redhead, red-headed widgeon, swamp widgeon, whistler, widgeon**

evans'-root n Also *evan root* [Folk-etym for *avens,* understood as proper name *Evans*]

Usu **water avens,** but also *Geum virginianum.*

1828 Rafinesque *Med. Flora* 1.220, *Geum virginianum*. . . Vulgar Names—Evan root, Avens, Chocolate root [etc]. . . The *Geum rivale* . . is more commonly employed in the north, and this species in the south. **c1873** in 1976 Miller *Shaker Herbs* 61, A receipt or formula book kept at Hancock [Massachusetts] . . from 1828 to 1846. . . included coriander, bloodroot, . . evans'-root *[Geum rivale]* . . and of course rhubarb. **1876** Hobbs *Bot. Hdbk.* 35, Evans root, Avens root, Geum rivale. **1911** *Century Dict. Suppl.,* Evans. . . A provincial corruption of *avens. Evans-root.* . . The water-avens, *Geum rivale.* **1945** *NY Folkl. Qrly.* 1.215 **NY,** Of evans' root we made our tea.

evaporator n

1 also *evaporator pan, evaporating kettle:* A shallow rectangular receptacle usu with wooden sides and metal bottom used on an **arch 2** in converting sugarcane juice or maple sap into syrup or sugar.

1822 *Farmer's Diary* (1823) C3ʳ *(DA)* **nwNY,** The evaporators are not removed during the summer, but only turned bottom upwards and exposed to the weather. **1892** *Outing* Mar 461/2 **nNY,** We draw near the blazing fire and watch the men pour into the great mysterious evaporators the sap which runs its tortuous course and comes out syrup at the other end. **1911** (1916) Porter *Harvester* 35 **IN,** Behind him came Betsy drawing the sap buckets and big evaporating kettles. *Ibid* 299, He picked up a half a dozen old white plates, saucers, and several cups, starting toward the evaporator. **1947** *PADS* 8.5 **VT,** *Evaporator.* . . An arch over which rests a partitioned pan usually equipped with flues beneath it into which the sap from the storage tank is introduced. . . By the time it reaches the last compartment, the liquid has evaporated so much that it is almost syrup. At that point it is closed off and boiled until it reaches the necessary boiling point of standard syrup. **1966–68** *DARE* Tape **FL**26, The last few years, we used an evaporator. It was a long, wide pan and the juice would run at one end . . and it went right out the other end—it was syrup; **CT**3, When we have enough to start the evaporator, we use a wood fire. . . As I showed you the evaporator outside, there are two pans; one is called a flue pan where the cold sap comes in through a special pump that we have; **MA**5C, The evaporators are all different capacities in boiling, one'll boil faster than another. **1969** *DARE* FW Addit **neKY,** Evaporator pan—where cane juice is boiled down in sorghum molasses making.

2 In the production of moonshine: =**boiler** n[1] **2.**

1968 *Foxfire* Fall–Winter 49 **TN,** *Still*—the container into which the beer is placed for boiling. Also called the *Evaporator* or *Boiler* or *Kettle* or *Cooker.*

evapulate v [Pronc-sp for *evaporate*]

1945 Saxon *Gumbo Ya-Ya* 298 **New Orleans LA** [Black], 'Another time,' said she, 'a rooster done appeared in my room. . . Then it disappeared—jest evapulated. Was I glad.'

Eve n [*Eve,* in the Bible, the first woman] Cf **Adam 1**

A woman one cannot identify; see quot.

1965–70 *DARE* (Qu. II26, *Joking ways of saying that you would not know who somebody is: "I wouldn't know him from ______.")* Infs **CA**81, **MD**24, **MI**28, **MN**2, 42, **MO**18, **NJ**68, **PA**167, **RI**1, **TX**74, Eve. [9 of 10 Infs female]

Eve-and-Adam n

=**Adam-and-Eve 1.**

c1938 in 1970 Hyatt *Hoodoo* 1.410 **cAR,** She got some *rattlesnake dust* . . an' she made some little bags an' she hung one undah dis arm an' one undah dis one, an' she went an' got some dat *Eve-an'-Adam dust* an' she place it on cousin right heah. . . Now, mah cousin wus crazy—she wus stone crazy. *Ibid,* The term *Eve-and-Adam* is more frequently used than Adam-and-Eve.

eve day n

1949 *AmSp* 24.108 **GA,** *Eve day.* . . New Year's Eve.

eveglo(a)m See **gloam**

even adj, adv, v Usu |'iv(ə)n|; also |'ivm̩|; **chiefly Sth** |'ibn̩, 'ibm̩| (cf Pronc Intro 3.I.17) Pronc-spp *ebbm, ebbn, eben, eb'm, eb'n, ebun, eeben*

Std senses, var forms.

1888 Jones *Negro Myths* 168 **seGA,** *Eeben,* even. **1891** *DN* 1.164 **cNY,** In general *n* is stable, but it is assimilated to *m* in . . [ivm] < *even,* [ɒvm] < *oven.* **1899** (1912) Green *VA Folk-Speech* 166, *Ebbm. . . Ebbn;* even. **1916** *Scribner's Mag.* Mar 354/1 **VA** [Black], Eben dat young Paul, he done made hisse'f skase. **1922** Gonzales *Black Border* 270 **sSC, GA coasts** [Gullah], 'E wouldn' eb'n gimme time fuh go home. **1929** Sale *Tree Named John* 111 **MS,** Ah ain' got narry piece uv line ner eb'm a straing. **1936** *AmSp* 11.236 **eTX,** In words of the first group—*eleven, even* . . the [v] > [b] in careless or illiterate speech, the following vowel is elided . . and then [n̩] > [m̩] by assimilation to [b]: ['lɛbm̩], ['ibm̩]. **1942** Hall *Smoky Mt. Speech* 96 **wNC, eTN,** *Eleven, even* . . [(ə)'lɛbm̩], ['ibm̩] . . (pronunciations said to be fairly common, but not heard). **1953** [see **evendown** adv].

even n Pronc-sp *e'en* [Engl and Scots dial]

Evening.

1917 in 1944 *ADD* **sWV,** *Even.* . . Evening. 'Good even' = Good evening. **1983** *MJLF* 9.1.38 **ceKY,** *E'en* . . evening. **1985** *DARE* File **WV,** Even—short for evening, any time after noon, in West Virginia.

even-and-even See **even-even**

evendown adj [Engl dial]

1899 (1912) Green *VA Folk-Speech* 166, *Even-down.* . . Downright; direct; plain; flat: an even-down lie.

evendown adv

Even.

1953 Brewer *Word Brazos* 30 **eTX** [Black], Many a preachuh rat heah in de Bottoms c'mit 'dult'ry, drunk his lickuh, an' ebun down swo' in de pulpit. *Ibid* 74, Dey ain't ebun down got no house for de preachuh to live in. *Ibid* 90, Dey ebun down go so far as to gib dey pappies an' dey mammies sass. **1957** in 1958 Brewer *Dog Ghosts* 36 **TX** [Black], He won't ebun down hab time to worry his own se'f!

evener n

1 On a horse-drawn vehicle: A pivoting bar or set of bars used to equalize the force from two or more **singletrees;** sometimes the whole apparatus including the **singletrees.** Note: A few *DARE* and *LAUM* Infs appear to use *evener* in the same sense as **singletree** or even to interchange their senses; this probably reflects confusion due to lack of familiarity with the implements or simply misunderstanding of the question. **chiefly Nth** See Map and Map Section Cf **doubletree, equalizer 1**

1850 U.S. Patent Office *Annual Rept. for 1849: Arts & Mfgr.* 371, I claim . . the exclusive use of said spring rests and "evener." **1872** (1876) Knight *Amer. Mech. Dict.* 1.813/2, *Evener.* A double or treble tree to 'even' or divide the work of pulling upon the respective horses. **1889** (1971) Farmer *Americanisms* 227, *Evener.*—The swing splinter-bar of a carriage. **1894** *Century Illustr. Mag.* 48.869, It is worth while remarking here that the "double-tree" is known in some Northern regions by an excellent descriptive name, the "evener." **1927** (1970) Sears *Catalogue* 1002, *Five-Horse String Out Plow Evener.* . . Main evener, 1¾x4½x54 in. Short evener, 1¾x3¾x25⅜ inches. Singletrees, 1⅜x2½x28 in. Doubletree, 1¾x4½x38 in. **1939** *LANE* Map 173, The term *evener* is the most common term in nearly all parts of New England for the cross bar that connects the two whiffletrees . . but is frequently applied to the whole assembly of whiffletrees and cross bar considered as a unit—usually in the singular form, but three times in the plural. . . Occasionally the term is used in both meanings by the same informant. **1950** *WELS ([Diagram shows evener connected to whiffletrees])* 36 Infs, **WI,** Evener; 1 Inf, Evener set; 1 Inf, This entire affair [including the whiffletrees] is referred to as an evener. **c1960** *Wilson Coll.* **csKY,** *Evener.* . . A doubletree or tribbletree. Very rarely used. **1965–70** *DARE* (Qu. L47, *The two moveable bars behind a team of horses are fastened to a longer piece; this is a ______*) 137 Infs, **chiefly Nth,** Evener; **TX**29, Three-horse evener; **OH**81, Two-horse evener; (Qu. L46, *Behind each horse there's a moveable bar [the leathers or ropes from the collar are fastened to it]—what would you call this?*) Infs **IL**33, **IA**46, **MI**97, **MO**19, **NY**189,

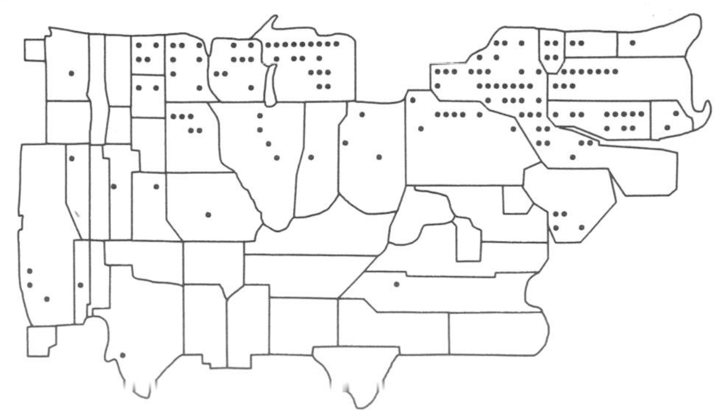

•evener 1 + varr (Qq. L47, L46)

OH81, Evener [*DARE* Ed: 2 Infs corrected this resp to *singletree;* 2 gave this resp also at Qu. L47]. **1973** Allen *LAUM* 1.215 (as of c1950), 5 infs, **IA, MN, SD,** Singletree... evener. *Ibid* 216, The device by which two—or more—horses are hitched to a buggy or wagon produces some semantic confusion... Several use *evener* for the third or equalizing bar and the plural *eveners* for the entire set. *Evener* competes with *doubletree(s),* with the latter slightly more frequent (82% to 54%). [Varr include] four-horse evener... pair of eveners... set of eveners... three-horse evener. **1982** *Greenfield Recorder* (MA) 27 Feb sec A 4, If a horse trotted along at a smart pace and hit one [=cradle hole], it would snap a harness or the bolt on the evener instantly.

2 A weapon. Cf **equalizer 2**

1949 *PADS* 11.6 **wTX** (as of c1920), *Evener*... A club, knife, or other aid a small man claims as an equalizer in a fight with a large opponent.

even-even adj Also *even-and-even* [Redup for intensification; perh infl by **even Stephen**]

1965–70 *DARE* (Qu. KK54, *Just about equal.. "They were both fast runners and it was _____ all the way."*) Infs **IL**11, **MS**61, Even-even; **LA**20, Even-even [FW: corr to *even Stephen*]; **OH**91, Even-even [FW sugg]; **AR**47, Even-and-even.

even full adj Cf **level full**

Completely full, brimfull.

1878 Taylor *Between the Gates* 233 **sCA,** An old-time preacher's election sermon would pack such a day even-full of doctrine. **1950** *WELS ("He had the box _____ of apples.")* 1 Inf, **ceWI,** Even full; *("The rain barrel is _____.")* 1 Inf, **cwWI,** Even full. [Both Infs of Ger extraction] **1970** *DARE* (Qu. LL28, .. *Entirely full: "The box of apples was _____."*) Inf **PA**242, Even full. [Inf of Ger extraction]

even-handed adj

Ambidextrous.

1965 in 1983 Johnson *I Declare* 52 **nwFL,** If you have a tendency toward misery in your arm .. it'll hesitate you unless you're "even-handed" and spell the hurtin' arm by ironing with the other.

evening n Pronc-sp *ebenin'*

A Forms.

1888 Jones *Negro Myths* 43 **seGA,** You member wuh me bin tell you las ebenin? **1901** *DN* 2.182 **KY** [Black], *Evening*.. ebenin'. **1922** Gonzales *Black Border* 299 **sSC, GA coasts** [Gullah glossary], Ebenin'—evening, evenings. **1939** *LANE* Map 76 *(Evening),* B[loch] records a pronunciation of *evening* with an initial glottal stop [ʔ] in fourteen cases... This presumably represents a form uttered in isolation. **1942** Hall *Smoky Mt. Speech* 64 **wNC, eTN,** Syncope of the vowel is usual in .. *battery* [ˈbætrɪ] .. *evening* [ˈivnən]. **1942** *Sat. Eve. Post* 3 Oct 68/3 **seSC,** It wouldn't be "evenin'," it would be "ebenin'"... All spirituals are sung in dialect.

B Sense.

Afternoon; the time of day between noon and twilight. [Engl dial] **chiefly Sth, S Midl** See Map

1790 *PA Packet & Daily Advt.* (Philadelphia) 5 Jan 3/1 **neKY,** It was .. dark from about two o'clock until about half after four in the evening. **1875** (1876) Twain *Tom Sawyer* 19 **MO,** He'll play hookey this evening. [Footnote:] South-western for "afternoon." **1886** Amer. Philol. Assoc. *Trans.* 17.45 **Sth,** Common Southern expressions... *evening* (afternoon). **1900** Harris *Reminiscences* 110 **TX** (as of 1834), The young people danced to that music from three o'clock in the evening till next morning. **1902** *DN* 2.233 **sIL,** *Evening*... The time between twelve, noon, and sundown. **1903** *DN* 2.312 **seMO. 1904** *DN* 2.418 **nwAR. 1908** *DN* 3.309 **eAL, wGA,** *Ev(e)nin(g)*... Afternoon... *Late this evening* is used to indicate any time from four o'clock till dark. **1909** *DN* 3.392 **nwAR. 1910** *DN* 3.457 **seKY,** *Evening*... Afternoon. Used by everybody. **1912** *DN* 3.575 **wIN. 1920** Hunter *Trail Drivers TX* 73 (as of 1879), That evening about four o'clock .. I saw a very high sand hill right on the edge of the old trail. **1923** *DN* 5.206 **swMO. 1930** *DN* 6.87 **cWV. 1934** *AmSp* 9.79 **nLA,** The word *evenin'*.. was commonly used to mean any time after noon and before supper or sundown. **1944** *PADS* 2.8 **Sth,** *Evening*... Afternoon, commonly the time of day between the midday and the end-of-day meals. *Good evening* is the common Southern salutation in the afternoon. **1946** in 1958 Brewer *Dog Ghosts* 56 **TX** [Black], Come ovuh to mah boss-man's ranch dis nex' comin' Saddy 'bout three o'clock in de evenin' time. **1946** *AmSp* 21.97 **sIL. 1962** Atwood *Vocab. TX* 48, *Between noon and night... Evening*.. is usually used. However, *afternoon*.. is also quite well known, and is apparently gradually replacing the older usage. **1965–70** *DARE* (Qu. A3, *The time between the middle of the day and supper time*) 166 Infs, **chiefly Sth, S Midl,** Evening; **AR**17, **KY**39, **NJ**69, **NC**49, Middle of the evening; **AL**24, **GA**22, **LA**18, Evening time; **IL**93, **MS**55, **MO**22, Mid (of the) evening; **NY**76, **NC**62, Shank of the evening; **AL**14, Late evening; **GA**55, Early evening. **1966–68** *DARE* Tape **AL**11, [Inf:] We'd have meeting in the morning, meeting in the evening, meeting at night. [FW:] Meeting in the evening—that's in the afternoon? [Inf:] Yes; **IN**3, That one evening .. they started to digging in. About the middle of the afternoon, about the time they got it open, where they thought they might see something, why, it begin to get dark.

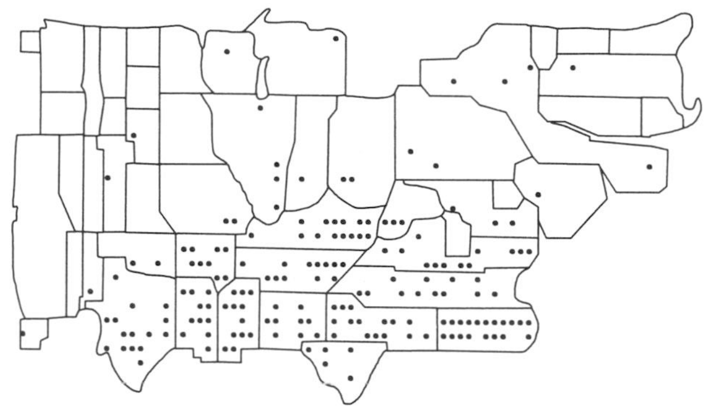

•evening B + varr (Qu. A3)

evening flier See **evening swallow**

evening grosbeak n

Std: a finchlike bird *(Hesperiphona vespertina)* once thought to sing only at evening. Also called **English parrot, German finch, hawfinch, sugarbird**

evening lily See **evening star 1**

evening primrose n

Std: a plant of any of several related genera; see below. Note: The latter two genera were formerly included in the first.

a A plant of the genus *Oenothera.* Also called **buttercup 5, glade flower, moonrose, primrose, rockrose, silent love, suncups, sundrops, treasure vine.** For other names of var spp see **butte primrose, coffee plant 2, cowboy lily 2, cure-all 2, fever plant, fluttermill 3, four-o'clock 2, German rampion, glade lily 2, golden candlestick 1, gumbo lily, king's cure-all, large rampion, night willow-herb, Ozark snowdrops, sand lily, scabious, scabish, scurvish, speckled John, summer rose-cup, tree primrose, wild beet, wild coffeeweed, yerba salada**

b A plant of the western genus *Camissionia.* Also called **primrose, suncups, sundrops.** For other names of var spp see **golden eggs, yellow cups**

c A plant of the genus *Calylophus.* Also called **primrose.** For other names of var spp see **creamcups 2**

evening-snow n

1 A gilia (here: *Linanthus dichotomus*). **CA** Also called **pigpens**

1897 Parsons *Wild Flowers CA* 50, *Evening Snow*... is one of the most showy of our gilias. **1903** (1950) Austin *Land of Little Rain* 53 **neCA,** The white gilias set their pale disks to the westering sun. This is the gilia the children call "evening snow." **1941** Jaeger *Wildflowers* 189, *Evening Snow*... When the plants occur in numbers, wide areas are in a few moments of waning daylight changed to a floral blanket of white. **1966** *DARE* (Qu. S26e) Inf **CA**2, Evening-snow—desert. **1976** Bailey–Bailey *Hortus Third* 666.

2 Sweet William *(Dianthus barbatus).*

1970 *DARE* (Qu. S26a, .. *Roadside flowers*) Inf **CA**208, Sweet William = purity flowers = evening-snow.

evening sparrow See **evening swallow**

evening star n [Prob because the flowers open in the late afternoon or early evening]

1 also *evening starburst, ~ lily:* Any of var chiefly western species of **stickleaf,** esp *Mentzelia decapetala.*

1915 (1926) Armstrong-Thornber *Western Wild Flowers* 302, *Evening Star—Mentzelia Lindleyi.* . . Slender plant . . with magnificent flowers, two and a half inches across, which open in the evening and remain open during the following morning. **1930** OK Univ. Biol. Surv. *Pub.* 2.73, *Mentzelia decapetala.* . . Showy Evening-lily. **1950** Stevens *ND Plants* 210, *Evening Star.* . . Flowers open in evening and resemble a cactus flower. **1967** Dodge *Roadside Wildflowers* 43 **SW,** *Evening Star.* . . Indians parched the seeds of some species and ground them into an edible meal. **1968** *DARE* FW Addit **CO**7, Evening star, evening starburst—*Mentzelia laevicaulis.*

2 =rain lily.

1959 Carleton *Index Herb. Plants* 42, *Evening star:* Cooperia pendunculata [sic]; Mentzelia laevicaulis. **1968** Barkley *Plants KS* 100, *Cooperia drummondii.* . . Prairie Lily, Eveningstar, Rain Lily.

evening swallow n Also *evening flier, ~ sparrow*

=nighthawk.

1951 *AmSp* 26.278, *Evening flier* (Nebr.) and *evening swallow* (Miss.) are alternative names for the nighthawk. **1965–70** *DARE* (Qu. Q20, . . *Kinds of swallows and birds like them*) 15 Infs, **chiefly east of Missip R,** Evening swallow; (Qu. Q3, . . *Birds that come out only after dark*) Inf **CA**2, Evening swallow; (Qu. Q21, . . *Kinds of sparrows*) Infs **IA**20, **NY**100, Evening sparrow.

evening thrush n

=wood thrush.

1951 *AmSp* 26.278 **NJ,** *Evening thrush* [denotes] the wood thrush in New Jersey.

evening trumpet flower n

=Carolina jasmine.

1901 Lounsberry *S. Wild Flowers* 424, Under the names also of evening trumpet-flower and Carolina wild woodbine is this lovely individual known. **1933** Small *Manual SE Flora* 1045, *Gelsemium.* . . Yellow-jessamine. Evening Trumpet-flower. **1971** Krochmal *Appalachia Med. Plants* 130, *Gelsemium sempervirens.* . . Common names: Yellow jessamine, Carolina jessamine, evening trumpet flower.

evenly adv [nEngl dial; cf *EDD*]

Even, at all.

1978 *DARE* File **appar KY,** And how they ever lived—and they didn't even know it. The girls didn't [know] that was big enough to remember, they didn't evenly know it.

even or odd See **odd or even**

even Stephen adj, adv Also sp *even Steven* [Cf 1983 *AmSp* 58.319–24] Cf **even-even**

Even, tied; on an equal basis, fifty-fifty.

1866 Smith *Bill Arp* 64 **GA,** Dick says you allowed members to exchange two hundred dollars of Confederate money for two hundred dollars of State money, "even Stephen." **1906** *DN* 3.135 **nwAR,** *Even Stephen.* . . "It's even Stephen. I believe they'll tie." **1908** *DN* 3.309 **eAL, wGA,** *Even Stephen.* . . Exactly even. **1914** *DN* 4.106 **KS,** *Even Steven.* . . Even;—in games. **1939** *Hench Coll.* **VA,** Let's trade even-Stephen = let's trade without either person getting something to boot. Let's trade and ignore any inequality in the trade. . . "This basket cost a bit more than the one I want to get; but let's exchange even-Stephen." **1949** *Sat. Eve. Post* 12 Mar 132/2 **NYC,** It occurred to me irresistibly that it would be only fair if I were to find a woman who could support me in the manner to which I'd become accustomed. Protection for support. Even Stephen. **c1960** *Wilson Coll.* **csKY,** *Even Steven.* . . Exactly equal in size, . . value, . . form, or achievement. **1960** Rockwell *Adventures* 21 **NY** (as of c1910), In the end it's all even Stephen, as we used to say when I was a kid—a little added here, some taken off there. **1965–70** *DARE* (Qu. KK54, *Just about equal . . "They were both fast runners and it was ______ all the way."*) 21 Infs, **scattered,** Even Stephen; **LA**20, Stephen even [FW: corr to *even Stephen*]; (Qu. EE38b, *If the game of tic-tac-toe . . comes out so that neither X nor O wins*) Inf **MI**103, Even Stephen; (Qu. II8, *When one person wants to share or divide something with another person . . "Let's ______ (on that)."*) Inf **MI**10, Go even Stephen. [15 of 23 total Infs young or mid-aged]

event n Usu |iˈvɛnt, ɨ-|; also **chiefly Sth, S Midl** |ˈiˌvɛnt, -ˌvɪnt|

Std senses, var forms.

1905 *DN* 3.101 **nwAR,** The most noticeable feature of the English spoken in Northwest Arkansas is recessive accent. . . [ˈivent]. **1908** *DN* 3.280 **eAL, wGA,** Recessive accent is noticeable in . . [ˈivɛnt]. **1914** *DN* 4.166, The following pronunciations . . show shift of emphasis to and protraction of the initial syllable. It is not enough to say that these forms illustrate a type of improper recessive accent. In the mouths of some speakers their first syllables are literally "stretched out". . . *e-vents.* **1936** *AmSp* 11.149 **eTX,** Careless speakers. . . are . . likely to shift the accent to the first syllable of . . *event.* . . When this shifting takes place, the second syllable bears secondary stress. **1941** *AmSp* 16.8 **eTX** [Black], *Event* [ˈiˌvɪ̃nt]. **c1960** *Wilson Coll.* **csKY,** Recessive accent. . . E-vent.

eventide n *somewhat old-fash*

Evening.

1851 Longfellow *Golden Legend* 290, Those same soft bells at eventide / Rang in the ears of Charlemagne. **1894** Frederic *Marsena* 159 **nNY,** The sun did well to spread that summer sky at eventide with all the pageantry of color the spectrum knows. **1950** *WELS (The time from about 4 p.m. to 6 p.m.)* 1 Inf, **WI,** Eventide; 1 Inf, Years ago we said eventide. **1967–68** *DARE* (Qu. A4, . . *When the sun goes out of sight*) Inf **IN**15, Eventide; (Qu. A5, *The time right after the sun goes out of sight, before it becomes all dark*) Infs **MO**9, **NJ**4, **OH**69, Eventide. [3 of 4 Infs old; 1 mid-aged]

even tree n Cf **evener 1**

=doubletree.

1983 *McDavid Coll.* (as of 1948) **cnNY,** Even tree = double tree.

ever adv Usu |ˈɛvə(r)|; also **chiefly Sth, S Midl,** *esp freq among Black speakers* |ˈɛbə| Pronc-spp *ebah, eb(b)er, iver, uver*

A Pronc varr.

1821 Cooper *Spy* 2.186 **nNY,** "He worse than ebber now," cried the . . African. **1823** Cooper *Pioneers* 1.194 **nNY,** As much tied to it as iver a thaving dragoon was to the pickets. **1888** Jones *Negro Myths* 68 **seGA,** Arter dat nobody ebber yeddy [=heard] um mek no mo prayer bout Det [=death]. **1899** Chesnutt *Conjure Woman* 136 **NC,** Is I eber tol' ou de tale er Sis' Becky en her pickaninny? **1901** *DN* 2.182 **KY** [Black], *Ever* . . ebah. **1905** Culbertson *Banjo Talks* 29 **SE** [Black], Yer's de pooties' sight dat uver I saw. *Ibid* 87, De beatenes' lot er chillen dat uver I did see. **1925** *DN* 5.357 **seGA** [Black], Al de ting an ting [=all the things] dat he ebber [ɛbə] had.

B Syntax.

Usu *ever* occurs between subj and verb; also, **chiefly Sth, S Midl, occas NEng,** *ever* precedes subj.

1867 Lowell *Biglow* 110 **'Upcountry' MA,** It'll be the long'st day ever *you* see. **1867** Twain *Jumping Frog* 15, Fellers that had travelled and been everywheres all said he laid over any frog that ever *they* see. **1871** (1892) Johnston *Dukesborough Tales* 58 **GA,** That ar the ontimeliest paddle that ever *I* seen. **1895** Murfree *Mystery of Witch-Face* 189 **TN,** She's the red-headedest gal ever I see. **1903** *DN* 2.302 **Cape Cod MA** (as of a1857), The biggest ever I saw. **1913** Kephart *Highlanders* 285 **sAppalachians,** Them's the travellinest hosses ever I seed. **1926** *DN* 5.385 **ME,** "Them is as good apples as ever I see." Obsol[escent]. **1930** Faulkner *As I Lay Dying* 4 **MS,** So I baked yesterday, more careful than ever I baked in my life. **1942** *Sat. Eve. Post* 7 Nov 79/1 **SC,** The young-'uns [=water turkeys] are the dangedest-lookin' an' the purtiest swamp babies ever you'll see between Cowcastle Crick an' Horse Savannah. **1960** Hall *Smoky Mt. Folks* 64, He was the crabbedest old feller ever I seed. **1976** Wolfram-Christian *Appalachian Speech* 99, That was the brightest light that *ever* I seen. . . That's the biggest rattlesnake *ever* I seen. . . Did *ever* a stray animal come to y'all's house and take up?

C Senses.

1 Always. [*OED ever* adv. 2 "*arch.* and *north. dial.*"] **chiefly Sth, S Midl**

1853 Bird *Nick of Woods* 321 **KY,** I hated you ever,—I hate you yet. **1928** Peterkin *Scarlet Sister Mary* 37 **sSC coast** [Gullah], I ever did say—company in de dark don' do for gals. *Ibid* 239, God knew he ever had tried to please the woman. **1930** Faulkner *As I Lay Dying* 16 **MS,** She was ever one to clean up after herself. **1933** Miller *Lamb in His Bosom* 15 **GA,** Her mother had named her Tillitha Cean, but ever she was called Cean. **1941** *Sat. Eve. Post* 10 May 36/3 **KY,** She was ever the scary one. **1942** Thomas *Blue Ridge Country* 50 **sAppalachians,** Twistin' the end of her apron like she ever did when she was warried.

2 When. Cf **ever and when, everwhen**

1933 Miller *Lamb in His Bosom* 130 **GA,** Men and women were the master-fools; ever he was grown, never would he marry!

3 As long as.

1968 *DARE* (Qu. A24, . . *"He's been hot-tempered from ________.")* Inf **PA**157, Ever I know him.

ever adj [Prob abbr for *every;* but cf *OED ever* adv. 4 "Ever where. *Obs.*"] **widespread, but chiefly Sth, S Midl, esp TX** See Map Cf **every** adv

Every; hence compounds *everone, everthing, everwhere(s),* etc.

1838 (1930) Phelps *Diary* 233 **IL,** They sure enough eat for they finished the whole, ever bit in just half an hour. **1893** Shands *MS Speech, Every* and *Ever. . .* A strange confusion of these two words exists in the speech of the uneducated; they say: "every since" and "ever man." **1894** Riley *Armazindy* 4 **IN,** She could raise the means to pay / Fer her farm-hands ever' day. *Ibid* 163, An' *ever*'body *ever*'wheres! *Ibid* 48, It peared-like ever'thing. **1908** *DN* 3.309 **eAL, wGA,** *Ever. . .* Every. Not so common as *evy.* **1915** *DN* 4.182 **swVA. 1923** *DN* 5.206 **swMO. 1930** Faulkner *As I Lay Dying* 66 **MS,** That's ever living thing the matter with Darl. **1933** Rawlings *South Moon* 15 **FL,** It's ever' man to his taste. *Ibid* 93, They comes ever' day. **1942** Hall *Smoky Mt. Speech* 64 **wNC, eTN,** *Everybody, everything,* and *everywhere* are most often . . ['ɛvɚˌbɑdɪ], ['ɛvɚθɪŋ], ['ɛvɚhwɝ]. **1946** McCullers *Member* 17 **AL,** That whole crowd give me the creeps. Ever last one of them. **1965–70** *DARE* (Qu. MM12a, *Other ways of saying 'in all directions'*) 71 Infs, **scattered, but less freq Atlantic,** Ever which way; 20 Infs, **chiefly Sth, S Midl,** (Scattered) everwhere; 13 Infs, **chiefly Gulf States,** Ever whichaway; 9 Infs, **Sth, S Midl,** Ever way; **KY**65, **MS**57, **OK**18, **TN**14, Ever direction; **VA**46, Everwheres; (Qu. MM12b) 16 Infs, **Sth, S Midl,** (All scattered, scattered, *or* flying) everwhere; 11 Infs, 7 **TX,** Ever which way (*or* whichaway); **FL**19, **KY**19, 60, 91, **MO**32, (Scattered) ever place; **AR**47, **LA**8, **TX**32, (In) ever direction; **NC**53, Ever way; **VA**15, Everwheres; (Qu. A15, *Something that happens only occasionally: "He comes around ________.")* Infs **FL**9, 19, 21, **MS**63, **TX**35, Ever now and then; **FL**35, **GA**44, **OK**53, **TX**13, 33, Ever so often; **NM**11, **SC**32, 51, Ever once in a while; (Qu. Y48, *To look in every possible place . . "I've ________.")* Inf **FL**31, Looked ever place; **KY**24, Looked everwhere; **MA**127, Searched everwhere; (Qu. KK40) Inf **MO**37, Ever once in a while; **MO**15, Ever other; (Qu. X48a, . . *"She must be ________ sixty")* Inf **TX**32, Ever bit of; (Qu. X48b) Infs **MO**23, 29, Ever bit sixty; (Qu. V6) Inf **WA**1, Everthing he touches sticks to his hands; (Qu. AA21) Inf **OK**18, Ever time she hollers frog he jumps; (Qu. FF18) Inf **FL**14, Painted everthing red; (Qu. GG22b) Inf **WV**18, Beats everthing; (Qu. KK2) Inf **FL**6, Liked by everone. **1966** *PADS* 46.25 **cnAR** (as of 1952), *Ever. . .* Every. "I stall them cows ever night." **1966–70** *DARE* Tape **CA**209, Mobile trailers, they're everwheres; **FL**35, Ever weekend; **MS**72, I was . . ever week over the place cow-hunting. **1976** Wolfram–Christian *Appalachian Speech* 99, And *ever* time I say something to her, she act like she's gonna kill me. . . We had *everthing* to eat.

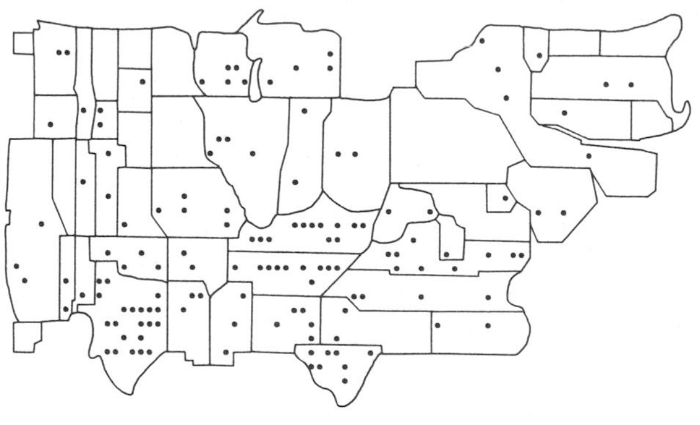

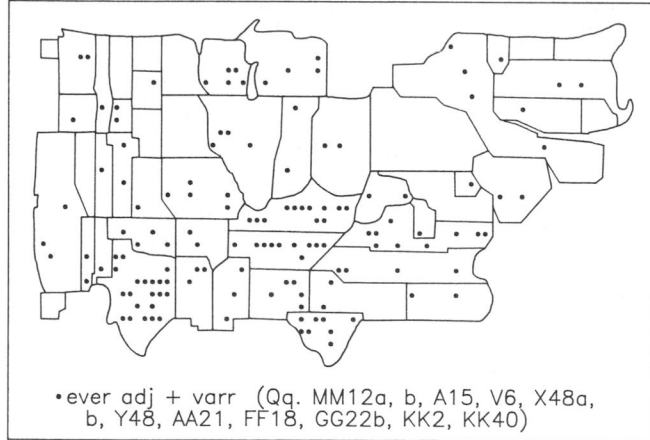

•ever adj + varr (Qq. MM12a, b, A15, V6, X48a, b, Y48, AA21, FF18, GG22b, KK2, KK40)

ever and always adv phr

Always; persistently.

1967 *DARE* FW Addit **sePA,** She was ever and always bringing me something.

ever and when adv phr Cf **everwhen**

Whenever, when.

1933 *AmSp* 8.1.49 **Ozarks,** *Ever an' when. . .* I'll go t' work ever an' when I git good an' ready, an' nary a minute sooner!

everbearing grape n

=**bird grape 1.**

1920 *Torreya* 20.23, *Vitis munsoniana. . .* Everbearing . . grape.

everbody See **ever** adj

everen See **everwhen**

everglade kite n, also cap E [*Everglades* land area in southern Florida + *kite*] **FL**

A small bluish-gray kite *(Rostrhamus sociabilis).* Also called **hook-billed hawk, marsh ~, snail ~, white-rumped kite**

1889 *Century Dict.* 2040, *Everglade kite, Rostrhamus sociabilis,* having a long, very slender, and much-hooked bill. **1895** U.S. Dept. Ag. *Yearbook for 1894* 1.218, The *everglade kite* is found within our borders in Florida only, where it is restricted to the middle and southern portions. **1942** U.S. Natl. Park Serv. *Fading Trails* 169 **FL,** In fact, there are only one or two spots in the entire State where, with luck, an Everglade kite may be seen. **1955** Forbush–May *Birds* 98.

evergreen n

1 Std: a conifer or nondeciduous broad-leaved tree.

2 A **club moss.**

1892 *Jrl. Amer. Folkl.* 5.105, *Lycopodium dendroideum* . . evergreen. Stratham, N.H. **1897** *Ibid* 10.147, *Lycopodium complanatum* . . evergreen, Oxford County, Me. **1898** *Ibid* 11.283, *Lycopodium complanatum* . . evergreen, Turner, Me. **1900** Lyons *Plant Names* 233, *Lycopodium obscurum* . . Evergreen. **1916** *Torreya* 16.236, *Lycopodium clavatum* . . Evergreen, Matinicus Id., Me. **1929** *Ibid* 29.149, All the Lycopodia were *"Evergreen,"* clavatum, complanatum, obscurum, being the most common.

3 =**orpine.**

1892 *Jrl. Amer. Folkl.* 5.96, *Sedum telephium* . . evergreen. Chestertown, Md. **1900** Lyons *Plant Names* 340, *Sedum telephium* . . evergreen.

4 See **evergreen onion.**

5 See **evergreen corn.**

evergreen cherry n Also *evergreen*

1 =**Carolina cherry.**

1893 *Jrl. Amer. Folkl.* 6.140 **GA,** *Prunus Caroliniana* . . evergreen. **1897** Sudworth *Arborescent Flora* 246 **TX,** *Prunus caroliniana. . .* Evergreen Cherry.

2 also *mountain evergreen cherry:* =**islay.**

1893 *Jrl. Amer. Folkl.* 6.140 **CA,** *Prunus ilicifolia* . . mountain evergreen cherry. **1897** Sudworth *Arborescent Flora* 247 **CA,** *Prunus ilicifolia. . .* Evergreen Cherry . . Mountain Evergreen Cherry. **1908** Britton *N. Amer. Trees* 512, The plant [=*Prunus ilicifolia*] grows rapidly. . . Among Californian common names for it are Holly-leaf cherry, Evergreen cherry. **1923** Davidson–Moxley *Flora S. CA* 207, *Evergreen Cherry. . .* Common on the lower hills throughout southern California. **1938** Van Dersal *Native Woody Plants* 330. **1979** Little *Checklist U.S. Trees* 213, *Prunus ilicifolia. . .* Evergreen cherry.

evergreen corn n Also *evergreen*

White sweet corn.

1856 Cozzens *Sparrowgrass* 82 **seNY,** She took out a package of seeds . . then handsful of beans, peas, . . sweet corn, evergreen corn, and other germs. **1966–69** *DARE* (Qu. I33, . . *Ears of corn that are just right for eating)* Inf **NJ**56, Evergreen corn; **NY**94, Evergreen corn—has white kernels; (Qu. I34, *If you don't have sweet corn, you can always eat young ________)* Inf **CT**12, Evergreen corn—all white; (QR, near Qu. I33) Inf **NH**12, Evergreen corn. **1974** *Burpee Seeds* 91/2, *Standard White Sweet Corn* . . *Burpee's White Evergreen. . .* Kernels retain their paper whiteness and flavor even when canned. **1976** Olds Seed Co. *Seeds* 11/1 **csWI,** *Golden or Bantam Evergreen. . .* Many attempts have been made to combine the sweetness, earliness, color and flavor of Golden Bantam, with the tender skin and large ear of the Evergreen. . . *Stowell's Evergreen. . .* remains long in the milk before ripening up.

evergreen grass n

1 A **fescue** (here: *Festuca elatior*).

1856 U.S. Dept. Ag. *Rept. of Secy. for 1855* 253 **swNC,** The evergreen-grass . . is very good for pasturing, through the fall and winter. **1878** Killebrew *Grasses TN* 186, *Meadow Fescue—Randall Grass—Evergreen Grass—(Festuca pratensis.)*

2 An **oatgrass** (here: *Arrhenatherum elatius*).

1889 Vasey *Ag. Grasses* 52, *Arrhenatherum avenaceum* (Evergreen Grass; Meadow Oat Grass; Tall Oat Grass).

evergreen magnolia n

A **magnolia** (here: *Magnolia grandiflora*).

1971 GA Dept. Ag. *Farmers Market Bulletin* 7 July 8/1, The southern magnolia also known as the evergreen magnolia, bull-bay and big-leaved magnolia . . is of the family Magnoliaceae and the species Magnolia grandiflora L. **1979** Little *Checklist U.S. Trees* 166, *Magnolia grandiflora—southern magnolia* . . evergreen magnolia.

evergreen millet n

=Johnson grass.

1889 Vasey *Ag. Grasses* 36, *Sorghum halepense* (Johnson Grass; Mean's Grass). . . In California it is best known as evergreen millet or Arabian evergreen millet.

evergreen oak n

Any of var oaks, such as:

a =laurel oak. Gulf States

1775 (1962) Romans *Nat. Hist. FL* 18, The principal [trees] however are . . Evergreen oak with oblong entire leaves, or live oak. **1833** Silliman *Sugar Cane* 19 *(DAE),* [The hammocks are] characterized by the natural growth of large evergreen oaks, . . magnolia and cabbage-palmetto. **1901** Mohr *Plant Life AL* 14, Spanish moss investing the huge limbs of venerable evergreen oaks (the laurel oak, mentioned by him [=Bartram] as *Quercus hemisphærica*). **1966–68** *DARE* (Qu. T10, . . *Different kinds of oak trees*) Infs **LA**18, **MS**16, Evergreen oak; **AL**20, Evergreen oak, stays green all winter—leaves do fall, but stay green.

b A **live oak** (here: *Quercus agrifolia*). **CA**

1845 Frémont *Rept. Rocky Mts.* 241 **nCA,** The prevailing tree [in the country west of the Sierra Nevada] was the evergreen oak, (which, by way of distinction, we shall call the *live oak*). **1846** (1848) Bryant *What I Saw in CA* 238, We crossed . . one or two small valleys or bottoms timbered with evergreen oaks, *(Quercus Ilex,)*. **1899** *Jrl. Amer. Folkl.* 7.99 **CA,** *Quercus agrifolia* . . scrub oak, evergreen oak.

c The Engelmann oak *(Quercus engelmanni).*

1922 Sargent *Manual Trees* 282, *Quercus Engelmannii. . . Evergreen Oak.* . . Low hills of southwestern California. **1938** Van Dersal *Native Woody Plants* 346, Oak, . . Evergreen *(Quercus engelmannii).* **1945** Wodehouse *Hayfever Plants* 79, Also of the Pacific coast is the evergreen . . oak (*Q. Engelmannii* Greene).

evergreen onion n Also *evergreen* **esp TX** Cf **everlasting onion**

An onion (here: *Allium cepa* Aggregatum Group).

1966–69 *DARE* (Qu. I5, . . *Onions that keep coming up without replanting year after year*) Infs **MI**93, **MS**72, **TX**36, 45, 69, 71, Evergreen (onions); **LA**2, Evergreen onions—you don't pull these up; **LA**33, Evergreen onions—in the garden; **AR**20, Evergreens; (Qu. I6) Inf **TX**32, Evergreen.

evergreen white oak n

Usu the Engelmann oak *(Quercus engelmanni),* but also the **blue oak 3.**

1894 *Jrl. Amer. Folkl.* 7.99 **CA,** *Quercus oblongifolia* . . evergreen white oak, live oak. **1897** Sudworth *Arborescent Flora* 161, *Common Names.* Engelmann's Oak. Evergreen White Oak. **1910** Jepson *Silva CA* 217, *Quercus Engelmannii. . .* The leaves remain on the tree until the appearance of the new leaves in the spring, whence the name "Evergreen White Oak." **1979** Little *Checklist U.S. Trees* 230, *Engelmann oak. . . Other common names*—evergreen white oak.

everhow adv [Reversed cpd] Cf Intro "Language Changes" I.1

However.

1932 Randolph *Ozark Mt. Folks* 236, In th' last few years o' my teachin', I tuck up with a different system—jest offered t' teach a ten-night school for twenty-five dollars flat, an' let 'em raise it ever'how they could. **1953** Randolph *Down in Holler* 64 **Ozarks,** *Ever-how* is not uncommon, and apparently means however. **1976** Wolfram–Christian *Appalachian Speech* 99, Say five or six of us boys, *everhow* many was in the . . , you know, lived close to us.

everies See **evers**

everlasting adj, adv **chiefly NEng, S Midl**

A As adj.

Infernal, damned; also used absol: tarnation, damnation. Cf **eternal B**

1904 *DN* 2.425 **Cape Cod MA** (as of a1857), *Everlasting. . .* An exclamation, as 'why the everlasting, see what he's done!' **1942** McAtee *Dial. Grant Co. IN* 25 (as of 1890s), *Everlasting* . . euphemism for an emphatic swear word; "You everlastin' idiot." **1951** *PADS* 15.66 **cwNH** (as of 1920s), *Everlasting. . .* Euphemism for a swear word. "I'll beat the everlastin' daylights out of you." **1954** *Harder Coll.* **cwTN,** Everlasting. . . euphemism for a swear word. **c1960** *Wilson Coll.* **csKY,** *Everlasting. . .* A term of reproach, almost equivalent to damned. **1970** *DARE* (Qu. NN17, *Something that keeps on annoying you . . "That ——— fly won't go away."*) Inf **VA**50, Everlasting.

B As adv.

Also *everlastingly:* Very, extremely; damned.

1832 in 1834 Smith *Letters Jack Downing* 95 **ME,** I had rather fight forty New Orleans battles than to govern this everlasting great country one year. **1848** in 1894 Lowell *Letters* 1.136 **MA,** It's everlasting hot to-day. **1872** in 1917 Twain *Letters* 1.201 **MO,** I have been so everlasting busy that I *couldn't* write. **1889** *Century Dict.* 2040, He is everlastingly stingy. **1891** Cooke *Huckleberries* 36 **NEng,** And then she was "everlastin' smart." **1968** *DARE* (Qu. LL37, *To make a statement as strong as you can: "I could have wrung her neck, I was so ——— mad."*) Inf **NC**82, Everlasting; **VA**31, Everlastingly [laughter].

everlasting n

1 Any of var plants, such as statice (*Armeria* spp) or **orpine,** but esp those suitable for drying, of the composite genera *Anaphalis, Antennaria, Gnaphalium, Helichrysum* and *Helipterum;* see quots. Cf **life everlasting, pearly ~**

1832 MA Hist. Soc. *Coll.* 2 ser 9.150 **VT,** *Gnaphalium . . polycephalum,* Everlasting [is indigenous to Middlebury, Vermont]. **1842** Kirkland *Forest Life* 2.144 **seMI,** Mrs. Lettsom's "everlastin'," . . is only a soft cooling herb much cultivated in these regions. **1848** in 1850 Cooper *Rural Hours* 310 **nNY,** Observed a broad field upon a hill-side covered with the white silvery heads of the everlastings. **1858** Holmes *Autocrat* 85 **NEng,** Perhaps the herb *everlasting,* the fragrant *immortelle* of our autumn fields, has the most suggestive odor to me of all those that set me dreaming. **1859** (1968) Bartlett *Americanisms* 138, *Everlasting. Life Everlasting. (Gnaphalium.)* So called from its medicinal properties (so the books say), but much more likely from the French "Immortelle," a similar plant, so named from the endurance of its flowers when dried. **1869** Fuller *Uncle John* 302 *(DAE),* They are your last flowers for this year, with the exception of . . a few Sun-flowers and Everlastings. **1893** Owen *Voodoo Tales* 6 **MO,** Instead of the flowers that bloomed to fade, stiff bunches of . . "everlastings" and bittersweet-berries peeped from under her great basket's-lid. **1899** Bergen *Animal Lore* 111 **nOH,** Tea made of the leaves and blossoms of "everlasting" *(Gnaphalium polycephalum)* is taken for colds and other mild diseases. **1900** Lyons *Plant Names* 340, *S[edum] telephium. . .* Everlasting. **1904** *DN* 2.425 **Cape Cod MA** (as of a1857), *Everlasting. . .* An aromatic herb. **1949** Moldenke *Amer. Wild Flowers* 207, In our gardens we cultivate several types of *"everlasting"* . . plants (*Gomphrena, Helichrysum, Helipterum, Ammobium,* etc.) **1967–69** *DARE* (Qu. S11, . . *Other names . . for: bachelor's button*) Inf **GA**70, Everlasting; (Qu. S26a, . . *Other wildflowers . . Roadside flowers*) Inf **VT**4, Everlasting; (Qu. S26c, *Wildflowers that grow in woods*) Inf **MN**2, Everlasting—a white weed; **PA**104, Everlasting flowers—white, yellow center, small center; (Qu. S26d, *Wildflowers that grow in meadows*) Inf **MI**45, Everlasting flower. **1967–68** *DARE* Wildfl QR Pl.211a Infs **SC**41, **WI**35, Everlasting(s). **1976** Bailey–Bailey *Hortus Third* 1245, Everlasting: *Anaphalis, Antennaria, Gnaphalium, Helichrysum, Helipterum.*

2 =pipewort.

1940 Clute *Amer. Plant Names* 258, *Eriocaulon* spp. Everlasting, . . button everlasting.

everlasting bread n

Bread made with **everlasting yeast.**

1979 Solomon–Solomon *Cracklin Bread & Asfidity* 16 **AL,** Our informants yielded some lovely names for breads: Everlasting Bread, a reference to the "starter" with religious overtones.

everlastingly See **everlasting** adj, adv **B**

everlasting onion n Cf **evergreen onion**

An onion (here: *Allium cepa* Aggregatum Group).

1967–68 *DARE* (Qu. I5, . . *Onions that keep coming up without re-*

planting year after year) Infs **CA**101, **ID**5, **IN**35, **WY**5, Everlasting onions.

everlastings exclam

In the game of **head and footer:** see quot.

1901 *DN* 2.139 **cNY,** *Everlastins*. . . In head and footer, said when one is to get down where his predecessor was.

everlasting yeast n [Because a remnant is always saved as a starter for the next preparation] **chiefly Cent, TX** See Map *somewhat old-fash* Cf **everlasting bread, sponge yeast**

Homemade yeast, a small portion of which is kept from one baking to the next.

1950 *WELS (What is used to raise bread before baking?)* 1 Inf, **cwWI,** Everlasting yeast. **1965–70** *DARE* (Qu. H17, . . *Different kinds [of yeast]*) 15 Infs, **chiefly Cent, TX,** Everlasting (yeast); **AR**38, Everlasting yeast—made at home; **KY**71, Everlasting yeast—old-fashioned; **NM**12, Everlasting yeast—kept back a piece of dough to make more; **OK**1, Everlasting yeast [distinguished from] that which you buy; **OK**19, Everlasting yeast—same as sponge yeast—made at home by adding a starter to potato water and sugar. [17 of 20 Infs old, 3 mid-aged] **1969** *DARE* Tape **AZ**11, I tried to get what my mother used to call an everlasting yeast. In other words, if you got your start, and it was nothing for the neighbors to borrow start, and then that way they would keep it going with one start and then another start, and if anything should happen to that, you could borrow one from your neighbor and get started again. **1978** Massey *Bittersweet Country* 30 **Ozarks,** *Old Ozarks Bread Recipe (with everlasting yeast)*—Add sifted white flour [to the yeast starter] to make a batter a little thicker than for pancakes. Cover and let stand overnight. . . In the morning take out about ½ cup of the new starter.

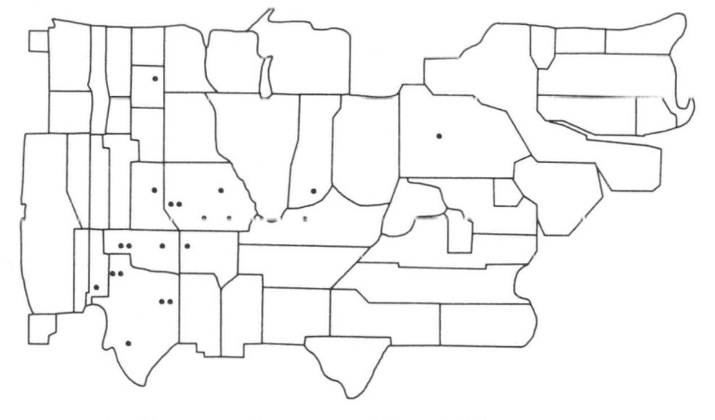

•everlasting yeast + var (Qu. H17)

everly adv [Scots, nEngl dial] **sAppalachians, Ozarks**

Always.

1916 *DN* 4.288 **sAppalachians,** It has everly been the custom. **1933** *AmSp* 8.2.29 **eKY,** The Singin' Fiddler told me, "I everly had a favorance for the Englishers." **1952** Brown *NC Folkl.* 1.538, *Everly*. . . Always, continuously. **1953** Randolph *Down in Holler* 65 **Ozarks,** *Everly* means always, or at least usually: "It's everly been Pap's way to holler a little, when he gits to drinkin'." **1968** Haun *Hawk's Done Gone* 305 **eTN,** He everly dabbed their mouths full of mud to see what size to make their gums.

evermore adv

1 Always, continually.

1928 Chapman *Happy Mt.* 44 **seTN,** How's a body to keep a home-place when it's evermore being peeled offen her?

2 Ever.

c1960 *Wilson Coll.* **csKY,** *Evermore* . . occasionally used for ever. . . "As soon as evermore I can, I will pay you."

3 Really, absolutely.

1933 *Sun* (Baltimore MD) 3 Jan 4 *(Hench Coll.),* [Advt:] When I like something I *evermore like* it—and I like *Chesterfield* Cigarettes. **1966** *DARE* FW Addit **MS,** Evermore don't like—a strong term meaning to particularly dislike.

evern conj [Prob contr of *ever* + **and** conj **B1**] Cf **iffen**

If ever.

1952 Brown *NC Folkl.* 1.538 **wNC,** *Evern*. . . Whenever, if. . . "Yes, and I'll put the law on you evern you do that."

everone See **ever** adj

evers exclam Also *everies, everys, everything(s), evreese* **[ever** adj + **-s** suff, commonly used in marbles and other games] Cf **abbers, nothings**

1 In marble play:

a A call to claim a privilege; see quots.

1890 *DN* 1.24 **KY,** To "take everys" or "evers" is to move around so as to get *every* "man" in range. **1892** *DN* 1.220 **MO,** *Evers* . . [is] used as in Kentucky. **1922** *DN* 5.187 **MA,** *Nothings*. . . A call which gave no privileges, whereas *everythings* gave all. **1935** *AmSp* 10.159 **seNE,** *Everts* [sic]. This may mean either of two things: the privilege of lining up the *commies* in a pot in a straight line so that more can be shot out; or the privilege of clearing away obstacles in order to insure a better shot. **1955** *PADS* 23.17 **cTN,** *Evers (everythings)*. . . A call that allows all liberties in making shots. **1963** *KY Folkl. Rec.* 9.3.63 **eKY,** *Demand for possession of all marbles knocked off square or out of ring when a shot is taken; this term is used in place of tribbles, doubles, etc*. . . everything, everythings. **c1970** Wiersma *Marbles Terms* **Chicago IL** (as of 1928), Everies. . . In playing the game described under "date", if a shooting marble stayed in the square in trying to oust a date, the first person to call out "everies" would get a chance to shoot the big marble out and upon hitting it, claim it for his own.

b A call to prevent an opponent from claiming a privilege.

1958 *PADS* 29.33 **WI,** *Evers*. . . A call to prevent an opponent from moving his marble. *Ibid, Evers on pards*. . . A call to prevent an opponent from shooting one's partner's marble.

2 =**dibs.**

1956 *AmSp* 31.38 **TN,** Of *aikies, evreese,* and *possy* (which I got from college students from New York City, Tennessee, and Maryland, respectively) . . I could find no trace.

ever see a lassie See **did you ever see a lassie**

eversharp n Also *eversharp pencil* [Trademark *Eversharp* fountain pen, 1932 →] **scattered, but esp N Cent, Upper MW, KS, MO** See Map

Any mechanical pencil.

[**1837** (1924) Higbee *Diary* 24 **Pittsburgh PA,** Stopped at jeweller's to purchase an ever-pointed pencil.] **1965–70** *DARE* (Qu. JJ10a, *Different kinds of pens and pencils*) 47 Infs, **scattered, but esp N Cent, Upper MW, KS, MO,** Eversharps; 15 Infs, **scattered, but esp N Cent, MO,** Eversharp pencils; **CT**5, Eversharp—brand name but used for mechanical pencils in general; **CT**9, Eversharp pencil—mechanical pencil; brand name became generic; **GA**86, Eversharp pencil—for any kind of automatic pencils; **ID**4, Eversharp pencil—used by schoolchildren for what some would call mechanical pencil; **IN**57, Eversharp—general term for any mechanical pencil; **KY**11, Eversharp—same as mechanical pencil; **MD**8, Eversharp—more modern word for mechanical pencil; **MD**49, Eversharp—any mechanical pencil; **NY**130, Eversharp pencil—old word; might be a brand name. [Of all Infs responding to the question, 36% were young or mid-aged; of those giving these responses, 61% were young or mid-aged.] [**1979** *Capital Times* (Madison WI) 3 May "Off Hours" sec 3/1, Each Sunday morning . . thousands of otherwise sane folk arm themselves with mugs of coffee and fists full of Eversharps.] **1979** *DARE* File **swMI,** When buying a pen & pencil set,

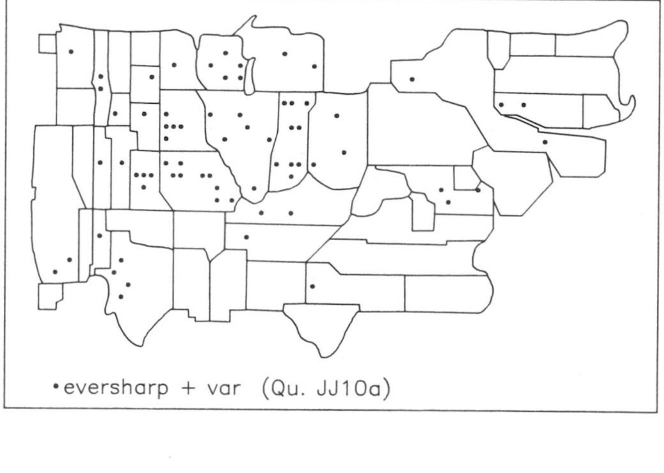

•eversharp + var (Qu. JJ10a)

the pencil is an eversharp and the pen is a fountain pen. Probably first heard the word . . about 45 years ago. Dad remembers standing in the . . shoe store waiting for a free eversharp. They gave them away with points for shoes. . . It was a brand name. Like all power saws are called skill saws, these pencils taking lead were called eversharp.

everthing See **ever** adj

everwhat pron [Reversed cpd] **chiefly sAppalachians, Ozarks** Cf Intro "Language Changes" I.1

Whatever.

1915 *DN* 4.179 **swVA,** Everwhat. **1923** *DN* 5.206 **swMO,** *Ever what*. . . "Ever whut you think'll be alright." **1927** *DN* 5.474 **Ozarks,** *Ever what*. . . "Ever whut you-all want done hyar now, we-uns shore will 'tend to hit." **1939** *Hall Coll.* **eTN,** "We'll do everwhat Jim wants to do." ("Whatever is used more than everwhat.") **1943** Chase *Jack Tales* 69 **wNC,** Told the doctor to take care of Big Jack, said he'd pay ever-what it cost when he came by that way again. **1944** *PADS* 2.42 **nwNC. 1952** Brown *NC Folkl.* 1.538, *Everwhat*. . . Whatever. . . General. **1958** *PADS* 29.9 **TN. 1968** Haun *Hawk's Done Gone* 40 **eTN,** Or squall out at me to bring him everwhat he had need for. **1969** *DARE* FW Addit **seGA,** Everwhat they do. **1971** *Foxfire* Winter 247 **neGA,** They was always prepared for ever what they had t' have. **1982** Ginns *Snowbird Gravy* 164 **nwNC,** They'd meet them in buggies and surreys and ever what they had. **1984** Burns *Cold Sassy* 306 **nGA** (as of 1906), Everwhat you done cain't be no worse than me lovin' you whilst I sat by her deathbed.

everwhen conj, adv Also *everen, everywhen* [Reversed cpd] **sAppalachians, Ozarks** Cf **ever** adv **C2, ever and when**

When, whenever.

1924 Raine *Land of Saddle-Bags* 77 **sAppalachians,** They told him an old woman across the valley had died with a shriek, ever when the man shot the picture with his rifle-gun. **1929** *AmSp* 5.18 **Ozarks,** *Ever-when*. . . "Ever-when you go a-foolin' roun' 'ith my gal you'll shore git hurted, an' hurted bad!" **1940** *AmSp* 15.53 **sAppalachians, Ozarks,** Ever(y)-when (whenever). **1943** Chase *Jack Tales* 14 **wNC,** I'm a-goin' to take the creek back up there closer to the house where your old woman can get her water everwhen she wants it. **1957** TN Folk Lore Soc. *Bulletin* 23.71 **TN,** We just put our dogs in atter one of the yearlin's. And they run hit and treed it. . . Everwhen we got there, why, I back-ridged [=went back along the ridge], got Jack's gun. **1966–69** *DARE* FW Addit **ceNC,** Everwhen—whenever; **OK**18, Everwhen I went. **a1975** Lunsford *It Used to Be* 158 **sAppalachians,** The word "everen" is used for whenever as, "Yes, and I'll put the law to you everen you do it."

everwhere conj, adv[1] [Reversed cpd] **esp sAppalachians**

Wherever.

1915 *DN* 4.179 **swVA,** Compound words sometimes exchange places: peckerwood, . . everwho, . . everwhere. **1939** *Hall Coll.* **wNC,** "Where do we go from here?" [=on a squirrel hunt]. . . "Everwhere the dog trees." **1969** *DARE* FW Addit **seGA,** Everwhere = wherever. "Everwhere they go."

everwhere adv[2] See **ever** adj

everwheres See **ever** adj

everwhich adj, pron Also *every which* [Reversed cpd] **chiefly sAppalachians, Ozarks**

Whichever.

1903 *DN* 2.312 **seMO,** *Everwhich*. . . Whichever. 'Everwhich way I turn I see trouble.' **1906** *DN* 3.135 **nwAR,** *Everwhich a*. . . "Everwhich a way I turn I meet him." **1908** *DN* 3.309 **eAL, wGA,** *Everwhich*. . . "Take everwhich (one) you want." **1915** *DN* 4.182 **swVA. 1927** *DN* 5.474 **Ozarks,** *Ever which*. . . "Ever which o' them 'ar saddles you-all want, jes' holler an' hit's yourn." **1930** *DN* 6.84 **cSC,** Idiomatic variations. . . *everwhich,* whichever. **1935** Hurston *Mules & Men* 142 **FL,** But every which a way he run de fire meet him. **1969** *DARE* FW Addit **ceNC,** Everwhich—whichever.

everwho pron Rarely *everywho* [Reversed cpd] **chiefly sAppalachians, Ozarks**

Whoever.

1905 *DN* 3.78 **nwAR,** *Everwho*. . . "Everwho done that didn't do a good job." Rare. **1915** *DN* 4.179 **swVA. 1919** *DN* 5.33 **seKY,** *Everwho*. . . "He give it to Cece or Mos, one, everwho I was with." **1926** *DN* 5.399 **Ozarks. 1930** *DN* 6.84 **cSC. 1934** (1970) Wilson *Backwoods Amer.* 107 **Ozarks,** They's a law in Arkansas pertectin' foxes, and if ary one should ever get caught it would be onfortunate for ever who owned the dawgs. **1939** *Hall Coll.* **wNC,** He thought that winder was open, everwho tried to get in here. *Ibid* **eTN,** Everwho hears that will be surprised. **1940** *AmSp* 15.53 **sAppalachians, Ozarks,** Ever(y)-who. **1953** Randolph *Down in Holler* 58 **Ozarks,** *Ever-who* is not uncommon. . . "We always give the prize to ever-who is the best dancer, even if they *ain't* no kin to the judges." The possessive form is sometimes heard, as "Them fellers stole ever-who's horse come down the road." **1958** *PADS* 29.9 **TN,** *Ever who*. . . whoever. **1966** *DARE* (QR p227) Inf **SC**3, Everwho's got the corn says, "How many?" **1976** Wolfram–Christian *Appalachian Speech* 99, And they said, "Everwho gets bloodied first won." **1990** *DARE* File **csWI** (as of c1940), Everwho.

every adj Pronc-spp *iv'ry;* **chiefly Sth** *ev(e)y, evuh, evv(a);* **chiefly Sth,** *esp among Black speakers, ebbery, ebry* Cf **ever** adj

Std senses, var forms.

1823 Cooper *Pioneers* 1.246 **cNY** [Black], Ebbery body know dat snap as good as fire. **1829** Tenney *Female Quixotism* 2.41 **Philadelphia PA** [Black], He don't want court fore ebbery body. **1842** in 1956 Eliason *Tarheel Talk* 310 **NC,** *Every*—evey. **1848** Lowell *Biglow* 7 **'Upcountry' MA,** Ev'y thin' thet's done. **1888** Jones *Negro Myths* 68 **GA** [Black], Eh tell ebry body. **1899** Chesnutt *Conjure Woman* 136 **NC,** Eve'ybody knows dat. **1901** *DN* 2.182 **KY** [Black], *Every* . . eb'ry. **1904** Day *Kin o' Ktaadn* 111 **ME,** Iv'ry schoolbye knows thot three ones make three. **1905** Culbertson *Banjo Talks* 108 **SE** [Black], You mummics ev'y one you see. **1908** *DN* 3.309 **eAL, wGA,** *Evy*. . . Every. Also *evything,* etc. **1909** *S. Atl. Qrly.* 8.44 **eSC** [Gullah], Ebrybuddy bemean um so 'im lef de settlement. **1917** Torrence *Granny Maumee* 49 [Black], Dat what de hoss say to me in my true dream ev'y night dis week. **1922** Gonzales *Black Border* 299 **sSC, GA coasts** [Gullah glossary], *Eb'ry*—every; *Eb'ryt'ing*—everything; *Eb'ryweh*—everywhere. **1927** Kennedy *Gritny* 26 **sLA** [Black], He mistake evvbody for somebody else. **1928** Peterkin *Scarlet Sister Mary* 37 **sSC coast** [Gullah], Evy time. *Ibid* 258, Evy night. **1931** *AmSp* 6.171 **eVA** [Black], [a mits əm pʌdı nıə ɛvı mitn nəıt]. **1941** in 1944 *ADD* **Sth,** Everybody. . . ['ɛvəˌbɑdı]. So long, evvabody. Radio. **1953** Brewer *Word Brazos* 90 **eTX** [Black], He come to preach evuh fo'th Sunday. **1966** *DARE* Tape **FL**42, Everybody ['ɛvıˌbɒdı].

every adv Also sp *ev'ry* Cf **ever** adj

Ever—used in phr *every since.*

1887 (1967) Harris *Free Joe* 136 **GA,** Ev'ry sence she wuz a little bit of a gal. **1893** Shands *MS Speech* 29, She has been here every since I can remember. **1916** *DN* 4.274 **NE,** *Every*. . . Ever. "Every since the beginning of the course." General. **1966** *DARE* (Qu. A24, . . *"He's been hot-tempered from ______."*) Inf **GA**4, Every since I know him. [Inf Black] **1970** *DARE* FW Addit **MS** [Black], Every since I knew him, every since he was a child. **1975** *DARE* File **SW,** Every since. [Said by Native American on nationally televised newscast]

every bit and grain adv phr

Fully, just.

1907 Wright *Shepherd* 273 **Ozarks,** You're every bit and grain as bad as the old crowd was. **1949** Hornsby *Lonesome Valley* 196 **eKY,** The clock was big as a wagon wheel, and the hands were every bit and grain as long as wagon spokes. **1952** Brown *NC Folkl.* 1.520, *Bit and grain, every*. . . Completely, all, just as. "He's every bit and grain as good as you are."—General. **c1960** *Wilson Coll.* **csKY,** *Bit and grain*. . . "He's every bit and grain as old as Grandpap."

every bit and grain n

All.

1952 Brown *NC Folkl.* 1.538 **wNC,** *Ever' bit and grain*. . . All there is of a thing. "I'll bet he's spent ever' bit and grain of his poor wife's savings." **1972** Cooper *NC Mt. Folkl.* 91, Every bit and grain.

everybody in free exclam For varr see quot [Abbr for *everybody who is out (may) come in free*]

In children's games of tag: **=all (in) free.**

1965–70 *DARE* (Qu. EE15, *When he has caught the first of those that were hiding, what does the player who is 'it' call out to the others?*) Infs **CO**21, **FL**14, **IN**69, **MO**27, **SC**34, **TX**62, Everybody('s) in free; **MO**35, Everybody come in; **MI**61, Everybody else in free; **MI**69, Everybody else's free; **MN**28, Everbody free; **PA**224, Everybody home free; **MI**45, Everbody out's in free; **OH**90, Everybody's out call in free.

everybody's darling n

=song sparrow.

1917 (1923) *Birds Amer.* 3.50, Song Sparrow *Melospiza melodia*. . . Everybody's Darling.

every constant adv phr [*constant,* perh malaprop for *instant,* but cf **constant**]

Constantly.

1940 Harris *Folk Plays* 48 **NC,** De wind hain't ris', but dere's somethin' a-shakin' dis whole place ev'ry constant. *Ibid* 292, Ev'y constant, *constantly, continually.* **1942** *Hench Coll.* **eNC,** I was invited by Mildred to go to an egg-nog party. But I don't know that I'll go because I'm down there every constant anyhow.

everyday adj [Cf std *everyday* ordinary, commonplace]

Special; worthy of continual attention.

1972 Cooper *NC Mt. Folkl.* 91, *Everyday gal*—steady sweetheart; jusem sweet.

every hair a rope yarn phr

See quot 1975.

1942 ME Univ. *Studies* 44.8.79 **eME,** "Every hair a rope-yarn and every drop of blood Stockholm tar." A thorough seaman. **1975** Gould *ME Lingo* 86, Every hair a rope yarn—Part of an old description of a very tough seaman: "Every hair a rope yarn, every finger a marlinspike, every drop of blood pure Stockholm tar, etc." Lingering phrases for a good man at his work.

‡every lasting one n

Every last one; everyone.

1946 in 1954 *Harder Coll.* **cwTN,** Every lasting one of them got the Whooping Cough.

every man in his own den n Also *den* [See quot 1883]

A children's game of tag, in which the sides try progressively to increase their numbers until all the players have been caught by one side; see quots.

1883 Newell *Games & Songs* 159 **neMA,** *Den.* . . Each boy represents a wild beast, and has a separate tree, which represents his "den." . . If a player can tag any one whom he has a right to capture, he takes him home to his own den, and the latter must help him to take the rest. **1891** *Jrl. Amer. Folkl.* 4.226 **Brooklyn NYC,** *Every man in his own den* is similar to [Red Lion]. . . Each [player] will . . select for his den a place not too near that of another. One player will then run out, and a second will try to catch him. The third player out will try to catch the first or second, and so on until the last one out, who may catch any player who is out of his den. When a player is caught, he goes to the aid of the one who catches him. . . The side that captures all the players wins the game. **1909** (1923) Bancroft *Games* 83, *Every man in his own den*—5 to 30 or more players. **1975** Ferretti *Gt. Amer. Book Sidewalk Games* 111, Another logical extension of tag is *Den,* in which the person who is "It" is the Hunter and those being pursued are a pack of wild beasts. Each animal has his own den: a step, a sidewalk square, a section of wall. As long as he stays there, he is safe.

every man jack n [**jack** n]

All men; each man.

1942 ME Univ. *Studies* 44.8.11, Sailors were called by their first names only. Their generic name was Jack. Collectively they were *every man Jack.* **1945** Colcord *Sea Language* 108 **ME, Cape Cod, Long Island,** *Jack* . . appears in a few shore phrases, such as "every man Jack," meaning every single one, all hands. **1949** Guthrie *Way West* 112, Tadlock had appointed other riders, until nearly every last manjack was gone. **1962** Fox *Southern Fried* 49 **GA, SC** (as of 1940s), I say all of us. You and me and all of us. Every man jack of us is guilty.

everys See **evers**

every since See **every** adv

everything(s) See **evers**

everything('s) drawing phr [Transf from naut use]

Everything is going well.

1916 Macy-Hussey *Nantucket Scrap Basket* 130 **eMA,** "Everything Drawing"—Making the best possible progress in any enterprise. It conveys the idea that, whatever a person may be doing, he has called to his assistance every available factor to facilitate his work, as the mariner trims every sail so that it may best catch the breeze and "draw". **1963** Haywood *Yankee Dict.* 55, *Everything's drawing*—A Yankee mariner's reply to the common question "How are you," if it so happens life is using him well just now. . . It came to be used not only as to a ship for which all was going well, but for a man who was functioning to the very best of his capabilities. But a true Yankee will reserve this answer for a friend he judges really wishes to know how the world is using him.

every way for Sunday See **Sunday, forty ways till**

everyways adv [*every* + *way* + **-s** adv-forming suff]

In every direction.

1967-68 *DARE* (Qu. MM12a, . . *"He shot into a flock of birds and they went* ______.*"*) Inf **MD**13, Everyways; (Qu. MM12b, . . *"When she was out on the dance floor, she broke her beads and they went* ______.*"*) Inf **MA**33, Everyways.

everywhen See **everwhen**

everywheres adv [*everywhere* + **-s** adv-forming suff]

Everywhere.

1867 Twain *Jumping Frog* 15, Fellers that had travelled and been everywheres. **1907** *DN* 3.187 **seNH,** *Everywheres.* . . Everywhere. **1920-44** in 1944 *ADD, Everywheres.* . . Very common, esp. in speech. **c1960** *Wilson Coll.* **csKY,** *Everywheres* . . common for everywhere. **1968-70** *DARE* (Qu. Y45, . . *To scatter in all directions*) Inf **MD**20, Went everywheres; (Qu. MM12a) Infs **MD**32, **VA**46, (Scattered) everywheres; (Qu. MM12b) Inf **MD**26, Scattered everywheres.

every whichaway(s) See **whichaway**

every whipstitch See **whipstitch**

everywho See **everwho**

‡every-year locust n [As distinct from the seventeen-year locust]

A **cicada.**

1967 *DARE* (Qu. R7, *Insects that sit in trees or bushes in hot weather and make a sharp, buzzing sound*) Inf **MO**38, The every-year locusts.

Eve's cup n Cf **Adam's cup**

A **pitcher plant** (here: either *Sarracenia flava* or *S. purpurea*).

c1873 in 1976 Miller *Shaker Herbs* 216, *Sarracenia purpurea.* . . Eve's Cup. . . Useful for its tonic and beneficial action on the stomach. **1876** Hobbs *Bot. Hdbk.* 35, Eve's cup . . Sarracenia flava. **1900** Lyons *Plant Names* 334, 335.

Eve's curse See **curse, the**

Eve's darning needle n

An **Adam's needle (and thread)** (here: *Yucca filamentosa*).

1892 *Jrl. Amer. Folkl.* 5.102 **neTX,** *Yucca filamentosa* . . Eve's darning needle. **1931** Clute *Common Plants* 80, Such names as Adam's flannel *(Verbascus thapsus)* and Eve's darning needle *(Yucca filamentosa)* must have been invented after the pair left the garden; at least they apparently had no use for flannel and darning needles earlier. **1949** Moldenke *Amer. Wild Flowers* 368, The leaves produce long and tough threads along their margins, with which the inrolled sharp tip of the leaf may be "threaded" to form a crude needle—hence the common names of *bearsthread* and *evesdarningneedle.*

Eve's necklace n

A **coral bean 2** (here: *Sophora affinis*).

1937 Stemen-Myers *OK Flora* 223, *Sophora affinis.* . . *Eve's Necklace.* . . Pod . . more or less constricted between the seeds. **1979** Little *Checklist U.S. Trees* 276, *Texas sophora.* . . *Other common names* . . Eves-necklace.

Eve's thread n

1 **=Adam's needle (and thread).**

1891 *Century Dict.* 7026, *Yucca.* . . From their sharp-pointed leaves with threads hanging from their edges, *Y. filamentosa* and *Y. aloifolia* are known as *Adam's needle and thread* and as *Eve's thread.* **1900** Lyons *Plant Names* 401, *Y. aloifolia.* . . Eve's-thread. . . *Y. filamentosa.* . . Eve's-thread.

2 A **day lily 1** (here: *Hemerocallis fulva*).

1894 *Jrl. Amer. Folkl.* 7.102 **WV,** *Hemerocallis fulva* . . Eve's thread. **1959** Carleton *Index Herb. Plants* 43, *Eve's thread:* Hemerocallis fulva.

evet See **effet**

evey See **every** adj

evil adj Pronc-sp *ebil*

A Form.

1901 *DN* 2.182 **neKY** [Black], *Evening*—ebenin'; *Ever*—*ebah; Every*—*eb'ry; Evil*—ebil.

B Senses.

1 Of persons: disagreeable, unpleasant, contentious. *chiefly among Black speakers* Cf **evil** v, **evilly**

1946 (1972) Mezzrow–Wolfe *Really Blues* 332, *Evil:* unpleasant, obnoxious, hostile, neurotic. **1959** *AmSp* 34.305, Of greater interest is the application of the adjective *evil* to persons, in the sense of 'unpleasant, disagreeable, sullen.' . . Among uneducated Negroes the word has no other use, and to the majority of educated Negroes this meaning is primary. Hence the statement 'He is evil' would probably be interpreted in a different manner by white and Negro residents of a city such as Washington, D.C. **1967–70** *DARE* (Qu. GG4, *Stirred up, angry: "When he saw them coming he got ______.*") Inf **SC**69, Evil; (Qu. GG18, . . *'Obstinate': "Why does he have to be so ______.*") Inf **PA**247, Evil; (Qu. GG35b, . . *"Because she couldn't go, she's been ______ all day."*) Inf **MS**88, Evil; (Qu. GG38, . . *Mean and bad tempered*) Infs **IN**19, **WA**9, Evil person; **MI**72, He is awfully evil, evil person; **VA**73, Evil. [5 of 7 Infs Black] **1980** Folb *Runnin' Down* 236 [Black], *Evil*—Mean. . . Violent. . . Worthless. **1982** Walker *Color Purple* 186 **GA** [Black], How Henrietta? Evil, say Sofia. Little face always look like stormy weather. But maybe she'll grow out of it. It took her daddy forty years to learn to be pleasant.

2 Of cattle: mean, ornery.

1968–70 *DARE* (Qu. K16, *A cow with a bad temper*) Inf **NY**107, Mean, evil; **VA**49, She's evil.

evil v [**evil** adj **B1**]

To brood.

1959 *AmSp* 34.306 [Black], Sporadically, *evil* may occur as an adverb and even as the base of a verbal: 'She was evilling,' i.e., brooding.

evil n

A hobgoblin.

1914 *DN* 4.159 **cVA**, *Evils*. . . Goblins; evil spirits. . . *Hants*. . . "The hants an' evils 'll getcha!"

evilly adv [**evil** adj **B1**]

Sullenly; broodingly.

1967 in 1973 Himes *Black on Black* 133 **NYC** [Black], "Go on, baby, you can be back in an hour with 'nuff bread so we can scoff." "I'se tired as you are," she said evilly. "Go sell yo' own ass to whitey, you luvs him so much."

evrage See **average**

evreese See **evers**

ev'ry See **every** adv

evuh, evv(a), evy See **every** adj

ewa adv [Haw *'Ewa* a district in southwest Oahu] **HI**

In the direction of 'Ewa; towards the southwest.

1938 Reinecke *Hawaiian Loanwords* 9, *Ewa* /'e,wɑ 'ɛ,vɑ/. . . In Hawaii, directions other than *mauka* . . and *makai* . . are usually indicated by the names of localities lying in either direction along the coast. In Honolulu these directions are *ewa*, toward the District of Ewa, and *waikiki*, toward Waikiki Beach, approximately S.W. and N.E. respectively. These are the directions given in the city directories. **1951** *AmSp* 26.22 **HI**, More common than the usual compass directions . . are *mauka* (towards the mountains) and *makai* (toward the sea). In Honolulu these are combined with the names of towns along the shore, *Ewa* and *Waikiki*. **1972** Carr *Da Kine Talk* 86 **HI**, Hawaiian Words Commonly Heard In Hawaii's English. . . *'Ewa*. The direction opposite from Waikiki and toward 'Ewa Plantation.

ewe n Usu |ju|; also **chiefly NEng, NY** |jiu, iu|; also **chiefly Sth, Midl,** *esp in rural areas, somewhat old-fash* |jo| (See Map); for addit varr see quots Pronc-spp *awe, eow, yo(e), yow(e)*

Std senses, var forms.

1890 *DN* 1.71 **LA**, *Yo:* ewe. **1899** (1912) Green *VA Folk-Speech* 166, *Eow*. *Ibid* 495, *Yoe*. . . Yow; yoe; eow; yowe. . . "Breeding yoes & a Ramm." **1908** *S. Atl. Qrly.* 7.346 **sSC coast** [Gullah], "The *Gullah* negro says . . *yowe* for *ewe*, like the Borderer and the Scotchman." **1909** *DN* 3.391 **eAL, wGA**, *Yo*. *Ibid* 406 **nwAR**, *Yo*. **1914** *DN* 4.83 **ME, nNH** [Rural], *Yow*. **1915** *DN* 4.193 **swVA**, *Yo*. . . *Ewe* is not heard. **1923** *DN* 5.225 **swMO**, *Yoe*. . . A ewe. **1930** Shoemaker *1300 Words* 69 **cPA Mts** (as of c1900), *Yowe*. **1931** *AmSp* 7.90 **eKY**, Hit were rainin' mightily, and he'd been out drivin' the yoes and the yearlin's up under the clifts. **1937** *AmSp* 12.104 **eNE**, A ram is often called a *buck* and a ewe a *yo*. **1941** Stuart *Men of Mts.* 187 **neKY**, He was tall like a bean-pole with a yowe neck. **1942** McAtee *Dial. Grant Co. IN* 72 (as of 1890s), *Yo*. **1942** Warnick *Garrett Co. MD* 2 **nwMD** (as of 1900–18), *Yo*. **c1960** *Wilson Coll.* **csKY**, *Ewe* /jo/ is almost universal; /ju/ would require explanation to many people. **1961** Kurath–McDavid *Pronc. Engl.* 157, Four types of pronouncing *ewe* are current in the Eastern States. . . /ju/ is common in the North and in parts of the North Midland, especially in urbanized areas where the word is normally acquired in school or through reading. . . /iu/ and /jiu/ are confined to the New England settlement area. . . The type of /jo/ is heard in all parts of the Eastern States. In the South and South Midland it has rather general currency, except among the cultured; in the North Midland it is common in rural areas . . in the North it has been largely abandoned, except in the Catskills, in northeastern New England, and on . . Nantucket, Martha's Vineyard, and Block Island. **1965–70** *DARE* (Qu. K62, . . *A female sheep*) 726 Infs, **widespread,** Ewe; 159 Infs, **chiefly Sth, Midl,** Yo [jo]; **MD**24, Awe [ɔ]. [Of all Infs responding to the question, 45% were comm type 5, 73% old, 36% gs educ or less, 66% male; of those giving the response *yo*, 61% were comm type 5, 81% old, 55% gs educ or less, 79% male.] **1976** Allen *LAUM* 3.254 (as of c1950), Nearly all U[pper] M[idwest] infs. offering this item have the common Northern and North Midland /ju/ pronunciation . . as a consonantal glide followed by [u] or by a rising diphthong with the stress upon [u]. . . The rural pronunciation /jo/ . . is a minor variant in the UM . . for 17 infs., mostly farmers, along the Canadian border and in the Midland speech territory of Iowa and Nebraska. An unexplained [jʉn] is in the speech of a Minneapolis Type I [=old, with little educ] inf., a Black with southern ancestry.

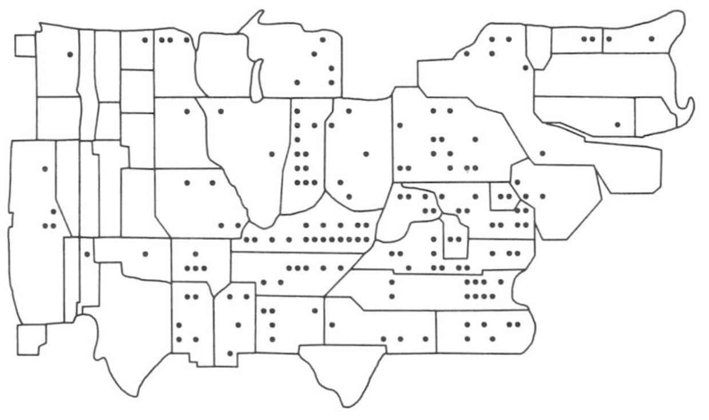

•yo (at ewe n) (Qu. K62)

ewe v

To give a **ewe-neck** to.

1848 (1855) Ruxton *Life Far West* 51 **NM,** The severities of a prolonged winter, with scanty pasture and long and trying travel, had robbed his [=the horse's] bones of fat and flesh, tucked up his flank, and "ewed" his neck.

ewe cat n Pronc-sp *yow cat*

A female cat.

1914 *DN* 4.83 **ME, nNH,** *Yow*. . . "A yow cat." **1931–33** *LANE Worksheets* **cCT,** All them York staters all talk about a ewe cat [jou kæt].

ewe-neck n, hence adj *ewe-necked* Pronc-spp *yo(e)-necked*

A horse's neck which is thin and concave.

1820 Irving *Sketch Book Crayon* 2.380 **seNY,** The animal he bestrode was a broken-down plough-horse . . with a ewe neck and a head like a hammer. **1858** Holmes *Autocrat* 298 **NEng,** Drawn by a rat-tailed, ewe-necked bay. **1899** (1912) Green *VA Folk-Speech* 495, *Yoe-necked*. . . Long and hollow neck like a yoe. **1936** McCarthy *Lang. Mosshorn* np [Range term], *Ewe-necked*. . . Applies to a horse with a long, thin neck resembling that of an ewe. **1942** McAtee *Dial. Grant Co. IN* 72 (as of 1890s), *Yo-necked* . . having a slender, decurved neck like a sheared yo; camel-necked horses of scrub stock were so described. **c1960** *Wilson Coll.* **csKY,** Ewe-necked /jo-/. . . Decurved neck. **1968** Adams *Western Words* 106, *Ewe-necked*.

ex n[1] Also *exle;* also sp *aix, eks, excel, x* [*OED ax, axe* sb.[2] "*Obs.* or *dial.*"] **chiefly Nth, esp NEng, NY** See Map Cf **ax** n, **exe**

An axle.

1648 in 1850 CT (Colony) *Pub. Rec.* 1.508, *An Inventory of the Estate of Thomas Nowell*. . . waine, wheeles, expinns, cops and pin. **1774** in 1906 Litchfield *Diary* 29 Dec 319 **MA,** I turnd out Some Exceltrees, for a Clock, out of Holley wood. **1867** Lowell *Biglow* xxvii **'Upcountry' MA,**

In most cases he [=the Yankee] follows an Anglo-Saxon usage. In *aix* for *axle* he certainly does. **1890** *DN* 1.6 **cNY,** The sound [ɛ] instead of [æ] . . in *catch, radish, eks* (=*axle*). *Ibid* 73 **NEng,** *Eks* (usually written X): axle. Extremely common. **1907** *DN* 3.187 **seNH,** *Ex.* **1910** *DN* 3.441 **wNY,** *Ex.* **1914** *DN* 4.72 **ME, nNH,** *Ex.* **1917** *DN* 4.391 **neOH,** *Ex.* . . The usual native word. *Axle* was comparatively rare. **1923** *DN* 5.206 **swMO,** *Ex.* . . Axle, specifically, of a wagon. **1929** *AmSp* 5.121 **eME,** There was "mud to the *exes.*" **1934** *Hanley Disks* **cMA,** The [stone] boat was hitched to the chains of the ex [ɛks] of the wheels; **swCT,** Wagon . . was pretty near up to the exles [ɛkslz]. **1939** *LANE* Map 188 **MA, VT,** Names for the *wagon axle* were incidentally recorded in connection with the verb *grease.* . . [7 infs], ex [ɛks]. *Ibid* **CT, MA, VT** [6 infs], Exle [ɛksl]. *Ibid* Map 173 **ceMA,** I found it was better to have a couple of length (sic) of chain back to the [ɛksl]. **1950** *WELS (The part of a wagon that has a wheel at each end)* 8 Infs, **WI,** Ex. **1954** *Harder Coll.* **cwTN,** *Axle* ['ɛksəl]. **1965–70** *DARE* (Qu. L48, *The part of a wagon that goes crosswise underneath and has a wheel at each end*) 49 Infs, **Nth, esp NEng, NY,** Ex; **ME5,** Concord ex; **NY24,** Front ex, hind ex; 30 Infs, **chiefly Nth,** Exle; (Qu. N41b, *Horse-drawn vehicles to carry heavy loads*) Inf **OR3,** Dead-ex wagon—no springs. **1967–68** *DARE* Tape **MI71,** A buckboard has no body. It's just slats from ex to ex [ɛks tu ɛks], from exle to exle ['ɛksl̩ tu 'ɛksl̩]; **CA100,** I come overland . . by horse 'n' buggy stage and the roads were just one-way roads in the springtime the mud was up to the exes in many places.

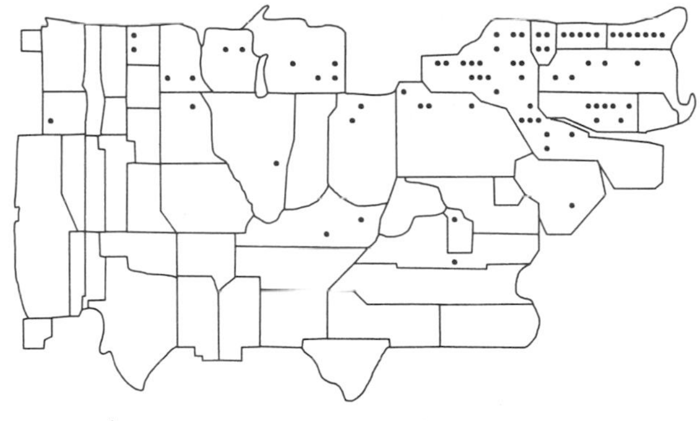

•ex n¹ + varr (Qq. L48, N41b)

ex n² Also *ex-note, ~-spot;* also sp *x* [From the Roman numeral for ten]

A ten-dollar bill; hence *double-ex* a twenty-dollar bill.

1942 Berrey–Van den Bark *Amer. Slang* 467.2, x, x-note, x-spot, *a ten-dollar bill.* **1966–69** *DARE* (Qu. U28b, . . *A ten-dollar bill*) Infs **MI110, NY227, RI17,** An ex; **MT4,** Ex-note; (Qu. U28c, . . *A twenty-dollar bill*) Infs **ID5, MA58,** Double-ex; **IL36,** Two ex's.

ex exclam [Prob abbr for *excuse*]

=king's ex.

1968 *DARE* (Qu. EE20, *When two boys are fighting, and the one who is losing wants to stop, he calls out, "______."*) Inf **LA15,** Ex.

ex- pref

Used to form joc or fanciful vogue-words; see quots.

1911 *DN* 3.543 **csNE,** *Expluderosity.* . . Willingness, obligingness. "Will you please pick up my pencil?" "With the greatest of expluderosity." **1913** *DN* 4.18 **NE,** *Expolagollucious.* Splendid, very fine, elegant. . . "That candy is expolagollucious." "Your new hat is really expolagollucious." **1937** (1958) Levin *Old Bunch* 67 **Chicago IL,** "How's business, Rudy?" he asked. "Exqualafadocious," Rudy replied. **1968** *DARE* (Qu. LL35, . . *"This cake tastes ______."*) Inf **CT15,** Exmalagocious ['ɛksmɑləˌgošus] = delicious.

exactly adv Usu |ɪg'zæk(t)lɪ, ɛg-| Pronc-spp **chiefly Sth, S Midl** *adzackly, adzac'ly, adzactly, edxactly, edzackly, edzactly, esac'ly, (e)zackly, ez(z)actly, 'xacly, zac(t)ly;* eye-dial sp *egg-zactly* Cf **edzact, prezactly**

Std senses, var forms.

1832 *Maysville* (Ky.) *Eagle* 2 Feb *(DA),* 'Edxactly,' giving the lawyer a knowing wink—Captain Rise he gin a treat. **1843** (1916) Hall *New Purchase* 228 **IN,** How it all was ezactly. **1844** Thompson *Major Jones's Courtship* 35 **GA,** My lord! thinks I, how could she tell it so zactly to half a second. **1846** (1973) Porter *Quarter Race* 85 **TN,** Your back looks adzactly like a blaze on a white oak. **1859** Marcy *Prairie Traveler* 211 **West,** No, not adzackly. **1864** (1868) Trowbridge *3 Scouts* 136 **TN,** That didn't happen esac'ly's I ca'c'lated. **1891** Page *Elsket* 140 **VA,** I had council, but not a la'yar, edzactly. **1893** Shands *MS Speech* 69, *Zackly.* . . Negro for *exactly.* **1894** Riley *Armazindy* 7 **sIN,** They's none / Knows adzac'ly *what* she done. **1903** *DN* 2.313 **seMO,** *Exactly.* . . Pronounced edzactly. **1904** Day *Kin o' Ktaadn* 101 **ME,** Figgered out edzackly how to work the thing. **1906** *DN* 3.164 **nwAR,** *'xac'ly.* . . "I couldn't tell you 'xacly what I paid." **1909** *DN* 3.391 **eAL, wGA,** *Zackly.* . . Exactly. **1915** *DN* 4.193 **swVA,** *Zacly.* . . Also *zactly.* **1917** Torrence *Granny Maumee* 51 [Black], Not ezackly. **1922** Gonzales *Black Border* 259 **sSC, GA coasts** [Gullah], Egg-zactly. *Ibid* 340, [Glossary:] *'Zackly*—exactly. **1929** Sale *Tree Named John* 46 **MS,** Zac'ly whut us gwine do fer 'im. **1936** *AmSp* 11.312 **Upstate NY,** In *exactly,* [gz] occurs 94 times; five times it is reduced to [z]. . . [t] included—30 [times] . . [t] omitted—69. **1940** *AmSp* 15.47 **sAppalachians, Ozarks,** Syncope . . occurs . . [in] d'reckly, ezackly. **1941** *AmSp* 16.12 **eTX** [Black], [t] is always omitted in such words as *directly, exactly* . . [ɛg'zæklɪ˔]. *Ibid* 15, The following . . is from the speech of a Negro man who . . can neither read nor write. . . [ə kẽɪnt ɛd'zæklɪ tɛl jə ʌĩn ɑz bɔ̃:n]. **1942** *AmSp* 17.156 **NYC, seNY,** Other consonantal losses include . . *exactly* [kt] 4 [infs], [k] 44 [infs]. **1942** Hall *Smoky Mt. Speech* 54 **wNC, eTN,** *Exactly* . . is often [(ə)'zæklɪ], as in . . 'Hit looks jus' zackly like him.' Only once was it heard as [ɛd'zæklɪ], a form . . apparently not widely used or known. **1958** Humphrey *Home from the Hill* 130 **TX,** What is yo problem ezzactly? **c1960** *Wilson Coll.* **csKY,** *Ezackly.* . . Humorous use for exactly.

exalted ppl adj Pronc-sp *'zalted*

A Form.

c1937 in 1972 *Amer. Slave* 2.1.54 **SC,** Course I knows my place in dis world; I 'umbles myself here to be 'zalted up yonder.

B Sense.

Hanged. [*exalt* raise high] **SW** *joc*

1934 (1940) Weseen *Dict. Amer. Slang* 97 [Cowboys and Westerners], *Exalted*—hanged. **1968** Adams *Western Words* 106, *Exalted*—Hanged. Almost any cowman is, in the words of one, "too proud of his Adam's apple to want to be exalted."

exaltification n [**-ification**]

Exaltation.

1841 (1952) Cooper *Deerslayer* 212 **nNY,** "And what exaltification"—the reader will have remarked that the Deerslayer had not very critically studied his dictionary—"And what exaltification would it be to me . . to be bedizened and bescarleted like a Mingo chief . . ?"

exaltify v [**-ify**]

To exalt.

1931 *AmSp* 6.269 **KY,** Redundant . . suffixes occur in . . temptify, exaltify. **1940** *AmSp* 15.51 **sAppalachians, Ozarks,** The suffix *-(i)fy* survives: argufy, . . exaltify.

example n [*OED example* sb. 1. c] *old-fash*

A sample.

1926 Roberts *Time of Man* 127 **KY,** I brought a little example of the sugar bread I made.

‡exasperate v [Malaprop]

To bleach.

1909 *S. Atl. Qrly.* 8.45 [Gullah], *Florida lime* [Footnote: *Chloride of lime,* used to bleach white goods.] is used in city laundries to *mo' quickah exasperate de clo'es.*

excape See **escape**

exceed v

1922 Gonzales *Black Border* 300 **sSC, GA coasts** [Gullah glossary], *Exceed*—succeed, succeeds, succeeded, succeeding.

excel See **ex n¹**

except(ing) prep, conj Usu |ɪk'sɛpt(ɪŋ), ɛk-|; also |ə'sɛpt, sɛp| Pronc-spp *'cep(e)n, 'cep'm, 'ceppin', 'cep(t), 'cepting, sep(s)*

A Forms.

1871 Eggleston *Hoosier Schoolmaster* 88 **IN,** They a'n't nobody come in here lately 'ceppin' the master. *Ibid* 116, 'Most everybody forgets God, 'cept Mr. Bosaw. *Ibid* 196, Hadn't seed nobody else, 'ceptin' Dr. Small. **1884** *Anglia* 7.269 **SE,** 'Ceppin' I fotch' you = unless I fetched you. **1894** Riley *Armazindy* 5 **IN,** Purtier girl you never seen— /

'Ceptin' she lacked schoolin'. **1899** (1912) Green *VA Folk-Speech* 375, *Sep, Seps*. . . "I knowed 'em all seps two." **1922** Gonzales *Black Border* 292 **sSC, GA coasts** [Gullah glossary], *'Cep' 'cep'm 'cep'n'*—except, excepts, excepted, excepting. **1927** Adams *Congaree* 18 **cSC [Black],** An' I ain't never say a word 'bout her, cepen I went to Pooch an' Big Daughter. **1937** *AmSp* 12.288 **nwVA,** [ə'sɛpt] for *except*. **1938** Matschat *Suwannee R.* 161 **nFL, sGA,** All grew up safe an' well, 'ceptin' one. **1939** in 1944 *ADD* **nwDE,** *Except*. . . [ə'sɛpt]. Freq[uent]. **1941** *AmSp* 16.8 **eTX** [Black], *Except,* [sɛp]. **1942** Hall *Smoky Mt. Speech* 54 **wNC, eTN,** There is occasional apheresis also in *except* . . [sɛpt]. **1965–70** *DARE* (Qu. LL31, . . *All but one: "Everybody's here now, ——— John."*) 38 Infs, **scattered,** 'Cep'; **MS**64, **OR**10, **PA**167, **SC**39, **TX**97, 'Cept; **KY**84, **MS**88, 'Cepting. **1966** *Wilson Coll.* **csKY,** Cept /sɛpt/ conj., except. **1966** *DARE* Tape **MS**15, Except [ɛk'sɛp].

B As conj.

Unless. **Sth, S Midl**

1845 Thompson *Pineville* 55 **cGA,** The first man that touches me, I'll whip, 'cept I die tryin'. **1884** [see A above]. **1899** (1912) Green *VA Folk-Speech* 375, *Sep, Seps*. . . "I don't know the place, and I can't find the way sep somebody shows me." **1906** *DN* 3.136 **nwAR,** *Excepting*. . . "I can't do it, excepting you help me." **1922** Gonzales *Black Border* 165 **sSC, GA coasts** [Gullah], Buzzut ent free 'nuf fuh light 'puntop nutt'n' 'cep'n' 'e dead. *Ibid* 217, Me cyan' ketch de dog 'cep'n' wunnuh fetch'um t'ru de ribbuh. **1962** Steinbeck *Travels* 224, "When do they get going?" He looked at his watch. "Except it's cold, they been coming in since dawn. It's quarter to. You get along and you won't miss nothing except it's cold."

exception n

A noteworthy example.

1906 *DN* 3.135 **nwAR,** *Exception of a*. . . "The Odd Fellows and the Rebekahs had an exception of a good time at their hall last Monday night."

exceptions n pl [*W3 "archaic"*]

Exception; offense.

1869 Twain *Innocents* 647, Many . . even took exceptions to the article. **1902** *DN* 2.234 **sIL,** *Exceptions*. . . Always used for exception, as designating something contrary to rule.

exchange n, v Pronc-sp *aschange*

A Forms.

1905 *DN* 3.101 **nwAR,** The most noticeable feature of the English spoken in Northwest Arkansas is recessive accent. . . ['ɛks,čenǰ]. **1939** in 1944 *ADD* **nwDE,** *Exchange*. . . Freq. aschange [əs'čenǰ].

B As verb.

=change v[1].

1966 *DARE* (Qu. K70, *Words . . for castrating an animal*) Inf **SC**9, Change, exchange; (Qu. K24, *What does the word "ox" mean around here?*) Inf **SC**9, A kind of quiet thing that for work you exchange a bull for, that is to say, to make an ox. [FW: (Ex)change must mean to castrate.]

exchange work v phr, n Also *exchange (help, labor), exchanging (work, help, labor);* for addit varr see quots **widespread, but less freq Inland Sth, Lower Missip Valley** See Map

=change work.

1950 *WELS (When a farmer gets help on his job from his neighbors in return for his help on their farms later on)* 15 Infs, **WI,** Exchange (work, help, labor); 11 Infs, Exchanging (work, help, labor). **1965–70** *DARE* (Qu. L5) 208 Infs, **widespread, but less freq Inland Sth, Lower Missip Valley,** Exchange (work, help, labor *or* time); 43 Infs, **chiefly Nth, N Midl,** Exchanging (work, help, labor *or* time); **IL**59, **IN**19, 69, **MO**15, **OK**14, Exchange of work (*or* help, labor); **IA**45, **PA**21, **UT**4, Help (*or* labor, work) exchange; (Qu. FF2, . . *Kinds of parties*) Inf **OH**27, Exchanging thrashing; (Qu. II13, *When you are friendly with people who live near you . . "We've always ——— with them."*) Inf **OK**18, Exchanged work.

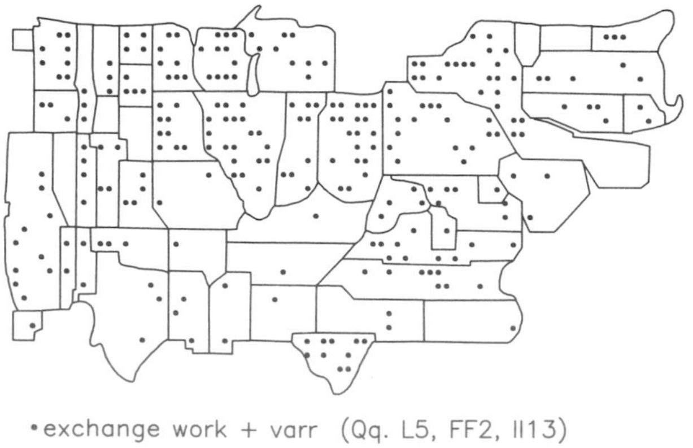

•exchange work + varr (Qq. L5, FF2, II13)

excursion n Pronc-spp *excussion, scussion, 'scusshun*

1893 Shands *MS Speech* 55, *Scussion*. . . Negro for *excursion*. **1922** Gonzales *Black Border* 324 **sSC, GA coasts** [Gullah glossary], *'Scusshun*—excursion, excursions. **1928** Peterkin *Scarlet Sister Mary* 112 **sSC** [Gullah], "Gone to town on de boat." "On de excussion?"

excuse v Usu |ɛk'skjuz|; also |skjuz| Pronc-spp *ixcuse, skuse, skuze* Cf Intro "Language Changes" I.7, IV.2

Std sense, var forms.

1891 Page *Elsket* 138 **VA,** Might be ixcused ef you jes consider dat smell. **1892** Stevenson *Across Plains* 71 **neNV,** [Quoting a native speaker:] Ex-cuse me, sir. **1893** Shands *MS Speech* 57, *Skuze* [skjuz]. Negro for *excuse* and *accuse;* as, "Skuse me for hittin' you, but you skused me of lyin'." **1936** *AmSp* 11.149 **eTX,** *Excuse* (verb) is often [skju:z]. **1940** in 1944 *ADD* **AR,** *Excuse*. . . *"Recess. Accent."* . . Excuse. Radio. **1941** *AmSp* 16.8 **eTX** [Black], *Excuse* (v.), [skju:z].

excuse n Usu |ɛk'skjus|; also |'skjus| Pronc-sp *skuse* Cf Intro "Language Changes" I.7

Std sense, var form.

1880 (1881) Harris *Uncle Remus Songs* 25, "I aint gwineter take no skuse," sez Brer Fox. **1893** Shands *MS Speech* 50, *Po' skuse for* [po skjus fʌ]. A negro phrase meaning *a poor substitute for* or *example of;* as, "He is a mighty po' skuse for a man."

excuse prep See **excusing** prep

excuse house n *euphem* Cf **escusada**

1970 *DARE* (Qu. M21b, *Joking names for an outside toilet building*) Inf TN53, Excuse house.

excuse-me-ma(a)m n

=thank-you-ma'am.

1933 *AmSp* 8.4.51 **NE,** *Excuse-me-mams* were bumps on the pioneer roads. **1936** Adams *Cowboy Lingo* 235, A bump in the road was humorously called an 'excuse-me-ma'am.'

excuse-us n

A gift in exchange for hospitality.

1938 Rawlings *Yearling* 113 **nFL,** Penny said, "Anyway, here's our excuse-us. Fresh venison." "And the hide," Jody said. "For a rug for you. . . " She lifted her hands in the air. Their gifts became at once of great value.

excusing prep Also *excuse, excusing of, ~for, scused;* freq aphet *scusin, skusin* **chiefly Sth** *esp among Black speakers*

Except (for), with the exception of, not counting.

1887 Page *In Ole VA* 199 [Black], The grettest gent'man in the county skusin him . . and the Colonel. **1898** Lloyd *Country Life* 136 **AL,** He don't buy no groceries, scusin a little sugar and flour and coffee. **1908** *DN* 3.309 **eAL, wGA,** *Excusin(g)*. . . Excepting. **1910** *DN* 3.458 **FL, GA,** "I washed the clothes in two waters, scused the billin' [*DARE* Ed: =*bilin*?]" (used only by blacks). **1916** *Scribner's Mag.* 353/1 **VA** [Black], I ain't got no entitle 'scusin' Ommirandy. **1922** Gonzales *Black Border* 232 **sSC, GA coasts** [Gullah], We come back—eb'rybody 'scusin' Silus' wife. **1927** Adams *Congaree* 58 **cSC** [Black], It ain't never been no place for crane, scusin' de big yaller crane Saber see, and dat ain't been no crane. **1928** Peterkin *Scarlet Sister Mary* 213 **sSC coast** [Gullah], Nobody, excusin Gawd, knows what's ahead o you. **1938** Rawlings *Yearling* 42 **FL,** I ain't done much today, excusin' fret and worry. **1952** Brown *NC Folkl.* 1.538 **c,eNC,** *Excuse*. . . Except. "I will work with anybody on this farm excuse him." . . *Excusing*. . . "Everything is clean excusing that spot on the rug." **1959** Lomax *Rainbow Sign* 40 **AL** [Black], We was so far out in the country it cost eight dollars for the doctor to come, 'scusin the medicine he might bring. **1964** Will *Hist. Okeechobee* xi **FL,** Excusing for—except for. **1969** Emmons *Deep Rivers* 52 **eTX** [Black], Then he heard a pow'-ful rumblin' and here come the rest of the body excusin' o' the head and arms. **1970** *DARE* (Qu. LL31, . . *"Everybody's here ——— John."*) Infs **FL**48, 52, Excusing. [Both Infs Black, coll educ] **1975** Thomas *Hear the Lambs* 80

nwAL, My husband Jake do keep a stiddy job at a dairy, and he have a little farm. He gives me what I wants excusin' a railroad ticket back heah to see my folks.

excusing conj [**excusing** prep]

Unless; without.

1922 Gonzales *Black Border* 161 **sSC, GA coasts** [Gullah], Him done tell me de wu'd two time, en' 'scusin' oonuh hab dat wu'd, oonuh yent fuh pass. [=He told me the word twice, and unless you have that word, you are not allowed to pass.] *Ibid* 265, You couldn' git no chickin' 'scusin' you git aig'. [=You couldn't get any chicken unless you got an egg.] **1936** in 1977 *Amer. Slave Suppl. 1* 1.277 **AL** [Black], Yer jess cain't breathe the air, excusin' you gits choked er somethin'.

excusing of See **excusing** prep

excussion See **excursion**

exe n [Pronc-sp for *ax*] Cf **ex** n[1]

1844 Thompson *Major Jones's Courtship* 48 **GA,** I told nigger Jim to git sum light-wood and the exe. **1867** Lowell *Biglow* xvii **'Upcountry' MA,** The Yankee has retained something of the long sound of the *a* in such words as *axe, wax,* pronouncing them *exe, wex* (shortened from *aix, waix*).

executive stone n Cf **worry stone**

=feeling stone.

1975 Gould *ME Lingo* 90, *Feeling stones*—Sometimes executive stones. . . A solace to high-strung businessmen.

exercise n Pronc-sp *exrecise*

A Form.

1941 in 1944 *ADD* **nWV,** *Exercise.* . . exrecise. Not always distinct.

B Sense.

An episode of paroxysms experienced by a participant in a religious revival meeting. **chiefly KY, TN** *hist* Cf **holy dance**

1804 in 1850 Gallaher *W. Sketch-book* 54 **seTN,** The only thing with us, which can be construed into disorder or extravagance, is the motions of the body under the exercise. In most of the cases, when the paroxysm begins to go off, the subject feels the strongest desire for prayer. **1807** McNemar *KY Revival* 34, The readiest way to keep clear of this extraordinary exercise, was to drown the soul in debauchery and vice. **1843** (1916) Hall *New Purchase* 365 **IN,** I've jist had a powerful exercise over thare in the Courthouse; and when I kim to, I couldn't see my bonnit no whare about. **1886** Smith *Hist. KY* 422, In the midst of religious services and enthused exhortation, the *exercises* of falling prostrate, jerking with nervous motions, and involuntary dancing, would begin. **1948** Dick *Dixie Frontier* 196 **swKY, TN** (as of 1800), These spiritual "exercises" burst into full flower.

exflunct v Also *exflunctify* [A humorously extravagant quasi-Latin elaboration of *flunk* to fail] *obs* Cf **-ification, -ify**

To cause to fail, render useless, overcome completely; hence ppl adj *exflunctified* and varr.

1831 *Louisville* (Ky.) *Public Advt.* 17 Oct. 2/3 *(DA),* Clear meat-ax disposition; the best man, if I a'nt, I wish I may be tetotaciously exfluncted! **1836** (1955) *Crockett Almanacks* 49 **wTN,** My throat and jaws were so exflunctoficated with the influenza that I even snored hoarse. **1839** *Chemung* (NY.) *Democrat* 30 Nov. *(DA),* The mongrel armies are prostrate—used up—exflunct*i*cated. **1840** U.S. Congress *Congressional Globe* 21 July 545/2 **IN,** [It has been widely proclaimed] that the Administration is bodaciously used up, tetotaciously exflunctified. **1844** Featherstonhaugh *Excursion Slave States* 71 **St. Louis MO,** Stranger, if that ar hoss don't go like a screamer, I'll give you leave to ex-flunctify me into no time of day at all. **1853** Bird *Nick of Woods* 274 **KY,** You exflunctified, perditioned rascal.

exhorter n

A lay preacher; also vbl n *exhorting* preaching, proclaiming the gospel.

1843 (1916) Hall *New Purchase* 366 **sIN,** All the *crack* preachers within a circle of three hundred miles were to be present, and also a celebrated African exhorter from Kentucky. **1845** in 1927 *IN Mag. Hist.* 23.202 **seIN,** He joined the church . . and was made class-leader, then exhorter, and then local preacher. **1901** Harben *Westerfelt* 253 **nGA,** I got hugged by a whole string of exhorters. *Ibid* 274, She hain't doin' one bit o' exhortin' that I kin see. I don't know whether she's in the vineyard [=a faithful Christian] or not. **1953** Brewer *Word Brazos* 4 **eTX** [Black], L.K. comed to chu'ch all day evuh Sunday, an' putty soon he come to be a exhorter (dat's a preachuh tryin' to git on foot preachin', you know). So putty soon dey calls 'im to pastuh a li'l ole chu'ch. **1967** *DARE* (Qu. CC10, . . *An unprofessional, part-time lay preacher*) Infs **KS**5, **TN**15, Exhorter; **PA**60, Exhorter [ɛg'zortɚ]; exhorter Jones. [All Infs old] **1971** Wood *Vocab. Change* 38 **Sth,** [A part-time preacher whose professional training may lie only in what he has read from the Bible goes under several names; nine are given in the questionnaire, and about the same number were volunteered.] *Ibid* 368, [Footnote:] Volunteered: *devil chaser, exhorter.*

exle See **ex** n[1]

exmalagocious See **ex-** pref

ex-note See **ex** n[2]

exoduser See **exoduster 1**

exodus oil n Cf *DJE oil of* ———

A conjure or magic concoction, used to drive people away.

1947 Ballowe *The Lawd* 197 **LA** [Black], "Whut you got? Conjuh?" "The bestes'. Hit's called Exodus Oil, an' hit's got go-way powder skunt a mile."

exodust v [*exodus* interpreted as a verb + epenthetic *t* (cf Intro "Language Changes" I.8)]

To leave quickly for a distant place.

1947 Ballowe *The Lawd* 197 **LA** [Black], He'll exodust so fur he'll never find his way back.

exoduster n

1 also *exody:* A Black person who left the South in the mass migration to the Northwest (esp Kansas) c1878–80. [*exodus* mass migration + excr *-t* + *-er* person associated with] *hist*

1880 *Galveston News* 26 March *(DA),* Thirty-three Ethiopian exodusters passed south today en route from Kansas to their old homes in Grimes country [sic]. *Ibid* 31 March *(DA),* Two caravans of exodusters, containing about a dozen wagons and fifty darkies of assorted sizes each, passed through here today en route for Kansas. **1882** *N.Y. Tribune* 21 June *(DA),* An exoduster was seen a while ago furrowing . . with a plough drawn by a cow. **1939** FWP *Guide KS* 57, It [=Kansas] was yet to receive the sudden flow of emancipated Negroes, known as "exodusters." **1941** *AmSp* 16.20 **KS** (as of 1890s), [Song lyric:] I'se gwine to jine the exodies that's makin' fo de Noff. **1959** Tallman *Dict. Amer. Folkl.* 105, In the spring of 1880 a group of Negroes from the South who sometimes called themselves the Exodusers [sic] founded a settlement in Kansas which they named Nicodemus. **1961** Sackett–Koch *KS Folkl.* 110, *Exoduster.* . . An ex-slave who came to Kansas in the great exodus from the South in 1879.

2 A refugee from a "dust bowl."

1941 *AmSp* 16.317 **KS,** The word [=*exoduster*] has been revived . . by an editor of the Topeka *Daily Capital.* In the issue of November 25, 1938, p. 4/1, occurred the sentence: 'Most of the exodusters from the Dust Bowl were not "rooted" anywhere.' And the caption of a letter, *ibid.,* December 20, 1938, p. 4/6, read: 'Protected Exodusters.' **1961** Sackett–Koch *KS Folkl.* 110, *Exoduster* . . was again applied to those who left the "dust bowl" in the '30's.

exody See **exoduster 1**

exparience See **experience**

expart See **expert**

expecially See **especially**

expect v Usu |ɛk'spɛkt, ɪk-|; also **chiefly Sth, S Midl** aphet |spɛk(t)| (See Map) Pronc-spp *expeck, ixpect, 'spec(k), 'spect, 'xspec'* Cf **suspect**

A Forms.

1853 Simms *Sword & Distaff* 203 **SC** [Black], I 'speck (expect) ef he bin yer, he would nebber le' maussa res'. *Ibid* **SC,** And he was always a giving to them persons from whom there was no sort of reason to ixpect to git any thing back again. **1867** Lowell *Biglow* 110 **'Upcountry' MA,** I 'xspec' to be nex' spring. **1871** (1882) Stowe *Fireside Stories* 168 **NEng,** In them days folks was brought up to spect trouble; they didn't look for no less. **1888** Jones *Negro Myths* 119 **seGA,** Me spec wen Mossa fire pon topper um, de deer mus be bin er bresh. **1893** Shands *MS Speech* 59, *Speck.* . . Used by negroes for both *expect* and *suspect.* **1915** *DN* 4.191 **swVA,** *Spec.* **1937** (1977) Hurston *Their Eyes* 60 **csFL** [Black], Ah specks to pay him. **1941** *AmSp* 16.8 **eTX** [Black], *Expect,* [spɛk]. **1941** O'Donnell *Great Big Doorstep* 9 **sLA,** Now I guess you gunna expeck him to find a house floatin down. **1942** Hall *Smoky Mt. Speech* 54 **wNC, eTN,** There is occasional apheresis also in . . *expect* . . [spɛk(t)]. **1965–70** *DARE* (Qu. JJ34, *When you decide it would be to your advantage to do something, you might say, "Yes, I ______ I'll be better off that way."*) 18 Infs, **chiefly Sth, S Midl,** 'Spec; **LA**3, 'Spect; (Qu. BB21) Inf **TX**98, I 'spec not; (Qu. NN1) Inf **OH**41, I 'spec; (Qu. NN4) Inf **TX**32, 'Spect not. **1968–69** *DARE* Tape **IN**9, I went into the carp'ry work o' buildin' houses and worked at that fer I 'spect twenty years; **IN**76, Oh, I 'spect . . last year we . . loaned seven hunderd 'n' fifty-one nonfiction books.

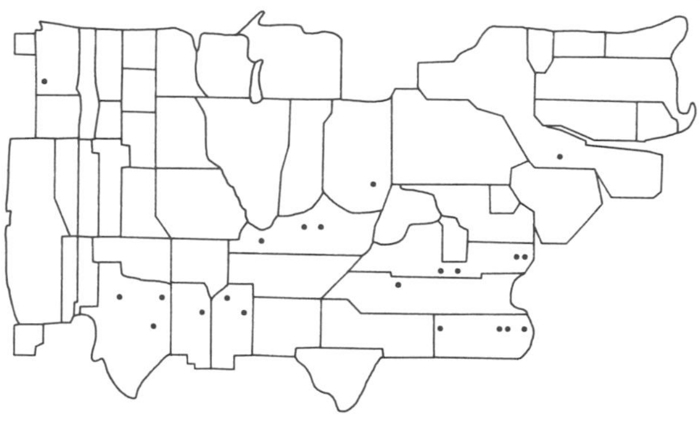

•'spec(t) (at expect A) + varr (Qq. JJ34, BB21, NN1, NN4)

B Sense.

To suppose, think, believe. [*OED expect* v. 6 "Now *rare* in literary use. The misuse of the word as a synonym of *suppose,* without any notion of 'anticipating' . . , is often cited as an Americanism, but is very common in dialectal, vulgar or carelessly colloquial speech in England."]

1763 in 1853 Jefferson *Writings* 1.186 **VA,** I say *has been,* because I expect there is one [=an opening] no longer. **1786** *Ibid* 506, I expect they [=pecan nuts] can always be got at Pittsburg. **1810** (1912) Dwight *Journey to OH* 11 **NJ,** There is a man today in Camptown where we stopt to eat, not oats but gingerbread, who enquired, or rather *expected* we were going to the Hio. **c1820** in 1956 *AmSp* 31.268 **Philadelphia PA,** In most parts of the world people *expect* things that are to come. But in Pennsylvania, more particularly in the metropolis, we *expect* things that are past. One man tells another, he *expects* he has had a very pleasant ride. . . I have indeed heard a wise man of Gotham say, he *expected* Alexander the Macedonian was the greatest conqueror of antiquity. **1828** Webster *Amer. Dict., Expect.* . . The common phrase, *I expect it was,* is as vulgar as it is improper. **1829–30** in 1927 *DN* 5.424, *Expect.* . . "I expect you left Richmond yesterday." **1836** Weston *Visit U.S.* 59 **NYC,** The word "expect" is indiscriminantely [sic] used for our words "believe," "suppose," "think," and "expect," as we use it. **1848** Bartlett *Americanisms* 131, *To expect,* instead of *suspect.* To suppose. . . A very common corruption. . . Nor is it confined to ourselves. **1889** Twain *CT Yankee* 129, Have you been questioned . . ? . . Well, I didn't expect you had. **1899** (1912) Green *VA Folk-Speech* 167, *Expect.* . . "I expect he went to town yesterday." **1902** *DN* 2.234 **sIL,** *Expect.* . . To suppose, or presume. **1907** *DN* 3.222 **nwAR. 1910** *DN* 3.441 **wNY. 1966–67** *DARE* (Qu. JJ37, . . *"I'm not sure, but I ______ that man is a thief."*) Inf **GA**3, Expect; (Qu. NN1, *Other words like 'yes': "Are you coming along too?"*) Inf **MI**67, I expect so—[used] regularly around here; (Qu. GG12, . . *"There she comes now. I ______ she would."*) Inf **SC**19, Expect. **1967–68** *DARE* Tape **IN**5, They will go back to their parents and say, "No, Mommy, that was real Santy Claus," and the mom would say, "Yes, I spect it was."; **IN**13, I expect . . he spent about, oh, six or seven hundred dollars every year; **IN**36, I spect I caught a hunderd big bluegills; **MI**66, I expect that . . the stones were gathered in this community; **TX**35, I don't think they ever had forty but they had, I spect . . , thirty-five.

experience n, v Pronc-spp *exparience, experence, experient, expurance, ixperance, 'sperience, speunce;* for addit varr see quots

Std senses, var forms.

1823 Cooper *Pioneers* 1.214 **cNY,** You have had great experunces in your life, Benjamin. **1837** Sherwood *Gaz. GA* 69, *Expeerunce,* experience. **1841** (1952) Cooper *Deerslayer* 58 **nNY,** My exper'ence would tell the same story. **1851** Hooper *Widow Rugby's Husband* 44 **AL,** I'll give you my ixperance after supper. **1852** in 1956 Eliason *Tarheel Talk* 310 **NC,** *Experience*—expurance. **1853** Simms *Sword & Distaff* 327 **SC,** Your ixperence is jest none at all in the way of business. **1856** *Knickerbocker* 48.433 **NEng,** A hull lot of fellers exparienced religion. **1867** Lowell *Biglow* 65 **'Upcountry' MA,** An' *my* experunce,—tell ye wut it's ben. **1871** (1892) Johnston *Dukesborough Tales* 58 **GA,** In all my experence, I has not seed jest sich a case. **1893** Shands *MS Speech* 59, *Speunce.* . . Negro for *experience,* both the noun and the verb. The past tense of the verb is *speunced.* **1922** Gonzales *Black Border* 329 **sSC, GA coasts** [Gullah glossary], *'Speriunce*—experience, experiences, experienced, experiencing. **1929** Sale *Tree Named John* 54 **MS,** John say 'spe'ence is the best teacher. **1934** *AmSp* 9.251, *Southern Mountain Accent* . . [of] a certain distinguished man of letters . . experience [ɪkspɪrəns]. **1937** in 1958 Brewer *Dog Ghosts* 84 **TX** [Black], Dey was habin' confession meetin' an' hit comed ole Joe's time to tell his 'sperience. **c1938** in 1970 Hyatt *Hoodoo* 1.182 **neFL** [Black], Now, for experient [Hyatt: experience], for self-experient about mahself, about mah wife—ah tole you about my wife. **1942** Hall *Smoky Mt. Speech* 65 **wNC, eTN,** Omission of [ɪ] is usual in . . experience [ɪk'spɪrəns]. **1953** Brewer *Word Brazos* 41 **eTX** [Black], So she wait till attuh all de res' of de brothuhs an' sistuhs gits thoo tellin' dey 'speriunce 'fo' she riz to tell her 'speriunce.

expert adj, n Pronc-spp *expart, spert*

Std senses, var forms.

1841 (1952) Cooper *Deerslayer* 40 **nNY,** I do not know that a hunter is less expart with the rifle. *Ibid* 230, They're expart enough in them sort of miracles. **1917** *DN* 4.417 **wNC,** *Spert,* n. . . expert.

expire v [Malaprop for *perspire;* cf Intro "Language Changes" I.10]

1966–68 *DARE* (Qu. X56a, *Other words for sweat*) Infs **IL**16, **TN**27, Expiring; **LA**2, Expiring [kspaɪr] or [ɪk'spaɪr]; (Qu. X56b, . . *Sweating very heavily*) Inf **SD**2, Expiring. [3 Infs gs educ, 1 Inf hs educ]

explanify v [*explain* + **-ify**]

To explain.

1891 Page *Elsket* 143 **VA,** I tolt 'em dyah in de cote-house ev'y wud jes like I have explanified it heah.

explification n [Blend of *explication* + **-ification**]

An explanation.

1843 (1916) Hall *New Purchase* 266 **IN,** "How is a child's spelling-book to be made any plainer?" "Why, sir, by clear explifications of the words in one column, by exemplifying illustrations in the other."

explode v[1] [Ext of *explode* to give sudden release to an emotion] **chiefly Nth, N Midl** See Map

To suddenly burst forth in laughter. Note: Responses to Qq. GG15 and KK11 suggest that, when used to describe the violent expression of anger, *explode* is not regionally restricted.

1950 *WELS (To have a sudden fit of laughter)* 4 Infs, **WI,** Exploded. **1965–70** *DARE* (Qu. GG30, *To suddenly break out laughing: "When he told her that, she just ______."*) 31 Infs, **chiefly Nth, N Midl,** Exploded; **MI**81, About exploded; **CA**15, Exploded in laughter; **CT**6, Exploded with laughter.

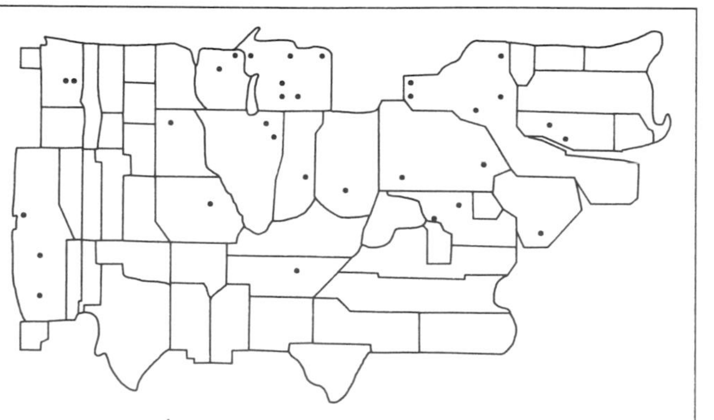

•explode v[1] + varr (Qu. GG30)

explode v[2] [Appar var of *explore*]

1979 *AmSp* 54.97 **sME** (as of c1900), *Explode.* . . Explore [*AmSp* Ed: "common" usage].

explore v, n Cf **explode** v[2]

To explode; an explosion.

1902 *DN* 2.234 **sIL,** *Explore*. . . Commonly used for explode. Explore. . . 'When the blast went off, it made a loud explore.'

explorer's gentian n Cf **hikers' gentian**

A **gentian** (here: *Gentiana calycosa*).

1959 Munz-Keck *CA Flora* 442, *G. calycosa*. . . Explorer's gentian. **1973** Hitchcock-Cronquist *Flora Pacific NW* 359, Explorer's g[entian], m[oun]t[ain] bog g[entian].

expluderosity, expolagollucious See **ex-** pref

export tobacco See **black tobacco 2**

‡exposable adj [Malaprop]

Disposable.

1968 *DARE* (Qu. G17, *Other kinds of towels*) Inf **GA**37, Exposable towel [laughter].

expose v [Prob blend of **expect** + *suppose*]

To suppose.

1895 *DN* 1.371 **eTN,** *Expose*. . . "I expose it's about a mile." **1987** *DARE* File **cwNC** (as of c1917), I heard *expose* used to mean 'suppose' by at least one person in Burke Co.

express v Pronc-sp *aspress* Cf Intro "Language Changes" IV.2

Std senses, var forms.

1936 *AmSp* 11.149 **eTX,** The accent is frequently shifted to the first syllable of *express* ['ɛksprɛs]. **1939** in 1944 *ADD* **nwDE,** *Express* . . aspress [ə'sprɛs]. Freq.

express wagon n For varr see quots **chiefly NEng, N Cent, West** See Map

A usu lightweight but capacious wagon used for prompt delivery of goods or people.

1856 *Spirit of Times* 20 Sept 36/2 **NY,** As I spoke an immense express wagon—"Harlem, Carmansville, and New York"—came lumbering down upon our frail wagon. **1859** (1968) Bartlett *Americanisms* 139, *Express wagon.* The wagon in which packages, boxes, etc., are taken to and from an express office. **1884** Barber *Diary* np **MA,** George Manning paid me .25 for use of express wagon. **1890** *Harper's New Mth. Mag.* 80.742/1 **East,** I saw the express carts this morning. **1910** *DN* 3.453 **seVT,** *Express-wagon*. . . Any light spring wagon having one seat and a long open body. **1914** *DN* 4.155 **Cape Cod MA,** *Express-wagon*. . . A four-wheeled, one-horse wagon, lighter than a farm-wagon, and usually equipped with two removable seats. **1948** Rittenhouse *Amer. Horse-Drawn Vehicles* 84, *Market or express wagon*. . . 1870. . . These rather top-heavy wagons were used in cities after the Civil War. Body was 86 by 45 inches, with lower side panels 12 inches high. . . Top . . was removable. . . Canvas sides. **1965-70** *DARE* (Qu. N41c, *Horse-drawn vehicles to carry light loads*) 32 Infs, **chiefly NEng, N Cent, West,** Express (wagon); **WA**3, Express delivery, package delivery; **CT**26, Two-seated express wagon; (Qu. N41b, . . *To carry heavy loads*) 10 Infs, **esp Nth,** Express wagon; (Qu. N41a, . . *To carry people*) Infs **GA**45, **MA**5, 74, **NV**8, **OH**41, Express wagon; **IN**58, Light express; **MA**58, Two- or three-seated express wagon. [39 of 43 total Infs old]

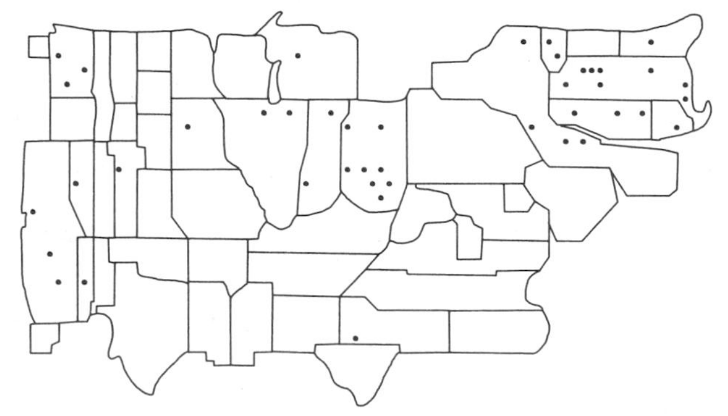

•express wagon + varr (Qu. N41a, b, c)

expurance See **experience**

exqualafadocious See **ex-** pref

exrecise See **exercise**

ex-spot See **ex** n[2]

exta'ornary See **extraordinary**

extension club n For varr see quot **chiefly Cent, N Cent**

An organization, usu associated with a university, for fostering continuing education in rural areas.

1965-70 *DARE* (Qu. FF22a, . . *Clubs and societies around here*) Infs **KS**5, **MO**1, 5, 20, 21, 37, Extension club(s); **MI**45, Extension club—connected with Michigan State [University]—its own Ladies Aid or Guild. . . Like an adult 4-H; **NE**4, Extension clubs—The Pine Ridge, Chadron Creek Ladies, etc; **NM**4, Extension clubs—they learned to work at different hobbies; **IL**102, **NE**3, Home extension club; **AR**52, Extension homemakers; **NY**121, Extension service; **IL**96, Home extension council; (Qu. W32, . . *A group of women that meet to sew together*) Inf **OK**47, There used to be a home demonstration club, but now it's an extension club; **MI**92, Home extension society—[a] modern group; (Qu. FF1) Inf **MO**1, Extension club; (Qu. FF2) Inf **MI**78, Extension clubs.

extermish v

To destroy completely.

1903 *DN* 2.351 **neOH,** *Extermish*. . . Contamination of exterminate and abolish. [*DARE* Ed: or blend of *exterminate* + *extinguish*?]

extinguisher moss n [See quot 1928]

A moss of the genus *Encalypta.*

[**1821** Gray *Nat. Arrangement Brit. Plants* 1.725, *Encalypta*. . . Extinguisher-moss.] **1928** *Torreya* 28.111 **NJ,** The moss in these cracks is *Encalypta streptocarpa* . . Extinguisher Moss, so named because the outer covering of the capsule has the shape of the metal extinguisher of the tallow "dip" of colonial days. **1956** Conard *Mosses* 52, *Encalypta*. . . Called Extinguisher Mosses because the calypta resembles a candle-extinguisher.

extra adj, n, adv Usu |'ɛkstrə|; also |'ɛkstri, -ɪ| Pronc-sp *extry* Cf **wuxtra** n, **-y**

A Forms.

1861 Holmes *Venner* 1.165 **wMA,** An extry number of p'oopils. **1891** *DN* 1.169 **cNY,** ['ɛkstri]. **1894** Riley *Armazindy* 10 **IN,** Extry waste o' sympathy. **1911** Wharton *Ethan Frome* 120 **wMA,** A dollar extry. **1928** *AmSp* 3.402 **Ozarks,** *Extra* is nearly always *extry.* **1934** *AmSp* 9.45 **Sth,** The tendency in rustic Southern speech is to substitute [ɪ] for [ə] in *stomach, organ, extra.* **1936** *AmSp* 11.160 **eTX,** Among older or less well educated people in rural districts . . *extra* . . [is] pronounced . . ['ɛkstrɪ]. **1938** Matschat *Suwannee R.* 30 **nFL, sGA,** Extry fond of long sweetnin'. **1941** *AmSp* 16.9 **eTX** [Black], *Extra* . . ['ɛkstrɪ]. **1942** Hall *Smoky Mt. Speech* 76 **wNC, eTN,** Words in which [ɪ] was heard . . extra, Florida, Georgia. **1965-70** *DARE* (Qq. D3, 12, 16, G6, L2, N15b, 16a, U15, W40, X43b, KK1a, 5, LL4, 35) 22 Infs, **scattered,** ['ɛkstrɪ]. [21 of 22 Infs hs educ or less] **1966-67** *DARE* Tape **MI**8, If you specialize then you don't have to have a great deal of extra ['ɛkstrɨ] machinery; **MA**5A, That man was an extra ['ɛkstrɪ] good chopper.

B As adj.

Excellent, unusually good. [Perh ellip for *extra good*] **chiefly Sth, S Midl**

1848 (1936) Thorne *Jrl. of Boy's Trip* 43 **NY,** Having gone 34 miles we had a sight at the Capitol which was not anything extra. **1851** Hooper *Widow Rugby's Husband* 120 **AL,** I find it's with liars, as with everything else, *if you want an extra article you must send to furrin* [=foreign] *parts.* **1851** (1852) Stowe *Uncle Tom's Cabin* 1.43 **KY** [Black], Her corn-cakes is n't extra, not extra now, Jinny's corn-cakes is n't. **1939** *Hall Coll.* **eTN,** *Extra*. . . Very good. "He was a extra hand to work." **1952** Brown *NC Folkl.* 1.538 **c,eNC,** *Extra*. . . Excellent, very good. . . "This cotton is extra." **c1960** *Wilson Coll.* **csKY,** Extra ['ɛkstrɪ]. . . Very good, excellent. **1966** *DARE* (Qu. KK1a, . . *Very good—for example, food: "That pie was ______."*) Inf **SC**3, Extra ['ɛkstri]; (Qu. KK5, *A very skilled or expert person—for example, at woodworking: "He's . . ______."*) Inf **GA**5, Extra.

C As noun.

1 Something very large.

1932 *Hanley Disks* **swCT,** The extras, they run a hundred to a basket. Them are the extremely large oysters. **1966** *DARE* (Qu. LL5, *Something impressively big: "That cabbage is really a ______."*) Inf **GA**7, Extra.

2 =**ethyl.** **chiefly Gulf States, Mid Atl** See Map Cf **high test**
1965–70 *DARE* (Qu. N15b, . . *Kinds of gasoline: A more expensive kind*) 26 Infs, **chiefly Gulf States, Mid Atl,** Extra; **DC**8, Extry; **LA**29, 44, **TX**27, Esso extra.

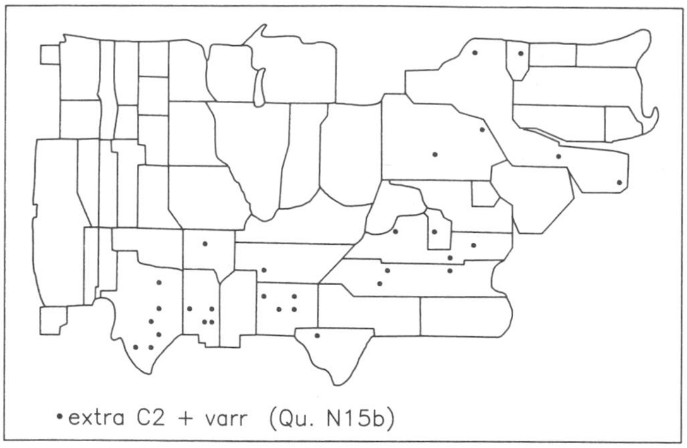

•extra C2 + varr (Qu. N15b)

‡extracize v
To extract.
1917 *DN* 4.411 **wNC,** *Extracize. . .* "I've done extracized them."

extract of hammer handle n *joc*
A nonexistent item used as the basis of a practical joke.
1966 *DARE* (Qu. HH14, *Ways of teasing a beginner or inexperienced person . . "Go get me ______."*) Inf **MI**10, Extract of hammer handle.

extraordinary adj Pronc-spp *exta'ornary, extrornary*
Std sense, var forms.
1841 (1952) Cooper *Deerslayer* 211 **nNY,** This is an extr'ornary garment, too; and extr'ornary things get up exta'ornary feelin's. **1890** *DN* 1.39 **csME,** *Extraordinary. . .* [ɪk'strɔdn̩eri] *(five syllables) and* [ɪk'strɔdneri], *not* [ɪk'strɔdn̩ri]. **1912** Green *VA Folk-Speech, Extrornary. . .* For extraordinary. **1959** *VT Hist.* new ser 27.135, *Extraordinary* ['stɔrdnæri] . . pronc. Rowland Robinson, *A Danvis Pioneer,* 90. Rare.

extra spoke n [Cf *fifth wheel*]
A misfit.
1950 *WELS (Somebody who doesn't seem to "fit in" or get along very well)* 1 Inf, **ceWI,** Extra spoke.

extrornary See **extraordinary**

extry See **extra**

‡exturbment n
A disturbance.
1970 *DARE* (Qu. JJ4, *A child who is always telling on other children*) Inf **NJ**69, Exturbment [ˌɛks'tɚbmənt]-maker. [Inf Black, old, gs educ]

exwance n [Pronc-sp for *advance*]
1922 Gonzales *Black Border* 78 **sSC, GA coasts** [Gullah], Uh buy'um en' pay t'ree dolluh' exwance on'um. *Ibid* 81, To recover her three dollars "exwance."

exwantidge n [Pronc-sp for *advantage*] Cf *DJE egvaantij*
1922 Gonzales *Black Border* 78 **sSC, GA coasts** [Gullah], Uh 'ooman tek uh exwantidge w'en uh yent binnuh study 'bout 'um. [=The woman took advantage [i.e., the opportunity] when I was not studying about [i.e., paying attention to] her.]

exwice n, v Also sp *agvice, egvice, egvise, exwise* [Pronc-spp for *advice, advise*] **Sth** *among Black speakers*
1922 Gonzales *Black Border* 274 **sSC, GA coasts** [Gullah], 'E nebbuh had my exwice een de back'uh 'e head! *Ibid* 300, [Glossary:] *Exwise*—advise, advises, advised, advising. **1927** Adams *Congaree* 14 **seSC** [Black], She give agvice and do everything she kin do to save her friend. *Ibid* 17, I mighty nigh done talk my heart out geeing agvice to dat gal. **1927** Kennedy *Gritny* 159 **sLA** [Black], You ain' got to gimme no egvice cuncernin' Dink. **1929** (1931) Faulkner *Sound & Fury* 314 **MS** [Black], Soon es Quentin need any of yo egvice, I'll let you know. **1929** (1951) Faulkner *Sartoris* 64 **MS** [Black], Dey egvised us to pick out a hole and stay dar fer a while. **1930** Stoney–Shelby *Black Genesis* 41 **seSC** [Black], "Waller in de sof' mud," he exwise 'em, "an' dem debbils can't git t'rough de dirt to bite you."

ey See **i**

'ey See **e** intj

eyah See **ayuh**

eye n[1]

1 also *stove eye;* In ref to a woodburning stove: see below. **chiefly Sth, S Midl** See Map Cf **damper 1, hook** n **4, key**
a freq attrib: A **cap** n[1] **2a.**
1905 *DN* 3.96 **nwAR,** *Stove-eye. . .* Stove-lid. 'Take off the stove-eye and put in some wood.' **1915** *DN* 4.242 **ceTN,** *Eye. . .* Lid (of a stove). **c1960** *Wilson Coll.* **csKY,** *Stove eyes. . .* Removable metal pieces on top of a cookstove. **1965–70** *DARE* (Qu. F10, . . *Wood-burning stoves . . the round flat pieces that you take out to put in the wood*) 147 Infs, **chiefly Sth, S Midl, esp Gulf States, TN,** Eye; **GA**1, **KY**20, **SC**1, Stove eye; **MS**22, Eye, cap; (Qu. F11, *The thing . . to remove the lids . . from a wood-burning stove when it is hot*) 41 Infs, **Sth, S Midl,** Eye lifter; **FL**9, **TN**1, 13, Eye hook; **GA**1, **SC**38, Eye key; **TX**9, Eye lift. **1968** *DARE* FW Addit **LA**21, Eye lift—the utensil to lift stove eyes with. **1971** *Foxfire* Spring-Summer 93 **nGA,** It [=a wood stove] has six circular eyes. The eyes and their partitions are easily removable for cleaning.
b The opening covered by the **cap** n[1] **2a.**
1939 *Hall Coll.* **eNC, wTN,** *Eye. . .* An opening in the top of a wood stove. **1966** *DARE* (Qu. F10) Inf **GA**8, Eye cap; (Qu. F11) Inf **AL**61, Eye lid-lifter; **NY**75, Stove-eye lid-handle.

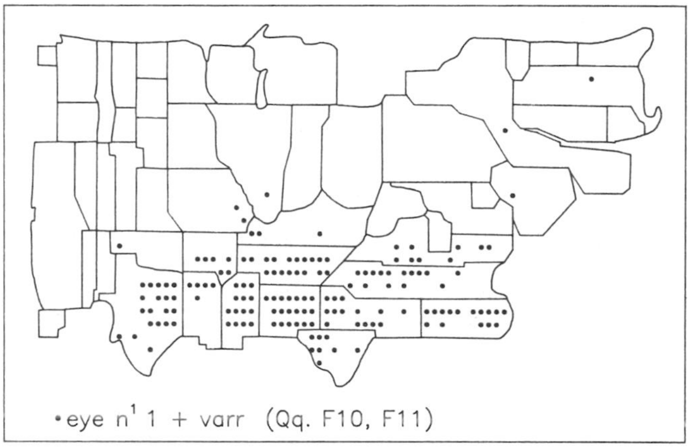

•eye n[1] 1 + varr (Qq. F10, F11)

2 Among railroad workers: a trackside signal.
1932 *RR Mag.* Oct 367, *Eye*—Signal. **1938** Beebe *High Iron* 220 [Railroad terms], *Eye:* Signal. **1943** *AmSp* 18.165 [Railroad terms], *Eye.* Signal. **1945** Hubbard *Railroad Ave.* 342, *Eye*—Trackside signal.

3 See **eye horse.**

4 In marble play:
a =**eye-drop.**
1955 *PADS* 23.17 **cwTN,** *Eye. . .* A marble game.
b A kind of marble resembling an eye.
1967 *DARE* (Qu. EE6d, *Special marbles*) Inf **OH**23, Eyes.
c See quot.
1976 *WI Acad. Rev.* Mar 8/1 (as of 1920s), A crockery marble called a "coffee" came in blue and in light brown (hence "coffee"). The color was glazed on the clay surface. Those parts of the marble that touched the firing-clay surface or other marbles developed an "eye" or spot: a ring in which there was very little or no glaze at all.

5 In children's games: see quot.
1915 *DN* 4.182 **swVA,** *Eye. . .* In games,—a (second, third, etc.) lease of life after being 'dead,' (that is, forced to retire).

6 The germ or embryo of a kernel of corn.
1986 Pederson *LAGS Concordance,* 1 inf, **neLA,** Eye—part of a corn kernel; 1 inf, **cwLA,** Eye—the kernel of a grain of corn.

eye n[2] [Calque from Haw *maka* mesh of a net, transf from *maka* eye]
Mesh.
1967 *DARE* (QR, near Qu. P13) Inf **HI**4, Trap wire with one-inch eye.

eyeable adj *arch*
Pleasant to look at.

1889 *AN&Q* 3.285/2 **NJ,** Eyeable, in the sense of *comely,* is a word I have heard in Camden County.

eyebait n

1 A small herring.

1884 Goode *Fisheries U.S.* 1.246 **N Atl,** The Lant is found in spring or early summer in the open sea, in the neighborhood of banks and shoals remote from land, as is also the sprat in Europe and the "brit," "eye-bait," or small herring in America.

2 See quot.

1889 *Century Dict.* 2104, *Eyebait*. . . Same as *brit*², 2. [*Ibid* 687, *Brit*². . . *1.* A young herring of the common kind, occurring in large shoals, and formerly classed as a separate species, *Clupea minima.—2.* A general name for animals upon which whales feed, as *Clio borealis,* etc.; whale-brit.]

3 Pieces of fish used as bait.

1985 *DARE* File, *Eyebait*—Used . . in South Carolina . . where it is said to refer to fish eyes used as bait; and in California, where the term refers to chum used as bait, possibly because fish heads figure so prominently in chum.

eyeball n

1 also *eyeballs:* Someone precious or dear. NC, SC

1952 Brown *NC Folkl.* 1.538 **cnNC,** *Eyeballs*. . . One's favorite person; "apple of the eye." "She . . is my eyeballs." . . Rare. **1954** *PADS* 21.27 **SC,** *Eyeball*. . . Someone dear, precious, especially a favorite child. "Dat chile 'e mammy eyeball." Also plural. **1966** *DARE* Tape **NC**38, Those are grandchildren. . . The little boy over there is my pride and joy; he's my eyeball. **1974** Betts-Walser *NC Folkl.* 7 **cnNC,** Eyeball: one's favorite person.

2 See quot.

1966 *DARE* (Qu. HH15, . . *Inexperienced person*) Inf **SC**10, Eyeball—one who looks on.

3 See quot. Cf **eyeballer**

1966 *DARE* (Qu. II35, *A person who is disliked because he seems to think he knows everything*) Inf **SC**10, Eyeball = know-it-all.

eyeball v

1 To look at intently; to stare at. *orig esp freq among Black speakers*

1901 *Harper's Mth. Mag.* Feb 443/1 **sCA,** "God!" burst from the lips of the man as he eyeballed his attendant. **1935** Hurston *Mules & Men* 160 **FL,** De cat . . was lookin' at de man, and de man was lookin' at de cat. God seen how they eye-balled one 'nother, so He ast de man, "Man, what is it between you an dis cat?" *Ibid* 173, De lion and John eye-balled one another for a minute or two. **1942** *Amer. Mercury* 55.223.85 **NYC** [Black], Whenever he was challenged by a hard-head or a frail eel on the right of his title he would eye-ball the idol-breaker with a slice of ice and put on his ugly-laugh. **1946** (1972) Mezzrow-Wolfe *Really Blues* 332, *Eyeball:* look, stare. **1950** *PADS* 14.28 **SC,** *Eye-ball*. . . To stare at, to glare at. Negro: "Look here, nigger, don't you eyeball me." " . . standin' outside dis window eyeballin' dat doll all day." Amos and Andy radio program, December 25, 1949. **1960** Wentworth-Flexner *Slang* 175, Eyeball. . . *Teenage and synthetic hipster use since c1950.* **1965-66** *DARE* FW Addit **MS,** Eyeballing—looking at something with great intensity. This word almost implies staring with one's mouth open. Occasional use. **1987** Jones-Wheeler *Laughter* 137 **Appalachians,** John . . had just got in a shipment of them big old round coconuts. . . and old Steamer kept eyeballing them things.

2 To measure by eye; to estimate.

1958 McCulloch *Woods Words* **Pacific NW,** *Eyeballing a line*—Making a preliminary survey by the eye, mostly by guess, not by instrument. **1961** *PADS* 36.27 **West** [Construction terms], *Eyeball*. . . To sight the alignment of forms, rafters, etc. with the eye to see if it is straight. **1966** *DARE* Tape **AR**33, Quite a bit of us . . use the term "eyeball". You just look at it [=rice] and determine from its color and the way the heads are drooped over . . that it's about ready for harvest. **c1970** *Thompson Coll.* **Detroit MI, Los Angeles CA** (as of 1946-60), *Eyeball*. . . In the machine industry: work not requiring micrometer accuracy is . . "eye-balled" when it is not necessary to bother with a steel rule. **1984** *MJLF* 10.150 **cnWI,** *Eye-ball*. . . To judge the alignment of timbers and buildings, to sight by eye without the use of instruments.

3 See quot. Cf **eyeball n 2, inspector**

1966 *DARE* (Qu. KK31, *To go about aimlessly looking for distraction: "He doesn't have anything to do, so he's just ——— around."*) Inf **SC**10, Eyeballing.

eyeballer n Cf **eyeball n 3**

A meddlesome person.

1920 Hunter *Trail Drivers TX* 300, An "eye-baller" is a person who pokes himself into other people's business. **1933** (1950) Allen *Cowboy Lore* 58 **SW,** *Eyeballer,* Anyone poking his nose into the affairs of others. **1936** Adams *Cowboy Lingo* 199.

eyeballing vbl n Cf **eye-opener**

1968 Adams *Western Words* 107, *Eyeballing*—The cutting off of the upper eyelids of cattle, a practice that was resorted to occasionally in the brush country to prevent cattle from going back into the brush. Not being able to protect their eyes from the brush, the animals were glad to stay in the open country.

eyeballs n

1 See **eyebright 3.**

2 See **eyeball n 1.**

eyeballs are floating phr

=back teeth are floating 1.

1970 *DARE* (Qu. BB20, . . *Overactive kidneys*) Inf **IL**118, My eyeballs are floating—when you wait too long.

eyebalm See **eyebright 3**

eyebane See **eyebright 5**

eyebreaker n

A **black gnat.**

1857 (1859) Olmsted *Journey TX* 404 **LA,** A black gnat, called the "eye-breaker," . . They were worse than all manner of musquitoes [sic], flies, or other insects.

eyebright n

1 A plant of the genus *Euphrasia.* [*OED eyebright* sb.¹, 1533 →]

1677 (1892) Hammond *Diary* 171 **MA,** Take Sage, Fennel, . . Eye-bright . . Steep them in White wine . . & use the water to wash the Eyes. **1778** Carver *Travels N. Amer.* 515 **MI, MN, WI,** *Herbs*. . . [include:] Balm, Nettles, Cinque Foil, Eyebright, Sanicle. **1789** Morse *Amer. Geog.* 53, Of the various aromatic and other kinds of herbs are . . eye-bright, sanikle. **1867** Beecher *Norwood* 60 **wMA,** A bed of trailing arbutus, a patch of eye-brights, a log covered with green moss,—these all seem to be of my family kin. **1950** Gray-Fernald *Manual of Botany* 1294, *Euphrasia*. . . *Eyebright.* **1959** Anderson *Flora AK* 422, *Euphrasia*. . . The species are known as Eyebright.

2 A **bluet 2** (here: *Houstonia caerulea*).

1894 *Jrl. Amer. Folkl.* 7.90 **wME, ceMA,** *Houstonia cærulea* . . eye-bright. **1928** Chapman *Happy Mt.* 311 **seTN,** *Eyebright*—a mountain flower known also as bluet or "Innocence"; of the madder family *(Houstonia cærulia).* **1940** Clute *Amer. Plant Names* 53.

3 also *eyeballs, eyebalm, eyeroot:* **=goldenseal 1. chiefly S Midl**

1830 Rafinesque *Med. Flora* 251, *Hydrastis canadensis*. . . *Vulgar Names*—Yellowroot, . . Eyebalm, &c. [*Ibid* 253, This plant is much used in Ohio, Kentucky, &c. for diseases of the eyes, the juice or an infusion are [sic] used as a wash, in sore or inflamed eyes.] **1876** Hobbs *Bot. Hdbk.* 35, Eye balm. . . Eye root, Goldenseal, Hydrastis Canadensis. **1933** *Jrl. Amer. Folkl.* 46.2 **Ozarks,** A weed called eye-bright is used for all minor eye trouble. **1968** *Foxfire* Summer 15 **nGA,** Its sometimes use as an eyewash gives it [=goldenseal] such names as eye-root and eye-balls. **1971** Krochmal *Appalachia Med. Plants* 144, *Hydrastis canadensis*. . . Common names: Goldenseal, eyebalm, eye-bright, eyeroot.

4 An **Indian tobacco** (here: *Lobelia inflata*).

1837 Darlington *Flora Cestrica* 15, *Inflated Lobelia. Vulgò*—Eye-bright. Indian Tobacco. **1876** Hobbs *Bot. Hdbk.* 35, Eyebright, Lobelia, Lobelia inflata. **1911** Henkel *Amer. Med. Leaves* 35, *Lobelia inflata*. . . Indian tobacco, . . eyebright. **1949** Moldenke *Amer. Wild Flowers* 244, Of interest because of its narcotic-poisonous juice is the *indian-tobacco,* . . also known as *gagroot, eyebright,* and *wild-tobacco.* **1971** Krochmal *Appalachia Med. Plants* 164, *Lobelia inflata*. . . Common names: Indian tobacco, . . eyebright.

5 also *eyebane:* A **spurge,** usu either *Euphorbia maculata* or *E. hyssopifolia.*

1876 Hobbs *Bot. Hdbk.* 35, Eyebright, Euphorbia hypericifolia. **1892** (1974) Millspaugh *Amer. Med. Plants* 147, *Euphorbia hypericifolia*. . . Com[mon] Names . . Spotted Eyebright. **1933** Small *Manual*

SE Flora 796, *C. hyssopifolia*. . . Eye-bane. **1950** Gray–Fernald *Manual of Botany* 972, *E. maculata*. . . Eyebane. **1970** Correll *Plants TX* 974, *Euphorbia nutans*. . . Eyebane.

6 A **rose pink** (here: *Sabatia angularis*).

1876 Hobbs *Bot. Hdbk.* 35, Eyebright, American centaury, Sabbatia [sic] angularis.

7 A **sundew** (here: *Drosera rotundifolia*).

1892 *Jrl. Amer. Folkl.* 5.92 **NH,** *Drosera rotundifolia*, eye-bright. **1959** Carleton *Index Herb. Plants* 43, *Eyebright* . . Drosera rotundifolia; [etc].

8 **=Indian pipe.**

[**1830** Rafinesque *Med. Flora* 2.243, *Monotropa uniflora*. . . Juice mixt with water deemed specific lotion for sore eyes.] **1900** Lyons *Plant Names* 252, *M[onotropa] uniflora*. . . Eye-bright. **1940** Clute *Amer. Plant Names* 42, *Monotropa uniflora*. . . Eye-bright.

9 A **speedwell** (here: *Veronica chamaedrys*).

1900 Lyons *Plant Names* 391, *V. Chamaedrys*. . . Eye-bright. **1940** Clute *Amer. Plant Names* 33, *Germander Speedwell*. . . Eyebright. **1959** Carleton *Index Herb. Plants* 43, *Eyebright* . . Veronica chamaedrys.

10 **=scarlet pimpernel.**

1959 Carleton *Index Herb. Plants* 43, *Eyebright:* Anagallis arvensis.

11 A **monkey flower** (here: *Mimulus moschatus*).

1959 Carleton *Index Herb. Plants* 43, *Eyebright* . . Mimulus moschatus.

12 A **forget-me-not 1a** (here: *Myosotis laxa*).

1959 Carleton *Index Herb. Plants* 43, *Eyebright* . . Myosotis laxa.

13 A **blue-eyed grass 1** (here: *Sisyrinchium angustifolium*).

1973 Hitchcock–Cronquist *Flora Pacific NW* 698, Blue-eyed grass, blue star, eye-bright. . . *S. angustifolium*.

eye cap See **eye** n[1] **1**

eye crutches n

1966 *DARE* (Qu. X23, . . *Joking words* . . *for eyeglasses*) Inf **OK**18, Eye crutches.

eye-drop n Also *eye-drops, eye-dropping(s)* **chiefly Nth**

In marble play:

a A shot in which a player attempts to strike his opponent's marble by dropping his shooter from the height of his eye; a game in which this kind of shot is used.

1958 *PADS* 29.33 **WI,** *Eye-drops*. **1966–69** *DARE* (Qu. EE7, . . *Kinds of marble games*) Inf **FL**37, Eye-dropping; **NY**209, Eye-droppings—hold shooter at eye and drop it straight down; **MI**89, Eye-drops; **NJ**22, Pigtail [or] eye-drop on the pigtail. Put three marbles down in [a] circle. Place one marble on top of the three. Stand up. Hold one marble up to the eye. Drop it. Any marbles knocked out of the circle, you win. **1968** *DARE* Tape **IA**27, [In] eye-drops you get it like that [=place the marble at the height of your eye] and then you go like that [=drop the marble on your opponent's marble]. **1973** Ferretti *Marble Book* 44 **seNY,** *Eye drops*. Dropping a shooter directly down on an object marble. A "luck" shot.

b See quot.

c1970 Wiersma *Marbles Terms* **Pacific NW** (as of 1931), Eye drop . . The marble is dropped onto other marbles, rather than being shot, from a point as far above the circle as it lay away.

eye-drops exclam Also *eye droppers, ~ droppings, high droppers*

In marble play: a call allowing a player to shoot an **eye-drop.**

1935 *AmSp* 10.159 **seNE,** *Eye-droppin's*. Saying this permits the player to drop his *shooter* vertically from the eye in an attempt to hit his opponent's *shooter*. **1958** *PADS* 29.33 **WI,** *Eye-drops*. . . A call claiming the right to a shot: the player holds his marble directly below his eye, sights straight down at the opponent's marble, and drops his in the attempt to hit it. **1962** *PADS* 37.2 **cKS,** *High-droppers*. A call used to claim the advantage of dropping one's marble on his opponent's. (Sometimes called *eye-droppers*.) **1968** *DARE* Tape **IA**27, And you can say "eye-drops" and "toe-drops."

eye fly n [Because it attacks the eyes of cattle] Cf **nose fly**

=face fly.

1967–68 *DARE* (Qu. R12, . . *Other kinds of flies*) Inf **CT**17, Eye flies (recent); **MO**5, Eye fly—a fly on cattle's eyes now; **OH**56, Eye flies [FW: like face flies]; **TN**6, Eye fly.

eye grass n *obs*

=yellow-eyed grass.

1830 Rafinesque *Med. Flora* 2.276, *Xyris*, L. *Eyegrass*. . . Roots and leaves used against lepra and diseases of the skin.

eye hoe n [*eye* hole]

See quot 1949.

1941 Perry *Hold Autumn* 77 **TX,** She could still eat more than a big man, and chop sprouts with an eye hoe along with the best hoe hand. **1949** *PADS* 11.6 **wTX** (as of c1920), *Eye-hoe*. . . A hoe whose blade has a hole in it for the insertion of a handle. **1965–68** *DARE* (Qu. L35, *Hand tools used for cutting underbrush and digging out roots*) Infs **OK**14, **TX**51, Eye hoe. **1986** Pederson *LAGS Concordance*, 1 inf, **cAL,** Eye hoe; 1 inf, **cwTN,** Earlier, hoecakes were made on an eye hoe.

eye hook See **eye** n[1] **1**

eye horse n Also *eye* [By metanalysis (cf Intro "Language Changes" I.2): *an eye horse* < *a nigh horse;* cf *OED eye* sb.[2], used for *nye*, a brood (of pheasants)]

=nigh horse.

1969 *DARE* (Qu. K32b, *The horse on the left side in plowing or hauling*) Inf **PA**178, Eye horse; **NY**155, Eye [ɔɪ].

eye hurt n

=strawberry blite.

1959 Carleton *Index Herb. Plants* 43, *Eye hurt:* Chenopodium capitatum (Blitum capitatum).

eye key See **eye** n[1] **1**

eyelasher n Cf **-er** affix **1, eyewink(er)**

1917 in 1944 *ADD* **sWV,** *Eye-lashers*. . . Eye-lashes.

eye lid-lifter, eye lift, eye lifter See **eye** n[1] **1**

eyelids, hang by one's v phr **NEast, esp NEng** *old-fash*

1 To be held in suspense; to be left untended or undecided; hence ppl adj phr *hung by the eyelids* left unfinished.

1780 in 1901 Clinton *Pub. Papers* 5.644 **NY,** So that the Vermont business still hangs by the Eyelids. **1792** in 1939 Morris *Diary* 2.366 **NY,** I find that no Decision was made down to the Evening of the ninth of January . . being in the whole eighteen Days that it had hung by the Eyelids. **1859** Smith *30 Yrs.* 454, Lettin' the whole country hang by the eye-lids—war and all. **1904** *DN* 2.426 **Cape Cod MA** (as of a1857), *Hung by the eyelids*. . . Unfinished.

2 also *hold on by one's eyelids, hang by one's eyelashes:* To be in a perilous situation.

[**1840** (1841) Dana *2 Yrs.* 61 **MA,** I tarred down all the head-stays, but found the rigging about the jib-booms, martingale, and spritsail yard . . the hardest. Here you have to hang on with your eye-lids and tar with your hands. *Ibid* 227, The fore royal [=a sail] . . fell to my lot . . [and] I found my hands full . . especially as there were no jacks [=crosstrees at the masthead] to the ship . . and nothing left for Jack [=a sailor] to hold on by, but his eyelids.] **1877** Fields *Underbrush* 11 **Boston MA,** I came by accident upon a magic quarto, shabby enough in its exterior, with one of the covers hanging by the eyelids, and otherwise sadly battered. **1945** Colcord *Sea Language* 72 **ME, Cape Cod, Long Island,** *Eyelids, hanging* or *holding on by the*. The seaman's vivid description of his situation aloft during a heavy gale. It has been adopted by landspeople to characterize any precarious situation. **1961** Cole *Idioms New Engl.* 36 (as of c1900), To hang by one's eyelashes.

eye-opener n Cf **eyeballing**

1968 Adams *Western Words* 107, *Eye openers*—Small sticks used to prop open the eyes of cattle. Eye openers had the same purpose as the practice of *eyeballing*.

eyereach n

An expanse of country which extends as far as the eye can see.

1903 (1950) Austin *Land of Little Rain* Pl. 22 **neCA,** Sagebrush . . is found only on . . open country, great space of pale sky, what the inhabitants call, "eye-reach," mountains hanging on the horizon in opalescent haze.

eyeroot See **eyebright 3**

eyes n [*EDD eye* sb.[1] 10] **chiefly Sth, S Midl**

Eyeglasses.

1965–70 *DARE* (Qu. X23, . . *Joking words* . . *for eyeglasses*) 10 Infs, **chiefly Sth, S Midl,** Eyes; **AL**8, **MS**86, **MO**14, **NC**68, **OH**90, **OK**42, My eyes.

eyes exclam
=eye-drops.
1987 *DARE* File **ceWI** (as of 1958), The call *eyes* was used to claim the right to drop your marble onto your opponent's marble from eye level. The call *no eyes* was used to prevent this privilege from being claimed.

eyeseed n [*OED, EDD*] Cf **eyestone 1**
A seed which, when put in the eye, is said to remove foreign matter.
1912 Green *VA Folk-Speech* 168, *Eye-stone*. . . Flax-seeds will do it [=remove foreign bodies from the eye] by mucilage formed. *Eye-seeds.*

eye seers See **seers**

eye-servant n [*OED eye-servant* →1832; cf Ephesians 6:5–6]
One who works adequately only when watched; also *eye-service* work poorly done.
1967 *DARE* (Qu. II20a, *A person who tries too hard to gain somebody else's favor*) Inf **LA8**, Eye-servant—if he works only when the boss is around. **1976** Rose *Doc. Hist. Slavery* 254, The phrase for work badly done in cases where an individual laborer's responsibility could not be readily discerned was "eye service," indicating that a particular slave performed well only so long as he or she was closely watched.

eyesies n Cf **bombsie(s)**
=eye-drop a.
c1970 Wiersma *Marbles Terms* **swMI** (as of 1973), *Eyesies*. . . Just like bombsies . . but drop marble right from eye. Helps to sight it better.

eyesight n [Perh malaprop or folk-etym for *inset* or *insert*]
1970 *DARE* (QR, near Qu. X23) Inf **FL48**, I got eyesights in my glasses. [FW: Inf refers to the insets in his bifocals.]

eyes in the breeches exclam [Perh *eye* hole or aperture] Cf *DS* W24b
1957 Battaglia *Resp. to PADS 20* **eMD,** *(Expressions . . of warning for a tear in the pants)* Eyes in the breeches.

eye stitcher n Also *eye stinger, ~ taker* [See quot 1950] **WI** Cf **ear sewer 1, snyder**
A **dragonfly.**
1950 *WELS (Other names for the dragonfly)* 1 Inf, **csWI,** Eye stinger; 1 Inf, **csWI,** Eye taker; [1 Inf, **cwWI,** Devil's darning needle—will sew your eyes shut if you don't behave.] **1950** *WELS Suppl.* **ceWI,** Eye stinger—dragonfly. **1968** *DARE* (Qu. R2, . . *Other names . . for the dragonfly*) Inf **WI48**, Eye stitcher.

eyestone n
1 A small piece of calcareous material used to absorb and remove foreign particles from the eye. Cf **eyeseed**
1866 (1881) Whitney *Leslie Goldthwaite* 35 **NEng,** If you don't do something quick, the cinder will get so bedded in . . that a dozen eyestones wouldn't draw it out. . . [She] produced the wonderfully chalky morsel. . . "Wet it in your own mouth". . . Then one thumb and finger was held to take it again, while the other made a sudden pinch at the lower eyelid, and, drawing it at the outer corner before it could so much as quiver away again, the little white stone was slid safely under. **1912** Green *VA Folk-Speech* 168, *Eye-stone*. . . A small body put into the eye to remove foreign bodies from the eye. **1926** Cady *Rhymes VT* 177, Our cupbord [sic] had a draw beneath / For twisted strings that dealt with teeth; / The fambly pincers, too, was there. . . And in the right hand corner lay / The eyestones that are mine today. **1947** (1964) Randolph *Ozark Superstitions* 140, One man told me that he had seen several of these eyestones, and that they looked like opals. You just wet the stone and slip it under the eyelid; in a few minutes it is supposed to draw any foreign substance out of the eye. **1968** *Yankee* Dec 46 **RI,** *Dear Oracle:* I have two eye-stones which were used years ago to put in your eyes to get out particles. A friend had them for 25 years and says they are still "alive" . . [because] she put them in a shallow dish with a little vinegar and water and bubbles came and they moved across the dish. . . *Answer:* "Eye-stones." From the shell of a small marine critter. Folks slipped 'em into an eye to remove dirt or other objects. . . We wouldn't bet they are still alive, but they'll work just the same.
2 An otolith from a fish such as the **freshwater drum.** Cf **jewelhead**
1927 *Jrl. Amer. Folkl.* 40.308 **PA,** Wearing the eye stones of fish in a bag around the neck as a protection against cramps in swimming is also easily understandable.

eye taker See **eye stitcher**

Eyetalian, Eyetallion See **Italian**

eyeteeth n pl
1 One's prized possessions—usu in phrr *to give* (or *bet, lose,* etc) *one's eyeteeth.*
1844 Stephens *High Life in NY* 1.190 **CT,** They talk about the Yankees having a nack of cheating people out of their eye teeth. **1856** Durivage *Three* 195 (Taylor–Whiting *Dict. Amer. Proverbs*), You'd hev' a fellur's eye teeth afore he knowed it, ef you wanted 'em. **1946** McAtee *Dial. Grant Co. IN Suppl. 3* 4, Eye-teeth. . . "He would give his eye-teeth to get Mary." **1955** Funk *Heavens to Betsy* 189, *To be skinned out of one's eyeteeth*—To be right royally hornswoggled, bamboozled or flim-flammed, that is, cheated or deceived. . . Whereas . . "to cut one's eye-teeth" indicates that one has reached . . years of discretion, . . "to be skinned out of one's eyeteeth" . . conveys the reverse impression, to be duped, to be made a fool. **c1960** *Wilson Coll.* **csKY,** *Eye-teeth*. . . A symbol of one's prized possession. "He'd give his eye-teeth for a buggy like that." **1966–69** *DARE* (Qu. HH22c, . . *"He's mean enough to ______."*) Inf **MN15**, Steal his grandmother's eyeteeth; (Qu. JJ20, . . *"I'm so sure, I'd ______."*) Infs **AR51**, **KY17**, Bet my eyeteeth (on that); **CA170**, Give my eyeteeth; (Qu. U39, *Somebody who has lost all his money: "During the Depression he ______."*) Inf **CO20**, Lost his mint, lost his eyeteeth; **MI18**, Lost his eyeteeth.
2 See quot. [Prob by confusion]
1968 *DARE* (Qu. X12, . . *Large front teeth that stick out of the mouth*) Infs **DE5**, **OH53**, Eyeteeth.

eyeteeth, cut one's v phr Also *have one's eyeteeth* (*cut* or *sharpened*); rarely *cut one's eyetooth* [Because the eyeteeth develop late and are therefore a sign of presumed maturity; cf quot 1948] **esp NEng** Cf **baby teeth, shed one's**
To reach (or have reached) the age by which maturity, experience, or shrewdness should have been gained.
1770 in 1931 Johnson *Papers* 7.670 **NYC,** His Lordship . . must have his Eye teeth & be a good State pilot in the Bargain. **1782** in 1874 Lee *Papers* 4.25 **VA,** He seems a sensible . . young man, and upon my word (according to the vulgar saying) he seems to have all his eye teeth about him. **1812** Paulding *Diverting Hist.* 96 **NEng,** He who gets the better of them in the way of bargaining, must have his eye teeth cut, and rise before day, I can tell him. **1843** (1846) Haliburton *Attaché* (1st ser) 2.142 **NEng,** They was men that had cut their eye-teeth, and that you couldn't pull the wool over their eyes. **1844** Haliburton *Attaché* (2d ser) 1.283 **NEng,** I warn't born yesterday, and I had my eye-teeth sharpened before your'n were through the gums. **1848** in 1935 *AmSp* 10.41 **Nantucket MA,** *Cut (one's) eye teeth*. . . *He has cut his eye teeth.* He is keen. **1853** Simms *Sword & Distaff* 214 **SC,** That won't be axing whether he's cut his eye-tooth or not. **1948** Funk *Hog on Ice* 185, *To cut one's eyeteeth*. . . The expression is somewhat literal, for the implication is that by the time a person has got his permanent set of canine teeth, has reached the age of twelve or fourteen, he has passed out of babyhood and has reached years of discretion.

Eyetie See **Itie**

eyewater n [Cf *OED eyewater* sb. d "gin"]
Liquor, esp illegal whiskey.
1940 *AmSp* 15.447 **TN,** *Eye water.* Liquor. "Eye water's more plentiful in Jackson County now than common." **1969** *DARE* (Qu. DD21c, . . *Illegally made whiskey*) Inf **GA72**, Thomson's eyewater. **1977** *AmSp* 52.115 **nGA,** Whiskey: . . devil's eye water.

Eyeway See **Iowa**

eyewink(er) n [Scots *eewink(er)* eyelash; *SND* 1808 → (at *ee* n., v.[1] 4)] **esp Midl**
An eyelash.
1872 Twain *Roughing It* 329 **MO,** One ear was sot back on his neck, 'n' his tail was stove up, 'n' his eye-winkers was swinged off. **1874** Clark *Out Hurly-Burly* 311 **DE,** I would prefer a Pitman without an eye-winker, or fuzz enough on him to make a camel's-hair pencil. **1896** Bergen *Current Superstitions* 66 **ME,** Put an eyewinker down inside your clothes, wish, and you'll get your wish. *Ibid* 67 **nwMA,** Put an eyewinker on the back of the hand, knock that hand with the other so as to throw the eyewinker over the shoulder, and at the same time wish. If the eyewinker is not seen again, the wish will come true. **1899** (1912) Green *VA Folk-Speech* 168, *Eyewinker*. . . An eyelash. **1903** *DN* 2.313 **seMO,** *Eye-winker*. . . Eyelash. **1906** *DN* 3.118 **sIN,** *Eye-winker.*

1909 *DN* 3.395 **nwAR,** *Eye-winker. . .* "He got his eye-winkers scringed off." **1916** Howells *Leatherwood God* 19 **OH,** He never moved a eye-winker. **1932** Randolph *Ozark Mt. Folks* 56, I've saw fellers pick up a pen keerless-like an' draw a bird afore you could bat a eyewinker. **1967–68** *DARE* (Qu. KK3a, . . *The perfect condition . . "It's done to ______."*) Inf **OH**72, A gnat's eyewinker; (Qu. KK50, . . *Down to the last detail*) Inf **WY**2, Down to a gnat's eyewink. **1978** *DARE* File **cnMA** (as of 1920), Eyewinker—this was the term I first learned for eyelash.

ey God See **i** prep

Eytie See **Itie**

ez See **as**

(e)zackly, ezactly, ez(z)actly See **exactly**

F

fa n [Abbr for *father* prob infl by *pa*] Cf **faddy, fafa**

1941 *LANE* Map 371 *(Dad, Pa)* 1 inf, **seNH,** [fa˂·], an older term of address.

faateman See **fattigmanns bakkels**

fabuh See **favor** n, v

faby bean n [Var of *faba;* cf **-y**]

The broad bean or faba bean *(Vicia faba).*

1969 *DARE* (Qu. I4, *What vegetables are less commonly grown around here?*) Inf **NY**216, Faby ['febi] beans.

fac See **fact A1**

face n

1 One's mouth—esp in phrr *shoot one's face, shut ~, feed ~.* Cf **head** n **B2**

1896 Crane *Maggie* 73 **NYC,** Shet yer face, an' come home, yeh old fool! **1896** (1898) Ade *Artie* 26 **Chicago IL,** If you open your face to this lady again to-night I'll separate you from your breath. **1917** Sinclair *King Coal* 200 **CO,** The marshal bade him "shut his face," and emphasised [sic] the command by a twist at his coat-collar. **1935** Sandoz *Jules* 365 **wNE** (as of 1880–1930), Oh, you just talk to hear your face go. **c1960** *Wilson Coll.* **csKY,** *Feed (one's) face. . .* Eat unmannerly, use rough manners, make unpleasant noises. **1965–70** *DARE* (Qu. X9, . . *"I wish he'd shut his ______ ."*) 12 Infs, **scattered,** Face; (Qu. II22, *Expressions to tell somebody to . . mind his own business*) Inf **CA**120, Shut your face; (Qu. HH7b, *Someone who talks too much, or too loud: "He's always ______ ."*) 13 Infs, **scattered,** Shooting (off) his face; (Qu. KK11, *To make . . a big fuss about something: "When we asked him to do that, he ______ ."*) Inf **ME**1, Just shot his face off; (Qu. H9, *If somebody always eats a considerable amount of food*) Inf **NY**88, Feeds his face; (Qu. H11a, *If somebody eats rapidly and noisily*) Inf **NY**92, Stuffs his face. **1979** Stegner *Recapitulation* 163 **UT,** How about just unostentatiously keeping your face shut?

2 Presence, immediate vicinity; sight—esp in phr *get out of one's face. esp freq among Black speakers*

1931 *PMLA* 46.1307 **sAppalachians,** Git out o' my face, or I'll slap ye into the middle of next week! **1942** *Amer. Mercury* 55.223.88 **Harlem NYC** [Black], Git out of my face, Jelly! **1965–70** *DARE* (Qu. II22, *Expressions to tell somebody to . . mind his own business*) Infs **AL**62, **GA**92, **MS**62, **NC**72, Get out of my face; **SC**10, Come out my face. [4 of 5 Infs Black]

3 Cheek, brazenness. [*OED face* sb. 7 1537 →]

1851 Burke *Polly Peablossom* 149 **MS,** How can you have the face to talk to me, arter saying what you sed? **1887** *The Lantern* 29 Jan 2/2 (*AmSp* 25.32) **New Orleans LA,** He has the face to think he's a masher. **1968** *DARE* (Qu. GG5, *When someone does something unexpectedly bold or forward, you might say: "Well, she certainly has a lot of ______ ."*) Inf **MN**38, Face.

4 In turpentine production: the cut surface of a tree, from which resin exudes; less freq, the surface which is to be cut.

1859 Perry *Turpentine Farming* 39, As the face goes up, we know the pines get smaller, and leave less of the natural surface to cut. *Ibid* 41, The faces of the pines with one box, after a few years, were much shorter, the trees were more thrifty, and the extremities sounder than the rest. **1935** Hurston *Mules & Men* 219 **FL,** [Footnote:] 10,000 "faces" in the turpentine woods, i.e. tree trunks that have been cut on one side to make the sap run from which turpentine is made. **1939** FWP *Guide FL* 378, The part of the tree to be cut is called the 'face.' **1941** *AmSp* 16.237 **GA,** When the *faces* are near the ground, a V-shaped instrument is used. . . The average turpentine farm consists of about eight *crops* or working units. A crop consists of 10,000 *faces.* **1968** *DARE* Tape **GA**23, In October you go by and you scrape all these faces off.

5 In logging:

a See quot.

1956 Sorden-Ebert *Logger's Words* 14 **Gt Lakes,** *Face,* The side of a load of logs on which it is loaded [i.e., logs are being added].

b See quot.

1958 McCulloch *Woods Words* 59 **Pacific NW,** *Face. . .* The front edge of a stand of timber.

6 See quots.

1944 *Hench Coll.* **cVA,** *Face*—The top layer of apples in an apple basket. **1961** *Ibid* **cVA,** *Face*—The top layer of fruit in a basket.

7 See **facer.**

8 A blossom of the **catalpa B1.** [From its appearance; see **catalpa** etym]

1965 *DARE* File **Milwaukee WI** (as of 1915), Faces—fallen catalpa flowers. Children's use.

face v

1 In packing fruit: to put the best-looking pieces in the top and bottom layers of the box or barrel; hence ppl adj *faced.* Cf **deacon** v **2, facer**

1903 *DN* 2.351 **neOH,** *Faced. . .* Of a basket of fruit, so packed as to make the best appearance, as with a layer of larger or finer fruit on top. **1905** *DN* 3.78 **nwAR,** The best apples, used to 'face' the tops and bottoms of barrels.

2 In logging: to cut out a slab preparatory to felling the tree.

1968 *DARE* Tape **NH**14, The next thing you do you face it, . . make your notch.

face board n Also *facer board* [*face* outer or finished surface; perh also infl by *baseboard*]

A baseboard.

1965–69 *DARE* (Qu. D37) Infs **IL**83, 84, Face board; **MS**55, Facer board.

face bowl n

A small wash basin.

1967 *DARE* File **HI,** [In a museum display:] Face bowl. **1977** *Ibid* **cnMA** (as of c1915), My grandmother (born in 1853 in southern New Hampshire, her mother from Cornwall, England) sometimes let us wash our hands in the face bowl kept in the kitchen. Called a basin by other people, the face bowl was considerably smaller than the regular Victorian wash bowl that came with matching pitcher; it probably held about a quart of water. **1985** *Ibid* **eTX,** The term is common here among blacks, "here" meaning East Texas. . . A west Texas faculty member in her 50's tells me that the *face bowl* was a pan, often white, used to wash the face. **1988** *NADS Letters* **seMI,** *Face bowl*—one black student from River Rouge . . says that she uses the term when she visits her grandmother, who lives in River Rouge.

face, buy on one's See **face, run one's**

facecloth n Also *facerag* **chiefly NEast, Sth**

A washcloth.

1902 (1969) Sears *Catalogue* 865, Unbleached Turkish Face Cloths. . . Size, 8 x 9½ inches. **1934** *AmSp* 9.267 **Upper MW,** [Resulting from] the tendency to use . . euphemisms . . *wash rag* becomes . . *face cloth.* **1939** *LANE* Map 141 **throughout NEng,** [*Face cloth* occurs frequently; *face rag* is common, but occurs less frequently.]

1965–70 *DARE* (Qu. G17, *Other kinds of towels*) Infs **FL**27, **GA**92, **NY**105, **RI**5, **MA**18, Facecloth; **FL**19, **PA**167, **SC**22, 42, 62, Facecloth = washcloth; **FL**18, Facecloth = bathcloth; **LA**23, Facecloth = washrag; **NH**6, Facecloth—not a towel; **NY**81, Facecloth—something to wash [your] face with; **SC**29, Facerag = washrag; a square one. **1966** *DARE* FW Addit **SC,** Facerag—a washcloth. **1967** LeCompte *Word Atlas* 146 **seLA,** Face cloth. [Used by 2 of 21 infs.] **1970** Tarpley *Blinky* 92 **neTX,** Face cloth [rare]. **1971** Bright *Word Geog. CA & NV* 155, *Face cloth* 10% [of 300 infs] . . *face rag* 4%. **1981** *NYT Mag.* 9 Aug 6/3 **RI,** We wash ourselves with facecloths, not washcloths.

faced See **face v 1**

faced camp See **half-faced camp**

face fly n [See quots 1964, 1980] **chiefly Nth, N Midl, esp N Cent** *chiefly rural* Cf **back fly, ear ~, nose ~**

An introduced fly *(Musca autumnalis).*

1964 Borror-DeLong *Intro. Insects* 503, The face fly, *Músca autumnàlis* . . , an important pest of cattle in the East and Midwest, gets its name from its habit of clustering on the face of cattle. **1965–70** *DARE* (Qu. R12) 60 Infs, **chiefly Nth, N Midl, esp N Cent,** Face fly; (Qu. R10) Inf **VA**7, Face fly; (Qu. R11) Inf **NC**35, Face fly. [Of all Infs responding to Qu. R12, 33% were comm type 5; of those giving this response, 77% were comm type 5.] **1967** *Hooker Co. Tribune* (Mullen NE) 28 Sept 4/4, [Advt:] Keep Your Cattle Feeding Instead of Fighting Flies! . . BRICON is deadly to Hornflies and Faceflies. **1970** *Sci. News* 30 May 532, A serious problem in the United States is the face fly, which breeds on cattle dung, then attacks the eyes of cattle. **1980** Milne-Milne *Audubon Field Guide Insects* 682, The larger and darker Face Fly . . resembles the House Fly but settles on cow rather than horse manure. It creeps into the nostrils and eyes of cattle and into horse fly wounds.

face, go on one's See **face, run one's**

face hurts, one's phr *joc*

1896 *DN* 1.416 **MD,** His face hurt him = he blushed.

face-lifting n [In allusion to the cosmetic procedure]

A hard blow to the face.

1968 *DARE* (Qu. Y11, . . *"You should have seen Bill go down. Joe really hit him a _______."*) Inf **PA**164, Face-lifting.

face log n Cf **face n 5**

In logging: see quot 1905.

1905 U.S. Forest Serv. *Bulletin* 61.39, *Head log.* . . The front bottom log on a skidway. (N[orthern] F[orest].) Syn.: face log. **1956** Sorden-Ebert *Logger's Words* 18 **Gt Lakes,** Head-log. . . Same as face-log.

face on adv phr

Head on.

1970 *DARE* (Qu. KK53, . . *"He ran ______ into a car."*) Inf **VA**46, Face on.

facer n Also *face* Cf **deacon v 2, face v 1**

In packing fruit: a good-looking piece of fruit placed in the top layer of a basket; a device for forming such a layer of fruit; a packer who places the best fruit in the top layer.

1905 *DN* 3.78 **nwAR,** Those apples will make good faces. **1940** *Hench Coll.* **VA,** *Facer* may refer to each apple in the top layer of a basket or barrel. It may also refer to that skilled packer who places the *facers* in an orderly layer before the other apples are piled on top and then the whole turned right side up. **1941** Writers' Program *Guide AR* 240, These workers select the most handsome peaches for use as "facers", which are placed in baskets atop orchard-run fruit. **1943** *AmSp* 18.75 **WI,** *Facer,* a sort of metal basin with a vertical flange of the same diameter as the top of a bushel basket. Into this are put carefully the apples which will appear on top when the customer sees the basket. These are, of course, the best looking, and are also called *facers.*

facerag See **facecloth**

facer board n [*facer* that which acts as a *face* or finished surface]

1 See **face board.**

2 A **clapboard B.**

1971 *AmSp* 46.170 **Chicago IL,** 'Protective boarded covering on the sides—not the roof—of a house': . . *facerboards.* [1 inf]

face, run one's v phr Also *buy (or go, travel) on one's face* *somewhat old-fash*

To gain credit on the basis of one's wits or appearance.

1839 *Spirit of Times* 5 Oct 368/3, The Picayune says there is a chap in New Orleans who has "run his face so often for drinks, that it is completely worn off." **1859** *Yale Lit. Mag.* 60 (1912 Thornton *Amer. Gloss.*), If you have not a ready tongue, and cannot travel upon your face, you had better, &c. **1870** Fowler *Wall St.* 237 **NY,** I had to get the hack-man to trust me, and 'ran my face' for a dinner that day. **1905** *DN* 3.17 **cCT,** *Run one's face.* **1907** *DN* 3.216 **nwAR,** *Run one's face.* **1908** *DN* 3.316 **eAL, wGA,** *Go on one's face.* . . To go free or on credit. **1942** McAtee *Dial. Grant Co. IN* 53 (as of 1890s), *Run one's face* . . use one's credit, buy on tick. **1965–70** *DARE* (Qu. U11, *If you buy something but don't pay cash for it, you might say, "I _______."*) Infs **AR**55, **IA**30, **MO**5, **PA**115, **TX**1, Run my face (for it); **MI**107, **OR**5, **TX**35, Ran my face; **VA**6, Bought it on my face. [7 of 9 Infs old]

facet See **faucet A1**

face tag n Cf **last tag, line ~**

A children's game of tag.

1901 *DN* 2.139 **cNY,** *Face tag.* . . The name of a game; the same as *last tag.* **1957** *Sat. Eve. Post Letters* **csMN** (as of c1895), When I was a child . . we called the games we played by these names: . . Face tag. **1969** *DARE* (Qu. EE33, . . *Outdoor games*) Inf **RI**12, Face tag. Fellow that's "it" turns around, crowd starts moving.

face, travel on one's See **face, run one's**

face up v phr

To keep one's chin up, be brave, cheerful.

1970 *DARE* (Qu. GG27a, *To get somebody out of an unhappy mood, you might say to him, "Everything's going to be all right, so ________."*) Inf **VA**101, Face up.

face wall n Cf **balanced wall, double stone wall**

A stone wall finished on one side with cut pieces of stone.

1934 *Hanley Disks* **seCT,** The face wall's got a face to it. . . It's built on one side, so to speak, and a balance wall is built on the middle and let your ends go where they will.

fâché adj |ˌfɑˈše| Pronc-sp *fawché* [Fr] **LA**

Angry.

1850 Garrard *Wah-to-yah* 242 **SW,** I tellee, this hos was fawché. **1967** LeCompte *Word Atlas* 344 **seLA,** [4 of 21 infs offered *fâchét* [sic] for 'angry'.] **1968** *DARE* (Qu. GG40, *Words . . meaning violently angry*) Inf **LA**32, Fâché [ˌfɑˈše]—used by English speakers.

facing bench n Also *facing seat*

Among Quakers: see quots.

1933 *AmSp* 8.1.13 **Philadelphia PA,** *The Facing-seats.* The two or three rows in the front of the Meeting-house, facing the congregation. In these seats sit the elders. **1940** Weygandt *Down Jersey* 305 **sNJ,** A man who in later years sat on the "facing bench" and preached in meeting. **1944** *PADS* 2.33 **NC,** *Facing bench.* . . The bench placed at the front of the Quaker church overlooking the assembly. The occupants of the facing bench face the audience. **1967** *DARE* (Qu. CC5, *Names for seats in a church, especially near the front*) Inf **PA**49, In Quaker Meeting House, the Elders sit on a facing seat.

fact n, v

A Forms.

1 pronc-spp *fac(k), fak.* [Scots dial, 1836 →; cf *EDD, SND*] **chiefly S Midl** Note: Among Black and some White speakers, this may be of independent formation rather than Scots origin. Cf Pronc Intro 3.I.22

1862 (1864) Browne *Artemus Ward Book* 64, In fack, Oberlin *is* the college. **1864** Sargent *Peculiar* 110 **VA,** The fak is, I'm in fur a hahnd at euchre. **1894** Riley *Armazindy* 7 **IN,** That-air fac' and nothin' less. **1899** (1912) Green *VA Folk-Speech* 168, *Fack.* . . A fact. **1908** *DN* 3.309 **eAL, wGA,** *Fac.* . . Fact. **1921** *DN* 5.118 **KY,** *Fer a fac'.* . . For a fact. **1937** *AmSp* 12.287 **wVA,** [fæks]. **1940** *AmSp* 15.47 **sAppalachians, Ozarks,** Almost as common is the dropping . . of a final letter, particularly of a final stop, usually a dental, especially when preceded by a stop: . . fack. **1941** Writers' Program SC *Folk Tales* 82, I know dat fo' a fac'.

2 pronc-sp *fect.*

1866 Lowell in 1944 *ADD* **NEng,** Our *fect* is only the O[ld] F[rench] *faict.*

B As noun.

See quot. [Ellip for *in fact, the fact is,* or similar phrr]

1831 in 1834 Smith *Life Jack Downing* 154 **ME,** But fact, after digging, and sawing, . . my patience got most wore out. **1899** Chesnutt *Conjure Woman* 23 **csNC** [Black], Fac', he got so biggity.

C As verb.

See quot.

1942 *Amer. Mercury* 55.223.95 **Harlem NYC** [Black], *I'm cracking but I'm facking*—"I'm wisecracking, but I'm telling the truth."

factory n, also attrib [Abbr for *factory cotton*] *old-fash* Cf **domestic 1**

See quots.

[1859 (1968) Bartlett *Americanisms* 140, *Factory cotton.* Unbleached cotton goods, of domestic manufacture.] **1896** *DN* 1.416 **IL, NY,** *Factory:* muslin. "Bleached factory." **1906** *Out West Mag.* Jan 50, The wagon waited under the maple trees by the door, its stout cover of unbleached "factory" bulging over the high curved hickory bows. **1907** *DN* 3.230 **nwAR,** *(Bleached) domestic*. . . Cotton cloth. . . It is a plain, smooth, bleached or unbleached cotton cloth, without any woven or printed design. Also called *factory.* **1910** *DN* 3.441 **wNY,** *Factory cloth*. . . Heavy muslin; sheeting. **1950** *WELS (Kinds of cloth commonly used for home sewing in your community)* 1 Inf, **cwWI,** Factory, chambray, pique, [etc]; 1 Inf, **seWI,** Factory cloth—[used] way back. **1953** Randolph *Down in Holler* 168 **Ozarks,** Maw made me a factory dress, an' dyed it yaller with hickory bark. **1982** Brooks *Quicksand* 261 **swUT** (as of c1922), She came home with a length of "Factory" long enough for a dress. . . This "Factory" was so named because it had been woven from local cotton into fabric at the local factory. It was a heavy piece—not as heavy as a wagon cover canvas—but heavier than most of the fabric which was used to line quilts. It was a rich cream, bordering on yellow, and had a sheen on the right side—a satin finish.

factory bean n

A bean grown for the canning factory.

1968 *DARE* (Qu. I20) Inf **DE**1, Factory beans are small beans that grow like bunch beans. They are less desirable than others, but are the chief commercial bean.

factory smoker n

A cheap cigar.

1968 *DARE* (Qu. DD7) Inf **WI**64, Factory smoker.

faculate v Cf **faculized, faculty** n

1889 (1971) Farmer *Americanisms* 232, *Faculate, To.*—A New England localism for to arrange; to put in order.

faculized adj Also *facultised* **[faculty** n**] chiefly NEng** *old-fash*

Versatile; endowed with many faculties or abilities.

1816 in 1819 Thomas *Travels W. Country* 118, This expression is a good match for that of "a well *faculized* person," so common in the eastern part of New-York state. **1871** (1882) Stowe *Fireside Stories* 53 **NEng,** She was one o' these 'ere facultised persons that has a gift for most any thing. **1882** (1971) Gibbons *PA Dutch* 51, New England women will not be willing to admit that they do not understand housework, and are not eminently "faculized." **1913** *DN* 4.56 **Cape Cod MA,** *Faculized* ['fækə͵laɪzd]. . . "Isn't she faculized? She can do anything she's o' mind to?" **1980** *DARE* File **Martha's Vineyard MA,** *Faculized,* meaning ingenious, or having all one's faculties alert and ready for any emergency, [is an example of words which are] all but extinct here but still linger with the elderly.

faculty n **chiefly NEng** *old-fash* Cf **faculized**

An ability to manage (esp domestic) situations; see quots.

1844 in 1847 Child *Letters from NY* 134, The want of self-reliance, and what in New-England is called "faculty" about common things, was partly to be attributed to Miss Adams's delicate health. **1859** Stowe *Minister's Wooing* 2 **RI,** She was . . said to have "faculty,"—a gift which . . commands more esteem than beauty, riches, learning, or any other worldly endowment. *Faculty* is Yankee for *savoir faire,* and the opposite virtue to shiftlessness. **1891** Cooke *Huckleberries* 4 **NEng,** "I'll see ef Potter faculty can't match Fyler grit," he muttered . . for the Potters had that trait which conquers the world far more surely and subtly than grit,—"faculty," *i.e.,* a clear head and a quick wit, and capacity of adaptation that wrests from circumstance its stringent sceptre, and is the talisman of what the world calls "luck." **1914** Furman *Sight* 38 **KY,** She were the smartest, most managing woman in these parts, and I never did have no faculty, and don't run her house like I ought. **1927** *AmSp* 3.134 **ME,** The New England contempt of lack of industry expresses itself in such locutions as having . . "no faculty."

faculty v Cf **feature** v **2**

To understand, comprehend.

1934 (1970) Wilson *Backwoods Amer.* 68 **Ozarks,** Henry can't faculty the workin' of them town telephones.

fad die exclam Also *had die* [See quots] **sAppalachians**

See quots.

1911 *DN* 3.538 **eKY,** *Fad die* = If I had to die, a phrase of asseveration; e.g., "*Fad die,* I'll do it." Also "had die." **1916** *DN* 4.297 **sAppalachians,** Words and phrases of asseveration, and "cuss"-words of Elizabethan England still survive. Among these we find . . "Fad die," . . (If I had to die!). **1931** *PMLA* 46.1309 **sAppalachians,** Fad die (if I had to die)!

faddy n [Alter of **father;** prob also infl by **daddy**] *old-fash* Cf **fa, fafa**

One's father.

1843 (1916) Hall *New Purchase* 258 **IN,** The landlady concluded that if I was *"faddywaddy,"* Aunt Kitty must be *"mammywammy."* **1905** *DN* 3.78 **nwAR,** *Faddy*. . . Diminutive form of *father*. . . 'Here's faddy and muddy!' Not uncommon.

fade v Freq with *away, out*

1 To leave a place; depart in haste; disappear.

1900 Ade *More Fables* 10, The Bookie told him to Back Up and Fade and do a Disappearing Specialty. **1932** *Atlantic Mth.* May 559, People are now apt to 'fade out' instead of departing. **1950** Lomax *Mr. Jelly Roll* 140 **LA,** Of course, nobody can go up against a knife in the hand of a man who know how to use it, but . . Coon Cant George . . walked in right then, pulled out that big .45 of his and the gentleman with the knife faded. **1966–68** *DARE* (Qu. Y19, . . *"It's about time for me to* _______.") Infs **MD**27, **MA**5, **TX**3, Fade away; (Qu. Y18, *To leave in a hurry: "Before they find this out, we'd better* _______*!"*) Inf **MA**5, Fade away; **MI**24, Fade out; (Qu. AA12, *If a man loses interest in a girl and stops seeing her, you'd say he* _______) Inf **MI**24, Faded out, pulled away, called it quits; **WI**52, Faded out. **1967** *DARE* Tape **TX**25, He . . keeps the steer from . . fading out from you, where you have a good jump at him.

2 To die. *joc, euphem*

1940 *AmSp* 15.447 **eTN,** *Fade.* To die. 'Aunt Mittie faded last night.' **1943** *LANE* Map 521 **Cape Cod MA,** Jocular or disrespectful synonyms of *died*. . . Faded out.

3 To take a nap.

1967 *DARE* (Qu. X41, *When you're going to sleep for a very short while, you might say, "I'm just going to* _______.") Inf **OR**4, Fade out.

faded midget n Also *midget faded rattlesnake*

A subsp of the **prairie rattlesnake** (here: *Crotalus viridis concolor*).

1968 Abbey *Desert Solitaire* 18 **seUT,** It is not after all the mighty diamondback, *Crotalus atrox,* I'm confronted with but a smaller species known locally as the horny rattler or more precisely as the Faded Midget. An insulting name for a rattlesnake, which may explain the Faded Midget's alleged bad temper. But the name is apt: he is small and dusty-looking, with a little knob above each eye—the horns. His bite though temporarily disabling would not likely kill a full-grown man in normal health. **1974** Shaw–Campbell *Snakes West* 235, The midget faded rattlesnake . . , found in eastern Utah, western Colorado, and the extreme southwest of Wyoming, seldom grows longer than two feet.

faded snake n [See quot 1974] **SW**

=glossy snake.

1930 OK Univ. Biol. Surv. *Pub.* 2.217, *Arizona elegans*. . . Faded Snake. (Western Oklahoma). **1947** Pickwell *Amphibians* 45, This genus has but one species, of which the representative in our region is . . the Western Glossy, or Western Faded, Snake. **[1974** Shaw–Campbell *Snakes West* 105, Adult glossy snakes. . . Their basic coloration is much like that of a gopher snake whose pattern has faded.]

fadedy adj Cf **flowerdy**

Somewhat faded.

1936 *AmSp* 11.355 **eTX,** Faded [sic] ['fedɪdɪ]. . . [In the] speech of East Texans who have been least influenced by school training.

fade out See **fade**

fader See **father** n

fady adj Also sp *fadey* Cf **fadedy**

Dull, faded.

1928 Chapman *Happy Mt.* 40 **seTN,** Before he [=a star] gets fadey with summer nights. **1955** Ritchie *Singing Family* 55 **seKY,** [The letter was] hard to read, too, yellow and fady.

fa-ence See **fence** n, v

fafa n [Alter of **father,** by analogy with *dada, papa*]
One's father.
1967 *DARE* (Qu. Z1) Inf **CA**6, Fafa.

fag n [Perh abbr for **faggot,** or perh an independent development from *fag* cigarette, through their early assoc with effeminacy; perh also assoc with Brit *fag* a public-school boy who acts as servant to an older boy] **scattered, but esp NY, PA, CA**
=**faggot.**
1923 (1927) Anderson *Hobo* 103, Fairies or Fags are men or boys who exploit sex for profit. **1927** *DN* 5.445 [Underworld jargon], *Fag.* **1932** Hemingway *Death in Afternoon* 448, Interested parties . . are continually proving that Leonardo da Vinci, Shakespeare, etc., were fags. **1934** *AmSp* 9.26 [Prison parlance], *Fag.* An effeminate man. **1957** Kerouac *On Road* 206, The car belonged to a tall, thin fag. **1965–70** *DARE* (Qq. HH38, 39) 16 Infs, **scattered, but esp NY, PA, CA,** Fag. [10 Infs young, 14 White, 14 male, 11 coll educ. Cf distrib of *DARE* Infs at **faggot.**] **1968** *DARE* Tape **NY**118A, Everybody played ball, and if you didn't play ball you were a fag. That was the classification. Either you played ball or you were a fag, and they really meant you were a fag.

fag v[1] [*OED fag* v. 6]
To beat, strike.
1834 *Life Andrew Jackson* 70, Fag him in the craw, hit him in the pudding bag. **1942** Berrey–Van den Bark *Amer. Slang* 322.5, *Beat; thrash* . . fag.

fag v[2] Also *fag along* [Prob from *fag* to tire] **chiefly West** Cf **fog** v[2] **1**
To move quickly; to depart hurriedly; hence vbl n *fagging.*
1920 Hunter *Trail Drivers TX* 300, Moving fast is "faggin'." **1933** (1950) Allen *Cowboy Lore* 58, *Faggin,* To get away from a place quick. **1942** *AmSp* 17.75 **NE,** A cowboy riding fast is *faggin' along.* **1942** Berrey–Van den Bark *Amer. Slang* 53.9, *Go Fast* . . fag, flicker (along). *Ibid* 58.6, *Depart Hurriedly* . . fag. **1960** Wentworth–Flexner *Slang* 176, *Fag along*—To ride fast. *Cowboy use. Still current.*

fagan n [Etym uncert, but cf **fergen**]
1968 McPhee *Pine Barrens* 45 **NJ,** Charcoal pits were actually above ground. They had the shape of beehives and were twenty feet high. . . The colliers dropped burning kindling into a hole in the top and then sealed it over. They poked holes in the sides with a stick called a fagan, and kept watch over the pit day and night.

faggart See **faggot**

fagging See **fag** v[2]

faggot n Also *faggart, faggy, fagot* [Perh from Engl dial *faggot* a term of abuse for a woman or child, transf to an effeminate or unmasculine man] **scattered, but esp NY, PA** *informal, freq derog* Cf **fag** n, **faggotty, faggy** adj Note: Both *fag* and *faggot* occurred occas in early 20th cent, but are now used esp freq in New York and Pennsylvania, chiefly by young speakers, most freq by well educ urban males. *Faggot* is more freq among Blacks, *fag* among Whites.
An effeminate or homosexual male.
1914 Jackson *Criminal Slang* 30, All the fagots (sissies) will be dressed in drag at the ball tonight. **1934** *AmSp* 9.288 [Black], *Faggart* (or *faggot, fagot*). A sexual pervert. **1936** Dos Passos *Big Money* 273 **NYC,** The first thing Margo thought was how on earth she could ever have liked that fagot. **1965–70** *DARE* (Qq. HH38, 39) 22 Infs, **scattered, but esp NY, PA,** Faggot; **GA**83, Faggy. [17 of 23 Infs young, 13 Black, 15 male, 10 coll educ. Cf distrib of *DARE* Infs at **fag** n.] **1970** Major *Dict. Afro-Amer. Slang* 52, *Faggot:* a male homosexual (derogatory). **1978** *NYT Mag.* 12 Mar 16, A heterosexual freshman at Stanford complained that he had always been called "faggot"—first in his Long Island, N.Y., high school and now in college—just because he liked to dress well and to iron his shirts.

faggotty adj [**faggot**]
Effeminate; homosexual.
1928 McKay *Home to Harlem* 36, And there is two things in Harlem I don't understan' / It is a bulldycking woman and a faggotty man. **1964** Bellow *Herzog* 238 **NY,** There was a certain faggotty prissiness in his speech.

faggy n See **faggot**

faggy adj [**fag** n]
Effeminate; homosexual.
1951 Salinger *Catcher* 5 **NY,** You could hear them [=football fans] all yelling, deep and terrific on the Pencey side, . . and scrawny and faggy on the Saxon Hall side. **1952** Brossard *Who Walk* 8 **NY,** Porter hated Harvard Men. . . He always said they were exotic and over-mannered and inclined to be faggy.

faghting See **fight A2**

fagiano n
A channel rockfish (here: *Sebastolobus alascanus*).
1953 Roedel *Common Fishes CA* 136, *Channel Rockfish. . . Unauthorized Names* . . fagiano.

fagot n[1] [Engl dial, from *fag(g)ot* a bundle of sticks]
A type of liver sausage.
1968 *DARE* (Qu. H43, *Foods made from parts of the head and inner organs of an animal*) Inf **PA**110, Pig liver and meat are wrapped in the apron (the tissue the intestines are wrapped in) and cut to size. Onions and sage are added to the liver. It's called fagots; (Qu. H65, *Foreign foods favored by people around here*) Inf **OH**80, Fagots—a Welsh liver sausage.

fagot n[2] See **faggot**

fahdoodle n [Var of 17th cent Brit *fadoodle* nonsense] Cf **flapdoodle 1**
Nonsense, rubbish, twaddle.
1955 Adams *Grandfather* 127 **NY** (as of 1870s), Say 'carcagne' to any of them and he would spin you a tale to make a woodcat's whiskers bristle. All fahdoodle, as I have warned you. *Ibid* 180, "All folderol and fahdoodle," Grandfather replied.

fahr See **fire**

faht See **fart**

faid adj [Pronc-sp for *afraid*] *Gullah*
1888 Jones *Negro Myths* 40 **GA coast** [Gullah], Buh Monkey faid fuh come down. **1922** Gonzales *Black Border* 75 **sSC, GA coasts** [Gullah], 'E 'faid 'e gwine drowndid. *Ibid* 300 [Glossary], *'F'aid*—afraid, afraid of. **1928** Peterkin *Scarlet Sister Mary* 138 **SC** [Gullah], I'm 'faid e might would catch cold.

failery n [*failer,* obs form of *failure*]
A failure.
1913 Johnson *Highways St. Lawrence to VA* 229 **DE** [Black], The late crop was a failery.

failing disease n [From the gradual loss of strength; see *OED fail* v. 3]
Tuberculosis.
1911 *DN* 3.538 **eKY,** *Failing-disease. . .* Consumption, tuberculosis. **1952** Brown *NC Folkl.* 1.538, Failing disease.

fail out v phr [*fail* + redund *out* perh by analogy with *flunk out*]
1910 *DN* 3.456 **seKY,** *Fail out. . .* Fail. "I failed out in three of my examinations."

fail up v phr
1 To become impoverished, go bankrupt. **NEng** *old-fash*
1890 Jewett *Strangers* 144 **NEng,** He'd failed up and got into trouble. **1893** Wiggin *Polly Oliver* 63, If compartment two [of a box holding household monies] had only met its rightful obligations, compartment three needn't have "failed up," as they say in New England; but as it is, poor compartment four is entirely bankrupt, and will have to borrow of the sugar-bowl or the ginger-jar. **1901** Freeman *Understudies* 203 **NEng,** The bank he kept it in has failed up, and he's lost every dollar.
2 To decline in health; to fall ill.
1914 *DN* 4.72 **ME, nNH,** The old jedge is failin' up pow'ful fast. **1959** *VT Hist.* new ser 27.135, *Fail up. . .* To lose energy; weaken. Rare. Windham.
3 To stop (doing something).
1907 *DN* 3.243 **eME,** My cow has failed up eating hay. **1942** in 1944 *ADD* **eWV.**

fain(s) See **fen**

faint n, usu pl Also sp *feint* [From the low alcoholic content] **S Midl** Cf **tailings**

In the production of whiskey: see quots.

1917 *DN* 4.411 **wNC,** *Faint*. . . Worthless residue in the "thumper" after distilling whiskey. **1968** *Foxfire* Fall–Winter 100 **nGA,** *Faints*—dead beer; or backings that steam has been run through in a thumper to strengthen a run. These are drained and replaced before each new run. **1974** Dabney *Mountain Spirits* xxi **Appalachians,** *Feints:* The leftover liquid in a thumper keg after a run. **1974** Maurer–Pearl *KY Moonshine* 117, *Faints*. . . (1) Low-proof distillate that comes through the condenser at the end of a run. . . (2) Heated slops used for setting mash.

faintified adj [*EDD* Suppl; cf **-ified**] **chiefly Sth** *somewhat old-fash* Cf **faintish, fainty 1**

Weak, faint.

1933 Rawlings *South Moon* 321 **nFL,** I felt faintified, thinkin' of all them people had died there. **1938** Rawlings *Yearling* 39 **nFL,** Don't go gittin' faintified on me. **1952** Brown *NC Folkl.* 1.538 **cnNC,** This hot-dry weather makes me feel sickly and faintified. **1966–69** *DARE* (Qu. BB6, *A sudden feeling of weakness*) Inf **TN**16, Faintified; **SC**27, Faintified—Negro [usage]; (Qu. BB16b, *If something a person ate didn't agree with him, he might just feel a bit* ———) Inf **NC**61, ['fendi,faɪd]. **1967** Will *Dredgeman* 92 **FL,** A fearsome situation! I was plumb faintified.

faintish adj Cf **fainty 1**

Weak, faint.

1965–68 *DARE* (Qu. BB6, *A sudden feeling of weakness*) Infs **MD**5, **OK**1, **PA**142, **SC**27, Faintish (spell); (Qu. GG26, *A feeling of weakness from fear: "When she saw the dog coming at her she got* ———*."*) Inf **NC**41, Faintish.

faint-out n

A feeling of weakness or faintness.

1965–66 *DARE* (Qu. BB6) Infs **OK**1, **SC**2, Faint-out.

faint over v phr

To fall over in a faint.

1954 *Harder Coll.* **cwTN,** Faint over.

fainty adj

1 also *fainty-sick:* Physically weak, faint. **chiefly Sth, S Midl** Cf **faintified, faintish**

1696 (1945) Dickinson *Jrl.* 60 **FL,** Many were sick and fainty. **1872** (1973) Thompson *Major Jones's Courtship* 37 **GA,** Jest then I cotch'd Miss Mary's eye—she was lookin her prettyest. I felt kind of fainty. **1899** (1912) Green *VA Folk-Speech* 168, I feel very fainty. **1926** Roberts *Time of Man* 208 **cKY,** You feel fainty-sick, don't you now? **1965–70** *DARE* (Qu. BB6, *A sudden feeling of weakness*) 10 Infs, **chiefly Sth, S Midl,** (Feel) fainty; **GA**23, **LA**6, 8, Fainty spell; **TX**4, Feeling fainty; (Qu. BB16b, *If something a person ate didn't agree with him, he might just feel a bit* ———) Inf **AL**16, Fainty; **TN**52, Fainty-sick; (Qu. BB38, *When a person doesn't look healthy, . . you'd say, "He looks* ———*."*) Inf **KY**94, Fainty.

2 Weak from fear. *somewhat old-fash*

1965–70 *DARE* (Qu. GG26, . . *"When she saw the dog coming at her she got* ———*."*) 27 Infs, **scattered,** (All) fainty; **DC**1, Scared and fainty. [24 of 28 Infs old]

3 Causing faintness. [*OED* →1683] *arch*

1899 (1912) Green *VA Folk-Speech, Fainty*. . . That causes a feeling of faintness. "These flowers have a fainty smell."

fainty-sick See **fainty 1**

fair adj Usu |fɛr, fɛə|; for varr see quots See Pronc Intro 3.I.1.b Pronc-sp *far*

A Forms.

1871 Eggleston *Hoosier Schoolmaster* 117 **sIN,** Thought may be you'd want somebody to see far play. **1922** (1926) Kephart *Highlanders* 421 **sAppalachians,** You can't fight a man fa'r and squar who'll shoot you in the back. **1927** Shewmake *Engl. Pronc. VA* 18, *Fair* . . in Virginia . . *fae-uh* seems to prevail. **1942** Hall *Smoky Mt. Speech* 24, [æ] occurs in . . fair. *Ibid* 25, [ɛ] frequently occurs [in] . . *fair*.

B Senses.

1 Fresh, pure. [*OED fair* a. 8. b "Now *rare*"; *W3* [1]*fair* 4. b *"archaic"*]

1858 Holmes *Autocrat* 3 **MA,** The rinsings of an unwashed wineglass spoil a draught of fair water. **1975** Gould *ME Lingo* 87, *Fair water*—Fresh water for cooking.

2 Plain, clear, obvious. [*OED fair* a. 17 "Now chiefly *dial*"; *W3* [1]*fair* 10 *"archaic"*]

1965 *Dict. Queen's English* 14 **NC,** The money was lying on the floor as fair as your hand.

3 Original, genuine. *obs*

c1820 in 1941 *AmSp* 16.157 **NY,** This is a copy but that is a fair thing. **1859** (1968) Bartlett *Americanisms* 140, *Fair*. Real, genuine; as, "This is not a chalk egg, it is a fair one." New York; a word mostly used by children.

4 Good, excellent—sometimes used in intentional understatements.

1938 *AmSp* 13.5 **seAR,** 'He was fair playing the piano.' That is, he was playing the piano very well. **1957** Beck *Folkl. ME* 67, In a land where living is hard and nature always seems to be against you . . [it is] felt that any good fortune is accidental. . . Therefore, one . . [says that a] bumper crop is "fair" . . and good weather is "fair, iffen it don't breeze on." **1968** *DARE* (Qu. KK1a, . . *Words meaning very good—for example, food: "That pie was* ———*."*) Inf **MD**47, Fair. **1975** Gould *ME Lingo* 87, Used by Mainers to understate excellence, *fair* usually means superb, wonderful, *finest kind*. "That's a fair piece of pie!" is equivalent to "That's the best pie I ever stuck a tooth in!"

5 Truthful, candid.

1936 Morehouse *Rain on Just* 232 **NC,** If I have much more toting and work to do, Euph, I'll be fair with you, some one will have to do for me. **1945** *Hall Coll.* **eTN,** Well, just to be fair, Jim, I don't do so hot with them [=French girls] for you know I can't speak French. **1985** *DARE* File **wNC** (as of c1910), The phrase "I'll be fair with you" was a favorite of my father. It always puzzled me just a bit, but I took it to mean "candid."

fair adv Cf **fairly** adv

1 Moderately. [*OED fair* adv. 7. b *"Obs."*]

1938 Matschat *Suwannee R.* 136 **nFL, sGA,** Pappy 'lowed as how hit was fair late in the fall, an' he an' Mammy was a-settin' up till all hours, a-yawnin'. **1943** Writers' Program NC *Bundle of Troubles* 72, He just couldn't stand her, but he forced himself to speak fair polite anyhow.

2 Squarely, fully.

1908 *DN* 3.309 **eAL, wGA,** He hit me fair in the face. **1935** Horwill *Mod. Amer. Usage* 125/2, *Fair*. In the sense of *completely, fully,* or *clearly, distinctly,* this word is now obs. in Eng., exc. in certain dial., but it is still current in Am. 'She threw a stone fair at the motorman' (i.e. straight at). **1966** *DARE* Tape **ME**26, They come to a cedar tree in the brook, that is, the brook was so high the cedar tree was in it then. And they struck that but they didn't strike it fair and it took 'em 'round it.

3 Scarcely, barely.

1894 Twain *Pudd'nhead Wilson* 234, It 'uz jes fair daylight when we passed our plantation.

4 =**fairly** adv **2.**

1926 Roberts *Time of Man* 18 **cKY,** I just wish you could 'a' seen Pappy . . a-whistlen to fair split his sides. **1960** Carpenter *Tales Manchaca* 107 **cTX** (as of c1915), My sister Portervine has a pomegranate hung in her mouth and she's fair choking to death.

5 =**fairly** adv **1.**

c1970 *DARE* File **IL,** It fair did rain; **Ozarks,** He was fair fat.

fair v See **fair off**

fair n [*fair* adj, used absol; *OED fair* sb.[2] 2 "Now *arch.* or *poet.*"] *old-fash*

A man's sweetheart.

1944 *PADS* 2.42 **NC,** *Fair*. . . Female sweetheart. Mitchell Co., N.C. Reported. **1952** Brown *NC Folkl.* 1.538, *Fair*. . . A female sweetheart. . . West[ern North Carolina].

fair away See **fair off**

fairce See **fierce** adj

fair down v phr Cf **fair off**

Of the wind: to decrease.

1939 *LANE* Map 92, 1 inf, **nNH,** [The wind is] fairing down.

fair fight n Also *fair fist and skull (fight)* Cf **fist and skull**

A fight without weapons—also used as an exclam.

1908 *DN* 3.309 **eAL, wGA,** *Fair fight*. . . A fight with bare fists. *Fair fist* *and skull (fight)*. . . A fight without weapons. **1942** McAtee *Dial. Grant Co. IN* 25 (as of 1890s), *Fair fight* . . cry of onlookers adjuring the use of fists only, no weapons. **c1960** *Wilson Coll.* **csKY,** Fair fight. . . A fight without weapons, a fist fight.

fairground v [Perh from *fairgrounds,* where rodeos are held] **SW**

To rope, throw, and tie a steer; hence vbl n *fairgrounding.*

1920 Hunter *Trail Drivers TX* 298, To "fair ground" is to rope an animal by the head, throw the rope over the back while still running and then throw the animal violently to the ground. **1929** Dobie *Vaquero* 289, About 1898 the whole of Southwest and West Texas went "hog wild" over roping contests. All the boys in the country were practicing at "fair grounding" (roping and tying) steers. **1933** (1950) Allen *Cowboy Lore* 58, *Fair Ground,* To rope an animal, . . then throw animal violently to the ground, where it usually lies long enough to be hogtied and branded.

fair-haired adj [By assoc with **white-haired**]

Specially favored—usu in phr *fair-haired boy.*

1909 *Sat. Eve. Post* 24 Apr 26/2, The old crowd of Fair-haired Correspondent Boys who hung to the ear of President Roosevelt with viselike grip dissolved, but a new one formed immediately which included the men who had been with Taft in his campaign. . . Presently the President [=Taft] let it be known that, though he will be glad to see his old friends occasionally in a personal way, there really is to be no new Fair-haired Organization. **1949** *Time* 14 Mar 30/1, Vishinsky was Stalin's newest fair-haired boy. **c1960** *Wilson Coll.* **csKY,** Fair-haired boy. . . A favorite. A rather modern word in the area, but the idea is old. **1969** *DARE* (Qu. JJ9, *Somebody who studies . . all the time*) Inf **NJ**54, Fair-haired boy, teacher's pet.

fairies' duster See **fairy duster**

fairies' table See **fairy table**

fairies' washing n

1966 *DARE* FW Addit **neME,** Fairies' washing—small, dew-covered spiderwebs in fields.

fairing See **fair off**

fairly adv Pronc-spp *farly, fyahly*

1 Really, fully, quite.

1873 Eggleston *Man of Honor* 192 **IN,** She was fairly frightened by her husband's tone and manner. She saw at a glance that he was in very serious earnest. **1883** Bunce *Don't* 41, Don't respond to remarks made to you with mere monosyllables. This is chilling, if not fairly insulting. Have something to say, and say it. **1891** Page *Elsket* 134 **VA,** He hollered tell dee say you could heah him two miles; he fyahly lumbered. **1893** Shands *MS Speech* 69, She [=a train] farly zuned [=went swiftly]. **1936** Morehouse *Rain on Just* 12 **NC,** Dolly inched slowly down the bank, her mouth fairly thirsting for the cold sweet milk. **1941** *LANE* Map 483 **nwCT,** He got in wrong before he fairly opened his mouth. [=He had scarcely opened his mouth before he offended me.] **1947** *Hench Coll.* **VA,** [Radio advt:] Put Kreml on your hair and your hair "fairly radiates" charm.

2 Virtually; almost.

1888 Censor *Don't* 74 *(Hench Coll.),* Don't shout every time you want to speak. Some boys fairly shout at playfellows who are only a few feet away. **1939** *Sun* (Baltimore MD) 10 Feb 6/3 *(Hench Coll.),* [Advt:] It Makes Grease Go So Fast Dishes Fairly Wash Themselves! **1966–68** *DARE* (Qu. LL30, . . *"He fell off the ladder and ______ [broke his neck]."*) Inf **GA**3, Fairly; (Qu. OO28a, . . *"John was so scared he ______ [all the way home]."*) Inf **KY**11, Fairly flew. **1969** *DARE* Tape **TX**69, Nigras just came into it thick and fast and the people fairly giving away their lovely houses. **1982** *Barrick Coll.* **csPA,** *Fairly*—*nearly.* "They fairly run up the hollow."

fairly adj Cf **poorly**

In good health, well.

1949 Webber *Backwoods Teacher* 32 **Ozarks,** Now Mrs. Caldwell said, "We're right fairly, thank you," but she was not cordial. "How're you all?" "Fairly. Fairly. Where's Mr. Caldwell at?"

fair maid n **Mid Atl**

=scup.

1873 in 1878 Smithsonian Inst. *Misc. Coll.* 14.2.27, *Stenotomus argyrops*. . . Fair-maid *(East Shore of Virginia).* **1884** Goode *Fisheries U.S.* 1.387, On the Virginia coast the Southern Scup is known as the 'Fair Maid.' **1902** Jordan–Evermann *Amer. Fishes* 437, On the New England coast it is usually called scup. . . Farther south it is the fair-maid. **1939** Natl. Geogr. Soc. *Fishes* 68, It is the . . maiden, fair maid, and ironsides in Chesapeake Bay. **1975** Evanoff *Catch More Fish* 208, The northern porgy . . is also called the fair maid, ironsides, and scuppaug. **1984** *DARE* File **Chesapeake Bay** [Watermen's vocab], Scup, porgy, maiden, fair maid.

fair off v phr Also *fair up;* less freq *fair (away)* **chiefly Sth, S Midl** See Map Cf **get fair**

Of the weather: to become clearer; hence ppl adj *fairing.*

1836 (1929) Willson *Journey* 29 May **NJ,** It was still rainy; towards night it faired away. **1859** (1968) Bartlett *Americanisms* 140, *Fair off, fair up.* To clear off, clear up. **1891** *PMLA* 5.170 **WV,** Fair off. **1895** *DN* 1.388 **MA,** Fair off. **1899** (1912) Green *VA Folk-Speech* 168, Fair up. **1909** *DN* 3.396 **nwAR,** Fair off. *Ibid* 411 **nME,** Fair off. **1917** *DN* 4.411 **wNC, SC,** Fair up. **1921** *DN* 5.120 **VT,** Fair off. **1930** *AmSp* 5.227 **NE,** Fair off. **1930** *DN* 6.84 **ceSC,** Fair off. **1933** Rawlings *South Moon* 226 **FL,** Hit'll soon fair off. Why didn't you wait? Seem to me you jest enjoy gittin' soaked to the hide. **1933** *AmSp* 8.1.49 **Ozarks,** Fair up. **1937** *AmSp* 12.287 **wVA,** The Shenandoah German may say . . "It's faired off some" for it's clearing up. **1939** *LANE* Map 89 **scattered, but chiefly ME, NH, VT,** Fairing up, fairing off, fairing. **1944** *PADS* 2.33 **NC,** *Fair off. Ibid* 55 **MO,** *Fair up;* **VA,** *Fair off.* **c1960** *Wilson Coll.* **csKY,** *Fair off* (or *up*). **1965–70** *DARE* (Qu. B7, *When clouds begin to decrease, you say it's ______*) 37 Infs, **chiefly Sth, S Midl,** Fairing off; 29 Infs, **chiefly Sth, S Midl,** Fairing up; **GA**84, **KY**83, **NY**8, **SC**20, **TN**14, Fairing; **GA**36, **MS**24, **SC**3, Going (*or* fixing) to fair off; **AR**1, **NC**49, (Looks like it) gonna fair off; **FL**19, **MS**63, **VA**13, Going (*or* beginning, fixing) to fair up; **MO**15, Fairing away; (Qu. B8) Inf **LA**9, Fairing off; **NC**67, About to fair up; (Qu. B13) Infs **KY**41, 86, Fairing up; **KY**37, Fairing off; **MO**5, Fairing away; (Qu. B18) Inf **GA**89, Fairing wind; (Qu. B19) Inf **KY**86, Fairing up; **MO**5, Fairing away.

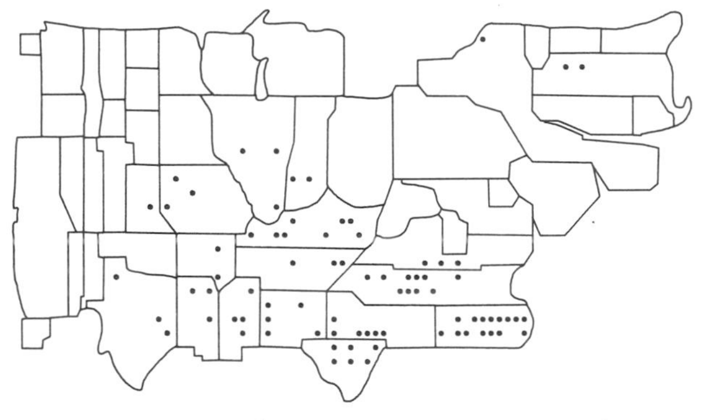

•fair off + varr (Qq. B7, B8, B13, B18, B19)

fair play adv phr

=fairly adv **1.**

c1885 in 1981 Woodward *Mary Chesnut's Civil War* 718 **SC** (as of 1865) [Black], Lord ha' mercy. She [=a white woman] say you bring me and Laurence [=a male slave] here to keep us from running away to de Yankees—and I say, 'Name o' God, ole Missis! If dat's it—what she bring Laurence and me for? She got plenty more. Laurence and me's nothing—to our white people. De ole soul fair play insulted me.

fair play exclam

In children's games: **=time out.**

1896 *DN* 1.416 **NY,** *Fair play:* for *king's excuse.*

fair shake n [Perh in ref to a *shake* of the dice in gambling, or the *shake* of the hands by which a bargain is sealed, or a *shaken* measure of grain (cf Luke 6:38)]

A fair chance; an equitable bargain.

1830 *Central Watchtower* (Harrodsburg, Ky.) 22 May *(DA),* Says I . . any way that will be a fair shake. **1845** Thompson *Pineville* 88 **GA,** He determined to have one "fair shake" at the birds. **1848** Bartlett *Americanisms* 132, *Fair Shake.* A fair trade; a satisfactory bargain or exchange. A New England vulgarism. **1889** (1971) Farmer *Americanisms* 232, *Fair Shake.*—A fair bargain. **1899** (1912) Green *VA Folk-Speech* 168, *Fair-shake*. . . Fair play; fair chance. **1914** *DN* 4.106 **KS,**

Fair shake . . = *square deal.* **1942** McAtee *Dial. Grant Co. IN* 25 (as of 1890s), *Fair shake* . . just treatment, a square deal. **1948** *Antioch Rev.* Autumn 160, I figger that's a fair shake [=a good bargain]. **1960** Wentworth-Flexner *Slang* 176, *Fair shake 1* An honest arrangement; a fair deal; a square deal. *2* An attempt or try under the same conditions given others. *Apparently in reference to dicing. Colloq. since c1825.* **1969** *DARE* (Qu. HH22c, . . *"He's mean enough* . . ———*."*) Inf **PA**219, Not to give his grandmother a fair shake.

fairs, no exclam [Var of *no fair;* cf **-s**]

1939 *Hench Coll.* **PA,** Exclamation in games: That's no fair. That's no fairs. No fair. No fairs. . . These expressions I heard always when I was a boy in Pittsburgh, shouted whenever a boy thought another boy wasn't playing correctly or fairly.

fair to middling adj phr, adv phr [In ref to grades of livestock] Cf **middling** adj

1 About average; slightly better than average—freq used to understate a feeling of good health.

1865 Browne *Artemus Ward Travels* 41 **Salt Lake City UT,** The men are fair to middling. They will never be slain in cold blood for their beauty, nor shut up in jail for their homeliness. **1892** *DN* 1.210 **seMA,** *Fair to middlin':* pretty well (of the health). Common in replying to the question "How are you?" **1906** Casey *Parson's Boys* 43 **sIL** (as of c1860), "How do you do, and how is Sister Ratcliffe to-day?" "Oh, fair to middlin', Brother Flint." **1906** *DN* 3.135 **nwAR. 1907** *DN* 3.237 **nwAR, seMO. 1910** *DN* 3.441 **wNY. 1954** *Harder Coll.* **cwTN,** *Fair to middling.* . . An answer to the question "How yens [=you ones] gittin' along?" When everything is neither good nor bad. **c1960** *Wilson Coll.* **csKY.**

2 Below average.

1939 *AmSp* 14.264 **IN,** Ill health or just 'puniness' is indicated by such expressions as 'jest tol'able only,' 'middlin',' 'fair to middlin',' [etc]. **1968-70** *DARE* (Qu. KK30, *Feeling slowed up or without energy*) Infs **GA**31, **MS**88, Fair to middlin'.

fair up See **fair off**

fair-weather Christian n Also *fair-weather churchgoer* **Nth**

A person who goes to church seldom if at all.

1950 *WELS* 4 Infs, **WI,** Fair-weather Christian; 1 Inf, Fair-weather churchgoer. **1968-70** *DARE* (Qu. CC7) Infs **NY**36, 145, 206, 220, **PA**223, 243, Fair-weather Christian; **PA**72, Fair-weather (+ name of religion).

fair wind n [From naut usage]

A safe journey; good fortune.

1851 (1976) Melville *Moby-Dick* 497, Let me square the yards, while we may, old man, and make a fair wind of it homewards. **1916** Macy-Hussey *Nantucket Scrap Basket* 131, "Fair Wind"—In wishing well a parting guest, one says, "A fair wind to you." It is used also in speaking of a streak of luck, as "he struck a fair wind."

fairy n

1 An effeminate or homosexual man. **widespread, but chiefly Nth, N Midl** See Map

1895 *Amer. Jrl. Psychology* 7.216, This coincides with what is known of the peculiar societies of inverts. . . [B]alls, where men adopt the ladies' evening dress, are well known in Europe. 'The Fairies' of New York are said to be a similar secret organization. **1923** (1927) Anderson *Hobo* 103, Fairies or Fags are men or boys who exploit sex for profit. **1950** *WELS (A womanish man)* 6 Infs, **WI,** Fairy. **1965-70** *DARE* (Qu. HH39, *A homosexual man*) 205 Infs, **widespread, but chiefly Nth, N Midl,** Fairy; (Qu. HH38, *A womanish man*) 47 Infs, **scattered, but chiefly Nth, N Midl,** Fairy; **FL**38, **IL**98, **MA**1, Fairy nice boy (*or* guy, man). **1971** Roberts *Third Ear* np [Black], *Fairy* . . a homosexual.

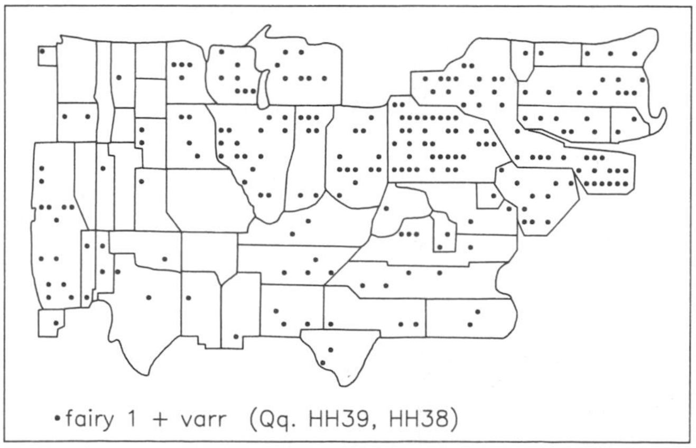

2 pl: A white columbine (here: *Aquilegia vulgaris*).

1896 *Jrl. Amer. Folkl.* 9.197, *Aquilegia vulgaris.* . . White variety, fairies, Norridgewock, M[ain]e. . . Pressed by schoolgirls and carried for a time.

3 =**snow angel.**

1967 *DARE* (Qu. EE26) Inf **CO**26, Fairy—an angel imprint.

fairy bell n, usu pl Also freq *fairy bells* [From the shape of the nodding flower]

1 also *fairy cap,* ~ *fingers,* ~ *thimbles:* A **foxglove 1** (here: *Digitalis purpurea*).

1900 Lyons *Plant Names* 136, *D. purpúrea* . . Fairy-bells . . Fairy-cap . . Fairy-fingers . . Fairy- thimbles. **1930** Sievers *Amer. Med. Plants* 29, Other common names [for *Digitalis purpurea*] . . fairybells.

2 A plant of the genus *Disporum.* For other names of var spp see **drops of gold, fairy lantern 2, mandarin, wartberry fairy bell**

1897 Parsons *Wild Flowers CA* 376, Fairy Bells. Drops of Gold . . we find . . one or more exquisitely formed little green bells hanging from the tip of each branch. **1933** Small *Manual SE Flora* 298, *Disporum.* . . Fairy-bells. **1963** Craighead *Rocky Mt. Wildflowers* 22, Fairybells. . . This plant is usually confused with Twisted-stalk *(Streptopus amplexifolius)* and False Solomonseal *(Smilacina racemosa).* **1967-69** *DARE* (Qu. S26b) Inf **CA**140, Fairy bells grow on eastern, moist, shady slopes. They are white, hang down, and look like Japanese lanterns; (Qu. S26c) Inf **CA**24, Fairy bells; (Qu. S26e) Inf **IL**37, Fairy bells or twisted stalks.

3 A **mariposa lily.**

1942 Whipple *Joshua* 174 **UT,** Thousands of fairy bells with lavender hearts, tossing their lovely heads.

4 =**Solomon's seal.**

1966 *DARE* Wildfl QR Pl.21 Infs **WA**10, 15, Fairy bells.

fairy-boats n

A **white water lily** (here: *Nymphaea odorata*).

1951 *PADS* 15.32 **TX,** *Castalia odorata* Aiton.—Fairy-boats; water queen.

fairy bread n Also *fairy club*

A mushroom of the genus *Craterellus.* Cf **fairy ring 1**

1902 McIlvaine-Macadam *1000 Amer. Fungi* 508, *Craterellus* . . are . . popularly associated with fairies. . . "Fairy rings," "Fairy Bread" and "Fairy Clubs" are titles belonging to them.

fairy butter n

A **witches' butter** (here: *Dacrymyces* spp).

1987 McKnight-McKnight *Mushrooms* 68, *Dacrymyces* (sometimes also called . . Fairy Butter) is usually smaller [than *Tremella mesenterica*], but otherwise almost indistinguishable in the field.

fairy candles n

A **bugbane 1.**

1933 Small *Manual SE Flora* 513, *C[imicifuga] racemosa.* . . Fairy-candles. . . Woods, various provinces. **1948** Wherry *Wild Flower Guide* 56, Fairy-candles. . . Desirable for the large wild garden. **1949** Moldenke *Amer. Wild Flowers* 419, Fairycandles, see *Cimicifuga racemosa.*

fairy cap See **fairy bell 1**

fairy circle n [From its common habit of growing in rings] Cf **fairy ring**

A juniper *(Juniperus communis).*

1892 *Jrl. Amer. Folkl.* 5.103, *Juniperus communis,* fairy circle. **1900** Lyons *Plant Names* 208. **1930** Sievers *Amer. Med. Plants* 25, *Common Juniper—Juniperus communis* . . Fairy circle.

fairy club See **fairy bread**

fairy creeper n

=**mountain fringe.**

1900 Lyons *Plant Names* 16, *A[dlumia] fungósa.* . . Climbing Fumitory, Mountain-fringe, . . Alleghany-vine, Canary-vine, . . Fairy-creeper. **1910** Graves *Flowering Plants* 197 **CT.** **1933** Small *Manual SE Flora* 549, *Fairy-creeper...* Rich woods and stream banks, .. N.C. to Tenn., Wis., and N.B. **1959** Carleton *Index Herb. Plants* 43.

fairy cross See **fairy stone**

fairy cup n

1 A **miterwort** (here: *Mitella diphylla*).

1893 *Jrl. Amer. Folkl.* 6.142 **NY,** *Mitella diphylla,* false sanicle; fringe cup; fairy cup. **1900** Lyons *Plant Names* 250, Fairy cup. **1910** Graves *Flowering Plants* 216 **CT.**

2 A cup fungus (*Peziza* spp).

1902 McIlvaine-Macadam *1000 Amer. Fungi* 560, *Peziza...* "Fairy Cups," they are called. **1908** Hard *Mushroom Edible* 503, *Peziza* .. are often beautifully colored and are called fairy cups, blood cups, and cup fungi.

fairydiddle n[1] [Var of *taradiddle;* perh infl by *fairy tale*]

Nonsense.

1936 *AmSp* 11.372 **NE,** 'Stop that fairydiddle!,' i.e., stop that flattering complimentary talk. To tell someone he 'talks fairydiddle' is to tell him, in a light refined way, that he talks nonsense.

fairydiddle n[2] See **ferrididdle**

fairy duck n [See quot 1936]

=**northern phalarope.**

1936 Roberts *MN Birds* 1.536, Northern Phalaropes *(Lobipes lobatus)* are graceful, dainty, gentle little birds, and the name "Fairy Duck," which has been applied to them, is very fitting, for their actions, as they swim lightly about, suggest tiny, elfin, Duck-like creatures. **1946** Hausman *Eastern Birds* 298, *Northern Phalarope—Lobipes lobatus...* Fairy Duck. **1955** Forbush-May *Birds* 211, *Northern Phalarope—Lobipes lobatus...* Fairy Duck.

fairy duster n Also *fairies' duster* [See quot 1937]

A low, bushy shrub *(Calliandra eriophylla)* with pink or reddish-purple flowers. Also called **false catclaw, false mesquite, huajillo 3, mesquitilla, mock mesquite, pink-flowered acacia, pink mimosa, yerba bonita**

1915 (1926) Armstrong-Thornber *Western Wild Flowers* 266, *Fairy Dusters* .. sometimes bloom when they are only a few inches high. **1937** U.S. Forest Serv. *Range Plant Hdbk.* B36, The plant also is sometimes called fairies' duster because the numerous stamens on their long, threadlike stalks form a plumelike cluster resembling a dainty feather duster. **1971** Dodge *100 Desert Wildflowers* 26, "Fairy duster" is a small, straggling bush, quite Japanesy in appearance. **1981** Benson-Darrow *Trees SW Deserts* 231, The fairy duster is one of the most valuable browse and erosion control plants of the Southwest. **1985** Dodge *Flowers SW Deserts* 45, The petite fairyduster adds much to the color and springtime atmosphere of the desert.

fairy fans n [See quot 1949]

A **farewell-to-spring** (here: *Clarkia breweri*).

1925 Jepson *Manual Plants CA* 674, *C[larkia] breweri...* Fairy Fans. **1949** Moldenke *Amer. Wild Flowers* 93 **CA,** In the same part of our area lives *E[uchardium] breweri,* the *fairyfans,* with inch-long, fan-shaped petals of a luminous pink color. **1976** Bailey-Bailey *Hortus Third* 280, *Clarkia Breweri...* Fairyfans.

fairy fingers See **fairy bell 1**

fairy flame See **fairy light**

fairy-fringe n

A **fringed orchid** (here: esp *Habenaria psycodes*).

1943 Peattie *Great Smokies* 196, There was .. a brilliant lilac-purple display from that splendid orchid, the fairyfringe. **1976** Bailey-Bailey *Hortus Third* 534, *Habenaria psycodes* .. Fairy-fringe.

fairy glow See **fairy light**

fairy lantern n

1 also *lantern of the fairies:* =**mariposa lily,** esp *Calochortus albus.* **CA**

1897 Parsons *Wild Flowers CA* 54, Hairbell. Lantern of the Fairies. White Globe-Tulip. *Calochortus albus.* **1911** Jepson *Flora CA* 98, *C[alochortus] amabilis... Golden Lily Bell...* Also called Cat's Ears and Fairy Lantern. **1954** CA Div. Beaches & Parks *Pt. Lobos Wild Flowers* 29, The White Fairy Lantern .. appears at Point Lobos about the last of April... Smooth stems .. produce .. hanging lantern-shaped flowers. **1967** *DARE* (Qu. S26a) Inf **CA**20, Fairy lanterns, or harebells, [are found] under poison oak; (Qu. S2) Inf **CA**31, Fairy lanterns; (Qu. S26c) Inf **CA**87, Fairy lanterns or air castle flowers. **1968** *DARE* File **CA,** Fairy lantern. An orchid-colored wildflower growing in mountain dells of the Sierra Nevada Mountains, north of Bakersfield.

2 A **fairy bell 2** (here: *Disporum smithii*). **CA, Pacific NW**

1911 Jepson *Flora CA* 110, *D[isporum] menziesii... Fairy Lantern...* Stream banks, Coast Range woods. **1942** Hylander *Plant Life* 560, The related Fairy Lantern of .. California to Washington bears broadly cup-shaped white flowers. **1973** Hitchcock-Cronquist *Flora Pacific NW* 689.

fairy light n Also *fairy flame, ~ glow, ~ spark*

=**will-o'-the-wisp.**

1950 *WELS (A small light that seems to dance over a swamp or marsh by night)* 1 Inf, **csWI,** Fairy sparks or fairy lights. **1967** *DARE* (Qu. CC16) Inf **NY**35, Fairy flame or fairy glow.

fairy lily n

1 =**zephyr lily,** esp *Zephyranthes atamasco.*

1891 *Century Dict.* 7033, *Z[ephyranthes] Atamasco,* found from Mexico to Pennsylvania, with rose-colored flowers, is cultivated under the name of *fairy-lily,* or *atamasco-lily.* **1933** Small *Manual SE Flora* 320, *Zephyranthes...* Zephyr-lilies. Fairy-lilies. Rain-lilies. **1955** *S. Folkl. Qrly.* 19.233, The term *fairy* in *Fairy Lily* (Atamasco atamasco) .. is a reference to the delicacy of the blossoms. **1964** Batson *Wild Flowers SC* 35, *Atamasco Lily, Fairy Lily...* Sizeable colonies of these bright flowers may be encountered.

2 =**rain lily.**

1961 Wills-Irwin *Flowers TX* 98, Bulbs of nearly all the Rain-lilies and Atamascos are marketed by seedsmen under such names as Star-lilies, Zephyr-lilies, Fairy-lilies, and Copper-lilies.

fairy loop n

A small cloth loop sewn into the yoke-seam on the back of a shirt.

c1970 *Hand Coll.* **Provo UT,** A group of girls will determine a time span that they will run a contest, and usually this would be a week. They were to pick a boy, usually in their class. The girl who gets the most of his "fairy loops" (hanging loops on the back of men's shirts) would be the one to marry him.

fairy paddle n

A **duckweed 1** (here: *Lemna trisulca*).

1936 McDougall-Baggley *Plants of Yellowstone* 36, *Fairypaddle (Lemna trisulca)* .. has an elongated plant body which is narrowed at the base into a stalk.

fairy picture n Also *fairy track, ~ work* [From the delicate, lacy pattern]

A pattern formed by ice on the inside of a window.

1967-69 *DARE* (Qu. B36) Infs **IL**5, **MO**10, Fairy pictures; **PA**128, Jack Frost with fairy pictures; **MO**19, Fairy tracks; **OH**72, Fairy work.

fairy platform n

A bracket fungus; see quot.

1911 (1916) Porter *Harvester* 314 **IN,** "There is a fine fairy platform... " The Harvester broke from a tree a large fan-shaped fungus, the surface satin fine, the base mossy, and explained to the Girl that these were the ballrooms of the woods, the floors on which the little people dance in the moonlight at their great celebrations.

fairy potatoes n

=**bladder campion.**

1898 *Jrl. Amer. Folkl.* 11.223, *Silene cucubalus* .. fairy potatoes, Auburndale, Mass.

fairy primrose n

1961 Douglas *My Wilderness* 19 **CO,** Close to the ground and perhaps no more than an inch high is the fairy primrose *(Primula angustifolia).* Its five-petaled flower is extremely fragrant. The corolla is magenta; the center is yellow. It is part of the treasure that this high Colorado country offers those who find exhilaration in dry, thin air and wind-swept ridges.

fairy ring n Cf **fairy circle**

1 A circle of mushrooms; one of the mushrooms in a circle; see quots.

1895 (1900) Arnold *Century Cook Book* 317, *The Fairy Ring Champignon (Marasmius oreades)*—This is one of the most common and easily recognized mushrooms, and in their season enough for a sauce may be gathered in almost any dooryard. **1898** in 1902 McIlvaine–Macadam *1000 Amer. Fungi* 38 **cwIN,** This mushroom . . grows luxuriantly in the pastures, generally in grand fairy rings, five, ten, fifteen feet in diameter. . . One fairy ring yields a bushel. **1901** *Plant World* 4.206, The Fairy Ring Mushroom *(Marasmius oreades).* On coming to eastern South Dakota eleven years ago, one very noticeable thing about the flora of the prairies was the great number of "fairy rings" to be found. **1924** *Torreya* 24.48 **NY,** We also found a "fairy ring" thirty feet in diameter containing scores of gemmed puffballs of unusual size. In the Middle West, the giant puffball sometimes grows in giant "fairy rings"! **1949** Palmer *Nat. Hist.* 66, *Fairy-ring Mushroom. Marasmius oreades.* . . Found usually in rings in grassy fields or on lawns or orchards from spring to fall and from year to year. Ring caused by exhaustion of available food from center. **1966–68** *DARE* (Qu. I37, *Small plants shaped like an umbrella that grow in woods and fields—which are safe to eat*) Inf **MN**36, Fairy ring; (Qu. S26e) Inf **WA**15, Fairy ring—a mushroom that grows big in a ring. **1987** McKnight–McKnight *Mushrooms* 166, *Fairy Ring Mushroom. Marasmius oreades.* . . Scattered, in groups or clusters (fairy rings) on grassy soil in lawns, parks, meadows, or shrubland.

2 A circular patch of grass on a prairie.

1950 Hitchcock–Chase *Manual Grasses* 402, *Ringgrass.* . . Perennial in loose tufts, . . sometimes forming large patches or "fairy rings". . . Plains, mesas, and dry hills, western Kansas and Wyoming to Texas and Arizona.

fairy shrimp n

A freshwater crustacean, esp of the genus *Eubranchipus.*

1935 Pratt *Manual Invertebrate Animals* 376, *Eubranchipus vernalis* . . Fairy shrimp. **1954** Borror–DeLong *Intro. Insects* 767, A fairy shrimp, *Eubranchipus.* **1966** *Wilson Coll.* **csKY,** *Fairy Shrimp*—small transparent shrimp found in sloughs or ponds which become dormant when they [=ponds] dry up.

fairy slipper n **chiefly West**

A bog orchid *(Calypso bulbosa).* Also called **deerhead orchid, fox slipper, lady's slipper, slipper orchid, Venus's-slipper**

1938 (1958) Sharples *AK Wild Flowers* 28, "Fairy Slipper." A monotypic genus. *C[alypso] bulbosa.* The "Fairy Slipper" is borne on a four-inch stem above a single pleated leaf. . . The whole [=flower] forms a dainty rose-hued slipper obviously fashioned for a fairy's foot. **1950** FWP *Guide ID* 66, A single lovely rose-purple bloom hanging at the end of a rosy stem gives to calypso its common name of fairy slipper. **1957** Roberts–Nelson *Wildflowers CO* 9, Fairyslipper. . . This slipper that would have decorated Titania's foot is one of the most beloved of our native flowers. **1963** Craighead *Rocky Mt. Wildflowers* 36, Fairyslipper is unique among the orchids of the area, though it could possibly be confused with the shootingstars. **1966** Goldstein–Byington *Two Penny Ballads* 157 **Philadelphia PA** (as of 1940s), Fairies live in the woods in wild flowers called fox-slippers or fairy-slippers, and come out and dance in the moonlight while the elves play music for them. **1966** *DARE* Wildfl QR Pl.40 Inf **WI**35, Fairy slipper. **1973** Hitchcock–Cronquist *Flora Pacific NW* 699, *Calypso* . . Fairy-slipper.

fairy's loving cup n

A **horn of plenty 2** (here: *Craterellus cornucopioides*).

1980 Marteka *Mushrooms* 86, *Craterellus cornucopioides.* . . Fairy's loving cup. . . Trumpet- or funnel-shaped, looks like empty cornucopia to some.

fairy smoke n

=**Indian pipe.**

1894 *Jrl. Amer. Folkl.* 7.93 **ME,** *Monotrapa* [sic] *uniflora,* fairy smoke. **1900** Lyons *Plant Names* 252.

fairy's paintbrush n Cf **Flora's paintbrush**

=**orange hawkweed.**

1940 Clute *Amer. Plant Names* 224, *Hieracium aurantiacum.* Fairy's paint-brush.

fairy spark See **fairy light**

fairy spuds n Cf **Eskimo potato**

=**spring beauty.**

1943 Fernald–Kinsey *Edible Wild Plants E. N. Amer.* 197, "Fairy-Spuds," *Claytonia caroliniana* and *C. virginiana.* . . The roundish, irregular roots . . varying from ½ to 2 inches in diameter, when boiled in salted water, are palatable and nutritious. **1974** Angier *Field Guide Edible Plants* 212, *Spring Beauty. . . Other names*—Groundnut, Fairy Spuds. . . It is for the starchy roots, however, that this wild edible is most famous. These small, potatolike tubers . . take a bit of digging, although where they are abundant just a few minutes with a pointed stick will amass a respectable meal. . . To me they have the flavor of especially choice little potatoes with overtones of cooked chestnut.

fairy stars n

A **woodland star** (here: *Lithophragma tenellum*).

1953 Nelson *Plants Rocky Mt. Park* 88 **cnCO,** *Fairy stars* or *slender woodland star* . . grows near Fern Lake.

fairy stone n Also *fairy cross* [See quot 1970] **chiefly Mid and S Atl**

A staurolite crystal.

1908 Fox *Lonesome Pine* 201 **KY,** She saw his gaze drop to the fairy-stone at her throat. **1940** Writers' Program *Guide VA* 610, Fairy Stone State Park . . was so named because of the small staurolite crystals, locally called fairystones, found in profusion in the area. **1942** Kennedy *Palmetto Country* 166 **nFL,** *Through the Days of Labor and Nights of Rest,/ The Charms of Fairy Stones Will Keep You Blest.* That sign hangs over the entrance of . . one of the typical Palmetto Country's cunjure shops. **1968** *DARE* (Qu. C26, *What special kinds of stone or rock are there in this part of the state?*) Inf **MN**33, Staurolite or fairy cross. It is formed by nature in the shape of a cross, and is only found in four places in the world; **NC**53, Fairy stone. **1970** *NC Folkl.* 18.49, Fairy or lucky crosses (found in North Carolina and Virginia and thought to have been dropped from the skies and then formed into crosses) are said to have magic properties to protect owners from witchcraft, sickness, and disasters. **1976** *Yankee* Aug 32/1, Fairy stone[s are] . . crystals of staurolite which occur in well-defined crosses here in Patrick County, Virginia. Legend has it that when Christ was crucified all the fairies' tears crystallized into these crosses.

fairy sword n

A **lip fern** (here: *Cheilanthes lindheimeri*).

1970 Correll *Plants TX* 58, *Cheilanthes Lindheimeri. . . Fairy swords.* Fronds scattered on a slender creeping rhizome, often forming extensive colonies . . ; blades ovate-lanceolate to elliptic-lanceolate, to 2 dm. long and 5 cm. wide, tripinnate or quadripinnate.

fairy table n Also *fairies' table*

1 A **meadow mushroom** such as *Agaricus campestris.*

1900 Lyons *Plant Names* 53, *A[garicus] campestris.* . . To this and other species, are given the names Fairies'-table, Pisky-stool, White-caps. **1968** *DARE* (Qu. I37) Inf **NY**41, "Fairy tables"—old-fashioned.

2 A **marsh pennywort** (*Hydrocotyle* spp).

1900 Lyons *Plant Names* 196, *Hydrocotyle* . . Fairy-table.

fairy thimbles See **fairy bell 1**

fairy track See **fairy picture**

fairy trumpet n

1 =**skyrocket.**

1953 Nelson *Plants Rocky Mt. Park* 128 **cnCO,** *Skyrocket gilia* or *fairy trumpet, Gilia aggretata* [sic]. **1968** *DARE* FW Addit **CO**7, Fairy trumpet *Gilia aggregata.* Phlox order and family, flower white. The red-flowered one is called Indian trumpet. Not found on the prairie.

2 A **horn of plenty 2** (here: *Craterellus cornucopioides*).

1980 Marteka *Mushrooms* 86, *Craterellus cornucopioides.* . . Fairy trumpet. . . *Cap:* 1 to 3 inches across; trumpet- or funnel-shaped.

fairy umbrella n Cf **devil's umbrella, frog umbrella**

A mushroom.

1968 *DARE* (Qu. I38, *Small plants shaped like an umbrella that grow in woods and fields—which are not safe to eat*) Inf **TN**26, Fairy umbrellas; (Qu. S18, *A kind of mushroom that grows like a globe . . sometimes gets as big as a man's head*) Inf **GA**38, "Fairy umbrellas"—a children's term.

fairy wand n [From the wandlike stem and raceme of white flowers]

=**blazing star 2.**

1933 Small *Manual SE Flora* 276, *C. luteum.* . . Fairy-wand. **1941** Walker *Lookout* 55 **eTN,** The staminate plants of fairywand . . [bloom] in April and May on the sides of the mountain. **1948** Wherry *Wild Flower Guide* 11. **1953** Greene–Blomquist *Flowers South* 6, Fairy- or Angel's-Wand. . . Flowers are borne in spike-like racemes. . . It . . is widely distributed in e. N.A. **1971** Krochmal *Appalachia Med. Plants* 82. **1976** Bruce *How to Grow Wildflowers* 172, *Chamaelirium luteum* . . hardly lives up to some of the dramatic common names applied to it—Devil's Bit, Blazing Star, Fairy Wand, Rattlesnake Root.

fairy waterlily n

A **floating heart 1** (here: *Nymphoides aquatica*).

1976 Bailey–Bailey *Hortus Third* 774, *[Nymphoides] aquatica.* . . Fairy water lily.

fairy work See **fairy picture**

fais See **feist** n

fais-dodo n |ˌfedoˈdo| Also sp *fait-do-do* [See quot 1931] **sLA** *rural* Cf **dodo, go**

A traditional dancing party arranged to accommodate entire families; see quots.

1926 *Times–Picayune* (New Orleans LA) 15 Aug mag sec 2 **csLA,** The country folk . . are coming to town for the fait-do-do, which in plain English . . is a good old country dance. . . The fait-do-do is the essence of the gay, the merry, the devil-may-care. . . Certainly, if one is at all concerned about the outer covering, it is at the fait-do-do that one must strut one's stuff. . . One may accuse the fait-do-do orchestra of anything, but no one can say that it has not rhythm . . sensitive to the regular rhythm, and swaying with it, they strut their fait-do-do, and sing the while. [**1931** Read *LA French* 38, *Fais-dodo.* . . A country dance; from the *fais dodo* "go to sleep," of children's speech. . . *Dodo* is formed from the initial syllable of *dormir,* "to sleep."] **1939** *AmSp* 14.198 **sLA,** Both the Cajun farmer and his town neighbors . . participate in the two important weekly activities—the Saturday night *fais-do-do* and the Sunday mass. . . The music for this dance is usually furnished by an accordion, a violin, and a metal triangle, which is struck with a rod. **1961** *PADS* 36.12 **sLA,** So far as evidence goes, certain usages are confined to the rural parishes as against New Orleans. Among these are . . *fais do-do.* **1967** LeCompte *Word Atlas* 277 **seLA,** *Large country dance which all the members of the family attend.* . . The most interesting response, though not much used in this area [=Lafourche Parish and Grand Isle], is the dialect word *fais-do-do* (go to sleep), from the lullaby to the children, who accompanied their parents to the dance and often slept there as the adults danced the night away. **1968** *DARE* (Qu. FF4, *Names . . for different kinds of dancing parties*) Inf **LA**32, [ˌfeɪdɪˈdou]; **LA**35, [ˌfedoˈdo]—for the whole town. They block off the streets and dance there. **1979** Hallowell *People Bayou* 76 **sLA,** If Cajun institutions were all to die, the *fais do-do*—a children's expression that means "take a nap"—would be the last to go. The literal meaning notwithstanding, the fais do-do is an occasion for the dancing that is as important to traditional Cajun life as freedom of movement in the marsh. In the old days families gathered en masse for weekend dances at someone's house, a different one each weekend. . . On that evening . . the children were put into a separate room and lulled to sleep by a quiet tune on a fiddle or accordion—hence fais do-do. The dancing went on for hours, sometimes right through to the next morning.

faist See **feist** n

fait' See **faith**

fait-do-do See **fais-dodo**

faith n, v Pronc-sp *fait'*

A Form. Cf Pronc Intro 3.I.17

1892 (1969) Christensen *Afro–Amer. Folk Lore* 13, An' de Tiger, to try de man fait' gen run 'e spear in 'e side, an' den holler de same ting as befo', an' de man gi' um de same arnswer 'gain.

B As noun.

An oath, pledge, promise. [*OED faith* sb. 8, 9. b 1382, c1320 →]

1968 *DARE* (Qu. DD11, *When somebody gives up drinking: "I hear he _______."*) Inf **CT**9, Took the faith.

C As verb. [*OED "Obs."*]

To put credence in.

1951 Craig *Singing Hills* 35 **swVA, nNC,** "No," she drawled. "I don't faith religion none." *Ibid* 183, "It's good for other things too," Granny explained to me later. "Most folks don't faith it none excepting just for whooping cough." *Ibid* 191, Presently we joined the others. I noticed the whooping was much better and I began to "faith" the Druids' medicine.

faith doctor n

One who cures physical ailments by means of charms, incantations, and (especially) the patient's confidence in his special abilities.

1828 Hall *Letters West* 340, Your *faith doctor* is one who practices without diploma, and vanquishes disease without drug or lancet. . . Every thing is accomplished by the potency of a charm, which is inoperative unless the patient has entire confidence in its efficacy, and thence arises the appellation of *faith* doctor. **c1938** in 1970 Hyatt *Hoodoo* 1.297 **seNC,** Well, before tha' mothah sent me de hospital, came old man name of Ole Man Stuckey—he's dead, he's a white fellah called a *faith doctor.* **1966–68** *DARE* (Qu. BB51a, . . *Cures for corns or warts*) Inf **AL**34, People around here cure them through a faith doctor. That's any person (including myself) who uses magic of a sort. It works for warts but not for corns; (Qu. BB51b, . . *'Magical' cures for corns or warts*) Inf **AR**21, Faith doctors could take them off; **NC**22, Faith doctors rubbed them; **TN**27, Faith doctor used to rub 'em; [he would] say something in his mind. You didn't hear it.

faithful adv

Thoroughly.

1891 Page *Elsket* 126 **VA** [Black], Yes, suh, I did. I whupped him faithful.

faith, hope and charity n

A party game; see quot 1925.

1905 *DN* 3.78 **nwAR,** *Faith, Hope and Charity.* . . The name of a young people's game. **1925** Geister *Ice-Breakers* 70, Faith, Hope, and Charity. Some of the men are sent from the room. Three girls named Faith, Hope, Charity stand behind chairs which conceal a man, preferably one with a beard. The men are brought in one by one and told that if they will choose one of the girls they will get a kiss. No matter which one they choose, they are seated in the middle chair, are blindfolded, and the man in the rear kisses them.

faith you exclam [Cf *EDD faith*] *arch*

Indeed! Yes!

1907 *DN* 3.187 **seNH,** *Faith you.* . . An asseveration.

fak See **fact A1**

fake v [Etym uncert; cf *OED fake* v.[2]]

1 To steal.

1906 *DN* 3.135 **nwAR,** We fake eggs every night and then roast 'em. **1942** Berrey–Van den Bark *Amer. Slang* 490.8, *Steal* . . fake.

2 See quots.

1930 Williams *Logger-Talk* 23 **Pacific NW,** *Fake up a batch of biscuits.* **1958** McCulloch *Woods Words* 59 **Pacific NW,** *Fake.* . . To *do* anything. *Fake for cake*—To work for a living.

fake alder See **false alder**

fakealoo n Cf **fakus**

See quots.

1930 Williams *Logger-Talk* 23 **Pacific NW,** *Fake:* The most used word in a logger's vocabulary; if he can't think of the name of anything instanter it's a *fake.* . . *Fake-a-loo:* The same word embroidered for greater euphony. **1958** McCulloch *Woods Words* 59, *Fakealoo*—Any thing or scheme for which a better name is lacking.

faker n Also sp *fakir* [Prob **fake v 1**] *somewhat old-fash*

A vendor of cheap or worthless articles, esp on street corners or at fairs; a swindler.

1882 in 1936 Poe *Buckboard Days* facing 99 **NV,** Notice: To Thieves, Thugs, Fakirs and Bunko-Steerers. . . If Found within the Limits of this City after Ten O'Clock P.M., this Night, you will be Invited to attend a Grand Neck-tie Party. **1915** *DN* 4.201, Two fakers are sleeping in the cooler tonight. **1927** *DN* 5.445 [Underworld jargon], *Faker.* . . A peddler who attracts a crowd by a speech, song, or acrobatic performance and then proceeds to sell them some wonderful article. **1949** *AmSp* 24.261, The business objective of the old medicine show *fakers* [of the American frontier] was to *hoodoodle* or defraud the public. **1968–69** *DARE* (Qu. U5, *Someone who sells small articles on a street corner*) Inf **IA**30, Faker—he's out to git you; **OH**65, Faker; **OH**79, Street faker—old-fashioned; **PA**202, Faker—we call them this even if they're honest; (Qu. V7, *A person who sets out to cheat others while pretending to be honest*) Infs **KY**24, **MI**92, **MN**10, **NJ**8, **NC**68, **PA**34, **SC**24, **WA**18, Faker. [11 of 12 Infs old]

fakus n Cf **dingus** n[1] **1,** *hocus*

1905 *DN* 3.66 **NE,** Indefinite expression applied to something, the name of which is not readily recalled . . fakus.

fall v

A Forms.

1 pres 3rd pers sg: usu *falls;* also *fall.*

1970 *DARE* Tape **VA**73, You stay in the game till your card fall.

2 past: usu *fell;* rarely *fall, falled, felled.*

1966–70 *DARE* (Qu. BB14, . . *"Just as she came to the door she ______."*) Infs **MO**9, **SC**10, 27, Fall out; (Qu. KK4, . . *"Everything . . ______."*) Inf **IN**61, Falled into place; (Qu. U39, . . *"During the depression he ______."*) Inf **PA**248, Felled.

3 past pple: usu *fallen;* also freq *fell,* rarely *falled, fellen.* Note: Evidence for transitive forms is very limited; see also **C1, 3** below.

1781 *PA Jrl. & Weekly Advt.* (Philadelphia) 16 May 1/3, One of the most common vulgarisms or blunders in the English language, is putting the preterite for the participle. This is taken particular notice of by Lowth, in his grammar, as after he had *fell* down, for *fallen.* **1835** (1851) [see **C2** below]. **1893** *DN* 1.277 **wCT,** [Infin:] fall [past, past pple:] fell. **1903** *DN* 2.293 **Cape Cod MA** (as of a1857), Many strong verbs use the same form for the past and past participle. This is true of . . *fall–fell.* **1940–41** Cassidy *WI Atlas* **nwWI,** They would 'a' fell. **1940** Richter *Trees* 46 **sOH** (as of c1800), It'd a fell out. **1954** [see **fall away** v phr **2**]. **1955** Roberts *S. from Hell-fer-Sartin* 172 **seKY,** Him and his brother-in-law had fellen out over a well. **1966** *DARE* Tape **AL**1, This tree had fell; **OK**19, He had fell off'n a broomcorn rack. **1967–69** *DARE* (Qu. B26) Inf **SC**34, Bottom's fell out; (Qu. AA10, . . *"He ______ her."*) Infs **GA**77, **KY**19, He's (really) fell for.

B Intr sense.

Also with *down, off;* Of the wind: to decrease in intensity; hence ppl adj *falling.* *somewhat old-fash*

1752 (1892) Washington *Daily Jrl.* 22 Jan 73, Ye Wind was fallen & in ye Night grew calm. **1827** Roberts *Narratives* 271, Towards evening . . the breeze began to fall off. **1965–70** *DARE* (Qu. B13, *When the wind begins to decrease, you say it's ______*) 15 Infs, **scattered,** Falling; **AK**2, **GA**80, **PA**197, **TN**44, Falling off; **OK**47, Falling down; (Qu. O19, *Different kinds or degrees of wind that are important when you're in a boat*) Inf **PA**74, Falling [wind]. [18 of 21 Infs old] **1966** Dakin *Dial. Vocab. Ohio R. Valley* 2.27, *Falling* is the predominant word along the Ohio River from the Hocking Valley to Columbiana County and in the Muskingum Valley, although other terms compete. *Falling* is rare in Ohio west of the Hocking and does not appear outside this state. **1973** Allen *LAUM* 1.156 **IA** (as of c1950), The wind is falling. [1 inf, old]

C Tr senses.

1 To cut down, fell (a tree); hence vbl n *falling,* often attrib. [*OED* "*Obs* exc. *dial.* or *U.S.*"]

1678 in 1904 New Castle DE Court *Records* 1.362, 3 falling axses. **c1770** in 1832–33 Boucher *Glossary* 50 **MD** [Archaic and provincial words], *Fall,* or cut down, a tree. **1805** in 1917 *DN* 4.379, Cut 60 logs for huts and worked at the canoes. This, considering we had only two falling-axes and three hatchets, was pretty good work. **1806** (1905) Clark *Orig. Jrls. Lewis & Clark Exped.* 5.8, They have fallen a number of small pine . . for the Seed which is in the bur of which they eate. **1835** (1930) Strang *Diary* 231 **NY,** I directed David to go around a[nd] fall a tree from the opposite shore to me. **1905** U.S. Forest Serv. *Bulletin* 61.37, *Falling ax.* An ax with a long helve, and a long, narrow bit, designed especially for felling trees. . . *Falling wedge.* A wedge used to throw a tree in the desired direction, by driving it into the saw kerf. **1914** *DN* 4.72 **ME, nNH,** *Fall.* . . To fell (a tree). **1919** *DN* 5.56 **Pacific NW,** He has a crew of men falling and bucking and a donkey to haul logs. **1923** *DN* 5.206 **swMO. 1925** *AmSp* 1.135 **Pacific NW. 1927** *AmSp* 2.354 **WV. 1954** *Harder Coll.* **cwTN,** Falling notch—a notch in a tree which makes it fall in the desired direction. **1966–69** *DARE* Tape **CA**172A, Dad would fall the trees; **CA**104, To fall that tree [FW: Inf also used *fell* in same sense.]; **ME**6, Ones that do the falling; **WA**30, A faller's a guy who falls trees. **1981** *DARE* File **ME,** They [=loggers] had each fallen a tree.

2 Of a horse: to unseat (a rider).

1835 (1851) Colton *Ship & Shore* 139, The servant-boy . . by way of apology . . told how an animal had falled him three times.

3 Of an animal: to give birth to (its young).

1899 (1912) Green *VA Folk-Speech* 169, Fallen. . . "A cow-calf that is fallen this year." Dropped. **1967** *DARE* (Qu. K11) Inf **MO**2, [She] fell a calf.

fall n

1 A terrace.

1899 (1912) Green *VA Folk-Speech* 169, *Fall.* . . A terrace. "There are three falls in the garden." **1938** FWP *Ocean Highway* 199 **SC,** Often considerable leveling and building up was done before construction of the house was started; some South Carolinians spent much effort to obtain the terraces or "falls" that were so fashionable for the river front. **1954** *Sun* (Baltimore MD) 19 May 14/3 *(Hench Coll.),* Here the ground has been terraced in six terraces, or "falls," which spill a carpet of grass down to the Washington Boulevard.

2 pl, but sg in constr: A stream.

1935 *AmSp* 10.154 **MD,** *Falls* (stream). Western Shore. **1942** Footner *MD Main* 36, In Maryland speech, "branch" is an inlet from tide water while "run" is the running stream that empties into it; a "falls" is a larger flowing stream.

3 In the bituminous coal mining industry: see quot.

1973 *PADS* 59.52 **sIL, IN,** The amount of coal dislodged by the explosion or *shot* . . [is called] fall.

4 A women's hairpiece, usu made of long hair, and worn to supplement one's own hair. *chiefly among young, well-educ, urban women*

1965–70 *DARE* (Qu. X1b) 102 Infs, **scattered, but least freq Sth,** Fall. [Of all Infs responding to the question, 11% were young, 31% coll educ, 6% comm type 1, 54% female; of those giving this response, 29% were young, 48% coll educ, 18% comm type 1, 74% female.]

5 See **fallfish.**

6 in phrr *take* (or *get*) *a fall out of:* To get the best of.

1889 Daly *Great Unknown* 29 *(DA),* But I really have been hard at work, Cousin Neddie—and I've stowed a lot. You just see me take a fall out of my 'Universal History.' **1913** London *Valley of Moon* 325 **CA,** "What are you going to do [to scare an animal away]?" "Yell the top of my head off. I'll get a fall outa whatever it is."

fall asleep v phr Also *fall on sleep* [Cf Acts 13:36, 2 Peter 3:4] *euphem* Cf *DS* BB56

To die.

1943 *LANE* Map 520 **neMA,** Fell asleep. **1947** *McDavid Coll.* **cSC,** Fall on sleep—die.

fall away v phr

1 To lose weight, usu as the result of illness; hence vbl n *falling away,* ppl adj *fallen away.* **scattered, but chiefly NEast** Cf **fall off** v phr **1**

1891 *Jrl. Amer. Folkl.* 4.125 **PA,** "Falling away" is cured, in a child, by placing it in the oven. **1939** Coffin *Capt. Abby* 248 **ME** (as of c1860), But two days later she is in the doldrums bad, and is afraid that 12 pounds is thin for a four-months' baby! He looks delicate to her! All fallen away to a cartload, as the Maine saying goes. **1941** *LANE* Map 459 *(Emaciated, peaked)* 2 infs, **csCT, csRI,** Fallen away; 1 inf, **seRI,** He fell away. **1950** *WELS (To lose weight)* 1 Inf, **cWI,** Fall away—used commonly among Kentucky people; 1 Inf, **csWI,** Fall away—used occasionally; 1 Inf, **swWI,** Fall away. **1954** *Harder Coll.* **cwTN,** 'E jist plumb fell 'way to nothin'. Don' gain no weight 'tall. **c1960** *Wilson Coll.* **csKY,** *Fall off* (or *away*). . . Lose weight. **1965–70** *DARE* (Qu. X51, . . *"He was sick all winter and ______."*) 17 Infs, **scattered, but chiefly NEast,** Fell away; **IL**97, Fell away to a shadow; (Qu. X50, . . *A person who is very fat*) Inf **IL**97, Fell away to a ton. [14 Infs old] **1970** *Thompson Coll.* **AL** (as of 1920s), He's fell away to nothing since he's been tryin to cook for hisself.

2 By ext: see quot. Cf **fall off** v phr **2**

1954 *Harder Coll.* **cwTN,** *Fall away.* . . To decline in health. "Since 'at baby come 'ere, 'at girl's fall away to nothin'." " 'Es just a-fallin' 'way little at time."

3 To go to shreds, disintegrate.

1930 (1935) Porter *Flowering Judas* 39 **TX,** Maybe someone had bewitched your linens, they fall away so fast in the wash.

fall-away n Also *fell-away* [*fall away* v phr apostatize; *OED fall-away* sb. *"obs."*]

1968–69 *DARE* (Qu. CC7, . . *A person who goes to church very seldom or not at all*) Infs **PA**93, 227, Fall-away; **IA**18, Fall-away—a Roman Catholic expression—if he used to go; **MN**12, Fell-away or dropout—Catholics say.

fall back v phr
To devolve on, fall to (as by lot or inheritance).
1915 *DN* 4.242 **eTN,** *Fall back to*. . . To revert to (one) as an obligation. "All the things fell back to Papa to sell."

fallback n
1 A horse that rears and falls backward.
1952 FWP *Guide SD* 84, *Fall-back:* a horse that deliberately falls backward with his rider.
2 also *backfall:* The action of a horse falling backward.
1936 Adams *Cowboy Lingo* 99, A 'fall back' or 'rear back' was when a horse reared on his hind legs, lost his balance, and fell backward. . . The 'throwback' was when the horse hurled himself backward intentionally, and this was the trick of a 'killer.' **1951** Grant *Cowboy Encycl.* 62, *Fall-back.* When a horse rears and falls backwards. This is different from the "throw-back," in that the action of falling is not intentional on the part of the horse. The fall-back or back-fall is dangerous for the rider.

fall bean n **eKY, wVA**
A cultivated var of *Phaseolus;* see quots.
1968–69 *DARE* (Qu. I20, . . *Beans . . grown around here*) Inf **KY**28, Fall beans—both bunch and pole varieties; **KY**37, Fall beans are the same as cranberry beans; **KY**40, Cream-colored fall beans [are] bunch beans; **KY**42, Red fall beans are red beans with green hulls; **KY**44, Fall bean—the hull is white with red streaks; (Qu. I15, . . *Beans that you eat in the pod . . [with] yellow pods*) Inf **VA**2, Fall beans; (Qu. I16, *The large flat beans that are not eaten in the pods*) Inf **VA**2, Fall beans. **1976** *Wanigan Catalog* 8, *Fall Beans*—Apparently a local name in Kentucky for a buff hort. Similar to October [bean]. **1981** *Broaddus Coll.* **ceKY,** Fall beans.

fall bird n
1967 *DARE* (Qu. R7, *Insects that sit in trees . . in hot weather and make a sharp, buzzing sound*) Inf **OH**28, Cicada; fall birds; (Qu. R8, . . *Creatures that make a clicking or shrilling or chirping kind of sound*) Inf **OH**28, Crickets; [they are] the same as fall birds.

fall-bird's nest n
=pinedrops.
1869 Fuller *Flower Gatherers* 190 *(DA),* The other flower he mentioned was the 'Albany Beech-drops,' or 'Fall-Bird's Nest.'

fall by See **fall in 2**

fall caterpillar n
=woolly bear.
1967 *DARE* (Qu. R27, . . *Kinds of caterpillars*) Inf **NJ**2, Fall caterpillars are brown and black and woolly. Much brown indicates a mild winter.

fall dandelion n
A **hawkbit 1** (here: *Leontodon autumnalis*).
1857 Gray *Manual of Botany* 236, *L[eontodon] Autumnale. . . (Fall Dandelion.)*. . . Common in E. New England Aug.–Oct. **1859** (1880) Darlington *Amer. Weeds* 202, Hawkbit. Fall Dandelion. . . This introduced plant is especially abundant in New England. **1892** Torrey *Foot-Path Way* 60 *(DA),* The names of these hardy adventurers [as] . . fall dandelion. **1966** *DARE* FW Addit **MA**6, Fall dandelion—blooms on leafy stalk; gold [with a] scragglier top.

fall down See **fall v B**

fall downstairs v phr Also *fall down the steps* [Ger *die Treppe herunterfallen* have one's hair cut; see quot 1980] **chiefly WI**
To get a haircut.
1950 *WELS (Joking terms for getting your hair cut: "I'm going to _______.")* 3 Infs, **cWI,** Fall downstairs. [All Infs of Ger descent] **1980** *DARE* File **neIL** (as of c1940), Seeing an acquaintance who had obviously just had a haircut it was not unusual to remark "I see you fell down the steps." These haircuts were evidently given by some member of the family rather than a professional barber. The end result was a choppy haircut which resembled stair steps. *Ibid* **cWI,** When I was a child (c1950) I often heard my parents and other adults mention jocularly that someone had "fallen downstairs." This didn't seem funny to me until it was explained that the expression simply meant "to get a haircut." *Ibid* **swWI** (as of 1930s), When I first taught school in Lafayette County, the German family I lived with said "you fall down the steps"—no, "you fall downstairs," I think it was—if you get a haircut. *Ibid* **swWI,** Years and years ago in Mineral Point they would always say that you "fell down the steps" if you got a haircut.

fall duck n
Any of var ducks esp noticeable in a particular locality during fall migration: see quots.
1830 Tanner *Narrative* 308, Fall duck, red neck. **1888** Trumbull *Names of Birds* 51, [Red-Headed Duck]. . . *Fall Duck.* **1923** U.S. Dept. Ag. *Misc. Circular* 13.15, *Pintail*. . . Fall duck (Calif.). *Ibid* 17, *Redhead*. . . Fall duck. *Ibid* 21 *Ring-necked Duck*. . . Fall duck (Minn.). **1951** *AmSp* 26.272, Recognized as *fall ducks* are: pintail (Saskatchewan, Calif.); baldpate (Wis.); green-winged and blue-winged teals (Athabaska, Alberta); canvas-back (Tenn.); redhead and ringneck (Minn.); greater scaup (Mich., Manitoba, Northwest Territories); lesser scaup (Mich., Manitoba, Saskatchewan, Alberta, Northwest Territories); bufflehead and ruddy duck (Athabaska, Alberta). **1982** Elman *Hunter's Field Guide* 202, *Ring-necked Duck*. . . *Common & Regional Names:* . . fall duck.

fallen away adj
1 Apostate; having abandoned allegiance. [*fall away* to apostatize] Cf **fall-away** n
1979 *Capital Times* (Madison WI) 29 Jan 4/3 **NYC,** [He] described her as a "fallen away Catholic, ambivalent about developments in the church."
2 See **fall away** v phr **1.**

fallen palate See **falling palate**

fallen weather n
=falling weather 1.
1946 Stuart *Tales Plum Grove* 154 **KY,** The smoke is blowing toward the ground. . . Last night, there was a ring around the moon. The mules have played in the barnlot all day. These are sure signs of fallen weather. **1950** Stuart *Hie Hunters* 67 **eKY,** Ye know the first day ye come out here how the smoke was goin' to the ground. That's a good sign of fallen weather! It's been a-gittin' colder every day.

faller n [**fall v C1**] **chiefly Pacific NW; less freq Upper MW, NEng**
In the timber industry: one who cuts down or fells trees.
1905 U.S. Forest Serv. *Bulletin* 61.37, *Faller*. . . One who fells trees. **1925** *AmSp* 1.135 **Pacific NW,** The chopper is a "faller" now, if his task is to fell trees. **1941** *Time* 11 Aug 16/2 **OR,** The faller (who chops and saws the tree). **1941** Writers' Program *Guide WA* 73, "Fallers" chopped the trees down, while "buckers" cut or "bucked" them into 24, 32, or even 40-foot lengths, using a crosscut saw or "Swede fiddle." **1967–68** *DARE* Tape **CA**104, A lot of fallers are not experts; **WA**24, Then they had fallers and buckers; them [=fallers] are the guys that falls the timber; **WA**29, I had worked several years in the woods as what they call a bucker; they have fallers and buckers; **WA**30, A faller's a guy who falls trees. **1968** *Recorder-Herald* (Salmon ID) 25 Jan 7/6, Mack Neely, faller for George Biggs on the Ulysses Overlook timber sale, cuts fallen Ponderosa pine into sections. **1969** Sorden *Lumberjack Lingo* 41, While both *faller* and *feller* have been used, by far the more commonly used word is *faller*. . . New England and Wisconsin prefer the word *faller;* in other areas, including Michigan, *feller* is just as common.

fall fever n [From its prevalence in the fall of the year] *?obs*
Typhoid fever; any remittent fever.
1774 (1957) Fithian *Jrl. & Letters* 4 July 1.129, With us in Jersey wet Weather about this time . . is . . a forerunner of Agues, Fall-Fevers, Fluxes, & our Horse-Distempers. **1831** Peck *Guide for Emigrants* 295 **MO,** It will be more exposed to fall fevers than an elevated and airy situation. **1889** *Century Dict.* 2194, *Fall fever, (a)* Typhoid fever. *(b)* Remittent fever.

fallfish n Also *fall* [See quot 1820] **chiefly east of Allegheny Mts**
A fish of the genus *Semotilus,* esp *S. corporalis* which is also called **chiven, corporal** n^2, **cousin trout, dace, horned dace 2, roach, windfish.**
1812 Henry *Campaign Against Quebec* 32 **ME,** Several of our company angled successfully for trout, and a delicious chub, which we call a fall-fish. **1820** Rafinesque *Ohio R. Fishes* 51, Baiting Fallfish. *Rutilus compressus*. . . A small fish from two to four inches long, called Fall-fish Bait-fish, Minny, &c. It is found in the Alleghany Mountains. . . The name of Fall-fish arises from its being often found near falls and ripples. **1850** *Knickerbocker* 36.105, He will squat under a big, projecting rock the live-long day; now soberly hauling up an eel, now a 'catty,' or a 'fall,' or a 'parch.' **1884** Goode *Fisheries U.S.* 1.617, The Fall-Fish—*Semo-*

tilus Bullaris. The "Fall-fish," "Chub," "Roach," or "Dace" is abundant in the streams of the Eastern and Middle States east of the Alleghanies. **1947** Dalrymple *Panfish* 321 *(DA),* The Fallfish, *Semotilus corporalis,* though much smaller, stands in about the same relationship to the Trout, in waters east of the Alleghanies. **1968** *DARE* (Qu. P3, *Freshwater fish that are not good to eat*) Infs **PA**73, 89, Fallfish; **PA**155, Whitefish. Some call them fallfish. **[1970** WI Acad. *Trans.* 58.293, *Semotilus corporalis* . . Fallfish. Appearance of the fallfish in the Cedar Cr., Thunder Bay District of Ontario, Canada is explained through the use of northern Lake Superior as a migration route. Not yet reported from Wisconsin waters.]

fall-from-grace n Cf **fall-away** n

1970 *DARE* (Qu. CC7, . . *A person who goes to church very seldom or not at all*) Inf **KY**84, Backslider, fall-from-grace. Methodists are backsliders, Baptists fall from grace.

fall grape n **chiefly sAppalachians**

A wild grape such as a **fox grape** and a **frost grape.**

1815 Drake *Natural View Cincinnati* 77 **sOH,** *Vitis labrusca,* L. *Fall grape.* **1966–69** *DARE* (Qu. I46, . . *Fruits that grow wild around here*) Inf **KY**28, Fall grape—sweet and good; **KY**50, Fall grape—large and sweet; **NC**44, Fall grapes are wild grapes; **VA**13, Fall grapes; (Qu. I53, *Other fruits grown around here*) Inf **GA**72, Fall grapes are the same as possum grapes. They make good jam and jelly.

fall grass n

1968 *DARE* (Qu. S8, *A common kind of wild grass that grows in fields: it spreads by sending out long underground roots, and it's hard to get rid of*) Infs **MD**29, 30, Fall grass; (Qu. S9, *Other kinds of grass that are hard to get rid of*) Inf **WV**13, Fall grass. It looks like crab grass.

fall herring n Also *fall shad* Cf **spring herring, summer herring**

A **hickory shad** (here: *Alosa mediocris*).

1814 in 1815 Lit. & Philos. Soc. NY *Trans.* 1.451, *Long-Island Herring. (Clupea mattowaca)* Called also . . fall herring. *Ibid* 452, Some call this fish . . the *fall shad.* **1861** Acad. Nat. Sci. Philadelphia *Proc.* 54, *Meletta mattowacca.* . . "Fall Herring." **1889** *Century Dict.* 2809, Fall herring, *Clupea mediocris,* . . rather common along the Atlantic coast of the United States from Florida to the Bay of Fundy, and of little economic value. **1896** U.S. Natl. Museum *Bulletin* 47.425, *Pomolobus mediocris.* . . Fall Herring. **1905** NJ State Museum *Annual Rept. for 1904* 94, *Pomolobus mediocris.* . . Fall Herring. . . This herring does not ascend the fresh waters to spawn, and is not a highly-valued food-fish.

fall in v phr

1 To go to bed.

1942 Berrey–Van den Bark *Amer. Slang* 251.3, *Go to bed* . . fall in. **1950** *WELS ("I'm going to bed.")* 1 Inf, **csWI,** Fall in. **1966–70** *DARE* (Qu. X40, . . *Other ways . . of saying, "I'm going to bed."*) Infs **CA**2, **FL**39, **IL**63A, **OH**61, **TX**33, **WI**60, Fall in; **VA**69, Falling in.

2 also *fall by, ~ up:* To arrive at a place.

1946 (1972) Mezzrow–Wolfe *Really Blues* 332, Fall in: *arrive on the scene.* **1970** Major *Dict. Afro-Amer. Slang* 52, *Fall by (in, up):* (1940s) act of arriving. **1977** *DARE* File **Columbia SC** [Black], We fell in here early this morning (from a long distance).

falling ppl adj See **fall** v **B**

falling vbl n

1 See **fall** v **C1.**

2 See **falling exercise.**

falling away See **fall away** v phr **1**

falling down n

1 See **falling exercise.**

2 pl: See quot.

1982 *DARE* File **TN,** Blacks in Memphis used to speak of friends who had the "fallin' downs," an affliction I never learned much about. Maybe epilepsy?

falling-down drunk adj phr

Thoroughly intoxicated.

1968–69 *DARE* (Qu. DD15, *A person who is thoroughly drunk*) Infs **CA**154, **NY**42, **OH**61, Falling-down drunk. **1981** Mebane *Mary* 169 **cnNC** [Black], But whenever we in Wildwood saw him, he was falling-down drunk. Yet he had this marvelous talent [of drawing].

falling exercise n Less freq *falling, ~ down* **chiefly KY** *hist* Cf **exercise B**

A dropping to the ground in uncontrollable ecstasy during a religious experience or conversion.

1807 McNemar *KY Revival* 26, The various operations and exercises . . were indescribable. The falling exercise was the most noted. **1824** Bishop *Hist. Church KY* 353, The first bodily exercise, which appeared in our worshipping assemblies, was *falling.* **1847** Davidson *Hist. Presbyterian* 137 **KY,** The spectacle of persons falling down in a paroxysm of feeling . . became now [=1801] so common as to receive a distinct title, and to be known as the *Falling Exercise.* **1850** Gallaher *W. Sketch-book* 32 **csKY,** The *falling down.* This was one of the forms of that *bodily exercise,* as it was then called, which accompanied this remarkable work.

falling fever n

Perh =**fall fever.**

1944 Wellman *Bowl* 153 **KS,** Me, that cured her of the fallin' fever an' the liver complaint! . . I used golden seal an' kingroot tea. She was up in five days.

falling-off place n

=**jumping-off place.**

1908 *DN* 3.326 **eAL, wGA,** The end of the world, a deserted or uninhabited region. Sometimes *fallin(g)-off place.*

falling off the roof See **fall off the roof**

falling palate n Also *fallen palate* Cf *DJE come down*

An enlarged and inflamed soft palate.

1901 *Jrl. Amer. Folkl.* 14.33 **KY,** For "fallen palate," the hair on top of the patient's head is grasped and pulled "till it pops," the patient at the same time being made to swallow twice. **1914** *Ibid* 27.246 **Sth** [Black], To cure "fallen palate," twist two locks of hair tightly on the top of the head, and wrap them with a string. **1970** Anderson *TX Folk Med.* 31, [To cure] *Falling palate* Flatten your hair and then pull on it. Drink alum and sweet milk. *Bastrop* [*County*]. Take black pepper and salt and put it on the handle of a teaspoon. Put the spoon down the affected person's throat. *Brazos* [*Co.*].

fallings n Cf **red dog, tailings**

Refuse, leavings.

1980 *McDavid Coll.* **WV** (as of 1940), Red dog—the burnt "fallings" from a coal mine: soapstone, slate, etc.

falling star n

1 Prob a **goatsbeard 1.**

1969 *DARE* (Qu. S26e) Inf **NC**60, Falling stars—2 ft. stem with fluffy balls which blow off in wind.

2 A type of fireworks.

1967 *DARE* (Qu. FF28) Inf **CA**1, Falling stars.

falling statues n

A children's game: =**statues.**

1966 *DARE* (Qu. EE33) Inf **MS**38, Falling statues.

falling weather n **chiefly Midl**

1 Weather characterized by rain, snow, hail, or heavy fog; conditions likely to produce such weather. [Prob in ref to falling barometric pressure] Cf **weather fall**

1732 (1849) Franklin *Poor Richard 1733* 7, *Windy and . . falling wea[ther].* **1838** (1852) Gilman *S. Matron* 172 **SC,** It looks like falling weather, and my old drab will come in well to-day. **1884** Baldwin *Yankee School-Teacher* 176 **VA** [Black], I'se done got de rheumatiz pow'ful dis season; been s' much fallin' wedder lately dat de damp hab sort o' got groun' inter my ole bones. **1899** (1912) Green *VA Folk-Speech* 169, *Falling-weather.* . . A rainy or snowy time. Weather in which rain, hail, or snow, may be expected. **1902** *DN* 2.234 **sIL.** **1903** *DN* 2.313 **seMO.** **1906** *DN* 3.118 **sIN.** **1916** *DN* 4.302 **IL, KS, NC, VA, WV.** **1933** *AmSp* 8.1.49 **Ozarks,** *Falling Weather.* . . Weather in which the smoke from the chimney comes down to the ground, indicating rain. **1938** *AmSp* 13.5 **seAR.** **1967–70** *DARE* (Qu. B5, *When the weather looks as if it will become bad, you say it's* ———) Infs **AL**52, **AR**53, **IN**3, **KY**26, 44, **NC**87, (Going to be) falling weather; (Qu. B6, *When clouds begin to increase, you say* . . ———) Inf **NC**39, It seems we're going to have falling weather; (Qu. B8, *When clouds come and go all day, you say it's* ———) Inf **AR**53, Liable to be some falling weather.

2 Autumn, fall. [Perh by assoc with the season]

1942 Thomas *Blue Ridge Country* 63 **sAppalachians,** It was in the falling weather. These hills . . were a blaze of glory. *Ibid* 157, When the leaves begin to drap [=drop] in the falling weather.

‡fall in hell with the wicked v phr

To be victimized.

1967 *DARE* FW Addit **LA**7, When you hire somebody these days, you done fell in hell with the wicked with your pocketbook.

fall in on v phr Cf **fall in 2**

To drop in on, pay a visit to.

1891 Johnston *Primes & Neighbors* 142 **cGA,** I am always glad when any one falls in on me as you have to-night. Have you any news?

fall mackerel n

A **chub mackerel.**

1824 *Shipping & Comm. List* 31 July (Pettigrew P.) *(DA),* Fall mackerel. **1842** DeKay *Zool. NY* 4.103, *The Fall Mackerel. Scomber grex*. . . In the autumnal months, this species appears in great numbers on our coast. **1890** *Century Dict.* 3561, Fall mackerel are simply tinkers, about 10 inches long, of wandering or irregular habits.

fall off v phr

1 To lose weight, usu as a result of illness. **chiefly Sth, S Midl** See Map Cf **fall away** v phr **1**

1805 in 1947 Bakeless *Lewis & Clark* 188, For some days past they were unable to wear their mockersons; they have fallen off considerably. **1908** *DN* 3.309 **eAL, wGA,** *Fall off*. . . To become thin, lose flesh. **1937** *Natl. Geogr. Mag.* 71.276 **MS,** I used to weigh 467 pounds, but I fell off to 426. **1946** *AmSp* 21.190 **eKY,** *Fall off,* to become thin. 'She's fell off somethin' turrible, last two–three months.' **1950** *PADS* 14.28 **SC,** *Fall off*. . . To lose weight. There is no necessary connotation of bad health. "She has fallen off some, and looks much better." **c1960** *Wilson Coll.* **csKY,** *Fall off* (or *away*). . . Lose weight. **1965–70** *DARE* (Qu. X51, . . *"He was sick all winter and ______."*) 156 Infs, **chiefly Sth, S Midl,** Fell off; **AK**1, Fell off to a shadow; **GA**33, Fell off till he was just skin and bone; **GA**72, Fell off a lot; **KY**24, Fell off weight; **KY**65, Fell off to skin and bones; **SC**26, Fall off; **DC**6, **VA**5, Has fallen off in weight (*or* so much you'd hardly know him). **1980** *Verbatim* 6.3.14 **MO,** Erma, your dress is loose. Did you fall off a little?

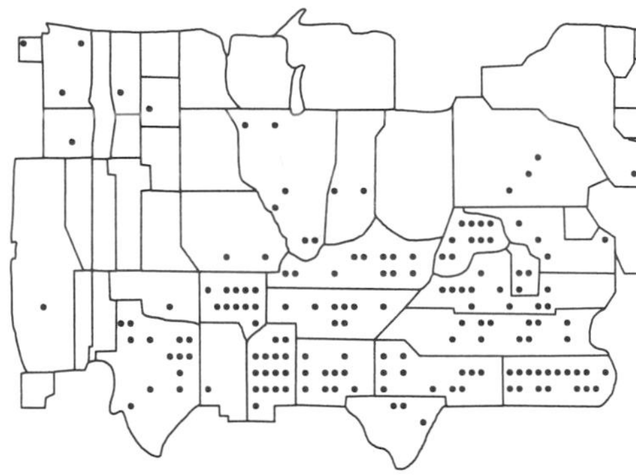

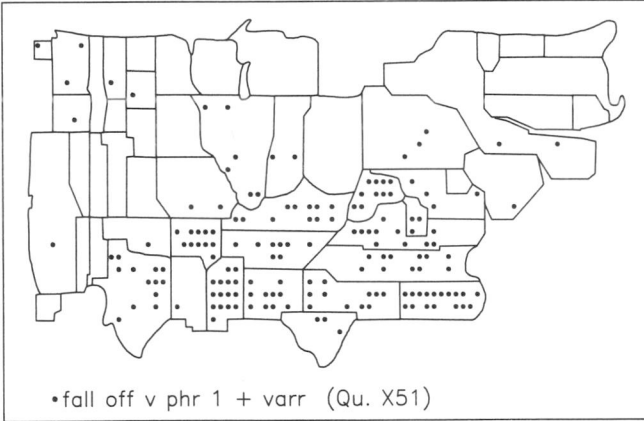

•fall off v phr 1 + varr (Qu. X51)

2 By ext: see quot. Cf **fall away** v phr **2**

1954 *Harder Coll.* **cwTN,** *Fall off*. . . To decline in health. "Aunt Marthy's shore [=sure] fell off a sight."

3 See **fall** v **B.**

4 See **fall off the roof.**

fall-off n [Abbr for **falling-off place**]

1967 *DARE* (Qu. C33, . . *Joking names . . for an out-of-the-way place, or a very unimportant place*) Inf **NY**31, A fall-off, a no-man's land.

fall off one's dinosaur See **fall out of one's cradle**

fall off the roof v phr Also *fall off* *joc, euphem*

To begin a menstrual period; hence vbl n *falling off the roof.*

1948 *Word* 4.3.184, Many of the terms [for menstruation] seem to defy classification. One of these, which is commonly used by high school and college girls is *to fall off the roof* (variants, *to fall off, to be off*). **1959** Thurber *Years with Ross* 12, We damn near printed a newsbreak about a girl falling off the roof. That's feminine hygiene, somebody told me just in time. You probably never heard the expression in Ohio. **1965–70** *DARE* (Qu. AA27, . . *A woman's menstruation*) 67 Infs, **scattered, but esp N Cent, NEast,** Falling off the roof; **CT**11, **GA**44, 55, 75, **MA**12, **RI**1, Fell (*or* fall) off the roof [Of all Infs responding to the question, 39% were young or mid-aged, 34% coll educ, 58% female; of those giving these responses, 52% were young or mid-aged, 53% coll educ, 78% female.]; **VT**16A, Kitty said, "I fell off the roof." I had no idea what she was talking about. What a stupid thing to say! **1972** (1974) Wilson *Playboy's Words* 101, *Fall off the roof*—A euphemism that has become a joke. *She fell off the roof* means that she has her menstrual period. **1978** *MJLF* 4.1.37 **cTX,** "I fell off the roof." I pushed my way into her house, "Fell off the roof? Whatever were you doing up there?" She laughed as she clutched at her stomach. "Haven't you ever heard that expression? It means I've started my period, silly."

fall on sleep See **fall asleep**

fall out v phr

1 To burst out laughing; to be tickled by something funny. **scattered, but esp Sth** *esp freq among Black speakers* Cf **fall out of one's cradle**

1946 (1972) Mezzrow–Wolfe *Really Blues* 332, Fall out: be tickled to death. **1965–70** *DARE* (Qu. GG30, *To suddenly break out laughing: "When he told her that, she just ______."*) Infs **CA**94, **IN**32, **LA**17, 23, **MS**21, **NY**235, **SC**69, Fell out; **MI**72, **MA**128, **MS**73, Fell out laughing; (Qu. GG31, *To laugh very hard: "I thought I'd ______."*) Infs **LA**28, **VA**46, Fall out; (Qu. FF21b, . . *"The first time I heard that one I ______."*) Inf **CA**94, Fell out. [5 of 12 Infs Black] **1967** *DARE* FW Addit **LA**3, To fall out laughing [means] to start laughing very hard. **1971** *Today Show Letters* **DC** [Black], She was so funny I fell out. **1973** *Patrick Coll.* **AL,** I like to fell out when he told me that-thar story. **1982** *Smithsonian* Oct 93 **eSC** [Black], Everybody includin' her is fallin' out laughin'.

2 To faint, lose consciousness. **chiefly Sth, S Midl** See Map *esp freq among Black speakers*

1884 Baldwin *Yankee School-Teacher* 112 **VA** [Black], Two of the deacons lift Aunt Molly and bear her to a bench by the rear door, where awaiting sisters fan her, and wipe her forehead, and watch her complete recovery. Aunt Molly has "fallen out." **1936** *Amer. Caravan* 154 **MS,** "Whuts the matter!" "A woman fell out! Fainted, Ah reckon. . . " **1959** Lomax *Rainbow Sign* 47 **AL** [Black], They tell me I shouted [at a revival meeting]. I musta did, because my clothes had all come a-loose when I come to myself. They tell me I just fell off the bench, just fell out. **1965–70** *DARE* (Qu. BB14, . . *"Just as she came to the door she ______."*) 32 Infs, **chiefly Sth, S Midl,** Fell out; **MO**9, **SC**10, 27, Fall out; **WI**30, In Arkansas, they "fall out"; (Qu. BB15, . . *Unconscious from a hard blow*) Inf **MD**9, Fell out—heard Negroes saying this; (Qu. BB6) Inf **MI**72, I'm going to fall out or pass out; (Qu. GG20, . . *"When those two got married, I . . ______."*) Inf **LA**17, Nearly fell out. [8 of 39 Infs Black] **1968** *DARE* FW Addit **Baltimore MD,** "To fall out"—common among Blacks.

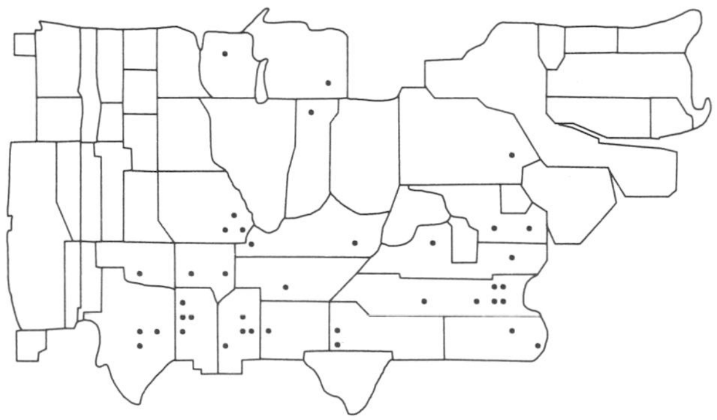

•fall out v phr 2 + varr (Qq. BB14, BB6, BB15, GG20)

3 See quot.

1970 Major *Dict. Afro–Amer. Slang* 52, *Fall out:* (1930's) to be surprised or overcome.

fall-out n [**fall out** v phr **2**]

A fainting spell.

1970 *DARE* (Qu. BB6, *A sudden feeling of weakness, when sometimes the person loses consciousness*) Inf **KY**86, Fall-out.

fall out of one's cradle v phr Also *fall out of one's crib, ~ high chair, fall off one's dinosaur* Cf **fall out** v phr **1**

Used in joc phrr to indicate that a joke is outdated; see quots.

1965–70 *DARE* (Qu. FF21b, . . *About old jokes people say: "The first time I heard that one . . ———."*) 20 Infs, **scattered,** I fell out of my (*or* the) cradle; 19 Infs, **scattered,** I fell out of my high chair; **FL**15, **MI**106, **NY**78, I fell out of my (*or* the) crib; **IN**75, **NJ**69, **NY**118, I fell off my dinosaur; **IL**97, I fell out of my crib laughing; **MI**76, I fell out of the cradle when my Grandpa told that; **IN**32, My Grampaw fell out of the cradle laughing; [**OH**38, **PA**94, I laughed so hard I fell out of my cradle]. **1983** *DARE* File **CO, ID, UT,** *(People say [of an old joke], "The first time I heard that one, ———."*) I fell off my dinosaur.

fallover n [Reversed cpd < *overfall;* cf Intro "Language Changes" I.1]

A waterfall.

1949 Arnow *Hunter's Horn* 303 **KY,** He couldn't climb out [of the canyon] now until he got to the fallover. . . He knew now that only a few feet away . . was Tucker Fallover, and that deep back in the wide warm room behind the water curtain the Tuckers had taken shelter.

fallow n, also attrib Usu |'fælo|; occas **esp NEast** |'fɑlo, -ə(r)| Pronc-spp *follow, falor, foller*

A Forms.

1782 in 1947 *AmSp* 22.35 **CT,** Coten brosh [?=cutting brush] in your falor. **1891** *DN* 1.116 **cNY,** [fɑlə, fɑlr] . . 'fallow'. **1895** *DN* 1.388 **ceNY,** *Foller* . . a fallow field. **1917** *DN* 4.401 **neOH,** I guess I'll make summer-foller out of that lot. **1968** *DARE* (Qu. L36) Inf **PA**103, ['fɑlo]; **PA**103A, ['fælo].

B Sense.

A piece of land on which trees have been cut. **chiefly NEast** Cf **chopping 1, cut-down n 1, slashing**

1782 [see **A** above]. **1819** Johnson *Letters from PA* 56, When the timber is cut down, ready for burning, it [=the cleared land] is called a fallow. **1845** *Knickerbocker* 25.388, Our western sky, . . much be-dimmed with the pervading smoke of fallow-fires. **1907** *DN* 3.243 **cME,** *Fallow.* . . A piece of ground where the trees are felled. **1909** *DN* 3.411 **neME,** *Follow.* . . A chopping. **1953** Van Wagenen *Golden Age* 30 **ceNY,** There are parts of the country where such a tract of felled timber is called a slashing, but in our local speech it was a "foller"—probably a variation of the old English term "fallow." *Ibid* 31, The fire would sweep across the foller in a line of swirling smoke and crackling flame, consuming the leaves and underbrush and smaller branches and leaving behind the fire-blackened stumps. **1968** *DARE* FW Addit **neNY,** I'm clearing me up a ['fɑlə].

fall-poison n

=**fly poison 1.**

1900 Lyons *Plant Names* 98, *C[hrospérma] muscaetoxicum.* . . Fall-poison. *Bulb* insecticide.

fall rose n

Any of several composite plants: see quots.

1892 *Jrl. Amer. Folkl.* 5.98, *Callistephus Chinensis,* fall roses. Mansfield, Ohio. **1896** *Ibid* 9.191, *Aster* (cultivated varieties), fall roses, Sulphur Grove, Ohio. **1950** *WELS Suppl.* **swWI,** Fall roses—small, late-blooming chrysanthemums. **1968–69** *DARE* (Qu. S25, . . *Small wild chrysanthemum-like flowers . . that bloom in fields late in the fall*) Infs **IN**28, **PA**77, Fall roses; (Qu. S11, . . *Other names . . for . . zinnia*) Inf **KY**40, Fall roses.

fall salmon n **Pacific**

Usu the **chum salmon,** but also the **chinook salmon.**

1850 Hines *Voyage Round World* 331 **OR,** In this country they are generally distinguished by the names spring-salmon and fall-salmon. **1882** U.S. Natl. Museum *Bulletin* 16.306, *O. chouicha. . . Chinnook* [sic] *Salmon; . . Fall Salmon (male); Spring Salmon; Winter Salmon.* **1940** Smith *Puyallup–Nisqually* 235 **WA,** The fall salmon, however, cannot be taken in quantity in the rivers until their flesh has deteriorated. **1960** Amer. Fisheries Soc. *List Fishes* 67, Salmon, fall—see salmon, chum.

fall shad See **fall herring**

fall snipe n **chiefly NEast**

=**red-backed sandpiper.**

1886 *Forest & Stream* 27.287/1, I should be glad to hear . . from any one who can tell me how far the use extends of the local name, "fall snipe," as applied to the . . young red-backed sandpipers . . that come upon the New England coast late in the autumn. I have heard the name used in the neighborhood of Portland, M[ain]e. **1888** Trumbull *Names of Birds* 182, At Pine Point, Me., Seaford, L. I., and Pleasantville (Atlantic Co.), N. J., [the Dunlin is called] *Fall Snipe.* **1917** (1923) *Birds Amer.* 1.237, *Red-Backed Sandpiper. . . Other Names.*—American Dunlin; . . Fall Snipe. **1925** (1928) Forbush *Birds MA* 1.416, *Pelidna alpina sakhalina . . Red-backed Sandpiper. Other names:* American Dunlin; . . Fall snipe; . . Winter Snipe. **1951** *AmSp* 26.273, *Fall snipe,* the dunlin (Maine, N.Y., N.J.).

fall sore n

1937 Johnson *Ante-Bellum NC* 73, The soil pollution around the cabins of these people also accounted for the scabies and impetigo, commonly known among them as "fall" and "spring" sores.

fall teal n

The blue-winged teal.

1923 U.S. Dept. Ag. *Misc. Circular* 13.13, *Blue-winged Teal. . . Vernacular Names. . . In local use. . .* Fall teal (Miss.). **1951** *AmSp* 26.273, By *fall teal,* we are to recognize the blue-winged teal southwardly (N.C., Miss., La., Texas). **1982** Elman *Hunter's Field Guide* 163, *Blue-winged Teal. . . Common & Regional Names:* . . fall teal.

fall up See **fall in 2**

fall weed n

An aster, such as *Aster ericoides.*

1891 *Jrl. Amer. Folkl.* 4.149 **ME,** One of the frequent Asters around rocks and the edges of thickets, with purple-white flowers, as I remember, she called simply *Fall-weed.* **1966** *DARE* (Qu. S21, . . *Weeds . . that are a trouble in gardens and fields*) Inf **NC**24, Fall weed. It has a white bloom late in the fall.

faloosie n [Var of **floozy** n[1]]

1936 *AmSp* 11.375, 'She is nothing but an old faloosie,' [is] said of a woman of loose morals.

falor See **fallow**

false adj Cf **bastard 2**

Of a plant or animal: resembling and sometimes mistaken for the "true" form. See also separate entries below

1884 U.S. Dept. Ag. *Rept. of Secy. for 1884* 326 **GA,** False-caterpillars, of which the Imported Currant-worm *(Nematus ventricosus)* is a familiar type. **1901** Lounsberry *S. Wild Flowers* 142, False elm . . often . . is strongly suggestive of an old elm. **1901** Howard *Insect Book* 310, Another very common and destructive insect belonging to this family is the so-called "false chinch-bug" *(Nyzius angustatus)* . . frequently mistaken by farmers for the true chinch-bug. **1931** Harned *Wild Flowers Alleghanies* 504, *False Boneset. . .* This plant resembles those of the genera [sic] Eupatorium but the leaves are alternate on the stem. **1966–67** *DARE* (Qu. S21, . . *Weeds . . that are a trouble in gardens and fields*) Inf **NY**34, False portulaca; (Qu. S26e, *Other wildflowers*) Inf **CA**9, False incense; (Qu. T16, *What kinds of trees are 'special' around here?*) Inf **ME**5, False hornbeam. **1968** *Swedesboro News* (NJ) 11 July 8/1, Vacationers fishing or swimming off the New Jersey shores this summer could easily sight or even meet a Dusky, Sharpnose or False Cat Shark.

false n

1 =**rough-box.**

1930 *DN* 6.81 **ceSC,** *False.* . . The wooden box in which a coffin is placed before it is lowered into the grave. Rare.

2 A falsehood, lie. [*OED false* sb. C. 2. c "*Obs.* exc. *arch.*"] Cf **true** n

1923 (1946) Greer–Petrie *Angeline Doin' Society* 2 **csKY,** If he [=a preacher] *had* told a *false,* Lum wanted to be able to tell . . about hit when he got home. **1927** Kennedy *Gritny* 20 **sLA** [Black], I ain' tellin' no false. **c1938** in 1970 Hyatt *Hoodoo* 1.12 **seGA** [Black], Dey'll go, prob'ly uptown an' tell a false' on me an' have me put in jail.

false albacore n

A **bonito 1** (here: *Sarda sarda*).

1947 Caine *Salt Water* 16, *Bonito. Sarda sarda* . . is also known as . . false albacore.

false alder n Also *fake alder*

A **winterberry** (here: *Ilex verticillata*).

1822 Eaton *Botany* 410, *Prinos . . verticillatus . .* winter berry, false alder . . leaves oval, serrate, acuminate, pubescent beneath. **c1873** in 1976 Miller *Shaker Herbs* 126, Fake Alder. Used with good effect in jaundice, diarrhea, gangrene, dyspepsia. **1930** U.S. Dept. Ag. *Misc. Pub.* 77.25, False alder . . is a shrub usually from 6 to 8 feet high . . with grayish bark and smooth twigs. **1960** Vines *Trees SW* 656, Common Winterberry. . . Also known under the vernacular names of . . False Alder . . and Virginia Winterberry.

false aloe n

1 An **agave** (here: *Agave virginica*).

1847 Wood *Class-Book* 539, *A. Virginica. False Aloe.* **1876** Hobbs *Bot. Hdbk.* 35, False Aloe, Agave Virginica. **1901** Lounsberry *S. Wild Flowers* 66, *False Aloe. . .* Although the custom is very prevalent, it is quite improperly that the agaves are called aloes and century plants. **1930** OK Univ. Biol. Surv. *Pub.* 2.56, False Aloe. Rattlesnake Master. **1976** Bruce *How to Grow Wildflowers* 287, *Agave virginica,* American Aloe, False Aloe, or Rattlesnake Master, is a yucca-like plant.

2 =**colicroot 2.** *obs*

1822 Eaton *Botany* 166 **MA,** *Aletris . . farinosa . .* false aloe. . . Here the inhabitants use the root as a tonic, which at the same time serves as a moderate cathartic. The root is intensely bitter. **1840** MA Zool. & Bot. Surv. *Herb. Plants & Quadrupeds* 208, *A. farinosa. . .* False Aloe. . . The root is very bitter, and in small quantities used as a tonic and stomachic.

false alumroot n

=**fringecup 2.**

1916 Parsons *Wild Flowers CA* 348, False Alum-root. . . *Tellima grandiflora.*

false angel wing n Cf **angel('s) wing 1**

A wing-shaped bivalve.

1974 Abbott *Seashells* 535, *Petricola pholadiformis . .* False Angel Wing.

false anise n

A **giant hyssop** (here: *Agastache foeniculum*).

1950 Stevens *ND Plants* 241, *Agastache anethiodora. . . False anise. . .* It has an anise-like fragrance when bruised for which it was used by the Indians. Not related to true anise.

false azalea n

A **mock azalea** (here: *Menziesia ferruginea*).

1938 (1958) Sharples *AK Wild Flowers* 88, *M[enziesia] ferruginea.* "False Azalea." One of the most beautiful shrubs of Southeastern Alaska.

false balm n

A **horsemint 1** (here: *Monarda clinopodioides*).

1937 Stemen–Myers *OK Flora* 453, *Monarda clinopodioides. . . False Balm. . .* On plains and prairies.

false banana See **banana B1**

false beechdrops n

A **pinesap** (here: *Monotropa hypopithys*).

1822 Eaton *Botany* 316, False beechdrops. . . Grows on roots of trees, &c. **1848** Gray *Manual of Botany* 274, False Beech-drops. . . Oak and pine woods, common, June–Aug. **1912** Mathews *Amer. Wild Flowers* 326, False Beech-drops or Pine-sap. . . The small vase-shaped flowers are light crimson-red more or less touched with yellow. **1941** Writers' Program *Guide WI* 345, Flowers rare to Wisconsin grow in the dampness: Indian pipe, false beechdrops. **1953** Greene–Blomquist *Flowers South* 85, False beech-drops and pinesaps are similar plants but lack the pure whiteness of the Indian-pipe.

false-belly n

The opossum's marsupial pouch.

1912 Green *VA Folk-Speech* 169, *False-belly. . .* The pocket in which a possum carries her young.

false bittersweet n

=**climbing bittersweet.**

1822 Eaton *Botany* 227, *Celastrus . . Scandens . .* (false bittersweet, staff tree. . . Retains its scarlet berries through the winter.) **1911** (1916) Porter *Harvester* 225 **IN,** The false and true bitter-sweet . . run riot here. **1936** IL Nat. Hist. Surv. *Wildflowers* 188, The Climbing Bittersweet is called by various names in different places, such as . . False Bittersweet. **1960** Vines *Trees SW* 660, Known also by the vernacular names of False Bitter-sweet [etc] . . the plant sometimes injures trees by constriction.

false box n

1 A **flowering dogwood** (here: *Cornus florida*).

1822 Eaton *Botany* 251, *Cornus . . florida* (false box, dogwood tree). **1960** Vines *Trees SW* 795, Vernacular names are . . False Box . . and White Cornel. **1974** (1977) Coon *Useful Plants* 119, *Cornus florida*—Flowering dogwood, . . false box.

2 also *false boxwood:* A tree *(Gyminda latifolia)* native to southern Florida and the Keys. Also called **Florida boxwood 2**

1897 Sudworth *Arborescent Flora* 281, *Gyminda. . . Common Names.* False Boxwood (Fla.) **1908** Britton *N. Amer. Trees* 632, *False Boxwood. . .* Evergreen trees with simple opposite leaves, and small greenish imperfect flowers. **1933** Small *Manual SE Flora* 819, *False-boxwood. . .* The dark heart-wood is heavy, and hard. **1979** Little *Checklist U.S. Trees* 142, *Falsebox. . . Other common names*—false-boxwood.

3 =**Oregon boxwood.**

1960 Vines *Trees SW* 666, *Pachystima* [sic] *myrsinites . .* is also known under the vernacular names of . . False-box [etc].

false boxwood See **false box 2**

false buckthorn n

A **gum elastic** (here: *Bumelia lanuginosa*).

1901 Mohr *Plant Life AL* 664, *Bumelia lanuginosa . .* False Buckthorn. **1940** Clute *Amer. Plant Names* 113, *Bumelia lanuginosa.* False Buckthorn. **1950** Gray–Fernald *Manual of Botany* 1145, *Bumelia lanuginosa . .* False Buckthorn. **1960** Vines *Trees SW* 833, *Bumelia lanuginosa . .* Vernacular names are . . False-buckthorn, and Blackhaw. **1976** Bailey–Bailey *Hortus Third* 190, *Bumelia lanuginosa . .* False Buckthorn.

false buckwheat n

=**climbing false buckwheat.**

a1862 (1864) Thoreau *ME Woods* 315, *Polygonum cilinode* (fringe-jointed false buckwheat). **1878** (1887) Jackson *Bits of Travel* 186 **MA,** Solid knitted and knotted banks of vines on either hand,—woodbine, groundnut vine, wild or "false" buckwheat.

false buffalo grass n

A mat-forming grass *(Munroa squarrosa)* native to the western US.

1894 *Jrl. Amer. Folkl.* 7.104, *Munroa squarrosa . .* false buffalo-grass. **1950** Hitchcock–Chase *Manual Grasses* 545, *False Buffalo Grass. . .* Forming mats as much as 50 cm. in diameter. **1970** Correll *Plants TX* 216.

false bugbane n [See quot 1901]

A plant of the genus *Trautvetteria.* For other names of var spp see **tasselrue**

1857 Gray *Manual of Botany* 7, *Trautvetteria. . . False Bugbane. . .* A perennial herb. **1901** Lounsberry *S. Wild Flowers* 183, *Trautvetteria Carolinensis. . .* It may be that this perennial herb is called false bugbane because at one time it was associated with the genus Cimicifuga, whose members have a reputed efficacy for expelling plant vermin, and are popularly known as bugbanes. **1931** Harned *Wild Flowers Alleghanies* 183, *False Bugbane. . .* More or less abundant along rivers and mountain streams. **1973** Hitchcock–Cronquist *Flora Pacific NW* 141, *Trautvetteria. . .* False Bugbane.

false caraway n

=**yampah.**

1961 Peck *Manual OR* 562, *P. Gairdneri. . . Western False Caraway. . . P. oregana. . . Oregon False Caraway. . . P. Bolanderi. . . Mountain False Caraway.* **1963** Craighead *Rocky Mt. Wildflowers* 130, *Yampa. . .* False Caraway . . has a parsnip flavor, raw; cooked it is sweet and mealy. **1973** Hitchcock–Cronquist *Flora Pacific NW* 335, *Perideridia. . .* Yampah; False-caraway. **1976** Bailey–Bailey *Hortus Third* 846.

false catclaw n [See quot 1937]

=**fairy duster.**

1931 U.S. Dept. Ag. *Misc. Pub.* 101.73, *False-mesquite . .* is a dwarfed, more or less prostrate shrub, known also as . . false catclaw. **1937** U.S. Forest Serv. *Range Plant Hdbk.* B36, False-mesquite, also known as . . false-catclaw because of its resemblance to the related . . catclaw *(Acacia gregii),* belongs to the mimosa family.

false chanterelle n [From the resemblance to *Cantharellus* spp]

1 A mushroom (*Hygrophoropsis aurantiacus*).

1908 Hard *Mushroom Edible* 200, *False Chanterelle* . . is generally labeled poisonous, but some good authorities say it is wholesome. **1942** Hylander *Plant Life* 58, The False Chantrelle [sic] . . is small and trumpet-shaped, quite inconspicuous in the copses it frequents because of its sombre yellowish color. **1987** McKnight-McKnight *Mushrooms* 154, *False Chanterelle*. . . On soil or decaying wood, including charred wood. . . Late summer and fall.

2 =**jack-o'-lantern** (here: *Omphalotus illudens*).

1981 Lincoff *Audubon Field Guide Mushrooms* 788, *Jack O'Lantern*. . . Also called the "False Chanterelle," and often mistaken for the Chanterelle, this is a species complex. **1985** Ammirati et al. *Poisonous Mushrooms* 291, *Omphalotus illudens*. . . *Common names*. . . False chanterelle. *Ibid* 292, It is sometimes mistaken for *Cantharellus cibarius* (chanterelle). . . *Cantharellus cibarius* is similar in color to *O. illudens*, but does not grow in dense, large clusters.

false cohosh n

1 =**blue cohosh 1.**

1822 Eaton *Botany* 227, *Caulophyllum* . . *thalictroides* (poppose [=papoose] root, false cohosh). **1840** MA Zool. & Bot. Surv. *Herb. Plants & Quadrupeds* 41, *Leontice thalictroides*, Poppoose Root, and False Cohosh. . . Blossoms in April and May.

2 A **bugbane 1** (here: *Cimicifuga racemosa*).

1971 Krochmal *Appalachia Med. Plants* 96, *Cimicifuga racemosa*. . . *Common Names*: . . false cohosh.

false coltsfoot n Also *false coltfoot*

A **wild ginger** (here: *Asarum canadense*).

1822 Eaton *Botany* 184, *Asarum* . . *canadense* . . white snake-root, wild ginger, false coltfoot. . . Root aromatic and stimulant. **1876** Hobbs *Bot. Hdbk.* 36, False coltsfoot, Canada snake root, Asarum Canadense. **1910** Graves *Flowering Plants* 157 **CT**, Sweet, False or Canada Coltsfoot. . . Readily cultivated, and makes a pleasing ground covering in rich shaded places. **1930** Sievers *Amer. Med. Plants* 19, False coltsfoot. **1974** (1977) Coon *Useful Plants* 70, False colt's foot . . has often been used as a substitute for "tropical" ginger.

false crawley n Cf **crawley root**

=**pinedrops.**

1876 Hobbs *Bot. Hdbk.* 36, False crawley, Albany beech drops, Pterospora andromeda. **1900** Lyons *Plant Names* 310. **1940** Clute *Amer. Plant Names* 228, *Pterospora andromedea* [sic]. False crawley, . . giant bird's-nest.

false damiana See **damiana 2**

false dandelion n

Any of var plants with flowers resembling dandelions (*Taraxacum* spp), but esp those of the genera *Agoseris, Microseris*, and *Pyrrhopappus*.

1894 *Jrl. Amer. Folkl.* 7.92, *Krigia amplexicaulis* . . False dandelion, W. Va. **1900** Lyons *Plant Names* 19, *Agoseris*. . . False Dandelion. *Ibid* 261, *Nothocalais*. . . Called also False Dandelion. *Ibid* 347, False Dandelion. . . Pyrrhopappus. **1935** (1943) Muenscher *Weeds* 503, *Hypochoeris radicata*. . . False dandelion. **1936** Winter *Plants NE* 167, *A[goseris] cuspidata*. . . False Dandelion. **1949** Moldenke *Amer. Wild Flowers* 183, Many other handsome plants . . could be mentioned . . , including . . *falsedandelions (Agoseris, Sitilias)*. **1966** *DARE* FW Addit **TX**44, False dandelion [*Pyrrhopappus multicaulis*]. **1972** Brown *Wildflowers LA* 212, *False Dandelion. Pyrrhopappus carolinianus*. **1973** Hitchcock-Cronquist *Flora Pacific NW* 478, *Agoseris*. . . False-dandelion; Mountain-dandelion; Agoseris.

false dogwood n

1 Either a **striped maple** or a **mountain maple** (here: *Acer spicatum*).

1822 Eaton *Botany* 154, *[Acer] striatum* . . striped maple, false dogwood, moose wood. **1840** Phelps *Lectures on Botany* 71, *Acer*. . . *striatum*, . . false dogwood. . . Small tree, with a greenish, striped bark. **1900** Lyons *Plant Names* 11, *A. Pennsylvanicum*. . . False or Striped Dogwood. **1940** Clute *Amer. Plant Names* 129, *Striped Maple*. . . False dogwood. *Ibid* 249, *Acer spicatum*. . . False dogwood.

2 A **soapberry** (here: *Sapindus saponaria*).

1897 Sudworth *Arborescent Flora* 295, *Sapindus saponaria*. . . *Common Names*. False Dogwood (Fla.) **1908** Britton *N. Amer. Trees* 665, The tree [=*Sapindus saponaria*] is known also as False dogwood. **1933** Small *Manual SE Flora* 828, *False-dogwood*. . . The light-brown heartwood is close-grained, hard, and heavy. **1976** Bailey-Bailey *Hortus Third* 1004.

false dragonhead n

1 also *false dragon*, ~ *dragon's-head*: A plant of the genus *Physostegia*. Also called **compass plant 6, dragonhead 2, lion's heart, obedience, obedient plant.** For other names of *P. virginiana* see **hinge flower, lady-by-the-lake, lion's mouth, Saint Margaret's flower, shellflower, toad's mouth**

1848 Gray *Manual of Botany* 329, *Physostegia*. . . *False Dragonhead*. **1895** Gray-Bailey *Field Botany* 354, False Dragon's Head. **1901** Lounsberry *S. Wild Flowers* 452, *False Dragon Head* . . makes no effort to rebound, but remains most obediently wherever it is put. **1931** Harned *Wild Flowers Alleghanies* 426, *False Dragon-head*. . . Flowers showy, pale purple. **1966** *DARE* (Qu. S26d) Inf **NC**10, False dragon. **1976** Bailey-Bailey *Hortus Third* 869, False dragonhead.

2 =**dragonhead 1.**

1949 Moldenke *Amer. Wild Flowers* 217, These plants are also known as *false-dragonheads, Dracocephalum*. **1950** Stevens *ND Plants* 243, *[Dracocephalum] parviflora* . . is also called false dragonhead.

false elm n [See quot 1901]

A **hackberry** (here: *Celtis occidentalis*).

1854 (1969) Thoreau *Walden* 218 **MA**, The *Celtis occidentalis*, or false elm. **1901** Lounsberry *S. Wild Flowers* 142, *C. occidentalis*, . . false elm, is so appropriately called, as often it is strongly suggestive of an old elm. **1960** Vines *Trees SW* 206, Vernacular names are Nettle-tree, False-elm [etc].

false everlasting n

A **groundsel tree** (here: *Baccharis douglasii*).

1954 CA Div. Beaches & Parks *Pt. Lobos Wild Flowers* 32, *Baccharis Douglasii* . . False Everlasting.

false flesh n

=**proud flesh.**

1973 Allen *LAUM* 1.365 (as of c1950), *Dead flesh* is a oncer [for *proud flesh*] in South Dakota, as is *false flesh* in North Dakota.

false foxglove n [Prob from a resemblance to *Digitalis*]

Any of numerous plants of the genera *Agalinus* and *Aureolaria* (both formerly included in *Gerardia*). Also called **foxglove 2a.** For other names of var spp see **autumn bells, cornflower 5, feverweed 1, feverwort 3, gall of the earth 1, golden oak 1, gold foxglove, kidney weed, lousewort, oak leach**

1822 Eaton *Botany* 289, *Gerardia* . . *flava* (false foxglove). **1848** Gray *Manual of Botany* 307, *Smaller False Foxglove*. . . Woods and barrens, from Ohio and Kentucky southward along the mountains. **1876** Hobbs *Bot. Hdbk.* 86, False foxglove, Golden oak, Gerardia Quercifolia. **1901** Lounsberry *S. Wild Flowers* 464, Smooth or entire-leaved false foxglove . . travels not further northward than Pennsylvania or Michigan. **1933** Small *Manual SE Flora* 1213, *Aureolaria*. . . *Yellow-foxgloves. False-foxgloves*. **1976** Fleming *Wild Flowers FL* 85, *False Foxglove (Agalinus fasciculata)* . . blooms from spring to fall in low grounds and along borders of marshes from Florida to Texas and Maryland.

false garlic n

A plant of the genus *Nothoscordum*, usu *N. bivalve* which is also called **crow poison 3, odorless onion.**

1903 Small *Flora SE U.S.* 264, *Nothoscordium* [sic] *bivalve*. . . In sandy soil. . . Spring. *False Garlic*. **1936** Whitehouse *TX Flowers* 8, *False Garlic* . . is one of the first flowers to appear in the spring on lawns, meadows, and roadsides throughout the Southern States. **1940** Steyermark *Flora MO* 68, False Garlic. . . Leaves bright green. . . Glades, rocky ledges, and prairies. **1961** Wills-Irwin *Flowers TX* 94, Crow-poison, sometimes known as False-garlic or Odorless-onion, . . makes an attractive early spring addition to any garden. **1972** Brown *Wildflowers LA* 18, *False Garlic* . . has no onion or garlic odor. . . It is closely related to the onion. **1975** Duncan-Foote *Wildflowers SE* 250, False-garlic. . . Perennial to 45 cm tall from a small bulb which has a faint odor of onions when fresh.

false goatsbeard n

A tall perennial plant *(Astilbe biternata)* which produces panicles of yellowish-white flowers. Also called **feather tree**

1900 Lyons *Plant Names* 52, *A. biternata*. . . Southeastern U.S. False Goat's-beard. **1901** Lounsberry *S. Wild Flowers* 216, *False Goat's Beard*. . . No goat's beard, it would seem was ever so pretty as the foamy, fleecy spray of this plant's bloom. **1949** Moldenke *Amer. Wild Flowers* 54, These falsegoatsbeards are among our largest herbs, 3 to 6 feet tall.

1975 Duncan–Foote *Wildflowers SE* 62, False Goat's-beard . . may be identified by the 3-lobed terminal leaflet.

false goldenrod n

1 A **goldenrod 1** (here: *Solidago sphacelata*).

1968 *DARE* FW Addit **VA**15, False goldenrod. Common roadside plant.

2 =**rabbit brush** (here: *Chrysothamnus* spp).

1924 *Amer. Botanist* 30.33, "Rabbit-brush" . . refers in common parlance of the west to the various species of *Bigelovia*. . . "Rayless or false goldenrod" are less frequently used. **1947** (1976) Curtin *Healing Herbs* 57, *False Goldenrod*. . . Chrysothamnus graveolens. . . Nothing so completely characterizes the landscape as the silvery-green foliage and storm of yellow bloom. **1963** Craighead *Rocky Mt. Wildflowers* 202, *Rabbitbrush*. . . *Other names:* False Goldenrod. . . This is a conspicuous, bushy, goldenrod-like plant. **1966** *DARE* Wildfl QR Pl.22 Inf **CO**7, False goldenrod.

false grape n [From similarity to plants of the genus *Vitis*]

1 A **Virginia creeper** (here: *Parthenocissus quinquefolia*).

1822 Eaton *Botany* 171, *Ampelopsis* . . *quinquefolia* . . false grape, creeper . . leaves in fives, toothed: stem rooting, climbing. **1900** Lyons *Plant Names* 277, Virginia Creeper . . False Grape. **1940** Clute *Amer. Plant Names* 131, *Virginia Creeper*. . . False grape.

2 A woody vine *(Ampelopsis cordata)* with somewhat grapelike leaves and fruit. Also called **coon grape 2, pepper vine, swamp grape**

1940 Steyermark *Flora MO* 349, *False Grape*. . . High-climbing vine having tendrils. . . The fruit . . turns . . finally turquoise blue. **1948** Stevens *KS Wild Flowers* 328, *False Grape*. . . Berries . . quite inedible to us, but a favorite fruit of the brown thrasher. **1973** Stephens *Woody Plants* 376, False grape. . . In the vegetative condition, this plant is often confused with *Vitis*.

false greasewood n

A **false indigo 1** (here: *Amorpha canescens*).

1931 U.S. Dept. Ag. *Misc. Pub.* 101.83, Leadplant *(A. canescens)*, known also as . . false greasewood, . . is a low, mostly spreading bush, 1 to 4 feet high.

false gromwell n

Std: a plant of the genus *Onosmodium*. Also called **marbleseed.** For other names of the common *O. virginianum* see **gravelweed 3, necklace plant, pearl-plant, wild Job's tears**

false guinea grass See **guinea grass 2**

false heart n

A condition of potatoes in which the centers are hollow.

1928 *Ruppenthal Coll.* **KS,** We saw false heart in potatoes in Pennsylvania more often than we have in Kansas.

false heather n

1 also *false heath:* =**beach heather.**

1822 Eaton *Botany* 308, *Hudsonia* . . *ericoides* (false heath). **1840** Phelps *Lectures on Botany* 104, *Hudsonia* . . *ericoides,* (false heath, . .) pubescent. **1900** Lyons *Plant Names* 194, *Hudsonia tomentosa* . . False Heather. **1910** Graves *Flowering Plants* 283 **CT**, *Hudsonia tomentosa* . . False Heather. **1951** Hough *Singing in Morning* 39 **Martha's Vineyard MA,** Dried beach heather—also known popularly as barren heath, ground cedar, poverty plant, and false heather—can be no worse than corn husks or seaweed [for mattress stuffing].

2 =**mountain heather.**

1938 (1958) Sharples *AK Wild Flowers* 101, *Phyllodoce*. . . Ericaceae. "False Heather."

3 =**minniebush.**

1901 Lounsberry *S. Wild Flowers* 382, False Heather. . . *Menziesia pilosa*. **1932** *Country Life* 62.66, Alleghany Manziesa [sic] (False Heather) blooms in May and June. The shrub grows from two to six feet high, and has grayish-brown, peeling bark which is generally black dotted.

false hellebore n

1 A plant of the genus *Veratrum*. Also called **corn lily 3a, elleber, skunk cabbage, varebells, white hellebore.** For other names of var spp see **cow cabbage, devil's tobacco 4, Indian poke, skunkweed**

1848 Gray *Manual of Botany* 476, *Veratrum*. . . *False Hellebore*. **1976** Bruce *How to Grow Wildflowers* 171, Closely related to the foregoing, but rather different in aspect, is *Veratrum viride,* the False-hellebore or "Indian Poke."

2 =**Indian cucumber root.**

1966 *DARE* Wildfl QR Pl.22 Inf **OH**14, False hellebore [*Medeola virginiana*].

false hemlock n

=**water parsnip.**

1966 *DARE* Wildfl QR Pl.149 Inf **OH**14, False hemlock.

false honohono See **honohono 2**

false horehound n

=**boneset 1.**

1972 Brown *Wildflowers LA* 201, *False-hoarhound* [sic] . . *Eupatorium rotundifolium*.

false hyacinth n

A **camas 1** (here: *Camassia scilloides*).

1946 Reeves–Bain *Flora TX* 23, *C[amassia] scilloides*. . . *False Hyacinth*. . . Thickets and meadows.

false indigo n

1 A plant of the genus *Amorpha*. Also called **indigo, indigo-bush, lead plant, plume locust, shoestrings.** For other names of var spp see **bastard indigo 1, devil's shoestring 5, false greasewood, leadwort, mock locust, polecat tree, rabbit bush, river forest, river locust, sachet bush, senna, spicebush, stinking willow, wild indigo, wild tea**

1822 Eaton *Botany* 171, *Amorpha* . . *fruticosa* (false indigo). **1857** Gray *Manual of Botany* 95, *Amorpha*. . . *False Indigo*. **1897** Parsons *Wild Flowers CA* 315, *False Indigo* . . is remarkable for its sickeningly fragrant foliage. **1940** Steyermark *Flora MO* 305, *False Indigo (Amorpha)*. Low or tall shrubby plants, woody at least at the base, with leafy stems. **1966** *DARE* FW Addit **CO**7, False indigo—purple amorpha. *Amorpha fruticosa*. **1976** Bailey–Bailey *Hortus Third* 69.

2 =**wild indigo.**

1843 Torrey *Flora NY* 1.188, *Baptisia australis*. . . *Blue-flowered False Indigo*. . . A common species in the Western States, and often cultivated in gardens. **1901** Lounsberry *S. Wild Flowers* 265, *Blue False Indigo*. . . *Baptisia australis*. **1936** IL Nat. Hist. Surv. *Wildflowers* 161, False Indigo is a name applied to many species of this genus which blacken in drying, showing the presence of a blue dye resembling indigo. **1944** ME Univ. *Studies* 59.36, *Leguminosae*. . . *Baptisia*. False Indigo. **1964** Batson *Wild Flowers SC* 62, *False Indigo: Baptisia alba*. . . Erect perennial herb up to 4 ft. high.

false ipecac See **wild ipecac**

false jack-in-the-pulpit n

=**wild calla.**

1966 *DARE* Wildfl QR Pl.4 Inf **ND**4, False jack-in-the-pulpit.

false jasmine n Also sp *false jessamine*

=**Carolina jasmine.**

1857 Gray *Manual of Botany* 296, *Gelsemium, Yellow (False) Jessamine*. **1971** Krochmal *Appalachia Med. Plants* 130, *Gelsemium sempervirens*. . . *Common Names:* . . false jasmine, false jessamine.

false koa n

A **lead tree** (here: *Leucaena glauca*).

1929 Neal *Honolulu Gardens* 133, The false koa is a common roadside shrub that here and there becomes a small tree. . . The leaves closely resemble the true leaves of the koa, while the flower heads are somewhat larger stemmed and larger than those of the koa. **1954–60** Hance et al. *Hawaiian Sugar* 2, False koa, *Leucaena glauca*. **1965** Neal *Gardens HI* 411, *False Koa*. . . Pods, which hang in clusters, are similar to those of the koa but contain more seeds, which are oblong and dark brown.

false lady's slipper n

A **helleborine** (here: *Epipactis gigantea*).

1916 Parsons *Wild Flowers CA* 394, *False Lady's Slipper. Epipactis gigantea* . . is closely related to the *Cypripedium,* and resembles it much in habit.

false lettuce n

A wild lettuce, such as *Lactuca floridana*.

1857 Gray *Manual of Botany* 240, *Mulgedium. . . False* or *Blue Lettuce.* **1901** Lounsberry *S. Wild Flowers* 488, Florida Lettuce. False Lettuce. *Lactuca Floridana.*

false lily of the valley n

An herb of the genus *Maianthemum.* Also called **bead ruby, wild lily of the valley.** For other names of var spp see **Canada mayflower, cowslip 5, deerberry f, dwarf Solomon's seal, elf-feather, heartleaf 4, heartleaf lily, heartleaf solomon's-plume, lily of the valley, mayflower, Oregon coltsfoot, two-leaved Solomon's seal**

1900 Lyons *Plant Names* 383, *M. Canadense. . .* False . . Lily-of-the-valley. **1931** Harned *Wild Flowers Alleghanies* 118, *False Lily-of-the-Valley. . .* A familiar little woodland plant. . . It is rather unfortunate that this plant should have been given the name . . for it is in no sense like it. **1950** Stevens *ND Plants* 106, *Maianthemum canadense. . .* False lily-of-the-valley. **1966–68** *DARE* (Qu. S26c, *Wildflowers . . woods*) Inf **PA**99, False lily of the valley; (Qu. S26e, *Other wildflowers*) Inf **MA**6, False lily of the valley. **1973** Hitchcock–Cronquist *Flora Pacific NW* 692, *M. dilatatum. . .* False lily-of-the-valley.

false loosestrife n

A plant of the genus *Ludwigia.* For other names of var spp see **marsh purslane, primrose willow, rattlebox, seedbox, spindle root, water primrose, water purslane**

1857 Gray *Manual of Botany* 132, *Ludwigia,* False Loosestrife. **1940** Gates *Flora KS* 214, *Ludwigia alternifolia . .* False Loosestrife.

false lupine n

1 A plant of the genus *Thermopsis.* Also called **buckbean 2, bushpea, golden banner, golden pea, prairie bean, yellow pea.** For other names of var spp see **Aaron's rod 1, buffalo pea 4**

1897 Parsons *Wild Flowers CA* 148, The false lupine very closely resembles the true lupines, but may be distinguished from them by the stamens. **1938** FWP *Guide ND* 14, In the Badlands grow the rabbit-brush, butte primrose, false-lupine, and prickly pear. **1963** Craighead *Rocky Mt. Wildflowers* 102, False Lupine can withstand drought and trampling, and is sufficiently unpalatable to game and livestock to thrive. **1974** Munz *Flora S. CA* 470, *Thermopsis. . .* False-Lupine.

2 A **wild indigo** (here: *Baptisia australis*).

1959 Carleton *Index Herb. Plants* 44, *False-lupine:* Baptisia australis; Thermopsis (v).

false mallow n

Any of var plants of the family Malvaceae as:

a A mallow, usu *Sida spinosa,* but also *Sida hermaphrodita.*

1822 Eaton *Botany* 360, *Napaea . . laevis . .* false mallows. **1876** Hobbs *Bot. Hdbk.* 36, False mallows, Sida spinosa. **1933** Small *Manual SE Flora* 850, *S[ida] spinosa. . . False-mallow.* **1959** Carleton *Index Herb. Plants* 44, *False-mallow:* Malvastrum (v); Sida Spinosa.

b A large shrub *(Malacothamnus fasciculatus)* with wandlike branches, native to California.

1897 Parsons *Wild Flowers CA* 220, *False Mallow . .* is a very handsome and noticeable shrub when in full bloom. **1915** (1926) Armstrong–Thornber *Western Wild Flowers* 290, *False Mallow. . .* A handsome shrub . . common in southern California.

c A plant of the genus *Malvastrum.*

1900 Lyons *Plant Names* 238, *Malvastrum. . .* False Mallow. **1939** Tharp *Vegetation TX* 62, False Mallow *(Malvastrum);* all regions. **1959** [see **a** above].

d =**globe mallow 1** (here: *Sphaeralcea* spp).

1930 OK Univ. Biol. Surv. *Pub.* 2.1.72, Bank Mallow. Scarlet False Mallow. **1949** Moldenke *Amer. Wild Flowers* 113, The *red falsemallow . .* is abundant on the prairies and plains. **1976** Bailey–Bailey *Hortus Third* 1063, *Sphaeralcea. . . Globe mallow, false m[allow].*

false maple n

=**box elder.**

1897 Sudworth *Arborescent Flora* 292, *Acer negundo californicum. . . Common Names. . .* False Maple (Cal.)

false marigold n

A **marsh marigold.**

1968 *DARE* (Qu. S22) Inf **PA**126, Yellow or false marigold.

false mayweed n

A **fetid marigold** (here: *Dyssodia papposa*).

1914 Georgia *Manual Weeds* 485, False Mayweed. . . A vile weed, which is gaining ground in the Eastern States. **1935** (1943) Muenscher *Weeds* 480, False Mayweed. . . Fields, new meadows, waste places.

false meadowsweet n

An **ocean spray** (here: *Holodiscus dumosus*).

1953 Nelson *Plants Rocky Mt. Park* 94, *False meadowsweet. . .* A shrub with pyramidal clusters of small white flowers and toothed leaves.

false mesquite n

=**fairy duster.**

1937 U.S. Forest Serv. *Range Plant Hdbk.* B36, False-mesquite, also known as bastard-mesquite . . because of its resemblance to the related mesquites (*Prosopis* spp.) belongs to the mimosa family. **1945** Benson–Darrow *Manual SW Trees* 156, *Calliandra eriophylla. . . False Mesquite.* **1971** Dodge *100 Desert Wildflowers* 26, False-mesquite . . in California . . is especially abundant along the east side of the Chocolate Mountains.

false miterwort n Also sp *false mitrewort*

A **foamflower,** esp the common eastern sp *Tiarella cordifolia* which is also called **coolwort 1, gemfruit, miterwort, Nancy-over-the-ground.**

1848 Gray *Manual of Botany* 150, *Tiarella . .* False Mitre-wort. . . The form of the pod, or rather pistil, . . is like that of Mitella, to which the name of *Mitre-wort* properly belongs. **1891** Jesup *Plants Hanover NH* 14, False Mitre-wort. . . Common in moist ground. **1901** Lounsberry *S. Wild Flowers* 217, False mitre-wort . . is one of the most pleasing of early bloomers. **1931** Harned *Wild Flowers Alleghanies* 217, False mitrewort . . is perennial, growing in colonies on shaded hillsides and along rich ravines. **1966** *DARE* Wildfl QR Pl.88 Inf **WA**10, False mitrewort.

false morel n [See quot 1942]

A **mushroom** of the family Helvellaceae, esp of the genus *Gyromitra* or *Helvella.* Also called **lorchel.** For other names of *Gyromitra* spp **see elephant's ear 6, snow morel.**

1942 Hylander *Plant Life* 58, Another common yellow-spored mushroom is *Gyromitra,* peculiar in the lobed and irregularly folded surface of the cap, which in some ways resembles the Morel Mushroom. . . The species known as False Morel, though considered edible by some authorities, has caused the death of many eaters. *Ibid* 640, False Morel, Gyromitra esculenta. **1972** Miller *Mushrooms* 215, *Gyromitra, Helvella, and Related Species. . .* The false morels are found throughout the growing season, but . . I would recommend . . never eating any false morel collected in summer or fall. **1975** Smith *Field Guide W. Mushrooms* 39, *Helvella (False Morels). . .* The best field characters are the . . coloration of the *Helvella* fruit body and . . of *Gyromitra.* **1985** Ammirati et al. *Poisonous Mushrooms* 119, When you consider the large number of people who eat false morels, the incidence of poisoning is rather low. *Ibid* 121, Species of *Gyromitra,* commonly called the false morels, are widely distributed in North America. **1987** McKnight–McKnight *Mushrooms* 43, *False Morels and Lorchels.* Family Helvellaceae. . . This family contains both edible and poisonous species.

false morning-glory n

A **heliotrope 1** (here: *Heliotropium convolvulaceum*).

1941 Jaeger *Wildflowers* 208, *False Morning-glory. . .* A low-growing, rough-hairy annual, with handsome, sweet-scented, morning-glory-like flowers, which open at sunset.

false nettle n

A nettlelike plant *(Boehmeria cylindrica)* but without stinging hairs. Also called **horse nettle 3, leatherleaf**

1936 Winter *Plants NE* 190, *Boehmeria cylindrica . .* False Nettle. **1937** Stemen–Myers *OK Flora* 102. **1940** Gates *Flora KS* 148. **1946** Tatnall *Flora DE* 104. **1963** Evers *IL* 50.32. **1966** *DARE* Wildfl QR Pl.45 Infs **OR**9, **WA**30, False nettle. **1970** Correll *Plants TX* 500.

false onion n

Appar a clam.

1945 Saxon *Gumbo Ya-Ya* 568 **LA**, *Unidentified Terms* 'Le sent bon'—false onion (bivalve).

false pass See **faux pas n**

false pennyroyal n

1 A blue-flowered plant *(Isanthus brachiatus)* of the mint family. Also called **blue gentian 1, fluxweed**

1822 Eaton *Botany* 320, *Isanthus . . cæruleus . .* blue gentian, false pennyroyal. . . Along the Hudson. . . Odour resembles the spikenard. **1861** Wood *Class-Book* 542, *False Pennyroyal. . .* Branching, leafy . . with the aspect of Pennyroyal. **1911** NJ State Museum *Annual Rept. for 1910* 664, *Isanthus brachiatus. . . False Pennyroyal.* **1931** Harned *Wild Flowers Alleghanies* 421, *False Pennyroyal. . .* Sandy soil along streams and dry fields. **1968** Barkley *Plants KS* 295, False Pennyroyal. Fluxweed.

2 A **pennyroyal** (here: *Hedeoma* spp).

1948 Stevens *KS Wild Flowers* 220, *Hedeoma. False Pennyroyal. . .* The herbage and flowers smelling of oil of pennyroyal. **1968** Barkley *Plants KS* 294, Hedeoma drummondii. . . False Penny Royal. . . Hedeoma hispida. . . Rough False Penny Royal. . . Hedeoma pulegioides. . . American False Penny Royal.

false pound n

The wide outer section of a **pound net.**

1976 Warner *Beautiful Swimmers* 126 **eMD,** Fish will . . swim . . into "false pounds" or "turnbacks." These are a pair of gracefully curved, heart-shaped wings supported by thirty-six more stakes that mass and concentrate the fish. A funnel at the apex of the turnbacks then leads the fish into a large circular "main pound."

false ragweed n

1 A **marsh elder** (here: *Iva xanthifolia*).

1935 (1943) Muenscher *Weeds* 506, *Iva xanthifolia. . .* False ragweed.

2 **=guayule.**

1939 Tharp *Vegetation TX* 72, False ragweed *(Parthenium);* all regions. **1970** Correll *Plants TX* 1627, *Parthenium Hysterophorus. . . False ragweed. . .* Locally very abundant in disturbed ground, Rio Grande Plains and s.e. Tex., less frequent . . elsewhere in the state.

3 **=burr sage.**

1945 Wodehouse *Hayfever Plants* 145, *Franseria* (False Ragweeds). The false ragweeds are similar and closely related to the true ragweeds and to the cockleburs. **1950** Stevens *ND Plants* 282, *Franseria acanthicarpa. . . False ragweed. . .* It looks much like common ragweed, but leaf segments are broader and pale green.

false redtop n

1 **=fowl bluegrass.**

1848 Gray *Manual of Botany* 597, *P[oa] serotina. . . False Redtop . .* Wet meadows and banks of streams, abundant everywhere northward. **1912** Baker *Book of Grasses* 205, *False Red-Top. . . Poa triflora.* **1950** Stevens *ND Plants* 59, *Poa palustris . .* False Redtop.

2 **=purpletop.**

1940 Gates *Flora KS* 138, *Triodia flava . .* False Redtop.

false rocket n [See quot 1936]

A **purple rocket** (here: *Iodanthus pinnatifidus*).

1857 Gray *Manual of Botany* 31, *Iodanthus. . . False Rocket.* **1900** Lyons *Plant Names* 202, *Iodanthus. . .* Purple or False Rocket. **1936** IL Nat. Hist. Surv. *Wildflowers* 132, *False Rocket. . .* The common name of this plant comes from the . . similarity to another plant with larger flowers, which is cultivated in gardens under the name Rocket. **1959** Carleton *Index Herb. Plants* 44.

false sandalwood n

=hog plum 1.

1900 Lyons *Plant Names* 400, *X[imenia] Americana. . .* False Sandalwood. . . *Flowers* and *wood* fragrant. **1908** Britton *N. Amer. Trees* 377, *Tallowwood . .* is also called . . False sandalwood. . . It is said to be used as a substitute for Sandalwood in the Eastern tropics.

false sanicle n

=miterwort.

1893 *Jrl. Amer. Folkl.* 6.142 **NY.** **1900** Lyons *Plant Names* 250, *Mitella diphylla . .* False Sanicle.

false sarsaparilla n Cf **sarsaparilla, wild ~**

1 A **spikenard,** either *Aralia nudicaulis* or *A. racemosa.*

1847 Darlington *Weeds & Plants* 156 *(DAE), A[ralia] nudicaulis. . .* Naked-stem Aralia. Sarsaparilla. False sarsaparilla. **1916** *Torreya* 16.239, *Aralia racemosa. . .* False sarsaparilla, Brown Co., Wis. **1968** *Foxfire* Summer 49 **nGA,** Aralia racemosa, called . . false sarsaparilla, . . is a tall, dramatic plant. . . The strong-smelling roots are dug in autumn. **1971** Krochmal *Appalachia Med. Plants* 54, *Aralia nudicaulis. . . Common Names: . .* false sarsaparilla.

2 Any of three **greenbriers:** *Smilax bona-nox, S. glauca,* or *S. waltheri.*

1861 Wood *Class-Book* 702, *S[milax] glauca. . .* False Sarsaparilla. **1914** Georgia *Manual Weeds* 83, *Smilax glauca. . .* False Sarsaparilla. **1940** Clute *Amer. Plant Names* 15, *S[milax] glauca. False Sarsaparilla. . . S. pseudo-China. . .* False sarsaparilla. . . *S. Walteri. False Sarsaparilla.* **1959** Carleton *Index Herb. Plants* 44, *False-sarsaparilla* [sic]: Smilax pseudo-chinensis.

false scabish n

=Barbara's-buttons.

1861 Wood *Class-Book* 457, *False Scabish. . .* Solitary long-stalked h[ea]ds of purplish fl[ower]s resembling a Scabish. **1940** Steyermark *Flora MO* 541, *False Scabish, Marshallia. . .* Limestone glades and bald knobs.

false shagbark n

=pignut.

1979 Little *Checklist U.S. Trees* 73, *Carya glabra . . red hickory . .* false shagbark.

false shaggy mane n [From the resemblance to **shaggy mane**]

A **desert inky cap** (here: *Podaxis pistillaris*).

1981 Lincoff *Audubon Field Guide Mushrooms* 815, *Desert Inky Cap. . .* Also called the "False Shaggy Mane." This is a characteristic desert mushroom.

false Solomon's seal n Also *false Solomon seal*

A plant of the genus *Smilacina.* Also called **false spikenard, Solomon's feather, Solomon's plume, wild lily of the valley, wild spikenard.** For other names of var spp see **fat Solomon, goldenseal 2, Jacob's ladder, Job's tears, plume lily, Solomon's zigzag, treacleberry**

1848 Gray *Manual of Botany* 490, *Smilacìna . .* False Solomon's Seal. **1897** Parsons *Wild Flowers CA* 22, The False Solomon's Seal is one of the prettiest plants in our woods in March, and in many places it almost hides the ground from view. **1924** *Torreya* 24.2, Well buried, two to six inches deep, one may find the horizontal rootstocks of the False Solomon's Seal or Wild Spikenard, *(Smilacina racemosa).* **1936** IL Nat. Hist. Surv. *Wildflowers* 58, False Solomon's Seal. . . There is really nothing false about this plant. It is called False merely because its leaves closely resemble those of the Solomon's Seal. In fact they are so similar that before the inflorescence appears it is very easy to mistake one species for the other. **1951** Voss–Eifert *IL Wild Flowers* 74, False Solomon's seal has none of the appearance of the true Solomon's seal. **1963** Craighead *Rocky Mt. Wildflowers* 27, False Solomonseal. *Smilacina racemosa.* **1966–69** *DARE* (Qq. S26a, b, c, e) 9 Infs, **NEast, N Cent,** False Solomon's seal.

false spikenard n

=false Solomon's seal, usu *Smilacina racemosa.*

1848 Gray *Manual of Botany* 491, *S. racemosa. . . False Spikenard. . .* Berries pale red, speckled with purple, aromatic. **1895** Gray–Bailey *Field Botany* 439, S[milacìna] racemòsa. . . False spikenard. **1910** Graves *Flowering Plants* 122 **CT,** False Solomon's Seal. . . Wild Spikenard. False Spikenard. **1936** IL Nat. Hist. Surv. *Wildflowers* 57. **1966** *DARE* Wildfl QR Pl.18 Inf **NH4,** False spikenard. **1968** *DARE* (Qu. S26a) Inf **MN14.**

false stargrass n

A **colicroot 2** (here: *Aletris farinosa*).

1822 Eaton *Botany* 166, *Aletris . . farinosa . .* false stargrass. **1900** Lyons *Plant Names* 21, *A. farinosa. . .* False Star-grass.

false strawberry n

A **cinquefoil.**

1961 Douglas *My Wilderness* 29 **CO,** Higher up, the vegetation changes. . . The false strawberry hugs the ground. **1966** *DARE* Wildfl QR Pl.92A Infs **NY91, WA10,** False strawberry.

false sunflower n

1 A **sneezeweed.**

1822 Eaton *Botany* 301, *Helenium . . autumnale* (false sunflower . .). At Hudson it grows in the mud of South Bay. **1911** *Century Dict.* 2774/3, *Helenium. . .* The best-known species, *H. autumnale, . .* is called *sneezeweed . .* [and] is also called *false sunflower.* **1936** Winter *Plants NE* 160, False . . Sunflower. In swamps and wet places westward to Ariz., Nev. and Oreg. **1961** Smith *MI Wildflowers* 417, *False Sunflower. . .* Aromatic, resinous perennial up to 2 m. tall.

2 =**oxeye** (here: *Heliopsis* spp).

1900 Lyons *Plant Names* 186, *Heliopsis*. . . False Sunflower. **1931** Harned *Wild Flowers Alleghanies* 569, *False Sunflower (Heliopsis helianthoides . .).* The . . name . . signifies sun-like in allusion to its flowers which are supposed to follow the course of the sun in its journey from east to west. **1938** FWP *Guide ND* 13, The showy oxeye or false-sunflower. **1950** Stevens *ND Plants* 283, *False Sunflower*. . . Heads orange yellow, 5–7 cm. wide. . . Roadsides, especially near woods or brush. **1976** Bruce *How to Grow Wildflowers* 236, The other plants which I want to discuss along with the wild sunflowers are members of the genus *Heliopsis,* Ox-eyes or False-sunflowers.

3 A **marsh elder** (here: *Iva xanthifolia*).

1935 (1943) Muenscher *Weeds* 506, *Iva xanthifolia*. . . False sunflower. **1940** Clute *Amer. Plant Names* 262, *Iva xanthifolia*. . . False sunflower.

false thistle n

A **button snakeroot 2** (here: *Eryngium leavenworthii*).

1951 *PADS* 15.37 **TX,** *Eryngium leavenworthii*. . . Purple thistle; false thistle.

false tinder fungus n

A common **conk** n[2] **1** (here: *Fomes igniarius*).

1948 Boyce *Forest Pathology* 394, The false tinder fungus causes more loss than any other wood destroyer of hardwoods.

false tobacco n Cf **Indian tobacco**

=**mullein.**

1957 McMeekin *Old KY Country* 206, It [=a back road] will have duckberry vines (bittersweet) and tall velvety false tobacco (mullein) and golden rod and Bouncing Bet.

false turkeytail n Cf **turkeytail**

A parchment fungus *(Stereum ostrea).*

1981 Lincoff *Audubon Field Guide Mushrooms* 497, False Turkey-tail. *Stereum ostrea*. . . Description: *Petal-like, leathery, with multicolored zones and smooth undersurface.* **1987** McKnight-McKnight *Mushrooms* 80, False Turkeytail. . . is very commonly mistaken for . . *Coriolus versicolor.*

false unicorn n

=**blazing star 2.**

1876 Hobbs *Bot. Hdbk.* 36, False unicorn, Helonias dioica. **1971** Krochmal *Appalachia Med. Plants* 82. **1974** (1977) Coon *Useful Plants* 173, *Chamaelirium luteum* . . false unicorn.

false unicorn root n

1 =**blazing star 2.**

1822 Eaton *Botany* 303, *Helonias* . . *dioica* . . (blazing star, false unicorn root.) **1892** (1974) Millspaugh *Amer. Med. Plants* 177, *False Unicorn Root*. . . *Rootstock* thick, abrupt, light colored, and furnished with many long roots from the base of the stem, and a number of fibrous rootlets from its thickest portion. **1930** Sievers *Amer. Med. Plants* 22, *Chamaelirium*. . . *Other common names*. . . False unicorn root, blazing-star.

2 =**colicroot 2.**

1892 (1974) Millspaugh *Amer. Med. Plants* 172, *Aletris farinosa*. . . *Com. Names*. . . *False Unicorn Root*. . . *Root* cylindrical-tuberous, more or less horizontal, giving off numerous fibres from its lower surface. **1910** Graves *Flowering Plants* 125 **CT,** False Unicorn-root. . . The rootstock is medicinal. **1971** Krochmal *Appalachia Med. Plants* 40.

false valerian n

A **golden ragwort** (here: *Senecio aureus*).

c1873 in 1976 Miller *Shaker Herbs* 196, *Senecio aureus*. . . False Valerian. **1901** Lounsberry *S. Wild Flowers* 534, *Senecio aureus* . . false valerian. **1914** Georgia *Manual Weeds* 508, The slender, creeping rootstocks of this plant [=*Senecio aureus*] are strong-scented, whence its name of False Valerian. **1971** Krochmal *Appalachia Med. Plants* 234, *Senecio aureus*. . . Common Names . . false valerian.

false varnish tree n

=**tree of heaven.**

1900 Lyons *Plant Names* 20, *Ailanthus glandulosa*. . . False Varnish-tree. **1960** Vines *Trees SW* 600, *Tree-of-heaven—Ailanthus altissima*. . . Vernacular names for the tree are Copal, . . False Varnish-tree, and Devil's Walkingstick.

false violet n [From the violetlike leaves]

=**dewdrop.**

1833 Eaton *Botany* 120, *Dalibarda*. . . *repens* . . false violet. . . Leaves simple, cordate, crenate. **1861** Wood *Class-Book* 341, *False Violet*. . . In low woods, Penn. to Can. **1942** Hylander *Plant Life* 298, Dewdrop or False Violet . . is one of the few flowers of the Rose Family with simple heart shaped leaves. **1950** Gray-Fernald *Manual of Botany* 864. **1976** Bailey-Bailey *Hortus Third* 361, *False Violet*. . . Woods, Que. and Ont., s. to Conn., N.C., Ohio, Mich.

false willow n

A **groundsel tree.**

1931 U.S. Dept. Ag. *Misc. Pub.* 101.158, *Seepwillow (B[accharis] glutinosa),* locally named false willow. **1933** Small *Manual SE Flora* 1398. **1937** U.S. Forest Serv. *Range Plant Hdbk.* B33, Seepwillow *[Baccharis glutinosa],* known locally as false willow. **1938** Van Dersal *Native Woody Plants* 68. **1966** Grimm *Recognizing Native Shrubs* 276. **1976** Bailey-Bailey *Hortus Third* 133, *Baccharis angustifolia*. . . False willow.

false wintergreen n

1 =**wintergreen,** usu *Pyrola rotundifolia.*

1848 Gray *Manual of Botany* 271, *Pyrola*. . . False Wintergreen. **1871** Burroughs *Wake-Robin* 75 *(DAE),* Here and there in the bordering a spire of the false wintergreen strung with faint pink flowers. **1974** (1977) Coon *Useful Plants* 218, *Pyrola rotundifolia*—False wintergreen. . . This is not, it should be noted, the true wintergreen which is *Gaultheria.*

2 =**pipsissewa.**

c1873 in 1976 Miller *Shaker Herbs* 216, *Pipsissewa—Chimaphila umbellata*. . . False Wintergreen.

false yarrow n

=**morning brides.**

1963 Craighead *Rocky Mt. Wildflowers* 200, *Chaenactis douglasii*. . . False Yarrow. . . This plant is often confused with Yarrow *(Achillea lanulosa)* or Dogfennel *(Anthemis cotula).* **1973** Hitchcock-Cronquist *Flora Pacific NW* 500, *Chaenactis* DC. False-yarrow; Chaenactis.

falutin adj [Abbr for *highfalutin*]

1966 *DARE* (Qu. HH35, *A woman who puts on a lot of airs: "She's too ——— for me."*) Inf **OK28,** Falutin. I'd like to buy her for what she's worth and sell her for what she thinks she's worth.

fambily, fambly See **family** n

fameflower n

A plant of the genus *Talinum.* Also called **flameflower 1, rock pink** For other names of var spp see **baby's breath 2f, rock portulaca, sunbright**

1891 *Century Dict.* 6169, *T[alinum] teretifolium,* a native of the United States from Pennsylvania to Colorado and southward, . . has been called fame-flower from the transitoriness of its elegant purple petals. **1938** FWP *Guide IA* 18, Clubmoss and rock mosses surround the bright pink fameflowers that hold tightly to the rocks in northwestern Iowa. **1941** Walker *Lookout* 47 **TN,** In little pockets . . grows a dainty wild flower with pink petals. . . This is fameflower. **1976** Bailey-Bailey *Hortus Third* 1095, *Talinum*. . . *Fameflower*. . . Fl[ower]s showy, ephemeral, mostly in erect terminal cymes or panicles.

famerly See **family** n

fam-fam n [Creole redup form of Fr *faim* hunger]

Hunger.

1955 Warren *Angels* 84 **New Orleans LA** [Black], I'm hongry. I got de ole fam-fam, and ain't no lie.

familious adj Also sp *fermilyus* [varr of *familiar*] *esp freq among Black speakers; arch*

Std senses, var forms.

1884 *Anglia* 7.271 [Black], To 'gin ter git kinder familious wid = to begin to get on familiar terms with. **1899** Chesnutt *Conjure Woman* 112 **csNC** [Black], Dey 'peared ter be sump'n fermilyus 'bout de mule's face. *Ibid* 206 **csNC** [Black], De mo' fermilyus dis yer Hannibal got, de mo' Chloe let her min' run on Jeff. **1921** *DN* 5.119 **KY,** Familious. **1922** *DN* 5.183 **GA** [Quoting Joel C. Harris], W'en you see niggers gittin' dat familious, you kin' 'pen' on dere campin' wid you de ballunce er de season.

family n Usu |'fæm(ə)li|; also **chiefly Sth, S Midl** |'fæmbli| (cf Pronc Intro 3.I.23); for addit varr see **A** below Pronc-spp *fambily, fambly, famerly, famly*

A Forms.

1862 (1864) Browne *Artemus Ward Book* 164, I immejitly commenst restin myself with my famerly. **1887** (1967) Harris *Free Joe* 105 **GA** [White], I'll . . make some inquirements about his famerly. **1891** Harris *Balaam* 140 **GA** [Black], I know it b'longded in de Flewellen fambly sence 'way back. **1894** Riley *Armazindy* 9 **IN,** Fambily of her own. *Ibid* 20, Jes like one fam'bly. **1899** Chesnutt *Conjure Woman* 42 **csNC** [Black], He wuz . . sorry fer ter break up de fambly. **1903** *DN* 2.313 **seMO,** Fambly. **1905** *DN* 3.57 **eNE,** *Fam(b)ly* (infrequent). **1906** *DN* 3.118 **sIN,** *Family*. . . Regularly pronounced *fambly.* **1907** *DN* 3.231 **nwAR, seMO,** Fambly. **1908** *DN* 3.309 **eAL, wGA,** Fam(b)ly. **1913** Kephart *Highlanders* 121 **sAppalachians,** Let ary thing go wrong in the fam'ly . . and we can't git a doctor up hyar less'n three days. **1915** *DN* 4.182 **swVA,** Fambly. **1925** *DN* 5.366 **GA,** [fɛmblɪ]. **1936** *AmSp* 11.238 **eTX,** *Family:* ['fæmlɪ] usually, but also ['fæmblɪ] (illiterate). **1950** Stuart *Hie Hunters* 11 **eKY,** Them last's a crazy fambly. **1959** *VT Hist.* new ser 27.135, Family ['fæmblɪ]. . . Occasional.

B Sense.

An organized group of Shakers or of Friends.

a1772 (1871) Woolman *Jrl.* 184, I accompanied some Friends in a visit to the families of Friends in Mount Holly [New Jersey]. **1832** Williamson *Hist. ME* 2.699, The Shakers live in families, having a community of goods, or all things common. **1837** (1966) Martineau *Soc. in America* 2.55, There are fifteen Shaker establishments or "families" in the United States. **1920** Howells *Vacation Kelwyns* 209 **NEng,** The Family will have to take them at the referees' valuation. **1977** Neal *KY Shakers* 18, To the Shakers a *family* was a group or class of members. For example, the Church or Senior family . . was composed of all members who had signed the covenant.

family duty n

Sexual intercourse between married people.

1928 *Ruppenthal Coll.* **KS,** He claimed to be not too old for family duty. **1930** *AmSp* 5.390, *Family duties*. . . Intercourse by a married couple.

family-favor See **favor** n

family home evening See **home evening**

family pie n

=**cobbler** n[1] **2.**

1896 *Daily News Cook Book* 329 **VA,** Blackberry Cobbler—This is a southern dish sometimes called "family pie." Take a yellow pudding dish, line it with pastry and fill with ripe, luscious blackberries or dewberries. . . Sprinkle with sugar and cover with a top crust. . . Bake slowly one-half hour and serve with cream or butter and sugar. **1967** *PADS* 47.6, *Family pie*—'cobbler' S M[idland].

family way, in a adj phr Also *in (the) family way* [*OED* 1796 →] *euphem somewhat old-fash*

Pregnant.

1931 *PMLA* 46.1322 **sAppalachians,** "Pregnant" also falls under the *index expurgatorius,* "in a family way" supplanting it. **1931** Randolph *Ozarks* 83, If no women are within hearing, a hillman may remark to a comparative stranger that his wife is *ketched,* or *knocked up,* or *in a family way,* but these phrases are not for use in mixed company. **1941** *LANE* Map 392 **throughout NEng,** The map shows adjectives and adjectival expressions applied to a pregnant woman . . [including] *in the family way (in a* ~, *in family way)*. . . The expression . . is regarded as old-fashioned by [5 infs]. **c1941** *Hall Coll.* **wNC, eTN,** [Inf] has heard old men use [the expression]: "That woman is doin' too much work, and her in a family way." *Ibid,* [Letter:] I was afraid for her to come for I have got her in the family way. **1952** Brown *NC Folkl.* 1.538, Louis's wife is in a family way again. **1965–70** *DARE* (Qu. AA28) 195 Infs, **widespread,** In a family way; 36 Infs, **scattered,** In the family way. [Of all Infs responding to the question, 63% were old; of those giving these responses, 73% were old.]

family whitefish n

1 A cisco.

1903 U.S. Bur. Fisheries *Rept. for 1904* 688 **Gt Lakes,** In some instances salt herring are sold under the trade name of "family white fish."

2 =**white sucker.**

1908 Forbes–Richardson *Fishes of IL* 86, They [=white suckers] are frequently salted for winter use, and are sometimes sold in our local markets under the name of "family whitefish."

family woman n [Cf **family way, in a**]

A pregnant woman.

1929 Faulkner *Sound & Fury* 89 **MS** [Black], *And when family woman look him in the eye in the full moon, chile born bluegum.* **1978** *DARE* File **csMA** (as of 1953), After a summer Sunday in the park, he said, "Did you ever see so many family women at once?"

famished ppl adj

Suffering for lack of something vital other than food.

1943 *LANE* Map 716 **seMA,** "I'm famished with the cold." Old-fashioned.

famly See **family** n

fan n

A bough of the palmetto palm or of the balsam tree.

1893 *Harper's New Mth. Mag.* May 894/2 **FL,** Expanses . . carpeted with flowers and ferns and the fans of the dwarf-palmetto. **1903** White *Forest* 43, Fell a good thrifty young balsam and set to work pulling off the fans. . . In the tent lay smoothly one layer of fans, convex side up, butts toward the foot. **1975** Newell *If Nothin' Don't Happen* 123 **nwFL,** He had him a shack built up, roofed over and sided up with palmetto fans, somethin' like a Indian chickee.

fan v

A Transitive senses.

1 with *out:* To defeat or overcome (in a fight).

1879 (1880) Tourgée *Fool's Errand* 261 **Sth,** When . . we met them in battle, there was always one satisfaction, whoever got "fanned out,"—it was always our own folks that did it. **1895** Harris *Mr. Rabbit* 187 **Sth,** He told a big tale of how he had met the great Brindle Dog in the road, and had fanned him out in a fair fight. **c1960** *Wilson Coll.* **csKY,** *Fan out*. . . Whip or overcome.

2 To strike, hit; to spank; hence vbl n *fanning.*

1908 Ruhl *Other Americans* 151, One dreams of . . a Broadway policeman marching down upon them leisurely with a night-stick and fanning them away. **1931** Steffens *Autobiog.* 213 **NYC,** You wonder why we fan these damned bums, crooks, and strikers with the stick. **1942** McAtee *Dial. Grant Co. IN* 25 (as of 1890s), *Fan* . . spank. **1950** *WELS (Exclamations of surprise . . "They're getting married next week." "Well ______!")* 1 Inf, **seWI,** Fan me with a brick! **c1960** *Wilson Coll.* **csKY,** *Fan*. . . To punish, spank; maybe create a breeze by the swiftness of the spank. **1968** *DARE* Tape **NY**61 [Black], My father, he fanned me one time, and I remember it till now. **1968** *DARE* FW Addit **MD**18, [He] fanned his pants. **1987** *DARE* File **csPA,** In local usage, I have recently heard (or remembered): fan = spank. 1940s, but occas. more recently. I well remember being threatened, "Do you want a fannin? Git the pot-stick."

3 with *out:* To scold.

1954 *Harder Coll.* **cwTN,** She was fanning me out for selling 36 of my little chickens. **c1970** *Halpert Coll.* **wKY,** Fan out—Same as bawl out, chew out, etc. "He fanned the kid out pretty bad." "If I were you, I'd fan him out about that."

4 To strike (a horse) so as to urge it on—esp by use of one's hat.

1915 in 1975 White *Git Along* 144 **West,** [Song lyrics:] Sez I "I'm yure man,/ Fur the bronk never lived that I couldn't fan." *Ibid* 147, [Footnote:] *Fan*—A bronc rider would often take his hat and "fan" the horse from side to side to show his complete mastery of the situation. Or he might sit there and "fan" himself to show his nonchalance. **1927** James *Cow Country* 230 **NW,** Todd . . stuck to his seat and fanned his pony on out to the open. **1937** *DN* 6.619 **swTX,** He is a skilful cowboy who rides the horse and *fans* him by whipping the pony with his hat. **1946** Mora *Trail Dust* 90 **sCA,** His chaps . . flap around plenty and plainly show the lower legs of the rider. They certainly help to fan that bronc. **1961** Adams *Old-Time Cowhand* 310, Fannin' a hoss with the hat used to allow the rider to ride better by its balance and was spectacular, but modern rodeos forbid quirtin', fannin', or even touchin' the animal with the hand.

5 To manipulate (a gun):

a By moving it from side to side while firing; by ext, to spray with bullets by moving the gun in this way; hence vbl n *fanning.*

1898 *Science Siftings* 15.79/1 *(DA),* The destructive area of the gun can . . be greatly increased by moving it gently from side to side while it is being fired. . . This process is known as fanning. **1901** Wilson *With the Flag* 2.472, It was our . . task to 'fan' this [=a wooded valley], as an American officer would say, by scattering a ceaseless shower of . . bullets throughout its length.

b By spinning it around the finger; see quot.

1901 Norris *Octopus* 258 **CA,** He "fanned" his revolver, spinning it about his index finger by the trigger-guard with incredible swiftness.

c By hitting the hammer with the hand rapidly and repeatedly; hence n *fanner,* vbl n *fanning.* **West**

1902 *Out West Mag.* 16.308, Wm. Martin, Esq., walked into the only ball of six he could find at a six-foot range; took it in good part and a short rib, and dispassionately cracked the "fanner's" skull with his fist. **1929** Dobie *Vaquero* 268 **SW,** To "fan" a gun the person gripped it in his left hand and with rapid passes of his right hand knocked back and released the hammer. The gun used in "fanning" had, of course, no trigger. A man might "fan" for pastime, but seldom for his life. **1932** *K.C. Star* 17 May *(DA),* Two Schools of Old-Time Gunmen—the 'Fanners' and the 'Thumbers.' **1939** FWP *Guide MT* 414, Fan the hammer. To fire rapidly with a single-action revolver on which the trigger catch has been filed down. **1948** *Popular Western* June 32/1 *(DA),* Degrew was fanning his triggerless Colt with the heel of his other hand. **1961** Adams *Old-Time Cowhand* 177, Fannin' was done by holdin' the gun in one hand in the usual way and strikin' the hammer back repeatedly with the heel of the other hand, thus bringin' the hammer to a full cock.

6 To stir. [Cf *EDD fan* v. 8 "To stir as with a whisk"]

1942 Whipple *Joshua* 198 **UT** (as of c1860), Clory was up before five o'clock, 'fanning the churn' so that the butter would come before the flies did.

7 To set (a door) open.

1953 *PADS* 19.10 **sAppalachians,** *Fan the door wide:* . . To keep the door open. "Don't fan the door wide, it's cold in here."

B Intransitive senses.

1 also with *about, out:* To move about quickly; to run. Cf **fan, turn on the**

1899 (1912) Green *VA Folk-Speech* 169, *Fan.* . . To stir about briskly: as, "She goes fanning about." **1905** (1909) Beach *Pardners* 130 **MT,** He saw I was drunk, and fanned out, me shootin' at him with every jump. **1942** Berrey–Van den Bark *Amer. Slang* 53.11, *Run* . . fan. **1952** Giles *40 Acres* 66 **KY,** We hadn't much more than got home when she came fanning down the road, out of breath from hurrying, her apron strings and bonnet tails flying.

2 Of an animal: to kick up the heels.

1967 *DARE* (QR p69) Inf **IA**8, The mule was a-fannin' for ten minutes. [FW: The mule was kicking with its hind legs at the Inf, who was lying on the floor. *Fanning* is the Inf's general term for a horse or mule kicking.]

3 See quot. Cf **fanfoot**

1970 Major *Dict. Afro-Amer. Slang* 52, *Fan:* to flaunt one's self.

fan exclam See **fen**

fan about See **fan** v **B1**

fan-cat n [*fan* to swing a baseball bat + **cat** n **3c**]

1966 *DARE* (Qu. EE11, *Bat-and-ball games for just a few players [when there aren't enough for a regular game]*) Inf **NC**30, Fan-cat.

fan-crested duck n Also *fanhead*

=**hooded merganser.**

1799 Barton *Fragments Nat. Hist. PA* 2, Mergus cucullatus. Fan-crested-Duck. **1897** *Outing* 30.58/1 *(DA),* The hooded merganser . . , generally termed 'fan-head' owing to its beautiful crest, is a fish duck and worthless for the table, but the drakes are lovely in their bravery of velvet-black and snow-white, and make handsome specimens if properly mounted. **1917** (1923) *Birds Amer.* 1.112, *Hooded Merganser. Lophodytes cucullatus. . . Other names. . .* Round-crested Duck; Fan-crested Duck; Tree Duck. **1944** Hausman *Amer. Birds* 511, Duck, Fan-crested —see Merganser, Hooded.

fancy n

1 A favorable impression. [Prob infl by phr *take a fancy to*]

1936 *AmSp* 11.316 **Ozarks,** *Make a fancy.* . . To make a good impression. 'Jim's a-tryin' t' make a fancy with Lucy tonight.'

2 A man's sweetheart. [*EDD fancy* sb. 2 "A lover, sweetheart"]

1941 *LANE* Map 400 *(His sweetheart)* 1 inf, **cnCT,** Some would say [fæntsɪ].

3 A kind of homemade candy.

1967 *DARE* FW Addit **WA,** Fancies—made with coconut, cherries, nuts, and peanut butter all rolled into balls and dipped in chocolate.

fancy adj

1 Requiring costume or masquerade. [Abbr for *fancy dress* a costume]

1836 in 1874 Hawthorne *Passages Amer. Note-Books* 23 **MA,** A Fancy Ball, in which the prominent American writers should appear, dressed in character. **1853** (1927) Rodman *Diary* 313 **MA,** The children are all at Bessy Morgan's fancy party this ev'g. **1966** *Jrl. Amer. Folkl.* 79.529 **Philadelphia PA,** Today the Mummers are represented by three groups of marchers: the Comic Clubs . . ; the Fancy Clubs (which got their start after the Civil War); and the string bands. . . In the Fancy Clubs the items which attract the most attention are the captain's capes. **1986** Curson *Guide's Guide* 445, Philadelphia is best known for its . . *Mummers Parade.* The magnificently costumed string bands, comics and fancy divisions strut for two-and-a-half miles along Broad Street.

2 Disreputable; of immoral sexual behavior.

1849 Foster *NY in Slices* 48, There are a few hundred of lawless boys and lazy 'fancy-men,' supported by their mistresses, who hang about the midnight oyster-cellars, and three-cent groggeries. **1907** *DN* 3.187 **seNH,** *Fancy house.* . . A house of bad repute. *Fancy woman.* . . A kept woman; a harlot. **1914** *DN* 4.106 **KS,** *Fancy woman.* . . Prostitute. **1935** Sandoz *Jules* 98 **wNE** (as of 1880–1930), Good enough looker too, and dressed in silks like a fancy woman, but she ain't that kind. She's refined. **1946** *PADS* 6.12 **NC, sVA,** *Fancy woman.* . . A woman of ill repute. **c1960** *Wilson Coll.* **csKY,** Fancy woman. . . A strumpet. **1965–70** *DARE* (Qu. W36, . . *A woman who uses a lot of cosmetics*) Infs **MS**23, 37, Looks like a fancy woman; (Qu. HH37, *An immoral woman*) Infs **AR**12, **ID**5, **NM**12, Fancy woman; **CA**110, Fancy lady. **1977** Didion *Book Common Prayer* 158 **New Orleans LA,** Came back down home around the time Lady married her fancy man?

3 Of domestic animals: suitable for breeding.

1870 Nowland *Early Indianapolis* 38, Knowing him to be a very irritable and passionate man, he set about getting up innocent charges against him. The first was that he thought it an insult to the people for a Kentucky lawyer, who, in his own State, was thought only fit for and did keep a "fancy horse," to offer himself to the intelligent citizens of Indiana, . . to represent them in the Legislature. [*DARE* Ed: The context does not provide conclusive evidence for the sense "stallion."] **c1960** *Wilson Coll.* **csKY,** Fancy horse. . . Euphemism for stud-horse or stallion.

4 Highfalutin, pretentious.

1954 *Harder Coll.* **cwTN,** *Fancy dude.* . . Jesting or sarcastic name for the preacher. . . Any person who acts superior. **1965–70** *DARE* (Qu. HH35, *A woman who puts on a lot of airs: "She's too ______ for me."*) 10 Infs, **scattered,** Fancy.

fancy Dan n

1 A flashily dressed man; a ladies' man. Cf **dapper Dan**

1943 *AmSp* 18.107, *Fancy Dan* (. . a dressy [baseball] player). **1950** *WELS (Different kinds of men's haircuts)* 1 Inf, **cnWI,** A fancy Dan's. **1969** *DARE* (Qu. AA6a, . . *A man who is fond of being with women and tries to attract their attention—if he's nice about it*) Inf **CA**169, Fancy Dan; (Qu. W38, *When a man dresses himself up in his best clothes, you say he's ______*) Inf **WI**64, A fancy Dan. **1973** Lomax *Mr. Jelly Roll* 49 **New Orleans LA,** Then you could observe the fancy Dans, dressed fit to kill.

2 In sports: a showy but undependable player.

1943 *AmSp* 18.107, *Fancy Dan* (a pitcher good in practice but sour in a game). **1949** Brandley in 1960 Wentworth–Flexner *Slang,* This is no time for 'Fancy Dans' who won't hit the line with all they have on every play. **1950** J. Dempsey *Championship Fighting* ii. 12 *(OEDS),* The amateur and professional ranks today are cluttered with . . 'fancy Dans'.

fancy doo-dad woman n

A woman who is overly prim or conscious of decorum; one who is **nasty-nice.**

1968 *DARE* (QR, near Qu. BB52) Inf **CA**36, Fancy doo-dad women wouldn't say "urine" if they had a mouthful.

fancy four n

A "game" played to music, as a substitute for dancing.

1904 (1913) Johnson *Highways South* 101 **GA,** The games of "Stealing Partners," "Twistification," and "Fancy Four" . . do not differ much from dancing, except in name. . . Fancy Four is a good deal like Twistification, only two couples instead of one do the dancing and promenading. Of co'se these games ain't regular dancing. . . They're Christian dancing. **1938** Matschat *Suwannee R.* 134 **sGA,** Dancing was not allowed, in deference to the preacher, but Stealin' Partners, Fancy Four, and Twistification were almost as good. All these romping games were played to music.

fancy mouse n [Folk-etym for **fence mouse**]

1966 Dakin *Dial. Vocab. Ohio R. Valley* 2.400, *Chipmunk. . . Fancy mouse* appears once in Knox County, Ohio. The informant says this is "because of the 'fancy' stripes on his back," but the name is without doubt an unrecognized relic of the Pennsylvania German *Fenzemaus.*

fandangle See **fandango 8b**

fandango n [Span] **chiefly SW**

1 A Spanish and Spanish-American dance in triple time, usu accompanied by castanets.

1807 in 1810 Pike *Expeditions* 207, [In New Mexico] we had a dance which is called the *Fandango.* **1872** Schele de Vere *Americanisms* 132, Certain authorities . . recognize in it [=*fandango*] an African word, believing that the dance and its name were both brought from Guinea to the West Indies by slaves, and that it had made its way from there back to Spain, which in its turn sent it to the American colonies. **1910** Hart *Vigilante Girl* 223 **CA,** There will be three or four more dances by couples—the *zorrita,* the *borrego,* and probably the *fandango.* **1967** *DARE* (Qu. FF5a, . . *Different steps and figures in dancing—in past years*) Inf **CA**8, Fandango.

2 The music to which the fandango is danced.

1843 (1916) Hall *New Purchase* 412, Up struck the piano—not with any of your new-fangled fandangos, but with those primitive movements—"Polly put the Kettle on" . . and so forth. **1883** Twain *Life on Missip.* (Boston) 403, Tilted pensively against the piano, a guitar—guitar capable of playing the Spanish Fandango by itself, if you give it a start.

3 A social gathering at which dancing is the main activity.

[**1774** in 1867 Peyton *Adventures* 104 **NM,** We heard the ceremony of marriage was to be followed by a dance or fandango, as the Spaniards call it.] **1844** (1954) Gregg *Commerce* 170, Respecting *fandangos,* . . this term, as it is used in New Mexico, is never applied to any particular dance, but is the usual designation for those ordinary assemblies where dancing and frolicking are carried on. **1856** (1928) Jaeger *Diary Fort Yuma* 103 **CA,** Had a fandango in the evening—fine time. **1892** *DN* 1.190 **TX,** *Fandángo* . . any dancing party or public ball of low order. **1949** Emrich *Wild West Custom* 169, At Santa Fe the early trappers and traders took in the fandangos and courted the señoritas.

4 Any rowdy or boisterous social gathering.

1848 (1855) Ruxton *Life Far West* ix, The Mexican fandango *is true to the letter.* It does seem difficult to understand how they contrived to keep their knives out of the hump-ribs of the mountaineers. . . I myself, with three trappers, cleared a fandango at Taos, armed only with bowie-knives. **1856** *Star* 19 Apr 2/3 (*Western Folkl.* 7.10) **Los Angeles CA,** There was a fandango at the house of Jesus Dominguez . . a sad affair, and affords a striking commentary upon the vicious and pernicious habits of wearing pistols and drinking liquor at fandangos. **1872** Schele de Vere *Americanisms* 133, Here [in the Eastern US], however, the idea of more than usual noise seems to be intimately connected with the term, and any very boisterous assembly, even a row, is familiarly called a *fandango.* **1920** Hunter *Trail Drivers TX* 234 (as of 1877), Dodge City was then a wide-open town. Gambling and fandangoes were in full blast. While we were there two men were killed in a saloon row. **1966** Giles *Great Adventure* 1 **NM** (as of 1830s), To the last man they were suffering a little or a lot from a final spree with Taos lightning, and sleepless from one last *fandango.* **1968** Adams *Western Words* 109, *Fandango.* . . The word was used by freighters and trappers to mean any kind of dance, and sometimes a boisterous gathering or a fight. **1969** *DARE* (Qu. FF16, . . *Local contests or celebrations*) Inf **CA**158, The fandango, on the 4th of July.

5 A dance hall or room for dancing. *?obs*

1890 Jefferson *Autobiog.* 59 **TX,** He kept a bar-room in conjunction with a fandango, a keno-table, and a faro-bank—by which means it seems he had endeavored to refine the depraved tastes of the citizens. *Ibid* 287, A 'fandango' . . [is] a place where Spanish girls sing and dance, and play the guitars and castanets.

6 attrib: See quots. [By assoc of dance halls with prostitution] *hist* Cf **fancy** adj **2**

1928 Ritchie *Forty-Niners* 237 **CA,** And there was Madam Jewsharp's fandango house. Now Madam Jewsharp was hardly a lady. . . But . . Madam Jewsharp ran a good house: no fights or loud swearing. **1955** Lewis *High Sierra* 264 **ceCA** (as of c1850), Few of the [mining] camps . . were long without their quota of ladies of joy, euphemistically termed "fandango girls." . . Some towns, to be sure, held out no welcome to the fandango girls, the citizens turning them away on their arrival.

7 also sp *fandangle:* An amusement device; see quots. **eMA**

1797 (1907) Bentley *Diary* 2.237 **MA,** [At Bunker's Hill] a Fandango is erected, which was invented at Haverhill. On two ropes a chain slides down hill to a place accommodated to receive it, with the person who dismounts below. **1906** Lovett *Old Boston Boys* 12, Here an effort was once made by the city to provide a few amusements for the public, and several swings were set up as well as two "fandangoes," as they were called,—long, wooden, open-framework structures, which revolved perpendicularly, with a swinging seat at each end holding perhaps four or five persons. One of these forecasts of the "Ferris Wheel" carried the victims to a height of forty or fifty feet, the other being much smaller, and made presumably for those more timid. **1933** *Hanley Disks* **Boston MA,** We'd have foot races, potato races, and fandangles—what they called the fandango—call it the windmill—aeroplane now they call it. . . [They'd have] fandangoes . . around—they call it the wheel now, ferris wheel now they call it.

fan dodge n [Prob var of *fantods;* cf **fantods 5**]

1958 McCulloch *Woods Words* 60 **Pacific NW,** *Fan dodge*—Dysentery.

fanega n Also sp *fanego* [Span] **SW**

One of several units of dry measure (see quots); by ext, a unit of land that can be sown with that amount of seed.

1808 *Amer. Reg.* 3.1.63, Its production the first year were 1500 fanegos of wheat, and 500 of corn. **1844** (1954) Gregg *Commerce* 108, Husbandmen rate their fields by the amount of wheat necessary to sow them, and thus speak of a *fanega* of land—*fanega* being a measure of about two bushels—meaning an extent which two bushels of wheat will suffice to sow. **1856** (1928) Jaeger *Diary Fort Yuma* 124 **sCA,** Had to leave 3 cargoes of flour & one fanega of beans. **1892** *DN* 1.190 **TX,** *Fanéga:* a dry measure, about two and a half bushels. By extension as much land as may be sowed with a fanega of seed. **1932** Bentley *Spanish Terms* 136, *Fanega.* . . A measure for dry matter, about 1.60 bushels. Rarely used except in communities of very intimate association and close business dealings between Mexicans and Americans. It is also used to signify the amount of land that may be sown by a fanega of seed.

fanent See **fornent**

fanfoot n [Cf **fan** v **B3**]

A woman who openly seeks sexual relations; hence v *fanfoot,* to "run around," seek sexual favors.

1935 Hurston *Mules & Men* 234 **LA** [Black], She all de time way from dat house—off fan-footin' whilst he workin' lak a dog! **1942** Hurston *Dust Tracks* 190 **FL** [Black], Fan-foot, what you doing with my man's hat cocked on *your* nappy head? . . Who's a whore? Yeah I sleeps with my mens, but they pays me. I wouldn't be a fan-foot like you—just on de road somewhere. Runs up and down de road from job to job making pay-days. **1948** Hurston *Seraph* 141 **FL,** What do Jim mean by listening to all that rigmarole from that fan-foot, that street-walker, that brick-bat for? **1960** Williams *Walk Egypt* 282 **GA,** She said instantly, fiercely, "Fan-Foot Alley can miss you this trip."

fanhead See **fan-crested duck**

faniggle See **finagle**

fanleaf palm See **fan palm**

fanlip orchid n

A **fringeless orchid** (here: *Habenaria peramoena*).

1948 Wherry *Wild Flower Guide* 32, *Purple Fanlip Orchid.* . . Lip fan-shaped, split into 3 triangular divisions which are shallowly toothed at tip.

fan mussel n

A pen shell.

1869 *Amer. Naturalist* 3.284, In Florida are numerous specimens of the Fan Mussels (Pinna) . . these submarine weavers spin a byssus, or beard, by which they attach themselves to the bottom of the sea. [**1974** Abbott *Seashells* 437, The pen shells are large, fragile, fan-shaped clams which live in sandy or mud-sand areas, usually in colonies.]

fanner n Pronc-spp *fanna(h), fannuh*

1 also *fanner basket:* A broad, flat basket, orig used for winnowing grain, later adapted to other purposes. **chiefly GA, SC** *old-fash*

1797 in 1916 Hawkins *Letters* 252 **GA,** I will give . . each a pestle and mortar, a sifter and riddle and fanner, an earth pot, pan and large wooden spoon. **1890** *DN* 1.58, *Fanner:* an open basket dishing out from the bottom upward, is sometimes heard in Charleston, S.C. Originally it was used to separate the chaff from the wheat, by tossing it up into the air and catching it as it fell down, thus allowing the wind to fan out the chaff. **1909** *S. Atl. Qrly.* 8.47 **SC** [Gullah], The broad, flat baskets woven of grass and palmetto fibers, that are used for winnowing rice, are *fannas* or *fannah baskits* [sic]. **1922** Gonzales *Black Border* 300 **sSC, GA coasts** [Gullah glossary], *Fannuh*—a wide, shallow basket used for winnowing beaten rice or separating the corn husks from the grist after grinding. **1930** Stoney–Shelby *Black Genesis* 46 **seSC,** An' she gots a fanner (basket) wid all kind o' t'ing in it. **1936** Smith–Sass *Carolina Rice* 62 **SC coast** (as of 1850s), On fine days there might be seen on the open ground before this house a large number of "fanner-baskets," and on each basket a folded blanket, and on each blanket a baby. **1950** *PADS* 14.29 **SC,** *Fanner*. . . A basket, especially a broad flat basket for carrying fruit or vegetables. Formerly used when rice was threshed out with flails, to toss the rice into the air and allow the wind to fan out the chaff. Also called *fanner basket.* **1966–68** *DARE* (Qu. L32b, *In early days, how was the grain separated from the chaff?*) Inf **GA**28, Cleaning rice is called fanning rice; the implement is called a fanner; **ME**1, Hand fanners—thin wood baskets filled with grain and shaken in the wind; **DC**5, Wheat fanner.

2 See **fan** v **A5c.**

fannie daddy n

See quots.

1939 Wolcott *Yankee Cook Book* 59, "Fannie Daddies". . . *The Cape Cod name for Fried Clams.* **1965** *Woman's Day Encycl. Cookery* 1.66, *Rhode Island. . . Fried Clams or Fannie Daddies*—3 eggs . . ¾ cup milk, 2 tablespoons melted butter, 1½ cups all-purpose flour, 1 teaspoon salt, 1 to 2 tablespoons fresh lemon juice, 3 cups shucked cherrystone or littleneck clams, drained.

fanning See **fan** v **A2, 5a, c**

fanning the breeze See **fan the breeze**

fannuh See **fanner**

fan out See **fan** v **A1, 3, B1**

fan palm n Also *fanleaf palm* [see quot 1910]

A palm of the genus *Washingtonia.* Also called **hula palm, Washington palm.** For other names of var spp see **petticoat palm, skyduster palm, thread palm, weeping palm, wild date**

1884 Sargent *Forests of N. Amer.* 217, *Washingtonia filifera*. . . Fanleaf Palm. **1897** Sudworth *Arborescent Flora* 105, *Neowashingtonia filamentosa. . . Common Names*. . . California Fan Palm (Cal.) . . Fanleaf Palm (Cal.) **1910** Jepson *Silva CA* 171, *Washingtonia. . . Fan Palm*. . . Trees with fan-shaped much folded leaves. **1957** Jaeger *N. Amer. Deserts* 114. **1968–70** *DARE* (Qu. T16, *What kinds of trees are 'special' around here?*) Infs **CA**79, 185, Fan palm. **1981** Benson–Darrow *Trees SW Deserts* 77, The fan palms are distinguished readily from the commonly cultivated date palms by the arrangement of the leaf blades.

fantad See **fantod**

fantail n

1 =**red-tailed hawk.**

1913 Bailey *Birds VA* 111, *Buteo borealis*. . . Fantail.

2 See quot.

1968 *DARE* (Qu. Q5, . . *Kinds of wild ducks*) Inf **MI**76, Fantail, pintail.

3 A mustang. [From the shape of the tail when the horse gallops] **West**

1937 *AmSp* 12.103 **eNE,** Fan-tail is a name for the mustang. **1941** Writers' Program *Guide WY* 462, *Fan tail* A wild horse. **1942** Berrey–Van den Bark *Amer. Slang* 916.14 [Western slang], *Range horse; mustang* . . broomtail, . . fantail, . . fuzztail, . . willowtail. **1944** Adams *Western Words* 57, *Fan-tail*—A wild horse, a horse with a long bushy tail.

4 A type of cigar: see quot.

1969 *DARE* (Qu. DD7) Inf **NY**196, A fantail—not wrapped at one end.

fan-tailed grackle n Also *fan-tailed crow blackbird*

=**great-tailed grackle.**

1898 (1900) Davie *Nests N. Amer. Birds* 352, *Great-tailed Grackle*. . . Called the Fan-tailed Crow Blackbird or Texas Grackle. **1928** Bailey *Birds NM* 659, The large . . Fantailed Grackles, have strikingly long, keeled, and graduated tails.

fan-tailed pigeon n

=**band-tailed pigeon.**

1951 *AmSp* 26.91, Among other instances in bird names are . . *fan-tailed pigeon* (Oreg.) for the band-tailed pigeon. **1969** *DARE* (Qu. Q7, . . *Game birds*) Inf **CA**136, Fan-tailed pigeon.

fantan n

A kind of yeast roll made of short strips of dough placed on their side in a muffin cup so that they open like a fan when baked.

1950 *WELS (Fancy home-baked rolls)* 1 Inf, **cWI,** Cloverleaf rolls, cinnamon rolls, fantans. **1959** (1977) Farmer *Cookbook* 341, Butter Rolls *or* Fantans. **1967–68** *DARE* (Qu. H19) Inf **MN**2, Fantan—a many-sectioned roll; (Qu. H32) Inf **KS**18, [ˈfænˌtænz]. **1973** Allen *LAUM* 1.278 **NE** (as of c1950), [Other kinds of bread made with flour] Fantans [1 inf].

fantastic n Also *fantastical;* pronc-sp *fantastikil* **chiefly NEast, Sth** *old-fash* Cf **antiques and horribles**

A mummer.

1838 *Bentley's Misc.* (Amer. ed.) 2.295 **NY,** "Fantasticals." [Footnote:] Some militiamen who parade in fantastic dresses to ridicule the "military," volunteers who sport very splendid uniforms. **1872** (1973) Thompson *Major Jones's Courtship* 40 **GA,** "My lord!" ses I, "Miss Mary, aint you skeered?" "Shaw, no, Majer," ses she, "its only the Fantastikils!" **1876** in 1966 *Jrl. Amer. Folkl.* 79.528 **Philadelphia PA,** [Newspaper item:] Local Affairs: On New Year's Day . . the Fantasticals or "Shooters" were out in full force during the whole day, and caused much boisterous amusement. **1899** (1900) Harris *On the Wing* 82, He dressed himself up after the style of the "Fantastics," as modern mummers were called in the South just prior to the war, donned a hideous mask and a wig and beard of long white hair. **1907** *DN* 3.243 **eME,** *Fantastics*. . . Antiques and horribles. **1908** *DN* 3.309 **eAL, wGA,** *Fantastic*. . . A mummer. Still in common use in the villages. . . *Fantastical*. . . Same as *fantastic.* Rare.

fantatolites See **fantod 4**

fan the breeze v phr, hence vbl n *fanning the breeze* Also *fan the fire*

To talk, chatter.

1946 *Western Folkl.* 5.387, One of the sailor's chief activities during his free time is *flapping his chops, . . fanning the breeze, beating his gums,* [etc]. **1966–67** *DARE* (Qu. HH7b, *Someone who talks too much or too loud: "He's always ______."*) Inf **MI**44, Fanning the breeze; (Qu. II15, *When somebody is passing by and you want him or her to stop and talk a while, you might say, "______."*) Inf **SC**21, Let's fan the fire.

fan the dust v phr

=**fan** v **B1.**

1970 *DARE* File **nwAR** (as of c1910), *Fan the dust.* When one traveled in a hurry he was . . fanning the dust.

fan the fire See **fan the breeze**

fantod n, usu pl |ˈfæntɑdz, -tɔdz| Also sp *fantad, phantod* [Etym unknown; cf *fantigue* a state of excitement, fit of temper]

1 A feeling of fidgety uneasiness; the creeps.

1876 (1954) Henry *Death of a Legend* 178 *(DAS),* Cole [Younger], what the Sam Hill is eating you? I dunno. You just got the fantods that's all. **1884** (1958) Twain *Huck. Finn* 86 **MO,** These was all nice pictures, I reckon, but I didn't somehow seem to take to them, because if ever I was down a little, they always give me the fan-tods. **1899** (1912) Green *VA Folk-Speech* 170, *Fantods*. . . Fidgets; restlessness; a state of anxiety or excitement. **1944** Wellman *Bowl* 135 **KS,** I couldn't even lay my hand down on that glass [=a cage holding a rattlesnake], it give me the fantods so bad. **1967** *DARE* (Qu. GG13b, *When something keeps bothering a person and makes him nervous, he may say: "It gives me the ______."*) Inf **TX**43, Fantods. **1968** Stegner *Edge* 156 **CA,** Michael's sermons gave me the phantods.

2 A feeling of depression; the blues.

1899 (1912) Green *VA Folk-Speech* 170, *Fantods*. . . A fit of the sulks or other slight indisposition, mental or bodily. **1942** Berrey–Van den

Bark *Amer. Slang* 283.2, *Dejection* . . fantad, fantod. **1969** *DARE* (Qu. GG34a, *To feel depressed or in a gloomy mood: "He has the ______ today."*) Inf **MA**58, High fantods.

3 A feeling of excitement, of high spirits.

1942 Berrey–Van den Bark *Amer. Slang* 266.1, *Excitement* . . fantad, fantod. **1969** *DARE* (Qu. BB47, *Feeling in the best of health and spirits*) Inf **NC**61, Got the ['fæntɔdz]!

4 also *fantatolites:* A minor or imaginary disease.

1839 (1969) Briggs *Advent. Franco* 1.249, You have got strong symptoms of the fantods; your skin is so tight you can't shut your eyes without opening your mouth. **1942** McAtee *Dial. Grant Co. IN* 25 (as of 1890s), *Fantod* . . indisposition, perhaps more feigned than real. **1968–69** *DARE* (Qu. BB28, *Joking names* . . *for imaginary diseases*) Infs **GA**59, **NJ**53, ['fæntɔdz]; **IL**88, **IN**22, ['fæntɑdz]; **NY**42, High fantatolites.

5 Looseness of the bowels. Cf **fan dodge**

1968 *DARE* (Qu. BB19) Inf **GA**59, The fantods.

fan, turn on the v phr Also *put on the fan* Cf **fan** v **B1**

To hurry; to move quickly.

1942 Berrey–Van den Bark *Amer. Slang* 53.11, *Run* . . turn on the fan. *Ibid* 58.6, *Depart hurriedly* . . turn on the fan. **1967–70** *DARE* (Qu. A19, *Other ways of saying "I'll have to hurry."*) Inf **TN**47, Turn on the fan; (Qu. A22, . . *"To start working hard."*) Infs **MO**22, **VA**30, Put on the fan; (Qu. Y20, *To run fast: "You should have seen him ______!"*) Inf **SC**55, Turn on the fan. [All Infs old; 3 of 4 Infs Black]

fanweed n **West**

A **pennycress** (here: *Thlaspi arvensis*).

1937 U.S. Forest Serv. *Range Plant Hdbk.* W189, This plant [=*Thlaspi arvense*], known locally as . . fanweed . . is now well distributed. **1938** *Frontier & Midland* 19.4 **MT**, Turnin' a furrow sober and earnest, like he was maybe plowin' under more'n jest the stubble and the fan-weed. **1941** *Torreya* 41.48, *Thlaspi arvense*. . . Fan-weed, Ovando, Mont. **1943** KS State Bd. Ag. *Report* 62.256.25, *Pennycress* . . also called *Fan-weed* and *Frenchweed* . . when eaten by dairy cattle, imparts a very disagreeable flavor to milk and butter. **1968** *ID Enterprise* (Malad City) 1 Feb 5/4, Other weeds creating problems are white top, blue mustard, fan weed, burdock, larkspur, wild oats and rye.

fanwort n

=water shield.

1933 Small *Manual SE Flora* 539, *C[abomba] caroliniana*. . . Fanwort. **1937** *Torreya* 37.97. **1950** Gray–Fernald *Manual of Botany* 642. **1970** Correll *Plants TX* 632.

far adv, adj[1] Usu |fɑr, fɑ|; also freq |fɝ|; occas |fʌ, fɜ| Pronc-spp *fare, fer, fur*

A Pronc varr.

1837 Sherwood *Gaz. GA* 69, *Provincialisms*. . . *Fare*, for far. **1843** (1916) Hall *New Purchase* 262 **IN**, It's [=a piano] as fur afore a fiddle, as a fiddle's afore a jusarp! **1860** Holmes *Professor* 86 **NEng**, He [was] as good as merried, so fur as solemn promises went. **1888** Jones *Negro Myths* 3 **GA coast**, From dat day to dis you kin nebber ketch Buh Alligatur sleep fur from de bank. **1892** *DN* 1.239 **MO**, *Fur side*. **1902** *DN* 2.235 **sIL**, On the fur side. **1905** *DN* 3.80 **nwAR**, *Fur side*. **1907** *DN* 3.187 **seNH**, *Fur*. . . Far. **1908** *DN* 3.313 **eAL, wGA**, *Fur-side*. **1916** Howells *Leatherwood God* 147 **OH**, That's all right as fer as it goes. **1941** *AmSp* 16.13 **eTX** [Black], *Far* . . [fʌ]. **c1960** *Wilson Coll.* **csKY**, *Far* in "How far?" is often [fɚ]. **1965–70** *DARE* (Qu. LL34, . . *"This is ______ we can go."*) 24 Infs, **scattered**, As fur as; 7 Infs, **scattered**, Fur (as); (Qu. V2b) 8 Infs, **scattered**, (As) fur as I could throw him [and varr—see *DS*]; (Qu. GG22a) Inf **CO**22, Fur as I'm going to go; (Qu. II22) Inf **LA**3, You done gone fur enough; (Qu. MM24) Inf **LA**7, Not fur; (Qu. MM25) Infs **IL**15, **IN**5, **LA**8, **MA**81, Fur (away, distance, way). **1966–70** *DARE* Tapes **CA**199, **FL**36, **IN**36, **SD**8, **TX**49, 50, 96, Far [fɚ]. **1967** *DARE* FW Addit **seAR**, It'd be that [fɜ] too [fɑr].

B Compar.

Usu *farther, further;* also:

1 pronc-spp *furder;* infreq *farder.* [*OED* "obs."] **chiefly Sth, S Midl**

1815 Humphreys *Yankey in England* 105, *Furder*, farther. **1851** Hooper *Widow Rugby's Husband* 47 **AL**, Afore I get any furder. **1899** (1912) Green *VA Folk-Speech* 172, Furder. Farder. **1906** *DN* 3.137 **nwAR**, *Furder*. **1908** *DN* 3.313 **eAL, wGA**, *Furder*. **1909** *DN* 3.411 **nME**, *Furder*. **1923** *DN* 5.207 **swMO**, *Furder*. **1934** *WV Review* Dec 77/2, We might think that the peculiar sounding *furder* which we sometimes hear for *further*, is an error. . . But this word, too, is a vestige of the past. **c1960** *Wilson Coll.* **csKY**, *Furder*. **1963** Edwards *Gravel* 89 **eTN** (as of 1920s), Though I ain't a sayin this fer it to go no furder, it looks to me like it uz Charlie's time. **1966** *DARE* Tape **MI**20, The farder ['fɑrdɚ] back you went the more crude they'd be. **1966** *DARE* FW Addit **NC**, ['fɝdɚ]. **1968** *DARE* (Qu. LL33, . . *Which is ______ from here?*) Inf **NC**33, Farther; futher (older); furder.

2 pronc-spp *far(r)er, ferrer, fur(r)er.* **chiefly Sth, S Midl**

1899 (1912) Green *VA Folk-Speech* 172, *Fer, ferrer, ferrest*. . . Fur, furder. Farder, farrer. **1908** *DN* 3.284 **eAL, wGA**, Farer. **1927** in 1983 Taft *Blues Lyric Poetry* 64 [Black], Crying won't make me stay / More you cry: the farer I'll ride away. **1940** *AmSp* 15.52 **sAppalachians, Ozarks**, Farer. **1952** Brown *NC Folkl.* 1.539, *Farrer, furrer:* . . *Farther, further*. *Ibid* 1.543, *Furer*. . . Illiterate. **c1960** *Wilson Coll.* **csKY**, *Farther* [fɚə], often, or [fɚr̩]. Also [fɑrr̩].

3 pronc-spp *futher;* also *fudder, fudduh, futter.* **chiefly Sth, S Midl** See Map

1922 Gonzales *Black Border* 302 **sSC, GA coasts** [Gullah glossary], *Fudduh*. **1923** *DN* 5.207 **swMO**, Futher. **1927** *AmSp* 3.8 **Ozarks**, *Fu'ther*. **1941** Stuart *Men of Mts.* 341 **neKY**, We'll get to Gadsden today and camp in the grove. We may get a little futter. **1941** *AmSp* 16.12 **eTX** [Black], ['fʌdə]. **1942** Hall *Smoky Mt. Speech* 42, [ʌ], without *r*, may appear in . . *further*. **1954** *Harder Coll.* **cwTN**, *Futher*. **1965–70** *DARE* (Qu. LL33, . . *Which is ______ from here?*) 35 Infs, **chiefly Sth, S Midl**, Futher ['fʌðɚ, -ə]; (Qu. LL34, . . *"This is all ______ we can go."*) Infs **DE**7, **FL**7, **TN**36, **WA**1, (The) futher; (Qu. Y52) Inf **LA**12, Move futher. **1968** *DARE* FW Addit **seGA, sIN, wKY**, ['fʌðɚ, -ə]. **1970** *Foxfire* Spring–Summer 31 **neGA**, M'dogs couldn't trail it no fudder an' . . I had t'quit. **1970** *DARE* Tapes **TX**87, 94, ['fʌðɚ]; **FL**47, ['fʌðə].

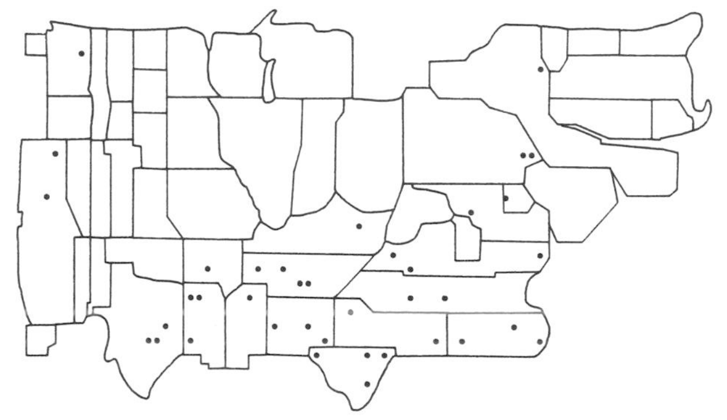

•far adv, adj[1] B3 + varr (Qq. LL33, Y52, LL34)

C Superl.

Usu *farthest, furthest;* also:

1 pronc-spp *fardest, furdest.*

1871 Eggleston *Hoosier Schoolmaster* 66 **sIN**, You'll find a bed in the furdest corner. **1895** *DN* 1.388 **OH**, *Fardest, furdest*. **1922** (1926) Kephart *Highlanders* 23 **sAppalachians**, Bushnell's the furdest ever I've been.

2 pronc-spp *far(r)est, ferrest, furrest.* **chiefly S Midl**

1899 (1912) Green *VA Folk-Speech* 172, *Fer, ferrer, ferrest*. . . For *far, farther, farthest*. **1908** *DN* 3.284 **eAL, wGA**, Abnormal comparisons . . farer, farest. **1940** *AmSp* 15.52 **sAppalachians, Ozarks**, Abnormal comparisons abound: farer, farest. **1952** Brown *NC Folkl.* 1.539, *Farrest, furrest:* . . Farthest, furthest. **c1960** *Wilson Coll.* **csKY**, Farthest ['fɚɪst] often. **1970** *DARE* (Qu. LL33, . . *New York or California —which is ______?*) Inf **DC**13, Farrest; (Qu. LL34, . . *This is* . . ______ *we can go*) Inf **MS**88, The farrest.

3 pronc-spp *farth(e)rest, ferthrest, furtherest.*

1833 in 1934 Frear *Lowell & Abigail* 51 **MA**, A boundless ocean met my farthrest gaze. **1837** Walker in 1940 Drury *Pioneers Spokanes* 25 **ME**, Retiring to the ferthrest corner of the room. **1849** in 1951 *AmSp* 26.182 **NC**, It was the fartherest from my intentions. **1895** *DN* 1.388 **NEng**, *Fartherest, furtherest:* for *farthest*. **1909** *DN* 3.396 **nwAR**, *Fartherest, furtherest*. **1939** *LANE* Map 49, [In contexts "Two miles was the ______ he could run," and "Boston is the ______ I've ever been," both *fartherest* and *furtherest* are common throughout New England.] **c1960** *Wilson Coll.* **csKY**, Farthest . . ['fɑrðə·ɪst]. **1962** Atwood *Vocab.*

TX 49, Of those who use the superlative form [in the context "The farthest one can go"], about one-third use a double suffix: *fartherest* or *furtherest.* **1965–70** *DARE* (Qu. LL33, . . *Which is ______ from here?*) 111 Infs, **scattered,** Fartherest; 53 Infs, **scattered,** Furtherest (away); **CO**47, Furtherest distance; (Qu. LL34) Inf **AL**24, The ['fɑðrɨs]; **GA**80, **IA**8, [This is] the furtherest. **1969** *DARE* Tape **MA**62, They could tell right off where the fartherest drop of water went; **TN**39, I really felt then . . that school would be the fartherest thing from my mind for quite a while.

4 pronc-sp *futherest.* **chiefly S Midl** Cf **B3** above

1954 *Harder Coll.* **cwTN,** *Futherest.* **1965–70** *DARE* (Qu. LL33, . . *"Which is ______ from here?"*) Infs **GA**77, **KY**36, 40, 60, 72, **SC**32, **VA**46, Futherest; (Qu. LL34) Inf **PA**150, Futherest.

5 pronc-sp *furderest.*

1968 Haun *Hawk's Done Gone* 63 **TN,** She was hid in the furderest corner that evening.

far adj[2] See **fair** adj

far adj[3] See **farrow** adj

far n[1] See **fire**

far n[2] [Pronc-sp for *fir*]

1909 *DN* 3.411 **nME,** *Far,* . . Fir.

faradiddle n [Prob var of *taradiddle* pretentious nonsense] =**flummadiddle 2.**

1944 Adams *Western Words* 63, *Fumadiddle*—A western term for fancy dress. *Faradiddle* and *fofaraw* are also used in this sense.

far, all the See **all the**

farblonjet adj |fə(r)'blʌnǰəd, -ɨt, fɑ(r)'blɔnǰəd, -ɨt| Also sp *farblondjet* [Yiddish *farblondzhen* to lose one's way, get lost, go astray] *in Jewish communities*

Lost, astray; confused, befuddled.

1968 Rosten *Yiddish* 111, *Farblondjet*—Pronounced *far*-blawn-*jit,* to rhyme with "car lawn kit." Slavic: "wander," "roam." Lost (but *really lost*), mixed-up, wandering about without any idea where you are. . . You can describe a meandering statement, a fouled-up presentation, a galloping *non sequitur,* a thoroughly confused *contretemps,* as one in which someone got really *farblondjet.* **1969** *DARE* (Qu. GG2, . . *"So many things were going on at the same time that he got completely ______."*) Inf **IL**99, [fə'blʌnǰəd]. [Jewish Inf] **1970** Feinsilver *Yiddish* 89, *Farblonjet* has a wonderfully expressive sound, which has been taken advantage of by TV comics. Not only did Danny Thomas devote a show to the topic "What Means *Farblonjet*?" but the word was even misused in a cartoon movie for kids in the line, "I'll *farblonje* him." . . That sentence should have been, . . "I'll make him get *farblonjet.*" **1978** *DARE* File **csWI** [Jewish speaker from New Jersey], I was really [fə'blʌnǰɨt] this weekend—I put the peanut butter in the refrigerator, and I even forgot my own address. **1984** *AmSp* 59.274, Four pronunciations [of the first syllable of *farblonjet*] are found in Jewish English [including /fə, fər, fɑr/ and] . . /[f]ɑ/. . . Three pronunciations [of the stressed syllable] are found in Jewish English: [ɔ], . . [ʌ], . . and [ə]. . . [In] the final syllable, this word has two morphemic variants in English: *-et* reflects Yiddish, but *-ed* is a Jewish English innovation.

farce v [*W3 "obs"*] *relic*

To stuff (poultry); to garnish (poultry); hence ppl adj *farced.*

1927 *AmSp* 2.354 **wcWV,** *Farce a goose* . . to stuff a goose for the table. "The girls farced the goose yesterday." **1940** *Hench Coll.* **cVA,** A farced turkey is a turkey decorated to look pretty when it is first brought in and laid on the table: decorated with little sprigs of green or something else, holly, etc. **1975** Gainer *Witches* 9 **sAppalachians,** My daughter-in-law knows little about cooking; she can't even farce a chicken.

farce adj See **fierce** adj

farchadet adj Also sp *farchadat* [Yiddish *fartshadet*]

Confused, befuddled.

1968 Rosten *Yiddish* 112, *Farchadat* Pronounced *far*-chah-*det,* to rhyme with "Car got it." Slavic: *chad* "smoke," "daze." 1. Dizzy, confused, dopey, "punchy." "That guy walks around all farchadat." **1968** *DARE* (Qu. GG2, . . *"So many things were going on at the same time that he got completely ______."*) Inf **PA**172, Farchadet [fɪ'čɑdɨd]. [Inf Black] **1987** *DARE* File **NYC** (as of 1955), In my house the word *farchadet* was frequently used in the sense of "confused" or "dopey." If, for example, I did something stupid such as bringing back the wrong brand of an item from the store my mother would say something like, "It looks like you're a bisl (=a bit) farchadet today," or "You're really farchadet." It was a word that one would often hear in the homes of one's Jewish friends as a disapproving comment made by mothers on the doings of their children.

farcoal See **fire coal**

fard See **forehead**

farder See **far** adv, adj[1] **B1**

fardest See **far** adv, adj[1] **C1**

Far-down n Also *Far-downer* [*far* in the North + *down,* prob for County Down in Northern Ireland] **esp in areas of Irish settlement** *formerly often derog, less so now* Cf **Corkonian**

An Irish-American whose family came from the north of Ireland.

1834 *Amer. Railroad Jrl.* 21 June 3.384/1 **MD,** The parties arrayed against each other are known as the *Fardowns* and the *Corkonians.* **1857** *Porter's Spirit of Times* 1.405/2 **NJ,** After a due devotion to the crathur [=whiskey], they formed into two hostile factions, called Corkonians and Far-downers, and had a regular pitched battle. **1940–41** Cassidy *WI Atlas* **csWI,** Far-down—Irish from Tip'rary [sic]; **swWI,** Far-down—a native of the north of Ireland; so-called by southern Irish. **1941** *LANE* Map 454 **seME,** ['fɑ·dæ̃ʊ̃nə] an Irishman from 'a certain part of Ireland'. **1943** Writers' Program MT *Copper Camp* 6, The "Far-Downs," as North-of-Ireland Protestants were known, shoveled and blessed themselves with their left hand. **1968** *DARE* Tape **PA**84, They were paid mourners. . . They'll cry and they're good hands at it. And they'd moan—this is keening. . . They were called the Far-downers . . the women who came. They had men mourners too. **1969** *DARE* (Qu. HH28, *Names . . for people of foreign background . . Irish*) Inf **PA**199, Far-downer.

fare n [Rel to *fare* a journey, expedition (obs), and *fare* to go, travel] **NEng, esp MA**

A catch of fish, esp that of a commercial fishing boat; also transf.

1707 in 1906 Essex Inst. *Coll.* 42.165 **MA,** The owners of such vessels . . Threaten him with further Damages in regard of loosing their last faires of fish. **1805** (1916) Putnam *Diary* 59 **MA,** Wm. Pindar's vessel arrived with a good fare of fish. **1871** (1882) Stowe *Fireside Stories* 221 **MA,** They was a-runnin' up to the Banks for a fare o' fish. **1904** *Eve. Post* (NY NY) 18 June Suppl 11/1 **MA,** The prices brought by the "fares," which are not passenger tariffs, but cargoes of fresh or salted fish. **1916** Macy–Hussey *Nantucket Scrap Basket* 131, "Fare"—The total catch, as "a big fare of fish." **1945** Colcord *Sea Language* 73 **ME, Cape Cod, Long Island,** *Fare.* . . A fisherman's catch of fish. Alongshore, a full fare may mean a bountiful crop, or gains in general.

fare v

Std sense, var form. Past: usu *fared;* also *fore.* [By analogy with *tear/tore, wear/wore* etc]

1946 *PADS* 6.14 **eNC** (as of 1900–10), *Fore:* . . Past tense of *fare.* "The crops *fore* bad during the drouth." . . Occasional among older people.

fare adv, adj See **far** adv, adj[1]

fare out v phr

1985 in 1986 *Barrick Coll.* **csPA,** "How'd you fare out?" [i.e., how well did you do?]

farer See **far** adv, adj[1] **B2**

farest See **far** adv, adj[1] **C2**

fare-thee-well n Also *fare-ye-well, fare-you-well, farewell*

1 in phrr *to* (or *for*) *(a) fare-thee-well:* See below. Cf *for fair* (at **for B4a(4)(a)**)

a To the utmost degree; thoroughly; in abundance.

1885 Cable *Dr. Sevier* 400 **LA,** And then it means . . some bacon and cornpone, and maybe a little coffee; and milk, . . and buttermilk to fare-you-well. **1915** *DN* 4.233 **cnOH** [College slang], I balled [sic] him out for *fare thee well.* **1942** McAtee *Dial. Grant Co. IN* 25 (as of 1890s), *Fare-ye-well, to a.* **1942** Warnick *Garrett Co. MD* 6 (as of 1900–1918), *Fare-ye-well, to a.* **1950** *WELS (“He bawled him out for ______”)* 9 Infs, **WI,** Fare-thee-well; 4 Infs, A fare-thee-well; 4 Infs, (A) fare-you-well; 1 Inf, To a fare-ye-well. **1954** *Harder Coll.* **cwTN,** *To a fare-thee-well* . . completely, entirely. **1965–66** *DARE* (Qu. LL27, . . *"The boss bawled him out ______."*; total Infs questioned, 75) 6 Infs, To a (*or* the) fare-you-well; **FL**25, **MS**71, To a fare-thee-well; **MS**6, To a fare-ye-well. **1974** (1975) Shaw *All God's Dangers* 56 **AL** [Black], He was layin it on him, flailin him. And he cleaned up TJ to a farewell.

b To perfection.

1940 *Sat. Eve. Post* 3 Feb 53 **sMS,** "Say she can play that fiddle, huh?" "To a fare-thee-well." **c1960** *Wilson Coll.* **csKY,** *Fare-you-(or thee)-well.* **1965–70** *DARE* (Qu. KK3a, *Words for the perfect condition—for example, in cooking: "It's done to ______."*) Inf **IL**111, Fare-thee-well; **CA**99, Fare-ye-well; **SC**44, Fare-you-well; (Qu. KK50, *When something is planned out carefully, down to the last detail: "He had it all worked out ______."*) Infs **CA**15, **LA**17, **MS**39, (Down) to a fare-thee-well; **IN**5, 68, **SC**44, (Down) to a fare-you-well; **IL**25, To a fare-ye-well.

2 A curt dismissal; a brush-off.

1967–70 *DARE* (Qu. II5b, *When you don't want to have anything to do with a certain person . . you might say, "I'd certainly like to give him the ______."*) Infs **DC**1, **NY**241, **SC**34, **VA**69, Fare-you-well.

3 A simple expression of courtesy.

1942 *New Yorker* 24 Oct 11/3 **OK,** He ordered the barefoot attendant to fill her [=a car] up, this being an order a colonel or anybody else can still give in that section without so much as a fare-thee-well, much less a ration card.

farewell n

1 also attrib: An aftertaste. [*OED farewell* sb. 3 1634–1759; *W3 "dial."*] **Midl**

1905 *DN* 3.70 **nwAR,** That medicine had a bitter farewell to it. *Ibid* 78, That medicine had a farewell whang to it. **1917** *DN* 4.412 **wNC,** *Farewell.* . . After taste. "That ain't got no bad taste; it has a leetle farewell to it as though it had campfire [=camphor] in it." **1927** *AmSp* 2.354 **wcWV,** That liquor has a good farewell. **1955** McAtee *Dial. Grant Co. IN Suppl. 6* (as of 1890s), *Farewell.*

2 See **fare-thee-well.**

farewell-summer n

1 also *farewell-to-summer, goodbye-summer, summer's farewell:* Any of several asters (*Aster* spp). **chiefly cAppalachians**

1894 *Jrl. Amer. Folkl.* 7.91 **WV,** *Aster diffusus* . . Gray, white devil, wire-weed, devil-weed, Old Virginia stick-weed, old-field-sweet, farewell-summer, nail-rod. . . *Aster* (a purple species), Good-by [sic] Summer, Lincolnton, N.C. **1900** Lyons *Plant Names* 51, Aster. . . Local names in America are Frost-flower, Good-bye-summer, Daisy (Ohio). **1931** Clute *Common Plants* 140, Several species of this tribe [=*Aster* spp] are called farewell-summer. **1940** (1978) Still *River of Earth* 174 **KY,** Mother brought out an armload of yellowrods, stickweed blooms, and farewell-summer Euly had stuck around in fruit jars. **1949** (1958) Stuart *Thread* 177 **eKY,** Above the blackboards and between the windows were decorations of autumn leaves, clusters of red shoe-make berries, bittersweet, pale-blue and white farewell-to-summer. **1968–70** *DARE* (Qu. S25, *What do you call the small wild chrysanthemum-like flowers . . that bloom in fields late in the fall?*) Infs **KY**47, **VA**28A, Farewell-summer; (Qu. S26a, . . *Roadside flowers*) Inf **VA**105, Farewell-summer; (Qu. S26e, *Other wildflowers*) Inf **VA**24, Summer's farewell. **c1969** *DARE* FW Addit **KY,** *Goodbye-summers* . . late blooming asters with a flower that has purple or lavender petals around a yellow center (either large-leaved aster, heart-leaved aster, red-stalked aster, late purple aster, or a combination).

2 **=goldenrod 1.**

1944 *Times Dispatch* (Richmond VA) 9 Aug 8/6 *(Hench Coll.),* The goldenrod, known also as *farewell Summer,* is blooming and the Joe-Pye-Weed is making ready to join the procession.

farewell-to-spring n Also *goodbye-to-spring* **chiefly West**

A summer-flowering plant of the genus *Clarkia.* For other names of var spp see **butterfly flower 4, deer horn 1, elkhorn 3, fairy fans, herald-of-summer, pink fairies, ragged robin, red ribbons, satin flower, summer's darling**

1897 Parsons *Wild Flowers CA* 240, Farewell to Spring. . . In early summer the rosy flowers of this *Godetia* make bright masses of color along dry banks and hill-slopes. **1902** *Out West Mag.* May 512 **CA,** I love the parted lips / Of that weird flower folk call "farewell-to-spring." **1915** (1926) Armstrong–Thornber *Western Wild Flowers* 318, These plants bloom in late spring, hence the pretty name, Farewell-to-Spring. **1948** *Nat. Hist.* June 260/2 **sCA,** Here was . . a Joseph's coat of golden poppies, blue lupine, white primroses, and mauve godetias, those tissue-petaled Farewells-to-Spring. **1967** *DARE* FW Addit **OR,** Farewell-to-spring. **1969** *DARE* (Qu. S26a, *What other wildflowers do you have around here . . Roadside flowers*) Inf **CA**150, Goodbye to spring. **1976** Bailey–Bailey *Hortus Third* 280, *Clarkia. . . Farewell-to-spring. Godetia.*

farewell-to-summer See **farewell-summer 1**

fare-ye-well, fare-you-well See **fare-thee-well**

far-gone adv phr

By all measure; far and away.

1940 *Sat. Eve. Post* 23 Nov 10/1 **sGA,** Trouble was known to be far-gone the best hound on the upper Suwannee River.

far horse n Also *far-side horse* Cf **far side**

=off horse.

1965–70 *DARE* (Qu. K32a, . . *The horse on the driver's right hand*) 36 Infs, **scattered,** Far horse; **IL**62, **MD**32, **MI**78, **OH**89, Far-side horse; (Qu. K32b, *The horse on the left side*) Infs **DC**5, **KS**20, **MI**113, **NY**23, 41, **PA**201, Far horse; **MO**38, **PA**230, Far-side horse. [For discussion of confusion of terms for right- and left-hand horses see notes at **off-horse.**]

farkis n Also *farko* [Perh varr of *Farcot's*] **SC**

A type of plow; see quot 1978.

1966 *DARE* (Qu. L18, . . *Plows . . present and past*) Inf **SC**26, ['fɔkɨs]—for siding cotton. **1977** *DARE* File **cSC** [Correspondence from Raven McDavid], Farko. **1978** *Ibid* **cSC,** *Farkis plow* . . now *Farcot's* plow [was] used to cut or open furrows, i.e. lay off rows; also for planting cotton and corn but no other crops. It had an adjustable foot to which the eagle was attached with a heel bolt which ran through the land slide [sic]. It is not to be confused with the turnplow, or Dixie plow, which was also known as the (Oliver) Dixie goober plow.

farkleberry n Also sp *fartleberry* [Orig obscure; *DA* sugg term might be rel to *sparkleberry; W3* sugg it is an alter of *whortleberry*] **chiefly Sth**

A **blueberry** (here: *Vaccinium arboreum*). Also called **bluet 1, gooseberry 2, sparkleberry, tree huckleberry, winter huckleberry, whortleberry**

1765 (1942) Bartram *Diary of a Journey* 14/1, Trees which naturaly grows there is . . very fine long-leaved pine[,] pitch pine[,] yapon[,] fartle berry[,] chinkapin. **1829** Eaton *Botany* 434, *Vaccinum. . . arboreum.* . . farkleberry. **1941** Walker *Lookout* 60 **TN,** Farkleberry, or winter huckleberry, is a common shrub whose . . fruit which ripens in autumn may remain on the trees throughout the winter. **1942** Tehon *Fieldbook IL Shrubs* 232, The Farkleberry ranges in dry sandy soils in open woods from Virginia to Florida and westward into Texas. In Illinois it grows only in the southern third of the state. **1979** Little *Checklist U.S. Trees* 292.

farko See **farkis**

farly See **fairly** adv

farm n

1 See quot.

1915 Poole *Harbor* 322, There are many 'farms' on the waterfront [of N.Y. Harbor], for a 'farm' is simply the open shore space in front of a dock.

2 See quot.

1975 Gould *ME Lingo* 88, *Farm*—Besides its agricultural meaning, *farm* has a lumbering context in Maine. The early woods operations used many horses, and . . *farms* were cleared for pasturing the animals all summer. These *farms* became regional offices, storehouses, and general headquarters for all timberland activity in a region. . . The term *farm* lingers for a place, an area, a headquarters.

3 freq in phr *farm in Texas* and varr: A very lucrative piece of land—used as a symbol of great wealth. *chiefly rural*

1965–70 *DARE* (Qu. KK62, . . *"I wouldn't do that for ______."*) Infs **IL**5, 11, **MN**36, **NJ**3, A farm; **IN**40, 76, A farm in Texas; **ME**16, A farm down east; **VA**11, A farm in Georgia; **GA**67, A farm in Texas and a seat in Congress. [8 of 9 Infs comm types 4 and 5; 7 of 9 Infs old] **c1970** *Halpert Coll.* **wKY,** Wouldn't do it for a farm in Texas.

farm v

1 To grow (a particular crop).

1980 Banks *First-Person America* 8 **eTX** (as of 1938), We . . grew our beef and farmed enough garden stuff to care for us. **1982** *Smithsonian* Oct 92 **eSC** [Black], Near 'bout everything our family eat, we either farmed it or caught it.

2 with *it:* To make a living by farming.

1942 ME Univ. *Studies* 56.67, Before the end of the War of the States coasting vessels . . were looked down upon by deep water sailors who called their crews "cow sailors," because along the coast of Maine they farmed it part of the year.

farm cheese See **farmer's cheese**

farmer n

1 A rustic, hillbilly; an unmannerly or otherwise objectionable person. **chiefly Nth, N Midl** See Map *somewhat more freq among younger speakers and coll educ speakers; derog* Cf **country** n **B2, hoosier B1**

1901 (1961) Greenough-Kittredge *Words* 285, In this country, *farmer*. . is sometimes jocosely applied to a 'greenhorn,' or to a person who has made himself ridiculous, particularly by awkwardness or stupidity. **1903** Lewis *Boss* 263, Me fadder aint such a farmer as to go leavin' his address wit' no one. **1958** *AmSp* 33.261 **Upper MW,** Next most frequent [after *hayseed* as a disparaging term for a farmer] . . is the word *farmer* itself. . . Precisely one third of the responses indicate this special [derogatory] connotation, but it may be observed that such responses occur more commonly in Northern than in Midland speech territory. **1963** *AmSp* 38.172 **KS** [University slang], An ill-mannered student with poor, unpolished manners: . . *farmer.* **1965-70** *DARE* (Qu. HH1, . . *A rustic or countrified person*) 80 Infs, **chiefly Nth,** (Old) farmer; **IL**29, **IN**80, Farmer boy; **IN**68, Hick farmer; **MD**17, Dumb farmer; [**MN**36, Farmer Jack; **MO**12, Farmer Jake;] **NY**22, Typical country farmer [Of all Infs responding to the question, 63% were old, 11% young, 32% coll educ; of those giving these responses, 48% were old, 24% young, 45% coll educ.]; (Qu. N12, . . *Somebody who drives carelessly or not well*) Inf **WI**57, Farmer; (Qu. AA6b, . . *A man who . . tries to attract [women's] attention—if he's rude*) Inf **IL**140, A farmer; (Qu. HH16, *Uncomplimentary words*) Inf **PA**185, Big farmer; (Qu. HH21, *A very awkward, clumsy person*) Inf **PA**108, Farmer; (Qu. II21, . . *Somebody . . without manners*) Inf **MI**106, Farmer. **1971** Bright *Word Geog. CA & NV* 194, *A rustic . . farmer* 15%. . . This term was generally considered neutral, but 5 San Franciscans and 1 informant from Yerington considered it derogatory.

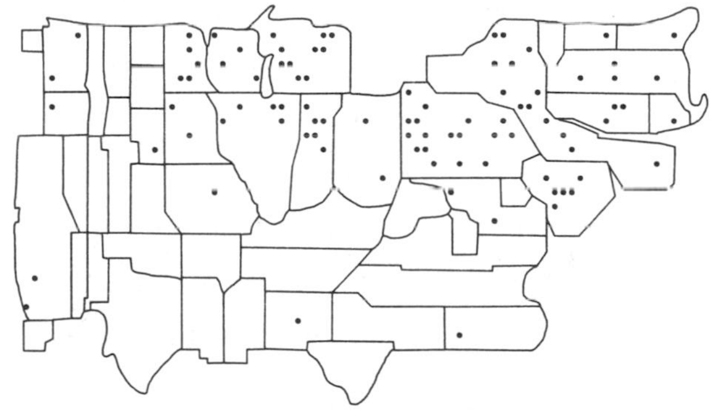

•farmer 1 + varr (Qq. HH1, N12, AA6b, HH16, HH21, II21)

2 also attrib; Esp among loggers: an incompetent worker. Cf **hoosier B2**

1930 Williams *Logger-Talk* 23 **Pacific NW,** *Farmer:* A fighting word quite dissociated from the idea of an agriculturist; to call a logger a farmer is to call him incompetent, stupid, stingy, cowardly, and a stench to the nostrils. **1949** *AmSp* 24.35 [Oil field jargon], An unsatisfactory driller may be called a *brake weight, farmer, Sears Roebuck,* or *synthetic* driller. **1958** McCulloch *Woods Words* 60 **Pacific NW,** *Farmer*—A poor logger. *Farmer eye*—An eye splice formed by stranding a cable and rerolling it to form an eye; frowned on by good loggers. *Farmer splice*—A splice showing poor workmanship. . . *Farmer's laydown*—An easy logging show. **1968** Adams *Western Words, Farmer splice*—In logging, a rough splice at the end of a cable forming a temporary loop. **1970** *DARE* Tape **MI**125, That was what they called a farmer log. . . They [=the farmers] just took the choice [part]; the rest got cut into [fire]wood.

3 also *farmer's;* attrib:

a Very large; oversized.

1968 *DARE* FW Addit **PA**81, A farmer's acre is larger than a regular acre; a farmer's mile is longer than a regular mile. **1970** *DARE* (Qu. LL4, *Very large: "He took a ______ helping of potatoes."*) Inf **OK**55, Farmer's.

b Homemade.

1950 *WELS (Kinds of sausage most eaten in your neighborhood)* 2 Infs, **ceWI,** Farmer('s) sausage; *(Home-grown and home-cured tobacco)* 1 Inf, **cWI,** Farmer knast [=Ger *Knaster* tobacco]—used by the German group.

farmer ball See **animal ball**

farmer bread n

1973 Allen *LAUM* 1.279 **ND** (as of c1950), *Farmer bread:* Round loaf baked on the bottom of the oven, not in a pan; apparently common with Finnish people here.

farmer cheese See **farmer's cheese**

farmer jake See **jake** n

farmer match n Also *farm match, farmer's ~* **chiefly Upper MW, Gt Lakes, NY, WV** See Map

A wooden match that can be struck on any rough surface.

1965-70 *DARE* (Qu. F46) 42 Infs, **chiefly Upper MW, Gt Lakes, NY, WV,** Farmer matches; 17 Infs, **chiefly Upper MW, WV,** Farmer's matches; **MN**16, 39, Farm matches. **1970** *DARE* File **IA,** Farmer matches. **1973** Allen *LAUM* 1.160 **Upper MW** (as of c1950), *Wood(en) matches* is concentrated in the Northern speech area; so is *farm(er('s)* [sic] matches, but with a heavier return in the Dakotas. [28% of the infs use the term *farm, farmer,* or *farmer's match.*]

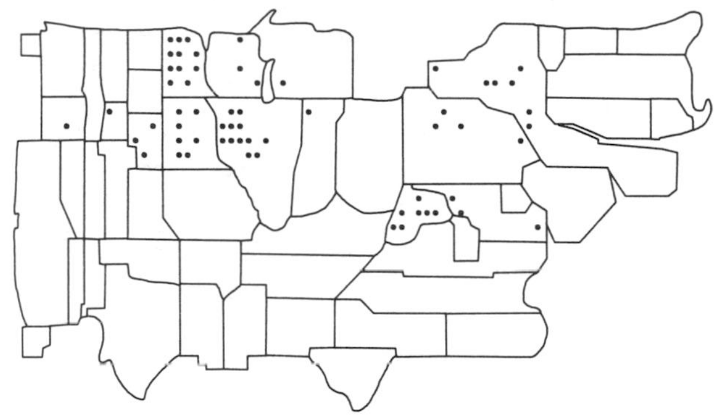

•farmer match + varr (Qu. F46)

farmer's See **farmer 3**

farmer's beef n Also *farmer's beast*

=**government beef.**

1967-68 *DARE* (Qu. P35a) Inf **WI**48, Farmer's beef; **MN**2, Farmer's beast.

farmer's bootjack n [**farmer 1**]

A wagon wheel.

1942 Whipple *Joshua* 369 **UT** (as of c1860s), He was sitting up with the heel of his boot caught in the spokes of a wheel ('the farmer's bootjack,' sneered at by cowboys).

farmer's cheese n Also *farm cheese, farmer ~*

A cheese similar to but sometimes dryer than cottage cheese, often pressed in a mold.

1966-69 *DARE* (Qu. H60, *The lumpy white cheese that is made from sour milk*) Inf **GA**75, Farmer's cheese, cottage cheese; **MD**28, Farmer's cheese [heard]; **NY**119, Farmer cheese; **NY**205, Farmer cheese—a harder cheese; **PA**49, Farmer [cheese]; smearcase [is] creamier; **MI**119, Farm cheese—pressed into a flat cake; (Qu. H61, *Other kinds of homemade cheese . .*) Inf **AR**38, Farmer's cheese—like cottage cheese, but dry. **1976** *DARE* File **csWI,** Grocery stores here carry farmer cheese, a white cheese made at least partially from skim milk. It is advertised as a low-fat cheese; **ceWI,** Farmer cheese—like cottage cheese. **1977** *Atlantic Mth.* May 61, I go back / to the kitchen to share / lox, farmer cheese, and bagel / with my father. **1980** *NY Times* (NY) 5 Mar sec C 4, Q. *Can you explain how cottage cheese, pot cheese and farmer's cheese differ?* A. They are all prepared similarly, the difference being in the wetness or dryness of the cheeses. . . Cottage cheese is one of the first stages, when the curd turns into a fairly firm but still wet mass. Pot cheese is left to drain for a longer period. . . Farmer's cheese and pot cheese are practically identical, except that farmer's cheese is generally molded.

farmer's foxtail n

A barley, either *Hordeum leporinum* or *H. murinum.*

1923 in 1925 Jepson *Manual Plants CA* 106, *H. murinum... Wall Barley. Farmer's Foxtail...* Very common and abundant. **1961** Thomas *Flora Santa Cruz* 86 **CA,** *H. leporinum...* Farmer's Foxtail. Common on grassy slopes and in disturbed areas.

farmer's haircut n

1984 *MJLF* 10.150 **WI,** *Farmer's haircut.* A closely trimmed cut which leaves a band of light skin contrasting with the tanned portions of neck and face, especially above the ears.

farmer's match See **farmer match**

farmer's oil n [**farmer 1**]

1958 *AmSp* 33.306 (as of c1920), Seeking ways to get rich quick, ministers, schoolteachers, and farmers invested life savings in wildcat drilling outfits. Every owner of a piece of land became a dedicated oil scout. This led to the name *farmer's oil* (comparable to fool's gold), applied to a blue shale derivative, black, viscous, which looked like oil but was absolutely worthless.

farmers' railroad n

A road made of planks laid crosswise on longitudinal timbers.

1939 FWP *Guide NC* 44, Many plank roads, or "farmers' railroads," were built between 1849 and 1860.

farmer's rice n [**farmer 4b**] Also called **rubs**

1967 *DARE* File **csWI,** Farmer's rice—a mixture of egg and flour made very stiff and put in soup the last few minutes of cooking time.

farmer's satin n [Infl by **farmer 1**]

A durable fabric of wool or a cotton blend with a satin-like finish.

1893 *Harper's New Mth. Mag.* Apr 668/2, The milliners' work, made of Canton flannel and farmer's satin, is often as stylish as if it was seen on Broadway. **1901** Norris *Octopus* 236 **CA,** She was dressed in what had been Mrs. Hooven's wedding gown, a cheap affair of 'farmer's satin.'

farmer's scrap n Cf **cook's piece, old maid's ~**

The last piece of food left on a plate.

1968 *DARE* (Qu. H71) Inf **MD**12, The farmer's scraps. [Laughter]

farmers' time n Cf **Alaska time, fast ~ 2, Indian ~, Jewish ~**

1940 Yoder *Rosanna* 199 **PA,** They were all in the carriage ready to go very soon after eight o'clock, farmers' time, and that is always at least a half hour fast.

farmer's wine n Cf **farmer's beef, farm liquor**

Whiskey, esp when illegally made.

1968 *DARE* (Qu. DD21c) Inf **NJ**23, Farmer's wine.

farmer wood n

1958 McCulloch *Woods Words* 60 **Pacific NW,** *Farmer wood*—a. Pulpwood worked up by a farmer or by a small logger operating on his farm. b. Small logs, typical of those taken off a farm woodlot.

farm for (the) half v phr Also *farm on half, ~ (the) halves* **chiefly PA** Cf **half farmer**

To work a farm in return for half of the proceeds.

1967–69 *DARE* (Qu. L3) Infs **PA**6, 37, 63, Farming for the half; **PA**56, 153, Farm for (the) half; **NY**176, Farming on halves; **PA**3, Farms on half; **GA**74, Farms on the halves.

farm-furnish store n [**furnish** n]

A store at which tenant farmers can purchase groceries and other necessities on credit against future crops.

1957 Faulkner *Town* 216 **MS,** The hardware and farm-furnish stores cluttered with garden and farm tools and rolls of uncut plow-line and sample sacks of slag and fertilizer.

farmhand n **NW, ND, SD**

A piece of farm machinery used to pick up hay.

1966–67 *DARE* (Qu. L16, *Machines used around here in handling hay*) Inf **OR**13, Farmhand—a big rig with teeth that scoops up hay; **ND**1, **SD**2, 5, **WY**1, Farmhand; (Qu. L11) Inf **SD**8, Buck it with a farmhand, put it into cocks; (Qu. L23, .. *Machinery.. used.. in putting in the seed*) Inf **OR**10, Farmhand staker. **1966–67** *DARE* FW Addit, Farmhand—a common name in Walhalla and Bismark, North Dakota and Eureka, South Dakota for the fork-like arrangement attached to the front of a tractor and used for picking up large bunches of hay; **WY**1, A tractor with a farmhand mounted on the front both picks up the hay and raises it to the top of the stack; **OR**11, Farmhand—a derrick mounted on a tractor. **1977** *DARE* File **sID** (as of 1950s), When my Idaho cousins spoke of a farmhand I assumed they referred to a hired man. Instead, it was a versatile piece of equipment they were talking about.

farm in Texas See **farm** n **3**

farm in the woods v phr Cf **farm liquor**

To operate an illegal still.

1972 *Foxfire Book* 305 **nGA,** If.. the sheriff had gotten a report about one of his [=a friend's] stills, he would.. [say], "I hear you're farmin' in th' woods." The moonshiner would know that that was a warning for him to watch his step.

farmisht adj [Yiddish]

Confused, jumbled, mixed up.

1982 Rosten *Hooray for Yiddish* 120, *Farmisht..* mixed up... Confused; all balled up. "I'm so farmisht I don't know whether I'm coming or going." **1983** *DARE* File **NYC,** That's where the page got all farmisht, as my mother would say. [Jewish speaker]

farm it See **farm** v **2**

farm liquor n Cf **farmer's wine, field whiskey**

1953 Randolph *Down in Holler* 243 **Ozarks,** Farm liquor... Ordinary homespun whiskey, neither aged nor artificially colored. "Hit's just common farm liquor, boys, but it sure has got the power!"

farm-market road See **farm-to-market road**

farm match See **farmer match**

farm on half, farm on (the) halves See **farm for (the) half**

farm steak n Cf **farmer 3a**

A large chopped steak.

1970 *DARE* FW Addit **nePA,** [On a restaurant menu:] Farm steak.

farm-to-market road n Also *farm-to-market;* rarely *farm-market road* **scattered, but chiefly Sth, Cent** See Map

A secondary road intended for local rather than through traffic.

1945 *Ault* (Colo.) *Progress* 7 June 1/5 *(DA),* He pointed out this would be for use on farm-to-market roads, not federal-aid highways. **1947** *Dly. Oklahoman* (Okla. City) 11 Aug. 11/5 *(DA),* A meeting will be held soon.. for the purpose of discussing Seminole county farm to market road projects. **1965–70** *DARE* (Qu. N29, .. *A less important road running back from a main road*) 35 Infs, **chiefly Sth, Cent,** Farm-to-market road; (Qu. N27a, .. *Kinds of unpaved roads*) Infs **GA**23, **MO**3, **TX**102, **WA**1, Farm-to-market road; **AL**39, Farm-to-market road—could be paved or unpaved, but usually small country roads; **NY**142, Farm-market road; (Qu. N18) Inf **TX**64, Farm-to-market; (QR, near Qu. N21) Inf **CT**17, Farm-to-market roads—old dirt roads built up and tar-topped by W.P.A.; (Qu. N23, .. *Kinds of paved roads*) Inf **SC**40, Farm-to-market; (Qu. N28, *A road that connects a big highway with stores and business places set back from it*) Inf **MO**4, Farm-to-market road.

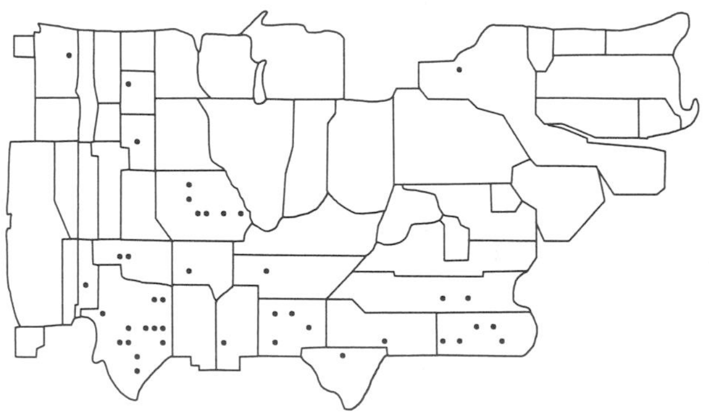

•farm-to-market road + varr (Qq. N29, N18, N23, N27a, N28)

farm-to-market wagon n [**farm-to-market road**]

1967 *DARE* (Qu. N41c, *Horse-drawn vehicles to carry light loads*) Inf **NY**23, Farm-to-market wagon.

farm with the bottle v phr

1967 *DARE* (Qu. DD12, .. *Expressions.. for a person who drinks steadily or a great deal*) Inf **OR**1, [He's] farming with the bottle.

faro for meddlers See **Pharaoh for meddlers**

farow See **farrow** adj

far piece n Also freq pronc-sp *fur piece*

1 A long distance. **scattered, but chiefly Sth, S Midl, N Cent** See Map

1932 Faulkner *Light in August* 1, I have come from Alabama: a fur piece. All the way from Alabama a-walking. A fur piece. **1938** Rawlings *Yearling* 10 **nFL,** "Hit were a mighty purty day to go," Penny said. " . . How come you to take out such a fur piece?" **1950** *WELS* 1 Inf, **cwWI,** A far piece; 1 Inf, **cWI,** A fur piece. **1962** Atwood *Vocab. TX* 48, The word *piece* . . ,in such phrases as a *little piece, a long piece, a far* (or *fur*) *piece, a good piece,* and so on, is well established in all parts of the state except the Trans-Pecos. **1965–70** *DARE* (Qu. MM25, . . *"Texas is a ——— [from here]."*) 86 Infs, **chiefly Sth, S Midl, N Cent,** Fur piece; 53 Infs, **chiefly Sth, Midl,** Far piece; **KY**65, Damn fur piece; **GA**84, Heck of a fur piece; **TX**76, Pretty fur piece; **DE**1, Right far piece; **TN**1, Far piece off; (Qu. LL33) Inf **TN**23, Fur piece; (Qu. MM1) Inf **VA**99, Not a fur piece. **1970** *DARE* Tape **TX**85, A fur piece back. **1974** Fink *Mountain Speech* 10 **wNC, eTN,** Hit's a fur piece from here. **1975** Gould *ME Lingo* 88, *Far piece*—Considerable distance. It's a *far piece* from Liverpool to Hong Kong!

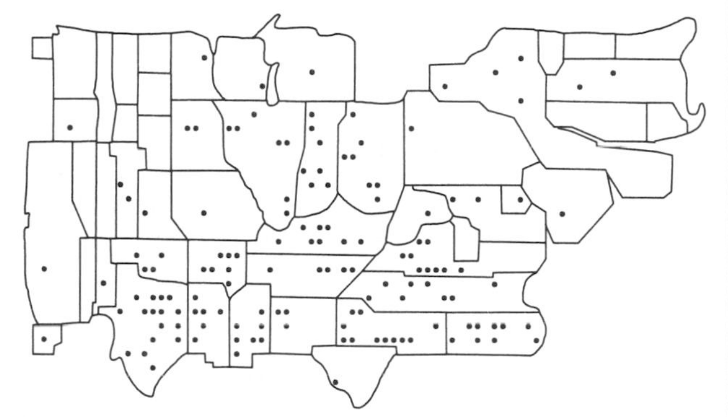

•far piece 1 + varr (Qq. MM25, LL33, MM1)

2 The most distant part of a specific piece of land.

1940 Faulkner *Hamlet* 53 **MS,** We walked up to Old Man Anse's to borrow a mule to finish the far piece with. **1975** Gould *ME Lingo* 88, *Far piece* . . the distant part of a Maine farm which folks to the west'ard might call the "back forty." A man going to work in the *far piece* would carry his *dinner.* (*Far* is sometimes *fur,* and *farthest* is often *fartherest.*)

farputst adj Also *farputzt* [Yiddish]

Dressed up.

1969 *DARE* (Qu. W37, *When a woman puts on her good clothes and tries to look her best*) Inf **IL**99, Farputzt [ˌfɚˈpɪtst]. [Jewish Inf] **1970** Feinsilver *Yiddish* 108, *Farputzt* (or *oysgeputzt*)—All dressed up, all decked out.

farr See **fire**

farrah See **father** n

farren n [Cf *EDD farren* a division of land, freq used for pasturage; cf also *farrow* to bear a litter of pigs]

1968 *DARE* (Qu. M15, *The place outdoors where pigs are kept*) Inf **GA**39, Hog farrens [ˈfærɪnts].

farrer adj[1] See **far** adv, adj[1] **B2**

farrer adj[2] See **farrow** adj

farrest See **far** adv, adj[1] **C2**

farrit See **forward** adj, adv

far room n [Perh var of **fire room**]

1983 *MJLF* 9.39 **ceKY,** *Far room* . . a parlor.

farrow adj, also used absol Usu |ˈfæro, ˈfærə|; occas |ˈfɑr-, ˈfɛr-, ˈfer-, ˈfærəl|; for addit varr see quots Also sp *farow;* pronc-spp *far, farrer* [Scots, Engl dial *farrow,* of unknown derivation; see *OED*] **chiefly NEast**

1 Of a cow: not producing milk.

1858 Hammett *Piney Woods Tavern* 131, If you ever see an old cow fed on bog hay and milked all winter, go farrer about June. **1892** *DN* 1.210 **neMA,** *Farow* [fero]. . . "A farow cow." **1929** *AmSp* 5.127 **ME,** A dry cow was "farrer" (farrow). **1931–33** *LANE Worksheets* **csCT,** She's farrow now, but I expect her to come in within a month; **swCT,** A farrow is a cow when she ain't coming in at all. **1966–69** *DARE* (Qu. K3a, *When a cow stops giving milk, you say she[′s] ———*) Inf **ME**1, [ˈfærə]; **NY**23, [ˈfɑro, fɑr]; **NY**160, [ˈfæɚrə]; **NY**189, [ˈfæɚrel]; **PA**222, [ˈfɑrə]; (Qu. K3b, *When a cow stops giving milk, you say she's a ———*) Infs **CT**13, **ME**9, 23, **MA**66, **NY**117, 148, **VT**9, Farrow cow; **IL**46, **ME**1, **MA**55, 58, 68, **OH**6, Farrow; **NY**72, If she dries up before she's bred, we call her a farrow cow, she's farrow an' dry.

2 Of a cow: unable to conceive.

1939 *LANE* Map 191, 1 inf, **cwCT,** A farrow [fɛ˞rə] cow is one that won't breed; 1 inf, **nwCT,** Farrow [fɑrʊ] cows are those that don't take when they're put to bull; 1 inf, **csCT,** [færo]—a cow that hasn't bred within two or three years. **1969** *DARE* (Qu. K3a) Inf **NY**219, She's far. [That means] she's been bred but she's not pregnant and not giving milk.

3 See quots.

1966 *DARE* (Qu. K1) Inf **ME**5, A [ˈfærə] cow—milking some, but not due to have a calf. **1971** *Down East* Nov 25, *Farrow* . . [is] used to describe a cow that is not having a calf this year. . . In Maine some people use *fallow* and *farrow* interchangeably, often making it sound like "farrer."

farrow v

Of a cow: to stop producing milk.

1968 *DARE* (Qu. K3a, *When a cow stops giving milk, you say she ———*) Inf **WI**29A, Farrowed—used in Indiana; old-fashioned.

farrow hen n [Prob by analogy with **farrow** adj]

Prob a hen that is not producing eggs.

1958 *VT Hist.* new ser 26.274, Doesn't know as much as a farrow hen.

farrowing house n Also *farrowing barn* [*farrow* to bear a litter of pigs] **chiefly Sth, S Midl**

A farm building used for the delivery of pig litters.

1966–70 *DARE* (Qu. M22) Infs **AL**2, **IA**6, **KY**49, 80, **MD**13, **MS**19, **VA**59, Farrowing house; (Qu. M15) Infs **GA**19, **IA**22, **IL**108, **NC**81, 87, Farrowing house; (Qu. M1) Infs **KY**72, **WI**63, Farrowing barn.

farruh See **father** n

farse See **fierce** adj

farsee v [Perh back-formation from *far-sight;* prob infl by *foresee*]

To foretell the future; hence n *farseer* one who is prescient.

1944 (1967) McNichols *Crazy Weather* 110 **SW,** "Will you give me an answer? Are you a farseer?" "Well, if I was, would I tell you!" roared the old man. "I can't ease my mind about Havek till I know for sure whether you're farseeing him coming here, or just guessing."

far side n [*OED* (at *far* a. 3) *"Obs."*] Cf **far horse, Indian side**

The right side of a horse.

1929 *AmSp* 5.63 **NE,** A horse is "broken" to be saddled and mounted on the left, the "near side," though an "Indian pony," one "Indian broken," is approached and mounted on the right or "far side."

far-side horse See **far horse**

farst See **forest**

fart n Pronc-sp *faht* *esp among young and mid-aged speakers*

Used of a person:

a As a generalized term of abuse, esp for a man.

1965–70 *DARE* (Qu. HH40, *Uncomplimentary words for an old man*) 20 Infs, **scattered,** (Old) fart; (Qu. BB53b, . . *A doctor who is not very capable*) Inf **DE**5, Old fart; (Qu. HH16, *Uncomplimentary words with no definite meaning*) Inf **LA**14, Old fart; (Qu. HH36, *A careless, slovenly woman: "She's just an old ———."*) Inf **PA**149, Fart; (Qu. LL3b, . . *"He's a little ——— old man."*) Inf **TX**98, Dried up fart. [16 of 23 total Infs young or mid-aged] **1968** Rosten *Yiddish* 14, *Alter kocker.* . . A crotchety, fussy, ineffectual old man. . . I make no special plea for *alter kocker,* but I certainly prefer *A.K.* to its English equivalent, "old fart." **1975** *AmSp* 50.58 **AR** (as of c1970), *Fart* . . One who is insincere, a faker. **1979** Lewis *How to Talk Yankee* [11] **nNEng,** "He's an awful old faht. Never been known to go anywhere without his necktie on." . . "She's an awful old faht; wants to wash your plate before you've et!"

b As a term of affection.

1967–68 *DARE* (Qu. Z12, . . *Joking words meaning 'a small child': "He's a healthy little ———."*) Inf **CO**39, Fart; (Qu. AA23, *Joking* *names that a woman may use to refer to her husband: "It's time to go and get supper for my ______.")* Inf **MD**5, Old fart. [Infs young and mid-aged] **1980** *DARE* File **csWI,** I was surprised to hear a middle-aged woman in one of my classes refer to her husband as "the old fart." She said it in front of the whole class while he was sitting right beside her, so she obviously intended it as some kind of endearment despite the fact that she was openly annoyed at him.

fart-box n

1968 *DARE* (Qu. X35, *Joking words for the part of the body that you sit on)* Inf **PA**76, Fart-box.

farth adj, adv Also *furth* [Back-formations from *farther, farthest, further, furthest*]

Far.

1895 *DN* 1.388 **NEng,** *Farth, furth:* positive from analogy to *farther, farthest.*

farther, all the See **all the**

fartherest See **far** adv, adj[1] **C3**

farthing n [*farthing* Brit and colonial Amer coin worth ¼ penny]

Fig: something of very small value.

1967 *DARE* (Qu. GG21b, . . *"Go ahead—I don't give a ______.")* Inf **NJ**2, Farthing; (Qu. HH20b, . . *"He doesn't amount to ______.")* Inf **NY**102, A farthing; (Qu. HH20c, . . *"He isn't worth ______.")* Inf **ME**6, A farthing. [All Infs old]

farthrest See **far** adv, adj[1] **C3**

fart in a whirlwind n For varr see quots

Fig: the most insignificant, impotent, or transitory thing.

[1734 in 1894 MA Hist. Soc. *Coll.* 6th ser 7.41 **MA,** As for his protest, if he shou'd set a f______t against a N.W. wind, how then?] **[1945** Adams *A. Woollcott* 71 (as of c1915), The critic captioned his article "Farce in a Gale of Wind." An alert proofreader caught it.] **1952** Brown *NC Folkl.* 1.405, Like a fart in a whirlwind. No more'n a fart in a whirlwind. **1963** Wright *Lawd Today* 54 **Chicago IL,** You'd last as long trying to overthrow the government as a fart in a windstorm. **1965–69** *DARE* (Qu. HH20b, . . *"He doesn't amount to ______.")* Inf **MS**64, A fart against a whirlwind; (Qu. HH20c, . . *"He isn't worth ______.")* Inf **NY**119, A fart in hell; **PA**202, A fart in a hailstorm. **1969** *DARE* FW Addit **csNY,** He don't amount to a fart in a gale of wind.

farting spell n

1 See quot.

1899 (1912) Green *VA Folk-Speech* 170, *Farting-spell. . .* A short space of time.

2 See quot.

1984 Wilder *You All Spoken Here* 13 **Sth,** Had a fartin' spell: Displayed bad temper; showed his ass.

fartknocker n

1 See quot.

1968 Adams *Western Words* 109, *Fartknocker*—What the cowboy calls any kind of hard fall, especially when thrown from a horse.

2 See quot.

1984 Weaver *TX Crude* 44, *Fartknocker.* Any obscure person. Equates to "whatsisname."

fartleberry See **farkleberry**

fartweed n [Perh because they are sometimes used as forage plants]

1 A **summer cypress** (here: *Kochia americana* var *vestita*).

1954 McAtee *Suppl. to Nomina Abitera* [4], *Kochia vestita.* Fart-Weed—West desert of Utah.

2 =**horsebrush 1.**

1954 McAtee *Suppl. to Nomina Abitera* [5], Tetradymia spp.—Fartweed, Utah.

farwell exclam [Pronc-sp for *farewell*] Cf Pronc Intro 3.I.1.b

1903 *DN* 2.313 **seMO,** *Farwell. . .* Farewell.

farzino phr Also sp *farziner, fezinah, forzino* [Pronc-spp for telescoped phrr *(as) far as I know*] **NEast** *obs* Cf **fortino**

As far as I know; perhaps; maybe.

1815 Humphreys *Yankey in England* 105 **CT,** *Forzino,* far as I know. **1848** Bartlett *Americanisms* 133, *Farziner.* A vulgar contraction of *far-as-I-know,* extensively used through New England and New York, including Long Island. **1859** (1968) Bartlett *Americanisms* 141, *Farzino,* or *Farziner.* **a1870** Chipman *Notes on Bartlett* 160 *(DAE), Forzino.* So far as I know.—Occasional in N[ew] E[ng]. **1872** Schele de Vere *Americanisms* 601, *Farziner,* a violent corruption of as *far as I know,* throughout New England and in parts of New York, but confined to the most ignorant classes, and rapidly disappearing. **1890** *DN* 1.73, *Fezinah* [fəˈzaɪnə]: a contraction of 'far as I know.' Equivalent to *perhaps, I guess so, for all I know.* An aged aunt of mine in Chicopee, Mass., who died fifteen years ago, used it constantly. 'It may rain tomorrow, *fezinah.'* Often in answer to a question, as, 'Will he come back soon?' 'Fezinah.'

faschnacht See **fastnacht**

faschtie See **fastnacht 2**

fascinator n Also rarely *fascination;* pronc-spp *vasarator, vascinator* (cf Pronc Intro 3.I.15) *old-fash* Cf **zephyr**

A head scarf, usu crocheted, knitted, or of lace.

1878 in 1925 Smith *Kate Douglas Wiggin* 35, [Letter:] Raining outside —Mother crocheting a fascinator—Phil reading the 'Pilot.' **1911** Wharton *Ethan Frome* 32 **wMA,** The lively young man . . drew forth a girl who had already wound a cherry-coloured "fascinator" about her head. **1917** *DN* 4.418 **wNC,** *Vascinator. . .* A woman's head-wrap. **1927** *DN* 5.479 **Ozarks,** *Zephyr,* n. A woman's wrap. . . A similar but more modern garment is known as a *fascinator.* **1931** *PMLA* 46.1317 **sAppalachians,** In the days when the fascinator was à la mode, [the pronunciation] "vascinator" was common. **1965–70** *DARE* (Qu. W3) 20 Infs, **scattered,** Fascinator; **NM**9, Fascination. [18 of 21 Infs old] **1967** *DARE* FW Addit **AR**52, Fascinator—a scarf worn by men over a cap. **1971** Bright *Word Geog. CA & NV* 160, There were 23 responses of *fascinator* [for a head scarf, tied under the chin], many of which were suggested. Fourteen of them qualified the word as old-fashioned. **1982** Brooks *Quicksand* 113 **swUT** (as of c1908), Two "drummers," or traveling salesmen, were in town with such notions as fascinators, ribbons, buttons, laces and yardage to sell. **1983** *MJLF* 9.1.60 **ceKY** (as of 1956), *Vasarator . .* something like a cap for women.

fash v [Scots and Engl dial; *OED* 1533 →; cf *OED, SND, EDD,* where the verb is tr, intr, and refl]

1 refl: To trouble oneself, worry; to put oneself out.

1870 *N&Q* 24 Sept 42.249 **sPA,** To *fash* oneself, to worry; good English, not obsolete perhaps, elsewhere. **1933** White *Dog Days* 213 **CA,** She [=a bulldog] had not fashed herself. She knew perfectly that sooner or later we always slowed. No use getting excited: speed was not her game. **1951** West *Witch Diggers* 12 **IN,** Don't you fash yourself about me, daughter. **1956** Settle *Beulah Land* 280 **WV** (as of 18th cent), Don't fash yourselves. **1967** *DARE* (Qu. GG23c, . . *Expressions [to tell someone to be patient])* Inf **OH**37, "Don't fash yourself." My mother said that.

2 To ruin, spoil.

1944 Adams *Canal Town* 331 **wNY** (as of 1820s), "That husband of yours has fashed his prospects well, this time," she began. "How?" . . "By his quarrel with Genter Latham."

fashed ppl adj [Perh **fash**]

?Astonished.

1968 *DARE* (Qu. GG20, *Expressions meaning 'very much surprised': "When those two got married, I was certainly ______.")* Inf **GA**67, [fæšt].

fashion n

Custom, habitual manner.

1893 Shands *MS Speech* 29, An old man once told me that it was always his fashion to shake his head during the preaching if he did not agree with the minister.

fashionable tour n *euphem*

A visit to a house (or houses) of prostitution.

1967 Cerello *Dakota Co. MN* 55 (as of c1900), Old man Stockton went on a fashionable tour at least once every two weeks. . . There was nothing wrong with going on a fashionable tour as long as your family didn't know about it. . . The only women who wore shop-made gowns were either . . rich or . . those who conducted fashionable tours. [Reported from six communities]

fashion, in good See **good fashion**

fasnacht, fasnak See **fastnacht**

fasola n, usu attrib [*fa* + *sol* + *la* names for tones of a diatonic scale] *somewhat old-fash* Cf **buckwheat note, do-re-mi 1, patent note, sacred harp singing, shape note**

In music: see quot 1960.

1933 *Musical Qrly.* Oct 397 **S Midl,** The "Fasola Folk," . . still number from about 30,000 to 50,000 souls. **1940** Writers' Program *Guide GA* 127, An interesting development of this rural music is the Sacred Harp singing, in which performers read from shaped-note song books with triangle, circle, square, and diamond standing respectively for *fa, sol, la* and *mi.* Because they begin by vocalizing the notes, the participants are called "fasola" singers. **1943** Powell *I Can Go Home* 72 **swGA,** We called it "do-ra-me" or "fa-so-la" singing. The Leader would announce the song, catch the key from the tuning fork, and lead off, carrying the tune, and the rest of us followed, whether we could sing or not. **1960** Scholes *Concise Dict. Music* 320/1, *Lancashire Sol-fa. . .* It is a method of solmization applied to the normal staff notation; the first 3 notes of every major scale are called *fa-sol-la,* and so are the second 3 notes, the remaining note being called *mi. . .* In the Amer. Colonies (and later the U.S.A.) it was called *Fasola* or, sometimes (from the special notation there used), *Patent Notes.*

fasset See **faucet A1**

fassnacht See **fastnacht**

fast Aleck n [Prob by analogy with *smart Aleck*]

A quick person.

1935 Hurston *Mules & Men* 217 **FL** [Black], Boy, he sich a fast Aleck, he grabbed de bridle and went down tuh de lot tuh ketch ole Bill.

fast brand n [*fast* unchangeable]

1968 Adams *Western Words* 109, *Fast brand*—A brand [on an animal] deep enough to be permanent; the opposite of *slow brand.*

Fast Day n **chiefly NEng**

A holiday, orig for the purpose of fasting and prayer.

1788 in 1873 May *Jrl.* 17 Apr 18 **CT,** After breakfast met numbers of people going to meeting, in their old clothes, it being fast-day. We were accosted by some sort of Sunday officer with, *"What makes you ride fast-days?"* **1860** Holmes *Professor* 150 **MA,** Hossback-ridin' a'n't for them,—except once a year,—on Fast Day. **1866** in 1911 Lowell *Poet. Wks.* 431/1 **MA,** As near to the present occasions of men / As a Fast Day discourse of the year eighteen ten. **1968** *Yankee* Apr 20 **NEng,** Fast days were observed widely a few generations ago, but always, as far as we know, by proclamation by some authority such as a Governor. **1969** *Ibid* Feb 42, Nineteen holidays are celebrated every year somewhere in New England. Seven of these are strictly Yankee affairs. Observed only in New England are: . . Fast Day, New Hampshire, fourth Monday in April. **1982** Brooks *Quicksand* 137 **swUT** (as of c1908), I knew all about the case . . even before the Fast Day when both men bore their testimonies and asked forgiveness of each other and the ward for their hot-tempered quarrel.

Fast Day cake n

=**fastnacht 1.**

1941 *LANE* Map 285 1 inf, **cCT,** Fast day cakes—all shapes, dropped from spoon.

fast daylight express See **fast train**

fasten v Also sp *fastne*

To take fast hold of, prevent from moving.

1888 Jones *Negro Myths* 91 **GA coast** [Gullah], Eh tell um fuh gard de well, an fastne ebrybody wuh come day fuh tief water. [=He tells him to guard the well, and hold everybody that comes there to steal water.]

fast express See **fast train**

fast freight See **fast train**

fast ground See **fastland**

fasthold n

1916 *DN* 4.275 **NE,** *Fasthold. . .* Blend of *fastness* and *stronghold.* One instance noted.

fast house n [*fast* immoral, promiscuous]

A brothel.

1929 Ellis *Ordinary Woman* 40 **CO** (as of early 1900s), We had clothes to deliver to the 'fast-house', where one mustn't go in. . . But we did. . . And this is what I remember: first, a strong sweet smell . . , several pretty girls . . , two men . . sitting there laughing. **c1938** in 1970 Hyatt *Hoodoo* 2.1074 **seLA,** Now, it's a *good-time house*—yo' see, dat's tuh draw . . de trade in faster—de *fast-house,* yo' know whut ah mean, fast women draws mens to 'em yo' see.

fastland n Also *fast ground* [*fast* secure] **chiefly C Atl coast**

Coastal land lying above high tidemark.

1680 in 1904 New Castle DE Court *Records* 1.504, Containing . . 724 acres of fast Land. **1765** Bartram in 1953 McMullen *Topog. Terms FL* 107, But between it and the common fast ground is a great swamp. **1862** U.S. Congress *Congressional Globe* 37th Cong 2d Sess 11 July 32.4.3264/2, Mr. *Lehman.* I ask the gentleman from New York . . to tell this house what he means by "fast land?" Mr. F.A. *Conkling.* I mean to refer to land originally above the ebb and flow of the tide. **1894** *DN* 1.330 **sNJ,** *Fast land:* upland near coast. **1940** Writers' Program *Guide MD* 411, The narrow strip of fastland along the southeast shore. **1956** *DE Folkl. Bulletin* Oct 22/1, Both the creek and the river are bordered by stretches of fast-land, which are covered by trees down to the water's edge. **1956** *Sun* (Baltimore MD) 7 Aug sec B2/2 *(Hench Coll.),* Fishing Creek, Md. . . Some 1,500 watermen of this isolated island community and those of nearby Taylors Island and the "fast" or mainland are eagerly awaiting the arrival of August 24 . . when the "new doctor" . . will arrive. **1976** Warner *Beautiful Swimmers* 8 **eMD,** "South of the Little Choptank [River]," the watermen tell you, "the fast land disappears." It is their way of saying that only isolated islands or small clumps of firm ground dot the vast marsh landscape of these parts.

fast line n See **fast train**

fast luck (oil) n

In **hoodoo n 1a:** a preparation supposed to bring good luck.

1931 *Jrl. Amer. Folkl.* 44.411 **LA** [Black], Fast Luck: Aqueous solution of oil of Citronella. It is put in scrub water to scrub the house. It brings luck in business by pulling customers into a store. . . Red Fast Luck: Oil of Cinnamon and Oil of vanilla, with wintergreen. Used as above to bring quick luck. **c1938** in 1970 Hyatt *Hoodoo* 1.652 **New Orleans LA,** He told me to go and get some *fast luck oil* . . oil of *van-van* and olive oil, and mix it up and rub your hands and it [will] bring luck to you . . in gambling. *Ibid* 2.1825 **New Orleans LA,** You could *dress* your place with *fast luck.* Scrub your place out every morning with *Red Devil Lye. . .* Then you sprinkle it all over with that holy water. Then you take your incense and you give it good smoke, all over it, and you sprinkle it with that *red fast luck* . . , all over the place and sugar. . . And you'll have more trade in there than you'll be able to wait on.

fastly adv [*W3 "archaic"*]

1 Firmly.

1927 *DN* 5.474 **Ozarks,** Brethren, you-all got t' stick *fastly* t' th' church o' Gawd!

‡**2** Quickly.

1968 McPhee *Pine Barrens* 60 **NJ,** Fred says "spragnum" for "sphagnum," "braken" for "bracken," and "fastly" for "quickly."

fast mail n See **fast train**

fast-mouthed adj [*fast* rebellious, flouting proprieties]

1970 *DARE* (Qu. II36b, *Of somebody who talks back or gives rude answers . . "She certainly is ______!"*) Inf **SC68,** Fast-mouthed [laughter].

fastnacht n Usu |'fasnat, 'fɔs-|; also |-nak(t), -naxt, -nət, 'fɔsə,nɔk, 'fasə,nak| Also sp *fasnacht, fawsnocht, fawstnacht, fosnacht, fossnock;* for addit varr see quots [PaGer *fasnacht* < Ger *Fastnacht* fast night (Shrove Tuesday)] **chiefly PA**

1 also *fastnacht kuche,* ~ *kucha:* A deep-fried raised doughnut traditionally made on Shrove Tuesday, preceding Lenten fasting. See Map

1872 Haldeman *PA Dutch* 57, German forms of food have furnished the vicinal English with . . *fawstnachts.* [Footnote:] Shrove-tide cakes—with the PG. pronunciation, except *st.* **1915** Thomas *Mary at Farm* 206 **PA,** "Fast Nacht Kuchen" (Doughnuts). . . Without fail, every year on Shrove Tuesday, or "Fast Nacht," the day before the beginning of Lent, these cakes were made. **1934** in 1944 *ADD* **cPA,** Fosnochkucha. **1935** *AmSp* 10.170 **sePA,** Other German words used in English are . . *fawsnocht (fastnacht) kucha,* molasses or honey doughnuts. **1937** *AmSp* 12.204 **sePA,** [Footnote:] Professor Struble quotes the form 'fawsnocht (or fastnacht) kucha,' molasses or honey doughnuts; but among the English-speaking people the form 'fasnacht' is generally used, meaning an ordinary doughnut. **1945** *AmSp* 20.254 **sPA,** In their own home district the regionalisms *ponhaus, snits, sots, fasnachts, Belschnickel,* and a host of others are accepted by the natives of Southern Pennsylvania quite as naively as quaint New England provincialisms are accepted in their own habitat. **1948** *AmSp* 23.130 **sePA,** A *doughnut* is usually called [fetkuxə] or [fɔ:snaxt]. **1949** Kurath *Word Geog.* 35, *Fossnocks* . . for a kind of doughnut (Pa. Ger. *fasnachskuche* 'Shrove-tide cakes'), [is current] from the Great Valley to the Alleghenies. **1950** Klees *PA Dutch* 424, Like Christmas cookies, these are made but once a year—on Fasnacht Day. . . The most delectable of the doughnut tribe, fasnachts are very like raised doughnuts; but they have no holes and instead of being round they are square, triangular, rectangular, or even quinquangular. **1957** Schönfelder *Deutsches Lehngut* 132, Fasnacht, fastnacht, fasnak, fassnacht, fawsnocht, fosnock, fossnock, fosnochkucha, fawsnochtkucha . . fawstnacht. **1964** Smith *PA Germans* 108, [On Shrove Tuesday] we made fritters, fried in hog grease, we called them 'fasch-nachts'. **1965–70** *DARE* (Qu. H28, *Different shapes or types of doughnuts*) Infs **PA**2, 18, 63, Fastnacht; **PA**143, Fastnacht—square, without a hole; **CA**167, **NY**105, Fastnacht kuchen; **MD**27, [Inf's sp:] Fosnacht ['fɔsnɑt]; **MD**28, ['fɔsnɑt]—square, with slits, or twisted into a knot; **MD**30, ['fɑsnɑt]—eaten on Shrove Tuesday; a fibrous dough, cut in strips or braided, fried in deep fat, eaten with molasses; **MI**51, [Inf's sp:] Fossnocks ['fɑsnɑks]; **NY**49, ['fɑsnaxts]; **VA**30, ['fɔsnəts]; (Qu. H26) Infs **PA**29, 150, Fastnacht; **PA**9, ['fɑsnɑts]; **PA**63, Before Lent, all old shortening, leavening, and oil had to be got out of the house; so they cooked them into doughnut cakes called fastnachts; **PA**159, ['fɔsənɔk]; **MD**27, [Inf's sp:] Fosnacht ['fɔsnɑt]—square shape with slits across it, made with yeast; made only in homes, usually by people of German background; **PA**203. Faustnacht; (Qu. H27) Infs **PA**13, 22, 88, 136, Fastnacht; **PA**52, Some call them ['fɑsənɑk]; **PA**242, ['fɔstnakt]; **VA**30, ['fɔsnəts]; (Qu. H30) Infs **PA**2, 40, 136, 159, Fastnacht. **1968** *Helen Adolf Festschrift* 35 **sePA,** The term *faasnachts* for 'molasses or honey doughnuts' is derived from Pennsylvania German *Faastnachtkuche.* **1973** Allen *LAUM* 1.282 **NE** (as of c1950), ['fas,nɑt] used by a Nebraskan of Illinois and Ohio parentage.

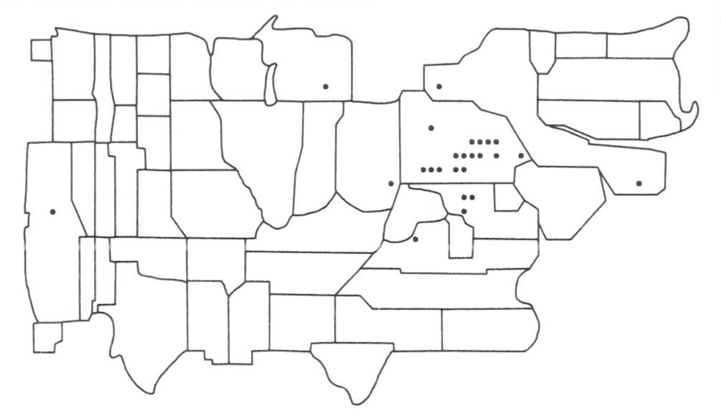

•fastnacht 1 + varr (Qq. H28, H26, H27, H30)

2 also *faschtie:* Transf: see quots.

[**1924** Lambert *PA Ger. Dict.* 54, Di alt Fâsnacht, said of that member of a family who rises last on Shrove Tuesday.] **1964** Smith *PA Germans* 108, The last person to get up on Shrove Tuesday was called "Old Faschtie," and the young folks all struggled to get up early to avoid being teased throughout the day. **1968** *DARE* (QR p43) Inf **PA**159, The one who got up late on Ash Wednesday was the fossenock ['fɔsənɔk].

fastne See **fasten**

fast passenger train See **fast train**

fast print n

Counterfeit money.

1968 *DARE* (Qu. U29) Inf **NY**92, Funny money; fast print.

fast shuffle n [*fast* marked by trickery + *shuffle* a manipulation of playing cards]

A bad bargain; an unfair transaction.

1966–70 *DARE* (Qu. LL23, . . *"These apples are wormy; I think you got ______ ."*) Infs **IL**135, **OK**9, **VT**16, A fast shuffle.

fast time n

1 Daylight saving time.

1937 *Lit. Digest* 1 May 9/1, Daylight-saving or, as it now is coming to be called, "fast" or "summer" time. **1942** *AmSp* 17.113 **SC,** The official terms (Eastern Standard and Daylight Saving) were, however, quite rare, especially in the country; they were frequently replaced by 'old time' and 'new time,' but most commonly by 'slow time' and 'fast time.' *Ibid* 281, ['Slow time' and 'fast time'] were commonly used by the Pennsylvania Dutch in eastern York County, Pennsylvania, as early as the summer of 1938. **1949** *Chesterton* (Ind.) *Tribune* 28 April 5/4 *(DA),* Yes, we are trying to fool the Lord going on fast time. But a lot of us will not get there even at that. **1968** *DARE* FW Addit **MD**20, Fast time—clock is moved forward one hour, as for daylight savings time. **1973** *Hardin Co. Independent* (Elizabethtown IL) 26 Apr 1/7, The last Sunday in April . . will mark the beginning of daylight saving time, commonly known as "fast time." **1975** Gould *ME Lingo* 89, In Maine, Daylight Saving Time is usually called *fast* time.

2 See quot. Cf **farmers' time**

1931 *AmSp* 6.466 **cnNE,** Central time is spoken of as "fast time," and mountain time as "slow time." Some sandhillers prefer to regulate their timepieces by "half time," meaning half an hour slower than "fast time" and half an hour faster than "slow time." . . Fast time is sometimes "long time" and, less frequently, "high time."

fast train n Also *fast line, ~ (daylight) express, ~ freight, ~ mail, ~ passenger train* **chiefly N Cent, Lower Missip Valley** See Map Cf **cannonball**

A train which operates at high speeds and stops only at major cities.

1881 *Chi. Times* 12 March *(DA),* The initiative in this competitive cutting of tariffs was taken by the Commercial Express Fast-Freight line. **1904** *NY Times* (NY) 11 May 3/1, He saw the fast freight approach at high speed. **1950** *WELS* 2 Infs, **WI,** Fast train; 1 Inf, Fast mail. **1953** Goodwin *It's Good* 159 **sIL,** The fast Daylight Express puffed to a stop. *Ibid* 160, The fast passenger train raced toward the Southland. **1965–70** *DARE* (Qu. N35) 18 Infs, **chiefly N Cent, Lower Missip Valley,** Fast train; **NJ**2, **OH**22, 72, 74, Fast line; **IL**71, **MI**2, Fast express; **LA**18, Fast passenger train; **NH**14, Fast freight; **MD**31, Fast mail. **1977** Adams *Lang. Railroader* 57, *Fast train—See* . . cannonball express, flyer, greased lightning [etc].

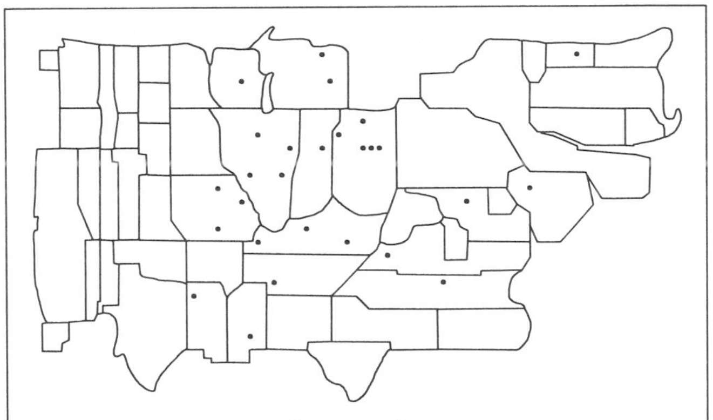

•fast train + varr (Qu. N35)

fat n[1] [Early form of *vat;* see *OED fat, vat*]

1 A vat. *arch*

1899 (1912) Green *VA Folk-Speech* 170, *Fat.* . . A large open vessel for water. A vat. Tan-*fat.*

2 also *fats:* In marble games: a square "ring" into (or out of) which the marbles are shot; a game played in such a ring. [Etym uncert] Cf **fat** adj[2], **fatty** n[1], **in the fat**

1890 *DN* 1.76 **NJ, NY,** A "fat" is a square ring a foot or so each way. **1950** *WELS* 1 Inf, **ceWI,** Fat. [Inf drew a square filled with an x.] In Two Rivers [about ten miles north] it is called [a] Big Ring. **1955** *PADS* 23.17 **AL,** *Fat.* . . A "ring" in the shape of a square. **1958** *PADS* 29.33 **WI.** **1963** *KY Folkl. Rec.* 9.3.61 **eKY,** *The squared pattern on which marbles are played:* . . fats: Johnson, Rowan, Greenup, Boyd [Counties]. *Ibid* 62, *The name of the area inside the lines of a square:* . . fats: Rowan [County]. **1967** *DARE* (Qu. EE7 . . *Kinds of marble games*) Inf **NV**3, Fats—[you] stood back of a line; [there was] a big round ring, and [you] hit all you could out of the ring.

fat n[2]

1 See quot. Cf **fat crab**

1904 *DN* 2.396 **MA,** *Fat*. . . The crabber's name for a soft-shell crab, or one which has shed its shell and is covered only with a thin, tender skin.

2 See quot.

1979 Hallowell *People Bayou* 117 **sLA,** She stood in her kitchen before a big bowl of . . crawfish tails. Nearby was a smaller bowl full of a greenish, semiliquid stuff. "That's the key to good etouffée. . . That's the fat and that's what makes your roux take on a special taste." The fat, as she calls it, is actually the animal's liver and pancreas.

fat adj[1]

1 Of wood: having a high resin content. Cf **fat pine, fatwood**

1705 Beverley *Hist. VA* 3.12, To make the Smoak less troublesome to their Eyes, they [=Indians] generally burn Pine, or Lightwood, (that is, the fat Knots of dead Pine) the Smoak of which does not offend the Eyes. **1808** *Thomas' MA Spy or Worcester Gaz.* (MA) 9 Nov 3/4, A pine post, fat with pitch, had taken fire. **1903** *DN* 2.351 **sePA,** *Fat*, . . Of pine wood[,] full of sap and without reference to its use in burning. **1969** *DARE* (Qu. T8, *Joints of pine wood that burn easily and make good fuel*) Inf **CT**28, *Fat knot*—we called it that in Alabama; **NY**219, Fat spruce. **1971** Wood *Vocab. Change* 13, With caution one can deduce that in frequency . . *fat splinters* . . would occur regularly in responses throughout the entire region [=Alabama, Arkansas, Florida, Georgia, Louisiana, Mississippi, Oklahoma, Tennessee].

2 Of people: well off, in a comfortable position.

1848 Judson *Mysteries NY* 114, *"Fat."* Rich. "Fat cull," a rich fellow. **1950** *Western Folkl.* 9.159 **nCA,** *You're fat.* Equivalent to slang, "You're in," or "You've got it made." **1968** *DARE* (Qu. U37, . . *Somebody who has plenty of money*) Inf **VA**8, Fat. **1970** Major *Dict. Afro-Amer. Slang* 52, *Fat* . . wealthy.

3 in phr *cut it fat* and varr: To overdo something; to go too far. ?*obs*

1838 Neal *Charcoal Sketches* 65 **NEng,** "If that ain't cutting it fat, I'll be darned!" growled Salix [after someone had taken advantage of him]. **1853** Curtis *Potiphar Papers* 131 **NYC,** It's bad enough to be uncomfortable in your own house without knowing why; but to have a philosopher of the Sennaar school show you why you are so, is cutting it rather too fat. **1856** Kelly *Humors* 88 (Taylor-Whiting *Dict. Amer. Proverbs*), [He] got married, and cut it very "fat."

4 Of a fish: see quot.

1930 *AmSp* 5.390, *Fat*. . . Used to describe certain fish, especially the herring, shad, or menhaden when they reach a state of perfect health between spawning seasons.

5 Of tobacco stems: see quots.

1967 Key *Tobacco Vocab.* **PA,** Fat stem—stems of the leaves which are not fully dried out. . . A fat stem is improperly cured. The mid-rib is still sappy. **1969** *DARE* Tape **KY**60, When a buyer sees that those stems (connected to the leaves in a hand) are not dry or that they're what we call fat, that reduces the value of the tobacco. . . It can have fat stems.

6 Meaningless; nonsensical. Cf **fatmouth** v

1970 *DARE* FW Addit **Memphis TN** [Among young Blacks], Fat talk—nonsense, meaningless talk.

fat adj[2] [*EDD fat* adj.[2] 1828 →] **chiefly Sth, S Midl** Cf **dead** adj **B4, stuck**

Of the **taw** in marble games: having stopped in the ring; also of a player: having shot the **taw** so that it stopped in the ring—also used as an exclam.

1843 (1916) Hall *New Purchase* 42 **sePA,** Go to baste! [?=base]—fat!—histings!—comins about! **1890** *DN* 1.24 **KY,** To "get fat" happens when a player's taw rolls into the ring and there are two or more men in it already. **1892** *DN* 1.219 **DC,** One's marble is *fat* when in playing "little ring" it stays in the ring when it ought to have come out. **1893** Shands *MS Speech* 29, If a player's *taw* stops in the ring, it is said to be *fat*. **1899** (1912) Green *VA Folk-Speech* 170, When the taw stopped in the ring it was *"fat"* and the player had to stop playing untill [sic] next game. **1908** *DN* 3.309 **eAL, wGA,** In marbles, when one's taw stops inside the ring he is said to be *fat*. *Stuck* is the term used in Texas. **1922** *DN* 5.186, *Fat*. . . Said of a taw which rolls inside the ring and stops there. The owner of a "fat" taw quits, removing his taw. **1955** *PADS* 23.15 **AL,** If the player who rolls into the ring has knocked out the marbles, he places them in the ring along with his taw, and his marble is called *fat* or *chuck*.

fat v, hence ppl adj *fatting* Also *fat up* *old-fash*

To fatten; to become fatter; also fig.

1840 Haliburton *Clockmaker* (3d ser) 137 **NEng,** They hadn't fatted up. **1859** Beecher *Plain & Pleasant Talk* 122 **cIN,** When the fatting hogs have eaten off the field . . they are turned into another. **1871** (1882) Stowe *Fireside Stories* 69 **MA,** He took it into his head that Huldy ought to have a pig to be a fattin' with the buttermilk. **1885** Twain *Huck. Finn* 29 **MO,** I says to myself, if a body can get anything they pray for, why . . can't Miss Watson fat up? **1892** *KS Univ. Qrly.* 1.96, *Fat up:* to increase a stake at cards. **1934** *Hanley Disks* **seMA,** You take her [=a cow] down and let her feed on them [salt] marshes, and if she's all run down and poor as a skunk up here in the high, dry land, take her down there and she'll fat right up. **1949** *AmSp* 24.108 **SC,** To fat my hogs. **1968** *DARE* (Qu. K58) Inf **CT**14, All your fatting pigs are either sows or castrated pigs. [Inf old] **1986** Pederson *LAGS Concordance*, 1 inf, **cwGA,** It really fats a hog.

fataga n [Var of **catawba**]

=**catalpa B2.**

1969 *DARE* (Qu. P6, . . *Worms* . . *used for bait*) Inf **GA**72, Fataga [ˌfəˈtagə]—feeds on cottonwood.

fatal adj

Complete; out-and-out—used as an intensifier.

1927 Kennedy *Gritny* 15 **sLA** [Black], People takin' me for a fatal rogue; an' I ain' had no way to convince 'um I was jes' try'n to do de w'ite folks wishes. *Ibid* 57, 'Twas like a fatal purrade goin' roun' Gritny.

fatal step, take the v phr Also *take the fatal plunge,* ~ *leap* *joc*

To get married.

1942 Berrey–Van den Bark *Amer. Slang* 359.4, *Marry; Be Married*. . . take the fatal step,—leap *or* plunge. **1965–70** *DARE* (Qq. AA15a, b, c) 12 Infs, **scattered,** Took the fatal step; **OH**11, Took a fatal step; **NM**5, **WI**63, Took the fatal plunge; **ID**5, Took the fatal leap.

fat and fine adj phr

=**fat and sassy 1.**

1968 *DARE* FW Addit **sLA,** "My, you really lookin' fat and fine." A high compliment, e.g. from a Black woman to a White girl.

fat and funky adj phr

Prob =**fat and sassy 1.**

1967 *DARE* FW Addit **SC,** *Funky*—stinky. Also in the set phrase "fat and funky."

fat and sassy adj phr Also *fat and saucy;* ~ *ragged; fat, ragged, and sassy*

1 In good health and spirits.

1843 (1916) Hall *New Purchase* 329, He was no inconsiderable a people himself, being very fat and very saucy. **1857** in 1939 *Hench Coll.* **CA,** As for my health I [have] but a few words to say about it—only that I am fat ragged and sassy. **1893** in 1901 *Independent* 53.3009/2 **NEng,** Fixed Clocks and Sewing Machines all through Southwest Missouri that winter; came out in the spring Fat and Raged [sic]. **1928** Peterkin *Scarlet Sister Mary* 287 **SC** [Gullah], You better listen to me; an' cat a plenty and get fat an' sassy again. **1939** *AmSp* 14.264 **sIN,** The person in good health is feeling 'fine as frog hair,' 'right peart,' or 'fat and sassy.' **1951** *PADS* 15.54 **nIN,** Fat and sassy. **1954** *Harder Coll.* **cwTN,** Fat and sassy. **1970** *DARE* (Qu. BB47, . . *"I'm feeling ______."*) Inf **IL**135, Fat 'n sassy. **1978** *DARE* File **sOH** (as of c1900), "How're you feelin' today?" "Fat, ragged, and sassy!"

2 Securely entrenched, and therefore arrogant.

1968 *Needles Desert Star* (CA) 14 Mar 2/1, The reason is obvious. These fat and sassy officials of the BIA do not intend to destroy their meal tickets.

fat around the heart adj phr

Afraid.

1935 Hurston *Mules & Men* 71 **FL** [Black], Jack . . put down five hund'ud and says, " . . You fat 'round de heart [Footnote: scared]. Bet some money."

fat as a match adj phr Also *fat as a buggy whip,* ~ *hen's forehead*

Thin; small.

1899 (1912) Green *VA Folk-Speech* 23, Fat as a match. **1939** FWP *ID Lore* 241, *Fat as a hen's forehead*—meager. **1942** McAtee *Dial. Grant Co. IN* 25 (as of 1890s), *Fat as a match* . . not fat at all. **1967** *DARE* (Qu. X49, . . *Very thin*) Inf **TX**23, Fat as a match; **WA**30, Fat as a buggy whip.

fat as God's pocket adj phr Cf *DS* AA28
Pregnant.
1931–33 *LANE Worksheets* **nwCT,** As fat as God's pocket.

fatback n
1 Fat meat from the back of a hog, with little or no lean. [See quot 1903] **chiefly Sth, S Midl; also NEast** See Map Cf **fat meat, flitch 1, salt pork**
[**1903** *Sears Cat.* (ed. 113) 18/1 *(DA),* Clear Back Pork. This pork is made from the fat backs of prime hogs, is free from lean and bone.] **1932** (1974) Caldwell *Tobacco Road* 6 **GA,** Soup Ada had made by boiling several fat-back rinds in a pan of water. **1942** (1960) Robertson *Red Hills* 65 **SC,** One of our cousins, who did not care for cowpeas and fatback, bowed his head and said: "Good God, look at this." **1949** Kurath *Word Geog.* 70, Less common terms are: *fat-back* (the upper part of a side of bacon) in the western parts of the Carolinas and the Virginia Piedmont. **1952** Giles *40 Acres* 104 **KY,** In the winter, just after hogs are killed, fresh pork is plentiful. During the summer there is side meat, jowls, and what we call fat back. Fat back is the fat, white, salted meat that is usually used for cooking. **1954** Armstrong *Satchmo* 214 **LA,** She . . bought . . a big slice of fat back and a big red onion. **1962** Atwood *Vocab. TX* 62, Other terms in occasional use in Texas include *bacon, side bacon, dry salt (bacon) fatback,* and *sowbosom.* **1963** *AmSp* 38.249, Midland . . *fatback* 'a kind of bacon' [seems to be penetrating southward through central Georgia]. **1965–70** *DARE* (Qu. H38, *Other words for bacon*) 157 Infs, **chiefly Sth, S Midl; also NEast,** Fatback; (Qu. BB34b, *What is a poultice made with?* total Infs questioned, 75) Inf **MS**1, Fatback meat; (Qu. BB50c, *Remedies for infections*) Inf **VA**41, White meat (fatback). **1969** *Weakley Co. Press* (Martin TN) 2 Oct 8, [Advt:] *Nice thick fat back* Lb. 29¢.

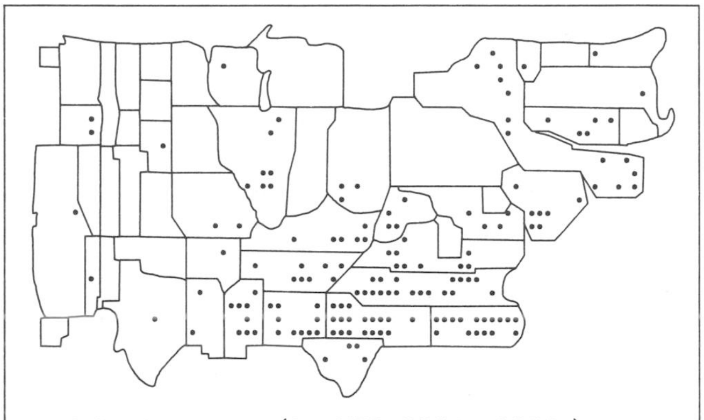

2 Any of var fish, as:
a =striped mullet. chiefly Mid Atl
1709 (1967) Lawson *New Voyage* 160 **NC, SC,** Fat-Backs are a small Fish, like Mullets, but the fattest ever known. They put nothing into the Pan to fry these. They are excellent sweet Food. **1884** Goode *Fisheries U.S.* 1.449, The name 'Fat-back' is also in use, but whether this name is used for Mullets in general, or simply for those in particularly good condition, I have been unable to learn. **1939** Natl. Geogr. Soc. *Fishes* 91, Another name, fatback, refers to its [striped mullet *(Mugil cephalus)*] broad round back. **1946** *PADS* 6.13 **neNC,** *Fat-back. . .* Fatty, bony fish used for oil and fertilizer. Pamlico. Common. **1966–68** *DARE* (Qu. P2) Infs **DE**1, 4, **MD**36, **NC**12, Fatback(s); (Qu. P3) Inf **NC**8, Fatback. **1966–69** *DARE* Tape **NC**25, Fatback; **NC**65, We used to fish on them porgy boats . . for them fatbacks for fertilizer. **1968–70** *DARE* FW Addit **DE, NC,** Fatback; **DE, VA,** Fatback [is the same as] jumping mullet; **eVA,** Fatback net—a fish net used for fatback.
b =menhaden. S Atl
1873 Smithsonian Inst. *Misc. Coll.* 14.2.33, *Brevoortia Menhaden. . .* fat-back and yellow-tail *(coast of North Carolina).* **1884** Goode *Fisheries U.S.* 1.569, In North Carolina occurs the name "Fat-back," which prevails as far south as Florida, and refers to the oiliness of the flesh [of the menhaden]. **1941** *Nature Mag.* 34. 138/2 **S Atl,** From North Carolina to Florida is heard the term fat-back, embodying a natural allusion to the oily nature of the flesh of the fish [=menhaden]. **1953** MD Dept. Educ. *Our Underwater Farm* 15, Menhaden are also known as alewives, bunkers, fatbacks, and bug fish. **1976** Warner *Beautiful Swimmers* 127, In New England it [=the menhaden] is the pogy; in the middle Atlantic states, the mossbunker; in North Carolina, the fatback.
c =bluefish 1.
1896 U.S. Natl. Museum *Bulletin* 47.946, *Pomatomus saltatrix* . . Fatback. **1946** LaMonte *N. Amer. Game Fishes* 42, *Bluefish—Pomatomus saltatrix. . .* Fatback. **1975** Evanoff *Catch More Fish* 127, Bluefish . . fat back.

fat ball n [By analogy with **fatcake**]
A kind of raised fried cake containing currants and raisins.
1965 *Woman's Day Encycl. Cookery* 1.48 **MI,** *Fat Balls.* ¼ cup shortening, ½ cup sugar, 1 egg . . 2½ cups potato water . . 1 cup currants, 1 cup raisins [etc].

fatbird n
=pectoral sandpiper.
1844 DeKay *Zool. NY* 2.242, [*Tringa pectoralis*] passes under the various names of *Meadow Snipe, Jack Snipe, Short-neck,* and according to Mr. Giraud it is called *Fat-bird* on the coast of New-Jersey. **1888** Trumbull *Names of Birds* 176. **1917** (1923) *Birds Amer.* 1.233, *Pectoral Sandpiper. Pisobia maculata. . . Other names. . .* Triddler; Hay-bird; Fat-bird; Short-neck. **1923** U.S. Dept. Ag. *Misc. Circular* 13.54, *Pectoral Sandpiper. . . Vernacular Names. . . In local use. . .* Fat-bird (N.J.)

fat-bread See **fatty-bread**

fatcake n [PaGer *fettkuche*] **chiefly PaGer area**
=friedcake 1.
[**1948** *AmSp* 23.130 [PaGer], A *doughnut* is usually called [fɛtkʊxə].] **1949** Kurath *Word Geog.* 35, Some expressions of Pennsylvania German origin are current not only in the still bilingual area in the eastern part of the state but also in sections where Pennsylvania German is now little used or extinct. . . *fat-cakes* . . for doughnuts (Pa. Ger. *fettkuche*), [is current] from the Great Valley to the Alleghenies. **1962** Atwood *Vocab. TX* 83, Terms of Pennsylvania German origin . . have not, as a rule, reached Texas at all. There are . . only two [occurrences] of *fatcakes.* **1968–69** *DARE* (Qu. H26) Inf **MD**27, Fatcake—made only in homes, usually by people of German background; it's a German dish; (Qu. H27) Infs **MD**28, **OH**81, Fatcakes; (Qu. H28) Inf **PA**203, Fatcakes—no holes, just dough. **1971** Wood *Vocab. Change* 45 **Sth,** *Fat cake* . . appear[s] occasionally. **1973** Allen *LAUM* 1.281 (as of 1950), Pennsylvania German *fat cake* is the term of 2 Midland respondents [in the Upper Midwest].

fat cat n
A children's game; see quot.
1924 *DN* 5.286 **Cape Cod MA,** 'Fat Cat' is a concentrated form of leap frog, where the leapers approach the side of a barn, and continue leaping upon one another.

fatch See **fetch**

fat char See **fat lake trout**

fatched See **fetch** v **A2**

fat-chewing n Cf **chewing match**
A gabfest; spirited conversation.
1957 *Daily Progress* (Charlottesville VA) 5 Feb 8/1 *(Hench Coll.),* Every once and again we get together for a little fat-chewing. **c1960** *Wilson Coll.* **csKY,** Fat-chewing . . Arguing, gossip. **1965–70** *DARE* (Qu. KK12, . . *"They got together yesterday and had a real ______"*) Infs **CA**213, **NY**131, **PA**66, **TN**52, **VA**42, **WV**7, 8, 13, 16, Fat-chewing.

fat crab n Cf **poor crab**
A crab which is almost ready to molt. Also called **green** adj **1, snot, white sign crab**
1905 U.S. Bur. Fisheries *Rept. for 1904* 411, As the crab approaches the shedding period it begins to show its condition by various external "signs," which are well known to the fishermen and are of great importance to them. The first indication is a narrow white line which appears just within the thin margin of the last two joints of the posterior pair of legs. This line is so narrow and so obscured as to be barely visible, but it is immediately detected by the expert, and the individual bearing it is classed as a "fat crab," or more vulgarly as a "snot." **1976** Warner *Beautiful Swimmers* 214 **eMD,** We call them greens or fat crabs mostly. **1984** *DARE* File **Chesapeake Bay** [Watermen's vocab], White sign crab—snot—fat crab.

fate n *old-fash*
A person whom one is fated to marry.
1856 Stowe *Dred* 1.25 **VA,** "I suppose you have heard of Miss Benoir, of

Baltimore. Well, she is my fate." "And are you really engaged?" "All signed and sealed, and to be delivered next Christmas." **1899** (1967) Chesnutt *Wife of Youth* 99, It had become fashionable [for wealthy mulatto women] . . to go traveling, ostensibly for pleasure, but with the serious hope that they might meet their fate away from home.

fat-eater n

=**verdin.**

1883 Nuttall Ornith. Club *Bulletin* 8.76, *Auriparus flaviceps*. . . In Texas . . [the bird's] yellow-daubed head has won it the name *Fat-eater.*

fat enough to kill adj phr [In ref to animals being fattened for slaughter]

Very fat.

1929 *AmSp* 5.121 **ME,** One putting on much weight was "in good order" or "fat enough to kill" or "fat as a hog in bootcherin' time." **1949** *PADS* 11.14 **wTX** (as of c1920), *Fat* enough to kill. (Very fat. Usually said of hogs, but occasionally said of people.) **1954** *Harder Coll.* **cwTN,** Fat enough to kill.

fat flitch n Cf **fatback 1, flitch 1**

Fat bacon.

1843 (1916) Hall *New Purchase* 121 **IN,** Pay came . . also in the shape of fat-flitch, cord-wood, eggs, and butter.

fat gourd n

See quot 1908.

1840 (1847) Longstreet *GA Scenes* 24 **GA,** I am perhaps . . the best man at a horse-swap that ever stole *cracklins* out of his mammy's fat gourd. **1899** (1912) Green *VA Folk-Speech* 170, Fat-gourd, a gourd used for holding lard. **1908** *DN* 3.309 **eAL, wGA,** *Fat-gourd.* . . A receptacle for grease, meat drippings, etc., originally a large gourd used for this purpose.

fathead n

1 also *fathead chub, ~ minnow, fat-headed minnow:* A cyprinid fish of the genus *Pimephales,* usu *P. promelas.* For other name of *P. promelas* see **blackhead minnow**

1820 Rafinesque *Ohio R. Fishes* 53, Fat-head. . . Its head is very remarkable, soft and fat all over. **1882** U.S. Natl. Museum *Bulletin* 16.158, *P[imephales] promelas* . . *Fat-head.* **1967** Cross *Hdbk. Fishes KS* 151, No other fish seems so . . nearly ubiquitous in Kansas as the fat-headed minnow. **1967–68** *DARE* (Qu. P7, *Small fish used as bait for bigger fish:*) Inf **MN**5, Fatheads; **MN**42, Fatheads; some call them flatheads; **MN**21, Fathead—a larger crappie minnow—[i.e., one which is] good bait for crappies. **1970** WI Acad. *Trans.* 58.280, *Pimephales promelas* Rafinesque—Fathead minnow—Locally common over the entire state. Frequently associated with turbid water. **1983** Becker *Fishes WI* 595, *Bluntnose Minnow. Pimephales notatus.* . . Other common names . . fat-head chub.

2 A California sheepshead *(Pimelometopon pulchrum).*

1882 U.S. Natl. Museum *Bulletin* 16.602, *Harpe pulchra [Pimelometopon pulcher]* . . Fat-head. **1946** LaMonte *N. Amer. Game Fishes* 92, *Pimelometopon pulcher* . . Fathead. **1953** Roedel *Common Fishes CA* 117, *Sheep-Head—Pimelometopon pulchrum—* . . Unauthorized Names: . . fathead, humpy.

fathead chub, fathead(ed) minnow See **fathead 1**

fat hen n [Prob **fat** v; cf *EDD fat-hen*]

1 A **saltbush** (here: *Atriplex patula* var *hastata*). **chiefly West**

1900 Lyons *Plant Names* 54, *Atriplex hastata* . . Fat-hen. **1911** Jepson *Flora CA* 143, *A[triplex] hastata*. . . *Fat-hen*. . . Herbage mealy, scarcely succulent. **1961** Thomas *Flora Santa Cruz* 150 **CA,** Fat Hen. . . Common in salt marshes along the coast . . , occasionally inland. **1973** Hitchcock-Cronquist *Flora Pacific NW* 96, *Atriplex patula* . . fat-hen.

2 also *hen-fat:* A **goosefoot,** usu *Chenopodium album* or *C. bonus-henricus.*

1900 Lyons *Plant Names* 95, *C[henopodium] album*. . . Fat-hen. . . *C. Bonus-Henricus*. . . Fat-hen. . . *C. rubrum*. . . Fat-hen. **1914** Georgia *Manual Weeds* 112, *Chenopodium album*. . . Fat Hen. **1935** (1943) Muenscher *Weeds* 205, Fat-hen. . . Annual; reproducing by seeds. **1940** Clute *Amer. Plant Names* 140, *C. album*. . . Fat hen. . . *C. Bonus-Henricus*. . . Fat hen. **1959** Carleton *Index Herb. Plants* 44, *Fat hen:* Atriplex (v); Chenopodium bonus-henricus. *Ibid* 60, *Hen-fat:* Chenopodium album. **1974** (1977) Coon *Useful Plants* 95, Fat-hen. . . Regarded by most users as better than . . common spinach.

3 =**shepherd's purse.**

1900 Lyons *Plant Names* 72, *B[ursa] bursa-pastoris*. . . Fat-hen.

father n Usu |ˈfɑðər|; also **esp eNEng, Mid Atl** |ˈfaðə, ˈfɑðə|; less freq |ˈfeðər, ˈfæ-, ˈfɒ-|; for addit varr see quots Pronc-spp *fader, fayther;* also *Gullah, farrah, farruh*

A Forms.

1888 Jones *Negro Myths* 22 **GA coast** [Gullah], Me farruh befo me blan plant tetter [=used to plant sweet potatoes]. **1896** *DN* 1.416 **NY,** *Father:* in Ontario Co., N.Y., sometimes pron. [feðər]. **1899** (1912) Green *VA Folk-Speech* 168, Fader. **1902** *DN* 2.234 **sIL,** *Fayther*. . . Pronunciation of father, when used, which is seldom. **1905** *DN* 3.56 **eNE,** The same vowel ([æ]) . . sometimes prevails in . . *father.* **1909** *S. Atl. Qrly.* 8.43 [Gullah], *Father* . . is [pronounced] *farrah.* **1922** Gonzales *Black Border* 302 **sSC, GA coasts** [Gullah glossary], *Farruh*—father, fathers. *Farruhlaw*—father-in-law, fathers-in-law. **1925** *DN* 5.347 **Boston MA,** [faðə] [is] not general—at least in the cultivated speech of Boston and the neighborhood—but, on the other hand, not uncommon. **1946** *AmSp* 21.231 **seNC** (as of c1900), The Irish *fayther* is found for father [in the speech of the Croatans]. **1950** *WELS Suppl.* **csWI,** Father [ˈfɔ˞ðɚ]; [this is the pronunciation of an elderly farmer of "Yankee" heritage]. **1961** Kurath-McDavid *Pronc. Engl.* 112, The free low vowel /ɑ ~ a/, as in . . *father* . . is confined to . . Eastern New England, Metropolitan New York, Virginia east of the Blue Ridge with adjoining parts of Maryland and North Carolina, and South Carolina-Georgia. Dialects in which postvocalic /r/ is in use have checked /ɑ/ . . in *father,* . . [except that in] Western Pennsylvania . . *father* . . [has] the phoneme /ɒ/. **1969** *DARE* (QR, near Qu. L65) Inf **CA**141, [ˈfɑdɚ]. **1976** Allen *LAUM* 3.20 (as of c1950), In *father* /ɑ/ is the normal vowel for all but two U[pper] M[idwest] infs. **1978** *DARE* File **Philadelphia PA** (as of c1960), My [fɑdɚ] said he would [rɑdɚ] not go. [Old, coll educ speaker; regular use.]

B Senses.

1 usu cap: Used by a woman to refer to her husband.

1941 *LANE* Map 374, [In context "I must ask my husband":] **nwCT,** Many people say *father;* **csMA,** *Father,* often used. **1966–67** *DARE* (Qu. AA23, *Joking names that a woman may use to refer to her husband*) Infs **MI**3, **MO**2, **OR**1, Father. **1973** Allen *LAUM* 1.336 (as of c1950), One instance of *Father* [for a husband who is also a parent] occurs in Iowa as the term used in talking to the children of the family.

2 freq attrib: A male animal kept for breeding purposes. *euphem* Cf **daddy 5, gentleman** n **B2**

1939 *LANE* Map 190 1 inf, **neRI,** *Father cow,* in speaking to children. *Ibid* Map 206 1 inf, **seCT,** [faðə pɪg], also used for *boar;* 1 inf **cnMA,** *Father,* also used for *boar.* **1966–68** *DARE* (Qu. K23, *Words used by women or in mixed company for a bull*) Infs **NY**107, **TX**75, Father cow; **OH**27, Father cow—I only heard that once; **MI**23, *Sire* is used by educated women, *father cow* or *top cow* by the common woman; (Qu. K22, *Words used for a bull*) Inf **NC**44, Father cow. (Qu. K68, . . *A goat that habitually strikes people with its horns*) Inf **NJ**50, He's a father goat. [5 of 6 Infs old]

3 God—used in exclams or imprecations. **chiefly Sth** *euphem*

1965–70 *DARE* (Qu. NN27a, . . *"My ______!"*) Infs **GA**13, **IL**51, **LA**25, **MI**28, **MS**6, **VA**11, Father; **GA**9, **IL**26, **TX**37, Heavenly Father; **AL**8, Fathers; (Qu. NN29a, . . *"Great ______!"*) Inf **SC**65, Father; (Qu. NN29c, . . *"Holy ______!"*) Infs **GA**12, **TN**26, Father.

4 Used as a title of respect, esp for a minister.

1892 (1893) Botume *First Days* 48 **seSC** (as of 1864), ["]Father["] for all leaders in church and society, . . [was the term] generally used. **1970** Vandiver *Revised Ed. Hist. Anderson Co.* 29 **SC,** "Father Humphreys", as he was affectionately called, once sitting through a wearsome [sic] session of Presbytery . . rose to his feet and exclaimed: "Fiddle-faddle! What's all this long talking about?" **1983** *McDavid Coll.* **SC,** *Father* was the title used for Presbyterian ministers in South Carolina in the 1840's: "Father Dickson of Greenville."

5 in var phrr used to warn a woman that her slip is showing: See quots.

1950 *WELS* 2 Infs, **WI,** You love your father better than your mother; 1 Inf, Father loves you best. **1965–70** *DARE* (Qu. W24a) Infs **MI**61, **PA**110, You like your father best; **NE**3, **PA**194, Your father likes you better than your mother; **IN**77, Your father likes you; **MA**38, Your father is thinking of you; **MA**69, Your father loves you; **NJ**16, Father loves you better; **NY**83, You think more of your mother than you do your father; **PA**1, Your father loves you better than your mother; **PA**96,

Your mother likes you better than your father; **PA**194, Your father likes you best; **VA**28, Your father loves you best. [10 of 12 Infs old, white, female]

father v Cf **daddy** v **2**

To admit paternity or responsibility.

1966 *DARE* (Qu. JJ40, *When you admit that you did something wrong and are willing to take the consequences, you might say: "It was my fault and . . ———."*) Inf **ME**5, I'm going to father it [laughter].

father and son n

1 A children's game; see quot.

1950 (1965) Richter *Town* 190 **OH** (as of c1900), [They were] playing Father and Son like simple-minded children. You played it in pairs, racing to a mark and back. Each had a switch. On the way over the son tried to birch the father and on the way back it was the father's turn if he could reach the son.

2 attrib; Of a business enterprise: small. Cf **ma and pa**

1943 Korson *Col Dust* 4, Some farmers, however, overcame this fear and operated small mines variously called "country banks," "wagon mines," "dog holes," "gopher holes," or "father-and-son" mines.

father bird See **mother bird**

father divine n [Perh in allusion to George Baker, also known as *Father Divine,* Black evangelist 1880–1965]

1967 *DARE* (Qu. CC13b, . . *The person who knows how to use a forked stick to find water*) Inf **MO**14, Diviner or father divine.

father graybeard n Also sp *father greybeard*

=**fringe tree.**

1937 *Torreya* 37.100 **VA,** *Chionanthus virginica* . . Father grey-beard.

father longlegs n

=**daddy longlegs 1.**

1792 Belknap *Hist. NH* 3.183, Father Long Legs, *Phalangium.* Several species. **1841** in 1886 Longfellow *Life of H.W. Longfellow* 1.380 **MA,** C———'s little girl . . saw a "father-long-legs" crawl over her pillow, and cried out to her mother, "Oh mamma, here's Mr. Longfellow in here!" **1864** (1873) Webster *Amer. Dict., Father-long-legs.* . . A species of spider . . ;—called also *harvest-man, shepherd-spider,* and *daddy-long-legs. U.S.* **1889** *Century Dict.* 2154, *Father-long-legs.* . . Same as *daddy-long-legs.*

father (up) the herd v phr

Among cowboys: to get cattle settled for the night.

1939 FWP *Guide MT* 444, *Father up the herd*—To get the herd bedded down at night. **1961** Adams *Old-Time Cowhand* 277, It was the duty of the day herders to have the cattle on the bedground and bedded down before dusk. This beddin' down was the formin' of the herd for their night's rest. . . [These cowboys were] said to "father the herd."

fathoms under adj phr

In a sound sleep.

1968 *DARE* (QR, near Qu. X46) Inf **CT**1, Fathoms under—deep asleep.

fat horse n

=**crease-back bean.**

1976 *Wanigan Catalog* 8, *Fat Horse*—See Creaseback[.] Known very early in the Upper Missouri River area. This seed looks like Great Northern.

fatigue n Usu |fə'tig|; also |fə'tɪg|; sp-pronc |'fæti,gju|; for addit var see quots Similarly, adj *fatigued* Pronc-sp *fatigg*

Std sense, var forms.

1911 *DN* 3.549 **NE,** In facetious usage—'fati,gued. **1930s** in 1944 *ADD* **WV,** [fə'tɪg] fa*tigg* n. Common or usual, but unknown in cent. N.Y. **1941** *LANE* Map 479 *(Tired)* 6 infs, **scattered NEng,** [fə'tigd]; 5 infs, **ME, MA, NH,** [fə'tɪgd]; 1 inf, **neMA,** [fə'tæɪgd]; 1 inf, **seNH,** ['fætɪgjuʷd]. **1964** *AmSp* 39.158 **Philadelphia PA,** The phenomenon [of /ɪ/ for usual /i/] is not confined to monosyllables, but may be heard also in such words as *colleague, fatigue,* and, particularly, *legal,* which rhymes with *wiggle.* **1967–68** *DARE* (Qu. X47, . . *Very tired*) Infs **DE**3, **LA**11, **MO**35, **VA**13, [fə'tɪgd]. **1989** *DARE* File, *Fatigue* is sometimes jocularly pronounced ['fæti,gju] or ['fætɪ,gju].

fat lake trout n Also *fat char, fat trout, fats* Cf **lean trout**

=**siscowet.**

1943 Eddy–Surber *N. Fishes* 96, Siscowet (Fat Trout) *Cristivomer namaycush siscowet.* . . Several specimens caught off Grand Marais had smaller swim bladders than the lake trout, with much thicker walls. . . This fish is extraordinarily fat and has a thick skin. **1983** Becker *Fishes WI* 330, *Siscowet. Salvelinus namaycush siscowet.* . . Other common names: fat lake trout, fat trout, fats, fat char. . . Commercial fishermen and buyers recognize . . at least four variants: . . *fat trout* (siscowet) [etc.] . . The higher fat content in the fish has an adaptive significance in buoyancy regulation.

fat light, fat lighterd, fat lighter(wood) See **lightwood**

fat man n[1] Cf **bad man 2**

1970 *DARE* (Qu. EE41, *A hobgoblin that is used to threaten children and make them behave*) Inf **MS**84, Booger man, snake man, fat man, crazy man.

fat man n[2] See **fattyman**

fat meat n **chiefly Midl; also Sth** See Map

=**fatback 1.**

1949 Kurath *Word Geog.* 70, Less common terms [for salt pork in the South and South Midland] are *fat-back* . . and *fat-meat.* **1956** Ker *Vocab. W. TX* 270, *Fat meat* (for boiling), a term of the Southern coastal area . . , is reported by [one informant]. **1957** Battaglia *Resp. to PADS 20* **eMD,** *(Dishes made with greens)* Fat meat and greens (boiled). **1965–70** *DARE* (Qu. BB50c, *Remedies for infections*) 20 Infs, **chiefly Midl,** Fat meat; 12 Infs, **chiefly Midl,** Fat meat [in var phrr—see *DS*]; (Qu. BB50a, . . *Remedies . . for a cough*) Infs **IN**54, **OK**11, Fat meat (around the neck); (Qu. BB50b, *Remedies for chest colds*) Inf **OK**11, Fat meat; **PA**133, Fat-meat poultice; (Qu. BB51a, . . *Cures for corns or warts*) Inf **AR**37, Rub with cooked fat meat, bury it; (Qu. BB51b, . . *'Magical' cures for corns or warts*) Inf **AR**37, Rub with cooked fat meat; **KY**72, Put piece of fat meat on them; (Qu. BB34a, . . *Remedies . . to bring a boil to a head;* total Infs questioned, 75) Infs **OK**1, 31, 42, (Piece of) fat meat; **MS**45, 60, 63, Put (some) fat meat on it; **GA**8, Lay piece of fat meat on it; (Qu. BB34b, *What is a poultice made with?* total Infs questioned, 75) Infs **AR**27, 39, **FL**26, **GA**3, **MS**20, **OK**13, (Piece of) fat meat; Inf **FL**8, Thin slice of hot fat meat. **1966** *DARE* Tape **AL**1, We had fat meat, we had our own hams.

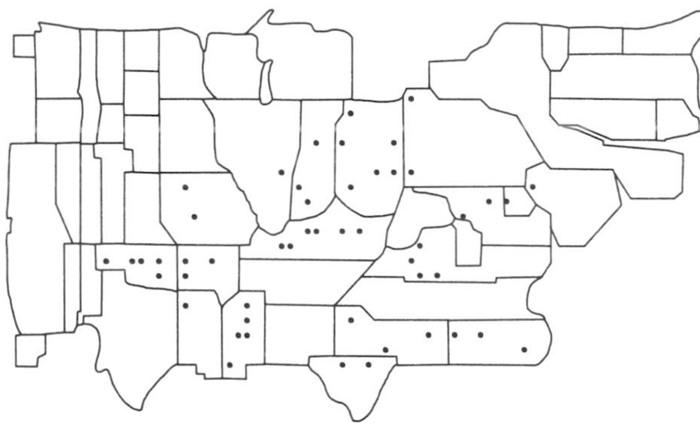

•fat meat + varr (Qq. BB50a, b, c, BB34a, b, BB51a, b)

fat morel n

A **morel** (here: *Morchella angusticeps*).

1973 *Foxfire 2* 54, Look for the fat morel, *M[orchella] angusticeps,* in oak, beech, or maple forests when the service berry . . is in bloom.

fatmouth v [Cf **fat** adj[1] **6**] *among Black speakers* Cf **badmouth** v

To talk too much; to blabber.

1968 *DARE* FW Addit **PA**66 [Black], Fat-mouth—to talk excessively. **1970** *Atlantic Mth.* May 61/1 [Black], They can no longer sit back and fat-mouth about it, because the country will be on fire. **1972** *New Yorker* 30 Dec 64/2 **NJ** [Black], "Steve Adubato figured he would establish himself as Defender of the Italians," Baraka told me. "But he didn't realize that he would have to out-fatmouth Imperiale." **1977** Smitherman *Talkin* 45 [Black], *Fat mouth,* to talk too much, especially about somethin you don't know nothin bout.

fat mucket n

A **freshwater clam** (here: *Lampsilis radiata*)

1949 Palmer *Nat. Hist.* 354, *Fat Mucket*. . . Shells a valuable source of pearl-button material. **1979** *WI Week-End* Apr 6, Do you know what a white heel splitter is? How about . . a fat mucket? **1982** U.S. Fish & Wildlife Serv. *Fresh-Water Mussels,* Fat Mucket . . *Lampsilis radiata.*

fat pine n [**fat** adj^{1} **1**]

1 A resinous pine tree, esp **longleaf pine.** Cf **pitch pine, rich pine**

1674 Josselyn *Two Voyages* 66, The knots of this Tree [=fir] and fat-pine are used by the *English* instead of Candles, and it will burn a long time. **1898** Sudworth *Forest Trees* 19, *Pinus palustris*. . . *Longleaf Pine*. . . *Names in use*. . . Fat Pine (Southern States). **1903** *DN* 2.313 **seMO,** *Fat-pine*. . . Pitch pine. **1906** *DN* 3.135 **swAR,** *Fat-pine*. . . A very resinous pine. **1939** FWP *Guide FL* 165, These houses, built of fat pine, were set on high land and well off the ground. **1971** Krochmal *Appalachia Med. Plants* 192, Fat pine. . . This pine in southern Appalachia is a valuable source of turpentine, pine oil, tar, pitch, and rosin.

2 The wood from such a tree, used as kindling or as a torch. **chiefly Sth, S Midl** See Map Also called **fatwood, lightwood**

1791 Bartram *Travels* 468 **SC,** Many people go out together on this kind of sport [=pigeon hunting], when dark; some take with them little fascines of fat Pine splinters for torches. **1849** Lanman *Letters Alleghany Mts.* 92 **wNC, eTN,** A couple of torches made of the fat pine. **1881** Pierson *In the Brush* 284 **Sth,** In case of a funeral, they [=slaves] assembled in large numbers from adjoining plantations, provided with pine-knots, and pieces of fat pine called light-wood, which when ignited made a blaze compared with which our city torch-light processions are most sorry affairs. **1949** Kurath *Word Geog.* 51, In the Southern area kindling wood is called *lightwood* . . , in the Midland *pine, fat-pine, pitch pine, rich-pine.* **1965–70** *DARE* (Qu. T8, *Joints of pine wood that burn easily and make good fuel*) 24 Infs, **chiefly Sth, S Midl,** Fat pine; **MA**42, Fat-pine knots; (Qu. D34, . . *Small pieces of wood . . used to start a fire*) Infs **MS**27, **VA**44, **WV**17, Fat pine; **NJ**56, Fat-pine roots.

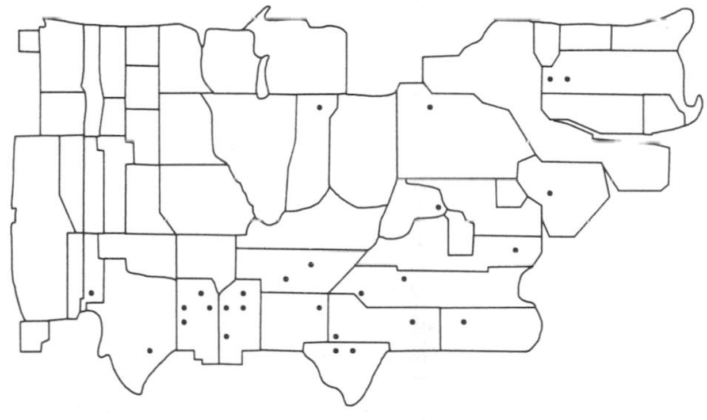

•fat pine 2 + varr (Qq. T8, D34)

fat pocketbook See **pocketbook**

fatpokes n [Perh by analogy with *slowpoke;* but cf **fat pork**]

1969 *DARE* (Qu. X50, *Names or nicknames for a person who is very fat*) Inf **GA**72, Fatpokes.

fat pork n Cf **salt pork**

=**fatback 1.**

1941 *LANE* Map 301, [Commentary] *Fat pork* and *Fried pork* mean (or meant) primarily 'fat salt pork' and 'fried salt pork'. **1968** *DARE* (Qu. BB51b, . . *'Magical' cures for corns or warts*) Inf **WI**44, A piece of fat pork bandaged on will bring the core out.

fat, ragged, and sassy See **fat and sassy**

fats n^{1} See **fat lake trout**

fats n^{2} See **fat** n^{1} **2**

fat Solomon n Cf **slim Solomon**

A **false Solomon's seal** (here: *Smilacina racemosa* var *amplicaulis*).

1923 in 1925 Jepson *Manual Plants CA* 249, *S[milacina] amplexicaulis*. . . *Fat Solomon*. . . Rootstock stout, elongated.

fatstick n [From the use of tallow in candlemaking]

A candle.

1943 Korson *Coal Dust* 133 **PA,** Pioneer miners had a curious way of telling time by candles. They estimated the time of day by the number of "fatsticks" burned.

fatstock n

Fattened and marketable livestock.

1970 *DARE* Tape **TX**87, You have . . your fatstock show, your rodeo here. . . You have . . your bulldogging of the calves, . . your steer wrestling, . . your bronc riding, . . your wild steer riding.

‡fatten food n [Prob for *fattening* or *fatting*]

A snack.

1970 Tarpley *Blinky* 188 **neTX,** *Food eaten between meals* . . fatten food.

‡fattening day n

1930 *DN* 6.87 **cnWV** [Lumber camp jargon], *Fattening day,* Saturday, or Saturday afternoon, spent in town, particularly after pay is received.

fattening hog n attrib

Extremely large.

1954 *Harder Coll.* **cwTN,** *Fattening hog post card*. . . A jumbo-sized post card.

fattening time n

The time when hogs and other animals are readied for butchering.

1980 *DARE* File **neTX** (as of c1930), On a big farm near Bonham, Texas . . Summertime = fattening time.

fatter than a settled minister adj phr

1914 *DN* 4.79 **ME, nNH,** *Settled minister, fatter'n a*. . . Very fat; in good condition.

fatticows, fattikows See **fetticus**

fattigmanns bakkels n Usu |'fɑtɪˌmɑn(z) (bɑkəlz)|; also |-mən(z)|; sp-pronc |'fɑtɪg-|; for addit var see quots Usu abbr *fattigmann;* also sp *faateman, fatti(g)mand* [Norw "poor man's cookie"] **chiefly in Scan settlement areas, esp MN, WI** Cf **fattyman**

A rich deep-fried cookie, often diamond-shaped.

[**1946** Harris *Cooking* 99, Swedish Klanneter or English Lovers' knots or Norwegian Fattigmandes Bakkles or Hungarian Csörege.] **1950** Oleson–Oleson *WI My Home* 11 (as of 1866), The name *"fattigmand"* (poor man) is a joke, for it is a very rich cookie. . . It was cut in squares or oblongs with a knife, and each square pricked with the knife-point. When *fattigmand* was baked in hot grease in a skillet, the square corners all turned up. **1950** *WELS* 2 Infs, **WI,** Fattigmannsbakkels; 1 Inf, Faateman—fried cake, poor man's cake. **1966** Tufford *Scandinavian Recipes* 25, *Fattigmand*. . . Roll out thin, cut in diamond shapes; make slit in center of each cookie and draw one corner through, making a knot. Fry in deep fat . . until golden brown. Dust with powdered sugar. **1966–68** *DARE* (Qu. H65, *Foreign foods favored by people around here:*) Inf **IA**13, Fattigmann ['fɑtɪˌmɑn]; **MA**50, Fattigmanns ['fatɪgˌmɑnz] [are] similar to shortbread cookie dough; slits made in the dough become a crescent when they are baked; **MN**28, Fattigmann ['fɑtimən]; (Qu. H63, . . *Desserts . . favored . . around here*) Inf **MN**30, Fattimand; **WI**72, Fattigmann ['fatiˌman]; (Qu. H28, . . *Types of doughnuts*) Infs **ID**5, **SD**3, Fattigmann ['fɑtɪˌmɑn]; (Qu. H32, . . *Fancy rolls and pastries*) Inf **MN**28, Fattigmann ['fɑtimən]. **1967** *DARE* Tape **MN**6, We also had fattigmann ['fɑtɪgmɑn], which is a good little cookie that is fried.

fatting See **fat** v

fat-to-my-Christ intj Also *fat-to-my-jassum*

See quots.

1955 Roberts *S. from Hell-fer-Sartin* 118 **seKY,** "Well," he said, "fat-to-my-jassum, we're all here, le's go!" *Ibid* 119, "Why, that's a toad frog." "Fat-to-my-Christ . . it looked big enough for a deer to me."

fat to the heart adj phr

c1970 *Halpert Coll.* **wKY,** Fat to the heart [is] said of a good healthy cow.

fat trout See **fat lake trout**

Fat Tuesday n [Transl of Fr *mardi gras*] **esp sLA**

Shrove Tuesday, the last day before Lent.

1941 Writers' Program *Guide LA* 107, Wherever the French influence has been felt there are masquerades of some kind. . . on Fat Tuesday in such outlying districts as Golden Meadow, many a Cajun trapper dons his wife's bonnet and a pair of rabbit-skin gloves in preparation for a spree. **1978** *Capital Times* (Madison WI) 8 Feb 6/2 **New Orleans LA,** Thousands turned out, as always, for the celebration of "Fat Tuesday," the day before the 40 days of Lenten penitence and sacrifice. **1979** *Ibid* 21 Feb 52/1, The classic Fat Tuesday foods are often in the doughnut line (fastnachts, beignets) because farewell to fat means farewell to deepfrying too. **1989** *DARE* File **seLA,** In my experience of living in New Orleans (1965–71), I not only heard the phrase "fat Tuesday" used in common parlance, I first met it there. I had no familiarity with French at the time, so "fat Tuesday" sounded strange and perplexing to me altogether. I would say that the familiar "mardi gras" is the usual expression, as in other places around the country, but one does hear "fat Tuesday."

fatty n[1] **[fat n[1] 2]** Cf **fattybox, fatty hole**

In marble games: **=fat n[1] 2.**

1963 *KY Folkl. Rec.* 9.3.61 **eKY,** *The squared pattern on which marbles are played:* . . fatty: Carter [County]. *Ibid* 62, *The name of the area inside the lines of a square:* fatty: Floyd, Perry, Pike, Johnson, Knott, Carter, Breathitt, Rowan, Greenup, Boyd, Morgan [Counties]. **1968–70** *DARE* (Qu. EE7, *What kinds of marble games are played or used to be played around here?*) Inf **WV5**, Fatty is played in a small square. A player knocks a marble out. If his stays in, he gets to shoot again. The one who shoots out the most marbles wins; **VA50A**, Nicks (small marbles) were put in a fatty [fædi] ([in] a row) and shot out with a shooter. Whoever hit the most out won.

fatty n[2]

=bobolink B.

1923 WV State Ornith. *Birds WV* 42, *Bobolink—Dolichonyx oryzivorus*. . . Fatties. . . They are fat even before they reach the rice fields, because boys used to shoot them along the lowlands beside the K. and M. tracks in Charleston, and the boys called them "fatties."

fatty arbuckle n Also *fatty arbuncle* [From Roscoe *"Fatty" Arbuckle* 1887–1933, silent film comedian; *arbuncle* is prob a blend of *arbuckle* + **carbuncle]**

A very fat person.

1966–69 *DARE* (Qu. X50) Inf **RI6**, Fatty arbuncle; **WA17**, Fatty arbuckle. [Laughter]

fattybox n **[fatty n[1]]**

1975 Ferretti *Gt. Amer. Book Sidewalk Games* 151 **ceMA,** Up in Boston, a version of Old Bowler is called *Fatty Box.* In this game, all players put their stakes into the square and, after choosing for "firsties," shoot. A player has to shoot a marble from the square, and his shooter has to remain in the square. If it fails to, he has to put back every marble he has already shot out.

fatty-bread n Also rarely *fat-bread* **chiefly S Midl**

1 =crackling bread; also cornbread shortened with or fried in lard.

1899 (1912) Green *VA Folk-Speech* 170, *Fat-bread*. . . Bread made of corn-meal, shortened with *fat,* or hog's lard. **1903** *DN* 2.313 **seMO,** *Fatty-bread*. . . A kind of shortened corn-bread. 'Fine as a fattybread.' A common expression meaning 'in fine condition.' **1906** *DN* 3.135 **nwAR,** *Fatty bread*. . . Corn bread containing scraps of fat left after lard is rendered from pork. **1908** *DN* 3.309 **eAL, wGA,** *Fatty-bread*. . . Same as *cracklin-bread.* **1940** (1978) Still *River of Earth* 212 **KY,** When the cushaws were boiling Mother got a bag of cracklings. She crisped a handful of rinds in the stove. "Six pones o' fatty bread I'm going to make," she said. **1949** Kurath *Word Geog.* 68, The term . . *fatty-bread* is common between the lower James and the Roanoke rivers, uncommon elsewhere. **1952** Brown *NC Folkl.* 1.271, *Fatty Bread*—Put on a pan of grease to heat. Mix a cup of meal and a pinch of salt, add water, form the dough into a cake and fry it in hot grease. **1958** *PADS* 29.9 **TN,** *Fatty bread.* **1971** Wood *Vocab. Change* 313 **FL,** *Fatty bread* [rare].

2 Transf: a very fat person.

1969–70 *DARE* (Qu. X50) Infs **KY42**, **TX106**, Fatty-bread.

fattycows See **fetticus**

fatty dodger n [Blend of **fatty-bread** + **corn dodger]**

=crackling bread.

1937 (1963) Hyatt *Kiverlid* 68 **sAppalachians,** "He's allus been the cravenest boy-child atter cracklin' bread . . ." "Alright, Granny," said the girl, "I'll make one fatty dodger."

fatty hole n **[fatty n[1]]**

A marble game.

1940 (1978) Still *River of Earth* 82 **KY,** The boys crouched on their knees to play fatty hole, the bright marbles spinning from rusty fists into the dirt pockets.

fattyman n Also *fat man* [Folk-etyms and pronc-spp for **fattigmanns bakkels]**

See quots.

1950 *WELS (Different shapes or sizes [of doughnuts])* 1 Inf, **cnWI,** Fat man—a flat cut fried in deep fat. **1968** *DARE* (Qu. H65, *Foreign foods favored . . around here*) Inf **WI64**, Scandinavian cookies . . fattyman.

fat up See **fat v**

fatwood n **[fat adj[1] 1] chiefly FL, GA** Cf **fat pine 2**

=lightwood.

1933 Rawlings *South Moon* 3 **nFL,** Light from a fat-wood hearth fire flickered through the small-paned windows on three sides of the cabin. **1942** Rawlings *Cross Creek* 335 **nFL,** I have seen no more beautiful thing in my life than my orange grove by night, lighted by the fatwood fires. **1965–70** *DARE* (Qu. D34, . . *Small pieces of wood . . used to start a fire*) Infs **FL27**, **GA19**, 27, 32, **OK18**, Fatwood; **AL6**, Fatwood knot; (Qu. T8, *Joints of pine wood that burn easily and make good fuel*) Infs **FL51**, **GA25**, **NJ67**, **PA49**, **SC53**, Fatwood. **1969** Lyons *My Florida* 45, Pitch-pine, called lighter-knots or fatwood, was one of the blessings of pioneer Florida. **1971** Wood *Vocab. Change* 25, [In eight Southern states] *fatwood* . . [is] mainly found in Florida and Georgia.

faucet n Usu |'fɔsɪt, 'fɑ-, 'fa-, -ət|; for varr see **A** below

A Forms.

1 |'fæsɪt|; pronc-spp *facet, fasset.* **scattered, but esp freq east of Missip R**

1892 *DN* 1.238, *Faucet.* Always pronounced [fæsɪt] in Kansas City. [*DN* Ed: Both [æ] and [ɔ] in Michigan . . and in New England.] **1905** *DN* 3.56 **eNE,** *Faucet* . . may show the same vowel [æ]. **1939** *LANE* Map 143, Pronunciations of the type of [fæsɪt] are described as natural or more common by . . [7 infs]; and as old-fashioned though still in use by . . [35 infs]. **1944** *PADS* 2.25 **NC, OH,** *Fasset* ['fæsɛt]. **1945** *PADS* 3.10 **CT, NY,** *Fasset.* **1961** Kurath–McDavid *Pronc. Engl.* 161, When *faucet* is used in these areas [=the North, including Metropolitan New York], it has the vowel /ɔ ~ ɒ/ of *law* or the /ɑ/ of *lot.* A variety of vowels are used in *faucet* in the Northern area . . : the /ɔ ~ ɒ/ of *law;* the /ɑ/ of *lot;* the /a/ of *car, half;* and the /æ/ of *bag.* /ɔ ~ ɒ/ predominates in cultivated speech and is rather common in the speech of the middle group. /æ/ is chiefly a folk pronunciation, but is still used by some elderly cultured speakers. . . [ɑ ~ a] sounds are less common. **1965–70** *DARE* (Qu. F27a) 34 Infs, **scattered, but esp freq east of Missip R,** Fasset; (Qu. F27b) 15 Infs, **scattered, but esp freq east of Missip R,** (Water) fasset; (Qu. F15) Inf **IL107**, **NY68**, Fasset. **1975** Gould *ME Lingo* 87, *Facet*—Maine plumbers like this pronunciation of faucet. As with *hurth* and harth amongst Maine masons, you'll find the plumbers about fifty-fifty *facet*-fawcet. **1976** Allen *LAUM* 3.259 (as of c1950), A pronunciation with fronted /æ/, . . survives weakly in the U[pper] M[idwest] in two lonely instances in North Dakota, although one Minnesotan recalls /fæsɪt/ as her parents' usual pronunciation.

2 |'fɔsɪp|; pronc-spp *fossip, fossup.*

1957 *Sat. Eve. Post Letters* **OK,** Fossup = faucet. **1960** *PADS* 34.63 **CO,** Fossip 'faucet'. . . These expressions are most likely to become old-fashioned, if they are not so already. **1968–70** *DARE* (Qu. F15) Inf **TN27**, Fossip; (Qu. F27a) Inf **KY85**, Fossip ['fɔsɪp]; **KY89**, Fossip ['fasɪp, 'fɔsɪp]; **TN27**, ['fɑsəp]; (Qu. F27b) Inf **TN27**, Fossip.

B Senses.

1 A fixture for turning water on and off, esp outside the house. **formerly chiefly Nth; now widespread, but less freq Mid and C Atl** Cf *spicket* (at **spigot**)

1841 Cist *Cincinnati* np **OH,** [Advt:] Brass Fossets of every description. **1879** *Scribner's Mth.* 18.156/2 **NYC,** The sinks and water faucets are within the tenements instead of being in the dark halls. **1902** (1969) Sears *Catalogue* 657/2, *Shower Bath Yoke*. . . This great life invigorator can be attached to any faucet. **1948** *AmSp* 23.34, While *faucet* is a book word throughout the [spɪkɛt] area (the extent of which outside the South needs to be investigated), it seems to be the common household word throughout most of the rest of America. **1949** Kurath *Word Geog.* 15, *Faucet* . . , which is in regular use among all social groups in the North, is encroaching upon *spicket* or *spigot* in parts of the Midland and the South. **1961** Kurath–McDavid *Pronc. Engl.* 161, *Faucet*. . . This term is largely confined to the North, including Metropolitan New York. The Midland and the South have the synonym *spicket, spigot.* **1965–70** *DARE* (Qu. F27a, . . *Inside the house*) 759 Infs, **widespread,** (Water) faucet; 34 Infs, **chiefly east of Missip R,** Fasset; **KY**85, 89, **TN**27, Fossip; (Qu. F27b, . . *Outside the house*) 502 Infs, **widespread, but less freq Mid and C Atl,** Faucet; 26 Infs, **scattered,** Outside (*or* outdoor, hose) faucet; 15 Infs, **chiefly east of Missip R,** (Water) fasset; **TN**27, Fossip; **MO**26, **ND**3, **NY**130, Water faucet. **1973** Allen *LAUM* 1.204 (as of c1950), In the eastern states a sharp distinction appears between Northern *faucet* and Midland and Southern *spigot/spicket.* But *faucet* has almost completely replaced *spigot* everywhere [in the Upper Midwest].

2 A tap on a barrel or similar container. **widespread, but less freq NEast, N Cent, West** See Map

1790 Deane *New Engl. Farmer* 21/2 **MA,** The mash tub should have a cock, or a tap and fauset fixed into its bottom. **1902** (1969) Sears *Catalogue* 598/1, *Wood Faucets,* made of selected hard maple. **c1960** *Wilson Coll.* **csKY,** Faucet, often /ˈfɑsɪt/. . . Tap or spigot to draw liquid from a barrel or cask. **1965–70** *DARE* (Qu. F15) 205 Infs, **widespread, but less freq NEast, N Cent, West,** Faucet; **IN**52, Cider faucet; **MO**16, Faucet-like; **IL**107, **NY**68, Fasset; **TN**27, Fossip. **1968** *DARE* Tape **MI**96, Later they had a pail . . with a little tap on it, a faucet . . you could use to get some water if you wanted to. **1973** Allen *LAUM* 1.204 (as of c1950), Although *faucet* is making some inroads upon the dominance of the *spigot/spicket* forms to designate the device on a barrel, the latter are not in a minority in any state [in the Upper Midwest].

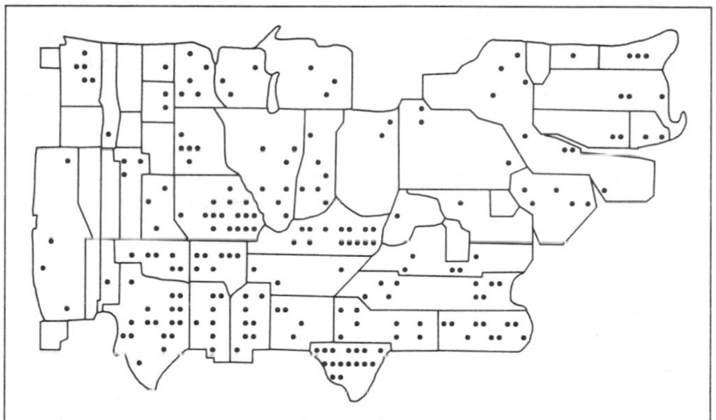

•faucet B2 + varr (Qu. F15)

fauch v[1] See **faunch**

fauch v[2] See **fetch v A1**

faught See **fight A3, 4**

fault n, v Pronc-sp **chiefly Mid and S Atl** *fau't;* also *fort* Similarly, adj *fau'ty* Cf Pronc Intro 3.II.27

A Forms.

1815 Humphreys *Yankey in England* 29 **NEng,** Well, Mister, if you don't understand plain English, that is'nt my fort. *Ibid* 105, *Fort,* fault. **1899** (1912) Green *VA Folk-Speech* 171, *Faut.* . . "It's your faut." . . *Fauty.* . . "The apples are all fauty this year." **1922** Gonzales *Black Border* 300 **sSC, GA coasts** [Gullah glossary], *Fau't*—fault, faults. **1946** [see **B1** below]. **1952** Brown *NC Folkl.* 1.539, *Fau't* [fɔt]. . . *Fau'ty.* . . *Faulty.* . . General. Mainly illiterate.

B As verb.

1 To criticize, blame, scold. **chiefly S Midl**

1702 (1972) Mather *Magnalia* sig C3r/2 **MA,** I have seldom seen that Way of Writing faulted. **1839** (1927) Trollope *Domestic Manners* 292, I'm not going to fault you. **1903** *DN* 2.313 **seMO,** He faulted me for everything I said or did. **1924** Raine *Land of Saddle-Bags* 103 **sAppalachians,** "He *faulted* her" (scolded). **1937** (1963) Hyatt *Kiverlid* 26 **KY,** I ha'n't faultin' Jed's Maw none. **1938** FWP *Ocean Highway* 189 **NC,** "Don't fault me if I'm scunnered" means "Don't blame me if I'm disgusted." **1946** *PADS* 6.13 **eNC,** "I don't fau't him for doing that." . . Occasional. Uneducated. **1968** *DARE* (Qu. II32, *To manage . . to shift the responsibility: "He . . tried to_______.*") Inf **VA**31, Fault someone else.

2 Of a hunting dog: to lose the scent or trail.

1936 (1951) Faulkner *Absalom* 238 **MS,** He and grandfather were sitting on a log now because the dogs had faulted. **1942** Faulkner *Go Down* 18 **MS,** Then they heard the fyce, not trailing now but yapping, about a mile away, then the nigger whooped and they knew the fyce had faulted. **1958** Humphrey *Home from the Hill* 52 **TX,** A new note was heard from the pack, a few puzzled whimpers, a whine, then a series of disappointed howls, a general howl, and, exhausted, you breathed, "Faulted."

3 ?To harm. [Cf *EDD fault* sb. 3 "Harm, injury, wrong"]

1943 Weslager *DE Forgotten Folk* 204, "And if you ever dream of a snake three nights straight, look out," adds the husband. "It means that someone who don't like you will presently fault you. The onliest way to keep him from faultin' you is to go out next day and kill a snake. That will break the spell."

faunce v [Prob < *vaunce,* obs aphet var of *advance* v]

To rush, to make a sudden, violent attack.

1858 in 1966 Boller *MO Fur Trader* 123, Knowing, that if a war party "faunced on us" the Indians would be attacked first.

faunch v Also with *along, around* Also sp *fauch, fawnch* [Orig uncert]

1 To rant, rave, rage; hence ppl adj *faunched, faunching* angry. **chiefly S Midl, West**

1911 *DN* 3.543 **NE,** The father fairly faunched when he found that his children had played truant. **1923** *DN* 5.206 **swMO,** *Faunch.* . . To rave, make an outcry against. **1930** Williams *Logger-Talk* 23 **Pacific NW,** *Faunching:* Raving angry. **1933** Williamson *Woods Colt* 168 **Ozarks,** It's jest once in a great while that George gits to foamin' an' faunchin', but law! when he does he's a reg'lar springtime flood. **1941** *AmSp* 16.22 **swIN,** *Fawnch.* To rage. **1942** Whipple *Joshua* 168 **UT** (as of c1860s), 'Laws,' said Willie, . . 'did you see that Marianne Snow a-faunchin' around?' *Ibid* 376, 'Quit your faunchin' around, then!' shrilled 'Sheba, clouting him over the ear. **1949** *PADS* 11.6 **wTX** (as of c1920), "That really made him faunch." Occasional. Uneducated. **1953** Randolph *Down in Holler* 243 **Ozarks,** A man in Stone County, Mo., was described as "poundin' on the table with his knife, just *a-fawnchin'* an' a-slaverin' for his victuals." **1958** *PADS* 29.22 **IN,** Mary Jane (being angry) was just "a-fauchin' ". **1960** Carpenter *Tales Manchaca* 50 **cTX,** But worse . . than a visitation from the Clootie himself were those faunching (as we say in my family), snorting, pawing-the-earth bulls. **1966** Giles *Great Adventure* 66 **West** (as of 1830s), Old Dan was faunchin' along. *Ibid* 117, Fouchette's face was dark and young Pete was in a faunching rage. **1982** *Smithsonian Letters* **sIN,** She was describing how upset and agitated and downright angry she was at her grandmother. . . she again said that she "was faunched."

2 To fret; to show irritation or impatience.

1970 *DARE* (Qu. GG14, . . *Someone who fusses or worries a lot*) Inf **IL**143, He faunches [ˈfɔnčɪz]. **1984** Weaver *TX Crude* 112, *Fawnching.* Complaining, sulking. . . "I want you to quit fawnchin' around this house and get out there." **1989** *DARE* File, The verb *faunch* is part of my vocabulary and was absorbed, I'm sure, from my grandmother's speech which reflected the late nineteenth & early twentieth century usage of south-western Kansas. Typical of this usage were such expressions as: "Jody was faunching to get done with it." *To faunch* here means to feel or show impatience in the eager or anxious anticipation of something.

faunch n [**faunch v 1**]

A rage.

1982 *Smithsonian Letters* **sIN,** My mother . . was relating an incident that happened when she was a young girl. . . She was describing how upset and agitated and downright angry she was at her grandmother. Finally, she slurted [sic] out that she was "just in a faunch". . . Thinking perhaps that I wasn't understanding correctly, I asked her to spell it. She immediately replied "f-a-u-n-c-h".

faunchy adj [**faunch v 2**]

1970 *DARE* (Qu. GG14, . . *Someone who fusses or worries a lot*) Inf **IL**143, He's always faunchy [ˈfɔnči].

faus(t) See **feist**

fausty See **feisty adj**

fau't See **fault**

faux pas n Pronc-spp and (often intentional) folk-etyms *false pass, fawks ~, folks ~, forks ~, fox(y) ~, folks paw, fo(o) pah, foo paw, fo par, fo paws, fore paw, fox paw(s)* [Fr "false step"] *chiefly among well educ speakers*

A social blunder; a botched job.

1882 Godfrey *Is. Nantucket* 65, You've made a reg'lar foopaw of it. **1916** Macy-Hussey *Nantucket Scrap Basket* 132, "Foopaw"—A bungling job; to make a foopaw of a thing is to make a mess of it. **1920** *DN* 5.77, The class of speakers employing jocular mispronunciations of French words and phrases is an educated class. It consists of newspaper humorists, students, and those . . with a . . knowledge of French, and a percentage of returned soldiers. *Ibid* 78, *Fox pass, fawks* or *folks pass, fo paws,* faux pas. "I made the fox paws of my life." **1920s** in 1944 *ADD* **cNY,** Fox-paw ['fɑkspɔ]. Humorous. Not uncommon. **1932** *AmSp* 7.332 [Johns Hopkins slang], *Fox pass*—a faux pas. **1942** Berrey-Van den Bark *Amer. Slang* 170.3, *Faux pas.* False pass, fawks pass, folks pass, fo-pah, fo paws, fox pass, fox paw, foxy pass. **1945** Colcord *Sea Language* 79 **ME, Cape Cod, Long Island,** *Foo-paw* . . the "forks pass" of the landsman is probably an educated quip by those who have studied French. **1950** *WELS (An embarrassing mistake: "Last night she made an awful______.")* 2 Infs, **cWI,** Foxy pass; 1 Inf, **seWI,** Fore paw. **c1960** Bailey *Resp. to PADS 20* **KS,** In my experience the people who would say *fox pass* are familiar with the French from which the expression comes and would actually say "faux pas" except facetiously on rare occasions. **1965-70** *DARE* (Qu. JJ41, . . *"Last night she made an awful______."*) 111 Infs, **widespread, but less freq S Midl,** Faux pas; **IN**5, **IA**41, Fox paw; **VA**93, Folks paw; **IN**48, Fore paw; **CA**53, Foo pah ['fupɑ]; **NJ**19, Fo par ['fopɑr] [Of all Infs responding to the question, 36% were coll educ; of those giving these responses, 66% were coll educ.]; (Qu. JJ42, . . *"He usually handles things well, but this time he certainly ______."*) Infs **NY**186, **OK**9, **TX**65, Made a faux pas.

faux pas v Pronc-sp *foo paw* **[faux pas n]**

To make a blunder; to fail.

1969 *DARE* (Qu. JJ42, . . *"He usually handles things well, but this time he certainly______."*) Inf **NC**61, Foo pawed ['fupɔd]—that's Shakespearian, dearie; (Qu. KK10, . . *"He didn't work it out carefully enough, and his plan______."*) Inf **NC**61, Foo-pawed.

favor n, v Pronc-sp *fabuh* Cf Pronc Intro 3.I.17

A Forms.

1922 Gonzales *Black Border* 300 **sSC, GA coasts** [Gullah glossary], *Fabuh* (n. and v.) favor, favors, favored, favoring.

B As noun.

1 Family resemblance. **Sth, S Midl** Cf **C1** below

1887 *Scribner's Mag.* 2.161 **AR** [Black], Reckon by her favor, dat ar's Haskett's gell comin' by. **1887** (1967) Harris *Free Joe* 207 **cGA,** They tell me that Hallie's husband an' the Yankee was mighty nigh the same age, an' had a sorter favor. **1902** *DN* 2.234 **sIL,** *Favor.* . . Personal resemblance; rarely, similarity. **1906** *DN* 3.135 **nwAR,** I can see the favor to you in that child. **1908** *DN* 3.309 **eAL, wGA,** You can see the family-favor in every one of the Satterwhites. **1910** *Atlantic Mth.* 105.277/2 **Appalachians,** Those girls are of a favor. **1930** *DN* 6.84 **SC.**

2 Appearance.

1881 Twain *Prince & Pauper* 83, The old Baron Morley, being mad, forgot the favor of his own countenance. **1899** (1912) Green *VA Folk-Speech* 171, *Favour.* . . Countenance; appearance; look; features.

3 A liking.

1941 in 1944 *ADD* **nWV,** We've kinda taken a favor to her.

C As verb.

1 To resemble, usu in appearance; to resemble one another. **[favor n B1] widespread, but chiefly Sth, S Midl** See Map

1887 Kirkland *Zury* 537 **IL,** *Favor.* . . To resemble. **1893** Shands *MS Speech* 29, *Favor.* . . In the sense of *to resemble,* Webster marks this word as obsolete, but it is still very largely used, with this meaning, by all classes of Mississippians. **1929** (1951) Faulkner *Sartoris* 26 **MS,** "I seed him on de street, and he looked bad; he jes' don't favor hisself," the visitor was saying. **c1938** in 1970 Hyatt *Hoodoo* 1.360 **swAL,** She swole up so until she didn't even favor herself. **1941** *LANE* Map 393 *(He looks like his father)* **scattered throughout NEng,** Favors. **1946** *AmSp* 21.190 **eKY,** Are you brothers? You don't favor. **1949** *AmSp* 24.188 **PA** (as of 1898), *Favor* in the sense to *resemble* and by extension to 'look like' is also in general use. **1954** *Harder Coll.* **cwTN,** *Banana melon* . . favors a banana. **1965-70** *DARE* (Qu. Z10, *If a child looks very much like his father, you might say, "He______ his father."*) 248 Infs, **widespread, but chiefly Sth, S Midl,** Favors; **SC**19, 26, Favor; (Qu. KK65) Inf **LA**8, They favor; they look alike. **1973** Allen *LAUM* 1.342 (as of c1950), *Favors* is uncommon [in the Upper Midwest]. **1979** *Antioch Rev.* 37.49 **MS,** I come by my size favoring Mama's people.

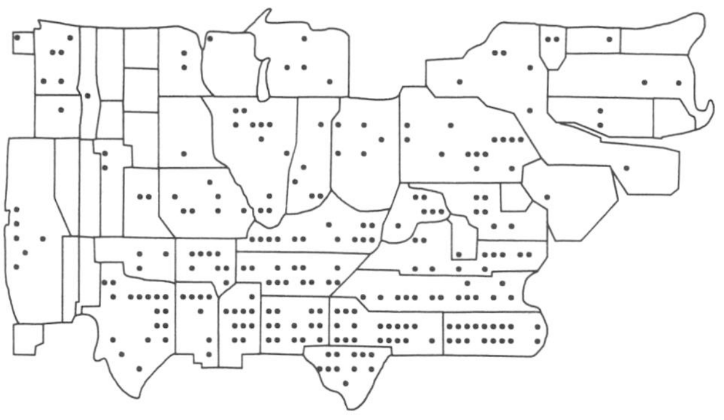

•favor C1 + var (Qq. Z10, KK65)

2 To indicate, give an appearance of, presage.

1938 FWP *Guide DE* 500, Hit favors rain right smart. **1949** *AmSp* 24.188 **PA** (as of 1898), I was told that carrying a rifle into the woods 'favored' hunting, and a similar use seems to have prevailed among the Jamaica negroes some fifty years ago.

3 See quot.

c1960 *Wilson Coll.* **csKY,** *Favor.* . . To like, to praise.

4 To spoil (a child).

1950 *WELS ("Everybody______ that child.")* 1 Inf, **seWI,** Favored. **1965-70** *DARE* (Qu. Z14a, *To give a child its own way or pay too much attention to it: "Everyone ______ that child."*) 11 Infs, **scattered,** Favors.

5 To curry favor with; to butter up.

1965-70 *DARE* (Qu. II20b, *A person who tries too hard to gain somebody else's favor: "He's always trying to ______ the boss."*) Infs **LA**11, **MN**12, 15, **MO**21, **VT**16, **WA**18, Favor; **WA**13, Favor [corr to "polish"]; (Qu. JJ3a, *When a school child makes a special effort to 'get in good' with the teacher in hopes of getting a better grade: "He's trying to ______ again."*) Inf **MA**8, Favor the teacher.

6 foll by infin: To want, desire. Cf **admire B2**

1948 Hurston *Seraph* 35 **wFL** (as of c1920), I'd favor to get some information on the marrying subject just as quick as I can. *Ibid* 43, Before we drive off, I favor to see that playhouse you used to play in.

favoraite See **favorite**

favorance n

1 Resemblance. **[favor C1] S Midl**

1914 Furman *Sight* 56 **KY,** You air the woman! I know you by your favorance to your talk. I allowed you would look that fair and tender. **1915** *DN* 4.182 **swVA,** *Favorance.* . . Resemblance (of features). **1939** *Hall Coll.* **wNC,** "Abe Lincoln sure showed a favorance for the Enloes." . . "She shows a favorance of his father," [said one informant, but] "She favors his father" is more common. **1953** Randolph *Down in Holler* 243 **Ozarks,** Soon as I seen the *favorance* betwixt them boys, I figgered they must be kin.

2 A liking, preference.

1933 *AmSp* 8.2.29 **KY,** I everly had a favorance for the Englishers. You see my grandsir come from that country. **1942** Thomas *Blue Ridge Country* 226 **sAppalachians,** You like this Circle Star quilt, Miss, you say:/ I have a favorance for this Flower Bed bright and fair.

favor-dance n

1906 *DN* 3.135 **nwAR,** *Favor-dance.* . . A dance at which dance-orders [=dance-programs] are not used. "I like a program-dance better than a favor-dance. You don't have to dance with one girl all the time then."

favorite n, adj Usu |'fev(ə)rət, -ɪt|; also **esp S Midl** |'fevor,aɪt, 'fevər,aɪt| Pronc-sp *favoraite*

A Forms.

1907 *DN* 3.231 **nwAR,** *Favoraite.* . . Favorite. **1908** *DN* 3.310 **eAL, wGA,** *Favorite.* . . Pronounced ['fevor,aɪt] by the illiterate. **1942** Hall *Smoky Mt. Speech* 75, *Favorite,* usually with [-ɪt], but sometimes with [-aɪt]. **1952** Brown *NC Folkl.* 1.539, *Favorite* ['fevo,raɪt]. . . Illiterate. **c1960** *Wilson Coll.* **csKY,** *Favorite* /'fevrɪt/ often or /'fevɚ,aɪt/ now largely for fun.

B As noun.

A friend. *old-fash*

1895 *DN* 1.371 **eTN,** Me an' Abernathy is great favorites. **1909** *DN* 3.396 **nwAR,** *Favorite. . .* Friend. "She is a great favorite of mine."

faw See **for**

fawché See **fâché**

fawid See **forehead** n

fawk See **fork** n

fawks pass See **faux pas** n

fawnch See **faunch** v

fawnfoot n Also *fawn's foot*

A **freshwater clam** (here: *Truncilla donaciformis*).

1979 *WI Week-End* Apr 6, Meanwhile such shellfish as the . . fawn's foot . . go right on living . . in the quiet waterways of the Mississippi. **1982** U.S. Fish & Wildlife Serv. *Fresh-Water Mussels,* [Wall chart:] Fawnfoot. . . *Truncilla donaciformis.*

fawn lily n [See quot 1894]

=dogtooth violet.

1894 Burroughs *Riverby* 26 **NEast,** A fawn is spotted, too, and "fawn lily" would be better than "adder's-tongue." Still better is the name "trout lily." **1941** Writers' Program *Guide WI* 16, In low-lying wooded lands . . the fawn lily expands large white flowers. **1949** Peattie *Cascades* 252 **Pacific NW,** The yellow glacier lily, Erythronium grandiflorum, is called fawn lily and lamb's tongue . . the glacier lilies prefer the eastern side [of the Cascade crest]. **1976** Bruce *How to Grow Wildflowers* xv, Members of the genus *Erythronium* are trout-lilies or fawn-lilies.

fawn's foot See **fawnfoot**

fawsnocht, fawstnacht See **fastnacht**

fawty See **forty**

fawwu'd See **forward** adj, adv

fay v Also with *in* [From *fay* to fit or join together] **chiefly NEng** *old-fash*

To fit, fit in, agree; to fill in (a gap).

1847 (1853) Thompson *Locke Amsden* 138 **VT,** I have no notion of spoiling sense to make it fay in with book rules. **1859** Elwyn *Glossary* 117, In New England they have a word, *to fay,* to fit: that *fays* nicely. **1867** Lowell *Biglow* 219 **MA,** Ther' 's gaps our lives can't never fay in. **1889** (1971) Farmer *Americanisms* 234, *Fay, to.*—To fit. "Your coat fays well." This obsolete form . . is still current in New England. **1906** P. Lowell *Mars & its Canals* 347 *(OEDS),* The explanation of the canals as threads of vegetation fays in with the one which has been found to meet the requirements of the blue-green areas.

fay n, also attrib [Aphet form of **ofay**] *chiefly among Black speakers*

A White person; a person displaying characteristics of White people.

1927 *Amer. Mercury* Aug 393 [Black], "What a lot of 'fays!" I thought, as I noticed the number of white guests. **1938** *AmSp* 13.152 **IN** [Black], *Fay.* A white person. **1942** Berrey–Van den Bark *Amer. Slang* 385.2, *White person* . . fay. **1946** Mezzrow & Wolfe *Really Blues* (1957) 62 *(OEDS),* He was the first fay boy I ever heard who mastered this vital foundation of jazz music. **1964** *PADS* 42.44 **Chicago IL,** *Black fay* is applied to the modern counterparts of Uncle Tom. *Fay* is commonly used by Negroes to designate Caucasians. **1970** *DARE* (Qu. HH34, *General words around here for a woman*) Inf **TN**53, Fay broad—any light-skinned woman, black or white. [Inf Black] **1971** Landy *Underground Dict.* 76, *Fay. . .* Derogatory term for a white person.

fayence See **fence** n, v

faygeleh n |ˈfeɪgələ| Also *feygel* Also sp *faygelah* [Yiddish *foygl* bird, *faygele* little bird; perh infl by **fag** n] *in Jewish communities*

A male homosexual.

1968 Rosten *Yiddish* 114, *Faygeleh. . .* Homosexual. Quite common (the word, not the libidinal arrangement) in the American-Jewish vernacular. A synonym for the English "fairy" or "fag." Jews use faygeleh as a discreet way of describing a homosexual—especially where they might be overheard. **1970** Feinsilver *Yiddish* 91, *Feygel* is also a girl's name and is the vulgar term for an effeminate man. **1978** *DARE* File **neNJ,** I couldn't determine whether my host was simply effeminate, or whether he was a real faygelah [ˈfeɪgələ]. [Inf Jewish] **1987** Elkin *Rabbi of Lud* 80 **NJ,** "This AIDS business is doing me in. . . There are eleven AIDS victims in the ground here." . . "What's all this about AIDS?" . . "I told him about eleven people," Shull said. "I never told him we're the Holy Faygeleh Sacred Burial Ground."

fay knight exclam [Perh reduced from "(on the) faith of a knight"; cf *OED fay* sb.[1] 6. b]

=king's ex.

1958 *PADS* 29.21 **AR,** When I was fourteen we moved to Fayetteville, Arkansas, in the Ozarks, and for the first time I heard the words "Fay Knight" used to halt a game temporarily. In Colorado and Nebraska children said "King's X."

fayther See **father**

faze v Also sp *fayz, phase, phaze* [Varr of **feeze** v]

Std sense, var forms.

1875 (1876) Twain *Tom Sawyer* 94, When pap's full [of liquor], you might take and belt him over the head with a church and you couldn't phase him. **1958** Humphrey *Home from the Hill* 55 **neTX,** The blood was spurtin out of that pig, only it didn't phaze him.

faze n [Var of **feeze** n]

1 A state of worry.

c1885 in 1981 Woodward *Mary Chesnut's Civil War* 152 **SC** (as of 1861), I was so uncomfortable—as soon as silence prevailed, I left the table. I made a good deal of commotion . . all to divert them from their madness or folly. And a man is always in such a faze about his dignity—what is due his own self-respect, &c&c&c, and so contemptuous of feminine folly!

‡2 An injury.

1894 *DN* 1.330 **c, sNJ,** *Faze*: to injure. As noun in "he went through and nary a faze."

fazzled adj [Cf *EDD fazle out* "to ravel out" (at *fazle* v., sb.)]

1913 *DN* 4.43, *Fazzled. . .* Tired. "I was just fazzled out." From *fagged* and *frazzled.*

F.D.R. n [For *Franklin Delano Roosevelt,* during whose administration many home improvements were made] **WV** Cf **federal building, Roosevelt**

An outdoor toilet building.

1968 *DARE* (Qu. M21b, *Joking names for an outside toilet building*) Infs **WV**3, 4, F.D.R.(s); **WV**2, F.D.R.s. A W.P.A. project was to make outside toilets.

fe intj [Twi *fẽẽ* a challenge to fight; cf *DJE fe*]

1892 (1969) Christensen *Afro-Amer. Folk Lore* 22, Fe! Fe! boy, tink you kin catch me, but you can't catch me!

feador See **fiador**

feared adj Also sp *feard, feart, feered* [Engl dial] Cf **afear(e)d**

Afraid.

1834 *Life Andrew Jackson* 208, This, gineral, was leavin an example which I'm feart your successors wont imitate. **1899** (1912) Green *VA Folk-Speech* 61, Are you feared to go? **1908** *DN* 3.285 **eAL, wGA,** *Afeard. . .* Also sometimes *feard.* **1933** Rawlings *South Moon* 44 **nFL,** She blurted, "Pa, what you been so feered of?" **1941** *LANE* Map 475 *(Afraid)* **scattered, but esp freq neNEng,** Feared. **1949** Webber *Backwoods Teacher* 10 **Ozarks,** I had a wooden-backed eraser in my hand. I was 'feared to th'ow it at his head. **1962** *Mt. Life* 38.1.17 **sAppalachians,** The *-d* and *-ed* endings of past forms of verbs are frequently pronounced *-t,* particularly when the ending is preceded by *l, m, n,* or *r.* A few such verbs are . . feared, feart [etc]. **1967–69** *DARE* (Qu. GG25, . . *"The children were ______ he was going to hurt them."*) Infs **AK**5, **CA**101, **IL**30, 92, **TN**6, Feared.

fearn n

A long-handled ladle or dipper.

1967 Cerello *Dakota Co. MN* 56, She used a silver fearn which was beautifully wrought. . . Did you dip with a cup or a fearn? . . Fill the fearn up but try not to spill it. . . She dipped a fearnful of soft-soap from the kettle. [2 infs, both elderly women of Engl-Scots heritage]

fearnought n, also attrib Also *fearnaught, fearnot, fearnothing* **chiefly NEast, esp NEng** *old-fash* Cf **dreadnought 1**

A heavy woolen fabric used chiefly for winter outer garments; a jacket made of such fabric.

1720 *Amer. Weekly Mercury* 17 Nov 3/2, Run away from *James Carroll* in *Maryland*. . . [a man wearing] a fear-nothing Coat. **1790** *PA Packet & Daily Advt.* (Philadelphia) 7 Jan 1/3, Now Opening for Sale . . cassimers, low priced narrow cloths, baize, flannel, fearnoughts. **1825** Neal *Brother Jonathan* 2.77 **CT,** He was fairly mounted upon the box, . . a ragged fear-nought great coat, loosely dangling over the seat. **1854** Smith, *'Way Down East* 57 **ME,** And as for cold weather, it [=a strong drink] will keep that out better than any double-milled kersey or fearnot great coat that I ever see. **1969** *Yankee* Feb 28, *Dear Oracle:* What in tarnation is a "fear-naught?" "They sit and eat their luncheon in stout fear-naughts on the dry oak leaves on the shore." I can't imagine what it is they are sitting on. . . Answer: *A fearnaught was a very heavy jacket.* **1975** Gould *ME Lingo* 89, Cold enough today for my *fear-nought!*

fearsome adj, adv

Powerful; powerfully, severely.

1935 (1944) Rawlings *Golden Apples* 122 **FL,** The sun's mighty fearsome this time o' year. **1942** *Sat. Eve. Post* 16 May 20/2 **eTN,** You'll never know how fearsome I have thirsted!

feart See **feared**

fease n ,v See **feeze** n, v

feast n [By analogy with **fest**] **scattered, but esp Nth, N Midl** *somewhat old-fash*

In combs: An informal get-together, a session.

1906 *DN* 3.137 **nwAR,** *Gabfeast*. . . A conversation carried on by several persons. "There was a gabfeast on the campus this morning." **1927** *AmSp* 3.133 **NE** [College slang], A summons from the scholarship committee is designated as . . "a gab feast." **1942** Berrey–Van den Bark *Amer. Slang* 191.1, *Conversation; discussion*. . . gabfeast. **1950** *WELS* 1 Inf, **cwWI,** Gabfeast. [Several Infs give *gabfest.*] **1965–70** *DARE* (Qu. KK12, *A meeting where there's a lot of talking: "They got together yesterday and had a real ______.")* 13 Infs, **scattered, but esp Nth, N Midl,** Gab feast; 13 Infs, **scattered, but esp Nth, N Midl,** Talk feast; **AR**3, Gossip feast. [24 of 27 Infs old]

feast adj See **feest**

feast in the wilderness n [Perh in ref to Matthew 15:33 "so much bread in the wilderness, as to fill so great a multitude"]

1950 *AmSp* 25.230 **cwMS,** *Feast in the wilderness.* Box-lunch supper.

feater See **feature** n

feather n Pronc-spp *fed(d)er, fedduh*

A Forms.

1899 (1912) Green *VA Folk-Speech* 171, *Feder*. . . A form of *feather.* **1922** Gonzales *Black Border* 301 **sSC, GA coasts** [Gullah glossary], *Fedduh*—feather, feathers. **1939** [see **B1** below].

B Senses.

1 A pen. [Cf Ger *Feder*]

1939 Aurand *Quaint Idioms* 13 [PaGer], Give me once your *fedder* (pen) and I will write my "John Henry."

2 usu pl: One's clothes, esp one's best clothes; fancy adornments.

1942 Berrey–Van den Bark *Amer. Slang* 87.6, *Best or most showy clothes* . . full *or* high feather. **1950** *WELS (Clothes in general)* 1 Inf, **seWI,** Fine feathers. **c1960** *Hall Coll.* **OR** (as of early 20th cent), She was all fuss and feathers. **1965–70** *DARE* (Qu. W39, *Joking ways of referring to a person's best clothes)* Infs **CT**1, 8, **IL**2, **IN**13, **NY**67, 83, **OK**9, Fine feathers; **CT**1, Best feathers; (Qu. W37, *When a woman puts on her good clothes and tries to look her best, you say she's ______)* Inf **NY**232, All starch and feathers; **PA**244, All silk and feathers; (Qu. W43, *Joking words . . for clothes in general)* Infs **KY**70, **NY**34, Feathers.

3 pl: One's bed.

1942 Berrey–Van den Bark *Amer. Slang* 86.2, *Bed*. . . the feathers. **1950** *WELS* 1 Inf, **csWI,** Hit the feathers; 1 Inf, **cWI,** I've got a date with the feathers. **1967–69** *DARE* (Qu. X40, . . *Other ways . . of saying, "I'm going to bed")* Infs **CA**36, **MI**47, **MA**58, **OR**3, **PA**223, Hit the feathers; **CO**33, Get in the feathers; **KY**24, Pound the feathers. [6 of 7 Infs old]

4 often in combs: =**dust bunny. esp Nth, N Midl** See map

1965–70 *DARE* (Qu. E20, *Soft rolls of dust that collect on the floor under beds or other furniture)* 11 Infs, **chiefly Nth, N Midl,** Feathers; **MI**100, Feathers of dust; **MI**108, **MA**14, **OH**65, Dust feathers; **OH**29, Cat feathers; **GA**46, Ghost feathers; **ID**5, Goober feathers; **NE**7, Goose feathers; **WA**6, Soldiers' feathers.

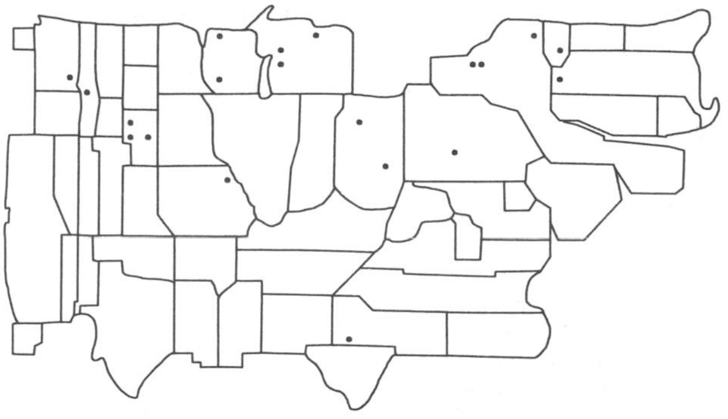

•feather n B4 + varr (Qu. E20)

5 Anything thought to resemble a feather; see quots.

1910 Maury *Trees KY* 28, The word "feather" is the name applied to the cone-shaped piece of figured wood in the crotch of a tree. **1967–70** *DARE* (Qu. B36, *Patterns formed by ice inside a window glass in winter)* Inf **WI**57, Feathers; **CA**87, Feathers and ferns; (Qu. JJ12, *Little flourishes that some people put on their handwriting or signature to make it look fancy)* Inf **GA**77, Tail-end feathers. **1969** *DARE* FW Addit **NJ,** A heavy feather or a light feather—where the boat's bow cuts through the water.

6 in phrr *in full* (or *high*) *feather:* In good condition, fine fettle, high spirits.

1855 Cooke *Ellie* 476 **VA,** No words can describe the serene effulgence of the Heartsease [=a family] appearance, when in full feather, and high spirits. **1865** Sedley *Marian Rooke* 186, All those choice and eccentric spirits, who were destined to be so cruelly interfered with . . were in high feather. **1883** Twain *Life on Missip.* (Boston) 27, Lax court morals and the absurd chivalry business were in full feather [when White men discovered the Mississippi]. **1889** (1971) Farmer *Americanisms* 256, *Full Feather.*—To be in full feather; that is, in good trim, condition. **1935** Sandoz *Jules* 228 **wNE** (as of 1880–1930), Then one day he came back in high feather, with a bottle of whiskey for himself and his friends. **1942** Berrey–Van den Bark *Amer. Slang* 128.1, Full feather, *best condition.* **1943** Writers' Program NC *Bundle of Troubles* 25, But Mr. Bullfrog, he jes strut by in high feather, payin' no mind to the women-folks atall.

7 in var fig phrr indicating anger, annoyance, distress, or retreat from a position, as:

a in phrr *drop* (or *lower*) *one's feathers:* To back down from a position. *obs*

1843 Thompson *Chronicles* 141 (Taylor–Whiting *Dict. Amer. Proverbs*) **GA,** Challenge him right here, now? Yes, and you'll see how he'll drop his feathers. **1855** Jones *Winkles* 103 (Taylor–Whiting *Dict. Amer. Proverbs*), Our haughty neighbors. . . must lower their feathers.

b in phr *with one's feathers cut:* Discomfited. *obs*

1859 Taliaferro *Fisher's R.* 74 **nwNC** (as of 1820s), I . . moseyed fur home, with my feathers cut.

c in phrr *get one's (tail) feathers up, get one's tail feathers in a downdraft:* To become angry, lose one's cool; to make angry. [From the ruffling of a bird's feathers when it is agitated or angered]

1952 Brown *NC Folkl.* 1.539, *Feathers, to get (one's), up*. . . To become angry, to make one angry. **1966** *DARE* (Qu. GG23c, . . *To tell someone to be patient)* Inf **SD**5, Don't get your tail feathers up. **1975** *DARE* File, Don't get your tail feathers in a downdraft = keep cool.

d in phr *up in feathers:* Annoyed, irritated.

1969 *DARE* (Qu. GG7, . . *"Though we were only ten minutes late, she was all ______.")* Inf **KY**65, Up in feathers.

e in phr *make one's feathers rise:* See quot.

1956 McAtee *Some Dialect NC* 15, *Feathers*. . . Hackles. "That way o'doin' made my feathers rise."

8 in phr *have feathers in the hair:*

a See quot. Cf **3** above.

1940 *AmSp* 15.334, *Feathers in the hair,* to have. To be sleepy.

b See quot.

1966 *NADS Letters* **sNM,** *Feathers in one's hair*. . . The last show of the 1954–55 radio season for the *Jack Benny Program,* date on or about

May 22, 1955, contained this expression in the script. Mary Livingston used the expression to mean 'pixilated' or 'a bit crazy.' The audience found the expression appropriate and laughed appreciatively. A student reports hearing the expression on other old time radio shows and glosses the term as 'flaky,' in the parlance of the day.

9 in var combs used to indicate flightiness, lack of substance or of common sense: See quots. **chiefly Nth, Pacific**

1942 Berrey-Van den Bark *Amer. Slang* 212.4, *Flighty; capricious . .* feather-minded. **1944** Adams *Western Words* 110, *Feather-headed*—Light-headed, with no brains. **1965–70** *DARE* (Qu. HH9, *A very silly or light-headed person*) 11 Infs, **chiefly Nth, Pacific,** Featherbrained; 8 Infs, **Nth,** Featherbrain; **CA**14, **CT**35, **NY**54, **RI**11, **SC**5, Featherhead; **ID**5, Featherpated; **CT**4, Feathertop; **AL**6, Featherweight; (Qu. HH3, *A dull and stupid person*) Infs **ID**5, **WY**5, Featherbrain; (Qu. GG42, *. . One who takes foolish chances*) Inf **CA**169, Featherhead.

10 See **feather cloud.**

11 pl: See **feathers, feathers, animal's feathers.**

feather v

1 Of milk or cream: to curdle or form flakes on the surface of coffee or tea.

1816 Pickering *Vocab.* 201, *To Feather. . .* This *colloquial* word . . is used in some parts of New England, to denote the appearance of curdled cream, when it rises upon the surface of a cup of tea or coffee, in the form of little flakes, somewhat resembling feathers. We say—The cream *feathers.* **1889** (1971) Farmer *Americanisms* 234, Cream *feathers* when it rises like flakes in tea. A New Englandism. **1890** *Critic* 21 June 314/1, A woman, it is said, can dress prettily and dance gracefully even if she cannot conjugate the Greek verbs in *mi;* and the ability to calculate an eclipse would not help her to keep cream from feathering in hot weather. **1937** [see **fly** v **B1**].

2 See quot. *obs* Cf **flybrush**

c1970 *DARE* File **MO, TX** (as of c1850–70), Feather—to cool the air by means of a peacock-feather fan suspended from the ceiling and actuated by a featherer [=a small boy].

3 also with *about, around*; Of a hunting dog: to move the hindquarters back and forth while hunting for a scent.

1892 *Field* 7 May *(OED),* In a lot of oats Saul feathered about, but could not find. **1966** *DARE* Tape **DC**9, We say hounds are 'feathering around' because they're on the ground and their sterns, their tail you know, their sterns are going back and forth. . . When the scent gets a little stronger, boy their sterns get to goin' a lot faster . . and you can just visually see that they're gettin' hotter an' hotter on the line.

4 To pamper, treat well; to curry favor with; hence ppl adj *feathered.*

1939 FWP *Guide KY* 439, She feathered him too much. **1940–41** Cassidy *WI Atlas* **swWI,** I was feathered here. **1968** *DARE* (Qu. II20b, *A person who tries too hard to gain somebody else's favor: "He's always trying to ______ the boss."*) Inf **MO**35, Feather.

5 with *in(to):* To attack. [See quot 1930; cf *SND feather* v. 5 *"Fig.:* to beat, chastise*"*] **S Midl**

1917 *DN* 4.412 **wNC,** *Feather into* (one). . . To attack, as with arrows piercing to the feather. "He feathered into him, feeding him lead." **1930** *AmSp* 5.425 **Ozarks,** When an Ozarker threatens to *feather into* somebody, he means that he is about to shoot this individual, or at least to attack him with serious intent. Horace Kephart traces this expression back to the days of the longbow in England, when to *feather into* a man meant to shoot him with such force that the feather at the butt of the arrow was buried in his body. **1931** *PMLA* 46.1308 **sAppalachians,** "Feather into one" means to attack him violently. **1934** (1970) Wilson *Backwoods Amer.* 64 **Ozarks,** There are . . picturesque survivals, such as *feathered into 'em,* a phrase which touches back into the romantic days of long bows and feathered arrows. **1952** Brown *NC Folkl.* 1.539, *Feather into. . .* To fight, to light into. **c1960** *Wilson Coll.* **csKY,** *Feather into. . .* Attack vigorously, tear into.

6 with *in(to)*; By ext: to do something vigorously.

1941 *AmSp* 16.22 **IN, MO,** *Feather in.* To do something vigorously. **1967** *Hall Coll.* **eTN,** Feather into, that means to fall into something and get right with it.

7 with *up:* To bristle, prepare to fight. [From the ruffling of feathers or rising of hackles when a bird or animal gets angry or ready to fight]

1935 Davis *Honey* 105 **OR,** He shot at the bear in the dark, and when daylight came he found blood on the ground, so he feathered up and trailed it across the mountains. **1952** Brown *NC Folkl.* 1.539, *Feather up to. . .* To show fight. "He feathered up to them big fellers eechin' [Brown: itching] for a fight."

feather about, feather around See **feather** v **3**

feather ball n [From the shape and consistency of the fruit]

A sycamore tree.

1956 Ker *Vocab. W. TX* 83, Sycamore. . . feather ball [1 inf].

feather ball, go to the v phr Cf **feather** n **B3**

To go to bed.

1950 *WELS* 1 Inf, **seWI,** I'm going to the feather ball. **1969** *DARE* (Qu. X40) Inf **IL**45, "Going to the feather ball"—for children.

feather bed n Also sp *fether bed*

1 also *feather tick, ~ tie:* A warm, thick bedcover, orig filled with feathers. **chiefly Nth** *old-fash*

1818 (1937) Guild *Jrl.* 263 **VT,** She came and turned down the fether bed and told me to get in next to the straw and put the fether bed on top. **1941** *LANE* Map 342 *(Quilt; comforter),* Other bed covers incidentally mentioned by the informants are the *feather bed,* which is now rare. . . 1 inf, **swCT,** 'Nobody hardly uses a [fɛðr bɛd] now, but I stick to mine.' **1950** *WELS Suppl.* 1 Inf, **swWI,** Feather tie. **1968–70** *DARE* (Qu. E16, *A padded covering used on a bed, mostly for warmth*) Infs **CT**2, **IA**33, **LA**43, **MI**119, Feather bed; **MN**23, Feather bed—old-fashioned; about eight inches thick, pulled up over [one]; **IL**98, **PA**176, Feather tick. [5 of 7 Infs old] **1973** Allen *LAUM* 1.228 **MN** (as of c1950), *Quilt* or *comforter. . .* featherbed [1 inf]. *Ibid* 230 **SD,** Featherbed [2 infs]: feather tick [2 infs]. [4 of 5 infs born before 1893]

2 also *featherbed plant:* =**musk grass.** [See quot 1847]

1807 (1923) Pursh *Jrl. Bot. Excursion* 4 Aug 50 **NY,** The Creek was coverd at its bottom with Chara, which the boatmen call Feather beds. **1822** Eaton *Botany* 234, *Chara vulgaris,* feather-beds. . . Odour disagreeable. Ponds and ditches mostly stagnant. **1847** Wood *Class-Book* 637, *C[hara] vulgaris.* Feather-beds. . . It appears in dense tufts, like a soft bed, undulating with the motion of the water. **1870** Ludlow *Heart of Continent* 377 **VT,** The vegetation of the moister portions chiefly consists of . . the *Chara,* or feather-bed plant. **1926** *Torreya* 26.4, *Chara* sp.—Featherbeds, Susquehanna River, Pa. **1939** *AmSp* 14.255, A plant belonging to the family *Characeae;* also called *featherbeds, stonewort,* and *horse watertail.*

3 =**shoveler.**

1911 *Forest & Stream* 77.173, (Spoonbill) *Spatula clypeata. . .* Feather-Bed, Delavan Lake, Wis., is an excellent name for this species whose size when picked is in such contrast to its apparent bulk in life. **1956** *AmSp* 31.185 **WI** [Facetious bird names], Feather bed—Shoveler. . . Because it is usually poor and therefore 'all feathers.'

4 A light, fluffy roll, sometimes deep fried.

1939 Wolcott *Yankee Cook Book* 147, Featherbeds. . . *A New Hampshire potato roll. . .* Place in pan and let rise until very light. **1947** Bowles-Towle *New Engl. Cooking* 207, *Featherbeds* [2-in squares of bread dough. After they have risen till they are very light, they are fried in deep fat.] Featherbeds are delicious when served with maple syrup.

5 See quot.

1950 *WELS (Names or nicknames for someone who is very fat)* 1 Inf, **cnWI,** Feather bed.

6 See quot. *joc*

1968 *DARE* (Qu. N27b, *When unpaved roads get very rough, you call them ______*) Inf **NJ**20, Feather beds.

featherbed plant See **feather bed 2**

feather bells n [See quot 1953] **Sth**

A plant of the genus *Stenanthium,* usu *S. gramineum.* Also called **feather-fleece**

1933 Small *Manual SE Flora* 277, *Stenanthium. . .* Featherbells. **1953** Greene-Blomquist *Flowers South* 6, *Featherbells . . (Stenanthium gramineum)* This is well named for when in full bloom, its large panicles resemble large, white feathers. **1972** Brown *Wildflowers LA* 16, *Featherbells. . .* Perennial herb up to 5 feet tall.

feather bluestem n

=**beardgrass** (here: *Andropogon barbinodis* or *A. saccharoides*).

1937 U.S. Forest Serv. *Range Plant Hdbk.* G14, Other local names, such as Torrey beardgrass . . feather bluestem . . are applied indiscriminately to these species [=*Andropogon barbinodis, A. saccharoides*].

feather bush See **feather peabush**

feather cloud n Also *feather* **chiefly Nth, N Midl**

1965–70 *DARE* (Qu. B10, . . *Long trailing clouds high in the sky*) 21 Infs, **chiefly Nth, N Midl,** Feather cloud; **NC**83, Feathers; (Qu. B11, *Other kinds of clouds*) Infs **IA**36, **ID**1, Feather clouds.

feather crown n Also *heavenly crown, angel wreath*

A ball of feathers found in a pillow (usu after someone's death).

1947 (1964) Randolph *Ozark Superstitions* 320, Another superstition which has to do with the welfare of the dead is the tale of the heavenly crowns, also known as feather crowns and angel wreaths. The idea is that when a very good and saintly person is dying, the feathers in the pillow form themselves into a crown, a kind of symbol of the golden crown which the dying person is soon to wear in Heaven. *Ibid* 321, The most finished type of feather crown . . is not shaped like a cap or doughnut at all, but rather like a large bun; these are very tightly woven, solid enough to be tossed about like a ball, and surprisingly heavy. [**c1960** *Wilson Coll.* **csKY,** Feathers form crown in pillow of sick person.] [**1961** *Mt. Life* Spring 45 **sAppalachians,** Feather pillows on which children died were often ripped open and searched for "crowns," little whorls of feathers forming a circle, which were considered to symbolize the fact that the child was in Heaven.] [**1966** Goldstein–Byington *Two Penny Ballads* 140 **PA,** If a sick child was sleeping on a pillow, feathers were said to be forming a ring inside the pillow. When the ring was completed the child would die.]

feather dalea See **feather peabush**

feather duster n

1 A Native American. [From the use of feathers in costume or headgear]

1907 Mulford *Bar-20* 103 *(DA),* I had a little argument with some feather dusters. **1911** Mulford *Bar-20 Days* 82 *(DA),* We'll see if two infant feather-dusters can lick the Bar-20.

2 A children's game; see quot.

1968 *DARE* (Qu. EE11) Inf **CA**73, Feather duster—the one who was "it" carried a feather duster and teased captives. An indoor game.

feathered ppl adj

1 See quot.

1937 *AmSp* 12.107 **eNE,** Potatoes with the outer skin partly rubbed off are said to be *feathered.*

2 See **feather** v **4.**

feathered elm n

An elm (here: *Ulmus americana*).

1910 Graves *Flowering Plants* 152 **CT,** *Ulmus americana*. . . Weeping or Feathered Elm.

featheredge n

1 Fiery spirit.

1891 *Harper's New Mth. Mag.* July 210/1 **West,** Let the pony have a little fun . . bucking round in a pretty lively fashion. . . This takes the feather-edge off him.

2 A fine point—also in phr *not to put a featheredge on it* to speak plainly.

1903 Lewis *Boss* 59 **NYC,** Not to put a feather-edge on it, I thought I'd run you over, an' see if they'd been fixin' you. **1961** Adams *Old-Time Cowhand* 30 **West,** There's been a few books on the subject wrote by men educated to a feather edge.

3 A style of men's haircut.

1944 Clark *Pills* 221 **Sth,** It was not until the First World War that the 'feather edge' haircut done with clippers came into popular style. **1965–70** *DARE* (Qu. X5, . . *Different kinds of men's haircuts*) 10 Infs, **scattered, but esp freq LA, TX,** Featheredge.

feathered out adj phr Cf **feather** n **B2**

1968 Adams *Western Words* 110, *Feathered out*—A cowboy's expression meaning *dressed up.*

feathered snake n [*feathered* dressed up, disguised + *snake* symbol of evil]

1930 *AmSp* 6.98 **cNY,** *Feathered snake:* A clever scoundrel. "This feathered snake will steal your money."

featherfew n Also sp *fetherfew*

=**feverfew 1.**

[**1676** Royal Soc. London *Philos. Trans.* 11.629 **VA,** Such Herbs as grow wild in *England,* and do not grow there, they plant, as *Wormwood, Fetherfew* [etc].] **1737** (1911) Brickell *Nat. Hist. NC* 20, In these Parts . . *Featherfew, Wormfeed* [sic], *Garden-Poppies,* none yet being discover'd growing Wild in this Province. **1868** Hale *If* 123 **MA,** It was a long featherfew, from her prize school-bouquet. **1916** *DN* 4.301 **sCT,** *Featherfew*. . . The feverfew *(Chrysanthemum parthenium):* wrongly designated as only Dial. Eng.

feather-fleece n [See quot 1953]

=**feather bells.**

1933 Small *Manual SE Flora* 277, *Stenanthium*. . . Feather-fleeces. **1953** Greene–Blomquist *Flowers South* 6, *Feather-Fleece (Stenanthium gramineum)* This is well named for when in full bloom, its large panicles resemble large, white feathers. **1976** Bailey–Bailey *Hortus Third* 1073, *Stenanthium*. . . *gramineum*. . . Feather-fleece.

feather flower n *obs*

Perh a **cockscomb 1.**

1881 (1967) Tourgée *Royal Gentleman* **VA,** The feather-flower, with its white plumes drooping.

feather geranium n

=**Jerusalem oak.**

1837 Darlington *Flora Cestrica* 177, *C[henopodium] Botrys*. . . Feather-Geranium. **1857** Gray *Manual of Botany* 364, *C[henopodium] Botrys.* (Jerusalem Oak. Feather Geranium.) **1894** Coulter *Botany W. TX* 3.368, Jerusalem oak. Feather geranium. **1936** Winter *Plants NE* 192, Feather Geranium. . . Found throughout the U.S. **1974** (1977) Coon *Useful Plants* 96, *Chenopodium botrys*—Ambrose, feather geranium.

feather grass n

1 =**needlegrass** (here: *Stipa* spp).

1791 in 1793 Amer. Philos. Soc. *Trans.* 3.161 **PA,** *Stipa,* Feather-grass. avenacea. **1822** Eaton *Botany* 481, *Stipa*. . . *avanacea* . . feather grass. **1933** Small *Manual SE Flora* 97, *Stipa*. . . Spear-grasses. . . Feather-grasses. **1936** Winter *Plants NE* 30, *Stipa*. . . Porcupine-grass. Feather-grass. **1950** Hitchcock–Chase *Manual Grasses* 447, *Stipa neomexicana*. . . New Mexican feathergrass.

2 =**velvet grass.**

1847 Darlington *Weeds & Plants* 396 *(DA), H. lanatus*. . . Velvet-grass. Feather-grass. White Timothy. **1894** *Jrl. Amer. Folkl.* 7.104, *Holcus lanatus* . . old white top, feather-grass, velvet grass. West Va.

3 =**red sprangletop.**

1854 *S. Lit. Messenger* 20.618/1, Sprigs of feather-grass, red-top, and ox-eye. **1901** Mohr *Plant Life AL* 376, *Leptochloa mucronata*. . . Feather Grass. . . Alabama. From the Coast plain to the Central Pine belt. Sandy fields.

4 =**switchgrass.**

1933 *Torreya* 33.82, *Panicum virgatum* . . Feathergrass, Marsh Id., La.

featherhead n Cf **featheredge 3**

1970 *DARE* (Qu. X5, . . *Different kinds of men's haircuts*) Inf **VA**46, Featherhead.

feather hyacinth n [See quot 1976]

A **grape hyacinth** (here: *Muscari comosum* or *M. racemosum*).

1897 *Jrl. Amer. Folkl.* 10.145, *Muscari racemosum* . . var. *plumatilis,* feather hyacinth, . . Sulphur Grove, Ohio. **1900** Lyons *Plant Names* 254, *M. comosum*. . . is called Feather Hyacinth. **1910** Graves *Flowering Plants* 121 **CT,** *Muscari racemosum*. . . Feather Hyacinth. . . Grassland near dwellings. **1976** Bailey–Bailey *Hortus Third* 746, *[Muscari] comosum*. . . Cv. *'Monstrosum'. Feather hyacinth.* Fl[ower]s all sterile, violet-blue, and cut into fine shreds. Cv. *'Plumosum'*. . . *Feather hyacinth.* Fls. reddish-purple, cut into long, fine shreds.

feather in(to) See **feather** v **5, 6**

feather, knocked for a adj phr [Perh blend of *knocked for a loop* + *knocked over with a feather*]

Greatly surprised.

1967 *DARE* (Qu. GG20, . . *"When those two got married, I was certainly ______ ."*) Inf **NJ**2, Knocked for a feather.

feather-legged adj [See quot 1950] **Sth, S Midl**

Cowardly; frightened.

1934 Stribling *Unfinished Cathedral* 56 **AL,** By God, I'm going down and organize every man on the outside against your damned feather-legged bunch! **1950** *PADS* 14.29 **SC,** *Feather-legged*. . . Having feathers on the legs; hence, of cocks, a poor fighter. (Gamecocks have clean legs.) Hence, afraid to fight; cowed. The slogan of Judge Ira B.

Jones, in his race for governor in 1912, was: "There are no feathers on my legs." *Ibid* 75 **FL,** *Feather-legged* . . cowardly. **1952** Brown *NC Folkl.* 1.539, *Feather-legged*. . . Frightened, cowardly. "I get sorta feather-legged when I get around her!" **1966–67** *DARE* (Qu. HH10, *A very timid or cowardly person: "He's ______."*) Inf **GA**12, Feather-legged [-lɛgəd]; (QR, near Qu. NN32) Inf **AL**32A, Someone who is frightened is feather-legged. **1972** Cooper *NC Mt. Folkl.* 91, Feather-legged—cowardly.

feather merchant n [*feather* symbol of lightness or ease]

1 A shirker; a cheat; one who is given a position without having worked for it.

1784 *Mass. Centinel* 15 May 3/1 **MA** *(DAE),* A couple of Feather Merchants were taken up here the last week for passing counterfeit French Guineas. **1812** *Beauties Brother Bull-Us* 52 **Sth,** [Connecticut is] an unreformed congregation of tories, made up of British pensioners, quacks, lawyers, and feather-merchants, rag-men, priests, pedlars, and horse jockies; a modern Babylon. **1944** Shulman *Feather Merchants* [v], Every soldier knows that "feather merchants" means civilians. **1945** *AN&Q* 5.8/1, *Feather Merchant:* Army-Navy expression meaning a "dope-off," a lazy person. **1946** *Western Folkl.* 5.384, *Feather merchant* is a general service-term for civilians. . . an enlisted man who receives a rate upon entering the service instead of working up from apprentice-seaman status, is likewise a *feather merchant.*

2 See quot.

1958 McCulloch *Woods Words* 60 **Pacific NW,** *Feather merchant*—A small logger [*DARE* Ed: =a logger who runs a small operation].

3 A silly or stupid person. Cf **feather** n **B9**

1968 *DARE* (Qu. HH9) Inf **CA**106, Feather merchant.

feather moss n

A moss of the genus *Hypnum.*

1890 *Century Dict.* 3869, *Feather-moss,* a name sometimes given to some of the larger species of *Hypnum.* **1961** Douglas *My Wilderness* 242 **nME,** A delicate feather moss grew only inches high.

‡**feather one's own end** v phr [Perh infl by *feather one's nest* + *further one's own end*]

To gain advantage by tricky or deceitful means.

1968 *DARE* (Qu. II33, . . *"I don't trust him, he's always trying to ______."*) Inf **DE**3, Feather his own end; old-fashioned.

feather party n **N Cent**

A gathering at which a turkey, duck, chicken, or other fowl is offered as a prize.

1967 *Northwest Signal* (Napoleon OH) 15 Nov 5/4, Deshler Eagles Auxiliary feather party, at Eagles Hall, 8 p.m. **1982** *NADS Letters* **seMI,** My parents . . explained that feather parties were a commonplace in Detroit in the 30's. Usually they were held in movie houses, but churches and fraternal organizations had them too. They were most frequent at Thanksgiving and Christmas. Feather parties were door prize giveaways. Numbered ticket stubs were drawn, and the holder of the matching half won a prize of a turkey or chicken—a *live* one, hence with feathers. **1985** *WI Alumnus Letters* **neIN,** Every year our volunteer Fire Dept. has a feather party. . . You play Bingo and the prizes you win are chickens and turkeys; **neIN,** Feather party—Three or four times a year, particularly before the holidays, they would have the parishioners [of the local Catholic church] sell raffle tickets as a fund raiser, and the prizes would be something with feathers such as turkeys, ducks, and chickens; **csWI,** Until recent years the law was very specific as to what was out-lawed by the anti-gambling statutes. So no one would say in public that their [VFW] post was having a raffle of dressed poultry. . . They referred to it among themselves as a "feather party." . . I first heard this used after World War II; **seWI,** A "feather party" was a clandestine gathering (for men only) to gamble. . . They were held before Thanksgiving, and the gambling supposedly was to win a turkey for a holiday dinner. . . I strongly suspect the gambling was on cock fights. [Addit letters from **IL, IN, OH, WI**]

feather peabush n Also *feather bush, ~ dalea, ~ plume*

An **indigo bush** (here: *Dalea formosa*) native to the Southwest.

1931 U.S. Dept. Ag. *Misc. Pub.* 101.85, *Feather peabush* . . known by a variety of local names, including . . little featherbush, . . grows commonly but usually scatteringly on dry plains and hills. **1938** Van Dersal *Native Woody Plants* 177, *Feather peabush*. . . A small, much-branched shrub; flowers April–October. **1970** Correll *Plants TX* 826, *Dalea formosa*. . . *Feather plume*. . . is reportedly a good browse. **1981** Benson–Darrow *Trees SW Deserts* 266, Feather dalea is attractive at flowering time, and sometimes it is planted as an ornamental.

feather rock n [In ref to its light weight]

Pumice.

1967 *DARE* (Qu. C26, . . *Special kinds of stone or rock . . in this part of the state*) Inf **OR**1, Feather rock—pumice.

feathers, come to a goat's house for See **goat** n **3**

feathers, feathers, [animal's] feathers n For addit varr see quots

A children's game; see quots 1953, 1973.

1953 Brewster *Amer. Nonsinging Games* 24 **NC,** Feathers. . . This is known also as Horns, Birds Fly, Ducks Fly, All the birds in the Wood, All the Horns in the Wood, etc. In this game the players are seated around a table. Each places both hands on top of the table and keeps them there as long as the thing named by the leader has no feathers. If the latter names something which has feathers, all must lift their hands quickly. When, for example, he calls, "Feathers, feathers, goat feathers!" anyone lifting his hands from the table must pay a forfeit. A forfeit must be given also if a player fails to lift his hands when he should do so or if he is slow in doing so. **1965** *DARE* File **sIN,** Feathers, feathers—a type of children's finger game. **1973** *Ibid* **sIN,** "Feather, feather, hen's feather" or "Feather, feather, cow's feather." All the children sit in a circle with forefingers extended and touching the ground in front of each child. The leader says "feather, feather, ______ feathers" and lifts his forefinger. If the animal named has feathers, the child lifts a finger. If it does not he keeps still. The leader calls rapidly, lifting his own finger each time. If the child makes a mistake and follows suit when the animal does *not* have feathers, he gets a two-fingered thump on his head. This game has been traditional in my family for three generations.

feathers, fine as adj phr Cf **feather B6** and *fine as frog hair* (at **frog hair 2b**)

In good shape; just right; fine.

1967 *DARE* (Qu. KK4, . . *"Everything is ______ now."*) Inf **NJ**1, Fine as feathers.

feathers in the hair, have See **feather B8**

feather-stripping bee n Also *feather-stripping party*

A gathering at which people prepare feathers for use in pillows by removing the quills.

1935 Sandoz *Jules* 115 **wNE** (as of 1888), There were literaries in the schoolhouses, husking bees, a feather-stripping party or two, and socials, sings, masquerades and dances. **1950** *WELS (Different kinds of parties)* 1 Inf, **ceWI,** Feather-stripping bee. **1970** *DARE* (Qu. FF2) Inf **MI**120, Feather-stripping party—old-fashioned. Neighbors meet at a farm and strip the shaft from the stem of feathers, to make pillows, etc. There is singing and games, jokes, etc., during the work.

feathers up, get one's See **feather B7c**

feathers, up in See **feather B7d**

feather tail n [Perh blend of **feather cloud** + **mare's tail**]

1968 *DARE* (Qu. B10, . . *Long trailing clouds high in the sky*) Inf **NY**99, Feather tails.

feather tick, feather tie See **feather bed 1**

feathertop n [See quot 1970]

An introduced ornamental grass *(Pennisetum villosum).*

1950 Hitchcock–Chase *Manual Grasses* 728, *Feathertop*. . . Cultivated for ornament, sparingly escaped in dry ground, Michigan, Texas, and California; introduced from Africa. **1961** Thomas *Flora Santa Cruz* 100, Feathertop. Occasional as weeds; San Francisco and Santa Cruz. **1970** Correll *Plants TX* 188, *Feathertop*. . . Panicles . . several cm. thick, softly fuzzy and pale-buffy- or tawny-white. **1976** Bailey–Bailey *Hortus Third* 838, *Feathertop.*

feather tree n Cf **plume tree**

=false goatsbeard.

1933 Small *Manual SE Flora* 596, *Astilbe*. . . Flowers very numerous, in spikes, racemes or panicles. . . *Feather-trees.* **1949** Moldenke *Amer. Wild Flowers* 54, In our area we have 33 genera . . including . . *feather-trees (Astilbe)* of the Blue Ridge Mountains.

feather up See **feather** v **7**

feather vine n [Prob from the plumose achene tails]

A **virgin's bower** (here: *Clematis drummondii*).

1951 *PADS* 15.31 **TX,** *Clematis drummondii*. . . Feather vine.

feather wands n

A **bugbane 1** (here: *Cimicifuga racemosa*).

1959 Carleton *Index Herb. Plants* 36, *Feather wands:* Cimicifuga racemosa.

featherweed n

A **cudweed 1** (here: *Gnaphalium polycephalum*).

1892 *Garden and Forest* 5.614, The omnipresent Life-everlasting is in northern New York called Feather-weed, because it is used by poor people to fill beds when feathers are lacking. **1892** *Jrl. Amer. Folkl.* 5.98, *Gnaphalium polycephalum* . . feather-weed. No. New York. **1930** U.S. Dept. Ag. *Misc. Pub.* 77.55, *Sweet Cudweed. . . Other common names. . .* Feather-weed, rabbit-tobacco. **1959** Carleton *Index Herb. Plants* 45, *Feather-weed:* Gnaphalium polycephalum.

feather white adj phr **chiefly NEng** Cf **feather** n **B5** quot 1969

Of the sea: turbulent, frothy, full of whitecaps; transf, of a person, extremely agitated, angry.

1924 *DN* 5.287 **Cape Cod MA,** The surface of the ocean when whipped by a heavy gale is said to be 'feather white.' And in truth one's imagination does not have to be strained very far to imagine the frothy surface as white feathers blown over a barn floor. **1966–68** *DARE* (Qu. O15, . . *Different kinds of waves*) Inf **MD**45, It's feather white—very big whitecaps; (Qu. GG40) Inf **ME**15, He was so mad he was feather white. **1975** Gould *ME Lingo* 89, *Feather white*—A wind-whipped sea, all whitecaps, is said to be *feather white.* Hence, some degree of agitation in a person: "He came all feather white to give me a piece of his mind!" **1979** *AmSp* 54.98 **swME** (as of 1899–1910), *Feather-white. . .* (Descriptive term for the sea) "All feather-white."

feather white, all of a adv phr

Quickly; so as to make the water **feather white.**

1935 *AmSp* 10.40 **Nantucket MA** (as of 1848), *That vessel comes all of a feather white.* Coming quickly.

feature n Pronc-spp *feater, feetur* *arch* Cf **creature A**

Std senses, var forms.

1846 Lowell in 1944 *ADD,* Featers. **1851** Hooper *Widow Rugby's Husband* 47 **AL,** My ugly feeturs came into play.

feature v

1 To resemble in appearance. **chiefly Sth, S Midl, ME** Cf **favor C1, future** v

1941 *LANE* Map 393 *(He looks like his father)* **scattered, but esp ME,** Features; 1 inf, **neME,** Features, rarely heard [old-fashioned]. **1965–70** *DARE* (Qu. Z10, *If a child looks very much like his father, you might say, "He ______ his father."*) Infs **GA**37, **MS**47, **MO**29, **NC**40, **WV**14, Features. [3 of 5 Infs Black] **c1970** Pederson *Dial. Surv. Rural GA (If the boy's behavior is similar to his father's, you would say that the boy ______ his father)* 1 inf, **seGA,** Features. [Inf Black] **1986** Pederson *LAGS Concordance* **Gulf Region,** [10 infs use *feature* as a verb in the sense "resembles."]

2 To imagine, comprehend, believe.

1934 *AmSp* 9.160, A teacher . . writes that . . She hopes that the vogue of expressions like *Can you feature that?* meaning 'Can you comprehend it?' will be short-lived. **1942** Berrey–Van den Bark *Amer. Slang* 171.2, Feature, *to comprehend, get a picture of, as "can you feature that!"* **1950** *WELS Suppl.* 1 Inf, **csWI,** I couldn't feature it = I couldn't believe it. **1951** *AmSp* 26.237, Strange, can you feature such a shrimp of a man as high brass? **1966** *DARE* (Qu. NN7, *Exclamations of surprise*) Inf **AR**41, Feature that! **1978** Doig *This House* 33 **MT,** Thought we couldn't see 'em behind those damned little lunchboxes, can ye feature that?

3 To strut, show off.

1970 *DARE* (Qu. Y22, *To move around in a way to make people take notice of you: "Look at him ______."*) Inf **FL**51, Featuring (said of men).

feaze n, v See **feeze** n, v

February n Usu |'fɛbru,(w)ɛri, 'fɛbju,(w)ɛri|; for varr see quots Pronc-spp *Febbywerry, Febiary, Febuary, Fibbywerry*

Std sense, var forms.

1837 Sherwood *Gaz. GA* 69, *Provincialisms. . . Febuary,* February. **1890** *DN* 1.38 **csME,** *February. . .* [fɛbruɛri], *rather than* [fɛbruɚi]. **1899** (1912) Green *VA Folk-Speech* 171, Febuary. **1915** *DN* 4.182 **VA,** *Febiary.* **1922** Gonzales *Black Border* 301 **sSC, GA coasts** [Gullah glossary], *Febbywerry, Fibbywerry*—February. **1936** *AmSp* 11.245 **eTX,** February [is pronounced] ['fɛbə,wɛrɪ], ['fɛb(ə),wɝɪ, 'fɛb(ə),wɛrɪ], ['fɛb,wɛɪ] [by Plantation-Type, Hill-Type, and Negro speakers, respectively]. **1939** *LANE* Map 65, [Many pronunciations occur: most freq ['fɛbju,(w)ərɨ]; less freq ['fɛbə,wərɨ]; infreq ['fɛbru(w)ɛrɨ]; also ['fɛbju,ærɨ], ['fɛbwərɨ], ['fɛbərɨ], ['fɛ˃bṛɨ˅], ['fibəwə˅ṛɨ˅].] Pronunciations of the type of [fɛb(ə)wərɨ] are regarded as older though still in use by . . [14 infs]. **1975** Morris–Morris *Usage* 239, The pronunciation FEB-roo-er-ee is preferable to FEB-yoo-er-ee, though the latter is heard with increasing frequency among otherwise literate speakers, especially among radio and television commentators. **1976** Allen *LAUM* 3.323 (as of c1950), In *February* the first retroflex glide /r/ is retained by slightly less than one-third of all U[pper] M[idwest] infs. in the pronunciation /fɛbruɛri/. Speakers with a Northern speech background seem more likely to retain it, as do Type III [=cultivated] speakers in Midland speech territory, but the evidence is not very strong.

febuh See **fever** n[1]

fect n[1] See **fact A2**

fect n[2]

1987 Jones-Jackson *When Roots Die* 139 **sSC coast** [Gullah], A number of idioms are still very much apparent in daily communication. . . Do the fect to you: cause harm to come to you.

fed(d)er, fedduh See **feather** n

federal building n Cf **F.D.R., government house**

An outdoor toilet.

1949 *AmSp* 24.108 **seSC,** *Federal Building. . .* Privy. **1962** Atwood *Vocab. TX* 53, A number of local, individualistic, and imaginative terms occur occasionally. [Footnote:] For example, *Chic Sale, Congress, Federal Building* (no doubt from unreconstructed Confederates). **1967** Faries *Word Geog. MO* 154, Federal Building (1 [informant]).

federal decoration n

1906 *DN* 3.135 **nwAR,** *Federal decoration. . .* Decoration day; May 30. "What day does federal decoration come this year?"

federation pike n [See quots 1887, 1889]

=**chain pickerel.**

1842 DeKay *Zool. NY* 4.225, *The Federation Pike. Esox tredecem-radiatus. . .* The flesh is savory and fine. **1887** Goode *Amer. Fishes* 277, Patriotic Americans of early Federal days called it the "Federation Pike," an allusion to the chain of thirteen linked rays, symbolical of the Federal union, which was stamped upon certain copper coins used during the last century. **1890** *Century Dict.* 4484, *Pike. . . Federation pike,* a pickerel, *Esox americanus:* so called in allusion to the bands with which its body is crossed and rays being often thirteen in number. **1935** Caine *Game Fish* 22, *Esox reticulatus. . .* Chain Pickerel. . . Federation Pike.

federation squirrel n [See quots]

The thirteen-lined **ground squirrel n b** *(Spermophilus tridecemlineatus).*

1890 *Century Dict.* 5882, *Squirrel. . . Federation squirrel,* the thirteen-lined spermophile, or striped gopher: so called in allusion to the thirteen stripes of the flag of the original States of the American Union. **1947** Cahalane *Mammals* 349, The 'thirteen-lined ground squirrel' is supposed to have thirteen stars and stripes. For this reason it is sometimes called the federation squirrel. The scientific name also means 'thirteen lines,' but the animal may have a few more or a few less. **1989** Gores *Wolf Time* 209 **MN,** The thirteen-lined ground squirrel, also called the federation squirrel because its patterns resembled stars and stripes.

fee v

1 To hire, employ. *old-fash*

1701 in 1870 Penn *Corresp.* 9.78, A lawyer sends me word he is offered to be feed against me by Col. Quarry, who is now come to do us all the mischief he can. **1804** Fessenden *Poems* 108, Although the bard, you may rely on't,/ Pleaded like lawyer, fee'd by client. **1843** *Amer. Pioneer* 2.370 **nwPA,** This decision was fatal to the settlers, few of whom were able to fee foreign counsel, or even to attend court on court at Philadelphia. **1967** *DARE* Tape **KY**3, A poor farmer may not have enough money to fee a good lawyer.

2 To give a gratuity to; to tip.

1925 Parrish *Perennial Bachelor* 221 **MD** (as of late 19th cent), How much do you think I ought to fee the driver?

fee-ance See **fiance**

feebee n [Perh var of **peewee**]

A small or cheap playing marble.

1970 *DARE* (Qq. EE6b, c) Inf **SC**68, Feebee or peewee—chalk marbles, very small.

feeble n [Echoic]

=**piping plover.**

1925 (1928) Forbush *Birds MA* 1.470, *Charadrius melodus*... Piping Plover... Feeble. **1955** MA Audubon Soc. *Bulletin* 39.444 **MA,** *Piping Plover*... Feeble.

feeble man n

The ring finger.

1950 *WELS (Nicknames for the fingers)* 1 Inf, **cnWI,** Third or ring finger or feeble man. **1986** *NADS Letters* **sNM,** *Feeble man*—Mothers with preschool children know this expression. It apparently occurs in a nursery rhyme that begins "Where is thumbkin?" **1988** *Ibid* **csMI,** *Feeble man*—'ring finger': widely known among my students. They attribute the source to the game 'Thumbkin' in which the names of the digits are: thumbkin, pointer, tall man, feeble man, pinkie. Feeble man is so called because it is the hardest to turn down toward the palm in isolation.

fee chaser n Cf **fee grabber**

1967 *DARE* (Qu. HH44, *Joking or uncomplimentary names for lawyers)* Inf **OR**6, Fee chaser.

feed v, hence vbl n *feeding* Cf **dress v 5, hand n B4**

In **hoodoo n 1a:** to give power to a magical object by offering or applying something to it as if to strengthen it.

1931 *Jrl. Amer. Folkl.* 44.372 **New Orleans LA** [Black], Write his name three times and put it on the sock. Place the dime on the name and the hair.. on the dime. Put a piece of "he" Lodestone on top of the hair and sprinkle it with steel dust. As you do this, say, "Feed the he, feed the she." That is what you call feeding the Lodestone. *Ibid* 412 **Sth,** Take a picture of St. Peter and put it at the front door and a picture of St. Michael at the back door. Put the Paradise seeds in little bags and put one behind each saint. It is known as "feeding the saint." **c1938** in 1970 Hyatt *Hoodoo* 1.456 **seSC,** You make dat up like a bag, and den you got'a put *John de Conker* and dis dime.. in the *chamber lye* and let it lay over all night... [D]en de next morning dey take and dey *feed* it and dey wear dat around dere waist. See, den nobody can't hurt cha... You feed that with that same *Hearts Cologne*. *Ibid* 558 **swTN,** Yo' takes a frog an' yo' kill him an'.. sews him up in a shammy skin, an' *feed* him with whiskey. Well, that's supposed to be a very, very nice *toby* fo' gamblin'. *Ibid* 578 **cwFL,** Go to a graveyard for a gambling *hand,* git dat *graveyard dirt* and sew it up into a bag, and puts dat lucky lodestone into hit... If yo' went to de graveyard, yo' *feed* it [=the bag] with whiskey, yo' puts whiskey on it; an' if you.. uses de lucky lodestone, yo' uses de *Hearts perfume* on it.

feed n

1 also rarely *feeding:* A meal, esp an abundant or elaborate one.

1839 Marryat *Diary* 1.197, Also, "will you have a *feed* or a *check*?"—A dinner, or a luncheon? **1845** Kirkland *Western Clearings* 131 **MI,** But if our good lady had been initiated into the fashionable notion of a "feed," she could not have provided more bounteously. **1905** Lincoln *Partners* 166 **NEng,** Talk about your feeds! Why, Brad, there was oysters, and soup, and lobster.. and turkey, and ice cream, and the Lord knows what. **1949** *PADS* 11.21 **CO,** *Feed*... A meal, usually a big feast in celebration of something. "The club had a feed." **1966–70** *DARE* (Qu. FF1,.. *What kinds [of 'socials'] are there?*) Infs **MN**38, **WA**1, Pancake feed; **CA**158, Crab feeds; **MN**38, Beef feed; **MI**4, Pig feed; (Qu. FF2,.. *Kinds of parties*) Inf **WA**18, Pancake feed; (Qu. FF16,.. *Local.. celebrations*) Inf **WA**13, Sportsman's fish feed; (Qu. H5) Inf **SC**70, Between-meal feed; (Qu. H70) Inf **TN**1, A git-together feed; **SC**26, Feeding; (Qu. FF3) Inf **MD**25, Feeds. **1967–69** *DARE* Tape **CA**5, The first thing they do, they have a feed; **GA**86, We would get anywhere from 75 to 125 rabbits on that hunt.. an' dress 'em,.. barbecue 'em... Then we'd all have a big feed there when it was over; **MA**47, We found a restaurant, and we got a feed.

2 Food (or drink) for human consumption; also fig. Cf **feed, off (of) one's 1**

1818 Fearon *Sketches* 194 **wPA,** I guess whiskey is all the feed we have on sale. *Ibid* 224, The small farmer.. raises a sufficient "feed" for his family. **1867** in 1919 Hale *Letters* 27 **NEng,** The cook is French and feed delicious. **1898** Westcott *Harum* 283 **cNY,** You want a change o' feed [=a change of friends] once in a while, or you *may* git the colic. **1966–68** *DARE* (Qu. H6,.. *"He certainly enjoys his _____."*) Infs **CT**5, **IL**9, **PA**131, **WA**18, Feed.

3 attrib: Providing food, that serves food.

1903 *Cin. Enquirer* 9 May 12/2 *(DA),* He was grinning broadly as he stepped into the feed shack and addressed me. **1909** Wason *Happy Hawkins* 304 *(DA),* We sidled into a feed-joint. **1910** Raine *B. O'Connor* 106 *(DA),* Jay Hardman's place, a tumble-down feed-station on the edge of town.

4 See quot.

1899 (1912) Green *VA Folk-Speech* 171, *Feed*... A certain allowance of provender given: as, a *feed* of oats.

5 A period of active eating; the signs of such a period.

1846 Thorpe *Mysteries* 35 **lower Missip Valley,** In the shade of yonder lusty oak you will perceive what arrow-fishermen call a "feed;" you see the bubbles.. come rushing upwards swiftly, like handfuls of silver shot. They are.. caused by the fish below, as they, around the root of that very oak, search for insects for food. **1968** *DARE* Tape **IN**36, Them catfish, they're kinda temperamental. They'll go on a feed. Then they'll just quit bitin' and you might just as well reel in and go home.

feed bag n [Transf from std sense "bag used for feeding an animal; nose bag"]

A meal; a place where one can get a meal; a container for a meal—also in phr *put on the feed bag* eat a meal.

1929 Burnett *Little Caesar* 219 **Chicago IL,** I'm ready for the feed-bag. **1937** Sandoz *Slogum* 17 **NE,** "Feed bag ready?" called Hank Short... "I got the biscuits in the oven," Gulla answered him. **1960** Wentworth–Flexner *Slang* 180, *Feedbag*.. A meal, as dinner. **1968** Adams *Western Words* 110, *Feed bag*... A cowboy's name for the mess house. A logger's name for his lunch pail. **1987** *DARE* File **Missip-Ohio Valleys** (as of c1960), *To put on the feed bag*—to have a meal.

feeder n

1 freq attrib: An animal being fattened for market.

1880 *Bradstreet's* 16 Oct 2/2 **ceMO,** The exception is the present scarcity of what are termed "feeders." **1905** U.S. Forest Serv. *Bulletin* 62.19, Cattle from the ranges of Arizona supply Phoenix with feeders. **1935** *AmSp* 10.270 [Stockyard terms], *Feeders*. Animals ready for fattening (feeding). **1941** *AmSp* 16.236 **NE,** *Feeders,* young cattle that can be fattened more. **1966–70** *DARE* Tape **SD**8, We raise feeder cattle too—for finishing in the corn belt... There was a feeder buyer here today; **CA**90, Feeder cattle are fed at local feed yards, shipped in by train; **KY**93, A feeder pig weighs about forty, fifty pounds; **CA**90, Feeder cattle; **FL**32, **SD**3, Feeder. **1967–70** *DARE* (Qu. K51,.. *A very young [pig]*) Infs **IA**1, **IL**59, **IN**67, **KY**93, **MI**78, **WI**63, Feeder (pig); (QR, near Qu. K52) Inf **MN**3, Feeder pigs are taken out at about thirty-five or forty pounds of weight; (Qu. K58, *A castrated pig*) Infs **IN**80, **OH**95, **WI**54, Feeder (pig); (Qu. L7, *Piece of land with a hay crop*) Inf **MN**2, Feeder farm; (Qu. M1,.. *Kinds of barns*) Inf **MO**32, Feeder barn; (Qu. M22) Inf **TX**8, Feeder barn.

2 One who buys animals to fatten for market.

1889 *Las Cruces* (N.M.) *News* 16 Nov. *(DA* at *feed lot),* [The new lower rate] allows Kansas feeders to ship from this territory or Arizona to their feed lots, fatten them and ship on to market. **1929** *AmSp* 5.57 **NE,** The term "feeder" is also applied to one, generally a farmer, who purchases "range cows" and fattens them for the market. **1946** *Chi. D. News* 23 Mar 3/1 *(DA),* Under a special rule, 'feeders' can purchase live animals, feed them for 30 days, slaughter them and collect the government subsidy. **1966** *DARE* Tape **SD**8, Feeders come out here and buy 'em. **1967** *DARE* (QR, near Qu. M12) Inf **CO**3, Feeders use more [fodder] than dairymen. **1968** Adams *Western Words* 110, *Feeders*—Cattle which are shipped or driven to the corn belt for fattening before marketing; also, men who feed such cattle.

3 See quot.

1969 Sorden *Lumberjack Lingo* 41 **NEng, Gt Lakes,** *Feeder*—A man who cared for the horses and stables in a logging camp.

4 One who eats (usu prodigious amounts).

1967–69 *DARE* (Qu. H9, *If somebody always eats a considerable amount of food, you say he's a _____*) Inf **CT**26, Big feeder; **OH**61, Good feeder; **WY**5, Heavy feeder; (Qu. H12,.. *Somebody [who].. leaves most of [his food] on his plate*) Inf **WY**5, Light feeder.

5 also *self-feeder:* A feed trough; a structure or device that allows animals to feed themselves rather than having to be fed. **chiefly Upper MW, N Cent, SE** See Map

1877 *Harper's New Mth. Mag.* Jan 267/2, Upon the other [side of the store] stood sturdily rakes and hoes, shellers and feeders, even more costly implements of agriculture. **1925** *Book of Rural Life* 9.5405, The grain and protein-rich supplement may be fed [to hogs], free choice, in separate compartments of the self-feeder, or a properly balanced mixture of grain and supplements may be self-fed. **1927** (1970) Sears *Catalogue* 1066, Thousands of hog raisers have installed these automatic feeders. The two sides prevent crowding, save labor and keep food clean. Feeder strongly made of high grade clear lumber. . . Shipped from factory near *Chicago.* **1965–70** *DARE* (Qu. K59) 53 Infs, **chiefly Upper MW, SE,** Feeder; 33 Infs, **chiefly Upper MW, SE,** Self-feeder; **GA**72, **IL**19, **MO**18, Hog feeder; **CA**36, Automatic feeder; **MS**74, Pig feeder; **OH**60, Dry feeders; **VA**40, Feeder trough; (Qu. M12) Inf **CA**124, Feeders; in the West they're called self-feeders; **IL**80, Self-feeder; **FL**32, Creep feeder, out in the pasture. **1968** *DARE* Tape **NJ**10, We have feeder wagons.

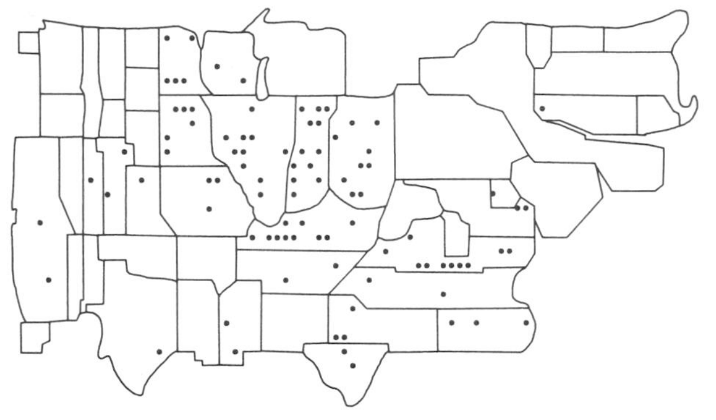

•feeder 5 + varr (Qq. K59, M12)

6 A hay chute in a barn.

1954 *Harder Coll.* **cwTN,** Feeder—a hay-hole. **1970** *DARE* (Qu. M5) Inf **TN**42, Feeder.

7 also attrib: An access road. **widely scattered, but less freq Atlantic**

1855 *Chicago Times* 25 Jan. 2/3 *(OEDS),* This road has many lateral roads as feeders to it. **1950** *WELS (A less important road going off from the main highway)* 1 Inf, **csWI,** Feeder road. **1965–70** *DARE* (Qu. N28, *A road that connects a big highway with stores and business places set back from it*) 11 Infs, **scattered but esp N Cent,** Feeder road(s); **IL**128, **NY**23, **OH**6, **TN**47, Feeder; **PA**107, Feeder line; (Qu. N29, . . *Names . . for a less important road running back from a main road*) 10 Infs, **scattered,** Feeder; 8 Infs, **scattered,** Feeder road; **CA**111, Feeder route. [30 of 33 Infs old] **1972** *DARE* File **Houston TX,** Feeder road. It feeds cars onto the highway, or from the highway to shops alongside. **1980** *Houston Chron.* (TX) 27 Jan 8, Along the Gulf Coast it's the feeder. Access road is the most common across the state.

8 Kindling wood.

1969 *DARE* (Qu. D34) Inf **KY**65, Feeder.

feed fish See **feed the fish(es)**

feed floor See **feeding floor**

feeding See **feed** v

feeding floor n Also *feed floor*

A hard floor on which feed for hogs is spread.

1868 IA State Ag. Soc. *Rept. for 1867* 104, Put them [=hogs] in small yards with . . a good plank *feed-floor.* **1925** *Book of Rural Life* 9.5402, [Caption:] *A Concrete Feeding Floor*—Hogs are naturally clean if given a chance to be so. Such an arrangement as the one shown here helps with this, and also prevents any loss of feed. **1967** *DARE* (Qu. K59, *What do pigs eat out of?*) Inf **IA**1, Feeding floors—just put the feed on the floor. **1973** Allen *LAUM* 1.188 **IA** (as of c1950), Feeding floor. [1 inf] **1988** *Atlanta Constitution* (GA) 30 Dec sec D 1/3 **ceGA,** He is moving toward the more lucrative enterprise of finishing all his own stock [=hogs] by building a $40,000 "feeding floor."

feeding lot See **feed lot**

feeding time n Also *feed time* **widespread, but chiefly Sth, Midl** See Map Cf **chore time, feed up**

The time of day when chores (not restricted to the feeding of livestock) are done.

1899 (1912) Green *VA Folk-Speech* 171, Come, you had better go to the 'cuppen,' it is feeding-time. **1902** *DN* 2.234 **sIL,** *Feedn-time.* . . The terms 'chores' or 'chore time' are not used. The women milk, get in wood, water, etc., while the men feed the stock; hence the term. **1906** *DN* 3.118 **sIN,** *Feedin' time.* . . Evening; time to feed stock. "Let's stop work; it's feedin' time." **1909** *DN* 3.396 **nwAR,** *Feedin' time.* **1939** *LANE* Map 217 *(Chore time)* **throughout NEng,** Feeding time; 3 infs, Feed time. **c1960** *Wilson Coll.* **csKY,** *Feeding time.* . . Time to feed and water the stock, milk the cows, etc. **1965–70** *DARE* (Qu. L4b, . . *Time . . to feed livestock, clean stalls, and so on*) 262 Infs, **chiefly Sth, Midl,** Feeding time; 15 Infs, **chiefly Sth, Midl,** Feed time. **1971** Wood *Vocab. Change* 36 **Sth,** In all [of the eight] states except Oklahoma the time when animals are attended to is first *feeding time* and second *time to feed.* **1971** Bright *Word Geog. CA & NV* 172, *Feeding time* 45% . . *chore time* 29%. **1973** Allen *LAUM* 1.258 (as of c1950), *Chore time* is the most common U[pper] M[idwest] expression, with a[n] . . average of 78%. . . *Feeding time,* . . with Northern orientation, has a 10% . . average.

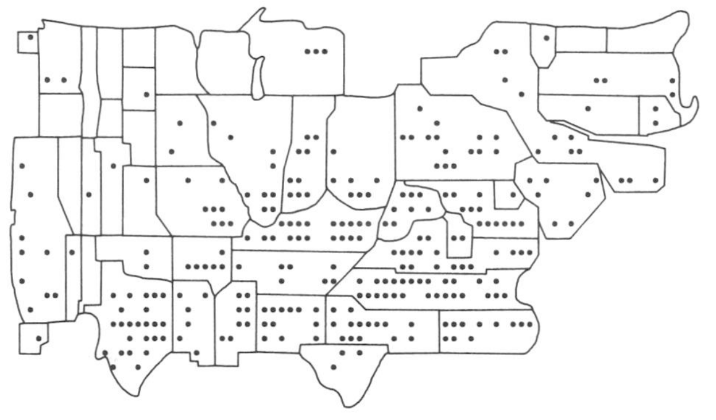

•feeding time + var (Qu. L4b)

feeding-up (time) See **feed up**

feed lead v phr Cf **feather** v **5**

To shoot (someone).

1917 *DN* 4.412 **wNC,** He feathered into him, feeding him lead. **1931** *PMLA* 46.1308 **sAppalachians,** Many terms for . . killing abound. And so: to "feed one hot lead," to shoot.

feedlot n Also *feeding lot* **chiefly N Cent, Upper MW**

A barnyard.

1940–41 Cassidy *WI Atlas* 1 Inf, **cWI,** Barnyard—some call it feeding lot. **1959** Faulkner *Mansion* 10 **MS,** If I was you and my cow was in Jack Houston's feed lot, I would take my rope and go and get it. **1965–70** *DARE* (Qu. M13, *The space near the barn with a fence around it where you keep the livestock*) 10 Infs, **chiefly N Cent,** Feedlot; **IL**128, Feeding lot; (Qu. M14, *The open area around or next to the barn:*) 20 Infs, **chiefly N Cent, Upper MW,** Feedlot; **IN**35, **NY**52, **PA**127, Feeding lot; (Qu. M15, *The place outdoors where pigs are kept*) Infs **IL**56, **IN**53, 67, **MO**34, Feedlot. **1968** *PADS* 49.13 **Upper MW,** *Feed(ing) lot* [for *barn yard*] (field informants, 7.7% [of 208]; students, 25% [of 100]) appears to be an innovation; this term usually designates an enclosure for feeding cattle to be fattened before they are sent to the packing houses.

feed off v phr

1 To clear (a field of its crop or remaining fodder) by turning stock into it to feed. Cf **hog C1**

1968 *DARE* (QR, near Qu. K80) Inf **NV**8, Feed it off—turn the stock out.

2 See **feed up 1.**

feed, off (of) one's adj phr [Transf from farm or ranch use, in ref to livestock] **chiefly Nth**

1 also *off one's food* (or *eats*): Unable to eat normally; slightly ill; indisposed.

1872 Holmes *Poet* 75 **MA,** A little "off my feed," as Hiram Woodruff would say. **1946** *Western Folkl.* 5.234 **wOR,** *He's off his feed.* No food pleases him; he has lost interest in life. **1948** Manfred *Chokecherry* 4 **nwIA,** Pa had flatly written in his last letter that Ma was failing, "she's been off her feed for a month." **1965–70** *DARE* (Qu. BB39, . . *"I'll be all right tomorrow—I'm just feeling ______ today."*) 9 Infs, **Nth,** Off (of) my feed; **MA**73, Off your feed; (Qu. BB41, *Not seriously ill, but sick enough to be in bed*) Infs **CA**53, 106, **NJ**58, **OH**72, **WA**30, Off his feed; (Qu. BB16b) Infs **WA**13, 30, Off his feed; **MI**68, Off his food; off his eats; (Qu. BB5) Inf **HI**1, Off my feed; (Qu. H12) Inf **NM**12, Off his feed.

2 Sulky, petulant.

1966 *DARE* (Qu. GG35b, . . *"Because she couldn't go, she's been ______ all day."*) Inf **ME**19, Off her feed.

feed one's face See **face n 1**

feed out v phr

To fatten (an animal) for market.

1946 *Harper's Mag.* Oct 311/1 **MO,** Now and then my father would have to borrow money to "feed out" the steers. **1967–69** *DARE* Tape **IA**1, They feed their hogs out. All hogs practically are fed out here; a few of 'em are sold as pigs, but not very often; **KS**14, He'll winter and feed out about 2,000 head of cattle; **MN**12, We feed them [=cattle] out; **PA**178, The heifers I mostly sell, and the steers I feed out for two years.

feed-stretcher See **stretcher**

feed the fish(es) v phr Also *feed fish, feed the goldfish* [Orig naut; *OED* 1870] *old-fash*

To vomit.

1928 *Ruppenthal Coll.* **KS,** *To feed the fish(es)*—(army) to be seasick and vomit in consequence. **1942** Berrey–Van den Bark *Amer. Slang* 130.32, *Vomit.* . . go feed the goldfish . . feed the fishes. **1943** *LANE* Map 504, 1 inf, **cnMA,** Feed the fishes. [Inf old] **1966–70** *DARE* (Qq. BB17, 18) Infs **CA**164, **MI**2, **MN**19, **NC**36, **NY**105, **OH**98, **VA**5, Feed the fish(es); **AK**8, Feeding fish. [7 of 8 Infs old] **1973** Allen *LAUM* 1.369 **IA, NE, SD** (as of c1950), Feed the fishes. [3 infs, all old]

feed time n

1 See **feeding time.**

2 The time when animals come out to feed; hence, the best time to hunt.

1926 *AmSp* 1.412 **Okefenokee GA,** They scarcely propose to hunt except when it is 'feed-time.' . . "The surest way ter tell when it's feed-time is ter know where the moon is. Whenever the moon's right straight overhead (south), they feed. Or when it rises or goes down, that's good feed-time."

feed tree n

1950 *PADS* 14.29 **SC,** *Feed tree.* . . A tree bearing fruit or berries, such as the persimmon or blackgum, which the opossum frequents to obtain food.

feed up v phr Also rarely *feed off* **chiefly Mid and S Atl** See Map

To do farm chores; spec, to feed and water livestock; hence n *feed-up time,* vbl n *feeding-up (time).*

1933 Miller *Lamb in His Bosom* 83 **GA,** He went out into the whipping wind to feed up, to milk Betsey and turn her out. **1939** *LANE* Map 217 *(Chore time)* 5 infs, **MA, NH,** Time to feed up; 2 infs, **MA,** Feeding-up time. [All infs old] **1965–70** *DARE* (Qu. L4b, *What do you call the time early in the morning and at night when you have to feed livestock, clean stalls, and so on? A person might say, "I've got to go now, it's ______."*) 14 Infs, **LA, NC, SC, VA,** Time to feed up; **GA**22, Go feed up; **SC**9, Time for me to feed off; **SC**34, Let's feed up; **NC**8, 24, 49, Feeding up; **FL**32, 50, **GA**17, **NC**13, 21, 81, Feeding-up time; **LA**10, **SC**12, 57, Feed-up time; (Qu. K60, *When somebody is going to give the pigs food, he says, "I'm going to ______."*) Inf **SC**12, Feed up; (Qu. OO33b, *Talking about doing chores: "This morning as usual we ______."*) Inf **VA**75, Fed up.

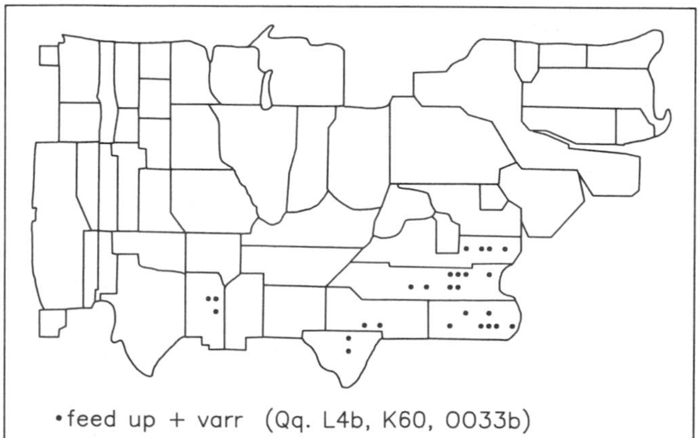

•feed up + varr (Qq. L4b, K60, OO33b)

feedway n **KY, VA**

The opening in a barn loft through which hay is thrown to animals below.

1968–70 *DARE* (Qu. M5) Infs **KY**75, **VA**14, 77, Feedway; **KY**80, Feedway—old-fashioned, for mules.

feed yard n

1 A feedlot.

1879 *Chi. Tribune* 14 May 7/4 *(DA),* The feed-yards in Chicago are extensive. **1966** *Roundup Record–Tribune* (MT) 10 Nov 1/4, This is the scene . . at the Stensvad feed yard . . pen after pen of sleek, fat cattle, others just beginning the 120 day ration to peak marketing condition. **1966–68** *DARE* Tape **CA**90, Feeder cattle are fed at local feed yards; **ID**3, Get 'em concentrated in one spot like on a feed yard.

2 See quot.

1969 *DARE* Tape **TX**70, The stores has feed yard[s] where you could turn your wagon and team, you know, put your wagon and team in there and they'd feed 'em for you.

fee grabber n **TN**

A law enforcement officer; a lawyer.

1967–70 *DARE* (Qu. V9, . . *A policeman*) Inf **TN**23, Fee grabber; (Qu. V10a, . . *A sheriff*) Inf **TN**23, Fee grabber—a deputy sheriff; (Qu. V10c, . . *A constable*) Infs **TN**23, 30, Fee grabber; (Qu. HH44, . . *Lawyers*) Inf **TN**53, Fee grabber. [**1968** *Foxfire* Fall–Winter 40 **nGA,** Despite the fact that the sheriffs at that time [=early days of prohibition] were paid on the "fee system," and thus their entire salary depended on the number of arrests they made, they did not go out looking for stills.] **1970** *Thompson Coll.* **cTN** (as of 1930s), Fee grabber. An officer paid so much a head for the criminals he dragged in.

feel v

1 See quot.

1906 *DN* 3.135 **nwAR,** *Feel, v. intr.* To feel like, be conscious of being. "They felt cheats and story-tellers."

2 To seem, appear.

1934 *Scribner's Mag.* Aug 97/3 **nFL,** I reckon I feel strange to you.

feel a breeze v phr Also *feel a draft, feel the breeze* (or *draft, wind*)

Used to warn a man that his pants are torn or that his fly is open—usu in interrog constrs.

1950 *WELS (Sly words of warning for a tear in the pants)* 1 Inf **swWI,** Feel the draft? Feel the breeze? **1965–70** *DARE* (Qu. W24b, *Sayings to warn a man that his pants are torn or split*) Infs **GA**59, **NJ**63, **OH**38, **VA**31, Do (*or* Don't) you feel a breeze? **TX**11, Are you feelin' a breeze? **IL**78, **NE**11, **NJ**40, **PA**134, Do (*or* Don't) you feel a draft? **WA**4, Can't you feel the wind? (Qu. W24c, *Sayings to warn a man that his trouser-fly is open*) Inf **NY**240, Feel a draft? [**NY**45, Don't you feel a little airy?] **1988** *NADS Letters* **csMI,** *Feel a draft*—widely used by my students from Lansing and Saginaw, but not elsewhere in the state.

feel a draft v phr

1 See **feel a breeze.**

2 To sense hostility or discrimination; see quots.

1957 Shapiro–Hentoff *Jazz Makers* 263, He [=Lester Young] is credited with having originated the widely used phrase (among Negro musicians mostly), "I feel a draft," which can mean the detection of Jim Crow in a person or a general feeling of not being wanted for other reasons. **1970** Major *Dict. Afro-Amer. Slang* 53, *Feel a draft:* the sensing of racism in a white person, especially when directed against oneself. **1986** *NADS Letters* **sNM,** *Feel a draft*—Completely unknown to New Mexicans. . . Widely used in California.

fee lark n [Var of **field lark**] **chiefly Lower Missip Valley** See Map

=meadow lark.

1893 Shands *MS Speech* 29, *Fee-lark.* . . The common name for *meadow-lark,* used by all classes in Mississippi. It is a corruption of *field-lark.* **1927** *DN* 5.474 **Ozarks,** *Feelark.* . . The meadowlark. Probably a contraction of field-lark. These birds are also known as medlars. **1934** Vines *Green Thicket* 60 **cnAL,** He had enough feathers from wild things to make a feather bed. . . He had a little old trunk nearly full of feathers and down from . . feelarks (field larks). **1949** *PADS* 11.6 **wTX** (as of c1920), *Field lark* ['fi,lɑrk]. . . A meadow lark. **1955** Warren *Angels* 189 **LA,** My heart lifted like a fee-lark. **c1960** *Wilson Coll.* **csKY,** Field lark ['fi,lɑrk] usually: The Eastern Meadowlark, common in farming areas. **1965–70** *DARE* (Qu. Q15, . . *Different kinds of larks*) 38 Infs, **chiefly Lower Missip Valley,** Fee lark; (Qu. Q7, . . *Game birds*) Inf **AR**28, Fee lark; (Qu. Q14) Inf **MS**81, Fee lark. **1970** *DARE* File **neTX,** Fee lark (field lark).

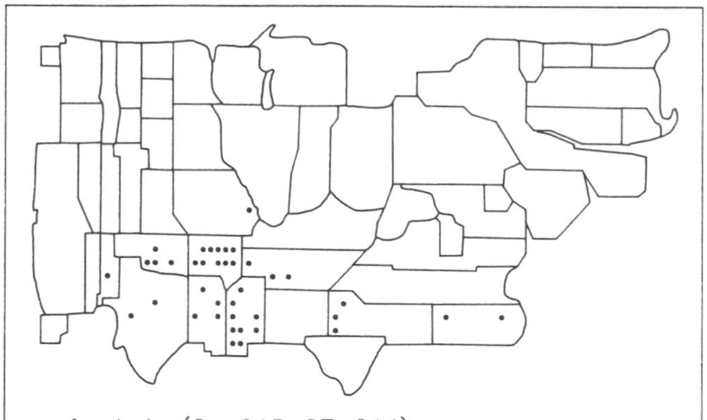

•fee lark (Qq. Q15, Q7, Q14)

feelay See **filé**

feeler n

1939 FWP *Guide TN* 139, A man called a "feeler" [at a Negro baptism] goes ahead of the minister with a pole, feeling the way for the others, so that there may be no "pit falls" [in the river or creek].

feel fine See **feel good**

feel for v phr

To want, like.

1907 (1970) Martin *Betrothal* 111 **sePA,** If you feel for some more supper, go to the cupboard and get a piece. **1940** Writers' Program *Guide MD* 8, 'Feel for' means to 'like', as in 'they all felt for peaches'.

feel for to See **feel to**

feel good v phr Also *feel fine* **chiefly Midl** *joc, euphem*

To be slightly drunk.

1927 Adams *Congaree* 84 **cSC** [Black], He missed the water and got hold of the whiskey glass, and he got to feeling good and commenced to preach. **1942** Berrey–Van den Bark *Amer. Slang* 106.7, *Drunk. . .* feeling . . good. **c1960** *Wilson Coll.* **csKY,** *Feeling good. . .* Beginning to feel the effects of one's drink. **1965–70** *DARE* (Qu. DD13, *When a drinker is just beginning to show the effects of the liquor, you say he's* ______) Infs **KY**10, **OK**13, **TN**44, **TX**36, **VA**33, Feeling fine; **FL**13, **IA**14, **MD**27, **MI**2, Starting to feel (pretty) good; **MD**42, Beginning to feel good.

feeling stone n Also *feely* Cf **executive stone, worry stone**

See quots.

1975 Gould *ME Lingo* 90, *Feeling stones*—Sometimes executive stones. Sea-washed small pebbles from certain Maine islands become so smooth it is pleasurable to rub them idly with the fingers. A solace to high-strung businessmen. Ye Olde Giftie Shoppes sell a lot of them every summer. **1977** *DARE* File **CA** (as of 1950s), My Dad used to carry a feely around in his pocket just because he enjoyed feeling its soft, cool smoothness. It didn't have to be an ocean or river stone; it could be one he had polished on a grinding wheel.

feel in one's bones v phr Also *have a feeling in one's bones*

To have a sense of certainty based on instinct rather than evidence.

[**1844** in 1884 Weed *Life* 2.123, It was in my bones all summer.] **1857** *Lawrence* (Kan.) *Republican* 11 June 4 *(DA* at *bone),* They feel in their bones, that, as American citizens, they have a right to it [political power]. **1868** (1871) Alcott *Little Women* 1.317 **MA,** Hannah "felt in her bones that it was going to be an uncommonly plummy day." **1912** Green *VA Folk-Speech* 172, Christmas is near, I feel it in my bones. **1947** *Sat. Eve. Post* 8 Mar 148/3, We have a feeling in our bones that this plan for the revival of Europe will not do so badly with American public opinion. **1965–70** *DARE* (Qu. GG12, *To have an inner feeling that something is about to happen: "There she comes now, I* ______ *she would."*) Infs **FL**38, **MN**16, **MS**88, **NJ**38, **PA**234, **RI**13, **VA**13, **WI**47, Felt (*or* could feel) it in my bones; **MA**5, [Had a] feeling in my bones.

feel like going v phr

1954 *Harder Coll.* **cwTN,** Feels like going. . . Feeling in good health and spirits.

feel of v phr [*OED feel* v. 2 1751 →; "now only *dial.* and U.S."] **chiefly S Midl, Sth** See Map Cf **taste of, smell of**

To touch, handle.

1817 in 1866 Essex Inst. *Coll.* 8.249 **MA,** My ears were frozen; and . . I felt of them. **1872** Burnham *Memoirs U.S. Secret Service* 225 **sOH,** "Feel of it. . . Put your hand in it," says she. **1884** Twain *Huck. Finn* 284, You come in here and feel of me if you don't believe me. **1907** *DN* 3.215 **nwAR, cCT,** *Of. . .* Used in the phrases "to feel of," "to taste of," "to smell of," etc., to signify a voluntary act. **1926** Roberts *Time of Man* 128 **cKY,** What I want to be a-feelen of a old calf for? **1936** *AmSp* 11.352 **eTX,** The use of the preposition *of* after verbs which in standard speech take the object directly is almost universal: *Taste of it, smell of it, feel of it.* **c1960** *Wilson Coll.* **csKY,** Feel of my big muscle. **1960s** *Hall Coll.* **wNC, eTN,** Feel of it now. **1965–70** *DARE* (Qu. KK57, . . *"That suitcase must weigh forty pounds. Just* ______ *it."*) 42 Infs, **chiefly Sth, S Midl,** Feel of it. **1967** *DARE* Tape **TX**5, An experienced farmer knows when to irrigate by just feeling of the soil.

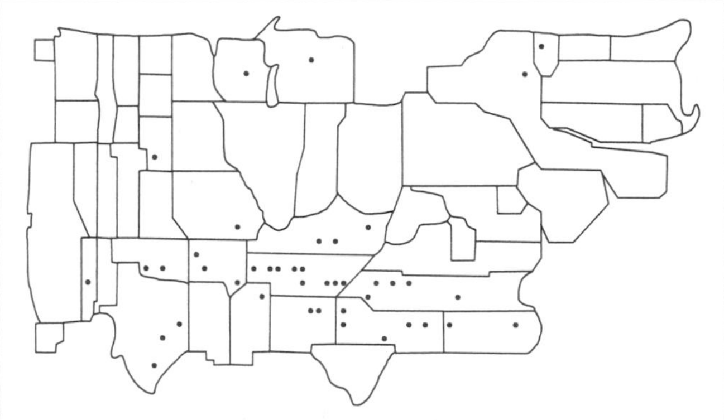

•feel of (Qu. KK57)

feel one's keeping v phr Also *feel one's keep(ings)* [*keeping* support, food, provision] **chiefly S Midl** *somewhat old-fash*

To be in good health and spirits; to feel confident, ambitious.

1927 *AmSp* 2.354 **wcWV,** *Feel his keeping* . . to be in excellent physical condition. "If he is feeling his keeping so well, give him some more work to do." **1942** Berrey–Van den Bark *Amer. Slang* 128.2, *Be in good health. . .* feel one's keeping. **1966–69** *DARE* (Qu. GG19a, *When you can see from the way a person acts that he's feeling important or independent: "He surely is* ______ *these days."*) Infs **AL**28, **AR**39, Feeling his keeping; **LA**12, He feels his keeping; **NJ**57, Feeling his keep (like a well fed animal); (Qu. KK28, *Feeling ambitious and eager to work*) Inf **GA**72, Feelin' his keepin'; **AR**31, Feelin' his keepin's. [5 of 6 Infs old]

feel the breeze, feel the draft See **feel a breeze**

feel the weight of the meeting v phr

Among Quakers: see quots.

1933 *AmSp* 8.1.13 **Philadelphia PA,** *To feel the weight of the meeting.* To get the judgment of the *solid* or *weighty* Friends [=those whose opinions are respected]. **1985** *DARE* File **csWI,** To "feel the weight of the meeting" is to feel a certain pressure both from senior Friends and from the Divine to accept a certain mode of thinking or course of action.

feel the wind See **feel a breeze**

feel to v phr Also rarely *feel for to*

To want, desire; to want to, feel inclined to (do something).

1837 *Knickerbocker* 10.249, We were only . . urging her to accept Mr. Lovejoy's offer. . . But somehow it seems as if she could not any way feel to it. **1859** (1968) Bartlett *Americanisms* 144, To *feel* to do a thing is an expression commonly used by some clergymen, for to feel inclined, to be disposed to do it. **1901** *DN* 2.139 **NY,** *Feel. . .* Desire; wish for. Used with infinitive, as "I feel to go." **1922** Brown *Old Crow* 81 **NEng,** I didn't go ag'in. I didn't feel to. **1931** *PMLA* 46.1304 **sAppalachians,** I feel to know that hit's true. **1948** Hurston *Seraph* 12 **FL,** If you had the sense that God give a june bug you'd feel glad that he feels to scorch [=escort] you to and from. **1974** Fink *Mountain Speech* 9 **wNC, eTN,** I didn't feel for to work. **1977** *DARE* File **csWI,** I don't care, I'll do it if I feel to.

feely See **feeling stone**

feenger See **finger**

feered See **feared**

feeren See **fern**

feery adj [Pronc-sp for *fiery*]

1887 *Scribner's Mag.* 2.474 **AR,** Headlights's dey calls 'er, kase of dem big feery eyes er hern.

fees See **feest**

feesh See **fish** n

feest adj Also sp *feast, fees* [Du *vies* dirty, filthy; particular, fastidious] **chiefly in Du settlement areas, esp NY, N Cent**

1 usu with *of:* Disgusted with; sated by; made nauseous by; nauseated; see also quot 1932.

1859 (1968) Bartlett *Americanisms* 142, *Feast.* A corruption of the Dutch *vies,* nice, fastidious. "I'm feast of it," is a literal translation of the Dutch *Ik ben er vies van,* i.e. I am disgusted with, I loathe it. A New York phrase, mostly confined to the descendants of the Dutch. **1903** *DN* 2.351, *Feest. . .* Used in Iowa, s.e., in the expression, 'I am feest of it.' Also, 'It makes me feest,' the word *feest* in this latter sentence being the equivalent of *sick* or *ad nauseam.* **1904** *DN* 2.396 **NY,** *Feest* [fist], *adj.* Sated. "I was feest of it," referring to maple sugar, of which the speaker had eaten a large quantity. The word or expression was formerly common in central N.Y., but is now almost obsolete. **1932** Smiley *Gloss. New Paltz* **seNY,** In speaking of something that he was almost afraid of Herb Smith used the expression that he was "feast of it". . . It seems to mean being afraid or more particularly leery of a thing or situation. **1933** *Ibid,* You ain't feast to eat anything she cooks. **1943** *AmSp* 18.111, Marjorie Heebink of Baldwin, Wisconsin, writes that 'The expression *I am fees* (with no *t*) *of that* is very common in this Dutch community. It is used to indicate strong repugnance, usually of food. **1966** *DARE* File **nNJ,** "I'm feest of that" means I'm revolted by that.

2 Untidy, unkempt; filthy.

1901 *DN* 2.140 **cnNY,** *Feest* . . Untidy, not clean. "Her house is just feest." St. Lawrence Co., N.Y.; heard from a lady who formerly lived in Canada. **1969** *DARE* (Qu. X52, . . *A person . . who had been sick was looking* ______.) Inf **MI**103, Fees [fis]. That's Dutch, meaning greasy, unkempt. [Inf old, of Du ancestry] **1985** *DARE* File **ceWI,** "That room is fees!" means that it is absolutely filthy. [Inf of Du ancestry]

feet See **foot** n **B1**

feeting n

1 also *feetning:* Footprints, tracks. [*EDD feetens, feetings* (at *footing* sb. 2 "A footprint")]

1663 in 1883 *Archives of MD* 1.472, They had pursued them [=Indians] towards Bush riuer and found them by their feeting to be fiue in number. **1894** *Century Illustr. Mag.* 47.855, In one of the witch stories by which Increase Mather unwittingly sowed seed for his son's Salem harvest, "the feeting of cattle," that is, cattle tracks, are found . . where no cattle have been. **1903** *DN* 2.297 **Cape Cod MA** (as of c1850), *Feeting. . .* Tracks, as *hens' feeting, cats' feeting.* **1966** *DARE* Tape **MA**110, An old, real old Cape Codder wouldn't speak of footprints out there, he'd talk about feetnin'.

2 See **footing.**

feet in the trough, have one's v phr

1968 *DARE* (QR, near Qu. Y52) Inf **AK**2, To have one's feet in the trough—to hold a government job.

feetning See **feeting 1**

feets See **foot** n **B2a(2)**

feetses See **foot** n **B2a(3)**

feetur See **feature** n

feet washing n See **foot washing**

feeze n, v Also sp *fease, feaze, pheese, pheeze* [Engl, Scots, Ir dial, from ME *fesen* to drive off, frighten] *old-fash* Cf **fizz** n[1]

A As noun.

A state of excitement or anxiety.

1647 in 1856 RI (Colony) *Records* 1.174, Larcenie. . . is a fraudulent and felonious taking away another man's personall goods, . . yett without making any assault vpon his person or putting him in a fease. **1846** Worcester *Universal Dict.* 533, *Pheese* . . a fit of fretfulness, is a colloquial, vulgar word in the United States. **1855** Lowell in 1892 *Atlantic Mth.* Dec 749/2, I am not used to being tied to hours or driven. I have always waited on the good genius, and he will not come for being sent after by express; so I am in a *feeze* half the time. **a1883** (1911) Bagby *VA Gentleman* 90, Willing rather to let things rot . . than to get into a Yankee stew and a New England fease the moment anything needs mending. **1889** *AN&Q* 3.107/1 **NYC,** "I am in a perfect pheeze about it," "I've been in a pheeze all day over it." **1899** (1912) Green *VA Folk-Speech* 172, *Feeze. . .* Worry; fret. To be in a *feeze,* to be in a state of excitement. *Feaze.* **1955** Adams *Grandfather* 161 **NY** (as of 19th cent), Canandaigua, New York, Grandfather began, was all of a feeze over the visit of the distinguished Miss Wright.

B As verb.

1 trans: To vex, trouble, faze.

1851 Hall *College Words* 204, A man writes cards during examination to 'feeze the profs'. **1886** [see **B2** below]. **1889** (1971) Farmer *Americanisms* 235, *Feaze, Feeze,* and *Pheeze, To.*—To vex. . . still commonly colloquial in the States, especially Virginia and the South. **1906** *Springfield W. Republican* 27 Dec. 1 *(DAE),* The gentlemen at the head of the Standard oil trust will not be feazed or troubled a bit by these revelations. **1907** Mulford *Bar-20* 137 **West,** "Same old story—lots of gold. Shucks, I've bit on so many of them rumors that they don't feaze me no more." **1940** (1942) Clark *Ox-Bow* 135 **NV** (as of 1885), "How would I know?" I asked again. It didn't feeze him.

2 intrans: To worry, fret.

1886 Amer. Philol. Assoc. *Trans.* 17.38, *To feaze, . .* in the South . . is still used intrans., meaning to be worried, fret, fume = to be in a feaze. . . It is also used trans. in the South in a sense close akin to disturb. **1889** *Century Dict.* 2172, *Feeze, feaze. . .* To fret; be in a fume; worry. **1968** *DARE* (Qu. GG27b, *To get somebody out of an unhappy mood, you might say to him, "Don't* ______.") Inf **NJ**16, Feeze [fiz]. [Inf old]

Feginny See **Virginia**

feint See **faint**

feist n Usu |faɪs(t)|; rarely |fist, faɪf, faɪšt| Also sp *fais(t), faus(t), feice, fice(t), fiest, fife, fise, fist(e), fouce, fyce, fyst(e), phyce* [Abbrs for Engl *fisting-hound, foisting-hound,* ult from *fist* to break wind]

1 freq attrib: A small dog of mixed breed; a cur. **chiefly Sth, SMidl** See Map on p. 384 *freq derog*

[**1770** (1925) Washington *Diaries* 1.371, A small foist looking yellow cur.] **1850** Garrard *Wah-to-yah* 64 **NM,** In our lodge were three huge curs and four cross fiı̄sts [sic]. **1855** *S. Lit. Messenger* 21.228/2, A young lady had a fist-dog (. . we spell it *fist,* because they are not much larger than a man's fist,) to which she was very much attached. **1886** Amer. Philol. Assoc. *Trans.* 17.39, *Fice* (fyce or phyce) is the name used everywhere in the South, and in some parts of the West, for a small worthless cur. **1890** *DN* 1.64 **KY,** *Fice* [faɪs(t)]. **1895** *DN* 1.371 **eTN,** *Fīst.* **1903** *DN* 2.313 **seMO,** *Fist* [fist]. . . Fise. **1908** *DN* 3.309 **eAL, wGA,** *Faus(t), faus(t) dog. . . faist, fais.* "Wun er deze yer lil fausez," is common among the negroes. *Ibid* 310, *Fice, fist. . .* Plural sometimes *fistes, faustes. . . Fice-dog. . .* Same as *fice.* **1934** *WV Review* Dec 77, Fiest. **1934** (1970) Wilson *Backwoods Amer.* 109 **Ozarks,** That ain't no hound—that's jest a fyste pup. **1938** Rawlings *Yearling* 2 **nFL,** Rip the bull-dog and Perk the new feice. **1940** Harris *Folk Plays* 47 **NC,** Hasselin' for breath. . . like a fouce dog. **1941** in 1944 *ADD* **nWV,** Fife [faɪf]. **1949** *Hall Coll.* **eTN,** *Fiste. . .* A little dog that stays around the house and keeps the varmints run off. He barks more than anything else. Just a 'scare dog' you might call him. **c1960** *Wilson Coll.* **csKY,** *Feist dog. . .* A mongrel or nondescript small dog, esp. one that is playful or nosey or always in the way. **1965–70** *DARE* (Qu. J1, . . *A dog of mixed breed*) 14 Infs, **Sth, S Midl,** Fice; **KY**42, **NC**44, Feist; **GA**6, **MS**69, Fice dog; (Qu. J2, . . *Joking or uncomplimentary words . . for dogs*) Infs **CA**22, **MS**33, **NC**81, **VA**40, 46, Fice; **SC**38, Fice dog; **CA**87, 99, Feist; **UT**4, [faɪšt]. **1973** Allen *LAUM* 1.243 (as of c1950), A sharply regional form [for a dog of uncertain antecedents] is *fice,* found almost exclusively in Iowa (24%) and twice in Nebraska (6%) but not elsewhere [in the Upper Midwest]. This word, sometimes appearing as *ficet* /fɑɪst/, is to be correlated with its derivative *ficety (feisty).* **1977** *Verbatim* Dec 7/2, [In the Gulf States] *fice* . . is usually not just a 'small mongrel dog,' but a 'noisy and contentious, dyspepsic little dog,' usually spelled *feist. . .* Indeed, many Southern folk speakers believe the *feist (fice/fyce)* is a breed apart, as distinctive as the Catahoula cur.

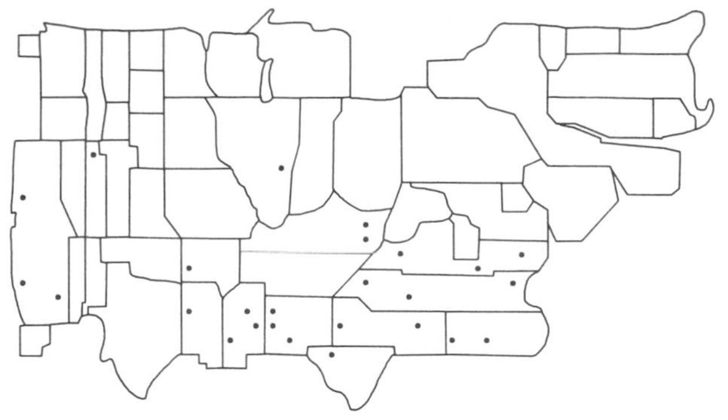

•feist n 1 + varr (Qq. J1, J2)

2 Transf: a person or animal that is irascible, touchy, or bad-tempered. *derog*

1915 *DN* 4.196 [Terms of disparagement], *Fice, fiste, fyst.* **1930** Shoemaker *1300 Words* 21 **cPA Mts** (as of c1900), *Fyst*—A child that is disrespectful to its elders. A small snarling dog. **1935** Davis *Honey* 60 **OR,** I'd watch this kid, too, if I was you. No tellin' when the little feist'll turn on you. **1937** *AmSp* 12.103 **eNE,** A bad-tempered horse may be called a *fyst* or a *bronk.* **1949** *PADS* 11.21 **CO,** *Feist, fist.* . . 1. A small dog, usually bad-tempered. . . 2. A bad-tempered person, esp. an ornery little child.

feist v [**feist n**] **sAppalachians** Cf **feisty adj 2**

To strut, flirt, move so as to draw attention to oneself.

1931 *PMLA* 46.1306 **sAppalachians,** Quit feistin' aroun' me; I'll slap the taste outn ye mouth. **1953** Randolph–Wilson *Down in Holler* 243 **Ozarks,** *Feist.* . . To behave coquettishly or provocatively. "Them Lee gals don't do nothin' but feist all the way home from school." **1954** *Harder Coll.* **cwTN,** Feist [faɪst]—To behave coquettishly or provocatively. **1966–69** *DARE* (Qu. Y22, *To move around in a way to make people take notice of you: "Look at him ________."*) Inf **KY**28, Feisting around; **NC**37, [fa:st].

feister n [Cf **feist v**]

1958 McCulloch *Woods Words* 60 **Pacific NW,** *Feister*—A no-good.

feisty adj Usu |ˈfaɪsti|; rarely |ˈfisti| Also sp *fausty, ficety, ficy, fiesty, fisty, fysty* [**feist n**]

1 Irascible, irritable; impertinent; frisky, mettlesome. **chiefly SMidl**

1890 *DN* 1.64 **KY,** He is fice-ty (frisky). **1895** *DN* 1.371 **eTN,** *Fīsty:* low, mean . . cross. "That cow is fisty." **c1900** in 1944 *ADD* **sIN,** Fysty. **1903** *DN* 2.313 **seMO,** *Fisty* [fisti] . . Impudent; self important. "He's too fisty to suit me." **1908** *DN* 3.310 **eAL, wGA,** *Fausty,* adj. Meddlesome, like a little fice. *Ibid* 311, *Fisty.* **1927** in 1944 *ADD* **WV,** Fiesty. **1949** *PADS* 11.21 **CO,** *Feisty.* . . Angry, looking for trouble. **1954** *Harder Coll.* **cwTN,** [Letter:] That little black calf of yours is fisty. He sucks every cow that goes in the lot. One morning I told mama it was fisty like you. **1965–70** *DARE* (Qu. Z16, *A small child who is rough, misbehaves, and doesn't obey*) Inf **TN**2, Feisty little brat; (Qu. J2, *Joking . . words . . for dogs*) **CA**99, Feisty dog; (Qu. GG39, . . *Looking for reasons to be angry*) **CA**4, **WA**1, Feisty; (Qu. KK27, *A very lively, active old person*) **KY**85, **OR**6, Feisty. **1973** Allen *LAUM* 1.358 (as of c1950), *Feisty,* found only in Iowa . . , is a clear South Midland term so restricted to speech that few of its users [in the Upper Midwest] are sure of its spelling. **1974** Fink *Mountain Speech* 9 **wNC, eTN,** *Ficsty* [sic] . . pert, impudent.

2 Acting so as to show off or draw attention to oneself; putting on airs; flirtatious, of questionable morals. **chiefly S Midl** Cf **feist v**

1906 *DN* 3.136 **nwAR,** *Ficety.* . . (Of a girl.) Tomboyish, fast. "She's too ficety for me." **1917** *DN* 4.412 **KS, KY, wNC,** *Feisty* means when a feller's stuck on hisself and wants to show off—always wigglin' about wanting everybody to see him. **1944** *PADS* 2.55 **MO,** *Feisty* [ˈfaɪstɪ]. . . Flirtatious, giddy; used to describe a vivacious girl whose morals the neighborhood is beginning to question. "I'd wear out a razor-strop on any girl of mine that was as feisty as them two of Rollo Brown's." **1954** *Harder Coll.* **cwTN,** *Feisty* . . [used] of a woman who moves around so that people will take note of her. **c1960** *Wilson Coll.* **csKY,** *Feisty.* . . Showing off, prossy. Also *ficy.* **1961** Sackett–Koch *KS Folkl.* 113, *Feisty.* . . (applied to girls). Wild—not in the sense of being "bad tempered," as sometimes the word is used in the South—saucy or overflirtatious. **1967** *DARE* FW Addit **AR**51, Feisty—prissing around, smarting about, can't sit still. **1969** *DARE* (Qu. Y22, . . *Make people take notice of you*) Inf **KY**85, He's feisty; (Qu. AA4a, . . *Eager to get married*) Inf **KY**5, Feisty [ˈfaɪsti]; (Qu. AA7a, . . *A woman who is very fond of men . . if she's nice about it*) Inf **MO**37, Feisty; (Qu. AA7b, . . *A woman who is very fond of men . . if she's not respectable about it*) Inf **KY**6, Feisty [ˈfaɪsti]; (Qu. HH35, *A woman who puts on a lot of airs: "She's too ________ for me."*) Inf **IL**73, Feisty.

3 Worthless.

1916 *DN* 4.347 **TX, KS,** *Feisty.* . . Worthless. "A little feisty thing."

4 See quot.

c1960 *Wilson Coll.* **csKY,** *Feisty.* . . Sometimes means nosey.

feisty n Also sp *fisty*

1 =**feist n 1.**

1939 *Hall Coll.* **wNC,** That fisty [ˈfaɪstɪ] he was just a-yelpin' like he was lookin' at 'im [=a bear].

2 See quot.

1954 *Harder Coll.* **cwTN,** Feisty; fisty: One who moves about hurriedly: "He's a fisty."

feisty britches n Also sp *ficety breeches* Cf **fiddle-britches**

See quots.

1906 *DN* 3.136 **nwAR,** *Ficety breeches* [faɪstɪ brɪčɪz]. . . Opprobrious epithet applied to a boy by other boys. **1955** Ritchie *Singing Family* 57 **seKY,** Hush, you scamp [=a young girl]. You don't have to holler so loud and act so crazy. Wait'll I catch up with you, little feisty-britches!

felee See **filé**

felicities n pl [Perh from *viscera*]

1909 *DN* 3.411 **neME,** *Felicities.* . . Entrails. A local use of the word.

fell v [Pronc-sp for *fail*] Cf Pronc Intro 3.I.3.d

1982 McCool *Sam McCool's Pittsburghese* 12 **PA,** Fell: the opposite of succeed, as in "I felled my driver's test again."

fell n See **fill** n^2

fella n^1 See **fellow**

fella n^2 See **felly**

fellah, fellar See **fellow**

fell-away See **fall-away**

fellen n See **felonwort**

fellen past ppl See **fall v A3**

feller n^1 See **fellow**

feller n^2 See **felly**

feller n^3, **fellern** See **felon**

fell-field n [Scots, nEngl dial *fell* a rocky hillside; a stretch of high, open untilled land] Cf **fell-piece**

1942 Peattie *Friendly Mts.* 172 **NEng,** Large areas above timber line are of bare rock. . . The only soil, found in small hollows or crevices, is thin and poor. These are sometimes called "fell-fields" or "barrens," and have a ragged, patchy plant cover.

felling See **felon**

felloe n Pronc-spp *fella, feller* [See Intro "Language Changes" IV.1.C]

Std sense, var forms.

1927 *AmSp* 2.354 **WV,** The fellers are all loose. **1954** *Harder Coll.* **cwTN,** Feller. **1967** *DARE* Tape **NY**27, That rim there is called a rim or a fella. You don't very often hear it called a fella, but that was another name for it.

fellon See **felon**

fellonwood See **felonwort**

fellow n Usu |ˈfɛloʊ, ˈfɛlə|; freq |ˈfɛlər| (see Pronc Intro 3.I.12.d) Pronc-spp *fella(h), fellar, feller, felluh*

A Forms.

1795 Dearborn *Columbian Grammar* 135, [In a list of "improprieties":] Feller for Fellow. **1837** Sherwood *Gaz. GA* 69, [In a list of 'provincialisms' to be avoided:] *Feller,* for fellow. **1860** Holmes *Profes-*

sor 38 **MA,** Give a fellah a fo'penny bun in the mornin', an' he downs the whole of it. **1891** (1967) Freeman *New Engl. Nun* 94, She married a real rich fellar from Bostown. **1906** *DN* 3.118 **sIN,** *Fellow*. . . Regularly pronounced *feller*. **1908** *DN* 3.310 **eAL, wGA,** *Feller*. **1922** Gonzales *Black Border* 301 **sSC, GA coasts,** [Gullah glossary], *Felluh*—fellow, fellows. **1933** *AmSp* 8.2.45 **neNY,** Excrescent [r] is not infrequent, as . . *fellow* [fɛlr], *follow* [fɑlr]. That practice, however, is old fashioned and today [fɛlə] and [fɑlə] are rapidly replacing the earlier forms. **1936** *AmSp* 11.161 **eTX,** In addition to the usual sound of [ə] in the final syllable, some . . words . . have [ɚ] in less literate speech. They are: . . *bellow, bellowed, fellow, shallow* [etc]. **1966–68** [see **B1** below].

B Senses.

1 A woman's sweetheart, beau.

1833 Neal *Down-Easters* 1.135 **NEng,** Nice putty stars, but lord you, as the gal said to her feller, if you could only see the bunch thats right over our front door. **1887** in 1950 *AmSp* 25.33 **New Orleans LA,** My feller tells me that Watermeyer . . is looking for a fuss. **1895** *DN* 1.388 **MA, NY,** A young woman's *feller* is the particular one who is "sparkin' " her—paying her attention with possible matrimonial intention. **1937** *AmSp* 12.237 **CO,** She has a feller. **1941** *LANE* Map 399 *(Her Sweetheart)* **throughout NEng,** Fellow, best fellow. **1966–68** *DARE* (Qu. AA3, . . *Names for a sweetheart*) Infs **GA**37, **MI**68, **SC**44, (My) fella; **AR**24, **VA**13, (My) fellow. [4 of 5 Infs old]

2 One, oneself—used by a speaker in reference to himself.

1902 *DN* 2.234 **swIL,** *Feller* . . one; oneself. **1907** *DN* 3.222 **nwAR, sIL,** *Feller* [fɛlə]. . . Fellow; one; one's self. **1916** *DN* 4.275 **KS, NE, NY,** *Feller, fellow*. . . Person: sometimes given feminine application, with reference to herself, by a woman. **1942** McAtee *Dial. Grant Co. IN* 25 (as of 1890s), *Feller* . . one's self; "Don't be too hard on a feller". **c1960** *Wilson Coll.* **csKY,** *Feller*. . . Oneself. "Where can a feller git a drink?"

3 A child.

1939 *Hall Coll.* **wNC, eTN,** While mother'd set and cyard wool, we'd set, little fellers, an' pick cotton seed [female inf]. . . The White Rock in olden times was called the Mother Mountain. I heerd that name when we was little fellows [male inf]. **1967** Wilson *Folkways Mammoth Cave No. 2* 18 **csKY,** Before baby blankets came into use, shawls were used to wrap the little fellows. **1980** *DARE* File, A colleague from South Carolina frequently used "fellows" to refer to his children.

4 A Black man. Cf **5** below

1842 Buckingham *Slave States* 2.29 **SC,** The men are usually called "boys," whatever may be their age; and very often "fellows." **1859** (1968) Bartlett *Americanisms, Fellow* or *Black Fellow*. A black man. Southern.

5 See quot. Cf **4** above

1941 Percy *Lanterns* 307 **nwMS,** When a Negro now speaks of a "man" he means a Negro; when he speaks of a "fellow" he means a white man.

6 A mythical person cited as an authority: see **as the feller says.**

fellow and a wench, a n

1952 Brown *NC Folkl.* 1.539, *Fellow, a—and a wench*. . . A pair of mismatched socks or stockings; that is, a companion and a noncompanion. I have heard the expression used only in reference to socks or hose, but I suspect that it may apply to a mismatched pair of any wearing apparel.

fellowly adj

Sociable, companionable.

1928 Chapman *Happy Mt.* 24, **seTN,** The Howards' farmstead was fere and fellowly with the countryside. *Ibid* 157, It might be the folks therein were fellowly, so he hollered, but the man that came to the door was a colored man, and Waits's manners so far forsook him that he turned and ran. **1940** Weygandt *Down Jersey* 72 **sNJ,** "The Man" said very little, but his slow smile, his slow movements, the angle at which he smoked his corncob, his pats and pretended reprimands of his dog . . made a background of human acceptance of the will of God that was engaging and fellowly.

fellowship v [By ext from use in ref to churches and church members]

1 To associate with, be on familiar terms with.

1861 *Atlantic Mth.* Feb (Schele de Vere *Americanisms* 238), No, thanky, Miss Randall, Dely Bligh aint such a fool as that yet; she hasn't never *fellowshipped* the minister, though he did court her . . considerably of a spell. **1878** (1887) Cooke *Happy Dodd* 368 **NEng,** 'Taint natur that a great lazy sozzlin' girl is one a woman will fellowship if she ain't noway related. **1884** Baldwin *Yankee School-Teacher* 21 **NY,** Didn't he now, Marun? (I can't Miss ye! Seems 's if I'd allers fellowshiped ye!) **1949** Webber *Backwoods Teacher* 16 **Ozarks,** Hit's all right to fellowship with him a little, of course.

2 See quot.

1946 Stuart *Tales Plum Grove* 158 **KY,** Before we really begin this service for a departed Brother . . we had better 'fellowship.' Now if any of you Brothers and Sisters know of anybody that you have anything against . . get up and tell us about it here.

fell-piece n Also *felled piece* [*fell* to cut down] Cf **cut-down n1, fell-field**

A piece of land from which the trees have been cut but not yet removed.

[**1839** Holmes *Rept. Aroostook R.* 54 **nME,** Some prefer to let the *"chopping," or trees that are fell, lie until the next spring.*] **1851** Sibley *Hist. Union* 98 **csME,** After the trees had been left to dry through a considerable part of the season, the 'cut-down,' or 'fell-piece,' was set on fire. **a1874** in 1949 *PADS* 11.31 **ME,** He worked the taxes in his bills / Upon a fell-piece that he cleared. **1912** Oak *Hist. Garland ME* 149, The "felled piece" having been cleared of the leaves and small limbs by fire, the work of hand-piling was next in order.

felluh See **fellow**

fellum See **felon**

felon n Pronc-spp *feller(n), felling, fellon, felm, fellum* Cf **bone felon, felony**

A severe inflammation, usu in a finger or toe and often involving a bone.

1840 in 1956 Eliason *Tarheel Talk* 310 **NC,** Felm. **c1890** in 1944 *ADD* **GA,** A bone-fellum. **1899** (1912) Green *VA Folk-Speech* 172, Fellon. **1941** Writers' Program SC *Folk Tales* 115, *Boon-feller*—bone-felon. **1943** *LANE* Map 512, 1 inf, **nwCT,** A felon is an exaggerated boil that starts on the bone; 1 inf, **seMA,** Felon, on the hand. **1950** *WELS* 43 Infs, **WI,** Felon. **1954** *Harder Coll.* **cwTN,** I'm a-gonna git t'at bone fellern ['fɛlərn] lanched [=lanced] today. **1965–70** *DARE* (Qu. BB30, *What do you call a hard, painful swelling [often on a finger] that seems to come from deep under the skin?*) 408 Infs, **widespread, but less freq Sth, Midl,** Felon; 219 Infs, **chiefly Sth, Midl,** Bone felon; 13 Infs, **scattered,** Fellum; 12 Infs, **chiefly S Atl,** Bone fellum; **KY**5, Bone ['fʌlɪŋ]; **MD**24, Bone felling ['fɛlɪŋ]; **VA**42, Joint felon; **KY**34, Joint fellum; [**NY**70, Thellum [Inf doubtful]]. [Of all Infs responding to the question, 69% were old; of those giving these responses, 75% were old.]

felon herb n [From its use in treating **felons**]

=**mugwort.**

1900 Lyons *Plant Names* 47, *Artemisia vulgaris* . . Felon-herb. **1910** Graves *Flowering Plants* 401 **CT,** *Artemisia vulgaris* . . Felon-herb. **1976** Bailey–Bailey *Hortus Third* 113.

felonweed n [From its use in treatig **felons**]

A **ragwort** (here: *Senecio jacobæa*).

1900 Lyons *Plant Names* 342, *Senecio Jacobæa* . . Felon-weed. **1967** *DARE* (Qu. BB50c, *Remedies for infections*) Inf **KY**34, Fellumweed—tall, dark green, with a long leaf (7–8 inches).

felonwort n Also *fellen, fellonwood* [From its use in treating **felons**]

A **bittersweet** (here: *Solanum dulcamara*).

1900 Lyons *Plant Names* 349, *S. Dulcamara*. . . Felonwort. . . Stipites dulcamarae, mildly narcotic, sedative. **1930** Sievers *Amer. Med. Plants* 11, *Bitter Nightshade*. . . *Other common names*. . . Felonwort. **1940** Clute *Amer. Plant Names* 51, *S[olanum] dulcamara*. . . Fellen, felonwort. **1959** Carleton *Index Herb. Plants* 45, *Fellen*. . . *Fellonwood*. . . *Fellon-wort:* Solanum dulcamara. **1973** Hitchcock–Cronquist *Flora Pacific NW* 412, Eurasian sp., widely intro in thickets, clearings, and open woods; bittersweet, . . felonwort.

‡felony n [Prob folk-etym or malapropism for **felon**]

1969 *DARE* (Qu. BB30, . . *A hard, painful swelling [often on a finger] that seems to come from deep under the skin*) Inf **CA**158, A felony.

felt leaf See **feltwort 1**

feltleaf willow n [See quot 1908]

A **willow** *(Salix alaxensis)* native to Alaska. Also called **diamond willow**

1908 Sudworth *Forest Trees Pacific* 236, Feltleaf willow, so called on account of the felt-like, woolly covering of its leaves, was known for over thirty years as a low shrub. It was only about eight years ago that it was found to become a tree. . . The yearling twigs are . . densely covered with white hairs . . ; later the twigs lose this covering. **1922** Sargent *Manual Trees* 157, *Feltleaf Willow. Leaves* . . coated above . . with thin pale deciduous tomentum and covered below with a thick mass of snowy white lustrous hairs persistent on the mature leaves. **1972** Viereck–Little *AK Trees* 112, Feltleaf willow is a preferred browse species of moose. . . It is reported that the inner bark has served as food for humans. **1979** Little *Checklist U.S. Trees* 258, *Feltleaf willow*. . . Almost throughout Alaska.

felt-plant n [See quot 1941]

A plant of the genus *Horsfordia*.

1941 Jaeger *Wildflowers* 143 **Desert SW,** *Yellow Felt-Plant. Horsfordia Newberryi*. . . The plants are covered with a dense, yellow felt of stellate hairs. **1957** Jaeger *N. Amer. Deserts* 264, In the pink-flowered felt-plants the stems may reach a height of almost 10 feet.

felt-thorn n [From its being both spiny and woolly]

=**horsebrush 1.**

1941 Jaeger *Wildflowers* 303 **Desert SW,** Bald-leaved Felt-thorn. *Tetradymia glabrata. Ibid* 306, Narrow-scaled Felt-thorn. *Tetradymia stenolepis*. . . Much-branched shrub, covered with a close-appressed white wool. . . Gray Felt-thorn. *Tetradymia canescens*. . . White Felt-thorn. *Tetradymia comosa.*

feltwort n

1 also *felt leaf:* =**mullein.** [From the woolly leaves]

1900 Lyons *Plant Names* 389, *V. Thapsus*. . . Feltwort. **1930** U.S. Dept. Ag. *Misc. Pub.* 77.42, *Mullein. . . Other common names*. . . Feltwort. **1967** *DARE* (Qu. S20) Inf **MI**67, Mullein—We used to call it felt leaf and Indian tobacco. **1971** Krochmal *Appalachia Med. Plants* 264, Feltwort.

2 A **green gentian** (here: *Frasera parryi*).

1959 Carleton *Index Herb. Plants* 45, *Felt-wort*. . . Frasera parryi.

fem n[1] [See quot]

1958 *PADS* 29.33 **WI,** *Fem: n.* A small marble, a *fiver*. . . Prob. from Norw. *fem,* five.

fem n[2] [Perh abbr for *effeminate*]

An effeminate man.

1969–70 *DARE* (Qu. HH38, *A womanish man*) Inf **IL**98, Fem; (Qu. HH39, *A homosexual man*) **CA**213, Fem.

female complaint n Also *female trouble euphem*

Any of various illnesses of women, usu related to reproductive functions.

1930 Faulkner *As I Lay Dying* 237 **MS,** "It's the female trouble," she says. . . "Ah," I says. "Have you got female troubles or do you want female troubles?" **1937** Sandoz *Slogum* 57 **NE** (as of 1900–20), She read to them, delicately, of the horrid appetites of husbands and of the dreadful female trouble and disease that followed. **1938** Hertzler *Horse & Buggy Dr.* 135 **KS** (as of early 20th cent), The complaints of women make up a large part of office practice. These are vaguely termed female complaints. . . By female complaints are generally understood disturbances of organs peculiar to women, but they do not include all diseases that women complain of. **1960** Williams *Walk Egypt* 254 **GA,** You reckon . . you can tell what a plant is good for by how it looks? Like liver-leaf for liver trouble, squaw root for female complaint . . ? **1968** *DARE* (Qu. X8, . . *Organs inside the body*) Inf **MI**75, Female trouble [laughter]. **1970** *Thompson Coll.* **AL** (as of 1930s), Female trouble . . genito-urinary ailments.

female fern n Cf **male fern**

=**lady fern.**

1795 Winterbotham *Amer. U.S.* 3.399, Among the native and uncultivated plants of New-England, the following have been employed for medicinal purposes. . . Moonwort, . . Female fern. **1843** Torrey *Flora NY* 2.493, *Asplenium Filix-fœmina*. . . Female-fern. . . Moist shady woods. **1900** Lyons *Plant Names* 51, *Asplenium Filix-foemina* . . Female Fern.

femmy adj, adv [Perh var of *effeminate*] Cf **fem** n[2]

1967–68 *DARE* (Qu. HH11a, *[A man] who is too particular or fussy*) Inf **WA**22, Femmy; (Qu. HH38, *A womanish man*) Inf **MN**28, Femmy-acting.

fen exclam Also *fain(s), fan, fend, fens, fin(s), finney, finns* [Aphet varr of *defend* forbid, or of *defense*] Cf **ven**

In marbles and other games: used (usu in comb phr) as a call to give one player a particular advantage or to deny an advantage to another.

1843 (1916) Hall *New Purchase* 42 **sePA,** Man-lay!—Clearings!—'fen!—knuckle-down! **1859** (1968) Bartlett *Americanisms* 145, *Fen.* A prohibitory exclamation used by boys in their games; as, "Fen play!" i.e. I forbid you to play, stop! **1883** Foote *Led-Horse* 62 **CO,** "What is it the boys say when they play marbles?—'Fend' something," she asked with fitful gayety. "Fend dubs?" Hilgard suggested. **1890** Howells *Boy's Town* 82 **sOH,** A great many points were always coming up: . . whether, when another boy's toy drove one marble against another and knocked both out of the ring, he holloed "Fen doubs!" before the other fellow holloed "Doubs!" **1890** *DN* 1.61 **Cincinnati OH,** *Fen:* to forbid; used especially by boys playing marbles. "Fen heist" [haɪst]: don't hoist or raise your hand while shooting. **1892** *DN* 1.219 **DC,** *Fen.* When you said "fen clarances" your opponent had no right to *clear* away the rubbish lying between his marble and yours. The phrase "fen everything" deprived your opponent of all privileges, such as *clarances.* When boys saw a dead animal they would say, "fen all round my family and spit out," and then would spit. **1895** *Searcher* 1.7/2 **CT,** In Connecticut, where I was "brought up" . . , we played the game of marbles . . with the aid of . . "fen inching"—(that is, shoot from where your "annie" lies, not an inch or two nearer the triangle). **1907** *German Amer. Annals* 9.375 **sePA,** Fen-Hext. No charming. Used in marbles meaning that your opponent must not make a cross on the ground to bewitch you. "You daren't do that; I said *fen-hext.*" **1915** in 1944 *ADD* **cNY,** 'No fin hunchin'!' = [Don't hoist or raise your hand while shooting]. **1940** *Qrly. Jrl. Speech* 26.266 **nwVA,** In a game, if a child misses, he may call "Finney slips" and have another turn. **1950** *WELS* 1 Inf, **WI,** Fan dubbs; 1 Inf, Fan. **1955** *PADS* 23.17, *Fen (fain, fend, vence, vent, vents, van, ven): interj*. . . (aphetic form of either *defend* or *prevent*). A call preceding another call, preventing or forbidding an advantage of the shooter. A common marble term. **1956** *AmSp* 31.37, *Fain, fains, fen, fens, fin, fins, vance, ven, venture, vents*—these are all recorded variants of the same word, which was probably originally *fend,* which is in turn, . . a shortened form of *defend* in its old sense of 'forbid.' **1958** *PADS* 29.33 **WI,** *Fan*. . . Same as *fen*. . . *Fan dubs*. . . Same as *fend dubs*. . . *Fin-flick*. . . *Fin* is a var. of *fen.* **1960** *DE Folkl. Bulletin* Oct 36/2, No fin fudgin (said to curb the marble-player who is too aggressive). **1968** *DARE* (Qu. EE17, *In a game of tag, if a player wants to rest, what does he call out so that he can't be tagged?*) Inf **NY**66, Fen! **1973** Ferretti *Marble Book* 45 **NYC,** *Fens!* Or Fins! or Finns! An all-inclusive call by which a player can suspend all rules until he has planned his shot.

'fen' v See **fend** v

fenagle See **finagle**

fence n, v Usu |fɛnts|; also |fɛns|; freq **esp eNEng, Sth** |fɛən(t)s|; freq **esp Sth, S Midl,** |fɪn(t)s|; occas |fæn(t)s, fens| Pronc-spp *fa-ence, fayence, fench, fince, fy-ence*

A Forms.

1911 *DN* 3.538 **eKY,** *Fence*. . . Pronounced fāyence. **1916** in 1944 *ADD* **sAppalachians,** Fy-ence, fa-ence. **1921** Haswell *Daughter Ozarks* 140 (as of 1880s), Take a'hould here, John, and help me throw this fince. **1922** Gonzales *Black Border* 301 **sSC, GA coasts** [Gullah glossary], *Fench*—(n. and v.) fence, fences, fenced, fencing. **1930** Stoney–Shelby *Black Genesis* 25 **seSC,** When de Garden is all fixed up an' de fench done, God laid down de gold tools he been workin' wid. **1942** Hall *Smoky Mt. Speech* 19, Words . . in which [ɛ] is often raised to or toward [ɪ]: . . fence. **c1960** *Wilson Coll.* **csKY,** *Fence* is often [fæns]. **1961** Kurath–McDavid *Pronc. Engl.* Map 9, Diaphones and Variants of /ɛ/ in *fence.* [The monophthong [ɛ] predominates in the North except in eastern New England, where [ɛə] is also current. Diphthongal [ɛə] and lower high-front [ɪ] prevail in the South, except in the Chesapeake Bay and Charleston areas, and in western South Carolina, where [ɛ] is current.] **1966** *DARE* (Qu. U40) Inf **SC**11, On the fence [fe˞ɪns]. **1976** Allen *LAUM* 3.300 (as of c1950), An analysis of the pronunciation of *answer, dance, fence,* . . reveals that only a small proportion (17%) of all infs. are recorded with /ns/ [as opposed to /nts/] in even one of these words, and most of these are in eastern Iowa and eastern Minnesota.

B As noun.

1 A fenced-in area.

1914 *DN* 4.106 **KS,** *Fence*. . . Field; pasture. "Put the cattle in the fence." **1967** *DARE* (Qu. M13, . . *Space near the barn with a fence around it*) Inf **SC**39, In the fence.

2 also *fencies:* See quot.

1968–69 *DARE* (Qu. EE11, *Bat-and-ball games for just a few players*) Inf **IL97**, Fence; **PA76**, Fencies—only three play; there is no running of bases.

C As verb.

With *with:* To share a fenced boundary with.

1959 *VT Hist.* new ser 27.135, *Fence with. . .* to have boundaries running side by side and a common fence between. Common. Southern Vermont.

fence adj See **fence-corner 2**

fence balk n Cf **balk 1**

See quots.

1917 *DN* 4.391 **neOH,** *Fence-balk. . .* The strip of uncultivated land left after the removal of a fence. **1927** *AmSp* 2.354 **WV,** *Fence-balk . .* the uncultivated ground when the fence is removed. "That fence-balk will have to be grubbed out."

fence breaker n Cf **fence lifter**

1966 Dakin *Dial. Vocab. Ohio R. Valley* 2.21 **KY,** Terms for severe rainstorms. . . [*fence breaker* 1 inf; *fence breaker and gulley maker* 1 inf].

fence-cap See **cap** n^1 **12**

fence-corner adj, adv Also abbr *fence*

Of illegitimate or uncertain ancestry; accidentally (bred).

[**c1937** in 1977 *Amer. Slave Suppl. 1* 1.153 **AL,** When we knowed we's free. . . Babies was bein born in fence-corners; anywhere.] **1950** *WELS (A dog of mixed breed)* 1 Inf, **ceWI,** Fence-corner breed; *(A horse that was not intentionally bred)* 1 Inf, **ceWI,** Fence-corner bred. [**1958** *Hand Coll.* **sIN** (as of c1920), When an illegitimate child was born, my father would say, "they found it in a fence corner."] **1967** *DARE* (Qu. Z11b, . . *A child of unwed parents*) Inf **MO5**, Fence-corner or hay-stack kid. **1973** Allen *LAUM* 1.345 **IA** (as of c1950), [Of an illegitimate child:] "If he were a horse, he'd be a 'fence colt.' "

fence cornering vbl n Also *fence worming* Cf **fencerow; fence worm, lay**

1968 Adams *Western Words* 110, *Fence cornering*—A style of bucking in which the horse zigzags in a manner resembling the zigzags of the frontier rail fence. Also called *fence-worming.*

fence-corner weed n

A **nightshade** (here: *Solanum triquetrum*).

1951 *PADS* 15.39 **TX,** *Solanum triquetrum. . .* Fence-corner weed.

fence crawler n

See quots.

1936 Adams *Cowboy Lingo* 74, A cow that could not be kept in a pasture by a fence was known as a 'fence-crawler.' **1938** FWP *Guide SD* 86, *Fence-crawler:* a breachy animal that cannot be held in a fence.

fencediver n

=**loon.**

1909 *DN* 3.411 **neME,** *Fencediver. . .* A loon.

fence hackee See **ground hackee**

fence law n Cf **fence viewer**

A law regulating the erection of fences to keep livestock out of fields.

1858 Warder *Hedges* 143, The courtesy of its [=the Cincinnati Law Library's] Directors has enabled me to gather the material for this exposition of the fence-laws of our country. **1944** Clark *Pills* 59 **Sth,** Few issues were so hotly debated as that of fence laws. **1956** *Hall Coll.* **eTN,** At that time we had what we called a Fence law. . . They'd split rails and build rail fences to protect their crops. The law was to build it five rails high, and if a cow brute broke over that, and it five rails high, the owner of the brute had to pay for the damage. **c1960** *Ibid,* Fence law—A law requiring owners of property to build a fence around their fields to protect them from cattle which were then allowed free, open range.

fence lifter n Cf **goose-drownder, gully washer, trash mover** and *DS* B24, 25

A very heavy rain.

1933 *AmSp* 8.1.49 **Ozarks,** Lesser showers [than *goose drownders*] are called *fence-lifters* or *gully-washers.* **1944** Adams *Western Words* 58, *Fence lifter*—A very hard rain, when, as Peewee Deewees used to say, "The weather gets plumb wholesale." **1954** *Harder Coll.* **cwTN,** Fence-lifter. . . A heavy rain.

fence lizard n

1 Either of two **swifts:** *Sceloporus occidentalis* or *S. undulatus.* [See quot 1900] For other names of *S. undulatus* see **alligator** n^1 **B2, alligator lizard 1, blue scorpion, granny hatchet, pine lizard, rustygut, rusty jack, scaly lizard, scorpion, scorpion lizard**

1869 *Amer. Naturalist* 3.478 **seCA,** A large Fence Lizard *(Sceloporus magister?),* eight inches long, began to frequent the trees March 20th. **1900** U.S. Natl. Museum *Annual Rept. for 1898* 373, The *Sceloporus undulatus,* or "Fence lizard," as it is commonly called, is abundant in dry and wild regions in the Alleghenian and Carolinian districts of the Eastern region. It is usually seen running on fences, logs, or trunks of trees with great activity. **1928** Pope–Dickinson *Amphibians* 43, *Pine Lizard. . .* Other common names are Common Swift, Brown Swift and Fence Lizard. **1955** *DE Folkl. Bulletin* Mar 17/1, As she stooped to pick up a certain piece [of firewood] she saw a blue-throated "scorpion lizard" (fence lizard) resting on it. The male lizard is thought to be poisonous. **1964** Lowe *Vertebrates* 161 **AZ,** Eastern Fence Lizard. . . climbs and suns on yuccas, trees, logs, rocks, fenceposts, etc. **1979** Behler–King *Audubon Field Guide Reptiles* 525, Western Fence Lizard *(Sceloporus occidentalis). . .* Frequents stone fences, fence posts, old buildings. *Ibid* 529, Eastern Fence Lizard *(Sceloporus undulatus). . .* Generally sunny locations: favors rotting logs.

2 Transf: see quot. Cf **fence-corner**

1968 *DARE* (Qu. HH37, *An immoral woman*) Inf **MD23**, A fence lizard. An old-fashioned word that implies she lies in fence corners.

fence lock n

1946 *PADS* 6.13 **NC** (as of c1900), *Fence lock. . .* An angle made by the interlocking rails of a fence. . . Common.

fence man See **fence viewer**

fence moss n

A **ball moss** (here: *Tillandsia recurvata*).

1951 *PADS* 15.28 **TX,** *Diaphoranthema recurvata. . .* Bunch, . . or fence, moss. It grows on . . wire fences.

fence mouse n Also sp *fensemaus, fenzemaus* **esp in Ger settlement areas** Cf **fancy mouse**

A **ground squirrel n b** or a **chipmunk** (here: *Tamias striatus*).

1857 U.S. Patent Office *Annual Rept. for 1856: Ag.* 75, In Northern Illinois, I have heard the German farmers very generally call it [the striped and spotted prairie-squirrel, *Spermophilus tredecimlineatus*] "Fence Mouse," which name they also apply to the Tamias striatus. [**1924** Lambert *PA Ger. Dict.* 191, Fensemaus . . chipmunk, (*fence-mouse*).] **1950** *WELS (Other names for the chipmunk)* 2 Infs, **WI,** Fence mouse. **1967** *PADS* 47.6 **cPA,** Fenzemaus, 'chipmunk'.

fence, on the adj phr

1 Ready to change into a different state or condition.

1968 *DARE* (Qu. H58) Inf **LA40**, On the fence. . . That's when it [=milk] is just about ready to go over; (Qu. K14, *Milk that has a taste from something the cow ate in the pasture*) Inf **LA40**, On the fence. That's when it's just beginning to sour.

2 Financially embarrassed.

1966 *DARE* (Qu. U40, *Somebody who is temporarily out of money: You might say, "At the moment he's ______."*) Inf **SC11**, On the fence.

fence post n

1 A toothpick. *joc*

1950 *WELS* 1 Inf, **seWI,** Fence post. **1968–69** *DARE* (Qu. G11) Inf **IL63A**, Fence post; **MN33**, Small fence post (father's term).

2 A household match. *joc* Cf *DS* F46

1943 *AN&Q* 3.120/1, Household Matches: Regional Names. . . I myself have heard them referred to as "cordwood," "fence posts," and "railroad ties".

3 in phr *deaf as a fence post:* See **post, deaf as a.**

4 in phr *hatched on a fence post:* See quot. Cf **fence-corner**

1968 *DARE* (Qu. Z11b, . . *A child of unwed parents*) Inf **IA31**, "Hatched on a fence post" if the father never showed himself. A put-off for further questions.

fence-post bird n

=**kingbird.**

1969 *DARE* (Qu. Q14, . . *Other names . . for . . kingbird*) Inf **MA30**, Fence-post bird.

fence-post hole n

A nonexistent item used as the basis for a practical joke.

1968 *DARE* (Qu. CC17, *Imaginary animals or monsters that people . . [use] to tease greenhorns*) Inf **WI**30, Wild fence-post holes!

fencer See **fence rider 1**

fence rail n

1 A very thin person.

[**1909** *DN* 3.380 **eAL, wGA,** *Thin as a (fence) rail. . .* Very thin, emaciated.] **c1960** *Wilson Coll.* **csKY,** Fence rail. . . A very thin, lanky person. **1966–70** *DARE* (Qu. X49) Infs **MA**75, **OH**48, 78, **PA**214, **WY**2, Fence rail.

2 A cattle brand consisting of a long horizontal line.

1961 Adams *Old-Time Cowhand* 261, The straight horizontal line, if long, like John Chisum's brand, which extended from shoulder to tail is, [sic] knowed as the "fence rail."

3 =**walking stick.**

1967 *DARE* (Qu. R9a, *An insect from two to four inches long that lives in bushes and looks like a dead twig*) Inf **LA**8, Fence rail.

fence rider n

1 also *fencer:* See quot 1968. **West**

1885 *Wkly. New Mexican Rev.* 12 Feb. 4/3 *(DA),* When one or more of the wires [about the ranch] are broken the ringing bells in the house signal the break, locating the same, thus saving the expense of the fence rider. **1913** *DN* 4.26 **NW,** *Fence rider. . .* One who rides around the big cattle enclosures and repairs the breaks in the fence, usually a cowboy. Used generally in the cattle-raising country. "The fence riders were gone for three days." **1968** Adams *Western Words* 110, *Fence rider*—A latter-day cowboy who keeps barbed-wire fences in repair; also called *fencer.* He rides leisurely along the fence, following a narrow, ever deepening trail that has been cut by many earlier trips. During his journey he watches for broken or loose wires, fallen posts, missing staples, water gaps that may have washed deep enough to allow cattle to get under the fence, open or tampered-with gates, and anything else that lessens the security of the fence.

2 See quot.

1929 *AmSp* 5.54 **NE,** When horses are being "broke," trained for riding, in the corrals, some of the men might perch themselves on the fence to watch the activity and are at the "opera," or are "fence riding." They are facetiously called "fence riders."

fencerow n, v Cf **fence cornering**

Of a horse: a style of bucking; to buck in such a way; see quot 1937.

1933 *AmSp* 8.1.28 **nTX,** *Fence-row.* A style of pitching. **1937** *DN* 6.619 **swTX,** The horse is *fence rowing* when he bows or humps his back and permits his front legs to come down together, first on one side and then on the other.

fence stretcher See **stretcher**

fence tag n

A children's game; see quots.

1891 *Jrl. Amer. Folkl.* 4.222 **Brooklyn NYc,** *Fence Tag.* Bounds are chosen along a fence. "It" gives the other players a chance to get over the fence, and chases them until he tags one of them, who becomes "it" for the next game. The players jump over the fence and back again, as they are pursued, but are only allowed to cross the fence within the bounds. **1909** (1923) Bancroft *Games* 85, *Fence Tag. . .* A certain length of fence is chosen. . . The one who is It gives the other players a slight start in which to vault over the fence, when he immediately vaults over and tries to tag them. This tagging may be done only when both players are on the same side of the fence. **1923** Acker *400 Games* 95, *Fence Tag. . .* The players start on one side of a fence; "it" on the other. "It" vaults the fence and tries to tag the players . . [who] dodge by going back and forth over the fence.

fence, up on top of the adj phr [Var of *on top of the world*]

1970 *DARE* (Qu. BB47, *Feeling in the best of health and spirits: "I'm feeling ______!"*) Inf **NC**83, Up on top of the fence.

fence viewer n Also *fence man* **chiefly NEng** *old-fash* Cf **field driver**

A local official who regulates the building of fences, inspects them, and settles disputes concerning them.

[**1657** in 1887 East Hampton NY *Records* 1.113 **NY,** It is farther ordered yt Tho Chatfeild is chosen to vew the fences yt they be kept sufisient accordinge to law.] **1661** in 1883 Dorchester MA *Town Rec.* 109, Fence viewers: for the necke of Land[,] Richard Withington [etc]. **1699** in 1880 Groton MA *Early Rec.* 118, For fence men Joseph laken [sic] and Joseph Cade [were chosen]. **1771** in 1914 Copley–Pelham *Letters* 125 **Boston MA,** She will apply to the Fence Viewers to have the Fences made upp. **1858** Warder *Hedges* 162 **WI,** Fence-viewers [are] to assign the portions to each occupant when they cannot agree. **1917** *DN* 4.379 **MA, KS,** The fence-viewer in country districts to-day is an officer (of whom there are usually three in each town) who determines the portion of fences to be built by each property owner, and who "views" fences that are put up to see that they conform to legal requirements. **1931–33** *LANE Worksheets* 3 Infs, **CT, MA, RI,** Fence viewer. **1940** Writers' Program *Guide NY* 546 (as of 1808), Local governmental offices included . . fence viewers. **1940** Writers' Program *Guide OH* 219 (as of 1800), Officially, he held only the office of 'fence viewer', but he kept the settlement together. **1975** Gould *ME Lingo* 90, *Fence Viewer*—A minor town official whose duties have largely become obsolete. In early days there was frequent dispute between neighbors as to how much of a line fence each should build and maintain. The board of three *fence viewers* would adjudicate. . . Although his day is done, the *fence viewer* is still a statutory town officer, and some towns still appoint them; an empty honor. A man who is busy as a *fence viewer* will not be doing much.

fence with See **fence C**

fence worm See **worm**

fence worming See **fence cornering**

fence worm, lay v phr [From the zigzag course of a **worm fence**] Cf **fence cornering, fence-row**

1873 Morrell *Flowers & Fruits* 304 **TX,** As I approached the house of my old friend Morrell, . . the horse . . commenced "pitching," or, as the old Texans sometimes said, "laying fence-worm."

fench See **fence** n, v

fencies See **fence B2**

fend v Also sp *'fen'* [Aphet forms of *defend*]

1922 Gonzales *Black Border* 301 **sSC, GA coasts** [Gullah glossary], *'Fen'*—fend, defend. **1927** Adams *Congaree* 37 **cSC** [Black], Kill him if he try to 'fend he-self. **c1938** in 1970 Hyatt *Hoodoo* 2.1477 **seGA,** Now, *Peelee,* ah want chew to 'fend dis case.

fend exclam See **fen**

fendue groier, fendu groijer See **vendue crier**

fenig(g)le See **finagle**

fennel n

A **sneezeweed** (here: *Helenium amarum*).

1935 (1943) Muenscher *Weeds* 495, Fennel, . . Sneeze-weed. . . Meadows, pastures, yards, waste places and roadsides. **1940** Clute *Amer. Plant Names* 260, *Helenium tenuifolium.* Fennel.

fennel-flower n

Std: A plant of the genus *Nigella* (esp *N. damascena*). Also called **devil-in-the-bush, jack-in-the-bush, jack-in-the-pulpit, lady-in-a-chaise, lady-in-the-green, love-in-a-mist, love-in-a-puzzle, maid-in-the-mist, ragged lady, ragged sailor, St. Catherine's flower**

fen orchid n Also *fen orchis*

A **twayblade** (here: *Liparis loeselii*).

1901 Mohr *Plant Life AL* 458, *Leptorchis loeselii. . .* Fen Orchis. **1910** Graves *Flowering Plants* 136 **CT,** *Liparis Loeselii. . .* Fen Orchis. . . Bogs, moist woods and wet shaded banks. **1936** Winter *Plants NE* 16, Fen Orchis. Tway-blade. Rare in Nebr. **1950** Correll *Native Orchids* 276, The Fen Orchid has a more restricted range in our region [=eastern United States] than its relative *L. lilifolia.* **1976** Bailey–Bailey *Hortus Third* 669, *Fen orchid. . .* Fl[ower]s to ½ in. across, whitish- or yellowish-green.

fens See **fen**

fensemaus See **fence mouse**

fensies exclam [Prob *fens* (at **fen**) + hypocoristic **-ies**]

=**king's ex.**

1977–78 Foster *Lexical Variation* 87 **NJ,** Minor responses include . . the truce term *fensies* (1).

fenuken n [Perh var of *penuche*]

1966 *DARE* (Qu. H80, *Kinds of candy often made at home around here*) Inf **MI**13, Fenuken [fə nukən].

fenzemaus See **fence mouse**

fer prep See **for**

fer v See **fuh**

fer adv, adj See **far** adv, adj[1]

ferce, ferceness See **fierce** adj

ferdarva adj [PaGer *verdarwe* spoiled < Ger *verdorben* past pple of *verderben*] **PaGer area**

Spoiled.

1939 Aurand *Quaint Idioms* 13 **PaGer area,** Children soon get *ferdarva* (spoiled) when you give them everything they want. **1968** *DARE* (Qu. H46, *When meat begins to go bad, so that you can't eat it*) Inf **PA**159, [fɛr'dɑrnəvə].

Ferdinand n [Ref to *The Story of Ferdinand* by Munro Leaf, 1936] *joc* or *euphem*

A bull.

1950 *WELS* 2 Infs, **WI,** Ferdinand. **1968–70** *DARE* (Qq. K22, 23) Infs **IN**30, **NY**36, (Old) Ferdinand; **RI**2, **TX**82, Ferdinand [laughter]. **1970** Tarpley *Blinky* 166 **neTX,** *Male cow (euphemism)* . . Ferdinand [rare]. **1973** Allen *LAUM* 1.244 **IA, MN, SD** (as of c1950), *Ferdinand,* perhaps not a term to survive, derives from the story *Ferdinand the Bull,* popular not long before fieldwork took place. [Of 5 Infs, 3 considered the term amusing, one called it old-fashioned.]

ferdutzt adj |fɛr'dutst, fə(r)-, -'dʌtst, -'dʊtst| [PaGer, Ger *verdutzt* past pple of *verdutzen* to bewilder, startle] **PaGer area**

1 Bewildered, nonplussed, confused.

1967 *DARE* FW Addit **PaGer area,** Ferdutzt [fɛr'dutst] mixed up. **1969** *DARE* (Qu. CC12b, . . *If a person has a lot of bad luck*) Inf **PA**209, Ferdutzt [fɚ'dʌtst].

2 Spoiled, botched, bungled.

[**1924** Lambert *PA Ger. Dict.* 162, *Verdutzt* . . mopish, sheepish, spoiled, despised.] **1985** *DARE* File **sePA,** You still hear [fə'dʊtst], meaning spoiled or botched.

fergen n [Perh rel to Scots *fargin* a piece of wood on the end of a pole to push out the sail of a boat] Cf **fagan**

1894 *DN* 1.330 **sNJ,** *Fergen:* centre pole in a charcoal pit, forming the central part of the "crib" [=pieces of cord-wood that form a column to support additional wood].

ferget, fergit See **forget**

Ferginny, Ferginyeh See **Virginia**

fergittery See **forgettery**

ferhex v [Ger *verhexen* to bewitch] **esp PaGer area**

To bewitch, put a curse on; hence ppl adjs *ferhexed, ferhext.*

1935 *AmSp* 10.170 **cPA,** 'He was ferhexed.' . . *hexing* implies the use of black magic. **1939** Aurand *Quaint Idioms* 14 **PaGer area,** Such a woman must be *ferhext* (bewitched; full of the "devil"). **1950** *WELS (Expressions . . for one person casting a "spell" over another)* 1 Inf, **cWI,** To ferhex; to put a curse on someone. [Inf of Ger ancestry] **1964** Smith *PA Germans* 151, In the Probst Gap area some people used to burn sulphur in the house. They thought they were *ferhext.* **1967–69** *DARE* (Qu. CC14, . . *Where one person supposedly casts a spell over another*) Infs **MD**30, **MI**93, **PA**4, Ferhex; (Qu. CC12b, . . *If a person has a lot of bad luck*) Inf **PA**14, Ferhexed. **1967** *DARE* FW Addit **PaGer area,** If someone has bad luck he is ferhexed [fɛr'hɛkst]. All know the term, many use it.

ferhoodle v, hence ppl adjs *ferhoodled, ferhudled, verhuddelt* |ˌfə(r)'hudəl, -'hʊdəl| [PaGer < Ger *verhudeln* to spoil by lack of care] **PaGer area**

1 To jumble; to botch. Cf **hoodle** v

1969–70 *DARE* (Qu. Y38, . . *"The things in the drawer are all _______."*) Inf **PA**223, [ˌfɚ'hudəld]; (Qu. JJ42, . . *"He usually handles things well, but this time he certainly _______."*) Inf **PA**242, Ferhoodled it.

2 By ext: to confuse or perplex.

[**1872** Haldeman *PA Dutch* 20, *Fərhúttələ,* v. intrans. 'Ich bin f'r-huttlt,' (I am confused, perplexed.)] [**1924** Lambert *PA Ger. Dict.* 164 , Verhuddle . . to tangle, confuse.] **1935** *AmSp* 10.170 **sePA,** Other German words used in English are . . *ferhudled,* mentally confused. **1939** Aurand *Quaint Idioms* 14 **PaGer area,** The boy is too young yet, and he gets all *ferhoodled* (tangled, or mix-up [sic]). **1968** *Helen Adolf Festschrift* 37 **sePA,** "I am so verhuddelt," meaning "I am mentally confused," is still a fairly common expression in the area. *Verhuddelt* is of course a direct borrowing from the Pennsylvania German dialect. **1967–70** *DARE* (Qu. GG2, . . *"So many things were going on at the same time that he got completely _______."*) Inf **PA**28, Ferhoodled [ˌfɚ'hudəld]—Dutch; **PA**242, [fə'hʊdəlt].

ferhoonse v, hence ppl adj *ferhoonsed* [PaGer < Ger *verhunzen* to spoil, botch, bungle] **chiefly PaGer area**

To botch; to mix up, disarrange.

[**1924** Lambert *PA Ger. Dict.* 164, *Verhunse* . . to spoil, botch, ruin.] **1950** *WELS Suppl.* **seWI,** The term [=*kroepfle*] may have been "ferhoonsed" by the local Plattdeutsche. Our local baker advertises them as "krupplich." **1970** *DARE* (Qu. KK70, . . *Out of proper shape: "That house is all _______."*) Inf **PA**242, [far'hʊnst]. **1977** *DARE* File **cPA,** Stay out of my workshop—I don't want it all ferhoonsed [fɚ'hunst] or [fɚ'hunsəld].

ferhudled See **ferhoodle**

ferlicue n Cf **cut up a curlicue, dido 1**

A shenanigan, prank.

1975 McDonough *Garden Sass* 112 **AR,** It weren't long, though, before he cut up some ferlicues, and got into a priminary [=predicament]; and so one morning he was found among the missing.

ferm See **fern**

fermilyus See **familious**

fermoose v [Var of **vamoose**]

1968 *DARE* (Qu. Y18, *To leave in a hurry: "Before they find this out, we'd better _______."*) Inf **NJ**28, [fɚ'mus].

fern n Usu |fɝn|; for varr see quots Pronc-spp *feeren, ferm, ferrn, firm*

Std sense, var forms.

1906 in 1944 *ADD* **nwAR,** *Fern.* . . ferrn, sometimes [fæən]. **1925–30** *Ibid* **eWV,** *Fern.* . . [fɛrn]. Common country pron. **1941** *Ibid* **nWV,** *Fern.* . . [fɚm] ferm, firm. **1942** Hall *Smoky Mt. Speech* 106, In Cades Cove *fern* was once ['firən]; in other cases this word was [fɪɚn], [fjëɚn]. **1960** Hall *Smoky Mt. Folks* 34, The cattle lived on mountain "feeren" (fern).

fernanth See **fornent**

fernanz exclam

=**fen.**

1976 *WI Acad. Rev.* Mar 9/1 (as of 1920s), Should an opponent shout "fernanz" (a possible distortion of "defense") before you shouted "rounds," your shooter could not be moved.

fern-bush n

1 A **sweet fern** (here: *Comptonia peregrina*).

1828 Rafinesque *Med. Flora* 1.115, *Comptonia asplenifolia.* . . Fern-bush. . . A small shrub from two to five feet high. **1869** Porcher *Resources* 357 **Sth,** *Fern bush.* . . An aromatic astringent used . . as a pleasant drink in the summer complaints of children. **1876** Hobbs *Bot. Hdbk.* 37, Fern bush, Sweet fern, Comptonia asplenifolia. **1900** Lyons *Plant Names* 113, *Comptonia peregrina* . . Fern bush. **1911** Henkel *Amer. Med. Leaves* 9, Fern bush. . . The present price . . is about 3 to 5 cents a pound. **1933** Small *Manual SE Flora* 410, *Fern-bush.* . . A characteristic plant of poor soil. **1974** (1977) Coon *Useful Plants* 190, Fern-bush. . . An old Indian-recommended cure for poison ivy.

2 An aromatic shrub *(Chamaebatiaria millefolium)* native to much of the western US. [See quot 1990] Also called **desert sweet, mountain misery, tansybush**

1915 (1926) Armstrong–Thornber *Western Wild Flowers* 230, *Fern-bush.* . . A pretty and unusual-looking shrub, . . the downy leaves . . arranged at intervals along the branches in soft feathery bunches **1931** U.S. Dept. Ag. *Misc. Pub.* 101.55, *Chamaebatiaria millefolium* . . fern-bush. . . is regarded in parts of Arizona as fair sheep and goat browse. **1952** Davis *Flora ID* 391, *Fern-bush.* . . Dry rocky areas. Idaho to Oreg., south to Ariz. and Calif. **1990** *Plants SW* (Catalog) 66, *Chamaebatiaria millefolium. Fernbush.* 8 ft. tall and just as broad with fernlike leaves as the name suggests. Whole plant is very fragrant.

3 A **mountain misery** (here: *Chamaebatia foliolosa).*

1931 U.S. Dept. Ag. *Misc. Pub.* 101.55, *Bearmat (Chamaebatia foliolosa),* also known as . . fernbush, . . is a low, . . evergreen shrub 1 or 2 feet high; its thrice-pinnate, fernlike leaves are 2 or 3 inches long. **1937**

U.S. Forest Serv. *Range Plant Hdbk.* B52, Bearmat, also known as . . fernbush, . . is a . . shrub occurring . . on the west slope of the Sierra Nevadas in California.

fernen(s)t, fernenth See **fornent**

ferngale n

1 A **sweet fern** (here: *Comptonia peregrina*).

1828 Rafinesque *Med. Flora* 1.115, *Comptonia asplenifolia*. . . Ferngale. . . A small shrub . . with many crooked branches and long horizontal roots. **1876** Hobbs *Bot. Hdbk.* 37, Fern gale, Sweet fern, Comptonia asplenifolia. **1900** Lyons *Plant Names* 113, *Comptonia peregrina* . . Fern-gale. **1911** Henkel *Amer. Med. Leaves* 9, Fern gale. . . has a fragrant, spicy odor and an aromatic, slightly bitter, and astringent taste. **1935** (1943) Muenscher *Weeds* 187, Fern gale. . . Eastern Canada to North Carolina, rare westward to Indiana. Native. **1971** Krochmal *Appalachia Med. Plants* 102, *Comptonia peregrina*—Common Names: . . ferngale.

2 =**sweet gale.**

1900 Lyons *Plant Names* 255, *M. Gale*. . . Fern Gale. **1940** Clute *Amer. Plant Names* 159, *Myrica gale*. . . Fern-gale.

fernhopper n **Pacific NW**

Among foresters: see quots.

1955 *Register-Guard* (Eugene OR) 27 Apr (*Western Folkl.* 15.202), *Fernhopper*—a West Coast forester. **1958** McCulloch *Woods Words* 61 **Pacific NW,** *Fernhopper*—A forester from Oregon State College. **1977** *WI State Jrl.* (Madison) 16 Jan sec 5 5/1 **Pacific NW,** The old-timers [among West Coast foresters] are "fernhoppers".

ferninst See **fornent**

ferninster n [Var of *fornenst* + *-er*] Cf **aginner, fornent 2**

One who habitually dissents.

1935 in 1944 *ADD* **SD,** America's ace ferninster predicts that Roosevelt will be swamped in the 1935 election. **1943** *Time* 8 Mar 13/1 **KS,** But the trouble with the Republican leaders in Congress . . is that they are just ferninsters. They are 'agin' everything and 'for' nothing.

fernleaf n [See quot 1963]

=**lousewort.**

1933 Small *Manual SE Flora* 1224, *Pedicularis*. . . Louseworts. Fernleafs [sic]. **1937** U.S. Forest Serv. *Range Plant Hdbk.* W142, Of the approximately 30 species of fernleaf (all perennial) occurring in the Western States, the majority grow in the mountains from the ponderosa-pine belt to above timber line. **1963** Craighead *Rocky Mt. Wildflowers* 176, The common name Fernleaf refers to the characteristic fernlike leaves. **1975** Duncan–Foote *Wildflowers SE* 178, *Fernleaf*. . . Members of this genus are perennials with pinnately-lobed leaves.

fern-leaf maple n

A cultivar of the Japanese maple *(Acer palmatum)*.

1967 *DARE* (Qu. T14, . . *Kinds of maples*) Inf **PA**40, Fern-leaf maple.

fernling adv [Prob Scots *fairlins,* Engl dial *fairlings* completely, absolutely]

Extremely.

1936 Morehouse *Rain on Just* 46 **NC,** "God damn it to yell," spat . . Emmet, fernling mad.

fern moss n

=**resurrection fern.**

1920 *Torreya* 20.91, *Polypodium polypodioides*. . . Other common local names are "fern moss," "moss fern," "tree fern"—from its epiphytic habit of growing on the trunks of trees.

fern snakeroot n Also *fern rattlesnake root, fern root* [From fernlike fronds and its efficacy in counteracting the effects of snakebite]

=**cinnamon fern.**

1738 (1841) Byrd *Westover MSS* 42 **VA,** We found in the low ground several plants of the fern root, which is said to be much the strongest antidote yet discovered against the poison of the rattle-snake. The leaves of it resemble those of fern, from whence it obtained its name. . . The root has a faint spicy taste, and is preferred by the southern Indians to all other counter-poisons in this country. **1739** (1946) Gronovius *Flora Virginica* 196, *Fern-Rattle-Snake-root.* **1775** Adair *Amer. Indians* 235 **SC,** Everyone carries in his shot-pouch, a piece of the best snake-root, such as the *Seneeka,* or fern-snake-root . . [which] will effect a thorough and speedy cure if timely applied. **1791** in 1793 Amer. Philos. Soc. *Trans.* 3.115, Osmunda *virginiana (Virginian Osmunda, Fern-Rattle-Snake-root).* **1975** Hamel–Chiltoskey *Cherokee Plants* 33, Fern-snake-root. . . *Osmunda cinnamomea*. . . For snake bites, chew root, swallow a portion and apply the rest to the wound, repeat as necessary.

fern weed n [From its lacy fernlike stalks and its tendency to grow wild]

Asparagus.

1951 *PADS* 15.29 **TX,** *Asparagus officinalis* L.—Fern weed. Asparagus has long run wild on vacant lots, in untended portions of old cemeteries, and along ditches.

ferreck v [Ger *verrecken*]

To die.

[**1924** Lambert *PA Ger. Dict.* 165, *Verrecke* . . pp verreckt, to die, kick the bucket.] **1967** *DARE* (Qu. BB42, *If a person is very sick* . . ______) Inf **IL**4, He might [fɛˈrɛk] (German word for *die,* used by the German farmers around Galena).

ferrer See **far** adv, adj[1] **B2**

ferrest See **far** adv, adj[1] **C2**

ferricadouzer n [Perh based on Lat *ferri-* iron + *ca-* intensifier (at **ker-**) + *douser* a heavy blow (at *OED douse* v.[1])]

1930 Shoemaker *1300 Words* 21 **cPA Mts** (as of c1900), *Ferricadouzer*—A sound beating given with an iron poker to unruly scholars of both sexes.

ferricked adj [Ger *verrückt*] **PaGer area**

Crazy.

[**1924** Lambert *PA Ger. Dict.* 166, Verrickt, out of place, deranged, crazy.] **1939** Aurand *Quaint Idioms* 14 **PaGer area,** He was *ferricked* (deranged), that was why the boys wanted to fool around with him so much. **1968** *DARE* (Qu. HH6, *Someone who is out of his mind*) Inf **PA**161, [gɑns fəˈrɑɪk] [=quite crazy]. **1985** *DARE* File **sePA,** [fəˈrʊkt], meaning crazy, is something you'd still hear in Reading, but probably not in Lancaster.

ferrididdle n Also sp *fairydiddle, ferrydiddle* [Etym unknown; but see quot 1945]

1 =**red squirrel.**

1893 *Jrl. Amer. Folkl.* 6.143, *Ferrydiddle,* a chickaree or red squirrel, *Sciurus hudsonius.* This is a common name in the mountains of Virginia. **1917** in 1944 *ADD* **sWV,** *Ferri-*[diddle], squirrel betw. gray & ground squirrel. **1931** *AmSp* 6.230 **neOR,** A 'ferrididdle' is a chipmunk. **1936** *AmSp* 11.372 **VA,** 'He is as quick as a fairydiddle.' . . A man . . said that it is not a flying squirrel, but a little ground squirrel, smaller than the common gray variety but larger than the chipmunk. It is striped, and 'when he runs, his tail points straight up in the air, and they're quick all right!' **1945** McAtee *Nomina Abitera* 50, Red Squirrel *(Sciurus hudsonicus . .)*—Fairy-diddle. . . Diddle in popular parlance means to copulate, so I assume there is a related significance in this name. **1984** *DARE* File, I first encountered fairydiddle [the response for chipmunk] . . from a sixty-year-old informant at a Zanesville, Ohio, talk about "Ohio Speech" to the local Kiwanis. He said he'd heard it in the Shenandoah Valley of Virginia and in Cincinnati, Ohio; only one other person ever volunteered it, a graduate student from the eastern panhandle of W. Va.

2 A flying squirrel (*Glaucomys* spp).

1983 *Audubon Mag.* Nov 14/1 **cOR,** "Fairy diddle" is one of several popular names . . for any of the three closely related species of flying squirrels that inhabit North America and Eurasia. . . a northern flying squirrel, *Glaucomys sabrinus*. . . the southern flying squirrel . . *Glaucomys volans*. . . *Petromys volans* is the Eurasian version of *Glaucomys.*

ferriner See **foreign**

ferrn See **fern**

ferro See **pharaoh**

ferryboat n Cf **canal boat**

1970 *DARE* (Qu. W11, *Men's low, rough work-shoes*) Inf **NY**232, Clodhoppers, ferryboats; (Qu. X38, *Joking names for unusually big or clumsy feet*) Inf **NY**232, Ferryboats.

ferrydiddle n See **ferrididdle**

ferry-flat n **esp Missip-Ohio Valleys, S Atl** *old-fash* Cf **flat** n[1] **3**

A **flatboat 1** used as a ferry.

1821 Schoolcraft *Jrl.* 84 **Missip Valley,** [I] was conveyed over in a ferry-flat, or scow. **1828** Flint *Condensed Geog.* 1.230 **Missip Valley,**

The ferry flat is a scow-boat, and when used as a boat of descent for families, has a roof, or covering. These are sometimes, in the vernacular phrase, called 'sleds.' **1859** (1968) Bartlett *Americanisms* 146, *Ferry-Flat.* A flat boat used for crossing, and sometimes for descending, the Mississippi River and its tributaries. **1884** *Harper's New Mth. Mag.* June 124 **Ohio Valley,** Of smaller vessels there were "covered sleds," "ferry flats," and "Alleghany skiffs." **1966** *DARE* Tape **SC**9, You put a ferry-flat there; **SC**10, A pull flat, you pull 'em; they got a long cable all the way across. Then you get in the flat, and then row 'em all the way across. Ferry-flat.

ferry wheel n [Folk-etym for *Ferris wheel*]

1967 *DARE* (QR, near Qu. EE32) Inf **CO**35, Ferry wheel.

ferschimmelt adj [PaGer < Ger *verschimmelt* moldy] Cf **ferhoodle, ferhoonse**

Confused, mixed up.

[**1924** Lambert *PA Ger. Dict.* 166, *Verschimmelt* . . mouldy.] **1968** *DARE* (Qu. GG2, *Expressions meaning 'confused, mixed up': "So many things were going on at the same time that he got completely ________.*") Inf **NY**118, Ferschimmelt.

ferschnapp oneself v phr [PaGer < Ger *verschnappen* to make a slip of the tongue]

See quots.

[**1924** Lambert *PA Ger. Dict.* 167, Verschnappe . . sich, to let the cat out of the bag.] **1970** *DARE* (Qu. JJ43, *To give away a secret or tell a piece of news too soon: "He wasn't supposed to know. Somebody must have ________.*") Inf **PA**242, Ferschnappt himself.

fersteh v Usu |fə(r)'ste, vər-, -'šte| For other prons, pronc-spp, and var forms see quots [Ger *verstehen* to understand] **Ger settlement areas**

To understand.

[**1924** Lambert *PA Ger. Dict.* 167, *Verschteh* . . . , pp verschtanne, to understand, comprehend.] **1950** *WELS (Other ways of saying "do you understand?")* [2 Infs, **WI,** Versteh(e)st du;] 1 Inf, Ferstay; 1 Inf, Forstay; 1 Inf, Fur stash to da [*DARE* Ed: perh for *Verstehst du da*]. **1965–70** *DARE* (Qu. NN5, *Other ways of saying 'Do you understand?'*) Infs **NY**18, 94, **OR**3, **PA**191, 227, (You) fersteh [fɚ'ste(ɪ)]; **IL**4, **NY**68, [fə'ɜtcɪ]; **MD**9, **PA**50, [fɔ'šte]; **MN**41, Versteh; **MI**69, ['fɚˌšte]; **PA**71, [fɔrstaɪ]; **PA**82, [fɛr'ste]; **IN**45, Do you [for'ste]; **PA**227, Do you [fəstei]; **IN**5, [vɪr'šte]; **NY**102, [vɚ'stejɑ]; [**IA**17, **MI**92, **NJ**2, **NY**105, Verstehen Sie; **WI**62, Verstehen; **IN**40, [vɚ'steən zi]; **NY**108, [vɨr'steɛn zi];] **MO**12, [vɚ'steɪstu]; **MO**26, [vɚ'štestu]; **WI**48, [vɛr'šteštu]; **MI**63, [nɪkst vɚ'ste]; [(Qu. JJ16) Inf **IL**48, [ˌvɚ'šteən]]. [**1970** Feinsilver *Yiddish* 150, *Farshteystu mir* Lit., you understand me—a phrase used in mid-sentence.] **1987** *DARE* File, I recall [fə'šte] being used in otherwise English conversation in Akron, Ohio, c1920, from people of German background (but not first-generation—at least second). It was certainly current in 1920.

ferthrest See **far** adv, adj[1] **C3**

fertili n [Back-formation from **fertilize** n, understood as pl]

1953 Randolph *Down in Holler* 48 **Ozarks,** Many hillfolk use fertilize as a noun, meaning commercial fertilizer; it seems to be a plural, as one often hears *these fertilize* or *them fertilize.* Sometimes a singular form *fertili* is used. . . [A] farm agent . . spoke often in favor of "choosin' the right *fertili,* an' then stickin' to it."

fertilize n [By apocope] **chiefly Sth, S Midl** See Map

Fertilizer.

1913 Johnson *Highways St. Lawrence to VA* 231 [Black], He'd paid his help and his fertilize bill. **1930s** in 1944 *ADD* **eWV,** 'I bought 4 tons of fertilize.' Common. **1942** Hall *Smoky Mt. Speech* 78 **wNC, eTN,** [Footnote, quoting c1937 diary:] We never heard of Fertalizer's untill I was 13 or 14 year's old, yet we made plenty to live on, and to spair, and now it takes all our crops to pay our Fertalize bills. **1946** *AmSp* 21.271 **neKY,** *Fertilize, n.* . . Common. **1955** *DE Folkl. Bulletin* 1.20/2, The corner store handles fertilize. **1965–70** *DARE* (Qu. L17, . . *Manure used in the fields*) 17 Infs, **chiefly Lower Missip Valley, S Atl,** Fertilize; **GA**52, **LA**10, **MS**72, **TX**32, Cow(pen) fertilize; **GA**17, **MS**81, Lot fertilize; **LA**10, Barnyard or henhouse fertilize; **TX**35, Chicken fertilize; **GA**52, Stable fertilize; (Qu. F23) Inf **VA**39, Fertilize bag. [2 of 23 Infs coll educ] **1968** *DARE* Tapes **FL**36, **IN**51, Fertilize. **1970** *Foxfire* Spring–Summer 27 **nGA,** When they first come out with fertilize, they'd even put it out in th' hill with a teaspoon. [*DARE* Ed: Speaker alternates between *fertilize* and *fertilizer.*]

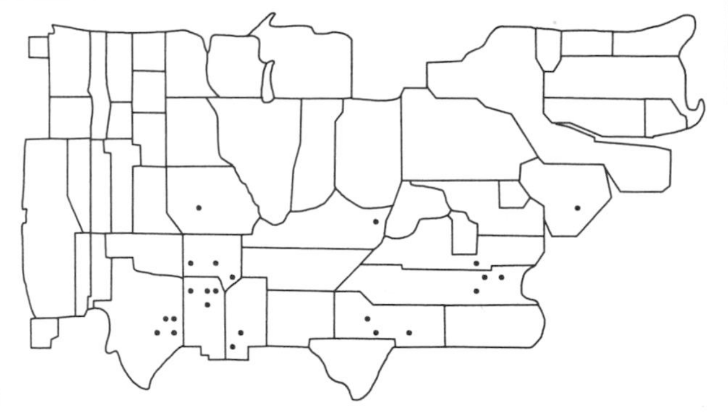

•fertilize + varr (Qq. L17, F23)

fes See **fess** v[1]

fescue n **chiefly S Midl, S Atl** See Map Note: While the grass itself is grown throughout the country, its use as fodder seems to be regionally concentrated.

A grass of the genus *Festuca.* Also called **bunchgrass 2.** For other names of var spp see **evergreen grass 1**

1878 Killebrew *Grasses TN* 188, *Tall Fescue Grass* . . [will] yield more nutritious matter per acre, when cut in flower, than any other grass. **1965–70** *DARE* (Qu. L9a, . . *Grass . . grown for hay*) 56 Infs, **chiefly S Midl, S Atl,** Fescue; **GA**72, 80, Fescue grass; **AZ**9, **OR**7, Alta fescue; **NC**73, **VA**14, Kentucky fescue; **MN**7, **SC**43, Meadow fescue; **AR**56, Kentucky 31 fescue; (Qu. L9b) Infs **AR**4, 40, **KY**75, **OH**35, 58, **SC**30, 34, **VA**24, Fescue; (Qu. L8) Infs **KY**9, **VA**105, Fescue; (Qu. L7) Inf **TN**37, Depends on what is planted; "my alfalfa, my fescue,"etc.

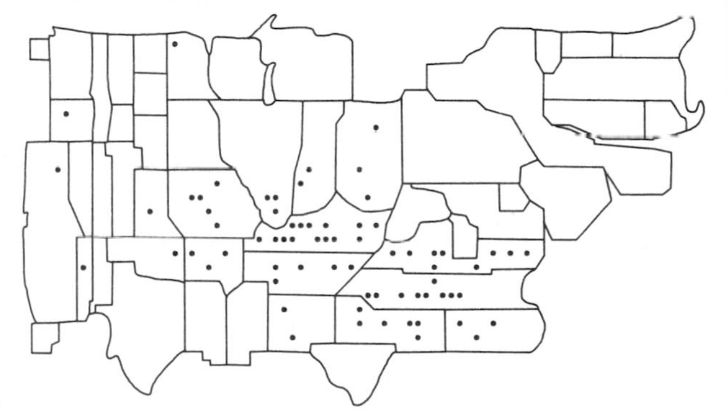

•fescue + varr (Qq. L9a, b, L7, L8)

fesper See **vesper**

fess n See **fessor**

fess v[1] Also sp *fes* [Aphet forms of *confess*]

Among students: to fail in recitation; to admit that one is not prepared to recite.

1834 *Military & Naval Mag.* 3.25, My first appearance before the Blackboard—that terror to all "fifth-section men;" that abomination of him who has to "'fess"—that delight of him who hopes to "fan." **1851** in 1951 *AmSp* 26.182 **NC,** I had Magnus Spencer to read over a greek lesson which I fessed on last week. **1859** in 1956 Eliason *Tarheel Talk* 135 **NC,** Prof Smith was to hear Sunday lesson. The class, to a man 'fessed.' When they were required to make up the lesson, they refused. **1939** Banning *West Point* 295 [Cadet Lingo], Fes. . . To fail completely in a recitation.

fess v[2] [Aphet form of *profess*]

To acknowledge, profess.

1953 Brewer *Word Brazos* 54 **eTX** [Black], Don' keer how haa'd Sistuh Sadie an' de membuhship of de Mt. Zion Chu'ch try, dey cain't in no-wise toll Pete off to de Christun faith. . . he ain't fessed religion yit.

fesse n |fɛs| [Fr]

1969 Cagnon *Franco-Amer. Terms* 223 **RI,** *Fesse,* . . [fɛs] Buttock.

"I'll slap you on the *fesses.*" "Did you fall on your *fesses?*" *Ibid* 222, The word *fesses* acquires its plural in [z], i.e., [fɛs^{ə}z], by analogy with such English words as "dresses" and "tresses."

fessed up adj phr [*EDD fess* adj "1. Of animals: bad-tempered, fierce. . . 4. . . Hence . . *Fessed* . . *Fessy* . . flurried, put out"]
Angry, excited.

1955 *DE Folkl. Bulletin* Mar 17/1, Referring later to having provoked her to anger, the young fellow told me, "She got all fessed up, but I didn't mean to fault her."

fessor n Also *fess(er)* [Abbrs for *professor*] **chiefly S Midl, Sth** *esp freq among Black speakers*
A male teacher.

1908 *DN* 3.310 **eAL, wGA,** *Fesser.* . . Professor. . . Every man that teaches is called a professor. **1930** *AmSp* 6.129 **AL,** "'Fessor" is in common use, even by the townsfolk. "'Fess" is less commonly, yet frequently heard. **1965–70** *DARE* (Qu. JJ1b) Infs **AR**39, **GA**45, 67, **MD**41, **MS**61, **SC**39, **TN**43, **TX**97, Fessor; **GA**45, **MO**22, **TN**53, Fess. [6 of 11 Infs Black] **1976** Garber *Mountain-ese* 29 **sAppalachians,** The fessor called Johnny inter his office fer throwin' spitballs.

fest n [Ger "festival, holiday"] **chiefly Nth** Note: Although *gabfest* occurs throughout the US, other combinations with *fest* are most freq in the Nth.
An informal meeting or celebration; a festival—usu used in comb.

1910 *Chicago Daily Maroon* 10 June 1/2 *(OEDS),* After the roll call a 'talk fest' was indulged in by some of the old timers. **1916** *DN* 4.353, [Article contains examples, chiefly from Nebraska, of words with the suff *-fest,* including *batfest, blarneyfest, eatfest, jawfest, smilefest, sobfest, walkfest, etc.*] **1918** *DN* 5.11, Chatfest. . . Egofest. . . Fun-fest. . . Gossipfest. **1922** (1924) Lewis *Babbitt* 16, If you get to be Gruensberg's secretary—and maybe you would, if you kept up your shorthand and didn't go sneaking off to concerts and talkfests every evening. **1963** Mencken–McDavid *Amer. Lang.* 255, Since the Civil War the chief contribution of German has been the domestication of the suffix *-fest.* It came in with *sängerfest* and *turnfest* in the early 1850s, but the manufacture of American analogues did not begin until 1900 or thereabout. **1963** McCarthy *Group* 22, She . . loved . . a good hen fest. **1965–70** *DARE* (Qu. KK12, *A meeting where there's a lot of talking*) 315 Infs, **widespread,** Gabfest; 47 Infs, **scattered, but chiefly Nth,** Talkfest; 18 Infs, **chiefly Nth,** (Blab, blabber, bull, chin, gabber, glab, hen, jab, jam, jaw, tongue, yak) fest; (Qu. O21, *When men out in seagoing boats get together for a visit and a cup of hot coffee, that's called a ______*) Infs **CA**108, **IL**9, **MD**5, **ME**16, **NH**18, **NY**122, Gabfest; (Qu. Y12a, *A fight . . mostly with words*) Infs **MI**68, **WA**18, Gabfest; **MN**15, Chewfest; (Qu. DD34) Inf **WI**40, Beerfest; **NY**226, Drinkfest; **NY**37, Rumfest; (Qu. EE21b) Inf **NY**92, Had a slugfest; (Qu. FF16) Inf **MI**120, Alpine Fest; **WI**76, Scandinavian Fest; **AK**8, Syttende Mai Fest; (Qu. FF23) Infs **MI**103, **NE**8, Gabfest. **1981** *AmSp* 56.207–13, [This article lists 69 compounds of *-fest,* collected especially from Illinois newspapers in 1979.]

fester n Also rarely *fester bump* **scattered, but esp Nth, N Midl**
A suppurating wound or sore; pus from such a sore.

1899 (1912) Green *VA Folk-Speech* 173, *Fester.* . . A small purulent tumour, a superficial suppuration resulting from irritation of the skin, the pus being developed in small vesicles of irregular figure and extent. **1942** Warnick *Garrett Co. MD* 6 **nwMD** (as of 1900–18), *Fester.* . . pus. **1965–70** *DARE* (Qu. X59, . . *Small infected pimples . . on the face*) Inf **ME**22, Festers; **ME**15, Some say fester; **NY**101, Festers, hickeys, blackheads; **VT**16, Fester, whiteheads; (Qu. BB33a, . . *A swelling under the skin . . that comes to a head*) Inf **MI**2, Fester; **MA**14, Festers—smaller than boils; **VA**71, A fester bump is smaller than a boil; (Qu. BB33b, . . *A swelling under the skin—if it is very big or serious*) Infs **NV**8, **OH**2, Fester; (Qu. BB35, *The yellowish stuff that comes out of a boil when the head breaks*) Infs **LA**3, **VA**13, Fester. **1973** Allen *LAUM* 1.364 (as of c1950), One South Dakotan uses both *boil* and *fester.*

fester v **chiefly Inland Nth, N Midl, CA** See Map and Map Section Cf **matterate**
Of a wound or sore: to secrete pus; hence ppl adj *festered.*

1899 (1912) Green *VA Folk-Speech* 173, *Fester.* . . To become a fester; generate pus. **1943** *LANE* Map 514 *(Wound; inflamed)* 2 infs, **MA, RI,** Festered; 1 inf, **CT,** Festering. **1950** *WELS (When pus . . comes out of an open sore, you say the sore is ______)* 14 Infs, **WI,** Festering; 3 Infs, Festered; *(When the skin around a sore . . is red and hot, you say it is ______)* 4 Infs, **WI,** Festering. **1965–70** *DARE* (Qu. BB36, *When there's an open sore and this yellowish stuff is coming out of it, you say it's ______*) 31 Infs, **chiefly Inland Nth, N Midl, CA,** Festering; 9 Infs, **chiefly N Midl,** Festered; **IL**126, All festered up; (Qu. BB37) Infs **IA**3, 22, **KS**16, **MN**42, **MA**14, **NV**8, **TX**31, Festered ear; (Qu. BB33a) Infs **IL**135, **WA**26, Festered; **NY**139, It festers; (Qu. BB29) Infs **MI**44, **SD**5, Festering; (Qu. BB30) Infs **FL**5, **PA**245, Festering; **MN**3, Festered; (QR, near Qu. Y44) Inf **NJ**9, Festered—of a wound with a splinter. **1985** *Amer. Jrl. Med.* Feb. 183, *Fester* . . to form pus.

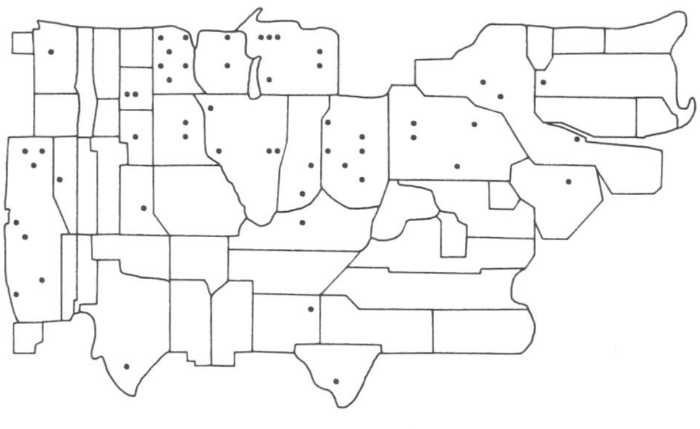

•fester v + varr (Qq. BB36, BB29, BB30, BB33a, BB37)

fester bump See **fester** n

festered ppl adj See **fester** v

festoon ground pine See **festoon pine 2**

festoon pine n [Perh from their use as Christmas decorations]
1 A spike moss (here: *Selaginella rupestris*).

1822 Eaton *Botany* 344, *[Selaginella] rupestre.* . . Festoon pine. . . Rocks and gravelly banks. **1832** in 1836 Traill *Backwoods Canada* 120, The Americans ornament their chimney-glasses with garlands of this plant, mixed with the dried blossoms of the life-everlasting (the pretty white and yellow flowers we call love-everlasting): this plant is also called festoon-pine. **1876** Hobbs *Bot. Hdbk.* 37, Festoon pine, Christmas evergreen, Lycopodium rupestre. **1900** Lyons *Plant Names* 341, *S. rupestris.* . . Festoon Pine.

2 also *festoon ground pine, ground festoon:* A **club moss,** such as *Lycopodium complanatum.*

1843 Torrey *Flora NY* 2.510, *Lycopodium complanatum.* . . Festoon Ground-pine. **1861** Wood *Class-Book* 811, *L. complanatum* L. *Festoon Ground Pine.* . . A trailing evergreen, common in woods and shady grounds. **1900** Lyons *Plant Names* 233, *L. complanatum.* . . Ground-festoon. **1938** Small *Ferns SE States* 418, This plant [=*Lycopodium flabelliforme*] has received many popular names, such as . . *Festoon-pine.* **1959** Carleton *Index Herb. Plants* 45, *Festoon-pine:* Lycopodium obscurum.

fetch v Usu |fɛč|; also **esp S Midl** |fɑč|; rarely |fɪč|
A Forms.
1 pres (exc 3rd pers sg): usu *fetch;* also **esp S Midl** *old-fash, fotch, fotches;* rarely *fauch.*

1789 Webster *Dissertations Engl. Lang.* 111, *Fotch* for *fetch* is very common, in several states, but not among the better classes of people. **1827** (1939) Sherwood *Gaz. GA* 139, [In a list of 'provincialisms' to be avoided:] *Fauch,* for fetch, or bring. **1851** [see **B2** below]. **1884** Murfree *TN Mts.* 251 **TN,** Ef ye brings away so much ez a leaf, or a stone, or a stick, ye fotches a curse with it. **1893** Shands *MS Speech* 30, *Fotch* . . Negro for *fetch* and *fetched.* **1906** *DN* 3.136 **nwAR,** *Fotch.* . . Fetch. "Fotch it along." "Fotch it up." **1923** *DN* 5.207 **swMO,** *Fotch.* . . To fetch. **1936** *AmSp* 11.275 **cTN,** Fotch me my bonnet. **1953** Randolph *Down in Holler* 37 **Ozarks,** I have heard *fotch* only as the preterite and past participle of fetch. But the old-timers tell me that fifty or sixty years ago it was used in other tenses . . [as in] "Fotch me that ax." **1954** *Harder Coll.* **cwTN,** "Go fotch a bucket of water." [Harder: Used by one family only.] **c1960** *Wilson Coll.* **csKY,** *Fotch.* . . Go and get. Now rare. Sometimes [fɑc], with [fɑct], past. **1960** *Hall Coll.* **wNC, eTN,** *Fetch.* . . [fɛtʃ], [fɪtʃ] with an older variant [fɑtʃ]. To carry. The older expression 'fotch' was reported to me by several people, but I never heard it.

2 past and past pple: usu *fetched;* also **esp S Midl** *fatched, fotch(ed), fo(t)cht;* rarely *fetch.*

1829 Kirkham *Engl. Grammar* 193 **Sth,** *Provincialisms.* Have you focht the water? **1843** (1916) Hall *Nw Purchase* 147 **IN,** Many's the . . turkey they fotch'd as a sort of present. **1872** Schele de Vere *Americanisms* 470, The very old participle, *fotch,* still continues in use among low people, and is very general among the negroes of the South. . . Nor is the hybrid *fotched* wanting. **1895** *DN* 1.376 **eTN,** *Fotch.* **1903** *DN* 2.314 **seMO,** *Fotch.* **1907** *DN* 3.231 **nwAR,** *Fotch.* **1908** *DN* 3.312 **eAL, wGA,** *Fotch(t), pret.* and *pp.* of *fetch.* Chiefly among the negroes. **1910** *DN* 3.458 **FL, GA,** *Fotch. . .* Fetched. **1918** *DN* 5.18 **NC,** *Fotched* for *fetched.* Mostly negro. **1926** Roberts *Time of Man* 141 **cKY,** You was fatched up. **1942** Faulkner *Go Down* 67 **MS,** She say maybe ifn we took and fotch that kettle . . , maybe . . yo mind might change. **1951** Porter *Ragged Roads* 75 **wOK,** By then some of the other men had made a table and fotch it in, an' placed wreaths of wild flowers on it. **1967** *DARE* (Qu. OO16a, . . *"You should have ——— [the hammer]."*) Inf **NJ**1, Fetch; (Qu. OO16b, . . *"I did bring the hammer, and I also ——— [a saw]."*) Inf **IL**31, Fetch; **NC**33, Fotch. **1967–68** *DARE* FW Addit **sGA, eTN,** *Fotch* used as preterite of *fetch.* **1972** *Atlanta Letters* **swGA,** He fotched in a load of firewood.

B Senses.

1a To go or come after and bring back. *somewhat old-fash*

1732 [see **fire, come to borrow**]. **1771** in 1887 Franklin *Complete Wks.* 1.59 **sePA,** There were . . canoes on the shore, and we made signs and hallow'd that they should fetch us. **1876** in 1969 *PADS* 52.51 **seIL,** Pa and Ma is talking about fetching Jen and the children home and keeping them. **1939** *LANE* Map 153 *([Go] bring)* **NEng,** [c110 infs gave the resp *(go) fetch* or accepted it without comment when it was suggested; 14 infs said it was obsolete, 8 that it was old-fashioned, 4 that it was rare, and 4 that it was used only to a dog.] **1970** *DARE* (Qu. U1a, *When you are going to a store . . to buy things, you say, "I'm going ———."*) Inf **IL**144, To fetch it. **1986** Pederson *LAGS Concordance* **Gulf Region,** [113 infs gave the responses *fetch* or *go fetch* for "go bring"; of these, 19 said that they did not use it themselves; 22 indicated that it was old-fashioned or obsolete, and 4 that it was used only for dogs (or other animals).]

b also with *up;* Of a dog: to collect and drive back (cattle).

1937 *Hall Coll.* **eTN,** [The dog's been learned] to fetch the cows. **1969** *DARE* (Qu. J8, *To tell a dog to attack an animal*) Inf **CA**131, Fetch 'em up—when you drive cattle.

2 To bring, cause to come; to carry, take. Note: this sense cannot always be distinguished from sense **1**.

1851 Hooper *Widow Rugby's Husband* 88 **AL,** It's enough to fotch sickness in the family! **1860** Holmes *Professor* 36 **NEng,** John arose and placed himself in a neat fighting attitude.—Fetch on the fellah that makes them long words!—he said,—and planted a straight hit with the right fist in the concave palm of the left hand. **1885** Twain *Huck. Finn* 89 **MO,** He told me when the roads forked I must take the right hand, and five mile would fetch me to Goshen. **1894** Twain *Pudd'nhead Wilson* 184, I persuaded myself this evening that I could fetch him around without any great amount of effort. **1899** (1912) Green *VA Folk-Speech* 173, Devil *fetch* you. **1901** Harben *Westerfelt* 7 **nGA,** Mis' Simpkins was at Lithicum's when a nigger fetched the note. **1902** *DN* 2.234 **sIL,** *Fetch. . .* To bring; the latter seldom used. **1939** *LANE* Map 153 **NEng,** 1 inf, He'd fetch on another hemorrhage; 1 inf, You fetch the water to a boil. **1958** *PADS* 29.10 **TN,** *Fetch:* To bring. "Fetch is [now] rarely used and then by very old people." **1965–70** *DARE* (Qu. OO16a, . . *"I was supposed to bring the nails—you should have ——— [the hammer]."*) 16 Infs, **scattered,** Fetched; **NJ**1, Fetch; (Qu. OO16b, . . *"I did bring the hammer, and I also ——— [a saw]."*) Infs **LA**12, **MA**73, **NC**33, **NV**2, **OH**44, **TX**37, Fetched; **IL**31, Fetch; **NC**33, Fotch; (Qu. Y14a, *To hit somebody hard with the fist*) Inf **NY**233, Fetch him down to earth; (Qu. Y30a, *To take something up and move it from one place to another—for example, a paper sack of groceries*) Infs **IL**110, **KY**5, **MA**56, **OH**56, Fetch. [23 of 26 total Infs old] **1968** *DARE* Tape **VA**27, Pulled these here logs to the railroad and from the railroad they fetched 'em to Cass. **1968** *DARE* FW Addit **IA**30, "He fetched me into the world" = he assisted my mother at my birth. **1973** Allen *LAUM* 1.395 (as of c1950), *Fetch,* the minor variant [for *bring*], clearly is on the way to obsolescence. A few Type I infs. [=old, with little educ] use it . . , fewer in Type II [=mid-aged, with approx hs educ], and none in Type III [=mid-aged, with coll educ]. A third of them consider it old-fashioned. **1986** Pederson *LAGS Concordance (I lugged)* 1 inf, **swGA,** Fetched it [=carried it]; 1 inf, **nwFL,** Fetch [has heard, wouldn't use]; 1 inf, **cnAR,** Fetch [wouldn't say]. *Ibid* 1 inf, **nwGA,** May I fetch you home [on foot].

3 To draw, pull; also fig.

1844 Thompson *Major Jones's Courtship* 28 **GA,** I spose you all know as how my friends is fotched me out to represent this county in the next legislater. **1885** Twain *Huck. Finn* 83 **MO,** The drift of the current fetched me in at the bottom of the town. **1967–68** *DARE* (Qu. E13, . . *"When the sun is too bright, you go to the window and ———."*) Inf **NH**14, Fetch the shade down; (Qu. O13) Inf **HI**2, Along the shoreline groynes are used to "fetch the sand in."

4 To draw (breath); by ext, to utter (a sigh, groan, or other inarticulate noise).

1848 (1855) Ruxton *Life Far West* 26 **NM,** But them diggings get too over crowded nowadays, and it is hard to fetch breath amongst them big bands of corncrackers to Missoura. **1875** Howells *Foregone Conclusion* 145, The girl . . fetched a long sigh. **1879** (1880) Twain *Tramp Abroad* 194, He fetched a prodigious *"Whoosh!"* to relieve his lungs and make recognition of the heat. **1889** (1971) Farmer *Americanisms* 237 **Sth,** I *fetched* a howl that you might have heard two miles. **1908** *DN* 3.310 **eAL, wGA,** *Fetch. . .* To bring forth, utter. Also in other senses. "He fotch such a yell that the woods fair trembled." The word is very common in rural speech, but is felt as an extreme vulgarism by the semi-educated. **a1910** (1924) Twain *Autobiog.* 2.243, She would slip up behind a person . . and . . fetch a war whoop that would jump that person out of his clothes. **1932** Faulkner *Light in August* 476 **MS,** I never made a sound; I don't know but I might have fetched a snore or two for him.

5 in phrr *fetch one a lick* and varr: To hit one.

1833 in 1834 Smith *Life Jack Downing* 229 **ME,** At that the Gineral fetched me a slap on my shoulder. **1853** *Putnam's Mag.* Feb. (Schele de Vere *Americanisms* 470) **Sth,** With an arm no bigger than the round of a chair, you *fetched* the old schoolmaster the famous lick, plump in the black of his eye. **1885** Twain *Huck. Finn* 50 **MO,** He . . fetched the tub a rattling kick. **1890** *DN* 1.67 **KY,** "I fotch him a slap with my hand" shows a frequent use of the word among the negroes. **1943** Wolfert *Torpedo 8* 81, Sometimes they'd find what they were looking for and fetch it a clout over the ears. **1975** Gould *ME Lingo* 91, He dared me, and I fetched him one!

6 To make, execute (a movement, blow, etc); by ext, to hurl (something).

c1880 in 1917 Twain *What is Man* 289, You steer along [on a bicycle] . . catch your breath, fetch a violent hitch this way and then that, and down you go again. **1884** *Anglia* 7.267 **Sth** [Black], To fetch er wipe wid = to strike with. **1892** Johnston *Mr. Fortner's* 153 **GA,** But I grabbed him [=a snake] by the tail, give him a whirl or two like a whip-thong, then, fetchin' a jerk, slung his head off. **a1910** (1924) Twain *Autobiog.* 1.237, Narrative should flow as . . a brook that never goes straight for a minute, . . sometimes fetching a horseshoe three-quarters of a mile around. **1937** (1963) Hyatt *Kiverlid* 13 **sAppalachians,** All suddent she fetched a lunge and bolted clear out'n the road and busted one of the saddle gyrts. **1939** *LANE* Map 153, 1 inf, **Cape Cod MA,** You take it (a swordfish) by the fin and fetch a cut under the fin. **1967** *DARE* (Qu. Y14a, *To hit somebody hard with the fist*) Inf **ME**16, He fetched a punch at [him]. **1986** Pederson *LAGS Concordance,* 1 inf, **cwMS,** [He] fetched it [=a stone] at him.

7 To strike, overcome, kill; also fig, to strike with amazement or indignation.

1869 Twain *Innocents* 37, "*Do* you think I could venture to throw a rock here in any given direction without hitting a captain of this ship?" "Well, sir, I don't know—I think likely you'd fetch the captain of the watch, may be." **1873** Beadle *Undeveloped West* 369, [He] killed him right in front of this car. Shot at him twice afore. Fetched him dead that time. **1875** Holland *Sevenoaks* 291 **NEast,** This is a world o' sorrer, an' when a feller comes to think of a lot o' women as is so hard pushed that they hanker arter Mike Conlin, it fetches me. It's worse nor bein' without victuals, an' beats the cholery out o' sight. **1875** (1876) Twain *Tom Sawyer* 66, **MO,** That'll fetch *any* wart. *Ibid* 94 "Maybe that whack done for *him!*" "No, 'taint likely, Tom. He had liquor in him. . . When pap's full, you might take and belt him over the head with a church and you couldn't phase him. . . But if a man was dead sober, I reckon maybe that whack might fetch him." **1877** (1878) Harte *Story of a Mine* 357 **CA,** I got another shot and fetched him. **1933** Williamson *Woods Colt* 244 **Ozarks,** You tell me when he's nigh enough for my shotgun to fetch him.

8 To move (someone) to acquiescence or admiration, impress favorably; to convince.

1860 Holland *Miss Gilbert* 471 **NEng,** I've always been hoping I should get converted under you. . . I thought you'd fetched me once, but somehow it didn't stick. **c1866** in 1932 Clemens *Twain Letter Writer* 18, "If a man compell thee to go with him a mile, go with him Twain." I have closed . . many a lecture . . with that. It always "fetches" them. **1872** in 1917 Twain *Letters* 1.193, I'll even "fetch" those Dutch Pennsylvanians with this lecture. **1889** (1971) Farmer *Americanisms* 237, When some potent argument is said to have influenced strongly, or *fetched* a man, "that *fetched* him" or that convinced him. This meaning is largely colloquial in America. **1896** Harris *Sister Jane* 24 **GA,** Why don't—[he] drop his wing and cut the double-shuffle around her? I lay that would fetch her. **1899** (1912) Green *VA Folk-Speech* 173, Money will fetch him, if persuasion will not. **1957** Hoggart *Auden* 36, To an American it [=the word *fetched*] is likely to mean also 'emotionally bowled over' (as when jazz enthusiasts say that a solo performer 'fetches' them).

9 To reach (a place), weather (a point of land), gain (an objective); to hold a course, arrive: hence *fetch it* to gain an objective.

1885 Twain *Huck. Finn* 89 **MO,** I'll fetch Goshen before day-light. **1904** *DN* 2.425 **Cape Cod MA** (as of a1857), *Fetch it*. . . To succeed in an attempt. 'He tried to carry three baskets at once but he couldn't quite fetch it.' **1905** Wasson *Green Shay* 83 **NEng,** The way it commenced to breezen on after dinner, I guess likely he was tickled enough to fetch the turf [Footnote: To come to land] again himself, leave alone towin' in no wracks. **1929** (1951) Faulkner *Sartoris* 80 **MS,** Hit passed me too fast fer me to tell whether they was anybody in hit a-tall or not. I asked when I fetched town who 'twas. **1930** Stoney–Shelby *Black Genesis* 151 **seSC,** Cloud o' dus' ebery which way. When a wind fetch across a field, look like de whole top o' de eart' is trabblind wid it. **1942** ME Univ. *Studies* 56.69, In trying to make the entrance to the harbor, if the wind was fair but light and there was a head tide . . , he couldn't always make it or *fetch (it)*. [Footnote:] Fig. Gain one's objective. **1945** Colcord *Sea Language* 74 **ME, Cape Cod, Long Island,** *Fetch, Fetch by.* To succeed in weathering a point of land. Ashore, it means to attain an objective. "He couldn't quite fetch (it)." **1975** Gould *ME Lingo* 91, He got there first and *fetched* the job.

10 also with *around;* Orig naut: to tack successfully; to change course.

1906 *Harper's Mth. Mag.* Sept 539, They will leave to-morrow, letting on to go south, but they will fetch around north all in good time. **1907** Twain *Chr. Sci.* 141, Mrs. Eddy. . . fetches around and comes forward and testifies again. It is most injudicious. For . . she seems to reverse the percentages. **1946** *PADS* 6.13 **NC,** *Fetch*. . . To bring a sail into the wind in making a tack. If the sail is successfully handled, the boat is said to have *fetched.* Pamlico. Common in sailing days, about 1900.

11 To bring as a price, sell for.

1739 in 1911 Davis *Colonial Currency* 3.276, As the old saying is, The first Value of any Commodity whatever, is what it will fetch. **1939** *LANE* Map 153 **NEng,** 1 inf, They fetch a better price; 1 inf, The property fetched a good price; 1 inf, It'll fetch a good price. **1950** Stuart *Hie Hunters* 181 **eKY,** These hides will fetch ye some money.

12 usu with *up:* To rear, bring up (a child). [Scots, nEngl dial] Cf **fetching-up 1**

1841 *Knickerbocker* 17.156, Harry Cott says he was 'fetched up' on Long Island. **1870** *Putnam's Mag.* Nov. **Sth** (Schele de Vere *Americanisms* 470), You were the child of a missionary, and from your cradle had been *fetched* up for the work. **1889** (1971) Farmer *Americanisms* 237 **Sth,** *To fetch* has also the sense of "to bring up," or "to educate"; thus, children are *fetched up* or *raised.* **1890** *DN* 1.67 **KY,** I was fotch up with the niggers. **1909** *DN* 3.396 **nwAR,** *Fotch up*. . . Brought up. Used by negroes and po' whites. Facetious with others. **1926** Roberts *Time of Man* 141 **cKY,** You look like you was fatched up in town. **1941** *LANE* Map 395, [In the context "She has brought up three children" *fetch up* is given by 38 infs, **chiefly nNEng;** 24 say it is obsolete, 4 that it is older but still in use, and 1 that it is uneducated; 1 inf says *fetch.*] **1966–69** *DARE* (Qu. Z17, . . *"All her children were ______ [on the farm]."*) Infs **IL47, IN16, MI68, NC40,** Fetched up; (Qu. II21, . . *"The way he behaves, you'd think he was ______."*) Inf **AL6,** Fetched up; **TN15,** [fɑčt]. [All Infs old] **1973** Allen *LAUM* 1.343 (as of c1950), Old-fashioned *fetched up* is a write-in response in Iowa . . and in North Dakota. **1975** Gould *ME Lingo* 91, They took two state children to *fetch up* along'th their own.

13 with *up* (or rarely *to*): To come or be brought to a sudden stop; to end up (in some place or situation); also fig. Cf **fetching-up 2**

1838 Neal *Charcoal Sketches* 96, I was soon fotch'd up in the victualling line—and I busted for the benefit of my creditors. **1859** (1968) Bartlett *Americanisms* 146, We often hear the phrase, "He fetched up all standing," that is, he made a sudden halt. It is a nautical vulgarism, the figure being that of a ship which is suddenly brought to, while at full speed and with all her sails set. **1867** Twain *Jumping Frog* 12, She'd always fetch up at the stand just about a neck ahead. **1904** *DN* 2.425 **Cape Cod MA** (as of a1857), *Fetch up all a standing*. . . To come to a sudden stop. **1905** *DN* 3.9 **cCT,** *Fetch up*. . . To come to a sudden stop. **1930** Faulkner *As I Lay Dying* 8 **MS,** The horse comes dropping down the slope . . and fetches up twenty feet away. **1939** (1962) Thompson *Body & Britches* 199 **NY,** The family . . left Nantucket before the Revolution and for the most part have not been seafarers since that date. Yet . . if they are brought up shortly, they will observe that they have "fetched up with a wet sail". **1942** ME Univ. *Studies* 56.30, A vessel that attempted to navigate near the shore in thick fog was likely to run on the rocks and *fetch,* or *bring up all astanding,* that is, with all sails set. [Footnote to *fetch up all astanding:*] Fig. To meet with an unforeseen and insurmountable obstacle. **1955** Adams *Grandfather* 131 **NY** (as of 1829), At last she rounded the point, reefed down to the thirds, scuttering like a mink out of a henhouse, and fetched to against Saunders' dock. **1965** *PADS* 43.26 **seMA,** *Fetch-up* used to mean *stop short* by 8 [of 9] informants. **1969** *DARE* Tape **MI109,** We used to say we'd fetch up on the Crow Bar; that's where we did sit occasionally. [*DARE* Ed: Inf is punning on *bar* a submerged sandbank and *bar* a drinking establishment.] **1975** Gould *ME Lingo* 91, He *fetched up* on a dead-end road.

14 also with *(a)round:* To restore to health or consciousness; to regain consciousness, "come around." [Cf *OED fetch (again)* (at *fetch* v. 2. d, 12. b) restore to consciousness]

1859 Taliaferro *Fisher's R.* 90 **nwNC** (as of 1820s), The poor 'oman fainted away, and we like to a nuver a fotched her to. **1884** *Anglia* 7.269 **Sth** [Black], To fetch one all right = to cause one to recover. **1889** Twain *CT Yankee* 136, You do feel so strange . . —like somebody that has been married on a sudden, or struck by lightning, . . and hasn't quite fetched around, yet, . . and can't just get his bearings. **1899** Chesnutt *Conjure Woman* 156 **NC,** He 'lowed mebbe he could kyo' 'im [=a horse] en fetch 'im roun' all right, leas'ways good 'nuff ter sell ag'in.

15 also with *on:* To give birth to; to deliver (a baby).

1931 Hannum *Thursday April* 9 **wNC,** All the more reason that he would be a good hand to fetch on a child. **1937** (1963) Hyatt *Kiverlid* 31 **sAppalachians,** The set o' them horns p'ints that she'll be a pow'ful fine milker when she fetches a calf.

16 with *away, loose:* To break loose, come adrift.

1840 (1841) Dana *2 Yrs.* 11, My hats, boots, mattress and blankets had all *fetched away* and gone over to leeward, and were jammed and broken under the boxes and coils of rigging. **1872** Twain *Roughing It* 288 **MO,** *She* never could tell when it [=a glass eye] hopped out, being blind on that side, you see. So somebody would have to hunch her and say, "Your game eye has fetched loose, Miss Wagner dear." **1942** ME Univ. *Studies* 56.34, In heavy weather, something was sure to *fetch away.* [Footnote:] To break; become unfastened.

17 To be about (to act).

1937 Sandoz *Slogum* 161 **NE** (as of c1900), "Smells like a herd a fetchin' to stampede it across the country at the stompin' of a gnat," an old cowpuncher said.

18 ?To express.

1981 Harper–Presley *Okefinokee* 68 (as of 1930), My wife . . said, 'The first time that ol' Uncle Johnny Wainwright' (that's the way she fetched it over) 'or ol' Uncle Eli Lee passes hyere, I expect them to take this wart off my finger.

fetch n[1] [Engl dial; *EDD fetch* sb.[1] "A spectre, wraith, apparition; a ghost, spirit." Quots suggest that the apparition is usu that of the person who sees it, and its coming is believed to portend his death.]

See quots.

1930 Shoemaker *1300 Words* 21 **cPA Mts** (as of c1900), *Fetch*—A spirit that foretells early death, a "token". **1965** *DARE* File **New Orleans LA** (as of c1901), A fetch is an apparition of oneself, portending one's death.

fetch n[2] Cf **drop C3**

An illegitimate or abandoned child.

1944 *Collier's* 114.13/1 **Harlem NYC** [Black], The child subject was sheltered by its grandmother who apparently was a professional granny accepting anywhere from twenty-five cents to a dollar a week for taking in drops, rustles, fetches or whatever you've a mind to call them.

fetch around See **fetch v B10, 14**

fetch a shingle off the house v phr

To take unfair advantage; see quot.

1953 Randolph-Wilson *Down in Holler* 218 **Ozarks,** A woodcutter came into the village restaurant, ordered a cup of coffee, and then produced a big sidemeat sandwich from his pocket. The outraged waitress stared at him. "Well," she said, "that's what I call fetchin' a shingle off'n the house!" I have heard the same expression applied to a man who drank from his own flask in a place where whiskey was being sold by the drink.

fetch away See **fetch v B16**

fetched ppl adj, adv Also *fetching* **chiefly S Midl** *euphem* Cf **dad** n[2]

Confounded, damned—used for emphasis.

1854 (1923) Holmes *Tempest & Sunshine* 144 **KY,** I've got such fetchin' big corns on my feet that I ain't goin' to be cramped with none of your toggery. **1856** Holmes *Lena Rivers* 113, The few negroes able to assist, thought "she needn't be so fetch-ed cross." **1927** *DN* 5.475 **Ozarks,** *Fetching*. . . This emphatic adjective is in very common use, but does'nt [sic] seem to mean anything in particular. The following sentence is typical: "Four o' them Tadlock boys jumped onter him t'once, but Jim he licked ever' fetchin' one of 'em." **1954** *Harder Coll.* **cwTN,** *Fetching*. . . In common use for emphasis, like blinking, blooming, etc. **1966** *DARE* (Qu. NN17, . . *"That ——— fly won't go away."*) Inf **NC**15, Fetched [fɛčɪt]. **1967** *Courier-Jrl.* (Louisville KY) 7 Jan **wTN,** I had not though of fetched . . in a month of Sundays. My mother said it lots of times . . when provoked. I remember it, too, as "dad fetch-ed."

fetched-on See **fotch-on**

fetch fire See **fire, come to borrow**

fetch grass n [Var of *vetch;* cf also *OED fitch* sb.[1]]

Perh a grass of the genus *Cynodon.*

1967 *DARE* (Qu. L9a, . . *Kinds of grass grown for hay*) Inf **LA**12, Fetch [fɛč] grass. That's a kind of Bermuda.

fetching See **fetched**

fetching stick n [**fetch v B1a**]

1978 Massey *Bittersweet Country* 136 **Ozarks,** For high shelves and hidden items nothing came in handier than a fetching stick—a stick with a long handle and a forked end. With it the merchant could reach the item he needed without having to climb a ladder.

fetching-up vbl n Also *fetch-up, fetchings-up*

1 Upbringing, rearing, esp "proper" upbringing. [**fetch v B12**]

1854 *Harper's New Mth. Mag.* 10.135/1 **VA,** The hero . . has come up to the state capital . . to . . rub off some of the rust which his back-woods "fetching-up" has thrown about his manners. **1967-70** *DARE* (Qu. II21, . . *"The way he behaves, you'd think he . . "*) Inf **IL**141, Had no fetchins-up; **MI**116, Didn't have any fetching-up [laughter]; **NY**231, "Ain't had no fetchin'-up," they say; **PA**138, Had no fetching-up; **WA**20, Don't have no fetching-up. **1975** Gould *ME Lingo* 91, A child shows his *fetchin' up* by his manners in public: "Show your fetchin' up—stop spilling your milk!" . . *Fetchin' up,* as applied to a child, is often shortened to *fetch-up;* "Now, be a good boy and show your fetch-up!"

2 A sudden stop; the jolt which results from such a stop; also fig. [**fetch v B13**]

1866 (1881) Whitney *Leslie Goldthwaite* 163 **MA,** It isn't the fall that hurts,—it's the fetch-up. **1897** *Outing* 30.558/2, Then [there was] a final lightning race down a precipice, with a dismembering "fetch-up" at the bottom. **1927** *Harper's Mth. Mag.* Dec 82 **CT,** They had both been born in this house, but India had been born longer ago than Flagg, so his fetch-up was the sharper.

fetch loose See **fetch v B16**

fetch on See **fetch v B15**

fetch-on See **fotch-on**

fetch round See **fetch v B14**

fetch-taked adj *euphem* Cf **fetched**

Blasted, damned.

1953 *PADS* 19.10 **sAppalachians,** *Fetch-taked*. . . Mild expletive used in speaking to dogs. "Begone, you *fetch-taked* dogs!" **1956** McAtee *Some Dialect NC* 15, *Fetch-taked*. . . Mild expletive.

fetch to See **fetch B13**

fetch up See **fetch v B12, 13**

fetch-up n See **fetching-up**

fetchy adj [**fetch v B8**]

1908 *DN* 3.310 **eAL, wGA,** *Fetching, fetchy*. . . Charming, attractive.

fether bed See **feather bed**

fetherfew See **featherfew**

fetid currant n [See quot 1848]

=**skunk currant.**

1848 Gray *Manual of Botany* 142, *R. prostratum*. . . *Fetid Currant*. . . The bruised plant and berries exhale an unpleasant odor. **1885** *Bot. Gaz.* 10.227 **Upper Peninsula MI,** In the colder and denser woods, where the white pine and hemlock were more common, the fetid-currant, *Ribes prostratum,* L'Her., frequently occurred. **1931** Harned *Wild Flowers Alleghanies* 220, *Fetid or Skunk Currant*. . . Cold wet places on the mountains. **1972** Viereck-Little *AK Trees* 154, Fetid currant. . . In spite of its strong odor, it makes excellent jelly.

fetid marigold n

1 A plant of the genus *Dyssodia.* [See quot 1857] Also called **dogweed 2.** For other names of var spp see **dog fennel 5, false mayweed, flea-weed 2, prairie-dog weed, prickleaf, stinkweed, yellow mayweed**

1857 Gray *Manual of Botany* 223, *Dysodia* [sic]. . . *Fetid Marigold*. . . Herbs, dotted with large pellucid glands, which give a strong odor; . . flowers yellow. **1906** Rydberg *Flora CO* 381, *Fetid Marigold*. . . On prairies, river valleys, roadsides and waste places. **1931** U.S. Dept. Ag. *Misc. Pub.* 101.165, Dogweeds, often called fetid-marigolds, comprise a group of about 20 species occurring in the West, mostly in the Southwest. **1970** Correll *Plants TX* 1680, *Fetid Marigold.* Strongly scented annual or perennial herbs. **1976** Bailey-Bailey *Hortus Third* 405.

2 A **chinchweed** (here: *Pectis angustifolia*).

1970 Kirk *Wild Edible Plants W. U.S.* 275, *Pectis angustifolia* . . Chinchweed, Fetid Marigold. . . The plant may be eaten raw, cooked, dried, or used for seasoning other food.

fetid shrub n

=**pawpaw** (usu *Asimina triloba*).

1897 Sudworth *Arborescent Flora* 200, *Asimina triloba*. . . Fetid Shrub (N.C.). **1911** *Century Dict. Suppl.,* Fetid-shrub. . . The papaw. **1960** Vines *Trees SW* 290, Vernacular names [of pawpaw] are Fetid-shrub and Custard-apple. **1974** (1977) Coon *Useful Plants* 60.

fetterbush n [See quot 1953 at **3**]

1 A **staggerbush** (here: *Lyonia lucida*).

1857 Gray *Manual of Botany* 254, *A[ndromeda] nitida,* . . the *Fetter-bush,* . . may grow in S. Virginia. **1860** Curtis *Cat. Plants NC* 95, *Fetter-Bush* (Andromeda nitida . .)—Found only in the Lower District in low Pine barrens. **1968** *DARE* (Qu. T5, . . *Kinds of evergreens*) Inf **GA**25, ['fɛdɚˌbʊš]—same as hoorah ['huˌrɔ] bush; (Qu. T15, . . *Kinds of swamp trees*) Inf **GA**25, Fetterbush. **1968** *DARE* Tape **GA**30, The real name for it, I think, is a fetterbush but we call it the hoorah bush.

2 as *mountain fetterbush:* An ericaceous shrub *(Pieris floribunda).*

1901 Lounsberry *S. Wild Flowers* 393, *Mountain Fetter-bush. Pieris floribunda*. . . It is only through the mountainous parts of its restricted range that this most exquisite of the fetter-bushes is found. **1933** Small *Manual SE Flora* 1003, Mountain fetter-bush. **1938** Van Dersal *Native Woody Plants* 186, *Mountain fetter-bush*. . . A small evergreen shrub with dense foliage.

3 A shrub of the genus *Leucothoe. Also called* **hemlock 3.** For other names of var spp see **black laurel 2, dog hobble 1, dog laurel, ivy, pepperbush, pipestem, pipewood, poison hemlock, Sierra laurel, sweetbells, switch-ivy, titi, white osier, white pepper**

1901 Mohr *Plant Life AL* 122, Where the hammocks merge into the alluvial lands, . . the silver-bell tree . . is found . . interspersed with . . evergreen fetterbushes *(Pieris nitida, Leucothöe axillaris).* **1942** Van Dersal *Ornamental Amer. Shrubs* 257 *(DA), Leucothoe catesbaei* . . is variously known as fetterbush, switch-ivy, doghobble, and ivy. **1946** Tatnall *Flora DE* 198, *Fetter Bush.* Common in wet thickets, throughout the Coastal Plain. **1953** Greene-Blomquist *Flowers South*

91, *Fetter-Bushes (Leucothöe)* The common name of the evergreen species of this genus alludes to their habit of growing in such thickets that it is difficult to walk through them. **1976** Bailey–Bailey *Hortus Third* 653.

fetticus n Also sp *fatticows, fattikows, fattycows, vettekost, vettikost* [Du *vettig kost* fatty or greasy food] **esp NY**

A **lamb's lettuce** (here: *Valerianella locusta*).

1848 Bartlett *Americanisms* 136, *Fetticus. Vettikost.* Vulg. *Fåttikows.* (Bot. *Valerianella* . .) Corn-salad, or lamb's-lettuce. A word used in New York. **1872** Schele de Vere *Americanisms* 83 **NY,** Vegetables were evidently not much to the taste of the old burghers, for it seems they called Corn-salad *(Valerianetta)* [sic] with biting irony *Vettikost,* something like rich fare, and their descendants, still retaining the dish, have as contemptuously allowed it to appear half classically as *Fetticus* or in ludicrous English disguise as *Fatticows.* **1889** *AN&Q* 4.22, The plant called corn-salad, or lamb-lettuce, is called *fetticus,* or *vettekost,* by gardeners. In the New York market I believe it is called fatty-cows. It appears to be the Dutch *vette kost,* "fat food;" but perhaps the *kost* is the same which appears in alecost, costmary, and other plant names. **1891** *Century Dict.* 6688, *V[alerianella] olitoria* . . is now often cultivated under glass as an early salad under the name of *fetticus.* **1935** (1943) Muenscher *Weeds* 438, *Valerianella Locusta.* . . Fetticus. . . Introduced . . as a salad plant. May–July.

fettiglich n [Prob Ger *fettig* fatty, greasy + redund *lich* -ly] Cf **fatcake**

A doughnut.

1967 *DARE* (Qu. H27) Inf **MO**12, In the fall of the year we call them ['fetiklɪx]. When [I] was a girl, children would mask and go from door to door saying ['fetixlɪx 'fetixlɪx]. People would give [us] doughnuts. [Inf of Ger background, in Ger community]

fettilock n [Pronc-sp for *fetlock;* cf Pronc Intro 3.I.23]

1917 *DN* 4.392 **neOH,** *Fettilock* [fetɪlɑk] . . Fetlock. Ashtabula Co.

fettle n [By lambdacism; cf Intro "Language Changes" IV. 4]

A fetter.

1932 *Hanley Disks* **cMA,** Fettles . . made of wood, looks like . . a little yoke made of bent wood and open so the top would come off and let it be around the creature's ankles and then fastened up again.

fetty n [Abbr and pronc-sp for **asafetida**]

1969 *DARE* (Qu. BB50d, *Favorite spring tonics*) Inf **MI**105, I used to wear a ['feti] bag around my neck during the winter; it smelled very strong. **1970** *DARE* FW Addit **MI**115, For diphtheria, you carry around your neck (on a string) a little sack of fetty.

feundu See **vendue**

feustering vbl n [Cf *EDD fooster* v. "to fuss or fumble about in a futile, purposeless way."]

1939 (1962) Thompson *Body & Britches* 503 **NY,** It is not so easy to explain a word used in Erie county to mean wasting time by puttering, *feustering.*

fever n Pronc-sp *febuh*

A Form. Cf Pronc Intro 3.I.17

1922 Gonzales *Black Border* 301 **sSC, GA coasts** [Gullah glossary], *Febuh*—fever, fevers.

B Senses.

1 often with *the:* Any illness characterized by fever—used in ref to whatever disease is prevalent at a particular time or place.

1822 in 1839 Mathews *Memoirs* 3.328 **NY,** Here we are—confidence restored—fever gone. . . I firmly believe you know nothing of the horrors of the yellow fever by newspaper report. **1885** *Wkly. New Mexican Rev.* 15 Jan. 1/3 *(DA),* If they [=Texas cattle] come over early in the season they may not bring the fever [*DARE* Ed: =**Texas fever**] with them. **1905** *DN* 3.97 **nwAR,** *The fever.* . . Typhoid fever. In Fayetteville and the other non-malarial parts of N. W. Ark., as in Morgantown, W. Va., typhoid is the most common kind of fever. **1937** *Hall Coll.* **eTN,** *Fever.* . . Any kind of fever, but especially typhoid. Sometimes the type of fever is specified, as e.g. "lung fever" (pneumonia, though one may also hear the expression "pneumonie"), brain fever, and bilious fever. "A sight of people died of the fever (typhoid) on this branch twenty-five er thirty year ago. Hit began when loggin' started and the stumps (o' trees) soured." **1953** *PADS* 19.10 **wNC,** *Fever.* . . Pneumonia. "Lige, he's took down with fever." **1961** Folk *Word Atlas N. LA* Map 1809, What do you call *The fever?*—yellow fever[,] 76%[;] *the* fever[,] 10%[;] others[,] 14%[:] scarlet fever[,] slow fever[,] typhoid fever[,] malaria[,] swamp fever.

2 with *the:* =**buck fever 1.**

1966 *DARE* (Qu. P36, *When a hunter sees a deer . . and gets so excited he can't shoot, he has* ______) Inf **FL**7, The fever. [That's] when he does want to go so badly.

fever and ague n Also *fever ague* Pronc-sp *fevernagy* Cf **ague**

1 A form of malarial fever characterized by chills and fever. *old-fash*

[**1658** (1857) Hull *Diaries* June 184, Much sickness in the southern colonies,—fevers and agues, of which many died.] **1671** (1912) Alvord–Bidgood *First Explor.* 187 **VA,** Perceute being taken very sick of a fever and ague every afternoon . . we resolved to leave our horses. **1751** in 1883 *Documents Colonial & Post-Revol. Hist. NJ* 7.601 **NJ,** This Town and my Situation in it have for 4 years past . . subjected me to the Fever & Ague. **1841** Kennedy *Texas* 1.66, Intermittent fever, or "fever and ague," as it is vulgarly termed, is the general penalty attached to settlements in the "bush," from the St. Lawrence to the Sabine. **1851** Burke *Polly Peablossom* 155 **nIL,** A tall, yellow-haired, fever-and-ague-looking youth. **1872** Schele de Vere *Americanisms* 432, *Ague* . . is rarely used without its companion, fever, and the two form the familiar *fevernagy* of the West. **1889** (1971) Farmer *Americanisms* 237, The *fever'n'ager* got fastened to me, and stuck jest like a Comanche on a mustang: the worse it jumps, the tighter he sticks, as if he was glued to the saddle. **1943** *LANE* Map 505 *(Fever and Ague),* Many informants declare that the disease . . is rare locally . . or entirely unknown. . . It is commonly regarded as a Southern disease, . . sometimes as Western. . . Several informants report that the disease was formerly prevalent but is now rare, or simply characterize it as 'an old-fashioned disease'. **1958** *DE Folkl. Bulletin* Oct 32/1, Fever-and-ager chills (ague). **1966–68** *DARE* (Qu. BB13, *Other words . . for chills and fever*) Inf **ME**5, Fever and ague ['eɪgju]; **MN**12, Fever ague ['ego]; **WA**6, Fever and ague [eɪg]; not here—in the South. It's ['eɪg,ju].

2 See **fever-and-ague worm.**

fever and ague seeds n Also *fever and ague blossom* [Perh from its appearing when **fever and ague** is most likely to be contracted] *obs*

Masses of plant or insect matter on the surface of still water; see quots.

1807 in 1810 Schultz *Travels* 1.25 **NY,** The lake is . . bordered with swamps . . which produce innumerable swarms of small butterflies. . . These insects cannot fly any great distance without resting, and a very light breeze off shore will prevent their regaining the land . . ; in consequence of which, they soon fall with outspread wings and cover the lake so completely as fully to justify the expression of its being *"in blossom."* . . The water . . will be found to be full of small particles which the boatmen call *fever and ague seeds;* but, in reality, are the eggs of certain insects. **1823** Cooper *Pioneers* 1.164 **NY** (as of 1793), I've drunk the Onondaga water . . when the fever-an-agy seeds was to be seen in it, as plain and as plenty as you can see the rattle-snakes on old Crumhorn. **1826** Flint *Recollections* 316 **LA,** I judge it to be vegetable matter, brought in by the *Bayou,* by which the lake communicates with the Mississippi, and like that singular appearance on the northern lakes, called "fever and ague blossoms"

fever-and-ague worm n Also *fever-and-ague, ager worm, egger* ~ Cf **fever worm**

A **woolly bear:** here, the larva of the isabella moth *(Isia isabella).*

1818 in 1824 Knight *Letters* 106, In the fields, a kind of foxtail grass here [in KY] becomes timothy; and our black-and-yellow caterpillar is named fever-and-ague. **1958** *DE Folkl. Bulletin* 1.31, When the "ager" worm in the fall has more black on his head than on his rear, you will have an open winter and a late spring. . . The "ager"—pronounced with a hard "g"—worm is the fever-and-ague worm, with a fuzzy brown body but black at both ends, which crawls about and is readily found during late August and early fall. **1968** *DARE* (Qu. R27) Inf **NJ**16, Egger [ɛgɚ] worms—this is the woolly bear.

fever and lurk(s) n [*EDD fever-lurk* "idleness, indolence, laziness" (at *fever* sb. 2)]

The "disease" of laziness.

1966–67 *DARE* (Qu. BB28, . . *Imaginary diseases: "He must have the* ______.") Inf **AL**10, Fever and lurk—too sorry to eat and too lazy to work; **KY**34, Fever and lurks—two stomachs to eat and neither would work.

fever bark See **fever tree**

feverbush n [From their use in treating fevers]

1 A **spicebush** (here: *Lindera benzoin*).

1778 Carver *Travels N. Amer.* 510 **WI, MI, MN, IA,** The *Fever Bush* grows about five or six feet high; . . and it bears a reddish berry of a spicy flavour. **1792** Belknap *Hist. NH* 3.97, *Spice-wood (laurus benzoin)* or as it is commonly called *Fever-bush,* is another species of the *laurus,* common in New-Hampshire. **1837** Darlington *Flora Cestrica* 253, *L. Benzoin. . .* Spice-wood. Wild All-spice. Fever bush. Benjamin tree. **1889** (1971) Farmer *Americanisms* 237, *Fever Bush (Laurus benzoin).* —The spice-bush, or wild allspice. Its bark is valued as a febrifuge. Mass. **1944** ME Univ. *Studies* 59.19, *Lindera. . .* Wild Allspice, Feverbush. *L. Benzoin. . .* Occasional and local. Damp woods and thickets on low ground. North central and southern York County [Maine]. **1945** Saxon *Gumbo Ya-Ya* 170 **LA,** Other things used for cure and prevention of illness included hair plant, button tree, fever bush. **1971** Krochmal *Appalachia Med. Plants* 160, Feverbush. . . The aromatic bark is used to treat dysentery, coughs, and colds.

2 A **winterberry** (here: *Ilex verticillata*).

1830 Rafinesque *Med. Flora* 253, *Black Alder, Fever bush, Winterberry. . .* Used in agues, fevers, debility, anasarca [etc]. **1892** (1974) Millspaugh *Amer. Med. Plants* 106, *Fever Bush. Ibid* 107, In intermittent fever it has often proved as generally applicable as Peruvian Bark. **1949** *Amer. Photography* 43.115/2, Probably the commonest of these are the two winterberries: the Virginia winterberry *(Ilex verticillata),* sometimes called black alder or feverbush, and the smooth winterberry *(Ilex laevigata).* **1974** (1977) Coon *Useful Plants* 64, *Ilex verticillata*— Winterberry, . . feverbush.

3 A **silktassel.**

1897 Parsons *Wild Flowers CA* 370, *G[arrya] Fremonti. . .* is the shrub usually spoken of as "quinine-bush," "fever-bush," etc. **1937** U.S. Forest Serv. *Range Plant Hdbk.* B81, All parts of the silktassels are permeated with an intensely bitter, quininelike substance. . . Fremont silktassel, locally called bearbrush and California feverbush. . . Tasseltree *[Garrya elliptica],* known also as feverbush.

fever deluxe n [Perh folk-etym for **fever and lurk(s)**]

1969 *DARE* (Qu. BB28, *Joking names . . for imaginary diseases: "He must have the ________.")* Inf **MA69,** Fever deluxe [fivə di'luks].

feverfew n

1 A plant *(Chrysanthemum parthenium)* with daisylike flowers. Also called **featherfew**

1790 in 1793 Amer. Philos. Soc. *Trans.* 3.177 **sePA,** Matricaria, Fever-few. Parthenium. Chamomilla. **1840** MA Zool. & Bot. Surv. *Herb. Plants & Quadrupeds* 127, *Chrysanthemum parthenium.* Feverfew. **1901** Mohr *Plant Life AL* 813, The herb, under name of 'feverfew,' is used medicinally. **1968** *DARE* (Qu. S25, . . *Wild chrysanthemum-like flowers . . that bloom in fields late in the fall)* Inf **PA99,** Feverfew; (Qu. BB50c, *Remedies for infections)* Inf **WV10,** Feverfew tea. Feverfew is a flower [whose] blossoms are boiled into a tea to combat fever.

2 A **false foxglove** (here: *Aureolaria pedicularia*).

1966 *DARE* Wildfl QR Pl. 201 Inf **NC28,** Feverfew.

3 A plant of the genus *Parthenium.* For other names of var spp see **guayule, prairie dock, wild quinine**

1900 Lyons *Plant Names* 276, *Parthenium . .* Feverfew. **1940** Steyermark *Flora MO* 532, *[Parthenium integrifolium; P. hispidum]* American feverfew. **1968** Barkley *Plants KS* 360, *Parthenium integrifolium . .* Feverfew. **1970** Correll *Plants TX* 1626, *Parthenium hispidum . .* Feverfew.

4 An agrimony (here: *Agrimonia eupatoria*).

1900 Lyons *Plant Names* 19, *A[grimonia] eupatoria. . .* Feverfew.

fever flower See **feverweed 1**

fever grass n [See quots] **SE**

Either **blue-eyed grass 1** or a **sneezeweed** (here: *Helenium amarum*).

1933 Small *Manual SE Flora* 327, *Sisyrinchium. . .* Blue-eyed grasses. Fever-grasses. **c1937** in 1972 *Amer. Slave* 2.171 **SC,** Some old folks use to make medicines out of herbs. I 'member my ma would take fever grass and boil it to tea and have us drink it to keep de fever away. **1955** *S. Folkl. Qrly.* 19.234 **FL,** A medicinal tea was made by boiling the plant and roots of *Fever Grass* (Sisyrinchium xerophyllum). **1970** *NC Folkl.* 18.15, For colds, drink "fever grass" root tea, sweetened with cane sugar. **1970** *DARE* (Qu. S21, . . *Weeds . . that are a trouble in gardens and fields)* Inf **FL50,** Fever grass; (Qu. BB22, . . *Home remedies . .* for constipation) Inf **FL49,** Make tea from fever grass. **1974** Morton *Folk Remedies* 71, *Fever Grass. . . Helenium amarum. . . South Carolina (Current use):* Some people break off below leaves, boil the entire top and drink "tea" for fever.

fever leg n

Perh a form of phlebitis.

1968 *Budget* (Sugarcreek OH) 25 July 15/2 **cwFL,** [He] is also hospitalized 3 weeks. Had a gland operation. Now he has what Dr.'s call a fever leg.

fever lily n [See quot]

A canna lily (here: *Canna indica* or *C. generalis*).

1974 Morton *Folk Remedies* 161, *Canna indica . .* and *C. generalis. . .* are grown in dooryards in the South Carolina Low Country and are called . . *"Fever Lily." . .* If an adult has a fever, a fresh canna leaf may be placed on the back of the neck. To "bring down" the fever of a small child, canna leaves are wrapped around the child's body.

fevernagy See **fever and ague**

fever plant n [See quots]

An **evening primrose** (here: *Oenothera biennis*).

1893 *Jrl. Amer. Folkl.* 6.142, *Œnothera biennis . .* fever-plant; coffee-plant. Eastern States. [Footnote to *fever-plant:*] Used as a diaphoretic in fevers. **1911** Henkel *Amer. Med. Leaves* 14, *Evening Primrose. . . Other common names. . .* Fever plant. . . It has been used for coughs and asthmatic troubles.

feverroot n [From their use in treating fevers]

1 =**horse gentian.**

1739 (1946) Gronovius *Flora Virginica* 23, Triosteospermum perfoliatum. . . *Feverroot & Cinque.* **1832** Williamson *Hist. ME* 1.123, The *Fever-root,* or *wild Ipecac,* occurs in limestone soils. . . It may be used for an emetic or cathartic. **1901** Mohr *Plant Life AL* 744, *Triosteum perfoliatum. . .* Tinker's Root. Fever Root. **1974** (1977) Coon *Useful Plants* 90, Fever-root. . . A decoction of this plant was used by the Cherokee Indians in fevers, colds, and female obstructions.

2 Prob a **water hemlock.**

1790 in 1793 Amer. Philos. Soc. *Trans.* 3.234 **VA,** I have heard this poisonous herb, called by the names of Wild-Carrot, Wild Parsnep, Fever-Root, and Mock-Eel-Root.

3 =**pinedrops.**

1830 Rafinesque *Med. Flora* 2.68, *Pterospora andromeda. . .* Fever Root, Albany Beechdrop. *Ibid* 69, The root is the officinal part. . . It is said to avail in all remittents, typhus, and nervous fevers. . . and often stops the fever in a few hours. **1959** Carleton *Index Herb. Plants* 45, *Fever-root:* Pterospora andromeda; Triosteum perfoliatum.

fever tick n [See quots]

The cattle tick (here: *Margaropus annulatus*).

1916 Benedict–Lomax *Book of TX* 104, The quarantine line . . marks the area below which cattle are subject to the "Texas fever" . . and must be inspected for the fever tick before being allowed to go farther north or west. **1926** Essig *Insects N. Amer.* 20, *The cattle tick, North American fever tick, or the Texas cattle fever tick, . .* is the most important cattle tick from the fact that it is the carrier of . . a protozoan parasite which causes Texas cattle fever. **1928** Metcalf–Flint *Destructive & Useful Insects* 788, *Texas-fever Tick. . .* It is the only means of spread of the disease known as cattle fever, tick fever, splenetic fever, or Texas fever, from sick animals to healthy ones. **1966–68** *DARE* (Qu. R23a, . . *Creatures that fasten themselves to the skin and suck blood)* Inf **LA12,** Fever ticks—get on cattle; **LA15,** Fever tick—a long, sharp tick with red spot; **CA87,** Both the grey tick and the red fever tick that burrows right in; **OK23,** Fever tick. **1966–70** *DARE* Tape **FL35,** The fever tick was the only one that was detrimental to cattle; **TX96,** Fever tick—a type of wood tick afflicting cattle.

fever tree n Also *fever bark* [See quot 1976]

A small tree *(Pinckneya pubens)* native to the southeastern United States. Also called **bitterbark 1, calico bush 2, Carolina bark, Florida bark, Georgia bark, maiden's blushes**

1830 Rafinesque *Med. Flora* 57, *Pinckneya pubens. . . Names. . . Vulgar.* Bitter Bark, Georgia Bark, Florida Bark, Fever-tree. *Ibid* 58, It has long been used in Georgia and Florida, in intermittent fevers with success, and found nearly equal to the officinal bark. **1868** (1870) Gray *Field Botany* 176, *Fever-Tree. . . P. pubens. . .* This plant is of the same tribe with the *Cinchona . .* and has similar medicinal (tonic) properties.

1884 Miller *Dict. Engl. Names of Plants* 231, *Pinckneya pubens,* bitter-bark-tree, Fever-tree of Georgia. **1897** Sudworth *Arborescent Flora* 337, *Pinckneya pubens. . .* Common Names. . . Fevertree (Ala.). **1933** Small *Manual SE Flora* 1253, *Fever-tree. . .* The numerous bright-pink foliaceous sepals make the plants conspicuous on the edges of swamps. **1976** Bailey–Bailey *Hortus Third* 874, *Fever tree. . .* Bark, called Georgia bark or fever bark, contains cinchonin and has been used in treatment of intermittent fevers. **1979** Little *Checklist U.S. Trees* 187, *Pinckneya. . . Other common names*—fevertree, fever-bark, Georgia-bark.

fevertwig n [From its medicinal use]

1 also *fevertwitch:* A **bittersweet** (here: *Celastrus scandens*).

1830 Rafinesque *Med. Flora* 206, *Celastrus scandens. . . Fever-twig. . .* Bark used, emetic, antisyphilitic, discutient; externally it expels indurated tumors, and the swelling of cow bags. **1876** Hobbs *Bot. Hdbk.* 37, Fever twig. . . Fever twitch, . . Celastrus scandens. **1930** Sievers *Amer. Med. Plants* 4, *American Bittersweet. . . Other common names. . .* Fevertwig, fever-twitch. **1960** Vines *Trees SW* 660, [Bittersweet is] known also by the vernacular names of . . Fever-twig, . . and Climbing-orangeroot.

2 A **bittersweet** (here: *Solanum dulcamara*).

c1873 in 1976 Miller *Shaker Herbs* 138, *Solanum dulcamara. . .* Woody Nightshade. . . Fever Twig. **1900** Lyons *Plant Names* 349, *S. Dulcamara. . .* Fever-twig. . . Mildly narcotic, sedative. **1940** Clute *Amer. Plant Names* 272, *Solanum dulcamara. . .* Fever-twig.

fevertwitch See **fevertwig 1**

feverweed n

1 also *fever flower:* A **false foxglove** (here: *Aureolaria pedicularia*). [See quot 1842]

1842 Buckingham *E. & W. States* 1.162 **ME,** The fire-weed, fever-weed, foxglove, . . [are] carefully collected and prepared for medicinal uses. **1900** Lyons *Plant Names* 131, *D[asystoma] Pedicularia. . .* Fever-weed. **1959** Carleton *Index Herb. Plants* 45, *Fever-weed:* Aureolaria pedicularia. **1961** House *Wild Flowers* 251, *Fever-flower. Aureolaria pedicularia. . .* Flowering in late summer, from the latter part of July to September.

2 A **button snakeroot 2** (here: *Eryngium aquaticum*). [*OED* 1855 →]

1971 Krochmal *Appalachia Med. Plants* 114, *Eryngium aquaticum. . . Common Names:* . . feverweed.

3 A vervain (here: *Verbena stricta*). [See quots]

1892 *Jrl. Amer. Folkl.* 5.102 **IL,** *Verbena stricta,* fever-weed. [Footnote:] Thought to be a specific for fever and ague. **1899** Bergen *Animal Lore* 116 **cIL,** A common vervain *(Verbena stricta)* is popularly known as "fever-weed" from its supposed efficacy as a remedy for fever and ague. **1961** Brown *NC Folkl.* 6.124 **cnNC,** A weed called "fever weed" will stop bleeding.

4 A **lamb's lettuce** (here: *Valerianella amarella*).

1967 *DARE* Wildfl QR Pl. 50c (Wills–Irwin) Inf **TX**34, Feverweed.

fever worm n [See quot 1899] **chiefly KY** Cf **fever-and-ague worm**

A **woolly bear,** usu the larva of the isabella moth *(Isia isabella).*

1872 MO State Entomol. *Annual Rept.* 142, It [=the tiger moth] occurs still more abundantly in the Southern swamps, where the larva is dubbed "Fever Worm" by the negroes, under the absurd impression that it is the cause of fever and ague. *Ibid* 144, Mr. Huron Burt, of Williamsburg [MO] informs me that this caterpillar [=the isabella moth] is also called "Fever-worm" in his neighborhood. As the miasma of the Southern swamps induces ague, and as the large black species is found abundantly in such situations, . . through ignorance . . some Ethiopean [sic], right from Dixie, has perhaps perpetuated the name in Missouri, by applying it to our more northern Hedge-hog caterpillar. **1899** Bergen *Animal Lore* 17 **cnKY,** Tawny and brown caterpillars are called "fever-worms." One must spit on meeting one of these to keep off fever. **1901** *Jrl. Amer. Folkl.* 14.35 **KY,** If you see a hairy caterpillar (called "fever worms" in some sections) spit on it, and it will save you a spell of fever. **1967–70** *DARE* (Qu. R27, . . *Kinds of caterpillars*) Inf **KY**5, Fever worm—same as a woolly worm; used to predict winter weather; **KY**9, Fever worm—brown and red fuzzy caterpillar; **KY**34, Fever worm—red and black, very fuzzy; **KY**68, Fever worm—forecast winter weather by [its] color; **KY**88, Fever worm—brown and black; **KY**94, Fever worms come in the fall; **TN**56, Fever worm.

feverwort n

1 =**horse gentian.** [See quot 1948]

1814 Bigelow *Florula Bostoniensis* 56 **MA,** *Triosteum perfoliatum. . . Feverwort. . .* Not very common. . . Flowers in June. **1861** Wood *Class-Book* 393, *Fever-wort. . .* Root large, fleshy, in much repute, having many of the properties of Ipecacuanha. **1891** Jesup *Plants Hanover NH* 19, Fever-wort. Horse-Gentian. **1948** Stevens *KS Wild Flowers* 357, Various vernacular names have been given to this species: . . feverwort, because in the early practice of medicine in this country an infusion of the leaves was used to increase secretions and induce sweating in cases of intermittent fever. **1974** (1977) Coon *Useful Plants* 90.

2 A **boneset 1** (here: *Eupatorium perfoliatum*). [See quot 1900]

1828 Rafinesque *Med. Flora* 1.174, *Boneset. . . Vulgar Names* . . Feverwort, Sweating-plant [etc]. **1900** Lyons *Plant Names* 155, *E[upatorium] perfoliatum. . .* Feverwort. . . Febrifuge, diaphoretic. **1930** Sievers *Amer. Med. Plants* 16. **1971** Krochmal *Appalachia Med. Plants* 118, Feverwort. . . is also considered . . febrifuge, diuretic, and astringent.

3 A **false foxglove** (here: *Aureolaria pedicularia*).

1966 *DARE* Wildfl QR Pl. 201 Inf **WA**15, Feverwort.

few adj Cf **few, a** adj phr

1933 in 1944 *ADD* **KY, VA, sWV,** *Few ways.* Short distance. . . Freq. Not observed in cent. or n. W. Va. or the adjoining part of Va.

few n

An expert; someone to be reckoned with.

1851 Burke *Polly Peablossom* 52 **MO,** It was that feller Arch Coony. . . Didn't you know that ar' hossfly? He's a few! *Ibid* 147 **MS,** That chap Arch Coony was er few in that line! He was the durndest, rantankerous hoss-fly that ever clum er tree! **1856** *Porter's Spirit of Times* 20 Dec 252/2 **MS,** Turkey Tom . . [is] a *few* in any kind of hunting, but especially death on turkies.

few, a adv phr

1 also *a little few:* A little, to some extent, occasionally.

1837–40 Haliburton *Clockm.* (1862) 177 *(OED),* You must lie a few to put 'em off well. **1851** Burke *Polly Peablossom* 50 **MO,** I've hearn o' mean folks in my time, an' I've preached 'bout 'em a few; but . . I've stopped talkin'. *Ibid* 167 **TN,** I will never forget him, or the service he rendered me in my "hour of great peril," although for a time he annoyed me not a few. **1865** in 1894 Lowell *Letters* 1.347 **MA,** I am . . a little few *(un petit peu)* vexed. **1954** Smith *Yazoo River* 226 **MS,** You see, then, I could afford to be perlite a few.

2 in phr *a few bit (the), a few of the:* Certainly, very.

1936 *AmSp* 11.278 **wVA,** A mountaineer, for emphasis, would say: 'The lake is a few of the pretty this morning,' or 'It's a few of the hot today, hain't it?' About as often one heard this variation: 'That feller's a few bit the lazy,' or 'I'm a few bit tired tonight.'

3 Very well.

1942 McAtee *Dial. Grant Co. IN* 25 (as of 1890s), *Few* . . excellently; "Mervil certainly can skate a few."

few, a adj phr [Engl dial] **Sth, S Midl**

Some—used in ref to a mass noun.

1910 *DN* 3.458 **FL, GA,** *Few,* adj. Some, a portion. "Will you have a few cabbage, or squash?" (at table). **1913** Kephart *Highlanders* 297 **sAppalachians,** I'll have a few more of them cabbage. **1934** *WV Review* Dec 77, Almost every one who is familiar with the common speech in West Virginia has at some time heard the phrase "a few cheese" [=a small amount of cheese]. **1941** Perry *Hold Autumn* 215 **TX,** We're fixin to run off a few sirup.

few bit (the), a; few of the, a See **few, a** adv phr **2**

fexatially adv Also *fexatiously* [Varr of *vexatiously;* cf **finatially**]

Completely, thoroughly.

1931 *PMLA* 46.1306 **sAppalachians,** Well, I'm fexatially (or fexatiously) whipped out. (That is, completely surprised, or astonished.) *Ibid* 1308, He's fexatiously beat!

feygel See **faygeleh**

fezinah See **fezzino**

F.F.V. n [Abbr for *first family* (or *families*) *of* (or *in*) *Virginia*] **chiefly Sth, esp VA** Cf **first family**

1 Any of the earliest or most prominent families to settle Virginia; a member or descendant of such a family.

1847 *Knickerbocker* 29.495, The only things we could make out among the unknown writing were a set of letters that looked like a disorderly F.F.V. . . A Virginia scion insisted that they were an abbreviation . . to represent 'First Family in Virginia.' **1870** (1871) Rae *Westward by Rail* 311, The man who, in the Old World, would be dubbed a viscount or a baron was known in the Old Dominion as an F.F.V., that is, he belonged to one of the First Families in Virginia. **1888** M. Lane in *America* 4 Oct. 15 *(DAE),* F.F.V.'s—We heard a good deal about these letters at about the time that the Civil War began. They mean First Families of Virginia. **1909** Porter *Options* 10, What Federal prison did Moore escape from, or what's the name of the F.F.V. family that he carries as a handicap? **1949** *AmSp* 24.28, In satirical allusion to their belief that the state was settled mainly by Englishmen of very high tone the Virginians have also been called *Cavaliers* and *F.F.V.'s.*

2 By ext: any socially prominent family; one who considers himself to be of the "best" society.

1967–70 *DARE* (Qu. II23, *Joking names for the people who are, or think they are, the best society of a community: The ______*) Infs **LA**17, **SC**54, **VA**58, 68, 91, F.F.V.

fi' See **five**

fiador n Also sp *feador, fiadore;* folk-etym sp *theodore* [Span] **West**

A cord attached to a hackamore; see quot 1951.

1936 McCarthy *Lang. Mosshorn* **West** [Range term], *Feador.* . . That part of a hackamore which is placed around the horse's neck. **1942** Berrey–Van den Bark *Amer. Slang* 915.3 **West,** *Bridle; Halter.* . . fiadore, theodore, *a braided horsehair cord passing from the front of the "bosal" up over the horse's head.* **1951** Grant *Cowboy Encycl.* 62, The fiador is a small doubled rope of either horsehair or sashcord that runs through the loops of the hackamore's brow band at the point just below and behind the ears. Then it goes around the neck, is knotted under the throat, and ends in another and lower knot, so tied that it will not slip over the heel button of the bosal. **1961** Adams *Old-Time Cowhand* 122, The word "fiador" is from the Spanish verb *fiar,* meanin' to answer for, to go surety for. . . Some Americans have corrupted it into "theodore." . . The main advantage of the fiador's its grip on the head of the hoss, and many times means keepin' the hoss and rider together because it's a safety device. **1981** *KS Qrly.* 13.2.66, *Fiador* . . a device consisting of a halter or hackamore and a rope, knotted to the romal that forms both a lead and a pair of closed reins; known also as a "theodore."

fiah See **fire** n

fiancé n Pronc-sp *fee-ance;* joc varr *finance, financy*

1920 *DN* 5.78 **NE** [Jocularized French words], There goes Miss Blank with her new finance. **1943** Writers' Program NC *Bundle of Troubles* 28, Miss Muskrat begin jumpin' straight up and down, and yellin': "Take him out, take him out! He's my financy!" **1984** Burns *Cold Sassy* 144 **nGA** (as of 1906), I couldn't think of anything worse . . than getting beat up by his wife's former fee-ance.

fib n

‡1 A smart aleck or rude person.

1968 *DARE* (Qu. II36a, *Somebody who talks back or gives rude answers: "Did you ever see such a ______?"*) Inf **NY**40, Fib.

2 An expulsion of gas from the intestines.

1966 *DARE* (Qu. X55b) Inf **MS**45, Fib.

Fibber McGee('s) closet n Also *Fibber McGee('s room)* [From *Fibber McGee* a radio show character (1935–50s)] **chiefly Nth, N Midl**

An untidy or overstuffed closet, cubbyhole, or room that serves as a catchall.

1966–69 *DARE* (Qu. D7, *A small space anywhere in a house where you can hide things or get them out of the way*) Infs **IL**34, **KS**19, **MT**2, **NE**2, 10, Fibber McGee's closet; **CA**99, Fibber McGee; **PA**128, Fibber McGee—if it's overstuffed; (Qu. E22, *If a house is untidy and everything is upset, you might say, "It's a ______!" or "It looks like ______."*) Inf **IN**1, Fibber McGee's closet; **CT**2, Fibber McGee's room—a room with everything in it, including old gifts that were never given, but might be given someday. **1975** Gould *ME Lingo* 110, *Gloryhole.* . . Nowadays, any catch-all that may be in constant disorder. A Fibber McGee closet. (If you don't remember Fibber McGee's closet, its contents fell into the room every time he opened the door.)

fibble adj [Pronc-sp for *feeble*]

1883 (1971) Harris *Nights with Remus* 211 **GA** [Black], How much er dish yer meat ought a fibble [Footnote: Feeble] ole man lak me ter take?

Fibbywerry See **February**

fibe See **five**

fibs exclam [Var of *fives,* by analogy with **thribs, fourbs**]

In children's games: see quots.

1912 Green *VA Folk-Speech* 173, *Fibs, num. adj.* Five. Dubs; thribs; fourses; fibs. **1935** *AmSp* 10.159 **seNE,** *Dubbs.* . . a particular . . [cry] which the player must utter in order to lay claim to two marbles knocked from the pot with a single shot. . . Likewise, *thribs, fourbs,* and *fibs* must be cried for three, four, or five marbles.

fice, ficet See **feist** n

ficety, ficy See **feisty** adj

fid n [Etym unknown; senses may have diff origins]

1 Orig naut: a conical pin of hard wood or metal used in splicing rope; a marlinspike.

1866 in 1938 Twain *Letters Sandwich Is.* 68, A fid is an instrument which the sailor uses when he splices the main brace on board ship. **1958** McCulloch *Woods Words* 61 **Pacific NW,** *Fid*—A short sharp steel tool used in splicing wire rope; a marlin spike. **1975** Gould *ME Lingo* 92, *Fid.* . . On shipboard a *fid* is a small, wooden *marlinspike.*

2 A wood or metal pin used to shorten or fasten a chain. **esp ME** Cf **fid hook**

1851 (1856) Springer *Forest Life* 107 **ME,** Having knocked out the "fid," which united the chain that bound the load, the log rolled suddenly upon him. **1900** Day *Up in ME* 45, He strung the chain 'round a good big rock / And found that he'd lost the little block / To catch the link; it's used instid / Of a hook and link, and it's called a fid. **1975** Gould *ME Lingo* 92, *Fid*—The upland *fid* is a metal pin used to shorten chain. One link is thrust through another, and a *fid* inserted. Ruel Norton once fidded a chain with his thumb, but only once. A farmer sometimes calls his *fid* a toggle, but the lobsterman's *toggle* . . is never called a *fid.*

3 See quot.

1930 Shoemaker *1300 Words* 22 **cPA Mts** (as of c1900), *Fid*—The key log in a jam.

4 A small piece of tobacco. *old-fash*

1848 Bartlett *Americanisms* 136, *Fid of tobacco.* A chew, or quid of tobacco. A word only used by those who make use of the weed. **1943** *AN&Q* 3.7/2 **NEng** (as of c1925), Fid (a small piece of tobacco).

5 A drink; a measure of alcohol.

1830 Ames *Mariner's Sketches* 24 **MA,** Their breakfast consists of coffee, strong enough to bear up a grape shot, with a 'fid' of gin that would infallibly overthrow any ordinary worshipper of Bacchus. **1866** in 1938 Twain *Letters Sandwich Is.* 63, He'd been among his friends having a bit of a gam, and had got just about one fid too much aboard, and his judgment had fetched away in the meantime.

fid v

To insert a **fid.**

1975 [see **fid** n 2].

fiddle n [From resemblance to a violin (or violin bow) in shape or manner of use]

1 Naut: see quot 1975.

1872 (1876) Knight *Amer. Mech. Dict.* 838, *Fiddle.* . . *(Nautical.)* A frame of bars and strings, to keep things from rolling off the cabin table in bad weather. **1975** Gould *ME Lingo* 92, *Fiddle*—A frame or railing to keep dishes from sliding off a ship's table in rough weather. **1979** *Yankee* Aug 83/2 (as of c1860), The table [of the whaling ship] had fiddles around the edges to keep dishes from sliding off.

2 See quot. Cf **fiddlehead n 2**

1968 Adams *Western Words* 111, *Fiddle*—A horse's head. The rider strives to keep a bronc from putting "his fiddle between his feet."

3 also attrib: =**fiddlehead n 1.**

1951 Graham *My Window* 176 **ME,** The shepherd's crook and bishop's crozier are to be seen in the new thrust for life of the fiddle fern in the woods. **1969** *DARE* Tape **NY**223, Did you ever eat ferns? . . When they're coming out early in the spring, they're . . rolled up very tight . . like . . the end of a fiddle . . and I'm not sure that they didn't call 'em little fiddles.

4 A farm implement with a strung bow used to broadcast seed. Cf **fiddle in**

[**1902** (1969) Sears *Catalogue* 686/1, This seeder has a light centrifugal wheel . . that is revolved rapidly in opposite directions by means of a bow.] **1969** *DARE* (Qu. L23, *What machinery is used around here in putting in the seed?*) Inf **IN**59, Hand fiddle, for grass seed; a grass seeder. [**1986** *NADS Letters* (as of c1922), I clearly recall . . my maternal grandfather using an implement he called simply a *fiddle* for sowing grain—undoubtedly oats. He was born in the 1860's on a farm in . . County Antrim [Ireland]. The implement consisted of an oblong box with an opening on the top through which it was filled with seed. . . The operating factor was a stick like a violin bow with a strong string attached to it. The string was wound once round a long spindle running through the middle of the box and fixed—below the box—to a wooden disk onto which the seed dropped from an opening in the bottom of the box and was widely and uniformly scattered as the "bow" was moved back and forth.]

5 in phr *give up one's fiddle* and var: see quot. [Perh in allusion to the stereotype of the long-haired musician]

1950 *WELS (Joking terms for getting your hair cut)* 1 Inf, **ceWI,** Gave up my fiddle . . couldn't find a fiddle.

fiddle v [From the arm motion]

1 To saw.

1905 *DN* 3.79 **nwAR,** *Fiddle wood*. . . To saw wood. Rare.

2 as vbl n *fiddling:* See quots. Cf **fiddle worm, grunt v 4**

1971 *Daily Progress* (Charlottesville VA) 12 July 1/7 *(Hench Coll.),* A Geneva, Ala., businessman outdistanced 117 other contestants in the second annual World's Championship Worm Fiddling Tournament at Caryville, Fla. . . Participants in worm fiddling, also called grunting or snoring, drive stakes into the soil and rub them with wood, causing vibrations that make the worms seek the surface. **1982** [see **grunt** v]. **1984** Wilder *You All Spoken Here* 42 **Sth,** Fiddlin', sawin': A trick to entice fishing worms to the surface by driving a stake in the ground and fiddlin', or sawin', on it with an iron bar or a stone; it's more heard of than done.

fiddle-a-ding n Cf **ding-a-ling**

1904 *DN* 2.425 **Cape Cod MA** (as of a1857), *Fiddle-a-ding*. . . A nickname for a trifling person.

fiddleback spider See **fiddle spider**

fiddle-box n Cf **box n 2**

A fiddle, violin.

1928 Chapman *Happy Mt.* 307 **seTN,** 'Tain't but a fiddle-box. **1959** *MI Hist.* 43.387 (as of 1880s), Nels Fredrickson, the best fiddler in [the logging] camp, was pumping away on his precious fiddle-box.

fiddle-britches n Cf **feisty britches**

1954 *Harder Coll.* **cwTN,** Fiddle-britches—A smart Aleck.

fiddle case n *joc* Also called **violin case**

An unusually large foot or shoe.

1942 Berrey–Van den Bark *Amer. Slang* 87.34, *Large Shoes*. . . fiddle cases. **1950** *WELS (Humorous or uncomplimentary names for big feet)* 2 Infs, **WI,** Fiddle cases. **1967** *DARE* (Qu. X38) Inf **MN**2, Fiddle case. **1970** Major *Dict. Afro-Amer. Slang* 53, *Fiddle-cases:* (1940's) shoes.

fiddle dance n

A community dancing party at which music is provided by a fiddler; hence n *fiddle dancing* dancing to the music of a fiddle.

1949 Webber *Backwoods Teacher* 107 **Ozarks,** The better-thought-of folks did not hold with "round dancing" or "fiddle dancing." The fiddle was still, to many, "the devil's music box." We heard of violent "fractions," even to the wrecking of all the furniture in a cabin, at a fiddle dance.

fiddledeedamn intj Also *fiddledeesticks* [Varr of *fiddledeedee, fiddlesticks*]

Damn! Fiddlesticks!

1969 *DARE* (Qu. NN8a, . . *"Oh ______, I've lost my glasses again."*) Inf **KY**60, Fiddle-dee-sticks! Fiddle-dee-damn!

fiddledeedee around v phr [Blend of *fiddledeedee* + *fiddle around*]

To meddle, fool around.

1963 Burroughs *Head-First* 175 **CO,** What with having a new calf, and her bag as big as an ordinary wash boiler and sore as a boil, . . that not-so-dumb four-legged female wasn't about to let us fiddle-dee-dee around with her teats for love or money.

fiddledeesticks See **fiddledeedamn**

fiddle-faddled ppl adj

Damned; darned.

1970 *DARE* (Qu. NN25b, *Weakened substitutes for 'damn' or 'damned': "Well, I'll be ______!"*) Inf **PA**242, Fiddle-faddled.

fiddle-fart v Also with *around* Also *fiddlefuck around* Cf **fiddle-foot v 2**

To fool around, waste time.

1975 *AmSp* 50.59 **AR** (as of c1970), *Fiddle fart around* . . Loaf, shirk responsibility. **1984** Weaver *TX Crude* 112, *To fiddlefuck around.* To dawdle, to waste time. "Boys, Grandmother was slow, but she was crippled and born blind. But you've been fiddlefuckin' around here for three hours and ain't accomplished Jack Shit." **1986** *NADS Letters* **cwPA,** Three local expressions . . *fiddle around, fiddle-fart around,* and *fiddle-fartin'* all carry the connotation of wasting time.

fiddle, fine as a adj phr [Var of *fit as a fiddle*] **now chiefly Sth, S Midl**

Very fine; in excellent health or spirits.

[**1811** *Thomas' MA Spy or Worcester Gaz.* (MA) 20 Mar 4/1, But pleasures are brittle as glass, Although as a fiddle they're fine.] **1836** Paulding *Book St. Nicholas* 78 **NY,** Pleasure sleighs, which, at that period, it was the fashion among the farmers to have as fine as fiddles. **1908** *DN* 3.310 **eAL, wGA,** *Fine as a fiddle*. . . Extremely fine. **1912** Green *VA Folk-Speech* 27, Fine as a fiddle. **1927** *AmSp* 2.354 **WV,** *Fine as a fiddle* . . in the best of spirits. **1967–69** *DARE* (Qu. BB47, *Feeling in the best of health and spirits: "I'm feeling ______."*) Infs **MO**19, **NE**6, **SC**55, Fine as a fiddle.

fiddlefish n

=**angel shark.**

1879 U.S. Natl. Museum *Bulletin* 14.67, *Squatina Dumerili* . . Fiddle-fish. **1889** *Century Dict.* 210/1, *Angel-fish*. . . Also called *monk-fish* and *fiddle-fish.*

fiddle flower n [From its shape]

A **bleeding heart 1** (here: *Dicentra spectabilis*).

1898 *Jrl. Amer. Folkl.* 11.222, *Dicentra spectabilis*, . . fiddle flower, Plymouth, Ohio.

fiddle-foot n

1 A skittish horse.

1944 Adams *Western Words* 58. **1968** Adams *Western Words* 111, *Fiddle-foot* . . a horse that prances around.

2 One who wanders.

1944 Adams *Western Words* 58. **1968** Adams *Western Words* 111, *Fiddle-foot*. . . A person who drifts, or has "itching feet." **1968** *DARE* (QR p169) Inf **CA**87, Fiddle-foot—a wandering person.

fiddle-foot v

1 Of a horse: to make skittish movements.

1958 Latham *Meskin Hound* 151 **cTX,** He . . spoke sullenly to his horse when the animal grew impatient and started fiddle-footing beneath him. "Be quiet, you fool!" he commanded.

2 with *around:* To fool around, move restlessly.

1963 Burroughs *Head-First* 66, Instead of going straight home, I fiddle-footed around, skipped rocks and launched fleets of last year's leaves on Butcherknife Creek. *Ibid* 139, But . . we fiddle-footed around most of the day, finishing up in the late afternoon.

fiddle-footed adj [By ext from *fiddle-footed* skittish (of a horse)]

Restless, given to wandering.

1941 *Sat. Eve. Post* 1 Mar 12/3 **TX,** Eb had his memories. There had been that taffy-haired Arkansaw girl . . And a brown-eyed one who came within a case card of heeling him. . . But Eb had been fiddle-footed. He had drifted down the country each time before things got too simmery. **1950** *PADS* 14.29 **SC,** *Fiddle-footed*. . . Restive, given to wandering. **1959** Robertson *Ram* 5 **ID** (as of c1875), Father at this time was restless and fiddle-footed and needed Win's stabilizing influence. **c1960** *Wilson Coll.* **csKY,** Fiddle-footed. . . Given to wandering, gadding about. **1966** FWP *Guide VT* 94, The Reverend George "Pearly" Gates, a fiddle-footed educator, moved from Vermont to Iowa. **1977** *Amer. West* 14.6.5 **NM,** None of them were feckless, fiddle-footed boys; neither were they yet stiff in the knee hinges.

fiddle, give up one's See **fiddle** n **5**

fiddlehead n, also attrib

1 The young uncoiling frond of any of var ferns, often eaten as greens; the fern itself. [From the resemblance to the scroll of a violin; *OED* 1882 →] **scattered, but chiefly NEng, esp ME** Also called **fiddleneck 3, fiddlestick**

1892 *Jrl. Amer. Folkl.* 5.105 **cME,** *Osmunda cinnamomea,* fiddleheads. **1943** *New Yorker* 10 Apr 59/2, Fiddleheads, those tiny fronds of common brake fern which are grown as a commercial crop in Maine and which enterprising vegetable dealers have carried for several seasons. **1960** Williams *Walk Egypt* 7 **GA,** Everywhere would be violets and cinquefoil and fiddlehead ferns. **1963** Zimmerman-Olson *Forest* 141 **WI,** *Interrupted Fern...* The first fern to appear in the spring with stout fuzzy "fiddleheads"—the unrolling leaves. **1966** *Aroostook Republican* (Caribou ME) 8 June 10/7, *Fiddleheads* Fresh Picked 3 lbs 1.00. **1966–69** *DARE* (Qu. I28a, .. *"Greens" .. that are eaten raw*) Inf **ME**20, Fiddlehead greens grow in wet places; spiral-shaped top is eaten; **MA**5, Some people use fiddleheads, but not natives; (Qu. I28b, .. *Greens that are cooked*) Inf **ME**9, Fiddleheads; **NH**12, Fiddleheads—brake ferns; **VT**13, Fiddlehead ferns. **1966** *DARE* Tape **ME**8, As the young leaves come up through the ground, before they open up, they're tightly coiled, shaped like the head of a fiddle. That's why they call 'em fiddle-heads. Ostrich fern and lady fern produce these... They call 'em [=places where fiddleheads are found] fiddlehead flats mostly; **ME**2, We called them fiddleheads. **1974** (1977) Coon *Useful Plants* 198, Here we have the useful royal fern, *Osmunda regalis,* of which the unfurling fronds are among those known as fiddleheads, which may be cooked and eaten. *Ibid* 199, *Pteridium aquilinum*—Bracken fern, .. fiddleheads (or necks). **1975** Hamel-Chiltoskey *Cherokee Plants* 33 **NC,** Fern-christmas, shield .. *Polystichum acrostichoides...* Fiddle heads [used] for food. **1979** *Yankee* July 146 **VT,** Each spring they would drop by the farm seeking permission to gather wild leeks, dandelions, fiddleheads, sorrel, and other wild greens.

2 attrib; also *fiddleheaded* adj; Of an animal: having a head shaped like a violin. Cf **fiddle** n **2**

1928 French *Ranchman NM* 38 (as of c1880s), There was an old fiddle-headed black and white cow . . , and as she blundered right on to us the look of surprise and dismay on her ugly face was ludicrous. **1940** Faulkner *Hamlet* 327 **TX,** How about that fiddle-head horse without no mane to speak of? For a saddle pony, I'd rather have him than that stocking-foot. **1968** Adams *Western Words* 111, *Fiddle-headed*—Said of a horse with an ugly-shaped head.

fiddlehead v, hence vbl n *fiddleheading* **esp ME**

To gather **fiddlehead** ferns.

1961 Douglas *My Wilderness* 283 **cnME,** We arrived in time to get fiddlehead ferns for supper. Trout Brook drains Lower South Branch Pond, and where its flanks are soggy is the place to look for fiddleheads. Someone had been "fiddleheading" before us. **1966** *DARE* Tape **ME**8, One of the popular pastimes in the spring of the year is going fiddleheading. **1975** Gould *ME Lingo* 92, Going *fiddleheading* ranks with goin' smeltin' as a Maine vernal outing of ritualistic importance.

fiddleheaded See **fiddlehead** n **2**

fiddleheading vbl n See **fiddlehead** v

fiddle in v phr [See quot] *old-fash* Cf **fiddle** n **4**

1917 *DN* 4.392 **IL, neOH,** *Fiddle in* (grass seed or oats)... To sow these with a seeding machine operated by a bow resembling a fiddle-bow. From the '80's on.

fiddle-ma-dab n [Nonsense word; cf **-ma-**]

1967 *DARE* (Qu. NN12b, *Things that people say to put off a child when he asks, "What are you making?"*) Inf **IA**11, Fiddle-ma-dab ['fɪdəlmə,dæb].

fiddleneck n

1 A plant of the genus *Amsinckia.* [From the curving flower] Also called **fireweed j, forget-me-not 1c, fuzzy britches, tarweed, woolly breeches.** For other names of var spp see **buckthorn weed, devil's lettuce, finger-weed, saccato gordo, yellow burnweed**

1898 *Jrl. Amer. Folkl.* 11.275, *Amsinckia* (sp.), fiddle-neck .. Cal. **1911** CA Ag. Exper. Sta. Berkeley *Bulletin* 217.978, Next of importance are the deciduous fruits, .. followed by the orange, .. filaree, burr clover, fiddle neck, tarweed and other spring flowers. **1915** (1926) Armstrong-Thornber *Western Wild Flowers* 428, *Fiddle-neck .. Amsinckia intermedia...* has bright flowers, but the foliage is dreadfully harsh. **1947** *So. Sierran* May 4/2 *(DA),* There were also... Desert Calico, .. Tidy-tips, Buckwheat, and Fiddle-neck. **1951** Martin *Amer. Wildlife & Plants* 413, Fiddlenecks are among the most common weedy plants of open slopes and fields of the Pacific states. **1967–68** *DARE* (Qu. S26a, .. *Roadside flowers*) Inf **CA**79, Fiddleneck—a yellow flower curves over like the neck of a fiddle; (Qu. S26d, *Wildflowers .. in meadows*) Inf **CA**24, Fiddleneck or tar plant—has a yellow flower, grows profusely in fields. **1968** *DARE* File **CA,** Fiddleneck—an orange colored wildflower growing on mountainsides north of Bakersfield. Common. **1973** Hitchcock-Cronquist *Flora Pacific NW* 386, *Amsinckia...* Fiddleneck. **1979** *Blair & Ketchum's Country Jrl.* Sept 86 **CA,** But the old windows still hold their morning tapestries .. a spring pasture flecked with wild mustard and fiddle-neck blossoms [etc].

2 **=scorpionweed.** [From the curving flower]

1911 Jepson *Flora CA* 342, *P[hacelia] tanacetifolia... Fiddle-neck.* **1936** McDougall-Baggley *Plants of Yellowstone* 104, *Fiddleneck (Phacelia)...* Mostly hairy plants with alternate leaves and showy, usually lavender or purple flowers. **1967–68** *DARE* (Qu. S26e, *Other wildflowers*) Inf **CA**4, Fiddleneck; **CA**41, Fiddleneck or phacelia. The blue one [with] a curving flower.

3 **=fiddlehead** n **1.** [From the coiled frond]

1943 Damon *Sense of Humus* 114 **NEng,** Nowadays even New Yorkers can have fiddle-neck greens (without the fun of gathering them), for they are being canned in Maine... But hadn't I heard that "fiddle-necks" are good to eat, and hadn't these things before they were boiled looked like "fiddle-necks"? **1974** (1977) Coon *Useful Plants* 199, *Pteridium aquilinum*—Bracken fern, .. fiddleheads (or necks)... Here the tender unfolding fronds are used . . , cooking until tender in salted water, and serving with butter.

fiddle of sticks n [From *fiddlesticks,* prob by analogy with *hill of beans, row of pins,* etc]

1969 *DARE* (Qu. HH20b, *Of an idle, worthless person you might say, "He doesn't amount to ______."*) Inf **MA**68, A fiddle of sticks.

fiddle on a broomstick exclam Also *fiddle up a gum tree*

Nonsense! Fiddlesticks!

1959 *VT Hist.* new ser 27.135, *Fiddle on a broomstick!* .. Rare. *Ibid* 164, *Fiddle up a gum tree!* .. Rare.

fiddler n

1 also *fiddler cat(fish):* A **channel catfish** (here: *Ictalurus punctatus*). **chiefly Missip-Ohio Valleys**

1908 Forbes-Richardson *Fishes of IL* 178, At Alton .. the smaller channel-cat *(I. punctatus)* is known as "fiddler," and fished for with special small nets. **1940** Wilson *Wabash* 186 **IN,** Fried chicken such as can be found nowhere else, .. fiddler catfish .. hickory barbecue .. roasting ears. **1953** Randolph *Down in Holler* 243 **Ozarks,** *Fiddler...* A small mottled or spotted catfish, with a forked tail. Some rivermen believe that the fiddler is a young channel cat *(Ictalurus locustris),* which it actually is, but many regard it as a distinct species. **1954** *Harder Coll.* **cwTN,** Fiddler or fiddler cat—a small catfish. Fiddler net—a fish net used to catch fiddler cats. **1957** Trautman *Fishes* 415 **OH,** Young less than 14.0″ long (colloquially called .. fiddlers) are bluish—or olivaceous-silvery dorsally, and silvery-white ventrally; these have few to many spots on body. **1968–70** *DARE* (Qu. P1, .. *Freshwater fish .. good to eat*) Infs **IL**83, **KY**75, 88, Fiddlers; **IA**29, Fiddler cat (the small channel cat); **IL**81, Fiddlers—small catfish about six inches; illegal size, but they're good eating; **IN**42, Fiddlers—small catfish; **KY**84, Fiddlers—one or two pound; (Qu. P14, .. *Commercial fish*) Infs **IN**42, **KY**11, Fiddlers. **c1970** *DARE* File **sIN,** On restaurant menus they are listed as *fiddlers,* never *fiddler catfish.* **1973** *Hardin Co. Independent* (Elizabethtown IL) 26 April 4/6, Friday Night Specials—Fiddler—Catfish Dinner—$2.50.

2 **=flicker** n² **1.** [See quots]

1881 Nuttall Ornith. Club *Bulletin* 6.184, *Colaptes auratus... Fiddler* (Cape Cod)... What "Yaffle" and "Fiddler" signify I have no idea. **1900** *Wilson Bulletin* 31.6, *Fiddler.* Cape Cod, Massachusetts. I feel pretty sure that this name is derived from the peculiar sew-saw [sic] motions indulged in by the males while courting the females during the early spring months. **1956** MA Audubon Soc. *Bulletin* 40.82, *Yellow-shafted Flicker...* Fiddler (Mass. Possibly from the see-saw movements of the male in its courting performance.)

3 See **fiddler duck 2.**

4 See **fiddle spider.**

fiddler bird n Cf **fiddling bird**

=white-throated sparrow.

1902 (1924) Johnson *New Engl.* 177, "A fiddler bird, the teacher calls it"... "Teacher says it says, 'Here I come fiddling, fiddling'; . . " The fiddler bird, or white-throated sparrow . . visits most parts of New England only in its spring and autumn migrations, but it is a summer bird in the mountains.

fiddler cat(fish) See **fiddler 1**

fiddler crab n

Std: a crab of the genus *Uca*. Also called **sand fiddler, soldier crab**

fiddler duck n

1 =**tree duck.**

1897 *Auk* 14.286 **LA,** *Black-bellied Tree-Duck.*—Commonly known as Fiddler Duck... *Fulvous Tree-Duck.*—Known as Yellow-bellied Fiddler Duck. **1911** *Forest & Stream* 77.173, *Dendrocygna autumnalis.* Fiddler Duck, La... *Dendrocygna bicolor.* Yellow-bellied Fiddler Duck... La. **1916** *Times-Picayune* (New Orleans LA) 26 March 2, *Redhead* (Marila americana), . . Fiddler Duck. **1923** U.S. Dept. Ag. *Misc. Circular* 13.38, *Fulvous Tree Duck... Vernacular Names... In local use...* Yellow-bellied fiddler duck (La.)

2 also *fiddler:* =**redhead.**

[**1897** *Auk* 14.286 **LA,** *Redhead.*—Commonly known as *Canard Violon,* because in flying it makes a noise like a violin, with its wings.] **1911** *Forest & Stream* 77.173/1, *Redhead...* Fiddler, Chef Menteur, La.; Fiddler Duck, Venice, La. **1916** *Times-Picayune* (New Orleans LA) 26 March 2, *Fulvous Tree Duck* (Dendrocygna bicolor)... Fiddler Duck. **1923** U.S. Dept. Ag. *Misc. Circular* 13.17, *Redhead... Vernacular Names... In local use...* Fiddler, fiddler duck (La.) **1982** Elman *Hunter's Field Guide* 199, *Redhead... Common & Regional Names:* . . red-headed broadbill, raft duck, fiddler.

3 A **goldeneye 1** (here: *Bucephala clangula*).

1923 U.S. Dept. Ag. *Misc. Circular* 13.22, *Glaucionetta clangula . . In local use...* fiddler duck (Ala.) **1962** Imhof *AL Birds* 153, *Bucephala clangula . . Other Names:* Fiddler Duck.

fiddler, pay the v phr Also *pay of the fiddler* [By analogy with *pay the piper*]

To suffer the consequences of one's acts.

1867 Edwards *Shelby & Men* 250 **M,** Those who dance must pay the fiddler, says an adage old as the Plymouth Rock blarney- stone at least. **1896** Harris *Sister Jane* 148 **cnGA,** I frittered away my wind a-cuttin' up capers in my young days, an' now I'm a-payin' of the fiddler. Ther's a turrible crick in my knee-jint. **1903** (1965) Adams *Log Cowboy* 114 **NM,** We were now paying the fiddler for lack of proper precaution. **1966–69** *DARE* (Qu. JJ40, . . *"It was my fault and I'm willing to ______."*) Infs **KY**60, **MA**6, **TX**28, **VA**15, **WA**18, Pay the fiddler.

fiddler's bitch n

Used as a symbol of intemperance, lack of moderation, extremes, esp in phr *drunk as a fiddler's bitch;* see quots.

1899 (1912) Green *VA Folk-Speech* 21, As drunk as a fiddler's bitch. **1908** *DN* 3.307 **eAL, wGA,** *Drunk as a fiddler's bitch...* Extremely drunk. Common. **1925** in 1953 Botkin *Treas. Railroad Folkl.* 227, I got drunker than a fiddler's bitch. **1931** *PMLA* 46.1304 **sAppalachians,** He wuz ez drunk as a biled owl, er a fiddler's bitch. **1967** *DARE* (Qu. H74a, . . *Coffee . . very strong*) Inf **WA**30, Stronger than a fiddler's bitch; (Qu. DD15, . . *Thoroughly drunk*) Inf **TX**11, Drunk's [a] fiddler's bitch. **1967** *DARE* Tape **WA**30, He [=a person] must have been hotter than a fiddler's bitch.

fiddler's damn n Also *fiddler's darn, ~ durn, ~ whoop* [By analogy with *tinker's damn* (or *dam*)]

Something of little or no value.

1898 Lloyd *Country Life* 148 **AL,** If the horse, or the man, is triflin or sorry stock himself, his family papers, pedigrees, registers and records jest simply aint worth a fiddler's durn in Texas. **1968–69** *DARE* (Qu. HH20b, *Of an idle, worthless person you might say, "He doesn't amount to ______."*) Inf **NJ**25, A fiddler's damn; **IN**82, Fiddler's darn; **IA**30, A fiddler's whoop.

fiddler's feist n [Euphem for **fiddler's bitch**]

1969 *DARE* (Qu. DD15, . . *Thoroughly drunk*) Inf **GA**72, High as a fiddler's feist.

fiddler's fountain n Cf **fountain B**

A type of firework; see quots.

1966 *DARE* (Qu. FF28, . . *Other kinds of fireworks*) Inf **NH**1, Fiddler's fountain. **1966** *DARE* FW Addit **cnMA,** We had many different kinds [of firecrackers]—cherry bombs, hammerheads, lady-fingers, . . fiddler's fountains (made a whistling noise).

Fiddler's Green n [Orig naut, now more widespread; *OED* 1825 →]

A paradise chiefly characterized by drinking and dancing.

a1891 (1924) Melville *Billy Budd* 16, That portion of the terraqueous globe providentially set apart for dance-houses, doxies and tapsters, in short, what sailors call a 'fiddler's green'. **1891** Farmer–Henley *Slang* 2.390, *Fiddlers'-Green . .* A sailor's elysium (situate on the hither and cooler side of hell) of wine, women, and song. **1912** Green *VA Folk-Speech* 173, *Fiddler's Green...* A place five miles the other side of hell. Sailors' Heaven; where there is fiddling and dancing all the time. **1939** (1962) Thompson *Body & Britches* 229 **NY** (as of 1820s), "Yep," they [=canal boatmen] would say, "when I die, I'm not going to stop at Heaven. I'm going fifteen miles beyond, to Fiddler's Green. We'll never be dry there, and there'll be fun on Saturday nights." **1951** Randolph *We Always Lie* 243 **Ozarks,** New neighbours in the Ozarks don't believe in Purgatory and they never heard of Limbo, but many of them refer occasionally to Fiddlers' Green, which is seven miles the other side of Hell. This place was originally set aside for fiddlers only, but . . [now there] are sailors and peddlers and tinkers in Fiddlers' Green, and a few cowpokes, and maybe a thin scatterin' of old soldiers. **1966** *DARE* FW Addit **ME**15, Fiddler's Green—imaginary place nine miles this side of Hell (fiddlers were an unsavory lot). **1970** *DARE* (Qu. CC9, . . *Words . . for hell*) Inf **OK**55, Fiddler's Green—actually that's ten miles on the other side of hell.

fiddlers in Hell, thick as adj phr Cf **Fiddler's Green**

Plentiful, numerous.

1914 *DN* 4.72 **ME, nNH,** *Fiddlers in Hell, thick as...* Very plentiful. **1919** *DN* 5.33 **KY,** *Fiddlers in hell...* Familiar figure, heard in "Thick as fiddlers in hell."

fiddler spider See **fiddle spider**

fiddler's spurge n [See quot 1976]

=**fire-on-the-mountain.**

1933 Small *Manual SE Flora* 803, Painted-leaf. Fiddler's-spurge. **1940** Clute *Amer. Plant Names* 223. **1976** Bailey–Bailey *Hortus Third* 462, *[Euphorbia] cyathophora... Fiddler's s[purge]...* L[ea]v[e]s variable, . . sometimes fiddle-shaped.

fiddler's trumpet n [See quot 1949] Cf **trumpet, trumpetleaf**

A **pitcher plant** (here: *Sarracenia drummondii*).

1933 Small *Manual SE Flora* 582, *Fiddler's-trumpet...* Sandy bogs, Coastal Plain, NW Fla. to Miss., and W Ga. **1949** Moldenke *Amer. Wild Flowers* 60, Spectacularly beautiful are the 1- to 4-foot long trumpets of the *fiddlerstrumpet...* The purple petals are fiddle-shaped.

fiddler's whoop See **fiddler's damn**

fiddle song n Also *fiddle sing*

A secular as opposed to a religious song.

1867 Allen *Slave Songs* x **sSC coast,** In other parts of the South, "fiddle-sings," "devil-songs," "corn-songs," "jig-tunes," and what not, are common. **1942** (1965) Parrish *Slave Songs* 15 **GA,** Then there are the "rags," the "fiddle" or "sinful" songs. These may be plentiful in the interior; but on the coast, where the Negroes are apparently more religious, they have been the most difficult to locate.

fiddle spider n Also *fiddleback spider, fiddler (spider)*

1 A **violin spider. scattered, but esp freq KY**

1965–70 *DARE* (Qu. R28, . . *Kinds of spiders*) Infs **IA**34, **IN**3, 45, **MI**104, Fiddle spider; **CA**80, Fiddleback spider—very venomous; **KY**35, **OK**25, Fiddleback spider; **KY**5, 11, 86, Fiddler (spider); **KY**65, 68, 75, 88, Fiddler—brown recluse (spider).

2 An unidentified spider.

1965 *DARE* (Qu. R28, . . *Kinds of spiders*) Inf **OK**46, Fiddle spider—[it has] a thing on its head shaped like a fiddle.

fiddlestick n

=**fiddlehead** n **1.**

1969 *DARE* (Qu. I28b, *Kinds of greens that are cooked*) Inf **MA**15, Brakes. Same as fiddlesticks.

fiddlestock intj [Var of *fiddlesticks*]

1849 in 1957 Old Farmer's Almanac *Sampler* 74, "Fiddlestock on your butcher's and baker's bills," Uncle Jeremy cries again.

fiddle up a gum tree See **fiddle on a broomstick**

fiddle worm n **AL**

Prob =**grunt worm.**

1967 *DARE* (Qu. P6, . . *Worms . . used for bait*) Inf **AL**32, Fiddle worm—a large worm up to a foot long; **AL**35, Fiddle worm—grew to almost a foot in length. **1971** Wood *Vocab. Change* 313 **AL**, Fiddle worm [volunteered by 1 inf]. **1986** *NADS Letters* **sNM**, *Fiddle worm*—A student reports her grandmother talking of these. Location: Dallas-Ft. Worth [Texas].

fiddling See **fiddle** v 2

fiddling bird n Cf **fiddler bird**

=**winter wren.**

1956 MA Audubon Soc. *Bulletin* 40.127, Winter Wren. . . Fiddlin' Bird (Maine. From its surprisingly sustained and melodious song.)

fiddlin'in' See **-ing**

fidge v [Perh from *fidget*, but cf *W3* "prob. alter of ³*fitch*;" *OED fidge* v. 1575-1883 "*Obs.* exc *dial.*"] *old-fash*

To act in a nervous manner; to fidget.

1916 *DN* 4.323 **KS**, *Fidge. . . =fidget.* "She will fidge a good deal about that matter."

fidgerty adj [Var of *fidgety*]

1954 *Harder Coll.* **cwTN**, [Letter:] If I miss Ye one letter I get fidgerty.

fidget n

1 usu pl; usu with *the;* also *fidges:* A feeling of uneasiness, nervousness; the creeps; an unspecified or imagined illness. **chiefly Sth, Midl**

1899 (1912) Green *VA Folk-Speech* 173, To have the *fidgets.* **1913** Johnson *Highways St. Lawrence to VA* 43 **csNY**, Listening to the sermons all day put me in a fidget. **1934** (1970) Wilson *Backwoods Amer.* 70 **Ozarks**, It is likely, too, that [the man of the backwoods] . . will term nervousness the *all-over fidges.* **1953** *PADS* 19.10 **NC**, I've got the *fidges* all over. I wish Lem would come home before the snow gets deep. **1954** *Harder Coll.* **cwTN**, All-over fidgets. **c1960** *Wilson Coll.* **csKY**, *Fidgets* (or *fidges*): Nervousness, expressed in a jerky or fidgety way. **1965-70** *DARE* (Qu. GG13b, *When something keeps bothering a person and makes him nervous, he may say: "It gives me the ______."*) 16 Infs, **chiefly Sth, Midl**, The fidgets; (Qu. A21, . . *"Now just slow down! Don't ______."*) Inf **FL**15, Be in such a fidget; **TX**4, Get in a fidget; (Qu. BB5, *A general feeling of discomfort or illness that isn't any one place in particular*) Inf **AR**27, The fidgets; (Qu. BB28, *Joking names . . for imaginary diseases*) Inf **AR**27, The fidgets; (Qu. GG11, . . *"That letter hasn't come and he's ______."*) Inf **DE**1, Got the fidgets. [All Infs old]

2 One who is fussy about trifles.

1837 F. Cooper *Recoll. Europe* I. 208 *(OED)*, He . . betrayed himself immediately to be a fidget. **1866** (1881) Whitney *Leslie Goldthwaite* 178 **NEng**, It's only a few fidgets that complain. **1880** Aldrich *Stillwater* 98 **NEng**, I hope you are not a fidget. . . a person who always wants everything some other way, and makes just twice as much trouble as anybody else. **1967-69** *DARE* (Qu. GG14, . . *Someone who fusses or worries a lot, especially about little things*) Infs **NY**32, 206, A fidget; (Qu. HH11b, *[A woman] who is too particular or fussy*) Inf **OH**22, A fidget. [All Infs old]

fidget v [*OED* 1785-1847]

To cause to be uneasy.

1898 Westcott *Harum* 378 **nNY**, "These people walking about fidget me," he said rather irritably. **1931-33** *LANE Worksheets* **swCT**, It fidgets me, but I can't do nothing.

‡fidgety n [**fidget** n 2]

1967 *DARE* (Qu. A21, *When someone is in too much of a hurry you might say, "Now just slow down! Don't ______."*) Inf **SC**32, Be in such a fidgety.

fidgie-gibbets n pl [Perh blend of *fidgets* + *flibbertigibbet*]

=**fidget** n **1.**

1970 *DARE* (Qu. GG13b, . . *"It gives me the ______."*) Inf **KY**85, ['fɪʤi,ʤɪbɪts].

fidgittyfudge intj

1859 Taliaferro *Fisher's R.* 85 **nwNC** (as of 1820s), "Pshaw! fidgitty-fudge!" said Uncle Davy.

fid hook n Cf **fid** n **2**

In logging: see quots 1905, 1958.

1851 (1856) Springer *Forest Life* 108 **ME**, He [=a logging teamster] examines the chains, lest they should part, and above all, . . the "fid-hook" and the "dog-hook," the former that it does not work out, the latter that it loose not its grappling hold upon the tree. **1905** U.S. Forest Serv. *Bulletin* 61.37, *Fid hook.* A slender, flat hook used to keep another hook from slipping on a chain. (N[orth] W[oods] L[ake] S[tates Forest].) **1958** McCulloch *Woods Words* 61 **Pacific NW**, *Fid hook*—a. A flat hook with a narrow slot and a movable tongue. It is used to tighten two ends of a chain and lock the connection. . . b. A flat hook without the tongue. In this case a link of chain is grabbed in the slot to make the lock in cinching up a load.

fidity See **asafetida**

‡Fido's going to get you phr Cf **dog** n¹ **B17c**

1967 *DARE* FW Addit **nwLA**, Fido's going to get you = you are becoming very tired. If you are *real* tired you spell it *phideaux.*

fiduddle v [Perh *fiddle* + intrusive syll]

To putter around.

1968 *DARE* (Qu. A10, . . *Doing little unimportant things: Somebody asks, "What are you doing?" and you answer, "Nothing in particular—I'm just ______."*) Inf **MD**17, Fiduddling [fɨdʌdlɪŋ].

fieh See **fire**

field n Usu |fi(ə)ld|; also **esp Sth, S Midl** |fi(ə)l|; for addit varr see quots Cf Pronc Intro 3.I.3.c, 3.I.22 Pronc-spp *fiel', filled* Cf **fee lark**

A Forms.

1899 Chesnutt *Conjure Woman* 18 **csNC** [Black], One er [=of] de fiel' han's died. **1922** Gonzales *Black Border* 301 **sSC, GA coasts** [Gullah glossary], *Fiel'*—field, fields. **1931-33** *LANE Worksheets* **cMA**, Field corn ['fil ˌkɔən]. **1939** *LANE* Map 120 *(Field)*, [In northern New England the dominant variants are of the types [fijld, fijɫd]; these pronunciations also occur in southern New England as do those of the type [fi(ə)ld]. [fiəl, fiil] occur infrequently.] **1942** Hall *Smoky Mt. Speech* 91, [d] is frequently unsounded after [n] or [l], as in . . field. **1966-70** *DARE* Tape **AL**24, Along about . . ten years old I went to [fijə] and chopped cotton; **GA**93, [fiəl]. **1970** *DARE* (Qu. I42, . . *Names . . for peanuts*) Inf **DC**12, Field [fɪ:l] peas. **1982** McCool *Sam McCool's Pittsburghese* 12 **PA**, Filled: a large open space, as in "The Pirates used to play in Forbes Filled."

B Senses.

1 See quot. Cf **old field**

1894 *DN* 1.330 **NJ**, *Field:* deserted farm overgrown with pine, scrub oak, and brambles. Some of these *fields*—the term is equivalent to *plantation*—are from a century to a century and a half old. Distinguishing names are Broomstick Ridge Field, Lawrence Field, etc. (Cape May County names).

2 See quot.

1981 *KS Qrly.* 13.2.66, *Field* . . fenced enclosure near a buckaroo camp where cattle are kept during trail drive.

3 In railroading: see quot 1945.

1932 *RR Mag.* Oct 367, *Field*—Yard. **1938** Beebe *High Iron* 220 [Railroad terms], *Field:* Classification yard. **1945** Hubbard *Railroad Ave.* 367, *Yard*—System of tracks for making up trains or storing cars. . . Also called *garden* and *field.* **1976** Gould *Blackie's RR Hdbk.* 9, *Classification Yard:* Field - Garden.

4 attrib; Of plants:

a Wild (rather than cultivated).

1789 Morse *Amer. Geog.* 53, Of the various aromatic and other kinds of herbs are . . field-dock, rock-liverwort. **1822** Eaton *Botany* 491, *[Trifolium] arvense* (rabbit-foot, field clover). . . Grows in dry pastures or barren fields. **1928** Aldrich *Lantern* 168 **NE**, Along the grassy roadway, one's skirts touched Queen Anne's lace, field mustard and yarrow. **1932** in 1957 Old Farmer's Almanac *Sampler* 289 **NH**, Field penny cress. **1965-70** *DARE* (Qu. I5) Inf **OH**102, Field onions; (Qu. I28a) Inf **NY**49, Field salad—green leaf, eaten in December; **VA**24, Field cress—like watercress; early in spring; hot; (Qu. I28b) Inf **MD**30, Field cress; (Qu. I37) Inf **MN**36, Field mushrooms; (Qu. I43) Inf **FL**27, Field hickory nuts; (Qu. I44) Inf **NY**128, Field strawberries; (Qu. I46) Infs **SC**46, 57, Field plum(s); **LA**3, Field plums—these are wild too; grow in clusters at edge of field; may be red or yellow; not as sour as wild plums; **SC**34, Field plums—red, yellow; on road banks; **NY**195, Field berries. **1967** *DARE*

Tape **KY**34A, [FW:] Do people still go out and gather greens in the spring? [Inf:] Yeah. . . [FW:] What kinds do they pick? [Inf:] Well they pick old-field lettuce. . . Field lettuce, you ever seen it?

b Grown primarily for livestock feed or for market; less than desirable for human consumption.

1772 in 1919 *MD Hist. Mag.* 14.362, I once tryed field Carrots [for livestock] under Heesons management without success. **1854** PA State Ag. Soc. *Rept. for 1853* 1.43, John H. Smith, Lancaster county, one-fourth acre field turnips. **1856** U.S. Patent Office *Annual Rept. for 1855: Ag.* 177 **cNY,** All who reside in this vicinity say that it ripens at least two weeks earlier than other field corn. **c1960** *Wilson Coll.* **csKY,** Field punkin. . . One raised for the stock, in the cornfield. . . Field punkin is the same as cow punkin. **1965–70** *DARE* (Qu. I34, *If you don't have sweet corn, you can always eat young* ______) 707 Infs, **widespread,** Field corn; (Qu. I20, *Other kinds of beans*) Infs **IA**12, **IN**30, **OH**55, **TX**36, Field beans; **AR**51, Field beans—commercial crop beans for canning; **IN**82, Field beans—same as soy beans; (Qu. I23) Inf **CT**17, Field punkins—used for punkin moonshine or cattle; **NY**209, Field punkins—yellow; **KY**34, Field squash—small, brown, ridgy; baked in oven; size of saucer; old-fashioned; **TX**33, Field squash—small and yellow; (Qu. I24; total Infs questioned, 75) Infs **AR**39, **MS**45, Field pumpkin; **NM**2, Field pumpkins—large, more watery [than pie pumpkins]; **OK**1, Field pumpkin—yellow and large; **OK**3, Field pumpkin—large, round; (Qu. I17, *Beans . . dark red when . . dry*) Inf **MA**15, Field beans; (Qu. I18, *Smaller beans . . white when . . dry*) Inf **MI**116, Field beans.

5 attrib; also *old-field;* Of animals: found in fields.

1819 *Plough Boy* 1.118/3 **IL,** This spider, which is supposed to be the tarantula, is much larger and darker colored than the common field spider. **1868** [see **field viper**]. **1967–70** *DARE* (Qu. P25) Inf **MO**26, Field snake; **VA**47, Old-field snake—high land.

fieldball n

1966 *DARE* (Qu. EE11, *Bat-and-ball games for just a few players*) Inf **MS**71, Fieldball.

field balm n

1 =**ground ivy 1.**

1900 Lyons *Plant Names* 174, *G. hederacea*. . . Ground Ivy, Field Balm [etc]. **1914** Georgia *Manual Weeds* 351, *Ground Ivy. . . Other English names:* Field Balm. . . Propagates by seeds and by rootstocks. **1973** Hitchcock–Cronquist *Flora Pacific NW* 402, Field balm. . . Eurasian weedy sp. of moist woods and thickets, often also in lawns.

2 Catnip.

1971 Krochmal *Appalachia Med. Plants* 184, *Nepeta cataria. . . Common Names:* Catnip, . . field balm, nip.

field bed n Also *field couch old-fash*

A bed made up on the floor; a **pallet.**

1851 (1969) Burke *Polly Peablossom* 189, The mammy made up a field couch upon the floor in front of the fire, to which she consigned all her guests. **1966–69** *DARE* (Qu. E18) Infs **CT**39, **ME**10, 16, Field bed [all Infs old]; **FL**23, Field bed—old-fashioned. **1973** Allen *LAUM* 1.231 **MN** (as of c1950), [Bed on the floor:] Field bed: for several people. [Inf old]

fieldbird n [See quot 1955 MA Audubon Soc.]

=**golden plover.**

1888 Trumbull *Names of Birds* 195, *Charadrius dominicus* . . In Maine at Ash Point, Field-bird. **1917** (1923) *Birds Amer.* 1.257, Golden Plover, *Charadrius dominicus dominicus*. . . Other Names.—American Golden Plover; . . Squealer; Field-bird; Pasture-bird. **1955** Forbush–May *Birds* 174, *American Golden Plover—Pluvialis dominica dominica* . . Field-bird. **1955** MA Audubon Soc. *Bulletin* 39.444, *American Golden Plover*. . . Field Bird (Maine, Mass. It resorts to grasslands more than do its relatives, except the Killdeer.)

field-bred adj *old-fash* Cf **field colt 1, pasture-bred**

Of a horse: not intentionally bred; mongrel.

1966–70 *DARE* (Qu. K43) 8 Infs, **scattered,** Field-bred; **MA**6, **VA**68, Field-bred horse; **WV**3, Field-bred—same as woods colt; **OH**35, Field-bred? [Inf queries]. [All Infs old; 10 of 12 Infs male]

field bunting See **field sparrow a**

field centaury n

A centaury (perh *Centaurium pulchellum*).

1969 *DARE* FW Addit **KY**5, Field centaury ['sɛntri]—used to ease menstruation pain (old-fashioned).

field chippy n Cf **chippy** n² **1, ground chippy, meadow chippy, winter chippy**

=**field sparrow a.**

1917 (1923) *Birds Amer.* 3.43, *Field Sparrow. . . Other Names*. . . Field Chippy. **1944** Hausman *Amer. Birds* 508, Chippy, Field—see Sparrow, Field. **1946** Goodrich *Birds in KS* 314, Colloquial name. . . Chippy, field . . Common name, A. O. U. Check-List. . . Sparrow, field. **1963** Gromme *Birds WI* 213, Field chippy.

field colt n **esp VA** Cf **woods colt**

1 also *old-field colt:* A horse that was not intentionally bred

1835 *S. Lit. Messenger* 1.582/1 **VA,** I could . . only remember that every untrimmed *old field* colt was a regular descendant of Eclipse. **1968** *DARE* (Qu. K43, *A horse that was not intentionally bred*) Infs **VA**24, 26, Field colt.

2 also *old-field(s) colt* (or *kid*), *field rabbit;* Transf: an illegitimate child.

1946 *PADS* 5.30 **VA,** *Oldfields colt*. . . Illegitimate child; in the southern Piedmont. **1966–70** *DARE* (Qu. Z11b, . . *Joking words for a child of unwed parents*) Infs **KY**6, **VA**18, 26, Field colt; **VA**31, Field colt (common); field rabbit; **VA**41, Old-field colt—heard long ago, not used now; **GA**9, Old-field kid. [5 of 6 Infs old] **1984** Wilder *You All Spoken Here* 98 **Sth,** Come-by-chance child: Illegitimate; woods colt; bush colt; catch colt; old field colt; outsider; volunteer; yard child; bantlin'.

field couch See **field bed**

field daisy n

=**oxeye** (here: *Chrysanthemum leucanthemum*).

1936 Winter *Plants NE* 160, *C[hrysanthemum] leucanthemum* . . Field Daisy. **1961** Smith *MI Wildflowers* 419, Field Daisy—*Chrysanthemum leucanthemum.* **1965–70** *DARE* (Qu. S7) Infs **IL**76, **KY**9, **OH**64, **VA**52, Field daisy; (Qu. S11) Inf **SC**11, Field daisy; (Qu. S26a) Inf **NY**123, Field daisies; (Qu. S26d) Infs **IA**13, **KY**35, **MI**9, 100, 108, **SC**2, **VA**43, Field daisy; **MI**17, White field-daisies, yellow field-daisies.

field dinner n *?obs* Cf **dinner on the ground(s)**

A picnic dinner out of doors.

1857 Stone *Life Howland* 282, "A field dinner and Rhode Island clam bake, . . " was announced to follow the services. *Ibid* 284, A company of fifty or more [e]merged from the orchard, in which they had partaken of their "field dinner."

field driver n Also *field drover* **NEng** *old-fash* Cf **fence viewer, hogreeve**

See quots 1859, 1931–33.

1694 in 1889 Manchester MA *Town Rec.* 1.56, John Elathorp & william Allen sen[ior]: weare chosen hawards or feld Drivers. **1826** Cushing *Hist. Newburyport* 119 **MA,** *Field Drivers,* Moses Somerby, Charles Toppan. **1859** (1968) Bartlett *Americanisms* 147, *Field-driver.* A civil officer, whose duty it is to take up and impound swine, cattle, sheep, horses, etc. going at large in the public highways, or on common and unimproved lands, and not under the charge of a keeper. **1888** Bryce *Amer. Commonwealth* 2.229, [There are] divers minor officers, such as hog-reeves (now usually called field drivers). **1931–33** *LANE Worksheets* **ceMA,** If a young fellow gets married they make him a field-driver (local term for fence-viewer). **1975** Gould *ME Lingo* 90, Most of the other town officers in the same category [as fence viewers] have lapsed the same way: *scalers* of bark, surveyors of shook, inspectors of spirits and vinegars, field drovers, *pound* keepers.

fieldfare n

=**robin.**

1946 Hausman *Eastern Birds* 456, *Turdus migratorius migratorius. . . Other Names* . . Fieldfare.

field gentry n [Perh folk-etym for **field centaury**]

1969 *DARE* (Qu. S26d, *Wildflowers that grow in meadows*) Inf **KY**5, Field gentry.

field gillyflower n

A **gilia** (here: *Gilia capitata*).

1967 Gilkey–Dennis *Hdbk. NW Plants* 337, *Gilia capitata. . . Field gilly-flower*. . . Flowers in dense terminal heads . . blue, rarely white or lavender.

field gopher n

1 A **ground squirrel** n **b** (here: *Spermophilus richardsoni*).

1970 *Western Folkl.* 29.172, *Field gopher* . . [is] used just for Richardson's ground squirrel.

2 A **meadow mouse.** Cf **gopher** n[1] **2c**
1970 *DARE* (Qu. P29) Inf **KY**84, Field gopher.

field hawk n **chiefly SE, C Atl**
Prob a **marsh hawk.**
1966–70 *DARE* (Qu. Q4) Infs **GA**6, **KY**21, **OR**13, **VA**79, Field hawk; **DE**4, Field hawk—small, about the size of a pigeon; **KY**11, Field hawk—feeds on mice; a small hawk, a little smaller than a blue-tail hawk; **LA**3, Field hawk—one with long wings that flies back and forth over fields; **LA**10, Field hawk—same as mice hawk; flies back and forth low across fields; **MD**25, Field hawk—looks like a big pigeon—brownish or black; may be the same as crow; **MD**34, Field hawk—one-third the size of a chicken hawk.

field holler See **holler** n[1] **C2**

field lark n **chiefly Sth, S Midl** See Map Cf **fee lark**
=**meadowlark.**
1874 Coues *Birds NW* 190, *Sturnella Magna.* Meadow-lark; Field-lark. **1880** Cable *Grandissimes* 42 **LA,** The call of the field-lark came continually out of the grass. **a1883** (1911) Bagby *VA Gentleman* 49, He enjoys . . shooting field-larks in the daytime and . . possum-hunting . . in the night. **1899** (1912) Green *VA Folk-Speech* 173, *Field-lark. . .* A bird generally called *"old field-lark."* **1917** (1923) *Birds Amer.* 2.434. **1936** Roberts *MN Birds* 2.290, *Sturnella magna . . Other name:* Field Lark. . . *Sturnella neglecta . . Other Name:* Field Lark. **1950** *PADS* 14.29 **SC,** *Field lark. . .* The meadow lark. **1954** *Harder Coll.* **cwTN,** Field lark. . . *Sturnella magna.* **1963** Gromme *Birds WI* 215. **1965–70** *DARE* (Qu. Q15, . . *Different kinds of larks*) 163 Infs, **chiefly Sth, S Midl,** Field lark; (Qu. Q7, . . *Game birds*) Infs **GA**77, **MD**13, Field lark; (Qu. Q14) Inf **AL**22, Field lark.

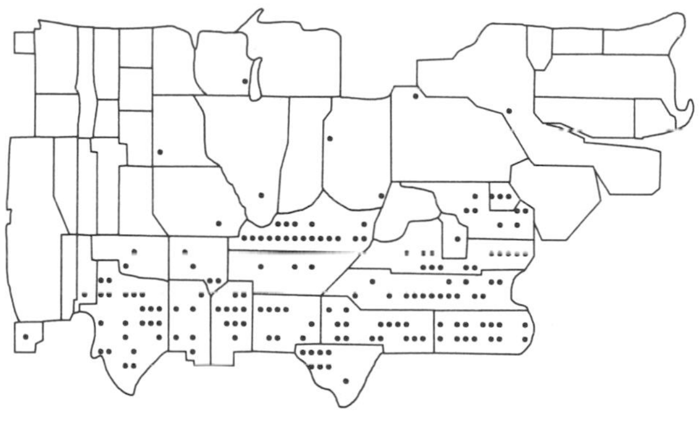

•field lark (Qq. Q15, Q7, Q14)

field lily n
1 A **dogtooth violet.**
1967 *DARE* (Qu. S11, . . *Names . . for . . dog-tooth violet*) Inf **ID**5, Field lily.
2 Appar a small-flowered **tiger lily.**
1967 *DARE* (Qu. S26c) Inf **OR**5, Field lily; (Qu. S26d) Inf **NE**11, Field lilies—small version of a tiger lily.
3 An unidentified plant of the genus *Lilium.* Cf **field B4a**
1968 *DARE* FW Addit **VA**15, Field lily. Common in meadows.

field lobelia n
=**Indian tobacco.**
1971 Krochmal *Appalachia Med. Plants* 164, *Lobelia Inflata . .* field lobelia.

field marlin n
=**hudsonian godwit.**
1888 Trumbull *Names of Birds* 210, Again, in New Jersey . . at Somers Point, *Field Marlin [Limosa haemastica].* **1917** (1923) *Birds Amer.* 1.240, *Hudsonian Godwit—Limosa haemastica . .* Field Marlin.

field martin n
=**kingbird.**
1810 Wilson *Amer. Ornith.* 2.66, [The] Tyrant Fly-catcher, or King-bird, *Muscicapa Tyrannus, . .* is the *Field Martin* of Maryland and some of the southern states, and the *King-bird* of Pennsylvania and several of the northern districts. **1859** (1968) Bartlett *Americanisms* 147, *Field Martin.* A name sometimes given in the South to the King-Bird. **1872** Schele de Vere *Americanisms* 379, The proud name of *King-bird* is very fairly given to the bravest of birds, the *Scissor-tail* (Tyrannus carolinensis). . . while in some parts of the South he is known as *Fieldmartin.* **1917** (1923) *Birds Amer.* 2.192. **1966–67** *DARE* (Qu. Q14) Inf **LA**7, Field martin; (Qu. Q20) Inf **DC**4, Fiel' martin—swift-flying bird, can whup a crow.

field mouse n **chiefly Nth**
=**meadow mouse,** esp *Microtus pennsylvanicus.*
1743 (1754) Catesby *Nat. Hist. Carolina* 2 [app] xxv, Beasts of which the same are in the Old World [include]. . . House-mouse, Field-mouse, Mole. **1792** Belknap *Hist. NH* 3.153, Field mouse *(Sorex araneus.)* **1832** Williamson *Hist. ME* 1.138, The three species of the *Mouse kind,* seen in our woodlands, are—1. the *shrew,*—2. the *ground,* and 3. the *field Mouse.* **1891** (1967) Freeman *New Engl. Nun* 167 **eMA,** A little field-mouse . . had appreciative notice from Jenny Wrayne. **1904** (1977) Porter *Freckles* 64 **IN,** [The snakes] liked neither the heat nor leaving the field-mice, moles, and young rabbits. **1928** Anthony *N. Amer. Mammals* 415, *Microtus pennsylvanicus. . . Names.*—Meadow Mouse; . . Field Mouse. **1961** Jackson *Mammals WI* 230, Field mouse. . . A . . mouse with rather small ears nearly concealed in the long loose fur, and with small black beady eyes. **1966–70** *DARE* (Qu. P29) Inf **CA**156, Field mouse—species of gopher and mouse together; **CA**168, Field mice—also called kangaroo mice; **IN**45, Field mouse—a little short-tailed rat; **KY**11, Gopher—like a mouse, also called gopher mouse, a field mouse; builds tunnels through the grass; **KY**75, Gophers—alternate name for field mice; **WI**12, Gopher—mice, field mouse most common; **WI**52, Field mouse; (Qu. P32, . . *Other kinds of wild animals*) Infs **KS**10, **MI**32, **NY**66, **OH**82, **PA**176, Field mouse. **1980** Whitaker *Audubon Field Guide Mammals* 495, *Meadow Vole* "Field Mouse" *(Microtus pennsylvanicus).*

field mouse-ear n
A **chickweed 1b.**
1840 MA Zool. & Bot. Surv. *Herb. Plants & Quadrupeds* 186, *Myosotis Virginiana,* Field Mouse-Ear, . . a troublesome weed in fields, among wheat, etc. **1976** Bailey–Bailey *Hortus Third* 248, *Cerastium arvense . .* Field Mouse-ear.

field mushroom n
A mushroom of the genus *Agaricus.* For other names of var spp see **frogstool, horse mushroom, meadow mushroom, toadstool**
1902 McIlvaine–Macadam *1000 Amer. Fungi* 728, The field mushroom *(A[garicus] campester) . .* deserves more than ordinary attention. **1908** Hard *Mushroom Edible* 310, *Agaricus arvensis. . . The Field or Horse Mushroom. . .* grows much larger than the common mushroom. **1942** Hylander *Plant Life* 57, The Field Mushroom . . prefers open fields and pastures where it displays its tan-brown cap, which often has a silky luster. **1968** *DARE* (Qu. I37, *Small plants shaped like an umbrella that grow in woods and fields—which are safe to eat*) Inf **MN**36, Field mushrooms. **1974** (1977) Coon *Useful Plants* 273, *Agaricus campestris*—The field mushroom. . . is actually the cultivated one, but a native form is *A. arvensis.* **1987** McKnight–McKnight *Mushrooms* 254, *Field Mushrooms. . .* Genus *Agaricus.*

field owl n
=**short-eared owl.**
1946 Hausman *Eastern Birds* 363, *Short-eared Owl. . . Other Names . .* Field Owl. . . This owl is most often seen in open country.

field pansy n Also *field violet*
A **johnny-jump-up** (here: *Viola tricolor*).
1848 Gray *Manual of Botany* 46, *V. tricolor. . . Field Pansy. . .* Dry hills and fields, Long Island and New Jersey. **1941** Walker *Lookout* 46 **TN,** Among this class of flowers is heartsease, or field pansy. **1969** *DARE* (Qu. S11) Inf **RI**15, Field violet—light blue.

field pea n Also *old-field pea* **Sth, S Midl**
A cultivated legume such as *Pisum sativum* var *arvense* or the **black-eyed pea;** rarely, a peanut.
1709 (1967) Lawson *New Voyage* 82 **NC, SC,** All the sorts of *English* Pease . . thrive very well in *Carolina.* Particularly . . the common *Field-Pease . .* yield very well, and are of a good Relish. **1785** (1925) Washington *Diaries* 2.363 **VA,** Sowed one Bushel and three Pecks of the Albany, or field Pea in the inclosure. **1903** *DN* 2.313 **seMO,** *Field-peas. . .* A kind of bean used for feeding stock. **1908** *DN* 3.310 **eAL, wGA,** *Field-pea, old field-pea. . .* A kind of cow-pea, so called because it is the only crop that will grow on the old or worn-out cotton fields. **1942**

Faulkner *Go Down* 157 **MS,** A big pot of field peas et clean empty on the stove, and him laying in the back yard asleep. **1949** Ahlgren *Forage Crops* 131, The field pea was brought to America by the early colonists, being reported first in Virginia in 1636. **1965** Needham–Mussey *Country Things* 140 **sVT,** For a laxative he would dig out a little of this gummy stuff, and roll it up in a round pellet not quite the size of a Canada pea or a field pea; that was one dose. **1965–70** *DARE* (Qu. I20, . . *Beans . . grown around here*) 14 Infs, **Sth, S Midl,** Field peas; **LA**32, A field pea looks like a black-eyed pea but is splotchy or variable in color; the hull isn't any true color either; **GA**17, Field peas—used for hog feed; **SC**70, Field peas are red peas with a black spot; (Qu. I19, *Small white peas with a black spot where they were joined to the pod*) Infs **AL**6, **AR**14, **FL**27, **NC**38, **TN**4, Field peas; **LA**14, These are similar to navy beans; I think 'field peas' is a misnomer; (Qu. I14, . . *Beans that you eat in the pod before they're dry*) Inf **AR**27, Field peas; **LA**33, Field peas—when they're young and tender; (Qu. I15, . . *Beans . . [with] yellow pods*) Inf **LA**24, Field peas; (Qu. I42, . . *Names . . for peanuts*) Inf **DC**12, Field peas; (Qu. L34, . . *Important crops grown around here*) Inf **MN**16, Field peas—heard of them; they're experimental in this area. **1976** *DARE* File **SC,** In Abbeville County we used the term *field peas* which were planted both for eating the small peas and turning under the vines for soil improvement.

field pine n

1 An **old-field pine** or similar pine. **chiefly SE, Gulf States**

1836 Simms *Mellichampe* 63 **SC,** He describes the field-pine as being "of inferior and frequently dwarf size". **1966–70** *DARE* (Qu. T17, . . *Kinds of pine trees*) 11 Infs, **Sth, Gulf States,** Field pine; **LA**18, Field pine—same as hill pine; [also called] shortleaf or bull pine; **LA**40, Field pine—a shortleaf pine that takes possession of the ground; **NC**24, Yellow or field pine; **TX**33, Field pine—[a] volunteer; **VA**43, Field pine = black back pine; **VA**70, Field pine—very low.

2 A **beach heather** (here: *Hudsonia ericoides*).

1900 Lyons *Plant Names* 194, *H[udsonia] ericoides*. . . Field Pine. **1959** Carleton *Index Herb. Plants* 46, *Field-pine:* Hudsonia ericoides.

field plover n

Either of two plovers: the **upland plover** or the **golden plover.**

1844 DeKay *Zool. NY* 2.247, The Grey Plover . . is known under the various names of . . Grass Plover, Upland Plover, and Field Plover. **1858** Baird *Birds* 690, This bird [=*Charadrius virginicus*], well known throughout the United States as the Bull-head, Field Plover, or Golden Plover, appears to be one of the species that inhabit . . the entire continent of America. **1917** (1923) *Birds Amer.* 1.247, Upland Plover, *Bartramia longicauda*. . . Other Names.—Bartramian Sandpiper; . . Field Plover; Highland Plover. *Ibid* 1.257, Golden Plover, *Charadrius dominicus dominicus*. . . Other names.—American Golden Plover; . . Field Plover; Greenback. **1932** Bennitt *Check-list* 28, *American golden plover. Pluvialis dominica dominica* . . field plover. **1955** Forbush–May *Birds* 174, *Pluvialis dominica dominica* . . Field Plover.

field rabbit See **field colt 2**

field road n **chiefly Sth**

A dirt road.

1900 Stockton *Afield* 21 **Philadelphia PA,** There was a field-road on this side of the pond . . , and proceeding along this they came to the bridge and got into the main road. . . the wheels were [now] on the hard road. **1966–68** *DARE* (Qu. N27a, . . *Different kinds of unpaved roads*) Infs **GA**63, **LA**34, **MS**1, Field road; **LA**26, Field road—[on] headlands, roads through fields of cane also called field roads.

fieldspar n [Folk-etym for *feldspar*]

1967–68 *DARE* (Qu. C26, . . *Kinds of stone*) Infs **NJ**2, **VA**13, Fieldspar.

field sparrow n [From the habitat]

Any of various sparrows, as:

a also *field bunting:* A common small sparrow *(Spizella pusilla).* Also called **field chippy, grass sparrow b, ground bird a, ground sparrow d, huckleberry bird, red-headed sparrow, rush sparrow, wood sparrow**

1810 Wilson *Amer. Ornith.* 2.121 **PA,** Field Sparrow. *Fringilla Pusilla.* **1839** Audubon *Synopsis Birds* 104, Emberiza pusilla. . . Field Bunting.—Field Sparrow. . . From Texas to Maryland, in Kentucky and the intermediate parts, during winter. **1844** Giraud *Birds Long Is.* 105, *Field Bunting*. . . The Field Sparrow. . . prefers pasture lands, dry grounds and corn-fields, and passes the most of its time on the ground. **1917** (1923) *Birds Amer.* 3.43, *Field Sparrow. . . Other Names.* . . Field Bunting. **1942** Peattie *Friendly Mts.* 197, To the left of the thrasher, waft in at regular intervals the dainty and sweet notes of the field or bush sparrow *[Spizella pusilla]*. **1946** Goodrich *Birds in KS* 314, Field chippy. **1946** Hausman *Eastern Birds* 608, Eastern Field Sparrow *Spizella pusilla* . . Other Names . . Field bunting. **1948** *Press-Gaz.* (Green Bay WI) 13 July 11/4, Birds that sang in the afternoon were the song, vesper and field sparrows. **1965–70** *DARE* (Qu. Q21) 44 Infs, **chiefly east of Missip R,** Field sparrow.

b =**vesper sparrow.**

1871 Burroughs *Wake-Robin* 16, Have you heard the song of the field sparrow? . . Wilson, I believe, calls him the grass-finch, and was evidently unacquainted with his powers of song.

c =**savannah sparrow.**

1944 Hausman *Amer. Birds* 526, Sparrow, Field (incorrect)—see Sparrow, Savannah.

field spur n

An unidentified burr; see quot.

1967 *DARE* (Qu. S15, . . *Weed seeds that cling to clothing*) Inf **SC**40, Field spur.

field swallow n [See quot 1946]

=**barn swallow 1.**

1946 Hausman *Eastern Birds* 415, *Hirundo erythrogaster*. . . Field Swallow. . . Very common about farms, or sweeping over fields and meadows. **1967** *DARE* (Qu. Q20) Inf **NY**1, Field swallow.

field violet See **field pansy**

field viper n Also *old-field adder* Cf **adder 1, field B5, viper**

Perh a **hognose snake.**

1868 Gregg *Life in Army* 264 **C Atl,** Like the old field adder, a little warmth of public patronage . . will restore their [=Northern and Southern traitors'] poisonous propensities. **1968** *DARE* (Qu. P25, . . *Kinds of snakes*) Inf **DE**1, Field viper—a striped snake; **DE**3, Field viper—not poisonous; a dirty brown and yellow color.

field whiskey n Cf **farm liquor**

See quot 1953.

1953 Randolph *Down in Holler* 243 **Ozarks,** *Field whiskey*. . . Common moonshine, not aged or colored. In Aurora, Mo., a woman told me: "Them boys was a-sellin' field whiskey right on Main Street, an' it a Sunday!" **1954** *Harder Coll.* **cwTN,** Field whiskey.

field yam-root n

A **carrion flower 1** (here: *Smilax herbacea*).

1920 *Torreya* 20.19, *Smilax herbacea*. . . Field yam-root, Manitowoc, Wis.

field yarrow n

A **ragwort** (here: *Senecio smallii*).

1968 *DARE* FW Addit **VA**15, Field yarrow (whose book name is Small's ragwort) was used to cure hollow-tail in cattle.

fierce adj Usu |fɪrs, fɪəs|; also **esp NEng** *old-fash* |fɝs| Pronc-spp *fa(i)rce, farse, ferce* Similarly, n *ferceness*

A Forms.

1815 Humphreys *Yankey in England* 105, *Fairce, farce,* fierce. **1841** (1952) Cooper *Deerslayer* 246, As for f'erceness, it's no great ricommend to a soldier. **1848** (1894) Lowell *Biglow* 169, The New England *ferce* for *fierce,* and *perce* for *pierce* (sometimes heard as *fairce* and *pairce*). **1894** *Century Illustr. Mag.* 48.868 **NEng,** Our Lake George people say *fairce,* and the word seems merely a broad sound of fierce. **1894** *DN* [see **B1** below]. **1918** *DN* 5.15 **seMA,** *Fierce* [fɝs].

B Senses.

1 Eager, excited, agitated. **NEng**

1894 *DN* 1.341 **wCT,** *Farse:* eager. "He's dretful farse to go fishin'." **1894** *Century Illustr. Mag.* 48.868 **NEng,** A *fierce* dog is dangerous. But "fairce" only means eager; a dog may be *fairce* to catch a rabbit, or *fairce* to get indoors on a cold night, and yet not be fierce, and so a man is said to be *fairce* to hear the news. **1966** *DARE* (Qq. AA4a,b, . . *Eager to get married*) Inf **ME**22, He's gettin' fierce! **ME**16, She's fierce to catch a man. **1975** Gould *ME Lingo* 92, It can mean agitated, as in "He was some fierce!"

2 Terrible; disagreeable in the extreme.

1907 Porter *Trimmed Lamp* 6, How can you wear a waist like that, Lou? . . It shows fierce taste. *Ibid* 210, But it's fierce, now, how cynical I am, ain't it? **1914** *DN* 4.106 **KS,** *Fierce*. . . Disagreeably extreme;—

applied to prices, heat, style, etc. **1915** *DN* 4.217, *Fierce,* disagreeable or below par. "Isn't the wind fierce?" "That's a fierce looking hat.' **1942** McAtee *Dial. Grant Co. IN* 25 (as of 1890s), *Fierce* . . extreme in an unpleasant or undesirable way, applied to a happening, a price, heat, cold, etc.

3 See quot.

1975 Gould *ME Lingo* 92, *Fierce*—A fairly mild Maine adjective, seldom meaning ferocious. . . But mostly it qualifies only slightly: a *fierce* (big) hunk of pie, a *fierce* (forced or unmeant) smile, a *fierce* (heavy) fog.

fierce adv

Extremely.

1963 *DE Folkl. Bulletin* Oct 40/2, It's fierce bad (with reference to illness, the weather, etc.)

fierro n [Span "iron; brand"] **SW** *?obs*

A brand affixed to an animal upon purchase.

1844 (1954) Gregg *Commerce* 132 **NM,** No matter how many proprietors a horse or mule may have had, every one marks him with a huge hieroglyphic brand, which is called the *fierro,* and again, upon selling him, with his *venta,* or sale-brand. **1857** Davis *El Gringo* 206 **Desert SW,** Each person has his own brand, with which he marks all his mules, horses, and other animals as soon as they come into his possession. . . This is called the *fierro,* or buying brand. **1892** *DN* 1.247 **TX,** *Fiêrro:* a brand or mark on cattle and horses. Old form of *hierro,* iron.

fiery thorn See **fire thorn**

fiery water n

1950 *WELS Suppl.* **nwIA,** Fiery water—the watery matter that often comes out of a sore with pus. The blisters of athlete's foot also have "fiery water" in them.

fiest See **feist** n

fiesta n [Span] **chiefly SW, esp CA, TX** Cf **fest**

A festival or celebration; see quots.

1844 (1954) Gregg *Commerce* 147 **NM,** These *carretas* . . [are] the 'pleasure-carriages' of the rancheros, whose families are conveyed in them to the towns, whether to market, or to *fiestas,* or on other joyful occasions. **1892** *DN* 1.190 **TX,** *Fiêsta:* a festival, formerly a holiday celebrated on the patron saint's day of a church, town or village. By extension any festivity, religious or national. Even a *corrida de toros,* a bull fight, is a *fiesta.* *Ibid* 248, In the plural *las fiestas* is synonymous with a fair, which generally lasts several days. **1907** White *AZ Nights* 161, "Well," insisted the first voice, "what in hell does Colorado Rogers mean by bustin' in on our song *fiesta* that way?" **1940** Writers' Program *Guide TX* 115, Notable among the observances [in San Antonio] is the Fiesta de San Jacinto, which is the brilliant climax of the city's social season. **1948** *Sat. Eve. Post* 31 July 16/2 **SW,** Reckon you came here to see our big fiesta, huh? **1965–70** *DARE* (Qu. FF16, . . *Local* . . *celebrations*) Infs **CA**18, 30, 65, **IL**64, **MN**42, **TX**20, Fiesta; **TX**27, Citrus Fiesta; **CA**211, Fiesta de las Rosas; **CA**142, Folsom Fiesta; **CA**145, Logging Fiesta; (Qu. FF2, . . *Kinds of parties*) Inf **CA**65, Fiesta party; (Qu. AA18, . . *Celebration after a wedding*) Inf **NY**241, Fiesta. **1968** Adams *Western Words* 111, *Fiesta*—A festival or celebration; now used to designate any party where Spanish food, decorations, or costumes are featured.

fiesta flower n [See quot 1897] **CA**

A plant of the genus *Pholistoma,* usu *P. auritum.*

[**1897** Parsons *Wild Flowers CA* 279, It is said that the dark-eyed señoritas of early days decked their ball-dresses with sprays of this flower [=*Pholistoma auritum*], which clung gracefully to the thin fabrics.] **1925** Jepson *Manual Plants CA* 812, *N. aurita*. . . *Fiesta Flower*. . . Corolla deep purple or violet, paler outside. **1949** Moldenke *Amer. Wild Flowers* 253, The *fiestaflower, Pholistoma aurita* [sic], has weak and straggling stems. . . The flowers are deep purple or violet. **1961** Thomas *Flora Santa Cruz* 283 **CA,** *P. auritum*. . . Common Fiesta Flower. . . *P. membranaceum*. . . White Fiesta Flower. **1976** Bailey–Bailey *Hortus Third* 864, *P. auritum*. . . *Fiesta flower*. . . Spring. Calif.

fiesty See **feisty** adj

fif See **fifth**

fife See **feist** n

fift See **fifth**

fifteen-cent-store n

=**five-and-ten 1.**

1971 Bright *Word Geog. CA & NV* 204, *Fifteen cent store* 5% [of 300 infs]. **1980** *DARE* File **cwCA** (as of c1955), Eating at the lunch counter in the fifteen cent store was considered a big treat for us, as children.

fifteen-day pickle See **fourteen-day pickle**

fifth adj, n Usu |fɪfθ|; freq |fɪθ|; also |fɪf(t)| Pronc-spp *fif(t), fith*

Std senses, var forms.

1891 *PMLA* 6.172 **TN,** *Fift* for *fifth* is heard. **1908** *DN* 3.310 **eAL, wGA,** *Fif(t), fith*. . . Fifth. **1936** *AmSp* 11.234 **eTX,** *Fifth* is usually [fɪθ]. **1939** *LANE* Map 63 **NEng,** [Pronunciations of the type /fɪfθ/ are most frequent; those of the type /fɪθ/ occur frequently, /fɪf/ occasionally, and /fɪft/ rarely.] **1942–43** in 1944 *ADD* **nWV,** *Fifth*. . . |fɪft|. **1952** Brown *NC Folkl.* 1.540, *Fift* [fɪft] *n.* and *adj*. . . *Fifth.* *Ibid* 541, *Fith* [fɪθ]. . . *Fifth.*—General. All classes. **c1960** *Wilson Coll.* **csKY,** *Fifth* [fɪθ] or [fɪft] much more common than [fɪfθ]. **1976** Allen *LAUM* 3.310 (as of c1950), Simplification of the unique /fθ/ cluster in *fifth* is effected in the speech of one-third of the U[pper]M[idwest] infs. . . The . . pronunciation, /fɪθ/, is that of about one-tenth of the infs. in Minnesota, South Dakota, and Nebraska. . . Both pronunciations [=/fɪft/ and /fɪf/] are social markers with their highest frequency among the least educated; and /fɪf/ may be Northern-oriented.

Fifth Avenue n [In ref to the street in New York City]

A place where people of wealth and high social standing live; the people who live there.

[**1857** *S.F. Call* 15 Mar. 1/2 *(DA),* Speaking of the *décolleté* style of dress in vogue in public assemblies in New York, he . . [terms the Upper Tendom] the class of the *'fifth Avenuedity!'*] **1858** *Porter's Spirit of Times* 3.409/3 **NYC,** The Fifth Avenue does not drive out or walk out on Sunday. They do not consider it to be in good taste, and they do not see why foolish working-people . . should not so consider it. **1946** *Coronet* Oct 129/1, Thousands of New Yorkers have found a way to lick postwar scarcities and high prices—and even satisfy Fifth Avenue tastes on a five-and-ten budget. **1967–68** *DARE* (Qu. II24, *Names and nicknames for the part of a town where the well-off people live*) Infs **IA**15, **IN**15, **MN**2, **NJ**48, **NY**100, **WI**30, 66, Fifth Avenue.

fifth calf n [See quot 1982]

Someone extra; one who doesn't fit in or belong.

1895 *DN* 1.396 **NEng,** *Fifth calf:* same as *fifth wheel.* [**1939** (1962) Thompson *Body & Britches* 497 **NY,** Unlucky as a fifth calf (because the mother has only four filling-stations).] [**1982** Brooks *Quicksand* 195 **swUT** (as of c1916), *Don't stand there like the fifth calf!* A cow can accommodate only four calves at a time. The fifth calf is simply doomed unless someone comes to his rescue and forces each of the others to surrender his place for a few minutes, at least.]

fifth day See **first day 1**

fifth month See **first month**

fifth moon n

See quot.

c1938 in 1970 Hyatt *Hoodoo* 1.188 **ceVA,** He tole de ole man dat he had to have a tub of hot watah, twelve o'clock at night but not at de full moon—when de moon wus goin' off. Well dat's when yo' git de *fifth moon.*

fifth quarter n *old-fash*

1 The hide and tallow (also sometimes the head and entrails) of a slaughtered steer.

1801 in 1841 Cist *Cincinnati* 188 **OH,** To kill beef cattle, the butcher to receive for his share the "fifth quarter." **1908** *DN* 3.310 **eAL, wGA,** *Fifth quarter*. . . The hide and tallow of a dressed animal. **1918** Waller *IL Pioneer Days* 75, *Fifth Quarter,* the hide and tallow of a beef. It was sometimes given to an expert rifleman at a shooting match in order to appease him for being ruled out of the game. **1951** Swetnam *Pittsylvania Country* 143 **PA** (as of c1800), Mike [Fink] hung around Pittsburg, where his marksmanship was so good he was often excluded from the shooting matches for beef. As a reward for not trying for the beef, Mike claimed the "fifth quarter" (hide and tallow), which he would trade for whiskey to treat the crowd. **1968** Adams *Western Words* 111, *Fifth quarter*—The hide and entrails of a slaughtered animal. **1978** Mayer *Beef Club* 5 **cSC** (as of 1840–1940), Everything that was not portioned out [to members in a **beef club**] was called the fifth quarter. This included tripe, melt, kidneys, tongue, brains, lights, heart, hide, and head. It was all kept by the producer of the steer.

2 The giblets of a fowl.

1908 *DN* 3.310 **eAL, wGA,** *Fifth quarter*. . . The small pieces of a dressed fowl, as the liver, gizzard, etc.

fifth-Sunday meeting n Also *fifth-Sunday rally*

A special religious service held when a fifth Sunday occurs in a month.

1937 (1963) Hyatt *Kiverlid* 49 **KY,** Lookit the time at Shady Grove at the Fifth Sunday Meetin', and hit wus the Footwashin' too, how she whiffeled right through the man's-door, brazen as gull, and took her seat on the man's side of the Meetin' House. **1975** Thomas *Hear the Lambs* 96 **nwAL,** Do you remember the fifth-Sunday rallies, when we sometimes received forty or fifty dollars at one rally? [**1982** *Foxfire 7* 39 **wNC,** They agreed to [let us] have foot washings and be in the association. . . We do it whenever there's a fifth Sunday in the month.]

fifth wheel n *joc*

Fig: one's wife.

1968 *DARE* (Qu. AA22, . . *"I have to go down and pick up my ________."*) Inf **NJ8,** Fifth wheel. A fifth wheel is the part of a wagon to make the axles turn. [It's] between the axles and wagon body.

fifty n Also *fifty-fifty* **IL, MI, WI**

A dice game.

1950 *WELS* 4 Infs, **WI,** Fifty; 1 Inf, Fifty = bunco; toss two dice; different combinations count accordingly. **1967–68** *DARE* (Qu. EE40, *What table games are played around here, using dice?*) Inf **IL4,** Fifty—like twenty-one; **WI68,** Fifty; **IL17, MI78,** Fifty-fifty; **MI44,** Progressive fifty; (Qu. DD37) **MI44,** Progressive fifty—played with dice. Used to be called bunco years ago.

fifty-fifty n

1 See **fifty.**

2 See quots. [From its being half ice cream and half frozen flavored water; perh orig a trademark]

1980 *DARE* File **sCA** (as of 1950s), What was known in Milwaukee as a *creamsicle* was called a fifty-fifty in Long Beach, California. Although fifty-fifty was definitely a commercial name, we used it as a generic to distinguish between a popsicle or ice-cream bar and a bar that was a popsicle on the outside and an ice-cream on the inside. *Ibid* **cwCA** (as of 1950s), A fifty-fifty was the shape of a fudgesicle, but it was made of vanilla ice cream covered by a thick layer of flavored (usually orange) frozen liquid similar to that in a popsicle, but thicker in consistency.

fifty-o n Also *fifty-oh, one-two-three-fifty-o* [See quot 1952] **NC**

A type of hide-and-seek; see quots.

1946 *PADS* 6.13 **eNC,** *Fifty-O (-oh).* . . A school game in which the leader counts aloud to fifty while the other children hide. The leader closes his eyes and stands with his back to those hiding. When he reaches fifty, which he shouts at the top of his voice, he opens his eyes and tries to tag each player before the player can touch base. Pamlico, around 1905. Common. **1952** Brown *NC Folkl.* 1.38, *Fifty-oh* . . is a form of 'Hide and Seek.' . . The counter . . counts to fifty, closing with a very loud "Fifty-oh!" He then says: "A bushel of wheat and a bushel of clover,/ All not hid can't hide over./ A bushel of wheat and a bushel of rye,/ All ain't hid holler 'I'." If anyone calls, the counting proceeds to fifty again. Then the counter begins hunting. . . The first player caught is counter for the second game. **1968** *DARE* (Qu. EE13a, *Games in which every player hides except one, and that one must try to find the others*) Inf **NC79,** Hoop and hide, hide and seek, one-two-three-fifty-o.

fifty-seven (varieties or variety) dog See **Heinz dog**

fifty-two scatter n Cf **fifty-o**

1968 *DARE* (Qu. EE13a, *Games in which every player hides except one, and that one must try to find the others*) Inf **MA1,** Fifty-two scatter; [you] count to fifty-two.

fig n[1] See **fig leaf**

fig n[2] [Perh var of **fid** n **4**]

A twist of tobacco.

1837–40 Haliburton *Clockmaker* (1862) 187 *(DA),* How are you off for tobacco? said Mr. Slick. Grand, said he, got half a fig left yet. **1851** (1857) Hawthorne *Twice-Told* 1.130 **MA,** The pedler . . sold him many a bunch of long nines, and a great deal of pigtail, lady's twist, and fig tobacco.

fig around v phr [Perh var of *frig* v]

To idle, waste time.

1966 *DARE* (QR, near Qu. A9) Inf **ME16,** Fig around [FW: Inf has heard this.] **1987** *NADS Letters* **cVT,** Fig around—This appears to be a contraction of "Frig around." A euphemism for "fucking around."

figeater n Usu |ˈfɪgˌitə(r)|; also |ˌfɪˈgetə| Pronc-spp *figater, fingater* [From their liking for figs] **Sth, esp SC**

1 The green **June beetle** *(Cotinus nitida).*

1869 U.S. Dept. Ag. *Rept. of Secy. for 1868* 90, In some of the southern States [these beetles] are so very destructive to ripe figs as to have acquired the local name of fig-eaters. **1889** *Century Dict.* 2207/2, *Fig-eater* . . a scarabæoid beetle, *Allorhina nitida.* (Southern U.S.) **1950** *PADS* 14.29 **SC,** *Figater* [fɪgˈetə]. . . The Junebug, a persistent *fig eater.* Charleston. **1966–67** *DARE* (Qu. R5) Inf **SC21,** June bug; figeater [is a] more common [name]. Some call them fingaters. Negro? [FW: Not restricted to Charleston]; **SC26,** Figeater; **SC43,** June bug; figeater. **1977** *DARE* File **seSC** (as of 1948), The term *figeater* [ˈfɪgˌitə], was used by a cultured Informant.

2 =**orchard oriole.**

1949 Sprunt–Chamberlain *SC Bird Life* 495, *Orchard Oriole: Icterus spurius* (Linnaeus). . . In the Aiken–Augusta region it was at one time called "Fig-eater." **1950** *PADS* 14.29 **SC,** *Figeater.* . . The orchard oriole.

figger See **figure** n, v

figger(y) four See **figure four**

fight v Usu |faɪt|; also **esp Sth, S Midl** |fa:t, fæɪt|; for addit var see quots Cf Pronc Intro 3.II.13

A Forms.

1 pres (exc 3rd pers sg): usu *fight;* rarely *fit, fout.*

1927 Shewmake *Engl. Pronc. VA* 25, [fəɪt]. **1938** Matschat *Suwannee R.* 163 **nFL, sGA,** He walked in the swamp a-hollerin' . . an' a-darin' the b'ars to come out an' fit. **1942** in 1944 *ADD* **cwVA,** *Fout.* . . Fight. . . [faʊt]. 'I'll no fout you.' Reported said by old [Black] man. **1954** *Harder Coll.* **cwTN,** *Fight.* . . Present: [fæɪt]. **1986** *DARE* File **nGA,** Fight [fa:t].

2 pres pple: usu *fighting;* also *faghting, fitting, fouting*

c1938 in 1970 Hyatt *Hoodoo* 2.1099 **cSC,** A home where a man an' his wife or his *sweetheart woman* always foutin' [Hyatt: fighting] an' quarrelin'. **1949** Dean *Diamond Bess* 15 **TX,** Folks is stirred up almost to the fittin' point. **1954** *Harder Coll.* **cwTN,** *Fight.* . . Pres. pple: a-faghtin', a-fittin'. 'Ey jis' a-fittin' up a storm.

3 past: usu *fought;* also *faught, fit, fout;* occas *fight, fitted.*

1818 Fessenden *Ladies Monitor* 172 **VT,** [In a list of "provincial" words to be avoided:] *Fit* for fought. **1837** Sherwood *Gaz. GA* 69, [In a list of "provincialisms" to be avoided:] *Fout,* for fought. **1893** *DN* 1.277 **wCT,** Fight—fit [for past and past pple.] **1903** *DN* 2.313 **seMO,** *Fit, past* and *pp.* of fight. **1905** *DN* 3.79 **nwAR,** *Fit, fout* [faʊt]. . . Fought. 'They fit and they fout.' **1906** *DN* 3.118 **sIN,** *Fit, pt.* and *pp.* of fight. **1908** *DN* 3.311 **eAL, wGA,** *Fit, pret.* and *pp.* of *fight.* **1912** *DN* 3.576 **wIN,** *Fit, pret.* and *pp.* of *fight.* Quite generally used in some country districts. **1922** Gonzales *Black Border* 301 **sSC, GA coasts** [Gullah glossary], *Fight*—fight, fights, fought, fighting. **1934** Carmer *Stars Fell on AL* 166 **AL** [Black], If that warn't a hant we fitted that night I don' know what it was. **1952** Brown *NC Folkl.* 1.542, *Fought* [faʊt]. . . Rare. **1953** Atwood *Survey of Verb Forms* 14, *Fought* /fɔt/ prevails in cultured speech everywhere; . . The form *fit* /fɪt/ . . occurs in the Hudson Valley, part of c.N.Y., and at some points in n.N.J. and n.e.Pa. . . [in] Type I speech. . . [It also occurs] along the upper Ohio and throughout n.W.Va. . . [,in] s.w.Va. and w.N.C., . . [and] in n.c.N.C. and throughout the Piedmont area of Va. . . The preterite *fout* /faut/ occurs at several points along the Delaware and in nearly all the communities of s.N.J. . . In s.e.Va. . . and in . . e.N.C. and n.e.S.C. . . , *fout* occurs solidly . . among Type I informants, and is used by about two thirds of the Type II informants. . . Both *fit* and *fout* occur rather often in w.S.C. and in . . [inland] Georgia. . . informants who do not use *fit* or *fout* . . invariably classify both as "old," "old-fashioned," "used by Negroes," and so on. Something over half the Negro informants in Md. and Va. use *fit;* all the N.C. Negroes use *fout.* . . in S.C. and Ga., two use *fought,* one *fit,* two *fout,* and three . . *fight.* **1954** *Harder Coll.* **cwTN,** *Fight.* . . Past: fit, faught (occas.), fought (occas.) **1955** Roberts *S. from Hell-fer-Sartin* 76 **seKY,** They fit and they fought and they fit and they fought. The red bull killed the other'n. **1965–70** *DARE* (Qu. EE21b, . . *"For a while those fellows really ________."*) 70 Infs, **scattered,** Fought (hard) [and var phrr]; **AR3, IN32,** Fit; **MI67,** Fought; we hear *fit,* probably lightly [=facetiously]; **VA43,** Fit like the devil; (Qu. OO24a—total Infs questioned, 75) 57 Infs, **scattered,** Fought; **MS69,** Fought; heard *fit* used by Negro maid; **NM11,** Fought, fit; **OK6,** Fit—[used by] oldsters; about gone now; (Qu. Y12b) Inf **KY19,** They fit like cats and dogs; **LA6,** They fit with their fists; **NY69,** Fit; (Qu. II11b)

Inf **CT**39, Fit like cats and dogs. **1968–69** *DARE* Tape **MA**58, We fit, you know, to make the world safe for Democracy, but I guess we didn't do a very good job; **VA**2, And throwed those coals out the window on the bear's back and they fit. [Inf quickly corrected herself and said "begin to fight."] **1969** *DARE* FW Addit **neNC,** *Fout* [fəʊt]. **1973** *PADS* 60.66 **seNC,** Only the oldest of our [12] informants (whose parents came from the Outer Banks) said /faut/; all the others said *fought*. . . It is my impression that the form has been dying out in North Carolina for some time; it was rare in the Neuse River area even during my childhood. **1975** Allen *LAUM* 2.18 **Upper MW** (as of c1950), Standard *fought* [as past of *fight*] is well-nigh universal among the infs. questioned. Only three instances of *fit* appear.

4 past pple: usu *fought;* also *faught, fight, fit, fitted, fout.*

1840 (1847) Longstreet *GA Scenes* 11, I was jist seein' how I could 'a' *fout.* **1843** (1916) Hall *New Purchase* 438 **IN,** I've fit ba'r afore. **1893** [see **A3** above]. **1903** [see **A3** above]. **1906** [see **A3** above]. **1908** [see **A3** above]. **1912** [see **A3** above]. **1944** *PADS* 2.9, *Fit:* pret. and p.p. of *fight.* Ala. [*PADS:* Also Va., N.C., S.C. In Harnett Co., N.C.: *fought* [faʊt]. Uneducated.] **1954** *Harder Coll.* **cwTN,** *Fight*. . . Past pple: fit, faught (occas.), fought (occas.) **1965–70** *DARE* (Qu. OO24b; total Infs questioned, 75) 53 Infs, **scattered,** Fought; **GA**1, 7, 9, 13, Fight; **NM**11, Fit; **MS**69, Fitted or fit (Negro). **1967–68** *DARE* FW Addit **TN**14, He'd a-fit for me; **csNY,** She's fit with them two boys.

5 ppl adj: Usu *fought;* also *fit.*

1954 *Harder Coll.* **cwTN,** Yer plum fit out [=exhausted from fighting]. They's jus' knocked down and dead as a dornail and fit out.

B Sense.

See quot. *obs*

1837 Sherwood *Gaz. GA* 69, [In a list of 'provincialisms' to be avoided:] *Fight,* for chastise.

fightable adj Cf **fighty**

Disposed to fight.

1935 Davis *Honey* 29 **OR,** Clay was hot and fightable, and it insulted him to be ordered off his work like an errand-boy playing stick-horse.

fight a circular saw v phr Also *fight a circle saw(mill)* **Sth, S Midl**

To fight against tremendous odds.

1898 Lloyd *Country Life* 111 **AL,** A man that wouldn't fight anything from a catamount up to a circular saw wasn't sigh high to a whirlwind in politics before the war. **1932** Randolph *Ozark Mt. Folks* 36, Buck was th' . . fighten'est feller ever come t' them parts. He'd fight a circle-saw an' turn it hissе'f, an' he warn't skeered o' nothin'. **1939** *Hall Coll.* **eTN,** *Fight a circle sawmill*. . . Tall talk for 'to be a hard fighter.' . . "He said he made it in his mind to never surrender. He could a fit a circle saw-mill." **1984** Wilder *You All Spoken Here* 44 **Sth,** He'd fight a circ'l saw: He'd tear up an anvil; he'd fight a steam sawmill.

fight-banterer n Cf **banter v 2**

One who dares or challenges others to fight.

1935 Davis *Honey* 39 **OR,** His oldest brother had been considerable of a fight-banterer and a devoted hand at breaking community dances up in a row.

fight eggs v phr Cf **egg picking**

1890 Howells *Boy's Town* 114 **swOH,** Most Easter eggs never outlasted Easter Day. As soon as the fellows were done breakfast they ran out of the house and began to fight eggs with the other fellows. They struck the little ends of the eggs together, and if your egg broke another fellow's egg, then you had a right to it.

fight, go on the v phr

To become belligerent.

1956 Gipson *Old Yeller* 140 **TX,** She [=a cow] was too crazy mad to be driven anywhere. . . If I ever let her know I was anywhere about, she might go on the fight.

fightified adj Also sp *fightyfied* **[fighty + -ified]**

=fighty.

1952 Brown *NC Folkl.* 1.540, *Fighty-fied:* . . Inclined to fight, easily angered.—General. Old people. **1984** Wilder *You All Spoken Here* 44 **Sth,** Fighty-fied: Inclined to fight; has a short fuse; easily angered.

fighting adj

1 Likely to provoke a fight.

1875 (1876) Twain *Tom Sawyer* 23, You're a fighting liar and dasn't take it up! **1917** Lardner *Gullible* 209, You know they's lots o' words that's called fightin' words. Some o' them starts a brawl, no matter who they're spoke to. **1923** *DN* 5.207 **swMO,** *Fightin' word*. . . An epithet the use of which ordinarily induces a fight. "He called me a fightin' word so's I whanged away an' busted 'im 'ith a rock." The term applies, usually to 'liar' and 'son-of-a-bitch.' **1967** *DARE* (Qu. DD21c, . . *Whiskey*) Inf **IA**11, Fighting liquor.

2 Bad-tempered; quick to anger. **chiefly Sth, S Midl**

1965–70 *DARE* (Qu. K16, *A cow with a bad temper*) 9 Infs, **Sth, S Midl,** Fighting cow; **TX**6, Fightin' hussy; **TX**105, Fightin'; (Qu. K68, . . *A goat that habitually strikes people with its horns*) Infs **LA**2, **MS**28, **OK**18, Fighting goat; **TX**6, Damn fighting billy; (Qu. C34, *Nicknames for . . districts*) Inf **MN**38, Fighting Irish; (Qu. HH28, . . *Nicknames . . for people of foreign background*) Inf **IA**11, Fighting Irish.

fighting adv **scattered, but chiefly Sth, Midl**

To the point of violence; extremely.

1941 *LANE* Map 472 **NEng,** Fighting mad [occurs infrequently]. **1965–70** *DARE* (Qu. LL37, . . *"I was so ______ mad."*) 19 Infs, **chiefly Sth, S Midl,** Fighting; (Qu. GG40, . . *Violently angry*) 15 Infs, **chiefly Midl,** Fighting mad; (Qu. GG4, *Stirred up, angry*) Infs **CA**94, 107, **GA**54, **IL**20, **KY**65, **LA**2, **WA**22, Fightin(g) mad; (Qu. DD15) Inf **TX**33, Fighting drunk.

fighting clothes on, have one's v phr

To be ready to quarrel.

1927 *Ruppenthal Coll.* **KS,** In Oklahoma the governor and the legislature have their fighting clothes on.

fighting eagle n

=fish hawk 1.

1969 *DARE* (Qu. Q10, . . *Water birds*) Inf **MA**21, Fishhawk = fighting eagle = osprey.

fightingest adj Cf **-est** **esp S Midl**

Most likely or eager to fight; scrappiest.

1871 (1882) Stowe *Fireside Stories* 209 **MA,** There was old Dick, Ike's bell-wether, was the fightin'est old crittur that ever yer see. **1909** *DN* 3.396 **nwAR,** "That's the fightingest old rooster I ever saw." The formation of superlative adjectives from present active participles is a common negroism. **1939** Rawlings in *Sat. Eve. Post* 25 Nov 62 **nFL,** Them game roosters was the fightingest things I ever laid eyes on. **1942** *Time* 13 Apr 78, As the mightiest, fightingest American, [Superman] ought to join up. **1942** *NY Times* (NY) 12 Nov 26/2, The Marine Corps doesn't have to convince its recruits that they have joined "the fightingest outfit." **1953** Randolph *Down in Holler* 60 **Ozarks,** Superlatives of this type are very numerous, such as *fightin'est, dancin'est, shootin'est* [etc]. **1974** Fink *Mountain Speech* 9 **wNC, eTN,** That's the fightin'est dog. **1976** Garber *Mountain-ese* 29 **sAppalachians,** He's the fightin'est man in town.

fighting jack n

A **pickerel.**

1938 FWP *Guide MN* 345, The lakes abound with game fish—walleyed pike, northern pike, called by the natives "fighting jack," and crappie.

fighting the bear vbl n

In the timber industry: see quot.

1968 Adams *Western Words* 111, *Fighting the bear*—Separating strips from boards in a sawmill. This is the job of the *bear fighter,* the man who works back the "edges" and separates all strips from the boards and directs them below to an endless chain that runs under the cage in which he works. These strips come rapidly, and the worker must be fast.

fight net n [Perh folk-etym for *fyke net*]

1966 *DARE* (Qu. P13, . . *Other ways of fishing*) Inf **GA**5, Fight net—has four-inch mesh, winged to open; [it's strung] all the way across a stream; [it's] illegal.

fight one's face v phr

Fig: to eat voraciously.

1950 Stuart *Hie Hunters* 138 **eKY,** "I feel like I could fight my face too," Peg said. "Gives a body a-hankerin' fer grub to walk up here."

fight one's hat v phr

To struggle uselessly.

1944 (1967) McNichols *Crazy Weather* 163 **SW,** I can think like an Indian sometimes, then I can think like a white man. But like now—I get caught in between—I don't know how to bring them two kinds of thinking together. I just get to fighting my hat, and I can't figger nothing.

fight one's head v phr Also *fight the bits*

Of a horse: to toss the head back and forth to resist restraint; fig, of a person: see quot 1968.

1968 Adams *Western Words* 111, *Fighting the bits*—Said of a horse that throws its head around when reined. Also said of an impatient or restless person. **1971** Green *Village Horse Doctor* 131 **TX** (as of 1940s), After looking at him [=a horse] carefully, I tried to open his mouth and he began to fight his head and run backwards.

fight piece n Cf **manners piece**

The last portion of food, which more than one person wants for himself.

1967 *DARE* (Qu. H71, *Words for the last piece of food left on a plate*) Inf **TX**33, Fight piece!

fight the bits See **fight one's head**

fight the tiger See **tiger**

fighty adj Cf **fightable, fightified**

Inclined or eager to fight.

1927 in 1944 *ADD* **WV**, *Fighty*. . . Pugnacious. **1965–69** *DARE* (Qu. K16, *A cow with a bad temper*) Infs **IN**63, **OK**1, **SC**47, Fighty; (Qu. GG41, . . *"You never did see such a ______ person."*) **SD**8, Fighty.

fightyfied See **fightified**

Figinny See **Virginia**

fig leaf n Also *fig* [Genesis 3:7]

A garment, esp one that covers the private parts.

1942 Berrey–Van den Bark *Amer. Slang* 87.2, *Clothes*. . . fig, fig leaf *or* leaves. *Ibid* 87.15, Fig leaf, *an apron*. **1966–67** *DARE* (Qu. W14, *Names for underwear . . men's—short*) Inf **CO**31, Briefs. Fig leaf—very brief; **NC**35, Fig leaf.

figmill n

A game played with checkers or counters on a diagrammed board.

1951 *Jrl. Amer. Folkl.* 64.303 **wNY**, This game [known in English as *merels, mills,* and *nine men's morris*], under the name of *figmill,* was played in the village of Clarence, in Erie County, New York, as recently as 1938. . . It was generally played on homemade boards . . but a combination game board made by the Carrom–Archarena Company . . had markings that could be used for the game. . . the markings we used consisted of alternating circles and diamonds connected by various ornamental lines. *Ibid* 305, The possibility that *figmill* stands for *pegmill* is suggested by the many variants of the name with the word *peg*. . . The second etymology that suggests itself offers a convincing meaning in the obsolete word *fig,* "to move briskly and restlessly; to jog to and fro," which exactly describes the motion of a playing piece when a "mill" [=a row of three counters on a line] has been made.

figur See **figure** n, v

figure n, v Usu |ˈfɪgjə(r)|; also freq |ˈfɪgə(r)| Pronc-spp *figger, figur, figyo*

A Forms.

1857 *Putnam's Mag.* 10.353/2 **NEng,** I can't stan' it, so I set to figgerin' on it out. **1861** Holmes *Venner* 2.301 **NEng,** If the' 's any mistake of figgers or addin' 'em up, it'll be made all right. **1899** (1912) Green *VA Folk-Speech* 173, *Figger, n.* Figure. . . Figur. *Ibid, Figger, v.* **1908** *DN* 3.310 **eAL, wGA,** *Figger*. . . Figure. **1909** *S. Atl. Qrly.* 8.43 **sSC coast** [Gullah], The elimination of *r* medial and final has several odd exceptions: in the words *doctor, picture, figure, mister, sister,* the final sound is turned to *o: docto, pitcho, figyo, misto, sisto.* **1936** *AmSp* 11.166 **eTX,** *Figure, figured* are [ˈfɪgjɚ], [ˈfɪgjɚd]; in illiterate speech [ˈfɪgə/ɚ(d)]. **1961** Adams *Old-Time Cowhand* 45 **West,** I sometimes wonder why the cowboy couldn't seem to resist usin' some figger of speech when a plain statement would serve his purpose. **1965–70** *DARE* (Qu. JJ34, . . *"I ______ I'll be better off that way."*) 38 Infs, **scattered,** [ˈfɪgɚ, -ə]; 24 Infs, **scattered,** [ˈfɪgjɚ, -ə]. **1968** *DARE* FW Addit **PA**81, Figure [ˈfɪgɚ]—a person's figure or a number, or the verb; **nePA,** Figure [ˈfɪgjʊɚ].

B As noun.

1 in phr *cut a figure* and varr: To make a conspicuous appearance; to play an important role.

1815 Humphreys *Yankey in England* 21, You, with another likely lad, must cut a figure behind her coach. **1833** U.S. Congress *Reg. of Debates* 8.3.3687 20 June **KY,** Not enough to cut any figure in this calculation. **1890** in 1937 Moses *Repr. Amer. Dramas* 31/2, A Captain is all very well on the frontier, but he doesn't cut much of a figure among the officers in Washington. **1899** (1912) Green *VA Folk-Speech* 173, Doesn't she cut a figger? **1907** *Scribner's Mag.* Apr 506/2, The poor figure cut in scholarship by the Rhodes scholars. **1939** *Hall Coll.* **eTN,** He [=a bear] was cuttin' a big figure 'n growlin'.

2 in phrr *go the big* (or *whole*) *figure* and varr: To do something grandly, thoroughly.

1831 *Boston Eve. Transcript* (MA) 28 Oct 2/2, The opponents of the existing militia system, who are not enlisted in the corps of *exempts,* are 'going it' at New York 'on the big figure.' **1837** Smith *Col. Crockett's Exploits* 30, When a man sets about going the big figure, halfway measures won't answer no how. **1848** Bartlett *Americanisms* 159, *To go the whole figure.* To go to the fullest extent in the attainment of any object. . . *To go the big figure.* To do things on a large scale. **1864** (1868) Trowbridge *Cudjo's Cave* 17 **TN,** The time may come when we will have to . . go the whole figure with the free North, or drift with the cotton states. **1917** James *Ivory Tower* 309 **NEast,** The . . momentous season, or scene, . . in which she goes the whole "figure."

3 in phrr *miss a* (or *the*) *figure:* To make an error.

1819 in 1884 Weed *Life* 2.12 **cNY,** Three, six, and nine months were the different periods some new-light prophets confidently asserted, would bring our valedictory; but they have missed a figure, for we now complete twelve months, and, if kind Heaven spares us life and ability to labor, we shall commence and complete another year. **1829** in 1956 Eliason *Tarheel Talk* 135 **nwNC,** Professors Mitchell and Olmstead have missed the figure as we say in the 'West Countree' in their speculations on the gold mines. **1839** Marryat *Diary in A.* II.235 *(DA),* When a person had made a mistake, or is out in his calculation, they say, 'You missed a figure that time.' **1877** Bartlett *Americanisms* 396, *To miss a Figure* is to commit a vital error.

C As verb.

1 To make arithmetic calculations. *old-fash*

1837 U.S. Congress *Congressional Globe* 25th Cong 1st Sess 27 Sept 5 app 247/2 **VA,** I . . cannot understand the [Treasury] Secretary's report. I figured upon its data until I threw down my slate in despair. **1865** U.S. Congress *Congressional Globe* 38th Cong 2d Sess 9 Feb 671/3 **NV,** I have not figured the number of square miles that there will be. **1899** (1912) Green *VA Folk-Speech* 173, *Figger*. . . To figure; to do sums. "Let me figger it out." *Ibid* 174, *Figure*. . . To set down, or reckon up in numerical figure; make a calculation of: as, to *figure up. Figure it out.* **1953** *Hall Coll.* **wNC,** He went a term or two to school there till he learned to read and write and figger some. **1955** Adams *Grandfather* 286 **NY** (as of 1830s), Well, I wouldn't expect it of you. Write nor figger, neither, I reckon. **1960** Carpenter *Tales Manchaca* 50 **cTX,** We weren't required to do much except read, spell, and figger.

2 usu with *on, upon:* To study, consider; hence vbl n *figuring* considering, preparing.

1877 Bartlett *Americanisms* 215, "Figure on that" means to consider it; to think it over. Western. **1942** Perry *Texas* 54, You realize how easy it is to sit by the fire in January and grow crops in your mind. But these things take a lot of figuring.

3 with *upon:* To count on, be confident about.

1889 (1971) Farmer *Americanisms* 238, You may figure upon getting a reply by return mail.

4 with *on, to:* To intend to, plan on. Cf **calculate B2**

1925 Hunter *Trail Drivers TX* 553 (as of 1916), "I've been figgerin' on writin' some recollections of my trail drivin' days," confided an old man to his friend. **1938** Rawlings *Yearling* 55 **nFL,** You figger on huntin' some on your way back? **1943** *LANE* Map 704, In the context *I intend to go soon* [*figure on* and *figure to* occur sporadically]. **1950** *WELS ("I ______ on buying one.")* 10 Infs, **WI,** Figure(d); 1 Inf, **cWI,** Kentucky people . . "Figure" on doing it. **1966** *DARE* (Qu. AA1, *When a man goes to see a girl often and seems to want to marry her, he's ______ her.*) Inf **OK**27, They're figuring on getting hitched. **1969** *DARE* Tape **CA**170, She figures on going back in some kind of newspaper work.

5 To expect, think, assume.

1898 Wister *Lin McLean* 12 **WY,** How many miles per hour do you figure that cayuse of yourn can travel? **1943** *LANE* Map 592, In the context *I think I'll have time, I think so* or the like, . . [*figure* is] described as old-fashioned [by three informants]. **1950** *WELS ("I ______ he'll come tonight.")* 1 Inf, **seWI,** Figure. **1955** Roberts *S. from Hell-fer-Sartin* 150 **seKY,** They's an Englishman come over from England oncet and . . the American people . . figured that he might be capable of taking a crew of men and working them. **1965–70** *DARE* (Qu. JJ34, .. *"I ______ I'll be better off that way."*) 64 Infs, **scattered,** Figure; (Qu. GG12, .. *"There she comes now, I ______ she would."*) 34 Infs, **scattered,** (Just) figured; (Qu. KK10) Inf **OK**18, [It] didn't work out like he figured it would.

6 also with *up:* To think out and conclude; to decide.

1946 *AmSp* 21.97 **sIL,** *Figgered,* calculated, concluded. **c1960** *Wilson Coll.* **csKY,** I figgered I had better plant my tobacco here. **1968** *DARE* Tape **IN**42, We figgered up that, well, farmers don't strike. . . So there's one way to beat it [=low corn prices]—we just built storage.

7 To regard a thing as.

1931–33 *LANE Worksheets* 1 inf, **cwCT,** We don't figure evening until it begins to get dusk.

8 To scheme.

1889 (1971) Farmer *Americanisms* 238, The next evening we came to a drove of small pigs and began to figure for one. Finally I stood behind a tree with a club; when the pig followed up I shot him with my stick. **1967** *DARE* (Qu. II33, .. *"I don't trust him, he's always trying to ______."*) Inf **MI**55, He's always figuring.

9 To deceive with numbers; to cheat by false calculation.

1977 *Foxfire 4* 129 **nGA,** I didn't know a thing about arithmetic. But I've learnt someway. You can't figger [*Foxfire* Ed: cheat] me out of nothing. I can figger with any of 'em.

10 in phr *figure (something) close:* See quots.

1951 *PADS* 15.54 **IN,** *Figure close.* . . Have a narrow escape. "That was figurin' it purty clost." **1954** *Harder Coll.* **cwTN,** *Figure (it) close.* . . Have a narrow escape. **c1960** *Wilson Coll.* **csKY,** *Figure close.* . . Have a narrow escape or barely make good on one's attempt to do something.

figure eight n [From the shape]

Anything thought to resemble the Arabic figure eight; see quots.

1940 *Cattleman* May 26 **West,** Another [roping] stunt is the "figure 8" which can be thrown to catch the forefeet of an animal in the lower part of the "8" while his head goes through the upper. **1949** Shaw *Cowboy Dances* 268, Cut a figure eight with the lady in the lead. . . Cut a figure eight with the gent in the lead. **1953** *NY Times* (NY) 23 Sept 33/4 **NYC,** *Figure Eight*—The part of the bridle that crosses over the nose and under the chin to keep the the [sic] horse's mouth closed. **1961** Adams *Old-Time Cowhand* 129 **West,** There were many styles in hobbles. . . there were the various carefully braided and ornamentally knotted or buttoned Spanish-California models and the more modern strap-buckle-and-ring, called a "figger eight." **1965–70** *DARE* (Qu. H28, .. *Shapes .. of doughnuts*) 10 Infs, **scattered,** Figure eight; (Qu. X3, .. *Hair up on .. [a woman's] head in a bunch*) Infs **AL**30, **CO**20, **CT**12, **GA**59, **MI**108, **NY**105, **TX**40, Figure eight; (Qu. FF5a, .. *Figures in dancing*) Infs **AR**47, **CA**166, **FL**19, **IN**49, **PA**69, Figure eight; **KY**23, 89, Cut the figure eight; (Qu. EE1) Inf **AR**47, Figure eight around the lady—a square dance; (Qu. N20, .. *A circular arrangement on one level at a big intersection*) Inf **CO**20, Figure eight.

figure eight v phr

To form a **figure eight** with; to cause to make the shape of a **figure eight.**

1967 Green *Horse Tradin'* 132 **swTX,** I brought her [=a mare] to the center of the pasture and figure-eighted her along in a little fox trot. **1967** *DARE* Tape **TX**25, [FW:] So, it's kind of like a figure eight, is it? [Inf:] Well no, well you can figure eight it but .. the hondo itself is platted more or less. [FW:] But it's got two holes in it; one to go over the saddle horn .. and one for the rope to go through. [Inf:] No, it's just one hole.

figure four n Also *figure of four, figure four trigger, figure-y four* Pronc-spp *figger(y) four*

The trigger of an animal trap which, when set, resembles an Arabic numeral four; the trap itself; also fig.

1785 (1930) Hazard *Jrl.* 76/2 **RI,** I made and Sott atrap [sic] with a figger 4 for quails. **1831** Audubon *Ornith. Biog.* 1.216, Many of them [=ruffed grouse] are taken alive in trap boxes during winter, although the more common method of catching or rather destroying them is by setting dead falls with a figure-of-four trigger. **1837** *NY Mirror* 18 Nov 165/1, The poor quail has to contend with. . . the figure-y 4 box-traps of vagabond hen-roost pilferers. **1838** Neal *Charcoal Sketches* 12, I often have the most beautiful notions .. but they're all lost for the want of a trap; an intellectual figgery four. **1853** *Putnam's Mag.* 1.408 **ceMA,** So bait your moral figure-of-fours to catch the Orson public. **1908** *DN* 3.310 **eAL, wGA,** *Figure-four.* . . A trap or set of triggers in the form of the figure 4. Pronounced [figə fo]. **1919** Wilson *Ma Pettengill* 243 **West,** Lew Wee . . made a figure-four trap, and put something for bait on the pointed stick and set the trap. **1943** *Hench Coll.* **cVA,** Figure-four trigger—a rabbit trap [illustr shows a long box with one end on the ground, the other balanced on the point of a figure-four-shaped stick]. When the rabbit eats the bait the device is released and the box falls down on the rabbit.

figurehead n [**figure C1** + **head** n **C1,** perh with pun on *figurehead* std sense]

One who works with numbers.

1945 Hubbard *Railroad Ave.* 342, *Figurehead*—Timekeeper. **1958** McCulloch *Woods Words* 61 **Pacific NW,** *Figure head*—To a logger, anyone who works with figures; a bookkeeper.

figure nine with the tail cut off n

1916 Macy–Hussey *Nantucket Scrap Basket* 131, "Figure Nine with the Tail Cut Off"—That is, nothing; of no account or consequence.

figure of four See **figure four**

figure of seven See **figure seven**

figure on See **figure C2, 4**

figure seven n Also *figure of seven* Cf **half-crop**

An earmark consisting of a notch shaped much like the Arabic numeral seven, used to identify cattle.

1946 Mora *Trail Dust* 197 **NEng** (as of 1734), Listen to this Record of Registry for a personal cattle brand in New England, in the early colonial period. . . "the ear-mark . . is . . a half cross cut of the under side of the left ear split or cut out about the middel of the Top of the ear, called by som a figger of seven." **1967** *DARE* (Qu. K18) Inf **LA**2, Earmarks include the smooth crop, upper figure seven or upper half crop, lower figure seven or lower half crop [cut on the upper or the lower edge of the ear]; **LA**7, Earmarks: poplar leaf, underbit, over figure seven [figə sɛbm̩], under figure seven, hole in one ear, smooth crop.

figure (something) close See **figure C10**

figure to See **figure C4**

figure up See **figure C6**

figure upon See **figure C2, 3**

figure-y four See **figure four**

figuring See **figure C4**

figwort n

1 A plant of the genus *Scrophularia.* Also called **heal-all 3.** For other names of var spp see **bee plant 2, brownwort, bullwort, California bee plant, carpenter's square 1, pilewort, scrofula plant, Simpson honey plant, square stalk**

1784 in 1785 Amer. Acad. Arts & Sci. *Memoirs* 1.464, Figwort. It is said, that swine that have the scab are cured by washing them with a decoction of the leaves. **1873** *Amer. Naturalist* 7.12 **Nth,** Certain of the fig-worts *(Scrophulariaceæ)* are narcotic poisons. **1901** Mohr *Plant Life AL* 717, *Scrophularia marilandica,* . . Maryland Figwort. . . New England west to . . Oregon, south to Florida. **1968** *DARE* (Qu. S26c) Inf **WI**64, Figworts.

2 **=self-heal.**

c1873 in 1976 Miller *Shaker Herbs* 182, *Prunella vulgaris.* . . Figwort. Stone Root.

figyo See **figure**

fike See **fyke**

filaree n [Var of AmSpan *alfilerillo*] **West**

Alfilaria.

1889 Vasey *Ag. Grasses* 102, *Erodium cicutarium* (Alfilaria). . . is known as storksbill, pin clover, pin grass, and filaree; it is neither a grass nor a clover, but belongs to the geranium family. **1914** Brininstool *Trail Dust* 141 *(DA),* They'll liven up and no mistake, When they hev browsed on filaree! **1946** Linsdale *CA Ground Squirrel* 457, Among the plants observed to be prominent as squirrel food on the Reservation are oats, acorns, windmill pink, filaree, and poor man's weather glass. **1966** *DARE* Wildfl QR Pl.119 Inf **OR**12, Filaree. **1966–69** *DARE* (Qu. S15, .. *Weed seeds that cling to clothing*) Inf **CA**79, [fɪlɚi]—a stiff seed with a spiral and a point; **WA**6, Filaree; (Qu. S26a, .. *Roadside flowers*) Inf **CA**4, **UT**7, Filaree; (Qu. S26e, .. *Wildflowers*) Inf **CA**115, [ˌfɪləˈri]—small, lavender, good food for sheep and cattle.

file n[1]

1984 Smith *SW Vocab.* 125, *File:* One soldier, an individual, one man in a single column in a military formation. The word also has a more personal usage: "He's a good old file," suggesting appeal, likeability, friendliness.

file n[2] [Prob from Du *feil,* var of *dweil* floor cloth, mop] **chiefly NY, NJ, PA** *old-fash*

A cloth used for wiping floors or tables; less freq a mop.

1850 (1852) Warner *Wide World* 2.232 **NY,** "You never touch your fingers to a file now-a-days,—do you?" "A file!". . . "Margery calls it a dishcloth, or a floorcloth, or something else." **1859** (1968) Bartlett *Americanisms* 147, *File.* A cloth used for wiping a floor after scrubbing. *File-pail,* or *Filing-pail.* A wash-pail. **1889** (1971) Farmer *Americanisms* 239, *File.*—What is known to English servants as a house-flannel, and a house-maid's pail, goes by the name of *file-pail,* or *filing-pail.* **1896** *DN* 1.417 **NY, PA,** *File* (v.): to scrub with a file (hand-mop). . . Albany Co., St. Lawrence Co. N.Y., Tannersville, Pa. **1983** *Lutz Coll.* **neNJ,** Some women in Bergen County, N.J. (the "Jersey Dutch" area) still know the word *file* for a cloth with which to remove dirt, especially a floor cloth. . . "After you file the floor, you wash out the file and hang it out on the grape arbor till you need it again." *Ibid,* [One inf] defined *file* as a mop rather than a floor-cloth for wiping up dirt. . . File the floor = mop the floor.

file v[1], hence vbl n *filing* [**file** n[2]] **chiefly NY, NJ, PA** *old-fash*

To wipe or mop floors or tables.

1850 (1852) Warner *Wide World* 2.232 **NY,** I've seen you file off tables down yonder a few times, ha'n't I? **1859** (1968) Bartlett *Americanisms* 147, *File-pail,* or *Filing-pail.* A wash-pail. **1896** [see **file** n[2]]. **1932** Smiley *Gloss. New Paltz* **NY,** "File the floor" means to mop or scrub it. **1968** *DARE* FW Addit **Kinderhook NY,** File the floor = mop the floor. Reported in common use by young as well as old speakers. **1983** [see **file** n[2]]. **1988** *DARE* File **eNY,** Filing the floor—A Mohawk Valley expression for washing the floor.

file v[2] [*file* to arrange in a particular order]

1958 *Think* Jan 10, Where most people *park* cars, residents of Trenton *rank* them and those in southern Delaware *file* them.

filé n |ˈfi,le| Also sp *filee;* pronc-spp *feelay, felee, filet* [AmFr < Fr *filer* to twist, spin] **LA**

1 also *filé gombo:* A seasoning consisting largely of ground sassafras leaves, used both for thickening and for flavor. Cf **gumbo filé 2**

1885 *Cuisine Creole* 18 **New Orleans LA,** Take the large bones from the pot, and add okra or a preparation of dried and pounded sassafras leaves, called filee. **1889** (1971) Farmer *Americanisms* 236, *Feelay.* The leaves of the sassafras prepared by being dried and powdered. A Louisianian term. **1946** Tallant *Voodoo* 101 **New Orleans LA,** One of her favorite *gris-gris* to break up such an affair was a mixture of gunpowder, mud from a wasp nest, flaxseed, cayenne pepper, BB shots, filé, bluestone and dragon's blood. **1953** Goodwin *It's Good* 152 [Black], I ate some gumbo over to Miss Farquhar's. It had . . lotsa okra in it, but Miss Farquhar said it was the felee that made it green and stringy. **1967** LeCompte *Word Atlas* 327, (Powder made from the dried leaves of the sassafras tree) 3 infs, **seLA,** *Filé gombo.* **1967–68** *DARE* (Qu. I35, . . *Herbs . . grown and used in cooking around here*) Inf **LA3,** [ˈfi,leɪ]—leaf of thyme and sassafras dried for gumbo; **LA37,** [ˈfi,le]. This is bought, not grown. **1967** *DARE* Tape **LA11,** You can use filé [ˈfi,le] if you want to. **1986** Pederson *LAGS Concordance,* 1 inf, **cLA,** File gumbo—ground up sassafras leaves; 1 inf, **neMS,** File gumbo—from sassafras leaves; [Seasonings:] 1 inf, **seMS,** File gumbo; 1 inf, **New Orleans LA,** File gumbo.

2 in combs *filé gombo,* ~ *gumbo:* A **gumbo 2** seasoned with the above. Cf **gumbo filé 1**

1952 Williams *Jambalaya,* [Song:] Jambalaya and a crawfish pie and [ˈfi,le] gumbo / 'Cause tonight I'm gonna see my ma cher a mio. **1967** LeCompte *Word Atlas* 299, (A brown soup of chicken shrimp, etc., thickened with file) 2 infs, **seLA,** *Filé gombo.*

filefish n Cf **triggerfish**

Any of several rough-skinned fish of the family Balistidae, esp of the genera *Alutera* and *Monacanthus.* For other names of var spp of these genera see **foolfish 1, hogfish c, horny cony, leather fish, sunfish, unicornfish**

1814 in 1815 Lit. & Philos. Soc. NY *Trans.* 1.467, *Tutmouthed file-fish. (Balistes broccus.)* With brown skin, serrated horn, and small mouthed [sic] turned up. **1839** Storer *Mass. Fishes* 174 *(DAE), Monocanthus Massachusettensis.* The Massachusetts File Fish. **1884** Goode *Fisheries U.S.* 1.171, File Fishes, *Balistidæ* are found everywhere in tropical and sub-tropical seas. . . The best known species on our coast is the Orange File Fish, *Alutera Schoepfii,* . . which is rather common in Southern New England and in the Gulf of Mexico. **1933** John G. Shedd Aquarium *Guide* 157, Family *Monacanthidae*—The filefishes. These slow-swimming fishes with rough leathery skins are common in all warm seas. **1960** Amer. Fisheries Soc. *List Fishes* 48, Balistidae—triggerfishes and filefishes.

filé gombo See **filé 1, 2**

filé gumbo See **filé 2**

file one's teeth for someone v phr

To prepare to take revenge on someone.

1961 Adams *Old-Time Cowhand* 83 **West,** If some kangaroo court found you guilty of breakin' a law of the range, you'd be bent over a wagon tongue and the chaps applied where they'd do the most good. If the man wieldin' 'em didn't like you and had been filin' his teeth for you, he could make 'em take the hide off.

file path n

A narrow path which requires walking single file.

1950 *WELS (A path through woods . . for people going on foot)* 1 Inf, **ceWI,** File path—term used when a teacher took children on a walk in the woods.

filer n

1966 *DARE* (Qu. L18, *Kinds of plows used around here, at present and in the past*) Inf **NC6,** [ˈfaɪlə]—a horse-drawn plow used to hill tobacco.

filer's two inches n Cf *DS* U15

1975 Gould *ME Lingo* 93, *Filer's two inches*—A new expression in Maine lingo, coming into use since the invention of the chainsaw; it means a gratuitous extra amount. Hardwood bolts for the turning mills were always handled in four-foot lengths, but the buyers found poorly filed chainsaws were "running" in the cut, and a man might start at 48 inches, but finish a couple of inches one way or the other. To be sure they got full 48 inches, they insisted on 50-inch bolts. Thus the *filer's two inches.* (Figure it out: poorly filed chainsaws waste 5⅓ cubic feet of every cord!)

file-tail n [From the similarity of the tail to a round, metal file]

An opossum (*Didelphis* spp).

1968 *DARE* (Qu. P31) Inf **NC53,** [ˈfal,teɨl]. **1968** *DARE* Tape **NC55,** File tail—a local name for the opossum.

file-tail rat n Also *file-tailed rat* [From the prominently-scaled tail]

A black rat *(Rattus rattus)* or a var thereof.

1927 Boston Soc. Nat. Hist. *Proc.* 38.356 **Okefenokee GA,** Sam Mizell calls it [=*Neotoma floridana*] 'Slick-tailed Rat,' perhaps in contradistinction to the 'File-tailed Rat' (*Rattus rattus rattus* and *R. r. Alexandrinus*). *Ibid* 368, A general name for these rats [=those named above] on Billy's Island and on both sides of the swamp is 'File-tailed Rat.' **1968** *DARE* FW Addit **GA22,** File-tail rat—one of the denizens of the Okefenokee.

filfil v [Redup form of *fill,* prob infl by *fulfill*] Cf **fill** v[1] **1** *Gullah*

See quots.

1922 Gonzales *Black Border* 301 **sSC, GA coasts** [Gullah glossary], *Filfil*—fulfill, fulfills, fulfilled, fulfilling; also fill, as to fill a pulpit. **1949** Turner *Africanisms* 235, *Reduplicated Forms.* . . [ˈfilfil] ('fill fill') 'to fill entirely'.

filibuster n *joc*

A gabfest, talk session.

1970 *DARE* (Qu. KK12, . . *"They got together yesterday and had a real ______."*) Inf **FL48,** Filibuster.

filibuster v **Mid and S Atl** *esp freq among Black speakers*

To talk garrulously, sometimes in an attempt to show off, to stall, or to divert attention from one's own error.

1970 *DARE* (Qu. A11, *When somebody takes too long about coming to a decision, you might say, "I wish he'd quit ______."*) Inf **FL51,** Filibustering; (Qu. HH7b, *Someone who talks too much, or too loud: "He's always ______."*) Inf **NC84,** Filibustering. Someone who tries to outtalk and put his point over regardless; (Qu. II31, . . *"He saw that he was wrong, so he started to ______."*) Inf **FL48,** Filibuster; (Qu. JJ45, . . *"We tried to pin him down, but he just kept ______."*) Inf **VA39,** Filibustering [laughter]. [All Infs Black]

fililoo See **fillilo bird**

filing See **file** v[1]

filione n Also *fliaum, flioma* [See quot 1887] **CA**

A **rockfish** (here: *Sebastodes pinniger*).

1882 U.S. Natl. Museum *Bulletin* 16.662, *S[ebastodes] pinniger. . . Fliaum; Orange Rock-fish. . .* Pacific coast, from Monterey northward; one of the most important species. **1887** Goode *Amer. Fishes* 267, Orange Rockfish. . . The Portuguese at Monterey know it by the name "Fliaum," a word of unknown origin. **1898** U.S. Natl. Museum *Bulletin* 47.1793, *Flioma; Orange Rockfish. . .* From San Diego to Puget Sound; . . constantly found in the markets. **1953** Roedel *Common Fishes CA* 126, *Orange Rockfish. . .* The most important species in the State in recent years. . . *Unauthorized Names:* canary, red rock cod, . . filione.

filipino See **philopena**

Filipinyock n [Perh blend of *Filipino* + *Hunyock*] *derog* Cf **hunyak**

A Filipino.

1942 *New Yorker* 17 Oct 19/2, Anyways, he happens to go under the name Joe—a Filipinyock. . . But still in all, he was strickly a wack from Wackland, that Joe.

fill n[1]

1 An embankment (as in road or railroad construction) built to fill or cross a low area.

1850 U.S. Congress *Congressional Globe* 31st Cong 1st Sess 4 Apr app 22.1.531/1 **KY,** It was like . . making deep cuts and large fills with a view to construct a railroad. **1884** *Lisbon* (Dakota) *Star* July 18 (1912 Thornton *Amer. Gloss.*), The fill will be 150 feet long. **1913** *Pacific Coast Avifauna* 9.46 **cCA,** On another occasion the author was acting as ditch tender . . and guarding a rather high fill that was carrying about all the water that could be crowded through the ditch. **1942** Rawlings *Cross Creek* 348 **nFL,** That distant line was a fill, a forty-foot sand embankment across the marsh between the St. John's River and the . . town of Mimms. . . The marsh had been even more desolate from the height of that untravelled, unfinished roadway. The fill ended . . in a forty-foot drop to a decrepit ferry that crossed the river. **1948** *CA Highways* Mar-Apr 12/1, A blanket of river bed sand and gravel is being laid as base for the fills.

2 A large portion; filling.

1966 *DARE* (Qu. LL4, . . *"He took a ______ of potatoes."*) Inf **OK**45, Big fill.

fill n[2] Pronc-spp *fell, filt* [Var of **thill**] **chiefly Nth** See Map

One of a pair of shafts on a buggy or other vehicle.

1795 J. Pettigrew *Let.* 23 Feb. (Pettigrew P.) *(DAE),* The young horse . . was not able to go on in the fills. **1845** in 1857 Webster *Private Corresp.* 2.202 **NEng,** He could not follow them, any more than a dray-horse can jump out of the fills. **1903** *DN* 2.292 **Cape Cod MA** (as of 1840), *Fills = thills.* **1905** *DN* 3.9 **cCT,** *Fills. . .* Thills. **1914** *DN* 4.154 **CT,** *Fill. . .* In *waggon* [sic] *fill,* shaft. **1939** *LANE* Map 171, *Fills* is described as the usual term by [7 infs]; as old-fashioned by [3 infs]; and as older though still in use by [19 infs]. **1949** Kurath *Word Geog.* 17, From New England to Lake Erie *fills* or *thills* . . is a common name in rural areas for the shafts of a buggy. *Fills* predominates over *thills* in the more conservative parts of New England and in the settlement area beyond the Hudson. **1950** *WELS (The two long pieces of wood in front of a buggy that the horse goes between)* 28 Infs, **WI,** Fills. **1965–70** *DARE* (Qu. L44) 81 Infs, **Nth,** Fills; **MI**97, Fill; **PA**132, Fells [fɛlz]. **1967** *DARE* Tape **MI**71, Some calls 'em fills, some calls 'em shavs. **1973** Allen *LAUM* 1.214 (as of c1950), The *thills* and *fills* reveal their New England and Hudson Valley origin by occurring chiefly in southern Minnesota and northern Iowa, with an extension of the less conservative *fills* into North Dakota. . . [One informant] pronounced *[fills]* as if 'filts'. **1984** *Shoppers' Herald* (Stevens Point WI) 18 Sept, [Advt:] *Auction. . . Tools & Equipment:* Anvil, power hammer, . . blow torch, horse fills, hundreds of tools.

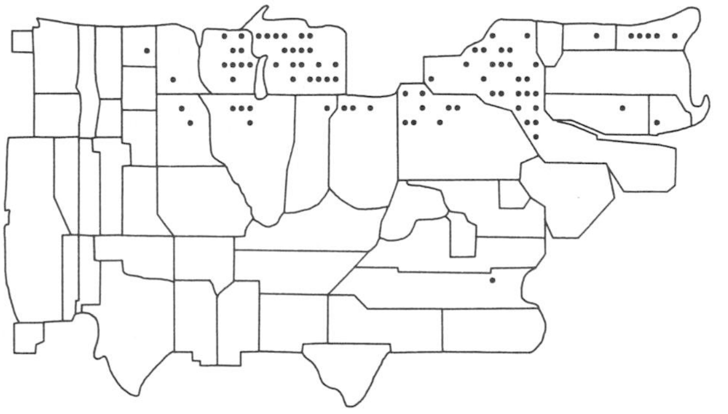

•fill n[2] + var (Qu. L44)

fill v[1]

1 To fulfill, carry out the promise or intent of. Cf **filfil**

1836 U.S. Congress *Congressional Globe* 24th Cong 1st Sess 19 Jan 3 app 50/2 **VA,** From age to age they [=Black people] have filled this saying [="Cursed be Canaan"].

2 In poker: to draw the card(s) needed to complete a full house, flush, straight, etc; to complete (a full house, etc) by drawing the necessary cards.

1875 Twain *Sketches New & Old* (Hartford) 74, His last acts [sic] was to go his pile on "Kings-*and*" (calklatin' to fill, but which he didn't fill), when there was a "flush" out agin him. **1884** Murfree *Where the Battle* 168 **TN,** The special Providence of filling a "bob-tail flush" at a critical juncture. **1903** *Out West Mag.* 18.726 **SW,** Give me the top one. If I do fill, look out for yourselves. **1928** *Amer. Mercury* Oct 136/2, I'd made maybe a straight flush, [h]a[ve] filled somehow anyway, and cleaned him!

3 also with *up:* To fool (someone); to provide with misinformation.

1879 (1880) Twain *Tramp Abroad* 256, These things are manifestly impossible . . they simply took your measure, and concluded to fill you up. They seem to have succeeded. **1903** *Eve. Post* (NY NY) 23 Sept 6/1 **NYC,** Filling up Mr. Jerome with large tales about dissatisfaction in the Citizens' Union. **1968** *DARE* (Qu. KK36, . . *A person who is easily fooled: "It's easy to ______."*) Inf **NY**122, Fill him.

4 To put stuffing in; hence ppl adj *filled.* Cf **filling 3**

1843 (1916) Hall *New Purchase* 43 **PA,** Our batter cakes, eggs and ham, . . steaks, filled chickens, plum puddings. **1977–78** Foster *Lexical Variation* 64 **NJ,** The verb *to fill* [a turkey] is rare and restricted to elderly informants.

fill v[2] [**fill** n[2]] *hist*

To pull, draw (a wagon or carriage).

1883 Amer. Philol. Assoc. *Trans.* 14.48, *Fill,* 'to draw.' This usage, derived from the old word *fills,* 'shafts,' is, so far as I know, confined to North Carolina.

filla-ma-loo bird See **fillilo bird**

filled ppl adj See **fill** v[1] **4**

filled n See **field**

filled cookie n **chiefly NEng** Cf **hermit 4**

A sandwich cookie usu with a cooked raisin or date filling.

1939 Wolcott *Yankee Cook Book* 270 **cMA,** Filled cookies. [Recipe calls for a filling of cooked raisins, sugar, cornstarch and water placed between two thin vanilla-flavored cookies and baked.] **1966** *DARE* (Qq. H29, 32) Inf **ME**2, Filled cookies. **1966** *Sanford Tribune* (ME) 28 Apr sec A 16, Luncheon menus for the pupils of St. Ignatius and Holy Family Schools. . . Friday: Crabmeat salad roll, pea soup, filled cookie. **1969** *Cape Cod Std.-Times* (Hyannis MA) 22 Jan 40, [School lunch menu:] Beef stew with whole vegetables, . . bread, butter, filled cookies and milk. **1978** *DARE* File **cnMA** (as of c1915), *Filled cookie*—A home-made, sandwich type cookie popular when I was a child in Massachusetts. The cookie part was plain sugar cookie, the filling usually raisins (cooked to a jam-like consistency). Filled cookies were more popular with children than with mothers, who knew it took three times as long to make them as plain cookies. **1988** *Ibid* **csWI** (as of c1940), Date cookies with a little mound of dates piled on the round base and then covered by a cap of dough before baking were *filled cookies* to us: *hermit* was a highfalutin word.

fillilo bird n Also *filla-ma-loo bird, fililoo ~, fillyloo ~, fillieloo* [Cf *EDD fillyloo* sb. "An uproar" and int. "An exclamation."] Cf **clew bird, elbedritsch, floogie bird, flu-fly bird**

See quots.

1899 (1912) Green *VA Folk-Speech* 174, *Filliloo-bird*. . . A mythic bird that sticks his bill in the sand and whistles in a mysterious way. **1939** Tryon *Fearsome Critters* 19, *The Filla-Ma-Loo Bird*—He always flies backwards. . . [Has] a turkey-like head on a long bottle-green neck . . a black right wing and a pink left one. . . The nest is usually built upside down. . . The call resembles the clank of a Johnson bar [on a steam locomotive] being shoved into reverse. **1950** *Hench Coll.* **cVA,** Fililoo bird—For ten or fifteen years, I have heard of this imaginary comic bird, a bird that flies backward because it doesn't want to see where it's going but simply wants to see where it's been. . . Often used to describe ultra-conservative people in education, religion, politics, etc. **1958** McCulloch *Woods Words* 62 **Pacific NW,** *Fillyloo bird*—A dirty bird often appearing in loggers' yarns; eats red pepper, flies backward for cooling purposes. **1966** *DARE* (Qu. CC17, *Imaginary animals . . that people . . tell tales about—especially to tease greenhorns*) Inf **WA**6, Filliloo [ˈfɪliˈlu] bird. Greenhorn must go out in the dark to get him; like a left-handed monkey-wrench. **1975** Gould *ME Lingo* 93, *Fillieloo*—Commonest of the imaginary feathered friends of Maine. Some say he doesn't care where he's going, but flies backwards so he can see where he's been. A more plausible explanation is that he flies backwards to keep the wind out of his face. His limited range (only in Maine) is explained by the great time it takes him to get anywhere; he always flies in slow motion.

fillilu n Cf **filliloo bird**

See quot.

1952 Brown *NC Folkl.* 1.540, *Fillilu* [ˈfɪlɪˌlu]. . . Some jocularly mysterious thing. . . When an inquisitive child (or adult) asks what one is doing, the answer may be: "I'm making a fillilu."—Granville county.

filling n

1 =**icing;** see quots. **esp Sth, S Midl** See Map Cf **frosting 1**

1965–70 *DARE* (Qu. H64, *The sweet covering . . on top of a cake*) 17 Infs, **esp Sth, S Midl,** Filling. **1986** Pederson *LAGS Concordance,* 1 inf, **cMS,** Filling—icing or frosting, not sauce [for pudding] or dip; 1 inf, **nwGA,** Cake filling.

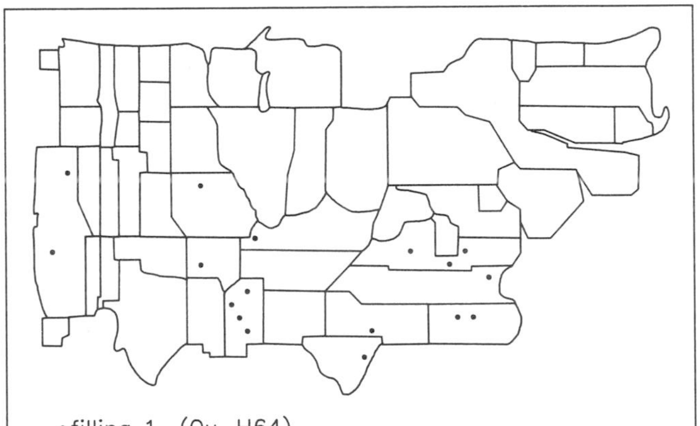

•filling 1 (Qu. H64)

2 also *filly:* See quots. **esp Sth, S Midl** Cf **frosting 2, icing**

1966–70 *DARE* (Qu. H66a, *The sweet liquid that you pour over a pudding*) Infs **AL**14, **GA**8, **KY**85, **MO**9, Filling; **TX**37, Filly. **1986** Pederson *LAGS Concordance* **Gulf Region** *(Sauce . . sweet liquid)* 11 infs, Filling; 1 inf, Filling—beaten eggs, sugar, baked—top of pudding; 1 inf, Filling—thick and sweet.

3 Poultry stuffing.

1907 *German Amer. Annals* 9.375 **sePA,** *Filling.* Stuffing, of a fowl. "I want some chicken and some more filling." . . fr. Pa. Ger. *fils'l;* Ger. *füllsel.* **1967** *DARE* (Qu. H37) Inf **PA**29, Filling—inside a turkey. **1977–78** Foster *Lexical Variation* 64 **NJ,** As a noun, *filling* is common [for turkey stuffing] in the Philadelphia Suburbs and in Newark and South Orange . . elsewhere it occurs only sporadically.

fillipeen(er) See **philopena**

fillit n, v [Pronc-sp for *fillet, filet*]

1975 Gould *ME Lingo* 93, *Fillit*—Plenty of Mainers properly say *fil-lay* for filet and fillet, but in the fisheries *fillit* is the right sound. Redfish are *fillited,* chowder is made from haddock *fillits.* The knife used is a *fillitin'*-knife.

fill one's shirt v phr

1923 *DN* 5.239 **swWI,** *Fill one's shirt.* . . To eat heartily. "We had a big supper, and maybe I didn't fill my shirt!"

fill-the-dootsy v phr

To fiddle around, putter.

1968 *DARE* (Qu. A10, . . *"What are you doing?"* . . *"Nothing in particular—I'm just ______."*) Inf **NY**56, Fill-the-dootsying. **1987** *NADS Letters* **sePA,** *Fill the dootsy:* my husband's late mother (b. 1923, Philadelphia, PA, high school, bank employee, white) used to say, when she saw him idling around the house or dawdling over his homework, "What are you doing? Just *fill-a-dootsyin'*?" This was always said in an indulgent tone, not one of real reproof.

fillum See **film**

fillumajig n [Var of *thingumajig*]

1968 *DARE* (Qu. NN12b, *Things that people say to put off a child when he asks, "What are you making?"*) Inf **CA**105, Fillumajig.

fill up n See **fill** v[1] **3**

filly n

1 See quot. *euphem*

1968 *DARE* (Qu. Z11b, . . *Joking words for a child of unwed parents*) Inf **LA**46, 'Filly' for a girl, 'colt' for a boy.

2 See quot. *joc, euphem* Cf **doe 2**

1967 *DARE* (Qu. M21b, *Joking names for an outside toilet building*) Inf **CO**38, Studs and fillies—two separate buildings.

3 See **filling** n **2.**

4 See **flying filly.**

filly dirt n Cf **foolish earth**

1930 *DN* 6.81 **cSC,** *Filly dirt.* . . Fuller's earth or kaolin, of which there are several deposits in the neighborhood of Wedgefield.

fillyloo bird See **filliloo bird**

film n Usu |fɪlm|; also freq |ˈfɪləm| (cf Pronc Intro 3.I.23); occas |ˈfɪəm| Pronc-spp *fil(l)um*

Std senses, var forms.

1899 (1912) Green *VA Folk-Speech* 174, *Fillum.* . . *Film.* . . as, a fillum over the eye. **1905** *DN* 3.103 **nwAR,** [fɪləmz]. **1933** *AmSp* 8.2.44 **neNY,** In the words *elm, film, athletic,* [ə] is sometimes present, giving the pronunciations [ɛləm], [fɪləm], [æθəlɛtɪk]. **1936** *AmSp* 11.166 **eTX,** In less literate speech, and in the speech of children, [ə] is intrusive also in *elm, film* [ˈɛləm], [ˈfɪləm]. **1942** Hall *Smoky Mt. Speech* 104, *Bulb* and *film* in all occurrences were [bʌəb] and [fɪəm]. **c1960** *Wilson Coll.* **csKY,** Film [fɪləm]—almost universal. **1968** *DARE* FW Addit **neNY,** How much do you charge for Polaroid [ˈfɪləm]? **1982** McCool *Sam McCool's Pittsburghese* 12 **PA,** Make sure we have filum for the camera.

filnut n

=**butternut 1.**

1971 Krochmal *Appalachia Med. Plants* 148, *Juglans cinerea. . . Common Names:* Butternut, filnut. **1974** (1977) Coon *Useful Plants* 154.

filt See **fill** n[2]

filth n [The base of std *filth* is *foul,* not *fill;* however, this may be a new formation, as sugg in quot 1924, on the basis of fill; cf *EDD filth* sb.[2] 4 "Weeds"] **sAppalachians, esp WV**

Underbrush, weeds, unwanted vegetation.

c1900 in 1944 *ADD,* **eOH. 1924** Raine *Land of Saddle-Bags* 103 **sAppalachians,** As *wealth* is the collective noun made from weal, and *stealth* is the thing one steals, and *spilth* what one spills, so *filth* in the mountains means the weeds or driftwood that fill up, and *blowth* is the mass of blossoms that blow. **1927** *AmSp* 2.349 **cwWV,** *Brush hook* . . a short heavy filth scythe. **1929** *WV Review* Oct 9/2, *Filth* for *weeds* or *brushwood.* **1930** *DN* 6.87 **cnWV,** *Filth land,* land not tilled and grown over with weeds and underbrush. Farmers frequently speak of "cutting filth" when they mean scything the grass and weeds on the rough hillsides. **1943** in 1944 *ADD* **cnWV,** If vigilance is relaxed, vice appears to spring up overnight like filth on a neglected farm . . I know we can [keep vice down] if we are as diligent as a good farmer in keeping the filth down on his farm. **1967** Key *Tobacco Vocab.* **TN** [In tobacco cultivating], Grass—filth.

filthy adj Usu |ˈfɪlθɪ|; occas |ˈfɪltθɪ|

A Forms.

1905 *DN* 3.57 **NE,** Very commonly it [=excrescent *-t*] is inserted in *fil(t)thy.* **1920** in 1944 *ADD* **cNY,** ['fɪltθi].

B Senses.

1 Extreme, acute. [Prob by analogy with *dirty shame*] Cf **filthy** adv

1966 *DARE* (Qu. LL36, *To make a statement much stronger: "Poor fellow. I think it's a ______ shame."*) Inf **WA**11, Filthy.

2 Wealthy. [Prob abbr for *filthy rich*]

1967–69 *DARE* (Qu. U37, *Words . . about somebody who has plenty of money*) Infs **CA**113, **TX**28, Filthy.

filthy adv *esp common among mid-aged and young speakers*

Extremely.

1843 *Knickerbocker* 21.122, His trousers [were] 'filthy dirty' and pulled up above the tops of his boots. **1940** M. Banning *Enough to live On* ix.168 *(OEDS),* He's filthy rich and didn't earn a cent of it. **1950** *WELS (Someone who has plenty of money)* 1 Inf, **cWI,** Filthy rich. **c1960** *Wilson Coll.* **csKY,** *Filthy dirty*—especially dirty. **1965–70** *DARE* (Qu. U37, *Words . . about somebody who has plenty of money*) 83 Infs, **scattered,** Filthy rich. [Of all Infs responding to the question, 25% were mid-aged, 9% young; of those giving this response, 36% were mid-aged, 16% young.]

filum See **film**

fimdiddle n Also *fimfaddle* Cf *DS* NN12b

1946 *PADS* 6.38 **VA,** *Fimdiddle* for a dingbat. (An evasive answer to "What is that? What are you making?") Salem, 1938. Rare. **1988** *DARE* File **csWI** (as of c1940), I've heard *fimfaddle to tie up a dingbat* as an expression used to avoid answering a child.

fimpted adj

1972 Claerbaut *Black Jargon* 64, *Fimpted . .* ugly, physically repulsive.

fin n [In ref to a fish's *fin*]

1 A kind of rough oar on a flatboat.

1843 (1916) Hall *New Purchase* 38 **OH,** Forwards were the fin-holes, and behind these . . were . . berths for the captain and mate. The *fins*—(improperly by some called *horns*)—where [sic] rude oars, . . and by these the ark was steered. . . The fins would . . sometimes play in a heavy sort of frolic to get us along faster; but usually they were idle.

2 See quot.

1956 Sorden–Ebert *Logger's Words* 14 **Gt Lakes,** *Fin,* A log fastened underwater to direct the course of logs floating down river.

3 in phr *on the fin;* Of fish: freshly caught.

1944 *PADS* 2.33, Fish are sold *on the fin* (in Shallowford, N.C.)—i.e., caught fresh for you on the spot.

fin exclam See **fen** exclam

fin' See **find**

finagle v, n Usu |fɪ'negəl, fə-|; also occas |fə'nɪgəl| Also sp *fanig-gle, fenagle, fenig(g)le, finigal, fin(n)agel, finaygle, phenagle* [Cf *EDD fainaigue* v. 3 "To deceive by flattery; to obtain by improper means, to cheat."]

A As verb.

Also with *around:* To wangle, maneuver; to obtain by devious means; hence vbl n *finagling,* n *finagler.* **widespread, but less freq W Midl** See Map *esp freq among young and mid-aged speakers*

1922 *DN* 5.147 **sePA,** *Finagler*—one who stalls until someone else pays the check. **1926** Anderson & Stallings *What Price Glory* 111 *(OEDS),* I'm a weary man, and I don't want any finnagelling from you. **1930s** in 1944 *ADD* **eWV,** He'll faniggle around some way to win. **1933** (1978) Cain *Fast One* 245 **Los Angeles CA,** Turn her over to me in the open and without any finaygling. **1936** *Writer's Digest* Oct 4, Discounting any possible editorial finageling . . the solid fact remains that opposing politically minded people do cancel subscriptions. **1942** *Sat. Eve. Post* 3 Jan 17 **Sth,** But anyway, all such finigaling was out in Texas. **1944** *ADD, Fenagle, -ig(g)le.* = *finagle.* **1949** *PADS* 11.6 **wTX** (as of c1920), *Finagle* [fə'nɪgəl]: *v.t.* To manage, often dishonestly. **1950** *WELS Suppl.* **neWI,** Finagle [fɪ'nagəl]. . . To obtain desired ends by unscrupulous means. **1965–70** *DARE* (Qu. II33, . . *"I don't trust him, he's always trying to ______."*) 56 Infs, **scattered, but less freq W Midl,** Finagle (around); 4 Infs, **scattered,** Finagle you (*or* one, someone, something); **GA**82, Finagle his way around; (Qu. U12, *If you . . made him lower the price, you might say, "I ______."*) Infs **PA**240, **RI**1, Finagled (with him); (Qu. V1) Infs **CT**40, **KS**3, **NJ**2, 55, **PA**82, (Some) finagling; **FL**27, **MN**6, Finagling going on; (Qu. II20b) Inf **CA**14, Finagle; (Qu. II32) Infs **NY**86, **VA**18, Finagle (his way out); (Qu. JJ3a) Inf **OK**9, Finagle a good grade; (Qu. JJ3b) Inf **CA**59, Finagler; (Qu. JJ45) Infs **FL**5, **GA**72, Finagling (around); (Qu. KK8) Inf **MS**1, Finagled his way in; (Qu. KK36) Inf **NY**93, Finagle him [41 of 74 Infs young or mid-aged].

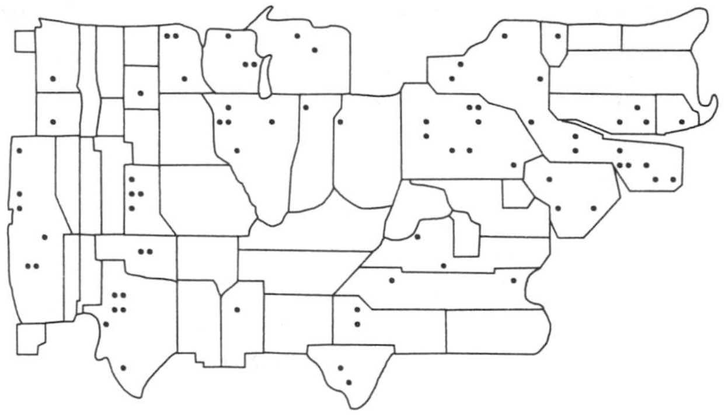

•finagle A + varr (Qq. II33, U12, V1, II20b, II32, JJ3a, b, JJ45, KK8, KK36)

B As noun.

1 An instance of wangling or chicanery.

1941 in 1944 *ADD,* [Newspaper headline:] Philatelic Fenagle.

2 See quot.

1939 *MLN* 54.292, That's the colloquial word I heard when I was a boy in the Carolinas, *fenagle, phenagling. . .* the meaning I grew up with, . . fuss and feathers over a small matter with fakery in it, a lackadaisical effort to sell a bargain, a small bargain. . . The etymology *fenagle (finagle)* < *Feinaigle* [=Gregor von Feinaigle (1765?-1819), German proponent of mnemonics who lectured (and was often ridiculed) in England and France] is submitted to the etymologists, for their perpension.

finakin See **finicking**

final adv

Finally, at last.

1897 Johnston *Old Times GA* 66, Final she got mad, and she fetched a flirt, she did. **1937** in 1944 *ADD,* When it comes to stretching out final for the grave-box.

finally adv Usu |'faɪnḷi|; also freq |'faɪnli| Pronc-sp *finely*

Std sense, var forms.

1941 *Sat. Eve. Post* 5 Apr 116/1 **OH,** He finely gets hisself into a stanch nobody'd ever seen on a ball field before. **1942** Hall *Smoky Mt. Speech* 60, Omission of the [medial] vowel is frequent . . Examples: . . finally. **1963** Edwards *Gravel* 8 **eTN** (as of 1920s), Finely, (that's the way we pronounce it in Speedwell,) I crave to pass along a tale. **1973** Gawthrop *Dial. Calumet* 108 **nwIN,** Pronunciations especially noted as substandard or unusual included . . the two-syllable pronunciation of *finally* /fainli/. **1984** Burns *Cold Sassy* 32 **nGA** (as of 1906), "Is she still hiccuppin'?" I whispered back. "No, it fine'ly stopped, thank the Lord."

finally at last adv phr [Redund]

In the end; finally.

1922 Gonzales *Black Border* 301 **sSC, GA coasts** [Gullah glossary], *Fin'lly at las'*—meaning at last, finally. **1926** Smith *Gullah* 35 **SC, GA coast,** *Fin'lly at las',* a full phrase for at last. **1953** Randolph *Down in Holler* 67 **Ozarks,** Sometimes a number of redundant adverbs . . are strung together for emphasis, as . . "finally at last I got tired of talkin' to them fellers."

finance See **fiancé**

finatially adv [*finally* + infixed syll, perh for emphasis] Cf **-ma-**

Completely, thoroughly.

1931 *PMLA* 46.1308 **sAppalachians,** I'm wore finatially to death!

finaygle See **finagle**

fince See **fence**

finch v [Perh blend of *filch* + *pinch*]
To snitch, pilfer.
1969 *DARE* (Qu. V5a, *To take something of small value that doesn't belong to you*) Inf **CA**169, Finched (filched).

find v
A Forms.
1 infin: usu *find;* pronc-spp *fine, fin'* (Cf Pronc Intro 3.I.22).
1848 Lowell *Biglow* 144 **'Upcountry' MA,** Fin', *find.* **1899** Chesnutt *Conjure Woman* 17 **csNC** [Black], Mars Dugal' did n' hab no 'casion ter fine no mo' fault. **1922** [see **A2** below]. **1984** Burns *Cold Sassy* 327 **nGA** (as of 1906), I have plan [=planned] it so you wont be the one to fine me.
2 past: usu *found* (pronc-sp *fount,* cf Pronc Intro 3.I.15); occas *fin', finded.*
1843 (1916) Hall *New Purchase* 433 **IN,** He backed in [a cave] a rite smart chance, yet arter a while he finded he could a kinder sorter stand up. **1922** Gonzales *Black Border* 301 **sSC, GA coasts** [Gullah glossary], *Fin'*—find, finds, found, finding. . . *Fin'um*—find, finds, found, finding him, her, it, them. **1950** [see **B2** below]. **1962** *Mt. Life* Spring 17 **sAppalachians,** The *-d* and *-ed* endings of past forms of verbs are frequently pronounced *-t,* . . [e.g.] *found, fount.*
B Senses.
1 To provide, provide for; to supply (esp room and board); hence vbl n *finding* and, freq, ppl adj *found* (often understood as n *found* (the cost of) room and board). **chiefly NEast, S Atl**
1631 in 1853 MA (Colony) *Rec. of Gov.* 1.85, [Every] man that findes a muskett shall . . haue ready . . 20 bullets, & 2 fathome of match. **1704** in 1886 Braintree MA *Records* 60, The Rvd Mr. Moses Fiske [shall] have a settled sallary of ninety pounds in or as money (he finding himself wood). **1801** in 1887 MA Hist. Soc. *Proc.* 2d ser 4.127 **MA,** Three Packets ply constantly from New Bedford to New York, and the same number to Nantucket. The rate of fare of the former is four dollars without, and Seven with finding supplies, for a passenger. **1833** (1925) Bagley *Diary* 25 **MA,** He is to find all the stuff [for making window sashes and frames]. **1834** Smith *Letters Jack Downing* 13 **NEng,** I get 12 dollars a month and found. **1888** Jones *Negro Myths* 13 **GA coast** [Gullah], Enty you bin tell me one day dat ef me kin ketch you in you bed you guine fine me? Now me done ketch you in de bed. Gimme de bittle [=victuals] you prommus me. *Ibid* 79, Buh Wolf [want to] see ef him couldnt mek rangement wid Buh Porpus fuh fine him een fish. **1908** *S. Atl. Qrly.* 7.345 **seSC,** *Find, to supply with victuals* . . is in common use: *Buh Sun,* in a well-known folk-tale, promised *Buh Fowl-hawk fuh fine um een bittle* [=Brother Sun promised Brother Fowl-hawk to provide him with victuals]. **1936** *Hench Coll.* **cVA,** Was it a party at which the hostess found the food, or did you all take things to it? **1937** Sandoz *Slogum* 179 **NE** (as of 1900–20), He discovered that in hard times . . five dollars a month and found can be big money to a man who dried out three years hand-running. **1940** (1941) Bell *Swamp Water* 11 **Okefenokee GA,** I'm my own man, now, since I'm a-paying my found. **1944** *PADS* 2.42 **sVA, eNC, wSC,** *Find.* . . To provide for; to furnish a renter with food and other necessities. **1950** *PADS* 14.29 **SC,** *Find.* . . To provide food, as for a party, a picnic. **1952** Brown *NC Folkl.* 1.540, *Find.* . . To supply a person (usually a worker) with provisions. **c1960** *Wilson Coll.* **csKY,** He gets $100 and found. **1975** Gould *ME Lingo* 100, *Found*—Room and board in addition to wages. . . A waitress will be paid so much a week and *found.* . . Newer tax and minimum wage regulations are bringing an end to this long-accepted Maine manner of engaging help; employers find it difficult to compute *found* to the satisfaction of tax collectors.
2 To give birth to—used esp of animals but also occas of humans. **chiefly Sth, S Midl** See Map *euphem*
1902 *DN* 2.234 **sIL.** **1903** *DN* 2.313 **seMO.** **1906** *DN* 3.118 **sIN.** *Ibid* 136 **nwAR.** **1907** *DN* 3.222 **nwAR.** **1908** *DN* 3.310 **eAL, wGA,** *Find, v. tr.* To give birth to: used of all domestic animals, but particularly of cattle. **1917** *DN* 4.412 **NC, KY.** **1926** *AmSp* 1.416 **Okefenokee GA,** The ol' gip [=female dog], when she finds [Footnote: Brings forth] pups, 'll be hongry. **1938** Matschat *Suwannee R.* 87 **GA,** "Freeman told me you used to bring all the children into the world, here in the swamp country." . . "Course, I do so now an' agin, when I keers to. I found my ten all alone, with the holp of the mister." **1941** Writers' Program SC *Folk Tales* 36, Budduh Woof, you know my sowah [=sow] hog fine eight pig las' night! **1946** *PADS* 6.13 **eNC,** *Find.* . . To give birth to. A euphemism. . . Common. **1950** *PADS* 14.29 **SC,** To give birth to, of persons or animals. "Liza fin' a chile last Wednesday." **1951** *PADS* 15.54 **IN.** **1965–70** *DARE* (Qu. K10, . . *A cow that is going to have a calf*) 17 Infs, **chiefly Sth, S Midl,** (She's) going to find a calf; **WY**1, Going to find a calve; **NC**8, Going to find; **NC**60, Will soon find a calf, **VA**70, Finding; (Qu. K11, *When a cow has a calf, you say she* ______) 16 Infs, **Sth, S Midl,** Found a calf; **FL**48, **GA**46, **VA**1, 7, (Has) found her calf; **SC**9, Find a calf; (Qu. K45, *When a mare has had a young horse, you say she has just* ______) Infs **FL**48, **GA**74, **KY**93, **MD**34, **MO**24, **NC**60, **SC**9, **VA**7, 46, Found a colt. **1968** *DARE* Tape **VA**2, His sow had found a litter of pigs.

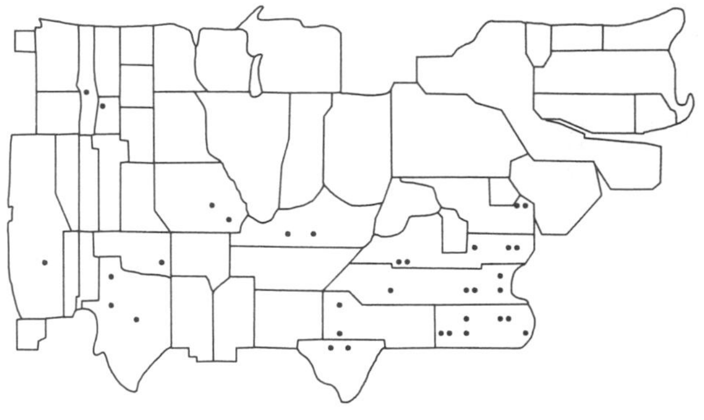

•find B2 + varr (Qq. K10, K11, K45)

3 also with *for:* To seek, look for. **HI**
1960 *Social Process* 66 **HI,** Find . . [meaning] seek. ["Error" made by 1 child of Japanese ancestry.] **1972** Carr *Da Kine Talk* 130 **HI,** "Wait, wait—I'm finding for the scissors in this drawer!" Still heard occasionally in Hawaii, even in the speech of Type IV [="Hawaiian near-standard"], . . the expression seems to point to a link with Melanesian pidgin.

find dog n Also *find hound* Cf **catch dog**
A hunting dog particularly skilled at locating its quarry.
1954 *True* June 66 **TX,** I usually get one or two 'find' dogs out of a litter, maybe a good 'catch' dog, and the rest I use for 'lead' and 'rally' dogs. A find dog has to have a good nose, and a catch dog is usually mean, or he gets that way in a hurry fighting wild stuff. **1966** *DARE* Tape **DC**9, [FW:] Are there some hounds that are very noticeably better at scenting than others? [Inf:] Oh, sure. . . When you've got a big pack of hounds . . you'll have certain hounds that are your find hounds. You can depend on them. . . If there's a fox around, they'll find it.

finded See **find A2**

finder n **chiefly Sth**
In children's games: the player who is **it.**
1966–68 *DARE* (Qu. EE13b, *In games in which all the others hide, the one who must try to find them, he's* ______) Infs **AL**30, **FL**6, 37, **SC**7, **VA**13, The finder; **ME**1, Finder (occasional use).

finders keepers n
1965–70 *DARE* (Qu. EE3, *Games in which you hide an object and then look for it*) 31 Infs, **scattered,** Finders keepers; 12 Infs, **scattered,** Finders keepers [FW sugg]; **IA**22, Finders keepers—hide an eraser, etc., for one person to find.

find for See **find B4**

find hound See **find dog**

finding See **find B1**

find out different v phr
To discover that one was wrong.
1966 *DARE* (Qu. JJ25, . . *"He thought he could take . . over, but I made him* ______*."*) Inf **ME**1, Find out different. **1978** *DARE* File **cnMA** (as of c1915), In response to a whining excuse for something unacceptable I had done, ending "Well, that's what I *thought,*" my mother might say, "When you get a little older, you'll find out different." **1988** *Ibid* **csWI** (as of 1930s), "If that's what you think, you'll find out different." In the same kind of chastising a young person was likely to be told, "If that's what you thought, you've got another think coming."

find rest v phr *euphem* Cf *DS* BB56
To die.

1911 (1916) Porter *Harvester* 199 **IN,** Aunt Molly found rest in the night. . . She will be buried to-morrow. **1987** *NADS Letters* **cwTN,** *Find rest:* I remember this one in reference to death: "He found rest." "She'll find rest in the hereafter," which is not quite the same thing, but that was common, too. I suspect the reinforcement of some old gospel songs, too.

find up v phr [Engl dial; cf *EDD find* v. 3]

To discover, find out.

1969 *DARE* FW Addit **CT,** I'll see if I can find up something.

fine adj

1 See quot.

1923 *DN* 5.234 **swWI,** *Fine boots*. . . High-heeled boots with tops of variously colored leather, and decorated with stars, or other ornaments. (Obs.) . . "Fine boots" were of calfskin, and were worn by men. They always fitted tightly, and the wearer might even have to soap his feet to put them on.

2 Citified; affected. *usu derog*

1939 *Hall Coll.* **eTN,** *Fine*. . . (Used in ironic and contemptuous sense of mountain people who 'put on airs' or act like city folk.) . . "People who talks proper around here are called fine people." "To try to act fine." **1969–70** *DARE* (Qu. HH2, . . *A citified person*) Inf **VT**16, Fine gentleman; [**IL**138, Mr. Fine].

3 High-pitched. Cf **coarse-talking**

1939 *Hall Coll.* **eTN,** *Fine*. . . High-pitched (of the voice). He talks fine. . . Contrasting word . . is *coarse:* "Your voice is too coarse." **1981** Howell *Surv. Folklife* 197, Most fiddle tunes consist of two strains of equal length: a high-pitched part sometimes referred to as the "Fine" and a low part known as the "Coarse." Each part is usually repeated once, but this practice varies from one performer to another. Most tunes begin with the "Fine" and end on the "Coarse" and are played over and over for as long as the dance demands or until the musicians give out. **1983** *MJLF* 9.39 **ceKY,** *Fine* . . high pitched (voice). **1984** Wilder *You All Spoken Here* 170 **Sth,** Coarse: He who sings coarse sings bass; the same for him who basted. A tenor sings fine and a soprano sings shallow.

fine v^{1}

1 also with *down, up:* To make fine, small; to refine, purify; to discipline, cultivate.

c1940 *Hench Coll.* **cVA,** To *fine down* may be used of thoroughbred horses, high-class people. . . "You break the average horse, but you fine-down a thoroughbred." . . "Life has fined her down so that though she is most mannerly she has little life left." **1949** *AmSp* 24.108 **neGA,** *Fine Up*. . . To chop up fine. 'Got that fined up.' **1960** Williams *Walk Egypt* 205 **GA,** "Babies is like a sifter," she declared. "They fine a woman's grain." **1963** Adamson *Household Hints* 232 **NEng** (as of late 1800s), *Hippocrates' Sleeve, How To Make*—This filtering bag is very useful for fining fluids and every woman who makes wine should have one.

2 Of rain: to fall in tiny drops.

1950 *PADS* 14.29 **SC,** *Fining*. . . Drizzling. "It's fining rain." So called because of the small or fine drops.

fine v^{2}

Std sense, var form. Past, past ppl: usu *fined,* also *founded.* [By confusion with *find/found*]

1859 (1968) Bartlett *Americanisms* 160, *Found.* Ignorant and careless speakers say, "The prisoner was found ten dollars," instead of he was *fined.* **1903** *DN* 2.314 **seMO,** He was convicted and found five dollars. **1906** *DN* 3.136 **nwAR,** *Find*. . . To fine. "They found him ten dollars and costs." Newton Co. "They founded him"—a Texas negroism. **1908** *DN* 3.312 **eAL, wGA,** "The mayor found him ten dollars and costs." Not unusual. **1962** Wilson *Folkways Mammoth Cave* 19 **csKY,** The jury found him ten dollars and costs.

fine-aired adj Cf **airy** adj^{1} **1, fine-haired**

1970 *DARE* File **IN,** *Fine-aired*—Elegant in manner. Current among older people.

fine and superfine See **fine or superfine**

fine as frog hair See **frog hair 2a, b**

fine cut adj phr, also used absol **chiefly Nth, N Midl** See Map *old-fash*

Of tobacco: cut into thin shreds for chewing.

1837 *Knickerbocker* 9.268, He ejected a quid from his mouth, that would have shamed in size the largest paper of Lorillard's fine-cut chewing tobacco. **1844** *Knickerbocker* 23.288, I thrust a ball of 'Mrs. Miller's fine cut,' . . between the sub-maxillary bone and its carnal casement. **1909** Porter *Roads of Destiny* 355, Have n't got a chew of fine-cut on you, have you? **1950** *WELS (Tobacco used for chewing . . in loose pieces)* 11 Infs, **WI,** Fine cut. **1965–70** *DARE* (Qu. DD1, *What different forms does chewing tobacco come in around here?*) 45 Infs, **chiefly Nth, N Midl,** Fine cut; **OH**16, Dark fine cut, light fine cut; **IN**73, Sweet Cuban fine cut. [45 of 47 Infs old]

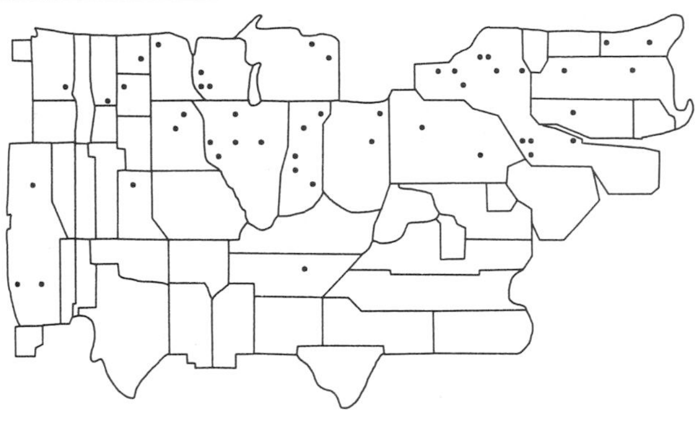

•fine cut + varr (Qu. DD1)

fine down See **fine** v^{1} **1**

fine feed n

1931–33 *LANE Worksheets* **nwRI,** Brown bread is made with rye plus Indian meal (shots) [*DARE* Ed: prob "shorts"] or fine feed (animal meal) plus molasses.

finefy See **finify**

fine-haired adj **chiefly Midl**

1 Cultivated; fastidious; too particular.

1873 Miller *Modocs* 162 **nCA,** He was, as an expression of the time went, a little too 'fine-haired.' He spoke too properly; he never "got on any glorious benders," with the western men, nor could he eat codfish, or talk about Boston. **1914** *DN* 4.106 **KS,** *Fine-haired*. . . Fastidious. "We can't please these fine-haired gentry." **1933** Williamson *Woods Colt* 56 **Ozarks,** Purty fine-haired them Starbucks is a-gittin', 'pears to me. I hear they got screens on their winders. **1950** *WELS (Somebody who is very particular or fussy)* 1 Inf, **nwWI,** Fine-haired. **1951** West *Witch Diggers* 21 **IN** (as of c1900), A dainty housekeeper. Fine-haired. A place for everything and everything in its place. **1954** *Harder Coll.* **cwTN,** *Fine-haired*. . . Of a woman: one who puts on her good clothes and tries to look her best.

2 Impressed with one's own importance; arrogant, conceited.

1901 *Congressional Record* 8 Jan 744/2 **MO,** The only reason that the hoodlums run any town on the American continent is that the fine-haired people, the self-styled "better classes," think they are better than other people. They are unwilling to be jostled by a hoodlum on the day of election. **1923** *DN* 5.207 **swMO,** *Fine haired*. . . Aristocratic, conceited. "He's a-gittin' right fine haired sence he heired that money." **1942** (1971) Campbell *Cloud-Walking* 112 **seKY,** It looked like Sabriny would rather had store-boughten goods. But Sabriny wasn't fine-haired like that and she was plumb satisfied with Sary's home made goods. **1951** West *Witch Diggers* 307 **IN,** Too damn good to spill out a word on us ordinary folks, too damn fine-haired to have a drink with us, too damn sanctimonious to listen to a funny story.

finely adv^{1} [Prob by overcorrection] *old-fash*

Well, excellently.

1852 (1925) Browning *Diary* 75 **KY,** Every thing has gone off finely. **1905** (1906) Low *Some Recoll.* 109 **NYC,** Where we went I do not know, but we must have driven fifteen or twenty miles, and I had never driven a horse before! But I did finely. **1911** (1916) Porter *Harvester* 28 **IN,** "How does it work?" "Finely!" **1939** Coffin *Capt. Abby* 191 **ME** (as of 1860s), Elias is well, stout and rugged. Has fleshed up since he left home and is getting along finely.

finely adv^{2} See **finally**

finely adj [Cf *EDD finely* adv. 2 "Used predicatively as a quasi-*adj.:* very well in health, convalescent."]

Fine, very good.

1859 (1931) Tuttle *CA Diary* 71 **WI,** All of us in high spirits and our team loo[k]ing finely.

fine moss n

1 A water plant *(Naias flexilis).*

1913 *Torreya* 13.226, *Naias flexilis*. . . Fine or chaffy moss, Lake Wapanoca, Ark.

2 =**musk grass.**

1913 *Torreya* 13.225, *Chara* sp.—Fine moss, New Richmond, Mich.

fine or superfine n Also *fine and superfine* [From a question asked in the game]

The game of *forfeits* (at **forfeit** n).

[**1897** (1952) McGill *Narrative* 137, Some of the boys were skilled in the dispensation of suitable redemption of these pawns, and when exhibited to them they inquire: "Fine or superfine?" and being told superfine (a lady's), she is told to go in a corner and say: "Here I stand on two little chips, Do come and kiss my sweet little lips," and to call a boy to do it. Another pawn is exhibited and 'tis pronounced fine only (a boy's), he is ordered to go in a cold corner and say: "In the cold I stand on my big toes, Do take me away before I froze," or this one of great elegance and signification: "You are required to bow to the prettiest, kneel to the wittiest and kiss the one you love best."] **1959** Lomax *Rainbow Sign* 36 **AL** [Black], We'd play a kissin game, like Fine and Superfine. . . One child would sit in a chair and . . we all say to the one in the chair, say, "Heavy, heavy hang over your head." Chair say, "Fine, superfine." They all say, "What shall Nora do to redeem this pawn?" The one in the chair say, "She shall get out there and call her somebody she like right well." **1966** *DARE* (QR, near Qu. EE9) Inf **DC**8, Fine or superfine: Players each give leader a small object. Leader holds it over the head of another player and says "Heavy heavy hangs over thy head." Guesser asks "Fine [from a boy] or Superfine [from a girl]?" Leader answers according to the source of the object: "Fine" or "Superfine." Guesser guesses source player's name. If right, wins; if wrong, pays a forfeit.

finer than frog hair See **frog hair 2a**

finest kind n, adj phr, adv phr, exclam Also *finest kind of pork* [Cf *DNE* 1965 →] **chiefly NEng, esp ME**

Used variously, as a general indication of approval; also used ironically; see quots.

1957 Beck *Folkl. ME* 134, "Frankie, I got news foah yew." "Eyah?" "Frankie; we're aground." "Well, isn't that just the finest kind naow." **1972** *NYT Article Letters,* "Finest kind"—used mostly by fishermen "Down East," usually to sign off a radio conversation between fishing boats. But I've heard it along the coast of South Carolina too—a kind of contraction for "Have the finest kind of—a day—weather—fishing—health" or whatever. **1975** Gould *ME Lingo* 94, *Finest kind*—Spoken as one word to designate the very best. Whatever it is, the *finest kind* cannot be surpassed. The *summer complaints* [=tourists] have picked this up and worked it to death. Ask a tourist how he slept if you want to hear him say *finest kind.* (Newfoundland may have a prior claim to *finest kind,* and the Maritimers use it as much as Mainers do.) **1978** Merriam *Illustr. Lobstering* 36 **ME,** *Finest Kind*—The ultimate comment on quality—of the weather, the price, and even in one case, describing a drywall company. . . May go out of use from overuse. **1979** Lewis *How to Talk Yankee* [12] **nNEng,** *Finest kind of pork.* This extension of the above [=*Finest kind*] is favored by coastal Mainers. Of obscure origin and having nothing to do with the flesh of the pig, it denotes appreciation of anything from a profitable haul while fishing to a jug of cider, to a good looking pan of biscuits. **1982** *DARE* File **coastal ME,** "Finest kind" . . can be used to describe anything from a good haul of fish, [to] a sermon by the preacher, a new car or an amorous affair. "Finest kind o' pork"—same as "finest kind." Used on the offshore islands mostly. **1983** Beyle *How Talk Cape Cod* 27, Anything good is the "finest kind [for the Portuguese on Cape Cod]."

fine up See **fine** v[1] **1**

fingater See **figeater**

finger n Usu |ˈfɪŋgə(r)|; also |ˈfiŋ-, ˈfɛŋ-, ˈfɪŋə(r)| Pronc-sp *feenger*

A Forms.

1934 in 1944 *ADD* **Sth,** Finger . . [fi]—fee-. **1935** *AmSp* 10.166 [PaGer], For *finger* . . one hears [fɪŋər]. . . The mispronunciation of *finger* . . disappears among the educated classes. **1942** Hall *Smoky Mt. Speech* 16, [ɛ^] or [ɛ] often occurs in . . *finger.* **1966** *DARE* FW Addit **swNC,** [ˈfɛŋgɚ]. **1986** *DARE* File **NYC,** The pronunciation [ˈfɪŋə] for *finger* is common in Brooklyn.

B Senses.

1 Anything thought to resemble a finger in shape, spec:

a See quots.

1917 *DN* 4.392 **IL, KY, NEng, NY, neOH,** *Finger*. . . One of the long curved rods on a cradle scythe to catch the grain so that it may be laid in the swath. **1960** Climax Molybdenum Co. *Manual* 47, *Fingers*—Inclined openings used to direct ore from cave to slusher drifts or grizzlies. **1965–70** *DARE* (Qu. B11, . . *Kinds of clouds*) Inf **NY**34, Fingers; (Qu. H32, . . *Fancy rolls*) Inf **GA**75, Cheese fingers; (Qu. H43, *Foods made from parts of the head and inner organs of an animal*) Inf **MN**35, Fingers—kidneys, etc. ground up, fried, served with vinegar and sugar; (Qu. T6, . . *Pointed leaves that fall from pine trees*) Inf **CT**6, Fingers [corrected to *needles*]; (Qu. FF14, . . *Firecrackers*) Inf **MA**28, Fingers. **1967** *DARE* FW Addit **CO,** Grain cradle [has] four fingers and one blade; cuttings [are] bound with straw by binders. **1976** Warner *Beautiful Swimmers* 80 **eMD,** "When we went to the floats in the morning we found that every one of the little crabs had shed its 'fingers,' and we called them 'buffaloes.' They were of no use whatever." . . A very rough wind will still cause floated crabs to . . purposely drop off a threatened limb at the socket.

b An oblong doughnut. **chiefly Upstate NY**

1967–70 *DARE* (Qu. H28, . . *Types of doughnuts*) Infs **CA**157, **NY**99, 109, Fingers; (Qu. H30, *An oblong cake, cooked in deep fat*) Infs **NY**5, 21, 109, 173, 210, **OH**102, Finger; **VT**16, Jelly finger. **1967** *DARE* FW Addit **nNY, NYC,** Fingers—oblong doughnuts; [also called] maple bars or planks.

c in interrog phr *Is your finger sore?* and varr: Used as a warning that one's trouser-fly is open. **chiefly Sth, S Midl**

1954 *Harder Coll.* **cwTN,** Finger too sore to button? **1966–69** *DARE* (Qu. W24c) Infs **AR**23, **NY**219, **SC**34, **TX**32, Is your finger sore? **AR**47, What's the matter, your finger sore? **GA**77, You got a sore finger? **IL**74, **OH**38, Are your fingers sore?

2 attrib:

a Of breads and pastries: long, slender.

1931–33 *LANE Worksheets* **ceCT,** Finger rolls—rolls used for frankfurters. **1958** (1972) Funk *Horsefeathers* 152, As applied to the modern bakery-made American product the name [=ladyfinger] is distinctly inappropriate. The name *finger biscuit,* also in early use, would be more fitting: the finger could be that of a heavyweight prizefighter. **1966** *DARE* File **cwCA,** Small "closed-face" sandwich oblong in shape—finger sandwich. **1966–68** *DARE* (Qu. H32, . . *Fancy rolls and pastries*) Infs **IL**9, **MN**3, **NY**49, Finger rolls; **NH**11, Finger rolls—long as a finger, sliced on the side, filled with tuna fish, etc; (Qu. H19, . . *Biscuits*) Inf **DC**7, Finger rolls—put in hot dog; **SD**3, Finger biscuits—add sugar and eggs to bread dough, put together in a pan; (Qu. H15, *Bread made with wheat flour*) Inf **SC**19, Finger bread—a biscuit about two by five inches, fried, but not cut, so as to hold good in the pan.

b Resembling a finger (or hand with fingers) in shape or function.

c1938 in 1970 Hyatt *Hoodoo* 2.1789 **New Orleans LA,** Dere's one of de roots [of an ash tree] grows right straight down in de ground lak dat [Hyatt: taproot]—it's called de *fingah root.* It looks jes' lak a person's fingah. **1939** *Eve. State Jrl.* (Lincoln NE) 16 Oct 3 *(Meredith Coll.),* The ground was . . worked twice, before planting. . . after planting the field was dragged four times by a 27 foot cultivator known as a finger weeder. **1949** Guthrie *Way West* 174, He stooped and grabbed two finger stones, thinking he would kill the grasshopper with them. **1953** Sun *(Baltimore MD)* 6 July 14/4 *(Hench Coll.),* The [railroad] terminal includes two crane piers, a grain pier, . . two coal piers, an ore pier, and miscellaneous smaller finger piers. **1965** *PADS* 43.25 **seMA,** Finger pier [=a wharf]. **1965–70** *DARE* (Qu. C17, . . *A small, rounded hill*) Inf **CA**211, Finger ridge—an extension of a ridge; (Qu. H56, . . *Kinds of pickles*) Inf **NY**65, Finger pickles (small); (Qq. I22a, b, . . *[Hot] peppers*) Infs **IL**76, **MA**2, **MI**34, **PA**245, **SC**4, Finger peppers; (Qu. O3, . . *Platform . . where boats . . tie up*) Inf **ME**10, Finger float—a collection of floats attached to one another for small boats in a quiet harbor; (Qu. P7, *Small fish used as bait*) Inf **SC**63, Finger mullet; (Qu. T17, . . *Kinds of pine trees*) Inf **CT**6, Finger pine; (Qu. FF14, . . *Firecrackers*) Inf **MO**2, Little finger firecrackers. **1968** Adams *Western Words* 112, *Finger loop*—In packing, a cinch loop. About 15 inches from the end of the cinch a round piece of leather 3 inches in diameter is sewed on, and two holes are punched through it. A leather thong is attached to it, leaving a 3-inch loop. The loop is used to secure the end of the latigo strap after cinching. **1976** Sublette Co. Artist Guild *More Tales* 160 **WY** (as of c1900), Onto each of these forked chain ends was also attached another chain. These chains came together under the center of the wagon. These chains ran into a "bitch link" which . . ran back to the next wagon after going through a "finger link".

3 in phr *one's fingers are all thumbs:* See **all thumbs.**

fingerberry n [Perh by assoc with **thimbleberry**]

A **raspberry** (here: *Rubus allegheniensis*).

1893 *Jrl. Amer. Folkl.* 6.141 **NY,** *Rubus villosus* . . finger berry; thimble berry. **1940** Clute *Amer. Plant Names* 229, *Rubus Alleghieniensis*. . . Finger berry.

fingerboard n Also *fingerpost*

A sign shaped like a finger, pointing the way to a specified destination; by ext, a place where such a sign would be useful; also fig.

1804 *Frederick-Town Herald* (MD) 11 Feb 3/1, Holding the finger board in a wrong direction for Carter's Mountain. **1845** in 1870 Drake *Pioneer Life* 235 **KY,** At their . . forks there were no finger boards, and not many living fingers to point out the true way to the puzzled traveller. **1886** *Chautauqua Assembly Annual* (Long Beach, Calif.) 10 *(DA),* The humble village pastor saw . . no finger-boards along life's highways to point the people thither [to knowledge]. **1894** Twain in *N. Amer. Rev.* 159.245, A literary swamp which has so many misleading fingerboards up as this book is furnished with. **1902** (1904) Rowe *Maid of Bar Harbor* 79 **ME,** If the old finger-post was torn down and buried in some secret place under the snow it was no great matter after all. **1968** McPhee *Pine Barrens* 59 **NJ,** An outsider needs a glossary to follow simple directions—for example, "Go down here about a mile and turn left at the fingerboard." A fingerboard is a place where several roads come together.

finger cactus n

A **pincushion cactus** (*Mammillaria* spp).

1967 *DARE* FW Addit **neCO,** Finger cactus—nipple cactus.

finger cap n [Cf Ger *Fingerhut*] Also called **sewing cap**

A thimble.

1967 Cerello *Dakota Co. MN* 58, In my day a very popular gift for a young lady was a finger cap. . . An elegant sterling silver finger cap with her initials engraved on it. . . My grandmother's finger cap was of ruby-colored glass. [Cerello: *Finger cap* was recorded in six communities.]

finger-cone pine n [From the long, slender cones]

A **white pine** (here: *Pinus monticola*).

1897 Sudworth *Arborescent Flora* 15, *Pinus monticola*. . . Finger-cone Pine (Cal.) **1908** Britton *N. Amer. Trees* 9, *Pinus monticola*. . . is also known as Silver pine, Finger-cone pine [etc]. **1976** Yepson *Trees* 270, *Pine, Western White* . . finger cone pine . . *P[inus] monticola.*

finger fly n

Perh a sweat bee (*Halictus* spp).

1965 *DARE* (Qu. R12, . . *[Common] flies*) Inf **MS**1, Finger fly—sits on the body when one sweats.

finger grass n

1 =**crabgrass 1.**

1820 in 1832 MA Hist. Soc. *Coll.* 2d ser 9.149 **VT,** [Plants . . indigenous in the township of Middlebury] Digitaria sanguinalis, . . Finger grass. **1857** MA State Bd. Ag. *Annual Rept.* 4.85, *Finger Grass, Common Crab Grass, (panicum sanguinale.)* . . This grass grows on waste or neglected cultivated grounds . . and is generally regarded as a troublesome weed. **1943** Peattie *Great Smokies* 168, In the first year after abandonment there is a one-year stage when horseweed and finger grass predominate. **1952** Strausbaugh-Core *Flora WV* 76, *D[igitaria] filiformis*. . . Finger Grass.

2 A grass of the genus *Chloris.* [See quot 1933] Also called **windmill grass**

1933 Small *Manual SE Flora* 114, *Chloris*. . . Tufted perennials or annuals with . . 2- to several often showy and feathery spikes aggregated at the summit of the stems. . . *Finger-grasses.* **1950** Hitchcock-Chase *Manual Grasses* 519, *Fingergrass*. . . may be locally abundant and then furnishes considerable forage. **1970** Correll *Plants TX* 238.

finger Indian grass n Cf **Indian grass**

A **big bluestem** (here: *Andropogon gerardii*).

1863 in 1865 IL Dept. Ag. *Trans.* 5.867, *Andropagan* [sic] *scoparius,* Broom, Beard-grass. *A. furcatus* . . Finger Indian-grass, are given as specimens of very worthless native grasses which make their appearance in old neglected farms, especially on light soils.

finger length See **finger's length**

fingerling n

1 A small firecracker. Cf **finger B1a** quot 1965-70.

1969 *DARE* (Qu. FF14) Inf **NY**209, Fingerlings—little ones.

2 See quot.

1950 *WELS (Nickname for the little finger)* 1 Inf, **ceWI,** Fingerling.

finger-nose n

The gesture of thumbing one's nose.

1932 *Hench Coll.* **cVA,** *Finger-nose*—A gesture made by putting the thumb on the nose and wiggling one's fingers. In its true meaning the gesture is one of contempt meaning "Kiss my ass." Often it is used to mean joking contempt. **1932** *Sun* (Baltimore MD) 31 Oct *(Hench Coll.),* As attempted justification for canceling the debts with a sneer, or grabbing a life line with one hand while making finger-noses with the other, this is all very well. But it hasn't much to do with scholarship.

finger oak n

A **red oak** (here: *Quercus falcata* [formerly *Q. digitata*]).

1950 Moore *Trees AR* 50, *Southern Red oak*. . . Local Names . . Finger . . Oak. . . *Leaves* vary extremely in size and shape, many types occurring on the same tree; may be pear-shaped with three lobes at the end, resemble the outline of a hand, or be elongated with several lobes, the center one being longest. **1976** Yepson *Trees* 261, *Oak, Southern Red* . . finger oak. . . This is a large tree with foliage of varying shape.

finger-pointing vbl n Cf **shunning**

1955 Warren *Angels* 121 **sLA** (as of c1860) [Black], The most feared punishment, past things like short pork rations or banishment from the Saturday night juba-pat, was the "finger-pointing," a kind of putting in Coventry, a system whereby no word except an order might be addressed to the culprit during the term of punishment, and at every encounter a pointed finger would accompany the wordless stare.

fingerpost See **fingerboard**

finger pulling n Cf **arm pull**

An Eskimo game of strength.

1973 *Theata* 1.1.9 **cAK,** The old games, such as the double high kick, single high kick, arm pulling and finger pulling have been passed down to the people of today and are still kept.

finger-rot n

A **spurge nettle** (here: *Cnidoscolus stimulosus*).

1974 Morton *Folk Remedies* 51, *Finger-rot*. . . *Cnidoscolus stimulosus*. . . Hairs on plant inject an irritant substance on contact with the skin, causing a fiery sensation and rash persisting several days.

fingers exclam Also *five fingers* Cf **fins 2**

1968 *DARE* (Qu. EE17, *In a game of tag, if a player wants to rest, what does he call out so that he can't be tagged?*) Inf **NY**44, Fingers! [means] crossed fingers; **NY**118, Five fingers.

fingers, go around one's See **elbow, go (all) around one's**

finger's length exclam Also *finger length*

In marble play: see quots.

1942 Berrey-Van den Bark *Amer. Slang* 665.6, Finger's length! two fingers' length! &c., *a call for permission to move the "shooter" a given distance from the "target" when it is too close to shoot.* **1955** *PADS* 23.19 **cwTN,** *Hand's length (finger's length, two finger's length, etc.)* . . A call that allows the shooter to move his marble or taw away from the defensive marble in order to allow greater freedom of movement. **c1970** Wiersma *Marbles Terms* **MI,** Finger length—a call entitling a player to move a finger's length closer to the target marble.

fingertip towel See **finger towel**

finger-toe n

=**Indian pipe.**

1966 *DARE* (Qu. S26e) Inf **SC**10, Finger-toes.

finger towel n Also *fingertip towel chiefly among women*

A small, freq decorative, towel usu reserved for guests.

1965-70 *DARE* (Qu. G17, . . *Other kinds of towels*) 26 Infs, **scattered,** Finger towel; **IL**63, **IA**25, **VA**28, Finger towel—for guests; **NY**67, Finger towel—a very small linen towel that is used in the guest bathroom; they usually have some sort of embroidery on them; 13 Infs, **scattered,** Fingertip towel; **CA**10, **GA**81, **IA**13, **NJ**19, 46, **PA**171, Fingertip towel—for guests; **MS**38, Fingertip towel—also finger towel; **MI**68, Fingertip towel—smaller than a finger towel, maybe a foot by fifteen inches; **IL**82, Fingertip towel—small, usually embroidered; **PA**40, Fingertip towel—very small; on dinner table. [46 of 51 total Infs female]

finger tree n

=**fringe tree.**

1955 *S. Folkl. Qrly.* 19.232 **FL,** Chionanthus Virginica . . , also called *Finger Tree,* . . is a sheet of pure white color . . in March before the foliage appears.

finger-weed n [Prob from the finger-like branched stems]

A **fiddleneck 1** (here: *Amsinckia intermedia*).

1935 (1943) Muenscher *Weeds* 377, *Amsinckia intermedia.* . . Finger-weed. . . Native to the Pacific Coast.

finicking adj Also sp *finakin, finickin, finnikin(g)*

Std senses, var forms.

1872 Schele de Vere *Americanisms* 471, *Finnikin, finniking,* . . are American corruptions of finical in frequent use. **1899** (1912) Green *VA Folk-Speech* 174, *Finickin.* . . Fussy; fastidious; unduly particular about trifles; overnice. Finakin.

finickity adj [Perh blend of *finicky* + *persnickity*] Cf Intro "Language Changes" I.8

Finicky.

1969 *DARE* (Qu. H12, *If somebody eating a meal takes little bits of food and leaves most of it on his plate, you say he* _____) Inf **NY**226, Is finickity.

finify v, hence ppl adj *finified* Also sp *finefy* Also with *off, up* [*fine* + *-ify* to make] *old-fash*

To make fine, adorn.

1847 (1962) Robb *Squatter Life* 73 **sMO,** But this new Jedge I ain't never seed, and ef he is the slicked up finefied sort on a character they pictur' him, I don't *want* to see him. **1889** (1971) Farmer *Americanisms* 240, *Finefied.*—Bastard American English for "made fine"; dandified. **1891** *Harper's New Mth. Mag.* Jan 221/1 **eTN,** But the wimmin folks air so gin over ter pride an' fixin's that they air obleeged ter set out a *table* all tricked up an' finified off. **1941** *LANE* Map 358 *(Dress up)* 1 inf, **seNH,** [fɪnɨfaɪ, ~ʌˑp].

finigal See **finagle**

fining comb n

1936 *AmSp* 11.317 **Ozarks,** *Redding Comb.* . . An ordinary coarse comb, with which the mountain woman *reds out* her hair. A fine-toothed comb is called a 'finin'-comb' or a 'booger-comb.'

finish v

To award a diploma to.

1968 *DARE* Tape **WI**23, When I graduated from high school we only finished twelve. [Inf old]

finish n **scattered, but esp Sth, S Midl**

A state of perfection.

1897 *KS Univ. Qrly.* (ser B) 6.87, *Do up brown:* to "do up" completely.—General. *Do to a finish:* same as last. **1965–70** *DARE* (Qu. KK3a, *Words for the perfect condition—for example, in cooking: "It's done to* _____*."*) Infs **NC**15, 35, **SC**11, **VA**29, A finish; (Qu. KK3b, *Something done perfectly—for example, a piece of work: "It's done to* _____*."*) Infs **CA**21, **GA**45, **LA**8, **ME**5, **MO**22, **NM**9, **TN**12, A (*or* the) finish; (Qu. KK50, . . *"He had it all worked out* _____*."*) Infs **CA**164, **CT**6, **GA**45, To the finish; **KY**40, **MO**32, **NM**9, (Down) to a finish.

finish in v phr

To complete the harvest of.

1968 *Budget* (Sugarcreek OH) 25 July 12/5 **cPA,** Farmers are finishing in the hay, and starting on the wheat.

finishing pan n

A stainless steel pan used in the final stage of boiling maple sap for syrup.

1968 *DARE* Tape **IN**36, Anymore I finish on a gas stove I got in my sugarhouse, in a finishin' pan—stainless steel pan,—and once you're done you just shut your fire off and it's not overcooked . . and every batch is consistent. **1980** *Milwaukee Jrl.* (WI) 1 Apr Accent sec 4 **seWI,** Trials must be taken every so often to see whether the liquid in the finishing pan has reached syrup stage—66% sugar content. **1987** *DARE* File **cWI,** You put the [maple] sap in the holding tank. A hose leads to a long, rectangular, flat, open pan that sits over the oven. The pan, about a foot deep, is the finishing pan. You cook the sap down, adding more slowly from the holding tank.

finishing stick n

A toothpick.

1966 *DARE* (Qu. G11) Inf **OK**18, Finishin' stick.

finishment n [**-ment**] *old-fash*

An end, conclusion; also fig.

1872 Eggleston *End of the World* 59 **Ohio Valley,** Ef this 'rithmetic preacher can't make a finishment of this sub*lu*nary speer by addition, he'll do it by multiplyin'. **1874** (1895) Eggleston *Circuit Rider* 46 **IN,** I tell you, he come plaguey nigh puttin' a finishment to me, though.

finish one's circle v phr Also *finish one's course,* ~ *out the row*

To die.

1968 Adams *Western Words* 112, *Finished his circle*—Said of a cowman who has died. **1968** *DARE* (Qu. BB56, *Joking expressions for dying: "He* _____*."*) Inf **CT**6, Finished his course; called home. **1984** Wilder *You All Spoken Here* 208 **Sth,** Rung the knell, finished out the row: Said "good mornin' " to Saint Peter.

Finlander hell n

A sauna.

1952 FWP *Guide SD* 77, Probably the most characteristic custom existing among the Finns today is their system of bathhouses—"Finlander hells," as they are popularly known.

Finn n

1 The Finnish language.

1968 *DARE* Tape **CA**103, He'd talk Finn to them.

2 attrib; Spec:

a Inhabited by people of Finnish heritage.

1966–67 *DARE* (Qu. C34, *Nicknames for nearby settlements*) Inf **WA**24, Finn Settlement; **WI**52, Finn Town; (Qu. C35, *Nicknames for . . parts of your town*) Infs **MN**2, **MT**1, Finn Town; (Qu. II25, . . *Nicknames for the part of town where . . foreign groups live*) Infs **MN**2, **OR**4, Finn Town.

b Used by Finnish loggers. Cf **Swede**

1969 Sorden *Lumberjack Lingo* 42 **NEng, Gt Lakes,** *Finn Grub Hoe* or *Finn Hoe*—A heavy hoe made from a shovel used for leveling tote roads. *Finn Saw*—A short saw with a bow-type handle, generally used to cut pulpwood. Same as bow saw, Swede saw.

finnagel See **finagle**

finnan haddie n Also, by folk-etym, *finny haddie* [*finnan,* var of a Scots place-name, prob *Findhorn,* but confused with *Findon* (see *OED*) + *haddie,* Scots dial var of *haddock*] **NEng**

Smoked haddock.

1907 *DN* 3.244 **eME,** *Finny haddie.* . . Finnan haddie. Doubtless an instance of popular etymology. **1932** (1946) Hibben *Amer. Regional Cookery* 170, Finnan Haddie in Milk *(Gloucester, Massachusetts). Ibid* 171, Finnan Haddie Soufflé *(New Bedford, Massachusetts).* **1939** Wolcott *Yankee Cook Book* 35, Finnan haddie is, strictly speaking, a Scotch and not a Yankee dish. It gets its title from the reputation of the haddock cured around Findon, a fishing village near Aberdeen, Scotland. Once our American supply was almost entirely imported, but now the great bulk of it, and some of the very finest, comes from New England. **1964** Amer. Heritage *Cookbook* 462, Finnan Haddie . . became common in New England as fishermen began to take haddock off the coast. **1967** *DARE* (Qu. H45, *Dishes . . that everybody around here would know, but that people in other places might not*) Inf **MA**50, [fɪnən hædi]. It's a smoked fish in a cream sauce.

finnegan v [Perh infl by **finagle**]

To cozen, persuade artfully.

1968 *DARE* (Qu. U12, *If you were buying something and you argued with the person selling it till you made him lower the price, you might say, "I* _____*."*) Inf **PA**70, Finneganed him out of it.

finnegan pin n

A nonexistent object used as the basis of practical jokes.

1967 *DARE* (Qu. HH14, *Ways of teasing a beginner or inexperienced* *person. . . "Go get me ———."*) Inf **MA**1, A finnegan pin in the muffler gear.

finnie v [*fin* var of **fen** exclam]

To lay claim to, latch on to.

1956 *AmSp* 31.36, Bill Burkhardt, of Concord, Massachusetts, said 'I've got dibs on that,' meaning 'That's mine.' Others said 'I finnie that,' 'I whackie that,' 'I kibbie that,' or 'I possy that'—all with the same meaning. **1968** *DARE* (Qu. V5b, *If you take something that nobody seems to own, you might say, "Before anybody else gets it, I'm going to ——— this."*) Inf **OH**87, Finnie.

finnikin(g) See **finicking**

Finnish taxi n

1984 *DARE* File **nMI,** Finns in the Upper Peninsula, in order to pay a lower automobile license fee, would extend the bed of a car to carry many people—for example, to church. This vehicle was a "Finnish taxi."

finns See **fen** exclam

finny haddie See **finnan haddie**

fin out adj phr [See quot 1916] **esp eMA** *old-fash*

Injured, ill; near death.

1916 Macy-Hussey *Nantucket Scrap Basket* 131 **MA,** "Fin Out"—"All in," as we say nowadays. A dying whale rolled over and showed his fin. So the whalemen used to say, when a man was very sick or badly hurt, "he was pretty nigh fin out." [**1938** Tripp *Flukes* 197 **New Bedford MA,** A cry rang out from all hands, "Fin out! the whale is dead."] **1939** (1962) Thompson *Body & Britches* 199, If they are "all in", they are "all stove up"; on Nantucket they would probably have said that they were "fin out". **1945** Colcord *Sea Language* 75 **ME, Cape Cod, Long Island,** When a whale rolls over to die, he is said to be fin out. In whaling communities the term means moribund. "Old Cap'n Peleg is nigh about fin out."

fins exclam

1 See **fen** exclam.

2 =king's ex. chiefly NYC Cf fingers

1967-68 *DARE* (Qu. EE17, *In a game of tag, if a player wants to rest, what does he call out so that he can't be tagged?*) Infs **NJ**43, **NY**37, 78, Fins! **NY**34, "Fins!" or "I got fins!" Cross your fingers to immune yourself from tagging; **NY**42, Cross the fingers and shout "fins!"; (Qu. EE20, *When two boys are fighting, and the one who is losing wants to stop, he calls out, "———."*) Inf **NY**68, Fins! **1975** Ferretti *Gt. Amer. Book Sidewalk Games* 176 **NYC,** Often, the fluidity of One-on-One basketball ebbing and flowing in the gutter . . was abruptly halted with "Time!" or "Fins!" to let cars pass through the court.

3 See quot.

1901 *DN* 2.140 **cNY,** *Fins. . .* In head and footer [=a game similar to leap frog], said when a boy is to get down at the mark.

fip n [Abbr for *fippenny bit* a coin worth about six cents that circulated in the eastern US before 1857] *arch*

Fig: the slightest thing; a trifle.

1897 *KS Univ. Qrly.* (ser B) 6.52, *Fip* . . a trifle. **1909** *DN* 3.411 **nME,** *Fip. . .* Five pence. "I don't care a fip." **1955** Adams *Grandfather* 54 **NY** (as of 1830s), He said he had paid to travel by steam and he wouldn't give a fip for any other way of travel.

fir balsam n **chiefly NEng**

1 =balsam fir, usu *Abies balsamea.*

1810 Michaux *Histoire des Arbres* 1.18, Abies balsamifera.—*Sylvir fir . . , Fir balsam . . , Balsam of Gilead tree . . ;* Dénominations également en usage dans la partie la plus septentrionale des États-Unis. **1848** (1864) Thoreau *ME Woods* 9, Delicate and beautiful specimens of the larch, arbor-vitae, ball-spruce, and fir-balsam. **1899** Jewett *Queen's Twin* 16 **ME,** Now, you see them little peakéd-topped spruces an' fir balsams comin' up over the hill all green an' hearty. **1966** *DARE* (Qu. T5, . . *Kinds of evergreens*) Infs **ME**5, **NH**4, Fir balsam; (Qu. T15, . . *Kinds of swamp trees*) Inf **ME**5, Fir balsam. **1976** Bailey-Bailey *Hortus Third* 2, *Abies . . balsamea. . . Balsam f[ir], fir balsam. . .* Yields Canada balsam.

2 See quot.

1909 *DN* 3.411 **nME,** *Fir balsam* . . Same as *blob,* q.v. *Ibid* 408, *Blob. . .* The resinous exudation from the fir tree.

fir club moss Also *fir moss*

A **club moss** (here: *Lycopodium selago*).

1824 Bigelow *Florula Bostoniensis* 386 **NH,** *Lycopodium Selago. . . Fir Club Moss. . .* On the highest summit of the White mountains. **1876** Hobbs *Bot. Hdbk.* 38, Fir club moss, Lycopodium selago. **1900** Lyons *Plant Names* 233, *L. Selago* . . , Fir Club-moss, Fir Moss. **1974** Welsh *Anderson's Flora AK* 6, *Fir Clubmoss. . .* Alpine and arctic tundra, heathlands, and woods; almost throughout Alaska and Yukon; eastward to the Atlantic and southward to Oregon, Montana, Michigan, and North Carolina; circumboreal. **1987** Hughes-Blackwell *Wildflowers SE AK* 112, Fir Clubmoss. . . Stems are upright and cylindrical and grow in tufts.

fire n, v Usu |faɪr, faɪə|; also **esp Midl** |fɑr|; also **esp Delmarva, sNJ,** |fɔr|; for addit varr see quots Pronc-spp *fahr, far(r), fiah, fieh, fiuh, foir, for*

A Forms.

1915 *DN* 4.182 **swVA,** *Far* . . Fire. **1917** Torrence *Granny Maumee* 39 [Black], Fieh. **1917** *DN* 4.409 **wNC,** That's the most *coggled up* [=rickety] far . . I ever seed. **1922** Gonzales *Black Border* 301 **sSC, GA coasts** [Gullah glossary], *Fiah*—(n. and v.) fire, fires, fired, firing. **1923** (1946) Greer-Petrie *Angeline Steppin'* 29 **csKY,** They didn't have no forplace. **1927** Shewmake *Engl. Pronc. VA* 42, *Fire. Fi-uh* prevails in Virginia. **1931** *PMLA* 46.1316 **sAppalachians,** "Farr" (fire). **1933** *AmSp* 8.1.32 **nTX,** Between pokin' the far and watchin' clo'es hung on a bob war fence, I had a handful. **1933** *AmSp* 8.2.28 **eKY,** A hot coal from the foir-place. **1933** Rawlings *South Moon* 9 **FL,** "We got the farr! You-all never figgered on the farr!" . . The fire crackled. **1936** *AmSp* 11.33 **eTX,** [Words] such as *fire, fired* . . are also often pronounced with [aː], [ɑː], [ɒː], or in illiterate speech even [ɔː]: [faːr], [fɑːr], [fɒːr], [fɔːr]. **1944** *PADS* 2.29 **eKY, wNC,** *Fire* [fɑr]. . . Common. **1950** Faulkner *Stories* 67 **MS,** Hit was like a fahr. **c1960** *Wilson Coll.* **csKY,** *Fire* is often [fɑr] or [fɑɪjə]. **1961** Kurath-McDavid *Pronc. Engl.* 122, Three different vowel phonemes are current in *wire, tired, fire:* . . The phoneme /ai/ . . (1) has general currency in the North, in the Hudson Valley with Metropolitan New York, and in East Jersey, (2) is nearly universal in the South . . , (3) predominates decidedly in Pennsylvania east of the Susquehanna . . , and (4) is rare in the South Midland, from West Virginia to the South Carolina line, though apparently preferred by cultured speakers. . . The merging of /ai/ with /ɑ/ before tautosyllabic /r/, which makes *fire, tired* homophonous with *far, tarred,* is a characteristic feature of Midland speech. . . The dialect of the Delmarva Peninsula and southern New Jersey is unique in that . . /air, ɑr, ɔr/, as in *wire, barn, corn,* coalesce in /ɔr/. **1967-68** *DARE* Tape **AZ**9, Fire [fɑɚ]; **FL**42, Fire [fɑ˅ə]. **1982** McCool *Sam McCool's Pittsburghese* 12 **PA,** There's a four alarm fahr on the South Side.

B As noun.

1 often in combs: Phosphorescence or **will-o'-the-wisp.** Cf **C4** below, **foxfire**

1965-70 *DARE* (Qu. CC16, *A small light that seems to dance or flicker over a marsh or swamp at night*) 31 Infs, **chiefly Nth,** St. Elmo's fire; 9 Infs, **scattered,** Swamp fire; **IN**22, **NY**30, 35, Marsh fire; **FL**39, **GA**74, Ball(s) of fire; **NY**123, Spirit fire; **ID**5, Wandering fire; **SC**11, Woods fire; **NJ**1, Fire wood—logs, primarily in swampy holes. **1975** Gould *ME Lingo* 94, *Fire*—Phosphorescence in salt water at night. Fishermen can establish the presence of fish by thumping a boat's side and watching the *fire* of the startled fish as they dart away. A school of herring can be followed by their *fire.*

2 Hell; the devil; spec: see below. **scattered, but chiefly Sth, S Midl**

a also attrib, often in phr *fire and brimstone* and varr: See quots.

1917 Torrence *Granny Maumee* 39 [Black], You shorely is on de way to de fieh but I'm goin' pluck you out ef it skins you alive. **1954** *Harder Coll.* **cwTN,** *Fire and brimstone* . . Euphemism for *Hell.* **1965-70** *DARE* (Qu. CC9, . . *"That man is headed straight for ———."*) 48 Infs, **chiefly Sth, S Midl,** Fire and brimstone; 12 Infs, **scattered,** Fire; **OH**76, Fires; **NY**121, **OR**4, Fire pit; **MO**38, **SC**21, Fire place; **NY**43, Fire and furnace; **AR**12, Fire works; (QR, near Qu. G11) Inf **NJ**21, Coon's quill—what the fire is it?; (Qu. CC8, . . *Names for the devil*) Inf **LA**20, Fire man; (Qu. NN26a, . . *Substitutes for 'hell': "Oh ———!"*) Inf **KY**19, Fire and damnation.

b in phrr *beat* (or *slap, whip*) *the fire out of someone:* See quots.

1960 Williams *Walk Egypt* 274 **GA,** Now if I find you been there, I'll whip the fire out of you. **1965-70** *DARE* (Qu. Y15, *To beat somebody thoroughly: "John really ——— that fellow."*) Infs **KY**75, **SC**3, 34, Beat the fire out of him; **SC**46, Slapped the fire out of him; (Qu. Y14b, *To hit somebody with the open hand*) Inf **FL**17, Slap the fire out of him.

c in phr *by fire:* Used as a mild oath.

1916 Lincoln *Mary-'Gusta* 25 **eMA,** "Don't be so profane. Remember you've just come from the graveyard." "Come from it! By fire! There was a time there when I'd have been willin' to go to it—yes, and stay."

3 Any of var children's games; see quots.

1891 *Jrl. Amer. Folkl.* 4.237 **Brooklyn NYC,** *Fire* is a game in which the new boy is made a fireman, who is sent in search of a fire; and when he cries out, as he has been instructed, "Fire! fire! fire!" the others come running from their engine-house, and salute him with a shower of stones. **1950** *WELS (Games . . played during your childhood),* 1 Inf, **ceWI,** "Fire" or "police"—a rather sadistic game in which "it" chases the other players with a stick. When he catches a player he has the privilege of hitting him as hard as he pleases.

‡4 See quot.

1896 *DN* 1.417 **RI,** *Fire:* a child's apron.

5 See quot.

1936 *AmSp* 11.315 **Ozarks,** *A Fire Of Wood.* . . A small 'jag' of firewood, just enough to cook one meal.

6 in phr *put a fire out:* See quot.

1952 Brown *NC Folkl.* 1.540, *Fire, to put a ——— out.* . . To set a fire to a field or the woods, generally with an incendiary intent. The standard meaning, to extinguish a fire, is also used.

C As verb.

1a To set on fire; to burn as a way of clearing land or driving out animals; hence vbl n *firing.*

1633 in 1855 New Plymouth Colony *Records* 1.23 **MA,** Also, whensoever any are justly occasioned to fire the same [woods] at any other time, they shall give warning thereof to the neighbours about them. **1709** (1967) Lawson *New Voyage* 17 **NC, SC,** Some *Sewee Indians* [were] firing the Canes Swamps, which drives out the Game. **1835** (1927) Evans *Exped. Rocky Mts.* 196, It is the oppinion of many well acquainted with the praries that the anual fall fireing of them by the Indian has caused the scarcity of timber. **1872** *Newton Kansan* 21 Nov. 2/3 *(DAE),* Cannot those whole-sale destroyers of property be held responsible for their . . intentional . . firing prairie. **1950** *WELS (The children were playing with matches and they ——— the shed)* 5 Infs, **WI,** Fired. **1956** *Hall Coll.* **eTN,** There was one herd of cattle at Gregory Bald and another herd at Thunderhead. The herders burnt off the brush on top of the mountain. If they hadn't fired, they couldn't have herded Smoky Mountain. **1968** *DARE* Tape **IN**3, They knew someone was firing them [=houses].

b To set on fire, burn. [Calque from Haw *ahi* n 'fire', v 'to burn']

1972 Carr *Da Kine Talk* 130 **HI,** "Pele, she no good! She only fire us." The semantic range of the noun *fire* has been extended to include the meaning of a verb, 'to burn'.

2 To apply heat to; spec:

a To sterilize, cauterize.

1940 (1942) Clark *Ox-Bow* 172 **NV** (as of 1885), He washed the wound clean with whisky, but told me they'd have to fire it to prevent infection. They . . slowly heated a pistol barrel red hot in the flame. Then Gil and Moore held me down while the wound was burned. **1951** *PADS* 16.27, *Fire.* . . To cauterize an injury [on a horse].

b with *out:* See quot.

1968 Adams *Western Words* 113, *Fire out*—To alter a brand to indicate change in ownership.

c also with *up:* To dry (tobacco) with artificial heat; hence vbl n *firing.* Cf **fire-cure**

1854 in 1910 Commons *Doc. Hist. Amer. Industrial Soc.* 1.212 **SC coast,** Clean corn and grate guano this Morning with all hands untill eight oclock Rain untill that time fired Tobacco ploughed with Nine plows and suckered Tobacco the Balance of the day. [**1941** Writers' Program *Guide SC* 367, The farmer himself stays home 'to fire up the barn'. Huge stacks of wood decrease rapidly as the curing fires burn day and night [in tobacco barns].] **1944** *PADS* 2.66 **S Midl,** *Fire.* . . To cure or dry out tobacco by means of a fire in the barn. *Ibid* **sVA,** *Firing.* . . keeping a fire in the barn for curing tobacco. **1966** *PADS* 45.12 **KY,** We fire our tobacco when the weather is rainy. **1967** Key *Tobacco Vocab.* 90 **NC,** When they get the barn full, then they fire up on it; **TN,** Some fire it up when it isn't curing right; **KY,** Fire it. **1970** *DARE* Tape **VA**40, We would fire that tobacco; **KY**72, Too much dampness . . is overcome a lot of times by firing it with gas, or coke, or wood.

d with *down:* To preserve, can.

1941 Smith *Going to God's Country* 40 **MO** (as of 1890), There were so many things to do in the winter. There was buchering [sic]. And lard to make. And sausage and sage to make. A lot of meat to be fired down in big jars for sumer use. A lot more . . hung up in the smoke house and smoked for sumer use too.

3 To tend a fire; to tend the fire of or for; to serve as a fireman on a locomotive, ship, etc.

1943 in 1953 Botkin–Harlow *Treas. Railroad Folkl.* 297, I was working in the [railroad] shop until I could persuade John Bailey to send me out firing again. **1947** *PADS* 8.6 **VT** [In maple sugar industry], *Fire.* . . To take care of the fire used in boiling the syrup. **1967–68** *DARE* Tapes **GA**22, I fired a pile-driver; **MI**54, Then I went firin' on the boats [in the Great Lakes]; **WA**24, He was firing donkey [=a donkey engine]; **TX**35, She wouldn't let me fire it [=a kettle of cane syrup] because I wouldn't fire it to suit her. She'd just fire it herself, but I'd cut pine and put it . . in for her.

4 Of sea water: to phosphoresce; hence vbl n *firing.* Cf **B1** above

1880 *Harper's New Mth. Mag.* Sept 511/2 **ME coast,** The schools [of fish] worked nearer the top at night, and their presence was betrayed by a phosphorescent "firing" in the water. **1905** Wasson *Green Shay* 70 **NEng,** Look how the water fires [Footnote: To sparkle with phosphorescence] to-night, will ye? **1978** Merriam *Illustr. Lobstering* 36 **ME,** *Firing*—Phosphorescence in the water caused by dinoflagellates (small marine organisms). On calm nights when they are active any motion in the water stirs them and causes a brilliant shining. The brightness makes looking for herring easier.

5 To throw, fling. **chiefly Nth**

1872 Schele de Vere *Americanisms* 471, *Fire,* to, a term very generally used for to throw. "The boys were firing stones at the house at a great rate, and, after a while, the negroes began firing back with rocks, chunks, and broken bricks." **1905** *DN* 3.9 **cCT,** *Fire.* . . To fling with the hand. **1907** *DN* 3.212 **nwAR. 1943** *LANE* Map 667 1 inf, **nwVT,** He fired a stone at the dog. **1951** *Eaton Coll.* **Washington Island WI,** I should have fired the eggs when I started to fall (instead of getting myself hurt). **1965–70** *DARE* (Qu. Y10, . . *He picked up a stone and ——— it at him)* 12 Infs, **chiefly Nth,** Fired; (Qu. C24b, . . *He took a stone . . and ——— [it])* Infs **NY**23, 209, **OH**3, 12, **WA**2, **WI**58, Fired; **MA**100, Throw, fire, scale, skip a stone.

6 also with *out:* To eject, kick out.

1885 *Milner* (Dakota) *Free Press* 25 Apr. 5/2 *(OED),* If . . the practice is persisted in, then they [pupils] should be fired out. **1897** Lummis *King of Broncos* 101 **NM,** He always guarded them [=his belongings] jealously against tramps who were "fired from the train" and haunted the cañon to "jump" another. **1922** *DN* 5.162, *Fire.* . . To expel or order from a classroom. **1927** *DN* 5.446 [Underworld jargon], *Fire.* . . To throw a man off a train. **c1960** *Wilson Coll.* **csKY,** *Fire.* . . To put someone out, bodily, from a place.

7 To reject, jilt (a person).

1941 *LANE* Map 407A *(She refused him)* 1 inf, **csCT,** *Fired him, bounced him,* jocular, quite common; 2 infs, **ceMA, cwVT,** Fired him. **1973** Allen *LAUM* 1.373 **IA** (as of c1950), [In context *She turned him down*] Fired him. [2 infs]

8 with *on* or *up:* To strike, hit, fight with.

1972 Claerbaut *Black Jargon* 64, *Fired (me) up* . . to strike another physically. . . *He fired me up! Ibid, Fired on* . . to hit or strike another physically: *The cat fired on him.* **1980** Folb *Runnin' Down* 56 **Los Angeles CA** [Black], Don' be callin' no ese [=Chicano] Cholo or Chico if you don' be knowin' d' dude, 'cause he'll righteously fire on you. *Ibid* 75, Got belligerent, wanted to thump [=fight]. . . So, I jus' fired on 'im. *Ibid* 237, *Fire (on one).* . . See *blaze on (one).* [*Ibid* 229, *Blaze on (one).* . . Hit one quickly or unexpectedly. . . Knock one down.]

9 To crack (a whip). [*DJE* 1828 →]

1967 *DARE* Tape **AZ**9, He raised the whip back and was just going to fire it.

10 also with *up;* Of crops: to turn yellow prematurely, from excessive rain, heat, or drought; hence ppl adj *fired* withered or dried out from such conditions; vbl n *firing.* **chiefly S Midl**

1770 (1925) Washington *Diaries* 1.394 **VA,** Why Corn in so short a drought shou[l]d fire so badly is difficult to Acc[oun]t for. **1800** in 1969 Herndon *Wm. Tatham Tobacco* 22 **VA,** The plant is subject to a malady called *firing.* This is a kind of blight occasioned by . . the too moist condition of the plant. **1856** in 1956 Eliason *Tarheel Talk* 271 **NC,** The corn on Belgrade is fired veary bad. **1902** *DN* 2.234 **sIL,** *Fired*. . . Blasted as by fire. Plants turned yellow by heat or drought are said to be *fired*. **1903** *DN* 2.313 **seMO,** *Fire*. . . To turn yellow prematurely as wheat or corn. Caused by drought or continued rain. **1906** *DN* 3.118 **sIN,** *Fired*. . . Colored as if burnt, as of autumn coloring. "The corn is fired." **1944** *PADS* 2.56 **MO,** "Dad says that north field of corn is sure to fire if it don't rain soon." Pike Co. Common. *Ibid*, 66 **S Midl,** *Fire*. **1954** *Harder Coll.* **cwTN,** Mah corn's done fared up. Won't make seed back. **c1960** *Wilson Coll.* **csKY,** *Fire*. **1966** *PADS* 45.12 **KY,** If you get too much rain late in the season, the tobacco may fire. **1966** *Russell Rec.* (KS) 11 Aug 7/2, Sorghums were in fair to good condition but dry weather was causing many fields to curl and some fields were firing.

11 with *up;* Of fog: to dissipate. Cf **burn v B3, Indian fire**

1967 *DARE* (Qu. B19, *When fog begins to go up into the air, you say it's* ______) Inf **TN**14, The fog's gonna fire up.

fire and brimstone See **fire B2a**

fire and tow n Rarely *fire in tow* [See quot 1984; cf *EDD* "of a hasty person: irascible" (at *fire* sb. 4) and obs proverb "*Do not put fire to flax* or *tow*" (*OED* at *fire* sb. A. 1. h)] **chiefly NEng, S Midl, Sth**

Fig; in phr *all fire and tow:* irascible, excitable.

[**1834** Davis *Letters Downing* 253 **NY,** They . . got up some letters full of fire, and toe, and brimstone, and bloody murder agin the Gineral.] **1838** (1843) Haliburton *Clockmaker* (2d ser) 152 **NEng,** To the court they are as cool as cucumbers. . . To the jury, all fire and tow and declamations. **1884** Jewett *Mate of Daylight* 7 **ME,** Just like Dan's nonsense, all fire and tow! [*DARE* Ed: In ref to a man who became angry and went out in a fishing boat in bad weather.] **1953** *PADS* 19.10 **NC,** *Fire and tow*. . . Hot-tempered. "She's all fire and tow." **1956** McAtee *Some Dialect NC* 15, *Fire and tow, all*. . . Excitable, hot-tempered. **c1960** *Wilson Coll.* **csKY,** *Fire in tow:* . . High-tempered, quick to explode. Said of cow, person, or any other creature. Also *fire and tow*. **1984** Wilder *You All Spoken Here* 14 **Sth,** *All fire and tow:* About to explode. "Tow" is a fiber of flax, hemp, and jute good for starting fires and used for patches in firing muzzle-loading rifles.

fire ant n [See quot 1980]

An ant, usu *Solenopsis geminata*.

1957 *Time* 18 Mar 84/3, The South, long inured to red bugs, screwworms, . . and other varmints, irritably recognized last week that it had a new pest on its hands: the fire ant. Reddish and only ¼-in. long, the fire ant has a peculiar talent: it chews a slit in the skin of its victim, lifts the skin with its mandibles, curves its abdomen under its body and injects a dose of fluid which causes fiery pain . . [and] raises angry welts. **1965–70** *DARE* (Qu. R18, . . *Kinds of ants*) 76 Infs, **chiefly Gulf States, S Atl,** Fire ant; (Qu. R17, . . *Big black ants that sting*) Infs **GA**46, **KY**24, **LA**18, 23, **SC**69, Fire ants; (Qu. R22, *Very small red insects . . that get under your skin and cause itching*) Inf **PA**168, Fire ants. **1980** Milne–Milne *Audubon Field Guide Insects* 831, *Fire Ant (Solenopsis geminata)*. *Ibid* 832, Fire Ants sting and bite, producing a burning sensation like fire, inspiring the common name. **1982** Heat Moon *Blue Highways* 136 **TX,** That stirred a conversation on methods of putting away kittens, and that led to methods of killing fire ants. The man beside me said, "I've got the best way to kill far ants, and it ain't by diggin' or poison." No one paid attention. Finally he muttered, "Pour gasoline into the hive."

fireback See **firebug 2**

fireball n

1 See quots.

1890 Howells *Boy's Town* 128 **sOH,** Maybe the boys nowadays do not throw fire-balls, or know about them. They were made of cotton rags wound tight and sewed, and then soaked in turpentine. When a ball was lighted a boy caught it quickly up, and threw it and it made a splendid streaming blaze through the air, and a thrilling whir as it flew. **1967** Williams *Greenbones* 13 **GA** (as of c1910), Someone shouted, "Fireball!" and a flashing ball spun out of the dark. It was the great ball of rags that Nin had seen, soaked for several days in kerosene, allowed to dry, now set alight. A circle of young men had formed, and the ball spun toward a tall light-skinned youth who caught it between both palms and cast it away almost before it touched, across the ring to a friend.

2 **=will-o'-the-wisp.** Cf **fire B1**

1966–68 *DARE* (Qu. CC16, *A small light that seems to dance or flicker over a marsh or swamp at night*) Infs **HI**9, **PA**133, Fireball; **MS**33, Fireball, foxfire, jack-o-lantern; **WI**64, Indians say *fireballs*, sailors say *St. Elmo's fire*, farmers say *foxfire*.

3 The maltese cross *(Lychnis chalcedonica)*.

1889 *Century Dict.* 2228/2, *Fire-ball*. . . The scarlet lychnis, *Lychnis Chalcedonica*. **1892** *Garden and Forest* 5.614, Red Lychnis . . in Ohio, Fireballs. **1892** *Jrl. Amer. Folkl.* 5.93 **OH,** *Lychnis chalcedonica*, sweetwilliam. . . Fire balls. Mansfield, O. **1959** Carleton *Index Herb. Plants* 46, Fire Ball: . . *Lychnis chalcedonica*.

4 **=summer cypress.**

1914 Georgia *Manual Weeds* 107, *Fireball. Kochia Scoparia*. *Ibid* 108, Wherever this plant is established as a weed it has usually first been cultivated in gardens for its bright coloring in autumn. **1935** (1943) Muenscher *Weeds* 213, Fireball. . . Widespread, but most common in fields; mostly on dry soils. **1959** Carleton *Index Herb. Plants* 46, *Fire ball:* Kochia trichophylla; Lychnis chalecedonica. **1964** Kingsbury *Poisonous Plants U.S.* 43, *Kochia scoparia*. Fireball. **1975** Logan *Land Remembers* 165 **swWI** (as of c1920), We argued half the summer about whether the red flowers should be called Indian paintbrush, red-hot poker, fireball, or scarlet cup.

5 A salmon egg.

1969 *DARE* FW Addit **AZ,** Salmon eggs [used for fish bait] are colored red; hence, their nickname *fireballs*.

fire basket n

A metal support for firewood in a fireplace.

1950 *WELS (The metal stands in a fireplace)* 1 Inf, **WI,** Fire basket. **1967–68** *DARE* (Qu. D32) Inf **IA**25, *Andirons* [is] old-fashioned, *fire dogs* [is] old-fashioned, *fire basket* [is] the modern thing; **MI**69, Fire basket.

fire birch n

=gray birch a.

1979 Little *Checklist U.S. Trees* 63, *Betula populifolia* . . gray birch . . *Other common names* . . fire birch.

firebird n

1 An oriole, usu the **Baltimore oriole.** [See quot 1808]

1778 in 1789 Anburey *Travels* 2.198 **CT,** The most remarkable are the Fire-bird, Hanging-bird, Blue-bird and Humming-bird. **1808** Wilson *Amer. Ornith.* 1.23, *Oriolus Baltimore*. . . *Baltimore Bird* is generally known, and, as usual, honored with a variety of names, such as Hangnest, Hanging-bird, Golden Robin, Fire-Bird (from the bright orange seen through the green leaves resembling a flash of fire). **1824** Irving *Tales of a Traveller* 2.357 **NY,** The fire-bird [Footnote: Orchard oreole] streamed by them with his deep red plumage. **1917** (1923) *Birds Amer.* 2.258, Baltimore Oriole. *Icterus galbula*. . . Other names.—Golden Robin; . . Fire-bird; Pea-bird. **1956** MA Audubon Soc. *Bulletin* 40.130, *Baltimore oriole*. . . Fire Bird (Mass., R.I.)

2 **=scarlet tanager.**

1844 DeKay *Zool. NY* 2.176, *The Black-winged Red-bird [Pyranga rubra]*, or *Fire-bird* and *Tanager*, as it is often called in this State, . . is a shy solitary bird, breeding in this State. **1917** (1923) *Birds Amer.* 3.79, *Piranga erythromelas* . . Firebird. **1917** *Wilson Bulletin* 29.2.83, *Piranga erythromelas*.—Fire bird. **1963** Gromme *Birds WI* 214, Firebird *[Piranga erythromelas]*.

fireboard n

1 A mantel over a fireplace. [See quot 1984] **chiefly S Midl** See Map *chiefly among speakers with little formal educ* Cf **mantelpiece**

1886 *S. Bivouac* 4.350 **sAppalachians,** Fire-board (mantle-piece). **1915** *DN* 4.183 **swVA,** *Fire-board*. . . Framework around a fire-place, usually a shelf. **1933** *AmSp* 8.2.28 **eKY,** To this day his folks cook at the open fireplace and cut pumpkin in rings and dry it on a stick suspended from the *foir-board* (the mantel). **1941** Writers' Program *Guide AR* 298, An ancient clock on the mantle above the fireplace ("fireboard," they call it). **1948** *AmSp* 23.194 **SC,** With little experience a speaker learns that the folk forms ['laɪtɚd], *lightwood*, and ['fɑɚ,boɚd], *fireboard*, do not have the prestige of the corresponding standard forms *kindling* and *mantelpiece*. **1949** Kurath *Word Geog.* 51, The South Midland, including the drainage basin of the Kanawha, has the distinctive expression *fire board*, which has spread down to the Atlantic between the Cape Fear and the Peedee rivers. **1955** Roberts *S. from Hell-fer-Sartin* 5 **seKY,** The fireboard above the archrock is covered with spools of thread, boxes of notions, a carbide lamp, and an old ticking clock. **c1960** *Wilson Coll.* **csKY,** *Fireboard*. . . Mantel or mantelpiece. Most common usage in area. **1965–70** *DARE* (Qu. D36, . . *The shelf over the fireplace*) 36 Infs, **chiefly S Midl,** Fireboard. [23 Infs were gs educ or less] **1984** *AmSp* 59.321, *Fire board* . . is clearly a sign of Scotch-Irish influence; *fire* *board* . . is recorded in the British Isles only in Ulster . . where it can still be heard.

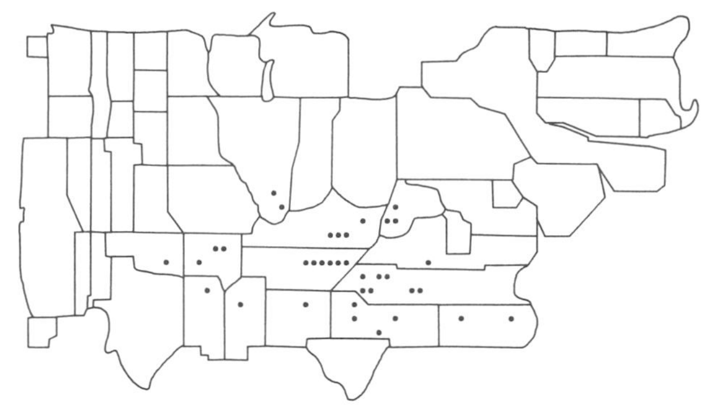

•fireboard 1 (Qu. D36)

2 See quot 1958.

1915 [see **1** above]. **1958** *PADS* 29.10 **TN,** *Fireboard:* Shelf above the fireplace. . . Sometimes *fireboard* seems to refer to the wood facing rather than the shelf of the fire place.

3 A covering for a fireplace opening; see quot 1974.

1857 (1949) Thoreau *Jrl.* 3 June **NEng,** Instead of . . sitting by the kitchen fire, you would be shown into a cold parlor, there to confront a fireboard. **1903** *DN* 2.297 **Cape Cod MA** (as of c1840), *Fireboard.* . . A wooden or sheet iron cover for the opening of a fireplace. **1938** FWP *Guide CT* 397, Raised paneling is used in the window blinds, fire boards, cupboards and doors. **1946** *PADS* 6.13 **NC, VA,** *Fire board.* . . A cover made of wood to conceal the fireplace when not in use. **1974** Lipman–Winchester *Folk Art* 191, During the summer season . . a fireboard served the practical purpose of sealing off the fireplace, keeping out dirt, soot and chimney swallows. Constructed of wide boards held together by sturdy battens on the back, the fireboard was always custom-made for its particular fireplace opening, and it was often painted by the same decorators who worked on the overmantels.

4 A piece of wood used as a platform on which to build a fire.

1938 Matschat *Suwannee R.* 184 **GA,** Diah lifted the fireboard from the bottom of the skiff, set it across the gunwales, and packed it with mud. Next, he gathered some . . branches . . [and] lighted his fire.

5 See quot.

1968 Adams *Western Words* 112, *Fire board*—In mining, a blackboard on which the *fire boss* . . indicates every morning the amount of gas present in different parts of the mine.

fire bob n [Cf *EDD bob* sb.[1] 9 "A small insect"] *obs*

=**firefly 1.**

1825 (1832) Pickering *Inquiries* 27 **MD,** I amused myself by observing the motions of the numerous "fire bobs" (flies) flashing in the air like candles.

fire, borrow See **fire, come to borrow**

fire boss n **Appalachians, West**

In coal mining: a safety inspector; see quots.

1883 Greeley *Glossary Coal Mining (DA), Fire-bosses* (U.S.A.), underground officials who examine the mine for gas, and inspect every safety-lamp taken into the colliery. **1917** Sinclair *King Coal* 30 **CO,** The "fire-boss" was supposed to make his rounds in the early morning, and the law specified that no one should go to work till he had certified that all was safe. **1938** *Sun* (Baltimore MD) 27 Aug 3/2 *(Hench Coll.),* In an address prepared for delivery at a conference of foremen, assistant foremen and fire bosses, called by Southwestern Virginia coal operators, Morton [=the Virginia State Labor Commissioner] thanked those attending for cooperation with his [safety] inspectors. **1968** Adams *Western Words* 112, *Fire boss*—In mining, an underground official who examines the mine for firedamp and has charge of its removal. **1970** *DARE* Tape **PA**245, There was what they called a fire boss. He was assistant mine foreman. **1973** *PADS* 59.36 **Appalachians, OH,** *Fire boss* . . a worker who carries a *safety lamp* throughout the *mine,* particularly to the working *faces,* before the day's work begins and shuts off all sections which are *gassy.*

firebox n

1 Any of var appurtenances of a wood-burning stove, spec:

a An ashpan. **esp Sth, S Midl**

1966–69 *DARE* (Qu. F12, *The flat metal piece below a wood-burning stove, to catch the ashes*) Infs **AR**38, **CA**132, **FL**8, **MO**32, **VA**22, **WV**3, Firebox.

b See quot.

1981 *KS Qrly.* 13.2.66, *Fire box* . . a low sand-filled wooden box frame on the floor of a bunkhouse that the wood stove sits in for protection against fire.

c A woodbin.

1966 *DARE* (QR, near Qu. F14) Inf **AR**17, Firebox—a place to store wood for the stove. **1986** Pederson *LAGS Concordance,* 1 inf, **nwAR,** Firebox—to put wood in.

2 A box in which a fire can be built. Cf **fire stand**

1960 Williams *Walk Egypt* 218 **GA,** Toy remembered the gathering under the trees, the fireboxes flaring in the dark and warning how Hell looked, the people shouting and praying, dancing in the aisles and jerking.

3 Fig: one's stomach.

1958 McCulloch *Woods Words* 62 **Pacific NW,** *Fire box*—Stomach; particularly the stomach of one who has just returned to camp from a week end in town.

fireboy n

In railroading: a fireman.

1916 *DN* 4.356, *Fireboy.* . . A locomotive fireman. Eastern. **1945** Hubbard *Railroad Ave.* 342. **1958** McCulloch *Woods Words* 62 **Pacific NW,** *Fire boy*—Fireman on a steam locie or donkey. **1976** Gould *Blackie's RR Hdbk.* 1.

firebrand n [Prob from the orange and yellow coloring]

The Blackburnian warbler *(Dendroica fusca).*

1917 (1923) *Birds Amer.* 3.137, *Dendroica fusca.* . . Firebrand.

fire-brew adj [Folk-etym for *fibroid*]

1937 in 1977 *Amer. Slave Suppl. 1* 1.331 **AL** [Black], A party by the name of Ira Bell Thomas suffered with fire-brew . . tumor in 1930.

firebug n

1 A **firefly 1. scattered, but chiefly Nth, PA** See Map Cf **lightning bug**

1789 Morse *Amer. Geog.* 62, Of the astonishing variety of *Insects* found in America, we will mention . . Fire Fly or Bug. **1877** J. M. Bailey *Folks in Danbury* 46 *(DA)* **NEng,** [The lamp] don't give more light than a fire-bug. **1939** *LANE* Map 238, 16 infs, **scattered NEng,** Firebug. **1949** Kurath *Word Geog.* 33, From the Susquehanna to the Allegheny River [in Pennsylvania] *fire bug* . . is a common expression for the lightning bug. *Fire bug* is probably a blend of *lightning bug* and *fire fly.* *Ibid,* Fig 142. [*DARE* Ed: The map shows *fire bug* concentrated in **PA,** occurring very rarely elsewhere in the eastern US. Apparently the *LANE* information was overlooked in compiling this map.] **1950** *WELS* 2 Infs, **seWI,** Firebug. **1965–70** *DARE* (Qu. R1) 36 Infs, **scattered, but chiefly Nth, PA,** Firebug. **1973** Allen *LAUM* 1.328, Wood reports it [=*firebug*] in the South, too, particularly in Mississippi, and Atwood finds it in Texas. [*DARE* Ed: Wood found *firebug* to occur in only 6% of the responses in **MS;** Atwood includes it in a list of words occurring only two to six

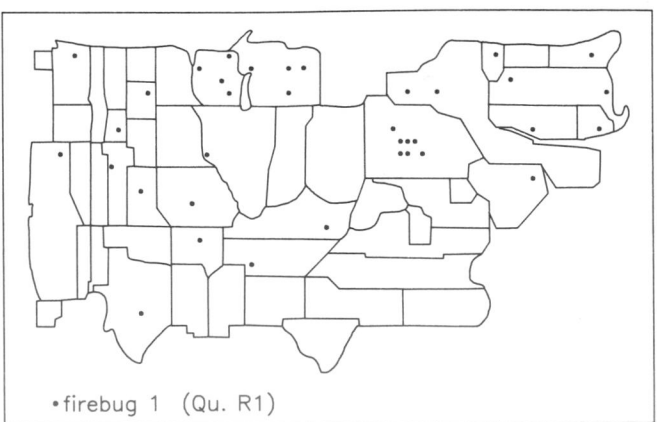

•firebug 1 (Qu. R1)

times.] Yet . . in the U[pper] M[idwest] its correlation is clearly Northern.

2 also *fireback:* =**harlequin cabbage bug.** [See quot 1980]

1924 U.S. Dept. Ag. *Farmers' Bulletin* 1371.18, The harlequin cabbage bug, also called the calico bug, fire bug, or terrapin bug, is about half an inch long and red, spotted with black. It is a southern insect, commonly found from Virginia to California, but often works northward. **1925** *Book of Rural Life* 1984, *Fireback,* one of the names by which the injurious *harlequin cabbage bug* is known. **1940** Teale *Insects* 188, Fire bug. . . Harlequin cabbage bug. **1949** *AmSp* 24.108 **nGA,** *Firebug*. . . A destructive species of insect, preying on cabbage leaves; same as *harlequin bug.* **1980** Milne-Milne *Audubon Field Guide Insects* 486, "Fire Bug". . . Jet-black with *bright yellow or orange marks above*. . . Nymph is shiny red and black.

fire bush n

1 A red-flowered shrub or small tree *(Hamelia patens)* native to southern Florida. [See quot 1953] Also called **scarlet bush.**

1933 Small *Manual SE Flora* 1258, *H[amelia] patens*. . . Sometimes popularly known as fire-bush on account of the red inflorescence. **1953** Greene-Blomquist *Flowers South* 121, Often called "firebush". . . The calyces as well as the branches of the inflorescences are also reddish in color. **1979** Little *Checklist U.S. Trees* 145, Firebush. . . Commonly a shrub in Fla. but recorded also as a small tree in Fla. Keys.

2 also *Mexican fire bush:* A **summer cypress** (here: *Kochia scoparia*). [See quot 1970]

1950 *WELS Suppl.* 1 Inf, **csWI,** Chicago fire—fire bush, Mexican fire bush; 1 Inf, **seWI,** Chicago fire—commonly, fire bush. **1968** *DARE* (Qu. S26e, *Other wildflowers*) Infs **MD**20, Fire bush. [FW: Fire bush is a green plant, with grass-like leaves; it turns red in the fall, lives until killed by frost.] **1970** Correll *Plants TX* 546, *Mexican fire-bush* . . is . . grown primarily for its globular dense habit and the foliage which turns purplish-red in autumn. Escaped from cult. in many areas of the U.S. **1976** Bailey-Bailey *Hortus Third* 626.

3 A **burning bush 1.**

1988 *DARE* File, [Radio:] Some people also call corkbark 'fire bush'.

fire cactus n [Perh from the color of the blossom]

Perh the firecracker cactus *(Cleistocactus baumanni).*

1969 *SC Market Bulletin* 24 July 4/4, Fire cactus, lg. cutting 75¢.

fire cake n *?obs* Cf **ashcake 1**

A rudimentary cake made of flour and water and baked before an open fire.

1777 in 1897 *PA Mag. Hist. & Biog.* 21.310, But why do I talk of hunger & hard usage, when so many in the World have not even fire Cake & Water to eat. **1906** *Pocumtuc Housewife* 22 **nwMA,** Make a paste like piecrust . . only use less lard. Roll out thin and cover plates with it. . . Put a row of flat irons around a brisk fire and set the plates against them. . . Brown [on both sides]. **1979** Amer. Heritage Soc. *Americana* Mar/Apr 70, [Glossary of military food:] *Fire cakes.* A crude flour-and-water concoction cooked on a heated stove. The term dates back to the Revolutionary War—fire cakes were eaten at Valley Forge.

fire cherry n [See quot 1896]

=**pin cherry.**

1896 *Jrl. Amer. Folkl.* 9.187, *Prunus Pennsylvanica* . . fire cherry, Franklin County, M[ain]e. . . Always appears on newly burned land. **1897** Sudworth *Arborescent Flora* 240, *Prunus pennsylvanica*. . . *Wild Red Cherry*. . . [Also called] Fire Cherry (N.Y.) **1937** *Hall Coll.* **eTN,** "The mountain's all kivered over with fire-cherry now" (several years after a fire). **1943** Peattie *Great Smokies* 162, When it is clean-cut or burned off, it is replaced by fire cherry, a worthless little weed of a tree under which the seeds of its noble predecessors do not readily germinate. **1944** ME Univ. *Studies* 59.26, *P[runus] pennslylvanica*. . . Pin, Wild Red, Bird, or Fire Cherry. Common; locally abundant in recent clearings, especially following fires. **1950** *WELS* 1 Inf, **cnWI,** *(Different kinds of wild cherries in your neighborhood)* Fire cherry, chokecherry, pin cherry. **1961** Douglas *My Wilderness* 172 **wNC,** The fire cherry and blackberry showed on open slopes. **1976** Bailey-Bailey *Hortus Third* 920.

fire, chew See **chew fire**

fire coal n Pronc-sp *farcoal* **chiefly S Midl**

A piece of charcoal; an ember.

1854 Shillaber *Life Partington* 310 **Boston MA,** O, you satan! see how you have tumbled my collar with your pesky nonsense; and my face burns like fire-coals. Right before a city gentleman too; O, for shame! **1899** (1912) Green *VA Folk-Speech* 174, *Fire-coal*. . . A coal of burnt wood. **1917** *DN* 4.412 **wNC,** *Fire-coal*. . . An ember. **c1938** in 1970 Hyatt *Hoodoo* 1.414 **seGA,** Yo' kin go in de left-hand side of yore fireplace an' take . . two fire coals an' . . put 'em in a little sack an' wear 'em in yore left pocket an' no one can't do yo' no harm. **1959** *Hall Coll.* **wNC,** Strain it [=moonshine] through them fire coals to take the vordegris [=verdigris] off. **1959** Roberts *Up Cutshin* 27 **eKY,** She would fill that thing full of dough, draw out the farcoals and make a place to set it, put it in the hot ashes. **1967** *DARE* FW Addit **LA**12, Fire coals ['faɪ,koUlz]—coals in the fireplace raked out to cook on. **1969** *Foxfire* Summer 13 **neGA,** The small box contained either "fire coals" (crushed charcoal) or a mixture of pokeberry juice and lime [for marking logs].

fire, come to borrow v phr For varr see quots **scattered, but esp S Midl**

To pay a very short visit.

1732 in 1893 MA Hist. Soc. *Coll.* 6th ser 6.212 **MA,** But he seem'd to come hither to fetch fire, & not to do business. **1831** in 1918 Ruffin *Papers* 2.31 **NC,** I shall be glad to see you in March: *do not come for a chunk of fire.* **1929** Dobie *Vaquero* 7 **SW,** If anybody wanted to "borrow" fire, he generally made his call brief. Hence arose the old saying, once common but now dying out, "You must have come after a chunk (or coal) of fire," in protest to a brief call. **1939** *AmSp* 14.265 **swIN,** 'Did you come to borrow fire?' . . [is] said to one making a call of very short duration. **1940** *AmSp* 15.446 **eTN,** To indicate a hasty visit. 'I came to borrow a coal of fire.' **1966-69** *DARE* (Qu. II14, *To pay a short visit: "Last night our new neighbors ______."*) Inf **TX**74, Came after a coal of fire; (QR, near Qu. II15) Inf **AR**3, "Did you come after a coal of fire?"—when people just stay a minute at your house. **1968** *DARE* FW Addit **ceVA,** If you pay a visit and your host suspects you've come to pay a very short call, he may ask, "Did you come to borrow a chunk of fire?" **1978** *AP Letters* **neGA** (as of c1900), Expressions . . of the pioneers . . from . . mountain and rural areas: . . A short visit brought the question, "Did you come after a chunk of fire?" **1989** *DARE* File **cAR,** My mother is very familiar with the expression "come to borrow a coal of fire" to mean that someone has come to the house for a specific purpose and leaves right away.

firecracker n

1 Appar a fuchsia.

1949 *WELS Suppl.* **csWI,** Firecracker was to us a house plant which had yellowish tipped red cylindrical blossoms about one inch in length and truly resembling firecrackers. These plants were not common, I think, for I remember seeing only two besides that of my mother.

2 See **firecracker flower 2.**

3 See **firecracker vine.**

4 A bean; see quots. [From the explosive sound of the flatulence produced] Cf **forty-four**

1956 Sorden-Ebert *Logger's Words* 14 **Gt. Lakes,** *Fire-crackers,* Beans. **1964** Clarkson *Tumult* 362 **WV,** *Fire-crackers*—Beans.

firecracker flower n [From the tubular red flowers]

1 also *firecracker plant:* A **brodiaea** (here: *Brodiaea ida-maia*).

1897 Parsons *Wild Flowers CA* 240, Upon the walls of such charming gorges the firecracker flower rears its slender stem and shakes out its bunch of brilliant crimson blossoms. **1911** Jepson *Flora CA* 100, *B[rodiaea] ida-maia*. . . Fire-cracker Plant. . . A showy and curious species. **1915** (1926) Armstrong-Thornber *Western Wild Flowers* 26, Fire-cracker Flower. . . bears a large cluster of six to thirteen flowers, one or two inches long, hanging on slender, reddish pedicels. **1949** Moldenke *Amer. Wild Flowers* 420, Firecrackerflower see *Brevoortia ida-maia* firecrackerplant. **1976** Bailey-Bailey *Hortus Third* 381, *Firecracker flower*. . . Perianth tube bright red. . . Ore., n. Calif.

2 also *firecracker, firecracker plant:* A **beardtongue,** either *Penstemon eatonii* or *P. utahensis.*

1941 Jaeger *Wildflowers* 231, *Eaton Firecracker. Penstemon Eatonii*. . . *Fl[ower]* scarlet. *Ibid* 234, *Utah Firecracker. Penstemon utahensis*. . . *Fl.:* scarlet-red. **1957** *Plateau* 30.32 **AZ,** Firecracker flowers *(Penstemon eatoni)* . . added their color to the background of red sandstone and red sand. **1957** Roberts-Nelson *Wildflowers CO* 41, *Penstemon eatoni*. . . "Firecracker plant" is an appropriate name. **1967** Dodge *Roadside Wildflowers* 65, One of these, *Penstemon eatoni,* is also known as Eaton's firecracker.

3 A **wild columbine** (here: *Aquilegia canadensis*).

1950 *WELS Suppl.* 1 Inf **csWI,** Firecracker flower. Wild columbine. It *does* bloom in late June and early July—red might seem fiery. **1988**

DARE File **csWI** (as of 1940s), *Firecracker flower* was one name for wild columbine in Dane County because they started to bloom around July 4.

firecracker plant n

1 See **firecracker flower 1, 2.**

2 =**red buckeye.** [See quot 1942]

1933 Small *Manual SE Flora* 822, *Ae[sculus] Pavia*. . . Firecracker-plant. Red-buckeye. Scarlet-buckeye. **1942** Van Dersal *Ornamental Amer. Shrubs* 191 *(DA)*, The red buckeye, *Aesculus pavia* . . has bright red clusters of small flowers that appear in March or April in the South and as late as June in the North. . . It is also known as scarlet buckeye and firecracker plant. **1960** Vines *Trees SW* 682, Some vernacular names in use for the plant *[Aesculus pavia]* are . . Firecracker-plant and Fish-poison-bush. **1979** Little *Checklist U.S. Trees* 46, *Red buckeye. . . Other common names* . . firecracker-plant.

3 The garden **sage** *(Salvia officinalis)*.

1950 *WELS Suppl.* 1 Inf **csWI,** Firecracker plant. . . Salvia. Bright red flowers that appear in late June and early July probably help these names in popularity. Salvia is a name not generally known.

firecracker vine n Also *firecracker* [Prob from the red flowers] Prob =**trumpet honeysuckle.**

1966 *DARE* Wildfl QR Pl.214A Inf **SC**41, Firecrackers; **WI**35, Firecracker vine. **1968** *DARE* FW Addit **LA**40, Firecracker vine—an occasional name for the vine called woodbine.

fire-cure v, hence ppl adj *fire-cured,* vbl n *fire-curing* Cf **air-cure, flue-cure**

To prepare tobacco by exposure to open fire and smoke.

1848 U.S. Patent Office *Annual Rept.* 170, The following experiment respecting the curing of tobacco . . shows that fire-curing is not necessary. **1881** U.S. Census Office *Prelim. Rept. Tobacco* 18, *Fire-cured fillers of the heavy tobacco districts* . . are employed in making a coarse, strong chewing-tobacco. **1940** [see **dark-fired**]. **1944** *PADS* 2.66 **sVA,** *Fire-cure*. . . To use artificial heat in the barn for curing tobacco. **1960** Heimann *Tobacco* 109, In addition to flue-curing, which applies heat without smoke, and the more natural air-curing, some tobaccos are smoked or fire-cured like smoked ham. **1966** *PADS* 45.12 **KY,** *Fire-cured*. . . Of tobacco: Cured by open fires on the floor of the barn. . . "They grow some fire-cured tobacco in the mountains." **1966–69** *DARE* Tape **KY**9, Other places, away from here, they're fire-cured; **FL**26A, Cigarette tobacco is fire-cured. . . You put it in the barn and have heaters you fire up and run the heat up so many degrees and cure it out in a week's time.

fired See **fire C10**

fire dart n

A **wax mallow** (here: *Malvaviscus arboreus*).

1982 Perry–Hay *Field Guide Plants* 66, *Malvaviscus arboreus*. . . Giant fire dart. . . *Flowers:* . . brilliant red, funnel-shaped but narrow at mouth like a loosely furled umbrella.

firedog n [*fire* + **dog** n[1] **B3**] **scattered, but esp freq sAppalachians, S Atl, Gulf States** See Map

=**andiron.**

1792 *Thomas' MA Spy or Worcester Gaz.* (MA) 1 Mar 3/1 **CT,** He soon disengaged himself [from the three ruffians], retreated to the hearth, caught a fire dog, which he threw with such force that he knocked down one of the ruffians. **1793** in 1956 Eliason *Tarheel Talk* 271 **NC,** Pr. fire Doggs. **1903** *DN* 2.313 **seMO.** **1907** *DN* 3.231 **nwAR, seMO.** **1933** *AmSp* 8.1.48 **Ozarks,** *Dog irons*. . . Rude andirons, made by the country blacksmiths. The term *firedogs* is also common. **1946** *PADS* 5.21 **VA,** *Firedogs* . . in the southern part of the Blue Ridge and all of the Piedmont. **1949** Kurath *Word Geog.* 51, *Fire dogs* [predominates] in South Carolina and the greater part of North Carolina. Scattered instances of *fire dogs* occur also in Eastern Pennsylvania, and the term is not unknown in New England. **1950** *WELS (The metal stands in a fireplace)* 13 Infs, **WI,** Firedogs. **c1960** *Wilson Coll.* **csKY,** *Firedogs*. . . Andirons; not so common as dogirons. **1965–70** *DARE* (Qu. D32) 114 Infs, **scattered, but esp freq sAppalachians, S Atl, Gulf States,** Firedogs; **FL**31, Firedog. **c1970** Pederson *Dial. Survey Rural GA* **seGA,** [39 of 64 infs offered *fire dogs* as the term for iron supports in a fireplace.]

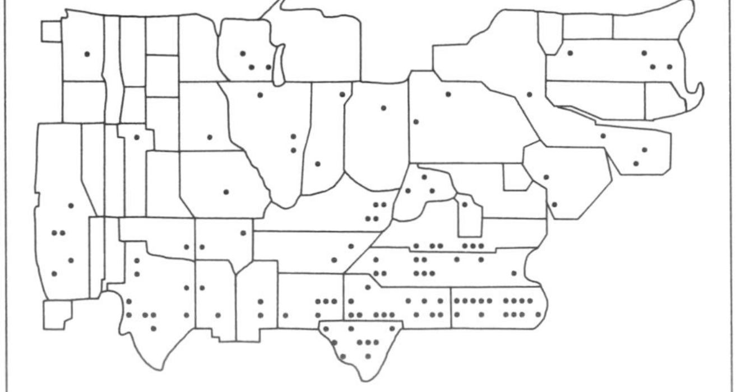

•firedog (Qu. D32)

fire down See **fire C2d**

fire-drawing See **draw fire**

firefang v, hence ppl adj *firefanged* [*OED* 1513 →; "*Obs.* exc. *dial.*" *OEDS* includes 1896 quot below.] *arch*

To become damaged by excessive heat.

1839 Buel *Farmer's Companion* 69 **NY,** The dung . . is apt to heat and become *fire-fanged.* **1896** VT State Bd. Ag. *Rept. for 1895* 15.72, There is danger if ensilage contains more than 25 per cent of dry matter that it will fire-fang in the silo. **1899** (1912) Green *VA Folk-Speech* 175, It has been so hot and dry that the corn is fire-fanged.

fire-fishing vbl n Cf **fire jack**

The practice of fishing at night, using fire for illumination.

[**1841** Bonnycastle *Canadas* 2.6, We went to see two of the *voyageurs* launch the canoe for the purpose of fire-fishing. This sport is pursued by placing over the bow a bundle of bark, pine-knots full of turpentine, or other combustible wood, and then paddling slowly over the water.] **1870** Nowland *Early Indianapolis* 97, He had several ways of fishing, but his favorite was fire-fishing. He would build a platform on the bow of his canoe; on this he would build a fire, the reflection of which would show him the fish at the bottom of the deepest water. **1936** *AmSp* 11.315 **Ozarks,** *Fire Fishing*. . . The practice of spearing or gigging fish at night, with burning pine knots for illumination. **1941** Writers' Program *Guide IN* 209 (as of c1820), Indian settlements were near by, and at night the lights of 'fire fishing' parties could be seen on the streams.

fire flag n

A large-leaved plant *(Thalia geniculata)* of the arrowroot family.

1975 Natl. Audubon Soc. *Corkscrew* 12 **FL,** *Fire Flags (Thalia geniculata)*—The large broad leaves atop slender stalks give this plant its name of "flag." During most of the year the light green foliage and tall bloom stalks (up to 10 feet) are a prominent feature of Florida's wet lands.

fireflower n

1 =**fire-on-the-mountain.**

1959 Carleton *Index Herb. Plants* 46, *Fire-flower:* Euphorbia heterophylla. **1975** Thomas *Hear the Lambs* 26 **nwAL,** Dat big red bloom by de chimley, it's a devil-in-de-bush, and some calls it de fire flower.

2 A **fireweed.**

1966 *DARE* Wildfl QR Pl.144B *[Chamaenerion angustifolium]*, Inf **MN**14, Fireflower. **1968** *DARE* (Qu. S26a, . . *Roadside flowers*) Inf **CT**11, Fireflower.

firefly n

1 A winged nocturnal light-producing insect of the families Lampyridae and Phengodidae. **widespread, but less freq Sth, S Midl** See Map Also called **candle fly, fire bob, firebug 1, glowworm, jack-o-lantern, lamp bug, lightning bug, light bug, will-o-the-wisp**

1682 in 1836 Carroll *Hist. Coll. SC* 2.74, There are in Carolina great numbers of Fire Flies, who carry their Lanthorns in their Tails in dark Nights. **1852** (1925) Browning *Diary* 52 **KY,** At night saw fire flies for first time this season. **1912** *DN* 3.581 **wIN,** *Lightnin(g)-bug*. . . A firefly. In some localities *firefly* is unknown. **1949** Kurath *Word Geog.* 17, *Fire fly* . . is a common rival of *lightning bug* in all of New England except western Vermont. . . In New York State, . . *lightning bug* . . has largely eliminated *fire fly*. . . [I]n New York and in Philadelphia *fire fly* has considerable currency among the better educated, since it is supported by literary usage. As far as Philadelphia is concerned, *fire fly* may be old in part, since the term appears on the conservative Jersey side of Delaware Bay. **1950** *WELS (A small insect that flashes light at its tail)* 14 Infs, **WI,** Firefly; 22 Infs, Firefly or lightning bug; 13 Infs, Lightning bug. **1962** Atwood *Vocab. TX* 58, *Lightning bug* . . is very heavily favored; the alternate *firefly* . . is distinctly an educated variant. *Ibid*

109, Lack of direct acquaintance with the rural scene probably also accounts for the increasing use of such book words as *firefly*. *Ibid* 122, [*Firefly* is included in a table showing highest frequency of usage in the younger groups of speakers.] **1965–70** *DARE* (Qu. R1) 288 Infs, **widespread, but less freq Sth, S Midl,** Firefly. **1973** Allen *LAUM* 1.328 (as of c1950), U[pper] M[idwest] infs. rather evenly divide their responses between older *firefly* and the Americanism *lightning bug*. . . *firefly* is more strongly favored by Type II speakers [=mid-aged, with approx hs educ] than by older and less educated Type I, though not by the small sample of college graduates. . . [In checklist responses] *firefly* dominates the Northern area and *lightning bug* the Midland area. *Ibid* 329, [One inf comments that *firefly* is] "One of those real swell persnickety names." **1977–78** Foster *Lexical Variation* 47 **NJ,** College-educated informants are . . perhaps twice as likely [as non-college-educated informants] to use *firefly*. . . The data . . supports the notion that *firefly* has positive cultural prestige but fails to find much evidence that the word is used by individuals to enhance their own social status.

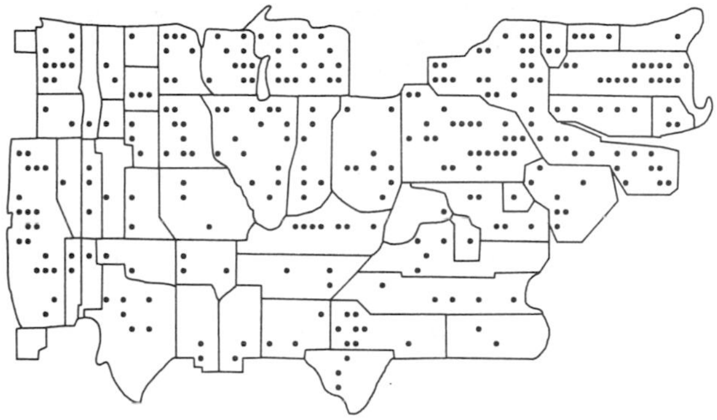

•firefly 1 (Qu. R1)

‡2 =cardinal 1.

1911 (1916) Porter *Harvester* 40 **IN,** "How long before you begin your house, old fire-fly?" he inquired of a flaming cardinal tilting on a twig.

3 Blue waxweed (here: *Cuphea viscosissima*).

1955 *S. Folkl. Qrly.* 19.235 **FL,** And the *Fire-Fly* (Cuphea petiolata) has attractive red flowers, suggestive of the light given off by the fire fly.

4 A kind of mushroom. Cf **jack-o-lantern**

1968 *DARE* (Qu. S19) Inf **WV7,** Firefly—the name of a mushroom. The 'fire' is the fungi growing on it that makes it glow at night.

fire grass n

1 A **fireweed** or similar plant. [See quot a1817]

a1817 (1822) Dwight *Travels* 4.61 **nNY,** Immediately after the fires, a species of grass springs up, sometimes called fire grass, because it usually succeeds a conflagration. **1969** *DARE* (Qu. S9, . . *Kinds of grass that are hard to get rid of*) Inf **MA**68, Fire grass.

2 A **beardgrass** (here: *Andropogon cabanisii*).

1971 Craighead *Trees S. FL* 200, Firegrass, *Andropogon cabonisii* [sic].

fireguard n Cf **fire stop**

A firebreak.

1874 McCoy *Cattle Trade* 217 **wKS,** An impassable barrier would be created between the unburned grass within the encircled tract, and that upon the outside of the 'fire-guard.' **1928** *Ruppenthal Coll.* **KS,** *Fire-guard*. . . On prairie, in fields, in forests,—a space made bare of combustibles, whether by plowing the land, or clearing off . . all vegetation. **1937** Sandoz *Slogum* 180 **NE** (as of c1900), The two had even ploughed all the fireguards. . . They cut the guards extra wide around the winter pasture and the hay flats, for the prairie was dry and the enemies plentiful. **1968** Adams *Western Words* 113, *Fireguard*—A firebreak made by plowing two parallel sets of furrows about 50 yards apart with four furrows in each set. The grass between the sets is burned by men trailed by water-laden wagons.

fire hangbird n [From the orange color of the male and the suspended nest] **esp NEng**

=Baltimore oriole.

1844 DeKay *Zool. NY* 2.139, The *Oriole, Hang-bird, Fire Hang-bird,* or *Golden Robin* . . is known under all these names. **1867** Holmes *Guardian Angel* 32 **NEng,** It was natural enough that Cyprian Eveleth should have called her the fire-hang-bird, and her little chamber the fire-hang-bird's nest,—using the country boy's synonyme for the Baltimore oriole. **1891** Cooke *Huckleberries* 179 **NEng,** More pernickity 'n a fire-hang-bird. **1932** Bennitt *Check-list* 58 **MO,** *Baltimore oriole. Icterus galbula* . . fire hang-bird. **1946** Hausman *Eastern Birds* 556, The Fire Hang-birds' long purse-like, gray, pendent nests are familiar objects dangling from long drooping elm branches along our roadways. **1956** MA Audubon Soc. *Bulletin* 40.130, *Baltimore oriole*. . . Fire Hangbird (Mass. The nest is suspended.)

fire hearth n Pronc-sp *fire herth* [*OED* c1440–1769] **chiefly Sth** *esp freq among Black speakers*

A hearth.

1966–70 *DARE* (Qu. D31, *In front of a fireplace there's usually stonework on the floor—what do you call this?*) Infs **DC**3, **GA**4, **LA**6, Fire herth; **AL**14, 61, **NY**90, Fire hearth. [5 of 6 Infs Black]

fire-hunt v, hence vbl n *fire-hunting* **chiefly Sth, Midl** Cf **fire-lighting** vbl n, **jacklight** v, **shine** v

To hunt animals at night by shining light in their eyes; also n *fire hunt*.

1814 *Sporting Mag.* 44.62/2, The method of approaching . . the red deer . . by means of *fire-hunting them*, (which is a well-known custom in the Southern Provinces of America, and in constant practice) is invaluable. **1844** Hawks *Advent. Boone* 21 **eTN,** Two people are always necessary for a fire-hunt. One goes before, carrying a blazing torch of pitch-pine wood . . , while the other follows behind with his rifle. **1859** Taliaferro *Fisher's R.* 155 **nwNC** (as of 1820s), I don' 'clude I'll fire-hunt no more. **1891** *Outing* Dec 236/1 **cMS,** No sooner had he eaten his supper each day than he began to importune the younger men of the party to join him in a "fire hunt". . . Beverly carried the gun, his chief the torch, consisting of "lightwood" knots blazing in the bowl of a long-handled frying pan. **1942** Rawlings *Cross Creek* 158 **nFL,** Now you know the law says you can't fire-hunt deer at night. **1966–70** *DARE* (Qu. P35b, *Illegal methods of shooting deer*) 14 Infs, **chiefly Sth, Midl,** Fire-hunting. **1966** *DARE* Tape **FL**37, [Inf:] I went with him fire-hunting at night. [FW:] Now what's that? [Inf:] Oh, at night take a headlight and go out and hunt deer.

fire insurance Christian n *joc*

1928 *Ruppenthal Coll.* **KS,** Fire insurance Christians . . persons whose value of Christianity is the belief that it will save them from fiery hell, or from punishment hereafter.

fire-in-the-bush n

A shrub of the genus *Chaenomeles.*

1940 *Hench Coll.* **cwVA,** *Fire-in-the-bush:* . . Either flowering quince or apple japonica—I'm not sure which. The one that has the blossoms inside the foliage. . . Heard the phrase in Arnold's Valley, which is near Natural Bridge.

fire in the hole exclam [See quot 1974 Maurer–Pearl]

Used among moonshiners as a warning that law officers are near.

1963 Carson *Social Hist. Bourbon* 110 **sAppalachians,** The arrival of federal men in the vicinity was announced by the cry, "Fi-i-i-ire in the hole!" the traditional warning of the moonshiner. **1974** Maurer–Pearl *KY Moonshine* 118, *Fire in the hole!* . . Local warning cry, especially on Coe Ridge in Cumberland County, Kentucky, and elsewhere near the Tennessee line, heard immediately after word has spread that the "law's in." Called in a high-pitched, far-carrying yodel, it is necessary to know the words in order to understand them. Adapted from the coal mines, where it is used to indicate that the fuse has been lit and a powder charge is about to explode. **1974** Dabney *Mountain Spirits* xxi, Fire in the hole = a term some moonshine families in Kentucky used to signal their men that the "law" was near.

‡fire in the mountains n

1967 *DARE* (Qu. EE1, *What games do children play around here, in which they form a ring, and either sing or recite a rhyme?*) Inf **CA**4, Fire in the mountains.

fire in tow See **fire and tow**

fire iron n

1 also *fireplace iron:* An **andiron.** **chiefly Gulf States, S Atl, N Cent** See Map

1871 (1882) Stowe *Fireside Stories* 5 **NEng,** He had brushed over and under and between the fire-irons. **1946** *PADS* 5.21 **VA,** *Fire irons* . . not common. **c1960** *Wilson Coll.* **csKY,** *Fire irons*. . . Andirons; the least-used term, so far as I can tell. **1965–70** *DARE* (Qu. D32)

18 Infs, **chiefly Gulf States, S Atl, N Cent,** Fire irons; **MA**55, Fireplace irons. **c1970** Pederson *Dial. Surv. Rural GA* **seGA,** [4 of 64 infs used *fire irons* to refer to metal supports for wood in a fireplace.] **1971** Bright *Word Geog. CA & NV* 143, Nevada had . . one [response] of *fire irons.*

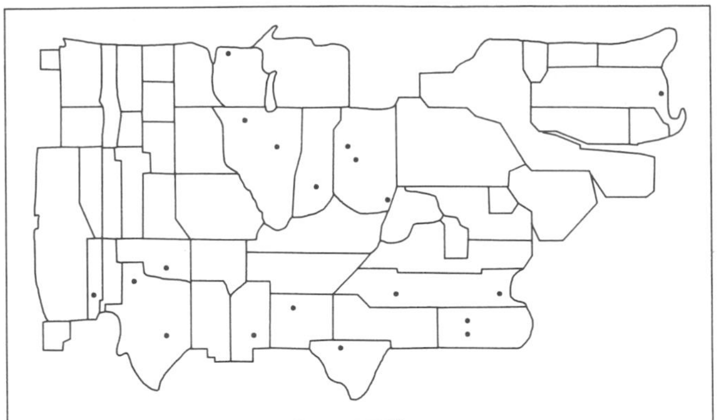

•fire iron 1 + var (Qu. D32)

2 A flatiron. **scattered, but esp Inland Sth**

1965–70 *DARE* (Qu. F29, . . *Irons—not electric—used around here for smoothing clothes after they're washed*) 14 Infs, Fire irons.

3 also *firing iron:* A gun.

1911 *DN* 3.550 **WY,** *Fire-iron(s),* gun. **1968** *DARE* (Qu. P37a, *Nicknames for a rifle*) Inf **CT**14, Firing iron; (Qu. P37b, *Nicknames for a shotgun*) Inf **CT**14, Firing iron; **MD**32, A shootin' iron, fire iron.

fire jack n [**jack** n]

=**fire pan.**

1933 Williamson *Woods Colt* 222 **Ozarks,** What makes the fire is in the middle o' the skift, pine knots burnin' in a fire jack, a kind of a iron basket on the end of a iron rod that sets down into the boat an' fastens there. The glare from the pine knots makes enough light for ye to see the fish, then down you jab with your gig pole.

fireleaf n

=**golden club 1.**

1927 Boston Soc. Nat. Hist. *Proc.* 230, *Orontium aquaticum* 'Never-wet'; 'fire-leaf.'

fire ledge n

A mantel over a fireplace.

1973 Allen *LAUM* 1.162 (as of c1950), Single instances of these appeared: . . *fire ledge* in Minnesota.

fire-lighting vbl n **esp NC** See Map Cf **fire-hunt**

Hunting animals at night by shining light in their eyes.

1849 Lanman *Letters Alleghany Mts.* 48 **nGA,** In killing wild animals he pursues but two methods, called "fire-lighting" and "still hunting." **1926** *AmSp* 1.411 **Okefenokee GA,** Then Jim wanted ter go fire-lightin' that night, but I wuz worried out an' stayed in camp. **1966–69** *DARE* (Qu. P35b, *Illegal methods of shooting deer*) Infs **NC**1, 3, 8, 12, 21, 60, Fire-lighting; **NC**6, Fire-lighting—using a flashlight.

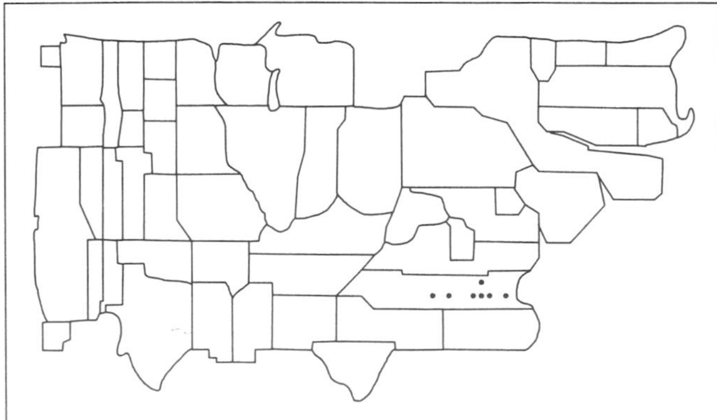

•fire-lighting (Qu. P35b)

fire lily n

1 An orange- to red-flowered liliaceous plant such as a **wood lily** (here: *Lilium philadelphicum*) or the common orange **daylily 1** *(Hemerocallis fulva).* [See quot 1931]

1871 (1882) Stowe *Fireside Stories* 179 **MA,** Every now and then a tall, straight fire-lily—black, spotted in its centre—rose like a little jet of flame. **1878** (1977) Stowe *Poganuc People* 211 **CT,** There, under the burning August sun, the ground shot up those ardent flower-flames well called fire-lilies. **1931** Clute *Common Plants* 42, Fire lily *(Lilium Philadelphicum)* . . [is] so called because these plants are among the first to appear in burned over tracts. **1959** Carleton *Index Herb. Plants* 46, *Fire-lily:* Hemerocallis fulva; Lilium philadelphicum.

2 =**squaw grass.**

1923 in 1925 Jepson *Manual Plants CA* 210, *X[erophyllum] tenax*. . . Fire-Lily. **1949** Moldenke *Amer. Wild Flowers* 315, One of the best known [lilylike plants] is . . *firelily*. . . The stem is 2 to 6 feet tall, and the uppermost 6 to 18 inches are occupied by a huge mass of several thousand white or cream-colored flowers. **1961** Thomas *Flora Santa Cruz* 116 **cwCA,** Fire Lily. . . Known from only two localities in the Santa Cruz Mountains. **1976** Bailey–Bailey *Hortus Third* 1176, *Fire lily*. . . B. C., s. to Wyo. and cent. Calif.

fire log n

=**backlog 1.**

1965–70 *DARE* (Qu. D33, *When you build a fire in the fireplace, what do you call the big log that goes behind the others?*) 18 Infs, **chiefly NEast, Missip Valley,** Fire log. **1967** LeCompte *Word Atlas* 151 **seLA,** [1 inf of 21 offered the term *fire log* for the large log burned at the back of the fireplace.]

fireman's cap n Also *fireman's helmet* [Perh from the color and shape of the corolla]

An introduced **coral tree** *(Erythrina crista-galli).*

1946 Reeves–Bain *Flora TX* 194, *E[rythrina] cristagalli* . . Fireman's Cap. **1960** Vines *Trees SW* 561, Cockspur Coral Bean. . . Some of the vernacular names in use are Fireman's Cap, Common Coral-tree, Cry-baby-tree, Dragon's Teeth, and Immortelle. **1961** Wills–Irwin *Flowers TX* 140, Fireman's helmet, . . a native of southern South America, with leafy flowering shoots and scarlet flowers from March to June, is commonly cultivated.

fire mantel n [Perh blend of **fireboard 1** + *mantel*]

The shelf over a fireplace.

1962 Atwood *Vocab. TX* 100, Some of the examples . . show only one occurrence each, . . but at any rate they demonstrate the sort of thing that is likely to happen when two synonyms are about equally prominent in the speaker's mind. . . *firemantel* (*fireboard* + *mantel*). **1972** *DARE* File **nwFL,** Fire mantel.

fire-new adj Also *firing-new* [Fresh from the fire or forge; *OED "arch";* 1594–1842] Cf **brand-fire-new**

Brand-new.

1790 (1955) Freneau *Prose* 257 **NYC,** As you will now . . receive your printing materials fire-new (as the phrase is) from Europe. **1848** Bartlett *Americanisms* 140, *Fire-new*. . . Instantly they are seized with a *fire-new* reverence for the Constitution and laws! . . *N. Y. Tribune* April 25th, 1848. **1906** *Harper's Weekly* 7 Apr 488, Mr. Foley began to do schoolboy poems in a fire-new and blood-curdling and criminal fashion of spelling. **1950** *PADS* 13.22 **sKY,** *Fire-new*. . . *Fire-new, brand-new, brand-fire-new, spit-fire-new* are all fairly common. "Jim driv in his spit-fire-brand-new car this evenin'." **1952** Brown *NC Folkl.* 1.540, *Firing-new*. . . Brand-new. **c1960** *Wilson Coll.* **csKY,** *Fire-new*. . . Very new, brand-new.

fire oil n Cf **coal oil, kerosene oil**

1949 *AmSp* 24.108 **Charleston SC,** *Fire oil*. . . Kerosene.

fire on See **fire C8**

fire one's shuck v phr [**fire C1a** + **shuck** n]

Fig: to light into someone; to criticize severely.

1951 Porter *Ragged Roads* 44 **OK,** They [=people who have a mean streak] flare up quickly when you least look for it; they will be good to you when they ought to fire your shuck.

fire-on-the-mountain n Cf **snow-on-the-mountain**

A red-bracted **spurge** *(Euphorbia cyathophora).* Also called **fiddler's spurge, fireflower 1, Mexican fire plant, milkweed, painted leaf, wild poinsettia**

1911 *Century Dict. Suppl., Fire-on-the-mountain.* . . A euphorbiaceous annual plant of the warmer regions of America, *Poinsettia heterophylla,* having bright red floral bracts. **1940** Clute *Amer. Plant Names* 167, Fire-on-the-mountain. *Euphorbia heterophylla.* **1957** *Sat. Eve. Post Letters* **MA,** Fire-on-the-mountain. **1976** Bailey–Bailey *Hortus Third* 462, *[Euphorbia] cyathophora.* . . *Fire-on-the-mountain.* . . Upper lvs. and bracts red or red-based. . . Often naturalized.

fire out See **fire C2b, 6**

fire oven n [From its being set directly into the fire, with coals both under and over it]

1966 *DARE* (QR p41) Inf **NC**44, Fire oven [is the same as] Dutch oven.

fire pan n Cf **fire jack, jacklight** n

See quots.

1826 Flint *Recollections* 339 **LA,** Two or three black boys carry over their shoulders fire-pans, being a grating of iron hoops, appended to a long handle, and filled with blazing torches of the splinters of fat pine. **1853** Hammett *Stray Yankee in TX* 37, A "fire-pan" is a kind of basket formed of pieces of iron hoops or straps, to which a long pole is attached as a handle. It is used in "fire-hunting." **1927** J. D. Freeman *When West Was Young* 70 *(DA),* The firepan was made of a steel basket fastened to a long, light piece of timber. **1933** Rawlings *South Moon* 101 **nFL,** Slippin' along in the dark, with my ol' fire-pan at the end of a pole over my shoulder, and the fat-wood splinters blazin' away.

firepiece n [Perh blend of *fire* + **mantelpiece**]

1970 *DARE* (Qu. D36, . . *The shelf over the fireplace*) Inf **OK**56, Firepiece.

fire pink n

1 A red-flowered **catchfly 1** (here: *Silene virginica*).

1848 Gray *Manual of Botany* 58, *S[ilene] Virginica.* . . *Fire Pink. Catchfly.* . . Open woods, from W. New York . . westward and southward. **1939** FWP *Guide TN* 22, Wild flowers common to much of Middle Tennessee are the . . dragonroot, firepink, Indian tobacco. **1943** Peattie *Great Smokies* 196, Nature plunged boldly ahead with her efforts to mingle vermilion with lilac, by adding everywhere the shooting stars of the fire pink, which is about as "pink" as the dress uniforms at Buckingham Palace. **1969** *DARE* (Qu. S26c, *Wildflowers that grow in woods*) Inf **TN**33, Fire pink. **1976** Bailey–Bailey *Hortus Third* 1045, *Fire pink.* Showy per[ennial]. . . N.J. to Minn., s. to Ga. and Okla.

2 An **Indian paintbrush** (here: *Castilleja coccinea*).

1898 *Jrl. Amer. Folkl.* 11.276, *Castilleja coccinea* . . fire pink, Monroe, Wis.

fireplace n

In the charcoal-burning industry: a place in the middle of the stacked wood in a kiln where the fire is started.

1966 *DARE* Tape **MA**5C, I helped to fill . . the charcoal kiln on my father's place. . . They'd pile around in a circle a tier of wood, and then they'd put in another tier . . and then in the very middle they made what they called the fireplace. They'd put in a lot of kindling.

fireplace iron See **fire iron 1**

fireplace shelf n Also *fire shelf* **chiefly Nth**

The shelf over a fireplace.

1941 *LANE* Map 328 **NH,** Fire shelf, fireplace shelf [1 inf each]. **1966** Dakin *Dial. Vocab. Ohio R. Valley* 2.38, *Fire shelf* [1 inf]. **1966–68** *DARE* (Qu. D36) Infs **AK**7, **IL**50, **MD**24, **MI**68, **MN**38, Fireplace shelf. **1973** Allen *LAUM* 1.162 (as of c1950), Single instances of these appeared: . . *fire shelf,* a rare New Hampshire term, in northwestern Iowa.

fireplace skillet n

A Dutch oven.

1967 *DARE* Tape **LA**6, [FW:] What do you call the one that's got legs on it? [Inf:] That's a fireplace [fɑ·pleɪs] skillet. . . Ain't that what we call a fireplace skillet, a oven? An' it's got a iron lid on it, an' you put your fire under the skillet. [FW:] And it's got three legs? [Inf:] Yes.

fire plant n

=**golden club 1.**

1938 Rawlings *Yearling* 33 **nFL,** "He's feedin' on the fire-plant." . . He pointed to the flat arrow-shaped leaves. . . "Hit's his spring tonic. A bear'll make for it first thing, time he comes out in the spring." *Ibid* 34, The drops of water on the leaves o' the fire-plant shinin' bright and red as a bull-bat's eyes.

fire-pole n

The long wooden handle of a **fire pan.**

1933 Rawlings *South Moon* 101 **FL,** And me balancin' the fire-pole under my right arm and h'istin' my rifle and takin' aim betwixt them two shinin' eyes.

fire popper n

A firecracker.

1949 *AmSp* 24.108 **cwSC,** *Fire poppers.* . . Firecrackers. **1966** *DARE* (Qu. FF13; total Infs questioned, 75) Inf **GA**3, Fire poppers.

fire rape See **fir rape 2**

‡fire rat n [Perh for *fire rack*]

=**firedog.**

1966 *DARE* (Qu. D32) Inf **GA**4, Fire rat; firedogs.

firerock See **firestone**

fireroom n [*SND* (at *fire* n. 7. [24]) 1700 →; "Now only *hist.*"] *old-fash*

A room heated by a fireplace.

1708 *Boston News-Letter* (MA) 5 Jan 2/2, There is a good Dwelling House, three Fire Rooms on a Floor . . to be Lett. **1899** Wilkins *Colonial Times* II.31 *(DA),* All the drawbacks to her delight was that Grandma should have the southwest fire-room. **1937** FWP *Guide RI* 137, They [=early Providence area houses] had usually one lower section called the fire-room, and a small half-story chamber above. **1939** McGuire *FL Cracker Dial.* 175, *Fire-room.* . . Sitting room, parlor (room with fireplace).

fire scald n

An opening in a forest caused by a fire.

1895 Murfree *Mystery of Witch-Face* 2 **TN,** A stretch of burnt, broken timber that goes by the name of "fire-scald." **1908** Fox *Lonesome Pine* 401 **KY,** Once he looked back from a "fire-scald" in the woods at the lonely cabin in the cove.

fire-set v

To set fire to.

1939 *Hall Coll.* **eTN,** They fire-set our fence.

fire shelf See **fireplace shelf**

fireshine n [By analogy with *sunshine, moonshine*]

The light from a fire.

1984 Doig *English Creek* 56 **nMT,** The McCaskill next to me here in the fireshine.

fire-shooting vbl n Cf **fire-hunt**

=**fire-lighting.**

1877 Habberton *Jericho Road* 95 **IL,** He had done "fire-shooting" near springs elsewhere.

fire snake n [See quot 1987] **WI**

A **red-bellied snake** (here: *Storeria occipitomaculata*).

1950 *WELS (Snakes found in your neighborhood)* 1 Inf, **ceWI,** Fire snake. **1968** *DARE* (Qu. P25, . . *Kinds of snakes*) Inf **WI**58, Fire snake. **1987** *DARE* File **csWI,** The Inf, a professional zoologist, knows the term *fire snake* for the northern red-bellied snake *(Storeria occipitomaculata),* having often heard it used in the field. It is so-called partly because of its bright red-belly, but also because it is often found in burned-over areas.

fire stand n Cf **firebox 2**

See quots.

1938 FWP *Guide DE* 508, The tabernacle and tents are lighted by electricity instead of the primitive fire-stands, which were elevated boxes of sand with blazing fat-pine lightwood knots. **1944** Footner *Rivers* 105 **MD,** These fire stands are still used at camp meetings. Little platforms are erected on a stand of tall posts, and thickly heaped with mud or sand. On such beds fires are kept burning to give light to the proceedings at night.

fire stick n

1 A poker for stirring a fire.

1637 in 1874 Williams *Letters* 80, Of all the natives [=Indians] in Boston, she is the worst used: is beaten with fire-sticks, and especially by some of the servants. **1896** Harris *Sister Jane* 100 **nGA,** Sister Jane, armed with the fire-stick (a heavy piece of metal weighing four or five pounds) . . was waving her weapon in the air and making an effort to get to the door. **1939** FWP *Guide NC* 98, The kitchen is a "cook room," the poker is a "fire-stick." **1952** Brown *NC Folkl.* 1.540 **c,eNC,** *Fire-stick*. . . A fire poker, generally of wood.

2 A large wooden match.

1967 *DARE* (Qu. F46, . . *The kind of matches you can strike anywhere*) Inf **NE**7, Fire sticks. **1973** Allen *LAUM* 1.160 **MN, ND** (as of c1950), *Kitchen matches* (that will strike anywhere). . . Fire sticks. [2 infs; 1 labels it old-fash]

3 also *firing stick:* A rifle.

1968–70 *DARE* (Qu. P37a) Inf **MD**22, Fire stick—[I] believe the Indians used the term; **TX**101, Firin' stick.

firestone n Also *firerock*

A hearth.

1941 *LANE* Map 329 **cCT,** Firestone, usual name for the hearth. **1966–68** *DARE* (Qu. D31, *In front of a fireplace there's usually stone-work on the floor—what do you call this?*) Inf **WA**18, Firerock; **MI**96, Firestone.

firestop n Cf **fireguard**

A firebreak.

1926 C. E. Mulford *Cassidy's Protégé* iv.41 *(OEDS),* The farms he had dreamed of were now no more than memories, their boundary furrows and fire-stops rank with triumphant bunchgrass. **1940** Writers' Program *Guide PA* 486, At intervals, long swathes, called 'fire stops,' have been cut through the forests.

firetail n [From the red-orange patches on the tail]

=redstart.

1917 (1923) *Birds Amer.* 3.167, Redstart. *Setophaga ruticilla*. . . Fire-tail. **1946** Hausman *Eastern Birds* 542, *Setophaga ruticilla* . . Firetail. **1953** Jewett *Birds WA* 578, *Setophaga ruticilla* . . Fire-tail. **1960** Williams *Walk Egypt* 15 **GA,** Birds were pouring over the mountains. Raccoon-marked yellowthroats, cheeky firetails, and little parulas hung from every twig.

fire thorn n Also *fiery thorn*

A thorny shrub of the genus *Pyracantha.*

1858 Warder *Hedges* 276 **OH,** Fiery Thorn . . is an evergreen with dark foliage and bright-red berries. **1900** Lyons *Plant Names* 119, *C. Pyracantha*. . . Fire Thorn. **1916** Bailey *Std. Cyclop. Horticult.* 2863/2, *[Pyracantha]*. . . *coccinea*. . . Firethorn. Fiery Thorn. Everlasting Thorn. **1941** Writers' Program *Guide LA* 443, Wooded stretches are dense with growth of oak, pecan, cypress, prickly-ash, locust, persimmon, and red-berried "firethorn." **1948** *Times-Picayune* (New Orleans LA) 5 Dec mag sec 2/2, It's a shrub of the rose family [and] . . it's sometimes called firethorn. **1960** Williams *Walk Egypt* 57 **GA,** She saw the periwinkles massed around the pump, . . the dog, Joe, panting under the firethorn. **1976** Bailey-Bailey *Hortus Third* 930, Firethorn.

fire tongs n pl Cf **firedog, fire iron 1**

c1970 Pederson *Dial. Surv. Rural GA,* [4 of 64 infs in southeast Georgia offered *fire tongs* as the term for iron supports for wood in a fireplace.]

firetop n [See quot 1974] Cf **fireweed e**

A **willow herb** (here: *Epilobium angustifolium*).

1893 *Jrl. Amer. Folkl.* 6.142, *Epilobium angustifolium,* fire-top; burnt weed. Penobscot River, Me. (lumbermen). **1974** (1977) Coon *Useful Plants* 196, *Epilobium angustifolium* . . purple fire top. . . Cotton from the seed pods makes an excellent tinder for campfires.

fire trail n

A firebreak.

1958 McCulloch *Woods Words* 63 **Pacific NW,** *Fire trail*—A cleared line around a slash area or other hazard, intended to prevent fire from escaping out of it. **1969** *DARE* Tape **CA**147, Most of it is done with . . bulldozers. . . Build a fire trail . . to keep the fire contained. You build a trail around the burning area.

fire up See **fire C2c, 8, 10, 11**

fire viewer n Cf **fire boss**

1968 Adams *Western Words* 113, *Fire viewer*—In mining, a person who examines the workings of a mine with a safety lamp.

fireweed n Cf **Mexican fireweed**

Any of var plants which colonize burnt-over areas, somehow suggest fire, or kindle readily or are used in the making of fire, as: **a** Carline thistle *(Carlina vulgaris).* *obs*

1784 in 1785 Amer. Acad. Arts & Sci. *Memoirs* 1.477 **neMA,** *Carlina*. . . *Fire-weed.* Blossoms white. It abounds in new plantations where the ground has been burnt over.

b A **wild lettuce,** such as *Lactuca canadensis.*

1792 Belknap *Hist. NH* 3.133, The fireweed, which spontaneously grows on all burnt land. This fireweed is an annual plant, with a succulent stalk and long jagged leaf; it grows to the height of five or six feet, according to the strength of the ashes. It bears a white flower, and has a winged seed, which is carried every where by the wind, but never vegetates, except on the ashes of burnt wood. **1814** Bigelow *Florula Bostoniensis* 184, *Lactuca elongata. Tall Lettuce*. . . This plant . . [i]s sure to appear in great abundance on grounds which are newly burnt over, and on this account it has received the name of *Fire weed* in the interior. **1900** Lyons *Plant Names* 212. **1940** Clute *Amer. Plant Names* 70, *Lactuca* . . *Canadensis*. . . Fire-weed.

c A plant of the genus *Erechtites.* For other names of *E. hieracifolia* see **butterweed 5, pilewort**

1822 Eaton *Botany* 457, *Senecio*. . . *hieracifolius* (fire weed . .). This plant springs up wherever land has been recently cleared of timber; and more particularly if it has been burned over. **1837** Darlington *Flora Cestrica* 498, Fire-weed . . is remarkable for its prevalence in newly cleared grounds,—especially in and around spots where brush-wood has been burned. **1892** IN Dept. Geol. & Nat. Resources *Rept. for 1891* 146, *Erechtites hieracifolia*. . . Fireweed. **1933** Small *Manual SE Flora* 1477. **1961** Thomas *Flora Santa Cruz* 375 **cwCA,** Toothed Coast Fireweed. . . In disturbed ground along the margins of redwood-Douglas fir forests. **1967–68** *DARE* (Qu. S21) Infs **KS**5, 15, Fireweed. **1973** Hitchcock-Cronquist *Flora Pacific NW* 511, *Erechtites*. . . Burnweed; Fireweed. Heads disciform, dull yellow or whitish.

d A **ragwort,** such as *Senecio aureus.*

1830 Rafinesque *Med. Flora* 2.262, *Senecio*. . . Groundsel, Fireweed. **1876** Hobbs *Bot. Hdbk.* 38, Fireweed, Erechthites [sic] hieracifolius [sic]. . . Erigeron Canadense. . . Senecio gracilis. **1900** Lyons *Plant Names* 342, *S. aureus*. . . Fireweed. **1940** Clute *Amer. Plant Names* 230, *Senecio aurens* [sic]. . . Fire-weed. **1959** Carleton *Index Herb. Plants* 46, *Fire-weed:* Datura stramonium; Epilobium angustifolia; Erigeron canadensis; Lactuca elongata; Plantago media; Senecio jacobaea.

e =willow herb, esp *Epilobium angustifolium.*

1857 (1864) Thoreau *ME Woods* 262, There were great fields of fire-weed *(Epilobium angustifolium)* on all sides. **1882** *Harper's New Mth. Mag.* 64.861 **NEng,** Those "pink spikes of the willow-herb," also called fire-weed. **1913** *Torreya* 13.11 **NY,** How soon we notice *Epilobium,* the fire-weed, with its . . purple flowers standing like sentinels where a fire has raged. **1942** *Natl. Geogr. Mag.* May 594, Eager to gather the blue lupines, pink roses, and magenta fireweed along the trail, Jo was not careful where she walked. **1949** Moldenke *Amer. Wild Flowers* 185, Everyone . . knows how the *fireweed* . . invades a woods on the heels of a forest fire. **1966** *DARE* Wildfl QR Pl.144A Infs **WA**10, 30; Pl.144B Infs **MI**57, **NH**4, **WA**10, 30. **1968** *DARE* (Qu. S26b) Inf **NY**75, Fireweed; (Qu. S26e) Inf **AK**7, Fireweed—reddish to pinkish. **1974** (1977) Coon *Useful Plants* 196, *Epilobium angustifolium*. . . Its name of fireweed comes from the fact that it seems always to come up quickly in any spot where there has been a fire. . . Further, cotton from the seed pods makes an excellent tinder for campfires. **1977** Churchill *Don't Call* 140 **nwOR** (as of c1918), The very young shoots of fireweed picked before the flowers appeared tasted something like asparagus when peeled but Mother didn't serve them often. They could be eaten raw, which Mother said was good because cooking often ruined the health-giving stuff in greens and vegetables.

f A **jimson weed** (here: *Datura stramonium*).

1873 Pratt *Flowering Plants* 2.104 **VA,** In Virginia, the Thorn-Apple is called Fireweed. **1900** Lyons *Plant Names* 132. **1930** Sievers *Amer. Med. Plants* 38, Fireweed . . is a very common weed in fields and waste places almost everywhere in the United States except in the North and West. **1959** [see **d** above].

g A **horseweed 1** (here: *Conyza canadensis*).

1876 [see **d** above]. **1904** Henkel *Weeds Used in Med.* 36, *Leptilon canadense*. . . (*Erigeron canadensis* . .). *Other common names.*—Horseweed, . . fireweed. **1930** U.S. Dept. Ag. *Misc. Pub.* 77.37, Fireweed . . is common . . throughout almost all of North America. **1959** [see **d** above].

h =orange hawkweed.

1898 *Jrl. Amer. Folkl.* 11.230, *Hieracium aurantiacum*. . . Fireweed, Dover, Me. **1970** *DARE* (Qu. S26d) Inf **MI**120, Fireweed—with reddish-orange bloom.

i A **snakeweed** (here: *Gutierrezia* spp).

1913 (1979) Barnes *Western Grazing* 236, In the southwest and on some of the ranges in the northern regions . . (Guttierezia) known locally as snakeweed, fireweed, turpentine weed, and possibly by other names. . . The flowers bear little white seeds that seem to be filled with a resinous substance which makes it burn like tinder. Hence the name fire or turpentine weed. **1942** *Torreya* 42.165, *Gutierrezia* spp.—Fireweed, lightning-brush, Utah.

j also *ranchers fireweed:* A **fiddleneck 1,** esp *Amsinckia intermedia.*

1914 Georgia *Manual Weeds* 336, *Amsinckia intermedia.* . . Fireweed. . . Corolla orange-yellow. **1925** Jepson *Manual Plants CA* 844, *A. douglasiana.* . . Also called Fireweed and Zaccato Gorda [sic]. **1935** (1943) Muenscher *Weeds* 377, Fireweed. . . Grain fields, gardens, orchards, meadows and waste places. Native to the Pacific Coast. **1970** Correll *Plants TX* 1302, *Amsinckia intermedia. . . Ranchers fireweed.* . . From w. Tex. and Ariz., n. to Ida. and westw. **1973** Hitchcock-Cronquist *Flora Pacific NW* 386, *Amsinckia.* . . Fiddleneck; . . Fireweed. . . Ranchers f[ireweed]. . . *A. intermedia.*

k =he-huckleberry 1.

1940 Clute *Amer. Plant Names* 257, *Cyrilla racemiflora.* Titi, . . burning-wood, fire-weed.

l =Oswego tea.

1966 *DARE* Wildfl QR Pl.189 Inf **OR**9, Fireweed.

m =cotton grass 1.

1969 *DARE* (Qu. S26b) Inf **NY**223, Fireweed or Alaskan cotton. Wild-flax-like, turns into milkweed-like seeds that float. Grows heavily in Alaska [where] they say Alaskan cotton. Here it's called fireweed. [It's] not cardinal flower.

firewheel n Also *Indian firewheel* [From color and shape of flower] **esp TX**

=gaillardia B, usu *Gaillardia pulchella.*

1933 Small *Manual SE Flora* 1461, *Gaillardia.* . . About 20 species, all except one North American.—Blanket-flowers. Fire-wheels. **1946** Reeves-Bain *Flora TX* 268, *G. pulchella.* . . Firewheel, Indian Sunburst. . . Open grounds; often cultivated for ornament, but also native locally. **1951** *PADS* 15.42 **TX,** *Gaillardia pulchella.* . . Blanket flower; firewheel; beach red-daisy. **1961** Wills-Irwin *Flowers TX* 241, Firewheel covers miles of roadsides in prairie districts from April to June with rusty red and innumerable flecks of yellow. **1967** *DARE* Wildfl QR Pl.223A Inf **TX**44, Looks like Indian firewheel. **1975** Duncan-Foote *Wildflowers SE* 222, Fire-wheel *Gaillardia pulchella.* . . Usually sandy soils; Fla into Ariz, s Neb, La, C[oastal] P[lain] of Ga, and sc Va.

fire willow n [See quots]

=Scouler willow.

1931 U.S. Dept. Ag. *Misc. Pub.* 101.15, *Scouler willow* . . , known also as fire . . willow, is one of the most common, abundant, and widely distributed willows in west North America. . . On areas denuded by fire it forms a thicket of a transition type until the climax conifer cover is reestablished. **1938** Van Dersal *Native Woody Plants* 252, *Salix scouleriana. . . Fire willow.* . . A pioneer in burned-over areas. **1960** Vines *Trees SW* 98, *Salix scouleriana.* . . Vernacular names are Black Willow, Fire Willow. . . It recovers well from grazing and comes back quickly on burned-over areas. **1972** Viereck-Little *AK Trees* 121, It is often called "fire willow" because of its rapid occupation of burned areas, forming blue-green thickets.

fireworm n [See quot 1926]

The larva of the tortricid moth *Rhopobota naevana.*

1884 U.S. Dept. Ag. *Rept. of Secy. for 1884* 395, This insect, the Fire-Worm, which had in previous seasons done so much damage, has this year been kept pretty well under control. **1926** Essig *Insects N. Amer.* 740, The cranberry blackhead *fireworm, Rhopobota naevana* . . when abundant cause the cranberry bogs to appear fire-swept. **1954** Borror-DeLong *Intro. Insects* 530, The cranberry black-headed fireworm, *Rhopobota naevana* . . is a serious pest of cranberry plantings in the Eastern states. **1968** *DARE* (Qu. R21, . . *Kinds of stinging insects*) Inf **NJ**52, Fireworm.

firing n [*OED* a1555 →]

Fuel.

1931-33 *LANE Worksheets* **sRI,** It was from the tug swamps that the old settlers got their firing.

firing vbl n See **fire C1a, 2c, 4, 10**

firing adv Cf **all-fired**

Extremely.

1968 *DARE* (Qu. LL37, . . *"I was so ______ mad."*) Inf **OH**41, Firing.

firing iron See **fire iron 3**

firing line n [From *firing line* the line from which fire is directed in a battle or in target practice] Cf *DS* HH14

An imaginary object used as the basis for practical jokes.

1921 *DN* 5.93 **AL,** The young soldier in our late war was sometimes sent for so many "yards of firing-line." **1923** *DN* 5.241, *Firing line.* Army.

firing-new See **fire-new**

firing stick See **fire stick 3**

firkin n **esp NEast** *old-fash*

A small container similar to a bucket or pail and often used for storage of foodstuffs, esp butter; see quots.

1636 in 1869 Winthrop *Life & Letters* 2.156 **eMA,** Many firkins of butter and suet. **1734** in 1885 Boston Registry Dept. *Records* 12.81, All Grain, Flower, Butter in Firkins, Pork, Beef, Cheese, Meat or Fish salted in Barrels . . may be sold. **1886** *Outing* 8.168/2 **NY,** We three managed to make him one [=a banjo] out of a butter firkin. **1939** *LANE* Map 129, *Firkin,* made of staves, usually tapering toward the top and covered, for butter or lard. [9 infs **nMA, VT, NH, ME**] **1939** Coffin *Capt. Abby* 117 **ME** (as of c1860s), No Maine woman could sail without her firkin of mincemeat any more than without her marriage certificate. **1960** Williams *Walk Egypt* 89 **nGA,** [There were] firkins of butter to make the biscuits fly. **1967-69** *DARE* (Qu. D10a) Inf **RI**1A, Butter firkins—wooden boxes to keep butter and carry it in; (Qu. F31) Inf **MA**72, Firkin—larger at the bottom than at the top; **NY**105, Firkin—oak bucket used for butter; (QR p42) Inf **NY**72, Firkin—a vessel for keeping butter in, just like a little barrel. **1968** *DARE* Tape **NY**73, He made butter tubs and firkins for butter. A firkin is like a small barrel. **1970** *DARE* FW Addit **csVA,** Firkin—a five-gallon metal container for lard.

fir lice n pl

1977 Jones *OR Folkl.* 101/2 (as of 1948), *Fir lice:* minute splinters from fir bark.

firm See **fern**

fir moss See **fir club moss**

firm peach n Cf **hard peach**

=clingstone.

1949 *AmSp* 24.108 **SC,** *Firm Peach.* . . Clingstone peach.

firnitree See **furniture**

fir pine n

=balsam fir.

1897 Sudworth *Arborescent Flora* 51, *Abies balsamea* . . Fir Pine. **1900** Lyons *Plant Names* [7], *Abies balsamea* . . Fir Pine.

fir-rape n

1 =beechdrops 1.

1876 Hobbs *Bot. Hdbk.* 38, Fir rape, False beech drops, Monotropa hypopitys. Fir rape, Beech drops, Orobanche Virginiana. **1900** Lyons *Plant Names* 198, *H[ypopitys] Hypopitys.* . . Fir-rape. *Ibid* 221, Epifagus Virginiana. . . Fir-rape.

2 also *fire rape:* A **pinesap** (here: *Monotropa hypopitys*).

1876 [see **1** above]. **1900** [see **1** above]. **1959** Carleton *Index Herb. Plants* 46, *Fire-rape:* Monotropa hypopitys.

first adj, adv Usu |fɝst, fɜst|; also **NYC, scattered Sth,** |fɜɪst|; for addit varr see **A** below Pronc-spp *fus(s), fust*

A Forms.

1829 Tenney *Female Quixotism* 2.84 **Philadelphia PA** [Black], Let me make noise fuss, for fright away ghos. **1843** (1916) Hall *New Purchase* 227 **IN,** He stops for the furst time. **1844** Thompson *Major Jones's Courtship* 74 **GA,** If I didn't have some real fust rate news to tell you, I don't blieve I could find time to rite now. **1861** Holmes *Venner* 2.173 **NEng,** I'll see y' darned fust! **1896** *DN* 1.463 **NYC,** Out of a hundred cases of guards on the elevated road at Eighty-first Street, eighty-one announced [etɪfʌɪst]. . . [This pronunciation] extends . . over the whole of Long Island, and through all the Sound cities of Connecticut, and up the valley as far as Hartford. **1899** Chesnutt *Conjure Woman* 23 **csNC** [Black], Fus', when de grapes 'uz gethered. **1903** *DN* 2.290 **Cape Cod MA** (as of a1857), Still in use, at least among old people, . . *fust* for *first.*

1905 *DN* 3.58 **eNE,** *Fust.* **1908** *DN* 3.313 **eAL, wGA,** *Fus(t).* **1927** Shewmake *Engl. Pronc. VA* 33, In words like . . *first,* . . Some speakers sound the *r,* and others omit it; but a third set of speakers pronounce these words with a sound approaching that of *oi.* The last-named pronunciation is common in New York and, in a slightly modified form, in some Southern states; but it is exceptional in Virginia. **1939** *LANE* Map 62, [The form [fɜst] predominates throughout **eNEng;** [fɚst] predominates in **wNEng** and is scattered in **eNEng;** [fʌst] is regarded as old-fashioned but is still used by several infs in **sVT, NH, sME;** [fɜɪs] was given by 1 inf in **swCT,** [fɜ̯ɪst] by 2 infs in **seCT;** the forms [fɜs] and [fɚs] are also recorded sporadically.] **1941** *AmSp* 16.7 **eTX** [Black], *First* is [fʌs]. **1942** *AmSp* 17.151 **NYC,** First. . . [ɝ] 57 [infs]—[ɜ] 12 [infs]—[ɜɪ] 20 [infs]. **1949** Turner *Africanisms* 264 **sSC coast** [Gullah], [fʌs]. **1966–70** *DARE* Tapes **FL**3, 20, [fɜɨst]; **MS**15, [fʌɪst]; **GA**51, [fʌst]; **TN**57, [fʊɪst]. **1976** Allen *LAUM* 3.312 **Upper Midwest** (as of c1950), When /st/ in *first* . . occurs before juncture followed by bilabial /m/ in *man,* only 10 scattered U[pper] M[idwest] infs. have simple /s/. . . But the articulatory interference provided by the following velar stop as in . . *first class* . . yields a situation in which more than one-third of the infs. have /fɚs/ instead of /fɚst/. But no regional or social patterns emerge.

B As adj.

1 Single, most basic—usu in neg constrs. Cf **first form thing**

1849 *NY Daily Tribune* (NY) 23 May 2/2, My knees, which I couldn't move the first inch. **1859** (1968) Bartlett *Americanisms* 150, *First.* One, single. An absurd use of the word, which has recently crept into the newspapers and public speeches from the colloquial language of the West, "I won't pay you the first red cent," i.e. I will not pay you a single cent. **1888** Jones *Negro Myths* 62 **GA coast** [Gullah], Buh Wolf mek up eh mine dat Buh Rabbit yent [=didn't] do de fus ting een de fiel. **1966** *DARE* (Qu. JJ15b, . . *"He doesn't know ______."*) Inf **ND**1, The first thing about it; **AR**16, The first thing; (Qu. LL14, . . *"This pond used to be full of fish but now there's ______ left."*) Infs **GA**19, **MS**69, Not the first one; (Qu. LL16, . . *"He doesn't know ______ thing about plumbing."*; total Infs questioned, 75) 11 Infs, **scattered,** The first thing; **AR**39, The first letter; **OK**48, The first principle; **GA**7, The first step. **1968** *Foxfire* Fall–Winter 23 **nGA,** I went looking, but I didn't see the *first* sang plant.

2 Eager, anxious.

1913 *DN* 4.56 **Cape Cod MA,** *First.* . . Eager. "I didn't give him a lift; he was altogether too first to ride." **1916** Macy–Hussey *Nantucket Scrap Basket* 131, "First"—Eager, anxious; as "he was quite first to go the voyage." This is a curious and, apparently quite local use of this word. **1965** *DARE* File **Milwaukee WI** (as of c1950), He was awfully first to go.

3 in var phrr indicating immediate success; see below. Cf *DS* A23

a *first crack (off the bat)* and varr.

1950 *WELS (He did it ______)* 5 Infs, **WI,** (At the) first crack; 1 Inf, First crack off the bat. **1951** Johnson *Resp. to PADS 20* **DE,** First crack off the bat. **c1960** *Wilson Coll.* **csKY,** *First crack off the bat.* . . At once or on the first try. **1960** Bailey *Resp. to PADS 20* **KS** (*"He did it ______."*) First crack off the bat, first crack out of the box, right off—all three [responses] very common. **1965–70** *DARE* (Qu. A23) 26 Infs, **scattered, but less freq N Midl,** First crack off the bat; 12 Infs, **scattered, but more freq Sth, Atlantic,** (At the) first crack; **VA**74, First crack of the bat.

b *first crack* (or *shot*) *out of the box, first shot* and varr. **chiefly Nth, N Midl**

1907 Lincoln *Cape Cod* 85 **MA,** I heard how you'd rung the bell the first shot out the box and was rolling in coin. **1908** *NY Eve. Jrl.* (NY) 29 Sep 9th ed 10 *(Zwilling Coll.),* The very first crack out of the box he came face to face with a bear. **1928** [see **c** below]. **1950** *WELS (He did it ______)* 3 Infs, **WI,** First crack out of the box; 3 Infs, First shot out of the box. **1960** Bailey [see **a** above]. **1965–70** *DARE* (Qu. A23) 15 Infs, **chiefly Nth, N Midl,** First crack out of the box; **MA**100, **NY**53, 89, 179, **RI**8, (At the) first shot; **CA**11, First crack on the box; **NY**67, First shot out of the box; **NC**25, First shot out of the locker; [**KY**67A, At the first cat out of the box].

c *first dash* (or *pop, rattle*) *out of the box* and var.

1909 *DN* 3.396 **nwAR,** *First dash out of the box* . . At the very outset. **1928** *Ruppenthal Coll.* **KS,** First dash (crack, throw) out of the box. . . At first chance; as soon as possible. **1942** Faulkner *Go Down* 92 **MS,** By God, you better find it first pop this time. **1950** *WELS (He did it ______)* 1 Inf, **WI,** First pop. **1967–70** *DARE* (Qu. A23) Infs **AR**53, **LA**15, **TX**43, 80, First rattle out of the box; **NY**56, **TX**4, **VA**39, First pop; **MS**1, First dash out of the box; **TN**4, First pop out of the box. **1968** Adams *Western Words* 113, *First rattle out of the box*—A cowboy's expression meaning *prompt action.*

C As adv.

1 Just now. [Cf Ger *erst*]

1950 *WELS Suppl.,* 1 Inf, **Milwaukee WI,** Used like *just*—I first came; 1 Inf, **Milwaukee WI,** I'm first going back; 1 Inf, **nwWI,** Have you got your buck and come back or are you first going out?

2 Before a particular event occurs; from now. [Engl dial; cf *EDD first* adv. 4]

1899 (1912) Green *VA Folk-Speech* 175, "Is that job finished?" "It won't be long first."

first n

In marble play: the chance to shoot first.

1932 *Hanley Disks* **swCT,** Sometimes it was a large ring and we'd say "My first." We'd knuckle down.

first along adv [Engl dial; cf *EDD first* adv. 5] Cf **first off**

At first.

1895 *DN* 1.388 **seMA.** **1907** Lincoln *Cape Cod* 265 **seMA,** The only trouble she made was first along, and that wa'n't her fault. *Ibid* 287, His being a millionaire and a stock-jobber was what scart me fust along.

first-and-last snake n

Prob a **king snake** (here: *Lampropeltis getulus*).

1968 *DARE* (Qu. P25, . . *Kinds of snakes . . around here*) Inf **MD**13, First-and-last snake—black [with] white spots, non-poisonous, [a] land snake, three to four feet long.

first base n Cf *DS* EE11

A substitute game when there aren't enough players for baseball.

1968 *DARE* Tape **LA**37, [FW:] You mentioned a game played with a baseball when you don't have enough people for a regular game. [Inf:] That's called first base. . . one guy's the catcher, one guy the pitcher, one guy's the first baseman, which is the one base we only have. . . there's two other guys, one play left field, no center fielder, and there's one guy on bat, and he . . hits 'til he's out. . . The catcher rotates, when he's out, to batter, pitcher rotates to catcher, and he goes in the field. . . Play it with a softball, usually.

first-best adj, adv

Foremost; in first place.

1858 Hammett *Piney Woods Tavern* 31 **NEng,** I was a most bunkum at it [=Latin] when I went to school, I tell you—gin'rally allowed to be the first best there was in the academy. *Ibid* 34, The old bank's a standin yet, and holds up it head among the first best. **1867** Lowell *Biglow* 2d ser 94 **'Upcountry' MA,** Where every fem'ly is fus'-best an' nary white man works. **1891** *Scribner's Mag.* 10.771, He has come out first best in the costly contest with those who would have revised nature.

first bottom See **bottom n 1b**

first breakfast n [Perh calque < Ger *erstes Frühstück,* or perh by analogy with **second breakfast**]

A breakfast eaten very early in the morning before a second meal eaten at the regular breakfast time.

1963 North *Rascal* 152 **WI** (as of 1918), On the fifth morning of my visit, Rascal and I joined the family at four A.M. for "first breakfast."

first breath of spring n

A **honeysuckle 2** (here: *Lonicera fragrantissima*).

1931 Clute *Common Plants* 139, In the shrubberies, the fragrant honeysuckle *(Lonicera fragrantissima)* sends forth a perfume that may well make the name of first-breath-of-spring a tangible thing.

first by day(, last by night) phr Also *first by night and last by day* **NYC**

In the game **hide-and-seek A:** see quots.

1957 *Sat. Eve. Post Letters* **NYC,** The "it" rules were "first by night and last by day." That is, the first or last one caught was "it." This game was great at night for the first one caught was "it" as opposed to daytime playing. The reason for this was because you could hide out longer at night and if you got caught first you deserved to be "it." **1968** *DARE* Tape **NY**118A, Some of the things they didn't know about hide-and-seek was "first by day, last by night." Now, nobody knows what that means. In other words, if you're caught first in the daytime, you get "it," you know, you have to go hide, but if you're caught last, at night, then you're "it." **1975** Ferretti *Gt. Amer. Book Sidewalk Games* 173 **NYC,**

"It" searches through the darkened bushes and weeds . . looking for prey. When he is found, "It" tags him, brings him back to base, and calls the other players in for the night. . . The one caught is then recognized as "It" for whatever game begins the new day tomorrow. He is known to be "first by day."

first-calf heifer n

A young cow that has had only one calf.

1950 *WELS (How is the word "heifer" used in your neighborhood?)* 5 Infs, **c,sWI,** First-calf heifer; 1 Inf, **ceWI,** Called "heifer calf" up to about 3 months old, then called "heifer," and with first calf called "first-calf heifer," with second calf a "second-calf heifer," from then on called a cow. **1967** *DARE* (Qu. K11) Inf **IA**8, A first-calf heifer—a cow who has had her first calf.

first chop See **chop** n³

first crack (off the bat) See **first** adj **B3a**

first crack out of the box See **first** adj **B3b**

first dark n Also *first dusk;* rarely *first evening, ~ night* **chiefly Sth, esp S Atl** Cf **first light**

Twilight.

1898 Lloyd *Country Life* 63 **AL,** Well, the old man drops me down about a mile from home. It was then first dusk. **1922** Gonzales *Black Border* 303 **sSC, GA coasts** [Gullah glossary], *Fus' daa'k, fus' dus'*—first dark, dusk, twilight in the evening. **1928** Peterkin *Scarlet Sister Mary* 303 **SC coast,** The day had been lowering and gray, and before the first dark fell, rain began. **1930** Woofter *Black Yeomanry* 53 **seSC,** *Fus' daak:* first dark, twilight. **1930** Stoney–Shelby *Black Genesis* 13 **seSC,** 'Taint a bit too soon, either, 'cause fus' dark like to ketch him. **1936** Morehouse *Rain on Just* 124 **NC,** In the evening . . with first dark the men began stepping recklessly in. *Ibid* 180, The crowd of them came just at first dusk. **1952** Giles *40 Acres* 160 **KY,** As first dark begins to settle down over us, a thrush lifts its song from the head of the hollow and lets it fall like a golden shower about us. **1967–69** *DARE* (Qu. A5, *The time right after the sun goes out of sight, before it becomes all dark*) Infs **LA**2, **MS**63, **SC**32, 62, First dark; **AL**14, First night; (Qu. A4, . . *When the sun goes out of sight*) Infs **AL**15, First dark; **GA**66, First dark—common, [but] I don't say it; **IL**37, First evening—a Southern term. **1974** (1975) Shaw *All God's Dangers* 66 **AL** [Black], First dark I got up to go. . . Stayed until about first dark, I decided I'd better be pullin out. **1977** *New Yorker* 17 Oct 45 **Sth,** There was always a little time that people call first dark. That was when she would go, with the help of the [walking] stick.

first dash out of the box See **first** adj **B3c**

first dawn See **first light**

first day n

1 often cap; Sunday. Similarly, *Second day* Monday, *Third day* Tuesday, etc. *chiefly among Quakers; old-fash exc in ref to days of worship* Cf **first month**

1655 in 1874 Williams *Letters* 292, Sir, the last first day divers of Boston merchants were with me. **1683** in 1861 MA Hist. Soc. *Coll.* 4th ser 5.85, The time desired you would please to appoint . . is on next fourth day. **1705** (1879) S. Sewall *Diary* 2.147 **MA,** I refer'd them to second-day Morning Decr 10. to meet at the Secretary's office. **1782** Crèvecoeur *Letters* 202 **MA,** *First Days* are the only seasons when it is lawful for both sexes to exhibit some garments of English manufacture. **1804** (1898) Hunt *Diary* 10 **PA,** Thomas Tucker's Store was rob'd on first day evening last. **1851** in 1983 *PADS* 70.54 **ce,sePA,** Polly Atkinson came to see mother last Thirdday. **1858** in 1983 *PADS* 70.51 **ce,sePA,** August 14th 1858 Sixthday morning. **1868** Channing *Recollections* 231 **RI,** I went frequently to hear him at the fifth-day (Thursday) meetings. **1873** in 1983 *PADS* 70.50 **ce,sePA,** Uncle George Walton brought Ellie Michener over to our place Seventhday forenoon. **1933** *AmSp* 8.1.13 **Philadelphia PA,** *First day, Second day,* etc. Used instead of Sunday, Monday, etc. **1940** *Time* 15 Apr 61 **PA,** Fifth Day Meeting on Thursdays in the . . Friends Meeting House. **1967** *DARE* Tape **PA**31, First Day school. **1968** *Burlington Co. Herald* (Mount Holly NJ) 8 Aug sec B 10/3, The speech [in the Quaker Meeting House] will be preceded by 11 a.m. Firstday School.

2 See quot. Cf **day clean**

1950 *PADS* 14.31 **SC,** *Fus' day*. . . First day. That is, broad daylight in the morning. Same as *day clean.*

3 See **first light.**

first daylight See **first light**

first dusk See **first dark**

firstest adj, adv [*first* + **-est 3**]

First.

1905 Culbertson *Banjo Talks* 28 **SE** [Black], Tell how de milyun wuz fustes' found. *Ibid* 118, De fustes' time he saw hit. **1940** *Time* 4 Nov 12/3, One of the most popular inhabitants of the train was Porter Foley, who could get there fustest with the mostest drinks. **1944** Henry *First Forrest* 18 **NC** (as of c1860), Legend has had its way the more with the story of Forrest because so much of his fame is folk fame. . . He is remembered chiefly . . not so much by what he did as by what he is supposed to have said—"Git thar fustest with the mostest men." Of course that wasn't just what he said. . . He said simply and directly—"Get there first with the most men," although doubtless his pronunciation was "git thar fust," that being the idiom of the time and place. **1974** Fink *Mountain Speech* 10 **wNC, eTN,** Who got there fustest? **1980** Bartlett *Familiar Quotations* 583, *Nathan Bedford Forrest* 1821–1877 —Get there first with the most men. [Footnote:] Erroneous version usually rendered: Git thar fustest with the mostest.

first evening See **first dark**

first family n Also *first folks* Cf **F.F.V.**

Any one of the earliest families to settle in an area; hence, a family of high social status, real or imagined.

1843 (1847) Field *Drama Pokerville* 13, There was a "heap" of taste in Pokerville, too, and it had its "first families." **1877** in 1939 Frazier *Negro Family* 415 **DC,** The 'fust families' of Washington Colored Society—keep a servant, two dogs, a tom cat and a rifle that saw service in 1776. **1909** *Atlantic Mth.* July 136 **VA,** I shall avail myself of the words furnished us by our Negroes, who are so wisely discerning in social matters. "First folks" are first folks, everywhere. The synonymous use of the word "quality" tells much. **1948** *Reader's Digest* Jan 52, No Boston First Family party is complete without some discussion of genealogy. . . Boston's First Families owe their present position to fortunes founded in the last century in shipping, railroading, textiles, mining or banking by indefatigable merchant grandfathers. **1950** *Western Folkl.* 9.141, The so-called elite in society were variously called *first folks, blue bloods,* and *Montebanks.* [Footnote to *first folks:* Used especially by the southern Negroes when referring to white people who demanded their respect.] **1969** *DARE* (Qu. II23, *Joking names for the people who are, or think they are, the best society of a community: the* ———.) Inf **NY**206, First Family.

first feasting n Cf **first footer**

1939 FWP *Guide MT* 152, The heart of it [=Hogmanay] however, is the ceremony of "first feasting," which takes place in the homes [of people of Scottish descent in Great Falls]. A table is set for guests, who arrive immediately after the beginning of the New Year. A blonde man must partake of the food first, and unless such a man is present, visitors may not enter.

first folks See **first family**

first-footer n [N Engl and Scots dial; cf *EDD, SND*]

The first person to enter a home on New Year's Day; a visitor on New Year's Day or another special occasion; also *first-footing* visiting or being the first to enter a home on New Year's Day.

1961 Sackett–Koch *KS Folkl.* 187, New Year's Day custom called "first-footing," which consisted of taking a basket containing wine and fruitcake and calling on all your friends early in the morning New Year's Day and having a drink of wine and a piece of fruitcake at each house. **1967** Cerello *Dakota Co. MN* 58, This shortbread is like my grandmother made to give to first footers when they came to call on Hogmanay. . . When we were first married and moved to Coates we had forty first footers call on us our first weekend in town. . . There was always something special about greeting first footers after the new year had begun. [Cerello: A custom brought by the Scotch-Irish settlers in the 1870s; now obsolescent.] **1967** *DARE* Tape **MN**2, Dad used to do what they always called first-footing. On New Year's he would be the first one to come in the door—[what] they'd call the first-footer. He would go out and come in with a bottle of wine and some pennies and some biscuits or cookies or something . . in his hand and then he'd give everybody a penny; that was supposed to be luck. . . They wanted somebody who was lucky to be the first footer. Dad was pretty lucky about winning things, and so he was usually the one that did the first footing.

first form thing n Also *form thing, first forn thing* [Perh from *first form* the lowest class in school (with assim of the *m* in *form* to *n* before *th*)] **chiefly Midl**

The most rudimentary thing; anything.

1914 *DN* 4.106 **KS,** *First form thing.* . . Rudiments. "She doesn't know the first form thing about music." Also *first forn.* **1923** *DN* 5.207 **swMO,** He don't know the first for'n thing 'bout raisin' hogs. **1948** *AmSp* 23.314 **sIL,** 'I haven't done a form thing today.' . . 'form' is a corruption of 'for'n' (foreign). Investigation turns up several users of the original phrase 'not a foreign thing.' . . Early Southern emigrants doubtless brought the phrase into southern and southeastern Illinois. **1952** Brown *NC Folkl.* 1.542, *Form (thing).* . . "I don't owe him a form thing."—General. Old people. **1960** Criswell *Resp. to PADS 20* **Ozarks** *(He doesn't know ——— about plumbing)* A form thing. **c1960** *Wilson Coll.* **csKY,** She didn't do the first form thing to help Aunt Mary with the washing. . . Didn't do a form thing. **1966** *DARE* (Qu. JJ15b, . . *"He doesn't know ———."*) Inf **AR**16, The first form thing.

first fowl-crow(ing) See **fowl-crow**

first going off n

The beginning.

1922 Gonzales *Black Border* 303 **sSC, GA coasts** [Gullah glossary], *Fus' gwinin' off*—first going off, at the beginning.

firsties n [-ies]

1 In children's games: the right to go first.

1975 Ferretti *Gt. Amer. Book Sidewalk Games* 153 **ceMA,** In this game, all players put their stakes into the square and, after choosing for "firsties," shoot. *Ibid* 226 **NYC,** Often in street games, *doing* is as much fun as *preparing*— . . choosing for "firsties," electing captains, planning strategies.

2 In **hide-and-seek A:** see quot. Cf **first by day(, last by night)**

1969 *DARE* (Qu. EE15, *When he has caught the first of those that were hiding what does the player who is 'it' call out to the others?*) Inf **MI**108, Firsties?

first in the ring, any old thing exclam

In marble play: see quot.

1958 *PADS* 29.33 **WV,** *First in the ring, any old thing:* . . A call announcing "that a boy had arrived at the marble playing site, and with himself shooting first, was willing to play with anyone at all".

first light n Also *first day(light), ~ dawn* **Sth** Cf **first dark**

Dawn.

1887 *Century Illustr. Mag.* 35.110 **LA,** "Befo' de wah, de plow gang had to be in de field long befo' sun up, all drawn up in line and ebery man a-hold of his plow, waitin' foh de first daylight to start." **1936** Morehouse *Rain on Just* 189 **NC,** Along the low ridge . . had come, between last dark and first dawn, one . . traveller. **1938** Matschat *Suwannee R.* 183 **sGA,** He would have prayed for light if he had known any more prayers; . . at last he saw it: . . A cold gray mist, the color of the first light, hung over the water. **1962** Faulkner *Reivers* 165 **MS,** The conductor waked us and we stood on the cinders at Parsham in the first light. **1964** Will *Hist. Okeechobee* 208 **FL,** At first light . . they started out. **1968–69** *DARE* (Qu. A1, . . *The time . . before the sun comes into sight*) Inf **IL**37, First light—a Southern term, heard near Biloxi, Mississippi; (Qu. A2, . . *When the sun first comes into sight*) Inf **GA**36, First daylight. **1984** Wilder *You All Spoken Here* 61 **Sth,** *First light, fus day:* When you can distinguish the horizon.

first line n

1985 *DARE* File **LA,** *First line*—The band and official mourners in a "jazz funeral."

first lunch n Cf **first breakfast**

1907 *DN* 3.244 **eME,** *First lunch.* . . Woodsman's early breakfast, eaten at 5 A.M.

firstly adj [Cf **first** adj **B2**]

Hasty.

1888 *Detroit Free Press* 29 Sept (Farmer *Americanisms*), I took down the gun and peppered Bill Bibbs. . . Mebbe we've been too *firstly* (hasty), but the Bibbs hain't never cum to talk it over.

first man n

The best man at a wedding.

1966 *DARE* (Qu. AA17, . . *Other people beside the bride and groom . . in a wedding party*) Inf **NC**33, Bridesmaids, first man.

first Monday n

1 The first Monday of each month, on which day a public auction, sale, and trading session is held.

1951 *New Yorker* 10 Feb 32/3 **TN,** Sometimes when she crossed the Square on a busy Saturday morning or on a first Monday, she would hold up one hand with the palm turned outward and stop all the traffic until she was safely across. *Ibid* 19 Nov 58/3 **TN,** Somebody else asked Hominy one time if he thought it right to take the boy to the square on First Monday, where he would be exposed to some pretty rough talk. **1967** *DARE* File **neAL,** We visited Scottsboro, Alabama for their "First Monday" sale day. . . Around the courthouse square . . [was] the most awesome collection of people, iron ware, glass, pictures, coffee mills, chickens, rabbits, . . clothes, chairs, auto parts, . . silver, shotguns, and only the Lord knows what else. . . The sale has been a tradition for many years and draws people from many states, and much of the crowd is made up of professional "trade-day" followers.

2 By ext: see quot.

1950 *PADS* 14.29 **SC,** *First Monday.* . . A poor, worn-out, bony horse or mule, such as come up for public auction on the first Monday of each month.

first month n *among Quakers* Cf **first day 1**

January. Similarly, *second month* February, *third month* March, etc.

1863 in 1983 *PADS* 70.54 **ce,sePA,** 2nd day 26th of 10th MO 1863. **1933** *AmSp* 8.1.13 **Philadelphia PA,** *First month, second month,* etc. Used instead of January, February, etc.

First National Bank n Cf **federal building, F.D.R.**

1967 *DARE* (Qu. M21b, *Joking names for an outside toilet building*) Inf **OR**2, First National Bank.

first night See **first dark**

first off adv phr

1 At first; right away. [*EDD first* adv. 5. (3). (a)] Note: *First off* in this sense was formerly considered non-std; it is now fairly widespread.

1879 (1880) Twain *Tramp Abroad* 193, First-off, I thought it would certainly give me the botts, but I don't mind it now. **1895** *DN* 1.397 **seNY,** I was there *first off.* **1950** *WELS (He did it ———)* 1 Inf, **WI,** First off. **1951** Johnson *Resp. to PADS 20* **DE,** First off. **c1960** *Wilson Coll.* **csKY,** *First off.* . . First, at first. **1965** Will *Okeechobee Boats* 8 **FL,** First off Disston built hisself some dredges. **1967–69** *DARE* (Qu. A23, . . *"He got the right answer ———."*) Infs **IN**75, **MD**49, **NY**1, **OH**49, **PA**209, First off. **1976** Warner *Beautiful Swimmers* 286 **eMD,** But, Lordy, didn't we have our troubles first off!

2 First of all, firstly.

1940 *Sat. Eve. Post* 20 July 25/1 [Black], He fust off ain't gwine b'lieve me. An' second off, he's gwine commence doin things. **1987** *DARE* File, Saying "First off" is a way of telling the listener that the speaker has a series of things to say, of which the first will be what immediately follows. This usage has increased especially in the past decade or two.

first of it adv phr

At first.

1966 *DARE* Tape **ME**18, I worked 'em all winter with them harnesses. They, first of it, they couldn't pull so much, not first of it.

first pop (or rattle) out of the box See **first** adj **B3c**

first reader n [Transf from *first reader* an elementary reading book] *joc*

See quots.

1930 *RR Man's Mag.* June 470, *First Reader*—Conductor's train book. **1932** *Santa Fe Employes' Mag.* Jan 34/2 [Railway slang], A conductor's train book is a *first reader.*

first run n Cf **frog run**

In maple sugaring: the earliest and best flow of sap in the spring.

1947 *PADS* 8.6 **VT,** *First run.* . . The first sap of the spring. All farmers are desirous of getting the first run, for this is of the best quality. The grade goes down as the season advances.

first shot n, usu pl, but sg or pl in constr **Sth, S Midl** Cf **foreshot**

In whiskey distilling: the first of the distillate to come from the condenser.

1840 *Daily Picayune* (New Orleans LA) 30 Aug 2/4, O, it's illigant, Mrs. Mahoney, and as strong as fust shot (strong whiskey) says Mrs. Casey. **1891** *Jrl. Amer. Folkl.* 4.168 **MO,** The first shots is the first run made when stilling, or the first whiskey that is run off when starting. **1911** *DN*

3.538 **eKY,** *First-shot*. . . The last [sic] and therefore strongest run of whiskey from the still. **1968** *DARE* Tape **NC54,** After your whiskey runs out [of the still], your first shot, I'd say 220 proof, . . then you can use the . . backins . . to make it how you want to drink it, 90 proof, or 100 proof. **1974** Maurer-Pearl *KY Moonshine* 118, *First shots*. . . The initial distillate which emerges from the flakestand as the stilling process begins. This liquor is high in esters, aldehydes, and fusel oil that make it undrinkable. "This 'ere still yet runnin' first shots." Also called "heads," "foreshots." **1984** Wilder *You All Spoken Here* 137 **Sth,** The initial trickles of high-proof booze that come from the worm, or condenser, are "first shots."

first shot (out of the box) See **first** adj **B3b**

first x See **x**

fis See **fist**

fise See **feist** n

fises See **fist**

fisgig n [Var of *fizgig* frivolous woman] *old-fash*

1899 (1912) Green *VA Folk-Speech* 175, *Fisgig*. . . A worthless fellow.

fisgig adj

1899 (1912) Green *VA Folk-Speech* 175, *Fisgig*. . . Frisky.

fish n, v, adj Usu |fɪš|; also **chiefly Sth, S Midl** |fiš|; occas |fɛš| Pronc-sp *feesh*

A Forms.

1893 Shands *MS Speech* 29, *Feesh* [fiʃ]. Illiterate white and negro pronunciation of *fish*. **1902** *DN* 2.234 **sIL,** *Feesh*. . . Pronunciation of fish. **1903** *DN* 2.313 **seMO,** *Feesh*. **1907** *DN* 3.231 **nwAR,** *Feesh*. **1923** *DN* 5.209 **swMO,** I been a-hankerin' for fresh feesh. **1923** (1946) Greer-Petrie *Angeline Doin' Society* 21 **csKY,** The only thing that saved him was gittin' hit feesh'd out afore hit went plum down. **1942** Hall *Smoky Mt. Speech* 15, There is a tendency in some speakers to use . . [i] in *fish, itch, little, stick, wick*. **1944** *PADS* 2.34, *Fish* [fɛʃ]. . . Common pronunciation among Negroes and uneducated whites in some parts of the South. **1957** *Sat. Eve. Post Letters* **ceIL,** In 1913-14 I taught in Oakland, Ill. where the children pronounced *fish* as though spelled 'feesh' and *initial* as 'ineetial.' **c1960** *Wilson Coll.* **csKY,** *Fish* is occasionally [fiš]. **1966-68** *DARE* Tape **IN36,** We got a pond over here I fish [fiš] in; **NC1,** We fished [fišt] that net every morning. We'd go out once a day to fish [fiš] that net.

B As noun.

1 Codfish. Cf *DNE*

1889 *Century Dict.* 2235 **eMA,** *Fish*. . . 5. The codfish: so called specifically by Cape Cod and Cape Ann fishermen, in distinction from fish of other kinds, as mackerel, herring, etc.

2 A gullible person, dupe, greenhorn; an undesirable person, jerk—often in phr *poor fish*. [Cf *OED fish* sb.[1] 3. a 1722 →; "a person . . whom it is desirable to catch"]

1900 *DN* 2.35 [College slang], *Fish*. . . A person easily fooled. **1915** *DN* 4.233 **neOH** [College slang], *Fish*. . . A gullible person; also used as a vague term of reproach or disapproval. "You poor fish." **1920** Fitzgerald *This Side of Paradise* 38, I'm tired of being nice to every poor fish in school. **1950** *WELS (Uncomplimentary words . . about a person)* 1 Inf, **WI,** Poor fish. **1956** Sorden-Ebert *Logger's Words* 14 **Gt Lakes,** *Fish*, Anyone who is good for a touch. A person who is easily fooled. **1967-69** *DARE* (Qu. U32, . . *A very generous person*) Inf **LA45,** A good guy; a live one; a fish; a mark; (Qu. AA21, . . *A husband who takes . . [orders] from [his wife]*) Inf **OH23,** Poor fish; (Qu. II34, *If you think somebody is trying to use you to his advantage: "I'm not going to be his ______."*) Inf **GA86,** Fish. **1982** *AmSp* 57.261 (as of c1926), *Fish*—New prisoner; recent arrival.

3 In marble play: see quots. **esp West**

1940 *Recreation* (NY) 34.110, [In a list of marbles games played throughout the country:] Fish. **1942** Berrey-Van den Bark *Amer. Slang* 665.1, Fish, *a game with a fish-shaped "pot"*; . . fish, *a fish-shaped "pot"*. **1949** *PADS* 11.21 **CO,** *Fish*. . . A marble game in which the marbles are shot from a fish-shape drawn on the ground to a lagging line about ten feet away. **1967-70** *DARE* (Qu. EE7, . . *Kinds of marble games*) Inf **CA32,** Fish—after lag; in an ellipsis [sic for *ellipse*]-shaped area; set up marbles inside ellipsis; both marbles have to go out or you are frozen; **CA118,** We drew a fish, then shot marbles out of it; **CA190,** Fish; **HI1,** Fish—[in] a ring shaped like a fish; **HI6,** Fish—draw outline of fish [for the] ring; **HI9,** Fish. [5 of 6 Infs young; the sixth is a recently retired high school teacher.] **1970** *DARE* Tape **CA190,** Fish is played with a fish-shaped ring, or circle, with several marbles set in a line inside of it. The players stand back and they try and hit one of the marbles of the fish with their shooter. Once they've shot it out, their marble's poison and they try and shoot the other player's marble, and once they've hit the other player's marble the game is ended; the other player is out of the game. **c1970** Wiersma *Marbles Terms* **cwMI,** Fish—A marble game in which the ring or pot is shaped like a fish.

4 also *fishskin*: A raincoat, esp an oilskin. [See quot 1968]

1903 (1965) Adams *Log Cowboy* 47, I rode to the lead, unfastening my slicker as I went, and on reaching the turned leaders [of a stampeding herd] . . flaunted my "fish" in their faces until they re-entered the rear guard of our string. **1958** McCulloch *Woods Words* 63 **Pacific NW,** *Fishskin*—A waterproof slicker worn by green hands or non-loggers; it tears so easily it is no good for woods work. **1968** Adams *Western Words* 113, *Fish*—The yellow oilskin slicker that all old-time cowboys kept neatly rolled and tied behind the cantle of their saddles, so called because of the slicker's trade-mark, a fish.

5 In well-drilling: see quots.

1932 *AmSp* 7.266, *Fish*. . . Anything lost in the hole that must be extracted or evaded before drilling can proceed. **1949** *AmSp* 24.37 [Oil field language], Whatever is caught with one of these [fishing] tools is called a *fish*. **1951** *PADS* 15.75, To *fish for tools lost in the hole* uses a metaphor that is also common in standard English, but the oil workman uses a noun *fish* meaning anything fished for. . . "Operators were preparing to drill by the fish." **1966** *DARE* Tape **OK29,** [Inf:] There's a lot of things can go wrong; you could twist off a drill pipe a lot of times. . . You mark it [=the twisted-off place] on your kelly, so that when you go back in . . you know exactly . . where the top of your fish is. [FW:] What do you mean by the fish? [Inf:] That's the part [of the twisted-off pipe] left in the hole.

‡**6** A jalopy. [Abbr for **fish horn**]

1969 *DARE* (Qu. N5, *Nicknames for . . an old . . car*) Inf **IL108,** Fish—from the sound of the horn.

C As verb.

1 tr: To catch or try to catch (fish); to fish for.

1950 *WELS Suppl.* **csWI,** To fish wall-eyes. **1966** *DARE* Tapes **MI21,** It makes it hard to fish whitefish; **MI32,** All they do is fish pike. **1968** *DARE* FW Addit **sLA,** You can't fish perch that way.

2 To use (a specific device) for catching fish; to fish with.

1966-68 *DARE* Tape **LA5,** We hardly ever fish a net over four-and-a-half foot front; **MI21,** Years ago, when they first started to fish hooks . . they used to take old nets and save the line on 'em and then they used to tie short . . snoods, they'd only be about around fifteen, sixteen inches long, that they'd put a big hook on; **MI29,** He fished trap nets. He fished mostly for suckers . . quite a few walleyes and a few whitefish too; **NC1** [see **A** above].

3 To be serviceable in fishing.

1966 *DARE* Tape **MI21,** A seven inch [mesh gill net] would fish just as good as any net.

4 To strengthen or repair (a spar) by applying a splint; hence generally, to mend; also v phr *fish on* to splice on. **esp NEast**

[**1626** Smith *Accidence* 3 **NEng,** Ready for . . fishing or spliceing the Masts or Yards. *Ibid* 13, A Jury-mast . . is made with yards, rouftrees, or what they can, . . fished together.] **1711** (1879) S. Sewall *Diary* 2.322 **MA,** Our Axel-tree . . broke quite off. . . Fish'd on a piece in the morning. **1840** (1841) Dana *2 Yrs.* 276, All hands were now employed in setting up the lee rigging, fishing the sprit-sail yard, lashing the galley, and getting tackles upon the martingale. **1909** *DN* 3.420 **Cape Cod MA** (as of a1857), *Fish*. . . To mend a broken spar, as a gaff, by fastening around it battens, that is, stout sticks of timber. **1942** ME Univ. *Studies* 56.67, In case of loss of masts or heavy spars which they could not replace or *fish* [Footnote: Repair with splints], . . they went into a foreign port for repairs. **1945** Colcord *Sea Language* 76 **ME, Cape Cod, Long Island,** To fish . . means at sea, to mend a spar by setting in a brace or splint. . . Alongshore, the word is used for mending jobs. "I want you should fish that clothes-horse for me today."

5 See quot 1945.

1840 (1841) Dana *2 Yrs.* 269 **NEast,** The whaler came in, and made a clumsy piece of work in getting her anchor. . . They were heave-ho-ing, stopping and unstopping, pawling, catting, and fishing, for three hours. **1945** Colcord *Sea Language* 76 **ME, Cape Cod, Long Island,** Fish also . . is applied . . to one of the processes of getting the anchor fast on the bow after weighing.

6 To doze.

1952 Brown *NC Folkl.* 1.540, *Fishing: pres. part.* or *adj.* Nodding, asleep.—General. Rare.

7 as vbl n; In rodeo parlance: see quots.

1968 Adams *Western Words* 114, *Fishing*—In rodeo, roping in such a way as to sweat a near miss into a fair catch; for example, throwing a wide loop that settles flat on a calf's neck and then falls clear around his neck. **1978** *WI State Jrl.* (Madison) 23 July Rodeo Section 7/2 **Madison WI,** Fishing—A common expression used in rodeo when the roper has thrown at an animal but has missed, and then by accident, or by flipping the rope, turns it into a legal catch.

8 in phr *fish in the right direction:* To be on the right track.

1959 *VT Hist.* 27.135, *Fish in the right direction*. . . To go in the right direction or toward a goal. Occasional.

D As adj.

Foolish, stupid. **[fish B2]**

1980 Banks *First-Person America* 105 **VT** (as of c1939), Only suckers work for a living. I know because I tried it. I worked in the stone sheds [where granite and marble are carved]. My brother Dante is still in there. I tell him he's fish but he don't listen.

fish and game club n **chiefly NEast**

A rod and gun club.

1967–69 *DARE* (Qu. FF22b) Infs **MA**1, 69, **NY**92, 146, 175, 190, Fish and Game Club; (Qu. FF22a) Inf **NY**219, Fish and Game Club Auxiliary.

fishback n [From the fin-like deflector]

In the tobacco industry: a stove which controls barn humidity during tobacco curing.

1966 *PADS* 45.12 **KY,** *Fishback*. . . "A fishback has got a heat deflector on it."

fish bait n

1 also *fish-bait worm, fishing bait:* **=earthworm. chiefly Midl, Sth**

1934 Carmer *Stars Fell on AL* 216, She might git some fishbait worms an' boil 'em and strain the water. **1949** Kurath *Word Geog.* 74, *Fish bait* and *bait worm* occupy smaller areas within the extensive *fish worm* and *fishing worm* areas of the Midland and the South, namely, (1) south-central Pennsylvania and adjoining parts of Maryland and (2) the western piedmont of North Carolina and adjoining parts of Virginia. **1966** Dakin *Dial. Vocab. Ohio R. Valley* 2.394, *Fish(ing) bait* is fairly common beside the usual red-worm in southern Kentucky. This term . . also has rare scattered use in Ohio and Illinois within the *fish worm/fishing worm* areas. **1967** Faries *Word Geog. MO* 111, The Southern and Midland *fish bait* . . , while in scattered usage, is most common south of the Missouri River. **1968–69** *DARE* (Qu. P5, . . *The common worm used as bait*) Infs **MD**29, **PA**166, **TX**67, Fish bait; **MS**11, Fishing bait. **1973** Gawthrop *Dial. Calumet* 73 **nwIN,** [Ten of one hundred twenty-five infs used the term *fish bait*].

2 See quot.

1966–67 *DARE* (Qu. X16, *Sticky mucus that forms in the nose—children's words for this*) Infs **GA**7, **TX**33, Fish bait. [Laughter]

fishbait tree n [Because the tree attracts the catalpa worm] Cf **fishworm tree**

=catalpa B1.

1966–67 *DARE* (Qu. T9) Infs **MS**38, **SC**46, Fishbait tree.

fishbait worm See **fish bait 1**

fish ball n

1 A deep-fried ball of shredded fish and mashed potatoes. **NEng** Cf **codfish ball**

[**1830** Child *Frugal Housewife* 62 **Boston MA,** There is no way of preparing salt fish for breakfast, so nice as to roll it up in little balls, after it is mixed with mashed potatoes, dip it into an egg, and fry it brown.] **1854** Shillaber *Life Partington* 100 **MA,** The breakfast was waiting for him, the fishballs were getting cold. **1896** (c1973) Farmer *Orig. Cook Book* 160 **MA,** *Fish Balls.* 1 cup salt codfish. 1 egg. 2 heaping cups potatoes. . . Take up by spoonfuls, put in frying-basket, and fry for one minute in deep fat. **1939** Wolcott *Yankee Cook Book* 30, Eating fish balls for Sunday morning breakfast is part of Boston's tradition, like reading the Transcript or taking visitors to see the glass flowers. **1944** Johnson *As Much* 7, Only in parts of New England do beans and brown bread come always for Saturday supper, and fish balls for Sunday breakfast.

2 A ball of chopped fish, egg, milk, etc, cooked in boiling water. **esp Scandinavian settlement areas**

1901 Kander *Settlement Cook Book* 116 **WI,** *Fish balls* . . raw fish . . egg . . bread crumbs . . milk. . . shape into balls. . . Drop into boiling, salted water. **1936** Farmer *Cookbook* 222, *Swedish Fish Balls.* Shape mixture [=fish, egg whites, cream, etc] in buttered tablespoon. Slip . . into boiling water. Cook 8 minutes. **1950** *WELS (Dishes made with fish)* 3 Infs, **WI,** Fish balls. **1965** Farmer *Cookbook* 131, Swedish Fish Balls. **1966** Tufford *Scandinavian Recipes* 72 **MN,** *Fiskeboller (Fish Balls)*—Remove scales from a good sized pickerel or other fish. . . Grind very fine . . adding a little sweet cream until mixture is of right consistency to form into balls. . . Boil fish balls 20 minutes. **1969** *DARE* (Qu. H45, *Dishes . . that people in other places might not [know]*) Inf **WI**76, Fish balls—especially Norwegian; **MN**11, Fish balls—boiled balls of herring. [Both Infs of Scan background, from Scan communities]

fish basket n Also *basket* **chiefly S Atl** See Map Cf **fish box 1, ~ pot, ~ wall**

Any of various types of fish trap; see quots.

1814 Brackenridge *Views of LA* 179 **LA,** There are various modes of stopping a crevasse [in a levee] . . ; they begin . . to drive double rows of piles gradually falling with the current so as to meet less resistance, until they unite, and thus form a semicircle like a fish basket. **1872** Schele de Vere *Americanisms* 351, The *Fish-Basket* of Pennsylvania . . designates a structure for taking fish. . . "Various species," says Professor S. S. Haldeman, . . "are abundantly caught . . in fish-baskets, made of lath-work, with diverging walls of stone." **1883** (1971) Harris *Nights with Remus* 383 **GA** [Black], Ole man Plato say dat de nigger on de River place w'at aint got a fish-baskit in de river er some intruss in a fish-trap aint got no 'count w'atsomever. **c1937** in 1972 *Amer. Slave* 2.244 **SC,** They had fish baskets, made of wooden splits, with an opening at the end like the wire baskets now used. **c1960** *Wilson Coll.* **csKY,** *Fish basket*—A slatted fish trap, usually baited. **1965–70** *DARE* (Qu. P13, . . *Other ways of fishing*) 11 Infs, **chiefly S Atl,** (Fish) basket(s); **FL**16, **SC**40, Wire basket; **AR**9, Fish baskets—illegal; **GA**76, Fish baskets—fish trap, built by Indians; **KY**23, Fish baskets—fish traps; **SC**3, Fish basket—a trap; **SC**31, Basket—used to be made of splits . . funnel-shaped . . made of wire now; **SC**32, Fish basket—a wire trap; **SC**40, White oak basket; **SC**57, Baskets—split baskets. **1969** *DARE* Tape **GA**84, He would fish with a fish basket in the summertime; **KY**16, We used to put baskets in the river. They'd . . make baskets outa splits . . of timber. **1972** Hilliard *Hog Meat* 86 **Sth,** The basket, or "trap," was particularly useful, since the angler wasted little time tending them.

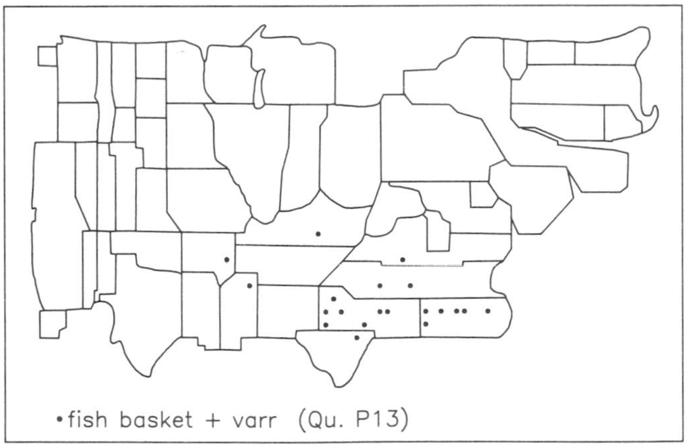

fish begonia n [From the spotted or scale-like appearance of the leaf]

A fibrous-rooted begonia: see quot.

1892 *Jrl. Amer. Folkl.* 5.96 **MA,** *Begonia maculata,* trout begonia. Bedford, Mass. fish begonia. Cambridge, Mass.

fish belly n

1 A fish peddler.

1967 Cerello *Dakota Co. MN* 59, We often called male[s] or females who sold fresh fish fish-bellies.

2 A second-rate prostitute.

1967 Cerello *Dakota Co. MN* 59, She was an old fish-belly and played around every young man, married or unmarried, that she could hook for a few dollars. . . A fish-belly never cared much hows [sic] they dressed;

she never had the quality of the really professional ladies who sold favors to men. [Cerello: Recorded from six communities.]

fish billy n

1957 Beck *Folkl. ME* 119, Along with each trawl tub went a short gaff to haul the larger fish aboard and a "fish billy" (a short, carved club) to kill the bigger fish before they could knock out the side of the boat or otherwise prove disagreeable.

fishbite n Cf **wedgie**

1988 *DARE* File **seID,** The act of lifting a person (from behind) by the belt, belt buckles, top of the underwear, the seat of the pants: Fishbite; **csWI,** Fishbite.

fish blankets n [Perh because small fish hide among its soft hairlike leaves]

=**hornwort 1.**

1920 *Torreya* 20.20 **SC,** *Ceratophyllum demersum* . . Fish-blankets. **1933** Small *Manual SE Flora* 509, *Ceratophyllum*. . . Fish-blankets. **1959** Carleton *Index Herb. Plants* 46, *Fish blankets:* Ceratophyllum demersum.

fish blossom n [See quot 1921] Cf **shadberry**

=**redbud.**

1819 (1970) Thomas *Travels W. Country* 67, *Cercis canadensis* fish blossom. **1921** Deam *Trees IN* 227, The redbud is the common name for this tree throughout the State. In one locality it was known as the fish blossom because the larger fish spawn when this tree is in flower. **1940** Clute *Amer. Plant Names* 255, *Cercis Canadensis.* Fish blossoms, red Judas-tree.

fish boil n Cf **fish fry**

A dish consisting of boiled fish, potatoes, and onions; the gathering at which this dish is served.

1952 Tracy *Coast Cookery* 67 **Chicago IL,** *Great Lakes Fish Boil*—On the shores of the Great Lakes a favorite outdoor or shore dinner is the fish boil—a meal in one kettle. **1968** *DARE* (Qu. H45, *Dishes* . . *that people in other places might not [know]*) Inf **WI60,** Fish boil; start potatoes boiling, add fish; the liquid must boil over three times before it's finished; use lake trout. I think this originated in Algoma. **1973** *WI State Jrl.* (Madison) 5 July sec 2 1, Steaming potatoes, onions, chunks of fresh whitefish or lake trout, hot coffee, cabbage salad, cherry pie . . —that's the fish boil. . . Fish boils were being held on this thumb of Wisconsin jutting out into Lake Michigan for as long as any of the natives can remember. **1987** *DARE* File, In Door County, Wisconsin, many restaurants advertise their fish boils; most are on Friday night, but some places have them other nights as well.

fish bone n [From the shape]

=**Indian bead.**

1967 *Living Museum* 29.107 **IL,** Because crinoids were so abundant and because a single stem sometimes contained several hundred individual plates, these stone buttons are among the most common fossils in Illinois. These so-called "Indian beads" or "fish bones" can be collected in most parts of Illinois.

fish bouquet n

1945 Saxon *Gumbo Ya-Ya* 317, In Louisiana graveyards the decorating is unrestrained. . . 'Fish bouquets,' flowers and wreaths made of garfish scales used to be favorites, but are seldom seen now.

fish box n

1 See quot. Cf **fish basket**

1965 *DARE* (Qu. P13, . . *Other ways of fishing*) Inf **TN53,** Fish box.

2 In ice fishing: a type of tip-up or tilt constructed from a box which is placed over the hole.

1967 *WI Conserv. Bulletin* Jan-Feb 12, The styles and types of tip-ups and fish boxes stagger the imagination: under-water tip-ups, heated box tip-ups, tip-ups with mousetraps, [etc].

3 A can containing fish; see quot.

1950 *PADS* 14.16 **SC,** "Fish box," a can of salmon, etc.

fish brant n

=**snow goose.**

1874 Long *Amer. Wild-Fowl* 243, The snow-geese are all called fish-brant, and as such are never pursued for the table.

fish bread n

1954 *Harder Coll.* **cwTN,** *Fish bread* . . made from fish scraps mixed with cornmeal. Common.

fish bug n

A **June beetle** (here: *Phyllophaga* spp).

1969 *DARE* (Qu. R5, *A big brown beetle that comes out in large numbers in spring and early summer, and flies with a buzzing sound*) Inf **KY11,** June bugs—green; fish bugs—brown.

fishburg n [Blend of *fish* + **hamburg 1**]

A fish sandwich.

1968 *DARE* File **csNY,** [On a menu at a lunch counter:] Hamburg, cheeseburg, fishburg.

fish burner n **AK**

A sled dog.

1967 *AK Sportsman* Nov 8 (Tabbert *Alaskan Engl.*), In Anchorage, the gas burners are running swift competition to the traditional fish burners in the field of sport. **1969** *AK Sportsman* Aug 25/3, It's easier to run a trap line on snowshoes than to worry about feeding a half dozen or more 'fish burners'. **1976** Vaudrin *Racing Alaskan Sled Dogs* 65 (Tabbert *Alaskan Engl.*), You can't have a wife making static about a new $300 dog. She's got to be the kind that when you bring home another fish-burner, . . she kisses you and wants to know why you didn't get two.

fish cake n

1988 *Barrick Coll.* **csPA,** Fishcakes—A type of "flip flop" or sandal with laminated rubber soles.

fish camp n Also *fishing camp*

1 A seasonal camp established by Indians for the purpose of fishing. **chiefly AK**

1806 (1905) Lewis *Orig. Jrls. Lewis & Clark Exped.* 4.200 **nwOR,** We arrived at a Cathlahmah fishing cam[p] of one lodge; here we found 3 men . . who from appearances had remained here some time for the purpose of taking sturgeon. **1902** U.S. Revenue Cutter Serv. *Rept. Nunivak* 80 **AK,** By the middle of October all the Indians living in the vicinity of Dall River had returned from their various fishing camps and taken up their quarters in the winter village at the mouth of the Dall. **1917** Stuck *Voyages Yukon* 183, The fish camp at Anvik, with its many tents, its smouldering fires and its swarming native people and dogs, is a picturesque sight. **1973** *Tabbert Coll.* **AK,** Fish camp—A temporary or semi-permanent habitation along a river or ocean where natives stay to lay up a winter's supply. **1979** Henzie *Biography* 56 **AK,** When water is right, everybody leave and get ready for fish camp.

2 A camp established for sport fishermen, esp a commercial operation supplying lodging and sometimes equipment to fishermen.

1897 *Outing* 30.374/2, We have the hunting camp, the fishing camp, the trapping camp. **1978** *New Yorker* 5 June 75, [She] told . . something of the recent history of her family as it had to do with a fishing camp maintained by them on the Au Sable River in Michigan. . . [T]hey run it now for paying guests. **1980** *Capital Times* (Madison WI) 26 Sept 18/1, Someone told him about a primitive fishing camp built by a Finn 40 miles northeast of Ely, Minn., on the Canadian border. . . [We] came up to spend a vacation here in one of the four cabins.

3 also *fisherman's camp:* A boat landing with rental equipment for fishermen. **Sth** See Map

1946 *Birmingham News-Age-Herald* 7 April 1-B/8 *(DA)* **AL,** Fishing camps where boats may be obtained are fairly well distributed about the fishing waters. **1964** Will *Hist. Okeechobee* 120 **FL,** Fish camps began

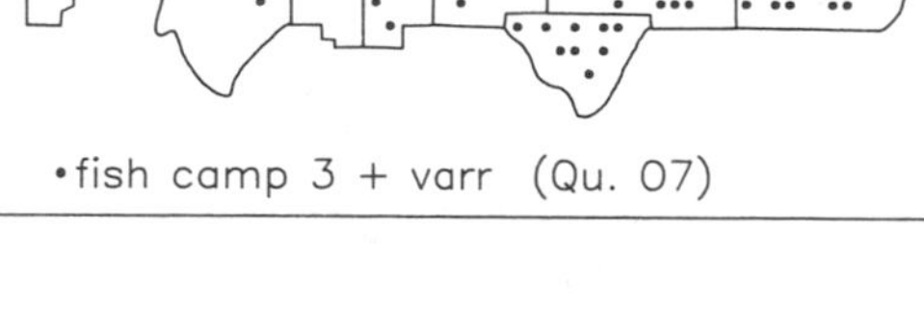

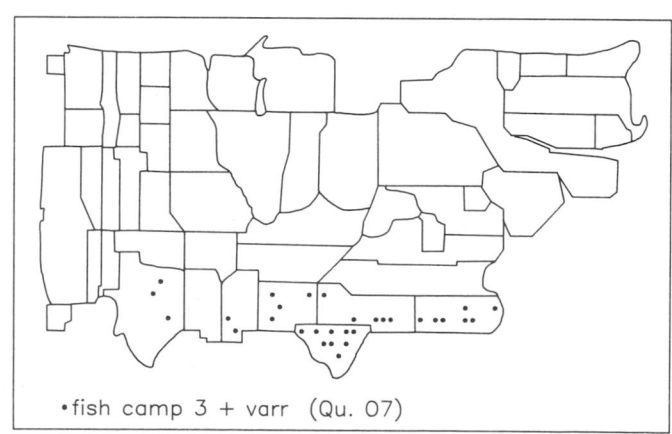

•fish camp 3 + varr (Qu. 07)

to spring up. . . A camp was nothing but a long, narrow shack built of palmetto thatch on a frame of cypress poles, or maybe it might be of tarpaper tacked on 2 x 4's. Offshore a bit, or even far out in the lake would be the skinning bench, a platform perched on spindly piles, roofed with cabbage leaves or tin. Sometimes a camp was a houseboat, with a covered porch on which the cats were skinned. These "floating rigs" became more common later on. **1965** *DARE* (Qu. O7, . . *A place where boats can be rented*) 15 Infs, 8 **FL,** Fish camp; 14 Infs, 7 **SC,** Fishing camp; **FL**1, Fisherman's camp.

4 By ext: see quots.

1980 *AmSp* 55.80 **NC, SC,** *Fish camp* [is] a term common in the Carolinas for a restaurant specializing in fish dishes. Carolina fish camps generally offer no facilities for fishing, nor are lakes necessarily nearby. . . Originally a *fish camp* . . was . . a place where . . one could go fishing. Often the lake on which the camp was situated provided the fish for a nearby restaurant, to which the term *fish camp* came also to be applied. Later, other fish restaurants, many having no lake to draw upon, took on the name *fish camp.* **1980** *DARE* File **swNC,** We were visiting in the . . area last month and noted numerous advertisements for "Fish Camps." These appeared to be road houses or restaurants specializing in fish and sea food dishes, although one of them advertised that it also served steaks.

fish car n [**car** n[2]] Cf **eel car**

See quot 1889.

1818 (1930) Hazard *Jrl.* 512/2 **csRI,** Son Benja[min] and Joseph M Taylor Carried the Lobster Potts and Fish Carr to the Pier and brought home a lode of Eal Grass. **1839** *Knickerbocker* 14.323 **NYC,** 'Tell me where you would sleep.' . . 'Up here in a fish-car, in the market.' **1867** De Voe *Market Ass't* 21 *(DA),* His early visit gave him the desired opportunity to select . . and *catch* the lively, jumping fish, which, ten minutes before, were swimming in the fish-cars. **1884** U.S. Natl. Museum *Bulletin* 27.1050, *Floating fish car.* . . A series of six wooden crates suspended in frame with floats on two sides. . . Used for preserving live fish at market. **1889** *Century Dict.* 2236, *Fish-car.* . . A box in which fish which have been caught are kept alive, designed to be towed in the water behind a boat. **1939** FWP *Guide FL* 200 **FL,** The *fish markets* . . line the waterfront [at Key West]. Each has its wharf, and tied to the various docks are crates called 'fish cars'. Here fish are netted, killed, and dressed in the buyer's presence. **1978** *Pioneer Amer.* June 89 **Missip Valley,** The *live-car* (also called *live-boat,* . . and *fish-car*) is a boat shaped structure made of widely spaced wooden slats. Water can circulate freely through the live-car, thus fish placed in it can be transported alive.

fish coop n

=fish shanty.

1889 *Century Dict.* 2236 **wNY,** *Fish-coop.* . . A box about three feet square used in fishing through ice. There is a hole in its bottom, which is placed over a similar hole in the ice. The fisherman crawls into the box, and, it being quite dark inside, can see to the bottom of the water, into which he lets down a decoy or lure by a string. When fish are attracted by the lure, he spears them. This device is used on lakes in western New York.

fish crane n Also *fish heron*

=great blue heron.

1917 *Wilson Bulletin* 29.2.78, *Ardea herodias.* . . Blue, fish or gopher crane, Fresno, Calif. **1932** Bennitt *Check-list* 14 **MO,** *Great blue heron.* . . Blue crane; fish heron; poor Joe. **1961** Ligon *NM Birds* 29, *Great Blue Heron.* . . The name Fish Crane, commonly applied to it, is a misnomer, since its food consists of a great variety of aquatic life. The fish on which these Herons feed are largely undesirable, such as carp and suckers. **1968–69** *DARE* (Qu. Q10, . . *Water birds*) Inf **IL**67, Fish crane; **MD**29, Fish crane—dips into water, catches fish.

fish crow n

1 A crow *(Corvus ossifragus)* commonly found near water, esp along the Atlantic and Gulf coasts. Also called **carrion crow 2, jackdaw**

1812 Wilson *Amer. Ornith.* 5.27, *Fish crow. Corvus ossifragus* . . is another roving inhabitant of our sea-coasts, ponds, and river shores. **1883** *Century Illustr. Mag.* 26.682/2 **NY,** The fish-crow fishes only when it has destroyed all the eggs and young birds it can find. **1916** *Times-Picayune* (New Orleans LA) 16 Apr 9, *Fish Crow* (Corvus ossifragus). Kopman found this smaller species abundant along the coast, but not inland. **1934** *Natl. Geogr. Mag.* 65.610/2 **sGA,** Was this, I wondered, a clever move to mislead such devourers of its eggs as the bear, raccoon, skunk, and fish crow? **1962** Imhof *AL Birds* 375, The Fish Crow eats nearly all kinds of food, but naturally much of its diet is marine life. **1968** *DARE* (Qu. Q11, . . *Kinds of blackbirds*) Inf **AK**1, Beach crow or fish crow.

2 also *(north)western fish crow:* **=northwestern crow.**

1858 Baird *Birds* 569, *Northwestern Fish Crow.* . . By the above name I wish to indicate a small crow from the northwest coast, which, though not much like the eastern fish crow, appears to possess its peculiar habits. **1953** Jewett *Birds WA* 470, *Corvus caurinus.* . . Other names: Fish Crow; Western Fish Crow; Northwestern Fish Crow.

fish-drownder n

A very heavy rain.

1968 *DARE* (Qu. B25, . . *"It's a regular ______."*) Inf **OH**87, Fish-drownder.

fish duck n

1 also *fisher duck, fishing ~:* **=merganser. chiefly Inland Nth** See Map Cf **fisherman 1**

[**1805** (1904) Lewis *Orig. Jrls. Lewis & Clark Exped.* 2.179, I have seen for the first time on the Missouri at these falls, a species of fishing ducks with white wings, brown and white body and the head and part of the neck adjoining a brick red.] **1813** (1824) Wilson *Amer. Ornith.* 8.126, The Smew, or White Nun. . . This is another of those Mergansers commonly known in this country by the appellation of Fishermen, Fisher Ducks, or Divers. **1858** Baird *Birds* 813, *Mergus americanus.* Goosander; Sheldrake; Fish Duck. **1917** (1923) *Birds Amer.* 1.111, Red-breasted Merganser. . . Other Names. . . Fishing Duck; Fish Duck; Red-breasted Sheldrake. **1950** *WELS (Wild ducks)* 3 Infs, **WI,** Fish duck; 1 Inf, Fish duck—so called because its flesh tastes of fish. **1965–70** *DARE* (Qu. Q5, . . *Wild ducks*) 21 Infs, **chiefly Nth,** Fish duck; **OR**13, Fisher duck; (Qu. Q10, *Other water birds*) 20 Infs, **chiefly Nth,** Fish duck; (Qu. Q9) Infs **MI**101, **WA**24, Fish duck; (Qu. Q8) Inf **TN**53, Fishing duck. **1975** Newell *If Nothin' Don't Happen* 231 **nwFL,** Some wood ducks went a-screamin' over and a couple of them little black-and-white fish ducks the Yankees call mergansers.

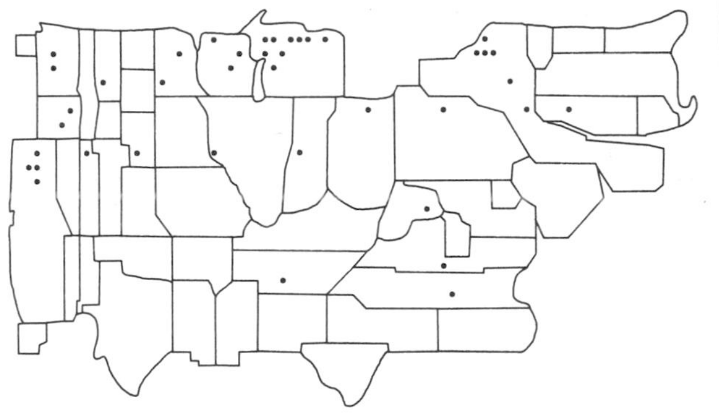

•fish duck 1 + varr (Qq. Q5, Q10, Q8, Q9)

2 =long-billed curlew.

1881 *Forest & Stream* 17.226, Sickle-billed curlew *(Numenius longirostris).* . . are plenty all winter on Savannah River and are there called "fish ducks" by the natives, but are not esteemed of value for table use.

3 =white-winged scoter.

1953 Jewett *Birds WA* 147, *Melanitta deglandi* . . Fish Duck.

fish eagle n Also *fishing eagle* [See quot 1955]

=fish hawk 1.

1917 (1923) *Birds Amer.* 2.94, Osprey—*Pandion haliaëtus.* . . Fishing Eagle. **1926** *AmSp* 1.419 **Okefenokee GA,** Shot a Fish Eagle fer 'im. [Footnote:] The specimen (a Fish Hawk) is still in his collection. **1946** Goodrich *Birds in KS* 315, Fish eagle . . osprey. **1950** *PADS* 14.29 **SC,** *Fish eagle.* . . The osprey. **1955** MA Audubon Soc. *Bulletin* 39.442, *Osprey.* Fish Eagle (. . . The bird preys almost exclusively upon fishes, and is eaglelike in appearance.) **1966–69** *DARE* (Qu. Q4, . . *Hawks . . found around here*) Inf **KY**11, Fish hawk—some call it a fish eagle; **WA**6, Fish eagle.

fish-eater n **chiefly Inland Nth, N Midl** See Map *derog* or *joc* Cf **mackerel-snapper**

A member of an ethnic or religious group (esp Roman Catholic) noted for eating fish.

1946 *Western Folkl.* 5.177 **MT,** Finns didn't mind being called "Fish Eaters" or "Herring Chokers," but they resented being called "Round Heads." **1949** *AmSp* 24.26 **MN,** Those of Duluth were once [called] *Fisheaters* because its only land connection with the world was provided by a precarious stagecoach line to St. Paul. **1950** *WELS (Nicknames for different religions)* 3 Infs, **WI,** Fish-eaters; 2 Infs, Fish-eaters—Catholics. **1965–70** *DARE* (Qu. CC4, . . *Nicknames . . for . . religious groups*) 66 Infs, **chiefly Inland Nth, N Midl,** Fish-eaters [most Infs specified Roman Catholics]; **GA**11, Fish-eaters—Catholics and Episcopalians; **MI**3, **MS**45, **NY**166, **WI**70, Fish-eaters [FW sugg; Infs have heard]; (Qu. HH28, . . *Nicknames . . for people of foreign background*) Inf **IL**29, Fish-eaters—Irish, if they're also Catholic; **MI**47, Fish-eaters—Finns; **WA**13, Fish-eaters—Norwegians; (Qu. FF23, . . *Joking names for . . clubs*) Inf **NY**131, Fish-eaters—Knights of Columbus. **c1971** Hall *Snake River Valley* **sID,** Fish-eaters—Catholics. [5 infs] **1989** *NY Times* (NY) 13 Dec 31/1 **cnMD** (as of 1930s–40s), [Newspaper column:] There was much amusement among Protestants about the Catholics eating fish every Friday, but the term of abuse around Union Square "fish eaters" seemed toothless enough.

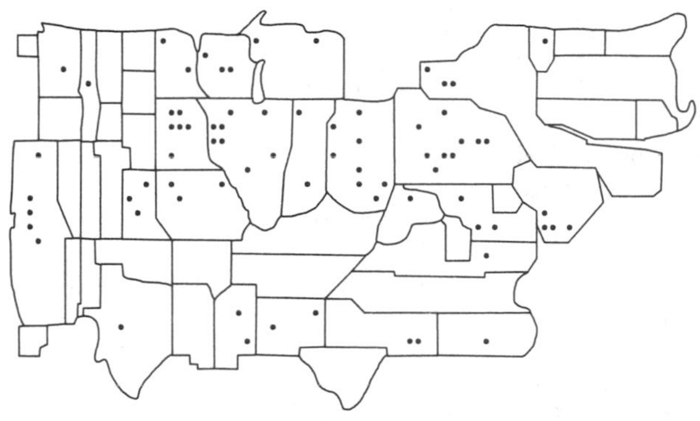
•fish-eater (Qq. CC4, FF23, HH28)

fish eel n

An eel *(Anguilla rostrata).*

1966–68 *DARE* (Qu. P1, . . *Freshwater fish . . that are good to eat*) Infs **LA**8, **MS**16, **TN**24, Fish eel; (Qu. P3, *Freshwater fish that are not good to eat*) Inf **LA**15, Fish eel; **LA**29, Eels—commonly called fish eels.

fish egg n [From the texture and translucence]

A globule of tapioca or sago pudding.

1922 *DN* 5.141 **sePA** [College slang], Seems to me we get nothing but fish-eggs for dessert lately. **1969** Sorden *Lumberjack Lingo* NEng, Gt Lakes, *Fish eggs*—Tapioca pudding.

fisher n

1 also *fisher cat,* ~ *fox,* ~ *weasel:* A marten (here: *Martes pennanti*). [See quot 1928]

1685 (1902) Budd *Good Order* 38 **NJ, PA,** The Commodities fit to send to *England* . . are the Skins of the several wild Beasts that are in the Country, as . . *Fisher, Bear,* [etc]. **1806** (1905) Clark *Orig. Jrls. Lewis & Clark Exped.* 4.88 **WA,** The *black Fox* or as they are more frequently called by the N West Trader *Fisher* is found in the woody country on this coast. **1825** in 1974 *Fauna Americana* 65, *Mustela canadensis. . . Pekan weasel. . .* The *fisher,* . . from the western states. *Fisher weasel* or *martin* of others. **1887** (1895) Robinson *Uncle Lisha* 153 **wVT,** I jedge the name of fisher an' black cat don't no ways imply to 'em. They don't ketch fish, an' consequentially they hain't fishers, an' though they be toll'able black, they don't resemblance the cat speshy [=species]. . . They're a overgrowed weasel or saple. **1928** Anthony *N. Amer. Mammals* 97, Fisher.—*Martes pennanti. . .* The Fisher is a large Marten and is said to have been so named . . because of its fondness for fish. In appearance it looks like an overgrown black Cat or a black Fox. It is one . . of the most feared members of the Weasel family. **1935** Pratt *Manual Vertebrate Animals* 273, *Martes pennanti. . .* Fisher. **1940** Richter *Trees* 11 **sOH** (as of c1800), The black cat of the forest that could see in the dark that some called the fisher fox. **1965–70** *DARE* (Qu. P32) 8 Infs, **Nth,** Fisher; **AK**1, Fisher—similar to a marten; **CA**105, Fisher—last one caught in 1908. Fast, climbing animal; cat-like, twenty-five pounds; **CA**145, Fisher—like a pine marten but three times as big; **MN**5, Fisher—like an otter; **NY**6, Fisher—like a fox, but more like a wolverine; dark in color, shorter than fox legs; **NY**71, Black cat = fisher; **NH**4, 14, Fisher cat. **1982** *Milwaukee Jrl.* (WI) 6 Jan sec 2 5/4, The fisher is a medium-sized mammal, weighing about 10 pounds. It has the build of a stocky weasel. The fisher is uniquely adapted to prey on porcupines. Their low bodies allow the fisher to attack the porcupine's face.

2 A **kingfisher** or similar bird.

1737 (1911) Brickell *Nat. Hist. NC* 209, The Dipper, or Fisher . . so called, from their dexterity in Fishing and catching small Fish, on which they feed. **1805** (1904) Lewis *Orig. Jrls. Lewis & Clark Exped.* 2.225 **MT,** The blue crested fisher, or as they are sometimes called the *Kingfisher,* is an inhabitant of this part of the country; this bird is very rare on the Missouri. **1969** *DARE* (Qu. Q10, *Other water birds*) Inf **MA**15, Fisher = the kingfisher.

fisher cat See **fisher 1**

fisher coon See **fisher raccoon**

fisher duck See **fish duck 1**

fisher fox See **fisher 1**

fisherman n

1 =merganser. chiefly C Atl coast

1737 (1911) Brickell *Nat. Hist. NC* 208, The Fishermen, so called, from their Dexterity in Fishing, . . are like a Duck, only they have narrow bills with sets of Teeth. They feed on small Fish and Fry, which they catch as they swim. **1813** [see **fish duck 1**]. **1968** *DARE* (Qu. Q5) Inf **NC**80, Fisherman (fish duck). **1968** *DARE* FW Addit **DE**7, Fisherman—a duck with a bill like a crow. He's almost black, has a dark bill and a topknot.

2 A porpoise.

1966 *DARE* FW Addit **seGA,** Fisherman—a porpoise or dolphin. [The term is] used on fishing boats, [where] it is considered bad luck to use the word *porpoise.* **1980** *DARE* File **Sapelo Is. GA** (as of 1953), "The Fisherman" is the only term used by Gullah fishermen for the porpoise. To use any other term is to invite the worst luck.

3 In well-drilling operations: see quot. **[fish B5]**

1903 *DN* 2.340 **wNY, wPA, WV,** *Fisherman. . .* An expert who gives his time to recovering 'stuck tools.'

fisherman's camp See **fish camp 3**

fisherman's hornpipe See **fisher's hornpipe**

fisherman's luck n **scattered, but more freq Sth, Midl**

Bad luck in fishing—often in phr *fisherman's luck, a wet ass, and a hungry gut* and varr.

1889 *Century Dict.* 8.2236, *Fisherman. . . Fisherman's luck,* getting wet and hungry, and catching no fish; poor luck. [Colloq.] **1899** (1912) Green *VA Folk-Speech* 27, Fisherman's luck, wet backside, and a hungry gut. **1942** McAtee *Dial. Grant Co. IN Suppl. 1* 4 (as of 1890s), *Fisherman's luck. . .* A stock response to the question, "What luck did you have?", was, "Fisherman's luck, a wet ass, and a hungry gut." **1965–70** *DARE* (Qu. P9, *When you're fishing but not catching any, you might say "________."*) 31 Infs, **scattered, but more freq Sth, Midl,** (Had *or* having) fisherman's luck; **MO**18, **NC**82, Fishermen's luck; **DE**4, **TN**26, Fisherman's luck, wet ass, and a hungry gut; **GA**77, Muddy rump and a hungry gut is the old fisherman's luck; **KY**84, Fisherman's luck, a wet tail, and a hungry gut; **NJ**1, Fisherman's luck, wet ass, and empty gut; [**SC**69, Fishing my luck, no fish, hungry guts]. **1984** Wilder *You All Spoken Here* 150 **Sth,** *Wet ass, hungry gut, an' nary a scale:* Fisherman's luck.

fisherman's moon n

A full moon.

1978 Mullen *Old Fishermen* 58 **seTX,** "A fisherman's moon is a full, clear moon". . . There were varying explanations as to why a full moon brought about good fishing, for instance: "On a full moon the shrimp was bunched together. When it decreased they seemed to spread out."

fishermen's coal n

1951 Morgan *Skid Road* 226 **cwWA,** The men spent hours combing the beach for bark ("fishermen's coal") and driftwood.

fishermen's court n

1939 FWP *Guide NC* 277, Here [=Gatesville] is annually held the Fishermen's (February) Court (3rd Mon. in Feb.) which developed, after slaves had been freed, as a day on which Negro labor was employed for the fishing season.

fishermen's net n

1967 *DARE* (Qu. B10, . . *Long trailing clouds high in the sky*) Inf **NC**38, Fishermen's nets.

fisher raccoon n Also *fisher coon*
=raccoon.
1850 Seymour *Sketches MN* 240, The wolf, the fox, the wolverine, the fisher raccoon, musk-rat, mink. **1960** Williams *Walk Egypt* 40 **GA,** He told me about this old fisher-coon he'd caught.

fisher's hornpipe n Also *fisherman's hornpipe*
A traditional dance.
1899 Garland *Boy Life* 209 **nwIA,** At last came the inevitable call for the "Fisherman's Hornpipe," or the "Devil's Dream," to which Joe Gilman jigged with . . energy and abandon. **1940** Writers' Program *Guide OH* 21, Settlers given to more rollicking entertainment found it in the taverns at night, dancing the money musk and the fisher's hornpipe. **1969** *DARE* (Qu. FF5a, . . *Different steps . . in dancing—in past years*) Infs **MA**48, 73, Fisher's hornpipe. [Both Infs old] **1969** *DARE* Tape **VT**13, We did the contras, fisher's hornpipe, and money musk. . . then there would be other contra dances with a little different changes.

fisher spider n Also *fishing spider* [See quots 1972 and 1980 Milne]
A spider of the genus *Dolomedes.*
1967 *DARE* (Qu. R28) Inf **CA**26, Fisher spider. **1972** Kaston *How Know Spiders* 188, *Genus Dolomedes*—Fishing Spiders—Most of the members of this genus live near water and have been reported catching small fishes as well as the aquatic insects on which they usually feed. **1980** Milne-Milne *Audubon Field Guide Insects* 894, Brownish-gray Fishing Spider—*(Dolomedes tenebrosus)*. . . Spider hunts widely, finding prey on water surface, in water, and on land. . . It occasionally seizes a small fish or tadpole that swims by. . . Six-spotted Fishing Spider—*(Dolomedes triton)*. **1980** Oates *Bellefleur* 21, He sometimes crouched for hours in the waist-high rushes, watching dragonflies and fisher spiders and whirligig beetles.

fisher weasel See **fisher 1**

fish eye n
1 =fish egg.
1929 *Ruppenthal Coll.* **KS,** *Fish eyes*—tapioca pudding (army usage). **1958** McCulloch *Woods Words* 63 **Pacific NW,** *Fish-eyes*—Poorly cooked tapioca.
2 See quot. Cf **frog-eye gravy**
1968 *DARE* FW Addit **Sth,** "String beans never tasted better than when cooked with ham hock on those old pots, with greasy fish-eyes on top when served"—spots of grease which float on top.

fisheye slick n
An area of smooth calm water.
1984 Wilder *You All Spoken Here* 143 **Sth,** *Dish ca'm:* Water as flat and calm as a dish. *Fish-eye slick:* A ca'm ca'm.

fish feeder n Cf **snake feeder**
A **dragonfly.**
1969 *DARE* (Qu. R2) Inf **PA**184, Fish feeder—long body, transparent wings, greenish blue body.

fish flake See **flake** n[1] **1**

fish fly n
1 An insect of the family Corydalidae: usu of the genus *Chauliodes,* but also of the genera *Neohermes* and *Nigronia.*
1866 *Prairie Farmer* 16 June 412/1 *(OEDS),* Large Fish Fly. **1901** Howard *Insect Book* 211, The so-called comb-horned fish-fly (*Chauliodes pectinicornis* L.) is the commonest form throughout the United States east of the Rocky Mountains. **1954** Borror-DeLong *Intro. Insects* 289, Fishflies . . belong to the genera *Chauliodes, Neohermes,* and *Nigronia.* . . Some of the fishflies have clear wings; other fishflies have the wings spotted. **1955** *Sci. News Letter* 14 May 313/2, The fishfly, which begins its slow, nocturnal flights about this time of the year, is among the earliest insects with complete metamorphosis, fossil records show.
2 =mayfly. chiefly Gt Lakes
1965-70 *DARE* (Qu. R4, *A large winged insect that hatches in summer in great numbers around lakes or rivers, crowds around lights, lives only a day or so, and is good fish bait*) 15 Infs, **chiefly Gt Lakes, Upper MW,** Fish fly; **IA**21, Fish fly—the Illinois chad fly; **MI**42, Fish fly—a lot of people call them mayfly too; **MI**80, Some people (strangers) call it a June bug; fish fly is more common; **MI**82, Fish fly—that's what they call 'em up north; **OH**67, Fish fly—same as Canadian soldier; **OR**5, Fish fly—light colored, more delicate than a moth. **1983** *Capital Times* (Madison WI) 12 July 2/1 **eIA,** Millions of smelly, sticky fish flies are making highways slick, blacking out windows and piling up a foot deep as they die in an annual invasion of Mississippi River towns. . . The flies, also known as mayflies and Mormon flies, infest the river towns annually.
3 =flesh fly.
1966-69 *DARE* (Qu. R12, *What other kinds of flies are common around here—for example, those that fly around animals?*) Inf **MI**14, Fish fly—a Lake Superior fly; a tremendous biter, right through your sock; **MI**37, Some call 'em beach flies, others call 'em fish flies. . . [It's the] size of a housefly, stings terribly, is speckled; **MN**14, Fish fly—a small one, like a horsefly; [it's] gray, can really bite; (Qu. R13, *Flies that come to meat or fruit*) Inf **WA**1, Fish fly—light tan body.
4 A **bluebottle fly.**
1969 *DARE* (Qu. R12, *What other kinds of flies are common around here—for example, those that fly around animals?*) Inf **RI**15, Fish fly—a bluebottle fly.

fish for love v phr Also *fish for fun,* ~ *sport joc*
To have poor luck in fishing.
1905 *DN* 3.79 **nwAR,** 'Have any luck?' 'No, I'm fishing for love.' **c1960** *Wilson Coll.* **csKY,** *Fishing for fun*—that is, having no luck; *fishing for love:* a humorous way of saying that fish are not biting. **1966-70** *DARE* (Qu. P9, *When you're fishing but not catching any, you might say, "________.")* Infs **IL**115, **TX**1, **VA**73, Fishing for love; **CA**65, **OR**13, Fishing for fun; **NC**33, Fishing for sport.

fish frog n Cf **spring peeper**
An unidentified frog.
1968 *DARE* (Qu. P21, *Small frogs that sing or chirp loudly in spring*) Inf **MD**20, Fish frogs.

fish fry n **scattered Missip-Ohio Valleys, Sth, S Midl** Cf **fish boil**
A dinner, usu held as a social event, at which fried fish is the main dish; fish prepared as it would be at such a dinner.
1816 in 1824 Knight *Letters* 66 **VA,** Fish-fries are held about once in a fortnight, during the fish season; when twenty or thirty men collect, to regale on whiskey, and fresh fish, and soft crabs just out of their sloughs, cooked under a spreading tree, near a running stream, by the slaves. **1890** *DN* 1.70 **LA,** *Fish-fry:* a sort of picnic, where the fish are caught and cooked on the grounds. **1892** *DN* 1.234 **KY. 1898** Canfield *Maid of Frontier* 168 **TX,** The young clerks and lawyers who formed the eligible population of Jonesboro concocted a "fish-fry" to take place on the banks of the Jim Ned. **1903** *DN* 2.313 **seMO,** *Fish-fry.* . . A picnic at which fried fish is the specialty. **1906** *DN* 3.136 **nwAR. 1908** *DN* 3.311 **eAL, wGA. 1950** *WELS (Dishes made with fish)* 1 Inf, **ceWI,** Fish fry, at taverns. **1954** *Harder Coll.* **cwTN,** *Fish fry.* . . A gathering of people at which quantities of fish are fried and eaten. **1965-70** *DARE* (Qu. FF1, . . *Kinds [of socials]*) Infs **CA**65, 160, **FL**10, **GA**23, **IL**15, **IN**19, 45, 61, **KY**36, **NY**104, 105, **OH**20, **SC**39, 58, **TX**104, **WI**47, 49, Fish fry; (Qu. FF2, . . *Kinds of parties*) Infs **GA**23, **NY**105, **OH**20, Fish fries; (Qu. H45) Inf **SC**46, Fish fry. **1970** Hyatt *Hoodoo* 1.690 **New Orleans LA,** A *fish fry* is a meal of fried fish served in a private home to the public. A sign with date, hours and cost of the meal is posted on the house or advertised by word of mouth. **1970** *DARE* FW Addit **cwTX,** Fish fry—A picnic where fish is cooked. **1978** *DARE* File **Madison WI,** [On a menu:] *Deep Fried Cod Fish Fry* $3.30—deep fried in our famous buttermilk breading.

fishfuddle tree n
=Jamaica dogwood.
1942 Amer. Joint Comm. Horticult. Nomenclature *Std. Plant Names* 486, *Piscidia* . . Fishfuddle tree. . . *[P.] communis* . . Florida F[ish-fuddletree]. **1951** Teale *North with Spring* 58, Florida is the land of the woolly-bucket tree, the buckwheat tree, the fishfuddle tree and the pondapple tree. **1979** Little *Checklist U.S. Trees* 200, Florida fishfuddletree.

fish geranium n [See quot 1865] Cf **fish begonia**
A cultivated geranium (*Pelargonium* x *hortorum*).
1865 IL State Ag. Soc. *Trans. for 1861-64* 5.581, I remarked to her, on viewing some fish geraniums in the window, how much their scent was like that emitted from the scales of a fresh fish. **1884** Baldwin *Yankee School-Teacher* 105 **VA** [Black], Aunt Molly paused once by the window to pinch off a rakish-looking sprout of her favorite "fish geranium," all aglow with great trusses of scarlet. **1976** Bailey-Bailey *Hortus Third* 834, *Pelargonium* x *hortorum* . . Fish geranium.

fishgig n Also *fishjig, fissgig* [Varr of *fizgig* harpoon] Cf **gig** n² **1**

A spear with barbed prongs used for fishing.

1702 in 1906 Essex Inst. *Coll.* 42.161 **neMA,** Inventory of Ship. . . a fis[h] gig. [*DARE* Ed: [h] supplied by 1906 ed.] **1866** *Atlantic Mth.* Mar 278/2 **PA,** They were prevented from ascending by what appears to have been an ordinary *fish gig.* Some of the witnesses described it as "like a pitchfork with blunt prongs." **1884** U.S. Natl. Museum *Bulletin* 27.863, [Heading:] Many-pointed fish-jigs. **1899** (1912) Green *VA Folk-Speech* 175, *Fissgig.* . . Fish-gig. An instrument with barbed prongs for striking fish.

fish grass n

=water shield.

1937 *Torreya* 37.97, *Cabomba caroliniana* . . fish-grass.

fish hawk n

1 also *fishing hawk:* An osprey *(Pandion haliaëtus).* **widespread, but chiefly Atlantic, NW** See Map Also called **fighting eagle, fish eagle, sea hawk**

1848 (1864) Thoreau *ME Woods* 27, As we stood upon the pile of chips by the door, fish-hawks were sailing overhead. **1950** *PADS* 14.75 **FL,** *Fish-hawk.* . . The osprey. **1950** *WELS (Hawks in your neighborhood)* 2 Infs, **c, cnWI,** Fish hawk; *(Water and marsh birds)* 1 Inf, **cwWI,** Fish hawk or osprey. **1965–70** *DARE* (Qu. Q4, . . *Kinds of hawks*) 126 Infs, **widespread, but chiefly Atlantic, NW,** Fish hawk; **DE**4, **MD**13, Fishing hawk; (Qu. Q10, *Other water birds*) 14 Infs, **chiefly Atlantic,** Fish hawk. **1975** Newell *If Nothin' Don't Happen* 43 **nwFL,** Them old bald-headed eagles set around waitin' for a fish hawk to catch him a fish. . . Lots of times they'll catch that fish in the air when the osprey drops it. "Osprey" is just Yankee for fish hawk.

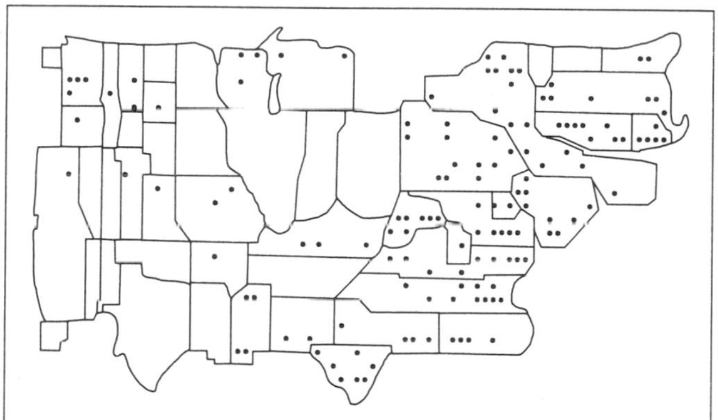

•fish hawk 1 + var (Qq. Q4, Q10)

2 =swallow-tailed kite. [See quot 1955]

1913 *Auk* 30.494 **Okefenokee GA,** *Elanoides forficatus.* . . 'Fish Hawk.'—Fairly common. **1955** *Oriole* 20.5 **GA,** *Swallow-tailed Kite.* —*Fish Hawk* (by misapprehension, this expert flyer drinking from the surface of the water while on the wing). **1962** Imhof *AL Birds* 167, *Swallow-tailed Kite.* . . *Other Names:* . . Fish Hawk.

fishhawk cactus n [Prob for *fishhook cactus* (at **fishhook 1**)]

A **barrel cactus** (here: *Echinocactus wislizeni*).

1896 *Jrl. Amer. Folkl.* 9.188, *Echinocactus Wislizeni* . . fish-hawk cactus, Ariz.

fish head n

1 A **turtlehead.** *obs*

1784 in 1785 Amer. Acad. Arts & Sci. *Memoirs* 1.464, *Chelone* . . Chelone. Fish-head. Snake-head. Blossoms in spikes; white. Common by fences and amongst bushes in moist land. August.

2 Used as an uncomplimentary epithet; see quots.

1950 *PADS* 14.75 **FL,** *Fish-head.* . . A person from the West Florida coast. **1950** Bissell *Stretch on River* 77 **eMO,** The way he carried on the time that fishhead from Nauvoo got himself drowned. **1970** *DARE* (Qu. HH28, . . *People of foreign background*) Inf **NY**239, Fish head—a West Indian Negro. **1979** *Oregonian* (Portland OR) 23 Sept sec A 1, "Fish-head" (a worker in a fish cannery).

3 See quot. [From the shape] Cf **fish tail 3**

1967 *DARE* (Qu. B11, . . *Kinds of clouds*) Inf **NC**48, Fish heads.

fish heron See **fish crane**

fishhook n

1 A sharply recurved plant spine—freq attrib, esp in phr *fishhook cactus;* used esp of cacti of the genera *Ancistrocactus, Echinocactus, Ferocactus,* and *Mammillaria.*

1875 *Amer. Naturalist* 9.20 **sUT,** "The fish-hook cactus," is found as a rarity in rocky clefts, at this season adorned with its bright red fruit. **1907** White *AZ Nights* 196, About this time Denton ran across some fish-hook cactus, which we cut up and chewed. They have a sticky wet sort of inside, which doesn't quench your thirst any, but helps to keep you from drying up and blowing away. **1913** *Torreya* 13.74, The central spine of a mature plant of *[Echinocactus] Wislizeni* is always very much *hooked,* hence this species is known as the fishhook cactus. **1924** Austin *Land of Journeys' Ending* 127 **AZ,** There are scores of variations of the bisnaga type, "niggerhead," "fish-hook," and "cushion" cacti, running to fat button shapes or short thickened cylinders, widely distributed through the Southwest. **1947** *So. Sierran* May 4/2 *(DA),* And last, rare and very beautiful, the Mohave Fishhook or Pineapple Cactus, *Echinocactus Polyancistrus,* with clustered iridescent magenta-pink blossoms. **1965** *Silver City Press Frontier* (NM) July 20, Not[e] the full grown century plant at left rear, complete with needle-sharp leaves and "fishhooks" along the edges, plus the center stalk which reaches a height of from 12 to 18 feet before blossoms appear. **1976** Bailey–Bailey *Hortus Third* 1235, Cactus. . . Fishhook: *Ancistrocactus Scheeri, Ferocactus, F. Wislizenii, Mammillaria.* **1985** Dodge *Flowers SW Deserts* 52, Fishhook Mammillaria. . . The long spines are curved at the tips giving the plant the appearance of being covered with unbarbed fishhooks.

2 pl: A **dogtooth violet** (here: *Erythronium americanum*).

1959 Carleton *Index Herb. Plants* 46, *Fishhooks:* Erythronium americanum.

3 See quot. Cf **fish head 3**

1968 *DARE* (Qu. B11, . . *Clouds that come often*) Inf **AK2A,** Fish hooks—small clouds with a hook on the end; a presage of storms.

fishhook cactus See **fishhook 1**

fishhooks intj Cf **gosh all hemlock**

Used to express surprise, disbelief, or disapproval.

1959 *VT Hist.* 27.135, Oh Fishhooks! . . Common.

fishhooks in one's pockets, have v phr Also *have one's pockets lined with fishhooks*

To be miserly.

1915 *Los Angeles Examiner* (CA) 19 Apr 2.2 *(Zwilling Coll.),* [In the cartoon "Indoor Sports":] You can't get a nickel out of him. He has his pockets lined with fish hooks. **1942** Berrey–Van den Bark *Amer. Slang* 376/6, *Be niggardly; stingy.* . . have fishhooks in one's pockets. **1950** *WELS (A stingy person)* 1 Inf, **cnWI,** [He] has one-way pockets; he has fishhooks in his pockets. **1960** Criswell *Resp. to PADS 20* **Ozarks** *("Stingy")* The expression, "he has fishhooks in his pockets," may have come from this area.

fish horn n

A simple horn used on fishing boats or by fish peddlers; by ext, any loud horn.

1856 Cozzens *Sparrowgrass* 38 **seNY,** Mrs. Sparrowgrass asked me who that was "blowing a fish-horn [=a bugle]?" **c1895** (1914) Norris *Vandover* 293 **nCA,** There were about twenty college men on top [of a coach] . . and they were blowing fish-horns. **1907** *DN* 3.187 **seNH,** *Fish-horn.* . . 1. Horn blown by a fish-pedler. . . 2. Any common horn. "Blow that fish-horn, will you?" **1910** *DN* 3.441 **cwNY,** *Fish-horn.* . . Horn used by a fish-peddler. **1931–33** *LANE Worksheets* **eMA,** Fish horn—a sort of noisemaker. **1932** *Hanley Disks* **swCT,** They blowed the great large fish horn they had and the farmers uptown or the owners heard the horn and down they'd . . drive . . with their horse and wagon. **1977** Adams *Lang. Railroader* 60, *Fish horn:* An electric horn on an electric or gasoline railcar.

fish house n

Orig a building for storing fish; now a place for processing fish and other seafood.

1650 in 1881 Boston Registry Dept. *Records* 2.102, Brother Salter had Libertie granted to sett up a Fish house. **1770** (1925) Washington *Diaries* 1.367 **neVA,** He . . is to have the use of the Fish House for his Salt, fish, &ca. **1877** Jewett *Deephaven* 224 **ME,** There were a few old buildings there . . ; some dilapidated fish-houses; and a row of fish-flakes. **1966** *DARE* Tape **FL**24, I went to work in the fish house. . . I handled many hundred thousands of shrimp; **MI**21, Every fish house used to have their barrels that they used to keep the fish guts in; **TX**14, [FW:] Then what do you do with 'em when you get in? [Inf:] Take 'em to the different fish houses. We got fish houses, oh, just about everywhere, that buy these [=shrimp]. **1978** *Capital Times* (Madison WI) 11 Apr 14/2 **eNC,** [He] had this old abandoned fish house on the Buxton harbor, just a slanted concrete floor and a shed.

fishing bait See **fishbait 1**

fishingbird n
=Carolina wren.
1931 Faulkner *Sanctuary* 2 **MS,** [Behind him the bird sang again, three bars in monotonous repetition.] *Ibid* 6, They call that Carolina wren a fishingbird. That's what it is. What I couldn't think of back there. **1976** Brown *Gloss. Faulkner* 46, Horace Benbow knows the book name but has trouble recalling the popular name, *fishingbird.* It is fortunate that Faulkner gives us the identification: I have never heard this name and cannot find it attested anywhere.

fishing camp See **fish camp**

fishing duck See **fish duck 1**

fishing eagle See **fish eagle**

fishing for love n Cf **fish for love**
1908 *DN* 3.311 **eAL, wGA,** *Fishing for love. . .* A young people's game.

fishing frog n
=goosefish.
1807 in 1846 MA Hist. Soc. *Coll.* 2d ser 3.55, The sting-ray, the skaite, and the goose fish, or monk, or fishing frog, are common. **1842** DeKay *Zool. NY* 4.162, The American Angler, *Lophius americanus,* . . [has] many popular names, such as Sea-Devil, Fishing Frog, Bellows-fish, . . and various others. **1927** (1930) *WNID, Fishing. . . f. frog,* the angler fish. **1933** John G. Shedd Aquarium *Guide* 162, *Lophius piscatorius*—Goosefish . . Fishing Frog.

fishing hawk See **fish hawk 1**

fishing pole reed n
Prob **=fishing rod.**
1971 GA Dept. Ag. *Farmers Market Bulletin* 10 Nov 8/2, "Please tell me what will get rid of fishing pole reeds. They are about to take over my place." . . "The pole people advised that you should cut down the reeds in early fall and spray any new shoots in the spring."

fishing rod n Cf **fish pole**
Perh a cane (*Arundinaria* spp).
1834 *Visit to TX* 192, They [=cane brakes] are tracts of land . . overgrown with the long reeds which we know in the Northern States as fishing rods. **1836** Edward *Hist. TX* 67, The undergrowth of the best lands in Texas is Cane. . . These canes, or reeds, are known in the Northern States as fishing rods.

fishing spider See **fisher spider**

fishing tug See **fish tug**

fishing warden See **fish warden**

fishing weed n *joc*
A weed that grows while a farmer is away fishing.
1969 *DARE* Tape **KY**53, They have quite a few fishin' weeds in their tobaccer every once in a while. . . They go fishin' an' let the weeds grow in their tobaccer.

fishing worm n **chiefly Midl** See Map Cf **fishworm**
=earthworm.
1885 Twain *Huck. Finn* 317, A hard piece of corn-crust . . was shot across the table, and took one of the children in the eye, and curled him up like a fishing-worm. **1905** *DN* 3.79 **nwAR,** 'Got any fishin'-worms?' . . [*Fish-worm* is] Less common than *fishin(g)-worm.* **1946** *PADS* 5.21 **VA,** *Fishing worm, fish worm* . . common everywhere except on Chesapeake Bay. **1949** Kurath *Word Geog.* 74, *Fishing worm* predominates (1) in an area extending from the lower Susquehanna southward on either side of Chesapeake Bay, including all of Delmarvia except the southern tip, (2) in Western Pennsylvania and adjoining parts of Ohio and West Virginia, and (3) in the Virginia Piedmont and adjoining parts of North Carolina. **c1960** *Wilson Coll.* **csKY,** *Fishing worm:* The common earthworm. Fish worm is about equally common. **1965–70** *DARE* (Qu. P5) 121 Infs, **chiefly Midl,** Fishing worm; (Qu. P6) Inf **NC**15, Fishing worm; (Qu. R27) Infs **IL**143, **OH**40, Fishing worm.

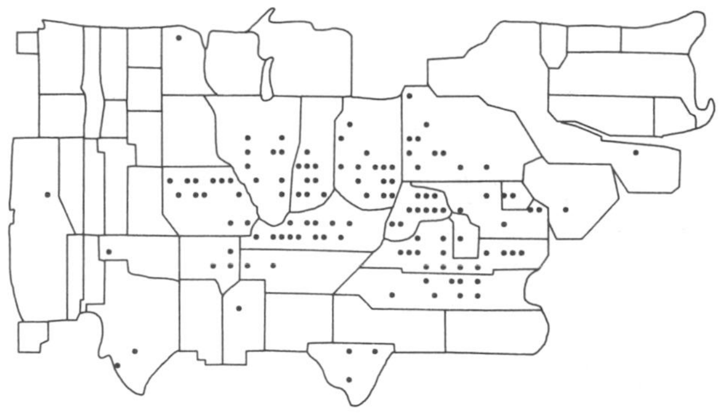
•fishing worm (Qq. P5, P6, R27)

fishin'in' See **-ing**

fish in the right direction See **fish C8**

fish-in-the-sea n Cf *DS* EE2
1950 *WELS (Games with an extra player: at a signal the other players change places, and the extra tries to get a place)* 1 Inf, **Milwaukee WI,** Fish-in-the-sea.

fishjig See **fishgig**

fish killer n
=giant water bug.
1972 Swan–Papp *Insects* 112, Variously called fish killers, electric light bugs, . . the . . giant water bugs are among our largest insects. . . Found in ponds and quiet pools in streams, they attack a great variety of aquatic insects, tadpoles, and fish (sometimes several times their size).

fish leech n
A **lamprey** (here: *Ichthyomyzon* spp).
1928 Baylor Univ. Museum *Contrib.* 16.9 **LA, TX,** The true Lamprey Eel is found in the same sections of country, but is known as the "Fish Leech."

fish locoweed n
=turkey mullein.
1902 (1974) Chestnut *Plants Indians* 363, A very low, gray weed . . known as "turkey mullein." . . A recent popular name which suggests the intoxicating action of the plant is "fish locoweed." The plant is altogether too commonly used both by the Indians and whites for catching fish.

fish mint n
=water mint.
1940 Clute *Amer. Plant Names* 25, *M. aquatica. . .* Fish mint.

fish moccasin n
Perh a **water snake.**
1967–68 *DARE* (Qu. P25, . . *Kinds of snakes*) Inf **LA**10, All the moccasins are poisonous except the fish moccasin; **LA**15, Fish moccasin.

fishmouth n [Prob from the shape of the flower]
Usu **=turtlehead,** but see quot 1968.
1876 Hobbs *Bot. Hdbk.* 38, Fish mouth, Balmony, Chelone glabra. **1930** Sievers *Amer. Med. Plants* 58, *Chelone glabra. . . Other common names. . .* Fishmouth, codhead. **1968** *DARE* FW Addit **VA**15, Fishmouth—common. The term covers a variety of plants, including purple gentian, skullcap, turtlehead. **1971** Krochmal *Appalachia Med. Plants* 84.

fish muddle See **muddle**

fish on a string n
A type of fireworks.
1968 *DARE* (Qu. FF28) Inf **NY**75, Fish on a string—shaped like a fish. When you touched it off it went *Zip!*

fish pea n [From its size and shape] Cf *DNE*
1975 Gould *ME Lingo* 95, *Fish peas*—Spawn, roe, caviar, haddock eggs, but usually when they are still massed within the membrane.

fish pirate n **AK**
See quot 1953.

1939 *AK Sportsman* July 27 (Tabbert *Alaskan Engl.*), More excitement is added to trap life by frequent visits of fish pirates when the fish are running heavy. **1953** *AK Sportsman* Feb 7/1, Fish pirates are fishermen. Some of them fish legitimately most of the time and steal from traps only when the fish are scarce or they find an opportunity too good to resist. Others make a career of garnering their fish illegally from streams, closed waters and fish traps. **1968** *DARE* Tape **AK6**, Here in the 1920s they had a very bad time with the fish pirates—these are boats that would go around and rob the fish traps.

fish poison n

1 also *fish-poison bush:* =**red buckeye.**

1802 Drayton *View of SC* 67 **SC,** Fish poison, horse chesnut, or buck's eye. (*Æsculus* Pavia.) Grows in high land. Its root [sic], is used as soap, for washing woollens; and if thrown into water, it has a property of stupifying the fish, so that they will lay on the top of the water, and may be taken with the hand; the Indians in this manner use it for catching fish. **1889** [see **2** below]. **1960** Vines *Trees SW* 682, Red Buckeye. . . Some vernacular names in use for the plant are Scarlet Buckeye . . and Fish-poison-bush. It is reported that . . the crushed fruit [is used] for fish poison.

2 A **mullein** (here: *Verbascum thapsus*).

1889 *Century Dict.* 2238, *Fish-poison. . . Lepidium Piscidium;* the mullen [sic], *Verbascum Thapsus;* and the red buckeye, *Aesculus Pavia.*

3 =**Jamaica dogwood.** [See quot 1962]

1889 *Century Dict.* 2238, Fish-poison. . . *Lepidium Piscidium.* **1962** Harrar-Harrar *Guide S. Trees* 381, *Florida Fishpoison-Tree. . .* An extract of the bark has been used . . to stupefy fish in order to catch them in nets more readily; hence the common name. **1979** Little *Checklist U.S. Trees* 200, Florida fishpoison-tree.

4 =**turkey mullein.**

[**1902** (1974) Chestnut *Plants Indians* 321, Several other plants are sometimes used . . with soap root . . , but none except the turkey mullein . . is equally effective. . . No ill effect has ever been noted as a consequence of eating fish caught by any of these "fish poisons."] **1961** Peck *Manual OR* 503, *Eremocarpus setigerus. . . Fish-poison. . .* Both sides of the Cascades, to Wash. and Calif.

5 also *fish poisoning:* See quots.

1950 *PADS* 14.75 **FL,** *Fish poison. . .* A type of blood poison which gets in the flesh from a wound by a fish fin. **1966** *DARE* (Qu. BB25, . . *Common skin diseases*) Inf **FL25**, Fish poisoning.

fish-poison bush See **fish poison 1**

fish poisoning See **fish poison 5**

fish pole n Cf **fishing rod**

=**horsetail 1.**

1920 *Torreya* 20.17, *Equisetum* spp.—Fishpoles, Traverse City, Mich.

fish pole, line, and sinker adv phr [Var of *hook, line, and sinker*]

1968 *DARE* (Qu. LL25, *Expressions meaning entirely, completely: "He sold out the whole place, ______."*) Inf **PA104**, Fishpole, line, and sinker.

fish pot n

Any of several types of fish trap; see quots.

1775 (1924) Cresswell *Jrl.* 69 **VA,** These fish pots are made by throwing up the small stones and gravel something like a mill weir, beginning at the side of the River and proceeding in a diagonal line, till they meet in the middle of the stream, where they fix a thing like the body of a cart, contracted where the water flows in just to admit the fish, but so contrived as to prevent their return or escape. **1872** (1876) Knight *Amer. Mech. Dict.* 2.874/1, *Fish-pot.* An open-mouthed wicker basket containing bait, and sunk in the haunts of fish to catch them. **1874** Collins *Hist. Sketches KY* 1.544, Requiring overseers . . to "work it" [=the Green River] with hands from the neighborhood—*i.e.* to remove all fish-pots. **1968** *DARE* (Qu. P13, . . *Other ways of fishing*) Inf **PA136**, Eel racks were called fish pots; **VA33**, Fish pot—a dam of loose rocks is made in a creek in the shape of the letter V, forcing current to drive the fish into it; the water goes up a ladder at the point, but the fish are stranded on the boards nailed across the ramp; they [=the dams] are hard to keep because they are easily washed out by rain storms.

fish pound n

A basket-like trap with wing nets which channel fish into the trap.

1859 in 1889 Huntington NY *Town Rec.* 3.447, Application of William Spriggs and Charles S. Hartt to put down fish pounds in Northport harbor for the purpose of catching fish. **a1870** Chipman *Notes on Bartlett* 151 *(DA), Fish-pound,* a net attached to stakes and used for entrapping and catching fish; a weare.—Conn. **1968–70** *DARE* (Qu. P13, . . *Other ways of fishing*) Inf **MD36**, Fish pound net—a series of nets that funnel into each other; the fish get confused and can't get out; copied from old Indian nets; **VA46**, Fyke—made of wire, like a fly trap; same as fish pound. **1984** *DARE* File **Chesapeake Bay** [Watermen's vocab], Pound net, pound trap, fish trap, fish pound, bay net, fyke, pound fyke.

fish rake n

An implement with multiple unbaited hooks for snagging fish.

1968 *DARE* (Qu. P13, . . *Other ways of fishing*) Inf **NY75**, Raking suckers—cut holes in the ice and use a snatch hook. Somebody drums on the ice to drive the fish. Snatch hook is sometimes called fish rake.

fish scale n, usu pl Cf **fish tail 3, mackerel sky**

A long, wavy cirrus cloud; see quots.

1956 *Hand Coll.* **cnOH,** "Mares' tails and fishes' scales / Make the sailors haul in their sails." Mares' tails and fishes' scales were terms used to designate high cirrus clouds in the form of streamers. **1967–69** *DARE* (Qu. B11, . . *Kinds of clouds*) Infs **NJ2**, **TX43**, Fish scales; **WV8**, Fish scales—long clouds with lines through; (Qu. B10, . . *Long trailing clouds*) Inf **IL58**, Fish scale. [All Infs old]

fish shanty n

A small building used as a shelter for ice fishing.

1964 Gould *Parables of Peter* 146 **ME,** I think a smelt shanty is a special thing. The art of angling from the private isolation of a fish shanty draws a man apart to such an extent that he is temporarily separated from the silliness and foibles of society, including laws. **1970** *DARE* Tape **MI120**, [Aux Inf:] Do you remember when our dad used to go ice fishin'? We had a shanty on Otsego Lake, and of course then you had to walk, it's about six, seven miles. . . and we had a fish shanty where you can sleep overnight, and cook your meals. [Inf:] Most of the boys 'round here at that time had fish shanties made . . so you could stay out there for a week at a time. **1977** *Sawyer Co. Rec.* (Hayward WI) 5 Jan 1/3 **nWI,** While the offenses are minor and range from not having a name or address on a fish shanty to possession of an untagged deer, . . the issue of Indian fishing and hunting rights is at stake.

fishskin See **fish B4**

fish slide n

See quot 1884.

1884 U.S. Natl. Museum *Bulletin* 27.1017 **VA,** *Fish-slide or trap. . .* A series of wooden slats set in a sloping frame. . . "A slide of this kind is set in the current of a shallow stream, its upper surface raised from the bottom at an angle of 25 to 30 degrees, the lower edge, which comes in contact with the water, facing up stream, and the top edge reaching above the water." **1889** *Century Dict.* 2238, *Fish-slide. . .* A fish trap for shallow rivers and low waterfalls: used in the southern United States.

fish stew n Cf **fish fry, muddle**

A picnic or party at which fish stew is eaten.

1930 *DN* 6.81 **cSC,** *Fish-stew. . .* A supper, usually in the swamp, at which is served fish-stew, rice, corn dodgers . . , and coffee. The stew is nearly always made of catfish. **1941** Writers' Program *Guide SC* 238, Fish stews on the banks of streams and lakes are part of the birthright of all—men and women, whites and Negroes, young and old.

fish tail n

1 See quot.

1933 *Hanley Disks* **Byfield MA,** This is what they call a fishtail, a kind of Indian arrow sometimes found.

2 A jazz dance step; see quot 1968.

1946 (1972) Mezzrow-Wolfe *Really Blues* 332, Fishtail: weaving motion of the buttocks during a dance. **1968** Stearns-Stearns *Jazz Dance* 12, [He] cut loose with the Fish Tail . . , a movement in which the buttocks weave out, back, and up in a variety of figure eights. *Ibid* 26, Snake Hips and the Fish Tail are compounded of Congo pelvic movements that would probably have shocked the white interviewers.

3 See quot. Cf **fish scale**

1968 *DARE* (Qu. B10, . . *Long trailing clouds high in the sky*) Inf **NJ39**, Fish tails.

fishtail blackbird n

Perh a **boat-tailed grackle.**

1968 *DARE* (Qu. Q11, . . *Kinds of blackbirds*) Inf **MD32**, Fishtail blackbird—the common word for the blue grackle.

fishtail hawk n
=swallow-tailed kite.
1873 *Amer. Naturalist* 7.202 **sIL,** Numbers of exquisitely graceful swallow-tailed kites or "snake hawks" (*Nauclerus forficatus,* also locally known as "fish-tail hawk") were seen. **1925** Bailey *Birds FL* 66.

Fish Town n Also *Fishville derog*
A section of a town or city associated with fish.
1967–70 *DARE* (Qu. C35) Inf **KY**76, Fish Town—along the river north of the business section; they fished and sold fish; **PA**88, Fish Town—old-fashioned; **PA**248, Fish Town—for Kensington; but I don't say this; **KS**14, Fishville; (Qu. C34) Infs **DE**1, **MI**40, Fish Town; (Qu. II25) Inf **KS**15, Fishville.

fish trap n Cf **fish car**
1912 Green *VA Folk-Speech* 175, *Fish-trap*. . . A box with holes in it to let in water into which live fish are put to be kept alive.

fish tug n Also *fishing tug* **MI**
A fishing boat; see quots.
1966–69 *DARE* (Qu. O10, . . *Other kinds of boats*) Inf **MI**2, Fishing tug; **MI**10, Fish tug—diesel powered, on Lake Superior; **MI**54, Fish tug; **MI**103, Fish tug—used by commercial fishermen; (Qu. O1, . . *A small rowboat*) Inf **MI**109, Fish tug. [FW: This is a common local term for a twenty to thirty foot powerboat that fishes commercially in Lake Michigan.] **1969** *DARE* Tape **MI**109, [FW:] How many are here in town still? [Inf:] Oh, there's only one boat that I would say is working regular. Well, he only works two days a week and his boat is up for sale. But those are a dime a dozen, fish tugs.

Fishville See **Fish Town**

fish wagon n Cf **fish horn**
1945 Hubbard *Railroad Ave.* 342, *Fish wagon*—Gas-electric car or other motorcar equipped with an air horn (which sounds like a fishmonger's horn).

fish wall n Cf **eel rack, fish pot**
1968 *DARE* (Qu. P13, . . *Other ways of fishing*) Inf **PA**155, Fish walls—called eel trap.

fish warden n Also *fishing warden* **NEng**
An officer empowered to enforce fishing regulations.
1790 *Mass. Acts & Laws* (1894) V.498 *(DAE),* Every town in this Commonwealth bordering on Merrimack river . . shall at their annual meeting . . choose by ballot, at least four suitable and fit persons, as fish wardens. **a1857** *Maine Rev. Statutes 1857* 309 *(DAE),* The towns of Thomaston, St. George, and Cushing shall . . choose . . fish wardens to have a general supervision over the fisheries of salmon. **1868** *N.H. Laws 1867–71* 132 *(DA),* Any town in this state . . may . . choose one or more fishing-wardens. **1975** Gould *ME Lingo* 95, *Fish warden*—The enforcement officer of the Department of Sea & Shore Fisheries. . . The inland wardens also police freshwater fishing, but are never called *fish wardens.* A Maine *fish warden's* jurisdiction not only extends to sea, but he can make inland arrests if, say, he finds a restaurant . . that is serving short lobsters.

fishweed n
1 =Mexican tea.
1916 *Torreya* 16.237, *Chenopodium anthelminthicum* L.—Fishweed, Revels I[slan]ds, Va. **1959** Carleton *Index Herb. Plants* 46.
2 =Jerusalem artichoke.
1943 Weslager *DE Forgotten Folk* 162, The following record of Cheswold herbs represents an ethnobotanical study of hitherto unformulated cures and applies only to the Cheswold Moors. . . Fishweed (Jerusalem Artichoke)[,] *Helianthus tuberosus* (N)[,] A tea to rid children of worms.

fish wheel n **Pacific NW, AK**
A wheel with nets, put in a stream to catch fish; sometimes used to help fish over a dam or waterfall.
1893 *Outing* 22.135/1 **nwOR,** A large salmon canning establishment is located at Celilo. In this building is a fish-wheel with nets which extend to the falls of the river, and automatically land the large salmon in the factory. Other wheels are outside on the rocks. **1908** Johnson *Highways Pacific Coast* 258 **OR,** "The salmon have been kind o' played out the last few years up here," said he, "and when a fish-wheel gets worn out or stove up we don't trouble to repair it, and there's seldom any new ones built." **1909** Marsh-Cobb *Fisheries of AK in 1908* 31 (Tabbert *Alaskan Engl.*), This year the first fish wheel to be erected and operated in the coastal waters of Alaska was put in the Taku River, about 10 miles above its mouth. . . The wheel had two dips, each 22 feet in width and hung with netting. **1967** *DARE* (Qu. P13, . . *Other ways of fishing*) Inf **WA**20, Fish wheel—like a big paddle wheel but there are nets instead of paddles. **1973** *Tabbert Coll.,* Fish wheel—Device used mainly by natives to take fish from a river. **1973** *Fairbanks Daily News-Miner* (AK) 15 June *(Tabbert Coll.),* Everyone's busy around here cleaning up and cutting poles for fish wheels. Looks like will [sic] have quite a few fishing this year.

fishwood n
A **burning bush 1** (here: *Euonymus americanus*).
1860 Curtis *Cat. Plants NC* 102, *Strawberry Bush.* (Euonymus Americanus, Linn.)—A shrub 2 to 5 feet high, . . and known by the names of *Burning Bush, Fish-wood* and *Bursting Heart,* besides the one first given. **1900** Lyons *Plant Names* 154. **1960** Vines *Trees SW* 661, [It is also] known under the vernacular names of Bursting-heart, Fish-wood, and Burning-bush.

fishworm n **widespread, but more freq Nth, N Midl, Cent** See Map Cf **fishing worm**
=earthworm.
1854 (1969) Thoreau *Walden* 223, I catch shiners with fish-worms. **1870** Emerson *Soc. & Solitude* 163, The savant is often an amateur. His performance is a memoir to the Academy on fish-worms, tadpoles, or spiders' legs. **1905** *DN* 3.79 **nwAR,** 'This year fish-worms have burrowed deeper than usual.'—Arkansas newspaper. [*Fish-worm* is] [l]ess common than *fishin(g)-worm.* **1939** *LANE* Map 236, *Fishworm* is described as the usual term by [7 infs], as rare by [1 inf]. . . 1 inf, **cMA,** The real name is *angleworm,* but we usually say *fishworm.* **1949** Kurath *Word Geog.* 74, *Fish worm* is common (1) in the upper Connecticut Valley and Worcester County, Massachusetts, (2) in the Dutch settlement area, and (3) in West Virginia. **1950** *WELS (The common worm used for bait)* 12 Infs, **WI,** Fishworm. **c1960** *Wilson Coll.* **csKY,** *Fish worm* is about [as] common [as *fishing worm*]. **1962** Atwood *Vocab. TX* 58, As in the coastal area of the Carolinas, *earthworm* . . is the most usual word for the annelid used for fish bait. . . There is some rivalry, however, from *fish worm . . , fishin(g) worm.* **1965–70** *DARE* (Qu. P5) 199 Infs, **widespread, but more freq Nth, N Midl, Cent,** Fishworm; (Qu. P6) Infs **IL**29, **IN**55, **MD**31, **NY**123, **OK**1, 18, 52, **PA**6, Fishworm; (Qu. R27) Inf **MI**24, Fishworms—in a dry summer they come up after rain; nightcrawlers; (Qu. B26, . . *"It's raining ———."*) Inf **OH**31, Fishworms. **1981** *Greenfield Recorder* (MA) 18 Apr sec A 4, When they [=robins] do pull up a lusty fish worm and get it down, . . they often sit kind of hunched up waiting.

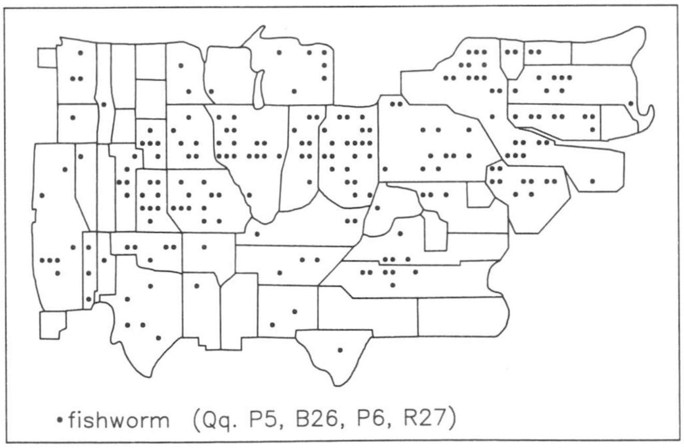

fishworm tree n [Because the tree attracts the catalpa worm] Cf **fishbait tree**
=catalpa B1.
1954 *Harder Coll.* **cwTN,** Fishworm tree, sometimes called bean tree, [is] a tree with large heart-shaped leaves, clusters of white blossoms, and long, slender seed pods.

fishy adj
Of a professional fisherman or whaler: dedicated to one's work, steadfast, persevering.
1889 *Century Dict.* 2238, *Fishy*. . . Plucky; brave; sturdy and enduring; thorough and faithful in duty: as, *fishy* to the backbone; a *fishy* man. [*Cent:* Fishermen's slang.] **1905** Wasson *Green Shay* 55 **NEng,** Fishing hard is a grand good fault, but you always want to rec'lect that there's

reason into everything, Asy, boy. You're doin' complete as it is, and you don't want to forgit that no matter how 'fishy' ever a man may be, he ain't going to stand everything, no more'n a horn spoon. **1939** (1962) Thompson *Body & Britches* 199 **seNY** (as of late 1900s), A [whaling] man who . . loves his work and seems born to it . . is *fishy.*

fiss around See **fissle around**

fissel n [Pronc-sp for *thistle*]

1928 *Ruppenthal Coll.* **KS,** *Fissel* . . f- for th- occasionally heard in *thistle.*

fissgig See **fishgig**

fissle around v phr Also *fiss around* [Scots, Engl dial *fissle,* to fidget, bustle]

To fool around, putter.

1967 *DARE* (Qu. A10, . . *Doing little unimportant things: Somebody asks, "What are you doing?" and you answer, "Nothing in particular—I'm just ______.")* Inf **OH**36, Fissling [fɪslən] (*or* fissing [fɪsən]) around; it means fooling around.

fist n[1] Pl usu |fɪsts|; also freq |fɪs(t)|; also **esp S Midl** |fɪs(t)ɨz|; for addit varr see **A** below Pronc-spp for pl, *fis(es), fist, fist(es)es* Cf **-es suff**[1] **1a, 2**

A Forms.

1891 *Jrl. Amer. Folkl.* 4.315 **csTN,** "Pot up yer weepons and fight it out with yer fisteses." **1919** *DN* 5.39 **TN,** *Fistes.* . . Fists. **1967** *DARE* (Qu. EE21b, . . *"Those fellows really ______.")* Inf **MO**8, Used their fists [fɪst]. **1967** *Wilson Coll.* **csKY,** [fɪstɪz]. **c1970** Pederson *Dial. Surv. Rural GA* **seGA,** [Of 61 infs who pronounced *fists,* 34 said [fɪst], 21 [fɪs·], 3 [fɪstɨz], 1 [fɪsɨz], 1 [fɪsts], 1 [fɪts].] **1976** Allen *LAUM* 3.312 **Upper MW** (as of c1950), *Fists* is . . /fɪsts/ by 37% of the 207 recorded infs., with a clear preference by the better educated. . . 12% . . [have] /fɪs·t/ as their plural form, but . . 52% . . [have] /fɪs/, often with a noticeable prolonged [s:]. No geographical contrast is apparent. **1981** *DARE* File **Augusta GA,** *Fists* n pl. Fist—20 infs; Fists—6 infs; Fis—5 infs; Fises—1 inf. **1986** Pederson *LAGS Concordance* **Gulf Region,** 70 infs, Fistes.

B Senses.

1 Handwriting; a signature. [*OED fist* sb.[1] 3 "Now only *jocular;*" 1553 →1864] **chiefly Sth** *somewhat old-fash*

1854 (1923) Holmes *Tempest & Sunshine* 13 **KY,** [He] told him there was no doubt that he could obtain a good school in that immediate neighborhood. "Your best way," said he, "will be to write a subscription paper. The people then see what for a fist you write, and half the folks in Kentucky will judge you by that." **1899** (1912) Green *VA Folk-Speech* 176, That's his *fist.* **1908** *DN* 3.311 **eAL, wGA,** *Fist.* . . Handwriting. **1915** *DN* 4.226 **wTX,** *Fist.* . . Handwriting. **1930** *RR Man's Mag.* June 470/1, *Fist*—Operator's handwriting. **1950** *WELS (When you sign your name to a check or a contract, you call it your ______)* 1 Inf, **ceWI,** Fist. **1966–69** *DARE* (Qu. JJ11, *Joking names for handwriting that's hard to read: "I can't make anything out of his ______.")* Infs **NC**4, 15, Fist; (Qu. JJ13, . . *Joking words . . for a name signed to a paper . . "I'll put my ______ on that.")* Infs **GA**5, 15, **KY**5, **NC**13, 15, Fist. [All Infs old]

2a An attempt, a "go"; one who makes an attempt, a "hand."

1838 (1852) Gilman *S. Matron* 46, He reckoned he should make a better fist at farming than edicating. **1880** Howells *Undiscovered Country* 87 **MA,** Mrs. Burton is really making a very pretty fist at a *salon.* **1891** *Harper's New Mth. Mag.* 83.578/1 **MA,** It's a long way, and I've noticed that this gal is a good fist at a knife and fork. **1894** *DN* 1.330 **NJ,** *Fist:* "to make a bad fist of it"; to make mistakes or do work incorrectly. **1911** (1916) Porter *Harvester* 149 **IN,** Someway I am making an awful fist of things. Everything I do is wrong.

b Spec: a poor attempt, failure, mess.

1833 Greene *Life Dr. Dodimus* 2.8 **NEast,** You had'nt ought to tax any thing . . seeing you've made such a fist of it. **1927** *AmSp* 2.354 **WV,** *Fist of it, to make a* . . to fail badly in an undertaking. "He certainly did make a fist of that."

3 A throw in the game of mumblety-peg.

1957 *Sat. Eve. Post Letters* **GA** (as of 1904), [Mumblety-peg as played in Macon] consisted of a long series of highly stylized throws. . . I remember the names of the first few throws. "Palms," "backs," and "fists" were made with one hand.

fist n[2] See **feist n**

fist v

To strike with the fist, slug.

1806 (1970) Webster *Compendious Dict.* 118, *Fist* . . to beat, strike or hold fast, with the fist. **1871** (1882) Stowe *Fireside Stories* 120 **MA,** Hokum was so mad at Toddy for speakin', that he was a fistin' on him. **1914** *DN* 4.72 **ME, nNH,** *Fist.* . . To strike. **1927** *DN* 5.474 **Ozarks,** Th' ol' woman she jes' *fisted* him sumthin' turrible. **1954** *Harder Coll.* **cwTN,** *Fist.* . . To beat with the fists. **1966–69** *DARE* (Qu. Y12b) Inf **LA**8, Fist it out with one another; (Qu. Y14a, *To hit somebody hard with the fist*) Infs **MO**20, **NY**68, Fist; (Qu. Y15, *To beat somebody thoroughly*) Inf **IN**77, Fisted; (Qu. EE21b, . . *"For a while those fellows really ______.")* Inf **MS**46, Fisted.

fist and skull adj phr, adv phr Rarely *fist and heel* **chiefly Sth, S Midl**

Of a fight: bare-fisted; without weapons.

1832 Hall *Legends West* 51 **TN,** They [=Indians] never come out boldly into the open field, and take a fair fight, fist and skull, as Christians do. **1908** *DN* 3.311 **eAL, wGA,** *Fist and skull, adj.* or *adv. phr.* Without weapons. "A fist and skull fight." **1935** Allen *Annals Haywood Co.* 268 **NC,** It was a great rendezvous for the people, where all the then sports of the day were engaged in, such games as pitching quoits, running foot races, shooting matches, wrestling, and, sometimes a good fist and skull fight. **1935** Davis *Honey* 184 **OR,** Since they were already on one another's nerves, they had a fist-and-heel fight about it. **1937** *Hall Coll.* **eTN,** They were fightin' fist and skull. **c1960** *Wilson Coll.* **csKY,** *Fist fight.* . . A fair fight, with no weapons, biting, or gouging. Same as a fist-and-skull fight. **1966–69** *DARE* (Qu. Y12b, *A real fight in which blows are struck*) Infs **AL**3, **NC**33, Fist-and-skull fight; **GA**77, Fist-and-skull knockout.

Fist City n Also *Fist Holler* **chiefly Sth, S Midl**

An imaginary place where disputes are settled by fistfights.

1936 *AmSp* 11.315 **Ozarks,** When two men are said to be 'goin' up *Fist Holler'* it means that they are about to have a fight. **1954** *Harder Coll.* **cwTN,** Fist Holler. **1967–68** *DARE* (Qu. Y12b, *A real fight in which blows are struck*) Infs **LA**18, **TX**51, (They) went to Fist City; **PA**93, Going to Fist City; **TX**18, Fist City—more a threat; **TX**23, Fist City. **1976** Lynn-Vecsey *Loretta Lynn* 92 **eKY,** So I warned any girl making eyes at Doo [=her husband] then, and I'm still jealous enough to warn 'em today . . you'd better walk a circle around us if you don't want to go to Fist City.

fiste See **feist n**

fistelow See **fistula**

fist(es)es See **fist n**[1]

Fist Holler See **Fist City**

fist stalk n Also *fist off*

=**club fist.**

1913 (1980) Hardy *OH Schoolmistress* 38 **swOH** (as of c1850), The game "fist-stock" [sic] had much the same ending [as William o' Trimpity] after a long preamble of questions and answers; the last hand is asked: What you got there? Bread and cheese./ Where is my share? The cat's got it./ . . Fee, faw, fun! The first one who speaks or laughs or shows his teeth will get a box and five nails. **1965** *DARE* File **sIN,** "Fist stalk" was played by my ancestors as they came down the Cumberland and Tennessee Rivers on flatboats in the late 18th century. The game (some called it "fist off") was passed on from generation to generation. After the "stalk" was made and only one person had a hand free, he said to the player whose hand was on top, "Take it off or knock it off," and that player could remove it voluntarily or have it knocked off. This was repeated until all hands were free, and a question-answer game followed.

fist-to-cuff fight n [Folk-etym from *fisticuff*]

1968 *DARE* (Qu. Y13, *A fist fight with several people in it*) Inf **VA**28, Fist-to-cuff fight.

fistula n Usu |ˈfɪst(j)ulə, ˈfɪstələ, ˈfɪsčələ|; also freq |ˈfɪst(j)ulo, ˈfɪstəlo|; less freq |ˈfɪsələ, ˈfɪsəlo|; for addit varr see quots Pronc-spp *fistelow, thistelow* Cf **cupola A, gondola 1**

Std sense, var forms.

1892 *DN* 1.233 **KY,** [fɪstjulo]. **1899** (1912) Green *VA Folk-Speech* 176, *Fistelow.* . . "He had a fistelow for five years." **1942** Hall *Smoky Mt. Speech* 77, *Fistula* . . [is] always pronounced with [o]: . . [ˈfɪstəˌlo]. **1950** *WELS (Diseases of horses)* 5 Infs, **WI,** Fistula; 1 Inf, Fistula, also called thistelow. **1965–70** *DARE* (Qu. K47, . . *Diseases . . [of] horses* *or mules)* 38 Infs, **scattered,** ['fist(j)ulə, 'fistələ, 'fisčələ]; 37 Infs, **scattered,** ['fist(j)ulo, 'fistəlo]; 4 Infs, ['fisəlo]; **IN**8, ['fistuli]; **IN**63, ['fistərol]; **MD**15, ['fiskjɨlə]; **MA**42, ['θɪsəlo]; **NY**97, ['tɪslə]; (Qu. BB33b, . . *A swelling under the skin—if it is very big)* Infs **AL**4, **RI**1, **TN**48, **WI**18, 47, Fistula; **KY**94, ['fisčəlo]; **MN**19, **TX**86, ['fistələ]; (Qu. BB33a) Inf **DC**3, ['fisələ]; **DC**3A, ['fistjʊlə]; (Qu. BB30) Inf **MN**37, ['fistiulə]. **1967** *Wilson Coll.* **csKY,** Fistula [fistəloʊ].

fisty See **feisty** adj, n

fit v[1]

A Forms.

Past and past pple: usu *fit;* also *fitted.* Note: The following data are limited to the sense 'to be of the correct size for;' in other senses the past and past pple *fitted* may show greater currency.

1935 Sandoz *Jules* 135 **wNE** (as of 1880–1930), Ma fried a steak that just fitted her big skillet. **1940** in 1944 *ADD* **swPA, nWV,** 'Last year it fit him.' Old illit. speaker. **1941** Daniels *Tar Heels* 276 **NC,** Wolfe . . was the voluble man who fit snugly into the politics of the place. **1950** *WELS ("When I tried these shoes on they ——— . . just right.")* 39 Infs, **WI,** Fit; 20 Infs, Fitted; *("If they hadn't ———, I wouldn't have bought them.")* 45 Infs, **WI,** Fit; 13 Infs, Fitted. **1953** Atwood *Survey of Verb Forms* 14, In the context "His coat (fitted) me" . . the inflected form *[=fitted]* is strongly favored [in New England]. . . In the M[iddle] A[tlantic] S[tates] and the S[outh] A[tlantic] S[tates], on the other hand, *fitted* predominates only in e. N.C. It also occurs alongside *fit* (in about equal numbers) in N.Y., n. N.J., the Chesapeake Bay area, and parts of e. Pa. and w. N.C. Elsewhere in the East the uninflected *fit* is universal, or nearly so. **1965–70** *DARE* (Qu. OO38a, . . *"When I tried these shoes on, they ——— just right."*) 855 Infs, **widespread,** Fit; 120 Infs, **widespread,** Fitted; (Qu. OO38b, . . *"I wouldn't have bought them if they hadn't ——— just right."*) 769 Infs, **widespread,** Fit; 211 Infs, **widespread,** Fitted. **1975** Allen *LAUM* 2.18 **Upper MW** (as of c1950), Although the eastern surveys clearly reveal the inflected preterit *fitted* as the favored form in New England, . . the Midland simple *fit* [in the context 'His coat ——— me.'] has so strongly expanded into Northern speech territory that four out of five of the infs. in all five states prefer the latter.

B Senses.

1 To make ready; spec:

a also with *up:* To prepare (soil) for planting; hence vbl n *fitting.*

1914 Sears *Productive Orcharding* 85, It is not always necessary that the land should be plowed. On lightish lands in particular it is often possible to fit them . . with some type of disc harrow. *Ibid* 86, The desirability of fitting the land as early in the spring as possible is very frequently overlooked by the orchard man. **1917** *DN* 4.392 **neOH,** *Fit.* . . To prepare soil for seed. Usually applied to the finishing processes. "This field is not fitted yet." "I am fitting for wheat this week." **1967** Key *Tobacco Vocab.* **CT,** *Fit up.* Of a field: to prepare for planting. "Fit up the fields." Fitting the ground means getting on the fertilizer. **1981** *Greenfield Recorder* (MA) 4 June sec A 9, He plowed and fitted the garden plot near the house ready for planting. . . Then one day soon, he said to her, "Won't you be a little late with your garden unless you start it very soon? I fitted it ready some time ago."

b To cut (firewood) to a particular size; hence ppl adj *fitted.*

1914 *DN* 4.72 **ME, nNH,** *Fit.* . . Cut wood to stove-size. "Fitted wood."

c See quot.

1969 Sorden *Lumberjack Lingo* 43 **NEng, Gt Lakes,** *Fit a saw*—To put a saw in good condition by jointing, setting, and filing the teeth.

2 in phr *fit too soon:* See **soon.**

3 in phr *fit one right in the neck:* To suit one exactly.

1968 *DARE* FW Addit **LA**15, [FW:] Is she nosy? [Inf:] That's exactly it. That would fit her right in the neck.

fit v[2] See **fight A1, 3, 4, 5**

fit n[1] [From *fight* v]

A fistfight.

1896 *DN* 1.417 **cNY,** *Fit* . . a fight.

fit n[2] [Abbr for *outfit*]

1972 Claerbaut *Black Jargon* 64, *Fit* . . dress; clothes; apparel. . . a suit; complete outfit.

fitch n [Var of *fitchew* polecat]

A **polecat** (*Mephitis* spp); or its fur.

1616 Smith *Descr. New Engl.* 30, Fitches, Musquassus, & diuerse sorts of vermine, whose names I know not. **1891** (1967) Freeman *New Engl. Nun* 91, I had a fitch tippet an' muff that cost twenty-five dollars. **1920** *DN* 5.81 **Seattle WA,** [Newspaper item:] Ermine, fox, lynx, wolf, fitch, reasonable while they last. **1942** Hale *Prodigal Women* 298 **MA** (as of early 1900s), Her mother's present, a small fitch fur, was, she thought, a measly little thing and she could not wear it by itself.

fitch v [Prob var of *filch,* but perh rel to Scots, nEngl *fitch* to shift, remove]

To filch, pilfer.

1943 *LANE* Map 566, Synonyms of *stole* (preterite), recorded in the context *Who swiped my pencil?* . . *Fitched.* [2 infs, **seME,** [fiʔtʃt, fitʃt]; 1 of the infs considers *fitched* rare.]

fitcher v, hence vbl n *fitchering,* ppl adj *fitchered* [*OED* 1865; appar a Cornish mining term]

In mining: to stop short, stick.

1899 (1960) Norris *McTeague* 266 **nCA,** From time to time he rapped the drill with a pole-pick when it stuck fast or fitchered. *Ibid* 272, Well I've mined some too. I had a hole in the ground meself, but she was silver; and when the skunks at Washington lowered the price of silver, where was I? Fitchered, b'God! **1945** *CA Folkl. Qrly.* 4.321 **CO** [Cornish terms used in mining camps], Fitchering, "dog in the hole": When the drill sticks. **1946** *Western Folkl.* 5.167 **MT,** Whenever a drill lurches suddenly from hard rock to soft, or into a small cavity . . without drilling a hole large enough to release the drill, old miners acquainted with the Cornish terminology say, "There's a Dutchman in the hole." "Fitchering" is the standard term.

fitchery adj [**fitcher** v]

In mining: see quot 1950.

1926 *Engin. & Mining Jrl.* 122.300/2 **MT,** In the Butte district the ground varies from very hard, tough rock and ore to loose fitchery ore and even to a clay or mud. **1950** *Western Folkl.* 9.37 **MT** (as of c1900), [Song parody:] Oh, the stope it was filled with gas, Maggie,/ And the ground it was fitchery as well. [Footnote: "fitchery" ground is usually soft or loose rock.]

fitch-fork n [Var of *pitch-fork*]

1941 O'Donnell *Great Big Doorstep* 330 **sLA,** By his looks he oney needs the horns and fitch-fork to be name Lucifer, and a harpoon on his tail.

fiten See **fitten** adj

fit for the fox farm See **fox farm, ready for the**

fith See **fifth**

fitified adj Also sp *fittified, fittyfied* [*fit* n + **-ified**] **chiefly Midl; also Sth** Note: Senses **1** and **2** are not always distinguishable.

1 Subject to fits; epileptic.

1822 in 1929 Phillips *Life Old South* 275, The fellow you bought of Tutt is fitified or subject to convulsions. **1894** Riley *Armazindy* 3 **IN,** Had to look / After her old fittified / Grand-aunt. **1899** (1912) Green *VA Folk-Speech* 176, *Fittyfied.* . . Subject to fits, spasms, or paroxysms. Fitty. **1903** *DN* 2.313 **seMO,** *Fitified.* . . Subject to fits. **1908** *DN* 3.311 **eAL, wGA,** *Fitified.* **1917** *DN* 4.412 **wNC,** *Fitified.* **1942** (1971) Campbell *Cloud-Walking* 56 **seKY,** She had always been fitified at certain times of the moon from laying in the moonlight a heap when she was a little youngun. **c1960** *Wilson Coll.* **csKY,** *Fitified.* . . Subject to epileptic or other seizures. **1963** Edwards *Gravel* 23 **eTN** (as of 1920s), "You wouldn't think he used to be fitified now, wouldje?" "No," said Ma. "He's completely outgrowed it, I think." They thought Uncle Jeems's mind was a little weaker than most grown people's because he took fits when he was younger. **1983** *MJLF* 9.1.39 **ceKY** (as of 1956), *Fitified* . . afflicted with fits.

2 Eccentric, erratic.

1902 *DN* 2.234 **sIL,** *Fitified.* . . 1. Hysterical; nervous. 2. Erratic; notional; fastidious. **1905** *DN* 3.79 **nwAR,** She's so fitified I hardly know how to get along with her. **1930** *DN* 6.84 **cSC,** *Fitified,* temperamental. **1937** Thornburgh *Gt. Smoky Mts.* 104, This spring flows normally for about ten months of the year. Often during October and November it is irregular and is referred to as the "fittified spring" by the mountain people. **1960** Hall *Smoky Mt. Folks* 57, *Fitified:* as in Fitified Springs: an intermittent spring.

fitn See **fitten** adj

fit one right in the neck See **fit** v[1] **B3**

fitout n [*fit out* v phr] *old-fash*
An outfit; the necessary equipment and provisions for an expedition; the equipping of an expedition.
1840 (1841) Dana *2 Yrs.* 140 **NEng,** Go-ashore jackets and trowsers [were] got out and brushed; pumps, neckerchiefs, and hats overhauled . . so that among the whole each one got a good fit-out. **1846** in 1924 *UT Geneal. & Hist. Mag.* 15.108, We were obliged to send down to Missouri . . to procure provisions, to make a necessary fitout for the great western expedition. **1905** Lincoln *Partners* 264 **seMA,** I know where we can buy a complete fit-out second-hand—pumps, pipes, diver's suit and the whole business. **1942** Whipple *Joshua* 1 **UT** (as of c1860), Dugway builders offered no guaranty that all of the fit-out, including wagon, oxen, grub, and humans, would reach bottom at the same point. **1947** Morgan *Great Salt Lake* 250 (as of c1850), The [Mormon] church felt the enormous responsibility that was theirs for helping the poor. The wealthy among the Saints could provide their own "fit-outs" and make their own way to Zion, though always in the organized companies that were the hallmark of Mormon immigration.

fitroot n Also *fit plant* [See quots 1830, 1910]
=**Indian pipe.**
1830 Rafinesque *Med. Flora* 243, Fitroot. . . Dried root in powder used in epilepsy and convulsions of children, dose a teaspoon full. **1876** Hobbs *Bot. Hdbk.* 38, Fit-root plant, Ice plant, Monotropa uniflora. **1910** Graves *Flowering Plants* 307 **CT,** Indian Pipe. . . Fit-root. . . The root is sometimes employed medicinally and has been used as a substitute for opium. **1931** Clute *Common Plants* 123, Fit-root *(Monotropa uniflora).* **1959** Carleton *Index Herb. Plants* 46, *Fit-plant:* Monotropa uniflora.

fitsroot n
A **milk vetch** (here: *Astragalus glycyphyllos*).
1950 Gray–Fernald *Manual of Botany* 911, *Fitsroot.* . . Roadsides and waste grounds, local, Mass. to Ind.

fitsy adj Cf **fitified, fitty** adj[2]
1930 Shoemaker *1300 Words* 22 **cPA Mts** (as of c1900), *Fitsy*—Subject to attacks of temper, uncertain.

fittable adj Cf **fitten** adj
Suitable.
1927 *AmSp* 3.139 **ME coast,** A thing deemed unsuitable was not "fittable."

fitted v[1] See **fit** v[1] **A, B1b**

fitted v[2] See **fight A3, 4**

fitten adj Also sp *fiten, fitn, fittin'* [Engl dial; pronc varr of *fitting*] **chiefly Sth, S Midl**
1 Fit, suitable; ready, prepared.
1798 Munford *Plays* 14 **VA,** After you declin'd, I thought I was the next *fittenest* man in the county. *Ibid* 37, An't I as *fitten* a *(hickups)* man as either of those? **1857** in 1956 Eliason *Tarheel Talk* 271 **NC,** The new ground . . is not fiten for cotten. **1893** Shands *MS Speech* 29, *Fitten.* . . This is used by illiterate whites for *fit.* **1902** *DN* 2.234 **sIL,** It aint fitn. **1903** *DN* 2.313 **seMO,** This dress isn't fitten to wear. **1906** *DN* 3.136 **nwAR,** He's not fittin' for that work. **1908** *DN* 3.311 **eAL, wGA,** *Fitten.* **1923** *DN* 5.207 **swMO,** *Fitten.* **1948** Hurston *Seraph* 31 **wFL** [Black], Even if Jim meant it [=to marry her], she was not fitten. **1952** Brown *NC Folkl.* 1.541, *Fitten:* . . Fit, suitable. "He ain't fitten to be a officer." **1966** *DARE* Tape **FL**36, Just ain't no water that's fitten to drink. **1967** *DARE* (Qu. I8, *When root vegetables get old and tough and are not good to eat)* Inf **LA**6, Not fitten to eat.
2 Good; beautiful; spec, of foods: pleasing.
1906 *DN* 3.118 **sIN,** These apples are mighty fittin'. **1909** *DN* 3.396 **nwAR,** That's fittin' to the taste. **1966–70** *DARE* (Qu. KK1a, . . *Words meaning very good . . "That pie was _______.")* Inf **IN**32, Right fitten; **TX**95, Fitten; (Qu. B1, *If a day is very pleasant, you say it's a _______ day.)* Inf **FL**29, Right [fɪtn̩]. **1967** Green *Horse Tradin'* 212 **swTX,** I started in on this barbeque, and it sure was fittin'. I began to brag on it.

fitten adv [**fitten** adj]
Properly, well.
1941 *Sat. Eve. Post* 10 May 112/2 **eKY,** I can't grub [out trees] fitten.

fittified See **fitified**

fittin' See **fitten** adj

fitting pres pple See **fight A2**

fitting vbl n See **fit** v[1] **B1a**

fit to be tied adj phr **chiefly Nth, N Midl, Mid Atl**
Very excited, agitated, or angry.
1950 *WELS (Very excited . . "When he saw them coming he was _______.")* 3 Infs, **WI,** Fit to be tied; *(Violently angry)* 3 Infs, **WI,** Fit to be tied. **1960** Bailey *Resp. to PADS 20* **KS,** Fit to be tied, riled up. **1960** Criswell *Resp. to PADS 20* **MO,** Old man Jones was so mad at that kid that he was fit to be tied. **1965–70** *DARE* (Qu. GG11, *To be quite anxious . . "The letter hasn't come and he's _______.")* 19 Infs, **chiefly Nth, N Midl,** Fit to be tied; (Qu. GG40, . . *Violently angry)* 16 Infs, **chiefly Atlantic,** Fit to be tied; (Qu. GG4, *Stirred up, angry)* Infs **CA**61, **MA**58, **WI**47, Fit to be tied; (Qu. GG6, . . *A person's feelings being hurt: "When she said she wouldn't go with him, he was quite _______.")* Inf **NY**241, Fit to be tied; (Qu. GG7, . . *Annoyed or upset)* Infs **IL**82, **RI**13, Fit to be tied; (Qu. GG35b, . . *Annoyed or disappointed . . "Because she couldn't go she's been _______ all day.")* Inf **WI**24, Fit to be tied. **1983** *Lutz Coll.* **neNJ,** Mary was fit to be tied because Bruce had not come to pick her up as he had promised.

fit too soon See **fit** v[1] **B2**

fitty adj[1]
1 =**fitten** adj **1.** [Prob *fit* adj + *-y; OED* 1589–1880; "*Obs.* exc. *dial.*"]
1913 Kephart *Highlanders* 229 **sAppalachians,** The words that man used ain't fitty to tell. **1917** *DN* 4.412 **wNC, TN,** It ain't fitty fer hell.
2 Healthy, fit. [Engl dial; *EDD fitty* adj.[1] 6 "In good health, well"]
1950 *WELS (He's feeling _______ this morning.)* 1 Inf, **csWI,** Fine and fitty.

fitty adj[2] [Engl dial; *EDD fitty* adj.[2]] Cf **fitified**
Subject to fits; eccentric.
1872 (1973) Thompson *Major Jones's Courtship* 205 **GA,** I really do blieve the baby is spasomy. Mercy on me! it jumps and twitches like it is fitty. **1899** (1912) Green *VA Folk-Speech* 176, *Fittyfied.* . . Subject to fits. . . Fitty. **1915** *DN* 4.214, *Fitty, fitified,* eccentric. **1927** in 1944 *ADD* **WV.**

fittyfied See **fitified**

fit up See **fit** v[1] **B1a**

fitweed n
Corydalis.
1947 (1964) Randolph *Ozark Superstitions* 110, "Mirandy" Bauersfeld tells of an Ozark granny who chewed up *fitweed* leaves and then thrust them into the patient's mouth. **1964** Kingsbury *Poisonous Plants U.S.* 153, *Corydalis* spp. Fitweed, corydalis, fumatory [sic]. . . Symptoms. . . Convulsive clonic spasms.

fitzy See **fizzy** n[1] **1**

fiuh See **fire**

five adj, n Usu |faɪv|; for varr see **A** below Pronc-spp *fi', fibe* Cf Pronc Intro 3.I.17
A Forms.
1899 Chesnutt *Conjure Woman* 14 **csNC** [Black], A nigger did n' mine [=mind] goin' fi' er ten mile in a night. *Ibid* 202, Ef we des [=just] set heah fo' er fibe minutes, she'll sta't up by herse'f. **1922** Gonzales *Black Border* 301 **sSC, GA coasts** [Gullah glossary], *Fibe, fi'*—five; "fibe dollah en' seb'nty-fi' cent.' " **1942** Hall *Smoky Mt. Speech* 44 **eTN, wNC,** Five . . [fa·v]. **1961** Kurath–McDavid *Pronc. Engl.* 109, In two rather sharply delimited areas of the South, (1) Virginia and adjoining parts of Maryland and North Carolina, and (2) the coastal belt of South Carolina, Georgia, and Florida, . . "fast" diphthongs with centralized beginning occur only before voiceless consonants, as in *twice, night,* and differ sharply from the "slow" diphthongs [a·^{ɛ}, a·^{ə}, ɑ·ɨ] current in these areas before voiced consonants, as in *five* [etc]. . . Northern [ʌɨ, ɐɨ] occurs in all positions; it is yielding ground to [aɨ] and has been largely replaced by it in southern New England and in the Hudson Valley. . . The most widespread variants [in the South] are [a·^{ɛ}] and [ɑ·^{ɛ}]. **1976** Allen *LAUM* 3.25 (as of c1950), Roughly two-thirds of the U[pper] M[idwest] infs. have this low-central [=aɨ] diphthong [in *five, twice, nine*]. . . That with a centralized first element, [ɐɨ], . . is preponderantly Northern . . and apparently is on the increase. . . [a^{ɨ}, ɑ^{ɨ}] . . appears chiefly in those parts of Nebraska and Iowa subject to some South Midland influence.

B As noun.

1 An inexpensive marble. Cf **fivefer**

1968 *DARE* (Qu. EE6b, *Small marbles*) Inf **LA**25, Fives—the cheapest, small china marbles.

2 A short rest; a break. [Abbr for *five-minute break*]

1966–69 *DARE* (Qu. O21, *When men out in seagoing boats get together for a visit and a cup of hot coffee, that's called a* ______) Inf **CA**111, Five; woodsmen too, called it a five; (Qu. X41, *When you're going to sleep for a very short while . . "I'm just going to* ______*."*) Inf **MN**10, Take a five; (Qu. X43b, *If you sleep later than usual . . "I* ______*."*) Inf **MT**4, Took another five; (Qu. A9, . . *Wasting time by not working on the job*) Inf **MI**80, Taking a five.

five-and-ten n

1 also *five-(and-ten-)cent store, five-and-dime (store)* and varr: Orig a store selling all items for five or ten cents; now, a store selling relatively inexpensive articles. **widespread, but more freq NEast, C Atl**

1879 in 1940 *Sat. Eve. Post* 10 Feb 22/2 **sePA,** No one knew there was a 5c store in this city until Friday night, and we managed to sell yesterday in one day $127.65. **1880** in 1940 *Sat. Eve. Post* 10 Feb 23/3 **nePA,** [Sign board:] Woolworth Bros. 5 & 10 Cent Store. **1907** Porter *Trimmed Lamp* 115 **NYC,** Did you ever notice me . . peering in the window of the five-and-ten? **1934** (1974) Farrell *Young Manhood* **Chicago IL** 17, A small American flag which he'd copped from the nearby five-and-dime store. **1942** Hale *Prodigal Women* 34 **MA,** They spent every cent of money they could beg, on college ices; jewelry in the 5-10-25 cent store; tin bangles that clattered on their arms, and necklaces in bright colors. **1962** Atwood *Vocab. TX* 122, [Table D:] Highest Frequency of Usage in the Younger Groups. . . [Includes] five-and-ten (store). **1965–70** *DARE* (Qu. U43; not asked in early QRs) 230 Infs, **widespread, but more freq NEast, C Atl,** Five-and-ten; 210 Infs, **widespread,** Five-and-ten-cent store; 173 Infs, **widespread, but more freq NEast,** Five-and-dime; 15 Infs, **scattered,** Five-and-dime store; 13 Infs, **scattered,** Five-and-ten store; **IL**13, **IN**34, Five-to-ten store; **AR**23, Five-cent store; **IN**35, Five-and-ten-to-a-dollar; **NY**207, Five-to-a-dollar store; **IN**73, **MI**101, Five-ten-cent store; (Qu. W36, . . *A woman who uses a lot of cosmetics*) Inf **NJ**16, A million-dollar baby from the five-and-ten-cent store. **1971** Bright *Word Geog. CA & NV* 203, *Five and ten* 37% . . *five and ten cent store* . . 10% . . *five and dime (store)* 20%. **1983** *Barrick Coll.* **csPA,** *Five and ten*—variety store; still used. I don't recall ever hearing "five and dime" in this area, except from outsiders.

2 A marble game.

1940 *Recreation* (NY) 34.110, [In a list of marbles games played throughout the country:] 5 and 10.

3 A children's ball game; see quot.

1977 *NY Times* (NY) 7 June 29/3 **Brooklyn NYC,** But one kid's stoopball is another kid's "five and ten," and instead of a kind of baseball it becomes a game of points, five points after the ball passes the first line from the stoop, 10 points if it goes past the second line.

five-cent nickel n [Orig to distinguish it from the three-cent nickel minted 1865–89]

A nickel coin worth five cents.

1875 *Chicago Tribune* (IL) 6 Nov 5/6 **MS,** He went to the bottom of his pockets, turned them inside out, but he could find nothing but a 5-cent nickel. **1910** *N.Y. Post* 8 Dec. 8 *(DAE),* Until recently the 'five-cent nickel' has for all practical purposes been the lowest unit of legal tender [in the West]. **1969** *DARE* (Qu. U22) Inf **IL**39, Five-cent nickel.

five-cent store See **five-and-ten 1**

five-come-in n Cf **five hundred 2**

A bat-and-ball game with fewer than the regulation number of players.

1967 *DARE* (Qu. EE11) Inf **SC**65, Five-come-in.

five-corns n pl, but sg or pl in constr

1 also *five-corn vine:* The cupseed *(Calycocarpum lyonii)* or its fruits.

1898 *Jrl. Amer. Folkl.* 11.222, *Calycocarpum* . . five corns [*Jrl.* Ed: So called from the seeds which children use as dice.], Southern Kentucky. **1954** *Harder Coll.* **cwTN,** *Five corns*—a weed. "Look lak [=like] sweet gum leaves, but lak a bushel; play hul-gul with it." *Five corn vine*—a weed. **1987** *DARE* File **cwTN,** The [five-corn] vine had several segments. From each segment grew a stem with a stamen that . . looked much like a bushel basket. . . This contained five kernels or "five corns," hard enough for children to play the guessing game of hully gully with them.

2 A game played with the seeds of **five-corns 1.**

[1898 see **1** above.] **1967** *DARE* (Qu. DD37, . . *Table games played a lot by adults*) Inf **KY**34, Five-corns. **[1987** see **1** above.]

five-corn vine See **five-corns 1**

five crimson doves n

A columbine (here: *Aquilegia canadensis*).

1967 Borland *Hill Country* 157 **nwCT,** The wild columbines now blooming in rocky places all through our area have been called five crimson doves. . . The "five crimson doves" name comes from the five deep spurs of the blossom, which might be likened to doves, I suppose.

five-dollar william (or willy) See **william**

five-eights rig n

A saddle with fittings for a single girth slightly forward of the center.

1961 Adams *Old-Time Cowhand* 111, [A saddle] with the cinch between the "rim-fire" and the "three-quarter" is a "seven-eights," and one between the "three-quarter" and the "center-fire" is a "five-eights" rig. Neither of these latter rigs is commonly used.

fivefer n Also *fiver, fivefor* [*five* + *for*] Cf **twofer**

An inexpensive marble sold in lots of five; a marble game.

1950 *WELS (Kinds of marbles: small ones)* 2 Infs, **WI,** Fivers. **1967–68** *DARE* (Qu. EE6c, *Cheap marbles*) Inf **IN**46, Twofers, threefers, fivefers; (Qu. EE7, . . *Marbles games*) Inf **TX**11, Fivefors.

five-finger See **five-fingers n**

five-finger(ed) creeper See **five-fingers n 3**

five-fingered grass n

1 also *five-finger grass:* **=cinquefoil.** [From the five leaflets of the digitate leaves]

1889 *Century Dict.* 2243, *Fivefinger*. . . Also called *cinquefoil* or *five-finger grass.* **1931** *Jrl. Amer. Folkl.* 44.413 **LA,** Five-fingered grass. Used to uncross. Make tea, strain it and bathe in it nine times. **c1938** in 1970 Hyatt *Hoodoo* 1.245 **seGA** [Black], Well, oftentimes fellahs carries a *lucky piece* in dere pocket. Maybe it be lodestone or *John de Conker* or *five-finger grass* or some kinda perfume in lodestone. **1946** Tallant *Voodoo* 217 **New Orleans LA,** *Five Finger Grass*—This plant has a leaf divided into Five Segments that many claim when hung up in the house or over a bedstead will bring restful sleep and ward off any Evil that five fingers would bring about. We make no claims to this effect and sell only as Genuine Five Finger Grass. Voodoos and certain Occults believe that each finger has a significance such as standing: 1 for *Luck,* 2 for *Money,* 3 for *Wisdom,* 4 for *Power,* 5 for *Love.* **1964** Smith *PA Germans* 26.131 **VA, WV,** *Cinquefoil* or five-finger grass [was used] for fever.

2 Perh a **crabgrass 1.**

1950 *WELS (Kinds of grass that are hard to get rid of)* 1 Inf, **swWI,** Five-fingered grass.

five-fingered ivy See **five-fingers n 3**

five-fingered Jack n [From the five leaflets of the digitate leaves + *Jack* (*OED* sb.[1] 32)]

A **cinquefoil** (here: *Potentilla canadensis*).

1898 *Jrl. Amer. Folkl.* 11.226, *Potentilla Canadensis,* . . five-fingered Jack, Auburndale, Mass.

five-fingered Joe n [Prob in ref to the five-pointed leaves, + *Joe* a fellow]

Appar a **Virginia creeper.**

1966 *DARE* (Qu. S26d) Inf **MA**6, Five-fingered Joe—non-poisonous ivy.

five-finger fern n

A **maidenhair fern** (here: *Adiantum pedatum*).

1913 London *Valley of Moon* 526 **CA,** Saxon drew Billy's eyes to a mossy bank of five-finger ferns. **1923** in 1925 Jepson *Manual Plants CA* 29, *A[diantum] pedatum* . . Five-finger Fern. **1938** (1958) Sharples *AK Wild Flowers* 5, A variety of the common "Maidenhair" [=*Adiantum pedatum*], sometimes called the "Five-Finger Fern," found in many parts of the United States. **1961** Thomas *Flora Santa Cruz* 60 **cwCA,** *A[diantum] pedatum* . . Five-finger Fern. **1974** Munz *Flora S. CA* 25.

five-finger grass See **five-fingered grass 1**

five-finger ivy See **five-fingers n 3**

five-fingers n Also *five-finger*

1 =cinquefoil.

1683 in 1861 MA Hist. Soc. *Coll.* 4th ser 5.113, For the mouth, we take strawberry-leaves, five-finger, violet, . . —of each, a like quantity boiled in spring water. **1782** Crèvecoeur *Letters* 256 **PA,** Five-fingers (a small plant resembling strawberries). **1824** Bigelow *Florula Bostoniensis* 204, *Potentilla simplex. . .* Common Cinquefoil or Fivefinger. **1897** Creevey *Flowers* 184, Norway Cinquefoil. Five-finger. **1941** Writers' Program *Guide WY* 23, Tucked into crevices and sunwarmed pockets on the high slopes, or bent by the wind on the drying prairie, are saxifrage, five-fingers, . . miner's candle, beardtongue, arnica. **1966** *DARE* Wildfl QR Pl.95 Inf **WA**10, Five-finger. **1976** Bailey–Bailey *Hortus Third* 904, *Potentilla. . .* Cinquefoil, five-finger.

2 A **ginseng B1** (here: *Panax quinquefolium*).

1830 Rafinesque *Med. Flora* 52, *Panax quinquefolium. . . Names. . . Vulgar. . .* Five-fingers. **1876** Hobbs *Bot. Hdbk.* 38, Five-fingers, . . Ginseng root, Panax quinquefolia [sic]. **1930** Sievers *Amer. Med. Plants* 30. **c1938** in 1970 Hyatt *Hoodoo* 2.985 **seGA,** Den ah goes down den inside of a kinda wet place an' hunt de—whut chew call de *five finger roots.* Well, when yo' git it, it be five—see, it's jest like five of yore fingers, called de *five finger roots.* **1971** Krochmal *Appalachia Med. Plants* 186, *Panax Quinquefolium L. . . Common Names:* American ginseng, . . five fingers, . . tartar root.

3 as *five-finger, five-finger(ed) creeper, five-finger(ed) ivy:* A **Virginia creeper** (here: *Parthenocissus quinquefolia*).

1893 *Jrl. Amer. Folkl.* 6.139 **NY,** *Ampelopsis quinquefolia,* five-fingered ivy; American joy. **1900** Lyons *Plant Names* 277, *P. quinquefolia. . .* Five-finger, . . Five-fingered Ivy. **1940** Clute *Amer. Plant Names* 131, *Virginia Creeper. . .* Five-fingered ivy, five-fingered creeper. **1960** Vines *Trees SW* 712, Vernacular names for the vine are . . Five-finger Ivy, Five-finger Creeper. **1961** Wills–Irwin *Flowers TX* 150, Perhaps the most common victim of confusion is Virginia-creeper or 5-finger-ivy.

4 A five-armed starfish. **NEng**

1850 (1852) Hawthorne *Scarlet Letter* 207 **MA,** She . . made prize of several five-fingers. **a1862** (1865) Thoreau *Cape Cod* 101 **eMA,** A few Star-fishes or Five-fingers *(Asterias rubens).* **1871** Townsend *Diary* 9 Aug (*AmSp* 23.298), Another bad enemy of the oyster is the starfish, called the 'five-fingers' north of Cape Cod. **1881** *Scribner's Mth.* 22.214/2 **ME,** The trap . . contains from one to a dozen [lobsters] of all sizes, and with them a few 'five-fingers' (star-fish).

five fingers exclam See **fingers**

five-foot yardstick n

An imaginary object used as the basis of practical jokes.

1969 *DARE* (Qu. HH14, *Ways of teasing a beginner . . "Go get me ______."*) Inf **MA**24, A five-foot yardstick. [Laughter]

fivefor See **fivefer**

five-holer See **-holer**

five-holes See **hole n 4**

five hundred n

1 A card game similar to euchre, in which a player wins by scoring five hundred points. **chiefly Nth, N Midl, but less freq eNEng, NW** See Map

1920 Lewis *Main Street* 195 **MN,** What do you say we go down to Jack Elder's and have a game of five hundred this afternoon? **1948** Faulkner *Intruder* 61 **MS,** Now it was no childhood's game of stakeless Five Hundred. It was more like the poker games he had overlooked. **1950** *WELS (Card games played a good deal in your neighborhood)* 34 Infs, **WI,** Five hundred. **1965–70** *DARE* (Qu. DD35, . . *Favorite card games*) 160 Infs, **chiefly Nth, N Midl, but less freq eNEng, NW,** Five hundred; **MT**4, Progressive five hundred; (Qu. FF2, *Kinds of parties*) Inf **PA**59, Five-hundred parties. **1969** *Richland Observer* (Richland Center WI) 22 May sec 1 10/4, Cards were played after the 1 p.m. luncheon with . . the five hundred prizes to Mrs. Raymond Marshall and Mrs. Bessie Bohmann.

2 also *five hundred up:* A bat-and-ball game played when there are not enough players for two full teams; see quot 1950. **esp West, Gt Lakes** See Map Cf **town ball, work-up**

1950 *WELS* 1 Inf, **csWI,** Five hundred—choose a pitcher and batter;

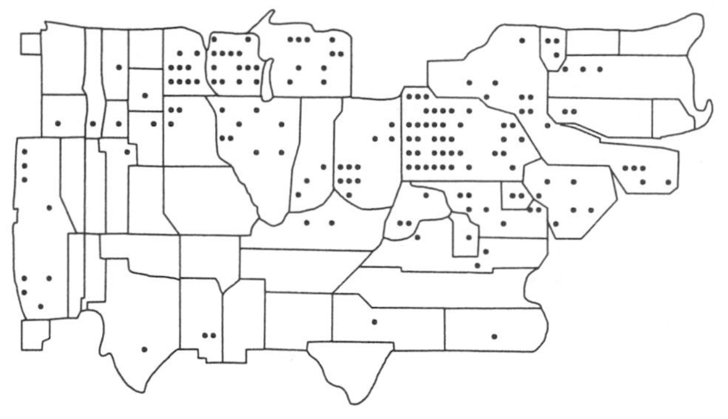

•five hundred 1 + varr (Qq. DD35, FF2)

ball pitched to batter who bats out to the other players. [For a ball] caught with one hand on the fly [the fielder earns] 200 points; caught with both hands, 100 points; caught on one bounce, 75; two bounces, 50; three bounces, 25; dead ball, no count. The two [with] high[est points] go to bat and pitcher; 1 Inf, **cWI,** Five hundred up; 1 Inf, **cwWI,** Fly or five hundred; flies count so much, bounces so much; roll along ground so much; any miss, you lose points. **1957** *Sat. Eve. Post Letters,* As a school teacher from 1910 to 1944 the following activities . . [were popular among my students] in the State of Washington and California . . 500 (a baseball game). *Ibid,* About ten years ago I played these games in Rochester, N.Y. . . hit the bat, five hundred, [etc]. **1965–70** *DARE* (Qu. EE11) 15 Infs, **esp West, Gt Lakes,** Five hundred. [7 Infs young, 5 mid-aged]

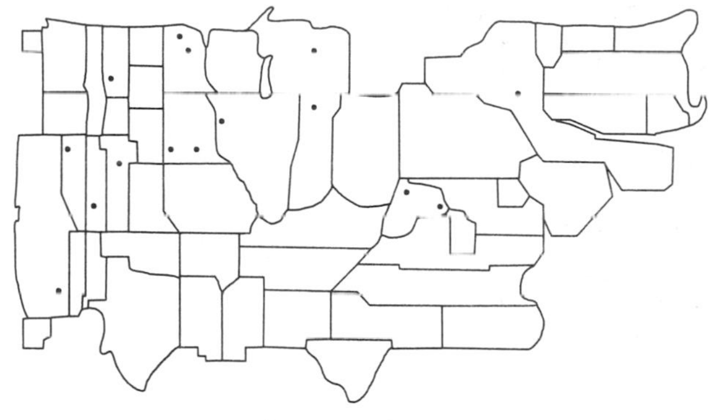

•five hundred 2 (Qu. EE11)

3 The "best" society; the area where the best society resides. [Var of *four hundred*] **chiefly Nth, N Midl**

1965–70 *DARE* (Qu. II23, *Joking names for the people who are, or think they are, the best society of the community: The ______*) 16 Infs, **chiefly Nth, N Midl,** Five hundred(s); **LA**3, **NJ**20, **NY**27, **ND**1, **PA**68, 220, Five hundred class (*or* club, crowd, group); **NY**68, They think they're one of the five hundred; **PA**242, Upper five hundred; (Qu. II24, . . *The part of town where the well-off people live*) Inf **NY**220, Five hundreds; **NY**227, Five-hundred row; **PA**130, In the five hundred; **FL**6, Where the five-hundred class lives.

4 in phr *like five hundred:* Very much, excessively. Cf **forty n B2**

1854 (1923) Holmes *Tempest & Sunshine* 12 **KY** [Black], We seen a bright light, and heard the niggers larfin like five hundred. **1968** *DARE* (Qu. X56b, . . *Sweating very heavily*) Inf **VA**24, Sweat like five hundred.

five hundred up See **five hundred 2**

five-leaved ivy n Also *five-leaf ivy, five leaves* [See quot 1901] **=Virginia creeper.**

1876 Hobbs *Bot. Hdbk.* 38, Five leaves, American Ivy, Ampelopsis quinquefolia. **1901** Lounsberry *S. Wild Flowers* 332, Five-leaved ivy. . . has five oblong-obovate leaflets, palmately arranged. **1940** Steyermark *Flora MO* 348, Virginia Creeper, Woodbine, Five-leaved Ivy *(Parthenocissus).* **1960** Vines *Trees SW* 711, *Parthenocissus vitacea. . .* Vernacular names are Five-leaf Ivy and Woodbine. *Ibid* 712,

Parthenocissus quinquefolia. . . Vernacular names for the vine are Woodbine, . . Five-leaf Ivy, and American Ivy. **1968** *DARE* (Qu. S26e) Inf **NC**53, Five-leaf ivy—not poisonous. **1973** Stephens *Woody Plants* 380, Five-leaved ivy. A vine, climbing by tendrils with sucker disks and by aerial roots to a height of 25m.

five-leaved jack n

A **jack-in-the-pulpit** (here: *Arisaema quinatum*).

1869 Fuller *Uncle John* 74, There is still another species of Arum found in the South, called *Five-leaved Jack.*

five leaves See **five-leaved ivy**

five-man n Also *five-man square*

A marble game played with five marbles.

1968 *DARE* (Qu. EE7, . . *Kinds of marble games*) Inf **IN**32, Five-man square. **1969** *DARE* Tape **KY**40, We used to play what they called five-man, in a little triangle shape. . . The one [=player] in the middle took five marbles to play it. . . There's two guys back here with two marbles, . . and you draw a line below that, and you call that the dead line; and if you hit below that line well you was dead, you was out of the game. And if you . . knocked a marble out of that game . . why, you won the game and you'd get to go back and shoot again.

‡five minutes of eleven, like adj phr [From the placement of a clock's hands at that time]

Very friendly, intimate.

1968 *DARE* (Qu. II3, *Expressions to say that people are very friendly toward each other: "They're ________."*) Inf **PA**151, Like five minutes of eleven—very close.

five old cat n

A variation, involving more players, of the bat-and-ball game **one old cat.**

1883 Eggleston *Hoosier Schoolboy* 10 **IN,** "Four old cat," "two old cat," and "five old cat" are, as everybody knows, played in the same way [as "three old cat"], the number of bases or holes increasing with the addition of each pair of players.

five-pot poison See **poison**

fiver See **fivefer**

five-sisters n [Perh because the leaves are often in whorls of five (despite the species name *quadrifolia*)]

A **loosestrife** (here: *Lysimachia quadrifolia*).

1900 Lyons *Plant Names* 234, *L. quadrifolia*. . . Five-sisters. **1940** Clute *Amer. Plant Names* 112, *Whorled Loosestrife*. . . Five sisters. **1959** Carleton *Index Herb. Plants* 46, *Five sisters:* Lysimachia quadrifolia.

five-spot n

1 A **baby blue-eyes** (here: *Nemophila maculata*). [See quot 1949]

1949 Moldenke *Amer. Wild Flowers* 253, The *fivespot, Nemophila maculata,* has white corollas beautifully marked with rows of purple dots radiating from the center to the large purple blotch at the end of each of the five lobes. **1959** Munz–Keck *CA Flora* 520, *Nemophila maculata* . . Fivespot. **1959** Carleton *Index Herb. Plants* 46, Five Spot: *Nemophila maculata.*

2 See **desert fivespot.**

fives-um See **-um**

five-ten n

A children's hiding game; hence exclam *five-ten on (someone)* a call used in such a game; see quots.

1955 Ritchie *Singing Family* 214 **seKY,** All right, we going to play five-ten. I'll count first and everybody hide, but not more'n a hundred feet away. **1968** *DARE* (Qu. EE15, *When he has caught the first of those . . hiding what does . . 'it' call out?*) Inf **DE**2, Five-ten on Johnnie!

five-ten-cent store See **five-and-ten 1**

five-ten on (someone) See **five-ten**

five tinkers n

A singing game in which players circle around a "father" and a "daughter" who, by responding to the lyrics of the song being sung, choose a male partner for the "daughter" who is then replaced by another girl from the circle.

1940 *Handy Play Party Book* 40, *Five Tinkers*—This game, once very popular in the hills of Tennessee, was one of a group of games called "Singing-in" games, used to pair off the company into congenial couples. It was in some places called "Hog Drovers".

five-toed shoe n *joc*

1969 *DARE* (Qu. W42b, . . *Men's square-toed shoes*) Inf **GA**77, Five-toed shoes.

five-toed woodpecker n

Perh a nuthatch.

1966 *DARE* (Qu. Q17) Inf **NC**44, Five-toed woodpecker.

five-to-ten store See **five-and-ten**

five-up n **chiefly S Midl** See Map *esp freq among Black speakers*

1965–70 *DARE* (Qu. DD35, . . *Favorite card games*) 15 Infs, **chiefly S Midl,** Five-up. [9 Infs Black]

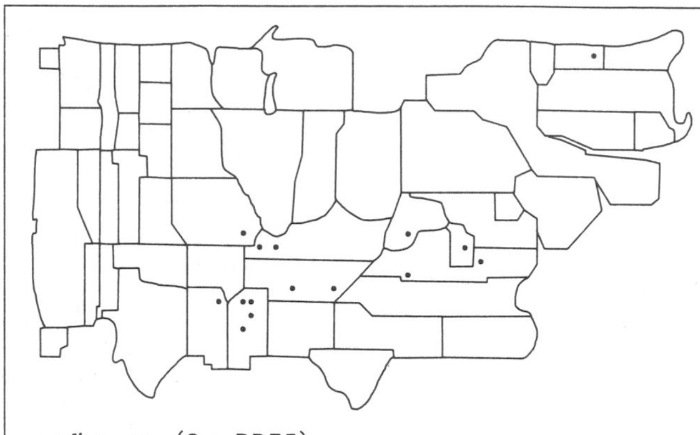

•five-up (Qu. DD35)

fix v

A Form.

Past: usu *fixed;* also *fix.* Cf Pronc Intro 3.I.22

1899 Chesnutt *Conjure Woman* 15 **csNC** [Black], Bimeby ole Mars Dugal' fix' up a plan ter stop it. *Ibid* 21, She fix' it so he kin eat all de scuppernon' he want. **1936** *AmSp* 11.350 **eTX,** Among unlettered people, 'He will fix you,' and 'He fixed you' are both expressed by 'He fix you.'

B Senses.

1 To arrange, put in order, prepare, as:

a also with *up:* To spruce up; to style (hair); to dress; hence ppl adj *fixed up.*

1820 *Thomas' MA Spy or Worcester Gaz.* (MA) 16 Feb [3/3], She with an angry and haughty tone replied, that *she had rather go to Hell than to Church* without having her hair fixed to please her. **1842** Dickens *Amer. Notes* 55/2, You call upon a gentleman in a country town, and his help informs you that he is "fixing himself" just now . . by which you are to understand that he is dressing. **1855** Cooke *Ellie* 15 **VA,** I wish you'd make haste, and not take so long to fix yo'-self in the mornin'. **1911** Harrison *Queed* 16 **Atlantic,** Sharlee . . going to the bureau began fixing her hair in the back before the long mirror. **1946** *PADS* 5.22 **VA,** *Fix up*. . . Get dressed up; fairly common. **1950** *WELS (When a woman puts on her good clothes and tries to look her best)* 1 Inf, **WI,** All fixed up in Sunday-go-to-meeting togs. **1965–70** *DARE* (Qu. W38, *When a man dresses himself up . . he's ________*) 9 Infs, **scattered,** (All) fixed up; (Qu. W37, *When a woman puts on her good clothes . . she's ________*) Infs **CA**178, **GA**6, **IN**28, **MD**35, **NY**119, **NC**30, 76, **SC**44, (All) fixed up; **PA**42, Fixed up to kill; (Qu. W36, . . *A woman who uses a lot of cosmetics*) Inf **IA**3, Fixed up like a fruit salad. **1978** *DARE* File **cSC,** In North Carolina uneducated speakers have their hair "fixed." "Refined" speakers have their hair "done."

b now usu with *up:* To straighten up (a room); to make (a bed); to tidy up.

1832 in 1836 Traill *Backwoods Canada* 82, One of their [=Americans'] most remarkable terms is to *"Fix."* Whatever work requires to be done it must be *fixed.* "Fix the room" is, set it in order. "Fix the table"—"Fix the fire," says the mistress to her servants, and the things are fixed accordingly. **1954** *Harder Coll.* **cwTN,** To fix the bed—to make up the bed. **1965–70** *DARE* (Qu. E21, . . *"I'm just going to ________ this* *room.'*) Infs **DE**3, **ME**20, **PA**1, **TN**1, 11, 52, Fix up; **NY**8, **NC**50, **PA**245, Fix it up; **LA**20, Fix up a little in; (Qu. KK49, . . *"I'm not going to give the place a real cleaning, I'll just* ______ *.'*) Inf **CT**27, Fix it up. [9 of 11 Infs old]

c To set (a dining table); hence ppl adj *fixed out.* **esp Sth, S Midl** See Map

1832 [see **b** above]. **1842** Dickens *Amer. Notes* 55/2, You inquire . . whether breakfast will be ready soon, and he tells you . . they were "fixing the tables:" in other words, laying the cloth. **1889** (1971) Farmer *Americanisms* 243, A table is *fixed out* when arranged for a meal. **1954** *Harder Coll.* **cwTN,** To fix the table—prepare the table for setting. **1965–70** *DARE* (Qu. G9, . . *To get the table ready for a meal*) 17 Infs, **esp Sth, S Midl,** Fix the table. [15 of 17 Infs old] **1984** Wilder *You All Spoken Here* 28 **Sth,** *Fix:* Arrange; set, as in "Fix the dinner table."

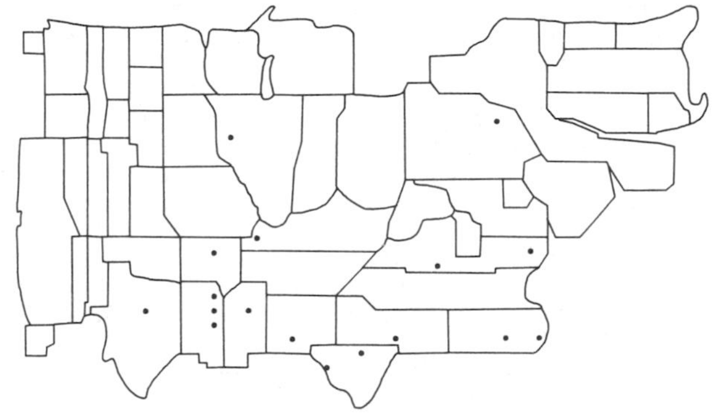

•fix v B1c (Qu. G9)

d To light (a fire or lamp); to tend (a fire).

1832 [see **b** above]. **1856** *Knickerbocker* Mar 270 **Boston MA,** Go ahead; I can hear you and fix the fire too. **1967–70** *DARE* (Qu. Y41a, *Expressions . . to tell someone to light a lamp*) Infs **PA**199, **TX**12, Fix; (Qu. Y43a, . . *To light a fire*) Inf **KY**85, Build, start, set, fix. **1968** *DARE* Tape **IN**3, They pitched them a tent and they was fixin' fire. **1984** Wilder *You All Spoken Here* 29 **Sth,** *Mend the fire, fix the fire:* Tend the fire.

e infreq with *up:* To prepare (a meal, food). **widespread, but more freq Sth, S Midl, N Cent** See Map Cf **get v C2, make v**

1839 Marryat *Diary* 1.197, Shall I *fix* your coat or your breakfast first? **1891** Harte *First Family* 2.34 **CA,** Mother'll fix you suthin' hot. **1940** Weygandt *Down Jersey* 297 **sNJ,** [It is a splashy business, that of the scoring and pressing out of corn. [*DARE* Ed: That is, pressing sweet corn out of the kernels.]] *Ibid,* In my boyhood I used to "fix the corn" not only for myself but, sometimes, for father and mother, and for certain guests. **1944** Howard *Walkin' Preacher* 109 **Ozarks,** You'll be gone every day to school and there'll be no one to fix his dinner, watch the fires and see that he sleeps regularly. **1954** *Harder Coll.* **cwTN,** To fix dinner—to prepare lunch. **1965–70** *DARE* (Qu. H7, . . *"I have to go and* ______ *supper."*) 273 Infs, **widespread, but more freq Sth, S Midl, N Cent,** Fix; **SC**9, Fix up [Of all Infs responding to the question, 70% were old; of those giving these responses, 57% were old.]; (Qu. H68, . .

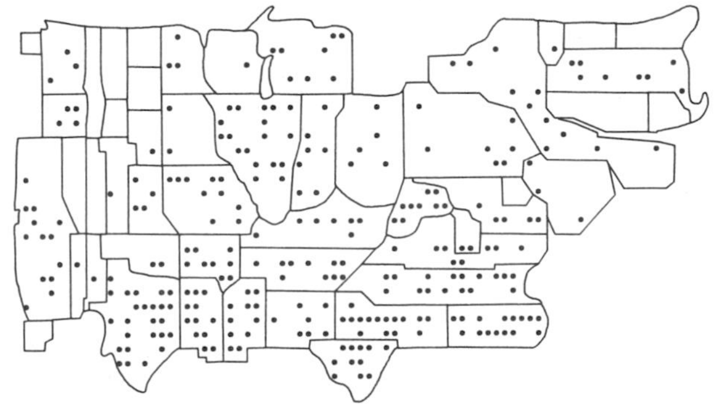

•fix v B1e + varr (Qq. H7, H68)

"She got out Sunday's roast and ______ *.'*) Infs **IL**61, **MI**106, Fixed it up. **1967** *Wilson Coll.* **csKY,** Fix = prepare a meal. **1967** *DARE* Tape **TX**32, I like to fix a couple of vegetables, some meat, and something for dessert. **1971** Bright *Word Geog. CA & NV* 180, *Fix [supper]* 22% [of 300 infs]. **1973** Cheever *Apples* 87, I . . serve my wife breakfast in bed. I try to fix her a nice breakfast, because this sometimes improves her disposition. **1978** *DARE* File **cSC,** One always "fixes" dinner, never "makes" dinner.

f infreq with *up:* To prepare (a beverage, esp coffee). Cf **cook v 1**

c1830 in 1949 Trollope *Domestic Manners* 414, You must fix me a drink. **1884** *Harper's New Mth. Mag.* 69.304/1 **NEng,** I'll hev to fix me up some thoroughwort tea. **1941** *LANE* Map 310 1 inf, **cwVT,** Fix the coffee. **1954** *Harder Coll.* **cwTN,** *Fix*—to prepare coffee. "Lots of times, I say 'fix,' but I [also] say 'put on' and 'make.'" **1960** Bailey *Resp. to PADS 20* **KS,** Fix some coffee. **c1960** *Wilson Coll.* **csKY,** *Fix coffee*—fairly common. **1965–70** *DARE* (Qu. H73, . . *"I think I'll go and* ______ *some coffee."*) 36 Infs, **scattered,** Fix; **AR**47, Fix some instant coffee. [22 of 37 Infs young or mid-aged] **1973** Allen *LAUM* 1.296 (as of c1950), *(I'm going to make some coffee) Fix,* listed only once in *LANE,* is . . slightly more popular in the U[pper] M[idwest], where it is scattered in the northeast quadrant and in Nebraska but not in Iowa and most of South Dakota.

2a also with *up:* To get ready.

1716 (1865) Church *King Philip's War* 42 **MA,** Capt. Church . . fixes for another Expedition. **1774** in 1906 Litchfield *Diary* 313 **MA,** About one oclock in the morning I got up to fix to go to Boston. **1828** (1935) Bolling *Diary* 237 **VA,** We met Albert on his way home from Richmond, where he has spent a fortnight to fix for the trip. **1837** Sherwood *Gaz. GA* 70, *Provincialisms. . . Fix* for fit or prepare. To *fix* is to fasten: to *fit* is to make ready, &c. **1857** in 1956 Eliason *Tarheel Talk* 271 **cnNC,** Today we have been busy fixing for company tomorrow. **1875** in 1923 Twain *Speeches* 55, You fix up for the drought. **1891** Cooke *Huckleberries* 1 **CT,** I don't want none o' Jake Potter's folks round, 'nd you may as well lay your account with it, 'nd fix accordin'. **1939** *Hall Coll.* **eTN,** Fixed to stay a week to bear-hunt. **1942** (1971) Campbell *Cloud-Walking* 22 **seKY,** Go long home to your pap now and fix for going to the school house. **1966–68** *DARE* (Qu. B5, *When the weather looks as if it will become bad, you say it's* ______) Inf **GA**4, Fixing up for a rain; **MD**31, Fixing up for bad weather; (Qu. B6) Inf **MO**38, Fixing for weather; (Qu. B14) Inf **LA**27, Fixing up for a storm. **1968** Adams *Western Words* 114, *Fixin' for high ridin'*—A cowboy's expression for preparing to leave in a hurry. **1978** *DARE* File **cSC,** If a carload of relatives arrives unexpectedly for Sunday dinner, the hostess may call her friends for help. "Girl, can you come and help? All these people I've got to fix for."

b with *for;* Spec: to lie in wait for.

1987 Jones-Jackson *When Roots Die* 139 **sSC coast** [Gullah], A number of idioms are still very much apparent in daily communication. . . De fix for you: lie in wait for you.

3 By ext from **2a;** in progressive, foll by infin: To be about (to); to plan or intend (to). **chiefly S Atl, Gulf States** See Map

1933 Rawlings *South Moon* 37 **nFL,** I'm fixin' to make me a few jugs, come fall, and my cane juice plentiful. **1944** *PADS* 2.9 **AL, NC, Upper SC, TN, VA,** *Fixing to. . .* In progressive tense system, followed by infinitive. . . About to, on the point of. "I was just fixin' to call on you." . . "Look at that child! He's fixin' to fall!" **1952** Brown *NC Folkl.* 1.541, *Fix. . .* To be on the point of doing something. "I was just fixing to go to see you."—General. All classes. **1960** Criswell *Resp. to PADS 20* **Ozarks,** *Fix*—to be on the point of. "I'm fixin' to go to town." Always common. Preparation not necessarily involved in this meaning. **1965–70** *DARE* (Qu. B5, *When the weather looks as if it will become bad, you say it's* ______) 16 Infs, **chiefly Sth,** Fixing to rain [and var phrr: see *DS*]; (Qu. B6) Infs **GA**7, **MI**108, **VA**38, Fixing to (become a *or* have a) storm; **GA**3, **MO**9, Fixing to rain; (Qu. B7) Infs **GA**13, **MS**24, 63, **TX**100, Fixing to break off (*or* clear up, fair off, fair up, have a pretty day); (Qu. B8) Inf **AR**1, A-fixing to do something; **CA**87, Fixing to rain; (Qu. B12) Infs **FL**24, **GA**36, Fixing to blow (*or* change); (Qu. B13) Inf **LA**7, Fixing to break off; (Qu. B15) Inf **TX**33, Fixing to come to a stop; (Qu. K10, . . *A cow that is going to have a calf*) Infs **GA**3, 7, **MS**1, **OK**43, **SC**57, **TX**33, Fixing to freshen; **GA**7, **MS**87, Fixing to come in; **GA**3, Fixing to foald; **LA**18, Fixin' to bring a calf; **SC**1, Fixin' to drop a calf; (Qu. W24c) Inf **AL**17, Horse fixin' to get out; (Qu. AA5, . . *A woman . . going after one certain man . . "She's* ______ *him."*) Inf **LA**2, Fixing to get her hooks in; (Qu. AA15b) Infs **GA**6, 23, Fixing to tie the knot (*or* get hitched); (Qu. AA15c) Inf **GA**23, Is fixing to get married; (Qu. AA28, . . *[A woman] is going to have a baby*) Inf **GA**23, Fixing to drop one; (Qu. KK7, *When wood . . is starting to decay*) Inf **GA28,** Fixing to rot; (Qu. KK20a, *Something that looks as if it might collapse any minute*) Infs **GA3, MS6,** Fixing to tumble (down); **MS88,** Fixing to fall down; (Qu. KK20b) Inf **GA7,** Fixing to go to the junk pile. **1966–69** *DARE* Tape **GA23,** It looks like it's fixing to fall off; **SC9,** When you get that done mash up, now you're fixin' to plant your rice; **SC10,** I ain't feel so good an' I would like to—I'm fixin' to go anyway to the doctor; **SC26,** You get the ol' skimmin' from a syrup mill . . fixin' to cook the syrup in the pot; **TX40,** She'd fix her some dough or some flour like she was fixin' to make biscuits; **TX49,** Look out, it's fixing to happen now; **TX68,** I was fixing to reach out and grab him.

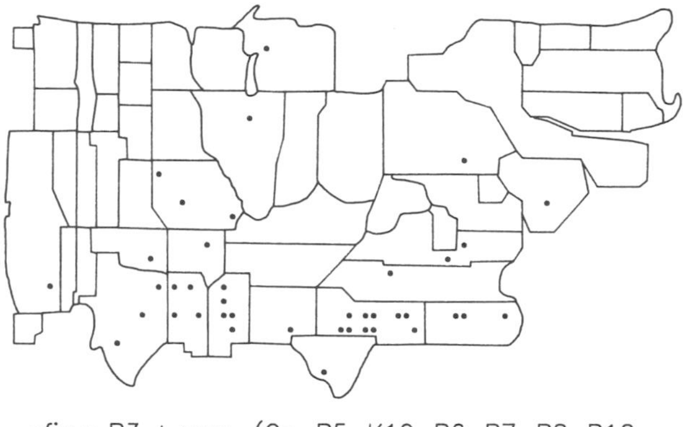

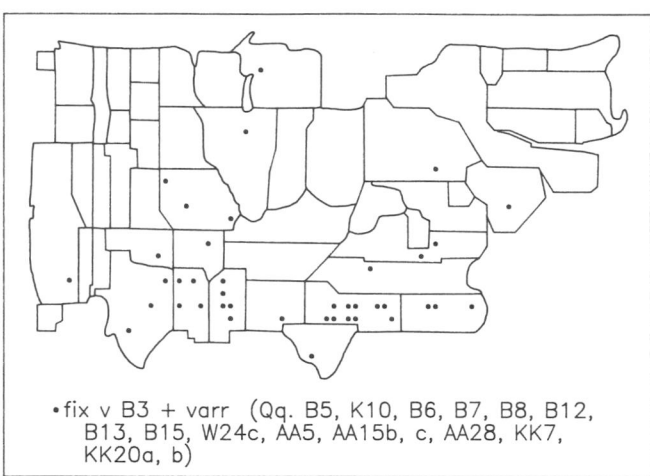

•fix v B3 + varr (Qq. B5, K10, B6, B7, B8, B12, B13, B15, W24c, AA5, AA15b, c, AA28, KK7, KK20a, b)

4 To thwart, frustrate (someone); to get even with, take vengeance on; to punish, kill:

a also with *off* or *out:* See quots.

1800 *Aurora* (Philadelphia PA) 8 April (1912 Thornton *Amer. Gloss.*), Have *fix'd* Randolph,—wish the other house would *fix* Mason. **1845** Thompson *Pineville* 57 **cGA,** You's fixed me off and made a widder of my wife and children. **1857** *Knickerbocker* Jan 68, I swore a big oath like to myself, that I'd fix that cussed varmint [=a coon] in less nor a week. **1891** Cooke *Huckleberries* 18 **CT,** Darned fool! what'd he want to be a-kitin' round in a narrer road this time o' night? Fixed me out, I guess. **1949** Webber *Backwoods Teacher* 227 **Ozarks,** "I'll fix her!" Sister Viny cried. . . "Whur does the ol' bitch think her man is at? I'll cuckle her 'fore she's a day older if I have to backslide to do it." **1951** *PADS* 15.66 **NH,** *Fix.* . . Punish. "I'll fix you." **1954** *Harder Coll.* **cwTN,** *Fix*—to punish. "I'll fix you." **1960** Criswell *Resp. to PADS 20* **Ozarks,** "Just let me get my hands on him—if I don't fix him." . . "I fixed myself when I turned down his offer; I'll never get another chance." **1968** *DARE* (Qu. GG22b, *When you have come to the end of your patience, you might say, "Well, that certainly ______."*) Inf **MD47,** Fixed me; **MO18,** Fixes me. **1976** Lynn-Vecsey *Loretta Lynn* 18 **eKY,** Mommy smoked and she drank coffee, but she wouldn't let none of us kids do it. And we wouldn't complain about it, or she'd fix us good.

b in phrr *fix one's clock* (or *flint, wagon*) and varr: See quots.

1836 (1838) Haliburton *Clockmaker* (1st ser) 59, If it had been me he had used that way, I'd a fixed his flint for him, so that he'd think twice afore he'd fire such another shot as that are again. **1846** (1973) Porter *Quarter Race* 190 **NY,** The time had come for him to walk into one on 'em [=polar bears] at laast, and fix his mutton for him right. **1908** *Collier's* 31 Oct 22/1, You know how an Indian is—the palefaces fixed his clock when they introduced him to firewater. **1942** McAtee *Dial. Grant Co. IN* 26 (as of 1890s), *Fix one's clock* . . effectively silence, finish, or even kill; "I'll fix his clock." **1942** Warnick *Garrett Co. MD* 7 **nwMD** (as of 1900–1918), *Fix one's clock* . . to prevent accomplishment by another. **1946** *PADS* 6.9 **eNC,** To knock out of the way; to settle "the hash of"; to threaten "to fix up the flint of a teaser." **c1960** *Wilson Coll.* **csKY,** *Fix one's clock* (or *stop one's clock*): . . Silence someone. Also . . *fix one's wagon.* **1975** Newell *If Nothin' Don't Happen* 122 **nwFL,** So I put a thirty-thirty in the burr of his ear and that fixed his clock. **1980** De Vries *Consenting Adults* 109 **IL,** If you don't keep the hell away from Colly I'll clean your clock. I'll fix your wagon, but good. **1981** *Burrick Coll.* **csPA,** "I'll fix his clock." Get even.

5 rarely with *up:* In the practice of **hoodoo n 1a:** to invest with magical power; to cast a spell on; hence n *fixer.* *among Black speakers* Cf **fixment n 3**

1923 Parsons *Folk-lore Sea Islands* 212 **csSC** [Gullah], As elsewhere [Footnote: North Carolina], "fix" is the usual term for practising black magic. You may "fix dem so dey couldn' stay home" or "so dey get crazy." **1928** Peterkin *Scarlet Sister Mary* 115 **SC,** Only Daddy Cudjoe, of all the old people left, knew any of the old secret ways. But he knew them well. He could fix July too. **1937** (1977) Hurston *Their Eyes* 127 **csFL** [Black], It's been singin' round here ever since de big fuss in de store dat Joe was 'fixed' and you wuz de one dat did it. **c1938** in 1970 Hyatt *Hoodoo* 1.66 **seNC** [Black], An' the man he *fixed* [Hyatt: *dressed*] a long hick'ry stick an' he tole this man, he said, "when this rabbit cross the road," he say, "you wan'a take this stick an' fling it af' tim [=after him]." *Ibid* 1.511 **NC** [Black], He married a girl here and this girl's mother seemed to be one of those fixers, you know, and she put those spells on this boy. *Ibid* 764, She thought she was fixing him—instead of fixing him fo' good, she was fixing him fo' bad. *Ibid* 2.1438 **FL** [Black], Said dey fix de place up. [Hyatt: Someone had put a spell on the house.] **1938** FWP *Guide MS* 27, If the trouble be insanity, boils, or constipation, the verdict is that a secret enemy has "fixed" him and nothing in the world but a powerful "toby" or "jack" (charm) can dispel this conjuration. **1946** Tallant *Voodoo* 190 **New Orleans LA,** Feltie Butler died a hoodoo death. . . Feltie had been *fixed.* *Ibid* 199, If the "fixer" is apprehended while placing some of the dreaded *gris-gris* on a neighbor's front porch and brought into court, the authorities cannot depend upon the victim to make any charge. He will practically always be too frightened. **1953** Goodwin *It's Good* 125 **sIL** [Black], Braxton, folks are saying somebody done fixed Big Chick. **1968–70** *DARE* (Qu. CC14, . . *One person supposedly casts a spell over another*) Inf **FL48,** Fix, conjure. They used to use these, but they're going out of style; **FL51,** "I'm going to *fix* you," but "Somebody *conjured* her."; **MS80,** Fixed; **MS88, MO29, PA172,** Fix; **SC68,** Fix—the main word here; **SC69,** Fix—the main word; also rooted, voodoo. [All Infs Black]

6 also with *out* or *up:* To make pregnant; hence ppl adj *fixed.* Cf **fix n 2**

1941 *LANE* Map 392 *(Pregnant)* 1 inf, **cNH,** Fixed out . . vulgar, used only by men. **1952** Brown *NC Folkl.* 1.541, *Fix.* . . To make pregnant.—Central and east [NC]. **1954** *Harder Coll.* **cwTN,** To fix her—to impregnate. **1968–69** *DARE* (Qu. AA28, . . *Joking . . expressions . . to say that another [woman] is going to have a baby*) Inf **NY108,** Fixed; **KY51, MO25,** Fixed up; **MA55,** Fixed out; **VA31,** She's been fixed; he's fixed her.

7 rarely with *over:* To castrate, spay; hence ppl adj *fixed,* vbl n *fixing.* **scattered, but chiefly Atlantic, Gt Lakes, CA** See Map

1939 *LANE* Map 210 *(Castrate),* [Occas, esp in **sNEng,** Fix; Fix over—rare]. **1950** *WELS (To make a female dog unable to breed, she must be ______)* 1 Inf, **WI,** Fixed; *(Words for castrating an animal)* 2 Infs, **WI,** Fixing. **1952** Brown *NC Folkl.* 1.541, *Fix.* . . To castrate or spay an animal.—General. Farmers mainly. **1962** Faulkner *Reivers* 26 **MS,** With a kind of incredulous yearning, like a fixed bull. **1965–70** *DARE* (Qu. J3a, *To make a female dog so that she can't breed, she must be ______*) 33 Infs, **esp NEast, Gt Lakes, Inland Sth, CA,** Fixed; (Qu. J3b, . . *Female cat*) 47 Infs, **esp NEast, Gt Lakes, Inland Sth, CA,** Fixed; **CA73, NJ28, OH15,** Fix; (Qu. K70, *Words . . for castrating an animal*) 35 Infs, **esp Atlantic,** Fix; (Qu. K58, *A castrated pig*) Infs **NJ29, PA235,** Fixed; **NJ21,** Fixed pig; (Qu. K25, *What is a 'steer'?*) Inf **NC3,** Bull that's been fixed. **1973** Allen *LAUM* 1.251 **IA, ND** (as of c1950), *Castrate.* . . fix [2 infs].

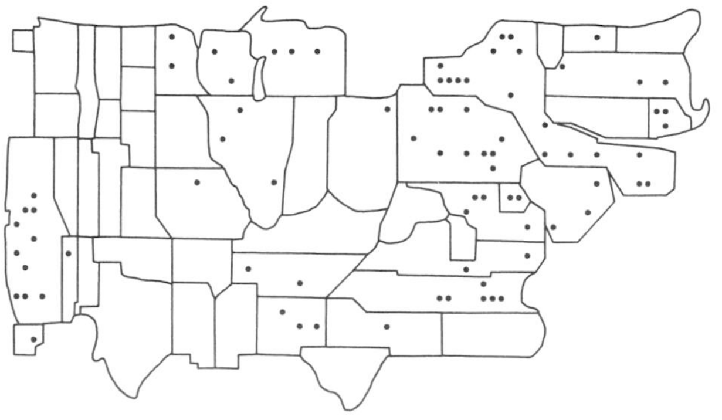

•fix v B7 + varr (Qq. J3a, b, K70, K25, K58)

8 in phr *any how you (can) fix it* and varr: No matter how you arrange it; any way you look at it.

1836 Crockett *Exploits* 125 *(DA),* If he had stolen the pennies . . in Louisiana, the people in Texas would have nothing to do with that affair, nohow they could fix it. **1843** (1916) Hall *New Purchase* 121 **IN,** I . . couldn't read a chapter in the Bible no how you could fix it, bless the Lord! **1859** (1968) Bartlett *Americanisms* 152, If I was an engineer, I'd clap on steam—I'd fire up, I tell you; you wouldn't get me to stop the engine, *no way you could fix it.* **1884** *Anglia* 7.266 [Black], Anyway you fix er thing = no matter how, &c. **1905** *DN* 3.2 **cCT,** *Any how you can fix it.* **1907** *DN* 3.208 **nwAR,** *Any how you can fix it.* . . In any way. **1908** *DN* 3.287 **eAL, wGA,** *Any way you fix it.* In any way whatever.

fix n

1a A situation, position, esp a bad situation, predicament—usu in phrr *in a* (*good* or *bad*) *fix.*

1809 (1814) Weems *F. Marion* 126 **SC,** They are in a mighty good fix. **1818** (1906) Fordham *Personal Narr.* 167 **KY,** The fire went out and it got quite dark. I was in a bad *fix,* as they say in the back woods. **1834** Caruthers *Kentuckian* 1.96 **VA,** You see he has the rogues in the city like a coon when he's treed; an old dog's better than a young one in such a fix. **1839** Marryat *Diary* 1.174, The Americans are never at a loss when they are in a *fix.* **1841** *Knickerbocker* 17.527 **TN,** I'm in a *fix,* and *no* mistake! **1960** Criswell *Resp. to PADS 20* **Ozarks,** Next time I come I'll be in a fix to stay longer. **1965–70** *DARE* (Qu. KK19, . . *"My sewing machine ——."*) Inf **GA**5, Is in a bad fix; **MS**69, Is in the worst fix; (Qu. U40, *Somebody who is temporarily out of money*) Inf **FL**25, In a bad fix; (Qu. BB42, *If a person is very sick*) Inf **SC**40, In a bad fix; (Qu. CC12b, . . *If a person has a lot of bad luck*) Inf **NC**77, A bad fix; (Qu. KK20a, . . *"That old shed is certainly ——."*) Inf **GA**23, In a bad fix.

b in phr *in a fix;* Spec: pregnant.

1927 *Ruppenthal Coll.* **KS,** In a fix—pregnant. **1927** *AmSp* 2.354 **WV,** That woman, is in a fix six months. **1954** *Harder Coll.* **cwTN,** *In a fix* . . pregnant. **1967–69** *DARE* (Qu. AA28, . . *Joking . . expressions . . that another [woman] is going to have a baby*) Infs **IL**15, **TX**42, **VA**18, 31, In a fix; (Qu. AA20, *A marriage that takes place because a baby is on the way*) Inf **IL**37, She's in a fix. **1975** Gainer *Witches* 9 **sAppalachians,** Miz Barb's in a fix agin.

2 Condition of body or mind, state of repair, usu good condition or repair—usu in phrr *in (good) fix* in good condition; fig wealthy; *out of fix* in bad condition, in poor repair; out of sorts, upset. Note: This sense cannot always be distinguished from **1a** above.

1839 *Spirit of Times* 27 Apr 90/3 **NC,** The filly is a keener, but looked out of fix. **1874** Woodruff *Trotting Horse* 113, In getting a whole stable of horses into fix to trot races, there will seldom be two whose treatment during their preparation ought to be the same. **1892** *DN* 1.230 **KY, MI,** "Out of fix" = out of health, out of humor, out of almost any normal condition of body or mind. **1898** Canfield *Maid of Frontier* 36, His horses are in good fix. **1902** *DN* 2.237 **sIL,** *In fix.* . . In running order, as a machine. *In good fix.* . . 1. In good condition, as livestock. 2. Well to do; in easy circumstances. **1906** *DN* 3.118 **sIN,** *Fix.* . . Condition. In fix or in good fix, "in good condition." So, out of fix, "in bad condition." *Ibid* 120, "The cattle are in good fix." "That man's in good fix (*i.e.* wealthy)." *Ibid* 149 **nwAR,** *Out of fix.* . . Tainted. "I never sell any meat that's out of fix." **1907** *DN* 3.223 **nwAR,** *In fix.* . . In running order. *In good fix.* . . In good condition, as live stock. **1965–70** *DARE* (Qu. KK19, . . *"My sewing machine ——."*) 35 Infs, **chiefly Sth, Midl,** (Is) out of fix; (Qu. GG7, . . *"Though we were only ten minutes late, she was all ——."*) Infs **AZ**6, **MD**17, Out of fix; (Qu. KK20b, . . *"Our old washing machine is ——."*) Infs **GA**72, **IA**36, **KS**19, **VA**66, 103, (Gone) out of fix; (Qu. KK70, . . *"That house is all ——."*) Inf **GA**5, Out of fix; (Qu. MM13, *The table was nice and straight until he came along and knocked it ——*) Inf **GA**5, Out of fix. **1968** Kellner *Aunt Serena* 113 **sIN** (as of c1910), "We don't need any of your put-in!" I began angrily, but Virginia soothed me. "Now don't get out of fix!" she said.

3 An evil spell. Cf **fix** v **B5** *among Black speakers*

c1938 in 1970 Hyatt *Hoodoo* 1.316 **NC,** He wanted to *hurt* her hisself so she would love 'im. So he took her [cut] fingernails an' her toenails an' put 'em in . . that tube an' . . put 'em in his trunk. . . [Later, a root doctor] told her *this was bad fix.* *Ibid* 1.761 **swAL,** And so the ole lady told him that . . she could cure him—yo' know, she could git him outa dis kinda *fix.* **1962** *Jrl. Amer. Folkl.* 75.313 **cNC,** Negroes who become insane, die under mysterious conditions, have strange afflictions . . are also thought to be under the influence of some form of evil magic. Local synonyms for the spell are "curse," "trick," "fix," "conjure," "root," and "hoodoo."

fixed See **fix** v **B6, 7**

fixed for See **fix** v **B2b**

fixed out See **fix** v **B1c**

fixed up See **fix** v **B1a**

fixen n Also sp *fixin* [*OED "Fixen . . obs. forms of Vixen"; EDD "Fixen . . Obs."*] *relic*

A vixen; a rascal, mischievous person.

1924 (1946) Greer–Petrie *Angeline Gits an Eyeful* 17 **csKY,** That child is . . the *antickest little fixin'.* **1963** Edwards *Gravel* 19 **eTN** (as of 1920s), Keep outen my pockets, you little fixen! **1969** *WV Hist.* 30.2.464, That trifling old *fixin* ain't worth a *haet!*

fixen vbl n See **fixing**

fixer See **fix** v **B5**

fixin See **fixen** n

fix, in See **fix** n **2**

fix, in a See **fix** n **1**

fixing n Pronc-spp *fixin', fixen*

1 A piece of equipment, implement, accessory.

1820 in 1904 Thwaites *Early W. Travels* 10.126 **TN,** "There wife," said he, "did you ever see such fixings?" He felt the paper, looked in a mirror . . , and gazed with amazement. **1828** Hall *Letters West* 304, These little fixens [=knife, flint, and steel] . . make a man feel right *peart,* when he is three or four hundred miles *from any body* or *any place.* **1844** (1954) Gregg *Commerce* 289 **NM,** Boxes . . filled with provisions, on the top of which is lashed a huge machine containing a mattress and all the other 'fixings' for bed furniture. **1848** Burton *Waggeries* 18 **Cape Cod MA,** They're playin' old hub with my garding grounds and oyster beds by scratchin' and rakin' 'em all over with them ar' darned anchors and grapnel fixins. **1859** Taliaferro *Fisher's R.* 129 **nwNC** (as of 1820s), I kep' in my pocket allers a tin water-tight fixin', which I toated my smokin' apperratus in. **1916** Kephart *Camping & Woodcraft* 1.110, An old campaigner is known by the simplicity and fitness of his equipment. He carries few "fixings," but every article has been well tested and it is the best that his purse can afford. **1919** *DN* 5.39 **eTN,** *Shootin' fixin's.* . . Guns, pistols, etc. **1924** Raine *Land of Saddle-Bags* facing 165 **Appalachians,** When she's "clean out o' bakin' powders, and has broke her needle, and wants a new dress," the "woman" takes her baby and a basket of eggs and rides to the little store five miles away to barter for groceries and "fixin's." **1926** *DN* 5.403 **Ozarks,** *Shootin'-fixin's.* . . Firearms. Heard only occasionally. **1928** *Ruppenthal Coll.* **KS,** *Fixin(g)s* . . materials to make cigarets as paper and tobacco. **1932** Randolph *Ozark Mt. Folks* 128, Even in the matter of china or tinware, or other household "fixin's", it is the man of the house who does the buying. **1940–41** Cassidy *WI Atlas* **seWI,** The grindstone had a fixing so you could turn it with your foot.

2 pl: Food.

1828 *Western Souvenir* 147, I feel powerful weak; but I don't like the fixens here, no how. **1860** in 1960 *Seattle Daily Times* (WA) 1 Jan mag sec 7 **cwWA,** Swan dined with Old Skipping, evidently a Clallam, "on mussel, skates, salmon and other Indian fixings." **1967** *DARE* (Qu. H6, . . *Food in general: "He certainly enjoys his ——."*) Inf **IL**9, Fixin's.

3 pl: Trimmings, extras, frills—used esp of foods. Cf **doing** n **1**

1840 Hoffman *Greyslaer* 2.58 **NY,** Add the salt and pepper fixings, and the king himself hasn't a slicker supper. **1858** *Mag. Travel* 179 **IA,** Mebby you think, boys, that this ere old gun wont shoot, cause she haint got any shiny fixens and fancy flumididdles on her. **1887** (1967) Harris *Free Joe* 217 **ceGA** [Black], Yassum, my young marster wuz des gone by sixteen year, kaze 'twa'n't so mighty long 'fo' dat, dat we-all sont 'im a great big box er fixin's en doin's fer ter git dar on he's birfday. **1905** *DN* 3.9 **cCT,** *Fixings.* . . Trimmings. **1907** *DN* 3.212 **nwAR, cCT,** *Fixings.* . . Trimmings. **1908** *DN* 3.311 **eAL, wGA,** *Fixin(g)s.* . . Prepared dishes, especially fancy dishes, desserts, etc. **1910** *DN* 3.441 **cwNY,** *Fixings.* . . Embellishments; relishes and sauces (of a dinner). **1948** *Democrat* 2 Dec. 1/2 *(DA)* **AL,** Wild turkey with all the fixings was served for dinner.

fixing vbl n See **fix** v **B7**

fix, in good See **fix** n **2**

fix it, any how you (can) See **fix** v **B8**

fixment n Cf **-ment**

1 See quot. [*EDD fixment* sb. 1 "The furniture of a house."]

1984 Wilder *You All Spoken Here* 32 **Sth,** *Fixments:* Furnishings.

2 A preparatory task.

1928 Chapman *Happy Mt.* 305 **seTN,** The girls went on with their spasm of dinner fixments.

3 in phr *put the fixment(s) on:* To render ineffective; to take revenge on. [Cf *EDD fixment* sb. 2 "A dilemma."] Cf **fix** v **B5**

1898 Lloyd *Country Life* 18 **AL,** A strong steady pull on the apron strings of the establishment will put the fixments on him and bring him to his knittin, and make him meek and gentle as any little kitten. **1943** Writers' Program NC *Bundle of Troubles* 24, I heerd the woods critters plottin' to put the fixment on Mr. Bullfrog, and I was there when his downfall come.

fix off See **fix** v **B4a**

fix one's clock (or flint, wagon) See **fix** v **B4b**

fix out See **fix** v **B4a, 6**

fix, out of See **fix** n **2**

fix over See **fix** v **B7**

fix up See **fix** v **B1a, b, e, f, 2, 5, 6**

fix-ups n pl [**fix** v **B1a**]

Fancy clothing or adornments.

1832 *Polit. Examiner.* (Shelbyville, Ky.) 8 Dec. 4/1 *(DA),* She says Mr. Bunker sit down, well I thought I would whilst she was getting her fixups off. **1836** *Pub. Ledger* (Philadelphia PA) 27 July, Down I came chewallop right on Deb's bonnet and her fixups, and overset the chair. **1873** Miller *Modocs* 126 **CA,** The lady who has the least amount of natural hair, has invariably the largest amount of artificial fix-ups on her head. **1968** *DARE* (Qu. W39, . . *A person's best clothes*) Inf **VA**16, Sunday fix-ups! [Laughter]

fixy adj [**fix** v **B1a**] **chiefly S Midl**

1 Particular about one's clothes or other personal items; overly concerned about personal appearance, vain.

1898 Lloyd *Country Life* 80 **AL,** Now as to clothes, old Mart ain't to say very fixy. **1933** *AmSp* 8.2.29 **eKY,** "She's not fixy like that young widder-woman over on Brushy." He leaned closer with scandalized expression . . "That widder-woman wears pink sun-bonnets." **1952** Brown *NC Folkl.* 1.541 **nwNC,** *Fixy. . .* Dressy, particular about clothes or arrangement of things in the house. **1953** Randolph–Wilson *Down in Holler* 244 **Ozarks,** *Fixy. . .* Well groomed, fastidious. A fixy girl is one who dresses with unusual care and "keeps her things nice." **c1960** *Wilson Coll.* **csKY,** *Fixy. . .* Dressy, particularly [sic] about one's face or complexion; sometimes about one's clothes. **1960** Criswell *Resp. to PADS 20* **Ozarks,** *Fixy. . .* Vain as to personal looks. **1968–69** *DARE* (QR, near Qu. AA7a) Inf **GA**57, Fixy—fussy about clothes; (Qu. HH35, *A woman who puts on lots of airs: "She's too ______ for me."*) Inf **IL**106, Fixy. [Inf old]

2 Transf: fancy.

1942 Thomas *Blue Ridge Country* 285 **sAppalachians,** All these here fixy contrapshuns [=electrical appliances]. **1951** West *Witch Diggers* 107 **sIN,** At first glance Christie saw that it was the kind of room his mother used to call "fixy." . . [There were] pictures, cushions, tidies, books. . . The soap . . had a paper frill about it, like a fancy cake. The chamber-pot lid was covered with a crocheted silencer.

3 Bossy, interfering.

1943 Writers' Program NC *Bundle of Troubles* 69, For years old Miss Nannie has tried to tell all the folks . . how to run their own critical affairs. Curious thing about it is that very few has ever stood up to the fixy old girl. [*Ibid* 71, Wasn't a doctor, lawyer, merchant, or grocer that she didn't try to boss.]

fiz n[1] See **fizz** n[1]

fiz n[2] See **phiz**

fizz n[1] Also sp *fiz*

1 A hurry; a state of excitement or agitation. [Engl and Scots dial; cf *EDD, SND*] **esp S Midl**

1897 *KS Univ. Qrly.* (ser B) 6.52 **KS,** *Fiz* . . hurry; as, Don't be in a fiz. **1938** *AmSp* 13.5 **seAR,** *Fizz. . .* A disturbed mental state. 'I was in such a fizz that I forgot my gloves.' An expression used chiefly by the older generation. **1960** Criswell *Resp. to PADS 20* **Ozarks,** *In a fizz*—To be very hurried and nervous. Very common. **c1960** *Wilson Coll.* **csKY,** *Fizz. . .* Hurry. "What's your fizz?" **1966–69** *DARE* (Qu. A21, *When someone is in too much of a hurry you might say, "Now just slow down! Don't ______."*) Infs **KY**20, 26, **SC**46, Be in such a fizz; (Qu. A22, . . *"She had only ten minutes to clean the room."*) Inf **OK**42, She's in a fizz.

2 See **fizzle** n **3.**

fizz n[2] See **phiz**

fizz v[1] [Scots dial] Cf **fizz** n[1] **1**

To bustle about.

1960 Carpenter *Tales Manchaca* 193 **cTX,** Meanwhile, Mamie was fizzing around the table, giving people this and asking if they didn't want that. Jim finally said, "Mamie, for God's sake, *light.*"

fizz v[2] Also with *out* [Abbr for *fizzle* v]

To fizzle out, fail.

1969 *DARE* (Qu. FF19, . . *A dull . . time: "The party was ______."*) Inf **VT**16, It fizzed out; (Qu. KK10, . . *Something failing . . " . . His plan ______."*) Infs **IN**7, **PA**167, Fizzed.

fizzer n

1 See **fizzle** n **3.**

2 See quot.

1914 *DN* 4.106 **KS,** *Fizzer* . . A soda fountain.

fizzle v [*OED "Obs."*; c1532–1739] **Sth**

To fart.

1908 *DN* 3.311 **eAL, wGA,** *Fizzle. . .* To break wind. **1967** *DARE* (Qu. X55b) Inf **LA**8, He done fizzled. **1969** *DARE* Tape **GA**74, Occasionally one o' those fat women or some old man would, in that hot weather an' everybody sweating, would fizzle. Then they'd go to fannin' . . with their hats, an' the women with the palmetto fans.

fizzle n

1 A fart. [**fizzle** v; *OED* 1598–1836-48] **Sth, S Midl** See Map

1908 *DN* 3.311 **eAL, wGA,** *Fizzle. . .* A breaking of wind. **1965–70** *DARE* (Qu. X55b, . . *Breaking wind from the bowels*) 10 Infs, **Sth, S Midl,** Fizzle. [All Infs comm type 4 or 5]

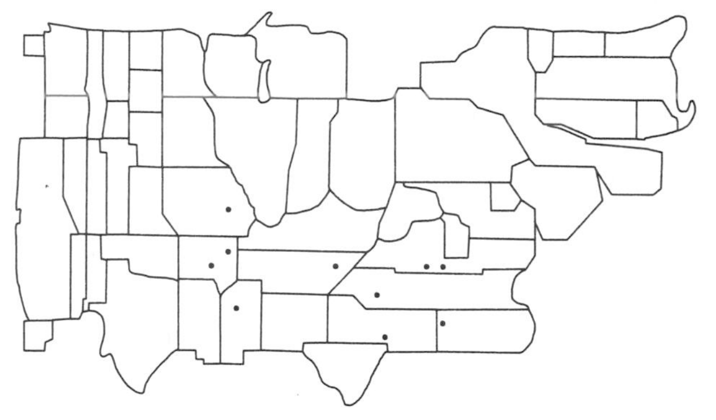

•fizzle n 1 (Qu. X55b)

2 =**fizz** n[1] **1.**

1968 *DARE* (Qu. GG11, . . *"The letter hasn't come and he's ______."*) Inf **OH**45, In a fizzle—that's not common any more.

3 also *fizz(er), fizzler, fizzle-out, fizzle-bomb, fizzy, frizzle:* A defective firecracker that burns with a fizzing sound.

1894 Frederic *Marsena* 154 **nNY,** I . . fired off these crackers one by one. Those which, by reason of having lost their tails, were only fit for "fizzes," I saved till after breakfast. **1914** *DN* 4.106 **KS,** *Fizzer. . .* A firecracker that explodes with a hiss. **1951** Johnson *Resp. to PADS 20* **DE** *(When a firecracker doesn't go off . . you call it a ______)* Fizzler. **1957** Battaglia *Resp. to PADS 20* **eMD,** A fizzer. **c1960** *Wilson Coll.* **csKY,** *Fizzler. . .* A firecracker that fails to pop. **1965–70** *DARE* (Qu. FF15, *When a firecracker doesn't go off, and you break it in the middle and light the powder, you call it a ______*) 79 Infs, **scattered, but chiefly Missip-Ohio Valleys, Upstate NY,** Fizzle; 78 Infs, **scattered, but more freq West,** Fizzler; 30 Infs, **scattered, but more freq Nth, N Midl,** Fizzer; 27 Infs, **scattered,** Fizz; 7 Infs, **scattered,** Fizzle-out; **CA**87, **IN**61, 75, Fizzy; Inf **MI**89A, Fizzle-bomb; **MD**20, Frizzle. **1968** *Daily Hampshire Gaz.* (Northampton MA) 3 July [np], These were fire crackers that hadn't exploded. We bent them in our fingers into U shaped "fizzers" so that the black powder showed. When lighted it made a loud "fizz."

fizzle-dizzle n [*fizzle* carbonated water + *dizzle* redup]
1967 *DARE* (Qu. BB22, . . *Home remedies . . for constipation*) Inf **CO**14, In eastern Colorado, fizzle-dizzle. [It's the] juice of a lemon, warm water, a pinch of baking soda.

fizzle-dust n Cf **frog hair 2a**
1897 *KS Univ. Qrly.* (ser B) 6.53, *Fizzle-dust:* something infinitesimal: 'fine as fizzle-dust.'

fizzle-out, fizzler See **fizzle** n **3**

fizzletown n
1969 *DARE* (Qu. C34, *Nicknames for nearby settlements*) Inf **IN**58, Fizzletown—for Maxinkuckee.

fizz out See **fizz** v²

fizzy n¹
1 also *fitzy:* The American **scoter** *(Melanitta nigra).*
1888 Trumbull *Names of Birds* 107 **MA,** The female (and young) [of the American scoter *(Oidemia americana)* are] . . known at Salem as Smutty Coot, at Chatham, same state, as Fizzy, and at Bellport and Moriches, L. I., as Broad-billed Coot. **1917** (1923) *Birds Amer.* 1.148, *Oidemia americana* . . Fizzy. **1923** U.S. Dept. Ag. *Misc. Circular* 13.28 **MA,** *American Scoter. . . Vernacular Names. . . In local use. . .* Fizzy (sometimes fitzy).
2 See **fuzztail.**

fizzy n² See **fizzle** n **3**

fizzy salts n pl
Epsom salts.
1966 *DARE* (Qu. BB22, . . *Home remedies . . for constipation*) Inf **SC**27, Fizzy salts—Epsom salts. Negro [term], from *physic.*

flabagate v [Var of *flabbergast* v, perh infl by *OED -ate* suffix³]
To confuse, flabbergast.
1834 *Life Andrew Jackson* 132, The Reverend diocesan . . ascrib'd all the victory . . tu him who, when rulers are good, makes 'em wise, when wicked, flabagates their understandins.

flabber See **flabber-mouth 1**

flabberdegaz n [Prob rel to *flabbergast* v; cf *OED flabberdegasky* v. *"Obs. nonce-wd."*]
Nonsense.
1918 *DN* 5.24 **NW,** *Flabberdegaz* . . . Talk; vain imaginings in speech. General, but rare.

‡flabbergast n
1966 *DARE* (Qu. HH21, *A very awkward, clumsy person*) Inf **SC**11, Flabbergast.

flabbergasted ppl adj Pronc-spp *flabergast(er)ed, flambergasted* Note: All of the following senses derive from std sense "astonished."
1 Exhausted. [Scots; see *DSL flabrigastit* "Worn out with exertion"]
1908 *DN* 3.311 **eAL, wGA,** *Flabergast(er)ed. . .* Exhausted, limp from exhaustion, run-down. "I am completely flabergasted to-day." **1941** *LANE* Map 482 1 inf, **sME,** [Flabbergasted] = *all in.* **1968** *DARE* (Qu. X47, . . *Other ways . . of saying, "I'm very tired."*) Inf **NY**107, Flabbergasted.
2 Annoyed, put out, disgusted.
c1960 *Wilson Coll.* **csKY,** *Flabbergasted. . .* Disgusted, chagrined, at one's wits end. **1966–68** *DARE* (Qu. GG7, . . *"Though we were only ten minutes late, she was all ______."*) Infs **ME**5, **NY**66, **PA**48, Flabbergasted.
3 Confounded, blasted, damned.
1856 Whitcher *Bedott Papers* 24 **NY,** Well, the hoss got stuck in one o' them are flambergasted snow-banks. *Ibid* 61, If there ain't Major Coon's wife, with that flambergasted old red hood o' hern on! **1967–69** *DARE* (Qu. NN25b, *Weakened substitutes for 'damn' or 'damned': "Well, I'll be ______!"*) Infs **NH**18, **NY**214, **OH**11, Flabbergasted.
4 Drunk.
1969 *DARE* (Qu. DD15) Inf **PA**188, Flabbergasted.

flabberjack n Cf **slippery jim**
1950 *WELS Suppl.* **csWI,** I heard the word flabberjack for ripe yellow cucumbers used for sweet pickles or left to spoil in the field.

flabber-mouth n
1 also *flabber:* The mouth.
1966 Giles *Great Adventure* 7 **West** (as of 1830s), [To a mule:] Git yer head up and quit snatchin' at them cactus! Ye'll git yer fool flabber-mouth full of them needles. **1967** *DARE* (Qu. X9) Inf **LA**8, Flabber ['flæbə].
2 One who talks too much.
1968 *DARE* (Qu. HH7a) Inf **CA**81, Flabber-mouth; **NV**7, Flabber-mouth; blabber-mouth.

flabble n
A fight.
1978 Doig *This House* 58 **MT** (as of c1945), Hear they had a little flabble down the street last night. Couple of fellows squared off and pushed each other around a little.

flabergast(er)ed See **flabbergasted**

flabuh v [Pronc-sp for *flavor;* see Pronc Intro 3.I.17]
1922 Gonzales *Black Border* 301 **sSC, GA coasts** [Gullah glossary], "Da' buckruh' hogmeat flabuh me mout' 'tell uh done fuhgit uh hab sin fuh kill'um"—That white man's pork flavored my mouth so that I forgot the sin I committed in killing the hog.

flack v [*OED* 1393–1876; *"Obs.* exc. *dial."*]
To flap, flutter; hence ppl adj *flacking.*
1806 (1905) Clark *Orig. Jrls. Lewis & Clark Exped.* 5.258 **cVA,** The beaver was flacking *(flapping their tails)* in the river about us all the last night. **1912** Austin *Woman of Genius* 10 **IL,** Flacking windmills on the straight horizons of the north, struck on my childish fancy as some sort of mechanical scarecrow to frighten away the homey charms of the wooded hills. *Ibid* 34, A loose board of the scaffolding . . flacking like a torn leaf. **1938** Matschat *Suwannee R.* 289 **nFL, sGA,** [Glossary:] Flack: to flutter or to strike a blow.

flac-soled adj [Etym unknown]
See quot 1976.
1929 (1954) Faulkner *Sound & Fury* 330 **MS,** She stood in the door for awhile with her myriad and sunken face lifted to the weather, and one gaunt hand flac-soled as the belly of a fish. [**1976** Brown *Gloss. Faulkner* 82, *Flac-soled. . .* The off-white color of the palm (sole) of Dilsey's [=a Black woman's] hand is apparently being compared to the similar color on the bellies of many fish.]

fladbrod See **flatbread**

flag n¹
Std: any of var monocotyledonous plants with more-or-less swordlike leaves such as those of the families Poaceae or Juncaceae (see **flagreed**), Iridaceae (see **blackberry lily, French iris, iris**), or of the genera *Acorus* and *Typha.*

flag n²
1 pl: =**capture the flag.**
1968 *DARE* Tape **NY**53, We played flags. Each team had a bundle of sticks. They were the flags. . . The object was to try to steal each others' supply without getting caught.
2 in var phrr referring to menstruation: See quots. *euphem* Cf **flag** v **3, flying baker**
1925 *AmSp* 1.24 **Chicago IL,** The function of menstruation is described by dozens of evasive terms, . . [including] "flying the red flag." **1942** Berrey–Van den Bark *Amer. Slang* 123.10, *Menstruate* . . fly the red flag. **1948** *Word* 4.185, Have the flag up. . . The flag's up. . . She has her flag out. **1954** *AmSp* 29.298 **Sth** [Vernacular of menstruation], *Flagging* (M[en], fraternity); *fly the bean flag* or *the red flag* (M[en], navy). **1965–70** *DARE* (Qu. AA27, . . *Expressions . . for a woman's menstruation*) 10 Infs, **scattered,** (Red) flag is out (*or* up); **OH**76, **OR**1, **PA**161, **SC**21, Flag day; **MD**15, **MN**16, **NY**10, **VA**41, Red flag; **DC**11, **MD**5, 9, **NY**87, Flag is flying; **IL**14, **PA**148, (Got her) flag out; **CO**47, **PA**170, She's got the flag on (*or* out); **MD**9, **WV**12, (She's) waving (*or* flying) the flag; **WA**33, Flying the red flag; **FL**2, Got the red flag up; **MI**10, Hang the white flag up; **IL**45, I'm waving my red flag; **NJ**56, Flag. **1971** *AmSp* 46.82 **Chicago IL,** Menstrual period . . *flag out, . . flagging, . . red flag, . . carrying a flag, . . flying Baker, . . flag day.*
3 A shirttail or underwear—used in var phrr to warn a person that it is showing.
1968 Adams *Western Words* 114, *Flag at half-mast*—Said of a cowboy whose shirttail is out—and he wouldn't be a cowboy if he didn't work with it out half the time. **1968–70** *DARE* (Qu. W24a, . . *Expressions . . to warn a woman slyly that her slip is showing*) Inf **CA**59, Your

flag is waving; **OH**90, Flag's out; (Qu. W24c, *Sayings to warn a man that his trouser-fly is open*) Infs **MA**9, **NJ**63A, Flag's at half mast.

4 A bill of paper currency. [Perh abbr for **Jewish flag**]

1965–70 *DARE* (Qu. U26, . . *A paper dollar*) Infs **MO**39, **SC**68, Flag; (Qu. U28a, . . *A five-dollar bill*) Inf **OK**13, Flag.

5 See quot.

c1970 Wiersma *Marbles Terms* **swMI,** *Flags*. . . A red, white, and blue marble.

6 See quot. Cf **handle** n **B3**

1932 *RR Mag.* Oct 367, *Flag*—An assumed name.

7 See **flag lot.**

flag v, hence vbl n *flagging*

1 To attract (game) by waving a piece of cloth; see quots.

1884 *Harper's New Mth. Mag.* 69.367/2 **MT,** I will give you a point or two on flagging antelope. . . you will have little trouble in decoying them within rifle range by displaying . . a little bright red flag. **1885** (1891) Roosevelt *Hunting* 194 **Plains States,** One method of hunting them [=antelope] is to . . "flag" them up to the hunters by waving a red handkerchief . . to and fro in the air.

2 To protect (a flock of sheep) by placing flags nearby to frighten away predators.

1952 FWP *Guide SD* 85, *To flag a bunch* [of sheep]: to place scarecrows about it to scare away coyotes. **1968** Adams *Western Words* 114, *Flagging*—In sheepherding, staking white flags around the flocks at night to frighten off coyotes. . . This practice is followed when there are too few herders to maintain a sufficient night guard.

3 in var phrr referring to menstruation: See quots. Cf **flag** n² **2**

1954 [see **flag** n² **2**]. **1965–70** *DARE* (Qu. AA27, . . *Expressions . . for a woman's menstruation*) 10 Infs, **scattered,** (She's) flagging. **1971** [see **flag** n² **2**].

flag a freight (train) v phr

To do the most rudimentary thing.

1968–70 *DARE* (Qu. JJ15a, *Sayings about a person who seems to you very stupid: "He hasn't sense enough to ______."*) Infs **KY**75, **VA**26, Flag a freight (train).

flag bird n

=**red-headed woodpecker.**

1917 (1923) *Birds Amer.* 2.155, *Melanerpes erythrocephalus*. . . Flag Bird. *General Description*. . . Red; . . black . . ; white.

flag day See **flag** n² **2**

flagfish n

A minnow-like fish *(Jordanella floridae)* native to Florida and Gulf Coast waters.

1955 Carr–Goin *Guide Reptiles* 77, Flagfish. . . A little, gray fish an inch or two long, with a dark blotch on the side. . . Dorsal fin with a single spine and 14–16 soft rays. **1960** Amer. Fisheries Soc. *List Fishes* 21, Flagfish . . *Jordanella floridae.*

flag flower n

A **flag** n¹.

1967–68 *DARE* (Qu. S24, *A wild flower that grows in swamps . . and looks like a small blue iris*) Infs **MD**30, **MN**2, Flag flower.

flag fly n

=**deerfly 1.**

1969 *DARE* (Qu. R12) Inf **NY**219, Flag fly—same as deer fly.

flag gill n

A type of gill net.

1967 *DARE* Tape **LA**5, There's flag gill which is nothing but loose webbing.

flaggings n [Etym uncert, but cf quot 1930]

See quots.

1914 Jackson *Criminal Slang* 33, *Flaggings*. . . Used by yeggs and hobos: Meat of any description, usually applied to cold victuals. Example: "If you are not a vegetarian, stay away from that man's burg, for flaggings is scarce." [**1930** Irwin *Amer. Tramp* 74, A tramp or beggar "flags" a citizen when he stops him to ask for charity.] **1964** Hargreaves–Foehl *Story of Logging* 17 **MI,** At noon, to save precious daylight, a meal called "flaggins" was brought out to the men, loaded on a sled or wagon. **1969** Sorden *Lumberjack Lingo* 43, **NEng & Gt Lakes,** *Flaggin's*—Dinner toted out to the woods on a sled by cookee. Standard fare consisted of kettles of roast beef and brown gravy and a couple of bushels of boiled potatoes and homemade bread.

flaggit adv [Var of *plegged* (at **plague**)]

1954 *Harder Coll.* **cwTN,** *Flaggit*. . . Very, quite. "Plumb messed up, flaggit dirty."

flaggity adj Also *fleggity* [**flaggit** + *y*]

1978 *DARE* File **cwTN,** Fleggity (or flaggity)—oh yes, my sister says that—means 'plaguy'. My mother used to say that.

flag-gone adj [Var of **plague-gone**] *euphem* Cf **flaggit**

Damned.

1954 *Harder Coll.* **cwTN,** 'Em people ain't got no flag-gone sense.

flag grass n

1 A **cattail 1.**

1848 Emory *Notes Reconnoissance* 92, [The island] was overgrown with willow, cane, Gila grass, flag grass, &c. **1857** Hammond *Wild N. Scenes* 145, [A moose] was feeding upon the lily pads and flag grass. **1910** *Auk* 27.388 **seLA,** Every summer these flats are covered by a dense growth of . . cat-tails or "flag-grass" *(Typha angustifolia).* **1913** *Torreya* 13.226, *Typha angustifolia* . . Flag grass, Mississippi Delta, La.

2 A **pondweed** (here: *Potamogeton americanus*).

1920 *Torreya* 20.18, *Potamogeton americanus*. . . Flag . . grass, Reelfoot Lake, Tenn.

flag is up (or out), the See **flag** n² **2**

flag lily n **chiefly Sth, S Midl**

An **iris.**

1884 Murfree *TN Mts.* 18, Among their roots flag-lilies . . and devil-in-the-bush mingled in a floral mosaic. **1892** *Jrl. Amer. Folkl.* 5.103, *Iris versicolor,* poison flag, flag-lily. **1951** *PADS* 15.28 **TX,** *Iris* spp. . . flag-lilies. **1966–67** *DARE* (Qu. S24, *A wild flower that grows in swamps . . and looks like a small blue iris*) Infs **LA**10, **MS**73, Flag lilies; **NC**14, 16, **NJ**4, Flag lily; (Qu. S11, . . *Other names for . . iris;* total Infs questioned, 75) Inf **NC**14, Flag lily.

flag line n

In tuna fishing: a long line trailing many hooks and having flags attached at intervals along the line.

1955 Day *HI People* 254, Smaller sampans . . may range for a thousand miles and stay out for days at a time. They operate flag lines as much as a mile long, to which are attached pendants dropping to depths of a hundred fathoms. Hooks are baited with frozen fish, or else the crew use aku to catch mackerel, which in turn become bait for the ahi (the prized yellowfin tuna or albacore).

flag lot n Also *flag* [From the shape]

See quots.

1986 *Daily Hampshire Gaz.* (Northampton MA) 3 Oct 3/5, Building on a flag may be approved by . . the City Council. *Ibid* 10 Oct 5/1, Flag lots . . [are] parcels of land with at least twice the normal lot size but inadequate frontage. **1986** *DARE* File **cwMA,** [Letter from the office of the Mayor of Northampton:] [A] "flag lot" . . is . . a parcel of land that is set back from the public roadway and shaped in such a manner that it is accessible only via an access strip. This strip of land does have frontage on the public roadway, but the frontage is smaller than the local requirement for construction of a single family dwelling. . . the configuration of a "flag lot" could take many forms, and . . several phrases have been coined by communities to describe . . [them]. They are: *pork chop lot, dog leg lot, axe handle lot, banner lot.*

flag one's kite v phr

See quots.

1944 Adams *Western Words* 60, *Flag his kite*—To leave in a hurry. **1984** Wilder *You All Spoken Here* 67 **Sth,** *Flag your kite:* Hit the breeze; get a hump on.

flag pawpaw n

A **pawpaw** (here: either *Asimina obovata* or *A. speciosa*).

1933 Small *Manual SE Flora* 531, *A. speciosa*. . . Flag-pawpaw. . . *Asimina obovata*. . . Flag-pawpaw. **1938** Van Dersal *Native Woody Plants* 64, *Flag pawpaw*. . . *A. speciosa*. . . A small shrub. **1953** Greene–Blomquist *Flowers South* 36, *Asimina obovata,* which is locally called "flag paw-paw," has leaves leathery, broadened upward, appearing before the flowers which are white to cream

flagrant adj [Perh malapropism, but cf *OED flagrant* a. 6 1450–1611]

1899 (1912) Green *VA Folk-Speech* 177, *Flagrant. . .* For *fragrant.* "A flagrant smell."

flagreed n

A **flag** n[1].

1941 Writers' Program *Guide IN* 38, The Kickapoo occupied rectangular bark houses in the summer and flagreed oval lodges in the winter.

flag rockfish n [From the pattern of color]

A **rockfish** (here: *Sebastodes rubrivinctus*).

1953 Roedel *Common Fishes CA* 127, *Flag Rockfish. . .* A distinctive color characteristic is the several bright red vertical bars against a light pink background. **1960** Amer. Fisheries Soc. *List Fishes* 37, Flag rockfish. . . *Sebastodes rubrivinctus.*

flagroot n **esp NEast** Cf **poison flagroot**

=**sweet flag** or its root.

1828 Rafinesque *Med. Flora* 25, *Acorus calamus. . . Vulgar Names*—Flag-root, . . Sweet Root, Sweet Rush. **1851** in 1892 Thoreau *Autumn* 77 **MA,** Flagroot . . looks like a cock's tail or a peacock's feather in form. **1881** Greene *Cape Cod Folks* 107 **seMA,** Grandma fed him with bits of unsweetened flag-root. **1931–33** *LANE Worksheets* **seMA,** Flagroot grows in fresh water; spindle is two inches long; you eat the spindle. You take it up when young and put it down [=preserve it] in sugar. **1969–70** *DARE* (Qu. S24) Inf **RI**17, Flagroot; (Qu. S26e) Inf **NJ**67, Flagroot or calamus root; it looks like carrot top but grows close to ground; it's a root for making tea for baby's stomach pain or for sweetening breath; (Qu. BB22, . . *Remedies . . for constipation*) Inf **VA**41, Flagroot tea. **1974** Morton *Folk Remedies* 21, *Calamus; Sweet Flag; Flag-root. . .* Root chewed to sweeten breath. . . Fresh root is boiled and decoction given . . to relieve "pain in the stomach."

flagrush n

=**sweet flag.**

1940 Clute *Amer. Plant Names* 249, *Acorus calamus. . .* Flag-root, flag-rush.

flag squirrel n Cf **federation squirrel**

The thirteen-lined **ground squirrel** n **b** *(Spermophilus tridecemlineatus).*

1961 Jackson *Mammals WI* 130, *Citellus tridecemlineatus tridecemlineatus. . . Vernacular names. . .* Flag squirrel (13 stripes and several "stars" suggest U.S. flag).

flag station n Also *flag stop*

A railroad station where trains stop only on request; hence an insignificant town.

1850 MA Genl. Court Comm. RR & Canals *Annual Rept. for 1849* 21, Whole number of way stations,—Nineteen, Whole number of flag stations,—Fifteen. **1871** Nelson *Pictorial Guide-Book* 21 **NE** (*AmSp* 12.320), We quickly reach the small flag-station of Jackson. **1943** Powell *I Can Go Home* 251 **SE,** A Negro woman got on with tickets to Williamsburg (a flag station in a Negro settlement seven miles beyond Arlington). **1950** *WELS (Joking names . . for . . an unimportant village)* 1 Inf, **WI,** Flag station. **1953** *AmSp* 28.47, When asked . . about the term *whistle stop,* a railroad man replied that it was a political term, that railroad men said *flag stop. . .* The more common term seems to be *flag station.* **1967–70** *DARE* (Qu. N39) Inf **SC**40, Flag station—a place where you could board the train by flagging it down; (Qu. N37, . . *A branch railroad that is not very important*) Inf **MS**83, Flag stop; (Qu. C33, . . *An out-of-the-way place, or a very unimportant place*) Inf **CT**42, Flag stop; (Qu. FF21b, . . *About old jokes people say: "The first time I heard that one . .* ______*."*) Inf **SC**40, New York was a flag station.

flag-stretcher See **stretcher**

flagtail deer n Also *flagtail*

=**whitetail deer.**

[**1928** Anthony *N. Amer. Mammals* 519, The sight of a White-tailed Deer bounding away, with the snowy white tail or "flag" flashing, is one of the most stirring spectacles.] **1966** *DARE* (Qu. P32) Inf **NM**3, White-tail deer—also called flagtail deer. **1982** Elman *Hunter's Field Guide* 461, *Whitetail Deer (Odocoileus virginianus)* Common & Regional Names: . . flagtail.

flag-waver n

1968 *DARE* (Qu. HH43b, *The assistant to the top person in charge of a group of workmen is called the* ______) Inf **CA**66, Small potatoes; big executive; big wheel; little Fauntleroy; the flag-waver.

flahr See **flower**

flail n **widespread, but chiefly Nth, N Midl** See Map *old-fash* Cf **frail** n

1 An implement for threshing grain, made of a wooden handle with a stout stick swinging freely from the upper end.

1732 *Weekly Rehearsal* (Boston MA) 3 Jan 2/2, An Ashes Pail,/ A threshing Flail,/ An iron Wedge & Beetle. **1863** (1864) Mitchell *My Farm* 78 **CT,** None but a few . . of a very ancient school, think now-a-days of . . pounding out their grain with a flail. **1939** *LANE* Map 128, Flail. [Offered in conversation by 7 infs] **1950** *WELS (In early days, how was the grain separated from the straw?)* 37 Infs, **WI,** (With) flails. [50 total Infs] **c1960** *Wilson Coll.* **csKY,** *Flail. . .* A jointed pole formerly used to thresh grain; remembered by very old people. **1965–70** *DARE* (Qu. L32a, *In early days, how was the grain separated from the straw?*) 243 Infs, **widespread, but chiefly Nth, N Midl,** (Beat, thrash, *etc,* with) flail(s); **MA**31, Hand flail; **TN**1, Flail-poles—long, long ago; **CA**105, By flails; (Qu. L32b, . . *How was the grain separated from the chaff?*) Infs **IL**4, **PA**116, 135, Flail(s); (Qu. L33, . . *Nowadays?*) Inf **MA**75, Flails; **NM**6, Flails then winnow.

2 See quot.

1967 *DARE* FW Addit **cnNY,** *Flail*—an iron instrument for breaking ice on a pond or lake.

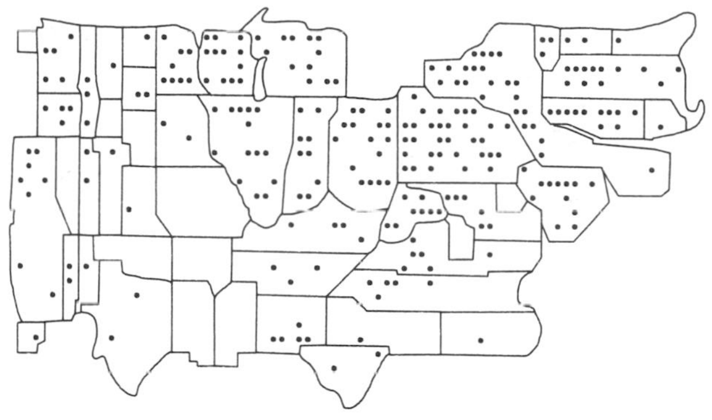

•flail n + varr (Qq. L32a, b, L33)

flail v, hence vbl n *flailing* Also with *out* **chiefly Nth, N Midl** *old-fash*

To thresh (grain) with a **flail** n **1.**

1950 *WELS (In early days, how was the grain separated from the straw?)* 10 Infs, **WI,** Flailed; by flailing. **1951** Johnson *Resp. to PADS 20* **DE,** By flailing. **1965–70** *DARE* (Qu. L32a) Infs **CA**36, **CO**22, **IA**6, **MD**32, **MN**4, Flailed; **IA**12, **NY**209, Flail(ed) out; (Qu. L32b) Inf **WA**4, Flailed; **IL**116, **NY**93, Flailing; (Qu. I13, *When you take dry beans out of the cover you are* ______ *them.*) Infs **NH**5, **OR**3, **PA**163, Flailing. **1967** *DARE* Tape **PA**14, Lay it down on the barn floor, flail it out, and get the seed.

flaish See **flesh** n

flake n[1]

1 also *fish flake:* A rack or platform for drying fish. **NEng**

1635 in 1862 Essex Inst. *Coll.* 4.93/2 **Salem MA,** Granted unto mr. John Holgrave fisherman three quarters of an acre . . for flakes. **1744** (1907) Hamilton *Itinerarium* 144 **neMA,** There is round the town [of Marblehead] above 200 acres of land covered with fish-flakes, upon which they dry their cod. **a1862** (1865) Thoreau *Cape Cod* 197 **seMA,** A great many of the houses here were surrounded by fish-flakes close up to the sills on all sides. **1933–34** *Hanley Disks* **Cape Cod MA,** Them fish were all pickled and salted before they came out of the vessel hold, and then they were taken right into water and washed out and put on those flakes; **seME,** That rack, they tell me, was all covered with fish flakes—that's racks to dry fish on. **1969** *DARE* Tape **MA**57, They had what they called fish flakes; they were these great big things like a table that were made of laths instead of boards and they put 'em out in the field, and they'd lay these flat fish on them head to tail and head to tail so they could get a lot on, with the skin down. **1975** Gould *ME Lingo* 96, *Flakes*—The wooden racks on which split fish are dried after salting.

2 in phr *on the flakes:* Dead; prepared for burial.

1945 Colcord *Sea Language* 76 **ME, Cape Cod, Long Island,** "On the flakes" is a fisherman's slang term for dead, "laid out." **1975** Gould *ME*

Lingo 96, *Flakes*—The wooden racks on which split fish are dried after salting; hence, a corpse laid out is *"on the flakes."*

3 A section of a building; see quots. [Cf *SND flake* n.[1] 1 "Framework of crossed slats, gen. portable and used as a fence, barricade . . Also in Eng. dial."]

1918 *DN* 5.16 **Martha's Vineyard MA,** They moved the church in flakes. **1933** *Hanley Disks* **Cape Cod MA,** "Then when Truro went down, why they took their houses down and . . rafted them over to Provincetown." "Take a whole house on a raft?" "No, 'twas taken down in flakes. They'd flake it, you know, and make a good solid raft of it, tied together, and watch their chance and go across [the bay]."

flake n[2] Also *flake stand* [*SND* 1743–1904] **sAppalachians**

In moonshining: a container filled with cold water through which a condensing tube is passed.

1953 *Hall Coll.* **eTN,** We left our flake stand settin' there. They [=the revenuers] knocked the flake stand down. **1968** *Foxfire* Fall–Winter 49 **nGA,** *Flake Stand*—the container through which water is constantly flowing for final condensation of the steam. Holds the worm, condenser, or radiator, depending on which apparatus is being used. **1969** *DARE* Tape **GA**72, Your flake stand—which is your coolin' or condensin' barrel where the steam is condensed into liquid. **1974** Maurer–Pearl *KY Moonshine* 118, *Flake* or *flakestand*. . . The container, filled with cold water, in which the condenser is immersed so that the alcohol vapor will condense. Usually a barrel or a drum.

flake v [**flake** n[1] **3**]

To take apart in sections.

1933 [see **flake** n[1] **3**].

flake cheese n

1986 *WI Dairy Recipes* 42, Cottage cheese has had many names: Dutch cheese, pot cheese, smearcase, country-style cheese, popcorn cheese, and flake cheese.

flake food n

Processed, dry breakfast cereal.

1968 *DARE* Tape **MI**84, I learned how to keep books. And I took a job at the Malta-Vita Company which was the first flake food company in Battle Creek.

flakes, on the See **flake** n[1] **2**

flake stand See **flake** n[2]

flake yard n [**flake** n[1] **1**] **NEng**

An area where **flakes** are set up.

1856 Reynolds *Peter Gott* 40 **neMA,** The owners of the vessels [in fishing districts] have a flake-yard in the vicinity of the landing places, to which the fish are carried on being landed. The flakes consist of three long poles laid upon crotched posts driven into the ground. These poles are placed parallel to each other, about two feet apart, and covered with brush; upon them the fish are spread. **1896** *New Engl. Mag.* 13.682, 'Flake yard,' store and fish-houses of a typical fish-curing establishment. **1915** (1916) Johnson *Highways New Engl.* 155 **neMA,** There I found everything very quiet, the buildings closed, the acres of flake yards, where the fish are dried, vacant, and almost no work being done. **1975** Gould *ME Lingo* 96, The flake yard is where *flakes* are arranged.

flam adj, v[1], n [*SND flam* v.[3] "To broaden out towards the top, of a ship's bow"; *flam* n.[5] "The form of a ship's bows so constructed."]

Broader at the top than the bottom, flaring; to flare; a flare.

1946 *PADS* 6.13 **eNC** (as of 1908), *Flam*. . . The five-degree slant in the sides of a small skiff. **1968** *DARE* (Qu. L13, *The kind of wagon used for carrying hay*) Inf **DE**1, A wagon with a flam rack, the rack flammed out. [It was] put on a regular wagon. [Inf old]

flam v[2] [Cf *EDD flam* sb.[3] "A heavy fall; a violent stroke."]

To fall heavily, crash into.

1900 Day *Up in ME* 26, Tied a rope around the pole and then he let her flam. **1904** Day *Kin o' Ktaadn* 60 **ME,** Forgot till he flammed on the ground nearly kilt. *Ibid* 154, 'T was something fierce to see them flam the dust.

flamant n [Fr "flaming"]

=wood ibis.

1911 *Forest & Stream* 77.174, *Ajaja ajaja*. Flamant, Gum Cove, La. **1916** *Times–Picayune* (New Orleans LA) 2 Apr 5, *Wood Ibis* (Mycteria americana). Flamant.

‡**flambastic** adj [Prob blend of *flamboyant* + *bombastic*]

1970 *DARE* FW Addit **Houston TX,** He fell for that flambastic stuff. [=He was duped by an incredible story.]

flambeau n

1 In cane sugar making: one of the kettles used for boiling the syrup. *hist*

1883 Silliman *Man. Sugar Cane* 33 *(DA),* The different kettles are as follows: the largest is called the *grande,* the next the *flambeau.* **1887** *Century Illustr. Mag.* 35.116/1 **LA,** In the course of the boiling [the sirup] is ladled successively into the others, called, in order, "the prop" or "proy," "the flambeau," the "sirop," and "the battery." *Ibid,* The "flambeau" [is so called] because the flames of the furnace strike it with most force.

2 also *flambeau lamp* (or *torch*): A torch, flare, or lamp, usu with an open flame. **chiefly Sth, S Midl**

1930 *DN* 6.81 **cSC,** *Flambeau*. . . A torch, usually made of a "fat lightwood knot." Common. **1940** (1978) Still *River of Earth* 91 **KY,** Leth had a flambeau made of a rag stuffed in a bottle of coal oil. **1940** in 1944 *ADD* **WV,** Lawbooks freq. mention 'flambeau lamps,' continuously burning natural-gas lights, as in front yards. **1969** Sorden *Lumberjack Lingo* 43 **NEng & Gt Lakes,** *Flambeau torch*—Tin twin-spouted torch resembling a double-spouted teapot. Generally used to light a road or landing. **1975** Newell *If Nothin' Don't Happen* 18 **nwFL,** We'd ride out through the Hammock on a dark night, holdin' a pine-knot flambeau up over our heads and lookin' under its light for a deer's eyes. To make the flambeau we'd split a fat light'd pine knot into splinters. **1982** *McDavid Coll.* **ceGA, cnFL,** Flambeau—A makeshift lamp. *Ibid* **ceGA,** Flambeau—Wavering flare used by highway dept., etc., to warn of accidents.

3 Transf: see quot.

1983 *Reinecke Coll.* 5 **LA,** *Flambeau*. . . ['flæm,bo] man wearing white smock sometimes hooded, who carries the gasoline torches which light the night parades at carnival. Also, the torches themselves.

flambeau lamp (or torch) See **flambeau 2**

flambergasted See **flabbergasted**

flamboyant-tree n Also *flamboyant* [Fr *flamboyant* flaming; see also quot 1982]

=royal poinciana.

1960 Vines *Trees SW* 544, The Flamboyant-tree is often confused with the tropical American poincianas. **1976** Bailey–Bailey *Hortus Third* 367, *[Delonix] regia*. . . Flamboyant. **1979** Little *Checklist U.S. Trees* 123, Flamboyant-tree. . . Cultivated for ornament in s. Fla. incl. Fla. Keys, persistent and escaping locally. **1982** Perry–Hay *Field Guide Plants* 24, *Delonix regia*. . . Flamboyant. . . *Flowers:* often before leaves, orchid-like, brilliant scarlet.

flambustious adj [Perh blend of *flamboyant* + *bustious,* var of obs Scots *busteous* boisterous, powerful, fierce]

Gaudy; exciting.

1868 in 1872 Schele de Vere *Americanisms* 602, *Flambustious,* a fictitious word made from *flam,* a lie, denotes something great and showy. "We will have a *flambustious* time." **1913** *DN* 4.18, *Flambustious.* Showy, gaudy, pleasant. . . "That dress is rather flambustious." "They have a flambustious window." "We had a flambustious time."

flam cake n [Prob Scots *flam* pancake, pastry] Cf **flamdonia, flannel cake**

Perh a pancake or corn cake.

1904 (1913) Johnson *Highways South* 242 **neVA,** [She mixed up a pan of batter.] *Ibid* 243, At length the "flam cakes" were fried.

flamdonia n Cf **flam cake**

1952 Brown *NC Folkl.* 1.541, *Flamdonia*. . . A pancake or lunch stand.

flamdoodle n, also attrib [Var of **flapdoodle,** perh infl by *flam* nonsense, rubbish]

1 Nonsensical talk.

1888 in 1971 Farmer *Americanisms* 244, We . . planted Uncle George in ship-shape and proper manner. We wasn't goin' to have any highfalutin' flamdoodle business over him. He wouldn't have laid quiet in his grave. **1915** *DN* 4.204, *Flamdoodle, flapdoodle,* empty talk. **1921** in 1952 Crane *Letters* 52 **Cleveland OH,** M. Ray will allow the Dada theories and other flamdoodle of his section run him off his track.

2 Frippery.

1902 Harben *Abner Daniel* 82 **GA,** Durned ef I don't like 'er better without a hat on than with all the fluffy flamdoodle that gals put on when they go out.

flame azalea n Cf **Florida flame azalea**

A deciduous **rhododendron** (here: *Rhododendron calendulaceum*) with yellow to orange-red flowers. Also called **flaming pinxter, honeysuckle 3, turkey beard**

1847 Wood *Class-Book* 376, *R[hododendron] calendulaceum. . . Flame Azalea. . .* A splendid flowering shrub, in mountains and woods, Penn. to Ohio. **1857** Gray *Manual of Botany* 268, *A. calendulacea. . . Flame-colored Azalea . .* [is a] shrub . . covered just when the leaves appear with a profusion of large and showy yellow or orange blossoms, usually turning to flame-color. **1941** Walker *Lookout* 48 **TN,** Flame azalea is also an exquisite creation in the acid soil area. **1947** *Natl. Geogr. Mag.* July 65/1 **SE,** Both of these, the Catawba Rhododendron and Flame Azalea, belong to the same group of plants, the Ericaceae or Heath Family. **1970** *DARE* (Qu. S26c) Inf **VA**101, Flame azalea. **1976** Bruce *How to Grow Wildflowers* 107, The third azalea in this color range to bloom (in early June) is perhaps the showiest of all—an Appalachian native that is one of the best known of the group: *R. calendulaceum,* the Flame Azalea. **1985** *NC Folkl. Jrl.* 33.37 **wNC** (as of c1912), The next to come in [in the spring, after the mayapple] was the fruit that grows on the "honeysuckle" or flame azalea. It is juicy, crisp, and tender, but does not have much flavor.

flame-crest n

=**golden-crowned kinglet.**

1917 (1923) *Birds Amer.* 3.220, *Regulus satrapa . .* Flame-crest.

flameflower n

1 =**fameflower.**

1936 Winter *Plants NE* 70, *Talinum. . .* Flame-flower. **1939** FWP *Guide TN* 22, Wild flowers common to much of Middle Tennessee are the . . dragonroot, firepink, Indian tobacco, lamb's lettuce, . . and the flameflower, which blossoms only on clear days. **1970** Correll *Plants TX* 609, *Flame-flower. . .* Flowers often showy.

2 A tall, orange-flowered plant *(Macranthera flammea).*

1972 Brown *Wildflowers LA* 168, *Flame Flower. Macranthera flammea. . .* Tubular bud opens into an irregular orange-yellow corolla.

flame lily n

1 A **wood lily** (here: *Lilium philadelphicum*). [See quot 1911]

1900 Lyons *Plant Names* 224, *L. Philadelphicum. . .* Flame . . Lily. **1911** *Century Dict. Suppl., Lily. . . Flame-lily,* the red lily, *Lilium Philadelphicum.* **1949** Moldenke *Amer. Wild Flowers* 323, A close second in popularity among our American lilies is the *wood lily, . .* also known as . . *flame lily.*

2 A **zephyr lily.**

1959 Carleton *Index Herb. Plants* 47, *Flame-lily:* Zephranthes [sic] (v).

flame-mallow n

A **globe mallow 1** (here: *Sphaeralcea coccinea*).

1959 Carleton *Index Herb. Plants* 47, *Flame-mallow:* Malvastrum coccineum.

flame maple n

A red-leafed maple, such as *Acer rubrum.*

1968 *DARE* (Qu. T14) Inf **PA**162, Flame maple—very red ones.

flame tree n

Any of var trees or shrubs with brilliant red, orange, or yellow flowers, usu of the genera *Caesalpinia* and *Delonix.*

1933 Small *Manual SE Flora* 666, *D[elonix] regia. . . Royal-poinciana. Flame-tree. . .* The massive clusters of large crimson or orange-colored flowers are conspicuous before the leaves unfold. **1949** Moldenke *Amer. Wild Flowers* 125, Anyone who has ever visited southern Florida will remember with pleasure the spectacular . . *flametree (Delonix regia),* whose huge masses of crimson flowers render it one of the showiest plants in the world. **1960** Vines *Trees SW* 543, *Caesalpinia pulcherrima. . .* Other vernacular names are . . Barbados-Pride, Flame-tree, and Dwarf Poinciana. *Ibid* 544, *Delonix regia. . .* Other vernacular names are . . Royal Poinciana, Flame-tree, and Peacock-flower. **1966** *DARE* (Qu. T16) Inf **FL**4, Royal poinciana, or "flame tree." **1976** Bailey–Bailey *Hortus Third* 1248, Flame tree: *Delonix, Brachychiton australis.*

flamfooted adj [**flam** adj]

1958 *DE Folkl. Bulletin* Oct 32/1, Flamfooted (the opposite of pigeon-toed).

flamigig n [Cf *EDD flam* sb.[1] "nonsense . . flattery"; *flammy* v. "To praise, pet, coddle"; *gig* sb.[6] 2 "Fun, frolic; a taunt, jibe."]

A flirtatious or affected mannerism.

1914 *DN* 4.72 **ME, nNH,** *Flamigigs. . .* Airs and graces; affectations. **1954** Forbes *Rainbow* 117 **NH** (as of early 1800s), When . . the driver offered her a seat beside him, as they do offer pretty girls in nice weather, she perked right up . . all ready to begin her flamigigs on him.

flaming cypress n [From the red flowers and the leaves that resemble those of the cypress vine]

A **standing cypress** (here: *Ipomopsis rubra*).

1966 *DARE* Wildfl QR (Wills–Irwin) Pl.36C Inf **TX**34, Flaming cypress.

flaming eucalyptus n

An unidentified plant.

1968 *DARE* (Qu. T16) Inf **CA**85, Flaming eucalyptus.

flaming fountain See **fountain B**

flamingo tongue n [See quots]

A seashell *(Cyphoma gibbosum)* found off the southeastern coast.

1974 Abbott *Seashells* 152, *Cyphoma gibbosum. . .* Flamingo Tongue. . . A rich cream-orange to apricot buff except for a small whitish rectangle on the back. . . Fairly common on searod gorgonians. **1983** *Miami Herald* (FL) 23 Jan sec G 6, The shell . . is a relative of the flamingo tongue, a small, white shell that supposedly looks like the tongue of a flamingo. If you catch a flamingo yawning, you'll know how the shell got its name.

flaming pinxter n

=**flame azalea.**

1869 Fuller *Uncle John* 60, The flowers are a reddish yellow, so bright it is often called the *Flaming pinxter.*

flaming poppy n

=**wind poppy.**

1897 Parsons *Wild Flowers CA* 129, *Flaming Poppy . .* is an exceedingly variable flower. **1976** Bailey–Bailey *Hortus Third* 1083, *Flaming poppy. . .* Fl[ower]s brick-red with purple center, to 2 in. across.

flaming sword n

=**ocotillo.**

1985 Dodge *Flowers SW Deserts* 42, *Ocotillo. . .* Flaming-sword. . . Blooms bright red.

flammy n Cf **flam cake**

A large biscuit.

1970 *DARE* (Qu. H19) Inf **VA**39, Flammy ['flæmɪ]—made of biscuit dough [in] one big piece. [It] didn't rise too much.

flander See **flounder** n

flanen See **flannen**

flang v See **fling** v **A**

flang n See **fling** n

flang-dang n [Redup var of *fling;* cf *whing-ding*]

A party with music; a shindig.

1937 in 1958 Brewer *Dog Ghosts* 98 **TX** [Black], A fiddler ebun down come from way down in Loozyannuh, on t'othuh side of de Red Rivuh, to play for dese Saddy night flang-dangs. **1949** *PADS* 11.6 **wTX** (as of c1920), *Flang-dang. . .* A play party; a shindig. **1953** Brewer *Word Brazos* 104 **eTX** [Black], All dey knowed was haa'd work, mean obuh-seers, chu'ch oncet a mont', big dinnuhs on a Sunday, Saddy night chu'ch suppuhs, an' string ban' flang-dangs.

flanger n

A kind of small boat; see quot.

1966 *DARE* (Qu. O10) Inf **ME**1, Flanger ['flæŋɚ]—flat-bottomed, holds three or four [people].

flange up v phr

To seal (an oil well) with a flange; by ext, to finish, complete.

1949 *AmSp* 24.34 [Oil field terms], A well that has been *completed, bottomed, finaled,* or *flanged up* begins *breathing, clucking, doing, flowing.* **1972** *DARE* File **neTX,** [Orig in oilfields, now generalized:] *Flange up*—To close off, finish.

flanigan cloth n [Prob var of **flannen**]

Perh flannel.

1974 Dabney *Mountain Spirits* 121 **nGA** (as of c1910), [In the distillation of moonshine:] When the liquor came out, we strained it through fire coals which we put on top of flanigan cloth in a little copper funnel.

flanin See **flannen**

flank n

1 The part of a herd of cattle following the **swing** and preceding the **drag** n **3;** a position to the side of the herd occupied by a cowhand.

1933 (1950) Allen *Cowboy Lore* 36, The cattle in that part of the herd [=following the point] are called swing cattle. . . Then follow the flankers, that part of the herd being called the flank. **1966** *DARE* Tape **NM**14, On a cattle drive we had two men in the lead and two in the swing and two in the flank—that was right next to the drag. **1971** Jennings *Cowboys* 229 **MT, WY,** *Flank*—One of the side positions in a drive. *Ibid* 235, *The Flank* was where the flank should be, between the belly and the hip of the herd, or about two-thirds of the way back.

2 See **flank girth 2.**

flank v

1 To look after, take care of.

1968 Coatsworth *ME Memories* 155, You "flank" a sick person when you look after him.

2 To throw a calf to the ground by reaching over its back and jerking on its flank; hence n *flanker* a cowhand who throws calves to the ground in this manner, vbl n *flanking.*

1920 Hunter *Trail Drivers TX* 297, "Flanking" consists in seizing the animal [to be branded] by the skin of the flank opposite to the cowboy, with his arm thrown over the animal's back; when the animal jumps with all four feet off the ground, the cowboy by a jerk throws it on its side. . . When the flanker and assistants have the animals stretched on the ground, they call out "hot iron." **1933** *AmSp* 8.1.29 **nwTX** [Ranch diction], *Flankin'.* Throwing an animal by flinging an arm over its back, catching its flanks, and jerking vigorously just as the animal jumps. **1958** Blasingame *Dakota Cowboy* 88, The ropers caught by the head and took the calf to the fire where "flankers" took over. These men threw a calf to the ground by reaching over his back, catching his opposite flank and rolling him over their knee. **1961** Adams *Old-Time Cowhand* 231, Sometimes, if he [=the roper] wanted to have some fun with the flankers, he'd rope a big calf by the neck and enjoy watchin' 'em try and wrastle it down. . . If the flankers, however, refused to flank the calf, to save face the roper might have to get down and wrastle 'im down 'imself.

flanken n [Prob Yiddish *flanken* sides or flanks of beef] *esp in Jewish communities*

A cut of beef similar to short ribs or flank steak.

1958 (1960) Grossinger *Jewish Cooking* 24, *Flanken Soup*—3 pounds plate flank[,] Beef bones [etc]. *Ibid* 61, *Boiled Flanken*—4 pounds flank[,] 2 tablespoons fat [etc]. **c1965** *DARE* File **Cleveland OH,** There were cellophane packages of meat in Cleveland supermarkets labeled *flanken.* **1967** *Watertown Daily Times* (NY) 14 June 31, [Advt:] *Roasts. . .* flanken chuck. **1968** *Times Herald Rec.* (Middletown NY) 12 June 61/1, [Advt:] Economical flanken ribs ea. lb. 59¢. **1968** *DARE* (Qu. H45, *Dishes made with meat . . that everybody around here would know, but that people in other places might not*) Inf **NY**119, Flanken. **1971** Isaac Singer in *New Yorker* 31 July 35 **NYC,** I picked out flanken in horseradish with boiled potatoes and lima beans. **1977** *DARE* File **Cleveland OH,** Flanken seems a little better grade of meat than hamburger, but not a really choice cut either. Most of the pieces were eight to ten inches long by about two by two, alternating meat and bone . . like two-inch ribs. It was very tasty and good, . . and medium tender cooked as pot roast in the oven. **1987** *Ibid* **NJ,** I grew up in Trenton and never heard of flanken ['flaŋkən] till I got married. My wife was Jewish and grew up in Piscataway. [Inf born 1948]; **NYC,** In the Bronx it was always pronounced ['flɑŋkən] never ['flæŋkən]. [Inf Jewish]

flanker n

1 also *flank rider;* In cattle-driving: a cowhand who rides at the **flank** n **1.**

1929 *AmSp* 5.72 **NE,** Two "hands" "heading" the side lines guarding the cattle on march, are "lead riders" or "point men," and those riders behind them at long intervals are "swing men" or "flank riders." **1933** (1950) [see **flank** n **1**]. **1966** *DARE* Tape **NM**14, The flankers were behind the swing men and just in front of the drag driver, to keep the cattle all in line, going in one direction. **1968** Adams *Western Words* 115, *Flank rider*—In cattle driving, a rider who stays about one-third of the distance of the length of the column of cattle behind the swing riders, and two-thirds of the distance behind the point riders.

2 See **flank** v **2.**

flank girth n **West**

1 also *flank cinch:* The rearward girth on a **double-rigged** saddle.

1922 Rollins *Cowboy* 123, Some Texans called the cinches "girths," and the rearward of them the "flank girth." **1955** Harris *Look of Old West* 248, [In diagram of a saddle:] Flank cinch ring. **1967** *DARE* (Qu. L53a, *The band that goes under a horse's middle to hold a saddle on*) Inf **TX**16, The back one is called a flank girth [gɚt]. **1968** Adams *Western Words* 115/1, *Flank girth*—What the Texan calls his hind cinch; always pronounced *girt.*

2 also *flank(-rigging):* A strap tightened far back around a rodeo horse or bull to provoke it to buck.

1961 Adams *Old-Time Cowhand* 111, The "flank riggin' " is a flank strap from the rear of the saddle, goin' far back on the flank of the hoss. Used in rodeos to make the hoss buck, it's also called a "scratcher cinch." **1967** *DARE* Tape **TX**25, They put a flank on a horse or a bull. . . It's supposed to make him buck harder. It fits in his flank, and therefore they call it a flank girt. . . The object is to make him buck a little harder.

flanking See **flank** v **2**

flank rider See **flanker 1**

flank rigging See **flank girth 2**

flannel See **flannel leaf**

flannel breeches n

A **baby blue-eyes** (here: *Nemophila phacelioides*).

1936 Whitehouse *TX Flowers* 111, *Baby Blue-Eyes. Flannel Breeches (Nemophila phacelioides)* forms a lovely carpet on banks and in moist woods.

flannel bush n [See quot 1941]

A shrub or small tree of the genus *Fremontodendron.* For other names of *F. californicum* see **leatherwood, silver oak, slippery elm**

1910 Jepson *Silva CA* 40, Flannel Bush . . is a diffuse though tall shrub in the Sierra Nevada. **1941** Jaeger *Wildflowers* 146 **Desert SW,** *California Slippery Elm. . .* Called "flannel-bush" because of the felt-like surface of the under sides of the small, fig-like leaves. **1962** Sweet *Plants of West* 27, *California Fremontia. . .* Also called Flannel Bush. . . Leaves have a brown soft fuzz underneath; flowers are a lovely yellow. **1979** Little *Checklist U.S. Trees* 138, *California fremontia. . . Other common names*—flannelbush, California flannelbush.

flannel cake n Also rarely *flannen cake* [*OED* (at *flannel* sb. 6) 1792; cf *EDD flannel* sb. 3 "A coarse oatcake"; *SND flannen bannock, flannen biscuit*] **chiefly Appalachians** See Map and Map Section Cf **battercake 1**

A pancake.

1847 Briggs *Tom Pepper* 1.112 *(DAE),* A very delicate species of food, which I tasted then for the first time, called flannel cakes. **1895** *DN* 1.388 **KY, NC,** *Flannen cakes.* **1932** (1946) Hibben *Amer. Regional Cookery* 21, *Flannel Cakes. . .* In Mississippi these are eaten for breakfast or supper with sausage or chicken hash; towards the end of the meal they are served with syrup. **1941** *LANE* Map 289 **sNEng,** *Flannel cake* [is used by 3 infs]. **1946** *PADS* 5.22 **VA,** *Flannel cake. . .* A pancake; mostly west of the Blue Ridge, also on Chesapeake Bay. **1949** Kurath *Word Geog.* 69, *Flannel cake (flannen cake)* seems to be an old Pennsylvania term. It is in regular use from the Susquehanna to the Alleghenies and in the adjoining part of Maryland, including Baltimore. It has been carried southward into the Blue Ridge and along Chesapeake Bay, and westward to the upper Ohio River. In the Pennsylvania German area and the vicinity of Philadelphia *flannel cake* still has some currency but has been yielding ground to *hot-cake* and *pancake.* **1951** *AmSp* 26.253 **NY,** Eastern Pennsylvania [words found in Upstate NY] . . *flannel cakes* (pancakes). **1953** *AmSp* 28.249 **sPA,** *Flannel Cakes. . .* Hot cakes, griddlecakes. Not applied to buckwheat cakes or corncakes. In general use. **1965–70** *DARE* (Qu. H20b) 17 Infs, **chiefly Appalachians,** Flannel cakes; **MD**17, Flannel cakes—same as pancakes, wheat cakes, and flapjacks; the standard wheat pancakes; **MD**28, Flannel cakes—usually made with sour milk and soda; **NY**1, Flannel cakes—made with corn meal; **PA**110, Flannel cakes are thick—[we] slice them; **VA**33, Flannel cakes are made of the same dough as waffles; **WI**49, Flannel cakes—

very puffy [Inf has read of them]; **WV8**, Flannel cakes—made thicker than flapjacks. **1973** Allen *LAUM* 1.283 **Upper MW** (as of c1950), *Flannel cakes,* an old Pennsylvania term likely to have been carried by the Scotch-Irish down the Shenandoah Valley, is used by . . [4 infs] with Midland backgrounds.

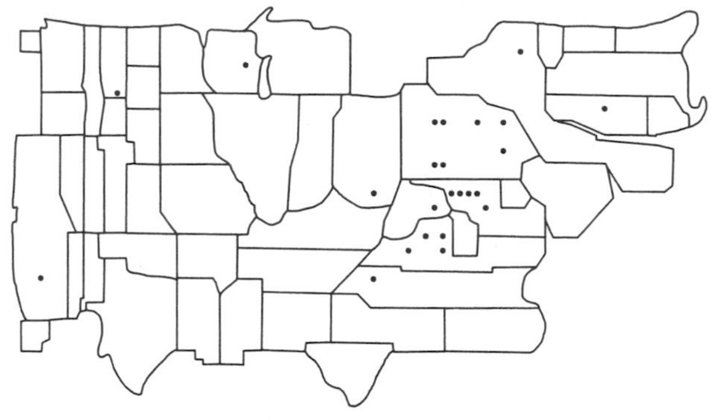

•flannel cake (Qu. H20b)

flannelface See **flannelmouth 2**

flannel feet n pl, but sg or pl in constr

Large feet; an awkward person.

1967–70 *DARE* (Qu. X38, *Joking names for unusually big or clumsy feet*) Inf **MA**122, Flannel feet; (Qu. HH21, *A very awkward, clumsy person*) Inf **MI**67, Flannel feet.

flannel flower n [Cf **flannel leaf**]

=**mullein.**

1876 Hobbs *Bot. Hdbk.* 38, Flannel flower, Mullein, Verbascum Thlapsus. **1891** *AN&Q* 7.210, Numerous fanciful names have been bestowed on the Mullein, such as *flannel-flower, hare's beard.*

flannel hash See **red flannel hash**

flannel leaf n Also *flannel, flannel plant,* ~ *weed* [See quot 1967]

=**mullein.**

1900 Lyons *Plant Names* 389, *V. Thapsus.* . . Flannel-leaf, Old-man's flannel. **1910** Graves *Flowering Plants* 349 **CT,** Flannel-leaf. . . The leaves, tops and flowers are used medicinally, and the leaves are often dried and smoked like tobacco for respiratory affections. **1931** Harned *Wild Flowers Alleghanies* 441, The basal leaves are mostly large, thick, pale green, velvety-hairy. . . The name "Flannel Plant" has often been applied to it. **1950** *WELS* 1 Inf, **cnWI,** Flannel plant; 1 Inf, **csWI,** American flannel. **1951** *PADS* 15.40 **TX,** *Verbascum thapsus* L.—Yellow-flowered mullein; poultice weed; flannel weed. **1961** Smith *MI Wildflowers* 337, Common Mullein, Flannel-plant. **1964** Batson *Wild Flowers SC* 102, *Mullein, Flannel-Plant.* . . Stout, densely wooly, erect biennial up to 7 feet tall. **1967** Borland *Hill Country* 157 **nwCT,** And the giant mullein . . is also called flannel-plant because of the soft, hairy texture of its gray-green leaves.

flannelmouth n

1 also *flannelmouth grunt, flannelmouth(ed) porgy:* A **grunt** n **1,** usu *Haemulon* spp. [See quot 1884]

1884 Goode *Fisheries U.S.* 1.398 **S Atl coast, Gulf states,** *The grunts or pig-fishes* . . are distinguished by the brilliant red color of the inside of the mouth and throat, from which they have sometimes been called Red Mouths or Flannel Mouths. . . The Red-mouth Grunt, *Diabasis aurolineatus* is probably the Flannel-mouthed Porgy, familiar to Florida fishermen. **1935** Caine *Game Fish* 81, *French Grunt. Haemulon flavolineatum.* . . *Synonyms* . . Flannel-mouth Grunt. Flannel-mouth Porgy. *Ibid* 83, *Gray Grunt. Haemulon macrostomum.* . . *Synonyms* . . Flannelmouth. **1946** LaMonte *N. Amer. Game Fishes* 63, [*The Grunts.* . . Bright red mouth lining in some.] *Ibid* 64, *Gray Grunt.* . . *Names:* Striped Grunt, Flannelmouth [etc]. . . Inside of mouth pale pink.

2 also rarely *flannelface:* An Irish person; a loudmouth, braggart. **chiefly Nth** derog

1870 in 1940 *America's Lost Plays* 4.74, You Irish flannel-mouth mick. **1912** Dreiser *Financier* 8 **Philadelphia PA,** Yah do, and I'll kick your head off, you flannel mouth. **1929** Ellis *Ordinary Woman* 202 **CO** (as of early 1900s), But soon George starts to complain that it was run by a bunch of 'red necks,' 'chaws,' 'flannel mouths,' 'Micks'—all names for Irishmen. **1931–33** *LANE Worksheets (Nickname for an Irishman)* 1 inf, **CT,** Flannel mouth—heard, not used; 1 inf, **MA,** [flæ̃əl] mouth; 1 inf, **MA,** [flænəl mɑoθ]. **1933** *AmSp* 8.4.51 **NE** (as of late 19th cent), A *flannel mouth* was one who talked much with little sense or who was a braggart. **1941** *LANE* Map 454, *(Nicknames for an Irishman) Flannel-mouth* [occurs sporadically, most often in **sNEng**]; *flannelface* [occurs once]. **1950** *WELS (Someone who talks too much or too loud)* 1 Inf, **ceWI,** Flannelmouth. **1964** *PADS* 42.39 **Chicago IL,** *Chawmouth* . . refers to the Irishman's talkativeness and parallels the more common *flannel-mouth.* **1966–67** *DARE* [(Qu. X9, . . *"I wish he'd shut his ______."*) Infs **IL**116, **MN**2, **PA**199, Flannelmouth;] (Qu. HH7a, *Someone who talks too much or too loud*) Infs **MI**26, **NY**7, Flannelmouth; (Qu. HH28, . . *Nicknames* . . *for* . . *Irish*) Inf **MI**65, Flannelmouth. **1968** Adams *Western Words* 115, *Flannelmouth*—A cowboy's name for a person who talks too much, a person who talks nonsense, or a braggart.

flannelmouth cat n Also *flannel-mouthed cat* [See quot 1889]

=**blue catfish 1.**

1882 U.S. Natl. Museum *Bulletin* 16.108, *I[ctalurus] lacustris.* . . Catfish of the Lakes; Great Fork-tailed Cat; Mississippi Cat; Florida Cat; Flannel-mouth Cat. . . Abundant in all large bodies of water. One of the largest of the cat-fishes, reaching a weight of 100 pounds. **1887** Goode *Amer. Fishes* 377, The Great Lake Catfish, *Ictalurus nigricans.* . . The young are sometimes called "Flannel-Mouth Cats." **1889** *Century Dict., Flannel-mouthed.* . . Having a mouth with the appearance of flannel: as, the *flannel-mouthed* cat, a fish *(Amiurus nigricans)* of the great North American lakes.

flannelmouthed porgy, flannelmouth grunt (or porgy) See **flannelmouth 1**

flannelmouth sucker n Also *flannelmouthed sucker* [See quot 1896]

A **sucker** (here: *Catostomus latipinnis*) native to the Colorado River basin.

1896 U.S. Natl. Museum *Bulletin* 47.174, *Catostomus latipinnis.* . . *Flannel-mouthed Sucker.* . . Lips very thick, greatly developed. **1902** Jordan–Evermann *Amer. Fishes* 47, *Flannel-mouth Sucker.* . . This sucker is known only from the Colorado River of the West, and its larger tributarics. **1963** Sigler–Miller *Fishes UT* 97, The flannelmouth sucker may be caught on hook and line and large individuals have had considerable economic importance in the past as a cheap food fish, at least in parts of Colorado. **1964** Lowe *Vertebrates* 144 **AZ,** The flannelmouth sucker is used as a baitfish along the lower Colorado River.

flannel mullein n

=**mullein.**

1948 Stevens *KS Wild Flowers* 190, *Flannel Mullein.* . . Biennial with hoary leaves and stems. **1967** Dodge *Roadside Wildflowers* 63 **SW,** *Flannel Mullein.* . . a conspicuous roadside perennial, grows singly or in colonies. **1973** Hitchcock–Cronquist *Flora Pacific NW* 442, Pl[ants] copiously tomentose. . . flannel m[ullein].

flannel plant See **flannel leaf**

flannelweed n

1 See **flannel leaf.**

2 A **golden aster 1** (here: *Chrysopsis longi*).

1950 Gray–Fernald *Manual of Botany* 1380, *C[hrysopsis] Longii.* . . *Flannelweed.* . . Leaves, stems, peduncle and involucres *densely and permanently silvery-lanate.* . . Dry sandy pine-barrens, S. Southampton County, Va.

flannen n Also *flannin, flanen, flanin* [Scots, Engl dial varr of flannel] **chiefly Sth, S Midl** *old-fash* Cf **flannel cake**

Flannel.

1805 (1904) Lewis *Orig. Jrls. Lewis & Clark Exped.* 2.159 **VA,** I had left my leather over shirt and had woarn only a yellow flannin one. **1806** in 1956 Eliason *Tarheel Talk* 310 **NC,** Flanin. **1815** *Ibid,* Flanen. **1895** *DN* 1.388, *Flannen:* for flannel. Common in N. C. and Ky. [*DN* Ed: and elsewhere in the South]. **1899** (1912) Green *VA Folk-Speech* 177, *Flannen.* . . Flannel. **1899** Chesnutt *Conjure Woman* 174 **csNC** [Black], She had tuk [=taken] . . a piece er [=of] red flannin. **1902** *DN* 2.234 **sIL,** *Flannen.* . . Flannel. **1923** *DN* 5.243 **LA,** *Flannens.* . . Flannels: among negroes. **1923** (1946) Greer–Petrie *Angeline Steppin'* 39 csKY, He wern't none too hot with a suit of red flannins on. **1929** Sale *Tree Named John* 6 **MS,** Tie a red flannin straing roun' 'er wais' fer strengt'. **c1938** in 1970 Hyatt *Hoodoo* 1.80 **cAR,** Then yo' take yore bone back . . an' yo' put chew [=you] a flannen rag aroun' it an' wear it in yore pocket. **1968** *DARE* File **sIN,** Flannen—old-fashioned.

flannen cake See **flannel cake**

flannin See **flannen**

flap n

1 **=flapjack 1.**

1969 *DARE* (Qu. H20b) Inf **OH**89, Flaps.

2 also *flapper:* One's mouth.

1965–70 *DARE* (Qu. X9, .. *"I wish he'd shut his ______."*) Infs **CO**15, **CT**19, **GA**13, **IN**35, **LA**12, **MO**23, **NM**2, **WI**13, (Big) flap; **GA**17, 75, **MD**12, **MO**2, **SC**29, (Big) flapper.

3 **=flop n 6a.**

1971 *Today Show Letters* **swPA** (as of c1900), My father (from Rhode Island) called them [=droppings of cow manure] "cow flaps" (obviously a shortening of "cow flapjacks"). **1975** Gould *ME Lingo* 67, On the farm, to step inadvertently on a pasture cow dropping or flap is to *cut your foot.*

flap-and-trap outing n Cf **flap** n[1] **2,** *trap* mouth

1968 *DARE* (Qu. W32, .. *A group of women that meet to sew together*) Inf **CT**11, A flap-and-trap outing—any group of women together.

flapboard n **West**

See quot 1968.

1926 Branch *Cowboy* 75 **TX,** The flap-board on the chuck-wagon had been let down, and a cold lunch was ready for the trail-drivers. **1968** Adams *Western Words* 115, *Flapboard*—The back of the chuck wagon, hinged at the bottom so that it can be let down to serve as a table.

flapcake n [Blend of **flapjack** + *pancake*]

=flapjack 1.

1835 Shirreff *Tour N. Amer.* 221 **MI,** Into one of these pans some small loaves were placed . . and in the other, batter-cakes, called flap-cakes, were prepared. **1962** Atwood *Vocab. TX* 100, *Flapcakes* (*flapjacks* + *pancakes* or *battercakes*) [occurs once]. **1967–68** *DARE* (Qu. H20b) Infs **MO**21, **NY**61, Flapcakes.

flapdoodle n [*OED* 1833 →; cf earlier *fadoodle* (a1670), *fopdoodle* (→1664)] Cf **fahdoodle, flamdoodle**

1 also *flapdaddle;* An imaginary food of fools; nonsense.

1862 *N.Y. Tribune* 22 Jan (*AmSp* 25.174), He then goes on . . to utter other flapdoodle for the nourishment of the Richmond mind. **1885** Twain *Huck. Finn* 212, He gets up . . and slobbers out a speech, all full of tears and flapdoodle. **1888** *Daily Inter-Ocean* 2 Mar (Farmer *Americanisms*), Possibly rich men will turn from sharp dealing, from debauchery, from *flap-doodle* fashion to a common-sense recognition of a situation. **1899** (1912) Green *VA Folk-Speech* 177, *Flapdoodle*. . . Food for fools. The stuff that fools are fed on. **1912** *DN* 3.575 **wIN,** *Flapdoodle*. . . Poppycock; bosh. "His speech was nothing but flapdoodle." **1915** *DN* 4.204, *Flamdoodle, flapdoodle,* empty talk. **1970** *DARE* FW Addit **OH**95, All that fancy financial flapdaddle. **1975** Gould *ME Lingo* 96, He gave me a crate of *flapdoodle* about lookin' for a dog.

2 Mischief.

1932 Stribling *Store* 471 **AL** [Black], I shouldn't be a-tall surprise' if'n dat Alex Cady di'n' come roun' dis ve'y night an' try some sawt o' flapdoodles wid us.

3 An uproar, fuss. [Infl by *flap* in same sense]

1980 *Capital Times* (Madison WI) 23 Sept 3/1, She created a giant-sized flapdoodle by issuing rules for 16,000 local school systems to teach basics . . in their students' strongest language.

flap-footed adj

1970 *DARE* (Qu. X38, .. *Unusually big or clumsy feet*) Inf **KY**94, Flap-footed.

flapjack n Also *flapperjack* [*OED* c1600 →]

1 A pancake. Also called **clapjack, flap** n[1] **1, flapcake, flapover, flat** n[1] **10, flatcake 1, flatjack, flip** n[1] **8, flipjack, flipper** n[1] **1, flopjack, flopover** n, **slapjack**

1789 *Thomas' MA Spy or Worcester Gaz.* (MA) 5 Mar, Danties [sic] of all sorts, too, are here. . . Pies, custards, cranb'ry tarts, and flapjacks. **1818** in 1920 *WI Mag. Hist.* 3.358 **VT,** My living at present is prety much as follows— . . Supper, Coffee—Flapjacks Beef and onions. **1825** Neal *Brother Jonathan* 1.272 **CT** (as of 1775), Hed'a been flat enough . . like a flap jack in a fryin' pan. **1899** (1912) Green *VA Folk-Speech* 177, *Flap-jack*. . . A pancake. Slapjack. **1937** Sandoz *Slogum* 114 **NE,** Them flapjacks 'd make good tug leather. **1941** *LANE* Map 289, *Flapjack, slapjack, flapover, flipper,* . . are widely used (especially *flapjack*), but are being replaced by *griddle cake, pan cake* or *fritter* and are therefore often felt as old-fashioned, crude, or amusing. **1950** *WELS Suppl.* **WI,** Flapjacks. . . Served in stacks with brown sugar, eaten only at dinner and supper. Same batter as pancakes (eaten for breakfast). **1962** Atwood *Vocab. TX* 62, *Battercake* and *flapjack* are obsolescent; *hotcake* and *pancake* are both gaining ground. **1965–70** *DARE* (Qu. H20b) 455 Infs, **widespread,** Flapjacks; **KY**44, Flapperjack. **1966** Dakin *Dial. Vocab. Ohio R. Valley* 2.325, From the standpoint of use in all parts of the Ohio Valley, *flapjack* and its close relative *slapjack* are the nearest approach to a regional term, but only in Ohio . . can it truly be called common. **1973** Allen *LAUM* 1.283 (as of c1950), *Flapjacks,* widespread but decreasing in New England, . . is also declining in the U[pper] M[idwest]. . . 19 infs . . consider the term archaic. It is sometimes characterized as relevant only to pancakes cooked outdoors, as on a camping trip.

2 A kind of fried bread or biscuit. **chiefly Midl** Also called **flatcake 2, jack** n, **slapjack**

1862 (1863) Winthrop *Canoe & Saddle* 6.116, Cakes of unleavened bread, hight flapjacks in the vernacular, confected of flour and the saline juices of fire-ripened pork, and kneaded well with drops of the living stream. Baked then in frying-pan, they stood now, each . . resting on its edge. **1927** *AmSp* 2.354 **cwWV,** *Flapjacks* . . biscuit dough baked without being cut into biscuits. "Break that flapjack for me. It is so hot that I cannot handle it." **1951** Grant *Cowboy Encycl., Flapjack.* A kind of bread, something like a pancake but larger and made of thicker dough. It is turned over by a quick flip of the frying pan. **1967–69** *DARE* (Qu. H14, *Bread that's made with corn meal*) Inf **KY**52, Corn flapjacks—fried; (Qu. H18, .. *Special kinds of bread*) Inf **MD**21, Scones—bread dough fried; also called flapjacks; not the same as pancakes, which are also called flapjacks; (Qu. H25, .. *Fried corn meal*) Inf **IL**103, Flapjacks; **VA**26, Flapjacks or flapperjacks; (Qu. H26, *A round cake of dough, cooked in deep fat*) Inf **MO**18, Flapjack—similar to a doughnut, but it is a little more of a bread dough; you cook it in grease; no hole in the center; not the same as a pancake.

3 A fruit turnover. Cf **applejack 4, fried puppy 1, jack** n

1954 *PADS* 21.27 **SC,** *Flapjack*. . . An apple turnover fried in deep grease, also called *fried puppy* in Anderson County. This may also apply to turnovers made of other dried fruits, as peaches, apricots. The word is sometimes also applied to any pancake or griddle cake. **1956** McAtee *Some Dialect NC* 16, *Flapjack* . . turnover pie fried in deep fat. **1968** *DARE* (Qu. H20b) Inf **VA**26, Flapjacks—made with apples. Some say *flapperjacks.*

flapjack cactus n [From the shape and thickness of the joint]

A **prickly pear** (here: *Opuntia chlorotica*).

1976 Bailey–Bailey *Hortus Third* 791, *[Opuntia] chlorotica. . . Flapjack cactus*. . . Joints orbicular to obovate.

flapjaw n

1969 *DARE* (Qu. HH7b, *Someone who talks too much*) Inf **CA**107, He's a flapjaw.

flapover n

=flapjack 1.

1941 *LANE* Map 289, *Flapjack, slapjack, flapover, flipper* . . are being replaced by *griddle cake, pan cake* or *fritter.*

flapper n

1 See quot. [Engl dial]

1930 Shoemaker *1300 Words* 22 **cPA Mts** (as of c1900), *Flapper*—A young wild duck, easily taken along the edge of mountain ponds.

2 A spatula. Cf **flipper** n[1] **2**

1966–70 *DARE* (Qu. F3, *When you're frying . . eggs—you turn them over with a ______*) Infs **FL**49, **OH**54, Flapper; **CA**2, Pancake flapper.

3 A large foot or shoe.

1968–70 *DARE* (Qu. X38, *Joking names for unusually big or clumsy feet*) Inf **OH**89, Flappers; **VA**9, Flappers; flapper-foot; (Qu. W42b, .. *Men's square-toed shoes*) Inf **NJ**63, Flappers.

4 See **flap** n[1] **2.**

flapperjack See **flapjack**

flapping eagle n
A dance step.
1965 Little *Autobiog. Malcolm X* 60 [Black], Circling, tap-dancing, I was underneath them when they landed—doing the "flapping eagle," "the kangaroo" and the "split."

flare v Pronc-spp *flar, flor* See Pronc Intro 3.I.1.b
A Forms.
1905 [see **B** below]. **1923** (1946) Greer-Petrie *Angeline Doin' Society* 4 **csKY,** Lights was a-florin' all over the place.
B Sense.
To display oneself ostentatiously. [Engl dial]
1905 Culbertson *Banjo Talks* 8 *(ADD)* [Black], Dey flar's an' flants.

flared adj
1918 *DN* 5.16 **Martha's Vineyard MA,** *Flared.* . . Somewhat deranged mentally. "Toward the last of his life he was kind o' flared. He wan't crazy, but he was queer actin'."

flare-tail n
An unidentified jay *(Cyanocitta).*
1969 *DARE* (Qu. Q16, . . *Kinds of jays*) Inf **NC**60, Flare-tail.

flash v
1 To splash. Cf **flosh** Cf *DJE*
1966 *DARE* (Qu. Y36, . . *"See if you can carry that water without ———."*) Inf **SC**10, Flashing; (Qu. Y45, . . *"When he opened the can, the beer ——— [all over the kitchen]."*) Inf **SC**10, He [=it] flash. [Gullah speaker]
2 also with *up:* To dress or act ostentatiously.
1969 *DARE* (Qu. W36, *What do people say . . about a woman who uses a lot of cosmetics?*) Inf **CA**134, Trying to flash up; (Qu. Y22, *To move around in a way to make people take notice of you: "Look at him ———."*) Inf **CA**134, Flash.
3 To vomit.
1936 *Hench Coll.,* Flash v.i.—to throw up. **1959** *AmSp* 34.156 **FL** [University slang], As a result of this state [=drunkenness], they may *flash* (vomit). **1968** *DARE* (Qu. BB17) Inf **PA**74, Flash his cookies.
4 To thresh.
1966 *DARE* (Qu. L32a, *In early days, how was the grain separated from the straw?*) Inf **MS**66, Thrashing; flashing.

flash n See **flesh** n

‡flash adv
Quickly.
1966 *DARE* Tape **MI**20, Get in and get out flash.

flasharity n [*flash* showy]
1968 Adams *Western Words* 115, *Flasharity*—A cowboy's term for a fancy riding outfit or fancy clothes.

flashcracker n
A firecracker.
1950 *WELS (Other names for firecrackers)* 1 Inf, **cWI,** Flashcrackers. **1967-70** *DARE* (Qu. FF14) Infs **DC**12, **WA**20, Flashcrackers.

flasher n
1 See quot. Cf **flash** v **2**
1966 *DARE* (Qu. U37, . . *Somebody who has plenty of money*) Inf NC3, A flasher or a spendthrift.
2 A firecracker that does not go off. [Perh from *flash in the pan*] Cf **flashcracker**
1968 *DARE* (Qu. FF15) Infs **NJ**8, **NY**123, Flasher.
3 =tripletail.
1857 Smithsonian Inst. *Annual Rept. for 1856* 260 **NYC,** *Lobotes surinamensis.* . . I saw a single specimen of this species in Fulton market last year. . . It did not seem to be known. The owner called it "flasher;" why it was so named, I was unable to learn. **1887** Goode *Amer. Fishes* 148, The 'Flasher' or 'Triple-tail' of New York, *Lobotes surinamensis,* . . is spoken of by various authors as the 'Black Triple-tail.' **1933** John G. Shedd Aquarium *Guide* 103, *Lobotes surinamensis* . . Flasher. **1933** LA Dept. of Conserv. *Fishes* 206, Elsewhere this species [=the Tripletail, *Lobotes surinamensis*] has been called Flasher . . and Black Grunt. **1946** LaMonte *N. Amer. Game Fishes* 57, *Tripletail—Lobotes surinamensis* . . Names: Flasher. **1960** Amer. Fisheries Soc. *List Fishes* 57, Flasher—see tripletail.

flashlighting n
=fire-lighting.
1967 *DARE* (Qu. P35b, *Illegal methods of shooting deer*) Inf **CO**47, Headlightin', spotlightin', flashlightin'—all shooting after dark is illegal in Colorado.

flashlight tag n
A game of tag played in the dark; see quot 1977.
1969-70 *DARE* (Qu. EE33) Infs **IL**116, **MI**106, Flashlight tag. **1977** *DARE* File **seWI** (as of 1950s), On summer evenings we played flashlight tag. We ran about in the dark until "it," who had a flashlight, tagged another player with the beam of light. That player then took the flashlight and became "it."

flash, make a v phr [Perh rel to *flash in the pan*]
To make a mistake.
1968-69 *DARE* (Qu. P9, *When you're fishing but not catching any, you might say, "———."*) Inf **LA**15, We made a flash; we gummed it up; (Qu. JJ42, *To make an error in judgment*) Inf **GA**77, [He] made a flash.

flash rider n
1968 Adams *Western Words* 115, *Flash rider*—A bronc buster who takes the rough edges off unbroken horses.

flash speed n [Cf *flash (off)* to evaporate rapidly]
The concentration of alcohol in whiskey at which the **bead** n **3** disappears rapidly.
1974 Dabney *Mountain Spirits* 133 (as of c1940), "What proof you want?" the moonshiners would inquire. . . "Just flash speed," the bootleggers often replied, meaning that when you shook the bottle, the bead would hang on top a bit and flash off. This would be around 85 proof.

flash up See **flash** v **2**

flashy adj[1]
1 also *fleshy;* Of a stream: in flood. [Cf *OED flashy* a. 1 "splashing"; →1611, and **flash** v **1.** The meaning and the form *fleshy* may be infl by *fleshy* fat (also pronc *flashy*)]
1923 *DN* 5.243 **wNC,** *Get fleshy* . . To rise: of water. **1983** *MJLF* 9.1.39 **ceKY,** *Flashy* . . fleshy, swollen (a creek), flush. *Fleshy* . . same as above.
2 Touchy, irascible. [Cf *OED flashy* a. 4 "Excited, impulsive, eager"; →1781]
1941 *LANE* Map 470 1 inf, **csRI,** Flashy = quick-tempered; 1 inf, **swVT,** Flashy . . 'angry'.

flashy adj[2] [*OED flashy* a. 2 "watery . . insipid . . *Obs.,*" prob ult from Lat *flaccus* flabby (cf *OED flash* a.[2] 2)] **VA**
Flat, insipid, bad tasting.
1872 Schele de Vere *Americanisms* 472, *Flashy* is used in the mountain regions of Virginia for everything that is not sweet and fruitful. "The peaches are flashy on account of the drought." **1889** (1971) Farmer *Americanisms* 244, *Flashy.*—In Virginia, used of anything that is unproductive, acid or sour. Thus, crab-apples, sloes, etc., would be called *flashy.* **1899** (1912) Green *VA Folk-Speech* 177, *Flashy.* . . Insipid; vapid; without taste or spirit, as food or drink. **1947** *Hench Coll.* **cVA,** Flashy: over-wet—said of vegetables or meat boiled in too much water.

flashy fry n [*flashy* showy + *fry* a young person]
1967 Cerello *Dakota Co. MN* 60, A flashy fry in my days was a no-good loafer who chased women. . . All the trouble in our town used to be caused by those flashy frys and their high-stepping women folk. [Reported in 4 of 19 communities studied]

flastergated adj [Var of *flabbergasted*] Cf **flabagate**
Astonished.
1967 *DARE* (Qu. GG20, . . *"When those two got married, I was certainly ———."*) Inf **AR**55, Flastergated; occasional use.

flat adj Cf **flat-footed** adj **2**
Unmixed, undiluted.
1968-69 *DARE* (Qu. KK61, . . *"Would you like milk or lemon in your tea?" "No thanks, I'll take it ———."*) Infs **GA**19, **KY**41, **NH**14, Flat.

flat n[1]
1 An area of relatively level ground, spec:
a also pl: A plain or **prairie. widespread, but less freq Missip-Ohio Valleys, Plains States**
1857 in 1924 *Jrl. Amer. Hist.* [New Haven] 44 **RI,** We passed some very pretty farms, situated on smooth flats. **1962** Atwood *Vocab. TX* 40,

[For] "flat, grassy country" . . [instances of] *flat(s)* . . are very scattered. **1965–70** *DARE* (Qu. C29, *A good-sized stretch of level land with practically no trees*) 129 Infs, **widespread, but less freq Missip-Ohio Valleys, Plains States,** Flat(s); **CA**99, **MT**4, Open flat(s). [*DARE* Ed: Some of these Infs may be referring to a more specific sense; see below.] **1968** *DARE* Tape **CA**89, There was one valley out there . . and that was a big, open flat and just clumps of brush here and there.

b A plateau or level hilltop.

1733 in 1905 *Colonial Rec. GA* 3.380 **Savannah GA,** The banks are about Forty Feet high, and on the Top a Flat, which they call a Bluff. **1891** Ryan *Pagan* 287 **WV,** Don . . was walking alone on one of the "flats," high up above the forge ravine. **1939** *LANE* Map 28 1 inf, **swVT,** *Flat,* often used for *interval,* but also for a level piece on a hill top; 1 inf, **swME,** *Flat,* low or on hill top; [3 infs, **New Brunswick,** *Flats,* higher up than an *interval;* never flooded]. **1954** *Harder Coll.* **cwTN,** *Flats*. . . High ground, a plateau. **1956** Ker *Vocab. W. TX* 77, High, flat land . . flats. [3 infs] **1967** *PADS* 47.6 **SW,** Flats 'high grassland'. **1969** *DARE* Tape **CA**145, The sand flats up on Mt. Shasta. **1983** *MJLF* 9.1.39 **ceKY,** *Flat* . . a level piece of land on top of a ridge or mountain.

c Low-lying alluvial land; **bottomland.**

1755 Evans *Geogr. Essays* **sePA,** *Sióto* is a large gentle River, bordered with rich Flats, which it overflows in the Spring. **1817** in 1918 IN Hist. Soc. *Pub.* 6.284 **cNY,** The river was larger and the current very moderate, the bank low and the flats large. **1856** Edwards *Statist. Gaz.* 431, A fine straight line [of road bed], over the widely expanded flats opposite the ancient village of Old Town, in Maryland. These are the finest bottom lands on the river. **1872** Schele de Vere *Americanisms* 177, Here [in the West], near the upper part of rivers, the new settler may meet with *flats,* . . which in America . . mean the alluvial lands close to a river, or very large shoals in the river itself. **1910** *DN* 3.441 **cwNY,** *Flats*. . . A low tract of land along the banks of a river or creek, flooded in time of high water. **1928** *AmSp* 4.125 **NE,** The "meadow" land is never "a meadow" but a "flat" or "hay-flat," depending on whether the land is flat and the water level near the surface of the soil. **1939** *LANE* Map 28, 1 inf, **ceMA,** *Flat,* a piece of low level land; 1 inf, **ceNH,** *Flats,* along a pond or lake; 1 inf, **neNH,** *River flat,* too low to be of any use. **1949** Kurath *Word Geog.* 61, In New York State and adjoining counties of Pennsylvania *flats* is the regular designation [for low-lying flat meadow lands]. This term is used to some extent also in northern East Jersey and in Eastern Pennsylvania as well as in the Virginia Piedmont and Tidewater. **1958** *KY Folkl. Rec.* 4.175, "Flats" is never used to refer to other than river bottoms. **1961** Folk *Word Atlas N. LA* 70, Among the terms listed as others [for low ground in a river valley]. . . *Flat* appeared once in each of these parishes: Jackson, Natchitoches, Red River, and Webster. **1965–70** *DARE* FW Addit **ME,** Flat—a low level treeless stretch of land near a river; **GA**20, Flats—an open low area in the woods, sandy but flooded in real wet times; **VA,** Flats—tree- and thicket-covered land along a river or creek; usually flat, not wet or water-covered unless in case of flood. (Common.) **1966–70** *DARE* (Qu. C6, . . *A piece of land that's often wet, and has grass and weeds growing on it*) Inf **FL**34, A gallberry flat; **IL**53, **LA**31, Flats; **TX**22, Flats—poorly drained areas; [they] are landmarks locally; (Qu. C9) Inf **MA**100, Flat; **OH**6, **NY**88, Flats; (Qu. C29) Inf **AK**2, Alluvial flats of several rivers. **1967** *DARE* Tape **TX**24, They had planned—to put that fort over there in that flat right across the draw from Uncle Bill's house; **MI**68, It's just like any low, watery section, flats. . . There was just a little . . incline that went down to it and then it was the flats . . section of the River Rouge.

d Low land between hills; a small, usu flat-bottomed, valley.

1894 in 1941 Warfel-Orians *Local-Color Stories* 595 **ID,** The flat is a little cup-shaped valley formed by high hills, like dark walls, shutting it in. **1949** *AmSp* 24.108 **nGA,** *Flat*. . . A level place, in hilly country. **1959** Robertson *Ram* 73 **ID** (as of 1875), Most of the buildings were wedged into draws or gulches between the hills. Where the gulches widened out they were called "hollers," and if the hollers leveled out enough they were called "flats." **1967–70** *DARE* (Qu. C19, . . *Low land running between hills*) 18 Infs, **scattered,** Flat(s). **1967** *DARE* FW Addit **TX,** Flat—a low expanse of land between hills. **1968** *DARE* Tape **CA**100, Flat—low land in a valley.

e often in combs: Used as a joc or derog nickname for a town or district. **chiefly NEast, West** See Map

1904 Day *Kin o' Ktaadn* 64 **ME,** "Patent-right" Belcher of Scarboro Flat. **1943** *LANE* Map 546 1 inf, **cVT,** Johnnycake Flat—jocular name for Stockbridge Common (a small plateau in the highest part of the village) explained by an anecdote about an unpopular townsman who was here 'crowned' with a freshly baked johnny-cake. **1965–70** *DARE* (Qu. C35, *Nicknames for . . parts of your town*) Infs **IL**38, **IA**46, **MA**17, 50, **NM**6, **NY**123, **TX**42, (The) Flats; **IL**5, **OK**25, Flat; **CT**29, **PA**245, **WA**3, 30, **CO**11, Codfish (*or* Irish, Sand, etc) Flats; **AZ**1, **CA**129, 195, **MD**26, **NM**11, **NY**93, **PA**115, Chloride (*or* Goose, North, Oakie, Potslayger's, *etc*) Flat; (Qu. II25, . . *Nicknames for the part of town where the poorer people . . live*) Infs **IA**46, **IL**36, **MD**24, **MA**53, **NY**149, **OK**27, **PA**185, **TX**40, Flats; **TX**18, **WA**8, Poverty Flats, **CO**15, Mexican Flats; **TX**81, Nigger Flats, **MD**26, Pot Liquor Flats; **GA**86, Flat; **WA**30, Starvation Flat; **NH**14, Wop Flat; (Qu. C34, *Nicknames for nearby . . districts*) **MA**68, **PA**184, Flat(s); **CA**137, 145, Jackass (*or* Rabbit) Flat; **WA**31, Tar Hill Flat; **PA**49, Penrose Flats; (Qu. II24, . . *Where the well-off people live*) Inf **MT**2, Mortgage Flat.

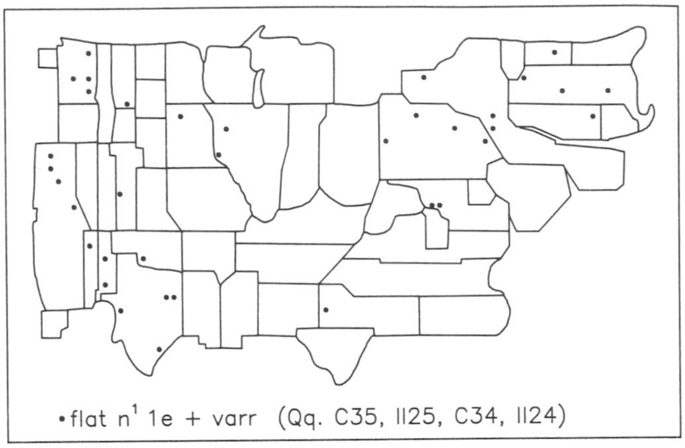

2a An alluvial tract alternately exposed and covered by the tide; a shallows.

1634 Wood *New Engl. Prospect* 43 **MA,** The Bay that lyeth before the Towne at low spring tyde, will be all flatts for two miles together. **1682** in 1940 *AmSp* 15.178 **VA,** Thence passing down the said Creeke and the maine Channell. . . untill it comes to the narrows, which goes into the Flatts agt Percimons Esson. **1786** (1925) Washington *Diaries* 3.5, The flats and creeks were froze, but that on the former dispersed with the tide when the Winds blew, the latter remained. **1898** *VA Mag. Hist. & Biog.* 6.250, From the mouth of Pagan creek there are extensive flats extending thirty, forty, fifty feet and more from the shore, preventing the easy loading of a vessel. **1905** *DN* 3.9 **cCT,** *Flats*. . . Low alluvial lands over which the tide flows. **1907** Lincoln *Cape Cod* 290, Did you ever see the tide go out over the flats? **1967** *DARE* (Qu. C29) Inf **WA**19, Tide flats—what the tide vacates. **1978** *DARE* File **cwCA,** The tide flats in Oakland have always been ugly because people throw old tires there, but recently someone has been "beautifying" the area by creating whimsical sculptures out of the tires and driftwood.

b By ext: a shallows in a river.

1755 Evans *Geogr. Essays* 26 **sePA,** At Fort du Quesne, at Paul's Island . . , and at a Flat between that and Logs Town, the Water is pretty rapid. **1846** Emmons *Agriculture NY* I.7, Flats and shallows are constantly recurring in the Mohawk, sometimes forming ripples. **1872** [see 1c above].

3 **=flatboat n 1a** or **b. chiefly Missip and Ohio R Valleys, SE coast**

1696 (1977) Dickinson *God's Providence* 60, A parcell of *Dutch Men* were killed who having been cast away on the *Bohemia* shoals in a flatt which they built escaped hither. **1782** *MD Jrl. & Baltimore Advt.* (MD) 10 Sept, A small *Flat,* or *Scow,* with one end broken. **1788** *KY Gaz.* 5 Apr [2/3] **Lexington KY,** The savages had in their possession a flat, in which eight or ten of them gave chace to the F[r]ench gentlemen. **1810** (1912) Dwight *Journey to OH* 60, We crossed the big Beaver . . It is generally, fordable, but is at present so rais'd by the rain, that a flat is used. **1838** (1852) Gilman *S. Matron* 106, A flat, well manned with negroes, turned the bend of the river, gently moving on the flooding tide. **1846** Thorpe *Mysteries* 120 **Ohio R,** He was lolling carelessly over the big "sweep" that guided the "flat." **1938** FWP *Ocean Highway* 131 **SC,** The vehicles, horses, cows, furniture . . were all put into great flats, some 60 by 20 feet, others even larger. **1956** Knipmeyer *Settlement Succession* 172 **LA,** All of the inland boats of Louisiana have flat bottoms, but only one kind is called a "flatboat". . . More commonly it is simply called a "flat." **1966–68** *DARE* Tapes **GA**25, They built what they called a flat. . . They hewed them timbers out . . and they put them together with pegs, they had no nails. . . It was large enough that you could drive your ox, horse, or whatever you was a-driving . . right up on it with the cart behind and take a long pole and push it across the river; **SC**16, Tote 'em to the flat; **SC**10, You get in the flat, and then row 'em all the way across; **SC**9, [Inf:] Tie 'em up then you call for the flat. . . [FW:] But the flat don't come in the field, though. [Inf:] No sir . . either the creek or the river. **1978** *Pioneer Amer.* June 82 **Missip Valley,** Although there are many flat-bottomed boats, there is only one flatboat. It is known by other names, such as *john boat, joe boat, scow,* and *flat.*

4a See **hay flat.**

b also *flat frame:* The rack on a **hay flat.**

1967–68 *DARE* (Qu. L13) Inf **AL**33, Flat frame; **WV**2, Flats are flat frames; [they are] put on ordinary wagons.

5 A **stoneboat.** Cf **flatboat n 2**

1950 *WELS* **ceWI,** Stoneboat; flat. **1965–70** *DARE* (Qu. L57, *A low wooden platform used for bringing stones or heavy things out of the fields*) 12 Infs, **chiefly Sth,** Flat.

6 **=flat tobacco.**

1892 *KS Univ. Qrly.* 1.96 **AR,** *Flat:* plug tobacco. **1923** *DN* 5.207 **swMO,** Got ary piece o' flat, Bill? **1966–70** *DARE* (Qu. DD1, *What different forms does chewing tobacco come in around here?*) Infs **IL**118, **MO**37, **TX**35, Flat; **MO**10, The flats; **NM**11, Plug—often called hammered flat; **WV**4, Flat—same as plug; **WV**16, Flat—cake or plug.

7 The truth. [Ellip for *the flat truth*] Cf **straight n**

1942 in 1944 *ADD,* That's the flat of it, & you can take my word. Radio.

8 A flatiron. **NEast** *old-fash*

1856 Whitcher *Bedott Papers* 53 **NY,** The times that critter has had my bake pans and my flats and my wash board, ain't to be numbered. **1889** Cooke *Steadfast* 118 **CT,** I've giv' her some ros'-berry leaf tea, an' put a hot flat to her feet. **1901** *DN* 2.140 **NY,** *Flat.* . . Flatiron. **1910** *DN* 3.441 **cwNY,** *Flat.* . . Flatiron. "She's going to put on her flats now." **1969** *DARE* (Qu. F29, . . *Kinds of irons—not electric*) Inf **RI**9, Just called it the iron or the flat; **RI**15, You warmed your flat and did your ironing. **1988** *DARE* File **cNY,** "Put the flat on the stove." Obviously what others would call a flatiron.

9 A type of whiskey still.

1972 *Foxfire Book* 332 **nGA,** These diagrams illustrate perhaps the simplest still of them all—the "deadman" or "flat."

10 **=flapjack 1.** [Abbr for **flatcake, flat car 1**]

1927 *DN* 5.446 [Underworld jargon], *Flats.* . . Griddle cakes. **1941** *AmSp* 16.233 [Among lumberjacks], *Flats.* The name for hotcakes or griddle cakes. **1958** McCulloch *Woods Words* 183 **Pacific NW,** *String of flats* . . Flapjacks. **1969** Sorden *Lumberjack Lingo* **NEng & Gt Lakes,** *Flat.* . . Pancake, griddle cake.

11 A herring split down the back for salting.

1905 U.S. Bur. Fisheries *Rept. for 1904* 687, In the preparation for salting the herring are cut either down the back or the belly, but usually the former. When cut down the back they are called "flats" and when cut down the belly they are termed "ciscoes."

12 also *flat trout:* **=cutthroat trout. MT**

1939 FWP *Guide MT* 119, Native blackspot trout ("flats") and Dolly Varden ("bulls") abound in northwestern lakes and larger streams. **1966** *DARE* (Qu. P1, . . *Freshwater fish . . that are good to eat*) Inf **MT**4, Flat trout.

13 See **flatfish 1.**

flat n²

1 An apartment, esp one occupying an entire floor and having a separate entrance. **chiefly Nth, N Midl, Pacific** See Map

1884 *N.Y. Herald* 27 Oct. 2/2 (*DA* at *elevated 2*), Commodious First Flat; Rent. $37. **1905** *NY Eve. Jrl.* (NY) 21 July 9th ed 8 *(Zwilling Coll.),* [Cartoon:] As Sul looked to James who is buying flats. **1934** *AmSp* 9.155, I have asked a number of persons from different localities their opinions, and I present some of their answers. . . "A flat is one story of a house and has a separate entrance." [Lawrence, Kansas.] "A flat is one half of a duplex." [St. Joseph, Missouri.] . . "A flat is a whole floor. . . " [Chicago.] "There are six flats in our dormitory, i.e., six different stairs. All that use one stair live in one flat." [Kearney, Nebraska.] "A flat has both a back door and a front door. . . " [Los Angeles.] "A flat has an individual hallway. . . " [South Dakota.] "A flat may be joined to other flats and have two stories." [Colorado Springs.] . . "A flat is a suite occupying a whole floor. . . " [Iowa City.] "A flat to me suggests a whole floor. . . " [Omaha.] **1964** *New Yorker* 26 Sept 48/3 **NYC,** They had, in fact, stayed in the flat there only a little more than a year . . ; they moved then to a floor-through in a decrepit but pleasant brownstone. **1965–70** *DARE* (Qu. D24, *Living quarters in a building where several other families live*) 49 Infs, **chiefly Nth, N Midl, Pacific,** Flat; (Qu. D26, . . *Kinds of apartments . . [Especially, small apartments]*) 27 Infs, **chiefly Nth, N Midl,** Flat; 13 Infs, **chiefly NEast,** Cold-water flat; **CA**166, **PA**134, One-room (*or* two-room, three-room) flat; **MN**36, One-bedroom (*or* two-bedroom) flat; **IL**50, Two-flat (*or* three-~, six-~); **WI**47, Walk-up flat.

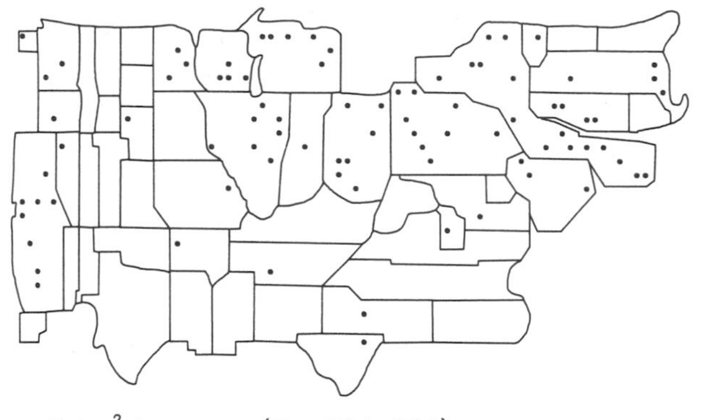

•flat n² 1 + varr (Qq. D24, D26)

2 An apartment building, csp one with two stories.

1934 *AmSp* 9.155, I have asked a number of persons from different localities their opinions, and I present some of their answers. . . "Flats are always two-story buildings." [Cheyenne, Wyoming.] "A flat is an apartment house with two stories. . . " [Hastings, Nebraska.] . . "A flat is larger than an apartment house." [Milwaukee.] . . "A flat is an apartment house with two stories." [Missoula, Montana.] . . "After an apartment house becomes old and run-down it is a flat." [Lincoln, Nebraska.] **1967–70** *DARE* (Qu. D23, *A house that is divided in two through the middle*) Infs **CA**15, **HI**1, **OR**4, Flat; **MO**7, 29, **TN**1, Two-family flat; **NY**105, Boston flat. **1970** *DARE* Tape **CA**185, That old four-family flat is still on Voliscious Street. **1971** *Today Show Letters* **seMI,** A structure with single apartments up and down—in Detroit it is called a flat.

flat v

1 To transport by **flatboat n 1a.** [**flat** n¹ **3**] Cf **flatboat** v

1753 in 1897 *Documents Colonial & Post-Revol. Hist. NJ* 19.237, William Richardson was employ'd . . to flat some wood to Philadelphia. **1770** (1925) Washington *Diaries* 1.380 **neVA,** Began to flat Stone round, as also to carry wood round for burning Lyme. **1845** in 1910 Commons *Doc. Hist. Amer. Industrial Soc.* 1.166 **coastal GA,** Having to cross two rivers, & a canal in flatting the crop from it. **1939** Griswold *Sea Is. Lady* 543 **sSC,** She was able to get the cotton all picked, bagged, and flatted to town before the rains came at last.

2 To flatten. Cf **sharp** v

1841 'Dow, Jr.' *Short Patent Sermons* 86 (*OEDS* at *get-up*), It flats right down, and stays there, like a junk of dough. **1940–41** Cassidy *WI Atlas* **swWI** [2 Infs], Rails flatted at the end. . . Flat it out.

flat and cold adj phr, adv phr Cf **cold** adv

1972 Cooper *NC Mt. Folkl.* 92, *Flat and cold*—unconscious; entirely; without any more to say.

flat around v phr

=flax v **2.**

1901 *DN* 2.140 **ceNY,** *Flat around.* . . *Stir,* hustle.

flat-ars(e) calm See **flat-ass calm**

flat as a flitter See **flitter** n¹ **2b**

flat-ass calm n Also *flat-ars(e) calm* **ME**

A condition of extreme calm at sea.

1975 Gould *ME Lingo* 97, *Flat-arse calm*—Absolutely no motion of wind and water. **1978** Merriam *Illustr. Lobstering* 38 **ME,** *Flat Ass Calm*—A condition existing when there is no wind, sea, or swell. This usually happens in the summer and frequently during a fog. Often pronounced "flat ars calm."

flatback n **esp VA** *?obs*

Prob a spotted **sucker** *(Minytrema melanops).*

1804 (1904) Clark *Orig. Jrls. Lewis & Clark Exped.* 1.111 **VA,** Cought upwards of 800 fine fish . . 1 Rock, 1 flat Back, 127 Buffalow. **1856**

Porter's Spirit of Times 27 Dec 271/1 **VA,** We have, in this region, the pike, perch, chub, mullet, and "flat-back," or *sucker.* **a1883** (1911) Bagby *VA Gentleman* 127, The fish are beginning to bite pretty well—one or two medium-sized flatback have been landed by Dr. X. *Ibid* 130, The "flatback," you know, is called "sucker" in some parts of the country, and, with its broad, mottled, green back, its large fins and black eyes, makes as pretty a fish as any that swim in our waters.

flatbedding vbl n

The process of setting out tobacco plants in level beds from which they are later transplanted to fields.

1968 *DARE* Tape **IN**11, First thing you have to do is start your beds [for tobacco seedlings]—you know what they call flat-bedding.

flat-bellied dress n

1942 Warnick *Garrett Co. MD* 7 (as of 1900–18), *Flat-bellied dress* . . child's dress having a plain fitting body and a gathered skirt.

flatbelly n[1]

=flathead catfish 1.

1908 Forbes–Richardson *Fishes of IL* 194, Other local names [for *Pylodictis olivaris*] are mud-cat, flat-belly, and nigger-belly. **1947** Dalrymple *Panfish* 200 *(DA),* Many are the colloquial names for it *[Pylodictis olivaris]*—Yellow Cat, . . Flat-belly, Nigger-belly, Goujon. **1983** Becker *Fishes WI* 728, *Flathead Catfish*. . . Other common names: . . flatbelly.

flatbelly n[2]

=belly-flop 2.

1968 *DARE* (Qu. EE29, *When swimmers are diving and one comes down flat onto the water, that's a* ______) Inf **IN**32, Flatbelly.

flatbill n

=paddlefish.

1956 Harlan–Speaker *IA Fish* 46, Paddlefish. . . Other Names— . . shovelnose cat, flatbill, and, incorrectly, spoonbill sturgeon.

flatboard n Cf **flatbottom n 1**

1931–33 *LANE Worksheets* **swCT,** *Flatboard*—Toboggan.

flatboat n

1 Any of var types of flat-bottomed boats, as:

a A large square-ended boat used to transport freight in shallow water. Also called **ark 1, broadhorn 1, flat n[1] 3**

1689 (1878) S. Sewall *Diary* 1.301 **MA,** Their flat Boat [in London] ly there which carry Seven Hundred Quarters of Matts, which they count seventy Tun. **1780** in 1875 VA *Calendar State Papers* 1.390 **VA,** He may procure Casks, and use the flat-boats to transport it. **1851** Cist *Sketches Cincinnati* 282, Flat-boats . . take down more or less bacon for the coast trade. **1902** Gordon *Recoll. Lynchburg* 88 *(DAE),* With varying frequency steamboats, flatboats, tugs, and grain and coal barges, are passed. **1968** *DARE* Tape **CT**4, In the old days before seventeen hundred . . they built here a series of seven warehouses where loads coming up the river were unloaded and transferred into flatboats which ran on a regular schedule way up in to northern Vermont; **IN**3, Flatboats transported timber and supplies down the Ohio River; **IN**10, One of 'em brought his family after the [Revolutionary] war was over, came down the Ohio river from Pennsylvania on a flatboat.

b A small boat, esp a narrow square-ended one. **chiefly Missip Valley, Ohio Valley** See Map

1938 Burman *Blow for a Landing* 256 **Missip Valley,** A gaunt-faced woman rowed past in a flatboat, its bow piled high with fox and otter skins. **1956** Knipmeyer *Settlement Succession* 172 **LA,** All of the inland boats of Louisiana have flat bottoms, but only one kind is called a "flatboat." . . Both ends . . are blunt, and the stern is always wider than the bow. . . The average boat is between twelve and fourteen feet long, and has a beam of about three feet. **1965–70** *DARE* (Qu. O2, . . *An old, clumsy boat*) 15 Infs, **chiefly east of Missip R,** (Old) flatboat; (Qu. O10, . . *Kinds of boats . . around here*) 10 Infs, **chiefly Missip Valley, Ohio Valley,** Flatboats; (Qu. O1, *A small rowboat, not big enough to hold more than two people*) Infs **AR**36, 55, **IL**108, Flatboat; **LA**31, Flatboat—blunt at both ends; (Qu. O9) Inf **MS**6, Flatboat. **1967** LeCompte *Word Atlas* 220 **seLA,** [10 of 21 Infs offered *flatboat* as the term for a small, flatbottomed, rectangular boat.] **1978** *Pioneer Amer.* June 83 **Missip Valley,** The flatboat could easily be adapted to carry an internal combustion engine, and in this modified form, it became extremely important to commercial fishermen. One design change doubled its length, and the average became about twenty-eight feet.

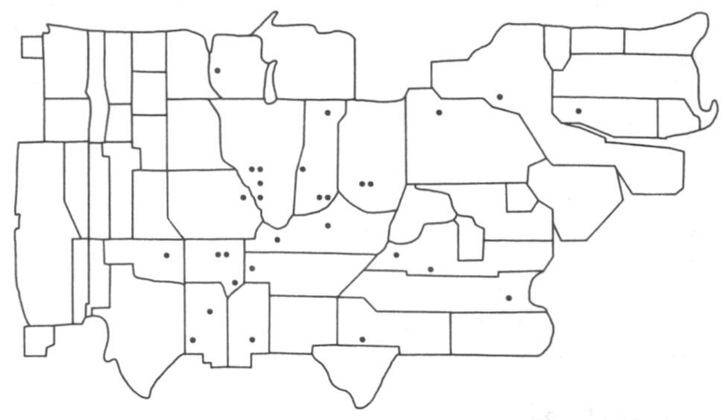

•flatboat n 1b + var (Qq. O2, O10, O1, O9)

2 A stoneboat. Cf **flat n[1] 5**

1967–69 *DARE* (QU. L57, *A low wooden platform used for bringing stones or heavy things out of the fields*) Infs **IL**4, **PA**232, Flatboat. **1973** Allen *LAUM* 1.219 **MN** (as of c1950), Flat boat. [Inf queries]

3 pl: Large feet or shoes.

1903 *Cin. Enquirer* 10 May IV.3/7 *(DA),* Don't you know a switchman oughtn't t' put his feet in flatboats? Don't you know you'll get your foot stuck in a tongue or a guard? **1968–70** *DARE* (Qu. X38, . . *Unusually big or clumsy feet*) Infs **KY**72, 74, **MN**18, Flatboats. **1969** *DARE* FW Addit **KY**66, Flatboats—joking name for big shoes.

flatboat v, hence vbl n *flatboating*

To transport by **flatboat n 1a;** to operate or work on a **flatboat n 1a.**

1858 *Natl. Intelligencer* (DC) 29 July 3/4, Fruit, which he flat-boated from Wheeling to [New Orleans]. **1858** Wilkie *Davenport* 194, Capt. May commenced flat-boating on the Ohio in 1822. **1862** Newell *Orpheus C. Kerr* 1.32 **NY,** [Abraham Lincoln] when he took to flat-boating . . was so tall and straight, that a fellow once took him for a smoke-stack on a steamboat. **1870** 'O. Optic' *Field & Forest* 279 *(DAE),* I took to the river for a livin'. I worked a choppin', a flat boatin' and firin' on a steamboat.

flatboot n Cf **flatboat n 3**

1970 *DARE* (Qu. X38, . . *Unusually big or clumsy feet*) Inf **KY**77, Flatboots.

flatbottom n

1 See quot. Cf **flatboard**

1917 *DN* 4.392 **neOH,** *Flat-bottom*. . . Short for *flat-bottom sled,* a sled with wide wooden runners for use in soft snow or mud. "It's so soft I think I'll use the flat-bottom today."

2 See quot.

1967–68 *DARE* (Qu. X38, . . *Unusually big or clumsy feet*) Infs **LA**11, **OH**72, Flatbottoms.

flat-bottom(ed) plow n Also *flat-bottomed turner,* ~ *turning plow, flat plow*

See quot c1960.

c1960 *Wilson Coll.* **csKY,** *Flat-bottomed plow*. . . Old-fashioned plows as contrasted with disc plows of today. **1969** *DARE* (Qu. L18) Inf **KY**6, Turning plows—disc and flat-bottom; **NY**219, Flat plow. **1986** Pederson *LAGS Concordance* **Gulf Region,** 4 infs, Flat-bottom plow; 1 inf, Flat-bottom turners—a type of breaking plows; 1 inf, Flat-bottom turning plow.

flatbread n Also *flatbrod, fladbrod* [Norw *flatbrød, fladbrød*] **chiefly Scan settlement areas**

A thin usu unleavened bread.

1876 Warner–Warner *Gold Chickaree* 37, Porridge and flad-brod and cheese . . were set on the table. **1950** *WELS (Kinds of fancy home-baked rolls and so forth in your neighborhood)* 1 Inf, **cwWI,** Flatbrod—Norwegian; *(Special kinds of bread)* 1 Inf, **swWI,** Flatbread—still eaten extensively by Norwegians. **1966–70** *DARE* (Qu. H18, . . *Special kinds of bread*) Inf **MN**6, Flatbread—very thin; use white flour; **MN**16, Flatbread—baked on the stove top; **SD**1, Flatbread—unleavened, baked on top the stove; **WI**53, Flatbread—Norwegian, old-fashioned; same as lefse; **WI**70, Flatbread—Norwegian; (Qu. H32, . . *Fancy rolls and pastries*) Inf **SD**8, Flatbread—fried bread dough; (Qu. H65, *Foreign* *foods*) Inf **IA**13, Flatbread—Scandinavian; **MN**13, Flatbread—baked on top of the stove and dried in the oven; break it up and put cream on it; Norwegian; **ND**2, Flatbread.

flat-break v, hence vbl n *flat-breaking* [Prob **flat** n[1] **1a** + **break** v**B1**] **Sth**

See quot 1946.

1946 *PADS* 6.13 **eNC,** *Flat-break land:* . . To plow all around a piece of ground with a turning plow, throwing all furrows toward the margin, ditch, hedge, etc. Pamlico. Occasional. **1965–68** *DARE* (Qu. L20) Inf **NC**80, Flat-breaking [is] when you plow it; (Qu. L19, *When you plow land . . that has never been plowed before, you've* ______; total Infs questioned, 75) Inf **MS**28, Flat-breaking. **1967** *DARE* Tape **TX**49, [When you're] layin' off ground, just use one [horse or mule]; breakin', flat-breakin', use two. **1986** Pederson *LAGS Concordance* 13 infs, **chiefly eTX, LA, MS, AL,** Flat-break(ing).

flat-break plow n

A plow used to **flat-break** land.

1986 Pederson *LAGS Concordance* 1 inf, **seTX,** Flat-break plows—designed to cut deep.

flatbrod See **flatbread**

flat bullhead n

A **bullhead 1b** (here: *Ictalurus platycephalus*) with a flattened head. Also called **flathead catfish 2, mud cat, snail cat**

1955 Carr–Goin *Guide Reptiles* 63, *Ameiurus platycephalus* . . Flat Bullhead. **1960** Amer. Fisheries Soc. *List Fishes* 18, Flat bullhead . . *Ictalurus platycephalus.*

flatcake n

1 =**flapjack 1.**

1968 *DARE* (Qu. H20b) Inf **IA**32, Flatcakes. **1986** *DARE* File **cOK,** *Flatcakes*—pancakes.

2 =**flapjack 2.**

1954 *PADS* 21.27 **SC,** *Flat cake.* . . A piece of biscuit dough flattened and baked on top of the stove. This is usually small, and baked for or by a child, but larger *flat cakes* have also been made in the same way. They are turned over and baked on both sides.

flat-cake tobacco See **flat tobacco**

flatcar n

1 =**flapjack 1.** Cf **flat** n[1] **10**

1936 (1947) Mencken *Amer. Lang.* 582 [Among tramps and hoboes], Pancakes are *flat-cars.* **1942** Berrey–Van den Bark *Amer. Slang* 784.1, Flatcars, flats, string of flats, *hot cakes.*

2 A large foot. Cf **boxcar 1, flatboat** n **3**

1968 *DARE* (Qu. X38, *Joking names for unusually big or clumsy feet*) Inf **WI**27, Flatcars.

flat-country people n pl

=**flatlanders.**

1967 *DARE* File **KY, TN,** [They are] flat-country people. I'm a mountain man myself.

flat-down adj Cf **flat-footed** adj **1, hard down** adj phr **3**

Plain, straightforward.

1940 *Hench Coll.* **cVA,** They don't talk this old-time flat-down talk anymore.

flat-face n

Prob a banjo or guitar.

1921 Thorp *Songs Cowboys* 163, While Randolph sits here by the fireside / With a "flat-face" on his knee.

flatfawm See **flatform**

flatfeet See **flatfoot** n **2b**

flatfish n [From the laterally compressed body]

1 Std: a fish of the order Pleuronectiformes. See also **flounder** n **B, sole, tonguefish**

2 also *flat;* Spec: a **flatfish 1** such as **winter flounder** or **summer flounder.** [*OED* 1710 →] **Atl coast, esp NEng**

1716 Church *Philip's War* 29 *(DAE),* They . . saw a vast company of Indians, . . some at Foot-ball, some catching Eels & Flat-fish in the water, some Clamming. **1790** (1905) Bentley *Diary* 1.156 **eMA,** The Season very open, & boats out in every place, successful in taking the flat fish, with which our harbour abounds. **1819** Dana *Geog. Sketches* 53, Those [=fish] most worthy of note [include] . . suckers, sturgeon, hickory shad, flat fish, salmon. **1879** U.S. Natl. Museum *Bulletin* 14.26, *Pseudopleuronectes americanus* . . Flat-fish. **1887** Goode *Amer. Fishes* 321, Next in importance to the Plaice, comes the Flat Fish, *Pseudopleuronectes americanus.* **1898** U.S. Natl. Museum *Bulletin* 47.2647, *Pseudopleuronectes americanus* . . Common Flatfish. **1933** John G. Shedd Aquarium *Guide* 71, Winter Flounder; Common Flatfish. . . The Flatfish . . is an equally important food fish along the Atlantic coast. **1939** Natl. Geogr. Soc. *Fishes* 42, *Winter Flounder.* . . The most remarkable feature of the flatfishes is their flatness. **1946** LaMonte *N. Amer. Game Fishes* 96, *Winter Flounder.* . . Names: Flatfish. **1968–69** *DARE* (Qu. P2, *[In saltwater areas] What kinds of saltwater fish caught around here are good to eat?*) Infs **CT**13, 17, 23, 26, **MA**40, **RI**6, 8, 15, Flatfish; **CT**39, Flats. **1972** Sparano *Outdoors Encycl.* 384, *Summer Flounder*—Common Names: . . flatfish. Scientific Name: *Paralichthys dentatus.* . . *Winter Flounder*—Common Names: . . flatfish. Scientific Name: *Pseudopleuronectes americanus.* **1982** Heat Moon *Blue Highways* 349 **ME,** From the CB [=Citizens' Band radio] we hear the day's prices for "flats" (flatfish).

3 A freshwater fish, as:

a A fish of the family Centrarchidae, usu any of several of the genus *Lepomis,* but see quots.

1935 Caine *Game Fish* 26, [Freshwater Game Fish:] Red-breasted Sunfish—*Lepomis auritus*—*Synonyms:* . . Flatfish . . Roach . . Sunfish. **1949** Caine *N. Amer. Sport Fish* 42, *Colloquial Names.* Lest the following list of names sound like something dreamed up in idle moments, it is best to explain that this plethora of nicknames cover the pumpkinseed and its six closely related cousins [=*Lepomis auritus, L. cyanellus, L. gulosus, L. megalotis, L. microlophus, L. punctatus*]. . . Bream or Brim, . . Flatfish. **1950** *PADS* 14.29 **SC,** *Flat fish.* . . Any fish of a short flat shape, as bream, warmouth, crappie, etc. **1966–69** *DARE* (Qu. P1, *What kinds of freshwater fish are caught around here that are good to eat?*) Inf **NH**14, Flatfish—same as panfish; (Qu. P3, *Freshwater fish that are not good to eat*) Infs **MA**6, Flatfish—same as pumpkin ['pʌŋkɨn] seed; **MA**68, Flatfish.

b A **gizzard shad 1** (here: *Dorosoma cepedianum*).

1956 Harlan–Speaker *IA Fish* 60, *Gizzard Shad.* . . *Other Names* . . flatfish. . . The gizzard shad is a flat, compressed, silvery fish that strongly resembles the other members of the shad family. **1983** Becker *Fishes WI* 273, *Dorosoma cepedianum.* . . Flatfish. . . Body oblong, deep, strongly compressed laterally.

flatfoot n

1 also attrib: =**buck-and-wing** n. Cf **flatfoot** v

1951 *DE Folkl. Bulletin* Oct 8/1 (as of c1870–1900), At night, a crowd of neighbors gathered and shucked the corn. They sang, talked, and danced the "flat foot" when their work was done. **1967–68** *DARE* (Qu. FF5a, . . *Figures in dancing—in past years*) Inf **SC**31, Flatfoot—buck dance; **VA**13, Flatfoot. **1967** *DARE* Tape **TX**49, [FW:] Was that a square dance, or what? [Inf:] Oh, just flatfoot dancing. Get together lots o' times and some feller 'd pat, you know? **1977** Nevell *Time to Dance* 188 **sAppalachians,** We just did the old buck and wing dances . . some call it 'flatfoot,' or 'cloggin,' 'buckdancin' ' but it's all the same.

2 Used as a derog nickname for:

a A sailor.

1835 *Knickerbocker* 5.23, While a man-of-war comes in at one end, we can slip out at the other. If this does not prove that Jemmy Flatfoot had a hand in laying out the coast of Africa, you may call me a marine. **1914** *DN* 4.150 [Navy slang], *Flatfoot.* . . A sailor. **1928** Nason *Sergeant Eadie* 41, I'll crown the flatfoot that gave me that basin.

b also *flatfeet, flatty:* A police officer. [With special ref to walking the beat]

1913 Stringer *Shadow* 48 **NYC,** By the time he had fought his way up to the office of Second Deputy he no longer resented being known as . . a "flat foot." **1921** *DN* 5.112 **CA,** *Flat-foot.* . . A policeman. **1926** Finerty *Criminalese* 20, *Flatty*—A plain clothes officer. *Ibid* 22, *Flatfeet*—Policeman. **1927** *DN* 5.446 [Underworld jargon], *Flatty.* . . A policeman. . . Also *flat-foot.* **1950** *WELS (Joking names or nicknames for a policeman)* 40 Infs, **WI,** Flatfoot. **1960** Bailey *Resp. to PADS 20* **KS,** There was only one policeman and he was called "the marshall," seldom "flatfoot," "the law" or "cop."

c also *flat-footed Dutch:* A German. Cf **flathead 4**

1967 *DARE* (Qu. HH28, . . *Nicknames . . for . . Germans*) Inf **TX**35, Flatfoot; **IA**3, Flat-footed Dutch—used in a heavily German community.

d An Irish person.

1968 *DARE* (Qu. HH28, . . *Nicknames for . . Irish*) Inf **VA**15, Flatfeet.

flatfoot v [**flatfoot** n **1**]

1976 Garber *Mountain-ese* 30 **sAppalachians,** *Flat-foot* (v) dance solo —When the fiddle played, all the old timers started to flat-foot.

flatfoot adj

=barefooted 1.

1986 Pederson *LAGS Concordance,* 1 inf, **swAL,** Flatfoot—black coffee.

flat-footed adj

1 Forthright, straightforward, emphatic. Cf **flat-footed** adv

1828 Royall *Black Book* 2.114 **VA,** He was one of your right down flat-footed ox-drivers. **1854** *Knickerbocker* 43.439 **TX,** A *'Flat-Footed Candidate'* for Justice of the Peace . . comes out . . with the following address. **1916** Thoburn *Std. Hist. OK* 2.712, The republican platform . . came out with a flat-footed declaration in favor of immediate statehood for Oklahoma. **1927** *AmSp* 2.354 **WV,** He stands flat-footed in that matter, and will not change his mind. **1928** *Ruppenthal Coll.* **KS,** Flat footed—emphatic; clear; unequivocal. **c1960** *Wilson Coll.* **csKY,** *Flat-footed:* adj. and adv. Plain, forthright; unequivocally.

2 Of food: plain, without further preparation or admixture. Cf **flat** adj

1952 *Hench Coll.* **cnVA,** I like them [=canned tomatoes] flat-footed out of a jar as much as any other way.

3 Unprepared, surprised.

1912 *Amer. Mag.* June 202/2 [Baseball terms], Flat-footed—Unprepared, caught napping. **1943** *Sun* (Baltimore MD) 19 Aug 9/2 *(Hench Coll.),* The pilot stood flat-footed, too bumbfounded [sic] to return the salute. **1945** *New Yorker* 25 Aug 15 **NYC,** Caught flat-footed, like everybody else. **1970** *DARE* (Qu. KK42b, . . *A person who does something very easily: "He could do that ______."*) Inf **TX**95, Standing flat-footed.

flat-footed adv Also *flat-footedly* [**flat-footed** adj **1**] **chiefly SMidl, Sth** Cf **cold-footed** adv

Firmly, frankly, bluntly.

1846 *NY Herald* (NY) 30 June 3/6, Mr. Pickens . . has come out flat-footed for the administration—a real red-hot democrat, dyed in the wool. **1884** Johnston *Old Mark* 171 **GA,** Well—devilish is the word, to come down flatfooted. **1898** Westcott *Harum* 343 **nNY,** Tenaker . . wanted to know flat-footed which side the fence I was on. **1903** *DN* 2.313 **seMO,** I told him flat-footed what I thought of him. **1906** *DN* 3.136 **nwAR,** *Flat-footed.* . . Bluntly. **1908** *DN* 3.311 **eAL, wGA,** *Flat-footed.* . . Plainly, bluntly, resolutely. **1912** *Eve. Post* (NY NY) 4 Jan 4/3, Evans . . told him flat-footedly that American ships would always exact . . punishment for disrespect to Americans. **1941** Percy *Lanterns* 293 **wMS** [Black], He wuz hoppin' mad en told him flat-footed to git out en stay out. **1960** Criswell *Resp. to PADS 20* **Ozarks,** She came out flat-footed against any plan to send the girls to the convention alone. **c1960** [see **flatfooted adj 1**]. **1966–70** *DARE* (Qu. JJ24, *To refuse firmly: "He wanted to get some more money, but this time I ______."*) Inf **GA**11, Told him flat-footed; (Qu. KK51, *Very plainly or abruptly: "I asked him ______ what he meant by that."*) Inf **GA**67, Flat-footed; **OK**18, [I] come right out flat-footed and asked him.

flat-footed Dutch See **flatfoot** n **2c**

flat-footed in the corn field adj phr

Ignorant, unsophisticated.

1966 *DARE* FW Addit **FL**8, Flat-footed in the corn field—descriptive of a country Negro who is Country Negro all the way—i.e. uneducated, lazy, nonchalant. "My maid's daughter, who is flat-footed in the corn field anyway, told me she just loves *guts* when she meant *tripe!*"

flat-footedly See **flat-footed** adv

flatfoot floozy n Also *flatfoot flooty*

A person with big feet.

1968–70 *DARE* (Qu. X38) Inf **GA**44, Flatfoot flooty; **MS**86, Flatfoot floozy.

flatfoot walk v phr

Of a horse: prob to execute the flatfoot walk, in which each forefoot is followed immediately by the diagonal hind foot.

1967 *DARE* Tape **TX**49, He wouldn't ride the old horse any faster than 'e could just flat-foot walk, 'flap, flap, flap, flap.'

flatform n Pronc-sp *flatfawm, flatfo'm* [Folk-etym for *platform*] **chiefly Sth, S Midl, NEng**

1892 *DN* 1.233 **KY,** *Flatform.* **1899** (1912) Green *VA Folk-Speech* 177, I saw him standing on the *flatform* when the train came in. **1917** Torrence *Granny Maumee* 52 **Sth,** I done give you de plankses in my flatfo'm an' I'm a-goin' to stan' on hit. **1922** Gonzales *Black Border* 301 **sSC, GA coasts** [Gullah glossary], *Flatfawm*—platform, platforms. **1934** *Hanley Disks* **csCT,** The flatform of the buggy was all open. **1952** Brown *NC Folkl.* 1.541, *Flatform* Platform.—Central and east. **1962** Faulkner *Reivers* 144 **MS** [Black], What we needs is to either move that flatform or that boxcar. **1966–70** *DARE* (Qu. D16, . . *Parts added on to the main part of a house*) Inf **LA**6, Used to be, the kitchen was not attached to the house; there was a flatform leading from one to the other; (Qu. L57, *A low wooden platform used for bringing . . heavy things out of the field*) Inf **NC**8, Flatform—old-fashioned for *platform;* **VA**49, Flatform. **1975** Gould *ME Lingo* 97, *Flatform*—A boarded area usually at a back door but not connected to the house or foundation. A walkway where mud and snow may be stamped off boots. **1979** *AmSp* 54.98 **seME** (as of 1899–1910), *Flatform.* **1986** Pederson *LAGS Concordance, (Porch)* 2 infs, **GA,** Flatform; *(Wharf)* 1 inf, **cnAL,** Flatform.

flat frame See **flat** n[1] **4b**

flat grass See **flat rush**

flathead n

1 A foolish, stupid person; hence adj *flatheaded.*

1884 Twain *Huck. Finn* 229 **Missip Valley,** Greenhorns, flatheads! **1919** *DN* 5.61 **CA, NM,** *Flat-head,* a foolish person. **1929** *Harper's Mth. Mag.* 385/2 **cnCT,** The speaker was a flatheaded idiot. **1942** Berrey–Van den Bark *Amer. Slang* 433.3, *Stupid person* . . flat-head. **1950** *WELS* 1 Inf, **eWI,** Dumbbell, dumb dora, flathead.

2 In logging: a **faller** or sawyer. [Perh from **flatheaded borer,** in allusion to the production of sawdust]

1917 *DN* 4.421 **wLA,** *Flathead.* . . A man who fells trees for the saw-mills. **c1974** Jones *Ozark Hill Boy* 15, [It] was a thriving mill town being made up of loggers, . . timber cutters (flat heads) who cut timber with cross-cut saws and axes, section hands (snipes) . . , the train crews . . and the mill hands.

3 Prob **=niggerhead.** Cf **hardhead 7, roundhead**

1950 *WELS (Other kinds of stones)* 1 Inf, **ceWI,** Flatheads.

4 Used as a nickname for a member of a particular ethnic or social group.

1956 Ker *Vocab. W. TX* 368, Jew (nicknames). . . Flathead [1 inf]. **1966** Dakin *Dial. Vocab. Ohio R. Valley* 2.453, There is ample evidence that it [=*hoosier*] was originally a pejorative term comparable to the *Flatheads* of the Illinois–Ohio lowlands. **1967–69** *DARE* (Qu. HH28) Infs **IL**17, **IN**32, **MO**39, [German:] Flathead; **WI**37, Dakota flatheads —a name given to German settlers of Dakota, Wisconsin. **1989** *NY Times* (NY) 13 Dec 31/1 **cnMD** (as of 1930s–1940s), [Newspaper column:] The many Lithuanians in the neighborhood were called, for some unfathomable reason, "flatheads."

5 An animal without horns; see quot.

1967–68 *DARE* (Qu. K12, *A cow that never had horns*) Inf **NY**2, Flathead; (Qu. P35a, . . *Deer shot illegally*) Inf **NY**92, A doe is a flathead.

6 See quot.

1969 *DARE* (Qu. I23, . . *Kinds of squash . . around here*) Inf **GA**72, Flatheads.

7 See **flathead catfish 1.**

8 See **flathead chub.**

9 See **flatheaded adder.**

10 See **flatheaded borer.**

11 See **flathead snake 2.**

12 See **flathead mockingbird.**

flathead adder See **flatheaded adder**

flathead catfish n

1 also *flathead, ~ cat:* A large, yellowish-brown, mottled catfish *(Pylodictis olivaris)* characterized by a flattened head, and native chiefly to the Mississippi and Ohio River drainages and the Gulf States. Also called **appaloosa** n[2], **bashaw, cushawn, flatbelly** n[1], **goujon, granny cat, hoosier B4, johnny cat, Mississippi bullhead, Mississippi cat, morgan cat, mud catfish, niggerbelly, Opelousas cat, pied cat, river cat, Russian cat, shovelhead cat, yellow cat**

1946 Stilwell *Hunting in TX* 108, Those flatheads on the West Pecos are fine fish . . practically "salted down" by the cold spring water. **1946** LaMonte *N. Amer. Game Fishes* 163, *Flathead Catfish.* . . Very abundant in the Lower Mississippi Valley, in large, sluggish rivers. **1947** *Watonga* (Okla.) *Republican* 31 July 1/4 *(DA),* Monday he was showing a live Flathead catfish in his back yard that he claims is the largest to be brought in. **1956** Harlan-Speaker *IA Fish* 112, The color of the flathead cat is dark to olive-brown with dark brownish mottlings on the sides. **1965-70** *DARE* (Qu. P1, . . *Freshwater fish . . that are good to eat*) Infs **AR**55, **IA**22, 29, **IL**81, 119, **KY**23, 53, **OK**25, Flathead(s); **OK**11, **TX**88, Flathead catfish; **MS**1, Yellow flathead; (Qu. P14) Inf **IL**81, Flatheads. **1968** *Julesburg Grit-Advocate* (CO) 7 Feb, Among the many fish caught in Nebraska each year are a number which are worthy of the Master Angler Award. . . Flathead catfish . . 49 pounds.

2 as *flatheaded cat:* =**flat bullhead.**

1877 U.S. Natl. Museum *Bulletin* 10.93, *Amiurus platycephalus. . . Flat-headed Cat.* . . North Carolina to Georgia. **1902** Jordan-Evermann *Amer. Fishes* 31, *Flatheaded Cat; Brown Cat* . . is regarded as a good food-fish. **1911** *Century Dict. Suppl., Cat*[1]. . . *Flatheaded cat,* the mud catfish of Carolina, *Ameiurus* [sic] *platycephalus.*

flathead chub n Also *flathead, flatheaded chub*

A silvery minnow *(Hybopsis gracilis)* with a broad, depressed head, often used for bait.

1882 U.S. Natl. Museum *Bulletin* 16.219, *P. gracilis. . . Flat-headed Chub.* . . Head small and short, its upper surface very broad and depressed. **1896** *Ibid* 47.326, *Flat-headed Chub.* **1956** Harlan-Speaker *IA Fish* 90, The flathead chub . . is a beautiful silvery minnow with large sickle-like fins. **1968** *DARE* (Qu. P1) Inf **MN**15, Flathead—a small fish. **1971** Brown *Fishes MT* 90, The flathead chub is probably an important forage fish for sauger, northern pike and channel catfish.

flatheaded See **flathead 1**

flatheaded adder n Also *flathead (adder), flathead snake* [See quot 1952]

=**hognose snake.**

1875 *Amer. Naturalist* 9.10 **NJ,** I have known the Flat-head Adder or Blowing Viper, *Heterodon platyrhinos,* to eat the heads of the common eel. **1888** *Pop. Sci. Mth.* 33.660, The blow-snake of Illinois is variously known in other localities as hog-nose, flat-head, viper, and puff-adder. **1952** Ditmars *N. Amer. Snakes* 34, Flat-headed "Adder". . . When frightened it flattens the neck . . its head also becomes broad and flat and is moved in threatening fashion, while the snake exhales the breath in sharp hisses. **1968-70** *DARE* (Qu. P25) Infs **CT**39, **MA**42, Flatheaded adder; **CT**13, Flatheaded adder—a puff adder; **VA**61, Flathead snake.

flatheaded borer n Also *flathead (sawyer)* [See quot 1926]

A larva of a buprestid beetle. Also called **hammerhead 7**

1882 (1903) Treat *Injurious Insects* 144, *The Flat-headed Apple-tree Borer.* . . In consequence of its immensely broad and flattened head, it bores a hole of an oval shape, and twice as wide as high. **1889** Edwards *Runaways* 16 **GA,** Isam displayed his simple tackle, . . cut a pole from a neighboring brake, and, peeling the bark from a fallen tree, picked out a handful of flatheads. **1905** Kellogg *Amer. Insects* 266, The whole [buprestid] larva is thus a footless whitish tadpole-like grub expressively known as a flat-headed . . borer. **1908** *DN* 3.311 **eAL, wGA,** *Flathead.* . . A wood-worm found burrowing in dead wood, especially dead pine trees. **1926** Essig *Insects N. Amer.* 395, The larvae [of the family *Buprestidae*] are known as flat-headed borers because of the greatly enlarged and flattened thoracic segments. **c1940** Eliason *Word Lists FL* 8, *Flathead:* A certain species of worms that infest dead pine trees a short time after the trees have been cut down. The worms are used for fish bait. **1949** Swain *Insect Guide* 130, Evidencing some confusion as to just what constitutes a "head," the popular name for the buprestid larva is "flatheaded borer." **1965-67** *DARE* (Qu. P5) Inf **FL**18, Flathead; (Qu. P6) Inf **AL**17, Flatheads—on pine; (Qu. P13) Inf **GA**5, Flathead sawyer ['sajə]. A white worm one inch long, lives in dead pines.

flatheaded cat See **flathead catfish 2**

flatheaded chub See **flathead chub**

flathead mockingbird n Also *flathead*

=**loggerhead shrike.**

1911 *Forest & Stream* 77.174, *Lanius ludovicianus.* Flat- Head, Galveston, Tex. **1968** *DARE* (Qu. Q14) Inf **LA**20, Flat-head mockingbird: [same as] shrike.

flathead sawyer See **flatheaded borer**

flathead snake n

1 See **flatheaded adder.**

2 also *flathead:* A small, glossy light brown snake *(Tantilla gracilis).*

1984 Tennant *Snakes TX* 86, Flathead snakes are probably the second most abundant . . of the small, soil-colored serpents that turn up in flower beds and gardens. . . The oak-juniper brakes of the central hill country are good flathead habitat.

flathead sturgeon n

=**shovelnose sturgeon.**

1956 Harlan-Speaker *IA Fish* 48, *Shovelnose Sturgeon—Scaphirhynchus platorynchus* . . *—Other Names*—Sand Sturgeon, . . flat-head sturgeon. **1983** Becker *Fishes WI* 227, *Shovelnose Sturgeon—Scaphirhynchus platorynchus* . . Other common names: hackleback, . . flathead sturgeon.

flat-heeled puncher n [From farmers' low-heeled boots]

1968 Adams *Western Words* 115, *Flat-heeled puncher*—An amateur cowboy; a farmer turned cowboy.

flatiron n, often attrib

Something that resembles a flatiron, as:

a A broad shallow boat with a pointed prow.

1886 *Outing* 8.58/1 **FL,** There are . . the 'pumpkinseed', and the 'flat-iron' models [of boats]. **1968** *DARE* (Qu. O1, . . *A small rowboat*) Inf **CT**17, Flatiron—pointed.

b The triangular plot of ground formed when two streets meet at an acute angle; a building erected on such a lot.

1966-68 *DARE* (Qu. C35, . . *Parts of . . town*) Inf **OH**41, Flatiron—that's the shape of N. Eighth St.; (Qu. N32, . . *Where roads cross*) Inf **ME**5, Where they branch it's the crotch in the road, and the triangular piece of land is the flatiron piece. **1968** *DARE* File **NC,** Flat iron building—A building shaped like a flatiron. Used with me to describe a building at a fork in a road. **1970** *DARE* Tape **CA**179, Flatiron building—exactly like an iron . . comes to a point . . like a triangle.

flatjack n **chiefly NEast** Cf *DNE*

=**flapjack 1.**

1830 Child *Frugal Housewife* 79 **MA,** Flat-jack, or fritters, do not differ from pancakes, only in being mixed softer. . . only most people prefer to have no sweetening put in them, because they generally have butter, sugar, and nutmeg put on them, after they are done. . . They are not to be boiled in fat, like pancakes. **1846** Howland *N.E. Econ. Housekeeper* 25 *(DA),* Common Flat-Jacks, No. 1. Indian Flat-Jacks, No. 2. 26 Indian Griddle Cakes, or Flat-Jacks, No. 3. Rice Flat-Jacks, No. 4. **1891** *AN&Q* 6.179/1, The terms fritters and flat-jacks are very common to Pennsylvania at the present time, and especially to the county of Lancaster. **1906** *Pocumtuc Housewife* 22 **MA,** *Flat-Jacks or Fritters.* . . Either flour, Indian or rye is good for flat-jacks. **1970** *DARE* (Qu. H20b) Inf **PA**239, Flatjacks.

flatland n, sometimes pl

1 A broad area of relatively level land; sometimes used by mountain dwellers as derog term for other areas. Cf **flatlander, flatwoods**

1735 *Springfield Rec.* II. 505 *(DAE),* In the Said Ledge Hill then over Rocky flatland we found a Small white marked & Renewed it. **1836** Hall *Statistics* 31 **Ohio R Valley,** That [water] which overflows the flat lands, will be stagnant, or flow gently backward in eddies. **1913** London *Valley of Moon* I.xi *(DAE)* **CA,** Beneath them stretched the flatlands to the bay. **1956** Ker *Vocab. W. TX* 77, High, flat land . . flat land. [2 infs] **1961** Folk *Word Atlas N. LA* map 209, Waste land where trees have been cut . . others . . flat land. **1965-70** *DARE* (Qu. C29, *A good-sized stretch of level land with practically no trees*) 45 Infs, **scattered exc NEng,** Flatland; Inf **NY**84, Stretch of flatland; **CO**18, **IN**35, **NY**31, Flatlands; (Qu. HH31, *Somebody who is not from your community, and doesn't belong*) Inf **NY**92, Flatland foreigner. **1980** *NADS Letters,* People in eastern Kentucky also frequently call the rest of the state the Flatlands (even though the entire state is rather hilly).

2 An area of low land between hills.

1965-70 *DARE* (Qu. C19) 11 Infs, **chiefly east of Missip R,** Flatland; **MO**26, Flatlands, (Qu. C20; total Infs questioned, 75) Inf **FL**7, Flatlands.

flatlander n **[flatland 1]**

A person from the plains; hence, from the perspective of mountain dwellers, an outsider, a hick, an incompetent person.

1958 McCulloch *Woods Words* 64 **Pacific NW,** *Flatlander*—A farmer; a workman who has moved from the prairie states; anyone not a mountain logger. **1961** *AmSp* 36.272 **West, Pacific NW** [Truck drivers' language], Notice the derogatory humor in the term *flatlander* for a reckless driver, expressing contempt for the outsider's inability to cope with our crooked mountain roads. **1967–68** *DARE* (Qu. HH1, . . *Nicknames for a rustic*) Inf **NY**7, Flatlander; (Qu. HH31, *Somebody who is not from your community, and doesn't belong*) Infs **AR**39, **CA**106, 197, **NY**7, Flatlander. **1976** Garber *Mountain-ese* 30 **sAppalachians,** We make a pile uv money sellin' our mountain dodads to flatlanders. **1980** *Verbatim Letters* **cwVT,** Flat-lander is another term to describe someone from Massachusetts, Connecticut, New York, or New Jersey who comes to Vermont to visit or to live. It definitely implies one from the southern part of the Northeast. **1982** Heat Moon *Blue Highways* 326 **NY,** Unlike some of the villagers—many from other states—the Bagleys showed no animosity toward "flatlanders" (anyone from outside the Green or White Mountains) who kept the town prosperous.

flatland plow n **NY, nPA** *old-fash* Cf **side hill plow**

A plow with a fixed moldboard, usable only on flat ground.

1968–70 *DARE* (Qu. L18, *Kinds of plows . . present and . . past*) Inf **NY**72, Flatland plow—stationary moldboard; **NY**75, Flatland plow—fixed moldboard; sidehill plow—moldboard turned over; **NY**117, Flatland plow—blade in the center; sidehill plow—blade hinged; **NY**224, 233, Flatland plow; **PA**103, Flatland plow—old-fashioned. [All Infs old]

flatly adv

Certainly, surely—used as a mild intensive.

1968 *DARE* FW Addit **nwLA,** Y'all flatly got the heat back here a-blowin'.

flat mail n

1959 McAtee *Oddments* 6 **NC,** *Flat mail* . . magazines.

flat net n Cf **balloon net**

A type of net used in catching shrimp.

1966–67 *DARE* Tape **SC**18, Balloon nets and flat nets are the two main types [of shrimp nets]; **TX**14, What we use most in the bays is what we call a flat net, and it spreads open and the bottom portion will drag on the bottom and it'll have a set of boards . . to spread it and then the top . . will have a cork line on it.

flat-nosed bony pike n *obs* Cf **bony pike**

=shortnose gar.

1842 DeKay *Zool. NY* 4.273, *The Flat-nosed Bony Pike. Lepisosteus platyrhincus.* . . This species is found in Florida and the western rivers, and will probably be found in some of their sources within this State.

flat-out adv Rarely *flat-up* **chiefly Sth, Midl** Cf **flat-footed** adv

Plainly, directly.

1934 (1943) *W2*, *Flat-out.* . . Openly, directly. *Dial.* **1945** *AmSp* 20.82 **TX,** I flat-out told him I wasn't about to carry him down to Santone. **1966–68** *DARE* (Qu. KK51, *Very plainly or abruptly: "I asked him ______ what he meant by that."*) Infs **AR**51, **MD**30, **WV**3, **SC**8, Flat-out; **DE**3, Flat-up. **1972** *Atlanta Letters,* I told her flat out.

flat-out adj

1906 *DN* 3.136 **nwAR,** *Flat-out.* . . Frank, direct. "Didn't I ask you the flat-out question, whether you were there?"

flat out v phr

To decrease in intensity or value; to fade out.

1939 *LANE* Map 92 *(The wind is ______)* 2 infs, **Martha's Vineyard MA,** Flatting out. **1942** Whipple *Joshua* 489 **UT** (as of c1860), When midnight came and Clory's [labor] pains had 'flatted out' . . the anxious sisters burned feathers to coax her back to fight. **1967** *DARE* FW Addit **MA**5, His business all flatted out to nothing. [Said of a man who made scythe snaths.]

flat plow See **flat-bottom(ed) plow**

flatrack wagon n

=hay flat.

1969 *DARE* (Qu. L13, *The kind of wagon used for carrying hay*) Inf **MI**101, A wagon called a flatrack wagon was underneath the hay rack.

flatrail fence n

See quot 1966.

1966 Dakin *Dial. Vocab. Ohio R. Valley* 2.102, The occasional terms *flat rail fence* and *split rail fence* are plainly contrasting names used to distinguish between the post and rail fence with hewn rails and any of the several types constructed of split rails. **1983** *MJLF* 9.1.39 **ceKY,** *Flatrail fence.* . . a post and railing fence.

flat rush n Also *flat grass*

=cattail 1.

1941 *Torreya* 41.45, *Typhaceæ.* . . *Typha latifolia* . . Flat grass, Santee Club, S. C. **1942** *Ibid* 42.157, *Typha* spp.—Queue de chat, flat rush . . Louisiana.

flat salt v phr, hence ppl adj phr *flat salted*

1933 *Hanley Disks* **neMA,** Father always bought every fall a lot of pollock and flat salted them himself out in our yard. . . Every night he would . . take them in and every morning he would put them out for a week or two. . . They weren't so salt as salt fish are now. They're sweet. . . He'd have barrels and poles, clothes poles, to go across, and then put them on that. . . [They had] what they called flat salted pollock. That was an eating fish without cooking.

flatter v^1 [Cf *OED flatter up* (at *flatter* v.^{1} 10) "to indulge unduly, pamper, 'coddle'. . . *Obs.*"]

To spoil, pamper (a child).

1968 *DARE* (Qu. Z14a, *To give a child its own way or pay too much attention to it: "Everyone ______ that child."*) Inf **LA**37, Babies, flatters.

flatter v^2 [Perh Scots and Engl dial *flatter* to float, flutter]

See quot.

1978 *Smithsonian* May 82 **Brooklyn NYC,** Allan speaks with humorous scorn, too, when he mentions a "zorro," a mumbler who never raises his flock [of pigeons] up at all but keeps "poking" or "flattering" his birds with the long pole, just enough to get them to fly from the roof to the top of the coop and back again, luring strays down without risking one bird.

flatter n^1

1 One who works on a **flatboat n 1a.** **[flat n^1 3]**

1933 Blair–Meine *Mike Fink* 106 **Missip Valley** (as of c1815), Come on, you flatters, you bargers, you milk-white mechanics, an' see how tough I am to chaw! **1941** Baldwin *Keelboat Age* 97 **New Orleans LA** (as of 1840s), The eyes she was makin' . . might fetch a greenhorn or a flatter.

2 See quot. [Perh **flat n^1 1e**] Cf **flatlander**

1966 *DARE* (Qu. HH18, *Very insignificant or low-grade people*) Inf **IA**46, Flatters.

flatter n^2 [*flat* to level]

A plank dragged over the surface of a tobacco field to prepare the ground for planting.

1967 Key *Tobacco Vocab.* **CT,** We call it a flatter; in the South it's a smoothing board.

flat tobacco n Also *flat-cake tobacco* Cf **flat n^1 6**

Chewing tobacco formed in flat cakes.

1953 Randolph–Wilson *Down in Holler* 244 **Ozarks,** *Flat 'backer.* . . Plug tobacco. **1954** *Harder Coll.* **cwTN,** We used to call it flat tobacco. **1967–69** *DARE* (Qu. DD1, . . *Different forms [of] . . chewing tobacco*) Inf **AR**47, Flat-cake tobacco; **KY**39, Flat or sweet tobacco—comes pressed in cakes about a half-inch thick.

flat-toned adj Cf **flat-down**

1940 *Hench Coll.* **cVA,** Flat-toned—downright, absolute. "That's flat-toned selfishness."

flattop n

1 An **ironweed:** usu *Vernonia noveboracensis,* but also *V. altissima.*

1822 Eaton *Botany* 508, *Vernonia noveboracensis,* flat top. **1832** MA Hist. Soc. *Coll.* 2d ser 9.157 **cwVT,** Vernonia noveboracensis, Flat-top. **1859** (1968) Bartlett *Americanisms* 218, *Iron Weed* . . called in the North-eastern States Flat Top, almost the only tall weed found in the beautiful "woods pastures" of Kentucky and Tennessee. Western. **1900** Lyons *Plant Names* 391, *Vernonia Noveboracensis* . . Flat-top. **1914** Georgia *Manual Weeds* 412, *Tall Ironweed or Flat-top. Vernonia altissima.* . . This great weed is the despair of the prairie farmer.

2 A **wild buckwheat:** usu *Eriogonum fasciculatum,* but also *E. plumatella.* **esp CA**

1911 CA Ag. Exper. Sta. Berkeley *Bulletin* 217.989, Wild Buckwheat. Flat Top. . . Honey light amber, of agreeable flavor, and subject to granulation. **1911** Jepson *Flora CA* 132, *E. fasciculatum*. . . Flat-top . . is the third most valued native bee-plant after White Sage and Black Sage. **1937** U.S. Forest Serv. *Range Plant Hdbk.* B75, Flat-top buckwheatbrush . . , also called . . flat-top, . . is common, sometimes even abundant, in canyons and on dry mountain slopes and mesas. **1941** Jaeger *Wildflowers* 34 **Desert SW,** *Flat-top. Eriogonum plumatella*. . . Ascending stems . . are peculiarly forked above and horizontally branched to form flattish "platforms." **1961** Thomas *Flora Santa Cruz* 143 **CA,** Flat-top. . . Native from Monterey County southward.

3 In logging: see quot.

1950 *Western Folkl.* 9.381 **nCA,** *Flat top.* A tree that has flattened out on top and signifies maximum growth in height.

4 See quot.

1967 *DARE* (Qu. X38, . . *Unusually big or clumsy feet*) Inf **TX**5, Flattops.

flat trout See **flat** n[1] **12**

flatty See **flatfoot** n **2b**

flat-up See **flat-out** adv

flatweed n

A **cat's ear 2** (here: *Hypochoeris radicata*).

1935 (1943) Muenscher *Weeds* 503, *Hypochoeris radicata*. . . Flatweed. . . Very abundant on the Pacific Coast.

flat wheel n

One who walks with a limp.

1931 *Writer's Digest* 11.41 [Railroad terms], *Flat Wheel*—A car wheel that has flat spots on the tread; also applied to an employee who walks lame or limps. **1938** Beebe *High Iron* 220 [Railroad terms], *Flat wheel:* A lame train employee. **1942** Berrey–Van den Bark *Amer. Slang* 431.3, *Cripple*. . . flat-wheel. *Ibid* 772.1 [Railroad terminology], Flat-wheel, *a lame person.* **1957** Battaglia *Resp. to PADS 20* **eMD,** *(When a person who is walking steps more heavily on one foot than the other)* Flat wheel. Recent. **1958** McCulloch *Woods Words* 64 **Pacific NW,** *Flatwheel*—A lame man.

flatwoods n pl, but sg or pl in constr

1 A level tree-covered area often low-lying and poorly drained. **chiefly Sth, S Midl**

1841 in 1940 *AmSp* 15.179 **VA,** Running up under the foot of the ridge to a large span oak tree and a forked sugar standing in a flat woods. **1849** *New Engl. Farmer* 1.235/1, A large portion of the land in Indiana, as well as some other of the Western States, is technically called "flat woods," "wet land," "black slashes," &c. **1866** Smith *Bill Arp* 122 **GA,** It won't buy the hide an tallow of [a] flatwoods heifer. **1903** *DN* 2.313 **seMO,** *Flat-woods*. . . Low-lying timbered lands, not swampy. **1936** *AmSp* 11.315 **Ozarks,** Flat-woods. . . The comparatively level timbered plateaus between the high ridges. **1938** FWP *Guide MS* 34, The Flatwoods, a narrow band of flat, poorly-drained land, sweeps in an open crescent around the western and southern margin of the Black Prairie and Pontotoc Ridge. **1939** FWP *Guide FL* 20, Flatwoods, common throughout the State, consist of poorly drained level areas, with a sour boggy soil. Although open forests constitute their chief vegetation, they contain an abundance of flowers. **1939** *Hall Coll.* **eTN,** [They] fought down into the flat woods at the point of the ridge. **1966** *DARE* (QR, near Qu. C29) Inf **FL**6, Flatwoods—lower than flatland, where trees grow and hold the water to form ponds and hammock places and cypress ponds; (Qu. C35, *Nicknames for . . parts of . . town*) Inf **AR**1, Flatwoods. **1975** Newell *If Nothin' Don't Happen* 172 **nwFL,** There was a heap of wildcats in the scrubs and bay heads and flatwoods along the edge of the Hammock.

2 See quot.

1933 *AmSp* 8.1.49 **Ozarks,** *Flatwoods*. . . Level lands which have been cleared of timber, as distinguished from the small prairies and *balds* which were treeless when the pioneers first came to the Ozarks.

flatwoodsman n Also pl *flatwoods folks* [**flatwoods 1**]

=**flatlander.**

1966 *DARE* (Qu. HH31, *Somebody who is not from your community, and doesn't belong*) Inf **AR**39, Foreigner, flatlander, flatwoodsman. **1967** *DARE* FW Addit **eTN,** Flatwoods folks—what the country people around Maryville call themselves. "Flatwoods folks are infinitely superior to mountaineers!"

flatwoods plum n

A **wild plum** (here: *Prunus umbellata*).

1960 Vines *Trees SW* 401, *Flatwoods Plum*. . . The fruit is used in considerable quantities for jellies and preserves. **1966** Grimm *Recognizing Native Shrubs* 147, *Flatwoods Plum*. . . *Range.* Southeastern North Carolina south to Florida, west to Texas, north in Mississippi Valley to Arkansas. **1979** Little *Checklist U.S. Trees* 216, *Prunus umbellata*. . . Flatwoods plum.

flaus n Also *flaws* [Ger "fleece, tuft"]

See quot 1967.

1950 *WELS Suppl.* **swWI,** [Inf] has known of people with German background who used the word *flaws* for rolls of dust. **1967** *DARE* (Qu. E20, *Soft rolls of dust that collect on the floor under beds or other furniture*) Inf **MI**68, Flaus [flaʊs].

flavor v

=**favor C1.**

1946 *AmSp* 21.190 **eKY,** *Favor,* sometimes *flavor* . . to resemble each other in appearance. . . 'Joline and Arwillie's sisters, but they don't flavor.'

flavor wart n

A taste bud.

1948 Manfred *Chokecherry* 66 **nwIA,** It's probably all in the recipe. Ma had one that raised the flavor warts on my tongue.

flaw n [*OED* 1513 →] **Atl coast, esp Mid Atl** *old-fash*

A sudden burst of wind, sometimes with rain.

1881 *Century Illustr. Mag.* 22.530/1 **NY,** The playful breeze freshens in flaws. **1899** (1912) Green *VA Folk-Speech* 178, *Flaw*. . . A sudden gust of wind. **1949** *AmSp* 24.108 **seSC,** *Flaw*. . . A squall; a sudden, brief, violent burst of wind and rain, generally over water. **1966–70** *DARE* (Qu. O12, *A disturbance caused by wind which seems to run and spread quickly along the surface of water*) Infs **MD**36, **NC**21, 23, 81, **SC**63, Flaw(s) (of wind); **NC**60, Flaw in water; (Qu. O19, . . *Kinds . . of wind that are important when you're in a boat*) Inf **MA**56, A flaw and a puff are about the same; a puff is a breeze that's steady and then lets up; (Qu. B14, *When the wind is blowing unevenly, sometimes strong and sometimes weak, you say it's* ______) Inf **MA**100, Coming in flaws, in puffs. [6 of 8 Infs old] **1971** Wood *Vocab. Change* 33 **Sth,** *Flaw* and *squall* are rare. **1976** Warner *Beautiful Swimmers* 265 **eMD,** He figured the wind at about twenty knots steady. "Some flaws . . come along, I guess we'll have plenty," he added.

flaws See **flaus**

flawy adj Usu |'flɔ(w)i|; also |'flɔri| (Cf Intro "Language Changes" I.8) [**flaw n**] **Atl coast**

Of the wind: gusty.

1805 (1808) Gass *Jrl.* 111 **WV,** The wind became flawy, and the sailing bad. **1881** *Century Illustr. Mag.* 22.530/2 **NY,** Pushing the yacht . . is often required in light, flawy wind. **1899** (1912) Green *VA Folk-Speech* 178, *Flawy*. . . Subject to sudden flaws or gusts of wind. **1966–69** *DARE* (Qu. B14, *When the wind is blowing unevenly, sometimes strong and sometimes weak, you say it's* ______) Inf **MD**43, ['flɔ-i]; **MA**55, ['flɔri]; **NC**25, ['flɔwi].

flax n

Std: a plant of the genus *Linum.* Also called **blue flax, yellow flax.** For other names of var spp see **blue buttercup, lint bells, sucker flax**

flax v

1 usu with *out:*

a To beat, thrash; also fig. [Appar in ref to the beating of flax; cf Engl dial *flaxen* to beat, thrash] *old-fash*

1839 *Daily Picayune* (New Orleans LA) 8 Mar 2/4 **NEng,** Now, it's my opinion, that if they du cum to hard blows the Maine boys 'll flax out them are Brunswickers like sixty. **c1849** Paige *Dow's Sermons* I.54 *(DA),* Either flax out your opponent, or give nature special fits in the undertaking. **1867** Lowell *Biglow* xlvii **MA,** *To flax* for *to beat.* **1900** in 1908 Handsaker *Pioneer Life* 43 **OR,** Yes you look like a votin for him again dont you when you and all the rest was flaxt outen your shoes when you voted for him before. **1916** Howells *Leatherwood God* 8 **OH** (as of 1820s), When the Spirit took him he roared so that he had the Hounds just flaxed out; you could n't ketch a yelp from 'em.

b To weary, tire; to become tired.

1891 (1967) Freeman *New Engl. Nun* 180, These dretful smart, handsome folks are just the ones that flax out sometimes. They ain't nothin' more'n Fourth of July fireworks; there's more sputter an' fizzle than anything else. **1903** *DN* 2.351 **neOH,** *Flax out. . .* To wear out; be weary. 'I'm all flaxed out.'

2 usu with *around:* To hurry, bustle. **chiefly Nth, esp NEng**

1841 *Daily Picayune* (New Orleans LA) 24 Mar 2/2 **VT,** I wish you'd flax round and git supper as fast as you can, 'cause I'm allfired hungry and tired tu. **1884** Baldwin *Yankee School-Teacher* 130, If you'll flax roun' an' hunt up some eggs, I'll be 'bleeged t' yer f'r once. **1903** *DN* 2.351 **cMA,** To flax around = to hurry and get one's work done or preparations made. **1905** *DN* 3.61 **eNE,** *Flax. . .* Hurry, be lively. "Flax round and get supper." **1909** *DN* 3.420 **Cape Cod MA** (as of a1857), Come, flax around and get cleared up. **1927** *AmSp* 3.138 **eME,** One who moved quickly was said to "flax around". **1935** Davis *Honey* 31 **eOR,** Clay put the signal fires out of his mind and flaxed down to try the sheep again. *Ibid* 32, So Big Beaver flaxed in and fixed them a world for them to keep themselves apart in. **1957** *Sat. Eve. Post Letters* **neKS** (as of 1900–08), I was told to "Flax around lively" or to see if I couldn't get dressed in "two shakes of a lamb's tail." **1974** Fink *Mountain Speech* 9 **wNC, eTN,** I'll flax around and git dinner. **1983** *DARE* File **ceWI,** Flaxing around—hurrying.

flax bellflower n Also *flax bell* [See quot 1840] *obs*

A **bellflower** (here: *Campanula rotundifolia*).

1822 Eaton *Botany* 216, *Campanula rotundifolia* . . flax bell-flower. **1839** in 1856 MI State Ag. Soc. *Trans.* 7.402 **sMI,** *Campanula . . rotundifolia,* Linn. Flax bell-flower. **1840** MA Zool. & Bot. Surv. *Herb. Plants & Quadrupeds* 109, As the stem leaves are long, linear, and give the plant the appearance of flax, it [=Scotch Bell] is sometimes called *Flax Bell.*

flax bird n [See quot 1955]

A **goldfinch 1** (here: *Spinus tristis*).

1823 Latham *Gen. Hist. Birds* 6.120, [American Goldfinch] feeds on the seeds of flax, alder, &c. and is called in the back parts of Carolina, the Flax Bird. **1931** *Randolph Enterprise* (Elkins W. Va.) 24 Sep. 5/4 *(DA),* We used to wonder why old folks of early days called the wild canary the 'beet bird' until this summer they eat [sic] our beet tops. They also called them flax birds. **1955** *Oriole* 20.13, *Goldfinch.—Flax Bird* (from feeding on the seeds of that plant).

flax blossom n

A **sea lavender** (here: *Limonium carolinianum*).

1966 *DARE* Wildfl QR Pl.166 Inf **SD6,** Flax blossom.

flax out See **flax** v **1**

flax seed n

A larva of the Hessian fly *(Mayetiola destructor).*

1862 in 1865 IL Dept. Ag. *Trans.* 5.485, Mr. Frick . . was kind enough to take me to a wheat stubble, full of Hessian flies in the 'flax seed' or pupa state. **1884** Kingsley *Std. Nat. Hist.* 2.410, The larvae [of the Hessian fly] . . assume the pupa state, called the flaxseed stage. **1886** *Times* (London) 18 Aug. 10/6 *(DA),* Pupae . . resembling small and rather elongated flax seeds . . are called 'flax seeds' in America.

flaxweed n

1 =**butter-and-eggs 1.**

1900 Lyons *Plant Names* 226, *L[inaria] vulgaris. . .* Flax-weed. **1936** IL Nat. Hist. Surv. *Wildflowers* 301, *Butter and Eggs. . .* Other names are Brideweed, Flaxweed, and Eggs and Bacon. **1959** Carleton *Index Herb. Plants* 47, *Flax-weed:* Linaria vulgaris; Sysimbrium sophia.

2 A **tansy mustard** (here: *Descurainia sophia*).

1959 [see **1** above].

flea v Also *flee* [Arch and Engl dial varr of *flay*]

1899 (1912) Green *VA Folk-Speech* 178, *Flea. . .* To flay off the skin. To skin. . . *Fleed. . .* Flayed; skinned.

flea n [Cf Ger *Flöhe* tiddledy winks (literally "fleas")]

1969 *DARE* (Qu. DD37, *Other table games played . . by adults*) Inf **MI93,** Flea—played with dice.

fleabag n

1 also *flea trap:* A bed or sleeping bag. *joc* or *derog*

1942 Berrey–Van den Bark *Amer. Slang* 86.2, *Bed* . . fleabag . . fleatrap. *Ibid* 86.7, *Sleeping bag* . . fleabag. **1968** Adams *Western Words* 115, *Fleabag*—A cowboy's name for his sleeping bag. . . *Flea trap*—A cowboy's name for his bedroll. **1976** Garber *Mountain-ese* 30 **sAppalachians,** Because we were broke, we had to sleep on a flea-bag in a cheap hotel.

2 also *flea house, ~ joint, ~ trap;* also attrib: A run-down hotel; by ext, a jail.

1931 Runyon *Guys* 94 **NY,** His room on the top floor of an old fleabag in Eighth Avenue that is called the Hotel de Brussels. **1946** Evans *Halo in Blood* 29 *(DAS),* The Laycroft Hotel, a flea trap on West Madison Street. **1966** *Natl. Observer* (Silver Spring MD) 30 May 8/4, He . . lived in oil-field shacks and fleabag hotels in dusty little Texas towns. **1969–70** *DARE* (Qu. V11, . . *Joking names . . for a . . jail*) Inf **CA**147, Flea joint; **TX**76, Flea house; **TX**76, 89, Fleabag. **1971** *AmSp* 46.77 **Chicago IL,** Shabby hotel: . . *flea bag, flea joint.* **1976** Gould *Blackie's RR Hdbk.* 18, Rooming house: flophouse—flea trap.

3 also *flea house:* A movie theater, esp one that is run down.

1951 *New Yorker* 30 June 22/1, [The movie] was unveiled at an owl show in a Forty-second Street flea bag. **1957** Battaglia *Resp. to PADS 20* **eMD,** *(Names . . for motion pictures)* Flea house. **1966** *DARE* (Qu. FF24, . . *Where people go to see motion pictures*) Inf **WA**16, Flea house.

4 also *fleabait, flea trap:* A low-grade animal, esp a dog; transf, a tramp.

1942 Berrey–Van den Bark *Amer. Slang* 120.11, *Dog* . . flea bag. **1961** Adams *Old-Time Cowhand* 322, There was the dog. Chances are he didn't look like a fighter and was nothin' but a lazy flea trap. **1961** Folk *Word Atlas N. LA* map 907, Worthless dog . . [less freq responses include] flea bag. **1968–69** *DARE* (Qu. J2, . . *Uncomplimentary words . . for dogs*) Infs **CT**21, **IL**86, **NC**63, **TN**31, Fleabag; (Qu. K44, *A bony . . horse*) Inf **LA**31, Fleabait; **MD**9, Fleabag; (Qu. HH19, . . *A tramp*) Inf **CA**117, Fleabag.

fleabait See **fleabag 4**

fleabane n Also *fleabane daisy*

A plant of either of two genera: *Erigeron,* which is also called **bugbane 4, cocash 1, daisy 2b, daisy fleabane, scabious, squawweed, whitetop, wild daisy,** or *Conyza,* which is also called **horseweed 1.** For other names of var spp of *Erigeron* see **cut-leaved daisy b, dryland daisy, frostweed 1, gold buttons 1, gorge daisy, kiss-me-and-I'll-tell-you, lace-button, mule-tail weed, oxeye daisy, poor Robin's plantain, rockslide daisy, rosebetty, seaside daisy, sweet scabious, vine daisy, whiplash daisy, white root, whitetop weed, whiteweed**

1784 in 1785 Amer. Acad. Arts & Sci. *Memoirs* 1.480, *Erigeron. . .* Fleabane. **1824** Bigelow *Florula Bostoniensis* 303, Annual Flea-Bane. **1847** Wood *Class-Book* 327, Canadian or Common Fleabane. **c1873** in 1976 Miller *Shaker Herbs* 175, Fleabane. **1889** (1971) Farmer *Americanisms* 246, *Flea-bane. . .* This is not the English plant of the same name, but is a medicinal herb, largely used in the well-known Shaker preparations, as an astringent and diuretic. **1901** Mohr *Plant Life AL* 48, Fleabanes . . and other tall, coarse composites are characteristic of the prairie flora. **1944** Howard *Walkin' Preacher* 228 **MO,** The congregation single-filed through mullein and fleabane daisy to the natural baptistry at the ford. **1966–67** *DARE* Wildfl QR Pl.239B Infs **CO**7, **WA**10, Fleabane daisy; **TX**34, Fleabane. **1967** *DARE* FW Addit **neCO,** Fleabane daisy—Coulter's daisy. *Erigeron coulteri.* **1967** *Ozark Visitor* (Point Lookout MO) Feb 6, Pussy-toes and fleabane dasies [sic] . . fringed my path. **1968** *DARE* (Qu. S26a) Inf **PA**99, Fleabane. **1974** (1977) Coon *Useful Plants* 108, Canadian fleabane.

flea-bit adj

1 See **-bit** suff.

2 See **flea-bitten.**

fleabite n Also sp *fleebite*

1 Fig: a very small amount; a trifle.

[a1651 (1912) Bradford *Hist. Plymouth* 1.24, Their former afflictions were but as flea-bitings in comparison.] **1775** in 1889 Washington *Writings* 3.248 **neVA,** One hundred thousand dollars will be but a flea-bite to our demands at this time. **1816** in 1915 *MD Hist. Mag.* 10.281 **sePA,** This Mountain . . is but a mere flea bite to travel over, to the Mountains . . in Virginia. **1844** Stephens *High Life in NY* 2.51, It aint a flee-bite to what I want. **1899** (1912) Green *VA Folk-Speech* 178, *Fleabite. . .* A relatively very small or insignificant quantity. **1949** *Sun* (Baltimore MD) 15 Dec 8/1 *(Hench Coll.),* A total of about 310,000,000 gallons is expected to come into the reservoirs. "It will last a couple of hours," Edward J. Clark, chief water engineer, said. "It's a fleabite."

2 See quot.

1944 *PADS* 2.66 **VA,** *Flea-bite. . .* Very small holes in the tobacco leaf caused by flea-bugs.

flea-bitten adj Also *flea-bit* Cf **schimmel**

Also in combs; Of a horse: having tiny dark flecks on a light coat.

1888 *San Francisco Weekly Examiner* 22 March (Farmer *Americanisms*), A spirited flea-bitten gray mare fell to my lot when the straws were drawn. **1899** (1912) Green *VA Folk-Speech* 178, *Flea-bitten, adj.* Colour of a horse; dark brown spots on a white surface; generally the sign of an old animal. "A flea-bitten mare." **1930** Shoemaker *1300 Words* 22 **cPA Mts** (as of c1900), "Flea bitten white", a type of white horse once very common in the Pennsylvania highlands. **1949** *PADS* 11.6 **wTX** (as of c1920), *Fleabit gray: adj.* White, flecked with small dark specks. "His horse is a fleabit gray." **c1960** *Wilson Coll.* **csKY,** *Flea-bitten* (or *-bit*) *gray . .* Gray with small spots. **1965–70** *DARE* (Qu. K38, *A horse of a dirty white color*) 29 Infs **scattered,** Flea-bitten; 7 Infs, **scattered,** Flea-bitten gray; **TN**14, Flea-bit; (Qu. K39, *. . Other names . . for horses according to their colors*) 6 Infs, **scattered,** Flea-bitten (gray, brown, or horse); **LA**2, Dapple-gray or blue-gray when they are young, but both colors turn to just gray or to flea-bitten gray [when they are old]; **NM**13, Flea-bitten gray—little red spots in white or gray; **CA**152, Flea-bitten horse—like a roan, but spots are more prominent; (Qu. K37, *. . A horse of mixed colors*) Infs **KY**49, **MO**37, Flea-bitten. [41 of 45 total Infs old] **1968** Adams *Western Words* 115, *Flea bitten*—A white horse covered with small brown freckles.

fleabrain n

A very silly or stupid person.

1969–70 *DARE* (Qu. HH3, *A dull and stupid person*) Inf **GA**72, Fleabrain; (Qu. HH9, *A . . silly or light-headed person*) Inf **MI**116, Fleabrain.

flea hop n

A dancing party; a dance step.

1942 Berrey–Van den Bark *Amer. Slang* 366.3, Dance; ball. . . flea-hop. **1968** *DARE* (Qu. FF4, *Names and joking names for different kinds of dancing parties*) Inf **KS**8, Flea hops—a little outdated; (Qu. FF5a, *. . Different steps . . in dancing—in past years*) Inf **IN**47, Flea hop.

flea house See **fleabag 2, 3**

flea in one's bonnet n [Blend of **flea in one's ear** + *bee in one's bonnet*]

1966–68 *DARE* (Qu. JJ27, *To give somebody a hint for his own good: "He had no idea that she was up to anything, but I put ______.'*) Infs **IL**50, **NJ**28, **NY**54, A flea in his bonnet.

flea in one's ear n [*OED* c1430 →] **chiefly NEast** See Map *old-fash*

A hint, warning, disquieting disclosure; a rebuke.

1822 Irving *Bracebridge* 1.229 **NY,** If you had taken a friend's advice, you'd never have come away from Doncaster races with a flea in your ear! **1927** *AmSp* 2.362 **wcWV,** To warn a friend against treachery. "I will put a flea in his ear when I see him again." [**1933** Cobb *Murder* 213 **seNY,** I think possibly I may have a flea to put in his ear.] **1948** Funk *Hog on Ice* 181, To be sent away with a flea in the ear indicated that one had received a sharp and stinging reproof or rebuff, often wholly unexpected. . . Now we use it to carry no greater meaning than that of warning. **1950** *WELS ("He didn't guess that she was up to anything, but I ______.")* 2 Infs, **WI,** Put a flea in his ear. **1954** *Harder Coll.* **cwTN,** Put a bug (flea) in his ear: To give a hint. **1965–70** *DARE* (Qu. JJ27, *To give somebody a hint for his own good: "He had no idea that she was up to anything, but I put ______.'*) 30 Infs, **chiefly NEast,** A flea in his ear. [25 Infs old]

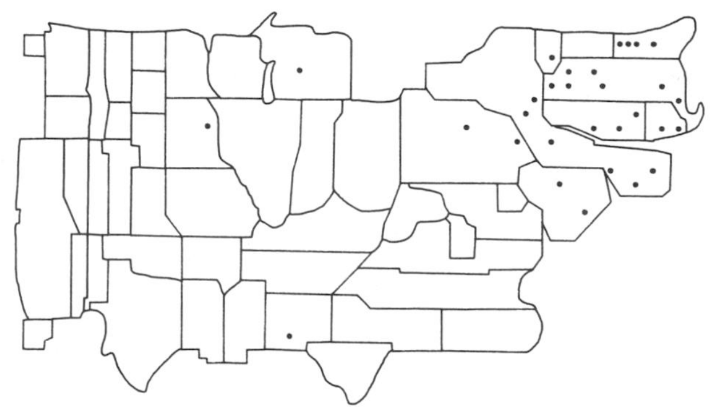

•flea in one's ear (Qu. JJ27)

flea joint See **fleabag 2**

fleak n[1] Also *fleek* [*OED fleak(e)* "obs. or dial. form of *flake*"] **S Midl**

A flake; a flat piece.

1933 *AmSp* 8.2.29 **KY,** The elder . . cyarved me a fleek (slice) of ham-meat the size of my pam (palm). **1941** *Hall Coll.* **wNC, eTN,** *A fleak of snow. . .* This expression is common. **1967** Key *Tobacco Vocab.* **KY,** When you bulk it down, it stays together . . and you can pick up a fleak of it. . . "He [=a buyer] pulls out a fleak."

fleak n[2] Also *fleck, flick* [*EDD flick* sb.[2] (also *fleck, fleek*) "The inside fat of a pig, which is melted down for lard."]

1899 (1912) Green *VA Folk-Speech* 178, *Fleak-fat. . .* Flake fat. The large flakes of fat in a hog's belly, from which the best lard is made. Fleck. Flick.

fleak v [**fleak** n[1]] **S Midl**

1 In making cane syrup: see quots; hence n *fleaking (point).* Cf **fleecing**

1936 Morehouse *Rain on Just* 153 **NC,** The molasses, so pretty with its fat brown breaking bubbles, boiled almost to the fleaking point. *Ibid* 156, "They're fleaking proper," roared young Emmet, testing the syrup. Just so much and no further should a good run of molasses boil. Boil to the fleaking so that a ladle full held up drips off in shield shaped drops. [**1966** *Record* (Columbia SC) 7 Dec sec B 1, Mrs. Schumpert announced when the syrup is ready. "See how it flakes," she said, holding up a ladel [sic] and letting the syrup pour slowly off. The syrup in a certain light, breaks off in infinitesimal layers.]

2 with *off* or *out:* To fall away gradually.

1939 *Hall Coll.* **eTN,** He fleaked off from Democracy [Hall: the principles of the Democratic Party]. **1942** Hall *Smoky Mt. Speech* 18, *Flake* was [flik] in the sentence, 'They fleaked out and left the church.'

fleaking (point) See **fleak v 1**

fleak off (or out) See **fleak v 2**

flea myrtle n [From the use of the dried plant as a flea repellent]

Prob a **wax myrtle** (here: *Myrica cerifera*).

1933 Rawlings *South Moon* 71 **FL,** He reached for a leaf of flea-myrtle and crushed its spiced sweetness against his nose.

fleaseed n

A plantain (*Plantago* spp).

1971 Krochmal *Appalachia Med. Plants* 196, *Plantago* L. spp. . . Common Names: . . fleaseed.

fleas, full of adj phr

Energetic, lively.

1967–69 *DARE* (Qu. KK28, *Feeling ambitious and eager to work*) Inf **NE**9, Itching to get started! Full of fleas! [laughter]; **NJ**57, Full of fleas. [Both Infs old]

fleas in one's nose, have v phr

?To have a foolish or erroneous idea. Cf **beans up one's nose**

1928 *Ruppenthal Coll.* **KS, PA,** "Mamma, I think there's candy up on that shelf." "Oh, you have fleas in your nose" is the response.

flea trap See **fleabag 1, 2, 4**

fleaweed n

1 A **blue curls 1** (here: *Trichostema lanceolatum*).

1911 CA Ag. Exper. Sta. Berkeley *Bulletin* 217.1022, *Trichostema lancealatum* [sic]. . . Flea Weed (Los Angeles County).

2 A **fetid marigold** (here: *Dyssodia papposa*).

1940 Clute *Amer. Plant Names* 258, *Dyssodia papposa.* Flea-weed.

‡**fleazy** adj [Perh var of *sleazy,* poss influenced by *flea*]

1968 *DARE* (Qu. KK6, *Something low-grade or of poor quality . . "I wouldn't buy that, it's ______.'*) Inf **NY**96, ['flizɪ].

fleck v [Var of *flick;* cf *EDD flick* v.[2] "Also in forms *fleck . . fleek*"]

To flick.

1887 Tourgée *Button's Inn* 124, 'You handle that as if there were eggs in it,' laughed the other, flecking the whip. **1889** Murfree *Despot* 424 **eTN,** He experimented with some delicate flecking touches of the bow. **1918** Sandburg *Cornhuskers* 50 **IL,** He lived flecking lint off coat lapels.

fleck n See **fleak** n^{2}

flecker n [Var of **flicker** n^{2} **1**]
1835 (1854) Kennedy *Horse-Shoe Robinson* 35 **VA** (Taylor–Whiting *Dict. Amer. Proverbs*), You shine like a flecker on a sunny day. **1899** (1912) Green *VA Folk-Speech* 179, *Flicker*. . . A woodpecker. Flecker. **1968** *DARE* (Qq. Q17, 18) Inf **PA**92, Flecker.

flee v^{1}
Std sense, var form. Past: usu *fled;* also *fleed.*
1949 *McDavid Coll.* **cnNY,** [hi 'flid ðə ˌkʌntrɪ].

flee v^{2} See **flea** v

fleebite See **fleabite**

fleece v
1 See quot. [*EDD fleece* v. 6 "To thrash, chastise, beat"]
1899 (1912) Green *VA Folk-Speech* 178, *Fleece*. . . To whip. Connected with the sense of taking off one's fleece: as, "I will fleece you."
2 To skin.
1971 *WI Conserv. Bulletin* Jan–Feb 22, First the carp are fleeced, eviscerated, decapitated, and split lengthwise.

fleech v [Scots and nEngl dial] **S Atl** *old-fash*
To coax, wheedle, flatter.
1938 FWP *Ocean Highway* 189 **NC,** "Fleech" means to flatter, not a complimentary term since the native is sparing with his praise. **1938** Matschat *Suwannee R.* 158 **GA,** But if I git married, I hain't my own man./ I'll have to fleech her jest as much as I can. **1952** Brown *NC Folkl.* 1.541, *Fleech*. . . To flatter.

fleecing vbl n [Prob < **fleak** v **1**]
In making cane syrup: see quot.
1973 *News & Courier* (Charleston SC) 25 Nov sec E 4, Women manning the skimmers dip them in the syrup and twirl to check for fleecing—that's when the syrup coats the skimmer and drips slowly.

fleed See **flee** v^{1}

fleek See **fleak** n^{1}

flees exclam
In marble play: used to defend an advantageous shooting position.
1963 *KY Folkl. Rec.* 9.3.66 **eKY,** *When Shooter Has Landed In A Good Shooting Position:* . . flees: Owsley, Knott, Lewis, Carter [Counties].

fleet adj [*OED* 1621 →]
1895 *DN* 1.388 **nwMA,** *Fleet:* shallow (of dishes). . . "O[ld-fash]."

fleet v [*OED fleet* v.^{1} 10 "To glide away like a stream . . change position imperceptibly"]
To slide along, "scoot."
1916 Macy–Hussey *Nantucket Scrap Basket* 132, "Fleet"—To move, especially to move over, to change the position of. **1945** Colcord *Sea Language* 77 **ME, Cape Cod, Long Island,** *Fleet* . . to move or slide along cautiously. . . "Fleet forrard, folks; there's too much cargo aft," said the deacon who wanted the front benches filled at prayer meeting.

fleet-footed preacher n
1971 Wood *Vocab. Change* 368 **Sth,** Volunteered [terms for "an unprofessional, part-time lay preacher"]: *devil chaser, exhorter, fleet footed preacher [etc.]*

fleeting See **flitting**

fleet out v phr [*fleet* a group of boats]
To form an organized group.
1970 *DARE* Tape **VA**112, When they [=crabs] fleet out like that, they get in a big fleet.

fleggity See **flaggity**

Flemish account n [*OED* 1785 →; cf *Flanders-fortunes* (*OED* at *Flanders* sb. 2) quot a1700 "of small Substance"]
An unsatisfactory accounting; a deficit, a smaller amount than is expected.
1756 in 1970 SC (Colony) *Doc. Indian Affairs* 2.151, I fancy there will be but a Flemish Account given. **1827** Cooper *Red Rover* 3.79, Then came the law, . . making a wreck at once of all the poor girl's hopes, and a Flemish account of my comfort. **1837** Smith *Col. Crockett's Exploits* 13, When the shaving shop [=bank] comes to make a Flemish account of her transactions, "the Government" will discover that he has not only lost the original deposite [sic], but a large body of the public lands to boot. **1950** *PADS* 14.29 **Charleston SC,** *Flemish account*. . . A small amount. "There's a Flemish account of butter on the table tonight."

flemish down v phr [*flemish (down)* to lay a rope down in a flat coil]
Fig: to lie down to sleep.
1966 *DARE* FW Addit **NM**12, Flemished down = laid [sic] down to rest. **1966** *DARE* (Qu. OO19a, . . *"He felt tired, so he went to the couch . . and ______ [down for a while]."*) Inf **NM**11, Flemished down.

flench See **flinch** v^{1}

Flerida See **Florida**

flesh n Usu |flɛš|; also **S Midl** |flæš, fleš|; occas |flɝš| Similarly, adj *fleshy* |flæši| Pronc-spp *flash, flaish, flersh, flursh*
A Forms.
1916 *DN* 4.340 **seOH,** *Flersh* (flesh). **1923** *DN* 5.207 **swMO,** *Flash*. . . Flesh. **1930s** in 1944 *ADD* **eWV,** [flɝš] flursh, flersh, n. Also *flaish,* almost [fleš]. **1931** *PMLA* 46.1315 **sAppalachians,** *E,* short, becomes highland *a* . . as in . . "flash" (flesh). **1942** Hall *Smoky Mt. Speech* 20, [æ] is common . . in . . *flesh, fleshy.* **1954** *Harder Coll.* **cwTN,** Does scrapin' on a grindstone make ye flash crawl? **1965** Carmony *Speech Terre Haute* 110 **IN,** /æ/, though heard fairly often in the folk and common speech of Monroe County, as in *She's too fleshy* [flæši], overheard in Bloomington recently . . does not occur in Terre Haute records. **1967** *Wilson Coll.* **csKY,** *Fleshy* [flæši]. **1985** *Amer. Jrl. Med.* 78.2.182 **eTN,** The flaish got strutted.
B Sense.
Weight, fat; condition—often in phrr *to make flesh, lose flesh.* Cf **fleshen up, flesh up**
1903 (1965) Adams *Log Cowboy* 16 **West,** The cattle were well shed and in good flesh for such an early season of the year. **1941** *LANE* Map 458, 1 inf, **nwCT,** He's making flesh = He's getting fat. **1952** Brown *NC Folkl.* 1.541, *Flesh, to carry*. . . To weigh more; to weigh heavier than one is supposed to.—Central and east [NC]. Old people. **c1960** *Wilson Coll.* **csKY,** *Fleshen up:* . . To put on weight or "flesh." **1965–70** *DARE* (Qu. K15, *A thin, bony . . cow*) Inf **IL**108, Poor in flesh; **MA**16, Cow in poor flesh; (Qu. K44, *A bony or poor-looking horse*) Inf **ME**12, Thin in flesh; **NC**49, Down in flesh; off in flesh; (Qu. X51, *To lose weight because of sickness: "He was sick all winter and ______."*) 11 Infs, **scattered,** Lost flesh; **MA**56, **MS**30, Lost a lot of flesh. [14 of 17 Infs old]

flesh v [Pronc-sp for *flush;* see Pronc Intro 3.I.5.d]
1969 *DARE* (Qu. P39a, *When a hunter or a dog finds a game animal and makes it start running, you'd say he ______ it*) Inf **RI**12, Fleshed; (Qu. P39b, *If the dog makes a bird or a covey fly, you'd say he ______*) Inf **RI**12, Fleshed it.

flesh crawl, make one's v phr **chiefly Sth, S Midl**
To make one's flesh creep, to cause one to shudder; also fig.
1875 (1876) Twain *Tom Sawyer* 59 **MO,** It makes my flesh crawl to hear you. **1893** Shands *MS Speech* 30, When cold chills run over one, especially if caused by some harsh or grating noise, one's flesh is said to crawl. In the greater portion of the United States the word *creep* is used instead of *crawl.* **1946** *PADS* 6.13 **eNC,** *Flesh crawl, to make the*. . . To make one shudder or quiver at the report or imagination of anything unpleasant to the nerves. . . Common. **1947** *PADS* 8.19 **eIA.** *Ibid* 25 **wNY.** *Ibid* 27 **MO.** **1952** Brown *NC Folkl.* 1.541, *Flesh crawl, to make the:* . . To make the flesh creep.—Central and east [NC]. Common. **1954** *Harder Coll.* **cwTN,** Does scrapin' on a grindstone make ye flash crawl? **c1960** *Wilson Coll.* **csKY.** **1968–70** *DARE* (Qu. GG13a, *When something keeps bothering a person and makes him nervous, he may say, "It ______ me."*) Inf **GA**67, Makes my flesh crawl; (Qu. II29b, . . *You might try to explain the unpleasant effect that person has on you: "He just ______."*) Infs **MS**88, **VA**71, Makes my flesh crawl.

flesh-creep n [From *make one's flesh creep*]
The shivers.
1930 *AmSp* 6.98 **cNY,** It's so cold it gives a body the flesh-creep.

fleshen up v phr [*EDD* (at *fleshen*)] **Sth, S Midl** Cf **flesh up**
To gain weight.

1912 Green *VA Folk-Speech* 178, He has fleshened up very much since he had that spell of sickness. **1939** *Sat. Eve. Post* 25 Nov 58/3 **FL,** I fleshened up again. **1952** Brown *NC Folkl.* 1.541, *Flesh, fleshen, up:* . . To take on weight, to become fat.—Central and east [NC]. Old people. **c1960** *Wilson Coll.* **csKY,** *Fleshen up:* . . To put on weight or "flesh." To become fleshy. **1971** *Today Show Letters* **sMS.** **1972** *Atlanta Letters* **nwGA,** "You've fleshened up a bit" [is] intended as a compliment. **1972** Cooper *NC Mt. Folkl.* 92.

flesh fly n [See quot 1901]

A fly of the family Sarcophagidae. Also called **carrion fly, fish fly 3**

1901 Howard *Insect Book* 163, This [=Sarcophagidae] is a large group of flies, comprising very many species and . . called "flesh-flies" because many of them live in the larval state in the bodies of dead animals. **1905** Kellogg *Amer. Insects* 343, Next to house-flies the commonest ones about houses and outbuildings are . . blow-flies or flesh-flies. **1928** Metcalf-Flint *Destructive & Useful Insects* 22, There are no insects that habitually live in the alimentary canal of man, but the eggs or small larvae of blue-bottle flies, flesh flies, . . and others may be swallowed with impure drinking water, milk or infested food. **1954** Borror-DeLong *Intro. Insects* 640, Flesh flies [=Sarcophagidae] are very similar to blow flies in appearance and habits and are generally quite common.

flesh fork n [*flesh* meat] *old-fash* Cf **fresh fork**

A long-handled fork used to lift meat from a large kettle.

1739 in 1906 *Colonial Rec. GA* 4.371, Several Wounds . . appeared on the Body, supposed to be done with a Flesh-Fork. **1845** T.J. Green *Texian Exped.* xvii.315 *(DAE),* The great diplomatist 'could . . hold his flesh-fork . . like a cook.' **1891** *Jrl. Amer. Folkl.* 4.126 **Buffalo Valley PA,** Boil some milk in a pan on the stove. By pricking the milk with a flesh-fork the witch can be made to appear. **1899** (1912) Green *VA Folk-Speech* 185, *Fresh-fork.* . . A large, three-prong iron fork, with a handle two feet or more long, for taking . . meat from a dinner-pot. . . Flesh-fork.

flesh, lose (or make) See **flesh** n **B**

flesh-naked adj

Stark-naked.

1948 Manfred *Chokecherry* 127 **nwIA,** Maybe even swimming together flesh-naked.

flesh up v phr **chiefly NEast** Cf **fleshen up**

To gain weight.

1931-33 *LANE Worksheets* **cCT,** He's fleshing up very fast; **cnMA,** He fleshed up. **1939** Coffin *Capt. Abby* 191 **ME** (as of 1860s), Elias . . has fleshed up since he left home. **1950** Robinson *Cardinal* 526 **seNY,** He was fleshing up slightly, but the additional weight served to insulate his nervous system against the jarring assaults of public office and private pain. **1952** Brown *NC Folkl.* 1.541, *Flesh, fleshen, up.*

fleshworm n

A blackhead.

1906 Gregory *Woman's Cookbook* 535 **appar Chicago IL,** The principal source of a bad complexion in otherwise healthy women is generally caused by comedos, commonly called flesh worms. **1968** *DARE* (Qu. X59, *What do you call the small infected pimples that form, usually on the face?*) Inf **IN45A,** Fleshworm.

fleshy adj[1] See **flesh** n

fleshy adj[2] See **flashy** adj[1] **1**

fletch See **flitch**

fleur-de-lis n [*OED* 14th cent →]

An **iris.**

1835 Hoffman *Winter in West* (NY) 1.145, The purple fleur-de-lis bloomed along the wet marshes. **1857** Gray *Manual of Botany* 460, *I. pumila,* . . the *Dwarf Iris* . . and *I. sambucina,* . . the common *Flower-de-Luce* (i.e. *Fleur-de-Lis*), are familiar in gardens. **1910** *Kindergarten-Primary Mag.* 10 June 312 *(DAE),* There were roses and lilies and violets and many other kinds of flowers, and in one corner a bed of purple fleur-de-lis. **1940** Steyermark *Flora MO* 90, *Blue Flag, Fleur-de-lis, Iris.* . . Flowers pale bluish-purple or lilac. **1941** Percy *Lanterns* 97 **MS,** They troop near the iris, which when coarsened by gardens some call fleur-de-lis, and others, who care nothing about names, flags. **1967** Dodge *Roadside Wildflowers* 5, *Rocky Mountain iris. Fleur-de-lis, snake-lily, water flag.* . . A truly American species. **1968-70** *DARE* (Qu. S24) Inf **CT8,** Fleur-de-lis; **PA234,** Wild fleur-de-lis.

flew('d) See **fly** v **A1**

flewed See **fly** v **A2, 3**

flewn See **fly** v **A3**

fliaum See **filione**

‡flibber digit n

1966 *DARE* File **csWI,** Flibber digit—the lock or closing usually described as a slide and turn-down lock.

flibbertigibbet n Also *flibbergibbet, flibbertigib, flibbertigibbety;* for addit varr see quots [*OED* 1549 →]

Std sense, var forms. Note: the variants ending in *-y* may have been intended as adjectives; cf **flibberty.**

1936 Reese *Worleys* 53 **MD** (as of 1865), [Black woman:] "Flibbo—gibbet." [White child:] "Flibber-gibbet?" "Yas Lady chile. Fire an' no linlins. He don' stick. He don' *stay.*" **1965-70** *DARE* (Qu. HH9, *A very silly or light-headed person*) 18 Infs, **scattered,** Flibbertigibbet; **CO34, WA1,** Flibbergibbet; **IL97,** Flibbertigibbert; **PA199,** Flibbertigib; **WA6,** Flibbertigibbety—if a girl [12 of 22 Infs coll educ]; (Qu. GG14, . . *Someone who fusses or worries a lot*) Inf **CT23,** Flibbertigibbet. **1967-69** *DARE* FW Addit **csPA,** Flibbertigibberty.

flibberty adj [**flibbertigibbet**]

Flighty, silly.

1954 Forbes *Rainbow* 16 **CT** (as of 1800s), They had two children. The oldest was a girl. Mitty let Jude give her the flibberty name of Leaf. **1984** Doig *English Creek* 122 **nMT,** "She's too young and"—my mother scouted for aptness—"flibberty. Leona is in love with the idea of men, not one man."

flibbity adj [Perh *EDD flip* adj. "Pliant, flexible"; but cf **flibberty**]

1952 Brown *NC Folkl.* 1.541, *Flibbity.* . . Limp; not crisp. "This bacon is mighty flibbity."—East.

flibdib n [Var of **flubdub** n 2]

1942 Warnick *Garrett Co. MD* 7 (as of 1900-18), *Flibdibs* . . ornaments on clothing.

fliche, flick n[1] See **flitch**

flick n[2] See **fleak** n[2]

flicka See **flicker** n[3]

flickem n Cf *flippum-jack* (at **flipjack**)

1940 *AmSp* 15.447 **eTN,** *Flickems.* Biscuit. 'Susie Jane cooks flickems of a morning.'

flicker v Also with *up* [From the *flickering* of a dying flame]

To fail; to faint; hence n *flicker* a faint.

1890 *DN* 1.64 **KY,** *Flicker* . . to fail, to back out. "He flickered to-day." **1900** Willard *Tramping* 393, *Flicker: noun,* a faint; *verb,* to faint or pretend to faint. **1903** *DN* 2.297 **Cape Cod MA** (as of a1857), *Flicker up.* . . To fail, to be unsuccessful. **1927** *DN* 5.446 [Underworld jargon], *Flicker.* . . To faint or to sham a faint.

flicker n[1] See **flicker** v

flicker n[2]

1 A brownish woodpecker (*Colaptes* spp) with black-barred back and black-spotted underparts. For other names see **butterbung, clape, English woodpecker 1, fiddler 2, flickertail 1, flitter** n[2], **flying auger, French woodpecker 2, gaffle woodpecker, gallie, goldenwing woodpecker, grasshopper woodpecker, graywacker, ground woodpecker, harry whicket, hammerhead 6, hickwall, high-holer 1, kippy woodpecker, northwestern woodpecker, partridge woodpecker, peckerwood, peerit, pe-ok, pigeon woodpecker, pique bois jaune, red-winged woodpecker, sapsucker, scythe-whetter, shad-spirit, silver-dollar bird, speckled woodpecker, taping bird, tapping bird, wake-up, weather hen, whafler, wheeler, whicker, wick-up, wild hen, will crisson, woodchuck, woodcock, woodpecker-lark, wood-peent, wood-pie, wood pigeon, wood-quoi, wood-wall, yacker, yaffle, yarrup, yecker, yellowhammer, yellow jay, yellow-winged woodpecker, yucker, zebec**

1808 Wilson *Amer. Ornith.* 1.53, It [=*Colaptes auratus*] has numerous provincial appellations . . , such as 'High-hole,' . . 'Piut,' 'Flicker,' by which last it is usually known in Pennsylvania. **1865** *Atlantic Mth.*

15.517/1 **nNY,** Another April comer . . is the Golden-Winged Woodpecker, *alias,* "High-Hole," *alias,* "Flicker," *alias,* "Yarup." **1872** Schele de Vere *Americanisms* 379, The *Yellow-Hammer* or *Flicker* (Picus amatus) . . is universally known as *Clape,* from a name bestowed upon him by the first settlers. **1890** *DN* 1.73 **sePA,** *Flicker:* the golden-winged woodpecker. Philadelphia. **1909** *DN* 3.396 **nwAR,** *Flicker. . .* The golden-winged woodpecker. **1916** Seton *Woodcraft Manual Girls* 312, *Flicker or Highhole (Colaptes auratus).* This large and beautiful woodpecker is twelve inches long. . . Its beautiful plumage and loud splendid "clucker" cry make it a joy in every woodland. **1916** *Times-Picayune* (New Orleans LA) 16 Apr 9, *Flicker* (Colaptes auratus). . . This, the state bird of Alabama, and the one member of our avian tribe that has been given over a hundred common or local names, is known to everyone who knows anything of birds. **1950** *WELS (Woodpeckers)* 20 of 50 Infs, **WI,** Flicker. **1965–70** *DARE* (Qu. Q17) 235 Infs **widespread, but more freq Nth, N Midl,** Flicker; **AR**48, Flicker—same as yellow-hammer; **CA**78, 140, **CO**7, Red-shafted flicker; **CO**7, **IA**3, **MO**25, Yellow-shafted flicker; **CA**3, Red flicker; (Qu. Q18) Infs **GA**18, **OH**16, Flicker.

2 =brown thrasher.

1950 *WELS (Brown thrasher)* 1 Inf, **csWI,** Flicker. **1967** *DARE* (Qu. Q14) Inf **MI**67, Flicker.

flicker n[3] Also *flicka* [*flick* to flip]

In marble play: see quots.

c1970 Wiersma *Marbles Terms* **swCA,** *Flicker*—type of shot, a snap of the thumb. "He got it on a flicker." *Ibid, Flicka*—variation on flicker. "He won it on a flicka."

flicker n[4] **sAppalachians**

Scrip issued by coal companies.

1943 Korson *Coal Dust* 72 **sAppalachians,** The same colloquial terms were used for scrip and store orders, such as "stickers," "clackers," "flickers," and "drag." **1967** *DARE* File **wKY,** *Flicker*—money made by mining companies, usually in coin form. Good for full value at company stores, ten cents less per dollar elsewhere. Especially in western Kentucky, this was the only pay coal miners got. **1973** *PADS* 59.37 [Bituminous coal mining vocab], *Flicker . .* scrip.

flickers n [*flicker* to flutter]

1968 Adams *Western Words* 116, *Flickers*—An earmark in which small, narrow strips are formed on the outer edge of the ear [of a cow] by cutting the ear parallel to the outer edge for a distance of about two inches.

flickertail n

1 =flicker n[2] 1.

1973 Allen *LAUM* 1.324 **Upper MW** (as of c1950), The flicker *(Colaptes aureatus luteus)* . . is . . [described] four times as *flickertail,* two occurrences of which are noteworthy as offered by North Dakota infs. who know the same word as a synonym for Richardson's ground squirrel.

2 also *flickertail(ed) gopher, flickertail squirrel:* A **ground squirrel n b** (here *Spermophilus* spp). [See quot 1943] **chiefly Upper MW, esp ND**

1890 *Brighton* (Colo.) *Reg.* 11 Jan. 4/1 *(DA),* The nickname of North Dakota is the 'flickertail state.' **1928** Anthony *N. Amer. Mammals* 204, *Richardson Ground Squirrel; Flickertail. . .* A medium-sized Ground Squirrel of rather uniform light yellowish to grayish coloration. **1943** Cahalane *Meeting the Mammals* 69 **WY,** If the squirrels observe any signs of danger they run to their homes, and with a last twitch of the tail disappear. This final gesture has given them another nickname—'flickertail.' **1946** Thompson *Amer. Daughter* 36 **ND,** As the wild rose was the official state flower, so was the gopher, commonly called the flickertail, its namesake. **1966–68** *DARE* (Qu. P29) Inf **MN**38, Flickertail—a South Dakota species; **MN**42, Flickertailed gopher; **MT**5, Gopher—little, brownish-gray, little short tail; also called flickertail gopher; **ND**9, Gopher—like a squirrel without a bushy tail; also called flickertail; the other gopher has stripes; **SD**8, Gopher—long body, striped; call them also flickertails; (Qu. P27) Inf **ND**1, Flickertail squirrel—like a squirrel but with a short tail; gray. **1973** Allen *LAUM* 1.322 (as of c1950), Richardson's ground squirrel (*Citellus richardsonii* Sabine) . . is usually known by *flickertail. . .* A dry-prairie rodent, it . . lacks stripes and is dusty gray with a cinnamon buff on the hairs. The common name describes its habit of rapidly flicking its tail.

3 in comb *Flickertail State:* North Dakota; hence *Flickertail* a North Dakotan.

1890 [see **2** above]. **1937** Shankle *Nicknames* 385/1, North Dakota is called the *Flickertail State* from the word flickertail. **1946** McWilliams *S. CA Country* 172, North Dakotans are 'flicker tails.' **1982** Heat Moon *Blue Highways* 276 **ND,** The nickname of North Dakota is the "Flickertail State." That morning I saw why. Mile after mile, the small ground squirrels stood at attention along the highway.

4 See **flickertail grass.**

flickertail(ed) gopher See **flickertail 2**

flickertail grass n Also *flickertail*

A barley (here: *Hordeum jubatum*).

1914 Georgia *Manual Weeds* 64, *Wild Barley. Hordeum jubatum. . .* flicker-tail. . . The long, barbed, reddish-golden awns become very brittle when ripe. **1935** (1943) Muenscher *Weeds* 160, Flicker-tail-grass. . . Biennial or perennial; reproducing by seeds.

flickertail squirrel See **flickertail 2**

Flickertail State See **flickertail 3**

flicker up See **flicker** v

flicket v [Engl dial]

To flutter.

1930 *VA Qrly. Rev.* 6.248 **S Midl,** Maristan Chapman, author of "The Happy Mountain," makes this comment: "A sense of onomatopoeia gives the mountain speech . . such turns as 'Yon's a bird flicketing in the laurel scrub."

flickie n [Perh rel to Du *flikken* to patch]

1983 *DARE* File **ceNY,** The type of denim jacket worn by farmers and other workmen was called a flickie.

flickity adj

1987 *DARE* File **nwMS,** Here are words . . that I collected in interviews with Black people in Marks . . back in the sixties: Flickity—(from *afflicted*) not intelligent.

flickup n [Var of **flicker** n[2] **1**]

1967 *DARE* (Qu. Q17, . . *Kinds of woodpeckers*) Inf **OR**5, Flickups.

flied See **fly** v **A2, 3**

flier n Also sp *flyer*

1 usu sp *flyer:* An express train. **chiefly Inland Nth, N Midl, West** See Map Also called **cannonball**

1888 *St. Louis Globe Democrat* 2 March (Farmer *Americanisms*), In spite of the strike, passenger trains, excepting what are known as the flyers, are running with reasonable regularity. **1907** *Scribner's Mag.* May 569 **Nth,** The "flyers" have the newest and best engines and cars. **1950** *WELS (A fast train that goes straight from one large city to another)* 4 Infs, **WI,** Flyer. **c1960** *Wilson Coll.* **csKY,** *Flyer. . .* A fast train; sometimes anything that goes fast. **1965–70** *DARE* (Qu. N35, *A fast train that goes from one big city to another without stopping at all the stations*) 76 Infs, **chiefly Inland Nth, N Midl, West,** Flyer; **GA**30, Dixie Flyer; **MD**31, Special Flyer; (Qu. N37, *Joking names for a branch railroad*) Inf **PA**82, Flyer; **IN**35, Ferdy Flyer; **WI**26, Callomine Flyer.

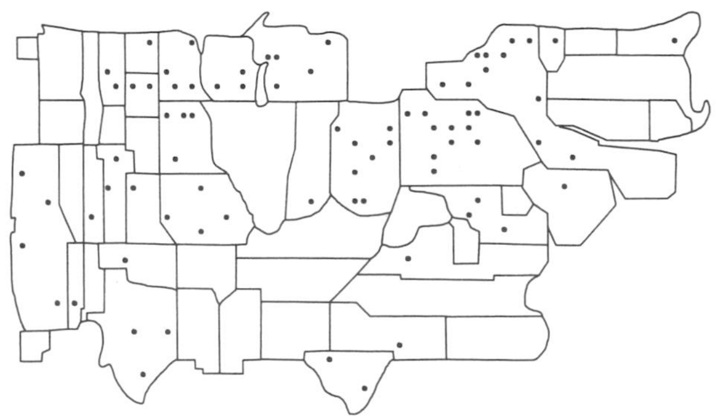

•flier 1 + varr (Qq. N35, N37)

2 A sunfish *(Centrarchus macropterus).* Also called **peacock sunfish, perch, round sunfish**

1896 U.S. Natl. Museum *Bulletin* 47.988, *Centrarchus macropterus . .* (Round Sunfish; Flier.) **1933** John G. Shedd Aquarium *Guide*

92, *Centrarchus macropterus* . . Flier. **1946** LaMonte *N. Amer. Game Fishes* 143, Flier—*Centrarchus macropterus.* **1966** *DARE* (Qu. P1, . . *Freshwater fish . . that are good to eat*) Inf **GA**16, Fliers. **1968** *FL Wildlife* July 13/1, There are at least nine species of native sunfishes, or panfishes, that attain catchable size in Florida. . . They include . . redbreast and flier, which range only as far south as central Florida.

3 See quot.

1884 Goode *Fisheries U.S.* 1.183 **ceME,** In Penobscot Bay they [=flounders] are taken in traps, or 'fliers,' as the fishermen call them shaped something like lobster-traps and baited.

4 See quot.

1914 *DN* 4.163 **Pacific NW,** *Flier.* . . A bad fall.

5 In ball games: a fly ball.

1967–69 *DARE* (Qu. EE11, *Bat-and-ball games for just a few players*) Inf **NC**63, Hitting fliers; **NY**28, Grounders and fliers.

6 In tobacco growing: see quot. Cf **flyings 2**

1899 U.S. Dept. Ag. *Yearbook* 435 **eOH,** Flyers, the first two bottom leaves, which are overripe and very trashy.

fliery adj [Perh blend of *fiery* + *fly;* cf **fly mad, fly up 1**]

1966–68 *DARE* (Qu. GG41, *To lose patience easily: "You never did see such a ______ person."*) Inf **MS**45, Fliery—he just flies up at anything; **OH**65, Fliery.

flies and grounders n Rarely *flies and rollers, fly and grounder*

=scrub.

1965–70 *DARE* (Qu. EE11, *Bat-and-ball games for just a few players*) 13 Infs, **chiefly Inland Nth, Midl east of Missip R,** Flies and grounders; **NY**98, High flies and grounders; **MO**33, Fly and grounder; **TX**28, Flies and rollers.

flies and skinners n **chiefly Gulf States, esp TX** See Map Cf **flies and grounders**

=scrub.

1965–70 *DARE* (Qu. EE11, *Bat-and ball games for just a few players*) 19 Infs, **chiefly Gulf States,** Flies and skinners; **LA**2, Flies and skinners—One man hits ball to others in the field. A fly is a high ball, a skinner is a ground ball.

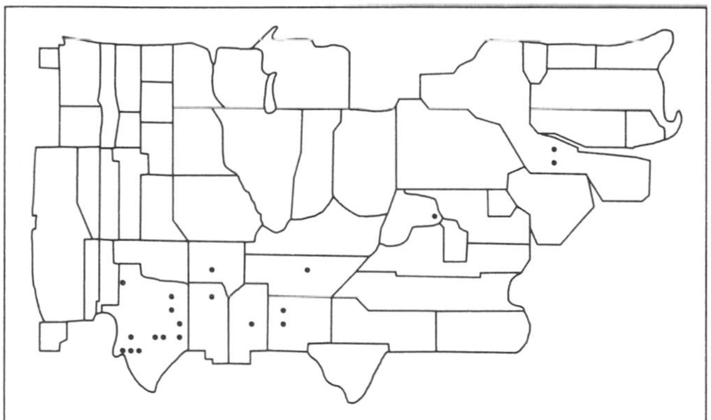

•flies and skinners (Qu. EE11)

flies-up See **fly-up** n

flight n [Cf *EDD flight* sb.[1] 3 "A collection of beings or things; a quantity; a crop"]

1957 Rose *Block Is.* 24 **RI,** As seaweed dries, its deterioration propensities render it a valued fertilizer. Hence, when great 'flights' were rolled up on the beach by storms, as soon as the tides were right, the farmers hastened to save it before it washed back in following tides.

flight v Cf **flight goose**

Of birds: to migrate.

1913 *DN* 4.1 **sME,** *Flight.* . . To fly, migrate. "The birds are flighting, have flighted."

flight goose n [See quot 1955] **esp ME**

=Hutchins's goose.

1835 Audubon *Ornith. Biog.* 3.17, That species [of Canada Goose] is distinguished there [=in Maine] by the name of *Flight Goose* and is said to be entirely migratory. **1888** Trumbull *Names of Birds* 4. **1923** U.S. Dept. Ag. *Misc. Circular* 13.36, *Hutchins Goose (Branta canadensis hutchinsii)* . . flight goose (Me.) **1951** *AmSp* 26.273, More generalized designations for Hutchins's goose, both indicating that it does not winter in the area concerned, are *southern goose* (Nova Scotia, Conn.) and *flight goose* (Maine). **1955** MA Audubon Soc. *Bulletin* 39.313, *Canada Goose.* . . Flight Goose (Maine. That is migratory goose, to distinguish Hutchins's Goose from the larger Canada Goose, which nests.)

flighty adj

1 Light-headed, silly, unstable. [*OED* 1768–74 →] **widespread exc Sth** See Map

1935 *AmSp* 10.171 **sePA,** *Flighty.* Applied to a person capricious, unsteady, untrustworthy. **1965–70** *DARE* (Qu. HH9, *A very silly or light-headed person*) 53 Infs, **widespread exc Sth,** Flighty; (Qu. GG41, *To lose patience easily: "You never did see such a ______ person."*) 13 Infs, **scattered exc Sth,** Flighty; (Qu. HH35, *A woman who puts on a lot of airs: "She's too ______ for me."*) Infs **KY**73, 80, **MN**6, Flighty; **AR**3, Highty-flighty; (Qu. AA7b, . . *A woman who is very fond of men . . if she's not respectable about it*) Infs **AK**1, **WV**20, Flighty. **1968** Kellner *Aunt Serena* 145 **cIN** (as of c1920), When they had fever, they turned flighty, or "light-headed as a dandelion gone to seed."

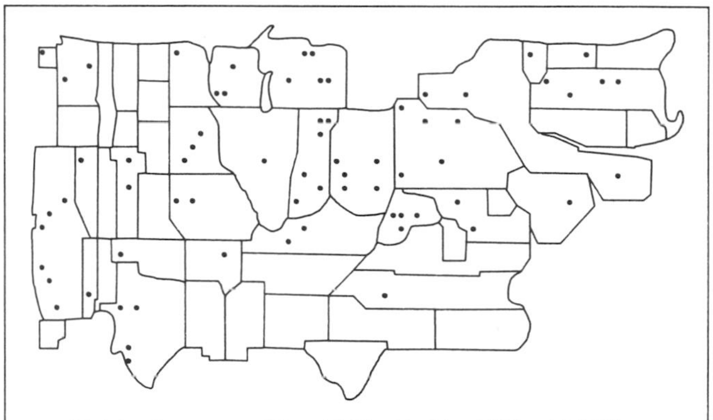

•flighty 1 + var (Qq. HH9, GG41, AA7b, HH35)

2 Of an animal: troublesome; skittish. [*OED* 1828]

1967 *DARE* FW Addit **MA**5, Flighty—used of young draft animals. [Inf old] **1969** *DARE* (Qu. K16, *A cow with a bad temper*) Inf **CT**26, Flighty. [Inf old]

3 See quot.

1933 *AmSp* 8.2.30 **KY,** He had one neighbor . . who was *flighty and drinlin'* (fragile and failing).

flimsy n [Folk-etym for *influenza*] Cf *DS* BB9, 10, 28

1954 *PADS* 21.27 **nwSC,** *Flimsy.* . . Influenza.

‡flimsy-flamsy adj [Perh redup of *flimsy* frivolous, superficial]

1966 *DARE* (Qu. KK46, . . *Expressions for taking things as they come and not worrying: "The whole family was sort of ______."*) Inf **FL**14, Flimsy-flamsy; [they] don't pay any attention.

flinch v[1] Usu |flınč|; also **Sth** |flinč, flɛnč| Pronc-sp *flench* Cf Pronc Intro 3.I.4.a

A Forms.

1934 *AmSp* 9.210 **Sth,** At times this vowel [=ı] becomes [iı], the second element being rather light. *Big, blink, . . flinch,* [etc]. **1960** Williams *Walk Egypt* 126 **GA,** The mule's hide flenched, questioning, under Peanuts' hands on the lines.

B Sense.

Tr; Of an animal: to drive off (insects) by making the skin quiver.

1960 Williams *Walk Egypt* 101 **GA,** The mule was flinching flies from its hide.

flinch n

1 A coward.

1936 *AmSp* 11.275 **cTN,** The flinch wouldn't fight.

2 In marble play: see quot.

c1970 Wiersma *Marbles Terms* **Grand Rapids MI,** Flinch—one player puts his foot directly next to the marble and then kicks his other foot against his first foot, causing the marble to roll with the object of hitting another player's marble. After a certain number of flinches . . the player is allowed to keep his marble if the flinches have been successful.

flinch v² [Perh blend of *filch* + *pinch*]
1966 *DARE* (Qu. V4, . . *Stealing . . "Yesterday someone ______ my watch."*) Inf **MI**24, Flinched.

flinchy adj [*flinch* to draw back, shrink]
Nervous, apprehensive.
1942 Hurston *Dust Tracks* 237 **FL,** But [Black] people had memories and told tales of what happened back there in Georgia, and Alabama and West Florida that made the skin of the young crawl with transmitted memory, and reminded the old heads that they were still flinchy.

flinder n [*OED* 1340 →; "*Obs.* exc. *dial.*"]
1938 Matschat *Suwannee R.* 289 **nFL, sGA,** Flinder: a butterfly. **1984** Wilder *You All Spoken Here* 59 **Sth,** *Flinder:* Butterfly; moth.

flinder v¹ [Scots dial, rare; perh US use is an independent back-formation from **flinders 1**]
To break into **flinders.**
1966 *DARE* (Qu. KK22, . . *Completely shattered: "The jug fell out of the window and was ______."*) Inf **NC**7, Flindered—broken to a million pieces. **1984** Wilder *You All Spoken Here* 158 **Sth,** *Flinder:* Break into small pieces.

flinder v² [Cf *DSL* "To flirt; to run about in a fluttering manner; also applied to cattle, when they break through enclosures, and scamper through the fields"] Cf **flinger along**
1886 Amer. Philol. Assoc. *Trans.* 17.45 **Sth,** To *flinder* (go fast).

flinder v³
To pester.
1981 Harper–Presley *Okefinokee* 78 **seGA** (as of 1929), Take him out where he expects to plough all day, he'll be slow. But if the flies flinders him, he'll work faster.

flinderation n See Intro "Language Changes" III.1
1 also pl: Destruction; **flinders 1.**
1883 (1971) Harris *Nights with Remus* 118 **GA** [Black], Hit's a blessin' dat dat ar platter is got mo' backbone dan de common run er crockery, 'kaze 'twould er bust all ter flinderations long time ago. **1908** *DN* 3.311 **eAL, wGA,** *Flinderation.* . . The state of being in flinders or fragments. Common. **1927** *AmSp* 2.354 **cwWV,** The wind blew the roof of the barn all to flinderation. **1954** *Harder Coll.* **cwTN,** Flinderation—complete destruction.
2 Tarnation; also used as a mild oath. Cf **thunderation**
1951 West *Witch Diggers* 22 **sIN,** "Peddling! Is that the way selling insurance strikes you, Uncle Wes?" "How in flinderation else?" **1954** *Harder Coll.* **cwTN,** Oh, flinderation and God-damn it to hell!

flindering adv Cf **flinder** v³, **flinderation**
Extremely.
1859 Taliaferro *Fisher's R.* 175 **nwNC** (as of 1820s), I was a-workin' fur 'Squire Freeman one flinderin hot day.

flinders n pl [*OED* c1450 →] **chiefly NEng, S Midl, Sth** *old-fash*
1 Fragments, splinters—usu in phr *break* (or *smash,* etc) *(all) to flinders.*
1843 Thompson *Major Jones' Courtship* 10 **GA,** I felt sort o' skeered, for fear them bominable criticks mought take hold of it and tare it all to flinders. **1848** U.S. Congress *Congressional Globe* 30th Cong 1st Sess 1 Mar 409/3 **MD,** [He] had riddled to flinders their young locofoco representative. **1878** (1977) Stowe *Poganuc People* 38 **CT,** Parson Cushing could knock that air [sermon] all to flinders. **1904** *DN* 2.425 **Cape Cod MA** (as of a1857), *Flinders.* . . Splinters. **1908** *DN* 3.311 **eAL, wGA,** *Flinders.* . . Fragments. The singular is not used. **1949** *Hench Coll.* **seVA,** He was speaking of a tree being struck by lightning and said that it was split into flinders. **1965–70** *DARE* (Qu. KK22, . . *Completely shattered: "The jug fell out of the window and was ______."*) Infs **AL**50, **OK**1, **SC**34, 39, **WV**4, 5, 14, Broke(n) (*or* busted, smashed) (all) to flinders; (Qu. KK21, . . *"They ran the wagon over the coffee pot and ______."*) Inf **GA**5, Mashed it all to flinders. [7 of 8 Infs old] **1975** Gould *ME Lingo* 98, My truck hit that chicken crate and stove it all to *flinders.*
2 in phr *like flinders:* In an extreme manner. Cf **flinderation 2**
1851 Burke *Polly Peablossom* 72 **MS,** I heard the all-firedest to do, . . and . . I spy my Sal er rarein' and er pitchin', . . and er shoutin' like flinders!

3 in phr *fly to flinders;* Fig: to lose one's temper.
1942 McAtee *Dial. Grant Co. IN* 26 (as of 1890s), *Fly to flinders* . . lose temper.

fling v
A Forms.
1 past: Usu *flung;* also *flang,* rarely *fling, flinged.*
1884 *Anglia* 7.252 [Black], *Pres.* fling—*Past.* flinged, fling'—*Pass. Part.* flinged. **1965** *Dict. Queen's English* 2 **NC,** He flang his coat over the chair. **1966–70** *DARE* (Qu. Y10, . . *"The dog came at him, so he picked up a stone and ______ it at him."*) 42 Infs, **scattered,** Flung; **IL**116, Flang; **MD**49, Some people say flang; **SC**10, Fling; (Qu. BB17) Inf **TX**35, He flung up. **1970** *DARE* FW Addit **IL**118, They flang him in the pokey.
2 past pple: Usu *flung;* rarely *flinged.*
1884 [see **A1** above].
B Senses.
1 with *up:* To vomit, throw up. **chiefly S Midl** *old-fash*
1908 *DN* 3.311 **eAL, wGA.** **1917** *DN* 4.412 **wNC.** **1931** Hannum *Thursday April* 170 **wNC,** But pap . . wouldn't swaller a drap of his licker efn hit was poured down him. He'd fling hit up first. **1939** *AmSp* 14.90 **cTN,** He's flinging up his supper. **1966** Dakin *Dial. Vocab. Ohio R. Valley* 2.484, Other neutral terms are attested only once or twice. These include . . *fling up.* **1967** *DARE* (Qu. BB17) Inf **TX**35, Flinging up. "He flung up."
2 To jilt, reject. *?obs*
1894 Twain *Pudd'nhead Wilson* 168, "Why, Tom, what do you mean? Has Rowena—" "Flung me? No, but the old man has."

fling n Pronc-sp *flang* (cf Pronc Intro 3.I.6.d) [Cf *OED fling* sb. 6. c, a1661; *EDD flink* 4. (1)] *euphem*
1954 *Harder Coll.* **cwTN,** Go and tell, for all I care. I don't give a flang.

fling-ding n
A heated argument.
1982 *Smithsonian Letters* **neVA,** The Commander and Hinky-dink [=unidentified staff member] were having a real fling-ding over that wee-woppy awning he put up.

flinged See **fling** v **A**

flinger along v phr [Perh var of **flinder** v²]
1941 *Hench Coll.* **eVA,** She says she hears it a lot around Gloucester and Middlesex Counties. E.g. "I just flingered along" = I really went fast.

flinghead n
=wood ibis.
1951 *AmSp* 26.92, One [instance] is the changing of *flinthead,* a widely used cognomen of the wood ibis, to *flinghead* in Florida.

fling line n
See quots.
1936 McCarthy *Lang. Mosshorn* **West** [Range terms], Flingline. . . A rope used for a lasso. **1961** Adams *Old-Time Cowhand* 127, His grass rope's called such names as . . "clothesline," "string," . . "fling line," "lass rope," . . or "Tom Horn."

fling up See **fling** v **B1**

flink v¹ [Var of *flinch,* perh infl by **flunk** v¹ **1;** cf *OED flinch* v.¹ 2 "To slink, sneak off."]
1 To act like a coward; to shirk one's duty.
1887 Custer *Tenting* 680 [Black], All the boys done bully, but Corporal Jackson—he flinked. The way he flinked was, to wait till the boys had drove the Injuns two miles, and then he hollered, 'Gin it to 'em!'
2 To play hooky, cut class.
1969 Kantor *MO Bittersweet* 152, 'I'm not going to school. I'm going to flink.' You remember that used to be slang for not going to school? . . My son and daughter tell me nowadays that it's merely 'cutting classes.'

flink v² [swEngl dial *flink,* to fling, toss, sprinkle]
To flick with the fingertips.
1978 *DARE* File **neMA** (as of late 19th cent), If you dipped your hand in water and then made a quick shaking gesture at a person you flinked water in his face.

flink n [Var of *fling*]
1916 Macy–Hussey *Nantucket Scrap Basket* 166, "I'm going out on a flink," meaning a good time.

flint n

1 also *flintie, flint marble:* A marble made of flint or other stone. **chiefly Midl, NY** Cf **agate 1**

1890 *DN* 1.76 **NJ, NY,** "Flints" are marbles made of flint, agate, or some colored stone. **1955** *Daily Progress* (Charlottesville VA) 10 Mar 24/1, The marbles used cost all the way from 10 of the "beanies" for a cent up to $1 or more for the "flints," or agates, commonly known as "aggies." **1955** *PADS* 23.18, *Flint*. . . A marble made of a hard substance, such as flint, agate, or stone. **1958** *PADS* 29.34 **NY,** *Flint*. . . "They cost 10¢ to 50¢". *Ibid,* **IL, MA,** *Flintie*. . . Dim. of *flint.* **1965–70** *DARE* (Qu. EE6d, *Special marbles*) 18 Infs, **chiefly Midl,** Flints; **OK**52, Red flints, twenty-five timers (red) flints; **KY**23, **MO**25, **OK**42, Flint marbles; (Qu. EE6a, . . *The big [marble] that's used to knock others out of the ring*) Inf **MO**25, Flint; (Qu. EE6b, *Small marbles*) Inf **FL**22, Flints. [18 of 22 Infs old] [**1969** *DARE* Tape **KY**23, They made those marbles outa flintrock.] **1973** Ferretti *Marble Book* 45 **NY,** *Flints.* Another name for aggies. **1973** Allen *LAUM* 1.404 **IA** (as of c1950), 1 inf, Flints.

2 A whetstone.

1970 Tarpley *Blinky* 134 **neTX,** Flat piece of stone for sharpening knives . . flint (4.0%) [of 200 infs].

3 See quot. *euphem* Cf *hen down* (at **down** n[3])

1915 *DN* 4.184 **swVA,** *Hen-flint*. . . Chicken dung.

flint corn n Also *flint maize* [See quot 1889] Cf **dent corn**

An **Indian corn** (here: *Zea mays* var *indurata*).

1705 Beverley *Hist. VA* 2.29, One looks as smooth, and as full as the early ripe Corn, and this they call *Flint-Corn.* **1802** Drayton *View of SC* 137, It consists of several varieties, of which the gourd and flint corn, are principally planted. *Ibid,* The *flint* is more hard and nourishing, and grinds more into grist. **1838** MA Ag. Surv. *Rept. for 1837* 20, The best kinds of flint corn weigh 60 lbs. to the bushel. **1874** (1895) Eggleston *Circuit Rider* 14 **sOH,** T'other eend [of a pile of corn] wuz the leetle, flint, hominy corn. **1883** *Encycl. Brit.* (9th ed) 15.309/2, The "Flint" varieties are most common east of Lake Erie and north of Maryland. **1889** *Century Dict.* 2271, *Flint*. . . Hard and firm, as if made of flint: as, *flint* corn or *flint* wheat. **1897** *Jrl. Amer. Folkl.* 10.147, *Zea mays,* . . (hard grains without dents), flint corn, Sulphur Grove, Ohio. **1911** *Century Dict. Suppl., Maize*. . . *Flint corn* . . has larger kernels incapable of popping with heat; the chit is surrounded by starchy matter, and this by a corneous envelop; the kernels are in from 8 to 16 rows in different varieties, but usually in 8. **1966–69** *DARE* (Qu. I34, *If you don't have sweet corn, you can always eat young_____*) Infs **CT**4, 17, **MA**42, **NH**5, Flint corn; (Qu. I33, . . *Ears of corn that are just right for eating*) Inf **CT**4, Flint corn. **1968** *DARE* FW Addit **NY**68, Flint corn—"They was just eight rows of kernels on the cob. And it was filled right out. They wa'n't no dent like they is in this dent corn." **1976** Bailey-Bailey *Hortus Third* 1182, *[Zea Mays]* Var. *indurata*. . . *Flint c[orn], flint m[aize].* Plants early-maturing, with tendency to produce 2 ears; ears long, cylindrical; grains hard, smooth, in 8–10 rows. An old var[iety].

flint, fix one's See **fix** v **B4b**

flinthead n

1 **=wood ibis.** [From the bare, shiny head] **esp FL, GA**

1913 *Auk* 30.491, *Mycteria americana*. . . Flinthead. **1938** Matschat *Suwannee R.* 97 **nFL, sGA,** A large flock of wood ibis swept slowly by. . . "Flintheads," he breathed. She nodded, recognizing the aptness of the name when the big birds strutted past with the last of the evening light falling full on their bare, featherless heads. **1950** *PADS* 14.75 **FL,** *Flint-head*. . . The gannet. **1951** *AmSp* 26.92, *Flinthead,* a widely used cognomen of the wood ibis. **1964** Will *Hist. Okeechobee* 149 **FL,** Up in the sky a Floridy stork, an old Flint Head, comes wingin' along overhead. **1966–68** *DARE* (Qu. Q10) Infs **FL**35, **GA**20, Flinthead.

2 See quot. Cf **niggerhead**

1970 *DARE* (Qu. C26, . . *Special kinds of stone*) Inf **VA**42, Flintrock or flinthead.

flintie See **flint 1**

flint maize See **flint corn**

flint marble See **flint 1**

flint match n [Perh from the use of flint in striking fire]

A friction match.

1968 *DARE* (Qu. F46) Inf **PA**134, Flint match.

flint mill, go through the v phr For varr see quots [Prob from the *flint mill* used in making portland cement]

To suffer severely; to have a bad time.

1960 Criswell *Resp. to PADS 20* **Ozarks,** *To have been through the flint mill* or *mills* meant to have worked almost to exhaustion. Usually plural. Common. "Well, I feel like I have been through the flint mills today working on that dam, and I'm going to bed." **1966–70** *DARE* (Qu. X52, . . *A person . . who had been sick was looking_____*) Inf **IL**114, Like he'd gone through the flint mill; (Qu. CC12b, . . *If a person has a lot of bad luck you might say, "He's been _____."*) Inf **NC**33, Run through the flint mill.

flintstone n [In ref to the hard crust]

1967 *DARE* FW Addit **cOR,** Flintstone—French bread, baked in a can.

flioma See **filione**

flip n[1]

1 A slingshot made with a forked stick and a rubber band. **Midl, Sth, esp AL** Cf **bean-shooter, flipper** n[1] **3**

1908 *DN* 3.311 **eAL, wGA,** *Flip*. . . Same as *slingshot* but not so commonly used. **1942** McAtee *Dial. Grant Co. IN* 26 (as of 1890s), *Flip* . . sling-shot. **1960** Criswell *Resp. to PADS 20* **Ozarks,** *Flip*. . . Nearly every boy had one of these forty years ago. . . This was the only term for the weapon. A sling-shot, with these people was much long[er] with the two ends held in the hand. **1968** *DARE* (QR, near Qu. EE41) Inf **AL**39. **1968** *DARE* Tape **AL**45, We call 'em [=slingshots] flips. **1968** *DARE* File **nAL,** Flip = a slingshot. **1968** Haun *Hawk's Done Gone* 15 **eTN,** He made her flips and shotguns and things like that.

2 A somersault or handspring. **chiefly Sth** Cf **flip-flop 1, 2**

c1960 *Wilson Coll.* **csKY,** *Flip*. . . A somersault. **1965–70** *DARE* (Qu. EE9a, *The children's trick of turning over rapidly straight forward close to the ground*) Infs **AL**8, 46, 52, **LA**37, **PA**247, A flip; **IL**138, 140, **LA**6, **VA**1, (Turning) flips; (Qu. EE9b, *If children jump forward, land on the hands, and turn over*) Infs **VA**1, 9, 13, (Turning) flips.

3 A state of turmoil.

1960 Wentworth-Flexner *Slang* 190, *Flip*. . . A minor or less tumultuous flap. **1967** *DARE* (Qu. KK52) Inf **MO**38, [I don't know] why he had to be in such a flip.

4 Used as an example of something worthless—usu in neg constrs. [*EDD not to care a flip* (at *flip* sb.[1] 2)] **chiefly Sth**

1965–70 *DARE* (Qu. GG21b, . . *"I don't give a _____."*) Infs **AL**6, 62, **GA**77, **MS**63, **NY**232, **TX**40, 53, **VA**46A, Flip; (Qu. HH20b, . . *"He doesn't amount to _____."*) Inf **GA**83, A flip; (Qu. HH20c, . . *"He isn't worth _____."*) Infs **GA**77, **TX**61, A flip; (Qu. KK17, . . *"It isn't worth _____."*) Inf **MS**56, A flip.

5 Used a as a mild oath.

1971 Brunvand *Guide Folkl. UT* 31, In a cultural climate that frowns on swearing, sham swear words and phrases or substitutes like "fudge," "flip," and "scrud" are heard.

‡6 A failure, flop.

1967 *DARE* Tape **AZ**1, And when I made a flip of the, ah, filling station and the restaurant, why, the laundry was about the only thing I knew.

7 See quot.

1968 *DARE* (Qu. H30, *An oblong cake, cooked in deep fat*) Inf **GA**62, Banana flip.

8 **=flapjack 1.**

1965 *DARE* (Qu. H20b, . . *Pancakes*) Inf **MS**62, Flips.

9 A cant hook.

1966 *DARE* Tape **MI**10, A cant hook, a most useful tool they employed with heavy timber became the flip or the crooked steel.

‡10 A cigarette.

1966 *DARE* (Qu. DD6b) Inf **SC**19, Flip.

flip adj

Nimble, agile, spry.

1941 *LANE* Map 461, 1 inf, **ceVT,** [Of either young or old people:] Flip; 1 inf, **swNH,** [Of elderly people:] Flip. **1973** Allen *LAUM* 1.353 **MN** (as of c1950), [Of a lively person:] 1 inf, Flip.

flip n[2]

A flippant, impudent, unsteady person; a flirt.

1915 *DN* 4.199, That little flip will give him a merry chase, I'm thinking. **1919** *DN* 5.66 **NM,** Those little flips wink at every boy they see. **1942** Berrey-Van den Bark *Amer. Slang* 398.3, *Impudent person . .* flip. *Ibid* 410.3, *Flighty person . .* flip, *a forward or flippant person.* **1955** Shapiro *Hear Me Talkin'* 347 **NY,** He's not a flip as far as business is concerned. **1965-70** *DARE* (Qu. II36a, *Somebody who talks back or gives rude answers: "Did you ever see such a ______?"*) 16 Infs, **chiefly C Atl, CA,** Flip; (Qu. AA7b, . . *A woman who is very fond of men . . if she's not respectable about it*) Inf **CA**196, A flip.

flip-flap n Cf Intro "Language Changes" I.3

1 **=flapjack 1.**

1942 Berrey-Van den Bark *Amer. Slang* 91.14, *Griddle cakes . .* flip-flaps.

2 A **hellgrammite 1.**

1889 *Century Dict.* 2272 **VA,** *Flipflap . .* the dobson or hellgrammite. **1901** Howard *Insect Book* 212, The names in use in Rhode Island alone for this insect. . . are: . . flip-flaps, alligators, . . and hell-diver. **1905** Kellogg *Amer. Insects* 226, But other names are. . . applied to the larva . . alone: . . flipflap [etc]. **1948** *Field & Stream* July 42/2 *(DA),* Various stages of the dobson are known as . . bogarts, hell-devils, flip-flaps, snake doctors and hell-divers.

3 See **flip-flop 1.**

4 See **flip-flop 2.**

5 See **flip-flop 3.**

flip-flop n

1 also *flip-flap:* A somersault.

1902 (1903) Lorimer *Letters* 245 **Chicago IL,** And when a fellow's turning flip-flops up among the clouds, he's naturally going to have the farmers gaping at him. **1929** *Liberty* 30 Nov. 43/1 *(OEDS),* Turning hand-springs and flip-flops all over the sawdust covered floor. **1940-41** Cassidy *WI Atlas* 1 inf, **swWI,** Flip-flap. **1960** *PADS* 34.51 **neCO,** *Colorado Localisms . .* used by at least two informants and . . in at least two different communities. . . Flip (flop) 'somersault.' **c1960** *Wilson Coll.* **csKY,** *Flip-flop. . .* A somersault, a flip. **1966-69** *DARE* (Qu. EE9a) Infs **IN**56, **OK**52, Flip-flop. **1973** Allen *LAUM* 1.392 **NE** (as of c1950), Flip-flop. [3 infs]

2 also *flip-flap:* A handspring; also fig. **esp N Midl, S Atl** See Map

1917 Garland *Son Middle Border* 22 **WI,** Once when the 'tumbling' in the little country 'show' seemed not to his liking, Frank sprang over the ropes into the arena and went around the ring in a series of professional flip-flaps. **1920s** in 1944 *ADD* **cNY,** Flip-flop. **1965-70** *DARE* (Qu. EE9b, *If children jump forward, land on the hands, and turn over*) 61 Infs, **scattered, but esp N Midl, S Atl,** Flip-flop; **OK**18, Turn flip-flops; (Qu. BB7) Inf **MI**100, My heart does flip-flops. **1969** *New Yorker* 12 Apr 100/2, Every time Lind or any other astronaut opens his mouth, the entire space industry turns flip-flops.

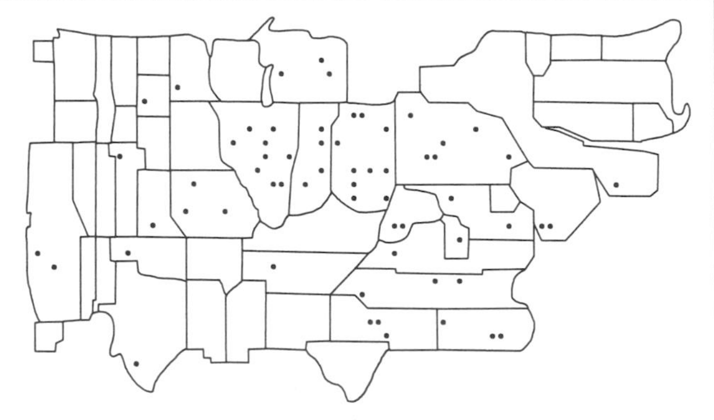

•flip-flop 2 + varr (Qq. EE9b, BB7)

3 rarely *flip-flap;* Fig: an abrupt reversal of opinion or policy—often in phr *do a flip-flop.*

1887 *Lantern* (New Orleans LA) 5 Feb 6/1 (*AmSp* 25.33), It has been a week of flip-flaps in local baseball circles. **1938** Hertzler *Horse & Buggy Dr.* 176 **KS** (as of late 19th cent), After watching us perform, the Professor did a flipflop and . . pled with us to abandon thoughts of general surgery and become laryngologists. **1948** *Time* 6 Dec 21/3, As Murray's attacks mounted in fervency, some old party-liners did some curious flip-flops.

4 An indecisive person.

1969 *DARE* FW Addit **ceNY,** He's a flip-flop—he's always changing sides.

5 **=belly-flop 1.** Cf **flop n 8**

1969 *DARE* (Qu. EE25, *When a child picks up his sled . . runs with it, and then throws himself down on it, that's a ______*) Inf **IL**61, Flip-flop.

6 A slipper or sandal (esp a rubber one with a toe thong) which flaps against the sole of the foot in walking.

1966-70 *DARE* (Qu. W8) Inf **PA**79, Flip-flops—for pools; (Qu. W13) Inf **GA**6, Flip-flops—rubber sandals; (Qu. W21) Infs **NJ**63, **VA**73, Flip-flops; **NY**89, Flip-flops—just slide feet in; **RI**15, Flip-flops—rubber, with thong. **1972** *New Yorker* 15 Apr 132/2 **FL,** A woman in Tampa said that her daughter had left home . . wearing a white blouse, pink pants, and green "flip-flops." **1981** *Seventeen Letters* **GA,** *Flip Flops*—Shoes you wear mostly during summer. **1986** Pederson *LAGS Concordance* **Gulf Region** *(Shoes)* 12 infs, Flip-flops. **1989** *Sierra* Mar/Apr 113 **UT,** I pull on my . . jacket . . and squish down to the kitchen area on flipflops that feel like two cold pieces of liver on my feet.

7 also *flip-floppy:* See quot.

1970 *DARE* (Qu. N5, *Nicknames for . . an old or broken-down car*) Inf **TN**53, Flip-flop; **VA**70, Milk wagon, Nellybelle, flip-floppy, Georgia buggy.

flip-it n Cf **flip-stick**

=cricket n^2.

1950 *WELS Suppl.* **seWI,** *Flip it*—Game where they take a long stick and hit a short tapered one.

flipjack n Also *flipjacker, flipperjack, flippum-jack*

=flapjack 1.

1907 *DN* 3.187 **seNH,** *Flipper-jack. . .* Jocose form of *flap-jack.* "I want flipper-jacks for breakfast." **1919** *DN* 5.36 **AR,** In the song "Sugar Hill":—Great big pan o' flippum-jacks,/ An' a little bit o' bottle o' wine,/ Great big jug o' 'lasses / To feed that gal o' mine. **1942** Berrey-Van den Bark *Amer. Slang* 91.14, *Griddle cakes . .* flip-jackers. **1966** *DARE* Tape **ME**2, Well, we made buckwheat pancakes as they called it. Flipjacks. **1970** *DARE* (QR near Qu. H20b) Inf **KY**85, Flipjacks.

flip one's cookies See **cookie** n^1 **4**

flip-over n

1 **=flip-flop 2.**

1966-68 *DARE* (Qu. EE9b, *If children jump forward, land on the hands, and turn over*) Infs **GA**1, 8, **NC**45, **OH**1, **PA**167, Flip-over.

2 **=flipper** n^1 **2.**

1970 *DARE* (Qu. F3, *When you're frying things . . you turn them over with a ______*) Inf **KY**85, Flip-over.

flip-over pie n

Perh a turnover.

1937 Sandoz *Slogum* 162 **NE** (as of c1900), Sometimes Libby made special dishes for him, a flip-over pie from the ends of the crust.

flipper n^1

1 **=flapjack 1. esp NEng**

1850 (1914) Kingsley *Diary* 114 **CT,** We arrived at the bar in time to . . get supper &c which consisted of flippers & fried pork. **1882** Hubbard *Moosehead Lake* 26 *(DA)* **ME,** Flippers, or 'flap-jacks,' are mixed like bread, except that a little more baking powder is used, and a good deal more water. **1941** *LANE* Map 289, *Flapjack, slapjack, flapover, flipper . .* are being replaced by *griddle cake, pan cake* or *fritter.* **1942** Berrey-Van den Bark *Amer. Slang* 91.14, *Griddle cakes . .* flippers.

2 A spatula. Cf **egg turner**

1950 *WELS* 2 Infs, **WI,** Flipper. **1965-70** *DARE* (Qu. F3) 26 Infs, **chiefly east of Missip R, SW,** Flipper; **NC**43, **SC**19, Egg flipper; **CA**162, Pancake flipper.

3 also *flipper-crutch, nigger-flipper:* A children's device using an elastic piece of wood or rubber bands to shoot small objects. Cf **bean-shooter, flip** n^1 **1**

1952 Brown *NC Folkl.* 1.234, *Flippers*—These were made from strong, springy wood like hickory or oak. A small limb or the trunk of a small tree was used. They were left round on one end for a handle. The other end was shaped off much like the half of a b[illegible]. They were held with one hand, while the other hand was used to hold a small pebble to shoot out for a distance of forty to fifty yards. Small boys used to use them in war games. **1970** Tarpley *Blinky* 230 **neTX,** Boy's weapon made of rubber strips on a forked stick . . 6% [of 200 infs] (nigger) flipper. *Ibid* 231, An unusual geographical distribution may be seen for *(nigger) flipper,* a name which appears to be used almost universally in Red River County but which is known in only three other counties. **1971** Bright *Word Geog. CA & NV* 158, *Slingshot . . flipper (crutch)* 2% [of 300 infs].

4 A handspring. Cf **flip** n^1 **2, flip-flop 2**

1967 *DARE* (Qu. EE9b) Inf **PA**35, Flipper.

5 In marble play: a shooter.

1969 *DARE* (Qu. EE6a) Inf **RI**12, Flipper—it could be an agate or a steelie or a china king.

flipper n^2 [Perh blend of **flip** n^2 + *flapper*]

1967–69 *DARE* (Qu. W36, . . *A woman who uses a lot of cosmetics*) Inf **IL**63A, Flipper; (Qu. HH34, . . *Words . . for a woman*) Inf **AR**47, Flipper; (Qu. HH35, *A woman who puts on a lot of airs*) Inf **IN**57, Flipper.

‡flippercanorious adj Cf **hippocanarious**

1911 *DN* 3.543 **NE,** *Flippercanorious. . .* Fine, grand; about the same as *scrumptious.* "I feel flippercanorious, to-day."

flipper-crutch See **flipper** n^1 **3**

flipperdinger n

1 A children's toy; see quots.

1963 *Chr. Sci. Monitor* (Boston MA) 26 Apr 6/6 **nwNC,** The folk industry's top seller is the flipperdinger. It is a reed blower which has a ball of corn-stalk pith that hovers over a jet of air. **1972** Cooper *NC Mt. Folkl.* 34, There were dolls, yarn balls, whistles, geehaw whimmydiddles or ziggerboos, rattle traps, noisemakers or bull roars and flipperdingers.

2 See quot.

1979 *DARE* File, In Mississippi a *flipperdinger* is a *tee-totter* or a *see-saw.*

flipperjack See **flipjack**

flippery floppery adv phr [Var of *flip-flop*]

In a loose, flapping manner.

1916 *DN* 4.275 **NE,** The fish went *flippery floppery.*

flippety-snippet See **flippy-wippet**

flippity adj Also *flipty* [Prob blend of *flip* or *flippant* + *uppity*]

Arrogant.

1967–69 *DARE* (Qu. HH35, *A woman who puts on a lot of airs: "She's too ______ for me."*) Inf **IL**54, Flippity ['flɪpəti]; **LA**8, Flipty ['flɪptɪ]; (Qu. II36b, . . *Somebody who talks back. . . "She certainly is ______!"*) Inf **LA**8, Flipty; (Qu. GG38) Inf **LA**8, Flipty person.

flippum-jack See **flipjack**

flippy adj [*flip* adj]

Silly, impudent.

1967–70 *DARE* (Qu. HH9, *A very silly or light-headed person*) Inf **AL**25, Flippy; (Qu. II36b, . . *Somebody who talks back. . . "She certainly is ______."*) Inf **IL**116, Flippy; **MA**53, [A] flippy one.

flippy-wippet n Also *flippety-snippet* [Nonce words based on *flip* adj, **flippy;** perh infl by **flibbertigibbet** and *snippet* a small scrap]

A silly, flighty person.

1949 Webber *Backwoods Teacher* 18 **Ozarks,** Last year they had a little ol' flippety-snippet that I don't reckon was no better'n she'd ort to abeen. Painted her face like a barn and acted uppity. **1968** *DARE* (Qu. HH9, *A very silly or light-headed person*) Inf **NY**92, Flippy-wippet.

flips exclam Cf **baby fingers, fudgings**

In marble play: a call to assert the right to move one's shooter.

1963 *KY Folkl. Rec.* 9.3.64, *The command to push or clip the shooter with one finger: . .* flips$_{[-]}$ Carter [Co.]

flipshot n

=**flip** n^1 **1.**

1982 Ginns *Snowbird Gravy* 131 **nwNC,** They showed me how to build a flip shot, a slingshot—some called 'em a flip shot.

flip-stick n Cf **flip-it**

=**cricket** n^2.

1969–70 *DARE* (Qu. EE10, *A game in which a short stick lying on the ground is flipped into the air and then hit with a longer stick, that's ______*) Infs **NC**84, **NY**190, Flip-stick.

flipty See **flippity**

flirch adj [nEngl dial *flurch* a large quantity]

Abundant.

1889 *AN&Q* 3.255/2 **NJ,** On the Cape May meadows flowers are said to be 'flirch' or abundant. **1894** *DN* 1.330 **sNJ,** *Flirch:* abundant.

flirt v Pronc-sp *flut* [*OED* 1583 →]

1 To move (something) with a jerk; to toss, flip. **Sth, S Midl**

1872 Twain *Roughing It* 288 **MO,** She could heft a bar'l of flour as easy as I can flirt a flapjack. **1888** Jones *Negro Myths* 81 **GA coast,** Buh Porpus sorter hump eh back an flut eh tail. **1937** in 1972 *Amer. Slave* 2.56 **cnSC,** I went often to the muster grounds at Kelton to see the soldiers drill and to flirt my curls at them. **1939** FWP *Guide FL* 456, They [=gamecocks] are tossed and 'flirted' to develop wing power, balance, style and punch. **1960** Criswell *Resp. to PADS 20* **Ozarks,** Flirt—to fling. . . I have not heard it elsewhere. Usually used only by women. Common. "I just flirted my skirt over my head and ran half dressed to church." **1968** *DARE* (QR, near Qu. M11) Inf **NC**80, So they [=cows] can't flirt their head around. **1969** *DARE* Tape **KY**23, Maybe one [=a marble] would be a-laying in the hole . . and this other fella was wanting to make that hole and some way he just squirrel his marble in there and it just flirt his'n out.

2 To flutter.

1952 Brown *NC Folkl.* 1.541, *Flirting at the heart. . . Fluttering* at the heart.

flirt n

1 A witty retort; a jibe. [*OED* →1726]

1897 Johnston *Old Times GA* 66, Final she got mad, and she fetched a flirt, she did, and as she fetched it, she fa'rly *sung* out, 'Well thank the good Lord, I ain't dead yit!'

2 See quot. [Cf *EDD flirt* sb. 8 "A slight shower"]

1975 Gould *ME Lingo* 98, *Flirt o' snow*—A light flurry, not enough to "make" any. Not so much as a *robin snow,* even.

flirty-eyed adj

Coquettish.

1943 Writers' Program NC *Bundle of Troubles* 25, Miss Muskrat . . set flirty-eyed on a stump . . all dressed up in a new fur coat.

flit v

1 To move to a different home; to assist (someone) in moving. [Scots, nEngl dial; *OED* 1504 →] Cf **flitting**

1843 (1916) Hall *New Purchase* 264 **IN,** A *nice* young gentleman engaged to be married . . is meditating "to flit" to a bran new settlement. **1882** (1971) Gibbons *PA Dutch* 380, Said an innkeeper, "The people come to flit them,"—to help them move. **1916** *DN* 4.343 **nMD,** *Flit. . .* To move house. **1930** Shoemaker *1300 Words* 22 **cPA Mts** (as of c1900), *Flitting*—Moving to a new abode.

2 To strut.

1967–70 *DARE* (Qu. Y22, *To move around in a way to make people take notice of you: "Look at him ______."*) Infs **MA**123, **NY**145, **OH**2, Flit; **NY**35, Flit around; **MN**33, Flit his feathers.

flit n [Perh var of **flirt** n **2**]

A flurry.

1828 in 1938 Gardiner–Gardiner *Chron. Old Berkeley* 278 **VA,** Wind continues, cloudy and flits of snow.

flitch n Pronc-spp *fletch, flick* [*OED* a700 →]

1 A cured side of pork; salt pork, bacon. **chiefly PA** See Map

1632 in 1855 New Plymouth Colony *Records* 1.7 **seMA,** A flich of bacon he was to haue at the rate of three powndes of beaver. **1795** (1976) Freneau *Poems* 10 **N Atl,** Down he took his hams and bacon flitches. **1852** (1854) Kennedy *Horse-Shoe Robinson* 273 **MD,** Into this narrow apartment the soldiers were now marched; . . sundry flitches of bacon, that hung upon the walls, were removed. **1872** Burnham *Memoirs U.S. Secret Service* 220, [He] . . went about the old "Queen City" [=Cincinnati] . . inquiring the price of hams and sides and flitches. **1935** *AmSp* 10.172 **sePA** (as of late 19th cent), *Flitch* was commonly used for bacon. **1949** Kurath *Word Geog.* 70, In the heart of Pennsylvania, from the Delaware to the Allegheny River, the expressions *flitch of bacon* and *flitch of side meat* are widely used for salt pork, and some in this area apply the term also to smoked *side meat. Flitch* has not spread beyond the boundaries of the state, although some of our informants on Delaware Bay are familiar with it. **1951** *AmSp* 26.253 **Upstate NY,** [Words from] Pennsylvania: . . *flitch* (bacon). **1952** Brown *NC Folkl.* 1.541, *Fletch. . . Flitch;* smoked bacon. **1965–70** *DARE* (Qu. H38, *Other* *words for bacon*) 19 Infs, **chiefly PA,** Flitch; **NJ**56, Smoked flitch; (QR, near Qu. BB50) Inf **MD**32, Fat meat is also called flitch. **1966** Dakin *Dial. Vocab. Ohio R. Valley* 2.336, The Pennsylvania term *flitch* is attested only once in Jefferson County [Ohio] on the upper river. **1967** Faries *Word Geog. MO* 103, *Salt pork . . flitch of bacon* (2 occurrences). **1969** Sorden *Lumberjack Lingo* 43 **NEng, Gt Lakes,** *Flitch. . .* The side of a hog salted and cured; a side of bacon.

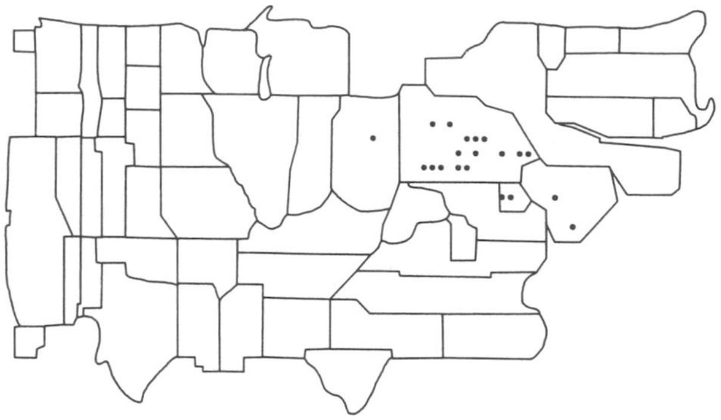

•flitch 1 + var (Qu. H38)

2 A slice or slab of flesh.

1805 (1904) Lewis *Orig. Jrls. Lewis & Clark Exped.* 2.178, The ballance of the party were employed in cuting the meat we had killed yesterday into thin fletches and drying it. **1805** in 1905 *Ibid* 3.325, The [whale] blubber . . was laid by in their cabins in large flickes for use. **1806** in 1905 *Ibid* 4.132, The sturgeon which had been previously cut into large fletches is now laid on the hot stones.

3 A slice or slab cut from a log, esp one with some of the bark remaining.

1748 in 1934 Eliot *Field Husbandry* 12 **CT,** I ordered therefore a Tree to be cut down across the Brook, and prepared Flitches instead of Plank which we set aslant, the upper end resting upon the Staddle that was fallen across the Brook. [Footnote to *flitches:*] Slabs or the outside pieces of sawed logs. **1944** *AmSp* 19.93, Experts saw 'flitches' of aero [=wood suitable for airplane structural members] out of any good log of the six species. **1969** Sorden *Lumberjack Lingo* 43 **NEng, Gt Lakes,** *Flitch. . .* A piece of lumber with bark on one or both sides.

4 See quot 1872.

1872 (1876) Knight *Amer. Mech. Dict.* 2.883, *Flitch. . .* One of several associated planks which are fastened side by side to form a compound beam. **1966** *DARE* Tape **ME**25, Made out of timbers, some of 'em had fifteen or twenty pieces, what we call . . double-flitched timber. A flitch is part of the timber. . . they're bolted together side by side [in building boats].

5 Appar a **firefly 1.**

1950 *WELS (A small insect that flashes light at its tail)* 1 Inf, **cnWI,** Firefly, lightning bug, flitch.

flitches n pl Cf **flux**

1968 *DARE* (Qu. BB19, *Joking names for looseness of the bowels*) Inf **LA**35 Flitches.

flitchet n [Perh var of Engl dial *flicket* a tatter, rag]

1968 *DARE* (Qu. W27, *What do you call a three-cornered tear in a piece of clothing from catching it on something sharp*) Inf **MD**37, Three-cornered flitchet ['flıčıt].

flitflats n pl

=all-overs 1.

1916 *DN* 4.323 **KS,** Give one the flitflats. . . To make one nervous. "He gives me the flitflats whenever he starts on that strain."

flitter n[1] [Var of *fritter*]

1 also *flitter cake:* A fritter; batter, often containing meat or fruit, fried in deep fat.

1837 Sherwood *Gaz. GA* 69, [In a list of 'provincialisms' to be avoided:] *Flitters* for fritters. **1903** *DN* 2.313 **seMO. 1906** *DN* 3.118 **sIN. 1919** *DN* 5.36 **KY. 1946** *PADS* 6.13 **eNC** (as of 1900–10), *Flitter. . .* A fritter, usually made of fried oysters and flour. . . Common. **1952** Brown *NC Folkl.* 1.541, *Flitter. . .* A fried meat cake of any kind. **1954** *Harder Coll.* **cwTN,** *Flitter. . .* A fritter . . of fried oysters and flour. **c1960** *Wilson Coll.* **csKY,** *Flitter. . .* A fritter, simple or elaborate, like a corn fritter. **1965–66** *DARE* (Qu. H22, . . *Flat pieces of food dipped in batter and fried in deep fat;* total Infs questioned, 75) Inf **MS**55, Flitter cakes; **GA**8, **MS**25, 46, 63, 72, **OK**1, Flitters. **1966** Dakin *Dial. Vocab. Ohio R. Valley* 2.323, The records quite commonly include the entry *fritter* or *flitter*—a dumpling-like product fried in deep fat rather than steamed. **1967** Faries *Word Geog. MO* 101, The informants list a variety of other words to identify [a small corn cake] . . *flitters, fritters, corn fritters* [etc].

2a also *flitter cake:* **=flapjack 1. chiefly S Midl** See Map Cf **fritter** n **1**

1848 Bartlett *Americanisms, Flitter* . . a pan-cake. **1905** *DN* 3.79 **nwAR,** I know a woman . . that calls pan-cakes 'flittercakes'. **1906** [see **2b** below]. **1919** *DN* 5.36 **KY. 1950** [see **2b** below]. **1954** *Harder Coll.* **cwTN,** [Syrup is] poured over flitters. **c1960** *Wilson Coll.* **csKY,** *Flitter. . .* Called also flitter-cake. **1965–70** *DARE* (Qu. H20b) 19 Infs, **chiefly S Midl,** Flitters; **KY**37, Flitter cakes. **1966** Dakin *Dial. Vocab. Ohio R. Valley* 2.328, People in the Mountains and in southern Kentucky generally, sometimes in the Bluegrass, and along the river in southeastern Ohio remember but apparently seldom use the old name *fritter* or *flitter*—a thin griddle cake, not the dumpling-like cake fried in deep fat like a doughnut. Where preserved in Ohio, this term always seems to be *flitter,* as it also is in the Mountains. **1967** Faries *Word Geog. MO* 102, Two expressions substituted by the informants are *flap jacks* . . and *flitters* (5 occurrences). **1971** Wood *Vocab. Change* 304 **Sth,** [82 of 1000 infs offered *flitters* for 'round, flat cakes made with white flour'.] **1973** Allen *LAUM* 1.283 **NE** (as of c1950), [1 inf offered *flitters* for 'griddle cakes,' and called it old-fashioned.]

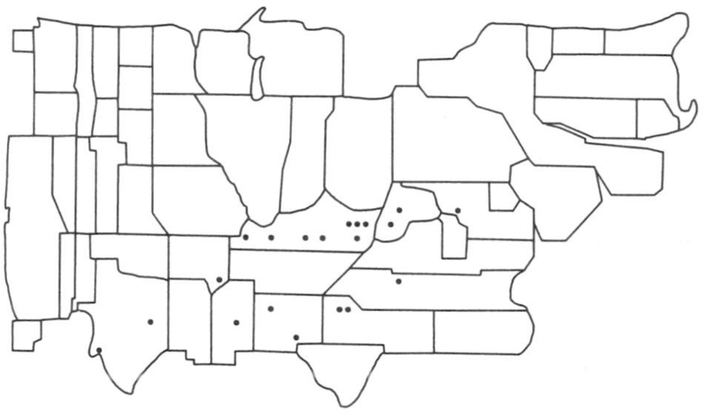

•flitter n[1] 2a + var (Qu. H20b)

b esp in adj phr *flat as a flitter:* Very flat.

1906 *DN* 3.118 **sIN,** He fell flat as a flitter. *Ibid* 136 **nwAR,** Flitter. . . Griddle-cake. The use of the word seems to be common only in the expression, "flat as a flitter." **1941** *AmSp* 16.21 **sIN. 1950** *PADS* 13.17 **cTX,** *Flitter. . .* A fritter. Uneducated. However, it is almost always *flitter* in the expression "as flat as a flitter," possibly because of the alliteration. **1968–69** *DARE* (Qu. KK21, . . *"They ran the wagon over the coffee pot and ______."*) Infs **GA**23, **KY**44, **LA**17, Mashed it flat as a flitter. **1970** *DARE* FW Addit **KY**85, Flat as a flitter—common. **1975** Preston *Proverbial Comparisons* 31 **sIN,** Flat as a flitter.

3 See quot. [Cf *pancake* in 1902 Farmer–Henley *Slang*]

1944 *PADS* 2.29 **KY,** *Flitter. . .* Pudenda muliebria. E. Ky. Rural. Common.

4 See quot.

1968 *DARE* (Qu. H27, . . *Joking names for doughnuts*) Inf **NY**88, Flitter.

5 **=fritter** n **2. Sth, S Midl**

1965–70 *DARE* (Qu. H14, *Bread that's made with cornmeal*) Inf **KY**25, Corn fritters; (Qu. H25, . . *Fried corn meal*) Infs **AR**55, **KY**40, 74, **VA**9, Flitters; **DE**2, **GA**70, **KY**74, **NC**1, Corn flitters; **MS**72, Cornmeal flitters; **GA**8, **MS**55, Fried (corn) flitters.

6 **=fritter** n **3.**

c1960 *Wilson Coll.* **csKY,** Flitter. . . Sometimes applied to a flat thin patty of mashed potatoes.

flitter n[2]

=flicker n[2] **1.**

1900 *Wilson Bulletin* 31.6, *Flitter.* Eastern Pennsylvania. A corruption of Flicker.

flitter n[3] [*flitter* v]

A flutter, tizzy.

1941 *LANE* Map 476–477 *(Excited, all nerved up)* 1 inf, **swCT,** All of a flitter.

flitter intj

Used as a mild expression of annoyance.

1954 *Harder Coll.* **cwTN,** Aw flitter. **1968** *DARE* (Qu. NN8a, *Exclamations of annoyance or disgust: "Oh ________, I've lost my glasses again."*) Inf **LA**28, Flitter.

flitter around v phr

1 To flit about.

1967 *DARE* (Qu. KK31, *To go about aimlessly looking for distraction: "He doesn't have anything to do, so he's just ________ around."*) Inf **MA**55, Flittering—[said] of women.

2 To strut. Cf **flit v 2**

1966 *DARE* (Qu. Y22, *To move around in a way to make people take notice of you: "Look at him ________."*) Inf **ME**13, Flitter around.

flitterbudget See **flutterbudget**

flitter cake See **flitter n[1] 1, 2a**

flittergibbet n Cf **flibbertigibbet, flutterbudget**

1967 *DARE* (Qu. W40, . . *A woman who overdresses*) Inf **MA**5, Flittergibbet; (Qu. AA7b, . . *A woman who is very fond of men*) Inf **MA**5, Flittergibbet; (Qu. HH9, *A very silly or light-headed person*) Inf **MA**5, Flittergibbet—old-fashioned.

flitterjig n [Ir dial, usu in phr *to flitterjigs* to pieces] *obs*

1865 Crockett *Life* 32, I scratched his face all to a flitter jig, and soon made him cry out for quarters in good earnest. The fight being over, I went on home.

flittermouse n [*OED* 1547 →; widespread in Scots and Engl dial]

1967 *DARE* (QR, near Qu. Q3) Inf **CO**7, Bats are flittermice.

flitter out v phr Cf **flicker v**

To fail.

1939 *AmSp* 14.90 **cTN,** He's flittered out at every job he's tried.

flitters n pl [*OED* 1620 → "Now *dial.*"; var of *fitters* fragments, infl by *flitter* to fly about, fly to pieces]

=flinders.

1789 *Amer. Museum* 6.296/2, Besides tearing your private character to flitters, [he] marks you out for the odium of the public, as an enemy to the liberty of the press. **1829** *MA Spy & Worcester Co. Advt.* (Worcester MA) 10 June 1/4 (citing *Boston Philanthropist*), [The bull had broken] [t]he most splendid mirror then in New England, . . all in flitters! **1863** U.S. Congress *Congressional Globe* 37th Cong 3d Sess 23 Feb 1197/1 **NH,** The northern part of the country . . will go into flitters and anarchy. **1905** *DN* 3.79 **nwAR,** It was just smashed to flitters.

flitter tree See **honey pond and flitter tree**

flittervish n [Cf Ger dial *Flittermaus, Fledawisch* a bat]

1950 *WELS (A very silly or light-headed person)* 1 Inf, **csWI,** Flittervish.

flittery adj [*flitter* v]

Flighty.

1966 *DARE* (Qu. HH9, . . *Silly or light-headed*) Inf **MT**3, Flittery.

flitting n Also *fleeting* [**flit v 1;** *OED* c1200 →; the form *fleeting* may be by confusion with **fleet v**] **chiefly PA** *somewhat old-fash*

1 The process or an occasion of moving to a different home.

1802 (1898) Hunt *Diary* 6/1 **sePA,** Went Thomas Evans's fleeting from waggon town [=Wagontown, PA] to the turnpike. **1870** *Nation* 28 July 56/2 **sePA,** It was the Scotch probably who furnished the word for the departure of a household—the "flitting." **1898** *Cosmopolitan* 192/1 **ME,** Two or three families departed by the same train. . . These mysterious flittings, like that of the famous Tartar tribe, roused a suspicion. **1935** *AmSp* 10.172 **sePA,** A few of the [old-fashioned English] terms are still in general use. . . *Flitting* in the sense of a family moving is another example. **1939** Aurand *Quaint Idioms* 24 **sePA,** We want you and the whole family to come and help us with the *flittin'* (moving) on April 1st. **1966** *DARE* File **cwPA,** "It's flittin' day" means "It's moving day." **1982** *Smithsonian Letters* **csPA,** The neighbours would pitch in and help with all the work of the move, the women bringing food, and the "flittin' " would become a social event. **1986** Hendrickson *Amer. Talk* 161, April first in [Pennsylvania] Dutch country is traditionally moving day, which is called *flittin' day.*

2 The entirety of the household goods of a family that is moving; a household in transit.

1907 *German Amer. Annals* 9.375 **sePA,** *Flitting.* Moving (of household goods.) "There goes Jones' flitting." **1916** *DN* 4.337 **sePA,** *Flitting.* . . Furniture, etc., moving from house to house. "We saw a flitting go by yesterday." **1917** in 1944 *ADD* **sWV,** [Flitting] = a moving van of household goods. **1940** Yoder *Rosanna* 29 **PA,** Several of the Amish men . . came with their wives to help load "the flittin'." The large cookstove was heavy; the kitchen cupboard was inconvenient to handle.

flixweed n [Etym unknown]

1 A **tansy mustard** (here: *Descurainia sophia*). [*OED* 1578 →]

1861 Wood *Class-Book* 234, *S. Sophia.* . . Flixweed. **1876** Hobbs *Bot. Hdbk.* 38, Flix-weed, Fine-leaved hedge mustard, Sisymbrium sophia. **1900** Lyons *Plant Names* 351. **1937** U.S. Forest Serv. *Range Plant Hdbk.* W182, Flixweed . . *Sisymbrium sophia.* **1950** Stevens *ND Plants* 156, *Flixweed.* . . has become extremely common . . especially in waste grounds about towns and small pastures. **1973** Hitchcock–Cronquist *Flora Pacific NW* 161, Alas[ka] to Cal, e to Atl; flixweed. . . *D[escurainia] sophia.*

2 =sand rocket.

1900 Lyons *Plant Names* 137, *Diplotaxis. . . muralis.* . . Flix-weed. **1959** Carleton *Index Herb. Plants* 47, *Flix-weed:* Diplotaxis muralis; . . Nasturtium officinale; Sisymbrium sophia.

3 Watercress.

1959 [see **2** above].

flo' See **floor**

float n

1 also attrib; also *floats, float copper,* ~ *mineral,* ~ *ore,* ~ *rock:* Ore or ore-bearing rock which has been redeposited at some distance from its original formation; also fig. Cf **float gold 2**

1814 Brackenridge *Views of LA* 148, That kind of ore called *floats,* being formed in large, irregular, but unconnected masses. . . The floats have no tiif [=tiff, sparry matter requiring separation with a pick], and are the most easily smelted. **1871** in 1872 U.S. Treas. Dept. *Mines* 212, A section of country twenty miles long and eight miles wide is covered with float quartz, some of which is reported very rich. **1873** Beadle *Undeveloped West* 333 **UT,** The first thing we look for is "float." This consists of mineral broken off from "croppings," or thrown out or washed out from fissures. **1876** in 1877 U.S. Treas. Dept. *Mines* 177, A point on the lode where some faint traces of float-mineral indicated the existence of ore beneath. **1880** Ingham *Digging Gold* 273 **SD,** The prospectors found 'float' rock at the base of the mountain. **1881** Raymond *Gloss. Mining* 36, *Float-ore,* water-worn particles of ore; fragments of vein-material found on the surface, away from the vein-outcrop. **1900** *Century Illustr. Mag.* 59.510/2, The literary float-rock . . all too often is taken for the vein. **1933** *Daily Progress* (Charlottesville VA) 6 Nov 1/3 *(Hench Coll.)* **CO,** The "look" extended into a 3-week's search. Then a piece of "float" was found. A float is a small piece of gold bearing ore chipped off from the main view [sic for *vein*] and washed away. **1966** *DARE* Tape **NM**15, They go along picking up this float 'n' panning it to see whether there's any gold in it. **1972** *Yesterday* 1.3.12 **nIL,** About the only "mining" today is by kids who sometimes find "float roack" [sic] along the creek and sell it to tourists. **1987** *DARE* File **csWI,** Float copper is sometimes found by farmers plowing in the formerly glaciated areas of Wisconsin. There is a large chunk of it in the UW Geology Museum in Madison.

2 =floating island 2.

1878 Guild *Old Times in TN* 396, And then came the fourth and final course, of fruit, wines, float, sillabub, and pickles. **1889** *Harper's New Mth. Mag.* 79.124/2 **Sth,** 'Drusy' in housewifely discomfiture . . without . . time to beat up a bowl of float. **1906** Gregory *Woman's Cookbook* 312, *Float.* **1956** McAtee *Some Dialect NC* 16, *Float* . . a thin custard topped with clumps of whipped eggwhite. **c1960** *Wilson Coll.* **csKY,** *Float* . . boiled custard, with floating whipped cream or egg white on top; also *floating island.* **1964** Wallace *Frontier Life* 127 **OK** (as of 1893–1906), At the right of each person's plate she placed a big goblet of rich "float," a concoction of sugar, eggs, ice cold milk, and vanilla extract, similar to modern milkshakes. **1968** *DARE* (Qu. H63, . . *Desserts*) Inf **MD**14, Apple float—egg custard with canned apples and lemon juice; white of eggs beaten in. Eaten back on the farm.

3 Any of various types of wheeled vehicle with a low platform for carrying heavy loads. **esp Sth**

1879 in 1924 Hearn *Creole Sketches* 79, Without, cotton-floats might rumble, and street-cars vulgarly jingle their bells. **1925** *Book of Rural Life* 4.2534, In this picture the hay is being brought from the field on what are known as floats, running very close to the ground. **1945** Saxon *Gumbo Ya-Ya* 147 **LA,** But within a week his brother was run over by a cotton float and instantly killed. **1967** *DARE* (Qu. L13, *The kind of wagon used for carrying hay*) Inf **TX**12, Float—a big flatbed, larger than a wagon, on wheels; (Qu. N11, *A very large truck used to haul freight*) Inf **LA**10, Float—for carrying soybeans and other things; including ones with closed trailer. **1982** *NADS Letters* **cNC,** At the U.S. Post Office here in Chapel Hill . . we have some large carts which the other fellows —mostly natives of Chapel Hill—refer to as "floats." . . They're about six feet long, and the end railings are about four feet high. The official name for it is a Nutter cart, from the name of the manufacturer.

4 **=stoneboat.**

1968 *DARE* (Qu. L57, *A low wooden platform used for bringing stones or heavy things out of the fields*) Inf **OH**70, Float.

5 also *plank float:* A platform of heavy planks used to smooth plowed ground or to surface a road or racetrack.

1911 *Century Dict.* 4.2274, *Float.* . . A timber drag used for dressing off roads, especially race-courses. **1952** *Sun* (Baltimore MD) 1 Dec sec B 17/1 *(Hench Coll.),* We used floats (heavy wooden drags) to get rid of most of the water [on a racetrack]. **1967–68** *DARE* (Qu. L20, *The implement used in a field after it's been plowed to break up the lumps*) Infs **IN**69, **MI**83, Float(s); **MI**97, Float—old-fashioned; **PA**116, Float —boards dragged over the ground; **PA**120, Plank float—after sowing, you pushed stones down so they would be out of the way of the cutter bar.

6 A floating pen or cage in which oysters or crabs are kept until ready for market. **Chesapeake Bay** Cf **crawl** n^2

1881 Ingersoll *Oyster-Industry* 244, *Float.*—A platform of planks, upon which oysters are piled and subjected to fresh water, before being taken to market. **1894** *DN* 1.330 **NJ,** *Floats.* . . (Oyster industry) pens of boards placed in fresh water, upon which oysters fatten during one tide. **1905** U.S. Bur. Fisheries *Rept. for 1904* 420, Every crabber has what is known as a float, a rectangular box approximately 10 or 15 feet long, 4 feet wide, and 2 feet deep, the sides and ends being constructed of laths, and the bottom of 6-inch planks. **1934** *Sun* (Baltimore MD) 6 Apr 6/2 *(Hench Coll.)* **MD,** The packers are building crab floats and erecting new crab shanties. **1942** *Ibid* 30 Apr 12/5 *(Hench Coll.),* We are willing . . that officials and inspectors from that State [=Maryland] visit the crabbing grounds, shedding floats and packing houses in Virginia. **1968** *DARE* FW Addit **swNJ,** Oyster floats. . . These were moored in fresh water. The oysters were dumped in these for a day or two to clean out their sand. It also made them swell up. **1976** Warner *Beautiful Swimmers* 10 **eMD,** Skill, hard work and infinite patience are required to hold [soft] crabs in "floats" or pens until they moult and successfully bring them live to market.

7 In charcoal burning: a piece of turf used to cover the heap of wood. [Cf *EDD float* v. 18 "To pare turf or stubble from land"] **NJ**

1894 *DN* 1.330 **NJ,** *Floats:* (charcoal industry) irregular sods laid on "four-foot lengths," over which sand is placed. **1968** McPhee *Pine Barrens* 45 **cNJ,** Colliers stacked cordwood in vertical tiers and covered the wood with chunks of sandy turf, known as floats.

8 See quot. Cf **floater 5**

1967 *DARE* (Qu. H30, *An oblong cake, cooked in deep fat*) Inf **IL**26, Floats.

‡9 See quot.

1985 McPhee *Table of Contents* 286 **ME,** He called the tracks of snowshoes floats.

float v

1 To flood (an area); also fig.

1667 in 1917 Topsfield Hist. Soc. *Town Rec.* 1.9 **neMA,** The Towne hath granted Liberty . . to make a dame . . to float there medow prouided it be no damige to the Towne. **1844** (1954) Gregg *Commerce* 57 **KS,** We now encountered a great deal of wet weather; . . the rain, at the same time, floating the plain to the depth of several inches. **1860** Hawthorne *Marble Faun* 1.130, A . . military band . . floating her [=a city] with strains. **1899** (1912) Green *VA Folk-Speech* 179, *Float* Flood; to cover with water. "All *afloat,*" filled with water. A child *floats* its bed at night.

2 also with *for:* To hunt (esp deer) at night from a boat with a bright light; to hunt in this way; hence vbl n *floating.* **NEast** Cf **fire-hunt**

1859 *Harper's New Mth. Mag.* 19.175/1 **nNY,** The usual method of hunting the deer in midsummer is by 'floating.' **1871** Burroughs *Wake-Robin* 80 **nNY,** Our guide proposed to conduct us to a lake . . where we could float for deer. **1885** *Outing* 7.80/2 **nNY,** "Kill any deers over there?" "No," said Carl; "we floated two nights, but it was terrible foggy." **1894** *Century Illustr. Mag.* 47.354/1 **NEast,** 'Jacking,' or 'floating,' for moose is seldom practised, from the difficulty found in getting close enough to flash the light on the game. **1930** Shoemaker *1300 Words* 23 **cPA Mts** (as of c1900), *Float*—"To float deer."

3 Of gold: to be washed away and lost during the process of extraction. Cf **float gold 1**

1873 Raymond *Silver & Gold* 17 **CA,** This shows that $5.85 [worth of gold] per ton 'floats,' which probably is at least 20 per cent. of the yield.

4 See quot.

1930 Shoemaker *1300 Words* 21 **cPA Mts** (as of c1900), *Float*—To "float a baby", to produce miscarriage.

5 To hold (crabs) in a **float** until they shed; to hold (oysters) in a **float** esp in fresh water to cause them to swell; hence vbl n *floating.* **[float n 6]**

1936 *Sun* (Baltimore MD) 15 Aug 6/1 *(Hench Coll.),* Other proposals were for . . the prohibition of "floating" green crabs and the establishment of breeding and hibernating grounds in the waters of both States. **1940** *Ibid* 21 Aug 22/2 *(Hench Coll.),* A delegation of oystermen from the Eastern Shore of Virginia . . protested an order of the Public Health Service . . outlawing floating oysters except in approved areas. **1948** *AmSp* 23.297 **Puget Sound WA,** To *float* oysters formerly meant to keep them on a float, so that they would continue in good condition till they could be processed or marketed; but the fresh harbor water distended or bloated them by its osmotic effect.

floatage n

In logging: see quots.

1958 McCulloch *Woods Words* 64 **Pacific NW,** *Floatage*—Logs spread over the surface of a river or lake. **1969** Sorden *Lumberjack Lingo* 43 **NEng, Gt Lakes.**

float blind n

A floating duck blind.

1969 *DARE* Tape **NC**76, Then we have float blinds; they can be so you can put a boat right inside of 'em; have rails that have bushes on 'em, or grass, make it look like an island. . . Some of 'em'll have boxes in 'em.

float boat n

Any of various sorts of broad, usu flat-bottomed boats of medium size.

1951 *Ford Times* Sept 37, A *float boat* is a shallow, wooden, scow-like craft, powered by an airplane engine and propeller, and steered with a long rudder. In Florida it is used by pleasure-bent fishermen to cruise the swamps and backwaters, but on the cranberry plantations of eastern Massachusetts . . it is technically, at least, a working boat. **1962** *Britannica Book of Yr. for 1961* 742, *Floatboat.* . . A slow-moving, flat-bottomed boat for leisurely viewing of the countryside. **1967** Faries *Word Geog. MO* 87, The expression *row boat* (90 percent) prevails . . to designate a large, flat-bottomed boat formerly used on rivers for taking farm or plantation produce to market towns or shipping points. . . Several expressions not mentioned by Kurath occur [including] *float boat.* **1970** *DARE* File **Madison WI,** Float boat = a pontoon boat. **1978** *DARE* File **Miami FL** (as of c1970), We'd go out a few miles in a float boat, then spend the day fishing as we drifted back toward land. This was a commercial operation, with the boat holding forty or fifty people. **1979** *Town & Country* 133 Aug 42/1, Even the river, spitting and snarling around her rubber floatboat, had no effect on her poise.

float copper See **float n 1**

floated gold See **float gold 2**

floater n

1 A representative elected by several counties grouped together. Cf **floaterial**

1853 *Texas State Gazette* 16 July (Farmer *Americanisms*), A candidate for floater in the district composed of the counties of Fayette, Bastrop, and Travis. **1888** *Congressional Record* 12 Dec 20.3 app 8/1 **IL,** [President Jackson] seems to have had in contemplation the Dudley scheme of purchasing floaters in "blocks of five" in the doubtful State of

Indiana. **1891** *Harper's New Mth. Mag.* 82.204/2 **TN,** He 'lows ez he's jes kem hyar along o' [=because of] Leonard Rhodes ez be a-'lection-eerin' fur floater fur the Legislatur'. **1952** *AmSp* 27.125 **TN,** It is found that the word 'floater' was used in our legislative enactments as early as the year 1851 in designation of a member of the House of Representatives of our General Assembly elected by a district composed of more than one county as distinguished from such members elected by the votes of a single county who were designated as Direct Representatives.

2 One who has no fixed home; an itinerant worker, tramp.

1873 Beadle *Undeveloped West* 455 **NM,** There are clerks, agents . . and perhaps fifty "floaters," making up the American population. **1899** *Boston Herald* 8 Sept. 6/2 *(DA),* Army 'floaters' without regular employment at home. **1919** *DN* 5.56 **WA,** *Floater*. . . Itinerant. In the winter when the floaters all drifted into Seattle. **1927** *AmSp* 2.281 [Prison lingo], *Floater*—A bum or hobo. **1930** Irwin *Amer. Tramp* 76, *Floater*—A migratory worker, one who moves from place to place, but who has some excuse for this in that he works occasionally. **1934** *Sun* (Baltimore MD) 11 Jan 1/5 *(Hench Coll.)* **Detroit MI,** He denied that the order marked the establishment of a policy designed to prevent the employment of transient or 'floater' labor. **1940** *RR Mag.* Apr 44, *Floater*—Same as *boomer.* **1949** *PADS* 11.21 **CO,** *Floater*. . . A man who never stays long on a job. **1967–69** *DARE* (Qu. Y28, *A person who loiters about with nothing to do*) Inf **NY**151, Floater; (Qu. HH20a, *An idle, worthless person*) Inf **WI**22, Floater; (Qu. HH31, *Somebody who is not from your community, and doesn't belong*) Infs **MN**3, **PA**135, **TN**6, Floater. **1967** *DARE* Tape **IA**8, Some floater come through and he's supposed to be a dynamite man.

3 A floating or partly floating log.

1873 Beadle *Undeveloped West* 718 **MN,** We generally knew of a coming [log] 'drive' a day or two beforehand, by the increase of 'floaters.' **1969** *DARE* Tape **KY**6, I tore up a barge one time . . on a floater coming upstream. . . It's a log. . . One end would be on the bottom and one end of it'll float up, just stick out of the water right at the top of the water.

4 An ice-cream float.

1920 *DN* 5.81 **Pacific NW,** *Floater*. . . A glass of malted-milk with a spoonful of ice cream in it.

5 A doughnut. [By analogy with **sinker**] Cf **float n 8**

1950 *WELS (Joking names for [doughnuts])* 1 Inf, **csWI,** Dunkers, floaters, sinkers.

6 also attrib: A cork or piece of wood used to buoy up the baited end of a fishing line; a float.

1966–69 *DARE* Tape **IN**36, A lot o' fellows 'll use a floater—a cork, you know, bobbin', and put their bait on that and cast it in; **WI**75, We fish with floaters; **MI**21, I was drifting, until one of the floater guys that was way outside of me coming in . . saw my distress signal so he came in and tried to tow me in to the island.

7 See quot. Cf **float n 6**

1968 *DARE* FW Addit **swNJ,** Floaters—oysters dumped in fresh water for a day or two to clean out their sand. The water makes them swell up. Hence, floaters or bloated oysters as compared to the smaller, firmer "salts."

8 A **freshwater clam** (here: *Anadonta* spp). Cf **strange floater**

1979 *WI Week-End* Apr 6, The very thinnest [shells], such as floaters, had little market value. **1982** U.S. Fish & Wildlife Serv. *Fresh-Water Mussels, [Floater]*. . . Flat Floater . . *A. suborbiculata*. . . Paper Floater . . *A. imbecillis*. . . Giant Floater . . *A. grandis.* **1982** *WI State Jrl.* (Madison) 22 Aug 3, Several of the clams that may be found in Wisconsin rivers include . . flat floater [etc].

floaterial adj Also sp *floterial* [**floater 1**] **TN**

Composed of or representing more than one district or county.

1952 *AmSp* 27.126 **TN,** Another paragraph . . mentions 'Floterial Districts' and gives an 1869 example of its use. **1970** *DARE* File **ceTN,** [He] is the floaterial representative from Knox County.

float fish v phr, hence vbl n *float fishing* [Prob from *float* bobber, but perh sometimes understood as *float* v, in ref to the boat; cf **drift fishing**]

To fish with bait suspended from a float or bobber, usu from a drifting boat.

1956 Harlan–Speaker *IA Fish* 206, Float fishing employs a bobber which holds the bait off the bottom. . . Float fishing is best accomplished by wading, although it can be done from a boat. **1966–70** *DARE* (Qu. P15, . . *Fishing that's done from a slowly moving boat*) Infs **AR**4, 56, **KY**11, Float fishing; **IA**29, Float fishing—if the boat drifts and you plug to the shore; **VA**33, Float fishing—boat just drifts; [**MO**20, Float; **NC**48, Floating; **TN**53, Floating fishing]; (Qu. P13, . . *Other ways of fishing . . besides the ordinary hook and line*) Inf **NJ**1, Float fishing; snell attached to a shingle, baited, thrown in the water; caught the fish, and raised the shingle, grabbed the shingle from the boat. Could be quite a chase. **1976** *NY Times* (NY) 24 Oct sec 5 8 **eNC,** The latter-named species [=pinfish] are most commonly used in the area when floatfishing for kings.

float for See **float v 2**

float gold n

1 See quot 1881. Cf **float v 3**

1873 Raymond *Silver & Gold* 17 **CA,** We have a yearly loss in 'float gold' alone . . of $84,960 from two single mills! **1881** Raymond *Gloss. Mining* 35, *Float-gold,* Pac[ific]. Fine particles of gold, which do not readily settle in water, and hence are liable to be lost in the ordinary stamp-mill process.

2 also *floated gold:* Gold which has been redeposited at some distance from the original vein. Cf **float n 1**

1858 (1941) Hafen *CO Gold Rush* 3 Sept 40, [Samples of gold] embrace the lump or "nugget" gold, as well as the float gold from the beds of the streams. **1873** Miller *Modocs* 204 **CA,** They had found only a few bars with float gold. **1883** Ingersoll *Knocking Round* 85 **Rocky Mts,** Therefore placer-gold is sometimes known as 'floated' gold. **1931** Willison *Here They Dug* 55 **CO,** At the mouth of the gulch soon to take his name, Gregory stops to dig for 'float' gold washed down from veins on the mountains above.

float house n **NW, AK**

A house built on a raft.

1940 White *Wild Geese* 187 **AK,** A raft of huge cedar logs was tethered to the precipitous side of a cliff, and on the raft stood a house and a flower garden. The house was a well-built structure, and . . possessed everything a land dwelling possessed. . . They rowed over to the float house. **1955** *Seattle Daily Times* (WA) 26 June mag sec 10, More and more of the floathouses now are going ashore. . . The houses stand on foundations of two huge logs each. The logs often are cut somewhat after the fashion of sleigh runners, for use when comes the day the house is to leave the water. **1956** *Chrysler Events* June 22 *(Hench Coll.)* **nwID,** Ask any native if these are boat-houses or house-boats and he'll answer emphatically, "Neither, they're float houses." **1967** *DARE* FW Addit **swWA,** Float house.

floating See **float v 2, 5**

floating battery n Also *battery* [From its fancied resemblance to a floating gun platform; cf **battery 1**]

=floating island 1.

1968 *DARE* Tape **GA**31, You'd have many years of decay that were floating in the water, little bushes would start growing in it. . . We call those floating batteries or floating mattresses. **1969** *Milwaukee Jrl.* (WI) 19 Jan pictorial sec 8 **FL,** Men from the Okefenokee wildlife refuge . . seem to know every battery and hammock (types of floating islands). **1981** Harper–Presley *Okefinokee* 136 (as of a1951), Batteries—small swamp islands. "I run on to one of them batteries. It's one of them things covered with broomstraw."

floating bridge n

=floating island 1.

1802 Ellicott *Journal* 124 *(DA),* This surprising floating bridge, or raft, is constantly augmented by the trees and rubbish, which the Chafalia draws out of the Mississippi. **1948** Dick *Dixie Frontier* 114 **LA,** In time ligneous material covered the wood, and often willow trees, many of them ten inches in diameter, grew up from these 'floating bridges,' as they were called.

floating cabin n Cf **float house**

1968 *DARE* FW Addit **swNJ,** Floatin' cabins were shacks on floats used by oystermen. They were towed to and tied up in a creek, and the men stayed in them while working an area. The buyers came around in big boats to buy the oysters.

floating floor n

=spring floor.

1922 (1926) Cady *Rhymes VT* 125, The meller [?=flexible] sills and floating floor [of a dance pavilion] / Made girls fall down and fellers roar.

floating fowl n Cf **flocking fowl**

Either the **greater scaup** or the **lesser scaup.**

1917 (1923) *Birds Amer.* 1.135, *Scaup Duck. Marila marila... Other Names.*—Mussel Duck; .. Floating Fowl. *Ibid* 136, *Lesser Scaup Duck... Other Names...* Names of the Scaup Duck with or without qualifying terms.

floating heart n

1 A plant of the genus *Nymphoides.* [See quot 1969] For other names see **bunch waterlily, fairy waterlily, fringe** n **1, fringed bogbean, fringed waterlily, heartleaf 1, water apple-blossom, water gentian, waterlily**

1848 Gray *Manual of Botany* 363, *Limnanthemum...* Floating Heart. **1857** Gray *Manual of Botany* 348, *Floating Heart... L[imnanthemum] lacunosum...* Shallow ponds, from Maine and N. New York to Virginia and southward. **1934** *Natl. Geogr. Mag.* 65.598 **seGA,** The small purple blossoms of watershield project above the wide-spread masses of its rounded, floating leaves, and the dainty white display of floatingheart nods over its own reflection in the water. **1938** FWP *Guide DE* 12, Ponds where water-lilies, spatterdocks, and floating-heart cover the surface—the edges surrounded with pickerel-weed and arrowhead. **1940** Writers' Program *Guide GA* 368 **seGA,** Other flowers that give variety to the waterways are the blue-flowered pickerelweeds, purple water shields, and dainty white floating hearts. **1968** *DARE* (Qu. S26b) Inf **GA**35, Floatin' heart. **1969** *DARE* Tape **GA**30, Floating heart—it's kinda like the white water lily .. the bloom comes right on the leaf .. an' you break it an' turn it over it looks just like a heart—the bottom side of the leaf. **1976** Bruce *How to Grow Wildflowers* 277, *Nymphoides*—Floating-heart. There are two native and one introduced species in this genus of small floating plants which look like miniature waterlilies.

2 A **bonnet B1.**

1968 *DARE* Tape **GA**48B, Floating heart—same as bonnet.

floating ice n

=**floating island 2.**

1968 *DARE* (Qu. H63) Inf **VA**33, Floating ice—custard with meringue.

floating island n

1 A floating mass of wood or vegetation formed in a lake or large river. **chiefly SE** Also called **floating battery, ~ mattress, ~ plain, ~ prairie, flottant** Cf **wooden island**

1791 Bartram *Travels* 88 **FL,** Pistia stratiotes... associates in large communities, or floating islands, some of them a quarter of a mile in extent... They are first produced on, or close to the shore, in eddy water, where they gradually spread themselves into the river. **1807** in 1810 Schultz *Travels* 2.32 **Lower Missip Valley,** *Floating Islands* are the same as the above [=wooden islands], being indifferently known by both names. **1849** Lyell *Second Visit* 2.143 **LA,** There is a floating island in it [=Lake Solitude], well wooded. **1874** in 1953 McMullen *Topog. Terms FL* 108, Floating islands .. are formed by the dead roots of the smart weed and other swampy vegetation torn up by the wind, and hurled upon the shore. A soil is formed, birds drop acorns upon the mass, and little trees make their appearance. A second wind sends the whole thing out on the lake, where it floats subject to every breeze. **1954** *Living Wilderness* 19.50.4 **Okefenokee GA,** They are large and small floating islands, formed by peat rising to the surface, on which small vegetation begins. **1968** Adams *Western Words* 116, *Floating island*—A detached mass of floating trees, logs, and accumulated debris formerly found in western rivers.

2 also pl; also *floating island pudding:* A dessert of pudding topped with whipped egg whites or cream. *old-fash*

1771 in 1887 Franklin *Complete Wks.* 4.415, At dinner .. we had a floating island. **1861** Holmes *Venner* 1.142 **wMA,** The marvellous *floating-island.* **1920** Lewis *Main Street* 334 **MN,** Kennicott was suspicious, but Aunt Bessie, serving the floating island pudding, agreed. **1932** (1946) Hibben *Amer. Regional Cookery* 248, *Floating Island* (Kansas). **1940** Mencken *Happy Days* 303 **MD,** I well remember his return from Kansas City, probably in 1889 or thereabout, with the first news that had ever reached Hollins street of a dessert called floating-island, then apparently a novelty in the world. **1950** *WELS (Kinds of pudding)* 1 Inf, **csWI,** Floating island. **c1960** *Wilson Coll.* **csKY. 1967–70** *DARE* (Qu. H63, .. *Desserts*) Infs **CA**97, **LA**11, **MA**98, **NY**12, 36, Floating island(s); **MI**51, My mother used to make floating islands: a thin custard, not set at all. [She] dropped spoonfuls of meringue onto the hot custard. The meringue remained intact and looked like white islands floating on a yellow sea. [All Infs old]

floating kidney n [Joc application of the term for a displaced kidney; cf **float** v **1**]

See quots.

1950 *WELS (Joking or nicknames for over-active kidneys)* 1 Inf, **seWI,** Floating kidney. **1967–69** *DARE* (Qu. BB20) Infs **CA**170, **KY**65, **MO**7, (Got *or* had) a floating kidney.

floating manna grass See **floating meadow-grass**

floating marsh n Cf **floating island 1**

1940–41 Cassidy *WI Atlas* 1 inf, **cwWI,** Floating marsh—a piece of ground so damp it was resilient; children would dance on it and make it shake.

floating mattress n

=**floating island 1.**

1968 [see **floating battery**].

floating meadow-grass n Also *floating manna grass*

A **manna grass** (here: *Glyceria fluitans*).

1857 MA State Bd. Ag. *Annual Rept.* 4.50, The *Floating Meadow Grass,* or *Common Manna Grass.* **1912** Baker *Book of Grasses* 208, Floating Manna-grass is often found in shallow, running water.

floating plain n

=**floating island 1.**

1791 Bartram *Travels* 89 **FL,** In great storms of wind and rain, when the river is suddenly raised, large masses of these floating plains are broken loose, and driven from the shores, into the wide water, where they have the appearance of islets.

floating prairie n **LA**

=**floating island 1.**

1941 O'Donnell *Great Big Doorstep* 118 **LA,** Some [=mules] bogged down way out in the floatin prairie. **1944** Kane *Deep Delta Country* 14 **sLA,** 'Floating prairie,' a growth out of a matted base suspended over water or liquid mud. **1967** LeCompte *Word Atlas* 226 **seLA,** Great areas of the southern section of .. [Lafourche Parish] are dotted with lakes and "floating prairies" *(flottant),* land-like masses in the process of being built up by the vegetation which they support.

float mineral (or ore) See **float** n **1**

float road n **Sth**

A channel or path cleared through a swamp so that logs may be floated.

1901 Montgomery *Reminiscences Mississippian* 115 **MS,** We paddled till dark... Next morning I determined to follow an old float road .. knowing that it would bring us to the brake from which the timber had been floated. **1905** U.S. Forest Serv. *Bulletin* 61.37 **Sth,** *Float road.* A channel cleared in a swamp and used to float cypress logs from the woods to the boom at the river or mill. **1923** *DN* 5.243 **LA,** *Float road.* In logging, a forest path chopped that flood water may carry rafts through.

float rock, floats See **float** n **1**

‡flob n

1968 *DARE* (Qu. HH40, *Uncomplimentary words for an old man*) Inf **MD**41, Flob [flɑb].

flobber v [Perh infl by *flop, flub*]

1967 *DARE* (Qu. JJ42, *To make an error in judgment and get something quite wrong: "He usually handles things well, but this time he certainly ______."*) Inf **KS**5, Flobbered ['flɑbɚd]. That's a word I haven't heard of for years.

flock n [Back-formation from *phlox* understood as pl]

1966–70 *DARE* (Qu. S26a, .. *Roadside flowers*) Inf **FL**16, Flock; (Qu. S26e, .. *Wildflowers*) Inf **PA**235, Flock—reddish flower, three foot tall.

flock by oneself v phr

See quots.

1897 *KS Univ. Qrly.* (ser B) 6.87 **neKS,** *Flock by one's self:* act in a reserved manner. **1927** *Ruppenthal Coll.* **KS,** To flock by one's self (themselves)—to be alone; also to be aloof from others, whether by choice or necessity.

flock duck n Also *flocking duck* [See quot 1889]

Either the **greater scaup** or the **lesser scaup.**

1888 Trumbull *Names of Birds* 55, *Aythya marila...* Again at Pleasantville, N.J., and at Crisfield, Md., *Flock-Duck.* *Ibid* 58, In Virginia at

Eastville and Cobb's Island it [=*Aythya affinis*] is the *Flock Duck.* **1889** *Century Dict.* 2276, *Flocking-fowl,* The blackheads or scaup ducks, *Aithyia* [sic] *marila* and *A. affinis* . . [are] called *raft-duck, flock-duck,* and *troop-fowl,* from the . . habit [of flocking]. **1917** (1923) *Birds Amer.* 1.135, Scaup Duck. *Marila marila*. . . Other Names.—Mussel Duck; . . Flock Duck; Shuffler. **1923** Dawson *Birds CA* 1807, Flocking duck. **1923** U.S. Dept. Ag. *Misc. Circular* 13.19, *Scaup Ducks* . . *In local use* . . flock ducks (N.J., Md., Va.) **1970** *DARE* Tape **VA47,** They shot flock ducks—redheads, bluebills mostly. **1982** Elman *Hunter's Field Guide* 205, *Greater Scaup (Aythya marila)* Common & Regional Names: broadbill, . . flock duck.

flock house n

A hen house.

1950 *WELS (Building for chickens)* 1 Inf, **csWI,** Flock house—occasional.

flocking duck See **flock duck**

flocking fowl n [See quot 1835]

A **scaup** or similar duck.

1835 Audubon *Ornith. Biog.* 3.226, In a few weeks these flocks are joined by others, for which reason the species is named in Kentucky the 'Flocking Fowl.' **1872** Coues *Key to N. Amer. Birds* 289, Greater Scaup Duck. . . Flocking Fowl. **1889** *Century Dict.* 2276, *Flocking-fowl,* . . a gunners' name in the United States of the blackheads or scaup ducks, *Aithyia* [sic] *marila* and *A. affinis,* from their flocking. **1953** *AmSp* 28.277, Older denominations of wild ducks . . *flocking fowl* (scaups, Ky.)

flog v

Of poultry: to beat with the wings.

1950 Stuart *Hie Hunters* 52 **eKY,** One rooster flogged another rooster for getting too near his hens. **1953** Randolph-Wilson *Down in Holler* 244 **Ozarks,** Of a woman with a black eye it was said that "She went out to the chicken-pen, an' the old crower flogged her in the face." Some people dislike guineas because they "flog the chickens away from the feed." **1954** *Harder Coll.* **cwTN,** *Flog*. . . Used chiefly with reference to domestic fowl.

flommuck n [Back-formation from **flummox** n, taken as pl]

A failure, fiasco.

1937 (1977) Hurston *Their Eyes* 171 **csFL** [Black], 'Cause Tea Cake ain't no Jody Starks, and if he tried to be, it would be uh complete flommuck.

flood v Cf **flood dam, splash**

In logging: see quot 1966.

1958 McCulloch *Woods Words* 64 **Pacific NW,** *Flood logs*—To move logs down a river by flooding the stream with water from a splash dam. **1966** *DARE* Tape **MI14,** The rivers going into Lake Superior aren't very big . . so they build dams across them and then flood the logs through these dams when they got the dam full of water.

flood dam n Also *flooding dam* Also called **splash dam** Cf **flood**

In logging: see quot 1905.

1879 *Lumberman's Gaz.* 2 Apr 3/3 **WI,** The great flooding dam at Little Falls . . has been completed. . . This will enable the loggers to bring out all the logs that can be got into the flowage of the dam, or below it, every year. *Ibid* 11 June 5/3 **WI,** They plan to build a flood-dam . . to flood the shallows, and then another season they will be able to get their logs out. **1904** *DN* 2.397 **NY,** *Flooding-dam*. . . Another name for a splash-dam. **1905** U.S. Forest Serv. *Bulletin* 61.49, *Splash dam.* A dam built to store a head of water for driving logs. . . [Also called] flood dam. **1956** Sorden-Ebert *Logger's Words* 14 **Gt Lakes,** Flood-dam.

flood gull n

1 **=oyster-catcher.** *obs*

1844 DeKay *Zool. NY* 2.217, The *Oyster-catcher* [=*Haemotopus palliatus*], or as it is better known among our gunners by the name of *Flood Gull,* is not very common.

2 A black skimmer *(Rhynchops nigra).*

1844 DeKay *Zool. NY* 2.297, *The Black Skimmer—Rhynchops nigra* . . The *Shearwater, Razor-bill, Cutwater, Skimmer, Flood Gull,* and *Skippang,* for it is known under all these names, reaches our coast from tropical America in May. **1913** Bailey *Birds VA* 18, *Rynchops nigra* . . *Black Skimmer.* [Flood Gull. Cut-Water]. **1951** *AmSp* 26.278, Connecting bird movements with those of the tide are the names *flood gull* (black skimmer, N.Y., N.J., Md., Va., Fla.), *tide gull* . . and *high-tide hen.* **1970** *DARE* (Qu. Q10, . . *Water birds*) Inf **VA52,** Flood gull—a black skimmer.

flooding vbl n

Menstruation.

1931 Hurston in *Jrl. Amer. Folkl.* 44.415. **1935** Hurston *Mules & Men* 342 **LA** [Black], Flooding [Footnote: Menstruation]. **1967-69** *DARE* (Qu. AA27) Infs **IN8, KY5,** Flooding; **SC40,** Flooding—Negro.

flooding dam See **flood dam**

floodwall n

A levee.

1968 *DARE* (Qu. O13, *A heavy stone structure* . . *that encloses and protects a harbor*) Inf **IN7,** Floodwall. **c1970** *DARE* File **nwIL. 1977** *DARE* File **Louisville KY.**

floogie bird n

=filliloo bird.

1948 *Sun* (Baltimore MD) 8 May 14/1 *(Hench Coll.),* Navy aviators today will slip temporarily into the role of the floogie bird, looking backward 37 years.

floogies, hot as adj phr [Var of **flugens** n, prob infl by *floogy* (at **floozy** n[1])]

Extremely hot.

1984 Wilder *You All Spoken Here* 143 **Sth,** *Hot as floogies:* Hot as a depot stove; floogies, or floozies, are promiscuous females.

floogy See **floozy** n[1]

flook See **fluke** v[1]

flookan n Also sp *flucan, fluken* [Cornish dial]

1 In mining: see quots.

1945 *CA Folkl. Qrly.* 4.320 **CO** [In a Cornish mining community], Flookan: A soft decomposed cross course. **1968** Adams *Western Words* 116, *Flookan*—In mining, flucan, a soft clay found between a vein and a wall.

2 By fig ext, in phr *put the flookan on one:* see quot.

1895 *DN* 1.388 **wNC,** *Fluken*. . . To put the *fluken* on one = to 'do him up'; to get the advantage of him, etc. It originated, as a phrase, in this manner:—A very dramatic murder trial was held in Lenoir, Caldwell County, in 1884, of two men who blockaded a half-dozen mica miners in a mine shaft and killed three of them. Several of the witnesses described the bodies as having had 'the fluken put on them.' *Fluken* is the name for the scaly, whitish soil dug from mica mines. Since then the phrase . . has been in common use in the region.

floor n Usu |flor, flɔr, floə, flɔə|; also **Sth,** *esp among speakers with little formal educ* |flo| Pronc-sp *flo'*

Std senses, var forms.

1873 Harte *Mrs. Skaggs* 146 **AL,** "Flo" was what the Colonel said. **1899** Chesnutt *Conjure Woman* 59 **csNC** [Black], Tenie, layin' on de flo'. **1908** *DN* 3.281 **eAL, wGA,** [flo]. **1922** Gonzales *Black Border* 301 **sSC, GA coasts** [Gullah glossary], *Flo'*—floor, floors, floored, flooring. **1927** Shewmake *Engl. Pronc. VA* 30, [A frequent pronunciation in the North, /flɔr/; the usual pronunciation in Virginia, /floə/.] **1931** *PMLA* 46.1303 **sAppalachians,** Such clipped forms as . . *flo' (floor),* and *yo' (your)* are rare. **1940** *AmSp* 15.48 **sAppalachians,** The Southern loss of final [r] occurs only in districts where lowland influence has crept in: flo', yo', mo'. **1966** *DARE* Tape **MS44,** [floʊ].

floor baby n Also *floor child* Cf **apron child**

See quots.

1950 *PADS* 14.29 **SC,** *Floor child, chile*. . . A child old enough to be put on the floor. **1968** *DARE* FW Addit **LA** [Black], Floor baby—a baby old enough to crawl.

floorboard n

A baseboard.

1957 Battaglia *Resp. to PADS 20* **eShore MD** *(Strip of wood* . . *along the bottom of a wall* . . *if the strip is more than eight inches)* Floorboard. **1965-70** *DARE* (Qu. D37, *The strip of wood about eight inches high along the bottom of the wall* . . *joining to the floor*) 16 Infs, **chiefly Inland Nth, N Midl,** Floorboard.

floor boss See **floorman**

floor child See **floor baby**

floor-flusher n [Folk-etym for **four-flusher**]

1967–70 *DARE* (Qu. U17, . . *A person who doesn't pay his bills*) Inf **MO**14, Floor-flusher; (Qu. II20a, *A person who tries too hard to gain somebody else's favor*) Inf **MI**116, Floor-flusher.

floorman Also *floor boss, floor manager*

In tobacco marketing: see quot 1966.

1966 *PADS* 45.12 **cKY,** *Floorman*. . . The straw boss on the warehouse floor. He sees that the baskets are properly lined up, and that the floor is kept in neat condition. . . "We keep our floorman on the year round." **1967** Key *Tobacco Vocab.* **MD, NC, TN,** Floorman; **GA, MO, TN,** Floor manager. **1970** *DARE* (Qu. HH43b, *The assistant to the top person in charge of a group of workmen*) Inf **NC**87, Floor boss. [Inf is a tobacco farmer.]

floor map n [Prob var of *floor mat*]

1945 Saxon *Gumbo Ya-Ya* 560 **LA,** Floor map: a rug.

floormat n

1 Fig: =**footstool 3.** Cf **doormat, footmat**

1966–70 *DARE* (Qu. II34, *If you think somebody is trying to use you to his advantage: "I'm not going to be his ______."*) Infs **NC**9, 26, **SC**69, Floormat; (Qu. II19, *When you think somebody has been put ahead of you . . you might say, "I'd rather quit than ______."*) Inf **VA**69, Be a floormat.

2 See quot.

1967 *DARE* (Qu. HH18, *Very insignificant or low-grade people*) Inf **MO**26, Floormat of society.

3 =**hogchoker.**

1984 [see **doormat**].

floor moss n

=**house moss.**

1967 *DARE* (Qu. E20, *Soft rolls of dust that collect on the floor under beds or other furniture*) Inf **NE**10, Floor moss. **1967** *DARE* File **csWI,** Floor moss—rolls of dust under furniture.

floor shoe n

1967 *DARE* FW Addit **swAR** [Black], ['flou͵šuz]—Sunday shoes, or shoes for wearing in the house.

floor-through n **NYC**

See quot 1968.

1964 *New Yorker* 26 Sept 48/3 **NYC,** They had, in fact, stayed in the flat there only a little more than a year . . ; they moved then to a floor-through in a decrepit but pleasant brownstone. **1968** *DARE* File **NYC,** Floor-through—an apartment which takes up an entire floor of a rather small apartment building. Common. **1970** *Harper's Mag.* 240.48/1 **NYC,** The trust she came into at twenty-one allowed her to live in a large floor-through.

floosie adj See **floozy** adj

floosie n See **floozy** n[1]

floozied up See **floozy up**

floozy adj Also *floosie, flucey* [Perh from Engl dial *floosy* fluffy, soft < *floose* (*flooze,* etc) varr of *floss* (though perh rather from *flue* fluff); cf **flossy** n, **flossy** adj]

1 Usu of a woman's appearance or clothing: showy, stylish, flashy.

1911 *DN* 3.543 **NE,** *Floozy,* [u, ʊ]. . . "Flossy," or "sporty." "You look floozy to-day." "What a floozy hat!" **1942** Berrey–Van den Bark *Amer. Slang* 37.10, *Beautiful* . . floozy. *Ibid* 233.10, *Stylish; "Chic."* . . floozy. **1967** *DARE* (Qu. W40, . . *A woman who overdresses or who spends too much on clothes*) Inf **TX**3, [She's] floosie ['flusɪ], overdressed. **c1970** *Halpert Coll.* **wKY,** *Flucey* . . fancy, frivolous; inclined toward flounces, frills, and furbelows. "That new girl next door sure is a flucey dresser." "Say, that [=a dress] is real flucey."

2 Of a woman: light-headed, highfalutin.

1942 Berrey–Van den Bark *Amer. Slang* 278.18, *Merry; Gay* . . floozy. **1967–70** *DARE* (Qu. HH9, *A very silly or light-headed person*) Inf **MI**103, Floozy—if a woman; silly; (Qu. HH35, *A woman who puts on a lot of airs: "She's too ______ for me."*) Infs **MI**67, 120, **NC**52, Floozy.

floozy n[1] Also *floosie, flusie, fluzie, fluzy, floogy* [**floozy** adj] *now usu derog* Also called **flossy** n

A woman, esp a young and attractive one; a woman of loose morals.

1905 *NY Eve. Jrl.* (NY) 31 Mar 9th ed 16 *(Zwilling Coll.),* [Cartoon:] He goes outside and finds a poor, skinny flusie almost frozen to death. **1911** *DN* 3.543 **NE,** *Floozy*. . . Defined by one contributor as a young woman to whom attention is paid, "John took his floozy to the baseball game;" by another as a term sometimes used of waitresses, or shopgirls. **1913** *DN* 4.28 **NW,** *Tommy*. . . A girl. Also called *calico, flūzy, chippy, molly, bunch of rags, bat,* all of which are not uncomplimentary in some circles. **1914** Jackson *Criminal Slang* 36, *Fluzie*. . . Current in the cosmopolitan demi-monde. A woman; a questionable female character. **1938** *Hench Coll.* **cePA** (as of 1912), *Floosie*—a girl, often a street-walker, an immoral girl. **1941** in 1977 Randolph *Pissing in the Snow* 132 **nwAR,** Shucks . . them cornfed floozies ain't been around much. **1949** *PADS* 11.6 **wTX** (as of c1920), *Floozy*. . . A whore. Occasional. **1953** *Daily Progress* (Charlottesville VA) 4 Aug 6/7 *(Hench Coll.),* There's a little bit of floozy in every nice girl. **1965–70** *DARE* (Qu. AA7b, . . *A woman who is very fond of men . . if she's not respectable about it*) 56 Infs, **scattered,** Floozy; (Qu. W36, . . *A woman who uses a lot of cosmetics*) 22 Infs, **scattered,** (Looks like a) floozy; **OH**29, Overdressed floozy; **KS**2, Painted floozy; **GA**59, Painted up like a floozy; (Qu. HH37, *An immoral woman*) 18 Infs, **scattered,** Floozy; (Qu. AA7a, . . *A woman who is very fond of men . . if she's nice about it*) Inf **FL**8, Floozy; (Qu. HH34, *General words . . for a woman*) Infs **AZ**15, **CA**15, 56, **MI**103, **MO**1, Floozy; (Qu. HH36, *A careless, slovenly woman*) Inf **HI**6, Floozy. **1968** *DARE* FW Addit **nePA,** If you're not a lady, you're a floozy. **1984** Wilder *You All Spoken Here* 143 **Sth,** Floogies, or floozies, are promiscuous females.

floozy n[2] [Prob joc deriv of *influenza*]

1968 *DARE* (Qu. BB28, . . *Imaginary diseases: "He must have the ______."*) Inf **NY**94, Floozy [laughter].

floozy up v phr, hence ppl adj *floozied up* [**floozy** adj or **floozy** n] Cf **floss up, flossied out**

1967–69 *DARE* (Qu. W30, *When a woman adds decorations to make something more attractive . . she might say, "It's too plain—I think I'll put on a few flowers to ______ it up."*) Inf **MI**68, Floozy; (Qu. W37, *When a woman puts on her good clothes and tries to look her best, you say she's ______*) Inf **GA**81, Floozied up.

flop v

1 To wave or flap (something).

1851 Hooper *Widow Rugby's Husband* 130 **AL,** As quick as a sheep can flop hit's tail! **1903** *DN* 2.291 **Cape Cod MA** (as of a1857), Short vowels frequently differed in quality. . . *o* for *a, flop.* **1917** *DN* 4.392 **neOH,** *Flop*. . . Flap (the wings) not necessarily with a noise, as of a bird flying. "The rooster flopped his wings and crew." "The hawk partly sailed and partly flopped his wings." . . Also N. Eng., Ill., Ia., South, Kan., Ky., N.Y. **1927** Adams *Congaree* 2 **cSC** [Black], De nigger stretch hisself and flop he whing three or four times an' create a dust. **1930s** in 1944 *ADD* **eWV,** The rooster flopped his wings. **1954** *Harder Coll.* **cwTN,** *Flop*. . . Move the wings. . . To wave something.

2 also with *over:* To change sides in a controversy; to make an abrupt change of character or position; hence n *flopper.* Cf **flop n 1, flip-flop 3**

1880 *Cleveland Leader* 8 June 1/7 *(OEDS),* On the twenty-fifth ballot the Florida flopper went to Sherman. **1889** *Century Dict.* 2278, *To flop over* . . to go over suddenly to another side or party; make a sudden change of association or allegiance. **1892** *Nation* 6 Oct 268/3 **NY,** His characters . . flop over and act in a way quite the reverse of what we had a right to expect. **1904** *Omaha Bee* 3 Sept. 6 *(OEDS),* A number of New York newspapers have flopped to the support of Parker. **1904** *Courier-Jrl.* (Louisville KY) 17 Aug 4/2, There are always floppers. The mere circumstance that somebody deserts his party and goes over to the other proves nothing. **1926** Cooper *Oklahoma* 123 *(DA),* Lawmakers who had been opposed to it 'flopped' to the other side.

3 To lie down, sleep; to spend the night.

1907 London *Road* 74 **CA,** 'Kip,' 'doss,' 'flop,' 'pound your ear,' all mean the same thing; namely, to sleep. **1913** *DN* 4.26 **NW,** *Flop*. . . To lie down. **1915** *DN* 4.244 **MT,** Boys, it's time to flop. **1930** *DN* 6.87 **cWV,** *Flop,* "Kin I flop here?" . . Means "May I sleep here for the night?" The question implies that the speaker, a man out of work, is asking for a job. The answer yes means that he stays some time. **1939** *Hall Coll.* **wNC, eTN,** Are you goin' to flop? **1959** Mailer *Advt. for Myself* 86 **NYC,** Why should they be flopping so near our house in a meadow? **1965–70** *DARE* (Qu. X40, . . *Other ways . . of saying, "I'm going to bed"*) Inf **MD**17, I'm going to flop; (Qu. OO19a, . . *"He felt tired, so he went to the couch . . and ______."*) 18 Infs, **scattered,** Flopped; **LA**18, Flopped over; (Qu. OO19b, . . *"He'll feel better after he* *has* ______.") Inf **NY**123, Flopped; (Qu. OO44a, . . *"He did nothing at all—he just* ______ *there."*) Infs **DE**3, **LA**25, **NJ**36, **NY**92, Flopped. **1968** Adams *Western Words* 116, *Flop*. . . A logger's term for . . going to bed.

4 To jilt, reject (a suitor).

1941 *LANE* Map 407A, 1 inf, **cwVT,** [She] flopped him.

5 To slop, spill. Cf **flosh** v

1969 *DARE* (Qu. Y36, . . *"See if you can carry that water without* ______ *[it all over]."*) Inf **CA**134, Flopping.

6 also with *over:* To faint. Cf **fall out** v phr **2**

1967–69 *DARE* (Qu. BB14, *To suddenly become unconscious and fall: "Just as she came to the door she* ______.") Infs **CT**37, **LA**25, **NY**31, **RI**4, Flopped; **NY**27, Flopped [laughter]; **NY**206, **TN**12, Flopped over.

‡**7** To fall down with laughter. Cf **fall out** v phr **1**

1968 *DARE* (Qu. FF21b, . . *"The first time I heard that one I* ______.") Inf **WI**29, Flopped.

8 To lose all one's money, go broke.

1966–69 *DARE* (Qu. U39, . . *"During the depression he* ______.") Infs **GA**13, **NY**109, 220, Flopped.

9 To move listlessly.

1969 *DARE* (Qu. Y21) Inf **TN**38, Flop along.

10 To flounce.

1969 *DARE* FW Addit **KY**37, She just done flop off and got married.

flop n

1 =**flip-flop 3.**

1880 *World* (NY NY) 22 Nov 5/1, Mr. Skinner's apparent flop on the railroad question is injuring his chances in the Speakership struggle. **1904** *Springfield* (Mass.) *W. Republican* 7 Oct. 2 *(DA),* That a flop by the most militant of the unionists is under contemplation has been denied. **c1960** *Wilson Coll.* **csKY,** *Flop*. . . A change in policy.

2 also *flop-up:* A rest, "lie-down"; a night's sleep.

1888 *Detroit Free Press* 15 Sept (1889 Farmer *Americanisms*), 'Stranger, did ye lope it?' (come on foot). 'Yes.' 'A mile or a sot-down?' [=half a day's travel] 'More'n that. About a dozen flop-ups.' **1967** *DARE* (Qu. OO19a, . . *"He went to the couch . . and* ______.") Inf **MN**10, Took a flop. **1968** Adams *Western Words* 116, *Flop*—What the sheepherder calls his morning and afternoon periods of rest and napping.

3 A bed or makeshift sleeping place, esp in a cheap lodging house; by ext, such a house. Cf *flophouse*

1910 D. Ranney *Autobiogr.* iv.70 *(OEDS),* You can get a bed in a lodging-house for ten cents, or if you have only seven cents you can get a 'flop'. **1916** *Amer. Mag.* May 14/1 **NY,** She said to tell you this ain't no hobos' flop, neither. **1925** *Lit. Digest* 11 July 50/1 **Los Angeles CA,** There's a couple of 'em [=missions] will give you a flop for nothing—if they ain't too full. **1955** *PADS* 24.120 **Chicago IL,** We are afraid to carry it around so we go up to my flop. **1966–67** *DARE* (Qu. E18, *A temporary or emergency bed made up on the floor*) Infs **MI**1, **NV**2, (A) flop. **1968** Adams *Western Words* 116, *Flop*. . . A logger's term for his bed. **1973** Allen *LAUM* 1.230 (as of c1950), 1 inf, **NE,** Flop [=bed on the floor].

4 also *floppy:* A fat, ungainly or slovenly person, esp a woman.

1936 O'Donovan *Bones of Contention* 70 **NYC,** She was a great flop of a woman. **1965–70** *DARE* (Qu. HH36, *A careless, slovenly woman: "She's just an old* ______.") Inf **TN**53, Flop; **WA**16, Floppy; (Qu. HH34b, *Disrespectful words . . for a woman;* total Infs questioned, 75) Inf **MS**56, Flop; (Qu. HH21, *A very awkward, clumsy person*) Inf **NJ**55, Flop.

5 A dull, unpleasant person; a misfit, failure.

1965–70 *DARE* (Qu. HH13, . . *Not very alert . . "He's certainly* ______.") Inf **NV**7, [A] flop; (Qu. HH16, *Uncomplimentary words . . "Don't invite him. He's a* ______.") Infs **CA**149, **MN**2, **NV**7, **OH**63, **VA**33, **WA**1, 11, Flop; (Qu. HH20a, *An idle, worthless person*) Inf **CT**16, Flop; (Qu. II20a, *A person who tries too hard to gain somebody else's favor*) Inf **LA**12, Flop; (Qu. II36a, *Somebody who talks back or gives rude answers*) Inf **KS**16, Flop.

6 in comb *cow flop:*

a A cow dropping; cow manure. Cf **flap 3**

1968–69 *DARE* (Qu. L17, . . *Manure used in the fields*) Infs **MD**9, **NY**82, 87, Cow flop; (Qu. BB50c) Inf **PA**227, Cow manure [is] also called a cow flop. **1968** *DARE* Tape **NY**45, Every morning he went out to the stable to put on the hot cow flop [on infected areas], and both arms healed up.

b Transf: see quot. Cf **horse-turd doughnut**

1940 Mencken *Happy Days* 136 **MD,** Even in the city a popular ginger-and-cocoanut cake, round in contour and selling for a cent, was called a cow flop.

7 A tumble, fall. **chiefly Nth, esp NEast** See Map

1950 *WELS ("He slipped . . and took quite a* ______.") 6 Infs, **WI,** Flop. **1965–70** *DARE* (Qu. Y1, . . *"He slipped on the steps and took quite a* ______.") 23 Infs, **chiefly NEast,** Flop.

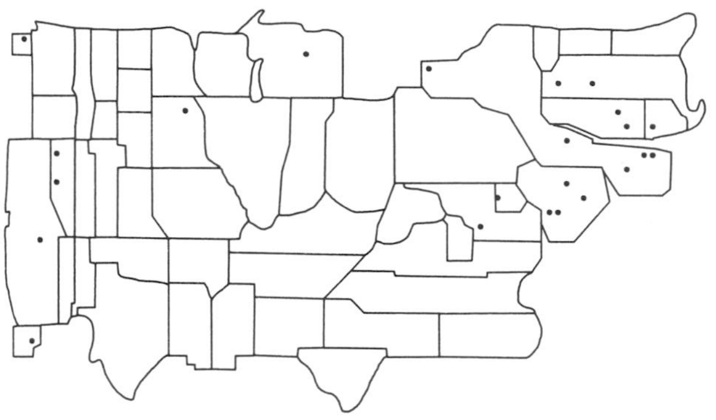

•flop n 7 (Qu. Y1)

8 =**belly-flop 1.** Cf **flip-flop 5**

1969 *DARE* (Qu. EE25, *When a child picks up his sled . . runs with it, and then throws himself down on it, that's a* ______) Inf **IL**57, Flop.

9 =**belly-flop 2.**

1968–69 *DARE* (Qu. EE29, *When swimmers are diving and one comes down flat onto the water, that's a* ______) Infs **MD**12, **MN**28, **MA**73, **NY**195, Flop. **1984** *DARE* File **UT,** Flop.

10 =**flip-flop 2.**

1969 *DARE* (Qu. EE9b, *If children jump forward, land on the hands, and turn over*) Inf **IN**81, Flop.

flop door n Cf **klop door**

1950 *WELS Suppl.* **eWI,** *Flop door*—outside cellar door.

flopdown n [From *flop* failure, perh by analogy with *letdown*]

1969 *DARE* (Qu. FF19, . . *A very dull or unenjoyable time: "The party was* ______.") Inf **GA**77, A letdown, flopdown.

flophouse n [Transf from *flophouse* a cheap lodging]

1 also *flop joint:* A cheap restaurant.

1967–69 *DARE* (Qu. D39, . . *A small eating place where the food is not especially good*) Inf **IL**57, Flop joint; **TX**26, Flophouse [laughter].

2 A prison. *joc*

1967 *DARE* (Qu. V11, . . *Joking names for a county or city jail*) Inf **TX**26, Flophouse—because you can stay there free.

3 also *flop wagon:* A caboose.

1977 Adams *Lang. Railroader* 26, *Caboose* . . flop wagon. *Ibid* 62, *Flophouse:* A caboose.

flopjack n

=**flapjack 1.**

1968 *DARE* (Qu. H20b) Inf **LA**24, Flopjacks. **1973** Allen *LAUM* 1.283 (as of c1950), 3 infs, **Upper MW,** Flopjacks. [2 infs label this old-fashioned.]

flop-jawed adj

=**wopper-jawed.**

1966 *DARE* (Qu. X6, *If a person's lower jaw sticks out prominently, you say he's* ______) Inf **GA**3, Flop-jawed.

flop joint See **flophouse 1**

flop over v phr See **flop** v **2, 6**

flopover n

=**flapjack 1.**

1968 *DARE* (Qu. H20b) Inf **NJ**19, Flapjacks, flopovers.

flopped out ppl adj phr

Listless, tired.

1970 *DARE* (Qu. KK30, *Feeling slowed up or without energy: "I certainly feel* ______.") Inf **TN**52, Flopped out.

flopper n

1 =**flipper** n[1] **2.**

1957 Battaglia *Resp. to PADS 20* **eMD** *(When frying food [for example, eggs] you turn them over with a ——)* Flopper, turner. **1966** *DARE* (Qu. F3) Inf **SD**1, Flopper.

2 =**flop** n **7.**

1969 *DARE* (Qu. Y1, . . *"He slipped on the steps and took quite a ——."*) Inf **MI**110, Flopper.

3 See **flop** v **2.**

4 A kalanchoe: see quots.

1953 Greene-Blomquist *Flowers South* 112, Flopper *(Kalanchoë Daigremontiana)*. . . One of the most interesting of leaf-propagating plants. **1976** Bailey-Bailey *Hortus Third* 622, *[Kalanchoe] pinnata. . . Floppers. . .* Easily prop[agated] by plantlets. **1982** Perry-Hay *Field Guide Plants* 122, *Kalanchoe pinnata. . .* Floppers. . . *Flowers:* pendent, in bunches, tubular and inflated.

floppy See **flop** n **4**

‡**floppy Joe** n [Var of **sloppy Joe**]

1968 *DARE* (Qu. H41, . . *Sandwiches . . in a round bun)* Inf **OH**38, Floppy Joe.

flop-up See **flop** n **2**

flop wagon See **flophouse 3**

Flora's paintbrush n [*Flora* goddess of flowers]

1 A **hawkweed** (here: *Hieracium aurantiacum*).

1894 *Jrl. Amer. Folkl.* 7.92 **ME,** *Hieracium aurantiacum,* . . Flora's paint brush, Oxford Co. and Penobscot Co., Me. **1959** Carleton *Index Herb. Plants* 47, *Flora's paintbrush:* Emilia sagittata (Cacalia coccinea); Hieracium aurantiacum.

2 A **tassel flower** (*Emilia* spp). [See quot 1929]

1929 Pope *Plants HI* 265, Flora's Paintbrush . . sometimes grows in the lawn grass and in the garden as a weed. . . *Emilia flammea.* . . Each stem is terminated by a few composite, tassel-like flower heads varying in color on different plants from *orange* to *scarlet.* **1959** [see **1** above]. **1965** Neal *Gardens HI* 854, *Floras paint brush. Emilia sonchifolia.* . . The plant . . is sometimes grown ornamentally, as is a similar species *[E. sagittata].* **1976** Bailey-Bailey *Hortus Third* 422, *[Emilia] javanica. . . Flora's-paintbrush.* . . Naturalized in s. Fla. The usual sp. in gardens.

Florida n Usu |ˈflɔrədə, florədə|; freq **esp Sth** |ˈflɑrədə|; also |-ɪdə, ɪdi|; for addit varr see quots Pronc-spp *Flerida, Floridy, Flur(r)idy*

Std sense, var forms.

1904 *DN* 2.423 **Cape Cod MA** (as of a1857), Floridy. **1914** *DN* 4.76 **ME, NH,** Floridy. **1925** Dargan *Highland Annals* 270 **sAppalachians** *(ADD),* Flurridy. **1931** *N. Amer. Rev.* May 433/1 **NY** (as of 19th cent), *Floridy, Arizony, Jarsey,* and the rest—in fifty rural districts, today, they flourish. You will hunt long before you hear one of them in town [i.e., New York City or Boston]. **1931** *PMLA* 46.1316 **sAppalachians,** Flerida. **1939** *LANE* Map 15, [Typical pronunciations: ˈflɑrədə, ˈflɒr-, ˈflɔr-, -ɨdə, -ɨdɪ.] Pronunciations with the last syllable of the type of [-dɨ] are regarded as older though still in use by . . [7 infs]. **1940** *AmSp* 15.50 **sAppalachians,** Flerida. *Ibid* 85 **eTN,** [flɑrɪdə]. **1942** Hall *Smoky Mt. Speech* 33, *Florida* [ˈflɑrɪdɪ]. **1942** *AmSp* 17.38 **seNY,** [Of 120 infs, 109 pronounced *Florida* with the stressed vowel [ɑ], 7 with [ɒ], 4 with [ɔ].] **1965** Will *Okeechobee Boats* 8 **FL,** Fluridy. **1966** *DARE* Tape **FL**37, [ˈflɔɚədi]. **1969** *DARE* FW Addit **MA**68, [ˈflɔɚɪdi, ˈflɔɚɪde]. **1970** *DARE* (Qu. BB25) Inf **FL**51, Florida sores [ˈflɑɚədə soz]. **1975** Gould *ME Lingo* 99, *Floridy*—The state. Mainers like to give the *y* sound to a final *a* in place names.

Florida anise-tree n Also *Florida anise*

An odorous, evergreen shrub or tree *(Illicium floridanum).* Also called **poison bay, polecat tree, purple anise, star-anise, star-bush, stinkbush, sweet laurel**

1830 Rafinesque *Med. Flora* 2.9, Florida Anisetree. . . Capsules ranged like a star around a central receptacle, bivalve, one-seeded. **1900** Lyons *Plant Names* 200, *I. Floridanum.* . . Florida Anise tree. . . *Bark* aromatic, tonic. **1960** Vines *Trees SW* 278, *Florida Anise* . . may be propagated by seeds or by cuttings of ripened wood. **1979** Little *Checklist U.S. Trees* 151, *Florida anise-tree.* . . Coastal Plain of nw. Fla. to c. Ala., s. Miss., and se. La.

Florida arrowroot n

=**coontie** or the starch which it yields.

1860 A.W. Chapman *Flora of Southern U.S.* 437 *(DAE),* The stem [of the coontie] abounds in starch, from which the Florida arrowroot is obtained. **1879** Pickering *Chronological Hist. Plants* 761 **FL,** [Footnote:] Z[amia] pumila was observed . . by Chapman, in "low grounds South Florida," and *Florida arrow root* procured from its trunk. **1891** *Century Dict.* 7028, *Z[amia] integrifolia (Z. pumila)* . . yields a starch known as Florida arrowroot. **1933** Small *Manual SE Flora* 1, *Zamia* . . Florida-arrowroots. **1971** Craighead *Trees S. FL* 200, Florida arrowroot . . *Zamia integrifolia.* **1976** Bailey-Bailey *Hortus Third* 1180, *Zamia pumila* . . Florida arrowroot.

Florida ash n

=**Carolina ash.**

1962 Kurz-Godfrey *Trees N. FL* 278, The Florida ash is a medium-sized tree, usually with a single trunk, which reaches at least 65 feet in height and 14 inches in diameter. **1979** Little *Checklist U.S. Trees* 135, *Fraxinus caroliniana* . . *Carolina ash* . . Other Common Names . . Florida ash.

Florida bark n Also *Florida quinine bark, ~ wild quinine*

=**fever tree;** also the bark of such a tree.

1830 Rafinesque *Med. Flora* 2.57, *Pinckneya pubens. Names. . . Vulgar.* Bitter Bark, . . Florida Bark, Fever-tree. *Ibid* 58, It has long been used in . . Florida, in intermittent fevers with success. **1876** Hobbs *Bot. Hdbk.* 20, Florida bark, Pinckneya pubens. **1889** *Century Dict.* 453, *Bark. . . Georgia, bitter, Carolina,* or *Florida bark* . . [has] the same properties as French Guiana bark. **1897** Sudworth *Arborescent Flora* 337, *Pinckneya pubens.* . . Common Names. . . Florida Quinine Bark (Fla.) **1940** Brown *Amer. Cooks* 127 **FL,** Florida wild quinine is called "Georgia bark."

Florida black duck See **Florida duck**

Florida blue jay See **Florida jay 1**

Florida boxwood n

1 An evergreen tree *(Schaefferia frutescens)* native to southern Florida. Also called **boxwood 3, white ironwood, yellowwood**

1908 Rogers *Tree Book* 366, *Florida Boxwood (Schaefferia frutescens)* . . grows on the Florida Keys, though the greed of lumbermen has narrowed its range materially. **1962** Harrar-Harrar *Guide S. Trees* 456, *Florida-boxwood.* . . A tree, sometimes 30′ to 40′ in height and 6″ to 10″ in diameter. **1979** Little *Checklist U.S. Trees* 272, *Florida-boxwood.* . . Rare on Fla. Keys.

2 =**false box 2.**

1971 Craighead *Trees S. FL* 200, Florida boxwood (false boxwood), *Gyminda latifolia.*

Florida cat n

=**blue catfish 1.**

1882 U.S. Natl. Museum *Bulletin* 16.108, *Great Fork-tailed Cat;* . . *Florida Cat.* . . One of the largest of the cat-fishes. **1896** *Ibid* 47.137. **1902** Jordan-Evermann *Amer. Fishes* 20, Blue cat. . . Florida cat, flannelmouth cat, etc. **1911** *Century Dict. Suppl., Cat,* n[1]. . . *Florida cat,* in Florida, the channel catfish, *Ictalurus furcatus.*

Florida chicken n Cf **Arkansas chicken**

A **gopher** n[1] **1a** (here: *Gopherus polyphemus*).

1952 [see **Georgia bacon**].

Florida clover n

=**Mexican clover.**

1883 Smith *Report for 1881 & 1882* 521, The Florida clover, or 'poor man's trouble,' is the greatest pest in the way of a weed. **1889** Vasey *Ag. Grasses* 103, *Richardsonia scabra* (Mexican Clover; Spanish Clover; Florida Clover; Water Parsley, [etc]). **1900** Lyons *Plant Names* 322, *Richardia scabra* . . Florida Clover.

Florida coffee n

A **coffeeweed 1.**

1833 *Richmond Enquirer* 2 July *(McDavid Coll.)* **VA,** Florida coffee. **1849** *Cin. Commercial* 10 Dec. 2/1 *(DA),* She ate some of the seeds and buds of what is called Florida coffee, the consequence of which was death. **1859** Gosse *Letters from AL* 212 **AL,** There is a plant now abundantly in blossom, which grows in neglected fields and such-like places. . . From its local name, Florida Coffee, I infer that these seeds are roasted.

Florida coffee bean See **coffee bean 2**

Florida dandelion n

A **green-eyes** (here: *Berlandiera pumila*).

1955 *S. Folkl. Qrly.* 19.233, *Green Eyes* . . [is] also known as *Florida Dandelion.*

Florida duck n Also *Florida black duck, Florida drake,* ~ *mallard*

A duck (*Anas fulvigula* and subspp) with mottled plumage, native to Florida and the Gulf Coast. Also called **black duck 1, dusky duck 2, English duck 4, Ireland mallard, Irish mallard, island duck, Mexican French duck, Mexican mallard, mottled duck, striped mallard, summer duck, summer French duck, summer mallard, Texas duck, Texas mallard**

1897 *Auk* 14.285 **LA,** *Anas fulvigula. Florida Duck.*—I took a pair of these ducks, with their nest and 7 eggs, on June 3, 1895, at Timbalier Island, on the southeast coast of Louisiana. **1898** (1900) Davie *Nests N. Amer. Birds* 79, *Florida Duck. Anas fulvigula.* . . This is a local, lighter colored species, which is resident in Florida. **1916** *Times-Picayune* (New Orleans LA) 26 Mar 2, *Florida Duck* (Anas fulvigula). . . This duck is a regular resident of the coast and islands of Louisiana. **1931** Read *LA French* 18, *Canard Noir D'Été* . . The Florida Duck *(Anas fulvigula).* **1946** Hausman *Eastern Birds* 139, Florida Duck *Anas fulvigula fulvigula.* **1954** Sprunt *FL Bird Life* 62, *Florida Duck: Anas fulvigula* . . Local Names: Florida Mallard. **1966** *DARE* (Qu. Q5, . . *Wild ducks*) Inf **FL**35, Florida drake; **FL**32, Florida mallard. **1969** Longstreet *Birds FL* 34, *Florida Duck.* Other names: Florida Black Duck. . . This 20- to 22-inch duck somewhat resembles the female mallard, when only its dusky brown back is seen.

Florida flame azalea n

A **rhododendron** (here: *Rhododendron austrinum*) similar to the **flame azalea.**

1953 Greene-Blomquist *Flowers South* 88, *Florida Flame-Azalea* . . has a limited distribution, being confined to n.w. Fla. It resembles the more northern flame-azalea *(R. calendulaceum).* **1976** Bailey-Bailey *Hortus Third* 952, *Florida flame a[zalea].* . . Fla. and adjacent Ga. and Ala.

Florida flip n Sth

=**Georgia skin (game).**

1935 Hurston *Mules & Men* 185 **FL,** The Florida-flip game was roaring away at the left. Four men playing skin game with small piles of loose change.

Florida gallinule n Cf **purple gallinule**

A gray ducklike bird *(Gallinula chloropus)* with a henlike red bill. Also called **bald coot 2, blue Peter 1, blue rail, bonnet walker, chickenfoot, gray pond-hen 2, king ortolan, king rail, king sora, marsh hen, marsh Peter, marsh pullet, meadow hen, moor hen, mud hen, mud pullet, pond chicken, pond fowl, pond guinea, pond hen, poule d'eau, red-billed mud hen, rice hen, summer coot, water chicken, water hen, wild hen**

1833 Bonaparte *Amer. Ornith.* 4.132, The Florida Gallinule, or Water Hen, . . is common in Florida and Jamaica on the streams and pools, and extends over a great portion of the southern continent of America. **1917** (1923) *Birds Amer.* 1.213/1, Florida Gallinules possess a wonderful repertoire in the matter of calls. **1950** *WELS (Water and marsh birds)* 1 Inf, **ceWI,** Florida gallinule. **1968-70** *DARE* (Qu. Q5, . . *Kinds of wild ducks*) Infs **GA**25, 35, Florida gallinule; **VA**47, Florida gallinule—a few occasionally; [they're] new to the area; (Qu. Q9, *The bird that looks like a small, dull-colored duck*) Inf **CA**78, Florida gallinule; (Qu. Q10, . . *Water birds and marsh birds*) Inf **WI**12, Florida gallinule—like a mud hen, colorful.

Florida grackle n

A subsp of the **purple grackle** *(Quiscalus quiscula aglaeus).*

1895 U.S. Dept. Ag. *Yearbook for 1894* 233, The common purple grackle *(Quiscalus Quiscula)* . . [has] two subspecies, the bronzed grackle *(Quiscalus q. æneus)* and the Florida grackle *(Quiscalus q. aglæus).* **1916** *Times-Picayune* (New Orleans LA) 16 Apr 9, *Florida Grackle* (Quiscalus quiscala aglaeus). . . This is the Louisiana form of the bird known as the purple grackle. **1932** Howell *FL Bird Life* 433, The Florida Grackle inhabits a variety of situations and adapts itself to very diverse conditions. **1938** Oberholser *Bird Life LA* 602, Florida Grackle—*Quiscalus quiscula.* **1945** *Natl. Geogr. Mag.* June 739, Along the central Atlantic coast is found its relative, the Purple Grackle; and in Florida, the Florida Grackle. **1954** Sprunt *FL Bird Life* 445, Florida Grackle: *Quiscalus quiscula.*

Florida heron n Also *Florida white heron*

=**great white heron 1.**

1898 (1900) Davie *Nests N. Amer. Birds* 113, *Ardea occidentalis.* . . This beautiful, majestic bird, known as the Florida Heron, . . is said not to be so abundant as in former years. **1917** (1923) *Birds Amer.* 1.183, *Great White Heron. . . Other Name.*—Florida Heron. **1946** Hausman *Eastern Birds* 99, *Great White Heron.* . . Florida Heron, Florida White Heron.

Florida Indian n *derog*

See quot.

1987 *NADS Letters* **SC,** My father . . referred to some blacks as *Florida Indians,* which I took to be derogatory and also as pointing out that these blacks were not as black as others he had encountered. If blacks were discussed in a good light, he would raise his eyebrow and say, "They must be some of those Indians, yeah, Florida Indians."

Florida jay n

1 also *Florida blue jay:* =**blue jay 1.**

1828 Bonaparte *Amer. Ornith.* 2.60, The Florida Jay [=*Garrulus floridanus*] . . is not confined to Florida, where it was first noticed by Bartram, being found also in Louisiana, and in the West extends northward to Kentucky. **1916** *Times-Picayune* (New Orleans LA) 16 Apr 9, *Southern Blue Jay* (Cyanocitta cristata florincola). Florida Blue Jay. **1917** (1923) *Birds Amer.* 2.219/2, In the peninsula of Florida the Blue Jay is smaller and his color is paler and duller. So here he is given the name of the Florida Bluc Jay *(Cyanocitta cristata florincola).*

2 A slender jay *(Aphelocoma cyanea)* native to Florida. Also called **scrub jay**

1894 B. Torrey *Fla. Sketch-Book* 62 *(DA),* The Florida blue jay (a smaller and less conspicuously crested duplicate of our common Northern bird), to which it bears little resemblance either in personal appearance or in voice. **1917** (1923) *Birds Amer.* 2.221, *Aphelocoma cyanea.* . . The Florida Jay is . . one of the few American birds whose range is restricted to a comparatively small area—in this instance, the peninsula of Florida. **1951** Teale *North with Spring* 59, Like the burrowing owls of the Kissimmee Prairie, these Florida or scrub jays underscore the geology of ornithology.

Florida laurel n

=**sweetleaf.**

1897 Sudworth *Arborescent Flora* 322 **FL,** *Symplocos tinctoria. . . Common Names.* . . Florida Laurel. **1908** Britton *N. Amer. Trees* 789, *Sweet Leaf.* . . is also called . . Florida laurel. **1950** Peattie *Nat. Hist. Trees* 551, Florida Laurel. . . *Range:* Northern Florida to Louisiana and southern Arkansas, and north to the Delaware peninsula. **1960** Vines *Trees SW* 840, Vernacular names are . . Florida-laurel, Dye-leaves, and Horse-sugar.

Florida lime n [Folk-etym]

1909 *S. Atl. Qrly.* 8.45 [Gullah], *Florida lime* is used . . to *mo' quickah exasperate de clo'es.* [Footnote:] *Chloride of lime,* used to bleach white goods.

Florida lobster n Cf **crawfish** n **B2**

A spiny lobster (family Palinuridae).

1942 Kennedy *Palmetto Country* 240 **FL,** Associated industries deal with shrimp, oysters, sponges, turtles, crabs, crawfish ("Florida lobster"), octopi, conchs, and other marine products. **1966** *DARE* (Qu. P19) Inf **FL**39, Florida lobster.

Florida longleaved pine See **Florida pine**

Florida longtail n Also *Florida sprig*

=**old-squaw.**

1940 Trautman *Birds Buckeye Lake* 198 **OH,** Old-squaw. . . For some unexplainable reason, the species in this area acquired the name of "Florida Longtail" and "Florida Sprig," and the name Old-squaw was seldom heard.

Florida mahogany n

=**red bay.**

1897 Sudworth *Arborescent Flora* 201 **FL,** *Persea borbonia. . . Common Names.* . . Florida Mahogany. **1908** Britton *N. Amer. Trees* 399, The Red bay or Sweet bay, known also as Florida mahogany, . . inhabits moist soil. . . The wood, used to a limited extent in carpentry, is strong, hard, red. **1933** Small *Manual SE Flora* 922, *Florida-mahogany.* . . The bright-red heart-wood . . is used for cabinet-work and construction. **1976** Bailey-Bailey *Hortus Third* 848.

Florida mallard See **Florida duck**

Florida maple n

Std: a maple *(Acer barbatum)* which frequently intergrades with *Acer saccharum.* Also called **hammock maple, sugar maple, sugar tree**

Florida moss n

=**Spanish moss.**

1888 Trumbull *Names of Birds* 75, A large bunch of 'Florida moss.' **1923** Parsons *Folk-lore Sea Islands* 198 **csSC,** The so-called Florida moss, which so heavily festoons the trees of the Carolinian shores. **1974** (1977) Coon *Useful Plants* 81, *Tillandsia usneoides*—Florida moss.

Florida myrtle n

A **stopper** (here: *Myrcianthes fragrans* var *simpsonii*).

1979 Little *Checklist U.S. Trees* 175, *Myrcianthes fragrans* var *simpsonii. . . Simpson stopper. . . Other common names . .* Florida myrtle.

Florida nighthawk n

A subsp of the **nighthawk** (here: *Chordeiles minor chapmani*).

1898 (1900) Davie *Nests N. Amer. Birds* 287, *Florida Nighthawk. . .* It is a somewhat darker-colored bird and is smaller than the common Nighthawk. **1916** *Times-Picayune* (New Orleans LA) 16 Apr 9, *Florida Nighthawk* (Chordeiles virginianus chapmani). **1969** Longstreet *Birds FL* 81, The Florida nighthawk has been placed on the honor roll of southeastern birds primarily because it destroys the boll weevil.

Florida nuthatch n

=**white-breasted nuthatch.**

1932 Bennitt *Check-list* 46 **MO,** Florida nuthatch. *Sitta carolinensis.* **1938** Oberholser *Bird Life LA* 431. **1954** Sprunt *FL Bird Life* 325, Florida Nuthatch: *Sitta carolinensis.* **1955** Forbush-May *Birds* 353, Florida Nuthatch—*Sitta carolinensis atkinsi.*

Florida pine n Also *Florida longleaved pine, ~ yellow pine*

=**longleaf pine.**

1896 Mohr-Roth *Timber Pines* 28, *Pinus palustris. . . Local or Common Names. . .* Florida Yellow Pine. . . Florida Pine. . . Florida Longleaved Pine. **1897** Sudworth *Arborescent Flora* 31, *Pinus palustris. . .* Florida Yellow Pine (Atlantic region). Florida Pine (Atlantic region). Florida Longleaved Pine (Atlantic region). **1951** Teale *North with Spring* 48, Broley's largest [eagle's] nest, perhaps the largest in America, is lodged in the top of a Florida pine near St. Petersburg. **1960** Vines *Trees SW* 26, Longleaf Pine. . . Vernacular names are . . Turpentine Pine and Florida Pine.

Florida purslane n Also *Florida pusley*

=**Mexican clover.**

1938 *Torreya* 38.1 **AL,** As soon as possible I . . found . . *Richardia scabra . .* known in this country as "Florida pusley" or "Mexican clover." **1969** *DARE* (Qu. S21, . . *Weeds . . that are a trouble in gardens and fields*) Inf **GA**84, Florida purslane, often called pusley.

Florida quinine bark See **Florida bark**

Florida rattler n

Prob a **diamondback rattlesnake.**

1970 *DARE* (Qu. P25, . . *Kinds of snakes*) Inf **FL**48, Florida rattler.

Florida room n **chiefly FL**

A room with large windows used as a living room or family room.

1958 *Washington Post* (DC) 16 Aug sec B 3/3 *(Hench Coll.),* [Advt:] *Glass-walled Florida room* with two magnificent floor to ceiling window-walls (entered from living room). **1966** *Haines City Herald* (FL) 31 Mar 4/3, The pastorium is an attractive house with four bedrooms, . . Florida room which opens on to the patio, and large kitchen. **1966-70** *DARE* (Qu. D13, *The room where you entertain company*) Inf **FL**8, Florida room—with lots of glass; **FL**27, Florida room—same as living room; **FL**35, Florida room, if screened; (Qu. D16, . . *Parts added on to the main part of a house*) Infs **FL**31, 33, Florida room; **FL**9, Florida room—like a porch, but closed in; **FL**51, Florida room—glassed-in room, usually with T.V., bar, casual furniture; (Qu. D15b, . . *Rooms . . in other people's houses*) Inf **FL**3, Florida room—enclosed porch. **1971** Wood *Vocab. Change* 48 **Sth,** The volunteered words *fireplace room* and *Florida room* have a reasonably wide distribution. **1978** *DARE* File **FL,** In many houses in Florida, there's a Florida room; it's situated so as to receive a maximum amount of sunlight. Screened windows run the length of the walls. The room is used much as a sun-porch or family room would be used. **1980** *DARE* File **FL,** A "Florida Room" . . is a room, not a screened porch. Generally off the kitchen or dining room, it does have screens on three sides, *but,* it also has jalousies. **1986** Pederson *LAGS Concordance,* 43 infs, 30 **FL,** Florida room.

Florida screech owl n

A subsp of the **screech owl** (here: *Otus asio floridanus*).

1889 U.S. Dept. Ag. *Rept. of Secy.* 376, The Florida Screech Owl *(Megascops asio floridanus)* inhabits the Gulf States from Louisiana to Florida, and extends north to South Carolina. **1913** *Auk* 30.504, *Florida Screech Owl. . .* Found in small numbers in the [Okefenokee] swamp. **1938** Oberholser *Bird Life LA* 332, The Florida Screech Owl is a fairly common permanent resident throughout Louisiana. **1955** Forbush-May *Birds* 264.

Florida sore n **FL**

A sore caused by impetigo.

1966-70 *DARE* (Qu. BB25, . . *Common skin diseases around here*) Inf **FL**5, Impetigo or Florida sores; old-fashioned; **FL**19, Enfantigo, or the Florida sores; **FL**51, Florida sores ['flɑrədə soz]; (Qu. BB49, . . *Kinds of diseases*) Inf **FL**39, Florida sores—kids got them on their legs—old-fashioned.

Florida sprig See **Florida longtail**

Florida vanilla n

The leaves of **vanilla plant.**

1891 *AN&Q* 6.225, The *Liatris odoratissima,* deer's tongue, is also used for this purpose. Its leaves are gathered and sold as *Florida Vanilla,* but this name is objectionable, since Florida has a species of true vanilla.

Florida waterlily n

=**banana waterlily.**

1933 *Torreya* 33.83, *Castalia mexicana . .* Florida waterlily.

Florida water rat n

=**round-tailed muskrat.**

1934 *Natl. Geogr. Mag.* 65.619/2, **FL, seGA,** The discovery of the Florida water rat in 1884 was a noteworthy event in the annals of American mammalogy, for the animal represents a distinct genus as well as species. It might be looked upon as a muskrat in miniature, with a rounded instead of a compressed tail. **1938** Matschat *Suwannee R.* 34 **sGA, nFL,** Maiden cane grows in dense green masses three or four feet high, and there rice rats and Florida water rats . . make their nests. **1957** Blair et al. *Vertebrates U.S.* 726, *Neofiber alleni . .* Florida water rat.

Florida white heron See **Florida heron**

Florida wild quinine See **Florida bark**

Florida wren n

=**Carolina wren.**

1887 Ridgway *N. Amer. Birds* 550, Larger, and darker colored [than the Carolina wren]. . . *T[hryothorus] ludovicianus miamensis . . Florida Wren.* **1917** (1923) *Birds Amer.* 3.191, The Florida Wren . . is found only in the peninsula of Florida, south of the Suwanee River.

Florida yellow pine See **Florida pine**

Florida yew n

An evergreen tree *(Taxus floridana)* native to Florida. Also called **stinking cedar, savin, yew**

1869 Porcher *Resources* 586, *Florida Yew (Taxus Floridana . .).* This tree should be examined for a resinous substance in the leaves, . . to see if they [sic] will diminish the circulation. **1885** *Bot. Gaz.* 10.253 **FL,** It is called *Savin,* or *Stinking Cedar* (the latter on account of its strong and disagreeable terebinthine odor when bruised), names also applied, I believe, to the Florida Yew *(Taxus Floridana),* a rarer tree, which is sometimes seen growing with it. **1901** Mohr *Plant Life AL* 34, The Florida yew *(Taxus floridana)* of the valley of the Apalachicola River in western Florida . . present similar striking instances of a strange localization. **1933** Small *Manual SE Flora* 12, *Florida-yew. . .* On account of its smaller size, limited distribution and comparative scarcity, it has not been used economically. **1979** Little *Checklist U.S. Trees* 283, *Florida yew. . .* Nw. Fla. . . Very rare and local.

Floridy See **Florida**

flosh v [Engl dial *flosh* to splash] **MD, VA** Cf **flash v 1**

To spill, splash; to cause to splash up, agitate.

1899 (1912) Green *VA Folk-Speech* 180, *Flosh. . .* To spill; shake over.

"Don't flosh the water on the floor." **1935** Glasgow *Vein of Iron* 75 **wVA,** I know very well what your grandfather meant when he used to say, 'If you flosh the water, you will have scum without fish.' **1968** *DARE* (Qu. Y36, . . *"See if you can carry that water without _____ [it all over]."*) Inf **MD44,** Floshing; (Qu. Y45, . . *"When he opened the can, the beer _____ [all over the kitchen]."*) Inf **MD44,** Floshed [flɑš].

flossed up See **floss up**

flossie See **flossy** n

flossied out ppl adj Cf **floss up, floozy up**

1969 *DARE* (Qu. W37, *When a woman puts on her good clothes and tries to look her best, you say she's _____.*) Inf **MA58,** All flossied out.

floss up v phr, hence ppl adj *flossed up* Cf **flossied out, floozy up**

To dress up; to decorate.

1967–70 *DARE* (Qu. W30, . . *"It's too plain—I think I'll put on a few flowers to _____ it up."*) Inf **VA106,** Floss; (Qu. W37, *When a woman puts on her good clothes and tries to look her best, you say she's _____*) Inf **SC34,** Flossed up.

flossy adj Cf **floozy** adj

Showy, flashy, slick; saucy, impertinent.

1889 *The Road* (Denver, Colo.) 28 Dec. 4/3 *(DA),* Phil, we have got it in for you if you don't quit being so flossy. **1913** *DN* 4.21 **NE,** *Flossy.* Gay, attractive. Usage widespread in Nebraska. "Those girls are a flossy lot." "You look pretty flossy." **1914** Brininstool *Trail Dust* 238 *(DA),* She had ol' Sagebrush locoed by the flossy talk she slung. **1914** *DN* 4.106 **KS,** *Flossy. . .* Pert; impudent. **1947** *Time* 21 July 10/3, In Muncie, Ind., the Chamber of Commerce called a halt to its flossy preparations for a Muncie Centennial when one Dorothea Bump gave the boys a quiet nudge: the city is still only 93 years old. **1966–69** *DARE* (Qu. W36, . . *A woman who uses a lot of cosmetics*) Inf **NC16,** She's flossy; she's floozy; she's a painted hussy; (Qu. W40, . . *A woman who overdresses or who spends too much on clothes*) Inf **NY165,** Too flossy; (Qu. HH35, *A woman who puts on a lot of airs: "She's too _____ for me."*) Inf **PA175,** Flossy.

flossy n Also *flossie, flozzy, fluzzy* [**flossy** adj; the forms with *z* are prob infl by **floozy** n[1]]

=**floozy** n[1].

1916 *DN* 4.344 **NC, PA,** *Flossie. . .* A girl. "During the junior promenade there were many visiting flossies on the Hill." **1937** Sandoz *Slogum* 70 **NE** (as of 1900–20), What was that high-farkin' Annette going around thundered up like a saloon keeper's flossie for? **1950** *WELS (A woman with the reputation of running after men)* 2 Infs, **WI,** Fluzzy. **1966** *DARE* (Qu. W36, . . *A woman who uses a lot of cosmetics*) Inf **MS7,** A flossy; **NE9,** Flozzy. [Both Infs old] **a1975** Lunsford *It Used to Be* 177 **sAppalachians,** The term "flossy" means a "fast" girl.

floterial See **floaterial**

flottant n [Fr "floating"] **sLA**

=**floating island 1.**

1903 *Scientific Amer. Suppl.* 55.22911/2, Occasionally some of the land is torn away and becomes an island. Such islands are known as *flottants* or floaters, by the Creoles, and are among the most picturesque sights of these Louisiana lakes. **1916** *DN* 4.346 **LA,** *Flottant. . .* Soft prairie with water underneath. **1961** *PADS* 36.12 **sLA,** [For a "marshy prairie," 20% of 70 infs offered the term *flottant.*] So far as evidence goes, certain usages are confined to the rural parishes as against New Orleans. Among these are . . *flottant.* **1967** LeCompte *Word Atlas* 226 **seLA,** [For "soft prairie with water underneath," 13 of 21 infs in Lafourche Parish offered the term *flottant.*] **1983** *Reinecke Coll.* 4 **LA,** *Flottant* ['flotɔ̃] an island like mass of aquatic vegetation.

flounder n Usu |'flaʊndə(r)|; also |'flæ(ʊ)ndə| Pronc-sp *flander* See Pronc Intro 3.I.1.h, 3.II.14

A Forms.

1936 *AmSp* 11.34 **eTX,** If a norm may be said to exist for this diphthong [=aʊ] in East Texas, it is [æʊ], but variations in the first element produce also [aʊ] and [æ˄ʊ]—all of these with various degrees of lengthening and nasalization. Examples: . . flounder. **1970** *DARE* (Qu. P2, . . *Saltwater fish*) Inf **MA123,** Flander ['flændə]; **VA47,** Flander.

B Sense.

Std: a **flatfish 1** of the families Bothidae or Pleuronectidae. For other names of var fishes see **diamond flounder, eel-back flounder, halibut B1, Monterey halibut, rusty dab, sand dab, sand flounder, sole 2, summer flounder, turbot, whiff, winter flounder, witch flounder**

flounder v[1], hence vbl n *floundering,* n *flounderer* **Gulf States**

To fish for flounder, esp at night using a torch and spear.

1938 FWP *Guide MS* 296, The equipment for "floundering" includes a spear and a torch or flambeau. On still, moonless nights the flickering yellow light of flambeaux illuminates the dark along the water's edge as the flounderers wade about in the shallow water spearing the fish. **1967** *DARE* (Qu. P13, . . *Other ways of fishing*) Inf **TX31,** Floundering, with light and spear. **1967** *DARE* Tape **TX18,** In the summer, why, we flounder, go flounderin'. Light a good, strong gasoline lantern, wade on the sand bars 'n' pick up an' gig flounder.

flounder v[2] [Perh causative use of *flounder* to thrash about ineffectually, or var of *founder* to disable] Cf **founder A**

See quot.

1938 Rawlings *Yearling* 93 **nFL,** If he walked around the edge of the pond, keeping a taut line, he might lead the bass into shallow water and flounder him at the edge.

flounder v[3] See **founder**

flounderer n[1] See **flounder** v[1]

‡flounderer n[2] [Perh by folk-etym]

A flounder.

1968 *DARE* (Qu. P2, . . *Saltwater fish*) Inf **LA22,** ['flaʊndərəz].

flounder house n [From its being thin and one-sided, like the fish] Also called **half-house**

See quots.

1940 Writers' Program *Guide VA* 192 **Alexandria VA,** Here and there are long narrow houses resembling halves of gabled houses, called locally 'flounder' houses. **1946** Davis *Alexandria Houses* 17 **VA,** The second type in Alexandria, is the "flounder" house of two stories with half a gable roof—that is, a half house formed as if a gabled structure were split down its center. **1969** Devlin *What Kind* 18 **VA,** The flounder house, or half-house as it is known outside of Alexandria, is not an accident.

floundering See **flounder** v[1]

flounder mouth n [In ref to the large mouth of the fish]

1968 *DARE* (Qu. X9, *Joking or uncomplimentary words for a person's mouth . . "I wish he'd shut his _____."*) Inf **NY43,** Flounder mouth.

flour n, v Usu |flaʊr, flaʊə|; for addit varr see **A** below Cf Pronc Intro 3.I.1.h, 3.II.14 and **flower** n

A Forms.

1891 *DN* 1.156 **cNY,** [flɑ·rɪn] . . [in] 'flouring mill'. **1939** *LANE* Map 134, [Typical pronunciations:] [flaʊə, flaʊwə, flaʊr̩, flæʊr, flɑᵊ, flɑʊr̩, flɑɔə, flɛ˅or]. **1944** *PADS* 2.29 **LA, NC,** *Flour, flower* [flær]. **1954** *Harder Coll.* **cwTN,** [flæɪr, flər, flɔr].

B As noun.

See **flour gold.**

flour barrel full, keep the v phr

To provide for one's family.

1929 Faulkner *Sound & Fury* 243 **MS,** If it's any satisfaction to you I'll quit work . . and let you and Dilsey keep the flour barrel full.

flour bread n [Scots dial]

1 Bread made with wheat flour. **now chiefly Sth** See Map

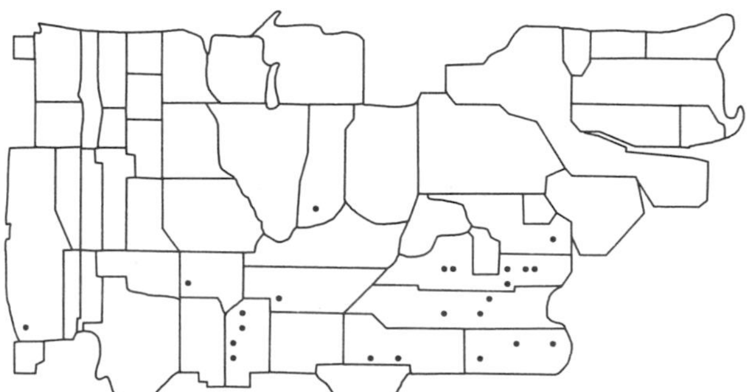

•flour bread 1 (Qu. H15)

1830 Child *Frugal Housewife* 82 **ceMA,** Flour bread should have a sponge set the night before. **1857** in 1924 *Jrl. Amer. Hist.* [New Haven] 18.49 **RI,** We got dinner . . consisting of dry flour bread. **1906** *Pocumtuc Housewife* 7 **MA** (?as of c1800), Johnny cake or hoe cakes are a good change from Rye and Indian bread. It is always best to keep flour bread in the house, but with a large family of farm hands or apprentices it cannot be eaten commonly. **1940** *AmSp* 15.51 **sAppalachians,** Flour-bread. **1941** *LANE* Map 281 *(Wheat bread)* 2 infs, **RI,** Flour bread. **c1960** *Wilson Coll.* **csKY,** *Flour bread. . .* Wheat bread rather than corn bread. **1965–70** *DARE* (Qu. H15, *Bread made with wheat flour*) 23 Infs, **chiefly Sth,** Flour bread. **1966** Dakin *Dial. Vocab. Ohio R. Valley* 2.312, *Flour bread* and *loaf bread* are neither very common and are used chiefly in the Mountains south of the Kentucky headwaters and scattered across southern Kentucky to the Mississippi. **1967** *DARE* File **cLA,** Flour bread. **1968** *DARE* Tape **GA**25, We didn't know what flour bread was until the turpentining come through this section.

2 A quick bread made with wheat flour; a large biscuit. **chiefly Sth, S Midl**

1934 Vines *Green Thicket* 59 **cnAL,** He was baking flour bread, boiling coffee, and frying young squirrels for breakfast. **c1938** in 1970 Hyatt *Hoodoo* 1.163 **neNC,** "A cake of bread, you know, like people used to bake bread to a fireplace, flour bread." "Flour bread?" "Yes, take and make it up like you gon'a make biscuits and put it on a griddle and sit it up to a fire . . and let it bake." **1944** *ADD* **NC, csUS,** *Flour-bread. . .* A flattened loaf of baked baking-powder-biscuit dough. **1958** *PADS* 29.10 **TN,** *Flour bread:* A kind of bread made from wheat. "Biscuit dough rolled thin and cut in four or five inch squares is referred to as flour bread." **1970** *DARE* (Qu. H19, *What do you mean by a biscuit?*) Inf **TN**49, Flour bread, made of flour, baking powder, shortening, milk or water, and soda. **1972** *Atlanta Letters* **neGA,** A hocake [sic] is a big flat piece of flour bread.

flour cake n [Engl dial]

A pancake.

1970 *DARE* (Qu. H20b) Inf **VA**66, Flannel cakes, flour cakes.

flour corn n Also *flour maiz*

A soft-grained var of **Indian corn.**

1763 LePage du Pratz *Hist. LA* 2.3, *Louisiana* produces several kinds of *maiz,* namely *flour-maiz,* which is white, with a flat, and shrivelled surface. **1917** Will–Hyde *Corn among Indians* 117 **Upper MW,** This green corn which was picked while in the milk and still soft . . was the common species of soft field-corn, known as flour corn. **1942** Castetter–Bell *Pima & Papago Ag.* 80 **SW,** This flour corn of early times was of three distinct colors—white, yellow and blue—the white most common, yellow next.

flour gold n Also *flour* **chiefly West**

Gold occurring in very fine particles.

1875 *Chicago Tribune* (IL) 16 Nov 7/6 **ND,** They prospected and found fine flour gold. **1904** (1969) Robins *Magnetic North* 292 **AK,** A few flakes of flour gold . . but no real 'pay'. **1939** FWP *Guide CA* 612 **sCA,** Experiments have been made in processing the lake bed's fine "flour" gold. **1939** FWP *Guide MT* 346, The flour (gold so fine it does not settle in the sluice box) was lost. **1941** Writers' Program *Guide UT* 349, For years he existed by washing out "flour" gold from the sandbars of the Colorado.

flour gravy n **now esp Sth, S Midl** Cf **cream gravy, thickened gravy, white gravy**

A gravy thickened with flour.

1917 *DN* 4.392 **neOH,** *Flour gravy. . .* Gravy made of milk, white flour, butter, and seasoning. . . Also N. Eng., Ill., N.Y., Kan., Ky. **1959** Faulkner *Mansion* 29 **MS,** He . . ate the sowbelly and flour gravy and undercooked biscuits. **1963** Owens *Look to River* 4 **TX,** With the taste of side meat and flour gravy still in his mouth, he went out to the long rows of corn. **1967–70** *DARE* (Qu. H37, . . *Words . . for gravy*) Infs **IL**91, **KY**69, 84, **LA**11, **MO**15, Flour gravy. [4 of 5 Infs old] **1978** Massey *Bittersweet Country* 206 **Ozarks,** After the chicken was done, Mother would always make flour gravy from the grease left in the frying pan.

‡flourish v *euphem*

To be pregnant.

1968 *DARE* (Qu. AA28, . . *Joking . . expressions . . to say that another [woman] is going to have a baby . . "She's ______ ."*) Inf **PA**96, Expecting; flourishing.

flour maiz See **flour corn**

flour-sifter snow n Cf **corn snow, hominy snow**

Snow which falls in small flakes.

1944 Walker *Winter Wheat* 212 **MT,** It was snowing again today, "a flour-sifter kind of snow" Mary Cassidy called it.

flow v, hence ppl adj *flowed* **chiefly NEng** Cf **flow** n[1] **1**

To flood.

1664 in 1899 Springfield MA *First Century* 2.62 (as of 1638), There was an Ancient Order . . requiring all that had ditches by the highway . . to keep them well scoured for the ready passage of the water that it might not pen up to flow the Meddowes. **1751** in 1934 Eliot *Field Husbandry* 61 **NEng,** If a *Swamp* be full of small Brush, and but few great Trees, the cheapest and best Way is to Flow it, and Kill it with the Water. **1883** *Century Illustr. Mag.* 26.650/2 **Cape Cod MA,** A brook is turned to run through it [=a cranberry field] . . so that the land can be 'flowed' in spring to kill insects, and in the fall for protection from frost. **1892** VT State Bd. Ag. *Rept. for 1891–92* 12.114, The areas of interval . . , or flowed lands, of the Otter Creek and some of its tributaries are very extensive. **1939** *Sat. Eve. Post* 10 June 37/2 **ceSC,** I opened all my rice-field trunks so that the flowed field inside would equalize the pressure from the outside, thus saving my banks. **1967** *DARE* Tape **MA**102, I can see why these boys handlin' my [cranberry] bog will say, "Well, shall we flow or shall we not flow?"

flow n[1]

1 The flooding of a rice field. Cf **flow** v

1856 Olmsted *Journey Slave States* 473 **GA, NC, SC,** The 'long flow' and the 'lay-by flow' are sometimes united, the water being gradually raised, as the plant increases in hight [sic].

2 A gust of wind. [Perh folk-etym for **flaw**]

1931–33 *LANE Worksheets* **seMA,** Flow and lull in the wind. If the lull is longer, the wind is decreasing. **1968** *DARE* (Qu. B14, *When the wind is blowing unevenly, sometimes strong and sometimes weak, you say it's ______*) Inf **NC**81, [It] blows in flows.

flow n[2] [Scots, nEngl dial "a bog, swamp"] Cf **vly**

In place names: a swamp or swampy pond.

1929 *AmSp* 5.161 **eNY,** Here and there in the lower Adirondack regions one finds small ponds which are called (on the map) *flows,* as: Alderbed Flow, . . Whitman Flow [etc]. . . The two words [=*flow, vly*] stand for the same thing—a swampy pond or swamp. **1968** *Courier–Freeman* (Potsdam NY) 21 Mar 14, [Advt:] *Camps* at Leonard Pond, Higley Flow, & Allens Flow.

‡flow adj [Perh *EDD flow* adj.[1] "windy, boisterous, stormy," but perh attrib use of **flow** n[1] **2**]

1967 *DARE* (Qu. B18, . . *Special kinds of wind*) Inf **MO**21, A high wind; a flow wind.

flowage n [**flow** v] **esp WI** Cf **backfill**

1 Water which has overflowed from a river or stream; floodwater.

1950 *WELS (Water from a river that spreads out and covers low land . . when a dam has been built)* 8 Infs, **WI,** Flowage. **1968** *DARE* (Qu. C9, *Water from a river that comes up and covers low land when the river is high*) Inf **MN**19, Flowage.

2 also *flowage lake:* A lake formed by the overflowing of a river or stream, usu caused by damming.

1879 *Lumberman's Gaz.* 2 Apr 3/3 **WI,** The great flooding dam at Little Falls . . has been completed. . . This will enable the loggers to bring out all the logs that can be got into the flowage of the dam, or below it, every year. **1948** *Wis. Fishing Regulations* 2 *(DA),* A closed season is established . . on all waters commonly known as the Chippewa Flowage. **1965** *Bee* (Phillips WI) 19 Aug 5/3, The dam . . is being constructed on Salters creek to create a flowage lake 5/8 mile long, 150 to 400 feet wide, with the water to be about 10 feet deep at the dam. **1966–68** *DARE* (Qu. C4a, . . *Fairly large body of fresh water*) Inf **WI**58, Gartszki Flowage, Wood's Flowage; (Qu. C7, . . *Land that usually has some standing water with trees or bushes growing in it*) Inf **ME**10, Beaver flowage—beavers flow the water back; Inf **WI**58, Flowage. **1968** *DARE* Tape **WI**30, Completed in 1953, this lake was. It has 23,000 acres of water which is about 15 miles long and about 5¼ miles wide at its widest point. . . It's called a flowage. **1979** *Capital Times* (Madison WI) 15 May 17/2, Because of his passion for sport fishing, the Greenwoods bought property on the flowage.

flowed See **flow** v

flower n Usu |'flaʊr, flaʊə|; also |flær, flɑr, flɔr|; for addit varr see **A** below Pronc-spp *flahr, flow'h* Cf Pronc Intro 3.I.1.h, 3.II.26 See also **flour**

A Forms.

1891 *DN* 1.154 **cNY,** [flɑwər] . . flower. **1927** Kennedy *Gritny* 20 **sLA** [Black], Put flow'hs on somebody grave. **1942** Hall *Smoky Mt. Speech* 46, Before *r* . . the second element [of the diphthong /ɑʊ/] is often reduced, suppressed, or converted to the consonantal glide [w]. . . Examples: . . *flower* [flæ:ɚ]. **1944** *PADS* 2.29 **nwNC, LA,** *Flour, flower* [flær]. **c1960** *Wilson Coll.* **csKY,** *Flower* is often [flær] or [flɑr]. **1961** Kurath–McDavid *Pronc. Engl.* 122, In *flower,* . . [d]isyllabic /flauə/, pronounced as [flaʊə ~ flawə ~ flæʊə ~ flæwə], is regular in areas where postvocalic /r/ is lost as such. Elsewhere disyllabic /flauɜ/ occurs beside the usual monosyllabic /flaur/, especially under heavy stress and in phrase-final position. A few speakers in eastern and western Pennsylvania have the /ɑ ~ ɒ/ phoneme . . [flɑɚ ~ flɑɚ]. **1968–70** *DARE* (Qu. R26) Inf **VA**7, [flæəɚ] lice; (Qu. FF14) Inf **IN**19, ['flɑɚ,pɑts]; (Qu. FF28) Inf **PA**237, [flaɚ] pot. **1976** Allen *LAUM* 3.33 (as of c1950), The weakening of the offglide to yield [ɑ^{ʊ}ɚ, ɑ^{ə}ɚ] appears in the speech of . . [1 Iowa and 5 Nebraska infs]. The eastern and western Pennsylvania phenomenon of complete loss of the glide appears in the form [flɑɚ] used by . . [1 Iowa and 5 Nebraska infs], and in the rounded variants [flɔɚ, flɒɚ] used by . . [4 Iowa infs]. **1982** McCool *Sam McCool's Pittsburghese* 12 **PA,** Flahr.

B Senses.

1 pl: Menstruation; see quots. [*OED* c1400 →; *"Obs."*] *euphem*

1925 *AmSp* 1.24 **Chicago IL,** The function of menstruation is described by dozens of evasive terms. . . The term "flowers" is another somewhat ornamental designation. **1953** Randolph–Wilson *Down in Holler* 106 **Ozarks,** A physician in Pineville, Missouri, asked a woman when she had last menstruated. "I ain't seen no flowers in four months," she told him. **1966–69** *DARE* (Qu. AA27) Infs **CA**65, **ME**5, 19, **NJ**1, (Got) the flowers; **AK**1, Flowers (among old-timers); [**RI**17, In flower]. [5 of 6 Infs old; the 1 mid-aged Inf labels this old-fash.]

2 in phr *in flower;* Of the moon: full.

1942 Perry *Texas* 139, Local beliefs, such as that a garden of peas planted when the moon is "in flower" will bloom profusely but make no peas.

flower v

1 To stain with menstrual discharge. [**flower n B1**]

1953 Randolph–Wilson *Down in Holler* 106 **Ozarks,** The wife of a state official once appeared . . with a large stain on her gown. "Law sakes," whispered an old woman in the audience, "the pore gal has done flowered her dress!"

2 To compliment, flatter.

1925 Dargan *Highland Annals* 106 **wNC,** I knew he was jest aflowerin' me.

flower attendant See **flower girl**

flower basket See **flowerpot 2**

flower bearer See **flower girl**

flower committee n Cf **flower girl**

A group of women who serve as attendants at a funeral.

1969 *DARE* File **MS,** If the deceased belonged to a popular organization of women, or if the family desired, a female organization was picked to be the flower committee . . called 'flower girls' in Texas and Oklahoma.

flower-cross n [From the shape of the flowers]

A **St. John's wort** (here: *Hypericum hypericoides* or *H. stans*).

1959 Carleton *Index Herb. Plants* 47, *Flower-cross:* Ascyrum (v).

Flower Day n [From the custom of giving flowers to friends on May 1st]

May Day; the first day of May.

1969 *DARE* (Qu. FF12a) Inf **CA**170, Flower Day.

flower-de-luce n [Var of *fleur de lis*] **esp NEng** *arch*

A **flag** **n**[1].

1640 in 1867 NH *Prov. & State Papers* 1.152, For the form of the toune, it is like a flower-de-luce. **1804** Fessenden *Poems* 48 **VT,** Nettles spring up flower-de-luces,/ If I am not ever thine. **1814** Bigelow *Florula Bostoniensis* 12 **MA,** *Iris Virginica.* . . Virginian Iris. Common blue flag or flower de luce. **1860** Holmes *Professor* 205 **MA,** By the side of the garden-flowers, . . dear to sketching maidens, of flower-de-luces and morning-glories. **1959** Carleton *Index Herb. Plants* 47, *Flower-de-luce:* Iris (v).

flowerdy adj Also *floweredy* [*flowered* adj + *-y*] Cf Intro "Language Changes" III.1 and **fadedy**

Decorated with a flower pattern.

1940 (1941) Bell *Swamp Water* 207 **Okefenokee GA,** My grave'll be right yonder under that sycamore, like as not, instead of some floweredy graveyard. **1960** Criswell *Resp. to PADS 20* **Ozarks,** Flowerdy cloth—cloth with large flowers printed on it. Once common—possibly no longer so. **1984** Burns *Cold Sassy* 255 **nGA** (as of 1906), Why shouldn't you . . wear a flowerdy dress if it might lift your grief a little?

flower fence n Cf *DJE*

=**pride of Barbados.**

1762 Gronovius *Flora Virginica* 65, Flower-fence. **1786** (1925) Washington *Diaries* 3.37 **VA,** Took the covering off the Plants in my Botanical garden, and found none living . . except some of the Acasce or Acacia, flower fence, and privy. **1923** Amer. Joint Comm. Horticult. Nomenclature *Std. Plant Names* 60, *Caesalpinia. . . pulcherrima* . . Flower-fence. **1933** Small *Manual SE Flora* 666, *Flower-fence.* . . Hammocks and pinelands, S. pen. Fla. and the Keys. **1949** Moldenke *Amer. Wild Flowers* 125, Many of the showiest of these are trees and shrubs, like . . *flowerfence (Poinciana).* **1979** Little *Checklist U.S. Trees* 68.

flowerfly n Cf **hover fly**

A fly of the family Syrphidae, often brightly colored and, as an adult, common about flowers.

1842 Harris *Treatise Insects* 414 **NEng,** Flower-flies . . are easily distinguished from the preceding flies . . by the smaller size of their winglets. **1954** Borror–DeLong *Intro. Insects* 621, *Syrphidae* . . Flower Flies. . . Many are brightly colored and resemble various bees or wasps. **1972** *Living Museum* 34.116, Other important predators of aphids are larvae of certain species of flower flies. . . Adults are black with bright yellow spots or bands on the abdomen and have one pair of transparent wings. Frequently seen hovering around flowers, these flies resemble small bees. **1980** Milne–Milne *Audubon Field Guide Insects* 671, *Toxomerus Hover Flies*—"Flower Flies" (*Toxomerus* spp.)

flower girl n Also *flower attendant,* ~ *bearer*

A member of a **flower committee.**

1967 *Smith Co. Pioneer* (Smith Center KS) 26 Oct 10/1, Flower bearers [at a funeral] were Odessa Schoeni, [etc]. **1968** *Muscatine Jrl.* (IA) 24 Apr 14/4, Flower attendants [at a funeral] were Mrs. Gene Lueders, [etc]. **1969** *DARE* File **TX, OK,** The girls would each have a spray . . of flowers and would line up a passageway from the top of the church steps to the funeral car . . and the coffin . . would be carried down this "aisle" of flower girls. At the cemetery they would do the same thing in reverse . . and then place flowers on the grave. . . This apparently is an old Texas and Oklahoma custom which is now about abandoned.

flower, in See **flower n B2**

flowering vbl n

1949 *McDavid Coll.* **cwNY,** *Go flowering* = pick wild flowers.

flowering box n Also *flowering box-berry*

=**mountain cranberry.**

1900 Lyons *Plant Names* 386, *V. Vitis-Idaea.* . . Flowering Box. **1940** Clute *Amer. Plant Names* 44, *V. Vitis-Idaea.* . . Flowering box-berry.

flowering cucumber n

Perh a **wild cucumber** such as *Echinocystis lobata.*

1966 *DARE* (Qu. S14, *Other prickly seeds*) Inf **MA**6, Flowering cucumber—roundish pod with four holes in the end, four seeds inside. The outside is covered with brambles. If one touches you, [it gives you a] bad sore.

flowering currant n

1 Any of several **currants B1:** in the eastern part of the US *Ribes americanum* or *R. aureum,* in the West *R. glutinosum, R. odoratum,* or *R. sanguineum.* Cf **flowering spice**

1824 Bigelow *Florula Bostoniensis* 90, *Ribes floridum. . . Large flowering Currant.* . . This is a common, wild currant. **1842** Kirkland *Forest Life* 2.142 **MI,** The flowering currant, a climbing shrub, [is] already strung with golden, clove-scented wreaths. **1889** *Century Dict.* 1405,

The flowering currant [is] *R[ibes] sanguineum,* the berries of which are insipid, but not, as popularly supposed, poisonous. **1892** *Jrl. Amer. Folkl.* 5.96, *Ribes aureum,* flowering currant. General. **1934** Haskin *Wild Flowers Pacific Coast* 135, Flowering currants and skunk cabbage are inseperably [sic] connected in my memory. **1950** *WELS (Shrub that gets covered with bright yellow spicy smelling blossoms early in spring)* 9 Infs, **WI,** Flowering currant. **1950** *WELS Suppl.* **csWI,** Flowering currant—I had always assumed this to be the same as Forsythia, but my dad says Forsythia has bigger, less fragrant blossoms. **1961** Thomas *Flora Santa Cruz* 192 **cwCA,** *R[ibes] glutinosum. . .* Flowering Currant. . . Common from San Francisco southward. **1973** Stephens *Woody Plants* 202, Flowering currant. . . *Ribes odoratum* is not abundant in any place. . . The fruit . . makes good jams and jellies and is sometimes used in pies.

2 =forsythia.

1950 *WELS Suppl.* **seWI,** Flowering currant—forsythia.

flowering dogwood n

A **dogwood 1:** either *Cornus florida,* which is also called **arrowwood b, boxwood 2, false box 1, Indian arrowwood, nature's mistake,** or *Cornus nuttallii* of the Pacific coast.

1843 Torrey *Flora NY* 1.290, *Cornus Florida. . .* Common Dogwood. Flowering Dogwood. **1880** *Harper's New Mth. Mag.* 61.78 **NEng,** The flowering dogwood has spread its layers of creamy blossoms. **1884** Sargent *Forests of N. Amer.* 91, *Cornus Nuttallii. . . Flowering Dogwood. . .* Generally in the dense shade of coniferous forests. **1968–69** *DARE* (Qu. S26e) Inf **RI**15, Flowering dogwood; (Qu. T16) Infs **VA**15, **WI**37, Flowering dogwood. **1969** *DARE* FW Addit **eNC,** Flowering dogwood. Common. **1979** Little *Checklist U.S. Trees* 97, *Cornus florida. . .* Flowering dogwood. *Ibid* 98, *Cornus nuttallii. . .* Flowering dogwood, western flowering dogwood.

flowering fern n [See quots 1938, 1942]

A fern of the genus *Osmunda.* Also called **rattlesnake fern.** For other names of var spp see **cinnamon fern, interrupted fern, royal fern**

1822 Eaton *Botany* 370, *Osmunda cinnamomea . .* flowering fern. **1829** Phelps *Familiar Lect.* 297, *Osmunda . . cinnamómea,* (flowering fern.) **1911** Waters *Ferns* 298, Flowering Fern.—*Osmunda regalis.* **1938** Small *Ferns SE States* 342, Although the phrase "flowering-fern," one of the popular names applied to this plant, is a botanical impossibility, it is apt. For, a patch of this fern in mature spore is often equal in pleasant effect to a bed of flowering plants. **1942** Hylander *Plant Life* 114, The Royal Fern *(Osmunda)* is often called the Flowering Fern because of its similarity to a flowering plant. **1976** Bailey–Bailey *Hortus Third* 803, *Osmunda . .* Flowering fern.

flowering maple n [From the maplelike leaves]

1 =dockmackie.

1913 *Torreya* 13.29 **NY,** *V[iburnum] acerifolium,* the "flowering maple," as it is called here, grows plentifully in the woods.

2 An **Indian mallow** (here: *Abutilon* spp).

1959 Carleton *Index Herb. Plants* 47, *Flowering-maple:* Abutilon (v). **1974** Munz *Flora S. CA* 562, *Abutilon. . .* Indian-Mallow. Flowering-Maple.

flowering moss n

1 =pixie moss.

1860 Curtis *Cat. Plants NC* 110, Flowering Moss. *(Pyxidanthera barbulata.)*—A very pretty, small, trailing evergreen. **1941** Writers' Program *Guide SC* 15, Here and there is found one of the loveliest little plants in the State—the pyxie, also known as flowering moss and pine barren beauty. **1976** Bailey–Bailey *Hortus Third* 932, *Pyxidanthera barbulata. . .* Flowering Moss.

2 A stonecrop: see quot.

1892 *Jrl. Amer. Folkl.* 5.96 **cnOH,** *Sedum (pulchellum?),* flowering moss.

3 A **moss pink** (here: *Phlox subulata*).

1892 *Jrl. Amer. Folkl.* 5.101, *Phlox subulata,* flowering moss. No. Ohio. **1959** Carleton *Index Herb. Plants* 47, *Flowering-Moss:* Phlox subulata.

flowering raspberry n Cf **white-flowering raspberry**

A **raspberry** (here: *Rubus odoratus*). Also called **mulberry, raspberry rose, thimbleberry**

1768 Miller *Gardener's Dict.* [np], *Rubus odoratus. . .* The Virginian flowering Raspberry, is commonly propagated in the nurseries as a flowering shrub. The flowers of this sort are as large as small Roses. **1814** Bigelow *Florula Bostoniensis* 123, *Rubus odoratus. . . Flowering Raspberry. . .* A superb, flowering shrub, commonly cultivated. **1848** Gray *Manual of Botany* 124, *Purple Flowering Raspberry. . . Petals rounded, purple rose-color. . .* Flowers very showy. **1901** Lounsberry *S. Wild Flowers* 236, *Purple-flowering Raspberry. . .* In bloom and fruit often at the same time, it appeared strikingly handsome. . . A delicious morsel especially when the road is long and dusty. **1924** Deam *Shrubs IN* 105, *Flowering raspberry. . .* Fruit maturing in midsummer, reddish, dry and scarcely edible. **1965** *Native Plants PA* 13, *Flowering Raspberry. . .* The fragrant purple-lavender 1-to-2-inch flowers appear in mid June. . . It deserves a corner in every garden. **1976** Bailey–Bailey *Hortus Third* 986, *Flowering raspberry, Purple-flowering r., Thimbleberry.*

flowering spice n Cf **flowering currant**

A **currant B1** (here: *Ribes aureum*).

1950 *WELS (Shrub that gets covered with bright yellow spicy smelling blossoms early in spring)* 1 Inf, **cWI,** Flowering spice. **1950** *WELS Suppl.* **csWI,** Flowering spice—alternate name for flowering currant; usage about evenly divided.

flowering spurge n

A **spurge** (here: *Euphorbia corollata*) with showy white petal-like appendages. Also called **bowman's root 1, forget-me-not 7, go-quick, Indian physic, milkweed, snake's milk, tramp's spurge, white spurge, wild hippo**

1848 Gray *Manual of Botany* 405, *E. corollata. . . Flowering Spurge. . .* Involucres very handsome on account of the white false lobes, which appear like petals. **1892** (1974) Millspaugh *Amer. Med. Plants* 148, The flowering spurge is a favorite medicine . . , being used as a purgative. **1912** Blatchley *IN Weed Book* 93, Flowering spurge . . exudes a milky, poisonous juice. **1949** Moldenke *Amer. Wild Flowers* 117, The flowering-spurge may be found in dry soil from Ontario and Minnesota to Florida and Texas. **1976** Bailey–Bailey *Hortus Third* 462.

flowering straw n

1 =wire lettuce.

1915 (1926) Armstrong–Thornber *Western Wild Flowers* 570, *Flowering Straw. Ptiloria pauciflora. . .* In the desert this is a very strange-looking, pale plant, . . with slender, brittle, gray stems, most of the leaves reduced to mere scales, and delicate, pale pinkish-lilac flowers. **1956** St. John *Flora SE WA* 471, *Stephanomeria. Flowering Straw. . .* Leafy-stemmed and branching herbs, with milky juice; upper leaves often reduced to bracts.

2 also *flowering straws:* A **skeletonweed,** usu *Lygodesmia aphylla.* [See quot 1949] **Sth**

1933 Small *Manual SE Flora* 1490, *L[ygodesmia] aphylla. . . Flowering-straws. . .* Coastal Plain, Fla. and Ga. **1936** Whitehouse *TX Flowers* 192, *Flowering Straw (Lygodesmia texana)* can nearly always be found in the prairie sections of the state from spring to fall. **1949** Moldenke *Amer. Wild Flowers* 182, *Lygodesmia aphylla. . .* The unexpectedness of finding . . very showy blossoms issuing from an apparently dead, or, at least, dormant naked stem has given rise to the name of *floweringstraws* for the plant. **1953** Greene–Blomquist *Flowers South* 143, Flowering-straw . . *(Lygodesmia aphylla)* belongs to the dandelion type of composites, of which there are several interesting and beautiful examples in the South.

flowering thistle n

A **prickly poppy** (here: *Argemone mexicana*).

1892 *Jrl. Amer. Folkl.* 5.92, *Argemone Mexicana . .* flowering thistle. Mansfield, O. **1900** Lyons *Plant Names* 44, *Argemone Mexicana. . .* Flowering-thistle. **1910** Graves *Flowering Plants* 197 **CT,** *Argemone mexicana. . .* Flowering Thistle. **1936** Whitehouse *TX Flowers* 34, *Yellow Prickly Poppy. . . (Argemone mexicana) . .* is also called bird-in-the-bush, . . flowering thistle, . . and Mexican thorn poppy.

flowering willow n

1 =desert willow.

1859 (1942) Patterson *Travel Diary* 188 **CO,** We find . . fringes of flowering willows. **1960** Vines *Trees SW* 929, *Desert-willow—Chilopsis linearis. . .* Also known under the vernacular names of Flowering-willow [etc]. . . These names arise from the fact that the flowers resemble those of the Catalpa-tree and the leaves are willow-like in appearance.

2 =willow herb.

1959 Carleton *Index Herb. Plants* 48, *Flowering-Willow:* Epiloblum [sic] angustifolium.

flowering wintergreen n [From the resemblance of the leaves to those of wintergreen]

=**fringed polygala.**

1822 Eaton *Botany* 398, *Polygala paucifolia,* flowering wintergreen. **1840** MA Zool. & Bot. Surv. *Herb. Plants & Quadrupeds* 77, Flowering Winter-green . . blossoms in May and June, in woods. **1897** Creevey *Flowers* 314, Fringed Polygala. Flowering Wintergreen. **1911** NJ State Museum *Annual Rept. for 1910* 525, Flowering Wintergreen. Gay-Wings. **1933** Small *Manual SE Flora* 767, Flowering-wintergreen. . . N. of Coastal Plain, Ga. to Ill., Man., Que., and Me. **1949** Moldenke *Amer. Wild Flowers* 50, Best known in the north is . . floweringwintergreen, or bird-on-the-wing. **1976** Bailey–Bailey *Hortus Third* 894.

flowerist n [*OED* 1694 →, but cf quot 1895]

A florist.

1895 *DN* 1.397 **NYC,** *Flowerist:* for *florist* by folk-etymology. **1913** Johnson *Highways St. Lawrence to VA* 144 **nePA,** They sell the berries to a man here who's a flowerist—has a flower house you understand—and he ships 'em to the cities.

flower louse n

An aphid.

1968 *DARE* (Qu. R26, . . *Small greenish lice that come on plants*) Inf **VA**7, Flower lice.

flower-of-an-hour n [In ref to the short blossoming time]

A plant *(Hibiscus trionum)* with short-lived dark-centered yellow flowers. Also called **black-eyed Susan 3, devil's-head-in-a-bush, modesty, shoo-fly, trailing hollyhock**

1822 Eaton *Botany* 306, Bladder ketmia, flower of an hour. **1939** *Natl. Geogr. Mag.* Aug 229/2, The dainty little flower-of-an-hour . . clothes waysides, roadsides, ditches, and waste places. **1967** *DARE* FW Addit **neCO,** Flower-of-an-hour—a cornfield pest. *Hibiscus trionum*

flower of gold n

=**goldenrod 1.**

1896 *Jrl. Amer. Folkl.* 9.193 **CA,** *Solidago* (any species), flower of gold.

flower-of-May n

A **false lily of the valley** (here: *Maianthemum canadense*).

1916 Keeler *Early Wildflowers* 28, The Flower-of-May appears in open, sunny woodlands.

flower-of-paradise n

A clammyweed (here: *Polanisia dodecandra*).

1966 *DARE* Wildfl QR (Wills–Irwin) Pl.13d Inf **TX**34, Flower-of-paradise.

flower pit n

A cold frame.

1967 *Wilson Coll.* **csKY,** *Flower-pit*—[Like a cucumber frame, four to five feet square] to keep potted plants from freezing over winter.

flowerpot n

1 A bouquet, nosegay. **chiefly VA, NC** [Engl dial (Gloucester). Note: *EDD flower-plot* (at *flower*) is an error for *flower-pot.*]

1940 *Qrly. Jrl. Speech* 26.265 **nwVA,** A woman who arranges flowers in a vase is "making a flower pot." **1942** *Hench Coll.* **swVA,** [Letter:] All of them call a bunch of flowers a "flower pot." **1952** Brown *NC Folkl.* 1.541, *Flower-pot.* . . A bouquet.—West. **1953** *PADS* 19.10 **sAppalachians,** *Flowerpot.* . . Bouquet. "You ought to see Aunt Bett's coffin; it looks like a flowerpot." **1959** *Hench Coll.* **cnVA,** [He] said . . "May I get you a flower pot?" When he brought it, it was a bouquet of flowers in his hand. **1966** *DARE* (Qu. G8, . . *"The bride carried a pretty ______."*) Inf **NC**33, Flowerpot. **1966** *DARE* File **swVA,** Flowerpot—a nosegay or bouquet. **1983** *MJLF* 9.1.39 **ceKY,** *Flower pot* . . a bouquet.

2 also *flower basket:* A firework which throws up a fountain of sparks. [*OED* 1842] **chiefly Nth, N Midl**

1965–70 *DARE* (Qu. FF28) 12 Infs, **Nth, N Midl,** Flowerpots; **NJ**2, Flowerpot—cone-shaped, sparkles out of tip; **NY**209, Flowerpot—round, not high off the ground; **PA**22, Flowerpot—lit and burst into many colors; **PA**113, Flowerpot—cone [-shaped], stuff shoots up; **SD**1, Flowerpot—pot which throws colored sparks; (Qu. FF14) Infs **IN**19, **NY**131, Flowerpots; **MI**103, Flower basket—a pyramid-shaped device.

flower strip n

=**grassplot.**

1968–70 *DARE* (Qu. N44, . . *The strip of grass and trees between the sidewalk and the curb*) Inf **MD**31, Flower strip; **TN**53, Tree strip; flower strip.

flower tree n

=**tulip tree.**

1969 *DARE* (Qu. T13, . . *Tulip tree*) Inf **KY**11, Flower tree.

flow'h See **flower**

flowing well n

A well from which the liquid flows without pumping, as:

a An oil well.

1865 *Atlantic Mth.* 15.393/2 **PA,** Oil announces itself . . in occasional happy instances by a rush of oil spouting to the top of the derrick. . . Such a well as this, known as a flowing well, is the best 'find' possible. **1887** Crew *Petroleum* 146 (*DN* 2.381), The first fountain well, or as it was afterwards universally called, flowing well, was struck . . and commenced to flow at the rate of three hundred barrels per day. **1904** Tarbell *Hist. Std. Oil Co.* 1.31 **PA,** The news [of the fall of Sumter in the Civil War] for the time blotted out interest even in flowing wells. **1939** FWP *Guide CA* 548, The northern wells are "stripping wells"—which draw the last remaining oil from the field—and the southern ones are "flowing wells" which produce oil without pumping.

b A water well.

1928 *AmSp* 4.126 **NE,** There is, also, . . the "flowing-well country," which is dotted with artesian wells. **1950** *WELS (Kinds of springs)* 1 Inf, **WI,** Two sulfur springs, one flowing well; 1 Inf, There are natural flowing wells within ten miles. **c1965** *DARE* File **swID,** My cousins lived on a farm that had a flowing or artesian well. We were fascinated by the everflowing water, but hesitated to drink it because of the sulphur smell. **1966** *DARE* Tape **NM**2, They've pulled the water down so low, why, we don't have many flowing wells now. **1967** *DARE* FW Addit **ceSC,** Flowing well—an artesian well.

flowsy adj Also sp *flowzy* [Prob var of *frowsy* (perh infl by *blowsy*), but cf *EDD flowsy* (at *flowse* adj.) "a slattern"]

Untidy, unkempt.

1950 *PADS* 14.29 **SC,** Flowsy ['flauzɪ]. . . Untidy; slovenly. **1953** Randolph–Wilson *Down in Holler* 244 **Ozarks,** That Tandy gal's hair looks kind of flowzy tonight. **1954** *Harder Coll.* **cwTN,** *Flowzy* . . disarranged, untidy.

flozzy See **flossy** n

flub v [*flub* to blunder, botch]

1 To disturb, confuse.

1968–69 *DARE* (Qu. BB40, . . *"All of a sudden he got up and left. What do you suppose ______ him?"*) Inf **MN**38, Flubbed; (Qu. GG2, . . *"So many things were going on at the same time that he got completely ______."*) Inf **CA**154, Flubbed.

2 with *around:* To fool around, kill time. Cf **flubdub** v **2, fub** v² **1**

1967 *DARE* (Qu. A10, . . *"What are you doing?" . . "Nothing in particular—I'm just ______."*) Inf **MA**82, Flubbing around.

flub a dub See **flub the dub**

flub around See **flub 2**

flubdub n

1 Nonsense, balderdash.

1888 *Detroit Free Press* Aug (Farmer *Americanisms*), By swiping out the flub-dub and guff, I guess we'll have room to put in the points. **1904** *Rochester Post–Express* 13 July 4 *(OEDS),* There is an immense amount of flubdub and nonsense and gush in this sort of talk. **1929** *Sun* (Baltimore MD) 5 Feb 1/1 *(Hench Coll.),* There was no flubdub whatever about this morning's business. **1947** Crane *Sins of NY* 259, He had, by intently listening to lawyers . . , acquired an astonishing hash of legalistic flubdub. **1952** *Daily Mirror* (N.Y.) 8 July 11/4 *(OEDS),* Maybe Mike Todd or Berle should take over the management of the conventions. . . They would remove much of the amateur flub-dub.

2 A bit of finery, ornamentation. Cf **flibdib, fluff-duff.**

1915 D. R. Campbell *Proving Virginia* 241 *(DA),* Thanks to Henrietta, you have plenty of pretty gowns and flub-dubs.

3 See quot.

1893 *KS Univ. Qrly.* 1.139 **ceMA,** *Flub-dub:* a snob, a pretender.

4 See **fubdub.**

5 An apple dumpling.

1941 *LANE* Map 292, 1 inf, **ceMA,** Flub-dub.

flubdub v

1 To blunder. Cf **flub the dub 2**

1968 *DARE* (Qu. JJ42, . . *"This time he certainly ______."*) Inf MN33, Flubdubbed.

2 with *around:* To fool around, stall. Cf **flub 2**

1966 *DARE* (Qu. KK11, . . *"When we asked him to do that, he ______."*) Inf **MA**6, Flubdubbed around—if he delayed. **1980** *DARE* File **eMA** (as of 1960s), If I complained about being late, my mother would say, "Of course you're late—you've been flubdubbing around instead of getting ready."

flub the dub v phr Also *flub one's dub, flub a dub, flub the dud*

1 To loaf, shirk one's duty.

1946 *AmSp* 21.238 [World War II slang], *Flubbin' the dub.* Loafing, goldbricking. **1960** Wentworth–Flexner *Slang* 193, *Flub the dub—1* To evade one's duty; to loaf. *2* To think and perform inefficiently and slowly. *Both meanings common W. W. II. use.*

2 To blunder, botch, fail.

1946 *Western Folkl.* 5.380, Anyone who is *on the ball* is alert, alive, thinking clearly. . . The diametric opposite of this is *to drop the ball,* or the more popular *flub the dub.* **1950** *WELS ("He usually handles things pretty well, but he certainly ______ this time.")* 1 Inf, **ceWI,** Flubbed a dub. **1959** *AmSp* 34.156 **FL** [College student jargon], He may fail; in his words, he *flubbed, flubbed up, flubbed the dub.* **1960** Wentworth–Flexner *Slang* 193, *Flub the dub.* . . To spoil or ruin by blunders or mistakes; to ruin or fail to take advantage of one's chances for success. **1965–70** *DARE* (Qu. JJ42, . . *"He usually handles things well, but this time he certainly ______."*) 14 Infs, 7 **S Midl,** Flubbed the (*or* his, a) dub; **KY**59, **LA**35, Flubbed the dud; (Qu. GG15, . . *A person who became over-excited and lost control, "At that point he really ______."*) Infs **MO**35, **VA**15, Flubbed the (*or* a) dub; (Qu. KK20b, . . *"Our old washing machine . . ______."*) Inf **MS**1, Flubbed the dub. **1976** Garber *Mountain-ese* 30 **sAppalachians,** If you try to outdo Marty, you are liable to flub your dub.

flucan See **flookan**

flucey See **floozy** adj

flue n[1] [*OED flue* sb.[2] 1 "*Obs.* . . A wooly or downy substance"; several quots ref to animal fur]

1899 (1912) Green *VA Folk-Speech* 180, *Flue.* . . Fur of an animal.

flue n[2]

1 A chimney, esp one that carries off smoke from a stove (rather than a fireplace). [*OED flue* sb.[3] 1 "In early use = *Chimney*"] **Midl**

1903 *DN* 2.313 **seMO,** *Flue.* . . Chimney into which a stovepipe enters. 'The house had n'ary chimney, but four or five flues.' Said of a well built house with no fireplaces. **1905** *DN* 3.79 **nwAR,** *Flue.* . . Chimney into which one or more stove-pipes pass. Never used of a chimney built with a fire-place. 'J. H. Eatherly will build a flue next week for the school-house in Happy Hollow.' Universal. **1954** *Harder Coll.* **cwTN,** *Flue.* . . The portion of a chimney that sticks out above the top of a house. . . A brick or stone structure through which smoke escapes from the house from stoves. **1973** Allen *LAUM* 1.159 **Upper MW** (as of c1950), *Flue,* . . [occurring 12 times] in Iowa and once in Nebraska, appears Midland oriented. [2 infs indicate that the flue is only one part of the chimney.]

2 in phr *one's flue draws strong:* See quot.

1967 *DARE* FW Addit **LA**14, [Heard from an "old Tennessee hill-dweller":] Her flue draws strong—said of a woman who is eager to get married.

3 One of the funnel-shaped throats in a **hoop net.** [Prob from its resemblance to a chimney flue, but cf *OED flue* sb.[1] "a kind of fishing net."]

1967 *DARE* Tape **LA**5, That's the first hoop . . and that has two flues in it or two throats, we call it. . . Just like a funnel.

4 Fig: one's gullet.

1903 (1965) Adams *Log Cowboy* 86, [We are] reaching the wagon in time for breakfast and lining our flues with Lovell's good chuck.

flue-cure v, hence ppl adj *flue-cured,* vbl n *flue-curing* Cf **air-cure, fire-cure**

To dry (tobacco) using indirect heat from ducts rather than exposure to direct heat.

1905 Odlum *Culture of Tobacco* 99 **SC,** In case of the flue-cured tobaccos, these barns would be too large to properly maintain the heat necessary. **1933** *Sun* (Baltimore MD) 2 Sept 7/5 *(Hench Coll.),* The money necessary to make these payments will be obtained from a processing tax on all flue-cured tobacco processed for domestic consumption. **1944** *PADS* 2.66 **S Midl,** *Flue-cure.* . . To cure by artificial heat passing through flues. **1960** Heimann *Tobacco* 151 **VA,** The essential feature of the cure was . . a thorough drying out of the leaves . . before the final intense heat was applied. . . this method—"flue-curing"—was not standardized until after the Civil War. **1966** *PADS* 45.13 **Lexington KY,** *Flue-cured.* **1967** Key *Tobacco Vocab.* **GA, NC,** Flue-cured. **1970** *DARE* Tape **VA**38, The flue-cured tobacco was cured the same way, cured by flue, mostly wood. Now most everybody cure by oil or gas.

flue, go up the v phr [*OED flue* sb.[3] 4 "*Up the flue* . . dead, collapsed"; 1821 →] Cf **flume, go up the,** *DS* BB56

To die.

1862 in 1943 Wiley *Life Johnny Reb* 130 **TX,** There is one thing Sure the war cant go on always I will either go up the flew or come home before a graitwhile.

flue pan n **NEng**

In the maple sugar industry: see quots.

1947 *PADS* 8.6 **VT,** *Flue pan.* . . A pan below the main pan of the evaporator in which there are many circulating partitions so that the sap can flow from flue to flue. **1968** *DARE* Tape **CT**3, As I showed you the evaporator outside, there are 2 pans. One is called a flue pan where the cold sap comes in through a special pump that we have.

flue-stretcher n

1970 *DARE* (Qu. HH14, *Ways of teasing a beginner . . for example, by sending him for a 'left-handed monkey wrench': "Go get me a ______."*) Inf **KY**84, Flue-stretcher.

fluff n

1 also *fluffy:* A soft roll of dust that collects under furniture; woolly dust. **chiefly Inland Nth, N Midl**

1950 *WELS (Soft rolls of dust that collect on the floor under beds or other furniture)* 1 Inf, **cwWI,** Fluff. **1965–70** *DARE* (Qu. E20) 13 Infs, **chiefly Inland Nth, N Midl,** Fluff; **NE**9, **NY**80, **OH**11, Fluffs; **NY**145, Fluffies.

2 A comforter. Cf **puff**

1969 *DARE* (Qu. E16, *A padded covering used on a bed, mostly for warmth*) Inf **MA**24, A fluff.

3 A tizzy, dither.

1970 *DARE* (Qu. GG7, . . *Annoyed or upset: "Though we were only ten minutes late, she was all ______."*) Inf **MS**80, In a fluff; in a huff.

fluff v

1 with *off:* To snub, jilt, shun. [Perh infl by *slough off*]

1946 *AmSp* 21.33 **TX** [College slang], *Fluff off* . . To snob [sic], slight, or to humiliate. **1967–69** *DARE* (Qu. Y51, . . *"He's not your kind—you'd better ______ him."*) Inf **CA**15, Fluff [him] off; (Qu. AA11, *If a man asks a girl to marry him and she refuses, you'd say she ______*) Inf **CA**107, Fluffed him off; (Qu. II6, *If you meet somebody who used to be a friend, and he pretends not to know you: "When I met him on the street he ______."*) Inf **IL**71, Fluffed me off.

2 with *off:* To waste time, shirk work.

1968 *DARE* (Qu. A9, . . *Wasting time by not working on the job*) Inf **NY**49, Fluffing off; (Qu. BB27, *When somebody pretends to be sick [often to get out of doing something] you'd say he's ______*) Inf **CA**53, Fluffing off.

3 with *up:* To tidy up. [Prob by ext from *fluff up* (a pillow or cushion)]

1967 *DARE* (Qu. E21, *Talking about a room that needs to be put in order, you might say, "I'm just going to ______ this room."*) Inf **IL**9, Fluff up.

4 See quot.

1970 *DARE* (Qu. Y37, *To make a place untidy or disorderly: "I wish they wouldn't ______ the room so."*) Inf **TN**53, Ruffle, fluff, rearrange.

fluffball n

A **puffball.**

1968 *DARE* (Qu. S18, *A kind of mushroom that grows like a globe*) Inf **MN**38, Fluffballs.

fluff-duff n Cf **flubdub n 2**

1968 Adams *Western Words* 108, *Fancy fluff-duff*—Anything fancy, from food to finery. For some of the ranch dances the ranch-women would make doughnuts, bake pies, and cook other fluff-duffs.

fluffer n

A **tedder.**

1969–70 *DARE* (Qu. L16, *Machines used . . in handling hay*) Inf **KY**27, Fluffer—the present-day term for a tedder, which is used to stir hay up; **KY**72, Fluffer—a tedder.

fluffgrass n

A low, tufted grass *(Erioneuron pulchellum)* native chiefly to the Southwest.

1942 Amer. Joint Comm. Horticult. Nomenclature *Std. Plant Names* 231, Fluffgrass . . *Triodia pulchella.* **1950** Hitchcock-Chase *Manual Grasses* 208, *Fluffgrass. . .* Panicle . . consisting of 1 to 5 nearly sessile relatively large white woolly spikelets. **1957** *Plateau* 30.34 **AZ,** In a few well localized areas fluffgrass . . , usually not more than three inches high, develops a stem with a cluster of leaves at the top. **1974** Munz *Flora S. CA* 970, *E[rioneuron] pulchellum. . .* Fluffgrass.

fluff off See **fluff v 1, 2**

fluff up See **fluff v 3**

fluffweed n

1 A **mullein** (here: *Verbascum thapsus*).

1940 Clute *Amer. Plant Names* 274, *Verbascum thapsus . .* fluffweed. **1959** Carleton *Index Herb. Plants* 48, *Fluffweed:* Verbascum thapsus.

2 A **dandelion 1.**

1968 *DARE* (Qu. S11) Inf **PA**89, Fluffweed.

fluffy See **fluff n 1**

flu-flux n [*flu* + **flux**] *joc*

1970 *DARE* (Qu. BB28, . . *Imaginary diseases: "He must have the ______."*) Inf **TX**92, Flu-flux.

flu-fly bird n

=**filliloo bird.**

1939 Tryon *Fearsome Critters* 19, *The Filla-Ma-Loo Bird. . .* [Also] called the Flu-fly Bird. *Ibid,* Low in intellectual curiosity, showing complete and consistent indifference as to where he's going. He prefers only to see where he's been; hence he always flies backwards.

flug n Also sp *phlug*

Dust or lint that collects in pockets, under beds, and in similar places; also fig.

1934 Wylie *Finnley Wren* 301 **neNJ,** The ones we talked about. Where are they now? What are they doing? Bitter fragments on the Lethe. Chips and gobbets. Human flug. **1952** *We're Not Married* [Movie] (*DAS* at *phlug*), Did you drop some flug in my cup? **1952** *San Francisco Examiner* (CA) 4 Dec 33/1, [Herb Caen's column, subtitle:] *Pocketful of flug.* **1970** *DARE* File, Flug [flʌ:g]—dust curls under furniture. Heard from "Southern people" in California. **1973** *San Francisco Chronicle* (CA) 19 Nov 29/1 [Herb Caen's column], In answer to questions from a few mildly interested readers, "phlug" is the stuff that collects in the pockets of aging suits and overcoats. **1980** *DARE* File **NYC** (as of 1930s), As for *phlug,* or *flug,* in high school and college this was (specifically) the lint that collected in the navel. **1982** *Smithsonian Letters* **KS,** A friend from Kansas calls the dust rolls "flug."

flugens n |ˈfluǰɪnz, -ǰɪns, -gɪnz, -žɪnz| Also *flugins, flujens, flujin, flugence, fluzions* **chiefly Sth** Cf **blixen; blugeons; floogies, hot as**

Hell, the dickens, tarnation—often in phrr *cold as (blue) flugens* and varr.

1830 *N. J. Chronicle* (Mt. Holly) 20 Aug. 2/2 *(DA),* 'Oh dad,' says he, 'I'm making money like flugens.' **1834** *Life Andrew Jackson* 62, The gineral thou't the glory of the nashion woud'n't shine bright enuff till he had brou't flugens among them [=the Indians]. **1850** Melville *White-Jacket* 123, It was cold as *Blue Flujin,* where sailors say fire freezes. **1859** Taliaferro *Fisher's R.* 204 **nwNC** (as of 1820s), But I was mad as flugence. **1893** Shands *MS Speech* 30, *Flugins* [fluǰɪnz]. . . "It is as cold as flugins." **1895** *DN* 1.388 **KY,** *Flugins:* in phrase "cold as blue flugins." **1898** Harris *Tales Home Folks* 129 **GA,** It's colder 'n Flujens. **1949** *PADS* 11.13 **wTX** (as of c1920), As *cold* as flugens. **1950** *PADS* 13.6 **Sth,** *Flugens* [ˈfludʒɪns]. **1954** Welty *Ponder Heart* 64 **MS,** It was hot as fluzions in that little front room. **1954** *PADS* 21.27 **SC,** *Flugins. . .* [ˈflugɪnz]—In the phrases "cold as flugins" "cold as blue flugins." The various ways in which this word is used have in common only the fact that it is always an intensive. Not common, but still heard.

flugens adv [**flugens** n]

Furiously, in a rush.

1834 *Life Andrew Jackson* 36, If they give you any jimber jaw be at 'em flugens, and make them scamper like monkeys before a fire.

flugins, flujens, flujin See **flugens n**

fluke n^{1} **Atlantic coast**

A **flatfish 2,** such as the **summer flounder.**

1906 NJ State Museum *Annual Rept. for 1905* 393, *Paralichthys dentatus. . .* Fluke. **1932** *Hanley Disks* **swCT,** And then we have another flat fish here we call the fluke. They are a large-mouth flat fish. They differ from our regular flat fish. They're a deep water fish. **1958** *Washington Post & Times Herald* (DC) 1 Aug sec D 5/3 *(Hench Coll.),* The skipper . . sadly announced there would be no wind strong enough to drift for "fluke." **1965–70** *DARE* (Qu. P2, . . *Saltwater fish . . good to eat*) 11 Infs, **Atlantic coast,** Fluke; (Qu. P14, . . *Commercial fishing*) Infs **MA**55, **VA**47, Fluke. **1969** *DARE* FW Addit **eNC,** Fluke—a flounder. **1972** Sparano *Outdoors Encycl.* 384, *Summer Flounder*—Common Names: . . fluke, flatfish. Scientific Name: *Paralichthys dentatus.*

fluke n^{2}

1 A flop, failure; a worthless person or thing. Cf **fluke v^{1} 2**

1928 *AmSp* 3.367 **Hollywood CA,** When a "cutter's" (film editor) deft eye and hand cannot help a picture that threatens to be a "fluke" and a "flop," . . [it] is called a "sick picture." **1942** Berrey-Van den Bark *Amer. Slang* 21.4, *Something Worthless. . .* fluke. **1966–68** *DARE* (Qu. FF19, . . *A very dull or unenjoyable time: "The party was ______."*) Inf **AR**3, A fluke; **PA**104, A flop, a flunk, or a fluke; (Qu. HH16, . . *"Don't invite him. He's a ______."*) Inf **MD**31, Fluke. Used to be common in [my] younger days.

2 A baseball pitch in which the ball is made to behave unexpectedly. Cf **fluke v^{1} 5**

1968 *DARE* Tape **NY**118A, A guy would pitch the ball with what they call a fluke. **1982** *WI State Jrl.* (Madison) 2 May sec 5 2/5 **NYC** (as of 1930s), A nun coached our stickball team and showed me how to pitch a "fluke," an arid spitball delivered with forked fingers.

fluke v^{1} Also sp *flook*

1 To steal.

1892 *KS Univ. Qrly.* 1.96 **IN,** *Fluke:* to steal.

2 To fail. Cf **fluke n^{2} 1**

c1902 Clapin *New Dict. Amer.* 190, *Fluke (to).* In college slang, to fail utterly. **1929** *AmSp* 4.340 [Vocab of bums], *Fluke*—To prove no good; to fail. **1942** Berrey-Van den Bark *Amer. Slang* 262.2, *Fail. . .* fluke. *Ibid* 837.4, *Not Pass; "Fail." . .* fluke.

3 To confuse, mix up.

1935 *Sun* (Baltimore MD) 22 Apr 4/5 *(Hench Coll.),* That wind and sand storm . . beat in upon the weather bureau so hard it flooked its forecasts for a string of days in succession.

4 also with *out:* To back out, renege.

1950 *WELS ("He said he'd help, but then he ______.")* 1 Inf, **seWI,** Fluked; *("At the last minute he ______.")* 1 Inf, **seWI,** Fluked out. **1952** Brown *NC Folkl.* 1.541, *Fluke. . .* To withdraw; to go back on one's word.

5 To pitch a **fluke n^{2} 2.**

1968 *DARE* Tape **NY**118A, The way you fluke the ball is you get a Spalding in your hand with your third finger, you go like that, and the ball does all kinds of weird tricks.

fluke v^{2} [Prob Engl dial *fluke,* to wheedle, cajole]

To flirt.

a1874 in 1949 *PADS* 11.31 **cME,** But now the flame you're "fluking" with,/ Perhaps is mostly "boughten."

fluked out ppl adj phr Cf **flunked out**

1961 Folk *Word Atlas N. LA* map 1406, Tired, exhausted . . others . . "fluked" out.

fluke, go up the v phr [Prob **fluke v^{1} 2** infl by **flume, go up the**]

c1902 Clapin *New Dict. Amer.* 190, *Fluke. . . To go up the fluke,* to fail in recitation or examination.

fluken See **flookan**

fluke out See **fluke** v[1] **4**

flukey See **fluky**

fluking ppl adj [See quot 1945] **NEng** Cf **fluting**

Sailing swiftly; rushing, darting about—often in phr *go (a-)fluking.*

1840 (1841) Dana *2 Yrs.* 306, We arrived on the following day, having gone 'all fluking,' with the weather clue of the main-sail hauled up, the yards braced in a little, and the lower studding-sail just drawing; the wind hardly shifting a point during the passage. **1900** Day *Up in ME* 22 (*AmSp* 41.21), Up [the ladder] he went afluking with them shingles on his hip. **1911** Shute *Plupy* 90 **seNH** (as of 1860s), She started 'n passed them jest flukin' 'n we both pulled and pulled. **1939** Coffin *Capt. Abby* 14 **ME** (as of 1860s), A big ship was built there... It came a-fluking down the river to the high stairway of the falls at Brunswick. **1945** Colcord *Sea Language* 77 **ME, Cape Cod, Long Island,** *Fluking, all a-.* Sailing fast and furiously. A whaleman's expression, from the speed of a whale driven by strokes of its powerful flukes, or tail-fins... The phrase has passed into shore speech, to mean rapid, unimpeded progress of any sort. **1968–69** *DARE* (Qu. MM12a, .. *"He shot into a flock of birds and they went ______."*) Inf **NY**96, [ə'flukɨn]; (Qu. MM12b, .. *"She broke her beads and they went ______."*) Inf **CT**22, Fluking. **1968** *DARE* File **RI,** *Aflukin', go,* to move in a fast manner, especially if not expected or if comical. A bustling old woman might go aflukin', or an old model T Ford. A mouse or an insect might go aflukin' across some cleared ground.

fluky adj Also sp *flukey*

Chancy, uncertain; esp of wind: gusty.

1937 *Sun* (Baltimore MD) 31 July 11/5 *(Hench Coll.),* The wind was so flukey that the first race was declared "no contest." **1966** *DARE* (Qu. B14) Inf **NC**17, Fluky or gusty. **1966** *DARE* FW Addit **neNC,** It's a fluky day.

flume, go up the v phr [Var of **flue, go up the**]

To meet with disaster, to die; hence adj phrr *(gone) up the* (or *a*) *flume* ruined, done for, doomed.

1865 *Eastern Slope* (Washoe, Nev.) 23 Dec. 3/1 *(DA),* The great Stockholder .. has in the classic language of the mines, 'gone up the flume.' **1872** Twain *Roughing It* 250 **MO,** You see, one of the boys has gone up the flume. **1875** *Scribner's Mth.* 10.277/1 **San Francisco CA,** If a man fails in business he is 'gone up a flume.' **1882** Twain *Stolen White Elephant* 101, Well, then, *that* idea's up the flume. We got to think up something else. **1889** Munroe *Golden Days* 124 **CA** (as of 1849), And, pard, he has moseyed with the map, and we're up a flume. **1890** *Denver Republican* 4 May 24/3 *(DA),* You frequently hear people say when a firm fails or great loss by fire is experienced, 'Well, they're gone up the flume.' **1966** Barnes–Jensen *Dict. UT Slang* 20, *Gone up the flume:* .. failed, come to grief. "Say, that mine's gone up the flume."

flumididdle See **flummadiddle**

flumix See **flummox** v

flummadiddle n Also *flumididdle, flumme(r)diddle, flummydiddle, fum(m)adiddle* [Perh elaboration of **flummery**]

1 See quots. **NEng** *?obs*

1857 *Harper's New Mth. Mag.* Sept 538/2 **NEng,** Flummadiddle is a compound mixture .. of .. stale bread, pork fat, molasses, water, cinnamon, allspice, and cloves. It is a kind of *mush,* baked in the oven. **1872** Schele de Vere *Americanisms* 338, Such is the *flummadiddle,* a holiday-mess of New England fishermen... It consists [primarily] of .. stale bread, pork-fat, molasses, cinnamon, allspice, and cloves .. baked in the oven and brought to the table hot and brown.

2 also attrib: Nonsense, foolishness—sometimes used as exclam.

1848 Thompson *Green Mt. Boys* 255 **eNY,** If a British General had not writ it, I should have called some of it nothing but damn flumididdle. **1854** (1923) Holmes *Tempest & Sunshine* 32 **KY,** What does she want of any more flummerdiddle notions? **1868** Brackett *Farm Talk* 70 **NEng,** What's the use of so much 'flummy-diddle'? Plain common sense is enough for any farmer's paper. **1903** *DN* 2.297 **Cape Cod MA** (as of a1857), *Flummydiddle...* Foolishness. **1942** *Sat. Eve. Post* 25 Oct 35/3 **Sth** [Black], An' does you try any fumadiddles, you is right away gwine happen to a catastrophe. **1942** in 1944 *ADD* [Black], [Radio:] NY, ['fʌmədɪdl̩]. **1970** *New Yorker* 11 Sept 33/3, What kind of fumadiddles is that brat of mine mixed up in now?

3 A frill, bauble, bit of finery.

1882 *Advance* 21 Sept 605/2 **Chicago IL,** Directions for .. crocheting all sorts of flummediddles. **c1939** in 1944 *ADD,* Then, all diked out in these fancy fumadiddles, what does he do? **1948** *Popular Western* June 104/2 *(DA),* I know a California vaquero feels positively naked if he don't have some fumadiddle about his get-up.

4 A doodad, thingamajig.

1897 *KS Univ. Qrly.* (ser B) 6.52, *Doofunny:* a thing not easily described, or thus mentioned to save description; .. thingumbob, .. fum-a-diddle. **1905** *DN* 3.66 **NE,** *Thingumbob, .. dingus, .. fummadiddle, .. jigger,* [etc]. **1931** *AmSp* 6.258, Indefinite names current in the Central West... fumadiddle.

flummergasted ppl adj [Var of *flabbergasted,* perh infl by **flummery**]

1893 Shands *MS Speech* 30, *Flummergasted...* Used by illiterate whites for *embarrassed,* or *befuddled.* In their parlance a man sometimes becomes *flummergasted* when he rises to make a speech, and so forgets what he wishes to say.

flummery n [Welsh *llymru* a gelatinous porridge of oatmeal or flour]

1 A sweet cold pudding thickened with starch or gelatin and usu including fruit. **chiefly NEng**

1763 in 1928 Watts *Letter Book* 173 **NY,** But you might as well have struck fire out of Flummery. **1853** (1982) Lea *Domestic Cookery* 128, *Blackberry Flummery.* Stew three pints of blackberries with one pint of sugar—soak a tea-cup full of ground rice—and .. stir in the rice .. until .. [the pudding] becomes thick. This should be eaten cold with cream. **1906** Gregory *Woman's Cookbook* 309, *Raspberry, Currant, Grape or Peach Flummery.* **1939** Wolcott *Yankee Cook Book* 195 **CT,** Blackberry Flummery. [Recipe consists of berries, water, sugar, cornstarch; it is served with sugar and cream.] **1952** Tracy *Coast Cookery* 104 **MA,** Flummery—Cornstarch pudding made with water and cooked fruit, served with cream and sugar. **1964** Amer. Heritage *Cookbook* 572, *Sister Abigail's Strawberry Flummery*—The Shakers were unusually attentive to the needs of their elders, and they developed a special diet, and special dishes, for the aged. This recipe is among the more popular of those dishes.

2 Nonsense, flattery, humbug; frippery. *old-fash*

1807 Irving *Salmagundi* 4.70, [Title:] *Flummery, from the mill of Pindar Cockloft, Esq.* Being a Poem with Notes. **1825** Neal *Brother Jonathan* 1.330 **CT,** I don't much like Bald Eagle's flummery, though. **1848** Bartlett *Americanisms* 146, *Flummery...* We use it only in the .. figurative sense [meaning 'flattery']. **1883** Twain *Life on Missip.* (Boston) 406, The Bridal Chamber .. whose pretentious flummery was necessarily overawing.

flummix, flummocks v See **flummox** v

flummocks n See **flummox** n

flummox v Also *flum(m)ix, flummocks, flummux, kerflommix, kerflummux, k'flummux, conflummox* [Engl dial and colloq; *OED* 1837 →] Cf **ker-**

1 To hesitate; to give way; to collapse.

1839 D. P. Thompson *Green Mountain Boys* xxiv.256 *(OEDS)* **eNY,** Well, if he should flummux at such a chance, I know of a chap .. who'll agree to take his place. **1843** (1847) Field *Drama Pokerville* 73 **MO,** "*Pre*haps," Parson Hyme didn't put it in to Pokerville for two mortal hours; and *pre*haps Pokerville didn't wiggle, wince, and finally "flummix" right beneath him! **1849** *NY Daily Tribune* (NY) 25 Apr 1/3, [Citing *Oyster War of Accomac:*] Be ye men of mighty stomachs,/ Men that can't be made to *flummux.* **1851** (1969) Burke *Polly Peablossom* 51 **MO,** I thought I should er flummuxed! The dogs they sidled back, an' Ike he cussed; an' I lay down an' rolled an' laughed sorter easy to myself, 'til I was so full I thort I should er bust my biler! **1890** *DN* 1.64 **KY,** "He ker-flummuxed to-day." "When they brought that in, I almost k'flummuxed." **1906** *DN* 3.143 **nwAR,** He kerflummuxed on the ice. **1908** [see **6** below].

2 To fail, blunder.

1851 Hall *College Words* 131, *Flummux.* To fail; to recite badly. **1905** *DN* 3.9 **cCT,** *Flummux...* To fail [Inf uncertain]. **1908** [see **6** below]. **c1960** *Wilson Coll.* **csKY,** *Flummox...* To fail badly.

3 To move in a clumsy manner, lumber.

1897 Robinson *Uncle Lisha's Outing* 18 **VT,** I went a kerflummuxin' daown yunder through the bushes right slap ontu a snag o' ducks 'at I might jes' 's well crep' up tu an' shot if I'd on'y 'spected they was there.

4 To back out, renege.

1914 *DN* 4.154 **NH,** *Flummux. . .* To back out of a trade. **1941** *LANE* Map 407B, 1 inf, **sVT,** I'll flummox, 'what a boy says to break the engagement.'

5 To do up, fuss with. *obs*

1877 Talmage *Crumbs* 270 **NYC,** Brushes . . with which heiresses . . flumixed their hair.

6 To cause to fail, to defeat; hence ppl adj *flummoxed* exhausted, beaten.

1899 [see **7** below]. **1905** *DN* 3.9 **cCT,** *Flummux* . . to thwart [Inf uncertain]. **1908** *DN* 3.326 **eAL, wGA,** *Kerflummux. . .* To fall in a heap, fail ignominiously; also to cause to fall or fail thus. **1983** *DARE* File **cwMA,** *Flummoxed*—I do not recall hearing it anywhere but around No. Leverett—we meant by it, "completely used up, at the end of our rope or tether, beat out, done up."

7 also with *up:* To confuse, bewilder, disconcert; hence ppl adj *flummoxed up.*

1893 Shands *MS Speech* 42, "I sho was kerflummuxed when dat aig struck me," a colored speaker who has been rotten-egged, might say. This word, however, is not in very general use in Mississippi. **1899** (1912) Green *VA Folk-Speech* 180, *Flummux. . .* To perplex; embarrass; bewilder; defeat. **1905** *DN* 3.9 **cCT,** *Flummuxed up. . .* Confused. In the expression 'to be all flummuxed up.' **1905** *DN* 3.62 **NE,** *Kerflummux. . .* Bewilder, daze. "I felt quite kerflummuxed." **1908** *DN* 3.326 **eAL, wGA,** *Kerflummux* . . to bewilder, muddle, disconcert. **1930** Shoemaker *1300 Words* 35 **cPA Mts** (as of c1900), *Kerflommixed*—Excited, overcome with surprise. **1942** Berrey-Van den Bark *Amer. Slang* 173.3, *Bewilder; perplex; baffle* . . conflummox . . flummix, flummocks, flummox, flummux. **1944** *PADS* 2.27 **cwNC, cwOH,** *Flummixed. . .* Excited, bewildered. **1960** Rockwell *Adventures* 338 **NY,** The editor of the *Post* in his shirt sleeves? I couldn't understand it. . . I was flummoxed.

8 with *around:* To waste time, mess around. Cf **flub 2**

1959 *VT Hist.* new ser 26.136, *Flummox around. . .* Waste time. **1978** *DARE* File **cnMA** (as of c1915), In response to a child who threw herself onto the floor and began kicking and crying because she didn't want to pick up her toys, I have heard a mother say "Now you stop flummoxing around and do what you're told."

flummox adv Also *kerflummux* [**flummox** v]

With a thud, heavily; hence v phr *go flummox* to fail in recitation.

1858 Avery *Harp* 11, The squirrel goes up and up, and he jumps from lim' to lim', . . and the first thing you know, he falls, and down he comes kerflummux. **1892** *DN* 1.215 **csMA,** *To fall kerflummux.* **1908** *DN* 3.326 **eAL, wGA,** He fell kerflummux off the bench. **1915** *DN* 4.203, *Flummox,* in colleges applied to a poor recitation. "I went flummox this morning in German."

flummox n Also *caflummux, flummocks, flummux* [**flummox** v] *somewhat old-fash*

1 A failure.

1851 Hall *College Words* 131, *Flummux.* Any failure is called a *flummux.* In some colleges the word is particularly applied to a poor recitation. At Williams College, a failure on the play-ground is called a flummux. **1905** *DN* 3.9 **cCT,** *Flummux. . .* A failure. [One inf] knows the expression 'sounds like caflummux.' **1907** *DN* 3.212 **nwAR,** *Flummux. . .* A failure. **1942** Berrey-Van den Bark *Amer. Slang* 837.3, *Failure* . . flummocks, flummox.

2 By ext: a stupid person. [Prob infl by *lummox*]

1941 *LANE* Map 465 *(Fool),* 1 inf, **seMA,** Flummux [flʌ·məks].

flummox around See **flummox** v **8**

flummoxed See **flummox** v **6**

flummox(ed) up See **flummox** v **7**

flummuck v [Cf *EDD flummock* v. 4 "To hurry and confuse"] Cf **flumucky**

See quot.

1834 Caruthers *Kentuckian* 1.29, Flummuck me if ever I want to be so fixed again; . . and, twist me, if I didn't feel as if I was about to be nicked.

flummux v See **flummox** v

flummux n See **flummox** n

flummydiddle See **flummadiddle**

flumucky adj [*EDD flommucky, flummocky* (at *flummock*) "slovenly . . untidy"; cf **flummox** v **7, flummuck**]

Confused, disordered.

1834 W. A. Carruthers *Kentuckian in N.Y.* II.215 *(OEDS),* Hang me if I don't think he's a little flumucky altogether about the head.

flunder away v phr

To fritter away, lose bit by bit.

1969 *DARE* (Qu. U39, *Somebody who has lost all his money: "During the depression he* ———*."*) Inf **GA**70, Flundered it away.

flunk v^1 [See *AmSp* 21.16-18]

1 also with *out, under:* To display cowardice, shrink, give in, give up; to shirk (a duty). Cf **flink**

1823 *Crayon* 3 *(DAE),* To joke in earnest, Gentlemen, we must have, at least, as many subscribers as there are students in College, or 'flunk out.' **1838** Neal *Charcoal Sketches* 46 **Philadelphia PA,** Why, little 'un, you must be cracked, if you flunk out before we begin. **1850** (1869) Watson *Camp-Fires* 414 **seSC** (as of 1783), They were, of course, exposed to the fire of the red-coats. . . But they did n't flunk a bit. **1859** Stowe *Minister's Wooing* 278 **NEng** [Black], *You* a man, and not stan' by your color, and flunk under to mean white ways! **1871** Cutting *Student Life* 22 **cwMA,** The fine for 'flunking' an appointment . . was two dollars. **1871** Hay *Jim Bludso* 9 **Missip Valley,** He never flunked, and he never lied,—/ I reckon he never knowed how. **1894** P. L. Ford *Hon. Peter Stirling* (1898) 355 *(OEDS)* **NY,** What will people say of me . . if my regiment flunks on September thirtieth? **1905** Lincoln *Partners* 304 **seMA,** We've flunked once, and, no matter how good the reason is, no more big jobs'll come our way. **1910** Hart *Vigilante Girl* 294 **CA,** I don't mean that he's flunking, for he's no coward.

2 with *around:* To waste time, idle.

1938 Rawlings *Yearling* 314 **nFL,** We'll flunk around 'til Christmas, and we'll go to the Christmas doin's at Volusia. Then after that we'll git down to work agin.

3 also with *out;* Of a plan: to fail, fall through.

1965-70 *DARE* (Qu. KK10, . . *"He didn't work it out carefully enough, and his plan* ———*."*) 13 Infs, **scattered,** Flunked; **CT**33, Flunked out. [13 of 14 Infs old]

4 To make an error in judgment. *old-fash*

1965-70 *DARE* (Qu. JJ42, . . *"He usually handles things well, but this time he certainly* ———*."*) 11 Infs, **scattered,** Flunked; (Qu. KK9, *When someone undertakes something too big for him to handle: "This time you've* ———*."*) Inf **MO**8, Flunked. [All Infs old]

5 See quot.

1967 *DARE* (Qu. KK63, *To do a clumsy or hurried job of repairing something: "It will never last—he just* ———*."*) Inf **AL**16, Flunked it.

6 See quot.

1969 *DARE* (Qu. GG9, *To suddenly embarrass somebody and throw him off balance: "When they told him what she had said about him, it certainly did* ——— *him."*) Inf **NC**69, Flunk.

flunk v^2 [Var of *plunk*]

To plunk down, shell out (money).

1965 *DARE* (Qu. U8b) Inf **MS**60, Flunk down.

flunk around See **flunk** v^1 **2**

flunked out ppl adj phr Cf **fluked out**

Tired out.

1941 *LANE* Map 481 *(Tuckered out)* 1 inf, **swME,** Flunked out. **1967** *DARE* (Qu. KK30, *Feeling slowed up or without energy: "I certainly feel* ———*."*) Inf **TN**23, All flunked out [laughter].

flunkey, flunkie See **flunky**

flunk out See **flunk** v^1 **1, 3**

flunk under See **flunk** v^1 **1**

flunky n Also sp *flunkey, flunkie* [*OED flunkey* sb.^{1} "A male servant in livery"; 1782 →]

1a A subordinate or menial worker.

1905 U.S. Forest Serv. *Bulletin* 61.37 **Pacific NW,** *Flunkey. . .* An assistant, usually either to the engineer of a donkey engine or to the cook in a logging camp. **1928** *Ruppenthal Coll.* **KS,** The unskilled worker in the garage who can do various little jobs when told what to do but has not skill to do any important work is often called a flunkey. **c1937** in 1977 *Amer. Slave Suppl. 1* 11.49 **NC** [Black], I wuz a flunkey [for the railroad] case [=because] I done most anything dey wanted me to do. **1960** Bailey *Resp. to PADS 20* **KS,** Flunky, shovel leaner, ditch-digger—refer to a common laborer. **1960** Criswell *Resp. to PADS 20* **Ozarks,** Flunky. . . A helper, errand boy, apprentice. Fairly common term from a good many years ago, still common. "If I hadn't given you a decent job, you would still be an undertaker's flunky."

b Esp: a cook's helper or waiter in a lumber camp or similar place.

1905 [see **1a** above]. **1906** *Eve. Post* (NY NY) 12 Sept 7/6, 'Flunkeys' in the Northwest do not wear uniforms; their work is to act as assistant cooks in mining and lumber camps. **1914** *DN* 4.163 **NW,** *Flunky.* . . In mining and logging camps, a waiter. **1915** *DN* 4.244 **MT,** There's the flunkey and his mules on the way to Hobson. **1920** *DN* 5.81 **NW,** *Flunky.* A table waiter, dishwasher and helper to the cook. Logging term. **1927** *DN* 5.446 [Underworld jargon], *Flunky.* . . A cook's helper at a construction camp. **c1930** Swann *Lang. Circus Lot* 8, *Flunkie:* Waiter in cookhouse. **1930** Williams *Logger-Talk* 17 **Pacific NW,** *Flunky:* Those who wait on table in the cookhouse dining room—whether male or female. **1938** (1939) Holbrook *Holy Mackinaw* 260 **Nth,** *Flunkey.* . . Cookhouse help. **1946** Peattie *Pacific Coast* 235, After the men had . . wolfed their grub, the flunkey hustled up and down the tables, picking up each dish, whanging it edgewise on the table, and thus emptying its left-over contents onto the oilcloth. **1950** *WELS (A cook's helper)* 4 Infs, **WI,** Flunky. **1956** Ker *Vocab. W. TX* 187, The cook's helper [on a ranch] is a *flunky* (2 [infs]). **1967** *DARE* Tape **WA**30, A flunky's a gal who waits on tables [in a lumber camp].

c In tobacco processing: see quot 1966. Cf **roustabout**

1966 *PADS* 45.13 **KY,** *Flunky.* . . A worker who keeps the strippers supplied with stalks of tobacco, and takes the full sticks of hands to the tobacco press. . . "I use one man for a flunky if I can spare him from stripping." **1967** Key *Tobacco Vocab.* **KY,** Flunky.

2 Fig: a stooge, doormat. **chiefly Sth, S Midl, esp lower Missip Valley** See Map *esp freq among Black speakers*

1965–70 *DARE* (Qu. II34, *If you think somebody is trying to use you to his advantage: "I'm not going to be his ______."*) 27 Infs, **chiefly Sth, S Midl, esp lower Missip Valley,** Flunky. [11 Infs Black]

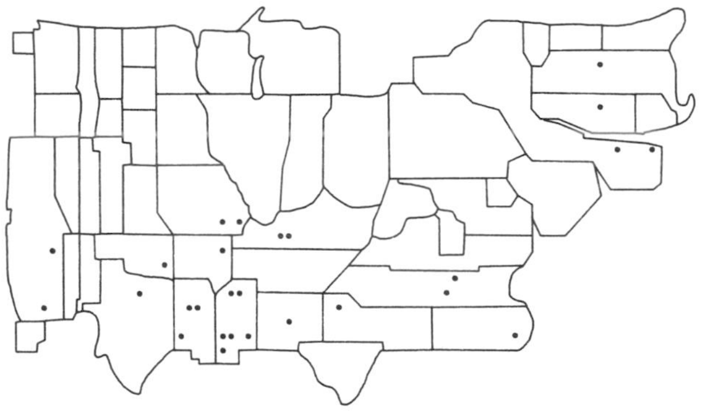
•flunky 2 (Qu. II34)

flurd n

1982 *Smithsonian Letters* **OK, TX,** Soft rolls of dust that collect in the house, an Oklahoma and Texas word is "flurd."

Fluridy See **Florida**

flurrididdle n [Var of **flummadiddle**]

=**flummadiddle 3.**

1935 Davis *Honey* 365 **OR,** There were several rocking-chairs carved with flurrididdles and adorned with quantities of brass tacks. **1970** *Thompson Coll.* **AL** (as of 1920s), She had all kinds of little flurrididdles hanging down from the shoulders.

Flurridy See **Florida**

flurry n

1957 Battaglia *Resp. to PADS 20* **eShore MD** *(Little flourishes that some people put on their handwriting)* Crooks, flurries—recent.

flursh See **flesh** n

flushed adj Also *flush* [Perh by confusion of *flush* affluent and *flush* to flow freely]

1967–69 *DARE* (Qu. U40, *Somebody who is temporarily out of money: . . "At the moment he's ______."*) Infs **MA**3, **NH**18, Flushed; **CT**40, Flush.

flusher n Cf **four-flusher**

1968 *DARE* (Qu. II20a, *A person who tries too hard to gain somebody else's favor: "He's an awful ______."*) Inf **MI**81, Flusher.

flusie See **floozy** n[1]

fluskatered adj Cf **flustrate, flusticated**

Flustered, upset.

1884 Baldwin *Yankee School-Teacher* 76 **VA** [Black], I neber feel s' sort or fluskatered as jess dis yer minit.

flusterate See **flustrate**

flusteration See **flustration**

flusterer n [See quot 1813]

=**coot** n[1] **1.**

1709 (1967) Lawson *New Voyage* 149, Black Flusterers; some call these Old Wives. They are as black as Ink. The Cocks have white Faces. **1813** Wilson *Amer. Ornith.* 9.62, [Footnote:] In Carolina they [=coots] are called *Flusterers,* from the noise they make in flying along the surface of the water. **1874** Coues *Birds NW* 543, If they [=*Fulica americana*] are surprised too far from their retreats to gain them in an instant, they splatter along over the water, half-flying—a habit which has gained for them in some districts the name of . . "Flusterers." **1917** (1923) *Birds Amer.* 1.214, Coot, *Fulica americana.* . . Other names.—American Coot; . . Flusterer; Blue Peter.

flusticated adj Also *fusticated* [Varr of *flustrated* (at **flustrate** v), perh infl by *intoxicated*]

Confused, befuddled, excited.

1835 Kennedy *Horse Shoe Robinson* I.78 *(DA),* [The English] listed you . . when you was flusticated with liquor. **1843** (1973) Porter *Big Bear AR* 98 **NC,** Being sorter flusticated like, . . I didn't notis perticlar where I sot. **1941** *LANE* Map 476–77 *(Excited, all nerved up)* 1 inf, **swCT,** Flusticated. **1942** Berrey–Van den Bark *Amer. Slang* 106.7, *Drunk* . . flusticated. *Ibid* 174.5, *Bewildered; confused; disconcerted* . . flusticated . . fusticated.

flustrate v, hence ppl adj *flustrated* Also with *up* Also *flusterate* [*OED* 1712 →. From *fluster,* prob on analogy of *frustrate.* The latter has perh had some influence on the meaning, but examples of usage do not support the frequent equation of the two words in dialect glossaries.] Cf **flusticated, fluskatered, flustration**

To confuse, upset, excite (someone).

1795 Dearborn *Columbian Grammar* 135, *List of Improprieties.* . . Flustrate for Frustrate. **1844** Thompson *Major Jones's Courtship* 30 **GA,** I's ben so flustrated bout this blamed muster, that I haint had no time to think of nothing else. **1899** Chesnutt *Conjure Woman* 19 **csNC** [Black], De han's on our own plantation wuz all so flusterated dat we fuhgot ter tell de noo han'. **1903** *DN* 2.297 **Cape Cod MA** (as of a1857), *Flustrated.* . . Confused. **1907** *DN* 3.206 **nwAR,** *Flustrated.* . . Confused. **1908** *DN* 3.311 **eAL, wGA,** *Flustrate.* . . To confuse, befuddle; chiefly in *pp.* **1910** *DN* 3.441 **cwNY,** Flustrated. . . Confused; embarrassed. **1912** Green *VA Folk-Speech* 180, *Flustrate.* . . To confuse; cause to flush and move or speak hurriedly and confusedly. **1927** *AmSp* 2.354 **cwWV,** *Flustrated up* . . very much excited. "He is all flustrated up over the trouble." **1941** *LANE* Map 476–77 **NEng** *(Excited, all nerved up)* 4 infs, Flustrated; 1 inf, Flustrated up. **c1960** *Wilson Coll.* **csKY,** *Flusterated.* . . Frustrated, chagrined. **1965–70** *DARE* (Qu. GG7, . . *"Though we were only ten minutes late, she was all ______."*) 33 Infs, **scattered,** Flusterated; **CA**123, **IL**45, **MS**67, **OK**1, **TX**1, **VA**42, Flustrated; (Qu. GG4, *Stirred up, angry: "When he saw them coming he got ______."*) Infs **CA**209, **IL**4, Flustrated; **KY**94, Flusterated; (Qu. GG13a, *When something keeps bothering a person and makes him nervous, he may say, "It ______ me."*) Infs **GA**74, 89, **IA**7, **KY**60, **MS**25, **NY**228, **VT**12, Flustrates; **GA**30, 77, **LA**12, **MI**107, **TX**1, **WI**49, Flusterates; (Qu. Y2, . . *"Losing all that money didn't seem to ______ him a bit."*) Infs **AL**3, **AZ**10, **GA**17, 77, **KY**68, **MS**1, **NY**219, **TX**4, Flusterate; **MS**10, Flustrate; (Qu. GG9, . . *"When they told him what she had said about him it certainly did ______ him."*) Inf **GA**77, Flusterate; **AR**55, Flustrate; (Qu. GG2, . . *"So many things were going on at the same time that he got completely ______."*) Infs **CO**11, **KY**30, **NY**117, **VA**39, **WY**3, Flusterated; **CO**21, **KY**28, 83, **VA**80, Flustrated; (Qu. P36, *When a hunter sees a deer . . and gets so excited he can't shoot,* *he* . . ———) Inf **NC**80, [Gets] excited, overanxious, flusterated; **IN**55, **OH**42, Gets flustrated; (Qu. GG26, *A feeling of weakness from fear: "When she saw the dog coming at her she got* ———*.*") Infs **GA**23, **MI**107, (All) flusterated; **NY**219, Flusterated and weak; (Qu. BB7, *A feeling* . . *with difficult breathing and heart beating fast*) Inf **CO**20, Flusterated, panicky; (Qu. AA4a, . . *A man who is very eager to get married*) Inf **IA**30, [He's] flustrated. **1984** Burns *Cold Sassy* 7 **nGA** (as of 1906), Mama was always fair, even when flustrated to distraction.

flustration n Also *flusteration* **[flustrate]**

1 Agitation, confusion.

1815 Humphreys *Yankey in England* 105, *Flustration,* extreme agitation. **1899** (1912) Green *VA Folk-Speech* 180, *Flusteration.* . . The state of being flustered; confusion; flurry.

2 Frustration.

c1960 *Wilson Coll.* **csKY,** *Flustration.* . . Frustration. **1984** Burns *Cold Sassy* 8 **nGA** (as of 1906), "Sister, I was fixin' to ast Pa for Ma's piano," she burst out. Tears of flustration wet her red face.

flut See **flirt** v

fluting ppl adj [Perh var of **fluking**]

1893 Shands *MS Speech* 16, *A flutin' and a flyin'.* . . A phrase used generally by the uneducated. When a man is moving rapidly in grand style, or succeeding remarkably well in any undertaking, he is said to be *a flutin' and a flyin'.*

fluts n [Var of **flux**]

1970 *DARE* (Qu. BB19, *Joking names for looseness of the bowels*) Inf **TX**92, [flʌts].

flutter v Also with *out* [*OED flutter* v. 6. a "To cause to flutter . . to agitate"; 1621 →]

To flush; to flush a (bird).

1834 Crockett *Narrative* 94 **TN,** My dogs. . . Poor fellows! many a time they looked for me, and wondered why I didn't come, for they knowed there was no mistake in me, and I know'd they were as good as ever fluttered. **1970** *DARE* (Qu. P39b, *If the dog makes a bird or a covey fly, you'd say he* ———) Inf **NC**87, Fluttered it; **VA**70, Fluttered it out.

flutterbudget n Also *flitterbudget* [*flutter, flitter* + **budget 3**]

A silly, flighty, or fretful person.

1967–69 *DARE* (Qu. GG41, *To lose patience easily: "You never did see such a* ———*.*") Infs **CA**22, **OH**5, Flutterbudget; (Qu. HH9, *A very silly or light-headed person*) Infs **CA**4, **MI**51, **NY**145, Flutterbudget; **ME**13, Flitterbudget.

flutterbutt n Cf **ass-up**

An unidentified **nuthatch.**

1970 *DARE* (Qu. Q23) Inf **CA**197, Flutterbutt.

fluttering mill See **fluttermill 2**

flutterment n

A disturbance, noisy scuffle.

1883 (1971) Harris *Nights with Remus* 195 **GA** [Black], You better b'leeve dey wuz a monst'us flutterment 'mungs de Guinnies.

fluttermill n

1 A mill powered by a **flutter wheel 1.** *obs*

1898 *Congressional Record* 25 Jan 31.8.223/1 **TN,** They will run their flutter mills and mixers and dope the flour to suit themselves. **1903** *DN* 2.313 **seMO,** *Flutter-mill.* . . A mill operated by a small undershot water-wheel. **1907** Cockrum *Pioneer IN* 325, A flutter mill was made by the water falling against the paddles which put the main shaft in motion by cogs.

2 also *fluttering mill:* A toy waterwheel. **chiefly Sth, S Midl**

1866 Smith *Bill Arp* 85 **GA,** The Choctaw children built their flutter mills. **1898** Lloyd *Country Life* 15 **AL,** I ambled off down to the branch where me and the other boys use to go fishin Saturday evenins and . . build flutterin mills. **1908** *DN* 3.311 **eAL, wGA,** *Flutter-mill.* . . A small undershot or overshot water wheel, a child's plaything. **1938** Rawlings *Yearling* 5 **nFL,** He had planned as long ago as Christmas, to make himself a flutter-mill. . . The palm-frond mill-wheel must just brush the water's surface. **1950** *PADS* 14.29 **SC,** *Flutter mill.* . . A toy made by children consisting of a *flutter wheel,* placed in a current of water so as to be turned by the current. **c1960** *Wilson Coll.* **csKY,** *Flutter-mill.* . . A child's toy water wheel, usually made of a cornstalk and run by a small stream's current.

3 An **evening primrose** (here: *Oenothera missouriensis*). [See quot 1936] **TX**

1936 Whitehouse *TX Flowers* 82, *Flutter-Mill.* . . Four broad yellow petals make up the cup-shaped portion of the flower. . . The seed-capsules at the base of the flower develop four broad papery wings. **1961** Wills–Irwin *Flowers TX* 164, Flutter-mill would probably brighten more gardens were it not so difficult to transplant. **1965** Teale *Wandering Through Winter* 150 **TX,** All across Texas, a host of . . names have been bestowed on the wild plants. . . They run from angel's trumpet . . to . . fluttermill . . and kiss-me-and-I'll-tell-you.

4 A windmill.

1949 *AmSp* 24.109 **neGA** [Black], *Flutter-mill.* . . Windmill.

flutter out See **flutter**

flutter owl n

An unidentified owl.

1967 *DARE* (Qu. Q1) Inf **CA**3, Flutter owl.

fluttersome adj Cf Intro "Language Changes" III.1

Fluttery.

1895 *Century Illustr. Mag.* 49.540, Beribboned, belaced, and very fluttersome. **1949** in 1986 *DARE* File **MS,** She was the most fluttersome woman I'd ever seen.

flutter wheel n

1 A usu small, rapidly turning waterwheel. *obs*

1818 U.S. Congress *Serial Set* 7 Doc 48 10, [An invention for] letting water on the flutter wheel [was patented July 1, 1817, by] Jarvis Smith, Queen's county, N.Y. **1859** (1968) Bartlett *Americanisms* 157 **West,** *Flutter-wheel.* A very small water-wheel, used where there is but . . little head of water. **1860** *Harper's New Mth. Mag.* Apr 609/2 **CA,** The 'flutter-wheel' . . consists of a wheel, sometimes thirty feet in diameter, the paddles of which are furnished with large buckets, made to catch themselves full of water at each revolution, and to discharge into a trough. **1872** (1876) Knight *Amer. Mech. Dict.* 2.894, *Flutter-wheel.* A water-wheel of moderate diameter placed at the bottom of a chute so as to receive the impact of the head of water in the chute and penstock. Its name is derived from its rapid motion. **1890** *Century Illustr. Mag.* 41.182 **CA,** It was an old-fashioned flutter wheel that propelled an upright saw.

2 =**fluttermill 2** or its wheel.

1874 Eggleston *Schoolmaster's Stories* 94 **PA,** "All the boys made little water-mills to be run by the force of the stream. We call them 'flutter-wheels.'" . . David explained it to her, . . showing the little cog-wheels, and the under-shot wheel that drove it. **1950** [see **fluttermill 2**]. **1968** *DARE* File **neAL,** *Flutter wheel*—A children's toy whittled out of wood; a little waterwheel which, set in running water, turns like a mill wheel.

flux n Also with *the* Also *bloody flux* **chiefly sAppalachians, lower Missip Valley** See Map

Diarrhea; spec dysentery.

1774 (1957) Fithian *Jrl. & Letters* 129, With us in Jersey wet Weather about this time . . is . . a forerunner of Agues, Fall-Fevers, Fluxes, & our Horse-Distempers. **1800** (1907) Thornton *Diary* 10.179 **PA,** The flux has prevailed a good deal this Summer. **1899** (1912) Green *VA Folk-Speech* 180, *Flux.* . . Bloody flux, dysentery. **1937** *Hall Coll.* **eTN,** To cure the flux drink a tea of sweet-gum bark, or take some mutton taller melted. **1937** in 1972 *Amer. Slave* 2.81 **SC,** I put my hand on any 'flux' man or woman and removes de pain, if dey have faith in my hand. **1950** *WELS (Looseness of the bowels)* 2 Infs, **WI,** (The) flux. **1965–70** *DARE* (Qu. BB19) 21 Infs, **chiefly sAppalachians and lower Missip**

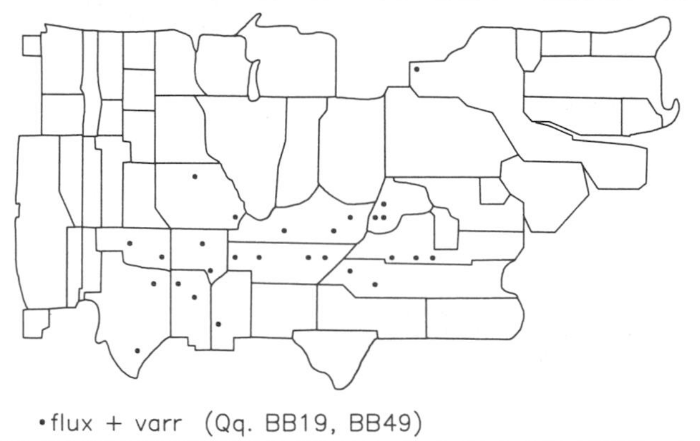

•flux + varr (Qq. BB19, BB49)

Valley, (The) flux; **VA**42, The bloody flux; (Qu. BB49, . . *Diseases*) Infs **KY**19, **TN**14, The flux; **TN**1, **VA**14, Flux = dysentery; **AR**52, Bloody flux. [22 of 27 Infs old; 9 label the term old-fash]

fluxroot n [**flux**]

1 =**butterfly weed 1.**

1828 Rafinesque *Med. Flora* 1.74, *Asclepias Tuberosa* . . Vulgar Names—Pleurisy root . . Flux root. **1876** Hobbs *Bot. Hdbk.* 39, Flux root, . . Asclepias tuberosa. **1940** Clute *Amer. Plant Names* 91, *Asclepias tuberosa*. . . flux-root. **1971** Krochmal *Appalachia Med. Plants* 70, *Asclepias Tuberosa* . . Butterfly milkweed . . fluxroot. **1974** (1977) Coon *Useful Plants* 72, *Asclepias tuberosa* . . fluxroot.

2 A **gentian** (here: *Gentiana catesbaei*).

1828 Rafinesque *Med. Flora* 1.211, *G[entiana] Heterophylla*. . . Sometimes called Flux-root and used for the Disentery [sic]. **1876** Hobbs *Bot. Hdbk.* 39, Flux root, Blue gentian, Gentiana Catesbaei.

fluxweed n [**flux**]

Any of several plants used as remedies for **flux,** such as **false mallow a, false pennyroyal 1,** or **butterfly weed 1.**

1887 *Courier-Jrl.* (Louisville KY) 1 May 20/7, It [=*Sida procumbens*] is known by the common name of 'Fluxweed,' and is used as a domestic remedy for flux or dysentery, and other bowel troubles. **1894** *Jrl. Amer. Folkl.* 7.96 **sIN,** *Isanthus cæruleus* . . flux-weed. **1968** Barkley *Plants KS* 295, Isanthus brachiatus. . . False Pennyroyal. Fluxweed. **1970** Correll *Plants TX* 1345, *Trichostoma brachiatum [Isanthus b.]* . . Fluxweed. **1975** Hamel-Chiltoskey *Cherokee Plants* 27, Flux weed . . *Asclepias tuberosa.*

fluzie See **floozy** n[1]

fluzions See **flugens** n

fluzy See **floozy** n[1]

fluzzy See **flossy** n

fluzzy-headed adj [Perh blend of *fluffy* + *fuzzy;* cf *EDD fluz(z* v. 3 "To crumple, ruffle"]

1954 *Harder Coll.* **cwTN,** *Fluzzy-headed*. . . Having untidy hair.

fly v

A Forms.

1 pres: usu *fly;* also *Gullah flew, flew'd.*

1896 Harris *Sister Jane* 137 **GA** [Black], She'll fly up an' flew at you. . . ef I know'd Miss Jane want gwine ter fly up an' flew'd at me, I'd come. **1922** Gonzales *Black Border* 301 **sSC, GA coasts** [Gullah glossary], *Flew*—fly, flies, flew, flying.

2 past: usu *flew,* also *flewed, flied, fly.*

1884 *Anglia* 7.252 [Black], *Pres.* fly—*Past.* flied, fly'—*Pass. Part.* flied. **1893** *DN* 1.277 **wCT,** *Flew* [for past and past participle]. **1899** Chesnutt *Conjure Woman* 147 **csNC** [Black], Little Mose flewed, en flewed, en flewed away. **1905** Culbertson *Banjo Talks* 29 **SE** [Black], Den de debil flewed off. **1922** Gonzales *Black Border* 302 **sSC, GA coasts** [Gullah glossary], *Fly*—flies, flew, flying. **1968** *DARE* (Qu. KK63, . . *"It will never last—he just* ________.") Inf **IA**27, Flied through it. **1975** Allen *LAUM* 2.79 (as of c1950), 1 inf, **wMN,** He flied off.

3 past pple: usu *flown,* often *flew,* also *flewed, flewn, flied*

1854 Riley *Puddleford People* 103, That great American eagle that has flew'd so long. **1865** Crockett *Life* 131, It had flew away. **1884** [see **A2** above]. **1893** [see **A2** above]. **1906** *DN* 3.118 **sIN,** He has flew the coop. **1954** Welty *Ponder Heart* 143 **MS,** She's flew the coop. **1966-67** *DARE* Tape **MA**6, He must've flew; **SC**19, They had flew across. **1968** McPhee *Pine Barrens* 60 **cNJ,** I could of flewn lots of times, but I never cared to. **1975** *DARE* File **csTX,** *Flewn* the coop seems especially prevalent here.

B Senses.

1 Of cream: see quot.

1937 *Hench Coll.* **VA,** Two Virginia expressions for the first beginning of cream to turn sour, as shown by the mottled formation it will make on the surface of hot coffee, even though to the taste it is not yet sour, are "the cream is flying," "the cream is feathering."

2 To cause to fly, flush.

1969 *DARE* (Qu. P39b, *If the dog makes a bird or a covey fly, you'd say he* ________) Inf **NY**151, He flew it.

fly n[1]

1 =**five hundred** n 2. Cf **fly ball, flies and grounders**

1950 *WELS (Bat and ball games . . when you don't have enough [players] for a regular game)* 1 Inf, **cwWI,** Fly or five hundred.

2 See quot.

1967 *DARE* FW Addit **MI**59, *Fly*—the no-draft vent window on a car. Heard in southern Indiana.

fly n[2]

1 See quot. [Abbr for **dragonfly**]

1970 *DARE* (Qu. R2, . . *Dragonfly*) Infs **DC**12, **MA**126, Fly. [Both Infs Black]

2 A dance step. **scattered, but esp PA** See Map *esp among younger speakers*

1966-70 *DARE* (Qu. FF5b) 23 Infs, **esp PA, WV,** Fly. [14 of 23 Infs young or middle-aged; 5 Black] **1968** Stearns-Stearns *Jazz Dance* 4, The best [of the popular dances of the late 1950s] were unrealized revivals: . . bits of the old Eagle Rock returned in the Fly. *Ibid* 191, A variety of Wings [=tap dances] began to emerge in the thirties: the Pump . . , the Pendulum . . , the Saw, the Fly. **1972** Jones-Hawes *Step it Down* 144 **eGA** [Black], *Fly.* Arms stretched out at full length and held stiffly are moved in a sailing motion (if the right arm goes up, the left arm goes down in the same axis). **1977** Smitherman *Talkin* 256, Popular dances [among Blacks], from roughly 1950 to the present: . . *boogaloo;* . . *emancipation; fly.*

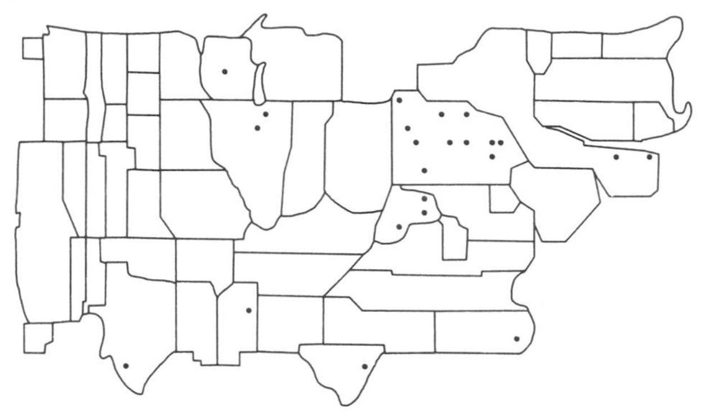

•fly n[2] 2 (Qu. FF5b)

3 In coal mining: a passage connected obliquely to a main passage. [Prob abbr for **shoo-fly**] Also called **slant**

1973 *PADS* 59.37 **sWV,** *Fly* . . = *slant.*

4 in phr *have no flies on one* and varr: To be active, alert, knowing.

1888 *Missouri Republican* 24 Feb (Farmer *Americanisms*), Persons who are capable of descending to New York and Boston English are fully justified in saying that there are no *flies* on St. Louis or the St. Louis delegation either. **1888** *Detroit Free Press* 25 Aug (Farmer-Henley *Slang*), *There ain't no flies on him,* signifies, that he is not quiet long enough for moss to grow on his heels, that he is wide awake. **1928** *AmSp* 4.123 **sIN. c1960** *Wilson Coll.* **csKY,** *No flies on* . . To be reliable, or counted on, to be right in style. **1968** *DARE* FW Addit **GA**63, "There are no flies on us!" = We're not moribund! **c1970** *Halpert Coll.* **wKY,** "There are no flies on me" is said when hurrying; also means "I'm pretty good."

fly n[3] See **vly**

fly agaric n Also *fly-blown agaric, fly amanita, flybane, fly cup, fly fungus, fly mushroom, fly poison amanita* [See quot 1943]

A **death cap** (here: *Amanita muscaria*).

1876 Hobbs *Bot. Hdbk.* 39, Fly agaric, Agaricus muscaricus. **1900** Lyons *Plant Names* 26, *A[manita] muscaria*. . . Fly Agaric, Flybane, Fly Fungus. **1924** *Torreya* 24.47 **NY,** Attention was called particularly to the two most deadly species . . and *Amanita muscaria,* the "fly agaric," which are accountable for most of the fatalities connected with mushroom eating. **1943** Fernald-Kinsey *Edible Wild Plants E. N. Amer.* 377, The *Fly-Amanita* . . , *Amanita muscaria* (because poisonous to flies), has a scaly bulb at base. **1972** Miller *Mushrooms* 32, *Amanita muscaria* . . "Fly Agaric". **1980** Smith-Weber *Mushroom Hunter* 170, *Fly Mushroom*. . . is the cause of considerable controversy because of certain cults, the members of which eat the fruiting bodies to experience the "visions" and other mental derangements its poisons . . produce. **1985** Ammirati et al. *Poisonous Mushrooms* 176, *Amanita muscaria. . . Common names.* Fly agaric, fly mushroom, scarlet fly cup, fly-blown agaric, fly poison amanita, fly amanita.

fly a kite v phr
1951 Johnson *Resp. to PADS 20* **DE** *(People who show off or make a big display: "When they give a party, they really ______ .")* Fly a kite.

fly amanita See **fly agaric**

fly and grounder See **flies and grounders**

fly around v phr
1 To hurry, bustle about; to make a display of haste.
1831 in 1834 Smith *Life Jack Downing* 154, **ME,** I flew round, and washed my face and hands. **1851** Hooper *Widow Rugby's Husband* 44 **AL,** Old 'oman, fly around, git somethin' for the squire and Dick to eat! **1892** Twain *Amer. Claimant* 177, Sailors don't fly around worth a cent unless you swear at them. **1905** *DN* 3.9 **cCT,** *Fly around. . .* To stir about, to be active. **1942** Warnick *Garrett Co. MD* (as of 1900–1918), *Fly around . .* act importantly. **c1960** *Wilson Coll.* **csKY,** *Fly around. . .* To be busy, usually too busy. **1967–70** *DARE* (Qu. A22, . . *"She had only ten minutes to clean the room, but she ______ [and had it done in no time].")* Infs **CT**17, **OH**23, **TN**4, Flew around; (Qu. GG14, . . *Someone who fusses . . a lot)* Inf **VT**11, Flew around like an old hen; (Qu. Y22, *To move around in a way to make people take notice of you: "Look at him ______ .")* Infs **MA**72, **VA**101, **VT**8, Fly around.
2 To flirt; to court.
1847 in 1956 Eliason *Tarheel Talk* 272 **NC,** I am in this Burgh [Greensboro] "flying around" a little bit among the fair sex. **1908** *DN* 3.311 **eAL, wGA,** *Fly around. . .* To court, pay attention to. "What girl is he flyin' around now?"

fly at v phr [*fly at* attack]
To set to work on vigorously, pitch into.
1954 *Harder Coll.* **cwTN,** He's jist a-flyin at 'at wood pile. Have'r cut up fore dark iffen he keeps a-hitten 'er. **1966–69** *DARE* (Qu. A22, . . *"She had only ten minutes to clean the room, but she ______ [and had it done in no time].")* Infs **CA**87, 163, **CO**11, **MT**3, **NY**92, Flew at it.

flyaway grass n [See quot 1912]
A **bentgrass 1** (here: either *Agrostis hiemalis* or *A. scabra*).
1857 MA State Bd. Ag. *Annual Rept. for 1856* 29, *Hair Grass,* or *Fly Away Grass, Tickle Grass, (agrostis scabra,) is another species.* **1912** Baker *Book of Grasses* 120, *Fly-away Grass. Agrostis hyemalis. Ibid* 119, The name Fly-away Grass is more appropriate as the seeds ripen, for the light panicles are soon broken by the wind and drift over the fields as the earliest tumble-weed.

fly away, Jack See **Jack and Jim**

fly back v phr
1923 *DN* 5.207 **swMO,** *Fly back. . .* To refuse to pull, as a balky animal.

fly ball n Cf **flies and skinners**
An informal bat and ball game; see quot 1967.
1967–70 *DARE* (Qu. EE11) Inf **NC**88, Fly ball. All men go out in the field except two, the batter and the catcher. The batter throws the ball up, then bat[s] it into the field. Whoever catches it gets to bat; if no one catches it, the batter gets another chance; **NY**51, 109, **SC**31, **VA**54, Fly ball. **1977** Taylor *Miro District* 128 **TN,** Later, in Irene's back yard, the three of us played fly-ball. . . I took up the bat and managed to get the fly-ball game going.

flybane See **fly agaric**

flybat n Also *flybatter* See Intro "Language Changes" III.4
A flyswatter.
1968–69 *DARE* (Qu. F47) Infs **CA**59, **VT**16, Flybat; **IN**79, **MD**21, Flybatter.

fly blister n Also *fly plaster*
A vesicant ointment, orig one made from Spanish fly (*Lytta vesicatoria*).
1869 Twain *Innocents* 167, A Jupiter with an eye out, or a Venus with a fly-blister on her breast, are not attractive features in a picture. **1883** (1971) Harris *Nights with Remus* 84 **GA** [Black], Dey'll come en dey'll go, en dey'll po' in der jollup yer en slap on der fly-plarster dar, en sprinkle der calomy yander, twel bimeby dat chile won't look like hisse'f. [=They [=doctors] will come and they'll go, and they'll pour in the jalap here and slap on the fly plaster there and sprinkle the calomel yonder till by and by that child won't look like himself.] **1898** Harper *Life Anthony* 1.129 **MA,** She went to a doctor for the first time in her life and was given a fly-blister and some drugs to put in whiskey. **1945** Saxon *Gumbo Ya-Ya* 194 **LA,** Rheumatism is treated with fly blister, an ointment made by mashing lightning bugs which have been soaked in alcohol. **1984** Wilder *You All Spoken Here* 170 **Sth,** *Fly blister:* Mustard plaster.

flyblow v [*OED* 1603 →; from *flyblow* the egg or maggot of a flesh fly]
To depreciate, taint the reputation of.
1904 *DN* 2.425 **Cape Cod MA** (as of a1857), *Fly-blow. . .* To slight, to attempt to depreciate. **1954** *PADS* 21.27 **SC,** *Flyblow. . .* To inform on, to report someone's bad conduct. An inebriated gentleman warned us boys: "Look here boys, don't you flyblow me."

fly-blown agaric See **fly agaric**

fly boss n
=**straw boss.**
1969 *DARE* (Qu. HH43b) Inf **RI**15, Fly boss.

flybresh See **flybrush**

flybroom n
=**flybrush.**
1945 Wilson *Passing Institutions* 16 **KY,** On special occasions, when company came of enough importance to warrant the opening of . . the front room, then the flybroom was brought out and put to use.

flybrush n Pronc-sp *flybresh* Also called **flybroom, flydriver, flyshooer, flywhip, flywhisk** Cf **fly fan**
Any of several devices used to drive away flies, esp at meals.
1833 Catlin *Indians* 1.113 *(DAE),* [The Indian's] fly brush [was] made of the buffalo's tail. **c1885** in 1981 Woodward *Mary Chesnut's Civil War* 757 **NC** (as of 1865), A fly-brush boy called Battis. His occupation in life was to stand behind the table and with his peacock feather brush flies. **1888** *Century Illustr. Mag.* 35.946 **cKY,** The abandoned fly-brush lay full across his face. **1927** *DN* 5.469 **Appalachians,** *Fly bresh.* A brush formerly used at table to drive away flies, sometimes artistically made of the plumes of pea-fowl. **1928** Aldrich *Lantern* 166 **NE,** [They] took turns in shaking the fly-brush with its long paper streamers over the tables. **1942** (1971) Campbell *Cloud-Walking* 68 **seKY,** Folks shoos the varmints offen the victuals and offen sick folks with a fly bresh made outen a little limb with the leaves left on it. **1953** *PADS* 19.10 **sAppalachians,** *Fly bresh. . .* Often it is made of paper which has been cut into strips and tacked to a long stick. **1954** *PADS* 21.27 **SC,** *Fly brush. . .* A mechanical *fly brush* was also used, with two revolving wings driven by a spring in the base. Still more elaborate affairs were swung from the ceiling and drawn back and forth by a string. The most glamorous *fly brushes,* used in the low country, were made of peacock feathers. **1955** *Hench Coll.* **csPA,** A fly brush is made thus: a folded newspaper is cut in strips up to near the edge, and then it is tacked to a stick. You wave it over dishes in the kitchen and over people sitting at table. **c1960** *Wilson Coll.* **csKY,** *Fly-brush. . .* A typical one was made with paper sewed on a peeled papaw limb and then cut into strips. **1968** *DARE* (Qu. F47) Inf **VA**13, Flybrush. . . Old-fashioned.

fly-by-night n [*OED* 1796 →]
A witch.
1903 Wasson *Cap'n Simeon's Store* 72 **ME,** Blowed ef 't wa'n't downright horrid the works them two ole fly-by-nights was into them days! **1927** *AmSp* 3.136 **ME,** A person suspected of being a witch was "an old fly-by-night."

fly camp n [*fly* piece of canvas forming the roof (or outer roof) of a tent]
A temporary camp.
1939 *AmSp* 14.236 **CO,** The branch camps attached to one of our mountain divisions of the CCC [are] referred to as *fly camps . .* not . . [because] the boys are engaged in . . fly eradication, but . . [because] their temporary quarters are the small, canvas tents called fly tents. **1945** Atwood *Rocky Mts.* 64, If long side trips from a headquarters camp must be made and an overnight stop is necessary, two men go together and lead a pack animal on which a light camp outfit has been placed. These are "fly camp trips." **1969** Sorden *Lumberjack Lingo* 44 **NEng and Gt Lakes,** *Fly camp*—A temporary camp.

flycatch n *hist* See Intro "Language Changes" III.4
=**winter wren.**

1806 (1905) Lewis *Orig. Jrls. Lewis & Clark Exped.* 4.133 **nwOR,** There are two species of the flycatch, a small redish brown species with a short tail. . . this is the same with that which remains all winter in Virginia where it is sometimes called the wren. the second species [of the fly-catch]. . . [is] yellowish brown on the back head neck wings and tail the breast and belley of a yellowish white; the tail is in proportion as the wren but it is a size smaller than that bird.

flycatch v Cf **catch flies, flycatcher 5, flytrap 8**

1967–70 *DARE* (Qu. X22, *To stare at something with your mouth open*) Infs **NY**34, **SC**70, [He's] flycatching.

flycatcher n

1 A passerine bird, as:

a Any of var birds of the family Tyrannidae such as the **chebec, crested flycatcher, kingbird, pewee,** or **phoebe.**

1796 Wansey *Excursion U.S.* 105 **NJ,** The birds in greatest plenty were partridge, . . fly-catchers, and wood-peckers. **1948** *Green Bay Press–Gaz.* (WI) 30 June 4/1, In summer they eat insects too, which they catch flycatcher fashion, that is, perched in one spot, and darting out at them when they come near. **1966–70** *DARE* (Qu. Q3, *Other birds that come out only after dark*) Inf **NY**66, Flycatcher; (Qu. Q14, . . *Other names . . for . . kingbird*) Infs **CT**5, **MI**65, **NJ**17, 21, Flycatcher; (Qu. Q20, . . *Birds like [swallows]*) Inf **KS**15, Flycatcher; **TX**84, Scissortail flycatcher; **FL**29, Dovetail flycatcher; (QR p117) Inf **MI**36, [We have] about 40 varieties of flycatcher; **TX**5, Flycatcher—forked tail, like a swallow; **VT**4, We also have flycatchers.

b Any of several warblers of the family Parulidae.

1862 NH Laws Statutes *Laws* 2609, If any person shall . . take, kill or destroy any of the birds called . . linnets, fly-catchers or warblers . . he shall forfeit . . one dollar. **1946** Hausman *Eastern Birds* 501, *Golden-winged Warbler. . . Other Names*—Golden-winged Flycatcher. *Ibid* 512, *Black-throated Blue Warbler. . .* Blue Flycatcher. *Ibid* 515, *Black-throated Green Warbler. . .* Green Black-throated Flycatcher. *Ibid* 540, *Wilson's Warbler. . .* Wilson's Flycatcher. *Ibid* 542, *American Red-start. . .* Redstart flycatcher.

c A **nuthatch.**

1966–67 *DARE* (Qu. Q23, *The insect-eating bird that goes headfirst down a tree trunk*) Infs **NC**36, **TN**13, **WA**6, Flycatcher.

d The blue-gray **gnatcatcher 1** *(Polioptila caerula).*

1844 Giraud *Birds Long Is.* 46, *Blue-Gray Gnat Catcher.* Blue-gray Flycatcher. . . Blue-gray Sylvan Flycatcher. **1917** (1923) *Birds Amer.* 3.223, *Polioptila caerula caerula. . . Other Names. . .* Small Blue-gray Flycatcher; Sylvan Flycatcher. **1946** Hausman *Eastern Birds* 466, Sylvan Flycatcher. . . Often dashing out in mid-air to snatch up an insect on the wing, flycatcher-wise.

e =**phainopepla.**

1917 (1923) *Birds Amer.* 3.97, *Phainopepla nitens. . .* Silky Flycatcher; Shining Crested Flycatcher; Shining Fly-snapper; Black-crested Fly-catcher. . . Sometimes thirty or forty of them may be seen in a flock, all engaged in catching flies.

2 =**bald-faced hornet.**

1939 *LANE* Map 240, 1 inf, **seNH,** Flycatcher, the white-faced hornet.

3 Prob a **green snake** (here: *Opheodrys vernalis*).

1968 *DARE* (Qu. P25, . . *Kinds of snakes . . around here*) Inf **CT**17, Flycatcher.

4 Any of var plants: see below. **chiefly SE**

a A **pitcher plant.**

1933 Small *Manual SE Flora* 582, *S. flava. . .* Fly-catchers. **1953** *S. Telephone News* **seGA,** The pitcher plant always receives special attention, as its local name of "fly catcher" would indicate. It grows in clumps . . , and eats insects which move down inside its blossom until they are trapped in a sticky gum exuded by the plant. **1966** *DARE* Wildfl QR Pl.83 Inf **WA**30, Flycatcher. **1966–68** *DARE* (Qu. S1) Infs **GA**35, **LA**40, **SC**2, Flycatcher; (Qu. S26b) Infs **GA**20, 35, Flycatcher; (Qu. S26c) Infs **FL**31, **PA**104, Flycatcher(s). **1968** *DARE* Tape **GA**30, Flycatcher, that's pitcher plant. **1972** Brown *Wildflowers LA* 61, *Fly Catcher. . . Sarracenia alata. . .* These hollow leaves . . have a zone of hairs so arranged that insects which get inside are unable to crawl out.

b A **tarflower** (here: *Befaria racemosa*).

1926 *Torreya* 26.6, *Bejaria* [sic] *racemosa. . .* Flycatcher, Jekyl [sic] Id, Ga. **1933** Small *Manual SE Flora* 992, *B[efaria] racemosa. . .* (Tar-flower, Fly-catcher.) **1953** Greene–Blomquist *Flowers South* 86, *Fly-catcher. . .* The buds and calyces are sticky and catch small insects. **1976** Bailey–Bailey *Hortus Third* 142.

c =**Venus's-flytrap.**

1803 Davis *Travels* 88 **SC,** In bogs, and marshy situations, is found the singular plant called the fly-catcher by the natives, and, I believe, *dionæ muscipula* by botanists.

5 =**flytrap n 8.**

1966–68 *DARE* (Qu. X9, . . *"I wish he'd shut his ______."*) Infs **NY**52, 66, **TX**1, 65, Flycatcher.

flycatch grass See **catchfly grass**

flycatch plant n

A **sundew** (here: *Drosera rotundifolia*).

1951 *PADS* 15.33 **TX,** *Drosera rotundifolia. . .* Flycatch-plant.

fly cup See **fly agaric**

fly door n

A screen door.

1882 'M. Harland' *Eve's Daughters* 377 *(DAE),* Where varieties of the *Musca Cæsar* . . do much abound, prudent housekeepers will put up 'fly-doors,' and keep their meats out of the way. **1967** *DARE* (Qu. D12) Inf **NJ**3, Fly door, in summer.

flydriver n

=**flybrush.**

1962 Carrell *Autobiog.* 28 **MA** (as of 1880s), Then with a fly driver, made from a . . slender peice [sic] of wood—and strips of news papers nailed to it—we would drive out flies.

flyer See **flier**

fly family n

A children's game; see quot.

1967 *DARE* (Qu. EE33) Inf **MI**65, The fly family—people [would] line up and a fella with a wet rag in his hand behind his back would go down the line saying to each in turn, "This is Mr. Horsefly," "Mr. Deerfly," "Mr. Butterfly." When he got to the one he wanted to hit, [he would say] "This is Mr. Letterfly" and try to hit his intended victim by the side of the head with the rag.

fly fan n Also called **flyminder, flyflap 1** Cf **flybrush**

A fan (hand or power operated) used to drive away flies, esp at meals.

1917 (1968) Phillips *Susan Lenox* 1.300 **Cincinnati OH,** They went into a large restaurant with fly fans speeding. **1952** [see **flyminder**].

fly-fish n **CA**

A **rockfish** (here: *Sebastodes rhodochloris*).

1887 Goode *Amer. Fishes* 266, The inexplicable name of "Fly-fish" is given to . . *Sebastichthys rhodochloris* by the fishermen at Monterey. . . It is one of the smallest species, rarely weighing more than a pound. **1898** U.S. Natl. Museum *Bulletin* 47.1809, *Fly-fish. . .* Off Monterey and San Francisco, in deep water.

flyflap n Also *flyflapper*

1 =**fly fan.** [*OED* c1440 →]

1899 (1912) Green *VA Folk-Speech* 181, *Flyflap. . .* Something to drive off flies. **1952** Brown *NC Folkl.* 1.541, *Fly-flapper. . .* A fan used to drive away flies. . . North [NC].

2 rarely *flyflip:* A flyswatter. **Sth, S Midl**

1965–70 *DARE* (Qu. F47) Infs **KY**34, **LA**2, 6, **MD**37, Flyflap; **FL**49, **KY**34, **NC**88, Flyflapper; **AR**54, Flyflip. **1966–69** *DARE* FW Addit **csGA,** *Flyflap*—a flyswatter; **eNC,** Flyflap. **1971** *Thompson Coll.* **Birmingham AL** (as of 1930s), Fly-flap. **1984** Wilder *You All Spoken Here* 52 **Sth,** *Give me a fly-flapper and I'll help you kill it:* Opinion registered of an outlandish hairdo, dress, or get-up.

fly-flower n **CA**

1 A **gold fields 1** (here: *Baeira chrysostoma*). [See quots]

1897 Parsons *Wild Flowers CA* 124, *Baeira gracilis. . .* In some localities this little plant is so much frequented by a small fly, which feeds upon its pollen, that it is called "fly-flower." **1915** (1926) Armstrong–Thornber *Western Wild Flowers* 550, *Gold Fields. . .* This is sometimes called Fly Flower, because in some places it is frequented by a small fly, which is annoying to horses. **1971** Dodge *100 Desert Wildflowers* 93, Horses graze *Baeria* avidly, but are annoyed by a small fly . . , giving the plant the name "fly flower."

2 =**Dutchman's breeches 1.**

1940 Clute *Amer. Plant Names* 121, *D. cucullaria. . .* Fly-flower.

fly-fly n

A **spurge nettle** (here: *Cnidoscolus stimulosus*).

1974 Morton *Folk Remedies* 51 **SC,** *"Fly-fly". . . Cnidoscolus stimulosus. . . (Current use):* Milky sap of root taken internally for "courage" [potency].

fly-foot n

1968 *DARE* (Qu. X37, *What words do you have to describe people's legs if they're . . not right?*) Inf **MD**15, Fly-foot—[When the] toes point out.

fly fungus See **fly agaric**

fly gallery n

The upper balcony in a theater.

1968 *DARE* (Qu. D40) Inf **VA**8, Fly gallery—upper.

fly gun See **flykiller 2**

fly honeysuckle n

Any of several spp of **honeysuckle 2** *(Lonicera),* but esp *Lonicera canadensis* which is also called **medaddy-bush** and **twinberry.**

1822 Eaton *Botany* 518, *Xylosteum. . . ciliatum,* . . fly-honeysuckle, twin-berry. **1848** in 1850 Cooper *Rural Hours* 70 **NY,** The fly-honeysuckle is in full leaf, as well as in flower. **1886** in 1919 Hale *Letters* 168 **RI,** Her celebrated fly-honeysuckle is all in flower. **1941** Walker *Lookout* 59 **TN,** The fly-honeysuckle . . is also a lovely creation to meet. **1944** ME Univ. *Studies* 59.55, *L[onicera] canadensis. . .* American Fly Honeysuckle. Common. Chiefly in moist or rather dry woods, often tolerating dense shade. Throughout [Maine]. **1952** Blackburn *Trees* 181, *L[onicera] Xylosteum.* European Fly-honeysuckle. *Ibid* 182, *L. oblongifolia.* Swamp Fly-honeysuckle. . . *L. villosa.* Mountain Fly-honeysuckle. . . *L. canadensis.* American Fly-honeysuckle. **1960** Vines *Trees SW* 953, *Lonicera utahensis. . .* The plant is also known as Fly Honeysuckle. *Ibid* 955, *Lonicera involucrata. . .* is also known under the vernacular names of . . Fly Honeysuckle . . and Inkberry. **1966** Grimm *Recognizing Native Shrubs* 263, Mountain Fly Honeysuckle. *Lonicera villosa. . .* American Fly Honeysuckle. *Lonicera canadensis. . .* Swamp Fly Honeysuckle. *Lonicera oblongifolia. . .* Involucred Fly Honeysuckle. *Lonicera involucrata.*

fly hot v phr Cf **fly mad, fly up 1**

To become suddenly and violently angry.

1942 Hurston *Dust Tracks* 29 **FL,** Papa always flew hot when Mama said that. *Ibid* 261, What did I do that for? He flew hot. In fact he was the hottest man in the five boroughs.

fly in v phr

To set to work vigorously, pitch in.

1895 Remington *Pony Tracks* 114 **SW,** William . . put the "grub," on a pack-saddle blanket and said, "Now, gemmen, fly in." **c1960** *Wilson Coll.* **csKY,** *Fly in. . .* To take a vigorous part in something, to pitch in. **1965–70** *DARE* (Qu. A22, . . *"She had only ten minutes to clean the room, but she ______ [and had it done in no time]."*) 13 Infs, **scattered,** Flew (right) in. **1971** *Foxfire* Spring–Summer 101 **neGA,** When somebody went t'build a house, ever'body flew in and helped'em.

flying ppl adj

Of cattle brands or geometric designs: having wing-like extensions.

1887 *Scribner's Mag.* 2.508/2, Words used in connection with . . life on the plains: . . *flying-brand.* **1894** *McClure's Mag.* 3.111/2, There is, first and simplest, the mere addition . . of flourishes to a plain letter to make a flying letter of it. **1961** Adams *Old-Time Cowhand* 260, A "flyin' brand" is one whose letter or figger has wings. **1967** *DARE* FW Addit **swOR,** Flying X—a quilt pattern with triangular patches at the ends of the crossed pieces.

flying adder n

A **dragonfly** of the family Cordulegastridae.

1951 Johnson *Resp. to PADS 20* **DE,** Flying adder. **1980** Milne-Milne *Audubon Field Guide Insects* 367, *Flying Adders (Family Cordulegastridae).* These large hairy dragonflies . . are brownish black with yellow markings.

flying ant n

A termite.

c1960 *Wilson Coll.* **csKY,** *Flying ants. . .* Termites, especially when they swarm in the spring.

flying auger n

=**flicker** n² **1.**

1911 *Forest & Stream* 77.174, *Colaptes auratus. . .* Flying Auger, Martha's Vineyard, Mass. **1956** MA Audubon Soc. *Bulletin* 40.82, *Yellow-shafted Flicker. . .* Flying-auger (Mass. From its looping flight, giving the appearance of boring a hole through the air.)

flying ax-handle See **ax-handle 2**

flying baker ppl adj phr [See quot 1948] Cf **flag** n² **2**

Menstruating; hence n *baker flying* menstruation.

1948 *Word* 4.183, Indirect allusion to red or blood also is made: *the gal's at the stockyards,* . . *the flag is up,* and *flying baker.* This last is common Navy parlance. . . In the Navy alphabet . . the B or baker flag is red, and when it is up it may mean . . 'Beware, keep off.' **1960** Wentworth–Flexner *Slang* 15, *Baker flying.* **1970** *DARE* (Qu. AA27) Inf **IL**135, Flyin' baker—from the Navy. A red flag. **1971** *AmSp* 46.82 **Chicago IL,** Menstrual period . . *flying Baker.*

flying-barked hickory n *obs*

=**shagbark hickory.**

1709 (1967) Lawson *New Voyage* 99, The third is call'd the Flying-bark'd Hiccory, from its brittle and scaly Bark.

flying board n

=**flying jenny 1a.**

1949 *AmSp* 24.109 **SC,** *Flying Board. . .* Flying jenny, a homemade merry-go-round, generally constructed of a board pivoted on a bolt driven into a stump.

flying buck See **buck fence**

flying bullfrog n

=**nighthawk.**

1950 *WELS (Other birds that come out only after dark)* 1 Inf, **seWI,** Nighthawk. . . jokingly called "flying bullfrog" on account of the booming noise when diving.

flying calamary n Also *flying squid*

A squid of the family Ommastrephidae. Also called **sea arrow**

1883 U.S. Natl. Museum *Bulletin* 27.189, *Ommastrephes illecebrosa,* . . the most common squid north of Cape Cod, . . is known as the . . 'flying calamary.' **1935** Pratt *Manual Invertebrate Animals* 690, *Ommastrephes* . . Sea arrows. Flying squids.

flying clipper n Cf **clipper 2**

=**mayfly.**

1968 *DARE* (Qu. R4, *A large winged insect that hatches in summer in great numbers around lakes or rivers, crowds around lights, lives only a day or so, and is good fish bait*) Inf **PA**115, Flying clipper—when in larval stage they live under stones.

flying colt See **flying horse 2**

flying disk n *joc*

1950 *WELS (Other names for pancakes)* 1 Inf, **cnWI,** Flapjacks, flying disks.

flying Dutchman n [In allusion to the legendary ship or captain so called, condemned to wander the seas forever]

1 A children's ring game; see quot 1967–69.

1949 Webber *Backwoods Teacher* 259 **Ozarks,** Children "got up games" in the yard. There were cries, out there in the lantern light . . which told of "three-deep" and "flying Dutchman." **1953** Brewster *Amer. Nonsinging Games* 95 **IN,** *Flying Dutchman.* **1957** *Sat. Eve. Post Letters* **ceTX** (as of c1938), Flying Dutchman—All players except two hold hands and form a large circle. The two others hold hands and run around the circle and hit two hands that are held together. These two must chase the other two around the circle trying to catch them before they get back to the vacant spot. **1967–69** *DARE* (Qu. EE33, . . *Outdoor games*) Inf **IA**36, Flying Dutchman—you all join hands, boy, girl, boy, girl. One couple is "it." They go around the outside of the circle, then touch some couple's hands. That couple chases the "it" couple around and tries to catch them before they get back to the vacant spot; **IL**80, Flying Dutchman [similar description except that the couples run in opposite directions trying to reach the vacant spot first]; **AZ**8, **NE**3, **PA**245, Flying Dutchman; (Qu. EE1, . . *Children . . form a ring, and either sing or recite a rhyme*) Infs **CO**21, **PA**22, **TN**35, Flying Dutchman; (Qu. EE2, *Games that have one extra player*) Inf **CA**154, Flying Dutchman.

2 See quot.

1950 *WELS (Names for different steps and figures in dancing)* 5 Infs, **WI,** Flying Dutchman.

3 =flying jenny 1a.

1953 Randolph-Wilson *Down in Holler* 244 **Ozarks,** *Flying Dutchman. . .* A primitive, homemade merry-go-round, also known as a *flyin' jenny.* **1965-70** *DARE* (Qu. EE32, *A homemade merry-go-round*) 20 Infs, **scattered,** Flying Dutchman. **1973** Allen *LAUM* 1.223 **Upper MW** (as of c1950), *Flying Dutchman* survives with 4 instances, 3 of which are in South Dakota.

flying filly See **flying horse 1b**

flying fish n

1 Std: a fish of the family Exocoetidae.

2 A **sea robin** (here: *Prionotus evolans*).

1862 Acad. Nat. Sci. Philadelphia *Proc. for 1861* 43, *Prionotus lineatus . .* "Flying Fish."

3 =flying gurnard.

1862 Acad. Nat. Sci. Philadelphia *Proc. for 1861* 43, *Dactylopterus volitans . .* "Flying Fish." **1882** U.S. Natl. Museum *Proc.* 5.616, *Cephalacanthus volitans . .* "Flying Fish." **1889** *Century Dict.* 473, *Batfish. . .* A name of the flying fish . . *Cephalacanthus volitans.*

flying fox n [From the reddish color]

=bittern.

1917 *Wilson Bulletin* 29.2.78, *Botaurus lentiginosus . .* flying fox, Indian River, Delaware. **1955** *AmSp* 30.179, For more or less rufescent coloration, the following species have won names including the term *fox:* bittern (*flying fox,* Del.)

flying frappy n

=flying jenny 1a.

1966 *DARE* (Qu. EE32) Inf **SC**10, Flying frappy.

flying ginny See **flying jenny**

flying gurnard n [See quot 1887]

A fish *(Dactylopterus volitans)* which resembles a gurnard. Also called **batfish 2, flying fish 3, flying robin, sea bat**

1879 U.S. Natl. Museum *Bulletin* 14.33, *Dactylopterus volitans. . . Flying Gurnard.* **1887** Goode *Amer. Fishes* 303, The most striking . . is the Sea-bat or Flying Gurnard, *Dactylopterus volitans,* which is remarkable on account of its enormous spreading fins. **1933** John G. Shedd Aquarium *Guide* 136, The flying gurnards. . . *Dactylopterus volitans.* **1960** Amer. Fisheries Soc. *List Fishes* 41, Flying gurnard . . *Dactylopterus volitans.*

flying handspring See **handspring a**

flying horse n

1a pl: **=flying jenny 1b.**

1882 (1971) Gibbons *PA Dutch* 46, Whitsuntide Monday is a great holiday. . . Now . . youths and girls . . visit the "flying horses." A number of seats are arranged around a central pole, and, a pair taking each seat, the whole revolves by the work of a horse. **1888** Gossler *Turnpike-Road* 78 **sePA,** There were all sorts of sideshows: flying-horses and carriages, that made their occupants sick as they whirled round and round. **1916** *DN* 4.268 **New Orleans LA,** *Flying horses. . .* A carousel or merry-go-round. Also Mass[achusetts]. **1946** Dadswell *Hey There Sucker* 102, Flying horses is the name applied at many southern amusement centers for the merry-go-round.

b also pl; also *flying filly, ~ mare, ~ nag:* **=flying jenny 1a.**

1949 *AmSp* 24.109 **SC,** *Flying Mare. . .* Flying jenny. **1966-70** *DARE* (Qu. EE32, *A homemade merry-go-round*) Infs **LA**8, **NC**4, 17, **PA**90, Flying horse; **FL**51, **IL**86, **NC**88, Flying mare; **SC**24, Flying filly; **SC**27, Flying nag. **1971** Wood *Vocab. Change* 368/2 **MS,** Volunteered [for a homemade merry-go-round] . . *flying horses.*

2 also *flying colt:* **=upland plover.** [See quot 1956]

1923 U.S. Dept. Ag. *Misc. Circular* 13.64 **NC,** *Upland Plover (Bartramia longicaude). . . In local use. . .* flying-colt. **1956** *AmSp* 31.187, The upland plover has had three extravagant animal metaphors applied to it—*flying horse* (Miss.); *flying colt* and *wild mare* (N.C.)—all because some of its cries suggest the whinnying of a horse.

flying jenny n Also *flying jinny, ~ jinnie, ~ ginny* **[jenny,** prob from its earliest form being a pole that was ridden astride (see **1a** quot 1946)]

1 An amusement device in which riders are whirled in a horizontal circle; a merry-go-round; spec:

a Any of various simple contrivances in which the riders supply the motive power. **chiefly Sth, S Midl** See Map Also called **flying board, ~ Dutchman 3, ~ frappy, ~ horse 1b, ~ sally, jenny, spinning jenny, whirling jenny**

1876 in 1969 *PADS* 52.52 **neIL,** We had a spring board flying jinnie etc we had lots of fun. **1916** *DN* 4.268 **New Orleans LA, NC,** *Flying jinny. . .* A home-made form of carousel. **1940** *Hench Coll.* **VA,** Flying jenny or jinny. [Drawing shows a pole with a rotating hub at the top, from which hang ropes or chains; children run holding on to these and are swung outwards by centrifugal force.] **1946** *PADS* 6.14 **eNC,** *Flying jenny. . .* A sixteen-foot pole five inches in diameter with a hole through the center. In this hole was a wooden or metal peg, which rested on a stump or some other wooden foundation. The jinny was rotated by some children while others rode it. **1954** *PADS* 21.28 **SC,** *Flying jinny.* **1958** *PADS* 29.10 **TN,** *Flying jinny. . .* It was a wheel or board on a post on which people rode round and round. **c1960** *Wilson Coll.* **csKY,** *Flying-jenny. . .* Sometimes made by cutting down a slender sapling and using the stump for the base, the rest of the tree for the moving part. **1965-70** *DARE* (Qu. EE32, *A homemade merry-go-round*) 107 Infs, **chiefly Sth, S Midl,** Flying jenny (*or* jinny); (Qu. EE31) Inf **GA**44, Flying jenny. **1966-67** *DARE* Tape **FL**8, The board that was put on this stump was a wide board . . , and a hole was bore into that, and then to hold onto the stump you'd need a long iron pin. . . The pin held it on the stump. . . It was known as a flying jinny. . . A child would sit on either end. It would just whirl round. . . A third person was usually needed to push; **TX**3, [Inf:] They called 'em flying jennies, where they turned round. [FW:] Was it something up on a pole, that they could go round on that way? [Inf:] Yes. . . It was a seat that turned around and around like that. **1969** *PADS* 52.52 **LA,** [Footnote to *flying jinnie:*] Saw off a straight, four or five-inch-thick tree about two and a half feet from the ground; whittle the top of the stump to form a pivot several inches high; trim the tree trunk to form a long pole; bore a hole through the pole at the point of balance; place the bored pole on the pivot. This piece of makeshift playground equipment was used as a combination seesaw and merry-go-round. **1980** *Foxfire 6* 201 **nGA,** Mack Dickerson remembers a small oak stump about four feet high. They used a plank with a hole drilled in the center. The flying jenny would last longer when they used axle grease.

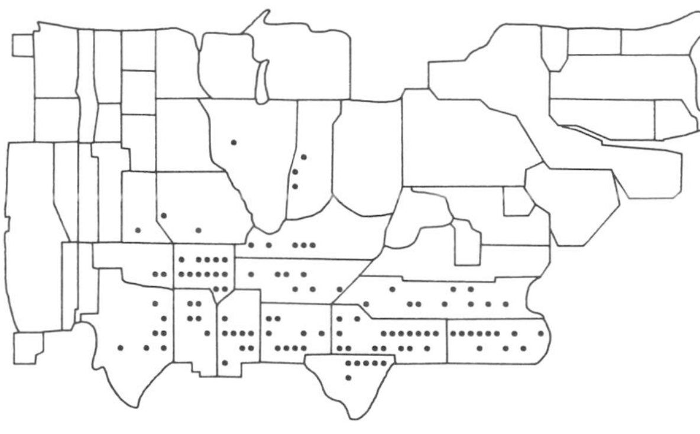

•flying jenny 1a + var (Qq. EE32, EE31)

b A carnival ride powered by an animal or motor. Also called **flying horse 1a**

1906 *DN* 3.136 **nwAR,** *Flying jinny. . .* A merry-go-round. Originally the propelling power was furnished by a mule. **1908** *DN* 3.311 **eAL, wGA,** *Flyin(g)-jinny. . .* A merry-go-round. Universal. **1939** FWP *Guide TN* 168 (as of c1869), Thoni designed and carved the first wooden animals to stand upon a "Flying Jenny" (merry-go-round). **1945** *Sat. Eve. Post* 9 June 17/3, Today, the carrousel—or "flying jinny" as she is known in the trade—is lighted by as many as 2200 electric bulbs. **1953** *AmSp* 28.116 [Carnival talk], *Flying Jenny.* **1959** Faulkner *Mansion* 317 **MS,** Them frustrated dogs [were] circling round and round the automobile like the spotted horses and swan boats on a flying jenny. **[1978** *AmSp* 53.198 **cwAR,** I can remember they had those merry-go-rounds pulled by a mule, a jenny. . . They had little double seats with a tent hung over it, and this jenny was inside.]

2 See quot.

1930 Shoemaker *1300 Words* 23 **cPA Mts** (as of c1900), *Flying-ginny* —A small wind-mill, sometimes used at mountain communities to draw water or run a chop-mill.

flying mantis n

1 Appar a **mayfly.**

1968 *DARE* (Qu. R4, *A large winged insect that hatches in summer in great numbers around lakes or rivers, . . lives only a day or so, and is good fish bait*) Inf **GA**25, Flying mantis.

2 Appar a **walkingstick.**

1968 *DARE* (Qu. R9a, *An insect from two to four inches long that lives in bushes and looks like a dead twig*) Inf **NY**80, Flying mantis.

flying mare n

1 See **flying horse 1b.**

2 Appar a **walkingstick.**

1969 *DARE* (Qu. R9a, *An insect from two to four inches long that lives in bushes and looks like a dead twig*) Inf **GA**72, Flying mare.

flying nag See **flying horse 1b**

flying out vbl n Cf *break out*

A rash, skin eruption.

1970 *DARE* (Qu. BB24, . . *A rash that comes out suddenly . . "He's got some kind of ______ all over his chest."*) Inf **VA**41, Flying out—old-fashioned.

flying pansy n

A **dog face** (here: *Colias eurydice*).

1926 Essig *Insects N. Amer.* 637, *The flying pansy . . Zerene eurydice . .* has a wing expanse of 25–50 mm.

flying robin n Also *flying sea robin*

=**flying gurnard.**

1873 in 1878 Smithsonian Inst. *Misc. Coll.* 14.2.21, *Dactylopterus volitans . .* Flying-robin. **1882** U.S. Natl. Museum *Bulletin* 16.738, *Cephalacanthus spinarella . .* Flying-robin. **1898** *Ibid* 47.2183, *Cephalacanthus volitans . .* Flying Robin. **1906** NJ State Museum *Annual Rept. for 1905* 384, *Cephalacanthus volitans . .* Flying Robin. **1933** John G. Shedd Aquarium *Guide* 136, *Dactylopterus volitans*—Flying Sea Robin. **1939** FWP *Guide FL* 30, 'Flying robins' that walk on their ventral fins.

flyings n pl

1 See quot 1953. [*OED* 1888 →]

1953 Randolph–Wilson *Down in Holler* 244 **Ozarks,** *Flyin's. . .* Short, coarse, hairlike wool, which flies or falls out of a carding mill. Frugal hillfolk used to knit socks out of flyin's; not so good as regular wool, but much cheaper. **1954** *Harder Coll.* **cwTN,** Flyings.

2 The lowest leaves of the tobacco plant. **chiefly Midl** Cf **flier 6, lugs, trash**

1940 *AmSp* 15.134 **KY,** *Flyings.* The lowest leaves of a Burley plant. **1941** *Sun* (Baltimore MD) 21 Jan 12/7 *(Hench Coll.)* **KY,** Leaf, lugs and flyings were showing unusual strength and in the majority of cases prices were from $2.30 to $10.70 higher. **1944** *PADS* 2.66 **S Midl,** *Flyings. . .* The lowest leaves, generally poor in quality but marketable. **1966** *PADS* 45.3 **cnKY,** The flyings and lugs were ideally suited to cigarettes. This brought about an inversion of prices for the several grades [after World War I]. **1967** Key *Tobacco Vocab.* **KY,** [Grade of] Burley tobacco—flyings; **MO,** Flyings, ground flyings; **TN,** 'Ground lugs' is the old word; 'flyings' [is a term introduced by] the Experiment Farm. **1968–70** *DARE* Tape **KY**35, The flyins an' trash we put together; they're just the light chaffy part of the tobacco; **KY**56, The bottom leaf . . is called the flying or trash; **KY**64, The grades are: flyings or trash which are the most ragged leaves, [etc]; **KY**72, Mostly it's trash or flyings; **KY**75, We usually make flyins which is the first we pull off the stalk out in the field; **OH**57, The top is the tip, of course. And down next is the . . bright leaf, then the next would be the lugs, then would be the red leaf, and then the flyings.

flying sally n

=**flying jenny 1a.**

1949 *AmSp* 24.109 **SC,** *Flying Sally. . .* Flying jenny.

flying saucer See **saucer**

flying sea robin See **flying robin**

flying shit-house n Cf **fly-up-the-creek 2, shitepoke**

=**bittern.**

1967 *DARE* (Qu. Q8, *A water bird that makes a booming sound before rain, and often stands with its beak pointed almost straight up*) Inf **MN**5, Shy-poke, flying shit-house.

flying spider n Also *fly spider*

Any of various spiders that float on a thread of silk, esp those of the family *Theridiidae.*

1871 *Amer. Naturalist* 5.148, *Flying Spiders. . .* One of the most curious habits of spiders is that of flying, as it is often called. **1911** *Century Dict. Suppl., Flying spider,* any one of many young spiders of the family *Theridiidae* and allied families. They are wafted through the air by long light threads of silk. **1960** Williams *Walk Egypt* 212 **nGA,** Flying spiders flung their final webs. Toy saw one hang twenty feet down from a pine-bough. A breeze came, and he rode it, swinging himself forty feet to a cedar limb. **1965–70** *DARE* (Qu. R28) 10 Infs, **scattered,** Fly spider; **MI**54, **MN**2, **MA**30, **WI**43, Flying spider. **1972** Kaston *How Know Spiders* 283, Flying Spiders.

flying squid See **flying calamary**

flying-squirrel apron n

1936 *AmSp* 11.315 **Ozarks,** *Flyin'-squirrel apron. . .* A long apron, like a dress but without sleeves. When it is untied in the back, the sides suggest the loose skin of the flying-squirrel.

flying the track See **fly the track**

fly-in-the-milk n

A mulatto.

1950 *PADS* 14.29 **ceSC,** *Fly-in-the-milk. . .* Offspring of one white and one colored parent.

fly-jig n Also *fly-jigger* Also called **jeep stick, whimmy-diddle**

A children's toy, consisting of a notched stick having at one end a blade which spins when something is rubbed over the notches.

1940 (1978) Still *River of Earth* 228 **eKY,** He . . [began] to stroke the knotched stick of a fly-jig. The wooden blade spun. It became a wheel. It hummed like a wasper. . . "I'll give you my fly-jigger," he said.

flykiller n

1 A flyswatter.

1967–70 *DARE* (Qu. F47) Infs **LA**33, **OR**3, **TX**51, **VA**47, Flykiller.

2 also *fly gun:* A children's toy; see quot.

1963 *Chr. Sci. Monitor* (Boston MA) 26 Apr 6/6 **Boone NC,** The flykiller, a combination of woods plus a metal screw, projects a wooden pellet missile with terrific force derived from pressure created by releasing a curved bow. **1980** *Foxfire 6* 200 **NC,** In Watauga County, North Carolina, numerous craft shops . . market a toy called a fly gun. A white-oak split propels a projectile out of the end of the toy. We could find no contacts who remembered seeing this toy as children.

fly-killer weed n

Prob=**fly poison 1.**

1954 *Harder Coll.* **cwTN,** Fly killer weed.

fly light v phr

Esp among railroad workers: to go without a meal; to work on an empty stomach.

1932 *RR Mag.* Oct 367, *Fly light*—Miss a meal. **1938** Beebe *High Iron* 221 [Railroad terms], *Fly light, to:* To go on duty after missing a meal.

fly loose v phr Cf **fly into**

To begin vigorously (to do something).

1975 *Foxfire 3* 267 **nGA,** I flew loose to digging that darn thing and it was the biggest root I ever got in my life over that small a top.

fly low v phr

To have one's trouser fly open.

1968–69 *DARE* (Qu. W24c, *Sayings to warn a man that his trouser-fly is open*) Infs **CT**36, **NY**70B, **VT**16, Flying low.

fly mad v phr Cf **fly hot, fly up 1**

To become suddenly and violently angry.

1917 *DN* 4.412 **wNC,** I don't know what the fraction [=ruction, quarrel] was, but he flew mad about something. **1923** (1946) Greer–Petrie *Angeline Steppin'* 43 **csKY,** The balance of them actors . . *flew mad,* and threatened to have Lum indited. **1941** *LANE* Map 472, 2 infs, **VT,** He flies mad. **1942** (1971) Campbell *Cloud-Walking* 184 **seKY,** He flew mad and . . hit old Mandy a crack across the back end. **1970** *DARE* FW Addit **nwPA,** He flew mad = he got mad, or flew into a rage.

flyminder n

=**fly fan.**

1952 Brown *NC Folkl.* 1.542, *Fly-minder. . .* A fly-fan. At Prestwould, . . Va., is still preserved Sir Peyton Skipwith's large mechanical fly-minder, which was operated by a slave boy who stood some distance from the table from which the flies were being kept away.

fly mushroom See **fly agaric**

fly off v phr

1 To become suddenly excited or angry. [Perh abbr for *fly off the handle*]

1966–70 *DARE* (Qu. GG15, . . *A person who became over-excited and lost control, "At that point he really ______."*) Infs **OH**87, **VA**73, Flew off; (Qu. KK11, *To make great objections . . : "When we asked him to do that he ______."*) Inf **FL**2, Flew off.

2 To suffer from diarrhea.

1966 *DARE* (Qu. BB19, *Joking names for looseness of the bowels*) Inf **FL**8, Flying off.

fly one over v phr Cf *bowl one over*

To astonish (someone).

1915 *DN* 4.242 **ceTN,** *Fly one over. . .* To overcome with surprise. "It flew me all over in a minute." **c1970** *Halpert Coll.* **wKY,** To fly one over = to overcome with surprise.

‡fly one's kite v phr

1968 *DARE* (Qu. GG15, . . *A person who became over-excited and lost control, "At that point he really ______."*) Inf **MD**41, Flew his kite.

flype v [Scots *flype, flipe* to fold back or inside out]

1937 *AmSp* 12.79 **NC,** A friend of mine who visited Greensboro, N.C., tells me that *flype* is used locally there. It is a verb describing the action of turning a stocking inside out in order to use the other side.

fly plarster See **fly blister**

‡flyplatter n

A flyswatter.

1968 *DARE* (Qu. F47) Inf **VA**9, Flyplatter [in conv].

fly poison n

1 also *fly poison flower:* A bulbous perennial *(Amianthium muscaetoxicum)* with mostly basal leaves and a raceme of white flowers. Also called **crow poison 1, fall-poison, poison lily, St. Elmo's feather**

1774 (1943) Amer. Philos. Soc. *Trans.* 33.135/1 **GA,** Took notice of a pretty species of Asphodelus called here by the Inhabitants Fly poison, having a long loose spike of white Flowers. **1857** Gray *Manual of Botany* 477, *Amianthium muscætoxicum. . . Fly-Poison. . .* Open woods, New Jersey and Pennsylvania to Kentucky and southward. **1943** Peattie *Great Smokies* 196, The curious big flypoison lit up the sward with flecks of white. **1953** Greene–Blomquist *Flowers South* 33, The fly-poison flower *(Amianthium muscaetoxicum).* **1966** *DARE* (Qu. S26b, *Wildflowers that grow in . . wet places*) Inf **SC**27, Fly poison. [*DARE* Ed: This Inf may refer instead to **fly poison 2.**] **1976** Bruce *How to Grow Wildflowers* 174, The only common name for this plant is "Fly Poison."

2 A **death camas** (here: *Zigadenus densus*).

1955 *S. Folkl. Qrly.* 19.233, *Osceola's Plume. . . Crow Poison* and *Fly Poison,* homelier epithets for this flower, are derived from the early use of the rootstalk as poison.

fly poison amanita See **fly agaric**

fly poison flower See **fly poison 1**

fly-poison plant n

=**apple (of) Peru 1.**

1941 Walker *Lookout* 52 **TN,** This is fly-poison plant, or the Apple-of-Peru. . . Before the use of wire screens . . country people depended on this plant for killing houseflies. The leaves and stems . . , after being crushed to a pulp, were mixed with sweet milk and set in a shallow pan. . . In about ten minutes after feeding on the mixture, houseflies begin . . to drop dead.

fly pudding n [Perh because it orig contained raisins]

1970 *DARE* (Qu. H63) Inf **CA**194, Fly pudding—peaches cooked and put in crust; like peach cobbler.

flyshooer n

=**flybrush.**

1968 *DARE* FW Addit **VA**12, *Flyshooer*—a wooden rod with a newspaper put across one end and sewed on. . . The paper was cut in strips . . and crimped with a case knife. "We used this brush to keep the flies off the dinner table. Someone had to stand and use the brush while others ate their dinner."

flyslapper n Cf **flyflap 2**

A flyswatter.

1968–69 *DARE* (Qu. F47) Infs **MA**38, 69, **PA**110, Flyslapper.

flysmacker n

A flyswatter.

1967–69 *DARE* (Qu. F47) Infs **IL**55, **MI**91, **OR**5, 13, **PA**176, Flysmacker.

flysnapper n

=**phainopepla.**

1895 C. C. Abbott *Birds About Us* II.75 *(DA),* Well . . did the flysnapper only make believe to launch out after insects? **1917** (1923) *Birds Amer.* 3.97, *Phainopepla.* Other Names.—Silky Flycatcher; Shining Crested Flycatcher; Shining Fly-snapper; Black-crested Flycatcher.

flyspatter n Also *flyspat* **chiefly NEast** See Intro "Language Changes" III.4

A flyswatter.

1928 *Ruppenthal Coll.* **KS,** Fly spatter . . a device to kill house flies. . . A person strikes at a fly to 'spat' or 'swat' the fly, and disable or kill it. **1966–69** *DARE* (Qu. F47) Infs **CA**6, **CT**18, **NY**75, 135, **PA**102, 119, Flyspatter; **PA**217, Flyspat; (Qu. EE41, . . *Used to threaten children*) Inf **MA**6, The flyspatter's going to get you and it's going to hurt.

flyspeck n

1 A small thing or quantity; a trivial imperfection.

1865 Stowe *House & Home* 290 **MA,** I would shut my eyes on fly-specks, and open them on the beauties of Nature. **1942** Berrey–Van den Bark *Amer. Slang* 21.2, *Something small or insignificant . .* flyspeck. **c1960** *Wilson Coll.* **csKY,** *Fly-speck. . .* A very small spot or quantity. Rare. **1968** *DARE* (Qu. HH12, *A person who is always finding fault about unimportant things*) Inf **CT**4, He's looking for flyspecks.

2 pl: Small, hard-to-decipher handwriting.

1967 *DARE* (Qu. JJ11, . . *"I can't make anything out of his ______."*) Inf **PA**49, Hen-scratches, flyspecks.

fly spider See **flying spider**

flysquatter n [Perh blend of *squasher* + *swatter*]

A flyswatter.

1967–68 *DARE* (Qu. F47) Inf **OH**4, Flysquatter—that sounds funny; **PA**136, Flysquatter—heard.

flyswapper n Also *flyswap*

A flyswatter.

1968–70 *DARE* (Qu. F47) Inf **KY**82, Flyswapper; **VA**9, Flyswap.

flyswat n **chiefly Sth, S Midl** See Intro "Language Changes" III.4

A flyswatter.

1940 Stuart *Trees of Heaven* 257 **eKY,** She takes a fly swat and shoos away the fat flies. **1950** *WELS ("If you don't do as I tell you, I'll get after you with ______.")* 1 Inf, **cWI,** A flyswat. **1965–70** *DARE* (Qu. F47) 54 Infs, **chiefly Sth, S Midl,** Flyswat. **1969** *DARE* FW Addit **cNC,** *Flyswat*—used for *flyswatter.*

flysweep n [Prob by analogy with **flybrush**]

See quot.

1973 Walker *In Love* 64, She was dressed like a flysweep! Not only was she raggedy, she was dirty! Filthy dirty, and with her filthy slip showing. She looked so awful she disgusted me.

fly the coop v phr [By ext from *fly the coop* leave suddenly, escape, elope]

1 To die, cease to function.

1954 Welty *Ponder Heart* 143 **MS,** In came Dr. Ewbanks. . . "You don't mean she's flew the coop?" he says. **1968–70** *DARE* (Qu. BB56, *Joking expressions for dying: "He ______."*) Infs **AK**8, **SC**70, Flew the coop; (Qu. KK20b, . . *"Our old washing machine is ______."*) Infs **MD**28, 34, (It) flew the coop.

2 To lose control of oneself, become angry.

1950 *WELS (When a person becomes over-excited, and loses control)* 1 Inf, **seWI,** Blow a fuse, fly the coop. **1968** *DARE* (Qu. GG15, . . *"At that point he really ______."*) Infs **LA**35, **MD**28, Flew the coop; (Qu. KK11, . . *"When we asked him to do that, he ______."*) Inf **LA**35, Flew the coop.

3 To go wrong.
1968 *DARE* (Qu. JJ42, *To make an error in judgment and get something quite wrong: "He usually handles things well, but this time he certainly ______.")* Inf **VA**15, Flew the coop.

fly the handle v phr
1944 *PADS* 2.57 **nwMO,** *Handle, to fly the*. . . To give up quickly. . . Common.

fly the track v phr, hence vbl n *flying the track* Cf **jump the track**
To abandon abruptly one's duty or allegiance; to go suddenly astray.
1847 U.S. Congress *Congressional Globe* 29th Cong 2d Sess 4 Feb 322/2, I had been accused of flying the track on the creed of the Democratic party. **1879** (1880) Twain *Tramp Abroad* 510, He is disposed to fly the track and avoid the implacable foe. **1910** C. Harris *Eve's Husband* 85 (*DA* at *track*), No man ever gets too old to fly the track in some way. **c1960** *Wilson Coll.* **csKY,** *Jump the track*. . . Violently quit something, blow up, change sides. Also *fly the track*. **1966** *DARE* (Qu. JJ42, . . *"He usually handles things well, but this time he certainly ______.")* Inf **NC**4, Flew the track.

fly-the-whip n
A children's game, perh crack-the-whip.
1971 *AmSp* 46.83 **Chicago IL,** Line and running games . . *fly-the-whip.*

flytime n
1a The season of the year when flies are troublesome.
1805 T. M. Harris *State of Ohio* 179 *(DAE),* [They are] called *'Buffaloe beats,'* because supposed to be occasioned by the resort of those animals thither in fly-time. **1865** Stowe *House & Home* 288 **NEng,** People . . shut up their rooms and darken their houses in fly-time. **1899** (1912) Green *VA Folk-Speech* 181, *Fly-time*. . . Summer. The time when animals are most annoyed by flies. **1947** Ballowe *The Lawd* 195 **LA,** It was fly time on the plantation. The cane had been laid by and the hands wouldn't be needed until corn picking and haying. **c1960** *Wilson Coll.* **csKY,** *Flytime*. . . The period in the summer when the houseflies are numerous or when biting flies attack the wild and domesticated animals. **1966** *DARE* Tape **ND**5, A horse never stops grazing; only in flytime he'll go on the scorious hills and face the wind.
b in var phrr: See quots.
1819 *KY Almanac for 1820* 29 **Lexington KY,** [He] has no more chance for the worth of his dollar, than a stump tail bull in fly time. **1851** Burke *Polly Peablossom* 72 **Sth,** Cuttin up shines worse nor er bob-tail bull in fly-time! **1898** Ford *Tattle-Tales* 12 **KY,** My Major [was] suffering worse than a docked horse in fly-time. **1899** (1912) Green *VA Folk-Speech* 39, Stand no more chance than a stump-tail bull in fly-time. **1967–68** *DARE* (Qu. U35, . . *Words meaning thrifty but not in a complimentary way*) Inf **IL**2, Tight as a bull's ass in flytime; (Qu. U36a, . . *A person who . . is greedy*) Inf **NJ**22, Tight as a bull's ass in flytime; (Qu. BB21, . . *Constipated*) Inf **NJ**39, Tighter than a bull's ass in flytime. **1978** *AP Letters* **neGA,** There are some [words] that are still used by old-timers, such as: . . Busy as a stump-tail cow in fly time.
2 Used as an exclam to warn a man that his trouser fly is open.
1967–69 *DARE* (Qu. W24c) Infs **CA**99, **IL**5, **NY**205, Flytime.

fly together v phr
To act as a unit; to hang together.
1969 *DARE* Tape **CA**134, If there's any tragedy or anything comes up, we're just the same as one—everybody flies together.

flytrap n
1 =spreading dogbane.
1828 Rafinesque *Med. Flora* 49, *Apocynum androsemifolium*. . . *Vulgar Names* . . Flytrap. *Ibid* 51, But small flies are often caught by inserting their proboscis between the fissures of the anthers . . ; they are often seen dead in that confined situation, after unavailing struggles. **c1873** in 1976 Miller *Shaker Herbs* 137, Flytrap. . . In conjunction with yellow parilla, it is excellent for dyspepsia. **1971** Krochmal *Appalachia Med. Plants* 50, Fly trap . . is a cardioactive drug.
2 A **pitcher plant;** see quots. **chiefly SE**
1860 *Charleston* (S.C.) *Mercury* 25 Dec. 1/8 *(DA),* Amair's Sarracenia or Fly Trap Bitters, The Great Southern remedy for Dyspepsia. **1876** Hobbs *Bot. Hdbk.* 39, Fly trap, Sidesaddle plant, Sarracenia purpurea. **1900** Lyons *Plant Names* 334, *S. flava* L. Southeastern U.S., . . Fly-trap. *Ibid* 335, *S. purpurea* L. Canada and eastern U.S. . . Fly-trap. **1913** *Torreya* 13.231, *Sarracenia minor*. . . Fly-traps, Santee Club, S.C. **1951** *PADS* 15.33 **TX,** *Sarracenia sledgei*. . . Trumpet-leaf flytrap.
3 =Venus's-flytrap.
1903 Small *Flora SE U.S.* 493, *Flytrap. Venus' Flytrap*. . . *Dionaea muscipula*. . . In sandy bogs, near the coast, eastern North Carolina and South Carolina. Spring. **1933** Small *Manual SE Flora* 580.
4 =jack-in-the-pulpit.
1970 *DARE* (Qu. S1) Inf **SC**67, Flytrap.
5 =cowherb.
1847 Wood *Class-Book* 192, *S. Vaccaria*. Fly-trap.
6 A spider's web.
1968 *DARE* (Qu. R29b) Inf **NJ**31, Flytrap.
7 A toad.
1940–41 Cassidy *WI Atlas* **seWI,** Flytrap—a toad (nickname).
8 One's mouth.
1834 *Life Andrew Jackson* 221, A million voices, with flytraps half open, cri'd hoora! **1837** Smith *Col. Crockett's Exploits* 57, The politician . . shut his fly trap, and turned on his heel without saying a word. **1913** London *Valley of Moon* 25 **CA,** If I'd knowed you was Bill Roberts there wouldn't been a peep from my fly-trap. **1919** *DN* 5.67 **NM,** *Trap,* the mouth. Sometimes called fly-trap. **1965–70** *DARE* (Qu. X9, . . *"I wish he'd shut his ______.")* 16 Infs, **scattered,** Flytrap; **CA**42, Big flytrap; [(Qu. X22, *To stare . . with your mouth open*) Inf **VA**31, Make a flytrap].
9 An unattractive, run-down establishment.
1909 Porter *Options* 71 **NYC,** Old Jerome was lingering long after breakfast . . before setting forth to his down-town fly-trap. **1969** *DARE* (Qu. D39, . . *A small eating place where the food is not especially good*) Inf **GA**89, Flytrap. **1978** *New Yorker* 6 Nov 41/3 **NY,** This is a deal involving millions, not like that flytrap [=a yard goods store] of yours.
10 The fly front on a pair of trousers. *joc*
1969 *DARE* (Qu. W24c, *Sayings to warn a man that his trouser-fly is open*) Infs **CA**132, 170, (Your) flytrap is open.

flytrap v [**flytrap** n **8**]
1968 *DARE* (Qu. X22, *To stare at something with your mouth open*) Inf **CT**7, To flytrap.

fly up v phr
1 also *fly up in the air:* To lose control of oneself; to become angry or excited.
1830 in 1834 Smith *Life Jack Downing* 94 **ME,** The Advertiser flies up, and says, you [sic] no business to be a republikin, you're a Jacksonite. **1884** Harris *Mingo* 203 **GA,** I skeer'd ter tell you, Mars. George; kaze you mought fly up en git mad. **1896** Harris *Sister Jane* 171 **GA,** An then she flew up like wimmen will. **1908** Lincoln *Cy Whittaker* 56 **MA,** You needn't fly up like a settin' hen. **1941** *LANE* Map 472 **cCT,** He flew up. **1949** Arnow *Hunter's Horn* 71 **KY,** An Pop, he'd jist fly up an tell her to mind her own business. **1950** *WELS (When a person becomes over-excited, and loses control)* 1 Inf, **cwWI,** Fly up. **1966–68** *DARE* (Qu. GG15, . . *Became over-excited and lost control, "At that point he really ______.")* Infs **MD**17, 20, Flew up; **MI**66, **MS**15, Flew up in the air; (Qu. KK11, . . *"When we asked him to do that he ______.")* Infs **GA**5, **LA**8, Flew up; **NJ**39, Flew up in the air; (Qu. GG41, *To lose patience easily*) Inf **MS**45, He just flies up at anything.
2 also *fly up to* (or *the*) *roost:* To go to bed. [From the behavior of chickens] **chiefly Sth, S Midl**
1923 *DN* 5.207 **swMO,** *To fly up* = to retire for the night. **1965–69** *DARE* (Qu. X40, . . *Other ways . . of saying, "I'm going to bed.")* Infs **AR**51, **OK**47, **TN**1, (I'm going to) fly up (to roost); **TN**23, Fly up the roost; **TX**35, Fly up for the night; **IN**82, Gonna fly up—derives from hens' flying up to roost. **1972** *Atlanta Letters* **Atlanta GA,** Since it is midnight, I guess I'd better fly up.

fly-up n Also *flies-up, fly-ups* Cf **flies and grounders**
A bat and ball game requiring only a few players.
1967–69 *DARE* (Qu. EE11) Infs **CA**118, **PA**196, 210, **WA**22, Fly-up; **IA**3, Fly-ups; **NY**118, Flies-up. **1975** Ferretti *Gt. Amer. Book Sidewalk Games* 190 **NYC,** A variation of Rotation is *Flies Up,* in which the rotation can be upset if a fly ball is caught by either the short-fielder or the outfielder. If, for example, the outfielder catches the ball on a fly, he becomes the batter.

fly-up-a-creek See **fly-up-the-creek 2**

fly up in the air See **fly up 1**

flyuppity adj [**fly up** v phr **1**]
Irascible.
1909 Wason *Happy Hawkins* 123, "An' you know 'at I don't like to beg no man to do anything; but you ought to see that I know that you're the usefullest man I ever had, an' you oughtn't to be so flyuppity," sez he.

fly-ups See **fly-up** n

fly-up-the-creek n **chiefly Sth, Midl**
1 =**green heron.**
1840 *Spirit of Times* 25 Jan 559/1 **MD,** He saw nothing but a bird, vulgarly called "a fly-up-the-creek," perched on a dead tree. **1893** *Advance* 3 Aug 588/4 **sOH,** One of the . . finds of the day was the nest of a green heron, often called "fly-up-the-creek." **1903** *DN* 2.313 **seMO. 1946** Hausman *Eastern Birds* 107, Other Names—Green Bittern, Little Green Heron, Fly-up-the-Creek. **1949** *AmSp* 24.27, *Fly-up-the-creek* is one of the many local names for the *shitepoke (Butorides virescens),* and the filthy habits of the bird give the term itself a very opprobrious smack. **1950** *WELS* 2 Infs, **WI. c1960** *Wilson Coll.* **csKY,** *Fly-up-the-creek. . .* The green heron.
2 also *fly-up-a-creek:* =**bittern.**
1904 Wheelock *Birds CA* 90, *American Bittern.—Botaurus lentiginosus. . .* It is called "Fly up the creek," . . "Bog-bull," and other names too unpleasant to mention. **1932** Bennitt *Check-list* 15, *American bittern. Botaurus lentiginosus* . . long-necked fly-up-the-creek. **1967–69** *DARE* (Qu. Q8, *A water bird that makes a booming sound before rain, and often stands with its beak pointed almost straight up*) Infs **PA**29, **TN**31, 35, **TX**11, Fly-up-the-creek; **KY**53, Fly-up-a-creek.
3 A **blue crane.**
1966–70 *DARE* (Qu. Q10, . . *Water birds*) Inf **NM**13, Cranes—also called fly-up-the-creeks; (Qu. Q23) Inf **TX**84, Blue cranes = fly-up-the-creeks.
4 An inhabitant of Florida. Cf **alligator** n[1] **B7**
1845 Cist *Cincinnati Misc.* 1.240/1, The inhabitants of . . Florida, [are called] Fly up the Creeks. **1888** Whitman *November Boughs* 70, Those from . . Florida . . [were call'd] Fly up the Creeks. **1946** McWilliams *S. CA Country* 172, Florida is the "fly-up-the-creek state." **1949** *AmSp* 24.26, *Fly-up-the-creek* . . for a Floridian.
5 A silly, flighty person; a **floozy** n[1].
1893 Shands *MS Speech* 30, *Fly up the creek. . .* This is quite a common term among the illiterate whites for a *shallow, silly person.* **1903** *DN* 2.313 **seMO,** *Fly-up-the-creek. . .* 'She is the fly-up-the-creek sort of girl.' **1907** *DN* 3.231 **nwAR,** *Fly-up-the-creek. . .* Foolish, light-minded. **1937** Sandoz *Slogum* 233 **NE,** Can't you find anything else to do with yourself besides chasing around after those Polish fly-up-the-cricks? **1939** FWP *Guide TN* 135, A person who changes his mind often is called a "fly-up-the-creek" or a "whip-around." **1947** Ballowe *The Lawd* 96 **LA,** He had been positive that he didn't want a fly-up-the-creek, nor one who would put all he earned on her back and holler for more to buy grub. **c1960** *Wilson Coll.* **csKY,** *Fly-up-the-creek* . . a giddy, unreliable person. **1966** *DARE* (Qu. HH37, *An immoral woman*) Inf **MS**15, Fly-up-the-creek.

fly up to (or the) roost See **fly up** v phr **2**

fly weed n
Perh =**apple (of) Peru 1.**
1969 *DARE* (Qu. S21, . . *Weeds . . that are a trouble in gardens and fields*) Inf **KY**43, Fly weed.

fly weevil n
The Angoumois grain moth *(Sitotroga cerealella).*
1768 in 1789 Amer. Philos. Soc. *Trans.* (2d ed) 1.274 **VA,** The *fly-weevil* . . destroys the wheat. **1790** *PA Packet & Daily Advt.* (Philadelphia) 30 Mar 1/4, Information . . for preventing damage to crops by insects; especially the Hessian-fly, the wheat-fly, or fly-weevil, the pea-bug, and the corn chince bug or fly. **1911** *Century Dict.* 2296, *Fly-weevil. . .* The Angoumois grain-moth *Sitotroga cerealella. . .* Southern U.S.

flywheel n
1968 *DARE* (Qu. EE9c, . . *Children spread their arms and turn over sideways*) Inf **NY**86, Flywheel, pinwheel.

flywheel stretcher n Cf *DS* HH14
An imaginary object used as the basis of a practical joke.
1921 *DN* 5.97, *Fly wheel stretcher.* Auto shop term.

flywhip n
=**flybrush.**
1945 Saxon *Gumbo Ya-Ya* 364 **LA,** Negro mammies . . fanning their wares with colorful *chasse mouches*—fly whips made of strips of vari-colored paper.

flywhisk n
=**flybrush.**
1936 (1951) Faulkner *Absalom* 31 **MS,** The . . house negroes to carry the parasols and flywhisks.

fly widow n
A **widow spider** (perh *Latrodectus variolus*).
1965 *DARE* (Qu. R28, . . *Kinds of spiders*) Inf **OK**11, Black widder, fly widder, brown widder.

flywood n
An unidentified plant.
1970 *NC Folkl.* 18.15, As cancer cure, take sheep sorrel . . and then add a bit of flywood tea.

f'm See **from**

f.m.c. See **free man of color**

f.m. highway n
=**farm-to-market road.**
1970 *DARE* (Qu. N29, . . *A less important road running back from a main road*) Inf **TX**89, F.m. highway—a farm-to-market highway.

fo adj See **four**

fo prep[1] See **for**

fo prep[2] See **fore** prep

fo conj See **fore** conj

foah adj, n See **four**

foah prep See **for**

foal n Also *foald, fold* Cf **foal** v
A Forms.
1915 *DN* 4.183 **swVA,** *Fold, n.* and *v.* Foal. **1967–70** *DARE* (Qu. K10) Infs **DE**3, **NY**9, In foald; (Qu. K45) Infs **NJ**69, **NY**163, **WI**52, Had a foald; **CT**25, In foald.
B Sense.
In phr *in foal;* Of a cow: pregnant. Note: *In foal* is std when applied to a mare.
1967–68 *DARE* (Qu. K10, . . *A cow that is going to have a calf*) Infs **NJ**53, **MO**17, [She's] in foal; **DE**3, **NY**9, In foald.

foal v
A Forms.
1 pres: usu *foal;* occas *foald, fold.* See Intro "Language Changes" I.8
1891 *DN* 1.166 **cNY,** [fold, foldɪd]. **1914** *DN* 4.106 **cKS,** *Fold. . .* To foal. **1915** *DN* 4.183 **swVA,** *Fold, . . v.* Foal. **1966** *DARE* (Qu. K10, . . *A cow that is going to have a calf*) Inf **GA**3, Fixing to foald.
2 past: usu *foaled;* also *foalded, folded.* Cf **-ed suff 1** See Intro "Language Changes" II.5
1795 in 1916 *New Engl. Hist. & Geneal. Reg.* 70.17 **MA,** My mare folded in ye barn tied up. **1805** (1898) Hunt *Diary* 11/1 **sePA,** Mare Foalded. **1902** *DN* 2.234 **sIL,** *Foalded.* Preterit. **1907** *DN* 3.222 **nwAR,** *Foalded, pret.* **1923** *DN* 5.235 **swWI,** The mare foalded in June. **c1960** *Wilson Coll.* **csKY,** *Foaled,* not a common word, is sometimes ['foldɪd]. **1966–68** *DARE* (Qu. K11, *When a cow has a calf, you say she* ———) Infs **GA**3, **NJ**25, Foalded.
3 past pple: usu *foaled;* also *foalded, folded;* rarely *foal* (prob by assim of final cons cluster). Cf **-ed suff 1**
1892 *DN* 1.210 **seMA,** The colt was folded at such a time. **1903** *DN* 2.314 **seMO,** The colt was foalded last May. **1907** *DN* 3.231 **nwAR,** *Foalded, pp.* **1908** *DN* 3.311 **eAL, wGA,** *Foalded, pp.* of *foal.* Common. **1923** *DN* 5.207 **swMO,** That colt was foalded las' spring. **1927** *Ruppenthal Coll.* **KS,** This colt was foalded . . in spring of last year. **1965–70** *DARE* (Qu. K45, *When a mare has had a young horse, you say she has just* ———) 650 Infs, **widespread,** Foaled (a colt); 115 Infs, **widespread,** Foalded (a colt) [Of all Infs responding to the question, 72% were old; of those giving this response, 83% were old.]; **MO**9, 20, Foal; (Qu. K43, *A horse* [illegible] *bred by accident*) Inf **FL**36, Accidently got foalded; (Qu. K10, . . *A cow that is going to have a calf*) Inf **LA**24, She's foalded. **1967** *Wilson Coll.* **csKY,** This little colt was foalded [foldɪd] last April.

B Senses.

1 Of a cow: to give birth; to give birth to.

1966 Dakin *Dial. Vocab. Ohio R. Valley* 2.235, [Expressions for *calve:*] *Foal (a calf)* (by two Kentucky informants.) **1966–68** *DARE* (Qu. K10, . . *A cow that is going to have a calf*) Inf **CA**90, Going to foal; **GA**3, Fixing to foald; **LA**24, She's foalded; (Qu. K11, *When a cow has a calf, you say she* ——) Inf **CA**90, Foaled; **GA**3, **NJ**25, Foalded.

2 Of a ewe: to give birth. *?obs*

1883 *Harper's New Mth. Mag.* Apr 652/2 **NEng,** The ewes are . . kept until they have foaled.

3 Fig: see quot.

1961 Adams *Old-Time Cowhand* 34 **West,** In this way new songs were foaled. *Ibid* 173, Many of 'em [=gunmen] didn't even belong to the West, but were foaled in the slums of Eastern cities.

4 To be delivered of a foal.

1967 *DARE* (Qu. K45, *When a mare has had a young horse, you say she has just* ——) Inf **MO**5, Been foaled.

5 To breed, impregnate.

1931 *PMLA* 46.1304 **sAppalachians,** I aim to foal that mare, come grass. **1966–68** *DARE* (Qu. K10, . . *A cow that is going to have a calf*) Inf **LA**24, She's foalded; (Qu. K43, *A horse . . bred by accident*) Inf **FL**36, Accidently got foalded.

foald n See **foal** n

foald v See **foal** v **A1**

foalded See **foal** v **A2, 3**

foalfoot n

=**coltsfoot 1.**

1876 Hobbs *Bot. Hdbk.* 39, Foles [sic] foot . . Tussilago farfara. **1900** Lyons *Plant Names* 381, *T[ussilago] Farfara*. . . Foal-foot. **1914** Georgia *Manual Weeds* 501, *Coltsfoot—Tussilago Farfara* . . Foalfoot. **1930** Sievers *Amer. Med. Plants* 24, Coltsfoot—*Tussilago farfara* . . foalfoot. **1931** Clute *Common Plants* 105, What particular foot should be associated with *Tussilago farfara* is hard to determine for among its vernacular names are . . foal-foot, and colt's foot.

foam n

1 =**sea-foam.**

1966 *DARE* (Qu. H80, *Kinds of candy . . made at home*) Inf **MO**1, Foam, sea foam.

2 Beer. Cf **suds**

1946 (1972) Mezzrow–Wolfe *Really Blues* 332, Foam: *beer.* **1968–69** *DARE* (Qu. DD25) Infs **CT**3, **IN**56, **MD**4, **RI**17, Foam.

foam bush n [See quot 1970]

An **ocean spray** (here: *Holodiscus discolor*).

1970 Kirk *Wild Edible Plants W. U.S.* 201, *Holodiscus discolor*. . . Foambush. . . The creamy-white flowers occur in large, dense masses. **1974** (1977) Coon *Useful Plants* 226, Foam bush. A spreading, much branched tall shrub found on the West Coast.

foam-eater n

Perh a **skimmer.**

1969 *DARE* (Qu. Q10, . . *Water . . and marsh birds*) Inf **NC**60, Foam-eater.

foamflower n [From the frothy appearance of the flower; *OEDS* 1895 →]

Any of var plants of the genus *Tiarella* (but esp *T. condifolia*) which have mostly basal heart-shaped leaves and small white flowers in loosely clustered racemes. Also called **coolwort 1, false miterwort.** For other names of var spp see **gemfruit, lace flower, Nancy-over-the-ground, sugar scoop**

1900 Lyons *Plant Names* 371, *T[iarella] cordifolia* . . Foam-flower. . . *Herb* reputed diuretic. **1910** Graves *Flowering Plants* 215 **CT,** Foam-flower. False Miterwort. Coolwort. . . A beautiful plant well worthy of cultivation. **1936** Morehouse *Rain on Just* 246 **NC,** No telling what might come forth, strong rank weeds, or a fairy white foam flower. **1949** Peattie *Cascades* 231, One of our constant companions as we climb . . is foamflower, whose loose raceme of very small white flowers is like a bit of airy fluff. **1966–70** *DARE* (Qu. S26a, c, e) Infs **MA**6, **PA**99, 234, **VT**4, **VA**52, Foamflower. **1967** *DARE* Wildfl QR Pl.88 Infs **MI**57, **OH**14, Foamflower. **1975** Duncan–Foote *Wildflowers SE* 60, Foam-flower. . . The flowers are in racemes, and white or pink tinged, except for the 10 yellow anthers.

foasty adj [Perh from Scots *vousty, voostie,* boastful, proud]

1897 *KS Univ. Qrly.* (ser B) 6.53 **AR,** *Foasty:* mannish, buckish.

foble See **fourble**

fobs n pl [Abbr for **fourbles;** cf Can *fobble* (*DN* 1.388)]

1955 *PADS* 23.18 **TN,** *Fobs.* . . Four marbles.

focht v See **fetch** v **A2**

focht n See **folk**

fock See **fork** n

fockit See **forked**

fo' day See **before-day**

fodder n

1 also attrib: The entire corn plant cured and used as livestock feed. Cf **fodder corn, shock fodder**

1907 U.S. Dept. Ag. *Farmers' Bulletin* 313.9, In the principal corn-growing States. . . The term "fodder" is applied to the entire plants as ordinarily cut and shocked. **1949** Arnow *Hunter's Horn* 324 **KY,** The tops of the sagging fodder shocks were tipped with gold. **1949** (1958) Stuart *Thread* 87 **KY,** I thought I was standing beside a fodder shock. It stood like a white wigwam before me. **1966** *DARE* (Qu. L30b, . . *Sheaves are set together in piles called* ——) Inf **FL**36, Fodder.

2 The blades and sometimes tops of corn plants cured and used as livestock feed. **chiefly Sth, S Midl** Also called **blade fodder** Cf **fodder** v, **fodder blade, ~-pulling, ~ stack**

1796 (1799) Weld *Travels* 105 **VA,** They feed their cattle upon fodder, that is, the leaves of the Indian corn plant. **1851** *De Bow's Rev.* 11.50 **ceLA,** We heretofore were in the habit of saving *fodder,* or the blades of corn. **1869** Porcher *Resources* 634 **Sth,** This [=feeding stalks and blades together] we regard as much better economy than to pull fodder and leave the whole stalks in the field. **1893** *Outing* Jan 274/1 **S Atl,** That afternoon [Zeke was] . . busy with his fodder (the blades of Indian corn which are stripped from the stalks, tied in small bundles, and later, when cured, into larger ones). **1903** *DN* 2.313 **seMO,** *Fodder.* . . Corn leaves cured by drying in the air. This word is not used for coarse feed in general as in the North. **1907** *DN* 3.231 **nwAR, seMO. 1908** *DN* 3.311 **eAL, wGA,** *Fodder.* . . The leaves of Indian corn cured in the air. The word is never used of any other kind of hay. **1922** Gonzales *Black Border* 302 **sSC, GA coasts** [Gullah glossary], *Fodduh*—fodder, used only for cured corn blades. **c1960** *Wilson Coll.* **csKY,** *Fodder and tops.* . . Blades of corn and sometimes the whole stalk above the ear, cut while still green, for stock food. **1965–70** *DARE* (Qu. L9b, *Hay from other kinds of plants*) Infs **MD**13, **TX**63, **VA**33, 46, Fodder; **VA**14, Fodder—the blades from the ear down, the tops from the ear up, the chucks or husks from the ear. It was cured, bundled, and stacked in the barn to be used like hay; **LA**12, **NC**54, Corn fodder. [*DARE* Ed: Some Infs may be referring instead to sense **1.**] **1969** *DARE* FW Addit **KY**40, Fodder—used for animal food—is the tops (the stalk and leaves above the ear) and the blades (the leaves below the ear).

3 Transf: the leaves of sorghum plants.

1869 Porcher *Resources* 658 **Sth,** Pull the fodder as you do corn fodder each day as you grind your canes. **1966–70** *DARE* Tape **AL**3, We'd pull the fodder off of the sorghum; **KY**90, They take a stick and knock all the fodder off and cut the heads off and they cut it down 'n put it in piles.

4 See quot.

1966–69 *DARE* (Qu. L8, *Hay that grows naturally in damp places*) Infs **MA**3, **NJ**2, Fodder; **NC**33, Fodder grass.

fodder v Cf **fodder-pulling**

To strip blades of corn for **fodder** n **2.**

1944 *PADS* 2.34 **wNC,** *Fodder.* . . To pull fodder. "When it gets through weathering, I'll finish foddering."

fodder bean n Also *fodder pea* **S Midl** Cf **shucky bean**

A shell bean dried in its pod.

1848 in 1910 Commons *Doc. Hist. Amer. Industrial Soc.* 198 **SC,** April . . 13, planted early peas and fodder peas. **1937** (1963) Hyatt *Kiverlid* 75 **KY,** Try some o' the fodder-beans, and here's greens an' hominy. Livin' is sorta pore this time a'year. **1949** Arnow *Hunter's Horn* 170 **KY,** He didn't like fodder beans much anyhow, and when he did eat them he wanted plenty of meat seasoning, but she couldn't help it if they were out of meat. **1981** Howell *Surv. Folklife* 106 **seKY, cnTN,** Dried beans, locally called fodder beans (also known as shucky beans or leatherbreeches), were prepared by cutting the whole beans into bite-size lengths then boiling them for a long time with a little fat meat for seasoning.

fodder blade n

A blade of corn used for **fodder** n **2.**

a1883 (1911) Bagby *VA Gentleman* 127, The corn has been topped, and stripped of its broad fodder blades. **1884** in 1973 *AmSp* 48.91 **nwGA,** When you crowd one of em [=a saddleback caterpillar] on a fodder blade you'd think that forty yaller jackets had stung you. **1943** Stuart *Taps* 271 **neKY,** It would look like livin to be able to walk through the corn in September when the fodder blades start a-turnin.

fodder corn n **chiefly Nth, esp NEng**

Corn grown for use as fodder (rather than for grain).

1856 Davis *Farm Bk.* 82 *(DA)* **AL,** Hauled up two loads wood & 1 of fodder corn. **1888** VT State Bd. Ag. *Rept. for 1877–78* 10.18, E.R. Towle spoke in favor of raising fodder corn. **1931–33** *LANE Worksheets* **csMA,** The other kind [than sweet corn] is fodder corn. **1940–41** Cassidy *WI Atlas* **neWI,** Fodder corn—gets no ears; used for animals. **1967–69** *DARE* (Qu. I34, *If you don't have sweet corn, you can always eat young* ———) Infs **ME**20, **MN**6, **MA**34, 72, 74, **NY**41, **VT**16, Fodder corn; **MA**55, Fodder corn doesn't have any ear on—it's cut green. Never heard of anyone eating it; **RI**1, Fodder corn—not eaten by people; (Qu. L34, . . *Important crops*) Inf **NY**24, Fodder corn.

fodder forker n **West** *derog*

A farmer.

1944 Adams *Western Words* 61, *Fodder-forker*—What the cowboy calls a hay hand or farmer.

fodder horse n Cf **horse bug**

=walkingstick.

1960 *Hench Coll.* **VA,** He called it a fodder horse "because in the fall of the year you will often find [it] on fodder." This specimen was a big one . . 3 or 4 inches long. It is very odd-looking. It climbs very slowly, colored gray, like a twig.

fodder house n Also *fodder hut*

A frame or building used for storing fodder.

1754 in 1922 Fries *Rec. Moravians* 1.106 **NC,** We thatched the fodder huts built in the 1st field yesterday. **1786** (1925) Washington *Diaries* 3.42 **VA,** This spot contained 16 A., 1 R., 24 P., including the fodder Ho[use]. **1805** Parkinson *Tour* 2.330, The usual method of preserving them [=tops and blades of corn] for the winter is to make what is termed a fodder-house, by setting up long-grained posts, and laying a rail upon the top; then placing other rails on the ground, leaning against what may be termed the ridge-tree; they then lay the tops on like thatch, and the blades are stored within the house. **1871** (1892) Johnston *Dukesborough Tales* 48 **GA,** The schoolhouse. . . stood in the corner of one of our fields (having formerly been used as a fodder-house), on the brow of a hill. **1895** Howells *Recollections* 148 **OH** (as of 1825), They made a kind of frame of poles, as for a tent, and thatched it, sides and top, with the corn tops placed with the tassel downward, so as to shed the rain and snow. This was called the fodder-house.

foddering n [*OED* 1601 →]

1914 *DN* 4.72 **ME, nNH,** *Fodderin' o' hay*. . . Sufficient to "feed up" once.

foddering time See **fodder time**

fodder pea See **fodder bean**

fodder-pulling vbl n **chiefly Sth, S Midl** Cf **fodder** v, **fodder-pulling time**

The process of stripping blades of corn for **fodder** n **2;** an occasion on which this is done.

1868 *Harper's New Mth. Mag.* Sept 486/1 **SC,** The "fodder pulling" had stripped the enormous corn-field to bare stalks. **1934** *Natl. Geogr. Mag.* 65.620 **seGA,** [Caption:] After "Fodder Pulling" Come Shucking and Shelling. **1938** in 1972 *Amer. Slave* 2.23 **SC,** I never didn' go to none of dem cornshuckin en fodder pullin en all dem kind of thing. . . Den dem kind of task was left to de men folks de most of de time cause it been so hot. **1948** Dick *Dixie Frontier* 173 **Sth,** Many schools ran for only a few weeks in the winter or for a short period in the summer after corn was "laid by" and before "fodder-pulling." **1963** Watkins–Watkins *Yesterday Hills* 75 **cnGA,** Hot weather made fodder-pulling one of the hardest jobs of the year. You reached up, pulled down the top of the stalk of the corn, and then stripped off the blades all the way to the dead leaves at the bottom. . . When you had a good handful of blades in each hand, you tied a hand, broke off the top of a cornstalk, and hung the little bundle on the stalk.

fodder-pulling time n **chiefly S Midl** Also called **fodder time 2**

Fall or late summer, when **fodder-pulling** is done.

1908 *DN* 3.311 **eAL, wGA,** *Fodder-pullin(g) time*. . . The time for pulling fodder, usually the first weeks in August. **1956** *Hall Coll.* **eTN,** Then in the fall, just before fodder-pullin' time, I got my new shoes. *Ibid,* The teachers would stop a couple of weeks for fodder-pullin' time. The people would pull fodder for feed. **1969** *DARE* Tape **GA**74, 'Possum hunting would be in what we called the fodder-pulling time. We would pull fodder during the day, wait for the dew to dampen that which had been pulled two days before, [and] tie it in bundles. **1984** Wilder *You All Spoken Here* 64 **Sth,** *Fodder pullin' time:* Late fall.

fodder seed n

Seed for **fodder corn.**

1936 *AmSp* 11.275 **TN,** *Fodder seed.* Corn. 'Have you planted your fodder seed?'

fodder shower n **SE**

A rain; see quots.

1947 *McDavid Coll.* **GA,** Fodder shower. **1966–68** *DARE* (Qu. B23, . . *A light rain that doesn't last*) Infs **GA**7, 31, **MS**72, Fodder shower. **1981** Pederson *LAGS Basic Materials,* 1 inf, **ceGA,** Fodder shower—when sun is shining, because you pull fodder only during the sunshine; 1 inf, **csMS,** Fodder shower—father's term; rains in small area; 1 inf, **cwFL,** Fodder shower—heavy, short duration; wets fodder; 1 inf, **seGA,** Fodder showers.

fodder stack n **Sth, S Midl** Cf **fodder house**

A conical stack of bundles of dried corn leaves, usu arranged around a central pole.

1738 (1841) Byrd *Westover MSS* 87 **SC,** There was a fodder stack . . in which the whole family sheltered themselves at night and in bad weather. **1788** (1925) Washington *Diaries* 3.424 **VA,** The Cart was drawing Rails for a fodder Stack. **1866** Smith *Bill Arp* 54 **GA,** The Governor . . is constrained to get on a fodder-stack pole. **1893** *Harper's New Mth. Mag.* 88.101/2 **wNC,** The great whitened cone of the fodder-stack gleamed icily in the purple air. **1912** Green *VA Folk-Speech* 181, *Fodder-stack*. . . The corn blades are tied in bundles to dry; then made into large *conical stacks* for keeping. **1939** Harris *Purslane* 92 **NC,** The wind rattled tan fodder stacks. **c1960** *Wilson Coll.* **csKY,** *Fodder stack*. . . A stack of bundles of fodder, with the tips of the bundles turned in toward the stack pole. [Wilson: An inf says he has not seen one in fifty years.]

fodder-stack-weed n Cf **fodder tea**

An unidentified plant used to make a medicinal drink.

1967 *S. Folkl. Qrly.* 31.298 **csKY,** Other teas included . . fodder-stack-weed (not yet identified).

fodder tea n Also *blade(-fodder) tea* Cf **blade fodder, fodder-stack-weed**

A medicinal tea made from **fodder** n **2.**

1869 Porcher *Resources* 632 **SC,** Blade tea is quite a favorite diaphoretic used recently by many in the Confederate States in fever—its anti-periodic properties doubtful. **1947** (1964) Randolph *Ozark Superstitions* 107, Boneset tea is a favorite remedy for chills, fever, and ague. . . Some people have great confidence in blade-fodder tea, especially if the fodder has been kept in a dry place. **1966–69** *DARE* (Qu. BB50a, *What are the favorite remedies around here for a cough?*) Infs **GA**8, 74, Fodder tea. **1970** *NC Folkl.* 18.25, Fodder tea was used to relieve measles.

fodder time n Also *foddering time*

1 The time of day when farm animals are tended.

1907 *DN* 3.222 **nwAR, sIL,** *Fodder-time*. . . The terms "chores" or "chore time" are not used. **1939** *LANE* Map 217, [Both *fodder time* and *foddering time* occur occas throughout NEng, but are more freq in nNEng. Labeled old-fashioned by two infs]. **1948** Davis *Word Atlas Gt. Lakes* app no. 60, [Time when farm animals are attended to:] Fodder time [6 infs out of 53, all in OH]. **c1960** *Wilson Coll.* **csKY,** *Foddering time*. . . Time to feed the stock. . . *Fodder time.*

2 =fodder-pulling time. chiefly S Midl

1954 *PADS* 21.28 **SC,** *Fodderin' time*. . . Time to pull fodder. Sumter County. **c1960** *Wilson Coll.* **csKY,** *Foddering time*. . . time to pull fodder. **1968** *DARE* Tape **NC**54, In fodder time they'd close the school down, an' fer two weeks, to pull fodder. **1984** Wilder *You All Spoken*

Here 132 **Sth,** *Foddering time:* Time to pull, or strip, the almost dried leaves from standing corn stalks.

fofaraw See **fofarraw** adj

fofarraw n Also *fufurraw, foofooraw, forforraw, froofraw, frufraw;* for addit varr see quots [Span *fanfarrón* braggart and Fr *fanfaron* blusterer; later forms perh infl by Fr *frou-frou;* see discussion in 1955 *AmSp* 30.96–98]

1 Baubles, trinkets, tawdry finery; hence *fofaraw house* brothel; also used as exclam to express contemptuous disagreement. **chiefly West**

1848 (1855) Ruxton *Life Far West* 191, Indian squaws . . strut about in all the pride of beads and fofarrow, jingling with bells and bugles, and happy as paint can make them. *Ibid* 202, First I had a Blackfoot—the darndest slut as ever cried for fofarow. **1850** Garrard *Wah-to-yah* 116 **sCO,** You've got so much 'fofarraw' stuck 'bout you, this child did'nt savy at fust! **1947** Guthrie *Big Sky* 87 (as of 1830s), A purty little whore at St. Louis, at a fofaraw house called a place of entertainment, she give it to me. **1947** Ballowe *The Lawd* 48 **LA,** "He look sorter cu'ious," one said under his breath. "Fooferaw," said another. "Nemmine [=Never mind]; Driver Green gwineter [=is going to] find out," said a third. **1948** Baumann *Old Man Crow's Boy* 37 **csID,** By then he . . had formed the habit of trading furs . . to Tatum at the store for fuforaw for his family, as well as supplies and traps. **1949** Emrich *Wild West Custom* 169 **NM,** They bought baubles and gimcracks, *forforraw* . . for their ladies and for themselves. **1955** *AmSp* 30.97, The different spellings it has amassed by this time include *fofar(r)aw, -ow, foofar(r)aw, -ow, -ah* (the *foo-* forms from the present century), and . . *forfarraw, froufraw, froofraw,* and *frufraw.* **1959** Tallman *Dict. Amer. Folkl.* 118, *Fofurraw* —A term, probably a corruption of "fanfaron," used for everything showy, effeminate and unessential by the trappers who kept away from civilization. **1966** Giles *Great Adventure* 98 **West** (as of 1830s), No squaw wanted any other squaw to have more than she did, in beads and shells and paint and foofooraw. **1968** Adams *Western Words* 117, *Fofarraw*—A trapper's and scout's word for anything fancy, such as fancy dress; also called *fufurraw.*

2 An uproar, fuss; hoopla.

1943 *Time* 18 Jan 65/3, Draft-age aliens, who were the center of one of the few big foofooraws yet kicked up about administration of the Selective Service Act. **1945** Webster *Town Meeting* 8 **eCT, RI,** It is a sensible land where romance does not flourish, and the picturesque froofraw of life is not appreciated. **1949** *Sat. Eve. Post* 12 Mar 6/4 **KS,** The refreshing thing about it is the lack of drumbeating and foo-foo-rah. **1954** *Time* 1 Mar 88/2, The Vatican's recent decision . . set off a foofaraw of petion[sic]-drafting, letter-signing, and complaining.

fofarraw adj Also sp *fofaraw, fofarrow* **West** *obs*

Vain, stuck-up.

1848 (1855) Ruxton *Life Far West* 26, Them white gals are too much like picturs, and a deal too 'fofarraw' (fanfaron). *Ibid* 107, American women are valued at a low figure in the mountains. They are too fine and "fofarraw." Neither can they make moccasins, or dress skins. **1941** Baldwin *Keelboat Age* 97 **LA** (as of early 19th cent), She had no business acting so fofarrow for she was jist a yaller gal. **1947** Guthrie *Big Sky* 265 **West** (as of 1830s), Too fofaraw, them bourgeways [=White women] are. I got things to do besides waitin' on a woman.

fog n[1] Also *fog grass* [Engl dial]

Grass left standing over the winter.

[**1895** *DN* 1.379 **eCan,** *Fog, fog-grass:* last year's grass standing in the fields in the spring.] **1899** (1912) Green *VA Folk-Speech* 181, *Fog-grass.* . . Long grass that remains on the land during the winter. **1903** *DN* 2.297 **Cape Cod MA** (as of a1857), *Fog.* . . Dead grass of the previous year at the bottom of mowing. **1913** *DN* 4.1 **ME,** *Fog.* . . Dry grass (such as is often burnt over in the spring). "There's lots of fog on your place."

fog n[2] Usu |fɔg, fɑg|; for addit varr see quots Cf Pronc Intro 3.II.9, 10

A Forms.

1890 *DN* 1.72 **New Orleans LA,** *Dog, hog, log* (with the vowel [ɔ]). A frequent pronunciation of these words; but *bog, fog* are always correctly pronounced [i.e., with the vowel [ɑ]]. **1891** *DN* 1.142 **cNY,** Before *g, ɔ* is usual in *'dog,' 'hog,' 'frog,' 'log,' 'fog,'* but ɑ sometimes occurs. **1905** *DN* 3.55 **NE,** Before *g, o* is almost universally *ɔ:*—*hog, log, dog, fog.* **1933** *AmSp* 8.2.44 **neNY,** [ɑ] is the usual sound of the vowel in . . *fog* [fɑg]. **1942** Hall *Smoky Mt. Speech* 32, These phenomena [=the raising and over-rounding or the diphthongization of /ɔ/] may be present . . in word-final position . . [as in] *fog.* . . There is occasional unrounding to [ɒ] [sic] and [ɑ] in *fog, foggy,* and *hog.* **1961** Kurath–McDavid *Pronc. Engl.* 163, [In the word *fog,*] /ɒ/ is regular in Eastern New England and in Western Pennsylvania. . . /ɔ/ is nearly universal in the Midland . . and rather common in Maryland, Virginia, and South Carolina. It is infrequent to rare in Eastern North Carolina, New York State, and Western New England. *Fog* with the vowel /ɑ/ . . is regularly used in Western New England, in New York State . . in Metropolitan New York . . , Philadelphia . . , and in Eastern North Carolina. In Virginia east of the Blue Ridge, in South Carolina, and in Georgia, /ɑ/ . . is definitely less common than /ɔ/. However, in Virginia and adjoining parts of Maryland all cultured speakers say /fɑg/. **1965** Carmony *Speech Terre Haute* 75 **IN,** Typical occurrences of [ɒɔ] are those in such words as *fog* [fɔ˕ɔg], [etc]. **1976** Allen *LAUM* 3.264 (as of c1950), In the U[pper] M[idwest] no . . clear pattern [of variation between /ɑ/ and /ɔ/ in *fog*] emerges. The field data do indicate, nevertheless, that fully rounded /ɔ/ is Midland-oriented. . . Fully unround /ɑ/, on the contrary, is somewhat stronger in Minnesota . . and North Dakota . . than in [Iowa, South Dakota, and Nebraska].

B Senses.

1 Steam.

1932 *AmSp* 7.267 **CA** [Oil field terms], *Fog.* . . Steam. **1932** *RR Mag.* Oct 367, *Fog*—Steam. **1938** Beebe *High Iron* 221 [Railroad terms], *Fog:* Steam.

2 in phrr of the pattern *to* ——— *up a fog:* To do something copiously. [By analogy with *to* ——— *up a storm*]

1939 *Hall Coll.* **wNC,** When I have a girl with me, I can sing up a fog. **1966** *DARE* (Qu. BB18, *To vomit a great deal at once*) Inf **GA3,** Puke up a fog.

3 Baker's bread. [From its color and insubstantial texture] Cf *DNE baker's fog* (at *baker*), *fog*

1966 *DARE* (Qu. H13, *Bread that is not made at home*) Inf **ME9,** Fog—joking.

fog v[1] Also with *up*

To smoke tobacco.

1859 Matsell *Vocabulum* 34, *Fog.* Smoke. **1925** *AmSp* 1.137 **Pacific NW,** When he [=a logger] leaves the cookhouse he "fogs-up" on his pipe. **1936** *AmSp* 11.275 **cTN,** Those girls are fogging. **1942** Berrey–Van den Bark *Amer. Slang* 112.3, *Smoke.* Blow a cloud, . . drag a smoke, . . fog.

fog v[2] [Perh var of **fag** v[2]] **West**

1 also *fog it:* To go fast, rush.

1893 (1958) Wister *Out West* 159 **TX,** To fog—to hurry, to scamper, to go quickly. **1927** James *Cow Country* 57 **West,** Being I didn't want to lose the cattle, I fogged in on them and kept 'em headed straight for the cutting-grounds. **1929** *AmSp* 5.76 **NE,** A fast running horse or man is "foggin'." **1930** *AmSp* 5.305 **NE,** *Fog*—Hasten. **1930** Knibbs *Songs Lost Frontier* 70 **West,** Bill Tandy, ridin' Hell's Delight, come foggin' into town one night,/ With three months' wages in his jeans, a clean shirt in his slicker. **1939** Rollins *Gone Haywire* 120 **MT** (as of 1886), With that the man, 'thout speakin' to me or givin' me chance to thank 'im, climbs on 'is bronc an' fogs it. **1961** Adams *Old-Time Cowhand* 70, If he couldn't . . cut 'em in the allotted time, he'd better get his hosses and . . fog it out of the country. *Ibid* 18, The first time he said somethin' 'round a tenderfoot a herd of questions came foggin' his way. **1962** *AmSp* 37.132 **nCA,** *Foggin', part[iciple].* Making a fast run on a logging railroad.

2 also with *up:* To attack, fire at; to fire (a gun) rapidly.

1914 Roberts *Rangers* 101 **TX,** Very soon the bullets began to fly at the robbers, . . and the Rangers kept "fogging" them, until they all quit their horses, and took cover. **1928** French *Ranchman NM* 48, Then Old Charlie and I made up our minds that it was up to us to fog him up a little and not to let Mr. Baca think he was the only man in the plaza who possessed ammunition. **1930** *Amer. Mercury* 21.455/2 [Racketeers' argot], They fixin' to hist me load, so I takes me heat an' fogs 'em. **1930** Raine–Barnes *Cattle* 133 **KS,** When in doubt they played trumps; that is to say, "came a-foggin'," not waiting for the other party to get into action. **1948** *Popular Western* June 20/2 *(DA),* I told you to get out of town once, or fog your guns the next time our trails crossed.

3 See quot.

1928 *Ruppenthal Coll.* **KS,** *To fog* . . to scold, complain, protest etc. vehemently. He fogged about the matter.

fog v[3]
1892 *KS Univ. Qrly.* 1.96 **KS,** *Fog:* to filch.

fog bird n
A marbled murrelet *(Brachyramphus marmoratus).*
1951 *AmSp* 26.275, *Fog bird* [is] the marbled murrelet in Washington, where this little seafowl is often nearly run over by the boats during foggy spells.

fogfruit See **frogfruit**

foggery n
A state of confusion.
1984 Wilder *You All Spoken Here* 157 **Sth,** *A-walkin' in a foggery:* Disoriented.

fog grass See **fog** n[1]

foggy adj
Of a person: dense, preoccupied; confused.
1931–33 *LANE Worksheets* **nwCT,** I'm so head foggy [hɛd fɑgɪ] today I don't know nothing. **1966–69** *DARE* (Qu. HH13, *Expressions meaning that a person is not very alert or not aware of things: "He's certainly ——.")* 15 Infs, **chiefly Atlantic,** Foggy; (Qu. GG2, *Expressions meaning "confused, mixed up": "So many things were going on at the same time that he got completely ——.")* Inf **RI**17, Foggy.

foghorn n
1 The nose. Cf **horn** n **4**
1942 Berrey–Van den Bark *Amer. Slang* 121.69, *Nose* . . foghorn. **1968** *DARE* (Qu. X14, *Joking words for the nose)* Inf **NY**107, Foghorn.
2 A loudmouth.
1969 *DARE* (Qu. HH7a, *Someone who talks too much or too loud: "He's an awful ——.")* Inf **CA**169, Foghorn.
3 A pipe. [Cf **fog** v[1]]
1964 Clarkson *Tumult* 362 **WV,** *Fog horn*—Smoking pipe.

‡**fogie** n [Perh *stogie* a cigar, infl by **fog** v[1] or *fogy*]
A cigar.
1969 *DARE* (Qu. DD6a, . . *Nicknames for cigars)* Inf **IL**51, Fogies.

fog it See **fog** v[2] **1**

fogle n [Perh Ger *Vogel* bird; but cf Engl dial *fugle* to whistle]
An audible backdraft made in a chimney by wind.
1967 Cerello *Dakota Co. MN* 60, You can get scared by the sound of fogles in a chimney. . . Fogles are usually caused by blustery northwesterly winds and are a sure sign of colder weather. . . Dad always said that a fogle could cause a chimney fire. [Cerello: Fairly common.]

fog light n
=**will-o'-the-wisp.**
1967–69 *DARE* (Qu. CC16, *A small light that seems to dance or flicker over a marsh or swamp at night)* Infs **MO**20, **TN**6, Fog light.

fog line n [From its being visible through fog]
1986 *DARE* File **swMT,** In Montana they call the white line along the outside edge of the road the "fog line." It keeps you from going into the borrow pit.

fog mull n [Perh Scots *mull* promontory, bluff (on analogy of *bank*)] **NEng, esp ME** Cf *DCan*
A heavy, stationary fogbank; also fig.
1905 Wasson *Green Shay* 39 **NEng coast,** All soul alone, he was, and right in the thick of a fog-mull, same's now. **1907** *DN* 3.244 **eME,** *Fog-mull*. . . Thick bank of fog. Used on the Maine coast. **1945** Colcord *Sea Language* 79 **ME, Cape Cod, Long Island,** *Fog mull.* Several days of intermittent fog without wind. **1950** Moore *Candlemas Bay* 26 **ME,** Say you're outside in a snowstorm or a fogmull, and you want to go into Boston Harbor. **1964** Gould *Parables of Peter* 154 **ME,** I think a Maine lobsterman . . would probably rather go to bed than . . compose somber verses about the difficulties he had in a fogmull. **1975** Gould *ME Lingo* 99, *Fog Mull*—Heavy fog, often with a drizzle but without wind. A man dazed or in his cups is described as being in a *fog mull,* rather than the customary description in other places of being "in a fog."

fogo n Also *fugo* [Engl dial; perh var of **hogo** n[1], infl by *fog*] **chiefly NEast** *old-fash*
An offensive smell.
1840 Haliburton *Clockmaker* (3d ser) 47 **NEng,** That word . . smelt so strong in his nose he had to take out his handkerchief, all scented with musk, to get clear of the fogo of it. **1890** *AN&Q* 4.211/2, Fogo, in the sense of a strong smell, is a rustic colloquialism. The word is not unlike *hogo* [< Fr *haut gout*] . . , in sense as well as in sound, but it may be akin to *fog,* a vapor. I have heard *fugo* used with a similar meaning. **1890** *DN* 1.21 **eMA,** *Fogo* [fogo]. A stench. Beverly and Salem, Mass. **1892** *DN* 1.215, *Fogo*. . . "I have heard *fugo* (pronounced [fiugo]) in . . New England. *Fogo* is common enough among North of Ireland people." **1968** *DARE* (Qu. X55b, *Words for breaking wind from the bowels)* Inf **PA**134, Fogo [fogo]—my father used to call them this.

fog out v phr Cf **foggy** adj
1967 *DARE* (Qu. JJ30a, . . *Expressions for forgetting something: "I ——.")* Inf **MN**1, Fogged out.

fog, raise the v phr
To celebrate uproariously, raise the roof.
1965–70 *DARE* (Qu. FF18, . . *A noisy or boisterous celebration. . . "They certainly —— last night.")* Inf **OK**13, Raised the fog! (Done something they had no business—probably had a fight); **SC**67, Raised the fog.

fog through v phr [From notion of 'cutting through the fog']
To think through, puzzle out (a problem).
1934 Smiley *Gloss. New Paltz* **NY,** Fog a thing through.

fog up v[1] See **fog** v[1]

fog up v[2] See **fog** v[2] **2**

fogweed n **Pacific**
An **orach** (here: *Atriplex expansa*).
1923 in **1925** Jepson *Manual Plants CA* 326, *A[triplex] expansa.* . . *Fog-weed*. . . Low alkaline areas of the interior. **1944** Abrams *Flora Pacific States* 2.82, *Atriplex expansa* var. *mohavensis*. . . Fogweed. **1961** Thomas *Flora Santa Cruz* 150 **CA,** Mohave Fog Weed. Rare as a weed in San Francisco; introduced from central California. May-July.

foh See **for**

fohty See **forty**

foir See **fire**

fold n See **foal** n

fold v See **foal** v **A1**

folded See **foal** v **A2, 3**

‡**folded money** n [Var of *folding money*]
Paper money.
1969 *DARE* (Qu. U19b) Inf **IL**43, They call it folded money.

folded pants n pl
Diapers.
1971 Adams *Cowman* 98 **West,** [He] had his folks buffaloed since before he quit wearin' folded pants.

‡**folderino** n [Perh joc var of *folderol*]
An absurd mechanical contrivance, gadget.
1900 Day *Up in ME* 39, Some new folderinos come 'long every day,/ All sorts of new jiggers to help git yer hay.

fold out See **fold up 2**

fold up v phr
1 Of a horse: to buck. **West**
1937 *DN* 6.619 **swTX,** When the bronco commences to buck, he *wrinkles his spine, unwinds, folds up,* or *boils over.* **1961** Adams *Old-Time Cowhand* 295 **West,** When a hoss started to buck there were a lot of slang expressions the cowhand used for a description of this act. The hoss "arches his back," "boils over," . . "folds up," [etc].
2 also *fold out:* To go to bed.
1967–70 *DARE* (Qu. X40, . . *Other ways* . . *of saying "I'm going to bed")* Infs **KY**94, **NE**11, Fold up; **MN**15, **MO**39, Fold out.

folk n Pronc-sp *focht*
A Pronc var.
1914 *DN* 4.106 **KS,** *Fochts* (guttural *ch* as in German). . . Folks.
B Gram forms.
1 Used with sg rather than pl reference.
a *folk.* [Back-formation from pl *folks*]
1867 Beecher *Norwood* 100 **NEng,** Wal, as near as I can see, it's a nigger sprouting and blossoming into a white folk.

b *folks.*

1894 [see **C1c** below]. **1903** [see **C1c** below]. **1905** [see **C1c** below]. **1909** *DN* 3.388 **eAL, wGA,** *White folks.* . . a single person. A negroism. **c1937** in 1972 *Amer. Slave* 2.1.67 **SC** [Black], De overseer was poor white folks . . and dat is one thing dat made him so hard on de slaves of de plantation. **1977** Dillard *Lexicon* 89 [Black], The young man [=a child born to a prostitute] is called White Folks by those of the ghetto community who are favorably disposed toward him.

2 pl: usu *folk, folks;* also double pl *folkses,* eye-dial sp *fowkses.* **Sth, S Midl** See Intro "Language Changes" II.3

1653 *Order Book* **VA** *(ADD),* There was a great many folkses in the house. **1843** (1916) Hall *New Purchase* 258 **IN,** The two old folkses. **1895** *DN* 1.371 **eTN,** *Folkses.* **1909** *DN* 3.396 **nwAR,** *Folkses.* **1927** *AmSp* 3.10 **Ozarks,** The word *folk* is never heard in the Ozark country, but *folks* and *folkses* are both common, and seem to be used interchangeably. **1929** Sale *Tree Named John* 30 **MS,** Ah been tellin' dese folkses. **1933** Rawlings *South Moon* 7 **FL,** Folkses mought o' got too thick for 'em here in Floridy. **1938** Matschat *Suwannee R.* 17 **seGA,** How many fowkses in New Yawk? **1945** Saxon *Gumbo Ya-Ya* 229 **LA,** My white folkses was never mean or crabbish. **1946** *PADS* 6.14 **eNC** (as of 1900–10), *Folkses. . . Folks,* people. Baby talk used by mothers to their children. Pamlico. Common. **c1960** *Wilson Coll.* **csKY,** Folkses. . . Folks, people. . . Usually humorous. **1960** Criswell *Resp. to PADS 20* **Ozarks,** Folkses. . . Usually, in direct address. Heard among some illiterate old-timers, now probably entirely gone. "Come on, folkses, let's go in and wake him up."

C Senses.

1a pl: One's family, relatives.

1637 in 1884 ME Hist. Soc. *Doc. Hist.* 3.117, Mr. Gibson is now going into the Bay to se somm of his Country folkes. **1884** Barber *Diary* 32 **MA,** Folks came home at 8:30 in Eve. **1894** *DN* 1.330 **NJ,** *Folks:* immediate family. **1905** *DN* 3.9 **cCT,** *Folks.* . . People, especially one's family. "How are your folks?" **1907** *DN* 3.212 **nwAR,** *Folks.* . . People, especially one's family. **1910** *DN* 3.441 **cwNY,** *Folks.* . . Immediate family. **1926** Roberts *Time of Man* 54 **KY,** "Are you lost from your folks?" . . "Yes ma'am. Tessie is my folks." **1928** Aldrich *Lantern* 48 **NE,** He wanted to know how all the Iowa Folks was. **1936** *AmSp* 11.315 **Ozarks,** His paw an' maw was folks—first cousins, I think they was. **1938** Rawlings *Yearling* 23 **nFL,** My folks runs to fairness [of complexion], too. **1954** *Harder Coll.* **cwTN,** *Folks, my.* . . Usually means the entire close family; can mean all relatives. **c1960** *Wilson Coll.* **csKY,** *Folks.* . . Relatives. **1965–70** *DARE* (Qu. Z8, . . *Your own immediate family group*) 168 Infs **widespread,** (My) folks; **KY**51, Home folks; (Qu. Z9, . . *Others related to you by blood*) 61 Infs **widespread,** (My) folks; **IL**102, My mother's folks; my father's folks; **MN**34, My husband's folks; (Qu. Z7, . . *Other relatives*) Inf **OH**98, Folks. **1971** [see **C1b** below].

b spec; in phrr *one's folks, the ~:* One's parents.

1926 *DN* 5.393 [Middle Western Speech], *(The) folks* . . may be restricted to the sense "my (our) parents." . . "The folks were in the hospital, and I had to look after my brothers and sisters." Pedantry sometimes corrupts the idiom, with laughable results; a certain young woman always says carefully "my folk." **1948** Manfred *Chokecherry* 4 **nwIA,** He wrote to tell his folks about the change. **1955** Potter *Dial. NW OH* 144, In all age groups *my folks* is commoner than *my parents* or *my family.* . . The least educated use *my folks* and *my parents* about equally, but the better educated groups prefer *my folks.* **1960** Bailey *Resp. to PADS 20* **KS,** Usually, I believe, "my folks" would mean "my parents," but certainly not always. I have myself used it also to mean "close relatives" and many time I have heard it used that way. I believe young people would be the ones most likely to . . mean "my parents." **1960** Criswell *Resp. to PADS 20* **Ozarks,** *My folks, our folks,* usually meant the immediate family and, now and then, simply parents. It could include more different relatives like uncles, aunts, cousins sometimes. **1971** Bright *Word Geog. CA & NV* 191, *Parents / immediate family / —parents* 56% . . *folks* 39% S[cattered]. . . Her *relatives / others related by blood /* —folks 10% P[attern] XI [=rural]. **1973** Allen *LAUM* 1.345 **Upper MW** (as of c1950), More than one-third of the infs. use simple *folks,* but sometimes only to refer to parents in contrast with other terms to include persons more distantly related.

c sg *folks:* One's wife or sweetheart.

1894 *DN* 1.330, *Folks.* . . In Connecticut I have heard men say "my folks," meaning strictly "my wife," though there were others in the family. **1903** *DN* 2.351 **nVT,** *Folks, n. pl.* as *sg.* The wife only. 'How are your folks? Well she ain't feeling very well this winter.' **1905** *DN* 3.79 **nwAR,** *Folks.* . . Sweetheart. 'I'm going to see my folks.' A students' expression.

2 pl: Transf: one's household, one's subordinates.

1823 *Nat. Intelligencer* 1 May 1/4 *(DAE),* [Yankee dialect:] *Our folks,* a term by which the whole family including servants, cats, and dogs, are alluded to. **1910** *DN* 3.441 **cwNY,** *Folks.* . . Tenant and his men who work a farm. "Our folks are going to begin plowing to-morrow."

3a pl: People considered to be like oneself; respectable people.

1839 Kirkland *New Home* 29 **csMI,** It's a rattle snake; the Indians call them Massisangas [sic] and so *folks* calls 'em so too. **1844** Sedgwick *Tales* 200 **NY** (1912 Thornton *Glossary*), There was considerable earthenware and silver tea-spoons, and it was evident they had lived like folks. **1871** (1882) Stowe *Fireside Stories* 176, All them Martha Vineyard Indians turned Christians, . . and they reely did settle down, and get to be quite like folks. **1894** *DN* 1.341 **wCT,** *Holler:* to shout. . . *Hollow* (as verb) is substituted by some when talking "afore folks." **1898** Westcott *Harum* 324 **nNY,** She'd been more like folks fer about a week mebbe 'n she had fer a long spell, an' I begun to chirk up some. **1903** *DN* 2.295 **Cape Cod MA** (as of a1857), *Act like folks.* . . To act with propriety.

b People of one's own community, people who "belong."

1851 (1852) Stowe *Uncle Tom's Cabin* 2.304, Miss Ophelia took Topsy home to Vermont with her, much to the surprise of that grave deliberative body whom a New Englander recognizes under the term *"Our folks."* **1860** in 1865 Thoreau *Letters* 190 **MA,** The genius of the mountains saw us starting from Concord, and it said, There come two of our folks. . . Get up a serious storm, that will send a-packing these holiday guests. **1926** *AmSp* 2.78 **ME,** You must be duly impressed [with the "local essence"], or you will be regarded as "tony" or "offish." Certainly you won't be regarded as "folks." **1943** Weslager *DE Forgotten Folk* 8, Among friends and neighbors, "our folks" corresponds to "you all" of the South. The question "Our folks going somewhere today?" means, "Going somewhere today, friends?" **1953** Randolph–Wilson *Down in Holler* 51 **Ozarks,** Folks is sometimes used to designate a member of the speaker's own kind or community, so that "he's folks" means "he's all right."

4 pl: Company, guests.

1869 *Harper's New Mth. Mag.* June 21, When my brain was at sixes and sevens,/ If my mother had 'folks' and ice-cream.

5 pl: Adults.

1968 *Sat. Eve. Post* 15 June 28/1 **AL,** He looks on the entire world as merely an extension of Barbour County, Ala., where he grew up—full of chillun and folks, some of them liars and cheats and no-counts, most of them decent people.

folks are as good as (the) people, (the) exclam

In cribbage play: see quot.

1965 *DARE* File **nMN** (as of c1945), When playing cribbage and the crib is no count—or has nothing in it—you naturally do not get to peg anything on the board. So, to make you feel good, or at least not as bad as you could for having a crib worth nothing, you move the back peg up to the front peg on the board. That is when you say "The folks are as good as the people." You move a peg, but of course it doesn't count anything. **1965** *DARE* File **IA,** Folks are as good as people.

folk school n

1968 *DARE* Tape **NC**54 (as of 1920s), Her husband had always planned on havin' a folk school somewhere. . . It was to learn you to carve, and . . learn you to farm. . . It give people jobs, and it learn 'em a trade . . older people learned to carve. They learned to survey, and dairy work, and just all kind of work.

folkses See **folk B2**

folks pass, folks paw See **faux pas** n

folla, foller v See **follow** v

foller n See **fallow** n

follow v Usu |ˈfɑlo|; also |ˈfɑlə|; also *old-fash* |ˈfɑlər|; less freq, **esp NEast** |ˈfɑli| (Cf Pronc Intro 3.I.12.d) Pronc-spp *folla, folluh, foller, folly*

A Forms.

1843 (1916) Hall *New Purchase* 113 **IN,** Crack away and I'll foller. **1848** Lowell *Biglow* 144 **'Upcountry' MA,** [Glossary:] Foller, folly, *to follow.* **1891** *DN* 1.117 **cNY,** [fɑlə, fɑlr] . . 'follow.' **1899** Chesnutt *Conjure Woman* 77 **csNC** [Black], Min' you follers de d'rections. **1899** Garland *Boy Life* 130 **nwIA,** Foller. **1901–07** in 1944 *ADD* **cVA,** To folla afteh Sayrah. **1910** Hart *Vigilante Girl* 145 **nCA,** That water follies the grade. **1922** Gonzales *Black Border* 302 **sSC, GA coasts** [Gullah glossary], *Folluh*—follow, follows, followed, following. **1933** *AmSp* 8.2.45 **neNY,** Excrescent [r] is not infrequent, as . . *follow* [falr]. That practice, however, is old fashioned and today . . [falə] . . [is] rapidly replacing the earlier [form]. **1933** Rawlings *South Moon* 9 **nFL,** You wa'n't afeerd to foller me, Py-tee? **1933** *Hanley Disks* **seMA,** An' I'd folly them to the pond. **1942** *New Yorker* 27 June 15/1 **NYC,** I don't know do they folly me around or what, those plainclothes policemen. **1960** Criswell *Resp. to PADS 20* **Ozarks,** [falɚ]—The usual pron. until a late date and still common. **1967** *DARE* FW Addit **TN**17, Follered ['falɚd].

B Senses.

1 To engage in (a trade or occupation), be habitually engaged with; to make a habit of. **chiefly S Midl**

1885 Grant *Personal Memoirs* 1.288 **sIL,** There were many men . . whose occupation had been following the river in various capacities, from captain down to deck hand. **1911** *DN* 3.538 **eKY,** He follows picking the banjo. **1912** *DN* 3.575 **wIN,** John is a carpenter, but I don't know what Sam follows. **1917** *DN* 4.412 **wNC,** "He follers pickin' the banjer." "What do you-uns foller for a livin'?" **1926** *DN* 5.400 **Ozarks,** Whut mout you-all foller for a living'? . . We-uns don't never foller a-takin' in strangers. **1926** Roberts *Time of Man* 120 **KY,** I heared tell about a man once that followed studyen the stars all his life. **1927** *DN* 5.469 **Appalachians,** To foller speakin or talkin, i.e., to make public speeches or addresses. **1927** *AmSp* 2.354 **WV,** He follers picking the banjo. **1937** *Hall Coll.* **wNC, eTN,** He follered trappin'. . . I followed huntin'. . . I don't follow drinkin'. **1951** Craig *Singing Hills* 30 *(Hench Coll.),* My host turned to me, "Do you follow praying?" he asked. I rightly judged that he meant for me to return thanks. **1966** *DARE* (Qu. DD12, . . *A person who drinks steadily or a great deal*) Inf **MS**71, [He] follows the bottle. **1968** *DARE* FW Addit **eMD,** To "follow the water" is to be a waterman.

2 To escort, accompany. Cf **carry B1**

1950 *WELS Suppl.* **cwWI,** [May I] follow you home?

follow n See **fallow** n

follow-cat n [**cat** n **1f**] Cf **follow-pot**

A tagalong.

1967–69 *DARE* (Qu. Y9, *Somebody who always follows along behind others: "His little brother is an awful ______.")* Infs **CA**120, **HI**8, **MI**40, **NY**20, **OH**48, Follow-cat; **NJ**3, Penny-dog; follow-cat.

follow horse n Also *follower* Cf **lead horse**

=**near horse.**

1966–70 *DARE* (Qu. K32b, *The horse on the left side in plowing or hauling*) Infs **FL**12, **GA**80, Follow horse; **GA**39, Foller horse; **PA**234, Follower [*DARE* Ed: All 4 Infs gave resp *lead horse* to Qu. K32a]; (Qu. K32a, . . *The horse on the driver's right hand*) Inf **MS**81, Follow horse. The wildest horses [are] put on the right. [For discussion of confusion of terms for right- and left-hand horses, see note at **near horse.**]

following ppl adj **chiefly coastal**

Of a wind or tide: moving in the direction of a ship's course.

1945 Colcord *Sea Language* 207 **ME, Cape Cod, Long Island,** In relation to navigation, fair (favoring) winds include: A following wind, one astern or from abaft the *quarter.* **1965–70** *DARE* (Qu. O18, . . *Currents or actions of the water*) 17 Infs, **coastal, esp Atl coast,** Following sea; **AL**22, Following sea shallows; (Qu. O19, . . *Kinds . . of wind*) Infs **CA**65, **CT**9, **OH**20, **RI**17, **VA**84, Following wind.

following the tongue vbl n

A method of setting one's course; see quot.

1961 Adams *Old-Time Cowhand* 277 **West,** The wagon boss set his direction by the North Star. At night, after locatin' this star, the chuckwagon tongue was pointed in the direction to be traveled the next day. This was called "followin' the tongue."

follow-master See **follow-my-master**

follow-me-boy oil n Also *follow-me-boy perfume, ~ water, follow me boys* (or *girls*) *powder, follow-me water* Cf *DJE oil of—*

Any of var preparations supposed to attract members of the opposite sex.

c1938 in 1970 Hyatt *Hoodoo* 2.1082, [From the catalog of the "Curio Products Company":] *Follow Me Boys or Follow Me Girls Powder.* This powder means just what it says. Girls, do you go to dances to just sit? Boys, do the girls give you the cold shoulder when you crave love and kisses? Then get wise and sprinkle this powder where it will do the most good. **1945** Saxon *Gumbo Ya-Ya* 540 **sLA,** *Prostitute's Lure*—Essences of vanilla, verbena, Jack honeysuckle, wintergreen, rosebud, and 'follow-me-boy' water. **1946** Tallant *Voodoo* 104 **New Orleans LA,** She invented Follow-Me Water; if a lady puts some of this on her handkerchief and waves the handkerchief in the face of a young man she likes he is sure to follow her. *Ibid* 179, You puts their names in a mixture of nine lumps of sugar, honey, a little strawberry syrup and some Follow-Me-Boy Oil. Mix all this in a plate and light a yellow candle in the middle of it. **1960** *Washington Post* (DC) 11 Nov C11 *(Hench Coll.),* There is [in New Orleans shops] war water, follow-me-boy perfume, success oil [etc].

follow-my-master n Also *follow-master* [Prob by analogy with *follow-the-*(or *-my-*) *leader*]

A children's game in which players must imitate the actions of a designated leader.

1880 *Harper's New Mth. Mag.* July 293/1 **NYC,** It was discovered . . that when the girl came to spend a Saturday with her cousins, she was available for "follow-my-master," and even for leap-frog. **1943** *AN&Q* 3.12/2 **NYC** (as of c1900), "Chiefs" were "bosses" or the leaders in our games of "follow-master" and the like.

follow-pot n Also *follow-pup, ~-tail* Cf **follow-cat, penny-pup, ~-pot, tag-tail** *DS* Y9

1950 *WELS (When a child always wants to follow somebody)* 1 Inf, **ceWI,** [He's a] follow-tail. **1968** *DARE* (Qu. Y9, . . *"His little brother is an awful ______.")* Inf **MN**33, Follow-pup; Inf **LA**25, Follow-pot.

follows(-up) See **follow-up**

follow-tail See **follow-pot**

follow-taw n [*(EDD) follow-tar, folly-~*]

=**follow-up.**

1968 *DARE* Tape **IA**40, Follow-taw—a marble game like tag where one player tries to hit and "kill" the other player's taw with his taw.

follow-the-arrow n

=**arrow chase.**

1966 *DARE* File **neIN,** Chalk the rabbit (Follow-the-arrow)—a kind of chase game. **1968** *DARE* (Qu. EE33, . . *Outdoor games*) Inf **NY**80, Follow-the-arrow. **1975** Ferretti *Gt. Amer. Book Sidewalk Games* 158 **DC,** *Follow the Arrow* . . is played in Washington, D.C. Two teams . . compete. One is prey; one, the hunter. Those being hunted lead off and every twenty or thirty feet draw an arrow to denote the direction in which they are going. Great pains are taken to be honest. . . The fun is in finding well-hidden arrows along the route.

follow-the-leader n

A marble game, either **peewee** or a variant.

1950 *WELS* 1 Inf, **seWI,** Follow-the-leader—same as peewee. **1958** *PADS* 29.34, *Follow the leader* . . 1. The same as *pee-wee* . . (Ohio, Wis.). 2. Similar to *pee-wee,* but with many calls and counter calls such as "knuckles down" and "roundsomes" (Ohio). **1967** *DARE* (Qu. EE7, . . *Kinds of marble games*) Inf **TX**5, Follow-the-leader.

follow-up n Also *follow-up marbles, follow-ups, follows(-up)* Also called **follow-taw, around-the-world 2**

A marble game; see quots 1940, 1958.

1940 Marran *Games Outdoors* 150, *Follow-up Marbles.* . . Players take turns shooting their taw marbles. The first player . . rolls his taw marble into the open space. The other players follow in turn and try to hit the taw marbles of each other. **1950** *WELS* 1 Inf, **WI,** Follows up—[played with] two players. [They] shoot at each other's shooters. **1958** *PADS* 29.34, *Follow-up(s).* . . A marble game for two (often played on the way between home and school): one player throws his marble ahead on the ground; if his opponent can hit it with a marble of equal value, he wins it (N.Y.) This could also be played with boulders but paid with commies (Ia.) **1963** *KY Folkl. Rec.* 9.3.60, *Game played by shooting at opponent's marble, his shooter, no boundaries:* . . follows: Johnson [Co], follows-up: Floyd, Mason, Knott, Breathitt, Rowan [Counties]; follow-ups: Carter [Co]. **1968** *DARE* (Qu. EE7, . . *Kinds of marble games*) Inf **WI**56, Follow-up.

folluh See **follow** v

folly n

A work party; **bee** n^2.

1968 *DARE* Tape **PA**70, At one of the follies that they had, that was scattering manure over the ground. A folly was called when they had the harvest time, the manuring time, plowing time, such as that.

folly v See **follow** v

folly ballad n
See quot 1949.
1949 Webber *Backwoods Teacher* 120 **Ozarks,** He gave us a "folly" ballad—a song with a nonsense chorus—and ended with, "Oh, I'm a 'roamer' gambler—." **1975** McDonough *Garden Sass* 187 **AR,** Sometimes even the rollicking old churchsongs were given secular words and became "folly ballads" or "giddy tunes."

f'om See **from**

foment v [For *ferment*]
1949 *McDavid Coll.* **cwNY,** Foments [FW:=ferments].

fonda n [Span] SW *arch*
A restaurant, inn.
1844 (1954) Gregg *Commerce* 288 **SW,** Fondas, however, are mere *restaurants,* and consequently without accommodations for lodging. **1860** *Star* (Los Angeles CA) 23 June 2/1 (*Western Folkl.* 7.10), The proprietor . . of each and every public eating house, fonda, or restaurant, bakery and brewery [is to pay] a monthly licence . . of five dollars. **1880** *Harper's New Mth. Mag.* 60.678/2 **NM,** He sits on the porch of the excellent *fonda,* or lounges in one of the great arm-chairs that the editor of the *Sentinel* provides for his visitors. **1940** Writers' Program *Guide NM* 113, *Fonda*. . . Inn. **1948** *Sat. Eve. Post* 18 Sept 134/3 **NM,** In that former *fonda* the mountain men and the teamsters celebrated in heroic fashion their return to civilization after months in the wilderness.

fonk v
1980 Folb *Runnin' Down* 109 **Los Angeles CA** [Black], To *style,* to *front off,* to *fiend,* to *high sign,* or to *fonk*—all . . mean to show off or upstage others.

fonky adj [Cf **funky**]
1968 *DARE* FW Addit **LA**34, Fonky ['fɔŋkɪ]—stupid, strange, a little "off."

fontis cat n Also folk-etym *funny sacks*
=chuck-will's-widow.
1938 *Oriole* 3.2.13 **Okefenokee GA,** In 1921 Marion Lee, who had spent most of his life on Billy's Island, gave me [=Francis Harper] an interesting bit of swamp folk-lore concerning the Chuck-will's-widow. In former years his father and uncles, on hearing this bird . . , would pronounce it "Fontis Cat," in order to scare the children. The latter corrupted the name into "Funny-sacks." They were afraid to venture outdoors after dark when this mysterious creature was calling. [Footnote to *Fontis Cat:*] Spelling phonetic; etymology undetermined.

food n Usu |fud|; also esp **wPA, sNY, nNJ** |fʊd|
Std sense, var form.
1931 *AmSp* 7.19 **swPA,** *Food.* Pronounced as though rhyming with *good.* (Widespread.) **1961** Kurath–McDavid *Pronc. Engl.* 155, The vowel /u/ of *two* is in general use in *food,* except for Pennsylvania and some adjoining districts. In Pennsylvania the /ʊ/ of *good* predominates west of the Susquehanna. . . In Eastern Pennsylvania, /ʊ/ is less common and sharply recessive. This pronunciation occurs also in the folk speech of northern New Jersey and the Catskills in New York State, and relics of /ʊ/ survive on Delaware Bay and in the Blue Ridge. . . It is probable that Pennsylvanian *food* with . . /ʊ/ . . is of Ulster Scots origin. **1968** *DARE* FW Addit **PA**142, [fʊd]. **1978** *DARE* File (as of c1930), When I was at Mount Holyoke, one of the housemothers (from southeast New York) always asked in a standard blessing that God bless this [fʊd] to our use. **1979** *DARE* File **nNJ,** [fʊd]—used jocularly.

food and bake sale See **food sale**

food choppers n pl Also *food grinders* *joc*
Teeth or false teeth.
1965–70 *DARE* (Qu. X13a, . . *Joking names . . for teeth*) Infs **GA**77, **IN**77, **MS**73, **OH**71, **OK**42, **WI**62, Food choppers; **TX**32, Food grinders; (Qu. X13b, *Joking names for false teeth*) 9 Infs, **scattered,** Food choppers.

‡fooder man n [Perh Scots *fouter,* used as a general term of abuse for a person]
1956 Ker *Vocab. W. TX* 435, An imaginary bad man that "gets" little children. . . Fooder man [1 inf, **nwTX**].

food grinders See **food choppers**

food locker n
A pantry.
1968 *DARE* (Qu. D8, *The small room next to the kitchen . . where dishes and sometimes foods are kept*) Inf **LA**23, Pantry; in older homes it's called a butler's pantry. Food locker—an old-fashioned term, used occasionally.

food, off one's See **feed, off (of) one's 1**

food safe See **safe**

food sale n Also *cooked food sale, food and bake sale* **chiefly Nth, esp NEast**
A money-raising activity at which donated food items are sold.
1966 *Bar Harbor Times* (ME) 9 June 4/1, June 15 and 16—Annual spring rummage and cooked food sale. **1966** *Carroll Daily Times Herald* (IA) 6 Sept 5/8, The circle will hold a food and bake sale at the October Women's Association meeting. **1967** *Tupper Lake Free Press & Herald* (NY) 3 Aug 1/3, The newly reactivated Boy Scout Troop . . will hold a food sale. **1967–68** *DARE* (Qu. FF1, . . *What kinds [of 'socials'] are there?*) Infs **CA**18, 30, **CO**43, **MN**33, **NY**70, Food sale. **1968** *Granville Sentinel* (NY) 27 June 1/2, A Holiday Bazaar . . will feature a food sale . . , gift articles, used clothing, white elephants and old jewelry. **1978** *DARE* File **cnMA** (as of 1920s), The term *bake sale* may be used now, but I was familiar with *food sale* for this church activity. **1979** *Capital Times* (Madison WI) 21 Feb 53/6, A food sale will also be held and will offer lefse, pies, cakes, . . jams and jellies for sale.

foo-foo n[1] Also sp *fu-fu* [Of West-African origin, rel to Ewe fu_1fu_1 yam, cassava, and coco boiled and pounded, and Fon *fufu* food made from maize, fish, and palm oil] Cf *DJE, DBE*
See quots.
[**1889** *Century Dict.* 2307/2, *Foo-foo.*.a negro name for dough made from plantains, the fruit being boiled and then pounded in a mortar.] **1926** Ashley *Yankee Whaler* 131, *Fu-fu:* Mush and Molasses. **1949** Turner *Africanisms* 193 [Gullah], ['Fufu] 'mush'; 'wheat flour made into a thin batter and cooked'.

‡foo-foo n[2]
1969 *DARE* (Qu. E20, *Soft rolls of dust that collect . . under beds or other furniture*) Inf **IL**45, My sister says ['fufuz].

foofooraw See **fofarraw n**

foogerboo v
1965 *DARE* (Qu. II33, *To get an advantage over somebody by tricky means: "I don't trust him, he's always trying to ________.")* Inf **MS**63, ['fugɚ,bu].

fool n[1]
1 in phr *fool for luck:* One who is particularly lucky. [Reanalysis of the proverb *A fool for luck and a poor man for children* (and varr), that is, "look to a fool for examples of luck. . . "]
[**1834** Crockett *Narrative* 89, The old saying—"A fool for luck, and a poor man for children."] **1875** *Chicago Daily Tribune* (IL) 8 Dec 1/4, [Headline:] A Fool for Luck. **1966** Barnes–Jensen *Dict. UT Slang* 16, Fool for luck . . one having a reputation for being lucky.
2 One with a particular aptitude and fondness for (some activity). [From sense 1 above, perh also infl by sense 3 below]
1937 *AmSp* 12.159, *A running fool* or *a swimming fool* . . [meaning] one who is devoted to running or to swimming and who is likely to win any race that he goes into . . [is not] known here in New England. **1939** (1973) FWP *Guide MT* 414, *Fool*—Person of more than ordinary aptitude; as "a ridin' fool" for an uncommonly good rider.
3 with *for, over* or *about:* One that has a passion for, is "crazy about" (someone or something). Cf **foolish adj 2**
1927 Boston Soc. Nat. Hist. *Proc.* 379 **Okefenokee GA,** A Deer is a fool about [very fond of] that. **1942** Berrey–Van den Bark *Amer. Slang* 353.11, *In love with* . . a fool for *or* over. **1951** *PADS* 15.54 **IN,** *Fool for, a*. . . Proficient in; very fond of. "A fool for runnin'." Susceptible to: "A fool for women." **1954** *Harder Coll.* **cwTN,** [Letter:] I would not give a nickel to see a dozen shows But Ollie Mae and Eddie are big fools over them. **c1960** *Wilson Coll.* **csKY,** *Fool for*. . . One interested in or proficient in something.
4 Foolishness. Cf *DBE*
1939 Griswold *Sea Is. Lady* 728 **sSC** [Gullah], I gots too much wuk fuh do, makin' de noo crap [=new crop], fuh study 'bout fool.
5 in phr *till I fool:* To the uttermost; totally.
1939 Griswold *Sea Is. Lady* 122 **sSC** [Gullah] (as of 1865), She [=a young Black woman] stood with her shoulder and hip toward the white

man [=a member of the family who had owned her] and looked him over with a mocking smile. Her voice came bold and shrill: "I *free,* hear! I ain' slabe no mo'. I free till I *fool!*" [**1989** *DARE* File (as of c1950), In Jamaican folk speech "till I fool" would mean "to the extreme, utterly."]

6 A stooge, sucker.

1954 *Harder Coll.* **cwTN,** *Fool. . .* A person who is used for an advantage. **1965–70** *DARE* (Qu. II34, *If you think somebody is trying to use you to his advantage: "I'm not going to be his ______.")* 16 Infs, **scattered,** Fool. [5 of 16 Infs young]

fool n² [Etym uncert; perh from **fool** n¹, and infl by *trifle,* a similar dessert] **esp NEast** *old-fash*

A dessert made of crushed, cooked fruit covered with custard or cream.

1839 Randolph *VA Housewife* 149, Gooseberry fool. **1895** *DN* 1.382 **NJ,** *Gooseberry fool:* an old-time dish of gooseberries and eggs; eaten with cream. **1939** Wolcott *Yankee Cook Book* 363, *Fool.* A dish of crushed fruit with whipped cream and sugar. **1952** Tracy *Coast Cookery* 104 **MA,** *Fool*—A dish of fruit, crushed or stewed, served with whipped cream and sugar.

fool v

1 with prep *around:* See below. Note: In std modern usage *around* is used as adv with *fool.*

a To hang around, flirt with (a woman).

1837 Greene *Glance at NY* (Farmer *Americanisms*), He mustn't come foolin' round my gal, or I'll give him fits. **1896** Freeman *Madelon* 102 **NEng,** He used to fool 'round her . . afore he went courtin' the parson's gal. **1954** *Harder Coll.* **cwTN,** *Fool (around). . .* To follow a woman around for sexual purposes; to dally sexually. "He's a-foolin' 'round that old hussy all time."

b To loiter, waste time (in a particular place). **scattered, but chiefly S Midl, Gulf States, Cent** See Map

1965–70 *DARE* (Qu. Y27, *To go about aimlessly, with nothing to do: "He's always ______ around the drugstore.")* 32 Infs, **chiefly S Midl, Gulf States, Cent,** Fooling.

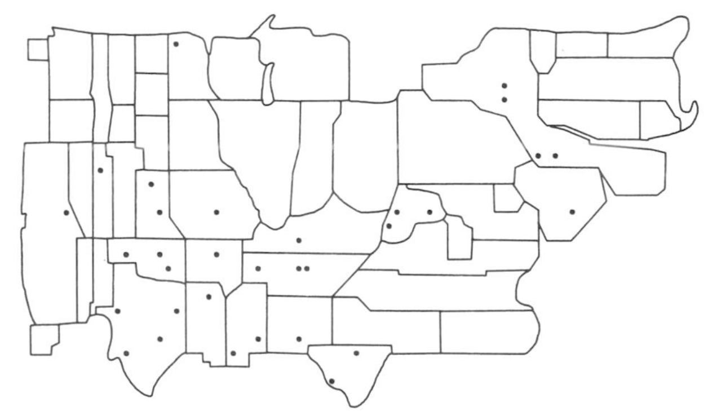

•fool v 1b (Qu. Y27)

2 In var specializations of std sense "to make a fool of, deceive":

a also with *around:* To trifle with someone's affections; to jilt, cheat.

1870 *Overland Mth.* Mar 288/2 **West,** Perhaps, foolin' is nateral to some women, and thar ain't no great harm done, 'cept to the fools. **1954** *Harder Coll.* **cwTN,** *Fool. . .* To stop seeing (a girl). "He went and fooled her after they been goin' together for over a year." **1965–70** *DARE* (Qu. AA11, *If a man asks a girl to marry him, and she refuses, you'd say she ______)* Infs **KY**89, **MS**63, **NC**2, **SC**7, 58, **TX**36, 38, Fooled him; (Qu. AA12, *If a man loses interest in a girl and stops seeing her, you'd say he ______)* Infs **AR**55, **LA**28, Fooled her; **PA**206, Fooled her around; (Qu. AA1, *When a man goes to see a girl often)* Inf **SC**58, [He's] trying to fool her, if he has no intention of marrying her. **1973** Allen *LAUM* 1.372 **MN** (as of c1950), She *turned him down. . .* [1 inf] Fooled him. **1984** Wilder *You All Spoken Here* 99 **Sth,** *Fooled her:* Promised to marry but didn't.

b To curry favor with.

1966–67 *DARE* (Qu. II20b, *A person who tries too hard to gain somebody else's favor: "He's always trying to ______ the boss.")* Infs **MI**24, **PA**28, **TX**26, 35, 38, Fool; **LA**8, Fool, soft-soap, tote milk to; (Qu. JJ3a, *When a school child makes a special effort to 'get in good' with the teacher . . : "He's trying to ______ again.")* Inf **MO**8, Fool [the teacher].

c To tease.

1967–70 *DARE* (Qu. Y7, *When one person never misses a chance to be mean to another or to annoy another: "I don't know why she keeps ______ me all the time.")* Inf **LA**6, Fooling; (Qu. GG3, *To tease: "See those big boys trying to ______ [that little one].")* Inf **VA**69, Fool. [Both Infs Black]

fool adj **formerly widespread, now esp Sth, S Midl**

Foolish, silly.

1805 (1833) Dow *Dealings of God* 193 **CT,** I showed the contrast of a gentleman and a fool *deist.* **1854** (1923) Holmes *Tempest & Sunshine* 12 **KY,** Tempest . . can hardly wait till I'm dead before she spends my money in fool fixin's. **1884** *Anglia* 7.262 **Sth, S Midl** [Black], *Er fool nigger* = a foolish negro. **1903** *DN* 2.314 **seMO,** 'That fool horse will run away if he gets a chance.' . . 'Let him kill his fool-self if he wants to.' **1907** *DN* 3.231 **nwAR,** He like to run his fool self to death. **1908** *DN* 3.312 **eAL, wGA,** *Fool. . .* Foolish. . . *Fool self.* Used in various reflexive phrases, "his fool self," "my fool self" [etc]. **1929** *AmSp* 5.119 **ME,** If a person's judgment were especially lacking he "might land in Augusty" (at the insane hospital); or he "gets more fool and *more* fool." **1939** (1973) FWP *Guide MT* 414, *Fool brand*—Brand too complicated to be described by a brief name. **1956** Gipson *Old Yeller* 38 **TX,** But there wasn't time to mess with a fool dog. **c1960** *Wilson Coll.* **csKY,** Where is that fool boy? **1966–68** *DARE* (Qu. K42) Inf **MS**21, A fool horse; (Qu. N12) Inf **GA**28, A fool driver [laughter].

fool adv **SC**

Foolishly, unreasonably.

1928 Peterkin *Scarlet Sister Mary* 259 **seSC** [Gullah], Do fo Gawd's sake, Doll, don' talk so fool. **1950** *PADS* 14.29 **SC,** *Fool sober. . .* Entirely and unreasonably sober. *Cold sober,* on the other hand, means *sober* in keeping with the seriousness of the occasion. **1966** *DARE* (Qu. N12, . . *Somebody who drives carelessly or not well)* Inf **SC**26, He drive fool. [Inf Black]

fool about See **fool** n¹ **3**

fool along v phr

To wander slowly, dawdle; also fig.

1866 Smith *Bill Arp* 44 **GA,** You get a government contract for a few thousand pounds, and you fool along with it, selling what you do make to these drug men at a bigger price. **1885** Twain *Huck. Finn* 285 **MO,** You turn back and fool along slow, so as to get to the house about the time you ought to. **1934** Vines *Green Thicket* 20 **nAL,** They fooled along and did not much try to reach the ferryman's house. **1966** Barnes–Jensen *Dict. UT Slang* 16, Fool along, to . . to proceed aimlessly and slowly.

fool around See **fool** v **1, 2a**

fool around the stump v phr Cf *DS* KK52

To beat around the bush.

1880 *Scribner's Mth.* 19.428/2 **NEng,** Thar aint no use in foolin' round the stump! . . I might jest as well come out with it, plain an' squar!

fool away v phr

To waste, fritter away (time or resources).

1942 Berrey–Van den Bark *Amer. Slang* 151.4, Fool away, *to spend . . foolishly. Ibid* 239.3, *Waste . .* fool away. **1943** *LANE* Map 568, 1 inf, **RI,** Fooling away his time; 3 infs, **ME, MA, VT,** Fooling his time away. **c1960** *Wilson Coll.* **csKY,** *Fool away. . .* Waste. "He fooled away a lot of money." **1966–68** *DARE* (Qu. A9, *What do you call wasting time by not working on the job?)* Infs **MD**41, **MN**22, Fooling (his) time away; **LA**11, **NC**5, Fooling away time; **FL**6, Fooling away; (Qu. A10, . . *Doing little unimportant things)* Inf **OR**13, Fooling away time; (Qu. A11, *When somebody takes too long about coming to a decision . . "I wish he'd quit ______.")* Inf **MO**21, Fooling the time away.

fool bird n

1 =**spruce grouse.**

1895 *Outing* 27.218/1, The spruce partridge. . . The Indians call them "fool birds," so easily are they caught.

2 See quot

1966 *DARE* (Qu. Q16, . . *Kinds of jays)* Inf **MI**10, Canada jay—also called the fool bird or the lumberjack.

fool-catcher n

An inferior kind of tobacco.

1920 Thomas–Thomas *KY Superstitions* 224, Do not buy tobacco of pawpaw color (motley color); it is called "fool-catcher."

fool duck n [Because they are thought to be easily caught]

1 =**ruddy duck.**

1888 Trumbull *Names of Birds* 111, Others at Detroit, and the 'punters' of St. Clair Flats, refer to the species [=ruddy duck] still as Fool-Duck, Deaf-Duck; and Shot-Pouch. **1917** (1923) *Birds Amer.* 1.152, Ruddy Duck. *Erismatura jamaicensis*. . . Other Names.—Dumpling Duck; Fool Duck; Sleepy Duck. **1942** Berrey–Van den Bark *Amer. Slang* 120.30, Fool duck, *the ruddy duck.* **1982** Elman *Hunter's Field Guide* 192, *Ruddy Duck: (Oxyura jamaicensis,* also classified as *Erismatura jamaicensis* . .) *Common & Regional Names:* . . fool duck.

2 =**redhead.**

1923 Dawson *Birds CA* 1801, *Redhead*. . . Fool Duck. **1982** Elman *Hunter's Field Guide* 199, *Redhead*. . . *Common & Regional Names:* . . raft duck, fiddler, fool duck.

fooler n

A pacifier.

1908 *DN* 3.312 **eAL, wGA,** *Fooler*. . . A nipple for consoling a baby. Also called *comforter.* **1968** *DARE* (Qu. EE34) Inf **GA**18, Fooler—a pacifier.

fool, feel like a v phr

1907 *DN* 3.187 **seNH,** *Feel like a fool, v. phr.* To be nervously exhausted, as from loss of sleep.

foolfish n

1 A filefish. [See quot 1842]

1842 DeKay *Zool. NY* 4.335, *Monocanthus* [sic] *broccus*. . . Our fishermen apply to it the whimsical name of *Fool-fish,* in allusion to what they consider its absurd mode of swimming with a wriggling motion, its body being sunk, and its mouth just on a level with the water. **1878** U.S. Natl. Museum *Proc.* 1.367 **NC,** *Alutera cuspicauda*. . . *Fool fish.* Rather common in Beaufort Harbor. Numerous specimens obtained. **1884** Goode *Fisheries U.S.* 1.171, The Orange File Fish, *Alutera Schoepfii,* also called "Barnacle-eater" and "Fool Fish," . . is rather common in southern New England and in the Gulf of Mexico. **1906** NJ State Museum *Annual Rept. for 1905* 358, File Fish. Thread File Fish. Fool Fish. **1933** John G. Shedd Aquarium *Guide* 157, *Monacanthus hispidus* . . Foolfish. . . *Ceratacanthus schoepfi* . . Foolfish. **1970** *DARE* (Qu. P4, *Saltwater fish that are not good to eat*) Inf **VA**55, Foolfish—flat, with sandpaper skin.

2 =**eel-back flounder.**

1884 Goode *Fisheries U.S.* 1.183 **MA,** At Salem . . they [=*Liopsetta putnami*] are also called "Fool Fish," because, in their anxiety for food, they will bite at any kind of bait, even at a rag. **1885** Kingsley *Std. Nat. Hist.* 3.279 **MA,** The *Pleuronectes glaber* . . is called fool-fish at Salem, because they are easily decoyed and bite even at a rag.

fool for See **fool** n[1] **3**

fool for luck See **fool** n[1] **1**

fool fowl n [See quot]

=**bittern.**

1955 *Oriole* 20.2, *American Bittern*. . . *Fool Fowl* (it stands still or "freezes" at the approach of danger; if seen it is regarded as a fool for braving the proximity of man).

fool hay n

1 A **witch grass** (here: *Panicum capillare*). [See quot 1890]

1890 *AN&Q* 5.101, Certain kinds of grass (as *Panicum vulgare*) in the far West produce such light hay (in proportion to its great bulk) that their product is called fool hay by the ranchmen, because they are *fooled* or deceived in estimating its weight. **1935** (1943) Muenscher *Weeds* 164, *Panicum capillare*. . . Fool-hay. . . Cultivated fields, pastures, roadsides and waste places. **1942** Berrey–Van den Bark *Amer. Slang* 119.7, Fool hay, *rough bent, also witch grass.*

2 A **bentgrass 1** (here: either *Agrostis scabra* or *A. hyemalis*).

1942 [see **1** above].

foolhead n [**head** n **C1a**] *derog*

A foolish or stupid person or animal; hence adj *foolheaded* foolish, stupid.

1903 *DN* 2.297 **Cape Cod MA** (as of a1857), That foolhead of a calf tipped his pail over. **1908** *DN* 3.312 **eAL, wGA,** *Foolheaded*. . . Foolish. **1915** *DN* 4.183 **swVA,** *Fool-headed*. . . Foolish. **1941** *LANE* Map 465, *Foolhead* [for a stupid person; freq throughout NEng]. **1942** Berrey–Van den Bark *Amer. Slang* 151.9, *Foolish; silly; witless* . . foolheaded.

fool hen n Also *fool's hen* [*fool* a stupid creature, in ref to its being easily killed]

1 =**ruffed grouse.**

1878 (1880) Stanley *Rambles* 144 **nwWY,** They will often sit or run by the road-side, and the driver slays them with his whip, or knocks them over with a club. From this remarkable trait they are frequently known as "fool-hens"—a suggestive title. **1942** Berrey–Van den Bark *Amer. Slang* 120.26, Fool hen . . *a grouse.* **1964** *Hand Coll.* **UT,** A child-bearing mother and father may not eat "fool hen," or the child will become a moron. **1978** *Outdoor Life* Sept 56, Remember the old stories about fools' hens? Early settlers in the Northeast regularly shot them when they needed fowl for stewing. Those birds were ruffed grouse.

2 =**spruce grouse. Nth**

1939 FWP *ID Lore* 239, Franklin grouse (known also as fool hens) are found chiefly in the extensive lodgepole pine areas. **1946** Hausman *Eastern Birds* 209, *Canada Spruce Grouse—Canachites canadensis* . . Other Names . . Fool Hen. **1961** Douglas *My Wilderness* 117 **nMN,** Where one portage climbs a sharp hill, a spruce grouse or fool hen went out ahead of us. **1963** Murie *Birds Mt. McKinley* 33 **AK,** *Spruce Grouse—Canachites canadensis*. . . Often called "fool hen," this grouse is exceedingly tame. **1966–67** *DARE* (Qu. Q7, . . *Game birds*) Inf **ME**8, Spruce grouse [is called] spruce hen or fool hen; [**MI**14, Spruce hen—up in Canada they're called fool hen; you can kill them with a club;] **MI**53, Spruce hen is also called the fool's hen; **MT**4, Franklin grouse is the fool hen; **SD**5, Fool hen—similar to grouse. **1975** Gould *ME Lingo* 99, *Fool hen*—The spruce grouse. . . A northern Maine game bird unwary enough to be called foolish. **1987** *DARE* File **ME,** A spruce grouse is called a fool hen. Any good bird dog wouldn't even bother with a fool hen. They don't taste good because all they eat is spruce buds. They have real dark meat.

3 =**dusky grouse.**

1923 Dawson *Birds CA* 1595, Fool hen. **1945** Mathews *Talking Moon* 112, Immature quail . . fly up into the trees . . like the dusky grouse in the Rockies called by the natives "fool hens."

4 See **fool quail.**

5 =**coot** n[1] **1.**

1945 Eifert *Birds* 56, "Fool hen", most hunters call the coot, or "mud-hen". **1962** Imhof *AL Birds* 215, American Coot—*Fulica americana*—Other Names: . . Foolhen.

fooling, do one a v phr

To trick, cheat someone.

1967 *DARE* (Qu. LL22, *Less than you should get: "They'll try to* . . ——— *every time."*) Inf **MO**8, Do ye a foolin'.

foolish adj

1 Dull, feebleminded. **chiefly Nth, esp NEast**

1895 *DN* 1.388 **wCT, MA, wNY,** *Foolish:* weak-minded, idiotic. **1909** *DN* 3.396 **nwAR,** *Foolish,* adj. Weak-minded, idiotic. **1954** *Harder Coll.* **cwTN,** *Foolish person*. . . A dull, stupid person. **1966–70** *DARE* (Qu. HH5, *Someone who is queer but harmless*) Infs **MA**75, **OH**61, Foolish; **GA**7, Funny, foolish; **MA**55, Foolish, simple, not all there; **MA**68, Simple, foolish, a little off; **NJ**43, A little foolish or queer; (Qu. HH6, *Someone who is out of his mind*) Inf **ME**5, One [local] retarded girl is called Foolish Annie W———; **ME**22, Gone nutty, foolish; (Qu. HH3, *A dull and stupid person*) Infs **LA**8, **ME**22, **SC**10, **WA**13, Foolish; **MA**68, Imbecile, foolish, feebleminded; (Qu. HH13, . . *Not very alert*) Inf **NY**68, Kinda foolish. **1973** Allen *LAUM* 1.356 **MN, SD** (as of c1950), Synonyms of *queer* . . range from . . "harmlessly psychopathic" to . . "loopy" and . . "misty in the peak." [2 infs offer *foolish*]. **1979** *DARE* File **cnMA** (as of 1920s), There was a feeble-minded fellow, who lived to a ripe old age, who was called by everyone in the town Foolish Nelson. I doubt that many knew his given name.

2 with *about* or *over:* Fond of, infatuated with. **chiefly Sth, S Midl** Cf **fool** n[1] **3**

1966–70 *DARE* (Qu. AA8, *When people make too much of a show of affection in a public place*) Inf **GA**28, Foolish about one another; (Qu. AA10) Inf **TX**95, [He] is nuts (or foolish) about [her]; (Qu. GG1a, . . *Very fond of*) Inf **GA**7, Crazy over, foolish about. **1972** Hall

Sayings Old Smoky 70 **wNC, eKY,** "She is plumb foolish over him." She loves him very much. Very common among old people. **1976** Wolfram–Christian *Appalachian Speech* 183, We always was foolish about gravy there at home, you know, and she always tried to fix it so we would like it, the way we all liked it.

3 Frail.

1924 Raine *Land of Saddle-Bags* 14 **sAppalachians,** I've had my health for nigh onto sixty years, but now I'm foolish [Footnote: Frail] and kind o' drinlin'.

foolish v

1 =**fool** v **2c.**

1907 Lincoln *Cape Cod* 280, I had considerable fun with Cap'n Jonadab over his not landing a rich husband for the Seabury girl. . . "Stop your foolishing," he says.

2 with *around:* To fool around.

1932 Randolph *Ozark Mt. Folks* 94, Pappy Lane he was all for follerin' 'em right up an' killin' ever'body, but we-uns jest kinder foolished round till we got him out o' th' notion. **1933** Williamson *Woods Colt* 66 **Ozarks,** He huddles on the edge of the bed, thinkin' of how he foolished aroun' an' let the sheriff take him.

foolish adv See Intro "Language Changes" II.8

1960 Criswell *Resp. to PADS 20* **Ozarks,** Foolish. . . Foolishly. By far the commonest usage for years and still probably so. "You're a talkin' foolish."

foolish n

Foolishness.

1938 Matschat *Suwannee R.* 124 **GA,** Mebbe ye know somethin' about the gov'ment nursin' trees, an' sich foolish. Be thar ary sinse to it?

foolish bone n

=**funny bone.**

1954 *Harder Coll.* **cwTN,** Hit my old foolish bone. Arm's went and gone sleep on me.

foolish curlew n

=**Hudsonian curlew,** esp its young.

1925 (1928) Forbush *Birds MA* 1.455, *Numenius hudsonicus. . . Hudsonian Curlew. . .* Other names: Jack Curlew; . . Foolish Curlew; Blue-legs. **1955** MA Audubon Soc. *Bulletin* 39.446, *Hudsonian curlew.* Blue-legs, Foolish Curlew (Mass. For birds of the year.) **1956** *AmSp* 31.300 **MA,** *Foolish curlew* (the young of the Hudsonian curlew, Mass.)

foolish earth n [Folk-etym for *fuller's earth*] Cf **filly dirt**

1968 *DARE* FW Addit **MD**15, Foolish earth—hard, compacted, impermeable soil, found especially at the bottom of a well.

foolish guillemot n

A **murre,** usu *Uria aalge aalge,* but also *U. lomvia lomvia.*

1828 NY Acad. Sci. *Annals Lyceum Nat. Hist.* 2.424, *Uria troile. . . Foolish Guillemot. . .* Common during winter on the coasts. **1835** Audubon *Ornith. Biog.* 3.142, The Foolish Guillemot . . lays only a single egg. **1844** DeKay *Zool. NY* 2.279, The *Foolish Guillemot,* or *Murre,* is a northern species. . . Large numbers of the eggs . . are annually brought to Boston for sale. **1899** Howe–Sturtevant *Birds RI* 27, *Uria lomvia. . . Foolish Guillemot. Brunnich's Guillemot.*—An irregular winter visitant along the coast. **1917** (1923) *Birds Amer.* 1.25, Murre. *Uria troille troille. . .* Other Names.—Foolish Guillemot. **1946** Hausman *Eastern Birds* 335, *Atlantic Murre—Uria aalge aalge . .* Foolish Guillemot, Guillem. **1955** Forbush–May *Birds* 243, *Atlantic Murre—Uria aalge aalge . .* Foolish Guillemot.

foolish house n [**foolish** adj **1**]

An insane asylum.

1920 Ade *Handmade Fables* 17 **IN,** Sometimes he feared that he was headed for the Foolish House.

foolishment n Pronc-sp *foolishmint* **chiefly Sth, S Midl** See Intro "Language Changes" III.1

Foolishness.

1918 *N.Y. Evening World* 4 Jan. 18/1 *(OEDS),* (title of verse) Foolishment. **1928** *Ruppenthal Coll.* **KS,** Foolishment . . esp used jocularly. **1929** Sale *Tree Named John* 30 **MS,** Whut . . kin' uv foolishmint is dat, anyhow? **1932** Randolph *Ozark Mt. Folks* 42, Thar ain't no sense in all this hyar foolishment—cuttin' paper dolls, an' playin' basketball, an' cookin' right in th' schoolhouse, an' all sich as that! **1945** Saxon *Gumbo Ya-Ya* 15 **sLA** [Black], It's time to cut out this foolishment, anyway. We is on our way to meet the Queen. **1958** Latham *Meskin Hound* 127 **cTX,** I've got a bellyful of your damned foolishment! **1984** Burns *Cold Sassy* 228 **nGA** (as of 1906) [Black], He say git on back to yo own church an' quit dis here foolish-ment.

foolkiller n

1 often cap: A mythical character whose business is to kill fools.

1853 Kennedy *Blackwater Chron.* 44, What a fool-killer he would make! **1888** *NY Tribune* (NY) 23 Dec 6/4, Now and then Niagara has ably assisted the fool-killer, by knocking out gentlemen who bid for fame by going over the Falls in a barrel. **1927** *Ruppenthal Coll.* **KS,** If the Fool killer came along, the town would be empty. **1939** Benét *Tales* 22, Whenever he heard of the death of somebody he didn't like, he'd say, "Well, the Fool-Killer's come for so-and-so," and sort of smack his lips. It was, as you might say, a family joke. **1948** *Georgia Rev.* 2.91, Yet by evening, the greatest Fool Killer / Known in the South let his zeal subside. **1968** Kellner *Aunt Serena* 155 **cIN,** The Fool Killer had become so real to me that I couldn't believe he wasn't. Whenever we had company, Aunt Serena would warn us in a stern whisper, "Now don't get rambunctious! . . " And if we did, she would say sharply, "Do I hear someone knocking?" **1974** Betts–Walser *NC Folkl.* 15, During the 1850's, a stout little man . . got so tired of the fools in North Carolina that he . . got himself a big club. Then, whenever he met up with a fellow saying or doing a silly, foolish thing, he pounded the rascal to the ground. Today there are wise citizens in North Carolina hoping for the Fool Killer to return.

2 A thing or situation that is dangerous to the foolish or unwary; esp, in logging: a tree or branch likely to fall or rebound on the logger. Cf **widow-maker**

1947 *Harper's Mag.* 195.80/1 **NEng,** A fool-killer . . was a live tree bent over by a fallen one so that when an unwary chopper drove an axe into it the tremendous tension, suddenly released, sent the tree splitting and charging up to catch him under the chin. **1950** *Western Folkl.* 9.117 **nwOR** [Logger speech], *Fool killer.* A piece of equipment which is unsafe; a situation which is obviously dangerous. **1950** *WELS (Joking names for a motorcycle)* 1 Inf, **seWI,** Foolkiller. **c1960** *Wilson Coll.* **csKY,** *Fool-killer. . .* A device that seems to take vengeance on meddlers. **1968** *DARE* (Qu. DD6b, *Nicknames for cigarettes*) Inf **AL**39, Foolkillers. **1968** *DARE* Tape **NH**14, A dead branch that could fall and hurt the logger when he hit the tree with the axe, or a leaning branch that could hit the logger when the tree fell—that's what they used to call a foolkiller. **1984** *MJLF* 10.150 **cnWI, ME,** *Fool killers.* Dead limbs that can become dislodged when a tree is cut and cause fatal injuries to a careless sawyer. . . General usage in Maine.

fool mallard n

=**gadwall.**

1940 Trautman *Birds Buckeye Lake* 186 **OH,** The Gadwall was more readily decoyed to "wooden blocks" . . and it was the only . . duck which frequently allowed the hunter to approach within shotgun range as it sat upon open water. Because of this tameness or stupidity . . the bird was justly called the "fool mallard."

fool off v phr

1 To waste (time); to putter.

1966–68 *DARE* (Qu. A10, . . *Doing little unimportant things*) Infs **LA**7, **MS**45, **NY**26, Fooling off time; **NY**86, Fooling off.

2 See quot.

1966–68 *DARE* (Qu. BB27, *When somebody pretends to be sick . . you'd say he's* ______) Infs **MS**45, **OH**82, Fooling off.

fool out v phr Cf **fool away**

To waste (time).

1937 (1963) Hyatt *Kiverlid* 15 **KY,** We cain't fool the day out when we've got the puttin' in of a piece to do.

fool over See **fool** n[1] **3**

fool plover n **NEng**

A **dowitcher.**

1923 U.S. Dept. Ag. *Misc. Circular* 13.51, *Dowitcher (Limnodromus griseus) . .* In local use . . fool plover (R.I.) **1925** (1928) Forbush *Birds MA* 1.396, *Limnódromus griseus . . Dowitcher.* Other names . . Fool Plover. **1956** *AmSp* 31.300 **RI,** Fool plover.

fool quail n Also *fool hen* [See quot 1917] **SW**

=**harlequin quail.**

1898 (1900) Davie *Nests N. Amer. Birds* 167, *Cyrtonyx montezumoe* [sic]. . . In Arizona this bird is known as "Fool Quail" or "Fool Hen."

1917 (1923) *Birds Amer.* 2.10, *Cyrtonyx montezumae* . . Other Names . . Fool Quail. *Ibid* 2.11, Mearns's Quail . . is a confiding bird and like some of its relatives has earned the name of "Fool Hen" by making no attempt to protect itself and by allowing itself to be killed with a stick or stone. **1928** Bailey *Birds NM* 223, *Mearns Quail: Cyrtonyx montezumae* . . This habit of "lying very closely" and taking flight only when nearly trodden on, is responsible for his name of "Fool Quail," and by its means . . he hides the conspicuous brown and black of his underparts. **1936** AZ Univ. *Genl. Bulletin* 3.85, A little larger and most remarkable of all in coloration, is the Mearn's quail *(Cyrtonyx montezumae).* Its black and white clownlike face might be thought responsible for its designation as the "fool quail," but in reality this term comes from its complete faith in the efficacy of its hiding. **1966** *DARE* (Qu. Q7, . . *Game birds*) Inf **NM3**, Fool quail—red-lookin' scoundrels.

fool's fumbling ball n Cf **layovers to catch meddlers**

1958 *PADS* 29.10 **TN**, *Fool's fumbling ball*. . . A joking, teasing, or even sarcastic expression used to reply to someone without answering his question: "What's that?" "It's a fool's fumbling ball to catch meddlers with."

fool's hen See **fool hen**

fool's hill n, sometimes cap

A state of complacent folly, esp the folly of youth, regarded as a barrier in the path to wisdom—often in phrr *climb (over) fool's hill* and varr.

1882 *Congressional Record* 12 Apr 2825/2 **AR**, Wise statesmen . . led her [=England] down from "fool's hill" [=a position of support for tariff protection]. **1923** Cook *50 Yrs.* 137, I had climbed almost over Fool's Hill, after groping in ignorance for quite a period in my earlier years. **c1935** Smiley *Gloss. New Paltz* **NY**, "Just starting up fool's hill" meaning foolishness not worked out. **1939** (1962) Thompson *Body & Britches* 498 **NY**, He's climbing Fool's Hill in a hurry: (showing the erratic conduct of an adolescent). **1946** *PADS* 6.38 **VA** (as of 1936), To go up *fool's hill.* (To live a care-free life. Said mainly of young people.) Salem. **1960** *Hench Coll.* **AL**, On top of fool's hill—at the age of 40 eager, alive, but unheeding of what's ahead. **1961** *Wall St. Jrl.* (NY NY) 20 Oct 16/2, "A lot of companies are being led down fool's hill," asserts A. R. Buchel . . here in Dallas. "Because of competition some executives and insurance departments have lost sight of the principles of good insurance." **1966** *DARE* (Qu. AA4b, . . *A woman who is very eager to get married*) Inf **MS16**, She's climbing fool's hill. **c1970** *Halpert Coll.* **wKY**, Climbing fools' hill = adolescence. **1981** *DARE* File **csMA, neCT** (as of 1940s), He's (just) having a hard time getting over fool's hill.

fool's huckleberry n

A **mock azalea** (here: *Menziesia ferruginea*). Also called **false azalea, rustyleaf, skunkbrush**

1915 (1926) Armstrong–Thornber *Western Wild Flowers* 350, Fool's Huckleberry—*Menziesia ferruginea.* **1956** St. John *Flora SE WA* 306, *Menziesia ferruginea* . . Fool's Huckelberry [sic]. **1972** Viereck–Little *AK Trees* 212, *Menziesia ferruginea* . . fools-huckleberry. . . Because of the leaf and flower size and shape, menziesia is sometimes confused with the huckleberries, but its fruit is not a berry. **1973** Hitchcock–Cronquist *Flora Pacific NW* 345, *Menziesia ferruginea*. . . Fool's huckleberry.

fool's light n [*OED fool's fire* 1631 (at *fool* sb. A. 7. b); *foolish fire* 1605 (at *foolish* a. 5)]

=will-o'-the-wisp.

1967 *DARE* (Qu. CC16, *A small light that seems to dance or flicker over a marsh or a swamp at night*) Inf **IL5**, Fool's light.

fool's mushroom n

A **death cap** (here: *Amanita verna*).

1987 McKnight–McKnight *Mushrooms* 238, *Fool's Mushroom. Amanita verna*. . . Flesh white; thick. Odor pleasant to nauseating; *poisonous—do not taste it.*

fool up v phr

To flirt, "fool around."

1933 Miller *Lamb in His Bosom* 129 **GA**, Why had he ever fooled up with her? . . Why had he kissed her that time?

foop v

To dance uninhibitedly.

1928 McKay *Home to Harlem* 30, When you were fed up with the veneer of Seventh Avenue . . you would go to the Congo [=a Black cabaret] and turn rioting loose . . ., fooping or jig-jagging the night away.

foo pah, foo paw n See **faux pas** n

foo paw v See **faux pas** v

fooper n

1968 *DARE* FW Addit **seMA,** Foopers ['fu:pəz]—a nickname for mully sobbers. Fried bread eaten at breakfast.

fooskie n [Du *voos* spongy, wooly, compressible + *-ke* dimin suff] *in Du communities*

A **dust kitten.**

1969 *DARE* (Qu. E20, *Soft rolls of dust that collect on the floor under . . furniture*) Inf **MI102**, ['fʊskəz]—a Dutch expression. **1979** *DARE* File **ceWI** (as of c1920), When I was a child we all called the balls of dust in corners and under beds 'fuskies' ['fʊskiz], a word I learned from my mother and her friends who spoke Dutch.

foot n Usu |fʊt|; occas |fʊət, fut, fʌt| Pronc-sp *fut*

A Pronc varr.

1897 Lummis *King of Broncos* 40 **NM**, He . . [had] a general build . . "like a two-futted brandin' iron." **1913** Kephart *Highlanders* 297 **sAppalachians,** I tuk my fut in my hand and lit out. **1930** *AmSp* 5.343 **TX**, *Could, coop, foot, roof, room* have [u]. **1931** *AmSp* 6.165, In the South, *roof, room, coop, couldn't, foot, stood,* etc. may have . . a short [u]. **1939** *LANE* Map 46, [[fʊ[ə]t] occurs throughout NEng; [fu[ə]t] is an occasional variant.] **1942** Hall *Smoky Mt. Speech* 37, [fʊət] *foot.* [Footnote:] Kephart . . notes that *u* occurs for *oo: fut* . . for *foot.* He apparently means [ʌ], although *foot* with this vowel was unknown to my informants.

B Gram forms.

1 sg: usu *foot;* also *feet.*

1922 Gonzales *Black Border* 301 **sSC, GA coasts** [Gullah glossary], *Feet*—frequently used for foot; as: "Snake bite da' gal 'pun 'e lef' han' feet"—The snake bit that girl on her left foot. **c1938** in 1970 Hyatt *Hoodoo* 2.1766 **New Orleans LA** [Black], (You put three glasses in a row.) Three glasses in a row but let one be roun' 'bout a feet apart. *Ibid* 1768, One feet deep.

2 pl:

a In most senses usu *feet;* also:

(1) *foots.*

1903 *DN* 2.314 **seMO,** *Foots*. . . 'The best white oak grows at the foots of the hills.' **1934** Carmer *Stars Fell on AL* 292, Brer dog asked brer rabbit was he foots coal. **1956** *AmSp* 31.109 [Army slang], Replacing plurals to the simple *-s*. . . *clubfoots.* **1967–69** *DARE* (Qu. X38, . . *Unusually big or clumsy feet*) Infs **GA23**, 59, **MO27**, Foots; **LA8**, Big clumsy foots.

(2) *feets.*

1927 Adams *Congaree* 6 **cSC** [Black], Sometime day [=their] feets in de air, sometimes dey horns. **1942** *Amer. Mercury* 55.223.92 **Harlem NYC,** If your feets don't hurry up and take you 'way from here you'll *ride* away. **1968** *DARE* FW Addit **LA** [Black], I want some house shoes to put on my feets at night. **1984** Burns *Cold Sassy* 289 **nGA** (as of 1906) [Black], My old feets, dey cain' make it back heah agin today.

(3) *feetses.* See Intro "Language Changes" II.3

1935 (1944) Rawlings *Golden Apples* 265 **FL**, I got to git my feetses washed good.

b As a unit of measure, also:

(1) *foot.* Note: This is an old and well-established usage, though often avoided as "incorrect;" see Intro "Language Changes" II.7.

1930 *AmSp* 5.266 **Ozarks,** The hillman's fondness for using the singular form as a pleural [sic] [is evidenced] in such words as *rod, cord, pound, foot, mile.* **1939** *LANE* Map 46, [In the context "The room is nine feet high," both *foot* and *feet* are current, but *feet* occurs less freq. in northern than in southern New England.] **1950** *WELS Suppl.* **seWI,** 16 foot long. Very common. **1960** Criswell *Resp. to PADS 20* **Ozarks,** "That post is about five foot high." Practically universal years ago . . still very common. **c1960** *Wilson Coll.* **csKY,** *Foot* is often a plural, as in earlier stages of English. **1966–69** *DARE* (Qu. V2b) Inf **SC21**, Two foot; (Qu. P25) Inf **NJ60**, Ten foot long. **1967–70** *DARE* Tapes **CA100**, 199, **IN45**, **MD51**, **TX14**, Foot. **1968** *DARE* FW Addit **eMD,** Ten foot of line.

(2) *foots.*

1966 *DARE* Tape **SC15**, Water be ten foots, sometime be five foots, sometime be three foot.

C Senses.

1 In mining: twelve inches measured along the ore-vein, regardless of width and depth. **West**

1860 *Californian* (Arcata) 30 May 2/3 *(DA),* The claims that I owned are not worth a straw, although parties in them sold ground adjoining for fifty dollars a foot. **1861** in 1917 Twain *Letters* 1.60, We have now got about 1,650 feet of mining ground—and if it proves *good,* Mr. Moffett's name will go in—if not, I can get "feet" for him in the Spring which *will* be good. **1862** in 1947 Chalfant *Gold* 61 **wNV,** He was not to be named in the same class with Uncle Ned, who owned about 100 feet in every ledge yet discovered. **1913** Goodwin *As I Remember* 234 **wNV,** "Sandy" Bowers, an illiterate and uncouth man in many ways, a rough miner, also owned twenty feet of the Gold Hill ground.

2 The leg. *Gullah* Cf *DJE*

1892 (1969) Christensen *Afro-Amer. Folk Lore* 8, Den Deer fit for kill 'e self. 'E say, "How! I hab four long foot, an' still Cooter git yere befo' me?" **1926** Smith *Gullah* 33, Deer hab long foot, him run fas'; Cootuh hab shawt foot, him trabble slow.

3 The main cutting unit of a plow, a bottom—usu in attrib phrr *single-foot plow, double-foot ~, three-foot ~,* etc. **chiefly sAppalachians**

1954 *Harder Coll.* **cwTN,** *Foot* . . the blade of a plow. **1965–70** *DARE* (Qu. L18, *Kinds of plows*) Infs **AL**2, **GA**72, 74, **NC**48, 54, **TN**14, Double-foot plow; **NC**37, 48, **TN**14, 16, Single-foot plow; **NC**37, **TN**16, **VA**7, Three-foot plow; **NC**37, **TN**7, Four-foot plow; **GA**77, Wooden-foot plow; (Qu. L20) Inf **GA**72, Double-foot; (Qu. L25) Inf **TN**7, Four-foot plow.

4 A footprint.

1942 Faulkner *Go Down* 124 **MS,** She so little and light she don't hardly make a foot on the ground.

5 in var phrr:

a *take one's foot in (one's) hand:* To set out walking; to set out in haste. [*SND* 1755 →] **Sth, S Midl**

1859 Taliaferro *Fisher's* 73 (Taylor–Whiting *Dict. Amer. Proverbs*) **NC,** I . . tuck my foot in my hand and walked all the way back to Old Bucksmasher. **1888** Jones *Negro Myths* 131 **GA coast,** Eh slip down de tree, an tek eh foot een eh han, an lean fuh de place way eh bin gwine. **1891** Page *Elsket* 132 **VA** [Black], I jes teck my foot in my han' an' come 'long way by myself. **1905** *DN* 3.97 **nwAR.** **1913** [see **A** above]. **1922** Gonzales *Black Border* 332 **sSC, GA coasts** [Gullah glossary], *Tek me foot in me han'*—meaning hastened, hurried, speeded up. **1927** *AmSp* 2.354 **WV,** "How are you going to get to town?" "I am going to take my foot in my hand." **1941** *Hench Coll.* **ceVA,** Why, take your foot in your hand and walk. **1952** Brown *NC Folkl.* 1.542, *Foot, to take (one's)—in (one's) hand:* phr. . . To depart, to set out walking. **1968–69** *DARE* (Qu. Y24, . . *"I can't get a ride, so I'll just have to _______.")* Inf **GA**89, Take my foot in my hand; **VA**11, Take my foot in hand and walk.

b *go foot:* To go to the foot of the class; to go to the tail end of the line in a game or contest. **chiefly Sth, S Midl**

1898 Lloyd *Country Life* 38 **AL,** Little Mary was most crazy to get back to school, sayin how she was in her a-b abs now, and if she missed another day she'd have to go foot, and the other scholars would laugh and poke fun at her. *Ibid,* She's all wrapped up in her books and it would most break her heart, I reckon, to go foot. **1905** [see **grin-go-foot**]. **1905** [see **headmark**]. **1944** Clark *Pills* 182 **Sth,** Luckless scholars went to the foot of the line for missing words. Sometimes humiliation at "going foot" was insufficient punishment and the master's flail fell heavily as a reminder that spelling was one of man's major achievements. **c1960** [see **headmark**]. **1968** [see **grin-go-foot**].

c *get* (or *put*) *one's feet under the table:* See quot.

1928 *Ruppenthal Coll.* **KS,** To get (or put) one's feet under the table [means] to eat; to board with; to sit at table with.

d *give (one) the foot* and var: To reject, dismiss. [Var of *give one the boot*]

1942 Berrey–Van den Bark *Amer. Slang* 67.3, *Oust or "bounce";* . . give the foot. **1970** *DARE* (Qu. AA11, *If a man asks a girl to marry him and she refuses, you'd say she _______*) Inf **OH**97, Gave him the foot (*or* boot); (Qu. II5b, *When you don't want to have anything to do with a certain person . . you might say, "I'd certainly like to give him the _______.")* Inf **VA**85, Foot; **VA**69, Bottom of my foot.

e *put one's foot up* and var: See quots. *among Black speakers*

1942 Hurston *Dust Tracks* 194 **FL,** "Dat's Big Sweet" my landlady told me. "She got her foot up on somebody." . . She was giving her opponent lurid data and bringing him up to date on his ancestry, his looks, smell, gait, clothes, and his route through Hell in the hereafter. . . My landlady explained to me what was meant by "putting your foot up" on a person. If you are sufficiently armed . . and know what to do with your weapons . . it is all right to go to the house of your enemy, put one foot up on his steps, rest one elbow on your knee and play in the family. That is another way of saying play the dozens . . [or] low-rate your enemy's ancestors and him. **1960** (1961) Oliver *Blues Fell* 128, If a particular person was the subject of enmity in a Negro folk community the offended man would 'put his foot up'—in other words, jam the door of his cabin with his foot and sing a blues that 'put in the Dozens' at the expense of his enemy, 'calling him out of his name'.

f *have one's* (or *one*) *foot in the road* and varr: To spend a great deal of time away from home. **esp Sth** Cf **in the street(s)**

1927 *Ruppenthal Coll.* **KS,** To have one's foot in the road means to travel much; to be much away from home or office or work, but has no necessary disparaging implication. **1950** *PADS* 14.78 **FL,** So *busy* my feets been in the road all day. Suwannee River backwoods speech. **1966–69** *DARE* (Qu. Y29a, *To 'go out' a great deal . . "She's always _______.")* Inf **TN**38, Got her big foot in the road; (Qu. Y29b, . . *A man who doesn't stay home much: "He's always _______.")* Infs **FL**5, **MS**37, Got his (or *one*) foot in the road. **1967** LeCompte *Word Atlas* 280 **seLA,** *Expression used to describe a person who is constantly visiting* . . [1 inf:] foot in the road.

g *have one's foot on the rail:* See quot.

1967 *DARE* (Qu. DD12, . . *A person who drinks steadily or a great deal*) Inf **NJ**2, He has his foot on the rail.

h *put one's foot on (something):* To count on, bet on (something).

1970 *DARE* (Qu. JJ20, *If you felt very sure about something. . . "I'm so sure I'd _______ it.")* Inf **TN**53, Put my foot on it.

i *on one's foot:* Pregnant. *Gullah* [Cf *SND heavy o' (the) fit* (at *fit* II. 10)]

1949 Turner *Africanisms* 233 [Gullah], [i ɒn ʃi fʊt] 'She is pregnant,' i.e., 'She is on her foot'.

j *my foot:* Used as an expression of disbelief or strong exception. Cf **dog's foot, the; foot** intj

1942 Whipple *Joshua* 298 **UT** (as of c1860), 'My foot!' snorted 'Sheba. **1966** Barnes–Jensen *Dict. UT Slang* 33, *Oh my foot!:* exclamation of unbelief. **1968** *DARE* FW Addit **csNC,** *My foot!*—used in conjunction with a statement the opposite of what you believe. "He wanted to marry her, my foot!"

k *in jolly foot:* See quot.

1986 Pederson *LAGS Concordance (Good-natured)* 1 inf, **csLA,** In jolly foot. [Inf Black]

foot v

1 To tread on, set foot in.

1937 (1977) Hurston *Their Eyes* 130 **csFL,** People who would not have dared to foot the place before crept in and did not come to the house. **c1938** in 1970 Hyatt *Hoodoo* 2.1494 **seGA,** An' jes' as dat terrapin crawl about why his mind is wonderin' [Hyatt: wandering], jes' keep on a wonder [Hyatt: wander] all de time, but he'll nevah *foot* yore place no mo'. **1981** Harper–Presley *Okefinokee* 79 **seGA** (as of 1929), Boys, I'm the best man ever footed Waresboro.

2 See quot. Cf **heel** v[2]

1941 Writers' Program *Guide WY* 462, *Foot*—To throw an animal by the foot.

foot intj Also *foot it* [Perh orig from *Christ's foot* (*OED* →1662), but perh infl by Fr *foutre;* understood as verb by some speakers] **chiefly Sth, S Midl** *euphem* Cf **cat's foot; dog's foot, the; foot** n **C5i**

Used as an expression of irritation.

1953 *New Yorker* 5 Dec 49/3 **MS,** And the lady was loading the Coca-Cola machine and says, "Oh, foot, I can't remember everybody." **1960** Criswell *Resp. to PADS 20* **Ozarks,** *Oh, foot* has always been a common interjection, a mild one usually. . . A woman's term always. **1961** Folk *Word Atlas N. LA* 240, [Mild expression of disgust:] Foot! **1966–70** *DARE* (Qu. NN8a, . . *"Oh _______, I've lost my glasses again.")* Infs **KY**72, **LA**3, **SC**8, 54, 59, **UT**6, Foot! (Qu. NN8b, . . *"This jar won't come open, _______ it.")* Inf **VA**69, Foot; (Qu. NN9a) Inf **SC**24, Oh foot; (Qu. NN9b) Inf **VA**39, Dog foot it; (Qu. NN25a, . . *"_______ it all!")* Inf **GA**83, Foot. **1970** Tarpley *Blinky* 300 **neTX,** [Mild expression of disgust:] Foot. **1972** *Atlanta Letters,* [A lady who] sometimes in despair needs a good strong word, but [who is] ever mindful of being a lady, uses "Oh foot in the branch!" **1979** *DARE* File **KS,** Oh, foot! I forgot it.

foot adz n Also sp *foot adze* **chiefly S Midl, West**

A long-handled **adz.**

1837 in 1858 Dewees *Letters TX* 214, We found a foot-adz. With this we dug a grave. **1908** *DN* 3.312 **eAL, wGA,** *Foot-adze*. . . Adze. Common. **1915** *DN* 4.183 **swVA,** *Foot-adze.* **1937** *Hall Coll.* **eTN,** Foot adze, or adze, made puncheon floors smooth. **1938** Stuart *Dark Hills* 248 **neKY,** I went out and took a broad ax, a couple of picks, a shovel and a foot-adz to the Hill Graveyard. **1952** Brown *NC Folkl.* 1.542, *Foot-adz.* **1956** Knipmeyer *Settlement Succession* 155 **LA,** The traditional tools are a hatchet, *arminette* (foot adze), . . "tee" (hand adze). . . The *arminette* is the regular long-handled adze with a straight blade. **1965–68** *DARE* FW Addit **cnOK,** Foot adz [æǰ]; **TN**26, ['fʊt ˌæd]. **1966–70** *DARE* (Qu. L35, *Hand tools used for cutting underbrush and digging out roots*) Infs **ID**1, **WA**8, **WV**7, Foot adz; **CO**47, Foot adz—has a hammer beater that you could drive a spike with on one end, a flat-bladed ax on the other end; also used for squaring timber; (Qu. L40) Inf **TN**62, Foot adz.

foot-and-a-half n [*EDD Suppl. foot-and-hawve*] *old-fash* Cf **half-over**

A children's game similar to leapfrog; see quots.

1901 *DN* 2.140 **NH,** *Foot-and-a-half.* . . The name of a game somewhat like Spanish fly. . . The player over whom the others leap is called the block. **1908** *DN* 3.312 **eAL, wGA,** *Foot and a half.* . . A jumping game. The players jump over the one who is 'down,' as in leap-frog, the difference being the length of the leap, as the game progresses. **1957** *Sat. Eve. Post Letters* **West coast,** Foot and a Half—A leap frog game—where leader leaps over a boys back—each time increasing distance to be cleared by a foot and a half—those failing drop out. *Ibid* **GA,** We had a game called "foot and a half". . . The player jumping the farthest became the "setter;" the one jumping the shortest distance, toed the base line and assumed a fore-and-aft position with his elbows on his knees. Then the "setter" from a running start leaped over the back of the bowed player. . . The bowed player then moved forward to the spot where the "setter" landed. . . The "setter" then named the number of jumps allowed. *Ibid* **NE,** Foot and a half.

foot and rail adv

Completely; lock, stock, and barrel.

1967 *DARE* (Qu. LL25, *"He sold out the whole place, ______."*) Inf **TN**12, Foot and rail.

foot-a-night n [In ref to its fast growth] Cf **yard-a-night**

A fast-growing plant such as **kudzu.**

1966–69 *DARE* (Qu. S21, . . *Weeds*) Inf **KY**53, Foot-a-night—because of their phenomenal growth rate; (Qu. K14, *Milk that has a taste from something the cow ate*) Inf **AL**3, Bitter, [as if from] grape vines, or kudzu vines, or foot-a-night. **1966** *DARE* Tape **AL**1, [FW:] It looks like a type of ivy that . . might cover all the trees. [Inf:] Oh, that's got two names. I never did know the right name for that. . . My mama always called it foot-a-night. Arkansas traveler and foot-a-night.

foot around v phr [Prob from *footer* or *footle;* cf **footy** adj]

To waste time.

1894 *DN* 1.330 **NEng,** "Footin around" . . [fut] = fussing, busying one's self uselessly. **1961** Hamner *Spencer's Mt.* 34 **VA,** "He's ready," chuckled Percy Cook "He's tired of footen around."

footback adv Also adv phr *on footback, by* ~ [By facetious analogy with *horseback; OED* 1589–1630] **esp S Midl**

On foot.

1899 (1912) Green *VA Folk-Speech* 182, *Footback.* . . On foot. **1939** FWP *Guide TN* 212, Rivertown people . . poured into Memphis by train, truck, rescue boat, and "footback". **1941** *Hench Coll.* **VA,** I went horseback but John went footback. **1952** Brown *NC Folkl.* 1.542, *Footback.* . . In jocular phrase: *on footback;* to walk. **1966–67** *DARE* (Qu. Y24, . . *"I can't get a ride, so I'll just have to ______."*) Infs **TN**23, **TX**32, Go footback; **OK**42, Go on footback.

football n

1 also *college football:* A dance step. *among Black speakers*

1970 *DARE* (Qu. FF5b, *Recent dance steps*) Infs **AL**60, 62, **IL**140, **MO**23, 30, **OH**103, **VA**39C, **WV**21, Football; **MO**30, College football. [All Infs Black] **1977** Smitherman *Talkin* 256 [Black], The names of most popular dances, from roughly 1950 to the present: . . *football* [etc].

2 A marble game; see quot.

1973 Ferretti *Marble Book* 102 **NYC,** *Football*—In this marbles game . . a football shape is drawn in the dirt, with a line connecting the two ends. Each player puts a marble on that line. Players attempt to knock the marbles off the line and out of the football. The game ends when all of the marbles are knocked out.

‡footboard n

A baseboard.

1969 *DARE* (Qu. D37, *The strip of wood about eight inches high along the bottom of the wall . . joining to the floor*) Inf **IL**102, Footboard.

foot burner n Also *foot warmer* **West** *joc* Cf **heel burner**

A **walking plow.**

1941 Writers' Program *Guide WA* 63, For ploughing, the farmer had only his back, his "foot-burner" (as the old-fashioned shallow plough was called), and his mules and oxen. **1958** *AmSp* 33.269 **eWA,** *Foot burner.* A walking plow, or single-bottom plow. **1967** *DARE* (Qu. L18, *Kinds of plows*) Inf **WY**1, A walking plow—a foot burner; **CO**19, A foot warmer.

foot comforter n

A padded slipper.

1967 *DARE* (Qu. W21, *Soft shoes that people wear only inside the house*) Inf **TX**9, Foot comforters—soft cloth, with padded soles.

foot, cut one's See **cut one's foot**

footed, well ppl adj phr [Var of *well heeled*]

1968 *DARE* (Qu. U37, . . *Somebody who has plenty of money*) Inf **LA**40, Well footed. [FW: Phrase also used in conversation]

footen See **footing**

‡footermans adv

On foot.

[**1968** Adams *Western Words* 118, *Footermans*—A term sometimes used by Wyoming cowboys for men afoot.] **1971** Jennings *Cowboys* 219 **MT,** Being as how no cowman would go footermans to heaven or to hell, the man and boy swung up on strange horses, and rode off together.

foot evil n Also *foot ill*

1 A disease affecting the feet of livestock. **esp Sth, S Midl**

1845 Frémont *Rept. Rocky Mts.* 259 **sCA,** Many animals are destroyed . . by a disease called the foot evil. **1870** IL Dept. Ag. *Trans. for 1868* 7.144, The disease known to stock-growers [*DARE* Ed: prob those in Texas] as foot-evil, or foules, to which our native cattle are occasionally liable. **1966–70** *DARE* (Qu. K28, . . *Diseases that cows have*) Inf **LA**8, Foot evil; **WV**13, Foot evil—get something between the two parts of the hoof; **VA**24, Foot ill; (Qu. K47, . . *Diseases . . [of] horses or mules*) Infs **AR**18, **TX**35, Foot evil; **MS**87, Foot evil—if the horse's hoof comes off.

2 Transf: see quot. *joc*

1938 *AmSp* 13.5 **seAR,** 'I have the foot-evil.' That is, my feet are tired.

footfeed n Pronc-sp *footfeet* [By analogy with earlier *handfeed*]

The accelerator of a car.

1966 *DARE* FW Addit **OK**27, *Footfeed*—accelerator in a car. **1972** McCormick *Vocab. HI* 71, *Footfeet.* . . Car accelerator. **1986** Pederson *LAGS Concordance* 2 infs, **neGA, csTX,** Footfeed. **1987** *DARE* File **seWI,** My parents called a car accelerator the footfeed; **csWI,** My father, who spoke German quite a bit, called the gas pedal the footfeet. *Ibid* **neKS,** My father and both his brothers said "footfeet" for gas pedal. They said "feet" not "feed."

footfree adj

Not tied down; footloose.

1837 Irving *Rocky Mts.* 1.36 **MO,** When a horse that is "foot free," is tied to one thus secured, the latter forms . . a pivot, round which the other runs . . in case of alarm. **1899** (1912) Green *VA Folk-Speech* 182, I am foot-free and can go where I please. **1920** Lewis *Main Street* 312, You used to be a pretty good sport yourself, when you were foot-free. **1969** *DARE* (Qu. KK60, *Having nothing in particular to do: "I'd just as soon go with you this afternoon—I'm ______ anyway."*) Inf **KY**11, Footfree.

foothill ash n

An ash (here: *Fraxinus dipetala*).

1925 Jepson *Manual Plants CA* 759, *Foothill Ash.* Shrub 5 to 15 ft. high. **1961** Thomas *Flora Santa Cruz* 271, **cwCA,** Foothill . . Ash. Dry slopes and hillsides in the vicinity of Uvas and Llagas Creeks.

foothills pine See **foothills yellow pine**

foothills snowdrops n
A **popcorn flower** (here: *Plagiobothrys nothofulvus*).
1961 Thomas *Flora Santa Cruz* 293 **cwCA,** *P. nothofulvus*. . . Foothills Snowdrops, Rusty Popcorn Flower. A common annual of grassy fields and slopes, San Francisco southward.

foothills yellow pine n Also *foothills pine*
=**ponderosa pine.**
1897 Sudworth *Arborescent Flora* 20, *Pinus ponderosa*, Bull Pine. . . Common Names. . . Foothills Yellow Pine *(P. Benthamiana)*. **1908** Britton *N. Amer. Trees* 27, It [=*Pinus ponderosa*] is also called . . Foothills pine.

foothold n Also, by folk-etym, *foothole* *old-fash* Also called **tip, toe rubber**
A light rubber overshoe which protects the toe and sole and is held in place by a strap around the heel.
1889 *Century Dict.* 2311, *Foothold*. . . A kind of light india-rubber overshoe, leaving the heel unprotected; a sandal. Sometimes called *tip.* **1914** Sears *Catalogue* 377, Profile. First Quality. Women's Foothold. **1950** *WELS (Kinds of rubber footwear)* 1 Inf, **cWI,** Footholds protect the sole, with straps fitting over the heel to hold them in place. **1979** *DARE* File **cnMA** (as of c1915), In the spring after the snow had gone but the streets were still muddy my grandmother used to wear footholes, which covered only the front part of her foot. A rubber strap slipped around her heel.

footie See **footy** adj

foot ill See **foot evil**

footing n Also *feeting, footen, footin* **esp NEast** *old-fash*
A stocking, sock.
c1850 in 1950 *WELS Suppl.* **csWI,** Footing [=stocking]. **1850** NH Hist. Soc. *Coll.* 6.221, The knitting of sale feetings has, with many females, superseded the braiding of straw. **1890** *Harper's New Mth. Mag.* 82.146/2 **seCT,** I had some o' the old blue feetin' layin' on my stockin' basket's if they was waitin' to be darned. **1894** *Century Illustr. Mag.* 47.855, In parts of New Hampshire the women speak of "selling feeting," that is, of disposing of the stockings they have knitted. **1914** *DN* 4.72 **ME, nNH,** *Footins*. . . Heavy, thick stockings. **1963** Adamson *Household Hints* 118 **NEng** (as of late 1800s), If the toes of the footings and woolen stockings feel stiff, they were not washed clean. **1977** Neal *KY Shakers* 5 **NY** (as of 1805), He suffered from frozen "footens" or socks and from shoes that were too small.

footing up See **foot up 1a**

foot it See **foot** intj

foot itch n Cf **dew poison, toe itch**
1954 *PADS* 21.25 **SC,** *Dew poison*. . . Ringworm on the feet, especially on the toes; athlete's foot; an infection caused by hookworm. . . In the PeeDee this is called *foot itch.*

foot jelly n Also called **toe jam**
1968 *DARE* FW Addit **cnFL,** [Heard from nurse's aide:] Foot jelly—the gummy substance that forms under and between the toes when feet go unwashed for a long time.

foot juice n [From the former custom of crushing grapes with the feet]
1967–70 *DARE* (Qu. DD27, . . *Nicknames . . for wine*) Infs **CA**15, 197, Foot juice.

footkisser n Also *footlicker* **Sth** Cf **ass-licker 1, bootkisser**
One who curries favor.
1966–70 *DARE* (Qu. II20a, *A person who tries too hard to gain somebody else's favor: "He's an awful ______."*) Infs **GA**12, **TX**79, 86, Footkisser; **SC**40, Footlicker; (Qu. JJ3b, *When a school child makes a special effort to 'get in good' with the teacher*) Inf **SC**40, Footlicker.

footkissing n Cf **blessing**
1967 *DARE* (Qu. II27, *If somebody gives you a very sharp scolding, you might say, "I certainly got a ______ for that."*) Inf **SC**65, Cussing out; footkissing; blessing out.

footless adj
1 See quot. [Scots *fitless* (var of *footless*) unsteady on the feet]
1968 *DARE* (Qu. DD15, *A person who is thoroughly drunk*) Inf **NJ**6, Stoned; stupefied; footless.
2 Futile, unrewarding.
1896 *DN* 1.417 **MA, cNY,** *Footless:* fruitless, unavailing. **1908** (1911) Gale *Friendship Village* 39 **WI,** "Life looks dreadful footless to me," she said.

footlicker See **footkisser**

footling ppl adj Cf **footy** adj **1**
Insignificant, small; measly.
1895 *DN* 1.382 **NJ,** *Footlin':* [small, insignificant]. **1969** *DARE* (Qu. LL2, . . *Too small to be worth much: "I don't want that little ______ potato."*) Inf **NJ**57, Footling ['fudlın].

foot-lock n [Folk-etym]
Fetlock.
1767 in 1917 Essex Inst. *Coll.* 53.135 **neMA,** Stray'd or stollen . . , a Bay Mare . . lame in the off Foot, about the Foot-lock Joint. **1899** (1912) Green *VA Folk-Speech* 182, *Foot-lock*. . . Tuft of hair growing beneath the pastern-joint of horses.

footlog n **chiefly Sth, S Midl**
A log serving as a footbridge.
1843 (1973) Porter *Big Bear AR* 130 **MS,** I husseled off to the hossin-gum and Jem to the foot log. **1873** Beadle *Undeveloped West* 446 **csCO,** An important bridge has been washed away, leaving only a foot-log, on which the passengers cross. **1883** Zeigler–Grosscup *Heart of Alleghanies* 292 **wNC,** Where the road comes down to its fords under the concealing chestnuts and oaks, long foot-logs reach from bank to bank. **1901** Harben *Westerfelt* 23 **nGA,** Sally fell off'n the foot-log into the creek this mornin' an' was drowned. **1948** Faulkner *Intruder* 5 **MS,** Halfway over the footlog . . all of a sudden the known familiar sunny winter earth was upside down. **1950** *PADS* 14.30 **SC. 1960** Criswell *Resp. to PADS 20* **Ozarks,** Foot-log. . . Usually a fallen tree that fell in the right place. Once universal, not nearly so common now. **c1960** *Wilson Coll.* **csKY,** *Footlog*. . . A log, hewn or not, across a stream to accommodate pedestrians. **1965** *Hall Coll.* **wNC,** The preacher, he tuck off and he run out there and started to cross the foot log, and he missed the foot log, he was runnin' so fast, and he run through the creek. **1966** *DARE* (QR, near Qu. EE36) Inf **OK**42, Footlog—a log used for a bridge.

footmat n
=**footstool 3.**
1966–70 *DARE* (Qu. II34, *If you think somebody is trying to use you to his advantage: "I'm not going to be his ______."*) Infs **NC**4, **VA**69, Footmat.

footmobile n *joc* Cf **ankle express, footback**
The feet.
1967–70 *DARE* (Qu. Y24, . . *"I can't get a ride, so I'll just have to ______."*) Infs **MO**29, **NY**240, Use my footmobile; **HI**7, Go on my footmobile.

footmop n
1902 *DN* 2.234 **sIL,** *Foot-mop*. . . Door-mat.

‡foot-off-and-foot-on n
A children's game.
1969 *DARE* (Qu. EE33, . . *Outdoor games*) Inf **NJ**55, Foot-off-and-foot-on.

foot-pie [From its shape; cf *EDD foot* sb. 6 "A closed tart or pie"]
1944 *PADS* 2.34 **cNC,** *Foot-pie*. . . An apple turnover (pastry).

foot rag n
A sock.
1961 Adams *Old-Time Cowhand* 73, A cowhand was mighty careful of his feet. . . His foot rags might not be much more'n a chinstrap to keep 'em from climbin' up his legs, but he tried to keep 'em clean.

foots See **foot** n **B2a(1), b(2)**

foot's horse n Cf **shank's mare,** *DS* Y24
The feet.
1883 *Harper's New Mth. Mag.* 66.946/1 **NYC,** The privilege of taking this trip on "foot's horse."

footsie n
A soft slipper.
1968 *DARE* (Qu. W21, *Soft shoes that people wear only inside the house*) Inf **PA**167, Footsies—made of terry cloth.

footsies exclam

In marble play: see quot.

1963 *KY Folkl. Rec.* 9.3.65, *Permission to kick the shooter to a more desirable destination when the shooter has been stopped by another player's foot:* footsies: Greenup [Co.]

foot slipper n

1952 Brown *NC Folkl.* 1.542, *Foot-slipper. . .* A slipper, a light shoe.—West[ern NC].

footsteps-of-spring n **esp CA**

A **sanicle** (here: *Sanicula arctopoides*).

1925 Jepson *Manual Plants CA* 698, *Footsteps-of-Spring. . .* Prostrate or decumbent, the plants 4 to 8 in. broad. **1954** CA Div. Beaches & Parks *Pt. Lobos Wild Flowers* 15 **cwCA,** Footsteps-of-spring compensates for its lack of pleasant aroma by adding attractive yellow splotches to the green grass of early March. **1961** Thomas *Flora Santa Cruz* 256 **cwCA,** Footsteps-of-Spring, . . Bear's Foot Sanicle. Open grassy slopes, windswept summits of coastal hills, and coastal bluffs. **1973** Hitchcock-Cronquist *Flora Pacific NW* 337.

foot stick n

A board set up at the foot of a grave.

c1938 [see **head stick**].

footstool n

1 The earth. [Isaiah 66:1] *old-fash*

1821 Dwight *Trav. New Eng.* (1823) III. 231 *(OEDS),* We felt a total superiority to all the humble beings who were creeping on the footstool beneath us. **1874** in 1917 Twain *Letters* 1.215, If there is one individual creature on all this footstool who is more thoroughly and uniformly and unceasingly *happy* than I am I defy the world to produce him. **1891** *Boston* (Mass.) *Jrnl.* 12 Sept. 5/1 *(OED),* I found Mauchline to be the most God-forsaken place on the footstool. **1906** *N.Y. Globe* 20 Feb. 8 *(OEDS),* This New York of ours, regarded by many the wickedest city on the footstool.

2 =**devil's footstool.**

1968-69 *DARE* (Qu. S18, *A kind of mushroom that grows like a globe . . sometimes . . as big as a man's head*) Infs **KY**18, **MD**4, **WI**70, Footstool(s).

3 Fig: a stooge, dupe. Also called **floormat 1, footmat, foot wiper** Cf **flunky 2**

1965-70 *DARE* (Qu. II34, *If you think somebody is trying to use you to his advantage: "I'm not going to be his ______.")* 26 Infs, **chiefly Sth, West,** Footstool. [11 of 26 Infs Black]

foot tub n **chiefly Sth**

A small tub, footbath.

1835 Haliburton *Clockmaker* 88 (*AmSp* 22.202), Afore me stood a china utensil with two handles, full of soup, about the size of a foot-tub. **1954** Armstrong *Satchmo* 234 **LA** (as of c1910), We used to take baths in the clothes washtub in the back yard, or else a foot tub. **1966** *DARE* (Qu. F31) Inf **NC**8, Foot tub—a wide, low bucket. Old-fashioned. **1967** *DARE* FW Addit **cLA,** *Foot tub*—a galvanized vessel between a water bucket and a washtub in size, which holds about three water buckets of water. The Inf said that the "right" name is *utility tub*—a term he read in a mail-order catalog. **1967** LeCompte *Word Atlas* 137 **seLA,** *Metal vessel for water . .* [1 of 21 infs] foot tub. [Footnote:] The "foot tub," the small #1 size tub, is often used as a bucket in this area. **1986** Pederson *LAGS Concordance,* 20 infs, **Gulf Region,** Foot tub.

foot up v phr

1a tr: To add up (an accounting), sum up; hence vbl n *footing up* accounting; also fig.

1828 Cooper *Prairie* 2.223, It is time to foot up the small reckoning, that has been running on for some time atwixt us. **1883** *Harper's New Mth. Mag.* 66.893/2 **NEast,** [He] was doing a little sum in social arithmetic. He was footing me up, as it were. **1906** *Eve. Post* (NY NY) 17 Nov 4/2, Some of the Russian newspapers observed . . the anniversary . . by footing up for the year the terrible roll of deaths by violence. **1907** Twain *Chr. Sci.* 259, We may now make a final footing-up of Mrs. Eddy, and see what she is.

b intr: To add up, come to a correct total; to amount to.

1854 'O. Optic' *In Doors & Out* (1876) 49 *(DAE),* Every thing foots up without the variation of a penny. **1861** (1955) Holmes *Brokenburn* 53 **LA,** As pork foots up $35 per barrel, the stealing is trying. **1861** *Chicago Daily Tribune* (IL) 19 July 1/2 **DC,** The value of those already received foots up over $25,000. **1883** Sala *Amer. Revisited* 2.86 **New Orleans,** I apprehend that his board-bill . . will "foot up" to something considerable. **1897** Twain *Following Equator* 145, Do you know what our crop is going to foot up? **1901** Roberts *Adrift America* 234 *(DAE),* Stowaways . . were turning up out of all sorts of holes and corners . . until they footed up a total of 17.

2 In seine fishing: see quot.

1964 Will *Hist. Okeechobee* 121 **FL,** If it [=the cork] submerged, it meant that the net was "bogged," hung up on grass or rocks. Then somebody would have to "foot it up," which meant to get it unsnagged while keeping the lead line down to prevent fish from escaping underneath.

foot warmer See **foot burner**

footwasher n

1 =**foot-washing Baptist.**

1954 *Harder Coll.* **cwTN,** *Foot-washers. . .* Nickname for "Old" Baptists. **1966-70** *DARE* (Qu. CC4) Infs **GA**11, 74, **IN**10, Footwashers.

2 =**footkisser.**

1954 *Harder Coll.* **cwTN,** *Foot-washer . .* asslicker.

foot washing n Also rarely *feet washing* **chiefly S Midl**

A rite in which church members, esp Primitive Baptists, wash one another's feet (in obedience to the Biblical injunction at John 13:14).

1905 *DN* 3.79 **nwAR,** *Foot-washing. . .* A religious ceremony practised by certain Baptist sects. 'Are you going to the foot-washing at Springdale?' Common. **1935** *AmSp* 10.36 **KY,** They sang *foot-washin'* hymns. **1937** [see **fifth-Sunday meeting**]. **1943** *Natl. Geogr. Mag.* 84.768/1 **sAppalachians,** One of the most interesting services is the "foot washin' " of the Primitive Baptists. This ceremony takes place once a year. **1945** *Harder Coll.* **cwTN,** [Letter:] Guess I'll have to go to foot-washing Sunday. **1947** *AmSp* 22.73 **IA,** Another unusual practice [among Mennonites] is the 'feet-washing' which concludes the communion service. **1953** Randolph-Wilson *Down in Holler* 245 **Ozarks,** *Foot-washing. . .* People take off their shoes and stockings, and wash each other's feet right in the church house. This is widely practiced by many of the Pentecostal sects, and by some backwoods Baptists. **c1960** *Wilson Coll.* **csKY,** *Foot-washing. . .* A religious rite among certain faiths, as the Primitive Baptists. **1982** *Foxfire 7* 39 **wNC,** We had some modern preachers that objected to a foot-washing church being taken into the Association.

foot-washing Baptist n **Sth, S Midl**

A member of a Baptist sect that practices **foot washing.**

1872 U.S. Congress *Congressional Globe* 42d Cong 2d Sess 30 May app 45.6.478/3 **nwGA,** I belong now to the Foot-Washing Baptists—the simplest form of the Christian faith. **1886** Amer. Philol. Assoc. *Trans.* 17.38 **eTN,** I heard . . a "foot-washing" Baptist preacher . . say, "Stone is the most *lastiest* . . material there is." **1949** Marshall *Little Squire Jim* 59 **cnNC,** Thag Totten . . was a church man, a Foot-washing Baptist, and a man of deep convictions. **1953** Brewer *Word Brazos* 34 **eTX** [Black], He de pastuh of de onlies' Foot Washin' Baptis' chu'ch in de Bottoms. **1966-70** *DARE* (Qu. CC4, . . *Nicknames . . for . . religious groups*) Infs **AL**10, 27, **GA**12, **KY**74, 76, **MS**33, **NC**36, **SC**28, 31, 39, 46, 58, **TX**18, Foot-washing Baptists; **GA**13, Foot-washing Baptists—meet once a year and wash their feet; [**TN**53, Footwash—said of Baptists].

foot-whack v

To run noisily.

1933 Williamson *Woods Colt* 236 **Ozarks,** Morgan gits in the lead an' goes foot-whackin' up the holler.

foot wharf n

A small wharf or dock.

1968 *DARE* (Qu. O3, *A small platform sticking out into the water where boats can tie up*) Inf **MD**13, A small one can be called a foot wharf.

foot wiper n

=**footstool 3.**

1942 Berrey-Van den Bark *Amer. Slang* 404.2, Foot-wiper . . *a submissive or downtrodden person.* **1969** *DARE* (Qu. II34, *If you think somebody is trying to use you to his advantage: "I'm not going to be his ______.")* Inf **NY**184, Foot wiper.

footy adj Also sp *footie, fouty* [*OED* 1752 →; "*dial.* and *colloq.*"; *SND* (at *foutie*) 1722 →. Prob ult from Fr *foutre* copulate] *old-fash*

1 Paltry, insignificant.

1870 *Nation* 11.57/1 **sePA,** A "fouty" thing was a trifling thing. **1894** *DN* 1.330 **NJ,** *Footy:* small, insignificant. **1929** Ellis *Ordinary Woman* 135 **CO,** At Christmas time he sent me a rose-colored velvet workbox, fitted with 'footie' tools, which bent at the slightest excuse.

2 Foolish, simple-minded.

1909 *DN* 3.420 **Cape Cod MA** (as of a1857), *Footy*. . . Simple-minded; lacking in judgment. **1940** *Qrly. Jrl. Speech* 26.265 **nwVA,** A *foolish thing* is "footy". **1941** *LANE* Map 464 (Awkward person, lummox) 4 infs, **MA, RI,** Footy-head. **1942** Berrey-Van den Bark *Amer. Slang* 152.5, *Insane; crazy* . . footy.

footy n Also sp *fouty* **NEng** *old-fash*

A **footy** thing or person.

1877 Bartlett *Americanisms* 230, *Footy, Fouty.* A mistake; a simpleton; a blunderer; any one slightly valued. Local in Massachusetts. **1889** *Century Dict.* 2313, *Footy*. . . Any one or anything slightly valued. . . Local, New Eng. **1894** *DN* 1.330 **ME,** *Footy* . . simpleton.

foozle v

To mess up, bungle, botch; to make an error.

1836 (1838) Haliburton *Clockmaker* (1st ser) 189, Do for gracious sake behave yourself; . . if you hav'n't foozled all my hair too, that's a fact, says she; and she put her curls to rights. **1922** (1926) Cady *Rhymes VT* 216, He seldom foozled, flunked or failed. **1942** Berrey-Van den Bark *Amer. Slang* 258.5, *Bungle; botch* . . foozle. *Ibid* 711.8, *Make a bad shot* [in golf] . . foozle. **1960** Wentworth-Flexner *Slang, Foozle* . . To entangle; to blunder or bungle; to make an error. . . *Still in use.* **1960** Bailey *Resp. to PADS 20* **KS,** Mr. Mencken said publishers are stupid, but that if I'd keep on sending the manuscript out I'd find a publisher who would not foozle it.

foozle n Also *fuzzle*

An old fogy.

1855 Thomson *Doesticks* 257 **NY,** One of the old foozles now wanted to talk spirit. **1898** Westcott *Harum* 247 **NY,** He was a slow, putterin' kind of an ole foozle, but on the hull a putty decent citizen. **1942** Berrey-Van den Bark *Amer. Slang* 409.1, *Stable or conservative person* . . die-hard, (old) dodo, . . (old) foozle . . (old) stick-in-the-mud. **1967** *DARE* (Qu. HH40, *Uncomplimentary words for an old man*) Inf **CA**15A, Fuzzle.

fop n **chiefly Nth**

A dandy, dude; a finicky man; hence adj *foppish.*

1950 *WELS (When a man puts on his good clothes and tries to look his best, you say he's ——)* 2 Infs, **WI,** Fop; *(A person who enjoys dressing up, or who spends too much on clothes)* 1 Inf, **csWI,** Foppish. **1966-70** *DARE* (Qu. AA6a, . . *A man who is fond of being with women and tries to attract their attention*) Inf **CA**4, Fop; (Qu. HH2, . . *A citified person*) Infs **MI**65, **NY**69, 232, **PA**234, Fop; (Qu. HH11a, . . *Too particular or fussy . . a man*) Infs **CA**24, **MA**58, **MS**8, **NY**145, **NC**30, Fop; (Qu. HH38, *A womanish man*) Infs **CA**4, **IA**5, **MI**51, **NY**60, **OR**4, **WA**13, Fop; **NJ**43, Foppish; (Qu. W41) Inf **NY**107, Foppish.

fop v

To dip or splash.

1943 Chase *Jack Tales* 79 **wNC,** Then that cat fopped its foot right smack in Jack's gravy, says, "Stop! Doll-ll-ll!"

fo pah, fo par, fo paws See **faux pas** n

foppish See **fop** n

for prep Usu stressed |fɔr, for, fɔ(ə)|, unstressed |fɚ, fə|; for addit varr see **A** below Pronc-spp *faw, fer, fo, fo(a)h, fuh, fur, f'r*

A Forms.

1848 Lowell *Biglow* 144 **'Upcountry' MA,** *Fer,* for. **1888** Jones *Negro Myths* 2 **GA coast,** Bimeby de fire, eh biggin fuh roll. **1889** Edwards *Runaways* 210 **GA,** Ef't had n' be'n fur sorryin' fur ther critter, I'd er busted wide open. **1890** *DN* 1.67 **KY,** *For* [fɔə]: sometimes [fə]. **1899** Garland *Boy Life* 159 **nwIA** (as of c1870s), I'll knock the everlasting spots offen 'im f'r two cents. **1914** *DN* 4.160 **cVA,** Thank yo' foah some damsons! **1923** *DN* 5.206 **swMO,** *Fer*. . . For. **1927** Shewmake *Engl. Pronc. VA* 41, *For it.* Some speakers would sound *r* . . ; others would say *faw it.* **1928** Peterkin *Scarlet Sister Mary* 153 **eSC,** Is dey anything I can do fo you? **1930** *AmSp* 5.353 **Philadelphia PA,** The sound is [oəɹ], first element very short, in *floor, board, order, course, for, morning.* **1940** *Sat. Eve. Post* 20 July 55/2 **GA,** Could I make private talk with you fo' just a minute? **1941** *AmSp* 16.6 **eTX** [Black], *For* is [fʌ:]. **1942** Hall *Smoky Mt. Speech* 34, As pronounced by older people, *for* is almost always [fɚ] stressed, [fɚ] unstressed; many younger people say [fɔɚ], [fɔɚ], [fɚ] unstressed. **c1960** *Wilson Coll.* **csKY,** *For* . . emphatic [fɚ], slurred [fə]. **1965** Carmony *Speech Terre Haute* 79, In the speech of some informants, such pairs as *horse* and *barn, for* and *far* occur with the same allophone, the slightly rounded [ɒ]. **1968** *DARE* FW Addit **New Orleans LA,** Aah, you don't even know what it's for [fʌ]; **NY**88, Usually [fɔɚ]; occasionally [fɜ] when stressed, [fɚ] when unstressed. **1969** Emmons *Deep Rivers* 101 **eTX** [Black], Her report of the candidates for baptism was always so many "foh de water."

B Gram functions.

1 Used with *to* to mark the infinitive in:

a An adverbial purpose clause. [*OED for* prep. 11. a "Now *arch.* or *vulgar*"; a1175-1774]

1637 (1972) Morton *New Engl. Canaan* 43, Many of them would begge Salte of mee for to carry home with them. **1813** (1940) Hartsell *Memora* 12.120 **TN,** Ther Came aney Express from General Jackson to General Cock for to reinforce his armey. **1845** Thompson *Pineville* 121 **GA,** This court's got as good ears as any man, but they aint for to hear no old woman's gabblement. **1893** Shands *MS Speech* 30, *For* [fə]. This preposition is still largely used by illiterate whites before an infinitive of purpose. "They say he went for to see." **1908** *DN* 3.312 **eAL, wGA,** "What did you come here for to do?" Common among the illiterate. **1915** *DN* 4.226 **wTX,** *For to do* . . still common. **1943** *LANE* Map 572, In the context *He came over to tell me about it* [*for to tell* occurs sporadically throughout New England but is most common in Maine and New Hampshire]. **1953** Atwood *Survey of Verb Forms* 34, *For to tell* occurs in all major portions of the M[iddle] A[tlantic] S[tates]. . . It is least frequent in e.N.Y. and most frequent in W. Va. . . In the S[outh] A[tlantic] S[tates] as far south as N.C. *for to tell* is used . . [frequently]. In S.C. and Ga. it is recorded much less frequently. **1960** Criswell *Resp. to PADS 20* **Ozarks,** *For to* . . in order to. Heard rarely fifty years ago, now probably extinct in this section. **1966** *DARE* (Qu. L43, *When somebody is going to get horses ready to work, he might say, "I'll —— the horses."*) Inf **SC**26, You mean for to work? Gear the horses up. **1966-70** *DARE* Tape **AL**14, You come an' hired me fer to pick cotton; **AK**8, That was for to have the oil for the river boats; **LA**8, Whatever it need on this tractor for to farm with, they have it; **MI**21, A tug came up here . . for to do some summer fishing; **NC**1, We had to take that net out the water an' . . spread it for to dry it; **VA**25, This room . . was built for to raise silkworms; **VA**40, That would be there until we get ready for to transplant; **VA**43, Don't have time enough for to grow a crop; **VA**52, For to keep her from knowing I had the gun, I took it apart. **1975** Allen *LAUM* 2.45 (as of c1950), The older *for to tell* is a minor old-fashioned variant in New England and New York but more common in the Middle Atlantic states and still viable in the North Central Atlas region. . . [But] only 11 U[pper] M[idwest] speakers have *for to tell,* nearly all in Minnesota.

b Other infinitival functions. [*OED for* prep. 11. b "*Obs.* in educated use"; a1225-1674]

1795 Dearborn *Columbian Grammar* 135, *List of Improprieties*. . . For to for To. **1838** (1843) Haliburton *Clockmaker* (2d ser) 305 **NEng,** If you go for to raise your voice at him, . . his Ebenezer is up in a minit'. **1845** Thompson *Pineville* 75 **cGA,** And then for to go and take Pete Hopkins's word all about it! **1899** Chesnutt *Conjure Woman* 20 **csNC,** She mought be able fer ter take de goopher [=conjuration] off'n him. **1931** *AmSp* 7.19 **swPA,** Sarah never liked for to have Jane wear mourning. **1961** *Mt. Life* Fall 9 **sAppalachians,** Ye jist might as well fer to set down an' set thar. **1966** *DARE* Tape **SD**8, The only way to straighten you out is for to git in your car. **1970** *DARE* (Qu. JJ30a) Inf **IL**141, I got for to do that.

2 Used instead of *to* to mark the infinitive. [This use is found in some Engl dial, but has prob been infl by one or more African languages; cf **fuh.** It is common in English-based creoles; cf *DJE fi*[3], *DBE for.*] *esp freq in Gullah, but also HI creole*

a In an adverbial purpose clause.

1829 Tenney *Female Quixotism* 2.84 **Philadelphia PA** [Black], Let me make noise fuss, for fright away ghos. **1838** [see **2b** below]. **1951** *AmSp* 26.15, From Negroes—whether the form is in origin an Africanism or a relic of early English usage—many white folk speakers along the South Carolina coast have taken *for* as the particle with the infinitive of purpose, as *he come for tell you* rather than the standard *to* or the widespread folk form *for to.* **1953** Atwood *Survey of Verb Forms* 34, Two Negro informants in coastal S.C. and one in coastal Ga. use the abbreviated *for tell.* **1966-68** *DARE* (Qu. AA4a) Inf **SC**10, Anxious for marry; (Qu. NN12a, . . *To put a child off when he asks too many questions: "What's that for?"*) Inf **VA**24, For shut your mouth. **1968** *DARE* FW Addit **MD**38, They use that machine for plant the corn. *Ibid*

Smith Is. MD, This boat is for catch oysters. **1971** Cunningham *Syntactic Analysis Gullah* 181, You got for blow for get through. . . [=] you have to blow to get through.

b In other infinitival functions.

1838 (1852) Gilman *S. Matron* 69 [Gullah], "How you been ax me for sing, Maus Lewis? Me an't got no voice for sing," answered Juba. **1887** (1967) Harris *Free Joe* 89 **cGA** [Black], It make yo' blood run col' fer lissen at 'im. **1922** Gonzales *Black Border* 155 **sSC, GA coasts** [Gullah], Ma tell me fuh git twenty-fibe cent' wut uh flour. **1930** Woofter *Black Yeomanry* 49 **seSC** [Black], Buh Wolf keep on fuh hollah [=Brother Wolf continues to holler]. **1941** Writers' Program SC *Folk Tales* 111, Ain't I tell you fuh leab dat sarpent 'lone? **1970** *AmSp* 45.234 [Hawaiian creole], Ask him for iron my shirt. **1971** [see **2a** above]. **1972** Carr *Da Kine Talk* 130 **HI,** "Dat's his business, fo' talk!" "We don't know what fo' do!"

3 following *like* and similar verbs: Used with the subject of an infinitival object clause. [By ext from the use of *for* to mark the subject of an infinitive clause in other uses: e.g. "it is rare for him to come"] **chiefly Sth, S Midl**

a1883 (1911) Bagby *VA Gentleman* 90, Perhaps you'd like for me to say England. **1904** *DN* 2.419 **nwAR,** I wouldn't like for the boys to use that saw. **1909** *DN* 3.346 **eAL, wGA,** I would like for you to go home with me. **1933** in 1956 Wolfe *Letters* 25 **NC,** I know you intended for me to eat them. **1938** Stuart *Dark Hills* 70 **neKY,** I'd like for you to go ahead. **1941** *AmSp* 16.17, 'They'd like for you to stay to supper' is the habitual idiom for any Southerner in Tennessee, Georgia, Alabama, and probably elsewhere in the South. To be sure, it does not often appear in print, . . but it occurs frequently in student papers, and . . before 1908 in familiar letters written by Southerners and in southern newspapers. **1966** *DARE* Tape **CA**2, I'd like for you to go. **1967–70** *DARE* (Qu. II4, . . *"I'd like . . ——— John Smith."*) Infs **GA**82, **NC**55, **TX**1, For you to meet (*or* know); **GA**30, For you to make me acquainted with; (Qu. OO43a) Inf **NY**10, She begged for me to stay. **1970** *Thompson Coll.* **Sth,** *For*. . . Used between a verb and an infinitive: like for (one) to, . . hate for (one) to, help for (one) to, etc. **1983** *Lutz Coll.,* When I heard classmates at Earlham College (Richmond, Ind.) use it, I thought it was just an error. Then I heard . . [the] head of the Department of English say something like, "I'd like for you to read the next two chapters."

4 Used with an adj or noun:

a To form adv phrr. Note: The following phrr are formed on the same pattern as std *for sure, for good (and all).* [From elliptical uses of *for* "as (being)"; e.g. *for certain* (arch *for a certain*) = "as being a certain thing"]

(1) *for certain:* See **certain B2.**

(2) *for true:* Really, for certain. **Sth**

1803 Davis *Travels* 99 **seSC** [Black], Too mush buckra come here to-day, for true! **1851** Burke *Polly Peablossom* 72 **MS,** The sperit it begin to move um for true. **1872** (1973) Thompson *Major Jones's Courtship* 146 **GA,** I tell you what, it was a live animal show for true. **1888** Jones *Negro Myths* 2 **GA coast,** Eh yeye shet. Eh duh sleep fuh true. [=His eyes are shut. He is sleeping for certain.] **1928** Peterkin *Scarlet Sister Mary* 212 **eSC** [Gullah], I'm heavy fo-true, but I'm well. *Ibid* 287, When a man finds out fo-true a 'oman is crazy bout em, he don' crave dat 'oman no mo. **1978** *DARE* File **New Orleans LA** (as of 1960s), *For true,* usually uttered as an exclamatory question to punctuate another's surprising or shocking remark, was common among Blacks and Whites.

(3) *for good;* In marble play: **=for keeps.** [*EDD for* prep. 1. (19)(b)]

1892 *DN* 1.220 **DC,** *To play for good:* to play for "keeps." **1895** *Searcher* 1.7/2 **CT,** In Connecticut . . we played the game of marbles . . either "for fun" or "for good." We did not use the phrase "for keeps." **1908** *DN* 3.312 **eAL, wGA,** *For keeps.* . . In games of marbles, for good. **1955** *PADS* 23.18 **TN,** *For good.* . . A marble game played in *earnest* [i.e., for keeps].

(4) *for fair:*

(a) Thoroughly, in earnest. [*EDD for* prep. 1. (17); cf **fair** adv **2, 5, fairly** adv **1**]

1900 Flynt & Walton *Powers that Prey* 180 *(OEDS),* They're goin' to railroad him for fair. The *World* says the police found the weapon on him. **1919** Kyne *Capt. Scraggs* 276 **CA,** If us three could get back to San Francisco with clean hands, I'd say lick the beggar an' lick him for fair. **1933** Caldwell *God's Little Acre* 136 **GA,** My white-haired boy is gone for fair. **1936** Morehouse *Rain on Just* 129 **NC,** Before the new moon we'll join with the Squealing Creek folks, and wash out our sins for fair. **1950** *WELS ("He bawled him out for ———.")* 17 Infs, **c,sWI,** Fair. **1957** Kerouac *On Road* 53, Then we danced and started on the beer for fair. **1968–69** *DARE* (Qu. W36, . . *A woman who uses a lot of cosmetics*) Inf **CA**166, Painted up for fair; old-fashioned; (Qu. CC12b, . . *If a person has a lot of bad luck you might say, "He's been ———."*) Inf **NY**43, Up against it for fair.

(b) In marbles play: **=for fun.**

1955 *PADS* 23.18 **TN,** *For fair.* . . A marble game not played in *earnest.* **c1970** Wiersma *Marbles Terms* **swMI,** For fair [4 infs]. **1973** Ferretti *Marble Book* 45, *For fair.* Playing only for the results of the game. All of the marbles won are returned, either to their owner or to the tournament. *Ibid* 138, All tournament play is for fair.

(5) *for common:* For everyday use, as the usual thing. [Scots dial]

1968 Kellner *Aunt Serena* 43 **sIN** (as of c1910), The parlor was never used "for common" but only for company.

(6) *for foolish:* Foolishly, like a fool.

1968 Kellner *Aunt Serena* 135 **sIN** (as of c1910), I'm s'prised your folks let you traipse up and down the road for foolish when you could be home helping out.

(7) *for free:* Without charge.

1942 *Cincinnati Enquirer* (OH) 31 Aug 2/2 *(Hench Coll.),* A hunert bucks' worth of work for free. **1942** *Sat. Eve. Post* 12 Dec 90/2 [Black], Railroads don't haul trash for free. **1943** *Sat. Eve. Post* 20 Feb 30/2, Something ought to be done about people who say "for free" when they mean gratis. **1966** *AmSp* 41.79 **IN,** The pleonastic usage *for free* seems virtually to have supplanted the adverbial use of *free* without a preposition. . . [e.g.] "install water meters in homes for free" . . "working for free" . . "It should really be done for free."

(8) *for soul:* Truly, really. *Gullah*

1922 Gonzales *Black Border* 303 **sSC, GA coasts,** [Gullah glossary], *Fuh sowl*—for truth, truly, used as emphasis; as: "'E fat fuh sowl"—He . . is . . very fat. **1930** Stoney–Shelby *Black Genesis* 73 **seSC** [Gullah], He nyam dem scrap [=ate those scraps] for sowl! (To repletion).

(9) *for real:* Really, for certain.

1950 *Richmond Times-Dispatch* (VA) 2 Nov 1/3 *(Hench Coll.),* That's no backfire. . . That's shooting for real. **1960** Wentworth–Flexner *Slang, For real.* . . Really. **1970** *DARE* (Qu. NN7, *Exclamations of surprise: "They're getting married next week? Well, ———."*) Infs **OH**103, **TN**54, For real! [Both Infs Black]

(10) *for all power:* For all one is worth.

1955 Roberts *S. from Hell-fer-Sartin* 108 **seKY,** And the next thing he lit onto a yearlin'—we call it a bull yearlin'—and it was just a-runnin' for all power.

b To form pleonastic or mildly intensive adj phrr—usu with *certain, sure, true,* and similar adjs. [By ext from phrr of the type illustrated in **4a** above]

1887 *Lantern* (New Orleans LA) 28 May 3/1 (*AmSp* 25.39), When a for-true doctor come to see him. **1937** *Hall Coll.* **wNC, eTN,** I'm not for sure. . . I'm not for certain. **1946** *AmSp* 21.271 **KY,** I think so, but I'm not for sure. **1960** J. Kirkwood *There must be a Pony* (1961) xii. 95 *(OEDS)* **sCA,** A good guy; a movie cop . . ; a for-real cop. **1965** *DARE* FW Addit **FL**18, The kids say, "Are you for real?" **1966** *AmSp* 41.79, You're not for real. **1966** *DARE* (Qu. NN2) Inf **AR**33, That's for certain. **1967** Green *Horse Tradin'* 77 **swTX,** I'm fo sho this is a different one, and I'm goin' tah buy huh. **1987** Rose *I Remember Jazz* 172, If that's for true . . I'm gonna buy you a box of cigars.

c following a pred noun or adj: Exceedingly, very. [From *for* in respect to, with replacement of the following abstract noun by the corresponding adj] Cf **done for** adv phr, **hell n 6**

1932 Randolph *Ozark Mt. Folks* 85, Th' hull thing worked jest like a ol' fashion rabbit gum, only bigger an' hell for stout. **1937** Sandoz *Slogum* 342 **NE,** A new brown car, advance 1932 model, small but hell-for-stout, he said proudly. **1958** McCulloch *Woods Words* 84 **Pacific NW,** *Hell for*—Exceedingly; as, "hell for strong." **1967** *DARE* (Qu. KK1a, . . *Very good . . "That pie was ———."*) Inf **PA**29, Hell for good. **1982** Cazden et al. *Folk Songs Catskills* 15 **NY,** This ain't nice fer purty, but it's hell fer stout. **1986** *NADS Letters* **nwAR,** My maternal grandparents, from Benton County, Arkansas, enjoyed telling about a neighbor of theirs who admiringly said of his wife, "She's not much for pretty, but she's hell for stout!" *Ibid* **swCA,** *For* preceded by an intensifier . . [is] common amongst country people particularly in the Southwest [US] i.e.: "Just built a new corn crib, she aint much for looks but Hell for stout" (strong).

5 Used after *say* and *think* when there is ellipsis of the complement. [Engl dial; perh from *for* 'as regards' with ellipsis of its object; cf "not that I know of" = "not so far as I know about the matter"] **VA**

1899 (1912) Green *VA Folk-Speech* 182, I'm not as old as you think for. **1947** *Hench Coll.* **seVA,** It's much colder than I thought for. This is as lovely a spot as you can think for. **1970** *DARE* FW Addit **VA**50, Smallpox was not catching like they said for.

C Senses.

1 After, in honor of (someone). [*OED for* prep. 7. c "now only *U.S.*"]

[**1800** H. Wells *Const. Neville* I. 7 *(OED),* Louisa . . had been named for the mother of Mr. Hayman.] **1863** Hawthorne *Our Old Home* 20, He had named his two children, one for Her Majesty and the other for Prince Albert. **1938** Damon *Grandma* 7 **CT** (as of late 1800s), My baby brother who had died the year before was named for him. **1941** *LANE* Map 394, [In the context *"We named the child______ his father"* both *after* and *for* are current, but *for* is more common in eastern than in western New England.] **1966** Dakin *Dial. Vocab. Ohio R. Valley* 2.221, *Named for* seems to be decidedly more common among women—despite the fact that *named after* is used more frequently throughout the Valley by a majority of more than two to one. **1971** Bright *Word Geog. CA & NV* 167, [In the context *"We named the child______ him"*] *after* 90% . . *for* 19%. **1975** Allen *LAUM* 2.63 (as of c1950), We named the child *after* him. . . U[pper]M[idwest] speakers in all groups so strongly prefer *after* that here *for* is clearly a receding form.

2 To the disadvantage of—used to indicate the person indirectly affected by some action. [Transl of Ger ethical dative] **chiefly PA**

1907 (1970) Martin *Betrothal* 104 **sePA,** It 's five years back already that he died for me. *Ibid* 107, The mare she got pink eye for me. **1914** *DN* 4.157 **sePA,** An ethical dative is often heard: "Little Thomas ran away for his mother again yesterday." **1931** *AmSp* 7.19 **swPA,** The cow died for me. **1934** *Language* 10.3 **sePA,** A sort of dative of disadvantage is commonly used (preposition *for*): *The baby died for us, Look out the bunny don't run away for you.* **1943** in 1944 *ADD* **neWV,** The horse died for us.

3 With, as regards.

1967 LeCompte *Word Atlas* 335 **seLA,** What's wrong for you? [1 of 21 infs] **1971** Cunningham *Syntactic Analysis Gullah* 39, You know that wouldn't agree for you.

4 Of, concerning.

1934 Smiley *Gloss. New Paltz* **NY,** There is more the matter with me than your mother had any idea for.

5 From.

1946 Stuart *Tales Plum Grove* 196 **seKY,** "I can't keep for worrying," Pa said. "Here I'm down sick and can't get out of bed."

6 in phrr *getting (on) for:* Coming close to, nearly (some specified time). [*OED get* v. 63. j 1861 →]

1940 *Sat. Eve. Post* 10 Feb 88/3 **NY** (as of 1836), It was getting on for twilight. **1954** Forbes *Rainbow* 164 **NEng,** It was getting for ten o'clock. **1979** *New Yorker* 26 Mar 35/1 **NY,** It was getting on for twelve when at last I began the homeward canter.

7 At, by (a specified time). [The LA examples may be infl by Fr use of *pour* to indicate the time of anticipated events. Cf Littré *Dictionnaire* 13.]

1961 *PADS* 36.11 **sLA,** *For eight o'clock* (at eight o'clock) [is used by 50% of infs]. *Ibid* 15, *For eight o'clock* may be a rendering of *pour huit heures.* **1967** LeCompte *Word Atlas* 381 **seLA,** To be at a certain place (at/for) eight o'clock. [7 of 21 infs used *for.*] **1968** *DARE* FW Addit **New Orleans, St Martinville LA,** "Janice said any time was all right so long as you were there for six." "She said she had to be there for six o'clock but she won't be there for six o'clock." **1979** *DARE* File **neWI** (as of 1950s), "I have to go to work for eight." "I'm going to the show for seven." Heard repeatedly.

8 See **what for (a).**

9 See **fore** prep.

for n See **fire**

for a little (bit) adv phr For varr see quot **chiefly S Midl** See Map

For a small amount; in response to a provocation—used to introduce a threat.

1965–70 *DARE* (Qu. JJ35b, *Other expressions . . when you have lost patience and are just about ready to tell somebody what you think of him*) 9 Infs, **chiefly S Midl,** For a little (bit); **FL**28, For a little bit I'd tell him all; **MO**6, For very little; **TN**53, For a damn little; **AR**51, **KY**41, **MO**39, **TN**13, Just for a little; **MO**37, For just a little; **MS**88, For little or nothing; **TX**40, For a little of nothing.

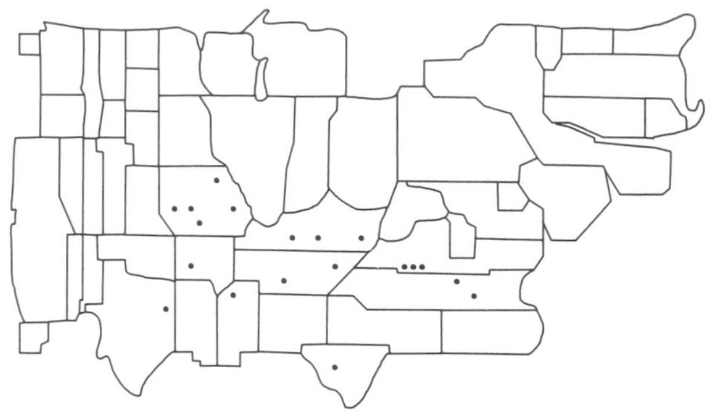

•for a little (bit) + varr (Qu. JJ35b)

for all conj phr

1 Despite the fact that, even though. [OED *for* prep. 23. b 1523 →; "Now *rare* in literary use"]

1845 Kirkland *Western Clearings* 44 **MI,** She's as proud as a peacock, for all she goes out to spin by the day. **1903** *DN* 2.351 **sePA. 1942** Whipple *Joshua* 8 **UT,** Wilhelmina at thirty-six was still silly and didn't seem to have improved much for all he had married her. **1951** Giles *Harbin's Ridge* 154 **eKY,** For all he hadn't liked the ridge school, seemed like he realized what he'd be missing. **1954** Welty *Ponder Heart* 142 **MS,** I ran back, but the laugh [on a dead woman's face] didn't go away—for all I went out of the room a minute, and for all Uncle Daniel sat still as a mouse, and for all the spirits of ammonia I offered her.

2 See quot.

1908 *DN* 3.312 **eAL, wGA,** *For all. . .* Whatever. "Don't swaller the seed for all you do."

for all adv phr [Scots dial]

Nevertheless, all the same.

1903 *DN* 2.351 **sePA,** *For all, adv.* Pronounced [fər'ɔl], or nearly [frɔl]. Nevertheless; however; used either at the beginning of a sentence or at the end. **1907** (1970) Martin *Betrothal* 108 **sePA,** I 'd sooner she 'd go as stay, for all. We're getting strangers Thursdays and we've made out to clean the kitchen to-morrow, so I don't know how long it will go before I can get time to make her a new dress already.

for all of me adv phr [Perh blend of obs *for me* as far as I am concerned + *for all I care*] **chiefly Nth**

1 For all I care, as far as I'm concerned.

1859 (1931) Tuttle *CA Diary* 80 **WI,** I came to the conclusion that the Antelope might live a little longer for all of me. **1893** Frederic *Copperhead* 83 **nNY,** He can go to the devil, an' take his sword with him, for all o' me! **1914** *DN* 4.72 **ME, nNH,** *Fer all o' me. . .* For all I care. **1951** Johnson *Resp. to PADS 20* **DE** (You can go ahead and do it ______) For all of me. **1955** Warren *Angels* 6 **KY,** Call hit whap-doodle fer all of me. **1960** Bailey *Resp. to PADS 20* **KS. 1965** *DARE* (Qu. GG21a, . . *"You can go ahead and do it______."*) 56 Infs, 40 **Nth,** For all of me [Of all Infs responding to the question, 64% were old; of those giving this response, 75% were old.]; (Qu. KK26, . . *"He can think what he likes . . ______ ."*) Inf **CA**2, For all of me.

2 Despite my efforts, for the life of me.

1967 *DARE* FW Addit **neNY,** I couldn't figure it out for all of me.

for all power See **for B4a(10)**

for any sake intj

1949 in 1986 *DARE* File, *For any sake*—My grandmother, age 82, says this continually instead of "for pity's sake" or "for heaven's sake."

forard(s) See **forward** adj, adv

forbid v

Std sense, var forms.

Past: usu *forbad(e);* also *forbid.*

1863 (1955) Holmes *Brokenburn* 251 **neLA,** I do not think he has even been angry until tonight, when Mamma forbid his going to church unless she or I went with him. **1941** *Hench Coll.* **ceVA,** [A Virginian] said "They forbid them to leave the land." She was talking about past time.

forby adj [Ger *vorbei* past, gone] Cf **all** adj²

1950 *WELS (Ways of saying that there's no more of something: "The potatoes are ______.")* 1 Inf, **seWI,** All; forby. [Inf of Ger and Scotch-Ir descent]

force n

1 in phr *no force:* It doesn't matter. [*OED force* sb.¹ 20 →1669]

[**1889** Twain *CT Yankee* 48, No force, said Merlin, hereby is a sword that shall be yours.] **1899** (1912) Green *VA Folk-Speech* 182, "No force;" no matter.

2 Importance, value—usu in neg constrs; hence *no force* of no value.

1887 *Scribner's Mag.* 2.476 **AR,** He wuz no force, nohow. Say he war blin' drunk w'en he tumbled outen the pilot-house. **1912** Green *VA Folk-Speech* 182, *Force*. . . Value; of use: "He is no force." **1961** Sackett-Koch *KS Folkl.* 113, *Force*. . . Worth; value. "He's not of much force."

forced draw n

1970 *DARE* (Qu. AA20, *A marriage that takes place because a baby is on the way*) Inf **TX**104, A forced draw.

forceps n Usu |ˈfɔrsɛps|; also |ˈfɔrsɪts| Cf Intro "Language Changes" IV.4

Std sense, var form.

c1960 *Wilson Coll.* **csKY,** [One informant] says [fɔrsɪts] for the instrument used by a dentist to pull teeth.

forceput n, also attrib [*OED* 1657 →; "Now *dial.*"]

An action about which one has no choice.

1927 *AmSp* 3.135 **ME coast,** A "forceput" marriage or "come by chance" child, were commonly spoken of.

for certain adv phr See **certain B2**

for certain adj phr See **for B4b**

for common See **for B4a(5)**

for cry-eye See **cry-eye**

for crying in the beer intj For varr see quot [Euphem for *for Christ's sake* or similar oaths; cf *for crying out loud*]

1966–68 *DARE* (Qu. NN31, *Exclamations beginning with the sound of 'cr-'*) Inf **MN**33, For crying in the beer (*or* cradle); **CO**39, For crying in a bucket; **WA**1, For crying in the sink.

for days adv phr

To a high degree.

1971 Roberts *Third Ear* np [Black], *For days*—an expression indicating extremes; e.g. . . he was fine *for days* (he was a very good-looking boy). **1981** *Pidgin To Da Max* np, *For days*. . . Plenty, a lot. Haole: "He certainly has long hair." Pidgin: "He get har fo' *days!*"

ford crossing n See Intro "Language Changes" I.4

1906 *DN* 3.136 **nwAR,** *Ford crossing*. . . Ford. "They varied from the ford crossing, it seems, and the wagon was overturned."

fore prep Pronc-sp *fo', for* [OE *fore;* now often felt as aphet form of *before*]

1 Of time: before. [*OED fore* prep. 2 →1601]

1795 Dearborn *Columbian Grammar* 135, *List of Improprieties*. . . Fore for Before. **1914** *DN* 4.72 **ME, nNH,** *'Fore wheelin' time* . . Before spring. **1922** Gonzales *Black Border* 285 **sSC, GA coasts** [Gullah], Tek care Stepney don' come een yo' house 'fo' wintuhtime! **1943** *LANE* Map 712 *(He will be well again ______)* 5 infs, **chiefly sNEng,** Fore long. **1958** Humphrey *Home from the Hill* 54 **neTX,** On comes the boar unsuspectin, an fore long you can hear him. **1966–69** *DARE* (Qu. A1, . . *The time in the early morning before the sun comes into sight*) Inf **AL**11, Fore sunup; **MD**19, Fore sunrise; **VA**26, Fore daylight; (Qu. A6, *What time is this?*) Inf **TN**34, Fifteen minutes fore eleven; **WA**2, Fore noon. **1975** McDonough *Garden Sass* 297 **AR,** We'd do it a day or two 'fore Christmas. . . On Christmas Day the older people they went to church 'fore day in the morning.

2 Before, by—used in oaths. [*OED fore* prep. 1. b c1435 →] **chiefly Sth** *esp freq among Black speakers*

1887 *Scribner's Mag.* 2.474/2 **AR** [Black], Whut ye got dar, Mist' Griffin? Looks like—fo' de Lawd, hit's a coffin! **1927** Adams *Congaree* 13 **cSC** [Black], 'Fore God! What make he [=made him] fine ole man Hall fi' dollahs? **1952** Caldwell *Lamp for Nightfall* 12 **ME,** Well, for and by God, she can and she is going to! **1957** Faulkner *Town* 369 **MS,** Fore God, men, run. It may already be too late. **1970** *DARE* (Qu. NN32, *Exclamations like 'I swear'*) Infs **FL**48, **NC**84, **SC**69, [I] 'clare fo' de Lord (*or* Lawd); **FL**48, 52, Swear fo' God. [All Infs Black]

fore conj Pronc-sp *fo'* [**fore** prep] Cf **afore**

Before.

1829 Tenney *Female Quixotism* 1.146 **Philadelphia PA** [Black], He get loose, and go off fore I come. **1901** Harben *Westerfelt* 6 **nGA,** I reckon it won't be long 'fore you move over on yore son-in-law's big farm. **1906** Casey *Parson's Boys* 60 **sIL** (as of c1860), Keep yer huff off'n that corn 'fore I larrup ye. **1929** Sale *Tree Named John* 93 **MS,** But 'fo' she kin do dat, she ha' t' shed her skin. **1940** Faulkner *Hamlet* 48 **MS** [Black], You fixing to get wet fo you get home. **1965–69** *DARE* Tape **CA**172A, It'd be dark fore he'd get back; **MA**92, Some . . from the old shop fore they tore it down; **AZ**6, 'Fore you go. **1966** *DARE* (Qu. A14) Inf **IL**113, 'Fore you can say Jack Sprat; (Qu. A21, . . *"Now just slow down! Don't ______."*) Inf **ME**16, Piss fore your water comes.

fore v See **fare** v

fore-and-aft adj [Prob because the tree so described, in contrast to a *corner tree,* stands with the line of survey extending both in front and behind]

In surveying; of a tree: standing on the line of survey.

1917 Kephart *Camping & Woodcraft* 2.66 **sAppalachians,** All trees that stand directly on the line of survey have two chops or notches cut on each side of them. . . These are called "sight trees" or "line trees" (sometimes "fore and aft trees"). **1928** in 1971 *Hench Coll.* **cVA,** Thence south 12 west at 585 feet crossing Mechum River at 1100 feet a large fore and aft oak, in all 1128 feet to center of Avon-Batesville Road.

fore-and-aft n See **fore-and-aft road**

fore-and-after n

1 A kind of square dance. [Perh from *fore-and-aft* lengthwise] **chiefly NEast** *old-fash*

1841 *S. Lit. Messenger* 7.767/2 **NYC,** The fiddler would be sawing away for life and death, and two or three couple [sic] in the floor—men and women—dancing fore and afters. *Ibid* 768/2, I was one of six sailors and women in a regular fore and after. **1848** Judson *Mysteries NY* 1.60, Cotillions, fore-and-afters, reels, and waltzes were danced. **1941** *LANE* Map 410, 1 inf, **seMA,** The fore-and-after—a square dance still held weekly in Brewster; 1 inf, **seMA,** The fore-and-after—an old quadrille with two couple [sic] facing each other.

2 Fig: see quot. [*Fore-and-after* a fore-and-aft rigged ship]

1975 Gould *ME Lingo* 99, *Fore-and-after* . . the term is held over in Maine speech for something that is trim, or perhaps a mite new-fangled and stylish. In this sense, "schooner-rigged" will more likely be heard.

fore-and-aft plank road n Also *fore-and-aft pole road*

In logging: a truck road paved with longitudinal planks or poles.

1958 McCulloch *Woods Words* 65 **Pacific NW,** *Fore-and-aft plank road*—The usual type of plank road, with two or three heavy timbers on each track, laid on stout cross pieces like ties. *Fore-and-aft pole road*— . . logs were laid lengthwise on cross ties. . . Flat surfaces were hewed on top, and an outside log was laid to make a curb so as to keep truck wheels in the tread. This type of road was used in the earliest days of truck hauling in the woods.

fore-and-aft road n Also *fore-and-aft*

In logging: see quot 1905.

1905 U.S. Forest Serv. *Bulletin* 61.37, *Fore-and-aft road.* A skid road made of logs placed parallel to its direction, making the road resemble a chute. (P[acific] C[oast] F[orest]) **1956** Sorden-Ebert *Logger's Words* 15 **Gt Lakes,** Fore-and-aft road, A skid-road in steep country for sliding logs into water. **1958** McCulloch *Woods Words* 65 **Pacific NW,** *Fore-and-aft*. . . A V-shaped trough made of logs, used for roading long distances or across swampy or other unfavorable ground.

forebay n

The overhanging section of the loft of a Pennsylvania German barn.

1938 *Hench Coll.* **VA,** The Valley Dutch call this overhanging part of a barn the forebay. **1950** Klees *PA Dutch* 395 **sePA,** To the south is the forebay, a projection of the upper story eight or ten feet over the lower. The forebay is often supported by the side walls and projecting ceiling beams. . . But often the forebay extends beyond the side walls and is supported by round pillars of field stone. **1967** *DARE* (Qu. M1, . . *Special kinds of barns*) Inf **PA**13, In Lancaster County, called forebay; (Qu. M13, *The space near the barn . . where you keep the livestock*) Inf **PA**3, Under the forebay—the overhang from the barn. **1975** *Professional Geogr.* 27.2.200, The typical Pennsylvania barn is a large structure of two or more levels with a simple gable roof. . . This barn's most characteristic feature consists of an upperlevel overhang referred to locally as a forebay (foreshoot). The forebay extends the full length of the long wall facing the barnyard.

fore-day See **before-day**

foredoor n [Engl dial; *OED* 1581 →]

The front door of a house.

1680 in 1866 NH Hist. Soc. *Coll.* 8.47, She laid bags under the threshold of the back door all the way and half way of the breadth of the fore door. **1767** in 1877 Boston Registry Dept. *Records* 3.223, Then measur'd from said Whittemores fore Door across to the N. W. Corner of said Whittemores other Land. **1877** Jewett *Deephaven* 34 **ME,** A system of barring and bolting for the wide "fore door." **1901** Jewett *Tory Lover* 64 **ME** (as of 1700s), My fore door . . is well sheltered, but I felt the wind.

forefather's cup n Also *forefather's pitcher* **esp NEng**

A **pitcher plant,** usu *Sarracenia purpurea.*

1818 MA Hist. Soc. *Coll.* 2d ser 8.171, Among the plants in the neighbouring towns, . . are . . the purple sarracenia, or, as it is here called, meadow cups and forefathers' pitcher. **1832** Williamson *Hist. ME* 1.126, *Meadow-cup,* called forefathers' pitcher, or Whippoorwill's shoes. **1876** Hobbs *Bot. Hdbk.* 39, Forefathers' cup, Side saddle plant, Sarracenia purpurea. **1893** *Jrl. Amer. Folkl.* 6.137, *Sarracenia purpurea,* . . forefather's cup, New England. **1896** *Ibid* 9.181, *Sarracenia purpurea,* . . forefather's pitcher, Me. **1933** Small *Manual SE Flora* 581, *S. purpurea.* . . Forefather's-cup. **1959** Carleton *Index Herb. Plants* 48, *Forefather's Cup:* Sarracenia (v).

Forefathers' Day n **chiefly NEng, esp MA**

A holiday observed on Dec 21 or 22 in commemoration of the landing of the Pilgrims at Plymouth in 1620.

1826 Morton *New Engl. Mem.* 48n, The 22d of December . . has long been observed at Plymouth . . in commemoration of the landing of the Fathers. . . [I]t has . . the . . appellation of *Forefather-Day.* **1855** Morton *New Engl. Mem.* 35n, The celebration of the landing on "Forefathers' Day," is not only attended at Plymouth, but at Boston, New York, Cincinnati, New Orleans, Charleston, Buffalo, Detroit, and perhaps some other places. **1885** *Harper's New Mth. Mag.* 71.476/2 **NYC,** Although for many a year the 22d of December has been known as Forefathers' Day, the date inscribed upon the pedestal of the "Pilgrim" is December 21. **1969** *Yankee* Feb 46, One other observance of New England origin is Forefather's Day. It is not a legal holiday but is celebrated . . on or about December 22. Ceremonies commemorate the landing of the Pilgrim Fathers at Plymouth in 1620 and for the space of a day or evening are a reminder for New Englanders everywhere of their heritage. **1977** *Yankee* Nov 260, This samp porridge bears a close resemblance to Plymouth succotash which is traditionally served in that Massachusetts community on Forefather's Day, December 21.

forefather's pitcher See **forefather's cup**

forefoot v **West** Cf **blocker** n[1]

To rope an animal by the front feet.

1928 French *Ranchman NM* 56 (as of 1885), The faster they ran the easier it was to forefoot them and throw them. In this forefooting of an animal [=a horse] it was always necessary to get both forefeet in the noose, otherwise you were liable to break the animal's leg. **1929** Dobie *Vaquero* 262, One of the neatest throws in common use is the *mangana,* which means catching an animal by the forefeet, "forefooting." **1933** (1950) Allen *Cowboy Lore* 11, *Fore-footing,* roping an animal by the front feet in order to throw same for handling. Hor[s]e stock are usually fore-footed—Cattle very rarely being fore-footed. **1937** Sandoz *Slogum* 339 **wNE,** The hand that could still spread a loop fast enough to forefoot a running yearling. **1958** Blasingame *Dakota Cowboy* 262 **SD,** A crazy little yearling jumped out of the roundup right beside me. . . Before I knew it, I had forefooted him—caught him by one leg and broke it.

foregoing ppl adj

Leading, prominent.

c1938 in 1970 Hyatt *Hoodoo* 2.1477 **seGA,** Ah'm going to speak three times to *Peelee.* Yo' know who dat is? (No, who is that?) Dat's one of de foregoin' angels—*Peelee.*

forehanded adj **chiefly NEng** *old-fash*

1 Foresighted, prudent, frugal; hence n *forehandedness.* [*OED* 1650 →; "Now only *U.S.*"]

1777 in 1854 Adams *Works* 9.454 **MA,** Here and there [one finds] a farmer and a tradesman, who is forehanded and frugal enough to make more money than he has occasion to spend. **1840** (1841) Dana *2 Yrs.* 478, Regular habits, forehandedness (if I may use the word) in worldly affairs, and hours reclaimed from indolence and vice . . follow in the wake of the converted man. **1864** Sargent *Peculiar* 61 **NEng,** Not being of a thrifty and forehanded habit, the Colonel's father never rose to the possession of more than three slaves at a time. **1880** *Harper's New Mth. Mag.* 62.81/1 **NEng,** He's got a sharp eye . . and he's forehanded as fury. **1892** *Harper's New Mth. Mag.* 84.428/2 **NYC,** In all these cities and in a hundred ways the observant traveller notes the same forehandedness. **1893** *Harper's New Mth. Mag.* 88.117/1 **ME,** I've always been forehanded; I never was caught so unprepared before. **1907** *DN* 3.187 **seNH,** *Forehanded.* . . Thrifty. "Gran'sir admired him because he was a forehanded man." **1935** Sandoz *Jules* 95 **wNE,** Forehanded, for once, he ordered a dozen.

2 Well-to-do, prosperous. [*OED* 1658 →; "Now only *U.S.*"]

1827 *Western Mth. Rev.* 1.446 **IN,** Her father had become, in the phrase of the country, 'forehanded, or well to do.' **1860** (1863) Olmsted *Journey* 230, A smaller proportion of the people live in a style corresponding to that customary among what are called in New England "fore-handed folks." **1880** (1883) Rollins *N. Engl. Bygones* 156, The wives of "forehanded" farmers and professional men were apt to be somewhat exalted. **1905** *DN* 3.9 **cCT,** *Fore-handed.* . . Provided for the future. **1905** *Eve. Post* (NY NY) 13 June 7/2, He became a very 'forehanded' man at one time, travelled about in private cars and gave other evidences of opulence.

3 See quot.

1895 *DN* 1.397 **NYC,** *Fore-handed:* energetic.

forehandedness See **forehanded 1**

forehead n Freq **esp NEng, NYC, Sth, S Midl** |'fɑrəd, 'fɔrəd|; also sp-pronc |'fɔr,hɛd, 'foə,hɛd|; for addit varr see quots Pronc-spp *fard, forrud* Cf **forward** n

Std sense, var forms.

1828 Webster *Amer. Dict.* np, *Forehead* . . ['fɔrhɛd], or rather ['fɔrɛd]. **1884** Lanier *Poems* 169 **sGA,** His forrud was creased with a turrible frown. **1922** Gonzales *Black Border* 302 **sSC, GA coasts** [Gullah glossary], *Forrud*—forehead, foreheads. **1936** [see **forest**]. **1936** *AmSp* 11.74 **Upstate NY,** In *forehead,* about three-quarters of the upstate speakers . . retain the [h], and give a secondary stress to the second syllable; of these speakers, 163 use [ɑ] in the first syllable, two use [ɑ], and there are no instances of [ɒ]. **1940** Stuart *Trees of Heaven* 236 **neKY,** The blood has rushed to my fard. **1941** *LANE* Map 485, [Most freq ['fɒ(ə)rəd, 'fɔrəd, -ɨd]; occas ['foə,hɛd, 'for,hɛd].] **1942** *AmSp* 17.153 **seNY,** Between vowels, *forehead* has [rh] 18, [r] 34, [h] 3. **1942** Hall *Smoky Mt. Speech* 33, The most striking thing here is the complete unrounding which the vowel often undergoes, as in . . *forehead* ['fɑrəd]. *Ibid* 72, There seems to be little tendency . . to restore the stress in *forehead* (though a few are reported to say ['fɔɚ,hɛd]). **1942** *Sun* (Baltimore MD) 22 Dec 14/3 *(Hench Coll.),* No dictionary to my knowledge lists *forehead* as it is commonly pronounced, "fore-head" to rhyme with "more dead." **1954** *Harder Coll.* **cwTN,** [fɑrd]. **c1960** *Wilson Coll.* **csKY,** [fɑrɪd] is more common than ['for,hɛd]; also ['fɔrɪd], almost [fɔrd]. **c1970** Pederson *Dial. Surv. Rural GA* **seGA,** [*Forehead* is usually ['fɔ(r),hɛd, 'fɔ(r),ɛd, 'fɑɚɨd], rarely [fɑɚd, fɑ·d].] **1976** Allen *LAUM* 3.287 **Upper MW** (as of c1950), The pronunciation . . /'fɔr,hɛd/ . . is easily predominant. . . /'fɔr,ɛd/ . . is the choice of but one out of ten. The third variant . . [=/'fɔrəd/] is also the choice of one out of ten infs.

forehobbled ppl adj Cf **forehopple**

Of a horse: having its forelegs connected with a short strap to prevent it from straying.

1935 Davis *Honey* 24 **sOR,** The horses were forehobbled and easy to catch.

forehopple n Cf **forehobbled, hopple** v

1844 (1954) Gregg *Commerce* 44 **KS,** The 'fore-hopple' (a leathern strap or rope manacle upon the fore-legs) being most convenient, was more frequently used [to secure the horses].

foreign adj Usu |'fɔrən, 'for-|; also **esp NYC,** |'fɑrən|; **esp sAppalachians** |'fɝən|; for addit varr see quots Pronc-spp *fur(r)in, furren, fureen* Similarly n *foreigner* Pronc-spp *ferriner, foreigneer, furriner*

Std senses, var forms.

1805 (1905) Clark *Orig. Jrls. Lewis & Clark Exped.* 3.185 **VA,** The articles . . cannot be an object of commerce with furin merchants. **1903** *DN* 2.314 **seMO,** [fɝɪnər]. **1907** *DN* 3.231 **nwAR,** [fɝɪnər]. **1911** *DN* 3.538 **eKY,** *Ferriner.* **1913** Kephart *Highlanders* 80 **sAppalachians,** A big furrin dog that I don't rightly know the breed of. **1915** *DN* 4.183 **swVA,** *Furriner.* **1927** Kennedy *Gritney People* **LA** *(ADD),* Furren. **1936** [see **forest**]. **1936** *AmSp* 11.73 **Upstate NY,** [In *foreign,* there were 15 instances of [ɔ], 3 of [ɑ], and 1 of [ɒ] among speakers in northern and western New York.] **1938** Stuart *Dark Hills* 143 **neKY,** Got a bunch of these damn foreigneers in here. **1938** Matschat *Suwannee R.* 105 **nFL, sGA,** Gre'-gre'-gran'paw brought it years and years ago from a fureen place—England, he called it. **1942** *AmSp* 17.38 **seNY,** [In *foreign,* there were 94 instances of [ɑ], 7 of [ɒ], and 7 of [ɔ] among speakers in New York City and Long Island.] **1942** Hall *Smoky Mt. Speech* 33, *Foreign* [fɝ·n], *foreigner* ['fɝənɚ] (both of which are used now only by aged, isolated, or illiterate speakers). **c1960** *Wilson Coll.* **csKY,** [fɔrɪn], [fɑrɪn], and, by older people, ['fɝɪn]; [fɝənəz], now used in fun. **1970** *DARE* (Qu. Z11b) Inf **FL**51, Foreigner ['fɑənə]. [Inf Black]

‡foreigner n

An illegitimate child.

1970 *DARE* (Qu. Z11b, . . *A child of unwed parents*) Inf **FL**51, An outside child; a foreigner. [Inf Black, coll educ]

foreknowing Jack n

1970 *DARE* (Qu. II35, *A person who . . seems to think he knows everything*) Inf **MO**23, Foreknowing Jack.

forelawn n

1967 *DARE* (Qu. N44, . . *The strip of grass and trees between the sidewalk and the curb*) Inf **OR**13, Forelawn—in California.

forelay v Also sp *forlay* **NEng** *old-fash*

1 To lie in wait for, ambush. [*OED* 1548 →; "*Obs.* exc. *dial.*"]

1892 *DN* 1.213 **Cape Cod MA,** *Forelay* or *forlay* ([fɔleɪ], with nearly equal accent on each syllable): to lie in wait for, head off. Heard last summer from a Cape Cod farmer who had in early life been a sailor.

2 To plan ahead; to prepare for. [*OED* 1605 → (in trans uses); "*Obs.* exc. *dial.*"]

1903 *DN* 2.297 **Cape Cod MA** (as of a1857), *Forelay* . . To make provision in advance. 'You better forelay and come home together.' 'When you see that kind of a sky you want to forelay for a storm.' **1907** *DN* 3.244 **eME,** *Forelay, v.i.* Provide for in advance.

3 To plan, intend.

1943 *LANE* Map 704 *(I intend to go)* 1 inf, **Cape Cod MA,** Forelaying.

forelog n Cf **backstick**

=forestick.

1867 Beecher *Norwood* 143 **wMA,** Barton was looking at the coals under the fore-log. **1880** (1883) Rollins *N. Engl. Bygones* 68, [The backlogs] were buried in embers, and then supplemented with a forelog. **1941** *LANE* Map 330, 11 infs, **scattered NEng,** *Fore log.* **1969** *DARE* (Qu. D34) Inf **KY**5, Forelog, middle log, kindling.

forenoon n [*OED* 1506 →] **esp Nth**

Morning, esp late morning; hence adv *forenoons* regularly in the mornings.

1805 (1904) White *Jrl.* 22 **MA,** We . . got out the lye all the forenoon, in the afternoon we got the kettle on to make some soap. **1859** (1931) Tuttle *CA Diary* 15.232 **WI,** We crossed this creek several times the forenoon. **1909** *Atlantic Mth.* July 137 **NW,** These neighbors . . speak of "forenoon, noon, and afternoon," we [Southerners] . . say . . "morning, evening, and night." **1939** *LANE* Map 77 **NEng,** *Forenoon* . . usually denotes the later part of the morning, from 7, 8, 9 or 10 o'clock to noon, or the period between breakfast and dinner. *Forenoon* normally has end stress, but level stress and initial stress (by contrast to *afternoon*) are common. **1946** *PADS* 6.14 **eNC.** **1950** *WELS (Between daylight and the middle of the day)* 34 Infs, **WI,** Forenoon. **1951** Johnson *Resp. to PADS 20* **DE,** Fore noon (old fashioned). **1954** *Harder Coll.* **cwTN.** **c1960** *Wilson Coll.* **csKY.** **1966** *Presque Isle Star–Herald* (ME) 9 June 8/2, [She was] with town children forenoons and rural children afternoons. **1967–68** *DARE* (Qu. A2) Inf **NY**93, After sunrise it's forenoon; (Qu. A3) Inf **CO**17, Afternoon; forenoon; **CT**17, Afternoon versus forenoon; **MI**76, Before twelve it's forenoon; **MN**2, Forenoon; (Qu. W22) Inf **CT**12, You'd wear a wrapper all forenoon; (QR p26) Inf **IA**9, Forenoon is the morning. **1967–68** *DARE* FW Addit **NY**104, Any time after 10:00 A.M. is the forenoon; **n,wNY,** Forenoon—common all over upstate New York for late morning; **MT, ND, SD,** People never say morning when referring to that time between breakfast and noon; they say forenoon. **1969–70** *DARE* Tape **IL**44, You get the biggest bulk of your eggs in the forenoon—there aren't near as many laid in the afternoon; **MI**115, We had two recesses, one the forenoon, one the afternoon.

forepappy n [Var of *forefather*]

=foreparent.

c1938 in 1970 Hyatt *Hoodoo* 2.1793, Yes, dese ole *receipts.* Mah ole mathah an' mah ole fathah learnt me, yo' know. Ah'm got 'em from mah *forepappies.*

foreparent n [*OED* (at *fore-* prefix 4. a) 1526] **chiefly S Midl**

An ancestor, forebear.

1906 *DN* 3.136 **nwAR.** **1917** *DN* 4.412 **wNC Mts.** **1922** (1926) Kephart *Highlanders* 429 **sAppalachians,** My foreparents war principally Scotch. **1926** *DN* 5.400 **Ozarks.** **1933** Williamson *Woods Colt* 43 **Ozarks,** His folks come from up beyond the Knob, where . . the old fore-parents used to kill ye for two bits an' give ye back twenty cents change. **1943** Weslager *DE Forgotten Folk* 204, My foreparents always used to say that dreams was the spirits talking. **1954** *Harder Coll.* **cwTN.** **c1960** *Wilson Coll.* **csKY.**

forepart n

1 The front portion of a thing. [*OED* c1400 →]

1714 (1882) S. Sewall *Diary* 3.26 **MA,** The Snow and Rain . . beat on the fore-part of the Calash. **1903** *DN* 2.297 **Cape Cod MA** (as of a1857), *Forepart* . . front. **1908** *DN* 3.312 **eAL, wGA,** The forepart of the wagon.

2 The early portion of a period of time. [*OED* 1614 →]

1804 (1904) Clark *Orig. Jrls. Lewis & Clark Exped.* 1.25, During the fore part of this Day it rained excessively hard. **1846** in 1924 *UT Geneal. & Hist. Mag.* 15.55 **NY,** In the fore part of February, 1846, several hundred families . . crossed . . the great Mississippi River. **1903** *DN* 2.297 **Cape Cod MA** (as of a1857), Come the forepart the day. **1908** *DN* 3.312 **eAL, wGA,** The forepart of the day. **1915** *DN* 4.183 **swVA.** **1931–33** *LANE Worksheets* **nwCT,** Morning is the forepart of the day; **cwMA,** The forepart of the evening. **1946** *PADS* 6.14 **eNC.** **1950** *WELS (Between daylight and the middle of the day)* 1 Inf, **cWI,** Forepart of the day; *(Right after dark)* 3 Infs, **WI,** Forepart of the night. **1953** Randolph–Wilson *Down in Holler* 219 **Ozarks,** It was about eight o'clock when Porter Lucas . . asked a farmer to have breakfast with him. "No, thank ye," said the man politely, "I done et, in the fore part of the day." **1954** *Harder Coll.* **cwTN.** **1960** Criswell *Resp. to PADS 20* **Ozarks,** Fore-part. . . Early part (of the day). . . Still common. **c1960** *Wilson Coll.* **csKY.** **1965–66** *DARE* Tape **NM**13, In the forepart of the eighties; **OK**1, The forepart of August. **1983** *MJLF* 9.1.39 **ceKY,** *Fore part of the night* . . from suppertime to bedtime or midnight.

fore paw See **faux pas** n

forereach v

1945 Colcord *Sea Language* 80 **NEast,** *Forereach.* To shoot ahead of another vessel. In shore speech, to get the better of another person.

foreroom n [*OED* 1728 →; "Now only *U.S.*"] **chiefly NEng** *old-fash* Cf **foredoor**

A parlor, living room.

1745 in 1915 NH *Prov. & State Papers* 33.321, I give . . to my beloved wife . . The following part in my dwelling house Namely the fore Room Next to the Street. **1880** (1883) Rollins *N. Engl. Bygones* 71, This was the "best-room," or, as my grandfather called it, the "fore" room. **1903** *DN* 2.351 **ME,** *Foreroom.* . . A front room. **1907** *DN* 3.187 **seNH.** **1929** *AmSp* 5.127 **ME.** **1932** *DN* 6.283 **swCT,** *Fore room.* "In plain people's houses this answers for a parlor till the girls begin to get beaus; then you don't call it a fore room any more." **1934** (1970) Wilson *Backwoods Amer.* 198 **AR, MO Ozarks,** We entered the foreroom and took places before an amiable fire. **1941** *LANE* Map 323, [*Fore room,* for the room where visitors are entertained, occurs 13 times, chiefly north of Massachusetts.]

fore-royal n

1945 Colcord *Sea Language* 80 **ME, Cape Cod, Long Island,** *Fore royal, the.* The early-morning mug of coffee on shipboard; the first cup alongshore. Just why it should be called after the topmost sail on the foremast is not known.

forerunner n

1 A **hickory shad** (here: *Alosa mediocris*).

1887 Goode *Amer. Fishes* 405, This species [=*Alosa mediocris*] is in some rivers called a "Forerunner," from the fact that it makes its appearance shortly before the Shad.

2 also, by folk-etym, *four runners:* See quots.

1923 Parsons *Folk-lore Sea Islands* 211 **csSC,** Names for the stars . . were limited. "Fore-runner" is the star "befo' Wenus," the morning star. **1943** Weslager *DE Forgotten Folk* 177, Constellations known as Job's Coffin, Four Runners, and Milkmaid's Path could also be readily recognized.

3 See quot.

1966 *DARE* (Qu. CC17) Inf **MD**15, Forerunner—a spirit that brings bad news. [It] knocks on doors, etc.

‡foresee v

1901 *DN* 2.140 **cnNY,** *Foresee*. . . Understand.

foreshot n, also pl

=**first shot.**

1808 in 1956 Eliason *Tarheel Talk* 271 **NC,** Put in half pint of spirits or a gill of fore shots. **1974** Dabney *Mountain Spirits* xxi, Foreshot: first whiskey to come out of the condenser at the beginning of a run.

foreside n

The front side; esp, in coastal areas, the part fronting the water.

1903 *DN* 2.297 **Cape Cod MA** (as of 1850s), *Foreside*. . . Frontside. **1946** Attwood *Length ME* 14, *Foreside*—Stretch of land facing the ocean. Falmouth Foreside.

forest n Usu |ˈfɔrəst, ˈfor-|; also **esp NYC, Sth** |ˈfɑrəst|; for addit varr see quots See Pronc Intro 3.I.2.b Pronc-sp *farst*

Std sense, var forms.

1936 *AmSp* 11.26 **eTX,** In words such as *Dorothy, forehead, foreign, forest . . ,* [ɒ] seems to be more general than [ɔ], though these words are frequently heard with an excessively rounded [ɔ] in the speech of uneducated people. *Ibid* 73 **Upstate NY,** [In *forest,* there were 11 instances of [ɑ], 12 of [ɒ] and 88 of [ɔ] among speakers in upstate NY.] **1939** *AmSp* 14.125 **ceTN,** [fɑrəst]. **1940** *AmSp* 15.146 **nwSC,** [In *forest,* there were 71 instances of [ɑ] to 4 of [ɔ] among 75 speakers in the Piedmont area of S.C.] **1941** *Sun* (Baltimore MD) *(ADD), Forest* . . pron. farst. **1942** *AmSp* 17.38 **seNY,** [In *forest,* there were 228 instances of [ɑ], 27 of [ɒ], and 19 of [ɔ] among speakers in the New York City area.]

forest chippy n [See quots] Cf **chippy** n² **1, field chippy**

The worm-eating warbler *(Helmitheros vermivorus).*

1929 Forbush *Birds MA* 3.203, *Forest Chippy*. . . Song, a torrent of *chips* not unlike those of Chipping Sparrow. **1946** Hausman *Eastern Birds* 499, *Worm-eating Warbler*. . . *Song*—Quite like the song of the Chipping Sparrow (hence the name Forest Chippy). **1955** Forbush–May *Birds* 411.

forestick n Also called **forelog, front stick**

The log at the front of a fire, usu smaller than the **backlog 1** and parallel to it.

1793 *Thomas' MA Spy or Worcester Gaz.* (MA) 7 Mar 3/2, He found his companion lying in a large body of live coals, her head on the backlog and knees on the forestick. **1825** Neal *Brother Jonathan* 1.33 **CT,** Watching the current of sparks, that rushed up the chimney, whenever the *"back log"* moved, or the *"forestick"* parted, in the fire. **1880** *Harper's New Mth. Mag.* 61.400/2 **NY,** The canoeist who has seen his dinner overturned by the burning away of a forestick or back-log . . seeks a stove. **1902** (1904) Rowe *Maid of Bar Harbor* 85 **ME. 1927** *AmSp* 2.354 **WV. 1938** Damon *Grandma* 24 **CT** (as of late 1800s), Next to be laid in its place well to the front, on the andirons, was the forestick. This, too, must not burn quickly, as its purpose was to hold the burning fuel in place. **1941** *LANE* Map 330, 20 infs, **scattered NEng,** *Fore stick.* **1953** Randolph–Wilson *Down in Holler* 245 **Ozarks,** *Fore-stick*. . . The log at the front of a fireplace. It is usually about half the size of the backlog. In building a fire, these two are put in position first, with smaller sticks between. **1954** *Harder Coll.* **cwTN. c1960** *Wilson Coll.* **csKY. 1968–70** *DARE* (QR, near Qu. D33) Inf **AR**56, Forestick—in front of the backlog; **OH**49, The forestick goes in front, the lash goes in the middle, the backlog in back.

forestiera n

Std: a shrub or tree of the genus *Forestiera.* For other names of var spp see **buckbrush 3f, chaparral B1, crooked brush 1, desert olive, devil's elbow, elbow bush 2, ironwood, pond brush, spring goldenglow, spring herald, stretchberry, swamp ash, swamp privet, tanglewood, whitewood**

forest man n

An imaginary figure used to frighten children; a boogeyman.

1966 Goldstein–Byington *Two Penny Ballads* 156 **PA,** If you should stay out after dark the forest man will take you away.

forest pine n

A pine, such as **shortleaf pine.**

1960 Vines *Trees SW* 25, *Pinus echinata* . . Vernacular names are . . Forest Pine . . Slash Pine, and Carolina Pine. **1966–67** *DARE* (Qu. T17, . . *Kinds of pine trees*) Infs **CA**1, **NC**33, 38, Forest pine.

foretop n

The hair growing on the front of the top of the head; the forelock of:

a A person; in earlier use esp an elaborate arrangement of hair on a woman's forehead. [*OED* c1290 →; "Obs."]

1771 *Mass. Spy* 21 March *(DAE),* An old fashioned lady, with a foretop of hair Cherokeed to imitate the Indian dress. **1842** *Amer. Pioneer* 1.431, I was still in Indian uniform, bare headed, my hair cut off close, except the scalp and foretop, which they had put up in a piece of tin. **1882** 'M. Harland' *Eve's Daughters* 197 *(DAE),* The girl . . devotes an hour a day . . to learning how to 'do' the fantastic scallops of her fore-top. **1927** *DN* 5.474 **Ozarks,** *Fore-top*. . . The fore-lock, a long lock of hair on the forehead. **c1960** *Wilson Coll.* **csKY,** *Foretop*. . . A lock of hair on front of head.

b An animal, esp a horse. [*OED* 1607 →]

1866 ME Dept. Ag. *Annual Rept.* 149, There are breeders . . who say that the foretop is not a distinguishing feature of this breed [of sheep]. **1917** *DN* 4.392 **IL, KS, KY, NEng, NY, OH, SC,** Foretop. . . The forelock on a horse's head. **1927** *AmSp* 2.354 **WV,** *Foretop* . . the hair between the ears of the horse. **1929** *AmSp* 5.126 **ME,** The horse's "foretop" was often braided. **1954** *Harder Coll.* **cwTN,** *Foretop*. . . The hair between the ears of a horse.

forevermore intj Also *forever* [Euphem for oaths beginning with *for* or **fore** prep **2**]

Used to express surprise.

1838 Kettell *Yankee Notions* 134, "Oh! forever!" he exclaimed. **1924** *DN* 5.267, For ever more. *Ibid* 285 **seNE,** Forevermore. **1950** Kimbrough *Innocents* 132 **IN,** "Forevermore." That is a word we said in Muncie when we were surprised. **1950** *WELS (Exclamations of surprise. . . "They're getting married next week." "Well, ______!")* 1 Inf, **csWI,** Forevermore! Old-fashioned. **1968–69** *DARE* (Qu. NN7) Infs **PA**74, **TX**74, Forevermore! (Qu. NN29a) Inf **MD**17, Forever!

for fair See **for B4a(4)**

forfeit n Cf **fine or superfine; heavy, heavy, what hangs over; tin tin**

Something surrendered as part of a game, to be redeemed by the performance of some trivial task; the task so imposed; hence *forfeits* a game involving such tasks.

1856 Holmes *Lena Rivers* 95 **KY,** Mr. Everett . . had joined in the game, claiming "forfeits" from Anna more frequently than was considered at all necessary. **1899** Champlin–Bostwick *Young Folks' Games* 348, *Forfeits,* a game played by any number of persons, in which articles given up by each of them are restored on the performance of some difficult or ridiculous feat. . . One of the players . . holds them over the judge's head one by one saying: "Heavy, heavy, what hangs over your head?" The judge then asks, "Fine or Superfine?" to which the other answers "Fine," if the owner of the forfeit is a boy, or "Superfine," if a girl. . . The judge then tells what the owner must do to get back his property. **1907** *DN* 3.244 **eME,** *Forfeits*. . . Game in which forfeits are imposed. An example of such a forfeit is this: "Kneel to the prettiest,/ Bow to the wittiest,/ Kiss the one you love the best." **1908** Lincoln *Cy Whittaker* 205 **NEng,** Did you ever play forfeits when you was little? Well, this is a forfeit game and you're It. You must bow to the prettiest, kneel to the wittiest, and kiss the one you love best. **1957** *Sat. Eve. Post Letters* **WI,** [In the game of tin tin:] If person laughs, he must give a forfeit. To redeem forfeit, starter hangs forfeit over player's head. . . Then fine is levied (eat a cracker, drink a glass of water, etc) and forfeit returned. *Ibid* **ceWI,** *Tin tin*—Parlor Game. Better known as *forfeits. Ibid* **cIL** (as of c1890), [In a list of games:] Forfeits. **1967** *DARE* (Qu. EE3, *Games in which you hide an object and then look for it*) Inf **NJ4**, Forfeit.

forfeit exclam

1967 *DARE* (Qu. EE20, *When two boys are fighting, and the one who is losing wants to stop, he calls out, "________."*) Inf **AL8**, Forfeit.

forfeits See **forfeit** n

for foolish See **for B4a(6)**

forforraw See **fofarraw** n

for free See **for B4a(7)**

for fun adv phr Also *for funs(es)* Cf **for B4a(4)(b), for play**

In marbles games: on condition that marbles taken will be returned (opposite of **for keeps**); hence n *funs(ies), funnies* a game played in this way.

1890 Howells *Boy's Town* 81 **OH** (as of 1840s), There were some mean-spirited fellows who played for fun. **1895** *Searcher* 1.7/2 **CT,** We played the game of marbles . . either "for fun" or "for good." **1935** *AmSp* 10.159 **seNE,** *Funs.* The opposite of *keeps*—all marbles are returned to their proper owners at the end of the game. **1942** Berrey–Van den Bark *Amer. Slang* 665.1, *Marbles. . .* Funs, funsies, *a game not "for keeps".* **1955** *PADS* 23.19 **cwAL, cwTN,** Fun. . . In phrases *for fun, in fun. Ibid* **cwTN,** *Funs. . .* Var of *fun.* **1957** *Sat. Eve. Post Letters* **cAR** (as of c1900), In playing marbles we used several terms such as "funnies" when we played for fun and "keeps" when we kept the marbles we knocked out of the ring. *Ibid* **cKY** (as of 1930s), [The marble game "Tennessee"] was usually played for "funs." **1962** *PADS* 37.2 **KS,** Those who play "for fun" do not play "for keeps." **1965–70** *DARE* (Qu. EE7) 9 Infs, **scattered,** For fun. **1966** *DARE* Tape **AL4**, We played [marbles] for funses. **1969** O'Connor *Horse & Buggy West* 83 **AZ** (as of 1910), It [=the marbles game **bullring**] was always a gambling game in that it was played for keeps, not for funs. **1970** *DARE* Tape **NC88**, That was quite a bit of fun as long as we were playin' for fun [instead of] . . for havin'. **c1970** Wiersma *Marbles Terms* **swMI,** For funs. *Ibid* **MA,** For funs. *Ibid* **swMI,** For fun. *Ibid* **swMI** (as of 1957), *Funsies:* Same as playing for funs. **1983** *MJLF* 9.1.40 **ceKY,** *Funs* . . playing marbles without gambling "for funs." In my youth only smaller children and sissies played "for funs."

forgainst prep Pronc-sp *forgenst* [Obs Scots dial]

1919 *DN* 5.33 **KY,** *Forgainst. . .* Against. "Over forgenst the mountain."

forget v Usu |fə(r)ˈget|; often |-ˈgɪt| Pronc-spp *fe'git, ferget, fergit, forgit, fuhget, fumget* Cf **get** v **A**

Std sense, var forms.

1815 Humphreys *Yankey in England* 105, *Forgit.* **1843** (1916) Hall *New Purchase* 521 **IN,** Bust my rifle—if I ever forgit you. **1884** *Anglia* 7.275 **Sth, S Midl** [Black], *To fergit off'n de mine* = to forget, to lose from memory. **1899** Chesnutt *Conjure Woman* 74 **csNC** [Black], I fe'git dat 'oman's name. **1908** *DN* 3.310 **eAL, wGA,** *Ferget. . .* Forget. Often pronounced *fergit.* **1927** Shewmake *Engl. Pronc. VA* 42, *Forgot.* Virginians usually, or certainly very often, say *fuhgot.* **1935** *AmSp* 10.293 **Upstate NY,** I have only a few instances of *forget,* but they show [ɪ] about as frequently as [ɛ]. **1953** *PADS* 19.11 **sAppalachians,** *Fumgot:* . . Forgot. Heard in Canoe, Ky.

forgetery See **forgettery**

forget it phr

1 Used as an exclam expressing rejection or denial.

1967–70 *DARE* (Qu. KK55c, *Other expressions of strong denial*) Infs **CO39**, **PA66**, 72, Forget it! (Qu. NN4, *Other ways of answering 'no': "Would you lend him ten dollars?" "________."*) Infs **AL62**, **CA142**, **NY132**, **OH63**, **PA66**, 72, Forget it! [4 of 7 Infs young, 2 Black] **1970** Bullins *Electronic* 85 **sCA** [Black], *Curt. . .* We'se friends . . and we been in some tighter things than you and me will ever be in. *Rich. . .* Well, forget it! **1970** Major *Dict. Afro-Amer. Slang* 55, *Forget it:* implies that the listener has not properly understood what is in question or being explained; example, "if you think this dictionary was easy to put together, *forget it!*"

2 also *forget it all:* Used as euphem for *damn it (all). among Black speakers*

1970 *DARE* (Qu. NN8b, . . *"This jar won't come open, ________ it."*) Infs **MO30**, **TN46**, Forget; (Qu. NN25a, *Weakened substitutes for 'damn' or 'damned': "________ it all!"*) Infs **DC13**, **KY92**, **MO30**, **NY236**, **TN46**, Forget. [All Infs Black, 3 young]

forget-me-not n

1 Any of numerous plants of the family Boraginaceae, as:

a also *wild forget-me-not:* A plant of the genus *Myosotis.* [*OED* c1532 →] Also called **mouse-ear, scorpion grass, scorpion weed.** For other names of *M. laxa* see **eyebright 12;** for other names of *M. scorpioides* see **love-me, snake grass**

1822 Eaton *Botany* 358, *Myosotis. . . arvensis* (forget-me-not). **1861** Wood *Class-Book* 562, *Myosotis. . . Forget-me-not. . .* Fl[ower]s never axillary. **1906** Rydberg *Flora CO* 292, *Forget-me-not. . .* In mountain meadows from Alb[erta] and Alaska to Colo[rado]. **1933** Small *Manual SE Flora* 1124. **1965–70** *DARE* (Qu. S23) Infs **IL44**, **OH28**, 66, Forget-me-not(s); (Qu. S26a) Infs **CA126**, **NY6**, **NC37**, Forget-me-not(s); (Qu. S26b) Infs **MI10**, **PA40**, 68, 176, **RI15**, Forget-me-not(s); **MA6**, Wild blue forget-me-nots; **OR1**, Wild forget-me-not; (Qu. S26c) Infs **CA200**, **NC1**, Wild forget-me-not(s); (Qu. S26d) Infs **AK7**, **CA24**, **NY88**, Forget-me-not(s); (Qu. S26e) Inf **CA9**, Wild forget-me-not; **VT10**, Forget-me-not. [*DARE* Ed: Some of these Infs may refer instead to other subsenses of **forget-me-not 1.**] **1966–67** *DARE* Wildfl QR Pl.182A Inf **WA10**, Forget-me-not; (Craighead) Pl.17.5 Inf **CO29**, Forget-me-not. **1976** Bailey–Bailey *Hortus Third* 749, Forget-me-nots are cultivated mostly outdoors and thrive in partly shady positions in moist soil.

b often *wild forget-me-not:* A **stickseed,** usu *Hackelia spp.* **West**

1897 Parsons *Wild Flowers CA* 334, The beautiful blossoms of the wild blue forget-me-not will be readily recognized by all lovers of flowers. **1915** (1926) Armstrong–Thornber *Western Wild Flowers* 424, *Wild Forget-me-not. . .* Beautiful flowers, resembling true Forget-me-nots, . . the most brilliant blue of any flower in Yosemite. **1968** *DARE* (Qu. S15) Inf **CA70**, Forget-me-not seeds. **1973** Hitchcock–Cronquist *Flora Pacific NW* 391, *Hackelia. . .* Stickseed; Wild Forget-me-not; Hackelia.

c A **fiddleneck 1,** esp *Amsinckia intermedia.* **West**

1897 Parsons *Wild Flowers CA* 128, Yellow Forget-me-not. . . *Amsinckia.* **1914** Georgia *Manual Weeds* 336, Yellow Forget-me-not. . . An unpleasant, hairy weed with sticky, bristly burs which make it a pest to California wool-growers. **1915** (1926) Armstrong–Thornber *Western Wild Flowers* 428, *Amsinckia intermedia. . .* These plants resemble white Forget-me-nots and are sometimes so called. **1935** (1943) Muenscher *Weeds* 377, *Amsinckia intermedia. . .* Yellow forget-me-not. . . Native to the Pacific Coast.

d A **popcorn flower,** usu *Plagiobothrys nothofulvus.* **Pacific**

1897 Parsons *Wild Flowers CA* 30, *Pop-corn Flower. White Forget-me-not. . .* The wild white forget-me-nots are among our most welcome flowers. **1911** *Century Dict. Suppl., Forget-me-not. . . White forget-me-not. . .* Some . . are included under the name . . *popcorn flower.* **1934** Haskin *Wild Flowers Pacific Coast* 301, *Plagiobothrys nothofulvus. . .* The white popcorn flower, or forget-me-not, grows in great abundance on dry open prairies from Oregon southward.

e =**hound's-tongue 1.**

1898 *Jrl. Amer. Folkl.* 11.275 **CA,** *Cynoglossum* (sp.), forget-me-nots.

f A plant of the genus *Cryptantha.* **West** Also called **hidden-flower, nievitas**

1900 Lyons *Plant Names* 267, White Forget-me-not. *Boraginaceae.* **1941** Jaeger *Wildflowers* 215, *Arched-calyxed* Forget-me-not. *Cryptantha recurvata. . .* Western Forget-me-not. *Cryptantha circumscissa. . .* Woody Forget-me-not. *Cryptantha racemosa. . .* Rough-stemmed Forget-me-not. *Cryptantha holoptera.* **1961** Thomas *Flora Santa Cruz* 290 **cwCA,** *Cryptantha. . .* White Forget-Me-Not. **1968** *DARE* (Qu. S26e) Inf **CA60**, Wild forget-me-nots—nievitas [in] Spanish. **1973** Hitchcock–Cronquist *Flora Pacific NW* 388, White Forget-me-not. Fl[ower]s gen[erally] borne in a series of sympodial, helicoid, naked or bracteate false spikes.

g A plant of the genus *Eritrichium.* **chiefly Rocky Mts** Also called **alpine forget-me-not**

1906 Rydberg *Flora CO* 286, *Eritrichium. . .* Mountain Forget-me-not. **1963** Craighead *Rocky Mt. Wildflowers* 156, *Eritrichium elongatum. . .* Dwarf Forget-me-not. . . A dwarf alpine cushion plant bearing a mass of brilliant blue or occasionally white flowers scarcely 1/4 in.

broad. **1973** Hitchcock-Cronquist *Flora Pacific NW* 391, *Eritrichium. . .* False or Alpine Forget-me-not.

h as *wild forget-me-knot:* A **lungwort** (here: *Mertensia lanceolata*).

1950 Stevens *ND Plants* 238, *Mertensia lanceolata. . .* Lungwort. Wild Forget-me-not.

2 also *wild forget-me-not:* =**bluet 2.**

1829 Eaton *Botany* 246, *Houstonia. . . caerulea . .* venus' pride, forget-me-not. **1892** *Jrl. Amer. Folkl.* 5.97, *Houstonia caerulea. . .* Forget-me-not. Kentucky. **1896** *Ibid* 9.190, *Houstonia caerulea, . .* forget-me-not, Oxford County, M[ain]e. **1911** *Century Dict. Suppl., Forget-me-not. . . Wild forget-me-not,* the bluet or innocence, *Houstonia caerulea.* **1949** Moldenke *Amer. Wild Flowers* 171, *Common bluets. . .* Among the plant's many popular names are *wild-forgetmenot [etc].* **1959** [see **3** below]. **1965-70** *DARE* (Qu. S11) 9 Infs, **scattered,** Forget-me-not(s); **VT**4, 13, Wild forget-me-nots; (Qu. S23) Inf **NY**21, Forget-me-nots, but real name bluets.

3 A **johnny-jump-up** or violet; see quots.

1832 Hale *Flora's Interp.* 65 *(DA),* Forget-me-not. *Viola cucula.* A species of the Violet common to America. Color blue. **1959** Carleton *Index Herb. Plants* 48, *Forget-me-not:* Ajuga chamaepitys; Houstonia caerulea; Omphalodes verna; Teuchrium [sic] scorodonia; Veronica chamaedrys; Viola tricolor. **1966** *DARE* (Qu. S3) Infs **MS**1, **NC**30, Forget-me-not.

4 A **blue-eyed grass 1** (here: *Sisyrinchium angustifolium*).

1897 *Jrl. Amer. Folkl.* 10.145, *Sisyrinchium angustifolium, . .* forget-me-not, Hartford, M[ain]e.

5 A **speedwell,** either *Veronica americana* or *V. chamaedrys.* [*OED* 1853 →]

1900 Lyons *Plant Names* 391, *V. Chamaedrys. . .* Forget-me-not. **1934** Haskin *Wild Flowers Pacific Coast* 325, *Veronica americana. . .* The pretty little speedwells are often called forget-me-nots. **1940** Clute *Amer. Plant Names* 33, *V. chamaedrys. . .* Eyebright, forget-me-not. **1966-68** *DARE* Wildfl QR Pl.199B Infs **CO**7, **MN**30, **WA**10, Forget-me-not(s).

6 A **Jacob's ladder** (here: *Polemonium reptans*).

1900 Lyons *Plant Names* 298, *P. reptans. . .* Bluebell, Forget-me-not. **1940** Clute *Amer. Plant Names* 228, *Polemonium reptans.* Blue-bells, for-get-me-not, Jacob's ladder.

7 usu *white forget-me-not:* =**flowering spurge.**

1936 IL Nat. Hist. Surv. *Wildflowers* 182, The Flowering Spurge. . . is frequently used . . under the name White Forget-me-not. **1940** Clute *Amer. Plant Names* 259, *Euphorbia corollata.* Emetic root, white forget-me-not.

forgettery n Also sp *forgetery, forgetory* [By facetious analogy with *memory*] *joc*

The faculty of forgetting; a poor memory.

1862 *Harper's New Mth. Mag.* 25.113/2, Her memory being rather a 'forgettery,' all she could say of the text was that 'it was sothin' 'bout dey was weighed in de balance an' come up missin'.' **1907** Lincoln *Cape Cod* 86, The sooner you box that fact up in your forgetory, the smoother 'twill be. **1911** *DN* 3.543 **NE,** "I have a good forgettery," "I'll store that in my forgettery." **1929** *Ruppenthal Coll.* **KS,** My forgetery has become better and my memory worse. **1967-68** *DARE* (Qu. JJ30a, . . *Expressions for forgetting something: "I ———."*) Inf **TN**12, Have a fine forgettery; (QR p94) Inf **CA**71, I've the best forgettery of everybody.

forgit See **forget**

for good See **for B4a(3)**

for greens See **green** n **3**

for having adv phr

In marbles games: =**for keeps.**

1970 *DARE* Tape **NC**88, That was quite a bit of fun as long as we were playin' for fun, but when we played for havin' I would always get out of the game.

forid See **forward** adj, adv

fork n Pronc-spp *fawk, fock*

A Forms.

1922 Gonzales *Black Border* 300 **sSC, GA coasts** [Gullah glossary], *Fawk*—(n. and v.) fork, forks, forked, forking. **1929** Sale *Tree Named John* 88 **MS,** De focks uv de road.

B Senses.

1 pl, but sg in constr: The point at which something, esp a road or stream, divides; a fork; the area around the confluence of two streams. **chiefly Sth, S Midl**

1645 in 1863 MA Hist. Soc. *Coll.* 4th ser 6.375 **swMA,** 2 of our Towne going downe the River . . were cast away, eather a litle before they came to the forks or at the first enterance. **1763** Roberts *Acct. FL* 12, The *Euchi* creek, on the forks of which is a village of the same name. **1805** (1905) Clark *Orig. Jrls. Lewis & Clark Exped.* 3.8 **VA,** The forks of this river is famous as a gig fishery. **1837** Sherwood *Gaz. GA* 69, [In a list of 'Provincialisms' to be avoided:] *Forks of Road,* fork. **1848** Bartlett *Americanisms* 148, *Forks.* In the plural, the point where a road parts into two; and the point where a river divides, or rather where two rivers meet. **1907** *DN* 3.212 **nwAR, cCT,** *Forks. . .* A place where a road parts into two. **1923** *DN* 5.207 **swMO,** *Forks. . .* The point where a road, trail, tree, stream or plant divides into branches. **1939** *Hall Coll.* **wNC, eTN,** We went on up the creek, we come to a forks. **1966-68** *DARE* (Qu. N32, *A place where roads cross at right angles*) Infs **GA**30, **MS**72, Forks of the road; **CO**33, Forks; **MD**31, Forks—where four roads intersect; a crossroads—where two roads intersect. **1971** *Foxfire* Spring-Summer 42 **nGA,** There was a forks of a road somewhere near a church.

2 The front arch of a saddletree.

1937 Sandoz *Slogum* 180 **NE,** She ordered a saddle of bright stamped leather for Ward, with a stout fork and plenty of good strings. **1958** *AmSp* 33.270 **eWA,** *Fork. . .* The tree of a saddle.

3 pl: The corner (of an animal's mouth).

1939 *Hall Coll.* **wNC,** So pretty soon I seen, well, just his [=a bear's] nose from about the forks of his mouth down. I cut direct at 'im. I was shootin' a thirty-thirty and I broke both of his underjaws, just snapped 'em in two.

4 A sawbuck.

1966-69 *DARE* (Qu. L59, *An implement with an x-frame to hold firewood for sawing*) Inf **NM**3, Forks; **GA**72, Saw fork.

5 A metal support for wood in a fireplace.

1967 *DARE* (Qu. D32) Inf **WA**27, Forks; wood irons.

fork v

1 To bestride (a horse). [*fork* the divergence of the legs] **chiefly West**

1903 (1965) Adams *Log Cowboy* 295 **West,** So fork that swimming horse of yours and wet your big toe again in the North Platte. **1920** Hunter *Trail Drivers TX* 300. **1929** Dobie *Vaquero* 294 **West,** He . . was one of the best cowmen that ever forked a horse. **1933** *AmSp* 8.1.28 **nwTX.** **1939** FWP *Guide MT* 414. **1939** FWP *ID Lore* 242. **1942** *AmSp* 17.74 **NE.** **1958** Blasingame *Dakota Cowboy* 250, Even Peavine, the crankiest old cowpuncher ever to fork a horse, laughed like a kid. **1958** *AmSp* 33.270 **eWA.** **1967** *DARE* FW Addit **nNY,** To *fork a cack* is to mount a saddle. **1968** *DARE* (Qu. OO27b, *Talking about riding horses: "All my life I've ———."*) Inf **CA**90, Forked horses.

2 with *up:* See quot. [Orig a mining term; *OED fork* v. 9 1702 →]

1940 *AmSp* 15.447 **eTN,** *Fork up.* To draw water. 'I fork up the water out of the well.'

forked ppl adj Usu |fɔrkt, forkt, fɔ(ə)kt|; also **esp Midl** |'fɔrkɪd, 'fɔ(ə)kɪd| Pronc-sp *fockit* See Intro "Language Changes" IV.3 Cf **forkity, forky**

A Forms.

1929 Sale *Tree Named John* 55 **MS,** Dey's all got a fockit tongue. **1965-70** *DARE* (Qq. CC13a, CC8) 18 Infs, **scattered, but esp Midl,** ['fɔ(r)kɨd, -əd]; **FL**22, **KY**51, ['forkt]; (Qu. X26b) Inf **IN**30, ['fɔrkɨd]-eyed; (Qu. KK11) Inf **KY**84, [fɔrkɪd]. **1966-68** *DARE* Tapes **AL**3, 45, ['fɔrkɪd]. **1967** *Wilson Coll.* **csKY,** [fɔrkɪd]. **1973** [see **forked end**].

B Senses.

1 Violent, remarkable.

1851 Burke *Polly Peablossom* 72 **MS,** The way they did hustle her about amongst the straw and shucks was forked! **1970** *DARE* (Qu. KK11, *To make great objections . . "When we asked him to do that, he ———."*) Inf **KY**84, Had a forked fit.

2 Of a cattle brand: see quot.

1931 (1960) Dobie *Open Range* 175, V-shaped prongs attached to some part of a letter make it "forked."

3 See quot.

1953 Randolph-Wilson *Down in Holler* 109 **Ozarks,** To describe a girl as *fork-ed* is to call her bold, brazen, "crazy about men."

forked chickweed See **chickweed 1c**

forked end n [*EDD* (at *fork* sb. 4)]

The lower half of the body; the legs and feet.

1862 in 1962 Truxall *Respects To All* 18 **PA,** Well in the first place we are all on our forked end and able for our allowance. **1973** in 1986 *Barrick Coll.* **csPA,** "I'm still on the forkèd end" [i.e., I'm still alive and walking]. **1985** *NC Folkl. Jrl.* 33.39 **wNC** (as of c1920), If someone asked her how she was feeling, she usually answered, "I've still got the fork-ed end down and am ready to go."

forked-eyed adj

1968 *DARE* (Qu. X26b, *If a person's eyes look in different directions, looking outward, he's* ______) Inf **IN**30, ['fɔrkɨd]-eyed.

forked-tail(ed) in combs See **forktail** entries and **fork-tailed** entries

for keeps adv phr Also *for keepses* [Prob Scots dial, though the only citation in *EDD* (at *keep* sb.[1] II. 17. (8)) is dated 1893] Cf **for B4a(3), for fun, keeps**

In marbles games: on condition that marbles taken will be kept; sometimes quasi-noun, a particular marbles game played for keeps.

1861 *Ladies' Repository* 21.627/1, Pay him! Nothing. He and I played for 'keeps,' and I was the best player and won all his. **1893** Shands *MS Speech* 30, In playing *for keeps,* each player puts a certain number of marbles in a ring, and each keeps all that he knocks out. **1899** (1912) Green *VA Folk-Speech* 249, To play marbles *"for keeps,"* each player to keep the marbles he wins. **1908** *DN* 3.312 **eAL, wGA,** *For keeps. . .* In games of marbles, for good. **1953** Brewer *Word Brazos* 24 **eTX** [Black], One Sunday he passes a bunch of li'l' ole boys on de plannuhtation playin' marbles for keeps. **1965-70** *DARE* (Qu. EE7) 43 Infs, **scattered, but more freq Sth, S Midl,** Play for keeps; **MS**90, Shooting for keeps; **NC**9, Play for keepses. **1966-69** *DARE* Tape **CA**172, There was another game too that they used to use when they played for keeps. . . [It] was to make a board and put holes near the bottom edge . . and the player would shoot . . for those holes, and if you went through the biggest hole with a marble you got one in return. If you went through the smallest . . you get six marbles. . . That was for keeps; **TX**30, I remember the expression, 'play for keeps.' [Aux Inf:], Yeah, that's where you'd knock the marbles out and keep 'em, you see; **WA**7, When you hit it with the marble and you launched at it, you kept that if you played for keeps. **c1970** Wiersma *Marbles Terms,* 10 infs, **MI, IA, KS, NJ, WA,** For keeps. **1973** Ferretti *Marble Book* 61, A city dweller who happens to be an expert shooter . . almost invariably will play "for keeps" with some fellows he may never see again. **1983** *MJLF* 9.1.39 **ceKY,** *For keeps* . . games in which players keep marbles they win, as opposed to "for fun."

fork hooks n pl [*OED fork* sb. 3. b *"(slang).* The fingers."; 1812 →]

1967 *DARE* (Qu. X32, *Joking . . words for the hands*) Inf **MI**72, Fork hooks, hooks, meat hooks.

forking stick n

A **dowsing rod.**

1968 *DARE* (Qu. CC13a, . . *To show where there's water underground*) Inf **MO**1, It's a forking stick they use.

forkity adj Cf Intro "Language Changes" III.1

Forked.

1930 Stoney-Shelby *Black Genesis* 108 **seSC,** Den he got a long soople saplin' wid a forkity end, an' he poked it up.

fork-leaf white oak n

=**white oak.**

1960 Vines *Trees SW* 149, *White Oak—Quercus alba—* . . Vernacular names are Stave Oak, Fork-leaf White Oak, and Ridge White Oak. **1971** Krochmal *Appalachia Med. Plants* 212, *Quercus Alba* . . fork-leaf white oak.

fork ridge n

A ridge which separates two confluent streams.

1939 *Hall Coll.* **wNC,** They turned right back down the Big Woolly Head Ridge, the fork ridge between the two forks of the left-hand fork of Deep Creek.

forks pass See **faux pas** n

forktail See **forktail hawk**

forktail cat See **forktail catfish 1**

forktail catfish n

1 as *fork(ed)-tail cat, fork-tailed ~, great fork-tail(ed) ~:* =**blue catfish 1.**

1882 U.S. Natl. Museum *Bulletin* 16.108, *I[ctalurus] lacustris. . .* Great Fork-tailed Cat. . . Caudal deeply forked, the upper lobe rather longer and narrower than the lower. **1933** LA Dept. of Conserv. *Fishes* 420, The Blue Cat. . . known also as the Great Fork-tail Cat. . . may be readily caught on trot lines baited with Crayfish or pieces of fish. **1956** Harlan-Speaker *IA Fish* 108, Blue Catfish. . . Other Names.—Chucklehead cat, forktail cat, great blue cat. **1969** *DARE* (Qu. P1) Inf **KY**49, Forked-tail cat.

2 =**white catfish.**

1946 LaMonte *N. Amer. Game Fishes* 163, *Ictalurus catus. . .* Fork-tail Catfish. . . Distinguishing Characteristics: Its deeply forked tail and its range. **1960** Amer. Fisheries Soc. *List Fishes* 53, Forktail catfish—see catfish, white. **1975** Evanoff *Catch More Fish* 94, The white catfish . . is also called the forktail catfish.

fork-tailed cat See **forktail cat 1**

fork-tailed gull n

=**Sabine's gull.**

1844 DeKay *Zool. NY* 2.312, The *Fork-tailed gull* is but an occasional visitor to our shores. **1946** Hausman *Eastern Birds* 319, *Sabine's Gull Xema sabini* . . Other Names—Fork-tailed Gull.

fork-tailed kite n Also *forked-tail kite*

=**swallow-tailed kite.**

1791 Bartram *Travels* 290, Falco furcatus, the forked tail hawk, or kite. **1894** Torrey *Fla. Sketch-Book* 138 *(DAE),* I descried some sharp-winged, strange-looking bird over our heads. . . A fork-tailed kite! **1946** Hausman *Eastern Birds* 180, Fork-tailed Kite. . . Tail long and very deeply forked. **1963** Gromme *Birds WI* 215, Fork-tailed kite. **1968** *DARE* Tape **GA**30, [FW:] What's the fastest bird in the swamp? [Inf:] The kite, the forked-tail kite.

fork-tailed petrel n Also *forked-tailed petrel*

Either of two petrels: *Oceanodroma furcata* of the Pacific coast, or *Oceanodroma leucorhoa,* found on both the Atlantic and Pacific coasts. The latter is also called **Mother Carey's chicken, stormy petrel, white-rumped petrel**

1835 Audubon *Ornith. Biog.* 3.435, The Forked-tailed Petrel is less numerous near the American coast than the species named after Wilson. **1844** Giraud *Birds Long Is.* 372, *Fork-tailed Petrel. . .* Length eight inches and three quarters, wing six. **1898** (1900) Davie *Nests N. Amer. Birds* 55, Fork-tailed Petrel. *Oceanodroma furcata. Ibid* 56, *Oceanodroma leucorhoa. . .* Leach's Fork-tailed Petrel at various seasons of the year wanders over a large portion of the watery expanse of the globe. **1917** (1923) *Birds Amer.* 1.85, *Leach's Petrel. . . Other Names.*—Common Fork-tailed Petrel; Leach's Fork-tailed Petrel. *Ibid* 86, Forked-tailed Petrel. *Oceanodroma furcata.* **1944** Hausman *Amer. Birds* 247, *Forked-tailed Petrel. . . Length*—8.60 inches. **1955** Forbush-May *Birds* 14, *Leach's Petrel. . . Other names:* Leach's Fork-tailed Petrel; . . Fork-tailed Petrel.

fork-tailed swallow n Also *forked-tail (barn) swallow, forktail ~*

=**barn swallow 1.**

1917 (1923) *Birds Amer.* 3.86/1, *Barn Swallow. Hirundo erythrogastra. . . Other Names.*—American Barn Swallow; . . Fork-tailed Swallow. **1965-70** *DARE* (Qu. Q20) Infs **AZ**9, **FL**22, **IL**7, **KS**15, **WI**61, Forktail swallow; **IL**32, Fork-tailed swallow; **MO**11, Forked-tail barn swallow; **CA**155, Forked-tail swallow.

forktail hawk n Also *forktail, forked-tail(ed) hawk*

=**swallow-tailed kite.**

1808 Ashe *Travels America* 159, Between ninety and an hundred American birds have been described by Catesby . . as follows: . . Fork-tail Hawk. **1844** DeKay *Zool. NY* 2.12, The *Swallow-tailed Hawk,* or *Fork-Tail,* is a southern species. **1850** U.S. Patent Office *Annual Rept. for 1849: Arts & Mfgr.* 621, Only two other birds he knew perform such a feat—the forked-tail hawk and the swift or chimney swallow. **1917** *Wilson Bulletin* 29.2.81, *Elanoides forficatus.*—Forked-tailed hawk, Hickman, Ky. **1955** *Oriole* 20.5, Swallow-tailed Kite. . . Fork-tail Hawk. **1962** Imhof *AL Birds* 167, *Swallow-tailed Kite. . . Other names:* . . Forked-tailed Hawk.

forktail swallow See **fork-tailed swallow**

forktail trout n
=**lake trout.**
1946 LaMonte *N. Amer. Game Fishes* 115, *Cristivomer namaycush*. . . Forktail Trout. **1972** Sparano *Outdoors Encycl.* 356, *Lake Trout*—Common Names: . . forktail . . Scientific Name: *Salvelinus namaycush.* **1975** Evanoff *Catch More Fish* 80.

fork-turn n
A place where a road divides into two branches.
1940 (1978) Still *River of Earth* 91 **KY,** We were on the road early next morning, going along with Father to the forkturn. **1953** Randolph–Wilson *Down in Holler* 52 **Ozarks,** When you come to the first fork-turn, take the left-hand prong.

fork up See **fork v 2**

forky adj [*OED* 1611 → (in comb *forkiness*)]
Forked, barbed.
1851 Hooper *Widow Rugby's Husband* 55 **AL,** A whole carryvan of blue-nose monkeys and forky-tail snakes. **1888** Jones *Negro Myths* 88 **GA coast,** De Debble . . wid eh forky tail, an eh claw. **1899** (1912) Green *VA Folk-Speech* 183, *Forky*. . . Forked.

forlay See **forelay**

form n [*OED* 1387 →] **appar chiefly Sth**
A long, backless bench.
1640 in 1850 CT (Colony) *Pub. Rec.* 1.449, Sixe cushions and one little forme. **1835** Ingraham *South-West* 1.194, They find themselves in a long, dimly-lighted apartment, without any article of furniture, except a backless form. **1893** (1900) Hale *New Engl. Boyhood* 25, They were simply long benches with what we call long "forms" in front. **1899** (1912) Green *VA Folk-Speech* 183, *Form*. . . A bench seat. **1932** Faulkner *Light in August* 112 **MS,** Eating, food, the diningroom, the ceremony of eating at the wooden forms.

form thing See **first form thing**

‡formulate v [Malaprop for *form*]
c1937 in 1977 *Amer. Slave Suppl. 1* 1.318 **AL,** Dem carriages would formulate in a long line and at de head would be de hearse.

fornent prep Usu |ˌfər'nɛn(s)t, -'nɪn(s)t|; for var prongs see quots Pronc-spp *fernen(s)t, ferninst, fornenst, fornin(s)t;* for addit varr see quots [Scots, nEngl, and Ir dial] **chiefly Midl**
1 also adv, adj: Opposite to, in front of, against, near; in front; opposite.
1823 *National Intelligencer* (*DN* 4.47), *Western Dialect . . fanent.* Opposite. **1829** Kirkham *Engl. Grammar* 192, *Vulgarisms. Common in . . Pennsylvania.* Furnentz—opposite. **1835** Crockett *Account* 123 **TN,** I walked with them to a room nearly fornent the old state-house. **1843** (1916) Hall *New Purchase* 79 **IN,** He lives rite fornence the tan house. **1911** *DN* 3.538 **eKY,** *Ferninst, prep.* Near to, adjoining. **1913** *DN* 4.58 **TN,** *Fornint, prep.* Close by; near. "The trail's over there fornint the house." **1917** *DN* 4.412 **wNC,** *Fernent, prep.* In front of. Also *ferninst.* **1918** *DN* 5.18 **NC,** *Fernent*. . . *Ferninst,* opposite. "He lives ferninst the hill." **1926** *DN* 5.400 **Ozarks,** *Fernent,* or *fernenst*. . . Beside, against, opposite. "His hat was a-layin' right fernent th' smoke-house." **1939** *Hall Coll.* **eTN, wNC,** "I crawled down through the alders by the river till I got fernint him." . . "The bear went up a tree ferninst us." Frequently used, especially by older people, . . according to a native woman resident. **1944** *PADS* 2.25 **cwNC,** Ferninst. . . Opposite to; against. *Ibid* 42 **wNC,** *Fornent, fornenst* [fɚ'nɛnt, -'nɪnt, -'nænt; -'nɛnst, -'nɪnst, -'nænst]: *prep.* Against, opposite. . . Common. *Ibid* 56 **MO,** Fornet [fɔr'nɛt]: *adj., adv.,* ((and *prep.*)) "We got fornet the other car before we knew who was in it." . . Very rare. **1952** Brown *NC Folkl.* 1.540 **wNC,** *Fernent, fernint* [fɚ'nɪnt, fɚ-]: *prep.* and *adv.* . . Opposite. *Ibid* 542 **wNC,** *Fornent, fornint: prep.* and *adv.* . . Opposite, in front of. **1964** *Mt. Life* Spring 54 **sAppalachians,** A few rare prepositions may be heard occasionally. . . *Fernenst* means *in front of* and *close by* at the same time but not as close as *against.* **1965–70** *DARE* (Qu. MM1, . . *'Opposite to' . . "The shed is ______ the barn."*) Infs **NC**35, **TN**3, 12, 14, Fernent; **KY**5, 25, 47, **MD**17, **VA**28, Ferninst; (Qu. MM6, . . *'Very close' . . "The house is ______ the park."*) Inf **IL**96, ['fɑrnɪst]; **IN**7, [ˌfɪr'nɪnst]; **TN**20, [fɚ'nɪnt]; (Qu. MM17, . . *Next to each other*) Inf **NY**42, Forninst each other—an Irish expression; (Qu. MM10, . . *"Is the car behind the house?" "No, I left it ______."*) Inf **IL**96, ['fɑrnɪst]. [5 of 13 total Infs call the term old-fash.] **1969** *DARE* FW Addit **NC,** "On the fernanth side of the hill." Used by older people. **1983** *MJLF* 9.1.39 **ceKY,** *Fernent* . . opposite.
2 Fig: opposed to, against. Cf **ferninster**
1862 (1864) Browne *Artemus Ward Book* 158, Axis him whether he's fur or fernenst slavery. **1915** *DN* 4.226 **wTX,** That is forninst my principles. **1960** Bailey *Resp. to PADS 20* **KS** *(I'm ______ him)* Forninst.
3 also adv: Beyond; behind; beneath.
1931 *PMLA* 46.1303 **sAppalachians,** A few words of more or less Scottish tincture follow: . . *fernent (ferninst),* near, or just beyond. *Ibid* 1306, Pole dirtied Lem's back (threw him) fernent the barn-lot. **1944** *PADS* 2.42, *Fornent, fornenst*. . . (Reported from S.C.: beneath.) **[1950** *WELS ("Where does she keep her broom?" "She stands it ______ the door.")* 1 Inf, **cwWI,** Hibernian—"ferninst."] **1952** Brown *NC Folkl.* 1.540, *Fernent, fernint*. . . Beneath.—South[ern NC]. . . *Fernenth: prep.* and *adv.* Opposite, beyond. "If it was me, I would put hit right yonder ferneth the sassafac bush."—West[ern NC]. **1968–69** *DARE* (Qu. MM4, . . *A short distance past . . "The mail box is just ______ the pine tree."*) Inf **VA**4A, [fə'nɨnt], out or beyond.

fornification See **-ification**

fornin(s)t See **fornent**

forn thing See **first form thing**

for play adv phr
In marble play: =**for fun.**
c1970 Wiersma *Marbles Terms* **swMI,** *For play:* (contrast to "for keeps") a ruling which allows the loser to re-possess all his lost marbles at the end of a game or series.

forrad, forrard(s) See **forward** adj, adv

for real See **for B4a(9)**

forr'ed, forrud adj, adv See **forward** adj, adv

forrud n See **forehead**

forsaken ppl adj [Cf *OED forsake* v. 2. b "to avoid, shun. *Obs.*"]
1929 *AmSp* 4.56 **Ozarks,** The word *forsake,* too, is in common use among the hillmen, who speak of a girl as *forsaken,* meaning that she has no suitors.

for soul See **for B4a(8)**

forstay See **fersteh**

for sure See **for B4b**

forsythia n
Std: a shrub of the genus *Forsythia.* Also called **blooming willow, flowering currant 2, golden bell, golden candlestick 2, jessamine, Scotch broom, sunshine bush**

forth and back adv phr, adj phr
Back and forth; for going back and forth.
1965 *DARE* File **cnIA,** I walked forth and back, forth and back, all night. **1968** *DARE* Tape **CA**100, We called it a drag saw because it dragged forth and back through. **[1977** Jones *OR Folkl.* 37 (as of early 1900s), A Sumpter assayer recalls the instance of a Cousin Jack [=Cornish miner] going into a shoe store and asking the clerk for *forth and back shoes.* The Cornish miner wanted shoes to wear from home to the mine and back.]

for that adv phr [Abbr]
For that matter, as far as that goes.
1941 Perry *Hold Autumn* 99 **TX,** I know the kids'll make a heap over this here runty calf; and Nona [=the speaker's wife] too, for that.

for the cry-eye See **cry-eye**

for the last longest adv phr
For a very long time.
1948 Hurston *Seraph* 33 **nFL** [Black], You ain't had no play-things out there for the last longest.

forthputting ppl adj [*OED* c1570 →; "Now chiefly *U.S.*"] **NEng** *arch*
Bold, forward, presumptuous.
1854 Hawthorne *Eng. Note-bks.* (1879) II.312 *(OED),* I should wrong her if I left the impression of her being forth-putting and obtrusive. **1878** *Atlantic Mth.* 41.307/2 **ME,** I'd ha' got my ears took off if I had been so forth-putting when I was little. **1883** Howells *Register* 19 **Boston MA,**

Do you think it was forth-putting at all, to ask him? **1887** (1895) Robinson *Uncle Lisha* 8 **wVT,** Loud and forthputting, there was Beri Burton, an uncouth giant. **1907** M. C. Harris *Tents of Wickedness* 14 *(DAE),* I have no patience with that forth-putting sort of person, always wanting to be 'of service' when there's a good looking girl about.

forthputting vbl n **[forthputting** ppl adj**] NEng** *arch*

Forwardness, presumption.

1856 Stowe *Dred* 1.153, Nina was as much annoyed at Clayton's silence, and his quiet, observant reserve, as with Carson's forth-putting. **1867** Lowell *Biglow* 2d ser 1.3 **'Upcountry' MA,** I say this . . to secure myself against any imputation of unseemly forthputting.

fortieth See **forty C**

fortifications n

1955 *PADS* 23.18 **cwTN,** *Fortifications*. . . A marble game.

for time conj phr

By the time.

1940 Harris *Folk Plays* 94 **NC,** Fer time I git het up in front, my hind parts is a-freezin'.

fortino adv phr Also sp *fortinah, fortiner, for-ti-'now, fortizno* [Pronc-spp for telescoped phr *for aught I know;* the var *fortizno* has prob been infl by the similar **farzino**] **chiefly NEng**

To the best of my knowledge, as far as I know.

1815 Humphreys *Yankey in England* 105 **CT,** *Fortino, fortizno,* for aught I know. **1823** Cooper *Pioneers* 1.210, The Presbyter'ans, and Congregationals, and Baptists too, for-ti-'now. **1848** Bartlett *Americanisms* 149, *Fortiner. (For-aught-I-know.)* This remarkable specimen of clipping and condensing a phrase . . is very common through New England, Long Island, and the rest of New York. **1890** *DN* 1.73, *Fortinah* [fɔət'aɪnə]: a contraction of 'for aught I know.' . . An aged New Haven lady remembers that her mother, who died forty-five years ago, used it occasionally. Mrs. Julia H. Wilson of New Britain, Conn., says that 'fortinah' was a frequent word with a Yankee servant in the employ of her father. . . Mrs. Wilson pronounces the *r*. . . Some friends of the said servant also used the word. **1892** *DN* 1.216 **swMA,** *Fortinah.*

fortnight n Also sp *fortni't* *old-fash* Cf **fortnightly club**

A period of two weeks. Note: While still widely recognized, *fortnight* is virtually obsolete in Amer colloq speech. It seems to have persisted longest east of the Mississippi River.

1859 (1968) Bartlett *Americanisms, Fortnight.* A Western man has remarked that this word is rarely heard in the new States, where, instead, they say "two weeks." **1898** Westcott *Harum* 323 **nNY,** The'd be spells fer a fortni't together when I couldn't any time of day git a word out of her hardly. **1959** *VT Hist.* new ser 27.136 **nwVT,** *Fortnight*. . . Occasional. **c1960** *Wilson Coll.* **csKY,** *Fortnight* . . known but not used. **1961** Folk *Word Atlas N. LA* map 109, Period of two weeks . . fortnight — 3% [of 275 infs]. Among the 19 not using *two weeks* only one is in the youngest group of informants. **1966–70** *DARE* (Qu. A15, . . *"He comes around ________."*) Inf **VA**71, Once in a fortnight (something the old folks say); (Qu. A16, . . *"I haven't seen him ________."*) Inf **DC**7, In a fortnight. [Both Infs old] **1973** Allen *LAUM* 1.151 (as of 1950s), *Fortnight* . . was added to the worksheets after the interviewing in Minnesota. Only 8.3% of the infs. in the other states offered the specific term *fortnight,* and more than half of those were in Iowa. Several considered the word old-fashioned or literary.

fortnightly club n Also *fortnightly*

A social group that meets every two weeks.

1950 *WELS (Clubs . . in your neighborhood)* 1 Inf, **csWI,** Fortnightly. **1965–70** *DARE* (Qu. FF1, . . *A kind of group meeting called a 'social'*) Inf **MO**26, Fortnightlies — for the children; (Qu. FF22a, . . *Clubs and societies . . for women*) Infs **IA**46, **IN**19, **MO**7, **NC**48, **NY**126, **OK**51, **WA**3, Fortnightly club; (Qu. FF22b, . . *For men*) Inf **DC**2, Fortnightly club.

fortni't See **fortnight**

for to See **for B1a**

for true See **for B4a(2), B4b**

‡fortune grass n

1969 *DARE* (Qu. L9a, . . *Grass grown for hay*) Inf **MO**37, Fortune grass.

fortune-teller n [From the practice of making a wish before blowing off the mature seed head]

A **dandelion 1** (here: *Taraxacum officinale*).

1900 Lyons *Plant Names* 365, *T. Taraxacum*. . . Fortune-teller. **1904** Henkel *Weeds Used in Med.* 13, *Taraxacum officinale*. . . *Other common names*. . . Fortune-teller. **1930** Sievers *Amer. Med. Plants* 26, *Dandelion*. . . *Other common names*. . . Fortune teller.

for-two-cents-plain n **NYC**

A serving of soda water; soda water.

1958 Golden *For 2¢ Plain* 81 **NYC,** It was time to enjoy a "for two cents plain," only now it is for five cents plain. I stood at the stand with its marble top, and . . asked the fellow to "put a little [=syrup] on the top." **1979** *DARE* File **NYC,** Perrier water is for-two-cents-plain for rich people.

forty adj, n Usu |'fɔrti, 'for-, 'fɔ(ə)-, 'fo(ə)-, -tɪ| Pronc-spp *fawty, fohty*

A Forms.

1922 Gonzales *Black Border* 300 **sSC, GA coasts** [Gullah glossary], *Fawty* — forty. **1928** in 1953 Botkin–Harlow *Treas. Railroad Folkl.* 233, Brakeman put you off thirty or fohty miles from nowhere. **1942** Hall *Smoky Mt. Speech* 35, In a number of words [o] rather than [ɔ] occurs before *r* . . ford, forty, four. **1942** *AmSp* 17.153 **seNY,** [In *forty-four,* both r's were pronounced by 41 infs; first r omitted by 1 inf; second r omitted by 7 infs; both r's omitted by 30 infs.] **c1960** *Wilson Coll.* **csKY,** Forty ['fɔrtɪ]. **1961** Kurath–McDavid *Pronc. Engl.* 121, Except for Pennsylvania and adjoining parts of New Jersey and Maryland, all areas have the /ɔ ~ ɒ/ phoneme . . in *forty*. . . In areas that preserve postvocalic /r/, the /ɔ/ vowel in *forty* . . is usually shorter than in other positions. . . In Upstate New York and Western New England the /ɔ/ of *forty* . . is extremely variable, [with the raised variants considered to be] . . positional allophones of /ɔ/. . . In Pennsylvania, Maryland, and New Jersey the /ɔ/ of *forty* . . must . . be regarded as an allophone of /o/. . . Western Pennsylvania has the phoneme /o/ in *forty.* **1964** O'Hare *Ling. Geog. E. MT* 175, A number of the informants do not seem to have a phonemic contrast of the type /or/; /ɔr/. Among those that do have such a contrast, there is little agreementas to the words in which one or the other occurs. No informant consistently differentiates 'four,' . . from 'forty.' **1967** *DARE* (QR p21) Inf **CA**15A, ['fɔti]. **1976** Allen *LAUM* 3.31 (as of c1950), [Map shows that the infs for whom the vowel of *four* is not higher than that in *forty* are chiefly in Iowa, Minnesota, and the eastern parts of South Dakota and Nebraska.]

B As noun.

1 A small tract of land, strictly one of forty acres. Cf **eighty** Note: Forty acres is the area of a quarter-mile square, the smallest substantial subdivision of a section of land, a one-mile square.

1845 Kirkland *Western Clearings* 70 **MI,** He'll want as much as one forty cleared right off. **1902** White *Blazed Trail* 9 **eMI. 1923** *DN* 5.234 **swWI,** A *forty* is the common unit of reckoning land. "How far is it over there?" "Oh, 'cross an eighty an' a forty." **1950** *WELS (A large piece of land under cultivation)* 2 Infs, **se,ceWI,** The back forty; the west forty. **1956** Sorden–Ebert *Logger's Words* 15 **Gt Lakes,** *Forty,* Smallest unit of acres which timber usually changes ownership. **1959** Faulkner *Mansion* 5 **MS,** Maybe he could still finish scratching that last forty. **1960** Criswell *Resp. to PADS 20* **Ozarks,** *Forty*. . . A tract of land . . containing forty acres. . . The usual term. **1961** Holbrook *Yankee Loggers* 121 **NEng. 1965–69** *DARE* (Qu. L6b, *A piece of land under cultivation — if it's several acres*) Inf **IA**8, South forty; **MI**67, Back forty; **OK**1, West forty; (Qu. T2b, . . *A piece of land covered with trees — if it's a large acreage*) Infs **MI**42, **WI**32, Forty; **MI**14, Forty of uncut timber; (Qu. C33, . . *An out-of-the-way place, or a very unimportant place*) Infs **MN**34, **WI**47, Back forty; (Qu. C35, *Nicknames for . . parts of your town*) Inf **CA**156, Indian Forty. **1967** *DARE* Tape **MI**54, He had a forty out here and another forty down on the lakeshore. **1967** *DARE* Tape **AL**20, When we built a home, we had a forty nearer the town. . . a forty acres. **1981** *DARE* File **Madison WI,** He's going up to look at a forty.

2 in compar phrr *as forty, like forty:* See quots.

1829 *Western Mth. Rev.* 2.643, As loving, as the Vermonter said, as *forty.* **1851** (1852) Stowe *Uncle Tom's Cabin* 1.117, I has principles, and I sticks to 'em like forty. **1854** (1932) Bell *Log TX-CA Trail* 234, The morning fairly, and gives a small indication of what it will be about noon — as hot as forty. **1897** *KS Univ. Qrly.* (ser B) 6.87, *(Like) forty:* for emphasis. — General. **1944** *Speleological Soc. Bul.* July 58/2 *(DA),* This stream is about 15′ wide with an average depth of 1½–2′, and goes like forty.

C As adj.

Used to express an indefinite, usu large, number; similarly *fortieth.* Cf **forty-eleven** adj, **forty-gallon Baptist, forty-gallons-of-soup, forty miles from nowhere, forty-rod, forty winks**

1851 Burke *Polly Peablossom* 95 **GA,** The dogs [were] a barkin and yelpin like forty thousand. **1871** Eggleston *Hoosier Schoolmaster* 33 **IN,** Her looks made Ralph's spirits sink to forty below zero, and congeal. **1872** Eggleston *End of the World* 110 **sIN,** You begin to fire off your forty-pound bomb-shell book-words. **1877** Jewett *Deephaven* 53 **ME,** I should have forty fits, if I undertook it. **1897** *KS Univ. Qrly.* (ser B) 6.87, *Fortieth:* same as "forty leventh" and "steenth."—General. **1902** Wister *Virginian* 162, I've a forty-dollar thirst. **1950** *PADS* 14.78 **FL,** *Forty* miles behind. Used with reference to an accumulation of work. *Ibid* 80, *Smell* him forty miles against the wind. Said of a person who needs a bath. **1961** Adams *Old-Time Cowhand* 185, He jes' swooped down like forty hen hawks on a settin' quail.

forty adv [Perh <*fortunate,* but cf **forty** n **B2**]

See quot.

1937 in 1970 Hyatt *Hoodoo* 2.1164 **eVA,** Chance is things is *not breaking so forty* with you? You don't handle the money good, do you? Seems like everything you put your hands to it's a failure?

forty acres n pl **Upper MW** Cf **acre-foot**

Extremely large feet.

1950 *WELS (Humorous or uncomplimentary names for big feet)* 4 Infs, **ce,seWI,** Forty acres. **1968–69** *DARE* (Qu. X38) Infs **MI**93, **MN**33, Forty acres.

forty axes n pl [Prob by metath from **aggie forti(e)s**]

1968 *DARE* (Qu. H74a, . . *Coffee . . very strong*) Inf **TX**52, Strong as forty axes; **IN**7, Strong as forty ['ɛksɪz].

forty-eleven adj, hence *forty-eleventh* Pronc-sp *forty-leven joc* Cf **forty** adj **C**

Indefinitely numerous.

1860 Holmes *Professor* 146 **MD,** On asking him what was the number of his room, he answered, that it was forty-'leven, sky-parlour floor. **1872** Schele de Vere *Americanisms* 313, A *forty-eleventh cousin* . . expresses an infinitesimal degree of relationship. **a1883** (1911) Bagby *VA Gentleman* 306, Perpetual motion, doubled and twisted, and tied, and turned, and tacked, and tangled into forty-'leven thousand double bowknots. **1897** *KS Univ. Qrly.* (ser B) 6.53 **KS,** *Forty-eleventh:* very distant; as a forty-eleventh cousin. **1908** *DN* 3.312 **eAL, wGA,** There was about forty-'leven mosquitoes on me. **1910** *DN* 3.441 **cwNY,** Forty-'leven. **1912** Green *VA Folk-Speech* 183, *Forty-eleventh cousin.* **1915** *DN* 4.183 **wIN,** Forty 'leven. **1954** *Harder Coll.* **cwTN,** Ain't no use a-goin' no forty-eleven mile. **1959** *VT Hist.* new ser 27.136, *More than forty-leven. . .* A large number. Occasional. **1960** Criswell *Resp. to PADS 20* **Ozarks,** *Forty-leven. . .* Fairly common for a long time and still probably used. Somewhat humorous expression. **c1960** *Wilson Coll.* **csKY,** *Forty-leven dozen.* **1968** *DARE* (QR p114) Inf **CT**14, Forty-eleven things to do. **1968** *DARE* Tape **MO**25, We had to walk forty-'leven times a day to the cellar.

forty-eleven n [From **forty-four** infl by **forty-eleven** adj]

1954 *Harder Coll.* **cwTN,** *Forty-elevens*—white beans, because of the amount of digestive gas supposed to be inherent in the beans.

forty-eleventh See **forty-eleven** adj

forty-five n

1 also pl: A card game in which the first person to gain 45 points is the winner. **NEast**

1880 W. B. Dick *Amer. Hoyle* 221 *(DAE),* Forty-five. **1966–70** *DARE* (Qu. DD35, . . *Favorite card games*) Infs **ME**1, 19, **MA**80, **NY**213, Forty-five. **1974** Gibson *Hoyle* 123, *Forty-five:* The modern form of *Spoil Five* . . played without the "spoil," scoring points for tricks instead. . . Individually, each trick counts 5 points, and the first player to reach 45 wins the game. . . This game is very popular in the Canadian Maritime Provinces. **1975** Gould *ME Lingo* 100, *Forty-five*—Also heard as *forty-fives;* a card game dearly loved in Aroostook County, introduced from the Maritimes.

2 See **forty-four.**

forty-five-ninety n [See quot 1966]

A large sausage.

1966 *DARE* Tape **MI**10, They [=loggers] were apt to call 'em forty-five-nineties, after a rather sizable rifle cartridge of the time. **1969** Sorden *Lumberjack Lingo* 44 **NEng, Gt Lakes,** *Forty-five-ninety*—Sausage.

forty-four n, usu pl Also *forty-four bean, forty-five* [*.44* (or *.45*) caliber cartridge, in reference to the shape and to the flatulence produced] Cf **forty-eleven** n

A bean.

1942 Berrey–Van den Bark *Amer. Slang* 91.73, *Beans* . . forty-fives, forty-fours. **1954** *Harder Coll.* **cwTN,** *Forty-four (bean)* (44's) . . navy bean. *Forty-fours* . . white soup beans; so called because white beans are supposed to create an exorbitant amount of gas in the stomach.

forty-gallon Baptist n, also attrib [Prob in reference to baptism by total immersion]

=deep-water Baptist.

1871 Eggleston *Hoosier Schoolmaster* 102 **IN,** The "Hardshell Baptists," or, as they are otherwise called, the "Whisky Baptists," and the "Forty-gallon Baptists," exist in all the old Western and South-western States. **1885** *Century Illustr. Mag.* 29.678 **nAL,** [I] don't keer ef ye do call 'im a Hardshell an' a Forty-gallon, an' a' Iron-Jacket Baptus. **1936** *Esquire* Sept 182/3 **KY,** I don't care if he does belong to the Forty Gallon Baptis and you are a Slab Baptis. **1940** Stuart *Trees of Heaven* 292 **neKY,** He was kicked out'n the Forty-Gallon Baptist Church. **1959** *IN Mag. Hist.* 55.233 (as of a1920), But it was not so much the daily routine which increased girths . . , it was the overtime extras: the Family reunions, . . the Old Baptist—Hardshell and Forty Gallon—Meetings, . . and Golden Wedding Celebrations.

forty-gallons-of-soup n

=great blue heron.

1956 *AmSp* 31.182 **NC,** The great blue heron has been labeled *forty gallons of soup* for its strong flavor.

forty-knot n

A chaff-flower (here: *Alternanthera repens*).

1876 Hobbs *Bot. Hdbk.* 39, Forty knot . . *Achyranthis repens.* **1889** *Century Dict.* 2346, *Forty-knot. . .* The *Alternanthera Achyrantha,* a prostrate amarantaceous weed of warm countries. It is said to have diuretic properties.

forty-leven See **forty-eleven** adj

forty miles from nowhere adv phr Also *forty miles the other side of nowhere* Cf **backside of nowhere, end of nowheres**

Far from any place of note, "out in the sticks."

1908 *DN* 3.312 **eAL, wGA,** *Forty miles from nowhere. . .* Far from any civilized or settled section. **1912** *DN* 3.576 **wIN,** We were over in Brown County last week, about forty miles the other side of nowhere. **1950** *WELS (An out-of-the-way place)* 1 Inf, **cnWI,** Forty miles from nowhere. **c1960** *Wilson Coll.* **csKY,** Forty (or any other) miles from nowhere.

forty miles of bad road n

Fig: An unattractive person or sight.

1970 *DARE* (Qu. X50, . . *A person who is very fat*) Inf **NJ**63A, Forty miles of bad road. **1989** *NADS Letters* **NY,** *40 miles of bad road.* When I attended college in the early 50's in upstate New York (with many people from the upper midwest), the term was used to describe someone (especially a female) who was especially unattractive. *Ibid,* While the chicken hawk lay there battered and broken, Leghorn [=a cartoon character] commented that he looked like *forty miles of bad road.* Also, since moving to middle Tennessee, I have actually heard the expression used by neighbors in reference to unattractive people or unsightly conditions of any kind. Moreover, a colleague . . from Memphis . . reports that she's heard the expression all of her life in reference to unattractive persons, usually in the context "she looks like forty miles of bad road." **1989** *DARE* File **Philadelphia PA,** You could tell she was having a hard time of it. By the time she got here, she looked like forty miles of bad road. *Ibid* **OK,** The phrase *forty miles of bad road* is used quite a bit. It means that whatever you're talking about is pretty bad. I always thought it referred to Oklahoma roads. . . You'd say a thing—a car or a house—looked like forty miles of bad road. You'd say it about a person too, but that's really an insult.

forty miles till Sunday See **Sunday, forty ways till**

forty miles to Borneo n

1901 *DN* 2.140 **seNY,** *Forty miles to Borneo. . .* The name of a game played on ice.

forty-rod adj, also used absol [Orig literally "capable of killing at forty rods" (see quot 1856), but later sometimes understood in other ways (see quot 1929)]

Very powerful—usu used of cheap liquor.

[**1856** Brewerton *War in KS* 254, The title is nothing more nor less than "rot-gut whisky," with an addenda [sic] about its "killing forty rods round a corner," which . . is an every-day remark in Missouri.] **1875** Twain *Sketches New & Old* (Hartford) 70, Trading for forty-rod whiskey, to enable you to get drunk and happy. **1896** Twain in *Harper's New Mth. Mag.* 93.524/1, Then he busted out and had another of them forty-rod laughs of his'n. **1909** (1922) Norris *Third Circle* 108 **CA,** And a mouthful of cold water, which the same we will thicken with forty-rod rye. **1929** *AmSp* 4.386 **KS,** The term *forty-rod whiskey* is said to imply that a man cannot walk more than forty rods after taking a drink of it, although another school of thinkers contends that a drink of this beverage actually causes the drinker to *run* forty rods before he can stop himself! **1931** Willison *Here They Dug* 235 **wCO,** The Odeon especially is notorious for its "forty-rod vitriol." **1934** *Sun* (Baltimore MD) 21 Apr 10/7 *(Hench Coll.),* Our Virginia neighbors have acquired so settled an appetite for corn likker that it has been found necessary to make provision for the manufacture of forty-rod. **1941** Writers' Program *Guide WY* 175, When the cowboys came to town . . they spent cash freely on '40 rod' whisky and other available entertainment. **c1960** *Wilson Coll.* **csKY,** *Forty-rod. . .* Whiskey of unusual potency. **1969** *DARE* (Qu. DD21b, . . *Bad liquor*) Inf **MA**58, Forty-rod.

forty-two n **chiefly TX** See Map

A game played with dominoes; see quot 1915.

1915 *DN* 4.226 **TX,** *Forty-two. . .* A state-wide game (said to have originated in Texas) played with dominoes. The sum of the "counters" (four-one, blank-five, two-three, six-four, and double-five) gives it the name "42." **1949** Perry *Granny Van* 153 **TX,** She always attended the regular meetings, at which . . the ladies played "42"—and . . Granny . . was a constant offender at . . advising her partner just which domino to play. **1954** *Harder Coll.* **cwTN,** *Forty-two. . .* A table game played with dominoes. **1960** Carpenter *Tales Manchaca* 39 **cTX** (as of c1880), We also played dominoes and forty-two, but we did not have a deck of regular playing cards in the house because Ma associated "spotted cards" with gambling and drunkenness. **1965–70** *DARE* (Qu. DD37, . . *Games played . . by adults*) Infs **AR**51, **OK**25, **TX**4, 18, 27, 29, 39, 40, 43, 53, 81, 89, 100, 104, Forty-two; (Qu. DD35) Infs **LA**18, **OK**11, **TX**13, Forty-two; **TX**3, Forty-two—a domino game; (Qu. FF2, . . *Kinds of parties*) Inf **TX**58, Forty-two games; one set of dominoes and two couples.

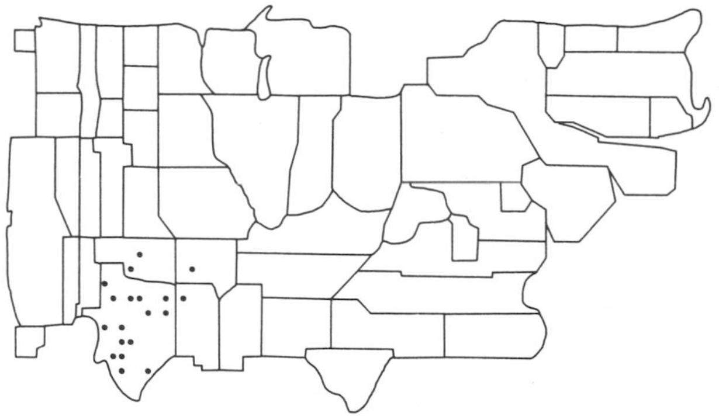

•forty-two + var (Qq. DD37, DD35, FF2)

forty ways for (or from, till, to) Sunday See **Sunday, forty ways till**

forty winks n pl **scattered, but less freq Sth, S Midl** See Map

A nap.

1942 Berrey–Van den Bark *Amer. Slang* 251.2, *Nap . .* forty winks. **1950** *WELS ("I'm just going to ______.")* 15 Infs, **WI,** Take (*or* catch, get, grab) forty winks. **c1960** *Wilson Coll.* **csKY,** *Forty winks . .* A short nap. **1965–70** *DARE* (Qu. X41, . . *"I'm just going to ______."*) 52 Infs, 7 **Sth, S Midl,** (Catch, take, get, grab, *or* nap) forty winks; (Qu. X40) Inf **NJ**2, Get forty winks; (Qu. X43b) Inf **NY**232, Caught forty extra winks.

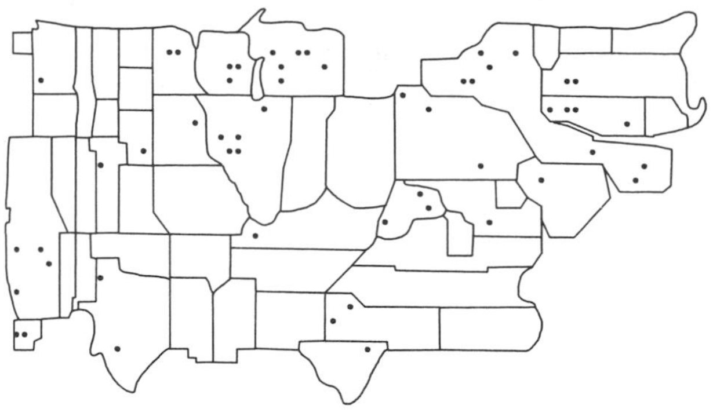

•forty winks + varr (Qq. X41, X40, X43b)

forward adj, adv Usu |ˈfɔrwərd(z), ˈfɔ(ə)wəd(z)|; also freq |ˈfɔrəd(z), ˈfɑwəd|; for addit varr see quots Also *forwards* Pronc-spp *for(r)ard(s), farrit, forid, forrad, forrud, fawwu'd, foward*

A Std senses, var forms.

1795 Dearborn *Columbian Grammar* 135, *List of Improprieties. . .* Forard. **1843** (1916) Hall *New Purchase* 281 **IN,** Touch then your "forrad" trigger and your ball is in the centre of the target. **1898** Westcott *Harum* 240 **Upstate NY,** 'Sore forr'ed?' I says, lookin' up at the driver. . . 'What's that?' says Price. . . 'I don't see anythin' the matter with his forehead.' he says. I looked up an' give the driver a wink. **1899** Edwards *Defense* 1 **GA,** I cussed 'er comin' an' goin', for'ards and back'ards, all erroun' an' straight through. **1899** (1912) Green *VA Folk-Speech* 183, *Forrud.* **1903** *DN* 2.291 **Cape Cod MA** (as of 1850s), The *w*-sound frequently assimilated or disappeared after a consonant . . *forrard = forward.* **1915** *DN* 4.183 **swVA,** *Forid.* Variant of *forward,* impudent. **1922** Gonzales *Black Border* 301 **sSC, GA coasts** [Gullah glossary], *Fawwu'd*—forward. **1926** Walrond *Tropic Death (ADD),* Farrit. **1927** Shewmake *Engl. Pronc. VA* 42, *Forward.* The standard pronunciation predominates, but *foward,* riming with *coward,* is used by some educated speakers. **c1940** Eliason *Word Lists FL* 4 **nwFL, c,cnNC,** *Forward* [fɑuwəd]. **1942** In 1944 *ADD* **eWV,** [fæ̞rd]. Rimes with Howard [hæ̞rd]. **1967** *Wilson Coll.* **csKY,** [ˈfɔrɔrdz]. **1967** *DARE* FW Addit **cwLA** [Black], [ˈfɑwəd]. **1970** *DARE* (Qu. KK51, *Very plainly or abruptly*) Inf **MO**22, Straight foward. **1973** *PADS* 60.54 **seNC,** (A mother and son whose ancestors came from the more conservative Outer Banks) gave the vowel the sound of the diphthong /au/ in one of the words [=*fought* and *forward*]. Neither used it in both. This is an infrequent but not unheard-of survival in the area surrounding the lower Neuse valley, as I know from my childhood.

B As adj.

Advanced, ahead, in var fig senses, as:

a Advanced toward some goal. [*OED* 1526 →]

1857 in 1956 Eliason *Tarheel Talk* 272 **NC,** I am forwarder with the crop this year than I ever have been befour. **1933** *Sun* (Baltimore MD) 27 Apr 8/2 *(Hench Coll.),* We are certainly somewhat "forrarder" on this thorny issue, though with a long way before us. **1945** Colcord *Sea Language* 82 **ME, Cape Cod, Long Island,** I can't seem to get any forrarder with this job. **1962** Faulkner *Reivers* 59 **MS,** But there we were. I mean, we were no forrader.

b Of crops or animals: well developed for their age or the season. [*OED* 1591 →]

1895 *DN* 1.371 **neTN, NEng,** I've got some forrard peaches. **1922** *DN* 5.184 **GA,** *Forward. . .* Early. "He hed done grabbed fo 'er [=four of] my forwardes' pullets." The same term is also applied to early vegetables.

c Of a child: precocious. [*OED* 1591 →]

1845 in 1934 Frear *Lowell & Abigail* 184 **MA,** She is a fine healthy little girl. . . She is quite forward—talks a good deal—is ever busy.

d Of a woman or female animal: far along in pregnancy.

1931–33 *LANE Worksheets* **swCT,** She's pretty forward with a calf [FW: Inf also used in ref to a woman.]; **nwCT,** She's pretty forward with child.

C As adv.

In prep phr *forward of:* In front of, in a forward direction from.

1838 (1932) Hawthorne *Amer. Notebooks* 29, Forward of the wardroom . . is the midshipmen's room. **1869** Twain *Innocents* 636, The water stands in deep puddles in the depressions forward of their after shoulders. **1891** Wilkins *Humble Romance* 165 *(DA)* **NEng,** Two little thin dancing curls . . just forward of her cap.

forward n Also *fawid* [Pronc-spp, sometimes by folk-etym, for **forehead**]

1914 *DN* 4.72 **ME, nNH,** *Forward*. . . Forehead. **1927** Kennedy *Gritny* 57 **sLA** [Black], A aw'inge flower wreath settin' 'cross her fawid. **1941** *LANE* Map 485, [The pronunciation [fɒ·wəd] occurs occasionally for *forehead.*] **c1970** Pederson *Dial. Surv. Rural GA* **seGA,** [Pronunciations of *forehead* include ten instances of the type ['fɔɚwɚd, 'fɑwɚd, 'fɔwəd, 'fa·wɨd]. 7 of 10 infs are Black.]

forward-behind adv

Backwards.

1969 *DARE* (Qu. MM2, . . *"Look, you've got your dress on ______ ."*) Inf **GA**77, Forward-behind.

forward of See **forward** adv **C**

forwards See **forward** adj, adv

for what I care adv phr [Var of *for all I care*] **S Midl**

As far as I'm concerned.

1966–70 *DARE* (Qu. GG21a, *If you don't care what a person does . . "You can go ahead and do it ______ ."*) Infs **MS**21, **MO**8, **SC**7, 19, **TN**48, For what I care.

for who laid the chunk See **who laid the chunk**

for why adv [Engl dial; *OED*→1700; *EDD* 1828–1896] **chiefly S Midl**

Why.

1871 (1892) Johnston *Dukesborough Tales* 34 **GA,** I had laid off in my mind to have gin you a duckin' this very day; and I'll tell you for why. **1877** Twain in *Atlantic Mth.* 40.443, I took No. 9. And I'll tell you for why. **1898** Lloyd *Country Life* 108 **AL,** The banker watches the merchant and the merchant watches the farmer and the farmer watches everybody. For why? **1926** Roberts *Time of Man* 70 **KY,** Croppen on the shares is a sight better contract and I'll tell you for why. **1930** *VA Qrly. Rev.* 6.246 **Ozarks. 1931** *PMLA* 46.1305 **sAppalachians,** If ye ax (ask) me on it I'll tell ye fer why. **1942** *Sun* (Baltimore MD) 29 Jan 13/2 *(Hench Coll.),* The U.S.G.A. has called off the tournament, for why I don't know. **1944** *PADS* 2.25 **cwNC,** He went down town, I don't know fer why. **1972** Carr *Da Kine Talk* 131 **HI,** "For why you tell lies?" . . [T]he Portuguese *para que* means literally 'for what?' A loan translation from the Portuguese and a confusion of the two standard forms *why?* and *what for?* might have brought *for why* into the local dialect. **1976** Garber *Mountain-ese* **sAppalachians,** I jist kaint understand fer why she wanted to marry a man like Joe.

forzino See **farzino**

fosnacht, fosnock See **fastnacht**

‡fossicate v

1953 Randolph–Wilson *Down in Holler* 245 **Ozarks,** *Fossicate*. . . To suffer from extreme heat, or lack of air, or both. A man from Yell County, Ark., said: "I like to a-fossicated down in town yesterday." Perhaps it is somehow connected with suffocate.

‡fossil-bustle n

1968 *DARE* (Qu. HH40, *Uncomplimentary words for an old man*) Inf **NC**82, Old fossil-bustle.

fossip See **faucet A2**

fossnock See **fastnacht**

fossup See **faucet A2**

foster on v phr

To force on; to compel to accept.

1957 *Hench Coll.* **MN,** [Radio:] This tight-credit program that the government has fostered on us is hard on business. *Ibid,* He will foster on us graduates who are second rate. **1958** *Ibid* **VA,** Is this the last of the group of guests fostered on you?

fotch See **fetch** v **A1, 2**

fotched See **fetch** v **A2**

fotched-on See **fotch-on**

fotches See **fetch** v **A1**

fotch-on ppl adj Also *fotched-on, fetch(ed)-on* **[fetch** v **A2] chiefly S Midl** Cf **brought-on**

1 Brought from outside, **boughten.**

1911 *DN* 3.538 **eKY,** *Fotch(ed)-on*. . . The same as brung-on. *Ibid* 537, *Brung-on*. . . Newly arrived or imported. **1913** Kephart *Highlanders* 285 **sAppalachians,** Damn this fotch-on kraut that comes in tin cans! **1924** Raine *Land of Saddle-Bags* 103 **sAppalachians,** We didn't have no fotch-on clothes when I was a-raisin'. **1926** *DN* 5.400 **Ozarks,** I caint stummick them fotch-on beans out'n cans. **1954** *Harder Coll.* **cwTN,** *Fotch-on*. . . Imported, not produced in the neighborhood. **1960** Williams *Walk Egypt* 265 **GA,** I don't mean none of these fetch-on kind comes in cans. **c1960** *Wilson Coll.* **csKY,** *Fetched on*. . . Something imported, bought at the store, not home-made. Also *fotch-on, fotched-on.* **1967** *DARE* (Qu. U2, . . *A piece of clothing not made at home*) Inf **TN**11, [ˌfɑčˈɔn]. Old-fashioned. [Inf old] **1983** *MJLF* 9.1.40 **ceKY,** *Fotched on* . . bought, as opposed to home made.

2 Of people, ideas, etc: coming from outside the community; strange, outlandish, highfalutin.

1914 Furman *Sight* 41 **KY,** Here's the fotch-on women [=teachers and nurses brought from outside the area]. **1943** Peattie *Great Smokies* 12, Though a "fotched-on" woman, one who came from the outside, there are few better qualified . . to tell the tale of mountain ways. **1952** Brown *NC Folkl.* 1.542, *Fotched-on*. . . Mainly of persons but sometimes of things: not of the community or section; educated; used in contempt. "He's one of them fotched-on school teachers, and knows everything." —West. Illiterate. **c1960** *Wilson Coll.* **csKY,** *Fotched on*. . . Term of contempt for some new-fangled or high-falutin thing or person. **1974** Fink *Mountain Speech* 9 **wNC, eTN,** I don't favor them fotch-on ideas. **1984** Wilder *You All Spoken Here* 156 **Sth,** *Fotched on:* Outlandish; said of something to be resented or distrusted.

fotcht See **fetch** v **A2**

fote, fo'teen See **four**

fouce See **feist** n

fo-uhteen See **four**

fouiller v [Fr]

1983 *Reinecke Coll.* 5 **LA,** *Fouiller* . . rummage. "I don't want you fouillering [fujɚɪŋ] in my drawer." Common in bi-lingual families 50 yrs ago.

foul adj [Engl dial] **S Midl** Cf **filth**

Overgrown with weeds.

1903 *DN* 2.314 **seMO,** *Foul*. . . Weedy or grassy as applied to a crop. 'We have had so much rain I couldn [sic] plow and my corn has got mighty foul.' **1908** *DN* 3.312 **eAL, wGA,** *Foul*. . . Weedy, grassy. "My cotton is awful foul." **1970** *DARE* Tape **KY**75, The ground sometimes would get real foul, and then they would have to go in with a rounder plow and bar this tobacco off, throw the dirt all away from it . . to cover up the grass an' stuff an' kill it.

‡foul v [Perh var of *fool* v]

To move listlessly; fool around.

1967 *DARE* (Qu. Y21, *To move . . slowly and without energy*) Inf **CO**47, Foulin' around.

foul line n

In marble play: **=taw line.**

1968 *DARE* (Qu. EE8, *The line toward which the players roll their marbles before beginning a game, to determine the order of shooting*) Inf **PA**130, Foul line; if you went over it, you were disqualified.

foul meadow grass See **fowl meadow grass**

found quasi-n See **find B1**

found v See **fine** v^2

foundation n

1 also pl: One's feet, esp large ones. **chiefly Sth, S Midl** *joc*

1936 *Scribner's Mag.* Oct 59 **neKY,** "Wear number ten shoes," says Flem. "I see you got a might little foundation, Mick." Flem laughs. **1967–69** *DARE* (Qu. X38, *Joking names for unusually big or clumsy feet*) Infs **KY**5, **SC**3, Foundation; **AL**16, **VA**9, Good foundation; **IL**19, **KY**28, **MO**15, **TN**1, Big foundations.

2 also *foundation log:* **=backlog 1.**

1967–68 *DARE* (Qu. D33, . . *The big log that goes behind the others*) Inf **MN**42, Foundation; **MA**4, Foundation log.

3 See quot.

1970 *DARE* (Qu. X35, *Joking words for the part of the body that you sit on*) Inf **KY**85, Foundation.

foundation log See **foundation 2**

founder v Also, by folk-etym, *flounder*

A Forms.

1950 *WELS (Diseases of horses)* 1 Inf, **cwWI,** Floundered. **1968–69** *DARE* (Qu. K28, . . *Diseases that cows have*) Inf **OH**43, Floundering; (Qu. K47, . . *Diseases . . [of] horses or mules*) Inf **NY**189, Floundered; **VA**33, Floundered—if they eat or drink too much. **1969** *DARE* FW Addit **MA**30, Floundered (capsized).

B Sense.

Of a person: to overeat; to make (oneself) ill by overeating; hence ppl adj *foundered.* Note: This term is std when applied to an animal.

1899 Garland *Boy Life* 110 **nwIA** (as of c1870s), The salt pork, when dipped in bread-crumbs, tasted so good that the boys nearly "foundered themselves," as Jennings used to say. **1905** *DN* 3.79 **nwAR,** I ate so much I almost foundered myself. **1915** *DN* 4.183 **swVA,** *Founder. . .* To overeat. **1944** Howard *Walkin' Preacher* 120 **Ozarks,** "Have to call the horse doctor fer ye," countered Lige. "You're afounderin' yo'rse'f." **1960** Hall *Smoky Mt. Folks* 65, Don't get foundered at that Democratic barbecue. **c1960** *Wilson Coll.* **csKY,** *Founder. . .* To suffer severely from overeating. Transferred to people who seem too greedy in their eating. **1966** *DARE* Tape **SD**3, Sometimes we eat too much—we founder ourselves. [**1968** *DARE* (Qu. BB21, *Other words for being constipated*) Inf **NY**79, Founded.] **1974** Betts-Walser *NC Folkl.* 7 **nwNC,** Founder: eat too much.

fount See **fine** v **A**

fountain n Pronc-sp *founting* See Intro "Language Changes" II.12

A Form.

1903 *DN* 2.321 **seMO,** Founting.

B Sense.

Also *flaming fountain, water ~:* A type of firework.

1965–70 *DARE* (Qu. FF28, . . *Kinds of fireworks*) 22 Infs, **scattered, but least freq Sth,** Fountains; **MO**37, Water fountains; **WA**13, Flaming fountain; (Qu. FF14) Infs **MS**8, **PA**74, **WA**16, Fountains.

four adj, n Usu **wNEng, Inland Nth, S Midl,** |for|; **eNEng** |foə|; **NYC** |fɔə|; **N Midl** |fɔr|; **Sth** |fo(ə)|; for addit varr see quots See Pronc Intro 3.I.1.e Pronc-spp *fo, fo-ah* Similarly adj, n, *fo'teen, fo-uhteen;* adj *fote*

Std sense, var forms.

1878 *Appletons' Jrl.* 5.414, In New England and Virginia they say *fō-ah, mō-ah . . ;* while in the region between they say *four, more.* **1899** (1912) Green *VA Folk-Speech* 183, *Fo'teen.* **1911** Saunders [see **four-flusher**]. **1922** Gonzales *Black Border* 302 **sSC, GA coasts** [Gullah glossary], Fo'teen. **1927** Shewmake *Engl. Pronc. VA* 29, Those who are less particular . . [say] *fo'teen . .* [as compared with the] *fo-uhteen* of cultivated and careful Virginia speech. **1941** *AmSp* 16.6 **eTX** [Black], Before *l* and *r,* I hear the diphthong [oʊ] as well as the lengthened [o:] . . *four.* **1941** Writers' Program SC *Folk Tales* 100, Hit wuz helt on duh fote Sunday. **1961** Kurath-McDavid *Pronc. Engl.* 120, In the South—from the Potomac to Georgia—*four . .* [is] usually pronounced as [fo·ə̯]. . . However, in the speech of the folk [foʊ] is common in the Virginia piedmont, [fo·] in South Carolina. . . [T]he cultured . . occasionally use disyllabic [foʊə]. . . The South Midland regularly has . . [fo·ɚ ~ foɚ]. . . In Eastern New England . . /foə̯/. . . In Western New England and Upstate New York . . /for/. . . In Metropolitan New York . . /fɔə̯/. **1965** Carmony *Speech Terre Haute* 112, /o/ is uniformly the vowel in *door, four,* and *hoarse.* **1976** Allen *LAUM* 3.31 (as of c1950), In *four, door, hoarse. . .* Although in the U[pper] M[idwest] the boundaries [between Northern /o/ and N Midland /ɔ/] are not so sharp, the chief contrast between these Northern and Midland variants has generally been retained.

fourble adj Also *foble, fourvel* [By analogy with *single, double,* etc] Cf **fourbles**

Quadruple—usu in combs; hence n *fourble,* in oil drilling, see quot 1932.

1914 *DN* 4.106 **KS,** *Fourvel. . .* Fourfold. **1932** *AmSp* 7.267 **CA,** Fourble. . . A *stand* of four joints of pipe. **1949** *AmSp* 24.37 **OK, TX,** In *fourble board,* the *r* is often lost and the word becomes ['fobl̩]. **1949** *PADS* 11.6 **wTX** (as of c1920), *Fourble-disc. . .* A plow with four discs. Uneducated. *Fourble-tree. . .* A pivoted bar to which four whiffletrees are attached. **1956** Ker *Vocab. W. TX* 179, For a bar to which three or four whippletrees [sic] are attached five informants report *tripletree, trebbletree, tribletree, fobletree, fourbletree* and *evener.* All five also report *doubletree.* **1962** Atwood *Vocab. TX* 52, A few informants volunteered terms for a longer bar [than a doubletree] in case there were three or more horses; these are *tripletree . . , trebletree . . , thribbletree . . ,* and *fourbletree.*

fourbles n pl [Prob < **fourble,** but perh understood as blend of *four + marbles*] Cf **fourbs, foursies**

In marble play: see quots.

1890 *DN* 1.24 **KY,** "Fourbles" (very rare), four marbles. **1955** *PADS* 23.18 **TN,** *Fourbles. . .* Four marbles. **c1970** Wiersma *Marbles Terms* **MI,** *Fourbles . .* four marbles.

fourble-tree See **fourble**

four-box baseball n **NYC** Cf **box ball**

A children's game; see quots.

1968 *DARE* Tape **NY**118, We used to play a lot of games with the boxes on the sidewalk. First we'd start with four-box baseball. . . Each player would stand four boxes away from each other and the person would pitch the ball into the fourth box, the box nearest the batter, and the batter would have to knock the ball, bouncing it first into the box nearest the pitcher, and no matter . . how many times the ball bounced, once it landed in that box that was nearest the pitcher, that was how many hits he got. There was another version where you had to bounce it in each of the boxes, so there was the second box, the third box, and then the fourth box and then the guy could hit it back. **1968** *DARE* (Qu. EE33, *Other outdoor games*) Inf **NY**119, Four-box baseball.

fourbs exclam [Abbr for **fourbles**] Cf **fibs, fobs, thribs**

In marble play: see quot.

1935 *AmSp* 10.159 **seNE,** *Fourbs . .* must be cried [to lay claim to] . . four . . marbles.

four-card flusher See **four-flusher**

four corner See **four corners 1**

four-cornered cat n Cf **four old cat**

A variation, involving more players, of the bat-and-ball game **one old cat.**

1888 *Cosmopolitan* 5.443, "One-cornered cat" . . was, therefore, forced to give way to a further development called "three-cornered cat," which in turn was followed by "four-cornered cat," and from this finally was developed the primitive "base-ball." **1940** Kennedy-Harlow *Schoolmaster* 228 **IN,** When this game [=two-cornered cat] was enlarged by the appearance of more players to Three- or Four-cornered Cat, it resembled Town Ball in some respects. In each, the runner could be either touched or crossed out; in each a batter could be retired either on a fly or first bounce, and a ball could be knocked in any direction; there were no fouls.

four-cornered pants n pl

Diapers.

1968 *DARE* (Qu. W19) Inf **NY**83, Four-cornered pants.

four corners n pl, but usu sg in constr

1 infreq sg; rarely *four-corner road:* A place where two roads cross; a crossroads. **chiefly Nth** See Map on p. 544

1851 (1976) Melville *Moby-Dick* 242, Some noted four corners of a great highway. **1857** *Spirit of Times* 13 June 226/3 *(DA),* Off the two cronies put for the 'Four Corners,' distant perhaps four miles. **c1938** in 1970 Hyatt *Hoodoo* 1.110 **csMD** [Black], If a man wants to sell hisself to the devil, why—if he wants to play a banjah . . good, he's to go to a *four-corner road* [Hyatt: crossroad] nine mornings. **1950** *WELS (A place where roads cross at right angles)* 12 Infs, **WI,** Four corners. [1 Inf labels it "rural."] **1965–70** *DARE* (Qu. N32) 85 Infs, **chiefly Nth,** (A) four corners; 11 Infs, **chiefly Inland Nth,** (A) four corner; (QR, near Qu. MM23) Inf **NY**219, There's a four corners at the center of town. **1975** Gould *ME Lingo* 100, *Four corners*—The usual Maine term for a crossroads. **1980** *Greenfield Recorder* (MA) 18 Oct A4, It's often more sensible to have only one name for a continuous road instead of one name to an intersection (Four Corners, old folks said).

2 A small town at a crossroads; hence fig, an insignificant or out-of-the-way place. **esp Gt Lakes** See Map

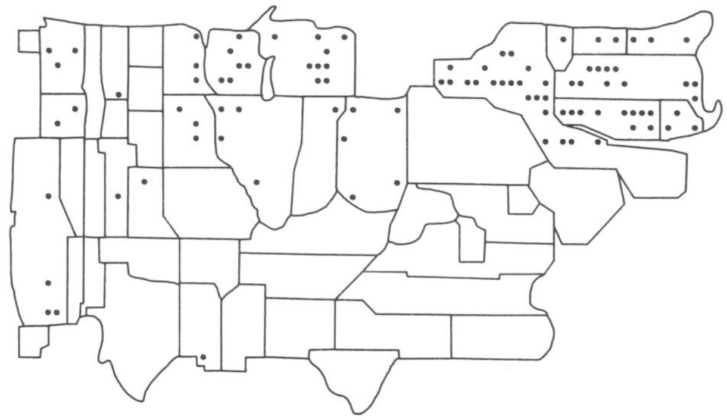

•four corners 1 + var (Qu. N32)

1867 Lowell *Biglow* 136 **'Upcountry' MA,** The Rev. Jonas Tutchel, in a recent communication to the Bogus Four Corners Weekly Meridian, has endeavoured to show that this is the sepulchral inscription of Thorwald Eriksson. **1879** Taylor *Summer-Savory* 138, You look for it [=the country store] at some lazy four-corners, within hearing of an anvil's ring, and the grind of a mill. **1937** FWP *Guide ME* 351, Rome, a 'four corners' is in the most rugged and least settled section of the Belgrade Lakes area. **1939** (1962) Thompson *Body & Britches* 485 **NY,** If he is really industrious, you may say of him as they do in Otsego County, "That young man will make his living on any four-corners". **1950** *WELS Suppl.* **csWI,** Four corners—out of the way place. **1965–70** *DARE* (Qu. C33) 21 Infs, 14 **MI, OH,** Four corners.

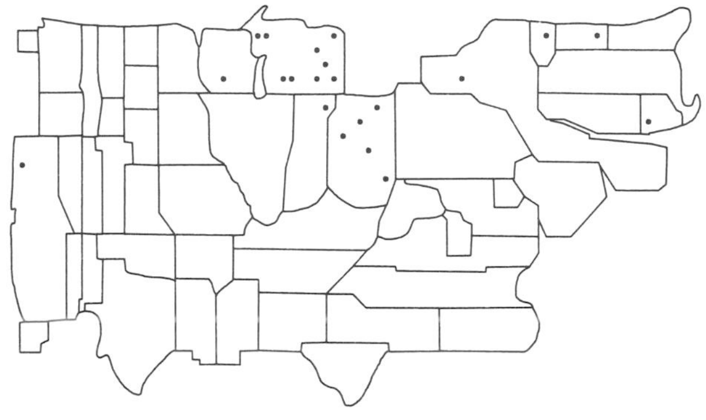

•four corners 2 (Qu. C33)

3 A dance step.

1967–70 *DARE* (Qu. FF5b, *More recent dance steps*) Infs **IL**141, **PA**66, **SC**65, Four corners. [2 Infs Black]

four-eyes n sg [In ref to the compound eye]

A **dragonfly.**

1968 *DARE* (Qu. R2) Inf **IL**27, A four-eyes.

four-five-six n **Pacific NW**

A game played with dice; see quot 1959.

1959 Hart *McKay's AK* 30, *Four-Five-Six:* A popular but illegal gambling game . . played with three numbered dice . . [and] similar to the card game "Twenty-One." . . Three of a kind and 4-5-6 are always winning throws. **1967** *DARE* (Qu. DD37, . . *Table games played . . by adults*) Inf **OR**10, Four-five-six—[with] dice; (Qu. EE40, . . *Table games . . using dice*) Inf **WA**22, Four-five-six.

four-flush n, also attrib [*flush* a poker hand in which all five cards are of the same suit] Cf **bobtailed flush**

A poker hand with four cards of the same suit (rather than the five required for a true flush); hence fig, something or someone that deceives or bluffs.

1887 J. W. Keller *Draw Poker* 35 *(DA),* If in opening a pot a player finds in his hand a pair and a four flush, or four straight, he may break his pair and draw to the straight or the flush. **1899** (1900) Ade *Fables in Slang* 12, But she always saw the same old line of Four-Flush Drummers from Chicago and St. Louis. **1904** *Eve. Post* (NY NY) 20 Feb 10/2, Mayor Harrison's assertion that the Sunday closing law is a 'four-flush' law—one that was meant to deceive and not meant for actual enforcement. **1913** *Official Rules of Card Games* 25, Without a pair, or a four-flush, or a four-straight, backing the hand is not justified by any odds he is likely to get in the betting.

four-flush v, hence ppl adj, vbl n *four-flushing* **[four-flush n]**

To act deceptively, bluff.

1896 (1898) Ade *Artie* 37 **Chicago IL,** "I thought he was going to fight." "Not that boy. He was four-flushin." **1901** 'J. Flynt' *World of Graft* 46 *(DAE),* They make a pinch o' some second-class old thief. . . That's what I call four-flushin'. **1942** Stegner *Mormon Country* 286 **UT,** A four-flushing holdup man named Gunplay Maxwell. **1970** *DARE* (Qu. BB27, *When somebody pretends to be sick . . you'd say he's* ______) Inf **NJ**64, Four-flushing.

four-flusher n Also *four-card flusher* **[four-flush v] scattered exc Sth, S Midl** See Map

One who deceives; a cheater, braggart, fraud—often used as a vague term of abuse.

1904 Number 1500 *Life in Sing Sing* 255 **NY,** *Four-flusher.* One who poses for effect. **1910** *New Outlook* 25 June 376, Though he was just home from Los Angeles with flying prizes won there, many doubted his intention, and one newspaper in the Hudson Valley called him a "four-flusher." **1911** Saunders *Col. Todhunter* 98 **MO,** You know it, you little fo'-card flusher, you! **1911** *DN* 3.543 **NE,** *Four-flusher.* . . Bluffer; one who cannot "make good." **1912** *DN* 3.576 **wIN.** **1919** *DN* 5.63 **NM,** *Four-flusher,* a person who pretends to have money. **1950** *WELS (A show-off)* 4 Infs, **WI,** Four-flusher; *(Other words for a cheater)* 3 Infs, **WI,** Four-flusher. **1960** Criswell *Resp. to PADS 20* **Ozarks,** Four-flusher. . . A bluffer. His bold, brassy appearance belies the reality. **1960** Bailey *Resp. to PADS 20* **KS,** *(A person who has no ambition and avoids work)* Four-flusher. **1965–70** *DARE* (Qu. V7, *A person who sets out to cheat others while pretending to be honest*) 19 Infs, **scattered exc Sth, S Midl,** Four-flusher; (Qq. U17, V1, V2a, **BB**53b, **HH**2, **HH**7a, **HH**8, **HH**17, **HH**20a, **HH**35, **II**18, **II**20a, **II**23, **II**32, **II**35, **JJ**3b) 28 Infs, **scattered exc Sth, S Midl,** Four-flusher; (Qu. II24) Inf **IN**73, Four-flushers' row.

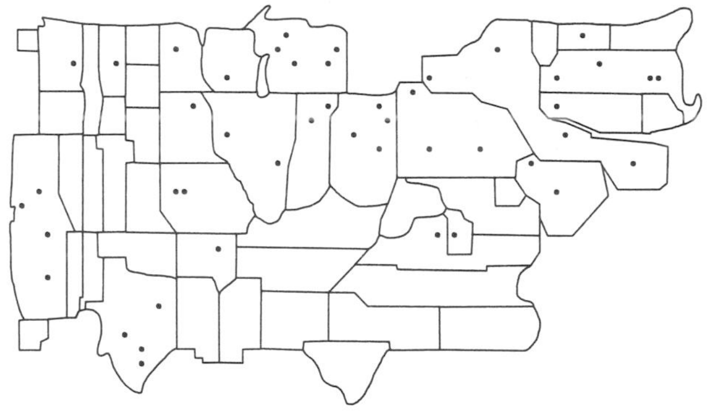

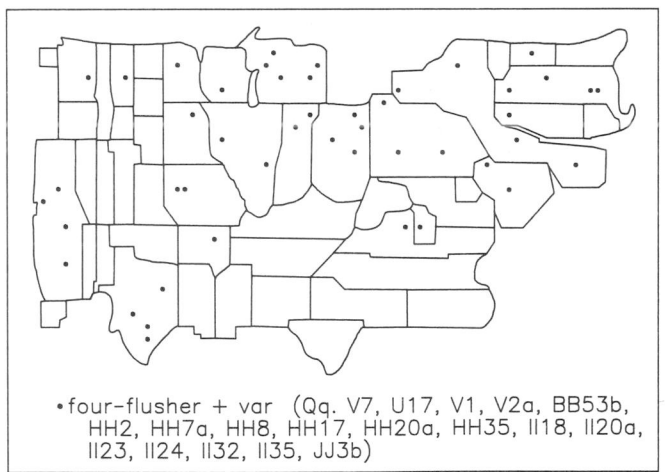

•four-flusher + var (Qq. V7, U17, V1, V2a, BB53b, HH2, HH7a, HH8, HH17, HH20a, HH35, II18, II20a, II23, II24, II32, II35, JJ3b)

four-flushing See **four-flush** v

four-foot plow See **foot** n **C3**

four-foot yardstick n

An imaginary object used as the basis for a practical joke.

1921 *DN* 5.94 **neOH,** Four-foot yard stick. **1966–68** *DARE* (Qu. HH14, *Ways of teasing a beginner . . for example, by sending him for a "left-handed monkey wrench": "Go get me* ______*."*) Infs **IL**7, **IN**30, **ME**13, **SC**19, A four-foot yardstick.

four-hand corner n Cf **four corners 1**

1968 *DARE* (Qu. N32, *A place where roads cross at right angles*) Inf **WI**30, A four-corners; in Adams County they say a "four-hand corner."

four-headed adj Cf **double-head(ed), two-headed**

In **hoodoo** n **1a**; having extraordinary mental power.

c1938 in 1970 Hyatt *Hoodoo* 2.1785 **New Orleans LA,** Some people call it *hoodooism* an' some jes' say, "Well, he's a—one dose *fo' haided* *people.*" . . People dat has a diff'rent mind to 'em—to mastah-mind people. . . Dey supposed tuh have de senses of fo' people.

four-hole marbles See **hole** n **4**

four-holer See **holer**

four-holes See **hole** n **4**

four-horse adj Cf **one-horse**

Of a farm: requiring four work animals.

1966 *DARE* Tape **GA**4, People . . run three-horse farm, four-horse farm, I run one farm [=one-horse farm]. . . That's just enough for one mule can tend.

four-leaf clover n

A highway cloverleaf.

1967–69 *DARE* (Qu. N20) Infs **AZ**15, **NY**12, 205, **VT**4, Four-leaf clover.

four-legged eel n Cf **two-legged eel**

=**congo snake 1.**

1928 Baylor Univ. Museum *Contrib.* 16.8 **LA, TX,** *Four-legged Eel.* This name distinguishes the Congo Snake from the . . Siren, which . . has only two limbs.

‡**four-legged word** n

A learned or polysyllabic word.

1961 Adams *Old-Time Cowhand* 14, When he heard some educated feller usin' them four-legged words that run 'bout eight to the pound, . . he'd have to ask 'im to ride over that trail again, and chew it finer so he could get the meanin'.

four-lined skunk n Cf **two-lined skunk**

=**spotted skunk.**

1961 Jackson *Mammals WI* 369, Spotted Skunks. . . *Vernacular names.* . . Four-lined skunk.

four-oarsman n [From the insect's use of its four hind legs to "row"]

A **water strider** of the family Gerridae.

1986 *Mod. Maturity* Apr-May 51 **NH,** I would . . view the quicksilver union of two worlds on which water striders ("four-oarsmen," we called them) sculled and over which dragonflies darted and hovered.

four-o'clock n

1 A plant of the family Nyctaginaceae, esp of the genus *Allionia, Oxybaphus,* or *Mirabilis.* [See quots 1987, 1950] Also called **umbrellawort.** For other names of var spp of *Mirabilis* see **green saucers, marvel of Peru, pretty-by-night, snotweed, wishbone bush**

1822 Eaton *Botany* 354, *Mirabilis. . . jalapa* (four o'clock . .) flowers heaped, peduncled; leaves glabrous. **1851** (1852) Stowe *Uncle Tom's Cabin* 1.38 **cCT,** Here also . . various brilliant annuals, such as marigolds, petunias, four-o'clocks, found an indulgent corner. **1897** Parsons *Wild Flowers CA* 208, *Mirabilis Californica.* . . When the heat of the day is over . . , the bright little four-o'clocks begin to open their myriad magenta-colored eyes. **1936** Whitehouse *TX Flowers* 19, *Small-Flowered Four-O'-clock (Allionia incarnata)* is very abundant in Southwestern Texas to Arizona and South America. **1950** Stevens *ND Plants* 135, *Allionia hirsuta. . . Hairy Four-o'clock. . . Allionia nyctaginea. . . Wild Four-o'clock. . . Allionia albida.* . . These plants are also known as umbrella-worts but the name wild four-o'clock seems fitting, since . . the flowers open in the evening. **1965–70** *DARE* (Qu. S1) Inf **IN**48, Four-o'clock; (Qu. S11) Infs **NY**54, **OH**49, **PA**198, Four-o'clock; (Qu. S21) Inf **PA**89, Four-o'clock; (Qu. S26a) Infs **CA**79, **NM**13, **TN**49, **WI**58, Four-o'clock(s); (Qu. S26b) Inf **IN**26, Four-o'clocks; (Qu. S26e) Infs **CA**24, **SC**63, 67, **TN**22, Four-o'clock. **1967** *DARE* FW Addit **PA**162, Marvel of Peru are four-o'clocks. **1970** Correll *Plants TX* 578, *Mirabilis. . . Four-o'clock.* . . About 60 species, entirely American. **1985** Dodge *Flowers SW Deserts* 43, Trailing Four-o'Clock. . . *Allionia incarnata.* . . Blossoms are usually showy and colorful.

2 also *wild four-o'clock:* An **evening primrose a** (here: *Oenothera biennis*).

1900 Lyons *Plant Names* 265, *O[enothera] biennis.* . . Four-o'clock. **1940** Clute *Amer. Plant Names* 93, *Common Evening Primrose.* . . Four o'clock. **1959** Carleton *Index Herb. Plants* 49, Four o'clock: *Oenothera biennis. Ibid* 125, *Wild four o'clock:* Oenothera biennis.

3 A **spiderwort** (here: *Tradescantia virginiana*).

1969 *DARE* FW Addit **KY**5, Four-o'clock—Virginia spiderwort *(Tradescantia virginiana).*

4 See quot.

1969 *DARE* FW Addit **KY**40, Four-o'clocks = bluebells. A yard flower.

5 in phrr *dead as four-o'clock* and varr: Dead. **sAppalachians**

1940 Oakley *Roamin' with the Roamin' Man of the Smoky Mountains* 29 *(Hall Coll.)* **eTN,** The bear kept going until reach [sic] top of tree, then fell out ded as fore o'clock in the morning. **c1950** *Hall Coll.* **eTN, wNC,** I let drive [=shot] at the bear and killed him deader'n four o'clock. **1960** Hall *Smoky Mt. Folks* 62, "He killed the bear dead as four o'clock." Also "deader'n four o'clock." Is it possible that this phrase is connected with the four o'clock plant, one of the nightshades, which is said to have been used . . as a fly poison? But more probably it refers to the hours of the dead, when ghosts walk, especially between midnight and dawn. **1969–70** *DARE* FW Addit **csVA,** Dead as four-o'clock—very dead; **seKY,** [Heard in conv referring to a horse that dropped in a race:] That horse was dead as four-o'clock afore he hit the ground. **1970** *DARE* Tape **VA**43, He gave 'im [=a calf] a shot, and I had to pay for him, and the next day she was just as dead as four-o'clock. **1986** Pederson *LAGS Concordance (Died—crude terms)* 1 inf, **ceTN,** Killed her deader than four o'clock—of a sow; 1 inf, **cTN,** Kill it dead as four o'clock—the hull on ringworm.

6 in phr *dumb as four-o'clock:* See quot.

1966 *DARE* (Qu. HH25, *One who never has anything to say: "What's the matter with him?"*) Inf **NC**36, He's dumb as four-o'clock.

7 in phr *it's four o'clock:* =**one o'clock, it's.**

1966 *DARE* (Qu. W24c, *Sayings to warn a man that his trouser-fly is open*) Inf **CA**2, It's four o'clock.

four old cat n Cf **cat** n **3c**

A variation, involving more players, of the bat-and-ball game **one old cat.**

1883 Eggleston *Hoosier Schoolboy* 10 **IN,** "Four old cat," "two old cat," and "five old cat" are . . played the same way, the number of bases or holes increasing with the addition of each pair of players. **1939** FWP *Guide IL* 532, Pictures from the time the game was called "Four Old Cat" through the present . . form part of the extensive collection [in a baseball museum].

four paws n pl

In logging: see quots.

1905 U.S. Forest Serv. *Bulletin* 61.35 **Pacific NW,** *Double Couplers.* Two coupling grabs joined by a short cable, used for fastening logs together. . . [Also called] four paws. **1958** McCulloch *Woods Words* 67 **Pacific NW,** *Four paws*—Double log grabs, hooks for fastening logs together in ground lead yarding. **1964** Clarkson *Tumult* 361 **WV,** *Double coupler*—Two sets of couplers or grabs fastened together with a short chain. Used on exceptionally large logs. *Syn.* four-paws.

four runners See **forerunner 2**

foursies n Cf **fourbles**

In marble play: a game played with or for four marbles.

c1970 Wiersma *Marbles Terms* **MI** (as of c1955), Foursies. . . A type of play in which four marbles are thrown out at once. This is sometimes used to begin the game. "Roll foursies." *Ibid* **swMI** (as of c1967), Foursies. . . Playing for four marbles. . . Today we'll play foursies. . . Using only four marbles as shooters. . . We'll play with foursies.

foursquare n

A children's ball game; see quot 1979.

1967–70 *DARE* (Qu. EE33, *Other outdoor games*) Infs **CA**4, **MO**30, Foursquare. **1979–88** *DARE* File **nCA** (as of 1950s), At recess we used to play foursquare. A square about six feet by six feet was drawn on the ground, then further divided into four squares. A player stood in each, and bounced a ball to another player, who had to bounce it to another without holding it or stepping out of bounds. *Ibid* **cCA** (as of 1960s). *Ibid* **cIA** (as of 1960s), Foursquare was my favorite game; **nwMA** (as of 1960s), There was a foursquare grid painted on the blacktop in the schoolyard. We would form a line to get to play. The squares were named King, Queen, Jack, and Joker. You would try to get the person ahead of you to miss a bounce, then they were out and you could move up into their place. The person out would go to the end of the line and someone could move into the Joker square. *Ibid* **csWI** (as of 1986), Kids I babysat for knew how to play foursquare.

fourteen-day pickle n Also *fourteen pickle, fifteen-day pickle* **chiefly Midl** See Map

A type of sweet-pickle made by a method that takes two weeks.
1963 Nichols *Freezing & Canning* 270, *14-Day Sweet Pickles*—Adaptation of an heirloom recipe long treasured in country kitchens. **1965–70** *DARE* (Qu. H56, . . *Kinds of pickles*) 19 Infs, **chiefly Midl, esp N Midl,** Fourteen-day pickles; **IL**134, Fourteen-day pickles—they're soaked in brine, heated, and changed every day; **OH**78, Fourteen-day pickles—they set two weeks; **PA**163, Fourteen-day pickles—sweet-pickles, in salt water for seven days, cover with boiling water for twenty-four hours . . [repeat four times]. Mix vinegar, sugar, and pickling spices, . . pour over. Do twice again; **PA**213, Fourteen-day pickles—it takes fourteen days to make it; **KY**37, Fourteen pickle; **ME**9, Fifteen-day pickles.

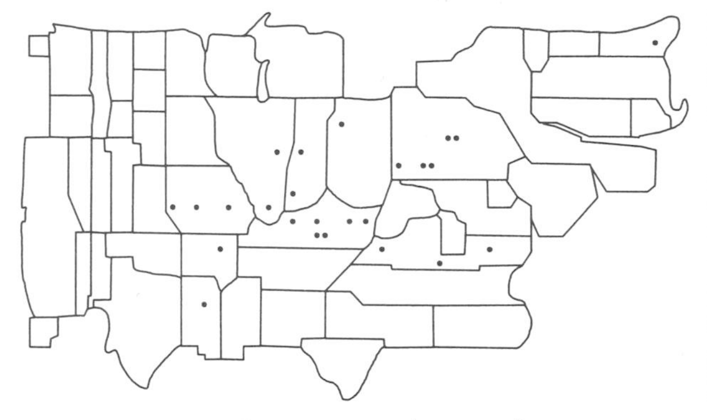
•fourteen-day pickle + varr (Qu. H56)

Fourth n Also *Fourth of July*
A celebration or party in honor of Independence Day.
1872 Eggleston *End of the World* 110 **sIN,** I kin rattle off . . big words picked up at Fourth-of-Julys. **1923** *DN* 5.207 **swMO,** We're aimin' on havin' a Fourth o' July down on the creek. *Ibid* 235 **swWI,** You goin' to the Fourth? **1969** *DARE* (Qu. FF16) Inf **KY**45, Are you going to the Fourth?

fourth cropper See **fourth hand**

Fourth day See **first day 1**

fourth hand n Also *fourth cropper* Cf **half hand 2, third and fourth farmer**
A tenant farmer who pays usu one fourth of the crop as rent; see quot.
1967–69 *DARE* (Qu. L3, *A man who lives on the farm and does the work, but divides the expenses and profits with the owner*) Inf **LA**8, A half hand if he's working on the halves, a fourth hand if he's working on the fourths; **LA**10, He might be a half hand (he puts up the labor) or a fourth hand (he furnishes everything); **MS**58, A fourth cropper gets three-fourths of the cotton, two-thirds of the corn; this man furnishes his equipment.

Four Thieves Vinegar n
In **hoodoo** n **1a** or **conjure** n **1:** see quot.
1931 *Jrl. Amer. Folkl.* 44.412 **LA** [Black], Four Thieves Vinegar. It is used for breaking up homes, for making a person run crazy, for driving off. It is sometimes put with a name in a bottle and the bottle thrown into moving water. It is used also to "dress" cocoanuts to kill and drive crazy. **c1938** in 1970 Hyatt *Hoodoo* 2.1512 **seLA,** Yo' git a . . dark, dark, red onion, an' cut it up in slices so dat yo' kin git it in a bottle. Yo' git whut dey call *Foah Thieves Vinegah.* Yo' po' dis in dere an' yo' write dese people name.

fourth month See **first month**

Fourth of July n
1 See **Fourth.**
2 Among loggers: see quot.
1958 McCulloch *Woods Words* 67 **Pacific NW,** *Fourth of July*—A shutdown. The term comes from the practice of laying off for a period after the Fourth of July until enough men sobered up to get the operation going again.
3 See quot.
1967 *DARE* File **csWI,** *Fourth-of-July*—the portulaca flower.

fourth-of-July plant n
The garden **sage** *(Salvia officinalis).*
1950 *WELS Suppl.* 1 Inf, **csWI,** Fourth-of-July plant. . . Salvia. Bright red flowers that appear in late June and early July probably help these names in popularity. Salvia is a name not generally known.

fourth-proof adj phr
Fig: powerful, vehement.
1846 (1847) Porter *Quarter Race* 17 **KY,** They used fourth-proof oaths with a volubility that would bother a congressional reporter. **1886** in 1923 Twain *Speeches* 137, Tons of A No. 1, fourth-proof, hard-boiled, hide-bound grammar.

fourth Thursday n
Menstruation.
1978 *MJLF* 4.1.38 **cTX,** *Euphemisms for menstruation.* . . One organization of girls . . contributed . . "the fourth Thursday," . . relating to the regularity of the event.

four-toed plover n
=**black-bellied plover.**
1917 (1923) *Birds Amer.* 1.256, *Black-bellied Plover—Squatarola squatarola* . . *Other Names.* . . Four-toed Plover. **1944** Hausman *Amer. Birds* 522, *Plover, Four-toed* . . Plover, Black-bellied. **1951** Pough *Audubon Water Bird* 328, Four-toed plover. . . Black-bellied plover.

four-toes n [From the shape of the flower head]
A **pussytoes** (here: *Antennaria plantaginifolia*).
1896 *Jrl. Amer. Folkl.* 9.191, *Antennaria plantaginifolia.* . . Four toes, . . Salem, Mass. **1900** Lyons *Plant Names* 37. **1940** Clute *Amer. Plant Names* 74, *A. plantaginifolia.* . . Four toes.

four-up n
1 also attrib: A team of four draft animals; hence adv, with a four animal team.
1942 Berrey–Van den Bark *Amer. Slang* 456.10, Four-up, four-up driver, *a driver of four teams.* **1967** Green *Horse Tradin'* 197, He knew he was going to have a little trouble; this was the reason he was working four-up instead of a single team. *Ibid* 203, I hooked them up for leaders and made me a four-up team.
2 A gambling game.
1931 Bradford *John Henry* 41 **Sth,** "Maybe you'd like to play a little seven-up?" "Four-up," said John Henry. " 'Cause seven-up takes jest dat much longer." . . "Four-up, coon-can, skin, or dices. Hit's all one and de same to me, and I plays you even."

fourvel See **fourble**

four ways for Sunday See **Sunday, forty ways till**

four-whiskered sea cat n [From the four barbels on the head]
=**gaff-topsail catfish.**
1933 LA Dept. of Conserv. *Fishes* 252, The Gaff-Topsail or Four-whiskered Sea Cat . . is a voracious feeder and by its bait stealing may become a great annoyance to the angler.

fout See **fight A1, 3, 4**

fouting See **fight A2**

foutory adj [*fouter, foutre* something or someone worthless or contemptible (chiefly Scots) < OFr *foutre;* cf **footy adj 1**]
1930 Shoemaker *1300 Words* 22 **cPA Mts** (as of c1900), *Foutory*—Flimsy, insignificant, contemptible.

fouty adj See **footy** adj

fouty n See **footy** n

foward See **forward** adj, adv

fowkses See **folk B2**

fowl n [By opposition to *chicken* in its older sense "young of the domestic fowl"]
An adult hen, esp one used for food.
1895 (1900) Arnold *Century Cook Book* 179, On young chickens there are pin-feathers; on fowls, there are long hairs. **1896** (c1973) Farmer *Orig. Cook Book* 215 **MA,** A *chicken* is known by soft feet, smooth skin, and soft cartilage at end of breastbone. . . In a *fowl* the feet have become hard and dry with coarse scales, and cartilage at end of breastbone has ossified. **1948** *Sun* (Baltimore MD) 5 Jan 10/2 *(Hench Coll.),* The term

"fowl" is not always understood by housewives. As used by the poultry trade "fowl" means hens weighing from about 3 to 6 pounds and usually over 1 year old. **1978** *Yankee* Sept 146/1 **seMA,** Dorothy uses fowl instead of chicken [for her chicken fricassee] because she prefers the stronger flavor, but if fowl is unavailable, she will use a large roasting chicken. **1979** *DARE* File **nCA,** My father always said that a fowl was just a very old chicken and that the only thing you could do with it was boil it. Then boil it some more and still find it tough. So I was surprised to find that grocery stores in Maine actually advertised fowl as though it were a delicacy. **1982** *DARE* File **coastal ME,** Fowl: never order stewing chicken by that name. Old chickens are always fowl.

fowl bluegrass n Also *fowl meadow bluegrass* Cf **fowl meadow grass**

A **bluegrass 1** (here: *Poa palustris*).

1950 Hitchcock-Chase *Manual Grasses* 124, *Poa palustris* . . Fowl Bluegrass. **1950** Stevens *ND Plants* 59, *Poa palustris* . . Fowl Bluegrass. **1952** Strausbaugh-Core *Flora WV* 134, *Poa palustris* . . Fowl Bluegrass. **1959** Munz-Keck *CA Flora* 1487. **1961** Peck *Manual OR* 99, *P[oa] palustris. . . Fowl Meadow Bluegrass.* . . Moist open ground.

fowl-crow n Also *first fowl-crow(ing)* *Gullah* Cf *DBE*

The time when the cock first crows; the very early morning, before dawn.

1888 Jones *Negro Myths* 161 **GA coast,** Las night, dis befo fus fowl crow, me bin er leddown een me bed. **1908** *S. Atl. Qrly.* 7.342 **seSC** [Gullah], The first division of the negro's day, *soon er mo'nin';* after which follow *fus' fowl-crowin', day-clean, sun-up,* [etc]. *Ibid* 343, "Buh Fowl-hawk mek plan fuh ketch de Sun een er trahp. . . W'en mo'nin' come, fus' fowl-crow' Buh Fowl-hawk pitch off de tree wey him *blan* [=is accustomed to] roos', an' sail fuh de spawt way de Sun *blan* sleep." **1922** Gonzales *Black Border* 303 **sSC, GA coasts** [Gullah glossary], *Fus' fowl crow*—first fowl crow—midnight, or soon thereafter. **1928** Peterkin *Scarlet Sister Mary* 59 **SC,** Every morning she got up at first fowl crow. . . The early mornings were chilly, but the shining stars made them beautiful. **1930** Stoney-Shelby *Black Genesis* 170 **seSC,** De nex' mornin' before fowl-crow she had him up, a-fixin' for de trip.

fowl hawk n Pronc-sp *fu'lhawk*

A **chicken hawk 1.**

1908 *S. Atl. Qrly.* 7.343 **sSC coast** [Gullah], Buh Fowl-hawk mek plan fuh ketch de Sun een er trahp. [=Brother Fowl-hawk made a plan to catch the Sun in a trap.] **1922** Gonzales *Black Border* 303 **sSC, GA coasts** [Gullah glossary], *Fu'lhawk*—fowlhawk. **1955** *Oriole* 20.5, *Sharp-shinned Hawk. . . Fowl Hawk* (Abbot, 1797; see Rhoads, *Auk,* 1918). **1970** *DARE* (Qu. Q4, . . *Kinds of hawks*) Inf **SC69,** Fowl hawk —looks almost like an eagle.

fowl house n Pronc-sp *fu'lhus'* **now esp SC** See Map

A hen house.

1767 in 1902 Singleton *Social NY* 44, Dwelling-house, stable, fowl-house and other necessaries. **1807** (1919) Bedford *Tour to New Orleans* 115 **VA,** Little huts few more than 10 feet square and more the resemblance of fowl-houses than human tenements. **1922** Gonzales *Black Border* 303 **sSC, GA coasts** [Gullah glossary], *Fu'lhus'*—fowl-house. **1945** FWP *Lay My Burden Down* 211 (as of c1864), I 'member when the Yankees come through. . . They burn the ginhouse, the shop, the buggy-house, the turkey-house, and the fowlhouse. **1966-67** *DARE* (Qu. M17, *A building where chickens or hens are kept*) 13 Infs, 11 **SC,** Fowl house.

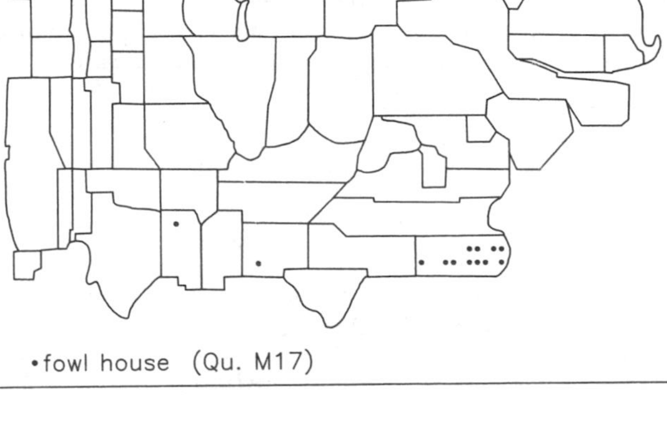

•fowl house (Qu. M17)

fowl manna grass n Cf **fowl bluegrass, fowl meadow grass**

A **manna grass** (here: *Glyceria striata*).

1950 Stevens *ND Plants* 58, *Glyceria striata. . . Fowl Manna-grass.* . . Often abundant in wet meadows and seepage areas. . . The nearly black grains are a characteristic feature of mannagrasses. **1961** Peck *Manual OR* 94, *G[lyceria] striata* . . Fowl Manna-grass. **1970** Correll *Plants TX* 123, *Glyceria striata.* . . Fowl Manna-grass.

fowl meadow n [Perh misinterpretation of *foul*] Cf **foul** adj, **fowl meadow grass**

1917 *DN* 4.385 **seME,** *Fowl-meadow.* . . Sour soil, needing to be treated with lime.

fowl meadow bluegrass See **fowl bluegrass**

fowl meadow grass n Also *foul meadow grass* [See quots 1751, 1786; but perh *foul meadow grass* is the original form] Cf **fowl meadow**

Either of two widely distributed grasses: a **manna grass** (here: *Glyceria striata*) or a **bluegrass 1** (here: *Poa palustris*).

1748 in 1934 Eliot *Field Husbandry* 12 **CT,** I then proceeded to sow Grass-Seed, such as red Clover, foul Meadow Grass, *English* Spear Grass, and Herd Grass. **1751** *Ibid* 61 **CT,** It is said . . That Fowl-Meadow Grass was bro't into a poor piece of Meadow . . by Ducks and other Wild Water-Fowl, and therefore called by such an odd Name. **1774** (1961) Adams *Diary* 28 Feb **MA,** Shall I try to introduce fowl Meadow And Herds Grass, into the Meadows? **1786** (1888) Cutler *Life* 2.264 **swMA,** *Fowl meadow-grass* is cultivated in wet meadows, produces great crops, and makes good cut-hay for cows. . . When the river . . overflowed its banks, [this meadow] . . was observed by the first settlers to abound with water-fowl, hence it was called fowl-meadow, and the grass *fowl meadow-grass.* **1889** Vasey *Ag. Grasses* 67, *Poa serotina* (Fowl Meadow Grass). . . This species is most common in the Northern States, particularly in New England, New York, and westward to Wisconsin. **a1890** (1944) Robinson *Hist. Morrill* 111 **csME,** Red-top, foul-meadow, and several other kinds [of grass] are native to this country. **1912** Baker *Book of Grasses* 205, Fowl Meadow-grass. *Poa triflora.* **1959** Munz-Keck *CA Flora* 1481, *G[lyceria] striata* . . Fowl Meadow Grass.

fox n

1 An attractive woman, *esp among Black speakers* Cf **foxy 3**

1963 *Freedomways* 3.53 **NYC,** Daddy, she was a real fox! **1963** Mencken-McDavid *Amer. Lang.* 745 [Argot of jazz musicians], A *cat* in hot pursuit of a *chick* or *fox* is said to *have his nose wide open.* **1967-70** *DARE* (Qu. HH34, . . *Words . . for a woman*) Infs **NY241,** 249, **SC65,** Fox; **MI72,** Fox—a real sharp-looking gal—looks good to the men; (Qu. Z6, . . *Affectionate words meaning 'sister'*) Inf **NY241,** Fox (she's a real fly chick; a together little chick); (Qu. AA7a, . . *A woman who is very fond of men . . if she's nice about it*) Inf **PA247,** She's a fox, if she's nice looking; (Qu. HH2) Inf **MI88,** Fox—a newer name for women. [5 of 6 Infs Black] **1970** Major *Dict. Afro-Amer. Slang* 55, *Fox:* (1940's-60's) a beautiful black girl. **1972** Claerbaut *Black Jargon* 64, *Fox* . . a very good-looking girl; beautiful female.

2 See quots.

1966-69 *DARE* (Qu. AA6b, . . *A man who is fond of being with women . . if he's . . not respectful*) Inf **ND3,** Wolf, fox; (Qu. HH38, *A womanish man*) Inf **NY35,** Dude, fox; (Qu. HH40, *Uncomplimentary words for an old man*) Inf **RI1,** Fogy, fox. **1981** *Seventeen Letters* **WA,** A very handsome or cute guy—Fox/Hunk.

3 See **fox and geese 1.**

4 See **fox and hounds 1.**

fox v

1 To make drunk; hence ppl adj *foxed.* [*OED* 1611 →] Cf **foxy 1**

1848 Worcester *Universal Dict., Fox.* . . To stupefy; to make drunk. **1899** (1912) Green *VA Folk-Speech* 183, *Fox.* . . To intoxicate; fuddle. **1928** *AmSp* 4.102 [Synonyms for "Drunk"], Foxed. **1942** Berrey-Van den Bark *Amer. Slang* 106.7, *Drunk* . . foxed.

2 To repair (a boot or shoe) by replacing or covering the foot with new leather and usu resoling; hence ppl adj *foxed;* vbl n *foxing.* [*OED* 1796 →] Cf **goose** v **1**

1846 Worcester *Universal Dict.* 292/2, Fox. . . To repair boots by adding new soles, and surrounding the feet with new leather. **1872** Schele de Vere *Americanisms* 481, When a new bottom is made and the boots are renewed half way up, it is called *goosing* boots, and *foxing,* when a new foot is made to old "uppers." The names are, however, not kept equally distinct in all the States. **1892** *AN&Q* 8.246/2, A pair of old boot-legs fitted to new *foot-parts* were said to be "foxed." Boots are not so generally worn now. . . It is long since I have heard the word . . [40 years ago]. It used to be very common in what was then "out West." **1912** Green *VA Folk-Speech* 183, *Fox.* . . To fit new feet to old boot-legs. . . To repair a shoe or boot by renewing nearly all the front upper leather.

3 To reinforce or decorate (shoes, trousers, etc) with a facing, usu of leather; hence ppl adj *foxed;* vbl n *foxing* a facing of this sort. [*EDD foxed* ppl. adj. 3]

1844 Kendall *Santa Fé Exped.* 2.104, His pantaloons were of cloth of the same colour, foxed with green morocco. **1853** Hammett *Stray Yankee in TX* 110, He was . . dressed . . in broadcloth pantaloons, seated and "foxed" with buckskin. **1865** (1889) Whitney *Gayworthys* 248 **NEng,** Say wore cloth boots with patent foxings. **1872** (1876) Knight *Amer. Mech. Dict.* 912/1, *Foxing.* . . Ornamental strips of a different material on the uppers of shoes. **1927** (1944) Russell *Trails Plowed Under* 2 **West** (as of 1870s), Maybe he'd wear California pants . . sometimes foxed, or what you'd call reinforced with buck or antelope skin.

4 Of an animal: to swivel (the ears) forward.

1944 Howard *Walkin' Preacher* 1 **csIA,** Suddenly Jinny [=a mule] foxed her ears. A quail whirred out of the plum thicket in yon draw.

fox across the river n Also *fox and the river, fox in the gully* **Sth**

A chasing game similar to **fox in the morning 1.**

1966–70 *DARE* (Qu. EE1, . . *Games . . in which . . [children] form a ring*) Inf **FL**28, Fox in the gully—two lines, on each side of the battle area. One [player] was the fox, the others tried to catch him; (Qu. EE12) Inf **TX**18, Run sheep run is also called fox across the river; it's played like pom-pom-pullaway; (Qu. EE33, *Other outdoor games*) Inf **VA**83, Fox and the river. **1968** *DARE* FW Addit **csLA,** Fox across the river—played across a ditch. Everybody gets on one side of the ditch except the one in the ditch—he is the fox. Somebody takes a chance and tries to cross the ditch. If he gets tagged, then he is the fox. If he crosses, he is safe.

fox and dog(s) See **fox and hounds 1**

fox and geese n Also *fox and goose*

1 also *fox:* A board game in which markers represent geese and a fox or foxes; usu the fox can capture geese by jumping them, while the geese try to hem in the fox so it cannot move or jump. [*OED* 1633 →]

1825 Neal *Brother Jonathan* 1.7 **CT,** Peters had beaten him . . first in argument . . ; then, at fox and geese; then, at morris; then, at checkers, or draughts. **a1874** in 1949 *PADS* 11.32 **cME,** She beat me bad at fox and geese,/ But I beat her at morris. **1949** (1958) Stuart *Thread* 96 **KY,** We made our fox-and-goose boards and we played with white, yellow, and red grains of corn. **1954** *Harder Coll.* **cwTN,** *Fox and geese.* . . Table game played with corn grains and on a specially made board. **1965–70** *DARE* (Qu. DD37, . . *Table games played . . by adults*) Infs **IL**73, **NY**101, **NC**31, 54, **PA**63, **VT**16, **WI**26, **WV**7, Fox and geese; **OK**1, **TN**14, **VA**27, Fox and goose; **AL**32, Fox and geese—two fox and twenty geese. Try to hem the fox up. If the fox jumps the geese, he takes [them]; (Qu. EE38a) Inf **IN**19, Fox and geese; **NC**72, Fox and goose; **VA**24, Fox; (Qu. EE39) Inf **NC**72, Fox and goose; **KY**89, Fox and geese; **KY**40, Fox and goose—old-fashioned. Two foxes and twenty-two geese. Geese would try to trap foxes while foxes tried to get geese. Played with corn kernels. **1967** *DARE* FW Addit **LA**1, Fox and geese—played with grains of corn or buttons on a cardboard court. The fox chased the geese and the geese tried to hem the fox in. **1969** *DARE* Tape **KY**5, Fox an' goose. . . Fox would be over here in this corner . . he could go anywhere he wanted to but the old goose, you'd have to move it a certain way all the time. **1980** *Foxfire 6* 285 **nGA,** *Fox and Geese* . . was usually played at the mill while people were waiting to have their corn ground. . . The miller was usually the fox and he was usually the winner because he got so much practice at it.

2 also *fox and the geese, ~ goose, fox-and-goose ring, fox-the-goose:* A tag game in which "foxes" chase "geese" in a wheel-shaped network of paths, usu marked out in deep snow. [Similar tag games, but without the marked paths, are called *fox and geese* in Engl dial] **chiefly Nth, N Midl, Plains States, Rocky Mts** See Map

1848 *Knickerbocker* 21.219, Recollections of early school-days; . . fox-and-geese in the deep snow, 'by the whole company.' **1950** *WELS* (*Games played in the snow*) 34 Infs, **WI,** Fox and (the) geese; 8 Infs, Fox and (the) goose; [1 Inf, Fox chasing the goose]. [Only 9 of 52 Infs did not mention this game; 22 described it as in quot 1953.] **1953** Brewster *Amer. Nonsinging Games* 54 **WI,** *Fox and Geese.* . . The base and the paths . . are made by trampling down the snow. . . The center spot . . is the "hen house." . . The "fox" tries to tag any "goose" who may try to stray from this safety zone. Both fox and geese must stay on the paths at all times. If the former succeeds in tagging a goose, the latter becomes a fox and must aid the captor. **1954** *Harder Coll.* **cwTN,** *Fox and geese.* **1965–70** *DARE* (Qu. EE26, . . *Games . . children play in the snow*) 286 Infs, **chiefly Nth, N Midl, Plains States, Rocky Mts,** Fox and geese; 15 Infs, **scattered N Cent, West,** Fox and goose; 8 Infs, 4 **MO,** Fox and the goose (*or* geese), **CA**136, Fox-and-goose ring; **IL**63, Fox-the-goose; (Qu. EE27, *Games played on the ice*) 14 Infs, **scattered Nth, N Midl** Fox and (the) geese; **NJ**1, Fox and goose; (Qu. EE2) Infs **IA**9, **MA**42, **NY**232, Fox and geese—played in snow; **CO**14, Fox and geese—a pie-shaped thing with alleys; (Qu. EE33) Inf **NY**52, Fox and geese—played in the snow. Tread a circle with spokes. The fox tried to catch somebody before they got back to the center hub; (Qu. EE1) Inf **MI**92, Fox and geese—winter game.

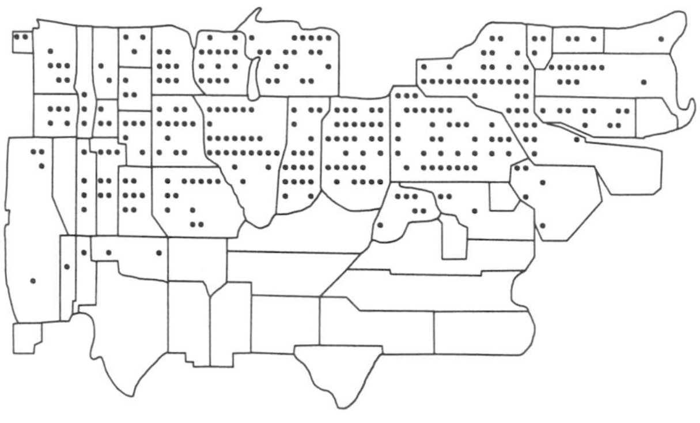

•fox and geese 2 + varr (Qq. EE26, EE27, EE1, EE2, EE33)

3 also *the fox and the goose:* A tag game in which the "geese" form a line and the "fox" tries to tag the hindmost "goose."

1885 Warner *Wide World* 315, There was a general call for "the fox and the goose." . . [The fox's] business was to catch the train of the goose, one by one, as each in turn became the hindmost; while *her* object was to baffle him and keep her family together, meeting him with outspread arms at every rush he made to seize one of her brood. **1909** (1923) Bancroft *Games* 92, *Fox and geese.* . . One player is chosen to be fox and another to be gander. The remaining players all stand in single file behind the gander, each with his hands on the shoulders of the one next in front. . . Only the last goose in the line may be tagged. . . A good deal of spirit may be added to the game by the following dialogue, which is sometimes used to open it: . . "Geese, geese, gannio!" . . "Fox, fox, fannio!" . . "How many geese have you today?" . . "More than you can catch and carry away."

4 =**fox in the morning 1.**

1952 Brown *NC Folkl.* 1.79, Three or four of the best runners challenge the crowd to a game of Fox and Geese. Bases are arranged and the challengers are foxes, while the rest of the players are geese. The foxes call from their base: "Goosey goosey gander!"/ Geese: Fox over yander./ Foxes: How many geese you got?/ Geese: More'n you can catch./ The geese all run out and the foxes chase them.

5 A children's ring game, perh **duck duck goose** or a variant of it.

1950 *WELS* (*Games in which the players form a ring and either sing or recite a rhyme*) 3 Infs, **WI,** Fox and geese; 1 Inf, Fox and goose. **1965–70** *DARE* (Qu. EE2, *Games that have one extra player—when a signal is given, the players change places, and the extra one tries to get a place*) 34 Infs, **scattered, but esp Nth, N Midl,** Fox and geese; (Qu. EE1, . . *Games . . in which they form a ring, and either sing or recite a rhyme*) Infs **IA**3, **NJ**6, **PA**71, Fox and geese; **OH**1, Fox and geese—like drop the handkerchief; **WI**47, Fox and geese—same game [as EE2]; **WI**70, Fox and geese—no rhyme or song. [Note: It is possible that some of these Infs are in fact referring to **fox and geese 2** or some other game.]

6 A children's game played in the water.

1906 *DN* 3.136 **nwAR,** *Fox and goose.* . . A game played in the water. **1967–69** *DARE* (Qu. EE28, *Games played in the water*) Infs **AL**2, **IL**45,

OH87, **PA**26, 104, Fox and geese; **MO**2, Fox and goose; **CO**21, Fox and geese—"it" [was] on bank, geese had to come out; **CT**5, Fox and geese—also played on dry land.

7 A children's hiding game.

1968–70 *DARE* (Qu. EE12, *Games in which one captain hides his team and the other team tries to find it*) Infs **CA**174, **MD**33, **NJ**48, **PA**134, Fox and geese [*DARE* Ed: Two Infs were doubtful about this resp.]; **CT**6, Fox and geese—one group of foxes tries to find group of geese; (Qu. EE13a, *Games in which every player hides except one*) Inf **KY**80, Fox and geese = hide-and-go-seek.

fox and geese come over n Also *fox and the geese and all come over*

=fox in the morning 1.

1937 in 1977 *Amer. Slave Suppl. 1* 1.246 **swAL,** The children of the plantation played ring games, "puss, puss in the corner", "next door neighbor", and "fox and the geese and all come over". **1968** *DARE* (Qu. EE33) Inf **NJ**28, Fox and geese come over—one man says to all others, "Come over," and others have to get past him without being tagged.

fox and goose See **fox and geese**

fox-and-goose ring See **fox and geese 2**

fox and hen n Cf **fox and geese 3**

=chickamy chickamy craney crow.

1953 Brewster *Amer. Nonsinging Games* 71, *Chickamy Chickamy Craney Crow* . . is known by many names . . [including] Fox and Hen. **1967** *DARE* (Qu. EE33, . . *Outdoor games*) Inf **KY**34, Fox and hen.

fox and hounds n

1 also *fox and (the) hound, fox and dog(s), foxes and dogs, dogs and fox, fox:* A game of pursuit, in which usu one player is given a head start and tries to outrun or elude the other players. [*OED* 1821 →] **chiefly Midl** Cf **hare and hound(s)**

1905 *DN* 3.79 **nwAR,** *Fox and dogs, fox and hounds*. . . Hare and hounds. Usual. **1938** Stuart *Dark Hills* 99 **KY,** When we played Fox and Dog, Big Andy was always the Fox. He could outrun the rest of us over the big meadows on the uplands, through the woods and down the hollows. **1953** Brewster *Amer. Nonsinging Games* 77 **IN,** *Fox*. . . The "fox" is allowed a few minutes (or a few yards) start, and then the "dogs" start in pursuit of him. Like a real fox, the former uses every possible trick to throw his pursuers off the trail. . . However, in some forms of the game, he must remain in full view at all times and may even be required to drop bits of paper or otherwise mark his trail as he runs. **c1960** *Wilson Coll.* **csKY,** *Fox and Hounds*—a chasing game. **1967–70** *DARE* (Qu. EE33, . . *Outdoor games*) Infs **AK**9, **GA**80, **MD**12, 34, **NJ**1, **PA**28, Fox and hound(s); **KY**11, 84, Fox and the hound; **MD**18, Fox and hounds—a boys' game. One boy is fox, others are hounds. The fox ran ahead, tried to hide. Hounds chased him till he fagged out and they caught him; **GA**75, Dogs and fox—one boy is fox, all others are dogs; they try to catch him; **MI**115, Dogs and fox; **VA**13, Foxes and dogs—similar to "chicken hawk"; **SC**32, Fox; all players chase one; (Qu. EE26) Inf **OH**15, Fox and hounds—in new snow—one player takes off and others follow his tracks; (Qu. EE16) Inf **AK**9, Fox and hounds; paper chase. **1968–70** *DARE* Tape **MD**12, Fox and hound is what they called it when I went to school; **MI**115, Dogs and fox, that was the name of the game. **1980** *Foxfire 6* 284 **nGA,** *Fox and Dogs* . . was a rough game usually played just by big boys. . . The fox would start running and try to find a small tree . . and climb it. The dogs would be chasing him. When they caught up with him and treed him, the person with the ax would come along and chop down the tree. If the fox could get away without getting caught, he'd start running again and climb another tree.

2 also *fox and hound:* **=fox and geese 2.**

1950 *WELS (Games played in the snow)* 1 Inf, **WI,**Fox and hounds. **1966–69** *DARE* (Qu. EE26, . . *Games . . in the snow*) Infs **AZ**1, **MO**37, Fox and hound(s); **MA**73, Fox and hounds—fox went through a maze of some kind. Hounds had to catch him; **OK**31, Fox and hounds—form two circles, one in the center of the other. Chase players over paths in the snow. [Note: Some of these Infs may be referring to sense **1**; see quot 1967–70, Qu. EE26, there.]

3 also *fox and hound, ~ the hounds:* A hiding game.

1968–70 *DARE* (Qu. EE12, *Games in which one captain hides his team and the other team tries to find it*) Infs **SC**54, **WI**12, Fox and hounds; **MD**31, Fox and hounds—one team hides, other team try to stir them out; each person tries to catch one of opposite sex and kiss and hug them; **NY**234, Fox and hound; (Qu. EE13a, *Games in which every player hides except one*) Inf **VA**99, Fox and hounds; (Qu. EE16, . . *Games that start with a special, elaborate method of sending the players out to hide*) Inf **SC**54, Fox and the hounds—used a whole block to play; five minutes head start for the foxes.

4 A marble game; see quot.

1966 *DARE* Tape **OK**42, Then we played fox and hounds. . . Just throw a marble out there and you shoot at me. Every time, if you hit me, well, the marble's yours. Just maybe we'd play all around the house.

fox and the geese See **fox and geese 2**

fox and the geese and all come over See **fox and geese come over**

fox and the goose See **fox and geese 2, 3**

fox and the hound(s) See **fox and hounds 1, 3**

fox and the river See **fox across the river**

fox and the tail n

A children's prank; see quot.

1968 *DARE* File **cDE,** Fox and the tail—children's game for fooling outsiders. A stick is dipped in the toilet; one boy runs with it and the others "try" to catch the fox by the "tail." They let the city boy catch him, and the fox jerks the stick out of his hand, leaving his hand fouled.

fox and the wahoo n

A children's outdoor game; perh a chasing game like **fox and hounds 1.**

1965–67 *DARE* (Qu. EE33, *Other outdoor games*) Infs **MS**30, **PA**59, Fox and the wahoo.

fox bait n Also *fox-farm bait, fox feed, ~ food, ~ meat* Cf **fox farm, ready for the; crowbait**

An old, broken-down horse.

1950 *WELS (Joking or uncomplimentary names for horses)* 2 Infs, **WI,** Fox bait; 1 Inf, Fox meat; 1 Inf, Fox-farm bait; [1 Inf, Bait for the fox farm]; *(A bony or poor-looking horse)* 3 Infs, Fox bait; 2 Infs, Fox meat; 1 Inf, Fox food. **1966–67** *DARE* (Qu. K44) Inf **IA**6, Fox feed; [**ME**23, Just right for the fox].

foxberry n

1 =bearberry 2.

1784 in 1785 Amer. Acad. Arts & Sci. *Memoirs* 1.444, *Arbutus*. . . *Fox-berry. Checkerberry*. . . The berries . . are sometimes eaten by children in milk. **1874** Ward *Trotty's Wedding* 213, Crushed ferns and the ruins of little foxberry blossoms that turned wax-white at the sight of her. **1911** Henkel *Amer. Med. Leaves* 20, *Arctostaphylos uva-ursi*. . . Fox-berry . . produces its pretty waxy flowers about May. **1930** Sievers *Amer. Med. Plants* 10, *Bearberry*. . . *Other common names*. . . Fox-berry, upland cranberry [etc].

2 A **frost grape** (here: *Vitis vulpina*).

1876 Hobbs *Bot. Hdbk.* 39, Fox berry, Frost grape, Vitis vulpina.

3 =partridgeberry.

1896 *Jrl. Amer. Folkl.* 9.190, *Mitchella repens*. . . Fox berry, Lynn, Mass. **1911** Henkel *Amer. Med. Leaves* 34, Foxberry . . has tonic, astringent, and diuretic properties. **1959** Carleton *Index Herb. Plants* 49, *Fox-berry:* Mitchella repens.

4 See quot.

1908 *DN* 3.312 **eAL, wGA,** *Fox-berry*. . . The berry on the common bramble.

5 A **mountain cranberry** (here: *Vaccinium vitis-idaea*).

1931 U.S. Dept. Ag. *Misc. Pub.* 101.136, Mountain cranberry, . . frequently called foxberry, . . is of some value as winter browse for reindeer and caribou in Alaska.

6 =French mulberry.

1970 Correll *Plants TX* 1339, *Callicarpa americana*. . . Foxberry, purple beautyberry.

fox bird n [From the reddish color]

1 =brown thrasher.

1955 *AmSp* 30.179, For more or less rufescent coloration, the following species have won names including the term *fox:* . . brown thrasher (*fox bird,* N.J.)

2 A **rufous-sided towhee.**

1955 *AmSp* 30.179, For more or less rufescent coloration, . . towhee (*fox bird,* N.Y.)

3 =black-crowned night heron.

1955 MA Audubon Soc. *Bulletin* 39.312, *Black-Crowned Night Heron. . .* Fox Bird (Maine. Again by erroneous transfer from the fox-colored bittern.)

fox-chase n Also *fox-hunt*

=fox and hounds 1.

1966–69 *DARE* (Qu. EE33, . . *Outdoor games*) Infs **GA**77, **NC**33, Fox-chase; **GA**72, Fox-hunt; (Qu. EE12) Inf **AR**47, Fox-hunt.

fox-colored finch See **foxy finch**

fox-colored sparrow See **fox sparrow**

fox-colored thrush n

=brown thrasher.

1731 (1754) Catesby *Nat. Hist. Carolina* 1.28, *Turdus ruffus. The Fox coloured Thrush. . .* This Bird is called in *Virginia* the *French Mock-Bird.* It remains all the year in *Carolina* and *Virginia.* **1917** (1923) *Birds Amer.* 3.179, *Brown Thrasher—Toxostoma rufum . .* Other Names. . . Fox-colored Thrush. **1946** Hausman *Eastern Birds* 453, *Brown Thrasher—Toxostoma rufum . .* Fox-colored Thrush.

fox dog n

A dog trained to hunt foxes; a foxhound.

1810 (1911) Bentley *Diary* 3.521 **MA,** We saw Guiney hens at one farm in Chelmsford, & a very fat fox dog at Dunstable. **1895** *Century Illustr. Mag.* 50.626/2 **KY,** I never sell a fox-dog; I consider him a member of my household. **c1937** in 1970 Yetman *Voices* 53 **TX,** We have bear dog, fox dog, and rabbit dog that mostly just go by the name of houn' dog. **1966–68** *DARE* Tape **GA**3, He's got fox dogs; **GA**9, I never have kept no fox dogs; **NY**32, [Inf:] I . . used to keep hunting dogs for foxes. [FW:] What kind of dogs were they? [Inf:] Fox dogs. . . They were bred for fox hunting.

foxed See **fox** v **1, 2, 3**

foxes and dogs See **fox and hounds 1**

foxey See **foxy**

fox-farm bait See **fox bait**

fox farm, ready for the adj phr Also *fit for the fox farm* [In ref to the feeding of horsemeat to foxes being raised for fur] **chiefly WI** Cf **fox bait**

Usu of an animal: old and broken-down.

1950 *WELS (A bony or poor-looking horse)* 3 Infs, **WI,** Ready (or fit) for the fox farm; 1 Inf, About ready for the fox farm. **1966–68** *DARE* (Qu. K44) Infs **IL**4, **IN**2, **WI**10, 14, 51, 61, Ready for the fox farm; (QR, near Qu. K44) Inf **WI**24, [In ref to a very old man:] He's ready for the fox farm.

fox feed See **fox bait**

foxfeet n

A **club moss** (here: *Lycopodium selago*).

1938 Small *Ferns SE States* 402, In addition to the common, fir-club-moss, the plant [=*Lycopodium selago*] is known as . . *Fox-feet.*

fox-finch See **foxy finch**

fox fire n [*OED* 1483 →. Prob orig meaning "deceptive fire"; cf *OED fox* sb. 2. b, **foxy 6**]

1a A luminescence appearing in or on rotting wood; the luminescent wood or fungus itself. **chiefly Sth, S Midl**

1824 Doddridge *Notes Indian Wars* 290 (as of c1770), If they had seen any thing like fire, between that and the fort, it must have been fox fire. **1885** Twain *Huck. Finn* 300 **MO,** What we must have was a lot of them rotten chunks that's called fox-fire and just makes a soft kind of a glow when you lay them in a dark place. **1890** *DN* 1.64 **KY,** *Fox-fire:* phosphorescent wood seen at night after continued rain. **1893** Shands *MS Speech* 30, *Fox-fire . .* Used by all classes. **1908** *DN* 3.312 **eAL, wGA. 1909** *DN* 3.396 **nwAR. 1910** *DN* 3.453 **seVT,** *Fox-fire. . .* Rare in this locality. **1941** Percy *Lanterns* 54 **nwMS,** To hunt in the mold of the wood-pile for the turquoise bits that were fox-fire. **1956** *Hall Coll.* **eTN,** Foxfire. "Hit glows of a night, kind of a rotten, doty wood. At night it will shine like fire." **c1960** *Wilson Coll.* **csKY,** *Fox-fire . .* A type of fungus on decaying wood that gives off a pale glow. **1965–70** *DARE* (Qu. CC16) 17 Infs, **chiefly Sth, S Midl,** Fox fire; **AR**52, Fox fire glows, but it's down on the ground phosphorus on rotten wood; **LA**31, Fox fire—this for the rotten wood that glows at night; **NY**219, Fox fire—that's on an old log—not over swamp; **SC**2, Fox fire seems to stay in one place. [*DARE* Ed: See note at **2** below, quot 1965–70.]

b Fig: a specious excellence or distinction; something insubstantial or inconsequential. *old-fash*

1853 *S. Lit. Messenger* 19.473/2 **MS,** After the first bustle of their coming with the fox-fire of their old reputations sticking to their gowns, it was generally found . . that the new importation would not suit the market. **1890** *Voice* 26 June *(DA),* About time sensible people quit frightening themselves with the fox-fire of a lot of office-thirsty politicians. **1890** *DN* 1.64 **KY,** We have an expression, "That is all fox-fire," meaning, of no consequence. **1909** *DN* 3.396 **nwAR.**

2 also *fox-fire light:* **=will-o'-the-wisp.**

1947 (1964) Randolph *Ozark Superstitions* 235, People who live near a little buryin' ground . . in Taney county, Missouri, have talked about such "fox-fire lights" for many years. A bluish light, they say, apparently about as high as a man's head, first appears among the gravestones and then slowly crosses the road. It moves about as fast as a man walking, I was told. **1950** *WELS (A small light that seems to dance over a swamp or marsh by night)* 2 Infs, **WI,** Fox fire. **1954** *Harder Coll.* **cwTN,** *Fox-fire . .* A small light that seems to dance over a swamp or marsh at night. **1965–70** *DARE* (Qu. CC16, *A small light that seems to dance or flicker over a marsh or swamp at night*) 132 Infs, **chiefly Sth, S Midl,** Fox fire. [*DARE* Ed: Since many Infs responded to Qu. CC16 with names for other mysterious lights, it is likely that many of these Infs were in fact referring to **fox fire 1a;** this was explicitly indicated for the 21 Infs accounted for at **1a,** quot 1965–70.]

3 A glow appearing around prominent points during an electrical storm; **St. Elmo's fire.**

1920 Hunter *Trail Drivers TX* 149, Talk about thunder and lightning! There is where you could see phosphorescence (fox fire) on our horse's ears and smell sulphur. **1941** Dobie *Longhorns* 96, The electricity played along the horn curves "as if they were lightning rods." . . Balls of fox fire ran around the wet brim of a cowboy's hat.

4 Perh a **standing cypress** (here: *Ipomopsis rubra*).

1911 (1916) Porter *Harvester* 228 **IN,** Everywhere flamed foxfire and cardinal flower.

5 =scarlet gilia. West

1956 St. John *Flora SE WA* 324, *Gilia aggregata. . . Fox fire. . .* Corolla scarlet, . . the lobes and throat maculate with deeper red or orange. **1963** Craighead *Rocky Mt. Wildflowers* 150, *Scarlet Gilia. . .* Foxfire. . . The brilliant red coloring immediately attracts attention. **1967** Dodge *Roadside Wildflowers* 58 **SW,** *Foxfire. . .* Color varies from brilliant red to pink and purple, even orange.

6 Prob **=glowworm.**

1968 *DARE* (Qu. CC16) Inf **GA**56, Fox fire ("glow worms").

fox-fire light See **fox fire 2**

foxflower n

A thrift (here: *Armeria leptophylla*).

1970 Kirk *Wild Edible Plants W. U.S.* 288, *Armeria leptophylla. . .* Thrift, Foxflower. . . The . . plant may be washed, boiled with seasoning, and eaten. . . It has been found at very high elevations . . in dry, rocky soil.

fox food See **fox bait**

fox frost n

1 See quot.

1949 *Hench Coll.* **VA,** *Fox-frost. . .* A heavy killing frost.

2 See quot.

1949 *Hench Coll.* **VA,** *Fox-frost. . .* Little pillars of ice that have during the night raised the loose top-surface of the ground. "When we were boys, and you'd come to a gall down a red-clay hillside, some mornings someone would shout 'Oh, fox frost!' "

foxglove n

1 Std: a plant of the genus *Digitalis,* esp *D. purpurea* [*OED* c1000 →] Also called **fairy glow 2**

2 Any of var plants of other genera in the family Scrophulariaceae as:

a =false foxglove.

1822 Eaton *Botany* 526, Foxglove [See pages] 266 *[Digitalis],* 289, 290 *[Gerardia].* **1901** Lounsberry *S. Wild Flowers* 463, *Dasystoma Pedicularia. . .* Among those plants that we know well are the foxgloves, holding their golden bloom through the autumn. **1913** *Torreya* 13.249 **NY,** The large purple foxglove, *Agalinus purpurea . . ,* with its snowy rose-colored flowers, was conspicuous in moist grassy places. **1959** Carleton *Index Herb. Plants* 49, *Fox-Glove: . .* Gerardia (v). **1967**

DARE Wildfl QR Pl.202 Inf **OH**37, Foxglove. **1968** *DARE* FW Addit **VA**15, Foxglove—woods, common; book term [is] *smooth gerardia (Gerardia laevigata).*

b A **beardtongue,** usu *Penstemon cobaea.* **TX**

1897 *Jrl. Amer. Folkl.* 10.52, *Pentstemon,* sp., foxglove, Tex. **1961** Wills–Irwin *Flowers TX* 200, *Wild-foxglove—Penstemon cobaea...* flowers in April and May. **1970** Correll *Plants TX* 1424, *Penstemon Cobaea... Fox-glove...* Common from the Rolling Plains to the Blackland Prairies, s. to the Gulf.

c A yellow-flowered perennial plant *(Brachystigma wrightii)* native to Arizona and New Mexico.

1960 Vines *Trees SW* 919, Wright Foxglove—*Brachystigma wrightii.*

3 A **pitcher plant** (here: *Sarracenia purpurea*). **esp nNEng**

1892 *Jrl. Amer. Folkl.* 5.92, *Sarracenia purpurea,* .. foxglove. N.H. **1896** *Ibid* 9.181, *Sarracenia purpurea* .. foxgloves, Woodstock, Me. **1898** *Ibid* 11.222, *Sarracenia purpurea* .. foxgloves, South Berwick, Me. **1929** *Torreya* 29.150 **ME,** Sarracenia purpurea was often *"Fox-glove,"* as well as "Pitcher Plant." **1959** Carleton *Index Herb. Plants* 49, *Fox-Glove:* .. Sarracenia purpurea.

4 also *foxglove vine:* **=trumpet creeper.**

1892 *Jrl. Amer. Folkl.* 5.102, *Tecoma radicans,* foxglove. Chestertown, Md. **1931** Read *LA French* 45, Some French natives of Louisiana apply this name to the Trumpet-Flower, which is also called .. Fox-Glove. **1960** Vines *Trees SW* 925, *Bignonia radicans...* Some of its vernacular names are .. Devil's-shoestring, Foxglove-vine, and Cow-itch.

5 A **pokeweed** (here: *Phytolacca americana*).

1900 Lyons *Plant Names* 287, *P[hytolacca] decandra...* Foxglove.

6 **=lady's slipper.**

1966 *DARE* (Qu. S26b) Inf **ME**24, Foxgloves—or lady-slipper—[grow] in the heath.

7 A **bellflower** (here: *Campanula trachelium*).

1900 Lyons *Plant Names* 77, *C[ampanula] trachelium...* Blue Fox-glove.

foxglove vine See **foxglove 4**

fox glow n Cf **fox fire 2**

1968 *DARE* (Qu. CC16, *A small light that seems to dance or flicker over a marsh or swamp at night*) Inf **PA**148, Fox glow.

fox grape n

1 A **grape** *(Vitis labrusca)* noted for the musky flavor of its fruit. Also called **coon grape 1, plum grape, skunk grape, swamp grape**

1638 in 1889 MD Hist. Soc. *Fund Pub.* 28.208 **MD,** I haue not seene as yett any white grape excepting the foxgrape wch hath some stayne of white. **1737** (1911) Brickell *Nat. Hist. NC* 92, The *Vines* that are Spontaneous and produce Grapes in *Carolina,* are of six Kinds, and are as follows, The *Fox-grape,* whereof there are four sorts, Two of which are call'd the *Summer-Fox-grape,* because they are ripe in *July.* **1832** MA Hist. Soc. *Coll.* 2d ser 9.158 **cwVT,** Vitis labrusca, *(Michaux.)*—Fox grape. **1889** (1971) Farmer *Americanisms* 252, *Fox Grape...* Its name is said to arise from its rank, fox-like taste. As, however, the juice, when fermented, is very intoxicating, it is more probable that its distinctive name is derived from the old English "fox," to intoxicate. **1893** Shands *MS Speech* 30, *Fox-grape...* The grape, commonly called *fox-grape* in Mississippi, is very small and very sour. It is also called *coon-grape* and *possum-grape.* **1913** Cather *O Pioneers* 29 **NE,** Stout as she was, she roamed the scrubby banks of Norway Creek looking for fox grapes and goose plums. **1942** Tehon *Fieldbook IL Shrubs* 186, The Fox Grape, which prefers woods along streams and bodies of water, ranges from New England to Illinois and south to Georgia. **1965–70** *DARE* (Qu. I46, .. *Fruits that grow wild around here*) 45 Infs, **chiefly C and S Atl, KY,** Fox grape(s); **PA**31, Wild fox grapes; **NJ**39, **PA**29, Fox grape; (Qu. I44, .. *Berries [that] grow wild*) Inf **FL**36, Fox grapes; (Qu. I53, *Other fruits*) Infs **GA**72, **PA**159, Fox grapes; (Qu. DD28b) Inf **NC**80, Fox grape wine. [*DARE* Ed: Some of these Infs may refer instead to **2** or **3** below.] **1966** *DARE* Tape **NC**25, Then they have the fox grape... They're just [a] single grape, that grows kinda single-like, much bigger with a tough hull.

2 **=frost grape.**

1792 Belknap *Hist. NH* 3.121, Of grapes we have two species. The *Black Grape (vitis labrusca)* and the *Fox-Grape (vitis vulpina.)* Of these there are several varieties. **1830** Rafinesque *Med. Flora* 2.132, *Vitis vulpina* .. It bears a multitude of vulgar names, such as .. Fox and Scupernong Grape. **1893** *Jrl. Amer. Folkl.* 6.139, *Vitis Cordifolia,* fox grapes. Ferrisburgh, Vt. **1906** *DN* 3.136 **nwAR,** *Fox grape...* A small, sour wild grape, ripe at the time of frost. **1960** Vines *Trees SW* 730, *Vitis vulpina* .. Vernacular names are Fox Grape. **1970** Correll *Plants TX* 1020, *Vitis vulpina* .. Fox grape.

3 **=muscadine grape.**

1900 Lyons *Plant Names* 395, *Vitis rotundifolia* .. Southern Fox Grape. **1946** *PADS* 6.14 **eNC,** *Fox grape:* .. A wild grape that grows in a cluster like the scuppernong; much smaller than the scuppernong. *(Muscadinia rotundifolia.)* Pamlico. Common. **1946** Tatnall *Flora DE* 173, *Vitis rotundifolia* .. Southern Fox Grape. **1954** *Harder Coll.* **cwTN.** **1960** Vines *Trees SW* 727, *Vitis rotundifolia* .. Vernacular names are Southern Fox Grape .. and Scuppernong. **c1960** *Wilson Coll.* **csKY,** *Fox grape.*

fox-grape winter n [**fox grape**] Cf **blackberry winter**

A period of cold weather in the spring.

1940 (1978) Still *River of Earth* 127 **KY,** "Even come spring," Grandma said, "we've got a passel of chills to endure: dogwood winter, redbud, service, foxgrape, blackberry... There must be seven winters, by count. A chilly snap for every time of bloom." **1941** *Sat. Eve. Post* 10 May 36/3 **KY,** We trembled in night chill, for it was fox-grape winter.

fox grass n

1 A **cordgrass** (here: *Spartina patens*).

1912 Baker *Book of Grasses* 162, Fox-Grass... *Spartina patens.*

2 A **beardgrass,** prob *Andropogon virginicus.*

1968–70 *DARE* (Qu. S9, .. *Kinds of grass that are hard to get rid of*) Inf **IN**19, Fox grass; **MA**100, Broom sage, poverty grass, fox grass—for dyeing.

foxhead n[1]

1 An unidentified flower.

1969 *DARE* (Qu. S26a, .. *Roadside flowers*) Inf **ID**5, Foxheads.

2 An unidentified shell.

1897 *Oölogist* 14.vii, *Showy Shells...* Fox head.

foxhead n[2]

1933 *AmSp* 8.1.49 **Ozarks,** *Fox-head...* Moonshine whiskey. There is a variety of rye which is called foxhead, and it may be that the name is somehow derived from this.

foxhole n Cf **hole n 4a**

In marble play: see quot.

1933 *Hanley Disks* **eMA,** Foxhole... small hole just scooped out with your heel.

fox horn n **chiefly S Midl** Cf **fish horn**

A small horn, often made from a steer's horn, used esp to call foxhounds.

1901 *Scribner's Mag.* 29.393/1 **sAppalachians,** While the begum [**=bee gum 4**] has given place to hickory bark when a cradle is wanted, baskets and even fox-horns are still made of that material. **1903** *DN* 2.351 **neOH,** *Fox-horn...* A fish-horn. **1936** *Scribner's Mag.* Oct 99/3 **neKY,** Buried on our mountain-top where only the fox-horns blow and the wind and hound-dogs bark. **1944** Howard *Walkin' Preacher* 255 **Ozarks,** The merrymakers came at ten o'clock tooting fox horns, ringing cowbells and firing shotguns. **1949** *Hall Coll.* **eTN,** *Fox horn...* A steer's horn used by hunters, especially fox hunters, to call their dogs. **1969** *DARE* Tape **KY**16, [FW:] If the chase [=fox hunt] is unsuccessful, how do you get the dogs to come back to you? [Inf:] We have what we call a fox horn, made outer a steer horn, and blow it, and .. most of 'em 'll come to you, that is if they've run any length of time.

fox horse n

=fox bait.

1950 *WELS (Joking or uncomplimentary names for horses)* **cwWI,** 1 Inf, Fox horse.

fox-hunt See **fox-chase**

foxing See **fox v 2, 3**

fox in the corner See **fox in the morning 1**

fox in the gully See **fox across the river**

fox in the morning n

1 also *fox in the morning (and) goose in the evening, fox in the corner, ~ morner, ~ wagon, ~ wall, ~ warner:* A tag game in which players try to avoid being caught by one or more "foxes" while running from one base to another. **chiefly S Midl** Also called **goosey goosey gander**

1901 in 1904 Porter *Cabbages & Kings* 19, This little literary essay I hold in my hands means a game of Fox-in-the-Morning. Ever played that, Frank, when you was a kid? . . This president man and his companion . . stand up over in San Mateo . . and shout: "Fox-in-the-Morning!" Me and you . . say: "Goose and the Gander!" **1940** Writers' Program *Guide VA* 141, Young people indulged in such games as . . 'fox in the warner.' **1946** TN Folk Lore Soc. *Bulletin* 12.1.18, Some of the mixed games required a good deal of running, as "Buzzard," "Base" and "Fox in the Morning, Goose in the Evening." **1952** Brown *NC Folkl.* 1.78, 'Fox in the Corner.' . . One player is the fox; all the others are geese. Both . . have homes. . . Fox: Fox in the corner./ Geese: Geese in the corner./ Fox: How many men you got?/ Geese: More than you're able to catch./ The geese then try to get to the fox's home. . . The fox catches as many as he can. *Ibid* 79, 'Fox in the Morner.' . . Fox: Fox in the morner./ Geese: Goose in the corner./ Fox: How many men you got?/ Geese: More than you can catch. **1953** Brewster *Amer. Nonsinging Games* 77 **AR,** *Fox in the Wall*. . . Bases are established at opposite ends. . . All the players except one . . take their place on one of these, and the "fox" . . [is] between the two bases. "Fox" and "geese" then carry on . . [a] dialogue. . . The "geese" then try to reach the other base without being caught. . . The last player to remain uncaught has the right to ask for "wagon room" (a clear space wide enough for a wagon to pass through). If it is granted, he makes a dash down this narrow passage to the other base. **1967–68** *DARE* (Qu. EE33, . . *Outdoor games*) Inf **AL**37, Fox in the morning and goose in the evening; **PA**28, Fox in the morning—a chase game; **VA**18, Fox in the morning—same as goose and the gander. You say "Fox in the morning / How many men?/ More than you can handle." Then the fox would try to catch the geese; **KY**80, Fox in the wagon—form two sides. "It" is in the middle. Run from side to side without getting caught by "it"; **VA**35, Fox in the wall—go from one tree to another without being caught by fox in the middle; if caught, then you're fox.

‡**2** =**fox and geese 2.**

1969 *DARE* (Qu. EE26, . . *Games . . children play in the snow*) Inf **PA**203, Fox in the morning—same as fox and geese.

fox in the wagon (or wall, warner) See **fox in the morning 1**

‡**fox in the window** n

1970 *DARE* (Qu. EE11, *Bat-and-ball games for just a few players*) Inf **VA**42, Fox in the window.

fox meat See **fox bait**

fox pass, fox paw(s) See **faux pas n**

fox plum n

A **bearberry 2** (here: *Arctostaphylos uva-ursi*).

1940 Clute *Amer. Plant Names* 38, *A[rctostaphylos] uva-ursa* [sic]. . . Fox-plum.

fox race n **S Midl**

A fox hunt.

1894 *Forest & Stream* 43.400/2 **TN,** But they had not gone 200yds on the fox race. **c1960** *Hall Coll.* **eTN, wNC,** Fox race. . . Pursuit of a fox with dogs, in a hunt. **1966** *DARE* Tape **AR**15, There's so many deer . . unless you have a dog that won't run a deer, it's hard to have a fox race unless you just happen to run across it before you do a deer.

fox sedge n Also *foxtail sedge*

A **sedge** (here: *Carex* spp).

1843 Torrey *Flora NY* 2.376, *Carex vulpinoidea*. . . Fox Sedge. . . Low grownds: common. *Ibid* 378, *Carex alopecoidea*. . . Fox-tail Sedge. . . Woods. **1961** Peck *Manual OR* 162, *Carex vulpinoidea* . . Fox Sedge.

fox slipper n

=**fairy slipper.**

1966 Goldstein–Byington *Two Penny Ballads* 157 **Philadelphia PA** (as of 1940s), Fairies live in the woods in wild flowers called fox-slippers or fairy-slippers, and come out and dance in the moonlight while the elves play music for them.

fox snake n [See quot 1952]

A light yellowish-brown **rat snake** (here: *Elaphe vulpina*) with dark brown dorsal blotches that is common in much of the upper Missip-Ohio Valleys. Also called **copperhead snake 2, pilot snake, pine snake, spotted adder, timber snake, wood snake**

1857 U.S. Patent Office *Annual Rept. for 1856: Ag.* 88 **nIL,** Meadow-mice. . . are also found in the stomachs of the milk-snake, . . and of the large fox-snake *(Scotophis vulpinus).* **1892** IN Dept. Geol. & Nat. Resources *Rept. for 1891* 499 **IN,** The fox snake appears to be moderately common in some localities. **1928** Pope–Dickinson *Amphibians* 54 **WI,** The Fox Snake can be easily distinguished . . by the blunt snout and the reddish tinge of the head. **1952** Ditmars *N. Amer. Snakes* 190, *Fox Snake*. . . It emits a strong-smelling secretion from glands at base of the tail. The odor is like that of a fox, hence the common name. **1968** *DARE* (Qu. P25) Inf **MI**76, Fox snake—also called wood snake and copperhead, but it's not a true copperhead.

fox sparrow n Also *fox-colored sparrow, foxy sparrow*

A rusty-colored sparrow *(Passerella iliaca).* Also called **foxtail 7**

1811 Wilson *Amer. Ornith.* 3.53 **PA,** [The] *Fox-Colored Sparrow, Fringilla Rufa*. . . frequents low sheltered thickets; . . scraping the ground, and rustling among the fallen leaves. **1839** Audubon *Ornith. Biog.* 5.512, *Fox-coloured sparrow. Fringilla iliaca*. . . This delightful songster is found abundantly on the Columbia River. **1865** *Atlantic Mth.* 15.521/2 **NY,** I have met here many of the rarer species, such as the . . Blue-Winged Swamp-Warbler, . . the Worm-Eating Warbler, the Fox-Sparrow, etc. **1940** Weygandt *Down Jersey* 25 **sNJ,** Small birds began to drift across our path. . . There were white-throats among them, and a bouncing big fox sparrow. **1948** *Pacific Discovery* Mar-Apr 18/1 **San Francisco CA,** The fox sparrow breaks the purple skin of the persimmon fruits with its stout bill, and eats greedily of the orange pulp. **1955** *AmSp* 30.179 **NJ,** Fox sparrow . . *foxy sparrow.* **1965–70** *DARE* (Qu. Q21) 54 Infs, **chiefly NEast, N Cent, less freq Mid and S Atl,** Fox sparrow.

fox squirrel n Rarely *foxtail squirrel* [See quot 1982]

A reddish-tinged squirrel: usu *Sciurus niger* and subspp, but also *S. apache.* Also called **cat squirrel 3, grinnie 3, red squirrel**

1682 (1836) Ash *Carolina* 73, There are . . the Red, the Grey, the Fox and Black Squirrels. **1737** (1911) Brickell *Nat. Hist. NC* 127, The *Fox-Squirrel,* so call'd, from its being the largest, and smelling like a *Fox.* **1834** Peck *Gaz. IL* 37, The gray and fox squirrels often do mischief in the corn fields, and the hunting of them makes fine sport for the boys. **1912** *Harper's Mth. Mag.* 126.14/1 **MO,** A fox-squirrel with his tail bent high like a shepherd's crook. **1933** Rawlings *South Moon* 7 **FL,** Seems to me they's cat-squirrels this side o' the river, 'stead o' fox-squirrels. **c1960** *Wilson Coll.* **csKY,** *Fox squirrel*. . . A large, reddish species of squirrel, considerably larger than the common gray squirrel. **1965–70** *DARE* (Qu. P27) 301 Infs, **widespread exc NEast, C Atl, West,** Fox squirrel; 18 Infs, **chiefly Cent,** Red fox squirrel; **GA**76, **IL**9, **KY**24, **MN**42, Gray fox squirrel; **AR**51, Black fox squirrel; **OK**15, Foxtail squirrel—larger than a gray squirrel. **1966–67** *DARE* Tape **LA**1, There's about as many cat squirrels as there is fox squirrels; **FL**16, We came up on one tree where there was five fox squirrels, and he killed all five of the fox squirrels. **1975** Newell *If Nothin' Don't Happen* 177 **nwFL,** Our fox squirrels are two or three times as big as cat squirrels and you find 'em more out in the piney woods. They're sort of yellowish brown and darker brown or black around the face. **1982** Elman *Hunter's Field Guide* 399, A fox squirrel's [=*Sciurus niger's*] tail is rust-edged. . . On the ground, a fox squirrel lopes in a manner reminiscent of the fox, and it has a luxuriant foxy plume, but it was probably named for the suffusion of red in its fur.

fox's tail n[1] See **foxtail 1**

fox's tail n[2] See **foxtail club moss**

foxtail n

1 also *fox's tail, foxtail barley, foxtail(ed) grass, foxtail weed:* Any of several grasses, esp of the genera *Alopecurus, Hordeum,* and *Setaria.* [In ref to the bristly spike] **chiefly N Cent, Upper MW, West** See Map

1822 Eaton *Botany* 168, *Alopecurus* . . foxtail. **1848** Gray *Manual of Botany* 574, *Alopecurus* . . Foxtail Grass. **1880** (1883) U.S. Census Office *Rept. Ag.* 961, *Hordeum murinum,* naturalized from the Old World, has become a great pest in California, where it is known as squirrel-grass, fox-tail, and white-oats. It is known in the Old World as wall-barley, and way-bent. **1912** Wooton–Standley *Grasses NM* 147, Its name [=squirrel-tail grass, *Hordeum jubatum*] is suggestive of its most pronounced characteristics, though it is not infrequent to hear it called "fox-tail grass." (The latter name should be reserved for . . species of *Chaetochloa* [=*Setaria* in part]. . . They resemble Italian millet somewhat.) **1950** Hitchcock–Chase *Manual Grasses* 268, *Hordeum juba-*

tum. . Foxtail Barley. **1950** *WELS (Other kinds of grass that are hard to get rid of)* 3 Infs, **WI,** Foxtail grass. **c1960** Criswell *Resp. to PADS 20* **Ozarks,** Foxtail. . . A late summer grass two feet tall or less with a blossom like a fox's tail. **1965–70** *DARE* (Qu. S9) 42 Infs, **chiefly N Cent, Upper MW,** Foxtail grass; **IL**19, 62, 80, Giant foxtail; **IL**25, Foxtails; **KY**47, Foxtailed grass; (Qu. S15, . . *Weed seeds that cling to clothing)* 24 Infs, **chiefly West, Upper MW,** Foxtail; **CA**31, 65, 105, 162, 170, **OR**3, **UT**10, Foxtails; **OH**33, **VA**30, Foxtail grass; **IA**13, Bristly foxtail; (Qu. S21, . . *Other weeds)* Infs **IA**8, 13, **KY**56, **MN**23, 38, **NE**1, **OH**22, 61, **WA**6, **WI**64, Foxtail; **IA**3, 8, **MO**18, Giant foxtail; **IL**6, Foxtails; **IL**4, Fox's tail; **NJ**45, Foxtail grass; **NC**80, Foxtail weed; (Qu. S14, *Prickly seeds, small and flat . . that cling to clothing)* Infs **CA**2, 204, 208, **UT**3, Foxtail; **CA**31, **OR**3, Foxtails; (Qu. S8, . . *Wild grass that . . spreads by sending out long underground roots, and it's hard to get rid of)* Infs **IL**70, **IN**26, 32, Foxtail; **IN**19, Foxtail grass.

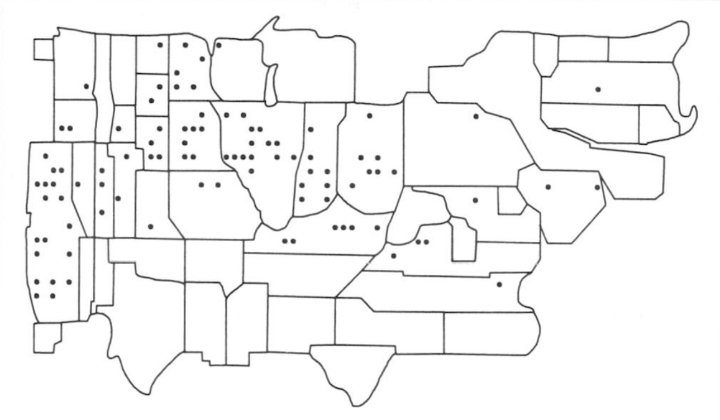

•foxtail 1 + varr (Qq. S9, S15, S21, S8, S14)

2 also *foxtail grass:* A **pondweed** (here: *Potamogeton pectinatus*).

1913 *Torreya* 13.226, *Potamogeton pectinatus*. . . Foxtail or foxtail grass, Currituck Sound, N.C.

3 The common reed *(Phragmites australis).*

1937 *Torreya* 37.95, *Phragmites communis*. . . Foxtail.

4 A **horsetail 1.**

1970 Kirk *Wild Edible Plants W. U.S.* 17, *Equisetum* species. . . Horsetails, Foxtail [etc].

5 See **foxtail pine.**

6 See **foxtail club moss.**

7 =**fox sparrow.**

1917 (1923) *Birds Amer.* 3.55, *Passerella iliaca iliaca*. . . Fox-tail. **1946** Hausman *Eastern Birds* 612, *Eastern Fox Sparrow*. . . *Other Names* . . Foxtail. . . Tail a richer, redder brown. **1955** *AmSp* 30.179 **DC, MI,** Fox sparrow . . *fox-tail.*

8 A palomino.

1968 *DARE* (Qu. K39, . . *Names . . for horses according to their color)* Inf **CA**101, Foxtails—pretty tan and white mane and tail; called palomino nowadays.

foxtail asparagus n

A **horsetail 1** (here: *Equisetum praealtum*).

1959 Carleton *Index Herb. Plants* 49, *Foxtail-asparagus:* Equisetum praealtum (E. robustum).

foxtail barley See **foxtail 1**

foxtail cactus n [Prob from the color of the spines]

A **pincushion cactus** (here: *Mammillaria alversonii*).

1940 Benson *Cacti AZ* 121, *Mamillaria* [sic] *Alversonii*. . . *Foxtail cactus*. . . Central spines . . white tipped with brown. **1941** Jaeger *Wildflowers* 165 **Desert SW. 1974** Munz *Flora S. CA* 311, *Foxtail Cactus*. . . Spines 12-16, straight, stout, divergent, dark above the white base.

foxtail club moss n Also *fox's tail, foxtail, foxtail moss*

A **club moss:** usu *Lycopodium alopecuroides,* but also *L. clavatum.*

1847 Wood *Class-Book* 626, *L[ycopodium] alopecuroides. Fox-tail Club Moss*. . . *Branches* simple, long, ascending, bearing a single sessile spike at top. **1900** Lyons *Plant Names* 233, *L[ycopodium] clavatum*. . . Foxtail. **1938** Small *Ferns SE States* 415, *L[ycopodium] clavatum*. . . Many popular names have become associated with this plant . . *Fox-tail* [etc]. **1946** Tatnall *Flora DE* 7, *Fox-tail Club-moss.* Coastal Plain species; common in Sussex County. **1959** Carleton *Index Herb. Plants* 49, *Fox's tail:* Lycopodium clavatum. **1968** McPhee *Pine Barrens* 130 **NJ,** Wherry pulled up another kind of moss and pointed out its spores, saying, "This is foxtail moss. The spores are explosive. The Chinese used them for gunpowder." **1970** Correll *Plants TX* 37, *Lycopodium alopecuroides* var *alopecuroides. Foxtail clubmoss*. . . Var. *pinnatum*. . . *Creeping foxtail clubmoss.*

foxtailed grass See **foxtail 1**

foxtail grass See **foxtail 1, 2**

foxtail moss See **foxtail club moss**

foxtail pine n Also *foxtail*

1 An upland pine *(Pinus balfouriana)* native chiefly to California. [See quot 1925] Also called **spruce pine**

1884 Sargent *Forests of N. Amer.* 191, *Pinus Balfouriana*. . . Foxtail Pine. Hickory Pine. **1897** Sudworth *Arborescent Flora* 18, *Pinus balfouriana*. . . Foxtail Pine (Cal.) **1925** Jepson *Manual Plants CA* 46, Foxtail Pine. . . Branches stout and rather short with half-drooping branchlets thickly clothed with short needles . . and thus resembling a fox's tail. **1948** *Pacific Discovery* Nov–Dec 20/2, At 10,000 feet elevation, where snow always lingers, may be found the foxtail pine *(Pinus balfouriana)* . . last of all the trees. **1959** Munz–Keck *CA Flora* 52, Foxtail Pine. . . Branchlets . . densely clothed toward ends with crowded lvs. **1970** *DARE* (Qu. T17) Inf **CA**208, Foxtail.

2 =**bristlecone pine.** [See quot c1945]

1897 Sudworth *Arborescent Flora* 18, Bristle-cone Pine. . . Common Names. . . Foxtail Pine (Cal. lit.) **c1945** U.S. Forest Serv. Rocky Mt. Region *Trees Native CO & WY* 4, *Bristlecone Pine*. . . Sometimes called "foxtail pine" because of the long, slender twigs clothed with needles which resemble the brush of a fox. **1960** Vines *Trees SW* 20, *Pinus* . . *aristata*. . . Other vernacular names are Fox-tail Pine and Hickory Pine. **1967** *DARE* (Qu. T17) Inf **CO**47, Foxtail.

3 Either **loblolly pine** or **shortleaf pine.**

1897 Sudworth *Arborescent Flora* 26, *Pinus taeda*. . . Foxtail Pine (Va., Md.) **1933** Small *Manual SE Flora* 5, *P[inus] echinata*. . . Short-leaf pine. Yellow-pine. Fox tail pine. **1960** Vines *Trees SW* 22, Loblolly Pine. . . Vernacular names are . . Fox-tail Pine [etc]. **1966–70** *DARE* (Qu. T5) Inf **DC**2, Foxtail pine; **DC**8, Foxtail; (Qu. T17, . . *Kinds of pine trees)* Infs **DC**5, **OH**25, **VA**79, 105, Foxtail.

foxtail rush n

A **horsetail 1** (here: *Equisetum arvense*).

1914 Georgia *Manual Weeds* 20, *Equisetum arvense*. . . Green Foxtail Rush. **1935** (1943) Muenscher *Weeds* 129, Foxtail-rush. . . Sterile stems green, . . branches in whorls, ascending, frequently branched again.

foxtail sedge See **fox sedge**

foxtail squirrel See **fox squirrel**

foxtail weed See **foxtail 1**

fox-the-goose See **fox and geese 2**

foxtooth n

Perh a vetch.

1967 *DARE* (Qu. S26e, . . *Wildflowers)* Inf **MI**69, Foxtooth—lavender, [with a] brush-like head or bloom.

foxtooth violet n

Prob a **dogtooth violet.**

1968 *DARE* (Qu. S26b, *Wildflowers that grow in water or wet places)* Inf **CT**17, Foxtooth violet.

foxy adj Also sp *foxey*

1 Moderately drunk. [**fox v 1**]

1899 (1912) Green *VA Folk-Speech* 183, *Foxy*. . . Drunk. **1939** *Hall Coll.* **eTN,** *Foxy*—feeling good from drinking liquor. . . "You were sure foxy last night when we left you." *Ibid,* [One inf] says it means "about half drunk" and that it [=the term] is used "lots and lots." **1962** *Mt. Life* 38.4.11 **sAppalachians,** The man who has drunk enough to glow, sing, and laugh freely but whose tongue might become twisted on a word now and then is "foxy." The "foxy" one has an "eetchin' heel" and likes to "find a little patch of fun."

2 Presumptuous, pushing.

1906 *DN* 3.136 **nwAR,** *Foxy*. . . Self-assertive, impertinent. "Don't get foxy around here." **1968** *DARE* (Qu. HH35, *A woman who puts on a lot of airs: "She's too ——— for me."*) Inf **IN**39, Hoity-toity; foxy. **1969** *DARE* FW Addit **Phoenix AZ,** Foxy—"uppish," "high on themselves." Old-fashioned.

3 Usu of a woman: stylish, attractive. Cf **fox n 1**

1913 *DN* 4.21 **NE,** *Foxy*. Stylish looking, attractive. Usage widespread in Nebraska. "She's a foxy looking little lady." **1942** Berrey–Van den Bark *Amer. Slang* 37.10, *Beautiful* . . foxy. *Ibid* 233.10, *Stylish* . . foxy. **1963** *Freedomways* 3.56 **NYC,** She was lookin' foxier by the minute. **1965** *DARE* (QR, near Qu. OO47) Inf **FL**18, Kids say a new hairdo is "foxy." **1967** Hendrix *Are You Experienced* (Phonodisc), [Song title:] Foxey Lady. **1970** Major *Dict. Afro-Amer. Slang* 55, *Foxy:* . . especially [of] black [women]. **1978** *DARE* File **WI,** At any state or county fair you can find "Foxy Lady" being sold, in any of several styles, as a slogan for adorning T-shirts.

4 Energetic, frisky; see also quot 1968.

1951 *PADS* 15.70 **nLA,** *Foxy*. . . Frisky. **1956** Ker *Vocab. W. TX* 349, [Words for a lively older person:] *Foxy man* [2 of 67 infs]. **1968** *DARE* (Qu. AA4a, . . *A man who is very eager to get married*) Inf **IN**8, Foxy; (Qu. BB47, *Feeling in the best of health and spirits*) Inf **IA**27, Foxy. **c1970** *Halpert Coll.* **wKY,** *Foxy* . . spry, full of life, [of] old people persistently lively. **1973** Allen *LAUM* 1.353 **SD** (as of 1950s), [An older person with unusual vigor and vitality is described as being "foxy" by 1 inf.]

5 Of tobacco leaves: see quot. [Specialized use of *OED foxy* adj. 3, denoting "various defects of colour and quality resulting from atmospheric conditions, improper treatment, etc."]

1967 Key *Tobacco Vocab.* **PA,** Foxy tobacco—[caused by a] virus [according to one inf]; foxy—the leaves get thin—the weather is too wet [according to another inf].

6 Scuffed.

1883 Twain *Life on Missip.* (Boston) 558, The scarecrow Dean—in foxy shoes, down at the heels; socks of odd colors, also "down." **1897** Twain *Following Equator* 326, He wore . . foxy shoes, imitation patent leather.

7 See quot. [*EDD foxy* adj. 1 "Of the weather, deceptive, uncertain"; cf *EDD fox-day* (at *fox* sb. 1. (2)), *foxing-day* (at *fox* v. 7)]

1967 *DARE* FW Addit **LA**3, 4, Foxy = cold. "It's really foxy outside this morning." Common.

foxy-eyed adj

Having piercing eyes (prob with an implication of cunning or shrewdness).

[**1859** Taliaferro *Fisher's R.* 118 **nwNC** (as of 1820s), I seen him cuttin' his fox eyes 'bout as I and Sally walked up to the meetin'-house door.] **1880** W.J. Florence in *Theatre* (U.S.) Oct. 215 *(OED),* The foxy-eyed party near us. **1969** *DARE* (Qu. X21b, *If the eyes are very sharp or piercing*) Inf **PA**184, Foxy-eyed.

foxy finch n Also *fox-(colored) finch*

=**fox sparrow.**

1839 Audubon *Synopsis Birds* 119, [The] *Fox-coloured Finch* . . [is] dispersed in winter throughout the Southern and Western Districts. **1889** *Century Dict.* 2355, *Fox-finch*. . . Same as *fox-sparrow*. **1917** (1923) *Birds Amer.* 3.55, *Passerella iliaca iliaca*. . . Foxy Finch. **1946** Hausman *Eastern Birds* 612, *Eastern Fox Sparrow*. . . *Other Names* . . Foxy Finch.

foxy goosey gander See **goosey goosey gander**

foxy grandpa n [See quot 1976]

An alert and crafty old man.

1950 *WELS (A very sly person)* 2 Infs, **WI,** Foxy grandpa. **1968** *DARE* (Qu. KK27, . . *"For his age, he's ———."*) Inf **PA**118, A foxy grandpa; (Qu. KK37, . . *A very sly person: "He's ———."*) Inf **NJ**33, A foxy grandpa. [**1976** Horn *World Encycl. Comics* 261, C. E. Schultze's *Foxy Grandpa* . . in which the kid-plagued parent cleverly turns the tables on the trick-playing kids . . captivated the public of the time [=1900].]

foxy pass See **faux pas n**

foxy sparrow See **fox sparrow**

fozy adj [Scots dial]

Of vegetables: pithy.

1968 *DARE* (Qu. I8) Inf **IA**30, Fozy ['fozi]—the same as pithy ['pɛθi].

f'r See **for**

fraction n

1 A disturbance, commotion, fracas. [*OED fraction* sb. 3 *"Obs."*] **S Midl**

1917 *DN* 4.412 **wNC,** *Fraction*. . . Ruction. "I don't know what the fraction was, but he flew mad about something." **1913** Kephart *Highlanders* 288 **sAppalachians,** I don't know how the fraction begun, but Os feathered into Dan and Phil, feedin' them lead. **1930** *AmSp* 5.426 **Ozarks,** *Fraction,* in the Ozarks, still means a quarrel or fight, just as it did in Shakespeare's day. **1949** Webber *Backwoods Teacher* 107 **Ozarks,** We heard of violent "fractions," even to the wrecking of all the furniture in a cabin, at a fiddle dance. **1952** Brown *NC Folkl.* 1.542, *Fraction*. . . A fight, disturbance.

2 A trying time.

1940 Harris *Folk Plays* 89 **NC,** I wa'n't thar when the Johnsons come after me . . and I had a fraction a-walkin' back. *Ibid* 94, [Stage directions:] *Ca'line* . . [is] twisting all the while. *Ella* is having a "fraction" pinning on the skirt.

3 in phrr *to a* (or *the*) *fraction:* Perfectly; to the highest degree.

1811 in 1869 Irving *Life & Letters* 1.201 **NY,** This place would suit you to a fraction. **1858** Bennett *Chronology of NC* 24, They both lived to a very old age, truthful, faithful, obedient and honest to a fraction. **1966–68** *DARE* (Qu. KK3a, *Words for the perfect condition . . in cooking: "It's done to ———."*) Inf **MO**38, A fraction; (Qu. KK50, . . *Down to the last detail: "He had it all worked out ———."*) Infs **DE**7, **VT**10, Down to a fraction; **DC**8, To the fraction. [All Infs old]

fractious adj

1 Unruly, contrary, irritable. **scattered, but chiefly Sth, Midl** See Map

1824 Irving *Tales of a Traveller* 2.30 **seNY,** The clown . . was a terribly peevish, fractious fellow, and always in ill humour. **1838** Ganilh *Mexico Versus TX* 46 **TX,** There is no mule, how fractious soever, which they cannot tame in three hours. **1873** Miller *Modocs* 187 **OR,** They lost at least ten minutes with a fractious mule, that for a time concluded not to be sinched again till it had taken rest. **1899** (1912) Green *VA Folk-Speech* 184, That child must be sick he is very fractious today. **1927** *DN* 5.474 **Ozarks. 1927** *AmSp* 3.138 **ME coast,** A cross, exacting child or person was "fractious." **1946** *PADS* 6.14 **eNC. 1954** *Harder Coll.* **cwTN. c1960** *Wilson Coll.* **csKY. 1965–70** *DARE* (Qu. K42, *A horse that is rough, wild, or dangerous*) 15 Infs, **chiefly Midl,** Fractious horse; (Qu. K16, *A cow with a bad temper*) 11 Infs, **scattered Sth, S Midl,** Fractious (cow); **SC**32, Nervous and fractious; (Qu. GG8, . . *A person [who] is very easily offended*) Infs **AL**33, **AR**22, Fractious; (Qu. GG35b, . . *Annoyed or disappointed*) Inf **MA**100, Fractious; (Qu. GG38, . . *Mean and bad tempered*) Inf **TX**104, Fractious; (Qu. GG41, *To lose patience easily: "You never did see such a ——— person."*) Infs **AR**52, **GA**89, **KY**89, **MS**8, 56, **NC**48, Fractious; (Qu. II36b, . . *Somebody who talks back or gives rude answers*) Inf **TX**95, Fractious. **1967** *DARE* Tape **KY**1, He won't take anything; he's fractious an' he gits mad. **1974** (1975) Shaw *All God's Dangers* 6 **AL** [Black], That little gray mare. His name was Silas and he was fractious. You had to treat him right, you didn't he'd play a trick on you.

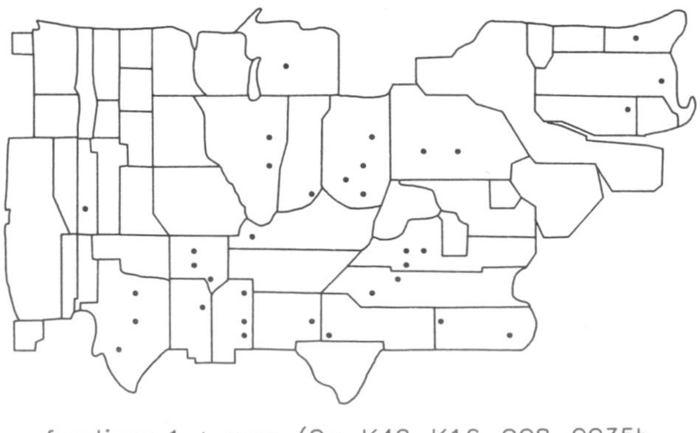

•fractious 1 + varr (Qq. K42, K16, GG8, GG35b, GG38, GG41, II36b)

‡2 Easily fractured.

1967 *DARE* (Qu. KK24, . . *"She broke her arm again: Her bones must be ———."*) Inf **LA**6, Fractious.

fragrant adj *joc, euphem*

Pregnant.

1967–69 *DARE* (Qu. AA28, *What joking or sly expressions do women use to say that another is going to have a baby?*) Infs **CA**123, **KS**10, **NE**9, **OR**1, **PA**229, Fragrant; **CA**169, **LA**14, **TN**38, Fragrant—a joking expression. **1967** *DARE* File, Fragrant—heard in Massachusetts.

fragrant balm n

=**Oswego tea.**

1895 Gray-Bailey *Field Botany* 352, *M. didyma*. . . Oswego Tea, Bee Balm, Fragrant Balm. **1910** Graves *Flowering Plants* 338 **CT,** Fragrant Balm. . . The herb finds some popular uses in medical practice, depending on its aromatic properties. **1940** Clute *Amer. Plant Names* 26, *Oswego Tea*. . . Fragrant balm.

fragrant hickory n

=**mockernut hickory.**

1960 Vines *Trees SW* 132, *Mockernut Hickory—Carya tomentosa*. . . Vernacular names are Whiteheart Hickory . . and Fragrant Hickory.

fragrant sumac n

Std: A widely-distributed **sumac** (here: *Rhus aromatica*) with a marked odor. Also called **agrillo 2, honeysuckle berry, Indian lemonade, lemita, lemonade berry, lemon sumac, polecat bush, quailbush, shoneehaw, skunkbush, smooth sumac, spicebush, squawberry, squawbush, stinkbush, stinking hazel, sweet-scented sumac, sweet sumac, threeleaf sumac**

fragrant wintergreen n

=**pipsissewa.**

1971 Krochmal *Appalachia Med. Plants* 90, *Chimaphila Umbellata*—Common Names: . . fragrant wintergreen.

fraid adj [Aphet form of *afraid*]

Afraid.

1927 Kennedy *Gritny* 67 **sLA** [Black], She ain' fraid to tell you. **1954** *Harder Coll.* **cwTN,** *Fraid*. . . Afraid. **1965–70** *DARE* (Qu. GG25, . . *"The children were ——— he was going to hurt them."*) 21 Infs, **scattered,** Fraid; (Qu. HH10, . . *Cowardly person*) 26 Infs, **scattered,** Fraid (of his shadow, of the dark, etc); (Qu. P36) Inf **NJ**69, Fraid; (Qu. AA4b) Inf **IL**141, Fraid of being an old maid; (Qu. DD17) Inf **MI**44, Fraid he isn't gonna get his share; (Qu. GG26) Inf **VT**5, Fraid; (Qu. HH11a) Inf **CA**120, Fraid he'll get dirty; (Qu. HH25) Inf **NJ**3, Fraid to talk. **1969–70** *DARE* Tape **KY**17, I'm always fraid; **VA**52B, He was that fraid. **1970** *AmSp* 45.77 [Black], 'Fraid not.

fraid n Cf **fright** n

See quots.

1902 *DN* 2.234 **sIL,** *Fraid*. . . Ghost; spectre. **1943** *LANE* Map 533, Names for the imaginary demons invoked to frighten children into obedience. . . 1 inf, **ceCT,** The fraids. **1955** Roberts *S. from Hell-fer-Sartin* 35 **eKY,** [Title:] The Boy That Never Seen a Fraid. *Ibid* 38, [Title:] Johnny That Never Seen a Fraid.

fraid cat See **fraidycat**

fraid hole n Also *fraidy hole* [**fraid** adj] **chiefly Cent**

=**cyclone cellar.**

1914 *DN* 4.163 **NW,** *Fraid hole*. . . A cyclone cellar. **1933** *AmSp* 8.1.49 **Ozarks,** *'Fraid Hole*. . . A cave in which people take refuge from severe windstorms—what used to be called a *cyclone cellar* in Kansas. **1944** Wellman *Bowl* 40 **KS,** He had been . . to the bottom of the 'fraid hole, into which he had gone to get a cool drink of buttermilk. **1963** *AmSp* 38.155 **NE,** Throughout the tornado area, these storm caves are referred to as *fraidy-holes*. **1966–67** *DARE* (Qu. D22, *Underground place to go in case of a violent windstorm*) Infs **KS**5, **OK**25, Fraid hole.

fraidy n

=**fraidycat.**

1930 (1935) Porter *Flowering Judas* 66, "All right, old fraidy," said Mrs. Whpple, "*He's* not scared. Watch *Him* do it." **1969** *DARE* (Qu. HH10, *A very timid or cowardly person: "He's ———."*) Inf **RI**11, A fraidy.

‡**fraidy** adj Cf **fraid** adj

Afraid.

1968 *DARE* (Qu. HH10, *A very timid or cowardly person: "He's ———."*) Inf **MD**41, Fraidy.

fraidycat n Also *fraid cat, fraidybug, ~calf* [**cat n 1f**]

A timid or easily frightened person.

1912 *DN* 3.576 **wIN,** *Fraid-cat*. . . A coward. **1917** *DN* 4.392 **neOH,** *Fraid-cat*. . . Coward. Only among children. **1929** (1931) Faulkner *Sound & Fury* 64 **MS,** Don't be a 'fraid cat. Come on. **1950** *WELS (A coward)* 10 Infs, **WI,** Fraidy cat; 1 Inf, **csWI,** Fraid cat. **c1960** *Wilson Coll.* **csKY,** *Fraidy cat*. . . A child's word for some person who is easily scared or is nervous. **1965–70** *DARE* (Qu. HH10, *A very timid or cowardly person: "He's ———."*) 102 Infs, **widespread,** Fraidycat; **CA**2, **CT**16, **MA**15, **NY**24, Fraid cat; **MD**40, Fraidybug; **WI**22, Fraidycalf; (Qu. Y9, *Somebody who always follows along behind others*) Inf **NY**23, Fraidycat.

fraidy hole See **fraid hole**

fraidy pants n

=**fraidycat.**

1950 *WELS (A coward)* 1 Inf, **ceWI,** Fraidy pants.

frail n [Engl dial, var of *flail* by rhotacism]

1 also *frailpole, frailstick:* A tool for threshing grain; a flail. **chiefly S Midl, NEast** See Map

1899 (1912) Green *VA Folk-Speech* 184, *Frail*. . . Flail. An implement for beating out grain, peas, and beans. **1902** *DN* 2.234 **sIL,** *Frail*. . . Flail. **1939** *LANE* Map 128, **seCT,** You thrash 'em with a frail; **csRI,** You thrash 'em with frails; **seNH,** Beans are threshed with a frail. **1945** TN Folk Lore Soc. *Bulletin* 11.3.1, The wheat was . . [threshed] with a "frail"—a twisted pole of hickory wood one end of which had been beaten with an axe until it was very soft. **1950** *WELS* 1 Inf, **swWI,** Frail. **1959** Roberts *Up Cutshin* 80 **eKY,** He was threshing that wheat with a big frailpole, what they allas used for it. **1965–70** *DARE* (Qu. L32a, *In early days, how was the grain separated from the straw?*) 16 Infs, **chiefly NEast, S Midl,** With frails (*or* a frail); **KY**6, 27, Frailpole; **SC**43, With a frailstick; **ME**19, Wood frail; (Qu. L32b) Inf **TN**14, Frailpole. [18 of 21 Infs old] **1979** Woolf *Woolfs VA* 11 **cnVA** (as of 1812), 1 cutting box and frails [$]2.10. **1983** *MJLF* 9.1.40 **ceKY,** *Frail* . . a flail.

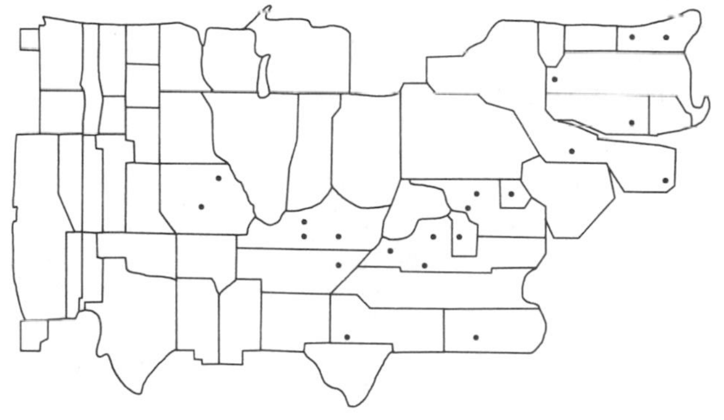

•frail n 1 + varr (Qq. L32a, b)

2 An instrument resembling a flail used as a weapon.

1950 *PADS* 14.30 **SC,** *Frail*. . . A long cudgel, a flail, usually for combat. **c1974** Jones *Ozark Hill Boy* 10 **AR** (as of c1920), The birds would flutter above the heap, having been blinded by the lights. The thorn bush frails went into action and the dead birds were gathered up.

frail v [**frail n**] **chiefly Sth, S Midl**

1 also with *out:* To thresh (grain).

1902 *DN* 2.234 **sIL,** *Frail*. . . To thrash as grain. **1907** *DN* 3.222 **nwAR.** **1927** *AmSp* 2.354 **WV,** We frailed out thirty bushles [sic] of wheat yesterday. **1954** *Harder Coll.* **cwTN,** *Frail it out over poles*. . . To separate grain from the straw; the custom still survives on a few farms. **1957** Battaglia *Resp. to PADS 20* **eMD** *(In early days, how was grain separated from the straw?)* Frail, tramp with oxen and horses. **1967–69** *DARE* (Qu. L32a) Inf **DC**8, Frail it; **KY**46, Hand frailed; **MO**38, Frailed it out; **TX**45, Frailed; **VA**24, Frailed with a frail; (Qu. L32b) Inf **MT**5, [By] frailing out. **1986** Pederson *LAGS Concordance* **chiefly TN** *(Oats is thrashed)* 1 inf, Frail; 1 inf, Frail it; 1 inf, Frailed it; 1 inf, Frailed oats out—before thrasher was available; 1 inf, If they raised oats, why, they frailed them.

2 To beat or strike (someone or something); to whip; hence vbl n *frailing.*

1851 (1879) Byrn *Life AR Doctor* 82, The old man plainly told her . . he would frail her worse than a dog would a pole-cat. *Ibid* 123, He . . did not like the thought of getting a frailing for it. **1883** (1971) Harris *Nights with Remus* 38 **GA** [Black], Mr. Man sa'nter out in de bushes en cut 'im a hick'ry, en he let in on Mr. Lion, en he frail en frail 'im twel frailin' un 'im wuz a sin. **1892** Harris *On Plantation* 64 **GA,** I'm a-thinkin' 'bout the frailin' I'm gwine to git. **1895** *DN* 1.375 **eTN, wNC, eKY. 1896** *DN* 1.417 **New Orleans LA. 1903** *DN* 2.314 **seMO. 1905** *DN* 3.79 **nwAR. 1906** Casey *Parson's Boys* 64 **sIL** (as of c1860), Let me hear another word like that out of ye, an' I'll 'frail ye till yer hide won't hold shucks! **1908** *DN* 3.312 **eAL, wGA,** I'll give you a frailin' if you don't mind. **1916** *DN* 4.302 **VA. 1917** *DN* 4.412 **IL, KY, NC, SC. 1928** Peterkin *Scarlet Sister Mary* 115 **SC,** He gave it a good frailing with a stout hickory stick. **1939** *Hall Coll.* **wNC, eTN,** One day I took that guitar outside and frailed it against the porch. . . I beat and frailed on the door. . . "He's been a-frailin' rocks all summer" (i.e., cutting stone). **1946** *PADS* 6.14 **eNC. 1950** *PADS* 14.30 **SC. c1960** *Wilson Coll.* **csKY,** *Frailing*. . . A sound thrashing or whipping. **1967–70** *DARE* (Qu. Y15, *To beat somebody thoroughly: "John really _____ that fellow!"*) Infs **CT**43, **TX**40, **VA**35, Frailed. [Inf **CT**43 is Black and has family from VA.] **1968** *DARE* FW Addit **swVA,** Whipping a misbehaving child is frailing him. **1986** Pederson *LAGS Concordance* **chiefly TN,** 1 inf, Take a paling and frail hell out of them; 1 inf, Frail the tar out of somebody; 1 inf, I'm going to frail you; 1 inf, Frail them—of killing birds with a limb; 1 inf, Frailing—using a club on someone; 2 infs, Frailing.

frail eel n [*frail* a girl or woman + *eel,* perh with connotation of elusiveness] *among Black speakers*

An attractive woman.

1942 *Amer. Mercury* 55.223.89 **Harlem NYC** [Black], I can get any frail eel I wants to. **1970** Major *Dict. Afro-Amer. Slang* 55, *Frail eel:* any good-looking woman.

frailing See **frail** v 2

frail out See **frail** v 1

frailpole, frailstick See **frail** n 1

fraish See **fresh** adj

fram v, hence vbl n *framming* [Etym unknown, but perh echoic (cf *slam, bam, wham*)] **S Atl**

To beat, strike, pound.

1933 Rawlings *South Moon* 259 **nFL,** Fram the chitlin's plumb outen 'em. **1933** Miller *Lamb in His Bosom* 84 **GA,** After a minute there was a framming of a fist on the front door and Dicie opened it. **1946** *PADS* 6.14 **eNC. 1950** *PADS* 14.30 **SC. 1952** Brown *NC Folkl.* 1.542. **1966–68** *DARE* (Qu. Y14a, *To hit somebody hard with the fist*) Inf **SC**3, Fram; (Qu. KK53, . . *"He . . _____ into a car."*) Inf **GA**31, Frammed. **1967** *DARE* FW Addit **SC,** I'll take this stick and fram the mush out you. . . He frammed him good. **1975** Newell *If Nothin' Don't Happen* 81 **nwFL,** We'd fram on the bottom or side of the skiff with a oar and make the mullet run so they'd hit the net and gill theirselves.

‡framalam n Cf **fram**

1968 *DARE* FW Addit **GA**52A, A ramshackledy car—a ['fræməlæm].

frame n

1 A skeleton; fig, an emaciated person or animal. **chiefly Sth**

1880 *Bradstreet's* 29 Sept 3/4, The north British farmers are finding it profitable to import what the American dealers graphically call "frames" to feed for the market. **1899** (1912) Green *VA Folk-Speech* 184, *Frame*. . . Skeleton. "She is nothing but a frame." **1913** *DN* 4.4 **ME,** *Frame*. . . The skeleton of an animal, bird, or fish. Used by trappers and hunters. **1966–69** *DARE* (Qu. K15, *A thin, bony, or poor-looking cow*) Infs **GA**72, 77, Quiltin' frame; **GA**72, Hay frames; **AL**2, Cow frame; **TN**26, Frame; (Qu. K44, *A bony or poor-looking horse*) Infs **AL**2, **WI**44, Frame; **SC**39, Quilting frame; (Qu. X49, . . *A person who is very thin*) Inf **LA**6, Nothing but a frame.

2 usu in comb: A rack to hold wood while it is being sawed; a sawhorse. **chiefly Sth, S Midl** See Map Cf **sawbuck**

1965–70 *DARE* (Qu. L59, *An implement with an X-frame . . to hold firewood for sawing*) 18 Infs, **chiefly Sth, S Midl,** Saw frame; **MS**1, **WV**13, Wood frame; **IN**32, Bucksaw frame; **VA**68, Cordwood frame; **SC**47, Frame; (Qu. L58, *An implement with an A-shaped frame . . that you put boards on to saw them*) Infs **GA**19, 28, A-frame; **NM**3, Frame; **GA**77, Saw frame. **1986** Pederson *LAGS Concordance* **Gulf Region** *(Sawbuck)* 13 infs, A-frame; 9 infs, Frame; 2 infs, X-frame; 1 inf, A jack frame—sawhorse, A-frame.

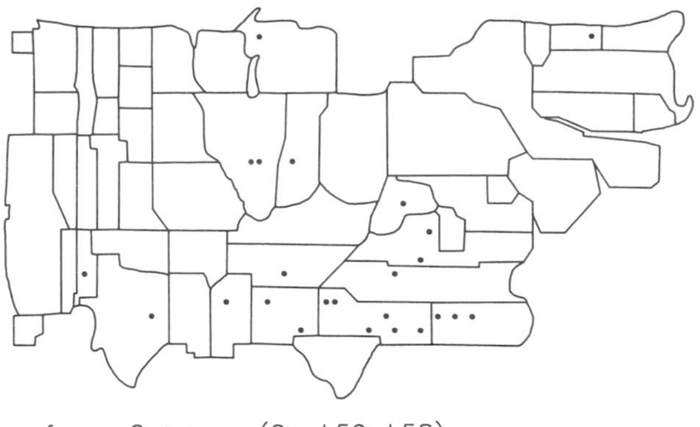

•frame 2 + varr (Qq. L59, L58)

frame sled n Also *framer* Cf **jumper, sliding sled**

A coasting sled.

1931–33 *LANE Worksheets* **nRI,** Frame sled—old-fashioned. **1943** *LANE* Map 573, A frame sled with post-supported seat and a device for steering. . . 4 infs, **RI, c,ceMA,** frame sled; 1 inf, **seMA,** Pointer, boy's sled; framer, girl's sled.

frame sleigh n Cf *DS* N40a, b

=bobsleigh.

1940–41 Cassidy *WI Atlas* **ceWI,** Frame sleigh—a sleigh consisting of two bobs held together by a lengthwise reach.

framming See **fram**

frampold adj [*OED* "*Obs.* exc. *dial.*"]

Of a horse: mettlesome, vicious.

1967 Jones *Peculiarities* 32 **wNC** (as of c1910), A dish-faced, white eyed horse was sure to be foolish and vicious, maybe even "frampold." ("Frampold" is a perfectly good old English word, now obsolete, which means such an animal was a mean, vicious and dangerous killer.)

fram pole n [**fram**]

A stick, prod.

1952 Brown *NC Folkl.* 1.542, *Fram-pole*. . . A weapon; a stick or some other object with which to beat one. "Goin' a get me a fram-pole and beat you up."—West and Duplin county. **1966** *DARE* (Qu. K27, . . *The sharp-pointed stick used to get oxen to move*) Inf **GA**3, A fram pole! [Laughter] A piece of brush (weed) with leaves and twigs on it.

France n [From the children's rhyme, "I see London, I see France, I see someone's underpants"]

1968 *DARE* (Qu. W24a, . . *Expressions . . to warn a woman slyly that her slip is showing*) Inf **WI**50, France is showing.

frances n [By assoc with *Fanny* nickname for *Frances,* and *fanny* buttocks] *euphem*

The buttocks.

1952 in 1960 Wentworth–Flexner *Slang* 199, It gives me a pain in the frances. **1969** *DARE* (Qu. X35, *Joking words for the part of the body that you sit on*) Inf **MA**20, Fanny, or frances, when they want to be polite.

‡Franciscan potatoes n pl

1968 *DARE* (Qu. H49, *Dishes made by boiling potatoes with other foods*) Inf **CA**59, Franciscan potatoes—cooked around a pot roast.

‡frandom, by adv phr [Perh blend of *by feel* + *at random*]

By ear; by instinct.

1968 *DARE* (Qu. KK48, *When you work something out as you go, without having a plan or pattern to follow: "I didn't have anything to go by, so I just did it _____."*) Inf **MO**10, By frandom ['frændɨm].

franic v [Prob < *frantic* adj] Cf **frantic**

To fret, worry; hence adj *franicky.*

1970 *DARE* (Qu. GG7, . . *Annoyed or upset: "Though we were only ten minutes late, she was all _____."*) Inf **VA**39A, Franicky—used by a Negro farmer; (Qu. GG27b, *To get somebody out of an unhappy mood, you might say to him, "Don't _____."*) Inf **KY**74, Franic.

frankfurt n Also *frankfurt sausage* Also sp *frankfort* [Abbrs for *frankfurter, frankforter* < Ger *Frankfurter* of Frankfurt] **chiefly NEast** See Map Cf **hamburg 1**

A cured and cooked sausage in a casing, often served on a long bun; a hot dog.

1899 *Chi. D. News* 16 May 5/4 *(DA),* Agar Bros.' Frankfurt Sausage, per lb. 7c. **1902** (1903) Lorimer *Letters* 127 **Chicago IL,** Only last week the head of our sausage department started to put out a tin-tag brand of frankfurts. **1941** *LANE* Map 283, 1 inf, **seMA,** Frankfort roll . . served with frankfort sausages; 1 inf, **seNH,** [fræŋkfɔət] roll . . with frankfort sausages. *Ibid* Map 304, 3 infs, **eMA,** Frankforts. **1965–70** *DARE* (Qu. H40, *A small sausage that is put into a long roll or bun to make a sandwich*) 42 Infs, **chiefly NEast** Frankfurt; **CT**39, Frankfort; (Qu. H18) Inf **MI**94, Frankfurt buns; (Qu. H32) Inf **RI**9, Frankfurt rolls. **1966** *Presque Isle Star-Herald* (ME) 9 June 9, [Advt:] Frankfort rolls. **1966** *Shopping Notes* (Yarmouth ME) 18 Aug 21, Skinless *Frankforts* 1 lb. Pkg. 59¢. **1969** *Cape Cod Std.-Times* (Hyannis MA) 22 Jan 9, [Advt:] 2 lbs Stop & Shop Frankforts 1.18. *Ibid* 13, [Advt:] Don't forget *Frankfort Rolls.*

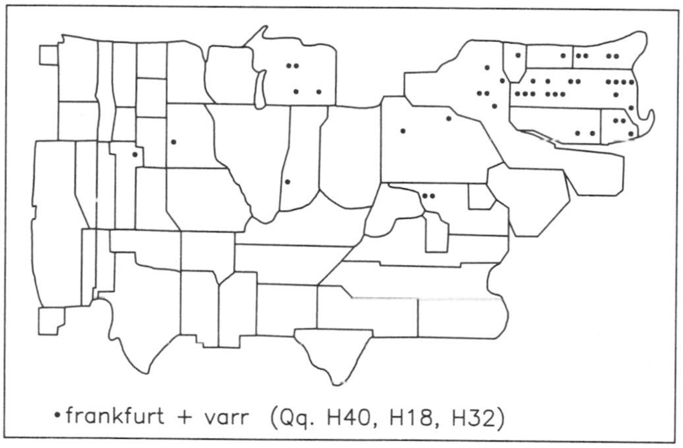

frankincense pine n [From the similarity of its resin to that of trees of the genus *Boswellia*]

=**loblolly pine.**

1785 Marshall *Arbustrum* 102, *Pinus Taeda. Virginian Swamp, or Frankincence* [sic] *Pine.* This grows to a pretty large size. **1803** Lambert *Descr. Pinus* 23, *Pinus Taeda. Frankincense Pine. . . Plains* consisting of dry sand, and sea coasts, in North America, are abundantly stocked with this species of Pine. **1858** Warder *Hedges* 249, The Frankincense or Loblolly, is a lofty American tree, often attaining eighty feet. **1897** Sudworth *Arborescent Flora* 26. **1901** Lounsberry *S. Wild Flowers* 6. **1952** Taylor *Plants Colonial Days* 56, The native evergreen tree, loblolly pine, bears bundles of three coarse needles. . . Old field pine and frankincense pine are other names sometimes used. **1960** Vines *Trees SW* 22, Loblolly Pine. . . Other vernacular names are Frankincense Pine [etc]. . . [It] is not usually worked for turpentine, because the flow of gum is checked quickly and labor costs are too high.

Franklin's gull n

Std: a black-headed **gull** (here: *Larus pipixcan*) usually found inland on freshwater. Also called **prairie dove, prairie pigeon, wet-weather bird**

Franklin tree n [After Benjamin *Franklin*]

A deciduous tree *(Franklinia alatamaha)* native originally to southeastern Georgia but now known only in cultivation.

1787 (1888) Cutler *Life* 1.273 **GA,** The Franklin tree is very curious. It is found only on one particular spot in Georgia. **1795** Winterbotham *Amer. U.S.* 3.392, *Flowering Trees, Shrubs, &c. . .* Franklin tree. **1942** Amer. Philos. Soc. *Trans.* 33.66/2 **GA,** A sand-hill bog . . about 1.7 miles northwest of Cox is believed to be the type locality of the famous Franklin tree *(Franklinia alatamaha)* . . which the Bartrams discovered here, apparently in association with the Georgia bark. **1976** Bailey–Bailey *Hortus Third* 485, *Franklinia alatamaha* . . Franklin Tree.

fransy See **franzy** n

frantic n

A fanatic.

1917 Torrence *Granny Maumee* 73 **Sth** [Black], I's a temp'unce man but I ain' no frantic. . . Well, suh, you got ter jine de frantics now.

franzied See **franzy** adj **1**

franzy n Also sp *fransy* [Engl dial varr of *frenzy*] **chiefly Sth, S Midl**

1899 (1912) Green *VA Folk-Speech* 184, *Fransy. . .* Violent agitation of mind approaching to temporary derangement of the mental faculties; distraction; madness. **1924** Raine *Land of Saddle-Bags* 98 **sAppalachians,** An excited state *franzy.* **1927** *AmSp* 3.139 **eME. 1938** Matschat *Suwannee R.* 145 **nFL, sGA,** Come fall, . . [a deer is] all in a franzy to get hitself a she-un. **1942** (1971) Campbell *Cloud-Walking* 19 **seKY,** She . . ought not get in a franzy fretting about a youngun being puny. **1952** Brown *NC Folkl.* 1.543, *Franzy.*

franzy adj [**franzy** n]

1 also *franzied:* Delirious; crazy; frantic. **Sth, S Midl**

1896 *DN* 1.417 **swNC,** *Franzy:* delirious. "The medicine made her franzy." **1937** in 1977 *Amer. Slave Suppl. 1* 8 **AL,** Paper said, 'Richard Amerson, franzy-minded, never no good for millinery service.' **1938** Matschat *Suwannee R.* 55 **nFL, sGA,** Must be tuk with a franzy spell. *Ibid* 145, We kept pets around till Pappy an' Mammy was nigh franzied. **1942** (1971) Campbell *Cloud-Walking* 40 **seKY,** She set down in the laurel bushes crying and getting all franzied. **1950** *PADS* 14.30 **SC,** *Franzy. . .* Delirious. **1952** Brown *NC Folkl.* 1.543, *Franzied. . .* Crazy.

‡**2** See quot.

1906 *DN* 3.136 **nwAR,** *Franzy. . .* Unpleasant, inferior.

franzy house n [**franzy** adj]

1 A brothel. [Perh infl by *fancy house* (at **fancy** adj **2**)]

1906 *DN* 3.136 **nwAR,** *Franzy house. . .* House of ill fame.

2 An insane asylum.

1938 Matschat *Suwannee R.* 106 **sGA,** Lessen ye be keerful ye'll be jest like Titterin' Tom, an' we-uns'll hev to shut ye up in a franzy house.

frap v Also *frop* [Engl dial]

To beat, strike.

1968 *DARE* (Qu. L32a, *In early days, how was the grain separated from the straw?*) Inf **NC**81, Beat it out by hand; frap it over a barrel. **1984** Wilder *You All Spoken Here* 48 **Sth,** Frap, frop: Strike with intent to gain attention or maim.

frappe n |fræp| [Sp-pronc for Fr *frappé* stirred, beaten up] **esp eMA** Cf **cabinet, milk shake, velvet**

A thick drink of ice cream, milk, and flavoring blended together.

1965–89 *DARE* File **csMA,** A *frappe* is the same as a *cabinet* or *velvet:* an ice cream milk shake; **cVA,** Frappe—a milk shake [with ice cream]. A [plain] milk shake is made without ice cream; **Cape Cod MA** (as of c1960), We used to sneak out of [summer] camp to buy frappes at a local ice cream parlor; **nCA,** Boston must be infamous for its milk shakes. Before visiting there in 1963 I was warned that if I wanted a *real* milk shake, one with ice cream, I had to order a frappe; **NYC** (as of c1953), In Brooklyn a famous ice-cream parlor featured a lengthy menu of ice-cream concoctions, one of which was the frappe. This was, as I recall, an elaborate ice-cream drink containing whipped cream, nuts, and cherries, but it wasn't a sundae because you drank it as well as spooned it; **wMA** (as of 1960s), A New England chain of ice-cream parlors served a frappe, which was a milk shake with ice cream. **1967** *DARE* (Qu. H45, *Dishes . . that everybody around here would know, but that people in other places might not*) Inf **MA**50, Frappe. **1979** *Yankee* Aug 86 **cVT,** I learned many things in Wyoming: that the words brook, soda, bag, and frappe, it turns out, do not exist, though creek, pop, sack, and milkshake do, luckily. **1980** Safire *On Language* 65 **ceMA,** Just south of Boston, ordering a milkshake would get you milk mixed with flavored syrup; no ice cream was included. "Frappe" was the order if ice cream was also desired. . . Incidentally, the French ending of frappe . . was never pronounced; it came out "frap." **1981** *New Yorker* 19 Jan 42 **csNY,** What I would really have liked was what we used to call a frappe in Binghamton. . . Out here [=California] called a milkshake.

frased See **freeze** v **A2**

Fraser fir n Also *Fraser pine*

Std: a fir tree *(Abies fraseri).* Also called **balsam 5, balsam fir, balsam tree c, blister balsam, blister pine, double balsam fir, double fir balsam, double spruce 2, healing balsam, lashhorn, mountain balsam, she-balsam, silver fir, southern fir**

frash v [Perh var of **fash 1**]
1953 *PADS* 19.10 **sAppalachians,** *Frash. . .* To upset or unnerve. "I was jest a-pranking. I didn't know it would frash her that way."

frash adj See **fresh** adj

frasher See **thrasher**

frassel See **frazzle** n **1**

‡frattling n
See quot.
1967 *DARE* FW Addit **CO**29, You frattling! Said by rough men to a fractious cow.

frau n [Ger] **chiefly Nth, Midl, West** See Map
A woman; a wife.
1919 Dreiser *12 Men* 41 **MO,** I'm going to have my little *frau,* my seven children, my chickens, dog, cat . . [and] my pipe. **1920** Lewis *Main Street* 306 **MN,** Be switched if sometimes I don't feel tempted to shine up to some girl that has sense enough to take life as it is; some frau that doesn't want to talk Longfellow all the time. **1939** Aurand *Quaint Idioms* 14 **sePA,** She is a very good-looking *frau* (wife). **1950** *WELS (Joking names that a man may use to refer to his wife: "I've got to go downtown and pick up my ______.")* 10 Infs, **WI,** Frau; *(Nicknames for a woman)* 2 Infs, **WI,** Frau. **1965–70** *DARE* (Qu. AA22, *Joking names . . [for one's] wife*) 37 Infs, **scattered Nth, Midl, West,** Frau; **PA**161, Mein frau; (Qu. HH34, . . *A woman*) Infs **CT**16, **IN**68, **MO**9, **MA**58, **WI**27, Frau. **1971** Bright *Word Geog. CA & NV* 111, Frau [2 infs].

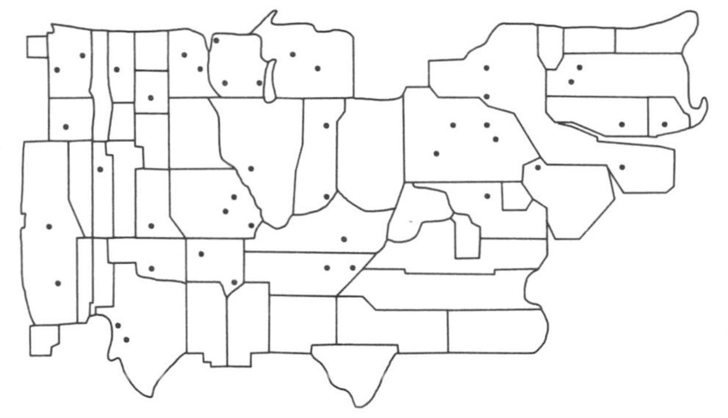

•frau + var (Qq. AA22, HH34)

fray n [*OED fray* sb.[1] 3 1382 →] **chiefly S Midl**
A fight or brawl; deadly combat.
1851 Hooper *Widow Rugby's Husband* 77 **AL,** I want you to present me and Ephraim Biddle for a 'fray. **1924** Raine *Land of Saddle-Bags* 135 **sAppalachians,** In a country where so many men carry weapons, . . heavy drinking . . result[s] in numerous "frays" . . and these frays generally prove fatal. **1927** *DN* 5.471 **sAppalachians,** *Fray. . .* A fight or brawl. **1929** *AmSp* 4.56, The good English word *fray,* meaning a fight with deadly weapons, is still common in the Ozark country. **1930** *VA Qrly. Rev.* 6.243 **S Midl,** Fray still carries its original meaning of a deadly combat. **c1960** *Wilson Coll.* **csKY,** *Fray. . .* A fight. **1967** *DARE* (Qu. Y12b, *A real fight in which blows are struck*) Inf **NC**41, A fray.

fray v
To fret, fuss.
1972 Cooper *NC Mt. Folkl.* 92, Frayed—fretted and cried, as a baby; was restless.

fraz See **frazzle** n **2, 3, 5**

frazed See **freeze** v **A2**

frazellating See **frazzellating**

frazle See **frazzle** v

frazzellating adj Also sp *frazellating* [**frazzle** n **1** + *-ate;* cf Intro "Language Changes" III.1]
=**frazzling** adj.
c1970 *Halpert Coll.* **wKY,** *Fraz(z)ellating . .* applied to no-good objects; absolutely nothing; not used to describe people, only things. "That frazzellatin' lamp!" . . "Haven't done a frazzellatin' thing all day."

frazzle v Also sp *frazle* [Engl dial] **chiefly Sth, S Midl** Cf **frazzled (out)**
1 also with *out:* To fray, unravel; to become frayed; also fig.
1884 Amer. Philol. Assoc. *Trans.* 14.48, *Frazle,* 'to unravel cloth'; used also of anything coming apart into strands. It is used everywhere in the South, and I was surprised to find that it was not in . . good use everywhere. **1890** *DN* 1.64 **KY,** "This cloth frays, or frazzles." To *frazzle out* is to fray out. **1896** Harris *Sister Jane* 344 **GA,** He's the genuine article, guaranteed not to rip in the seams or frazzle at the sleeves. **1899** (1912) Green *VA Folk-Speech* 184, *Frazzle. . .* To fray; wear out to threads, or small splinters. **1922** Gonzales *Black Border* 302 **sSC, GA coasts** [Gullah glossary], *Frazzle*—(n. and v.) frazzle, fray.
2 To whip (someone).
1889 in 1983 Zeigler *Lexicon Middle GA* 90, I'd a whirled in on you and I'd a frazzled you out so that you'd a ben thankful to be let take it all back. **1893** Shands *MS Speech* 31, If a switch be worn into shreds on some one, the switch is said to be *frazzled,* and the person whipped is also said to be *frazzled;* hence the word also means *to whip.* **1905** *DN* 3.80 **nwAR,** *Frazzle. . .* To whip severely.

frazzle n [**frazzle** v]
1 also *frassel:* A frayed end, shred, remnant. **chiefly Sth, S Midl** Cf **frazzling** n
1872 U.S. Congress *Congressional Globe* 42d Cong 2d Sess 30 May app 6.578/2 **GA,** They went out and got big long brushes, as big as these chair posts, and they whipped them all into frassels. **1890** *DN* 1.64 **KY,** This cloth frays. . . Look at the frazzles! **1899** (1912) Green *VA Folk-Speech* 184, *Frazzle. . .* A substance worn to threads, or small splinters. **1903** *DN* 2.314 **seMO,** The coat was worn to a frazzle. **1907** *DN* 3.231 **nwAR, seMO,** *Frazzle, frazzling. . .* A remnant or shred. **1908** *DN* 3.312 **eAL, wGA,** *Frazzle.* **1922** [see **frazzle** v **1**]. **1966–68** *DARE* (Qu. W25, *When a woman is cutting out a dress to sew, what do you call the little scraps of cloth left over?*) Inf **LA**18, Frazzles; (Qu. W26, . . *A piece of clothing . . used until it gets thin;* total Infs questioned, 75) Infs **MS**73, **NC**16, Worn to a frazzle.
2 also *fraz, frozzle;* Fig: a state of exhaustion or nervous excitement—freq in phr *worn to a frazzle* completely exhausted.
1859 Taliaferro *Fisher's R.* 203 **nwNC** (as of 1820s), After they had beaten each other into a "frozzle," and "inter mince-meat," they were parted by their "seconds." **1865** in 1897 Church *U.S. Grant* 318, Tell General Lee I have fought my corps to a frazzle. **1884** *Anglia* 7.271 **Sth, S Midl** [Black], *Wo' ter er frazzle* = worn out. **1908** *DN* 3.312 **eAL, wGA,** I was worn to a frazzle. **1910** Hart *Vigilante Girl* 294 **CA,** I reckon his nerves are all of a frazzle. **1950** *PADS* 14.30 **SC,** *Fraz. . .* "I'm worn to a fraz." **1954** *Harder Coll.* **cwTN,** *Fraz . .* worn out condition. **1956** McAtee *Some Dialect NC* 17, I'm worn to a fraz. **1960** Criswell *Resp. to PADS 20* **Ozarks,** I was worn to a fraz when the dance was over. **1965–70** *DARE* (Qu. X47, . . *Very tired*) 9 Infs, **scattered,** Worn to a frazzle; **GA**77, Wore to a frazzle; (Qu. GG22a) Inf **KY**75, You've wore my patience to a frazzle; (Qu. KK30) Inf **DC**11, Worn to a frazzle; (Qu. A21, *When someone is in too much of a hurry . . "Now just slow down! Don't ______."*) Inf **OH**36, Get in a frazzle; (Qu. GG7, . . *Annoyed or upset: "Though we were only ten minutes late, she was all ______."*) Inf **NY**241, In a frazzle.
3 also *fraz:* A very small amount.
1950 *PADS* 14.30 **SC,** *Fraz. . .* A very small portion or amount. **1953** Randolph-Wilson *Down in Holler* 245 **Ozarks,** "That there fish weighed sixteen pounds an' a frazzle" means that it weighed a trifle more than sixteen pounds. **1954** *Harder Coll.* **cwTN,** *Frazzle . .* a small amount.
4 By ext: see quot.
1968 *DARE* (Qu. E20, *Soft rolls of dust that collect on the floor under beds or other furniture*) Inf **OH**61, Frazzles.
5 also *fraz, frizzle:* A state of perfection; rarely, a condition of being overdone (as in cooking). [Perh infl by **frizzle** v] Cf **fraction 3, frizzle** n[1]
1897 *KS Univ. Qrly.* (ser B) 6.87, *Do to a frazzle:* same as *[do up brown].* **1959** *VT Hist.* new ser 27.136 **neVT,** *Done to a frizzle* (also frazzle). . . Overdone or almost overdone. Common. **1966–70** *DARE* (Qu. KK3a, . . *The perfect condition . . in cooking: "It's done to ______."*) Infs **IN**40, **WA**18, A frazzle; **KY**16, A fraz [fræz]; (Qu. KK3b, *Something done perfectly . . a piece of work: "It's done to ______."*) Inf **MO**3, A frazzle; (Qu. KK50, . . *Planned out carefully, down to the last detail: "He had it all worked out ______."*) Infs **GA**72, **NY**219, **ND**3, **SC**24, 34, **VA**25, 39, (Down) to a frazzle; **GA**72, To a frizzle; **KY**16, Down to a fraz.

frazzled (out) ppl adj [**frazzle** v]

1 also *frizzled:* Frayed, worn; disheveled. **chiefly Sth**

1872 U.S. Congress *Congressional Globe* 42d Cong 2d Sess 30 May app 577/3 **GA,** The ends of the switches were all frazzled. **1887** (1967) Harris *Free Joe* 177 **GA,** Her hair was of a reddish-gray color, and its frazzled and tangled condition suggested that the woman had recently passed through a period of extreme excitement. **1908** *DN* 3.312 **eAL, wGA,** My coat was all frazzled out. **1909** Porter *Options* 2 **Sth,** The drooping white mustache, slightly frazzled at the ends. **1956** Gipson *Old Yeller* 13 **TX,** Nothing was left hanging to the pole but the frazzled ends of the snapped blades [of bear grass]. **1966** *DARE* (Qu. W26, *When a piece of clothing has been used until it gets thin and breaks, you'd say it was* ______; total Infs questioned, 75) Inf **DC**4, Frizzled.

2 Fig: physically or emotionally exhausted; upset. **chiefly Sth, S Midl**

1883 *Amer. Philol. Assoc. Trans.* 14.48 **Sth,** *All frazled out,* figuratively used, [is] about equivalent to 'used up.' **1895** *DN* 1.371 **eTN,** *Frazzled out.* **1905** *DN* 3.80 **nwAR,** Frazzled out. **1908** *DN* 3.312 **eAL, wGA,** After this long day's tramp I was completely frazzled. **1911** Ferber *Dawn O'Hara* 15, No woman—not even a frazzled-out newspaper woman—could receive the love and care that they gave me. **c1960** *Wilson Coll.* **csKY,** *Frazzled*. . . Fatigued, worn out, tired. Usually adds *out.* **1960** Carpenter *Tales Manchaca* 56 **cTX,** I needed all such windfalls, for I often was too frazzled to think clearly. **1966–70** *DARE* (Qu. X47, . . *Very tired*) Inf **CT**27, All frazzled out; **MI**10, Frazzled; (Qu. GG2, . . *'Confused, mixed up': "So many things were going on at the same time that he got completely* ______.*"*) Inf **IN**75, Frazzled; (Qu. GG7, . . *Annoyed or upset: "Though we were only ten minutes late, she was all* ______.*"*) Inf **MO**23, Frazzled. **1972** Cooper *NC Mt. Folkl.* 92, Frazzled—very tired.

3 Drunk. Cf *DS* DD15

1928 *AmSp* 4.102, *Synonyms for "drunk"* . . frazzled. **1942** Berrey–Van den Bark *Amer. Slang* 106.7, *Drunk* . . frazzled. **1977** Adams *Lang. Railroader* 64, *Frazzled:* Drunk.

frazzle-headed adj [**frazzle** n **1**; cf **frazzled (out) 1** quot 1887] **S Midl**

Having tousled or unkempt hair.

1953 Randolph–Wilson *Down in Holler* 245 **Ozarks,** A frazzle-headed person is one whose hair looks ragged at the edges, either uncombed or not properly cut. **1954** *Harder Coll.* **cwTN,** *Frazzle-headed* . . of a person with ragged hair. **1983** *MJLF* 9.1.40 **ceKY,** *Frazzle headed* . . [having] messed up hair.

frazzle out See **frazzle** v **1**

frazzle, worn to a See **frazzle** n **2**

frazzling n [**frazzle** n] **chiefly Sth, S Midl**

=**frazzle** n **1, 2.**

1899 (1912) Green *VA Folk-Speech* 184, *Frazlings*. . . Threads of cloth torn or unravelled. **1907** *DN* 3.231 **nwAR,** *Frazzle, frazzling*. . . A remnant or shred. **1965** *DARE* FW Addit **MS,** People frequently say that they are just worn to a frazzle or frazzling. This means . . completely worn out or tired.

frazzling adj [**frazzle** n **1, 3**] **Sth, S Midl**

1 Trifling, measly; darned; hence adv *frazzling* darned—used as an intensifier.

1906 *DN* 3.136 **nwAR,** He won't do a frazzlin thing. **1941** Street *In Father's House* 34 **seMS,** I'd give it all to her. Ever frazzlin' cent. **1954** *Harder Coll.* **cwTN,** *Frazzling* . . small. **c1970** *Halpert Coll.* **wKY,** Hasn't done a frazzlin' thing. *Ibid,* He's so frazzlin' lazy.

2 See quot.

1954 *Milwaukee Jrl.* (WI) 14 Mar sec 4 4/7 **Ozarks,** Frazzlin' worm, the last worm in the can.

frazzling adv See **frazzling** adj **1**

freak n

1 A social affair or celebration; a party. *old-fash*

1887 Eggleston *Graysons* 57 **cIL,** He was a good teller of amusing stories,—so that he easily came to be a leader in all the frolics and freaks of the town. **1941** *LANE* Map 414 **ceME,** *Social gathering*. . . *Freak,* old term for *blowout.*

2 An unusual saddle; see quots. **West**

1936 Adams *Cowboy Lingo* 47, Saddles . . with an unusual bulge or roll were 'freaks,' 'form-fitters,' or 'bronc saddles.' **1967** *DARE* Tape **TX**25, Freak . . refers to a saddle girt or cinch or somethin'. Something that's unlawful or unusual.

3 An effeminate man; a homosexual. **esp Sth, S Midl** *esp freq among Black speakers*

1942 Berrey–Van den Bark *Amer. Slang* 405.1, *Effeminate man or masculine woman; homosexual* . . freak. **1956** Longstreet *Real Jazz* 150, *Freak* is homosexual. **1965–70** *DARE* (Qu. HH38, *A womanish man*) Infs **IN**45, **MS**1, **TX**1, 91, Freak; (Qu. HH39, *A homosexual man*) Infs **DC**8, **MS**80, **NY**241, **SC**68, **TN**53, **TX**1, **VA**41, Freak. [5 of 10 Infs Black] **1968** *Current Slang* Fall 25 **sCA** [Black], *Freak*. . . A child molester or homosexual. **1970** Major *Dict. Afro-Amer. Slang* 55, *Freak:* (1920's) one who practices socially unaccepted forms of sexual love. **1972** Claerbaut *Black Jargon* 64, *Freak* . . a homosexual.

freaking ppl adj [Perh var of *frigging*] *euphem*

1966 *DARE* FW Addit **cnMA,** Freakin'—a cuss word, milder than *friggin',* used as an adjective.

freakish adj [**freak 3**]

Effeminate; homosexual.

1930 *AmSp* 6.158 **NYC,** *Freakish* is used to describe an effeminate man or a mannish woman. **1946** (1972) Mezzrow–Wolfe *Really Blues* 332, Freakish: *homosexual, perverted, weird.*

freality n [Perh blend of *free* + *liberality*]

1899 (1912) Green *VA Folk-Speech* 184, *Freality*. . . Liberality. "Give to us with a freality."

freckled lily n Also *freckle lily* [From the spotted perianth] **ME**

=**wood lily.**

1897 *Jrl. Amer. Folkl.* 10.145, *Lilium Philadelphicum,* . . freckled lily, South Berwick, Me. **1929** *Torreya* 29.149 **ME,** Lilium Philadelphicum [was] *"Freckled Lily,"* and children were warned not to look into them lest they also freckle. **1966** *DARE* (Qu. S26a) Inf **ME**7, Freckle lilies—also called tiger lily.

frecklehead n

Perh an immature **red-headed woodpecker.**

1966 *DARE* (Qu. Q17, . . *Kinds of woodpeckers*) Inf **SC**26, Frecklehead—head black and white, speckled like a guinea.

freckle lily See **freckled lily**

free adj

1 Quick, unrestrained.

1903 (1965) Adams *Log Cowboy* 51 **West,** Throwing the two bunches [of cattle] together, we drifted them a free clip towards camp.

2 Of games and sports: having looser rules than the standard version of the game.

1967–68 *DARE* (Qu. EE11, *Bat-and-ball games for just a few players [when there aren't enough for a regular game]*) Inf **PA**148, Free ball; (Qu. EE28, *Games played in the water*) Inf **MN**2, Free catch—like volleyball, two teams.

3 Frank, truthful.

1917 Torrence *Granny Maumee* 55 **Sth** [Black], Ef you wan' me to he'p you den be free wif me.

free adv

Freely, unconstrainedly, abundantly.

1939 *Hall Coll.* **wNC,** They used to make it [=liquor] free. They used to make it purty free. People would come in here after it. **1984** Wilder *You All Spoken Here* 163 **Sth,** *Free:* Freely, as "I done et so free o' fish my stumick rises an' falls with the tide."

free exclam

1 also *free (for) all:* A call used in the game **hide-and-seek A;** see quots. Cf **all (in) free, free home, home free, in free**

1951 *PADS* 15.54 **IN,** *Free* . . or *in free*. . . A cry in games, the result of which was already decided, by an individual who desired to surrender without penalty, so as to shorten that particular phase of the play. **1966–69** *DARE* (Qu. EE15, *When he has caught the first of those that were hiding what does the player who is 'it' call out to the others?*) Infs **IA**3, **IL**63, **MI**93, **OH**1, 87, **PA**28, 29, **SD**3, **TX**53, **WA**18, Free; **CT**19, Free for all. **1977–78** Foster *Lexical Variation* 79 **NJ,** Calls to signal the freeing of captured players . . *free all* (1) [inf]. *Ibid* 80, Essex County preserves the older, Northern *free.*

2 also *I'm free;* In the game of tag: a call for time out.

1950 *WELS (In a game of tag, if you want to rest, what do you call out so* *that "it" can't catch you?)* 1 Inf, **cWI,** We used to say "free." **1967–69** *DARE* (Qu. EE17) Infs **IL**45, **MI**67, **MN**38, **MO**20, 26, **OH**82, **OR**4, **PA**22, 162, 203, **WA**22, Free; **OH**65, I'm free.

free n[1]
1972 *Yesterday* 1.4.28 **WI,** Hide-and-Go-Seek . . was always played in the alley. . . 'Free' was the goal, usually a telephone pole.

free n[2] See **free peach**

free all See **free** exclam **1**

free-clean n Cf **clean-peel, free peach**
=**freestone 2.**
1968 *DARE* (Qu. I51, *The kind of a peach where the hard center is loose*) Inf **SC**57, Free-cleans.

freedom See **freedom cut**

freedom bunch n
A children's game; see quot.
1950 *WELS (Games in which every player hides except "it," who must try to find the others)* 1 Inf, **csWI,** Freedom bunch.

freedom cut n Also *freedom*
=**Afro** n.
1968–70 *DARE* (Qu. X5, . . *Names . . for different kinds of men's haircuts*) Inf **PA**66, Freedom cut—worn by Negro males; long, unstraightened, and without a part; **PA**239, Bush, freedom, Afro—all mean the same thing.

Freedom War n
The American Civil War.
1937 in 1979 *Amer. Slave Suppl. 2* 1.364, I went dere atter de Freedom War. **1969** McDavid *Unpleasantness* 202 **Sth,** The terms . . [Afro-Americans] use are predominantly those of their white neighbors: *Civil War, Confederate War, War Between the States.* One [of 40 Black infs], however, went beyond local tradition to call it *Freedom* War.

free-for-all n
See quots.
1942 Berrey–Van den Bark *Amer. Slang* 439.1, *Woman of easy morals . .* free-for-all. **1967–68** *DARE* (Qu. AA7b, . . *A woman who is very fond of men . . if she's not respectable about it*) Inf **CA**36, A free-for-all; (Qu. HH37, *An immoral woman*) Inf **OR**3, Free-for-all.

free for all exclam See **free** exclam **1**

free gold n **chiefly CA**
Gold occurring naturally in an uncombined form; also gold which has been freed from its original matrix by erosion.
[**1870** Pine *Beyond the West* 107, In the granite district of the Upper Arkansas, quartz gold is found in simple combination, "free" as in California.] **1881** Raymond *Gloss. Mining* 37, *Free-milling.* Applied to ores which contain free gold or silver, and can be reduced by crushing and amalgamation, without roasting or other chemical treatment. **1897** Twain *Following Equator* 687, There was no paying way of getting anything out of such rock but the coarser-grained "free" gold. **1969** *DARE* Tape **CA**113, They were mining the free gold in the rivers and in these sections and when they came to the quartz they weren't able to handle the quartz; **CA**120, We have just a little mine down there that's got small quartz stringers with free gold. **1969** *DARE* FW Addit **CA**114, Free gold—gold that's separated from the quartz and has washed down into streams. The gold that is panned out of streams. Also called placer gold.

free grass See **free range**

free gratis adv phr Also *free gratis for nothing* [Redund; cf Intro "Language Changes" I.4] *joc*
Without charge, free.
1843 (1916) Hall *New Purchase* 375 **IN,** I read of a quack doctor once, who used to give his advice free gratis for nothing to any one what would *buy* a box of his pills. **1883** [see **gore** n[1] **1**]. **1928** *Ruppenthal Coll.* **KS,** You can get seeds free gratis for nothing by writing to the Secretary of Agriculture. **1931–33** *LANE Worksheets* **cwCT,** I got that free gratis. **1952** Brown *NC Folkl.* 1.543, *Free gratis. . .* Free; gratis.—General. Illiterate. Not common. **c1960** *Wilson Coll.* **csKY,** *Free gratis for nothing:* A humorous tautology for *free.* **1966** Barnes–Jensen *Dict. UT Slang* 16, They let me into the ball game free gratis. **1967** *DARE* (Qu. U15, . . *If the seller puts in a little extra to make you feel that you're getting a good bargain, you call that* ______) Inf **MO**11, Free gratis.

free hand n
1952 Brown *NC Folkl.* 1.543, *Free hand. . .* One who is liberal, generous.

freehanded adj Also *freehan'*
=**freehearted 1.**
1899 (1912) Green *VA Folk-Speech* 184, *Freehanded. . .* Free to give; openhanded. **1922** Gonzales *Black Border* 302 **sSC, GA coasts** [Gullah glossary], *Freehan'*—freehanded, generous, liberal. **1929** *AmSp* 5.129 **ME,** A person might be . . "freehanded," "good-hearted." **1965–70** *DARE* (Qu. U32, . . *A very generous person: "He's* ______.*"*) 18 Infs, **scattered,** Freehanded.

freehearted adj [*OED* 1398 →]
1 Generous. **chiefly Sth, S Midl, NEast** See Map
1914 *DN* 4.72 **ME, nNH,** *Free-hearted.* **1923** *DN* 5.207 **swMO,** *Free hearted. . .* Liberal, generous. **1941** *Hall Coll.* **wNC,** Windy Bill, you're too free-hearted with your money. **1946** *AmSp* 21.190 **eKY,** She's an awful free-hearted old soul. **1947** *AmSp* 22.156 **sIN. 1950** *WELS (A generous person: "He's* ______.*")* 3 Infs, **WI,** Free-hearted. **c1960** *Wilson Coll.* **csKY. 1965–70** *DARE* (Qu. U32, . . *A very generous person: "He's* ______.*"*) 185 Infs, **chiefly Sth, S Midl, scattered NEast,** Freehearted; (Qu. U31, . . *A person who spends money very freely;* total Infs questioned, 75) Infs **MS**1, 60, 63, Freehearted; (Qu. II19, *When you think somebody has . . been given something you deserved, you might say, "I'd rather quit than* ______.*"*) Inf **IA**30, Be freehearted.

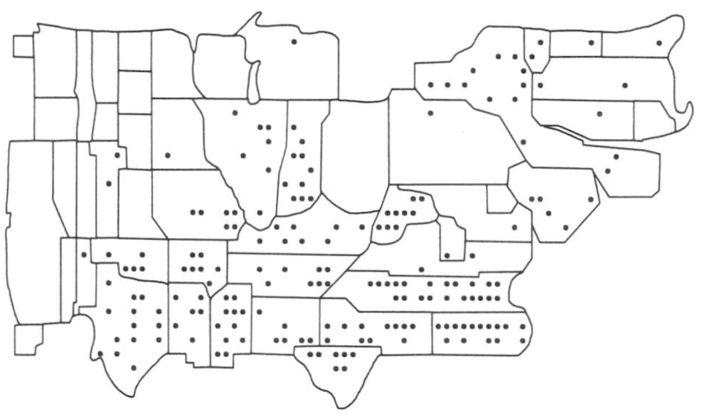

•freehearted 1 + var (Qq. U32, U31, II19)

2 See quot.
1941 *LANE* Map 468 *(Good-natured)* 1 inf, **ceMA,** Free-hearted.

freeholder n [*freeholder* one who owns a freehold estate] **NJ**
An elected official in charge of county affairs.
1887 NJ Laws *Revised Statutes Suppl.* 1111, The boards of chosen freeholders of the counties of Union and Somerset shall so change the course of Green brook . . as that it shall cross said street. **1968** *DARE* FW Addit **NJ**22, He has been a freeholder (this is a sort of county councilman) for years. **1969** *DARE* Tape **NJ**54, Take them over to the county building, . . have . . the freeholders meet and greet the class. **1979** *DARE* File **neNJ,** A freeholder is an elected county official, an administrator of counties. There's a board of freeholders, properly called a "board of chosen freeholders." They exist in every county in New Jersey, as far as I know. It could come from "free" as opposed to being a slave, but I think it probably comes from "fee," which designated ownership of land. A fee-holder was a land-owner, and ownership of land was a qualification for voting.

free-holy See **frijol(e)**

free home n, exclam Cf **free** exclam **1, home free**
=**hide-and-seek A;** the call used in the game.
1967–68 *DARE* (Qu. EE13a, *Games in which every player hides except one, and that one must try to find the others*) Inf **MN**2, Hide-and-seek, free home; (Qu. EE15, *When he has caught the first of those that were hiding what does the player who is 'it' call out to the others?*) Infs **MN**2, **NY**70, **PA**45, 148, **WI**52, Free home.

free hotel n Also *free motel* *joc* Cf **boarding house**
=**hotel B2.**
1942 Berrey–Van den Bark *Amer. Slang* 466.11, *Jail . .* free flop *or* hotel. **1966–70** *DARE* (Qu. V11, . . *Joking names . . for a . . jail*) Infs

SC10, 40, **TX**26, 106, **VA**42, Free hotel; **FL**51, Free motel. [4 of 6 Infs Black]

free hunt exclam

In children's games: =**free** exclam **1.**

1933 *Hanley Disks* **nwCT,** They'd call you in—free hunt, y'know. If they didn' nobody call you in, you stayed hidden.

free issue n **Mid Atl** *old-fash* Cf **issue**

1 also *free issue Negro, issue(-free Negro):* A Black or mixed-race person free by individual manumission or birth; spec, a child of a White woman and a Black man.

1887 Page *In Ole VA* 40 **eVA,** Dese heah free-issue niggers don' know what Christmas is. **1891** Page *Elsket* 127 **VA,** The old fellow [=a former slave] launched out into diatribes against the "free issues," who, he declared, expected to be "better than white, like white folks ain' been free from sense de wull begin." **1927** Adams *Congaree* 59 **cSC** [Black], De ole folks says dat de way dey come to be Free Issues dat white womens were dey mammy and niggers were dey daddy, and de law ain't 'low de chillun of a white ooman to be a slave; and a new lookin' race of goose eye niggers was created, and dey had minds of dey own and ways of dey own. Dey was discounted by white folks and dey was scorned by niggers. **1950** *PADS* 14.30 **SC,** *Free issue*. . . Offspring of white woman and Negro man. Sand hills of central S.C. and Pee Dee. **1952** Brown *NC Folkl.* 1.554 **c,eNC,** *Isshy* ['ɪšɪ]. . . A child born of a white mother and a Negro man. I have heard *isshy-free Negro,* referring to a slave that had been *issued* his freedom. **1963** Berry *Almost White* 34, Almost as bad is the term "Issues," which is applied to a group long known in Amherst County, Virginia, and whose counterparts are found up and down the Blue Ridge region of that state. Issue is a shortened form of Free Issue, a name by which the free colored, before and after the Civil War, were differentiated from those Negroes whose freedom derived from the war. **1968** *DARE* (Qu. HH29a) Inf **VA**25, Issue—claim Indian descent, but it is believed they are descendants of free issue niggers who came in 1618 or 1619.

2 also *old free issue, issue free:* =**issue.**

1927 Adams *Congaree* 56 **cSC** [Black], Him and Saber been seinin' back dere wid a gang of dem Free Issues. **1939** Frazier *Negro Family* 237 **NC,** [Footnote:] One old woman described their attitude toward the emancipated blacks as follows: "The tribe is all mixed up now more than they used to be. During the old times we [=people with Indian, Black, and White ancestry] had a separate feeling. We did not belong to the Negro or the whites. . . We was what was considered the 'Old Free Issue,' and those just freed was the 'New Free Issue.' They did not have much [Frazier: racial] mixture. They did not like us and we did not like them." **1939** FWP *Guide NC* 336, In Welsh Creek township . . are several hundred so called "Free-issues," people of mixed Indian, white, and Negro blood, whose ancestors were woodsmen when turpentine was profitably produced in this region. **1970** *DARE* (Qu. HH29a, . . *People of mixed blood—part Indian*) Inf **VA**35, Issue frees ['ɪšə,friz]—live on the Virginia-North Carolina line in Halifax County near Virgilina; (Qu. HH29b, . . *People of mixed blood—part Negro*) Inf **VA**42, Free issue—almost white, [with] straight black hair, thin lip, blue or brown eyes; (Qu. W40) Inf **VA**39, Issue free—[wears] hat, jewelry, the works.

3 as *new free issue:* A Black person freed by the Civil War.

1939 Frazier [see **2** above].

free issue Negro See **free issue 1**

free land See **free range**

free lot n

A vacant lot.

1976 *WI Acad. Rev.* March 9/1 (as of 1920s), Before school, recess, after school, and on weekends were times to try one's luck or skill with marbles, often on Milwaukee's "free lots" unused and unattended real estate.

freemale n [Perh folk-etym for *female*]

1922 Gonzales *Black Border* 302 **sSC, GA coasts** [Gullah glossary], *Freemale*—female, females. **1939** Griswold *Sea Is. Lady* 577 **sSC** [Gullah], An' as fuh dat freemale I jes' ain' gwine pay'um no mind.

free man of color n Also *free woman of color, free person of color,* abbr forms *f.m.c., f.w.c.* **chiefly LA** *hist* Cf **free issue 1**

A Black person not a slave; a person having one Black and one White parent.

1810 *Whitney's New Orleans Directory for 1811* app [2], Derniere Recensement—Last Census. *De la ville de la Nouvelle-Orleans—Of the city of New-Orleans.* Blancs, whites, 4507—Gens de couleur libres, free persons of colour, 3332—Esclaves, slaves, 4386—Total, 12,225. **1832** *New Orleans City Directory* np, Adam Lucile, f.w.c. 68 Espagne. . . Adams Gabriel, victualler, 188 Grands Hommes. . . Adams Christopher, f.m.c. cordwainer, 111 Moreau. **1840** *Daily Picayune* (New Orleans LA) 16 Aug 2/2, Bazile Croker, *f.m.c.* sworn. Witness is owner of a slave. **1882** *Century Illustr. Mag.* 1.605/2 **LA,** The following relates to the sad and silent 'f.m.c.' ('free man of color'). **1929** *Amer. Mercury* 16.284/1 **New Orleans LA** (as of 1880s), They found what they were after, his great-great-grandfather's name, and following it like an overweighted tail to a tugging kite, the letters f.m.c., branding him irrevocably as a Negro, a free man of color. **1967** *DARE* Tape **LA**14, The French mulattoes are a very interesting group that began to be given their freedom from the very earliest days of this settlement. The children of French people by Negro slaves . . were turned into what were called f.m.c. or free men of color or f.w.c., . . free women of color. . . They have developed a very interesting and different civilization of their own. They do not intermingle with the Whites and they do not intermingle with the Negro. They are *Colored,* . . the word that they prefer for that. They don't like the word "French mulatto," but . . they are called that . . by White people. Their daughters go to good convent schools. All of 'em practice the Catholic religion very assiduously.

freeman's base n [By analogy with *prisoner's base*]

1905 *DN* 3.80 **nwAR,** *Freeman's base*. . . Prisoner's base. Little Rock.

free motel See **free hotel**

free peach n Also *free* [Abbrs]

=**freestone 2.**

1940–41 Cassidy *WI Atlas* **nwWI,** Free peach. **1941** *LANE* Map 267 **csMA, cNH, cnVT,** Free. **1965–70** *DARE* (Qu. I51) Infs **CA**63, **NY**70, **OK**17, **SC**21, 29, Free peach; **ME**5, **PA**128, Free. **1971** Wood *Vocab. Change* 43, *Free peach* . . occur[s] occasionally on either side of [the Mississippi River]. **1973** Allen *LAUM* 1.306 (as of c1950), One Minnesotan on the Iron Range has the rare *free peach.*

free person of color See **free man of color**

free range n Also *free grass,* ~ *land* **West**

Public rangeland; unenclosed grassland.

1888 *Century Illustr. Mag.* 35.510, In our northern country we have "free grass"; that is, the stockmen rarely own more than small portions of the land over which their cattle range, the bulk of it . . still the property of the National Government. **1912** Mulford–Clay *Buck Peters* 186 **TX,** Outlying free range had been thoroughly combed. **1929** *AmSp* 5.53 **NE,** There is now little "open range" land, "free land," land open to any rancher or ranchers who care to enjoy it, in Nebraska; consequently there is little or no "free water" or "free grass." **1944** Adams *Western Words* 62, *Free grass*—The open range of the early days; also called *free range.* **1947** *Steamboat* (Colo.) *Pilot* 13 Feb. 8/4 *(OEDS)* **CO,** Then sheep commenced to come for a share of the free range. **1948** *Dallas Morning News* 5 Dec. (Book Sec.) 8/1 *(DA),* The two brothers had established a ranch—on free grass—south of the Nueces River. **1970** *DARE* Tape **TX**89, Well, in those days [when Inf's grandparents settled in Texas] everything was open range, free range, 'n' they grew cattle, horses.

free-running barn n Cf **free stall**

1969 *DARE* (Qu. M1) Inf **NY**209, Free-running barn—no stanchions.

free school n

A school operated at public expense and open to all children of a district; a public school.

1635 in 1886 Neill *Virginia Carolorum* 113 **eVA,** A learned and honest man to keep . . a free school, for the education and instruction of the children of the adjoining parishes. **1711** *Boston Rec.* 75 *(DAE),* Inspectors of the Free Gramer School. **1837** (1966) Martineau *Soc. in America* 3.164, One needs but go from a charity-school in an English county to a free-school in Massachusetts, to see how different the bare acquisition of reading and writing is. **1930** *DN* 6.87 **cWV,** *Free school,* public school, a term widely used in this vicinity. It originated evidently in the distinction drawn in the time within the recollection of men now living when there were . . only pay- or subscription-schools. **1935** Allen *Annals Haywood Co.* 212 **NC,** In 1839, the system of public schools called the "free schools" began . . on the basis of raising by taxation twenty dollars in each district in the county to be matched by forty dollars from the State fund. **1939** *Hall Coll.* **wNC,** Didn't have grades then. Went until we completed the free-school books. **1950** *WELS (A school that any child can go to without paying)* 1 Inf, **cwWI,** Public or free school. **1967**

DARE (Qu. JJ2a, *A child . . in the lower grades*) Inf **TN**23, He's in free school—when grade school was tuition-free and high school was paid.

free seeder n Cf *DS* L24

A **volunteer** crop.

1951 Johnson *Resp. to PADS 20* **DE** *(A crop [or part of a crop] that springs up and grows by itself from old seed)* Free-seeder.

freeseed n Also *freeseed peach* **esp Appalachians** See Map

=**freestone 2.**

1949 Kurath *Word Geog.* Fig 129, [There are seven instances of *free-seed peach,* five in W. Virginia, one in s. Ohio, one in e. N. Carolina.] **1962** Atwood *Vocab. TX* 100, *Freeseed (freestone + clear-seed)* [occurs only once]. **1966–70** *DARE* (Qu. I51, *The kind of a peach where the hard center is loose*) 17 Infs, **scattered, but esp Appalachians,** Freeseed. **1967** *PADS* 47.6 **sPA,** Free seed peach. **c1970** Pederson *Dial. Surv. Rural GA,* 1 inf, **seGA,** Freeseed.

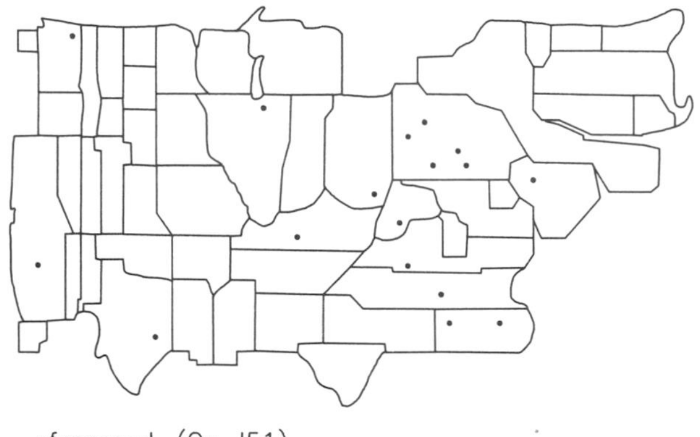

•freeseed (Qu. I51)

free stall n, freq attrib **chiefly Nth**

In a dairy barn, a stall without a stanchion.

1968 *Volette* (Martin TN) 24 Apr 6/2, An ultra-modern dairy unit . . is now undergoing the finishing touches at the Experimental Station here. . . Besides the milking parlor there are two freestall barns, two haybarns, and a silo. **1968–69** *DARE* (Qu. M1, . . *Kinds of barns . . according to . . the way they are built*) Infs **CT**24, **MA**25, **OH**70, Free-stall barn; **MN**16, Free-stall barn has stalls for cattle; **MA**47, Free-stall barn—individual bed for each cow; **WI**63, Free-stall housing barn; **VT**2, Free-stall housing barn—open in center, no posts; roof supported by arches and trusses; [**MA**37, Free-housing barn;] (QR, near Qu. M11) Inf **MA**16, [There are] free stalls in some stables now—cows run loose. **1979–80** *DARE* File **sID,** Free-stall barns make it easy to feed and clean up after your cattle. *Ibid* **csWI,** A free-stall barn is about 24 feet wide with a ten foot alley in the middle, with seven foot sections on each side and partitions every four feet. The stalls are raised above the alley, so the manure drops into the alley making the barn easy to clean. The cows eat from a bunk or a conveyor belt, so they can eat whenever they want. This gives them more freedom and saves the farmer labor.

freestone n

1 See **freestone water.**

2 also *freestone peach:* A peach whose flesh easily separates from the seed. **[stone] widespread, but least freq Sth** See Map Also called **clearseed, free peach, freeseed, open peach, press peach** Cf **clingstone**

1847 (1979) Rutledge *Carolina Housewife* 159, *Peach Leather.* Take a peck or two of soft freestone peaches. **1848** Bartlett *Americanisms* 85, When the stone readily separates from the peach, they are called *free-stones.* **1949** Kurath *Word Geog.* 72, *Free-stone peach* is current in the greater part of the Midland and in the entire New England settlement area. It is the regular expression in West Virginia and the Shenandoah Valley and has survived to some extent in the westernmost parts of Virginia and the Carolinas. As an innovation it appears now also in Tidewater Virginia and on the North Carolina coasts. **1950** *WELS (The kind of peach with the hard center loose)* 48 Infs, **WI,** Freestone (peach). **c1960** *Wilson Coll.* **csKY,** *Freestone* or *freestone peach.* **1962** Atwood *Vocab. TX* 60, A considerable majority of Texas informants in all areas speak of a *freestone peach.* **1965–70** *DARE* (Qu. I51) 805 Infs, **widespread but least freq in Sth,** Freestone. **1968** *DARE* Tape **GA**69, It was a freestone peach, meaning that . . you could break it open with your hand an' the meat would leave the seed. **1971** Bright *Word Geog. CA & NV* 183, *Free-stone (peach)* 96% [of 300 infs]. **1973** Allen *LAUM* 1.306 (as of c1950), For the peach whose pit is easily separated from the flesh the U[pper] M[idwest] term is *freestone* or *freestone peach,* common also in New England and the Midland area of the eastern United States.

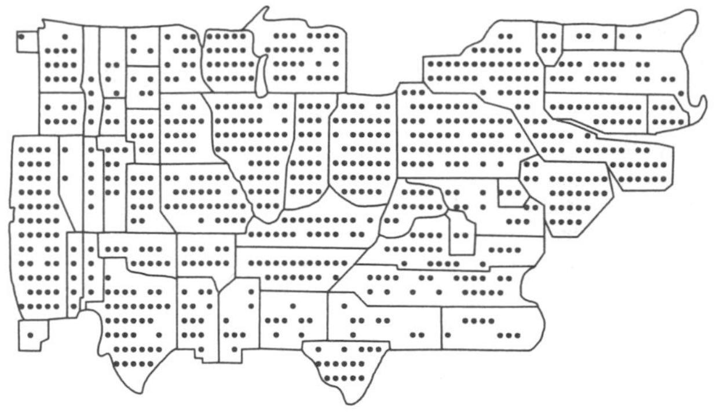

•freestone 2 (Qu. I51)

freestone spring n **[freestone water]**

See quots.

1902 *DN* 2.235 **sIL,** *Freestone-spring.* . . Soft-water spring. **1907** *DN* 3.222 **nwAR, sIL,** *Freestone-spring.* . . Soft-water spring.

freestone water n Also *freestone* **chiefly S Midl**

Water containing little or no dissolved minerals, soft water.

1727 in 1940 *AmSp* 15.263 **VA,** Crossing ye Sd. branch . . by a place called ye freestone cave. **1805** (1904) Lewis *Orig. Jrls. Lewis & Clark Exped.* 2.269, Springs . . wer[e] very cold and freestone water. **1883** Zeigler-Grosscup *Heart of Alleghanies* 347, The park is richly favored with springs, both of mineral and soft freestone water. **1902** *DN* 2.235 **sIL,** *Freestone-spring.* . . Soft-water spring. *Freestone-water.* . . Water from a freestone spring. **1905** *DN* 3.80 **nwAR,** *Freestone water.* . . Soft water, pure water, water free from mineral matter. Common. **1939** FWP *Guide TN* 317, A great spring in the back yard discharges 7 million gallons of pure freestone water daily. **c1940** *Hall Coll.* **eTN,** *Free-stone water.* . . "Any clear water without mineral properties." "Hit's just pure water; hit runs over the white rocks." [Hall: [Second inf] distinguished 'free-stone water' from 'slate water.']

free time exclam **[free** exclam, perh infl by *time out*]

=**free** exclam **2.**

1968 *DARE* (Qu. EE17, *In a game of tag, if a player wants to rest, what does he call out so that he can't be tagged?*) Infs **CA**59, **PA**165, Free time.

freeway n **widespread, but esp West** See Map

An expressway or four-lane divided highway.

1939 *Sun* (Baltimore) 16 Jan. 5/7 *(OEDS)* **MD,** Construction of freeways, either elevated or on the ground, would be necessary to facilitate movement of traffic in and out of Washington [D.C.] **1943** *Life* 15.21.118/2 **sCA,** Almost everybody in Los Angeles has some pet plan for rebuilding large parts of the city after the war and opening up new "freeways" (express auto highways). **1965–70** *DARE* (Qu. N16a,

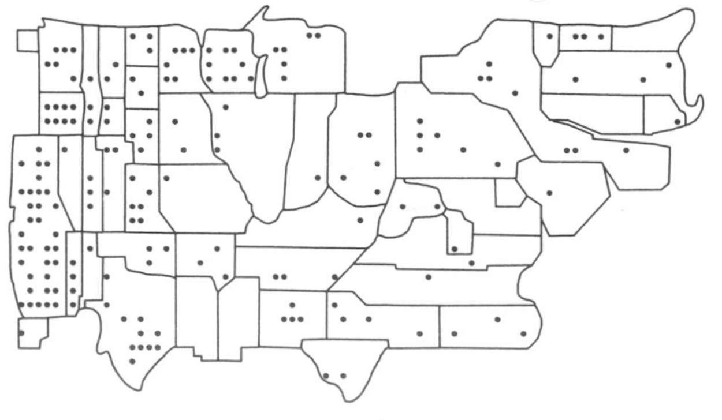

•freeway + var (Qu. N16a)

Names for a highway with two lanes on each side and a separation down the middle) 176 Infs, **widespread, but esp West,** Freeway; **CA**86, Super freeway.

free wheel adj **MD**

Of vehicles: not confined by tracks.

1929 *Amer. City* July 144/1 **Baltimore MD,** Before the ban [on parking], free wheel traffic moved at the rate of 6.18 miles per hour. **1936** *Sun* (Baltimore MD) 26 Aug 20/1 (*AmSp* 24.305), Tracks will be removed from the span and it will be redecked and made available for free-wheel traffic only. **1945** *Sun* (Baltimore MD) 3 Nov 8/1, Reduce the number of streetcars by the substitution of free-wheel vehicles—trackless trolleys and busses.

free woman of color See **free man of color**

freeze v

A Forms. [Cf similar forms in *EDD*]

1 infin: usu *freeze;* also *friz, froze.*

1906 *DN* 3.137 **nwAR,** I'm about to friz. **1927** Adams *Congaree* 31 **cSC** [Black], It look like my heart guh froze [=was going to freeze] I been so frighten.

2 past: usu *froze;* also *freeze(d), frozed;* also **chiefly Sth, S Midl** *friz* and, *esp among Black speakers, frez;* rarely *frased, frazed, freezen, frozen, fruz.*

1794 (1914) Clark *Jrl.* 444 **VA,** A very cold night last frased hard. **1867** Lowell *Biglow* 26, I friz down right where I wuz. **1893** Shands *MS Speech* 31, *Frez. . .* Negro for *froze.* **1906** *DN* 3.118 **sIN,** *Friz, pt.* and *pp.* **1908** *DN* 3.313 **eAL, wGA,** *Friz, pret.* and *pp.* of *freeze. Frez* is also used. **1931** *PMLA* 46.1319 **sAppalachians,** The strong preterite with change of vowel is common: . . "friz," or "fruz" (froze). **1943** *LANE* Map 648 **sME, sNH, sRI,** The map shows the preterite of *freeze* (*froze, freezed,* rarely *frozed, friz*). [4 infs report *friz,* three calling it old-fashioned, one jocular.] **1952** Brown *NC Folkl.* 1.543, *Frez* [frɛz]. . . Past tense and past participle of *freeze. . .* Old people. Rare. **1953** Atwood *Survey of Verb Forms* 14, *Froze* is with rare exceptions the only form used in N. Eng. and the M[iddle] A[tlantic] S[tates]. . . *Freezed* . . is a fairly common variant. . . *Frozed* . . is about as common as *freezed. . . Friz* . . occurs only rarely. . . *Frez* . . occurs [rarely]. . . Other preterite forms used by one or two informants each are: *frozen . . freezen* . . and *frazed. Ibid* 40, *Chiefly Southern* [verb forms include] . . freezed. *Ibid* 41, Forms that may be classed as primarily rustic include the following preterites: . . freezed, frez, friz, frozed. . . *Frez* . . [is] considerably more frequent among Negroes than among white informants. **1954** *Harder Coll.* **cwTN,** *Freeze. . .* Past: froze, friz (occ.) **c1960** *Wilson Coll.* **csKY,** *Friz* (p. and p.p.) **1962** *Mt. Life* 38.1.16 **sAppalachians,** Verbs which retain either the strong preterites of Middle English or variant preterites of the English dialects . . *Present*—freeze[,] *Past*—friz[,] *Past Participle*—friz [etc]. **1966–70** *DARE* (Qu. OO15a, . . *"I was so cold my ears nearly* ———*."*) Infs **NC**78, **SC**9, Freeze; **SC**26, Freeze off; **IL**93, Freezed; **CA**9, **GA**31, **IN**82, **MS**71, **OK**13, Friz; **MA**5, Friz off my head; **VA**26, Frizzed; **NC**1, 49, 60, **TX**56, Frozed (off); **GA**92, **MO**10, Frozen; (Qu. B36) Inf **NJ**69, The window freezed over. **1968** *PADS* 50.40 **swTN** [Black], For the past tense of *freeze,* /froz/ is almost the only form used outside the South. In the South the most frequently used variants are /frizd, frozd/, both of which are primarily used by type I informants [=those with little formal educ]. Other variants, which occur sporadically, are /frɪz, frɛz, frozən, frizən/. In this study /froz/ is used by all of the informants except one; one type I informant has /frozən/. **1975** Allen *LAUM* 2.19 (as of c1950), With a single exception *froze* . . is the preterit form exclusively found in the U[pper] M[idwest]. The rare variant *friz* . . is used by one rural Iowa Type II speaker [=mid-aged, with approx hs educ] . . in South Midland territory.

3 past pple: usu *frozen;* also *freeze(d), froze;* also **chiefly Sth, S Midl** *frez, friz;* occas *frizen, frozed.*

1837 Sherwood *Gaz. GA* 69, *Provincialisms. . . Frozed* and *freezed,* for frozen. **1893** Shands *MS Speech* 31, *Frez. . .* Negro for . . *frozen.* **1903** *DN* 2.293 **Cape Cod MA** (as of 1850s), Many strong verbs use the same form for the past and past participle . . *freeze—froze.* **1906** [see 2 above]. **1908** *DN* 3.313 **eAL, wGA,** *Friz. . . Frez* is also used. **1923** (1946) Greer-Petrie *Angeline Doin' Society* 22 **csKY,** Everything will be frez up solid by mornin'. **1943** *LANE* Map 648 **NEng,** The past participle of *freeze* was recorded . . in the following cases: [29 instances of *frozen,* 28 of *froze*]. **1954** *Harder Coll.* **cwTN,** *Freeze. . .* Past pple: froze, friz (occ.) **c1960** *Wilson Coll.* **csKY,** *Friz* (p. and p.p.) . . froze (p.p.) . . frizen (p.p.) **1965–70** *DARE* (Qu. OO15b, . . *"If he had been out last night he would have* ——— *his ears."*) 301 Infs, **throughout US,** Froze; 13 Infs, **scattered,** Froze [in var phrr]; **KY**5, 37, **MD**43, **NC**60, **VA**38, **WI**47, Frozed; **SC**9, 26, Freeze (off); **MS**44, Freezed; **KY**94, Some people would say frez [frɛz]; **MS**69, 71, **NY**34, Friz. **1975** Allen *LAUM* 2.19 (as of c1950), Occasional recording of the past participle [in the Upper Midwest] . . yields . . eight [instances] of *froze.*

4 ppl adj: usu *frozen;* also *froze;* also **chiefly Sth, S Midl** *friz;* occas *freezed, frizzed, frozed;* rarely *frozent.*

1805 (1965) Lewis *Jrls.* 206, Saw the Standing water froze over. **1838** Neal *Charcoal Sketches* 75 **Philadelphia PA,** "It's raining friz potatoes," observed Linkum. **1906** *DN* 3.137 **nwAR,** Things were all friz up this morning. **1931–33** *LANE Worksheets* **seMA,** The lake is froze up. **1933** *AmSp* 8.1.24 **sAppalachians,** *Acrost, . . suddent,* and *frozent.* **1965–70** *DARE* (Qu. B34, *When a pond . . becomes entirely covered with ice, you say it is* ———) 115 Infs, **widespread,** Froze over; 44 Infs, **scattered,** Froze (solid); 30 Infs, **scattered,** Froze [in var phrr]; **GA**3, **MD**40, **NC**78, **NY**61, Frozed [in var phrr]; **MS**60, **NJ**69, Freezed over; **OK**13, Friz (over); **KY**76, Friz—old-fashioned; **MI**68, I've even heard "friz over" and "frizzed over"; (Qu. B33b, . . *"The pond is just* ——— *over."*) 69 Infs, **scattered,** Froze; 15 Infs, **scattered,** Froze [in var phrr]; **NC**78, 81, **NY**61, Frozed (over); **OK**13, Friz; (Qu. B33a) Inf **AZ**7, Tank's froze over; (Qu. B36) Inf **NC**49, Window's frozed over. **1968** *DARE* (QR facing p85) Inf **GA**52, Was I friz. **1968** *DARE* Tape **CT**2, The first corn we planted got froze; **AK**9, It's all froze; **IN**12, I'm nearly froze to death. **1974** Fink *Mountain Speech* 9 **wNC, eTN,** The river was friz over solid.

B Senses.

1 To intimidate; to snub.

1876 Harte *Two Men* 93 **CA,** Why, the first day I came here on business, the old man froze me so that I couldn't thaw a deposit out of my pocket. **1967** *DARE* (Qu. II6, *If you meet somebody who used to be a friend, and he pretends not to know you: "When I met him on the street he* ———*."*) Inf **IL**20, Froze me.

2 =**frost v 2.**

1967 *DARE* (Qu. NN7, *Exclamations of surprise: "They're getting married next week? Well,* ———*."*) Inf **AL**30, Wouldn't that freeze you [FW: heard].

freeze n

1 A sherbet-like frozen dessert.

1967 *Rockport Pilot* (TX) 30 Mar sec 1 3, [Advt:] Freeze[,] Silver Valley[,] Half Gallon . . 39¢ Featuring: Cherry Vanilla And Cocoanut Pineapple. **1969** *DARE* (Qu. H63) Inf **CA**113, *Freeze*—a favorite Mexican dessert; colored ice, sort of like sherbet.

2 also *freeze and melt, freeze-out:* A children's game played in various ways; see quots. Cf **statues**

1966 *DARE* File **Boston MA,** *Freeze* is something like *Ten Steps.* **1970** *DARE* (Qu. EE33) Inf **FL**48, *Freeze*—"It" tells the player "Take one baby step," or "Take three giant steps." Player says "Mother, may I?" and tries to carry out orders before "it" shouts "Freeze" and he must stop where he is; **FL**51, Freeze—you tell someone to freeze and he must stop where he is; more an endurance test than an actual game; **SC**68, Freeze—you just told someone to freeze, even just walking down the street; **MO**30, Freeze; **OH**46, Freeze-out—like statues. **1975** Ferretti *Gt. Amer. Book Sidewalk Games* 167, *Freeze and Melt.* "It" stands in the center of a circle of other players, who move, wheel about, and advance on "It" until he yells, "Freeze!" Then, they have to stop exactly where they are and in position. . . If "It" detects someone moving . . he points him out, and that is the signal for all other players to pummel the mover. If "It" does not detect a move, he can permit the frozen to move again by shouting, "Melt!" Then, the process is repeated. *Ibid* 209, Another game . . is Statues, known also in the eastern part of the country as *Freeze.* "It" . . grabs the player's arm and pulls him or her into the street. . . That player has to remain still and in the position in which he has landed.

3 Unfriendly treatment; the cold shoulder.

1942 Berrey-Van den Bark *Amer. Slang* 352.1, *Slight; snub. . .* The chill, . . the cold shoulder, . . the freeze. **1953** Boyle AP column 9 Apr *(DAS),* Women are quick to put the freeze on free loaders. **1967** *DARE* (Qu. II5b, *When you don't want to have anything to do with a certain person because you don't like him, you might say, "I'd certainly like to give him the* ———*."*) Inf **TX**27, Freeze.

freeze and melt See **freeze n 2**

freeze-cat n

1 also *freezy-cat:* One who cannot tolerate the cold. **[cat n 1f]**

1942 Whipple *Joshua* 465 **UT** (as of c1860), Mebbe I'm a freeze-cat, but *I'm going home!* **1989** *DARE* File **IA** (as of 1980), I knew a woman dating a man from Florida who didn't want to go outside in wintertime and she called him a freeze-cat; **WI** (as of 1969), When I first moved here I picked up the phrase freezy-cat from my Wisconsin friends, meaning one who has a low tolerance for cold.

2 See quot.

1958 McCulloch *Woods Words* 67 **Pacific NW,** *Freeze-cat*—A pole-cat.

freezed See **freeze** v **A2, 3, 4**

freeze down to See **freeze on to**

freezen See **freeze** v **A2**

freeze off v phr

c1970 *DARE* File **eTX,** In rural communities in Nacogdoches County, *freeze off* means to freeze.

freeze on to v phr Also *freeze (down) to, freeze on* **chiefly NEast, S Midl**

To take hold of; to hold tight to.

1840 Haliburton *Clockmaker* (3d ser) 40 **CT,** This is the way, freeze down solid to it, square up to it, as if you was a-goin' to have an all-outdoor fight of it. **1851** Hall *College Words* 135 **MA,** We *freeze* to apples in the orchards, . . and alas! some even go so far as to *freeze* to the ladies. **1867** Twain *Jumping Frog* 12, He would grab that other dog jest by the j'int of his hind leg and freeze to it. **1867** Crawford *Mosby* 241 **VA,** Before the match was applied to the wagons containing the officers' baggage, our men *froze* on the valises, and brought them away. **1902** (1904) Rowe *Maid of Bar Harbor* 239 **ME,** And she froze to the idea right off. **1924** *DN* 5.290, *Freeze on to*. . . To hold tightly. "If the ball comes your way, you freeze on to it." **1927** *AmSp* 2.354 **WV,** I froze onto the pair of shoes that I bought at the sale. **1950** *WELS ("If I ever see another one of these, I'll certainly ______ it.")* 2 Infs, **WI,** Freeze on to. **1954** *Harder Coll.* **cwTN,** *Freeze onto*. . . To hold fast. **c1960** *Wilson Coll.* **csKY,** *Freeze on* (or *onto*). . . To cling to, sometimes very nervously. **1966–68** *DARE* (Qu. V5b, *If you take something that nobody seems to own, you might say, "Before anybody else gets it, I'm going to ______ this."*) Infs **NC**33, **NY**100, Freeze on to; **DC**1, I froze on to that one.

freeze-out n

1 A period of freezing weather that is extremely destructive to crops.

1968 *DARE* Tape **CA**36, We could tell when Florida would periodically have a freeze-out down there . . because our prices would be higher.

2 The freezing of shallow lakes and the resultant killing of fish and other aquatic life.

1972 *WI Conserv. Bulletin* 37.6.6, Winterkill or "freezeouts" of Wisconsin waters is an age-old story. . . If the lake is shallow and rich in plant life, the demand for oxygen very often exceeds the supply in midwinter months. A winterkill of fish life and aquatic organisms is the result.

3 See **freeze** n **2.**

freeze owl n Cf **shivering owl**

Prob =**screech owl.**

1981 Harper–Presley *Okefinokee* 96 (as of a1951) **seGA,** Jack added that the "freeze owl" will not holler anymore if someone throws salt in a fire.

freeze tag n Also *frozen tag* **chiefly Nth**

A children's tag game in which a player cannot be tagged as long as he is completely motionless, or in which a player must remain motionless from the time he is tagged by "it" until he is freed by another player.

1967 *DARE* FW Addit **eOR,** Freeze tag. **1968** *DARE* (Qu. EE33) Inf **NY**94, Freeze tag—one is "it," the others run around; when "it" touches somebody he has to freeze until somebody else comes around and touches him; **WV**10, Freeze tag—same as stoop tag. . . "It" has to hold a base while trying to tag other people. If he tries to catch another person they can stoop or freeze for any length of time and he can't catch them. If he goes away from the base, untagged people can go in and recapture tagged people; **NY**28, **PA**163, Frozen tag. **1972** *Yesterday* 1.3.32 **WI** (as of c1920), In freeze tag you couldn't be tagged if you "froze," only while you were moving. **1975** *Ford Times* Mar 22 **MI,** Freeze tag. **1981** Pederson *LAGS Basic Materials* **Gulf Region,** 3 infs, Freeze tag; 1 inf, Freeze tag—if you touch a person, you have to "freeze," and someone else must "unfreeze" you; 1 inf, Freeze tag—"freeze" when tagged. [This question was asked chiefly in urban areas.]

freeze to See **freeze on to**

freeze-up n **chiefly AK** Cf **break-up 1**

The freezing of bodies of water which renders them unnavigable; the time at which this occurs.

1876 *Oregon Weekly Tribune* (The Dalles) 29 Jan. 3/2 *(OEDS),* We hope to see the day when . . all the inhabitants east of the Cascades will not be detrimentally affected by any freeze-up which may occur. **1901** Grinnell *Gold Hunting* 93 **AK,** We cannot get much out before freeze-up this year, but ought to do fairly well next summer. **1959** Hart *McKay's AK* 31, *Freeze-up:* The time of the year when sea ports are icebound and all bodies of water are frozen. This condition does not exist in most coastal ports of southeastern and south central Alaska which are open the year around. **1973** *AK Mag.* 39.1.16/2 **cwAK** (as of c1904), At the approach of freeze-up, the whole town was getting ready for the annual Arctic Brotherhood Ball.

freezy-cat See **freeze-cat 1**

freightbird n

=**crested flycatcher.**

1910 Wayne *Birds SC* 101, *Myiarchus crinitus*. . . This bird has many local names and among them "Freight Bird." **1950** *PADS* 14.30 **s,cSC,** *Freight bird*. . . The southern crested flycatcher. **1954** Sprunt *FL Bird Life* 291, *Myiarchus crinitus*. . . Local Names: Freight-bird.

freighter n

1 One who transports goods overland in a **freight wagon. chiefly West** *old-fash*

1852 *Knickerbocker* 39.224 **CA,** The freighters were . . impatient of delay. **1884** Shepherd *Prairie Exper.* 200 **WY, MT,** The freighters are a special class, who have much to tell of the glories of the road in the days gone by. **1907** White *AZ Nights* 229, A freighter without the fear of God in his soul. **1935** Davis *Honey* 309 **OR,** A freighter traveled it, hauling ore and concentrates from some placer mines around Burnt River. **1937** Sandoz *Slogum* 17 **NE,** Libby . . whipped thick cream into the salad dressing with a fork—not for the freighters . . but for the Slogum table. **1966** *DARE* Tape **ID**2, How many freighters was killed by the Indians; **MT**5, I knowed quite a few o' them old freighters, and this one fella drove . . sixteen head o' horses in his team.

2 =**freight wagon.**

1885 *Century Illustr. Mag.* 31.65/1 **CO,** Heavily loaded freighters were lurching in, every mule straining in his collar. **1929** *Randolph Enterprise* (Elkins, W. Va.) 14 Nov. 1/3 *(DA),* The Conestoga Wagon, known as the freighter, hauled travelers, too. **1968–70** *DARE* (Qu. N41b, *Horse-drawn vehicles to carry heavy loads*) Infs **CA**171, 207, **IN**42, Freighter.

3 See quot.

1967–68 *DARE* (Qu. N11, *A very large truck used to haul freight, new cars, and other big loads*) Infs **MN**35, **MO**3, **OR**10, Freighter; **MN**19, Road train freighter.

4 See quot.

1925 in 1979 *DARE* File **NH,** [Letter to *DN* Ed:] *Freighters*—Men who go to Labrador, cod-fishing.

freighting wagon See **freight wagon**

freight one's pack v phr Cf **pull one's freight**

To leave (a job).

1958 McCulloch *Woods Words* 67 **Pacific NW,** *Freighting his pack*—A man quitting camp with his packsack on his back.

freight team n **West** *old-fash*

Two or more draft animals harnessed to a **freight wagon;** the animals and wagon together.

1860 in 1937 *Colorado Mag.* 14.207, Met a freight team here [=near the Platte bluffs], returning from Denver with oxen. **1923** E. G. Wade *Early Days at Paonia* (MS) 3 **CO** *(DA),* Samuel Wade hired freight teams. **1966–69** *DARE* Tape **CA**138, All freight came in here by freight teams. They had two wagons usually and maybe twelve, fourteen horses; **CA**159, About sixteen freight teams on that haul; **WA**2, Freight team—a twelve-horse team which brought supplies before the railroad was built. **1967** *DARE* FW Addit **eOR,** Freight team—a team of horses to pull logs, wagons, etc.

freight wagon n Rarely *freighting wagon* **chiefly West** See Map

A large, sturdy wagon used to carry heavy loads.

1855 Barnum *Life* 69 **CT,** My father . . ran a freight wagon to Norwalk. **1880** Ingham *Digging Gold* 307 **cwSD,** In this Black Hills forwarding business there are regularly employed one thousand four hundred large freight wagons. **1910** Hart *Vigilante Girl* 122 **CA,** Behind them [were] freight-wagons, with lines of mule teams and long strings of pack-mules. **1965–70** *DARE* (Qu. N41b, *Horse-drawn vehicles to carry heavy loads*) 22 Infs, **chiefly West,** Freight wagon; **AZ**3, Freighting wagon; (Qu. N41a, . . *Horse-drawn vehicles . . to carry people*) Infs **CA**147, 203, **WA**31, **WY**4, Freight wagon(s); **CA**97, Freight wagon—pulled by two or four horses; very large, with moveable sides; (Qu. N11) Inf **WA**1, Freight wagon. [No Infs young] **1966–70** *DARE* Tape **CA**205, I didn't travel in a covered wagon . . my dad drove a six-up team and a freight wagon, but it wasn't a covered; **NM**13 (as of c1880), It took a lot of beef to supply the miners. There was nothing, only freight wagons, and what bacon . . and stuff of that kind that they got, had to come from the Missouri River, freighted, in here; **MT**5, Me and my dad freighted quite a bit here too. I used to go with him with freight wagons; he'd take one wagon, me another.

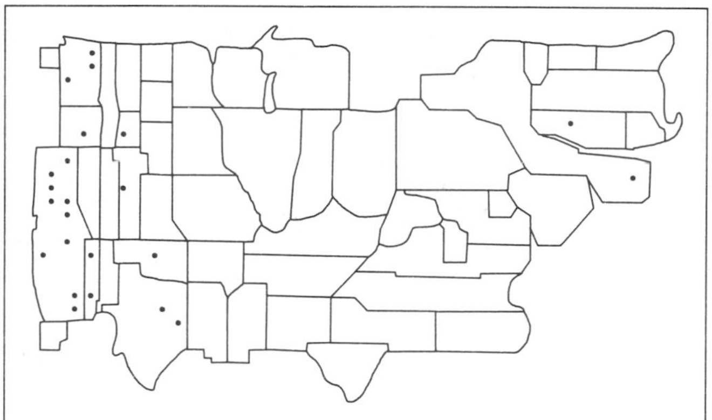

•freight wagon + var (Qq. N41a, b, N11)

freindschaft n Usu |ˈfraɪn(d)ˌšaft| Also sp *freinschaft, freundschaft* [PaGer var of Ger *Freundschaft* friendship] **PaGer area**

One's relatives; an extended family.

1872 Haldeman *PA Dutch* 57, In English conversation one may hear expressions like "He belongs to the *freindschaft*" (he is a kinsman or relation). **1882** (1971) Gibbons *PA Dutch* 22, Weddings are also highly festive occasions, but they are confined to the "freundschaft," and to much smaller numbers. **1914** *DN* 4.157 **sePA,** The 'freinschaft' is the 'relationship.' **1939** Aurand *Quaint Idioms* 14 **sePA,** Ei, such a big *freundschaft.* **1950** Klees *PA Dutch* 422, With all the friends and the *freindschaft* (relationship) too dropping in between Christmas and New Year, . . the . . cake boxes brimming over with cookies were soon emptied. **1967–68** *DARE* (Qu. Z28, . . *Immediate family*) Inf **PA**152, [fraɪndšɔft]; (Qu. Z9, . . *Others related to you by blood*) Inf **PA**18, [ˈfrɔnˌšɔft]—Dutch; **PA**55, 148, [ˈfraɪnˌšaft].

frejol See **frijole**

French n Usu |frɛnč|; also |frænč, frinč|

A Forms.

1934 *AmSp* 9.211 **Sth,** Words having standard [ɛn] . . generally have [in] before [tʃ]. . . *French.* **1954** *Harder Coll.* **cwTN,** *French* [fræntʃ] *harp.* **c1960** *Wilson Coll.* **csKY,** *French* is often /fræntʃ/.

B As noun.

1 See **frenching.**

2 A children's game involving twelve progressively difficult maneuvers with a ball.

1968 *Chicago Tribune* (IL) 15 Sept mag sec 78, We'll play French. . . we've got girls . . that can go all the way thru French—12 steps—and never drop the ball. Throw the ball against the building once and catch it without a bounce. That's one. Throw it again, twice, and catch it on one bounce. That's two. Now throw it above your head, clap your hands and catch it. Three times. That's—got the idea? Ever play French left-handed?

French aunt n Cf **German aunt**

A flighty woman.

1967 *DARE* (Qu. HH30) Inf **MN**2, French aunt—giddy and flighty.

French ball See **ball** n[1] **3**

French bean n Also *French string bean* Cf **green bean, Italian bean**

A cultivated bean *(Phaseolus vulgaris).*

1890 James *Mother James' Cooking* 146, *French Beans a la Maitre d'Hôtel.* Pick, string, and cut up the beans. . . Put . . Bechamel sauce into a stewpan with . . butter, . . parsley, little nutmeg, mignonette pepper, salt, and the juice of half a lemon. . . When well mixed throw in the beans, and toss the whole. . . *French Beans, with Fine Herbs.* Boil the beans as above [etc]. **1900** Lyons *Plant Names* 284, *Phaseolus vulgaris.* . . French String Bean. **1968** *DARE* (Qu. I14, *Kinds of beans that you eat in the pod before they're dry*) Inf **MN**12, French bean. **1976** Bailey–Bailey *Hortus Third* 854, *Phaseolus vulgaris.* . . French bean.

French blackbird n

=**bobolink B.**

1826 Flint *Recollections* 243 **MO,** I saw early in the spring a flock of those merry and chattering birds, that we call a bob-a-link, or French black-bird. **1956** MA Audubon Soc. *Bulletin* 40.130, *Bobolink.* . . French Blackbird (Mass. As a distinctive kind of blackbird.) **1957** *AmSp* 32.181 **MA,** French blackbird . . Bobolink.

French candy n *old-fash*

See quot 1950.

1950 *PADS* 14.30 **SC,** *French candy.* . . Any sort of candy in the shape and size of bonbons, such as chocolate drops, gum drops, etc., and including the small boxes of assorted bonbons and chocolates. French candy was contrasted with stick candy. Obsolescent. **1956** McAtee *Some Dialect NC* 17, *French candy* . . candy in small pieces as contrasted to stick candy; came to the stores in five-gallon buckets; hence, bucket candy. **1968–69** *DARE* (Qu. H82b, *Kinds of cheap candy that used to be sold years ago*) Infs **CA**105, **PA**210, **VA**18, 26, French candy; **VA**13, French candy—little balls, half to three-quarters of an inch in size; old-fashioned; mostly peppermint and cinnamon; **IN**7, French mixed candy.

French clover n

1 A clover (here: *Trifolium incarnatum*).

1826 *New Mo. Mag.* XVII.II.252 *(DA),* In one part of the country, you find the English walnut, and the French walnut; . . in another, the English clover, and the French clover. **1889** Vasey *Ag. Grasses* 82, *Trifolium incarnatum* (French clover) . . has been introduced and tried to some extent for cultivation. **1936** Winter *Plants NE* 97, *Trifolium incarnatum.* . . French Clover.

2 A globe amaranth (here: *Gomphrena globosa*).

1892 *Jrl. Amer. Folkl.* 5.102 **nOH,** *Gomphrena globosa,* French clover.

French cruller n [**cruller**]

A **cruller** with an esp distinct twist.

1965 *Rhinelander Daily News & New North* (WI) 12 Aug 14/3, [Advt:] *Bakery Dept. Elm Tree French Crullers*[,] Pkg. Of 12[,] 39¢. **1970** *DARE* (Qu. H26, *A round cake of dough, cooked in deep fat, with a hole in the center*) Inf **PA**239, Crullers (also called French crullers) and twists . . refer to the different shapes; (Qu. H28, *Different shapes or types of doughnuts*) Infs **CA**184, **NY**237, French crullers. **1979** *DARE* File **WI,** A French cruller is, I think, probably made of the same sort of dough as raised donuts, and is about six times longer than it is wide, twisted like a rope, fried in hot fat, and often glazed.

French doughnut n

A light, deep-fried cake which is especially sweet and is freq crimped or twisted in shape.

1950 *WELS (Different shapes or sizes [of doughnuts])* 2 Infs, **WI,** French doughnuts. **1966–69** *DARE* (Qu. H28) Infs **CA**11, **IL**97, French doughnuts; **CA**118, French doughnuts have a different taste and texture but are shaped like a regular doughnut; **IL**20, French doughnut—hollow, light, and fluffy; **IL**49, French doughnut—fluted; **ND**10, French doughnut—twisted; (Qu. H32) Inf **HI**32, French doughnuts—light and rippled; (Qu. HH30) Inf **WA**1, French doughnut. **1971** *AmSp* 46.79 **Chicago IL,** Light, glazed doughnut: *French doughnut.*

French drake n

Either the American **merganser** or the **red-breasted merganser.**

1957 *AmSp* 32.181, French drake . . Red-breasted merganser, . . American merganser.

French dry clean v phr, n *joc*

See quots.

1950 *WELS* 1 Inf, **cwWI,** French dry clean—turn shirt wrong side out and wear it. **1953** *AmSp* 28.144 **cFL,** Baths involving only a portion of the body are variously called *cat bath, spot bath, French dry clean.*

French duck n

1 =mallard.

1814 in 1815 Lit. & Philos. Soc. NY *Trans.* 1.134, Anas boschas. . . The French, or gray duck, is much larger than the common. **1820** in 1822 Morse *Rept. Indian Affairs* 2.32 **WI,** Throughout this north-western country, are . . several kinds of ducks, as the black, French (resembling the tame) wood duck, &c. **1889** *Century Dict.* 1789 **LA,** *French duck,* the mallard. **1957** *AmSp* 32.181, I first heard the name *French duck* for the mallard in Louisiana. . . *French duck* . . has been heard in Alabama and Mississippi also. **1983** *Reinecke Coll.* 5 **LA,** *French Duck* . . mallard. The mallard is circumpolar, and is the ancestor of most domesticated ducks, including Rouen ducks, which have the same plumage as the wild of the species. La. French, "canard français."

2 =white-winged scoter.

1957 *AmSp* 32.181, French duck. . . White-winged scoter . . Lake Huron.

French fiddle n Cf *DS* FF7, **French harp 1**

A harmonica.

1941 *LANE* Map 413, 1 inf, **swNH,** French fiddle, old-fashioned jocular term.

French flat n **NYC** *hist*

One floor of a house which has been divided for subleasing.

1879 Stockton *Rudder Grange* 67 **NYC,** He . . was now keeping house in a French flat in the upper part of the city. **1882** McCabe *NY by Sunlight* 250 **NYC,** In the lower part are a number of tenement-houses, but above 34th street the upper floors of the buildings are laid off in "French flats," some of which are elegant and stylish. **1938** Hart *New Yorkers* 176, Many of the reasonably well to do of the city lived in Greenwich Village, in apartments then [c1870] known as "French Flats" which were separately sublet floors of what previously had been private houses. There was, at first, only one door bell for the entire house; callers rang one or more times according to the floor on which their hosts dwelt.

French frog n [Prob in ref to the fact that frogs' legs are considered a delicacy in France] **CA, NV**

A frog.

1968–69 *DARE* (Qu. P21, *Small frogs that sing or chirp loudly in spring*) Inf **CA**105, French frogs; (Qu. P22, . . *A very large frog that makes a deep, loud sound*) Inf **CA**120, French frogs—big ones; **CA**156, French frogs; **NV**8, French frogs—the large edible frog; local name.

French gentian n [Perh var of fringed gentian]

A **gentian** (here: *Gentiana crinita*).

1940 Clute *Amer. Plant Names* 260, *Gentiana crinita.* French gentian. **1959** Carleton *Index Herb. Plants* 49, *French Gentian:* Gentiana crinita. **1968** *DARE* (Qu. S26c, *Wildflowers that grow in woods*) Inf **PA**176, French gentian.

French goose n

1 =Canada goose.

1923 U.S. Dept. Ag. *Misc. Circular* 13.35 **LA,** *Branta canadensis canadensis. . . Vernacular Names. . . In local use. . .* French goose. **1957** *AmSp* 32.181 **LA,** *French goose* for the Canada goose. **1982** Elman *Hunter's Field Guide* 269, *Canada Goose. . . Common & Regional Names* . . French goose.

2 See quot.

1981 in 1986 *Barrick Coll.* **cPA,** *French goose*—pig stomach; hog maw (a common dish; the stomach is cleaned, filled with sausage, potatoes and cabbage, and roasted).

French grass n [Cf *EDD*]

1 A **scurf pea** (here: *Psoralea onobrychis*).

1911 *Century Dict. Suppl., Grass. . . French grass. . .* The sainfoin psoralea, *Psoralea Onobrychis,* an American plant somewhat resembling the sainfoin, found from Ontario to South Carolina and westward to Missouri. **1936** IL Nat. Hist. Surv. *Wildflowers* 164, French Grass—*Psoralea Onobrychis. . .* Some species of *Psoralea* have edible tuberous roots, but not the French Grass. **1940** Steyermark *Flora MO* 300, French Grass *(Psoralea Onobrychis . .).* **1959** Carleton *Index Herb. Plants* 49, *French grass:* . . Phalaris arundinacea; Psoralea onobrychis.

2 A **canary grass** (here: *Phalaris arundinacea*).

1912 Baker *Book of Grasses* 94, Under the names of Ribbon-grass, . . and French grass, a variety of the Reed Canary [=*Phalaris arundinacea*] was planted in the gardens of earlier days. **1959** [see **1** above].

French grunt n

A **grunt 1** (here: *Haemulon flavolineatum*).

1898 U.S. Natl. Museum *Bulletin* 47.1306, *French Grunt. . .* One of the most strongly marked species. **1902** Jordan–Evermann *Amer. Fishes* 427, *French Grunt. . .* Usually found on sandy shores, and is taken in traps, seines, or with the hook. **1935** Caine *Game Fish* 82, The French grunt is one of the most beautiful, as well as the smallest, of the grunts. **1960** Amer. Fisheries Soc. *List Fishes* 166.

French harp n

1 A harmonica. **chiefly W Midl, TX, Cent** See Map

1891 Riley *Swimmin'-Hole* 11 **IN,** A slice of worter-melon's like a frenchharp in theyr hands. **1905** *DN* 3.80 **nwAR,** *French harp. . .* Harmonica. Common. **1908** *DN* 3.313 **eAL, wGA. 1912** *DN* 3.568 **MS, MO. 1915** *DN* 4.183 **swVA. c1940** *Hall Coll.* **wNC, eTN,** I was told of an accomplished player . . known as 'French Harp' Slim, who . . has made some phonograph records. **1958** Humphrey *Home from the Hill* 51 **neTX,** And from his jumper pocket he would draw his battered old French-harp . . and sound a chord. **c1960** *Wilson Coll.* **csKY,** French harp. **1965–70** *DARE* (Qu. FF7, *A small musical instrument that you blow on, and move from side to side in your mouth*) 182 Infs, **chiefly W Midl, TX, Cent,** French harp; (Qu. HH30) Infs **KY**78, **TX**1, **VA**42, French harp. **1973** Allen *LAUM* 1.207 (as of c1950), *Mouth harp* . . dominates the Midland speech area [in the Upper Midwest] except for the extreme southeastern sector, where South Midland speech is typical and where the accepted form is *French harp.* **1986** Pederson *LAGS Concordance (Harmonica)* 336 infs, **chiefly inland Gulf Region, eTX,** French harp(s).

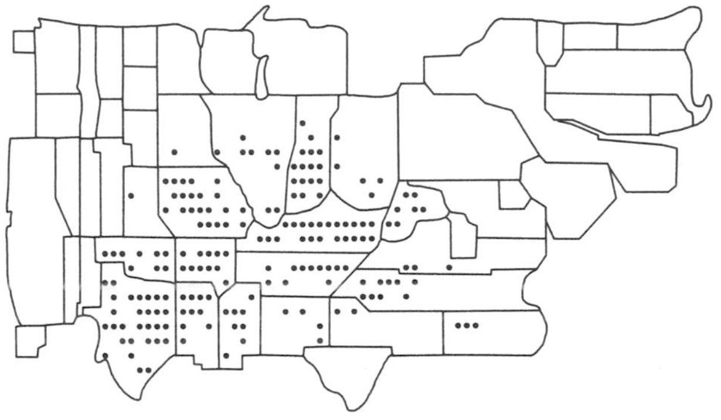

•French harp 1 (Qq. FF7, HH30)

2 A jew's harp.

1965–70 *DARE* (Qu. FF8) Infs **AL**10, **AR**47, **IL**60, 82, **KS**18, **MS**84, **PA**94, 247, **WA**18, French harp. **1971** Wood *Vocab. Change* 40 **Sth,** A harp with a kind of tine which is plucked while one blows against it, is known first as a *jew's harp* and second as a *juice harp. . . French harp* is not reported in Florida [but occurs occasionally in the other seven Sthn states investigated]. **1986** Pederson *LAGS Concordance (Jew's harp)* 5 infs, **Gulf Region,** French harp(s).

French hen n

A **ruffed grouse.**

1957 *AmSp* 32.181 **LA,** *French hen* for the ruffed grouse.

French hospitality n Cf **Dutch** adv

Minimal or nonexistent hospitality; see quot.

1968 *DARE* (Qu. HH30) Inf **CA**66, French hospitality—you pay for it.

French ice-cream soda n

1968 *DARE* FW Addit **Brooklyn NYC,** French ice-cream soda—an ice-cream soda with whipped cream added.

Frenchie See **Frenchy** n

frenching n Also *(black) French, dry-weather ~*

A plant disease of uncertain origin that causes leaves to narrow, thicken, curl, and turn white, and that especially affects tobacco and cotton.

1856 U.S. Patent Office *Annual Rept. for 1855: Ag.* 231 **FL,** Indian corn, however, is subject to "French;" and, in this case, the disease has been attributed to some imperfection of the soil. **1888** *Congressional Record* 12 May 4069/2 **MS,** Then it [=the cotton plant] begins to blight; then comes frenching and the shedding of squares and formes. **1940** *Newsweek* 12 Aug 47/1, If seedlings of Turkish tobacco are grown in fluids containing the drug [=sulfanilamide], the result is a condition similar to "frenching," a disease which has baffled plant experts for 250 years. **1957** *KY Folkl. Rec.* 3.64, In some parts of Western Kentucky it is called walloon; in other parts of the state, black french, dry weather french, frenching. **c1960** *Wilson Coll.* **csKY,** *Frenching. . .* A disease of tobacco plants that develops when the soil is too wet. **1966** *PADS* 45.13 **KY,** *French. . . = mosaic. . .* "We don't have many diseases, but I have seen some french." *Frenching. . .* A [tobacco] disease of obscure cause. The tips of the leaves turn white and the leaves become narrow and curled at the edges. Adequate fertilization will prevent the disease. . . "Frenching is not a problem around here." **1967** Key *Tobacco Vocab.* **GA, MO, PA, TN,** French. **CT,** Frenching.

French iris n [Perh in allusion to the *fleur-de-lis*]

A **flag** n[1].

1966 *DARE* (Qu. S24, *A wildflower that . . looks like a small blue iris*) Inf **ME**12, Blue lily or French iris.

French knot n [In ref to a needlework stitch that forms a small raised dot] Cf **gooseflesh**

1970 *DARE* (Qu. X58, *When you are cold, and little points of skin begin to come on your arms and legs, you have _____*) Inf **IL**135, French knots.

French love, hotter than adj phr Cf **Dutch love, hotter than**

1967 *DARE* (Qu. B3, *If a day is very hot, you say it's . . _____*) Inf NY34, "Hotter than French love," my father said.

French lozenger n [**lozenger**] Cf **Irish plum**

1941 *LANE* Map 257 **cwVT,** French lozengers, jocular name for onions.

frenchman n [See quot 1895] **VA**

In tobacco growing: see quots.

1688 in 1693 Royal Soc. London *Philos. Trans.* 17.948 **VA,** *Frenchmen* they call those Plants, whose Leaves do not spread and grow large, but rather spire upwards, and grow tall; these Plants they do not tend, being not worthy their Labour. **1895** (1896) Bruce *Economic Hist. VA* 1.439, [Tobacco] plants which had been guarded from injury . . showed . . a tendency to lag in their growth and to take a spiral shape. For this reason they were always referred to as "Frenchmen," a people who were associated in the Virginian mind with tallness and attenuation in form. **1899** (1912) Green *VA Folk-Speech* 185, *Frenchman. . .* Tall, spindling tobacco plants of a useless quality. **1944** *PADS* 2.66 **eVA,** *Frenchman; pl. Frenchmen. . .* Stalk(s) with short, erect small leaves and worthless as to quality.

Frenchman from Cork n *joc*

1941 *LANE* Map 454 *(Nicknames for an Irishman)* 1 inf, **cCT,** Frenchman from Cork.

Frenchman's buttons n

A **phlox** (here: *Phlox pilosa*).

1940 Clute *Amer. Plant Names* 228, *Phlox pilosa.* Frenchman's buttons.

Frenchman's style adv phr

=**catercorner B.**

1943 *LANE* Map 547 **seVT,** Walking Frenchman's style—crossing an intersection diagonally.

French melon n

A muskmelon (*Cucumis melo* or var thereof).

1797 Imlay *Western Terr.* 242, The seeds of water-melons are placed like those of the french melons. **1973** Allen *LAUM* 1.314 (as of c1950), Twice *sugar melon* appears as a synonym for *muskmelon,* as does *French melon* in a French bilingual community in Minnesota.

French mockbird See **French mockingbird 1**

French mocker See **French mockingbird 2, 6**

French mockingbird n

1 also *French mockbird:* =**brown thrasher.**

1731 (1754) Catesby *Nat. Hist. Carolina* 1.28, *The Fox coloured Thrush . .* is called in *Virginia* the *French Mock-Bird. . .* It sings with some variety of Notes. **1797** (1905) Latrobe *Jrl. of Latrobe* 111 **VA,** We stopped, and saw two of the birds, called the French mocking bird. **1810** Wilson *Amer. Ornith.* 2.22, The first, or Brown Thrush, from its inferiority of song being called the French, and the other the English Mocking-bird. A mode of expression probably originating in the prejudices of our forefathers; with whom every thing *French* was inferior to every thing *English.* **1877** Bartlett *Americanisms* 70, *Brown Thrasher (Turdus rufus.) . .* In Maryland, it is called the French Mocking-bird. **1917** (1923) *Birds Amer.* 3.179, *Brown Thrasher. . . Other Names. . .* French Mockingbird. *Ibid* 181, The song of this Thrasher . . suggests the Catbird's. **1942** McAtee *Dial. Grant Co. IN* 27 (as of 1890s), *French mockingbird . .* the brown thrasher *(Toxostoma rufum).* **1957** *AmSp* 32.182, French mockingbird . . Brown thrasher . . General [distribution of the name over the geographic range of the bird].

2 also *French mocker:* =**loggerhead shrike. S Atl, Gulf States**

1908 *DN* 3.313 **eAL, wGA,** *French mocker, French mocking-bird. . .* The butcher bird. Also called *loggerhead. . .* There is a superstition that this bird would speak French if its tongue were split. **1916** *DN* 4.345 **FL, GA,** *French mocking bird.* The butcher bird. **1950** *PADS* 14.30 **SC,** *French mockingbird. . .* The loggerhead shrike. **1957** *AmSp* 32.182, French mockingbird . . Southern shrike . . General [distribution of the name over the geographic range of the bird]. **1968** *DARE* (Qu. Q14, . . *Shrike*) Inf **GA**65, Butcher bird; French mocker; **LA**15, 29, Butcher bird; also called French mockingbird.

3 =**yellow-breasted chat.**

1957 *AmSp* 32.182 **AL, KY,** French mockingbird . . Yellow-breasted chat.

4 A **crested flycatcher** (here: *Myiarchus crinitus*).

1957 *AmSp* 32.182 **NC,** French mockingbird . . Great crested flycatcher.

5 =**summer tanager.**

1957 *AmSp* 32.182 **SC,** French mockingbird . . Summer tanager.

6 also *French mocker:* =**catbird 1.**

1966–67 *DARE* (Qu. Q14, . . *Catbird*) Infs **MS**6, **TX**37, French mocker; **DC**4, French mockingbird—imitates all birds.

French mulberry n

A **beauty-berry** *(Callicarpa americana)* with clustered usu red-purple fruit. Also called **Bermuda mulberry, bunchberry 3, foxberry 6, Mexican mulberry, sourberry, sour bush, sow-berry, Spanish mulberry, turkeyberry**

1860 Curtis *Cat. Plants NC* 87, *Bermuda or French Mulberry.* (Callicarpa Americana . .). Quite common in light soils and dry, open woods of the Lower District. **1897** *Jrl. Amer. Folkl.* 10.52, *Calicarpa* [sic] *Americana . .* French mulberry, Miller County, Mo. **1936** Whitehouse *TX Flowers* 118, *French Mulberry . .* is a low shrub 3–6 ft. high. **1950** *PADS* 14.30 **SC,** *French mulberry. . .* The Indian mulberry. **1969** *DARE* FW Addit **eNC,** French mulberry—a plant common on Hatteras Island. The standard name is American beautyberry. **1976** Bailey–Bailey *Hortus Third* 201.

French nettle n Also *French needle* [*EDD* (at *French* adj. 2. (10))]

A **dead nettle 1** (here: *Lamium purpureum*).

1959 Carleton *Index Herb. Plants* 49, French-nettle: *Lamium purpureum.* **1970** *DARE* (Qu. S14, . . *Prickly seeds, small and flat, with two prongs at one end, that cling to clothing*) Inf **KY**74, French needle—yellow flower; same as French nettle.

French pear n

Perh =**serviceberry.**

1967 *DARE* (Qu. I46, . . *Fruits that grow wild*) Inf **MI**53, French pear—sweet purplish berry. This *may* also be called Juneberry.

French peckerwood n Cf **French woodpecker, peckerwood**

=**pileated woodpecker.**

1957 *AmSp* 32.182 **IN,** French peckerwood . . Pileated woodpecker.

French pheasant n

=**hooded merganser.**

1957 *AmSp* 32.182 **MD,** French pheasant . . Hooded merganser.

French philopena See **philopena**

French pink n [Cf *EDD*]

1 =**cornflower 1.**

1896 Jewett *Pointed Firs* 132 **ME,** There was little trace of her flower garden except a single faded sprig of much-enduring French pinks.

1896 *Jrl. Amer. Folkl.* 9.191, *Centaurea Cyanus*. . French pink, Sulphur Grove, Ohio, Ala. **1900** Lyons *Plant Names* 89, *Centaurea cyanus*. . . French Pink. **1959** Carleton *Index Herb. Plants* 49, French-Pink: Centamea [sic] cyanus. **1967** *DARE* (Qu. S11, . . *Bachelor's button*) Inf **OR**5, French pink.

2 A **catchfly 1** (here: *Silene armeria* or *S. caroliniana*).

1893 *Jrl. Amer. Folkl.* 6.138, *Silene Armeria,* dwarf French pinks. Brunswick, N[ew] Y[ork]. **1966** *DARE* Wildfl QR Pl.53 Inf **WA**30, French pink.

French pony n [*French pony* a small, wiry horse used by Fr settlers in the Great Lakes region]

1930 Shoemaker *1300 Words* 23 **cPA Mts** (as of c1900), *French Pony*—A person of medium size, small boned, commonly supposed to be of Huguenot origin.

French pursley n

A **spurge** (here: *Euphorbia maculata*).

1897 *Jrl. Amer. Folkl.* 10.143, *Euphorbia maculata* . . French pursley, Sulphur Grove, Ohio.

French pusley n Cf **pussley**

The garden portulaca.

1892 *Jrl. Amer. Folkl.* 5.93 **sVT,** *Portulaca grandiflora* . . French pusley.

French sheet n

Prob a short-sheeted bed.

1906 *DN* 3.137 **nwAR,** *French sheet*. . . A bed which has been disarranged as a joke.

French sole n Cf **English sole**

The arrowtooth **flounder** *(Atheresthes stomias).*

1953 Roedel *Common Fishes CA* 57, *Arrowtooth Halibut*. . . Locally abundant. . . *Unauthorized Names* . . French sole.

French sparrow n [Cf *EDD* (at *French* adj. 3. (11))]

Prob =**English sparrow.**

1965–67 *DARE* (Qu. Q21, . . *Kinds of sparrows*) Inf **LA**2, English sparrow or French sparrow or town birds; **MS**63, French sparrow.

French spinach n

Garden orache *(Atriplex hortensis).*

1950 Stevens *ND Plants* 131, *Atriplex hortensis*. . . French Spinach.

French string bean See **French bean**

French tag n [Cf *EDD* (at *French* adj. 1. (6))]

See quots.

1891 *Jrl. Amer. Folkl.* 4.222 **Brooklyn NYC,** *French Tag.* In this game bounds are agreed upon, within which are numerous fences, high stoops, etc. Those who are pursued run up the steps and jump the fences to avoid being tagged, and the first caught becomes "it." . . Any one who is seen to go outside the bounds is at once declared to be "it" by the pursuer. **1909** (1923) Bancroft *Games* 96, *French Tag. 4 to 60 or more players. Indoors; out of doors*—In this form of tag certain boundaries are agreed upon beyond which players may not run, though they may climb or jump over any obstacles within the boundaries.

French turtle n Cf **caouane**

An unidentified turtle.

1968 *DARE* (Qu. P24, . . *Kinds of turtles*) Inf **LA**34, French turtle or yellowbelly.

French violet n

An unidentified violet.

1967 *DARE* (Qu. S11, . . *Blue violet*) Inf **LA**14, French violet.

Frenchweed n

1 A **galinsoga** (here: *Galinsoga ciliata*).

1935 (1943) Muenscher *Weeds* 490, *Galinsoga ciliata*. . . Frenchweed. . . Gardens, cultivated fields and waste places. . . Widespread.

2 A **pennycress** (here: *Thlaspi arvensis*).

1936 McDougall–Baggley *Plants of Yellowstone* 67, *Pennycress (Thlaspi arvense)*. . . Also known as *Frenchweed.* **1937** U.S. Forest Serv. *Range Plant Hdbk.* W189, This plant, known locally as bastard-cress, devilweed, fanweed, Frenchweed, stinkweed, treacle-mustard . . is now well distributed. **1943** KS State Bd. Ag. *Report* 62.256.25, *Pennycress* . . , also called *Fan-weed* and *Frenchweed*. . . when eaten by dairy cattle, imparts a very disagreeable flavor to milk and butter. **1968** *DARE* (Qu. K14, *Milk that has a taste from something the cow ate in the pasture*) Inf **MN**16, It has a bad taste—from Frenchweeds, a little broad-leafed plant; (Qu. S21, . . *Weeds . . that are a trouble in gardens and fields*) Inf **MN**23, Frenchweed or stinkweed.

French woodpecker n [Cf *EDD* (at *French* adj. 3. (12))] Cf **French peckerwood**

1 =**California woodpecker.**

1851 Woods *16 Months* 83, I have seen but few birds among the mountains of California. The large French woodpecker is the most common. It feeds upon the acorn, of which it lays up immense supplies after they have fallen from the trees. **1957** *AmSp* 32.182 **CA,** French woodpecker . . California woodpecker.

2 =**flicker** n² **1.**

1900 *Wilson Bulletin* 31.6, *French Woodpecker.* New Hampshire. Probably derived from the mongrel term, French-pie, which is one of the local names in common use in some parts of England for the Great Spotted Woodpecker. **1957** *AmSp* 32.182 **NH,** French woodpecker. . . Yellow-shafted flicker.

Frenchy adj

1 See quot. Cf **French aunt**

1900 *DN* 2.37 **New Orleans LA,** *Frenchy*. . . 1. Light-headed, foolish (of a man). 2. Forward, flirtatious (of a woman).

2 as *frenchy;* also *frency, frensy:* See quots. Cf **frenching.**

1889 *AN&Q* 3.285/2 **NC,** In North Carolina, land which suddenly and unaccountably fails to produce crops is said to *french;* such land is *frenchy.* **1918** *DN* 5.18 **NC,** *Frensy, frency,* withered, dry, as leaves of cotton or tobacco.

Frenchy n Also sp *Frenchie* **chiefly Nth, N Midl, West** See Map Cf **frog n B2**

A French person or person of French descent.

1942 Berrey–Van den Bark *Amer. Slang* 385.8, *Frenchman* . . Frenchy. **1945** Colcord *Sea Language* 63 **ME, Cape Cod, Long Island,** Frenchmen: at sea they are "Frenchies." **1950** *WELS (Nicknames for . . French)* 5 Infs, **WI,** Frenchy. **1956** Gold *The Man Who* 3 **wPA,** *There* he is on the midway, Grack the Frenchie, talking for his countstore. **1965–70** *DARE* (Qu. HH28, *Names and nicknames . . for people of foreign background*) 76 Infs, **chiefly Nth, N Midl, West,** Frenchy—French; **NY**249, **WA**16, Frenchy—Creole. **1970** Tarpley *Blinky* 256 **neTX,** *Nicknames for Acadian French or Louisiana French* . . Frenchie [listed as one of four "other responses"].

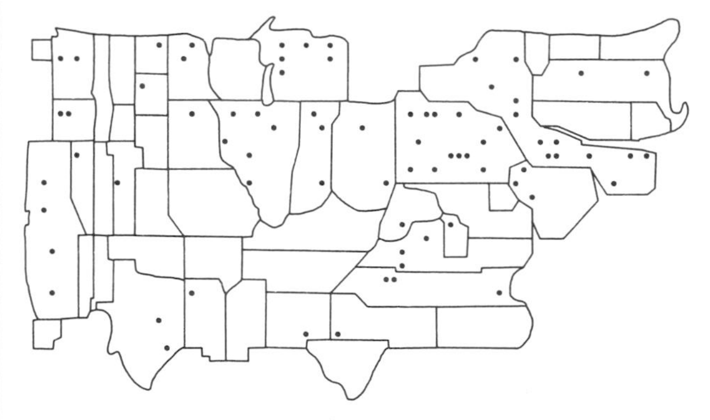

•Frenchy n (Qu. HH28)

frency See **Frenchy** adj **2**

freno n |'freno| [Span *freno* bridle or bit] **SW**

A bridle; a bit.

1933 (1950) Allen *Cowboy Lore* 61 **West,** *Spanish Words Used on the Range*. . . *Freno*—Bridle. **1944** Adams *Western Words* 62, *Freno (fray' no)*—This term means most often a bit, but it can mean the whole bridle, with the bit included.

frensy See **Frenchy** adj **2**

fresh adj Usu |frɛš|; also **esp S Midl** |fræš, freš|; for addit varr see quots Pronc-spp *fraish, frash, fresh*

A Forms.

1913 Kephart *Highlanders* 94 **wNC,** I've . . seed sign a-plenty and it's spang fraish. **1916** *DN* 4.340 **seOH,** The sound of *r* is usually inserted between certain *u* or *e* sounds and *sh* . . [as in] *fersh* (fresh). **1931** *PMLA* 46.1315 **sAppalachians,** *E,* short, becomes highland ɑ . . as in "frash" (or "fraish"). **1942** Hall *Smoky Mt. Speech* 20, [The vowel] [æ] is common also in . . *fresh*. . . The shift toward [e] . . is . . occasional in . . *fresh* [freɪ·ʃ]. . . *Fresh* is sometimes . . [frʌʃ]. **1961** *Mt. Life* Fall 9 **sAppalachians,** A *breath* o' frash air.

B Senses.

Of food, esp meat:

a Not salted or preserved with salt. Cf **fresh n 4**

1899 (1912) Green *VA Folk-Speech* 185, *Fresh*. . . Not salt, salted or pickled. . . *Fresh-meat*. . . Unsalted pork, beef, mutton to distinguish from bacon. **1927** *Ruppenthal Coll.* **KS,** *Fresh* adj, applied to . . unsalted butter. **1967** *DARE* (Qu. H45) Inf **SC**46, Fresh ham—one not cured.

b Salted, but not smoked or dried.

1905 *DN* 3.80 **nwAR,** *Fresh mackerel*. . . New salt mackerel. **c1970** Pederson *Dial. Surv. Rural GA (Meat from the side of a hog, that is salted but not smoked)* 1 inf, **seGA,** Fresh meat.

fresh n

1 An increased flow of water in a stream; a flood. **chiefly Sth, S Midl** Cf **freshet n 2**

1608 Smith *True Relation* 6 **VA,** The freshes by reason of the Rockes have left markes of the inundation 8. or 9. foote. **1738** *VA Gaz.* (Williamsburg) [Purdie-Dixon] 14 Apr 3/2, There was so great a Fresh in the River, occasion'd by excessive hasty Rains, that a great deal of Damage was done thereby. **1834** in 1956 Eliason *Tarheel Talk* 272 **NC,** The letter miscaried at the time of the last fresh. **1884** Amer. Philol. Assoc. *Trans.* 14.48, *Fresh* for 'freshet *or* overflow,' . . is still common among the lower classes of the South. **1906** Johnson *Highways Missip. Valley* 173 **MO,** The river put a terrible sediment on the bottoms this year—more than I've seen in any fresh for a long time. **1923** *DN* 5.207 **swMO.** **1937** *Hall Coll.* **eTN,** Come a fresh and knocked hit out. **1966–70** *DARE* (Qu. B24, . . *A sudden, very heavy rain*) Inf **MS**2, A fresh; (Qu. B27, *A sudden rush of water coming from heavy rain*) Infs **MS**2, **SC**9, **VA**42, **WV**7, Fresh; **VA**38, Going to have a fresh in the river; (Qu. C9, *Water from a river that comes up and covers low land when the river is high*) Infs **MS**2, **NC**87, **VA**38, Fresh; **VA**69, Fresh coming in; **SC**1, Fresh water.

2 A freshwater stream or swamp, esp one that flows into or adjoins a tidal river. **MD, VA**

1612 Smith *Map VA* 13, It groweth like a flagge in low muddy freshes. **1649** in 1940 *AmSp* 15.263 **VA,** Bounded . . upon a ffresh. **1794** in 1940 *AmSp* 15.263 **VA,** Thence crossing the main fresh. **1859** (1968) Bartlett *Americanisms* 162, *Fresh*. . . Used locally in Maryland for a stream distinct from the tide water. **1884** Amer. Philol. Assoc. *Trans.* 14.49, In Virginia it [=*fresh*] means also 'a small tributary of a larger river.' **1899** (1912) Green *VA Folk-Speech* 185, *Fresh*. . . A brook of fresh water; a small tributary stream; a current of fresh water running into tide-water. **1931** Embrey *Waters of State* 146 **VA** (*AmSp* 15.263), As a *fresh, i.e.,* freshwater stream, [the Rappahannock] runs its course . . to just below the fall line at Fredericksburg.

3 pl: The part of a tidal river immediately above the mingling of fresh and salt water; land adjoining such water. **C Atl**

1652 in 1940 *AmSp* 15.264 **VA,** Eight hundred Acres of Land . . Upon the South Side and within the ffreshes of Yorke river. **1683** in 1792 Belknap *Hist. NH* 3.5 **C Atl,** The Dutch inhabit those parts of the Province that lie on or near the Bay, and the Swedes the freshes of the Delaware. **1705** Beverley *Hist. VA* 2.6, The Damage occasion'd by these worms may be . . avoided. . . by running up into the Freshes with the Ship . . during the Five or Six Weeks, that the Worm is thus above Water. **1741** Oldmixon *Brit. Empire* 1.298 **sePA,** The River *Delaware,* above and below the Falls for a good Length, is called the *Freshes,* and near the Mouth are the *Marshes.* **1792** Belknap *Hist. NH* 3.5 **C Atl,** *Freshes* was understood to distinguish those parts of a river, below all the falls, where the fresh water which comes down from above is stopped by the flowing of the sea, and at the ebb, resumes its natural course; and which therefore, rises and falls with the tide. **1859** (1968) Bartlett *Americanisms* 162, The lands in Talbot County, Md., are divided into freshes and salts. **1899** (1912) Green *VA Folk-Speech* 185, *Freshes*. . . A stream or current of fresh water running into tide-water.

4 rarely *fresh meat:* Meat that is not preserved, esp freshly butchered pork; hence *freshie* a piece of fresh. **chiefly Sth**

1849 (1914) Kingsley *Diary* 39 **CT,** [We] had half of a beef sent aboard which as a fresh was quite a treat. **1883** (1972) McDowell *Dialect Tales* 83 **MS,** Never did she sit you down to her table unless she had "fresh," an' maybe a couple o' chickens besides. **1895** *DN* 1.388 **wCT, wNY,** *Fresh* . . butcher's meat, in distinction from salted or other meat. **1899** (1912) Green *VA Folk-Speech* 185, *Fresh*. . . Meat of a freshly killed hog; spareribs, chines, sausage. **1930** *DN* 6.81 **cSC,** *Fresh*. . . Newly-butchered pork. At "hog-killing time," one sends one's neighbor a basket of fresh,—spare-ribs, backbone, sausage, liver-pudding, and souse. Common. **1938** Rawlings *Yearling* 317 **nFL,** The bears is like to be our salvation for fresh this year. **1943** Writers' Program NC *Bundle of Troubles* 74, Mistah Whitt say he pay me with fresh meat, sech as liver, and jowls, and haslets, and foots, and backbone, and some sa'sage, and chittlin's. **1950** *PADS* 14.30 **SC,** *Fresh*. . . Any fresh meat, as game, etc. "Take dis meat sack an yo' gun, and git goin'. I ain't eat fresh in Gawd knows when." **1984** Wilder *You All Spoken Here* 90 **Sth,** Freshies, freshlets: Specific pork parts including brains, liver, lights, heart, chitlins that can't be set back and stored; unlike hams, shoulders, and slabs of bacon, they must be consumed immediately after hog killin'. **1986** Pederson *LAGS Concordance,* 1 inf, **cnFL,** Pan of fresh—pan of fresh meat.

fresh v

1 with *up:* To freshen, refresh.

1852 (1854) Kennedy *Horse-Shoe Robinson* 60 **cVA,** Put a sprinkling of salt in a bucket o' water, . . it sort of freshes the cretur up like. **1966** *DARE* (Qu. W30, *When a woman adds decorations to make something more attractive . . "I think I'll put on a few flowers to ______ it up."*) Inf **NC**33, Fresh.

2 with *up:* To become more cheerful, cheer up.

1969 *DARE* (Qu. GG27a, *To get somebody out of an unhappy mood, you might say to him, "Everything's going to be all right, so ______."*) Inf **GA**77, Fresh up.

3 Of a cow: =**freshen 2.**

1923 *DN* 5.207 **swMO,** *Fresh*. . . To freshen, as a cow upon dropping a calf. **1966–69** *DARE* (Qu. K10, *Words used about a cow that is going to have a calf*) Infs **SC**3, 34, 40, [Is] freshin(g); **GA**72, She's supposed to fresh; **VA**24, Going to fresh; (Qu. K11, *When a cow has a calf, you say she ______*) Infs **MN**7, **PA**178, 191, Freshed; **KS**17, Freshes; **GA**87, Is freshing.

4 To rain very hard. [Cf **fresh n 1**] Cf *DS* B24, 25

1884 Smith *Bill Arp's Scrap Book* 139 **GA,** And it aint done freshin' yet, for the frogs are croakin' and the air is full of swet and the salt sticks together and the camphor bottle is cloudy.

fresh bacon See **fresh side**

fresh cook n [**fresh** adj **B1**]

1890 *DN* 1.19 **NEng,** *Fresh:* in the phrase 'a fresh cook,' that is, one who uses little salt.

freshen v

1 freq with *up;* Of the wind: to increase.

1899 (1912) Green *VA Folk-Speech* 185, *Freshen*. . . To revive; to increase: the wind *freshens.* **1903** *DN* 2.294 **Cape Cod MA** (as of a1857), *Freshen up*. . . To blow hard. **1933** Rawlings *South Moon* 238 **FL,** The wind freshened and within an hour it was plain that most of the front would have to be abandoned. **1939** *LANE* Map 91 *(The wind is getting stronger),* [*Freshening* is used by 20 infs, *freshening up* by 2, chiefly along the eastern coast; 2 infs remark that it is used at sea.] **1966–69** *DARE* (Qu. B12, *When the wind begins to increase, you say it's ______*) Infs **FL**27, **IL**23, **MA**40, **NC**62, **OH**28, **TN**11, Freshening (up); **NH**5, A-freshening; (Qu. O19) Inf **SC**4, Freshening. [All Infs old] **1973** Allen *LAUM* 1.155 **IA** (as of c1950), The wind is freshening up. [1 inf]

2 Of a milk cow: to begin to produce milk after giving birth to a calf; hence, to give birth, be about to give birth. Cf **come fresh, fresh v 3**

1924 *DN* 5.295 **NH,** *Freshen*. . . To calve. **1927** *AmSp* 2.354 **WV,** The cow will freshen next month. **1932** (1974) Caldwell *Tobacco Road* 4 **GA,** Lov had told her that cows were not any good until they had been freshened. **1950** *WELS (When a cow has a calf, you say she ______)* 31 Infs, **WI,** (Has) freshened; *(A cow that is going to have a calf)* 32 Infs, **WI,** Going to freshen. **c1960** *Wilson Coll.* **csKY,** *Freshen*. . . Have a calf. **1965–70** *DARE* (Qu. K11, *When a cow has a calf, you say she ______*) 271 Infs, **widespread,** Freshens; 38 Infs, Freshened; 13 Infs, Has (just) freshened; **SC**30, Done freshened; (Qu. K10, . . *A cow that is going to have a calf*) 286 Infs, **widespread,** (She's) going to (*or* due to, about to, etc) freshen; 15 Infs, **scattered,** (She's) freshening; **OH**70, **WA**18, (She) freshens; **IA**1, Farmers with milk cows would use "going to freshen" or "she freshens"; **NY**233, **MI**27, (She's) bred to freshen; **NY**68, Time for her to freshen; **VT**16, She hasn't freshened yet. **1967–69** *DARE* Tape **MN**11, She [=a cow] was about to freshen; **MA**32, She hadn't freshened; finally did freshen, calf came dead. **1973** Allen *LAUM* 1.246 (as of c1950), The act of giving birth to a calf is indicated by three main groups of terms in the U[pper] M[idwest]: those with *calf* or *calve . . .,* those with *come,* and those with *fresh* or *freshen. . . Freshen* [has] . . a frequency of 29%.

3 To cleanse, free from impurities.

1942 (1960) Robertson *Red Hills* 188 **SC,** Brer Rabbit went to sunset prayer meeting to get himself freshened with the Lord.

4 To plow between rows of plants to keep the soil loose and weeds down.

1966 *DARE* Tape **GA**1, Every so often, maybe every ten days or two weeks, you'd go back and freshen . . around that cotton; corn the same way. . . Every time you'd plow it you'd put on a little bigger plow and a little wider sweep, which would throw more dirt to your cotton and your corn, till you plowed that middle plumb out.

freshener n

1 A moisture-resistant container; a bread box.

1968 *DARE* (Qu. D9, *To prevent bread and cake from drying, you put them in a* ______) Inf **MD**35, Freshener.

2 A cow which is about to calve. [**freshen 2**]

1967 *DARE* (Qu. K10) Inf **MN**4, She's heavy with calf; about due; a freshener or springer.

freshen up See **freshen v 1**

fresher n[1] [**fresh v 3**]

A cow which is about to calve or has recently calved.

1950 *WELS (A cow that is going to have a calf)* 1 Inf, **cWI,** A fresher. **1968** *DARE* (Qu. K1, *A cow that is giving milk*) Inf **LA**20, A fresher, when she's just started giving milk.

fresher n[2]

1901 *DN* 2.140 **Buffalo NY,** *Fresher. . .* Another name for prisoner's base.

freshet n

1 A small stream of fresh water. [*OED* "*Obs.* exc. *poet.*"]

1648 in 1940 *AmSp* 15.264 **VA,** On the end of a branch of the Pagan Bay Creek called the Freshet. *Ibid,* Upon a freshett called Moyses Run. **1956** Settle *Beulah Land* 5 **WV** (as of 18th cent), Where there is a cut, there will be a freshet; beyond the freshet, a spring branch; beyond the branch, a creek; beyond the creek, a river. **1967** *DARE* (Qu. C1, . . *A small stream of water not big enough to be a river*) Inf **OR**1, Freshet. **1973** Allen *LAUM* 1.237 (as of c1950), 2 infs, **MN,** Freshet [=small freshwater stream].

2 A usu sudden overflowing of a river; a flash flood. **chiefly Atlantic, Nth** See Map Cf **fresh n 1**

1784 (1888) Cutler *Life* 1.100 **ceNH,** The freshet in the river . . was so sudden that cattle on his intervale were in danger of being drowned. **1858** in 1956 Eliason *Tarheel Talk* 272 **NC,** We had a big freshit here the water got to the top of the Husk floor in the old mill. **1883** (1969) Leigh *GA Plantation* 267 **seGA,** The great enemies of the rice-planter are volunteer and freshets; . . [freshets are] floods, which come down from the hilly country in spring and autumn, and put the plantations under water. **1939** *LANE* Map 29, 1 inf, **swCT,** If they were plowed they'd wash away in a freshet; 1 inf, **cCT,** The meadows . . are sometimes flooded by freshets. **1965** *Amherst Rec.* (MA) 29 July 7/2, Several areas [along a river] . . might prove troublesome in a spring freshet or sudden rise in the river. **1965–70** *DARE* (Qu. B27, *A sudden rush of water coming from heavy rain*) 40 Infs, **chiefly Atlantic, Nth,** Freshet; (Qu. C9, *Water from a river that comes up and covers low land when the river is high*) 18 Infs, **chiefly Atlantic,** Freshet; (Qu. C2) Inf **FL**17, [The river is] having a freshet. [No Infs young, 49 of 60 Infs old] **1966–68** *DARE* Tape **NM**12, When these freshets would come, strong rains, the streets were washed out; **GA**11, Not too many oysters this past year because we had a freshet; **CA**100, They went to dairying . . until we had the big freshet, sixty, sixty-four. . . took most of the cattle . . drowned 'em and washed 'em out. **1988** *DARE* File **ME** (as of 1980), The St. John is known as a freshet river because of its large watershed. It could be sunny where you are but raining somewhere higher up in the watershed. This causes the river to suddenly and unexpectedly rise, then fall again as the effects of that rain go downriver.

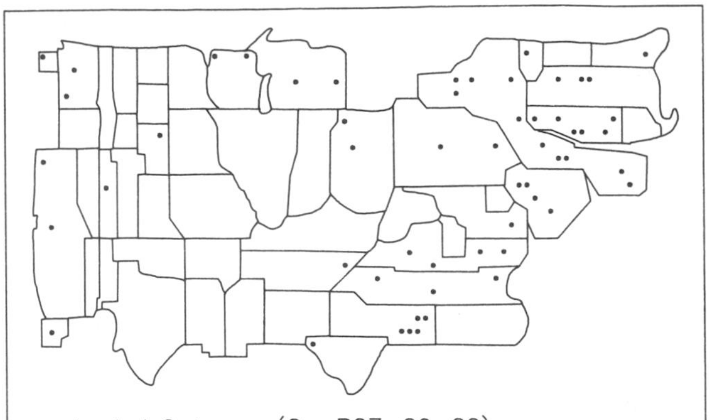

•freshet 2 + var (Qq. B27, C9, C2)

fresh fork n [Var of **flesh fork**]

1899 (1912) Green *VA Folk-Speech* 185, *Fresh-fork. . .* A large, three-prong iron fork . . for taking out . . cooked meat from a dinner-pot, or other boiler while cooking. Flesh-fork.

fresh fried potatoes n pl Also *fresh fries* **esp N Cent** See Map Also called **raw fried potatoes**

Raw potatoes thinly sliced and fried in a small amount of oil or fat.

1965–70 *DARE* (Qu. H47, *Kinds of fried potatoes favored around here*) 17 Infs, **esp N Cent,** Fresh fried (potatoes); **IN**19, 23, Fresh (fries). **1971** Lewis *Nothing Shadow* 38 **SD** (as of late 19th cent), Sometimes the potatoes were "fresh fried" but these were an emergency dish, not a first choice. Peeling, slicing, and frying the raw potatoes took much longer to prepare than what came to be called later "hashed browns." **1981** *DARE* File (as of 1930s), My father, who had grown up in Nebraska, was fond of fresh fried potatoes, so we had them often, especially on camping trips.

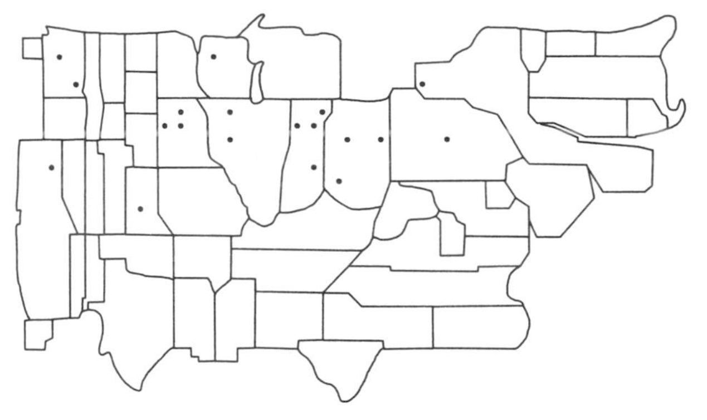

•fresh fried potatoes + varr (Qu. H47)

fresh frog n Cf **French frog**

Perh a **spring peeper.**

1967 *DARE* (Qu. P21, *Small frogs that sing or chirp loudly in spring*) Inf **PA**28, Fresh frog.

fresh grass n

A grass that grows in fresh rather than salt water.

1966 *DARE* (Qu. L8, *Hay that grows naturally in damp places*) Inf **ME**5, Fresh grass—any wild grass like swamp grass, bluejoint, [as opposed to] salt grass.

fresh hand at the bellows n [See quot 1975]

See quots.

1942 Berrey–Van den Bark *Amer. Slang* 790.4, A fresh hand at the bellows, *said when the wind freshens, esp. after a calm.* **1975** Gould *ME Lingo* 101, *Fresh hand at the bellows*—A sudden increase in wind for sailing, like having a new pumper on the blacksmith's bellows. An interesting term since it shows a land expression going to sea.

freshie See **fresh n 4**

freshlets n pl [Perh blend of **fresh n 4 + haslet**]
See quot 1984.
1940 Harris *Folk Plays* 107 **NC,** You can bring me 'long some 'taters, and purserves, and some cracklin's, and some freshlets next hog-killin'. **1984** [see **fresh n 4**].

fresh meat n
1 See **fresh** n **4.**
2 See quot.
1966 *DARE* (Qu. HH15, *A very inexperienced person*) Infs **SC**11, 21, Fresh meat.

fresh onion n
A green onion.
1965–70 *DARE* (Qu. I6, *The kind of onions that come up fresh early in the year, and you eat them raw*) Infs **AR**52, **CA**57, **FL**31, **GA**23, **IL**12, **OH**66, **WA**27, Fresh onions; **OK**27, They call them fresh onions when sold; (Qu. I7) Inf **MO**36, Fresh onions. **1971** Wood *Vocab. Change* 369 **Sth,** Volunteered [as a term for edible spring onions]: *fresh onions.* **1986** Pederson *LAGS Concordance,* 10 infs, **Gulf Region,** Fresh onions; [1 inf, **swTN,** Fresh spring onions].

fresh salt n [*fresh* not containing salt]
An imaginary commodity used as the basis for a practical joke.
1969 *DARE* (Qu. HH14, *Ways of teasing a beginner or inexperienced person—for example, by sending him for a 'left-handed monkey wrench': "Go get me ______."*) Inf **NC**61, Fresh salt.

fresh side n Also *fresh (side) bacon, ~ side pork* Cf **fresh** adj **B, salt side**
Meat from the side of a hog, that is not smoked and usu not salted.
c1955 Reed–Person *Ling. Atlas Pacific NW (Salt pork)* 1 inf, **nwWA,** Fresh side pork. **1966–70** *DARE* (Qu. H38, *Other words for bacon*) Inf **CO**27, Fresh side, same as side meat; **CO**40, Fresh side; **CO**11, Fresh bacon—not smoked; **KY**84, Fresh side bacon—not cured; **WA**31, Fresh side pork—from the side that isn't cured.

fresh up See **fresh** v **1, 2**

freshwater clam n Also *freshwater mussel* **chiefly NEng**
A bivalve usu of the family Unionidae but also of the family Sphaeriidae. For other names see **buckhorn 9, bullhead 3, butterfly 2, deertoe, eggshell 2, elephant's ear 8, elktoe, fat mucket, fawnfoot, floater 8, grandma** n **B3, hackleback 2, hatchetback, heelsplitter, ladyfinger, lilliput, mapleleaf, monkey face, Ohio River pigtoe, papershell, pigtoe, pimpleback, pistolgrip, pocketbook, purple pimpleback, rock pocketbook, rockshell, salamander mussel, sheepnose, slippershell, slop bucket, snuffbox, spectacle case, spike, squawfoot, strange floater, three horn, three ridge, wartyback, washboard, yellowback**
1843 DeKay *Zool. NY* 5.188, *Unio. . .* The shells of this and the other genera are popularly known under the names of *Freshwater clams* and *mussels.* **1849** Dana *Geology* 27 *(DA),* The fresh-water clam *(Unionidae).* **1903** (1950) Austin *Land of Little Rain* 59 **eCA,** Seyavi and the boy lay up in the caverns of the Black Rock and ate tule roots and fresh-water clams. **1965–70** *DARE* (Qu. P18, . . *Shellfish . . around here*) 20 Infs, 17 **NY, NEng,** Freshwater clams; **ME**8, **MS**66, **OH**82, Freshwater mussels. **1966** *DARE* Tape **ME**8, Here they just call 'em [=mussels] freshwater clam. **1975** Gould *ME Lingo* 101, *Fresh-water clams*—Maine does have a bivalve in inland waters, not eaten by humans but admired by muskrats.

freshwater cod n
=burbot.
1956 Harlan–Speaker *IA Fish* 157, *Burbot, Lota lota. . .* It is also known locally as . . fresh-water cod.

freshwater drum n
A **drum 1** (here: *Aplodinotus grunniens*). Also called **bubbler 1, buffalo perch 1, croaker** n[1] **1a(3), crocus** n[2] **b, drummer 3, freshwater sheepshead, gaspergou 1, gou, gray bass 3, gray perch 1, grinder 2, growler** n[1] **2, grunt** n **2, grunter 2a, jewelhead, lake sheepshead, mussel-eater, perch, sheepshead, silver bass, thunder-pumper, white perch**
1879 U.S. Natl. Museum *Bulletin* 14.45, *Haploidonotus grunniens. . .* Fresh-water Drum. **1897** *Outing* 30.435/2, Most abundant of these was the 'sheepshead' (freshwater drum), a good-looking, silvery fish, somewhat like the lake shad. **1966** WI Acad. *Trans.* 55.115, The freshwater drum or sheepshead is abundant in the lower Wisconsin and in the Mississippi Rivers. It is frequently caught on hook and line. **1970** *Ibid* 291, Freshwater drum—Common in the lower Wisconsin R., the Mississippi, the St. Croix upstream to the St. Croix Falls Dam. Sporadic in some large lakes of southern one-half of state. Abundant in L. Winnebago. **1972** Sparano *Outdoors Encycl.* 369, Freshwater drum. . . *Aplodinotus grunniens.*

freshwater herring n
1 A **whitefish** (here: *Prosopium williamsoni*).
1882 U.S. Natl. Museum *Proc.* 5.90 **WA,** *Coregonus Williamsonii. . .* are the "fresh-water herring" of Mill Creek.
2 =peamouth.
1902 Jordan–Evermann *Amer. Fishes* 73, In the Snake River this minnow [=*Mylocheilus caurinus*] . . is locally known by the misleading names "fresh-water herring" and "whitefish."
3 A **cisco** (here: *Coregonus artedi*).
1974 WI Univ. *Fish Lake MI* 13, *Lake Herring—Coregonus artedii* . . common names: . . freshwater herring.
4 A **mooneye** (here: *Hiodon tergisus*).
1983 Becker *Fishes WI* 284, *Hiodon tergisus. . .* Other common names . . freshwater herring.

freshwater lobster n **esp NEng**
=crawfish n **B1.**
1819 Evans *Pedestrious Tour* 243 **NH speaker in LA,** The craw-fish, which naturalists say is a fresh water lobster, here passes under the banks of the Mississippi . . and comes up through the earth into the fields. **1844** DeKay *Zool. NY* 6.23, *Astacus bartonii. . .* This little *Craw-fish,* or *Fresh-water Lobster,* is exceedingly common in most of the mountain streams of this and the adjoining states. It has been noticed . . in Carolina, and . . in Massachusetts. **1857** (1864) Thoreau *ME Woods* 237, Here were plenty of the shells of crayfish, or fresh-water lobsters, which had been washed ashore. **1966** *DARE* (Qu. P19, *What do you call the small, freshwater crayfish around here?*) Inf **ME**8, Freshwater lobster. **1975** Gould *ME Lingo* 101, *Fresh-water lobster*—The word crayfish is a no-no in Maine. . . But . . the state does have small native crayfish in certain inland waters. They don't grow to any size, and because we are not allowed to say *crayfish,* we call them *fresh-water lobsters.*

freshwater marsh hen n Also *freshwater mud hen* Cf **saltwater marsh hen**
Either of two birds: the **Virginia rail** or a **king rail** (here: *Rallus elegans*).
1835 Audubon *Ornith. Biog.* 3.27, The Fresh-water Marsh-Hen is abundant in South Carolina. **1844** Giraud *Birds Long Is.* 208, This species [=*Rallus virginianus*] is found in the course of the year throughout most parts of the United States—frequenting the borders of the sea shore, as well as the fresh water streams of the interior, for which it seems to have a great predilection. It is known to gunners and sportsmen by the name of Fresh Water Marsh or "Mud Hen." **1888** Trumbull *Names of Birds* 129, *Virginia Rail. . .* Known to some of the inhabitants along the sea-coast of New Jersey by the name of the *fresh-water mud-hen.* **1917** (1923) *Birds Amer.* 1.203, King Rail. . . [Also called] Fresh-water Marsh Hen. *Ibid* 205, Virginia Rail. . . [Also called] Fresh-water Marsh Hen; Long-billed Rail. **1938** Oberholser *Bird Life LA* 198, Perhaps its [=*Rallus elegans'*] hen-like voice has earned for it the name of 'fresh water marsh hen.'

freshwater marsh wren n
A **marsh wren** (here: *Cistothorus stellaris*).
1839 MA Zool. & Bot. Surv. *Fishes Reptiles* 315 **MA,** Fresh-water Marsh Wren, *Troglodytes brevirostris,* . . is known to boys by its song, *chip-a-day-day,* which is so often heard in the meadows. **1917** (1923) *Birds Amer.* 3.194, *Cistothorus stellaris. . .* Other Names.—Fresh-water Marsh Wren. **1946** Hausman *Eastern Birds* 449, *Short-billed Marsh Wren—Cistothorus stellaris. . .* Fresh-Water Marsh Wren.

freshwater meadow hen n Cf **freshwater marsh hen**
A **king rail** (here: *Rallus elegans*).
1923 U.S. Dept. Ag. *Misc. Circular* 13.40, *Rallus elegans. . . Vernacular Names. . . In local use. . .* Fresh-water meadow-hen (Long Id., N.Y.)

freshwater mosquito n
A mosquito; see quot 1946.

1946 *PADS* 6.14 **eNC,** *Fresh-water mosquito*. . . A long-legged, slender mosquito that has a sharp bite. *(Anopheles maculipennis.)* Pamlico. Common. **1968** *DARE* (Qu. R15a, . . *Names . . for mosquitoes*) Inf **DE**4, Salt marsh mosquitoes and freshwater mosquitoes.

freshwater mud hen See **freshwater marsh hen**

freshwater mussel See **freshwater clam**

freshwater sheepshead n

=**freshwater drum.**

1933 LA Dept. of Conserv. *Fishes* 363, Fresh Water Sheepshead. . . *Aplodinotus grunniens.* **1946** LaMonte *N. Amer. Game Fishes* 148, *Aplodinotus grunniens*. . . Fresh-water Sheepshead. **1947** Hubbs-Lagler *Fishes Gt. Lakes* 95, Freshwater sheepshead—*Aplodinotus grunniens.*

freshwater tad See **tad**

freshwater tailor n Cf **saltwater tailor**

A **hickory shad** (here: *Alosa mediocris*).

1884 Goode *Fisheries U.S.* 1.608, In the Potomac the species [=*Clupea mediocris*] is called the 'Tailor Shad,' or the 'Fresh-water Tailor.' **1902** Jordan-Evermann *Amer. Fishes* 102.

freshwater terrapin n Cf **saltwater terrapin**

=**wood turtle.**

1842 DeKay *Zool. NY* 3.15, *The Wood Terrapin. Emys insculpta*, . . is also called the *Fresh-water Terrapin.* **1884** Goode *Fisheries U.S.* 1.152, The marsh and river Tortoises constitute a large group, well represented in North America. It includes . . the Fresh-water Terrapins.

fresh yeast n

1 Homemade yeast. *old-fash*

1973 Allen *LAUM* 1.284 **MN, SD** (as of c1950), A few scattered infs. preserve various terms for the kinds of homemade liquid or sponge yeast used before the advent of the commercial cake variety. . . Older names include . . *fresh yeast* [3 infs].

2 =**compressed yeast.**

1965-70 *DARE* (Qu. H17, . . *Kinds [of yeast]*) Infs **GA**15, **LA**31, **MT**1, Fresh yeast and dry yeast; **IL**98, 107, **MN**42, Fresh yeast, also called cake yeast; **IA**47, Fresh yeast—baker's yeast, in cakes; **MI**18, Fresh yeast has to be refrigerated, comes in a cake; **MN**1, Fresh yeast—a cake of yeast; **TX**10, **VT**3, Fresh yeast—yeast cakes; **WI**64, Fresh yeast—oblong chunks are packaged. [7 of 12 Infs coll educ]

fresno n [Span "ash tree"]

1 An ash of the genus *Fraxinus.* **SW**

1913 Wooton *Trees NM* 131, *Fraxinus*. . . Fresno. *Ibid* 128, *The Mountain Ash* Fresno *(Fraxinus velutina).* **1945** Benson-Darrow *Manual SW Trees* 259, *Fraxinus velutina*. . . Fresno. **1960** Vines *Trees SW* 860, Gregg Ash *Fraxinus greggii*. . . Other vernacular names are Fresno, . . and China. *Ibid* 862, Single-leaf Ash *Fraxinus anomala*. . . Vernacular names are Dwarf Ash and Fresno. *Ibid,* Berlandier Ash *Fraxinus berlandieriana*. . . Local names for the tree are . . Fresno, and Mexican Ash. *Ibid* 863, Velvet Ash *Fraxinus velutina*. . . Other names are Arizona Ash, . . and Fresno. **1970** Correll *Plants TX* 1194, *Fraxinus americana*. . . White Ash, Fresno. *Ibid* 1195, *Fraxinus Berlandieriana*. . . Mexican Ash, Fresno. . . *Fraxinus velutina*. . . Velvet Ash, . . Fresno. **1979** Little *Checklist U.S. Trees* 134, *Fraxinus*. . . Other Common Name—fresno. **1981** Benson-Darrow *Trees SW Deserts* 186, *Fraxinus velutina*. . . Arizona Ash, Fresno.

2 often cap; also *fresno scraper;* pronc-spp *fresnol, freznal, frisno:* A horse-drawn scoop for moving dirt, freq used in road building. [From the name of the manufacturer, *Fresno* Agricultural Works, Fresno CA] **chiefly West, Cent** *old-fash* Also called **horse scoop, slip shovel, slusher**

1893 *Irrigation Age* Apr 359/1 *(DA),* This work was done by four-horse Fresno scrapers. **1911** Wright *Barbara Worth* 322 **CO,** Teamsters left their teams and Fresnos on the Company works. **1959** Robertson *Ram* 228 **ID** (as of c1900), Driving a four-horse fresno scraper in the bottom of a twenty-foot cut, with the dust so thick that one could scarcely see or breathe. **1959** *AmSp* 34.151, *Frisno* (['frɪzno]) is current in the Southwest. . . Informants from Oklahoma to Louisiana give precedence to *frisno, slip,* and *scoop,* . . over . . *scraper*. . . An East Texas informant . . offers *fresnol* as a local variant. **1966-70** *DARE* Tape **CA**201, They had what they'd call Fresno scrapers—a couple o' horses, three horses on 'em; **IA**8, A rig you put four horses on, it's a long scraper affair, six or eight feet long. It has one handle on it and it has kind of rockers on the ends of it to roll. . . When you lift up on that handle, it'll roll up on them rockers and dump, see. That's a Fresno; **OK**29, A Fresno is horse-drawn, by a team of horses, and it's one of our primitive methods for movin' dirt. Most all the railroads been built with Fresnos. It was just a scoop pulled by horses. **1967** Green *Horse Tradin'* 102 **TX,** Mule skinners, who were driving the fresnoes that were being used to build the highway roadbed. **1967-69** *DARE* (Qu. L41, *A device for moving dirt*) Inf **CO**22, Fresno; **LA**29, ['frɪzˌnoʊ]—pulled by a mule, had two wheels; **TX**71, ['frɪzˌno]; **WA**8, Fresno—used with horses; **WY**1, Fresno—horse-drawn road-building machinery. **1978-79** *Midwest Lang. & Folkl. Newsl.* 1-2.19 **KS** (as of 1920s), Freznal.

fress v [Ger *fressen* to devour greedily (usu used of animals)] **PaGer area and areas of Yiddish infl**

To eat greedily; to snack.

1916 *Judge* 12 Aug np **NYC,** Their buyer was mad at us like anything because he got indigestion trying to *fress* himself to death at our expense. **1939** Aurand *Quaint Idioms* 11 **sePA,** My husband—he always had such a good *abedit* (appetite) but now he don't *fress* (eat) much anymore. *Ibid* 14, Them kids *fress* (eat) just like hogs. **1967** *DARE* (Qu. H11a, *If somebody eats rapidly and noisily, you say he* ______) Inf **PA**18, Fresses like a pig. **1968** *Helen Adolf Festschrift* 35 **sePA,** The verb *to fress* (Pennsylvania German *fresse*) is used by many people in the area when they wish to indicate that someone has eaten to excess or like an animal. **1968** Rosten *Yiddish* 120, Did you ever see anyone fress like that? **1987** *Jrl. Engl. Ling.* 20.169 **ePA,** *Fress* 'to eat too much, to eat sloppily'. . . Of the eighteen informants [of 100 questioned] who responded with this variant six are under 30. . . Four other informants said that they know the word, but ascribe to it the meaning 'to snack, to eat between meals'. Two of the speakers who volunteered the form when given the traditional definition likewise maintained that it could possess this second sense. Thus, *fress* seems to be acquiring an additional meaning in the region.

fresser n [Ger *Fresser* glutton; cf **fress**] **PaGer area and areas of Yiddish infl**

A glutton; one with a large appetite.

1916 *Judge* 27 May np, Every minute the check was going up! They wasn't penny pikers; they was dollar *fressers.* **1967** *DARE* (Qu. H9, *If somebody always eats a considerable amount of food, you say he's a* ______) Inf **PA**18, Fresser. **1968** Rosten *Yiddish* 120, Don't act like a fresser. **1980** *DARE* File **Chicago IL** [Jewish speaker], You certainly don't need to worry about your son's appetite—he's quite a fresser.

fret v **chiefly Sth**

1 To tease; to vex, torment (someone or oneself).

1899 (1912) Green *VA Folk-Speech* 185, *Fret*. . . To worry; annoy. "Don't fret the child, but let him alone." **1928** Peterkin *Scarlet Sister Mary* 208 **eSC,** We ought not to fret em if we can help it. **1938** Matschat *Suwannee R.* 56 **nFL, sGA,** Must fret him powerful. **1941** Perry *Hold Autumn* 23 **TX,** "It ain't frettin me," Sam said, "cause I'm just goin to plow it out." **1943** *LANE* Map 498 *(Don't worry)* 2 infs, **cnCT, cVT,** Don't fret yourself. **1967-70** *DARE* (Qu. GG3, *To tease: "See those big boys trying to* ______ *[that little one]."*) Infs **VA**24, 37, Fret; (Qu. GG9, *To suddenly embarrass somebody and throw him off balance: "When they told him what she had said about him, it certainly did* ______ *him."*) Inf **KY**85, Fret; (Qu. GG13a, *When something keeps bothering a person and makes him nervous, he may say, "It* ______ *me."*) Infs **VA**69, 101, Frets; (Qu. GG35a) Inf **TX**33, Fret not thyself. **1968** *DARE* FW Addit **csNC,** It does it just to fret you.

2 To waste or fritter away (time).

1969 *DARE* (Qu. A9, . . *Wasting time by not working on the job*) Inf **NY**167, Fretting time.

fret-lip n

A **fringeless orchid** (here: *Habenaria peramoena*).

1950 Correll *Native Orchids* 95, *Habenaria peramoena*. . . *Common names:* Purple Fret-lip. **1976** Bailey-Bailey *Hortus Third* 534, *Purple fret-lip*. . . Fl[ower]s rich violet-purple, showy, lip 3-lobed.

fretted ppl adj Freq with *up:* also *fret up* **[fret v 1]** Cf **fretty**

Troubled, distressed, anxious.

1928 Peterkin *Scarlet Sister Mary* 100 **eSC,** He was worried and fretted, so he forgot himself. **1941** *LANE* Map 476-77 *(Excited, all nerved up)* 23 infs, **chiefly ME, NH,** Fretted up; 3 infs, **sNH, neMA,** Fretted. **1943** Weslager *DE Forgotten Folk* 153, He had a little accident, kind o' like, a few days before and is all fret up. **1970** *DARE* (Qu. GG11, *To be quite* *anxious . . "The letter hasn't come and he's ______.*") Inf **KY**85, Fretted.

fretty adj Also *frettish* *old-fash*

Fretful, irritable.

1890 *DN* 1.19 **NH,** *Fretty:* fretful. **1890** *DN* 1.78 **csCT,** *Frettish* is a form familiar to an old lady in New Haven. **1892** *DN* 1.216 **NC, TN. 1899** (1912) Green *VA Folk-Speech* 186, The child must be sick he is very fretty to-day. **1914** *DN* 4.154 **NH** (as of late 19th cent). **1952** Brown *NC Folkl.* 1.543, *Fretty.* . . Fretful. . . Rare.

fret up See **fretted**

freundschaft See **freindschaft**

frez See **freeze** v **A2, 3**

freznal See **fresno 2**

friar n

A **silversides,** usu *Menidia menidia.*

1873 in 1878 Smithsonian Inst. *Misc. Coll.* 14.2.30, *Chirostoma notata.* . . Silver-sides; friar *(New England).* Maine to Florida. **1884** Goode *Fisheries U.S.* 1.456, The most important species [of sand smelt] on the Atlantic side is the Green Smelt of the Connecticut coast, *Menidia notata,* also called in some parts of New England the "Friar." **1983** Becker *Fishes WI* 769, *Brook Silverside. Labidesthes sicculus.* . . Other common names: silverside, . . friar. . . In the Mississippi River and Lake Michigan drainage basins in Wisconsin.

fricole See **frijole**

friction match n **Nth** *old-fash*

A match that is ignited by striking on any rough surface.

1843 in 1957 Old Farmer's Almanac *Sampler* 99 **NH,** Lest the busy old author of all jar and jangle come along with his friction match and blow you sky-high. **1850** Emerson *Repr. Men* 153 **MA,** Men of the senses . . believe that mustard bites the tongue, that . . friction-matches are incendiary. **1891** Welch *Recoll. Buffalo* 76 **wNY,** There was no friction or locofoco matches in those days. **1967–69** *DARE* (Qu. F46, . . *The kind of matches you can strike anywhere*) Infs **MI**96, **MA**5, **NY**209, **WA**19, Friction matches. [All Infs old]

Friday patch n

1967 *DARE* (Qu. L6a, . . *A piece of land under cultivation—less than an acre*) Inf **TX**35, Friday patch. It's bad luck to not finish a job on Friday, so this is the size you can finish.

fridge n Also sp *frig* [Abbr for *refrigerator*] **chiefly Nth, N Midl, West** See Map Cf **frigidaire**

A refrigerator.

1942 Berrey–Van den Bark *Amer. Slang* 86.1, Frig, *a refrigerator.* **1965–70** *DARE* (Qu. D10b, *The place to keep food cool if it is run by electricity or gas*) 35 Infs, **chiefly Nth, N Midl, West,** Fridge; (Qu. D9, *To prevent bread and cake from drying, you put them in a ______*) Inf **CA**59, I just chuck everything like that into the fridge.

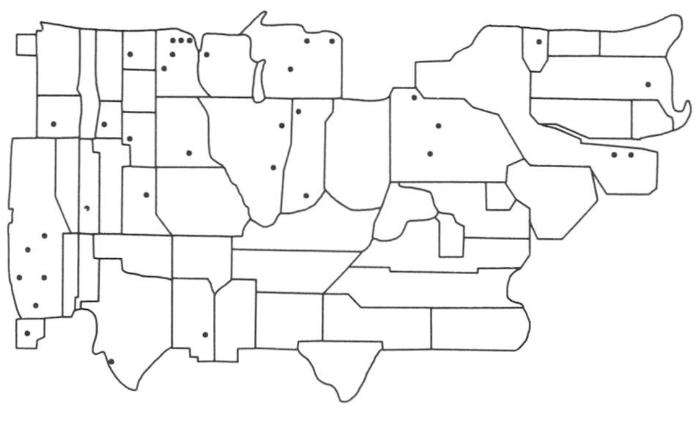

•fridge n (Qq. D10b, D9)

‡fridge v

To evade, dodge (an issue).

1966 *DARE* (Qu. JJ45, . . *"We tried to pin him down, but he just kept ______."*) Inf **MS**21, Fridging out of it.

fried adj [Perh by analogy with *boiled, stewed*] *old-fash* Cf *DS* DD14, 15

Drunk.

1926 G. Spencer, *Univ. of Va. Mag.,* Oct., 16/2 *(DAS),* Princeton has completed the idiom of the cuisine by adding *fried* to *boiled* and *stewed,* meaning intoxicated. **1928** *AmSp* 4.103, Terms [for *drunk*] taken from the preparation of food—"basted," "canned," "fried," "boiled," "potted," "preserved," "pickled," "soused." **1942** Berrey–Van den Bark *Amer. Slang* 106.7, Fried, fried on both sides, fried to the gills *or* hat. **1950** *WELS (A person who is very drunk)* 1 Inf, **cWI,** Fried.

fried apron n Also *fried rag*

See quot 1908.

1908 *DN* 3.313 **eAL, wGA,** *Fried-apron.* . . A flannel cloth soaked or 'fried' in hot grease and hung like an apron over the chest for protective and curative purposes in treatment of croup, colds, etc. **1968** *DARE* (Qu. BB50b, *Remedies for chest colds*) Inf **GA**33, Fried rags! Mix turpentine, kerosene, beeswax; soak a woolen cloth in it. It *has* to be wool. [People] used to think it had to be red! [Inf **NJ**16, Fry a rag.]

fried bacon frog See **fry-bacon frog**

fried ball n Cf **fried hole**

=**doughnut hole.**

1969 *DARE* (Qu. H28, *Different shapes . . of doughnuts*) Inf **MO**33, Fried ball, fried doughnut ball.

fried biscuit n

=**fried bread 1.**

1931–33 *LANE Worksheets* **Newport RI,** Fried biscuit—raised bread dough fried in deep fat, cut while gas is still in it or it is hard and soggy. **1950** *WELS (Special kinds of bread)* 1 Inf, **seWI,** If bread was short and the housewife knew it would not be baked by mealtime, she used to cut off small biscuit-sized pieces of the dough, pat them flat, and fry them slowly on a greased griddle until lightly browned on both sides. These fried biscuits were served hot and buttered. **1968** *DARE* (Qu. H28) Inf **IN**41, Fried biscuit—with biscuit dough. **1973** Kluger *Wild Flavor* 22 **csIN,** The Nashville House menu always includes sassafras tea. . . baked apple butter, fried biscuits, and hickory-smoked country ham.

fried-bosom shirt See **fried shirt**

fried bread n Note: Some of the following quots are not clearly distinguishable as to sense.

1 also *fry bread:* Yeast-bread dough cut into pieces and deep-fried. Cf **Baptist cake, huffjuff, morning glory, spider bread**

1836 (1930) Phelps *Diary* 228 **IL,** The fourth day of July I gave a feast to all the squaws, we boiled corn and had some fried bread, a favorite dish with them. **1895** *DN* 1.387, Dough from the regular batch of bread, fried instead of baked; eaten hot, with molasses. . . [This] was called simply *fried bread.* **1941** *LANE* Map 284 **NEng,** Pieces of raised bread dough fried in deep fat. . . *fried bread* [6 infs]. **1966–69** *DARE* (Qu. H18, . . *Special kinds of bread*) Inf **CO**40, Fried bread—from light bread dough; cut off a hunk and deep-fat fry (or boil) it; **MT**5, Fried bread; **NH**6, Fried bread—add shortening to extra bread dough, fry for breakfast. Some added jelly in the center of the dough; (Qu. H19) Inf **CA**132, Fried bread—use bread dough or baking powder biscuit dough. Let it raise and then fry; (Qu. H20b) Inf **SC**43, Fried bread; **SC**70, Fry bread. **1976** *LaCrosse Tribune* (WI) 8 Apr 17/4, The resulting fry bread is similar to bakery bismarcks, but less sweet and more airy. **1986** Pederson *LAGS Concordance,* 1 inf, **seAL,** Fried bread—lump of doughnut dough, no hole.

2 also *fry bread:* Quick-bread dough patted into rounds and fried. **esp SW**

1950 *WELS (Foods made with dough and cooked in deep fat)* 1 Inf, **cwWI,** Indian fry bread (Winnebago) is fried bread—pieces of dough pulled off and fried or sautéed. Fry bread is made with baking powder. **1968** *DARE* (Qu. H18, . . *Special kinds of bread*) Inf **CA**94, Fried bread—same ingredients as tortilla: flour, baking powder, salt, water; fried in deep oil. **1989** *DARE* File, Navajo fry bread—bread mixture basically like biscuits and deep fried. It is served with honey or sometimes like a taco—open-face—with meat and vegetables. **1989** *NYT Mag.* 26 Nov 36/4 **neAZ** (as of c1935), They ridiculed the Navajo customs, the ceremonials, the Navajo diet of mutton stew, fry bread and blue corn meal mush. **1989** *Sierra* Mar-Apr 69 **UT,** The Navajo taco. . . An acre of fry bread, a bushel of beans, a furlong of cheese, a firkin of lettuce. . . God knows what else. **1990** *NY Times* (NY) 7 Jan 12, [Headline:] *Savory Fried Bread of New Mexico* [Text:] Indian fry bread (also called Navajo fry bread)... [contains] flour, salt, baking powder, water and sometimes lard... [and is] deep-fried.. until golden brown... Indian fry bread dough is plucked into golfball-size lumps, which are patted into 9-inch rounds that are a half inch thick.

3 also *fry bread:* =**fried corn-bread. chiefly Sth**

1966–67 *DARE* (Qu. H14, *Bread that's made with cornmeal*) Inf **LA**12, Fried bread—hot-water bread made in a skillet. Hot-water bread is made with boiling salted water so the meal would stick; **SC**9, Fry bread is fried corn bread—round, flat; (Qu. H25, .. *Fried cornmeal*) Infs **AL**15, **NC**41, Fried bread; **SC**9, Fry bread. **1986** Pederson *LAGS Concordance,* 1 inf, **ceTN,** Fried bread—hoecake, cornbread; 1 inf, **nwGA,** Fried bread—cornbread; 1 inf, **cnGA,** Fried bread—type of hoecake that is thin and cooked in ashes; 1 inf, **seGA,** Fried bread—similar to pancake, made with meal; 3 infs, **ne,ceFL, cnTN,** Fried bread.

3 French toast.

1942 McAtee *Dial. Grant Co. IN* 27 (as of 1890s), *Fried-bread*.. slices of bread dipped in an egg-and-milk batter and fried; French toast. **1956** McAtee *Some Dialect NC* 17, *Fried bread*... French toast. **1968** *DARE* FW Addit **Baltimore MD,** Fried bread—[used] in reference to French toast.

friedcake n

1 also *fry cake:* A cake formed in various shapes and fried in deep fat; a doughnut, **cruller. chiefly Nth, esp Gt Lakes, Upstate NY** See Map *somewhat old-fash*

1839 Walker in 1940 Drury *Pioneers Spokanes* 139 **ME,** We had roast beef, .. fried cakes, bread, butter, cheese, and hulled corn. **1895** *DN* 1.388 **eMA. 1910** *DN* 3.441 **wNY. 1937** *AmSp* 12.102 **eNE. 1941** *LANE* Map 284 **widespread throughout NEng,** *Fried-cake*.. is described as ring-shaped.. ; as twisted.. ; as ball-shaped.. ; as diamond-shaped.. ; and as oblong... *Fried-cake* is often regarded as old-fashioned. **1950** *WELS* 29 Infs, **WI,** Fried cake; 5 Infs, **WI,** Fry cake. **1961** *AmSp* 36.29 **nOH,** The incidence of *friedcake*.. declines in frequency with the youth and the cultivation of the informant. **1965–70** *DARE* (Qu. H26, *A round cake of dough, cooked in deep fat, with a hole in the center*) 102 Infs, **chiefly Gt Lakes, Upstate NY,** Friedcake; **MI**18, **OH**15, **WI**20, Fry cake [Of all Infs responding to the question, 70% were old; of those giving these responses, 82% were old.]; (Qu. H27, .. *Joking names for doughnuts*) 16 Infs, **esp Gt Lakes,** Friedcake; **MI**22, **MN**1, **SD**3, Fry cake [12 of 19 Infs old]; (Qu. H28, .. *Types of doughnuts*) 10 Infs, **esp Nth,** Friedcakes [7 of 10 Infs old]; (Qu. H29, *A round cake, cooked in deep fat, with jelly inside*) Infs **MO**1, **PA**234, (Filled) friedcake. **1971** *AmSp* 46.172 **Chicago IL,** *Fried cake. Ibid* 180, [*Fried cake* occurs] only in the speech of.. informants of age 56 and over. **1973** Allen *LAUM* 1.281 (as of c1950), Northern *fried cake*.. survives in the U[pper] M[idwest] only in the first settled parts of the Northern speech area; several of the infs. declare it to be old-fashioned... One [informant] volunteered that *fry cake* was the "old usage." **1989** *NY Times* (NY) 7 Aug sec 2 34/3, But I generally prefer just the plain fry cake, the kind you break in half and dunk in your coffee.

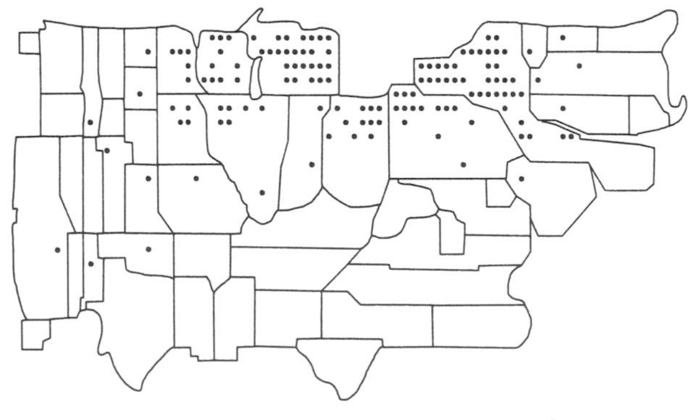

•friedcake 1 + varr (Qq. H26, H27, H28, H29)

2 also *fry cake:* A pancake.

1887 Freeman *Humble Romance* 251 **MA,** I thought I'd.. fetch a few of these fried cakes. I thought mebbe Alferd would relish 'em fur his breakfast. **1906** *DN* 3.137 **nwAR,** *Fried cake*... A thick, flat griddle-cake consisting of dough similar to that from which bread or biscuits are made. **1966–69** *DARE* (Qu. H20b, .. *Other names.. for pancakes*) Infs **IL**71, **MN**3, **OH**24, **OR**3, **SC**43, Friedcakes; **MI**13, Fry cakes—heard, though not as much as griddle cakes. **1973** Allen *LAUM* 1.283 **Upper MW** (as of c1950), *Fried cakes* is reported in this sense [=pancakes] by 3 widely scattered infs.

3 =**fried corn-bread.**

1967–70 *DARE* (Qu. H25, .. *Fried cornmeal*) Inf **IL**134, Corn cakes, friedcakes; **MO**21, Friedcakes.

fried chicken n *joc* Cf **Arkansas chicken,** *DS* H38

See quot 1944.

1903 (1965) Adams *Log Cowboy* 123, He helped himself to a third piece of "fried chicken" (bacon). **1944** Adams *Western Words* 62, *Fried chicken*—A sarcastic name for bacon which has been rolled in flour and fried.

fried-chicken mushroom n Cf **hen of the woods, hickory chicken**

An edible mushroom *(Lyophyllum decastes).*

1981 Lincoff *Audubon Field Guide Mushrooms* 768, Fried-chicken Mushroom. *Lyophyllum decastes*... When it is cooked, this abundant edible tastes like fried chicken. **1987** McKnight-McKnight *Mushrooms* 163, *Fried Chicken Mushroom. Lyophyllum decastes*... Edible and reportedly good.

fried corn n

See quots.

1966–70 *DARE* (Qu. H50, *Dishes made with.. corn*) Infs **GA**70, 79, **KY**22, 48, **TN**5, 24, Fried corn; **GA**10, Fried corn—cooked until most of the liquid is gone; **LA**11, Fried corn—cut off the cob and fried with milk and butter; **TX**102, Fried corn—off the cob, fried slowly; **OK**56, Fried corn and tomatoes. **1972** Hilliard *Hog Meat* 48 **Sth,** Corn was utilized in myriad ways. During early summer, while still green, it was boiled on-the-cob, cut off the cob and creamed (called "fried corn"), and roasted in the shuck.

fried corn-bread n **chiefly Sth** See Map Also called **fried bread 3** Cf **corn pone 1, fried mush**

Bread made from cornmeal and fried rather than baked.

1965–70 *DARE* (Qu. H25, .. *Fried cornmeal*) 15 Infs, **chiefly Sth,** Fried corn-bread; **AR**14, Fried corn-bread—fried on top of the stove; **FL**19, Fried corn-bread—scald the meal rather than put milk in it.

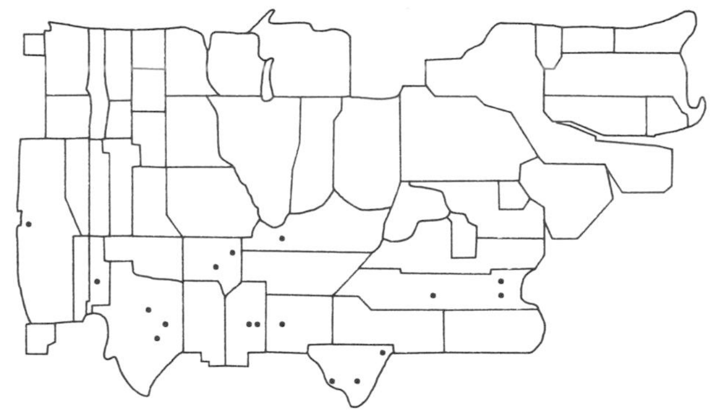

•fried corn-bread (Qu. H25)

fried corn(meal) mush See **fried mush**

fried dough n

=**fried bread 1.**

1941 *LANE* Map 284 **RI,** Pieces of raised bread dough fried in deep fat... *Fried dough* [2 infs]. **1966–69** *DARE* (Qu. H26) Inf **AK**3, Fried dough—made of bread dough, with yeast in it; **MA**6, Fried dough—bread dough fried in a pan with maple syrup; (Qu. H28) Inf **CT**39, Fried dough—just a chunk of dough.

fried dumpling n

See quots.

1941 *LANE* Map 284 **Portland ME,** Various types of cakes fried in deep fat... *Fried dumplin'* [1 inf]. **1968** *DARE* FW Addit **NY**45, *Fried dumplings*—an old Yankee dish eaten for breakfast. Made with flour and baking powder, kept in boiling water [sic] for exactly ten minutes.

fried egg n

1 also *fried-egg flower:* A **prickly poppy** (here: *Argemone platyceras* var *hispida*). [See quot 1915]

1915 (1926) Armstrong-Thornber *Western Wild Flowers* 162, Flowers . . with delicately crumpled, white petals and beautiful golden centers. . . The flowers are often quite broad and flat, and then are sometimes given the prosaic name of Fried-eggs. **1924** Austin *Land of Journeys' Ending* 52 **AZ,** About this season, too, the crêpe-petaled thistle poppy, the "fried-egg flower" of the cow-boy, makes a lovely whiteness over sandy patches.

2 See quot.

1966 *DARE* (Qu. S11) Inf **NC**44, Cactus—fried egg.

3 =frypan ball.

1969 *DARE* (Qu. H82b, *Kinds of cheap candy that used to be sold years ago*) Inf **MI**108, Fried egg—a small tin pan with a yellow center.

fried-egg flower See **fried egg 1**

fried hasty pudding See **fried pudding**

fried hog n Cf **fried pork**

=fried meat.

1967 *DARE* (Qu. H38) Inf **TX**26, Fried hog.

fried hole n

A doughnut; a **doughnut hole.**

1901 *DN* 2.140 **cNY,** *Fried-hole*. . . Fried-cake. **1941** *LANE* Map 284 **nwMA,** *Fried hole,* jocular term . . for the ring-shaped doughnut [1 inf]. **1950** *WELS* 1 Inf, **csWI,** Fried holes. **1960** Bailey *Resp. to PADS 20* **KS,** Nicknames for doughnuts . . fried holes, sinkers. **1966–69** *DARE* (Qu. H27, . . *Joking names for doughnuts*) Infs **GA**3, **RI**12, Fried holes; **CA**157, Fried hole—heard once; **NY**21, Fried hole [FW sugg]; **NY**96, Fried hole [laughter]; (Qu. H28) Inf **MI**106, Fried holes.

fried marble n [See quot c1970] Also called **American fried**

A crazed marble; one with a mesh of internal cracks.

1969 *DARE* (Qu. EE6c, *Cheap marbles*) Inf **PA**203, Fried marbles. **c1970** Wiersma *Marbles Terms* **NJ, NY,** Fried marbles—marbles which have been heated in a heavy skillet until the interior is a mass of cracks; **MI,** Fried marbles—marbles that have been heated up and as a result are cracked, commonly used as shooters; **MI,** Fried marbles . . have been subjected to boiling water and cold water in rapid succession and . . as a result have fracture patterns.

fried meal mush See **fried mush**

fried meat n Also *fry-meat* Cf **fried pork, fry 2**

Bacon.

1928 Peterkin *Scarlet Sister Mary* 39 **SC,** De mush is done now, an' de fry-meat is brown. **1966** Dakin *Dial. Vocab. Ohio R. Valley* 2.337 **eKY,** Bacon sliced and fried is *fried meat.* **1967–70** *DARE* (Qu. H38, . . *Bacon*) Infs **SC**29, **VA**74, Fried meat.

fried mush n Also *fried corn(meal) mush, fried meal mush* **chiefly Nth, Midl, West** See Map

Cornmeal that is boiled, then cooled, sliced, and fried.

1846 (1917) McClellan *Mexican War* 32 **PA,** For our Christmas dinner we had a beefsteak and some fried mush. **1936** Lutes *Country Kitchen* 205 **MI,** In winter, breakfast took on new meaning, for then the fried mush, johnnycake, or ordinary plain bread gave way to buckwheat cakes. **1941** *LANE* Map 288, Corn meal mush is sometimes sliced and fried. It is then called . . *fried mush* [3 infs]. **1950** *WELS (Fried cornmeal)* 28 Infs, **WI,** Fried mush. **c1960** *Wilson Coll.* **csKY,** *Fried mush*. . . Ordinary corn-meal mush, allowed to cool, then sliced and fried. **1965–70** *DARE* (Qu. H25) 435 Infs, **chiefly Nth, N Midl, West,** Fried mush; 16 Infs, **Nth, N Midl,** Fried cornmeal mush; **MI**68, **MN**33, Fried corn mush; **MO**32, Fried meal mush; (Qu. H23) Inf **OK**1, Fried mush.

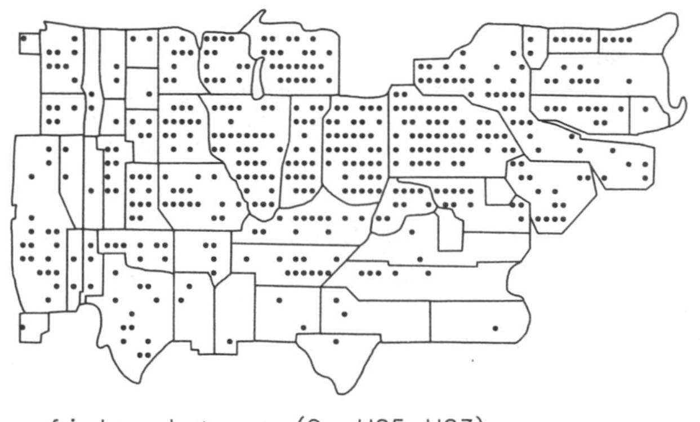

•fried mush + varr (Qq. H25, H23)

fried nothing n

=fried bread n 1.

1941 *LANE* Map 284 **ceCT,** Pieces of raised bread dough fried in deep fat. . . *Fried nothings* [1 inf].

fried nut n

1941 *LANE* Map 284, 1 inf, **seNH,** *Fried nuts,* older term for *doughnuts.*

fried pie n

1 often in combs; also *frying pie:* A turnover, usu fruit-filled, fried in deep fat. **chiefly Sth, S Midl, NEng** See Map

1905 *DN* 3.80 **nwAR,** *Fried pie*. . . A fruit pie fried in a deep vessel filled with fat. **1905** *DN* 3.80 **NH. 1936** Morehouse *Rain on Just* 78 **NC,** Granny Elvy settled back . . , a dish of fried pies in one hand, a pan of ash cakes close by. **1941** *LANE* Map 284 **NEng,** *Fried pie (=turnover)* [25 infs]. **1950** *WELS (Foods made with dough and cooked in deep fat)* 1 Inf, **cwWI,** Fried pies. **1954** *Harder Coll.* **cwTN,** *Fried pie*. . . Pie cooked in deep fat, usually in combined forms: fried chocolate pie, fried apple pie, fried peach pie. **1966–70** *DARE* (Qu. H32, . . *Fancy rolls and pastries*) Infs **GA**85, **MO**16, 17, **MA**69, **SC**32, 42, **TX**17, 33, **VA**74, Fried pies; **TN**57, 66, Fried fruit pies; **MO**17, Fried peach pies; (Qu. H29, *A round cake, cooked in deep fat, with jelly inside*) Infs **IL**30, **MA**58, Fried pie; **OH**37, Fried pie—fruit-filled and fried; (Qu. H30, *An oblong cake, cooked in deep fat*) Infs **MO**37, **TX**29, 62, Fried pie; **MA**6, Fried pie—Mother's term; with mincemeat, jelly, applesauce filling; (Qu. H63, *Kinds of desserts*) Infs **AR**56, **KY**5, **SC**29, Fried pies. **1966–68** *DARE* Tape **IN**3, Dried apple pie was pretty good eating, especially when they made frying pies out of 'em; **OK**19, We called that [=a pie made of a circle of dough folded over fruit filling and fried in a skillet] fried pies and lots of times we had that for breakfast on Sunday morning; **MA**5, He used to take fried pies . . when he went out burning charcoal; **AL**20, That's a great Southern dish, . . fried pies. . . Take any kind of fruit that you might have, like a pie . . and instead of puttin' it in the oven, you just fry it. **1967** *Good Old Days* Jan 25 **GA** (as of c1910), We who lived farther carried our sausage and biscuits, fried pies, baked sweet potatoes, etc. in lunch baskets, tin buckets or shoe boxes.

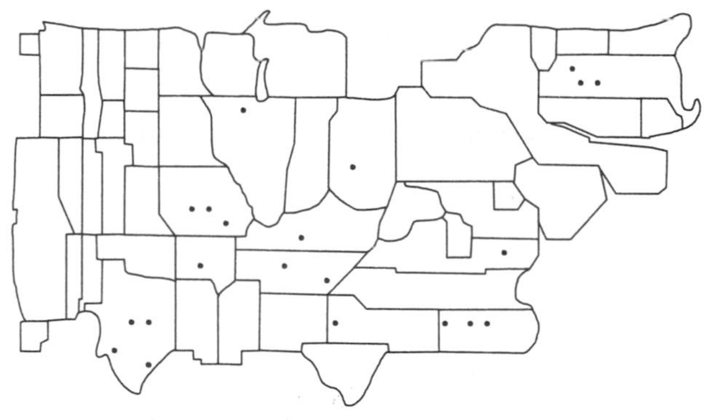

•fried pie 1 + varr (Qq. H32, H29, H30, H63)

2 See quot.

1954 *Harder Coll.* **cwTN,** *Fried pie*. . . Pan pie.

fried pork n Cf **fried hog**

Fried salt pork.

1941 *LANE* Map 301, *Fat pork* and *fried pork* mean (or meant) primarily 'fat salt pork' and 'fried salt pork'. [*Fried pork* occurs frequently in wCT, rarely elsewhere in NEng.] **1944** *AmSp* 19.124 **MA,** *Fried pork* . . does not mean whatever pork is fried. . . Fried pork is small thin slices of salt pork . . fried in a frying-pan crisp or not crisp according to local or personal taste.

fried pudding n Also *fried hasty pudding*

=fried mush.

1906 *Pocumtuc Housewife* 6 *(DA)* **MA,** In summer fried pudding is too heating. **1941** *LANE* Map 288 **NEng,** Corn meal mush is sometimes sliced and fried. It is then called . . *fried (hasty) pudding* [6 infs].

fried puppy n

1 =**fried pie 1.**

1951 *PADS* 21.27 **SC,** *Flapjack*. . . An apple turnover fried in deep grease, also called *fried puppy* in Anderson County.

2 =**hush puppy 1.**

1966 *DARE* (Qu. H25, . . *Fried cornmeal*) Inf **AL**1, Fried puppies.

fried rag See **fried apron**

fried roll n

=**fried bread 1.**

1950 *WELS (Other foods made with dough and cooked in deep fat)* 1 Inf, **ceWI,** Fried rolls.

fried shirt n Also *fried-bosom shirt* *old-fash* Also called **boiled shirt**

A heavily starched shirt.

1898 Lloyd *Country Life* 135 **AL,** And then you can see some good old brother . . with his store bought clothes and his fried shirt on. **1905** *DN* 3.80 **nwAR,** *Fried shirt*. . . Facetious for a freshly starched and ironed shirt. Common. **1912** *DN* 3.576 **wIN.** **1914** *DN* 4.106 **KS.** **1942** (1960) Robertson *Red Hills* 46 **SC,** We have worn fried-bosom shirts with a collar button and no collar if we have chosen to.

friend n

1 A common-law marriage partner. [Cf *OED friend* sb. 4 "A lover or paramour of either sex. *Obs*."] Cf *DJE*

1968–70 *DARE* (Qu. AA19, . . *A man and woman who are not married but live together*) Infs **TN**43, **WV**16, Great and good friends; **VA**72, Dear friends; **MO**17, Just friends.

2 Menstruation.

[**1893** Farmer–Henley *Slang* 3.73/2, *Friend* (or *Little Friend*). . . The menstrual flux . . whose appearance is sometimes announced by the formula 'My little friend has come.'] **1948** *Word* 4.3.185, *List of Expressions* [for menstruation]. . . My friend is here. . . The girl friend, to have the girl friend. [In spoken use among women.] **1965–70** *DARE* (Qu. AA27) Infs **IL**45, **MN**33, **NJ**23, **NY**89, 250, (My *or* her) friend; **NY**51, 76, My girl friend; **CT**11, **NY**83, Got my friend; **PA**170, 225, Have your (*or* my) friend; **PA**93, Little friend; **KY**59, My friend's come. [Of 13 Infs, 5 are young, 6 mid-aged; 11 female; all hs or coll educ.] **1982** Walker *Color Purple* 161 **GA** [Black], Just when I think I've learned to live with the heat, the constant dampness, . . my friend comes. . . Right after her mother's death, Olivia got *her* friend.

friend around v phr Cf **friend with**

To keep company, pal around.

1945 *Eaton Coll.* **Milwaukee WI,** Her and me used to friend around.

friend-girl n [Reversed compound; cf Intro "Language Changes" I.1]

A girl friend; similarly *friend-boy* a boy friend.

1930 *AmSp* 5.390 [Lingo of N Atl fishermen], *Friend-girl*. . . Girl friend, sweetheart. **1941** *S. Rev.* 7.68 **TN,** "Come along, come along," he said. "We've only got four days left, and you'll want to tell your friend-girls you learned to ride." She jerked one hand loose from his hold and slapped his hard cheek. She screamed, "Friend-girl? You never heard me say, Friend-girl. What black nigger do you think you're talking down to?" **1974** (1975) Shaw *All God's Dangers* 73 **AL** [Black male speaker], My daddy had no conveniences for me to enjoy myself with my friend-girls. **1977–79** *DARE* File **Baton Rouge LA** [Among Black students and faculty members], Friend-boy, friend-girl; **sID** (as of 1960s), In college we thought it was nice to have friend-boys, but, given a choice, would always have preferred to have boy-friends.

friendly n

A social gathering, usu informal.

1942 Berrey–Van den Bark *Amer. Slang* 365.1, *Social entertainment; party*. . . friendly, *a gathering of friends.* **1968** *DARE* (Qu. FF1, . . *Kinds [of 'socials']*) Inf **AL**42, Friendlies; (Qu. FF22a, . . *Clubs and societies . . for women*) Inf **AL**42, Friendlies.

friendly crab n

A wharf crab *(Sesarma cinereum).*

1981 Meinkoth *Audubon Field Guide Seashore* 652, Range: Chesapeake Bay to Florida and Texas. . . This crab [=*Sesarma cinereum*] . . is often called the "Friendly Crab" because of its habit of climbing into boats.

‡**friends and enemies** n phr

A children's game; see quot.

1968 *DARE* (Qu. EE12, *Games in which one captain hides his team and the other team tries to find it*) Inf **GA**18, Cowboys and Indians; friends and enemies.

friendship quilt n Also *friendship coverlet, ~ top*

A quilt whose top has been pieced (and usu also quilted) by a group of friends for one person, usu in honor of a specific occasion.

1940 Writers' Program *Hands that Built NH* 188, Similar to the "Album" was the "Friendship" coverlet, often more interesting than beautiful because of the latitude allowed in both design and coloring. The finished product was a medley . . since each block . . was the contribution of some friend. **1949** Ickis *Quilt Making* 52, There is a group of antique quilts we know today as the Friendship Quilts. They were made by exchanging patterns among a circle of friends, each of whom would complete a batch of blocks using her own individual design made on a basic motif that had been chosen for the quilt as a whole. **1954** *Harder Coll.* **cwTN,** Friendship top. . . A quilt that is sewed and donated by friends. **1972** *Foxfire Book* 149 **nGA,** The most captivating custom . . was that of the Friendship Quilt. This was a quilt much like the others . . with the added feature of a number of names embroidered on the squares themselves. . . "The name of everyone that pieced a square was supposed to be put on the quilt." . . Such quilts were made . . whenever a young person . . got married, when a neighbor lost his house by fire, for a newborn child in the neighborhood, or just for a keepsake.

friend with v phr Cf *DJE friend* v

To become friends with.

1937 (1977) Hurston *Their Eyes* 228 **csFL,** Since Tea Cake and Janie had friended with the Bahaman workers in the 'Glades, they . . had been gradually drawn into the American crowd. **1942** Hurston *Dust Tracks* 194 **FL** [Black], Lucky for me I had friended with Big Sweet.

frier See **fryer** n[1]

frig n See **fridge** n

frig v Also with *around, away* [Cf *OED frig* v. "*Obs*. . . To move about restlessly."] Cf **diddle** v **5, futz** v **1**

To fool around, putter; to fidget.

1940 Hemingway *For Whom the Bell Tolls* 272, We do not let the gypsy nor others frig with it [=a gun]. **1965** *DARE* File **neWI,** You spend your whole day frigging away at that kind of job. **1966** *DARE* FW Addit **nME,** To frig around—to fool with, toy with, bother, disturb. **1969** *DARE* (Qu. A11, *When somebody takes too long about coming to a decision . . "I wish he'd quit ______."*) Inf **WI**75, Friggin' around. [FW: very common here both among men and women] **1975** Gould *ME Lingo* 102, *Frig*—A word with four-letter nuance almost everywhere except Maine. Here, it means fiddle around, dawdle, fidget, fuss, fondle idly, putter. A Maine lady of unimpeachable gentility once . . said [her husband] would sit "frigging with his necktie."

frigate hawk n [Infl by *frigate bird*]

=**man-o'-war bird.**

1967 Will *Dredgeman* 83 **FL,** Overhead soars the frigate hawk or man-of-war bird, black and fork-tailed.

frigate mackerel n

=**bonito 1.**

1935 Caine *Game Fish* 53, *Bonito*—*Sarda sarda*. . . Frigate Mackerel.

frigate pelican n Cf **frigate hawk**

=**man-o'-war bird.**

1835 Audubon *Ornith. Biog.* 3.495 **Sth,** The Frigate Pelican. *Tachypetes Aquilus. Ibid,* About the middle of May, . . [on] the Florida Keys, the Frigate Pelicans assemble in flocks of from fifty to five hundred pairs or more. **1883** U.S. Natl. Museum *Bulletin* 27.164, *Tachypetes aquila.* Frigate Pelican; Man-o-war Hawk. . . North to California, Texas, Florida, and (casually) Long Island. **1925** (1928) Forbush *Birds MA* 1.171, *Fregata*. . . Frigate pelican. **1946** Hausman *Eastern Birds* 95, *Man-O'-War Bird*—*Fregata magnificens*. . . Frigate Pelican. **1962** Imhof *AL Birds* 79, *Fregata magnificens*. . . Frigate Pelican.

frig away See **frig** v

frigging ppl adj, adv

Trifling; annoying; darned.

1930 Dos Passos *42nd Parallel* 58 **MN,** Station agent's so friggin tough in this dump. **1965** *DARE* File **neWI,** All these frigging [i.e., trifling, trivial] little jobs. **1966** *DARE* FW Addit **nME,** *Friggin'*—a milder cuss word used as an adjective. **1968** *DARE* (Qu. NN17, *Something that keeps on annoying you . . "That ______ fly won't go away."*) Inf **NH**14, Frigging. **1979** Lewis *How to Talk Yankee* [12] **nNEng,** *Frigging. . .* Abominable. "I can't get this frigging halter on right." **1984** Doig *English Creek* 244 **nMT,** Drop the next frigging load right on that fork!

fright n Cf *DS* EE41, **fraid** n

1943 *LANE* Map 533, Names for the imaginary demons invoked to frighten children into obedience. . . 1 inf, **ceCT,** The frights.

frightment n Cf Intro "Language Changes" III.1, **-ment**

Fright.

1926 *DN* 5.400 **Ozarks,** Joe he lowed th' young-un war burnt t' death, but 'pears t' me like she jes' died fr'm frightment.

frigidaire n [Trademark] **widespread, but less freq Inland Nth, PA, West** See Map Cf **fridge** n

A gas or electric refrigerator.

1926 *Publishers' Weekly* 110.964/2, Vacuum cleaners, frigidaires, radios. **1958** Humphrey *Home from the Hill* 146 **TX** [Black], "Git out of that frigidaire, boy," she said. "I'll let you know when yo dinner's ready." **c1960** *Wilson Coll.* **csKY,** *Frigidaire. . .* A name for any electrical refrigerator. **1965–70** *DARE* (Qu. D10b, *The place to keep food cool if it is run by electricity or gas*) 107 Infs, **widespread, but less freq Inland Nth, PA, West,** Frigidaire; (Qu. D9) Inf **ME**1, Frigidaire; (Qu. D10a) Infs **MO**9, **OK**56, Frigidaire; (Qu. M18) Inf **KY**34, Frigidaire. **1966–68** *DARE* Tapes **FL**41, **NY**61, Frigidaire. **1986** Pederson *LAGS Concordance,* 15 infs, **Gulf Region,** Frigidaire. [In three instances the FW notes that the word is used generically.]

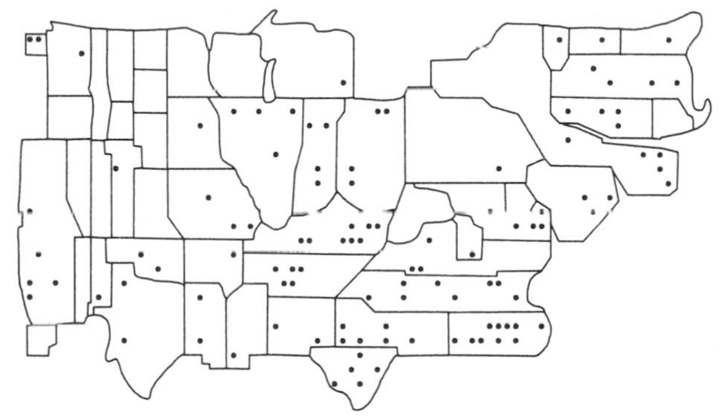

•frigidaire (Qq. D10a, b, D9, M18)

frigidaire watermelon n

=icebox melon.

1986 Pederson *LAGS Concordance* **Gulf Region** *(Watermelons)* 1 inf, Frigidaire watermelon—small, one person can eat; 1 inf, Frigidaire watermelons. [Both infs old]

frigolito See **frijolillo 1**

frijole n |ˌfri'holi, -le| Also *frejol, fricole, frijol, frijole bean;* pronc-sp *free-holy* [Span *frijol* kidney bean] **chiefly SW** See Map Also called **Mexican strawberry**

A kidney bean or similar bean.

1831 Beechey *Narrative* 2.50, A plentiful supply of cold fricole beans, bread, and eggs. **1856** (1929) Jaeger *Diary Fort Yuma* 221 **sCA,** Patro Mandus arrived from Caborca also & brought in some frijoles & corn. **1892** *DN* 1.190 **TX,** *Frijól, -es* (also *fréjol*). **1945** Thorp *Pardner* 273 **SW,** There was one staple item in the Southwestern cowboy's diet which it would be sinful to overlook, and that was the lowly *frijole* (free-holy) bean. **1962** Atwood *Vocab. TX* 60, The commercial term *pinto beans . .* is current all through the state. . . The older regional word is the Spanish *frijoles . .* which shows the highest frequency in Southwest Texas . . but which is also well known in the West and part of the Central area. It is nonoccurrent in East Texas, Arkansas, and Louisiana. **1965–70** *DARE* (Qu. I17, *Beans . . that are dark red when they are dry*) Infs **AZ**12, **CA**97, **TX**3, 6, 29, 67, Frijoles; **AZ**15, [fri'hole] beans; **NM**12, In English a frijole is a pinto bean; **TX**4, 69, [fri'holi(z)]; **CA**24, ['friholiz]; (Qu. H50, *Dishes made with beans . . that everybody around here knows, but people in other places might not*) Infs **CA**11, 54, 85, **CO**27, **NY**105, **TX**5, Frijoles; **NM**12, [fri'holiz] and chili; **TX**10, Frijoles—Mexican beans; **TX**69, ['friˌholi] beans; (Qu. H65, *Foreign foods*) Infs **CO**5, **NM**12, Frijoles; (Qu. I20) Infs **CA**50, **TX**5, 67, Frijoles.

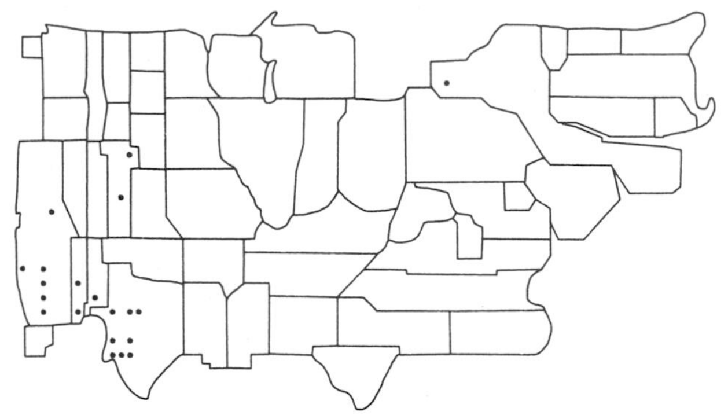

•frijole + varr (Qq. I17, H50, H65, I20)

frijole-eater n *derog* Cf *DS* HH28, **beaner 2, chili eater**

A Mexican.

1963 Mencken–McDavid *Amer. Lang.* 374, [The term *greaser*] has had . . various rivals, *e.g., pepper-belly . .* which embodies an obvious allusion to the Mexican cuisine, as do *chili eater* and *frijole eater.*

frijolillo n [AmSpan; dimin of Span *frijol* bean] **SW**

1 also *frigolito, frijolilla, frijol(l)ito:* An evergreen shrub/tree *(Sophora secundiflora).* Also called **big-drunk bean, coral bean 2, mescal bean, mountain laurel, whiskey bean**

1886 Havard *Flora W. & S. TX for 1885* 500, *Sophora secundiflora. . .* (Frijolillo; Coral Bean.) **1892** *DN* 1.190 **TX,** *Frijolíllo:* a large shrub of the family *Leguminosæ,* with bright red, very poisonous beans *(Sophora secundiflora).* **1936** NM Univ. *Biol. Ser.* 4.5.54 **NM,** *Broussonetia secundiflora,* known as "mountain laurel," and also by the Spanish names *frijollito* and *frijolilla.* It is a beautiful evergreen shrub with glossy dark green leaves, common in the Guadalupe Mountains southwest of Carlsbad. **1951** *PADS* 15.34 **TX,** *Sophora secundiflora* Lagasca.—Mountain laurel; frijolillo; whiskey bean; mescal bean. **1960** Vines *Trees SW* 569, Other vernacular names are . . Frigolito, Frijollito, Frijolillo [etc]. **1979** Little *Checklist U.S. Trees* 276, *Mescalbean. . . Other common names . .* frijolito, frijolillo.

2 A **locoweed** (here: *Oxytropis lambertii*).

1947 (1976) Curtin *Healing Herbs* 90, The *frijolillo,* or little bean, [is] so-called after the beanlike seeds this herb produces. Its fruit is contained in swollen pods that allow the seeds to rattle against their interiors when they are shaken.

frijol(l)ito See **frijolillo 1**

frill n [Engl dial; cf *EDD frill* sb. 2, *OED frill* sb.[1] 3]

1899 (1912) Green *VA Folk-Speech* 186, *Frill. . .* A piece of fat on a hog's entrails; the omentum.

frilled lace cactus See **lace cactus**

frilly adj [*frill* an affectation]

Highfalutin, affected; snobbish.

1967–70 *DARE* (Qu. HH35, *A woman who puts on a lot of airs*) Infs **IL**7, **KY**73, Frilly.

fringe n

1 also *water-fringe:* A **floating heart 1** (here: *Nymphoides peltata*). [See quot 1976]

1959 Carleton *Index Herb. Plants* 49, *Fringe:* Nymphoides peltatum [sic]. **1976** Bailey–Bailey *Hortus Third* 774, *[Nymphoides] peltata. . . Water-fringe. . .* Corolla bright yellow, . . lobes fringed.

2 also *corn fringe:* Corn tassel.

1966–69 *DARE* (Qu. I31, *When a corn stalk is well grown, what comes out at the top?*) Infs **MI**34, 106, (Corn) fringe.

‡fringe v [Malaprop]

To singe.

1967 *DARE* (Qu. NN20b, *Exclamations caused by . . a slight burn*) Inf **LA**8, I fringed my hand. **1967** *DARE* FW Addit **LA**8, After you pick a chicken, you put it over a fire to fringe it.

fringe bush See **fringe tree**

fringe cup n

1 A **miterwort** (here: *Mitella diphylla*).

1893 *Jrl. Amer. Folkl.* 6.142 **NY,** *Mitella diphylla,* false sanicle; fringe cup; fairy cup. **1949** Peattie *Cascades* 231 **Pacific NW,** Fringe-cups are common all along the way.

2 A perennial plant *(Tellima grandiflora)* native to western North America. Also called **false alumroot**

1911 Jepson *Flora CA* 199, *Tellima grandiflora*. . . Fringe-cups. **1916** Parsons *Wild Flowers CA* 348, Fringe-cups. . . *Tellima grandiflora.* **1959** Anderson *Flora AK* 283. **1961** Thomas *Flora Santa Cruz* 191 **cwCA. 1976** Bailey-Bailey *Hortus Third* 1100.

3 =woodland star.

1961 Peck *Manual OR* 406, *Lithophragma*. . . Fringe-cup. **1963** Craighead *Rocky Mt. Wildflowers* 72, *Lithophragma parviflora*. . . Fringe-cup. **1973** Hitchcock-Cronquist *Flora Pacific NW* 189, *Lithophragma*. . . Fringecup.

fringed bogbean n Also *fringed buckbean*

A **floating heart 1** (here: *Nymphoides peltata*).

1940 Clute *Amer. Plant Names* 227, *Nymphoides peltatum*. . . Fringed bogbean. **1959** Carleton *Index Herb. Plants* 50, *Fringed buckbean:* Nymphoides peltatum.

fringed orchid n Also *fringed orchis, fringe orchid*

Std: an orchid of the genus *Habenaria.* Also called **bog orchid, fairy-fringe, monkey face, rein orchid.** For other names of var spp see **bog candle, bog torch 2, dead-man's-fingers 3, fringeless orchid, frog arrow, frog spear, frog spike, gall of the earth 6, heal-all 1, hold-still, hook-eye orchid, meadow pink, moon-set, orange plume, plume of Navarre, plume-royal, pride-of-the-peak, ragged orchid, rattlesnake master, satyr orchid, scent bottle, shin-plasters, snowy orchid, soldier's plume, Solomon's seal, water-spider orchid, wild hyacinth, wood orchid**

fringed polygala n

Std: a **milkwort** (here: *Polygala pauciflora*) with wintergreen-like leaves and usu rose-purple flowers. Also called **babies' feet, babies' slippers 1, bird-on-the-wing, chicken-on-the-wing, dove-on-the-mountain, flowering wintergreen, gaywings, Indian pink, lady's slipper, little pollom, maywings, satin flower, snakeroot**

fringed sagebrush n Also *fringed sage*

A **sagebrush** (here: *Artemisia frigida*).

1950 Stevens *ND Plants* 291, *Artemisia frigida*. . . Fringed Sage. **1960** Vines *Trees SW* 966, Fringed Sage-brush—*Artemisia frigida.*

fringed spruce n

The bristlecone fir *(Abies bracteata).*

1897 Sudworth *Arborescent Flora* 56 **ID,** *Bristle-cone Fir*. . . Fringed Spruce. **1908** Britton *N. Amer. Trees* 85, *Abies bracteata*. . . This, the most peculiar, as well as the rarest of the North American Fir trees, is also called . . Fringed spruce.

fringed waterlily n

A **floating heart 1** (here: *Nymphoides peltata*).

1940 Clute *Amer. Plant Names* 227, *Nymphoides peltatum*. . . Fringed water lily. **1959** Carleton *Index Herb. Plants* 50, *Fringed-waterlily:* Nymphoides peltatum.

fringeless orchid n Also *fringeless orchis*

A **fringed orchid** (here: *Habenaria integra* or *H. peramoena*); see quot 1901.

1901 Lounsberry *S. Wild Flowers* 80, *H. peramoena,* fringeless . . orchid. . . The flower's lip has not the delicate fringe which makes so attractive its near relative. **1949** Moldenke *Amer. Wild Flowers* 386, In moist meadows . . is found the *fringeless* or *great purple orchis, B[lephariglottis] peramoena.* **1950** Correll *Native Orchids* 81, *Habenaria integra*. . . *Common names:* Yellow Fringeless-orchid. *Ibid* 95, *Habenaria peramoena*. . . *Common names:* Purple Fringeless-orchid. **1976** Bailey-Bailey *Hortus Third* 534, Fringeless orchid.

fringe orchid See **fringed orchid**

fringepod n

A plant of the genus *Thysanocarpus.* Also called **lacepod**

1911 Jepson *Flora CA* 191, *Thysanocarpus curvipes*. . . Fringe-pod. **1925** Jepson *Manual Plants CA* 447, Fringe-pod . . [is] frequent in the open hill country of Cal., 100 to 5000 ft., n. to B.C. and Ida. **1941** Jaeger *Wildflowers* 82 **Desert SW,** Fringe-Pod. *Thysanocarpus curvipes eradiatus.* **1973** Hitchcock-Cronquist *Flora Pacific NW* 180, *Thysanocarpus*. . . Fringepod.

fringe tree n Also *fringe bush*

A white-flowered deciduous tree *(Chionanthus virginicus).* **chiefly Sth, S Midl** Also called **bridal-veil tree, father graybeard, granddaddy graybeard 2, grandfather's beard 1, granny graybeard, graybeard, old-man's beard, poison ash, shavings, snowflower tree, sunflower tree, white ash, white fringe**

1731 (1754) Catesby *Nat. Hist. Carolina* 1.68 **NC, SC,** *Amelanchior* [sic] *Virginiana*. . . The Fringe Tree. On the Banks of Rivulets and running Streams this Shrub is most commonly found. **1759** (1775) Burnaby *Travels* 7, The woods are beautified with fringe-trees, flowering poplars, etc. **1806** (1905) Lewis *Orig. Jrls. Lewis & Clark Exped.* 6.213, The fringe tree has cast the corolla and it's [sic] leaves have nearly obtained their full size. **1838** (1852) Gilman *S. Matron* 145, She stood bowing to the various salutations, graceful as a fringe-tree, whose white tassels wave in the clustering forests. **1894** Torrey *Fla. Sketch-Book* 216 *(DAE),* The fringe-bush, likewise, stood here and there in solitary state. **1899** (1912) Green *VA Folk-Speech* 186, *Fringe-tree*. . . A tree, the bloom of which looks like lace. **1941** Walker *Lookout* 61 **TN,** Fringe-tree, or Old Man's Beard . . builds snowlike spots in many places on top of the mountain. **1943** Peattie *Great Smokies* 166, The sourwood, the fringe bush, and the mountain laurel, are understory trees. **1968** *DARE* (Qu. T15) Inf **MD**30, Fringe tree—flower looks like white tissue paper cut in fringes. Seed is flat and purple; (Qu. T16) Inf **PA**74, Fringe tree—has white fringe on it when in bloom.

‡fringy-minded adj [*fringe* an outer edge]

Mentally confused; senile.

1975 Thomas *Hear the Lambs* 114 **nwAL,** The po' old soul has got fringy-minded . . and he go all over this town totin' his sack. I bet he don't know where he's at.

frisk n

Appar an aphid.

1968 *DARE* (Qu. R26, . . *Small greenish lice . . on plants*) Inf **LA**15, Frisk—comes on cotton, so small you can't hardly see 'em.

‡friskin n

A type of bread.

1968 *DARE* (Qu. H20b) Inf **DE**4, Friskins—used on the [clam dredging] boat. Made out of white flour and eggs. A special kind of white bread.

frisky adj

‡1 Highfalutin, snobbish. Cf **frilly**

1966 *DARE* (Qu. HH35, *A woman who puts on a lot of airs: "She's too ——— for me."*) Inf **MS**6, Frisky.

2 Of weather: brisk, fresh.

1950 *WELS (Words to describe a clear, cold winter day)* 3 Infs, **eWI,** Frisky.

frisno See **fresno 2**

fritillary n Also *fritillaria*

Std: a plant of the genus *Fritillaria.* For names of var spp see **bronze bells, brown bells, brown lily, buttercup 3, checker lily, chocolate lily, crocus n[1] 2d, Eskimo potato, Indian rice, leopard lily, mission bells, modest lily, pink bell, red bells, rice root, snake lily, snowdrop, sourdough lily, speckled-hen lily, spider lily, squaw lily, stink bells, tiger lily, toad lily, yellow bells**

fritter n

1 also *fritter cake:* A pancake, often with slices of fruit cooked in the batter. [Cf Engl dial *frit* a kind of pancake, and *fritter* a small pancake containing currants] **chiefly Sth, S Midl, NEast** See Map Cf **flitter n[1] 2a** Note: It is not always possible to distinguish between the std *fritter* that is fried in deep fat and the cake that is fried on a griddle.

1690 (1878) S. Sewall *Diary* 1.313 **MA,** George Monk brought in a Dish of Fritters, but Major Hutchinson, Mr. Addington, and my self eat [sic] none of them. **1891** *AN&Q* 6.179/1, The terms fritters and flat-jacks are very common to Pennsylvania at the present time, and especially to the county of Lancaster. **1911** Shute *Plupy* 65 **NH,** Poor Plupy was promptly restricted to butter on his fritters. **1949** Kurath *Word Geog.* 20, In Maine, New Hampshire, and Essex County, Massachusetts, *fritter* is still often used in this sense, but *griddle cake* is taking its place. **1965–70** *DARE* (Qu. H20b, . . *Other names . . for pancakes*) 30 Infs, **chiefly Sth, NEast,** Fritters; **PA**41, **SC**56, **WI**49, Apple fritters; **LA**40, Banana fritters—pancake dough with bananas sliced in it; **SC**56, Peach fritters; [**LA**31, Fritters—this is made with deep fat; **MA**40, Fritters—cooked in deep fat; **PA**131, Fritters—this is different, is fried in deep fat rather than on the grill]; (Qu. F3, *When you're frying things—for example, eggs—you turn them over with a ______*) Inf **VA**9, Fritter turner; [(Qu. H18) Inf **LA**28, Fritters—pancake batter fried crisp in deep fat; made with flour; they are ruffled around the edge]. **1972** *PADS* 58.20 **cwAL,** *Pancakes* (14) is most frequent, but . . *fritter cakes* (1), and *wheat cakes* (1) are also found. **1973** Allen *LAUM* 1.283 (as of c1950), *Fritters* [for *pancakes*] . . appears in the U[pper] M[idwest] in and around that part of east central Nebraska having a New York state orientation.

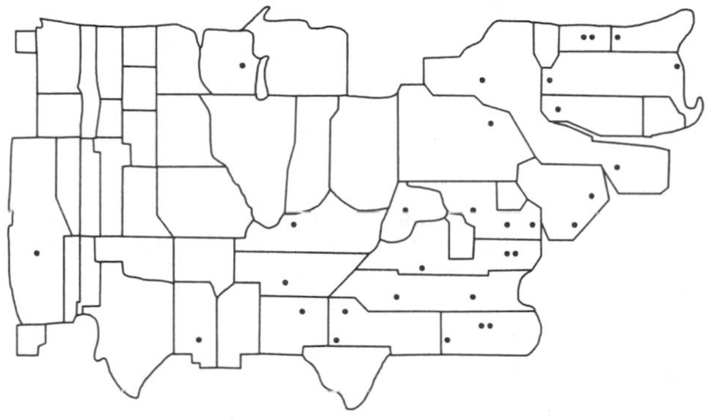

•fritter n 1 + varr (Qq. H20b, F3)

2 also *corn(meal) fritter:* A fried cornmeal cake. **scattered, but chiefly Sth, S Midl** See Map

1791 Bartram *Travels* 152 **FL,** They also mix it [=flour made from the root of the **China brier**] with fine Corn flour, which being fried in the fresh bear's oil makes very good hot cakes or fritters. **1847** (1852) Crowen *Amer. Cookery* 235 **NY,** *Corn Meal Fritters.* **1950** *WELS* (*What does 'fritter' mean?*) 1 Inf, **ceWI,** Fritter—corn dough fried in a pan with small amount of grease. **1965** *PADS* 43.25 **seMA,** 1 inf, Corn fritters [for corn bread]. **1965–70** *DARE* (Qu. H25, . . *Names . . for fried cornmeal*) 32 Infs **scattered, but chiefly Sth, S Midl,** (Corn) fritters; **IL**57, **MD**37, Cornmeal fritters; **TN**52, **VT**16, Fried fritters; (Qu. H14, *Bread that's made with cornmeal*) Infs **AL**52, **DC**7, **MD**12, **NC**8, 30, **PA**66, **SC**22, **VA**1, Corn fritters; **GA**11, **TN**37, Fritters; (Qu. H20b) Infs **MD**17, **PA**41, **VT**16, Corn fritters. **1967** *DARE* Tape **SC**46, [FW:] Did you ever have any kind of corn fixin's that you would fry in deep fat? [Inf:] Fritters. Corn fritters, yeah. **1973** Allen *LAUM* 1.280 **IA** (as of c1950), Other types of corn bread. . . corn fritters. [1 inf]

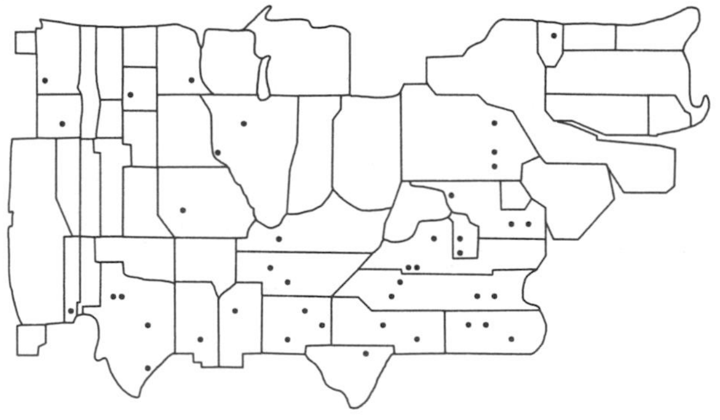

•fritter n 2 + varr (Qq. H25, H14, H20b)

3 See quot. [Prob by ext from **1**]

c1960 *Wilson Coll.* **csKY,** *Fritter*. . . Sometimes applied to a flat, thin patty of mashed potatoes.

fritter v

1969 *DARE* (Qu. AA8, *When people make too much of a show of affection in a public place—for example, "There they were at the church supper ______ [with each other]."*) Inf **CA**169, Frittering.

fritter-brained See **fritter-minded**

fritter cake See **fritter n 1**

fritter-fretter n [Redup of *fretter*]

One who frets or worries a lot.

1950 *WELS* (*Names or nicknames for someone who worries a lot or . . about little things*) 1 Inf, **seWI,** Fritter-fretter.

fritter-minded adj Also *fritter-brained* **S Midl**

Scatterbrained, flighty; hence n *fritter-mindedness* foolishness.

1928 Chapman *Happy Mt.* 15 **seTN,** First you know you'll be fritter-minded as an outlander. **1929** *AmSp* 5.18 **Ozarks,** *Fritter-minded.* . . Frivolous, erratic. "Them city gals is all kinder fritter-minded, 'pears like." **1931** Hannum *Thursday April* 83 **wNC,** Thursday April persuaded Joe to buy him a fiddle. Joe fussed and fumed at such fritter-mindedness and said it was a sight of nonsense. **1942** (1971) Campbell *Cloud-Walking* 72 **seKY,** When Sary saw she wasn't fritter-minded she told her how she made different patterns on her loom. **c1970** *Halpert Coll.* **wKY,** "Most fritter-brained youngster in that family." "I never saw an old fellow quite so fritter-brained."

fritter tree See **honey pond and flitter tree**

frittle n [By lambdacism from *fritter*]

=**fritter n 1.**

1970 *DARE* (Qu. H20b, . . *Names . . for pancakes*) Inf **VA**69, Frittles.

‡fritty n

1968 *DARE* (Qu. X55b, *Words for breaking wind from the bowels*) Inf **NY**109, Fritty, fart, stinker.

Fritz n [Ger nickname for *Friedrich*]

A German.

1932 Dos Passos *1919* 62, Joe . . told 'em how they were prisoners there like they were fritzes. **1946** *AmSp* 21.246 [Army speech], 'Heinie,' 'Fritz,' and 'squarehead' were relatively rare [as nicknames for Germans during WWII]. **1967–69** *DARE* (Qu. HH28, *Names . . for people of foreign background: German*) Infs **CA**145, **CT**16, **LA**11, **NY**22, **PA**94, **VT**12, Fritz. [5 of 6 Infs old]

fritz around v phr Cf **frig** v, **futz (around)**

To gad about, fool around.

1969 *DARE* (Qu. Y29b, *A man who doesn't stay home much: "He's always ______."*) Inf **MI**103, Fritzin' around.

fritz, on the adj phr, adv phr [Orig unknown] **chiefly Nth** See Map Cf **kaput**

Out of order; in (or into) a state of disrepair or ruin.

1903 R. L. McCardell *Conversat. Chorus Girl* 15 (*OEDS*), They gave an open air [performance] that put our opera house show on the Fritz. **1905** (1906) Green *At the Actors' Boarding House* 359 **NYC,** What with me ketchin' 'em cookin' spaghetti on the gas an' tearin' up the bed-spreads to use fur makeup towels, they're puttin' the place on the fritz! **1919** Kyne *Capt. Scraggs* 73 **CA,** I got my arms left, even if my feet is on the fritz. **1950** *WELS* (*"My sewing machine is ______"*) 8 Infs, **WI,** On the fritz. **1965–70** *DARE* (Qu. KK19, . . *Temporarily out of order:*

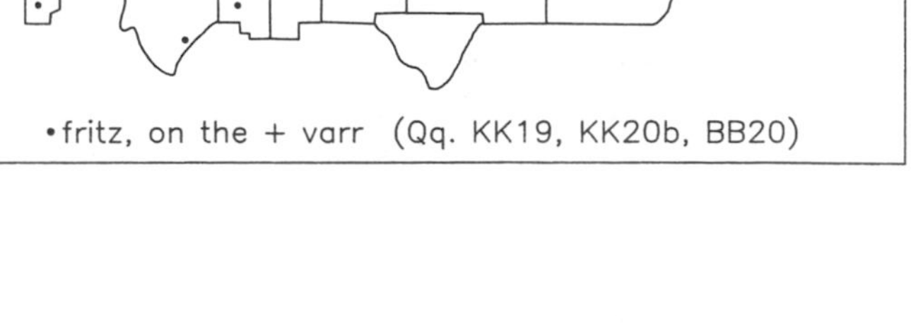

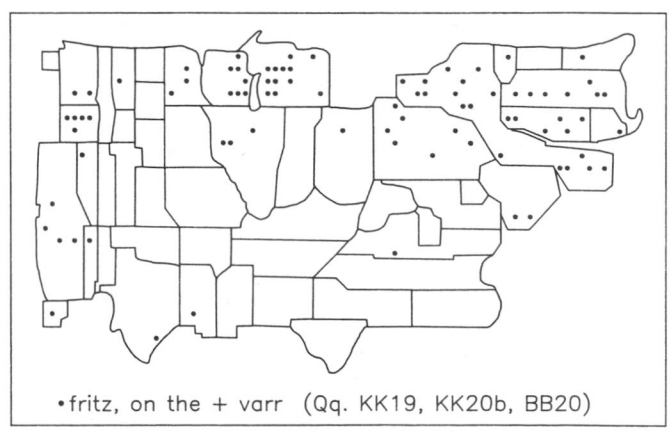

•fritz, on the + varr (Qq. KK19, KK20b, BB20)

"My sewing machine ______.") 75 Infs, **chiefly Nth,** Is on the fritz; **MA**54, Went on the fritz; (Qu. KK20b, *Something that looks as if it might collapse any minute: "Our old washing machine is ______."*) 10 Infs, **Nth,** On the fritz; [**NY**86, Fritz;] (Qu. BB20, . . *Overactive kidneys*) Inf **AZ**2, Waterworks on the fritz. **1980** *Milwaukee Jrl.* (WI) 3 July Green Sheet 2/1 **nwOH,** Today our TV set began acting up with the picture all scrambled. Dad fiddled with the controls, as he always does, but finally said: "This time it's really on the fritz. We'll have to call the repairman."

frivel See **frivol**

frivle-fravle n [Redup of **frivol**]

Trivial chatter; a frivolous or showy display.

c1885 in 1981 Woodward *Mary Chesnut's Civil War* 26 **SC,** The bride, my cousin. . . So very large and handsome and strong. So covered with a frivle fravle of finery. *Ibid* 56, Man after man came and interrupted the conversation with some frivle fravle, but we held on. *Ibid* 242, Mr. Chesnut has gone to Richmond. And now there is nothing but frivle fravle talked in this house.

frivol v Also sp *frivel* [Back-formation from *frivolous*]

To do something unimportant or frivolous; to waste time; to squander.

1866 (1881) Whitney *Leslie Goldthwaite* 56 **NH,** They will come, and frivel about the gates, without ever once entering in. **1928** *Ruppenthal Coll.* **KS,** He inherited a good farm but soon friveled it away. **1950** *WELS (Wasting time by doing unimportant or useless things)* 1 Inf, **csWI,** Frivoling. **1966** *DARE* (Qu. A10, . . *Doing little unimportant things . . "I'm just ______."*) Inf **FL**3, Frivolin'.

friz See **freeze** v **A1, 2, 3, 4**

frizen See **freeze** v **A3**

frizzed See **freeze** v **A4**

frizzle v [Blend of *fry* + *sizzle*]

To fry, esp with a sizzling sound; also fig; hence ppl adj *frizzled.*

1851 (1852) Stowe *Uncle Tom's Cabin* 1.39, Aunt Chloe . . presiding . . over certain frizzling items in a stew-pan. **a1864** (1871) Hawthorne *Passages Fr. & Ital. Note-Books* 2.161, Where the sun had the fairest chance to frizzle me. **1899** (1912) Green *VA Folk-Speech* 186, *Frizzle. . .* To fry. **1947** Bowles–Towle *New Engl. Cooking* 101, *Frizzled smoked beef. . .* Put one tablespoon butter in a skillet and frizzle the beef in it. **1953** Piercy *Shaker Cook Book* 100 (as of c1840), In one little manuscript volume we find recipes for forty-one ways of "preparing substantial and tasty egg dishes," ranging from boiled, baked, coddled, battered and steamed to dropped, fried, smothered, frizzled, puffed and potted eggs.

frizzle n[1]

=**frazzle** n **5.**

1959 [see **frazzle** n **5**]. **1969** *DARE* (Qu. KK50, . . *Planned out carefully, down to the last detail: "He had it all worked out ______."*) Inf **GA**72, To a frizzle.

frizzle n[2] See **frizzled chicken**

frizzle n[3] See **fizzle** n **3**

frizzle n[4] See **frazzle** n **5**

frizzled ppl adj[1] [Var of *frazzled*]

1 See **frazzled (out) 1.**

2 also with *up:* Wrinkled, withered. [Prob infl by *shriveled*]

1968–70 *DARE* (Qu. LL3a, *Shrunk, dried up: "These apples are all ______."*) Infs **CA**121, **FL**52, **IA**46, Frizzled (up).

frizzled ppl adj[2] See **frizzle** v

frizzled chicken n Also *frizzle, frizzled fowl, frizzly chicken* [*frizzled* curled]

A domestic fowl having feathers that curl outward or backward.

1849 *New Engl. Farmer* 1.309/2, The Frizzled fowl has its feathers pointed forward, so that it cannot run amongst grain. **1854** PA State Ag. Soc. *Report* 163, The immediate progeny of foreign importations, comprising, in the tribe of barn-yard fowls, . . the Frizzle; the Creely and the Creepy. **1931** *Jrl. Amer. Folkl.* 44.380 **LA,** Many persons keep a frizzled chicken in the yard to locate and scratch up any hoodoo that may be buried for them. These chickens have, no doubt, earned this reputation by their ugly appearance—with all of their feathers set in backwards. **1945** Saxon *Gumbo Ya-Ya* 537 **sLA,** Keep a frizzly chicken around you at all times. If someone hoodoos you, the chicken will dig it up. **1951** *New Yorker* 10 Feb 36/3 **TN,** The children had gone back to look at her half-grown collie dog and the two hounds, at the old sow and her farrow of new pigs, and at the frizzliest frizzly chicken Aunt Munsie [=a Black woman] had ever had. **1966** *DARE* Tape **GA**12, The feathers do stand up. . . It's been a long, long time since I've seen frizzled chickens.

frizzled up See **frizzled** ppl adj[1] **2**

frizzly chicken See **frizzled chicken**

‡**frizz up** v phr[1] [Abbr for **frizzle** v]

To fry quickly.

1966 *DARE* FW Addit **neWA,** Frizz 'em up—to fry thin slices of onion or potato.

frizz up v phr[2] [Cf *OED frizzle* to adorn with frills, "*Obs.*"]

To decorate, trim, pretty something (up).

1969 *DARE* (Qu. W30, . . *"It's too plain—I think I'll put on a few flowers to ______ it up."*) Inf **NC**76, Frizz.

'fro n [Abbr for **Afro**] *among Black speakers*

1970 *Current Slang* Fall 7 [Black], *'Fro. . . An Afro hair style.* **1970** *DARE* (Qu. X5, . . *Kinds of men's haircuts*) Inf **OH**102, 'Fro. [Inf Black] **1970** *Time* 14 Dec 40, One G.I. summed it up: " . . The regs [=Army regulations] say you can grow your hair *this* long, but the first sergeant says he don't care what the regs say, because he don't like no black man with a 'Fro." **1972** Claerbaut *Black Jargon* 64, *Fro . .* a large, bushy hairstyle popular among black people. **1986** Pederson *LAGS Concordance* **Gulf Region,** 8 infs, Fro; 2 infs, Curly fro; 1 inf, Freedom fro. [This question was asked chiefly in urban areas.]

‡**froach** n

1891 *Jrl. Amer. Folkl.* 4.159 **neMA,** *Froach.*—A piece of clumsy and imperfect needle-work; what would elsewhere be termed a botch.

frock n **chiefly Upstate NY, nNEng** See Map

A men's outer garment, esp a work jacket, often made of denim.

1840 (1841) Dana *2 Yrs.* 450, Away went . . the duck frocks, for tarring down rigging. **1856** in 1862 Colt *Went to KS* 36 **NY,** The driver being a small man with a blue frock on. **1904** *DN* 2.397 **NY,** *Frock. . .* In St. Lawrence Co. the name for a blouse or short coat bound at the waist with a band. **1934** *Hanley Disks* **seVT,** That was in the days when the men wore frocks. . . Just straight, right down. . . [They wore them] to work in, or if they were going to town. . . They were [woven of] blue and white threads. **1940–41** Cassidy *WI Atlas* 1 Inf, **seWI,** Frock—a work jacket. **1950** *WELS (Men's outdoor coats and jackets)* 1 Inf, **csWI,** Frock—short. **1966–70** *DARE* (Qu. W4) Infs **NY**107, 121, 232, **VT**12, Frock; **ME**6, Frock—rare; **ME**23, Frock—denim, goes just past waist; **MA**5, Frock—long, coverall garment, light-weight, made of denim; **NH**14, Frock—just a jacket, belt-high, any material; **NY**22, Frock, work frock; **NY**96, Frock—worn in warm weather; **ME**21, Frock—denim, waist-length; **MA**24, Frock—a jumper; made of denim . . , some hip-length. **1975** Gould *ME Lingo* 102, *Frock*—Usually barn *frock.* A jacket for barn work usually made of the same material as overalls. . . Most farm homes had . . a *frock* hook in the shed so that smelly barn clothes didn't come into the house.

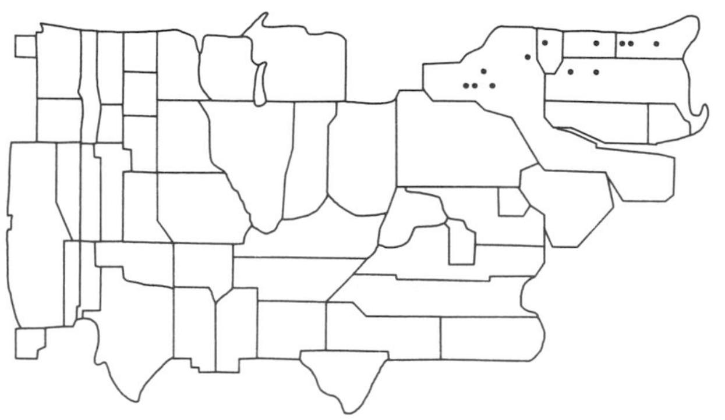

•frock + var (Qu. W4)

frocked up ppl adj Also *frocked out*

Dressed up, dolled up.

1966–68 *DARE* (Qu. W37, *When a woman puts on her good clothes and tries to look her best, you say she's* ______) Inf **GA**8, Frocked up; **GA**59, All frocked up, frocked out.

froe n [From *dull as a froe* (at **dull** adj **3b**)]

1935 Hurston *Mules & Men* 221 **FL,** One real good one Ah got down in Tampa, and one ole froe. [Footnote:] A damaged pocket knife.

frog n Usu |frɔg, frɑg|; also |frɔʊg|

A Forms.

1944 [see **B1** below]. **1961** Kurath–McDavid *Pronc. Engl.* 164, The incidence of . . /ɔ ~ ɒ/ and /ɑ/ in . . *frog* is much the same as in *fog.* [*Ibid* 163, /ɔ/ [in *fog*] is nearly universal in the Midland, . . and rather common in Maryland, Virginia, and South Carolina. . . the vowel /ɑ/ . . is regularly used in Western New England, in New York State . . , in Metropolitan New York . . , in the Philadelphia area, and in Eastern North Carolina. In [eastern] Virginia . . , in South Carolina, and in Georgia, /ɑ/ is not infrequent, but definitely less common than /ɔ/. However, in Virginia and adjoining parts of Maryland all cultured speakers say /fɑg/.] **1989** *DARE* File **wNC** (as of c1910), The pronunciation [frɑg] was often considered an affectation (and thus avoided). But [fɑg] was used by most well-educated speakers.

B Senses.

1 A toad. **chiefly Sth, S Midl** Cf **dry-land frog, land frog, toad-frog**

1908 *DN* 3.313 **eAL, wGA,** *Frog.* . . Toad. Very common. **1913** Kephart *Highlanders* 295 **sAppalachians,** In the Smokies a toad is called a frog or a toad-frog. **1927** *DN* 5.478 **Ozarks,** The word frog is used with reference to both frogs and toads. **1944** *PADS* 2.9 **AL,** *Frog* [frɔʊg]. . . A toad. **1965–69** *DARE* (Qu. P23, . . *The animal similar to the frog that lives away from water*) Infs **AL**53, **LA**37, **MD**18, **MS**63, Frog. **1973** Allen *LAUM* 1.326 **ND** (as of c1950), [1 inf uses *frog* for the common garden toad.]

2 also *froggy:* A French person; a person of French heritage. [Abbr for **frogeater;** *OEDS* 1778 →] **chiefly NEast, N Cent, Pacific** See Map *sometimes derog* Cf **crawfish n B3**

1872 Schele de Vere *Americanisms* 82, This arose not from a tendency to underrate, as when Frenchmen were dubbed Froggies. **1929** *AmSp* 4.340 [Vagabond argot], *Frog*—A Frenchman. **1932** Dos Passos *1919* 60, Even the dogs looked like frog dogs. *Ibid,* For Chris' sake, can't you c—s see that's a frog cop? **1950** *WELS (Nicknames for . . French)* 32 Infs, **WI,** Frogs. **1955** Greene *Quiet Amer.* 241, Don't go, Fowler. . . I can't talk to those Froggies. **1955** *AmSp* 30.175, American troops already had such elegant words as *frog* and *kraut* for others of their Allies and enemies. **1965–70** *DARE* (Qu. HH28, . . *Nicknames . . for people of foreign background: . . French*) 120 Infs, **chiefly NEast, N Cent, Pacific,** Frog; **CA**166, Froggy—old-fashioned; (Qu. HH28, . . *French-Canadian*) 7 Infs, **chiefly NEast,** Frog; (Qu. HH28, . . *Creole*) Inf **NY**213, Frog. [Of all Infs responding to Qu. HH28, 50% were male; of those giving these responses, 67% were male.]

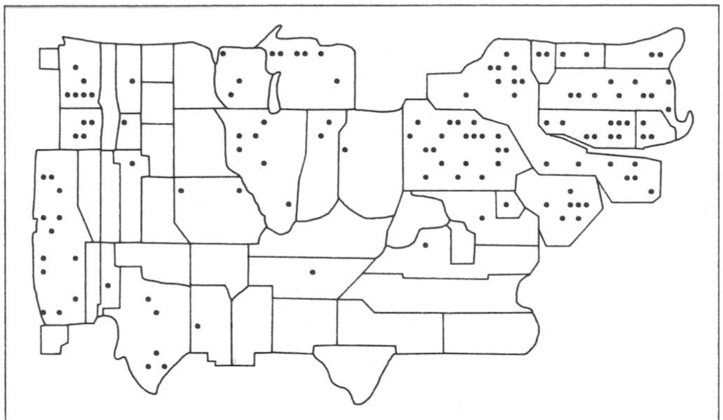

•frog n B2 + var (Qu. HH28)

3 The knot in the upper arm formed when the biceps muscle is flexed; a lump in the arm caused by a blow. **esp Sth, S Midl**

1858 *S. Lit. Messenger* 26.121/2, I warnt afeard that somebody was goin to hert me, for I has bonier knuckles than most men and you know the size uv the frog in my arm. **1899** (1912) Green *VA Folk-Speech* 102, *Frog.* . . The biceps muscle in the arm when made to move and swell by contraction is called "frog." **1949** *PADS* 11.6 **wTX,** *Frog.* . . A knot on a muscle made by a blow. **c1970** *Halpert Coll.* **wKY** 24, A sharp blow on your arm will cause a frog to appear. **1983** *Reinecke Coll.* 5 **LA,** *Frog.* . . A muscular knot or contraction in the arm resulting from a well-placed blow. Common in playground: "Watch I give 'im a frog on the arm."

4 Used in nicknames for small or out-of-the-way places; see quots. Cf **dog** n[1] **B8**

1859 in 1934 *AmSp* 9.318 **UT,** 'Frogtown' is a satellite, or suburb, whence grog and other luxuries . . are dispensed to thirsty soldiers. **1925** Krapp *Engl. Lang.* 1.162, Negro sections of cities have sometimes received distinctive names, as . . Frog Town, Frog Hollow. **1935** *AmSp* 10.80 **seMO,** Satirical reference [is] made to that nondescript neighborhood on the outskirts of a town. . . If a swamp, pond, or slough is near at hand, *Frogtown* may be used. **1950** *WELS (Nicknames for nearby cities, villages, or districts)* 1 Inf, **cwWI,** Frogtown district . . used to be a marsh or slough there; 1 Inf, **cwWI,** Frogtown. **1959** McAtee *Oddments* 10 **NC,** *Slang Names of Parts of Chapel Hill*—Not including real-estate names, but only those that are, or have been, current among the people. . . Frog Level. **1965–70** *DARE* (Qu. C33, *What joking names do you have for an out-of-the-way place, or a very unimportant place?*) Inf **MA**6, Frog Hollow; (Qu. C34) Infs **AL**30, **NJ**22, **RI**5, Frog Holler; **NC**46, Frog Level; **SC**56, Prosperity was formerly Frog Level; **NY**227, South of here they had a Frog Pond where [a woman] was buried; **MA**68, Frog Village; **MO**16, **NC**67, **PA**156, Frogtown; **AL**15, Frogtown—has liquor and gambling; (Qu. C35, *Nicknames for . . parts of your town*) Infs **IA**45, **NY**92, Frog Hollow; **VA**5, Frog Level—low land, wet in spring, frogs heard there first; **NC**10, Frog Pond; **LA**20, Frogamore; **AL**23, **KY**60, Frogtown; **DE**3, Frogtown—old-fashioned, no longer heard; **MN**33, Frogtown—a wet area with an abundance of frogs; old-fashioned; **MO**21, Frogtown—a lot of water stood there; **PA**216, Frogtown—used to be a swampy area filled with frogs; (Qu. II25, . . *The part of a town where the poorer people . . live*) Inf **KY**60, Frogtown; **FL**18, Frogtown—lower class, wrong side of the tracks; **MO**21, Frogtown—where the poor people live. **1980** *Capital Times* (Madison WI) 2 Dec 1/4, The people of Morrisonville [WI], an unincorporated community of 400—affectionately known as "Frogtown"—raised the money for the decorations themselves.

5 A codger, fogy.

1970 *DARE* (Qu. HH40, *Uncomplimentary words for an old man*) Inf **WV**21, Frog.

6 See quots. [See quot 1983]

1968 *DARE* (Qu. H18) Inf **LA**40, Italian bread—small loaves are called frogs, and it is made in other sizes and shapes of loaves. **1983** *Reinecke Coll.* 5 **LA,** *Frog.* . . a fist-sized hard-crust bread roll, usually deeply creased. From La. French "grenouille" translated.

7 See quot.

1968 *DARE* (Qu. X16, *Sticky mucus that forms in the nose—children's words for this*) Inf **LA**35, Frogs.

8 The palm of the hand. [Transf from *frog* the pad of the sole of a horse's foot]

1940 (1978) Still *River of Earth* 91 **KY,** Leth loaned me two marbles again. . . I held them in the frog of my hand, clicking them together.

9 =leather apron.

1947 Bowles–Towle *New Engl. Cooking* 246, First we have told how to prepare Sugar on Snow, or leather aprons or frogs, if you prefer the country names.

10 Fig: a rapid boil.

1982 Heat Moon *Blue Highways* 389 **DE,** She put a small pot of water on to heat. . . After ten minutes when the water still had not come to a boil, she said, "See if we have a frog in the pot." I looked. "No frog but a million bubbles."

frog v

1 To move or cause to move somewhat in the manner of a frog, spec:

a also with *it:* To walk hurriedly; to jump from place to place. **NEng**

1908 Lincoln *Cy Whittaker* 378 **NEng,** "How'd you get here?" "Walked," cackled Bailey. "Frogged it all the way." **1967–69** *DARE* (Qu. Y24, . . *"I can't get a ride so I'll just have to* ______.") Infs **MA**68, 72, Frog it. **1974** *AmSp* 49.62 **sME** (as of c1900), *Frog.* . . Hurry—"He frogged to town." **1975** Gould *ME Lingo* 102, *Frog it*—To cross a swampy place by jumping like a frog from hummock to hummock.

b See quot.

1968 *DARE* (Qu. EE36, *To climb the trunk of a tree by holding on with your legs while you pull yourself up with your hands*) Inf **VA**26, Frogging up the tree.

c also with *it:* To walk a canoe; to move (a floating) canoe by walking alongside it.

1975 Gould *ME Lingo* 102, *Frog it*. . . To walk a canoe through water too shallow to float it with a person aboard. Also, to take a canoe through white water that is either too dangerous or in which the canoeist is timid. A good woodsman will run the rapids; a novice will *frog it.* **1979** McPhee *Giving Good Weight* 146 **NEng,** In summer . . the water is so shallow over some stretches of rock and gravel that canoers have to frog their canoes—walk in the water beside them.

d To cause (a vehicle) to lurch forward.

1971 *DARE* File **OK** (as of 1920s), Frog (a truck)—to put a truck in neutral gear, race the motor, then quickly shift into forward gear, making the truck leap forward like a frog. Necessary in bringing equipment to drilling rigs in oil fields where there were no roads. **1982** *Smithsonian Letters* **OK,** My informant was an . . oil field worker in Seminole County, Oklahoma, in the 1920's when these fields were opening up. To move a truck across a muddy field, they would "frog" it, i.e. rev the motor and throw it into gear suddenly so the truck would jerk a few more feet. They would then repeat the process.

2 See quot. Cf **frog walk.**

1937 *DN* 6.619 **swTX,** When a rider *frogs* a horse, he mounts him, and then proceeds to calm him or to correct his *frog walking.*

3 also with *up:* To cheat (someone); to be deceived, confused.

1934 *AmSp* 9.289 **PA** [Black], *Frog up.* To be confused; to be fooled. **1966** *DARE* (Qu. LL23, *Cheated, treated dishonestly: "These apples are wormy, I think you got ________ ."*) Inf **SC**26, Frogged—old-timey. [Inf Black]

4 freq with *around:* To fool around, loaf, waste time.

1950 *PADS* 14.78 **FL,** Froggin' around in the rain. Prowling around in the rain. Hernando County. **1968** *DARE* FW Addit **csNY,** Frogging around—moving about aimlessly and slowly. **1969** *DARE* (Qu. A9, . . *Wasting time by not working on the job*) Inf **GA**78, Froggin', goofin'.

Frogamore See **frog n B4**

frog around See **frog v 4**

frog arrow n [*arrow* from the distinctive flower stalk] Cf **frog spear, frog spike**

A **fringed orchid** (here: *Habenaria integra* or *H. nivea*).

1950 Correll *Native Orchids* 81, *Habenaria integra*. . . *Common names:* . . Golden Frog-arrow. *Ibid* 89, *Habenaria nivea*. . . *Common names:* . . White Frog-arrow. **1976** Bailey–Bailey *Hortus Third* 534, *[Habenaria] nivea*. . . *White frog-arrow.*

frog bed See **frog bench**

frog belly n

A **pitcher plant** (here: *Sarracenia alata*).

1972 Brown *Wildflowers LA* 61, *Frog Belly—Sarracenia alata*. . . is one of our interesting insectivorous plants.

frog-belly pickle n

1968 *DARE* (Qu. H56, . . *Kinds of pickles favored around here*) Inf **NH**15, Sweet or frog-belly pickles—made of sliced ripe cucumbers.

frog bench n Also *frog bed* Cf **frogstool**

A **toadstool** or mushroom.

1986 Pederson *LAGS Concordance,* 3 infs, **FL, LA, MS,** Frog bench; 1 inf, **eFL,** Frog beds.

frogbit n Also *frog's bit*

A water plant *(Limnobium spongia)*. Also called **horseshoe 2** Cf **frog spit 1, 2**

1843 Torrey *Flora NY* 2.263, *Hydrocharis cordifolia*. . . Heart-leaved Frog's-bit. . . Braddock's bay near Lake Erie. **1866** *Treas. Bot. s.v. (DA),* Frog-bit, American, *Limnobium.* **1894** Coulter *Botany W. TX* 3.422, *Limnobium* (American Frog's-bit). **1950** Gray–Fernald *Manual of Botany* 94, *Limnobium*. . . Frog's-bit.

frog bonnet(s) n

=**pitcher plant.**

1933 Small *Manual SE Flora* 580, *Sarracenia*. . . Frog-bonnets. **1942** Hylander *Plant Life* 250, The eastern Pitcher Plant *(Sarracenia)*—also called Frog Bonnet and Bog Bugle—has a basal rosette of "pitchers."

frog bread n Also *toad-frog bread* [From the notion that frogs eat mushrooms and toadstools] *among Black speakers*

A **toadstool** or mushroom.

c1938 in 1970 Hyatt *Hoodoo* 1.72 **seGA** [Black], Dere's de stuff whut chew call *frog bread*. . . It's somethin' grows in de woods. . . It spreads yo' know as it gits up outa de ground—it spread kind round like a parasol. *Ibid* 562 **ceSC** [Black], It's little ole stuff dat come up in de groun'—yo' know, we call it *toadfrog bread.* It's a little white thing [Hyatt: mushroom] dat grows up an' after which it die an' it goes to a dust. **1966** *DARE* (Qu. I38, *Small plants shaped like an umbrella . . which are not safe to eat*) Inf **SC**9, Frog bread; **SC**26, Toadfrog bread. [Both Infs Black] **1986** Pederson *LAGS Concordance,* 1 inf, **cGA,** Frog bread. [Inf Black]

frog buttons n

A **duckweed 1** (here: *Lemna* spp).

1933 Small *Manual SE Flora* 249, *Lemna*. . . Duckweed. Frog Buttons.

frog catcher n *hist*

=**black-crowned night heron.**

1791 Bartram *Travels* 293, A[rdea] clamator, corpore subceruleo, the quaw bird, or frogcatcher. **1796** Morse *Amer. Universal Geog.* 1.212, Quaw bird or Frog Catcher, *Ardea clemata.* **1832** Williamson *Hist. ME* 1.150, There are several others, the genus of which is not known; as the *Frog-catcher,* also the Hagdel, of a dark brown colour, about as large as a Murr, though its feathers are longer.

frog-choker See **frog-strangler**

‡frog-cooler n Cf **frog ice**

The first thin layer of ice that covers a pond in winter.

1968 *DARE* (Qu. B33a) Inf **OH**87, Frog-cooler; [(Qu. B33b) Inf **NJ**39, Frogs will be under ice].

frog dipper n [From the size and shape]

A **jack-in-the-pulpit.**

1967 *DARE* (Qu. S1, . . *Other names . . for the jack-in-the-pulpit*) Inf **NC**41, Pitcher plant, frog dipper.

frog-drownder See **frog-strangler**

frog duck n

=**hooded merganser.**

1913 *Auk* 30.503, *Lophodytes cucullatus*. . . 'Frog Duck.' . . Sometimes it is found with the Wood Ducks on the prairies. **1955** *Oriole* 20.5, *Hooded Merganser*. . . Frog Duck. **1982** Elman *Hunter's Field Guide* 228, *Hooded Merganser*. . . *Common & Regional Names:* . . frog duck. [*Ibid* 230, It [=the hooded merganser] prowls quiet pools for frogs, tadpoles, crawfish, snails, insects, and a few fry.]

frogeater n [In ref to the French custom of eating frogs' legs] **chiefly Nth** *usu derog* Cf **frog n B2**

A French person.

1842 (1844) Sealsfield *Life New World* (transl. Hebbe & Mackay) 81, The British had sovereign contempt for the French soup and frogeaters. **1919** in 1983 Truman *Dear Bess* 293 **MO,** For my part I've had enough *vin rouge* and frogeater victuals to last me a lifetime. **1950** *WELS (Nicknames for . . French)* 1 Inf, **cwWI,** Frogeaters. **1966–70** *DARE* (Qu. HH28) Infs **MI**65, **NJ**45, **NM**12, **NV**7, **NY**57, 209, **PA**234, **WA**30, Frogeater.

frog egg n Also *frog eye* [From the texture and translucence] =**fish egg.**

1928 *Ruppenthal Coll.* **KS,** *Frog eggs* . . (army) tapioca pudding. [Also] frog eyes. **1969** Sorden *Lumberjack Lingo* 15 **NEng, Gt Lakes,** Frog-eggs, Tapioca.

frogeye n

1 also *frog's eye:* =**bug eye** n[1]; hence adj *frog-eyed* having a round or bulging eye.

1929 *AmSp* 5.121 **ME,** Prominent eyes were spoken of as . . "frog's eyes." **1967–70** *DARE* (Qu. X21a, . . *Eyes . . if they stick out*) Infs **CO**47, **GA**82, **NY**236, **PA**94, **VA**46, Frogeyes; **NY**205, Frog's eyes; **DC**13, **FL**33, **GA**17, **MD**17, **MA**1, **PA**179, 244, **TN**3, **TX**13, Frog-eyed; (Qu. X21c, *If the eyes are very round*) Infs **LA**20, **WY**2, Frogeyes.

2 See **frog-eye gravy.**

3 In moonshining: =**bead** n **3.** Cf **goose eye**

1969 *DARE* Tape **GA**72, You kin shake it lightly an' they'll pop up there big—we call 'em frogeyes, an' drake's eyes, sometimes.

4 See quot.

1969 *DARE* (Qu. EE6c, *Cheap marbles*) Inf **KY**11, Frogeyes—clay with a spot in 'em.

5 pl: Eyeglasses.

1967 *DARE* (Qu. X23) Inf **WA**22, Specs, four-eyes, frogeyes.

6 See **frog egg.**

frog-eyed See **frogeye 1**

frog-eye gravy n Also *frog-eye* [See quot 1942] **chiefly S Midl** =**red-eye gravy.**

1940 *AmSp* 15.447 **eTN,** *Frog Eye.* Red gravy. **1942** *AmSp* 17.170 **sIL,** *Frog-eye gravy* . . the gravy left in the skillet after frying ham. The black particles that slough off the meat in the frying process appear to simulate a frog's eye as they float in the globules of grease. . . This locution . . is said to be used in Missouri, and something similar is frequently referred to as 'hush-puppy' in Tennessee and Florida. **1946** *AmSp* 21.99 **sIL,** In older times, rarely now, *brindle gravy,* sometimes called *frogeye gravy,* was a popular dish; a dash of water in a little hot ham grease in the skillet did the trick. **1970** *DARE* (Qu. H37) Inf **KY**71, Frog-eye gravy—if made with ham.

frogfruit n Also *fogfruit*

A plant of the genus *Phyla,* usu *Phyla nodiflora* or *P. lanceolata.* For other names of *P. nodiflora* see **carpet grass 3, mat grass, turkey-tangle**

1822 Eaton *Botany* 519, *Zapania nodiflora,* fog-fruit. **1897** Creevey *Flowers* 20, Fog-fruit. *Lippia lanceolata.* . . A creeping plant, with range from Pennsylvania southward and westward. **1931** Dayton *Important Browse* 140, In addition there are about four western species of the herbaceous fog-fruit genus (*Phyla* spp.), which some authors merge in Lippia. **1936** IL Nat. Hist. Surv. *Wildflowers* 271, The Fog Fruit is found in moist or wet soil usually near streams. **1937** Stemen–Myers *OK Flora* 439, *Lippia lanceolata.* . . Fog-fruit. **1938** Madison *Wild Flowers OH* 112, Frog Fruit. *Lippia lanceolata.* **1940** Steyermark *Flora MO* 455, Fog-fruit *(Lippia).* **1965** Teale *Wandering Through Winter* 150 **TX,** All across Texas, a host of . . names have been bestowed on the wild plants. . . [They include] frog fruit, good mother, . . and widow's tears. **1970** Correll *Plants TX* 1331, *Phyla.* . . Frog-Fruit. . . *Phyla nodifera.* . . *Common Frog-Fruit.* **1976** Bailey–Bailey *Hortus Third* 865, *Phyla.* . . *Frogfruit.* . . Fr[uit] dry, of 2 nutlets.

froggy adj

Chipper, frisky.

1969 *DARE* (Qu. BB47, *Feeling in the best of health and spirits: "I'm feeling* ——— *."*) Inf **GA**72, Froggy.

froggy n See **frog** n **B2**

froggy-head adj [*froggy* var of *foggy,* perh infl by *groggy*]

Befuddled, inattentive, groggy.

1970 *DARE* FW Addit **VA**42, I felt froggy-head and didn't remember nothing he was a-telling me.

froggy in the meadow (or middle, millpond) See **frog in the meadow**

frog hair n

1 =**cotton grass 1** (here: *Eriophorum gracile* or *E. viridi-carinatum*).

1898 *Jrl. Amer. Folkl.* 11.282, *Eriophorum gracile* . . and *Eriophorum polystachyon* . . frog-hair, Oxford Co[unty], M[aine].

2a also *frog's hair:* Something very small; a minute measurement or detail—usu in phrr *fine as* (or *finer than*) *frog hair* very thin or fine. **chiefly Sth, S Midl**

1897 *KS Univ. Qrly.* (ser B) 6.53 **SC,** *Frog-hair:* something infinitesimal, as, 'fine as frog-hair.' **1927** *Ruppenthal Coll.* **KS,** *Frog's hair, split frog's hair*—simile of extreme fineness. "That's as fine as frog's hair, as split frog's hair." **1927** *AmSp* 2.354 **WV,** Those scratches are finer 'n frog hair. **1965–70** *DARE* (Qu. KK50, *When something is planned out carefully, down to the last detail: "He had it all worked out* ——— *."*) Infs **AR**31, **GA**9, To a frog's hair; (Qu. KK55a, *To deny something very firmly: "No, not by a* ——— *."*) Inf **TX**5, Frog hair. **1968** *Foxfire* Fall-Winter 24 **nGA, cwNC,** Fine as frog's hair.

b Transf; in adj, adv phrr *fine as frog hair* and varr: Excellent; very well.

1905 *DN* 3.79 **nwAR,** *Fine.* . . 'I'm getting along fine.' *Fine as frog-hair.* . . Extremely fine. **1916** *San Francisco Call & Post* (CA) 17 Jan 10 *(Zwilling Coll.),* [In cartoon:] You look fine as frog's hair. **1939** *AmSp* 14.264 **sIN,** The person in good health is feeling 'fine as frog hair.' [Footnote: *Var.* 'fine as frog hair quartered' or 'fine as frog hair split in the middle.'] **1946** *PADS* 6.38 **swVA,** As fine as *frog hair.* ((Excellent.)) **1950** *WELS ("How are you?")* 1 Inf, **cwWI,** Fine as frog fuzz. **1950** *PADS* 14.78 **FL,** Fine as frog hair. Hernando County simile in answer to "How are you?" **1965–70** *DARE* (Qu. BB47, *Feeling in the best of health and spirits: "I'm feeling* ——— *."*) Infs **CA**106, **DE**2, (As) fine as frog('s) hair; (Qu. GG29, *To be in a good or pleasant mood: "This morning he seems to be feeling* ——— *."*) Inf **TX**11, Fine as frog hair; (Qu. KK50, *When something is planned out carefully, down to the last detail: "He had it all worked out* ——— *."*) Infs **AL**43, 50, **GA**7, **IN**5, 13, **KY**60, **MI**106, **NJ**16, Fine as (a) frog hair; **GA**3, Fine as frog's hair.

3 Something imaginary or nonexistent.

1952 Brown *NC Folkl.* 1.412, As scarce as frog hair. **1966** *DARE* (Qu. HH14, *Ways of teasing a beginner* . . *for example, by sending him for a 'left-handed monkey wrench': "Go get me* ——— *."*) Inf **AR**22, A frog-hair brush.

4 See quot.

1967 *DARE* (Qu. E20, *Soft rolls of dust that collect on the floor under beds or other furniture*) Inf **TX**45, Frog hair.

frog hawk n

1 =**marsh hawk.** [See quot 1917]

1917 (1923) *Birds Amer.* 2.64, *Circus hudsonius.* . . Frog Hawk. . . Frogs are found on the menu of this bird. **1946** Hausman *Eastern Birds* 197, *Marsh Hawk.* . . *Other Names* . . Frog Hawk. **1955** MA Audubon Soc. *Bulletin* 39.442, *Marsh Hawk.* . . Frog Hawk (Mass. Frogs were found in 15 of those [601] stomachs.)

2 =**red-shouldered hawk.**

1955 *Oriole* 20.5, Red-shouldered Hawk. . . Frog Hawk; Hen Hawk.

Frog Hollow See **frog** n **B4**

frog-hop n Also *frog-leap* Also called **rabbit jump, squirrel's jump**

A short distance.

1950 *WELS (A short distance)* 1 Inf, **cwWI,** A frog-hop. **1966** *DARE* (Qu. MM24, . . *"The river is just a* ——— *from the house."*) Inf **OK**27, One good frog-leap.

froghopper n

1 =**spittlebug.** [See quots 1968, 1980]

1882 VT State Bd. Ag. *Rept. for 1881–82* 7.77, Dr. Cutting spoke of the frog hopper, usually known as the spittle bug on grass. **1884** *Boston Jrl.* 11 Oct. 2/4 *(DA),* Billions of insects have been killed by the electric lights in the Capitol at Washington. . . They comprise . . hornets, butterflies, moths, cicadas, froghoppers [etc]. **1965** Teale *Wandering Through Winter* 46 **CA,** As a kind of dessert, these Indians also ate the froth of the spittlebugs, or froghoppers, which is slightly sweet when made on certain plants. **1968** *WI Conserv. Bulletin* Mar-Apr 30, They are called spittle insects because the frothy white masses resemble spittle. They are called frog-hoppers because of the belief that tree frogs spit out these foamy "suds," and because the nymphs have large heads and bulging eyes, similar to frogs. **1980** Milne–Milne *Audubon Field Guide Insects* 495, *Froghoppers.* . . Spittlebugs . . hop about like tiny frogs on plants and shrubs, where they feed.

2 One who moves awkwardly. Cf **frog** v **1**

1970 *DARE* (Qu. FF4, . . *Kinds of dancing parties*) Inf **NJ**64, Froghoppers' dance—that is, awkward dancers.

frog house n

1 See quot 1908.

a1883 (1911) Bagby *VA Gentleman* 48, [He must] make frog-houses over his feet in the wet sand. **1908** *DN* 3.313 **eAL, wGA,** *Frog-house.* . . A small cave or hollow mound made in dampened sand by children, usually by heaping the sand about the bare foot. Toads often appropriate these 'houses' as hiding places.

2 also *toad-frog house:* A **toadstool** or mushroom. Cf **frog table, frog umbrella**

1986 Pederson *LAGS Concordance,* 6 infs, **Gulf Region,** Frog house; 3 infs, **GA, FL,** Toad-frog houses.

frog ice n Cf **cat ice, frog-cooler**

1969 *DARE* FW Addit **wKY,** Frog ice—the first thin layer of ice on a pond or lake.

frog in the meadow n Also *frog in the middle* (or *millpond, sea*), *froggy in the meadow* (or *middle, millpond*) [*OED* 1801 →] **chiefly S Midl**

A children's tag game played in a circle and with a rhyme that is sung or chanted; see quots.

1883 Newell *Games & Songs* 171 **Philadelphia PA,** Frog in the sea,/ Can't catch me?/ Played like the preceding [viz: children stand in a ring and chant the rhyme, and at the last word all stoop down; a child in the center tries to tag another child before he or she stoops]. **1905** *DN* 3.80 **nwAR,** *Frog in the middle*. . . a children's game. Common. 'Frog in the middle,/ I can't get him out./ Take a little stick / And stir him all about./ If you can't stir him out / Kick him out, kick him out.' **1940** (1978) Still *River of Earth* 198 **KY,** We could hear bare feet whispering on the floor. They played frog-in-the-middle, making out there were a full dozen in the ring. **1966–70** *DARE* (Qu. EE1, . . *Games . . in which . . [children] form a ring, and either sing or recite a rhyme*) Inf **NM9,** Froggy in the meadow—the one in the center tries to break out; those who let him out must take his place; **MO8,** Frog in the meadow—we just joined hands and one sat down in the center; **VA9,** Froggy in the meadow; **KY84,** Froggy in the middle; **AL10,** Froggy in the millpond; (Qu. EE2, *Games that have one extra player*) Inf **TN16,** Froggy in the meadow. **1966** *DARE* Tape **AL3,** "Frog in the millpond, can't get out, take a little skip . . an' start 'im out." . . The churning circle 'round a child in there, an' that's the froggie. **c1970** *DARE* FW Addit **swVA,** Froggy in the meadow—"Froggy" sat blindfolded in a circle of other players. They went around him chanting the rhyme; then he tried to catch them. **1974** Betts–Walser *NC Folkl.* 3 **cNC,** Frog in the Mill Pond. A large circle is drawn, and *It* is blindfolded and put in the circle, along with all the other players. The object of the game is for *It* to catch the other players, who cannot leave the circle. The game is started by taunting *It* with "Frog in the mill pond,/ Can't get out./ Take a little stick / And stir him all about."

frog-in-throat n

=**pied-billed grebe.**

1955 MA Audubon Soc. *Bulletin* 39.310, *Pied-billed Grebe*. . . Frog-in-throat (Maine. Query: from guttural notes?)

frog it See **frog** v **1a, c**

frog lantern n

1 as *frog's lantern:* See quot.

1909 *S. Atl. Qrly.* 8.48 **SC** [Gullah], The *ignis fatuus* is a *frog's-lantu'n.*

2 See quot.

1950 *PADS* 14.30 **Charleston SC,** *Frog lantern*. . . A rectangular doughnut or cruller, pierced by slits, as if to permit the passage of light.

frog leaf n

=**water shield.**

1900 Lyons *Plant Names* 68, *B[rasenia] purpurea*. . . Frog-leaf.

frog-leap See **frog-hop**

frog lily n [See quot 1931]

=**spatterdock.**

1869 Fuller *Flower Gatherers* 204 *(DA),* It flourishes best in dull, stagnant pools, and is often called the *Frog-lily.* **1889** *Harper's New Mth. Mag.* 78.860/2 **DE,** From its filthy habits it [=the yellow nuphar] has been called, with some justice, the frog-lily. **1931** Clute *Common Plants* 111, The frog lily *(Nymphaea advena)* is better named, for frogs delight to rest on its round floating leaves. **1936** IL Nat. Hist. Surv. *Wildflowers* 91, In some localities this plant is called Spatterdock, Cow Lily or Frog Lily. **1959** Carleton *Index Herb. Plants* 50.

frogmouth perch n Also *frog-mouthed perch*

A **rock bass** (here: *Ambloplites rupestris*).

1935 Caine *Game Fish* 24, *Rock Bass*. . . *Synonyms* . . Frog-mouthed Perch. **1949** Caine *N. Amer. Sport Fish* 28, *Rock Bass*. . . Its overly-large, bass-like mouth seems . . inadequate to the demands of its appetite. . . *Colloquial Names*. . . Frogmouth Perch.

frog one's eyes v phr

1946 *PADS* 6.14 **swVA,** *Frog the eyes*. . . To blink the eyes as a frog does in rain. Said of a surprised, naive person.

frog one's sides v phr

See quots.

1939 *AmSp* 14.90 **eTN,** *Frogging his sides.* Eating heartily. 'He's frogging his sides.' **c1970** *Halpert Coll.* **wKY, eTN,** To frog one's sides = to eat heartily. "He's froggin' his sides."

frog orchestra n

1960 Carpenter *Tales Manchaca* 60 **cTX** (as of c1894), We serenaded them first with a "frog-orchestra"—each girl singing a different song simultaneously.

frog owl n

Prob a barred owl.

1967 *DARE* (Qu. Q2) Inf **LA2,** Frog owl or swamp owl.

frog-peep n Cf *DS* A4, 5

=**first dark.**

1892 (1893) Botume *First Days* 128 **seSC** [Black] (as of c1864), The dial [=clock face] of the contrabands [=ex-slaves] was: . . "W'en de sun stan' straight ober head"—"At frog peep"—"When fust star shine."

frog pillow n Cf **frog bench**

A **toadstool** or mushroom.

c1938 in 1970 Hyatt *Hoodoo* 2.1805 **neSC,** [Goofer dust is] made outa dis ole thing dey call—maybe yo' have seen 'em—dey grows in de woods. Dey grows up in a kind of a big top-like—a *frog pillah,* seen [sic] like de *frogbread.*

frog plant n

1 also *frog's bladder,* ~ *mouth, frogs' throats:* An **orpine** (here: *Sedum telephium*). [See quots 1892, 1899]

1892 *Jrl. Amer. Folkl.* 5.96, *Sedum Telephium* . . frog's mouth; frog's bladder. N.Y./ . . frog-plant. N.H./ frogs' throats. Bedford, Mass. [Footnote to *frog-plant:*] Because of a children's custom of blowing up a leaf so as to make the epidermis puff up like a frog. **1899** (1909) Earle *Child Life* 389, From the live-for-ever, or orpine . . , we made frogs, or purses, by gently pinching the fleshy leaves between thumb and forefinger, thus loosening the epidermis on the lower side of the leaf and making a bladder which, when blown up, would burst with a delightful pop. The New England folk-names by which this plant is called, such as frog-plant, blow-leaf, pudding-bag plant, show the wide-spread prevalence of this custom. **1950** Gray–Fernald *Manual of Botany* 734, Live-forever. Garden-O[rpine]. Frogplant.

2 A **toadstool** or mushroom. Cf **frogstool**

1970 *DARE* (Qu. I38, *Small plants shaped like an umbrella that grow in woods and fields—which are not safe to eat*) Inf **NJ69,** Frog plant.

Frog Pond See **frog** n **B4**

frog rain n Also *frog storm* [Cf **frogs, rain**] Cf **frog-strangler**

A very heavy rain.

1954 *Harder Coll.* **cwTN,** *Frog storm*. . . A heavy rain: frogs fall to the ground. **1969** *DARE* (Qu. B25) Inf **TN37,** Frog rain.

frog run n [Because frogs come out of hibernation at this time] **VT** Cf **bud run**

In maple sugar production: the last run of sap.

1947 *PADS* 8.6 **VT,** *Frog run*. . . The last run of the season. The name is derived from an idea common among farmers that when the frogs are first heard the season is over. **1959** *VT Hist.* new ser 27.155, *Frog-run*. . . In maple sugaring, the run which comes after the frogs have been heard croaking; the last run. Common. **1979** *DARE* File **VT,** My father-in-law, who used to farm and sugar with his father, explained "frog run" to me. "If the season was real late, during the last run sometimes you could hear the peepers," he said. "The old timers used to call it a frog run, but by that time half of 'em had their buckets pulled and washed up, anyway."

frog rush n

=**toad rush.**

1840 MA Zool. & Bot. Surv. *Herb. Plants & Quadrupeds* 203, *Juncus bufonius.* Frog Rush. A low plant densely growing in wet places, forming almost a turf.

frog's bit See **frogbit**

frog's bladder See **frog plant 1**

frog's breadth n [Prob blend of *hair's breadth* + **frog hair 2a**] Cf **gnat's eyebrow**

1966 *DARE* (Qu. KK50, *When something is planned out carefully, down to the last detail: "He had it all worked out ______."*) Inf **AR31,** To a frog's breadth.

frog's eye See **frogeye 1**

frog's hair n

1 A spike rush. Cf **cunt-hair grass**

1895 *DN* 1.388 **wMA,** *Frog's hair:* the plant *Eleocharis acicularis,* and other allied species. **1941** *Torreya* 41.46 **MA,** *Eleocharis acicularis . .* Frog's hair.

2 See **frog hair 2a.**

frog shit See **frog spit 1**

frogskin n [In ref to the green back] **scattered, but esp Sth, S Midl** See Map Cf **buckskin 3**

A piece of paper money, esp a dollar bill.

1902 *DN* 2.274, *'Frogskins,'* used in Virginia for paper money or 'greenbacks.' **1906** *NY Eve. Jrl.* (NY) 29 Jan 8, Some unkind person offered him a bunch of frog skins to fight the giant again. **1950** *WELS (Joking names for a paper dollar)* 7 Infs, **WI,** Frogskin; *(It cost 100 ______)* 3 Infs, **WI,** Frogskins. **c1960** *Wilson Coll.* **csKY,** *Frogskin. . .* Any kind of bill: $1, $5, $10, $20. **1963** Edwards *Gravel* 141 **eTN** (as of 1920s), "Got to buy shells with this here frogskin," and he exhibited a new, crisp dollar bill. **1965–70** *DARE* (Qu. U26) 46 Infs, **scattered, but esp Sth, S Midl,** Frogskin; (Qu. U19a, . . *Money*) Infs **GA**89, **SC**3, Frogskin(s); (Qu. U28a, . . *A five-dollar bill*) Inf **CA**197, Frogskin; (Qu. U28c, . . *A twenty-dollar bill*) Inf **KY**80, Frogskin.

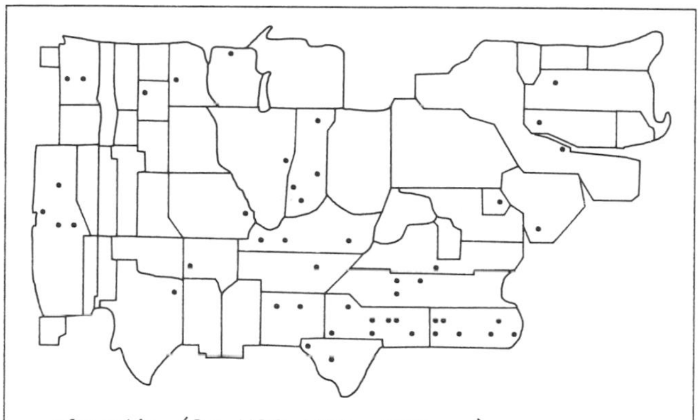
•frogskin (Qq. U26, U19a, U28a, c)

frog's lantern See **frog lantern 1**

frog's legs n pl

Bowed legs.

1969 *DARE* (Qu. X37) Inf **NY**210, Frog's legs.

frog slime See **frog spit 1**

frog's mouth See **frog plant 1**

frog spayer n *joc* Also called **snake jabber, toad stabber**

A sharp-pointed shoe.

1967 *DARE* (Qu. W42a) Inf **TN**14, Frog spayer [laughter].

frog spear n [Cf **frog arrow**]

A **fringed orchid** (here: *Habenaria nivea*).

1933 Small *Manual SE Flora* 373, *G[ymnadeniopsis] nivea. . .* Frog-spear. **1950** Correll *Native Orchids* 89, *Habenaria nivea. . . Common names . .* Frog-spear. **1976** Bailey–Bailey *Hortus Third* 534.

frog spike n [Cf **frog arrow**]

A **fringed orchid** (here: *Habenaria clavellata*).

1933 Small *Manual SE Flora* 374, *G[ymnadeniopsis] clavellata. . .* Frog-spike. Green rein-orchid. **1950** Correll *Native Orchids* 65, *Common names:* Small Green Wood-orchid, Frog-spike [etc]. **1976** Bailey–Bailey *Hortus Third* 533.

frog spit n

1 also *frog shit, ~ slime, ~ spittle:* Any of various algae, such as *Spirogyra,* which form slimy masses on the surface of water. For other names of *Spirogyra* see **frogum, watersilk** Cf **froghopper 1**

1892 *Jrl. Amer. Folkl.* 5.106, *Spirogyra* and allied confervaceae, frog-spit. U.S. **1898** *Bot. Gaz.* 26.258 **NH,** *Spirogyra,* sp., frog slime. **1945** McAtee *Nomina Abitera* 6, The term frog-spit, applied to the floating masses formed chiefly by filamentous algae, is in some localities transformed to frog-shit. **1950** *PADS* 14.30 **SC,** *Frog spittle. . .* Spirogyra. Also called *watersilk, frogum.* **c1960** *Wilson Coll.* **csKY,** *Frog-spit. . .* Algae on the surface of ponds.

2 A **duckweed 1** (here: *Lemna minor*).

1929 *Torreya* 29.149 **ME,** Lemna minor, *Frog-spit.*

3 also *froth-spit:* A frothy spittlelike mass produced by a nymph of a **froghopper 1.**

1899 (1912) Green *VA Folk-Speech* 186, *Frog-spit. . . Froth-spit.* A froth seen on pine bushes in the spring, from which may-flies are said to be hatched.

frog spittle See **frog spit 1**

frog-squat n

A squatting position with knees splayed out.

1961 Adams *Old-Time Cowhand* 10 **West,** When he hunkered down to take comfort in a frog squat, the first thing he did was jerk a leaf out of his prayer book [=cigarette papers] and commence bundlin' up a new life of Bull Durham [=tobacco].

frogs, rain v phr For varr see quot 1965–70 [Prob from frogs' coming out in numbers in heavy rain, as if it were "raining frogs"; cf **frog rain** and std *rain cats and dogs*] **chiefly Sth, S Midl** See Map Cf **bullfrogs, rain** and **toadfrogs, rain**

To rain heavily.

1965–70 *DARE* (Qu. B26, *When it's raining very heavily, you say, "It's raining ______.")* 25 Infs, **chiefly Sth, S Midl,** (Little) frogs; **SC**22, 26, Down frogs; **NC**3, **SC**46, Frogs and tadpoles; **MO**21, Cats and dogs and frogs; **KY**5, Cats and frogs; **NY**34, Frogs and happy [sic] toads; **AL**11, Tadpoles and frogs; **FL**37, Toads and frogs. **1979** *NY Rev. Books* 19 July 24/2 **KY,** It never rained any frogs.

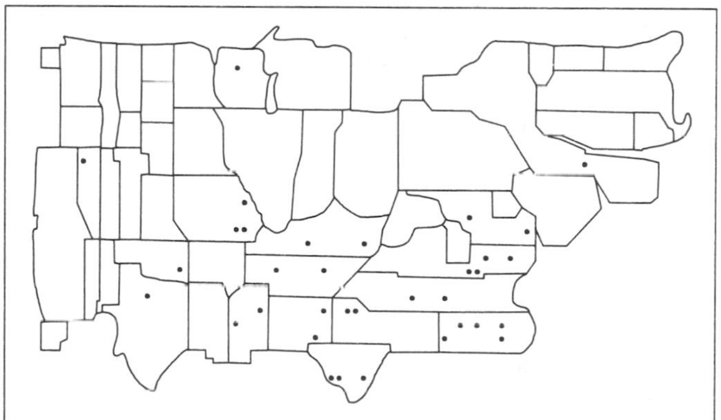
•frogs, rain + varr (Qu. B26)

frogstabber n

1 =**great blue heron.**

1955 MA Audubon Soc. *Bulletin* 39.312, *Great Blue Heron. . .* Frog-stabber (Maine. It eats frogs and sometimes impales rather than grasps prey with its beak.)

2 See **frogsticker (knife).**

frogs' throats See **frog plant 1**

frogsticker (knife) n Also *frogstick, frogstabber* [Cf *EDD Suppl. stick-frog*] **chiefly Sth, S Midl** See Map Cf **pigsticker, toadstabber**

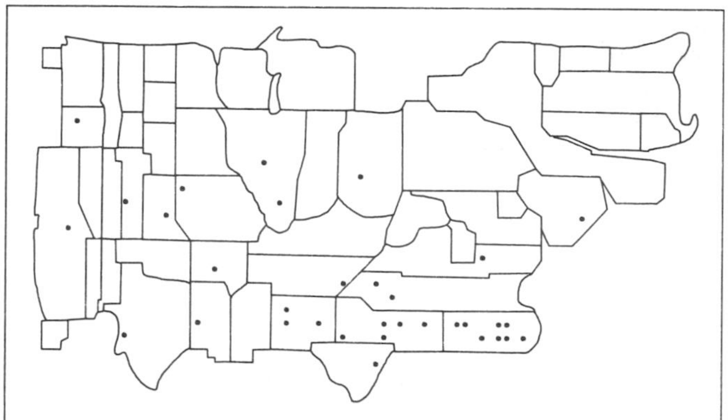
•frogsticker (knife) + var (Qu. F39)

A pocketknife, esp one with a long blade.

1836 Simms *Mellichampe* 2.152 **SC**, Wait a bit, till I . . find my frog-sticker, which has somehow tumbled out of the belt. **1892** *DN* 1.230 **KY**, *Frog-sticker.* **1893** Shands *MS Speech* 71, *Frog-sticker*. . . in Mississippi it is used as a disparaging name for any kind of pocket-knife. **1905** *DN* 3.80 **nwAR**, *Frog-sticker.* **1906** Casey *Parson's Boys* 137 **sIL** (as of c1860), I jerked out my frog-sticker on the run and bled him [=a deer]. **1908** *DN* 3.313 **eAL, wGA**, *Frog-sticker.* **1912** *DN* 3.576 **wIN**, *Frog-sticker.* **1923** *DN* 5.243 **LA**, *Frog-sticker.* **1927** *AmSp* 2.354 **WV**, *Frog-sticker.* **1929** Dobie *Vaquero* 259 **TX**, I also killed one wolf with a rock and another with a frog-sticker knife tied on the end of a stick. **1940** *Hall Coll.* **wNC, eTN**, Frog-stick. **1949** *PADS* 11.6 **wTX**, *Frog-sticker*. . . Uneducated. **1951** *PADS* 15.54 **sIN**, *Frogsticker.* **1965–70** *DARE* (Qu. F39, *A large pocket knife with blades that fold in and out*) 31 Infs, **chiefly Sth**, Frogsticker; **CO**11, **TX**69, Frogstabber. **1968** *Ozark Visitor* (Point Lookout MO) Mar, One of those long bladed knives that boys call "frog stabbers."

frogstool n **chiefly Sth, S Midl** See Map Cf **frog bench**

A **toadstool** or mushroom.

1855 Baldwin *Party Leaders* 337 **AL**, [Banks] that had sprung up, like frog-stools, all over the Union. **1895** *DN* 1.370 **TN**, *Frog-stools:* toad-stools. **1899** (1912) Green *VA Folk-Speech* 186. **1905** *DN* 3.80 **nwAR**, *Frog-stool*. . . Common. **1908** *DN* 3.313 **eAL, wGA. c1938** in 1970 Hyatt *Hoodoo* 2.1810 **seGA** [Black], Dey git some of dose *frogstools* an' we take de heart outa dat *frogstool*, bound it in a wool cloth, an' yo' may *spike* dat again . . wit *Heart Cologne.* **c1960** *Wilson Coll.* **csKY. 1965–70** *DARE* (Qu. S19, *Mushrooms that grow out like brackets from the sides of trees*) 52 Infs, **chiefly Sth, Midl**, Frogstools; (Qu. I38, *Small plants shaped like an umbrella . . which are not safe to eat*) 46 Infs, **chiefly Sth, S Midl**, Frogstools; (Qu. S18, *A kind of mushroom that grows like a globe*) 12 Infs, **Sth, S Midl**, Frogstool(s); (Qu. I37, . . *[Similar plants] which are safe to eat*) Infs **LA**9, **NC**79, 81, **NJ**69, **VA**71, Frog-stools.

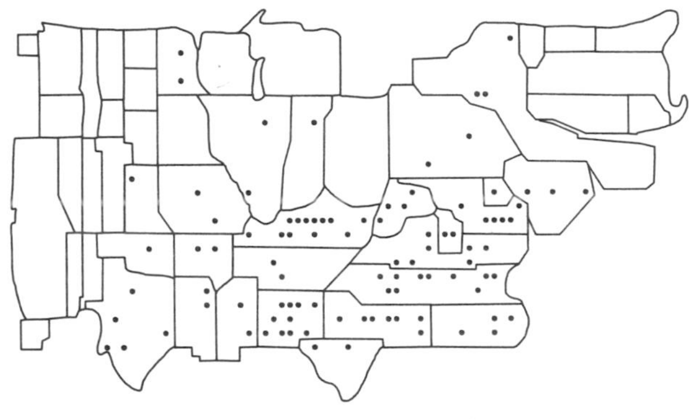
•frogstool (Qq. S19, I38, S18, I37)

frog storm n

1 =**blackberry storm.** [Because frogs have come out of hibernation by this time]

1936 *AmSp* 11.315 **Ozarks**, *Frog storm*. . . The first bad weather in the spring, after a warm period. The term *whip-poor-will storm* is synonymous.

2 See **frog rain.**

frog-strangler n Also *bullfrog-strangler, frog-choker, frog-drownder* **chiefly Sth, S Midl** See Map Cf **goose-drownder, toad-strangler**

A very heavy rain.

1951 *PADS* 15.70 **nLA**, *Frog-strangler*. . . A flood rain. **1962** *Chronicle of the Horse* 7 Dec 18 **WY** (*AmSp* 38.303), At five o'clock, the skies . . began to blacken with thunderheads, and at six, the heavens opened, and the rains came, not just rains, but a frog strangler. **1965–70** *DARE* (Qu. B25, . . *Joking names . . for a very heavy rain*) 15 Infs, **chiefly Sth, S Midl, TX**, Frog-strangler; **VA**44, Frog-choker; **TX**4, Frog-drownder. **1971** Wood *Vocab. Change* 33 **Sth**, Informants volunteered *(bull) frog strangler.* **1975** Newell *If Nothin' Don't Happen* 105 **nwFL**, I was wonderin' whether I'd make it before the rain—a real frog-strangler makin' up to the southeast.

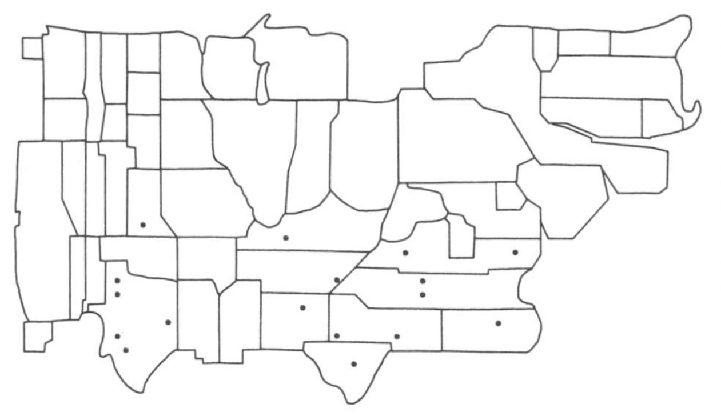
•frog-strangler + varr (Qu. B25)

frog table n Cf **fairy table 1**

A **toadstool** or mushroom.

1970 *DARE* (Qu. I38, *Small plants shaped like an umbrella . . which are not safe to eat*) Inf **VA**48, Frog tables [laughter].

Frogtown See **frog** n **B4**

frogum n

A **frog spit 1** (here: *Spirogyra* spp).

1950 *PADS* 14.30 **SC**, *Frog spittle*. . . Spirogyra. Also called . . *frogum.*

frog umbrella n Cf **bulltoad's umbrella, fairy ~**

A **toadstool** or mushroom.

1966–67 *DARE* (Qu. I38, *Small plants shaped like an umbrella . . which are not safe to eat*) Infs **MI**34, **SC**43, Frog umbrellas. **1986** Pederson *LAGS Concordance*, 1 inf, **eFL**, Frog umbrellas—toad-stools, mushrooms.

frog up See **frog** v **3**

Frog Village See **frog** n **B4**

frog walk v phr **West**

Of a horse: to buck or pitch.

1915 in 1975 White *Git Along* 145 **West**, [Song:] He shore is frog walkin' he heaves a big sigh,/ He only lacks wings fur tuh be on the fly. **1937** *AmSp* 12.153 **swTX**, On cold mornings practically all young broncos pitch a little or *frog walk* when first mounted. **1937** [see **frog** v 2]. **1961** Adams *Old-Time Cowhand* 300 **West**, A hoss which jumped 'bout with arched back and stiffened knees at a pretense of buckin' was said to "crow hop," "cat back," "pussy back," "frog walk," or "goat." **1964** Jackman–Long *OR Desert* 93, To describe a bucking horse: "He's frog walkin'."

frog willow n

Perh a **sandbar willow** (here: *Salix exigua*).

1937 FWP *Guide ID* 64, Baskets . . are made from twigs or slender sprouts of certain willows. Favorite material is taken from a squat variety of willow called the "frog willow" ("Yah-gwa-tsa-seeve").

frolic n

1 A lively country party, usu with games and dancing. **chiefly S Midl**

1794 *Wheeley's Baptist Ch. Minutes* Jan. (N.C. Univ. MSS.) *(DAE)*, An accusation was Brought Forward against John Sykes Concerning His Being at a Frollick Danceing and Behaveing himself in a very unbecoming manner. **1903** *DN* 2.314 **seMO**, *Frolic*. . . A country dance. **1908** *DN* 3.313 **eAL, wGA. 1927** Adams *Congaree* 29 **cSC** [Black], You sees her kind ever day, in churches and frolics. **1933** *AmSp* 8.1.49 **Ozarks. 1967–69** *DARE* (Qu. FF4, . . *Kinds of dancing parties*) Infs **GA**77, **KY**23, 34, Frolic. **1973** Allen *LAUM* 1.377 (as of c1950), [For] an informal dance . . *frolic* is a oncer in Iowa. **1981** Harper–Presley *Okefinokee* 57 **seGA** (as of a1952), Old-fashioned square dancing or frolics seem to have been held all through the Okefinokee region as far back as any one can remember.

2 A **bee** n[2]; see quot 1943.

1775 (1903) Patten *Diary* 337 **NH**, Jamey and Bob cut fence loggs for Mr. Shed it was a frolick. **1837** (1966) Martineau *Soc. in America* 2.99, Everyone has heard of the "frolic" or "bee," by means of which the clearing of lots, the raising of houses, the harvesting of crops is achieved. **1907** *German Amer. Annals* 9.375 **sePA. 1943** Weslager *DE Forgotten*

Folk 152, Now and then a wood-chopping "frolic" is held when the men gather by invitation to help a neighbor cut wood for winter use. In former years these frolics were held for corn husking, cutting and pitching hay, picking fruit, plowing, etc. The men who were invited to participate did not expect any financial remuneration for their labor inasmuch as each had the right to have a frolic of his own in the event that he needed extra help for a specific task. The man at whose farm the frolic was held was expected to furnish a big dinner for his guests. **1968** *Budget* (Sugarcreek OH) 25 July 14/4, Joe J. Zooks have a frolic today to tear down their old barn. **1968** *DARE* (Qu. FF2, . . *Kinds of parties*) Inf **OH**81, Frolics—to move furnishings or clear off a burned barn.

frolic v

Of a female animal: to be in heat.

1912 *DN* 3.576 **wIN,** *Frolic*. . . To experience menstruation. Said of animals when they are receptive to breeding.

frolicate v [**frolic n 1**]

1933 *AmSp* 8.1.49 **Ozarks,** *Frolicate*. . . To disport oneself at the back hill dances, which are called frolics. "I seen you-uns a-frolicatin' over t' Booger Holler."

frolicking ppl adj [*frolic* v]

Rollicking, gay.

1966 *DARE* (Qu. FF17, . . *A very good or enjoyable time: "We all had a _____ last night."*) Inf **AL**5, Frolicking time.

from prep Pronc-spp *frum, frun, f'm;* **chiefly Sth,** *esp freq among Black speakers, f'om, fum*

A Forms.

1883 (1971) Harris *Nights with Remus* 243 **GA** [Black], Brer Rabbit, whar'bout our bread comin' frun? **1891** *PMLA* 6.172 **TN,** We hear . . *frum* for *from*. **1892** *DN* 1.238 **MO,** *From* [frəm], even in stressed positions. **1893** Shands *MS Speech* 31, *Fum*. . . Negro for *from*. **1898** Westcott *Harum* 19 **NEng,** I had my old umbrel'—though it didn't hender me f'm gettin' more or less wet. **1899** Chesnutt *Conjure Woman* 16 **csNC** [Black], Some ha'rs [=hairs] fum a black cat's tail. **1908** *DN* 3.313 **eAL, wGA,** *Fum*. . . From. **1922** Gonzales *Black Border* 302 **sSC, GA coasts** [Gullah glossary], *F'um*. **1927** Shewmake *Engl. Pronc. VA* 42, *From*. Even when stressed . . this word is often called *frum*. **1928** Peterkin *Scarlet Sister Mary* 297 **sSC** [Gullah], I don' know whe e come f'om, an' I don' know whe e's gwine. **1942** Hall *Smoky Mt. Speech* 28, *From* varies [ɑ], [ɒ], [ʌ].

B Senses.

1 Away from. [*OED from* prep. 5. b "Now only in *from home*"]

1819 (1915) Mason *Pioneer West* 40 **MO,** Called to see Gatewood. . . He was from home. **1833** (1847) Lundy *Life & Travels* 39 **NJ,** Arrived at dusk at the house of Captain Bird, who was then from home. **1986** Pederson *LAGS Concordance,* 1 inf, **sMS,** [She is] from her home.

2 As a result of.

1847 Hurd *Grammatical Corrector* 35, *From,* for *by;* as, "He was injured from a fall." "He should profit from advice." **1943** *LANE* Map 519, *What he died from* [occurs infrequently]. **1960** *PADS* 34.65 **CO,** Died *from* [in a list of terms more common in the speech of younger than older informants]. **1971** Bright *Word Geog. CA & NV* 48, Pattern I . . [includes] *died from. Ibid* 46, In Pattern I occurrence in Southern California is in the Desert area only; . . the Northern California limits . . extend . . to Monterey on the coast and down the San Joaquin Valley inland. **1975** Allen *LAUM* 2.66 **Upper MW** (as of c1950), [In the context] I don't know what he died *of*. . *from,* which has a scanty 4.5% frequency in New England, has approximately a 25% frequency in Wisconsin and in the U[pper] M[idwest] is used by one-third of the infs. **1986** Pederson *LAGS Concordance,* 68 infs, **Gulf Region,** Died from.

3 in phrr *out from here* (or *there*): Out of here (or there). **esp Lower Missip Valley, eTX**

1891 Harris *Balaam* 121 **GA,** I make up my min' dat . . I better git out fum dar. **1965–70** *DARE* (Qu. Y18, *To leave in a hurry: "Before they find this out, we'd better _____."*) Infs **SC**34, **TX**98, Get (*or* git) out from here; **LA**11, Scoot out from here; (Qu. NN22b, *Expressions used to drive away children*) Inf **NM**11, Get out from here; (Qu. NN22c, *Expressions used to drive away a dog*) Infs **AR**51, 52, **MS**30, 57, **NM**11, **SC**34, **TX**32, 104, Get (*or* git) out from here. **1965** [see **get out** exclam].

4 in phr *from off:* Off of.

1937 *Esquire* 7.37/1 **neKY,** Mom hooked the bale from off the nail.

5 in phr *off from:* Off of. **chiefly Nth**

1943 *LANE* Map 724 **scattered NEng,** [In context "He fell off the horse"] Off from. **1950** *WELS (He broke his leg when he fell _____ the ladder)* 3 Infs, **WI,** Off from. **1965–70** *DARE* (Qu. X56b, . . *Sweating very heavily*) Inf **NY**75, Water just run off from him; **NY**88, Water run off from him in bucketsful; (Qu. MM20, . . *He took his coat _____ the chair*) Infs **MI**92, **MA**68, **NE**1, **WI**11, Off from; (Qu. MM21, . . *"Get _____ my land."*) Inf **GA**1, Off from. **1975** Allen *LAUM* 2.68 **Upper MW** (as of c1950), The full phrase *off from* [in the context "He fell off the horse"] comes from only two Midland speakers.

6 For, after; in recognition of. [*OED from* prep. 13 1596 →] *old-fash*

1941 *LANE* Map 394 *(Named after his father)* 1 inf, **neMA,** From him. **1986** Pederson *LAGS Concordance,* 5 infs, **nAL, nGA, sMS,** Named from [someone].

7 For; with respect to.

1893 Shands *MS Speech* 20, I didn't blame him from crying when that man hit him. **1943** in 1944 *ADD* 235 **csVA,** 'Of course I don't blame them from doing that.' Old, educated speaker.

8 in phr *sick from one's stomach:* =**at** prep **2.**

1975 Allen *LAUM* 2.65 (as of c1950), Sick *at* the stomach. . . Two instances of highly graphic *from his stomach* are in the Dakotas. **1986** Pederson *LAGS Concordance,* 1 inf, **ceTN,** Sick from his stomach.

9 in phr *help from:* To avoid, refrain from. [Perh by analogy with *keep from doing,* etc]

1927 Kennedy *Gritny* 58 **sLA** [Black], Can't help from knowin' w'at I know. **1942** *Sat. Eve. Post* 3 Oct 16, [Title:] I Can't Help From Cryin'. **1943** in 1944 *ADD* **sWV,** I could not help from hearing a group of girls talking.

10 in phrr *not to know from nothing* and varr: Not to know anything; to be stupid. [Prob Yiddish, see quot 1970 Feinsilver; but cf such phrr as *know down from up, know one from Adam* (at **Adam 1**), *know A from beans* (at **A from B, not to know**)]

1936 *Mademoiselle* Mar 43/1, I find I belong to the wrong gender to take part in such confabulations, and know from nothing. **1945** Manfred *Boy Almighty* 162 [Jewish speaker], Them San [=sanatorium] dietitians, they don't know from nuthin'. **1965–70** *DARE* (Qu. JJ15b, . . *A person who seems . . very stupid: "He doesn't know _____."*) 49 Infs, **chiefly east of Missip R, also Pacific coast,** From nothing; **AL**25, **IL**20, 25, **NY**39, 228, From beans; **IL**100, **WI**34, From Adam; **IL**11, **WI**30, From straight up; **PA**74, From little green apples; **MN**2, From a hill of beans [Of all Infs responding to the question, 32% were comm types 1–3, 75% hs or coll educ; of those giving these responses, 51% were comm types 1–3, 90% hs or coll educ.]; [(Qu. FF19) Inf **PA**247, This party ain't from nothing;] (Qu. HH16) Inf **MS**64, He don't know from nothing. **1968** Stegner *Edge* 75 **CA,** I don't know from nothing about any MG. **1970** Feinsilver *Yiddish* 311, He don't know from nothin'. This is the form in which *er veyst nisht fun gornisht* made its entry a generation or more ago. It has since been showing up in more sedate forms like "He doesn't know from nothing"; "He knows from nothing". **1970** *DARE* Tape **MI**112, She didn't know from anything about it. **1975** Gould *ME Lingo* 102, "Dumb? She don't know from nothin'!" This is at least one notch dumber than knowing nothing at all.

from a to izzard See **izzard**

fromety See **frumenty**

from off See **from B4**

front v Also with *off among Black speakers*

To show off, put on airs; hence n *fronter* one who puts on airs.

1970 *DARE* (Qu. AA8, *When people make too much of a show of affection . . "There they were at the church supper _____."*) Inf **OH**103, Fronting; (Qu. II23, *Joking names for the people who are, or think they are, the best society of a community: the _____*) Inf **WV**21, Fronters. [Both Infs Black] **1971** Roberts *Third Ear* np [Black], *Front* . . to put on airs; e.g. He was *fronting* like that because he knew she was listening. **1972** Claerbaut *Black Jargon* 64, *Fronting v.* to exhibit false behavior; create a facade; to fake: *He's just fronting, man.* **1980** Folb *Runnin' Down* 109 **Los Angeles CA** [Black], Terms like to *style,* to *front off* . . to *high sign* . . all of which mean to show off or upstage others.

front adj Cf **back** adj, **house B1b**

Of a room or living space: best, formal, reserved for company (not necessarily located at the front of the dwelling)—usu in comb *front room.*

1914 *DN* 4.72 **nNH, ME,** *Front-room*. . . Parlor. **1923** *DN* 5.207 **swMO,** *Front room*. . . The main room of a dwelling. **1929** *AmSp*

5.127 **ME,** The "front" or "fore room" was the parlor. **1941** *LANE* Map 323, Most New England houses built more than a generation ago have one 'best' room set aside for use on special occasions only (*the parlor, front room, fore room, drawing room, great room,* or *best room*). [*Front room* was offered by 44 infs, chiefly in sNEng.] **1942** (1971) Campbell *Cloud-Walking* 5 **seKY,** Sary didn't have a glass window in her cook room like in her front house. *Ibid* 74, It showed . . the four beds with fine weaved coverlids that Sary had in her front house. **1959** Sanders *Echoes* 5 **swAR,** One room was used for every-day and the other, we called the "front room," was used only when company came. This room had our finest [possessions]. **c1960** *Wilson Coll.* **csKY,** *Front room* (or *front bedroom*). . . The guest room or bedroom, not necessarily in the front of the house. **1965–70** *DARE* (Qu. D13, *The room where you entertain company*) 100 Infs, **widespread,** Front room; **CA**19, 71, **FL**15, **MN**30, Front parlor; (Qu. D3, *A room for visitors to sleep in;* total Infs questioned, 75) Infs **MS**72, **OK**1, 3, Front bedroom; (QR, near Qu. D16) Inf **FL**49, The main bedroom is the "front bedroom"; the other . . is called the "back bedroom," even if it's on the front of the house. **1967–68** *DARE* FW Addit **MA**5, That Christmas she built a fire in the front room, which had been Grandmother's parlor, and we had to stay in the sitting room; **IA**30, Front room—the "nicer" living room of the house, shut off, not used much. **1983** Mebane *Mary Wayfarer* 167 **NC,** I knew that "respectable" black folk always set good store in cleanliness and order in the "front room." I had sat in innumerable front rooms when I went to visit the parents of my eighth-graders.

frontage road n Also *front(al) road* **chiefly West, Upper Missip Valley** See Map

A street that parallels a highway, used for local traffic and for access to businesses set back from the highway.

1965–70 *DARE* (Qu. N28, *A road that connects a big highway with stores and business places set back from it*) 73 Infs, **chiefly West, Upper Missip Valley,** Frontage road; **CA**91, Business frontage road; **WI**51, Front road; **IA**32, Frontal road. **1980** *Houston Chron.* (TX) 27 Jan 8/4, Frontage road used to have some statewide popularity but is now limited to the Lower Rio Grande Valley.

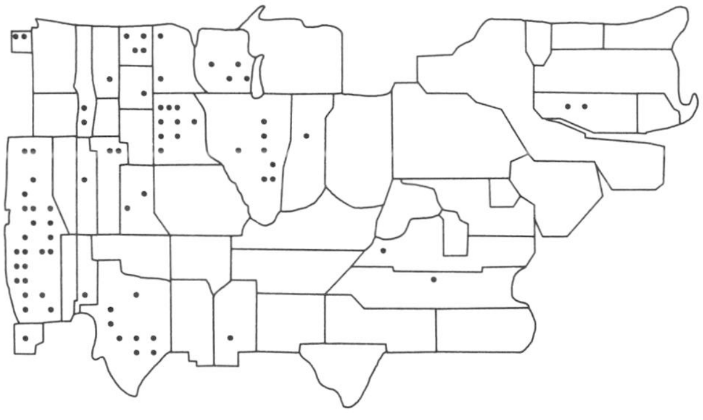

•frontage road + varr (Qu. N28)

front door n

1 also *front doors:* A movement in the children's game of jump rope; see quots; also quasi-adv. Cf **back door 3**

1943 TX Folkl. Soc. *Pub.* 18.198 **seTX,** The proficient jumper learns . . to enter and run out at will, either "front door" or "back door." **1961** *Western Folkl.* 20.179, *Front door*—Running in when the rope is turning toward the jumper. **1968** *DARE* File **seID,** Front door—turning the jump rope toward the jumper so she must run under the rope as it turns. **1979** *DARE* File **nCA** (as of 1950s), Jumping front doors was easier than back doors because you had an extra half second or so to ready yourself for the first jump after running in. With back doors, the jump was the very first thing. **1986** Pederson *LAGS Concordance,* 1 inf, **swTN,** *Front door*—running in with rope "towards you." [This question was asked chiefly in urban areas.]

2 One's trouser-fly—used in warnings; see quot.

1965–70 *DARE* (Qu. W24c, *Sayings to warn a man that his trouser-fly is open*) Infs **CA**166, **KY**77, **OH**53, (Your) front door's open; **NC**41, Front door open.

front doors See **front door 1**

fronter See **front** v

frontis n [Abbr for *frontispiece*]

The mantel over a fireplace.

1949 Kurath *Word Geog.* 52 **NC,** In the vicinity of Raleigh, North Carolina, the strictly local term *frontis* is in use.

front jockey See **jockey**

frontland n [*front* land that abuts (a body of water, a road)]

1941 Writers' Program *Guide LA* 9, The arable lands of the high elevation sloping away from the river compose the "frontlands."

front log See **front stick**

front name n

A first name, given name.

1877 Bartlett *Americanisms* 235, *Front Name.* Christian name. "The familiar manner in which the telegraph handles my *front name,*" i.e. in calling him Ben. **1893** (1958) Wister *Out West* 159, Texas Vocabulary. . . Front name—first name. **1908** Lincoln *Cy Whittaker* 317 **NEng,** After a few weeks' acquaintance we Bayporters almost invariably address people by their "front" names. **1928** *Ruppenthal Coll.* **KS,** I don't even know his front name. **1943** McAtee *Dial. Grant Co. IN Suppl. 2* 8 (as of 1890s), *Front name* . . given name. **c1960** *Wilson Coll.* **csKY,** *Front name.* . . One Christian name or the first of two given names.

front off See **front** v

front porch n

1 also *front yard:* One's stomach, esp a large one. Cf **back porch**

1921 Thorp *Songs Cowboys* 26 **CO,** You wouldn't know 'til mornin' that you had really dined / And taken in a lot of stuff your in'ards couldn't grind./ But you get the first reminder . . / When that "Frenchy" stuff starts quarrelin' down in your "front yard." **1942** Berrey–Van den Bark *Amer. Slang* 121.6, *Paunch; potbelly* . . front porch. **1969** *DARE* (Qu. X53a, . . *An oversize stomach*) Inf **CA**166, Front porch.

2 A woman's breasts.

1967 *DARE* (Qu. X31) Inf **MI**42, Front porch.

front road See **frontage road**

front room See **front** adj

front seat, get on the v phr

1896 *DN* 1.417 **nOH,** *Front seat:* "To get on the front seat," to have a very good time.

front stick n Also *front log*

=**forestick.**

1941 *LANE* Map 330 **NEng,** *Fore log, fore stick, front log* [5 infs] and *front stick* [1 inf] denote a smaller piece (sometimes described as longer than the back log) laid in front of the back log. **c1960** *Wilson Coll.* **csKY,** *Front stick.* . . Same as forestick: the front stick or log laid on the andirons. **1983** *MJLF* 9.40 **ceKY** (as of 1956), *Front stick* . . a fore stick.

front strip n Cf *DS* N44

The strip of land between the sidewalk and the street.

1966 *DARE* File **Pittsburgh PA** (as of c1940), Front strip—the "parking" or "boulevard."

front yard n

1 A wealthy section of town.

1970 *DARE* (Qu. II24, . . *The part of a town where the well-off people live*) Inf **SC**69, Front yard; Sugar Hill; [(Qu. II25, . . *The part of a town where the poorer people* . . *live*) Inf **SC**69, Back yard].

2 See **front porch 1.**

front yard fence n

A picket or slat fence.

1931–33 *LANE Worksheets* **ceMA,** Because the slats weren't up to a point, that would be a front yard fence. **1939** *LANE* Map 115 **NEng,** In New England the *picket fence* is often built around a dwelling; hence it is also called *front yard fence* [6 infs], *door yard fence, yard fence* and *lawn fence.*

froofraw See **fofarraw** n

frop See **frap**

fros' See **frost** n **A1**

frosses See **frost** n **A2**

frost n

A Forms.

1 sg: pronc-sp *fros'*.

1922 Gonzales *Black Border* 302 **sSC, GA coasts** [Gullah glossary], *Fros'*—frost.

2 pl: pronc-spp *frostes, frosses.* [Cf **-es suff[1] 1**]

1912 Green *VA Folk-Speech* 186, We have heavy frosses these mornings. **1924** Raine *Land of Saddle-Bags* 97 **sAppalachians,** Frost*es,* . . nest*es,* ghost*es,* in which cases the *es* forms a second syllable. **1969** *DARE* Tape **GA**22, A few light [frɔstɪz].

B Senses.

1 Something with a discouraging or chilling effect, as:

a Something which discomfits one; see quot. [**frost v B**]

1906 *DN* 3.137 **nwAR,** *Frost.* . . An unanswerable hit or retort. "That's a frost on him."

b See quot.

1939 *AmSp* 14.90 **eTN,** *Frost.* A quarrel between lovers. 'Lida and Oscar had a big frost last night.'

c A failure, dud.

1942 Berrey–Van den Bark *Amer. Slang* 262.1, *Failure* . . frost. **1950** *WELS ("The party was ________.")* 1 Inf, **cWI,** A frost. **1968** *DARE* (Qu. FF19, . . *A very dull or unenjoyable time: "The party was ________.")* Inf **NY**123, A frost.

2 See quot.

1965 Francis *Engl. Lang.* 121, A drink made by beating up milk, flavoring, and ice cream is variously known as a *frappe,* a *cabinet,* a *frost,* or a *milk shake* in different parts of the country.

frost v

A Form.

3rd pers sg: usu *frosts;* also *frostes.* [Cf **-es suff[1] 3a**]

1945 in 1954 *Harder Coll.* **cwTN,** I have some pretty peaches on the trees if it frostes they will fall off. **c1960** *Wilson Coll.* **csKY,** Frostes.

B Sense.

Also with *off:* To discomfit or irritate (someone).

1913 *DN* 4.10 **MN,** *Frost.* . . To surprise. "Wouldn't that frost you?" **1965–70** *DARE* (Qu. NN7, *Exclamations of surprise: "They're getting married next week? Well, ________.")* Infs **KY**60, **MI**13, 18, 25, 28, 109, **OR**6, **PA**104, **VT**16, **WI**67, Wouldn't that frost you! (Qu. GG22b, *When you have come to the end of your patience . . "Well, that certainly ________.")* Inf **IN**1, Frosts me off.

frost apple n

An apple that ripens after a frost.

1974 Peden *Speak to Earth* 108 **IN,** I am thinking about the old apples in the orchards, the horseapple, the sheep-nosed apple, the Vandiver, . . the Grinstone and the Frostapple.

frost aster n [From its blooming late in the fall]

Any of var asters (*Aster* spp); see quots.

1941 Walker *Lookout* 53 **TN,** Frost aster *[Aster linarifolius].* . . Until the coming of frost and then . . until November winds begin to blow. **1951** Voss-Eifert *IL Wild Flowers* 235, (Frost Aster. Frostweed) *Aster pilosus.* **1972** Brown *Wildflowers LA* 186, *Fall or Frost Aster. Aster ericoides.* . . September into November.

frostbird n

1 Any of three plovers:

a also *frost plover:* **=golden plover.** [See quots] **esp NEast**

1844 Giraud *Birds Long Is.* 214 **seNY,** It [*=Pluvialis dominica*] is better known to our gunners by the name of "Frost Bird," so called from being more plentiful during the early frosts of autumn. **1844** DeKay *Zool. NY* 2.213, *The Golden Plover.* . . As they appear in the greatest numbers after a sharp frost, they are popularly known under the name of *Frost-bird.* **1876** *Forest & Stream* 7.149/1 **Long Is. NY,** The frost bird comes next. He arrives late in the fall, and lives more in the fields than on the shore. . . He is of a frosted color, white with little dark spots, and is good for the table. **1917** (1923) *Birds Amer.* 1.257, *Golden Plover.* . . *Other Names.* . . Frost-bird. **1951** *AmSp* 26.275, *Frost bird* indicates one which comes in numbers at about the time of the first heavy frosts. It has been applied mostly to shore birds, as . . common kittiwake (Mass.); golden plover (Mass., N.Y., Pa., N.J., Nebr.; also frost plover, N.Y.); black-bellied plover (R.I., N.Y.), upland plover and dunlin (Mass.); and stilt sandpiper (N.J.) **1955** MA Audubon Soc. *Bulletin* 39.444, *American Golden Plover.* . . Frost Bird (Mass., R.I. As being associated with frosty weather.)

b **=upland plover.**

1849 Herbert *Frank Forester's Field Sports* 1.94, Bartram's Tatler. . . Upland Plover, . . Frost-bird, Grass Plover. **1951** [see **1a** above]. **1956** MA Audubon Soc. *Bulletin* 40.17, *Upland Plover.* . . Frost Bird. . . Probably through confusion with the Golden Plover, a shore bird also often seen in uplands.

c **=black-bellied plover.**

1899 Howe–Sturtevant *Birds RI* 54, Black-bellied Plover. . . Frost-bird. **1923** U.S. Dept. Ag. *Misc. Circular* 13.68 **seNY, RI,** *Black-bellied Plover.* . . *Vernacular Names.* . . *In local use.* . . frost-bird (for the young). **1951** [see **1a** above].

2 The black-legged **kittiwake.**

1932 Howell *FL Bird Life* 261, *Atlantic Kittiwake* . . Frost Bird. **1946** Hausman *Eastern Birds* 318, *Atlantic Kittiwake.* . . *Other Names* . . Frostbird. . . While with us in winter it is found mostly at sea, not often approaching the shore. **1951** [see **1a** above]. **1956** MA Audubon Soc. *Bulletin* 40.22, *Common Kittiwake.* . . Frost Bird . . (Mass. It is a winter visitor.)

3 Either the **red-backed sandpiper** or the **stilt sandpiper.**

1951 [see **1a** above]. **1956** MA Audubon Soc. *Bulletin* 40.19 **MA,** *Red-backed Sandpiper.* . . Frost Bird.

frostbiter n

One who sails a pleasure boat long after others have stopped on account of cold weather.

1934 *Sun* (Baltimore MD) 18 Dec (*AmSp* 11.104), Frostbiters are dinghy sailors. They 'will fight it out along the New York, Rhode Island, and Massachusetts shores throughout the winter, dodging ice cakes and apparently enjoying it.' **1937** FWP *Guide RI* 132, Even winter's icy blasts fail to discourage a few of the more hardy, and a class termed 'frostbiters' engages in competition as long as open water remains.

frost blow n Also *frost blossom* [See quot 1849] Cf **frost aster**

An aster (here: *Aster ericoides*).

1849 Lyell *Second Visit* 1.53 **ME,** There were also golden rods, everlastings, and asters in profusion; one of the asters being called "frost blow," because flowering after the first frost. **1940** Clute *Amer. Plant Names* 76, *A. ericoides.* . . Frost-blow. **1959** Carleton *Index Herb. Plants* 50, *Frost blow:* Aster ericoides. **1967** *DARE* FW Addit **KY**34, Frost blossom—the fall aster.

frost boil n

1 A defective spot in pavement caused by frost; see esp quot 1970. **chiefly Upper MW** Cf **frost heave,** *DCan*

1951 *AmSp* 26.233, *Frost boil,* a defect in highway paving caused by cold weather . . was used in a discussion of road conditions in Nebraska in . . 1948. **1968** *DARE* (Qu. N30, . . *A sudden short dip in a road*) Inf **MN**35, Frost boil—the dip or bump made by the action of frost in certain soil types (sand, etc). **1969** WI Statist. Reporting Serv. *Report* 5 May, The country roads are all frost boils. **1970** *DARE* File **WI,** Frost boil—a break, usually circular, which develops in blacktop pavement when frost works up through it in spring. **1973** Allen *LAUM* 1.400 **Upper MW** (as of c1950), [For *a hole in a road:*] One Minnesotan . . and one South Dakotan . . volunteer *frost boil.*

2 See quot.

1961 Douglas *My Wilderness* 217 **nNH,** Bigelow Lawn is a mass of polygons. Some call them frost boils. The working of frost, the freezing and thawing of water, pushes and moves the rocks. They end up forming polygons. Some polygons may have nothing but bare soil in the center. The more developed ones have a center of sedges, grasses, or rushes.

frost bug n

Appar a **katydid.**

1969 *DARE* (Qu. R8, . . *Creatures that make a clicking or shrilling . . sound*) Inf **KY**5, Frost bugs—shaped like a cricket, but green.

frost duck n

Either of two ducks: the **white-winged scoter** or the **ruddy duck.**

1951 *AmSp* 26.275 **OH,** *Big frost duck* [is used for] . . the white-winged scoter, and *little frost duck* . . for the ruddy duck. . . both of the birds owe their *frost* names to their often being observed to arrive immediately after a sharp, frosty night.

frosted-trunk tree n

Prob a **chalk maple.**

1969 *DARE* (Qu. T14, . . *Kinds of maples*) Inf **GA**80, Frosted-trunk tree—a maple with a white trunk.

frostening n [Var of **frosting 1**] Cf **icening**

Frosting.

1968 *DARE* (Qu. H64, *The sweet covering spread on top of a cake*) Inf NY70, ['frɔsnɪŋ].

frostes n See **frost** n **A2**

frostes v See **frost** v **A**

frostfish n

1 A **tomcod** (here: *Microgadus tomcod*). [See quot 1884] **chiefly NEast**

1634 Wood *New Engl. Prospect* 32, Th'Frostfish and the Smelt. **1795** Sullivan *Hist. ME* 21, The people have tom cod, or what they call frost fish, . . in great plenty. **1864** Acad. Nat. Sci. Philadelphia *Proc. for 1863* 233, There are two very distinct species found along the Eastern coast. . . The second is the "tom cod" or "frost fish" of the people. **1884** Goode *Fisheries U.S.* 1.223, The Atlantic Tom Cod, *Microgadus tomcod*, . . in various places south of Cape Cod, . . is known as the Frost Fish, owing to the fact that it becomes most abundant in the early part of the winter. **1931–33** *LANE Worksheets* **ceRI,** Frostfish. . . same as whiting. **1966–70** *DARE* (Qu. P2, . . *Saltwater fish . . [that are] good to eat*) Infs **ME**6, **NY**66, Frostfish; (Qu. P14, . . *Commercial fishing . . what do the fishermen go out after?*) **NJ**67, Frostfish (or whiting).

2 A **smelt** (here: *Osmerus mordax*).

1871 *Amer. Naturalist* 4.717 **NJ,** Professor George H. Cook, State Geologist, sent to the author of this paper a number of 'frost-fish' or 'smelt' *(Osmerus mordax).* **1883** U.S. Natl. Museum *Bulletin* 27.472 **N and Mid Atl,** *Osmerus mordax. . . Smelt; Frost-fish. . .* This is a food-fish of great excellence. **1906** NJ State Museum *Annual Rept. for 1905* 115, The Smelts.—*Osmerus mordax* . . Frost Fish.

3 A **cisco** (here: *Coregonus hoyi*).

1887 Goode *Amer. Fishes* 490, It [=*Coregonus hoyi*] is known as "Frost fish" in some parts of New York.

4 =**hake 1a** (here: *Merluccius bilineatus*).

1908 NJ State Museum *Annual Rept. for 1907* 188, *Merluccius bilinearis. . .* They are called frost fish at that locality [=Asbury Park NJ], as they are found washed ashore in numbers at times during the night.

5 =**Menominee whitefish.**

1935 Pratt *Manual Vertebrate Animals* 39, *Prosopium quadrilateralis* . . frostfish. **1946** LaMonte *N. Amer. Game Fishes* 122, *Prosopium quadrilaterale. . .* Frostfish. **1974** WI Univ. *Fish Lake MI* 31, *Prosopium cylindraceum* . . common names: . . frost fish.

frost flower n Cf **frostweed**

1 An aster (*Aster* spp); also fig. [From its blooming late into the fall] Cf **farewell-summer 1**

1860 Holmes *Professor* 59 **MA,** That kindly sentiment which all of us feel for old men's first children,—frost flowers of the early winter season. **1896** *Jrl. Amer. Folkl.* 9.191, *Aster* (all forms), . . frost flowers, N.H. **1929** *Torreya* 29.151 **ME,** Asters were *"Frost flowers."* **1937** Coffin *Kennebec* 278 **ME,** The white everlasting roses crowd up to my pasture bars, frost-flowers climb up the ledges to the pines that are centuries old. **1950** *WELS* 1 Inf, **swWI,** Frost flower—a wild aster. It will freeze exactly twenty-one days after they first bloom in the fall. **1964** Batson *Wild Flowers SC* 116, *Frost-flower: Aster pilosus. . .* Fall. Maine to Georgia. **1966–68** *DARE* (Qu. S25, . . *Small wild chrysanthemum-like flowers . . that bloom in fields late in the fall*) Inf **MD**17, Frost flowers; **NC**36, Frost flowers or asters; (Qu. S26c, *Wildflowers that grow in woods*) Inf **NC**35, Frost flower—blue, comes up about time of first frost.

2 A **rockrose** (here: *Helianthemum canadense*).

1940 Clute *Amer. Plant Names* 224, *Helianthemum Canadense.* Frost-flower.

3 A **crownbeard** (here: *Verbesina virginica*).

1940 Clute *Amer. Plant Names* 275, *Verbesina virginica* . . frost-flower.

4 Ice crystals resembling a flower.

1960 Bailey *Resp. to PADS 20* **KS** *(Ice that forms patterns inside a window glass in winter)* Frost flower. **1967** *DARE* (Qu. B36, *Patterns formed by ice inside a window glass in winter*) Inf **ID**5, Frost flowers.

frost grape n [Because it sweetens after a frost]

Any of var grapes [see quot 1862], but usu either *Vitis riparia* or *V. vulpina,* both of which are also called **arroyo grape, chicken grape, riverbank grape,** and **winter grape.** In addition *V. vulpina* is also called **August grape, bullet grape, bull grape, foxberry 2, fox grape 2, muscadine grape, possum grape, raccoon grape, scuppernong, sweet-scented grape**

1769 in 1789 Amer. Philos. Soc. *Trans.* 2d ed 1.261 **NJ,** The frost or winter grape is known to every body, both the bunches and berries are small, and yield but little juice. **1859** (1968) Bartlett *Americanisms* 77, *Chicken Grape.* The River Grape, or *Vitis riparia;* also called Frost Grape. **1862** U.S. Patent Office *Annual Rept. for 1861: Ag.* 481, The common names given to this species [=*Vitis labrusca*] and æstivalis and *V. cordifolia* are not uniformly constant. All three are called in different sections "Frost grape" and "Fox grape," and both æstivalis and *cordifolia* are often named "Frost grape" and "Chicken grape" in the middle States. . . The Frost grape has long, compound racemes, with a smaller thinner skin, and fruit more acid. **1905** *DN* 3.10 **cCT,** *Frost grape. . .* A small, sour wild grape. **1913** Johnson *Highways St. Lawrence to VA* 54, There's grapes in the woods, too—summer grapes and frost grapes. . . If I'm where the frost grapes are after they are ripe I eat 'em right out of hand. **1944** ME Univ. *Studies* 59.42, *V[itis] riparia. . .* River-bank or Frost Grape. **1966** *DARE* (Qu. I46, . . *Fruits that grow wild around here*) Inf **NH**5, Frost grape—small and sour. **1969** Kantor *MO Bittersweet* 312 **MO,** You bend close to read tiny signs. Frost Grape, Day Flower, Red-Bud Tree. **1976** Bailey–Bailey *Hortus Third* 1163, *[Vitis] riparia. . . River-bank g[rape], frost g[rape]. . . [Vitis] vulpina. . . Winter g., frost g., chicken g.* High-climbing vine, sometimes confused with *V. riparia. . . Fr[uit]* black and glossy, very acid but becoming sweet after frost.

frost grass n

1 =**fluffgrass.** [See quot]

1933 Jaeger *CA Deserts* 165, After spring rains the little frost grass *(Triodia pulchella)* comes up in enormous quantities and, true to its common name, makes the desert . . appear as if covered with frost.

2 An unidentified grass.

1968 *DARE* (Qu. S9, . . *Kinds of grass that are hard to get rid of*) Inf **NJ**52, Frost grass.

frost gull n

Either Bonaparte's gull *(Larus philadelphia)* or the black-legged **kittiwake.**

1925 (1928) Forbush *Birds MA* 1.89, *Bonaparte's Gull. . . Frost Gull. Ibid* 90, With the first warm days of April . . comes the . . Bonaparte's Gull. . . In autumn the immature birds appear. **1932** Howell *FL Bird Life* 260, *Bonaparte's Gull. . .* Frost Gull. **1951** *AmSp* 26.275, *Frost gull* signifies Bonaparte's gull in Massachusetts and the common kittiwake in Alaska. **1956** MA Audubon Soc. *Bulletin* 40.22 **MA,** *Bonaparte's Gull.* Frost Gull. . . *Common Kittiwake. . .* Frost Gull. . . It is a winter visitor.

frost heave n [*heave* a raised place or swelling] **chiefly NEng** =**frost boil 1.**

1967–68 *DARE* (Qu. N30, . . *A sudden short dip in a road*) Inf **MA**72, Frost heave; **NY**48, Frost heave, in New Hampshire; not permanent, made of ice. **1967** *DARE* FW Addit **VT,** Frost heaves—bumps in the road, caused by a freezing cold. **1979** *DARE* File, Along roads in Maine and Massachusetts one frequently sees signs saying "Frost Heaves," warning drivers that rough surfaces are ahead. **1989** *Yankee* 53.3.160 **NEng,** It's that time of year again when the little orange signs appear by the roadside: "Frost Heaves." . . Drivers unfamiliar with our roads are in for a rude shock, not to mention some serious front-end work. There is a frost heave in front of our house that is four inches above grade on one side and four inches below on the other. It extends completely across the roadway, like a tank trap.

frosting n

1 =**icing. widespread, but chiefly Nth, N Midl, West** See Map and Map Section Cf **filling 2**

1828 Webster *Amer. Dict.* np, *Frosting. . .* The composition resembling hoar-frost, used to cover cake, &c. **1920s** in 1944 *ADD* **cNY,** *Frosting* all but invariable. **1965–70** *DARE* (Qu. H64, *The sweet covering spread on top of a cake*) 451 Infs, **widespread, but chiefly Nth, N Midl, West,** Frosting; **AZ**1, **OH**89, **OK**19, Cake frosting. **1971** Bright *Word Geog. CA & NV* 180, *Frosting* 76% [of 300 infs].

2 =**icing.**

1967 *DARE* (Qu. H66b, *The sweet liquid that you pour over ice cream*) Inf **WA**27, Sauce, frosting, syrup. **1986** Pederson *LAGS Concordance* **Gulf Region** *(Sauce . . sweet liquid served with pudding)* 4 infs, Frosting.

3 Fig: anything considered desirable, special, extra.

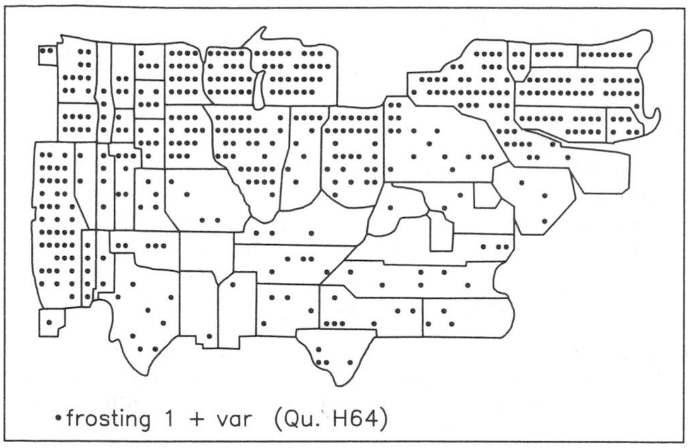

1967–69 *DARE* (Qu. U15, *When you're buying something, if the seller puts in a little extra . . you call that ______*) Inf **NY**133, The frosting on the cake; (Qu. GG22b, *When you have come to the end of your patience, you might say, "Well, that certainly ______."*) Inf **WA**28, Takes the frosting off the cookie; (Qu. II23, *Joking names for the people who are, or think they are, the best society of a community*) Inf **IN**70, The frosting on the cake.

frost lily n

A **zephyr lily.**

1959 Carleton *Index Herb. Plants* 50, *Frost-lily:* Cooperia (v).

frostmat n

A desert plant *(Achyronychia cooperi).*

1941 Jaeger *Wildflowers* 66, *Frost-mat. . . Achyronychia Cooperi. . .* The mats, which appear as if covered with frost crystals, are sometimes 1 ft. across. Sandy areas of the Colorado and eastern Mohave deserts; to Ariz. and Baja Calif.

frostmint n [See quot 1948]

=dittany.

1948 Wherry *Wild Flower Guide* 112, *Frost-mint (Cunila origanoides). . .* The common name refers to conspicuous curly ribbons of ice which develop at the bases of old stems on frosty mornings. **1949** Moldenke *Amer. Wild Flowers* 421, Frost-mint see *Mappia origanoides.*

frost off See **frost v B**

frost plant n [See quot 1822]

A **rockrose** (here: *Helianthemum canadense*).

1822 Eaton *Botany* 238, *Cistus . . canadensis* (rock rose, frost plant . .). In Nov. and Dec. of 1816, I saw hundreds of these plants sending out broad, thin, curved ice crystals, about an inch in breadth from near the roots. **1847** Wood *Class-Book* 181, *H. Canadense. . . Frost Plant. Rock Rose. . .* In dry fields and woods, Can. to Flor. **1876** Hobbs *Bot. Hdbk.* 40, Frost plant, Frost weed, Helianthemum Canadense. **1911** *Century Dict. Suppl.*

frost plover See **frostbird 1a**

frost smoke n

1966 *DARE* FW Addit **ME**16, Frost smoke—great clouds of steam coming off water in cold weather.

frost snipe n

1 Either of two sandpipers:

a =stilt sandpiper.

1876 *Forest & Stream* 7.68 **NJ,** *Tringa himanopus,* Frost snipe. **1917** (1923) *Birds Amer.* 1.230, *Stilt Sandpiper. . . Other Names. . .* Frost Snipe. **1951** *AmSp* 26.275, *Frost bird* indicates one which comes in numbers at about the time of the first heavy frosts. . . Upland plover and dunlin [=red-backed sandpiper] . . and stilt sandpiper. . . are named also *frost snipe* in New York, New York and Pennsylvania, and Connecticut and New Jersey, respectively; the willet also is a frost snipe in New York. **1956** MA Audubon Soc. *Bulletin* 40.20 **CT,** *Stilt Sandpiper. . .* Frost Snipe.

b =red-backed sandpiper.

1923 U.S. Dept. Ag. *Misc. Circular* 13.56, *Red-backed Sandpiper. . . Vernacular Names. . . In local use. . .* Frost snipe (Long Id., N.Y., Va.) **1951** [see **1a** above]. **1970** *DARE* (Qu. Q10, . . *Water birds*) Inf **VA**52, Frost snipe—a red-backed sandpiper—in area only during the winter.

2 =upland plover.

1951 [see **1a** above].

3 A **willet** (here: *Catotrophorus semipalmatus*).

1951 [see **1a** above].

frost the cookie v phr [Cf **frost v B**]

To be the limit; to be the last straw.

1966 *DARE* (Qu. GG22a, *When you have come to the end of your patience*) Inf **WA**33, That frosts the cookie.

frostweed n Cf **frost flower**

1 A **fleabane** (here: *Erigeron philadelphicus*).

1828 Rafinesque *Med. Flora* 1.162, *Erigeron philadelphicum. . . Vulgar Names*—Skevish, Scabish, . . Frostweed, Fieldweed, Squawweed, &c. **1959** Carleton *Index Herb. Plants* 50, *Frost-weed:* Aster ericoides; Erigeron philadelphicus; Helianthemum canadense.

2 =rockrose.

1837 Darlington *Flora Cestrica* 313 **PA,** Rock Rose. Frost weed. . . Prof. *Eaton* and Dr. *Bigelow* have noticed the formation, in freezing weather, of curiously curved ice-chrystals [sic] near the root of H. *canadense.* **1843** Torrey *Flora NY* 1.77, Frost-weed. Frost-wort. **1891** Coulter *Botany W. TX* 24, *H[elianthemum] Canadense,* . . the common "frost-weed" of the Atlantic States, occurs in eastern Texas and may be found within our eastern limit. **1931** Fassett *Spring Flora* 110, *Helianthemum. Frostweed.* **1942** (1960) Robertson *Red Hills* 200 **SC,** She massed plants with golden blossoms . . blazing gold foxglove, moth mullein, wild wood sorrel, frostweed, [etc]. **1944** ME Univ. *Studies* 59.43, *H[elianthemum] canadense. . .* Frostweed. *Ibid, H. Bicknellii. . .* Hoary Frostweed. **1976** Fleming *Wild Flowers FL* 56, *Frostweed (Helianthemum corymbosum). . .* Although most blossoms appear in March and April, frostweed blooms throughout the year.

3 An aster (*Aster* spp).

1896 *Jrl. Amer. Folkl.* 9.191, *Aster* (all forms) frost weed, Paris, M[ain]e. **1914** Georgia *Manual Weeds* 432, *Aster ericoides. . .* Steelweed, Frostweed [etc]. **1926** Roberts *Time of Man* 144 **KY,** Ellen bought a fresh ribbon for her dress and a bit of lace for her throat and blossomed anew with the frostweeds . . that lingered far into October. **1967** *DARE* (Qu. S21, . . *Weeds . . that are a trouble in gardens and fields*) Inf **SC**32, Frostweed; (Qu. S25, . . *Small wild chrysanthemum-like flowers . . that bloom . . late in the fall*) Inf **TN**6, Roadside asters or frostweed. **1976** Bruce *How to Grow Wildflowers* 254, In late September and October the fields and waysides of eastern North America turn white with the flowers of a group of some six species of asters which are called in many old wildflower manuals "frostweeds."

4 A **crownbeard** (here: *Verbesina virginica*).

1933 Small *Manual SE Flora* 1443, *P[haethusa] virginica. . .* Frostweed. Tickweed. Indian-tobacco. **1950** Gray–Fernald *Manual of Botany* 1495, *V. virginica. . .* Tickweed, Frostweed. **1970** Correll *Plants TX* 1657, *Frostweed. . .* rays and disk whitish. . . late summer-fall.

5 =dittany.

1940 Clute *Amer. Plant Names* 221, *Cunila origanoides.* Frost weed.

frostwort n

1 A **rockrose** (here: *Helianthemum canadense*). [See quot 1948]

1830 Rafinesque *Med. Flora* 2.209, *Cistus Canadensis. . . Frostwort, Rock rose. . .* The roots throw off small white icicles. **1843** Torrey *Flora NY* 1.77, *Frost-weed. Frost-wort. . .* Dry sandy woods and hillsides. . . Sometimes employed as an astringent and tonic. **1848** Bartlett *Americanisms* 150, *Frostwort. (Cistus Canadensis.)* A medical plant prepared by the Shakers and used for its astringent and tonic properties. **1864** *Catalogue of Herbs* **swME,** *Frostwort*—Helianthemum Canadense. **1948** Wherry *Wild Flower Guide* 68, *Frostwort. . .* The common name refers to the development, on frosty mornings, of striking ice ribbons around the shrubby stem bases. **1974** (1977) Coon *Useful Plants* 97.

2 A **buttercup 1** (here: *Ranunculus bulbosus*).

1900 Lyons *Plant Names* 316, *R. bulbosus. . .* Bulbous Buttercup, . . Frostwort.

frosty adj

Of a horse: streaked or mottled with white.

1966–67 *DARE* (Qu. K38, *A horse of a dirty white color*) Inf **MS**72, A frosty horse, a dapple gray; (Qu. K39, . . *Names . . for horses according to their colors*) Inf **AL**33, Frosty—partly red, partly white.

frosty n
=**frostfish 1.**
1933 *Hanley Disks* **swCT,** Frosty—frostfish, the tom cod.

frosty aster n Cf **frost aster**
An aster (here: *Aster ericoides*).
1956 in 1969 *DARE* File **swMN** [Flora of Pipestone Natl. Monument], Aster, Frosty. . . Aster ericoides.

frosty-beak n [See quot 1923]
=**mallard.**
1923 U.S. Dept. Ag. *Misc. Circular* 13.8, *Mallard. . . Vernacular Names. . . In local use. . .* Frosty-beak (Ill.). . . The names frosty-beak [etc] . . are applied to late migrants thought to be a race distinct from the fall flight. **1951** *AmSp* 26.275, Here also should be listed *frosty beak* for mallards of a late flight at Browning, Illinois. **1982** Elman *Hunter's Field Guide* 150, *Mallard. . . Common & Regional Names:* . . frosty-beak.

froth v Also with *up* Cf **frothy 1**
Fig: to be very angry—usu in phr *froth at the mouth.*
1928 *Ruppenthal Coll.* **KS,** To froth or foam at the mouth—to grow violently angry; to fly into a passion. **1942** McAtee *Dial. Grant Co. IN* 27 (as of 1890s), *Froth at the mouth* . . manifest anger. **c1960** *Wilson Coll.* **csKY,** *Froth at the mouth. . .* Be very angry. **1975** Gould *ME Lingo* 103, *Froth*—One who is angry will be said to froth, or froth up, no doubt as a mad dog.

froth-spit See **frog spit 3**

froth up See **froth**

frothy adj [Cf **froth**]
Angry.
1944 Adams *Western Words* 62, *Frothy*—Angry. **1971** Jennings *Cowboys* 167 **MT, WY** (as of 1877), So here you are saying good-bye to your whole damn herd and everything you worked for all these years, just because you had to get all frothy that day we come in and ast for a little time to sniff for gold.

froufrou adj [Fr "a rustle, swishing sound"]
See quots.
[**1945** Saxon *Gumbo Ya-Ya* 565, [Creole colloquialisms:] 'Frou-frou'—giddy.] **1968** *DARE* (Qu. W29, . . *Things that are sewn carelessly . . "They're ______."*) Inf **LA**20, They sewed it frou-frou [ˌfruˈfru] [laughter].

froughy See **frowy** adj[1]

frounce v [Var of *flounce*] Cf Intro "Language Changes" IV.4
To move suddenly; to flounce.
1899 (1912) Green *VA Folk-Speech* 180, She frounced out of the room.

frousty adj [Perh var of **frowzy**]
1 Musty, moldy. [Engl dial; cf *EDD frowsty* adj. 1] Cf **frowy** adj[1] **2**
1915 *DN* 4.214, This cellar smells frousty. **1928** Chapman *Happy Mt.* 50 **seTN,** His frousty brown coat wrinkled over his shoulders.
2 See quot. [Cf *EDD frowsty* adj. 2 "Dull, heavy-looking; peevish, crusty"]
1952 Brown *NC Folkl.* 1.543, *Frousty. . .* Slouchy, disorderly.—West[ern NC].

frouzy See **frowzy**

frow v [Perh back-formation from **frowy** adj[1]]
To foul, dirty, spoil.
1960 *VT Hist.* new ser 28.116 [Proverbs], It's a bad bird that frows its own nest. It is an ill bird that fouls its own nest.

frowey See **frowy** adj[1]

frowl n
=**murre.**
1917 (1923) *Birds Amer.* 1.25, *Murre—Uria troille troille* . . Foolish Guillemot; Guillem, or Gwilym; . . Frowl. **1946** Hausman *Eastern Birds* 335, *Atlantic Murre Uria aalge aalge. . .* Frowl.

frowsicating ppl adj [Cf Engl dial *frowze* to rumple] Cf **frolicate, frowzly,** Intro "Language Changes" III.1
Frolicking.
1881 Tourgée *Royal Gentleman & Zouri* 473 **Sth** [Black], "Hush yer mouf now, an' go an' tak keer o' dem frowsicatin' chillen." . . The child ran . . down the pathway to where "dem frowsicatin' chillen" were playing under a big persimmon tree.

frowsled, frowsly See **frowzly**

frowy adj[1] Also sp *froughy, frowey* [*frough, frow* brittle, fragile] **chiefly NEng**
1 Esp of wood: spongy, brittle; inferior. *arch* Cf *DS* KK7
1816 Pickering *Vocab.* 97, *Froughy* . . is in very common use in many parts of *New England. . .* It is doubtless a corruption of *Frough. . .* "*Frough;* loose, spungy; *Frough* wood; brittle." *Ray's North Country Words.* **1857** (1949) Thoreau *Jrl.* 10.14 **MA,** A lumberer called some timber "frowy." **1889** (1971) Farmer *Americanisms* 255, *Froughty* [sic—prob erron for *froughy*].—Spongy, brittle, or, in fact, applied to anything that is of inferior quality. A North of England provincialism, and colloquial in New England.
2 Rancid; spoiled; musty, foul-smelling. Cf **frousty 1, frowzy**
1848 Bartlett *Americanisms* 150, *Frough. Froughy. . . 'Froughy* butter,' is rancid butter. *[Froughy]* . . is in common use in many parts of New England. **1866** Stowe *Little Foxes* 253 **NEng,** Mrs. Dayton is a decent housekeeper, and so her bread be not sour, her butter not frowy. **1913** *DN* 4.4 **ME,** *Frowy. . .* Partly decomposed and ill-smelling. **1916** *DN* 4.302 **CT, MI, MA,** *Frowy. . .* Rancid. **1932** *DN* 6.283 **CT,** *Frowy plate.* "One with grease under the glaze; when it is warm you can smell it." **1941** *LANE* Map 306, Meat that has begun to decay or 'go bad'. . . 1 inf, **ceMA,** *Frowy,* mother's term for spoiled sausage meat or for salt pork beginning to smell; 1 inf, **swMA,** *Frowy,* of pork. *Ibid,* 12 infs, **chiefly swNEng,** Frowy [of rancid butter]. **1943** *AN&Q* 3.7/2 **NEng** (as of c1925), Frowey (spoiled). **1959** *VT Hist.* new ser 27.136, *Frowey. . .* Rancid, as in lard or butter. Rare. Washington; Windsor. **1965** Needham–Mussey *Country Things* 135 **VT,** One time he come out in the morning, and the air was frowy with skunk, and he said it smelled like an automobile had been by. **1973** Allen *LAUM* 1.287 **nwIA** (as of c1950), *Frowy,* recorded once . . is a . . reflection of a New England minor variation. . . Its range of meaning seems to include both that of *rancid* and that of *spoiled.*

‡frowy adj[2] [Perh var of *frowzy* slovenly, unkempt; but cf Engl dial *frow* an untidy, messy woman]
Unkempt, frowzy.
1970 *DARE* (Qu. W41, . . *Someone . . who always dresses carelessly*) Inf **NY**232, [ˈfraʊi].

frowzle n [Cf *OED frowze* sb. "*Obs. . .* ? A wig of frizzed hair worn by women" and *frowze* v. "*Obs.* exc *dial. . .* To curl, frizz, . . rumple."] Cf **frazzle-headed**
Often in combs; In ref to hair: a tousled or frizzy condition.
1892 Freeman *Young Lucretia* 40 **MA,** If she wants to have her own hair all in a frowzle, an' look like a wild Injun, she can. **1930** Shoemaker *1300 Words* 52 **cPA Mts** (as of c1900), *Strubbly*—"Frowzle headed", unkempt. **1942** Berrey–Van den Bark *Amer. Slang* 121.46, *Unkempt hair.* Frowzletop. **1958** *Sat. Eve. Post Letters* **sIN** (as of 1910–20), Frowzle-headed.

frowzly adj Also *frowsled* Also sp *frowsly* [Prob < **frowzle,** but cf *tousled, tously*] **esp NEng**
Disheveled, unkempt.
1872 in 1919 Hale *Letters* 111 **MA,** Both these Fräuleins had short frowsly hair. **1901** *Harper's Mth. Mag.* 102.665/1 **MA,** Look at the poor thing's hair! Only see how frowsly it is. **1904** Day *Kin o' Ktaadn* 33 **ME,** Grimy and frowsled and ragged and sore. **1958** *Sat. Eve. Post Letters* **sIN** (as of 1910–20), Frowzly; tacky.

frowzy adj Also sp *frouzy* Cf **frowy** adj[1] **2**
Musty, stale, foul-smelling.
1773 in 1887 Franklin *Complete Wks.* 5.197, It is the frouzy, corrupt air from animal substances. **1969** *DARE* (Qu. X17, . . *A damp cellar that had been shut up for some time would smell ______*) Inf **CT**27, Frowzy [ˈfraʊzi].

froze See **freeze** v **A1, 3, 4**

frozed See **freeze** v **A2**

frozen v See **freeze** v **A2, 3, 4**

frozen exclam [Cf **freeze tag**]
1969 *DARE* (Qu. EE17, *In a game of tag, if a player wants to rest, what does he call out so that he can't be tagged?*) Inf **RI**15, Frozen!

frozent See **freeze v A4**

frozen tag See **freeze tag**

frozy adj

?Frozen (with fear).

c1938 in 1970 Hyatt *Hoodoo* 1.XL **seLA,** Well, they had diff'rent—all kinds of animals come [=that came] out of human beings in a jar. Well, I see some frogs, I see some lizards. . . I left there, I was kind of *frozy.* I was scared—didn't know the way out, had to take me back on across the roofs.

frozzle See **frazzle n 2**

frufraw See **fofarraw n**

fruit n

1 Preserved or cooked fruit, usu apples; fruit sauce, usu applesauce. **chiefly S Midl**

1902 *DN* 2.235 **sIL,** *Fruit.* . . Cooked or preserved fruit on the table. The word sauce is never used. **1907** *DN* 3.222 **nwAR.** *Ibid* 231 **nwAR, seMO,** *Fruit.* . . Sauce; preserves. Seldom applied to fresh fruit. **1941–43** in 1944 *ADD* **WV,** *Fruit.* . . = Applesauce. Not applied to other stewed fruits served at meals. . . At the table, fruit = applesauce only. Apples are the only fruit commonly available. **1960** Hall *Smoky Mt. Folks* 60, *Fruit:* (as in West Virginia) at the table usually refers to stewed apples: "Have some of the fruit."

2 Fresh apples.

1917 in 1944 *ADD* **sWV,** Stewed fruit = apple sauce. **1939** *Hall Coll.* **eTN,** People in Elkmont had a sight of fruit to sell in the fall. [Hall: *Fruit* usually means apples.] **1974** Fink *Mountain Speech* 10 **wNC, eTN,** *Fruit* . . applies to apples only. "Have some fruit."

3 Onions. *?joc*

1969 Sorden *Lumberjack Lingo* 45 **NEng, Gt Lakes,** *Fruit*—Onions.

4 The kernel of a nut. Cf **goody 1**

1966–69 *DARE* (Qu. I41, *The part of the nut that you eat*) Infs **CO**3, **GA**72, **IN**1, **MD**37, **MO**14, Fruit.

fruit v

1953 Randolph–Wilson *Down in Holler* 246 **Ozarks,** *Fruit.* . . To result in, to produce an effect. "I told ye this God damn' hog-stealin' wasn't no good! Now it's fruited, an' here we are in the jailhouse!"

fruit basket n

A game with an extra player in which the participants exchange seats—also used as an exclam in the game; in var phrr, as:

a *fruit basket.*

1919 Elsom–Trilling *Social Games* 95, *Fruit Basket.* . . The players . . arrange themselves in chairs placed in a circle. They must then be numbered 1, 2, 3, 4. . . the ones are oranges; the twos are apples; the threes are bananas; the fours are lemons. . . ["It"] calls out . . [the names of two fruits] whereupon . . [those players] quickly exchange seats. . . ["It"] endeavors to secure a seat for himself. . . If ["It"] . . should call out "Fruit Basket!" the whole company must exchange seats. **1950** *WELS (Games with an extra player)* 3 Infs, **WI,** Fruit basket. **1960** [see **b** below]. **1965–70** *DARE* (Qu. EE2, *Games that have one extra player—when a signal is given, the players change places, and the extra one tries to get a place*) 41 Infs, **scattered,** Fruit basket.

b *fruit basket turnover* and varr. **chiefly Gulf States, Inland Sth** See Map

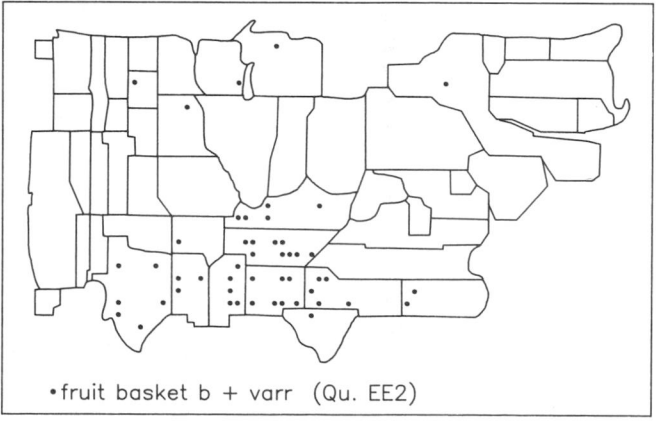

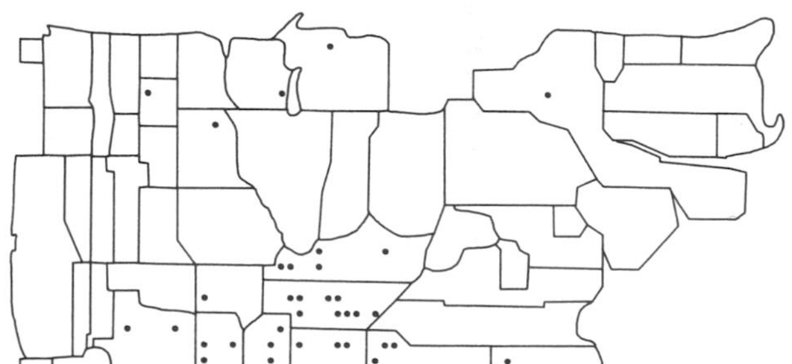

•fruit basket b + varr (Qu. EE2)

1905 *DN* 3.80 **nwAR,** *Fruit-basket (turned over).* . . The name of a game called in New England *'stage-coach.'* Common. **1957** *Sat. Eve. Post Letters* **eCO** (as of 1920s), Games I remember . . Going to New York; Fruit Basket Turn Over. **c1960** *Wilson Coll.* **csKY,** *Fruit Basket* (or *Fruit Basket Turn Over*). . . A group game with an extra player; in exchanging places, It often gets a chair and leaves someone else as It. **1965–70** *DARE* (Qu. EE2) 45 Infs, **chiefly Gulf States, Inland Sth,** Fruit basket turnover; **TX**101, Fruit basket turned over; **LA**3, **SC**34, Turn over the fruit basket; **WI**47, Fruit basket overturned. **1966** *DARE* Tapes **AL**3, 6, Fruit basket turnover.

c *fruit basket upset* and varr. **scattered, but chiefly Inland Nth, N Midl** See Map

1950 *WELS (Games with an extra player)* 17 Infs, **WI,** Fruit basket upset. **1954** *Harder Coll.* **cwTN,** *All change places*—same as *upset Grandma's fruit basket.* **1965–70** *DARE* (Qu. EE2) 89 Infs, **scattered, but chiefly Inland Nth, N Midl,** Fruit basket upset; 17 Infs, **scattered, but esp ePA,** Upset (the) fruit basket.

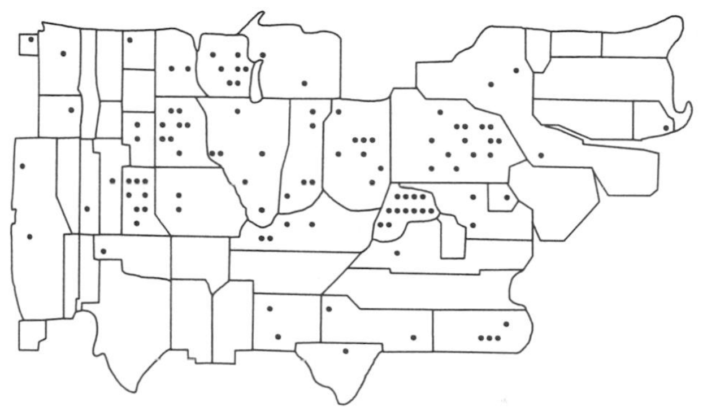

•fruit basket c + varr (Qu. EE2)

d *fruit basket (ex)change, ~ scatter, ~ tipover, ~ upside down.*

1950 *WELS (Games with an extra player)* 1 Inf, **cwWI,** Fruit basket scatter. **1966–70** *DARE* (Qu. EE2) Infs **NC**2, 16, **VA**75, Fruit basket (ex)change; **TN**14, **TX**90, Fruit basket upside down; [**WI**66, Tip the fruit basket]; **WI**70, Fruit basket scatter; **MN**37, Fruit basket tipover. **1970** *DARE* Tape **TX**89, Fruit basket upside down. Everybody'd have a seat except one. They'd call out "fruit basket upside down" and everybody would have to change seats. **1982** Brooks *Quicksand* 28 **swUT** (as of c1901), The fruit basket tipped over! At this signal every person in the room had to scurry to a new seat.

fruit basket turnover See **fruit basket b**

fruit basket upset See **fruit basket c**

fruit basket, upset the v phr

To spoil one's plans.

1953 *PADS* 19.10 **NC,** No, we can't go now; with Tom a-coming, he's upset the fruit basket. **c1960** *Wilson Coll.* **csKY,** *Upset the fruit basket.* . . Spoil some plan.

fruit basket upside down See **fruit basket d**

fruit bird n

Perh an **English sparrow.**

1966 *DARE* (Qu. Q21, *Different kinds of sparrows*) Inf **NM**13, Some are called fruit birds.

‡fruitcake n [In ref to the varicolored candied fruits in the cake]

1968 *DARE* (Qu. J5, *A cat with fur of mixed colors*) Inf **PA**74, Fruitcake.

fruit cave n [**cave n 1**]

=fruit cellar.

1865 IL Dept. Ag. *Trans.* 5.207, A Fruit Cave.—Mr. Coe had just completed a fruit cellar or cave. . . The walls are of limestone, eighteen inches thick, . . the lower . . [story] is sunk in the hill, the upper part is to be covered with earth, roof shapen, and turfed with blue grass. . . In one corner will be a bin of ice, which will add to its coolness. **1968** *DARE* (Qu. M19, *A place for keeping carrots, turnips, potatoes . . over the winter*) Inf **IN**30, Fruit cave.

fruit cellar n **chiefly Upper Missip Valley** See Map on p. 594

=cellar n[1] **B1.**

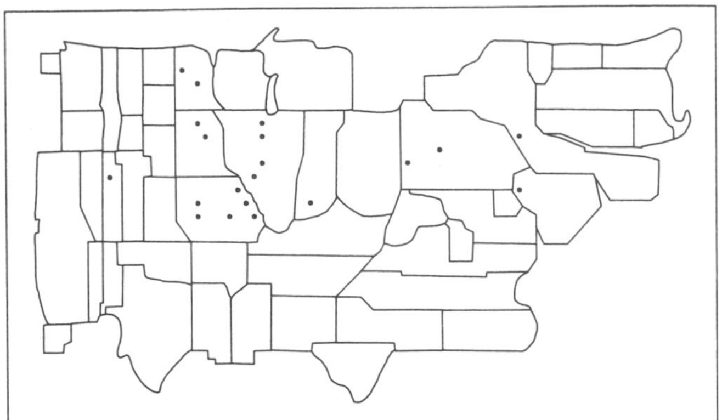

•fruit cellar (Qq. M19, D22)

1865 [see **fruit cave**]. **1965–70** *DARE* (Qu. M19, *A place for keeping carrots, turnips, potatoes . . over the winter*) 18 Infs, **chiefly Upper Missip Valley,** Fruit cellar; (Qu. D22, *Underground place to go in case of a violent windstorm*) Infs **MO**7, **PA**196, Fruit cellar. **1973** Allen *LAUM* 1.171 **MN** (as of c1950), [For a *storeroom:*] Fruit cellar [1 inf].

fruit-eater n

The Japanese white-eye *(Zosterops japonica japonica).*

1967 *DARE* (Qu. Q14) Inf **HI**2, White-eye or fruit-eater. [**1972** Berger *Hawaiian Birdlife* 225, The captive White-eyes ate fruit (e.g., papaya, avocado) placed in the cage, and Eddinger also observed wild birds . . eating the fruits of the introduced Chinese banyan.]

fruit hog n Cf **fruit tramp**

1950 *PADS* 14.75 **FL,** *Fruit-hog. . .* An orange picker.

fruit jar n [From its use as a container for moonshine]

Homemade whiskey.

[**1953** Randolph–Wilson *Down in Holler* 252 **Ozarks,** Others have referred to the hill people as . . *fruitjar suckers.*] [**c1960** *Wilson Coll.* **csKY,** Humorists declared that drinkers of [moonshine whiskey or home-brew] had developed fruit-jar noses, with a sore across the nose where the edge of the top of the jar irritated the skin.] **1966** *Wilson Coll.* **csKY,** *Fruitjar drinker. . .* A drinker of moonshine (which was put in fruit jars). **1968** *DARE* (Qu. DD21c, *Nicknames for . . illegally made whiskey*) Inf **SC**54, White lightning, booze, corn whiskey, fruit jar.

fruit soup n [Norw *fruktsuppe,* Sw *fruktsoppa*] **Upper MW**

A sweet soup made of cooked dried fruits and thickened with sago or tapioca, freq served cold.

1950 *WELS (Kinds of soup favored in your neighborhood)* 1 Inf, **cWI,** Scandinavians enjoy fish soups and fruit soup; 1 Inf, **cWI,** Fruit soup is made by Scandinavians. It is served hot or cold. **1952** Tracy *Coast Cookery* 174 **ND,** Norwegian Fruit Soup [includes water, sugar, prunes, raisins, sago, cinnamon]. . . Serve either hot or cold with small sweet rusks. **1966–69** *DARE* (Qu. H36) Inf **MI**94, Fruit soup; **MI**108, Fruit soup—made with prunes, raisins—a Scandinavian soup; **MN**17, Fruit soup—prunes, raisins, currants, dried apples; **WI**76, Sweet soup—cherry or raspberry juice and prunes, raisins, and little round tapioca—now called fruit soup; (Qu. H63, . . *Desserts*) Inf **MN**14, Fruit soup; (Qu. H65, *Foreign foods*) Infs **MN**6, 37, Fruit soup—Norwegian; **ND**2, Fruit soup—Swedish; all kinds of cooked fruit, thickened with tapioca.

fruit tramp n **West** *sometimes derog* Cf **fruit hog**

A migrant worker who follows the fruit harvest.

1918 *DN* 5.24 **cWA,** *Fruit-tramp. . .* A picker who follows the fruit harvest north and into the high valleys; implies careless workmanship. **1930** Irwin *Amer. Tramp* 81, *Fruit Tramp.*—A migratory worker who travels from orchard to orchard or from one fruit-producing region to another. . . The word "tramp" is almost a misnomer here, since many of these men are well-to-do, steady workers. **1941** Writers' Program *Guide CO* 240, These workers [=migrant peach-pickers], often referred to as "fruit tramps" are paid both by the day and on a piecework basis. **1971** Bright *Word Geog. CA & NV* 194, *Migratory worker. . . fruit tramp* 16% [of 300 infs].

frum See **from**

frumenty n Also sp *fromety, frumty;* pronc-spp *furmety, furmity* [*OED* ?a1400 →] **Mid Atl** *old-fash*

See quot 1859.

1637 (1972) Morton *New Engl. Canaan* 45 **MA,** But . . hee must eate some furmety before hee goe. **1705** Beverley *Hist. VA* 3.4.13, *Homony* . . is *Indian* Corn soaked, broken in a Mortar, husked, and then boil'd . . to the consistence of Furmity. **1859** (1968) Bartlett *Americanisms* 163 **MD,** *Fromety, frumty.* Wheat boiled with milk, to which sugar and spice are added. **1883** Amer. Philol. Assoc. *Trans.* 14.49 **Sth,** *Frumenty, fromety,* or *furmity,* 'wheat boiled in milk, to which sugar and spice are added'; used in Maryland, Virginia, North Carolina, and other Southern States. . . I cannot find that it is now known anywhere in the North. **1899** (1912) Green *VA Folk-Speech* 188, *Furmety. . .* Wheat boiled in milk and seasoned. **c1902** Clapin *New Dict. Amer.* 197, The *fromety* is especially well known in Maryland, where the word is, however, commonly pronounced *furmety.*

frump n [*frump* a dowdy, uninteresting person]

An unpleasant person; a boor.

1919 *DN* 5.66 **NM,** *Frump,* a loud person. **1969** *DARE* (Qu. HH16, *Uncomplimentary words with no definite meaning . . "Don't invite him. He's a ______."*) Inf **PA**219, Frump.

‡frump and a snitchel n

1969 *DARE* File **KY** (as of 1940s), 'A frump and a snitchel' is a short distance (e.g., down the road).

frumty See **frumenty**

frun See **from**

fruz See **freeze** v **A2**

fry n

1 A portion of meat suitable for frying; a frying chicken or "fryer."

1893 Shands *MS Speech* 33, *Give a fry off of one's liver. . .* This phrase is used by negroes to indicate a very great desire for something; as, "She would give a fry off of her liver for that house." **1927** *Ruppenthal Coll.* **KS,** Fry. . . [A] young fowl . . fried or otherwise cooked for food; by extension, the live fowl which may be so prepared. "We were presented with two excellent fries." **1965** *DARE* FW Addit **FL,** Fries—raw chickens. "You-all want any fries today?"[Asked by a delivery man in a store.]

2 Meat that is fried, esp bacon. **chiefly Sth, S Midl** Cf **fried meat**

1893 Shands *MS Speech* 45, Menses [=men], take a seat and have some of the fry. **1905** *DN* 3.80 **nwAR,** *Fry. . .* Fried meat. 'Pass the fry.' Common. **1908** *DN* 3.313 **eAL, wGA,** *Fry. . .* Fried meat. **1915** *DN* 4.226 **wTX. 1923** *DN* 5.207 **seMO,** *Fry. . .* Fried bacon. **1967** *DARE* (Qu. H38, *Other words for bacon*) Inf **LA**11, Hillbillies call it "fry." **1971** *Today Show Letters* **MS,** "Pass the fry." Refers to fried bacon, sausage, and so forth.

3 Gravy made from the drippings of fried ham. Cf **fryings**

1966 *DARE* (Qu. H37) Inf **NC**20, Fry—the gravy from ham; old-fashioned. **1970** *DARE* FW Addit **cVA,** Fry—gravy made of fried-ham drippings and water; old-fashioned.

4 The testicle of an animal, usu when fried for food—usu in combs *calf fry, lamb ~,* and varr; see quots. [Cf *EDD* fry sb.[2] 1] Cf **mountain oyster**

1889 Whitehead *Steward's Hdbk.* 420, *Rocky Mountain oysters,* Lamb's fries. **1937** *AmSp* 12.104 **eNE,** The testicles of lambs are eaten by some people and referred to as *lamb fries* or *oysters.* **1942** McAtee *Dial. Grant Co. IN Suppl. 1* 5 (as of 1890s), *Fry . . lamb fries,* meant lamb's testicles, either fresh or prepared for eating. **1949** Emrich *Wild West Custom* 180, Rocky Mountain oysters, the "lamb fries" available at gelding time, were simply tossed into the ashes of an outdoor fire, like potatoes. **1950** *WELS (Dishes made with lamb or mutton)* 1 Inf, **nwWI,** Lamb fries. **c1960** *Wilson Coll.* **csKY,** *Lamb fries. . .* Testicles of castrated animals served as food. Also called *hog mollies.* **1979** *Daily Forum* (Maryville MO) 7 Mar **nwMO, swIA,** Dennis Jeffers is the acknowledged expert on preparing and cooking the morsels, and his friends anticipate for months his annual oyster fry. . . Wayne Valentine says . . "We couldn't have fries if we didn't have him to cook them." **1981** *KS Qrly.* 13.2.67, *Fries* . . testicles of castrated calves and lambs kept for preparation as special dish; "calf fries" and "lamb fries."

fry-bacon frog n [Echoic] Also *fried bacon frog*

A treefrog.

1922 Gonzales *Black Border* 302 **sSC, GA coasts** [Gullah glossary], *Fry-bakin* [sic] *frog*—the small pond frogs, whose constant cry is interpreted by the Negroes as "fry-bacon, tea-table; fry-bacon, tea-table."

1932 Wright *Life-Hist. Frogs* 248, *Hyla cinerea. . . Common Names. . .* Fried Bacon Frog. . . It is a very slim, smooth, green frog. It may have side stripe, . . or have no stripe.

fry bread See **fried bread 1, 2**

fry cake n

1 See **friedcake 1, 2.**

2 See quot.

1958 McCulloch *Woods Words* 68 **Pacific NW,** *Fry cake*—A miserable mixture of dough and water and anything else left in the grub box, cooked in a frying pan . . when grub is about to run out.

fryer n[1] Also sp *frier*

1 A frying pan, skillet.

c1950 *WELS Suppl.* **swWI,** *Chicken fryer*—A pan with a rounding [sic] bottom, sloping sides, has a cover of its own; much steam pressure on inside. **1966** *DARE* FW Addit **OK**15, *Chicken fryer*—cooking utensil for frying. Made like a skillet, but has no vents for pouring grease, cover fits tight. **1967–70** *DARE* (Qu. F1) Infs **AL**58, **GA**46, **TN**52, Fryer; **GA**88, Fryer—if electric; **MN**1, Chicken fryer. **1972** [see **frying pan 1**]. **1973** Allen *LAUM* 1.199 **Upper MW** (as of c1950), *Frying pan. . .* frier. [3 infs]

2 A small pepper.

1968 *DARE* (Qu. I22c) Inf **NJ**26, Fryers—small, hot or sweet.

fryer n[2] [*fry* young fish]

A small bait fish; a minnow.

1939 *LANE* Map 234 *(Minnow)* 2 infs, **seMA,** Fryers.

frying kettle See **fry kettle**

frying pan n

1 A usu shallow metal pan with a handle, used for frying foods. **widespread exc W Midl** See Map Cf **frypan, spider**

1633 in 1867 NH *Prov. & State Papers* 1.77 **NH,** 1 frying pann. **1787** *KY Gaz.* 24 Nov 2/3 **cnKY,** For sale . . frying pans. **1888** Billings *Hardtack* 133 **eMA,** To fry it necessitated the taking along of a frying-pan. **1962** Atwood *Vocab. TX* 103, A *frying pan* is very generally thought to be lighter, or thinner, or smaller, or shallower than a *skillet,* and there is no reason why both terms should not survive. **1965–70** *DARE* (Qu. F1) 465 Infs, **widespread exc W Midl,** Frying pan; **CA**21, **MI**102, (Cast-)iron frying pan; **LA**17, Drip-drop frying pan; (Qu. F2, . . *The light metal pan for frying;* total Infs questioned, 75) 35 Infs, Frying pan; **AR**26, Aluminum frying pan; **MS**63, Little frying pan. **1970** *DARE* Tape **VA**96, I think of frying pan [as] a light one that you fry something hurriedly in [as distinguished from a cast-iron skillet]. **1971** *AmSp* 46.171 **Chicago IL,** [32 of 37 infs say *frying pan* for a "utensil for frying eggs."] **1972** *PADS* 58.15 **cwAL,** *Frying pan.* Midland *skillet* (15) is most frequent, but *frying pan* (9), *frier* (2), and *fry pan* also occur. **1973** *AmSp* 48.55 **Upper MW,** Common use of Midland *skillet* in supermarket promotion is helping to eliminate the already archaic Northern *spider,* and, for Northern users of . . *frying pan,* apparently is even effecting the replacement of that term by *skillet.*

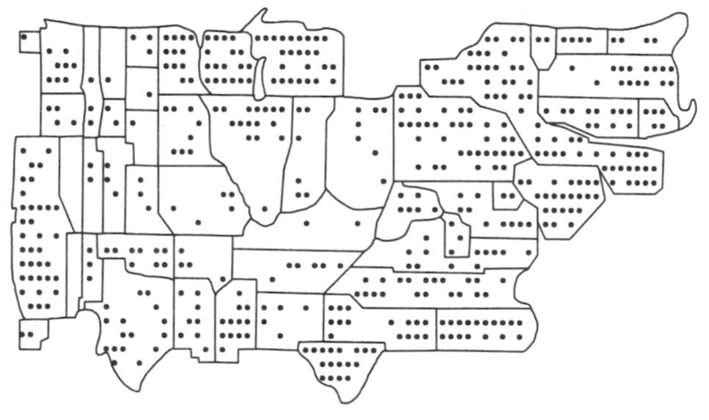

•frying pan 1 + varr (Qq. F1, F2)

2 Hell.

1966 *DARE* (Qu. CC9, . . *"That man is headed straight for ______.")* Inf **MT**3, The frying pan.

3 usu in phr *draw the frying pan* and varr: A children's hiding game; see quots.

1950 *WELS (Hiding games that start with some special, elaborate way of sending the players out to hide)* 3 Infs, **WI,** (I'll) draw the frying pan; 1 Inf, Poke the frying pan; *(Games in which every player hides except "It," who must try to find the others)* 1 Inf, Frying pan; 1 Inf, Draw the frying pan. **1966–69** *DARE* (Qu. EE16, *Hiding games*) Inf **AL**3, I'll draw the frying pan; **IL**97, Frying pan; (Qu. EE33, *Other outdoor games*) Inf **MN**42, I'll make the frying pan, who'll put the wiener in—one [player] stood, eyes closed, and drew a circle in the air, saying "I'll make the frying pan." Then one of the others jabbed him in the back and he had to guess who did it.

4 pl: A California poppy (here: *Eschscholtzia lobbii*).

1925 Jepson *Manual Plants CA* 403, *E. lobbii. . .* Frying-pans. **1949** Moldenke *Amer. Wild Flowers* 26, A species known as *fryingpans* . . has mostly basal leaves, leafless flower stalks, and light yellow flowers 1 to 2 inches wide. **1976** Bailey–Bailey *Hortus Third* 448, *Frying-pans. . .* Foothills of Sierra Nevada, Cent. Calif.

frying pie See **fried pie 1**

fryings n pl

Drippings; fat and juices drawn from meat during cooking, used as flavoring or shortening.

1937 *AmSp* 12.102 **eNE,** *Sop* is used . . for meat gravy made by dashing water into the fryings in a hot skillet. **1941** in 1944 *ADD* **VA** [Black], ['fraɪ-ɪnz]. **1942** *Ibid* **nWV,** Meat fryin's. **1966** *Wichita Eagle* (KS) 9 Apr sec 2b 1, From Mrs. Tibbie Patterson . . comes a note saying she had 8 quarts of meat fryings to give to anyone who will call for them. That ought to make a wonderful lot of homemade soap! **1967** *DARE* Tape **CA**21, We have bacon every morning so I have lots of fryings and as you say there's plenty of fat on it. **1968** *DARE* (Qu. H21, . . *The sweet stuff that's poured over [pancakes]*) Inf **MN**13, Fryings with cream and sugar mixed in.

frying size adj, also used absol Also *frying sized* **chiefly Sth, S Midl**

1 Of chickens: of the proper size and maturity for killing and frying.

1904 (1972) Harben *Georgians* 119, They was the best fryin' size I ever raised. **1927** *AmSp* 2.354 **WV,** *Frying size* . . young chickens large enough to kill. **1946** Wilson *Fidelity Folks* 80 **csKY,** You recall . . the old-fashioned country home, with its well-stocked smokehouse and with plenty of frying-sized chickens running around. **1954** *Harder Coll.* **cwTN,** *Frying size. . .* Young chickens old enough to kill.

2 Of a person: young—used esp in ref to girls. Cf **chicken n 3b**

1873 (1969) Smith *Bill Arp's Peace Papers* 249 **GA,** When I wer a fryin size chicken the biggest thing out was a trip to Augusty. **1896** *DN* 1.417 **TX,** *Frying size:* half grown (of girls). "A young lady, fryin size." **1908** *DN* 3.313 **eAL, wGA,** *Fryin(g)-size(d). . .* Applied to half-grown children. "There were half a dozen fryin'-size girls there." **1909** *DN* 3.396 **nwAR,** *Fryin' size. . .* Half-grown (of girls). "Now I wish that you girls back there, fryin' size misses on the back seat, would keep still long enough for me to bring some words of light to this dying congregation." **1915** *DN* 4.226 **wTX,** *Frying-size. . .* The younger set. **1960** Criswell *Resp. to PADS 20* **Ozarks,** *Frying size. . .* The adolescent stage of young people. **1961** Adams *Old-Time Cowhand* 124, Ropin's . . the most difficult of all cowboy attainments, and an expert started learnin' while he was fryin' size, and kept practicin' till he'd sacked his saddle.

frying skillet n Also *fry skillet*

=frying pan 1.

1970 *DARE* (Qu. F1, . . *A heavy metal pan that's used to fry foods*) Inf **DC**12, Frying skillet. **1970** Tarpley *Blinky* 94 **neTX,** Fry skillet [used by 2 of 200 infs]. **1986** Pederson *LAGS Concordance (Frying pan) 3 infs,* **AR, TX,** Frying skillet.

fry kettle n Also *frying kettle* **NEng**

A large, heavy kettle for deep-fat frying.

1875 (1969) Coffin *Caleb Krinkle* 138 **MA,** Little Maid . . rolled the dough, cut it . . , doubling and twisting the pieces, then handed them over to Deborah, who put them into the fry-kettle [to make doughnuts]. **1939** *LANE* Map 131, 26 infs, 24 in **ME, NH,** Fry-kettle; **RI, CT,** 2 infs, Frying kettle. [4 infs specify its use as a doughnut kettle; 2 add that it has a bail; 1 calls it a spider kettle, with three legs, used in fireplaces.]

fry-meat See **fried meat**

fry-meat preacher n [*fry meat* (at **fried meat**) prob because it is served to the preacher in return for his preaching] Cf **chicken preacher, gospel bird**

1970 *DARE* (Qu. CC10, . . *An unprofessional, part-time lay preacher*) Inf **NC**85, Chicken-eater, fry-meat preacher. [Inf Black]

fry out v phr, n

1982 WI Acad. *Trans.* 70.85/2 **WI,** In Calumet, Manitowoc, and Sheboygan counties, residents *fry out* rather than "cook out," when cooking bratwursts over coals. There exists the corresponding noun *A fry out,* to which one may be invited. **1989** *DARE* File **ceWI,** We didn't say "barbeque." We'd have a fry out. We'd fry out, or we'd have a fry-out. I'd say fry out where you'd say barbeque.

frypan n **chiefly Atlantic, Inland Sth, West** See Map

=**frying pan 1.**

1857 (1864) Thoreau *ME Woods* 323, A good outfit for . . an excursion . . into the Maine woods . . [includes] two tin dippers, three tin plates, a fry-pan. **1895** *DN* 1.374 **KY, NC, TN,** A skillet is a fry-pan with legs. **1907** White *AZ Nights* 75, A yearlin' carcass, half-skinned, lay near, and the fry-pan was full of meat. **1939** *LANE* Map 132 *(Frying pan),* 1 inf, **seMA,** Skillet = fry pan; 1 inf, **neMA,** Old people always called a fry pan a creeper; 1 inf, **wRI,** Fry pan, mother's term. **1950** *WELS* 1 Inf, **cwWI,** Iron frypan. **1963** *AmSp* 38.210, [In Sears-Roebuck catalogs:] *Frying pan, skillet,* and the once-colloquial *fry-pan,* present a more complicated catalog history, and, as far as Sears is concerned, *skillet* is the preferred trade term. As of 1962, however, the electric *fry pan* threatens to all but displace its competitors. . . The term *fry pan* rarely occurs before the 1950s. **1965–70** *DARE* (Qu. F1) 69 Infs, **chiefly Atlantic, Inland Sth, West,** Frypan; **CT**12, **NY**226, Electric frypan; **NC**79, Iron frypan; (Qu. F2, . . *The light metal pan for frying;* total Infs questioned, 75) Infs **MS**1, 73, Frypan. **1972** [see **frying pan 1**]. **1973** Allen *LAUM* 1.199 **Upper MW** (as of c1950), *Fry pan,* apparently an innovation, is scattered, but since the survey seems to have grown in popularity. **1986** Pederson *LAGS Concordance* **Gulf Region,** 46 infs, Frypan(s); 10 infs, Electric frypan.

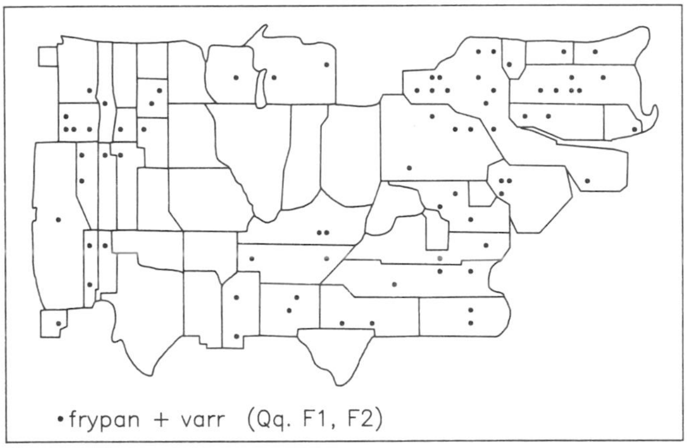

frypan ball n *old-fash* Cf **fried egg 3**

A round candy in a small metal container shaped like a frying pan.

1967–69 *DARE* (Qu. H80, *Kinds of candy often made at home around here*) Inf **CT**12, Frypan balls; [(Qu. H82) Inf **OH**61, Eggs in frying pans; **NY**199, Frying pan of candy—a non-edible frying-pan-shaped thing with little goodies in it; **NY**34, Frying pans—small metal frying pans, usually tin, filled with a colored creamy mixture similar to cake icing; eaten with a tiny tin spoon.]

fry skillet See **frying skillet**

fub v[1] [Var of *fob* to obtain by fraud or deceit]

1 To cheat, deceive.

1967 Cerello *Dakota Co. MN* 61, Father always taught us that it was sinful to fub anyone. . . Some people thrive and enjoy fubbing older persons such as we. [*Fub* heard in seven of nineteen communities studied.]

2 also vbl n *fubbing;* In marble play: see quot. [*EDD fub* v. 1]

1955 *PADS* 23.18 **TN,** *Fub. . .* To move the hand forward unfairly. . . *fubbing. . .* The act of moving the hand forward unfairly.

fub v[2]

1 usu with *around:* To waste time doing unimportant things; to putter or fool around; to fuss. **chiefly ME** Cf **flub 2**

1902 Day *Pine Tree Ballads* 142 **ME,** The high-priced doctors . . fubbed an' fussed. **1914** *DN* 4.72 **ME, nNH,** *Fub raound* [sic] *v. phr.* Fuss, bother. **1926** *DN* 5.387 **ME,** *Fub around. . .* To be busy without accomplishment. "The carpenter fubbed around here all day." Common. **1975** Gould *ME Lingo* 103, *Fub . .* to accomplish something in a left-handed manner. . . "Joe will fub around with a motor until he gets it running." "He fubbed around all forenoon, and anybody else could have done it in ten minutes."

2 See quot. Cf **flubdub** v **1**

1975 Gould *ME Lingo* 103, *Fub*—To bungle. . . "He fubs everything he touches."

3 In marble play: see quot.

1955 *PADS* 23.18 **cwTN,** *Fub. . .* To allow a marble to slip from the hand while in the act of shooting.

fub around See **fub** v[2] **1**

fubb n [**fub** v[2] **1**]

A waste of time; puttering.

1900 Day *Up in ME* 69, Can't own up that I approve it; seems too much like fubb and fuss.

fubbing See **fub** v[1] **2**

fubdub n Also *flubdub* [Cf **fub** v[2] **1**]

A **fussbudget 1,** fuddy-duddy.

1904 Day *Kin o' Ktaadn* 46 **ME,** Jawed at by ev'ry old fub-dub in town. **1979** Lewis *How to Talk Yankee* [12] **nNEng,** *Fubdub* or *Flubdub . .* one with a complusive [sic] personality, an old *faht.* "Jess is such an old fubdub—he can't stand to have one tool out of place on his workbench."

fubs exclam [**fub** v[2] **3**]

In marble play: a call used when one has accidentally dropped the shooter and lays claim to a second chance.

1955 *PADS* 23.18 **cwTN,** *Fubs.* A call made to nullify the error [*DARE* Ed: Letting the marble slip from the hand while shooting]. . . *Fen fubs.* Call forcing the act to remain as a shot.

fuck bug n

Perh a **love bug.**

1968 *DARE* (Qu. R30) Inf **LA**26, Fuck bugs—little orange and black bugs that come out in great numbers, always coupled, during the summer (last of July, first of August).

‡fuck bump n Cf **bump** n **1, love bump, nature bump**

An inflamed pimple.

1970 *DARE* (Qu. X59) Inf **TX**98, Acme [sic], blackheads, fuck bumps.

fuck the dog v phr, hence vbl n *fucking the dog* Cf **dog** v **8**

To loaf, shirk work; to malinger.

1942 Berrey–Van den Bark *Amer. Slang* 248.3, *Idle; loaf; loiter . .* fuck the dog. **1965–69** *DARE* (Qu. A9, . . *Wasting time by not working on the job*) Infs **MS**1, **WI**75, Fucking the dog; **WI**36, Fucking the dog—used to be used by hired men on the farm; (Qu. A10, . . *Doing little unimportant things*) Infs **MO**27, **OR**1, Fucking the dog; (Qu. BB27, *When somebody pretends to be sick . . you'd say he's ______*) Inf **OR**1, Fucking the dog; (Qu. KK31, *To go about aimlessly*) Inf **MO**27, Fuckin' the dog. **1970** *DARE* FW Addit **MI**112, Fuck the dog—to goldbrick, feign illness (to get out of work). **1984** Weaver *TX Crude* 93, *Fuckin' the dog. . .* Wasting time and loafing on the job. "Mike is the world champion at fuckin' the dog. I found him yesterday asleep under a truck with his sunglasses on and his hands wired to the driveshaft so it'd look like he was workin'."

fucky-knuckle adv phr Cf **duck knuckle**

In marble play: see quot.

1970 *DARE* File **KS** (as of 1890), Shooting with the taw cradled against the index finger so that the taw was pushed out with the thumb was called shooting fucky-knuckle.

fud n Also *fuddy* [Varr of *fuddy-duddy*]

An ill-natured or unpleasant person.

1968–70 *DARE* (Qu. GG38, *Somebody who is usually mean and bad tempered: "He's an awful ______."*) Inf **CA**81, Fud; (Qu. HH40, *Uncomplimentary words for an old man*) Inf **KY**80, Old fuddy. **1987** Stegner *Crossing* 24 **MA,** Wasn't it *luck* that What's-His-Name Jesperson went to Washington to work for Harold Ickes, and that we had been picked to take his place? He was such a fud.

fudder See **far** adv, adj[1] **B3**

fuddle-britches n

1953 Randolph-Wilson *Down in Holler* 246 **Ozarks,** *Fuddle-britches. . .* A wisecracker, a smart aleck. Cf. *Arkansas Gazette,* May 3, 1942. Perhaps sometimes it means a practical joker. Otto Ernest Rayburn (*Ozark Guide,* Eureka Springs, Ark., Autumn, 1950, p. 41) refers to "some clownish fuddle-britches who had humor bred in his bones."

fud-duddy See **fuddy-dud** n

fudduh See **far** adv, adj[1] **B3**

fuddy See **fud**

fuddy-dud n Also *fud-duddy* [Var of *fuddy-duddy*] **chiefly NEast**

A fussy or finicky person; a flighty or ineffectual person.

1914 *DN* 4.72 **ME, nNH,** *Fuddydud,* or *fuddyduddy. . .* Fussy person. **1952** McCarthy *Groves of Academe* 187 **NY,** "You old fuddydud," she finally teased him. **1966** *DARE* (Qu. HH40, *Uncomplimentary words for an old man*) Inf **ME**13, Fuddy-dud—said about young or old; **SC**24, Fuddy-dud; **MA**59, Fud-duddy. **1975** Gould *ME Lingo* 103, *Fuddy-dud*—Maine preference for fuddy-duddy, but used with more latitude than is found in the dictionaries. A person who is a *fuddydud* is a *niddy-noddy* [=an erratic, flighty person].

fuddy-dud v Also with *around* Also *fuddy-duddy* [**fuddy-dud** n] **chiefly ME**

To putter; to be ineffectual.

1941 *AmSp* 16.228, *Fuddy-duddy* . . was often used as a verb by a native of the state of Maine . . in the sense of 'to act in a foolish or ineffectual manner' as early as 1904. . . "George Thompson was fuddy-duddying around the Library basement." **1975** Gould *ME Lingo* 103, To *fuddydud around* suggests namby-pamby, perhaps a ladylike approach to a man's job. It can relate to abstractions; one *fuddyduds* about coming to grips with a problem.

fudge v, hence vbl n *fudging,* n *fudger* Cf **hudge** v

In marble play: to cheat; spec, to move the hand forward in an illegal way when shooting—also used as an exclam.

1849 *Daily Picayune* (New Orleans LA) 5 May 2/1, It reminds us of boys playing marbles; one cries, '. . no fudging; if you fudge it shan't count.' **1890** *DN* 1.24 **KY,** To "fudge" is to *poke* or something similar. *Ibid* 65, *Fudge* . . said when a player . . shoves his hand towards the marble at which he is shooting. **1892** *DN* 1.220 **MO,** To *fudge* is to cheat [at marbles]. **1896** *DN* 1.417 **NY,** "No fudgin's," a term in marbles. **1901** *DN* 2.140 **NY,** "No fudgins" = "mustn't crawl up." **1905** *DN* 3.61 **NE.** *Ibid* 80 **nwAR.** **1909** *DN* 3.396 **nwAR,** *Fudger. . .* One who *fudges* in a game of marbles; a cheat. *Fudgins. . .* A quick forward thrust of the hand in playing marbles so as to bring the marble nearer its object before releasing it. "No fudgins." **1915** *DN* 4.226 **wTX.** **1922** *DN* 5.187 **KY,** *Fudge* . . this is against the rules. **1934** *AmSp* 9.75 **ND,** *Fudging.* **1950** *PADS* 14.31 **SC.** **1955** *PADS* 23.18 **cwTN,** *Fudge. . . Fudger. . . Fudging.* **1958** *PADS* 29.34 **GA, WA, WI,** *Fudging.* **1962** *PADS* 37.2 **cKS.** **1963** *KY Folkl. Rec.* 9.3.65, *Attempt to get a more forceful shot by pushing the shooting hand forward when shooting:* fudge [in 17 counties]. **1966–70** *DARE* Tape **KY**76, **NM**6, 9, **TX**1, Fudge; **AZ**8, No fudging! **GA**13, He could say "free shooter" and then he could fudge; **OK**42, I say *venture fudge* [and] you can't fudge; **SC**32, He'd have to hold still when he'd shoot . . he couldn't fudge; **WA**6, One of our worst sins [in marble games] was fudging. **1967–68** *DARE* (QR, near Qu. EE7) Infs **CO**3, 7, 14, 42, 47, **CA**65, Fudging—going over the (lag *or* dead) line; **CO**28, Fudging—cheating in marbles. **1967–68** *DARE* FW Addit **cwLA,** Fudging—when your knuckles cross the line; **neLA,** Fudging—pushing fist ahead in marble game; **CO,** Fudging—scooting your hand forward from point where your marble landed, to shoot. **1973** Ferretti *Marble Book* 45, *Fudging.* Easing your hand over the ring line before shooting. . . Also used as a general term for cheating.

fudge n [**fudge** v]

In marble play: an instance of moving the hand forward illegally—also used as an exclam.

1958 *PADS* 29.34 **OK,** *Fudge. . .* An instance of fudging; "a fudge, if noticed, lost the player his turn." **1966** *DARE* Tape **GA**13, *Benching* meant that you couldn't shoot a slinging shot or a fudge shot. **1968** *DARE* FW Addit **CO,** If caught [fudging], the other player calls *fudges!*

fudge intj **chiefly Nth** *esp freq among women*

Used as an expression of annoyance, disgust, exasperation, etc.

1856 Whitcher *Bedott Papers* 155 **NY,** O fudge! that's nonsense—every one ought to be willing to exercise their gift, you know. **1924** *DN* 5.267 [Exclamations], *Fudge:* (oh)—(vex[ation], disap[pointment]). **1936** *WV Review* Aug 346/2 **WV,** Short expletives that can be shot out for any reason, or for no particular reason . . [include] Fudge. **1943** *LANE* Map 600, 5 infs, **MA, RI, VT,** Fudge! [One inf characterizes *fudge* as used chiefly by women.] **1950** *WELS (Exclamations showing great annoyance)* 1 Inf, **ceWI,** Oh fudge. [Inf male] **1966–70** *DARE* (Qu. NN8a, . . *"Oh ______, I've lost my glasses again."*) Infs **CA**2, **MI**82, **NY**123, 139, **WA**33, **WI**67, Fudge; (Qu. NN9a, . . *"______. The electric power is off again."*) Inf **MI**76, Fudge; (Qu. NN26a, *Weakened substitutes for 'Hell': "Oh ______!"*) Infs **MI**122, **WA**33, Fudge. [7 of 8 Infs female]

fudger See **fudge** v

fudgers See **fudgings**

fudging See **fudge** v

fudgings exclam Also *fudgers* Cf **fudge** v

See quots.

1958 *PADS* 29.34 **IA,** *Fudgings. . .* A call to get one's opponent's permission, in standing-up marble games, to get down on one's knees and use a thumb shot. **1963** *KY Folkl. Rec.* 9.3.64 **neKY,** *The command to push or clip the shooter with one finger:* . . fudgers.

Fudginny See **Virginia**

fu-fu See **foo-foo** n[1]

fufurraw See **fofarraw** n

‡fug-bugget n [Var of **fussbudget**]

1966 *DARE* (Qu. HH11a, *Someone who is too particular or fussy—if it's a man*) Inf **AL**6, Fug-bugget.

fugo See **fogo**

fuh prep See **for**

fuh v Also sp *fer* [Prob Afr, see quot 1949; cf *DJE fi* particle introd infin[3] 2] *Gullah* Cf **for B2**

Used as an aux verb expressing obligation, intention, prediction, or conditionality; sometimes used as a verb marker without further meaning.

1922 Gonzales *Black Border* 69 **sSC, GA coasts** [Gullah], Punkin skin' nigguh fuh beat black nigguh en' black nigguh ent fuh beat'um back, enty? *Ibid* 199, Uh bin ketch cootuh een me time, . . but uh yent fuh ketch no t'undah en' no lightnin'. **1941** Writers' Program SC *Folk Tales* 77, She fer bolt she door . . She bed down she fire, en she fall in she bunk. But she ain't fer out she light. *Ibid* 78, But w'en she hit dat bed, trubble bin fer start. *Ibid* 79, He mos' fer tear he fodder house do' down, but he ain fer stroy [=destroy] dat hant. *Ibid* 111, Bad luck fuh follow we now. **1949** Turner *Africanisms* 212, In Gullah, [fɑ] is used before another verb and is most accurately rendered in English by 'intend to,' 'choose to,' 'must,' or 'should': [ɒɪ ẽ no fɑ go fə no flɒwə; dɛm fɑ brɪŋ ɔm tu mi] 'I don't intend to go for any flour; they must bring it to me'; [ɪf ɒɪ fɑ go ɒf tu wɪlyʌm fə dɪ flɒwə] . . 'If I should go off to Williams' for the flour.' **1984** Joyner *Down by Riverside* 152 **SC coast** (as of 1930s), De hant [is] woorser at de full o' de moon. Maum Nellie fer testify it start way cross de fiel'. *Ibid* 153, Uncle Murphy he witch doctor en he bin tell me how fer fend 'em off.

fuhget See **forget**

Fuhginny, Fujinny See **Virginia**

fuik See **fyke**

fu'lhawk See **fowl hawk**

fu'lhus' See **fowl house**

full adj Usu |fʊl|; occas |fʌl, ful|

A Forms.

1931 *AmSp* 6.396 **TX,** A pronunciation of "full" making it rhyme with "dull" and "cull" instead of with "wool" and "pull" is not infrequent in the neighborhood of Fort Worth. **1941** in 1944 *ADD* **WV,** |ful|.

B Senses.

1 also in phr *in full;* Pregnant. Cf **foal n B**

1967 *DARE* (Qu. K10, . . *A cow that is going to have a calf*) Inf **NY**2, Full; **NY**24, She's full; she's in full. [Both Infs old] **1986** Pederson *LAGS Concordance (Pregnant)* 1 inf, **seLA,** Full—joking.

2 Drunk. [chiefly Scots dial; cf *EDD*]

1872 *Chicago Tribune* 14 Dec. *(DAE),* [He might] improve it by saying: 'Fellers, I ain't full.' **1899** (1912) Green *VA Folk-Speech* 187, *Full*. . . Filled with liquor; drunk. **1899** (1977) Norris *McTeague* 83 **CA,** "Let 'um alone," joined in Frenna . . ; "he's full, anyhow." **1920** Hunter *Trail Drivers TX* 455 (as of 1869), Here we found a store and plenty of "booze," and some of the boys got "full." **1927** *AmSp* 3.136 **ME,** Intoxication was indicated by such terms as "tight," "full," "hot," [etc]. **1965–70** *DARE* (Qu. DD13, *When a drinker is just beginning to show the effects of the liquor, you say he's* ______) Infs **AL**39, **GA**17, Full; **NM**3, **TN**6, **VA**27, Getting (pretty *or* too) full; (Qu. DD14, *When a person is partly drunk, "He's* ______*."*) Inf **NE**8, About full; **LA**15, **TX**32, **SC**32, (Getting) full; **CO**32, **MD**26, **VA**24, 87, Pretty (*or* sociably) full; (Qu. DD15, . . *Thoroughly drunk*) Infs **MN**10, **SC**69, **WA**6, Full; [**IL**37, Full to the gills; **WI**44, Full up to the brim]. **1969** Sorden *Lumberjack Lingo* 45 **NEng, Gt Lakes,** *Full*—Dead drunk.

full adv

1 Very much. *old-fash*

1914 *DN* 4.73 **ME, nNH,** *Full*. . . "Liz is full hun'somer than what Vieny is." "I'm full better'n what you be, Joe Buck!"

2 Entirely, quite, fully.

1924 Raine *Land of Saddle-Bags* 199 **sAppalachians,** Ye'll find a heap more that's full as good. **1931–33** *LANE Worksheets* **swCT,** *Casket* is used full as much as *coffin*. **1941** *Time* 17 Mar 32/1, Then Carol tramped full down on the accelerator. **1966–68** *DARE* (Qu. LL26b, . . *Words meaning 'entirely'* . . *"He's Irish* ______*."*) Infs **GA**1, **IN**5, Full Irish.

full n See **full beam**

full v

1 Of the moon: to become full. **chiefly Sth, S Midl**

1794 in 1889 Drinker *Extracts Jrl.* 237 **Philadelphia PA,** The moon fulled this morning about 8 or 10 o'clock, and rose this evening near the same hour. **1839** (1969) Briggs *Advent. Franco* 1.95 **NY,** The honey moon had fulled and waned. **1899** (1912) Green *VA Folk-Speech* 187, The moon fulls next Monday night. **1924** Raine *Land of Saddle-Bags* 104 **sAppalachians. 1938** Matschat *Suwannee R.* 129 **GA,** Then, one night when the moon was fullin', the womern who ruled 'em had a dream. **1953** *PADS* 19.11 **NC,** We will plant cucumbers when the moon fulls. **c1960** *Wilson Coll.* **csKY. 1970** *DARE* Tape **VA**38, After the moon maybe done fulled.

2 also with *up:* To fill (something); also ppl adj *fulling*. [*EDD* 1641 →, *DJE* 1797 →] **chiefly among Black speakers**

1872 Schele de Vere *Americanisms* 476, *Full*. . is often heard in the South for *filled,* and almost exclusively used by the negroes, who sometimes improve it in their way by saying *fulled*. **1888** Jones *Negro Myths* 7 **GA coast,** Buh Rabbit . . full him calabash long water. **1892** (1969) Christensen *Afro-Amer. Folk Lore* 26, Wolf hab full up 'e tub wid fish, an' 'e start for home. **1909** *S. Atl. Qrly.* 8.50 **sSC coast** [Gullah], The chambermaid *fulls* the waterbucket. **1922** Gonzales *Black Border* 303 **sSC, GA coasts** [Gullah glossary], *Full*—fill, fills, filled, filling. **c1938** in 1970 Hyatt *Hoodoo* 1.678 **seGA,** "Now, Cal," she says, "yo' talk about a place bein' full," she says, "ah'm gon' a full up mah rooms. . . Ah'm gon'a burn these buzzard feathers in kerosene . . an' . . ah'll git plenty roomers." **1966** *DARE* (Qu. N14, . . *Where you* . . *get gasoline put into a car*) Inf **SC**9, A fulling ['fulɨn] station. **1977** Dillard *Lexicon* 109, The adjective *full* becomes the verb *full,* not *fill,* in the Black English vernacular basilect.

3 See quot.

1911 *DN* 3.550 **WY,** "Horses full the corral," the corral is full of horses. "Potatoes full the wheelbarrow," the wheelbarrow is full of potatoes.

full and plenty adv phr

Amply, richly.

1882 (1971) Gibbons *PA Dutch* 196 **sePA,** Mrs. C.'s father was a miller, and perhaps lived more "full and plenty" than some of his neighbors.

full as rather adv phr

Preferably, just as soon as.

1969 *DARE* File **csME** (as of 1920s), "I'd full as ruther [sic] be outside"—said by a lobsterman dressed in oilskins, when invited to come in out of a storm.

full bank adj phr Also *at full banks*

Of a river: filled to the capacity of its channel.

1968 *DARE* (QR, near Qu. B18) Inf **CT**2, A full river is "at full banks." **1984** *Lutz Coll.* **NJ,** [She] was telling me about a small girl who fell into a brook. She said there had been a heavy rain and "the brook was full bank" . . meaning, of course, full to the tops of the banks.

full beam n Also *full (headlight)*

=**high beam 2.**

1967–69 *DARE* (Qu. N10 . . *The bright and dim lights on a car*) Inf **LA**3, Full and dim; **MA**40, Dimmers and full headlights; **NJ**55, Dimmers and full beam.

full butt adv phr

1912 Green *VA Folk-Speech* 187, *Full-butt*. . . With full force; point blank: "He ran full-butt against the wall."

‡full cheese n

A person of influence or importance.

1968 *DARE* (Qu. HH17, *A person who tries to appear important, or who tries to lay down the law in his community: "He'd like to be the* ______ *around here."*) Inf **MD**26, Full cheese.

full chisel adv phr Also sp *full chizel,* ~ *chizzle* [Etym unknown] **esp NEng** *arch*

At top speed.

1830 in 1834 Smith *Life Jack Downing* 93 **ME,** T'other [dog] arter him full chisel. **1846** in 1848 Lowell *Biglow* 2 MA, Hosy he cum down stares full chizzle. **1871** (1882) Stowe *Fireside Stories* 69 **MA,** Parson Carryl he driv into the yard, full chizel. **1942** Berrey–Van den Bark *Amer. Slang* 53.1, Full blast, - butt, - chisel.

full cock, on adj phr [*full cock* the position of the hammer of a gun when ready to be fired]

Fig: ready, prepared.

1935 Davis *Honey* 167 **OR,** They looked too substantial and pious to be capable of lying themselves, but they were on full cock to catch anybody else doing it.

full dark n Cf **black dark, first dark**

Nighttime; the dark of night.

1928 Chapman *Happy Mt.* 9 **seTN,** It was full dark now, . . [with] but one thin slice of day on the far edge of Big Gully Hill. **1942** Faulkner *Go Down* 118 **MS,** It was full dark when he tied the mare to Lucas' fence. **1949** Arnow *Hunter's Horn* 278 **KY,** Now git on, so's you can git back before full dark.

full ear n **West**

1936 McCarthy *Lang. Mosshorn* np **West** [Range terms], *Full-ear*. . . An unbranded calf or yearling with no earmark.

full-eye n

A bulging eye; a popeye.

1966 *DARE* (Qu. X21a, . . *Eyes* . . *if they stick out*) Inf **SC**10, Full-eye.

full-face cam n

A nonexistent object used as the basis of a practical joke.

1967 *DARE* (Qu. HH14, *Ways of teasing a beginner* . . *for example, by sending him for a 'left-handed monkey wrench': "Go get me* ______*."*) Inf **MA**1, A full-face cam. On cars, for a full-face cam, put a half-face cam in backwards.

full-feed v

1935 *AmSp* 10.270 [Stockyard jargon], To *full-feed*. To feed as much as the animal will eat.

full-handed adj [Cf *EDD full-handed* (at *full* adj. 7 (3)) "In good circumstances"] **S Midl**

Well supplied; prosperous.

1917 *DN* 4.412 **wNC, KY,** *Full-handed*. . . Well supplied; well to do. "He was a full-handed man—had a-plenty." **1927** *AmSp* 2.354 **WV,** I am full-handed now as far as help is concerned. **1954** *Harder Coll.* **cwTN,** *Full-handed*. . . Well supplied.

full headlight See **full beam**

full house n

1977 *DARE* File **SE,** Everywhere we went, restaurants served what they called a full house. It was a bowl of chili with a tamale in the center.

fulling See **full v 2**

full moon n [In ref to the 28-day cycle] *euphem* Cf *DS* AA27

Menstruation.

1954 *AmSp* 29.298 [Vernacular of menstruation], *Full moon* [used by women].

full night n Cf **black night**
=**full dark.**

1962 Faulkner *Reivers* 72 **MS,** Already you could see the moonlight. It would be full night when we reached Ballenbaugh's.

full noon n Cf **full dark**
Afternoon.

1969 *DARE* (Qu. A3, *The time between the middle of the day and supper time*) Inf **NY**227, Full noon.

full of oneself adj phr [*OED* (at *full* adj. 3) 1737 →] **chiefly Sth, Midl** See Map
Self-important; confident; **biggity** adj.

1965–70 *DARE* (Qu. GG19a, *When you can see from the way a person acts that he's feeling important . . "He surely is ______ these days."*) 27 Infs, **chiefly Sth, Midl,** Full of himself; **TX**36, Full of hisself; (Qu. GG29, *To be in a good or pleasant mood: "This morning he seems to be feeling ______ ."*) Inf **NC**84, Full of himself; (Qu. HH35, *A woman who puts on a lot of airs: "She's too ______ for me."*) Infs **GA**67, **MS**49, Full of herself; (Qu. HH41, *Someone who has a very high opinion of himself;* total Infs questioned, 75) Inf **FL**25, Full of himself. **c1970** *Halpert Coll.* **wKY,** *Full of oneself . .* presumptuous, harmlessly conceited. "I was feeling sort of full of myself when I started that job." **1976** Ryland *Richmond Co. VA* 371, Full of himself—self-confident.

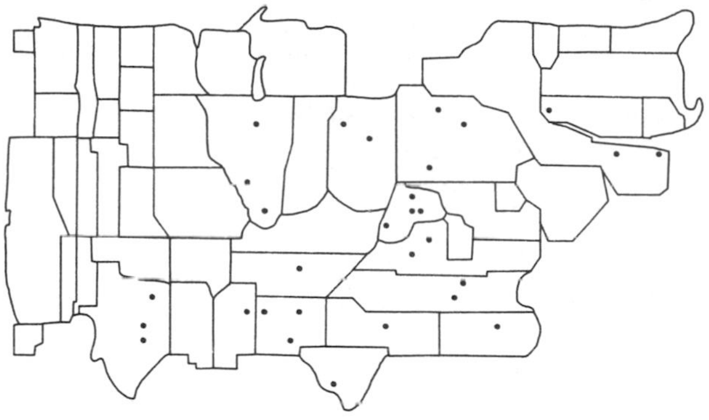

•full of oneself + varr (Qq. GG19a, GG29, HH35, HH41)

full-pot n [Prob echoic]
=**bittern.**

1951 *AmSp* 26.92 **SC,** A Gullah cognomen for the great bittern, *full-pot* (S.C.), has been interpreted to mean of the right size to fill a cooking pot. On the contrary, this is probably only another of the many names for this species that are in imitation of its queer vocalization.

full run n
In maple syrup production: see quot.

1947 *AmSp* 22.152 **wPA,** *Full run.* The total period when the sap is usable, or the entire *season.*

full split adv phr *old-fash* Cf **full chisel, full stick**
At full speed; recklessly.

1848 Bartlett *Americanisms* 152, *Full Split.* With the greatest violence and impetuosity. . . In common use in the United States in familiar language. **1892** *DN* 1.236 **Kansas City MO,** *Lickity-split* and *full-split:* at full speed.

full stick adv phr [*stick* a throttle lever]
=**full split.**

1914 *DN* 4.80 **ME, nNH,** He's goin' full stick.

full stroke adv phr
At full speed; at maximum capacity of the engine.

1969 *DARE* Tape **KY**6, When the head to your tow starts out, you just got to drive her [=a steamboat] full stroke.

full up adj phr
1 Satiated; completely full.

1906 *DN* 3.137 **nwAR,** *Full up. . .* Full. **1908** *DN* 3.313 **eAL, wGA,** *Full up. . .* Very full. **1914** *DN* 4.73 **ME, nNH,** *Full up. Ibid* 159 **cVA. 1922** Gonzales *Black Border* 303 **sSC, GA coasts,** [Gullah glossary], *Full'up*—filled up. **1923** *DN* 5.207 **swMO,** I'm full up 'ith y'r cussin'. **1939** *AmSp* 14.90 **eTN,** He's full up on corn coffee. **c1960** *Wilson Coll.* **csKY,** Full up. **1965–70** *DARE* (Qu. LL28, *Expressions meaning entirely full: "The box of apples was ______ ."*) 43 Infs, **scattered,** Full up. **1985** *DARE* File **cwIN,** A motel with a "no vacancy" sign is "full up." And I've heard this term among the best educated of my Midwestern friends.

2 Fully occupied; overburdened.

1906 *DN* 3.137 **nwAR,** *Full up. . .* Full, occupied, busy. "We're full up, we've got so many new goods." "I'm just full up with work." **1908** *DN* 3.313 **eAL, wGA,** *Full up . .* busy.

full up v phr[1] [*full* to shrink and thicken (wool) by using moisture and heat] **esp NEng**
Of fabric, esp wool: to shrink.

1943 *LANE* Map 660 *(Shrank)* 3 infs, **cwCT, ceVT, cwNH,** Fulled up. **1967** *DARE* (Qu. OO37a, . . *"The first time my wool socks were washed they ______ ."*) Inf **MA**5, Fulled up.

full up v phr[2] See **full** v **2**

fully adv
Certainly, decidedly, surely.

1902 *DN* 2.235 **sIL,** *Fully. . .* Certainly; most decidedly. . . 'He fully is, does, will, etc.' **1903** *DN* 2.314 **seMO,** *Fully. . .* Decidedly. 'Are you going.' [']I fully am.' This . . is quite common. **1966** *DARE* (Qu. NN14, *When you doubt something that somebody has said, and you want to be sure that it is true, you say: "Is that really so?" He answers: "______ .";* total Infs questioned, 75) Inf **MS**35, Fully.

fully colored adj [See quot]

1950 *PADS* 14.31 **SC,** *Fully colored. . .* Neither sallow nor black, but ruddy brown. The color of the *Fulah* Negroes of French West Africa. Probably from *Fulah* colored, with the aid of folk etymology.

fulmar n Also *fulmar petrel*
Std: a gull-like seabird *(Fulmarus glacialis).* Also called **gluttonbird, goose** n **B1, hagdon, marbleheader, noddy, oil-bird, sea horse, striker**

fulton cat n Also *fulton* Cf **blue fulton**
1 =**blue catfish 1.**

1908 Forbes–Richardson *Fishes of IL* 179, It [=*Ictalurus furcatus*] is commonly known as the "Fulton" or "blue cat" by Mississippi River fishermen. **1967** Cross *Hdbk. Fishes KS* 210, The blue catfish, which is more often called the "fulton," "white fulton," or "white cat" in the Kansas region, occurs fairly commonly in the Missouri River.

2 =**eel catfish.**

1933 LA Dept. of Conserv. *Fishes* 421, The Eel Cat, Willow Cat or Fulton Cat.

fuluk n [Perh var of *fulica* genus of birds comprising the coots]
A **coot** n[1] 1.

1966 *DARE* Tape **SC**15, Fuluk ['fu'luʔ], you call them fuluk, on that marsh to sleep. Then by the lamp or the fire, they cannot run, they cannot move. Then we take that switch and lick them at the neck, kill them, put 'em in a sack. . . And that, we call that lick coot.

fum See **from**

fumadiddle See **flummadiddle**

fumble n
Often in combs: An awkward fumbling person; hence adjs *fumble-fingered, fumble-fisted* awkward.

1903 *DN* 2.297 **Cape Cod MA,** *Fumble heels. . .* One who trips or falls easily. **1941** *LANE* Map 464 *(Awkward person)* 1 inf, **neMA,** He's an old fumble; 2 infs, **sME, ceNH,** Fumble-head. **1960** Criswell *Resp. to PADS 20* **Ozarks,** Fumble fist—someone clumsy with his hands. Fairly common once. **1966–69** *DARE* (Qu. HH21, *A very awkward, clumsy person*) Inf **TX**74, Fumble-butt; **IL**96, Fumble-fingered; **MI**67, Fumble-fingers; **FL**36, Fumble-fisted; **GA**89, Fumble-foot.

fum-fidgets and hoo-daddles n
A feeling of jittery unease; the **all-overs.**

1980 *DARE* File (as of 1956), A friend from Knoxville, Tennessee, visiting in Madison, Wisconsin, felt nervousness and discomfort one day, and remarked that she had "the fum-fidgets and hoo-daddles."

fumget See **forget**

fummadiddle See **flummadiddle**

fump v [Echoic; perh var of *thump*]

To strike, thump.

1943 Chase *Jack Tales* 11 **wNC,** Jack he picked him out a rock and cut-drive at the giant in front—fumped him right in the back of the head.

fun v **chiefly Sth, S Midl**

1 tr: To tease, trick, fool (someone).

1931 *AmSp* 6.267 **KY,** I'm not funnin' ye. **1936** *Scribner's Mag.* Oct 61/1 **neKY,** I didn't believe he had any graves out here when he told me. I thought he was just funning me a little. **1960** Williams *Walk Egypt* 77 **GA,** The postmaster stood in the weeds, funning Tom. **1968** *DARE* (Qu. GG3, *To tease: "See those big boys trying to ______ that little one."*) Inf **LA**17, Kid, fun, [if] in a humorous vein. **1968** *DARE* FW Addit **cNJ,** I was only funning you.

2 intr: To jest, joke, play; hence vbl n *funning* playing jokes, n *funning* a joke.

1885 Howells *Rise Lapham* 187 **MA,** She was far from epigram in her funning. **1888** Jones *Negro Myths* 135 **GA coast,** Buh Wolf, him say: "You mek mistake. Me no bin gwine hot [=hurt] you. Me dist bin er fun." **1890** *DN* 1.19 **NH,** 'I'm only funning' (=joking). *Ibid* 78 **LA.** **1892** *DN* 1.216 **NC, TN.** **1893** Shands *MS Speech* 31, *Fun.* . . Used by all classes as a verb, *meaning to joke* or *jest.* **1899** (1912) Green *VA Folk-Speech* 188, *Funning.* . . Jesting; joking; the playing of sportive tricks. **1904** Day *Kin o' Ktaadn* 158 **ME,** If ye did it for funnin' I'll eat your heart! **1909** *DN* 3.396 **nwAR.** **1961** *Mt. Life* Fall 29 **sAppalachians,** I knew Mama was funning with us. **1964** Will *Hist. Okeechobee* xi **FL,** *Funning*—joking. **1966–69** *DARE* (Qu. GG32a, *To habitually play . . jokes on people: "He's always ______."*) Infs **FL**30, **GA**89, **MN**2, **NY**199, Funning. **1973** Allen *LAUM* 1.408 **NE** (as of c1950), We said it just as a funning. **1984** Burns *Cold Sassy* 146 **nGA** (as of 1906), Knowing what I knew . . , all this funning and politeness gave me the creeps.

funal See **funeral**

funbox n [*fun* jest, ridicule + **box** n **5a**]

An object of ridicule.

1938 Rawlings *Yearling* 28 **nFL,** Jody burst out laughing. "That's right," she said. "Make a fun-box outen me." **1960** Williams *Walk Egypt* 123 **GA,** Like he says, we don't belong to make a fun-box of Tom.

funeral n Usu |fjun(ə)rəl|; occas **chiefly Sth** |fjunəl| Pronc-spp *fun'al, fune'l, funer'l, funerald, funeyul, funeyun, fun'l, fun'ral, fun'rul*

A Forms.

1827 in 1956 Eliason *Tarheel Talk* 311 **NC,** Funal. **1853** *Ibid* 273, Was her funerald preached at the burying, if not I would like to know when it will be. **1870** Harte *Luck Roaring Camp* 66 **neCA,** Fun'l. **1904** Day *Kin o' Ktaadn* 213 **ME,** The gait of a well-regulated fun'ral percession. **1906** *DN* 3.137 **nwAR,** *Funeral* [fjunrəl]. **1922** Gonzales *Black Border* 303 **sSC, GA coasts,** [Gullah glossary], *Fun'rul.* **1927** Kennedy *Gritny* 142 **sLA** [Black], I gotta go yonder dis evenin', an see 'bout de funeyun. . . lay 'uh away, yonder in potter's fiel'. *Ibid* 143, Money w'at goin' puhvide de carriage for all dem niggers to ride in; an' give Tempe a good-lookin' funeyun like people. *Ibid* 235, None y'all ain' goin' to Gussie funeyul tomorrow? **1940** *Sat. Eve. Post* 24 Feb 77/1 **TX** [Black], De finest fun'al. **1941** *AmSp* 16.10 **eTX** [Black], ['fjũnl]. **1943** Writers' Program NC *Bundle of Troubles* 76, I's done paid fer a big funer'l. **1969** Emmons *Deep Rivers* 82 **eTX** [Black], Her dead body was so palpably in the toils of the Devil that it took "four horses to get that hearse outn' her yard on the day of her fune'l."

B Senses.

1 also *preaching funeral:* A funeral sermon; a memorial service freq held some time after the death. **esp S Midl**

1859 (1968) Bartlett *Americanisms* 164, *Funeral.* "To preach a funeral." In some parts of the West, the funeral sermon is preached, not at the time of the burial, but long after, sometimes even a year after the death of the person. The custom arose, probably, from the difficulty of obtaining a competent "preacher" in a thinly settled country. After so long an interval, "preaching the funeral," which is almost always accompanied by a feast, becomes rather an occasion of merrymaking than of lamentation. **1894** *DN* 1.331 **NJ.** **1899** (1912) Green *VA Folk-Speech* 187. **1903** *DN* 2.314 **seMO,** *Funeral.* . . A service in memory of the dead; not a burial service. Funerals are often preached weeks or even months after the 'burying.' **1909** *DN* 3.396 **nwAR,** His funeral was preached Sunday, but he's been dead nearly a year. **1927** *DN* 5.469 **sAppalachians.** **1942** McAtee *Dial. Grant Co. IN* 27 (as of 1890s). **1942** Warnick *Garrett Co. MD* 7 **nwMD** (as of 1900–18). **1953** *PADS* 19.13 **sAppalachians,** *Preaching funeral: n.* A memorial service in the summer for those who die during the year. . . When a visiting minister came later during good weather the "funeral was preached." **c1960** *Wilson Coll.* **csKY.** **1986** Pederson *LAGS Concordance,* 1 inf, **swAL,** Funerals—performed 6 mo. to 1 year after burying.

2 in phr *preach one's funeral:* To rebuke, scold someone. **esp S Midl**

1905 *DN* 3.91 **nwAR,** *Preach one's funeral.* . . To administer a harsh rebuke to. 'If he does that, I'll preach his funeral.' **1909** *DN* 3.359 **eAL, wGA.** **1942** Warnick *Garrett Co. MD* 12 (as of 1900–1918). **c1960** *Wilson Coll.* **csKY,** *Preach one's funeral.* . . Criticize bitterly. **1968** *DARE* (Qu. II27, *If somebody gives you a very sharp scolding*) Inf **IN**42, [I] got my funeral preached.

3 Something felt to be one's concern or responsibility, spec:

a in phr *none of one's funeral:* See quots.

[**1854** *Oregon W. Times* 25 Nov. (Th.) *(DA),* A boy said to an outsider who was making a great ado during some impressive mortuary ceremonies, 'What are you crying about? It's none of your funeral.'] **1872** Schele de Vere *Americanisms* 239, "This is *none of your funeral,*" is heard quite frequently as an indirect rebuke for intermeddling, with the ludicrous undercurrent of thought, that the troublesome meddler has no right to be crying at a strange man's funeral. **1895** *Century Illustr. Mag.* 50.674/1 **ID,** We don't know for certain it was them, and it's none of our funeral, anyhow. **1916** Bower *Phantom Herd* 200 *(DA),* She's none of my funeral; I don't know her from Adam. **1927** *AmSp* 2.354 **WV,** If he gets into trouble over the matter, it is none of my funeral. **1942** McAtee *Dial. Grant Co. IN* 27 (as of 1890s).

b in phr *it's one's (own) funeral:* See quots.

1870 U.S. Congress *Congressional Globe* 41st Cong 2d Sess 18 Apr 42.3.2780/3 **sePA,** Mr. Painter then addressing you, said, "This is not my funeral." **1908** White *Riverman* 63 **MI,** "I can stand it if you can," returned Newmark. "I doubt it," said Orde grimly. "However, it's your funeral. Come on, if you want to." **1960** Criswell *Resp. to PADS 20* **Ozarks,** Well, go ahead and try it if you want to. It's your funeral, not mine. **c1960** *Wilson Coll.* **csKY,** *Funeral.* . . An affair of any sort, esp. one not wanted. "Go ahead and do what you want to; it's your funeral." **1966–69** *DARE* (Qu. GG21a, *If you don't care what a person does, you might tell him, "You can go ahead and do it ______."*) Infs **CT**21, **MD**17, **MI**26, **MA**6, **NJ**57, **NY**228, **OH**33, **RI**11, **WA**11, 22, It's your funeral; **RI**13, It's your funeral, not mine; **AK**5, **WI**47, It's your own funeral.

‡**funeral clean** adj phr

As clean as if prepared for a funeral.

1968 *DARE* (Qu. KK34, . . *Very neat and clean: "Her house always looks ______."*) Inf **VA**5, Funeral clean [laughter].

funeral clothes n pl Also *funeral suit* *joc*

One's best clothes.

1967–69 *DARE* (Qu. W39, *Joking ways of referring to a person's best clothes*) Infs **OH**87, **PA**130, Funeral clothes; **NE**11, Funeral clothes [laughter]; **KS**5, Funeral suit [laughter]; **WI**50, Funeral suit; [**MN**1, Say, where's the funeral? (Qu. W38, *When a man dresses himself up in his best clothes*) Infs **IL**135, **MD**16, Going to a funeral; **WA**20, On his way to a funeral.]

funerald See **funeral**

funeral door n *old-fash*

See quots.

1973 *AmSp* 48.69, In the Genesee valley of New York State there are certain kinds of two-story houses that have a set of nonfunctional French doors on the ground floor facing the street. They are not provided with steps. . . [At one time] they were used for the removal of the dead. The doorsills were three to four feet up from the ground, so that the pallbearers could stand beneath the open doors and have the coffin placed on their shoulders at relatively even keel. . . These doors nowadays are called *lych doors.* . . The lych-door is perhaps better known as a *funeral door.* . . the latter term is used in Massachusetts. **1976** *Yankee* July 24/2 **neNY,** On the front of the house was the main door leading into the living room, and on the side was a door leading into the dining room. The natives called this door the "funeral door." Why? *Answer* . . the funeral or coffin door was wider than other doors to allow space for the bearers. Folks didn't want to open these doors except for a funeral. **1976** *DARE* FW Addit **PA,** Old houses here have two front doors, one to the living room and one to the parlor. The parlors fell out of use around the turn of the century and these parlor doors were no longer used [except for] . . funerals when . . the bodies were carried out of the house through the parlor door. They soon began to be called the *funeral door,* although with the present use of funeral homes, the term only exists in the speech of old people.

funeral, it's one's (own) See **funeral B4b**

funeralize v, hence vbl n *funeralizing* **[funeral B1] Sth, S Midl**

To hold a funeral or memorial service for (someone); to perform funeral rites; see also quot 1895.

1859 (1968) Bartlett *Americanisms* 164 **Sth,** *To Funeralize.* To perform the clerical duties preparatory to a funeral. **1895** *DN* 1.371 **eTN,** "The bereaved parents whom we are funeralizing to-day." [*DN* Ed: Bartlett and DeVere give the impression that only the deceased is "funeralized."] **1917** *DN* 4.420 **LA.** **1935** *AmSp* 10.36 **eKY,** They *funeralized* their dead long after the *buryin'* so that the *Elder . .* might be present to *improve the occasion* (eulogize the departed). **1949** Guthrie *Way West* 57 **MO** (as of 1847), He preached his head off and wouldn't take pay. Said preachin' was one thing and funeralizin' another. **1953** *PADS* 19.11 **NC,** *Funeralize the dead. . .* To hold memorial services every year during the summer months, at which time several ministers preach sermons eulogizing those who have been dead for many years. **1966** *DARE* Tape **SC**25, They always ['fjunə,laɪz] these people. **1969** Emmons *Deep Rivers* 107 **eTX** (as of c1900) [Black], "Fune'lizing" a colored person then was a multiple affair. Beginning at the home of the deceased, mourners and friends would accompany the body to the church, then to the lodge, perhaps even to the homes of some friends of the family, and would conclude the procession, along with the day, at the cemetery. At every stop, services would be held, friends would speak words of comfort to the mourning relatives and loud praises of the departed. **1986** Pederson *LAGS Concordance,* 1 inf, **cAR,** Funeralizing —preacher speaking at funeral.

funeralizing n **S Midl, esp KY** Cf **funeral occasion**

=**funeral B1.**

1942 (1971) Campbell *Cloud-Walking* vii **seKY,** I went to neighborhood "gatherings," to "workings," . . to "meetings," "funeralizing." **1953** Randolph-Wilson *Down in Holler* 246 **Ozarks,** *Funeralize. . .* To hold a funeral or memorial service; the *funeralizin'* is often postponed for months or even years after the actual buryin'. **1959** Roberts *Up Cutshin* 56 **eKY,** This gave rise to long protracted meetings . . and what came to be called funeralizings. Simply stated, this last custom was the preaching of the funerals in good weather of all those who had died during the long winters when ministers could not be called. **c1960** *Wilson Coll.* **csKY,** *Funeral. . .* A funeral service held long after the burial; sometimes called a funeralizing.

funeral meeting See **funeral occasion**

funeral, none of one's See **funeral B4a**

funeral occasion n Also *funeral meeting*

=**funeral B1.**

1914 Furman *Sight* 35 **KY,** Never till that day of the funeral occasion, one year atter Evy died, did she ever give in. **1942** (1971) Campbell *Cloud-Walking* 165 **seKY,** It got to be the mountain fashion to have just the burying when a person died and then call a funeral meeting after anyways one planting and harvest had passed since the burying took place.

funeral pie n [Because it is freq served after a funeral in PaGer tradition] **PA**

A raisin pie; rarely, a prune pie.

1949 Brown *Amer. Cooks* 723 **PA,** A raisin pie with a latticed top is still called Funeral Pie, because it appears at all wakes worthy of the name. **1950** Klees *PA Dutch* 417, The name "funeral pie" is given to both raisin and prune pie, possibly because their dark color suggests mourning. These were the pies invariably served at the huge dinners that followed the funerals in the old days. **1960** Korson *Black Rock* 292 **PA,** Cold boiled ham and chicken were two favorite meats served at old-time funerals. The most popular pie was raisin, which came to be called "funeral pie" because it was served so often. **1967** *DARE* FW Addit **sePA,** Raisin pie—called funeral pie—is served only after a funeral here. **1968** *DARE* (Qu. H63, . . *Desserts . . favored . . around here*) Inf **PA**143, Funeral pie—crumbs on top; [made with] raisins. **1980** *NY Times* (NY) 30 Apr sec C 4/5 **PA,** A few weeks ago I took our children to Pennsylvania and one menu listed "funeral pie." The waitress said it was made of raisins.

funeral, preach one's See **funeral B2**

funeral suit See **funeral clothes**

funer'l, funeyul, funeyun See **funeral**

fungo n [Origin uncert; perh from Scots *fung* to pitch, toss, fling]

1 A fly ball or grounder hit by a batter who tosses the ball himself; the game played by hitting such fly balls to fielders.

1867 Chadwick *Base Ball Reference* 138 *(DA),* Fungoes.—A preliminary practice game in which one player takes the bat and tossing the ball up hits it as it falls. . . It is useless as practice in batting, but good for taking fly balls. **1888** *Cosmopolitan* 5.443, The first form of play was what we now call "fungo-hitting;" that is, he hit the ball in the air for his companions to catch. **1891** *Jrl. Amer. Folkl.* 4.232 **Brooklyn NYC,** *Fungo. . .* One boy is chosen for batsman, and the others stand around at some distance from him. A base ball is used, and the batsman throws it in the air, and then bats it out to the fielders, who endeavor to catch the ball "on the fly." **1947** Jones *Evergreen Land* 178 **WA,** He liked better being called . . the best horseshoe pitcher in the State, or the best fungo batter. **1970** *DARE* (Qu. EE11, *Bat-and-ball games for just a few players*) Inf **NJ**64, Batting fungoes ['fʌŋoz]. **1982** [see **2** below].

2 also *fungo bat:* A light bat, often with an enlarged end, used in such a game.

1937 *AmSp* 12.243, *Fungo-bats* are made of a light, tropical wood, and are about the thickness of a heavy broomstick. They are used only to hit 'flies' to outfielders for practice, and to propel 'grounders' at infielders in practice. **1938** Farrell *No Star* 123 **IL,** Every so often the man hitting out the flies and using the fungo bat Uncle Al had brought with them would bat him an easy fly or grounder. **1982** Safire *What's the Good Word* 71, In ordinary baseball usage, it [=*fungo*] seems to be attached to the implement—the "fungo bat"—and not to the act or the result. A coach says, "I'll hit some fungoes (fungos?)," meaning he will hit practice drives (grounders as well as flies) with a special narrow-handled bat, tossing the ball up himself rather than having it thrown to him. . . It became a verb well within my memory—let's say, the 1950's or 1960's. *Ibid* 74, The original fungo bat was a lightweight bat of willow, the handle of which . . ended in a mushroom-shaped knob.

fungo v **[fungo n]**

To hit a fly ball or **fungo** n **1.**

1938 Farrell *No Star* 123 **IL,** Uncle Al was out farther with the men, catching long flies that were being fungoed out there. **1960** Wentworth-Flexner *Slang* 205, *Fungo. . .* To bat fungos. **1982** [see **fungo** n **2**].

fungo bat See **fungo** n **2**

fungus twat-knot n

1954 McAtee *Suppl. to Nomina Abitera,* Fungus Twat-Knot—The burn made on Engelmann Spruce *(Picea pungens)* by the red-hot fungus.

funk n **chiefly S Midl**

1 An offensive odor; a musty, stale smell; body odor.

1806 (1970) Webster *Compendious Dict.* 126/2, *Funk. . .* offensive smell. **1899** (1912) Green *VA Folk-Speech* 188, *Funk. . .* A strong and offensive smell. **1917** *DN* 4.412 **wNC,** *Funk. . .* An offensive smell. "Open up the door and let the funk out." **1938** *AmSp* 13.152 **IN** [Black], *Funk.* Body odor, especially the odor arising from a crowd assembled in a poorly ventilated place. **1953** Randolph-Wilson *Down in Holler* 88 **Ozarks,** *Funk,* meaning a disagreeable odor, . . is still used in the Ozarks. **c1960** *Wilson Coll.* **csKY,** *Funk. . .* A bad odor from something spoiled, like funked tobacco. **1968** Baldwin *Tell Me* 117 **NYC** [Black], No one, in those days [=early 20th cent], desired to be "funky": funk was a bad smell, it was the invincible odor which filled our house, the very odor of battle, the battle waged by the living in the midst of death.

2 Mold, mildew, decay. Cf **funk** v

1877 in 1957 *KY Folkl. Rec.* 3.60, Free from any evidence of mold or funk (decay). **1937** *Hall Coll.* **eTN,** "Barrels get funk if ye don't smoke 'em." "Meal makes funk."

funk v, hence ppl adj *funked* **chiefly S Midl, esp KY** Cf **funk** n **2**

Usu of tobacco: to become moldy or mildewed; to rot.

1879 in 1957 *KY Folkl. Rec.* 3.61, Too much casing will cause your tobacco to funk. **1892** *DN* 1.230 **KY,** *Funked:* rotten. Used only of tobacco. **1902** *DN* 2.235 **sIL,** *Funked. . .* Molded or mildewed. Used only as a past participle. **1907** *DN* 3.222 **nwAR,** *Funked. . .* Molded or mildewed. **1942** Chevalier *Drivin' Woman* 304 **VA,** So when they take it down and pile it into the bulk, of course it rots—funks, the buyers call it. **1966** *PADS* 45.13 **Lexington KY,** *Funked. . .* Of tobacco: Rotted.

Funked tobacco turns black and has an undesirable smell. . . "They sometimes buy funked tobacco to make snuff." **1967** Key *Tobacco Vocab.* **NC,** *Funked* means mold[y] or overheated; **MO,** Funked.

funky adj Also sp *funkey* **[funk n]**

1 Having a strong or disagreeable odor, spec:

a Musty, moldy, mildewed, rancid. **chiefly Sth, S Midl**

1899 (1912) Green *VA Folk-Speech* 188, *Funky.* . . Having a bad smell. **1906** *DN* 3.118 **sIN,** *Funky.* . . Mouldy, old. "This butter's funky." *Ibid* 137 **nwAR,** *Funky.* . . Musty. **1908** *DN* 3.313 **eAL, wGA,** *Funky.* . . Musty, foul-smelling. **c1940** *Hall Coll.* **eTN, wNC,** "Funky scent in whiskey barrels"; "It smells funky as hell" [of "something starting to rot like old mouldy grass"]. **1953** Randolph–Wilson *Down in Holler* 88 **Ozarks,** Speaking of some stale milk, a woman near Branson, Missouri, told me: "It ain't sour, but it's got a feeble funky scent." **1965–70** *DARE* (Qu. X17, . . *A damp cellar that had been shut up for some time would smell* ______) 20 Infs, **chiefly Sth, S Midl,** Funky; **TN**13, A-funky [7 of 21 Infs Black]; (Qu. KK7, *When wood . . is starting to decay inside, you'd say, "It's* ______ *inside."*) Inf **AR**56, Funky. **1967** Key *Tobacco Vocab.* **TN,** "Smells funky"—a mildew smell. **1986** Pederson *LAGS Concordance* **chiefly Lower Missip Valley, AL,** [45 infs offered or accepted *funky* in reference to the bad smell, or occasionally taste, of stale or spoiled food.]

b Having noticeable body odor; see quots. *esp among Black speakers*

1929 Wolfe *Look Homeward* 41 **NC,** He remembered . . her [=a Black woman's] strong smell, black and funky. *Ibid* 85, The exquisite smell of the South, clean but funky, like a big woman. **1929** *NY Sunday News* 3 Nov (*AmSp* 6.158), *Funkey* is used to describe the odor of perspiration, as "a funkey old man." **1954** *PADS* 21.36 **SC,** *Shake a funky sock.* . . To dance. . . The body odor of vigorous dancers accounts for this usage. **1962** Baldwin *Another Country* 4 **Harlem NYC,** They knew . . why his hair was nappy, his armpits funky. **1963** Baraka *Blues People* 219, The adjective *funky* . . once meant to many Negroes merely a stink (usually associated with sex). **1970** *DARE* FW Addit **seLA,** I have a further bit of evidence that *funky* refers to the odor of unwashed sexual organs, especially or particularly female sexual organs. One of my musician friends heard one black girl insult another by calling her "funky-butt." **1986** Pederson *LAGS Concordance* **Gulf Region,** [Numerous informants report that *funky* refers to strong or offensive body odor, such as sexual odors or those of people who don't bathe often enough. A number of infs. consider the word "crude," "not nice," or "not polite"; several note that it is used especially by Blacks.]

2 Having a bad taste.

1967 *DARE* (Qu. K14, *Milk that has a taste from something the cow ate*) Inf **TX**40, Funky. **1986** [see **1a** above].

funky chicken n **chiefly Sth, S Midl** *esp among Black speakers* **=chicken n B7.**

1965–70 *DARE* (Qu. FF5b, . . *Recent dance steps*) 12 Infs, **chiefly Sth, S Midl,** Funky chicken; (Qu. FF5a) Inf **PA**247, Funky chicken—in Philadelphia. [All Infs Black, 6 of 13 Infs young] **1986** Pederson *LAGS Concordance* **Gulf States,** Funky chicken. [4 of 5 infs White] **1989** *Isthmus* (Madison WI) 3 Nov 19, [Comic strip:] I saw the funky chicken on *Soul Train* [=a TV music-and-dance show that plays music by Black groups] and I've been trying it. [Drawing shows a young girl imitating a chicken by flapping her arms up and down with her legs bent outward.]

funky house n **[funky 1]**

1968 *DARE* (Qu. M21b, *Joking names for an outside toilet building*) Inf **MD**31, Funky house.

fun'l See **funeral**

fun-makers' bench n [Prob by analogy with and in contrast to **mourner's bench]**

1954 *Harder Coll.* **cwTN,** *Fun-makers' benches.* . . Seats near the back door of the church.

funnel n Usu |ˈfʌnəl|; for varr see quot

A Forms.

1965–70 *DARE* (Qu. F9, *To get a liquid through a narrow opening . . you'd pour it through a* ______) Inf **MS**63, [ˈfʊrnəl]; **VA**53, [ˈfʌndʊl].

B Senses.

1 A stovepipe; a chimney. **Nth**

1836 (1940) Arnold *Diaries* 127 **VT,** Carried stove funnel to Mr. Howlands. **1907** *DN* 3.187 **seNH,** *Funnel.* . . Stove pipe. "The funnel got red hot after he filled the stove up." **1949** Kurath *Word Geog.* 22, *Funnel* . . for the stove pipe (from Massachusetts Bay to eastern Maine and northwestward to the upper Connecticut Valley). **1966** *DARE* (Qu. DD9b, *Of a person who smokes a great deal . . "He smokes like a* ______*."*) Infs **MT**2, **WA**1, Funnel.

2 =hay chute.

1951 Johnson *Resp. to PADS 20* **DE,** Funnel—hay chute. **1967–68** *DARE* (Qu. M5, *What do you call the hole for throwing hay down below?*) Infs **MD**32, **PA**37, Funnel.

3 A narrowing tubular opening in a fish net or trap. Cf **fyke**

1966 *DARE* Tape **ME**17, Some have hake mouth, some have funnel hoops. . . funnel hoop is five inches, hake mouth is six; **NC**1, This net sits between them and looks like a funnel. . . this pocket, this tunnel, funnel we called it. **1969** *DARE* (Qu. P13, . . *Other ways of fishing*) Inf **MI**109, Funnel net. **1975** Gould *ME Lingo* 104, Part of a lobster trap is the funnel.

4 A whirlpool.

1966–68 *DARE* (Qu. C8, . . *A place in a stream where water flows round and round and draws things in toward the center*) Infs **MI**12, **OH**41, 81, **WV**8, Funnel.

5 A spigot on a barrel.

1966–68 *DARE* (Qu. F15) Inf **AL**11, Funnel; a cut-off; **FL**33, A funnel; [FW: corr to] faucet; **OH**41, Funnel; [FW: corr to] spigot.

6 See quot. Cf **funnel** v

1934 (1940) Weseen *Dict. Amer. Slang* 276, *Funnel*—A heavy drinker.

funnel v Also *funnel it down,* ~ *in* **chiefly Sth, S Midl** See Map

To drink excessively or too fast; hence n *funneler*

1906 *DN* 3.137 **nwAR,** "He don't drink; he funnels it down." **1950** *WELS* (*"He doesn't just drink, he* ______*."*) 3 Infs, **WI,** Funnels it down. **c1960** *Wilson Coll.* **csKY,** *Funnel it down.* . . Drink a lot and too fast and hoggishly. *Ibid, Funneler.* . . One who drinks too much too fast. **1965–70** *DARE* (Qu. DD17, *To drink a great deal, or too fast: "He doesn't just drink, he* ______*."*) 52 Infs, **chiefly Sth, S Midl,** Funnels it down; 44 Infs, **chiefly Sth, S Midl,** Funnels; **AL**16, **AR**56, **GA**84, **MS**30, **NY**66, Funnels it in; **IN**13, Funnels down; **OK**13, Just funnels it down.

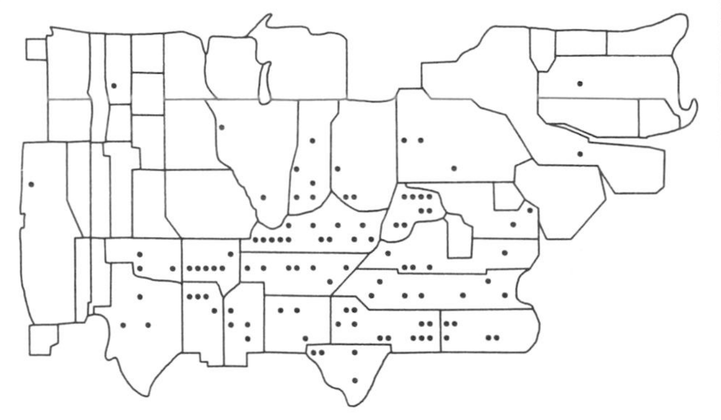

•funnel v + varr (Qu. DD17)

funnel cake n

A fried cake made by pouring batter through a funnel into deep fat.

1950 Klees *PA Dutch* 424, Today funnel cakes are rarely come upon. . . A thin batter was run through a funnel on to deep fat. As the forefinger held under the spout of the funnel was removed, the batter was dropped upon the fat in ever enlarging spirals. When the cake was fried on one side, it had to be turned over. **1967–68** *DARE* (Qu. H20b, . . *Other names . . for pancakes*) Inf **PA**40, Funnel cakes; **PA**18, Funnel cakes—[put] dough through funnel into hot fat; **PA**159, Funnel cakes—in deep fat; like a waffle, not doughy; **PA**5, Funnel [cake]—a Dutch word; (Qu. H28, *Different shapes or types of doughnuts*) Infs **PA**40, 159, Funnel cake; **PA**52, Funnel cake—in deep fat, strange shapes. **1976** *New Yorker* 4 Oct 113 **Adamstown PA,** Funnel cake is a plateful of twisted dough that has been cooked in oil, covered with powdered sugar, and served piping hot—a regional specialty that some connoisseurs believe to be of about equal harm to the fingers, the clothing, and the stomach lining.

funnel drinker n [**funnel** v]
1967–68 *DARE* (Qu. DD17, *To drink a great deal, or too fast: "He doesn't just drink, he ______."*) Infs **CA**105, **TN**16, Is a funnel drinker.

funneler See **funnel** v

funnel gang n Also *funneling gang* [**funnel** v]
A set of people who drink frequently, often to excess.
1950 *WELS* (*"He doesn't just drink, he ______."*) 1 Inf, **csWI,** He joined the funnel gang. **1965–70** *DARE* (Qu. DD17, *To drink a great deal, or too fast: "He doesn't just drink, he ______."*) Infs **IL**29, **LA**28, **MD**26, **MN**42, **MA**6, **OH**47, 50, **OK**11, 18, Joined the funnel gang; **AL**4, **LA**18, **ND**3, **OK**42, **TX**66, **VA**35, Joined the funneling gang; **CO**47, **NC**61, **NY**94, Belongs to the funnel gang; [**LA**15, Joined the funnel wagon;] (Qu. DD12, . . *A person who drinks steadily or a great deal*) Inf **WV**2, Belongs to the funnel gang. **1966** *PADS* 46.26 **AR,** *Funnel gang*. . . A group that drinks whiskey together.—"Now don't you go and join no funnel gang." **1967** *DARE* FW Addit **sPA,** He belongs to the funnel gang—he just pours it.

funnel gun n [Perh in ref to a blunderbuss-type gun with a bell muzzle]
1968 *DARE* (Qu. P37b, *Nicknames for a shotgun*) Inf **MD**31, Funnel gun.

funnel it down, funnel it in See **funnel** v

funneling gang See **funnel gang**

funnel lily n
A blue-flowered liliaceous plant (*Androstephium coeruleum*).
1948 Stevens *KS Wild Flowers* 29, *Blue Funnel-lily*. . . They are unusual . . in having a corona like a Narcissus. **1975** Zwinger *Run River* 203 **UT,** A funnel-lily sends up lead-colored leaves and stems, topped with a spray of blue-striped white-petaled flowers. **1976** Bailey–Bailey *Hortus Third* 74, *Blue funnel lily*. . . Kans. to Tex.

funnel-web spider n Also *funnel-webbed spider*
A spider of the family Agelenidae.
[**1895** Comstock–Comstock *Manual Insects* 31, The funnel-web weavers . . are long-legged, brown spiders.] **1913** Comstock *Spider Book* 582, The members of this family [=Agelenidae] spin sheet-like webs, which are usually furnished with a tubular retreat; this suggests the common name funnel-web spiders for the family. **1954** Borror–DeLong *Intro. Insects* 797, The web of the funnel-web spiders is somewhat sheetlike, but is shaped like a funnel. **1967** *DARE* (Qu. R28) Inf **CA**26, Funnel-webbed spider.

funnies See **for fun**

funning See **fun** v 2

funning boy n
A good-time companion.
1947 Ballowe *The Lawd* 180 **LA,** Quit pesterin' me. Ah had you jess fer a funnin' boy. When Ah gits married hit'll be to a man, like one o' the rollers.

funny adj
1 Slightly drunk; tipsy.
1942 Berrey–Van den Bark *Amer. Slang* 106.7, *Drunk* . . funny. **1967–69** *DARE* (Qu. DD13, *When a drinker is just beginning to show the effects of the liquor, you say he's ______*) Infs **IL**104, **MO**37, **TX**103, (Getting) funny; (Qu. DD14, *When a person is partly drunk, "He's ______."*) Inf **NJ**25, Funny.
2 In a playful mood.
1907 Lincoln *Cape Cod* 288 **MA,** Stop joking. I'm not funny to-night.
3 See quot.
1946 *PADS* 6.14 **NC,** *Funny*. . . Pretty, as applied to a baby. Salter Path, near Moorehead City, N.C. Older people.
4 Finicky, fussy.
1968–70 *DARE* (Qu. HH11a, *Someone who is too particular or fussy —if it's a man*) Infs **LA**20, **VA**54, (Too) funny; (Qu. HH11b, . . *If it's a woman*) Inf **LA**20, Too funny.
5 Of a man: effeminate; homosexual.
1967–68 *DARE* (Qu. HH38, *A womanish man*) Inf **NY**111, Funny one; (Qu. HH39, *A homosexual man*) Inf **MO**14, Funny fellow. **1972** Claerbaut *Black Jargon* 65, *Funny* . . homosexual-like; having homosexual tendencies.

funny n
1 A peculiar aspect of a thing; a strange thing.
1890 *DN* 1.19 **NH,** 'The funny of it was, that ______.' *Ibid* 78, **Boston MA, CT. 1892** *DN* 1.216 **cwNC,** *Funny* . . *n*. . . "Not common, but I have heard it once or twice."
2 A joke, trick.
1950 *WELS* (*"He's always telling ______."*) 1 Inf, **WI,** A funny; 1 Inf, Making funnies; recent—an old phrase rejuvenated by radio, I think. **1952** *WI State Jrl.* (Madison) 16 Oct 19 **GA,** [In the comic strip "Pogo":] Cut the funnies an' git a can-opener. **1966** *DARE* (Qu. GG32a, *To habitually play* . . *jokes on people: "He's always ______."*) Inf **MI**3, Pulling funnies; (Qu. FF20, . . *"He's always telling ______."*; total Infs questioned, 75) Inf **MS**46, Funnies. **1970** *New Yorker* 17 Oct 148/2, I hear he's a lawyer now, restricted, I suppose, to sneaking in a funny now and then in his summation to the jury.
3 pl: In marble play
a See quot. [Cf **for fun**]
1966 *DARE* Tape **WA**6, When you had shot an even number of marbles—six or four, whatever—and you would ask for funnies, I suppose that was based on "refunds," because you got half the marbles back which you had shot.
b See **for fun.**

funny bone n
1 The part of the elbow over which the ulnar nerve passes and which produces a peculiar tingling sensation when hit. [From the "funny" feeling one gets when the ulnar nerve in the elbow is struck; perh also by punning assoc with *humerus* the upper-arm bone which articulates at the elbow] **widespread, but less common eNEng, Midl, West** See Map and Map Section Cf **crazy bone, foolish bone**
1893 Shands *MS Speech* 31, *Funny-bone*. . . A name used . . by all classes to mean that particular bone in the elbow that is generally called *crazy-bone* in other parts of the United States. **1899** (1912) Green *VA Folk-Speech* 188, Funny-bone. **1903** *DN* 2.314 **seMO,** *Funny-bone*. **1906** *DN* 3.118 **sIN. 1908** *DN* 3.313 **eAL, wGA,** *Funny-bone*. . . Universal. **1923** Paine *Comrades* 148, The heavy end of the mop-handle smote him a crack on the funny-bone. **1950** *WELS* 24 Infs, **WI,** Funny bone. **c1960** *Wilson Coll.* **csKY. 1965–70** *DARE* (Qu. X33) 570 Infs, **widespread, but less common eNEng, Midl, West,** Funny bone.

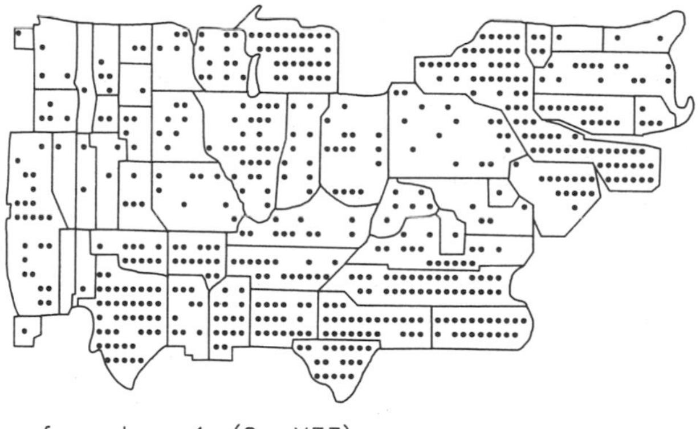

•funny bone 1 (Qu. X33)

2 in phrr *strike one's funny bone* (or *spot*): To impress one as being humorous.
1906 Casey *Parson's Boys* 242 **sIL** (as of c1860), When the brother stopped and spat so suddenly "it struck their funny-spots," as William said, and they giggled right out in meeting. **1955** in 1958 Brewer *Dog Ghosts* 38 **TX** [Black], One of de tales dat Unkuh Josh allus tol' dat struck mah funnybone was de one 'bout a big baseball game dey hab down to Beeville one Nineteent' of June day.
3 See quot.
1949 *AmSp* 24.109 **SC,** *Funnybone*. . . Wishbone. [*AmSp*: Charleston and Newberry cos., S.C.]

funny cake n [Prob so called because the ingredients are not mixed in the usual way, and because it is as much a pie as a cake] Cf **dump cake**

A single-crust pie made in two distinct layers; see quot.

1965 *Woman's Day Encycl. Cookery* 9.1356 **sePA,** *Funny Cake*—Pastry for 1-crust 9-inch pie, unbaked. *Lower part* [consists of sugar, cocoa, water, vanilla] *Upper part* [consists of sugar, shortening, egg, milk, flour, baking powder, vanilla]. . . Mix [ingredients for lower part]. Pour mixture into pie pan. Mix [ingredients for upper part]. Pour mixture over cocoa mixture. Bake.

funny eye n Also *funny hoop* [*funny* var of **funnel n 3**]

See quots.

1949 *McDavid Coll.* **cwNY,** Funny eye—the opening in a lobster pot. **1975** Gould *ME Lingo* 103, *Funny eye*—A twig of a tree bent to form the eye ring in the head of a lobster trap, now available in metal. It derives from funnel eye, because that part of a lobster trap is the funnel. Sometimes *funny eye* is *funny hoop.*

funny-minded adj Cf **curious-minded**

Strange, peculiar.

1943 Writers' Program NC *Bundle of Troubles* 166, Miss Essie was allus pow'ful funny-minded, from jes a chile on up. **1954** *Harder Coll.* **cwTN,** Funny minded. . . Same as *curious minded.*

funny sacks See **fontis cat**

funny spot See **funny bone 2**

fun'ral, fun'rul See **funeral**

funs(ies) See **for fun**

fur n^1

1 Dust that collects under furniture. Cf **fur baby**

1967 *DARE* (Qu. E20) Infs **CO**13A, **LA**9, **SC**46, Fur.

2 See **fur piece** n^1.

fur n^2 [Engl dial; by apoc from **furrow**] **Sth, S Midl**

1915 *DN* 4.183 **swVA,** *Fur. . .* Furrow. **1936** *AmSp* 11.161 **eTX,** Another group of words . . lose their final vowel sound entirely in illiterate speech. . . They [include] . . *furrow* . . [fɚ:]. **1941** *AmSp* 16.10 **eTX** [Black], *Furrow* . . [fʌ:]. **1942** Hall *Smoky Mt. Speech* 81 **wNC, eTN,** Often the unstressed vowel is lost, as in [fʌ·ɚ] *furrow.* **1954** *Harder Coll.* **cwTN,** *Furrow* [fɚ]. **1970** *DARE* Tape **KY**84, Where these fur lines crossed, that's where you made your tobacco hill.

fur adv, adj See **far** adv, adj^1

fur prep See **for**

fur baby n [**fur** n^1 **1**] Cf *DS* E20

A ball of dust.

1968 *DARE* File **St Louis MO,** *Fur baby*—used among librarians in recent years.

fur-bearing trout n

An imaginary creature used as the basis for practical jokes.

1969 *DARE* (Qu. CC17, *Imaginary animals . . that people . . tell tales about—especially to tease greenhorns*) Inf **VT**16, Fur-bearing trout. They've mounted trout and put like little fur coats on them. Then they go and tell the city slickers that there are fur-bearing trout like this in the lake.

furce See **fuss** n, v

furder See **far** adv, adj^1 **B1**

furderest See **far** adv, adj^1 **C5**

furdest See **far** adv, adj^1 **C1**

fureen See **foreign**

furer See **far** adv, adj^1 **B2**

fur fly, make the v phr [By ext from std sense "to fight scrappily"]

To do something vigorously.

1927 *AmSp* 2.354 **WV,** *Fur fly, to make the* . . to secure results quickly. "I tell you, he made the fur fly when he did begin." **1967** *DARE* (Qu. A22, . . *'To start working hard': "She had only ten minutes to clean the room, but she ______.'*) Inf **NE**11, Made the fur fly; (Qu. KK29, . . *"He was slow at first, but now he's really ______.'*) Inf **NE**11, Making the fur fly.

furge n, v [Cf *SND foorich* "Bustle, confusion . . to bustle, to get excited"]

1959 *VT Hist.* new ser 27.136, *Furge:*. . . A state of worry. . . To worry or scold. Rare.

furiation n Also *furynation*

=**fury.**

1904 Day *Kin o' Ktaadn* 55 **ME,** Then he'd squirt like furynation 'tween them old pipe teeth of his. **1917** *DN* 4.392 **neOH,** *Furiation. . .* Fury, in the phrase, *like furiation.* General. **1959** *VT Hist.* new ser 27.136, *Furiation!* . . Rare.

furin See **foreign**

furiosity n Cf **furiation**

A rage, fury.

c1938 in 1970 Hyatt *Hoodoo* 1.286 **MD** [Black], Man! I wus in a furiosity! I wus furious! I wus in a furious shape!

furmety, furmity See **frumenty**

furnace n

1 Fig: hell. *euphem*

1965–70 *DARE* (Qu. CC9, . . *"That man is headed straight for ______.'*) 21 Infs, **scattered,** [The] fiery furnace; **CA**82, **IA**11, **PA**25, Furnace; **PA**134, Big furnace; **NY**43, Fire and furnace.

2 A tobacco pipe.

1940 *AmSp* 15.335 **NE,** A pipe is a *hod, smokestack, . . furnace, chimney,* [etc].

3 A heavy smoker. [From phr *to smoke like a furnace*] Cf **chimney B2**

1967–69 *DARE* (Qu. DD9a, . . *A person who smokes a great deal: "He's a ______.'*) Infs **MA**5, **NY**217, **PA**177, Furnace.

furnentz See **fornent**

furnish n Also *furnishing(s)* **MS**

Groceries and supplies provided on credit to a tenant farmer by a plantation owner or merchant.

1938 FWP *Guide MS* 27, The standard rations the furnishing men allow the tenant Negro are a peck of corn meal, three pounds of salt meat, two pounds of sugar, one pound of coffee, one gallon of black molasses, and one plug of . . chewing tobacco. *Ibid* 105, This food and other necessities, obtained on credit during the crop season, is called "furnishings". It must be paid for out of the tenant's share of the crop at harvest time. **1941** Faulkner *Men Working* 75, They been used to running one of them furnish accounts and them rich furnish merchants add three hundred per cent to . . their accounts. **1950** *AmSp* 25.230 **MS,** *Furnish, n.* Groceries provided on credit to the tenant by the plantation owner. **1954** Smith *Yazoo River* 176 **MS,** The merchant protected his investment of "furnish" for a planter through a crop-lien system. The farmer gave the merchant a mortgage on his growing, or to be planted, crop as security.

furnishing n

1 See **furnish.**

2 Among Mennonites: the selection and purchase of household articles for a young woman who is to be married.

1907 (1970) Martin *Betrothal* 102 **sePA,** Preparations for the furnishing party and expeditions to town to buy the furniture for Ellie's parlor. *Ibid* 114, The event regularly known in Lancaster County as "furnishing" is, next to marriage, the most auspicious time in a young girl's life. As soon as her parents have "furnished" for her, she is expected to . . "keep comp'ny" with one especial "Friend," whom, as soon as convenient, she marries, and then the furniture of her parlor is taken with her into her own new home.

furnishings See **furnish**

furniture n Usu |'fɝnəčr, 'fɜnəčə|; also |-čur, -čuə, -tjur|; for addit prones see quot 1981 Pronc-spp *firnitree, furnitur', furnishure*

A Forms.

1824 in 1956 Eliason *Tarheel Talk* 311 **nw,cnNC,** *Furniture*—firnitree. **1890** *DN* 1.38 **csME,** *Furniture*—[fɜnɪčʊə], *rather than* [fɜnɪčə]. **1891** (1967) Freeman *New Engl. Nun* 95, An' her furnitur' was all stuffed, an' kivered with red velvet. **1933** in 1944 *ADD* **VA,** Furnishure. Quite general pron. east of Blue Ridge, but not west of it. **1972** *Atlanta Letters* **cwGA,** Someone will say, "I'm going to buy some new furniture." If *culture* and *picture* are pronounced cul-chure and pic-chure, certainly *furniture* should be furni-chure. **1981** Pederson *LAGS Basic Materials* **Gulf Region,** [Pronunciations of the type ['fɝnɨtʃɚ, 'fɜnɨtʃə] are most common; those of the type ['fɝnɨˌtj(u)ɚ, -ˌtɪʊɚ] are also frequent, as are ['fɝnɨtɚ, -tʊɚ]; others, such as ['fɜɨnɨtʃə, -tʉə, 'fɝntʃɚ] also occur.]

B Sense.

The cooking equipment and utensils used with or on a cook stove. *old-fash*

1844 (1940) Arnold *Diaries* 167 **VT,** Went to Walpole with Mary Ann to select cook stove—one was 30 dols. with furniture. . . 1 spider—cast iron pot and dish kettle with tin covers. **1902** Sears *Catalogue* 580, *Stove Furnishing Sets. . .* The first figure in stove size designates the size furniture that fits the stove. [*DARE* Ed: A list of available pots, pans, and utensils follows.]

furnucle n [By metath from *furuncle*]

1970 *NC Folkl.* 18.30, To cure sores, caused by boil-like "furnucles" on legs and arms.

fur piece n[1] Also *fur joc*

A wig or toupee.

1967 *DARE* (Qu. X1a, . . *False hair, worn by men*) Inf **MN**2, Fur piece. **1972** Claerbaut *Black Jargon* 65, *Fur* . . a female wig; a hairpiece for women: *She's wearing the fur.* See also *rug.*

fur piece n[2] See **far piece**

furren See **foreign**

furrer n[1] Cf **-er** affix **1**

1899 (1912) Green *VA Folk-Speech* 188, *Furrer. . .* Fur of animals.

furrer n[2] See **furrow**

furrer adv, adj See **far** adv, adj[1] **B2**

furrest See **far** adv, adj[1] **C2**

furrin(er) See **foreign**

furrow n, v Usu |'fɝo(ʊ)|; also |'fɝə, -i, -ər| (cf Pronc Intro 3.I.12.d); for addit varr see quots Pronc-spp *furrer, furry* Cf **fur** n[2]

Std senses, var forms.

1848 Lowell *Biglow* 144 **'Upcountry' MA,** Furrer, *furrow.* **1936** *AmSp* 11.159 **eTX,** The vowel in the final syllable . . is usually [ə]. . . fellow, furrow, harrow [etc]. **1939** *LANE* Map 123, [Both ['fɜroʊ] and ['fɜrə] are widespread; [fʌro, fʌrə] are less freq but not uncommon.] **1942** Warnick *Garrett Co. MD* (as of 1900–1918), Words ending in "row" were often pronounced "ry" as in borry, furry, harry. **1942** Hall *Smoky Mt. Speech* 81, [fɜrə]. **1967** *Wilson Coll.* **csKY,** Furrow [fərər]. **1970** *DARE* Tape **IL**114, Just make a furrow ['fɝi], plow it out, and drag your log up back and forth. **1976** Allen *LAUM* 3.36 **Upper MW** (as of c1950), In *furrow* . . the dominant type . . is . . /fɝo/. . . A much less common, though widely scattered, variety is . . /fɜro/. . . A third and rare variety . . is marked by [ʌ] or [ə] with a conspicuous consonantal /r/ glide to the final vowel.

furrow-hopper n

Prob =**clodhopper 1.**

1939 (1962) Thompson *Body & Britches* 497 **NY,** [Proverb:] Walk like a furrow-hopper.

furrow horse n [Cf **fur** n[2] and Scots, nIr dial *fur-horse*] Cf **far horse, land horse**

In plowing: the horse that walks in the freshly made furrow.

1967–70 *DARE* (Qu. K32a, *With a team of horses . . the horse on the driver's right hand*) Inf **NJ**21, Furrow horse, since used in plowing and field work; opposite is upland horse or up horse; **OH**22, Furrow horse—in plowing [FW: opposite is land horse]; **VA**105, Furrow horse [FW: opposite is hillside horse]; (Qu. K32b, *The horse on the left side in plowing*) Infs **NY**62, **OH**77, Furrow horse; **MD**34, Furrow horse—walks in the furrow that's been made. [*DARE* Ed: For discussion of confusion of the terms for right- and left-hand horses see note at **off horse.**]

furrow off v phr

To mark off in furrows in preparation for planting.

1966 *DARE* Tape **ME**6, I just furrow it off and drop the potatoes.

furrow out v phr esp **NEng**

To plant in furrows; hence n *furrowing-out plow.*

1835 (1930) Sewall *Diary* 163 **ME,** Finished furrowing out the corn one way of the ship. **1965** Krauss–Alexander *Grove Farm* 284 **HI** [Speaker from **CT**], I suppose you're going to finish furrowing out mauka today? **1966** *DARE* (Qu. L18, *Kinds of plows*) Inf **NH**12, Furrowing-out plow—small, makes trench to plant potatoes, etc.

furry See **furrow**

furs(e), furss See **fuss** n, v

furst See **first** adj, adv

furth See **farth**

furthenough adv [Prob blend of *further* + *enough*]

1979 *AmSp* 54.98 **swME** (as of 1899–1910), *Furthenough. . .* Far enough.

furtherest See **far** adv, adj[1] **C3**

fur to make kittens' mittens n [Var of **cat's fur to make kitten britches**]

1967 *DARE* (Qu. NN12a, *Things that people say to put off a child when he asks too many questions: "What's that for?" [Pronounce 'fur']*) Inf **OR**6, Fur to make kittens' mittens.

fury n

Used as a euphem for *hell, the devil,* etc—esp in phr *like fury* vigorously.

1804 in 1929 Weems *Mason Locke Weems* 2.297 **MD,** I mean to push on like Fury thro' the *Interiors* of N. & S. Carolina. **1856** Whitcher *Bedott Papers* 289 **NY,** A churnin' away like fury. **1950** *WELS (If a house is untidy, and everything is upset, you say it looks like ______)* 1 Inf, **csWI,** Fury. **1963** *Hall Coll.* **eTN,** So everyone is working like fury but me; I am not doing anything but bossing when I am around the other boys at work. **1966** *DARE* (Qu. DD9b, *Of a person who smokes a great deal you might say, "He smokes like a ______."*) Inf **DC**3, Like fury. **1966–68** *DARE* Tape **MI**3, [The snow] come down like fury; **CA**80, Run like fury. **1967** *DARE* (Qu. NN26a, *Weakened substitutes for 'hell': "Oh ______!"*) Inf **TN**23, Fury!

furynation See **furiation**

furze n [Var of *fuzz;* prob infl by *fur*]

1927 Kennedy *Gritny* 22 **sLA** [Black], W'en her chile was bawn, 'stid it havin' natchal furze und' de arms an' on de ches', like people got; de thing had duck feathers growin' on him. **1937** *AmSp* 12.231 **NJ,** Negroes use *furze* in the sense of 'hair, fuzz.' **1940** Stuart *Trees of Heaven* 81 **neKY,** The milkweed furze is flying . . like the soft down picked from geese and let go to a light blowing wind.

fus See **first** adj, adv

fused ppl adj [Aphet var of *confused*]

1970 *DARE* (Qu. GG2, *Expressions meaning 'confused, mixed up': "So many things were going on at the same time that he got completely ______."*) Inf **VA**75, Fused.

fusee n Also *fuser* Also sp *fuzee* [By ext from *fusee* signal flare]

See quots.

1951 *PADS* 15.66 **NH,** *Fuzee. . .* This name of a railroad flare was applied also to an unexploded firecracker which was broken open and the contents ignited. **1965–70** *DARE* (Qu. FF15, *When a firecracker doesn't go off, and you break it in the middle and light the powder, you call it a ______*) 29 Infs, **scattered,** Fusee; **TN**65, Fuser.

fush n [Cf **fush out**] **NEng** *old-fash*

Nonsense—freq used as an intj.

1890 *AN&Q* 5.18/1 **MA,** *It is all fush* is much like *it is all fudge.* **1907** *DN* 3.188 **seNH,** *Fush!* . . Bosh! "O fush! What nonsense!" **1937** Crane *Let Me Show You VT* 33, Bliss Perry . . recalls how his father could load the most ordinary language with profane implications. "Fush to Bungtown!" was one of his favorite bits of fireworks. **1959** *VT Hist.* new ser 27.136, *Fush to Bungtown!* . . Obsolescent.

fush out v phr **NEng** *old-fash*

To fail, come to nothing; to die out.

1859 (1968) Bartlett *Americanisms* 165, *To fush out.* To come to nothing. **1890** *AN&Q* 5.18/1 **MA,** To *fush out* means to come to nothing, to fail. **1907** *DN* 3.188 **seNH,** *Fush out. . .* To fail. "He tried to go into that business and fushed out completely." **1939** *LANE* Map 92 *(The wind is going down)* 1 inf, **seME,** Fushin' out, lettin' go, of wind suddenly ceasing. **1968** *Yankee* Dec 172 **NEng** (as of 1830), It's gonna moderate by then and this gale will fush out. **1975** Gould *ME Lingo* 104, *Fush out*—A strictly *down east* expression meaning to play out, give up, cease and desist. A wind *fushes out* to calm. Exuberance over a new church *fushed out* when the committee got the contractor's estimate.

fushy adj **[fush]**

?Senseless, nonsensical.

1890 *AN&Q* 5.18/1, *A fushy affair* is a common expression in Central New Hampshire.

fuss n, v Usu |fʌs|; also **chiefly S Midl** |fɝs| Pronc-spp *furce, furs(e), furss*

A Forms.

1871 Eggleston *Hoosier Schoolmaster* 63 **IN,** You're a makin' a blamed furss about nothin'. **1887** (1967) Harris *Free Joe* 62 **nwGA,** Make 'aste, Jess, and don't make no furse. **1892** *DN* 1.233 **KY,** *Fuss.* Sometimes pronounced [fɝs]. **1903** [see **B3** below]. **1911** *DN* 3.538 **eKY,** *Fŭss. . .* Pronounced furs. **1914** *DN* 4.106 **KS,** *Furse. . .* Fuss. **1931** *PMLA* 46.1316 **sAppalachians,** *Fuss* often becomes "furse." **1937** *AmSp* 12.286 **wVA,** Occasionally . . [fɜrs] . . [is] heard for . . *fuss.* **1940** [see **C4** below]. **1945** Saxon *Gumbo Ya-Ya* 560 **sLA,** Furce—fuss.

B As noun.

1 =fussbudget. esp NEng

1861 in 1961 *VT Hist.* 29.66, Grandmother Young came. A real old fuss. **1875** Howells *Foregone Conclusion* 98 **RI,** I *am* a fuss, and I don't deny it. **1880** Aldrich *Stillwater* 98 **NEng,** "I hope you are not a fidget." "A what?" "A fuss, then,—a person who always wants everything some other way, and makes just twice as much trouble as anybody else." **1968** *DARE* (Qu. HH11a, *Someone who is too particular or fussy—if it's a man*) Inf **CT**9, [A] fuss.

2 A dispute or quarrel; a fight. **[fuss v C3] scattered, but chiefly Sth, Midl** See Map

1863 in 1951 *AmSp* 26.182 **NC,** Had a bitter fuss with Means. **1908** *DN* 3.313 **eAL, wGA,** *Fuss, n.* and *v.* Quarrel. **1927** Adams *Congaree* 24 **cSC** [Black], She started to carryin' tales to de Lord on He son. She mighty nigh create a fuss 'twix 'em. **1930** *DN* 6.84 **cSC.** **1942** McAtee *Dial. Grant Co. IN* 27 (as of 1890s). **1942** Warnick *Garrett Co. MD* (as of 1900–18). **1954** *Harder Coll.* **cwTN,** *Fuss. . .* A quarrel, disturbance. **1961** *New Yorker* 22 Apr 86 **TX,** [Newspaper headline:] Home fuss ends with man's death. **1965–70** *DARE* (Qu. KK15, *A disagreement or quarrel: "They had ______ about where the fence was to be."*) 155 Infs, **scattered, but chiefly Sth, Midl,** A fuss; (Qu. Y12a, *A fight . . mostly with words*) 52 Infs, **chiefly Sth, S Midl,** Fuss; **SC**3, Fuss fight; **TX**31, Verbal fuss; (Qu. Y13, *A fist fight*) Infs **KY**19, **TX**42, (Family) fuss; (Qu. KK13) Inf **MO**4, A pretty fuss; (Qu. KK14) Infs **IN**13, **TX**31, Fuss. **1967** *DARE* Tape **AL**26, I fought for it. . . we had a big fuss here not too long ago.

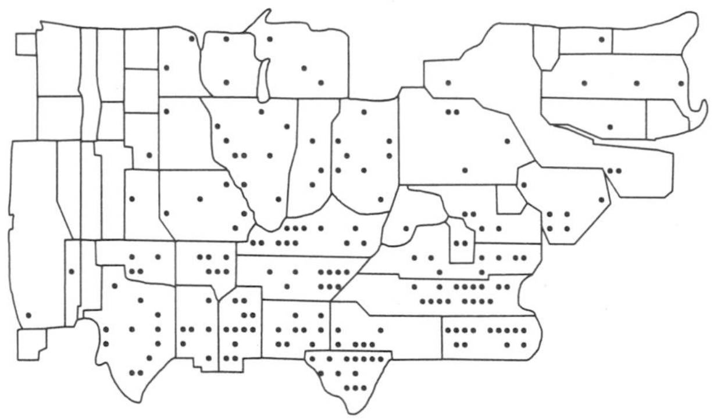

•fuss n, v B2 + varr (Qq. KK15, Y12a, Y13, KK13, KK14)

3 A loud noise; a noisy disturbance. **chiefly Sth, S Midl** See Map

1903 *DN* 2.314 **seMO,** *Furse. . .* A noise. 'I heard some kind of a furse, like a horse crossing a bridge.' 'That machine makes a queer furse.' **1939** *Hall Coll.* **wNC,** "And the bear sort of made a ugly fuss, and Johnny he hollered loud an' tried to scare the bear away." [Hall: Fuss—used of a sound made by a man covered by a bear hide to scare people.] **1965–70** *DARE* (Qu. KK16, *A great noise or disturbance: "I wish they'd stop making that awful ______."*) 65 Infs, **chiefly Sth, S Midl,** Fuss; (Qu. FF18, *A noisy or boisterous party: "They certainly last night."*) Infs **AR**24, **NC**1, Made a fuss; **VA**37, Raised a lot of fuss; (Qu. H11a, *If somebody eats rapidly and noisily, you say he ______*) Inf **AR**26, Makes a heap of fuss. **1986** Pederson *LAGS Concordance,* 1 inf, **cGA,** Making a fuss—of squeaking appliance needing oil; 1 inf, **nwMS,** An awful fuss—a lot of noise.

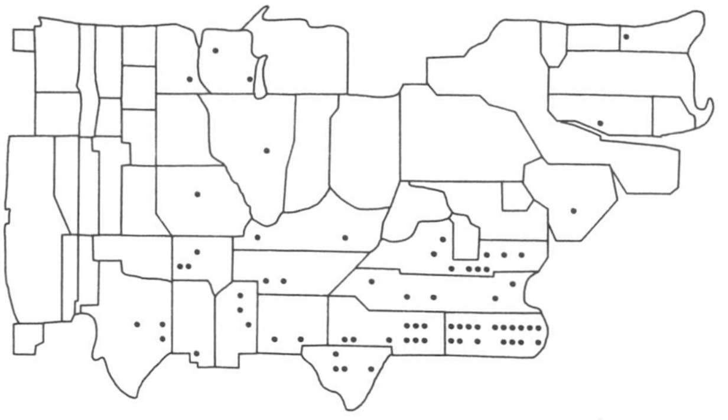

•fuss n, v B3 + varr (Qq. KK16, H11a, FF18)

4 By ext: a talkfest.

1966 *DARE* (Qu. KK12, *A meeting where there's a lot of talking: "They got together yesterday and had a real ______."*) Inf **FL**33, Fuss.

C As verb.

1 with *up:* To dress up; to decorate; hence ppl adj *fussed up.*

1874 Ward *Trotty's Wedding* 162, I wonder why girls fuss up and boys don't? **1875** Stowe *We & Neighbors* 69 **NYC,** I told her the way she is beginning—of petting Mary, and fussing up her room with carpet and pictures . . —would n't work. **1908** Fox *Lonesome Pine* 197 **KY,** Were they sorry she had not come back putting on airs and fussed up with ribbons and feathers . . ? **1941** *LANE* Map 358 *(Dress up)* 1 inf, **ceCT,** Used only of men: . . fuss up. **1967–70** *DARE* (Qu. W30, . . *"It's too plain—I think I'll put on a few flowers to ______ it up."*) Infs **MI**68, **MS**83, **NY**195, Fuss. **1969** *DARE* (Qu. W38, *When a man dresses himself up in his best clothes, you say he's ______*) Inf **PA**189, All fussed up; (Qu. W43) Inf **NY**220, All ragged out; all dressed up; all fussed up.

2 To court, date; hence vbl n *fussing* dating. *old-fash*

1900 *DN* 2.38 [College slang], *Fuss. . .* 1. To call on a lady. 2. To pay much attention to one of the opposite sex. **1924** *DN* 5.290, *Fuss. . .* To go out with girls. "Jack's out fussing tonight." **1940–41** Cassidy *WI Atlas* **cWI,** Fuss—to court. **1959** *VT Hist.* new ser 27.136, *Fussing expedition. . .* Courting. Rare. Orleans. **1969** *DARE* (Qu. AA1, *When a man goes to see a girl often and seems to want to marry her, he's ______ her.*) Inf **IL**47, Fussing. Used on the University of Wisconsin campus in 1914; used the same as *dating* would be used. **1980** *Observer* (Oberlin Coll.) 30 Oct, *How did the directory get the name "Fussers" anyway?* The . . name comes from "fussing," an old slang word for dating. . . [In] 1911 . . sophomore men advised freshman men to get "fussing permits."

3 To quarrel, argue contentiously; to pick a fight; hence vbl n *fussing* quarreling. **chiefly Sth, S Midl** See Map

1908 [see **B2** above]. **1914** *DN* 4.159 **cVA,** *Fuss. . .* To pick quarrels. **1931** *PMLA* 46.1308 **sAppalachians,** As would be expected, many terms for fussing, fighting, and killing abound. **1942** Warnick *Garrett Co. MD* 7 **nwMD** (as of 1900–1918), *Fuss. . .* quarrel. (Slang). **1954** *Harder*

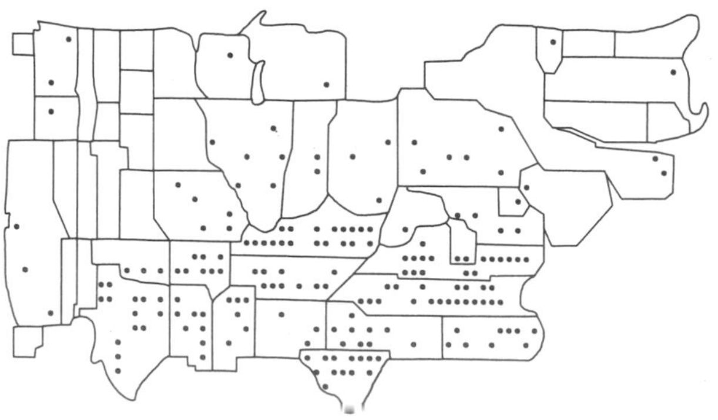

•fuss n, v C3 + varr (Qq. KK13, Y12a, II11a, b)

Coll. **cwTN,** *Fuss. . .* To quarrel. **c1960** *Wilson Coll.* **csKY,** *Fuss. . .* To quarrel, esp. without any cause. **1965–70** *DARE* (Qu. KK13, *Other words for arguing: "They stood there for an hour ______.")* 170 Infs, **chiefly Sth, S Midl,** Fussing; **TN**65, Fussing about it; **PA**203, Fussing and fibbing; **OK**20, **OR**6, **MS**56, **TN**13, **TX**60, (And) fussed; (Qu. Y12a) Inf **VA**5, Fussing and scrapping; (Qu. II11a, *If two people don't get along well together*) Inf **NC**55, [They] fuss and fight; (Qu. II11b, *If two people can't bear each other at all, you'd say, "Those two are ______.")* Inf **TN**24, Always fussing; **GA**72, Fuss. **1984** Burns *Cold Sassy* 67 **nGA** (as of 1906), The farmer was mad. . . I could still hear those two fussing after I passed the foundry.

4 usu with *at,* rarely *with:* To scold, nag. **chiefly Sth, S Midl**

1916 *DN* 4.268 **IL, KS, LA, NC,** *Fuss. . .* To scold. "My mother is going to fuss (at) me." **1940** Stuart *Trees of Heaven* 11 **neKY,** Don't you know your Pa comes to the house and furses with me every time you go out with the gun? **1961** *New Yorker* 22 Apr 86 **TX,** [He] started fussing at me and told me to get out. **1966** *DARE* (Qu. Y8, *To keep after a person so as to get him to do things: . . "She's always ______."*; total Infs questioned, 75) Inf **FL**8, Fussing at him; (Qu. II27, *If somebody gives you a very sharp scolding*) Inf **AR**24, Fussed at me; **LA**17, Fussing and cussing. **1967–68** *DARE* Tape **LA**25, He killed a little bird and I fussed at him; **SC**31, My children are always fussin' me about gettin' up on chairs. **1976** Wolfram–Christian *Appalachian Speech* 97, She'll probably give me a whippin' or I'll get fussed at. **1986** Pederson *LAGS Concordance,* 1 inf, **cLA,** They [sic] fussing at me.

5 also with *up:* To agitate, annoy, anger, upset; hence ppl adj *fussed (up).* **chiefly Nth, N Midl, CA** See Map

1916 *DN* 4.275 **IA, MA, NE, PA, VA, WV,** *Fussed. . .* Nervous, confused. "Mary was terribly fussed when the instructor called on her." **1927** *AmSp* 2.354 **WV,** She got all fussed up when the lawyers began to cross-examine her. **1932** Dos Passos *1919* 66 **VA,** The old man gave Joe a mean look and the kid sisters giggled and Joe went away feeling fussed. **1940** White *Wild Geese* 95 **OR,** Now that he had got over being mad he could see she had a lot of excuse for getting fussed up. **1941** *LANE* Map 476–77 *(Excited, all nerved up),* When a person is waiting in nervous suspense for an expected event. . . 1 inf, **ceMA,** *Fussed up.* **1966–70** *DARE* (Qu. GG7, . . *Annoyed or upset: "Though we were only ten minutes late, she was all ______.")* 21 Infs, **chiefly Nth, N Midl,** Fussed (up); (Qu. A21, *When someone is in too much of a hurry you might say, "Now just slow down! Don't ______.")* Inf **PA**13, Get fussed up; (Qu. Y2, . . *"Losing all that money didn't seem to ______ him a bit.")* Inf **IN**32, Fuss; (Qu. GG2, . . *"So many things were going on at the same time that he got completely ______.")* Infs **CT**15, **PA**140, **RI**1, **SD**3, **TN**12, Fussed (up); (Qu. GG4, *Stirred up, angry*) Infs **MA**6, **OH**5, 44, (All) fussed up; **IL**5, Fussed; (Qu. GG9, *To suddenly embarrass somebody. . . "When they told him what she had said about him it certainly did ______ him.")* Inf **TN**12, Fuss; **MA**5, He was fussed; **MI**18, He sure became fussed; (Qu. GG11, . . *"The letter hasn't come and he's ______.")* Inf **CA**163, Fussed up; (Qu. GG13a, *When something keeps bothering a person. . . "It ______ me.")* Inf **MA**100, Fuss; **PA**242, Fusses—Pennsylvania Dutch; (Qu. GG14, . . *Someone who fusses or worries a lot*) Inf **MD**23, Fussed up; (Qu. GG24, . . *To frighten: "Now don't let those fellows ______ you.")* Inf **AR**22, Fuss you up; (Qu. GG26, . . *"When she saw the dog coming at her she got ______.")* Inf **OH**16, Fuss up [*DARE* Ed: Inf freq assimilated final consonants]. [35 of 36 total Infs old]

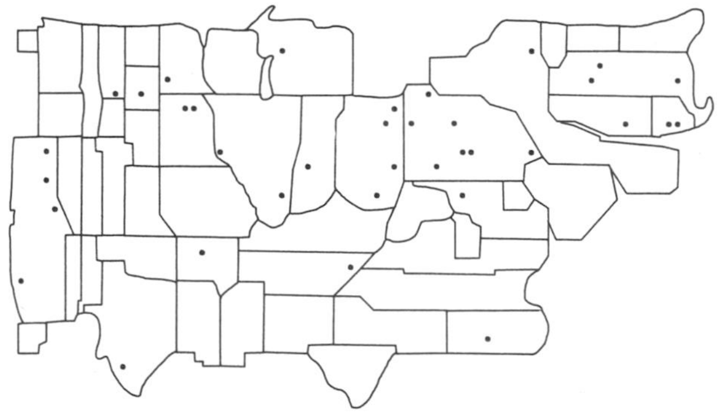

•fuss n, v C5 + varr (Qq. GG7, A21, Y2, GG2, GG4, GG9, GG11, GG13a, GG14, GG24, GG26)

6 also with *about, around:* To fool around, loaf. **Nth** Cf **futz 1**

1943 *LANE* Map 568 *(Loafing)* 3 infs, **CT, MA,** Fussing around. **1950** *WELS (Wasting time by doing unimportant . . things)* 2 Infs, **WI,** Fussing around. **1965–70** *DARE* (Qu. A10, . . *"What are you doing?" . . "Nothing in particular—I'm just ______.")* Infs **CT**17, **MI**50, 65, **NH**5, **NJ**2, **NY**220, **OH**23, **PA**209, Fussing around; **MI**22, 81, Fussing; **IA**16, Fussing about; (Qu. Y27, *To go about aimlessly, with nothing to do*) Inf **OH**84, Fussing; (Qu. NN12b, *Things that people say to put off a child when he asks, "What are you making?")* Inf **NY**73, Oh, just fussin'. **1968** *DARE* Tape **CA**100, Fussing around.

7 with *over* or *up:* See quots.

1892 Twain *Amer. Claimant* [Preface], This is an attempt to pull a book through without weather. . . Nothing breaks up an author's progress like having to stop every few pages to fuss-up the weather. **1969** *DARE* (Qu. A11, *When somebody takes too long about coming to a decision, you might say, "I wish he'd quit ______.")* Inf **MA**17, Mucking it over; fussing it over.

fuss adj, adv See **first** adj, adv

fuss about See **fuss** v **C6**

fuss-a-budget See **fussbudget**

fuss around See **fuss** v **C6**

fuss-ass See **fuss-butt**

fuss at See **fuss** v **C4**

fuss-box n **[box n 5a] chiefly Mid and S Atl** See Map
=fussbudget 1.

1950 *WELS (Somebody who is very particular or fussy)* 1 Inf, **csWI,** Fuss-box. **1965–70** *DARE* (Qu. GG14, . . *Someone who fusses or worries a lot, especially about little things*) 11 Infs, **chiefly Mid and S Atl,** Fuss-box; (Qu. GG16, *Words for finding fault, or complaining: "You just can't please him—he's always ______.")* Inf **NC**82, An old fuss-box; (Qu. HH11a) Infs **GA**6, **MD**47, **MA**30, **SC**26, **TX**74, Fuss-box; (Qu. HH11b) Infs **GA**6, 84, **MD**47, **MA**30, **PA**13, Fuss-box; (Qu. HH12, *A person who is always finding fault about unimportant things*) Inf **FL**52, A fuss-box.

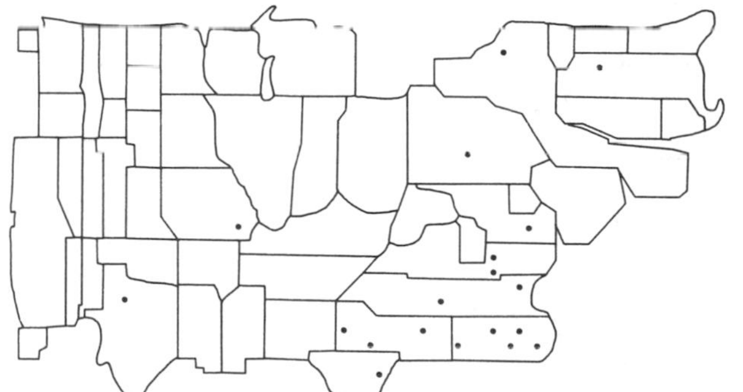

•fuss-box + var (Qq. GG14, GG16, HH11a, b, HH12)

fuss-bucket, fuss-buddy See **fuss-bug**

fussbudget n Rarely *fuss-a-budget, fussy-budget* **[budget 3]**

1 One who worries about trifles; a fretful, finicky or overly critical person. **chiefly Nth, N Midl, West** See Map

1904 *DN* 2.397 **cNY,** *Fuss-budget. . .* A nervous, fidgety person. **1907** *DN* 3.188 **seNH,** *Fuss-budget. . .* A person who makes a great ado about small matters; a fussy person. **1950** *WELS (Somebody who is very particular or fussy)* 19 Infs, **WI,** Fussbudget; *(Someone who . . worries about little things)* 19 Infs, Fussbudget. **1959** *VT Hist.* new ser 27.136, *Fussbudget. . .* A fussy person; one who makes much ado about trifles. Common. **1965–70** *DARE* (Qu. GG14) 264 Infs, **chiefly Nth, N Midl, West,** Fussbudget; **NY**25, 28, Fussy-budget; **NY**68, Fuss-a-budget [Of all Infs responding to the question, 33% were coll educ; of those giving this response, 45% were coll educ.]; (Qu. HH11a) 107 Infs, **chiefly Nth, N Midl, West,** (Old) fussbudget; [**NJ**22, Fusspodget;] (Qu. HH11b) 122 Infs, **chiefly Nth, N Midl, West,** (Old) fussbudget; **WA**22, Female fussbudget; (Qu. HH12, *A person who is always finding fault about unimportant things*) 33 Infs, **chiefly Nth, West,** Fussbudget; (Qu.

A18, . . *A very slow person: "What's keeping him? He certainly is ______!"*) Inf **RI**14, A reg'lar old fussbudget.

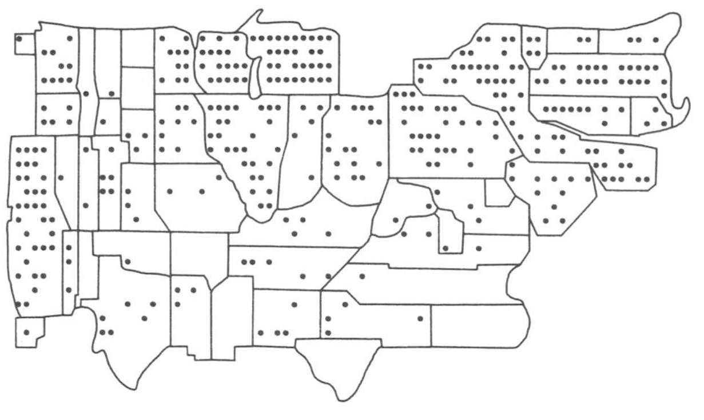

•fussbudget 1 + varr (Qq. GG14, HH11a, b, HH12, A18)

2 An ill-tempered person.

1927 *AmSp* 3.138 **eME,** A cross, exacting child or person was . . a "fussbudget." **1966–69** *DARE* (Qu. GG27b, *To get somebody out of an unhappy mood . . "Don't be a ______."*) Inf **NC**36, Fussbudget; (Qu. GG38, *Somebody who is usually mean and bad-tempered: "He's an awful ______."*) Infs **AL**30, **CA**169, Fussbudget; (Qu. GG39, *Somebody who seems to be looking for reasons to be angry: "He's a ______."*) Inf **IL**78, Fussbudget.

fuss-bug n Also *fuss-bucket, ~-buddy, fussy-bug*
=fussbudget 1.

1967–69 *DARE* (Qu. GG14, . . *Someone who fusses or worries a lot, especially about little things*) Infs **PA**133, **TX**43, Fuss-bug; **RI**4, Fussy-bug; **IN**32, Fuss-bucket; **NY**228, Fuss-buddy; (Qu. HH11a, *Someone who is too particular or fussy—if it's a man*) Inf **RI**4, Fussy-bug; (Qu. HH11b, . . *If it's a woman*) Inf **PA**75, Fuss-bug.

fuss-butt n Also *fuss-ass*
=fussbudget 1.

1967–68 *DARE* (Qu. HH11a, *Someone who is too particular or fussy—if it's a man*) Inf **TX**31, A fuss-butt; (Qu. HH11b, . . *If it's a woman*) Inf **MN**35, Fuss-ass—a dirty expression.

fuss-button n **chiefly PA, N Cent, Upper MW** See Map
=fussbudget 1.

1950 *WELS (Someone who . . worries about little things)* 6 Infs, **WI,** Fuss-button; *(Somebody who is very particular or fussy)* 4 Infs, Fuss-button. **1965–70** *DARE* (Qu. GG14) 16 Infs, **esp N Midl,** Fuss-button; (Qu. HH11a) 9 Infs, **esp PA, N Cent, Upper MW,** Fuss-button; (Qu. HH11b) 8 Infs, **esp PA, N Cent, Upper MW,** Fuss-button; (Qu. HH12, *A person who is always finding fault about unimportant things*) Infs **OH**78, **PA**167, Fuss-button.

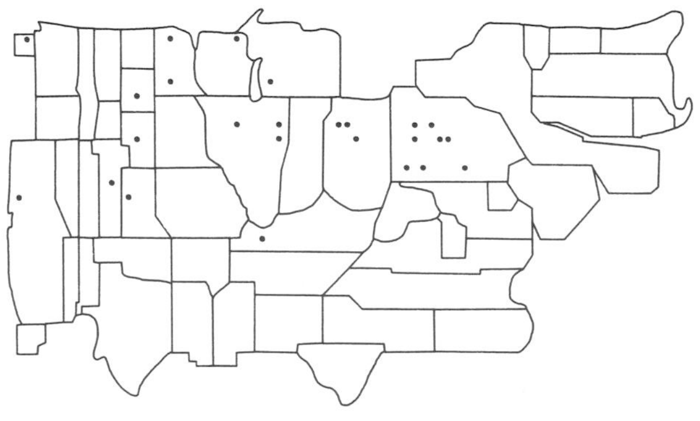

•fuss-button (Qq. GG14, HH11a, b, HH12)

fuss-cat n [**cat** n **1f**]
1 =fussbudget 1.

1942 Berrey–Van den Bark *Amer. Slang* 406.2, *Complainer; fault-finder. . .* fuss-cat. **1950** *WELS (Someone who . . worries about little things)* 1 Inf, **WI,** Fuss-cat; *(Somebody who is very particular or fussy)* 1 Inf, Fuss-cat. **1967–70** *DARE* (Qu. GG14) Infs **MA**100, **NJ**1, **NY**52, **VA**46, Fuss-cat; (Qu. HH11b) Infs **MA**15, **NJ**1, Fuss-cat; (Qu. HH12, *A person who is always finding fault about unimportant things*) Inf **MA**15, Fuss-cat.

2 also *fussy-cat:* **=fussbudget 2.**

1916 *DN* 4.269 **New Orleans LA,** *Fusscat. . .* A scold. **1966–70** *DARE* (Qu. HH22a, *A mean or disagreeable person*) Inf **FL**11, Fuss-cat; (Qu. II11b, *If two people can't bear each other at all, you'd say, "Those two are ______."*) Inf **KY**78, Like two old fussy-cats.

fussed See **fuss** v **C5**

fussed up See **fuss** v **C1, 5**

fussful adj [**fuss** n **B2**]
Quarrelsome, at odds.

c1938 in 1970 Hyatt *Hoodoo* 1.549 **New Orleans LA** [Black], If you put that [=a hoodoo device] under a woman's bed, she ain't going to be much service to her husband—her and her husband [will] be fussful all the time.

‡fuss-gadget n
=fussbudget 1.

1970 *DARE* (Qu. GG14, . . *Someone who fusses or worries a lot, especially about little things*) Inf **TN**65, Fuss-gadget; (Qu. HH11a, *Someone who is too particular or fussy—if it's a man*) Inf **TN**65, Fuss-gadget.

fuss-hunter n Also *fuss-maker* [**fuss** n **B2**] Cf **fight-banterer**
One who seeks to make quarrels.

1947 Ballowe *The Lawd* 96 **LA,** He couldn't abide a nagger, a fuss-hunter, a sloppy critter who wouldn't keep his house clean. **1965–70** *DARE* (Qu. HH26, *A person who is always ready to stir up trouble*) Inf **VA**46, Fuss-maker; (Qu. JJ4, *A child who is always telling on other children*) Inf **MS**61, Fuss-maker.

fussing See **fuss** v **C2, 3**

fuss-maker See **fuss-hunter**

fussock n [Engl dial *fussock* a stupid person; here perh infl by *fussy*]
A finicky person.

1969 *DARE* (Qq. HH11a, b, *Someone who is too particular or fussy*) Inf **MA**68, A [ˈfʌsək].

fuss over See **fuss** v **C7**

fuss-pot n [**pot**]
1 =fussbudget 1. chiefly NEast exc nNEng See Map

1965–70 *DARE* (Qu. GG14, . . *Someone who fusses or worries a lot, especially about little things*) 15 Infs, **chiefly N and C Atl,** Fuss-pot; (Qu. HH11a, *Someone who is too particular or fussy—if it's a man*) 15 Infs, **CT, NJ, NY, PA,** (Old) fuss-pot; (Qu. HH11b, . . *If it's a woman*) 12 Infs, **chiefly CT, NJ, NY, PA,** (Old) fuss-pot; (Qu. HH12, *A person who is always finding fault about unimportant things*) Infs **CT**6, **KY**40, **NY**118, Fuss-pot. **1967** *DARE* Tape **TX**27, Oh, you little fuss-pot!

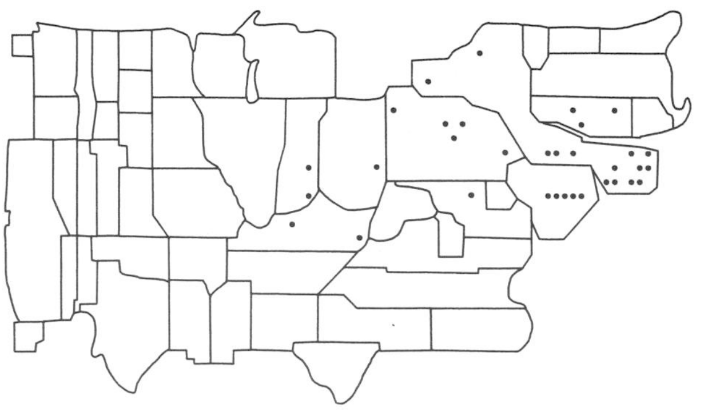

•fuss-pot 1 + var (Qq. GG14, HH11a, b, HH12)

2 =fussbudget 2.

1954 *Harder Coll.* **cwTN,** *Fusspot. . .* Someone who seems to be looking for reasons to be angry. **1969** *DARE* (Qu. GG39) Inf **KY**40, Fuss-pot.

fuss up See **fuss** v **C1, 5, 7**

fuss with See **fuss** v **C4**

fussy adj

Touchy, easily offended.

1973 Allen *LAUM* 1.358 **MN, NE** (as of c1950), [For *touchy:*] fussy [3 infs].

fussybody n [Prob infl by *busybody*]

1967 *DARE* (Qu. HH40, *Uncomplimentary words for an old man*) Inf **NY**24, Just an old fussybody.

fussy-budget See **fussbudget**

fussy-bug See **fuss-bug**

fussy-cat See **fuss-cat 2**

fussy-gussy See **fuzzy-guzzy 1**

fussy-head n [**head** n **C1a**]

=**fussbudget 1.**

1967 *DARE* (Qq. HH11a, b, *Someone who is too particular or fussy*) Inf **NY**24, Fussy-head.

fust See **first** adj, adv

‡fustered adj [Var of *flustered,* perh infl by **fuss** v **C5**]

1969 *DARE* (Qu. GG7, *Words meaning annoyed or upset: "Though we were only ten minutes late, she was all ——.")* Inf **IN**73, Flustered; fustered.

fustes(t) See **firstest**

fusticated See **flusticated**

fustrate v [Var, by dissim, of *frustrate*]

1966 *DARE* (Qu. GG13a, *When something keeps bothering a person and makes him nervous, he may say, "It —— me.")* Inf **SC**7, Fustrates.

fusty bump n [**bump** n **1**] Cf **fuck bump**

An inflamed pimple.

1968 *DARE* (Qu. X59, . . *The small infected pimples that form usually on the face*) Inf **DE**3, Fusty bumps, if they're on a young person, pin-jinnets [on an older person]; **MD**35, Fusty bumps.

fut See **foot** n

fute n [Perh *fute,* Scots var of *fout* a fool, simpleton; cf **foolish curlew**]

=**Eskimo curlew.**

1844 Giraud *Birds Long Is.* 274, In the vicinity of New York it is known by the name of "Futes"—in the Eastern States it is called "Doe Bird." **1888** Trumbull *Names of Birds* 204, Eskimo Curlew [=*Numenius borealis*]. At Stratford, Conn., and on Long Island . . *Fute.* **1917** (1923) *Birds Amer.* 1.254, Fute. **1956** *AmSp* 31.300, [For the etymology of *fute*] we are confronted with a choice between 'whistler' and 'simpleton' derivations. I am now inclined to the latter, because epithets of similar meaning are not rarely bestowed upon shore birds. Consider: *fool plover . . ; foolish curlew . . ; foolish godwit.*

futer See **future** n

futher See **far** adv, adj[1] **B3**

futherest See **far** adv, adj[1] **C4**

futsch adj [Ger *futsch* ruined, done for] Cf **kaput**

Finished, done for.

1968 *DARE* (Qu. KK20b, *Something that looks as if it might collapse at any minute: "Our old washing machine is ——.")* Inf **MN**36, Futsch. German slang. More common than *kaput* here. **1968** *DARE* FW Addit **csMN,** *Futsch* seems to have the sense of "clobbered," as it is used when you declare in a card game too. **1989** *DARE* File **NYC** (as of 1960), I used to play pinochle with a group of what were to me "old men." I distinctly remember one man who, when taking a trick, would forcefully lay his card on top of the others on the table and exclaim "futsch!"

futter See **far** adv, adj[1] **B3**

future n Pronc-spp *futer, futur*

Std senses, var forms.

1777 in 1956 Eliason *Tarheel Talk* 311 **NC,** Futer. **1845** Thompson *Pineville* 81 **cGA,** We'll try to take care of you for the futer. **1861** Holmes *Venner* 2.298 **wMA,** I wish to come to an understandin' as to the futur'. **1887** Freeman *Humble Romance* 260 **MA,** In futur I'm a-goin' to cook my vittles myself. **1927** *AmSp* 2.484 (as of early 19th cent), There are many instances of vowel *weakening* [sic] [in the tales of James Fenimore Cooper], especially of final syllables. . . Forms like *natur', . . creatur', . . futur', . .* are common.

future v [Folk-etym var of **feature** v **1**]

To resemble in appearance or behavior; to **favor C1.**

1967–68 *DARE* (Qu. Z10, *If a child looks very much like his father, you might say, "He —— his father.")* Inf **LA**8, Futures [Inf Black]; [**GA**44, Heard Negroes say "They future sho' looks alike."] **c1970** Pederson *Dial. Surv. Rural GA (If a boy is similar in appearance to his father, you would say that the boy —— his father)* 1 inf, **seGA,** Futures [inf Black]; *(If the boy's behavior is similar to his father's you would say that the boy —— his father)* 1 inf, **seGA,** Futures [inf White]. **1986** Pederson *LAGS Concordance,* 1 inf, **ceAL,** Futures his father—they say.

futz v, hence vbl n *futzing* Usu |fʌts|; rarely |futs| [Etym uncert; cf Ger *furzen* to fart, and see quot 1985 *Jewish Lang. Rev.* at **1**] **esp Nth** Cf **putz**

1 usu with *around,* rarely *about:* To fool around, idle, waste time. Cf **fuss** v **C6**

1932 Farrell *Young Lonigan* 119 **Chicago IL,** Studs kept futzing around until Helen Shires came out with her soccer ball. **1937** (1958) Levin *Old Bunch* 80 **Chicago IL,** There was a fellow that never wasted time. No fuzzy futzing around. **1943** *AmSp* 18.43 **NYC,** I myself have heard this expression [=*futz around*] employed by adolescent Negro and Italian boys. The Yiddish [=*arumfartzen*] does get around. As with the word 'nertz,' . . 'futz' has undergone an internal change to make it less obviously vulgar. . . The German word is *furzen.* **1950** *WELS ("He doesn't have much to do today, so he's just ——.")* 1 Inf, **ceWI,** Futzing around. **1967–68** *DARE* (Qu. A10, . . *Doing little unimportant things*) Inf **IN**68, Futzing around; **NY**34, Futzing; **CA**15, ['futsɪŋ] around; it may be Yiddish; (Qu. KK31, . . *"He doesn't have anything to do, so he's just —— around.")* Inf **PA**46, ['fʌtsɪŋ]; **PA**82, Futzing. **1976** *NY Times* (NY) 31 Oct sec D 32/5 **NY,** I futz about, move things, think up another pose, reposition the camera. **1985** *NYT Mag.* 1 Dec 16, The president . . discussing presummit maneuvering, told a group of wire-service reporters that the time had come to "stop this *futzing* around." **1985** *Jewish Lang. Rev.* 5.316, One possibly correct explanation of these meanings [of *futz*] if [sic] that they result from emulation of *fuck:* if *fuck* 'to copulate' = *futz* 'to copulate' and if *fuck around* means 'to idle, loaf, etc.', then *futz* acquires the[se] meanings . . by analogy. . . Another explanation . . is that the verb *futz* is a euphemism of *fuck.* Thirdly, there is the possibility of Yiddish influence. *Ibid* 318, Eastern Ashkenazic English *fart around* is a translation of [Eastern Yiddish] *arumfartsn zikh.* . . [I]f Yiddish or Eastern Ashkenazic English is relevant in any way, there must have been either deliberate phonological change or blending. . . I suggest . . that Eastern Ashkenazic English *fart around* is indeed relevant [to the etymology of *futz around*]. **1988** *DARE* File **ceWI** (as of c1920), When I was a child, my Uncle Fred often said, "You kids! Quit futzing ['fʌtsɪŋ] around!" or "Don't futz with that!" My mother, as well as others in our town, also used the expression; many of us still say it. I always thought it must be a euphemism for that other word, and I think it comes from the German.

2 with *with:* To mess with; to tinker or trifle with.

1974 *Esquire* 81.4.106/2, [Dan] Rather protested this caprice. He would film what he damn well pleased. . . Nobody futzes with Dan Rather and gets away with it. **1980** *Chr. Sci. Monitor* (Boston MA) 4 Mar 16/1, In spring there is the garden. In fall the leaves. But in winter, unless you're into igloo-making, futzing with the snowblower, or carving out figure eights on the pond, what is there to mess with? **1984** *Wall St. Jrl.* (NY NY) 26 Jan 19/3, [Advt:] Macintosh was designed for anyone who handles, collects, distributes, interprets, organizes, or otherwise futzes with information. **1988** *DARE* File **csWI,** Don't futz with it; you might break it. **1988** [see **1** above].

futz about, futz around See **futz 1**

futzing See **futz**

futz with See **futz 2**

fuyk See **fyke**

fuzee See **fusee**

fuzz n[1]

1954 *Harder Coll.* **cwTN,** *Fuzz.* . . A small amount. "He turned the stove up a fuzz."

fuzz n² [Var of *fuss* (cf **fuss** v **C5**), perh infl by *fuzz* a blurred effect] Cf **fuzzed up**
A state of confusion or perplexity.
1950 *WELS (There were so many things happening at once that she got all ——)* 1 Inf, **cWI,** In a fuzz.

fuzz n³ Also *fuzzer*
=**fusee.**
1966–69 *DARE* (Qu. FF15, *When a firecracker doesn't go off, and you break it in the middle and light the powder, you call it a ——*) Infs **CO**3, **IL**43, **PA**104, **SC**21, 58, Fuzz; **IN**69, Fuzzer.

fuzz v¹ [Prob var of **fuss** v **C6,** perh infl by **futz**]
1950 *WELS (Wasting time by doing unimportant . . things)* 1 Inf, **csWI,** Fuzzing around.

fuzz v² [Imit; var of *fizz*]
To spew out in an effervescent manner.
1969 *DARE* (Qu. Y45, . . *"When he opened the can, the beer —— [all over the kitchen]."*) Infs **IL**72A, **MA**40, Fuzzed.

fuzzball n
1 A ball of household dust.
1950 *WELS (Soft rolls of dust that collect on the floor under . . furniture)* 1 Inf, **swWI,** Fuzzballs. **1966–68** *DARE* (Qu. E20) Infs **MI**18, **MN**16, **NY**28, Fuzzballs. **1988** *Isthmus* (Madison WI) 25 Mar 17/1 **csWI,** Of course, you can choose to live in a hovel where fuzzballs grow to alarming size under the bed and where strange fungi sprout from yellowing pizza boxes.
2 =**puffball.** [*OED* 1597 →]
1967 *DARE* (Qu. S18, *A kind of mushroom that grows like a globe . . sometimes gets as big as a man's head*) Inf **WY**3, Fuzzball; puffball.
3 A dense or stupid person.
1967 *DARE* (Qu. HH13, *Expressions meaning that a person is not very alert or not aware of things: "He's certainly ——."*) Inf **MI**67, A fuzzball.

fuzz-brained adj
Stupid.
1969 *DARE* (Qu. HH3, *A dull and stupid person*) Inf **MA**58, Fuzz-brained.

fuzz bunny n Cf **dust bunny**
See quots.
1965 *DARE* File **Philadelphia PA,** Fuzz-bunnies—dust collected under the bed, behind doors, etc. **1968–69** *DARE* (Qu. E20, *Soft rolls of dust that collect on the floor under beds or other furniture*) Infs **MI**104, **OH**87, Fuzz bunnies.

fuzz-button n [Var of **fuss-button**]
1968 *DARE* (Qu. GG14, . . *Someone who fusses or worries a lot, especially about little things*) Inf **KS**7, Fuzz-button.

fuzz-buzz n [Redup form of *fuzz;* infl by **fussbudget** and varr]
=**fussbudget 1.**
1968 *DARE* (Qu. GG14, . . *Someone who fusses or worries a lot, especially about little things*) Inf **PA**82, Fuzz-buzz.

fuzzed up adj phr [Var of *fussed up* (at **fuss** v **C5**)]
1941 Percy *Lanterns* 61 **nwMS,** They seemed dreadfully fuzzed-up over peanuts. **1967–69** *DARE* (Qu. GG2, *Expressions meaning 'confused, mixed up': "So many things were going on at the same time that he got completely ——."*) Inf **MA**46, Fuzzed up; (Qu. GG4, *Stirred up, angry: "When he saw them coming he got ——."*) Inf **LA**2, Fuzzed up; (Qu. KK39, . . *"Because of the storm, the pond was all ——."*) Inf **MD**47, Stirred up; fuzzed up. **1971** Dwyer *Dict. for Yankees* 26 **Sth, S Midl,** *Fuzzed- up*—Disturbed, excited.

fuzzer See **fuzz** n³

fuzz face n
A boy; a young man who has not developed a beard.
1927 *DN* 5.447 [Underworld jargon], *Fuzz face.* . . A young tramp. **1958** McCulloch *Woods Words* 68 **Pacific NW,** *Fuzz face*—A boy.

fuzzhead See **fuzzy-head**

fuzzle n¹ See **foozle** n

fuzzle n² [Prob var of *fizzle*]
A failure.
1928 *Ruppenthal Coll.* **KS,** We made a fuzzle of last night.

fuzzle n³ [Ger *Fussel* fluff, fuzz, piece of lint; prob also infl by *fuzz*]
See quots.
1968 *DARE* (Qu. E20, *Soft rolls of dust that collect on the floor under beds or other furniture*) Inf **NY**77, Fuzzles; **WI**71, [ˈfuzəlz]. **1969** *DARE* FW Addit **cwIL,** [ˈfʌzəlz]—soft rolls of dust under the bed. Used by all the old Dutchmen (Germans) around here.

fuzzled ppl adj [Cf *OED fuzzle "Obs.* . . To intoxicate, . . confuse, muddle."] *arch* Cf **bumfuzzle**
Confused, perturbed.
1834 Davis *Letters Downing* 304 **NY,** Folks use to call him *old Sile,* when he'd come in all kiver'd with mud, and a considerable fuzzled—he was a willin, good-natur'd critter as ever was, but plagy knowin. **1894** Twain *Pudd'nhead Wilson* 389, Why, with a person pecking at *me* that way, I should get that fuzzled and fuddled that ——.

fuzzle-wuzzle See **fuzzy-wuzzy 3**

fuzztail n Also *fizzy, fuzzy* **West** Cf **broomtail 1**
A horse; see quots.
1929 *AmSp* 5.66 **NE,** "Fuzzies," range horses, "broomies" and "broom tails," range mares, are slang names for "ponies." A "fuzz tail" is a fiery horse; a "broom tail" a gentle old mare. **1937** Sandoz *Slogum* 55 (as of 1900–20), "She's touchy and mean as one a them fuzz-tail mustang colts," a browned man from Arizona complained. **1940** Writers' Program *Guide NV* 76, *Fuzztail* . . a cowboy's horse. **1940** Writers' Program *Guide NM* 113, *Fuzzies*—Poor quality horses. **1942** Berrey-Van den Bark *Amer. Slang* 916.14, *Range horse; mustang.* . . fizzy, fuzztail, fuzzy. **1958** *AmSp* 33.270 **eWA,** *Fuzztail.*

fuzzy n
1 See **fuzztail.**
2 See quot 1950.
1950 *WELS (Soft rolls of dust that collect on the floor under . . furniture)* 1 Inf, **cwWI,** Fuzzies. **1967–69** *DARE* (Qu. E20) Infs **CA**11, 80, **DE**4, **MA**27, **NJ**23, **OH**90, **PA**163, Fuzzies.
3 Prob a **tick trefoil.**
1968 *DARE* (Qu. S15, . . *Weed seeds that cling to clothing*) Inf **WI**37, Fuzzy. [It's] green, oval, smooth and fuzzy.

fuzzy ant n
=**cow-killer ant.**
1933 Jaeger *CA Deserts* 58, Those furry-backed insects which so energetically wander about on the sands, and which are known as fuzzy ants or cow-killers, are really solitary, parasitic wasps.

fuzzy-ball n [Prob from the shape and texture of the fruit]
A **sycamore.**
1969 *DARE* (Qu. T13) Inf **KY**11, Fuzzy-ball.

fuzzy bear n
=**woolly bear.**
1968–70 *DARE* (Qu. R27, . . *Kinds of caterpillars . . around here*) Infs **IA**46, **VA**101, Fuzzy bear; [**PA**79, Fuzzy woolly bear].

fuzzy britches n
=**fiddleneck 1.**
1970 *DARE* (QR, near Qu. I28) Inf **KY**77, Wild greens—fuzzy britches. **1973** Kluger *Wild Flavor* 72 **sIN,** To . . a fellow greens- hunter from another town nearby, "woolly britches" are "fuzzy britches".

fuzzy bug n Cf **fuzzy bear**
Prob =**woolly bear.**
1969 *DARE* (Qu. R27, . . *Kinds of caterpillars . . around here*) Inf **NY**186, Fuzzy bug.

fuzzy-dud n [Var of **fuddy-dud**]
=**fussbudget 1.**
1968 *DARE* (Qu. GG14, . . *Someone who fusses or worries a lot, especially about little things*) Inf **CT**19, A fuzzy-dud; (Qq. HH11a, b, *Someone who is too particular or fussy*) Inf **CT**19, A fuzzy-dud.

fuzzy-foot n
A mushroom *(Xeromphalina campanella)* found in dense clusters on rotting coniferous stumps and logs.
1981 Lincoff *Audubon Field Guide Mushrooms* 809, Fuzzy Foot. *Xeromphalina campanella.* . . Base covered with dense tuft of long, bright, tawny hairs.

fuzzy-guzzy n [Redup of *fuzzy*]

1 also *fussy-gussy:* A **cudweed 1** (here: *Gnaphalium obtusifolium*). [See quot 1911]

1892 *Jrl. Amer. Folkl.* 5.98, *Gnaphalium polycephalum...* Fuzzy-guzzy, Mansfield, O[hio]. **1900** Lyons *Plant Names* 176, *G. obtusifolium...* Fuzzy-guzzy. **1911** *Century Dict. Suppl., Fuzzy-guzzy...* The common everlasting, *Gnaphalium obtusifolium,* so called from its fuzzy appearance. **1959** Carleton *Index Herb. Plants* 50, *Fussy gussy:* Gnaphlium [sic] polycephalum.

2 See **fuzzy-wuzzy 3.**

fuzzy-head n Also *fuzzhead* [See quot 1932]

Either the **hooded merganser** or the **red-breasted merganser.**

1923 U.S. Dept. Ag. *Misc. Circular* 13.6 **FL,** *Red-breasted Merganser... Vernacular Names... In local use...* Fuzzyhead. *Ibid* 7, *Hooded Merganser... Vernacular Names... In local use...* Fuzzyhead. **1932** Howell *FL Bird Life* 158, *Hooded Merganser... Other Names:.. Fuzzyhead... Adult male:* Narrow, fan-shaped white head crest. **1982** Elman *Hunter's Field Guide* 228, Hooded Merganser... Fuzzhead. *Ibid* 230, Red-breasted Merganser... Fuzzyhead.

fuzzy mouse See **mouse**

fuzzy mullein n

A **mullein** (here: *Verbascum thapsus*).

1897 *Jrl. Amer. Folkl.* 10.52, *Verbascum Blattaria,..* slippery mullein (in distinction from fuzzy mullein, *V. Thapsus*), Southold, L[ong] I[sland]. **1968** *DARE* (Qu. S20, *A common weed that grows on open hillsides: It has velvety green leaves close to the ground, and a tall stalk with small yellow flowers on a spike at the top*) Inf **PA**126, Fuzzy mullein; also called musk mullein. If you bend it down and touch the ground, and go back a week later, it will point towards your true love.

fuzzywog n Cf *DS* E20, **golliwog**

1950 *WELS Suppl.* **csWI,** Fuzzywogs—rolls of dust under furniture.

fuzzy worm n Cf **fuzzy bear**

=woolly bear.

1967–70 *DARE* (Qu. R27,.. *Kinds of caterpillars.. around here*) Infs **MI**103, **TX**32, **VA**79, **WI**37, Fuzzy worm; [**AL**38, Fuzzy worm—a common term for all kinds].

fuzzy-wuzzy n [Redup of *fuzzy*]

1 A **woolly bear** or similar caterpillar. Cf **fuzzy bear**

1967–69 *DARE* (Qu. R27,.. *Kinds of caterpillars*) Infs **NC**38, **WI**48, Fuzzy-wuzzy; **GA**89, Fuzzy-wuzzy—a big reddish brown caterpillar; **MN**42, Woolly bear—also called fuzzy-wuzzy.

2 **=chaparral broom.**

1961 Thomas *Flora Santa Cruz* 345 **cwCA,** *B[accharis] pilularis* DC. var. *pilularis...* Dwarf Chaparral Broom, Fuzzy-Wuzzy. Coastal bluffs, hills, and sand dunes.

3 also *fuzzle-wuzzle, fuzzy-guzzy:* See quot 1950. Cf **fuzz bunny**

1950 *WELS (Soft rolls of dust that collect.. under beds or other furniture)* 1 Inf, **WI,** Fuzzy-wuzzies—used sometimes by children; 1 Inf, Fuzzle-wuzzles. **1968** *DARE* (Qu. E20) Inf **MN**42, Fuzzy-wuzzies. **1973** *DARE* File **cnMA** (as of c1900), Fuzzy-guzzy—a dust roll under the bed.

f.w.c. See **free man of color**

-fy See **-ify**

fyahly See **fairly** adv

fyce See **feist** n

fy-ence See **fence** n, v

fyke n |faɪk| Also *fyke net* Also sp *fike, fuik, fuyk* [Du *fuik* a bow-net] **orig chiefly NY, NEng; now chiefly C Atl coast** Cf **hoop net**

A funnel-shaped net kept open by a series of hoops and often equipped with wing nets designed to funnel the fish or other catch to the mouth of the net.

1832 in 1867 De Voe *Market Asst.* 197 **NYC,** While some men were rowing up Newtown Creek.. they discovered a sea-dog stealing bass from a fuik of a bass-net. **1859** (1968) Bartlett *Americanisms* 165, *Fyke.* (Dutch, *fuik,* a weel, bow-net.) The large bow-nets in New York harbor, used for catching shad, are called *shad-fykes.* **1895** *DN* 1.388 **MA, NY,** *Fyke, fuyk:* a fish-net. **1899** (1912) Green *VA Folk-Speech* 174, *Fike.* **1915** (1916) Johnson *Highways New Engl.* 276, Farther down the river lots of fish are caught in pounds and fike nets. **1940** Weygandt *Down Jersey* 173 **sNJ,** I had found.. funnel-shaped fish traps that bore the Hollandish name of *fykes* all along the Delaware. **1966–70** *DARE* (Qu. P13,.. *Other ways of fishing*) Inf **DE**4, They fish for eels with a fyke—a basket-type object with hoops and funnels; **ME**16, Fyke—put a set of nets and stakes [to] set off a beach in low tide;.. two arms (twenty to thirty feet) guide fish into the fyke in high water; pick them up at low tide; **MD**34, Fyke—a net stretched across stakes on the bottom of a river; it channels fish into the funnel end, which is then pulled in; **MD**36, Fyke net—barrel-shaped funnel.. confuses fish and they can't get out; **NJ**31, Fyke [faɪk]—used here as a trap for fish or turtles; [it] leads the critter into an inner compartment through a funnel; sometimes they had several wings; **NJ**39, Fyke means a trap made of net for fish or turtles; **NJ**53, Fyke. **1968** McPhee *Pine Barrens* 133 **NJ,** Snapping turtles in the Pine Barrens are sometimes a foot and a half long and almost as wide... Pineys trap them in fykes, and fry their delicious white meat. **1969** *DARE* Tape **WI**75, [FW:] You mentioned a fyke net. What's that? [Inf:] That's just a.. variation of the hoop net.. but it's just a little bit different; they have.. a little lead that brings the fish in.

fyst(e) See **feist** n

fysty See **feisty** adj

G

g' See **give A1b, 2c**

ga- See **ker-**

gab n[1] [Scots, nEngl dial var of *gob* mouth] **now esp Gt Lakes, Upper MW** See Map *joc* Cf **gabber** n[1]

The mouth, esp as the organ of speech.

1908 *DN* 3.313 **eAL, wGA,** *Gab*. . . mouth. "Shut up your gab." **1909** *S. Atl. Qrly.* 8.39 **sSC coast** [Gullah], Something to taste [=put a taste in] your gab. **1924** Marks *Plastic Age* 100, Close your gabs, everybody. *Ibid* 197, He shoots off his gab as if he knew everything. **1934** Stribling *Unfinished Cathedral* 10 **AL,** "Hush your gab," snapped Northrup. **1965–70** *DARE* (Qu. X9, . . *"I wish he'd shut his _______."*) 15 Infs, **scattered, but esp Gt Lakes, Upper MW,** Gab; (Qu. HH7b) Inf **MI**44, Gab is always going; (Qu. II22) Inf **MN**10, Shut your gab.

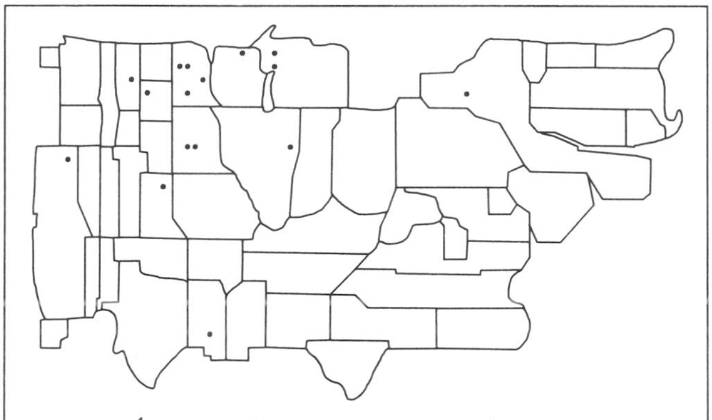

•gab n[1] + varr (Qq. X9, HH7b, II22)

gab n[2] [*SND* 1822 →; cf *gab* to talk] Cf **gabber** n[2]

1965–70 *DARE* (Qu. HH7a, *Someone who talks too much or too loud*) Infs **AR**3, **CO**15, **IL**7, **MT**2, **NC**35, **RI**17, **WA**1, 13, Gab. [All Infs old]

gabber n[1]

=**gab** n[1].

1967–68 *DARE* (Qu. X9, *Joking or uncomplimentary words for a person's mouth*) Infs **CA**22, **MN**37, **NJ**33, Gabber.

gabber n[2] Also *gabbler* [*gab* to talk]

=**gab** n[2].

1935 Porter *Flowering Judas* 164, He wondered who the man was, a strange voice, but a loud and ready gabbler as if maybe he was trying to sell something. **1965–70** *DARE* (Qu. HH7a, *Someone who talks too much or too loud*) 48 Infs, **scattered,** Gabber; (Qu. KK12) Inf **GA**17, Gabbers' meeting. [Of all Infs responding to Qu. HH7a, 63% were old; of those giving this response, 81% were old.]

gabber napper n [Var of **gallinipper 1a**]

1970 *DARE* (Qu. R15b, *Any names for an extra-big mosquito?*) Inf **VA**70, Gabber napper.

gabblement n [*OED* 1833 →; cf **-ment**] **Sth**

Chatter.

1845 Thompson *Pineville* 121 **GA,** This court's got as good ears as any man, but they aint for to hear no old woman's gabblement, 'thout its [sic] under oath. **1872** Schele de Vere *Americanisms* 476, In the South the word [=gab] is strengthened by being lengthened into *gabblement,* but only in its lowest sense. **1872** (1973) Thompson *Major Jones's Courtship* 185 **GA,** The galls [=girls] got round, and sich a everlastin gabblement as they did keep up. **1984** Wilder *You All Spoken Here* 165 **Sth,** *Jawed:* Gabbled; gobbled; talked; prated. *Gabblement:* An exhibition of the preceding.

gabbler See **gabber** n[2]

gabble racket n Also *gobble ratchet* [These and other similar Engl dial forms are folk-etyms of ME *Gabrielle rache,* from the name of the archangel + *rache* trackhound.] Cf **Gabriel's hounds**

1950 *PADS* 14.31 **SC,** *Gabble racket, gobble ratchet*. . . The honking sound made by wild geese flying by night; employed with various supernatural meanings, as of witches' chatter on broomstick flights; anciently believed to be the crying of unbaptized children doomed to wander in space until Judgment Day.

gabboon See **goboon**

gabby bird n [See quot 1950]

The Carolina parakeet *(Conuropsis carolinensis).*

1930 Shoemaker *1300 Words* 24 **cPA Mts** (as of c1900), *Gabby bird*—The Carolina paroquet, once plentiful in central Pennsylvania. **1950** (1965) Richter *Town* 153 **OH** (as of c1900), Moughty few ever heerd gabby birds a talkin'. They'd sooner wear them on their hats, the purtiest birds you ever laid eyes on. A kind of poll parrot, not very big. I've seed the trees red and yaller and blue with them. They'd talk to each other like humans.

Gabe n [Abbr for *Gabriel*] Cf **Adam**

In var prov phrr: see quots.

1968 *DARE* (Qu. KK62, . . *"I wouldn't do that for _______."*) Inf **IN**41, Gabe. **1975** Preston *Proverbial Comparisons* 32 **sIN,** To have as many X's as Gabe's got oats. Old fash.

‡**gabe** v

1948 *McDavid Coll.* **cnNY,** *Gabe*—to drink (alcoholic drinks). [Used by an 85 year old retired farmer and carpenter.]

gaberel See **Gabriel**

Gabe's off-ox n [Cf **Gabe** n]

=**Adam's off-ox 1.**

1967 *DARE* (Qu. II26, . . *"I wouldn't know him from _______."*) Inf **TX**18, Gabe's off-ox.

gabfeast See **feast** n

gaboodle See **caboodle**

gaboon See **goboon**

gabootzt adj [PaGer *gebutzt*]

Cleaned.

1939 Aurand *Quaint Idioms* 14 [PaGer], I was clean *gabootzt* (cleaned "clean") when I went to that house.

Gabriel n Pronc-spp *gab(e)rel, Gabrull*

A Forms.

1922 Gonzales *Black Border* 303 **sSC, GA coasts** [Gullah glossary], *Gabrull*—Angel Gabriel—he of the horn. **1956** [see **B** below]. **1968** *DARE* (Qu. W2) Inf **AK**8, In Gabr'el's gown.

B Sense.

Usu not cap; Among loggers: =**dinner horn.** [From the horn carried by Gabriel as the herald of the Last Judgment]

1956 Sorden–Ebert *Logger's Words* 15 **Gt Lakes,** *Gaberel* . . dinner-horn. **1964** Hargreaves–Foehl *Story of Logging* 59 **MI,** *Gabriel*—A long tin horn which "cookee" blew to call the shanty boys to their "hash." The gabriel sometimes was as long as eight feet!

Gabriel barn n [Perh folk-etym for *gable barn* or *gambrel barn* (at **gambrel roof**)]

1969 *DARE* (Qu. M1, . . *Different or special kinds of barns*) Inf **NY**176, Gabriel ['gebriɛl] barn (also a hay barn).

Gabriel's gown, in adj phr [Cf **Adam 4**]

Naked.

1968 *DARE* (Qu. W20, *If somebody has no clothes on at all*) Inf **AK**8, In Gabr'el's gown.

Gabriel's hounds n pl [*OED* ?16 . . → (at *Gabriel*); see also *EDD* at *Gabriel('s hounds*]

The supposed cause of **gabble racket.**

1912 Green *VA Folk-Speech* 189, *Gabriel's Hounds, n. pl.* Their cry heard in the air at night. [**1967** Stewart *Gabriel Hounds* 26 **Britain,** Gabriel Hounds are supposed to be a pack of hounds that run with Death, and when someone's going to die you hear them howling over the house at night. I've an idea myself that the idea must have come from the wild geese—have you heard them? They sound like a pack of hounds in full cry overhead, and the old name for them used to be 'gabble ratchet.']

Gabriel's trumpet n [From the shape of the flower and perh the poisonous nature of the plant]

A **jimson weed** (here: *Datura meteloides*).

1951 *PADS* 15.39 **TX,** *Datura meteloides.* . . Jimson weed; . . Gabriel's . . trumpet.

Gabrull See **Gabriel**

gabut See **kaput**

gad n[1] [ME *gad* (metal) spike]

1 also *gad stick:* A stick or whip, esp for driving oxen or punishing children. **chiefly east of Missip R** *old-fash*

1848 in 1968 Bartlett *Americanisms* 165, I looked around and saw where the three had set down on a log. I measured the length of the foot, and found where they had cut a big gad. **1894** *DN* 1.331 **sNJ,** *Gad* . . small whip used to drive cows to pasture. *Ibid* 341 **wCT,** *Gad* . . sometimes *whip* in general, but oftener a whipstock without lash, made of a young shoot of ironwood or hardbeam *(Carpinus Americana).* **1906** *DN* 3.137 **nwAR,** *Gad.* . . A stick. "If you don't quit that, I'll get a gad." **1906** Casey *Parson's Boys* 256 **sIL** (as of c1860), Mrs. Flint . . met the Parson as he strode into the house with gad in hand. **1917** *DN* 4.392 **IL, IA, KS, NH, OH, NY, VT,** *Gad.* . . A whip,—usually cut from a tree and suggesting stiffness (like a goad), though used as a whip. **1930** Shoemaker *1300 Words* 24 **cPA Mts** (as of c1900), *Gad*—A whip for driving cattle, or punishing children. **1939** *LANE* Map 179 *(Whip, goad),* 26 infs, **esp wNEng,** Gad. [2 infs described *gad* as rare; 5 infs as obsolete or old-fashioned] **1941** *Ibid* Map 398 *(Switch [for punishing children]),* 4 infs, **wNEng, Long Is,** Gad. [2 infs described the term as old-fashioned] **1948** Hedrick *Land Crooked Tree* 20 **MI** (as of 1870s), Two boys with blue-beech gads, five or six feet long, stood foot to foot, each thrashing the other in alternate strokes. **1949** Kurath *Word Geog.* 56, Oxen are little used as draft animals nowadays, but many of the older country folk still remember the ox goad, a stout pointed stick with a lash. There are many different terms for it in different parts of the Eastern States: . . *gad* in Western New England, on Long Island, in northern Pennsylvania, in northern West Virginia, and on Delaware Bay. **1952** *DE Folkl. Bulletin* 1.12/2, A twig used to punish a youngster was always referred to as "a gad to skutch th' young 'un." **1965–70** *DARE* (Qu. K27, . . *The sharp-pointed stick used to get oxen to move*) 10 Infs, **scattered east of Missip R,** Gad; **GA**77, Gad stick. **1975** Gould *ME Lingo* 105, *Gad*—Maine farm word for the goad or goadstick used in teaming oxen.

2 See quot 1940.

1940 Writers' Program *Guide NV* 76, The buckaroo's spurs are referred to as *steel, gads, hooks, gut lacers,* or *chihuahuas.* **1968** Adams *Western Words* 123.

3 See quot. [*DNE* 1894 →]

1975 Gould *ME Lingo* 105, The forked alder stick used to bring trout home from the brook by the gills is also a *gad:* "That's the prettiest gad o' trout I ever saw!"

gad v

To prod or whip with a **gad** n[1] **1;** to goad.

1906 *DN* 3.118 **sIN,** *Gad.* . . To punish; to whip, as a child. "I bet he gads him good." **1975** Gould *ME Lingo* 105, [Gad] is also a verb; to *gad* an ox, or to *gad* somebody figuratively into action.

gad n[2] Also *gadder* [Cf *gadabout*] *derog*

A runabout, busybody.

1867 Hill *Homespun* 161, All the town gads and gossips . . loiter, and talk, and listen in this most convenient place of public reception [=the country store]. **1884** Grant *Average Man* 45, Mamma is always complaining about my being such a gad down there . . but I can't see the harm of seeing people naturally. **1907** *German Amer. Annals* 9.376 **sePA,** *Gad.* . . A run-about; gossip. (Usually of women.) "There goes that good-for-nothing gad." **1915** *DN* 4.199, *Gad,* an idle woman. "The old gad! She would do well to stay at home and take care of her child." **1916** *DN* 4.337 **PA,** *Gad.* . . A talkative person. **1930** Shoemaker *1300 Words* 25 **cPA Mts** (as of c1900), *Gadder*—A trapesing, gossiping woman, a "gadabout".

gad n[3] Also sp *gadd* [Prob abbr for **gadwall]**

See quot 1930.

1930 Shoemaker *1300 Words* 27 **cPA Mts** (as of c1900), *Gad*—the Wild Goose. **1940** Richter *Trees* 47 **sOH** (as of c1800), Then you give us special treats like gadd or duck.

gadder n[1] See **gad** n[2]

gadder n[2] [Var of *gad* euphem for *God*]

1942 Whipple *Joshua* 62 **UT** (as of c1860), Here every man *will love his neighbor.* . . Or else, by gadder, we'll shoot him! *Ibid* 457, By gadder, Jake, you do the prayin' and I'll do the fightin'!

gadder v, n[3] See **gather**

gaddle See **gadwall**

gaddop, gaddup See **get up** v phr **1**

gaddy See **gadwall**

gaden See **garden**

‡**Gadfly** n Cf *DS* C33

1906 *DN* 3.137 **nwAR,** *Gadfly.* . . Facetious name applied to a small or remote hamlet or railway station.

gadling rod n [Perh rel to **gad** n[1]]

A divining rod.

1969 *DARE* (Qu. CC13a, . . *A forked stick that's used to show where there's water underground*) Inf **GA**74, Gadlin' rod—made of peach wood; (Qu. CC13b) Inf **GA**74, Gadlin' rod operator.

gadnipper See **gallinipper**

gad stick See **gad** n[1] **1**

gadwall n Also *gaddle, gaddy, gadwale, gadwall duck, gadwell* [*OED* 1666 →; etym unknown]

A gray to grayish-brown duck *(Anas strepera)* similar in size to the **mallard.** Also called **blating duck, creek duck, fool mallard, German duck, glissom duck, gray duck b, gray widgeon 1, prairie mallard, redwing, shuttlecock, specklebelly, Welsh drake, widgeon**

1814 Wilson *Amer. Ornith.* 8.121 **Sth,** The Gadwall . . is a very quick diver. **1839** Audubon *Synopsis Birds* 278, Gadwall Duck. . . Breeds in Texas, and westward to the Columbia River, Fur Countries, and sometimes in the States of New York, Massachusetts, and Maine. Rather common in autumn and spring in the middle Atlantic districts; more so in the Southern and Western States. **1887** *Amer. Field* 27.3/2 **CO,** The bulk of the birds after the teals leave are widgeons and gadwalls. **1888** Trumbull *Names of Birds* 24, *Gadwall* (spelled also "Gadwell," "Gadwale," etc.) . . Used at Chicago even by marketmen and gunners. **1894** *Harper's New Mth. Mag.* 89.456/2 **ND,** The air was now full of flying birds—mallards, . . butterballs, gadwalls, widgeon, and canvas-backs. **1923** U.S. Dept. Ag. *Misc. Circular* 13.10, *Vernacular Names. In general use.* Gadwall (also spelled gadwell, gadwale, sometimes shortened to gaddy). **1950** *WELS (Kinds of wild ducks)* 1 Inf, **ceWI,** Gadwall. **1967–70** *DARE* (Qu. Q5, . . *Kinds of wild ducks*) Infs **IA**3, **IL**9, **VA**47, 52, 79, Gadwell; **CA**136, Gadwell [gædwəl]; **CA**140, Gadwall; **UT**4, Gaddle. **1982** Elman *Hunter's Field Guide* 147, Hunters also mistake gadwalls for baldpates. . . Since the gaddy is the only surface-feeder with a substantially white speculum, it should be easy to identify on a freshwater hunting marsh.

gaff n, v Pronc-spp **chiefly NEng** *gaft, garft;* **appar chiefly West** *gav,* pl *galves* [*OED gaff* sb.[1] 1. a "An iron hook; a staff . . armed with this"; a1300 →]

A Forms. [Cf Intro "Language Changes" I.8; see also *EDD* (at *gaft*), *DNE*]

1827 Cooper *Red Rover* 3.151, The ship in sight carries a naked gaft. **1905** [see **C1** below]. **1933** [see **C2** below]. **1945** Colcord *Sea Language* 84 **ME, Cape Cod, Long Island,** A gaff is . . a pole with a hook in the end, used to lift fish on board a fishing-vessel. This is the source of a 'longshore verb, to gaft. **1961** [see **B1** below]. **1969** *DARE* (Qu. P13, . . *Other ways of fishing*) Inf **VT**16, Seine, nets, spear, gaft—all illegal. **1974** [see **C1** below]. **1975** Gould *ME Lingo* 105, *Gaff*—Usually pronounced *garft.*

B As noun.

1 The spike of a spur; a spur. [*OED gaff* sb. 3. a "A steel spur for a fighting cock"; 1688 →]

1810 Pike *Expeditions* 3rd app 36 **SW,** A sort of jack-boot . . to which are fastened the spurs, by a rivet, the gaffs of which are sometimes near an inch in length. **1933** [see **C2** below]. **1961** Adams *Old-Time Cowhand* 92, Them hooks, or galves, as he called 'em, were mighty necessary in his work.

2 In logging: see quots.

1956 Sorden–Ebert *Logger's Words* 15 **Gt Lakes,** *Gaff,* The steel hook on a pike pole. **1958** McCulloch *Woods Words* 69 **Pacific NW,** *Gaff*—The pointed or business end of a pike pole used by boom men in shoving logs around a pond. It has both a spike and a spur. **1968** Adams *Western Words* 123, *Gaff*. . . In logging, the steel point of the pike pole, consisting of a screw point and a spur.

3 =**gad** n[1] **1.**

1966–68 *DARE* (Qu. K27, . . *The sharp-pointed stick used to get oxen to move*) Infs **NC**53, **OK**20, **PA**127, Gaff.

4 A swelling or protuberance; see quot. [Perh by ext of *W3* [3]*gaff* 4. a "something painful or difficult to bear"]

1969 Sorden *Lumberjack Lingo* 46 **NEng, Gt Lakes,** *Gaff*. . . A tender or sore spot on an animal's body due to an improperly fitted harness. . . A swelling on a tree trunk. . . A protuberance or swelling of almost any kind.

5 See quot. [Perh rel to *guff;* cf *gaffe*]

1966 Barnes–Jensen *Dict. UT Slang* 17, *Gaff*. . . unbelievable talk.

C As verb.

1 with *onto:* To get hold of. Cf **gaffle** v

1905 Wasson *Green Shay* 65 **NEng,** Them folks there to the Island have got the taste of blood amongst'em now in good shape, and seems 's though their cal'lation was this winter to 'touch up' everything in sight,—blame' lucky if they don't gaft [Footnote: Seize] onto the gear and whole shootin' match, clip and clean! **1974** *AmSp* 49.62 **swME** (as of c1900), He gafted onto some money.

2 To spur.

1933 *AmSp* 8.1.28 **nwTX,** *Gaff* (often pronounced *gav*). To spur. Also a noun: *give him the gaff.* **1968** Adams *Western Words* 123, *Gaff*—To spur a horse.

3 To rescue someone from the water with a boathook or similar implement. [By ext from *gaff* to land a fish with a gaff]

1950 Moore *Candlemas Bay* 19 **ME,** If Johnny Allen hadn't come along in his punt and gaffed him out, Guy would have died there. **1975** Gould *ME Lingo* 105, *Gaff*. . . To grab or rescue. . . When a largish summer lady slipped on a gang-plank and needed assistance, Tim Mosely described his alert response this way: "I just garft her and steered her into the bo't on her belly."

gaffel See **gaffle v 1**

gaffer n[1] [*OED* 1575 → as a title for a man respected for age or position; in the present sense 1841 →; see also *EDD*]

A senior or head workman; a foreman or **straw boss.**

1894 *DN* 1.335 [Glass industry term], *Gaffer:* one who finishes bottle by putting mouth upon it. **c1930** Swann *Lang. Circus Lot* 9, *Gaffer:* The circus manager, the big boss. **1930** Williams *Logger-Talk* 17 **Pacific NW,** *Gaffer:* Foreman. **1958** McCulloch *Woods Words* 69 **Pacific NW,** *Gaffer*—A side rod [=the man in charge of one side or unit of a logging operation] or foreman. **1966–68** *DARE* (Qu. HH43a, *The top person in charge of a group of workmen, the* ———) Infs **NY**59, **WA**11, Gaffer; (Qu. HH43b, *The assistant to the top person*) Inf **WA**11, Gaffer. **1968** Adams *Western Words* 123, *Gaffer*—A logger's name for the general superintendent. A miner's name for the shift boss

gaffer n[2], **gaffer woodpecker, gaffle** n See **gaffle woodpecker**

gaffle v [Cf **gaff C1**]

1 also sp *gaffel:* To grasp, seize; to take hold of and carry; to steal, swindle; to arrest. **chiefly NEng**

1900 Day *Up in ME* 24, Gaffled up his britches' slack. *Ibid* 142, Gaffle your peavies. **1902** Day *Pine Tree Ballads* 218 **ME,** [In a square dance call:] Gaffle holt an' gallop for an eight hands round. **1914** *DN* 4.73 **ME, nNH,** *Gaffle*. . . Take or seize hold of. **1940** *Sat. Eve. Post* 10 Feb 9/1 **NY,** He paid Chadd . . for tending the stable, gaffling the swill out of the kitchen to the hogs . . and helping Mrs. Mott. *Ibid* 79/1, I kind of gaffled five dollars out of him, and probably he don't like it. [**1964** in 1982 *DNE,* He gaffled a big bark pot, an iron pot, out o' the after room, an' he gaffled that un overboard.] **1967** Maurer–Vogel *Narcotics* 357, *Gaffel.* 1. To shoplift or steal. 2. To arrest.

2 with *on(to)* or *up:* To take hold of (something); to take possession of (something). **appar NEng**

1900 Day *Up in ME* 90, Jest gafflin' up a couple boards / I sashayed out deerectly to'ards. **1907** *DN* 3.244 **csME,** *Gaffle on to*. . . Possess oneself of hastily, or without formality. "I gaffled on to that in a hurry." **1945** Colcord *Sea Language* 84 **ME, Cape Cod, Long Island,** *[Gaff]* is the source of a 'longshore verb, to . . gaffle on to something. "I'm goin' to gaffle on to that last piece o' punkin pie." **1975** Gould *ME Lingo* 105, A group of men *gaffle* or *gaffle* onto a heavy object and all lift together. The boss-man will say, "Allright, now, all hands gaffle on!"

gaffle woodpecker n Also *gaffer (woodpecker), gaffle* [See quots 1900, 1956] Cf **yaffle**

=**flicker** n[2] **1.**

1900 *Wilson Bulletin* 31.6, *Gaffle Woodpecker.* Hudson, Massachusetts. Perhaps a provincial corruption for "gaffer"—a talkative old man. . . Or a corruption of "Yaffle." **1927** Forbush *Birds MA* 2.292, Northern Flicker. Other names . . Gaffer woodpecker. **1955** Forbush–May *Birds* 291, *Northern Woodpecker*. . . Gaffer Woodpecker. **1956** MA Audubon Soc. *Bulletin* 40.82, *Yellow-shafted Flicker*. . . Gaffer (Mass.); Gaffle (Conn.); Gaffle Woodpecker (Mass. Names apparently adapted from those of the Green Woodpecker, the most similar European species; "yaffle," a British folk name for that bird, refers to its "laughing" note.)

gaff onto See **gaff C1**

gaff-top See **gaff-topsail catfish**

gaff-topsail n

1 See **gaff-topsail catfish.**

2 See **gaff-topsail pompano.**

gaff-topsail catfish n Also *gaff-topsail, gaff-top* [See quot 1887]

A chiefly marine catfish *(Bagre marinus)* of the Atlantic and Gulf coasts. Also called **blue catfish 3, four-whiskered sea cat, joe cat, saltwater catfish, sea catfish, sea kitten, turd-rustler**

1882 U.S. Natl. Museum *Bulletin* 16.111, *AE[lurichthys] marinus*. . . *Sea Cat-fish; Gaff-top-sail.* Dusky bluish, silvery below. **1887** Goode *Amer. Fishes* 379, The Gaff-topsail Catfish, . . which ranges from Cape Cod to Florida, is found chiefly in brackish water. . . It is known . . at Brunswick, Ga., as "Gaff-topsail," in allusion to the shape of the first dorsal fin. **1906** NJ State Museum *Annual Rept. for 1905* 165, The Gaff Topsail Cat Fishes. . . Dr. C. C. Abbott records this fish from the lower Delaware waters, though it is unusual out of salt-water. **1933** LA Dept. of Conserv. *Fishes* 250, But we happen to have in Louisiana . . two Marine Catfishes . . , the Gaff Topsail . . and the Hardhead. *Ibid* 253, The Hardhead has four "whiskers" or barbels on his lower jaw instead of two as in the Gaff-top. **1955** Carr–Goin *Guide Reptiles* 61 **FL,** Gafftopsail Catfish. . . A broad-headed, silvery-blue catfish with a forked tail. . . Only 4 barbels on head. **1966–70** *DARE* (Qu. P2, *[In saltwater areas] What kinds of saltwater fish caught around here are good to eat?*) Infs **LA**31, 37, Gaff-topsail catfish; **TX**14, 88, Gaff-top; (Qu. P4, *Saltwater fish that are not good to eat*) Inf **TX**19, Gaff-top. **1968** *DARE* FW Addit **csLA,** *Gaff-top*—a saltwater catfish with high dorsal fin. **1973** Knight *Cook's Fish Guide* 381, Gafftopsail—Catfish, Gafftopsail.

gaff-topsail pompano n Also *gaff-topsail* [In ref to the dorsal fin]

A **pompano:** esp *Trachinotus glaucus,* but also *T. falcatus* or *T. rhodopus.*

1882 U.S. Natl. Museum *Proc.* 5.270, *Trachynotus* [sic] *glaucus*. . . *Gaff-top-sail Pompano*. . . Not rare; reaches a weight of two pounds; a food-fish of mediocre quality. **1887** Goode *Amer. Fishes* 203, The Banner Pompano, *T. glaucus,* . . is not rare along the Carolina and Gulf coasts, and . . at Pensacola, wherever it is known as the 'Gaff-topsail Pompano,' it is held in low esteem. **1902** Jordan–Evermann *Amer. Fishes* 314, *Gaff-topsail Pompano. Trachinotus glaucus.* This beautiful fish is found from Virginia to the Caribbean Sea. **1911** U.S. Bur. Census *Fisheries 1908* 314, Other species [of *Trachinotus*] found on our eastern coast are the "old-wife," or "gaff-topsail pompano," the "round pompano," or "Indian River permit." **1935** Caine *Game Fish* 112, *Round Pompano. Trachinotus falcatus.* . . Gaff-topsail Pompano. **1960** Amer. Fisheries Soc. *List Fishes* 30, Gafftopsail pompano. . . P[acific]. . . *Trachinotus rhodopus.* **1973** Knight *Cook's Fish Guide* 381, Gafftopsail . . or Pompano, Gafftopsail.

gaft See **gaff**

gag n

Either of two **groupers 1 b:** usu *Mycteroperca microlepis,* but also *M. venenosa.*

1884 Goode *Fisheries U.S.* 1.413, There appear to be . . at Key West, as well as in Bermuda, various local forms closely related to this [=a rockfish], one of which is known by the name "Gag." **1896** U.S. Natl. Museum *Bulletin* 47.1177, *Mycteroperca microlepis.* . . *Gag.* . . Along the coast of Florida it is generally abundant on the banks and reefs, and is an important food fish. **1902** Jordan–Evermann *Amer. Fishes* 392, *M[ycteroperca] microlepis,* the gag, occurs from Beaufort, North Carolina, and around the coast of Florida to Pensacola. . . At Key West it is a common fish at all times, reaches a weight of 10 pounds, and is highly esteemed. **1935** Caine *Game Fish* 69, Gag. *Mycteroperca microlepis. Ibid* 77, *Yellow-fin Grouper. Mycteroperca venenosa.* . . *Synonyms* . . Gag. **1946** LaMonte *N. Amer. Game Fishes* 52, *Gag. Mycteroperca microlepis.* . . Chiefly offshore on banks and outside reefs. *Ibid* 53, *Mycteroperca venenosa.* . . *Names* . . Gag. **1960** Amer. Fisheries Soc. *List Fishes* 31, Gag. . . *Mycteroperca microlepis.*

gaga See **grandma** n **A13**

gage v [Aphet form of *engage*] *Gullah*

To engage; hence ppl adj *gaged,* n *gagement.*

1888 Jones *Negro Myths* 130 **GA coast,** Ebry body roun de settlement blan gage um fuh mek de music fuh dem fuh dance. One day eh bin gwine fuh keep eh gagement fuh play at er party. [=Everybody around the settlement would engage him to make the music for them to dance to. One day he was going to keep his engagement to play at a party.] **1922** Gonzales *Black Border* 303 **sSC, GA coasts** [Gullah glossary], *Gage*—engage, engages, engaged, engaging; hire, hired, etc. **1966** *DARE* (Qu. AA4a, . . *A man who is very eager to get married . . "He's ______."*) Inf **SC**10, 'Gaged [FW: from *engaged*].

gaggle v [Pronc-sp for *gargle*]

1952 Brown *NC Folkl.* 1.544, *Gaggle* ['gægl]. . . *Gargle.*—Central and east. Illiterate.

gagrish n [PaGer *gegrische, gegreisch* yelling]

A loud cry.

1939 Aurand *Quaint Idioms* 14 [PaGer], Stop your *Gagrish* (loud cry); you ain't goin' to be kill't.

gagroot n [See quot 1889]

=Indian tobacco.

1876 Hobbs *Bot. Hdbk.* 40, Gag root, Lobelia, Lobelia inflata. **1889** *Century Dict.* 2429, *Gagroot.* . . The *Lobelia inflata,* so called from its emetic properties; more usually known as *Indian tobacco.* **1901** Lounsberry *S. Wild Flowers* 486, Indian tobacco . . or gag-root. . . Its stem and leaves . . have been used in domestic practice as an emetic. **1919** (1923) House *Wild Flowers NY* 280, *Lobelia inflata.* . . The different names given in different localities (Gagroot, . . Asthma Weed, etc.) give some idea of the herbal character of the species. **1949** Moldenke *Amer. Wild Flowers* 244, Of interest because of its narcotic-poisonous juice is the . . *gagroot.* . . It . . was at one time used by herb doctors in the treatment of asthma. **1971** Krochmal *Appalachia Med. Plants* 164.

gahdeen See **guardian**

gahm See **gaum** n[1]

gahp See **gape**

gaieta See **galleta**

gaillardia n Usu |gəˈlɑrdiə|; also occas |gəˈlɑrdə|; pl occas |gəˈlɑrdiz| Pronc-sp *golardia*

A Forms.

1950 *WELS Suppl.* **csWI** (as of 1930s), *Gaillardia*—pronounced [gə'lɑrdə]. The only person I ever heard call it a [gəlɑrdiə] was a schoolteacher. *Ibid* **ceWI,** Those are [gəlɑrdiz]. **1979** Stegner *Recapitulation* 21 **UT,** God pity the woman. . . as she walked. Ass over teacup into a fountain or a bed of golardias.

B Sense.

Std: a plant of the genus *Gaillardia.* Also called **bandanna daisy, beach daisy, blanket flower, brown-eyed Susan 2, firewheel, Indian blanket, joe bell flower, Navajo blanket flower, sand dollars.** For other names of var spp see **Indian sunburst, niggertoe, pincushion daisy**

gaily adj Also sp *galy, gayly* [Scots, nIr, nEngl dial; see *EDD* (at *gaily*) and *SND* (at *geylies*)] **S Midl**

1 Of a horse: lively, spirited.

1773 (1957) Fithian *Jrl. & Letters* 177 **VA,** When a Horse is frolicsome & brisk, they, say at once he is "gayly." **1884** *Anglia* 7.271, Er gaily ridin'-hoss = A spirited riding-horse. **1899** (1912) Green *VA Folk-Speech* 192, *Gayly.* . . Spirited: as a *gayly* horse. *Galy.* **1903** *DN* 2.314 **seMO,** *Gaily.* . . Lively. 'That horse is mighty gaily.'

2 also adv; Of a person: well, in good health.

1903 *DN* 2.314 **seMO,** In response to 'How do you do?' the response is often 'Gaily!' **1917** *DN* 4.412 **wNC,** *Gaily.* . . Well. "The folks is gaily." **1926** *DN* 5.400 **swMO, nwAR,** *Gaily.* . . In good health. "My chaps [=children] is all right peart an' gaily now." **1931** *PMLA* Dec 1319 **Appalachians,** "I'm as gaily as a gal, but not half so pretty." (Answer to a salutation.) **1934** (1970) Wilson *Backwoods Amer.* 67 **AR, MO,** I hope the folks over your way is all gayly. **1939** *Hall Coll.* **eTN,** Do you feel *gaily* tonight? **1940** *AmSp* 15.52 **Appalachians, Ozarks,** We're all tol'able gaily (well, in good health) over to our place. **1944** *PADS* 2.23 **sAppalachians,** I'm as gaily as a buck. (Feeling in excellent spirits.) **1952** Brown *NC Folkl.* 1.544, *Gaily.* **1953** Randolph–Wilson *Down in Holler* 246 **Ozarks,** *Gaily.* . . In good spirits, or good health. **1954** *Harder Coll.* **cwTN,** Gaily. **1972** Cooper *NC Mt. Folkl.* 92, *Gayly.*

gain v

To fatten (an animal).

1931–33 *LANE Worksheets* **ceVT,** Gain . . cause to gain weight. Speaking of a man taking care of cattle during the winter: He gained them.

gain, on the adj phr **Nth, esp NEast**

In the process of recuperating or improving.

1850 Mitchell *Lorgnette* 1.57 **NY,** The town is certainly on the gain in these matters. **1894** (1934) Robinson *Danvis Folks* 18 **VT,** Their mother . . had been ill for weeks with an intermittent fever, but was now "on the gain." **1943** *LANE* Map 496 **CT, MA, VT,** On the gain. **1950** *WELS (Someone who has been very sick and is getting better)* 2 Infs, **WI,** On the gain. **1968–70** *DARE* (Qu. BB46) Infs **MI**92, **MA**38, **NH**14, **NY**150, 191, 234, On the gain. [4 of 6 Infs old]

gaited adj [Etym uncert]

1951 *PADS* 15.70 **nLA,** *Gaited.* . . Tired, weary. "I've worked so hard today I am gaited."

gaiter n [By ext from *gaiter* an ankle-high shoe, usu with elastic panels on the sides]

A low shoe or overshoe.

1908 *DN* 3.313 **eAL, wGA,** *Gaiter.* . . A low cut shoe. **1941** *LANE* Map 366 *(Low shoes)* 1 inf, **cMA,** Gaiters . . low shoes. **1950** *WELS (Rubber footwear)* 3 Infs, **WI,** Gaiters. [Described as old-fashioned by 1 Inf] **1966–69** *DARE* (Qu. W8, . . *Low canvas-top shoes with rubber soles)* Inf **MO**17, Gaiters; (Qu. W11, *Men's low, rough work-shoes)* Infs **MS**6, **NC**61, Gaiters; (Qu. W13, . . *Kinds of rubber footwear;* total Infs questioned, 75) Inf **GA**1, Gaiters—same as overshoes: low tops, not to work in.

gait on, get a v phr

To hurry up.

1963 in 1982 *Barrick Coll.* **csPA,** Gait, get a, on—*hurry up* "She'll have to get a gait on."

gal n Usu |gæl|; also |gjæəl| Also sp *gall*

A Forms.

1840 [see **gal** v]. **1934** *AmSp* 9.212 **Sth,** *Gal* [gjæəl]. **1941** *AmSp* 16.7 **eTX** [Black], [gjæəl].

B Sense.

=girl n **B.**

1922 Gonzales *Black Border* 222 **sSC, GA coasts** [Gullah], Gal, ef you tek off dat middle-blouse een dis house befo' dese mans, you will sho' hab sin. [*DARE* Ed: The speaker is a woman.]

gal v, hence vbl n *galling*

=**girl** v.

1840 Haliburton *Clockmaker* (3d ser) 31, I am a-goin' down to Sy Tupper's to . . spend the evenin'.—Exactly, said he, goin' a-gallin'; I know'd it. . . She is rich . . that gall. **1920** Hunter *Trail Drivers TX* 300, Going courting is "goin' gallin'." **1927** *DN* 5.474 **Ozarks,** *Gal. . .* To seek feminine society. "Th' boys allus goes a-gallin' of a Sunday." *Gallin'* is somewhat more respectable than *tom-cattin',* but considerably less so than *sparkin',* which latter term frequently implies serious matrimonial intentions.

galak v, hence vbl n *galaking* Also sp *galack* [Back-formation from *galax,* understood as pl] **Appalachians**

To gather **galax** or other ornamental greenery to sell to florists; hence n *galaker* one who gathers such greenery.

[**1901** Lounsberry *S. Wild Flowers* 402, To many that have never seen the blossoms [of galax] these leaves are familiar, for the mountain people pick them by the million, and tie them into little bunches of a hundred each which later are sent to florists in different parts of the country.] **1940** in 1944 *ADD* **NC,** 'Galakers' Finish Chopping Earlier. . . 'Galaking' is a year-round occupation. **1941** *AmSp* 16.31 **NC,** To a vast, scattered army of North Carolina *galakers* Christmas is in the air. *Galaking* is the business of collecting decorative greens, the term being derived from galax leaves. **1974** Fink *Mountain Speech* 11 **wNC, eTN,** *Galack* . . to gather galax or other ornamental greens. "They are going galacking." **1976** Garber *Mountain-ese* 32 **Appalachians,** *Galacking* . . picking greens—In the spring the wimmen git their baskets and go galackin' together.

galamander n Also *galander, gerrymander* **ME** [Perh fanciful varr of *salamander;* cf **katydid**]

See quot 1975.

1965 *Yankee* Oct 26/2 **ME,** Visiting recently in Vinalhaven, Maine, I saw an old vehicle they called a "galander." I could not imagine how such a thing could hoist great long blocks of granite, which it's supposed to do. **1975** Gould *ME Lingo* 105, *Galamander*—A wagon with very large wheels, equipped with derrick so huge blocks of granite may be underslung and transported from the quarry. The Rev. W.H. Littlefield, once pastor of Vinalhaven's Union Church, is credited with inventing the device, although smaller vehicles had earlier used somewhat the same principle for moving heavy ship timbers. Restored *galamanders* may be seen on exhibition at Vinalhaven and Franklin. **1981** *DARE* File **Vinalhaven ME,** Gerrymander, with a hard /g/—used on the island of Vinalhaven Maine for the large, horse-drawn wagon used to haul granite blocks from a quarry. An old man there pointed to an old wagon . . , told me that was its name & spelling. **1982** *Ibid* **csME,** The "galamander" mentioned . . was similar to that used in the lumber camp; two great wheels seven or eight feet high with a heavy axel [sic] from which heavy loads such as stone slabs or logs could be slung for hauling.

gala-nipper See **gallinipper 1**

ga-lant See **gallant**

galax n |ˈgelæks, -lɪks| Cf **galak**

A low-growing evergreen plant *(Galax aphylla)* native from Virginia to Georgia. Also called **beetleweed, carpenter's leaf, coltsfoot 5, galaxy, pine-barren-beauty, skunk cabbage, wand flower**

1857 Gray *Manual of Botany* 262, *Galax. . .* A smooth herb, with a thick matted tuft of . . rootstocks, . . sending up round-heart-shaped crenate-toothed and veiny shining leaves. **1901** Lounsberry *S. Wild Flowers* 402, As we see the galax blossoms pluming themselves along some shaded bank, we feel that they are a truly splendid assemblage. . . It is, however, with the leaves that our thoughts linger longest. . . It was Mrs. Kibbee . . who first recognized their decorative value and sent them out from North Carolina. **1915** *Torreya* 15.17 **GA,** People who know the galax only through its popular use for decorative purposes are not likely to become acquainted with its distinctive odor. **1941** Walker *Lookout* 53 **TN,** Galax . . is more highly prized for its . . evergreen leaf than for its . . white flowers. . . Harlan P. Kelsey was perhaps the first man to introduce galax leaves to the northern florists for decorative purposes. **1961** Douglas *My Wilderness* 173 **wNC,** The galax, with shining green leaves, was turning bronze. **1966** *DARE* Wildfl QR Pl.60a Inf **WA30,** Galax. **1966** *DARE* (Qu. T16) Inf **NC36,** Galax leaves—area famous for it. **1982** Ginns *Snowbird Gravy* 203 **nwNC,** Mother said, "The last bread flour is gone. You better take Ray and go to Stone Mountain and pull some evergreen galax." **1990** *DARE* File **MN,** At the florist's where I worked some thirty years ago, employees always looked forward to the arrival of a new supply of shiny galax [ˈgelɪks] leaves from North Carolina.

galax out v phr [**galax** n; cf **galak**]

To get by galaking.

1952 Brown *NC Folkl.* 1.544, *Galax out. . .* To earn money by gathering galax. "Well, I've galaxed out a pair of shoes this week."

galaxy n [See quot 1911]

=**galax.**

1900 Lyons *Plant Names* 166, *G[alax] aphylla* . . called also Galaxy. **1901** Lounsberry *S. Wild Flowers* 402, *Galaxy. . .* As we see the galax blossoms . . , we feel that they are a truly splendid assemblage, a veritable milky way; and, since their name suggests it, we do not hesitate to connect their sparkling . . forms with some of the mysterious wonder we accord to the stars, blink-blinking against their sombre background. **1911** *Century Dict. Suppl., Galaxy. . .* Same as *galax* . . a play upon that name. **1931** Harned *Wild Flowers Alleghanies* 378, *Galaxy. . .* The name of this small plant probably . . [refers] to its milk-white flowers. **1949** Moldenke *Amer. Wild Flowers* 158, But probably few of us have seen this plant—the *galaxy* . . —growing in its native haunts. **1976** Bailey–Bailey *Hortus Third* 492.

gal 'bacco n [*gal* girl + aphet form of *tobacco*]

1939 *AmSp* 14.90 **TN,** *Gal 'bacco.* Snuff. 'She bought a box of gal 'bacco at the store.'

gal boy n

1 A tomboy; a mannish woman.

1848 Bartlett *Americanisms* 153, *Gal-boy.* In New England, a romping girl; called also a *tom-boy.* **1942** Berrey–Van den Bark *Amer. Slang* 405.3, *Masculine woman* . . gal-boy.

2 An effeminate boy. **Sth**

1881 Tourgée *Royal Gentleman & Zouri* 513 **Sth,** He might have a pony, a dog—anything but a doll. He was afraid he was going to grow up a "milksop sort of gal-boy, anyhow." **1898** Lloyd *Country Life* 30 **AL,** By this time you have seen a few "gal boys," as Aunt Nancy Newton calls them, but I ruther like a real, genuine, natural, healthy boy—one that can travel all the gaits and cover all the ground. It don't look natural and right for a boy to be as good and gentle and sweet as a girl. **1929** Sale *Tree Named John* 67 **MS,** Aunt Betsey laughed and said, "He's tellin' you de trufe now, Miss Sallie. En you cain' keep 'im a baby all de time, you cain't," and then she went to the kitchen. Uncle John laughed and said, "Let him go"; he wasn't going to have "no gal-boy" around him.

gald v, now usu as ppl adj *galded* (also sp *gallded*) [Back-formation from *galded,* pleonastic past pple of *gall;* cf **-ed suff 1;** *OED* 1555–1633 *"Obs."*] **chiefly Sth, S Midl** Cf **galding n**

To chafe, make sore by rubbing.

1795 Dearborn *Columbian Grammar* 135, [List of improprieties:] Galded for Gall'd. **1903** *DN* 2.314 **seMO,** *Galded. . .* Galled. 'That horse is badly galded.' **1907** *DN* 3.231 **nwAR, seMO,** *Galded.* . . Galled. **1908** *DN* 3.313 **eAL, wGA,** *Galded, pret.* and *pp.* of *gall.* **1912** Green *VA Folk-Speech* 190, A galded back. . . A galded shoulder. **1949** *PADS* 11.6 **wTX** (as of c1920), *Galded. . .* galled. **1954** *Harder Coll.* **cwTN,** [Of a horse with a gall on its neck:] He's galded and scalded; cut holes in pad to keep from hurting. **1956** *AmSp* 31.146 **IN** (as of 1890s), *Galded* (galled). **1961** Adams *Old-Time Cowhand* 9, Neither did a cowhand propose to get 'imself "galded" followin' a mule's tail from behind a plow. **1963** [see **galding** n]. **1966** *Wilson Coll.* **csKY,** *Gallded. . .* The collar gallded the horse's neck.

galding n [**gald;** cf *OED gald* v. quot 1684]

A sore caused by chafing; a gall.

1963 Watkins–Watkins *Yesterday Hills* 131 **cnGA,** Sometimes a man's crotch became so "galded" that he could hardly walk, and some used flour as a powder to help cure the "galding."

gale n[1] [From *gale* a strong wind; cf *SND gell* n.[2] 4 (var of *gale*) "A romp, spree, merry-making; a drinking bout. Phr. *on the gell,* on the spree" and *EDD gell* sb.[2] 3, with five exx from Scotl]

A state of excitement or merriment—esp in phrr *in a gale, in the gales.*

1838 *S. Lit. Messenger* 4.65/2 **VA,** On the way Wirt was in "a great gale;" his spirits high, his hopes buoyant, his gaiety of heart overflowing. **1859** (1968) Bartlett *Americanisms* 165, *Gale.* Among the ladies, a state of excitement; as, "Mrs. A——— was in quite a gale on New Year's Day." **1872** Schele de Vere *Americanisms* 476, Gale is in New England and in the South not unfrequently used to denote a state of pleasant excitement. "The children were in such a gale, it took us nearly an hour to get them to bed, and then they could not sleep for a long while." **1905** *DN* 3.10 **cCT,** *Gale*. . . A good time. 'We had a perfect gale.' **1929** *AmSp* 5.18 **Ozarks,** *In the gales*. . . Cheerful, optimistic, hilarious. "I knowed Paw was in th' gales—he was a-laughin' so's you could see his liver an' lights."

gale v [**gale** n[1]]

1913 *DN* 4.4 **ME,** *Gale*. . . To lead in boisterous fun-making. . . "Then she got to galing it."

gale n[2] [sEngl dial (*EDD gale* sb.[2] 1)]

1930 Shoemaker *1300 Words* 27 **cPA Mts** (as of c1900), *Gale*—An old bull recently gelded.

gale bird n

=**northern phalarope.**

1956 MA Audubon Soc. *Bulletin* 40.21, *Northern Phalarope*. . . Gale Bird (Mass. At home in stormy weather.)

galebury See **gallberry**

galette n Pronc-sp *gaulette* [Fr "(sea) biscuit"; *DCan* 1843 →]

See quots.

[**1859** in 1869 Chicago Acad. Sci. *Trans.* 1.154 **Canada,** *Galette* is the only form of bread used on a voyage, that is, when voyageurs are so fortunate as to have any flour at all. It is made in a very simple style:—the flour bag is opened, and a small hollow made in the flour, into which a little water is poured, and the dough is thus mixed in the bag; nothing is added . . [the cook] kneads it into flat cakes, which are baked before the fire, in a frying pan, or cooked in grease.] [**1903** White *Forest* 169 **Canada,** A big fire and a clothes-rack of forked sticks and a sapling, an open-air change, a lunch of hot tea and trout and cold galette and beans, a pipe—and then the inevitable summing up.] **1940–41** Cassidy *WI Atlas* 1 inf, **ceWI,** Galette, large flat biscuit made with sour milk and saleratus. **1986** Pederson *LAGS Concordance* **seLA, seMS,** 1 inf, Galette—fried bread; an old French term; 1 inf, Galette; 1 inf, Galette—some called hoecake; dough rolled flat; 1 inf, Galette—fried dough; 1 inf, Galette—fried bread; 1 inf, Galette—a flatbread. **1988** Erdrich *Tracks* 7 **ND,** A guest must eat. . . She found flour for gaulette.

‡**gal gravy** n [Perh *gal* girl, in ref to its paleness or weakness]

1966 *DARE* (Qu. H37, . . *Words . . for gravy*) Inf **FL33,** Gal gravy ['gæl 'greɪvi]—white, without color.

Galilee n [Because the Jews were slaves under the Romans in *Galilee*] Cf **homeland**

The southern US; see quot.

1954 Armstrong *Satchmo* 230 **New Orleans LA** (as of 1922) [Black], There was no place for colored people to eat on the train in those days, especially down in Galilee (the South). Colored persons going North crammed their baskets full of everything but the kitchen stove.

galingale n

1 Std: a plant of the genus *Cyperus.*

2 A sedgelike plant *(Dulichium arundinaceum).* Also called **three-way sedge**

1822 Eaton *Botany* 269, Galingale. . . Culm 3-cornered, leafy: spikelets spreading, about 6-flowered. Wet. **1832** MA Hist. Soc. *Coll.* 2d ser 9.149 **cwVT,** Dulichium spathaceum . . Galingale. **1840** MA Zool. & Bot. Surv. *Herb. Plants & Quadrupeds* 254, Galingale. . . A common, large, leafy, tough grass . . scarcely eaten by cattle. **1933** Small *Manual SE Flora* 141, *Sheathed-galingale*. . . Swamps, springy places, and pond-margins.

galinsoga n

Std: a weedy plant of the genus *Galinsoga.* Also called **German weed, quickweed.** For other names of var spp see **devil's buckwheat, Frenchweed 1, Peruvian daisy, raceweed**

galknipper See **gallinipper**

gall n[1] [Prob from the bitterness of the berries]

The **gallberry** tree or shrub.

1860 Curtis *Cat. Plants NC* 60, I[lex] glabra. . . This and the next species [=*Ilex coriacea*] are evergreen shrubs, . . called . . sometimes *Galls*, . . apparently derived from their black bitter berries. This is . . very common in the Branch swamps of the Lower District, and giving [sic] its name of Galls or Gall-bays to the low places chiefly occupied by it.

gall n[2] Also sp *gaul* [Transf from *gall* a sore caused by chafing]

1 also in combs *cane gall, cypress ~, muckle ~:* An area of low boggy ground, often supporting a dense thicket of cane, bushes, or small trees. [*EDD gall* sb.[2] 6 "A barren or unfertile spot in a field, through which springs of water constantly ooze up"] **esp S Atl** Cf **baygall**

1763 in 1952 *AmSp* 27.282 **SC,** The Fountains taking their Rise from the Mountains, in seeking their Way towards the Ocean, wherever they met with either Resistance or Cavity they bedded, and thereby formed the immense Number of Morasses, Savannahs, Cane and Cypress Galls, that are every-where interspersed in the Country. **1773** in 1953 McMullen *Topog. Terms FL* 115/1, Crossed a run in a Small Gall. **1812** Stoddard *Sketches LA* 125 **FL,** The second are called cypress galls, the soil of which is mostly composed of sand. They produce a kind of swamp cypress, as also plenty of wild grass. **1827** Williams *View W. FL* 53, The third kind of swamps are those spongy tracts, where the waters continually ooze through the soil, and finally collect in streams and pass off. These are properly termed galls, sometimes sour, sometimes bitter lands. . . When their foundation is alluvial matter, it is usually very thin, like quagmire: the land may be shaken for acres in extent. When the base is sand, it is always a lively quicksand, very dangerous for cattle. **1892** (1969) Christensen *Afro-Amer. Folk Lore* 38, Den 'e gone in de t'ick wood, gone 'longside de gaul [Footnote: swamp]. **1930** Woofter *Black Yeomanry* 53 **seSC,** *Gaul:* swamp. **1949** *AmSp* 24.109 **seSC,** *Gall*. . . A swampy hollow on high ground. **1954** *PADS* 21.28 **SC,** *Gall*. . . A low wooded area; an area overgrown with bushes or low trees, as a *muckle (myrtle) gall.* Eastern and coastal region. *Ibid* 33, *Muckle gall, cane gall.*

2 also in comb *clay gall:* An infertile or eroded patch in a field; also adj *galled.* [*EDD gall* sb.[2] 7 "*pl.* void spaces in coppices; spots of land in a field where the crop of corn or grass has failed"] **Sth, S Midl, esp VA**

1813 Taylor *Arator* 223 **VA,** Providence has blest our shallow soil with a capacity of suddenly throwing up thickets, constituting a bountiful provision for manuring and curing galls and gullies. *Ibid* 224, A caput mortuum of a galled and gravelly hill side. **1883** Amer. Philol. Assoc. *Trans.* 14.49 **SC,** Galled spots in a field are places where the soil has been washed away, or has been so exhausted that nothing will grow. The word is common in South Carolina, and perhaps generally in the South. **1884** Baldwin *Yankee School-Teacher* 8 **VA,** The scanty pastures set in thickets of pines, with red "galls" cropping out unexpectedly, and deep gullies where the soil had baked in the sun's fierce heat and cracked like earthquake seams. **1898** Harris *Tales Home Folks* 25 **GA,** Where the ridge and the hunt entered the woods there was what is known as a "clay gall," a barren spot, above two acres in extent. **1925** Glasgow *Barren Ground* 121 **VA,** Far beyond him, where a field had been abandoned because it contained a "gaul," or barren spot, where nothing would grow, she could just discern the scalloped reaches of the broomsedge. **1940** *Hench Coll.* **VA, KY,** The other day Shepperton . . told me he had heard a man—a farmer in the County—call gulleys in one of his badly washed fields *galls*. . . Two or three of the men spoke up, one or two from Virginia and one . . from Kentucky and said they knew the word well in this sense. **1944** *PADS* 2.7 **cAL, NC, VA,** *Clay gall*. . . Clay land from which the good soil has been washed. "It's a strange thing that the cotton on the rich lands this year is poor, but that on the clay galls is excellent."

gall n[3] See **bergall**

gall n[4] See **gal** n

gallace See **gallus** adj

gallant v Usu |g(ə)'lænt| Pronc-sp *ga-lant, g'lant* [*OED gallant* v. II 1672 →] **chiefly Sth, S Midl**

To court or flirt; to gad about, esp with members of the opposite sex; to escort (someone); hence vbl n *gallanting.*

1859 Elwyn *Glossary* 51, *Gallanting.* Wandering about in gayety and enjoyment; applied chiefly to the associations of the sexes. "He's gone a gallanting," is common in New England. **1859** in 1956 Eliason *Tarheel Talk* 273 **NC,** I would like to know. . . what girl you was gallanting around. **1883** (1971) Harris *Nights with Remus* 149 **GA** [Black], He galanted 'roun' 'mungs um, same lak one er dese yer town chaps. **1888**

Johnston *Mr. Absalom Billingslea* 200 **GA,** I were jest a-ridin' pe-rusin' about, Missis Rainwater. . . Ef you can't do no better, I'll ga-lant you that fur. **1892** Harris *On Plantation* 80 **GA,** I'm a-gwine dis night a gallantin' out wid you! [A line from a hog-caller's song] **1916** *DN* 4.347 **nwTX, LA,** *Gallanting.* . . Going off on a pleasure trip. La., with accent on the second syllable. **1942** in 1944 *ADD* **cWV,** ['glæntɪn]. He's g'lantin' her. **1951** *PADS* 15.70 **nLA** Words . . used mostly by the older persons of the villages and rural areas. . . *G'lant.* . . To . . "wait on" a girl. Said of a man who "dates" a girl. "I see that Harry has been g'lanting Louise lately." **1968** *Filson Club Hist. Qrly.* 42.158 **KY,** When an eldress wrote of a company of men and women coming from Russelville "to gallant over the premises," she probably meant "roam idly accompanied by the other sex."

gallases See **gallus** n

gallberry n, also attrib Also sp *galebury* [Prob from the bitterness of the berries, but perh from their use, like oak galls, in dyeing] **chiefly Sth**

A **holly** n^{1} **1** or its berries: *Ilex glabra* or *I. coriacea* which is also called **baygall bush, gall** n^{1}, **gallbush 1, highbush gallberry, inkberry, sweet gallberry.**

1709 (1967) Lawson *New Voyage* 97 **NC, SC,** Gall-Berry-Tree, bearing a black Berry, with which the Women dye their Cloaths and Yarn black; 'tis a pretty Evergreen, and very plentiful. **1763** (1925) Washington *Diaries* 1.190 **neVA,** The first quarter abounding in Pine and Galebury bushes. **1859** Perry *Turpentine Farming* 9 **NC,** After this, the land needs no cultivation, but every kind of turf should be turned over, such as low bush huckleberry, gallberry, . . and broom-sage grass. **1860** Curtis *Cat. Plants NC* 60, *Gallberry.* (I. glabra . .). This and the next species [=*Ilex coriacea*] are evergreen shrubs, indiscriminately called by the above name, . . apparently derived from their bitter black berries. **1901** Lounsberry *S. Wild Flowers* 314, *I[lex] glabra,* . . gallberry, . . grows well from Louisiana and Florida to Massachusetts. **1933** Rawlings *South Moon* 16 **FL,** Her hair grew thick and low, the shining black of gallberries. **1962** Kurz–Godfrey *Trees N. FL* 205, The large or sweet gallberry *[Ilex coriacea]* is more often seen as a shrub than a tree. It is not uncommonly associated with the shrubby, bitter gallberry, *Ilex glabra.* **1965–70** *DARE* (Qu. C6, *What do you call a piece of land that's often wet, and has grass and weeds growing on it?*) Inf **FL**34, Gallberry flat; (Qu. C30, *What do you call loose, dark soil?*) Inf **SC**43, Gallberry land; (Qu. F36, *Other kinds of brooms that people use around here*) Inf **GA**23, Gallberry broom; **MS**72, Gallberry broom—for sweeping yard; **SC**19, Gallberry bush broom—used for the yard; (Qu. H21, *What do you call the sweet stuff that's poured over these cakes?*) Inf **GA**36, Gallberry honey; (Qu. I44, *What kinds of berries grow wild around here?*) Inf **FL**17, Gallberries for brown dye—poisonous; **FL**19, 21, 27, **GA**11, **LA**40, Gallberries; (Qu. S26b, *Wildflowers that grow in water or wet places*) Inf **GA**5, Gallberry; (Qu. T15, *What kinds of swamp trees do you have?*) Inf **NJ**69, Gallberry (bush)—black, bitter-tasting berry. **1966** *DARE* Tape **NC**24, About six or eight birds [=quail] got up and they got about that high off the ground and swung around a little gallberry bush, we call 'em—that little evergreen bush with little black berries on it in the winter time; they feed on those sometimes when . . feed is real scarce, . . but not if they can get something else. **1976** Bailey–Bailey *Hortus Third* 590, *Large gallberry.* . . Evergreen shrub, to about 15 ft.

gallberry child n [In ref to its being conceived in the (gallberry) bushes] Cf *DS* Z11a, b

1981 Harper–Presley *Okefinokee* 140 **sGA** (as of a1951), *Gallberry child*—A child born out of wedlock.

gallberry railroad n Cf **huckleberry train**

1965 *DARE* (Qu. N37, . . *A branch railroad that is not very important or gives poor service*) Inf **FL**18, Gallberry Railroad—here; [it] passed [gallberry] bushes and got nickname.

gallbush n

1 The **gallberry** tree or shrub. [See quot 1728 Byrd] **Mid Atl**

1728 in 1886 NC *Colonial Rec.* 2.802, They measured . . 16 chains and 70 links to a Gall Bush. **1728** (1922) Byrd *Descr. Dismal* 18 **VA, NC,** In many parts [of the Dismal swamp] . . grows an evergreen shrub very plentifully, that goes by the name of a gall-bush. It bears a berry which dyes a black colour, like the gall of an oak, from whence it borrows its name. **1853** Simms *Sword & Distaff* 89 **SC,** The gall-bushes, which are apt to associate with it [=hurrah bush], mass themselves together with a luxuriance of top, which effectually closes every aperture of sight. **1966** *DARE* (Qu. T5, . . *Kinds of evergreens*) Inf **NC**21, Gallbush.

2 =**sweet gale.**

1899 (1912) Green *VA Folk-Speech* 190, Gall-brushes [sic]. . . A sort of myrtle growing in marshy places; bog-myrtle. Gale. **1900** Lyons *Plant Names* 255, *M[yrica] Gale.* . . Gall-bush. **1940** Clute *Amer. Plant Names* 227, *Myrica Gale.* Gall-bush. **1946** *PADS* 6.14 **eNC,** *Gall bush.* . . A small evergreen bush (about three feet high) that grows abundantly in low flat lands. Bears berries. *((Myrica gale?))* . . Common.

gallded See **gald**

gallding See **gaulding**

galled See **gall** n^{2} **2**

gal-leg See **girl-leg**

gallerp See **gallop**

gallery n [Fr *galerie; OED* a1500 → (see esp sense 2, 1509 →), but US distrib suggests reinforcement from LaFr] **chiefly Gulf States, AR, TX** See Map

A porch, veranda, or balcony.

1784 (1925) Washington *Diaries* 2.283 **VA,** The dwelling House is to be 36 feet by 24, with a gallery of 7 feet on each side of the House. **1845** (1968) Simms *Wigwam & Cabin* (1st ser) 109 **MS,** I threw down the broad-axe . . and went towards the gallery (piazza) where the old man was sitting. **1903** *DN* 2.314 **seMO,** *Gallery.* . . Porch; veranda. **1905** *DN* 3.80 **nwAR,** *Gallery.* . . Veranda, porch, piazza, portico, balcony. **1908** *DN* 3.314 **eAL, wGA,** *Gallery.* . . A veranda or porch. Also called piazza. . . All these terms are used, but *gallery* is perhaps the commonest in colloquial usage. *Front gallery, back gallery, side gallery,* are used to designate the position of the veranda. **1911** *DN* 3.538 **eKY. 1916** *DN* 4.269 **New Orleans LA, NC,** *Gallery.* . . Used indiscriminately for: porch, stoop, veranda, balcony. **1923** *DN* 5.197 **swMO,** We was a-settin' out yander on the gallery a-smokin' an' a-jawin' one another. **1931** Faulkner *Sanctuary* 169, They reached Memphis in midafternoon. . . Popeye turned into a narrow street of smoke-grimed frame houses with tiers of wooden galleries. **1933** *AmSp* 8.1.31 **nwTX,** *Gallery.* Porch. **1938** *AmSp* 13.319, In the South, as represented by Virginia, Florida, Louisiana, and Texas . . a *gallery* is always roofed, otherwise is equivalent to porch but belongs rather higher in the social or architectural scale. It is recognized as a local term but is liked and is in general use. **1945** Saxon *Gumbo Ya-Ya* 156 **LA,** Creole houses often faced these patios, were built with their backs on the street. . . There were always balconies above—still known as 'galleries' in New Orleans. **1954** Armstrong *Satchmo* 160 **LA,** The place we lived in had two porches . . but we called them "galleries," as the word "porch" was unheard of to us then. **c1960** *Wilson Coll.* **csKY. 1965–70** *DARE* (Qu. D17, . . *The platform, sometimes with a roof, that's built on the front or the side of a house*) 52 Infs, **chiefly Gulf States, AR, TX,** Gallery; **LA**3, Gallery—on old homes; usually across the front; may have upper and lower gallery [FW: ['gælɚɪ]; rapid pronc is ['gæːrɪ]]. [*DARE* Ed: 22 of 53 Infs indicated that this was the older term.] **1990** Pederson *Regional Matrix* 452 **Gulf Region,** [The map shows 180 instances of *gallery,* scattered, but chiefly in **sAL, MS, LA, eTX.**]

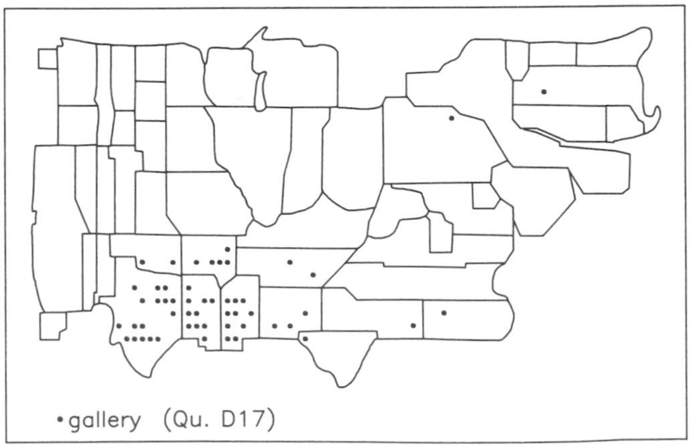

galleta n Also *galleta grass* Pronc-spp *gaieta, gietta grass* [Span *galleta* hardtack]

A forage grass of the genus *Hilaria,* esp *H. jamesii,* native chiefly to the Southwest. Also called **tobosa.** For other names of var spp see **black grama 2, curly mesquite 1, mesquite, southwestern buffalo grass, wire grass**

1856 in 1948 *Western Folkl.* 7.10 **swCA,** Here there is also plenty of fine bunch grass, differing from and superior to the galleta. **1856** *Wide West* (S.F.) Oct. 4/6 *(DA),* Galleta grass. **1872** *Overland Mth.* Aug 146/1 **sAZ,** The coarse, dry bunch-grass or *gaieta,* never abundant on this route, was unusually scarce that summer. **1889** Vasey *Ag. Grasses* 34, *Hilaria Jamesii* (Gietta Grass). . . This is one of the characteristic grasses of the arid districts of Texas, New Mexico, and Arizona. . . Relished by cattle. **1913** (1979) Barnes *Western Grazing* 43 **AZ, NM,** This area may properly be classed as a semi-desert country with considerable grass, mostly . . species of Hilaria known variously as Galleta (guy-et-ta), black bunch grass and curly mesquite. **1919** Chase *CA Desert* 196, About ten o'clock I found a few scraps of blue-stem (galleta grass) and burro-weed . . and we stopped to rest and lunch. **1937** U.S. Forest Serv. *Range Plant Hdbk.* G70, Galleta. . . grows on mesas, plains, and deserts. . . Galleta grass . . in . . northwestern . . New Mexico . . often forms practically pure stands which cover many miles of terrain. **1968** Abbey *Desert Solitaire* 29 **seUT,** Descend to the alkali flats of Salt Valley and you find an entirely different grouping: shadscale, . . budsage, galleta-grass. **1974** Munz *Flora S. CA* 975, *Hilaria. . . Galleta.* Stiff perennial grasses with solid culms and narrow blades.

galleta grass See **galleta**

‡galley-endways adv [Prob blend of **galley-west** + **endways**]
=**galley-west.**

1902 Day *Pine Tree Ballads* 129 **ME,** I can slat him galley-endways and not use one-ha'f my strength.

galleywampus adj [Prob blend of **galley-west** + *wampus*] Cf **catawampus** adj

1967 *DARE* (Qu. MM13, *The table was nice and straight until he came along and knocked it* ______) Inf **CA**9, Galleywampus.

galleyway n
=**cellarway.**

1968 *DARE* (Qu. D20, *Names for a sloping outside cellar door*) Inf **NJ**17, Galleyway.

galley-west adv, adj Also *galley-west'ard, gilly-west* Also sp *gally-west* [Varr of Engl dial *collywest(on)* contrarily, askew] **chiefly Nth** See Map Cf **high, west, and crooked**

Into confusion, in all directions, completely away; crooked—usu in phrr *knock galley-west, go galley-west.*

1875 in 1917 Twain *Letters* 1.250, Your verdict . . has knocked what little [critical penetration] I *did* have gally-west! **1901** *DN* 2.140 **NY,** "John knocked him gally-west," i.e., gave him a telling or finishing blow. **1902** Munn *Rockhaven* 3 **N Atl,** Thinkin' I'd set the price high 'nough ter knock him galley west. **1903** *DN* 2.351 **seIA,** *Galley-west (to knock). . .* To give a finishing or knockout blow. **1904** Day *Kin o' Ktaadn* 124 **ME,** And Joe throwed galley-west'ard the duds the crew had hung. **1909** *DN* 3.411 **ME,** *Galley west. . .* Used with the verb *to knock.* **1941** *AmSp* 16.22 **IN,** *Galley-west and crooked.* **1965–70** *DARE* (Qu. MM13, *The table was nice and straight until he came along and knocked it* ______) 29 Infs, **chiefly Nth,** Galley-west; **CA**164, Galley-west an' crooked, **PA**230, Gilly-west; (Qu. MM12a, . . *'In all directions' . . "He shot into a flock of birds and they went* ______*."*) Infs **MA**24, **NY**22, 105, **OR**4, Galley-west; **CA**136, All galley-west; (Qu. MM12b, . . *She broke her beads and they went* ______) Inf **CA**102, Galley-west. **1968** *DARE* File **KS,** Swat him galley-west. [To a remote place.] **1977** Cheever *Falconer* 108 **NEng,** He stopped so abruptly that several men banged into him, scattering the dream galley-west.

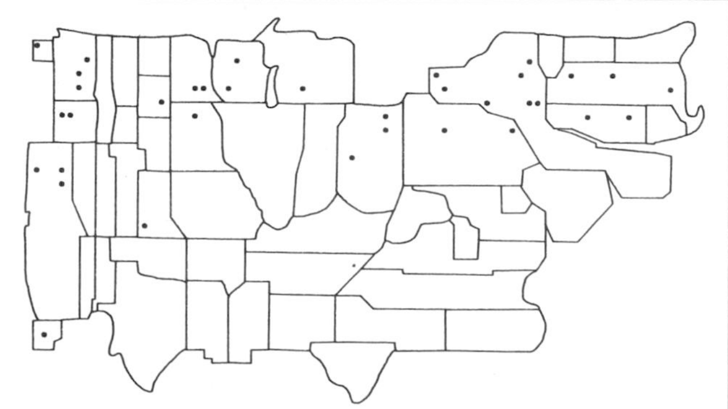

•galley-west + varr (Qq. MM13, MM12a, b)

galleywobbles n [Var of **gollywobbles,** infl by *galley* ship's kitchen]

1949 *AN&Q* 8.136, A Navy acquaintance . . reports *galley-wobbles* as the form in use [for *stomach-ache*] among sea-going men.

gallflower n [See quot 1901]
A **gentian** (here: *Gentiana quinquefolia*).

1901 Lounsberry *S. Wild Flowers* 428, *Gentiana quinquefolia. . .* Through these parts of the country the mountain people call it the gall-flower because its juices are so bitter. **1940** Clute *Amer. Plant Names* 57, *G. quinquefolia. . .* Gall-flower. **1959** Carleton *Index Herb. Plants* 50, *Gall-flower:* Gentiana quinquefolia.

gallices See **gallus** n

gallie n [Cf *EDD galley-bird* the green woodpecker]
=**flicker** n^2 **1.**

1900 *Wilson Bulletin* 31.6, *Gallie.* Northern New Jersey. Pretty generally so called by the bird nesting boys. . . Evidently an abbreviation of the old English title, "Galley-bird," which according to Charles Swainson in "Provincial Names of British Birds," is the Sussex name for a woodpecker. The old time supposition was that all of this tribe were doomed to "incessant toil and slavery:" hence the term.

gallied See **gally**

gallihoot v, hence vbl n *gallihooting* Also *galliflute* Also sp *gallyhoot* Cf **callyhooting, scallyhoot**
To gallivant; to go rapidly.

1921 Thorp *Songs Cowboys* 73 **TX,** And I went a-galliflutin' [downhill on a bicycle] like a crazy lightnin' streak. **1941** *AN&Q* 1.133/1, The word "gallihooting"—without the last letter, of course, is current in southern Indiana. It appears to be related to "gallivanting." [**1950** *PADS* 14.18 **SC,** *Callihootin . . , cahootin', gallihootin: . .* At high speed, same as "lickety-split."] **1966** *Good Old Days* Jan 23/1 **IN** (as of 1890s), One Mom continued to scold, saying, "Sally, I am ashamed of you. Off gallyhooting around and leaving little Annie to mind the dishes."

galling See **gal** v

gallinipper n Also *galknipper, gallinapper, gallon dipper, ~ nipper, gan(ni)nipper, gollynipper, gullynapper, gurnipper;* for addit varr see quots [Etym unknown; the orig form has clearly been much altered by folk-etym and other processes, but cf **gally** v.]

1 Any of several insects, as:

a A large mosquito of the genus *Megarhinus* or *Psorophora,* esp *P. ciliata.* **chiefly Sth, S Midl, esp S Atl** See Map on p. 620 Also called **gabber napper, galliwopper, granny-nipper 1** Cf **horse mosquito** Note: Some of these mosquitoes do not bite.

1634 Wood *New Engl. Prospect* 46, The third is Gurnipper which is a small blacke fly no bigger than a flea; her biting causeth an itching upon the hands or face, which provoketh scratching. **1709** in 1851 Prot. Episc. Hist. Soc. *Coll.* 64 **NJ,** Poor brother Jenkins was baited to death with musquitoes, and blood thirsty Gal-Knippers, which would not let him rest night nor day. **1801** *Port Folio* (Oldschool) 1.40/3 **Philadelphia PA,** Musquitos, Ants and Gnats, begin / With Fire-flies to assail his skin,/ Of Gallinippers too a monstrous host. These Gallinippers . . / Who toil not for themselves, or earn their food,/ But suck the hungry peasant's blood,/ 'Mongst tiny gnats a giant race. **1810** Cuming *Sketches* 275 **cwMS,** There are but few musquitoes on the dry part, but a low, drowned point . . swarms with them, and many of the largest size, called gannipers. **1831** *Daily Eve. Transcript* (Boston MA) **NY,** I have been pricked by a stiletto—by the gallon-nipper, by the blood-sucker, and the hornet. **1834** *Life Andrew Jackson* 115, It was good for 'em it warn't in July. Had it bin, the Kentuckians mite've bin spar'd, as the gallinippers . . wou'd've settled the hash, and the gineral woud've lost all the glory without a shot. **1890** Howells *Boy's Town* 31 **OH,** Fiery dragons could not have kept them out; gallynippers, whatever they were, certainly did not. **1901** Howard *Insect Book* 102, The mosquitoes of [the genera] *Megarhinus* and *Psorophora* are very large, and include the forms known in various parts of the country as gallinippers. **1906** Casey *Parson's Boys* 67 **sIL** (as of c1860), Some lusty "Gallinippers"—so called, the victim had explained to the boys because at each "nip" they took a gallon—were trying to puncture his bronzed skin. **1930** Stoney-Shelby *Black Genesis* 179 **seSC,** Skeeter an' gallinipper jine han's to tek place o' dem, an' suck we blood. **1960** Criswell *Resp. to PADS 20* **Ozarks,** Gallnipper is used for a large insect which may be a very large mosquito, but it does not seem to me to be that. **1965–70**

DARE (Qu. R15b, *Any names for an extra-big mosquito?*) 152 Infs, **chiefly Sth, S Midl, esp S Atl,** Gallinipper; 13 Infs, **chiefly Sth, S Midl,** Gallinapper; **AR**32, **MO**8, 19, Galnipper; **SC**2, Gallinipper ['gælınıpə]; gallon dippers ['gæləndıpəz], as a child; **IL**69, Gollynipper; **IL**114, Gullynapper.

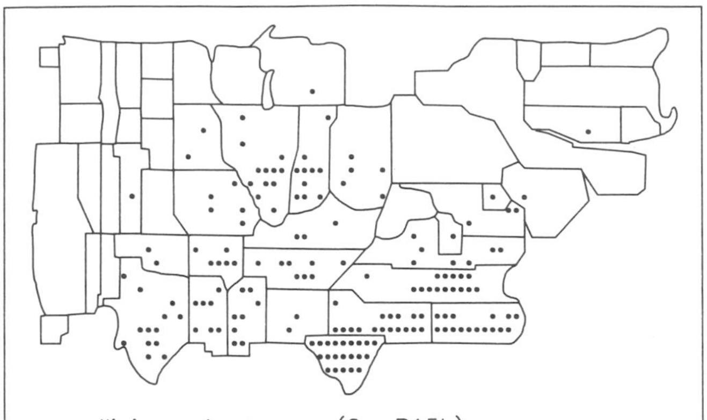
•gallinipper 1a + varr (Qu. R15b)

b A large biting fly such as those of the genus *Stomoxys.* *obs* Cf **Georgia piercer**

1674 Josselyn *Two Voyages* 122, There is another sort of fly called a Gurnipper that are like our horse-flyes, and will bite desperately. **1790** *PA Packet & Daily Advt.* (Philadelphia) 11 Oct 3/4 **PA,** A ganninipper is a kind of large horse-fly, frequent in pine woods, the sting of which is extremely poisonous as well as painful. **[1829** Mactaggart *3 Yrs. in Canada* 1.186, The gadnipper, a large species of gadfly, is also common, but not so troublesome as those above described.] **1862** *Harper's New Mth. Mag.* 25.737/1, The *Stomoxys georgina*—"Georgia Piercer," or "Gallinipper"— . . if curses could annihilate it, would soon be driven from off the earth.

c =crane fly.

1906 *DN* 3.137 **nwAR,** *Gally-nipper*. . . An insect resembling, but larger than, a mosquito. **1930** Shoemaker *1300 Words* 26 **cPA Mts** (as of c1900), *Gala-nipper*—A huge insect of the mosquito type, but harmless. **1938** Brimley *Insects NC* 314, *The Crane Flies.* Long-legged flies somewhat resembling mosquitoes in general appearance, but without scales on the wings and often much larger, being then sometimes mistaken for giant mosquitoes and called gallinippers. None however can bite or suck blood. **1938** *Hench Coll.* **VA,** Gallinippers. . . Great big mosquitoes with long trailing legs. **1940** Teale *Insects* 153, A common insect often mistaken for a large and ferocious mosquito . . is the crane fly. . . Its gangling, awkward, threadlike legs trail, behind it when it flies. In the sandhill country of northern Indiana, we used to call crane flies "gallinippers" and thought they were giants of the mosquito tribe. **1942** McAtee *Dial. Grant Co. IN* 27 (as of 1890s), *Gallinipper* . . a long-legged fly (crane-fly) sometimes seen in houses; the folk etymology differs from that of N.I.D. connecting the word with galley, being gal nipper; crane-flies, however, do not bite; the word is not used for the real biters—mosquitoes—as usually reported elsewhere. **1950** *WELS Suppl.* **WI,** Gallynapper—large mosquito, three times the size of a mosquito; fly size, but very slender in shape, like mosquito. **1953** Randolph-Wilson *Down in Holler* 246 **Ozarks,** *Gallynipper*. . . The original gallynipper was a gigantic mosquito, according to the old-timers. The term is applied to other flying insects, particularly the crane flies *(Tipulidae),* which look like mosquitoes, but are nearly two inches long. **1963** TN Folk Lore Soc. *Bulletin* 29.82, *Bugs*—The general name for small life is *bugs.* This term includes *spiders; grand-daddies* or *daddy-longlegs; crane-flies* or *gallinippers;* . . and others not so picturesquely named.

d A dragonfly.

1967 *DARE* (Qu. R2, *What other names do you have around here for the dragonfly?*) Inf **MO**11, Galnipper. **1987** *DARE* File, In . . some records which I [=Gordon Wood] collected . . in the 1940s, I have come across . . *gallinipper* (dragon fly) from Escambia County, Alabama.

2 Transf: see quot.

1944 Duncan *Mentor Graham* 126 **IL,** Many a rural gallinipper hove in, a "dominacker" rooster under his arm to put up to fight for drinks.

gallious See **gallus** adj

gallito n [Span "little rooster"]

1 A long-spurred **violet** such as *Viola pedunculata.* **CA** Cf **rooster**

1906 Parsons *Wild Flowers Calif.* 124 *(DA),* The Spanish-Californian children knew them as "gallitos." **1920** Rice *Calif. Wild Flowers* 57 *(DA),* They are seen but to be loved, and they may be called Violets, Pansies, Johnny-Jump-Ups, or by the Spanish children's name of Gallitos.

2 A **prairie coneflower** (here: *Ratibida columnifera).*

1936 Whitehouse *TX Flowers* 173, *Niggerhead, Thimble Flower (Ratibida columnaris)* is also called . . "gallitos."

3 A **ball moss** (here: *Tillandsia recurvata).*

1970 Correll *Plants TX* 356, *Tillandsia recurvata. . . Gallitos.* Plants typically in dense ball-like clumps, rarely more than 15 cm. tall.

galliwopper n [Perh blend of **gallinipper 1a** + **golly-whopper]**

1967-69 *DARE* (Qu. R15b, . . *Names for an extra-big mosquito)* Infs **GA**77, **IA**8, Galliwopper.

gallnipper See **gallinipper**

gall of the earth n

1 A **false foxglove** (here: *Aureolaria flava).* *obs*

1804 Michaux *Voyage à l'Ouest* 161 **KY,** Au milieu de ces graminées, croit une grande variété de plantes, parmi lesquelles dominoient alors: la *Gerardia flava, gall of the earth.* [=In the midst of these "barrens" grow a great variety of plants, among them . . *Gerardia flava, gall of the earth.*]

2 =rattlesnake root (here: *Prenanthes* spp, esp *Prenanthes serpentaria).* [See quots 1830, 1869, 1974]

1830 Rafinesque *Med. Flora* 2.253, *Prenanthes. . . Gall of the Earth.* . . Many sp. . . Root and milk very bitter, used in dysentery. **1848** Gray *Manual of Botany* 249, *N[abalus] Fraseri. . . Gall-of-the-earth.* . . Dry sandy or sterile soil, S. New England to Penn. and southward. **1869** Porcher *Resources* 477, *Gall of the Earth.* . . The root is excessively bitter; it is used in domestic practice in South Carolina as a tonic. . . *P[renanthes] serpentaria.* **1892** (1974) Millspaugh *Amer. Med. Plants* 94, *Prenanthes serpentaria. . . Gall-of-the-earth. Ibid* 94/2, As Gall-of-the-earth, it has been known in domestic practice from an early date. . . A decoction of the root has been found useful in dysentery, anemic diarrhoea, and as a stomachic tonic. **1896** *Jrl. Amer. Folkl.* 9.193, *Prenanthes* (any species), gall of the earth, Southern M[ain]e. **1910** Graves *Flowering Plants* 413 **CT,** *Prenanthes serpentaria.* . . Gall-of-the-earth. . . *Prenanthes trifoliolata.* . . Gall-of-the-earth. . . *Prenanthes altissima.* . . Gall-of-the-earth. **1946** Tatnall *Flora DE* 283, *P. trifoliolata. . . Gall-of-the-Earth.* Infrequent, in woods. **1974** (1977) Coon *Useful Plants* 115, *Prenanthes alba* . . gall-of-the-earth. . . It makes a bitter tonic and has been used for dysentery.

3 A **wild lettuce** (here: *Lactuca floridana).*

1840 MA Zool. & Bot. Surv. *Herb. Plants & Quadrupeds* 120, At the South, another species, there indigenous, *S[onchus] Floridanus,* . . is used as a remedy for the poison of the rattlesnake, and is called *Gall of the Earth.* **1848** Craig *(OED), Gall of the earth,* a name given in North America to the plant *Sonchus floridanus,* a species of the Sow-thistle. **1911** *Century Dict. Suppl., Gall-of-the-earth. . . (a)* Any plant of the genus *Nabalus,* especially *N. serpentarius.* See *Prenanthes. (b) Lactuca Floridana* of the eastern United States. *(c) Pterospora andromeda* [sic], more properly called *pine-drops.*

4 A **pinedrops** (here: *Pterospora andromedea).*

1876 Hobbs *Bot. Hdbk.* 40, Gall of the earth, Prenanthes Fraseri. Gall of the earth, Albany beech drops, Pterospora andromeda [sic]. **1900** Lyons *Plant Names* 310, *P[terospora] Andromedea.* . . Gall-of-the-earth. **1911** [see **3** above]. **1940** Clute *Amer. Plant Names* 228, *Pterospora andromedea.* . . Gall-of-the-earth.

5 A **gentian** (here: *Gentiana quinquefolia).* Cf **gallflower**

1940 Clute *Amer. Plant Names* 57, *G[entiana] quinquefolia.* . . Gall-of-the-earth. **1950** Gray-Fernald *Manual of Botany* 1161, *G[entiana] quinquefolia.* . . Stiff G[entian], Ague-weed, Gall-of-the-earth.

6 A **fringed orchid** (here: *Habenaria orbiculata).*

1959 Carleton *Index Herb. Plants* 50, *Gall-of-the-earth:* Habenaria obiculata [sic].

gallon n

A Form.

Sg used as pl (usu when preceded by a quantifier). Cf **foot n B2b**

1899 Chesnutt *Conjure Woman* 13 **csNC** [Black], Mars Dugal' made a thousan' gallon er [=of] scuppernon' wine eve'y year. **1936** (1947) Mencken *Amer. Lang.* 462, The general disregard of number [in "the common speech"] often shows itself when the noun is used as object. . . Especially when preceded by a numeral, such words as . . *gallon* . . retain their singular form. **1968** *DARE* Tape **IN**23, They made gallons and gallons of sorghum molasses. . . And maybe we'd have thirty gallon of sorghum made. . . Sometime maybe we had thirty gallons of sorghum; **IN**36, They'd give 'bout four gallon at a milking, some of 'em. **1976** Wolfram-Christian *Appalachian Speech* 117, Studies of some non-mainstream varieties of English have indicated there is a pattern in which the plural form typically represented by -s (or -es) in spelling, is occasionally absent . . In A[ppalachian] E[nglish], . . the pattern is limited almost exclusively to nouns of weight and measure when preceded by a quantifier . . [Examples include] two gallon of moonshine; three, four gallon of that; so many gallon.

B Sense.

A unit of dry measure. [sEngl dial; *EDD gallon* sb.[1] 1]

1906 *DN* 3.137 **nwAR,** *Gallon*. . . Both a *dry* and a liquid measure. "How much are June apples a gallon?" "New Irish potatoes are thirty cents a gallon." Universal.

gallon dipper (or nipper) See **gallinipper**

gallon of electricity n Also *gallon of prop-wash*

A nonexistent item used as the basis for practical jokes.

1968-69 *DARE* (Qu. HH14, *Ways of teasing a beginner or inexperienced person—for example, by sending him for a 'left-handed monkey wrench': "Go get me______.")* Inf **IN**42, Gallon of electricity; **IL**54, Gallon of prop-wash.

gallop v Pronc-sp *gallerp;* rarely interpreted as *gall up* (cf Jamaican creole interpretation of *develop* as *devel up* in Cassidy *Jamaica Talk* 5)

A Forms.

1883 (1971) Harris *Nights with Remus* 220 **GA** [Black], 'T wuz a whole team er spotted horses, en dey went gallin'-up des lak de yuther horses. [Footnote:] Galloping. **1909** *S. Atl. Qrly.* 8.51 **sSC coast** [Gullah], 'E spuh 'e hoss, an' come er gallin-up de road. **1923** (1946) Greer-Petrie *Angeline Doin' Society* 18 **csKY,** She'd make him a good wife, 'stid of gallerpin' around on them hosses.

B Sense.

Of water: to boil rapidly. [Engl dial]

1980 *DARE* File **ceNE,** [Label on package of Morton's corned beef brisket:] Bring water to boil and reduce heat immediately to simmer, making sure water does not gallop.

galloper n Cf **galloping goose**

1945 Hubbard *Railroad Ave.* 343, *Galloper*—Locomotive, the *iron horse.*

galloping consumption n Also *galloping catarrh, ~ con(sumpt), ~ fever, ~ T.B.*

A virulent form of **consumption.**

1914 Furman *Sight* 33 **KY,** Evy, her onliest little gal, was took. She died of the breast-complaint; some calls it the galloping consumpt'. **1950** *WELS (Nicknames . . for tuberculosis)* 3 Infs, **WI,** Galloping consumption; [All Infs identify this as old-fashioned]; 1 Inf, Galloping con, if progress of disease is very rapid. **1965-70** *DARE* (Qu. BB10, . . *Names or nicknames . . for tuberculosis*) 48 Infs, **scattered, but least freq Nth, West,** Galloping consumption; **NY**66, Galloping catarrh; **IL**5, Galloping fever; **SC**34, Galloping T.B. **1969** Kantor *MO Bittersweet* 19, The whole devil's dictionary of diseases—They called them by various names. Called them galloping consumption, febrile shakes . . or just plain plague. **1973** Van Noppen-Van Noppen *Western NC* 105, [An]other well-known disease of the area, in the vernacular, [was] . . "gallopin' consumption."

galloping dandruff n Also *crawling dandruff, mechanized ~, mobilized ~, traveling ~, walking ~* *joc* or *euphem*

Head lice.

1940 *AmSp* 15.447 **eTN,** *Crawling dandruff.* Head-lice. 'The baby's head is full of crawling dandruff.' **1965-70** *DARE* (Qu. R25, . . *A head louse, or body louse*) Infs **AL**62, **MN**2, **NY**34, 66, 84, 183, **TX**40, 42, **VT**16, **WI**48, 61, **WV**14, Galloping dandruff; **GA**72, **SC**69, **TX**37, Crawling dandruff; **PA**223, Mechanized dandruff; **OK**25, Mobilized dandruff; **VT**16, Traveling dandruff; **TX**35, Walking dandruff.

galloping fence n Also *galloping rail fence* **esp Mid Atl** Cf **jack fence, stake-and-rider fence**

A type of rail fence; see quots.

1896 *DN* 1.417 **NC,** *Gallopin, gallopin-fence:* fence made of rails stuck in the ground criss-cross. **1915** *DN* 4.183 **VA,** *Galloping fence*. . . A fence of rails set in the ground at about forty-five degrees, crossing each other at the opposite end. Such fences were formerly used on steep hills. **1959** *Hench Coll.* **wVA,** [Legend on postcard:] The variety of rail fences in this area are Snake, Post and Rail, and Galloping or Rabbit. **1967-68** *DARE* (Qu. L62, *A fence made of split logs*) Inf **SC**32, Galloping (rail) fence—two posts at each joint, put close together; stack the rails alternately; **SC**34, Galloping fence, alternately stack rails between two posts close together; **SC**39, Galloping fence [FW sugg; Inf has heard but can't describe.]; **VA**14, Gallopin' fence; (Qu. L65, . . *Other kinds of fences*) Inf **SC**30, Galloping fence—two posts, and logs are laid running in opposite directions between the posts; better for low places, as high water would float away a crooked fence. **1971** Wood *Vocab. Change* 370 **GA,** Galloping fence [volunteered in response to query about a kind of wooden fence]. **1986** Pederson *LAGS Concordance,* 1 inf, **cnGA,** Galloping fence—laid out in zigzag fashion.

galloping fever See **galloping consumption**

galloping Gertie n Cf **galloping goose**

1967 *DARE* (Qu. N37, *Joking names for a branch railroad that is not very important or gives poor service*) Inf **WA**20, Galloping Gertie.

galloping goose n **West** *joc*

1 A small, makeshift, or decrepit passenger train, engine, or piece of rolling stock; see quots.

1942 Berrey-Van den Bark *Amer. Slang* 774.16, *Trolley car*. . . gallop [sic] bathtub *or* goose. **1945** Hubbard *Railroad Ave.* 343, *Galloping goose*—A shaky section car. **1950** *Western Folkl.* 9.117, *Galloping goose.* A passenger-speeder operating on a set schedule over a logging railroad. **1950** Howe *Rocky Mt. Empire* 49 **CO** (as of 1930s), The Southern's miracle machinists procured an aged Rolls-Royce automobile engine, fashioned a ten-passenger cab on trucks behind it, and articulated a baggage car to that. Out on the main line this clattering nonesuch instantly acquired the name and fame of "Galloping Goose." **1952** FWP *Guide SD* 86, *Galloping goose:* A gas propelled, combined express and passenger railroad car, distinguished by striped front. **1958** McCulloch *Woods Words* 69 **Pacific NW,** *Galloping goose*—a. Any small steam or diesel locie which does not run smoothly. b. A three- or four-wheeled old time steam traction engine used to pull heavy log carts in the California pine country. c. A loose-joined speeder [=rail motor car] or crummy [=caboose]. **1962** *AmSp* 37.133 [Logging railroad language], *Galloping goose*. . . Any steam or diesel locomotive which does not run properly. **1966-68** *DARE* (Qu. N37, . . *A branch railroad that is not very important or gives poor service*) Infs **MN**16, 33, **MT**4, **NE**10, **UT**4, Galloping goose. **1966-67** *DARE* Tape **ND**3, On the way back we were coming across a railroad crossing, and my gosh, here comes the old galloping goose and—with passengers on—it's what they call a galloping goose here; **WA**30, [Inf:] A speeder is a four-wheeled thing like a galloping goose. . . Maybe it's twelve, fourteen feet long or maybe longer. Isn't a hand car. It's got an engine, a car engine in it, sides on it, windows in it. Transports men back an' forth to work. [FW:] What's a galloping goose? [Inf:] That's the same thing only a little bit bigger. **1967** *DARE* FW Addit **CO,** [Radio:] I came here because my husband was a mining engineer and we came in on the little galloping goose. . . That was forty-two years ago.

2 Transf: an airplane.

1942 Berrey-Van den Bark *Amer. Slang* 757.1, *Airplane*. . . galloping goose.

galloping rail fence See **galloping fence**

galloping T.B. See **galloping consumption**

galloptious See **galluptious**

gallow See **gallus** n

gallows n

1 A frame for hanging or supporting something, as:

a also pronc-sp *gallus:* A support for shocks of corn or other grain, made by fastening several adjacent stalks together.

1862 IL Dept. Ag. *Trans.* 5.160, I selected the gallows stalks, or breaks of my shocks [of sorghum]. **1872** (1876) Knight *Amer. Mech. Dict.* 936/2, *Gallows* . . The central core of four corn-stalks interlaced diagonally, and bound at the intersection, forming a *stool* or support for cut corn, which is bound around it to form a *shock.* **1923** *DN* 5.208 **swMO,** *Gallus hill* . . One of the hills of corn used as a support for a shock of fodder. **1938** *Reader's Digest* Aug 124/2, First you find the four central hills in an area 14 hills square, bend down the tops, and tie them all together. The "gallus" thus formed, which is not to be cut until the fodder is hauled in, is the core of the shock, and provides something against which to lean the first armfuls of fodder. **1971** *DARE* FW Addit **MI,** *Gallows*—the four middle stalks of corn tied together at the top to form the basic support of a corn shock. These were cut when the shock was tipped over for the ears to be husked. [Inf suggests that the word is old-fashioned.]

b usu *gallows frame;* In mining: a frame over a shaft supporting the hoisting mechanism.

1858 (1868) Stone *Put's Original* 29 **West,** When first I went to mining,/ I was uncommon green,/ With a "gallus" rig I went to dig, and claimed a whole ravine. **1877** U.S. Treas. Dept. *Mines for 1875* 148 **NV,** When the fire abated, so as to permit me to get to the shaft, I found that the heavy timbers of the gallows-frame, partially burned, had fallen down the shaft. **1879** *Scribner's Mth.* Oct 811/1, There being every indication that wealth is just beneath their picks, they erect over the shaft [of a Colorado lead mine] a frame-work of heavy timbers, called a "gallows," and hang in it a large pulley. **1926** *AmSp* 2.87/1 **West,** The cage [for lowering and raising men and ore] hangs on steel *cables* run over a *shive wheel* which is supported by a *gallows frame.* **1929** *AmSp* 5.146 **CO** [Mining terms], The support for the hoisting machinery is called the *gallows frame.* **1969** *DARE* Tape **CA**128, Well, a head frame is just a thing with the wheels up on top, see, where the cables from the hoist go over the top of this frame and they're tied onto your skips to let 'em down underground. . . Or a gallows frame—a lot of 'em call 'em gallows frames. **1971** Brunvand *Guide Folkl. UT* 33, Here . . is a partial list of mining . . terms collected from one Park City miner. . . Gallows frame.

c also *hog-gallows:* A frame used to hang a hog carcass. [Austr Engl; *AND* 1847 →]

1899 (1912) Green *VA Folk-Speech* 190, *Gallows.* . . A pole supported on forks on which hogs are hung to dry after killing and cleaning. **1930** Shoemaker *1300 Words* 29 **cPA Mts** (as of c1900), *Hog-gallows*—A trestle where hogs are hung after slaughtering. **1939** *Daily Progress* (Charlottesville VA) 22 Dec 5/2 *(Hench Coll.),* Gradually, the "gallows" is decorated with three or more carcasses. The men dissect the hogs and the meat is set in a safe place to cool. **1946** *PADS* 6.15 **NC,** [The gambrel is] inserted between the bone and the tendon of the hind legs of a hog to suspend the hog from a device called a *gallows.* **1982** *Barrick Coll.* **csPA,** Gallows [gálas]. . . In Perry County, the three-poled frame used for hanging hogs at butcherings is called a *gallows.*

d See quot.

1982 *Barrick Coll.* **csPA,** Gallows ['gæləs]—upright frame and cross-pieces at front and rear of a hay-wagon.

2 See **gallus** n.

gallows adj See **gallus** adj

gallows v See **gallus** v

gallowses See **gallus** n

gallows frame See **gallows** n **1b**

gallows up See **gallus** v

gall ring berry n

An **inkberry** (here: *Ilex glabra*).

1913 *Torreya* 13.232, *Ilex glabra.* . . Gall ring berry, St. Vincent I[slan]d, Fla.

gall shirt n [Prob var of **gauze shirt**] **Sth** *chiefly among Black speakers; somewhat old-fash*

1970 *DARE* (Qu. W15, *A shirt-length undergarment worn by women*) Infs **FL**48, **SC**70, **TN**53, Gall shirt; **FL**51, Undershirt—old people used to wear them till May; gall shirt [is] the right name; **VA**35, Gall [gɔəl] shirt—like men's vest; **VA**69, Gall shirt—same as undershirt: long, lightweight, knitted undershirt; can't buy [them] anymore; **VA**73, Gall shirt [gɒl šɜt]—older women wear them. Slipover [is the same thing]. [6 of 7 Infs Black] **c1971** Agee *Student Talk* 4 **GA,** (Sleeveless undergarment) 7 Infs, Gall shirt.

gall up See **gallop**

galluptious adj Also sp *gal(l)optious, galopshus, goloptious, goluptious;* for addit varr see quot 1913 [*OED goluptious* 1856 →; cf **ker-**] *old-fash*

Excellent, delightful, delicious.

1895 *DN* 1.389 **seNY,** *Galloptious:* splendid, excellent. **1910** Porter *Strictly Business* 120, To know your own power . . —say, girls, it's galluptious. **1913** *DN* 4.18 **NE,** *Galoptious.* Delightful, luscious, a general superlative. Facetious. . . "Isn't this a galoptious day?" *Galloptious. . . Galopshus. . . Globsloptious.* . . "That's mighty globsloptious cake." *Goberslooptious. . . Gobsloptious. . . Goloptious. . . Goluptious.* **1942** Berrey–Van den Bark *Amer. Slang* 29.4, *Excellent; first-rate.* . . galoptious. *Ibid* 135.6, *Delicious; "tasty".* . . galoptious. *Ibid* 277.6, *Pleasant, delightful.* . . galoptious. **1942** McAtee *Dial. Grant Co. IN* 27 (as of 1890s), *Galloptious* . . splendid.

gallus n, usu pl *gallus(s)es* Usu |'gæləsɪz|; also occas |'gɑ-, 'gɛ-| Pronc-spp *gallases, gallices, gallowses, goluses* Also sg *gallows,* rarely *gallow* [Var of *gallows,* but in US often interpreted as a distinct word; widespread in Brit folk use in var forms—see *OED gallows* sb. 6, *EDD gallows* sb. 6]

1 A suspender; the strap of a pair of overalls. *old-fash* Cf **one-gallus(ed)**

1806 *Spirit of Pub. Jrls.* 154, It must be very handy to have shoulder-straps instead of gallowses—besides *gallows* is an ugly name. **1836** (1838) Haliburton *Clockmaker* (1st ser) 127 **NEng,** Chock full of spring like the wire eend of a bran new pair of trowser gallusses. **1843** (1916) Hall *New Purchase* 329 **IN,** He always appeared . . with . . one "gallus" hard strained to keep up his greasy and raggy breeches. **1892** *DN* 1.230 **KY,** *Gallows* [gæləs]: suspenders [*DN* Ed: pl.? or sing. [gæləs], pl. [gæləsɪz], as elsewhere?]. **1899** (1912) Green *VA Folk-Speech* 190, *Gallowses.* . . Gallases. Goluses. **1902** *DN* 2.235 **sIL,** *Galluses.* **1903** *DN* 2.297 **Cape Cod MA** (as of a1857), *Galluses.* **1905** *DN* 3.10 **cCT,** *Galluses.* [Considered rare by one inf, unknown to the other two]. *Ibid* 81 **nwAR,** *Gallows* [gæləs]. . . Suspenders. **1906** *DN* 3.118 **sIN,** *Gallusses.* **1908** *DN* 3.314 **eAL, wGA,** *Gallus(es).* **1909** *DN* 3.411 **cnME,** *Galluses.* **1910** *DN* 3.441 **cwNY,** *Galluses. Ibid* 453 **seVT,** *Gallus(es).* **1914** *DN* 4.73 **ME, nNH,** *Galluses.* **1923** *DN* 5.207 **swMO,** *Gallus.* . . A suspender. **1927** *AmSp* 2.355 **wcWV,** *Galluses* . . suspenders. . . *Gallus strop* . . the straps of a pair of suspenders. **1932** (1974) Caldwell *Tobacco Road* 128 **GA,** He stepped into his overalls, put one arm through a gallus, and reached into his pocket for another match. **1941** *LANE* Map 363 *(Suspenders)* **NEng,** Galluses is described as the usual term by . . [2 infs]; as a jocular term by . . [4 infs]; as rare by . . [4 infs]; as older or old-fashioned though still in use by . . [91 infs]; and as old-fashioned but natural by . . [3 infs]; 1 inf, **swCT,** *Galluses,* made of cloth: 'Them's the kind I used before I could afford suspenders.'; 1 inf, **nwCT,** *Galluses,* 'old style suspenders'; 1 inf, **nwCT,** [ə səspendr] has two buttonholes at the end of each strap, [ə gæləs] only one; 1 inf, **ceCT,** *Galluses* with straps three inches wide; 1 inf, **csMA,** 'one [gæləs] on each shoulder'; 1 inf **csNH,** *Galluses,* hand-knitted. [Most proncs of *galluses* are of the type [gæləsɪz]; 18 infs in northern New England have proncs with [ɑ] or [a] in the first syllable, and 3 infs have [ɛ]. A few infs offer the sg *gallus.*] **1946** *PADS* 5.23 **VA,** *Gallowses.* . . common. **1950** *PADS* 14.31 **SC,** *Gallus.* . . Also pl. *galluses.* **1954** *PADS* 21.28 **SC,** *Gallices* [-ɪ-]. . . Galluses. A pronunciation of the Dutch Fork. **1965–70** *DARE* (Qu. W7, *If a man doesn't use a belt, what does he wear over his shoulders to hold up his trousers?*) 299 Infs, **widespread, but esp Sth,** Galluses; **CO**20, **SC**2, 40, Gallus; **MO**34, Gallow ['gælo]. [Of all Infs responding to the question, 65% were old; of those giving these responses, 79% were old.]

2 Transf: see quot.

1949 *AmSp* 24.109 **SC,** *Galluses.* . . Pie crust laid in thin strips.

3 See **gallows** n **1a.**

gallus v Also *gallows (up)*

To raise or support (trousers) with suspenders.

1896 *DN* 1.417 **c,wNY,** *Gallows* (v.): "He gallowsed [gæləst] up his breeches." **1909** *DN* 3.396 **nwAR,** *Gallus.* . . To raise trousers by means of suspenders.

gallus adj Also *gallace, gallious, gallows* [Engl dial; see *EDD gallows* adj. 10, 11] *old-fash*

1 Rakish, dashing; hence adv *gallusly.*

1848 in 1968 Bartlett *Americanisms* 166, Lizzy, you're a *gallus* gal, any how! . . Look, what a *gallus* walk she's got. **1859** *Unsworth's Burnt Cork Lyrics* 11, It's about one of the old boys, so gallious and so fine,/ For he drove an omnibus on the Knickerbocker line. **1869** Twain *Innocents* 439, Camels are not beautiful, and their long under lip gives them an exceedingly "gallus" expression. **1872** Twain *Curious Dream* 14, She . . has a kind of swagger in her gait and a 'gallus' way of going with her arms akimbo. **1877** Twain in *Atlantic Mth.* 40.592/2, The marvelous stove-pipe hat . . with its poor pathetic old stiff brim canted up "gallusly" in the wrong places. **1899** (1912) Green *VA Folk-Speech* 190, *Gallows.* . . Reckless; dashing; showy: as, "What a gallows walk she's got." **1916** *DN* 4.315 **Appalachians** [Folk song dialect], *Gallace* ['gæləs]. . . "I'll give you a husband both gallace and gay."—The Rich Margent.

2 Fine, excellent.

1858 in 1946 *AN&Q* 6.108/2 **NYC,** *Bob.*—"How's your ice cream?" *Tom.*—"Gallus! How's yourn?" **1890** *DN* 1.73, *Gallus* [gæləs] . . : excellent. . . New England and New York. "A gallus old time." **1923** *DN* 5.235 **swWI,** *Gallus*. . . Excellent, very fine, of a thing. . . "She set up a gallus dinner." "That was a gallus piece of meat."

gallus bridge n [Prob **gallows** n **1,** but perh infl by **gallus** n **1**]
Perh a suspension bridge.
1941 *LANE* Map 363 *(Suspenders)* 1 inf, **neMA,** Cf. [ə gæləs brɪdʒ].

gallusly See **gallus** adj **1**

gall weed n
1 A **gentian** (here: *Gentiana quinquefolia*). [See quot 1900]
1876 Hobbs *Bot. Hdbk.* 40, Gall weed, Five flowered gentian, Gentiana quinquefolia. **1900** Lyons *Plant Names* 171, *G. quinquefolia*. . . Gall-weed. . . *Plant* bitter, tonic. **1940** Clute *Amer. Plant Names* 57, *G. quinquefolia*. . . Gall-weed.
2 =**butter-and-eggs 1.**
1959 Carleton *Index Herb. Plants* 50, *Gall-weed:* Linaria vulgaris.

gally v, hence ppl adj *gallied* [*OED* 1605 →; "Now only *dial.* and in the whale fishery"] **MA**
To frighten, confuse.
1846 (1968) Browne *Etchings Whaling* 454, However, he steadily refused to move an inch till he knew what I was "gallied" at. I insisted that I was by no means *gallied*, though I was considerably *struck*. **1851** (1976) Melville *Moby-Dick* 379 **MA,** That strange perplexity of inert irresolution, which, when the fisherman [sic] perceive it in a whale, they say he is *gallied*. [Footnote to *gallied:*] To common land usages, the word is now completely obsolete. When the polite landsman first hears it from the gaunt Nantucketer, he is apt to set it down as one of the whaleman's self-derived savageries. **1895** *DN* 1.389 **seMA,** *Galleyied* [sic]: confused. **1916** Macy-Hussey *Nantucket Scrap Basket* 133 **Cape Cod MA,** "Gally"—To frighten, to terrify; more often used in the perfect participle from [sic] "gallied," meaning nervous, uncertain as to what to do next, "rattled"—applied to a whale when alarmed. **1938** Tripp *Flukes* 211 **MA,** The boat, which was being propelled by oars, was soon outdistanced by the "gallied," or frightened whales. **1968** *DARE* (Qu. GG2, *Expressions meaning 'confused, mixed up'*) Inf **MA**40, Gallied.

gally adj [**gall** n² **2;** *OED* 1602 →]
1899 (1912) Green *VA Folk-Speech* 190, *Gally*. . . Characterized by galls or naked spots, where no grass will grow.

gallyhoot See **gallihoot**

gallynapper, gallynipper See **gallinipper**

gallywampus n [Perh **gally** v + **wampus**] Cf **catawampus** n **1, wampus cat**
1950 *AR Hist. Qrly.* 9.70 **MO,** In central Missouri there are tales of the great gally-wampus, described as a kind of amphibious panther, which leaps into the water and swims like a colossal mink. One man told me that his grandfather's corn-patch near Jefferson City, Missouri, was ruined by a gally-wampus which "come down the creek so fast he couldn't stop at the Big Bend, an' skidded right on down the valley through the cornfields." I said nothing, but evidently looked a bit incredulous, for the old man hastened to explain. "Of course it was high water, or maybe a big wind, that flattened the corn thataway. But Grandpa always said it was the gally-wampus done it. The gally-wampus was kind of a joke, in them days."

gally-west See **galley-west**

galnipper See **gallinipper**

galook, galoop See **galoot**

galoopus n **Ozarks** Cf **filliloo bird, gallywampus**
An imaginary bird; see quot 1953.
1953 Randolph-Wilson *Down in Holler* 247 **Ozarks,** Galoopus. . . A fabulous bird, like a great black eagle, said to lay square eggs. The old-timers tell tourists that the *galoopus* was once common in southwest Missouri. The astounding productivity of the soil in certain areas is attributed to the dung of the galoopus bird. **1954** *Milwaukee Jrl.* (WI) 14 Mar 4.4/7 **Ozarks,** Willipus-wallupus and galoopus, strange critters found only in the hills.

galoot n Also *galook, galoop, galout* [Perh *ga* var of **ker-** + *loot* Scots var of *lout; OED* 1812 → in ref to a soldier or sailor] *usu derog, occas affectionate*
A person, usu a male.
1865 Browne *Complete Wks.* 323 **NEng,** Wake, Bessy, wake,/ My sweet galoot! **1871** Hay *Jim Bludso* 11 **Missip R,** I'll hold her nozzle agin the bank / Till the last galoot's ashore. **1887** Custer *Tenting* 49, The eyes of the old galoots started out of their heads and they vamoosed the ranche, I can tell you. **1908** *DN* 3.314 **eAL, wGA,** *Galoot*. . . A fool, a simpleton. **1919** *DN* 5.69 **NM,** *Galout,* an awkward fellow. "He is surely the greatest galout in school." **1922** in 1975 White *Git Along* 106 **AZ,** Here's an ugly brute from the cattle chute,/ Press along to the Big Corral./ The big galoot's got a bottle in his boot. **1926** Finerty *Criminalese* 26, *Galoot*—Used contemptuously for an awkward person. **1931** *Sun* (Baltimore MD) 29 May 12/7 *(Hench Coll.),* Every time a fellow puts his light out because he thinks it's a bum world you discover that he was a crazy galoot without sense enough to live normally. **1950** *WELS (Uncomplimentary word for an old man)* 1 Inf, **cWI,** Old galoot. **1965-70** *DARE* (Qu. HH21, *A very awkward, clumsy person*) 14 Infs, **Nth, N Midl,** Galoot; **NM**6, Big galoot; **NJ**39, **NY**111, **NC**16, **PA**13, Galook; **MA**33, Galoop; (Qu. HH20a, *An idle, worthless person*) Inf **SD**3, Lazy galoot; (Qu. HH40, *Uncomplimentary words for an old man*) **VA**101, Galoot; (Qu. NN9b, . . *"He's run off with my hammer again, ______!"*) Inf **VA**5, Crazy galoot. [19 of 23 Infs old] **1980** Banks *First-Person America* 81 **OR** (as of 1938), I saw one poor galoot . . come into one place with not enough clothes on him to flag a handcar.

galopshus, galoptious See **galluptious**

galore n [From *galore* adj; common in Engl dial (cf *EDD galore* sb. 2)] Cf **glory** n²
A great quantity—also in phrr *to* (or *by the*) *galore.*
1848 (1855) Ruxton *Life Far West* 65 **MO,** The wild and dissipated mountaineers get rid of their last dollars in furious orgies, treating all comers to galore of drink. **1869** Hale *Ingham Papers* 15 **CT** (as of 1826), The little boys took galore of apples and of doughnuts. **1947** Guthrie *Big Sky* 138 **NW,** There's a galore of 'em [=Rocky Mountain sheep] beyond the Yellowstone. **1966-69** *DARE* (Qu. LL9b, . . *All you need or more—for example, of clothes: "She's got clothes ______."*) Infs **MO**15, 19, **SD**5, To galore; **MN**42, **NY**70, By the galore.

galory See **glory** adj

galoshers n pl Also *gloshers* [Pronc varr of *galoshes*]
1954 *Harder Coll.* **cwTN,** *Gloshers*. . . Rubber footwear. **c1960** *Wilson Coll.* **csKY,** *Galoshers.*

galout See **galoot**

galuptzi See **golumpki**

galvanize n
1 The zinc coating on iron; by ext, nickel plating. Cf **fertilize**
1917 *DN* 4.412 **wNC,** *Galvanize*. . . Nickel plating. "The galvanize wore off my pistol." **1940** Stuart *Trees of Heaven* 315 **KY,** There was a washpan layin there. Boliver grabbed it and seized it with his teeth. The galvanize flew off in tiny white flakes.
2 also *galvanized:* Galvanized iron.
1966-70 *DARE* (Qu. F30, *What is a pail made of?*) Inf **MO**8, It's usually made out of granite or galvanized; **MT**5, Tin or galvanized; **NY**70, Galvanized, granite; **OH**96, Galvanized, wood; **VA**45, Made of galvanized or plastic; (Qu. D30, *The strip of . . metal that covers the ridge of a roof*) Inf **WA**21, Galvanized, galvanized tin. **1986** Pederson *LAGS Concordance* **Gulf Region,** 2 infs, (Water) bucket made of galvanize; 1 inf, Most common bucket is galvanize; 1 inf, "Bucket" is tin, plastic, or galvanize; 1 inf, Milk pails made of galvanize; 1 inf, Pipe made of galvanize; 1 inf, Water buckets made of galvanized or aluminum; 1 inf, Bucket made of galvanized or granite; 1 inf, It's made out of galvanized; 1 inf, Galvanize banding on barrels.

galvanizer n
In railroading: one who inspects cars.
1932 *RR Mag.* Oct 367, *Galvanizer*—Car inspector. **1938** Beebe *High Iron* 221 [Railroad terms], *Galvanizer:* Car inspector. **1940** Cottrell *Railroader* 127. **1976** Gould *Blackie's RR Hdbk.* 2.

galves See **gaff** n, v

galy See **gaily**

galygumber n
=**white sweet clover.**
1937 U.S. Forest Serv. *Range Plant Hdbk.* W123, White sweetclover, known also as . . galygumber, . . is a robust biennial herb.

gam n^1 [Perh abbr for obs Engl *gammon* lively talk, chatter] **chiefly NEng** Cf **mug-up** n

A sociable visit, orig between whaling crews at sea. Note: The sense "a school of whales," often taken as the original sense, appears to be merely a fig use; cf quot 1850 and **gam v 1** quot 1926.

1846 (1968) Browne *Etchings Whaling* 76, When two whalers meet on any of the whaling grounds, it is usual to have "a gam," or mutual visit, for the purpose of interchanging the latest news, comparing reckoning, discussing the prospect of whales, and enjoying general chit-chat. **1850** Cheever *Whale & Captors* 205, *Gam* is the word by which they designate the meeting, exchanging visits, and keeping company of two or more whale ships, or a sociable family of whales. Thus we *gammed* two days on the New Zealand whaling ground with the Niantic of Sag Harbor. **1916** Macy-Hussey *Nantucket Scrap Basket* 132, "Gam"—A social visit and talk. Originally this term was applied to a school of whales, and its use by the whalemen is doubtless derived from that source. . . The word was used both as a noun and as a verb, and it is still very frequently heard among Nantucketers. One says, "I met so-and-so today, and we had a grand gam together," or "we gammed for an hour or more." **1941** *LANE* Map 419, 1 inf, **cCT,** [hæv ə gæ·m], old whalers' term meaning [hæv ə 'tɔk fɛst]. **1945** Colcord *Sea Language* 86 **ME, Cape Cod, Long Island,** *Gam* . . alongshore, a long, friendly chat. "Come over after supper and have a gam." **1965–70** *DARE* (Qu. O21, *When men out in seagoing boats get together . . that's called a* ______) Infs **CT**4, **ME**16, **MA**5, 40, 56, 62, 72, **NY**123, **RI**17, **WA**8, Gam. [9 of 10 Infs old] **1975** Gould *ME Lingo* 106, *Gam*—This word means a school of whales; it was given an additional meaning by Maine sea captains who used it to describe a gathering of home folks in foreign ports. In Singapore, Rio, Liverpool, the captains (and families, if present) would visit together and have a talk-fest. One evening during each regatta of the Friendship Sloop Society is devoted to a skipper's *gam.*

gam v **chiefly NEng**

1 also *gam it:* To engage in a **gam** n^1 (with); hence vbl n *gamming.*

1849 Cooper *Sea Lions* 1.114, I see no reason why we should not be neighbourly, and 'gam' it a little, when we've nothing better to do. **1850** [see **gam** n^1]. **1853** in 1938 Tripp *Flukes* 99, These 24 hours commences with calm pleasant weather, Gam'ed with the *Monongahela,* Seabury Master. **1890** *Century Illustr. Mag.* 40.510/2 **Nantucket MA,** If the door still refuses to yield [you] are informed that probably the postmistress has . . gone "gamming." **1906** *Harper's Mth. Mag.* 112.841/2 **MA,** The Portuguese skipper of the *Conwell* came over with a boat's crew and gammed with us. **1916** [see **gam** n^1]. **1926** Ashley *Yankee Whaler* 131, *Gamming:* Visiting, as practiced between whaleships at sea, also said of Sperm Whales when they are herded and not in motion. **1941** *LANE* Map 419 *(Chat),* [*Gam* was given by one RI inf and 8 infs from Gardiners Is., Martha's Vineyard, and Nantucket Is. Four infs offerred it spontaneously, 2 acknowledged it when prompted, and 3 reported it as a sailors' term they had heard others use. Two of the Nantucket infs said that it was 'originally applied to whales.'] **1968** *DARE* (Qu. II15, *When somebody is passing by and you want him or her to stop and talk a while, you might say, "______.")* Inf **MA**40, Come in and gam awhile.

2 To engage (another ship) in a **gam** n^1.

1892 *Sun* (NY NY) 1 May sec 3 1/2 (as of 1876), On Sept. 20 we met the bark Atlantic . . and "gammed" her. **1938** Tripp *Flukes* 53 **MA,** While cruising, we gammed the Brig "Isabella," Captain Blossom, and there I found two of my shipmates.

gam n^2 See **grandma** n **A13**

gama (grass) n Also *gamma grass*

A grass of the genus *Tripsacum,* usu *T. dactyloides.* Also called **gemma grass, sesame grass**

1833 *Amer. Railroad Jrl.* 2.526/2 **NC,** I promised to send you some account and description of the Gama Grass. **1894** Coulter *Botany W. TX* 491, *T[ripsacum] dactyloides. . . Gama grass. . .* Low land, eastern Texas and eastward. **1910** Graves *Flowering Plants* 48 **CT,** *Tripsacum. . .* Gama Grass. . . Sometimes used for fodder in the South. **1930** Duffus *Santa Fe Trail* 134, They [=oxen] were not as adaptable as mules and it was hard to get them to eat the buffalo grass or gamma grass which was the only forage beyond the Arkansas River. **1939** Tharp *Vegetation TX* 44, Gama *(Tripsacum dactyloides)* occurs as an important constituent of the eastern portion . . and occasionally along low moist soil northward and westward. **1948** Wolfe *Farm Gloss.* 136, *Gama Grass*—A grass slenderer than corn and has a tassel resembling the corn tassel and the seed are [sic] borne in the tassel. Thought by some to be one of the ancestors of Indian corn. **1968** Radford et al. *Manual Flora Carolinas* 166, *Tripsacum. . . Gamma Grass. . .* Grain red, broadly conical. . . Late May-Nov.

gamass See **camas 1**

gambel See **gambrel roof**

Gambel crown sparrow See **Gambel's sparrow**

Gambel oak n [William *Gambel,* 19th-cent Amer ornithologist]

Std: an often shrubby oak *(Quercus gambelii)* native to the western US. Also called **encino, mountain oak, pin oak, scrub oak, shin oak, white oak**

Gambel partridge, Gambel quail See **Gambel's quail**

Gambel's finch See **Gambel's sparrow**

Gambel's quail n Also *Gambel partridge, ~ quail, Gambel's partridge, ~ plumed quail, ~ valley quail*

A gray to grayish-brown plumed quail *(Callipepla gambeli)* native chiefly to the Southwest. Also called **California quail 2, desert quail, helmet quail**

1851 Acad. Nat. Sci. Philadelphia *Proc. for 1851* 221 **TX,** Gambel's Quail, or Partridge, . . is much disposed to seek the farms, if any be within reach, and to cultivate the acquaintance of man. **1858** Baird *Birds* 645, *Gambel's Partridge. . .* This fine species belongs chiefly to the Rocky mountain region, from the Upper Rio Grande to the Colorado river. **1874** Coues *Birds NW* 435, There is as yet little cultivated grain in Arizona; but doubtless some future historian will have to . . speak of Gambel's Quail as frequenting old corn and wheat-fields. *Ibid* 438, Compared with the Eastern Quail . . , from the sportsman's stand-point, Gambel's Plumed Quail is more difficult to kill. **1904** Wheelock *Birds CA* 122, Early in the morning during the months of March and April, the love note of the Gambel Partridge may be heard from the underbrush. **1917** (1923) *Birds Amer.* 2.9, *Gambel's Quail. . . Other Names.* . . Gambel's Valley Quail. **1948** *AZ Highways* Apr 11, The Gambel Quail is one of the proudest and most beautiful of desert birds. **1965** *Silver City Press Frontier* (NM) 14, A variety of birds are found . . also ducks, dusky grouse, chukars, Gambel quail and band-tailed pigeon. **1966** *DARE* (Qu. Q7, *Names and nicknames for other kinds of game birds around here*) Inf **NM**6, Gambel quail. May be same as chukar quail; **NM**13, Fool-hen, Garble's [sic] quail, white-top quail. **1982** Elman *Hunter's Field Guide* 95, A Gambel's quail is apt to weigh 5 or 6 ounces and have a length of 9½ to 11 inches.

Gambel's sparrow n Also *Gambel's finch, ~ white-crowned sparrow, Gambel (crown) sparrow, ~ white-crowned ~*

A western race of the **white-crowned sparrow** (here: *Zonotrichia leucophrys gambeli*).

1861 U.S. Army Corps Topog. Engineers *Rept. Colorado R.* 5.6, *Zonotrichia gambelii,* . . Gambel's finch. Above Fort Yuma. **1869** *Amer. Naturalist* 3.183 **sCA,** Large flocks of Gambel's Finch *(Zonotrichia Gambelii),* and other species, flitted among the hedges. **1901** Grinnell *Gold Hunting* 15/1 **AK,** Every morning I hear the plaintive song of the Gambel's sparrows from the bushy thickets on the hillsides. **1917** (1923) *Birds Amer.* 3.36, Gambel's Sparrow. . . The lores [sic] is entirely white, thus making the white-colored stripe over the eye continuous to the bill. **1933** Jaeger *CA Deserts* 97, Like a glad harbinger of the glorious, sunny, winter days to come, the Gambel white-crowned sparrows appear from the north early in November. **1953** Jewett *Birds WA* 647, *Gambel White-crowned Sparrow. . .* Other names: Gambel Crown Sparrow. **1964** Lowe *Vertebrates* 246 **AZ,** Gambel's Sparrow. . . Very common transient in brushy places anywhere. Abundant winter resident in weeds about tall brush. **1968–69** *DARE* (Qu. Q21, *Different kinds of sparrows around here*) Infs **AZ**15, **CA**41, Gambel sparrow.

Gambel's valley quail See **Gambel's quail**

Gambel('s) white-crowned sparrow See **Gambel's sparrow**

gambering roof See **gambrel roof**

gamble See **gambling stick**

gamble cord n **[gambrel 1]** Cf **gambling string**

The hamstring of an animal by which its carcass is hung to be dressed.

1968 *DARE* Tape **MI**125A, When you get that . . done, you'd turn it [=a hog carcass] around, cut the legs out, the—[Inf **MI**125:] Gamble ['gæmbəl] cords—[Inf **MI**125A:] Gamble cords, put the gamble stick in there, and you'd spread 'em apart and you'd have another handle, see.

gamble roof(ed) See **gambrel roof**

gamble stick n

1 See **gambling stick.**

‡2 A divining rod. [From its similarity to a **gambrel 1,** perh with pun on *gamble* v]

1967 *DARE* (Qu. CC13a, . . *A forked stick that's used to show where there's water underground*) Inf **AR**55, Gamble stick—[made] out of peach-tree limbs.

gamble weed n

A **sanicle** (here: *Sanicula crassicaulis*).

1911 Jepson *Flora CA* 290, *S[anicula] menziesii. . . Gamble-weed. . .* Shady woods of the hills . . , common. **1961** Thomas *Flora Santa Cruz* 256 **cwCA,** *S[anicula] crassicaulis. . .* Gamble Weed. Fairly common throughout the Santa Cruz Mountains.

gambling stick n Also *gamble (stick), gambling rod, gamlin pole, gamlin stick, gim(b)lin' stick* [Varr, some perh by folk-etym, of **gambrel 1**] **chiefly Sth, S Midl** Cf **gambling string**
=**gambrel 1.**

1899 (1912) Green *VA Folk-Speech* 190, *Gamble* . . gambrel. **1915** *DN* 4.183 **VA,** *Gamblin' stick.* **1938** Stuart *Dark Hills* 212 **eKY,** Here was where we had to watch the dogs to keep them away from the clean sweet-smelling hog bodies, hanging to a scaffold with a gambling stick sharpened on both ends and run under the leaders of each hind leg. **1940** *Hench Coll.* **eVA,** A gamlin stick is put through both legs of a hog. *Ibid* **swVA,** Gimblin' or gimlin' stick. **1946** *PADS* 6.14, **eNC,** *Gamble. . . Gambrel.* A fifteen-inch stick sharpened at the ends and inserted between the bone and the tendon of the hind legs of a hog to suspend the hog from a device called a *gallows.* Pamlico. Common. (In s. Va. and c. N. C. called *gambling stick.*) **1947** Steed *KY Tobacco Patch* 37, A gambling-stick is inserted under the strong tendon of a hind foot and another buttonhole slit is punctured on the corresponding tendon of the other hind foot. **1950** *PADS* 14.31 **SC,** *Gamblin' stick.* **1952** Brown *NC Folkl.* 1.544 **wNC,** *Gambling-stick.* **1968** *DARE* Tape **IN**51, We scalded the hogs and scraped 'em with knives . . took 'em out and scraped the hair off of 'em and we hung 'em on the pole, gamlin' ['gæmlɪn] pole we called 'em, and then we gutted 'em; **MI**125, First we'd kill that hog . . , stick it, bleed it, bring it over here to the bench, and you had a barrel set on a slope—you'd scald half of it to a time, the back end first, then they'd reverse, see, put that gamble ['gæmbəl] in here and then—[**MI**125A:] The gamble stick is a—looked like a boomerang. . . It went over a pole on that same gamble stick . . spread out, and then you could clean it. **1968** *DARE* File **VA,** Gambling stick, gambling rod. **1970** *Foxfire* Spring-Summer 18 **nGA,** *Skinning And Dressing:* . . Skin out both hind legs, and make a small slice between bone and tendon and insert the gambling stick. . . Hang the coon up. **1972** *Foxfire Book* 192 **nGA,** When the hide was scraped clean, the hamstring was exposed on both hind legs, and a gambling stick sharpened on both ends—or a singletree—was slipped behind the exposed tendons. The hog was then strung up on a strong pole. **1976** *PA Folklife* Spring 29, The term *gambling sticks* . . is the usual way of naming gambrel or gammon sticks [on salebills issued between 1968 and 1975], those denominations being practically unknown.

gambling string n Cf **gambling stick, gamle**
=**gamble cord.**

1950 *PADS* 14.31 **SC,** *Gambling strings. . .* The tendons on the hind legs of slaughtered animals by which they are suspended by means of a *gambrel* for evisceration. **1954** *Harder Coll.* **cwTN,** *Gambling strings* . . tendons (esp. in heel?)

gambrel n

1 also *gambrel(ing) stick, gambril, gammerill;* In butchering: a stick, usu bent, used to spread and hang a carcass. [*OED* 1547 →; all the varr listed here are found also in Engl dials] Cf **gamble cord, gambling stick, gammon** n³

1764 *Boston Gaz. & Country Jrl.* (MA) 6 Feb 3/2, He first knock'd her down with a Gammerill, then run a Fork into her Neck. **1848** U.S. Patent Office *Annual Rept. for 1847* 526, His [=a hog's] hind legs are stretched open with a stick called a gambril and the hog is borne off by three men. **1875** Holland *Sevenoaks* 43 **wNEng,** I allers sleep hangin' on a gambrel, between two slabs. **1910** *DN* 3.453 **seVT,** *Gambrel-stick.* **1946** McAtee *Dial. Grant Co. IN Suppl. 3* 5, *Gambrel.* **1948** *AmSp* 23.317 **MN** [Packing plant language], *Gambrel stick. . .* Pole for fastening hogs on a rail. **1968** *DARE* File **KY,** Gambrel stick. **1982** Ginns *Snowbird Gravy* 37 **nwNC,** "What is a gambreling stick?" "The thing you hang it up with. Hang it up in the cherry tree." **1984** *DARE* File **ceWI,** My father (b. 1920) and his hunting partner (b. 1906) use a gambrel ['gæmbrel] when they skin and butcher deer. It's a carved stick with a bend in it, similar in shape to a boomerang, but with less of an angle. They poke it through the hind legs of the deer down close to the feet and use it to hang the deer upside down from a rafter in the garage.

2 See **gambrel roof.**

gambreling stick See **gambrel 1**

gambrel roof n, also attrib Also *gambering roof, gamble* ~, *gambrel* Also sp *gambel, gambril* [From **gambrel 1,** either directly or through Engl dial *gambrel* hock; in either case the ref is to the bent shape of the rafters] **chiefly Upstate NY, NEng** See Map

A roof with two slopes on each side, the lower steeper than the upper; hence adj *gambrel-roofed, gamble-*~ having such a roof.

1737 in 1926 *Old-Time New Engl.* July 21/2 **Boston MA,** One Tenement two Stories upright, with a Gambering roof, three Rooms on a Floor. **1779** in 1886 MA Hist. Soc. *Proc.* 2d ser 2.466 **MA,** The Queens Pallace was a gambril ruft house. **1845** Judd *Margaret* 33 **ME,** Here and there was a house in the then new style, three-storied, with gambrel roof, and dormar [sic] windows. **1848** Bartlett *Americanisms* 153, *Gambrel.* A hipped roof to a house, so called from its resemblance to the hind leg of a horse which by farriers is termed the *gambrel.* **1855** Mitchell *Fudge Doings* 1.129 **NY,** There are . . houses with gamble-roofs, and mossy, mouldy-looking, dormer-windows. **1891** (1900) French *Otto* 160 **AR,** You can see . . a score of gambrel-roofed white houses. **1910** *DN* 3.453 **seVT,** *Gambrel roof.* **1922** Foster-Carter *Farm Buildings* 76, The gambrel roof is the most popular type and is practical for all average conditions. A comparison with the gable roof shows a greater hay-loft capacity. . . The gambrel roof is sometimes erroneously termed "curb" roof or "hip" roof. **1941** *LANE* Map 348, 1 inf, **cCT,** [gæmbḷ rʊf]; 1 inf, **RI,** [gæmbrḷ ruft haʊzɪz]; 1 inf, **csMA,** [gæmbrəl rʊf]. **1950** *WELS* 11 Infs, **WI,** Gambrel roof. **1965-70** *DARE* (Qu. M1, . . *Kinds of barns*) 16 Infs, **chiefly Upstate NY, NEng,** Gamble-roof barn; **NY**113, 123, Gambrel-roofed barn; **OH**10, Gambrel barn; **NY**230, Gamble-roofed barn; (Qu. D1) Inf **DC**1, Gambrel-roof houses in Maryland to avoid taxes—counted as one story for tax purposes. **1976** Wells *Barns U.S.A.* np **Cape Cod MA,** This barn is of gambel roof design with a full cellar under. *Ibid* **nIN,** The gambrel roof formed with bent rafters gives the needed space.

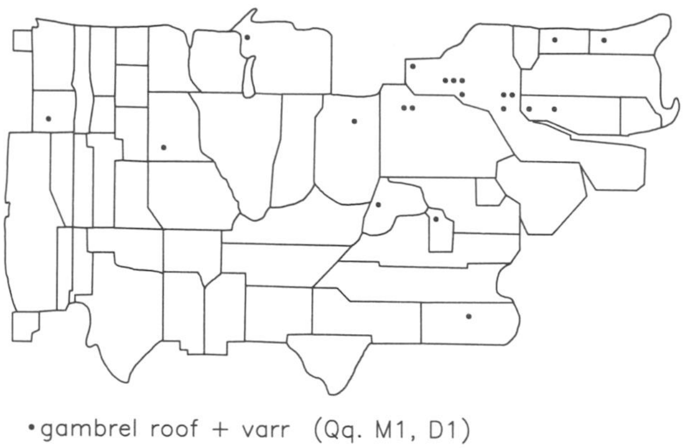

•gambrel roof + varr (Qq. M1, D1)

gambrel stick See **gambrel 1**

gambril n

1 See **gambrel 1.**

2 See **gambrel roof.**

game n *chiefly among Black speakers*

A pattern of behavior designed to outdo or manipulate others.

1884 *Anglia* 7.264, To put er game on = to get the better of. **1970** *DARE* (Qu. AA6a, . . *A man who is fond of being with women and tries to attract their attention*) Inf **NY**241, Got a beautiful game; got a tough game; his game is together; (Qu. GG3) Inf **NY**249, Run that game on; (Qu. II33) Inf **NY**238, Run a game. [All Infs Black] **1972** Claerbaut

Black Jargon 65, *Game* . . a manipulative attempt: *to run a game*. . . the process of attracting a member of the opposite sex; the courting process. **1977** Smitherman *Talkin* 257, *Game,* a series of shrewd maneuvers, a "story" for obtaining what one wants; also, by extension, a style of carrying and expressing oneself that enables someone to manipulate people and achieve a desired end. **1977** Dillard *Lexicon* 88 [Black], To keep another pimp from copping his girls, or to refrain from "blowing" them himself, each player has a *game*—romance . . or violence. **1980** Folb *Runnin' Down* 71 **Los Angeles CA** [Black], The vernacular expressions to *game someone* or to *run a game on someone*—to outwit, outsmart, or outdo another—convey the sense of contest and the power plays implicit in much teenage behavior.

game v [*OED game* v. 2. c *"slang. . . Obs."*]

1 To mock, delude.

1899 (1912) Green *VA Folk-Speech* 191, *Game, v.* To make game of, to turn into ridicule; make sport of; mock; delude or humbug. **1934** (1943) *W2* 1030/3, *Game. . .* To make fun of; ridicule; humbug. *Southern U.S.* **1942** in 1944 *ADD* **cGA.**

2 also *game on:* To act deceitfully or manipulatively; hence vbl n *gaming. chiefly among Black speakers* Cf **game** n

1970 *DARE* (Qu. II33, *To get an advantage over somebody by tricky means: "I don't trust him; he's always trying to ______."*) Inf **NY238,** Game on me; (Qu. JJ19, *If somebody has dishonest intentions, or is up to no good, you might say, "I think he's got ______."*) Inf **NY238,** He's trying to game on us. [Inf Black] **1971** Landy *Underground Dict.* 86, *Game. . .* Be dishonest, untruthful, defensive; con; stick to a story when everyone knows it is not valid or passable—eg. Don't game me. **1980** Folb *Runnin' Down* 70 *Los Angeles CA* [Black], Ain' nothin' happ'nin' 'cept a whole lotta frontin' and gamin' goin' on down here [in South Central]. The brothers—and d'sisters too—they be tryin' to keep on top, get over any way dey kin. *Ibid* 71, To *game someone* . . to outwit, outsmart, or outdo another.

3 with *after:* See quot. Cf **game** n

1972 Claerbaut *Black Jargon* 65, Game . . to attract a member of the opposite sex: *to game after her.*

game ball n

1897 (1952) McGill *Narrative* 143 **ceSC,** There was an outdoor sport called "game ball," played against the house and engaged in by boys and young men. For this purpose there was a ball yard at everybody's house, using the hall chimney-end as a battery or the sides of large barns. . . The ball with which we played was made of India rubber strings with woolen yarn wound around it and covered with soft dressed deer hide . . The game was played in two parties, two or four on a side and sometimes more. There were two lines marked out on each side of the ball yard from the battery, by which the play ground was extended on each side and within these lines the ball must fall.

game chicken n [Euphem] **esp S Midl**

A gamecock.

1846 *Spirit of Times* 18 April 1/1 *(DAE),* We shipped your Game Chickens by the 'Courier' on Saturday last. **1850** Gallaher *W. Sketchbook* 71 **TN,** Game chickens were in high repute, and were objects of much attention. **1896** Read *Jucklins* 26 **NC,** What do you know about game chickens? **1967–70** *DARE* (Qu. K76, *What other kinds of poultry are raised around here?*) Infs **KY35, VA111,** Game chickens; **KY23,** Game chickens—the roosters used in cockfighting; **SC40,** Game chickens—bred for fighting; pit—where game chickens fight. **1970** *DARE* File **KY,** Game chicken, species of chickens raised for fighting.

‡game hog n

An illegally shot deer.

1967 *DARE* (Qu. P35A, *Names or nicknames for any deer shot illegally*) Inf **CO41,** Game hog—one shot by a pot-hunter. No sportsmanship of the hunter.

game of India See **India**

game on See **game v 2**

gamick See **gammick**

gaming See **game v 2**

gam it See **gam v 1**

gamle v [Prob back-formation from *gamlin stick,* var of **gambling stick**]

1940 *Hench Coll.* **eVA,** *Gamle. . .* To put the gamlin stick in. E.g. Help me gammel [sic] this hog.

gamlin pole (or stick) See **gambling stick**

gamma See **grandma** n **A13**

gamma grass See **gama grass**

gammer See **grandma** n **A13**

gammerill See **gambrel 1**

gammet n, v Also sp *gammut* [*EDD gammet* sb. "Fun, frolic, sport; a game, joke, whim, trick"; v. "To play, frolic . . ; to deceive, hoax, 'take in' "; cf **gammick**]

See quots.

1899 (1912) Green *VA Folk-Speech* 191, Children when engaged in a very active and noisy game of play, were said to be in a *gammut* of play. Merriment; fun. **1926** *AmSp* 1.413 **Okefenokee GA,** So I motioned ter 'im; we understood all these gammets [Footnote: Tricks?], yer know, ermong us. He knowed jest whut I wanted 'im ter do, er whut it wuz. **1984** Wilder *You All Spoken Here* 192 **Sth,** Projeckin'; gammetin': Assling; cutting up; frolicking; pranking; piddling.

gammick v Also sp *gamick* [Varr of Engl dial *gammock;* see *OED, EDD*] Cf **gammet**

To play, frolic.

1919 *DN* 5.34 **KY,** *Gammick. . .* To play, gambol (of children). **1969** *DARE* FW Addit **neNC,** Gamicking—?frolicking about.

gamming See **gam v 1**

gammon n^{1} Also *bacon gammon* [*OED gammon* sb.^{1} 2 a1529 →]

See quot 1953.

1788 in 1873 May *Jrl.* 64 **OH,** Amongst the solids were bacon gammon, venison tongues, roast and boiled lamb. **1953** Randolph–Wilson *Down in Holler* 247 **Ozarks,** *Gammon. . .* Sometimes it means bacon, or salt sidemeat.

gammon n^{2} [See *OED gammon* sb.^{4}]

Idle or deceptive talk.

1848 Bartlett *Americanisms* 153, *Gammon.* Humbug; deceit; lies. Any assertion which is not strictly true, or, professions believed to be insincere; as . . 'that's all gammon;' meaning . . that's all a farce. **1953** Randolph–Wilson *Down in Holler* 247 **Ozarks,** Gammon. . . Idle talk, untruths.

gammon v [**gammon** n^{2}]

To trick, deceive, fast-talk; hence n *gammoner.*

1834 *Life Andrew Jackson* 241 **NEng,** I'm afear'd you are gammon'd by your hangers on, and that they impose on you. **1847** Paulding–Paulding *Amer. Comedies* 235 **ePA,** I'm annihilated—swept off to the last penny—cleaned out—diddled—gammoned—bit—cheated! **1848** Bartlett *Americanisms* 153, *Gammon. . .* 'I believe you're gammoning,' . . meaning, you are jesting with me. **1953** Randolph–Wilson *Down in Holler* 247 **Ozarks,** Gammoner. . . A talkative, unreliable person.

gammon n^{3} Also *gammon stick, ~ rod* [Perh var of **gambrel 1,** perh by assoc with **gammon** n^{1}]

=gambrel 1.

1874 McCoy *Cattle Trade* 312 **MO,** Then comes one or more men and insert a strong gammon, of four or more feet in length, in the hocks beneath the hamstrings of the hinder legs. In the middle of the gammon stick a flat iron hook is adjusted. **1940** *Hench Coll.* **cVA,** [Letter:] My step father who was raised on a farm near Staunton tells me that "gammon" is the word, a "gammon stick" being used to pass between the heavy tendon and the bone of the hog's hind feet when it is hung on the crossbar. **1976** [see **gambling stick**]. **1982** *Barrick Coll.* **csPA,** *Gammon rod*—notched rod used to hold carcass open during butchering. *Gammon stick*—idem.

gammoner See **gammon v**

gammon rod, gammon stick See **gammon** n^{3}

gammut See **gammet**

gammy See **grandma** n **A13**

‡gamologer n

1965 *DARE* (Qu. HH17, *A person who tries to appear important*) Inf **OK9,** Big [gəˈmɔlɪǰɚ].

gancho n Also *gaucho* [Span *gancho* hook, shepherd's crook] **chiefly West**

1 A sheephook.

1892 *DN* 1.248 **TX,** *Gaúcho*. . . The hook and crook such as the shepherds use in the miracle play of the *Pastores,* so common on both sides of the Rio Grande, at the *Noche Buena* = Christmas. **1940** Writers' Program *Guide NV* 78, *Sheep ropes* are used to tie ewes that do not at first claim their lambs, and a *gancho* is the sheep hook for catching the animals. **1968** Adams *Western Words* 124, *Gancho*—In sheepherding, a shepherd's crook.

2 also *gauch iron, gaunch* (or *gouch*) *hook:* An iron bar with a crook; see quots.

1892 *DN* 1.190 **TX,** *Gaúcho:* a crooked iron for branding horses. **1936** Adams *Cowboy Lingo* 151, The hook used in lifting the heavy lids of the cooking vessels were 'gouch-hooks' or 'gaunch-hooks.' **1968** Adams *Western Words* 125, *Gauch iron*—An iron bar with a hook on it, used in branding.

gander n[1] [*OED gander* sb. 2 1553 →] **NEng**

An awkward, gangling person; a rubberneck.

1903 *DN* 2.298 **Cape Cod MA** (as of a1857), *Great gawking gander*. . . A gawky person. **1941** *LANE* Map 459 *(Emaciated, peaked)* 1 inf, **swME,** He's a gander (a very thin person). *Ibid* Map 464 *(Awkward person, lummox)* 3 infs, **nNEng,** Gander; 5 infs, **nNEng,** (Gawky or gawking) gander.

gander v

1 also with *around, off:* To wander about staring; to stroll; to look at, examine; hence vbl n *gandering.* [Engl dial "to wander aimlessly"; cf *OED, EDD*]

1903 *Cin. Enquirer* 9 May 13/1 *(DA),* Gander—To stretch or rubber your neck. **1930** Shoemaker *1300 Words* 27 **cPA Mts** (as of c1900), *Gander off*—To wander away aimlessly. **1931** *AmSp* 7.108 [Underworld argot], (To) go gandering. . . To be out looking for someone or something. "We went gandering for a peterman." Sometimes known as "playing the bird with the long neck." **1939** *AmSp* 14.239 **sCA** [Hotel slang], *To gander.* To examine. **1940** *AmSp* 15.204 [Words used in *Variety*], *Gandering.* Visiting or sightseeing. **1941** *LANE* Map 463 *(Awkward, clumsy)* 1 inf, **swME,** He's always ganderin' 'round. **1948** Manfred *Chokecherry* 132 **nwIA,** I've never yet gandered an old cowboy thriller. **1984** Doig *English Creek* 17 **nMT,** I was surprised to glance ahead and learn that Mouse [=a horse] and my father were halted, and my father was gandering back to see what had become of me.

2 See quots. [Cf Engl dial *gander-month, ~ moon* the month of (or after) a wife's confinement; see also *OED gander* v. 1. a quot 1687 "To go a gandering, whilst his Wife lies in"]

1952 Brown *NC Folkl.* 1.544, *Gander*. . . To remain near one's pregnant wife. **a1975** Lunsford *It Used to Be* 172 **sAppalachians,** "Gandering" is a term describing a husband expecting his wife to bear him a baby and he has to stay around home a good deal. He says he is just gandering because the gander sets on the nest while the goose is away.

3 with *around:* See quots. [Cf **2** above]

1940 Richter *Trees* 183 **sOH** (as of c1800), No, a man could gander around and have his pleasure and then wander off free as a hawk. **1968** *DARE* FW Addit **VA,** *Ganders around* = is courting. Old-fashioned.

gander n[2] **[gander v 1]**

A look, peek; a watchful eye—esp in phr *take a gander.*

1914 Jackson *Criminal Slang* 36, Take a gander at this dump as we pass. **1938** FWP NYC *NY Panorama* 156, "Keep a gander on the visiting fireman." **1942** Berrey–Van den Bark *Amer. Slang* 137.1, *Sight; look; glance*. . . gander. **1948** *AmSp* 23.235 **NE,** I'm just taking a gander. **1969** *DARE* Tape **MA**58, Here's . . an expression that I don't know as I've heard anywhere except up here: instead of "take a look" or "to take a look at," "take a gander." **1971** *Scientific Amer.* Oct 74/2, [Advt for a car:] Take a gander at the see-through door below. See that corrugated piece of steel?

gander around See **gander v 1, 3**

gander berry n Cf **gooseberry 2**

A **blueberry 1.**

1933 *AmSp* 8.1.49 **Ozarks,** *Gander berry*. . . A large variety of huckleberry or blueberry.

gander bumps n pl [Var of **goose bumps 1**]

1969 *DARE* (Qu. X58, *When you are cold, and little points of skin begin to come on your arms and legs, you have_____*) Inf **KY**65, Gander bumps [laughter].

gander grass n

1 =**knotweed.** Cf **goose grass 1b**

1933 Small *Manual SE Flora* 454, *Persicaria*. . . Smartweeds. Gander-grasses. **1953** Greene–Blomquist *Flowers South* 28, *Smartweeds, Gander-Grasses (Polygonum)* . . are familiar plants to anyone who has wandered about in marshy places in late summer and autumn.

2 A **virgin's bower** (here: *Clematis virginiana*).

1940 Clute *Amer. Plant Names* 256, *Clematis Virginiana.* Gander grass.

gander-gut n

One who is thin and awkward; hence adj *gander-gutted* thin, gangling.

1941 *LANE* Map 463 *(Awkward, clumsy)* 1 inf, **csNH,** Gander gutted. *Ibid* Map 464 *(Awkward person, lummox)* 1 inf, **seME,** Gander gut, one who is both skinny and awkward; 1 inf, **seME,** Gander gut. **1959** *VT Hist.* new ser 27. 137, *Gander gutted*. . . Thin. Rare.

gandering See **gander v 1**

gander-legged adj

Having thin, awkward legs like a gander.

1872 (1973) Thompson *Major Jones's Courtship* 186, They say he's a monstrous grate, long, gander-legged feller, and may be 'bonimation ugly for all I know. **1970** *DARE* (Qu. X37, . . *People's legs, if they're noticeably bent, or uneven, or not right)* Inf **IL**114, Gander-legged.

gander off See **gander v 1**

gander party n *?old-fash*

A party of men only.

1867 Lowell *Biglow* lviii **'Upcountry' MA,** *Gander-party:* a social gathering of men only. **1889** (1971) Farmer *Americanisms* 259, *Gander-party.* A vulgarism for a party of men. Variants are *gander-gang; stag-party.* The term may be compared with the phrase "to go into the buck-hutch," and conversely with "hen-party," "grass-widow," etc. **1900** Munn *Uncle Terry* 154 *(DA)* **ME,** If you and I have any outing on the yacht, we must make up a gander party.

gander pulling n Also *gander pull, goose pulling* **chiefly S Midl, Sth** Cf **chicken pulling**

A "sport" in which mounted men try to pull the head off a live gander; hence n *gander puller* one who participates in this activity.

1818 Fearon *Sketches* 247 **KY,** They have also another practice . . called "gander pulling." This *diversion* consists in tying a live gander to a tree or pole, greasing its neck, riding past it at full gallop, and he who succeeds in pulling off the head of the victim, receives the laurel crown. **1835** *S. Lit. Messenger* 1.645/2 **KY,** Of the most conspicuous *"minora sidera"* the Kentuckian horsedrover, the horsejockey, the ganderpuller, might be mentioned. **1835** Longstreet *GA Scenes* 121, He laid off his gander-pulling ground, on the nearest suitable unappropriated spot. **1843** (1846) Haliburton *Attaché* (1st ser) 2.58, It puts me in mind of "Gander Pulling." **1885** Murfree *Prophet of Smoky Mts.* 103 **eTN,** They were making ready for the gander-pulling, which unique sport had been selected . . as likely to insure the largest assemblage possible . . to hear the candidates prefer their claims. **1889** (1971) Farmer *Americanisms* 259, *Gander pulling.*—A brutal game, peculiar to Texas fancy. **1894** *Harper's New Mth. Mag.* 89.629/2 **WV,** That queerest of all sports, the gander-pull. **1944** Duncan *Mentor Graham* 75 **KY** (as of early 1800s), The worst that ever happened on Brush Creek was gander pullings. **1945** Saxon *Gumbo Ya-Ya* 571 **sLA,** *Gander-pulling*—Head of a gander was plucked and greased. Horsemen tried to pull head off. **1947** *Time* 17 Mar 25/1, A fortnight ago, sportsmen at South Carolina's Branchdale Jockey Club revived the ancient sport of goose pulling.

ganders n [Var of *janders* (at **jaundice**), perh by confusion with *glanders*]

1968–69 *DARE* (Qu. BB23, *The disease where the skin becomes a yellowish color)* Inf **TX**65, Jaundice, ganders—same thing; **VA**27, Yellow ganders ['jɛlə ˌgændɚz].

gander-shanked adj Also *gander-shanky* Cf **bandy-shanked**

Thin, gawky; also n *gander-shank(s)* a thin or awkward person.

1865 Crockett *Life* 240 **TN,** Job Snelling, a gander-shanked Yankee, . . had been caught somewhere about Plymouth Bay. **1941** *LANE* Map 459, Recorded as nicknames for an awkward person . . but properly denoting one who is tall and thin . . 1 inf, **swME,** Gander shanks.

1942 Whipple *Joshua* 535 **UT,** Come! All you long-legged, gander-shanked, bow-legged, sway-backed, brush-headed pieces of humanity. **1949** *McDavid Coll.* **wNY,** *Gandershank*—a gangling/gawky adolescent. **1968** *DARE* (Qu. X49, *Expressions used about a person who is very thin*) Inf **NY**73, Gander-shanky, or a regular gander-shanks.

gander skunk n

A **skunk;** see quot.

1968 *DARE* (Qu. P26, *Names and nicknames around here for a skunk*) Inf **IN**3, Gander skunk ['gændɚ skʌŋk]. [FW: denotes one with a broad white stripe]

gander snipe n

=**great blue heron.**

1930 Shoemaker *1300 Words* 25 **cPA Mts** (as of c1900), *Gandersnipe*—The great blue heron. **1940** Richter *Trees* 69 **sOH** (as of c1800), Once it [= a path] even came out at a half open place on the river where the sun on the water blinded you and a big old gandersnipe waded on his stilts in the shallows. *Ibid* 153, Marrying wasn't like what you expected when you were young and foolish as a gandersnipe. **1956** *AmSp* 31.183, In *gandersnipe* (great blue heron, Pa.), the fun is in the second part; for so large a bird to be called a snipe (which it actually resembles in shape), a modifier indicating its large size is necessary, and the country choice of *gander* seems entirely satisfactory.

gander teeth n Also *gander's teeth* [See quot 1901]

A **sensitive brier** (here: *Schrankia uncinata*).

1901 Lounsberry *S. Wild Flowers* 257, *Gander Teeth. Morongia uncinata.* . . In return for being stepped on, it gets between his [=the southern mountaineer's] toes and fastens there its innumerable little prickles. **1940** Clute *Amer. Plant Names* 21, *S[chrankia] uncinata.* . . Gander teeth. **1941** Writers' Program *Guide OK* 366, From early spring to late fall colorful wild flowers are abundant here—Spanish larkspur, Virginia creeper . . and the pink-flowered brier or cat's claw, locally known as gander's teeth.

Gandertown n

Used as a nickname for a section of a town.

1939 FWP *Guide KY* 355 **cKY,** The section of the town [=Bloomfield] lying on the western side of the dividing creek was known as Gandertown because in early days the young men in this region indulged in gander pulling. **1970** *DARE* (Qu. C35, *Nicknames for the different parts of . . town*) Inf **KY**75, Gandertown on the river; the backwater from each flood of the Green River came there.

gander vine n

A **virgin's bower** (here: *Clematis virginiana*).

1933 Small *Manual SE Flora* 525, *C[lematis] virginiana.* . . Gander-vine. **1949** Moldenke *Amer. Wild Flowers* 7, Best known in the East is *C. virginiana,* the . . *gandervine.* **1960** Vines *Trees SW* 269, *Clematis virginiana.* . . Vernacular names are Devil's Darning Needle . . and Gander-vine.

gandy See **gandy dancer 1, 2**

gandy dancer n [Prob from *Gandy* Mfg. Co. (see quot 1945) + *dancer* one who works with rhythmic motions]

1 also *gandy, gandy hand:* A laborer on a railroad construction or maintenance crew; a pick-and-shovel worker; also vbl n *gandy dancing.*

1923 (1927) Anderson *Hobo* 93, A "gandy dancer" is a man who works on the railroad track tamping ties. **1927** *DN* 5.447 [Underworld jargon], *Gandy dancer.* . . A laborer on a railway steel gang. **1929** *AmSp* 5.172, [Letter to the *New York Sun:*] Even an old-fashioned gandy dancer like myself can understand why a flock of down-and-outs on the Bowery will stand in line for hours waiting for a handout. . . Gandy dancing is not considered a very honorable profession. . . But . . every year I offer up a prayer of Thanksgiving that I have never had to stand in a handout line. **1930** Irwin *Amer. Tramp* 83, *Gandy.*—A railroad section hand or labourer. . . The word was used as far back as the 1860's, when thousands of Irish labourers worked on the first trans-continental railroad, and it may be that one of these workers coined the word . . *Gandy Dancer.*—See "gandy". **1933** *AmSp* 8.3.26 [Prison terms], *Gandy dancer.* Section hand. [*AmSp:* From the rhythmic up-and-down motion of workers pumping a handcar. Tramps will tell you that the handcar sings *Gándy-dancer gándy-dancer gándy-dancer* as it clips along over the rails.] **1945** Hubbard *Railroad Ave.* 344, *Gandy dancer*—Track laborer. Name may have originated from the gander-like tremulations of a man tamping ties, or from the old Gandy Manufacturing Company of Chicago, which made tamping bars, claw bars, picks, and shovels. **1956** Sorden–Ebert *Logger's Words* 15 **Gt Lakes,** *Gandy-dancer,* Pick-and-shovel man. Same as a road monkey or a worker on a track crew. Same as gandy-hand. **1967** *DARE* Tape **ID**6, They were the section laborers. They were gandy dancers. . . They were the lower-paid group; **ID**9, [FW:] What do you call these guys who work on these crews and these handcarts, say, that you see going up and down there? [Inf:] Well, the term is still alive and has been, for, oh, a good century or more. They're called gandy dancers; **ID**10, Gandy, a gandy dancer . . is a common term all over this part of the country. He is the laborer who goes out with a pick and shovel and either builds a new road bed or repairs an old one and lays the track. **1978** Doig *This House* 282 **MT** (as of c1965), A railroad worker retired from tending the tracks which coiled between Ringling and Sixteen, Leo was a thick slab of a man whom it was uproarious to think of in the nickname of that job, a *gandy dancer.*

2 also *gandy;* By ext: a tramp or other undesirable character; see quots.

1942 Berrey–Van den Bark *Amer. Slang* 461.3, Gandy dancer. . . *a petty crook.* **1942** *Sat. Eve. Post* 31 Oct 69/2 **NV,** The blanket stiff and gandy dancer no longer drink cheap whisky or gin. **1969–70** *DARE* (Qu. HH19, *Other words or nicknames for a tramp*) Inf **MA**89, Gandy; **GA**72, Gandy dancer; (Qu. HH28, *Names and nicknames . . for people of foreign background. . . Italian*) Inf **PA**234, ['aɪtæljən] gandy dancers.

3 Among truck drivers: see quots.

1942 *AmSp* 17.103 [Truck driver lingo], *Gandy dancer.* Weaving truck. **1971** Tak *Truck Talk* 69, *Gandy dancer:* a weaving truck.

gandy dancing, gandy hand See **gandy dancer 1**

gang n

1 A herd, pack, or litter of animals. **appar now chiefly S Midl** *old-fash* Note: The 1657 quot which *DAE* and *DA* assign to this sense appears rather to illustrate the Engl dial sense "a walk or pasture for cattle" (*OED gang* sb.[1] 4. c, *SND gang* II. 3).

1709 (1967) Lawson *New Voyage* 60 **NC, SC,** We were got about half way, (meeting great Gangs of Turkies). **1804** (1808) Gass *Jrl.* 52, This day we saw several gangs or herds, of buffaloe on the sides of the hills. **1804** (1904) Lewis *Orig. Jrls. Lewis & Clark Exped.* 1.180 **SD,** Saw a large gang of Goat on the hills. **1820** in 1908 MO Hist. Soc. *Coll.* 3.18 **NJ,** Four of our party went in pursuit of a *gang of elk* which we observed. **1834** in 1839 Townsend *Narr. Rocky Mts.* 44 **NE,** This afternoon, we came in sight of a large *gang* of the long-coveted buffalo. **1902** *DN* 2.235 **sIL,** *Gang.* . . Brood, flock, litter, or drove. (The latter when applied to hogs.) **1905** *DN* 3.81 **nwAR,** *Gang.* . . Pack. 'A gang of wolves are reported in the neighborhood of Franklin, Sharp County.' Common. **1908** *S. Atl. Qrly.* 7.345 **SC** [Gullah], A group . . of beasts is universally known by the old Anglo-Saxon term, *gang* . . a gang of sheep, or fowls, a gang of pa'tridges. **1939** *Hall Coll.* **wNC,** So I'd went down the mountain and run my dog into a big gang of turkeys. **1956** *Ibid* **eTN,** We had a gang of sheep there. . . He went up there and found a gang of wolves eatin' a bunch of sheep.

2 A large amount; a large number.

1934 *AmSp* 9.288 **PA** [Negro university slang], *Gang* . . an intensive, taking the place of 'very great' or 'very much,' as in *That dog has a gang of luck!* **c1937** in 1972 *Amer. Slave* 2.145 **SC,** [They] didn't do a thing but ketch (catch) a gang o' fowl and gone on. **1965–70** *DARE* (Qu. LL8b, . . *A large number . . of cousins: 'She has a whole ______ of cousins.'*) 36 Infs, **scattered,** Gang. **1968** *DARE* Tape **NJ**33, There's a gang of stuff up there. **1970** Major *Dict. Afro-Amer. Slang* 57, *Gang:* (1930's–50's) a large amount of anything. **1974** *AmSp* 49.62 **swME** (as of c1900), Gang. . . Large group "There was a gang of fish in the net."

3 A fishline to which several hooks are attached; a trot-line.

1857 *Spirit of Times* 20 June 246/2 *(DA),* We were fully equipped with rods, reels, flies, trolling gangs, spoons, gaffs, and landing nets. **1876** *Fur, Fin, & Feather* Sep. 143 *(DA),* He has taken bass with the fly, spoon, gang, live minnow, and belly of yellow perch. **1879** U.S. Natl. Museum *Bulletin* 14.96, Minnow-gang. Property of J. H. Nichols, Syracuse N. Y. **1883** Eggleston *Hoosier Schoolboy* 109 **IN,** They got a "gang," or, as they called it, a "trotline," to lay down in the river for catfish, perch, and shovel-nose sturgeon.

4 See quot.

1975 Gould *ME Lingo* 106, *Gang*—The number of traps a lobsterman will haul at one time. With several hundred out, he can't get to them all in one day, so he'll divide them into *gangs* and haul a *gang* each morning.

5 in combs: A bottom on a plow. [From *gangplow* a plow with at least two bottoms working as a unit to turn parallel furrows]

1967–70 *DARE* (Qu. L18, *Kinds of plows*) Inf **IL**65, Eight- or twelve-gang plows; **KY**64, Two- or three-gang plow has two or three bottoms; **NY**230, One-gang plow, two-gang plow; **OH**22, Tractor with two- to eight-gang plow bottoms; **OH**70, Multiple-gang plow.

gang v [Scots, nEngl dial]

To go.

1899 (1912) Green *VA Folk-Speech* 191, What are you doing ganging about in that way? **1957** Beck *Folkl. ME* 81, Wild geese, wild geese, gangin' out to sea:/ All good weather it will be.

gan-gan See **grandma** n **A13**

gang bird n [**gang** n **1**]

See quots.

1953 *PADS* 19.11, *Gang bird*. . . A bird that travels with others, such as a goldfinch. Used in Davidson Co., N.C. **1955** *Oriole* 20.13 *Goldfinch*. . . *Gang Bird* (as being often seen in flocks).

gange v |gænǰ| [Cf *OED gange* v. 1 "To protect (a fish-hook . .) with fine wire"]

To fasten a fishhook to a line; by ext, with *onto:* to grab, latch onto (something).

1889 *Century Dict.* 2450, *Gange*. . . To fasten (a fish-hook) to the end of a section of line called the *ganging*. **c1902** Clapin *New Dict. Amer.* 200, *Gange*. . . In the South-West, to attach a hook to a line or snell. **1969** *DARE* (Qu. V5b, *If you take something [of small value] that nobody seems to own, you might say, "Before anybody else gets it, I'm going to ——— this."*) Inf **RI**15, Gange [gænǰ] onto.

gangeon See **ganging**

gange onto See **gange**

gang harve n [*EDD harve* sb.[1] a harrow] Cf **Dixie boy (plow)**

1969 *DARE* (Qu. L18, *Kinds of plows*) Inf **NC**68, Gang harves, like a boy dixie but with a switchfoot on it—a reversible foot to throw dirt downhill no matter which way the plow goes.

ganging vbl n Cf **gang** n **3**

Perh fishing with multiple hooks.

1968 *DARE* (Qu. P13, . . *Other ways of fishing*) Inf **NY**80, Ganging—illegal.

ganging n Also *gangeon, gangion* [Abbr for *ganging line* < *ganging* or *gangion* a short length of heavy, often wire-wrapped line connecting a fishhook to the main line]

See quot 1975.

[**1925** *DN* 5.332 **Nfld,** *Ganging line* (ǰ). A strong, small cotton line, like herring net twine.] **1950** Moore *Candlemas Bay* 127 **ME,** The fish-house was a junk heap of old and new rope, canvas, laths, engine parts, bolts and screws, gangion, open cans of paint with brushes dried up in them. **1975** Gould *ME Lingo* 106, *Ganging*—Pronounced *gan-jing* or *gain-jing*. Older and complete dictionaries have this word, but it survives in Maine with no great relationship to their definitions. . . Today in Maine it means the twine from which a fishing line is made. . . *Ganging* makes a cod line in one size, and in the smaller cunner-size it's great for kite strings. . . The final *g* of *ganging* is always carefully pronounced . . even though *ganging* is often misspelled (as seldom as Mainers write it) as *gangion* and *gangeon.*

gangler n [Cf *gangling*]

1969 *DARE* (Qu. HH21, *A very awkward, clumsy person*) Inf **TX**74, Gangler.

gangle-shanked adj

1969 *DARE* (Qu. X37, . . *Words . . to describe people's legs if they're noticeably bent, or uneven, or not right*) Inf **IL**96, Gangle-shanked.

gangling bird n

A **pewee.**

1934 Vines *Green Thicket* 60 **cnAL,** He had enough feathers from wild things to make a feather bed. . . He had a little old trunk nearly full of feathers and down from . . ganglin' birds (or peewees).

gangway n

1 Among railroaders: see quots.

1932 *RR Mag.* Oct 368, *Gangway*—Space between rear cab post of locomotive and tender. **1938** Beebe *High Iron* 221 [Railroad terms], *Gangway:* The rear portion of a locomotive deck. **1976** Gould *Blackie's RR Hdbk.* 4, *Gang way:* Space between tender and cab.

2 Among loggers: see quot.

1956 Sorden–Ebert *Logger's Words* 15 **Gt Lakes,** *Gang-way,* The incline plane upon which logs are moved from the water into a sawmill.

gank-gutted adj [By assim from **gant-gutted**] **FL**

=**gant-gutted.**

1932 *Harper's Mth. Mag.* June 26/1 **FL,** "You talkin' about that gank-gutted woman left jest now?" **1933** Rawlings *South Moon* 190 **nFL,** You got the biggest belly for sich a gank-gutted creeter.

gannet n

1 Std: a sea bird of the family Sulidae, in the US usu *Morus bassanus* which is also called **booby** n[1] **1, Jan van Gent, mud buzzard, sea gannet, white gannet, winter gannet.**

2 =**wood ibis.** [See quot 1938] **esp FL**

1874 Coues *Birds NW* 513, *Wood Ibis*. . . In Florida it is sometimes called the "Gannet". **1910** Wayne *Birds SC* 10, The Snake Bird or "Water Turkey" *(Anhinga anhinga)* and the Wood Ibis *(Mycteria americana)* are locally known on this coast as "Gannets." **1917** (1923) *Birds Amer.* 1.179 **FL,** "Goard Head" [sic] . . and "Gannet" are the appellations given to these birds by many swamp-dwellers to whom the name Wood Ibis is unknown. **1938** Oberholser *Bird Life LA* 75, *Wood Ibis*. . . Its bare head has given it the name of 'flinthead', and its general appearance that of 'gannet', by which name it is known in some localities. **1954** Sprunt *FL Bird Life* 41, *Wood Ibis*. . . *Local Names* . . Gannet. **1969** Longstreet *Birds FL* 28, *Gannet*. . . The wood ibis begins to nest in Florida in midwinter, from 6 to 100 feet up in trees.

3 =**ruddy turnstone.**

1888 Trumbull *Names of Birds* 186, *Arenaria interpres*. . . In New Jersey . . at Tuckerton, *Gannet.*

4 =**anhinga.**

1910 [see **2** above]. **1955** *Oriole* 20.1.1 **GA,** *Anhinga.*—*Gannet* (in the Southeast, this term is rather widely applied to large water birds).

5 =**white ibis.**

1910 Wayne *Birds SC* 25, *Gaura alba*. . . *White Ibis*. . . The local name of this species is "Gannet."

6 =**double-crested cormorant.**

1970 *DARE* Tape **VA**112, We always call 'em a gannet . . an' if somethin's on the water he'll just . . open his mouth an' scoop it right up . . it got a great big stout bill, it's kinda crooked . . we call 'em nigger geese too, 'cause they're black.

7 also *gannet-gut;* Fig: see quot. [*OEDS* 1929 →]

1979 Lewis *How to Talk Yankee* [13] **nNEng,** *Gannet* or *gannet-gut* . . a prodigious eater, like the bird from which the term derives.

gannet-mullet n

A **mullet:** prob a small **mullet** four inches or less in length.

1888 Jones *Negro Myths* 15 **GA coast** [Gullah], Eh lef in de boat some leely [=little] gannet-mullet an catfish wuh eh no want.

gannet striker n

Either the Caspian **tern** (here: *Sterna caspia*) or the **royal tern. chiefly VA**

1913 Bailey *Birds VA* 6, *Caspian Tern*. . . Gannet Striker. *Ibid* 7, *Royal Tern*. . . Gannet Striker. *Ibid* 8, There is practically no difference made by the local watermen between this [=*Sterna maxima*] and the former species [=*Sterna caspia*], both being called Gannet Strikers. **1917** *Wilson Bulletin* 29.2.75, *Sterna caspia, Sterna maxima.*—Gannet striker, Wallops I[slan]d, V[irgini]a. **1951** Pough *Audubon Water Bird* 329, Gannet striker. *See* Royal and Caspian tern. **1955** *Oriole* 20.1.8, *Caspian Tern.*—*Gannet Striker* (as a large kind of striker). **1969** Longstreet *Birds FL* 69, *Royal Tern.* Other names . . *Gannet Striker* (Virginia).

gannies See **gonnies**

ganninapper, ganninipper, gannip(p)er See **gallinipper**

ganny n[1] See **gonnies**

ganny n[2] See **grandma** n **A13**

ganser n [Aphet form of *merganser*]

1970 *DARE* (Qu. Q5, . . *Kinds of wild ducks . . around here*) Inf **VA**43, Ganser—eats fish. [Same as] fish duck—not fit to eat.

gansey n [Engl dial *gansey (EDD),* var of *OED guernsey* sb. 2. a; also in Newfoundland (*DNE* 1843 →)] Cf **guernsey**

A knitted jacket or sweater.

1899 (1912) Green *VA Folk-Speech* 191, *Gansey*. . . A knitted, woollen shirt. **1909** *DN* 3.411 **ME,** *Gauzy* [sic]. . . A knitted jacket similar to a sweater. A corruption of *guernsey*. [**1925** *DN* 5.332 **Nfld,** *Gansey*. . . A sweater.] **1968** *DARE* (Qu. W4, . . *Names . . for men's coats or jackets for work and outdoor wear*) Inf **NJ**16, Gansey [gænzi]—wool, machine-knit; button, pockets on side.

gant adj [Arch and dial Engl pronc-spp for *gaunt* (see *OED* at *gaunt, EDD* at *gant* adj)]

Thin, undernourished, tired.

1890 *DN* 1.6 **cNY,** The sound *æ* in *gaunt*. **1891** *PMLA* 6.163 **WV,** Gaunt [pronounced *gænt*]. **1899** Garland *Boy Life* 204 **nwIA,** At last even the "gantest" of them [=field hands] filled up. **1912** Green *VA Folk-Speech* 21, As gant as a grayhound. **1913** [see **gant-lot**]. **1935** in 1944 *ADD* **cNY,** 'I feel pretty ga'nt after that long walk' = tired. **1950** *WELS Suppl.* **csWI,** He'd be a big fish, but he's not filled out right; see—he's gant in through here. **c1960** *Wilson Coll.* **csKY,** *Gaunt,* not often heard now, is usually /gænt/. **1965–70** *DARE* (Qu. X52, . . *You'd say that a person like that [=thin] who had been sick was looking ______*) Infs **IL**135, **MI**10, **NY**7, **TX**23, Gant; **LA**14, Gaunt —but [gænt] is common; (Qu. K44, *A bony or poor-looking horse*) Inf **OH**35, Gant; (Qu. BB38, *When a person doesn't look healthy . . you'd say, "He looks ______."*) Inf **NY**7, Gant. **1967** [see **gant-lot**]. **1967** *DARE* FW Addit **OR,** [gænt]. **1968** Moody *Horse* 18 **nwKS** (as of c1920), Don't you figure she's too weedy in the legs and ga'nt in the belly to ever make a good milk cow? **1976** Garber *Mountain-ese* 33 **Appalachians,** He's a tall, gant lookin' man.

gant v Also with *up, out* [**gant** adj] Cf **gaunt** v

To make or become thin, to starve; transf, to tire, vex; hence ppl adjs *ganted (up)* thin, starved, *ganted out* tired out.

1861 Holmes *Venner* 2.72 **NEng,** The "gaänted-up," long-legged animals. **1887** *Scribner's Mag.* Oct 475/2 **AR,** [The baby] looks right puny an' ga'nted. **1917** *DN* 4.412 **wNC, KS,** Gant them cattle up; get the grass out of them so they can travel. **1927** *AmSp* 2.355 **WV,** *Gant* . . to give hard usage. "Gant those cattle up, so they won't be carrying so much grass." "He was riding a ganted horse." **1932** Smiley *Gloss. New Paltz* **NY,** John Yeaple told . . of finding his cat in the rumble seat . . where it had been from Sunday to Friday. When it came out he said it wasn't even 'ganted.' **1942** Whipple *Joshua* 240 **UT,** The audience cinches up its belt (does a man good to 'gant' up now and then!) stands upon its shoeless feet, and sings. **1944** Wellman *Bowl* 239 **KS,** He felt it was a weakness in him that he could not clear his mind of this kind of unprofitable thinking. It "ganted" him like a horse living on loco weed, which has no power of nourishment and only makes the animal start and stare and snort—and go crazy in the end. **1947** Guthrie *Big Sky* 136 **MT,** They'll git ganted up some, too, carryin' empty paunches. **1951** Giles *Harbin's Ridge* 100 **KY,** That's what eat into her an' ganted her up an' give her the sharp tongue she's got. **1961** Adams *Old-Time Cowhand* 155, Poor calves were said to be . . "ganted." **1967–69** *DARE* (Qu. X51, *To lose weight . . "He was sick all winter and ______ [quite a bit]."*) Infs **MA**5, 30, Ganted up. **1969** *DARE* Tape **CA**163, If there's a drastic change in the water . . lots of times the cattle won't drink for two or three days; then they gant all up and they look like the dickens. **1979** Lewis *How to Talk Yankee* [13] **nNEng,** "Don't Pete look awful?" "Ayuh, he's all ganted out. That boss of his drives him somethin' fierce." **1982** *Smithsonian Letters* **ME,** *Ganted,* from "gaunt". "We didn't have enough feed last winter, so the cattle were ganted."

gantered ppl adj [Var of *ganted* ppl adj from **gant** v]

1930 Shoemaker *1300 Words* 26 **cPA Mts** (as of c1900), *Gantered*—A horse in poor condition from overwork, or lack of food.

gant-gutted adj [**gant** adj; cf Engl dial *ganty-gutted* (*EDD* at *gant* adj. 2)] Cf **gank-gutted**

Thin, undernourished.

1912 Green *VA Folk-Speech* 191, *Gant-gutted;* lean in the flank. **1937** Sandoz *Slogum* 27 **NE** (as of 1900–20), Tie me fer a gant-gutted longhorn if I can figger this dump out. *Ibid* 244, Lancaster—that gant-gutted land attorney for the Diamond B. **1967** Will *Dredgeman* 117 **FL,** Big boned he was, hollow cheeked, ga'nt gutted, tanned like a Seminole.

gant-lot n [**gant** v] **chiefly Appalachians**

See quot 1913.

1913 Kephart *Highlanders* 93 **sAppalachians,** [Footnote:] *Gant-lot:* a fenced enclosure into which cattle are driven after cutting them out from those of other owners. So called because the mountain cattle run wild, feeding only on grass and browse, and "they couldn't travel well to market when filled up on green stuff: so they're penned up to git gant and nimble." **1917** *DN* 4.412 **wNC,** *Gant-lot*. . . An enclosure for cattle, to prevent their fattening on grass. Also N. Eng., Ky. **1931** *PMLA* 46.1304 **Appalachians,** The gimpson weeds in that 'ere gant-lot air ez thick ez redheads (woodpeckers) in a dead'nin' (clearing). **1952** Brown *NC Folkl.* 1.544. **1967** *Hall Coll.* **ceTN,** *Gant lot*. . . A pen made of rails to hold cattle until their owners came to pick them up. Not being free to range, they would lose weight and therefore be called "gant." **1974** Fink *Mountain Speech* 11 **wNC, eTN.**

gant out (or up) See **gant** v

ganty See **gaunty**

gap n[1]

1 A pass or valley cutting into a mountain ridge. [*OED gap* sb. 5 1555 →] **widespread, but esp Appalachians** See Map Cf **notch, water gap, wind gap**

1750 in 1898 Filson Club *Pub.* 13.49 **cVA,** This Gap may be seen at a considerable distance. **a1817** (1821) Dwight *Travels* 2.366 **wNEng,** The hills . . separate suddenly, and form a gap of a width just sufficient to allow a passage for the road. **1848** Bartlett *Americanisms* 154, *Gap*. . . It is applied to such openings in a mountain as are made by a river or even a high road. Thus the *Water-Gap;* and, in Virginia, *Brown's Gap, Rockfish Gap,* &c. **1930** Shoemaker *1300 Words* 27 **cPA Mts** (as of c1900), *Gap*—An opening in mountains through which a stream or "run" usually flows. **1932** *DN* 6.229, *Gap.* Rather an obvious topographical word, but not much used in the U.S. except in the South. In New England *notch* is more usual, in New York *pass*. The West, for some reason, seems to follow the latter usage. **1939** *LANE* Map 36 *(Ravine, notch)* 1 inf, **CT,** [gæᵊp]. **1940** *AmSp* 15.34 **VA,** Low places suitable for passage through the mountains. . . *Gap* is perhaps the most common [term]. **1960** Hall *Smoky Mt. Folks* 57, *Gap:* a depression on a ridge, as in Newfound Gap. **1965–70** *DARE* (Qu. C15, *A place in mountains or high hills where you can get through without climbing over the top*) 202 Infs, **widespread, but esp Appalachians,** Gap; **TN**30, **WV**3, 13, Low gap; (Qu. C19, . . *Low land running between hills*) Infs **CT**2, **ID**1, **IN**7, **MA**34, Gap. **1967** *Painesville Telegraph* (OH) 7 Oct 14/5, Down South . . the notches are called gaps. **1972** Cooper *NC Mt. Folkl.* 92, *Gap*—a mountain pass.

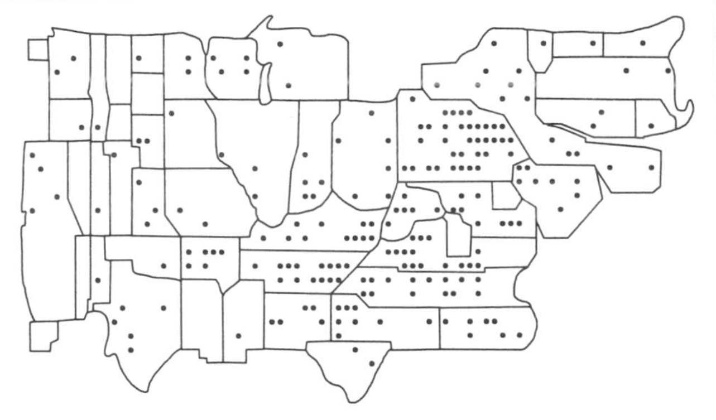

•gap n¹ 1 + var (Qq. C15, C19)

2 pronc-sp *gyap:* An opening in a fence, freq one closed with moveable bars or some other makeshift arrangement; hence, a gate. **now chiefly S Midl, Sth** Cf **water gap**

1636 in 1881 Boston Registry Dept. *Records* 2.12, [They] shall raynge theire payle upon each of their grounds streight from the corner of William Wilkes his house, or from the upper poast of his garding gap. **1698** in 1894 Providence RI Rec. Comm. *Early Rec.* 6.199, The Gapp or barrs where we did use to goe into the orchard. **1836** *S. Lit. Messenger* 2.162 **VA,** On every side I was met by gates, drawbars, and *gaps*—the necessary appendages in the economy of Virginian idleness. **1859** (1968) Bartlett *Americanisms* 167, *Gap*. . . An opening in a fence. A *slip gap* is a place provided in a fence, where the bars may be slipped aside and let down. **1899** (1912) Green *VA Folk-Speech* 191, *Gap*. . . A break or opening, as in a fence, or wall. **1910** *DN* 3.453 **VT,** *Gap*. . . An opening in a fence. "The cows went in through the gap." A "gap" may be entirely open, or it may be fitted with a gate or with bars. **1922** Gonzales *Black Border* 305 **sSC, GA coasts** [Gullah glossary], *Gyap*—gap, gaps, as in a fence or hedge. **1942** *Sat. Eve. Post* 5 Sept. 18/3 **cFL,** He can sit on a gap, which is what the cow people call a corral gate, and let the cowboys run—actually run—a herd of cattle past him. **1967** *PADS* 47.27 [Southern farm terms in Faulkner's *Go Down, Moses*], *Gap. . .* The word *gap* seems to refer to any break in a fence where a gate is not used. . . The gap is sometimes wide enough to allow a wagon to pass through it, in which case only three or four strands of barbed wire are generally used for closing the gap. If the gap is to be only wide enough for a person or animal to pass through, it is often closed with wooden poles called bars. **1968** *DARE* (Qu. N31, *A place in a road where animals regularly go across*) Inf **NC**55, A gap where they let the stock across. **1968** *DARE* FW Addit **MD**20, Gap—large gate in fence. **1984** Wilder *You All Spoken Here* 69 **Sth,** They let the gap down: The situation wherein you can't cross the road because of too much oncoming traffic.

3 Transf: a fence-panel. Cf **milk gap**

1954 *Harder Coll.* **cwTN,** *Gap. . .* Several planks or palings nailed to crosspieces to form a segment or panel of a fence or pen.

4 The mouth. Cf **gape C1, 2** *joc*

1915 *DN* 4.244 **MT,** *Gap,* Mouth. "Shut your gap." **1960** Wentworth–Flexner *Slang* 208, *Gap. . .* The mouth. **1965–70** *DARE* (Qu. X9, . . *"I wish he'd shut his ______."*) Infs **IN**13, **KS**7, **MN**39, **MT**5, **NE**8, **TX**18, Gap; (Qu. X10b) Inf **TX**18, Shut your gap.

5 Fig: an opportunity to say, propose, or agree to something.

1953 Randolph–Wilson *Down in Holler* 247, *Gap. . .* Used figuratively to mean opening, opportunity, encouragement. "Henry must have give them fellers some kind of a gap, or they wouldn't have said nothin' about makin' counterfeit money." **1954** *Harder Coll.* **cwTN,** *Gap. . .* Any opening, opportunity, or encouragement.

6 A trouser fly. *joc* Cf **gaposis**

1965–70 *DARE* (Qu. W24c, *Sayings to warn a man that his trouser-fly is open*) Inf **AR**55, Close the gap; **SC**40, Your gap's open.

gap v, n[2] See **gape**

gap-and-swallow n [*gap* var of **gape B1**] **esp NEng** *joc* Cornmeal mush or other soft or insubstantial food.

1939 Wolcott *Yankee Cook Book* 165, "Gap and Swallow" was another venerable emergency dish, not unlike Hasty Pudding. **1940–41** Cassidy *WI Atlas* **ceWI,** Gap-and-swallow [gæp m 'swɒlo], Nickname for mush and milk. **1941** *LANE* Map 288 *(Corn meal mush)* 1 inf, **swCT,** [gæp ən swɒlŭ]; 1 inf, **sRI,** [gæp m swɔlə]; 1 inf, **cnMA,** ['ga·p ən 'swɒlo]; 1 inf, **sME coast,** ['gæ˄p m̩ 'swɒ˜ᵊlə], made of wheat flour. **1947** Bowles–Towle *New Engl. Cooking* 104, Gap and swallow pudding, tipsy parson, and garden sass all have the "native and puckery flavor" which Lowell felt was characteristic of New England speech. **1968** *DARE* (Qu. H24, . . *Names or nicknames . . for boiled cornmeal*) Inf **CA**87, Gap-an'-swaller ['gæp æn ˌswɔlɚ] grub—applied to any soft food or soup, etc., that didn't have to be chewed. **1989** *DARE* File **RI,** My aunt [born 1889] used the phrase *ga'p and swallow* for the slightest of pick-up meals, nothing to satisfy you. Crackers and water, tea with a used teabag, or cold potatoes and a stalk of celery are examples made up by me to indicate her sense.

gape v, n Usu |gep|; also freq |gæp|; occas **esp S Midl** |g(j)a(r)p, gɛp|; **NEng** also |gɑp, gap| Pronc-spp *ga(h)p, garp, gearp(e), gyap, gyarp*

A Forms.

1806 (1970) Webster *Compendious Dict., Gape,* [a as in ask] *v.i.* to open the mouth, yawn, stare. **1858** Stearns *Practical Guide Pronc.* lv, Give the *a* the Italian sound also in *gape, laugh, father.* **1890** *DN* 1.41 **ME,** *Plant,* like *gape* . . with [ɑ]. *Ibid* 239 **cwMO, MI, NEng,** *Gape. . .* [gæp]. **1893** *DN* 1.273–75, [From 70% to 80% of 57 infs from **eNEng** use the vowel [ɑ] in *gape.* From 20% to 30% of 13 infs from **eVA** use [ɑ] in *gape.* 11% of the 86 infs from the North and West had [ɑ] in *gape.*] **1899** (1912) Green *VA Folk-Speech* 193, *Gearp. . .* To stretch open. A girl said to one who was fastening her dress: "Pin it so it won't gearp." *Ibid* [see **B2** below]. **1903** [see **B2** below]. **1907** *DN* 3.188 **seNH,** *Gape* [gap]. **1922** Gonzales *Black Border* 305 **sSC, GA coasts** [Gullah glossary], *Gyap*—gap, gaps. . . gape, gapes, gaped, gaping. **1954** *Harder Coll.* **cwTN,** [gɛps]. **1961** *Mt. Life* Spring 6 **sAppalachians,** Frequently *r* is inserted in other words: . . *garp* (gape). *Ibid* Spring 18 **sAppalachians,** His daughters . . inspect each other carefully to see that their "pettiskirts" don't gyarp. **1967** *DARE* (Qu. W24c, . . *To warn a man that his trouser-fly is open*) Inf **MA**5, ['gɑpɪn]. **1968** [see **B2** below].

B As verb.

1 To stare stupidly with the mouth open; also, of physical objects, to come or stay open, like an unclosed mouth. [*OED gape* v. 3 c1290 →] Cf **gaup v 1**

1806 [see **A** above]. **1899** [see **A** above]. **1902** (1904) Rowe *Maid of Bar Harbor* 65 **ME,** Go into yer breakfast right off, an' don't stand there gapin' like a stuck pig. **1906** *DN* 3.119 **sIN,** *Gap at. . .* To stare at. "Don't be gappin' at me." **1965–70** *DARE* (Qu. X22, *To stare at something with your mouth open*) 327 Infs, **widespread, but less freq NC, SC,** Gape; 149 Infs, **widespread, but chiefly east of Missip R, esp NC, SC,** Gap; **MA**75, [gɑp]; **MA**122 [ga·p]; **ME**21, [gapɪn] with his mouth open.

2 To yawn; hence vbl n *gapping* yawning; adj *gapey* (pronc-sp *gearpy*) inclined to yawn. [*OED gape* v. 6 c1440 →; "Now *rare* in southern Eng. and in literature; common *colloq* in midland and northern districts"]

1869 Twain *Innocents* 117, We gaped and yawned and stretched. **1885** Twain *Huck. Finn* 66, Pretty soon he gapped, and stretched himself, and hove off the blanket. **1892** *DN* 1.239 **cwMO,** *Gape:* to yawn. Universally pronounced [gæp] in Kansas City. [*DN* Ed: So in Michigan . . and not unknown in New England.] **1899** (1912) Green *VA Folk-Speech* 193, *Gearpe. . .* Pronounced very broad; to yawn. *Gearp.* Gyarp. *Ibid* 193, *Gearpy. . .* [Gyɑɑpee.] Inclined to gearp. "I think I am going to have a chill, I feel very gearpy." **1903** *DN* 2.297 **Cape Cod MA** (as of a1857), *Gap* [gæp]. . . To yawn. **1907** *DN* 3.188 **seNH,** *Gape* [gap]. . . To yawn. "You could see he was tired; he gaped so." *Ibid* 206 **nwAR,** *Gap* [gæp]. . . To yawn. **1908** *DN* 3.314 **eAL, wGA,** *Gap* [gæp]. . . To yawn. **1926** *AmSp* 2.81 **ME,** *Gape* is "garp." (A Maine man never uses the word "yawn.") **1942** in 1944 *ADD* 242 **ME,** [gɑp], v. = yawn. **1950** *WELS (He was getting sleepy and he started to ______)* 9 Infs, **WI,** Gap [gæp]. **1954** *Harder Coll.* **cwTN,** *Gape. . .* To open the mouth wide and take deep breaths. " 'E gapes all the time. Mus' be a-gettin' sick, or sumpin'." **1965–70** *DARE* (Qu. X46, *When a person's getting sleepy and opens his mouth wide and takes a deep breath, that's a ______*) Infs **AR**3, **LA**20, 35, **ME**5, **MA**56, **MS**60, **MO**39, **NJ**21, **NY**70, (He's) gapping; **VA**9, Oh, don't swallow me when you's a-gapping; **SC**7, People used to say this, "Excuse me for gapping"; **IL**57A, He's always gaping; **ME**15, Some say, "He [ga·pt]"; **DE**2, Yawn—some people say gapping! **LA**20, That's gapping; **TN**50, Used to say gaping. **1966** *Wilson Coll.* **GA,** *Gap* . . yawn . . gappin' [gæpɪn] or yawning. **1968** *DARE* Tape **GA**8, He breathed twice deeply and gaped and he was gone. **1968** *DARE* File **RI,** Gahp [ga:p]—to yawn. From my mother's family in Middletown, R.I. This would be the ordinary form for me to use in the family circle; yawn would seem learned. **1982** *Barrick Coll.* **csPA,** Gap . . *yawn.*

C As noun.

1 A yawn; hence *the gapes:* a fit of yawning. [*OED gape* sb. 1 1535 →; *the gapes* (*OED* at *gape* sb. 3. b c1815 →) prob in joc allusion to sense **C2** below] *old-fash*

1885 Twain *Huck. Finn* 58, I took a good gap and a stretch. **1899** (1912) Green *VA Folk-Speech* 193, *Gearp. . .* When a person yawns often he is said to have the *gearps.* **1965–70** *DARE* (Qu. X46) 133 Infs, **widespread, but less freq west of Missip R,** Gap; 24 Infs, **scattered, but less freq west of Missip R,** Gape; **GA**72, He's got the gapes; **VA**31, He had the gaps [gaps]. [Of all Infs responding to this question, 11% were young, 24% mid-aged, 64% old; of those giving these responses, 3% were young, 20% mid-aged, 77% old.]

2 usu pl; often with *the:* A disease of young poultry (caused by the **gapeworm**), which makes them seem to yawn continually. [*OED the gapes* (at *gape* sb. 3. a) 1799 →] **chiefly Midl** See Map on p. 632

1902 (1904) Rowe *Maid of Bar Harbor* 64 **ME,** Let's take a squint at them dead chickens. Like as not they wa'n't killed at all,—died o' the gapes, maybe. **1903** *DN* 2.297 **Cape Cod MA** (as of a1857), *Gaps. . .* A disease of chickens. **1908** *DN* 3.314 **eAL, wGA,** *Gaps* [gæps]. . . A disease of chickens, in which the chicken gapes continually. **1915** *DN* 4.183 **swVA,** *Gaps* [gɛəps]. . . A disease of young chickens. **1923** (1946) Greer–Petrie *Angeline Doin' Society* 22 **csKY,** I told them ladies if the gaps ever got amongst thar brood. **1926** Roberts *Time of Man* 142 **KY,** Then she would—say it had gaps—twist a bit of bluegrass top down into its throat and swab out the worms, drawing them up clinging to the grass brush. **1941** Percy *Lanterns* 325 **nwMS,** What cures gapes in baby chicks. **1954** *Harder Coll.* **cwTN,** *Gapes* [gɛps]—A disease of chickens; they say they got a worm in throat. **1965–70** *DARE* (Qu. K78, *What diseases do chickens commonly get around here?*) 22 Infs, **chiefly Midl,** (The) gaps; **KY**40, Take the gaps [gæps]—They gap every breath til they die; **MA**15, [gæps]—hasn't been seen for a while. Little chickens sometimes have little worms; you take a feather with kerosine on it and stick it down his throat to kill the worm; **NJ**56, The gaps—You twist a horsehair down into chicken's throat (like Roto-Rooter) and pull it up and it's full of worms; **GA**74, **NY**105, **OH**44, **PA**116, (The) gapes; **OH**55, Gap. **1968** [see **gapeworm**]. **1982** *Barrick Coll.* **csPA,** Gaps—a disease of chickens.

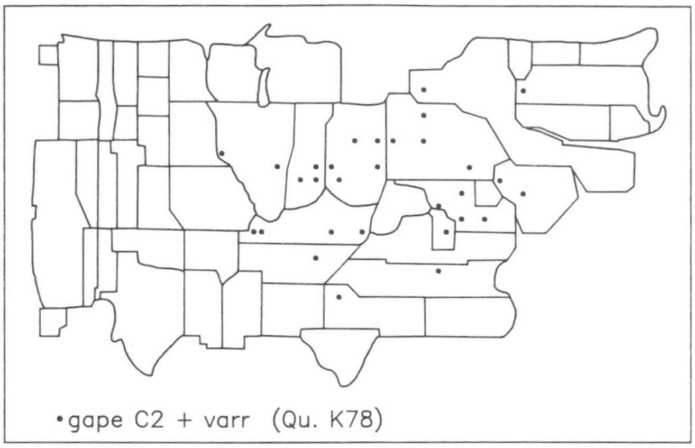

•gape C2 + varr (Qu. K78)

gaper n **Pacific Coast**

1 also *gaper clam:* A clam of the genus *Tresus.* For other names of var spp see **coho clam, horse clam, Washington clam**

1879 U.S. Natl. Museum *Bulletin* 14.257, "Gapers" *(Schizothoerus nuttalli . .).* Oregon. **1889** [see **2** below]. **1974** Abbott *Seashells* 491, *Tresus nuttalli . .* Pacific Gaper. Washington to Baja California. . . Shell with a prominent gape at the posterior end. . . *Tresus capax . .* Alaskan Gaper. . . Kodiak Island, Alaska to Monterey, California. . . Very common on most sand and mud beaches in Puget Sound. **1981** Meinkoth *Audubon Field Guide Seashore* 570, The Gaper Clam lives in a burrow as much as 36″ (1 m) deep. . . Gapers are used both as human food and as fish bait. **1981** Rehder *Audubon Field Guide Seashells* 756, *Tresus nuttallii. . . Hind end broad, rounded, with a large gap for siphons. . .* Commonly known on the Pacific Coast as the Gaper, this species lives . . under the surface in sand. . . The related Alaskan Gaper *(T. capax) . .* is about the same size.

2 A **Washington clam** (here: *Saxidomus* spp).

1889 *Century Dict.* 2453, *Gaper. . .* A gaping clam. . . On the Pacific coast of the United States the term *gaper* is applied to various similar bivalves, as species of *Glycymeris, Saxidomus,* and *Schizothaerus.*

gapeworm n

A nematode worm *(Syngamus trachea)* which inhabits the trachea of var fowl and causes **gape C2.**

1895 (1969) Ward *Catalogue* 217/3, Gape Worm Extractor. . . quickly removes, without injury to the chick, the worms . . from the windpipe. **1925** *Book of Rural Life* 2267, When gapeworms are present, the ground on which the young chicks were located . . should be plowed and limed. **1967** *Merck Vet. Manual* 1175, Gapeworms may produce local irritation, but the chief damage is caused by . . interference with respiration. . . This produces gasping, choking and shaking of the head. **1968** Haun *Hawk's Done Gone* 328 **eTN,** He give me fifteen turkeys and twenty-five chickens the next spring. . . One took the gapes but I twisted up a hair and put down its throat and pulled the gapeworm out.

gapey See **gape B2**

gaposis n *joc*

See quot 1960.

1960 Wentworth-Flexner *Slang* 208, Gaposis. . . A mythical disease, the symptom of which is a customary gap in one's clothing, as between buttons or when one's shirt and trousers or blouse and skirt do not properly meet. *A synthetic commercialism.* **1965–70** *DARE* (Qu. W4) Inf **CA**59, Jumper—blue denim, waist-length, may cover belt so [there's] no gaposis; (Qu. W24b, *Sayings to warn a man that his pants are torn)* Inf **CA**155, He's got gaposis; (Qu. W24c, *Sayings to warn a man that his trouser-fly is open)* Inf **TX**33, Gaposis; **AR**27, Got gaposis. **1988** *DARE* File **cwCA** (as of 1950s), My mother used to try to get rid of the "gaposis" [gæp'osɪs] in a garment she was making if she found that a blouse didn't lie flat between the button holes, or a zipper didn't come clear up to the waistband.

gapper n

A **cottonmouth** (here: *Agkistrodon piscivorus leucostoma*).

1958 Conant *Reptiles & Amphibians* 187, *Western Cottonmouth. . .* The habit of holding the mouth open has earned it the names of "gapper" and "trapjaw."

gapping See **gape B2**

gappings n pl

Wages.

1947 *True* 32.102 **New Orleans LA** [Black], Their [=musicians'] tips were so great until they did not have to even touch their nightly gappings.

gapseed n [*gap* var of **gape;** *OED gapeseed* sb. 1 1598 →]

In joc phrr referring to someone who is staring stupidly: See quots.

1942 McAtee *Dial. Grant Co. IN* 27 (as of 1890s), *Gap-seed . .* a common query to those deemed to stare was "Any ______ to spare?" **1943** McAtee *Dial. Grant Co. IN Suppl. 2* 8, The 1942 list should have included the word "sell" as a substitute for "spare." **1968** *DARE* (Qu. X22, *To stare at something with your mouth open)* Inf **IN**30, Sowing gapseed.

gar v [Cf *OED gar* v. "Chiefly *Sc.* and *north. dial.* . . 2. To make, to cause"]

1 To cause or compel to (do something).

1928 Chapman *Happy Mt.* 89 **seTN,** I'd gar him get a hair-cut under the law. *Ibid* 312, [Glossary:] Gar—to compel, force, make.

2 See quot. [Perh infl by **jar** (as in *ajar, on the jar*)]

1952 Brown *NC Folkl.* 1.544 **cnNC,** *Gar* [g(j)ɑ]. . . To open wide. "Gar your mouth open, son, so I can see your throat." "Don't gar that door; it's already too cold in here."—Granville county.

gar n Also *garfish* Pronc-spp *geaar, gyar* Cf Pronc Intro 3.I.16

1 A freshwater fish of the genus *Lepisosteus,* native chiefly to the South and Missip-Ohio Valleys. Also called **garpike.** For other names of var spp see **alligator gar, gilly gar, longnose gar, shortnose gar**

1765 (1942) Bartram *Diary of a Journey* 38, 'Tis full of large fish, as cats, garr, mullets, and several other kinds. **1772** in 1924 Phillips *Notes B. Romans* 124 **FL,** There is also a fish called the Gar Fish or Allegator Fish from the Shape of its head and teeth, by the french Called poisson armé. **1870** Nowland *Early Indianapolis* 41 (as of 1821), The river abounded with a fish called gar, which was unfit for anything but feeding hogs. **1899** (1912) Green *VA Folk-Speech* 191, *Gar. . .* A fish. Pronounced with hard *g,* and broad *a, geaar.* **1929** *AmSp* 5.18 **Ozarks,** *Gyar-broth. . .* Soup made of the worthless fish called gar. **1933** LA Dept. of Conserv. *Fishes* 392, Gars are especially conspicuous . . because of their curious habit of breathing air. **1949** *Chicago Daily Tribune* (IL) 16 Feb sec 2 2/1, It also may save some motorist from joining the garfish and snakes in a muddy canal. **c1960** *Wilson Coll.* **csKY,** *Garfish* (or *gar*). . . Not eaten by most people in the area. **1965–70** *DARE* (Qu. P3, *Freshwater fish that are not good to eat)* 185 Infs, **chiefly Sth, Missip-Ohio Valleys, TX,** Gar(fish); **MD**38, Freshwater gar; (Qu. P1, *What kinds of freshwater fish are caught around here that are good to eat?)* Infs **LA**7, 8, 10, 14, 15, 20, 34, **SC**26, Gar(fish); (Qu. P14, *If commercial fishing is done around here, what do the fishermen go out after?)* Infs **LA**14, 15, 20, 34, Gar(fish). **1967–68** *DARE* Tape **IN**45, We . . caught a gar about three feet long and . . tied it to a willow bush. The gar drowned; they'll drown 'cause they're . . not really a fish; they have gizzards. . . We dressed that gar and cooked some of it, and ate it and took gar meat to the neighbors—steaks—found out later that they didn't eat it. We ate ours. . . It tasted pretty good; **LA**8, But now when we go fishing and when we catch gar and German carp and goggle-eye perches and grunters . . we keep some and put 'em in deep freeze, and we eat 'em in the winter time.

2 A **needlefish** of the family Belonidae, esp *Strongylura* spp. [*OED* 1440 →]

[**1624** Smith *Genl. Hist. VA* 172 **Bermuda,** Some of them yet knowne to the *Americans,* as the Purgoose, the Cauallo, the Gar-fish, Flying-fish and Morerayes.] **c1735** Catesby *Carolina* II.30 *(DAE), Acus maxima, squammosa, viridis.* The green Gar-Fish. **1807** in 1846 MA Hist. Soc. *Coll.* 2d Ser 3.57, There are the bill fish and the gar; the latter opening a small mouth; the former opening its mouth like a snipe; being in other respects like each other. **1884** Goode *Fisheries U.S.* 1.459, The peculiar green color of the bones is said to prejudice many people against them. I have myself tasted the American Gar-fish and found it exceedingly palatable; and I cannot doubt that at some future time they will be highly prized by our people, as they richly deserve to be. **1906** NJ State Museum *Annual Rept. for 1905* 204, *Tylosurus marinus. . .* Gar. . . A good food-fish, but avoided usually on account of the greenish color of the bones and flesh, especially by the ignorant, who regard it as poisonous. **1909** Holder–Jordan *Fish Stories* 69, On the Florida reef there are myriads of garfishes... Long, slender, needle-like, they lie, often motionless, their long teeth-lined beaks giving them a savage appearance. *Ibid* 70, These gars were not over a foot in length. **1946** LaMonte *N. Amer. Game Fishes* 18, *The Needlefishes.* Genera: *Strongylura; Ablennes. Names:* Gar [etc]... There are several species in the Atlantic, running from our southern limit to Maine and including the Gulf of Mexico; and several in the Pacific, running north to Point Conception. **1966–70** *DARE* (Qu. P4, *Saltwater fish that are not good to eat*) Infs **GA**28, **MS**73, **VA**55, Gar; **LA**37, **VA**110, Garfish.

garabanzo See **garbanzo**

garage n Usu |gə'rɑž, 'rɑǰ|; for addit varr see quots Pronc-spp *gararge, garr-ridge, g'ra(r)j*

A Forms.

1916–20s in 1944 *ADD* **cNY,** [g(ə)rɑdʒ]. **1930s** in 1944 *ADD* **eWV,** Gararge. Common pron. **1940** *AmSp* 15.369 **nePA,** *Garage* [grɑdʒ] (one syllable). **1975** Gould *ME Lingo* 107, When automobiles began to appear, Mainers reserved *garage* for the mechanics' shops where repairs were made... In those days *garage* was pronounced garr-ridge, to rhyme with carriage. In the early 1920s the ladies and girls affected a new hair-do.. dubbed the "cootie garage.".. Radio was blossoming, and Maine speech began to be nationalized by it. The fad of cootie garages thus taught Maine people to say *g'rarj.* **1988** *DARE* File **nwMA,** I grew up in western Massachusetts saying "I left it in the g'rarj [grɑɚǰ]" (perhaps influenced by my father who is from eastern Mass.); now though, I say g'raj [grɑǰ].

B Sense.

A children's tag game; see quot.

1970 *DARE* Tape **CA**68, Then garage is much different... You have to pick any car and if the person in the middle says the [name of that] car, the person—any people on this side—run over to the other side and the other side runs over to this side if they have that car.

garage apartment n **scattered, but esp TX, AL, SC**

An apartment either converted from a garage or next to or over a garage.

1965–70 *DARE* (Qu. D26,.. *Different kinds of apartments [Especially, small apartments]*) 54 Infs, **scattered, but esp TX, AL, SC,** Garage apartment. **1985–87** *NADS Letters,* [Responses from twenty individuals, chiefly in the South, South Midland, and Southwest, indicate that *garage apartment* refers to a living space either converted from a garage or added at the side of or over a garage.] **1986** Pederson *LAGS Concordance,* 3 infs, **LA,** Garage apartment. **1986** *Tuscaloosa News* (AL) 22 Apr 23, *Forest Lake*.. 3 bedroom, 1 bath, plus rented garage apt. in rear. **1988** *Austin Amer.–Statesman* (TX) 8 Mar sec A 1, A neatly dressed young gunman slipped into the garage apartment of a Texas Christian University student.

garage door is open phr *joc* Cf **barn door 2b**

1965–70 *DARE* (Qu. W24c,.. *To warn a man that his trouser-fly is open*) Infs **AL**60, **GA**92, **IL**137, Garage door is open; **PA**66, Your garage door's open. [All Infs Black]

‡garagette n [*garage* + *-ette* dimin suff]

=**garage apartment.**

1966 *DARE* (Qu. D26,.. *Names.. for different kinds of apartments [Especially, small apartments]*) Inf **SC**6, Garagette.

garambullo n [MexSpan] **SW**

=**wolfberry** (here: *Lycium* spp).

1913 Wooton *Trees NM* 134, The *Garrambullo (Lycium torreyi)* is a shrub 3 to 5 feet high, common in the valleys of the southern end of the State. **1931** U.S. Dept. Ag. *Misc. Pub.* 101.142, *Lycium spp...* These bushes are common and characteristic and a wealth of vernacular names has been bestowed upon them, including.. garambullo. **1960** Vines *Trees SW* 916, *Lycium torreyi...* is also known by.. Garambullo.

garantogen n Also *garent oguen, garentoquen, garentoquere, grantogen* [See quot 1830]

A **ginseng B1** (here: *Panax quinquefolium*).

1743 (1946) Gronovius *Flora Virginica* 147, *Panax foliis ternis quinatis...* Sinensibus Ginzeng, Iroquæis Garent Oguen. **1830** Rafinesque *Med. Flora* 52, *Panax quinquefolium...* Ginseng-root,.. Garantogen. *Ibid* 55, The Huron tribes call this root *Garantogen,* meaning root like a man. **1900** Lyons *Plant Names* 273, *P[anax] quinquefolius* [sic]... Garentoquen (Iroquois), Grantogen. **1940** Clute *Amer. Plant Names* 265, *Panax quinquefolia* [sic]. Garantogen, tartar root. **1971** Krochmal *Appalachia Med. Plants* 186, *Panax Quinquefolium...* Garantogen, garentoquere,.. grantogen.

garapata n [Span *garrapata* tick] **SW**

Usu a tick of the family Ixodidae, but see quot 1889.

[**1836** Latrobe *Rambler in Mexico* 31 **Mexico,** Every leaf, every spray holds its myriads of *garapatos,* a species of wood bug.] [**1846** *Dollar Newspaper* (Philadelphia PA) 10 June 4/3 **Mexico,** They may meet with a few bloody-minded mosquitoes, an occasional *garapata,* or a wild Mexican in the chapparels.] **1889** *Century Dict.* 2454, *Garapata, garrapata...* The Spanish-American name of any tick of the family *Ixodidae;* also, especially, of the sheep-tick, a dipterous insect, *Melophagus ovinus.* **1934** Morris *Digging in Southwest* 19 *(DA),* There are more *garapatas* than ever.

garapata bean n [**garapata** + *bean*]

1912 Freeman *Southwestern Beans* 578 *(DA),* Garaypata or Mexican Tick Bean.. takes its name from the flecked markings of the seed coat, which somewhat resemble those on castor beans and on certain varieties of ticks which occur in Mexico.

gararge See **garage**

garb n[1], v Usu |gɑ(r)b|; also **esp S Midl, Sth** |gjɑ(r)b| (see Pronc Intro 3.I.16) Pronc-spp *gearb, gyarb*

Std senses, var forms.

1900 in 1944 *ADD* **Richmond VA,** The lady of the house receives you in a tasteful *gearb.* **1917** *DN* 4.413 **KY, wNC, SC,** *Gyarb...* garb. **1923** (1946) Greer–Petrie *Angeline Steppin'* 37 **csKY,** Walkin' around in a gyarb like that. **1924** (1946) Greer–Petrie *Angeline Gits an Eyeful* 6 **csKY,** She.. *gyarbs* herse'f like a right young gal. **1939** *Hall Coll.* **neTN,** *Garb...* [gjɑrb] Garb, clothes... He was dressed in an awful gyarb.

garb n[2] See **gob** n[1]

garbage collector n Also *garbage sandwich joc*

A large sandwich with many ingredients.

1968 *DARE* (Qu. H42, *The kind [of sandwich] in a much larger, longer bun, that's a meal in itself*) Inf **MN**33, Garbage collector. [Laughter] **1971** *Today Show Letters* **seNJ** (as of 1940s) [Black], To his [=Dr. Cassidy's] list I would like to add a name that my family and numerous friends used for this sandwich in the early 1940's in.. Atlantic City, N.J... The Italian Store across town sold "Submarine" sandwiches. We re-named them "Garbage" sandwiches, because everything was thrown *in* (instead of thrown *out*[)].

garbage mover See **trash mover**

garbage night n Cf **cabbage night**

1987 *DARE* File **Cincinnati OH** (as of c1935), Garbage night—The night before Halloween, when children dump garbage on the porches of people's houses.

garbancillo n Also *garbanzilla* [MexSpan; dimin of *garbanzo*]

A **milk vetch** (here: *Astragalus mollissimus* or *A. wootonii*).

[**1887** KS State Bd. Ag. *Report* 2.209, The Spanish name for the plant is Garabanzillo... The botanical name is *Astragalus mollissimus.*] **1937** U.S. Forest Serv. *Range Plant Hdbk.* W41, *Astragalus mollissimus* [was named] garbanzilla from its resemblance to the chickpea, Spanish "garbano" [sic] *(Cicer arietinum),* which is used in Spain as food. **1970** Correll *Plants TX* 847, *Astragalus Wootonii...* Garbancillo.

garbanzo n, also attrib Also *garabanzo, garbanza, garboza* [Span] **orig SW**

=**chick-pea 1.**

1844 Kendall *Santa Fe Exped.* II.225 *(DA),* The lower cup was generally filled with mutton broth, having a piece of the meat left within it, and also a quantity of garbanzos, or large Spanish peas. **1908** North *Mother of CA* 22, Around the present mission are.. fields where peas and *garbanzas*.. thrive most wondrously. **1942** Castetter–Bell *Pima & Papago Ag.* 196, It has been reported that *garbanzos* will endure a temperature of 13° F. without being injured. **1966–69** *DARE* (Qu. I20, *Other kinds of beans*) Inf **CA**22, Garabanzos—look like a nasturtium seed; **CA**136, Garbanzo [gɑr'bænzo]; (Qu. I18, *The smaller beans that are white when they are dry*) Inf **FL**11, Garbanza [gə'bænzə] beans—little, white, round, hard; used in salad or bean soup; (Qu. I19, *Small white beans with a black spot*) Inf **MI**110, Garboza beans; (Qu. H56,.. *Kinds of pickles*) Inf **CA**118, Pickled garbanza [ˌgɑr'bɑnzə] beans. **1976** Bailey–Bailey *Hortus Third* 271, *Garbanzo...* Widely cult. for the nutritious seeds.

garbed out See **garb out**

garbill n Also *garbill duck* [See quot 1889]
=merganser.
1888 Trumbull *Names of Birds* 73 **IL,** Gar-bill [is] . . indiscriminately applied to mergansers in general. **1889** *Century Dict.* 2454, *Gar-bill*. . . A merganser; a sawbill or fish-duck: so called from the long slender beak. [*Century:* Local, U.S.] **1923** U.S. Dept. Ag. *Misc. Circular* 13.5, *Red-breasted merganser*. . . Garbill (Ill.); garbill duck (La.) **1982** Elman *Hunter's Field Guide* 230, Red-breasted Merganser. . . Common & regional names . . garbill.

Garble's quail See **Gambel's quail**

garboon See **goboon**

garb out v phr, hence ppl adj phr *garbed out* [Cf *OED garb* v. b]
1944 *PADS* 2.56 **MO,** *Garb out*. . . To dress or overdress. "Here he comes all *garbed out* in his best bib and tucker." Several rural sections.

garboza See **garbanzo**

garbroth n, also attrib Pronc-spp *gyar-broth* **chiefly Sth, S Midl**
Broth made from the **gar** n **1**—usu used in compar phrr to represent what is poor, worthless, or despicable.
1832 Paulding *Westward Ho* 1.185 **KY,** The Gar-broth people are cluttering up the country. *Ibid* 2.100, If I hadn't sooner eat *garbroth* with a real nigger, may I never see a tree. **1893** Owen *Voodoo Tales* 32 **SW** [Black], One time dey wuz er man dat wuz meaner'n gyar-broth. **1899** (1912) Green *VA Folk-Speech* 191, A gar is looked on as a particularly poor fish for food, and broth made from it is very mean; applied to persons is worse still. "He is as mean as gar-broth." **1912** *DN* 3.586 **wIN,** *Poor* (or *thin*) *as gar broth.* **1927** *AmSp* 2.355 **WV,** That man treats his family meaner'n gar broth. **1941** Percy *Lanterns* 66 **nwMS,** It is bitter as gar-broth. **1950** *PADS* 14.31 **SC,** *Gar-broth*. . . Only in the simile "mean as garbroth." **1953** Randolph–Wilson *Down in Holler* 174 **Ozarks,** *Mean as garbroth* is common, but here the word [*=mean*] signifies no more than poor or inferior, since the hillman feels that gars are unfit for human food. Worn-out land is often said to be *as mean as garbroth* or *as thin as garbroth.* **1967–68** *DARE* (Qu. HH22b, . . *"He's meaner than ______."*) Infs **IN**39, **WI**22, Gar broth; (Qu. U41b, . . *"He's poor as ______."*) Inf **SC**43, Garboth ['gɑəbɔθ] [sic]—my father used it. **1982** Heat Moon *Blue Highways* 395 **Chesapeake Bay,** We have no poor except those that choose to be—those that would be poor as gar broth anywhere.

gardaloo n [Appar from Scots *gardyloo!* a cry to warn passersby before throwing slops from the window]
A noise expressing contempt; a raspberry.
1955 Adams *Grandfather* 175 **NY** (as of c1880), "A loud and scornful gardaloo offended the peaceful night." "I know what a gardaloo is," John said quickly, and delivered what, in modern parlance, would be called a Bronx cheer. "Precisely," Grandfather replied, though he was not too well pleased. He enjoyed puzzling us with his archaisms.

gardeen See **guardian**

garden n Usu |'gɑ(r)dən|; also **Sth, S Midl,** *once common, now old-fash* |'gjɑ(r)dən|; also **esp NEng** |'gɑ(r)dɪŋ| (cf Pronc Intro 3.I.16, 20) For further detail, see esp quots 1931, 1939, 1961 Pronc-spp *gaden, garding, gearden, gyaa'd'n, gya(r)den, gyardin* Cf **-ing**
Std sense, var forms.
1636 in 1881 Boston Registry Dept. *Records* 2.12, The upper poast of his garding gap. **1837** Sherwood *Gaz. GA* 70, [In a list of "Provincialisms" to be avoided:] *Garding,* garden. **1858** Stearns *Practical Guide Pronc.* lxxvii, Be especially careful *not* to interpose it in the following. Say, . . garden *[not]* gyarden. **1890** *DN* 1.67, *Garden:* pronounced *gyaden,* by old Virginians. Kentuckians say *gaden.* **1890** *PMLA* 5.199 **ceVA,** The consonants *g* and *k* are palatalized as in Charleston. One hears (. . gjarden . .). This pronunciation is of course not general. Some consider it vulgar and avoid it, but it can be heard in the best families. **1893** Shands *MS Speech* 32, The pronunciation of *c* and *g,* as if followed by a vocalic *y* just before the letter *a,* is of frequent occurrence in the language of the lower classes of Mississippi, and is sometimes heard even in the conversation of cultivated people. . . *gyarden* for *garden.* **1899** (1912) Green *VA Folk-Speech* 193, *Gearden*. . . With hard *g.* **1907** *DN* 3.193 **NH,** Garding. *Ibid* 2.344 **eME,** *Garding.* **1917** *DN* 4.413 **wNC,** *Gyarden*. . . Also S. Car., Ky. **1922** Gonzales *Black Border* 305 **sSC, GA coasts** [Gullah glossary], *Gyaa'd'n*—garden, gardens. **1923** (1946) Greer–Petrie *Angeline Doin' Society* 18 **csKY,** Gyardin. **1931** *AmSp* 6.169 **VA,** Today pronunciation of the . . [gjɑdn] type is not often heard in the speech of business and professional men, if we except Episcopal ministers. However, certain gentlemen of the old school, many ladies of the old families, debutantes who have attended Episcopal institutions, professional Virginians and parvenus are fond of the sound. **1934** *Hanley Disks* **seME,** Garden [gɑrdɪŋ]. **1939** *LANE* Map 121 *(Vegetable garden),* [Most proncs are of the type [gɑ(r)d(ɪ)n]. 11 infs offer proncs of the type [gɑ(r)dɪŋ]; 2 of these are labeled "affected" proncs, one "refined," and one "a slip of the tongue." A number of infs, chiefly **sNEng,** use a fronted g, which 9 infs follow with a front glide; 2 **CT** infs palatalize the initial consonant. Proncs of the type [gædn] are given by two infs, one of whom considers it old-fashioned.] **1942** Hall *Smoky Mt. Speech* 94 **wNC, eTN,** In the speech of older people, this glide [j] is very common after [k] or [g] before [ɑɚ]; for example, in . . *garden.* **1950** *PADS* 14.34 **SC,** *Gyarden*. . . Dialect pronunciation of *garden*. . . A survival of an eighteenth century pronunciation which is still heard in the coastal area, especially in Charleston, but only sporadically in the remainder of the state. **1961** Kurath–McDavid *Pronc. Engl.* 175, The pronunciation of *garden* as /gjɑdɪn/ is especially common (1) between the Potomac and the James in Virginia and (2) in the Low Country of South Carolina, where it occurs on all social levels, although it is clearly recessive. Some cultured informants, indeed, use this regional pronunciation with some pride. In eastern North Carolina and in the Upcountry of both of the Carolinas, /gjɑdɪn ~ gjɑrdən/ is largely restricted to folk speech. **1967** *DARE* FW Addit **LA,** [gjɑ:dn] Old-fashioned Negro usage. [Inf is old, reports that her generation laughed at this pronc.]

garden balm n
=lemon balm.
1889 *Century Dict.* 433, *Balm*. . . The garden- or lemon-balm . . is *M[elissa] officinalis.* **1903** Porter *Flora PA* 270, *Melissa officinalis*. . . *Garden* . . *Balm*. . . In waste places, thickets and woods. **1930** Sievers *Amer. Med. Plants* 8, Garden balm. . . is lemon scented. **1961** Thomas *Flora Santa Cruz* 296 **cwCA,** Garden . . Balm. Roadsides and shaded canyons, most common in the central portion of the Santa Cruz Mountains. **1974** (1977) Coon *Useful Plants* 160, Garden balm. . . has long been known for its sweetness and possible medicinal values.

garden catchfly n
A **catchfly 1** (here: *Silene armeria*). Also called **French pink 2, mice pink, mock sweet William, none-so-pretty, old maid's pink, pretty Nancy, sweet Susan, sweet William catchfly, wax plant**
1847 Wood *Class-Book* 191, *S[ilene] Armeria. Garden Catch-fly*. . . A popular garden flower. **1950** Gray–Fernald *Manual of Botany* 633, *Garden* . . *Catchfly*. . . Cult. and esc. to roadsides and waste places. **1976** Bailey–Bailey *Hortus Third* 1043, *Garden c[atchfly]*. . . Naturalized in N. Amer.

gardener's garters n
1 A **ribbon grass** (here: *Phalaris arundinacea* var *picta*).
1889 *Century Dict.* 2456, *Gardener's-garters*. . . A variety of canary-grass, *Phalaris arundinacea,* with variegated leaves. **1899** (1909) Earle *Child Life* 390 **NEng,** A particularly disagreeable sound could be evoked by every boy, and (I must acknowledge it) by every girl, too, by placing broad leaves of grass—preferably the pretty striped ribbon-grass, or gardener's garters—between the thumbs and blowing thereon. **1912** Baker *Book of Grasses* 94, Under the names of Ribbon-grass, . . Gardeners' Garters, . . and French-grass, a variety of the Reed Canary was planted in the gardens of earlier days. **1950** Hitchcock–Chase *Manual Grasses* 556, *Ribbon grass.* Blades striped with white. . . Grown for ornament in gardens; also called gardener's garters. **1976** Bailey–Bailey *Hortus Third* 854, *[Phalaris] arundinacea*. . . Var. *picta*. . . Gardener's-garters.
2 A **giant reed a** (here: *Arundo donax* var *versicolor*).
1959 Carleton *Index Herb. Plants* 51, *Gardener's garters:* Arundo donax; Phalaria arundinacea.

gardener snake See **garden snake**

garden hackle n [*hackle* part of an artificial fishing fly]
The common worm used as bait.
1950 *WELS (What do you call the common worm used for bait?)* 1 Inf, **WI,** Garden hackle. **1966–70** *DARE* (Qu. P5) Infs **MA**32, **NC**33, **NY**52, 233, Garden hackle. **1984** Wilder *You All Spoken Here* 196 **Sth,** Garden hackle—earthworms skewered on hooks.

garden house n [Also Engl dial; *OED garden-house* 1. b 1886] **chiefly Mid Atl** See Map

A privy.

1899 (1912) Green *VA Folk-Speech* 191, *Garden house*. . . A privy, as they are usually built in a garden of a country-house. **1946** *PADS* 5.23 **VA,** *Garden house*. . . A privy; common everywhere except the southern part of the Piedmont. **1948** *AN&Q* 8.172 **VA,** I remember seeing an old Negro . . clean a privy on my aunt's farm. He told me he was "movin' de honey from de garden house." **1949** Kurath *Word Geog.* 53, *Garden house,* in Virginia and northeastern North Carolina. **1954** *PADS* 21.28 **SC,** *Garden house.* **1956** McAtee *Some Dialect NC* 18, Garden house. **1965–70** *DARE* (Qu. M21b, *Joking names*) 13 Infs, **chiefly Mid Atl,** Garden house; **NC**21, Little garden house; (Qu. M21a, *An outside toilet building*) Infs **MD**22, **NC**41, 87, **SC**39, **VA**33, 70, Garden house. **1971** *DARE* FW Addit **nwMD,** Garden house. **1984** Wilder *You All Spoken Here* 176 **Sth,** Gardenhouse lilies: Day lilies. Often planted about privies. **1986** Pederson *LAGS Concordance (Privy)* 3 infs, **nTN, c,cwGA,** Garden house; 1 inf, **ceTN,** Garden house—grandmother's term; 1 inf, **cGA,** Garden house—would be a nice name for it; 1 inf, **neTX,** Garden house—polite; more delicate term.

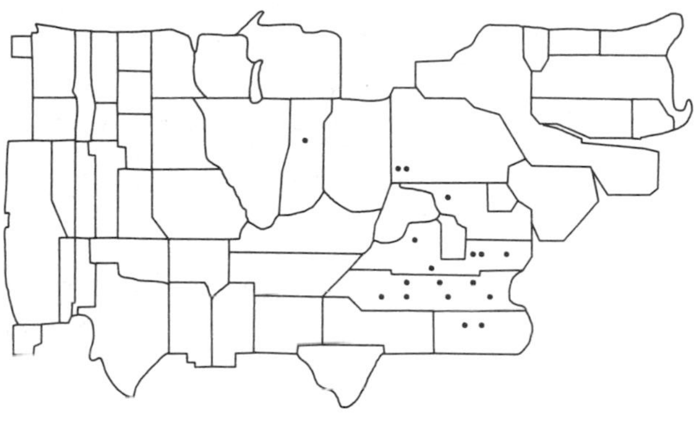

•garden house + var (Qq. M21a, b)

garden huckleberry n

1 A **nightshade** (here: *Solanum melanocerasum*). Note: This plant was formerly considered a var of *Solanum nigrum.*

1910 Graves *Flowering Plants* 345 **CT,** *Solanum nigrum*. . . This plant has recently been somewhat extensively advertised in seed catalogues as Garden Huckleberry, and it is claimed the ripe berries are entirely safe and wholesome either fresh or cooked. The testimony is somewhat conflicting. **1935** (1943) Muenscher *Weeds* 414, *Solanum nigrum.* . . Poisonous when eaten, although certain cultivated forms are grown under such names as "garden huckleberry" . . for the berries which are used in preserves. **1950** Stevens *ND Plants* 247, *Garden Nightshade*. . . The plant called . . garden huckleberry, is a stouter form of this species. **1967** Harrington *Edible Plants Rocky Mts.* 286, A husky, large-fruited form of this species [=*Solanum nigrum*] is fairly common in cultivation under the name of . . "garden huckleberry. . . " Many people eat these fruits without harm . . , but even this garden form has been reported to have occasionally caused illness. **1969** *DARE* (Qu. I53, *Other fruits grown around here*) Inf **IL**31, Garden huckleberry. **1976** Bailey-Bailey *Hortus Third* 1055, *[Solanum] melanocerasum.* . . *Garden huckleberry*. . . Perhaps of garden origin. . . Ripe berries edible, with flavor of a bitter tomato; cooked as a vegetable or used in preserves and pies.

2 A **ground cherry** (here: *Physalis neomexicana*).

1947 (1976) Curtin *Healing Herbs* 188 **NM,** Physalis neomexicana. . . *Garden Huckleberry*. . . And to this day, seed catalogues intended for the Plains states, where fruit is scarce, advertise the seeds under the name of garden huckleberry to be grown for preserving.

gardening spot See **garden spot**

garden oriole n

=**orchard oriole.**

1967 *DARE* FW Addit **AR**49, Garden orioles—darker than Baltimore orioles.

garden patience n

A **dock** n[1]: *Rumex patientia* or **curled dock.**

1892 (1974) Millspaugh *Amer. Med. Plants* 143, *Rumex crispus*. . . *Garden Patience*. . . grows in cultivated ground, and along roadsides, everywhere in the eastern section of the United States. **1900** Lyons *Plant Names* 327, *R[umex] Patientia*. . . Europe, nat. locally in U.S. . . Garden Patience. **1910** Graves *Flowering Plants* 157 **CT,** *Rumex Patientia*. . . Garden . . Patience. . . Sometimes cultivated for spring greens. **1971** Krochmal *Appalachia Med. Plants* 218, *Rumex crispus* . . garden patience. . . The roots of this plant are reportedly valuable as an astringent and mild laxative. **1974** (1977) Coon *Useful Plants* 214, *Rumex crispus* . . garden patience. . . A ten-minute cooking of the young leaves gives a delicious vegetable.

garden pea n Cf **field pea**

The common cultivated pea *(Pisum sativum).* Also called **English pea, green pea 1, sugar pea, sweet pea**

1822 (1972) Deane *New Engl. Farmer* 322/2, Garden pease are harvested by picking them off as they ripen; but field pease must unavoidably be harvested all at once. **1891** Jesup *Plants Hanover NH* 12, Additional plants of this order: *Coronilla varia* . . , *Pisum sativum* (Garden Pea), besides others. **1910** Graves *Flowering Plants* 257 **CT,** *Pisum sativum*. . . Garden Pea. . . Waste places as an escape from cultivation. **1950** *WELS (Kinds of peas grown in your neighborhood)* 11 Infs, **WI,** Garden pea(s). **1954** *PADS* 21.26 **SC,** *English peas*. . . Also called *sugar peas* . . , *green peas, garden peas*. . . *English peas* are purveyed commercially and widely sold under the name *green peas.* All four of these terms are used generally in South Carolina, with the possible exception of *sugar peas.* **1967–70** *DARE* (Qu. H49, *Dishes made by boiling potatoes with other foods*) Inf **DE**2, New potatoes and garden peas; **GA**17, White potatoes, snap beans, garden peas in soup; (Qu. H50), Inf **CO**5, Garden peas; (Qu. I14, *Kinds of beans that you eat in the pod before they're dry*) Inf **GA**28, Garden peas; (Qu. I20) Inf **NC**87, Garden peas. **1968** *DARE* Tape **CA**100, For many years they raised . . garden-pea seed and shipped it all over the world. **1989** *DARE* File **wNC** (as of c1916), Garden peas—this was the usual term for the small green peas that were a frequent vegetable as part of lunch and dinner, fresh in the summer, in commercial cans in other seasons.

garden salad n

=**salad.**

1942 [see **garden sauce**].

garden sarse (or sass) See **garden sauce**

garden sass stuff See **garden stuff**

garden sauce n Pronc-spp *garden sarse,* ~ *sass* **[sauce]** *old-fash*

Garden vegetables, produce—sometimes used to refer to particular kinds of vegetables.

1791 *Amer. Museum* 10.179, For want of garden sauce, they . . eat more flesh than is consistent with their health or his purse. **1817** in 1918 IN Hist. Soc. *Pub.* 308 **NY,** They ascertained the quantity we wanted . . four or five pounds, besides some garden sauce. **1833** Neal *Down-Easters* 1.91, I wanted cabbage or potaters, or most any sort o' garden sarse. **1893** Shands *MS Speech* 32, *Garden-sass*. . . Used by negroes and illiterate whites for *vegetables.* It means exactly the same as *garden-truck,* which is a well-known term. **1908** *DN* 3.314 **eAL, wGA,** *Garden-sass*. . . Vegetables, particularly greens, salads, etc. The simple form *sass* is rarely used. **1914** *DN* 4.73 **ME, NH,** *Garden-sass.* **1923** *DN* 5.208 **swMO,** *Garden sass*. . . Fresh vegetables or small fruit from the garden. **1941** *LANE* Map 253 *(Garden vegetables), Garden sauce* is generally used, by those to whom the term is still natural, as the equivalent of *garden vegetables;* but some informants restrict the use of this term to particular kinds of vegetables. Thus *garden sauce* is said to include only small vegetables . . [by 2 infs], or only radishes . . [by 1 inf], radishes and lettuce . . [by 1 inf], lettuce, peas and beans . . [by 2 infs], or lettuce, peppers and celery . . [by 1 inf]. One informant . . states that when he says to a child, 'Go out and get a little garden sauce', he expects him to bring whatever happens to be growing. Another . . describes *garden sauce* as an old term for cooked vegetables. [132 infs, **throughout NEng,** Garden sass; 27 infs, **throughout NEng,** Garden sauce. Of these, 24% regarded the term as older or old-fashioned but still in use and 28% regarded it as obsolete.] **1942** Hall *Smoky Mt. Speech* 33, An old woman of Catons Grove called green vegetables ['gɑɚdn̩ ˌsæs] (the usual expression is ['gɑɚdn̩ ˌsælɪt]). **1944** *PADS* 2.43 **sVA, NC,** Garden sass. **1946** *AmSp* 21.98 **sIL,** Only a genuine old timer speaks of *garden sass* now. **1950** *WELS,* 6 Infs, **WI,** Garden sass. **1966–68** *DARE* (Qu. I2, *What general word do you have for vegetables?* total Infs questioned, 75) Inf **FL**27, Garden sass [sæs] [heard]; **ME**5, Garden sass [sæs]—carrots, parsnips, beets; (Qu. I30, . . *Names for rhubarb*) Inf **OH**65, Garden sass. [All Infs old]

garden seed n [Euphem for *God sakes* or similar phr]
In phrr *for* (or *my*) *garden seed:* See quots.
1942 Berrey–Van den Bark *Amer. Slang* 194.6, *Oaths; expletives* . . for garden seed! **1965** *DARE* File **TX,** For garden seed! A popular exclamation during World War I. **1966** *DARE* (Qu. NN27a, *Weakened substitutes for 'God': "My ______!"*) Inf **AL**6, Garden seed.

garden smother n
Perh a **knotweed.**
1968 *DARE* (Qu. S21, . . *Weeds . . that are a trouble in gardens and fields*) Inf **VA**25A, Garden smother—tiny bloom, small tender-looking plant.

garden snake n Also *gard(e)ner snake*
=**garter snake 1.**
1958 Conant *Reptiles & Amphibians* 130, In the more humid East, Garter (sometimes called "garden") Snakes may occur almost anywhere. **1966–68** *DARE* (Qu. P25, *What kinds of snakes are found around here?*) Inf **MD**18, **MI**32, **MN**5, Gardener snake; **CA**72, **NY**80, **PA**76, Gardner snake. **1981** Vogt *Nat. Hist.* 152 **WI,** The eastern garter snake, garden snake, or grass snake is a medium-sized slender snake. **1986** Pederson *LAGS Concordance,* 15 infs, **Gulf Region,** Garden snake(s). **1989** *New Yorker* 5 June 32/3 **VA,** All over the street there are dead garter snakes—"garden snakes" most of the people in town stupidly call them.

garden spot n Also *gardening spot* [Also in Engl dial; see *EDD* (at *garden* sb. 2)]
A small plot for growing things, usu vegetables.
1687 in 1889 Plymouth MA *Records* 1.190 **eMA,** From thence we are bound by goodman Watsons garden spot. **1794** MA Hist. Soc. *Coll.* 3.250, The dwelling houses in Boston have an advantage above most of the large towns on the continent with respect to garden spots. **1896** Jewett *Pointed Firs* 147 **ME,** We all three regarded with deep interest . . the barns and garden-spots and poultry. **1939** *LANE* Map 121 2 infs, **wMA,** Garden spot. **1965–70** *DARE* (Qu. L6a, . . *A piece of land under cultivation—less than an acre*) 38 Infs, **scattered, but less freq NW, Upper MW,** Garden spot; **GA**45, Gardening spot; (Qu. I1, . . *The garden where you grow carrots, beans, and such things, to eat at home*) Infs **MA**25, **OH**89, 90, **TX**62, **WA**27, Garden spot. **1966–70** *DARE* Tape **FL**19, They [=snakes] came through that garden spot . . through a neighbor's yard and through our garden; **KY**85, We didn't raise much, only just a garden spot out here, it was all in cotton; **MI**29, Then I have a little garden spot and I usually plant about a dozen tomato plants, a few green onions. **1973** Allen *LAUM* 1.303 (as of c1950), 1 inf, **NE,** Garden spot. **1986** Pederson *LAGS Concordance (Vegetable garden)* 16 infs, **Gulf Region,** Garden spot(s).

garden stuff n Also *garden sass stuff* [*OED* a1687 →] **scattered, but chiefly Nth**
Garden vegetables.
c1644 in 1869 Winthrop *Life & Letters* 2.460 **MA,** All sorts of English fruits & garden stuffe, prosper very well heere. **1731** in 1930 Winslow *Amer. Broadside* 163/2 **MA,** An old Black Muff,/ Some Garden Stuff,/ A Quantity of Burrage. **1803** in 1852 U.S. Congress *Debates & Proc.* 8th Cong 2d Sess 1505, The inhabitants [of St. Bernardo, LA] . . are Spaniards . . who content themselves with raising fowls, corn, and garden stuff for the market at New Orleans. **1891** (1967) Freeman *New Engl. Nun* 403, We ain't got anything but garden-stuff. **1899** (1912) Green *VA Folk-Speech* 191, *Garden-stuff.* . . Plants growing in the garden; vegetables for the table. **1923** Herrick *Lilla* 265 **WY,** You've got your bees and your chickens and garden stuff. **1934** (1970) Wilson *Backwoods Amer.* 62 **Ozarks,** They'd cooked up 'most ever'thing—deer meat, fried ham, sausage, turkey and chickens and all sorts of gyarden stuff. **1941** *LANE* Map 253 *(Garden vegetables)* 26 infs, **scattered NEng,** Garden stuff; 1 inf, **ceVT,** Garden sass stuff. **1950** *WELS,* 6 Infs, **WI,** Garden stuff. **1966** *DARE* (Qu. L34) Inf **ME**12, Garden stuff. **1973** Allen *LAUM* 1.302 **Upper MW** (as of c1950), Of the minor variants *garden stuff* has greater vitality, with several occurrences in all states but Iowa, where there is only one. **1986** Pederson *LAGS Concordance (Vegetables)* 11 infs, **Gulf Region,** Garden stuff.

garden truck n [**truck** n] **scattered, but esp freq Nth, Midl**
Garden vegetables.
1804 (1808) Gass *Jrl.* 70, The Rees . . had left . . some garden truck, such as squashes. **1883** (1971) Harris *Nights with Remus* 13 **GA** [Black], W'en Brer Rabbit . . see de colluds, en de sparrer-grass, en de yuther gyardin truck growin' dar, hit make he mouf water. **1889** Twain *CT Yankee* 218, A gentleman could kill a free commoner and pay for him—cash or garden-truck. **1905** *DN* 3.23 **cCT,** *Truck.* . . Produce, as garden *truck.* **1907** *DN* 3.219 **nwAR,** *Truck.* . . Produce, as garden *truck.* **1911** (1916) Porter *Harvester* 83 **IN,** Here he raised corn for his stock, potatoes, and coarse garden truck. **1932** Randolph *Ozark Mt. Folks* 116, Some folks raised th' madder 'long with their gyarden-truck. **1941** *LANE* Map 253 *(Garden vegetables)* Infs in 65 communities, **scattered NEng,** Garden truck. **1950** *WELS* 9 Infs, **WI,** Garden truck. **1966** *DARE* (Qu. I2, *What general word do you have for vegetables?* total Infs questioned, 75) Inf **NM**2, Garden truck. **1969** *DARE* Tape **ID**14, My father raised various garden truck. **1973** Allen *LAUM* 1.302 **Upper MW** (as of c1950), *(Garden) truck* is still active in the western fringe. . . Neither *sauce* nor *truck* is known to younger infs. [7 infs gave *garden truck,* 2 infs, *truck.*] **1986** Pederson *LAGS Concordance* 4 infs, **Gulf Region,** Garden truck.

garden worm n **chiefly Nth** See Map
=**earthworm.**
1941 *Nature Mag.* 34.137, Garden-worm (Boston, Mass.) **1965–70** *DARE* (Qu. P5, *What do you call the common worm used as bait?*) 19 Infs, **chiefly Nth,** Garden worm(s); (Qu. P6, *Other kinds of worms also used for bait*) Infs **IL**115, **MI**54, **MA**74, 80, **NY**57, 191, Garden worm. **1966** Dakin *Dial. Vocab. Ohio R. Valley* 2.394 **IL, IN, KY, OH,** *Garden worm* is recorded once from each state. **1989** Mosher *Stranger* 93 **nVT** (as of 1952), I assured him that this time we'd use garden worms instead of flies and go up the burn, as my father called the small stream that ran out of the gore, where no doubt the brook trout would be biting.

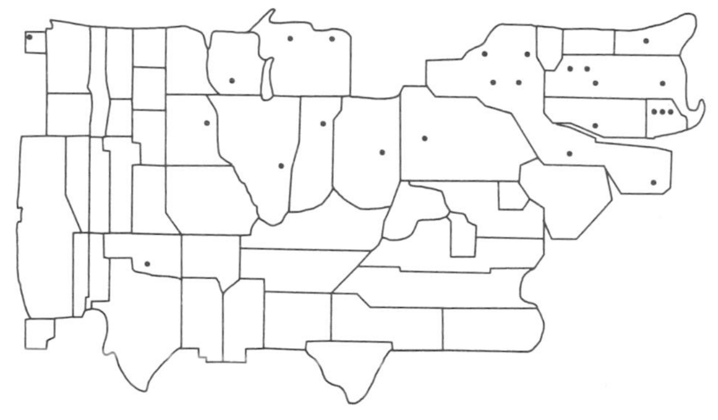

•garden worm (Qq. P5, P6)

garder snake See **garter snake 1**

garde-soleil n [LaFr]
1 A **bittern** (here: *Botaurus lentiginosus*). [See quot 1931]
1883 *Amer. Naturalist* 17.432, From its [=*Botaurus lentiginosus*] common attitude of rest, with its bill pointing straight up, . . it has gained the names "look-up" and "garde soleil." **1917** *DN* 4.422 **LA,** *Biorque.* The American bittern . . also called *sungazer, garde-soleil,* and *snake eater.* [**1931** Read *LA French* 40, *Garde-Soleil.* . . Sun-Gazer or American Bittern (*Botaurus lentiginosus* Montag.); it has the habit of standing on one leg and gazing by the hour at the sun. Hence the French have named this bird *garde-soleil,* which is an aphetic form of *regarde-soleil,* "Look at the sun." . . Garde-soleil is pronounced as if written *gar-soleil.*]
2 A sunbonnet. [Fr *garde* guard against + *soleil* sun]
1968 *DARE* (Qu. W2, *What do you call a cloth bonnet worn by women for protection from the sun?*) Inf **LA**33, Garde-soleil [ˌgɑɚ-so'le^{I}].

gardien See **guardian**

garding See **garden**

gardner snake See **garden snake**

garent oguen, garentoquen, garentoquere See **garantogen**

garfish See **gar**

garft See **gaff** n, v

garget n Also *garget plant, ~ root, gargit, gargot weed* [From its use in treating garget in animals]
=**pokeweed** or its root.

1778 Carver *Travels N. Amer.* 517, *Gargit* or *skoke* is a large kind of weed, the leaves of which are about six inches long. **1784** in 1785 Amer. Acad. Arts & Sci. *Memoirs* 1.447, *Phytolacca. . .* Garget. *Cunicum. Skoke.* American *Nightshade. . .* Common by road sides. July. **1832** Williamson *Hist. ME* 1.127, [Footnote:] *Garget* is a different vegetable from Poke, as farmers assure me, for *Garget-root* is good for milch kine, when the bag is diseased and the milk curdled. **1861** Wood *Class-Book* 610, *Phytolacca. . .* Poke. Gargot-weed. **1870** U.S. Dept. Ag. *Rept. of Secy. for 1869* 43, In all accounts of "hog cholera," . . tobacco, asafoetida, garget-root, mandrake, and all the poisons of the apothecary shop are administered. **1894** Coulter *Botany W. TX* 372, *P[hytolacca] decandra.* (Common poke or skoke, garget, pigeon berry.) **1910** Graves *Flowering Plants* 171 **CT,** Garget. . . The root is externally applied to caked udders of cows, and the berries are sometimes employed to color vinegar. **1929** *Torreya* 29.150, Phytolacca was always *"Garget"* given in B. & B., and used for cows which had garget. **1969** *DARE* (Qu. K28, *What are the chief diseases that cows have around here?*) Inf **MA**68, Garget ['gɑɚ,gɛt] . . herbs from the garget plant to cure disease. **1983** *MJLF* 9.40 **ceKY,** *Garget* . . a medicinal herb.

gar hole, get in a v phr [**gar** n **1**] Cf **garbroth**

See quot 1989.

1986 Pederson *LAGS Concordance,* 1 inf, **cwAL,** Get in a gar hole [means] having bad luck—old saying. **1989** *DARE* File **coastal MS,** To get in a gar hole is to have bad luck. A gar will hover just above the holes where other fish are. If you're catching gar when you're fishing, you're having bad luck because you're probably fishing for bass but gar are taking your bait.

garibaldi n [After Ital revolutionary Giuseppe *Garibaldi* (1807–82), whose followers wore red shirts]

An orange-red **demoiselle 1** *(Hypsypops rubicunda)* of the California coast. Also called **goldfish 1, red perch**

1882 U.S. Natl. Museum *Bulletin* 16.610, *Garibaldi.* Uniform deep scarlet, unmarked. . . Coast of California, south of Point Concepcion; common about rocky islands. **1884** Goode *Fisheries U.S.* 1.276, On the California coast occurs a species, *Pomacentrus rubicundus,* conspicuous by reason of its uniformly deep crimson or orange coloration, which is usually known as the 'Garibaldi' among the Italians. **1909** Holder–Jordan *Fish Stories* 47 **CA,** Graceful of shape, debonair, a "sea orange," . . the Garibaldi is to the manner born, and . . the very young are living sapphires. . . As they grow, they take on yellow tints, which gradually spread . . until in adult life the Garibaldi is a reddish yellow, a blaze of red gold against the sea. **1939** Natl. Geogr. Soc. *Fishes* 230, The garibaldi, which attains a length of 14 inches, is one of the largest of the demoiselles. **1960** Amer. Fisheries Soc. *List Fishes* 33.

garjack n Cf **jackfish**

=alligator gar.

1818 in 1933 LA Dept. of Conserv. *Fishes* 403, It is a voracious fish. Its vulgar names are . . Garjack, etc. **1973** Knight *Cook's Fish Guide* 381, Garjack—Gar, Alligator.

garland flower n Also *garland lily* [*OED* 1866 →; see quot 1965] **HI**

=ginger lily.

1889 *Century Dict.* 2457, *Garland-flower. . .* A common name for species of *Hedychium,* . . plants . . with delicately colored and very fragrant flowers. **1929** Pope *Plants HI* 49, White ginger, or garland flower, *Hedychium coronarium,* was named by the botanist Koenig. **1965** Neal *Gardens HI* 252, *Ginger lily, garland flower. . . Hedychium coronarium. . .* In Hawaii, the flower is even more popular than the yellow ginger for leis and has resulted in a lei industry involving 100,000 to 200,000 dollars. **1976** Bailey–Bailey *Hortus Third* 546, *Hedychium. . . Ginger lily, garland l[ily]. . .* Ginger lilies require rich soil and plenty of water. . . *[H.] coronarium. . . Garland flower, . . ginger l[ily]. . .* Naturalized extensively in trop. Amer. Zone 9.

garlic n Pronc-spp *garlac, garlet*

A Forms.

1983 *MJLF* 9.40 **ceKY,** *Garlac* . . a medicinal herb. *Ibid, Garlet* . . a wild onion, used as a green.

B Sense.

Also *wild garlic:* A **pennycress** (here: *Thlaspi arvense*). [See quot 1950]

1940 Clute *Amer. Plant Names* 273, *Thlaspi arvense. . .* Wild garlic. **1950** Stevens *ND Plants* 155, *Thlaspi arvense. . .* is often called "garlic" because of the pronounced odor caused by a substance that is also present in onions.

garlicky adj **chiefly DE, MD, NJ, VA** See Map and Map Section Cf **bitter adj 1, grassy, leeky, oniony, weedy**

Of milk: having a bad flavor from something the cow has eaten, esp any of various plants of the genus *Allium.*

1899 (1912) Green *VA Folk-Speech* 191, *Garlicky. . .* Smelling or tasting of garlic. In the spring, when the cows run out, the milk has a "garlicky taste." **1965–70** *DARE* (Qu. K14, *Milk that has a taste from something the cow ate in the pasture—you say, "That milk is ______."*) 23 Infs, **chiefly DE, MD, NJ, VA,** Garlicky.

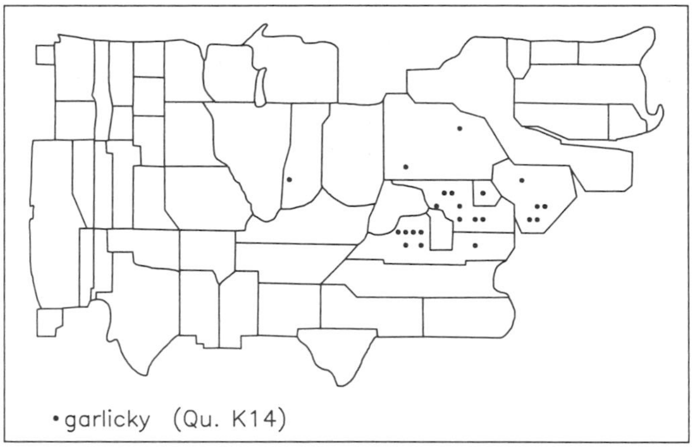

garlic weed n

The guinea-hen weed *(Petiveria alliacea).*

1970 Correll *Plants TX* 601, *Garlic-weed. . .* Perennial erect herbs with the odor of garlic. . . In dense thickets and open woods in extreme S. Tex., . . also Fla.

gar-mouth v, n attrib [**gar** n **1**]

1984 Weaver *TX Crude* 55, *To gar-mouth.* To spout empty threats and imprecations. "I'll knock your ass up so high you'll have to climb a stepladder to shit!" is a classic gar-mouth line.

garney n

See quots.

[**1867** Smyth *Sailor's Word Book* 336, *Garney.* A term in the fisheries for the fins, sounds, and tongues of the cod-fish.] **1931–33** *LANE Worksheets* **neMA,** Garney. . . Offal; liver and lights of fish. . . "All that collection of material was the garney and was shared up among the crew."

garoo n Also *caroo* [See quot 1946]

=whooping crane 1.

1917 (1923) *Birds Amer.* 1.198, *Grus americana. . . Other Names. . .* Garoo. **1946** Hausman *Eastern Birds* 229, *Whooping Crane. . .* Garoo. . . Loud, ringing, whooping calls, like the syllables *kewrook,* or *garoo,* from whence comes one of its common names. **1963** Gromme *Birds WI* 213, Caroo (Whooping Crane).

garp See **gape**

garpike n

=gar n 1.

1820 Rafinesque *Ohio R. Fishes* 73, This fish [=*Lepisosteus spatula*] bears . . the names of . . Alligator Gar, Alligator fish, Jack or Gar Pike. **1872** King *Mountaineering* 185, Savage fishes, of the garpike type . . are among the prominent water-fossils. **1883** *Harper's New Mth. Mag.* 66.515/2, The gar-pike of Western lakes. **1908** Forbes–Richardson *Fishes of IL* 30, Garpikes are abundant throughout the Mississippi, Rio Grande, Great Lake, and Appalachian regions. **1933** John G. Shedd Aquarium *Guide* 29 **IL,** The gar-pikes are long pike-like fishes armored with large, hard plates or scales. . . They are found only in the waters of North America. **1967–69** *DARE* (Qu. P3, *Freshwater fish . . not good to eat*) Infs **MI**71, 99, 108, Garpike. **1983** Becker *Fishes WI* 244, *Longnose Gar. . .* Other common names . . garpike, common garpike.

garpin n

=grayling.

1949 Caine *N. Amer. Sport Fish* 92, Montana grayling. . . *Colloquial Names. . .* Garpin.

ga'rr See **gather**

garret n

1 An attic or top-floor room. **scattered, but esp Nth** *old-fash* Cf **up garret**

1637 in 1865 MA Hist. Soc. *Coll.* 4th ser 7.119 **neMA,** In the garrett noe particion, but let there be one or two lucome windowes. [Footnote to *lucome:*] Luthern [sic]. **1799** in 1851 U.S. Congress *Debates & Proc.* 7th Cong 2d Sess 12.1408 **sePA,** I . . thought it was the best way of making the business easy, to . . put their arms into the garret. **1844** Thompson *Major Jones's Courtship* 89 **GA,** I do believe the niggers is skowered every spot from the garret to the dore-steps. **1899** Garland *Boy Life* 21 **nwIA** (as of c1870s), The children slept above in the garret, close to the stovepipe. **1904** *DN* 2.425 **Cape Cod MA** (as of a1857), *Garret*. . . Attic. **1941** *LANE* Map 345, The map shows the terms *attic* and *garret.* Both words are common throughout New England, but *garret* appears to have lost much ground in the last fifty years. Many informants have given it up, others who still use it regard it as old-fashioned. **1946** *PADS* 5.23 **VA,** *Garret*. . . The top story of a house; common. **1946** *PADS* 6.45 **ME. 1947** *PADS* 8.24 **wNY,** *Garret:* Rare. **1965–70** *DARE* (Qu. D4, *The space up under the roof, usually used for storing things*) 99 Infs, **scattered, but esp Nth,** Garret; (Qu. D7, *A small space anywhere in a house where you can hide things or get them out of the way*) Infs **NJ**2, **WI**47, Garret; (Qu. Y48, *To look in every possible place*) Inf **NY**233, Searched from cellar to garret. [Of all Infs responding to Qu. D4, 71% were old; of those giving this response, 88% were old.] **1973** Allen *LAUM* 1.168 **Upper MW** (as of c1950), The minor contrasting variant [of *attic*] is *garret,* with a frequency of 8.3% largely based upon the higher frequency of 19% in Iowa and 11% in Nebraska. . . *garret* is . . a disappearing term. **1982** *Barrick Coll.* **csPA,** Garrett [sic]—preferred over attic until ca. 1960.

2 By ext: the upper balcony in a theater.

1966 *DARE* (Qu. D40) Inf **MA**10, Garret.

garr-ridge See **garage**

garrupa n Also *garruta* [Port *garoupa;* cf **grouper**] **CA**

Any of several **rockfish** of the genus *Sebastodes,* but esp *S. atrovirens* or *S. nebulosus.*

1882 U.S. Natl. Museum *Bulletin* 16.662, *S[ebastodes] atrovirens*. . . *Garrupa.* Olive-green, marbled with darker. . . Coast of California; generally abundant, especially southward. *Ibid* 672, *[Sebastodes] vexillaris*. . . *Garrupa.* Bright pale yellowish-red. *Ibid* 676, *S[ebastodes] nebulosus*. . . *Garrupa.* Ground color blue-black of varying shade. **1887** Goode *Amer. Fishes* 261, Rockfish. . . In the southern part of California, the name "Garrupa" or "Grouper" is in common use, especially for the olivaceous species [=*Sebastodes atrovirens*]. This is a Portuguese word, and belonged originally to the species of *Epinephelus* and related genera. *Ibid* 264, The Speckled Garruta, *Sebastichthys nebulosus,* is known as "Garrupa" and "Rock-cod." **1898** U.S. Natl. Museum *Bulletin* 47.1797, *Sebastodes atrovirens*. . . Garrupa. **1929** Pan-Pacific Research Inst. *Jrl.* 4.4.7 **sCA,** *Epinephelidae.* The Sea Bass; Groupers; Garrupas.

garsh See **gorsh**

garter See **garter snake 1**

garter pink n

=**sleepy catchfly.**

1933 Small *Manual SE Flora* 507, *S[ilene] antirrhina*. . . *Garter-pink*. . . Waste places, cult. grounds, and roadsides.

garter snake n Cf **red-bellied garter snake**

1 also *garter;* pronc-sp *garder snake:* A snake, often brightly striped, of the genus *Thamnophis.* [See quot 1958] Also called **garden snake, water snake.** For other names of var spp see **grass snake 2, mouse snake, ribbon snake, striped snake**

1769 (1906) Smith *Tour Great Rivers* 41 **NY,** We saw Two Garter Snakes and one of our savages snapt his Gun at 4 Wolves. **1806** (1905) Lewis *Orig. Jrls. Lewis & Clark Exped.* 4.216, The garter snakes are innumerable & are seen entwined arround each other in large bundles of forty or fifty lying about in different directions through the praries. **1842** DeKay *Zool. NY* 3.45, The Striped Snake. . . is known under various popular names, such as . . *Slow Garter, Swamp Garter, Water Garter,* . . *&c.* **1885** Twain *Huck. Finn* 302, We can get you some garter-snakes. *Ibid* 306, [We] grabbed a couple of dozen garters and house-snakes. **1949** *Scientific Mth.* 68.57/2, One professional snake-swallower . . prefers snakes of the green and ring-neck species in performing his act since, as he maintains, these are not "nasty" like the garter snake and other kinds. **1958** Conant *Reptiles & Amphibians* 129, *Garter Snakes*. . . Like the fancy garters that were once fashionable for supporting a gentleman's socks, most of these snakes are longitudinally striped. **1965–70** *DARE* (Qu. P25, . . *Kinds of snakes*) 473 Infs, **widespread,** Garter snake; **AR**42, **NC**21, 85, **WA**17, Green garter-snake; **AL**22, **KY**65, **PA**29, 121, 126, 240, Garder snake. **1981** Vogt *Nat. Hist.* 146 **WI,** Butler's garters. . . emit a strong-smelling musky odor, but it is less offensive than that delivered by eastern garter snakes.

2 =**coral snake 1a. FL**

[**1791** Bartram *Travels* 276, There are many other species of snakes in the regions of Florida and Carolina, as the water snake, black snake, garter snake, copper belly.] **1894** U.S. Natl. Museum *Proc.* 17.334, *Elaps fulvius*. . . in south Florida. . . is known under several names, as . . "garter snake," and "candy-stick." **1923** *Copeia* 105, So few people in Florida . . believe that the Coral Snake *(Micrurus fulvius),* commonly called "garter" snake, is poisonous. **1951** Teale *North with Spring* 65 **FL,** The coral snake is known as the "garter snake." **1958** Harper *Travels William Bartram* 628, [In reference to quot 1791 above:] Snake, garter: perhaps Coral Snake *(Micrurus fulvius fulvius . .)* rather than Eastern Garter Snake *(Thamnophis sirtalis sirtalis . .)*

garvey n [Perh from the name *Garvey*] **chiefly C Atl coast, esp NJ**

A small scow.

1881 Ingersoll *Oyster-Industry* 244, *Garvey.*—A small scow, used to plant oysters, and take them up in for market. (Barnegat, New Jersey.) **1894** *DN* 1.331 **ceNJ,** *Garvey:* a small scow. (Barnegat region). **1945** Beck *Jersey Genesis* 49 **sNJ,** "Know what a garvey is, don't you?" he asked. . . "A garvey's a boat, sort of like a scow, same at both ends. A Barnegat boat—right?" **1965–70** *DARE* (Qu. O1, . . *A small rowboat*) Inf **DE**4, Garvey—square on both ends; (Qu. O2, . . *An old, clumsy boat*) Inf **VA**47, Garvey; (Qu. O10) Inf **NJ**39, Garvey—flat bottom, square bow, but concave at bow; used to be sailed with leg of mutton rig; now all have outboards or converted automobile engines; could run on wet grass—very slight draft. **1970** Rogers *Grandma's Is.* 11 **sME,** Alec Twombly with his garvey boat towed them to Yarmouth.

gas n

=**conk** n[3] **1;** hence *gashead* one who wears a **conk;** also transf; see quot.

1972 Claerbaut *Black Jargon* 65, *Gas* . . a processed or straightened hairstyle. See also do, mop, process. *Ibid, Gashead*. . . 1. one who has a processed or straightened hairstyle. 2. a black person who is a traitor to the pride of his race: *He's a real gashead.*

gashel n [PaGer *Geeschel, Gayschel* < Ger *Geissel*]

A whip.

1930 Shoemaker *1300 Words* 27 **cPA Mts** (as of c1900), *Gashel*—A raw-hide whip. **1939** Aurand *Quaint Idioms* 15 [PaGer], Pap got the *gashel* (raw hide whip) after the son-of-a-gun.

gashly adj [Arch and dial Engl form of *ghastly; OED* 1633 →, *EDD*] *arch*

Ghastly.

1885 Twain *Huck. Finn* 77 **MO,** Come in, Huck, but doan' look at his face—it's too gashly. **1887** *Scribner's Mag.* 2.476 **AR,** Jeff looked like he was jes' gittin' up by a spell er sickness, them days—p'int blank gashly. **1899** (1912) Green *VA Folk-Speech* 192, *Gashly*. . . Ghastly; horrible; dreadful; deadly.

gasoline buggy n Also *gas wagon*

An automobile.

1938 Hertzler *Horse & Buggy Dr.* 82 **KS** (as of early 20th cent), For those who did not drive one, automobiles were an unmitigated nuisance and often provided even dangerous situations. . . when they [=horses] met the unknown gas wagon they were not frightened but utterly terror-stricken. **1940** Writers' Program *Guide OH* 270, A local inventor, Dr. L. E. Custer, built an electric runabout in 1899; three years later as many as four 'gasoline buggies' could be seen on the streets in the course of a few hours.

gaspagon, gaspa(e)rgoo, gasper See **gaspergou**

gaspereau n

An **alewife** (here: *Alosa pseudoharengus*).

[**1873** in 1878 Smithsonian Inst. *Misc. Coll.* 14.2.33, *Pomolobus pseudoharengus* Gaspereau (British provinces).] **1896** U.S. Natl. Museum *Bulletin* 47.426, *Pomolobus pseudoharengus*. . . Gaspereau . . Atlantic coast of the United States; abundant. **1902** Jordan–Evermann *Amer. Fishes* 103, *Pomolobus pseudoharengus*. . . is known also as . . Gaspereau. . . It is found on our Atlantic coast from the Carolinas northward and is very abundant. **1960** Amer. Fisheries Soc. *List Fishes* 58, Gaspereau—see alewife.

gaspergou n Also *caspergou, gaspagon, gaspa(e)rgoo, gasper (goul), gaspew-gow, gaspregou* [LaFr *casseburgau;* see quot 1941 and 1945 *AmSp* 20.277–80] See also **gou**

1 =**freshwater drum. LA, TX** See Map

1807 in 1810 Cuming *Sketches* 302 **LA,** Marsalis gave us a tolerably good supper . . of coffee, bread and butter, sliced bacon, and a fine dish of gaspar-goo, the best fish I had yet tasted of the produce of the Mississippi. **1851** *De Bow's Rev.* 11.56 **LA,** We will now enter upon a list of the *Fishes. . . Pike; Gaspagon; Cotton Fish; Trout. Ibid* 615, The principal streams in and bordering the parish, are the Amite, Comite, Redwood. . . The trout, . . gaspew-gow, catfish, &c. abound in all these waters. **1854** Wailes *Rept. on Ag. & Geol. MS* 335, Ichthyobus . . Gaspaergoo. **1884** Goode *Fisheries U.S.* 1.370, The Fresh-Water Drum . . Southwestward, in Louisiana, Texas, and Arkansas . . is always known as the "Gaspergou." **1931** Read *LA French* 22, *Casburgot* or *Casseburgau.* . . 1. Fresh-Water Drum (*Aplodinotus grunniens* . .). 2. Common Sheepshead (*Archosargus probatocephalus* . .). . . Those who are not familiar with French corrupt *casburgot* into *gaspergou.* **1941** Writers' Program *Guide LA* 688, *Gaspergou*—Local corruption of Casseburgau, the fresh-water drum, *aplodinotus grunniens.* It is so called because it feeds on large bivalves of the genus *turbo* (Fr. *burgau*), which it breaks (Fr. *casser*) with its teeth. **1967–69** *DARE* (Qu. P1, . . *Freshwater fish . . good to eat*) Infs **LA**3, 8, 10, 14, 15, 26, 44, **TX**1, 9, 62, Gaspergou; **TX**27, Gaspergoul; **TX**26, Gaspers; **LA**34, Caspergou; (Qu. P2, . . *Saltwater fish . . good to eat*) Inf **LA**40, Gaspergou; (Qu. P3, *Freshwater fish . . not good to eat*) Inf **TX**37, Gaspergou; (Qu. P14, . . *Commercial fishing . . what do the fishermen go out after?*) Infs **LA**3, 26, 34, **TX**9, Gaspergou. **1969** *DARE* File **LA,** Gaspergou . . the Freshwater Drum fish. **1983** *Reinecke Coll.* 5 **LA,** *Gaspergou* ['gæspə͵gu]. . . Freshwater Drum, or according to some, also the common sheephead. General in former sense among fishermen and seafood dealers. From La. Fr. "Casse-burgot" or barnacle-cracker, with same meaning.

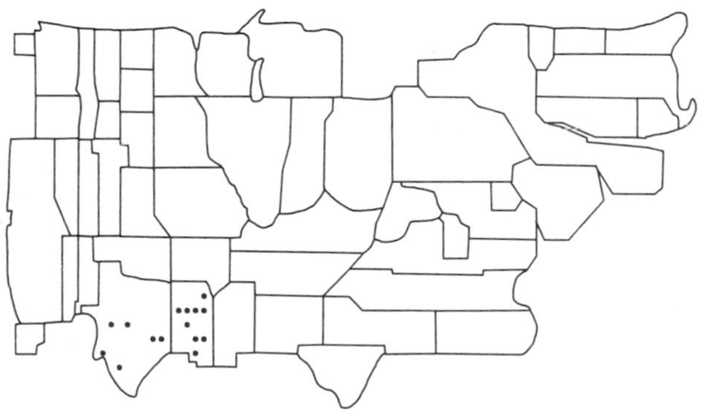

•gaspergou 1 + varr (Qq. P1, P2, P3, P14)

2 A **sheepshead** (here: *Archosargus probatocephalus*).

1885 *Outing* 5.336/2 **LA,** There are . . *gaspergoos*—an Indian word meaning "fish," and applied to anything fishy, from the delicate sheep's-head to the nasty mud-suckers of the Mississippi. **1900** *Land of Sunshine* 13.435, The *Gaspregou* or Sheepshead . . is a big, lean, tough, bony fish common in Texas rivers, but mostly below El Paso. **1931** [see **1** above]. **1983** [see **1** above].

3 A fish of the family Catostomidae:

a A **white sucker** (here: *Catostomus commersoni*).

1885 [see **2** above].

b =**buffalo fish.**

1887 Goode *Amer. Fishes* 438, The "Buffalo-fish," *Bubalichthyinæ,* . . are found mainly in the river channels of the Mississippi and its tributaries. . . The name "Gaspergou" is shared by these fishes with the fresh-water drum.

gastakutus n [Pseudo-Lat; cf **diacumbelicum, diasticutis, gyascutus**]

Appar some sort of digestive disorder; see quot.

1906 Sinclair *Chip* 94 **MT,** Maybe Mame an' the rest uh them Beckman kids can eat sech truck without comin' down in a bunch with gastakutus, but I'd hate t' tackle it myself.

gas wagon See **gasoline buggy**

gat n [*gat* a channel or opening to the sea; *OED* 1723 →]

1930 Shoemaker *1300 Words* 24 **cPA Mts** (as of c1900), *Gat*—A natural sink filled with water, that has an outlet to a creek or river.

gat brush n [**gat**]

A **river birch** (here: *Betula nigra*).

1930 Shoemaker *1300 Words* 27 **cPA Mts** (as of c1900), *Gat brush*—A black Birch which grows at eddies or gats, or low ground along streams.

gate n

1 Fig: a rejection, dismissal—in phrr *give (one) the gate* and varr.

1918 Witwer *Baseball to Boches* 143, "I wanna speak to you in private, Jeanne," I says to her. "Give this hick the gate!" **1922** Lewis *Babbitt* 119 **Upper MW,** If any of us were to indulge in it here, he'd get the gate so fast it would make his head swim. **1924** Marks *Plastic Age* 273, I guess his girl has given him the gate. **1941** *LANE* Map 406 *(She gave him the mitten),* [9 infs, scattered **NEng,** (She) gave (*or* give) him the gate]. **1950** *WELS (I'd like to give him the ______)* 15 Infs, **WI,** Gate; *(If a girl breaks her engagement . . she ______)* 3 Infs, Give(s) him the gate; *(If she . . refuses [to marry him])* 2 Infs, Give him the gate. **1951** *Sat. Eve. Post* 8 Dec 44/1, There's no reason why he should be fired . . or given the gate. **1965–70** *DARE* (Qu. II5b, *When you don't want to have anything to do with a certain person because you don't like him, you might say, "I'd certainly like to give him the ______."*) 157 Infs, **scattered,** Gate; **MA**16, Show him the gate; [**IA**5, Keys to the gate;] (Qu. AA11, *If a man asks a girl to marry him and she refuses, you'd say she ______*) 48 Infs, **chiefly Nth, Atlantic,** Gave (*or* give) him the gate; **LA**28, **TX**54, Showed him the gate; (Qu. AA12, *If a man loses interest in a girl and stops seeing her, you'd say he ______*) 22 Infs, **chiefly Nth, Atlantic,** Gave (*or* give) her the gate; **WV**2, Gave her gate; (Qu. Y51, . . *"He's not your kind—you'd better ______ him."*) Inf **NY**93, Give him the gate.

2 also *gates;* Fig: a jazz musician or enthusiast; by ext, any person—freq used as a term of address. [In punning ref to the swinging of a fence gate, but prob also infl by **gator 3**] Cf **cat** n **1c, d**

1936 Armstrong *Swing that Music* 77, "Swing it, Gate," one of them will sing out and that will be a "sender" to them and they'll all go into their music. . . That "sender," "Swing it, Gate," . . came from me. . . I started calling the other boys, "Gate," too. . . and now "Gate" is a word swing players use when they call out to one another. **1937** *AmSp* 12.180, A jazz musician . . if he can 'swing' particularly well . . may be addressed as 'Gate.' **1938** *AmSp* 13.152 **IN** [Negro college slang], *Gates.* Fellow. **1938** FWP NYC *NY Panorama* 161, *Swing, gate!* is an exhortation to a *solid sender* to *take a Boston* or let go with all the *riffs* . . in his repertoire. **1939** *Collier's* 8 Apr 33/3, You've handicapped your tunes with stuff no gate wants to play. **1946** (1972) Mezzrow-Wolfe *Really Blues* 232 (as of 1933), Louis . . wrote: "Say Gate. . . how wonderful your records are." *Ibid* 246, I finally got the story out. "Wow!" Zutty yelled. "This is it, ain't it gate!" *Ibid* 333, Gate: *form of greeting.* **1960** Wentworth-Flexner *Slang* 209, *Gate. . . 2* An able swing musician. *Wide swing use c1935–c1943. Prob. a shortening from "gator" or "alligator," reinforced by "swing like a gate." . . 4* Any male; esp. a hep one. . . *5 = cat. . . Some jive and swing use, c1935–c1942, often in admiration of a musician or as direct address to a fellow devotee. . . Pop. by comedian Jerry Colonna, on Bob Hope's radio program during W.W.II. Colonna always greeted the audience with a rhyme in synthetic jive on "gates." Thus "Greetings, gates,/ let's deliberate," "Greetings, gates,/ Sorry I'm late." Thus also was the jive greeting "Greeting, gate(s)" popularized.*

3 Fig: a trouser fly. Cf **barn door 2b**

1966–70 *DARE* (Qu. W24c, *Sayings to warn a man that his trouser-fly is open*) Infs **FL**8, **KS**15, **KY**70, **OK**28, Gate's open; **MO**29, You left the gate open; **LA**37, Barn gate's open.

gate horse n

1944 Adams *Western Words* 64, *Gate horse*—A cowboy stationed at the corral gate for any purpose.

gate-lifter n *joc* Cf **rooter**

A hog's snout.

1927 *DN* 5.447 [Underworld jargon], *Gate lifter. . .* A pig's snout, stewed or fried. **1969** *DARE* (Qu. K61, . . *The pig's nose*) Inf **KY**49, Gate-lifter—when he gets big and can with his snout force his way out of the hog lot through the fence. **1970** *Thompson Coll.* **AL** (as of 1920s), Gate-lifter . . hog snout.

gate night n **esp NEast** Cf **cabbage night, doorbell night**

A night, usu the night before Halloween, in which young people engage in var pranks, esp the removing of gates.

1904 *DN* 2.397 **OH, PA,** *Gate-night*. . . The night before Hallowe'en, i.e., the night of 30th Oct., when gates are carried off by children. **1954** *Hench Coll.* **NYC,** Where they grew up, Halloween night was known as *gate night,* the night youngsters took front yard gates off their hinges. **1985** *NADS Letters* **seNY** (as of c1945), *Gate night* was a great night! . . Some time before Halloween . . my Garfield St. gang of two or three young males, aged 10–14, would go . . to "enemy territory"—Webster Avenue. There . . we'd sneak up on front gates, unhinge them, furtively drop them on the ground or place them on a lawn, then wing away in the dark. . . This took place in . . a working class neighborhood of modest single and two- or three-family homes. *Ibid* **cwNJ** (as of 1950s), On gate night he and his friends would take gates off their hinges and throw them in neighboring yards to confuse people. [He] also remembers taking bean poles from farm fields and using them to overturn outhouses on gate night. **1988** *DARE* File **seNY** (as of 1960s), The night before Halloween was called *gate night.*

gater See **gator**

gate road n

1941 *Hench Coll.* **cVA,** Seen on signs . . on roads around Gordonsville, Va. A gate road is a road running in through a large estate to the main house and yard; literally to the gate of the yard or grounds around a main house. For instance the gate-road of the estate called Rocklands . . is at least a mile long. Finally you come to the large gate of the inner grounds—the grounds of the house itself.

gates See **gate**

gates-ajar collar n Also *gates-ajar*

A wing collar.

1943 *AN&Q* 3.151/1, "Gates Ajar": Poke Collar. I have recently seen the stiff white collar with the projecting corners—commonly called a poke collar—referred to as the "gates ajar." The fashion itself, of course, goes back to the nineties, at least. How old . . is this name . . and is it by chance only a regional expression? **1948** Idell *Great Blizzard* 91 **NYC** (as of 1884–5), Mr. Rogers was a triumph of impressiveness in tailed coat and winged collar, which he identified, respectively, as "shad-belly" and "gates-ajar." **1968** *Needles Desert Star* (CA) 15 Feb 2/2, Paw had been prevailed on to . . encase himself in stripped [sic] pants, a claw hammer coat, boiled shirt with a gates-a-jar collar. There was not going to be any thing cheap about this affair.

gate-stretcher See **stretcher**

gate tree n

A **goldenrain tree** (here: *Koelreuteria paniculata*).

1941 Writers' Program *Guide IN* 236, New Harmony has thousands of 'gate' trees, which flower in June, shedding their blossoms in a golden rain. These hardy, round-topped trees *(Koelreuteria paniculata),* native to China and Korea where they are called the 'Tree of the Golden Rain,' were introduced by William Maclure a century ago and planted near the gate of the Owen–Maclure home; hence the local name 'gate' tree. **1982** Heat Moon *Blue Highways* 410 **IN,** New Harmony in June piles up with the sprinkle from golden rain trees, here called "gate trees."

gather v, n Usu |'gæðə(r)|; also |'gɛðə(r)|; also |'gjɛðə| Pronc-spp *gadder, ga'rr, gedduh, gedr, gether, giedder, gither*

A Forms.

1805 (1965) Ordway *Jrls.* 266, Our Intrepters wife found and gethered a fine persel of servis berrys. **1829–53** in 1956 Eliason *Tarheel Talk* 311 **NC,** *Gather*—gethering 1829 . . , gethered 1851 . . , gedring 1852 . . , gadder 1852 . . , githering 1853. **1858** Stearns *Practical Guide Pronc.* lix, Say . . găth'er *[not]* gĕth'er. **1884** *Anglia* 7.270 **Sth, S Midl** [Black], *To giedder yo' mine tergyudder* = to collect your thoughts. **1891** *PMLA* 6.172 **TN,** I once heard an ignorant young fellow entertain a fireside company with: "Getherin' up shells from the sea-sure." **1892** *DN* 1.233 **KY,** *Gather* [gjɛðə]. [*DN* Ed: Often in Michigan; so 'gethers,' in sewing.] **1899** (1912) Green *VA Folk-Speech* 194, *Gether*. . . To gather. *Gethers*. . . The pleats of a woman's dress. *Gethering*. . . Gathering. **1905** *DN* 3.56 **NE,** Cases where [æ] is likely to become very close, passing into [ɛ] . . *gather.* **1906** *DN* 3.137 **nwAR,** *Gether.* **1908** *DN* 3.281 **eAL, wGA,** [gɛðə]. **1909** *S. Atl. Qrly.* 8.43 **sSC coast** [Gullah], In . . *gather, whether,* the formula [of alteration in Gullah] is *ga'rr, w'e'rr.* **1917** *DN* 4.392 **neOH,** [gɛðɚ]. **1922** Gonzales *Black Border* 303 **sSC, GA coasts** [Gullah glossary], *Gedduh*—gather, gathers, gathered, gathering. **1923** *DN* 5.208 **swMO,** *Gether*. . . To gather. **1939–43** *LANE* Maps 90, 252, 414, 512, [Throughout New England proncs of *gather* and *gathering* n with [ɛ] and varr are roughly four times as common as those with [æ] and varr.] **1976** Allen *LAUM* 3.277 **Upper MW** (as of c1950), An analogous variation appears in the pronunciation /gɛðɚ/ for *gather,* recorded in the free conversation of [two] Type I Iowa infs. **1976** Ryland *Richmond Co. VA* 371, Gether—gather.

B As verb.

1 To collect maple sap from the trees; hence vbl n *gathering* the operation of collecting sap (often used attrib); n *gathering* the sap collected at one time. Cf **dip v 2**

1917 *DN* 4.392 **neOH,** *Gather, gether*. . . To collect (maple sap). "He gethered all day yesterday, and is boiling today." Also N. Y., N. Eng., Ky. *Gathering, gethering*. . . In collecting maple sap, the act of collecting once from every tree in the sugar-bush; also, the amount so collected. "There were twenty barrels in the first gathering, and three gatherings in the one run." **1927** *AmSp* 2.355 **WV,** *Gathering* . . the amount collected each time. "We are boiling the last gathering of sugar water this morning." **1947** *PADS* 8.6 **VT,** *Gathering pail*. . . A galvanized iron bucket into which the sap from the sap buckets is emptied. *Gathering sled*. . . The bobsled used for transporting the sap from the trees. *Gathering tank*. . . A tank into which the buckets attached to the trees are emptied. The design of it is such that the sap will not spill out. . . In the earlier days it was made of wood. . . *Gathering tub*. . . A gathering tank made of wood. **1965** Needham–Mussey *Country Things* 40 **VT,** Nowadays they use a big gathering tub on a sledge. **1966** *DARE* Tape **NH6,** What we call a gathering tank on a wooden sled the horse drew.

2 To take, pick up (a single thing). [Cf *OED gather* v. 4. d 1715 →] **esp S Midl**

1845 Thompson *Pineville* 182 **GA,** "Gather him up, boys," said the judge; "the sentence of the law must be executed!" **1859** (1968) Bartlett *Americanisms* 168, To *Gather.* (Pron. *gether.*) Universally used in the West for to take up; as, "I gathered a stick." **1887** *Scribner's Mag.* 2.480 **AR,** Git shet of 'er now, an' we kin gether the chile an' light out. **1903** *DN* 2.314 **seMO,** *Gather*. . . To take. 'He gathered his hat and left.' **1926** Roberts *Time of Man* 179 **cKY,** He drew away from her and arose, gathering his hat from where it lay on the floor.

3 Of cream being churned: to come together (in lumps of butter); hence n *gathering* the stage of churning at which lumps of butter form. Cf **come B1**

1965 Needham–Mussey *Country Things* 66 **VT,** After the cream swells it starts to break. . . Then after it breaks it will gather. The three stages are the swell, the breaking, and the gathering. When it gathers, it gathers into lumps.

4 with *in* or *up:* To come together, meet.

1904 *DN* 2.418 **nwAR,** *Gather in*. . . To assemble, collect. 'The neighbors gathered in.' **1969** *DARE* Tape **IL69,** There will be a gang which'll gether up an' go to that place.

5 To fill with pus, come to a head; hence ppl adj *gathered* having an abscess; n *gathering* a boil, abscess, now esp one in the ear. [*OED gathering* vbl. sb. 3 c1000 →] **chiefly Midl, NY** See Map *old-fash*

1872 in 1983 *PADS* 70.34 **ce,sePA,** By this time my gathering got so bad that I was obliged to have a poultice on it which Matilda made for me, from vaxcinnation. **1899** (1912) Green *VA Folk-Speech* 192, *Gather*. . . To suppurate. . . *Gathering*. . . A suppuration; an abscess. **1902** *DN* 2.235 **sIL,** *Getherin*. . . A boil or rizin. **1906** *DN* 3.137 **nwAR,** *Gether*. . . "The risin' *gethered* to a head." **1942** Warnick *Garrett Co. MD* 7 (as of 1900–1918), *Gathering*. . . boil or other sore containing pus. **1944** *PADS* 2.56 **MO,** *Gatherin'.* **1949** *AmSp* 24.109 **SC,** *Gathering*. . . A boil ('North Carolina name'). **1954** *Harder Coll.* **cwTN,** *Gather to a head*. . . To abscess. *Gathering*. . . A boil or abscess. **1965–70** *DARE* (Qu. BB37, *When . . [pus] comes out of a person's ear, he has a ______*) 28 Infs, **chiefly Upstate NY, N Midl,** Gathering (in his ear); **NY**209, **UT**12, **NJ**41, Gathering in his (*or* the) head; **IA**7, Gathering in the ear; **PA**126, Gathering of the ear; **NJ**41, Head-gathering; 14 Infs, **chiefly N Midl,** Gathered ear; **KY**51, Gathered head [Of all Infs responding to the question, 65% were old; of those giving these responses, 87% were old.]; (Qu. BB33a, . . *A swelling under the skin . . that comes to a head*) Infs **DC**8, **IL**72, **NE**10, **WV**16, Gathering; (Qu. BB30, . . *A hard, painful swelling [often on a finger] that seems to come from deep under the skin*) Inf **NJ**53, Gathering; (Qu. BB36, *When there's an open sore and this yellowish stuff is coming out of it, you say it's*

———) Inf **CA**59, Gathered; (Qu. K7, *What sickness can a cow get in her udder—for example, if she's left unmilked too long?*) Inf **NJ**53, Her bag would gather. **1983** *MJLF* 9.1.40 **ceKY,** *Gathering* . . a boil before it comes to a head.

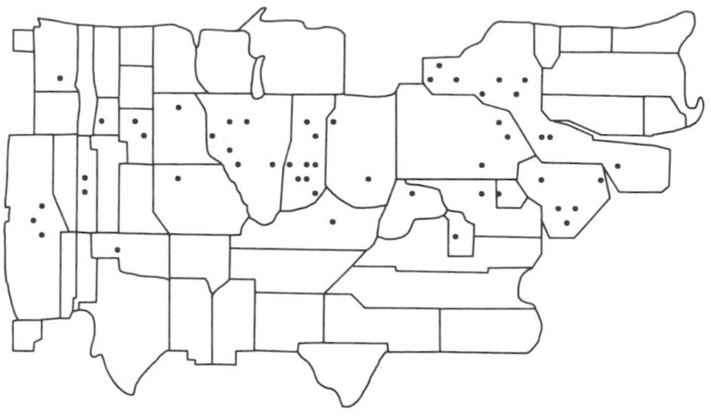

•gather B5 + varr (Qq. BB37, K7, BB30, BB33a, BB36)

6 Of weather:

a intr; also with *up:* To grow cloudy.

1903 *DN* 2.294 **Cape Cod MA** (as of a1857), *Gather*. . . To get thick. 'It's gatherin to-day.' **1939** *LANE* Map 90 *(Clouding up)* 9 infs, **eNEng,** Gathering; 1 inf, [əgɛðrɪn]; 1 inf, Gathering for a change; 1 inf, Gathering for a storm; 3 infs, Gathering up for a storm. **1950** *WELS (When clouds begin to increase, you say it's* ———*)* 1 Inf, **WI,** Gathering; 1 Inf, Gathering up; [1 Inf, Clouds are gathering; 2 Infs, Storm (is) gathering]. **1965–70** *DARE* (Qu. B6, *When clouds begin to increase, you say it's* ———) Infs **AL**6, **CA**125, **IL**39, **TX**51, **VA**13, **WI**47, Gathering; **NY**41, Gathering for a storm; **KY**88, **NC**81, **OK**1, Gathering up; **IA**29, Gathering up for a storm.

b tr: To threaten.

1965–70 *DARE* (Qu. B6, *When clouds begin to increase, you say it's* ———) Infs **AL**23, **CO**2, Gathering a storm; **OH**87, Gathering a rain.

C As noun.

The animals collected in a roundup. [Cf *OED gather* sb.[1] 1. a 1555]

1944 Adams *Western Words* 64, *Gather*—Cattle brought together by the roundup. **1945** Thorp *Pardner* 247 **SW,** On the beef roundup, the gather was trimmed of all stock except what was to be trailed to market. A beef herd of good size . . might contain twenty-five hundred head. **1958** Latham *Meskin Hound* 151 **cTX,** Jim and Sugar ought to be bringing their hog gather down the draw.

gathered See **gather B5**

gather in See **gather B4**

gathering See **gather B1, 3, 5**

gather up See **gather B4, 6a**

gatling gun n [By joc ext from *Gatling gun* a rapid-fire gun consisting of a rotating cluster of barrels, patented by R.J. Gatling in 1862]

1969 *DARE* (Qu. FF14, . . *Kinds of firecrackers*) Inf **IN**58, Gatling gun.

gatlins, by intj Cf *DS* NN7, 8, 9

1903 (1965) Adams *Log Cowboy* 202 **West,** But the steers were wild, long-legged coasters, and came through between us like scared wolves. . . 'Here they come and there they go; just an even thousand, by gatlins!'

gator n Also sp *gater, 'gatuh* [Abbr for *alligator*] **chiefly S Atl, Gulf States**

1 An alligator.

1844 *Knickerbocker* 23.407, The 'gator is n't what you may call a han'some critter. **1886** *Outing* 8.60/2 **sFL,** The natives often feed their dogs and hogs boiled 'gator meat. **1893** Shands *MS Speech* 32, *Gater* [getə]. Negro for *alligator.* **1922** Gonzales *Black Border* 122 **sSC, GA coasts** [Gullah], Ef da' 'gatuh bite you 'e gwine spile 'um [=a shirt], en' no use fuh t'row 'way uh shu't. **1934** Carmer *Stars Fell on AL* 198, Two-Toe is a red-eyed 'gator and about fourteen feet long and he can knock a mule into the water with just one flip of his tail. **1936** *AmSp* 11.20 **eTX,** Careless speakers omit the first two syllables from *alligator,* so that it is pronounced ['getɚ], ['geɪtɚ]. **c1940** Eliason *Word Lists FL* 8 **wFL,** *'Gator.* **1941** *AmSp* 16.5 **eTX** [Black], Alligator is simply ['gjetə]. **1966** *DARE* Tape **SC**15, Make me go and get de gator an' kill de gator. **1968** *DARE* FW Addit **seGA,** Gator ['getɚ]. The word "alligator" is rarely heard here.

2 An inhabitant of Florida, esp a student at the University of Florida. Cf **alligator** n[1] **B7**

1937 Shankle *Nicknames* 541, The members of the athletic teams of the University of Florida . . are popularly designated *The Alligators* and *The Gators.* **1959** *AmSp* 34.154 **FL,** Like college students the world over, Gators [=students at the University of Florida] have created their own lingo. **1963** *AmSp* 38.271 **KS** [American Indian student slang], Floridians are known as *gators,* and an individual (Seminole) may be a *gator boy* or a *gator girl.*

3 A jazz enthusiast; a "hep" person. Cf **alligator** n[1] **B5, gate 2**

1942 Berrey–Van den Bark *Amer. Slang* 576.29, *"Swing" enthusiast* . . gate, gator, hep-cat. **1960** Wentworth–Flexner *Slang* 210, *'Gator* . . =alligator; cat. *Some Negro use since c1925. Some jive use c1935–1942. . . Some swing use c1935.* **1970** Major *Dict. Afro-Amer. Slang* 57, *Gator:* (1920's) short for Alligator; one male friend to another.

4 =**alligator** n[1] **B10;** also the player who is "it" in this game. Cf **bully-gator**

1966–70 *DARE* (Qu. EE28, *Games played in the water*) Inf **FL**14, Gator—one person catches the others, then the next one caught is it; **GA**3, Chasing the gator—same as tag, but the one who has to catch others is called "gator"; (Qu. EE13b, *In games in which all the others hide, the one who must try to find them, he's* ———) Inf **GA**23, The gator. **1986** Pederson *LAGS Concordance,* 1 inf, **nwFL,** Gator—played in pool.

5 See quot.

1967–70 *DARE* (Qu. W42a, . . *Men's sharp-pointed shoes*) Inf **NC**41, Gators; **NY**240, Gators—with alligator leather.

6 in phr *a gator bit (a woman):* A woman's menstrual period has started.

1978 *MJLF* 4.1.38, On occasion, euphemisms [for menstruation] also provide a source of ribaldry. One evening down South, for example, as wedding guests tossed rice and confetti at the departing bride and groom, the maid of honor elbowed the best man. "Some wedding night this will be," she giggled. "A 'gater [sic] bit Lucy."

gator bait n **chiefly Sth**

1 =**alligator bait 2.**

1970 Tarpley *Blinky* 265 **neTX,** *Teasing and derogatory names for Negroes* . . 'gator bait. **1970** *DARE* (Qu. HH28, . . *People of foreign background* . . *Negro*) Inf **TN**43, Gator-bait. **1986** Pederson *LAGS Concordance (Negro)* 1 inf, **cAR,** Gator bait—derogatory.

2 See quot.

1959 *AmSp* 34.154 **FL,** To men students, good-looking or popular girls are . . *gator bait.*

gator bonnet See **alligator bonnet(s)**

gator-faced adj

Having a long face and large mouth.

1942 Hurston in *Amer. Mercury* 55.223.94 **Harlem NYC** [Black], *Gator-faced*—long, black face with big mouth. **1942** Hurston *Dust Tracks* 144 **FL,** It is an everyday affair to hear somebody called a . . 'gator-faced . . so-and-so!

gator flea n Cf **alligator** n[1] **B3**

=**hellgrammite 1.**

1968 *DARE* (Qu. P6) Inf **GA**41, Gator fleas—a pinching insect; (Qu. R21, . . *Other kinds of stinging insects*) Inf **GA**25, Gator flea. **1969** *DARE* FW Addit **Okefenokee GA,** 'Gator flea = a hellgrammite. Probably from appearance, looking vaguely like a diminutive alligator. They develop in water. No symbiotic relation to the alligator, however.

gator hole See **alligator hole**

gator nest n

See quot.

1964 Will *Hist. Okeechobee* 80 **FL** (as of 1922), After this the men had to sleep in their glade boats or on heaps of sawgrass cut and piled till above the water—"gator nests" they called them.

gator-nosed boat n

See quot.

1969 *DARE* FW Addit **Okefenokee GA,** 'Gator-nosed boat—a shallow, flat-bottomed, blunt-ended boat used by fishermen, etc., in the Okefenokee Swamp.

gator snapper See **alligator snapper**

gator tail n

1 A type of saw: see quot.

1950 *PADS* 14.31 **SC,** *Gator tail*. . . A single-handed crosscut saw. So called from its general shape.

2 Perh **=golden club 1.**

1966 *DARE* (Qu. S26e, *Other wildflowers*) Inf **SC**19, Gator tail—a weed.

gator trout n Also *alligator trout*

A **weakfish** (here: *Cynoscion nebulosus*).

1935 Caine *Game Fish* 144 **Sth,** *Spotted Weakfish. Cynoscion nebulosus*. . . *Synonyms:* Alligator Trout . . Gator Trout.

gator turtle See **alligator turtle**

'gatuh See **gator**

gaub See **gob** n[1]

gauber-grubber See **goober-grabber**

gauber See **goober** n[1] **1**

gauch iron See **gancho 2**

gaucho See **gancho**

gaufre n [Either directly from Fr *gaufre* waffle, or through Engl dial (cf *OED gofer, EDD gaufer*)]

See quots.

1890 *DN* 1.59, *Gaufre* (waffle) is still in use among the negroes, and is a relic of the early Huguenot French. **1945** Saxon *Gumbo Ya-Ya* 35 **LA,** Among the most famous of the cake vendors were the Gaufre Men or Shaving Cake Men. . . the Gaufre Man announced his approach by beating on a metal triangle. . . The last Gaufre Man . . never revealed the secret of his thin, crisp, cone-shaped pastries. . . *gaufres* are now unknown in New Orleans. **1950** *PADS* 14.32 **SC,** *Gofer*. . . Waffle. Negro usage. St. John's Parish, Berkeley County. A Huguenot French survival.

gaul See **gall** n[2]

gaulding n Also sp *gallding* Cf *DJE gaulin*

=night heron.

1925 Bailey *Birds FL* 38, Black-crowned Night Heron. . . Gallding. . . Yellow-crowned Night Heron. . . Gallding.

gaulette See **galette**

gaum v[1] |gɔm, gɑm| Also sp *gawm, go(r)m, gome* [*EDD gaum* v.[3]; *OED gaum* v.[2] a1796 →]

1 freq with *up:* To smear (with something sticky); to daub, dirty; also fig; hence ppl adj *gaumed up* smeared. **formerly widespread, now chiefly Appalachians** See Map

1859 (1968) Bartlett *Americanisms* 168, Put the child's apron on, and don't let her gaum herself all over with molasses. **1883** (1971) Harris *Nights with Remus* 379 **GA** [Black], He run ter de cubbud en des gawm hisse'f wid 'lasses. **1890** *DN* 1.70 **LA,** "The baby is all gaumed up with molasses." [*DN* Ed: Also on Cape Cod: [gɑm] or [gɔm].] **1895** *DN* 1.371 **TN,** Gawmed up, covered with litter. **1899** (1912) Green *VA Folk-Speech* 202, Look how you have gormed your face. **1905** *DN* 3.81 **nwAR,** 'He's gotten his clothes gawmed up.' Rare. **1907** *Harper's Mth. Mag.* 116.46/1, His funeral, which consisted of him being burnt and the other Injuns gauming their faces with his ashes and howling like wildcats. **1909** *S. Atl. Qrly.* 8.46 [Gullah], To daub, or to smear, to beslop one's self with spilled victuals or grease, is to *gorm* or *gaum yo'sef.* **1913** *DN* 4.1 **ME,** *Gorm.* **1915** *DN* 4.183 **swVA,** I'm all gommed up. **1916** *DN* 4.345 **TN,** *Gom* . . *=gorm.* **1923** *DN* 5.208 **swMO,** *Gaum*. . . Usually followed by 'up.' **1923** *DN* 5.235 **swWI,** *Gaum.* **1942** *AmSp* 17.171 **sIL,** *Gaum* . . [gɔm]. **1944** *PADS* 2.56 **MO,** *Gaum* [gɔm]. **1950** *PADS* 14.33 **SC,** *Gorm, gaum.* **1952** in 1968 Haun *Hawk's Done Gone* 289 **TN,** Don't mind about the mud. The porch is done gormed up. **1965–70** *DARE* (Qu. Y39, . . *"The children have been eating candy and they've got their faces all ______."*) 15 Infs, **chiefly Appalachians,** Gaumed up; **KY**42, **TN**13, 30, 58, [gɑmd] up; **MA**5, [gɔmd əp]; **FL**10, 27, [gɔmd]; **KY**24, Gaumed; (Qu. Y40a, . . *Sticky stuff: "I've got to wash my hands, they're all ______."*) Infs **KY**24, **VA**24, Gaumed up; **AR**51, ['gɔmd ˌəp]; **VA**11, [gamd] up. **1971** *DARE* File **VT** (as of c1910), "Don't gaum over the line" meant don't let your paint brush or crayon go outside the marked line. **1972** Cooper *NC Mt. Folkl.* 92, *Gormed, Gaumed*—messed up. **1974** Fink *Mountain Speech* 11 **wNC, eTN,** *Gaum; gom* . . to smear.

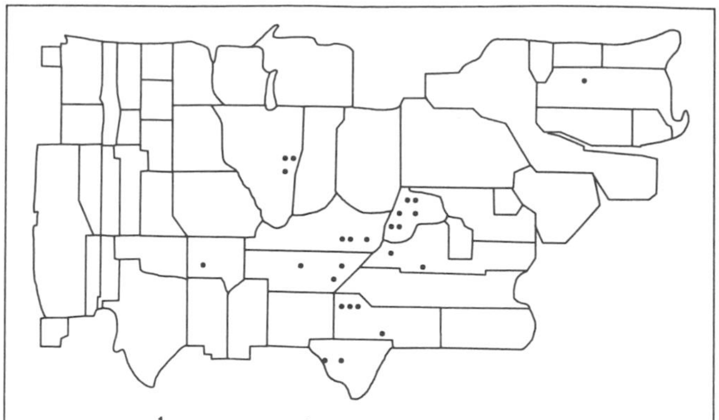

•gaum v[1] 1 + varr (Qq. Y39, Y40a)

2 To stick, cause to adhere. [Prob infl by *gum* v]

1911 *DN* 3.544 **NE,** *Gom, gaum* [ɔ]. . . "My eyes were gaumed together." **1914** *DN* 4.106 **KS,** *Gaum, n. & v.* Gum. **1926** Roberts *Time of Man* 16 **KY,** The whole place was lined with these-here little brown ants, all gaumed into the dinner. **1961** [see **3** below].

3 freq with *up,* also with *around:* To disarrange, mess up, confuse; hence ppl adj *gaumed up;* also fig. **chiefly S Midl, esp KY**

1913 Kephart *Highlanders* 294 **sAppalachians,** If the house be in disorder it is said to be all gormed or gaumed up, or things are just in a mommick. **1924** (1946) Greer-Petrie *Angeline Gits an Eyeful* 5 **csKY,** Them folks wuz expectin' to git all gormed up with cuckle burrs and brors [=briers]. **1932** Randolph *Ozark Mt. Folks* 33, I'd orter o' knowed better, but my head was all gaumed up with sparkin'. **1941** *AmSp* 16.22 **sIN,** Gom. **1942** (1971) Campbell *Cloud-Walking* 17 **seKY,** Pulling off theirs and Sabriny's dresses to save them from getting gaumed up with wrinkles. **1949** Arnow *Hunter's Horn* 155 **cKY,** He reminded himself to recollect to tell her that she must never leave a turn of corn untied; the rats had already been in it and spilled it and gomed it around. **1950** *PADS* 14.33 **SC,** *Gorm, gaum*. . . To render untidy, as the dress, clothing. **c1960** *Wilson Coll.* **csKY,** *Gaum,* or *gorm* or *gom* /gɑm/. . . To mess up. **1961** Sackett-Koch *KS Folkl.* 113, *Gaum*. . . This has a common meaning also of "mix" or "put together." **1969** *DARE* FW Addit **KY**6, Gaumed up—messy, mixed up, confused, referring to the contents of a drawer or room as "all gaumed up." **c1970** *Halpert Coll.* 27 **wKY, wTN,** *Gawm up* = to mess up or mix up. **1970** *DARE* FW Addit **MA**78, My people, etc., used to say, "so gormed that he couldn't talk straight!" **1972** Cooper *NC Mt. Folkl.* 92, Gommed—messed; disarranged; ruined. . . Gormed, gaumed—messed up. **1983** *MJLF* 9.1.40 **ceKY,** *Gaum* . . to mess, smear.

4 with *into:* See quot.

1927 *AmSp* 3.138 **ME coast,** A child was told not to "gorm" into food, . . when eating hastily and taking large mouthfuls. **1949** Arnow *Hunter's Horn* 281 **cKY,** I'd better start putten this stuff away fore th youngens wake up—they'd be a messen an a gomen into everthing.

gaum n[1] Also sp *gahm, go(r)m, gome* [**gaum** v[1]] **chiefly Sth, S Midl, but also NEng**

1 A mess; a state of stickiness or disorder. [**gaum** v[1] **1, 2, 3**]

1899 (1912) Green *VA Folk-Speech* 202, *Gorm*. . . A mess; all sticky. In a gorm. *Gaum.* **1915** *DN* 4.183 **swVA,** *Gom*. . . State of uncleanness from dirt, oil, etc.,—applied to machinery as well as hands and face. "See your hands, what a gom you're in!" **1915** *DN* 4.226 **wTX,** *Gahm*. . . A sticky mess. "You're making a gahm out of that candy." **1949** Arnow *Hunter's Horn* 276 **cKY,** Shit-fire, Suse, . . you're a droppen kernels in th hulls. . . Why, Lucy wouldn't have made such a gome. **1950** *PADS* 14.33 **SC,** *Gorm*. . . A mess; a state of confusion, disorder. **1960** *Courier-Jrl.* (Louisville KY) 1 Oct sec 2, But we impart a more subtle meaning to mess, in that we apply it to a mixture, or a gorm, of food that has been boiled in a pot, and served up all greasy, bubbly, or mushy. **1969** *DARE* (Qu. Y37, *To make a place untidy or disorderly*) Inf **GA**72, Make such a gaum [gɒm]; (Qu. Y38, *Mixed together, con-*

fused: "The things in the drawer are all ———.") Inf **KY**24, In a gaum; **KY**25, A-gaum; in a gaum; in a mess. **1982** *Smithsonian Letters* **cnKY** (as of 1930s), If the crock of cake batter slipped from a mother's hands and splattered all over the floor, she would ejaculate in disgust, "Look what a gorm I've made!"

2 By ext: something sticky; filth.

1914 *DN* 4.106 **KS,** *Gaum, n. & v.* Gum. **1946** *AmSp* 21.96 **sIL,** As a child in Southern Illinois, I often heard my mother, whose forebears came from the Appalachia country in the first quarter of the nineteenth century, use *gaum* to describe anything smeary spilled on the kitchen floor. *Gaum* still enjoys a limited use here. **1961** *Mt. Life* Spring 7 **sAppalachians,** *Gorm* (grime; often the *r* disappears completely, leaving *gom*). **1968** *DARE* (Qu. Y40b, . . *Sticky stuff. . "They're all covered with ———."*) Inf **IN**39, Gaum.

3 Fig: a botched job, a blunder.

1933 *AmSp* 8.1.49 **Ozarks,** *Gorm. . .* A mess, a muddle, a poor job. A house badly built, or a dress badly tailored, may be described as jest a plumb gorm. **1950** *PADS* 14.32 **SC,** *Gorm. . .* An awkward deed; a stupid deed; a blunder. "To commit a gorm."

4 A large quantity.

1883 (1971) Harris *Nights with Remus* 194 **GA** [Black], Dey aint no tellin' de gawm dat ole nigger kin eat. He look shaky, . . yit w'ence he set hisse'f down whar dey any vittle, he des nat'ally laps hit up. **1913** *DN* 4.1 **ME,** *Gorm. . .* A large amount. "I put a gorm of worms on the hook." **1939** *Esquire* Sept 54/3 **nwAR,** When he had let what he deemed was a sufficiency of blood out of the incised vein, he called to Elvira to bring a spoon of "sut" from off the back of the fireplace and a "gaum" of spiderwebs from somewhere or other.

5 Blood. [Prob by confusion with *gore*]

1942 Thomas *Blue Ridge Country* 253 **sAppalachians,** Them holes is where the McCoys stobbed Uncle Ellison and there's the stain of his gorm.

gaum v² Also sp *gawm, gorm* [*EDD gaum* v.⁴ "To stare idly or vacantly . . gape . . be stupid, awkward"] **chiefly NEng** Cf **gauming** adj

1 with *around:* To move awkwardly or clumsily.

1892 *DN* 1.210 **eMA,** *Gormy* or *gormin' around* [gɔm-]. Said of a horse that "gawks" in stable or harness. **1909** *DN* 3.411 **nME,** *Gawm around. . .* To move around in an awkward way.

2 also with *up:* To make an awkward job of (something); to bungle, cobble up. [Perh infl by **gaum** v¹ **3**]

1941 *LANE* Map 463 *(Awkward, clumsy)* 1 inf, **sRI,** He [gɔmz] everything up. **1966–69** *DARE* (Qu. KK63, *To do a clumsy or hurried job of repairing something: "It will never last—he just ———."*) Infs **KY**40, **ME**22, Gaumed it up. **1969** *DARE* FW Addit **KY**6, Referring to a pre-fabricated house, Inf said it wouldn't last because the contractor "just gaumed it up." **1975** Gould *ME Lingo* 114, *Gorm. . .* A favorite Maine word . . meaning to behave in a stupid, awkward manner. . . A man who bungles a job has gormed it.

3 with *around:* See quot; also vbl n *gauming.*

1971 *DARE* File **Cape Cod MA,** "Gawming" . . was not unknown . . in my childhood, 1902–1915+. . . Gawming was used in this sense, "Oh I just went down town gawming around," meaning to look around to see what one could see or hear what one could hear. . . "Gawming" could have been a variation of "gawking."

gaum n² Also sp *go(r)m* Also *gaumhead* [*EDD gaum* sb.³; *OEDS gom* sb.⁴] **nNEng** Cf **gaumy** adj²

A clumsy person; a lout.

1941 *LANE* Map 464 *(Awkward person, lummox)* 5 infs, **VT, ME,** Gaum; 1 inf, **nwMA,** Gaumhead. **1975** Gould *ME Lingo* 114, *Gorm*—Pronounced gawm. . . A clumsy oaf. . . A boy with two left hands is a *gorm.* **1977** *Yankee* Jan 113 **csME,** If it happens that you're so conked out that you trip on your way out the door, you might feel like a *lummox*—which is a clumsy oaf—in other words, a *gom.* **1979** [see **gaumy** adj²].

gaumandize v Also *gormandize* [Cf *gormandize* to eat gluttonously] *Gullah* Cf **gaum** v¹ **4**

To eat messily; see quot.

1909 *S. Atl. Qrly.* 8.47 **seSC,** *Gaumandize,* sometimes *gormandize,* meaning not *to eat . . gluttonously,* but, like a child, *to daub and to spatter one's self with victual.*

gaum around v phr¹ See **gaum** v¹ **3**

gaum around v phr² See **gaum** v² **1, 3**

gaumed up See **gaum** v¹ **1, 3**

gaumhead See **gaum** n²

gauming vbl n See **gaum** v² **3**

gauming adj Also sp *gawming, gorming* [**gaum** v²; cf *EDD gauming* (at *gaum* v.⁴)] **chiefly nNEng**

=**gaumy** adj².

1899 Garland *Boy Life* 340 **nwIA** (as of c1870s), He rode a "gauming" sorrel colt, with a bewildering series of gaits. **1909** *DN* 3.411 **nME,** *Gawming. . .* Awkward. **1914** *DN* 4.73 **ME, nNH,** *Gormin'. . .* Clumsy, stupid. **1926** *DN* 5.387 **ME,** *Gorming.* **1926** *AmSp* 2.80 **ME,** Anything clumsy is termed "gorming," whether it be a horse that walks on a flower bed, a person who breaks something, or a piece of furniture that takes up too much room. **1927** *AmSp* 3.135 **ME coast,** An awkward or clumsy man was a "gump" a "gawk" or "gowk," a lout, "a great gorming lummox," a "greenhorn." **1941** *LANE* Map 463 *(Awkward, clumsy),* A *gauming* person is ungraceful in his movements . . , ungainly in his general behavior but not in appearance . . , tall and awkward . . , or clumsy at work and play. [*Gauming* is reported from the majority of communities in **eVT, NH** and **ME** and from 3 infs in **neMA.** 3 infs, 2 in **MA,** restrict the term to horses. 1 inf, **ceVT,** is quoted for the superlative [gɔ·mɨnɚst].] **1959** *VT Hist.* new ser 27.137, *Gawming. . .* Clumsy. Common. **1965** Gould *You Should Start* 72 **ME,** She . . caught the sleeping Charley with one of her great, gorming, flat boots, and she mowed a swath with him right out through into the kitchen. **1970** *DARE* FW Addit **NH,** Gormin' . . used by my grandmother (cWWI). "She was a great gormin' girl." Overgrown. Clumsy. **1971** *DARE* File **Cape Cod MA,** My mother always used the word [=*gawming*] to denote *big* and *awkward.* Her ancestors came from Londonderry, Ireland via Londonderry N.H. to Londonderry, Vermont. **1975** Gould *ME Lingo* 114, A mother may call at her son, "Get your big gormin' hands out o' that cookie jar!"

gaum into See **gaum** v¹ **4**

gaumish adj [Perh rel to **gauming** adj, **gaumy** adj²]

See quot.

1969 *DARE* (Qu. BB5, *A general feeling of discomfort or illness*) Inf **NY**226, Gaumish ['gɔmɪš]—Father used this term.

gaum up v phr¹ See **gaum** v¹ **1, 3**

gaum up v phr² See **gaum** v² **2**

gaumy adj¹ Also sp *gormy* [*EDD gaumy* (at *gaum* v.³); *OED* 1881 →]

1 Sticky, smeared, dirty. **scattered, but esp Appalachians** See Map

1899 (1912) Green *VA Folk-Speech* 202, *Gormy. . .* Smeary; sticky. *Gaumy.* **1950** *PADS* 14.33 **SC,** *Gormy, gaumy. . .* Smeared, soiled. **c1960** *Wilson Coll.* **csKY,** *Gaumy. . .* Messy, smeared, dirty. **1965–70** *DARE* (Qu. Y40a, . . *Sticky stuff: "I've got to wash my hands, they're all ———."*) 20 Infs, **esp Appalachians,** Gaumy; **TN**4, ['gɔmɪ]; **TN**13, ['gɑmɪ]; (Qu. Y39, . . *"The children have been eating candy and they've got their faces all ———."*) Infs **IL**105, **WV**18, Gaumy; (Qu. W36, . . *A woman who uses a lot of cosmetics*) Inf **CA**50, Looks gaumy. **1975** Gould *ME Lingo* 114, A recipe for red-flannel hash says to "mix it loose but not gormy." **1984** Wilder *You All Spoken Here* 163 **Sth,** *Gaumy. . .* In disorder; soiled; gummy, like a child eating peanut brittle.

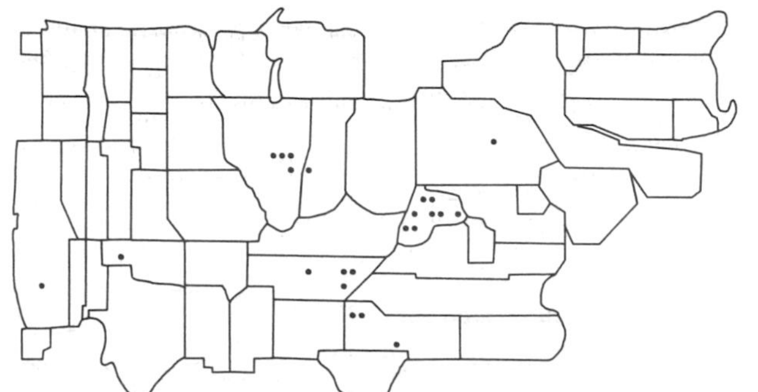

•gaumy adj¹ 1 + var (Qq. Y40a, W36, Y39)

2 Untidy.

1892 *KS Univ. Qrly.* 1.96 **AR,** *Gaumy:* not neat. **1950** *PADS* 14.33 **SC,** *Gormy, gaumy.* . . Untidy; when a lady's stockings wrinkle around the ankle she is said to have *gormy* ankles.

gaumy adj[2] Also sp *gawmy, gomy, gorm(e)y* [**gaum** n[2]; cf *EDD gaumy* (at *gaum* sb.[3])] **chiefly nNEng, esp ME**

Awkward, inept, stupid.

1892 [see **gaum** v[2] **1**]. **1940–41** Cassidy *WI Atlas* **ceWI,** Gaumy . . awkward [said of a coat]. **1941** *LANE* Map 463 *(Awkward, clumsy)* [16 infs, **VT, NH, ME, eMA,** Gaumy]. **1966** *DARE* FW Addit **ME**15, *Gaumy*—clumsy. **1970** *DARE* FW Addit **MA**78, "Gomy" meaning the clumsy way that I was trying to help my father. **1972** *NYT Article Letters* **ME,** When we're awkward, we're "gawmy". **1975** Gould *ME Lingo* 114, Anybody who stumbles over his own feet is *gormy.* The illustrative colloquy runs thus: "Ain't he the boy broke your plow, smashed your cart, lost the 40-quart can down the well, and got your Edie in a family way?" "Ayeh." "Gormy cuss, ain't he?" **1979** Lewis *How to Talk Yankee* np **ME,** *Gawmy* . . clumsy, awkward. Also *gawm* . . oafish person. This is an ubiquitous and essential downeast term. When Winston dropped the fishing trip's supply of beer down the well, his brother called him a *gawmy* bahstud, as he was. **1982** *Smithsonian Letters* **ME,** *Gormey:* Awkward, or, by extension, embarrassing. **1982** *DARE* File **coastal ME,** Gawmy: clumsy or repulsive.

gaunch hook See **gancho 2**

gaunt v Cf **gant** v

1 also *gaunt up:* To make thin; hence ppl adj *gaunted.*

1864 in a1972 *Hench Coll.* **cVA,** [Letter:] My horse, so far, stands very well; she is a little gaunted but *that* is of small importance. **1887** *Outing* 10.115.2, Jim, do you want to gaunt Peg-leg for a race, or will you give him his ration? **1890** Shields *Big Game* 476, A gorged Wolf is not fast, . . but when properly 'gaunted,' few horses can catch a Gray Wolf. **1914** *DN* 4.106 **KS,** *Gaunt.* . . To emaciate;—used with *up.* "He gaunted up the cattle." **1935** Sandoz *Jules* 78 **NE** (as of 1880–1930), Hans . . a gay, whistling cavalier on a plough-gaunted horse. **1967** Williams *Greenbones* 41 **GA** (as of c1910), I see your horses. They're gaunted, aren't they? Is that because you don't feed them anything but grass?

2 with *down:* To become thin.

1966 Giles *Great Adventure* 132 **West** (as of c1840), Driant gaunted down, but he crawled on his horse every morning and hung on.

3 with *in:* See quot.

1914 *DN* 4.155 **Cape Cod MA,** *Gaunt in.* . . To be concave. (Applied only to animals.) "What a big-boned horse that is—see how he gaunts in there in the flank!"

gaunt down See **gaunt 2**

gaunted See **gaunt 1**

gaunt in See **gaunt 3**

gaunt up See **gaunt 1**

gaunty adj Pronc-sp *ganty* [*gaunt* adj and **gant** adj] *?obs*

Thin, lean.

1772 in 1912 Thornton *Amer. Gloss.* 355 **MA,** A mare is described as "a ganty lofty carriage Beast."—Advt., *Mass. Gazette,* Jan. 30. **1823** Cooper *Pioneers* 2.327 **cNY,** Hounds should be gaunty to run well.

gaup v Usu |gɔp, gɑp|; rarely |gaʊp| Also sp *gawp* [Engl dial; *OED* 1682 →]

1 To stare with the mouth open; to stare stupidly; hence n *gawper,* one who stares. **chiefly NEast, Gt Lakes** See Map

1897 in 1919 Hale *Letters* 321, Leaving the three English gawping on the rocks. **1907** *DN* 3.188 **seNH,** *Gawp.* . . To stare with open mouth. "Who are you gawping at, you numskull?" **1909** *DN* 3.411 **nME,** *Gawpin'.* . . Gawking. **1917** *DN* 4.392 **OH,** *Gaup* [gɔp]. . . Gape, stare with open mouth. "Don't stand gauping at it." . . Also N. Eng., Ill., Ia., N.Y., Kan. **1927** *AmSp* 3.139 **ME coast,** If staring at someone, a child was told not to "gawp." **1939** *Fortune* July 102/1 **NYC,** Patrolman Dunnigan then called to the janitor . . to keep the gathering gawpers away from the gun on the floor. **1941** *LANE* Map 450, 1 inf, **swVT,** [gɔ˅·pɨŋ], daughter's term, = *gaping;* 1 inf, **cnVT,** 'A hayseed stands [gɔ˅·pɨŋ] around.' **1942** Whipple *Joshua* 376 **UT,** Well, come in! Come in! What y'u gawpin' out there for? **1949** Webber *Backwoods Teacher* 78 **Ozarks,** Make her quit gawpin' at me! **1959** *VT Hist.* new ser 27.137, Gauping ['gɔpɪŋ]. . . Occasional. Rural areas. **1965–70** *DARE* (Qu. X22, *To stare at something with your mouth open*) 31 Infs, **chiefly NEast, Gt Lakes,** Gaup; **AR**3, **MA**47, **MI**81, **NC**33, **VT**16, [gɔp]; **CT**1, Person is ['gɔpɪŋ]; **MI**75, **UT**3, [gɑp]; **WI**76, ['gɑpɪŋ]—he'd stand there and gaup; **MS**1, [gaʊp]; (Qu. KK31, *To go about aimlessly looking for distraction: "He doesn't have anything to do, so he's just ______ around."*) Infs **NY**24, ['gɑpɪŋ]. **1966** Barnes–Jensen *Dict. UT Slang* 17, *Gawp:* . . to overstare at strange sights. **1978** Doig *This House* 311 **MT** (as of c1970), Makes me spooky to think of everybody gawping down at me like that.

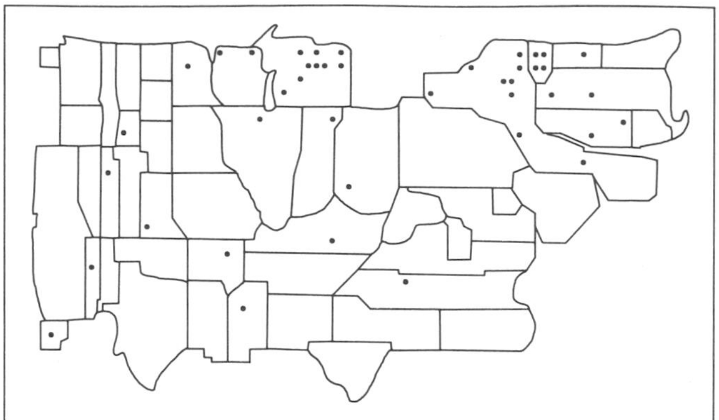

•gaup v 1 + var (Qq. X22, KK31)

2 To yawn.

1955 Ritchie *Singing Family* 166 **seKY,** We were so sleepy we could hardly live, but we moaned and stretched and gawped and finally got awake enough to know what day it was.

gaup n [**gaup** v]

1 See quot.

1941 *LANE* Map 464 *(Awkward person, lummox)* 1 inf, **cwME,** [gɔ˅·k, gɔ˅·p].

2 See quot.

1970 *DARE* (Qu. X46, *When a person's getting sleepy and opens his mouth wide and takes a deep breath, that's a ______*) Inf **SC**66, Gap, gaup.

gaupy adj [**gaup** v **1**]

1941 *LANE* Map 450 *(A rustic)* 1 inf, **nwMA,** A gaupy [gɔ˅·pɨ]-lookin' feller.

gauster v |'gɔstə(r)| Also sp *goster* [*EDD gauster* v. 1 "To bully . . to be turbulent . . to brag"] Cf **snollygoster**

To boast, to act in an overbearing manner; hence n *goster(er), gowster* a boastful, overbearing person, bully; n *gostration* arrogant speech or behavior.

1829 in 1931 *AmSp* 7.96 **wVA,** *Gostering,* pr. part. Imperious, boasting. Variant—Gaustering. West. **1840** U.S. Congress *Congressional Globe* 21 July 545/2 **IN,** Why have we witnessed manifestations of what must here, I suppose, be called chivalry, but which, in the hoosier State, the boys would call *gostration?* **1864** U.S. Congress *Congressional Globe* 13 Apr 1556/1 **IN,** With the blustering gostration of the cock[, he] would scare the enemy to death without a fight and save his powder. **1894** *DN* 1.331 **NJ,** *Goster:* to domineer. *Gosterer:* one who boasts or brags. **1915** *DN* 4.201 [Terms of disparagement], *Goster, gosterer,* a domineering person. "My husband might better be a gosterer than a drunkard." **1937** (1963) Hyatt *Kiverlid* 37 **KY,** Huh! . . him just a-gosterin' about my old snags [=bad teeth], and tellin' 'em here to keep adostin' [=dosing] me on that bottle o' draps thar. **1952** Brown *NC Folkl.* 1.544 **cnNC,** *Gauster* ['gɔstə]. . . To domineer. **1972** Kochman *Rappin'* 373 **Chicago IL** [Black], Perhaps the most outstanding and visible attribute possessed by . . gowsters is antisocial aggression. . . "Don't mess with that cat, he's a gowster."

gauze See **gauze shirt**

gauze grass n

A **muhly grass** (here: *Muhlenbergia uniflora*).

1912 Baker *Book of Grasses* 114, Gauze-grass is so small and delicate that it hides beneath one's feet, and hundreds of the plants may grow unnoticed by the margin of a brook where taller grasses have been gathered. *Ibid* 115, *Gauze-grass. Sporobolus uniflorus.* . . Maine to Michigan, south to New Jersey.

gauze hawk n Cf **mosquito hawk**
A **dragonfly.**
1968 *DARE* (Qu. R2, . . *Other names . . for the dragonfly*) Inf **NC**49, Gauze hawk.

gauze shirt n Also *gauze (vest)* **chiefly Atlantic** *old-fash* Cf **gall shirt, gores shirt**
A light, vest-like undershirt.
1965–70 *DARE* (Qu. W15, *A shirt-length undergarment worn by women*) Infs **MI**78, **MA**14, **NJ**3, 7, **NY**145, **OH**98, **SC**26, Gauze shirt(s); **NC**79, **SC**10, Gauze; **SC**46, Gauze vest—first used years ago. [8 of 10 Infs old] **1978** *DSNA Letters,* Gauze shirt . . I heard the term when I was a child from my grandmother. . . Gauze shirt was a type of undershirt worn by men and infants . . the kind without sleeves, and with a low neckline (similar to a vest or tanktop worn by basketball players), made of a very thin transparent fabric [that] resembled the gauze that was kept in her medicine cabinet.

gav See **gaff** n, v

gaved See **give A3c**

gavel n
A pile of grain; see quot 1926.
1851 in 1892 Thoreau *Autumn* 61 **MA,** He [=a farmer] used the word gavel to describe a parcel of stalks cast on the ground to dry. **1899** Garland *Boy Life* 278 **nwIA** (as of c1870s), Running to the gavel, he scuffled it together with his feet, while he jerked a handful of the wheat from the sheaf with his left hand. A swift whirl of the band, a stooping clutch, and he rose with the bundle on his knee. A sudden pull, a twist, a twirl over his thumb, and the first bound sheaf dropped into the stubble. . . Swiftly the gavels turned to sheaves behind him. **1926** (1961) Garland *Boy Life* 434 **nwIA,** *Gavel:* the loose mound of grain left by the cradle or the reaper, lying in an oblong heap with the heads all one way and the butts all another. A continuous line of gavels was called a *swath.* **a1945** *McDavid Coll.* **NY,** Gavel—a loose pile of grain in the field.

gaven See **give A3c**

gave out See **given out**

gavilan n [Span *gavilán* sparrow hawk]
A **chicken hawk 1.**
1892 *DN* 1.248 **TX,** *Gavilán:* a chicken-hawk; a species of *falconidæ,* not identified.

Gawd See **God**

Gawdfrediamonds See **Godfrey**

Gawja See **Georgia**

gawk v Also *gawk around* [*EDD gawk* v.[2] "with *about:* to wander aimlessly about"]
To act in an awkward or stupid manner; to wander about aimlessly.
1941 *LANE* Map 463 *(Awkward, clumsy)* 4 infs, **scattered NEng,** Gawking; Map 464 *(Awkward person, lummox)* 3 infs, **scattered,** Gawking gander. **1965–70** *DARE* [(Qu. X22, *To stare at something with your mouth open*) 374 Infs, **widespread, but less freq SE,** Gawk;] (Qu. Y21, *To move about slowly and without energy*) Inf **MN**10, Gawking; (Qu. Y22, *To move around in a way to make people take notice of you*) Inf **MO**9, Gawking around; (Qu. Y27, *To go about aimlessly*) Inf **ME**21, Gawking; (Qu. Y29b, . . *A man who doesn't stay home much: "He's always ______."*) Inf **PA**244, Gawking around; (Qu. KK31, . . *"He doesn't have anything to do, so he's just ______ around."*) Infs **NY**96, **TX**10, Gawking.

gawk n Also *gowk* [*EDD gawk* sb.[2]]
1 also *gawkhead:* A foolish, awkward person; a simpleton.
1837 (1966) Martineau *Soc. in America* 1.299 **appar AL,** They proved "such gawks," that they were unable to learn. **1872** Twain *Roughing It* 61, Well it was not funny, and there was no sense in those gawks making themselves so facetious over it. **1899** (1912) Green *VA Folk-Speech* 192, *Gawk.* . . A stupid, awkward fellow; a fool; a simpleton; a booby. **1915** *DN* 4.199, *Gawk,* an awkward fool. "Who's that gawk coming up the street?" In general usage. **1923** *DN* 5.235 **swWI,** *Gawk.* . . A gawky man, never a woman. . . "He's a regular gawk—all hands and feet." **1926** Finerty *Criminalese* 26, *Gawk*—An awkward simpleton of either sex. **1926** *DN* 5.387 **ME,** *Gawk.* . . An ungainly person. Rare. **1927** *AmSp* 3.135 **ME coast,** An awkward or clumsy man was a "gump" a "gawk" or "gowk." **1930** Shoemaker *1300 Words* 25 **cPA Mts** (as of c1900), *Gawk*—A lanky, ungraceful young fellow. **1941** *LANE* Map 450 *(A rustic)* 3 infs, **RI, MA,** (Country) gawk. *Ibid* Map 464 *(Awkward person, lummox)* [*Gawk* is common **throughout NEng, but esp in ME;** 1 inf, **sVT,** Gawkhead.] **1965–70** *DARE* (Qu. HH21, *A very awkward, clumsy person*) 27 Infs, **scattered,** Gawk; **NY**241, Dumb gawk; (Qu. HH1, . . *A rustic or countrified person*) Infs **MA**11, 47, Country gawk; **MI**4, **SD**1, Gawk.
2 Transf: see quot.
1974 *AmSp* 49.62 **swME** (as of c1900), *Gawk.* . . Something in poor taste "It was a gawk of a name he had."
3 =**black-crowned night heron.**
1911 *Forest & Stream* 77.174, *Nycticorax nycticorax naevius.* . . Gawk . . St. Vincent Island, Fla.
4 in phr *hunting the gawk* (or *gowk*): See quot. [Brit dial *gowk* cuckoo; cf *EDD gowk* sb.[1] 3. (3) "*to hunt the gowk* . . to send any one on a fool's errand"] Cf *DS* CC17
1944 *PADS* 2.43 **NC,** *Gawk, gowk, hunting the:* . . A sport like "snipe-hunting," in which unsuspecting strangers are dupes left to "hold the bag." Swain Co., N.C.

gawk around See **gawk** v

gawkey See **gawky**

gawkhead See **gawk** n **1**

gawkified adj [*gawky* adj + **-ified**]
1941 *LANE* Map 463 *(Awkward, clumsy)* 5 infs, **scattered NEng,** Gawkified.

gawkward adj [Blend of *gawky* + *awkward*]
See quots.
1913 *DN* 4.43, *Gawkward.* . . Gawky. **1941** O'Donnell *Great Big Doorstep* 273 **LA,** The gawkward little spirit is the cause of it all.

gawky n Also sp *gawkey* [*EDD gawky* sb. 3] **esp NEng** Cf *DS* HH1
=**gawk** n **1.**
1825 Neal *Brother Jonathan* 2.144 **NEng,** Great, long, slab-sided, simple "gawkeys" from the country. **1941** *LANE* Map 450 *(A rustic)* 4 infs, **chiefly wNEng,** (Country) gawky; 1 inf, **nwVT,** *Gawky,* 'one that stands gaping at the high buildings in a city'. *Ibid* Map 464 *(Awkward person, lummox)* [*Gawky* is recorded in 50 communities, **widespread throughout NEng, except ME** (where there are only 2 cases). It is found also with various adjectives, as "a regular gawky," "a great ~," "an old ~," and "a backwoods ~."Four infs say it is old-fashioned or rare. One inf, **RI,** defines: "A gawky's a halfwit."]

‡gawky-eyed adj [*gawky* adj]
1968 *DARE* (Qu. X21a, . . *Words . . used to describe people according to their eyes—for example, if they stick out*) Inf **VA**34, Gawky-eyed.

gawkyish adj [**gawky n**]
1941 *LANE* Map 463 *(Awkward, clumsy)* 1 inf, **eCT,** Gawkyish = countrified.

gawm v[1] See **gaum** v[1]

gawm v[2] See **gaum** v[2]

gawm n See **gum** n[1], v[1]

gawming adj See **gauming** adj

gawmy adj See **gaumy** adj[2]

gawnicus See **goonus**

gawny See **gooney**

gawp v See **gaup** v

gawper See **gaup** v

gawt See **get** v **B1a**

gay adj
1 Among Quakers, Amish, and other religious groups: worldly; not adhering to traditional customs; hence v phr *go gay:* to abandon traditional ways for those of the dominant culture. **esp PA**
1798 in 1912 Thornton *Amer. Gloss.* 357 **Philadelphia PA,** Her dress was pretty nearly that marked as *"gay quakers";* she wore a white gown, white gloves, green petticoat, and drab cloak. **1888** Gossler *Turnpike-*

Road 71 **PA,** Permit me to recall the Quaker Meeting-House. . . The attendance was much larger fifty years ago than now. During the interval they [=the Friends] have become "gay," or "gone West," or "over to the majority." **1935** *AmSp* 10.169, Two special expressions, for which there are no good American equivalents, are in use among the 'plain' people (i.e., those who wear the plain garb of the Mennonites, Amish, and other religious sects): *to go gay,* meaning to become worldly in the sense of attending dances, card parties, movies, or participating in other forbidden pleasures; and *to put off the church,* meaning to excommunicate. **1950** Klees *PA Dutch* 284, Occasionally there is magic in the phraseology, as in the case of the Amish girl who was expelled from meeting because she married a Reformed youth and "went gay." **1967** Williams *Greenbones* 190 **GA** (as of c1910), "Dancer? Thought Quakers didn't approve of dancing?". . . "I call him [=a horse] Dancer because I'm a Gay Quaker. Some call us Fat Quakers, George Washington did." **1967** *DARE* Tape **PA**30, By the plain person's standard I am gay, I am dressy and they are plain. But if you would go from me and go to one of the free type worship churches like the. . . tabernacle type groups who still dress in a modern fashion, they are still gay or dressy. And you can go into the Mennonite person who does not abide by the plain dress, the colorless coat, broad-rimmed [sic] hat and he is still considered to be a gay individual. He is still not a plain person. **1976** Flexner *America Talking* 269, The earliest Pennsylvania Dutch (and Quakers) called themselves *the plain people* as early as the 1680s and called the Pennsylvania Calvinists and Lutherans *the gay people.*

2 Sassy, impudent—used in phr *get gay* to get out of line in one's behavior.

1896 W.C. Gore in *Inlander* Jan. 147 *(OEDS), Get gay,* to joke boisterously; to show off; to act 'smart'. **1899** (1900) Ade *Fables in Slang* 109, The Copper, perceiving that he had come very near getting Gay with our First Families, Apologized for Cutting In. **1903** (1965) Adams *Log Cowboy* 268 **NM,** "It's nothing," said he; "just a couple of punchers, who had been drinking a little, were eating a snack, and one of them asked for a second dish of prunes, when the waiter got gay and told him that he couldn't have them,—'that he was full of prunes now.' " **1928** Peterkin *Scarlet Sister Mary* 214 **SC,** Her effort to get gay met with a dead silence. **1955** McAtee *Dial. Grant Co. IN Suppl. 6* np, *Gay:* . . saucy. "Don't get gay with me." **1974** *DARE* File **cwWI** (as of c1952), *Get gay* . . be saucy or impudent. "Now don't get gay with me." **1976** Flexner *America Talking* 162, In the 1890s, *gay* not only meant happy and carefree but informal, and *to get gay* with someone meant to take liberties, to be a little too brash even as Victorianism receded.

gay-cat See **cat** v 1

gayfeather n [See quots 1901, 1974]
=blazing star 3.

1822 Eaton *Botany* 336, *Liatris . . spicata* . . gay feather, button snakeroot. **1830** Rafinesque *Med. Flora* 2.237, *Liatris.* . . Many vulgar names, *Backache root,* . . *Gayfeather, Rough root,* &c. **1881** *Lib. Universal Knowledge* VI.493 *(DA), Gay-feather,* the common name for the *Liatris scariosa* and *L. spicata.* **1901** Lounsberry *S. Wild Flowers* 501, *L[iatris] scariosa,* . . gay feather, . . produces its flowers in rounded, compact and slender-peduncled heads quite distant from each other on the stem. . . The plant itself is known to grow quite six feet tall. **1941** Walker *Lookout* 50 **seTN,** Wild ginger, . . gayfeather, . . and purple gerardia are abundant. **1968** *DARE* FW Addit **CO**7, Gay feather *(Liatris punctata)*—Blazingstar, Button Snakeroot. **1968** Pochmann *Triple Ridge* 106 **cWI,** In August purple *Liatris spicata* lives up to its local name, gayfeather, and lifts my spirits. **1974** (1977) Coon *Useful Plants* 113, Gay-feather. . . Tall and brilliant when in bloom, it is. . . listed as being medicinally valuable.

‡gaylap n

1966 *DARE* (Qu. K23, *Words used by women or in mixed company for a bull)* Inf **GA**7, Gaylap ['gelæp].

gayly See **gaily**

gaywater n

1968 *DARE* (Qu. DD21c, . . *Whiskey, especially illegally made whiskey)* Inf **SC**64, Gaywater.

gaywings n [From the petal-like sepals which form "wings"]
=fringed polygala.

1848 in 1850 Cooper *Rural Hours* 86 **NY,** As for the May-wings, or "gay-wings," they are in truth one of the gayest little blossoms we have. **1893** *Jrl. Amer. Folkl.* 6.140, *Polygala paucifiora.* . . Gay wings. Ferrisburgh, Vt.; N. Y. **1900** Higginson *Outdoor Studies* 36 **MA,** Some early plants . . are still found near Worcester in the greatest abundance . . the pretty fringed Polygala, which Miss Cooper christened "Gay-Wings." **1933** Small *Manual SE Flora* 767, *Fringed Polygala. Gay-wings.* . . Moist woods and ravines. **1964** Campbell *Great Smoky Wildflowers* 18, *Gay Wings.* . . The attractive orchid-pink flowers . . are seen in April. **1966** *DARE* Wildfl QR Pl.125b Infs **MI**57, **WI**35, Gaywings. **1968** *DARE* (Qu. S26c, *Wildflowers that grow in woods)* Inf **PA**99, Gaywings.

gazabo n Usu |gə'zebo|; also |gə'zibo| Also sp *gaze(e)bo, gazubo* *usu derog*

A person, fellow, guy, esp an awkward, strange, or stupid one; see quots.

1889 *AN&Q* 4.53/1, Gazeebo. . . Colloquially, it sometimes means a laughing stock, or a gazing stock. In the latter sense I have heard it in Philadelphia, but I think it is Anglo-Irish in its origin. **1896** (1898) Ade *Artie* 44 **Chicago IL,** Who does I meet comin' out o' the house but a cheap gazabo. **1897** *KS Univ. Qrly.* (ser B) 6.87 **MO,** *Gazubo:* a "jaw" [*DARE* Ed: appar misprint for *jay* "a green, conceited fellow"]. From "gaze about(?)." **1911** *DN* 3.544 **NE,** *Gazábo.* . . An officious person; an odd, queer, or stupid person. "He's a regular gazabo," "I went down town, and some gazabo directed me to the wrong place," "See that gazabo, with his hat on in church." **1913** London *Valley of Moon* 134 **CA,** Take it from me, she's a wise gazabo. **1932** *AmSp* 7.332 **MD** [Student slang], Gazabo—a fellow. **1947** Paul *Linden* 124 **MA,** "Would that have anything to do with *dementia praecox,* or whatever the old gazabo from Malden said she had?" **1964** De Vries *Reuben* 157 **CT,** "They're not our sort, Frank, the gazebos who go in for that," said Mrs. Punck, using a term that rolled us back in time to about the year the Lizzie come out, 1926. **1968** *DARE* FW Addit **NY,** Gazebo [gə'zibo]—a rough guy. **1971** *Today Show Letters* **New Orleans LA,** Gazabo [gə'zebo]. . . An uncomplimentary term applied to a person. In our family vocabulary it means "clumsy, stupid" and was probably introduced to our southern household by my father who grew up in western New York state.

gazook n **esp West** *derog*
=gazabo.

1911 *DN* 3.550 **WY,** *Gazook,* vaguely uncomplimentary epithet, about the same as "gazabo." **1918** *DN* 5.24 **WA,** *Gazook-strap.* . . A leather thong attached to a handle, used to punish rule-breakers in "frat" houses. **1919** *DN* 5.69 **NM,** *Gazook,* a gawky person. "There comes the old gazook again." **1966** Barnes-Jensen *Dict. UT Slang* 17, *Gazook* . . an awkward one. **1969** *DARE* (Qu. HH17, *A person who tries to appear important)* Inf **NY**141, Head gazook [gə'zʊk].

gazpacho n Pronc-spp *gispachi, guspachy*

Std sense, var forms.

1939 Berolzheimer *U.S. Cookbook* 216 **Sth,** Florida guspachy salad. **1949** Brown *Amer. Cooks* 118, *Florida Gispachi.* . . This is a version of the Spanish "gaspacho" with the name Americanized to "Gispachi" and sometimes "Guspachy." It's one of the original dishes of the Florida cuisine.

gazubo See **gazabo**

gazunga tree n

See quot.

1982 *Smithsonian Letters* **swLA,** The "Bettywood tree." . . Surely it is the same tree today known to surveyors as a "Gazunga" tree. I tripped over this strange one several years ago in a surveyor's field notes. When asked, he replied that a Gazunga tree was any prominent tree used as a survey mark where the surveyor didn't recognize the type. The better training in botany a surveyor had, the fewer Gazunga . . trees he would encounter.

geaar See **gar** n

gear n

1 usu pl: Harness. **now chiefly Sth, S Midl**

1648 in 1850 CT (Colony) *Pub. Rec.* 1.508, *An Inventory of the Estate of Thomas Nowell* [includes] . . 2 horse collars, and other geares. **1776** in 1901 *Documents Revol. Hist. NJ* 1.104, *Stolen . . one mare and horse. . . both the abovesaid creatures used to the gears.* **1886** *S. Bivouac* 4.349 **sAppalachians,** Gears (harness). **1887** *Scribner's Mag.* 2.476 **AR,** "They jes' puttin' the gears on the mewls." **1902** *DN* 2.235 **sIL,** *Gears.* . . particularly wagon harness. **1903** *DN* 2.314 **seMO,** *Gears.* **1906** *DN* 3.119 **sIN,** Put the gears on the horses. **1907** *DN* 3.222 **nwAR,** *Gears.* **1908** *DN* 3.314 **eAL, wGA,** *Gear(s).* . . Harness, especially the simple harness used in plowing. **1915** *DN* 4.183 **swVA,** *Gears* . . harness. **1938** Faulkner *Unvanquished* 270, The horses too gathered in a tight group beyond them. . . One of them stamped and blew his breath and jangled his gear. **1966** Dakin *Dial. Vocab. Ohio R. Valley* 2.290, *Gears* (occasionally *gear* or *gearing*) used as a noun in the expression *put the gears on* . . [is] common everywhere in Kentucky and quite common in the interior counties in Illinois. **1966–69** *DARE* (Qu. L43a) Infs **KY**52, **NC**31, **SC**43, Put the gears on.

2 pl: Legs.

1940 *AmSp* 15.83 **swPA, nWV,** *Gears,* legs.

gear v

1 usu with *up;* rarely with *out:* To harness (an animal); to rig a wagon or carriage; to get animals in harness. **[gear n 1] chiefly Sth, S Midl** See Map

1854 in 1983 *PADS* 70.34 **ce,sePA,** Geared the greys up went to the mill to get them broke for ploughing. **1858** in 1983 *PADS* 70.34 **ce,sePA,** Cleard off after breakfast geared our carriage I went to the springs. **1859** (1864) Browning *Hunter* 199 **wMD,** The ostler had my team geared, and ready to hitch up. **1890** *DN* 1.76 **NJ,** *Gear.* . . To harness. **1890** *AN&Q* 4.249/2, *Gear up* a horse. In New Jersey the phrase I have heard used is invariably "gear out." *Ibid* 4.280/2 **nwTN,** We *gear up* horses here. **1892** *DN* 1.233 **KY,** *Gear up.* . . To harness. **1905** *DN* 3.81 **nwAR,** I reckon we'd better go out and gear up. **1933** Williamson *Woods Colt* 5 **Ozarks,** I jest geared up the old mare. **1948** Faulkner *Intruder* 96 **MS,** The men [would] . . catch and gear up the mules. **1954** *Harder Coll.* **cwTN,** Gear up the horses or mules. **1962** Faulkner *Reivers* 74, The . . mule skinners . . met the wagons at both edges of the bottom, with two and three and (when necessary) four span of already geared-up mules. **1965–70** *DARE* (Qu. L43a, *When somebody is going to get horses ready to work, he might say, "I'll ______ the horses."*) 38 Infs, **chiefly Sth, S Midl,** Gear up; 18 Infs, **chiefly S Midl, Appalachians,** Gear; **SC**26, Gear the horse up; **LA**7, Gear them up. **1966** Dakin *Dial. Vocab. Ohio R. Valley* 2.290, The origin of *gear, gear up* used in the Valley is unquestionably the South Midland and the South. . . The informants' comments make it quite clear, however, that (except possibly for southernmost Illinois) *gear (up),* etc., are not often used even if known as older expressions or as the usage of others. . . Some who actually use these terms—both above and below the Ohio—do so only in reference to the special rig used in plowing.

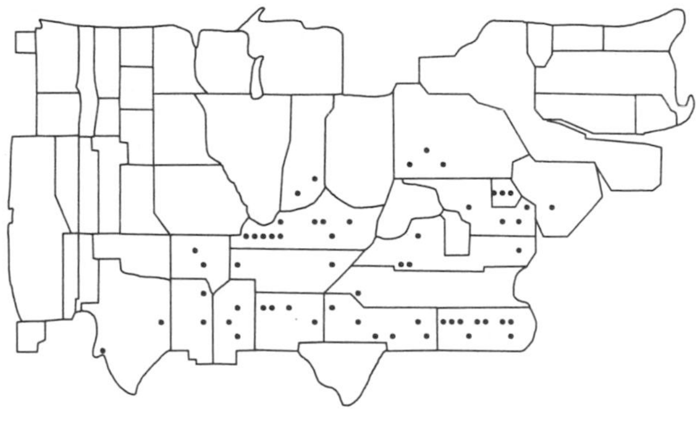

•gear v 1 + varr (Qu. L43a)

2 To fight.

1889 *AN&Q* 3.287/1 **NJ,** *Gear.* . . This word is also used as a synonym for "fight." In Gloucester Co., N.J., I have often heard "*gear* him" used, meaning "fight him."

gearb See **garb** n[1], v

geard See **guard**

geardeen See **guardian**

gearden See **garden**

gear grinder See **gear jammer**

gear house n Also *gear room, ~ shed* **esp Sth, S Midl**

A farm building used to store equipment.

1892 *Courier-Jrl.* (Louisville KY) 4 Oct 4/4, Noticing a wooden peg, almost rotten, in a block which supported one corner of an ancient gear-house, Mr. Orr concluded to investigate. **1954** *Harder Coll.* **cwTN,** *Gear house.* . . Farm building where work equipment is kept. **1967–68** *DARE* (Qu. M22) Inf **LA**22, Gear house; **SC**40, Gear house, gear room; **LA**15, Gear shed. **1986** Pederson *LAGS Concordance* **chiefly AL, GA,** [11 infs offered *gear house* for a shed used for storing tools, harness, etc.]

gearing n Also *gearings* [Engl dial]

=**gear n 1.**

1846 (1973) Porter *Quarter Race* 61, Put Sam on a horse, his legs clasped round its neck, his head towards the tail, and his arms clasped round the animal's hams, and at ten paces off you would swear he was an *old set of patent gearing.* **1870** Beadle *Utah* 200 *(DAE),* Great quantities of leather, gearing, cavalry equipments, clothing. . . were sold for one-tenth their value. **1902** *DN* 2.235 **sIL,** Gearins. . . Harness, particularly wagon-harness. **1907** *DN* 3.222 **nwAR,** *Gearins.* **1966** [see **gear** n **1**].

gear jammer n Also *gear grinder*

One who drives a truck or other heavy vehicle; also *gear jamming* driving such a vehicle.

1939 FWP *Guide MT* 308, Instead of the traditional "skinners" driving six-and-eight-horse teams, the Woodworth [lumber] operators have "cat skinners" and "gear jammers" to wrangle the big loop. **1950** *Western Folkl.* 9.381 **neCA** [Lumberjack language], *Gear jammer.* Refers usually to a truck driver. **1958** McCulloch *Woods Words* 69 **Pacific NW,** Gear grinder . . A truck driver. **1959** Martin *Gunbarrel* 23 **WY,** We had a lingo all our own in Yellowstone . . the bus drivers [were called] "gear jammers." **1969** *AmSp* 44.204 [Truckers' talk], *Gear jammer.* . . Truck driver. **1969** *DARE* (Qu. N11, *A . . large truck used to haul freight*) Inf **CA**147, Gear jammer, they call the driver. **1969** *DARE* Tape **CA**147, I first went, as my current expression is, gear-jamming [=driving a truck].

gear out See **gear v 1**

gearp(e) See **gape**

gearpy See **gape B2**

gear room, gear shed See **gear house**

geart See **girt**

gear up See **gear v 1**

geboodle n [Var of **boodle** n **2b**]

1950 *WELS (Words used for money)* 1 Inf, **WI,** Geboodle.

geddap See **get up** v phr **1**

gedduh See **gather**

geddup See **get up** v phr **1**

geddy up See **get up** v phr **1**

gedr See **gather**

gee v[1]

1 Used as a command to a draft animal to turn right (or, less freq, to turn left, go faster, stop, or back up). Cf **gee horse, haw** v

1848 Bartlett *Americanisms* 155, *Gee.* A term used by teamsters to their horses and oxen, when they wish them to go faster. It is also used in directing oxen to the right or off-side. **1908** Fox *Lonesome Pine* 19 **KY,** Git up—Whoa—Haw—Gee, Gee! **1943** *AK Sportsman* Apr 11 (Tabbert *Alaskan Engl.*), The lead [sled] dog will stay on the trail and heed the commands of "Gee!", "Haw!" and "Whoa!" **c1960** *Wilson Coll.* **csKY,** *Gee* . . to the right. **1962** Atwood *Vocab. TX* 77, Gee . . Call for a horse to go right (one informant says left). **1968–70** *DARE* (Qu. K34, . . *To make . . horses stop*) Infs **NY**65, **TX**82, Gee; (Qu. K36b, . . *To make a horse go backwards*) Inf **NY**65, Gee. **1969** Sorden *Lumberjack Lingo* 47 **NEng, Gt Lakes,** *Gee and Haw*—Commands used by oxen and horse drivers to indicate to the animal which way to turn. Gee means turn to the right; haw, turn to the left. **1970** *DARE* Tape **CA**199, [FW:] What sort of things would you have to talk to them to make them? [Inf:] Well, each one had a name. Like if you wanted 'em to come this way you'd holler—Old Larry was near leader—you'd holler, "Whoa, back Larry; come here Dan." Old Larry'd kinda back up and old Dan'd come right on around and if you wanted to go the other way you'd holler, "Whoa, back Dan; gee Larry." Old Dan'd kinda back up and old Larry'd go right on that way.

2 with *up* or *off:* To get up, move off—usu used as a command to draft animals; hence fig, to stir up.

1890 *DN* 1.65 **KY,** Gee up: same as "g'lang" [for *go along,* to a horse in plow or wagon.] **1909** *DN* 3.397 **nwAR,** Gee up = get up. **1927** Adams *Congaree* 20 **cSC** [Black], But I can't gee up my friends for you. **1931–33** *LANE Worksheets* **CT,** *Gee off.* . . "Men used to sharpen butt (=?poke in the rump) when they didn't gee off good." **1939** *LANE* Map 223 *(Calls to horses: Get up!)* 1 inf, **seME,** Gee up.

gee v[2]

Usu in neg constrs:

a To suit, fit.

1872 Schele de Vere *Americanisms* 478, Gee . . The term employed in driving a wagon, has been transferred to other transactions also, and people say in Pennsylvania, "That won't *gee,*" when they wish to express that something will not serve the purpose. **1884** Lanier *Poems* 169 **GA,** And he was a-wurken' appearently / A 'rethmetic sum that wouldn't gee. **1899** (1912) Green *VA Folk-Speech* 193, To agree; suit; fit. "That won't gee." **1934** Carmer *Stars Fell on AL* 223, We might live here for weeks and never see him. . . But if your hours don't gee with his—well, he goes his way. . . That's all there is to living here.

b also *gee horse(s):* Of people: to agree, to get on well with each other. **chiefly Sth, Midl** See Map

1889 *Century Illustr. Mag.* 39.225/2 **C Atl,** Me and the president did n't gee. He had n't no fault to find with me; but I did n't like his ways, and I quit. **1892** *DN* 1.236 **MO,** Gee . . to suit. "They don't gee worth a cent" = they don't get along well together. **1899** (1912) Green *VA Folk-Speech* 193, To get on well with a person. "They gee very well." **1903** *DN* 2.314 **seMO,** He and his partner couldn't gee. **1906** *DN* 3.119 **sIN,** Him and me couldn't *gee.* **1909** *DN* 3.397 **nwAR,** Gee . . "We didn't gee a little bit." **1944** *PADS* 2.56 **MO, NC, SC, VA,** *Gee.* . . To agree, to get along well together. **1946** *AmSp* 21.97 **sIL,** To gee . . to be in accord. **1965–70** *DARE* (Qu. III1a, *If two people don't get along . . you'd say, 'They don't* ______) 44 Infs, **chiefly Sth, Midl,** Gee; 7 Infs, **Sth,** Gee horses; **NC**4, Gee horse; **KY**65, **TN**13, Gee together; **VA**26, Gee very well; (Qu. KK67) Infs **LA**14, **OH**57, Gee; (Qu. KK68) Inf **NC**30, Don't gee.

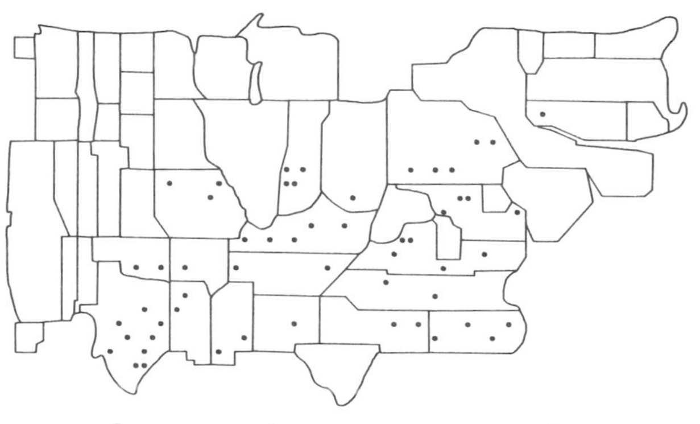

•gee v² b + varr (Qq. III1a, KK67, KK68)

gee v³ See **give A1b, 2c**

gee n See **gee horse**

gee and haw See **gee-haw v 2**

gee buck exclam Also *gee buzz, ~ fuzz, ~ rod, ~ Christmas* Cf **gee whillikers, gee whiz**

Used as an expression of surprise or enthusiasm.

1895 *DN* 1.376 **TN,** Gee buck! See all them bees drowned in the honey! **1895** (1969) Crane *Red Badge* 2.28, Gee rod! how we will thump 'em! **1901** White *Westerners* 11, "Gee Christmas!" ejaculated Billy, and laughed loudly. **1905** *DN* 3.61 **NE,** *Gee buzz.* . . Exclamation of surprise. **1906** *DN* 3.137 **nwAR,** *Gee fuzz.* . . Goodness! A mild exclamation. **1966** *DARE* (Qu. NN30) Inf **NC**36, Gee buck in Boston.

gee-buck v, hence vbl n *gee-bucking* [Cf **gee** v¹ **1, buck** n¹ **1d**] **csNH** Cf **hookey-bobbing**

To hitch a ride on the back of a sleigh either by hanging on to it or tying one's sled to it; hence n *gee-buck* a ride behind a sleigh, a sleigh on which to hitch a ride, n *gee-bucker* one who hitches a ride in such a way.

1986 *Yankee* Dec 18, Growing up in Manchester, New Hampshire, was good, especially in the winters of the early twentieth century. Plenty of snow and cold weather to enhance such sports as gee-bucking, double-runner coasting, and ice skating. **1988** *DARE* File **csNH** (as of early 20th cent), "Gee-bucking" . . is the practice of children hitching a ride on the tail-end or the runners of a moving horse-drawn sleigh, with or without the driver's knowledge. *Ibid,* We'd hook the rope of our sled . . to the turned up runner end of the delivery sleds. . . When we wanted to quit, we'd let go of our rope. With luck it wouldn't slag [sic]. If it did, . . you'd just run alongside and try to unhook your sled and walk back or catch another "Gee-Buck." You'll hear [about this] from many "Gee-Buckers." *Ibid,* We youngsters were always happy to "buck a ride" on the log carriers. . . We kids would shout "Gee-Buck coming—let's buck a ride." . . The driver . . would speak to the lead horse, "Gee Buck, got kids who want a ride." *Ibid,* We used to jump on the running boards [of sleighs], . . and this was called gee-bucking. *Ibid,* When I was a youngster . . kids gee-bucked for excitement. . . To be sure, gee-bucking was a "no-no", but that's why it was so exciting.

gee buzz See **gee buck** exclam

geech v Cf **gooch, goose v 2**

To tickle.

1950 *PADS* 14.31 **SC,** *Geech.* . . To tease by touching about the ribs. Applies only to susceptible or *geechy* persons.

geechee n Also sp *geechy, geejee, guichy* [Prob from *Ogeechee* River, but cf quot 1945 at **1** below] **chiefly S Atl** *sometimes derog*

1 also *geechy Negro:* A Black person from the South Carolina, Georgia, or north Florida coast, esp one with very dark skin or one who speaks Gullah; the Gullah dialect itself; rarely adj *geechee* having such characteristics.

1923 Parsons *Folk-lore Sea Islands* 91 **SC,** "De cow-doctor come aroun', hollerin' 'Tea-cat!' " "No, Baby, you talk jes' like a Guichy. You mean de conductor come roun', hollerin' 'Ticket!' " "Yeah, das what I mean." **1926** *Natl. Geogr. Mag.* Sept 278, Among the negroes living on the Ogeechee River a patois, developed in antebellum days, has persisted. . . The "Geechee" negro speaks in a sort of staccato and always seems excited when talking. His patois is encountered all along the Georgia coast. **1942** Kennedy *Palmetto Country* 240, A peculiar lot are the Negroes who man the pogy (menhaden) fishing boats—some are Geechees from South Carolina, while others are from the West Indies. **1945** *New Yorker* 8 Sept 20/2 **nFL,** Creecy was a Geechee . . blacker than the soot in the fireplace. **1945** *PADS* 3.13, The dialect known as Gullah or Geechee is spoken by a large number of ex-slaves and their descendants who live in the coastal region of South Carolina and Georgia, both on the Sea Islands and on the mainland nearby. [Footnote:] The word "Geechee" ("Geejee") . . is very probably derived from the name of another tribe and language of Liberia, among the different pronunciations of which are the following: [gitʃi], [gidʒi], [gitsi], [gisi], etc. **1950** *PADS* 14.31 **SC,** *Geechee, geechy.* . . A low country term for a Negro. . . "Wild Negroes fresh from Africa used to be put on Ogeechee river plantations in Georgia to mix with the hands there until they learned the minimum of white man's ways, that is, wearing clothes, a few English words, etc. Thus, a *geechy* Negro means a Negro from an *Ogeechee* plantation." **1960** Williams *Walk Egypt* 186 **GA,** She wondered if he was a Geechee, a Gullah-talker. Yellow Tom had told her once, "A Geechee be's a cross 'tween the Devil and a rattlesnake." **1970** *DARE* FW Addit **PA,** Geechee ['geči] [sic], a really dark Negro. [*DARE* Ed: young Black Inf] **1986** Pederson *LAGS Concordance,* 1 inf, **neFL,** Geechee—a low-down nigger; 1 inf, **nwFL,** Geechee—very black Negroes; Blacks resent this; 1 inf, **seFL,** South Carolina Geechees—Negroes from the Ogeechee River Delta in South Carolina [sic]; 1 inf, **csGA,** Geechee is a black nigger; 1 inf, **csGA,** An old Geechee—he doesn't speak as I do; 1 inf, **csGA,** Geechees—people that can't talk good; 1 inf, **csGA,** A saltwater Geechee—doesn't talk plain. **1988** *DARE* File **ceGA** (as of 1970), When I asked my Black high school students what they wanted to be when they grew up, one girl said she wanted to be a telephone operator. A classmate responded "You be too Geechee for that." He meant that people would not be able to understand her. If I had trouble understanding them, my students would say "You don't know Geechee."

2 Any person from coastal South Carolina or Georgia.

1946 (1972) Mezzrow–Wolfe *Really Blues* 333, [Glossary:] Geechee: *Southerner from Georgia.* **1951** *AmSp* 26.14, *Geechee* is commonly used, with mildly insulting connotations, by up-country South Carolinians as a nickname for any low-countryman, especially one from the Charleston area. **1977** *DARE* File **GA,** In Georgia, geechee meant anyone, Black or White, from the Savannah area. **1983** Neuffer–Neuffer *Correct Mispronc.* 68 **eSC,** A Geechee is a tidewater South Carolinian whose speech is "different"—some say influenced by Gullah—in the pronunciation of such words as shrimp, milk, house, Charleston, boat. In fact, it's almost another language, called Charlestonese by writer Frank Gilbreth (alias Lord Ashley Cooper) in his *News and Courier* column, "Doing the Charleston." **1986** Pederson *LAGS Concordance,* 1 inf, **cnGA,** Geechee—A Savannah white.

3 See quots.

1916 *DN* 4.345 **FL,** *Geechee*. . . A negro from the Islands, as from the Bahamas. **1972** *DARE* Tape **MA**58, Geechee . . it's a British subject from some of the offshore islands down below Florida . . they're brown and they don't talk very good.

geechee lime See **Ogeechee lime**

geechee twister n

1966 *DARE* (Qu. P6, *Other . . worms . . used for bait*) Inf **GA**3, Geechee twister.

gee Christmas See **gee buck** exclam

geechy n See **geechee**

geechy adj **[geech] chiefly S Atl** Cf **goochy**

Ticklish, nervous.

1923 *DN* 5.243 **NC,** *Geechy*. . . Goosey. **1930** *DN* 6.84 **cSC,** *Geechy,* goosey. **1950** *PADS* 14.32 **SC,** *Geechy*. . . Goosey, very nervous, unusually sensitive to geeching or tickling.

geechy negro See **geechee 1**

geedicker n Cf **chee-dee**

=**English sparrow.**

1969 *DARE* (Qu. Q22, . . *The common sparrow*) Inf **KY**11, Geedicker [*DARE* Ed: Inf has heard].

geed up adj phr [Perh **gee** v[1] **1** (to stop)]

Lame.

1968 Adams *Western Words* 125, *Geed-up*—A cowman's term for lame or out of commission.

geedus See **geetus**

gee fuzz See **gee buck** exclam

gee-haw v Pronc-sp *gee-ha* [**gee** v[1] **1** + **haw** v]

1 =**gee** v[1] **1;** also transf.

1965–70 *DARE* (Qu. K36a, . . *To make a horse go faster*) Inf **CA**72, Gee-haw; (Qu. K36b, . . *To make a horse go backwards*) Inf **AL**14, Gee ha. **1967** *DARE* FW Addit **LA,** Gee-haw—to get going, to operate, as of a motor that won't run. "I can't get it to gee-haw."

2 also *gee and haw, gee-hi:* =**gee** v[2] **b. chiefly Sth** See Map

1954 in 1958 Brewer *Dog Ghosts* 82 **TX** [Black], De word fin'ly gits 'roun' 'bout what a haa'd customer Brothuh Williams is to gee-haw wid. **1965–70** *DARE* (Qu. II11a, *If two people don't get along . . you'd say, "They don't ______."*) 39 Infs, **chiefly Sth,** Gee-haw; **KY**21, Gee-haw much; **GA**86, Gee-haw together; **OK**9, Gee-hi; (Qu. KK58) Inf **LA**35, Gee-haw; (Qu. KK67) Infs **AL**25, **LA**3, Gee-haw. **1970** *DARE* FW Addit **TX**79, Gee-haw [ʤihɔ] meaning to agree or understand; used commonly. **1984** Wilder *You All Spoken Here* 35 **Sth,** *Gee and haw together:* What a couple in harmony do.

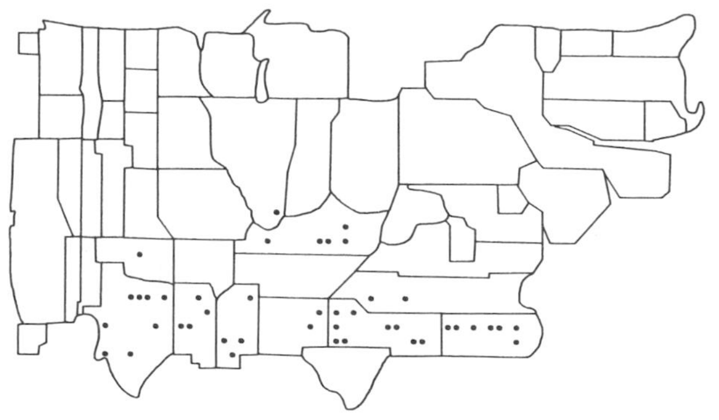

•gee-haw v 2 + varr (Qq. II11a, KK58, KK67)

3 See quot.

1942 McAtee *Dial. Grant Co. IN* 28 (as of 1890s), *Gee-haw* . . with us it meant to be irresolute, to pursue an undecided course; "gee-hawin' around and gettin' nowhere."

gee-haw n

1 See **gee horse.**

2 See **gee-haw whimm(e)y-diddle.**

3 in phr *do a gee-haw:* =**gee-haw** v **2.**

1967 Fetterman *Stinking Creek* 80 **seKY,** We lived together forty-five years, but we just couldn't do a gee-haw. We even got a divorce.

gee-haw adj See **gee-hawed**

gee-hawed adj Also *gee-haw, gee-ho-hawed, gee-jaw(ed), gee-hoppled, gee-whackerjawed, gee-whopped* [**gee** v[1] **1** + **haw** v] **esp Inland Nth** Cf **squee-hawed, whee-hawed**

Lopsided, awry.

1911 *DN* 3.544 **NE,** Gee-whackerjawed . . Askew, or awry. **1915** *DN* 4.218 **NE,** Your hat is gee-whackerjawed. **1957** *DE Folkl. Bulletin* Oct 28/1, Gee-hoppled (lopsided). **1965–70** *DARE* (Qu. KK70) Infs **IL**92, **NY**230, **OH**16, Gee-jaw; **AK**5, **ID**5, Gee-haw; **NY**146, **OH**29, Gee-hawed; **IL**39, Gee-ho-hawed; **NC**82, Gee-jawed; (Qu. MM13) Inf **OH**29, Gee-haw; **CA**61, Gee-whopped.

gee-hawing vbl n

See quot c1960.

1907 Wright *Shepherd* 99 **Ozarks,** All this here gee-hawin', balkin', and kickin' 'mongst th' married folks. **c1960** *Wilson Coll.* **csKY,** *Gee-hawing*. . . Going nowhere, working at cross purposes. Gee—to the right, Haw—to the left.

gee-haw whimm(e)y-diddle n Also *gee-haw* **sAppalachians, esp wNC** Also called **idiot stick, jeep stick, lie detector, ziggerboo**

A wooden folk toy; see quots.

1963 *Chr. Sci. Monitor* (Boston MA) 26 Apr 6/6 **nwNC,** The whimmydiddle . . was used in China and Sweden. . . Cherokee Indians knew the whimmydiddle as the hoodoo stick. In Tennessee it's a ziggerboo, and Georgians know it as a gee-haw. Ohio folks call it a lie detector. . . The gee-haw whimmydiddle is a notched stick with a whirlygig on the end that "gees" or "haws" seemingly at command. Pressure of the finger or thumb on the top side of the notches does the trick. **1966** *DARE* FW Addit **NC**33, Gee-haw whimmeydiddle—A toy manufactured in Boone, N.C. [consisting of] two pieces. [One is] a stick with a propeller on the end and several notches back from the [propeller] end. [The second piece is] another stick. The object is to cause the propeller to spin by rubbing the second stick along the notches of the first. **1970** *DARE* FW Addit **KY, TN,** Gee-haw whimmydiddle ['ʤi,hɔ 'hwɪmɪ,dɪdl]—A toy consisting of a notched stick with a smaller stick on the end, which rotates to left or to right according to how the notches are rubbed with another stick. **1972** Cooper *NC Mt. Folkl.* 34, The children's Christmas toys and gifts were mainly homemade. There were dolls, yarn balls, whistles, geehaw whimmydiddles or ziggerboos, rattle traps, noisemakers or bull roars and flipperdingers. **1979** *DARE* File, Geehaw whimmydiddles are common folk toys in Western North Carolina, but I did not know about them in my childhood in Kentucky over a half century ago. **1980** *Foxfire 6* 253 **nGA,** Some people call them "gee-haw whimmy diddles." [*Foxfire* Ed: The "gee haw" part of the name that many people use comes from the fact that you can make the propeller go in either direction, just as the same commands make a mule or steer turn to the right or the left.]

gee-hi See **gee-haw** v **2**

gee-ho-hawed See **gee-hawed**

gee-hoppled See **gee-hawed**

gee horse n Also *gee, gee-side horse;* rarely *gee-haw* **scattered, but esp N Cent, Gt Lakes** See Map on p. 650

=**off horse.**

1940–41 Cassidy *WI Atlas* **neWI,** Gee horse. **1962** Atwood *Vocab. TX* 56, Gee (horse) [usually means] the one on the right. **1965–70** *DARE* (Qu. K32a, *With a team of horses, what do you call the horse on the driver's right hand?*) 33 Infs, **scattered, but esp N Cent,** Gee horse; 24 Infs, **scattered, but esp N Cent,** Gee; **CT**29, **IL**87, **MS**19, **NC**36, Gee-side horse; **AK**4, Gee and haw; (Qu. K32b, *The horse on the left side in plowing or hauling*) Infs **CA**193, **IL**7, 9, **IN**27, **MI**101, **NY**107, Gee; **AL**43, **IN**72, **MD**40, **PA**59, 232, Gee horse; **NY**142, Gee-haw. [For discussion of confusion of terms for right- and left-hand horses see note at **off horse.**] **1986** Pederson *LAGS Concordance* **Gulf Region** *(Horse on left)* 1 inf, Gee horse; 1 inf, Also the gee horse and the haw horse; 1 inf, Gee horse—on the right; 1 inf, Gee horse or haw horse; 1 inf, The gee horse—horse on the left; 1 inf, The gee horse—lead horse, walked in furrow.

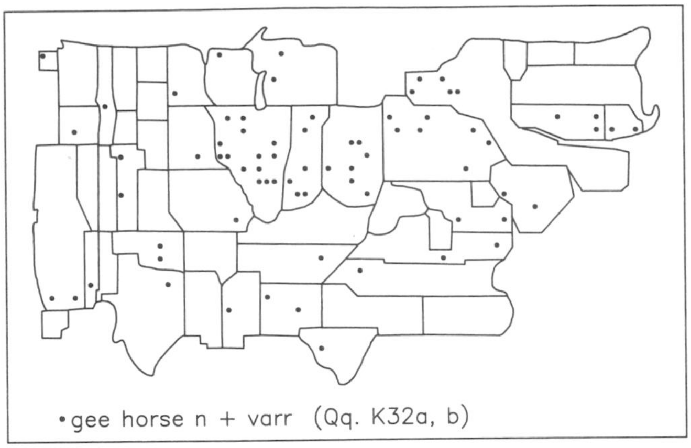

gee horse(s) v phr See **gee** v² **b**

Geehosofat See **Jehoshaphat**

gee-jaw(ed) See **gee-hawed**

geejee See **geechee**

geek n [Echoic]
=**killdeer.**
1968 *DARE* (Qu. Q14, . . *Other names* . . *for* . . *killdeer*) Inf **PA**165, Geek [gik].

geekus crow intj [Euphem for *Jesus Christ*]
1924 *DN* 5.267 **ME** [Exclamations in American English], Geekus crow.

gee line n [**gee** v¹ **1**]
A guide line or rein; see quot.
1897 (1952) McGill *Narrative* 79, Thus equipped with four horses geared to his wagon, on Tuesday at daylight, the wagoner in clean clothes, and proud of his calling, mounts the wheel saddle horse, seizes his long "gee" line, pops his whip, and punching his off wheel horse with his foot, we are soon on the road for Charleston.

geemany See **jiminy**

geemenetti, geemenety See **jiminetty**

Gee-mi-my See **Jemima**

geeminy See **jiminy**

gee-muckle-dun n Cf **muckle dun**
1967 *DARE* (Qu. K38, *A horse of a dirty white color*) Inf **OH**31, Gee muckle-dun ['ji 'mʌkəl,dən].

geenavy See **genavy**

gee off See **gee** v **1**

gee pole n [**gee** v¹ **1**] Cf *DCan*
A pole affixed to a dogsled, by which it is guided.
1902 U.S. Revenue Cutter Serv. *Rept. Nunivak* 161 **AK,** A "gee-pole" is attached to the forward end [of a sled] for [steering]. . . When a "gee-pole" is used the driver walks in front of the sled and steers it with one hand, and in order to allow him room to walk without interfering with the dogs a long line is used to attach the rear dog of the team to the sled. **1913** *Outing* 61.525/1 **AK,** Following me came the dogs driven by the man at the "gee-pole," who also wore snowshoes.

gee rod See **gee buck** exclam

‡geese gee n
1968 *DARE* (Qu. EE6b, *Small marbles or marbles in general*) Inf **OH**77, Geese gees [gisgiz]; (Qu. EE6c, *Cheap marbles*) Inf **OH**77, Geese gees.

geese hair See **goose hair**

geese poomples n pl *joc*
=**goose pimples.**
1950 *WELS* (*When you are cold and little points of skin stick up on your arms and legs*) 1 Inf, **scWI,** Geese poomples (jocular).

geeses See **goose** n **A**

gee-side horse See **gee horse**

gee stick n
A light pole connecting the bridles of a pair of draft horses.
1915 *DN* 4.183 **VA,** *Gee-stick*. . . A stick or pole fastened to the bit of the "off" horse (on right) and then to the "lead" horse (on left) in such a way that the "lead" horse guides. **1970** *DARE* File **KY**75, When two horses are used in plowing, only one horse is driven. The other horse is guided by the gee-stick, a piece of wood 3–4′ between the two horses. The gee-stick pushes or pulls the undriven horse, depending [upon] how the driven horse is turned.

geetar See **guitar**

geetas, geetis, geets See **geetus**

geet up See **get up** v phr **1**

geetus n Usu |'gidəs| Also sp *geedus, geetas, geetis, geets*
Money; rarely, power.
1942 Berrey–Van den Bark *Amer. Slang* 559.1, *Geetus* . . money. **1949** (1961) Partridge *Underworld Dict.,* Geetas or geetis . . The criminal has a slang term for almost every denomination of money. Money in general, he refers to as . . geetis. **1960** Wentworth–Flexner *Slang* 211, Geedus, geetis, geetus . . Money. c1935. *Underworld Use.* 1943: "The pitchmen must give the store a 40% cut on the 'geedus' . . " Zolotow, Sep. 13. *Pitchman use.* **1965–70** *DARE* (Qu. U19a, *Words* . . *for money*) Infs **AR**56, **CA**119, **TX**83, 98, Geetus ['gidəs]; **CA**59, ['gitəz]; TX54, ['gidɪs]. **1970** Major *Dict. Afro-Amer. Slang* 58, Geets (1940s) power or money or both.

gee up See **gee** v **1**

gee-whackerjawed See **gee-hawed**

gee whillikers intj Also *gee whillikins;* for addit varr see quots
=**gee whiz.**
1851 Burke *Polly Peablossom* 52, Jewhilliken, how he could whip er nigger! **1856** *Town Talk* (S.F.) 20 July 1/1 *(DA),* Gee-whitaker! what a kurchy she made, and bowed so low that I nearly fell outer my dickey onto the floor. **1857** *Knickerbocker* 5.50 Nov 435, And great Gewhilikins! *was n't* the snow peppering down! **1859** in 1956 Eliason *Tarheel Talk* 273 **NC,** Geewhilekins! how it did rain. **1871** Eggleston *Hoosier Schoolmaster* 50, "Gewhilliky crickets!" **1872** Schele de Vere *Americanisms* 611, *Jerusalem!,* a favorite New England exclamation. . . In the West it is, as usual, improved to suit the louder taste of the people, and becomes Jewhillikin. **1889** (1971) Farmer *Americanisms* 261, Geewhilikens! An exclamation of surprise equivalent to, and used in the same manner as Whew! Great Caesar! and other objurgations. Western; also jeewhilikens. **1890** *DN* 1.61 **OH,** Gee Whittaker! an exclamation of surprise . . [Also common in New England]. **1893** Shands *MS Speech* 32, Gee Whittaker! . . Exclamation of surprise, used by all classes . . used in Cincinnati, and . . in New England. **1906** *DN* 3.143 **nwAR,** Jeewhillikins. **1908** *DN* 3.324 **eAL, wGA,** Jeewhilligins. **1924** *DN* 5.279, Gee whillicats . . gee whillikers . . gee whillikins . . gee whittakers. **1945** Thorp *Pardner* 113 **SW,** "Gee wickles!" he said, . . "All the born liars don't live in New Mexico, do they!" **1950** *WELS (Exclamations)* 1 Inf, **WI,** Gee whitaker; 1 Inf, Gee whillikers; 1 Inf, Gee willikins; 1 Inf, Jee wooligans. **1956** Eliason *Tarheel Talk* 189 **NC** (as of 1859), There are . . weakened oaths and imprecations, distorted or consciously disguised variants of once mouth-filling phrases . . *gee whilikins* . . used undoubtedly with no realization of [its] original significance. **c1960** *Wilson Coll.* **csKY,** Gewhillikins: A sonorous but harmless and rather meaningless byword. **1965–70** *DARE* (Qu. NN30) 139 Infs, **scattered,** Gee whillikers; 18 Infs, **scattered,** Gee whillikins; **HI**13, **MI**66, **MA**5, **NC**55, **NY**7, 219, **PA**15, 82, Gee whittakers; **DE**7, **PA**113, Gee whinickers; **FL**35, **IA**43, Gee willikers; **NY**66, 209, Gee willikins; **MO**19, Gee gosh whittakers; **WA**1, Gee whilliker; **SC**19, Gee whillikin; **SC**3, Gee whippers; **PA**108, Gee whittigans; **KY**10, Gee willy whickers; **CA**87, Jumpin' gee whillikers; (Qu. NN6b) Infs **SC**45, **TX**33, Gee whillikers; (Qu. NN7) Inf **IL**135, Gee whillikins; (Qu. NN8a) Inf **NY**109, Gee whillikers.

gee whiz intj Also *gee whiskers, ~ whizzikers;* for addit varr see quots Cf **gee whillikers**
Used as an exclam of surprise, enthusiasm, emphasis, etc.
1885 W.T. Gray *Bad Boy at Home* 8 *(at back) (OEDS),* Gee wiz! but they do put on stile in New York. **1888** *Judge* 1 Sept. 334 *(DAE),* Geewhitz. **1890** *DN* 1.61 **OH,** Gee whizz! . . an exclamation of surprise. **1893** Shands *MS Speech* 32, Gee Whiz! . . Exclamation of surprise, used by all classes . . [also] used in Cincinnati. **1908** Johnson *Highways Pacific Coast* 154 **nCA,** Give me a few local rangers and I'd

nab every herder that sticks his nose across the line. Geewhizacar! I'd catch more trespassers in six months than they would in a hundred years. **1924** *DN* 5.279, Gee whiz . . gee whizzle. **1928** *AmSp* 4.87, Slang and profanity, when traced to their origins, are often found to be allusive . . *gee whiz* . . being [a] euphemistic variation . . of . . Jesus. **1950** *WELS* 8 Infs, **WI,** Gee whiz; 1 Inf, Gee whiskers. **1961** (1964) Salinger *Franny* 86, Well, gee whizz. I'm only trying to make polite bathroom talk. **1965–70** *DARE* (Qu. NN30) 706 Infs, **widespread,** Gee whiz; **KY**60, **NY**94, **TX**10, **WI**30, Gee whiskers; **MD**32, **NY**34, **PA**237, Gee whizzikers; **RI**1, Gee whizzikus; **LA**25, Gee whizzit; **SC**3, Gee wizard; (Qu. NN6b) 18 Infs, **scattered,** Gee whiz; (Qu. NN6a) 12 Infs, **scattered, but esp Nth,** Gee whiz; (Qu. NN8a) 12 Infs, **scattered, but esp Nth,** Gee whiz; (Qu. NN7) Infs **CA**164, **IL**9, **MS**35, **UT**3, Gee whiz; (Qu. NN21a) Infs **AR**52, **MS**6, **MO**1, **MA**4, Gee whiz; (Qu. NN21c) Infs **CA**17, **KS**2, 18, **OK**31, Gee whiz. **1966–69** *DARE* Tape **CA**117, And I thought, gee whiz, I've got a transistor radio, why not use it; **MI**15, Well, gee whiz, you hate to spend three dollars just to go in and picnic in an area for maybe a few hours.

gee whiz n [Trademark] **chiefly Sth**

A type of plow or harrow.

1965 U.S. Patent Office *Official Gaz.* 821.TM75/1, SN 188, 975. Gee-whiz Tool Corporation, Memphis, Tenn. Filed Mar. 18, 1964. *Gee-Whiz.* For Hand Tool for Many Purposes—Namely, Edging Lawns, Pruning, and the Like. First use May 5, 1961. **1965–70** *DARE* (Qu. L18) Inf **GA**72, Horse-drawn gee-whiz; from five to seven feet—adjustable; **GA**77, Gee whiz—one mule [and] several little plows; **GA**84, Gee whiz—triangular frame; had spikes [and] one horse; **MS**66, **NC**37, Gee whiz; (Qu. L20) Inf **LA**2, Side harrow—also called gee whiz [*DARE* Ed: primary stress on *gee*]; used for cultivating when corn is young.

gee-whiz candy n

1969 *DARE* (Qu. H82b, . . *Cheap candy . . sold years ago*) Inf **MA**69, Gee-whiz candy—long stick-candy which tasted like butterscotch.

gee whizzikers See **gee whiz** intj

gee-whollicker n Also *gewholliper* [*gee* emphatic expletive + varr of **walloper**]

Something remarkable.

1953 Randolph–Wilson *Down in Holler* 247 **Ozarks,** Gee-whollicker. . . A wonder, a marvel, something amazingly large or fine, or otherwise surprising. **c1960** *Wilson Coll.* **csKY,** Gewholliper . . Something extraordinary or large or surprising.

gee-whopped See **gee-hawed**

gee wizard See **gee whiz**

gee wooligans See **gee whillikers**

geez See **jeez**

geik n [Ger *Geige* violin, fiddle] **PaGer area**

A homemade fiddle.

1924 Lambert *PA Ger. Dict., Geik.* . . Fiddle, violin. **1930** Shoemaker *1300 Words* 26 **cPA Mts** (as of c1900), *Geik.* . . A homemade fiddle. **1939** Aurand *Quaint Idioms* 15 [PaGer], The important musical instrument at a country dance is a *geik* (fiddle).

geiss n [Cf *SND guise* n. 3 "A masquerade"]

1930 Shoemaker *1300 Words* 24 **cPA Mts,** *Geiss*—A mask worn by highwaymen.

geld n See **gilt 2**

geld v

=**gig** v^2 **1.**

1987 Jones-Jackson *When Roots Die* 153 **sSC coast** [Gullah], We had manage to catch many bushel . . of fish with four-prong or three-prong gig. . . Just use a little tar for light by night, and we gelds fish in the water. . . Catch em by stick em with that fork.

gelding n [Transf from *gelding* castrated horse] **chiefly Nth, N Midl** See Map Cf **gilt 2**

A castrated pig.

1965–70 *DARE* (Qu. K58, *A castrated pig is a* ______) 41 Infs, **chiefly Nth, N Midl,** Gelding.

gelding tobacco n [With pun on *gelding* a castrated animal and *cut* to castrate] *joc*

1975 Gould *ME Lingo* 108, *Gelding tobacco*—Cut plug, for smoking.

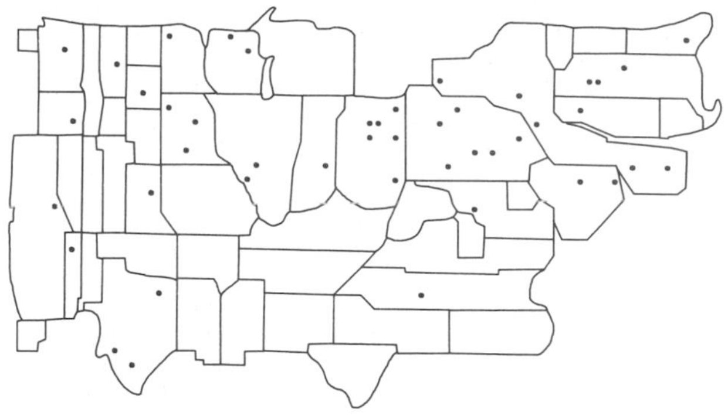

•gelding (Qu. K58)

gell See **girl** n

gelle interrog exclam [Ger dial *gelle* Isn't that so?] Cf **ainna**

As a tag question: Isn't that so? Don't you agree?

1968 *DARE* Tape **MN**36, [Inf:] These are German-American expressions . . there's the expression of *gelle* that's still used by high school and young people. . . I think it's from the old Swabian expression of "gelt" meaning "not so." They still use that. . . You say something, an' then you say "gelle." [FW:] Would it be like, "Do you agree with me?" [Inf:] Ja. [FW:] That means "Isn't that so?" [Inf:] At the end of a sentence . . you'd say something and then you'd say "gelle?"

gellybobbles n Cf **gollywobbles**

=**collywobbles 2.**

1949 *AN&Q* 8.136, In the September 14, 1949, issue of the *Smoker,* alumni paper of the Class of 1921 of Dartmouth College, the Editor . . uses the word *gellybobbles*—for *stomach-ache.*

gellyon n [Prob blend of *gelding* + *stallion*] Cf **rig**

1930 Shoemaker *1300 Words* 24 **cPA Mts** (as of c1900), *Gellyon*—A partly castrated horse.

gelt n^1 See **gilt 2**

gelt n^2 *Gullah*

Girth.

1909 *S. Atl. Qrly.* 8.51 **seSC,** The turning . . of *r* into *l,* as *gelt* for *girth* . . are all characteristics of *Gullah.* **1922** Gonzales *Black Border* 303 **sSC, GA coasts** [Gullah glossary], *Gelt* . . girth, girths.

gelt v [**gelt** n^2] *Gullah*

To fasten with a girth.

1888 Jones *Negro Myths* 111 **GA coast,** Buh Rabbit trow de saddle on de horse and gelt um tight.

gem n **chiefly Nth** *old-fash*

A muffin baked in a pan with sections, each having a rectangular outline with a rounded bottom.

1875 *Carson Valley News* 20 Feb. *(DA),* Take, for example, the gem pans, which must be good tools to work with. **1882** Peck *Peck's Sunshine* 82, His [=a dog's] head is about as big as a graham gem, and runs down to a point not bigger than a cambric needle, while his ears are about as big as a thumb to a glove. **1929** *Mod. Priscilla Cookbook* 23, *Gems* are identical with muffins, but baked in pans of special shape—long and narrow with rounded bottoms. **1931–33** *LANE Worksheets* **csMA,** *Graham gem.* . . A biscuit of graham or rye (round). **1939** Wolcott *Yankee Cook Book* 159, Maine oatmeal gems. *Ibid* 160, Graham Gems. **1965–70** *DARE* (Qu. H14) Inf **CT**39, Corn gems; **WI**20, Cornmeal gems; (Qu. H15) Inf **CT**39, Graham gems; (Qu. H18) Infs **AZ**8, **ME**11, Gems; **TN**23, Corn gems; (Qu. H19) Inf **IA**36, Graham gems. [5 of 6 Infs old] **1973** Allen *LAUM* 1.278 **Upper MW** (as of c1950), Gems [3 infs **IA,** 1 inf **MN**]; Graham gems [2 infs **NE**]. **1977** *DARE* File **cMA** (as of c1915), We used to make a distinction between muffins and gems. Muffins were baked in a tin as they are now. Gem tins were shaped so that they turned out rectangular muffins with a curved boat-like bottom. Graham gems were the most popular.

g'em v See **give A1b**

gemeinde n [See quot 1988] Cf **House Amish**

In Mennonite communities: see quot 1988.

1968 *Budget* (Sugarcreek OH) 25 July 15/6, West gemeinde was at Mrs. Ella Hochstetler's, Sunday. Will be there again in two weeks. East gemeinde will be at Jess M. Duckworth's next Sunday. Middle gemeinde will be at Levi J. Masts' next Sunday. [**1988** *NADS Letters, Gemeinde* is the standard German variant of the Pennsylvania German *gmee/gmay* [gme:/ġme:]. . . The form *gemeinde* is not usual in such reports [as in quot 1968]; as a rule you find *gmee/gmay.* Both are switches to the first language of the Old Order Amish. . . Meaning: 1) religious congregation; 2) social community; 3) church service. . . Old Order Amish settlements are divided into church districts . . [which] are as a rule named according to their relative position: *middle district, east district,* . . etc. Each district holds its own church service. . . In the case of . . [quot 1968], the church service of the West district was held at Mrs. Ella Hostetler's. *Ibid, Gemeinde* is used for all German-speaking church communities; thus, the parson will begin his sermon: "Liebe Gemeinde!" (Dear Community). *Ibid, Gemeinde* is an Amish word—they don't meet in church but in each other's homes. In Amish dialect the word is *Gemäe.* It can be translated as "gathering."]

gemenee See **jiminy**

gemfruit n

A **foamflower** (here: *Tiarella cordifolia*).

1822 Eaton *Botany* 487 *[Tiarella] cordifolia* . . miter-wort, gemfruit. **1847** Wood *Class-Book* 280, *T[iarella] cordifolia.* Mitre-wort. Gemfruit. **1900** Lyons *Plant Names* 371, Gem-fruit. **1971** Krochmal *Appalachia Med. Plants* 250, Gem fruit . . is reputed to be useful as a tonic and diuretic.

geminettae, geminetti See **jiminetty**

geminy fit See **jiminy fit**

gemma grass n

=**gama grass.**

1890 Gunter *Miss Nobody* iv. (1891) 47 *(DA),* The mesa is bare of everything for five hundred yards but gemma grasses.

gem'man See **gentleman** n

gemminy See **jiminy**

gen v See **give A1c**

gen conj See **gin** conj[1,2]

gen'al See **general**

gena'lly See **generally**

genavy n |ǰə'nevi|, |gɪ-| Also sp *geenavy, genavey* [Perh *ge-, ji-* emphatic affix + *navy* fleet, gathering]

A large number; a group.

1926 Fulton *Writing Craftsmanship* 436, He tells me that there was "a whole genavy of ducks on the flats yesterday morning,"—and I know he means an uncountable number. . . Others than he use the expression, but it seems peculiar to one small locality. **1942** Berrey–Van den Bark *Amer. Slang* 20.3, *Large amount; many. . .* genavy. **1946** *PADS* 6.15 **Pamlico Co NC,** *Geenavy* [ǰə'nevi]. . . A large number. Jocular . . common. **1951** *DE Folkl. Bulletin* 1 Mar 4, *Genavey. . .* Every part and parcel. **1968** *DARE* (Qu. FF26, . . *A large group of people at a . . gathering)* Inf **NJ**20, Great genavy [gɪ'nevi]; (Qu. LL8b, . . *"She has a whole ——— of cousins."*) Inf **NJ**20, Genavy; **DE**1, Genavy [ǰɨneɪvɪ].

general adj, n Usu |'ǰɛn(ə)rəl|; also |ǰɪnərəl|; **chiefly Sth** |'ǰɛnəl, ǰɪnrəl| Pronc-spp *gen'al, gineral, ginerl, ginnel, ginnerl, ginral, gin'ul*

A Forms.

1815 Humphreys *Yankey in England* 78, The gineral telled me to cum. *Ibid* 105, *Gineral, Gin'ral, General.* **1834** Davis *Letters Downing* 6, Don't forgit my face, and the Gineral's face; and let the likenesses be good and natural. **1887** (1967) Harris *Free Joe* 418 **GA,** First hit was Giner'l Jackson an' the bank. **1893** Shands *MS Speech* 33, *Ginral* [ǰɪnrəl]. . . Negro for *general,* both noun and adjective. **1903** *DN* 2.314 **seMO,** General Babtiss [ǰɪnrəl]. **1907** *DN* 3.188 **NH,** *Gineral* . . general. **1908** *DN* 3.315 **eAL, wGA,** *Ginnel, ginnerl* . . general. **1915** *DN* 4.177 **VA,** *Ginerl* (general). **1922** Gonzales *Black Border* 303 **sSC, GA coasts** [Gullah glossary], *Gin'ul* . . general. **1926** *DN* 5.377, *Gineral, gin'ral,* general. **c1960** *Wilson Coll.* **csKY,** General /ǰɪn(ə)rəl/. **1968** *DARE* Tape **WI**75, As a gen'al ['ǰɛnəl] rule. **1968** *DARE* FW Addit **TN,** ['ǰɪ·nrəl 'stor].

B As adj.

Usual.

1968 Haun *Hawk's Done Gone* 69 **eTN,** He drew her eye to him, like general.

C As noun.

The sum of expenses incurred in a fishing expedition; see quots. **NEng** *hist*

1763 in 1917 Colonial Soc. MA *Pub.* 19.383, From this Sum . . deduct the great General, which is Salt, Bait, Candles, Ballast, Boots etc. . . From the Crew's 5/8 . . is to be deducted the small General so called, being for Wood and Provisions of all Sorts, paid for by the Crew. **1848** in 1935 *AmSp* 10.40 **Nantucket MA,** *Big general.* The largest bill of a fishing vessel. **1889** *Century Dict.* 2482, *Great generals,* the general charges furnished by the owner of a fishing-vessel, including wood, water, lights, knives, salt, bait, etc. . . *Small generals,* the general charges furnished by the crew of a fishing-vessel, as the provisions, lines, hooks, etc. [*Century* Ed: New England] **1904** *DN* 2.425 **Cape Cod MA** (as of a1857), *Generals. . .* Some of the expenses of a fishing voyage are divided equally among the crew, such as food and the cook's wages; these are called *small generals.* Other expenses are divided in proportion to each man's catch of fish, as bait, salt, and barrels; these are called *great generals* or *big generals.*

generally adv Usu |'ǰɛn(ə)rəli|; also |'ǰɪnərəli|; **chiefly Sth** |'ǰɛnəli, ǰɪnlɪ, 'ǰɛnərli| Pronc-spp *gena'lly, generly, gin(e)rally, giner'lly, gin'ly;* for addit varr see quots

Std senses, var forms.

1843 (1916) Hall *New Purchase* 147 **IN,** When all the circumstansis was illustrated, it was ginerally found the white was agressur. **1884** Murfree *TN Mts.* 315 **TN,** He jes' war constant in lettin' his friends, an' folks ginerally, off 'thout hevin' 'em fined. **1886** [see **in generally**]. **1898** Westcott *Harum* 7 **nNY,** I gen'ally prefer to settle out of court. **1908** [see **in generally**]. **1910** Hart *Vigilante Girl* 144 **nCA,** "And do you carry much this way?" "No, this way we don't carry much. When we do, it's gin'ly coin to pay off the fellers." **1921** Haswell *Daughter Ozarks* 28 (as of 1880s), But most ginnerly folks has got to callin' of me 'Parson'. **1931** *PMLA* 46.1311 **Appalachians,** I gin'rally usually takes a dram o' mornin's. **1933** Rawlings *South Moon* 130 **nFL,** 'Twa'n't no more of a fight than they gin'rally gits into. **1942** Hall *Smoky Mt. Speech* 19, [ɛ] is often raised to or toward [ɪ] [in the word] . . generally. **1954** *Harder Coll.* **cwTN,** ['ǰɛnɚli]. **1967** *DARE* FW Addit **AR**54, ['ǰɪnlɪ]. . . Usually. He most generally comes back about dinnertime. **1968** *DARE* Tape **WI**75, They ['ǰɛnəli] fish 'em. **1976** Garber *Mountain-ese* 48 **Appalachians,** *Jinely* . . usually[.] Jinely he's a real mild mannered man.

generally always adv phr Also *always generally* [*EDD* 1875]

Usually.

1864 (1868) Trowbridge *3 Scouts* 55 **TN,** Wal, I gene'lly always have. But a man can't stand everything! **1898** Westcott *Harum* 13 **nNY,** You can't most alwus gen'ally tell. **1927** *AmSp* 3.7 **Ozarks,** I most generly allus rocks them 'tarnal dogs off'n th' place. **1934** (1970) Wilson *Backwoods Amer.* 198 **AR, MO,** Mr. Richmond generally always comes in after his mail Tuesday afternoon. **1989** *DARE* File **csWI,** I know a man (a hardware dealer) who habitually says "generally always" without being aware of the contradiction.

general muster See **muster**

general work n

A roundup.

1944 Adams *Western Words* 64, *General work*—A term sometimes used in referring to a roundup.

generate v

1966 *PADS* 46.26 **AR,** *Generate. . .* To be born. "I don't know where Granpa Chandler was generated at."

generation n **chiefly Appalachians** *old-fash*

A family, esp an extended family; a race or kind.

1899 (1912) Green *VA Folk-Speech* 194, *Generation. . .* Family; race; kind. **1915** *Harper's Mth. Mag.* 131.437/1 **eKY,** The visitor to the Cumberlands is sure to be struck by the use of the word "generation" without temporal significance and as an exact synonym of "breed" or "race." For example, "Thar's a powerful generation o' them Holmeses." **1931** Randolph *Ozarks* 73, The word *generation,* as used in the Ozark country, has nothing to do with temporal succession, but means a race or breed. **1935** Hurston *Mules & Men* 131 **FL** [Black], God, please do somethin' 'bout dat snake. . . He's killin' up our generations. **1937–39** *Hall Coll.* **TN,** *Generation. . .* A large family; family in large sense. "John Wear settled on Wallands Creek and raised a generation of children." *Ibid,* "Altogether there are only twenty-two boys in the Guilliams generation." (The 22 includes both brothers and cousins.) *Ibid,* I he'ped a party run his generation back [Hall: = trace his family] not long ago. **1942** (1971) Campbell *Cloud-Walking* 27 **seKY,** So's it was just in the generation for Sary to love learning and want her younguns to get a heap of knowledge. **1967** Fetterman *Stinking Creek* 37 **KY,** A big family—or a big 'generation', as mountain people put it. **1968** *DARE* (Qu. Z8, . . *Immediate family group*) Inf **GA**44, Generation; (Qu. Z9, . . *Others related to you by blood*) Inf **GA**23, My whole generation. **1972** Hall *Sayings Old Smoky* 73, *Generation.* A large family; family (in a broad sense); kind; breed; the people of the same period, or living at the same time. *Ibid,* The whole Morgan generation claimed to be half-Indian, and partly Black Dutch.

genie n [Cf *SND Jennie* prop. n. "Also . . *Jean(n)ie; Genny.* . . A generic term for a country girl"]

1930 Shoemaker *1300 Words* 27 **cPA Mts** (as of c1900), *Genie.* . . A dearly beloved person.

genius n Usu |ˈjinjəs|; also infreq |ˈjinəs| Pronc-sp *genus*

A Form.

1858 Hammett *Piney Woods Tavern* 169, My good old mother . . first discovered my wonderful genus. *Ibid* 172, I ain't much faith in yer bein' a genus. **1902** [see **B** below].

B Sense.

See quot. [Perh infl by *ingenious*]

1902 *DN* 2.235 **sIL,** *Genius* [jinəs]. . . Synonymous with dofunny. [*Ibid* 233, *Dofunny.* . . Any effective or labor-saving mechanical contrivance, particularly if novel.]

gensang, genseng See **ginseng 1**

genson n [See quot 1948]

A **horse gentian** (here: *Triosteum perfoliatum*).

1900 Lyons *Plant Names* 378, *T[riosteum] perfoliatum.* . . Genson. . . *Root* febrifuge, cathartic, deobstruent. **1940** Clute *Amer. Plant Names* 55, *Horse Gentian.* . . Genson. **1948** Stevens *KS Wild Flowers* 357, *Triosteum perfoliatum.* . . Various vernacular names have been given to this species . . the corruptions of gentian—ginseng, genson, because Triosteum has sometimes been used in this country as a tonic, substituting for the officinal, European yellow gentian. **1959** Carleton *Index Herb. Plants* 51, *Genson:* Triosteum perfoliatum.

gentian n

Std: a plant of the genus *Gentiana.* For other names of var spp see **agueweed 2, blind gentian, bottle gentian, closed gentian, creeping wintergreen 2, dumb foxglove, explorer's gentian, fluxroot 2, French gentian, gallflower, gall of the earth 5, gall weed 1, harvestbells, hikers' gentian, moss gentian, mountain gentian, pine-barren gentian, sampson's snakeroot, soapwort gentian, striped gentian, swamp gentian** Note: Included in the above are the separate genera *Gentianella* and *Gentianopsis* of some authors.

gentile n **esp UT**

Esp among Mormons: a non-Mormon.

1838 *Test* (Rushville, Ill.) 12 Dec. 3/3 *(DA),* It was intimated from the Head Quarters of the Mormons, they ought not to pay their debts—that the 'gentiles were bound to support the chosen people of God.' **1889** (1971) Farmer *Americanisms* 261, *Gentile.* . . Amongst Mormons, a contemptuous epithet of all persons outside the Mormon Church, regardless of "color, or previous condition of servitude." **1942** Whipple *Joshua* 28 **UT,** And Thy sacred name, O Lord, save us from profaning it, as is the unholy habit of the gentiles. **1966** Barnes–Jensen *Dict. UT Slang* 17, Since about 1838 the Mormons have called every person who does not belong to their church, a Gentile irrespective of his religion. **1967–69** *DARE* Tape **ID**6, [FW:] tell me somethin' about the early Mormons around here. . . [Inf:] They were religious, they were hard workers, and on the whole I considered 'em good neighbors, even though I was a gentile; **ID**7, One Mormon would do something and so they'd blame 'em all. . . And then . . one gentile would do something and they'd blame all of us. **1968** *DARE* (Qu. CC4, . . *Nicknames . . for various religions or religious groups*) Inf **UT**10, Gentiles—for all others [*DARE* Ed: i.e., non-Mormons; Inf is a Mormon].

gentle v **esp S Midl**

To soothe, calm (a person or animal); to tame (an animal); hence n *gentler;* see quot 1944.

1735 in 1896 *VA Mag. Hist. & Biog.* 3.356 **VA,** Y'r colts have not been gentled any, so that Charles can't lead them up. **1889** (1971) Farmer *Americanisms* 261, *Gentle, to.* . . To ease; soften; or soothe. **1903** *DN* 2.314 **seMO,** *Gentle.* . . To quiet. 'He gentled the horse.' **1926** *AmSp* 1.414 **Okefenokee GA,** 'Had that fawn in a crocus-sack, with 'is haid stuck out. When we got home an' let 'im out, he wuz jest as gentle. They're an easy thing ter gentle. **1927** *AmSp* 2.355 **cwWV,** *Gentle* . . to tame. "He gentles animals well." **1942** (1971) Campbell *Cloud-Walking* 18 **seKY,** Nelt gentled her worries. "Rest your mind about them boys." **1944** Adams *Western Words* 64, *Gentler*—An animal used to *neck* [=be tied] . . to a wilder one to subdue the latter until he becomes more tractable. A horsebreaker.

gentle down v phr

To become calm.

1906 *DN* 3.137 **nwAR,** *Gentle down.* . . To become calm. "His horse gentled down."

gentle hawk n Cf **gentle sparrow**

=**broad-wing.**

1946 Hausman *Eastern Birds* 192, *Broad-winged Hawk.* . . *Other Names* . . Gentle Hawk. . . A very unsuspicious, rather phlegmatic hawk which does not ordinarily molest small birds and will scarcely attack humans who intrude upon its nest.

gentleman n Pronc-spp *gem'man, gintleman, juntleman;* for addit varr see **A** below

A Forms.

1 sg: usu *gentleman;* for varr see quots.

1821 Cooper *Spy* 2.66, All alone wid a gem'man. **1858** Hammett *Piney Woods Tavern* 140 **TX** [Black], Only de ole gempleman. **1893** Shands *MS Speech* 32, *Gemman.* . . Negro for *gentleman.* **1922** Gonzales *Black Border* 308 **sSC, GA coasts** [Gullah glossary], *Juntlemun*—gentleman, gentlemen. **1926** Smith *Gullah* 35 **sSC, GA coasts,** *Juntleman* (gentleman).

2 pl: usu *gentlemen;* also *gentlemens;* for addit varr see quots. Cf Intro "Language Changes" II.3

1781 in 1956 Eliason *Tarheel Talk* 311 **c,cnNC,** *Gentlemen*—gintlemen. **1837** (1976) Simms *Martin Faber* 96 **SC** [Gullah], You truss Tom, mossa—he's de one for de gemplemans. **1858** Hammett *Piney Woods Tavern* 308 **TX** [Black], "Breffus [=breakfast] am ready, genelum," said that person. **1887** (1967) Harris *Free Joe* 135 **GA** [Black], "Why gentermen!" exclaimed Abe, "how *kin* she be dead?" **1923** *DN* 5.208 **swMO,** Gentlemens. **1956** *AmSp* 31.109 [Army speech], The double plurals *mens* and *gentlemens* are heard regularly in Negro speech. **1965–70** *DARE* Tape **FL**14, Gentlemens; **GA**39, Now, if there's any questions, gentlemens; **MS**86, We are hoping to have a nice little jail that will hold ladies and gentlemens; **MO**8, Most of our teachers were ladies and then we had two gentlemens. [Two Infs Black, two White]

B Senses.

1 Used as a form of address to a man whose name is not known.

1965–70 *DARE* (Qu. II10b, *Asking directions . . on the street . . you'd say to a man: "Say, ______, how far is it to the next town?"*) Infs **AL**33, **FL**52, **MO**23, **NC**55, Gentleman.

2 often attrib, esp *gentleman cow:* A male animal, esp one kept for breeding purposes. **chiefly Nth, N Midl** See Map *euphem* Cf **daddy** n **5, father** n **B2, he** n **1**

1855 Hammett *Wonderful Advent.* 111, I remember . . in my younger days . . to have been put in a state of great bodily peril by a pugnacious gentleman turkey, who had evidently taken umbrage at a flaming red and yellow silk dress that constituted my infantile apparel. **1859** (1968) Bartlett *Americanisms* 168, *Gentleman turkey.* . . A turkey cock. The mock modesty of the Western States requires that a male turkey should be so called. **1912** *DN* 3.576 **wIN,** *Gentleman cow.* . . A bull. The term is used by squeamish women. **1931** Randolph *Ozarks* 79, The names of male animals must not be mentioned when women are present. . . Many Southerners use *ox, male-cow,* or even *gentleman-cow* instead of the English word *bull.* **1931–33** *LANE Worksheets* **CT,** Gentleman cow. *Ibid* **VT,** Gentleman heifer. **1937** *Hall Coll.* **wNC,** Let me blaze that gentleman [=a bear] by the right of the ear. **1946** *PADS* 5.23 **VA,** *Gentleman cow.* . . A bull . . in the presence of women. **1946** *PADS* 6.15 **eNC,** *Gentleman cow.* **1949** *PADS* 11.21 **CO,** *Gentleman cow.* **1950** *WELS (Words used by women or in mixed company for a bull)* 25 Infs, **WI,** Gentleman cow; 1 Inf, Gentleman; *(Words for a bull)* 11 Infs, **WI,** Gentleman cow; 4 Infs, The gentleman; *(A male breeding* *pig)* 5 Infs, **WI,** Gentleman pig. **1965–70** *DARE* (Qu. K23) 146 Infs, **chiefly Nth, N Midl,** Gentleman cow; 10 Infs, **chiefly Nth, N Midl,** Gentleman; **MD**34, **NJ**65, Gentleman of the herd; **MD**48, Cow's gentleman friend; (Qu. K22) 11 Infs, **chiefly Nth, N Midl,** Gentleman cow; **IL**90, **IN**35, **NY**8, **WI**77, Gentleman (of the herd); **NJ**8, Gentleman of the family; (Qu. K52) Infs **MI**116, **ND**1, Gentleman pig; **VA**46, Gentleman—the polite word; gentleman hog [FW: laughter]. **1967** *DARE* Tape **ID**14, [FW:] Any special words . . that your mother or anyone used for, say, a bull . . ? [Inf:] A lot of 'em call it a gentleman cow.

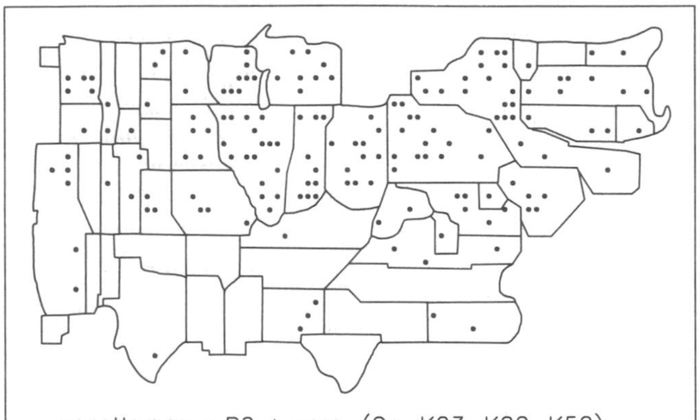

•gentleman n B2 + varr (Qq. K23, K22, K52)

gentleman intj Also *gentlemen* Pronc-sp *gentulmen*
Used as an exclam of astonishment.
1902 *DN* 2.235 **sIL,** *Gentlemen. . .* Used in exclamation denoting astonishment, or when anything extraordinary is beyond description. "George don't git mad very often, but when he does git mad—Gentlemen!!!" **1907** *DN* 3.222 **nwAR, sIL,** *Gentlemen.* **1950** *PADS* 14.75 **FL,** *Gen-tul-men. . .* An exclamation of surprise, particularly of agreeable surprise. **1968** *DARE* (Qu. NN29a, *Exclamations beginning with 'great': "Great ______!"*) Inf **PA**134, Jehosaphat gentleman!

gentleman cow See **gentleman** n **B2**

gentlemanfied adj Cf Intro "Language Changes" III.1
Gentlemanly; gentlemanlike.
1937 (1977) Hurston *Their Eyes* 114 **csFL** [Black], You'se noble! You's du most gentlemanfied man Ah ever did see. You'se uh king!

gentleman's breeches n
=**Virginia bluebells.**
1898 *Jrl. Amer. Folkl.* 11.275, *Mertensia Virginica . .* gentleman's breeches, Plymouth, Ohio.

gentleman's cane n [See quot 1894]
A **prince's-feather** (here: *Polygonum orientale*).
1894 *Jrl. Amer. Folkl.* 7.97, *Polygonum orientale, . .* gentleman's cane, Mansfield, O[hio]. . . The stems cut by children into canes. **1897** *Ibid* 10.54, *Polygonum orientale, . .* Gentleman's cane, . . Sulphur Grove, Ohio. **1911** *Century Dict. Suppl., Gentleman's-cane. . .* The prince's-feather, *Polygonum orientale.* **1959** Carleton *Index Herb. Plants* 51, *Gentleman's cane:* Polygonatum orientale.

gentleman's sorrel n Also *gentlemen's sorrel*
A **sheep sorrel** (here: *Rumex acetosella*).
1892 *Jrl. Amer. Folkl.* 5.102, *Rumex acetosella. . .* Gentlemen's sorrel. Cambridge, Mass. **1900** Lyons *Plant Names* 327, *R[umex] Acetosella. . .* Gentleman's Sorrel. **1940** Clute *Amer. Plant Names* 138, *R[umex] acetosella. . .* Gentleman's sorrel.

gentlemen intj See **gentleman** intj

gentlemen-and-ladies n
A **shooting star** (here: *Dodecatheon meadia*).
1940 Clute *Amer. Plant Names* 112, *D[odecatheon] meadia. . .* Gentlemen and ladies. **1959** Carleton *Index Herb. Plants* 51, *Gentlemen-and-ladies:* Dodecatheon meadia.

gentlemens See **gentleman** n **A2**

gentlemen's hats n
A **catchfly 1** (here: *Silene noctiflora*).
1892 *Jrl. Amer. Folkl.* 5.93, *Silene noctiflora,* gentlemen's hats. Gilsum, N[ew] H[ampshire].

gentlemen's sorrel See **gentleman's sorrel**

gentler See **gentle** v

gentle sparrow n Cf **gentle hawk**
=**pinewoods sparrow.**
1968 *DARE* (Qu. Q22) Inf **GA**25, Gentle sparrow (nickname for pine sparrow).

gentulmen See **gentleman** intj

genuine adj Usu |'ǰɛnjuwən, -wɨn|; also freq **chiefly Sth, SW** |'ǰɛnju,aɪn, 'ǰɪnɪ,waɪn|; for addit varr see quots Pronc-spp *genyuwine, gineine, ginniwine, ginnywine*
Std sense, var forms.
1843 (1916) Hall *New Purchase* 54 **IN,** 'Tisn't nun of your spice-wood or yarb stuff, but the rele gineine *store* tea. **1892** Smith *Day at Laguerre's* 184 **VA,** It's a pleasure, Kurnal, a gen-u-ine pleasure, zur, to meet a man of yo' calibre. **1898** Harris *Tales Home Folks* 274 **nGA,** Why, hit's the ginnywine coffee! **1908** *DN* 3.314 **eAL, wGA,** *Genyuwine. . .* Genuine. Sometimes pronounced [ǰɪn-ɪ-waɪn]. **1919** *DN* 5.36 **AR,** *Ginniwine. . .* Genuine, stressed on the final syllable. **1922** *DN* 5.134 **West,** The oxytone pronunciation of . . [genu'ine] is usually not jocular but dialectal. **1941** *LANE* Map 308, The map shows the word *genuine,* regularly recorded in the phrase *Genuine maple syrup. . .* The word *genuine* is usually stressed on the first syllable, often (especially in forms of the type of [dʒɛnjuwaɨn]) with a secondary stress on the last syllable. Level stress and end stress were recorded occasionally. . . Transcriptions of the type of [dʒɛnjuin, -juɨn] generally represent trisyllabic forms: that is, the sequence [ui, uɨ], etc., is not intended as a diphthong. . . The word *genuine* in the given context is unnatural to many of our informants. Some say they would never apply this word to maple syrup. **c1960** *Wilson Coll.* **csKY,** Genuine ['ǰɛnyu,aɪn] is rather common. **1968** *DARE* FW Addit **CA**105, ['ǰɛnju,aɪn]. **1976** Allen *LAUM* 3.287 (as of c1950), In the U[pper] M[idwest] the two pronunciations of *genuine,* both of which are common in New England among the various groups of speakers, provide a fairly sharp social contrast and a bare hint of a geographical contrast. The more common pronunciation is marked by a secondary stress on the final syllable and an accompanying retention of the free vowel—or diphthong—/ɑi/, as in /'ǰɛnju,wain/. Although two-thirds of the UM infs. have this, it is hardly a prestige form. . . Contrasting /'ǰɛnjuwɪn/, with weak stress on the final syllable, exhibits higher social acceptance.

genus See **genius**

genyuwine See **genuine**

geoduck n Also *goeduck, gooey duck, gweduck* [Chinook Jargon]
1 A large edible clam *(Panope generosa)* native to the Pacific coast. **Pacific coast, esp WA** Also called **giant clam**
1883 U.S. Natl. Museum *Bulletin* 27.239, *Glycimeris generosa . .* is a Pacific coast species, known as the "Geoduck." . . It is found in sheltered localities on the coast, from Puget Sound to San Diego. . . The Geoduck is said to be of very fine flavor, but too rich to be used constantly for food. **1903** *Scientific Amer. Suppl.* 55.805/1, In Alaskan waters is found a monster clam, the 'geoduck,' one of which would afford a meal for several persons. **1911** *Century Dict. Suppl., Goeduck* ['goidʌk]. . . [*Century* Ed: Also *geoduck;* from a native name.] **1947** Jones *Evergreen Land* 104 **WA,** G-w-e-d-u-c-k-s is the way Webster spells it. . . But around here we call them gooey-ducks. . . A gooey-duck . . is a very large kind of clam that is found only around Puget Sound. It's got a neck four or five feet long, and the shell is maybe six inches in diameter. They weigh up to eight or nine pounds sometimes. **1948** *Nat. Hist.* 57.165/3 **nwWA,** The shovel was laid aside, and two skillful hands reached into the ooze to lift the great geoduck gently from its home. **1966–67** *DARE* (Qu. P18, . . *Kinds of shellfish . . around here*) Inf **WA**11, Gooey duck . . clam with long neck; **WA**20, Gooey duck; (QR, near Qu. Q9) Inf **WA**32, Gooey duck [FW: in conv]. **1974** Abbott *Seashells* 542, *Panopea generosa . .* Geoduck (Goo-ee-duck). **1981** Rehder *Audubon Field Guide Seashells* 820, The Geoduck is supposedly one of the finest eating clams on the West Coast, but it is relatively scarce and difficult to dig out, so is not often sought.
2 A **Washington clam** (here: *Tresus nuttalli*).
1949 Palmer *Nat. Hist.* 360, *Washington Clam. . .* Siphons tough, but

flesh is delicious. . . Called "geoduck" but this name should correctly be applied to *Panope generosa.*

geoducker n

One who digs for **geoducks.**

1948 *Nat. Hist.* 57.190/2 **Puget Sound WA,** It would not only be poor sportsmanship but also illegal to jab a fishhook into a bivalve's projecting part and let the wounded animal draw down with it into the mud a cord or stick for the geoducker to follow in his digging.

geoducking vbl n Pronc-sp *gooeyducking*

Digging for **geoducks.**

1948 *Nat. Hist.* 57.162/1 **Puget Sound WA,** All this was before we went gooeyducking.

george v

1986 *WI Alumnus Letters* **neIL,** I myself have heard people use *george* as a verb with a meaning somewhat more benign than 'cheat'; rather, 'wheedle' or 'jolly' (vb.). Most recently from a native of the Chicago area . . about five years ago . . ; he said something like, "The lasagna was stone cold, and I griped about it; they were terribly apologetic, and I georged 'em out of an extra piece of pie."

George called phr

1978 *MJLF* 4.1.38 **cTX,** Euphemisms for menstruation—Some women personify the event: "Mother Nature," "Granny's coming," "Aunt Minnie is visiting," "George called."

george walker n [Prob var of **tom walker**]

A stilt; also *george walking* walking on stilts.

1945 Saxon *Gumbo Ya-Ya* 572 **LA,** George Walkers was a local name for stilts. *Ibid, George Walking* . . stilt walking.

George Washington n Also *Washington;* for addit varr see quots [From the portrait on the bill] Cf **Abraham Lincoln**

A one-dollar bill.

1950 *WELS (Joking names and nicknames for: a paper dollar)* 1 Inf, **WI,** Portrait of George Washington; 1 Inf, Washington. **1965–70** *DARE* (Qu. U26) 10 Infs, **scattered,** George Washington; **IN**75, **MI**97, **MA**1, Washington; **AL**8, George; **PA**245, George Washing; **AL**27, George Washington's picture. **1969** *DARE* FW Addit, **KY**47, George Washington. **1986** Pederson *LAGS Concordance,* 2 infs, **FL,** George Washingtons.

George Washington poke n Also called **cut the pie, frying pan 3, Washington punch**

A children's game.

1950 *WELS (Hiding games that start with some special, elaborate way of sending the players out to hide)* 1 Inf, **cWI,** The Waukesha cousins had a variation on our frying pan game called *George Washington poke.* "It's" back was a cherry pie. **1969** *DARE* (Qu. EE16) Inf **IL**45, George Washington poke. [FW sugg]

George Washington washout n

1970 Tarpley *Blinky* 54 **neTX,** *Very heavy rain that doesn't last long. . .* George Washington washout.

Georgia n Usu |ˈǰɔ(r)ǰə|; also **esp Sth, S Midl** |ˈǰɔ(r)ǰi|; for addit varr see quots Pronc-spp *Gawja, Georgie, Georgy* Cf Intro "Language Changes" IV.1.b.

Std sense, var forms.

1851 Hooper *Widow Rugby's Husband* 79 **AL,** I give it the Georgy set [=a maneuver against an opponent's eye], and then brought a raunch [=made a wrench], and commenced feelin' for the strings [=eye-strings]! *Ibid,* I fixed everything partickler, by the old Georgy rule, and fetched another raunch. **1884** Lanier *Poems* 172 **GA,** Folks was mighty big fools / That 'ud stay in Georgy ther lifetime out. **1904** *DN* 2.423 **Cape Cod MA** (as of a1857), *Georgia* [pronounced] (Georgy). **1908** *DN* 3.314 **eAL, wGA,** Georgy. . . Georgia. **1938** L.N. Jones 'Swappin' Fever' **MO** *(ADD),* Pa he wants me to learn to play 'Marchin' through Georgy.' **1939** *LANE* Map 14, *Georgia. . .* Pronunciations with the second syllable of the type of [-dʒɜ] are regarded as older though still in use by . . [12 infs]. 1 inf, **cnVT,** [dʒɔ· dʒɜr] I think. **1940** *Sat. Eve. Post* 6 Jan 15/3 **seMS,** "I was just thinking," Jud began, as always, "'bout a tale my pa told me 'bout the folks when they first came to Mississippi, up to ol' Jasper County, from Gawja." **1949** Arnow *Hunter's Horn* 295 **KY,** "Did you know we had green Georgie onions big enough to eat?" Suse called back. **1968** *DARE* Tape **GA**61, [ˈǰoɚǰi]. **1972** *Atlanta Letters* **GA,** I thought of another Georgie phrase. **1984** Burns *Cold Sassy* 242 **nGA** (as of 1906), They 'as ten or twelve fam'lies in our wagon train, takin' thangs south to sell in Washin'ton, Georgie.

Georgia bacon n

A **gopher** n[1] **1a** (here: *Gopherus polyphemus*).

1952 Carr *Turtles* 339, The importance of this animal [=*Gopherus polyphemus*] in the lives of the poorer rural people of Florida and south Georgia . . would not be easily overestimated. One has but to look over the list of half-facetious vernacular names for the gopher—Florida chicken, Georgia bacon, and any number of others—to get a hint of its local economic role.

Georgia bark n [See quot 1931] **chiefly SE**

=fever tree, or its bark.

1810 Michaux *Histoire des Arbres* 1.30, Pinckneya pubens *Georgia bark. . . Georgia bark tree* (Quinquina de la Géorgie), nom donné par moi à cet arbre, qui n'en a aucun dans le pays. [Pinckneya pubens *Georgia bark. . . Georgia bark tree* (Quinine of Georgia), name given by me to this tree, which doesn't have one in the country.] **1869** Porcher *Resources* 442 **Sth,** *Georgia Bark. . .* Very useful in intermittent fever. Dr. Law, of Georgia, cured six out of seven cases with it. . . The attention of those residing where it may be found is invited to it as a substitute for quinine. **1901** Lounsberry *S. Wild Flowers* 476, Georgia Bark. Calico Bush. . . The natives seek this shrub, or small tree, that they may peel its bark to use as a substitute for quinine. **1931** *AmSp* 6.418, It was not until 1810 . . that . . Michaux, discovering that in reality there were two species of this [=cinchona] in the Southern States, named the second *Georgia bark,* because the bark of the new species, like that of the cinchona or bark tree, has medicinal properties. **1940** Brown *Amer. Cooks* 127 **FL,** Florida wild quinine is called "Georgia bark." **1942** Amer. Philos. Soc. *Trans.* 33.66/2, A sand-hill bog . . about 1.7 miles northwest of Cox is believed to be the type locality of the famous Franklin tree . . which the Bartrams discovered here, apparently in association with the Georgia bark. **1979** Little *Checklist U.S. Trees* 187, Georgia-bark. . . Extreme s. S.C. . . , Ga., and n. and nw. Fla.

Georgia boy n

1 =marsh hawk.

1911 *Forest & Stream* 77.174, *Circus hudsonius.* Georgia Boy, Santee, S. C.

2 See **Georgia hopper** n.

Georgia buggy n

1 also *Georgia wagon:* A wheelbarrow or pushcart. **chiefly Sth, S Midl** See Map

1918 *DN* 5.18 **NC, SC,** *Georgia buggy* . . wheelbarrow. **1948** *AN&Q* 8.185, "Georgia buggy." Are your readers familiar with this term as American slang for *wheelbarrow?* **1965** Bradford *Born with the Blues* 120 **Sth** [Black], [He] is working as one of those 'push an' pull 'em' human derricks who drives one of those Georgia buggies downtown in the garment district [of New York City]. **1965–70** *DARE* (Qu. L41) 9 Infs, **Sth, S Midl,** Georgia buggy; **IA**31, Georgia buggy—Southern name; niggers use [it]; **MD**42, Georgia buggy—what niggers say; **WV**2, Georgia buggy—Negroes who came from Georgia brought this term. [3 of 12 Infs Black] **1986** Pederson *LAGS Concordance* **Gulf Region,** [49 infs, 42 of them White, offer the term *Georgia buggy,* most saying it is the same as or similar to a wheelbarrow; some say that it is a two- (rarely four-)wheeled cart used for hauling heavy loads such as bricks, cement, or dirt. 1 inf, **ceTN,** calls it a *Georgia wagon.*]

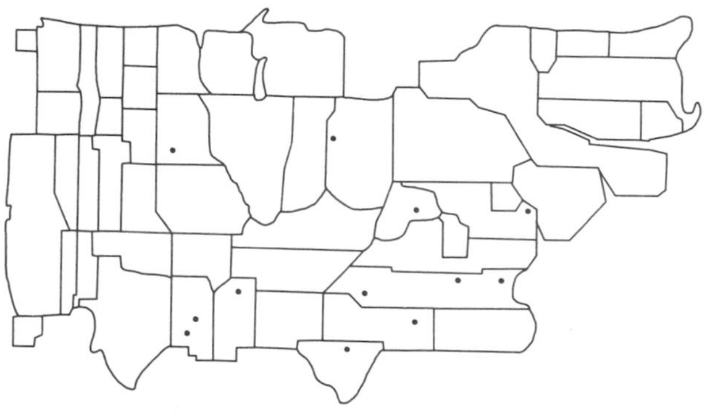

•Georgia buggy 1 (Qu. L41)

2 See quot.
1970 *DARE* (Qu. N5, *Nicknames for an automobile, especially an old or broken-down car*) Inf **VA**70, Georgia buggy.

Georgia cabin n Cf **dog run, dog trot**
1950 *PADS* 14.32 **SC,** *Georgia cabin...* A two-room cabin with an open runway, called a *dog run* or a *dog trot* between the two rooms.

Georgia cane n
A **giant reed a** (here: *Arundo donax*).
1939 Tharp *Vegetation TX* 43, Georgia cane *(Arundo donax)* grows abundantly in marshes... It has little if any forage value. **1970** Correll *Plants TX* 115, *Georgia cane...* Planted for erosion control along roads and in dune areas.

Georgia chicken n Cf **Arkansas chicken**
Salt pork.
1971 Wood *Vocab. Change* 369, Georgia chicken [volunteered in response to query about meat from sides of hog, salted but not smoked]. **1979** Solomon–Solomon *Cracklin Bread & Asfidity* 101 **AL,** *Saw-Mill Gravy and Georgia Chicken.* Soak fatback in cold water a few hours. Pour off. Dredge slices in flour. Fry, as chicken, turning often. Pour off most of grease. Stir in some flour, brown, then add water, let boil up, add black pepper.

Georgia crawler See **Georgia wiggler**

Georgia ham n *joc*
=**August ham.**
1971 Roberts *Third Ear* np [Black], *Georgia ham . .* watermelon.

Georgia holly n
A **holly** n[1] **1** (here: *Ilex longipes*).
1960 Vines *Trees SW* 652, *Georgia Holly. Ilex longipes...* Wide-spreading shrub or tree to 23 ft. **1970** Correll *Plants TX* 996, *Georgia Holly...* In woods, often on sandy banks of streams... From N.C. and Tenn., s. to Fla. and Tex.

Georgia hopper n Also *Georgia boy* Cf **Georgia thumper**
1968 *DARE* (QR, near Qu. R5) Inf **GA**20, Georgia hopper—it's a large grasshopper. **1986** Pederson *LAGS Concordance (Grasshopper)* 1 inf, **nwAL,** Georgia hopper; 1 inf, **seFL,** Georgia boy.

Georgia horse bed n
c1937 in 1970 Yetman *Voices* 40 **ceTX** [Black], Dey didn't bother to have much furniture, 'cause us in dere only to sleep. Us have homemake bench and "Georgia Hoss" bed with hay mattress.

Georgia ice cream n *joc*
Grits.
1972 *DARE* FW Addit, Georgia ice-cream is ground hominy; jocular; current. **1979** *DARE* File **Tallahassee FL,** Georgia ice cream is cracked, mill-ground corn—called "grits." **1984** Wilder *You All Spoken Here* 83 **Sth,** *Georgia ice cream:* Grits. **1986** Pederson *LAGS Concordance,* 1 inf, **neFL,** Georgia ice cream—grits.

Georgia jumper See **Georgia stock**

Georgia major n [*Georgia* the state + **major**] *joc* or *derog* Cf **colonel B1**
One who puts on airs or affects dignity or rank.
1844 Thompson *Major Jones's Courtship* 186 **GA,** It is now *"vexata questio"* (as the Lawyers say) with gentlemen of the 'Sword and Plume' whether you intend to extend your prohibition to 'Georgia Majors' and their subalterns—whether there are to be any exceptions to universal smooth faces? **1854** *Wide West* (S.F.) 27 Aug. 2/5 *(DA),* Digger Indians... are seen in the streets here; the gentlemen in attire bordering on the summer costume of the Georgia major. **1858** Hammett *Piney Woods Tavern* 123 **TX,** We had another old chap on board, Majer Rogers; and though he wasn't a Georgy Majer, he was jolly enough for one. **1950** *PADS* 14.32 **SC,** *Georgia major...* A pretentious fellow. A Georgia major's uniform is said to be a pair of spurs and a paper collar.

Georgian stock See **Georgia stock**

Georgia piercer n *obs* Cf **gallinipper 1b**
A large biting fly (here: *Stomoxys georgina*).
1862 *Harper's New Mth. Mag.* Nov 737/1, The . . "Georgia Piercer" . . if curses could annihilate it, would soon be driven from off the earth.

Georgia pine n
=**longleaf pine** or the wood of such a pine.
1796 (1855) U.S. Congress *Debates & Proc.* 4th Cong. 2d Sess. 2789, No. of feet of Georgia pine planks for decks. 85,930. **1857** Vaux *Villas & Cottages* 143, The other living-room, which should be library and dining-room in one, might appropriately be finished with Georgia pine. **1884** Sargent *Forests of N. Amer.* 202, *Pinus palustris...* Long-leaved Pine... Georgia Pine. **1896** Mohr–Roth *Timber Pines* 28, *The Long-leaf Pine... Local or Common Names...* Georgia Pine (Del.) **1919** (1922) Cady *Rhymes VT* 57, Paid, Georgia pine for culvert beams;/ He'd better bought some chocolate creams. **1933** Small *Manual SE Flora* 4, *Georgia-pine...* A timber tree of the first importance, and the principal source of rosin and turpentine in the U.S. **1971** Krochmal *Appalachia Med. Plants* 192, *Pinus Palustris... Common Names:* Longleaf pine, . . Georgia pine.

Georgia plow(stock) See **Georgia stock**

Georgia plume n
A large shrub or small tree *(Elliottia racemosa)* native to Georgia.
1987 *Nature Conserv. News* 37.3.28 **GA,** A recent one-acre purchase... enhances protection for . . Georgia plume *(Elliottia racemosa),* a small understory tree known for its upright, feathery flowers and blazing orange-red autumn foliage.

Georgia rattlesnake (melon) See **rattlesnake melon**

Georgia red wiggler See **Georgia wiggler**

Georgia roll n
1954 *PADS* 21.28 **SC,** *Georgia roll...* A method of moving a heavy, oblong object, as a bale of cotton, by lifting one end, balancing it on the lower edge, and rotating it so that the lower end rolls on the ground.

Georgia scooter stock See **Georgia stock**

Georgia skin (game) n **chiefly Sth** *esp among Black speakers*
A card game; see quots.
1935 Hurston *Mules & Men* 307 **LA,** *Georgia Skin Game.* Any number of "Pikers" can play at a time, but there are two "principals" who do the dealing. Both of them are not dealing at the same time . . when the first one who deals "falls" the other principal takes the deal... The principals draw the first two cards. The pikers draw from the third card on. Unless a player or players want to "scoop one in the rough," he can choose his own card which can be any card in the deck except the card on top of the deck and that one goes to the dealer. The dealer charges anything he pleases for the privilege of "scooping," the money being put in sight. It is the player's bet. After the ones who wish to have scooped, then the dealer begins to "turn" the cards... And the pikers choose a card each from among those turned off to bet on... When all . . have their bets down . . the dealer . . turns them [=the cards] until . . a card like the one he is holding falls... Then the players cry "hold 'em" until the player selects another clean card... The fresh side bets are down and the chant "turn 'em" and the singing "Let de deal go Down" until the deck is run out. **1947** *True* 32.105, [Footnote:] Georgia skin . . is played with widely differing rules in various sections of the South. Basically, it is an adaptation of Faro. The biggest pay-off is on the last card dealt. **1954** *Ebony* July 60/1, A Saturday night house rent party where I tried to pick up extra dough shooting craps or playing Georgia Skin took care of the rest of my money. **1970** Major *Dict. Afro-Amer. Slang* 58, *Georgia skin . .* a card game similar to Gin Rummy. **1970** *DARE* (Qu. DD35, . . *The favorite card games that people play*) Inf **SC**68, Georgia skin—lose their life playing this. [Inf Black] **1977** Dillard *Lexicon* 95, Jelly Roll Morton's Library of Congress conversations with Alan Lomax give some indication as to how important gambling on pool and card games was to Blacks in the southern city at the turn of the twentieth century. Among the games he mentions is the *Georgia skin game.*

Georgia stock n Also *Georgia jumper, Georgian stock, Georgia plowstock, ~ scooter stock* **chiefly Gulf States, AR, OK** See Map
A plowstock to which various appurtenances, such as shovels or teeth, can be attached; hence *Georgia stock (plow), Georgia plow* a plow having such a stock.
1843 Cotting *Essay on Soils* 51, By properly cultivating the soil, abandoning *that rude misshapen uncooth thing,* the remnant of ignorant barbarism, called a "Georgia plough," and substituting the improved implements of Europe, and the Northern States, . . the eye would no longer be pained at the sight of "gullied hills" and barren wastes. **1891** *Memphis Appeal-Avalanche* (TN) 25 Apr 5/6, [Advt:] Headquarters for Single and Double Georgia Stocks, Wood and Iron Double Shovels[,] Eye and Handled Planters' Hoes. **1902** (1969) Sears *Catalogue* 478/2, Our

Steel Beam Georgia Stocks combine lightness and strength. **1944** Clark *Pills* 110 **Sth,** They were selling the very same implements . . Georgia scooter stocks, side harrows. *Ibid* 281, Piled high around the foot of the counters . . were the so-called "plow irons" or the detachable shares which went with the homemade or shop-designed iron "Georgia" stocks. **1965–70** *DARE* (Qu. L18) 19 Infs, **chiefly AR, OK, TX,** Georgia stock; **AR**33, **MS**9, 72, Georgia stock plow; **AL**31, Georgian stock; **MS**4, Georgia plowstock; **AL**33, Georgia jumper; (Qu. L25) Infs **AL**31, **LA**31, Georgia stock. **1967** *DARE* Tape **TX**49, The only plow we had was what we called a Georgia stock, a wooden beam and a wooden foot. There was a heel bolt went through the foot of the Georgia stock and through the plow on top and you take a hammer and hit that tight and take the ground and do the plowing. **1986** Pederson *LAGS Concordance (Plow)* 52 infs, **chiefly coastal Gulf Region,** Georgia stock(s); 1 inf, **ceTN,** Georgia plow—same as grasshopper; 1 inf, **csAL,** Georgia plowstock.

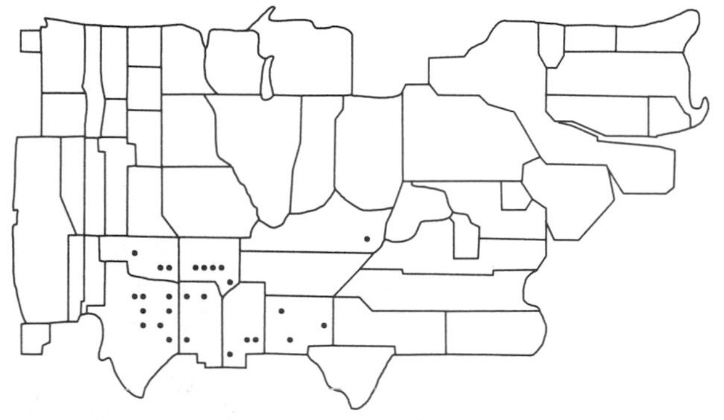

•Georgia stock + varr (Qq. L18, L25)

Georgia thumper n Also *Georgia stumper* **esp FL** Cf **Georgia hopper**

A **lubber grasshopper** (here: *Romalea microptera*).

c1940 Eliason *Word Lists FL* 8, *Georgia thumper:* A large grasshopper, having a black color with gold marking here and there on him. This grasshopper has a very bad odor, and birds and other insect-eaters will not bother one after it gets a week or so old. **1968** *DARE* (Qu. R6) Inf **GA**25, Georgia thumper (a big one). **1986** Pederson *LAGS Concordance (Grasshopper)* 7 infs, **nFL,** Georgia thumper(s); 1 inf, **cnLA,** Georgia stumper.

Georgia torch n

1951 Carter–Ragusin *Gulf Coast* 221, At night the darkness retreated before the "Georgia torches," blazing pine knots in containing cages, and from the luster of moon upon water.

Georgia wagon See **Georgia buggy 1**

Georgia wiggler n Also *Georgia crawler, ~ red wiggler* **chiefly S Atl** See Map Cf **African wiggler, red wiggler**

A worm used for bait.

1965–70 *DARE* (Qu. P6, . . *Worms . . for bait*) 9 Infs, **chiefly S Atl, esp SC,** Georgia wiggler; **FL**34, Georgia red wiggler; **LA**14, Georgia crawler. **1970** Tarpley *Blinky* 178 **neTX,** *Worm used for fish bait. . .* Georgia wiggler. **1971** Wood *Vocab. Change* 36 **Sth,** For a large worm used in fishing . . *Georgia wiggler* or *wiggler* is the first choice [of terms] in Georgia, Alabama, and Florida; it is the second choice in the other states. **1986** Pederson *LAGS Concordance (Earthworm)* 2 infs, **ceTX,** Georgia wiggler(s).

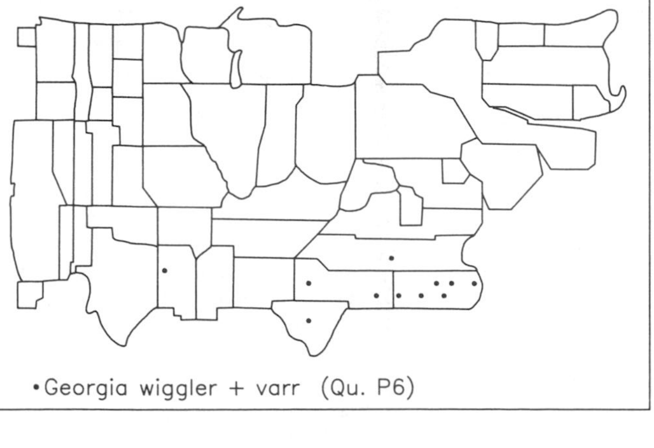

•Georgia wiggler + varr (Qu. P6)

Georgie, Georgy See **Georgia**

geound See **gown** n

gerardia n

Std: any of var plants which formerly constituted the genus *Gerardia,* but which are now included in the genera *Agalinus* and *Aureolaria:* see **false foxglove.**

gerfingle n

1973 *San Francisco Examiner* (CA) 2 Dec mag sec 1/1, You know those little rolls . . of crud that form under beds? Those . . are "gerfingles."

German n [Abbr for *German cotillion*]

1 A quadrille-like dance consisting of a series of steps and figures with frequent change of partners.

1863 (1889) Whitney *Faith Gartney* 170 **MA,** It was very agreeable . . to dance the "German" with the nicest partner in the Monday class. **a1883** (1911) Bagby *VA Gentleman* 73, I would show ankles higher than a circus rider, or a White Sulphur belle dancing the German. **1910** Hart *Vigilante Girl* 243 **nCA,** The repertoire of a ball-room belle of that day necessitated a familiarity with many dances—the waltz . . also "The German," as the cotillion was called. **1922** (1926) Cady *Rhymes VT* 229, " 'Twould pain me less," he said, "to hear / That angels danced the german." **1931–33** *LANE Worksheets* **CT,** *German. . .* A dance, the series of steps like a cotillion. "We used to have the German when I was an undergraduate." *Ibid* **MA,** *German. . .* A waltz in which you exchange partners. **1965–70** *DARE* (Qu. FF5a, . . *Different steps and figures in dancing—in past years*) Inf **SC**2, German—with partners and figures, but more sedate than [an] ordinary square dance; part of the high point of the dance; **SC**5, Germans—start several couples dancing, then stop music and all choose another partner from those not dancing; keeps people mixing around; **SC**11, Germans.

2 A dancing party. Cf **German favor**

1853 Curtis *Potiphar Papers* 26 **NYC,** The supper over, the young people . . descended to the dancing-room for the "German." This is a dance commencing usually at midnight or a little after, and continuing indefinitely toward daybreak. **1863** (1889) Whitney *Faith Gartney* 87 **MA,** "The girls" came in and called her down into the parlor,—about pretty looks, and becoming dresses, and who danced with who at the "German" last night. **1888** *Louisville Courier-Journal* 16 Feb (Farmer *Americanisms*), The flower german given last Friday evening by Mr. and Mrs. Louis Hite to Miss Maria Hopkins of St. Louis was the most elegant german ever given in this city. The favors were all flowers. After each figure the lady would be presented with a bunch of rare flowers. **1909** Porter *Options* 189, He had a vocabulary of about three hundred and fifty words that he made stretch over four germans a week. **1947** Perry *Cities of Amer.* 53, It is at this club's germans that the daughters of Baltimore's bon ton make their debuts. **1948** *AmSp* 23.249 **TX,** *German. . .* All-night dance. **1966–67** *DARE* (Qu. FF4, . . *Different kinds of dancing parties*) Infs **SC**5, 54, Germans; (Qu. FF16, . . *Local contests or celebrations*) Inf **NC**88, June German—big dance held in June with five or six bands; held in Rocky Mount, NC; two or three warehouses opened up; Whites would have their dance on Friday; Negroes on Monday.

3 A children's sidewalk game; see quot. Cf **box ball**

1975 Ferretti *Gt. Amer. Book Sidewalk Games* 82, And then there is German, which seems to have originated in Paterson, New Jersey, where it is still played. It has its beginnings in Box Ball; a wall and a sidewalk are necessary. . . German is played with teams, usually three men to a side, but often two. A member of the batting team stands in the sidewalk square designated as the batter's box and slams or very lightly tosses his spaldeen against the wall. . . The members of the other team stand in the squares marked Single, Double, and Triple and have to field the ball cleanly as it comes to them.

German aunt n Cf **French aunt**

1967 *DARE* (Qu. HH30) Inf **MN**2, German aunt—she's rather fat and countryish.

German bass See **German carp**

German bat-ball n

1968 *DARE* (Qu. EE11, *Bat-and-ball games for just a few players*) Inf **GA**33, German bat-ball, any number can play.

German bee n Also *German hornet*

A dark-colored honey bee *(Apis mellifera).*

1930 Shoemaker *1300 Words* 25 **cPA Mts** (as of c1900), *German Bee*—The small, wild black bee of the mountains. **1970** *DARE* (Qu. R21, . . *Other kinds of stinging insects*) Inf **VA**38, German bee—likes tree sap; German hornet—same as German bee.

German blackbird n Cf **German sparrow**

Perh a **starling** (here: *Sturnus vulgaris*).

1970 *DARE* (Qu. Q11, . . *Kinds of blackbirds*) Inf **VA**38, German blackbird.

German brown trout n Also *brown German, German brown, ~ trout*

=brown trout 1.

1904 *Salmon & Trout* 212, We have twenty-four . . salmon-trouts in the waters of North America, to which should be added . . the brown or German trout. **1949** Caine *N. Amer. Sport Fish* 75, *Brown Trout. . . Colloquial Names* . . German Brown Trout. *Ibid* 76, The brown trout . . was introduced in 1883 from Europe . . and for some time . . was known as the . . German Trout. **1956** Harlan-Speaker *IA Fish* 56, *Brown Trout. . . Other Names*—German brown, brownie. **1966-70** *DARE* (Qu. P1, . . *Freshwater fish . . that are good to eat*) 12 Infs, **scattered,** German brown trout; **CA**195, **CO**9, 38, **ID**3, **PA**176, **WY**1, German brown(s); **CO**12, German trout; (Qu. P2, *[In saltwater areas] . . Saltwater fish . . [that] are good to eat*) Inf **OR**5, Brown German. **1975** Evanoff *Catch More Fish* 80, The brown trout . . is also called . . German brown trout. . . Now it is found in most of our northern and mountain states. **1983** Becker *Fishes WI* 291, *Brown Trout. . .* Other common names: German brown trout, German trout.

German buzzard n

=black vulture.

1957 *AmSp* 32.182, *German buzzard* (Md.) . . black vulture.

German carp n Also *German bass, Germany carp*

The common carp *(Cyprinus carpio).*

1884 U.S. Natl. Museum *Bulletin* 27.1173, A desirable food-fish was needed for the inland waters of our Western and Southern States, and the German carp was found to meet this want. **1887** *Amer. Field* 27.6/1 **NE,** The waters of Nebraska are . . adapted to the cultivation of bass, wall-eyed pike and German carp, the latter of which have made prodigious growth. **1946** LaMonte *N. Amer. Game Fishes* 156, German Carp . . in many localities . . are considered to have higher nuisance than game qualities. **1966-70** *DARE* (Qu. P1, . . *Freshwater fish . . that are good to eat*) Infs **LA**8, **SC**7, **VA**43, German carp; (Qu. P3, *Freshwater fish that are not good to eat*) Infs **IN**18, **MA**15, **SC**31, 40, **VA**79, **WI**12, German carp; **MA**32, Germany carp. **1966-67** *DARE* Tape **LA**5, A German carp, he's red-lookin', somethin' like a goldfish I'd say, rich color to 'em an' they're a little slimmer built than what a buffalo is; **LA**8, Now when we go fishing now, when we catch gar n' German carp . . we keeps 'em an' put 'em in deep freeze. **1983** Becker *Fishes WI* 418, *Common Carp. . .* Other common names . . German carp, . . German bass.

German clover n

=red clover.

1970 *DARE* (Qu. L9a) Inf **VA**57, German clover; (Qu. L9b) Inf **VA**40, German clover; **VA**75, German clover—same as red-top clover.

German club n [**German 2**]

A social club whose members sponsor dancing parties.

1884 *Century Illustr. Mag.* 27.657/1 **DC,** But those who think that society exists only for dancing have ample opportunities for their amusement in the constant number of balls given by the different german clubs in public halls. **1893** *Harper's New Mth. Mag.* Feb 366/1, On Friday of this gala week is held the Carnival german. The Carnival German Club is composed of twenty-five society men, who give the german by subscription. **1909** Porter *Options* 188, Willie and I belonged to the same german club and athletic association. [**1968** *DARE* (Qu. FF22b, . . *Clubs and societies around here—for men*) Inf **AL**42, German club.]

German cob n

1970 *DARE* (Qu. P1, . . *Freshwater fish . . that are good to eat*) Inf **NC**87, German cob.

German coffee cake n **Nth**

See quots.

1941 *AN&Q* 2.55 **Philadelphia PA,** If you ask for coffee cake in San Francisco, you get the plain cake with a crumbly brown top, made in a large flat square and cut into strips—"German coffee cake," we used to call it. **c1965** Randle *Cookbooks* (Ask Neighbor) 32 **OH,** German coffee cake. [*DARE* Ed: Made with alternating layers of batter and a nut mixture] **1967-68** *DARE* (Qu. H32, *Names . . for . . pastries*) Inf **IL**12, German coffee cake; **WI**58, German coffee cake—"kuchen"; (Qu. H18, . . *Special kinds of bread*) Inf **IL**3, German coffee cake.

German duck n

=gadwall.

1844 DeKay *Zool. NY* 2.343, *Gadwall. . .* In New-Jersey, it is called the . . *German Duck.* **1844** Giraud *Birds Long Is.* 306 **seNY,** At Egg Harbor a few are seen almost every spring and autumn, and are there known by the name of . . "German Duck." **1888** Trumbull *Names of Birds* 24, *Gadwall. . . German Duck* at Egg Harbor. I have made numerous inquiries [for this name] among the Jersey coast duckers, but have found no one who remembered having heard [it].

German favor n

A small gift given at a **German 2.**

1931-33 *LANE Worksheets* **nwCT,** *German favor. . .* Gift presented to each guest at a dance; favors always called German favors.

German finch n

=evening grosbeak.

1957 *AmSp* 32.180, *German finch* . . the evening grosbeak at Portland, Oregon, since this unfamiliar species, when noticed at all, was deemed one of the importations of the bird cranks.

German fried potatoes n pl Also *German frieds, ~ fries* **chiefly Nth, N Midl, West** See Map Cf **American fried potatoes, Dutch fried potatoes**

Sliced potatoes, either raw or cooked, fried in a skillet.

1950 *WELS* 1 Inf, **ceWI,** German fries. **1960** Bailey *Resp. to PADS* 20 **KS,** German fries: large pieces. **1965-70** *DARE* (Qu. H47, *Kinds of fried potatoes*) 54 Infs, **chiefly Nth, N Midl, West,** German fried; **VA**33, German fried potatoes; **NJ**64, German frieds; **NY**1, 45, 123, **OH**98, German fries; (Qu. H49, *Dishes made by boiling potatoes with other foods*) Inf **AR**55, German fried potatoes. **1988** *DARE* File **WI,** German fried potatoes are raw potatoes which are sliced and then fried, whereas American fried potatoes are boiled first.

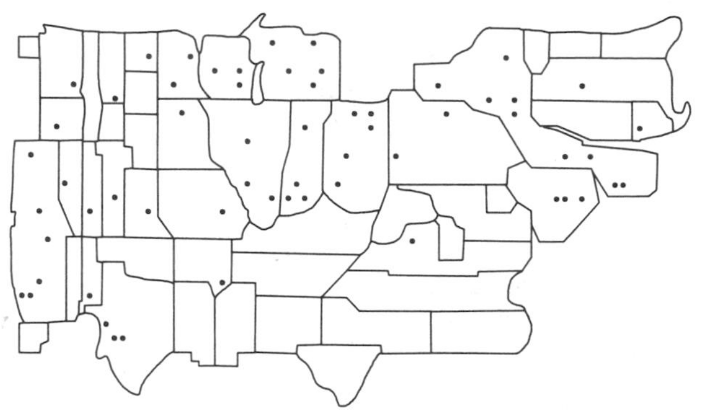

•German fried potatoes + varr (Qq. H47, H49)

German fries See **German fried potatoes**

German goiter n *joc* Cf **Milwaukee goiter**

An oversized belly, esp one resulting from drinking; also one having such a belly.

1935 Pollock *Underworld Speaks* np, *German goitre* . . a beer drinker with a big belly. **1942** Berrey-Van den Bark *Amer. Slang* 121.7, *German or Milwaukee goitre* . . drunkard's paunch. **1950** *WELS* 4 Infs, **WI,** German goiter. **1965-70** *DARE* (Qu. X53a, . . *An oversize stomach*) Infs **IL**114, **OH**32, **UT**7, German goiter; [**PA**148, Goiter;] (Qu. X53b, . . *Oversize stomach . . from drinking*) Inf **WI**60, German goiter.

German goose n

A **loon** (here: *Gavia immer*).

1956 *AmSp* 30.181, German goose. Common loon. Pa. **1957** *AmSp* 32.182, *German goose* (common loon, Pa.) indicates an unusual kind of goose, and very properly so, the bird being no goose at all.

German hornet See **German bee**

German hot potato salad See **German potato salad**

German ivy n [See quot 1868]

A **ragwort** (here: *Senecio mikanioides*) naturalized in California.

1864 (1873) Webster *Amer. Dict.* 721/3, *German ivy,* a creeping plant, with smooth, succulent stems, and fleshy, light-green leaves; a species of groundsel or *Senecio.* **1868** (1870) Gray *Field Botany* 194, *S[enecio] scandens,* cult. as house plant under the name of *German Ivy,* but is from Cape of Good Hope, and resembles Ivy only in the leaves. **1925** Jepson *Manual Plants CA* 1155, *German Ivy.* Stems twining and thus climbing over shrubs and trees to a height of 5 to 20 ft.; leaves ivy-like. **1959** Munz–Keck *CA Flora* 1252. **1961** Thomas *Flora Santa Cruz* 374 **cwCA,** German Ivy. . . In moist areas along streams or on shaded slopes. **1976** Bailey–Bailey *Hortus Third* 1036, *German ivy. . .* Tall-twining per[ennial]. . . naturalized in . . Calif.

German potato salad n Also *German hot potato salad, German style potato salad* **chiefly Gt Lakes, N Cent, esp WI** See Map

A dish consisting primarily of cooked sliced potatoes, bacon, onion, and a vinegar dressing, usu served hot.

1940 Brown *Amer. Cooks* 650 **ND,** *German Hot Potato Salad* Add salt, pepper, and pork drippings (bacon drippings are very good) and a small amount of water to 1 quart sliced raw potatoes. Stew until potatoes are tender. . . pour sweetened vinegar over all. **1955** (1956) Clark *Best Cookery Middle W.* 51 **MO,** Mrs. Fred Gunby's Hot German Potato Salad. **1965–70** *DARE* (Qu. H65) 10 Infs, **esp Gt Lakes, N Cent,** German potato salad; **MN**42, German potato salad—a hot potato salad, lots of vinegar; **WI**11, 20, German style potato salad; **WI**13, German style potato salad—hot, with bacon in; [**IL**82, **IN**3, **NY**194, **PA**18, Hot potato salad (German);] (Qu. H45) Inf **NY**194, Hot German potato salad—cold boiled potatoes, lots of cabbage, covered with sauce made from lean pork, vinegar, and salt; (Qu. H47) Inf **WI**49, German potato salad—with bacon; (Qu. H49) Infs **IL**91, **MN**14, German potato salad; (Qu. HH30) Infs **MO**14, **WI**28, German potato salad.

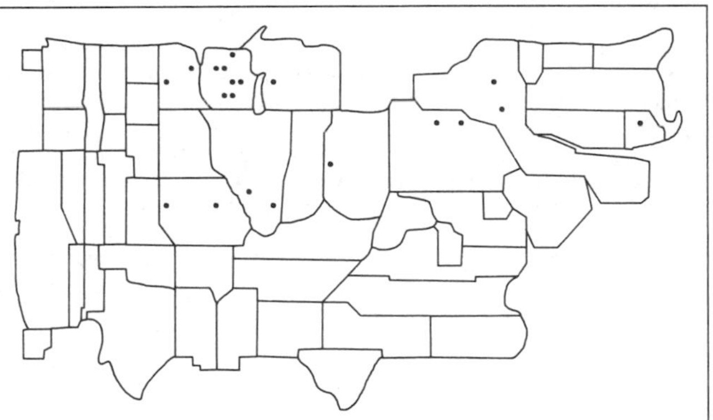

•German potato salad + varr (Qq. H65, H45, H47, H49, HH30)

German rampion n

An **evening primrose a** (here: *Oenothera biennis*).

1939 Medsger *Edible Wild Plants* 199, Oenothera biennis. The Evening Primrose is native. . . Formerly cultivated . . for its edible roots. . . it was recommended to American gardeners under the name of German Rampion. **1959** Carleton *Index Herb. Plants* 51, *German rampion:* Oenothera biennis. **1976** Bailey–Bailey *Hortus Third* 780, *German rampion. . .* E[astern] N[orth] Amer[ica]. Roots may be eaten as a vegetable, and the shoots in salads.

German snipe n

=**dowitcher.** Note: This name is freq cited in later sources, but all instances appear to be based directly or indirectly on this quot; there is no evidence that the bird was actually called *deutscher* or *duitsch* as some later sources allege, again appar on the basis of this quot.

1888 Trumbull *Names of Birds* 161, These names Dowitch and Dowitcher meant originally that this was the Dutch, or German, snipe *(Duitsch, Deutscher),* and were probably employed to distinguish [it] . . particularly from the *"English"* snipe. . . Colonel J. H. Powel, of Newport, R.I., writes (1885) of hearing it called *German snipe* on Long Island "some twenty-five years ago."

German sock n

A thick woolen sock.

1902 (1969) Sears *Catalogue* 970, 40 cents for German Socks. The heaviest made to Wear Inside of Boots. **1911** in 1914 Stewart *Letters* 126 **WY,** They never travel without their German socks. They are great thick things to wear on the outside of their shoes. **1916** Kephart *Camping & Woodcraft* 1.161, Dress the feet with soft woolen socks, and over these draw a pair of long, thick "German socks" that strap at the top. **1964** Jackman–Long *OR Desert* 132 **OR,** 'German socks' aren't sold much anymore in Oregon. These were heavy wool, about like felt. Worn with thin socks inside, and some heavy rubbers over the German socks, they were fine for cold winter weather. **1969** Sorden *Lumberjack Lingo* 47 **NEng, Gt Lakes,** *German socks*—Warm woolen lumberjack socks.

German sparrow n

A **starling** (here: *Sturnus vulgaris*).

1950 *WELS* 1 Inf, **ceWI,** German sparrow—a starling.

German style potato salad See **German potato salad**

German trout See **German brown trout**

German weed n

=**galinsoga.**

1967 Borland *Hill Country* 182 **nwCT,** Most of the weeds in the garden, though, are simply weeds . . galinsoga or German weed, purslane, . . and quack grass! *Ibid* 254, The German weed, as we call it, . . is a pest if there ever was one.

German whippoorwill n Cf **Dutch whippoorwill**

=**chuck-will's-widow.**

1957 *AmSp* 32.182, For the chuck-will's-widow, *German whippoorwill* (Tenn.)

German woodpecker n Cf **flag bird**

=**red-headed woodpecker.**

1957 *AmSp* 32.182, *German woodpecker* (redheaded woodpecker, Texas) refers to the bird's showing the colors—red, white, and black—of the flag of the former German Empire.

Germany n Also *three feet off to Germany, three steps to* ~

A children's sidewalk game; see quot.

1975 Ferretti *Gt. Amer. Book Sidewalk Games* 202, Another version [of Red Rover] has the two teams but no middleman. . . This second version, the most common both in this country and in Great Britain, is called *Germany* in some cities. . . In addition, there is *Three Steps to Germany,* also called *Three Feet off to Germany,* which is essentially a Red Rover game.

Germany carp See **German carp**

gerrymander See **galamander**

gert See **girt**

gesundheit intj Pronc-spp *kasunti, sundheit* [Ger, literally "health"] **widespread, but chiefly Nth, N Midl, West** See Map Cf **scat**

Used as an expression of good will toward one who has sneezed.

[**1911** *Century Dict. Suppl., Zur gesundheit* . . a good wish addressed by Germans to one who has just sneezed.] **1914** *Everybody's Mag.* 31.484 **NYC,** "Saved your life," he murmured mechanically, as one suffixes "Gesundheit" to a sneeze. **1934** Stone *Studien* 32, The word *Gesundheit!* ist [sic] known however in another connection in America. Most children learn that it will be said to them when they sneeze. It is usually said in this connection only to children. **1942** Nash *Good Intentions* 124, Mr. Weaver said "A cashew," and the man said "Gesundheit." **1948** *AmSp* 23.108 [German language influences in Illinois], *Gesundheit.* **1950** *WELS (What people say to somebody when he sneezes)* 33 Infs, **WI,** *Gesundheit.* **1952** TN Folk Lore Soc. *Bulletin* 18.83, An interesting variation [of *gesundheit*] showing the adaptation and Americanization of the German word is found in Mississippi. There, the term used is "kasunti." **1965–70** *DARE* (Qu. NN18) 467 Infs, **widespread, but chiefly Nth, N Midl, West,** Gesundheit; **PA**142, **TX**88, Sundheit; **PA**28, Gesundheit, das geht in an old hund's leib; **DC**8, ['gʌn,zaɪt].

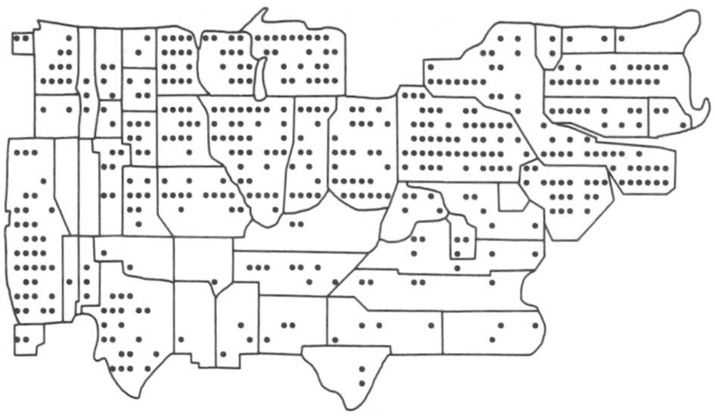

•gesundheit + varr (Qu. NN18)

Christensen *Afro-Amer. Folk Lore* 18, I gots no use for dem. *Ibid* 34, At lars' 'e see 'e gots for go. **1908** *S. Atl. Qrly.* 7.335 **sSC coast** [Gullah], Yo' gawt de fryin'-pan; me gawt de fush. **1922** Gonzales *Black Border* 248 **sSC, GA coasts** [Gullah], I gots to git anodduh lady. **1939** Aurand *Quaint Idioms* 30 [PaGer], You *gotta watch out.* **1942** Faulkner *Go Down* 136 **MS** [Black], We gots a jug in de bushes. **1968** *DARE* FW Addit **NY96**, *Gotta go in and see Polly Jones*—joking way of saying, "I have to go to the bathroom." **1986** *DARE* File **OK,** She gots one. **1986** Pederson *LAGS Concordance,* 1 inf, **swGA,** They gots hall steps inside; 1 inf, **seLA,** Every pond I've got gots a spring in it.

b as quasi-infin, equivalent to *have,* in neg and interrog constrr with aux *do.*

1938 Rawlings *Yearling* 24 **FL,** Do we got to wait for Pa to eat breakfast? **1965** *DARE* File **csWI,** "I don't got to do that!" "I don't got any." [Used by] younger people; colloquial. **1982** *Barrick Coll.* **csPA,** Got my pocketbook? **1986** Pederson *LAGS Concordance* **Gulf Region,** 1 inf, He don't got no church; 1 inf, You don't got to have the whole thing; 1 inf, We don't got; 2 infs, What time do you got? **1986** *DARE* File **OK,** Do you got it? I don't got it.

2 See quot.

1970 *AmSp* 45.234 [Hawaiian creole], *Get* for standard *have got: My boyfriend get mumps* 'My boyfriend has got the mumps.'

C Tr senses.

1 To acquire by study. [*OED* 1582 →] *old-fash*

1899 (1912) Green *VA Folk-Speech* 194, *Get. . .* When children prepare their lessons and get them ready for recitation [they] are said to *get their lessons.* **1929** Suckow *Cora* 20 **IA,** Pretty soon school'll begin, and then you won't let me stay with Cora because you'll think I've got lessons to get. **1966** *DARE* (Qu. JJ8) Inf **FL33,** Get your lessons.

2 also with *up:* To prepare, put together (food or a meal). **widespread, but less freq S Atl, Gulf States** See Map Cf **fix** v **B1e, make** v

1870 *Nation* 28 July 56/2, "It's time to get piece" was the way of saying it was time to prepare luncheon. **1871** in 1983 *PADS* 70.35 **ce,sePA,** I got home at four o'clock and got my supper to myself. **1903** (1965) Adams *Log Cowboy* 280 **NM,** There was a little woman at the ranch . . and I was helping her get up dinner. **1939** *Hall Coll.* **wNC,** *Get up* (a meal). . . To prepare (a meal). . . We come back to camp an' got up dinner an' lay down and slept that evenin'. **1941** *LANE* Map 310, In the phrase (I am going to) make some coffee, the following verb [is] recorded. . . *Get,* either 'make' (in the general sense) or 'fetch.' [16 infs, chiefly **sNEng**] **c1960** *Wilson Coll.* **csKY,** *Get. . .* To prepare, as a meal. **1965–70** *DARE* (Qu. H7, . . *To prepare a meal . . "I have to go and ______ supper."*) 349 Infs, **widespread, but less freq S Atl, Gulf States,** Get; **MO**15, 16, Git; **IN**70, Get the; **MA**65, Get up. **1971** Bright *Word Geog. CA & NV* 180, I'm going to get supper.

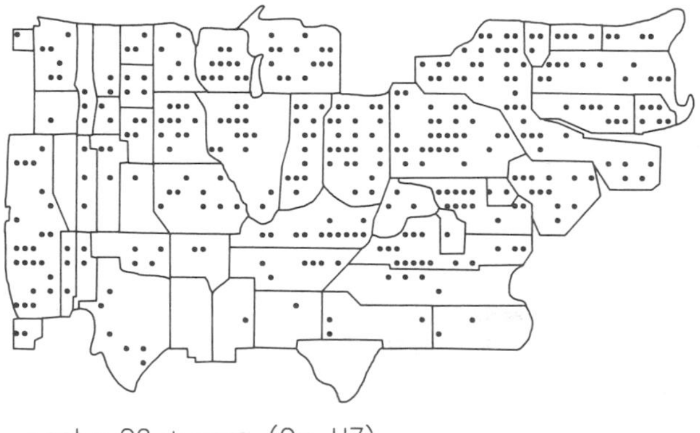

•get v C2 + varr (Qu. H7)

3 To hunt and kill (a game animal); to pursue and usu kill (a person).

1853 P. Paxton *Yankee in Texas* 118 *(DA),* [A Texan] does not kill his game, he *saves* or *gets it,* or *makes it come.* **1891** *Outing* Dec 246/2, Rum had so far "got him dead." **1914** *DN* 4.163 **Pacific NW, ID, MT, WY,** *Get. . .* To kill, esp in revenge. **1918** *DN* 5.24 **NW,** *To get. . .* "To do" or to revenge oneself on someone. "I've been laying for him for years; to-day I got him." General. **1922** Rollins *Cowboy* 52, Billy the kid, at twenty-three years of age, had committed twenty-three murders, and had made the question of his extermination a political issue in New

get v

A Forms.

1 pres (exc 3rd pers sg indic): usu *get;* infreq *gets;* pronc-spp *gid, git(s).*

1791 in 1956 Eliason *Tarheel Talk* 311 **cnNC,** *Get* . . git. **1798** (1922) Manning *Key of Libberty* 14 **NEng,** Therefore no person can posess property without labouring, unless he git it by force or craft. **1843** (1916) Hall *New Purchase* 433 **IN,** Keep rite even on strate ahead till you gits to Rock-Ford. **1872** [see **D1a** below]. **1890** *DN* 1.68 **KY,** *Git:* for *get.* [*DN* Ed: Also in New England.] Frequently used. "Git my hat." **1917** *DN* 4.393 **neOH,** *Git, v. i.* There is a tendency to specialize this form. People who would ordinarily use *get* might say, "You git!" **1927** Shewmake *Engl. Pronc. VA* 18, Get (git). This historical pronunciation should be pondered by all who are tempted to assign every slipshod pronunciation to negro influence. **1929** (1954) Faulkner *Sound & Fury* 141 **MS,** Hit's de folks dat says de high watter cant git dis fur dat comes floatin out on de ridge-pole, too. **1935** Sandoz *Jules* 18 **wNE,** "Can't git a glim of the light from down here fur as you can smell a lily in a nest of skunks," the cook explained. **1946** *AmSp* 21.97 **sIL,** *Git,* get. **c1960** *Wilson Coll.* **csKY,** Get as /gɪt/ is almost regularly used. **1965–70** *DARE* (Qu. J8) 11 Infs, **esp Sth,** Git 'im (*or* 'em); **LA**44, **NC**44, Git; **MO**13, Git him; (Qu. A19) Inf **MO**39, Gid up 'n' go. **1965–70** [see **D1a** below]. **1971** Metcalf *Riverside Engl.* 29 **sCA,** We seem to encounter increasing influence of Midlands and Southern pronunciations from the East [in the] . . spread of *git* for *get.*

2 pres 3rd pers sg indic: usu *gets;* also pronc-sp *gits.*

1843 (1916) Hall *New Purchase* 228 **IN,** He gits another chap to help. **1901** Harben *Westerfelt* 6 **nGA,** When Liz gits 'er head set she cuts a wide swathe. **1969** *DARE* (Qu. KK27, . . *"For his age, he's ______."*) Inf **MO**32, Really gits around.

3 past: usu *got;* rarely *git(ted), gotten;* pronc-sp *gut.*

1843 (1916) Hall *New Purchase* 372 **IN,** I never rub'd my back agin a collige, nor git no sheepskin. **1848** Lowell *Biglow* 122 **'Upcountry' MA,** Poppiler enthusiasm gut so almighty pressin'. **1884** Smith *Bill Arp's Scrap Book* 15 **nwGA,** When he gotten over it he laughed sorter weakly. **1922** Gonzales *Black Border* 51 **sSC, GA coasts** [Gullah], Maussuh ride de train. 'E come. 'E git off W'ite Hall deepo, 'e git 'pun 'e hawss. **1957** in 1958 Brewer *Dog Ghosts* 35 **TX** [Black], She was sinkin' mo' an' mo' evuhday an' de onlies' thing dat gitted her back on her feet was dat one day . . Sistuh Susie Jones . . comed ovuh to see her.

4 past pple: usu *got, gotten;* also *git;* pronc-sp *gut.*

1848 Lowell *Biglow* 138 **'Upcountry' MA,** He could read a Bible he 'd gut. [**1893** *DN* 1.277 **wCT,** [Pres] git—[past and past pple] got (pron. [gɔt], never [gʌt]).] **1922** Gonzales *Black Border* 273 **sSC, GA coasts** [Gullah], *Stepney* would'uh git dis po' ole body.

B Syntax.

1 Past pple *got* used:

a as pres indic, equivalent to *has/have got, has/have;* also, *chiefly among Black speakers, gots;* pronc-sp *gawt;* in phr *got to* freq pronc-sp *gotta.* [By ellipsis of *has/have;* the *-s* in *gots* is appar the *-s* of the std 3rd pers sg indic, extended, as often in non-std speech, to other pres indic forms.]

1849 *Knickerbocker* 34.12 **NY,** They got no principles. They got no platform to stand onto. **1890** *DN* 1.73 **NEng,** Observe the common New England phrase, "I got it" = I have it; of course shortened from "I've got it." "I have it" is hardly popular; it sounds literary. **1892** (1969)

Mexico. Incidentally, the sheriff, elected to "get" him, loaded a weapon and "got" him. **1924** Raine *Land of Saddle-Bags* 142 **Appalachians,** Gathered around your coffin, your family and kinsfolk reason that his next move will be to kill your brother, so they decide to "get" him before he shoots any more of the family. **1937** *Hall Coll.* **wNC,** *Get*. . . To kill (an animal). "First the panther came across, and later the bear. I got both of 'em."

D Intr senses.

1a To leave, depart; to clear out—often used in imper.

1872 Schele de Vere *Americanisms* 604, Git, and git out, is the uniform pronunciation of *get* among the people of the West. In California, near the town of Henroost Camp, is another settlement called *Git up and Git.* **1899** Garland *Boy Life* 141 **nwIA,** Rance let him up. "Now you let us alone," he said, "and git out o'here." **1917** [see **A1** above]. **1933** Rawlings *South Moon* 144 **FL,** Syl Jacklin asked, "How long you studyin' to give him to git?" **1942** *AmSp* 17.71 **Rocky Mts** (as of 1867), 'You git,' is the most emphatic notice that can be given to any luckless chap to leave the room or ranch, or to escape a revolver. **1953** *PADS* 19.11 **sAppalachians,** No, I can't stay no longer; I've got to git. **1954** *Harder Coll.* **cwTN,** *Git* . . go away, leave from where one is. "Got to git." **1957** Beck *Folkl. ME* 87, Usually when someone tells a story that tops the others one man will remark, "Eah, well I'd best be gittin' on." **1965–70** *DARE* (Qu. NN22c, *Expressions used to drive away a dog*) 279 Infs, **widespread,** Git; **MO**19, 35, Gid ouda there(, you son of a goat); (Qu. NN22b, *Expressions used to drive away children*) 80 Infs, **scattered,** Git; **MO**19, Gid out; (Qu. NN22a, *Expressions used to drive away . . flies*) 21 Infs, **scattered,** Git; 8 Infs, Get; **MO**26, Gid ouda here; (Qu. NN22d, *Expressions used to drive away animals other than dogs*) 21 Infs, **scattered,** Git; 6 Infs, Get; (Qu. Y20, *To run fast*) 16 Infs, **chiefly Sth,** Git; **NY**219, 232, **OH**46, **OK**15, **SC**21, **VA**109, Get; (Qu. Y18, *To leave in a hurry*) 13 Infs, **chiefly Sth,** Git; **FL**11, **IN**61, **KS**5, **ME**9, **NJ**69, **OH**70, **VA**42, Get; (Qu. Y19, *To begin to go away*) Infs **MI**120, **OH**71, 87, **PA**126, Get; **KS**12, Get for home. [Further exx throughout *DS*] **1966** *DARE* Tape **MI**29, When the weather got stormy, they really had to get for home.

b spec: See quot. Cf **gesundheit, scat**

1909 *DN* 3.403 **nwAR,** *Git!* . . Addressed to the Devil or his angels, who try to creep into the body of the person sneezing.

2 =**get up** v phr **1.**

1864 *Harper's New Mth. Mag.* 29.565/2 **neMO,** "George," after belaboring the mules till he was tired, and telling them to "git" till he was hoarse, would lean back in his seat and think. **1965–70** *DARE* (Qu. K36a, . . *To make a horse go faster*) Infs **IL**59, **IN**67, **OH**3, **TX**41, **WI**10, Git.

3 with following noun: To become, approach. [Cf Brit usage *He's getting an old man* = He's becoming an old man]

1908 Fox *Lonesome Pine* 100 **KY,** The Lord's been on my side an' I gits a better Christian every year. **1967–69** *DARE* (Qu. A1, *What do you call the time in the early morning before the sun comes into sight?*) Inf **KY**31, Getting daylight; (Qu. H58, *Milk that's just beginning to become sour is* ______) Inf **TN**1, Getting clabber; (Qu. L4b, *What do you call the time early in the morning and at night when you have to feed livestock, clean stalls, and so on? A person might say, "I've got to go now, it's* ______*."*) Inf **KY**43, Getting daylight. **1986** Pederson *LAGS Concordance,* 1 inf, **neFL,** After I got [=became] a young woman.

get n

1 The profit or "take" of an endeavor. [*OED get* sb.[1] 1 "What is got; gain, booty, earnings. *Obs.* exc. *dial.*"]

1942 Berrey-Van den Bark *Amer. Slang* 470.1, *Booty* . . get, goods, grab. **1960** Wentworth-Flexner *Slang* 212, *Get*. . . Profit; the "gate." **1975** Gould *ME Lingo* 108, *Get*—The catch or take of a fishing vessel; hence, the degree of success attending any venture or effort: "He ran for office and had a fair get, but he lost."

2 Offspring; a child, children. [*OED get* sub.[1] 2. a "Now only of animals"; 2. b "*Sc.* and *north.* In contemptuous use = brat"; *OEDS get* sb.[1] 2. b "Also *spec.* a bastard, hence as a general term of abuse"]

1936 Morehouse *Rain on Just* 109 **NC,** And where those twins? . . What breed of man your man there to let you treat his get so careless? **1972** (1974) Wilson *Playboy's Words* 122, *Get*—One's children, in rural and deliberately offensive slang: "I want you and your get off this land by sundown."

3 pronc-sp *git:* A distance to be traveled. Cf *fur piece* (at **far piece**)

1934 *Hanley Disks* **swNH,** Two looks and a long sight and a smart git. [*DARE* Ed: Inf says this was Southern Whites' answer during the Civil War to Northerners' question of "how fur" it was to some place.]

4 =**get-up** n **1.**

1948 Manfred *Chokecherry* 56 **nwIA,** An' come back showin' me you still got some git an' gumption t'yuh besides all that fop readin' an' educatin' you're doin' to yerself. **1967–68** *DARE* (Qu. HH27b, *Of a very able and energetic person who gets things done you might say, "He's got lots of* ______*."*) Inf **WI**27, Git; (Qu. KK28) Inf **OH**1, Full of git.

get about v phr **esp Sth, S Midl**

To move around; to move in a conspicuous way; to gad about.

1965–70 *DARE* (Qu. Y23, . . *To . . get yourself in motion: "I was so stiff I could hardly* ______*."*) Infs **LA**8, **MO**29, **NC**62, **TX**32, 37, **VA**74, Get about; (Qu. Y22, *To move around in a way to make people take notice of you: "Look at him* ______*."*) Infs **AR**55, **SC**58, Get about; (Qu. Y29b, . . *About a man who doesn't stay home much: "He's always* ______*."*) Inf **TX**26, Getting about. **1986** Pederson *LAGS Concordance,* 1 inf, **ceTX,** Get about—get around; 1 inf, **nwGA,** Able to get about; 1 inf, **csGA,** Can't hardly get about.

get across See **get over**

get a fall out of See **fall** n **6**

get a glow on See **glow**

get a hump, get a hump on (oneself) See **hump** n **5**

get all over one v phr

To irritate, unnerve (one).

1966–67 *DARE* (Qu. GG13a, *When something keeps bothering a person and makes him nervous, he may say, "It* ______ *me."*) Inf **GA**6, Gets all over me; (Qu. II29b, *Or you might try to explain the unpleasant effect that person has on you: "He just* ______*."*) Inf **TX**29, Gets all over me.

get-along n Also *get-away joc* Cf **hitch** n[1] **2**

The leg; the hip.

1941 *AmSp* 16.22 **swIN,** *Get-alongs.* Legs. 'Get up on your get-alongs.' **1949** *PADS* 11.21 **CO,** *Git-along*. . . Leg. Used only in the expression "I've got a hitch in my git-along." **1965–70** *DARE* (Qu. BB1, . . *He steps more heavily on one foot than the other*) Infs **CA**59, **NE**11, [Has] a hitch in his get-along; (Qu. BB3b) Inf **WA**26, Hitch in your get-away; (Qu. BB28) Inf **TX**79, Hitch in the get-along. **1987** *DARE* File **cwCA,** My father, who was born and raised in Idaho, says he has a hitch in his get-along if his leg or hip is stiff, making it difficult to walk.

get along with v phr

To be employed by.

1958 McCulloch *Woods Words* 90 **Pacific NW,** How are chances to get along with you?—How's chances for a job?

get an edge on See **edge B2**

get asleep See **get awake**

get awake v phr [Cf Ger *wach werden* to wake up, to become, get awake] **chiefly PA** See Map *among PaGer speakers* Cf **get grown**

To wake up; hence, by analogy, *get asleep* to fall asleep.

1862 (1922) Jackson *Col.'s Diary* 67 **PA,** I had merely got asleep and some of the company had not got asleep at all. **1866** in 1983 *PADS*

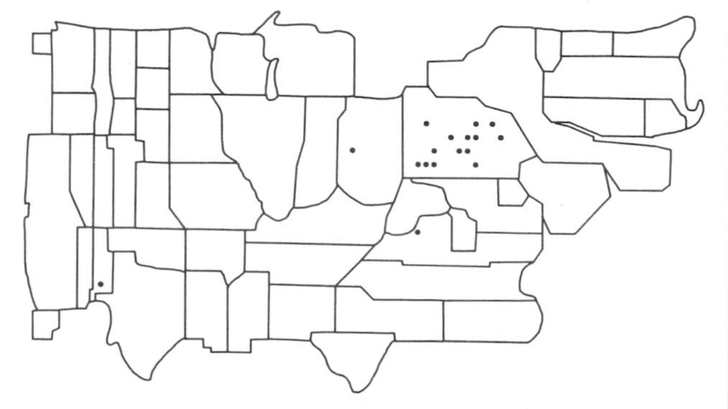

•get awake + varr (Qq. X42, 0032b, JJ26)

70,35 **ce,sePA,** *Get awake*. . . We got awake about one & two. **1934** *Language* 10.3 **PA,** *Get awake* is always used for *wake up;* cf. German *wach werden.* **1935** *AmSp* 10.167 **PA,** Such expressions as the following seem quite 'Dutchy' to an outsider, but to the great mass of people of the region they are the accepted currency of daily speech. . . "I stood up late this morning, though I usually get awake about five o'clock." **1953** Atwood *Survey of Verb Forms* fig 20 *(Woke up)* 29 infs, **chiefly PA,** Got awake. **1965–70** *DARE* (Qu. X42, *What other way do you have to say "I stopped sleeping at six o'clock."*) 12 Infs, **chiefly PA,** Got awake; (Qu. OO32b, *If a person can't sleep steadily but keeps on waking, he might say, "Every night this week I've _____ [several times]."*) Infs **PA**14, 44, 154, 175, 188, Got awake; **OH**93, **PA**72, 202, Gotten awake; **NM**11, I got awake; [**PA**130, Gotten awoke]; (Qu. JJ26) **PA**135, Get awake. **1966** Dakin *Dial. Vocab. Ohio R. Valley* 2.528, The phrase *got awake* . . is also rarely used only in Ohio. It appears in Tuscawaras [sic] County and again west of the Scioto in Champaign County. **1987** *NADS Letters* **cOK,** The expression *got awake* is supposed to be of Pennsylvania German origin, but I have met one man here whose grandmother was born in Germany who says *got awake.*

get away v phr See **get off** v phr **1**

get-away n See **get-along**

get away with v phr

1 To get the advantage of; to overcome.

1887 Kirkland *Zury* 537 **IL,** *Get away with.* To vanquish, conquer, excel, defeat, surpass, consume. **1893** *KS Univ. Qrly.* 1.139, *Get away with:* to overcome . . as 'He got away with me.' **1908** *DN* 3.314 **eAL, wGA,** *Get away with*. . . To get the advantage of, play a joke on, fool. "You can't get away with me." **1909** *DN* 3.352 **eAL, wGA,** You can't beat me playing dominoes. It's jest your nigger-luck that gets away with me.

2 To embarrass, upset, discomfit. **S Midl, Sth** Cf **get off with**

1905 *DN* 3.81 **nwAR,** *Get away with*. . . To humiliate. "That got away with him." Common. **1911** (1916) Porter *Harvester* 469 **IN,** "My! wouldn't that get away with some of my foxy neighbours," she said. "Me to have a 'phone like they do." **1952** Brown *NC Folkl.* 1.544 **c,eNC,** *Get away with*. . . To embarrass. **1956** McAtee *Some Dialect NC* 18, *Get away with:* . . embarrass. **c1960** *Wilson Coll.* **csKY,** *Get away with*. . . Embarrass. "I sure got away with her by telling about her new beau." **1965** *DARE* FW Addit **MS,** *Got away with him* . . embarrassed or caused mild discomfiture. **1965–70** *DARE* (Qu. GG9, *To . . embarrass somebody*) Infs **AL**41, **TN**26, Get away with; (Qu. GG22b, *When you have come to the end of your patience, you might say, "Well, that certainly _____."*) Inf **MO**23, Did get away with me. **c1970** *Halpert Coll.* **wKY,** *Get away with*. . . It got away with me so bad: = embarrassed.

get behind v phr Also *get in* (or *down, right*) *behind* **chiefly Sth, S Midl, esp S Atl** See Map

To put pressure on; to bring influence to bear on.

1896 *DN* 1.417 **FL,** *Get in behind:* follow up closely; question closely; punish. "The judge got in behind him and he acknowledged stealing." "If he does that again, I'll get in behind him." **1909** *DN* 3.397 **nwAR,** *Get in behind.* **1965–70** *DARE* (Qu. Y6, . . *To put pressure on somebody to do something he ought to have done but hasn't*) 13 Infs, **chiefly Mid and S Atl,** Get behind him; **GA**89, **SC**2, 3, 21, Get in behind him; **NC**86, Get down behind him; **SC**24, Get in behind; **KY**19, Get right behind him.

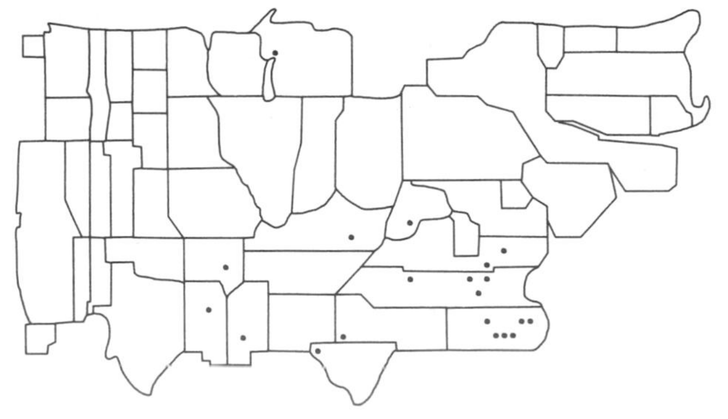

•get behind + varr (Qu. Y6)

get beyond one's business v phr

1884 *Anglia* 7.264 **Sth** [Black], To git beyant yo' biznis = to be above yourself.

get britches on v phr

1908 *DN* 3.314 **eAL, wGA,** *Get britches on*. . . In chess or checkers, to move a piece so as to attack two pieces at once so that both of them cannot escape.

get by v phr

=**get away with 2.**

1989 *DARE* File **eNC** (as of c1900), When Bill heard what they said about him, it certainly got by him.

get-by n

A sufficiency.

1978 *Natl. Geogr. Mag.* Mar 420 **AR,** "It [=his livelihood] ain't much," he says, "but it's a git by."

get country v phr

1966 *DARE* (Qu. Y18, *To leave in a hurry: "Before they find this out, we'd better _____!"*) Inf **AR**40, Get country.

get down v phr

1 To descend; spec: see below. [Prob reinforced in some areas by Fr *descendre;* but cf *OED get* v. 57. a]

a To dismount from a horse or step out of a vehicle—used in var phrr as an invitation to visit. **esp Sth, S Midl**

1931 *PMLA* 46.1307 **Appalachians,** Git down an' stay all night with us, stranger. **1966–68** *DARE* (Qu. II15, *When somebody is passing by and you want him . . to stop and talk a while*) Infs **GA**30, **LA**32, Get down and come in; **VA**5, Get down and rest your saddle; **MT**5, Get down and set awhile; **NM**4, Ranchers used to say, "Oh say, get down, come on in, stay all night." They still say "get down," even when one comes in a car. **1968** *DARE* FW Addit **LA**32, The Inf says that the expression *get down and come in* dates from the days when people rode horses, and the adverb (down) was carried over from one form of transportation where it was appropriate (get down from a horse) to another where it was not (get down from a car). Her observation that it is used more often by French speakers correlates favorably with Prof. Atwood's surmise that "get down" could be a literal translation of French *descendre.* **1969** *DARE* Tape **KY**16, He . . rid up and she knowed him, said, "Get down, preacher, and come in." **1983** *Reinecke Coll.* **LA,** *Get down* . . leave your vehicle and enter a house or property; analogous use "descendre" in La. French. **1986** Pederson *LAGS Concordance,* 1 inf, **swLA,** Get down and come on in—formerly common.

b To step off a public conveyance. **esp LA**

1962 Atwood *Vocab. TX* 76, The expression *want to get down* [=get off a bus] is very scattered in Texas, but in rural southern Louisiana becomes quite regular. **1968** *DARE* (Qu. JJ31a, *What you'd say to a bus driver: "Please stop at the next corner—I want _____."*) Inf **LA**35, To get down. **1969** *DARE* FW Addit **wNY,** I've heard "to get down" [from a bus] in Buffalo. **1976** Dillard *Amer. Talk* 52, The Louisiana resident *gets down* (from the French *descendre*) *from* rather than *off* a bus or river boat. **1986** Pederson *LAGS Concordance,* 1 inf, **seLA,** I want to get down; 1 inf, **New Orleans LA,** Where I want to get down.

2 also with *on, with;* rarely *get down to the ground:* To give one's attention to (something); to begin to do something; to do something vigorously or well; hence n *get-down* the beginning of something. *esp freq among Black speakers*

1914 *DN* 4.107 **KS,** *Get down*. . . To settle oneself (to a task). "Get down and dig." **1965–70** *DARE* (Qu. II9, *If several people have to contribute in order to pay for something, you say, "Let's all _____."*) Inf **NY**238, Let's get down; (Qu. JJ36, *To work out a plan . . "Mary knows more about that, you and she can _____ together."*) Inf **NY**238, Get down on [it]. **1971** Roberts *Third Ear* np [Black], *Get down* . . to do something in a bigger way; to put the intensity of "soul" into dance movements; e.g. He got down last night at the party. **1971** Landy *Underground Dict.* 87 [Black], *Get down with it*. . . Start to do something; be serious about doing something. **1976** *Harper's Weekly* 65.18 **TN** [Black], When you want something to begin, just say, "Let's get on with the get down." **1977** Smitherman *Talkin* 55, From doctor to ditchdigger, all classes and manner of black folk done always got down on the same soulful jams and latest steps. *Ibid* 72, Black vocabulary cuts across generational, sexual, educational, occupational lines. . . Musicians and dancers hope to achieve a spirit-catharsis by *gittin down.* *Ibid* 247, To "get down" is to do something vigorously, such as dance, sing, work, talk, or do exercises like these. . . I. Get Down on *Pronuncia-*

tion. . . II. Get Down on *be/non-be.* **1980** Folb *Runnin' Down* 239 **Los Angeles CA** [Black], *Get down, get down to the ground* 1. Do something exceptionally well. 2. Engage in something with great zest. 3. Initiate some activity. 4. Conduct serious business. *Ibid, Get down with* 1. Enjoy. 2. Get involved with.

3 To fight. *among Black speakers*

1971 Landy *Underground Dict.* 87 [Black], Get down. . . Fight . . thump. **1980** Folb *Runnin' Down* 104 **Los Angeles CA** [Black], Come out of your coat and get down! Some of these fight expressions are ritual challenges that have been in the vernacular for years; others are made up on the spot.

4 Of wind: to decrease. Cf **get up** v phr **5**

1965–70 *DARE* (Qu. B13, *When the wind begins to decrease, you say it's* ______) Infs **CT**25, **OK**13, **VA**100, Getting down.

5 =**go down** v phr **2.**

1986 Pederson *LAGS Concordance,* 1 inf, **cMS,** Ready to get down—grandmother said; 1 inf, **nwAL,** Ready to get down—if she's ready to deliver.

6 in phrr *get down sick, get down with:* To fall ill; to come down with (a disease). Cf **come down 2, down sick**

1966–68 *DARE* (Qu. BB44, . . *About a person just starting some sickness—for example, pneumonia: "He* ______ *pneumonia."*) Infs **LA**25, **MS**73, Got down with. **1986** Pederson *LAGS Concordance,* 1 inf, **ceTX,** Get down sick; 1 inf, **nwGA,** She never did get down with it [=catch the flu]. **1988** Lincoln *Avenue* 57 **wNC** (as of c1940) [Black], When Addie got down sick the last time, Nick gave Bonus the money he needed.

get-down n See **get down** v phr **2**

get down behind See **get behind**

get down on See **get down** v phr **2**

get down sick See **get down** v phr **6**

get down to hardpan See **hardpan 2**

get down to the ground See **get down** v phr **2**

get down with v phr

1 See **get down** v phr **6.**

2 See **get down** v phr **2.**

get fair v phr **esp Sth, S Midl**

=**fair off.**

1966–68 *DARE* (Qu. B7, *When clouds begin to decrease, you say it's* ______) Infs **LA**18, **MS**72, Beginning (*or* going) to get fair. **1970** Tarpley *Blinky* 50 **neTX,** *The weather has been bad, but now it is . . getting fair.* [*DARE* Ed: This is one of six responses comprising 13 percent of the total.] **c1970** Pederson *Dial. Surv. Rural GA,* 1 inf, **seGA,** Gettin' fair. **1986** Pederson *LAGS Concordance,* 1 inf, **cGA,** It's beginning to get fair; 1 inf, **csTN,** Gets fair; 1 inf, **nwLA,** Got fair. **1989** *DARE* File **New Orleans LA,** When the sky begins to clear off after a storm, you hear people say that it "gets fair."

get gay See **gay** adj **2**

get-go n Also *git-go* *esp freq among Black speakers*

The start, beginning.

1970 *AmSp* 45.77 **PA** [Black], I was 'spicious of him from the "get-go." **1970** Major *Dict. Afro-Amer. Slang* 58, *Get go (gitgo):* the beginning. **1970** *DARE* (Qu. A23, *To do something at the very first try: "He got the right answer* ______.") Inf **MO**29, From the gitgo. **1979** *DARE* File **Columbia SC** [Black], He was aginst me from the get-go. **1982** *Los Angeles Times* (CA) 25 July sec 1 20/3 **OH,** I thought she was attractive from the git-go. **1984** Wilder *You All Spoken Here* 67 **Sth,** These are hard-core fans who've been with this band since the get-go.

get gone v phr **chiefly Sth, S Midl** See Map

To leave, depart; to disappear.

1906 *DN* 3.137 **nwAR,** *Get gone. . .* To depart. "He hadn't got gone when I came." **1942** (1971) Campbell *Cloud-Walking* 58 **seKY,** Mace was too took back to say ary word and too plumb anxious to get gone from where he never had no business at. **c1960** *Wilson Coll.* **csKY,** Get gone. **1963** Edwards *Gravel* 159 **eTN** (as of 1920s), Davey must have been waiting for some time and he was ready to pay and get gone. **1965–70** *DARE* (Qu. Y18, *To leave in a hurry*) 14 Infs, **chiefly Sth, S Midl,** Get gone; **AR**31, **GA**28, Git gone; (Qu. A19) Inf **SC**32, Get gone; (Qu. Y19) Infs **GA**7, **KY**28, 90, **SC**44, 58, Get gone; (Qu. Y20) Inf **VA**54, Get gone; (Qu. NN22b) Inf **SC**34, Get gone; **GA**28, You all will just have to get gone; **GA**7, **IN**83, **MS**1, **TX**104, Git gone; (Qu. NN22c) Infs **IN**15, **LA**2, **MS**16, **NC**31, **TN**23, **WV**13, Git gone. **1965** *DARE* FW Addit **NC,** After you get gone, I'll write. **1986** Pederson *LAGS Concordance* **Gulf Region,** 1 inf, It got gone—of a strawberry pie; 1 inf, Would throw a stick and say get gone; 1 inf, Get gone—to make him accelerate after starting; 1 inf, Get gone—means "be on my way"; 1 inf, Wait until I get gone; 1 inf, Got gone—of a cat that died or ran away.

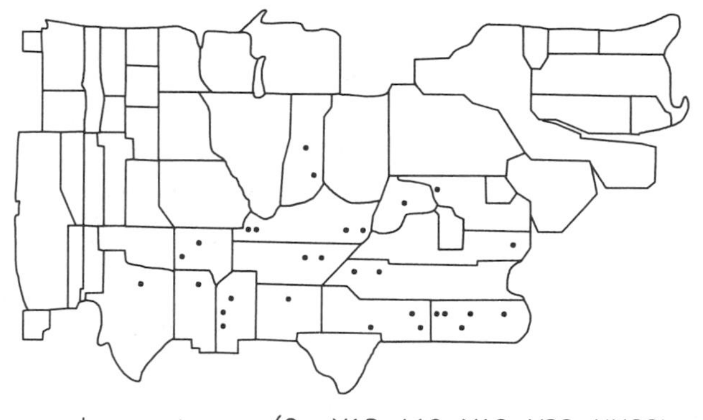

•get gone + varr (Qq. Y18, A19, Y19, Y20, NN22b, NN22c)

get goss See **goss**

get grown v phr Also *get up grown* Cf **get awake, get gone**

To grow (up).

1966 *DARE* Tape **AL**11, When I got grown . . [I] had a house. **1967** *DARE* (Qu. OO23a, *About a child growing: "Billy has to have new clothes—during the summer he* ______.") Inf **PA**57, Got grown. [**1976** Wolfram–Christian *Appalachian Speech* 97, My older sister, she used to have these birfday parties when she got sixteen.] **1986** Pederson *LAGS Concordance* **Gulf Region,** 55 infs, Get (*or* got) grown; 1 inf, Got growed; 1 inf, Get up grown; 1 inf, Got up grown; [1 inf, Got up to grown].

get happy See **happy** adj **1**

get hat v phr Cf **hat up**

1971 Roberts *Third Ear* np [Black], *Get hat!* an imperative urging one to leave; get out! . . *Got hat* . . left hurriedly.

gether See **gather**

get high behind v phr

1 To hurry; to get to work.

1938 *AmSp* 13.4 **seAR,** *'Get high behind'*—(hurry!) **1944** *AmSp* 19.231 **NW** [Shipyard terms], *Get high behind.* Bend over and put your shoulder to the wheel. **1949** *PADS* 11.7 **wTX** (as of c1920), *Get high behind. . .* To proceed with despatch. **1966** *DARE* (Qu. JJ26, *If somebody has been doing poor work or not enough, the boss might say, "If he wants to keep his job he'd better* ______.") Inf **AR**13, Get high behind [laughter]. **1989** *DARE* File **cAR,** *Get high behind* is very common, you hear that *all* the time. It means "get a move on." Mother said that to me every morning, sometimes twice—it depended on my state of sluggishness. I'd be in bed and she'd put her head in the room and tell me I'd better "get high behind."

2 To become impatient; to get angry.

1966 *DARE* (Qu. GG23c, . . *To tell someone to be patient*) Inf **NM**9, Just don't get high behind. **1966** *DARE* FW Addit **OK**51, "She got high behind"—She got angry.

get home See **home E**

get hunk(y) See **hunk** adj **2**

get in behind See **get behind**

get in honey See **honey** n **4**

get into it v phr

To quarrel.

1976 Lynn–Vecsey *Loretta Lynn* 107 **eKY,** Me and Betty Sue are really close, but we can get into it sometimes. She still likes to do opposite things, just to be mean. . . But if I'm around—watch out! We can get into it pretty good.

get it off on See **get off** v phr **3**

get next to v phr

1 To win the favor of; to curry favor with.

1903 *DN* 2.351 **OH,** *Get next to*. . . To get into the good graces of a person. **1942** Berrey–Van den Bark *Amer. Slang* 291.4, *Curry favor; toady* . . get next to. **1967–70** *DARE* (Qu. II20b, *A person who tries . . to gain . . favor*) Infs **AL**30, **IN**76, **MA**71, **NJ**68, **TN**53, Get next to; (Qu. JJ3a, . . *To 'get in good' with the teacher*) Inf **PA**247, Get next to the teacher.

2 To borrow, filch.

1903 *DN* 2.351 **OH,** *Get next to*. . . Borrow. **1908** K. McGaffey *Show-Girl* 28 *(DA)*, Some hussy got next to all my toothpicks and I had to use a hairpin for a liner.

3 To embarrass, discomfit.

1966–70 *DARE* (Qu. GG9, *To suddenly embarrass somebody and throw him off balance: "When they told him what she had said about him, it certainly did ______ him."*) Infs **MS**39, **NC**84, Get next to; (Qu. BB40, *If you're inquiring about somebody acting strangely: "All of a sudden he got up and left. What do you suppose ______ him?"*) Inf **GA**82, Got next to. **1986** Pederson *LAGS Concordance*, 1 inf, **neFL,** Get next to him—annoy him; 1 inf, **nwGA,** I let it get next to me—bother me; 1 inf, **ceTN,** Got next to me—worried me; 1 inf, **cwFL,** Got next to me—bothered me.

4 To feel friendly toward; to tolerate.

1968–70 *DARE* (Qu. II29a, *An unexplainable dislike that you feel from the first moment you meet a person: "I don't know why, but I just can't ______ him."*) Inf **NY**239, Get next to; (Qu. II29b, *Or you might try to explain the unpleasant effect that person has on you*) Inf **PA**82, I just can't get next to him.

get off v phr

1 also *get away:* To acquit oneself well.

1893 Shands *MS Speech* 32, *Get off*. . . Used by illiterate whites to mean to acquit one's self well in any undertaking; as, "Mr. Smith did not get off in that speech like he usually does"; i.e., did not do himself as much credit as usual. **1934** *AmSp* 9.289 **sePA** [Black], *Get off.* Used with the same sense as *get away* [i.e., to distinguish oneself; to make a hit].

2 To do (something) well.

1927 *AmSp* 2.355 **cwWV,** *Get it off* . . to tell a story well. "He got that story off to perfection." **1934** *AmSp* 9.290 **sePA** [Black], *Get your stuff off.* To display one's knowledge or ability; to say what you have to say; to tell your story.

3 in phr *get it off on:* To play a joke on.

1927 *AmSp* 2.355 **cwWV,** *Get it off* . . to play a joke on some one. "John has never liked me since I got it off on him at the party last year."

get-off n

An excuse.

c1938 in 1970 Hyatt *Hoodoo* 1.252 **NYC,** I didn't want to go with her. . . So I told her, "You know they say that church is condemned. You know my husband ain't here and I'm afraid something might happen and there would be nobody here to take care of the children." So that was my get-off to keep from going with her.

get off (on) one's case See **case** n[1] **7**

get off with v phr Cf **get away with 2**

To embarrass, discomfit.

1966–67 *DARE* (Qu. GG9, *To suddenly embarrass somebody . . "When they told him what she had said about him, it certainly did ______ him."*) Infs **GA**6, **LA**2A, **MS**45, Get off with.

get on v phr Also *get onto*

To reproach, find fault with.

1967 *DARE* Tape **AR**52, They wanted somebody from the farm to make a recording, and so the one that they chose from Arkansas was me. So I felt real thrilled to be feted ['fid̥ɨd] in the *Arkansas Free Press* the next morning and they said, the headline was that "She mixes raising six children and farm work with ease." And I got onto 'em about that. I said, "I didn't say it was easy!" **1974** Fink *Mountain Speech* 11 **wNC, eTN,** *Get on:* accuse, berate. "She got on him about drinking." **1976** Garber *Mountain-ese* 33 **Appalachians,** *Get-on* . . accuse, chide—The boss is allers bad to git on the office boy fer ever bad job he does.

get one in the harness See **harnessed, get oneself**

get one's ashes hauled See **ashes 2**

get one's bait back v phr

1975 Gould *ME Lingo* 109, *Get your bait back*—To catch just enough fish to match your bait expense; to break even. The expression is transferred variously. A boy who is wayward or subnormal may be compared: "Eyah, the lad's a problem—Henry didn't get his bait back on him." The expression is often used for a very small baby: "Weighed four pounds—hardly more'n got his bait back."

get one's chin out v phr

To become angry.

1940 (1942) Clark *Ox-Bow* 22 **NV,** You couldn't play long with a man acting like that without getting your chin out. . . I was getting riled myself.

get one's company v phr

1908 *DN* 3.314 **eAL, wGA,** *Get one's company*. . . To punish one, chastise one. "You better mind, or I'll get your company."

get one's ducks in line (or a row) See **duck** n **B9**

get one's Dutch up See **Dutch** n **4**

get one's ears set back (or down, out) See **ears lowered, get one's**

get oneself a cook v phr Also *get oneself a housekeeper;* for addit varr see quot 1965–70 **scattered, but esp Sth, S Midl** See Map *joc* Cf **boss, get oneself a**

Of a man: to get married; to seek a wife.

c1960 *Wilson Coll.* **csKY,** *Get himself a cook*. . . To seek a mate, often with cookery as a major goal. **1965–70** *DARE* (Qu. AA15b, . . *Joking ways . . of saying that a man is getting married*) 29 Infs, **esp Sth, S Midl, SW,** Got himself a cook; 10 Infs, **scattered,** Got himself a housekeeper; **AR**24, **CA**2, **FL**15, **MI**42, **SC**19, 26, **TX**40, 45, Got (him) a cook; **IL**102, **MS**29, 70, **TX**40, **SC**26, Got (*or* found) him a housekeeper; **FL**8, Taken on a cook, an old lady; **LA**8, Got himself a washwoman; **ND**2, Got himself a cook and housekeeper; **OK**18, Took on a cook; **TX**87, Got a new laundress; got a new baker.

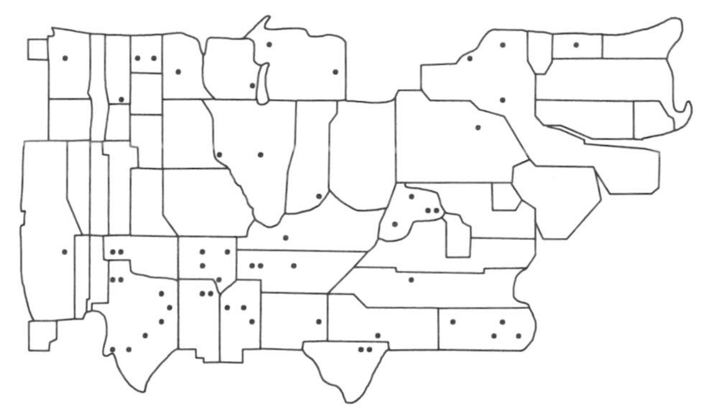

•get oneself a cook + varr (Qu. AA15b)

get one's feet under the table See **foot** n **C5c**

get one's ginger up See **ginger** n **2**

get one's hips up on one's shoulders See **hip** n[1] **2**

get one's hundreds See **hundred B4**

get one's name in the pot See **pot**

get on in with v phr

To ingratiate oneself with.

1965–70 *DARE* (Qu. II20b, *A person who tries too hard to gain somebody else's favor*) Infs **IL**9, **MS**84, **MA**123, Get on in with; **PA**247, Get on in tight with. [3 of 4 Infs Black]

get on one's case See **case** n[1] **7**

get on one's high keys See **high keys, be on one's**

get on the front seat See **front seat, get on the**

get onto v phr

1 To put pressure on.

1965–70 *DARE* (Qu. Y6, . . *To put pressure on somebody to do something he ought to have done but hasn't*) Infs **AR**37, **IN**82, **KY**28, 63, 68,

NC49, Get onto him; **CA**53, Get onto him about that; (Qu. JJ26, *If somebody has been doing poor work or not enough, the boss might say, "If he wants to keep his job he'd better ______ .")* Inf **MA**40, Get onto himself.

2 See **get on.**

get out v phr

1 To cut or fashion from raw timber.

1818 (1920) Clark *Diary* 2314 **CT,** The men have all come to get out the shingle and get on the roof. **1836** (1928) Underwood *Jrl.* 32.149 **MA,** I made a contract with some workmen to get me out timber and build me a store. **1856** in 1862 Colt *Went to KS* 93 **NY,** Husband meets father at the cornfield to get out fencing. **1899** (1912) Green *VA Folk-Speech* 194, *Get out.* . . To prepare, cut out and get timber ready. "To get out spokes for a wheel." "To get out timber for a ship." **1969** *DARE* (Qu. L54, . . *He was* ______ *firewood*) Inf **MA**16, Getting out. **1970** *DARE* File **cMA,** Let's see, was it shingles they got out there [=at a mill]?

2 To cut or bring in (a crop).

1837 (1930) Sewall *Diary* 186 **ME,** Getting out buckwheat. [*DARE* Ed: For two days before he had been cutting buckwheat.] **1840** in 1956 Eliason *Tarheel Talk* 273 **NC,** The crop of wheat I expect the thrasher / In afew day [sic] to get it out. **1968** *DARE* Tape **IN**13, Them days you done all the farm with horses and sometimes you got out 10 acres of corn, you was doing well . . with three good horses.

3 Of fire: to break out.

1941 *Sat. Eve. Post* 31 May 106/3 **neKY,** I remembered, when a fire got out, how we . . prayed for rain . . fighting fires that got out every March.

4 To shuck (corn).

1984 Wilder *You All Spoken Here* 132 **Sth,** Get out: When it's too wet to plow and corn needs to be shucked, farmers often come indoors and get out, or shuck, ears of corn.

get-out n Pronc-sp *git-out*

=**all get-out.**

1838 Neal *Charcoal Sketches* 12 **sePA,** We look as elegant and as beautiful as get out. **1876** in 1969 *PADS* 52.52 **seIL,** Cold as git out last night. **1952** Brown *NC Folkl.* 1.413, As mean as get-out. **1958** Taylor–Whiting *Dict. Amer. Proverbs* 151, *Get out.* Hum-sick as git out . . as easy as . . as mean as . . as impudent as . . as contented as . . as lonesome as . . etc. **1970** *DARE* (Qu. HH22b, . . *"He's meaner than* ______ *.")* Inf **KY**85, Get-out.

get out exclam Also *get out from here* Cf **go 'way**

See quots.

1942 McAtee *Dial. Grant Co. IN* 28 (as of 1890s), *Git out* . . exclamation of surprise or incredulity; "______, you don't mean it". **1942** Warnick *Garrett Co. MD* 7 **nwMD** (as of 1900-18), *Get out,* . . exclamation of surprise. **1956** McAtee *Some Dialect NC* 18, *Git out.* . . Expression of incredulity. "Git out, you don't mean it." *Dial.* **1965** *DARE* FW Addit **MS,** "Oh, git out from here!" An expression like "You don't say!" used after a mildly surprising or shocking bit of news. Used primarily by Negroes.

Get-Out-and-Push See **G.O.P.**

get out from here v phr

1 See **from B3.**

2 See **get out** exclam.

get out of one's face See **face** n **2**

get over v phr Also *get across among Black speakers*

To succeed, get by; to achieve a goal by whatever means are necessary; see quots.

1971 Roberts *Third Ear* np [Black], *Get over* . . to maneuver oneself into a more favorable position with another; to make oneself better. **1972** Claerbaut *Black Jargon* 66, *Get over* . . to succeed; get by: *I can get over without studying too much.* **1980** Folb *Runnin' Down* 77 **Los Angeles CA** [Black], I know you hafta have education to get over, but if you can't confront with the world outside, you can't say you schooled. *Ibid* 117, [If] somebody be steppin' fast dey . . takin' care o' business. . . Pimpin' hard, gettin' over. *Ibid* 128, Survival . . is the ultimate name of the game . . "to communicate . . to bullshit 'em, to con someone, to use your mind to overcome them. Dat's how you get over." . . the endgame is to *get over,* to *get across* . . to get what you can, to be successful at what you do. . . on a literal or psychological level. . . "All life is a game. You . . tryin' get over with your conversation, your fists, whatever you got." **1982** Naylor *Women of Brewster Place* 60 **NYC** [Black], Along with the countless other disillusioned, restless children of Ham with so much to give and nowhere to give it, she took her talents to the street. And she learned to get over, to hook herself to any promising rising black star. **1986** *Atlantic Mth.* 257.6.48 **sChicago IL** [Black], Another northern ghetto term that comes from southern town life is *getting over* which . . means, roughly, doing what is necessary to survive and, if possible, succeed. While it does not cover violence, it would apply to hustling as well as to more legitimate pursuits.

get religion v phr **chiefly Sth, S Midl** Cf *get happy* (at **happy** adj 1), **get through**

To experience religious conversion; to accept a religious faith; also fig.

1772 (1900) Fithian *Jrl.* 1.22 **cNJ,** We have had a considerable stir of religion in college since you went away, Lewis Willson is thought to have got religion. **1843** (1916) Hall *New Purchase* 365 **cIN,** Lord bless you, most powerful time—and it's there I've jist got religion. **1884** *Anglia* 7.261, To git 'ligiun = to become religious. **1890** *DN* 1.68 **KY,** *Git 'ligion:* negro for "to get religion." **1903** *DN* 2.314 **seMO,** *Get religion.* . . To become converted. 'The meeting lasted ten days and thirty people got religion.' **1905** *DN* 3.10 **cCT,** *Get religion.* **1906** *DN* 3.119 **sIN,** *Get religion.* . . To accept a religious faith. "He's got religion." **1907** *DN* 3.231 **nwAR. 1927** *AmSp* 2.355 **cwWV,** I got religion when I was sixteen. **c1960** *Wilson Coll.* **csKY,** *Get religion.* . . "Profess religion," join the church; trans., change one's point of view and support some movement previously opposed or neglected. **1967** *DARE* Tape **LA**8, That where I got my religion at.

get right v phr Cf **get religion**

To achieve a state of spiritual peace.

1920 Hunter *Trail Drivers TX* 191, I . . belong to the old M.E. [=Methodist Episcopal] Church South and I am proud of her record as a church. I am thankful for my own record that I have lived to get right and do something. . . The boys that have passed over the Divide . . I hope they got right.

get right behind See **get behind**

gets See **get** v **A1, 2**

get shed (or shet, shut) of See **shut** adj

get someone told v phr

To tell someone off.

1983 Mebane *Mary Wayfarer* 224 **NC** [Black], You know she always would get anybody told. She'd tell them exactly what was on her mind. Saturday night she was probably drinking and started getting somebody told and he couldn't take it.

get-ta See **goetta**

get the go-by See **go-by** n

get there v phr

1 also *get there Eli, ~ Ely, ~ with both feet:* To succeed conspicuously; to do something well or quickly.

1884 Nye *Baled Hay* 49, They were high-toned, and they got there. **1887** F. Francis Jr. *Saddle & Mocassin* viii.144 *(DA),* He 'got there with both feet' at starting. **1894** *Congressional Record* 17 Apr 26.4.3804/2 **IL,** He told Mr. Smith, the Democratic candidate for county clerk, that if he would agree to appoint him deputy, he would hustle for him, and he thought Mr. Smith would "get there." **1940** *AmSp* 15.336, The *Journal* of December 24, 1882, 1/7, attributed the popular saying 'He got there, Ely' to a race horse named Ely. This slang expression was said to be a revival. **1941** *AmSp* 16.153, When I was a boy in the Kentucky mountains, this figure [=*He got there Eli*] was in common use. But it was always used in the present tense, with the meaning of doing something well, or quickly. For example, 'Fine, boys; that's getting there Eli.'

2 See **get up there.**

get-there n

Ambition; energy.

1898 Westcott *Harum* 169 **nNY,** Charley's a likely 'nough boy some ways, but he hain't got much 'git there' in his make-up. **c1902** Clapin *New Dict. Amer.* 202, *Get there* . . used substantively, as embodying the sum of qualities necessary to attain one's object. "The much esteemed get there quality." **1969** *DARE* (Qu. HH27b, *Of a very able and energetic person who gets things done you might say, "He's got lots of* ______ *.")* Inf **NY**219, Git-there. **1969** *DARE* Tape **NY**219, She [=a pony] has a lot o' git-there in her and she's a good traveler.

get there Eli, get there Ely, get there with both feet See **get there** v phr **1**

get the wrong sow by the ear v phr Also *get the wrong bull* (or *cow*) *by the tail;* for addit varr see quots [*OED* (at *sow* sb.[1] 3. a) 1562 →; cf *OED pig* sb.[1] 11]

To act on the basis of a misapprehension; to be seriously mistaken.

1731 Cooke *MD Muse* 9, Bacon, Who by the Ear wrong Sow had taken. **1793** in 1807 Alsop *Echo* 58 **CT,** They've caught the wrong pig by the ear. **1843** (1846) Haliburton *Attaché* (1st ser) 2.31 **NEng,** Tell your friend . . she has got hold of the wrong cow by the tail in gettin' hold of you. **1901** Harben *Westerfelt* 223 **nGA,** 'Oh,' said I, 'you've got the wrong sow by the ear; a wagon went whizzin' by here a minute ago like it was shot out of a gun.' **1905** *DN* 3.10 **cCT,** *Get the wrong pig by the tail.* . . To make a mistake in selection. **1906** *DN* 3.137 **nwAR,** *Get the wrong bull by the horns.* . . To be defeated by a person whom one has expected to defeat; to attack the wrong person. "He got the wrong bull by the horns when he tackled me." **1927** *AmSp* 2.355 **cwWV,** *Get the wrong bull by the tail* . . to tell the wrong story, or to give an unsatisfactory explanation. "I got the wrong bull by the tail when I was explaining the matter to my friends." **1954** *Harder Coll.* **cwTN,** Get the wrong cow by the tail . . be embarrassingly mistaken. **c1960** *Wilson Coll.* **csKY,** *Get the wrong bull (cow, bear, pig, etc.) by the tail* . . tackle the wrong problem or person.

get through v phr

1 See quot. Cf **get religion**

1890 *DN* 1.65 **KY,** At protracted meetings the "mourners" . . "git through" when they profess conversion.

2 To be dismissed from a job.

1989 *DARE* File **csMA** (as of 1950s), "She's leaving at the end of the week." "Did she quit her job?" "No, she got through."

getting n

A load or portion that can be moved at one time; a helping of food.

1913 Kephart *Highlanders* 283 **sAppalachians,** You can git ye one more gittin' o' wood up thar. **1934** (1970) Wilson *Backwoods Amer.* 67 **AR, MO,** One more gettin' of fodder. **1940** in 1944 *ADD* **wAR,** [Radio:] I noticed you had 3 gittin's [of potatoes]. **1971** Dwyer *Dict. for Yankees* 26 **Sth, S Midl,** *Gittin'*—A load, lot, a helping of food, i.e., "He et three gittin's of taters."

getting for See **for C6**

getting one's hundred See **hundred B4**

getting on for See **for C6**

getting-place n

Used in evasive reply: see quots.

1893 Shands *MS Speech* 33, *Gittin place.* . . The general name for the place where anything has been, or can be, obtained, used by negroes and illiterate whites in the following connection: "Whar did yo' git dem cloze, nigger?" "Got 'em at de gittin place." This is meant as a witty retort, and is said in order to crush the questioner and stop further inquiries. **1908** *DN* 3.314 **eAL, wGA,** *Gettin(g)-place.* . . Used in evasive answers. "Where did you get that?" "At the getting-place." *Gitn* is the common pronunciation. **1972** Cooper *NC Mt. Folkl.* 89, At the getting place—where such things are obtained.

gettup See **get up** v phr **1**

get under one's hide See **hide** n[2] **4**

get up v phr

1 also pronc-spp *gaddup, geddy up, git up;* for addit varr see quots: Go!—used as a command to a work animal to go or go faster. Cf **gee** v[1] **2**

1849 in 1941 Chittick *Ring-Tailed Roarers* 248 **AL,** Git up, you lazy Injun [=a horse]! **1887** F. Francis Jr. *Saddle & Mocassin* vii.123 *(DA),* Get up!—get up . . he says. . . and once more the horses resume their gait. **1910** *DN* 3.442 **cwNY,** *Git up.* . . Often for "get up." Emphatically, as a command to a horse to go ahead. "Git up there!" **1917** *DN* 4.393 **neOH,** *Git up.* . . Get up! (to a horse). Also Vt., N.H., Ill., Ia., Kan., N.Y. **1939** *LANE* Map 223, *Get up!* The type of [gɪtʌp] is sometimes regarded as old-fashioned. . . All calls . . are used by some both . . to start the horses and . . to make them go faster. [*Get up* is widespread throughout NEng.] **1949** Kurath *Word Geog.* 65, Calls for Driving Horses. . . The call *get up!* (in various pronunciations), chirping, and clucking are in rather general use throughout the Eastern States. **1951** *PADS* 15.66 **NH,** *Giddap.* . . Get up; command to horses to go ahead. **1954** *Harder Coll.* **cwTN,** *Gaddop* [gædəp] . . call to make horses or mules go faster. **1956** Ker *Vocab. W. TX* 201, Call to horses to make them go . . geddup . . geet-up . . gettup . . get up . . giddap . . giddi-ap . . giddup . . git up. **c1960** *Wilson Coll.* **csKY,** *Get up!* To horse to make him go forward. *Ibid, Giddap* . . to horse to make him go forward. **1965–70** *DARE* (Qu. K36a, . . *To make a horse go faster*) 502 Infs, **widespread,** Giddup; 173 Infs, **widespread,** Giddy-ap; 60 Infs, **scattered,** Giddap; 47 Infs, **scattered, but esp SE,** Get up; 28 Infs, **scattered,** Giddy-up; 23 Infs, **chiefly Sth, S Midl,** Git up; **IN**82, **NC**52, 79, **NJ**16, Gaddup; **CA**138, 208, **MA**75, Geddup; **MI**27, 49, 64, Gid-dep; **IA**2, **NY**93, **TN**35, Git-ap; **MA**68, **TX**105, Geddap; **PA**204, Geddy-up; **SC**9, Get up, horse; **CA**100, Giddup, giddup; **KY**62, Giddup there; **NC**53, Giddy-up, boy; **MD**26, Git up here; **MD**29, Git up there; **IL**44, Gi-up; (Qu. K33, . . *How do you make [horses or mules] start?* total Infs questioned, 75) 12 Infs, **chiefly FL,** Giddup; **DC**1, **FL**6, **OK**1, 10, 14, 18, 52, Get up; **AR**29, 40, **GA**14, **MS**1, 19, Git up; **NM**3, **OK**8, 49, Giddap; **OK**27, **UT**3, Giddy-up; **OK**20, Geddup; **MS**53, Gid up; **FL**37, Giddyap. **1966** Dakin *Dial. Vocab. Ohio R. Valley* 2.277, The regular call to urge horses when driving them is *get up!* everywhere in the Ohio Valley. . . *Get up!* is pronounced with varied patterns of stress, intonation, and syllabication, and with individual differences in vowel and consonant patterns as well. These seem to have little distributional significance. The most common pronunciations are those of the types: [ˌgɪt'ʌp], [ˌgɛt'ʌp]. These are about equally common. The several other most frequent, in order of frequency are: [ˌgɪ'dʌp], ['gɪdˌʌp], ['gɛdˌʌp], ['gɪdˌæp], and [ˌgɪ'dæp]. *Gitty, giddy, geddy up!* . . also appear. **1967–69** *DARE* Tape **CA**135, 136, [Inf **CA**136:] When the mountain started boilin' up, why, he jumped in the old Ford and started hollerin', "Get up, get up, get up, get up." [FW:] He got in his Ford and he was hollerin' that? . . [Inf **CA**135:] Cuz he thought he had his horse, he hadn't had the car too long, I guess . . cars were just comin' in; **NV**2, Today . . the fella gets up on the seat and he grabs the lines and he says [gjɑp] . . the old teamster, he clucked.

2 To gather, collect (wood, crops, people, etc); to round up, drive (animals). **chiefly Sth, S Midl** Cf **get out** v phr **2**

1827 (1930) Sewall *Diary* 120 **WV,** Mr. Sudduth and myself busily engaged in getting up wood. **1830** (1930) Phelps *Diary* 209 **IL,** Today . . Wm. starts away to St. Louis on a keel boat to get up goods for his Father. **1939** *Hall Coll.* **wNC,** *Get up.* . . To gather (wood for a fire). . . We . . had our wood to get up after dark, and we all out a-pickin' up wood. **1953** *Ibid* **wNC,** *Get up.* . . To gather, collect (dogs, men, wood, etc.) "So I got up the dogs and joined the parties." *Ibid, Get up.* . . To roust, start, find. . . In the meantime they got up another bear that they run all day. . . And we got up two. **1966** *DARE* Tape **AL**13, Then in the evening we had to get up our wood, go cut wood an' bring it in, an' get up our water; **MS**75, [Inf:] We'd have to git up cows, you know. [FW:] What does that mean, "get up cows?" [Inf:] Go out in the bushes 'long the creeks an' get 'em out the bushes an' drive 'em up to the lot. **1968–70** *DARE* (Qu. L15, *When you are putting hay into a building for storage, you say you are* ______) Infs **DE**5, **VA**75, Getting up hay; (Qu. L43a, *When somebody is going to get horses ready to work . . "I'll* ______ *the horses."*) Inf **TX**82, Get up. **1968** Adams *Western Words* 126, *Getting up the horses.* . . Driving the saddle horses from the range or pasture to camp or headquarters in preparation for the roundup. **1970** *DARE* Tape **MI**113, We used to get up a pile of poles and small logs. **1986** Pederson *LAGS Concordance,* 1 inf, **cnGA,** Get up a lot of flowers [=pick flowers]; 1 inf, **nwMS,** I might get up some old things to interest you.

3 with *off (of);* Fig: to relinquish (something) reluctantly.

1970 *DARE* (Qu. U18, *If you force somebody to pay money that he owes you, but that he did not want to pay, you might say, "I finally made him* ______.") Inf **NY**235, Get up off; **DC**11, Get up off of it. [Both Infs Black] **1986** Chapman *New Dict. Amer. Slang* 164/1, *Get up off* something. . . *Army.* To relinquish something; to make something available. *He was able to convince the supply sergeant to get up off some fuel.*

4 See **get** v **C2.**

5 Of wind: to increase. **chiefly Sth, S Midl** See Map Cf **get down** v phr **4**

1946 *PADS* 5.23 **VA,** *Getting up.* . . Of the wind, rising; not common. **c1960** *Wilson Coll.* **csKY,** *Getting up* . . wind rising. **1965–70** *DARE* (Qu. B12, *When the wind begins to increase, you say it's* ______) 18 Infs, **chiefly Sth,** Getting up; **GA**71, 84, **KY**20, **MD**32, **OK**42, Wind's getting up; [**MO**38, Getting up a gale;] **GA**80, Getting up into a breeze.

1968 *DARE* FW Addit **NC,** *Getting up* . . used to refer to a rising wind. "There's a breeze getting up."

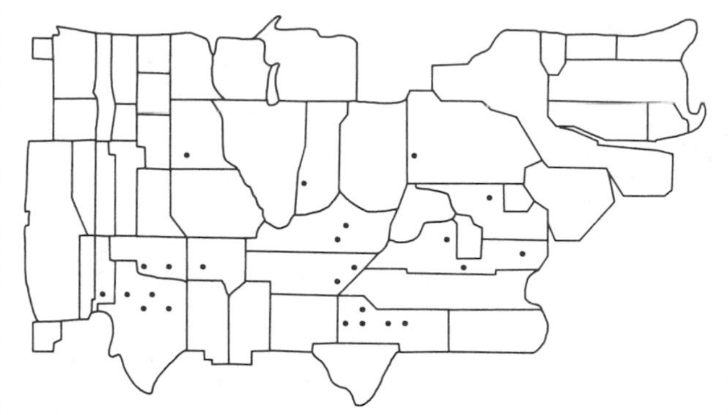

•get up v phr 5 + varr (Qu. B12)

6 To do (chores).

1966–70 *DARE* (Qu. L4b, . . *Time* . . *to feed livestock, clean stalls, and so on*) Inf **MS**19, Time to get up the chores.

get-up n

1 also *giddi-up, get-up-and-dust, get-up-and-get(-it):* Energy, initiative, ambition. [Varr of *get-up-and-go*]

1841 'Dow, Jr.' *Short Patent Sermons* 86 *(OEDS),* It flats right down, and stays there, like a junk of dough—no get up to it. **1863** *Ladies' Repository* Aug 477/1, In vain I tried to convince him that there was some 'get-up' in the animal. **1884** (1890) Peck *Peck's Boss Book* 183, The adjutant . . felt that his position demanded a horse that had some git-up-and-git. **1887** Kirkland *Zury* 537, Get up. . . Spirit, spunk; pluck in action, motion, or appearance. **1908** *DN* 3.314 **eAL, wGA,** *Get-up-and-get*. . . Energy, activity. Usually pronounced *git-up-an'-git.* "He's got plenty of git-up-an'-git about him." **1914** *DN* 4.107 **KS,** *Get-up*. . . Energy; enthusiasm. Also get up and go. **1917** *DN* 4.392 **OH,** *Get up and dust* . . energy, activity. . . "That man has some get-up-and-dust." Also N.Eng., Ky., Ia., Kan., Neb. **1926** *DN* 5.387 **ME,** *Git-up-and-git*. . . Enterprise. Common. **1927** *AmSp* 3.134 **ME,** The New England contempt of lack of industry expresses itself in such locutions as having "no get up and get." **1946** *PADS* 6.15 **NC, VA,** *Get-up*. . . Initiative. . . "He has no get-up." **1954** *Harder Coll.* **cwTN,** *Getup*. . . Initiative. **c1960** *Wilson Coll.* **csKY,** *Get-up-and-go* . . same as get-up-and-get. **1965–70** *DARE* (Qu. HH27b, *Of a very able and energetic person* . . *"He's got lots of______."*) 24 Infs, **scattered,** Get-up; **CO**34, **FL**16, **NY**209, **OH**72, **SC**5, 45, Get-up-and-git; **CT**16, **MA**5, **MS**73, **PA**126, **WI**65, Get-up-and-get; **CO**17, Git-up; **MO**35, Spunk and git-up; **IA**9, Get-up-and-dust; (Qu. Y21) Inf **PA**104, Has no get-up-and-git; (Qu. GG37) Inf **FL**16, Get-up-and-get; **SC**11, Get-up-and-git; **KY**94, Git-up; (Qu. KK28) Infs **CA**157, **MS**80, **TX**40, 54, Full of git-up-and-git; **KY**92, Full of git-up. **1969** Emmons *Deep Rivers* 4 **eTX** [Black], She explains her pep and energy by saying, "Some folks have just natchelly got the giddiup." **1986** Pederson *LAGS Concordance,* 1 inf, **swMS,** A get-up piece—a fast dance tune; 1 inf **csGA,** Poor trash—didn't have no get-up-and-get-it.

2 An outfit, usu of clothing. *usu derisive*

1899 (1912) Green *VA Folk-Speech* 194, *Get-up*. . . Equipment; dress; appearance; style. **1920** Lewis *Main Street* 333, Wasn't that the darndest get-up he had on? **1944** *PADS* 2.56 **MO,** *Get-up*. . . Clothing; an uncomplimentary term. "She's got on the darndest get-up I've ever seen on any mortal." **1954** *Harder Coll.* **cwTN,** *Get-up*. . . Clothing. Uncomplimentary form. **c1960** *Wilson Coll.* **csKY,** *Get-up*. . . Dress, outfit. **1965–70** *DARE* (Qu. W43, . . *Joking words* . . *for clothes*) Infs **FL**8, **MO**5, **NC**47, Get-up; (Qu. HH35) Inf **OK**48, Lavish in her get-up. **1976** Garber *Mountain-ese* 33 **Appalachians,** *Get-up* . . costume, ensemble—You should uv seed the git-up Kate wuz wearin' at the Halloween party.

3 See quots. [Cf *get up* to organize, often extemporaneously]

1916 *DN* 4.343 **MD,** *Get-up*. . . Makeshift arrangement. "We had some kind of a get-up instead of the regular programme." Gen'l south. **1944** *PADS* 2.56 **MO,** *Get-up*. . . A party. . . An activity.

get up and dig (or dust) v phr See **get up and get** v phr

get-up-and-dust n See **get-up** n **1**

get up and get v phr Also *get up and dig, get up and dust* [Varr of *get up and go*] Cf **get up** v phr **1**

To leave in a hurry; to move rapidly; also fig.

1863 (1922) Jackson *Col.'s Diary* 98 **PA,** As it had been a long time since our boys had "been in town before" they just made things "get up and dust." **1864** B. Cotton *Songster* 10 *(OEDS),* Monsieur will be invited to just 'get up and get'. **1889** Edwards *Runaways* 218 **GA,** Folk as es gittin' erway f'om er cyclone ain't expected ter move erbout in style. . . All they wants ter do es ter git up an' git tell the things blows over. **1889** (1971) Farmer *Americanisms* 265, *To git up and dust,* i.e., to use the utmost expedition in departing. **1893** Shands *MS Speech* 32, *Get up and dust*. . . An expression, used mainly by negroes, meaning to leave in a great hurry, to go away swiftly. This expression occurs also in Kentucky and Tennessee. **1903** Fox *Little Shepherd* 284 **eKY, wVA,** A voice bellowed from the rear, . . "Git up and git, boys!" That was the order for the charge. **1906** *DN* 3.117 **sIN,** *Get up and dig*. . . To rush; to race; to hurry. "Watch this horse get up and dig." **1909** *DN* 3.397 **nwAR,** *Get up and dig*. . . To rush, race, hurry. "You'll have to get up and dig if you beat him." **1917** *DN* 4.392 **OH,** *Get up and dust*. . . Be energetic. . . "If you get a living here, you have to get up and dust." . . Also N. Eng., Ky., Ia., Kan., Neb. **1951** *PADS* 15.66 **NH,** *Get up and get*. . . Leave quickly. **1966** *DARE* (Qu. A20, *Joking ways of telling somebody to hurry*) Inf **AR**38, Get up and git. **1966** Barnes–Jensen *Dict. UT Slang* 18, It's daylight—git up and git, boys.

get-up-and-get(-it) See **get-up** n **1**

get-up-and-goes n pl

1969 *DARE* (Qu. BB19, . . *Looseness of the bowels*) Inf **GA**72, Get-up-and-goes; (Qu. BB20, . . *Overactive kidneys*) Inf **GA**72, Get-up-and-goes.

get up grown See **get grown**

get up off (of) See **get up** v phr **3**

get up there v phr Also *get there, get up there in age* (or *years*), *climb up there* **scattered, but esp N Cent, C Atl** See Map

To grow old.

1965–70 *DARE* (Qu. X48b) 38 Infs, **scattered, but esp N Cent, C Atl,** Getting up there; 12 Infs, **chiefly Inland Nth,** Getting there; **CA**166, **PA**29, 63, Getting up there in age; **DE**3, **MI**47, Climbing up there; **NC**47, Getting on up there; **PA**3, Getting up there in years; **PA**131, Getting way up there; (Qu. X48a) Inf **OH**22, Getting up there.

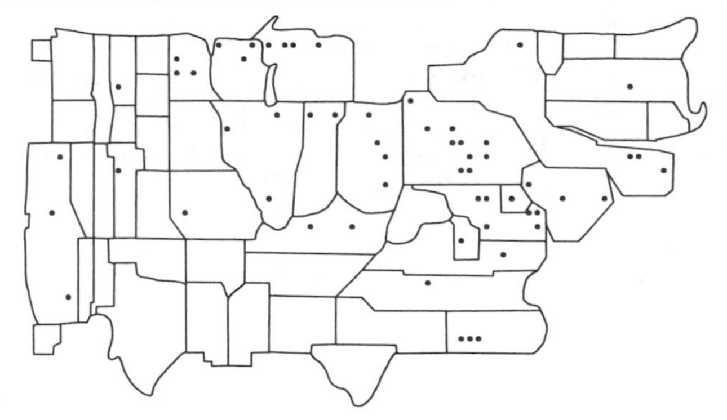

•get up there + varr (Qq. X48a, b)

get up with v phr

To catch up with; to get in touch with, meet.

1970 *DARE* Tape **FL**50, That's the reason you never can get up with your work. There's always something to do on a farm. **1971** *Today Show Letters* **seNC,** I would ask a person to make a telephone call. They would say "I'll see if I can get up with them." **1984** Wilder *You All Spoken Here* 103 **Sth,** Get up with: Come upon, meet, assemble with. **1989** *DARE* File **cNC,** Now current are such statements as "I'll get up with you later," meaning "catch up with." Meant literally; no hint of revenge or the like.

get with v phr Also *get with it*

To fight (someone).

1939 *Hall Coll.* **wNC,** *Get with*. . . To fight. (In this use, *get* receives secondary accent, and *with* primary accent). "He'll get with a feller," i.e., he'll fight a fellow, he's a good fighter . . in frequent use by men; never heard from women. **1970** *DARE* (Qu. Y12b, *A real fight in which blows are struck*) Inf **NJ**67, Getting with it.

geurl See **girl** n

gewgaw n Cf **hewgag 1**

A large tin horn used by members of **E Clampus Vitus.**

1904 Farish *Gold Hunters* 83 **CA,** When the gewgaw, a big horn, rang out, for miles around miners came, stores and banks and places of business were quickly closed and all their managers soon repaired to the "Clampus Hall." **1941** (1948) Dane–Dane *Ghost Town* 238 **CA,** Then . . [the Clampers] had the Hewgag or Gewgaw, or Dumb Bull as it was first called, the great tin horn that the Royal Grand Musician blew to announce that a candidate was caught and that they'd be a special meeting to initiate him.

gewgawed adj [Prob var of **gee-hawed**]

1967 *DARE* (Qu. KK70, *Something that has got out of proper shape: "That house is all _______.*") Inf **OH**24, Gewgawed.

gewhillikins, gewhilliky See **gee whillikers**

gewholliper See **gee-whollicker**

geyser daisy n [In allusion to the geysers of Yellowstone National Park]

A **goldenweed 1** (here: *Haplopappus uniflorus*).

1936 McDougall–Baggley *Plants of Yellowstone* 122, *Geyser-daisy (Pyrrocoma uniflora)*. . . Each stem bears only 5 or 6 or fewer leaves and usually only one head.

g.g. See **grandma** n **A13**

ghor See **gore** n **2**

ghos(es) See **ghost**

ghost n Pronc-sp *ghos* Pl usu *ghosts;* also *ghos(es), ghost(s)es, ghosties* Cf **-es** suff[1] **1a**

A Forms.

1829 Tenney *Female Quixotism* 2.84 **Philadelphia PA** [Black], For fright away ghos. **1893** Shands *MS Speech* 28, *-es*. . . The plural form, ending in *es,* is given to nearly all words ending in *t,* by negroes; as *postes, ghostes, hostes. Ibid* 56, Dat was sutenly a *sho nuff* ghos'. **1927** *DN* 5.470 **Appalachians,** Plurals in *-es* for *-s:* . . ghostes. **c1938** in 1970 Hyatt *Hoodoo* 1.19 **seNC** [Black], My uncle, he was awful scared of ghos'es. **1944** *PADS* 2.56 **AL,** *Ghostes* ['gostəz]. . . Rather common. . . [*PADS* Ed: also Va., N.C., Texas. Uneducated.] **1945** Saxon *Gumbo Ya-Ya* 302 **LA,** I put black pepper 'round the sills of all my doors. That stopped him; that always chases ghostses. **1954** in 1958 Brewer *Dog Ghosts* 117 **TX** [Black], Come in contact wid a lots of bad ghos'es. **1954** *Harder Coll.* **cwTN,** *Ghost* . . pl. *Ghosties.* **c1960** *Wilson Coll.* **csKY,** Ghosts ['gostɪz]. **1968** *DARE* (Qu. CC17) Inf **VA**31, Ghosties. **1968** *DARE* FW Addit **GA**18, [Colored people] call them ['gostɪz]. **1970** [see **B3** below]. **1986** Pederson *LAGS Concordance* **Gulf Region,** 37 infs, Ghostes; 2 infs, Ghostes—Black (*or* Negro).

B Senses.

1 in var combs referring to a cemetery: See quots. *joc* Cf **bone orchard**

1950 *WELS (Cemetery—Joking names)* 1 Inf, Ghost convention; 1 Inf, ghost land; 1 Inf, ghost walk; 1 Inf, ghost yard. **1965–70** *DARE* (Qu. BB61b, . . *Joking names for a cemetery*) Infs **KY**11, **MN**2, Ghost town; **NY**123, Ghost factory; **NY**167, Ghost garden; **CO**27, Ghost hollow; **IA**3, Ghost land; **LA**11, Ghost yard; [(QR, near Qu. CC17) Inf **CA**202, Ghost hollow—a place where ghosts walk at night].

2 also *ghost in the graveyard:* a variety of **hide-and-seek A.**

1967–69 *DARE* (Qu. EE13a) Inf **IA**45, Hide-and-seek—ghost, if you play the same game at night; **NY**28, Ghost—players hiding make wild noises. **1988** *NADS Letters* **csMI,** *Ghost in the graveyard*—My students . . reminded me of . . [this] version of hide-and-seek, which is quite common around Michigan (Lansing, Detroit, Grand Rapids all report it). The rules . . are the same as for hide-and-seek, but the game is played at night. It also goes by the name "bloody murder," I assume because the game elicits a good deal of screaming as people are surprised in the dark by fellow players.

3 Long underwear. [Perh from the usu white color]

1970 *DARE* (Qu. W14, *Names for . . underwear . . men's—long*) Inf **SC**68, Ghosts [gos].

4 A small whirlwind. Cf **dust devil 1**

1970 *DARE* (Qu. B18, . . *Special kinds of wind*) Inf **FL**48, Baby cyclone—like minute twisters, not destructive—some call them ghosts. Just hit in one spot and kick up dust.

5 See **ghost feather.**

6 See **ghost light.**

ghost baseball n

1969 *DARE* (Qu. EE11, *Bat-and-ball games for just a few players*) Inf **NY**161, Ghost baseball.

ghost bird n

1 =**yellow-breasted chat.**

1895 *Std. Dict. Engl. Lang.* (Funk) 761, *Ghost-bird*. . . [Local, U. S.] The American yellow-breasted chat *(Icteria virens).*

2 also *ghost owl:* =**snowy owl.** [See quots 1956, 1959]

1945 Mathews *Talking Moon* 28 **nOK,** One extremely hard winter a snowy owl drifted to my ridge. . . Eventually the crows hounded the northern ghost-bird . . , harassing him from daylight to darkness. **1956** MA Audubon Soc. *Bulletin* 40.81, *Snowy Owl*. . . Ghost Owl (Maine. . . Name from its whiteness and silent flight.) **1959** *Names* 7.114, For its white color, . . the snowy owl has been dubbed both ghost owl and ghost bird.

3 =**great black-backed gull.**

1956 MA Audubon Soc. *Bulletin* 40.22, *Great Black-backed Gull*. . . Ghost Bird (Mass.)

4 The American **egret.** [See quot]

1959 *Names* 7.114, For its white color, the American egret is known as . . ghost bird in Illinois.

5 =**sanderling.** [See quot]

1965 Teale *Wandering Through Winter* 155 **TX,** Sanderling flocks—in fall so white that natives call them "ghost birds"—followed the wash of waves on the beaches.

ghost bush n

An **Adam's needle (and thread)** (here: *Yucca filamentosa*).

c1960 *Wilson Coll.* **csKY,** Ghost-bush. . . The common yucca (Yucca filamentosa); called elsewhere bear grass or devil's shoestring.

ghost cord n

In breaking horses: see quots.

1922 Rollins *Cowboy* 152, The hackamore . . might, like the bit, have allied with it an illicit companion, the "ghost cord," a thin string tied about the tongue and gums, and thence passed below the lower jaw and up to the rider's hand. This string with its ingeniously devised ties was, in competent hands, an instrument of either mental diversion or extreme cruelty. **1944** Adams *Western Words* 65, Most ranchers frown upon the breaker who uses a ghost cord, since it has a tendency to make an outlaw of the horse.

ghost crab n [See quots]

A light-colored crab *(Ocypode quadrata).* Also called **sand crab**

1901 Arnold *Sea-Beach* 282, The . . ghost-crab. . . is colored almost exactly like the sand, and this mimicry, together with its fleetness, makes it interesting to note and difficult to capture. **1937** *Natl. Geogr. Mag.* 71.205 **NJ,** We have stumbled on a community of ghost crabs . . and well do they deserve their name. . . Their pale, yellowish-gray carapaces match the beach so exactly that when they are stationary it is almost impossible to see them. They are betrayed only by their swift movements as they glide over to the beach wrack. **1981** Meinkoth *Audubon Field Guide Seashore* 654, They are called Ghost Crabs with good reason; they blend closely with the sand on which they live, and are very swift. They seem to appear from nowhere, run and suddenly disappear again. **1983** Fox *At the Sea's Edge* 183, The ghost crab is a nocturnal scavenger that can still be seen roaming the beach in the early dawn.

ghost duck n

1 =**bufflehead 2.**

1955 MA Audubon Soc. *Bulletin* 39.316, *Buffle-Head*. . . Ghost Duck (Maine. . . In reference to its "supernatural" ability in diving at the flash of an old-time gun or the twang of a bowstring, quickly enough to avoid the missile.) **1959** *Names* 7.110, Prodigious divers have . . won spirit names . . ghost duck, for the bufflehead in Maine and for the pied-billed grebe in South Carolina.

2 =**pied-billed grebe.**

1959 [see **1** above].

ghostes See **ghost**

ghost-faced bat n

A leaf-chinned bat *(Mormoops megalophylla).*

1980 Whitaker *Audubon Field Guide Mammals* 305, *Ghost-faced Bat. . . Folds of skin across chin* from ear to ear make it unique in North America. . . Only in s Texas and s Arizona.

ghost feather n Also *ghost, ghost fart, ~ manure, ~ turd* Cf **feather n B5**

=dust bunny.

1965–70 *DARE* (Qu. E20, . . *Rolls of dust that collect . . under beds or other furniture*) Inf **GA**46, Ghost feathers; **NC**48, Ghost manure; **MI**1, Ghost turds; **MI**108, Ghosts. **1981** *AmSp* 56.145, *Ghost turds.* Surveying my class for terms for *dust bunnies,* one of my students reported *ghost turds.* She . . thought it was idiosyncratic to her immediate family. **1982** *Smithsonian Letters* **IA,** For dust balls under beds, "ghost farts." That term came from my husband's college roommate, and quickly became a favorite in our circle of friends.

ghost fire See **ghost light**

ghostfish n

Any of various fishes, as:

a A **wrymouth** (here: *Cryptacanthodes maculatus*). [See quot 1933] Cf **gray ghost**

1873 in 1878 Smithsonian Inst. *Misc. Coll.* 14.2.19, *Cryptacanthodes maculatus. . .* Ghost-fish; wry-mouth. Nova Scotia to Cape Cod. **1882** U.S. Natl. Museum *Bulletin* 16.780, *Wry-mouth; Ghost-fish.* Light brownish, with several series of smallish dark spots, . . body sometimes *("inornatus")* entirely immaculate. **1889** *Century Dict.* 2506, *Ghost-fish. . .* A whitish variety of *Cryptacanthodes maculatus.* See *wry-mouth.* **1898** U.S. Natl. Museum *Bulletin* 47.2443 **N Atl,** *Cryptacanthodes maculatus. . .* (Wry-mouth; Ghost-fish.) Labrador to Long Island Sound. . . The ghost-fish form *(inornatus)* occasionally seen, is doubtless an albino. **1933** John G. Shedd Aquarium *Guide* 152, *Cryptacanthodes maculatus. . .* Generally the specimens are brown, but occasionally one is found almost pure white. These pale individuals are called Ghostfish. **1960** Amer. Fisheries Soc. *List Fishes* 58, Ghostfish —see wrymouth.

b See quot.

1902 Jordan–Evermann *Amer. Fishes* 86, *Ten-pounder. Elops saurus. . .* The young are . . long, thin, and transparent, passing through a metamorphosis analogous to that seen in the conger eels. . . During these stages, the young of this species, . . and other fishes which undergo similar changes, are the so-called "ghost-fishes" which are sometimes thrown up on the beaches in large numbers by the waves.

c The leptocephalus stage of an eel.

1915 Bryan *Nat. Hist. HI* 221, The larvae of eels are so different from the adults that some of them have been described as an entirely separate and distinct group called . . ghost fishes. . . The little transparent larvae, or ghost fishes, . . make their way upstream and across country to the ponds and lakes . . , where they grow up to be eels.

ghostflower n

1 **=Indian pipe.** [From its whiteness]

c1873 in 1976 Miller *Shaker Herbs* 173, *Monotropa uniflora. . .* Ghost-flower. **1897** *Jrl. Amer. Folkl.* 10.49, *Monotropa uniflora, . .* ghost-flower, S. Berwick, Me. **1898** *Ibid* 11.273, *Monotropa uniflora. . .* Ghost flower, Farmington, Me. **1899** Going *Flowers* 260 *(DA),* In July pine-roots give a home and a maintenance to some curious parasitic plants—"pine-drops," "pine-sap," and "Indian pipe" or "ghost-flower." **1901** Lounsberry *S. Wild Flowers* 375, *Ghost Flower. . .* Its small nodding flowers are shaped like a pipe, and its look is ghost-like, the plant being quite without the grains of chlorophyll which produce the green colouring matter we are so accustomed to seeing in foliage. **1915** (1926) Armstrong–Thornber *Western Wild Flowers* 358, An odd plant, all translucent white, . . this . . is also called Ghost-flower. **1936** IL Nat. Hist. Surv. *Wildflowers* 227, Stems, leaves and flowers are white—so white that the plant is sometimes called . . Ghost Flower. **1966** *DARE* Wildfl QR Pl.152b Inf **MN**14, Ghost-flower . . corpse plant. **1974** (1977) Coon *Useful Plants* 217, *Monotropa uniflora . .* Ghost-flower. . . appears sort of ghost-like in the dense woods where it grows.

2 **=phantom orchid.**

1914 Saunders *With Flowers in CA* 222, The Professor called my attention to some upright gleams of light. . . "The ghost-flower," he remarked. Nothing could have been better named—the delicate slender pencils of white a foot high or more, seemed indeed like sheeted floral phantoms.

3 A **desert snapdragon** (here: *Mohavea confertiflora*). **Desert SW**

1941 Jaeger *Wildflowers* 244 **Desert SW,** Ghost-Flower. *Mohavea confertiflora. . .* The odd form of the large, silky corolla makes it unique among desert flowers. **1959** Carleton *Index Herb. Plants* 51, *Ghost-flower:* Mohavea confertiflora; Monotropa uniflora. **1974** Munz *Flora S. CA* 816, Ghost Flower. . . Colo. and Mojave deserts . . to L. Calif., Ariz., Nev.

ghosties See **ghost**

ghost in the graveyard See **ghost B2**

ghost light n Also *ghost, ghost fire, ~ lamp, ghost(l)y light, ghost's light* [*OED* (at *ghost*) 1897] Cf **fox fire 2**

=will-o'-the-wisp.

1950 *WELS* 2 Infs, **WI,** Ghost light. **1956** Rayford *Whistlin' Woman* 6 **AL,** Call it fox-fire, call it swamp-fire or ghost-fire. . . It is still there. The old ghosts of the ancient Indians keep their holy fire going, yet. **1965–70** *DARE* (Qu. CC16) 9 Infs, **scattered,** Ghost light; **NC**4, Ghost; **IN**32, Ghost lamp; **NY**66, Ghost's light; **FL**18, Ghostly light; **MO**15, Ghosty light.

ghost lizard n [Prob from its whitish color]

A cave-dwelling blind salamander *(Typhlotriton spelaeus).*

1958 Conant *Reptiles & Amphibians* 240, *Typhlotriton spelaeus. . .* The "ghost lizard" of Ozark caves and grottoes. The whitish or pinkish adults sometimes have faint traces of orange on tail, feet, and lower sides of body.

ghostly light See **ghost light**

ghost manure See **ghost feather**

ghost minnow n

A **silversides** (here: *Labidesthes sicculus*).

1956 Harlan–Speaker *IA Fish* 158, *Labidesthes sicculus. . .* is also called the ghost minnow . . and other names that describe its slender, silvery, and virtually transparent appearance.

ghost owl See **ghost bird 2**

ghost pipe n

1 **=Indian pipe. esp WI**

1928 Johnstone *Story of Pittsfield* 25 **neWI,** *The "Indian Pipes" or "Ghost Pipes". . .* The little waxy blossoms are shaped exactly like little clay pipes. . . The legend tells that "they are left along the forest ways by phantom chiefs who return from long star trails." . . Whether "ghost pipes" or not they are getting rare and hard to find. **1966** *DARE* Wildfl QR Pl.152b Inf **WI**35, Ghost pipe . . Indian pipe. **1969** *DARE* (Qu. S26e, *Other wildflowers*) Inf **WI**78A, Indian pipe (also "ghost pipe").

2 A **broomrape 1** (here: *Orobanche fasciculata* or *O. uniflora*).

1936 McDougall–Baggley *Plants of Yellowstone* 113, The Western ghostpipe *(Thalesia fasciculata)* . . grows attached to the roots of sage-brush, buckwheat, and perhaps other plants. **1948** Wherry *Wild Flower Guide* 123, Ghost-pipe *(Orobanche uniflora). . .* Stem scaly, creeping in litter around a parasitized root, sending up stalks a few inches high, bearing solitary lavender 2-lipped flowers. **1966** *DARE* Wildfl QR Inf **CO**7, Ghost pipe . . Thalesia uniflora. **1968** Barkley *Plants KS* 318, Ghostpipe. In woods, parasites on tree roots.

ghost plant n

1 A **tumbleweed** (here: *Amaranthus albus*). [See quot]

1887 *Science* 9.32, Dr. Newberry has told us that it [=*Amaranthus albus*] is also known as the 'ghost plant' in allusion to the same habit, bunches flitting along by night producing a peculiarly weird appearance.

2 **=Indian pipe.** [See quot 1949]

1941 Writers' Program *Guide WA* 507, As the forest closes in, its shade encourages the growth of ghost plants. **1949** Peattie *Cascades* 232, The best known of these strange, saprophytic denizens of the forest is the Indian pipe or ghost plant. . . The whole plant is waxy or pearly white, which accounts for the name ghost plant. **1963** Zimmerman–Olson *Forest* 182, *Indian Pipe. . .* This all-white plant is also known as ghost plant. **1966** *DARE* Wildfl QR Pl.152b Infs **MI**57, **WA**15, Ghost plant.

3 A **sagebrush** (here: *Artemisia* spp).

1959 Carleton *Index Herb. Plants* 51, *Ghost-plant:* Artemisia (v).

4 A **broomrape 1** (here: *Orobanche* spp).

1970 Kirk *Wild Edible Plants W. U.S.* 77, *Orobanche fasciculata* and related species. . . Broom Rape, Ghost Plant. . . They are not green, even though they are flowering plants, but vary from yellow to yellowish brown to white.

ghosts(es) See **ghost**

ghosts' eve n Cf **cabbage night**

1980 *DARE* File **neTX** (as of c1930), Night before Hallowe'en = ghosts' eve.

ghost shiner n [Because the fish lacks pigmentation]

A **shiner** (here: *Notropis buchanani*).

1929 OK Univ. Biol. Surv. *Pub.* 1.3.69, Ghost shiner. . . *Notropis buchanani*. . . Coloration a bare ghost-like remnant of that seen in subspecies *volucellus*. **1956** Harlan–Speaker *IA Fish* 99, The ghost shiner is seemingly. . . confined to the Mississippi River, but may be more widespread downstream. **1967** Cross *Hdbk. Fishes KS* 139, Ghost shiners usually occupy gentle eddies adjacent to strong currents, in the main channels of rivers. **1983** Becker *Fishes WI* 570, *Ghost Shiner*. . . General lack of pigmentation accounting for common name.

ghost shrimp n Cf **fairy shrimp**

A soft-bodied crab (here: *Callianassa affinis* or *C. californiensis*).

1939 Natl. Geogr. Soc. *Fishes* 239, *Callianassa californiensis*. . . The ghost shrimp . . lives in burrows in the mud and sand. . . It is a very soft-shelled crustacean, more or less transparent. **1981** Meinkoth *Audubon Field Guide Seashore* 622, *Beach Ghost Shrimp (Callianassa affinis)*. . . White to pink. . . S. California to Baja California. *Ibid* 623, *Bay Ghost Shrimp (Callianassa californiensis)*. . . Whitish, with yellow swimmerets and yellow bristles. *Carapace* . . transparent on sides, gills visible. . . S. Alaska to Baja California. **1982** Sternberg *Fishing* 126, *Ghost shrimp*. . . Although called shrimp, they are actually soft-bodied crabs that burrow into sand or mud flats of estuaries. *Ibid* 127, The ghost shrimp . . reaches 5 inches in length.

ghost's light See **ghost light**

ghost tree n

1 An **indigo bush** (here: *Dalea spinosa*). [See quot]

1915 (1926) Armstrong–Thornber *Western Wild Flowers* 246, *P[arosela] spinosa,* the Smoke Tree or Ghost Tree, of western Arizona, is almost leafless, with grayish or whitish branches.

2 See quot.

1953 Jewett *Birds WA* 360, The coast pygmy owl occurs. . . from the . . alder swamps near Nisqually to the ghost trees of the burned areas on Mt. Rainier. . . A pygmy owl . . was sighted about 30 feet above the ground on the branch of a ghost tree.

ghost turd See **ghost feather**

ghostweed n

A **spurge** (here: *Euphorbia bicolor* or *E. marginata*).

1897 *Jrl. Amer. Folkl.* 10.143 **cTX,** *Euphorbia marginata* . . milkweed, ghost-weed, snow-on-the-mountain. **1936** Whitehouse *TX Flowers* 66, *Ghost-weed (Euphorbia bicolor)*. . . bears rather unusual flowers which yield a poisonous honey. **1976** Bailey–Bailey *Hortus Third* 463, *[Euphorbia] marginata*. . . *Ghostweed*. . . Lvs . . white-margined; cyathia [sic] . . with broad, white, petal-like appendages. . . The latex is very corrosive to the skin, and may cause severe burns or dermatitis.

ghosty light See **ghost light**

ghy See **go** v **A4c**

ghyard See **guard**

gi See **give A1b, 2c**

gia See **grandma** n **A13**

giant See **giant cracker**

giant bass See **giant sea bass 1, 2**

giant bird's nest n [Prob from the resemblance to *Monotropa* spp; cf **bird's nest 5**] **West**

A **pinedrops** *(Pterospora andromedea)*.

1900 Lyons *Plant Names* 310, *P[terospora] Andromedea*. . . Giant Bird's-nest. **1915** (1926) Armstrong–Thornber *Western Wild Flowers* 360, Springing from a mass of matted, fibrous, astringent roots. . . it is also called Giant Bird's-nest and Albany Beechdrops. **1936** Winter *Plants NE* 107, Giant Bird's Nest. Pine-drops. Rare in canyons and dense moist draws in the Yellow Pine region of western Nebr. **1949** Moldenke *Amer. Wild Flowers* 156, Gigantic . . is the pinedrops or giant birdsnest. . . The . . stems rise to a height of 4½ feet and are densely covered with sticky hairs. **1963** Craighead *Rocky Mt. Wildflowers* 136, Giant Birds-nest. . . appears to be all stem with whitish flowers hanging downward like bells. **1976** Bailey–Bailey *Hortus Third* 926, *Giant bird's-nest.* To 3 ft. . . Summer.

giant black sea bass See **black sea bass 2**

giant cactus n

=**saguaro.**

1884 Sargent *Forests of N. Amer.* 90, *Suwarrow. Saguaro. Giant Cactus*. . . Wood . . used in the region almost exclusively for the rafters of adobe houses, for fencing, and by the Indians for lances, bows, etc. **1896** *Jrl. Amer. Folkl.* 9.188 **AZ,** *Cereus giganteus* . . giant cactus. **1912** Raine *Brand Blotters* 236 **AZ,** Greasewood and giant cactus struggled from the parched earth. **1940** Benson *Cacti AZ* 78, The . . name giant cactus is also in common usage, particularly in the United States outside of Arizona, where saguaro is all but unknown. **1976** Bailey–Bailey *Hortus Third* 224, *Giant cactus* . . To 60 ft. high and 2 ft. thick. **1985** Dodge *Flowers SW Deserts* 15, Giant Cactus. . . Largest of all the U.S. cactuses, this species occurs only in southern and western Arizona . . and sparingly in extreme southeast California.

giant cedar n

A **red cedar** (here: *Thuja plicata*).

1857 Gray *First Lessons* 152, Over twelve hundred layers have actually been counted on the stump of an aged tree, such as the Giant Cedar or Redwood of California. **1923** Abrams *Flora Pacific States* 1.71, Giant Cedar. . . A handsome tree, attaining a maximum height of 60–70 m. and a diameter of 5 m. **1959** Anderson *Flora AK* 26, Giant Cedar. . . A valuable tree, the wood is soft, brittle, aromatic, light reddish-brown and very durable. **1967** Gilkey–Dennis *Hdbk. NW Plants* 36, *Giant cedar*. . . Coast Ranges, Cascades, and along Columbia River. **1976** Bailey–Bailey *Hortus Third* 1109, *Giant cedar*. . . needs protection from strong winter winds.

giant chinquapin n Also sp *giant chinkapin*

A **chinquapin B3** (here: *Castanopsis chrysophylla*).

1910 Jepson *Silva CA* 239, The Giant Chinquapin . . is distributed from the outer Coast Ranges of Mendocino County to . . northwestern Siskiyou, thence northward along the Cascades to the Columbia River. **1923** Abrams *Flora Pacific States* 1.515, Giant Chinquapin. . . Tree 15–45 m. high, with a trunk 1–2 m. in diameter. **1939** Medsger *Edible Wild Plants* 110, The Giant Chinquapin . . is a tree. . . The nut, less than half an inch long, has quite a hard shell. **1959** Munz–Keck *CA Flora* 901, *Giant Chinquapin*. . . Burs chestnutlike, . . seeds . . hard-shelled, with sweet kernel. **1967** Gilkey–Dennis *Hdbk. NW Plants* 88, *Giant chinquapin*. . . Leaves . . golden-brown to pale yellow beneath, . . dark green above. **1973** Hitchcock–Cronquist *Flora Pacific NW* 74. **1979** Little *Checklist U.S. Trees* 78, *Castanopsis chrysophylla*. . . Giant chinkapin.

giant clam n

=**geoduck 1.**

1883 U.S. Natl. Museum *Bulletin* 27.239, *Glycimeris generosa*. . . is a Pacific coast species, known as the . . "Giant Clam." . . Said to be of very fine flavor, . . one animal is sufficient for an entire meal. *Ibid* 263, Giant Clam. Pacific coast, in rivers and estuaries, from Puget Sound to San Diego. Not . . very abundant at any point.

giant cracker n Also *giant (firecracker)* **chiefly Nth** Cf **baby giant**

A large firecracker.

1877 *Harper's New Mth. Mag.* Jan 298/2, Tom explained how the colt had been frightened . . at a giant cracker. **1965–70** *DARE* (Qu. FF14) 26 Infs, **chiefly Nth,** Giant crackers; 18 Infs, **chiefly Nth, Pacific,** Giants; 17 Infs, **chiefly Nth, CA,** Giant firecrackers; **WA**13, Big giants, little giants. **1967** Borland *Hill Country* 210 **NE,** Firecrackers came in all sizes, from the tiny "lady crackers," not much bigger around than the lead in a pencil, to "giant crackers" that could blow up a barn.

giant forget-me-not n

=**hound's-tongue 1.**

1940 Steyermark *Flora MO* 444, *Giant Forget-me-not (Cynoglossum)*. *Ibid* 446, *Giant Forget-me-not (Cynoglossum virginianum)*. . . The one or several flower-sprays borne at the top of the stem.

giant hyssop n

Std: a plant of the genus *Agastache*. Also called **horsemint 3.** For other names of var spp see **false anise, mosquito plant**

giant milkweed n

=**crown flower.**

1929 Neal *Honolulu Gardens* 254, *Giant milkweed (Calotropis gigantea)*. . . A large shrub. . . The abundant milky juice is said to furnish a remedy for leprosy. **1965** Neal *Gardens HI* 698, *Giant Milk-*

weed. . . was a great favorite of the Hawaiian queen, Liliuokalani. . . The milky juice may burn or irritate the skin.

giant ragweed n Also *great ragweed*

Std: a **ragweed** (here: *Ambrosia trifida*). Also called **bloodweed, buffalo weed, hogweed 2a, horse cane, horseweed 3, kinghead, richweed, wild hemp**

giant reed n

Either of two similar plants:

a also *giant reed grass:* A clump-forming grass *(Arundo donax)* naturalized chiefly in the South and Southwest. Also called **gardener's garters 2, Georgia cane**

1889 Vasey *Ag. Grasses* 60, *Arundo Donax* (Giant Reed Grass). . . Well established on the borders of the Rio Grande River, . . and . . recommended for cultivation. **1923** Davidson-Moxley *Flora S. CA* 55, *Giant Reed*. . . Perennial, 2-3 meters tall. **1933** Small *Manual SE Flora* 120, Stem as much as 6 m. tall, branching, the rootstocks thick, rough and knotty. . . *Giant-reed.* **1968** Radford et al. *Manual Flora Carolinas* 61, *Giant Reed*. . . Grain not seen. . . Roadsides and waste places. **1976** Bailey-Bailey *Hortus Third* 115, *Giant reed*. . . Often planted to control erosion. **1985** Dodge *Flowers SW Deserts* 32, The common reed and its close relative giantreed *(Arundo donax)* . . are . . found in marshes and stock tanks, along irrigation canals and on river banks throughout the desert country of the Southwest.

b The common reed *(Phragmites australis).*

1939 Tharp *Vegetation TX* 45, Giant Reed *(Phragmites communis)* is abundant in fresh or slightly brackish marshes or shallow water along the coast and inland. **1970** U.S. Ag. Research Serv. *Selected Weeds* 80, *Giant reed*. . . Marshes, banks of lakes and streams, and most wet wastelands. . . Throughout all the United States excepting the inland areas of the South Atlantic and the South Central States.

giant reed grass See **giant reed a**

giant sea bass n

1 also *giant bass:* A large fish *(Stereolepis gigas)* of the southern California coast. Also called **black sea bass 2, jewfish, sea bass**

1935 Caine *Game Fish* 94, *Promicrops itaiara*. . . is frequently believed to be the same as the California black sea bass or giant bass *(Stereolepis Gigas)*, but such is absolutely *not* the case. **1946** LaMonte *N. Amer. Game Fishes* 45, *Stereolepis gigas*. . . Giant Bass, Giant Sea Bass. . . Said to reach 600 pounds. **1947** Caine *Salt Water* 9, The giant sea bass is the largest member of the bass family on the Pacific coast and is. . . also known as . . giant bass. **1955** Zim-Shoemaker *Fishes* 108, Giant Sea Bass. . . This popular game fish also has some commercial importance as a food fish. **1973** Knight *Cook's Fish Guide* 376, Bass *(s[alt]w[ater])* . . Black Sea or Giant Sea.

2 also *giant bass:* A **jewfish** (here: *Epinephelus itajara*).

1935 Caine *Game Fish* 94, *Jewfish. Promicrops itaiara*. . . Giant Bass. Giant Sea Bass. **1946** LaMonte *N. Amer. Game Fishes* 45, *Spotted Jewfish*. . . *Names* . . Giant Sea Bass, Giant Bass. . . Present most of the year off rocky shores and often around pilings, etc. **1972** Sparano *Outdoors Encycl.* 382, Probably the largest of the groupers, the giant sea bass is not the gamest of fighters. . . It . . is most abundant in Florida waters and off the Texas Gulf Coast.

3 =**skilfish.**

1960 Amer. Fisheries Soc. *List Fishes* 51, Bass, . . giant sea . . see also skilfish.

giant snake n

Perh =**glass snake.**

1966-68 *DARE* (Qu. P25, *What kinds of snakes are found around here?*) Inf **MS**11, Giant snake; **NC**49, Giant snake—breaks if you hit it on head.

giant steps n Also *giants, giant steps and baby steps, (take a) giant step, giant stride* **chiefly NEast** See Map Also called **elephant steps, may I**

A children's game: see quot 1975.

1957 *Sat. Eve. Post Letters* **seMI** (as of 1930), Giant steps. *Ibid* **neNJ** (as of 1920s), Giant steps. *Ibid* **cwNJ** (as of 1920s), Giant steps. *Ibid* **sePA** (as of 1937-47), Giant steps. *Ibid* **NYC** (as of 1945-51), Giant step. **1965-70** *DARE* (Qu. EE16) 5 Infs, 4 **PA**, Giant steps; **PA**16, May I or Giant Steps—both terms used; **PA**247, Giant steps: Could be played on front steps. He [=the leader] would give a command. The person could not respond without saying, "May I?" Sort of like a manner-teaching game; 6 Infs, 5 **NY**, Giant step; (Qu. EE33) Infs **CT**5, **MO**30, **VT**16, Giant step; **NH**15, Giant step—Children walk toward another who says, "Allen, you take one giant step," . . the person about to step must first say "May I?" or he goes back to the beginning; **CT**11, 23, **FL**5, **NY**186, Giant steps; **ME**15, Giant steps and baby steps; **NY**80, Take a giant step; **CA**166, Giants. Just like "May I." You take giant steps; **HI**9, **IN**5, Giant stride. **1966** *DARE* File **ceMA,** Giant steps [children's game]. **1975** Ferretti *Gt. Amer. Book Sidewalk Games* 204, Giant Steps as it is known almost everywhere is also called *Steps* in Connecticut and *May I?* in Chicago. This is also a sidewalk-to-sidewalk game across a street. . . The object is to stay "It" as long as possible. "It" has the option of determining how each player on the opposite sidewalk can move and how far. "It" asks, "Is everybody ready?" When all agree, he says "Beverly may take two baby steps." Beverly then takes two steps into the street toward the other curb, *but only* after she asks, "May I?" Moving before asking automatically sends the stepper all the way back to where he or she began. **1977-78** Foster *Lexical Variation* 42 **NJ,** The game known as *Giant Steps, Mother, May I?,* or *May I?* . . is evidently a girl's game, as suggested by the distribution of informants knowing two names, knowing no name, and giving faulty responses. *Ibid* 43, *Giant Steps* seems to be more common in North Jersey.

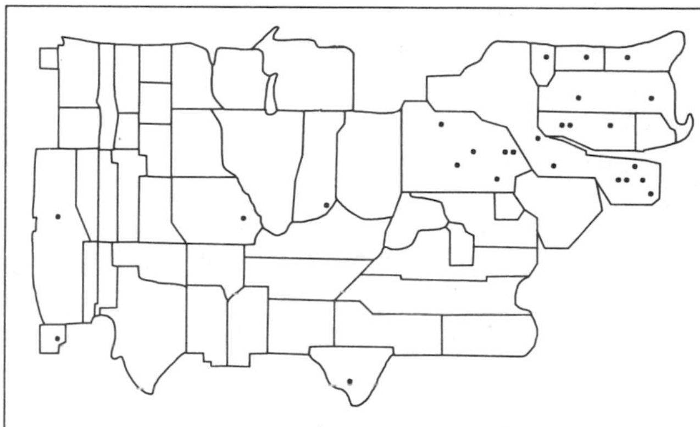

giant water bug n

A large aquatic bug of the family Belostomatidae. Also called **electric light bug, fish killer, toe biter**

1901 Howard *Insect Book* 278, *The Giant Water Bugs*. . . include the largest of living bugs, are strictly aquatic in their early stages and are predatory in habits. **1926** Essig *Insects N. Amer.* 366, *Belostomatidae.* Giant Water Bugs. *Ibid* 367, *The giant water bug* . . , *Lethocerus americanus* . . , is a giant brown bug varying from 45 to 60 mm. in length and from 20 to 25 mm. in width. **1940** Teale *Insects* 152, The giant water bug fastens her eggs with waterproof glue to the back of the male. **1964** Wigglesworth *Insects* 318, The giant water-bugs . . have the forelegs modified like a pair of wide pincers for seizing prey. **1980** Milne-Milne *Audubon Field Guide Insects* 463, To obtain air, giant water bugs raise the tip of the abdomen to the water surface and extend 2 tail-like breathing tubes.

giasticutus See **gyascutus**

gib v See **give A1a, 2c, 3b**

gib n See **jib** n

gibbet v [*gibbet* to execute by hanging]

1914 *DN* 4.73 **ME, nNH,** *Gibbet*. . . To beat, punish, hurt severely. "You, Si, come in outa thar, or by gravy, I'll gibbet ye!"

giblets n pl [Engl dial]

1886 *S. Bivouac* 4.349 **sAppalachians,** Giblets (fragments, tatters). **1899** (1912) Green *VA Folk-Speech* 195, *Giblets*. . . Rags; tatters. Torn to *giblets.*

gibraltar n **chiefly NEng**

A kind of candy; see quot 1886.

1831 in 1968 Hawthorne *N. Hawthorne* 1.126 **neMA,** I send Susannah's Gibraltars. . . If she has any sort of conscience she will send me back some sugar-plums. **1883** *Harper's New Mth. Mag.* 67.459/2 **neMA,** It is uncertain if he were stimulated to that nomenclature by the gibraltars and the silver pieces that Mr. Morley invariably bestowed upon him. **1886** Bates *Old Salem* 64 **MA,** The Gibraltar . . is a white and delicate candy, flavored with lemon or peppermint, soft as cream at one stage of its existence, but capable of hardening into a consistency so stony and so unutterably flinty-hearted that it is almost a libel upon the rock whose name it bears. The Gibraltar is the aristocrat of Salem confectionery. **1957** *Sat. Eve. Post Letters* **NH,** I think that Salem "Gibraltars" are still made in Salem. . . They were not too hard to bite and came in two flavors, peppermint and lemon. **1967** *Good Old Days* June 4 **Buffalo NY,** Gibraltars, rock-candy on strings. **1977** *Yankee* Feb 22 **Salem MA,** There's no better way to become acquainted with Gibraltars than to eat one. . . The candy . . seemed slightly harder than an after-dinner mint, properly peppermintish, and altogether admirable.

gice See **joist**

gick n

‡**1** A hick.

1966 *DARE* (Qu. HH1, . . *A rustic or countrified person*) Inf **OK**45, Country gick.

‡**2** A sticky substance.

1969 *DARE* (Qu. Y40b, . . *Sticky stuff: "I've got to wash my hands. They're all covered with ______.*") Inf **CA**170, Gick.

gid v^{1} See **get** v **A1**

gid v^{2} See **give A2e**

giddap, giddep, giddiap See **get up** v phr **1**

giddi-up See **get-up** n **1**

giddledehike See **gillagahike**

giddup, giddy-ap See **get up** v phr **1**

giddy-gapper n

1968 *DARE* (Qu. NN12b, *Things that people say to put off a child when he asks, "What are you making?"*) Inf **MD**9, Giddy-gapper.

giddy-headed adj [*OED* 1575 →]

1899 (1912) Green *VA Folk-Speech* 195, *Giddy-headed.* . . Having a giddy head; frivolous; volatile; incautious. **1965–70** *DARE* (Qu. HH9, *A very silly or light-headed person*) Infs **AL**19, **AR**33, **MI**26, **MS**30, **NC**31, 36, **VA**101, Giddy-headed.

giddy-up See **get up** v phr **1**

giedder See **gather**

gien See **give A2a**

gietta grass See **galleta**

gif See **give A1a, 2c**

giffy See **givey 1**

gift n [Engl dial]

1899 (1912) Green *VA Folk-Speech* 195, *Gifts.* . . White specks on finger-nails, which have been superstitiously supposed to foreshadow gifts. Sometimes called, also, "a sweetheart."

gift child n

1969 *DARE* (Qu. Z11b, *Nicknames and joking words for a child of unwed parents*) Inf **IL**70, Some kind of gift child.

gig n^{1} [*EDD gig* sb.^{6} 2 "Fun, frolic; a taunt, jibe; a trick"]

1970 *DARE* (Qu. GG32a, *To . . play tricks or jokes on people: "He's always ______.*") Inf **PA**236, Pulling a gig.

gig v^{1} Also with *back*

1 To back down. [*gig* to move backwards and forwards]

1900 Garland *Eagle's Heart* 297 **swCO,** The broncho-busting contest Mose declined. "How's that?" inquired Haney, who hated to see his favorite "gig back" at a point where his courage could be tested. **1901** *DN* 2.140 **cNY,** *Gig.* . . "He gigged there." Backed out at that point from his undertaking. **1904** *DN* 2.397 **nwAR,** *Gig.* . . To draw back. **1914** *DN* 4.107 **KS,** *Gig back.* . . To back down. Also *gig.* "He will gig if faced in the matter."

2 In logging: to return to one's starting point; to travel up and down along a river; hence n *gig(ging) trail* a trail along a river bank. [Prob a fig use of *gig back* to return (a saw carriage) to its starting point]

1956 Sorden–Ebert *Logger's Words* 15 **Gt Lakes,** *Gig.* . . To move up and down along the river's edge. *Ibid* 16, *Gig-back.* . . A river term meaning to go back to the head of a stretch of rapids to run through it again. . . To go back to the beginning of a haul over an iced road by a short-cut which might carry an empty sleigh but would not be suitable for a load. . . *Gigging-trail,* A trail along the side of a stream used to follow log drives. **1969** Sorden *Lumberjack Lingo* 47 **NEng, Gt Lakes,** *Gigging home*—Walking back toward camp on the gig trail. Walking upstream after the drive is over. *Gig trail* or *Gigging trail.*

gig n^{2}

1 =**fishgig.**

1705 Beverley *Hist. VA* 34, At each End of the Canoe stands an *Indian,* with a Gig, or pointed Spear. **1813** (1932) Schillinger *Jrl.* 72 **OH,** Went fishing, kill'd two with gigs. **1838** (1955) *Crockett Almanacks* 122 **wTN,** After providing himself with a "gig," or long spear, much used in the adjacent rivers, he started anew upon this perilous voyage. **1895** *DN* 1.389 **wFL.** **1899** (1912) Green *VA Folk-Speech* 195. **1905** *DN* 3.81 **nwAR,** *Gig.* . . Fish-spear. Common. **1923** *DN* 5.208 **swMO.** **1930** Shoemaker *1300 Words* 24 **cPA Mts** (as of c1900). **1952** Brown *NC Folkl.* 1.234, Gigs made from dining forks and umbrella ribs were used in catching fish and frogs in ditches and other shallow water. **1953** *Hall Coll.* **wNC,** Put a light up in the front end of a canoe . . and take a gig and go out and gig fish of a night. **1966–69** *DARE* (Qu. P13) Inf **MS**47, Gig fishing; **LA**37, Flounder gig. **1967** *DARE* Tape **TX**18, We usually make a two- or three-tined gig. Cause when we hit these big redfish . . if you don't have a good one, he'll bend it all to pieces for you. . . The best thing we've ever found is a pitchfork. . . and your center tine, you usually cut it off about an inch shorter than the others and grind a good point on it. . . no barbs or anything. **1968** *DARE* FW Addit **FL,** Gig, a ten foot spear with four prongs like arrowheads at the end; used to kill snakes, throw at fish. **1982** *Barrick Coll.* **csPA.** **1982** Sternberg *Fishing* 114, *Gigs,* or spears, are 3 to 5 inches wide, with three to six barbed tines mounted on a long handle. Speared frogs are used as cut-bait.

2 A goad. Cf **jig** n

1966 *DARE* (Qu. K27, . . *The sharp-pointed stick used to get oxen to move*) Inf **NC**26, Gig or spear.

gig v^{2}

1 To fish with a **gig** n^{2} **1;** hence vbl n *gigging,* n *gigger* one who uses such a **gig,** also the **gig** itself.

1803 (1965) Lewis *Jrls.* 36 **VA,** We fixed some spears after the indian method but have had too much to attend to of more importance than gigging fish. **1872** Schele de Vere *Americanisms* 339, *Gigging* . . is in Virginia still used to denote night-fishing with a three-pronged spear, as it was done in the days of Captain John Smith. **1895** *DN* 1.389 **wFL,** *Gig* . . to spear, generally fish or frogs, though anything run through with a sharp instrument is said to be *gigged.* **1899** (1912) Green *VA Folk-Speech* 195, *Gigging.* . . The act of taking fish with a gig. **1905** *DN* 3.81 **nwAR,** *Gig.* . . To spear (fish). . . Common. **1923** [see **3** below]. **1934** (1970) Wilson *Backwoods Amer.* 116 **Ozarks,** The giggers go barefoot or don wading boots, . . and select a long and relatively narrow stretch of river leading up to a pool of convenient shallowness. **1953** [see **gig** n^{2} **1**]. **1963** Watkins–Watkins *Yesterday Hills* 55 **cnGA,** Me and Rufe . . gigged bullfrogs and et the legs. **1965–70** *DARE* (Qu. P13) 84 Infs, **chiefly Sth, S Midl,** Gig; 22 Infs, **chiefly NMidl,** Gigging; **NC**53, Gig carp; **SC**40, Day gigging; night gigging; (Qu. P15) Inf **MO**36, Gigging. **1966–67** *DARE* Tape **AR**36, A friend of mine went with me one night to gigging. . . or spearing, either one you might wanna call it; **FL**16, There's two ways to catch frogs. That's either by giggin' 'em—at night you go along with a light and shine their eyes and gig 'em. . . Giggin' and shootin' is the two methods of catchin' frogs. . . Giggin' is usin' a harpoon, a three-prong gigger; **TX**18, Real often we find redfish and trout and gig those also. **1982** *Barrick Coll.* **csPA.**

2 To cheat.

1914 *DN* 4.163 **KS,** *Gig.* . . To cheat . . "Say, didn't you gig me a little on the price of that room?" **1934** (1940) Weseen *Dict. Amer. Slang* 98, *Gig*—To cheat; to swindle.

3 To prod, spur, or annoy.

1923 *DN* 5.208 **swMO,** *Gig.* . . To spear a fish, to prod with a pole, to annoy with suggestive remarks or practical jokes. **1944** Adams *Western Words* 65, *Gig* . . to use the spurs. **1967–68** *DARE* (Qu. Y7, . . *To be mean to another or to annoy another: "I don't know why she keeps ______ me all the time!"*) Infs **LA**14, **MO**25, Gigging.

4 To surprise.

1966 *DARE* (Qu. GG20, . . *'Very much surprised': "When those two got married, I was certainly ______.*") Inf **WA**16, Gigged.

gig n^{3}

1969 Sorden *Lumberjack Lingo* 47 **NEng, Gt Lakes,** *Gig.* . . A gadget like a wheelbarrow but with a runner instead of wheels.

gig n^{4} See **jig** n

gig back See **gig** v^{1}

gigger See **gig** v^{2} **1**

giggie n [Perh **gig** v^2 **3**]

1985 in 1986 *Barrick Coll.* **csPA,** "He slid off the road and got tight." . . The same person asked his neighbor to give him a *giggie* [push] to get loose.

gigging vbl n See **gig** v^2 **1**

gigging trail See **gig** v^1 **2**

gigi See **guigui**

gig trail See **gig** v^1 **2**

gig turner n [*gig* a light, two-wheeled carriage]

1982 *Smithsonian Letters* **cwIL,** One student interviewed an old lady locally born of Scotch-Irish descent whose grandfather had come from Kentucky in 1840's. When asked what she called a severe storm, her answer was, "A gig turner."

G.I. haircut n Also *G.I. (cut)* **scattered, but more freq C and Mid Atl, SE** See Map

A very short haircut.

1941 *AmSp* 16.165 [Army slang], G.I. haircut. One-inch trim. **1950** *WELS (Joking terms for . . hair cut: "I'm going to ________.")* 1 Inf, **WI,** Get a G.I. **1957** *NYT Mag.* 2 June 26/1, The Crew Cut is the big brother of what was once ridiculed as a G.I. haircut but was carried over into civilian life, with a dash of nostalgia by millions of now-graying men. **1965-70** *DARE* (Qu. X5, . . *Different kinds of men's haircuts*) 72 Infs, **scattered, but more freq C and Mid Atl, SE,** G.I.; **PA**134, **VA**9, G.I. cut; **CA**138, G.I. haircut.

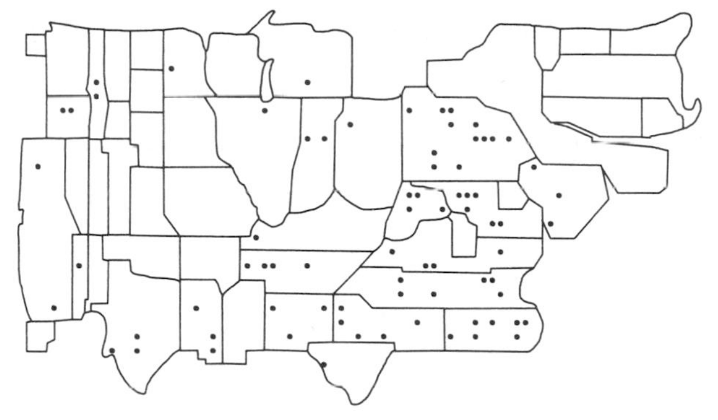

•G.I. haircut + varr (Qu. X5)

Gila n Usu |'hilə|; sp-pronc |'gilə|

A Forms.

1944 Kenyon-Knott *Pronc. Dict.* 184, *Gila* ['hilə]. **1989** *DARE* File **CA,** We used to laugh at visitors who talked about ['gilə] monsters rather than ['hilə] monsters.

B Senses.

1 See **Gila trout 1.**

2 See **Gila woodpecker.**

3 See **Gila monster 1.**

Gila monster n

1 also *Gila:* A brightly colored, venomous lizard *(Heloderma suspectum)* native chiefly to the Desert Southwest. [See quot 1877]

1877 Hodge *Arizona* 226 **sAZ,** There are many varieties of the saurian lizard species. . . There is one variety, however, peculiar to Arizona, found principally in the Gila River valley, and locally known as the Gila monster. **1904** Burdick *Mystic Mid-Region* 61, The Gila monster *heloderma horridum* . . is found in the southern portion of the Colorado Desert. This huge lizard is like the chameleon in one respect: it changes its color to conform to its surroundings. **1948** *Calif. Acad. Sciences News Letter* Oct. 2 *(DA),* The villain of the piece [is] a Gila monster, only venomous lizard in the United States. **1961** Douglas *My Wilderness* 85, Arizona also has many different species of lizards, but only two are poisonous—the Gila monster and the Mexican beaded lizard. **1969** *DARE* (Qu. R21) Inf **TX**66, Gila monster. **1979** Behler-King *Audubon Field Guide Reptiles* 547, Gila Monsters. . . Their bite, although rarely fatal to humans, serves to overpower animal predators and prey. **1987** *Smithsonian* 18.5.80 **Desert SW,** About 98 percent of the year the surface of the desert is too hot or cold for the Gilas. . . The Gila is extreme in this regard, but other lizards cope with the desert in somewhat the same fashion.

2 The collared lizard *(Crotaphytus collaris).*

1928 Baylor Univ. Museum *Contrib.* 16.10, Collared Lizard. . . Many persons in West Texas, mistaking it for the *Heloderma suspectum* . . call it . . *Gila Monster.*

3 The banded gecko *(Coleonyx variegatus).*

1928 Baylor Univ. Museum *Contrib.* 16.10, Banded Gecko. . . Many west Texans believe this lizard to be the young of the *Gila Monster* and call it by that name.

Gila trout n

1 also *Gila:* The Colorado chub *(Gila robusta).* [See quot 1911]

1852 (1854) Bartlett *Personal Narr.* 2.192 **sAZ,** A number of the fish called by Major Emory the "Gila trout" were caught near our camp. **1896** U.S. Natl. Museum *Bulletin* 47.226, *"Gila Trout".* . . have revived after being several hours out of the water and having become perfectly dry and stiff. **1900** *Land of Sunshine* 13.436 **sAZ,** The Gila is a hump-back chub, about a foot and a half long, with a low, large mouth and a long, broad tail. It is popularly known as . . Gila Trout . . ; and is about as poor eating as a fish can be. **1911** *Century Dict. Suppl., Gila. . . Gila trout,* a name sometimes applied to *Gila elegans,* a cyprinoid fish found in the Gila river: unlike and unrelated to the trout. **1963** Sigler-Miller *Fishes UT* 72, *Gila robusta.* . . Gila trout. . . will take a spinner, doughball, or worm readily and constitutes a "sportfish" for youngsters in parts of its range.

2 A **trout** *(Salmo gilae)* native to Arizona and New Mexico.

1957 Blair et al. *Vertebrates U.S.* 64, *Salmo gilae.* . . Gila trout. Recognized by numerous tiny black spots above L[ateral] l[ine]. **1964** Lowe *Vertebrates* 137 **AZ,** Gila Trout. . . The Arizona Game and Fish Department, alarmed over the rapid disappearance of the species, is attempting to restore this native fish through artificial propagation and restocking.

Gila willow n

A **seepwillow** (here: *Baccharis glutinosa*).

1931 U.S. Dept. Ag. *Misc. Pub.* 158 **SW,** *Seepwillow . . ,* locally named . . Gila . . willow, . . is a bush . . 3 to 12 feet high, with viscid willowlike leaves. **1937** U.S. Forest Serv. *Range Plant Hdbk.* B33, Seepwillow, known locally as . . Gila . . willow, . . is a graceful, willowy shrub.

Gila woodpecker n Also *Gila* [See quot 1928]

A fawn-colored woodpecker *(Centurus uropygialis)* with black-and-white barred back, native chiefly to the Desert Southwest. Also called **carpintero, saguaro woodpecker**

1858 Baird *Birds* 111, *Centurus uropygialis. . . Gila Woodpecker.* . . This very distinct species combines the peculiar characteristics of both *C. carolinus* and *flaviventris.* **1898** (1900) Davie *Nests N. Amer. Birds* 276, *Gila Woodpecker.* . . Though breeding in mesquite and cottonwood trees, they show a great preference for groves of giant cactus. **1917** (1923) *Birds Amer.* 2.163, It is, of course, comparatively easy for the Gila to make a way through the fiber of the cactus. **1928** Bailey *Birds NM* 381, The common name of the Gila Woodpecker was bestowed on account of its abundance in the valley of that river up which it ranges from Arizona into New Mexico as far as the town of Gila. **1957** Jaeger *N. Amer. Deserts* 200, *Gila Woodpecker.* . . A bird of the tree-cactus country, . . [it] feeds on mistletoe berries, cactus fruits, and insects. **1961** Douglas *My Wilderness* 81 **AZ,** The gila woodpecker comes here looking for the saguaro cactus, where it will drill for a nest, using it a season or so and then leaving it for the tiny elf owl to occupy. **1965** Herlan *NV Highway Bird Watcher* 35, *Gila Woodpecker.* . . is the only desert woodpecker which displays a white wing patch.

gild See **gilt 2**

Gilderoy's kite, higher than adv phr Also *higher than Gilroy's kite* [Appar in allusion to the 17th cent Scottish robber Gilderoy, of whom a ballad reports "They hung him high aboon the rest."]

Very high.

1869 Twain *Innocents* 192, The first time she took her new toy into action she got it knocked higher than Gilderoy's kite—to use the language of the pilgrims. **1887** (1895) Robinson *Uncle Lisha* 60 **wVT,** Tew drinks on't clear 'ould knock a feller higher 'n Gilderoy's kite. **1923** *DN* 5.238 **swWI,** *Higher than Gilderoy's kite.* . . Very high; or a simple intensive. "He knocked him higher 'n Gilderoy's kite." **1958** *VT Hist.* new ser 26.272, Higher than Gilderoy's kite. (Gilroy's kite).

Gilead fir n *obs* Cf **balm of Gilead 2b**
A **balsam fir** (here: *Abies balsamea*).
1859 (1968) Bartlett *Americanisms* 20, *Abies balsamea*. . . is also called Canada Balsam and Gilead Fir.

gilflirt See **gillflirt** n

gilgadget, gilhickey See **gillgadget**

gilhool(e)y See **gillgadget**

gilia n
Std: a plant of the chiefly western genus *Gilia;* also any of var plants formerly included in *Gilia* and now listed in such genera as *Allophyllum, Collomia, Eriastrum, Gymnosteris, Ipomopsis, Langloisia, Leptodactylon, Linanthastrum, Linanthus, Microsteris,* and *Navarretia.* For other names see **bird's eye 2, desert calico, evening-snow 1, field gillyflower, goldeneye 3, ground pink 2, Indian trumpet, lilac sunbonnet, mustang clover, pinkspot, prickly phlox, prickly sage, rock rose, scarlet gilia, skunkweed, standing cypress, stardust, starflower, stickerbush, stinkweed, threadflower, tiny trumpet, whisker brush, white mountainweed, whorl phlox, wild bouvardia**

‡giliqua n
1968 *DARE* (Qu. M21b, . . *An outside toilet building*) Inf **NY**92, Giliqua ['gɪlɪ,kwa].

Gill n[1] See **Gill-over-the-ground**

gill n[2] Also *gillie, gillipin, gilly(chick)* [Cf *SND gillygacus, gillygawkie* a silly person, and *gilly-gawpus* a fool]
A fool, dupe, rube.
1889 (1971) Farmer *Americanisms* 264, *Gilly*. . . An idiot; a soft pate. **1911** *DN* 3.544 **NE,** *Gillie,* [g]. . . Term of slight disparagement; a rather stupid or foolish person. **1915** *DN* 4.202, *Gilly,* a simpleton. "You gilly! Didn't you know mustard would burn your tongue?" **1927** *DN* 5.447 [Underworld jargon], *Gill*. . . A credulous person. **1930** Shoemaker *1300 Words* 24 **cPA Mts** (as of c1900), *Gilly*—An easily led, or quickly corrupted person. **c1930** Swann *Lang. Circus Lot* 9, *Gills:* Farmers, country people, etc. **1936** Fellows–Freeman *This Way* 119, "Rube" was not the only word by which circus folk stigmatized the townsmen. They were also called "gillipins" or "gills," "jays," and "saps." **1940** *Sat. Eve. Post* 10 Feb 88, You are a gillie all right. **1955** Adams *Grandfather* 18 **NY** (as of 1830s), Ever hear of Adams Basin, you gillychick?

gillagahike n Also *giddledehike* Also sp *gilligahike* Cf **gillgadget, gilligan hitch**
Any of various machines used in logging: see quots.
1950 *Western Folkl.* 9.121 **nwOR** [Sawmill workers' speech], *Giddledehike.* A motor vehicle used to stack lumber; usually called a hyster, which is a trade name. **1958** McCulloch *Woods Words* 70 **Pacific NW,** *Gillagahike (also spelled gilligahike)*—a. Any rig used in doing a peculiar or odd job. b. Any machine to roll up heavy lines. c. A motor speeder. d. A small donkey, as for example, one used on a little incline to haul men and supplies up the hill to the Larkin camp at Nalpee, Washington.

gill-creep-by-the-ground See **gill-over-the-ground**

gilley whipper n
1972 *Atlanta Letters* **GA,** Gully washer or Gilley whipper—Bad rain storm.

gillflirt n Also sp *gilflirt, jillflirt* [*OED* 1632 →] *old-fash*
See quots.
1859 Matsell *Vocabulum* 37, *Gilflirt.* A proud, capricious woman. **1902** *DN* 2.257 **sIL,** *Jill-flirt*. . . A wanton. **1942** McAtee *Dial. Grant Co. IN* 73 (as of 1890s), *Gillflirt* . . a heartless wanton. N.I.D. labels the word Archaic. I heard it used by a factory worker from the East.

‡gillflirt v Cf **gillflirted** adj **2**
To foul up.
1958 McCulloch *Woods Words* 70 **Pacific NW,** *Gilflirt* [sic]—To get all fouled up in horse logging.

gillflirted adj Also sp *jillflirted*
1 Of a woman or female animal: having the vulva injured, usu in giving birth; hence n *jillyflirt* one so injured.
1902 *DN* 2.237 **sIL,** *Jill-flirted*. . . Having the vulva lacerated in delivery. **1930** in 1977 Randolph *Pissing in the Snow* 191 **Ozarks,** They was afraid . . maybe she'd be jill-flirted for life. **1964** *PADS* 42.17 **csKY,** *Gillflirted* ['dʒɪl-]. . . A term applied to a mare that was ruptured in giving birth to a colt. **1974** in 1982 *Barrick Coll.* **csPA,** *Jilly-flirt*—mare with no membrane between anus and vagina.
2 Fouled up; hence adv *gillflirtedly* incompetently.
1959 *IN Mag. Hist.* 55.3.234 (as of c1920), September was a month of half-measures during which living creatures jillflirtedly tried everything and completed little. The amazing part of it was that most everything was delightful! **1987** *DARE* File **nVA,** Gillflirted—messed-up (of a situation or machinery).

gillgadget n Also *gilhickey, gilhool(e)y, gillhicket* Also sp *gilgadget* Cf **doohickey 1**
A thingamajig; a special device or contrivance.
1934 (1940) Weseen *Dict. Amer. Slang* 338, *Gadget*. . . Gilgadget is a variant. **1942** Berrey–Van den Bark *Amer. Slang* 75.4, *Contrivance; Indefinite object:* . . gilhickey. **1947** in 1960 Wentworth–Flexner *Slang* 214/2, I forgot to press the hickeymadoodle on the gilhooley. **1950** *Western Folkl.* 9.117 **nwOR** [Logger speech], *Gilhooly.* Term applied to a method of extracting logs from behind stumps and other obstructions. **1954** *PADS* 21.28 **SC,** *Gillhicket*. . . Any small mechanical device, monkey wrench, special screwdriver, etc. **1954** *PADS* 21.28 **SC,** *Gillgadget*. . . A thingumbob, a dingus.

Gill-go-by-the-ground See **Gill-over-the-ground**

Gill-go-over-the-ground See **Gill-over-the-ground**

gillhicket See **gillgadget**

gillie See **gill** n[2]

gilligahike See **gillagahike**

gilli-galoo fish n Cf **gilly-gilloo bird**
An imaginary fish.
1939 Tryon *Fearsome Critters* 63, *The Whiffenpoof* (Sometimes called the Gilli-Galoo Fish). . . A tasty fish, found only in perfectly round lakes. . . To catch him . . bore a square hole in the water. Bait . . with a bit of cheese. . . When he emerges, spit tobacco-juice in his eye. This will make him so swell with rage that he won't be able to withdraw into the hole.

gilligan hitch n Cf **gillagahike**
1984 Weaver *TX Crude* 94, *A Gilligan hitch.* Name used for any method of binding with a chain. "Hell, throw a Gilligan hitch on it, and let's go!"

gillipin See **gill** n[2]

Gill-over-the-ground n Also *Gill;* also sp *Jill;* for addit varr see quots [*OED* 1597 →] **scattered, but esp NEast**
=**ground ivy 1.**
1864 *Catalogue of Herbs* **swME,** *Gill run*—Glechoma hederacea. **1876** Hobbs *Bot. Hdbk.* 42, Gill-go-over-the-ground, Ground ivy, Nepeta glechoma. **1889** *Century Dict.* 2513, *Gill*. . . [*Century* Ed: Short for *gill-creep-by-the-ground,* or *gill-run-over-the-ground,* homely names for the plant in which *gill* is a familiar application of the feminine name.] The ground ivy, *Nepeta Glechoma. Ibid* 2514, *Gill-over-ground, gill-over-the-ground*. . . The ground-ivy, *Nepeta Glechoma.* **1892** *Jrl. Amer. Folkl.* 5.102, *Nepeta Glechoma*. . . Gill-over-the-ground. E. Mass. **1894** *Ibid* 7.96, *Nepeta Glechoma*. . . Gill-run-over-the-ground, Conn. **1897** *Ibid* 10.53, *Nepeta Glechoma*. . . Gill-run-over-grass . . Cambridge, Mass. **1900** Lyons *Plant Names* 174, *G[lechoma] hederacea*. . . Gill-over-the-ground, . . Gill-go-by-the-ground, Gill-run. **1929** *Torreya* 29.150 **ME,** Nepeta glechoma . . *"Gill-go-over-the-ground."* **1933** Small *Manual SE Flora* 1154, *G[lechoma] hederacea*. . . Ground-ivy. Gill-over-the-ground. **1940** Clute *Amer. Plant Names* 26, *N[epeta] hederacea*. . . *Gill-over-the-ground.* Gill-go-by-the ground, gill-run-over. **1959** Carleton *Index Herb. Plants* 68, *Jill-o'er-the-ground.* **1961** Douglas *My Wilderness* 193 **MD,** The tiny gill-over-the-ground, with small blue flowers, is everywhere. *Ibid* 252 **nME,** Deep in the floor litter one will find. . . long tangled creepers of ground ivy with their small, rounded leaves and purplish blossoms—the plant known as gill-over-the-ground or runaway-robin. **1967** Borland *Hill Country* 130 **nwCT,** The little creeping mint called . . gill-over-the-ground is thriving and loaded with blossoms. The gill, as we always call it, is an insistent creeper. **1967-70** *DARE* (Qu. S8) Inf **PA**53, Gill-over-the-ground; (Qu. S9) Inf **PA**234, Gill-go-over-the-ground; (Qu. S21) Inf **IL**55, Gill-on-the-ground; **NY**107, Gill-run-over-the-ground; (Qu. S26e) Inf **PA**35, Gill-over-the-ground. **1973** Hitchcock–Cronquist *Flora Pacific NW* 402, *G[lechoma] hederacea*. . . Gill-over-the-ground.

gill poke See **jill poke**

Gill-run(-over-grass), Gill-run-over(-the-ground) See **Gill-over-the-ground**

gilly n See **gill** n[2]

gillychick See **gill** n[2]

gillyflirt n

1901 *DN* 2.140, *Gillyflirt*. . . Gillyflower. Otsego Co., N.Y.

gilly gar n [Perh var of *billy gar*]

Prob either a **longnose gar** or a **shortnose gar.**

1966 *DARE* (Qu. P3, *Freshwater fish that are not good to eat*) Inf **MO**7, Gilly gar.

gilly-gilloo bird n

A **yellowlegs** (here: *Totanus flavipes*).

1923 U.S. Dept. Ag. *Misc. Circular* 13.61, *Lesser Yellowlegs*. . . *Vernacular Names*. . . *In local use*. . . Gilly-gilloo bird . . (Mo.) **1932** Bennitt *Check-list* 30 **MO**, Lesser yellow-legs. . . Gilly-gilloo bird. **1970** *DARE* FW Addit **nwPA**, As much sense as a gilly-gilloo bird.

gilly g'lieu n Cf **gilli-galoo fish, gilly-gilloo bird**

1958 McCulloch *Woods Words* 70 **Pacific NW**, *Gilly g'lieu*—A hunting cabin or shack.

gilly-west See **galley-west**

gilpin, go (a-) v phr [Perh in allusion to William Cowper's ballad "John Gilpin" (1782)]

To move fast.

1891 *PMLA* 6.173 **TN**, We have the two expressions, *go kitin'* and *go gilpin'*, both of which mean about the same thing . . 'to go rapidly.' . . To *go gilpin* is a common expression which I take to be derived from the story of "John Gilpin's Ride." **1893** Shands *MS Speech* 33, Go a gilpin [go ə gɪlpɪn]. Used by all to mean *to go fast*. . . In Mississippi the phrase is never used without the insertion of *a* between *go* and *gilpin*. It may be a corruption of *go-a-galloping* or *go-a-yelping*.

Gilroy's kite, higher than See **Gilderoy's kite, higher than**

gilt n

1 A young sow, esp one that has not yet been bred.

1890 *DN* 1.70 **LA**, *Gilt:* a sow with her first litter of pigs. Very common among the farmers of northern Louisiana. **1917** *DN* 4.412 **NC**, *Gilt*. . . A female shoat. [*DN* Ed: General among hog-raisers.] **1950** *WELS* 2 Infs, **cw,seWI**, Gilt. **c1960** *Wilson Coll.* **csKY**, *Gilt*. . . A young sow. **1965–68** *DARE* (Qu. K51, . . *Pigs . . very young one*) Infs **KS**15, **MN**17, **OR**10, Gilt; **MD**13, Gilt—a young sow not yet bred; (Qu. K51b, *A half-grown pig;* total Infs questioned, 75) Inf **MS**58, Gilt—after they breed they are called sows; (Qu. K51c, *A full-grown pig;* total Infs questioned, 75) Inf **FL**12, Gilt—a female before she has pigs; (Qu. K58) Infs **CA**87, Gilt—the young sow pigs; **NC**8, Gilt—a female pig; **WI**24, Gilt [gɛlt]—a young female; sow—female after littering. **1966** *DARE* FW Addit **MS**4, Gilt—unbred sow. **1969** *DARE* Tape **CA**163, They had some very fine hogs, so I bought a couple of gilts. A gilt is a young sow. **1973** Allen *LAUM* 1.250 (as of c1950), 20 infs, **IA**, Gilt . . a female hog; 1 inf, **MN**, Gilt . . a female hog; 6 infs, **IA**, Gilt: . . terms for a young sow. . . 1 inf, **IA**, [Gilt] An unbred 'sow.'

2 also *gelt, gild, geld:* A male hog, usu one that has been castrated. [Prob by confusion with *gelt* past pple of *geld*] Cf **gelding**

1950 *WELS* (*A castrated pig*) 2 Infs, **c,swWI**, Gilt; 1 Inf **swWI**, Gelt. **1965–70** *DARE* (Qu. K58, *A castrated pig*) Infs **CO**7, **MA**5, **NC**36, **NY**160, **OH**6, 75, 89, **PA**75, 218, **WA**5, **WY**5, Gilt; **OH**22, Gilt—or is that female? **PA**59, **NY**206, **TX**33, **VA**33, Gelt; **IL**7, Gild; **CA**152, Gild [Inf doubtful]; **CA**195, **PA**56, Geld; (Qu. K52, *A male pig kept for breeding*) Inf **MN**40, Boar, gilt; **WA**3, Gilt—A young male before breeding age.

gimbal v

See quot.

1968 *DARE* Tape **NJ**31, [Inf:] 'Cause when that sea hits 'em they gimbal ['gɪmbl̩] and if you don't top 'em [=pilings] they'll settle an' you'll have your walkway all crooked. [FW:] When they gimbal, you mean they give and wiggle back and forth? [Inf:] Yeah.

gimbal-jawed adj Pronc-sp *jimble-jawed* [*gimbal* n] Cf **jimberjawed**

Having a long, loose, or sagging lower jaw; fig, loquacious.

1859 (1968) Bartlett *Americanisms* 169, *Gimbal-jawed* or *jimber-jawed*. One whose lower jaw is loose and projecting. **1889** (1971) Farmer *Americanisms* 264, *Gimbal-jawed* or *gimber-jawed*. . . Idiomatically, to talk with loquacity; or, in slang parlance, "nineteen to the dozen." **1945** Colcord *Sea Language* 87, Alongshore, gimbal-jawed means having a protruding or wabbling lower jaw. **1950** *PADS* 14.41 **SC**, *Jimble-jawed*. . . Having a long face with a sad expression. "Whut makes you look so jimble-jawed?" **1966** *DARE* (Qu. X6, *If a person's lower jaw sticks out prominently*) Inf **GA**15, Gimbal-jawed ['ǰɪmbl̩].

gimberjawed See **jimberjawed**

gimbler, grease a See **gimlet, grease a**

gim(b)lin' stick See **gambling stick**

gimini See **jiminy**

gimlet v [*gimlet* to bore as with a gimlet]

To ride a horse so as to make its back sore.

1922 Rollins *Cowboy* 125, These men [=heavy riders] could cling to the bucker and throw the rope as successfully as could their "lighter-riding" brothers, but they "gimletted" or "beefsteaked" far more horses' backs and tired far more ponies. **1929** *AmSp* 5.64 **NE**, If he is a "light rider" . . he does not "gimlet" . . the horse, make its back sore, as does the "hard rider."

gimlet-assed, gimlet-ended See **gimlet-hammed**

gimlet, grease a v phr Also *grease a gimbler*

In fig phr: See quot.

1969 *DARE* (Qu. JJ15a, . . *"He hasn't sense enough to ______ ."*) Infs **AR**28, **IL**5, **KY**84, **NY**199, Grease a gimlet; **IL**96, Grease a gimbler.

gimlet-hammed adj Also *gimlet-assed, ~-ended*

Having thin thighs or hips.

1929 Dobie *Vaquero* 239, At a distance, one of them with arched neck, distended nostrils, and flowing mane and tail looked graceful, even magnificent, but near at hand he was likely to appear gimlet hammed and narrow chested. **1968** Adams *Western Words* 126, *Gimlet-ended*. . . A cowboy's description of someone with small hips. **1985** Ladwig *How to Talk Dirty* 11 **Ozarks**, Gimlet-assed . . thin. **1986** Pederson *LAGS Concordance*, 1 inf, **cnAR**, Gimlet-ended—wide top, narrow at end; [used of a] person too.

gimlet seed n

1970 *DARE* (Qu. HH14, *Ways of teasing a beginner or inexperienced person . . : "Go get me ______ ."*) Inf **KY**91, Gimlet seeds [laughter].

gimlet stick n [Prob by folk-etym]

=**gambrel 1.**

1963 Watkins–Watkins *Yesterday Hills* 96 **cnGA**, After the hair was removed, the farmer stuck a hickory gimlet stick about two feet long under the leaders in the hog's hind legs.

gimme v See **give A1d**

gimme n attrib Also sp *gimmie* [Pronc-spp for *give me;* because cigarette papers were formerly given free to purchasers of loose tobacco]

Given as an advertising or promotional gesture.

1941 Perry *Hold Autumn* 71 **TX**, Sam bought . . a can of dime tobacco and some gimme papers for himself. **1984** Wilder *You All Spoken Here* 195 **Sth**, *Gimmie paper:* Same as above [=a book, or pack, of cigarette papers]. **1989** *DARE* File **cTX**, The baseball-type caps bearing the names of feed, or farm implement or oil companies . . and which they give away, are called gimme caps.

gimme bird n

=**screech owl** (here: *Otus asio floridanus*).

1945 Saxon *Gumbo Ya-Ya* 549 **LA**, When 'Chouette' (screech owl) or 'Gimme Bird' sings around a house, it means there will be a death in the house.

gimmie See **gimme**

gimp n [Prob from *gimp* braid or fishing line stiffened with wire] **chiefly NEng**

Courage, spirit.

1901 *Munsey's Mag.* 24.587/2, Sort of took the gimp out of you, didn't it? **1927** *AmSp* 3.135 **ME**, When unpleasantly surprised, an old person said "it took the gimp all out of me." **1931–33** *LANE Worksheets* **cwMA**, He's got lots of gimp in him. **1948** Manfred *Chokecherry* 104

nwIA, Cor taunted, "I told you, Wilbur. He's never had any gimp of his own." **1968–69** *DARE* (Qu. GG37, . . *Brave or courageous: "He's got plenty of______."*) Inf **CT**13, Gimp; (Qu. HH27b, . . *A[n] . . able and energetic person . "He's got lots of ______."*) Infs **CT**13, **MA**15, Gimp. **1969** *DARE* FW Addit **NY,** She [=a horse] had the gimp and the get there. She had what it took.

gimpy adj **[gimp** n]
Spirited, lively.
1889 (1971) Farmer *Americanisms* 264, *Gimpy*. . . As used colloquially for sprightly or active, this word . . may be classed among Americanisms. **1941** *LANE* Map 461 *(Lively, spry),* 15 infs, **NH, ME, VT,** Gimpy; 1 inf, **swME,** Gimpy, of horses.

gimson weed See **jimson weed**

gin n See **gin pole 1**

gin v[1] Also sp *jin* [From rapid circular motion, prob as in the action of a cotton gin]

1 with *about, around;* To chase about, stir up (cattle).
1884 Aldridge *Ranch Notes* 88 **scKS,** The boss of the range has appointed two of his men to help to hold the herd, and also to prevent everybody from rushing in, as soon as the cattle are rounded up, and 'ginning them around,' as he would call it, so that no one can work properly, and the calves all get separated from their mothers, making it impossible to tell to whom they belong. **1929** Dobie *Vaquero* 225, Ten men are a small crew to handle a herd of 4500 cattle, especially when the cattle are hungry, thirsty, and feverish from having been ginned about. **1931** (1960) Dobie *Open Range* 306, Gin about . . Chase around. *Ibid* 243, He did not want them "ginned about" any more than was necessary.

2 also with *up:* To stir up, get (something) going.
1887 F. Francis Jr. *Saddle & Mocassin* vii.124 *(OED),* The Apaches were out to beat hell . . And they *were* ginning her up, and making things a bit lively, that's a fact! **1938** *AmSp* 13.5 **AR,** *Gin*. . . To act vigorously. 'The team ginned it last night in their scrimmage.' **1970** *DARE* File **FL, VA,** I'll see if I can gin [ǰɪn] up this meeting.

3 also with *around:* To work rapidly, bustle about.
1902 *DN* 2.235 **sIL,** *Gin* [ǰɪn]. . . To work rapidly. This word, as used, seems to convey the idea of *ability* to turn off work with ease and rapidity. **1931** *AmSp* 7.91 **eKY,** No, the babe's still puny but Marthy's a-ginnin' around'! **1942** Perry *Texas* 136, Many of our local expressions derive from our close association with cotton. If a man is seen doing something in great haste, we say that he was "really ginnin'." **1970** *DARE* (Qu. A19, . . *"I'm late, I'll have to ______."*) Inf **TX**80A, Gin [ǰɪn] around.

4 usu with *around, about:* To move around, fiddle about; to do odd jobs; hence n *ginner* errand boy. Cf **jim** v
1930 *DN* 6.84 **cSC,** *Ginnin' around,* moving about. **1939** *AmSp* 14.156 **WV,** There is a verbal colloquialism 'to gin (or jim) around' which means 'just to dabble around, to fool around, to fiddle around.' 'Well, what have you been doing during the holidays?' Answer: 'Oh, just ginning (or jimming) around.' **1940** *Qrly. Jrl. Speech* 26.265 **VA,** An *errand boy* in Wise or Lee counties is a "ginner," and a boy "gins" for someone when he *runs an errand.* **1967–68** *DARE* (Qu. A10, . . *Doing little unimportant things . . "I'm just ______."*) Infs **OH**31, 38, Ginning around. **c1970** *Halpert Coll.* 26 **wKY, nwTN,** Ginnin' around . . = killing time pretending to work. **1976** Garber *Mountain-ese* 34 **Appalachians,** *Gin* . . do odd jobs—Josh don't have no job atall, he jist likes to gin around the house. *Ibid* 48, We har'd him as a part-time hand jist to jin about the farm. **1981** *High Coll.* **ceKY** (as of c1930), I wasn't doing much—I was just *ginning around.*

5 To beat or reprimand; to fight; hence vbl n *ginning.* Cf **gin-rollers, be put through**
1938 *AmSp* 13.5 **AR,** 'They gave him a good ginning.' That is, they gave him a severe reprimand or beating. The expression has its origin in the threshing process of a cotton gin. **1972** Claerbaut *Black Jargon* 66, *Gin* . . to fight; scuffle.

gin conj[1] Also *gen* [Scots, nEngl dial; ult origin uncertain] **chiefly Appalachians**
If, whether.
1922 (1926) Kephart *Highlanders* 271 **sAppalachians,** I'll ax the woman gin she can git ye a bite. *Ibid* 328, [He] . . regarded the crowd with an expression of "Tetch me gin ye dar!" **1931** *PMLA* 46.1303 **sAppalachians,** *Gin,* if. **1934** *WV Review* Dec 78, [Archaic words still used in West Virginia include] *gin* for *if.* **1944** *PADS* 2.43 **NC, SC,** Gen, gin [gɪn] . . if.

gin prep [Scots dial; aphet form of *again*] Cf **gin** conj[2], **again C2, against B1**
By (a specified time).
1899 (1912) Green *VA Folk-Speech* 196, *Gin*. . . Against a certain time; by: as, "I'll be there gin five o'clock." Hard *g*. **1903** *DN* 2.314 **seMO,** *Gin* or *agin*. . . Against; by. 'I'll be there gin five o'clock.'

gin conj[2] Also *gen* [Scots, nEngl dial; aphet forms of *again.* The sense development has prob been influenced by **gin** conj[1].] **Sth, S Midl** Cf **gin prep, again D, against C1**
Before, by the time that; when.
1884 *Anglia* 7.261, Negro speech contains many archaisms . . Use of *'gin, 'ginst* in expressions of time or as conjunctions, *'gin I come.* **1907** Wright *Shepherd* 17 **swMO,** Hit'll be plumb dark 'gin I git home. **1908** *DN* 3.314 **eAL, wGA,** *Gin, ginst*. . . Against, before, by the time. "You better be thu that work gin I get back." **1918** *DN* 5.18 **NC,** Agin, by the time that, before. "Do it agin I come back." Also *gin.* **1931** *AmSp* 7.93 **eKY,** She wuz plum drug-out 'gin she got there with that young 'un on her hip. **1944** *PADS* 2.43 **NC, SC,** *Gen, gin* [gɪn]. . . After, when. . . "Gin I work all the week, I'm jest too tired to dress up uv a Sunday." **1949** Webber *Backwoods Teacher* 233 **Ozarks,** The ol' man [=the devil]—he's a serious thing an' a heap o' folks will find it out gin he gets holt of 'em and starts roastin' 'em. **1958** *PADS* 29.10 **TN,** *Gin:* When, as soon as. "Gin I get home it will be time to feed the turkeys." **c1960** *Wilson Coll.* **csKY,** *Gin*. . . By the time that: "Gin I get there, it will be dark." **1974** Fink *Mountain Speech* 11 **wNC, eTN,** It'll be dark 'gin I get home.

gin v[2] See **give A1c, 2a, 3a**

gin about See **gin** v[1] **1, 4**

gin around See **gin** v[1] **1, 3, 4**

ginched adj
Lame.
1982 *DARE* File **swNH,** Ginched (gimpy, lame).

gine See **go** v **A4c**

Ginee See **Guinea** n[1]

gineine See **genuine**

gineral See **general**

ginerally See **generally** adv

ginerl See **general**

ging n [*OED* a1100 →; *"Obs."*] *obs*
1899 (1912) Green *VA Folk-Speech* 196, *Ging*. . . Company; people. Gang.

ginger n

1 Std: a plant of the genus *Zingiber;* also the spice derived from such a plant.

2 Spirit, energy, temper; often in phrr *get one's ginger up, full of ginger* and varr. *somewhat old-fash*
1843 (1846) Haliburton *Attaché* (1st ser) 1.261, Curb him [=a horse] up, talk Yankee to him, and get his ginger up. **1888** *World* (N.Y.) 13 May (F.) *(DA),* Your spinal column is requiring a hinge, and . . considerable ginger is departing from your resolution to bear up and enjoy yourself. **1897** *KS Univ. Qrly.* (ser B) 6.88, *Ginger:* spunk.—General. **1905** *DN* 3.61 **NE,** *Ginger*. . . Life, energy . . "He needs a little ginger." **1908** *DN* 3.315 **eAL, wGA,** *Ginger*. . . Life, snap. "He lacks ginger." **1942** Warnick *Garrett Co. MD* 7 **nwMD** (as of 1900–1918), *Ginger*. . . temper. "She's got her ginger up this morning." **c1960** *Wilson Coll.* **csKY,** *Ginger*. . . Temper, spiritedness. **1965–70** *DARE* (Qu. KK28) 16 Infs, **chiefly Nth,** Full of ginger; **CA**164, Full of pep and ginger; **PA**234, Full of piss and ginger; (Qu. Y22) Inf **OH**6, He's full of ginger; (Qu. BB47) Infs **CA**4, **GA**59, **NY**196, 232, **OH**72, **WI**76, Full of ginger; (Qu. HH27b) Infs **MS**21, **MA**4, Ginger; **GA**77, Full of ginger; (Qu. KK27) Infs **CA**24, **KY**59, Full of ginger; (Qu. AA7b) Inf **PA**175, Full of piss and ginger; (Qu. GG5) Inf **IA**17, Ginger; (Qu. GG29) Inf **CO**21, Full of ginger. [28 of 33 Infs old]

3 also *gingerbread,* also in var phrr: Used as a mild oath. [Prob euphem for *Jesus*]
1865 in 1894 Lowell *Letters* 1.348, There, by ginger! I meant to give the merest hint of a sentiment, and I have gone splash into a moral. **1903** *DN* 2.297 **Cape Cod MA,** *Ginger!* . . Exclamation upon touching something hot. **1907** *DN* 3.206 **nwAR,** *Ginger!* **1916** Porter *Just David* 309, 'Well, by ginger!' exclaimed the man again. **1924** *DN* 5.268, *Ginger:* by

———, oh ———, ——— pop (all surp[rise]). **1930** *VA Qrly. Rev.* 6.241 **S Midl,** I says, 'We can, by ginger!' **1966–68** *DARE* (Qu. NN27a, . . *Substitutes for 'god'*) Inf **NH**5, By ginger! (Qu. NN30) Inf **NH**5, By ginger! (Qu. NN31) Inf **NY**65, Ginger creepers! (Qu. NN32) Inf **MA**5, By gingerbread! [All Infs old] **1983** *DARE* File **ceWI,** Ginger blue—an exclamation.

4 =coltsfoot 1.

1900 Lyons *Plant Names* 381, *T[ussilago] Farfara*. . . Ginger. . . A cough remedy. **1930** Sievers *Amer. Med. Plants* 24, *Coltsfoot. . . Other common names*. . . Ginger. **1959** Carleton *Index Herb. Plants* 52, *Ginger* . . Tussilago farfara.

5 =wild ginger.

1970 Kirk *Wild Edible Plants W. U.S.* 209, *Asarum* species. . . Wild Ginger, Ginger. . . Any of the species have a rootstock that may be used as a substitute for commercial ginger.

ginger adj [Back-formation from *gingerly* adv; *OED* 1600 →; "*Obs.* exc. dial."]

Cautious.

1968 *DARE* File **Boston MA,** "If we're ginger about it, the cord may stay up." Common usage.

ginger berry See **ginger plum**

gingerbread See **ginger** n **3, ginger cake 2**

ginger cake n

1 also *gingy cake:* A cake or cookie flavored with ginger. **esp Sth, S Midl**

1831 (1940) Motte *Charleston to Harvard* 53 **SC,** Those days of ginger-cakes and four-pennies are gone. **1859** Taliaferro *Fisher's R.* 186 **nwNC** (as of 1820s) [Black], What the people would have done for "gingycakes" at their musters and public gatherings I can not tell, had it not been for clever Josh. **1896** Harris *Sister Jane* 351 **GA,** I'll bet a thrip to a ginger-cake that Mary got you in a corner out there in the garden and asked you to marry her. **1899** Chesnutt *Conjure Woman* 18 **csNC** [Black], He wuz 'er ole nigger, er de color er a gingy-cake. **1908** Fox *Lonesome Pine* 141 **KY,** On election days the country people would bring in gingercakes made of cane-molasses. **1910** *DN* 3.442 **cwNY,** *Ginger-cake*. . . A plain sweet cake seasoned with ginger; gingerbread. **1937** Johnson *Ante-Bellum NC* 103, "Nigger Josh Easly" is doing a thriving business with his "gingy cakes." **c1960** *Wilson Coll.* **csKY,** *Gingercakes* . . Actual cakes of gingerbread, made from thick dough and baked like biscuits. **1967–69** *DARE* (Qu. H32) Inf **KY**5, Ginger cake; (Qu. NN12a) Inf **PA**27, Go home and tell your mother she's baking ginger cakes.

2 also *gingerbread;* also adj: A medium yellow-brown color—usu in ref to people of mixed blood.

1880 Tourgée *Bricks* 71 **NC,** There were three or four hundred scholars, of all ages, sizes, and colors—black, brown, white apparently, and all shades of what we used to call 'ginger-cake'. **1912** Green *VA Folk-Speech* 196, *Ginger-bread*. . . A colour. "Ginger-bread negro." [**c1937** in 1972 *Amer. Slave* 2.128 **SC,** My father was a ginger-bread colored man, not a full-blooded nigger. Dat's how I is altogether yellow.] **1967–69** *DARE* (Qu. J5, *A cat with fur of mixed colors*) Inf **RI**15, Brown and black with yellow hairs called "gingerbread," [as opposed to] "calico," with distinct patches; (Qu. HH29b, . . *People of mixed blood—part Negro*) Inf **SC**40, Ginger cake—an intermediate shade of skin of Negroes.

3 A piece of manure.

1968 *DARE* (Qu. L17 . . *Names* . . *for manure*) Inf **PA**169, Ginger cakes.

ginger drink See **ginger water**

ginger leaf n

1 A **wintergreen** (here: *Gaultheria procumbens*).

1903 *DN* 2.297 **Cape Cod MA** (as of a1857), Ginger leaf . . wintergreen. **1941** *Torreya* 41.51.

2 =turkey mullein.

1900 Lyons *Plant Names* 147, *E[remocarpus] setigerus*. . . California. Ginger-leaf. **1911** *Century Dict. Suppl., Ginger-leaf*. . . Same as turkey mullen.

ginger lily n [*OEDS* 1900→] **esp HI**

A plant of the genus *Hedychium,* esp *H. coronarium.* Also called **garland flower**

1929 Neal *Honolulu Gardens* 84, *Ginger lily, garland flower (Hedychium coronarium* . . *).* This plant grows wild in damp places. **1930** Degener *Ferns of HI* 117, Flowers of both kinds [=*Hedychium flavescens* and *H. coronarium*] of gingerlilies are gathered and strung into fragrant garlands, or *lei* [sic]. **1933** Small *Manual SE Flora* 361, *Hedychium coronarium* . . *Ginger-lily*. . . has become naturalized in marshes in eastern Ga. and along the Mississippi River below New Orleans, La. **1953** Greene–Blomquist *Flowers South* 154, *Ginger-lily (Hedychium coronarium)*. . . Several large, fragrant, butterfly-like flowers . . stand erect from a terminal bract, while the old flowers droop. **1965** Neal *Gardens HI* 252, *Ginger lily, garland flower*. . . *Hedychium coronarium*. . . The white ginger differs from the yellow in having pure white flowers with a more pleasing odor. . . In Hawaii the flowers are a source of perfume produced commercially. **1982** Perry–Hay *Field Guide Plants* 120, *Hedychium gardneranum* . . ginger lily. . . Perennial herbs noted for their showy flowers and fragrance. . . Summer.

ginger pine n [See quot 1910]

=white cedar.

1884 Sargent *Forests of N. Amer.* 179, *Ginger Pine.* Oregon, Coos bay, south to the valley of the Rogue river . . ; California, valley of the upper Sacramento river. . . A large tree of the first economic value. **1894** *Jrl. Amer. Folkl.* 7.99, *Chamaecyparis Lawsoniana*. . . Ginger-pine, Oregon and No. Cal. **1897** Sudworth *Arborescent Flora* 82, *Port Orford Cedar*. . . Common Names. . . Ginger Pine (Cal.) **1910** Jepson *Silva CA* 152, By lumbermen it [=Port Orford cedar] is sometimes termed "Ginger Pine" on account of the spicy fragrance.

ginger plum n Also *ginger berry*

A **wintergreen** (here: *Gaultheria procumbens*) or its berry.

1903 *DN* 2.297 **Cape Cod MA** (as of a1857), Ginger plum . . the berry of the wintergreen. **1940** Clute *Amer. Plant Names* 40, *Wintergreen.* . . Ginger-berry. **1941** *Torreya* 41.51, Ginger plum. **1959** Carleton *Index Herb. Plants* 52, *Ginger-berry:* Gaultheria procumbens. **1969** *DARE* (Qu. S26c, *Wildflowers that grow in woods*) Inf **MA**57, Ginger plum.

gingerroot n

1 =coltsfoot 1.

c1873 in 1976 Miller *Shaker Herbs* 159, *Coltsfoot*. . . Ginger Root. . . The leaves should be collected at full size, . . and the root immediately after the leaves mature. **1894** *Jrl. Amer. Folkl.* 7.92 **MN,** *Tussilago Farfara* . . ginger-root. **1930** Sievers *Amer. Med. Plants* 24, *Coltsfoot*. . . *Other common names*. . . Ginger-root. **1940** Clute *Amer. Plant Names* 274, *Tussilago farfara*. . . Ginger-root.

2 A **wild ginger** (here: *Asarum canadense*).

1910 Graves *Flowering Plants* 157 **CT,** *Asarum canadense*. . . Ginger-root. . . The rhizome is used medicinally and an oil from it is used in perfumery. **1966** *DARE* Wildfl QR Pl.46 Inf **MN**37, Ginger root . . wild ginger; **WA**10, Ginger root . . wild or Indian ginger. **1969** *DARE* (Qu. S16) Inf **IL**44, Ginger root.

ginger-tailed adj

1912 *DN* 3.576 **wIN,** *Ginger-tailed*. . . Poor in quality. Applied to animals, especially cattle. "I don't want to buy any of those ginger-tailed steers of yours."

ginger water n Also *ginger drink* Cf **belly whistle, hayfield drink, switchel chiefly NEng**

A drink made of water, molasses, vinegar, and ginger.

1912 *DN* 3.569 **cNY,** *Switchel*. . . A drink made of water, vinegar, molasses, and ginger. In Connecticut and Vermont called *ginger water;* in New Jersey, *belly whistle.* **1922** (1926) Cady *Rhymes VT* 38, I went and kicked the tedder / And give the ginger drink a blow. **1933** *Hanley Disks* **ceMA,** Ginger-water . . switchel. *Ibid* **neMA,** Ginger-water . . molasses and ginger. **1941** *LANE* Map 312, 1 inf, **nwCT,** Switchel = ginger water, water with molasses, ginger and a little vinegar. **1966** *DARE* Tape **NH**6, My son used to say switzel, or ginger, ginger water they used to call it. It had the vinegar and ginger. I think it had about a teaspoonful of ginger and a tablespoonful of vinegar, and oh, 'bout a quarter cup of sugar to a quart or so of water.

gingle n

A **jingle shell** (here: *Anomia simplex*).

1881 Ingersoll *Oyster-Industry* 244, *Gingles.*—Various species of *Anomia.* (Long Island sound.)

gingy cake See **ginger cake 1**

gin house n **chiefly S Atl** Cf **cotton gin**

A building in which cotton is ginned.

1827 (1939) Sherwood *Gaz. GA* 116, At three or four gin-houses much of the cotton raised in the vicinity, and in Burke, was cleaned. **1860** Hundley *Social Relations S. States* 134, . . His gin-house not unfrequently costs twice as much as his mansion. **1945** FWP *Lay My Burden Down* 211 [Black], I 'member when the Yankees come through. . . They burn the ginhouse, the shop, the buggy-house, the turkey-house, and the fowlhouse. **1967–68** *DARE* (Qu. M1, . . *Kinds of barns*) Inf **SC**57, Gin house—on some farms; (Qu. M22, . . *Buildings . . on farms*) Inf **SC**40, Gin house—on large farms only; ginned for themselves and for others too. **1986** Pederson *LAGS Concordance* 6 infs, 4 **GA,** Ginhouse; 1 inf, **cGA,** Ginhouse shelter.

gin job See **gin work**

gin juniper n

A **juniper** (here: *Juniperus communis*).

1960 Vines *Trees SW* 37, *Juniperus communis*. . . Vernacular names are Horse Savin . . and Gin Juniper. . . The fruit is used . . as a common constituent of Holland gin.

gink n *usu derog*

A guy, fellow.

1908 *NY Eve. Jrl.* (NY) 3 Mar 10 *(Zwilling Coll.),* [In cartoon:] Whos [sic] the gink with the brush [=beard]. **1910** *Sat. Eve. Post* 22 Oct 12/3 **NYC,** I don't believe that all these ginks have got coin enough to support one good game. **1913** *Sat. Eve. Post* 17 May 9/1, That's the stuff! You don't want the gink's ring. **1916** in 1983 Truman *Dear Bess* 183 **MO,** I shall mail this at Denison, Texas. I think there's a gink watching me do this. **1918** in 1953 Botkin–Harlow *Treas. Railroad Folkl.* 238, Gink or Gandy Stiff. . . occasionally labored, a day or two at the most. **1919** *DN* 5.66 **CA, NM,** *Gink,* an awkward, stupid person. "The old gink, he has charged me too much." **1927** *DN* 5.448 [Underworld jargon], *Gink*. . . A tramp who occasionally works. **1950** *Western Folkl.* 9.117 **nwOR** [Logger speech], *Gink.* A man who lives so far back in the woods the owls cross with his chickens. **1967–69** *DARE* (Qu. HH1, *Names and nicknames for a rustic or countrified person*) Inf **MI**108, Country gink; (Qu. HH2, *Names and nicknames for a citified person*) Inf **MD**2, City gink; (Qu. HH16, *Uncomplimentary words with no definite meaning*) Infs **NH**14, **VT**4, Gink; (Qu. HH40, *Uncomplimentary words for an old man*) Inf **IL**5, Gink. **1981** *DARE* File **cnMA** (as of c1915), *Gink* [gɪŋk] was in my childhood vocabulary. "This crazy old gink with his hat on the back of his head was standing in a doorway saying hello to everyone who went by." **1982** *Barrick Coll.* **csPA** (as of 1940s), *Gink* . . person; man. . . "I seen that gink before." **1983** De Vries *Slouching* 46 **ND,** The pearl-gray spats on his feet . . were a memento of those days as a spiffy gink.

gin'ly See **generally** adv

gin mill n [*gin* alcoholic liquor + *mill,* with punning allusion to *gin* a type of mill] **esp NEast**

A bar, saloon or nightclub, esp a lower-class one or one where alcohol is sold illegally.

1865 *Phila. Sun. Mercury* 3 Sep. 4/2 *(DA),* Ruby Nose Peg then came forward and said that she was the proprietor of an unlicensed gin mill. **1867** in 1935 Twain *Notebook* 50, Business mostly gin-mills—that is for soldiers. **1945** in 1953 Botkin–Harlow *Treas. Railroad Folkl.* 166, Coupons in the book could be used as a medium of exchange at almost any store or gin mill on or near Railroad Avenue. **1948** *Reader's Digest* Nov 117/1, Chicago's once invisible police, . . to be discovered mainly in gin mills and horse parlors. **1965–70** *DARE* (Qu. DD30, . . *A place where liquor is . . sold . . illegally*) Infs **MA**123, **NJ**6, 8, 9, 21, 55, 64, **NY**47, 87, **PA**234, **IL**11, Gin mill. **1967** *DARE* File **neNY,** Gin mill—a bar. **1970** Major *Dict. Afro-Amer. Slang, Gin mill:* a run-down nightclub, especially where a jazz musician finds himself working, grudgingly.

ginnel See **general** adj

ginner n[1] [Aphet form of *beginner;* cf *OED ginner* sb.[1] "*Obs.*"] Cf **ginning** n

1969 *DARE* (Qu. HH15, *A very inexperienced person*) Inf **NC**61, Ginner.

ginner n[2] See **gin** v[1] **4**

ginnerl See **general** adj

Ginney See **Guinea** n[1]

ginnie sack See **gunny sack**

ginning n Cf **ginner** n[1]

1899 (1912) Green *VA Folk-Speech* 196, *Ginning*. . . Beginning.

ginning vbl n See **gin** v[1] **5**

ginniwine See **genuine**

Ginny n[1] See **Guinea** n[1]

ginny n[2] [Perh by analogy with *John* toilet]

A chamber pot.

1968 *DARE* (Qu. F38, *Utensil kept under the bed for use at night*) Infs **PA**77, 163, Ginny [ʤɪni].

Ginny Gall See **Guinea** n[2]

ginnywine See **genuine**

gin out See **given out**

gin pole n Cf **gin** v[1]

1 also *gin;* Esp in logging: a pole, spar, or framework from which hoisting tackle is suspended. [*OED gin* sb.[1] 8. a "a crane"; 1447–8 →]

1905 U.S. Forest Serv. *Bulletin* 61.38 [Logging terms], *Gin pole.* A pole secured by guy ropes, to the top of which tackle for loading logs is fastened. **1920** *DN* 5.81 **Pacific NW,** *Gin pole.* Pole sunk in ground with pulley block on top. Used in loading logs. **1938** (1939) Holbrook *Holy Mackinaw* 261, *Gin pole.* A short spar, used for loading and unloading logs. **1942** *AmSp* 17.221, *Gin pole.* **1950** *Western Folkl.* 9.117 **nwOR** [Logger speech], *Gin pole.* A single pole or A-frame elevated at an angle to form a derrick for loading telephone poles, piling, or small logs. **1951** *PADS* 15.77, The oil man has borrowed . . *gin pole* [from the lumber man]. **1956** Sorden–Ebert *Logger's Words* 16 **Gt. Lakes,** Gin-pole, 1. A short spar, used instead of a jammer for loading and unloading logs. 2. Any of the three poles of a hoisting gin. 3. A single pole held in a vertical position by guys, which support a block and tackle used for lifting logs. **1956** *AmSp* 31.150 **Pacific NW,** *Gin* . . a pole used to load logs. **1958** McCulloch *Woods Words* 70 **Pacific NW,** *Gin*—Short for gin pole. *Gin pole*—An almost endless variety of rig-ups using a pole or two for loading logs. **1982** *Barrick Coll.* **csPA,** *Gin pole*. . . Pole similar to circus tent pole used in raising barn frames.

2 **=stack pole.**

1967 *Amer. Agric. & Rural New Yorker* 164.4.60, [In a list of old words not now commonly known:] Mrs. Sara Rhodes, who sent in the word, "ginpole," said that a ginpole was a pole for binding a loose load of hay. **1986** Pederson *LAGS Concordance,* 1 inf, **cTN,** Gin pole—stack pole.

3 A horizontal sweep.

1969 *DARE* FW Addit **ceKY,** *Gin pole* or *cane mill sweep*—pulled by mule though most use tractors [to power a sorghum-crushing mill].

4 A pile or post; see quot.

1964 *DARE* File **seMN,** [Text to a picture postcard:] Red Wing's picturesque boathouse village on the Mississippi River consists of over 200 floating boathouses. The tall poles are called "gin poles" which keep the boathouses and booms in place.

ginral See **general** adj

gin'rally See **generally** adv

gin-rollers, be put through v phr [In ref to the rollers in a cotton *gin*] Cf **flint mill, go through the**

Fig: see quot.

1952 Brown *NC Folkl.* 1.544, *Gin-rollers, to be put through:* . . To be subjected to rough or unpleasant treatment.—Granville county.

gins See **give A1c**

ginseng n Usu |ˈʤɪn,sæŋ|; for varr see **A** below Pronc-spp *gensang, genseng, gins(h)ang, jensang, jinshang, jinshard* [Chinese *jen*[2]*–shen*[1]]

A Forms.

1756 in 1898 Hamilton *Letters to Washington* 1.259, As they were digging some Roots of Ginsang [they] heard the tread of feet Crossing a dry Run. **1794** in 1835 MA Hist. Soc. *Coll.* 1st Ser 4.53 **MA,** Sharrack, Peter, and others . . had been gathering . . the genseng root for the European market. **1819** Dana *Geog. Sketches* 85 **OH,** *Of the Herbaceous Indigenous* productions, trees, and shrubberies of natural growth, divers species . . are useful in medicine and the arts; such as . . sassafras, spice wood, gensang. **1832** MA Hist. Soc. *Coll.* 2d ser 9.153 **cwVT,** Panax quinquefolia, Ginseng. **1894** *Jrl. Amer. Folkl.* 7.89 **VT,** *Aralia quinquefolia*. . . Ginshang. **1900** Lyons *Plant Names* 273, *P[anax] quinquefolius*. . . Ginseng, American Ginseng, Jinshang (U.S.) **1913** *DN* 4.54 **ceNY,** *Ginseng* [ˈʤɪn,šæŋ]. **1922** (1926) Cady *Rhymes VT* 259 **VT,** Go look for ginshang near the wet / And see what kind of dock you get. **1939** *Atlantic Mth.* 164.537/1 **eKY,** I . . carried a little mattock through the woods and dug ginsang. **1950** *WELS Suppl.* **nWI,** Ginseng . . ginsang, ginshang—forms of word used in Wis[consin]. **1954** *Harder Coll.* **cwTN,** Ginseng ['dzɪn,sæŋ]. **1966** *DARE* Wildfl QR Pl.132b Inf **AR**44, Ginseng [ǰɪnsɛŋ]. [FW: Approaches [ǰɪnsæŋ].] **1967–70** *DARE* (Qu. I35, *What kitchen herbs are grown and used in cooking around here?*) Inf **PA**235, Ginsang ['ǰɪnsæŋ]; (Qu. S26c, *Wildflowers that grow in woods*) Infs **KY**68, 82, Ginsang; **MO**38, Ginsang ['ǰɪn,sæŋ]; **TN**13, Jensang ['jɛn,sæŋ]; (Qu. S26d, *Wildflowers that grow in meadows*) Inf **VT**10, Wild ginsang [ǰɪnsæŋ]; (Qu. S26e, *Other wildflowers not yet mentioned*) Infs **KY**24, 35, Ginsang; **VT**13, Ginshang ['ǰɪŋšæŋ]—they dig root; (Qu. BB50d, *Favorite spring tonics around here*) Inf **NJ**56, Ginsang ['ǰɪnsæŋ] tea. **1968** *DARE* FW Addit **NY**88, Ginseng ['ǰɪŋšæŋ]. **1968** *DARE* Tape **WI**58, ['ǰɪŋšæŋ]. **1971** Krochmal *Appalachia Med. Plants* 186, *Panax quinquefolium. . . Common Names* . . gensang, ginseng, . . jinshard. **1988** *DARE* File **WI,** Ginseng hunters in northern Wisconsin often use the pronunciation ['ǰɪn,sɪn] when speaking of the plant they gather.

B Senses.

1 Std: a plant of the genus *Panax* or its root. Also called **sang.** For other names of var spp see **devil's walkingstick 3, five fingers 2, garantogen, groundnut B4, ninsin, redberry, tartar root**

2 A **spikenard** (here: *Aralia californica*).

1911 Jepson *Flora CA* 285, *A[ralia] californica. . . Ginseng.* Stems . . 6 to 10 ft. high, from a large rootstock with milky juice. **1923** Davidson–Moxley *Flora S. CA* 266, *California Spikenard. Ginseng. . .* Frequent along mountain streams at middle altitudes.

3 A **horse gentian** (here: *Triosteum perfoliatum*).

1948 Stevens *KS Wild Flowers* 357, *Triosteum perfoliatum. . .* Various vernacular names have been given to this species . . the corruptions of gentian—ginseng, genson, because Triosteum has sometimes been used in this country as a tonic, substituting for the officinal, European yellow gentian.

ginshang See **ginseng A**

ginst See **against**

gintleman See **gentleman** n

gin'ul See **general** adj

gin up See **gin** v[1] **2**

gin work n [**gin** v[1] **4**] Cf **jim work**

Miscellaneous tasks; odd jobs; hence *gin job* such a task.

1938 Stuart *Dark Hills* 330 **neKY,** I do my gin work on Sunday. **1939** *AmSp* 14.156 **WV,** A student applying for part-time work is asked: 'What kind of work have you ever done?' . . He answers: 'Gin-work' (Cabell County). At first I thought he meant he had worked around a cotton gin, but later learned that 'gin-work' means any sort of odds and ends that a 'handy-man' generally does. **1981** *High Coll.* **ceKY** (as of c1930), *Gin-job* . . odd job. . . "I got some gin jobs to do this evening. You want to help me cut the grass?"

gip n[1] See **gyp** n[1]

gip n[2] See **gyp** n[2]

gippo See **gyppo** n

gippy See **gyppy**

gipsen snow n [Perh for *gypsum*]

1915 *DN* 4.183 **VA,** *Gipsen snow. . .* A slight snowfall.

gipsy face See **gypsy fowl**

gipsy flower See **gypsy flower**

gipsyweed See **gypsyweed**

girasticutus See **gyascutus**

gird See **girt**

girdle n Also *girdle belt*

A saddle or harness girth.

1965–70 *DARE* (Qu. L53a, *The band that goes under a horse's middle to hold a saddle on*) Infs **IL**65, **KY**80, 93, **MO**21, **NJ**53, **SC**34, **WI**21, Girdle; **SC**7, Girdle belt; (Qu. L53b, . . *If it's part of a work harness*) Infs **GA**74, **MO**17, **NJ**53, **PA**3, 13, Girdle. **1966** *DARE* Tape **MI**34, Every time I buckled a girdle she'd pick me up by the seat of the pants. . . She never let anybody buckle . . the saddle without givin' 'em a good shake up.

‡girdle snake n [Perh for **garter snake**]

1968 *DARE* (Qu. P25, . . *Kinds of snakes* . . *around here*) Inf **MO**4, Girdle snake.

girl n Usu |gɝl, gɜl|; also **chiefly Sth, S Midl** |gjɝl, gjɜl|; **NYC** |gɜɪl| Pronc-spp *gell, geurl, goil, gyirl;* for addit varr see quots

A Forms.

1805 in 1956 Eliason *Tarheel Talk* 311 **NC,** *Girl*—garl. **1835** in 1956 Eliason *Tarheel Talk* 311 **NC,** Gairl. **1842** in 1956 *Ibid, Girl. . .* gill. **1871** Eggleston *Hoosier Schoolmaster* 95 **sIN,** That blessed gyirl. **1884** Baldwin *Yankee School-Teacher* 35 **VA,** I heap rudder play wid de geurls! **1890** *DN* 1.67 **KY,** *Girl* [gɜl]. Not infrequently [gjɜl]. **1891** (1900) French *Otto* 161 **AR,** Dat ar's Haskett's gell comin' by. **1899** Edwards *Defense* 28 **GA,** De little gyurl fum 'cross de street. **1899** (1912) Green *VA Folk-Speech* 196, *Girl. . .* Pronounced *gearle,* with hard *g.* **1908** *DN* 3.281 **eAL, wGA,** The intrusive *y* in . . gyirl . . is only heard sporadically. **1927** *AmSp* 2.356 **WV,** *Gyrl* . . written form for girl. "Those gyrls are painted too much to please me." **1928** *NY Times* (NY) 12 Aug 8.6/2, "Goil," "poil,""thoid," so frequently heard in New York, are much older. **1931** *AmSp* 6.170 **VA, NC,** A less noticeable palatalization of [g] and [k] before [æ], [ɛ] and [ʌ:] is common in the speech of men and women of all ages and both races in Virginia and North Carolina. . . *Girls* is frequently [gʲʌ:lz]. **1934** *AmSp* 9.212 **Sth,** Some speakers [in Georgia and parts of North Carolina] pronounce [ɝ] followed by [l] as a triphthong [ʌɪə]. *Girl, twirl, world,* etc. **1941** *AmSp* 16.7 **eTX** [Black], [gʌ:l], [gʌɪ˞l]. **1942** Hall *Smoky Mt. Speech* 41 **eTN, wNC,** [ɝ] is lowered and retracted . . by some speakers in . . *girls* [gʌɚlz]. **1950** *PADS* 14.34 **SC,** *Gyarden, kyar, gyrl. . .* [A] pronunciation which is still heard in the coastal area, especially in Charleston, but only sporadically in the remainder of the state. **c1960** *Wilson Coll.* **csKY,** Some old people said [gjɝl]. **1961** Kurath–McDavid *Pronc. Engl.* 108 **NYC,** The diphthongal [ɞɪ] of *girl* is kept apart from the [ɔɪ] of *boil,* except by some less educated speakers in Metropolitan New York (especially Brooklyn).

B Sense.

Used as a term of address between Black women.

1970 *DARE* Tape **TN**46, An' girl, that heat got unbearable. [*DARE* Ed: Inf and FW Black] **1977** Smitherman *Talkin* 255, *Girl,* used between black women, as in "Girl, let me tell you bout this." **1978** *AP Letters* **cSC** [Black], If a carload of relatives arrives unexpectedly for Sunday dinner, the hostess may call her friends for help. "Girl, can you come and help. All these people I've got to fix for."

girl v, hence vbl n *girling* [*OEDS* 1787 →]

Of men: To visit women; to go courting.

1931 Steffens *Autobiog.* 1.8 **CA** (as of c1870), Cowboys . . used to come shouting on bucking bunches of bronchos into town to mix with the teamsters, miners, and steamboat men in the drinking, gambling, girling, fighting, of those days. **1931–33** *LANE Worksheets* **cCT,** *Girling* . . to go courting. A man has gone off a girling. **1940–41** Cassidy *WI Atlas* **cwWI,** *Girling* . . used today. Old folks used *sparking, courting,* (Inf is a 65 year old farmer). **1959** *VT Hist.* new ser. 27.137, *Go girling. . .* To go out with a girl. Rare. **1961** *McDavid Coll.,* 1 inf **cOK,** Girling—courting. **1968** *DARE* (Qu. AA1) Inf **MI**78, He's gone girling; old-fashioned. **1975** Gould *ME Lingo* 109, *Girlin'*—Said of a boy conducting a courtship: "Jimmie's out girlin' tonight."

girl-leg (spur) n Also *gal-leg*

A type of spur; see quot 1944.

1944 Adams *Western Words* 64, *Gal-leg,* A spur with a shank in the shape of a girl's leg. **1958** Blasingame *Dakota Cowboy* 168, Then, without any urging from my girl-leg spurs, he . . bounced into stiff-legged, hell-to-set bucking, zig-zagging as he went.

girls-and-boys n Cf **boys-and-girls 1**

Either of two similar plants: **Dutchman's breeches 1** or a **squirrel corn** (here: *Dicentra canadensis*).

1893 *Jrl. Amer. Folkl.* 6.137, *Dicentra Canadensis* and *Dicentra cucullaria* called respectively (?) ladies and gentlemen. Franklin Centre, P[rovince] Q[uebec]. girls and boys. Vt. **1910** Graves *Flowering Plants* 198 **CT,** *Dicentra canadensis. . .* Girls-and-Boys. . . The tubers are medicinal.

girt n Also *gird, gert, geart* [Varr of *girth; OED* 1563 →; "in use chiefly in the 17th and 18th c."] Cf Pronc Intro 3.I.17 **chiefly NEng, Sth, S Midl** See Map

A girth used to secure a saddle or harness.

1806 (1970) Webster *Compendious Dict.* 131/1, *Girt*. . . a bandage for a saddle. **1899** (1912) Green *VA Folk-Speech* 193, *Geart*. . . Girt. . . Saddle-*geart*. **1903** *DN* 2.314 **seMO,** Your saddle-gert needs tightening. **1906** *DN* 3.119 **sIN,** Tighten the saddle girts. **1907** *DN* 3.231 **nwAR, seMO,** Gert. **1908** *DN* 3.314 **eAL, wGA,** *Gert, girt.* **1922** Gonzales *Black Border* 303 **sSC, GA coasts** [Gullah glossary], *Girt'*—girth, girths. **1933** *AmSp* 8.1.28 **wTX,** Girt. Saddle girth. Ranch people said *cinch* or *girt,* never girth. **c1960** *Wilson Coll.* **csKY,** *Girt* . . girth, cinch. **1965–70** *DARE* (Qu. L53a) 72 Infs, **chiefly Sth,** Girt; 27 Infs, **chiefly NEng, S Atl,** Belly girt; 10 Infs, **scattered,** Saddle girt; **TX**16, Flank girt; **MA**37, Belly girts; **IA**31, Gird [gɚd]; (Qu. L53b) 56 Infs, **chiefly Sth,** Girt; 32 Infs, **chiefly NEng, S Atl,** Belly girt; **ME**5, On a one-horse wagon or a buggy there is also a [šɑv] girt; **TX**33, Working girt. **1967** *DARE* Tape **TX**25, [FW:] What's the difference between a cinch and a girt? [Inf:] 'Ere's not any difference. **1983** *MJLF* 9.1.41 **ceKY,** *Girt* . . a girth, a band put around a horse's middle to hold the saddle on.

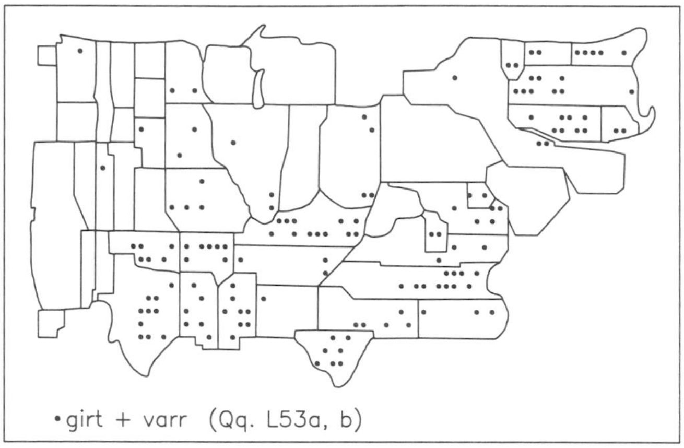

G.I.'s n pl Also with *the* Also *G.I. sickness, ~ trots*
Diarrhea.

1946 *AmSp* 21.247 [Army speech in the European theater], *The G.I.'s* is—or are—diarrhea; the phrase is a contraction, probably, of 'the G.I. trots.' The malady is cured or aggravated by a *G.I. pill.* **1947** *AmSp* 22.215, G.I., Is it not . . possible that the G.I.'s (diarrhea) might have derived from a service medical designation for *gastro-intestinal?* In any event, the later use of the term was a reflection upon service food and general cleanliness. **1965–70** *DARE* (Qu. BB19) 11 Infs, **esp TX, Sth,** (The) G.I.'s; **IL**97, **NY**34, 183, **TN**44, G.I. trots; **NY**66, G.I. sickness. [12 of 16 Infs male]

gism See **jism**

gispachi See **gazpacho**

giste See **joist**

git v See **get** v **A1, 3, 4**

git n See **get** n **3**

git-ap See **get up** v phr **1**

gitar See **guitar**

git-box n Also *gitbucket, git-fiddle, git-flip* [Abbr for *guitar* + **box** n **2,** *bucket, fiddle, flip*]
A guitar.

1935 Hurston *Mules & Men* 113 **FL,** De git Fiddles was raisin' cain over in de corner. **1936** *AmSp* 11.315 **Ozarks,** *Git-flip*. . . Humorous name for guitar. **1937** *AmSp* 12.181 [Jazz slang], *Gitbox.* Guitar. **1946** (1972) Mezzrow–Wolfe *Really Blues* 333 [Glossary], Git-box: guitar. **1958** Latham *Meskin Hound* 72 **cTX,** There's a git-fiddle dance over to Grit Saturday night. **1969** *DARE* (Qu. D40) Inf **CA**118A, [Guitar=] Git-fiddle. Comes from 'git your fiddle and play it.' **1974** Fink *Mountain Speech* 11 **wNC, eTN,** *Git-box* or *git-fiddle* . . guitar. **1977** Cheever *Falconer* 187 [Black], "I made a big decision," said Chicken . . "I'm going to sell my gitfiddle." **1982** *Barrick Coll.* **csPA,** *Git-fiddle*—humorous word for *guitar.* **1984** Weaver *TX Crude* 113, *Gitfiddle, or gitbucket.* A guitar. "That Chet Atkins can make that gitfiddle stand up and talk."

git-go See **get-go**

gither See **gather**

gitlet n [Prob Scots, nEngl dial *get* brat, bastard; dimins *gettling, gytling,* etc] Cf **get** n **2**
An illegitimate child.

1927 Kennedy *Gritny* 152 **sLA** [Black], Cindy didn't pay no mind to what they said about her, "good as she felt wid all dat fam'ly o' gitlets" (illegitimates) to take care of her when they grew up big enough to work.

git-out See **get-out** n

G.I. trots See **G.I.'s**

gits See **get** v **A1, 2**

gittar See **guitar**

gitted See **get** v **A3**

gitter See **guitar**

git up See **get up** v phr **1**

give v

A Forms. [All of these types of non-std forms occur also in Scots or Engl dial, though it is possible that some have developed independently in the US.]

1 pres: usu *give(s);* also:

a *gib,* rarely *gif. among Black speakers; old-fash*

1823 Cooper *Pioneers* 1.243 **cNY** [Black], Gib anoder shillin, Billy. **1884** *Anglia* 7.252 **Sth, S Midl** [Black], *Pres*. . . gib, gif. *Ibid* 269, *To gib it to 'um good*=to chastise them well. **1899** Chesnutt *Conjure Woman* 80 **csNC** [Black], He could n' gib no 'count er hisse'f. **1922** [see **A1b** below].

b *gi, gee;* also, in combs, *g'. among Black speakers; old-fash*

1922 Gonzales *Black Border* 303 **sSC, GA coasts** [Gullah glossary], *G'em*—give, gives, gave, giving him, her, it, them. *Ibid, Gi', gib'*—give, gives, gave, giving. **1927** Adams *Congaree* 17 **cSC** [Black], I mighty nigh done talk my heart out geeing agvice to dat gal of Riah's.

c *gin(s), gen.* **chiefly Sth, S Midl**

1859 Taliaferro *Fisher's R.* 116 **nwNC** (as of 1820s), I nuver gins a thing up as long as there's a pea in the gourd. **1871** Eggleston *Hoosier Schoolmaster* 121 **sIN,** A man what can gin up his gal on account of sech a feeling. **1888** Jones *Negro Myths* 43 **GA coast,** Den de snake tell um eh guine gen um some money nex day. **1899** Chesnutt *Conjure Woman* 77 **csNC** [Black], You take dis home, en gin it ter de cook. **1909** in 1914 Stewart *Letters* 41 **WY,** He was full of surprise they didn't "git some cherry bark and some sasparilly and bile it good and gin it to him." **1914** *DN* 4.159 **VA,** *Gin*. . . To give. "Gin it toe [sic] me."

d in comb *give me:* often *gimme.*

1837 Sherwood *Gaz. GA* 70, *Provincialisms*. . . *Gim me,* for give me. **1843** (1916) Hall *New Purchase* 172 **sIN,** No! no! no! I say, gim me the sperit. **1884** (1958) Twain *Huck. Finn* 33, Don't gimme no sass. **1931** *AmSp* 6.204 **MO,** *Gimme one.* **1966–67** *DARE* (Qu. Y41b) Inf **SC**55, Gimme some juice; (Qu. OO7b) Inf **DC**8, Gimme.

2 past: usu *gave;* also:

a *gin, gien, gun. old-fash*

1815 Humphreys *Yankey in England* 97, 'Tis she. The very she, I gin the shellers tu. **1838** (1852) Gilman *S. Matron* 169, They is . . more handsomer than Mrs. Whitney's that she gin six dollars for at Charleston. **1848** Lowell *Biglow* 144 **'Upcountry' MA,** Gin, *gave.* **1851** Hooper *Widow Rugby's Husband* 47 **AL,** The crowd gin the most tremenjus . . howl. **1887** (1967) Harris *Free Joe* 58 **GA** [Black], Marse Compton gun me a letter. **1893** Shands *MS Speech* 33, *Gin*. . . A negro form for *gave.* **1895** *DN* 1.397 **CT, MA, NY,** He gin me four dollars. **1899** (1912) Green *VA Folk-Speech* 196, *Gin*. . . Past tense of give. . . "I gin him one." For *given:* "Had gin it to her." **1899** Chesnutt *Conjure Woman* 20 **csNC** [Black], He gin Henry a big drink er w'iskey. *Ibid* 76, She gun 'im some stuff. **1905** *DN* 3.10 **cCT,** *Gin*. . . Gave or given. "He gin me a crack side of the head." **1907** [see **A3a** below]. **1908** *DN* 3.314 **eAL, wGA,** *Gin, pret.* and *pp.* of *give.* "She gin me a look that made me proud." **1909** *DN* 3.411 **nME,** *Gin*. . . Gave. **1913** Kephart *Highlanders* 284 **sAppalachians,** Preterite . . gi'n or give. **1924** Raine *Land of Saddle-Bags* 207 **Appalachians,** I gien it teas all night. **1927** *DN* 5.474 **Ozarks,** Doc he gin her some powders an' draps. **1951** Johnson *Resp. to PADS 20* **DE,** *("She ______ me a loaf of her homemade bread.")* Old-fashioned: guv, gun. **1952** Brown *NC Folkl.* 1.544, *Gin* [gɪn]. . . Past tense (and past participle) of *give*. . . General. Illiterate. *Ibid* 548, *Gun*. . . Past participle (and past tense) of *give.* **1953** [see **A2b** below]. **1969** *DARE* (Qu. U8b) Inf **CT**36, Gin ten dollars.

b *give.* *esp freq among speakers with little formal educ*

1836 (1955) *Crockett Almanacks* 52 **wTN,** But presently he give over completely choked to death. **1844** Stephens *High Life in NY* 2.39, I was . . scared . . they wouldn't print my letters agin, arter I give them the mitten so slick. **1893** Shands *MS Speech* 33, *Give*. . . Used even by educated people for gave. **1902** [see **A2d** below]. **1907** [see **A2d** below]. **1908** [see **A3b** below]. **1910** *DN* 3.442 **cwNY,** *Give, pret.* of *give.* "She give me a dish of it." **1913** [see **A2a** above]. **1936** (1951) Faulkner *Absalom* 237 **MS,** The nigger never give me a chance to tell him. **1953** Atwood *Survey of Verb Forms* 15, The uninflected *give* /gɪv/ [for the past] occurs in nearly two thirds of the communities investigated in N. Eng., with no particular concentration except that this form is uncommon in R.I. and c. Mass. . . *give* is used by something like from two thirds (Pa.) to over nine tenths (Va. and N.C.) of Type I [=poorly educ infs]. . . Sixteen N. Eng. informants, mostly in N.H. and Me., and two Southern informants use the form *gin* /gɪn/; nearly all of them also use *give* or *gave* or both. The form *gin* is characteristically an older . . form. Two Southern informants state that *gin* is "used by Negroes," yet none of the Negro informants offer that form (*give* being almost universal among them). One Negro . . uses the weak form *gived* /gɪvd/ [for the past]. **1965–70** *DARE* (Qu. OO7a, . . *"Yesterday was John's birthday, so everybody ______ [him presents].")* 109 Infs, **scattered exc Pacific, but esp Sth, S Midl,** Give; (Qu. U8b, *Similar expressions meaning "I paid ten dollars for it."*) 69 Infs, **scattered exc Gt Lakes, Pacific,** Give. [Of all Infs responding to Qq. OO7a and U8b, 24% and 25% respectively were gs educ or less; of those giving this response, 56% and 60% respectively were gs educ or less.] [Further exx throughout *DS;* Infs **widespread]** **1966–69** *DARE* Tape **CA**137, The last time she was over, I give her one; **FL**45, So they sent 'em over to America 'n' they give 'em a monthly pension; **IL**4, We came out and we give 'em a lunch then; **PA**17, They knowed he didn't kill the deer. I give it to him; **MI**32, I took off my lamp and battery, and give him back the belt. **1975** Allen *LAUM* 2.19 **Upper MW** (as of c1950), Two forms appear as preterits of *give* in the U[pper] M[idwest]—historical *gave* and uninflected *give.* Three-fourths or more of the infs. in all five states typically say *gave,* but in the folk speech of the Type I's [=old, with little educ] *give* retains strength. . . Eastern *gin* and *gived* do not appear in the UM data. **1981** *PADS* 67.44 **neMN,** Standard *gave* is usual . . and *give* frequent. . . *Give* [is stronger] among Type I [=less well educ] informants. **1982** *Barrick Coll.* **csPA,** *Give*—p.t. and p.p. of *give.* "They give me a hard time when I was up there." "You haven't give yourself much time."

c *gee, gi(b), gif, given;* also, in combs, *g'.* *among Black speakers; old-fash*

1853 Simms *Sword & Distaff* 315 **SC** [Black], Maussa owe me for dat ossifer [=officer's] coat . . , he gee way to de Doctor, to dis day. **1884** *Anglia* 7.252 **Sth, S Midl** [Black], *Past*. . . gib, gif, given. **1922** [see **A1b** above].

d *guv.*

1851 Burke *Polly Peablossom* 50 **MO,** Ever sense that feller . . guv me a brass picayune . . I've stopped talkin'. **1884** *Anglia* 7.252 **Sth, S Midl** [Black], I guv him two cents. **1893** Shands *MS Speech* 34, *Guv* [gʌv]. A negro form for *gave.* **1902** *DN* 2.235 **sIL,** *Give,* or *guv.* Preterit of give. **1906** Casey *Parson's Boys* 147 **sIL** (as of c1860), After he wuz dead, his wife guv the boots to the oldest boy. **1906** *DN* 3.139 **nwAR,** I guv it to him. **1907** *DN* 3.212 **nwAR,** *Give, guv*. . . Did give. **1943** *LANE* Map 649 *(Gave)* 1 inf, **cwCT,** Guv. **1951** [see **A2a** above]. **1967** *DARE* (Qu. OO7a) Inf **IA**12, Guv.

e *gived, gi'd.*

c1938 in 1970 Hyatt *Hoodoo* 1.235 **csNC** [Black], He gi'd her another bottle of roots. **1966–67** *DARE* (Qu. OO7a) Infs **LA**8, **MS**69, Gived. **1986** Pederson *LAGS Concordance,* 2 infs, **neAR, seGA,** Gived. [Both infs Black]

3 past pple: usu *given;* also:

a *gin, gun.* *old-fash*

1795 Dearborn *Columbian Grammar* 135, *List of Improprieties*. . . Gin for Given. **1815** Humphreys *Yankey in England* 105, *Gin,* given, gave. **1844** Stephens *High Life in NY* 1.212, You've gin me a first rate edecation for your parts. **1893** *DN* 1.277 **wCT,** Give—[past, past pple:] give—[much less frequently:] gin. **1899** [see **A2a** above]. **1899** Chesnutt *Conjure Woman* 109 **csNC** [Black], Primus . . went down . . ter a dance gun by some er de free niggers down dere. **1905** [see **A2a** above]. **1907** *DN* 3.212 **nwAR,** *Gin*. . . Gave, given. **1908** [see **A2a** above]. **1914** *DN* 4.73 **ME, nNH,** *Gin.* Given. **1915** (1916) Johnson *Highways New Engl.* 233, The musters was gin up while I was a little boy. **1927** *AmSp* 3.139 **ME,** The older people spoke of . . "gin" (given). **1952** [see **A2a** above].

b *give, gib.* **scattered, but esp Sth, S Midl** See Map *esp freq among speakers with little formal educ*

1899 Garland *Boy Life* 4 **nwIA** (as of c1870s), I'd jest about give you up. **1901** Harben *Westerfelt* 5 **nGA,** After all the advice I've give the foolish girl! **1907** Lincoln *Cape Cod* 146, I've got some gasoline. . . Has yours give out? **1908** *DN* 3.315 **eAL, wGA,** *Give, pret.* and *pp.* of *give.* "I would 'a give it to her if she had 'a ast me for it." Common. **1933** Rawlings *South Moon* 296 **nFL,** I've give that job to Zeke. **1939** Griswold *Sea Is. Lady* 509 **sSC** [Black], I hope my Sabeyuh [=Savior] is gib me mo' bettuh sanse dan foolish wirgin by dis time! **1965–70** *DARE* (Qu. OO7b, . . *"I would've ______ [one too]."*) 122 Infs, **scattered, but more freq Sth, S Midl,** Give; **PA**230, Give him [Of all Infs responding to the question, 29% were comm type 5, 24% gs educ or less; of those giving this response, 51% were comm type 5, 59% gs educ or less.]; (Qu. F32, . . *"A water pipe must have ______."*) Inf **OK**53, Give way; (Qu. K45, . . *She has just ______*) Inf **MO**17, Give birth to a colt; (Qu. BB54, *When a sick person is beyond hope of recovery, you'd say he's [a] ______*) Infs **MO**19, **OK**31, (Just) give up; **AL**34, Give up all hopes; **OK**18, We've give up on him; (Qu. DD11, . . *"I hear he ______."*) Inf **NC**82, Has give up the booze; (Qu. JJ43, . . *"Somebody must have ______."*) Inf **MO**38, Give him a secret. **1966–67** *DARE* Tape **MS**72, Mom told me she had give Audrey some of it; **TX**1A, She never has give it back. **1975** Allen *LAUM* 2.19 **csMN** (as of c1950) [Black], [One inf] has *give* also as a participle. **1982** [see **A2b** above].

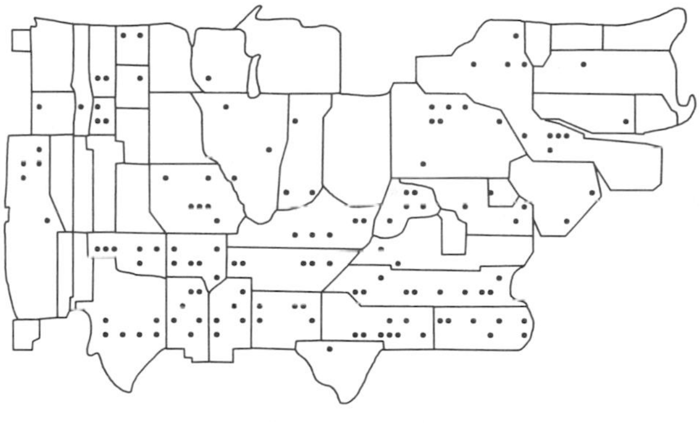

•give A3b + varr (Qq. 007b, F32, K45, BB54, DD11, JJ43)

c *gave, gaved, gaven.*

1965–70 *DARE* (Qu. OO7b, . . *"I would've ______ [one too]."*) 100 Infs, **widespread,** Gave [Of all Infs responding to the question, 29% were comm type 5, 24% gs educ or less; of those giving this response, 49% were comm type 5, 56% gs educ or less.]; (Qu. F32, . . *"A water pipe must have ______."*) Inf **CA**196, Gave out. **1966** *DARE* Tape **MS**71, He never had gave anybody any trouble. **1975** Allen *LAUM* 2.19 **neIA** (as of c1950), *Give:* Inf. uses 'gave' as participle. **1986** Pederson *LAGS Concordance,* 2 infs, **cnLA, csTX,** Gaven; 1 inf, **csLA,** Gaved.

d *guv, gived.*

1884 *Anglia* 7.269 **Sth, S Midl** [Black], *Like hit wer' guv* = as it was given. **c1938** in 1970 Hyatt *Hoodoo* 1.27 **swTN** [Black], Yo' take a pitcher—dis wus gived to me in a vision. **1950** *WELS ("I wish she had ______ me some cookies.")* 1 Inf, **seWI,** Guv—old-fashioned. **1967–69** *DARE* (Qu. OO7b, . . *"I would've ______ [one too]."*) Inf **KY**7, Gived; **MI**67, I've heard "guv," the old slang term, in the Southern Negro. **1986** Pederson *LAGS Concordance,* 1 inf, **cnGA,** Gived.

B Senses.

1 As a calque of Ger *geben* to give, in var idiomatic uses as: see below. **chiefly PaGer area**

a in phrr *it gives* and varr: There is, there are. [Cf Ger *es gibt*]

1882 (1971) Gibbons *PA Dutch* 390, "I guess it will give a gust," is said in Lancaster County. **1907** *German Amer. Annals* 9.377 **sePA,** "I think it will give rain to-night." . . "Give snow," "give hail," also used. **1935** *AmSp* 10.168 [English of the Pennsylvania Germans], The local weather prophet looks at the clouds and thinks . . 'It gives spritzers' (showers), or 'It gives thundergusts.' **1939** Aurand *Quaint Idioms* 24 **PaGer area,** What does this *give;* a parade or *what? Ibid* 25, Do you think it will *make,* or *give,* rain? **1948** *AmSp* 23.109 **swIL** [German language influences], I think it will give rain. . . It may give a war. . . It gives an election tomorrow.

b in phr *give good-bye:* To bid (someone) farewell. [Cf Ger dial *ade geben* to say good-bye]

1907 *German Amer. Annals* 9.376 **sePA,** *Give*. . . Say, especially in phrase below. "I must go and give him good-by." . . fr. Pa. Ger. *good-by gewa*. **1914** *DN* 4.158 **sePA,** You can . . 'give him good-bye.' **1937** *AmSp* 12.287 **nwVA,** The Shenandoah German may say . . 'Give me good-bye.' **1953** *AmSp* 28.246 **csPA,** Other PaG expressions common in this predominantly Scotch-Irish area are *to give someone goodbye* ('I went to the station to give him goodbye'), *what for* . . , [etc].

c To make, turn out to be.

1907 *German Amer. Annals* 9.376 **sePA,** *Give*. . . Prove to be; turn out as. "He'll give a good doctor." . . fr. Pa. Ger. idiom; also Ger.

2 with *to:* To favor (a leg). **esp Sth, S Midl**

1965-70 *DARE* (Qu. BB2, *If a person is careful not to put much weight on his injured leg, you might say he was ______ that leg*) Infs **FL**10, **NC**47, **NM**9, **TN**16, **TX**37, Giving to; **AL**4, Gives to; **LA**15, Give to; [**NC**22, Giving; **KY**11, **OK**11, **VA**69, Giving in to; **OK**25, Giving away to; **NC**52, Giving way to;] (Qu. BB1, *When a person has been injured so that when he walks he steps more heavily on one foot than the other: "He ______ ."*) Inf **MS**6, Gives to one leg.

give a hate, not to See **hate** n

give away v phr See **give way**

giveaway n, also attrib Also *give-way*

Any of var games in which players try to get rid of their playing pieces; also fig.

1872 *Newton* (Kansas) *Kansan* 19 Dec. 2/2 *(DAE),* We are decidedly opposed to the give-away game. **1899** Champlin-Bostwick *Young Folks' Games* 160, Give-Away, or the Losing Game, a game having the same moves and rules as checkers, in which the player who first gets rid of all his men wins. *Ibid* 181, Give-away Chess. . . The give-away game differs from the ordinary one in this, that a player must invariably take a man when offered. **1908** *DN* 3.315 **eAL, wGA,** *Give-way*. . . A child's game at drafts in which the object is to get rid of one's men as rapidly as possible, the one first exhausting his forces being the winner. Each player must 'jump' at every opportunity. **1950** *WELS,* 1 Inf, **WI,** *Give-away*. . . A marble game. **1954** *Harder Coll.* **cwTN,** *Give-away*. . . A table game played with checkers in which opponents try to see which can lose all his checkers first. **1966-68** *DARE* (Qu. EE7, *What kinds of marble games are played or used to be played around here?*) Inf **CA**2, Giveaway; **IN**49, Giveaway—see how many you could lose.

gived See **give A2e, 3d**

gived out See **given out**

give down v phr

1 Of a cow: to let (milk) flow; to yield milk—often used as a command.

1878 *Scribner's Mth.* 15.382, Give down! Give down—my crumpled brown! **1894** Frederic *Marsena* 128 **nNY,** One beast put her hoof square in his pail, and another refused altogether to "give down," while the rest kept up a tireless slapping. **1908** *DN* 3.315 **eAL, wGA,** Ole Sook won't give down her milk till the calf sucks. **1910** *DN* 3.442 **cwNY,** That old cow won't give down her milk. **1932** Randolph *Ozark Mt. Folks* 32, Ol' Muley give down lashin's o' milk that night. **1966** *DARE* FW Addit **DC, WI,** Give down. . . Of a cow: to release her milk to a milker. (Cows sometimes refuse to do so, or to do so for certain persons.) Also as an exclamation to the cow: "Give down!" Wisconsin—regular term; D.C. —one informant. **1970** *DARE* (Qu. K3a, *When a cow stops giving milk*) Inf **PA**235, Won't give down; (Qu. K4) Inf **TX**89, A stripper is a cow that doesn't give down her milk. **1982** Ginns *Snowbird Gravy* 127 **nwNC,** If you talk ill to her or grumble or hit 'er or anything, she won't give 'er milk down.

2 To admit.

1917 *DN* 4.412 **IL, wNC,** *Give down*. . . To admit; confess. "He'll give it down at last."

3 To be overcome with weariness, break down.

1938 Stuart *Dark Hills* 125 **KY,** The first time I had been to Camp Knox I gave down on marching the eight miles and carrying the heavy pack. . . But I weighed 145 pounds now and could carry two such packs as Staggers had done. **1966** *PADS* 46.26 **AR,** *Give down*. . . Break down; become inoperative.—"I was thinking my nerves would give down on me."

give good-bye See **give B1b**

give in v phr

1 To submit, render (something, as an accounting) to someone in authority. [*OED give* v. 59. e 1602 →] **esp S Atl**

1809 in 1956 Eliason *Tarheel Talk* 273 **NC,** 7 Bushels Corn you gave in that you had taken. **1904** (1972) Harben *Georgians* 6 **nwGA,** Three or four countrymen . . passed into the court-house to give in their taxes. **1928** Peterkin *Scarlet Sister Mary* 339 **SC,** The deacons appointed Wednesday night, for Mary to come and give in her experience and they invited all the people to hear them decide if her vision meant that her sins were forgiven. **1946** *PADS* 6.15 **eNC** (as of 1900-10), *Give in (taxes):* . . To list property for taxation. Pamlico. Common. **c1960** *Wilson Coll.* **csKY,** *Give in*. . . List one's property for taxation.

2 To make a contribution. [Prob by analogy with phrr such as *chip in, pitch in,* etc]

1968-70 *DARE* (Qu. II9, *If several people have to contribute in order to pay for something, you say, "Let's all ______ ."*) Infs **MS**88, **NC**63, **NY**93, 156, Give in.

given out adj phr Usu *give out* Also *gave out, gived out, gin out* [*give out* to be overcome by exhaustion] **chiefly Sth, S Midl** See Map

Tired out, exhausted, broken down.

1852 Stansbury *Expedition* 202, He . . had engaged to bring in a "give-out" mule which we had left behind. **1871** Eggleston *Hoosier Schoolmaster* 195 **sIN,** He had felt kyinder gin aout by the time he got to the blacksmith's shop. **1902** *DN* 2.235 **sIL,** *Give out*. . . Exhausted. Used of persons or things. **1907** Wright *Shepherd* 12 **Ozarks,** 'Taint no wonder 't all, God rested when he made these here hills; he jes naturally *had* t' quit, fer he done his beatenest an' war plumb gin out. **1920** Hunter *Trail Drivers TX* 211, The Indians had just as soon have these lame or given-out cattle as any. **1923** *DN* 5.208 **swMO,** I'm plumb give out. **1929** Dobie *Vaquero* 279 **West,** He [=a horse] was "give out." I had overtaxed his strength; neither he nor I had had a swallow of water or a bite to eat since daylight. **1933** Rawlings *South Moon* 36 **FL,** She's been beddin' sweet pertaters. I mean, she's give out. Field work's too hard on her. **1939** *Hall Coll.* **wNC,** I told her I was starved and froze and give out. **1954** Roberts *I Bought Dog* [22] **sAppalachians,** My legs are give out and I dont have to run after you any more. **1965-70** *DARE* (Qu. X47, *What other ways do you have of saying, "I'm very tired, at the end of my strength"?*) 55 Infs, **chiefly Sth, S Midl,** Give out; **OH**98, About give out; **MD**36, **NC**62, Just (about) give out; **MO**35, Tired and give out; **MO**9, **NC**79, 86, **SC**29, Given out; **FL**19, **TN**52, Just (about) given out; **CA**162, Gave out; **GA**6, Gived out; (Qu. BB5, *A general feeling of discomfort or illness*) Inf **VA**52, Give out; (Qu. KK19, *If a machine or appliance is temporarily out of order*) Inf **NC**1, Is give out; (Qu. KK20b, *Something that looks as if it might collapse any minute*) Infs **KY**91, **NC**40, **NY**9, Give out; **CA**2, **LA**12, **NY**206, (About) given out; (Qu. KK30, *Feeling slowed up or without energy: "I certainly feel ______ ."*) Infs **AL**25, **KY**65, 91, (All) give out; (Qu. LL17, *Ways of saying there's no more of something: "The potatoes are ______ ."*) Infs **SD**8, **VA**80, Give out; **MA**98, Given out. **1967** *DARE* Tape **AZ**4, He was ridin' a give out horse. **1968** Kellner *Aunt Serena* 109 **cIN** (as of c1920), I felt dauncy, peakèd, weak as water, give out, puny, and light-headed as a dandelion gone to seed. **1975** Newell *If Nothin' Don't Happen* 46 **nwFL,** I was so give out I could hardly drag around. **1986** Pederson *LAGS Concordance* **Gulf Region** *(Tired; worn out)* 187 infs, Give out; 22 infs, Given out; 5 infs, Gave out.

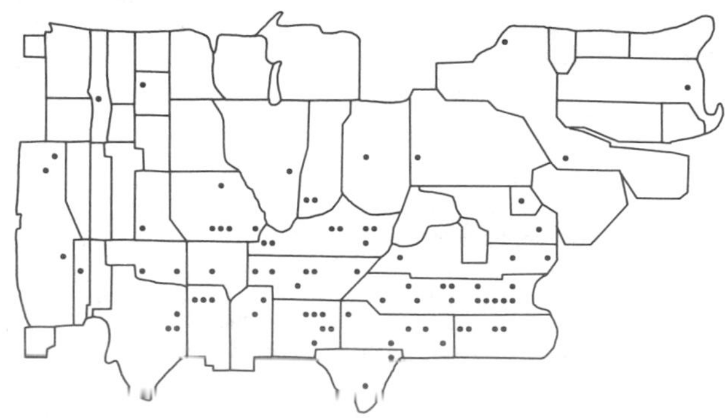

•given out + varr (Qq. X47, BB5, KK19, KK20b, KK30, LL17)

give one down (the) country (or river, road) See **down the country, give one**

give one goss See **goss**

give one gowdy See **gowdy**

give one no house See **house B6**

give (one) the foot See **foot n C5d**

give (one) the gate See **gate**

give one the go-around See **go-around n 1**

give one the go-by See **go-by** n

give one the go-sign See **go-sign**

give one the highball See **highball** n **3**

give one the high-hat See **high-hat** n **2**

give out v phr **chiefly S Midl, Sth**

1a To announce, make known; to give as the general report. [*OED give* v. 62. a c1340 →] Cf **give-out n 1**

1902 [see **1b** below]. **1903** *DN* 2.314 **seMO,** There was no meetin given out for next Sunday. **1907** *DN* 3.231 **nwAR,** *Give out. . .* To announce. **1908** *DN* 3.315 **eAL, wGA,** They give out a meetin' at Boyd's school-house for next Sunday. **1910** *DN* 3.442 **cwNY,** *Give out. . .* To announce (from the pulpit). **1923** *DN* 5.208 **swMO,** *Give out . .* to announce. "Has the Deacon give out his text?" **1931** Hannum *Thursday April* 6 **wNC,** "Now I reckon you could have as many men as you've got fingers—" "Do have," corrected Dolsy, complaisantly. "I've heerd as much give out." **1932** Randolph *Ozark Mt. Folks* 54, He'd give out that he'd teach them branches [=subjects] ever-when they was wanted. **1942** (1971) Campbell *Cloud-Walking* 38 **seKY,** Then Nelt spoke up to the boys and give out what to do. **1952** Brown *NC Folkl.* 1.545, *Give out. . .* To acknowledge, to accept as; generally in the passive. "He's given out to be the best shooter in this section."—General. Old people. **1984** Wilder *You All Spoken Here* 166 **Sth,** Give out: Announce; acknowledge, as "Short-tail Bob is give out to be the bes' squirrel dog aroun' here."

b Esp: to read out the lines of a hymn before the congregation sings them; by ext, to pronounce words to be spelled. [*OED give* v. 62. b 1712 →] **chiefly S Midl, Sth** Cf **line out**

1871 Eggleston *Hoosier Schoolmaster* 39 **sIN,** I 'low they'll appint the Squire to gin out the words to-night. **1899** (1912) Green *VA Folk-Speech* 197, To *give out* the lines of a hymn to be sung. **1902** *DN* 2.235 **sIL,** *Give out. . .* To announce, as 'To give out the lesson,' or 'To give out a hymn.' A hymn was usually read in full by the preacher before singing. **1946** *PADS* 6.15 **NC, VA,** *Give out. . .* To call out words to be spelled in a contest. . . Common. **1947** *PADS* 8.14 **IN,** *Give out* [=to call out spelling words]. **1954** *Harder Coll.* **cwTN,** *Give out. . .* Call out words, make a statement. **1956** McAtee *Some Dialect NC* 18, *Give out:* . . call the words in a spelling match. **c1960** *Wilson Coll.* **csKY,** *Give out. . .* To pronounce words to be spelled. **1976** Ryland *Richmond Co. VA* 371, *Give out . .* lead, as in speaking the lines of a hymn one by one as they are to be sung ("line out" the hymn.)

2 with *of:* To run out of (something). [*give out* to be overcome by exhaustion]

1972 *Atlanta Constitution* (GA) 2 Jan mag sec 7, When you don't have . . no money coming in [to the city treasury] is when your pot's getting low. You about give out of money to pay the police. **1973** *Patrick Coll.* **AL** (as of a1946), Give out—We give out of gas. The gas gave out. **1986** Pederson *LAGS Concordance,* 1 inf, **seAR,** Give out of sugar—run out of sugar.

3 To give up; spec:

a To abandon or postpone (a course of action).

1760 (1925) Washington *Diaries* 1.140 **neVA,** After several efforts to make a plow after a new model . . [I] was feign to give it out, at least for the present. **1832** in 1956 Eliason *Tarheel Talk* 153 **NC,** It is not my custom to give out doing a good thing after I once undertake it. **1899** (1912) Green *VA Folk-Speech* 197, He thought at first he would go, but at last he gave it out. **1903** *DN* 2.314 **seMO,** *Give out. . .* To give up; to decline. 'He gave out going when it began to rain.' **1906** *DN* 3.119 **sIN,** *Give out. . .* To postpone. "He's give out goin." **1908** *DN* 3.315 **eAL, wGA,** *Give out. . .* To give up, postpone. "We've done give out goin'." **1923** *DN* 5.208 **swMO,** *Give out. . .* To change one's mind, as "I've done give out a-gorn." **1927** *AmSp* 2.355 **cwWV,** He has given out the notion of going to college this year. **1976** Garber *Mountain-ese* 34 **Appalachians,** Ma has completely give out ever gettin' Ellie Mae married off.

b also with *on:* To despair of (someone); to give up hope of seeing (someone).

1854 in 1983 *PADS* 70.35 **ce,sePA,** We gave him out nearly. **1938** Rawlings *Yearling* 9 **nFL,** I near about give you out, son. **1952** Brown *NC Folkl.* 1.544 **c,eNC,** *Give out. . .* To lose hope that something (favorable) will occur. "I can't wait for that man any longer; I give him out." **c1960** *Wilson Coll.* **csKY,** *Give out. . .* To lose hope for someone lost or ill. "We give him out when we couldn't find him." **1983** *MJLF* 9.1.40 **ceKY,** *Gave you out . .* gave up looking for you. **1984** Wilder *You All Spoken Here* 166 **Sth,** Clara Della give out on seein' you ag'in, so she up an' lef' out of here with a fruit tree salesman.

4 To be open and communicative.

1968 *DARE* (Qu. HH24, *Somebody who doesn't talk very much*) Inf **OH49,** Doesn't give out.

give out adj phr See **given out**

give-out n **esp sAppalachians** Cf **give out** v phr **1a**

An announcement.

1917 *DN* 4.412 **wNC,** *Give-out. . .* Announcement. "I didn't hear no give-out at meetin'." Also Ill. **1926** *DN* 5.400 **Ozarks. 1931** *PMLA* 46.1319 **sAppalachians. 1944** *PADS* 2.19 **sAppalachians,** *Give-out. . .* An announcement. "I hyerd no give-out about it." [*PADS* Ed: Also, reported from upper S.C.] **1960** Williams *Walk Egypt* 283 **nGA,** Nah, I ain't heard no give-out. Now tell. **1972** Cooper *NC Mt. Folkl.* 89, A give-out—an announcement.

give out of See **give out** v phr **2**

give out on See **give out** v phr **3b**

give over v phr [*OED* (at *give* v. 63. g) *"Obs."*]

To give in; to yield (to someone).

1965–69 *DARE* (Qu. Z14a, *To give a child its own way or pay too much attention to it: "Everyone ______ that child."*) Infs **MS59, OH70, TN30, WV18,** Gives over to; (Qu. JJ23, *To refuse to give in or yield: "He tried to scare me off but I ______ ."*) Inf **AR47,** Didn't give over to him; (Qu. JJ25, *To show somebody that you're the boss: "He thought he could take the place over, but I made him ______ ."*) Inf **MS6,** Give over; (Qu. JJ40, *When you admit that you did something wrong and are willing to take the consequences, you might say: "It was my fault and I'm willing to ______ ."*) Inf **LA8,** Give over; **NC79,** Give over—change your mind about it.

giver n

c1970 Wiersma *Marbles Terms* **MI,** *Giver,* a marble of inferior quality that one has no fear of losing in a game.

gives n

c1970 Wiersma *Marbles Terms* **MI,** When hit, marble must be given up. 'He lost it on gives.'

give the gate See **gate**

give to See **give B4**

give up v phr

1 To acknowledge; to admit. **chiefly S Midl** Cf **give out** v phr **1a**

1851 Hooper *Widow Rugby's Husband* 150 **AL,** She may force them "to haul in their horns, and give up that there's other people knows something, besides theyselves." **1923** *DN* 5.242 **KY,** *Give up to be. . .* To admit; concede. "John Horseley's give up to be the knowin'est man in these parts." **1936** *AmSp* 11.63 **seWV,** He was given up (cried up, reputed) to be a good writer. **1952** Brown *NC Folkl.* 1.545, *Giv(en) up to be. . .* Acknowledged to be, accepted as.—General. Old people. **1955** Roberts *S. from Hell-fer-Sartin* 179 **seKY,** She was give up to be as good as any man in the country at rail splitting. **1956** *Hall Coll.* **TN,** He was give up to be the best bear dog in this country. **c1960** *Wilson Coll.* **csKY,** *Given up to be. . .* Regarded as. "She's given up to be the prettiest girl around here." **1965** Will *Okeechobee Boats* 16 **FL,** Cap'n Hall was give up to be one of the best pilots on the rivers. **1974** Fink *Mountain Speech* 11 **wNC, eTN,** He's give up to be the best doctor in town.

2 with *to:* To indulge, give in to. Cf **give over**

1967–68 *DARE* (Qu. Z14a, *To give a child its own way or pay too much attention to it: "Everyone ______ that child."*) Infs **MI47, VA27,** Gives up to.

give up one's fiddle See **fiddle** n **5**

give up to See **give up** v phr **2**

give way v phr Also *give away* [By ext from std *give way* to yield to force]

To fail, shrink away.

1923 *DN* 5.208 **swMO,** *Give way*... To play out, to become exhausted. That spring gives way in dry weather. **1954** *Harder Coll.* **cwTN** (as of 1945), *Give away*.. grow weaker. "[He] says it is his heart that is giving away." **1966** *DARE* (Qu. BB31, *When a swelling begins to get less, you say it's ______;* total Infs questioned, 75) Inf **FL**8, Giving way.

give-way n See **giveaway**

givey adj

1 also *giffy;* also sp *giv(v)y;* Of weather: humid, muggy, damp; by ext, moist, pliable. [Cf *EDD give* v. II. 9 "Of things: to be covered with moisture; to become moist or soft from damp or fermentation, to 'sweat.'.. Hence *Givey* or *Givy*... Of the ground: damp, soft, full of moisture."] **chiefly Mid and S Atl**

1829 *VA Lit. Museum* 1.457 *(OEDS), Givy,* 'muggy'. The weather is said to be givy when there is much moisture in the atmosphere. **1859** (1968) Bartlett *Americanisms* 170, *Givy.* A term applied to tobacco leaves, in a certain condition of their preparation for market. **1899** (1912) Green *VA Folk-Speech* 197, *Givey*... Damp, moist; "givey weather," said of damp weather. **1915** *DN* 4.183 **VA,** *Givey*... Soft; moist:—of earth. **1942** (1965) Parrish *Slave Songs* 41 **GA coast,** "Giffy".. on Sapelo means damp. **1949** *AmSp* 24.109 **SC,** *Giffy* ['gɪfɪ]... Damp and cold ('Negro'). **1950** *PADS* 14.32 **SC,** Giffy [gɪfɪ]... Cloudy and damp, applied to the weather. **1954** *PADS* 21.28 **Charleston SC,** Giffy... Of lumber, waterlogged and unfit for use. **1965** in 1983 Johnson *I Declare* 52 **nwFL,** It's givvy weather... Cloudy, hazy, hot, clammy. Damp, but not quite raining. Givvy weather. "Clothes won't get hard dry" when it's givvy weather... They "give" when you take them off the line. **1967** Key *Tobacco Vocab.* **KY, MO,** *Givey weather*.. moist weather which makes dry tobacco leaves pliable. "It takes givey weather" [to strip tobacco]. **1969** *DARE* FW Addit **NC,** It's givey and sticky. [FW: Talking about a hot, humid day.] **1986** Pederson *LAGS Concordance,* 1 inf, **neGA,** A givey morning—damp, unpleasant—not always [=necessarily] cool.

2 Unsteady.

1895 *DN* 1.371 **KY, NC, TN,** *Givey:* unsteady. "That table's givey." **1926** *DN* 5.400 **Ozarks,** *Givey*... Unsteady. "Th' big cheer's a-gittin' a leetle givey lately." **1984** Wilder *You All Spoken Here* 17 **Sth,** *Givey:* Unsteady, as a just-dropped calf or a bar patron.

3 ?Yielding, not firm.

1968 *DARE* Tape **GA**69, The peach that they grow... it's tough, it's spongy, an' it's givey and it does look exceptionally good in the can.

4 Generous.

1963 *DE Folkl. Bulletin* Oct 40/2, *Give-y* (generous). **1970** *DARE* (Qu. U32,.. *A very generous person*) Inf **VA**74, Givey.

givvy, givy See **givey 1**

gizzard n

Innards, guts; usu fig: courage, spirit, life.

1892 Johnston *Mr. Fortner's* 103 **GA,** [Gus] had never had any gizzard. **1898** Johnston *Pearce Amerson's Will* 203 **cGA,** [Wilie Amerson wants Hannah in a] distracted bad way. I'm obleeged to acknowledge that it make [sic] me see more gum in Wilie, and more gizzard, as the sayin' is, than I thought he have. They tell me he never seemed to keer so pow'ful much for his wife. **1908** *DN* 3.315 **eAL, wGA,** *Gizzard*... The seat of one's courage... Life: in the specific phrase 'to save one's gizzard.' "I couldn't reach it to save my gizzard," i.e., 'no matter how hard I tried.' **1942** McAtee *Dial. Grant Co. IN* 28 (as of 1890s), *Gizzard*.. life. "I couldn't do it to save my ______". **1958** McCulloch *Woods Words* 71 **Pacific NW,** *Gizzard*—Any insides of man or machine. **c1960** *Wilson Coll.* **csKY,** *Gizzard*... One's life. "I wouldn't speak to him to save my gizzard." **1961** Adams *Old-Time Cowhand* 194, Needle's friends wasn't shore of his nerve... Deep down in their gizzards they didn't think he had any sand in his craw.

gizzard (chad) See **gizzard shad 1**

gizzard fish n

1 A **whitefish** (here: *Coregonus clupeaformis*). **Gt Lakes**

1911 *Century Dict. Suppl., Gizzard-fish*... A whitefish, *Coregonus clupeiformis* [sic], found in the Great Lakes. **1974** WI Univ. *Fish Lake MI* 12, *Coregonus clupeaformis*... Common names: whitefish,.. gizzard fish, grande coregone (French). **1983** Becker *Fishes WI* 335, *Lake Whitefish*... Other common names.. gizzard fish.

2 A **gizzard shad 1** (here: *Dorosoma cepedianum*).

1968 *DARE* (Qu. P3, *Freshwater fish that are not good to eat*) Inf **DE**3, Mud shad or gizzard fish.

gizzard shad n

1 also *gizzard (chad):* A fish of the genus *Dorosoma:* either the **threadfin shad** or, commonly, *D. cepedianum* which is also called **flatfish 3b, gizzard fish 2, hairy back, hickory shad, jack shad, lake shad, mud shad, Norwegian herring, river herring, sawbelly, shad, skipjack, white-eyed shad, white shad, winter shad.**

1820 Rafinesque *Ohio R. Fishes* 40, Spotted Gizzard... Vulgar names Gizzard, Hickory Shad, White Shad, &c. **1884** Goode *Fisheries U.S.* 1.610, The names "Gizzard Shad" or "Hickory Shad" refer to the peculiar muscular stomach. **c1902** Clapin *New Dict. Amer.* 204, *Gizzard-shad.* (1) A North-Carolina term for the alewife. (2) A fish of the Ohio (Chatoessus ellipticus), common in Cincinnati, and so called because it possesses a muscular stomach resembling the gizzard of a gallinaceous fowl. **1933** LA Dept. of Conserv. *Fishes* 215, *The Atchafalaya Gizzard Shad. Signalosa atchafalayae*... This Gizzard Shad is to be distinguished from the ordinary Gizzard Shad, *Dorosoma cepedianum*..., by the fact that it has a much longer last ray of the dorsal fin than has the latter species. **1940** Writers' Program *Guide NM* 18, A peculiar type of gizzard shad, with a gizzard very similar to that of a hen, is found in Pecos Valley. **1966–67** *DARE* (Qu. P2.. *Saltwater fish caught around here [that] are good to eat*) Inf **NC**15, Hickory shad or gizzard shad; (Qu. P3, *Freshwater fish that are not good to eat*) Inf **NC**15, Gizzard chad; **SC**40, Gizzard shad—like roe shad, but real skinny; **SC**43, Gizzard shad. **1979** Hallowell *People Bayou* 116 **sLA,** Crawfish are surprisingly fussy about bait. They.. prefer gizzard shad. **1983** Becker *Fishes WI* 276, The gizzard shad is not esteemed as food by man because of its soft, rather tasteless flesh and numerous fine bones. In the past, however, there has been a limited market for this species where a cheap fish was sought.

2 An **alewife** (here: *Alosa pseudoharengus*).

1857 *Harper's New Mth. Mag.* Mar 442/1 **NC,** The refuse fish commonly taken are sturgeon,.. gizzard-shad or ale-wife. **1899** (1912) Green *VA Folk-Speech* 197, *Gizzard-shad*... A name for alewives. **c1902** [see **1** above].

3 A **mooneye** (here: *Hiodon* spp).

1971 *WI State Jrl.* (Madison) 29 Aug sec 4 5/3, I'll admit to being a little disappointed when it turned out to be a lowly mooneye, also, I think, known as a shiner or a gizzard shad.

gizzard string, pop one's v phr Cf **earstring**

=**bust a gut 1.**

1928 Peterkin *Scarlet Sister Mary* 84 **SC** [Gullah], You like to a popped you gizzard-string a-tryin to get July.

gizzle n Cf **guzzle**

=**goozle** n **1;** also fig.

1946 Faulkner *Sound & Fury* (App.) 84 **MS,** "He cut up all Benjy's dolls." Caddy said. "I'll slit his gizzle." **1960** Williams *Walk Egypt* 183 **GA,** "[They].. nigh-about hanged him." "Nigh? Why didn't they *do* it?" "More gizzle than guts, I reckon." **1968** *DARE* (Qu. X7,.. *Names for the throat*) Inf **MD**35, Gizzle.

glab v [Perh back-formation from **glabber** infl by *gab;* but cf *EDD glab* sb. 1 "Foolish, idle talk"]

1941 *LANE* Map 419 *(Chat)* 1 inf, **swME,** *Glab,* older term; 1 inf, **swME,** *Blob, gab, jawp, glab, buzz,* very old slang terms.

glabber v [Scots, Engl dial; cf *EDD glabber* v. 1 "To chatter, jabber, gabble"]

1900 Day *Up in ME* 157, When it [=a forest spook] blitters and glabbers the long night through.

glab-fest n [**glab** + **fest**] Cf **glib-glab**

1968 *DARE* (Qu. KK12, *A meeting where there's a lot of talking: "They got together yesterday and had a real ______."*) Inf **NY**69, Glabfest.

glacier duck n

=**harlequin duck.**

1932 Howell *FL Bird Life* 153, *Eastern Harlequin Duck*... *Other Names*.. *Glacier Duck*... Breeds in Iceland, southern Greenland, Baffin Island, and northern Labrador. Winters on the Atlantic coast south to Long Island, and casually to South Carolina and Florida. **1953** Jewett *Birds WA* 144, *Western Harlequin Duck*... Other Names.. Glacier Duck.

glacier lily n **West**

=dogtooth violet.

1915 (1926) Armstrong–Thornber *Western Wild Flowers* 28, *Glacier Lily . . Erythronium parviflorum. . .* Around Mt. Rainier these beautiful plants often grow in large patches at the edge of the snow. **1936** McDougall–Baggley *Plants of Yellowstone* 39, *Glacierlily (Erythronium grandiflorum). . .* The flowers bloom very early while the snow is still melting. **1954** Sharpe *101 Wildflowers* 4 **nwWA,** Glacier lily. . . A common and attractive flower, forming dense, short-lived fields of yellow at the very edge of melting snowbanks. **1961** Douglas *My Wilderness* 20 **nCO,** Before timber line is reached, gooseberries and currants are thick. In this zone are glacier lilies as bright and gay as those on the American Ridge in the Cascades. **1966** *DARE* (Qu. S11, . . *Other names . . for . . dog-tooth violet*) Inf **WA**15, Glacier lily. **1973** Hitchcock–Cronquist *Flora Pacific NW* 690, *Erythronium. . .* Glacier-lily.

glacier pine n

Perh a **white pine** (here: *Pinus monticola*).

1935 Davis *Honey* 222 **OR,** They made camp in a grove of glacier-pine, and suffered from the cold.

glad clothes n pl Also *glads;* for addit varr see quots [Varr of *glad rags*]

One's best clothes.

1901 *DN* 2.140 **NY,** To put on one's glad clothes. **1903** *Cin. Enquirer* 10 May IV.3/1 *(DA),* In the Evening you can put on your Glads and drink $47 worth of Vintage Wines and take in two or three Theaters. **1905** *Dly. Chron.* 11 Jan. 4/5 *(DA),* Only when starvation stares him in the face will he relinquish his 'glad clothes,' as the cowboys call them. **1954** Weingarten *Amer. Dict. Slang* 153, *Glad rags. . .* Variants are *glad garments* (1902): *glad raiment* (1906). **1970** *DARE* (Qu. W39, *Joking ways of referring to a person's best clothes*) Inf **VA**42, Glad duds.

glade n

1 An area of low swampy land. [By ext from *glade* a relatively open area in a forest] **esp Midl and S Atl**

1644 in 1940 *AmSp* 15.266 **VA,** Thence . . unto a Small White oake and a Pocickerry that Stands in the Glade and then paralell to the Glade or white Marsh. **1789** Morse *Amer. Geog.* 413 **NC,** Interspersed through the other parts, are glades of rich swamp. **1818** in 1934 *FL Hist. Qrly.* 13.28, The glades or Savannas are tracts a little lower than the palmetto land, and in winter are covered with water from a few inches to several feet in depth. They extend, with great variation of length and breadth through the whole country, sometimes forming long and narrow vistas through the pineland covered with luxuriant and nutritious herbage and in places, spreading into ponds or lakes many miles in extent only dry in the warmest seasons. **1828** in 1938 Gardiner–Gardiner *Chron. Old Berkeley* 263 **VA,** This country is flat and wet, the land clothed with white oak, elm, hickory and maple, for fifteen miles the bottom is interspersed with glades. **1837** (1962) Williams *Territory FL* 50, [Dry Creek] has an excessive crooked course among the mangroves, which terminates in a drain from the Glades. **1859** (1968) Bartlett *Americanisms* 170, *Glades.* Everglades; tracts of land at the South covered with water and grass. So called in Maryland, where they are divided into wet and dry *glades.* **1872** Schele de Vere *Americanisms* 480, *Glade. . .* In the South the term is often used as a shorter substitute for *everglades,* the tracts of land covered with water and grass, which are so called from Maryland down to Florida. **1964** Will *Hist. Okeechobee* 69 **FL,** White hunters tried to copy it [=the Seminole cypress dugout] with a flimsy, cranky boat of half inch cypress boards, and a poor imitation it was at best—glade boats they were called. **1966–70** *DARE* (Qu. C7, . . *Land that . . has some standing water with trees*) Inf **AR**52, Oak glade; (Qu. C35) Inf **FL**24, Glade land—in glades with saw grass on it; **FL**48, The glade—a farming section. **1986** Pederson *LAGS Concordance,* 1 inf, **neAR,** Glade—soft land in wintertime—low-lying; 1 inf, **neLA,** Glade—more or less a swamp; 1 inf, **neAR,** Sand glade.

2 An area of open water surrounded by ice. **NEng**

1698 (1878) S. Sewall *Diary* 1.472 **MA,** A considerable quantity of Ice went away last night: so that now there is a glade of water along by Governor's Island about as far as Bird Island. **1806** (1970) Webster *Compendious Dict.* 131/1, Glade . . an opening in a wood or in ice. **1864** Nichols *40 Yrs.* 1.18, I used to skate miles up and down the Connecticut river, and when thirsty, creep carefully to the edges of the air-holes, or 'glades,' in the ice, and drink. **1872** Schele de Vere *Americanisms* 480, *Glade,* the name given originally to a part of the water which is not frozen over, though surrounded by ice—from the analogy to the *glade,* an opening in the woods—has been subsequently applied in New England to smooth ice also.

3 Smooth ice. [Perh because it looks like open water] **esp NEng**

1828 (1970) Webster *Amer. Dict.* np, *Glade. . .* Smooth ice. *New England.* **1859** (1968) Bartlett *Americanisms* 170, *Glade.* In New England, smooth ice. **1872** [see **2** above]. **1905** *DN* 3.10 **CT,** *Glade . .* smooth ice. **1969** *DARE* (Qu. B33a, *The first thin ice*) Inf **NY**210, Glade.

4 A grove or thicket.

1968–70 *DARE* (Qu. C28, *A place where underbrush, weeds, vines and small trees grow . . so that it's nearly impossible to get through*) Inf **NJ**21, Glade; (Qu. T1, . . *A bunch of trees growing together in open country*) Infs **MI**108, **TN**46, Glade. **1986** Pederson *LAGS Concordance (Maple grove),* 1 inf, **seAL,** Glade.

glade devil n

The collared lizard *(Crotaphytus collaris),* about which some fabulous lore has grown up; see quot 1926. Cf **hoop snake**

1926 TX Folkl. Soc. *Pub.* 5.65, The glade devil inhabits the Ozark Mountains of Missouri and Arkansas. It is a large lizard that. . . lives around and under flat stones in open woods and is noted for its prowess and ferocity. According to the stories, it . . will chase a person even though he may be riding a horse and it can always outrun the horse. It bites with its teeth and stings with its tail and has a loud bark that can be heard for miles. . . It is to be understood that the glade devil . . is poisonous. **1928** Baylor Univ. Museum *Contrib.* 16.11, The cognomen *Glade Devil* is applied to it [=*Crotaphytus collaris*] in parts of southern Missouri and Arkansas. **1945** McAtee *Nomina Abitera* 22.

glade flower n

=evening primrose a.

1940 Clute *Amer. Plant Names* 265, *Oenothera Missouriense. . .* Glade flower. **1959** Carleton *Index Herb. Plants* 52, *Glade-flower:* Oenothera (v).

glade lily n

1 A **wood lily** (here: *Lilium philadelphicum*).

1894 *Jrl. Amer. Folkl.* 7.102 **WV,** *Lilium Philadelphicum. . .* Glade-lily. **1911** *Century Dict. Suppl., Lily. . . Glade-lily,* the red lily. **1940** Clute *Amer. Plant Names* 12, *Wood Lily. . .* Glade-lily. **1949** Moldenke *Amer. Wild Flowers* 322, This lily, known also as *glade lily, . .* lives in dry woods and thickets from Maine and Ontario south to North Carolina and West Virginia, blossoming in June and July.

2 An **evening primrose a** (here: *Oenothera missouriensis*).

1940 Steyermark *Flora MO* 376, *Missouri Primrose, Glade Lily. . .* Flowers showy, lasting but a day, the long calyx-tube resembling a flower-stalk. **1970** Correll *Plants TX* 1129, *Oenothera missouriensis. . . Glade-lily. . .* Flowers opening near sunset. . . Limestone knobs, prairies and dry hillsides.

glade mallow n

A coarse malvaceous plant *(Napaea dioica)* with maple-like leaves and small white flowers.

1848 Gray *Manual of Botany* 69, *Glade Mallow. . . N[apaea] dioica. . .* Limestone valleys, Penn., southward to Augusta Co., in the Valley of Virginia, . . west to Ohio and Illinois. **1884** *Amer. Naturalist* 18.724, The glade mallow is a dioecious plant. **1900** Lyons *Plant Names* 257, Glade Mallow. . . A perennial herb with small white dioecious flowers. **1931** Fassett *Spring Flora* 110 **WI,** *Glade Mallow. . .* Moist places and along railroads, north to Dane and Vernon Counties. **1951** Voss–Eifert *IL Wild Flowers* 162, In spite of the fact that glade mallow often grows along railroad tracks, it is almost as well concealed in these haunts as it would be in some forest glade. **1963** Gleason–Cronquist *Manual Plants* 464, Glade-mallow. . . Fl[ower]s very many in a large terminal panicle. **1976** Bailey–Bailey *Hortus Third* 754, *Glade mallow. . .* Early summer. Ohio, w. to Ill. and Minn.

glade owl n

The barred owl *(Strix varia).*

1925 Bailey *Birds FL* 76, *Strix varia alleni (Hoot owl, Cat owl, Glade owl).* Sadly lacking, would we think our glade hammock especially, if we did not include among its feathered inhabitants a pair of these fine birds.

glade tick n

Perh a wood tick.

1968 *DARE* (Qu. R23a, *Insects or other creatures that fasten themselves to the skin and suck blood—on land*) Inf **MD**18, Glade tick.

gladey See **glady**

glad garments, glad raiment, glads See **glad clothes**

glady adj Also sp *gladey*
Of land: infertile, with shallow, rocky soil.
1966 *PADS* 46.26 **AR,** *Gladey*. . . Slatey. "I dug it out of a gladey place." **1968** *DARE* File **AL,** Glady land [gledi]. . . Poor shallow soil with rock near the surface. Poor for cultivation.

glahm v See **glom** v[1]

glahm n See **glom** n[1]

glaikit adj Also sp *glaiket, glaked, glakid* [Scots dial]
Stupid, careless, foolish.
1889 (1971) Farmer *Americanisms* 266, *Glakid.*—*Glaikit,* in Lowland Scotch, is given by Jamieson as unsteady; giddy; stupid; and with the last of these meanings *glakid* is used in Pennsylvania. **1916** *DN* 4.275 **NE,** *Glakid, glaked*. . . Heedless, careless; as a *glaked* child. "I don't see what makes that child so glaked." **1952** Brown *NC Folkl.* 1.545, *Glaiket, glaikit* ['glekɪt]. . . Lazy, careless, foolish.—Rare.

glair See **glare** adj

glaked, glakid See **glaikit**

glam v See **glom** v[1]

glam n See **glom** n[1]

glance fish n
=**opah.**
1896 U.S. Natl. Museum *Bulletin* 47.954, *Lampris luna*. . . *Glance Fish*. . . Color a rich brocade of silver and lilac, rosy on the belly; everywhere with round silvery spots. **1902** Jordan–Evermann *Amer. Fishes* 326, The opah. . . is found in the open waters of the Atlantic and Pacific. . . It is called . . glance-fish. . . and is one of the choicest food-fishes. **1911** *Century Dict. Suppl., Glance-fish*. . . A common name of *Lampris luna*, . . the opah.

g'lang See **go along**

g'lant See **gallant**

‡glare n[1] [*glare* to shine brightly]
1967 *DARE* (Qu. N10, . . *Bright . . lights on a car*) Inf **MN**2, Glares for brights.

glare n[2] [Cf *SND glaur* n.[1] 6 "Slippery ice . . ; slipperiness"; *OED glare* sb.[2] a "Frost, icy condition *(obs.)*"; perh infl by *glare* dazzling light]
An expanse of slick ice—usu in phr *glare of ice.*
1854 Cummins *Lamplighter* 96 **MA,** You noticed how everything was covered with ice, this morning. . . The side-walks were . . a perfect glare. **1878** Beadle *Western Wilds* 457 **CO,** In ten minutes the road was a glare of ice, our wrappings stiff as armor. **1903** *DN* 2.297 **Cape Cod MA,** *Glare*. . . In expression 'glare of ice,' a surface of glare ice. **1907** *DN* 3.206 **nwAR,** *Glare*. . . In the expression, a "glare of ice," a surface of glare ice. **1968–69** *DARE* (Qu. B33a, *The first thin ice that forms over the surface of a pond or pool: "There's just a ______ of ice."*) Infs **IN**7, **NY**179, Glare.

glare adj Also sp *glair* Cf **black ice 2, glare** n[2]
Glassy; slick—now usu in comb *glare ice* a coating of smooth, slippery ice.
1832 Williamson *Hist. ME* 1.100, The rain sometimes freezes as it falls; covers the face of the earth with a glare ice, and adorns the trees with glistening pendants. **1856** Olmsted *Journey Slave States* 345, A congealed pool of rosin . . firm and glair; varying in color, and glistening like polished porphyry. **a1861** (1880) Eastman *Poems* 188 **VT,** When the ice was glare, the girls would stay / And share in our glorious fun. **1869** Stowe *Oldtown Folks* 73 **MA,** We was clear down in a well fifty feet deep, and the sides all round nothin' but glare ice. **1872** King *Mountaineering* 89, Looking down the glare front of ice. **1876** Warner–Warner *Gold Chickaree* 281 **NEast,** The sidewalks are in a state of glare ice this morning. **1891** (1967) Freeman *New Engl. Nun* 160, The roads were glare and slippery with it [=ice], and so were the door-yards. **1903** [see **glare** n[2]]. **1907** [see **glare** n[2]]. **1949** *Sat. Eve. Post* 16 April 178/3, There were times when sudden thaws turned the highway to glare ice.

glare of ice See **glare** n[2]

glarmy adj Cf **gaumy** adj[2]
1968 Coatsworth *ME Memories* 133 **cME,** "Glarmy" means clumsy

glass n Usu |glæs|; also **esp eNEng** |glɑs, glas|; also **scattered** |dlæs| [The change of gl > dl by assimilation is common in Engl (but not Scots or Ir) dial; see *EDG* 251]
A Forms.
[**1828** Webster *Amer. Dict.* np, [In "Pronunciation of Words":] *Gl* are pronounced as *dl.*] **1891** *DN* 1.167 **cNY,** A *g* is heard as *d* in [spaɪdlæs] < *spy glass.* **1936** [see **glory** n[1] **A**]. **1941** *LANE* Map 311, [For *glass,* prons of the type [glæs] are the most common throughout NEng; in eNEng the types [glas, glɑs] are also common, but they are rare in wNEng. Prons of the type [dlæs] are scattered esp wNEng; they are entirely lacking in ME. There are only three instances of the type [dlas], of which one is in ME.] **1942** *AmSp* 17.33 **seNY,** Glass—12 [infs have [æ]] 4 [infs have [a]] 1 [inf has [ɑ]]. Glasses—36 [infs have [æ]] 3 [infs have [a]] 0 [inf has [ɑ]]. **1961** [see **dance**]. **1976** Allen *LAUM* 3.319 (as of c1950), Before /l/, as in *glass . . ,* an initial velar [g] is likely to experience fronting . . or even to move to the palatal tongue position of /ɟ/ or alveolar /d/. In the U[pper] M[idwest] this extreme fronting in *glass* shows a possible Northern orientation as well as some preference by the less educated infs.
B Sense.
See **glassie.**

glass bait See **glass minnow**

glass can n
=**can** n **1.**
1959 *VT Hist.* new ser 27.137, *Glass cans*. . . Jars for canning. Occasional. **1974** Maurer–Pearl *KY Moonshine* 115, *Can*. . . In the Southern mountains, a half-gallon fruit jar. Also called "glass can" . . usually used only to hold liquor.

glass cat n
=**cat's-eye 1.**
c1970 Wiersma *Marbles Terms* 4 **UT** (as of 1965), Glass cat. . . A cat's eye marble.

glass cloth See **glass towel**

glass eel n
See quots.
1911 *Century Dict. Suppl., Glass-eel*. . . A young conger-eel. The young do not resemble the adults: they are elongate, thin, and have very small heads. **1983** Becker *Fishes WI* 257, *American Eel. Anguilla rostrata*. . . Transformed or "glass eels" with general shape of an eel, eyes pigmented but body transparent.

glassey See **glassie**

glass eye n[1] Cf **glassie**
1965–70 *DARE* (Qu. EE6d, *Special marbles*) 22 Infs, **scattered,** Glass eyes; (Qu. EE6a, *Names for different kinds of marbles—the big one that's used to knock others out of the ring*) Infs **CT**23, **IN**14, Glass eyes; (Qu. EE6b, *Small marbles or marbles in general*) Inf **MA**128, Glass eyes.

glasseye n[2] Also *glass-eyed pike*
=**walleye.**
1818 *Amer. Monthly Mag. & Crit. Rev.* 2.247/1 **cNY,** Glass-Eye—*Perca vitrea,* with the pupils of the eyes appearing like the semi-globes of glass in the decks of vessels. . . Found in the Cayuga Lake. **1856** *Porter's Spirit of Times* 1 Nov 142/3 **IL, IN,** The northern pike, . . in point of capacity, . . ranks next to the muscalonge among our lake fishes, being better flavored though not quite so firm as the Pike-Perch or Glass-Eye. **1870** (1871) *Fur Fin & Feather* 212 **cNY,** *Cayuga Lake*. . . The same party took eleven salmon trout, two black bass, and two glass-eyed pike. **1884** Goode *Fisheries U.S.* 1.417 **wGt Lakes,** The names 'Glass-eye' and 'Yellow Pike' are sometimes heard. **1933** LA Dept. of Conserv. *Fishes* 368, The Wall-eyed Pike. . . has received many popular names, among which are Pike Perch, . . Glass-eye. **1947** Dalrymple *Panfish* 217 *(DA),* The names which allude to Old Bleary's odd-looking eyes are certainly logical enough: i.e., Glass-Eye, White Eye, and of course his most common names, Walleye, or Wall-Eyed Pike. **1975** Evanoff *Catch More Fish* 87, The walleye *(Stizostedion vitreum)* is also called . . glasseye. **1983** Becker *Fishes WI* 871, *Walleye*. . . Other common names . . glasseye. . . Eyes silvery in life; a reflecting layer (tapetum lucidum) causes glowing in dark.

glasseye snapper n
A **snapper**-like saltwater fish *(Priacanthus cruentatus).*
1960 Amer. Fisheries Soc. *List Fishes* 26, Glasseye snapper . . *Priacanthus cruentatus.* **1973** Knight *Cook's Fish Guide* 391, Snapper . . Glasseye (. . g[oo]d).

glassie n Also *glass* Also sp *glass(e)y* **widespread, but more freq Nth, N Midl, West** See Map Cf **clayie, crystal B**

A marble made of glass.

1908 *DN* 3.315 **eAL,** *Glass.* . . A playing-marble made of glass. **1922** *DN* 5.187 **MA, MN,** *Glassy.* . . A glass marble. **1935** *AmSp* 10.159 **NE,** *Glassies.* Glass marbles of various sizes and descriptions. **1955** *PADS* 23.19, *Glassey (glassie, glassy).* . . A marble made of glass. . . The taw, or offensive marble. **1958** *PADS* 29.34, *Glassie* . . some report "clear glass"; others, "glass with whorls of color inside." **1963** North *Rascal* 51 **WI** (as of 1918), Here were glassies and steelies and one real agate marble. **1965–70** *DARE* (Qu. EE6d, *Special marbles*) 233 Infs, **widespread, but more freq Nth, N Midl, West,** Glassie; (Qu. EE6a, . . *The big one that's used to knock others out of the ring*) 9 Infs, **chiefly Nth,** Glassie; (Qu. EE6b, *Small marbles or marbles in general*) 8 Infs, **scattered,** Glassies; (Qu. EE6c, *Cheap marbles*) 8 Infs, **scattered,** Glassies; (Qu. EE7, . . *Kinds of marble games*) Inf **MA**11, Put marbles in ring, snap glassie, and try to knock others out; **MA**71, One player would put his glassies on a certain spot. **1966–69** *DARE* Tape **CA**172, All the schoolboys played marbles. . . They'd go to school with their pockets full of dough babies and compies and glassies. . . The glassies were made of glass; **IL**12, We used . . what we call a shooter marble which more 'n likely was a glassie. And we also used glassie marbles. . . Glassies . . if I remember right, you could buy for six for a penny; **WA**6, We had glassies and agates and crocks; **WI**29, Glassies . . they were made of glass. **1970** *Thompson Coll.* **GA** (as of c1920), *Glassie* . . A clear marble having colored bands spiraling from pole to pole. **c1970** Wiersma *Marbles Terms,* 10 infs, **chiefly MI,** Glassie. [Most of the infs said that a glassie is clear; four added that it is a large marble. Those who went into more detail were about evenly divided on whether it is colored or colorless and whether it has opaque inclusions.] **1976** *WI Acad. Rev.* June 20/1 (as of 1920s), We had little use for "glassies," the clear glass marbles which contained colored ribbons. **1983** Santiago *Famous All Over Town* **Los Angeles CA** 55, "Just a damn minute," I told myself and tried again, a medium-hard shot, five feet away. This time I connected like a cannonball and the glassie flew out the door.

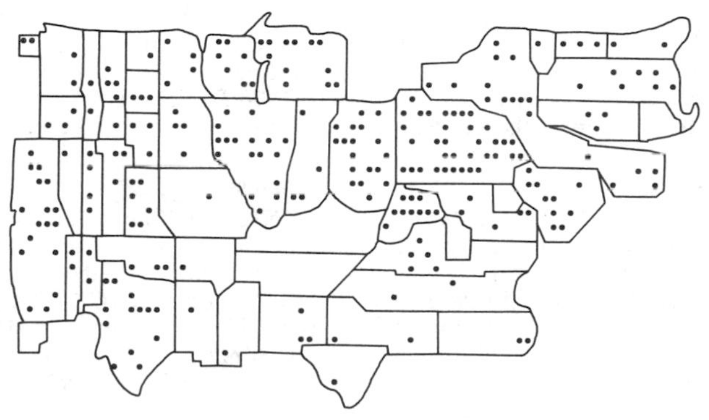

•glassie + varr (Qq. EE6a, b, c, d, EE7)

glass knothole n

1975 Gould *ME Lingo* 109, *Glass knothole.* . . A theodolite, transit, and the navigator's sextant. Captains shot the sun through a *glass knothole.*

glass lizard See **glass snake**

glassmaker n

A **dragonfly.**

1950 *WELS Suppl.* 4 Infs, **WI,** Glassmaker (dragonfly).

glass minnow n Also *glass bait*

A **silversides** such as *Menidia beryllina.*

1916 *DN* 4.345 **FL,** *Glass bait.* Silvery minnows, bait, or shiners. "We all use glass bait now while they run." **1955** Carr–Goin *Guide Reptiles* 80, *Menidia beryllina* . . Freshwater Glass-minnow. . . A silvery-greenish, streamlined little fish. **1966** *DARE* (Qu. P7, *Small fish used as bait for bigger fish*) Inf **FL**4, Glass minnows [glæs ˈmɪnɚz].

glass shrimp n

A **grass shrimp** (here: *Palaemonetes vulgaris*).

1982 Sternberg *Fishing* 126. *Grass Shrimp.* Some species of grass shrimp live in fresh water; other are found only in salt water. They are called *glass shrimp* because of their transparent appearance.

glass snake n Also *glass lizard* [See quot 1979] **chiefly Sth, S Midl**

A lizard without legs, of the genus *Ophisaurus.* Also called **brimstone snake, candy snake, grass snake 3, horn snake 2, joint snake, legless lizard**

[**1709** (1967) Lawson *New Voyage* 139 **NC,** We now come again to the Snakes. The Brimstone is so called, I believe, because it is almost of a Brimstone Colour. They might as well have call'd it a Glass-Snake, for it is as brittle as a Tobacco-Pipe, so that if you give it the least Touch of a small Twigg, it immediately breaks into several Pieces.] **1737** Royal Soc. London *Philos. Trans. for 1736* 39.258 **NC,** *Cæcilia maculata:* The Glass-Snake. **1793** Morse *Amer. Universal Geog.* 1.199, Glass Snake—Anguis ventralis. . . A small blow with a stick will separate the body, not only at the place struck, but at two or three other places, the muscles being articulated in a singular manner, quite through to the vertebra. They . . are numerous in the sandy woods of the Carolinas and Georgia. **1842** Buckingham *Slave States* 1.535 **GA,** Some of the harmless snakes of the country were seen on the rails or zig-zag fences of the road, one of which, called the glass-snake, appeared to be of peculiar brightness. **1894** U.S. Natl. Museum *Proc.* 17.320 **FL,** The "glass snake" has received its name because the tail is so very brittle. Ignorant people believe that the broken pieces are able to join together again. **1925** TX Folkl. Soc. *Pub.* 4.46, The so-called glass snake. . . is quite willing to sacrifice its tail in order to save its life. **1939** FWP *Guide FL* 29, Another lizard is the so-called . . 'glass' snake. **1939** FWP *Guide KY* 15, Less known are the several varieties of skinks and the fabulous glass or joint snake, which can shed its tail when attacked. **1941** Writers' Program *Guide AL* 24, Glass snake . . legless lizard. **1950** *WELS (Kinds of snakes found in your neighborhood)* 1 Inf, **cWI,** Glass snake. **1966–70** *DARE* (Qu. P25, . . *Kinds of snakes* . . *around here*) Infs **FL**27, **MO**11, **NC**27, 80, **SC**66, **TN**22, **WI**6, Glass snake; (Qu. CC17, *Imaginary animals or monsters that people around here tell tales about—especially to tease greenhorns*) Inf **TN**22, Glass snake—shatters when you hit it, then rejoins itself together; **OH**47, Glass snake. Hit and break it in two. It crawls around and finds itself. **1979** Behler–King *Audubon Field Guide Reptiles* 544, When held, this lizard squirms and wriggles vigorously in an attempt to escape. If the tail is grabbed or takes a blow, it may shatter into several pieces—hence the name glass lizard. **1981** Vogt *Nat. Hist.* 116 **WI,** The glass lizard, or glass snake, as it is often called, is a large limbless lizard up to 75 cm in length, about two-thirds of the length is tail.

glass towel n Also *glass cloth* **chiefly Nth** Cf **cup towel**

A towel used for drying glassware; a dish towel; hence *glass toweling* material for making such a towel.

1939 *LANE* Map 140 *(Dish towel)* 1 inf, **seCT,** Glass towel; 1 inf, **RI,** Glass toweling, bought in stores; 1 inf, **RI,** Glass towel; 1 inf, **RI,** Glass cloth, a finer grade; 1 inf, **csMA,** Glass towel; 1 inf, **neMA,** Glass towel, for glass. **1967–70** *DARE* (Qu. G16, *What do you dry dishes with?*) Inf **MN**11, Glass towels—a less linty, finer material; **MA**98, Glass towels of fine soft linen; **NY**37, Glass towel—smaller, linen; **NY**41, Glass towels—linen; (Qu. G17, *Other kinds of towels*) Infs **CA**126, 134, Glass towel; **MA**64, Glass towels—softer than linen towels, usually had stripes.

glass weed n [*OED* 1568 →]

A **glasswort.**

1955 in 1966 Goldstein–Byington *Two Penny Ballads* 144 **PA,** The juice of a glass weed will cure poison ivy.

glasswort n

Std: a plant of the genus *Salicornia.* Also called **glass weed, mutton-sass, pickleweed, saltgrass, sausage grass.** For other names of var spp see **cactus** n[1] **B2, lead grass, marsh tea, orange weed, pigeon's foot, prickly grass, saltweed, sea cress, spear grass, wild coral**

glassy See **glassie**

glassyass adj

1975 Gould *ME Lingo* 110, *Glassyass*—Sometimes given the sound of *glarssy-arse.* It is a variant for *flatarse* to describe an absolute calm at sea, but perhaps even a little flatter than *flatarse.*

glassy lizard n Cf **glass snake**

A **skink** such as *Eumeces tetragrammus;* see quot.

1928 Baylor Univ. Museum *Contrib.* 16.14, Short-lined Skink. . . The adult is one of the "Glassy Lizards."

glaucous gull n
Std: a large **gull** *(Larus hyperboreus).* Also called **harbor gull b, ice gull, owl gull, minister, white minister, white-winged gull**

glaum v See **glom** v^{1,2}

glaum n See **glom** n^{1,2}

glauming See **glom** v^{1} **3**

glawackus n Also sp *glawaucus* **CT**
An imaginary monster.
1939 *AmSp* 14.238 **CT,** The *glawackus,* according to a United Press item from Glastonbury, Connecticut, January 22, 1939, is the name given by townspeople to a mysterious beast that has kept the community terrified for some weeks. It is said to resemble a lion, a cougar, a panther, a boar, or even an overgrown police dog. Skeptics doubt its existence. **1968** *DARE* (Qu. CC17) Inf **CT**11, [glə'wɔkəs]—looks like a big dog. You put straw over a sawhorse and put it around on Halloween to scare people away. They think your creation is the real glawaucus. [FW: Inf's grandmother always made one]; **CT**19, [glə'wɔkəs]—story circulated by [a] local man about [a] monster. **1968** *DARE* Tape **CT**13, There's a wild animal around here that people claim they see, they call it the glawaucus . . when they see it they can't describe it so maybe they've had too much moonshine. It don't bother anybody. Might be a lynx that came down from Canada.

glaze v [Var of *graze*]
1923 *DN* 5.208 **swMO,** *Glaze. . .* To strike a glancing blow, or to graze with a blow. **1961** *Mt. Life* Spring 6 **sAppalachians,** In a few words *r* is substituted for *l* . . glaze (graze, meaning to scrape).

glazie n [Prob var of **glassie**]
1971 Bright *Word Geog. CA & NV* 116, [Marble terms:] 1 inf, Glazies.

gleam v [Var of *glean*]
1899 (1912) Green *VA Folk-Speech* 197, *Gleam. . .* To collect in fragmentary parcels; pick up here and there. Glean. **1970** *DARE* (Qu. L28) Inf **KY**80, [A sickle was used] when they used to gleam [glim] it by hand.

gleed n Also sp *glede* [*OED* c950 →; "Now only *arch.* or *dial.*"] *arch* Cf **fire, come to borrow**
1847 Longfellow *Evangeline* 75, The wind seized the gleeds and the burning thatch. **1930** Shoemaker *1300 Words* 27 **cPA Mts** (as of c1900), Glede. . . A red hot coal carried on a small tongs from one pioneer cabin to another to start fires.

glib adj [Prob by ext from *glib* fluent, voluble; but cf *OED glib* a. 1 "Of movement: Easy, unimpeded. Now *rare* exc. *dial*"] **chiefly S Midl**
Brisk, vigorous, spry; hence adv *glib(ly).*
1934 (1970) Wilson *Backwoods Amer.* 83 **AR, MO,** The boy leads his damsel back to the starting point, swings her around glibly, and the assembled party sings again the chorus. **1946** *AmSp* 21.271 **KY,** *Glib. . .* Briskly, quickly, vigorously. In the dark I overtook a man who looked around and said (mentioning a cripple): 'Hello, Gene—Oh! I thought you was Gene Hargis, but I didn't think Gene would be walkin' along so glib.' **1953** Randolph–Wilson *Down in Holler* 155 **Ozarks,** *Glib,* in the Ozarks, does not refer particularly to speech. It means active, brisk of movement. Rose O'Neill, of Day, Missouri, heard a neighbor say: "Granny's eighty-seven year old, but she's still glib as a quail." **1956** *Hall Coll.* **cwNC,** The old man was perty glib. *Ibid,* You are glibber than I am, so you go to the far pen. **1967–69** *DARE* (Qu. KK27, *A very lively, active old person: "For his age, he's ______.")* Infs **GA**72, **TX**37, **WI**44, Glib. **1986** Pederson *LAGS Concordance (Quite lively),* 11 infs, 8 **TN,** Glib.

glib n Cf **glibber, glib-glab**
1965–66 *DARE* (Qu. X9, *Joking or uncomplimentary words for a person's mouth. . . "I wish he'd shut his ______.")* Infs **FL**2, **MS**45, **OK**13, Glib.

glibber n Cf **glib n, glib-glab**
1966 *DARE* (Qu. HH7a, *Someone who talks too much, or too loud: "He's an awful ______.")* Infs **MS**45, Glibber.

glib-glab v [Cf *SND glibber-glabber* "to talk idly and confusedly"; *EDD glib* v, "to talk rapidly and volubly"] Cf **glab**
1968 *DARE* (Qu. KK13, . . *Arguing: "They stood there for an hour ______.")* Inf **NY**70, Glib-glabbing.

glibly See **glib** adj

glick v [Perh Ger *glücken* to prosper, but cf *click* to succeed, go well]
1914 *DN* 4.158 **PA,** *Glick. . .* To come out right. (From *glück*?)

glicker n [Perh var of *clicker,* but cf **glick**]
1970 *DARE* (Qu. EE6a, *Names for different kinds of marbles—the big one that's used to knock others out of the ring)* Inf **PA**242, Real big one—glicker.

glider n
A sled.
1968 *DARE* (Qu. EE24a, *When there's snow, children go down the hill on a ______)* Inf **PA**152, Glider.

glim n
1 A look, glimpse. [Scots dial]
1899 (1912) Green *VA Folk-Speech* 198, *Glim. . .* Glimpse; glance. **1935** Sandoz *Jules* 18 **wNE** (as of 1880–1930), "Can't git a glim of the light from down here fur as you can smell a lily in a nest of skunks," the cook explained. **1948** Manfred *Chokecherry* 78 **nwIA,** They won't get a glim at my hoofs.
2 also *glimmer:* A lamp, lantern or other source of light; the light emitted by such a source. [*OED* a1700 →] **esp Nth, West** *old-fash*
1902 (1904) Rowe *Maid of Bar Harbor* 97 **ME,** "Where's the witch?" . . "Give us a glim!" **1911** *DN* 3.544 **NE,** *Glim* . . Light. "Give me a glim." "Douse the glim." **1912** *DN* 3.576 **wIN,** *Glim. . .* Light. **1927** *AmSp* 3.13, *Glim* . . survives among seafarers with the meaning 'illumination.' **1931** *AmSp* 7.108 [Underworld argot] *Glim. . .* A light or a match. "Douse the glim, there!" **1932** *RR Mag.* Oct 368, *Glim*—Switchman's lantern. **1938** *AmSp* 13.315 [Jargon of garage men], *Glimmers.* Headlights. **1945** Hubbard *Railroad Ave.* 344, *Glimmer. . .* Locomotive headlight. **1950** *WELS Suppl.* 1 Inf, **WI,** Glim—for electric light. **1965–70** *DARE* (Qu. Y42, *Expressions for putting out a lamp or light)* 21 Infs, **scattered, but chiefly Nth, West,** Douse the glim; **NY**166, Douse the glimmer; (Qu. Y41a, . . *To tell someone to light a lamp or lantern: "______ the lamp.")* Inf **PA**234, Light the glim; **MI**92, Turn off the glim; (Qu. Y41b, . . *Light an electric light: "______ the light.")* Inf **CA**65, Turn up the glim; **ME**13, Years ago—turn on the glim; (Qu. N10, . . *The bright and dim lights on a car)* Inf **CA**211, Glims. [24 of 26 Infs old] **1976** *DARE* FW Addit **seME,** Morning glim . . the first light along the horizon before the sun becomes visible.
3 also *glimmer:* An eye; by ext, eye-glasses.
1889 (1971) Farmer *Americanisms* 266, *Glims* (Cant). Among the fraternity in England, a *glim* is respectively a light, a lamp, or a pair of spectacles. Among their American *confrères,* however, the name is especially given to the eyes. **1901** *Bulletin* (San Francisco CA) 27 Aug 4 *(Zwilling Coll.),* Then Graves soaks [=socks] him on the glim. **1904** *NY Eve. Jrl.* (NY) 9 Sep 12 *(Zwilling Coll.),* They might have these "particular" pugs wear colored glims. Then they couldn't tell a "smoke" from a lilly [sic] white scrapper. **1906** *DN* 3.138 **nwAR,** *Glims. . .* Eyes. "I didn't get my glims on it." **1919** *DN* 5.41 [Hobo cant], *Glims. . .* Spectacles. **1927** *DN* 5.448 [Underworld jargon], *Glim. . .* The eye. *Ibid, Glims. . .* Spectacles. **1966** *DARE* (Qu. X20, *What other words do you have for a black eye?)* Inf **MS**71, His glimmers are blacked.

glimmer n See **glim 2, 3**

glimmer v [Transf from *glimmer* to emit an intermittent light]
Of the eyes: to suffer a flickering sensation.
1984 *Annals Internal Med.* 100.6.900 **cwAL,** *My eyes glimmer and feel bleary* is as good as scintillating scotoma of migraine.

‡glimp n
A condition of poor health.
1970 *DARE* (Qu. K44, *A bony or poor-looking horse)* Inf **VA**70, Got the glimp [laughter].

glimpse v, n Usu |glɪm(p)s|; also occas |dl-| Pronc-spp *glimp, glimpsh*
Std sense, var forms.
1883 (1971) Harris *Nights with Remus* 209 **GA** [Black], I aint kotch a glimp' un 'er. **1887** (1967) Harris *Free Joe* 185 **cGA** [White speaker of little educ], I got a right good glimp' un 'er. **1917** *DN* 4.412 **wNC,** *Glimpsh. . .* Glimpse. **1936** [see **glory** n^{1} **A**]. **1941** O'Donnell *Great Big Doorstep* 131 **sLA,** 'Come in here and take a glimp at something nice, you all,' he said.

glinn n Also sp *glin* [Prob from **glim 2,** infl by *glint;* cf *DNE glim,* also *glin, glynn* "Glow . . seen over a distant ice-field"] **ME**

A bright streak in the sky; hence v phr *glinn up* of the weather: to show such a streak.

1903 Wasson *Cap'n Simeon's Store* 53 **ME,** Them gulls, too, has been bunchin' in the Cove here for a gale o' wind all day, and you take that 'ere glinn tonight; ef that wa'n't a proper forerunner, then I'm a tormented farmer! **1905** Wasson *Green Shay* 196 **ME,** Take a s'utheaster, and 't ain't onnach'al to look for more or less of a sundown-glinn [Footnote: A lightening up close to the horizon], so's they might be able to git a sight acrost for a secont or two. **1939** *LANE* Map 89 *(Clearing up)* 1 inf, **swME,** *Glinning up,* when a glinn (a bright streak in the sky) appears through the clouds. **1957** Beck *Folkl. ME* 82, An easterly glin, sure sign of a wet skin. **1975** Gould *ME Lingo* 110, *Glin, glinn*—A certain glint of light on the horizon, usually seen in cold weather, a portent of storm: "See a sea glin, catch a wet skin."

glissant n [Fr "sliding, slippery"]

A dumpling.

1949 in 1986 *DARE* File **nwMI,** *Glissants. . .* Heard many times in Upper Peninsula of Michigan—especially from people of French descent. "We will have chicken and glissants [gli'sɑnts] (dumplings)."

glissom duck n

=**gadwall.**

1923 U.S. Dept. Ag. *Misc. Circular* 13.10, *Gadwall. . . Vernacular Names. . . In local use. . .* Glissom duck (Calif.)

glister n See **glyster**

glister v [*OED* c1380 →; "*arch.* and *dial.*"]

To glitter, sparkle.

1975 Gainer *Witches* 10 **sAppalachians,** I saw a light glister a mile away.

gloam n Also *glom, glowm;* prob by folk-etym, *gloom* [*SND gloam* n.]

Twilight—usu in combs *evegloam, morngloam* and varr.

1928 Chapman *Happy Mt.* 111 **seTN,** The rain driveled to a smirr . . so that by eveglôm the rain quit. *Ibid* 312, Glôm—twilight. . . Mornglôm—the morning twilight, an hour before full dawn. **1938** Matschat *Suwannee R.* 123 **nFL, sGA,** She'd had to pass the old bury'n ground at mornglowm. **1944** *PADS* 2.47 **wNC,** *Morn-gloam. . .* The first light of morning. **1951** Craig *Singing Hills* 101 *(Hench Coll.)* **swVA, nwNC,** I sat by the spring. . . I watched eve-gloom come. *Ibid* 130 *(Hench Coll.),* That night Dale and I sat before Cap Dickey's house as even-gloom came. **1952** Brown *NC Folkl.* 1.537 **wNC,** *Evening glom . .* The melancholy close of day(?) **1965** *Dict. Queen's English* 10 **NC,** *Morngloam:* First light of day. When morngloam broke he was standing at the window.

globbered adj Also *globber* Cf **clabber** n[1] **1, v 1**

Of milk: curdled.

1950 *WELS (Milk that becomes thick as it turns sour)* 1 Inf, **cWI,** Globbered. **1969** *DARE* (Qu. H59) Infs **MA**69, **NY**220, Globbered; **NY**135, Globbered milk. **1973** Allen *LAUM* 1.291 **Upper MW** (as of c1950), Variants [for *curdled milk*] probably due to confusion with *clabber milk* are . . *globber milk* (known once in Minnesota), and *globbered milk* (twice in northern Iowa).

globe n

=**apple (of) Peru 1.**

1897 *Jrl. Amer. Folkl.* 10.51, *Nicandra physalodes, . .* globe, Sulphur Grove, Ohio.

globe amorette n

A **bead lily** (here: *Clintonia umbellulata*).

1933 Small *Manual SE Flora* 296, *X[eniatrum] umbellulatum. . . Globe-amorette. . .* Woods and hillsides, . . Ga. to N.Y. **1949** Moldenke *Amer. Wild Flowers* 333, *Globeamorette. . .* Its 5 to 15 flowers are borne in a dense terminal onionlike umbel. **1953** Greene–Blomquist *Flowers South* 10, *Globe-amorette. . .* Since it is not common, it is always thrilling to discover this lily.

globe apple n

A **ground cherry.**

1981 Stratton *Pioneer Women* 64 **KS** (as of late 19th cent), There were . . wild gooseberries, chokeberries, pawpaws, . . and hickory nuts, if you went far enough to get them, but the one lone fruit on the prairie was the globe apple, which was made into preserves.

globe-berry n Cf **netted globe-berry**

=**wild balsam** (here: *Ibervillea* spp).

1970 Correll *Plants TX* 1511, *Ibervillea. . . Globe-berry. . .* Fruit globose; seeds swollen.

globe cactus n

A **barrel cactus** (here: *Echinocactus horizonthalonius*).

1851 (1864) Reid *Desert Home* 90 **NM,** They were dark-green masses, of different sizes—the largest of them about the size of a beecap. They looked like a number of huge hedge-hogs rolled up, and presenting on all sides their thorny spikes. . . I knew they were the *globe cacti.*

globe dogwood n

=**buttonbush 1.**

1940 Clute *Amer. Plant Names* 255, *Cephalanthus occidentalis. . .* Globe-dogwood.

globefish n

1 Any of var fishes of the families Tetraodontidae and Diodontidae.

1743 (1754) Catesby *Nat. Hist. Carolina* 2.28, *Orbis laevis variegatus. The Globe-Fish.* This Fish . . has received its Name from the Form, which is almost globular. . . These Fish are found in *Virginia* and many other parts of *America.* **1842** DeKay *Zool. NY* 4.329, The Lineated Puffer. *Tetraodon laevigatus. . .* Brown Globe-fish. **1884** Goode *Fisheries U.S.* 1.170, [The members of the bellows-fish family] are summer visitors from a warmer climate, and . . are chiefly important to curiosity hunters. They are known by such names as "Swell Fish," "Bottle Fish," . . "Globe Fish," . . "Porcupine Fish," and "Blower." **1889** *Century Dict.* 2540, *Globe-fish. . .* A gymnodont plectognath fish of either of the families *Tetrodontidae* [sic] and *Diodontidae.* These fishes are so named from their capacity for inflating themselves by swallowing air, the whole body or much of it becoming blown up like a balloon. In some cases, as that of *Diodon,* the fish assumes an almost perfectly globular form. **1898** U.S. Natl. Museum *Bulletin* 47.1734, *Spheroides testudineus. . . Globe Fish. . .* Ranging occasionally northward in the Gulf Stream as far as Newport. **1933** John G. Shedd Aquarium *Guide* 160, *Cheilichthys testudineus. . .* Globefish.

2 An **ocean sunfish** (here: *Mola mola*).

1842 DeKay *Zool. NY* 4.330, *The Small Globe-fish. Acanthosoma carinatum. . .* Body vertically oval, being higher than long. *Ibid* 331, This little fish, so remarkable for its form, was first noticed on our coast by Dr. Mitchill. **1906** NJ State Museum *Annual Rept. for 1905* 368, *Mola mola. . .* Ocean Sun Fish. . . Globe Fish. . . Body ovate, strongly compressed, short, deep and lower profile more convex. . . The young are very different in appearance, with a much compressed deep body. **1960** Amer. Fisheries Soc. *List Fishes* 58, Globefish . . see also sunfish, ocean.

3 A lumpfish (here: *Cyclopterichthys glaber*).

1960 Amer. Fisheries Soc. *List Fishes* 41, Globefish. P[acific]. *Cyclopterichthys glaber.*

globeflower n

1 Std: a plant of the genus *Trollius.* For other names of var spp see **buttercup 7, crowfoot 1d**

2 =**buttonbush 1.**

1784 in 1785 Amer. Acad. Arts & Sci. *Memoirs* 1.409, *Cephalantus foliis oppositis ternisque. . . Globe-Flower Shrub. Pond Dogwood. Button Bush.* The florets form a perfect globe, and when the fruit stalk is separated it does not readily appear in what part of the globe it was inserted. . . Common in watery swamps and pond-holes. **1828** Rafinesque *Med. Flora* 1.100, *Cephalanthus occidentalis. . .* Globe flower. *Ibid* 101, Flowers . . forming round balls of a cream white color, and sweet scented, fringed all over by the protruding Stamina and styles, nearly as large as a walnut. **1901** Lounsberry *S. Wild Flowers* 475, *Globe Flower. Ibid* 476, More sweet than that of the others is its luscious fragrance, and quaint enough the little florets look closely packed in balls. **1924** Deam *Shrubs IN* 291, This species [=*Cephalanthus occidentalis*] has many common and merely local names. The name "globeflower" seems to be the most appropriate one we have heard. **1942** Tehon *Fieldbook IL Shrubs* 250, *Globeflower. . .* The flowers are borne in globular heads of as many as 200 flowers each. **1974** Morton *Folk Remedies* 39, *Globe Flower. . .* Root "tea" is gargled and swallowed to relieve throat irritation. **1979** Little *Checklist U.S. Trees* 82.

globe lily n **esp CA** Cf **globe tulip**

A **mariposa lily** (here: *Calochortus albus*).

1923 in 1925 Jepson *Manual Plants CA* 237, *C[alochortus] albus. . . White Globe Lily. . .* Wooded slopes and cañons. **1949** Moldenke *Amer. Wild Flowers* 320, *White globelily. . .* The petals are white or pale pink, their margins not fringed, and the gland is shaped like a crescent moon. **1954** CA Div. Beaches & Parks *Pt. Lobos Wild Flowers* 29, White Fairy Lantern is also known as globe lily. Smooth stems . . produce alternate lily-like leaves and hanging lantern-shaped flowers at the tips of the stems. **1974** Munz *Flora S. CA* 921, *Globe-lily. . .* Shaded, often rocky places in woods or brush.

globe mallow n

1 A plant of the genus *Sphaeralcea.* **esp SW** Also called **false mallow d, sore-eye poppy.** For other names of var spp see **desert hollyhock, desert mallow, flame-mallow, prairie mallow, mal de ojos, moss rose, rose-of-sharon, wild geranium, wild hollyhock**

1900 Lyons *Plant Names* 353, *Sphaeralcea. . .* Globe Mallow. . . Southwestern U.S. **1915** (1926) Armstrong–Thornber *Western Wild Flowers* 291, Salmon Globe Mallow. Sphaeralcea pedata. **1932** Rydberg *Flora Prairies* 541, *Globe Mallow. . .* Petals 5, golden, pink, or scarlet, usually notched. **1949** Curtin *By the Prophet* 80 **SW,** When in spring bloom, . . several . . species of globemallow are highly decorative along roadsides and in the fields. **1970** Correll *Plants TX* 1042, *Globe Mallow. . .* Several of the species are browsed to some extent by domestic and wild grazing animals. **1985** Dodge *Flowers SW Deserts* 44, *Globemallow. . .* Several species flower in spring and again after the summer rains.

2 A plant of the genus *Iliamna.* Also called **wild hollyhock.** For other names of var spp see **maple-leaved mallow, mountain hollyhock**

1940 Clute *Amer. Plant Names* 46, *S[phaeralcea] remota. Globe Mallow.* Maple-leaved globe mallow. **1951** Abrams *Flora Pacific States* 3.84, *Iliamna rivularis. . .* Stream-bank Globe-mallow. *Ibid* 86, *Iliamna longisepala. . .* Chelan Globe-mallow. . . *Iliamna latibracteata. . .* California Globe-mallow. . . *Iliamna Bakeri. . .* Baker's Globe-mallow. **1973** Hitchcock–Cronquist *Flora Pacific NW* 292, *Iliamna . .* Globemallow. Fl[ower]s racemose, pink to lavender, rather showy.

globes n

The globe amaranth *(Gomphrena globosa).*

1892 *Jrl. Amer. Folkl.* 5.102 **sVT,** *Gomphrena globosa. . .* Globes.

globe-skimmer n Cf **skimmer**

A **dragonfly** (here: *Pantala flavescens*).

1933 Bryan *Hawaiian Nature* 172, Our commonest species [of dragonfly] is one found so widespread around the world that it is called "The Globe-skimmer." . . These take advantage of any little puddle of water in the lowlands to breed, which is the reason why this species is so abundant, even in the driest localities. The scientific name is *Pantala flavescens.*

globe tulip n Cf **globe lily**

Any of var **mariposa lilies,** but esp *Calochortus albus.*

1897 Parsons *Wild Flowers CA* 54, *White Globe-Tulip. Calochortus albus. . .* Just before the oncoming of summer, . . the graceful stalks . . begin to hang out their delicate, white satin globes. **1901** *Land of Sunshine* 15.334 **swCA,** I once found in Eaton's Cañon a fine specimen of the globe tulip, Calochortus albus, with four petals and four sepals, instead of the customary three. **1915** (1926) Armstrong–Thornber *Western Wild Flowers* 56, The members of the genus Calochortus. . . fall into three groups: Globe Tulips, with nodding, globular flowers, and nodding capsules [etc]. **1959** Carleton *Index Herb. Plants* 52, *Globe-tulip:* Calochortus (v).

globe willow n

1966 *DARE* (Qu. T16, *What kinds of trees are 'special' around here?*) Inf **NM**9, Globe willows (may be native).

globsloptious See **galluptious**

Glocca Morra, how are things in phr For varr see quot [Allusive use of lyrics from a popular song; see quot 1966]

How are things in your neighborhood?

1965–70 *DARE* (Qu. MM22, *If you are talking to a friend . . and you want to inquire about his neighborhood, you might ask, "How are things ______?"*) 18 Infs, **chiefly Nth, N Midl,** In Glocca Morra; **GA**84, In Blacamora; **IL**9, In Glackamala; **RI**13, In Glockamorgan; **WI**27, In Guatemala. [**1966** Ewen *Amer. Pop. Songs* 152, How Are Things in Glocca Morra?, words by E.Y. Harburg, music by Burton Lane (1946). Irish ballad introduced by Ella Logan in the musical play *Finian's Rainbow* (1947).]

glom v^1 Also *gla(h)m, glaum, glomm(er), glomb* [*EDD glaum* v. 1 "To grasp, clutch at, snatch . . ; freq. with *at*"; *SND glaum, glam* v. (also *glaam, glom*) "1. To snatch, grab . . 2. To seize . . with the jaws; to eat greedily."] Cf **glom** n^1

1 To seize, grab at, steal; to arrest; hence n *glommer.*

1907 London *Road* 131, We . . discovered that our hands were gloved. 'Where'd ye glahm 'em?' I asked. **1916** [see **2** below]. **1919** Kyne *Capt. Scraggs* 83 **CA,** Why, we'll sail her in ourselves—me an' you—an' glom all the salvage for ourselves. **1919** *DN* 5.41 [Hobo cant], *Glaum. . .* To steal. *Glaumed, to be,* to be arrested. **1923** *DN* 5.208 **swMO,** *Glaum . .* to seize or grab all of anything, especially victuals. "Bill glaumed the whole pie." **1927** *AmSp* 2.276 **cwCA,** *Glomm . .* seize greedily. **1927** *DN* 5.448 [Underworld jargon], *Glom. . .* To steal. Also pronounced "glaum" and "glam." *Ibid, Glaumed, to be. . .* To be shanghaied, strong-armed, or arrested. **1930** Williams *Logger-Talk* 24 **Pacific NW,** *Glom:* Grab. **1931** *AmSp* 6.438 **OK** [Convict's jargon], *Glom. . .* To make a grab for. **1942** Berrey–Van den Bark *Amer. Slang* 461.13, Purse snatcher . . glommer. **1944** *PADS* 2.54 **swMO,** *Berry-glaumer* ['bɛrɪˌglɔmɚ]. . . A person who can pick strawberries very rapidly. **1966–69** *DARE* (Qu. V4, . . *"Yesterday somebody ______ my watch."*) Inf **KS**16, Glommered; (Qu. V5b, . . *"Before anybody else gets it, I'm going to ______ this."*) Inf **MI**24, Glom; (Qu. OO42a, *About stealing money: "He admitted that he ______ [the money]."*) Inf **NY**133, Glommed.

2 with *on (to):* To grab, get hold of, latch on to.

1916 *DN* 4.275 **NE,** *Glom. . .* To take, grab, 'swipe.' "He glommed onto my book." "Glom an apple." Often used by newsboys. **1950** *WELS ("If I ever see another one of these, I'll certainly ______ it.")* 3 Infs, **WI,** Glom on to. **1965–70** *DARE* (Qu. V5b, *If you take something that nobody seems to own, you might say, "Before anybody else gets it, I'm going to ______ this."*) 22 Infs, **chiefly wGt Lakes, Pacific,** Glom onto; **AK**9, **WI**71, Glom on to; (Qu. V4, *Other words for stealing something valuable—for example, a watch: "Yesterday somebody ______ my watch."*) Infs **CA**15, 185, **MA**58, Glommed on; (Qu. II18, *Someone who joins himself on to you and your group without being asked and won't leave*) Inf **AK**5, Glommed on. **1978** Doig *This House* 194 **MT** (as of c1955), I bet she thinks she glommed onto something when you came to that school. **1981** *Badger Herald* (Madison WI) 1 Oct 4/2, Most of them are probably glomming onto food stamp applications, selling second cars and advertising in "employment wanted" columns.

3 vbl n *glauming:* See quot. Cf **hooky bobbing**

1957 *Sat. Eve. Post Letters* **ceND,** From that [=*glaum*] came, I suppose, the word in general use in a Scandinavian community in Nelson County, North Dakota in the years 1906–10, when I was a school child there. The word was *glaumming* [sic], and we all "went glaumming" frequently in winter as that was to catch rides on moving bob sleighs (pulled by a team of horses) usually by running after them until one could get a foot firmly planted on a rear runner, and a hand on the sled box. Thru my adult years I've . . found only one woman, contemporary in age, who said she and her friends "went glaumming" (and used that very term) in childhood some place in Wisconsin.

4 To jab, poke.

1941 Stuart *Men of Mts.* 253 **neKY,** He [=a child] would kick me in the ribs and say: "Get up hossy! . . " And when he would say "Whoa back" he would glomb me in the eyes with his fingers like he was trying to stop a horse.

5 To devour greedily.

1966 *DARE* (Qu. GG1b, . . *"He ______ ice cream."*) Inf **AR**31, Glommed.

glom n^1 Also *glommer* Also sp *gla(h)m, glaum* [Cf **glom** v^1]

A hand.

1938 *AmSp* 13.156 **CA** [Aeroplane Factory English], *Glom.* A hand. **1960** Wentworth–Flexner *Slang* 217, *Glom, glaum, glahm. . .* A hand, considered as a tool for grabbing. . . [Also] *—mer.* **1966–68** *DARE* (Qu. X32, *Joking or uncomplimentary words for the hands—you might say, "Those are mine. You keep your ______ [out of them]."*) Infs **MI**2, 10, 20, 27, Gloms; **MI**20, Glams; **WA**3, Glommers; (Qu. AA5, *If a woman seems to be going after one certain man that she wants to marry: "She's ______ him."*) Inf **WI**27, Got her gloms on.

glom v^2 Usu with *up* Also sp *glaum* [Perh var of **gaum** v^1 **3,** infl by **glom** v^1]

To tangle up, make a hash of.

1923 *DN* 5.208 **swMO,** *Glaum. . .* To tangle. **1927** *AmSp* 2.355 **wcWV,** *Glom . .* to mess. "He has glommed everything up." **1966** *DARE* (Qu. KK63, *To do a clumsy or hurried job of repairing something: "It will never last—he just ——.")* Inf **ME**22, Glommed it up.

glom n² Also sp *glaum* [Cf **glom** v²]

A confused mass; a "gob."

1923 *DN* 5.208 **swMO,** *Glaum. . .* A snarl, a tangle, a confused mass. **1967** *DARE* (Qu. U38a, *Words referring to a great deal of money: "He's got —— [of money].")* Inf **AR**51, Gloms; (Qu. U38b, *Words referring to a great deal of money: "He made a —— [of money].")* Inf **AR**51, Gloms.

glom n³ See **gloam**

glomb See **glom** v¹

glomm See **glom** v¹

glommer n

1 See **glom** v¹ **1.**

2 See **glom** n¹.

glommer v See **glom** v¹

glommox n Also *glummicks* Cf **glom** v²

1894 *DN* 1.331 **NJ,** *Glommox, glummicks:* a muss, or a conglomeration of matter.

glom on (to) See **glom** v¹ **2**

glom up See **glom** v²

glook See **cluck** n

gloom See **gloam**

glooms n pl Also with *the*

Low spirits, the blues.

1968–70 *DARE* (Qu. GG34a, *To feel depressed or in a gloomy mood: "He has the —— today.")* Infs **CT**9, **IN**5, **NY**38, **OH**42, Glooms; (Qu. GG35a, *To sulk or pout: "It won't do any good to —— about it.")* Inf **NY**249, Go into glooms.

gloria n

1 A **bindweed 1.** Cf **glory** n¹ **B4**

1966 *DARE* (Qu. S5, *Other names around here for the wild morning glory)* Inf **FL**27, Gloria.

2 A summer onion.

1966 *DARE* FW Addit **WA**6, *Gloria*—a summer onion, white, somewhat pointed.

gloria daisy n

A **black-eyed Susan 2.**

1968 *DARE* (Qu. S7, *A kind of daisy, bright yellow with a dark center, that grows along roadsides in late summer)* Inf **MD**24, Gloria daisy. [FW: New name for this flower—Inf learned it at state fair.]

gloried, glorited See **glory** v **A**

glory n¹ Usu |'glori, 'glɔri, -ɪ|; also rarely |dl-|

A Form.

1828 Webster *Amer. Dict.* np, [In "Directions for the Pronunciation of Words":] *Gl* are pronounced as *dl;* glory is pronounced dlory. **1936** *AmSp* 11.236 **eTX,** [g] > [d] . . by assimilation to the following [l]. Examples: . . glad, glass, gleam, glimmer, glimpse, globe, glory, glum, glutton. [dlæd], [dlæ˞s], etc.

B Senses.

1 Heaven—freq in euphem phrr referring to death, esp *go to glory.*

1851 (1852) Stowe *Uncle Tom's Cabin* 1.51 **KY** [Black], I don't know when I'll be gone to glory. **1867** Allen *Slave Songs* 49 **SC, GA,** Brudder George is a-gwine to glory, Take car' de sin-sick soul. **1932** *RR Mag.* Oct 368, *Glory . .* death by accident. **c1937** in 1972 *Amer. Slave* 2.51 **SC,** They all dead and gone to glory long time ago. **1938** Rawlings *Yearling* 54 **nFL,** I'd ought to be dead this minute and gone to glory. **1942** *Sat. Eve. Post* 3 Oct 68 [Gullah], Dis train lebe for Glory,/ Lebe mawnin, nyune en' night. **1943** *LANE* Map 521 *(Kicked the bucket)* 1 inf, **seMA,** Gone to glory. **1953** Brewer *Word Brazos* 68 **eTX** [Black], She come to be 'bout ninety-nine yeahs ole an' her husban' an' two chilluns done gone on to glory long yeahs befo'. **1965–70** *DARE* (Qu. C34, *Nicknames for nearby settlements, villages, or districts)* Infs **NC**31, 34, Loafer's glory; **MD**31, Buzzard's glory; (Qu. BB56, *Joking expressions for dying: "He ——.")* Inf **AL**30, About to go to old glory; **VA**41, **MI**96, Gone to glory; **PA**35, Passed on to glory. **1982** Walker *Color Purple* 186 **GA** [Black], Well, say Sofia, Mama fight the good fight. If there's a glory anywhere she right in the middle of it.

2 Used in var exclams; see quots. [*glory be* is abbr for "Glory be to God!"; in some other cases *glory* appears to be euphem for *heaven(s)* or *God*]

1924 *DN* 5.268, *Glory:* (oh) —, — be to God, — to God, — hallelujah (all [express] joy). **1936** *WV Review* Aug 346, Even among people deeply religious we may hear at times . . Glory be . . Glory behold. **1965–70** *DARE* (Qu. NN6a, *Exclamations of joy)* 33 Infs, **scattered,** Glory be [27 of 33 Infs old]; **GA**7, **MS**6, **NE**11, **NC**41, **OH**41, Oh glory; **IN**40, **MS**16, **MA**127, **NY**96, Glory; **MO**5, Glory for me; (Qu. NN29a, *Exclamations beginning with 'great': "Great ——!")* Infs **MI**3, **NJ**28, 54, Glory; **NJ**54, Glory be; (Qu. NN26a, *Weakened substitutes for 'hell': "Oh ——!")* Infs **CO**4, **NC**55, Glory; (Qu. NN28a, *Exclamations beginning with 'good': "Good ——!")* Infs **NC**82, **SC**67, **VA**46, Glory; (Qu. NN6b, *Expressions of joy used mostly by children)* Inf **GA**72, Glory be; (Qu. NN7, *Exclamations of surprise)* Inf **NY**223, Glory be; (Qu. NN29b, *Exclamations beginning with 'land': "Land ——!")* Inf **PA**138, Sakes, glory be; (Qu. NN32, *Exclamations like 'I swear' or 'I vow': "I ——.")* Inf **CT**36, Swear to glory.

3 also *glory load;* In railroading: a string of empty cars.

1932 *RR Mag.* Oct 368, *Glory*—String of empties. **1976** Gould *Blackie's RR Hdbk.* 6, *Train (of empties):* Glory load.

4 also *glory vine:* A **bindweed 1.**

1967–69 *DARE* (Qu. S5, *Other names . . for the wild morning glory)* Inf **NY**183, Climbing glory; **IA**8, Glory; **IL**11, Glory vine.

5 See **glory hole** n **1.**

glory v

A Form.

Past: usu *gloried;* rarely *glorited.*

1914 *DN* 4.73 **ME, nNH,** *Glorit. . .* Glory. "She glorited in it."

B Sense.

To boast about. [*OED glory* v.¹ 2 →1673]

1913 Kephart *Highlanders* 312 **sAppalachians,** I'm a hillbilly, all right, and they needn't to glory their old flat lands to me!

glory adj Also *galory* [Varr of *galore*]

1967–68 *DARE* (Qu. LL9b, . . *All you need or more . . : "She's got clothes ——.")* Infs **MD**26, **NC**40, Glory; **AR**47, Galory [gəˈloə˞ɪ].

glory n² [Perh infl by std *glory*]

=**galore.**

1966–69 *DARE* (Qu. LL9b, . . *All you need or more . . : "She's got clothes ——.")* Infs **KY**53, **MS**1, **MO**18, **TX**36, To glory; **SD**2, By the glory.

glorybind n

=**bindweed 1.**

1942 Amer. Joint Comm. Horticult. Nomenclature *Std. Plant Names* 275, Glorybind. *Convolvulus.* **1963** Craighead *Rocky Mt. Wildflowers* 149, *Convolvulus arvensis. . . Other names:* Bindweed, Glorybind.

glory bone n

=**funny bone 1.**

1968 *DARE* (Qu. X33, *The place in the elbow that gives you a strange feeling if you hit it against something)* Inf **VA**9, Glory bone.

glory-hallelujah v

To speak to in the manner of an evangelist preacher.

1874 (1895) Eggleston *Circuit Rider* 323 **sOH** (as of c1810), You see I know all about you, and it's no use for you to glory-hallelujah me.

glory hole n

1 also *glory:* A storage place, esp one where odds and ends are cached. [Prob transf from naut use as a space between decks used for storage] Cf **hellhole**

1870 (1898) Whitney *We Girls* 50 **MA,** You can bring out your old ribbon-box. . . It's a charity to clear out your glory-holes once in a while. **1918** Lincoln *Shavings* 180 **eMA,** Any more money kickin' around this glory-hole that you want me to put to your account? **1941** *LANE* Map 344 *(Pantry)* 1 inf, **RI,** *Glory hole,* daughter's jocular term; 1 inf, **eMA,** *Glory,* 'just a family word' for the pantry. **1945** Colcord *Sea Language* 87, The strong room on old-time ships, where specie and treasure were kept. On modern steamships, it is a slang term for the living-quarters of the cooks and stewards. Alongshore, it means a locker for odds and ends, a disorderly one being implied. **1954** *WELS Suppl.* **seWI,** *Glory hole*—the term for the cupboard cubbyhole. **1967** *DARE* FW Addit **nPA,** Glory hole . . a place where you can stick things away to hide them and get them out of the way. **1968–69** *DARE* (Qu. D7, *A small space anywhere in a house where you can hide things or get them out of the way*) Inf **AL**43, Glory hole—Inf has heard, old-fashioned; **NY**223, Glory hole—any place where you can tuck things out of the way; **PA**115, 119, **RI**1, Glory hole. **1975** Gould *ME Lingo* 110, *Gloryhole*. . . Nowadays, any catch-all that may be in constant disorder. **1979** *DARE* File **cnMA** (as of c1915), At my father's uncle's house there was a deep, large closet in the dining room known as the glory hole. Things lost for years sometimes turned up in the glory hole.

2 In mining: see below. **chiefly West**

a A large, often funnel-shaped surface excavation, esp one formed about a vertical shaft through which material is withdrawn.

1909 (1910) *WNID, Glory hole*. . . *Mining*. An open pit produced by surface mining. **1939** FWP *Guide CA* 521, A glory hole is an open excavation without shafts or tunnels, enabling its operators to recover a large quantity of ore at minimum expense. **1948** *NV Highways and Parks* July–Aug 30/1, A landmark around Virginia City . . is . . the "Glory hole." There are several of them. These are huge, gaping surface excavations 150 to 200 feet deep and many hundreds of feet in diameter, cut right into the flank of the mountain. . . However, the holes got so big that raising the ore to the road surface became a problem. . . Caving of waste material into the hole also added to the difficulties. As a result "glory holeing" as it was called eventually ceased altogether. **c1965** Climax Molybdenum Co. *This is C.M.*, At Climax, a caving system of mining is used. . . The visible result of this type mining is called the "Glory Hole"—a tremendous cavity on the face of the mountain produced by literally pulling the insides out of the peak. **1966** Barnes–Jensen *Dict. UT Slang* 19. **1968** Adams *Western Words* 127, *Glory hole*. . . In mining, an open excavation formed by drawing off ore through an underground passage. An open pit produced by surface mining. **1968** [see **glory hole** v phr]. **1989** *DARE* File **cCO,** [Mining Engineer:] A glory hole's got the shape of a morning glory. [*DARE* Ed:] You mean like a funnel? [M.E.:] Exactly.

b A hole, pocket, or mine containing especially rich ore.

1914 *DN* 4.163 **SW,** *Glory-hole*. . . In mining, a hole which contains rich mineral deposits. **1929** Ellis *Ordinary Woman* 39 **CO** (as of early 1900s), The ore here runs in pockets and a few, a very few, have been fortunate enough to run into one of the glory holes. **1940** Writers' Program *Guide AZ* 369, He found impaled on the point a gold nugget that weighed more than half a pound. It was the top of a small glory hole that yielded over $100,000 worth of ore besides what was stolen by the hordes of "boomers" who rushed to the spot. **1943** Writers' Program MT *Copper Camp* 28 **swMT** (as of 1876), The joke was getting ancient now. Pity was mingled with mirth. "Parks' Gloryhole," they called his mine. **1989** *DARE* File **sID, wMT,** A glory hole is an especially rich vein of ore.

c A stope, esp a deserted one.

1918 *DN* 5.25 **ID,** *Glory-hole*. . . A deserted stope in a mine. **1968** *DARE* Tape **AK**6, The glory hole was a big cavern in a big hole in the ground where they had taken the ore out. **1989** *DARE* File **nwID** (as of 1975), In a silver mine I worked in we used *glory hole* to mean a large underground room or stope, particularly one from which the pickings had been lean.

glory hole v phr, hence vbl n *glory holing;* also *glory mining*

To mine by means of a **glory hole 2a** or **b.**

1929 Burns *Tombstone* 381 **csAZ,** Near the old lamppost is the cavelike aperture of the Million Dollar stope, so called because in this tunnel beneath the town the Grand Central mine 'gloryholed,' taking out $840,000. **1948** [see **glory hole** n **2a**]. **1960** *McGraw–Hill Encycl. Sci. & Tech.* 8.481/1, Glory-holing is an underhand stoping method occasionally used to develop funnel-shaped excavations in large ore bodies. **1968** *DARE* Tape **NV**8, [Inf:] If they could get down lower . . and just take that whole mountain out with this machinery—glory mining they call that. [FW:] This . . mine . . works on the glory hole principle too. They're taking that whole mountain. They take down from underneath and then it keeps collapsing down.

glory load See **glory** n[1] **B3**

glory mining See **glory hole** v phr

glory vine See **glory** n[1] **B4**

glory wagon n

A caboose.

1945 Beebe *Highball* 207, It is caboose, crummy, way car, . . glory wagon, . . and shanty.

gloshers See **galoshers**

glossie n Cf **glassie**

A type of marble.

1968 *DARE* (Qu. EE6c, *Cheap marbles*) Inf **MI**78, Glossies—[term used by] Inf's grandson in South Bend, Indiana. **c1970** Wiersma *Marbles Terms* **MI,** *Glossie* . . a glazed clay marble . . better than common marbles.

glossy ibis n

1 Std: a dark-plumaged ibis *(Plegadis falcinellus)*. Also called **black bec-croche, black curlew, bronze curlew, green ibis, liver**

2 =**white-faced ibis.**

1923 Dawson *Birds CA* 1926, *The White-faced Glossy Ibis*. . . The Glossy Ibis should be regarded solely as a work of art. **1928** Bailey *Birds NM* 101, In November, 1906, we made camp at Glenwood, . . and near by, . . perched on a dooryard fence, to our astonishment we discovered two stuffed Glossy Ibises. **1964** Phillips *Birds AZ* 8, *Plegadis chihi*. . . *Glossy Ibis*. . . The "white face" is inconspicuous.

glossy snake n [See quot 1974]

A smooth-scaled, burrowing snake *(Arizona elegans)* native to the Southwest. Also called **elegant bullsnake, faded snake, gopher snake 3**

1947 Pickwell *Amphibians* 45, The representative in our region is . . the Western Glossy, or Western Faded, Snake. **1957** Jaeger *N. Amer. Deserts* 102, On the Colorado Desert the most commonly seen reptiles include the . . glossy . . snake. **1974** Shaw–Campbell *Snakes West* 104, The glossy snake . . , whose body reflects glisteningly any nearby light, . . can be confused at first glance with the gopher snake. **1979** Behler–King *Audubon Field Guide Reptiles* 590, *Glossy Snake*. . . Resembles Gopher and Great Plains Rat snakes but has *smooth glossy scales* rather than keeled scales.

glove, give one the v phr [Var of **mitten, give one the**]

1968 *DARE* (Qu. AA11, *If a man asks a girl to marry him and she refuses, you'd say she* ______) Inf **OH**82, Gave him the glove.

glove orange n

A tangerine.

[**1976** Bailey–Bailey *Hortus Third* 276/2, Tangerine . . segm[ent]s 10–14, readily separating from each other and from the smooth, loose, thin skin. . . Among the c[ulti]v[ar]s are . . 'Kid Glove.'] **1977** *DARE* File **MA,** Yesterday he [=Inf's husband] was completely taken aback when I talked about "glove oranges"—tangerines. In Springfield where we lived a while and later in Pittsfield those words were used and it was considerably later that I first heard the word tangerine. **1987** *Ibid* **wMA,** We agreed the name "glove orange" meant oranges so easily handled one could wear kid gloves and not soil them; **csWI,** Tangerines are called *glove oranges* by two friends from the East.

glove sponge n

A sponge *(Spongia tubulifera)* of relatively little commercial value.

1879 Hyatt *Commercial Sponges* 19, I have frequently employed the reef or Glove Sponge. **1881** Ingersoll *Oyster-Industry* 244, *Glove sponge*.—One of the poorest grades of Florida commercial sponges, *Spongia tubulifera*. **1884** U.S. Natl. Museum *Bulletin* 27.124, The American species and subspecies are as follows: *Spongia officinalis* Linn., subsp. *tubulifera*—Glove Sponge; *S. graminea* Hyatt—Glove Sponge. . . The finest quality of American Sponge is the Sheepswool, the remaining grades being all quite inferior to it. **1901** Arnold *Sea-Beach* 104, Five species of commercial sponges are taken from Florida waters. They are graded by the trade . . as the "sheepswool," "yellow," "grass," "velvet," and "glove." **1935** Pratt *Manual Invertebrate Animals* 93, The American variety, the so-called glove sponge, is one of the least valuable commercial sponges.

glowbug See **glowworm**

glowering adj Also *glowery* [*glower* to stare sullenly]

Of weather: cloudy or threatening.

1939 *LANE* Map 88 *(A cloudy day)* 1 inf, **swMA,** Glowering. **1969** *DARE* (Qu. B5, *When the weather looks as if it will become bad*) Inf **NY**162, Glowery.

glowfly See **glowworm**

glowm See **gloam**

glowworm n Also *glowbug, glowfly* **scattered, but esp Nth, West**

=**firefly 1,** esp the female; also the larva of such an insect.

1737 (1911) Brickell *Nat. Hist. NC* 168, The *Glow-worm* has Wings, and it shines in the dark like Fire. **1781** Peters *Genl. Hist. CT* 259, The Glow-bug both crawls and flies, and is about half an inch long. These insects fly in the summer evenings, nearly seven feet from the ground, in such multitudes, that they afford sufficient light for people to walk by. **a1862** (1864) Thoreau *ME Woods* 184, It was . . a white and slumbering light, like the glowworm's. **1912** Coblentz *Phys. Study* 9, In some localities the mating of the glow-worm *(Phengodes)* is said to occur in the daytime. **1939** *LANE* Map 238, Lightning bug, firefly and firebug denote a winged insect 'with a light in its tail.' The glow worm is regarded as the same insect, but is usually described as wingless [by 9 infs]. One informant says the glow worm is the wife (i.e. the female) of the firefly. **1946** (1972) Mezzrow-Wolfe *Really Blues* 76, The halo that started to shape around my conk was so big and bright, I felt like an overgrown glow-worm. **1956** Ker *Vocab. W. TX* 237, 2 infs, Glow worm; 1 inf, Glow fly. [*DARE* Ed: The most common response is *lightning bug.*] **c1960** *Wilson Coll.* **csKY,** *Glow-worm. . .* A larva that gives off a weak light. **1966-70** *DARE* (Qu. R1, *What do you call the small insect that flies at night and flashes a light at its tail?*) 21 Infs, **scattered, but esp Nth, West,** Glowworm; **PA**182, Glowbug; (Qu. R27, *What kinds of caterpillars or similar worms do you have around here?*) Infs **IL**35, **NY**105, Glowworm; (Qu. P5) Inf **TN**14, Glowworm; (Qu. P6, *Other kinds of worms also used for bait*) Infs **IN**35, **NY**142, **TN**37, **VA**43, Glowworm. **1971** Bright *Word Geog. CA & NV* 188, *Lightning bug—firefly* 52% [of 300 infs] . . *glowworm* 22%. . . At the time this material was collected, the song "Glowworm" was very popular and apparently accounted for many of these responses. Several qualified their response as not the same thing as *lightning bug. . .* Few had really seen one. Those who were familiar with them had usually seen them elsewhere. **1973** Allen *LAUM* 1.329 **NE** (as of c1950), Inf. considers this [=*firefly*] and 'glowworm' as names for the same insect. . . [Another inf says:] "Some people call 'em [=lightning bugs] 'glowworms.' "

glue n^{1}

1 Tree gum. [*OED glue* sb. 3. b *"Obs."*]

1912 Green *VA Folk-Speech* 198, *Glue. . .* The gum that run [sic] out of some fruit trees when the bark is broken: Peach-*glue;* Cherry-*glue.*

2 Any sticky substance; hence adjs *gluey, glued up* **chiefly Sth, S Midl, NEast** See Map Cf **all** adj^{1} **2**

1899 (1912) Green *VA Folk-Speech* 198, *Gluey. . .* Like glue; sticky. **1965-70** *DARE* (Qu. Y40b, *Other words referring to sticky stuff: "I've got to wash my hands. They're all covered with ———."*) 14 Infs, **chiefly Sth, S Midl,** Glue; (Qu. Y40a, *Other words referring to sticky stuff: "I've got to wash my hands; they're all ———."*) Infs **GA**12, 30, **KY**40, 94, **MA**6, 56, **NY**66, **VA**39, Gluey; [**GA**3, Gluey [glu^{I}] up;] **NY**33, Glue; **AL**34, **GA**30, 82, **NC**82, Glued up; (Qu. Y39, . . *"The children have been eating candy and they've got their faces all ———."*) Infs **LA**11, Glued up; **CA**184, Gluey.

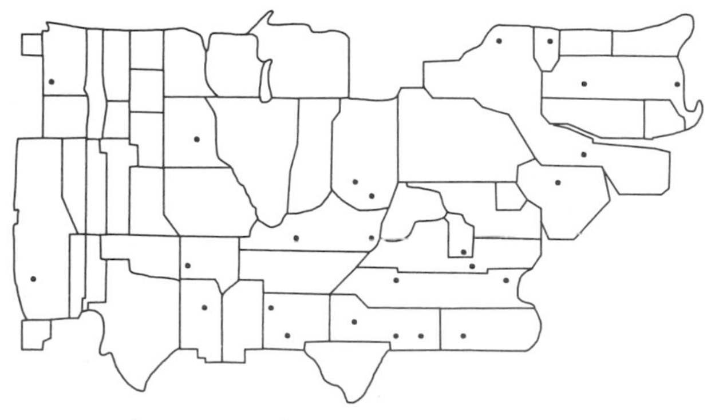

•glue n^{1} 2 + varr (Qq. Y40a, b, Y39)

glue n^{2} Also *gluey* [Perh by metath from *gool* (at **goal**); cf also **goalie 2**]

1988 *NADS Letters* **csMI,** *Glue*—One of my white students from a suburb of Detroit responded to the query regarding names for "home base" with this term. The spelling indicates the pronunciation /glu/. Of course, she had no idea how to spell it. Another student, *black* from *Detroit,* indicated the common term for her was *gluey* /glui/.

glued up See **glue** n^{1}

glue leaf n

A **bedstraw** (here: *Galium trifidum*).

1933 *Torreya* 33.84, *Galium trifidum. . .* Glue-leaf, Libby, Mont.

gluey adj See **glue** n^{1} **2**

gluey n See **glue** n^{2}

glummerin n

1902 *DN* 2.235 **sIL,** *Glummerin. . .* A darkening. Obfuscation.

glummicks See **glommox**

glumpi See **golumpki**

glup v [Echoic; perh by metath for *gulp*] Cf **glut** v

1968-70 *DARE* (Qu. H11b, *If he makes a noise with his food, he ———*) Infs **MI**82, **VA**39, Glups; **KY**5, Glups his food; (Qu. DD17, *To drink a great deal, or too fast: "He doesn't just drink, he ———."*) Inf **VA**39, Glups.

glut n^{1} See **glut** v

glut v [*OED glut* v.^{2} "Now *rare*"; cf also *EDD glut* sb.^{3} 4]

To gulp down, devour greedily; also fig; hence n *glut, glutter* a glutton.

1943 *Esquire* Feb 105/3 **neKY,** He's glutted a small fortune down his gullet. **1954** *Harder Coll.* **cwTN,** *Glut* . . a glutton. **1966-70** *DARE* (Qu. H9, *If somebody always eats a considerable amount of food, you say he's a ———*) Infs **GA**8, **KY**28, 41, **TN**27, Glutter; **VA**48, 56, Glut; (Qu. H11a, *If somebody eats rapidly and noisily, you say*) Inf **FL**9, He's a glut; (Qu. DD12, . . *A person who drinks steadily or a great deal*) Inf **FL**48, Glut; (Qu. DD17, *To drink a great deal, or too fast: "He doesn't just drink, he ———."*) Infs **FL**48, **IL**140, Gluts; **MS**16, Gluts it down; **TN**50, Glutting it.

glut n^{2} **chiefly Sth, S Midl**

A wooden wedge, used esp in splitting wood.

1806 (1905) Lewis *Orig. Jrls. Lewis & Clark Exped.* 4.20, We have also found this wood usefull to us for ax handles as well as glutts or wedges. **1847** in 1870 Drake *Pioneer Life* 70 **swOH** (as of c1800), When I got a tough log the wedges and "gluts" would fly out on being struck a hard blow. **1883** (1971) Harris *Nights with Remus* 37 **GA** [Black], He 'uz rippin' up de butt cut, Mr. Man wuz, en he druv in his wedge en den he stuck in de glut. **1887** Kirkland *Zury* 537 **IL,** Glut. . . A wooden wedge used in splitting logs. **1899** (1912) Green *VA Folk-Speech* 198. **1903** *DN* 2.315 **seMO,** *Glut. . .* A large wooden wedge. Used in connection with iron wedges in splitting large logs. **1906** *DN* 3.119 **sIN,** *Glut.* **1908** *DN* 3.315 **eAL, wGA,** *Glut.* **1946** *PADS* 6.15 **NC, VA,** *Glut. . .* Now replaced by the iron wedge. **1958** McCulloch *Woods Words* 71 **Pacific NW,** *Glut*—A heavy hardwood wedge used to follow steel wedges in getting an extra lift in falling trees. Also used in splitting redwood. **c1960** *Wilson Coll.* **csKY,** *Glut.* **1966** *DARE* Tape **AL**11, [FW:] Did the wooden wedges [for splitting logs] have a special name? [Inf:] Glut. **1967-68** *DARE* FW Addits **AR, SC, VA,** Glut. **1972** *Foxfire Book* 116 **nGA,** A second glut is driven into the crack still further down the trunk, and when the first falls out, it is driven into the crack beyond the second and so on, leapfrogging the gluts, until the trunk falls in half. **1983** *MJLF* 9.1.41 **ceKY.** **1985** in 1986 *Barrick Coll.* **csPA,** Dogwood is real hard wood. You take a tree like this an' cut it up, sharpen the pieces to make gluttons [sic], for splitting other wood. **1986** Pederson *LAGS Concordance* **Gulf Region,** 1 inf, Glut—a wedge used to split rails; 1 inf, Glut—a homemade wedge; 1 inf, Glut—wooden piece narrow at end; 1 inf, Gluts—wooden wedges to brace splits in logs; 1 inf, Gluts—used in making pickets.

glut n^{3}

1914 *DN* 4.73 **ME, nNH,** *Glut. . .* Saucy or impertinent answer.

glut herring n [See quots 1902, 1976]

A **herring** n^{1} **1** (here: *Alosa aestivalis*) of the Atlantic coast. Also called **alewife, blackbelly 1, blueback herring, English herring, kyack, rail herrin, sawbelly, sprat, summer herring, whitebait**

1882 U.S. Natl. Museum *Bulletin* 16.267, *C[lupea] aestivalis. . . Glut Herring. . .* Best distinguished by the black peritoneum. . . Atlantic coast. **1887** Goode *Amer. Fishes* 394, The *C[lupea] aestivalis* is the "Glut Herring" of the Albemarle and the Chesapeake. **1902** Jordan-

Evermann *Amer. Fishes* 104, *Pomolobus aestivalis. . .* Southward it is sometimes exceedingly abundant, hence the name "glut herring." **1911** U.S. Bur. Census *Fisheries 1908* 47, The "glut herring" . . is less abundant and much less valuable as a food fish than *P[omolobus] pseudoharengus.* **1939** Natl. Geogr. Soc. *Fishes* 64, Any discussion of the abundance of the alewife must include the glut herring also, because the two are seldom, if ever, listed separately in statistical tables. **1955** Carr–Goin *Guide Reptiles* 42 **FL,** Glut Herring. . . A moderate-sized, laterally compressed, silvery fish. **1976** Warner *Beautiful Swimmers* 127, *Alosa aestivalis. . .* Watermen call it the glut herring; the name is a wry comment on the price it usually fetches.

glut shoe n [**glut** n^2]

1953 Randolph–Wilson *Down in Holler* 248 **Ozarks,** *Glut shoes* are homemade footwear, so called because they are made on a straight last which looks like a glut. A *glut shoe* fits either foot; there are no rights and lefts.

glutter See **glut** v

glutton n

1 **=wolverine.** [*OED* 1674 →]

a1782 (1788) Jefferson *Notes VA* 55, There remains then the buffalo, red deer, fallow deer, wolf, roe, glutton, . . and water rat. **1872** McClellan *Golden State* 239 **wCA,** The badger, raccoon, glutton, skunk, . . seals and sea lions, are also found either in the rivers or bays of the coast of California. **1916** Kephart *Camping & Woodcraft* 1.262 **NC,** The wolverine, also called glutton, carcajou, skunk bear, and Indian devil, is the champion thief of the wilderness. **1928** Anthony *N. Amer. Mammals* 114, The name Glutton has been given to the Wolverine because of the supposed greediness of the animal. There is little to show that it is any more greedy than other carnivores. **1949** Palmer *Nat. Hist.* 597, *Glutton. . .* Found in wooded areas principally but now greatly reduced in range. **1980** Whitaker *Audubon Field Guide Mammals* 580, The Wolverine was once popularly called the "Glutton"; . . but its truly voracious appetite may be an adaptation for survival where food is often scarce.

2 A miserly, greedy person. **chiefly Sth, S Midl** [By ext from std sense]

1965–70 *DARE* (Qu. U36a, *Words and expressions about a person who saves in a mean way or is greedy in money matters: "He's an awful ———."*) Infs **AR**3, **FL**17, **OK**9, 20, **VA**73, Glutton; (Qu. U36b, *Words and expressions used to describe a person who saves in a mean way or is greedy in money matters: "She certainly is ———."*) Infs **FL**17, 48, Glutton; **KY**5, **OK**9, Glutton for money.

gluttonbird n

=fulmar.

1904 (1910) Wheelock *Birds CA* 19, *Pacific Fulmar. . .* Its common names are . . Gluttonbird, Giant Petrel. Of these "Gluttonbird" seems to apply to this vulture of the sea. Its food consists of dead flesh, fish, fowl, . . upon which it gorges until unable to fly.

glutz See **klutz**

glyster n Also sp *glister* [*OED clyster* 1398 →; varr *glyster, glister* c1440 →]

An enema; an enema-syringe.

1912 Green *VA Folk-Speech* 198, *Glister. . .* An injection by the rectum. **1930** Shoemaker *1300 Words* 25 **cPA Mts** (as of c1900), Glyster —A syringe made from a bladder attached to a hollow goose quill. **1935** *AmSp* 10.172 **sePA,** *Glyster* [was commonly used] for a syringe made from a bladder.

gnabble v [*OED gnab(b)le* "var. *knabble, Obs.*"] Cf **knabbler**

1899 (1912) Green *VA Folk-Speech* 198, *Gnabble. . .* To nibble.

gnat-ball n

1 A swarm of gnats.

1953 Randolph–Wilson *Down in Holler* 248 **Ozarks,** *Gnat-ball. . .* A dense swarm of gnats or other small flying insects. A woman told me, "When that child was two year old, he stuck his head in a gnat-ball, an' he's been kind of sickly ever since."

2 A gall formed by a gall gnat (family Cecidomyiidae).

1954 *Harder Coll.* **cwTN,** *Gnat-ball. . .* Gall on oak and hickory trees. Break one open and it's full of gnats.

gnat butter n Also *gnat bread* Cf **duck butter 1**

See quots.

1908 *DN* 3.315 **eAL, wGA,** *Gnat-butter. . .* Decayed skin tissue. **1944** *PADS* 2.43 **sVA,** *Gnat-bread. . .* Smegma. **c1960** *Wilson Coll.* **csKY,** *Gnat-bread. . .* Smegma. **1981** *AmSp* 56.16, I found several other users of the term [=*duck butter*] in its preputial sense (all of my informants happen to come from Southern states, coastal or inland, including Oklahoma). The synonyms *gnat butter* and *nut butter* also turned up.

gnatcatcher n

1 A bird of the genus *Polioptila.* For other names of *P. caerulea* see **chay-chay 1, flycatcher 1d, moss bird** [See quots 1844, 1904]

1839 Audubon *Synopsis Birds* 46, *Culicivora. . . Gnat-Catcher.* Bill of moderate length. **1844** DeKay *Zool. NY* 2.109, *The Blue-Grey Gnatcatcher. . .* This lively little Gnatcatcher is found . . in Louisiana about the middle of March, and in this State [=NY] is seen in the early part of May. . . It is exceedingly active in its movements, and is perpetually on the wing in search of the smaller winged insects, and particularly of mosquitoes. **1869** *Amer. Naturalist* 3.474, Not found westward of this [=the Colorado] valley . . [was] the lead-colored Gnatcatcher. **1883** *Century Illustr. Mag.* Sept 685/1, The nest of the humming-bird and the little gray gnat-catcher. **1904** (1910) Wheelock *Birds CA* 356, *Western Gnatcatcher. . .* Mr. Chamberlain writes . . in . . March, 1901, as follows: "The name Gnatcatcher is misleading as regards the diet of this species, for I have repeatedly seen one tackle a butterfly almost as large as himself, and bag his game too. I think, however, his food is largely made up of the eggs and larvae of insects." **1934** *Natl. Geogr. Mag.* 65.596/1, Gnatcatchers as a group are active and vivacious little birds. **1965** Bailey–Niedrach *Birds CO* 637, The rather inconspicuous little gnatcatchers—well named, since they take insects upon the wing—breed from Cañon City southward. **1967–69** *DARE* (Qu. Q14) Inf **NC**67, Gnatcatcher; (Qu. Q17) Inf **GA**65, Gnatcatcher; (Qu. Q23) Inf **KY**31, Gnatcatcher.

2 also *gnatcatcher bug:* A **dragonfly.**

1949 *AmSp* 24.109 **nwSC,** *Gnatcatcher; gnatcatcher bug. . .* Dragonfly.

gnat-fly n [Redund; cf Intro "Language Changes" I.4]

1914 *DN* 4.155 **Cape Cod MA,** *Gnat-fly. . .* Gnat. **1967–69** *DARE* (Qu. R10) Infs **MD**32, **MA**68, **MO**34, Gnat-flies; **TX**11, Gnat-fly.

gnat's bristle See **gnat's eyebrow**

gnats, catch See **catch flies**

gnat's eyebrow n Also *gnat's heel, ~ eye, ~ bristle;* for addit varr see quots **chiefly Sth, S Midl, West** See Map For distrib of major varr, see quot 1965–70 and Map Section

Used as an example of something small, fine, or neat—often in adv phr *(down) to a gnat's eyebrow* and varr, down to the last detail; exactly, precisely.

1840 *Spirit of Times* 9 May 109/2 **SC,** Well, now, the main thing is to learn the fust thing fust—you must learn to march fust. . . Well fellas, you went that lock-step to a nat's heel, just now. **1897** in 1950 *PADS* 13.13 **AL,** The name fits the man to a gnat's heel. **1903** *DN* 2.315 **seMO,** *Gnat's heel. . .* Something quite small. 'It fitted to a gnat's heel,' that is, perfectly. **1905** *DN* 3.81 **nwAR,** *Gnat's bristle, ~ ear. . .* A fine point. 'He's got things down to a gnat's bristle.' **1906** *DN* 3.119 **sIN,** There ain't room fer a gnat's heel here. **1908** *DN* 3.315 **eAL, wGA,** *Gnat's heel, gnat's toe-nail. . .* Any thing very small. "It fitted to a gnat's toe-nail," i.e., perfectly. **1915** *DN* 4.183 **swVA,** *Gnat's heel, to a. . .* Precisely. **1935** Davis *Honey* 69 **OR,** I set down and figured it out, and it'll work right down to a gnat's tail. **1940** White *Wild Geese* 189 **NW** (as of 1890s), He's got to drop his tree to a gnat's hair, or all his other calculations are no good at all. **1942** *AmSp* 17.131 **IN,** *To a gnat's heel* (exactly). **1952** Brown *NC Folkl.* 1.545, *Gnat's bristle. . .* Something very small or insignificant.—General. **1954** *Harder Coll.* **cwTN,** Sharp enough to split the hair on a gnat's ass. **c1960** *Wilson Coll.* **csKY,** Fine as a gnat's whiskers. *Ibid, Down to a gnat's bristle*—Something done exactly and meticulously. **1965–70** *DARE* (Qu. KK50, . . *"He had it all worked out ———."*) 23 Infs, **chiefly West,** (Down) to a gnat's eyebrow; 12 Infs, **esp S Atl,** Down to a gnat's heel; 11 Infs, **esp lower Missip Valley,** (Down) to a gnat's bristle; **CA**101, **KY**5, **MO**11, **MT**4, **OR**10, **TX**9, 13, (Down) to a gnat's eye; **IN**83, **NC**82, Down to the gnat's eye; **CA**138, 155, Down to a gnat-eye; **AL**3, **CA**157, **GA**3, **KS**18, **OH**66, **OR**14, (Down) to a gnat's ear; **FL**28, **PA**167, **TX**5, (Down) to a gnat's eyelash; **SD**5, **TX**19, Down to a gnat's ass; **KY**60, **TN**26, Down to a gnat's hair; **LA**8, 20, To a gnat's tail; **OR**1, Down to a gnat's balls; **VA**1f, Down to a gnat's prick; **WY**2, Down to a gnat's eyewink; (Qu. KK3a, . . *"It's done to ———."*) Infs **AR**3, **LA**16, Gnat's bristle; **OH**72,

Gnat's eye-winker; (Qu. KK3b, . . *"It's done to ______."*) Infs **OR**1, Gnat's ass; **AR**55, Gnat's bristle; **NE**4, Gnat's eyelash; (Qu. KK55a, . . *"No, not by a ______."*) Inf **PA**208, Gnat's eyelash; (Qu. KK55c, *Other expressions of strong denial*) Inf **MO**10, Not by a gnat's bristle; (Qu. LL1, . . *"I only took a ______ one."*) Inf **MS**56, Not bigger than a gnat's eye. **c1970** *Halpert Coll.* 20 **wKY, nwTN,** Everything has to be done to a gnat's eyebrow. . . (=exactly to a hair). **1982** *DARE* File, In reference to a yard that was all mowed & neat, "It's like a Gnat's whisker!" [I tho't it was cat's whisker, but apparently not!] [This expression was used by a lady, late 60's, who was born & raised in eastern Nebr., & has lived in eastern part of Iowa about 40 yrs.; farm wife.]

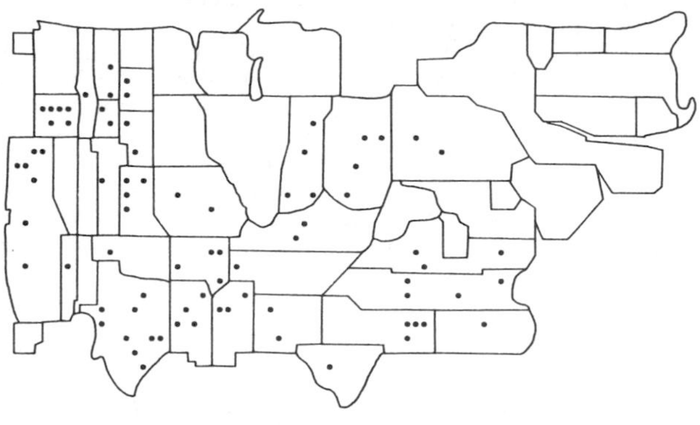

•gnat's eyebrow + varr (Qq. KK50, KK3a, b, KK55a, c, LL1)

gnat smoke n

Appar a smoky fire built to ward off gnats.

1959 Roberts *Up Cutshin* 6 **eKY,** She would tell a story at the ends of corn rows . . and of an evening around a gnat smoke in the yard.

gnatty-tail adj

Unkempt and disreputable.

1948 Hurston *Seraph* 187 **FL,** Look out for that bridge! Don't kill me about that gnatty-tail gal!

gnaw n

See quot.

1938 Rawlings *Yearling* 101 **nFL,** Penny pointed out a bear gnaw. . . "I've watched a bear at it . . many a time. He'll stretch up and he'll claw. He'll turn his head sideways and he'll nag and gnaw. Then he'll back up and rub his shoulders agin the resin."

gnir n Also *gnyr* Cf *DS* E20

Dust; a ball of dust.

1959 *VT Hist.* new ser 27.137, Gnyrs [nɝz]. . . Dust under the bed. Occasional. **1973** *San Francisco Examiner* (CA) 2 Dec Sunday Punch sec 1/1, The late Robert Benchley . . called it [=the stuff that collects in the pockets of old suits and overcoats] "gnir," and described it as being "specially constructed for adhering to candies."

gnome's gold n [From the many small, orange-colored fruits]

A **bittersweet** (here: *Celastrus scandens*).

1933 Small *Manual SE Flora* 818, *C[elastrus] scandens. . . Gnome's gold. . .* The ripe fruits are used for interior decoration in winter. **1960** Vines *Trees SW* 660, *Celastrus scandens. . .* Known also by the vernacular names of . . Gnome's-gold, Waxwork.

gnurl See **knurl**

gnyr See **gnir**

go v

A Forms. [Cf similar forms in *EDD*]

1 pres (exc 3rd pers sg): Usu *go;* sometimes *goes.*

1843 (1916) Hall *New Purchase* 150 **IN,** Then I goes to the fire and sits down to cook my duck . . Lets git a leg or two [of deer] for Mrs. Carltin afore they goes. **1966–68** *DARE* Tape **GA**30, These wild bees goes up in the trees; **SC**12, Some people goes down there. **1967** *DARE* FW Addit **AL,** The use of the third person singular morpheme with any pronoun; "I goes shopping on Mondays." Negro—almost exclusively.

2 pres 3rd pers sg: Usu *goes;* sometimes *go.*

1922 Gonzales *Black Border* 304 **sSC, GA coasts** [Gullah glossary], *Go*—go, goes, going, gone, went. **1933** Rawlings *South Moon* 52 **nFL,** Seems like ever' thing go along better when you do what's natural. **1967** *DARE* Tape **LA**12, That's the way it go.

3 infin: Usu *go;* also:

a *went.* [Perh in part by ext from *to went* = to have gone; see **A7b** below]

1890 *DN* 1.7 **cNY,** *Went* was sometimes used as the infinitive also. **1986** Pederson *LAGS Concordance,* 1 inf, **seAL,** How'd the question went? 1 inf, **seAL,** Was a bunch of us used to went places; 1 inf, **nwLA,** Never did went back; 1 inf, **csTX,** I used to went there.

b *gone.*

1949 Turner *Africanisms* 275 **seSC** [Gullah], After I gone out a couple of night . . I have to gone down in there and get it out. . . Then I have to go to her [in] the morning.

4 pres pple: Usu *going;* also:

a pronc-spp *gwine, guine, gwyne, gwa(i)n, gwi'.* **chiefly Sth, S Midl** *esp freq among Black speakers*

1787 in 1956 Eliason *Tarheel Talk* 311 **cnNC,** *Going*—guine. **1795** Dearborn *Columbian Grammar* 135, *List of Improprieties. . .* Gwyne for Going. **1834** *Life Andrew Jackson* 238 **ME,** I . . was jist a gwine tu tell all about it. **1845** Thompson *Pineville* 66 **GA,** Whar upon yeath can they be gwine in sich a hurryment? **1853** Hammett *Stray Yankee in TX* 25, "Massa Dave," asked old Cæsar, "aint you a-gwain to fetch Bose along?" **1887** Page *In Ole VA* 465, Yes, suh, I gwi' tell him. **1887** (1967) Harris *Free Joe* 12 **GA,** It hain't a-gwine to hurt you. **1890** *DN* 1.68 **KY,** *Gwine* [gwaɪn]: for *going. Goin'* of the Southern whites becomes *gwine* in the negro's mouth. **1893** Owen *Voodoo Tales* 177 **MO** [Black], Yo' ain't gwine ter flusteh me wid queschins. **1893** Shands *MS Speech* 34, *Gwine. . .* The common negro form for *going.* Used throughout the South. **1899** (1912) Green *VA Folk-Speech* 211, I gwine right away. **1901** *DN* 2.182 **KY,** *Going* . . gwinc. [Negro.] **1903** *DN* 2.315 **seMO,** There's gwine to be trouble here right soon. **1906** *DN* 3.139 **nwAR,** *Gwine. . .* Facetious for *going.* **1908** *DN* 3.318 **eAL, wGA,** *Gwine. . .* Going. A negroism, but often used by the white people in rural districts. **1922** Gonzales *Black Border* 305 **sSC, GA coasts** [Gullah glossary], *Gwi, gwine*—going, going to. **[1928** see **go down** v phr **2.]** **1931** *PMLA* 46.1319 **Appalachians,** "Gwine," and "a-gwine" do not necessarily derive from negro speech, and belong to earlier English speech. They are common enough among the illiterate. **1940** *Sat. Eve. Post* 24 Feb 77/1 **New Orleans** [Black], Dis gwan be de finest fun'al. **1950** *PADS* 14.34 **SC,** When used as an auxiliary, *gwine* is often pronounced *gwi',* with or without a nasalized *i.* **1953** [see **A4c** below]. **1967** *DARE* File **ceLA,** Gwine [gwaɪn] . . going—common, Negro. **1976** Garber *Mountain-ese* 37 **Appalachians,** We haint gwine to have much yield on our tater crop this year.

b pronc-spp *gon(e), goan, gorn, go', goun, guh.* **scattered, but chiefly Sth, S Midl**

1899 Garland *Boy Life* 171 **nwIA** (as of 1870s), Steve ain't a-go'n' to pitch into him yet. **1909** *DN* 3.411 **nME,** *Gōn. . .* Going. **1914** *DN* 4.73 **ME, nNH,** *Gone?* or *You gone?* Are you going already? **1916** Howells *Leatherwood God* 9 **OH,** You think you're just goun' to die. **1922** Gonzales *Black Border* 304 **sSC, GA coasts** [Gullah glossary], *Go* . . going. *Ibid, Gone* . . going. **1923** *DN* 5.204 **swMO,** I'm aimin' on a-gorn come Christmas week. **1927** Adams *Congaree* 4 **sSC** [Black], When dey guh finish? **1942** Faulkner *Go Down* 99 **MS** [Black], "Ah'm goan home," he said. **1952** [see **B** below]. **1960** Williams *Walk Egypt* 28 **GA** [Black], You gon puts in a garden. **1965–70** *DARE* (Qu. K10) Inf **LA**12, Gone come in; **MS**81, She's gone calve; she's gone get done; TN53, She's gone drop; (Qu. U17) Inf **LA**6, He mus' ain't gone pay me; (Qu. X40) Inf **TN**52, Gone lie down; gone stretch out; (Qu. KK26) Inf **AR**52, Ain't gone bother; (Qu. NN11) Inf **GA**54, I'm gone. **1966** *DARE* Tape **AL**24, Yes ma'am, he gone [gon] take it. **1979** *Ms.* Oct 20/2 **SC** [Black], I'm go wash your mouth out with Octagon soap! **1984** Burns *Cold Sassy* 5 **nGA** (as of 1906), Don't you care what folks are go'n say? **1987** Jones-Jackson *When Roots Die* 92 **sSC coast** [Gullah], On this Christian journey / The way ain't gone be easy on us children.

c pronc-spp *gine, ghy.*

1914 *DN* 4.159 **VA,** *Gine* . . going. "Iah gine; yo gine?" **1938** Faulkner *Unvanquished* 22 **MS,** "What we ghy do now?" Ringo said. **1953** Atwood *Survey of Verb Forms* 35, *Goin'* /goɪn/ is of course much more common than *going* /goɪŋ/. . . There are 16 occurrences of *gwine* / gwain/ in N. Eng., all northeast of the Merrimack. Elsewhere in the East this form does not occur until we reach the Chesapeake Bay area. . . In Delmarva, e. Va., N.C., S.C., and coastal Ga. *gwine* becomes fairly common in Type I [=older, old-fashioned, poorly educ infs] (one third to one half of the informants in most of the area use it) and also occurs occasionally in Type II [=younger, more modern, better educ infs]. . . A similar form without /w/, /gain/, is current on the Eastern Shore of Va. and in n.e. N.C. around Albemarle Sound and the lower Neuse River.

d in phr *going to* + infin (rarely with redund *to*): pronc-spp *gointa, gonter, gwinter, goina, gonna, gunna.*

1884 *Anglia* 7.267 **Sth, S Midl** [Black], *Aint gwinter* = am not going to. **1916** *DN* 4.341 **KS, LA, MA, NE, OH,** *Gonna.* Contraction of *going to.* **1918** *DN* 5.20 **NC,** *Gonna,* going to. **1932** Stong *State Fair* 255 **IA,** You gointa put the trophy in there with him? **1941** O'Donnell *Great Big Doorstep* 9 **sLA,** Now I guess you gunna expeck him to find a house floatin down. **1942** Faulkner *Go Down* 13 **MS,** I gonter tell you something to remember. **1945** O'Hara *Pipe Night* 63 **PA,** I never said I was gunna make you laugh. **1950** Faulkner *Stories* 689 **MS** [Black], He can't come to breakfast this morning because he gonter to be whuppin Genl Smith at Tallahatchie Crossing about that time. **1952** Brown *NC Folkl.* 1.543, Goin' a get me a fram-pole and beat you up. **1953** Atwood *Survey of Verb Forms* 35, In *going to* there are almost innumerable phonetic reductions of the types [goɪntə, goɪnə, gonə, gʌnə, gənə]. **1965–70** *DARE* (Qq. B5, B6, K10, X40, BB54) 87 Infs, **scattered,** Gonna be nasty [and var phrr; see *DS*]. [Further exx throughout *DS*]

e in phr *I'm going to* + infin: pronc-spp *Aminah, Ima, Imo.*

1954 *PADS* 21.18 **SC,** "I am going to . . " has become step by step: [aɪm gonə], [aɪ monə], [aɪmõ, aɪmo]. Such departures from standard speech are probably more or less general in the South. **1970** Abrahams *Deep Down* 195 **Philadelphia PA** [Black], I'm gonna walk the water for you. God is surely with me, 'cause I'ma walk the water. **1977** Smitherman *Talkin* 95 [Black], Well, baby, if you just give me a chance, Ima have it together pretty soon. **1978** Kalibabky *Hawdaw* 2 **neMN,** Aminah: A personal declaration to promote action with willful intent. "If I find out dat you drank da las' beer, aminah kill you!" **1980** *DARE* File **MI,** *Imo*—Reduction of *I'm going to.* I heard this in Ann Arbor, Nov 5, 1980, from a Black maid who had been working for my host for 30 years.

5 vbl n: Usu *going;* rarely *gwinen.* [*going* + **-ing**]

1928 Peterkin *Scarlet Sister Mary* 180 **SC** [Gullah], Den, I'll stay, Si May-e. I didn' know you'd feel so bad about my gwinen. *Ibid* 213, "Gwinen down don' worry me non 't all," Mary boasted.

6 past: Usu *went;* also:

a *goed.*

1884 *Anglia* 7.252 [Black], To the regular forms of the Irregular verbs as used by the whites, the Negro adds the following forms of his own. . . *Pres.* go—*Past.* goed (cf. Scotch), gone. **1909** in 1914 Stewart *Letters* 219 **WY,** We goed very fast as the wind. **1933** Rawlings *South Moon* 6 **FL,** The next day they was gone. . . No man kin say where they goed.

b *gone, go.* *esp Gullah*

1884 [see **6a** above]. **1888** Jones *Negro Myths* 44 **GA coast** [Gullah], Buh Snake . . gone to him house in de swamp berry bex [=very vexed]. **1892** (1969) Christensen *Afro-Amer. Folk Lore* 16, So 'e han' 'e Free Paper to Sis' Cat an' gone. **1922** [see **A2** above]. **c1937** [see **C10** below]. **1966** *DARE* Tape **SC**15, I gone there one night. **1971** Cunningham *Syntactic Analysis Gullah* 53, C[reole:] She got up and gone. E[nglish:] She got up and left.

7 past pple: Usu *gone* |gɔn|; also:

a |gon, gɑn|; pronc-spp *gorn, gown.*

1824 in 1956 Eliason *Tarheel Talk* 311 **wNC,** *Gone*—gown. **1896** *DN* 1.417 **c,wNY, NYC,** *Go:* ppl. *gone* sometimes pron. [gɑn]. **1911** *DN* 3.538 **eKY,** *Gone.* Pronounced gorn. **1950** Hubbell *Pronc. NYC* 84, Before /n/, the usual vowels are /ɑ/ and /ɑə̆/. . . The pronunciation of *gone* varies: /ɔə̆/ predominates, but /ɑə̆/ is also frequent, particularly in less cultivated speech. **1952** Brown *NC Folkl.* 1.546, *Gone* [gon]. . . Survival of an older pronunciation. . . —Harnett, Robeson, and Sampson counties. **c1960** *Wilson Coll.* **csKY,** *Gone* is [gɔn] . . or [gon] occasionally.

b *went.* Cf **A3** above

1832 (1919) Irving *Jrls.* 144, I have only went along yonder by the edge of the prairie. **1837** Sherwood *Gaz. GA* 72, You ought not to have *went* is improper; it should be have *gone.* **1883** Twain *Life on Missip.* (Boston) 450, The unpolished [Southerners] often use "went" for "gone." It is nearly as bad as the Northern "had n't ought." This reminds me that a remark of a very peculiar nature was made here . . (in the North) a few days ago: "He had n't ought to have went." **1890** *DN* 1.7 **cNY,** The principal parts *go, went, went* (*have went* for *have gone*) [were reported]. **1893** *DN* 1.277 **wCT,** *Go* . . went [=past, past pple] (*gone* in p.p. is confined to adj. use, = 'away,' 'not longer present'). **1895** *DN* 1.376 **KY, NC, TN,** *Went* = gone. **1906** *DN* 3.163 **nwAR,** *Went.* . . Common among the uneducated for "gone." "Jim hasn't went yet." "I'd a went if I'd ben you." **1909** *DN* 3.387 **eAL, wGA,** *Went.* . . Common even among educated persons. "I would 'a' went, but I didn't think you would be there." **1966–69** *DARE* Tape **CA**89, And they had went down; **CA**107, Must a went down a hunderd feet; **CA**156, He could a went . . down there; **MI**22, If he went past once, he must a went a past a dozen times; **SD**8, Pork has went down in consumption. **1967–69** *DARE* (Qu. BB56) Inf **MI**47, Has went over the hump; (Qu. JJ16) Inf **KY**53, It's went through. **1975** Allen *LAUM* 2.79 (as of c1950), For 12 Type I infs. [=old, with little educ] and 7 Type II's [=mid-aged, with approx hs educ] the past participle of *go* is *went.* . . Inf. 138 also has *went* in "We'd a like to went," where it probably is the participle and not the infinitive. **1976** Wolfram–Christian *Appalachian Speech* 81, Her home had went, I guess, 50 yards or more from its foundation. *Ibid* 83–84, [Past as participle . . 66 examples of *went* in 123 occurrences of the participle of *go.*] **1981** Pederson *LAGS Basic Materials* **Gulf Region,** [*Went* for *gone* in such contexts as "I've went" is widespread.]; 2 infs, Ought to went (=ought to have gone); 1 inf, They'd have had to went (=would have had to have gone). [*DARE* Ed: *to went* appears to represent *to have went* (=*to have gone*) with assimilation or omission of *have.*]

c rarely *go.*

1922 [see **A2** above].

B Syntax.

Pres pple foll by infin without *to.* **chiefly Sth** *esp freq among Black speakers* For addit exx see **A4b** above Note: It is possible that in some cases the *to* has been lost by phonetic reduction.

1853 Simms *Sword & Distaff* 76 **SC** [Black], John Sylvester nebber guine le' Joe Bossick put he dirty . . paw 'pon him shoulder agen! **1872** Schele de Vere *Americanisms* 607, *Gwine,* instead of *going,* is the uniform pronunciation of the negroes in the South. "I ain't a gwine do no such thing!" **1887** Page [see **A4a** above]. **1908** *S. Atl. Qrly.* 7.333 **SC** [Gullah], Me Ha'tym [Footnote: *Hard-times;* a given name], sho' gwine ketch jawb een rock-fiel' [Footnote: Phosphate rock-fields]. **1931** Faulkner *Sanctuary* 271 **swTN** [Black], I ghy leave it here by the door. **1949** Turner *Africanisms* 225 [Gullah], Usually . . the future [of the verb *go*] is indicated by prefixing the word *going* to the verb *go* without *to.* **1952** Brown *NC Folkl.* 1.545, *Go'* [gõ]. . . Going as part of a verb phrase. "I'm go' spank you if you don't stop crying."—Central. Many persons who use it are unaware that they do.

C Senses.

1 To walk; esp to be "up and about" (after an illness, etc). [*OED go* v. 1 a1000 →; *"Obs."*] **chiefly Sth, S Midl** See Map

1856 in 1956 Eliason *Tarheel Talk* 157 **NC,** I hurt my back this week so that I can hardly go. **1944** *PADS* 2.43 **eNC,** *Go.* . . To walk. . . Rare. **1965–70** *DARE* (Qu. Y23, *Expressions meaning to move yourself or get yourself in motion: "I was so stiff I could hardly ______."*) 18 Infs, **chiefly Sth, S Midl,** Go. [9 Infs mid-aged; 9 old] **1979** *DARE* File **wNC** (c1915–20), When I finished cleaning house I was so tired I could hardly go.

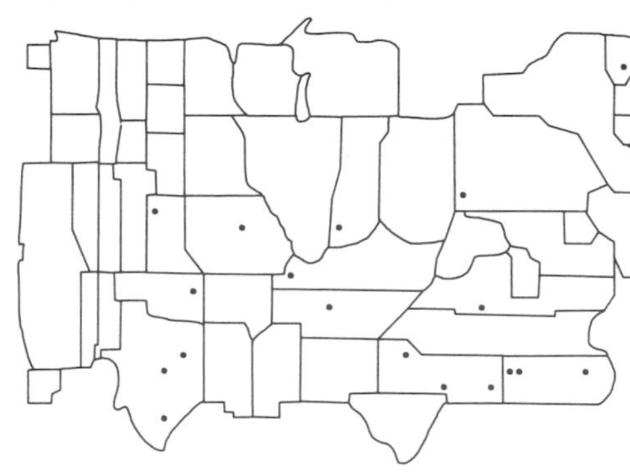

•go v C1 (Qu. Y23)

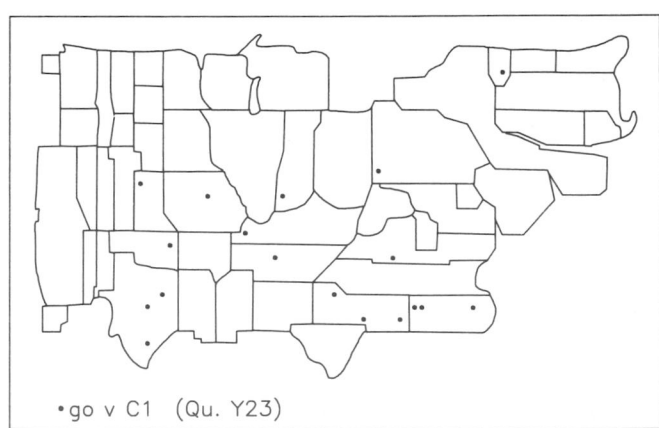

2 foll by *to* + vbl n (rarely infin): To begin, set about. **scattered, but esp Sth, S Midl**

1834 in 1968 *Filson Club Hist. Qrly.* 157 **csKY,** A company of sisters go to scutching flax today. **1862** in 1967 *DARE* File **AR,** [Letter:] John

Tyree . . has gone to making hats with John Vickers. **1884** Smith *Bill Arp's Scrap Book* 80 **GA,** There are as many female dudes as males, and they ought to marry I reckon and go to raising fools for market. **1937** *Hall Coll.* **eTN,** He went to killin' 'em (bear) when he was twelve year old. **1939** *LANE* Map 242, 1 inf, **CT,** We look out in the warm weather when we're haying, and if there are spider webs on the grass we go to mowing. **1958** McCulloch *Woods Words* 71 **Pacific NW,** *Go to logging* —To start logging. **1967** *DARE* FW Addit **AR,** Go to—inchoative. . . "I could go to cuttin' billets." **1967–70** *DARE* Tape **CA**196, They had Saturday night dances. . . Anybody with a little babies . . put the kids to sleep. Kids went to cryin', stop dancin' an' took care of 'em; **KY**23, We set this plant [=tobacco], try to go to setting about the fifteenth of May; **LA**40, She [=a mare]. . . went to backin'; **MI**52, My sister went to nursing; **SC**46, The first bale of cotton came, we'd leap on it an' go to playing; **TX**1A, Listen now, don't go to tell me to do this and do that. Just let me do it in my own way; **TX**5, And they have lately gone to canning it and shipping it out. **1972** Green *More Horse Tradin'* 180 **swTX,** I went to asking him what he wanted for his horses. **1984** Wilder *You All Spoken Here* 169 **Sth,** Gone to: Begun, as "It's gone to rainin' on the golf course a-ready."

3 To make, go on (a journey, ride, etc); to travel (a road).

1794 (1936) Parry *Jrl.* 34.391 **PA,** I was dissuaded very much from going this trip—it was counted very dangerous. **1843** (1916) Hall *New Purchase* 121, They are forced to go a few journeys. **1962** Carrell *Autobiog.* [37] **ceMA** (as of 1880s), Once every winter along about February, our school would go a sleigh ride. We hired a pung drawn by two horses. **1976** Wolfram–Christian *Appalachian Speech* 97, *Go* . . travel. . . Half the time, in '17, you couldn't go the road.

4 To wager; to bet (someone something).

1831 *Boston Eve. Transcript* (MA) 16 Dec 2/2, ["]Well,["] said the "Cotton man," ["]what will you go now?" "Go," said the farmer, . . "I'll go the whole hog." **1839** (1840) Simms *Border Beagles* 65, I'll go a quart and a dozen cabanas upon it. **1846** (1973) Porter *Quarter Race* 179 **SC,** I knows Bill well, and I'll go you an independent on his beating yon feller bad. **1860** Greeley *Overland Journey* 163, The main or drinking-room was also occupied by several blacklegs as a gambling-hall, and their incessant clamor of "Who'll go me twenty?" **1875** [see **fill** v[1] **2**].

5 To accept the offer of (someone), take (someone) up on an offer.

1902 White *Blazed Trail* 169 **eMI,** "Surely you won't refuse to be my guest here!" . . "Wallace," said Thorpe, "I'll go you." **1909** Porter *Options* 40, "Believe I'll go you," he said, brightening . . "I'll accept the invitation gladly." **1919** Kyne *Capt. Scraggs* 61 **CA,** I'll go you, Scraggs.

6 foll by infin: To intend, mean (to do something)—usu in neg constrs. **chiefly Sth, Midl**

1861 Holmes *Venner* 1.42 **wMA,** "Didn' go to, Sir." "Didn' dew 't o' purpose, Sir." **1883** Twain *Life on Missip.* (Boston) 449, Many of them [Southerners] say, "I did n't go to do it," meaning "I did n't mean to do it." **1884** *Anglia* 7.269 **Sth, S Midl** [Black], *Not ter go ter do* = not to intend. **1884** Baldwin *Yankee School-Teacher* 196 **VA** [Black], Jinny won't go f'r t' hab nobody [to stay with her]. **1892** *KS Univ. Qrly.* 1.96 **KS,** *Go to* . . to intend to, as in, I didn't go (for) to do it. **1897** (1952) McGill *Narrative* 32 **SC,** Before he could rise Davy came running up and saying in a sorrowful way, "Oh, Cousin Sam, I didn't go to do it." **1903** *DN* 2.315 **seMO.** **1906** Casey *Parson's Boys* 284 **sIL** (as of c1860), Oh, mother, *mother!* where are you? I didn't go to hurt the dog. **1907** *DN* 3.231 **nwAR, seMO.** **1908** *DN* 3.315 **eAL, wGA,** . . "I didn't go to do it." Universal. **1912** Green *VA Folk-Speech* 199. **1942** McAtee *Dial. Grant Co. IN* 28 (as of 1890s). **1942** Warnick *Garrett Co. MD* 7 **nwMD** (as of 1900–18). **1946** *PADS* 6.15 **NC, VA,** *Go to do*. . . To intend. Used negatively. "I didn't go to do that." **1960** (1962) Lee *Mockingbird* 201 **AL,** No suh, I didn't go to be. **1966** *DARE* File **cMS,** *Go* . . intend (illit.)—I didn't go to do it. I went to do it. I did go to do it. **1967** *DARE* FW Addit **LA**12, I didn't go to do it. **1976** Garber *Mountain-ese* 22 **Appalachians.** **1976** Ryland *Richmond Co. VA* 371. **1983** *MJLF* 9.1.41 **ceKY.**

7 foll by *with* + noun: To become of, be the matter with (someone)—usu in interrog constrs. **chiefly Sth, Midl**

1837 Sherwood *Gaz. GA* 70, *Gone with,* become of—what is *gone with it* or with him, for become of it or him. **1875** (1876) Twain *Tom Sawyer* 17 **MO,** What's gone with that boy, I wonder? **1882** Harte *Flip* 92 **CA,** Are ye moonin' agin with yer secrets? What's gone with ye? **1892** *KS Univ. Qrly.* 1.96 **OH,** *Go with:* to become of, as in, What has gone with my hat? **1914** *DN* 4.114 **KS,** *Went with*. . . Became of. "I don't know what went with that hammer." **1916** 'Bower' *Phantom Herd* 9 *(DAE),* Say, old-timer, what's gone with all the cattle and all the punchers? **1938** Rawlings *Yearling* 76 **nFL,** You got him [=a raccoon]. Good. That's what's been goin' with my hens. **1942** *Hench Coll.* **swVA,** [Letter:] Instead of "what became of anything?" they would say "what went with it." **c1960** *Wilson Coll.* **csKY,** What's gone with Jim? **1980** *New Yorker* 18 Feb 31 **KY,** "Did you ever find out what went with your little white cat?" Mama asks. "No. I think maybe he got shot," Sandra says.

8 To endure, to "stomach"—usu in neg constrs.

1830 *IL Mth. Mag.* Nov. 74 *(DA),* 'I can't go it, sir!' replied the dandy, strutting up and down. **a1883** (1911) Bagby *VA Gentleman* 72, Then again, I couldn't have gone the ancient costume. It is picturesque, does well for marble, and for historical paintings in oil, but it is sadly unfit for a citizen of Buckingham or Prince Edward. **1886** Stockton *Casting Away* 99, We've now eat two meals with the passengers, and me and my mates is agreed that that's about as much as we can go. **1895** (1969) Graham *Stories of Foot-hills* 235, I can't quite go the Methodist doctrine. **1912** Mathewson *Pitching* 214, I cannot "go" young ball-players who attempt to become the bootblacks for the old ones. **1913** *DN* 4.10 **MN,** (Can't) *go* (a person or a thing). . . (Can't) endure, stand, or put up with. "He likes her, but he can't go her sister." **1942** McAtee *Dial. Grant Co. IN* 28 (as of 1890s), "I can't go that kind of vittles". "I can't go sich actions". **1942** Warnick *Garrett Co. MD* 7 **nwMD** (as of 1900–1918), The meat was so rare that I couldn't go it. **1947** Ballowe *The Lawd* 62 **LA,** When even the Duppy couldn't go another piece [of food], Unc' Brutus leaned back for a nap. **c1960** *Wilson Coll.* **csKY,** I just can't go his queer ways. **1965–70** *DARE* (Qu. II29a, *An unexplainable dislike . . : "I don't know why, but I just can't ——— him."*) 34 Infs, **scattered, but esp Nth,** Go. **1967** *DARE* FW Addits **OK,** *Go* . . tolerate, esp of food. "You may like rhubarb pie, but I can't go it"; **OK,** I just can't go English peas; **NY,** I can't go dirt. **1968** Kellner *Aunt Serena* 197 **IN,** He got mad because the apple pie had nutmeg in it, and he never could go nutmeg.

9 in phrr *go to ride, ~ walk:* To go riding, walking.

1934 *Hanley Disks* **NH,** I went to ride on Monday. [Inf old] **1937** *AmSp* 12.287 **nwVA,** The Shenandoah German may say . . 'Would you go to ride?' for would you like to ride. **1940** in 1944 *ADD* **NC,** Will you go to walk? Assoc. Press. **1975** *DARE* File **cMA** (as of c1915), Go to walk, go to ride = go for a walk, ride: I grew up saying this.

10 To suffice for, last (someone).

c1937 in 1972 *Amer. Slave* 2.1.113 **SC,** One give this; one give that. Handle 'em light! . . Gone you till Saddy. [=They lasted you until Saturday.] **1970** *DARE* FW Addit **cwPA,** I try to bring enough food to go me (=last me)—old fashioned.

11 Of food: to be digestible—usu in neg constrs.

1965–70 *DARE* (Qu. H69, *When food is hard on your stomach, you say that it ———*) Inf **ME**2, Didn't go well; **NC**88, Doesn't go so well; **MO**39, Don't go.

go n

1 with *the:* The current fashion or usage—usu in phr *all the go.*

1848 Bartlett *Americanisms* 157, *The Go.* The mode; the fashion. 'This is all the go.' **1858** *Salem* (Ill.) *Advocate* 26 May 3/2 (*DA* at *donation* 10), Donation Suppers seem to have become all 'the go,' during the past winter. **1859** Taliaferro *Fisher's R.* 115 **nwNC** (as of 1820s), An old-fashioned "seven-handed reel" was the only go. **1899** (1912) Green *VA Folk-Speech* 65, All the go. . . The fashion. "Broad-brim hats are all the go." **1908** Johnson *Highways Pacific Coast* 134 **sCA,** When I come here, cattle, sheep and hogs were all the go. There was very little soil cultivated; but gradually it got to be a great wheat country. **1961** Sackett–Koch *KS Folkl.* 207, There was usually a big meal served, especially for the relatives; and then of course shivarees were the go always. **1968** *DARE* Tape **NY**55, I remember I used to wear a high-top shoe . . and they were all the go.

2 An agreement, a deal. Cf **go v C5**

1878 Harte *Man on Beach* 61, "Then it's a go?" . . "It's a go." **1887** Kirkland *Zury* 537 **IL,** *Go*. . . A bargain struck, a decision arrived at. **1897** Flandrau *Harvard Episodes* 233, 'I'll help you with your English . . and your Latin. Is it a go?' Haydock held out his hand. **1914** Atherton *Perch of the Devil* 195, 'It's a go. . . Shake.' And she gave his hand a hearty grasp. **1953** Brewer *Word Brazos* 102 **eTX** [Black], "De nex' time you heahs me cuss in de pulpit, Ah'm gonna gib you a whole sweet potato pie." "Awright," say li'l' Ned; "dat's a go."

3 also pl, but sg in constr; In children's games: the privilege of having the first turn. [Cf *go* a turn in a game]

1883 Eggleston *Hoosier Schoolboy* 36, The player who won the last game has the "go"—that is, he first puts down a grain of corn at any place where the lines intersect. . . Then the other player puts one down. **1922** *DN* 5.187 **KY,** *Go*. . . The start. Also *goes.* "The goes is usually determined by first seeing who can shoot closest to a mark."

4 =go-by n.

1966–70 *DARE* (Qu. II5b, *When you don't want to have anything to do with a certain person because you don't like him, you might say, "I'd certainly like to give him the ——.")* Infs **CT**37, **IL**4, **KY**19, 83, **MS**6, **MA**7, **VA**29, Go.

goad n Usu |god|; also **esp nNEng** |goəd, gord| Pronc-spp *go(a)rd, gore*

A Forms.

1825 [see **B** below]. **1834** [see **B** below]. **1914** [see **B** below]. **1929** *AmSp* 5.126 **ME,** The oxen were directed with "goa(r)ds." **1939** *LANE* Map 179 *(Whip; goad)* [Proncs of the type [goəd] or, less freq, [goɚd] are nearly universal in Maine and New Hampshire and common in Vermont; in southern New England proncs of the type [go(ʊ)d] are much more common.] **1965–70** *DARE* (Qu. K27, *What do you call the sharp-pointed stick used to get oxen to move?)* 148 Infs, **widespread,** (Ox) goad; 11 Infs, **chiefly NEng, Gt Lakes,** Gord; **CA**199, **ME**14, 19, **MI**27, 47, **NH**14, Gord stick. **1973** Allen *LAUM* 1.205 **Upper MW** (as of c1950), *Goad, gad,* and the phonetic variants with /r/ seem to have a distinct Northern orientation in contrast with the apparent Midland distribution of the minor variants *prod* and *prodding pole. Ibid* 206, 4 infs, Goad stick; 5 infs, Goard stick; 2 infs, Gore stick.

B Sense.

In comb *goad stick:* A goad used esp to drive oxen. **chiefly Nth**

1825 Neal *Brother Jonathan* I.159 **CT,** I fetches it a rap, with my goard stick. **1834** Smith *Letters Jack Downing* 46 **ME,** A farmer ort to stick to his ox bows and goard sticks. **1839** *Knickerbocker* 13.298 **ME,** A small man, . . holding a goad-stick in his hand, entered the room. **1869** Twain *Innocents* 58, They banged the donkeys with their goad-sticks. **1914** *DN* 4.152 **ME,** *Goard stick*. . . Goad stick. Penobscot valley. **1939** *LANE* Map 179 *(Whip; goad)* 59 infs, **chiefly ME, NH,** Goad stick. **1956** Sorden–Ebert *Logger's Words* 16 **Gt Lakes,** *Goad-stick,* Hickory rod from four to six feet long with a sharp steel point on one end used in driving oxen. **1958** McCulloch *Woods Words* 71 **Pacific NW. 1965–70** [see **A** above]. **1965** Gould *You Should Start* 54 **ME,** I thought about Uncle Elijah's goad-stick. This was a smooth maple wand, neither rigid nor supple—"souple," as he said it—with the handle end well worn from long years of holding in his calloused hand, and it was used for teaming the oxen. **1973** [see **A** above].

goadie See **goody**

goad stick See **goad B**

go against v phr

1 To encounter.

1903 (1965) Adams *Log Cowboy* 76 **West,** We went into the parlor. Say, fellows, it was a little the nicest thing that ever I went against. Carpet that made you think you were going to bog down every step.

2 Of food: to disagree with.

1965 *DARE* File **seME,** Go against . . of food, disagree with. "Everything he et went against him." [Inf:] I was familiar with this [phrase] as a boy in Vermont and New Hampshire. **1969** *DARE* (Qu. BB16a, *If something a person ate didn't agree with him)* Inf **NY**163, It went against his stomach.

go-ahead adj *old-fash*

Energetic, progressive.

1834 *Sun* (NY NY) 20 Mar 2/2 [The 'frail sisters'] were next called up to the bar, accompanied (as a kind of counsel, we suppose) by the 'man wot sings Zip Coon, on the *go-ahead* principle.' **1854** Smith *'Way Down East* 239, A real go-ahead sort of a fellow as ever I met with. **1877** in 1937 Ruede *Sod-House* 229 **PA,** He don't seem to be a very go-ahead boy. **1898** Frederic *Deserter* 103, Asa had made a good exchange in getting such an industrious and go-ahead chap as Job Parshall in Mose's place. **1899** (1912) Green *VA Folk-Speech* 199. **1905** *DN* 3.10 **cCT,** *Go ahead*. . . Progressive. **1915** (1916) Johnson *Highways New Engl.* 118, My wife was one of them regular go-ahead women before she was took sick.

go-ahead n

1 A flat-heeled, thonged sandal. **chiefly CA, HI** Cf **flip-flop n 6**

1962 *AmSp* 37.288, *Go-aheads*. . . Japanese *zori* or the American adaptation, thong sandals. **1967–68** *DARE* (Qu. W21) Inf **GA**59A, Go-aheads [term used by] Americans in Japan; **HI**1, Go-ahead (indoors or out) . . [same as] zoris . . Japanese slipper with piece between big toe and next toe. **1972** McCormick *Vocab. HI* 73, *Go-ahead*. . . Sandal with piece between toes. **1972** Carr *Da Kine Talk* 90 **HI,** Zōri, the low Japanese thong slippers often called "go-aheads" and "grass slippers," are worn by men and women of all ethnic groups and for many more occasions than in Japan. **1978** *DARE* File **nCA** (as of 1950s), During the summer we wore rubber thongs if any shoes at all. We called them flip-flops, but to some of our friends they were go-aheads or zoris.

2 =bigmouth buffalo. [Perh var of **gourdhead buffalo**]

1967 *DARE* Tape **LA**5, You got two different kinds of buffalo. . . You got what you call the raised-back, . . then you got the go-ahead. The go-ahead, I believe he do get bigger than what the raised-back would.

go-ahead signal See **go-sign**

goak v

1939 FWP *ID Lore* 242, *Goak* . . to goad.

goal n Usu |gol|; also **chiefly Nth** |gul|; rarely |guld, gold| Pronc-spp *gool, goold*

A Forms. Note: The form *gool* is largely confined to the sense illustrated at **B** below (which see for further quots), and is often felt to be a distinct word from std *goal.*

1896 *DN* 1.418 **NY,** Gool: for *goal.* **1907** *DN* 3.244 **eME,** Goold. **1914** *DN* 4.73 **ME, nNH,** Gool . . Goal. **1924** *DN* 5.288 **Cape Cod MA,** Gool. **1943** *LANE* Map 585 [For *goal* proncs of the type [goʊl] and [guwl] are found throughout New England. In Maine [guwl] is almost universal, while in southern New England the two types are about equally common. 14 scattered infs offered proncs of the type [guwld] and two of the type [goʊld]. Five infs offered the compounds *gool-line* or *gool-post,* but two distinguished between *gool,* used in children's games, and *goal,* used in football. One said that *goal* was the word used in most games, "but in hide-and-seek the place you get to is the *goold.* There's a *d* on that; I never supposed they was the same thing."]

B Sense.

A base used in playing tag or a similar game; a game that involves such a base—sometimes used as exclam in such a game. **chiefly Nth** See Map Cf **base B1, 2, dare base, prisoner's base, stink base**

1876 Whitney *Sights & Insights* 1.148 **MA,** Emery Ann says: 'You can't play tag continual, without a gool to run to!' **1884** *Harper's New Mth. Mag.* Jan 304/I, A sort of shinney . . or what we used to call, when we were boys, 'gool.' I suppose we meant goal, or golf. **1899** Garland *Boy Life* 53 **nwIA** (as of the 1870s), To play "gool" or "pom-pom pullaway" upon the frozen ponds. These games could be played with skates, quite as well as in any other way. **1904** Day *Kin o' Ktaadn* 227 **ME,** A-taggin gool with bullets in this red hot game of "Kill." **1907** *DN* 3.188 **NH,** *Gool*. . . Base; goal. "He's got to touch the gool first." *Ibid* 244 **eME,** Gool. **1917** Garland *Son Middle Border* 126 **IA** (as of 1870s), We built fires at the edges of the swales and played "gool". **1943** *LANE* Map 585 *(Goal),* The map shows the word *goal.* In the speech of our informants this usually denotes the base in hide-and-seek, run-sheep-run and other children's games . . , to which the players must run in order to escape being caught by the one who is "it." **c1960** *Wilson Coll.* **csKY,** *Goal*. . . Term used in games; rather modern. Older use was *home* or *home base.* **1965–70** *DARE* (Qu. EE14, . . *Where . . 'it' has to wait and count while the others hide)* 140 Infs, **chiefly Nth,** Goal; 46 Infs, **chiefly Nth,** Gool; **NJ**4, Home goal; (Qu. EE13b, *In games in which all the others hide, the one who must try to find them, he's ——)* Inf **OR**3, Goalkeeper; (Qu. EE15, *When he has caught the first of those that were hiding what does . . 'it' call out to the others?)* Inf **ME**19, Calls "gool" when he sees a player; **MI**103, At the beginning, the one who was it called out, "All round goal is caught." If the it-person saw a player and touched goal, he'd say, "Tick the goal on —— (person's name)";(Qu. EE17, *In a game of tag, if a player wants to rest)* Inf **CT**12, He gets to a goal and stays there. **1978** *DARE* File **cMA,** We always said "my goal" in hide and seek. [Inf old] **1979** Lewis *How to Talk Yankee* [14] **nNEng,** *Gool* . . goal. Where you try to get when playing tag and other games. **1981** *NADS Letters* **MI,** [Gool] denotes a marker (such as a tree or fence-post) which a tired player may hold on to in order to indicate that he has temporarily withdrawn from the game and is not to be tagged. Generally, only one player may be 'on gool' at a time. **1988** *DARE* File **csMN,** Gool was a place, for example a tree, clothesline pole, gutter, dirt patch, etc., where one would be safe, couldn't be tagged, when he/she and a bunch of kids were playing a game of tag. Often, upon reaching the designated place, the person would yell "Gool!" He/she couldn't be tagged while touching gool. *Goal* was also used, but in the standard sense of place to aim toward.

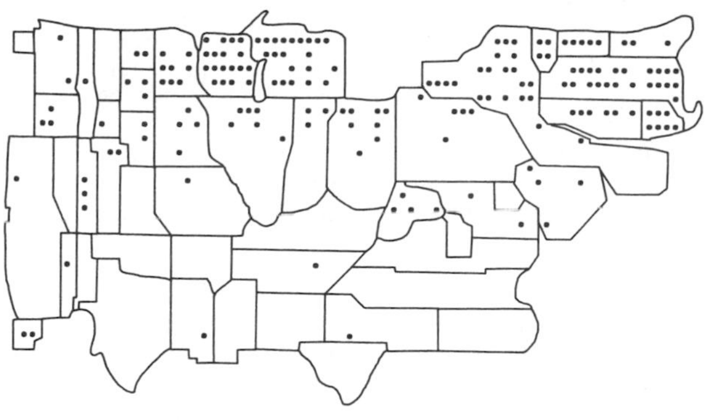

•goal B + varr (Qq. EE14, EE13b, EE15, EE17)

goalie n Pronc-sp *goolie* **[goal]**

1 In hiding games: the player who must find the others, "it."

1966–69 *DARE* (Qu. EE13b) Inf **MI**2, Goolie; **NY**98, Goalie, goolie [FW: Inf was doubtful about both responses.]; **NY**219, Goolie.

2 See quot. Cf **goal B**

1950 *WELS Suppl.* **IL,** *Goalie*—An alternative form applied to the tree used in games—*not* a nickname for the goal-keeper as in hockey and soccer.

‡3 See quot.

1969 *DARE* (Qu. EE18, *Games in which the players set up a stone, a tin can, or something similar, and then try to knock it down*) Inf **NY**219, Goolie. [FW: Inf was doubtful.]

4 In marble play: the shooter.

1969 *DARE* (Qu. EE6a, *Names for different kinds of marbles—the big one that's used to knock others out of the ring*) Inf **PA**213, Goalie.

go all around one's elbow (or thumb) to get to one's thumb (or elbow) See **elbow, go (all) around one's**

go along v phr Pronc-spp *go'long, g'lang* Cf **get up** v phr **1**

Get up!—used to command a horse to move or to go faster; to say "go along!"

1852 Bristed *Upper Ten Thousand* 28 **NY,** G'lang, old fellow. **1887** Freeman *Humble Romance* 139 **NEng,** Israel g'langed to the horse, an' put the whip over her, but she jest jogged right along. **1890** *DN* 1.68 **KY,** *G'lang:* for *go along,* to a horse in plow or wagon. **1899** Garland *Boy Life* 65 **nwIA** (as of c1870s), The hired man flung the cover shut and called *"Glang there, boys."* Back and forth across the wide field Lincoln moved. **1909** *DN* 3.397 **nwAR,** *G'lang*. . . Get up. To a horse in plow or wagon. **1939** *LANE* Map 223 *(Calls to horses: get up!), Go along!* The type of [go læŋ] is often regarded as old-fashioned. . . All calls . . are used by some both (a) to start the horses and (b) to make them go faster. . . Usage appears to vary from person to person rather than from one region to another. [Nine infs use *go along* in sense (b), six in sense (a), and four in both.] **1949** Kurath *Word Geog.* 66, Calls for Driving Horses. . . On lower Chesapeake Bay and especially in Eastern North Carolina *go along!* and *go on!* are used in this sense [=*get up! come up!*] **1965–66** *DARE* (Qu. K36a, *What do you say to make a horse go faster?*) Inf **MA**5, Go 'long; **MA**58, [gəˈlæːŋ, gəˈlɔːŋ]. **1967** Faries *Word Geog. MO* 95, *Calls for driving horses. . . Go on!* (83 occurrences [out of 700 infs]) and *go along!* (51 occurrences) are current in the western portion of the Northern Plains and in the Southwest Plains.

goal-sticker n, similarly vbl n *goal-sticking* Also *goal-sucker* Also sp *gool-sticker, ~-sticking*

See quots.

1949 in 1986 *DARE* File, *Goal-sucker* . . pronounced *gool* . . a term applied to timid participants in games such as grey wolf and hide-and-seek, who refuse to adventure far from the goal. **1950** *WELS Suppl.* **csWI,** Goolsticker—someone who stays so near to gool while he is "it" that the others have poor chance of coming in free. Those who have already come in taunt him by shouting "Goolsticker, goolsticker, goolsticker!" **1968** *DARE* (Qu. EE13b, *In games in which all the others hide, the one who must try to find them, he's* ______) Inf **NY**98, Goolsticker. **1981** *NADS Letters* **seMI,** The terms 'gool-sticking' or 'sticking on gool' mean 'being allowed to remain on gool rather than having to relinquish it to another player who subsequently arrives (with the first player having to re-enter play).' This term is well established in suburban Detroit, where I grew up, but when I mention it to people from other parts of the country, they don't seem to know it.

goan See **go** v **A4b**

go-and-come n

1952 Brown *NC Folkl.* 1.545, *Go and come, a (great)*. . . Confusion. ["]There was a great go and come over at Harry's house last night."—Central and east.

go-and-fetch-it n

Ready cash.

1898 Westcott *Harum* 226 **NEng,** He liked good things, Andy did, and didn't scrimp himself when they was to be had—that is, when he had the go-and-fetch-it to git 'em with.

goard See **goad**

goardhead See **gourdhead 1**

goardseed corn See **gourdseed corn**

go around v phr

To scold.

1946 *Harder Coll.* **cwTN,** [Letter:] [I] was about to go around you for not writing.

go-around n

1 in phr *give one the go-around:* To avoid someone; to reject, jilt someone.

1965–70 *DARE* (Qu. II5b, *When you don't want to have anything to do with a certain person . . "I'd certainly like to give him the* ______*."*) 20 Infs, **scattered but esp Sth, S Midl,** Go-around; (Qu. AA11, *If a man asks a girl to marry him and she refuses, you'd say she* ______) Infs **KY**85, 89, Gave him the go-around; (Qu. AA12, *If a man loses interest in a girl and stops seeing her, you'd say he* ______) Inf **SC**29, Gave her the go-around.

2 A merry-go-round.

1958 McCulloch *Woods Words* 71 **Pacific NW,** *Go-around*—Short for merry-go-round. **1967–68** *DARE* (Qu. EE32, *A homemade merry-go-round*) Infs **MI**67, **VA**1, Go-around.

3 A state of confusion.

1958 McCulloch *Woods Words* 71 **Pacific NW,** *Go-around* . . a confused situation.

go around one's elbow (or thumb) to get to one's thumb (or elbow) See **elbow, go (all) around one's**

go around the horn See **horn, go around the**

go ashore to windward v phr

1916 Macy–Hussey *Nantucket Scrap Basket* 133 **Cape Cod MA,** "Go Ashore to Windward"—Said of a person who would go wrong with no excuse.

goat n

1 The pronghorn *(Antilocapra americana)* or the mountain goat *(Oreamnos americanus).*

1759 in 1849 Darlington *Mem. John Bartram* 217, I have lately been reading *Hennepin's Travels*. . . He often mentions they were sustained by killing *goats.* **1789** Morse *Amer. Geog.* 490, He had killed 500 goats by running them down. **1805** in 1852 U.S. Congress *Debates & Proc.* 9th Cong 2d Sess 1136, This goat . . may from its swiftness prove to be the antelope, or it possibly may be a goat which has escaped from the Spanish settlements of New Mexico. **1843** (1973) Farnham *Travels Prairies* 28.291, Have you any meat? Come, I've got the shoulder of a goat, (antelope); let us go back to your camp, and cook, and eat, and talk awhile. **1848** (1855) Ruxton *Life Far West* 20, I hobbled the old mule and was approaching some goats, . . 'Hurraw, Dick!' I shouts, 'hyar's brown-skin acomin,' and off I makes for the mule. [Footnote to *goats:*] Antelope are frequently called "goats" by the mountaineers. **1872** Schele de Vere *Americanisms* 371, The *Pronghorn* (Antilocapre [sic] americana) is not a true antelope, because it sheds its horns, and has its name from the fact that each horn has a prong jutting out of it. It is called . . *Goat* by the fur-traders. **c1902** Clapin *New Dict. Amer.* 205, *Goat.* A name applied, among fur-traders, to the prong-horn antelope. **1948** *Hungry Horse News* (Columbia Falls, Mont.) 24 Sep. 7/2 *(DA),* Grizzly season also opens October 1, and goats can be hunted for five days from that date. **1982** Elman *Hunter's Field Guide* 519, Until the spotting scope was focused, they were uncertain whether it was a goat or another white sheep.

2 In railroading: a yard engine; hence n *goat herder;* n *goat feeder;* see quots. [See quot 1940]

1918 *DN* 5.25 **eWA, nID,** *Goat*. . . A switch engine at a roundhouse. **1931** in 1953 Botkin–Harlow *Treas. Railroad Folkl.* 308, [Bill] was a drunken savage foreman on the goat that Time-Check was riding that night. **1940** Cottrell *Railroader* 127, *Goat*—A yard switch engine; it usually butts cars around the yard. **1945** Hubbard *Railroad Ave.* 344, *Goat feeder*—Yard fireman. **1958** McCulloch *Woods Words* 71 **Pacific NW,** *Goat*. . . A switch engine. **1976** Gould *Blackie's RR Hdbk.* 1, *Engineer (yard engine only):* Goatherder.

3 in phrr *come to the goat's house for wool* and var: See quots.

1946 *PADS* 6.38 **eNC,** To come to the goat's house for wool. [*PADS* Ed: To ask a person for something which he would not be expected to have.] **1956** McAtee *Some Dialect NC* 18, Come to the goat's house for wool. **1972** *Atlanta Letters* 17 **GA,** My father had a standard reply when approached for money, 'Now you've come to a goat's house for feathers.'

4 in var combs used as nicknames for towns or parts of towns: See quots. Cf **billy-goat hill**

1965–70 *DARE* (Qu. C35, *Nicknames for the different parts of . . town*) Inf **AL**6, Goat hill; **FL**21, Goat hill—here, a nice section of Apalachicola; **NJ**28, Goat hill is roughly the same place [as gabby row, where people were very close and there was much talking over the fence]; many goats raised here; **KS**19, Goat's gulch—sort of a canyon which ran through a certain part of town . . now called Angora Heights, since it has been developed; (Qu. C34, *Nicknames for nearby settlements, villages, or districts*) Inf **NC**78, Goat town or goat woods [FW: for Buxton, an isolated town of small population]; **NC**81, Goat town; **OH**61, Goatsville; (Qu. II24, . . *Nicknames for the part of a town where the well-off people live*) Inf **OH**65, Goat hill.

goat v, hence vbl n *goating*

See quots.

1933 *AmSp* 8.1.28 **TX,** *Goatin'*. [Of a horse:] Pitching with stiff-legged short jumps. **1936** Adams *Cowboy Lingo* 99, A horse which jumped about with arched back and stiffened knees at a pretense of bucking was said to 'crow-hop.' 'Cat-back' and 'goat' were also terms for half-hearted pitching. **1962** Atwood *Vocab. TX* 56, Only an occasional informant speaks specifically of *goating, crowhopping, sunfishing,* and so on—terms that are probably familiar in rodeo circles.

goatbeard See **goatsbeard**

goatberry n [See quots 1931, 1937] Cf **goat nut**

=jojoba.

1916 *Torreya* 16.238, *Simmondsia californica.*—Goat-berry, Gila Valley, Ariz. **1931** U.S. Dept. Ag. *Misc. Pub.* 101.94, *Jojoba . .*, known by a variety of vernacular names, including . . goat-berry, . . is a bushy-branched and spreading shrub. . . said to be the chief source of feed for wild goats and deer on some of the large islands off the California coast. **1937** U.S. Forest Serv. *Range Plant Hdbk.* B148, Jojoba . . is also locally called . . goatberry, . . alluding to the nutlike fruit.

goatbush n

A densely-branched, spiny shrub *(Castela texana)* of the Southwest. Also called **allthorn 2, amargoso, bisbirinda**

1876 Hobbs *Bot. Hdbk.* 42, Goat bush, Castela Nicolsoni. **1886** Havard *Flora W. & S. TX for 1885* 515, Goat Bush. . . Common on the gravelly bluffs of the lower Rio Grande from Eagle Pass downward. **1903** Small *Flora SE U.S.* 679, *Castela*. . . Low rigid spinescent shrubs, with spreading branches and very bitter bark and wood. . . Goatbush. **1911** *Century Dict. Suppl., Goatbush*. . . A prickly shrub . . growing in the southwestern United States and northern Mexico. **1938** Van Dersal *Native Woody Plants* 85, *Goatbush*. . . Resistant to cattle as a hedge. **1960** Vines *Trees SW* 600, *Castela texana*. . . Vernacular names are Bisbirinda, Amargosa, and Goat-bush.

goat chicory n

A **false dandelion** (here: *Agoseris glauca*).

1963 Craighead *Rocky Mt. Wildflowers* 187, *Agoseris glauca*. . . Goat Chicory. [*Ibid* 189, The plant is moderately grazed by livestock, domestic sheep being especially fond of it.]

goat dandelion n

1 A **dwarf dandelion 1** (here: *Krigia biflora*).

1948 Wherry *Wild Flower Guide* 128, *Goat-dandelion (Krigia biflora)*. . . Plant smooth, grayish green, a foot or so high. Rays bright orange.

2 A **goatsbeard 1.**

1966 *DARE* (Qu. S26d, *Wildflowers that grow in meadows*) Inf **MI**31, Goatsbeard—goat dandelion. **1967** Dodge *Roadside Wildflowers* 100 **SW,** *Goat Dandelion*. The noticeable feature of this common plant is its enormous seed head resembling that of a huge dandelion. . . *Tragopogon dubius.*

3 A **false dandelion** (here: *Pyrrhopappus carolinianus*).

1975 Hamel–Chiltoskey *Cherokee Plants* 31, Dandelion, goat. . . *Pyrrhopappus carolinianus*. . . Drink tea to purify blood.

goat feeder See **goat** n 2

goatfish n

1 Std: a fish of the family Mullidae. For other names of var spp see **kumu, moana, red mullet, weke**

2 **=hake 1a.**

1975 Gould *ME Lingo* 110, *Goatfish*—The hake; from the hake's somewhat goatlike chin whiskers.

goat grass n

An introduced weedy grass of the genus *Aegilops.*

1931 U.S. Dept. Ag. *Yearbook* 277, Goat grass. . . was first reported from the vicinity of Trousdale, Kans., in 1917. . . Its continued spread has forced a recognition of its importance as a weed in wheat fields. **1935** (1943) Muenscher *Weeds* 172, *Aegilops cylindrica*. . . Goat-grass. A winter annual grass introduced from Russia. . . It has recently become troublesome in wheat fields of south central Kansas and adjacent Oklahoma. **1940** Gates *Flora KS* 120, Aegilops cylindrica. . . Goat Grass. Wheat fields and waste places in towns and along railroads. **1950** Gray–Fernald *Manual of Botany* 136, *Aegilops*. . . *Goat-Grass*. . . Becoming a troublesome weed. **1970** U.S. Ag. Research Serv. *Selected Weeds* 32, *Aegilops cylindrica*. . . *Jointed goatgrass*. . . Naturalized from Europe. Throughout approximately the south central and southwestern areas of the United States, east into Illinois and Indiana; distinct areas in Nevada, Washington, Oregon, and New York. **1973** Hitchcock–Cronquist *Flora Pacific NW* 613.

goathead n Also *goat's head* **chiefly SW** See Map

=puncture vine.

1961 Wills–Irwin *Flowers TX* 144, Goat-head. . . Each carpel with 2 stout divergent spines and 2 or more smaller ones. **1966–70** *DARE* (Qu. S15, . . *Weed seeds that cling to clothing*) 27 Infs, 12 **TX,** Goat-head(s); (Qu. S14, *Other prickly seeds . . that cling to clothing*) Infs **OK**18, **TX**5, 35, Goathead(s); **CO**20, Goat's head; (Qu. S21, . . *Other weeds . . that are a trouble in gardens and fields*) Inf **OK**28, Goatheads. **1967** *DARE* Tape **AZ**1, [FW:] Burrs and stickers? [Inf:] Most of 'em is called goatheads. **1970** Correll *Plants TX* 905, *Goat Head.* [*Ibid* 906, The spiny mericarps are a nuisance to both man and beast, injurious to bare feet and automobile tires, and occasionally fatal to stock if eaten.] **1982** *NADS Letters* **neOK,** The plant whose seed pod is . . known as *bullhead* (also *goathead* or *goat's head*) is *Tribulus terrestris,* Calthrop Family. **1983** *DARE* File **nCO,** The scientific name of "goathead" . . is *Tribulus terrestris.*

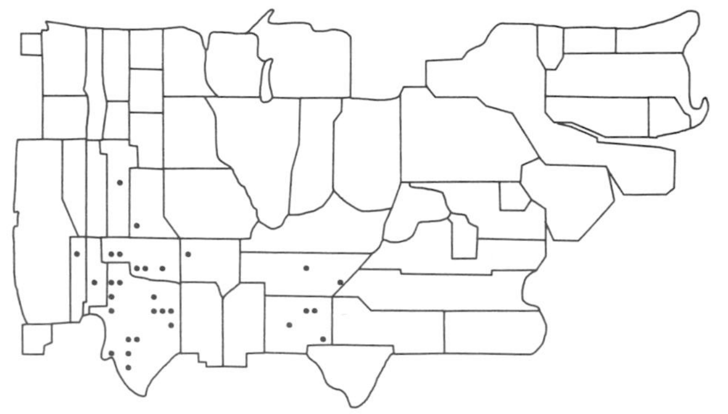

•goathead + var (Qq. S15, S14, S21)

goathead porgy See **goatshead porgy**

goat herder See **goat** n 2

goat house n Cf **courthouse 2,** *DS* M21b

1970 Tarpley *Blinky* 148 **neTX,** *Outdoor toilet*— . . other responses . . goat house.

goating See **goat v**

goat meat n Also *goat mutton euphem*
The flesh of deer killed out of season.
1937 *DN* 6.620 **TX,** Deer meat killed out of season is, euphemistically, *goat meat.* **1953** Randolph–Wilson *Down in Holler* 199 **Ozarks,** Contraband venison is always *goat mutton.*

goat nut n Cf **goatberry**
=jojoba.
1859 in 1863 CA Acad. Sci. *Proc.* 2.21, *Simmondsia pabulosa. . . Goat Nut. . .* An evergreen bush, or shrubby tree. . . The goats and deer . . are exceeding fond of both the fruit and leaves, and seem to live mostly upon them. **1925** Jepson *Manual Plants CA* 607, *Goat-nut. . .* Capsule . . somewhat acorn-like, rather less than 1 in. long. **1941** Jaeger *Wildflowers* 139 **Desert SW,** *Goat-Nut. . .* The oily nuts, which taste much like filberts, were long an important article of food among Indians and Mexicans. **1962** Sweet *Plants of West* 24, *Goat Nut. . .* forms a very good stock feed on heavily grazed lands. **1974** (1977) Coon *Useful Plants* 138, Goat nut. . . At one time, the bitter nuts were prepared as a coffee substitute, while the oil in the nuts has been used in the manufacture of hair oil, or as a substitute for beeswax in various products. **1981** Benson–Darrow *Trees SW Deserts* 118, In California it [=*Simmondsia chinensis*] is known as goat nut. . . The seeds are palatable.

goat prairie n
See quots.
1970 *WI State Jrl.* (Madison) 23 Aug sec I 7/5, Most of our bits of remnant prairie are high lime prairies, often called goat prairies, which were too steep or rocky to exploit profitably. [Private communication from the author: Now current among ecologists, and originated among farmers.] **1972** *DARE* File **swWI,** Goat prairie . . a type of small prairie on southwest slopes of high limestone lands in the driftless area. . . Similar sites in the area [=town of Bangor] are commonly called goat prairies . . so called because difficult to climb to.

goat roper n
See quots.
1983 *DARE* File **ID,** *(Names and nicknames for a rustic or countrified person)* Goat roper. **1989** *Ibid* **neTX,** A common name for rough or redneck types is *goat roper.*

goatsbeard n Also *goatbeard* Cf **false goatsbeard**
1 A plant of the genus *Tragopogon.* [See quot 1840; *OED* 1548 →] Also called **billy-goat beard, oyster plant, salsify, vegetable oyster.** For other names of var spp see **goat dandelion 2, Jerusalem star, morning sun, old man's beard**
1791 in 1793 Amer. Philos. Soc. *Trans.* 3.176/1, Tragopogon porrifolius. Goatsbeard. **1822** Eaton *Botany* 488, *Tragopogon. . . porrifolium* (vegetable oyster, goat-beard, salsify. . .) **1840** MA Zool. & Bot. Surv. *Herb. Plants & Quadrupeds* 120, Goat's Beard. . . is named . . on account of the long, hairy beard of the seeds. **1876** Hobbs *Bot. Hdbk.* 42, Goat's beard, . . Tragopogon porrofolius [sic] and var. *Ibid* 75, Goats' beard, Tragopogon pratensis and species. **1910** Graves *Flowering Plants* 410 **CT,** *Tragopogon. . .* Goat's Beard. . . The root is medicinal. **1931** Fassett *Spring Flora* 158 **WI,** *Goat's Beard. . .* Fields and roadsides, local. **1943** Fernald–Kinsey *Edible Wild Plants E. N. Amer.* 371, *Goat's-beard. . .* Flowers resembling large dandelion-heads, yellow or purple. **1966–68** *DARE* (Qu. S21, . . *Other weeds . . that are a trouble in gardens and fields*) Infs **OH**80, **WI**17, Goatsbeard; (Qu. S26d, *Wildflowers that grow in meadows*) Inf **MI**31, Goatsbeard. **1967** Harrington *Edible Plants Rocky Mts.* 220, *T[ragopogon] pratensis* and *T. dubius,* . . often called . . "goatsbeard," are preferred by some to the purple-flowered one. **1976** Bailey–Bailey *Hortus Third* 1120, Goatsbeard.
2 A plant of the genus *Aruncus.* For other names of var spp see **sea-foam, wild spiraea**
1843 Torrey *Flora NY* 1.199, *Spiraea Aruncus. . . Goat's-beard.* . . Flowers very numerous. . . On the Catskill mountains. **1868** (1870) Gray *Field Botany* 121, *Goatsbeard.* Rich woods from New York S. and W., also in some gardens. **1915** (1926) Armstrong–Thornber *Western Wild Flowers* 226, *Goat's Beard. . .* The minute, cream-white flowers are crowded closely along the many sprays which make up the very loose cluster, . . the effect . . being exceedingly airy and graceful. **1941** Walker *Lookout* 50 **TN,** Goatsbeard adorns the mountainside. **1959** Anderson *Flora AK* 295, Aruncus. . . Goat's Beard. . . Widely distributed. **1964** Campbell *Great Smoky Wildflowers* 58, *Goat's-Beard. . .* occurs at elevations up to 5,500 feet and . . makes an attractive display in May and June. **1968** *DARE* (Qu. S21, . . *Other weeds . . that are a trouble in gardens and fields*) Inf **AK**1, Wild spiraea/goatsbeard; (Qu. S26c, *Wildflowers that grow in woods*) Inf **PA**99, Goatsbeard. **1976** Bailey–Bailey *Hortus Third* 114, *Goatsbeard. . .* Attractive because of the upright panicles of many small flowers.
3 =dwarf dandelion 1.
1900 Lyons *Plant Names* 16, *Adopogon. . .* Dwarf Dandelion, Goat's-beard. **1901** Lounsberry *S. Wild Flowers* 488, *A[dopogon] dandelion,* . . goat'sbeard, produces a solitary flower-head about an inch in breadth. **1906** Rydberg *Flora CO* 404, *Adopogon. . .* Goat's Beard. **1940** Clute *Amer. Plant Names* 70, *K[rigia] amplexicaulis. . .* Virginia goat's-beard. *K[rigia] dandelion. . .* Dwarf goat's-beard. **1949** Moldenke *Amer. Wild Flowers* 178, Another lovely plant which blooms only in the morning is the *Virginia goatsbeard, Cynthia virginica.*
4 A **virgin's bower** (here: *Clematis drummondii*). [See quot 1936] **TX**
1936 Whitehouse *TX Flowers* 28, *Clematis drummondii. . .* The seeds mature in a few weeks, and soon the vine is covered with . . plumes. . . These plumes are elongated, persistent styles and are responsible for many common names given to the vine, including . . goat's beard. **1951** *PADS* 15.31 **TX,** *Clematis drummondii. . .* Goat's beard. **1960** Vines *Trees SW* 266, *Clematis drummondii. . .* Vernacular names for the plant are Texas Virgins-bower, . . Goat Beard.

goatsbeard lichen n
An unidentified lichen.
1939 FWP *Guide MT* 408, The overhanging hemlocks and cedars are festooned with goatsbeard lichen.

goat seed n
Perh a **goat's rue.**
1937 in 1977 *Amer. Slave Suppl. 1* 1.87 **AL,** Iffen dey got sick dey used goat seed.

goatsfoot n
=goutweed.
1859 (1880) Darlington *Amer. Weeds* 151, *AE[gopodium] Podagraria. . .* Goat's foot. Goat weed. Herb Gerarde. . . [It] has made its appearance in some parts of Pennsylvania, and proves to be a nuisance not easily abated. **1861** Wood *Class-Book* 388, *Goats-foot. . .* Strong, tenacious, creeping roots hard to eradicate. **1940** Clute *Amer. Plant Names* 100, *Goutweed. . .* Goat's-foot. **1959** Carleton *Index Herb. Plants* 53, *Goat's foot:* Aegopodium podograria [sic].

goat's hair n [Scots, nEngl dial]
A layer of clouds with a streaky, curly appearance.
1942 Berrey–Van den Bark *Amer. Slang* 70.5, Goat's-hair . . a mass of small hairlike cirrus clouds, said to portend a storm. **1945** Hamann *Air Words* 27, *Goat's hair.* Cirrus cloud. **1968** *DARE* (Qu. B11, . . *Other kinds of clouds that come often around here*) Inf **NH**14, When the sky is all curly and wrinkly, folks say the goat's hair is up.

goat's head See **goathead**

goatshead porgy n Also *goathead porgy, goatshead porgee*
A **porgy** (here: *Stenotomus caprinus*).
1882 U.S. Natl. Museum *Bulletin* 16.929, *A[rgyrops] caprinus. . . Goat's Head Porgee. . .* Profile steep, with a strong depression above eye; the snout rather pointed. **1884** Goode *Fisheries U.S.* 1.393, A species closely related to the Scup is the "Goat's-head Porgy" of the Gulf of Mexico, *Stenotomus caprinus.* **1898** U.S. Natl. Museum *Bulletin* 47.1345, *Otrynter caprinus. . . caprinus,* like a goat, the species having been sent in under the name "goat-head porgy," which was a misunderstanding of the name "jolt-head porgy," which is *Calamus bajonado.*

goat's house for wool, come to the See **goat n 3**

goat, son of a n For varr see quot
1965–70 *DARE* (Qu. NN24, *Humorous substitutes for stronger exclamations: "Why the son of a ______!"*) 9 Infs, **scattered,** Goat; **VA**102, Backwoods goat; **MO**19, Billy goat.

goat's rue n
A plant of the genus *Tephrosia.* Also called **catgut 1, devil's shoestring 1, hoary pea, turkey pea.** For other names of *T. virginiana* see **Dolly Varden 3, rabbit pea, shoestrings, wild sweet pea, wild pea**
1791 in 1793 Amer. Philos. Soc. *Trans.* 3/175/2, Galega virginiana. Goats-rue. **1822** Eaton *Botany* 285, *Galega. . . virginiana . .* Goat's

rue. . . Sandy alluvion. **1843** Torrey *Flora NY* 1.167, *Goat's Rue*. . . Flowers . . about the size of a pea-blossom, dull yellow handsomely tinged with purple. **1869** Porcher *Resources* 218, *Goat's Rue*. . . The roots . . are now employed in popular practice as a vermifuge. **1897** IN Dept. Geol. & Nat. Resources *Rept. for 1896* 646, *C[racca] virginiana*. . . Goat's Rue. . . Sandy hillsides. **1910** Graves *Flowering Plants* 251 **CT,** Goat's Rue. . . The roots are sometimes used medicinally. **1942** *AmSp* 17.134 **PA,** The herb . . goat's rue. . . grows widely in Pennsylvania. **1947** (1964) Randolph *Ozark Superstitions* 194, Some women in Washington county, Arkansas, are loud in praise of Devil's-shoestring as a remedy for menorrhagia . . the name is sometimes applied to goat's rue, a weed which the Choctaw Indians use in poisoning fish. **1968** Pochmann *Triple Ridge* 222 **cWI,** In July *Tephrosia* blooms there; goat's-rue is the unromantic name for this lovely flower of apricot and gold. **1976** Bruce *How to Grow Wildflowers* 284, *Tephrosia virginiana,* because of its enormously long root, is known as Cat-gut and Devil's Shoestring as well as Goat's-rue.

goatweed n

1 **=goutweed.**

1859 [see **goatsfoot**]. **1900** Lyons *Plant Names* 17, *A[egopodium] Podagraria*. . . Goat-weed. **1948** Wherry *Wild Flower Guide* 163, *Goat-weed*. . . Used as an edging in some gardens.

2 Prob **=goat's rue.**

1873 MO State Entomol. *Annual Rept.* 147, The Goat-weed occurs very sparingly in the immediate vicinity of St. Louis, and not till we reach Highland, Illinois, on the Vandalia railroad, is it found in profusion.

3 also *billy-goat weed:* A croton (*Croton* spp). **esp TX**

1913 *Torreya* 13.231, *Croton engelmannii*. . . Goat-weed, . . Marksville, La. **1939** Tharp *Vegetation TX* 60, Goat-weed (*Croton* spp.) . . Present in all regions. **1942** *Torreya* 42.162, *Croton capitatus*. . . Billy-goat weed. **1946** Reeves–Bain *Flora TX* 81, *C[roton] lindheimeri*. . . (Goatweed.) Rather coarse weedy annual. **1967–68** *DARE* (Qu. S21, . . *Other weeds . . that are a trouble in gardens and fields*) Infs **TX**33, 35, 51, Goatweed.

4 Sweet broomwort *(Scoparia dulcis).*

1933 Small *Manual SE Flora* 1187, *S[coparia] dulcis*. . . Goat-weed.

5 A **St. John's wort** (here: *Hypericum perforatum*). **West**

1934 Haskin *Wild Flowers Pacific Coast* 215, All who know the pestiferous goat-weed, . . —a most obnoxious plant from Europe, and now all too common here—will recognize the present form. **1952** Davis *Flora ID* 473, *Goatweed*. . . An introduced weed, hard to eradicate, and reported to be poisonous to stock. **1964** Kingsbury *Poisonous Plants U.S.* 171, Goatweed. . . Aggressive weed in dry ground of roadsides, pastures, and ranges. **1966–67** *DARE* Wildfl QR Pl. 131A Inf **OR**12, St. John's wort—goatweed; **WA**10, St. John's wort—klamath weed or goat weed. Noxious. **1967** *DARE* (Qu. S26e, *Other wildflowers not yet mentioned*) Inf **OR**5, Goatweed. **1974** (1977) Coon *Useful Plants* 148, *Hypericum perforatum* . . goatweed.

6 An **indigo bush** (here: *Dalea frutescens*).

1951 *PADS* 15.35 **TX,** *Dalea frutescens*. . . Goat weed. The way . . goats devour every morsel of this perfect bouquet of pansy purple, the plant will not last long outside of tightly fenced areas.

goatweed butterfly n Also *goatweed emperor* [See quot 1892]

A leafwing butterfly *(Anaea andria).*

1870 MO State Entomol. *Annual Rept.* 125, The Goat-weed Butterfly —*Paphia glycerium.* **1892** IN Dept. Geol. & Nat. Resources *Rept. for 1891* 389, The Goat Weed Butterfly. . . The larvae feed upon species of Croton. **1902** Holland *Butterfly Book* 192, The Goatweed Butterfly. . . The insect ranges from Illinois and Nebraska to Texas. **1911** *Century Dict. Suppl., Emperor*. . . *Goatweed emperor,* a nymphalid butterfly, *Anaea andria,* whose larva feeds on the goatweed: found in the western United States from Illinois to Texas. **1981** Pyle *Audubon Field Guide Butterflies* 652, *Goatweed Butterfly*. . . Habitat: Farmyards, canals, country roads, fallow fields, swamps, pine barrens, wood edges, and prairie groves.

goat whisker n

Prob a goatee.

1962 Faulkner *Reivers* 173 **MS,** You got too much name, . . You want something quick and simple to answer to around here until you can raise a white mush-tash and goat whisker like old Possum there, and earn it.

goat with v phr [Perh var of *court*]

c1950 *McDavid Coll.* **cwNY,** *Goating with:* courting. Inf a farmer's wife, about 70 years old. The term is local and is *not* an error for *going with:* the Inf said *going with* was a newer term.

go-away sign See **go-sign**

gob n[1] Also *gaub;* rarely *garb* [*OED* 1382 →]

1a A lump or mass, often of some sticky matter.

1823 in 1913 *DN* 4.47, *Yankee dialect*. . . *gob* . . Bulk. A large body. **1840** (1847) Longstreet *GA Scenes* 56, Who do you call an impudent huzzy, you nasty, good-for-nothing, snaggle-toothed gaub of fat, you? **1892** *KS Univ. Qrly.* 1.96 **KS,** *Gob,* or *gaub;* a shapeless mass, as, a gob of mud, then sportively, gaubs of wisdom. **1894** *DN* 1.341 **wCT,** *Gob:* a small quantity of any matter in a plastic state; *e.g.* a gob of mud. **1899** [see **1b** below]. **1908** *DN* 3.314 **eAL, wGA,** *Gaub* [gɔb]. **1912** *DN* 3.567 **cNY,** *Gob*. . . Small piece of anything; often something in a plastic state. **1940** Mencken *Happy Days* 158 **MD,** "The Moose Hunters" . . was not printed in one gob, but spread through *Chatterbox* in installments. **1956** McAtee *Some Dialect NC* 18. **c1960** *Wilson Coll.* **csKY,** *Gob*. . . A small quantity of something in a plastic state, like a gob of mud. **1965–70** *DARE* (Qu. LL4, *Very large: "He took a ——— . . of potatoes."*) 19 Infs, **scattered exc NEast,** (Big *or* great) gob; (Qu. X50, . . *A person who is very fat*) Infs **AL**3, **KY**65, **MS**1, **NC**55, **SC**34, Gob of fat (*or* lard); **GA**1, 43, Big gob (of fat); (Qu. LL6b, . . *"I'll put in just a ——— of butter."*) Infs **CA**208, **NY**205, **OK**48, (Small) gob; (Qu. NN29a, . . *"Great ———!"*) Infs **IN**42, **KY**70, Gobs of goose grease; **IL**45, Big gobs of greasy grimy gopher guts; **IL**119, Gobs; **WA**22, Gobs of goodness; **OR**3, Gobs of shit; **TX**70, Gobs of turkey feathers. **1985** Keillor *Lake Wobegon* 172 **MN,** Of all the people you'd want to see touch a giant gob, Darla was No. 1. She yanked her hand back just as Brian said, "Snot on you!" but she already knew.

b Esp: a mouthful; a swallow of food or drink.

1899 (1912) Green *VA Folk-Speech* 199, *Gob*. . . A mouthfull. **1965–70** *DARE* (Qu. DD2, *The portion . . of tobacco chewed at one time*) 13 Infs, **scattered exc Sth,** Gob; (Qu. DD18, *A drink of liquor, or the amount of liquor taken in one swallow*) Inf **MO**32, Gob; (Qu. DD20, *A big drink;* total Infs questioned, 75) Inf **OK**1, Quite a gob of it.

2 usu pl: A large amount; a great number. **widespread, but less freq NEast** See Map

1851 Hooper *Widow Rugby's Husband* 153 *(DA)* **AL,** If he . . is a judge of talent, Smith has got it, and that in great gobs! **1859** Taliaferro *Fisher's R.* 41 **nwNC** (as of 1820s), A heap uv groanin', gobs uv shoutin' and cryin', goes a grate ways toads settin' off a meetin'. **1871** Eggleston *Hoosier Schoolmaster* 29 **sIN,** He's wuth lots and gobs of money. **1887** *Harper's New Mth. Mag.* Dec 35/1 **VA,** It mought be well tuh do lots and gobs of things I ain' never tried. **1892** [see **1a** above]. **1894** *Century Illustr. Mag.* 48.872/1 **IN,** The poor-white's phrase for a great quantity is sometimes "gobs," sometimes "lots and gobs," or rather "lots and *gaubs,*" with a long hold on the last note. He also says "the whole gob" for all of anything. **1902** *Emporia Gazette* 29 July *(DAE),* There is nothing but harmony, great gobs of sticky harmony, between the *Gazette* and the *Journal.* **1905** *DN* 3.61 **NE,** *Gobs*. . . Large quantities. Always used in plural. "She has gobs of dough." **c1960** *Wilson Coll.* **csKY,** Gobs. . . Lots of, like money. **1965–70** *DARE* (Qu. U38a, . . *"He's got ———[of money]."*) 110 Infs, **widespread exc NEast,** Gobs; **MS**1, Gob; **IN**15, Oodles and gobs; (Qu. LL8a, . . *"He's got ——— of time."*) 78 Infs, **scattered,** Gobs; **AZ**1, Gobs and gobs, **IN**15, Oodles and gobs; (Qu. LL9a, . . *"We've got ——— of apples."*) 57 Infs, **scattered exc NEast,** Gobs; **WI**66, Heaps and gobs; **MO**21, Oodles and gobs; **CA**208, Whole durn gob; (Qu. LL8b, . . *"She has a whole ——— of cousins."*) 11 Infs, **chiefly middle Missip Valley,** Gob; **KY**23, Garb; (Qu. U37, . . *Somebody who has plenty of money*) Inf **MI**68, Got gobs; (Qu.

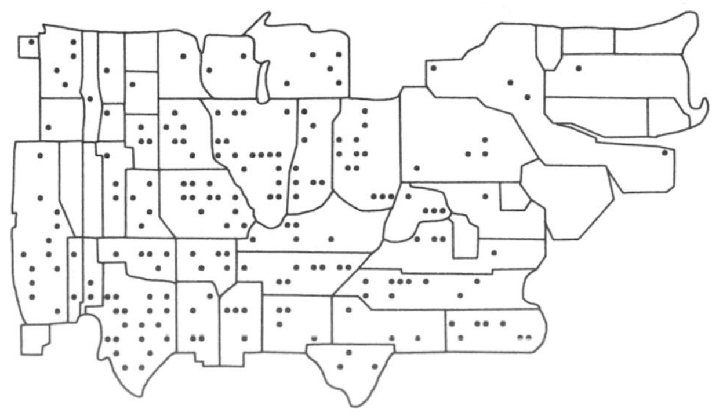

•gob n[1] 2 + varr (Qq. U38a, LL8a, LL9a, LL8b, U38b, U37, BB18, FF26, LL9b, LL10)

U38b, . . *"He made a ______ [of money].")* Infs **AL**2, **CO**20, 46, **IL**5, **IN**49, **KS**16, **TN**52, **TX**54, Gob; (Qu. BB18, *To vomit a great deal*) Inf **WY**2, Vomit gobs; (Qu. FF26, . . *"There was quite a ______ at the auction.")* Inf **TN**12, Gob of people; (Qu. LL9b, . . *All you need or more*) Infs **MO**9, **OK**18, **TX**10, Gobs; (Qu. LL10, . . *"They made too much noise, so he sent the whole ______ home.")* Inf **MO**30, Gob; **IL**135, Gob lot.

gob n² [*OED* a1550 →; prob ult of Gael orig]

The mouth; the face.

1893 *KS Univ. Qrly.* 1.139 **KS,** *Gob:* mouth, 'Hit him on the gob.' **1912** *DN* 3.567 **cNY,** *Gob*. . . Mouth. "Open your gob." **1967** Cerello *Dakota Co. MN* 61, He had a gob full of feed and nevertheless he kept right on talking. . . He always has his big gob going, chewing snuff or tobacco. . . He's got a big red Irish gob full of freckles. **1974** *ME Sunday Telegram* (Portland) 21 July sec D 2/4 **Brooklyn NYC,** *Gob*—Mouth, as in "shut your gob."

gob n³ Also attrib [*OED* 1839 →]

In mining (esp coal mining): waste rock; an abandoned part of a mine, often filled with waste.

1939 FWP *Guide IL* 431, Piled near each [coal] mine is the refuse of the process, the gob pile, which, frequently set ablaze by spontaneous combustion, lights the near landscape with a weird flicker. **1945** *CA Folkl. Qrly.* 4.320 **CO** [Mining terms], *Gunny or old gob:* Disused workings, open stope. . . One Cousin Jack told me he had heard "old gob" used in Arizona almost exclusively but did not know if it originated there. **1947** Natl. Coal Assoc. *Gloss.* 11, *Gob*—Waste material; a place where the waste material is stored; the worked out portions of the mine, sometimes partially filled with such material. *Ibid, Gob fire*—Spontaneous combustion of fine coal and slack in the gob. *Ibid, Gob pile*—An accumulation of waste material such as rock or bone. **1958** *Post* (Pittsburgh PA) 19 Nov 9 *(Hench Coll.),* Theodore A. Gall . . said a smouldering mine gob pile adjacent to his property is making it uninhabitable. **1973** *PADS* 59.37 [Bituminous coal mining vocab], *Gob* . . waste material, usually not including large rock, which may be left in the *mine* in piles, inside a *gob entry*. *Ibid, Gob entry* . . a short, dead-end, passage *driven* into a *pillar* or into a rock side for the disposal of *gob*. *Ibid, Gob wall* . . a wall of stone or other *stopping* material constructed alongside the *rib* behind which *gob* is disposed of. **1980** Banks *First-Person America* 84 **IL** (as of 1939), Some of the waste material is thrown into the places just mined out, and this part of the mine is known as the "gob."

gob v [Prob *gab* v infl by **gob** n²; cf *OED gob* v.² "dial. . . To prate, brag"]

?To chatter or nag.

1954 *Harder Coll.* **cwTN,** *Gob:* gab—"quitchie [=quit your] gobbin'."

go back v phr Cf **go-back** adj **1**

To revert to the wild state, deteriorate; also fig.

1947 Jones *Evergreen Land* 75 **WA,** About half the orchards had "gone back," as they say, and no new ones were being set in. **1965–70** *DARE* (Qu. KK64, . . *The part of a city that was once very fine, but isn't anymore*) Infs **ME**5, **PA**71, Going back; **CT**4, Gone back. **1968** *DARE* Tape **NJ**47, [The peach trees] were going back, they weren't producing well . . They were dying out.

go-back adj

1 also used absol: Having reverted to the wild state; growing wild on land once cultivated. Cf **go back** v phr

1904 *NY Post* (NY) 30 July 3/1, Vagrant grass, called by the natives [in the West] 'go-back,' because it has gone back from the breaking-up process that was given by the settlers years ago. **1914** *DN* 4.107 **KS,** *Goback land*. . . Land once cultivated but long since neglected. "The grass is generally ranker on goback land than on prairie sod." **1950** Reeves *Man from SD* 217, All told we've broken a hundred and fifty acres of go-back sod for flax. **1967** *DARE* (Qu. C28) Inf **CO**18, Go-back ground; let to go back to weeds.

2 in comb *go-back road;* In logging: a return road for empty sleds or other conveyances. Cf *gig(ging) trail* (at **gig** v¹ **2**)

1905 U.S. Forest Serv. *Bulletin* 61.38 [Logging terms], *Go-back road.* A road upon which logging sleds can return to the skidways for reloading, without meeting the loaded sleds en route to the landing. (N[orthern] F[orest]). **1914** *DN* 4.73 **ME, nNH,** *Go-back road*. . . Road to lumber-camp; "turn-out." **1942** ME Univ. *Studies* 57.39, At a large camp . . it is necessary to have a second road available upon which the empty sleds may return to the camps and woods. This is known as a "go-back" road. . . It is cheaper to construct a second road of low quality than to . . maintain the number of turn-outs required [on a single road]. **1958** McCulloch *Woods Words* 71 **Pacific NW,** *Go-back road*—The other end of a come-back road; the road that empties take when going back to the woods from the log dump; or that cats take when going out to yard in more logs to the landing.

go back on v phr

Of food: to disagree with (one).

1942 McAtee *Dial. Grant Co. IN* 29 (as of 1890s), *Go back on* . . fail to agree with; a food one formerly could, but no longer can, tolerate was said to have gone back on him. **1956** McAtee *Some Dialect NC* 19. **c1960** *Wilson Coll.* **csKY,** *Go back on*. . . Disagree with, as food.

go-back road See **go-back** adj **2**

go-backs n pl

A condition in children, characterized by failure to gain weight.

1863 *Young Parson* 154 *(DA),* [The child] only had the op-nemma, that's the gobacks. **1892** *Jrl. Amer. Folkl.* 5.107, Go-backs . . a disease of babies in Virginia. If the baby does not make an acceptable gain in height and weight, it may have the go-backs. The cure is obtained by hanging the string with which the measuring was done on the hinge of the gate, and as the string by gradual decay passes away, so passes away the go-backs. **1897** *Jrl. Amer. Folkl.* 10.79 **PA,** Go-backs . . child's consumption.

gobbed up ppl adj phr Cf **gob** n¹ **1a**

1966–69 *DARE* (Qu. Y39, . . *"The children have been eating candy and they've got their faces all ______.")* Infs **NE**11, **NY**23, 166, Gobbed up.

gobbin v Also *gubbin* [Cf *OED gobbon* v "Obs. . . To cut into gobbets" and Engl dial *gubbins* fragments]

1975 Gould *ME Lingo* 110, Mainers . . have also developed "gobbin" and "gubbin"; to break off into chunks *(junks)* or *gobbets.*

gobble v¹ Also with *on to* [By analogy with **glom** v¹ **2,** *latch,* and similar words]

To grab, seize.

1849 in 1856 Hall *College Words* 228 **CT,** *Gobble*. . . To seize; to lay hold of; to appropriate. . . Alas! how dearly for the fun they paid,/ Whom the Proffs *gobbled,* and the Tutors too. **1966** *DARE* (Qu. V5b, . . *"Before anybody else gets it, I'm going to ______ this.")* Inf **WA**4, Gobble on to it; (Qu. V5a) Inf **WA**4, Gobbling on to.

gobble v² Also with *together, up* [Prob *EDD gobble* v. 3 "To do anything in a hasty or superficial manner"; appar var of *cobble*]

To mend or patch hastily.

1950 *WELS (When a woman wants to sew up a torn place quickly)* 1 Inf, **cwWI,** Gobble up the hole. **1965–70** *DARE* (Qu. W28, . . *To sew up a torn place quickly*) Inf **OH**29, Gobble it; **MA**98, Gobble it up; **RI**1, Gobble it up for now; (Qu. KK63, *To do a clumsy or hurried job of repairing something*) Inf **MO**15, Gobbled it together; **RI**1, Gobbled it up.

gobble v³ Cf **gobbed up**

1913 *DN* 4.42, *Gobble*. . . To collect in 'gobs.' "Stir up the cream or it will get gobbled all over the pitcher."

gobble n

=**gob** n¹ **2.**

1970 *DARE* (Qu. LL9a, . . *"We've got ______ of apples.")* Inf **VA**39, Gobbles.

gobble flies v phr Cf **catch flies**

1967 *DARE* (Qu. X22, *To stare at something with your mouth open*) Inf NY24, Gobble flies; (Qu. X46, *When a person's getting sleepy and opens his mouth wide and takes a deep breath*) Inf **NY**24, Gobble flies.

gobble on to See **gobble** v¹

gobbler n [Perh by assoc with *goblin*] Cf **turkey goblin**

1968 *DARE* (Qu. EE41, *A hobgoblin that is used to threaten children*) Inf **MD**25, Gobbler; **VT**5, Watch out for the gobblers.

gobble ratchet See **gabble racket**

gobbler's knob n Also *gobbler hill*

Used as a nickname for an out-of-the-way place.

1935 *AmSp* 10.80 **MO,** With its hills, hollows, and swamps, southeast Missouri is well adapted to propagation of the *Podunk* idea. . . Emerging from Nigger-Wool Swamp, one is likely to find himself in the vicinity of Gobbler's Knob. **1968–69** *DARE* (Qu. C34, *Nicknames for nearby settlements, villages, or districts*) Inf **MD**32, Gobbler Hill . . [a] hill where turkeys were once kept in [the] nearby village of Cherry Hill; **PA**205, Gobbler's Knob; (Qu. C33, *What joking names do you have for an out-of-the-way place, or a very unimportant place?*) Inf **OH**79, Gobbler's Knob; (Qu. C35, *Nicknames for the different parts of your town or city*) Inf **NY**92, Gobbler's Knob.

gobble together, gobble up See **gobble** v²

gobboon See **goboon**

gobby n See **gorby**

gobby adj [**gob** n¹ **1a**]
Fat, lumpy; sticky.
1949 *PADS* 11.21 **CO,** *Gobby*. . . Too fat and lumpy in the hindquarters. Used to describe steers and people. **c1960** *Wilson Coll.* **csKY,** *Gobby* . . too fat. **1966–69** *DARE* (Qu. X50, *Names or nicknames for a person who is very fat*) Infs **GA**7, **MO**15, Gobby; **AR**18, Gobby fat. **1974** Peden *Speak to Earth* 21 **cIN,** I remember the vinegar bee. . . It was kind of yeasty stuff; particles of it would go up and down and some settled on the bottom of the jar. . . It was kind of gobby-lookin' stuff.

go-behind n
1969 *DARE* (Qu. Y9, *Somebody who always follows along behind others: "His little brother is an awful ________.")* Inf **IL**48, Go-behind.

gobernadora n [MexSpan]
=**creosote bush.**
1897 Parsons *Wild Flowers CA* 191, *Creosote-Bush. Gobernadora.* . . The most plentiful shrub growing in our southern desert region. **1920** Saunders *Useful Wild Plants* 202, Two other western plants are valuable . . for the healing of . . the saddle gall. One is an ill-smelling shrub . . variously called Creosote-bush, Greasewood . . and . . Gobernadora. **1945** Benson–Darrow *Manual SW Trees 208, Creosote bush. . . is called also gobernadora.* **1960** Vines *Trees SW* 574, Gobernadora. . . is poisonous to sheep, is not eaten by cattle, but is consumed by various small mammals and antelope. **1981** Benson–Darrow *Trees SW Deserts* 123.

gobersloptious See **galluptious**

go-billy n Cf **go-cart, go-devil** n **2**
1914 *DN* 4.73 **ME, nNH,** *Go-billy*. . . Any kind of wheeled vehicle.

goblin n¹
A freshwater **sculpin** of the genus *Cottus.*
1884 Goode *Fisheries U.S.* 1.259, In the lakes and streams of the Northern States are numberous species of *Uranidea* and allied genera, . . called "Bull-heads," "Goblins," "Blobs," and "Muffle-jaws."

goblin n² [Perh infl by *gobbling*]
1966–68 *DARE* (Qu. K75, *A male turkey*) Infs **IA**22, **WA**3, Goblin.

gobly-gossit n [Imit]
=**black-crowned night heron.**
1955 MA Audubon Soc. *Bulletin* 39.312, *Black-crowned night heron*. . . Gobly-gossit (Mass. Said to be from the notes, thus possibly from the collective clamor of a heronry.)

gob meat n [Perh **gob** n¹ **1a**] Cf **gobby** adj
1947 *McDavid Coll.* **cnFL,** *Gob meat*—fatback.

goboon n Usu |gɑ'bun| or |'gɑbun|; also |gar'bun|; for addit varr see quots Also *goboon can* Also sp *gabboon, gaboon, garboon, gobboon* [Blend of **gob** n¹ **1b** + *spittoon*] **chiefly Nth, West** *old-fash*
A cuspidor.
1930s in 1944 *ADD* 257 **NY,** [gɑ'bun], [gəbun]. A city w[or]d. **1942** *Sun* (Baltimore MD) 25 June 2/4 *(Hench Coll.),* If members cannot learn to expectorate straight enough without a rubber mat under the 'gaboon,' then we ought to get a bigger bucket for them. **1942** *Sat. Eve. Post* 17 Jan 27/3 **NC,** A brass gaboon is just inside the entrance to his suite, an invitation to visitors to dunk the glow before entering the presence. **1944** in 1975 White *Git Along* 112 **West,** The ugly baboon is a half-breed loon. . . / He makes his biscuits in a goboon. [*DARE* Ed: var stanza of "The Big Corral," a song by Romaine Lowdermilk]. **1949** Algren *Man with Golden Arm* 44 **Chicago IL,** For Antek held to . . the old ways. . . There was plenty of butchershop sawdust along the floor and an old-fashioned golden goboon for every four bar stools. **1958** McCulloch *Woods Words* 71 **Pacific NW,** *Gobboon*—Some early day bunkhouses were fancy enough to have spittoons, called gobboons. **1965–70** *DARE* (Qu. DD5), 34 Infs, **chiefly Nth, West,** Goboon; **IL**71, **MN**8, **WI**19, [gɑ'bun]; **IL**81, **MA**72, **WI**48, ['gɑbun]; **MA**62, [gɑ'bun]; **NM**11, [gɒ'bun], [gɔ'bun]; **MI**65, [gæ'bun], ['gæbun]; **IL**135, Goboon can; **CA**15, **MA**58, **MI**44, **PA**74, 134, 165, **WI**48, 51, Garboon [usu [gɑr'bun]]. [Of all Infs responding to the question, 65% were old; of those giving these responses, 76% were old.] **1969** Sorden *Lumberjack Lingo* 46 **NEng, Gt Lakes,** *Gabboon*—Spittoon or cuspidor. Found only in better bunkhouses.

gobsloptious See **galluptious**

go by v phr
1 also in phr *go by and stop:* To stop at, to visit. **Sth** Cf **by** prep **1, come by 2**
1816 Pickering *Vocab.* 98 **NC,** Mr. B. asked me to stop and dine with him *when I was passing his house,* by saying, 'Will you *go by* and dine with me.' When I mentioned this singular expression to some gentlemen afterwards, I was told it was often used. Its origin is very natural. When a gentleman is about riding a great distance through that country, where there are few great roads, and the houses or plantations are often two or three miles from them, a friend, living near his route, asks him to *go by* his plantation, and dine or lodge with him. But in a town, or when one is passing before the door, the expression is peculiar. **1827** (1939) Sherwood *Gaz. GA* 139, *Go by,* for call, or stop at. **1886** Amer. Philol. Assoc. *Trans.* 17.46 **Sth,** List of common Southern expressions—many of them vulgarisms—that have not, so far as I know, either old English or provincial English authority. . . *To go by* ("Won't you *go by* and stop"). **1899** (1912) Green *VA Folk-Speech* 198, *Go*. . . Go by: to leave the public road and take road by the owner's house. To call; to stop at. "Will you go by and get dinner with me." **1914** *DN* 4.159 **VA,** *Go by* . . = *come by:*—used only in future tense: "Won't yō go by?" **1976** Ryland *Richmond Co. VA* 371, *Go by*—visit; "Go by the house before you leave." **1984** Wilder *You All Spoken Here* 106 **Sth,** *Go by:* Stop by, as "Let's go by my place and have a drink."
2 To pass the prime; to become exhausted, spoiled, obsolete; hence ppl adj *gone by,* rarely *gone by with.* **NEng**
1902 (1904) Rowe *Maid of Bar Harbor* 238 **ME,** Them old duds! Why, nobody goes to see them now. They're all gone by. **1926** *DN* 5.387 **ME,** *Gone by*. . . Spoiled by decay. "The bananas are gone by," "The corn is gone by" (meaning it is past its season). Common. **1931–33** *LANE Worksheets* 1 inf, **ceVT,** *Going by*. . . All used up—no good any longer. "I'm going by." Used only with first person. **1951** Graham *My Window* 203 **ME,** They [=lilies of the valley] are going by a little. I don't think they'll keep long. **1959** *VT Hist.* new ser 27.138 **VT,** *Gone by with*. . . Over with; finished. Occasional. **1965–70** *DARE* (Qu. I8, *When root vegetables get old and tough*) 11 Infs, **NEng,** Gone by [10 of 11 Infs old]; (Qu. H46, *When meat begins to go bad . . you say it's ________*) Inf **ME**7, Gone by; (Qu. KK20a, *Something that looks as if it might collapse any minute*) Inf **ME**5, Gone by; (Qu. KK20b) Inf **MA**68, Gone by; (Qu. KK64, . . *The neighborhood is sort of ________*) Inf **MA**24, Gone by. **1988** *DARE* File **nwMA,** "This flower is going by" means the flower is withering, dying. I would also use this of vegetables that have gone bad.

go-by n *somewhat old-fash*
Avoidance, disregard—usu in phrr *give one* (or *get*) *the go-by.*
1855 Douglass *My Bondage* 248 **MD,** I judge from these circumstances, that Covey deemed it best to give me the go-by. **1887** (1967) Harris *Free Joe* 192 **GA,** Trouble hits some folks and glances off, and it hits some and thar it sticks. I tell you what, them that it gives the go-by ought to be monst'ous proud. **1899** (1912) Green *VA Folk-Speech* 199, *Go-by*. . . A passing without notice; an intentional disregard, evasion, or avoidance, in the phrase, *to give,* or *get the go by.* **1899** (1977) Norris *McTeague* 81 **San Francisco CA,** Now that he's rich and prosperous, . . he gives me the go-by; he's played me for a sucker. **1907** *DN* 3.212 **nwAR, cCT,** *Give one the go by*. . . To leave one in the lurch. **1908** *DN* 3.315 **eAL, wGA,** *Go-by*. . . A cut dir[e]ct. Often used in the phrase 'to give one the go-by,' i.e., 'to neglect, leave out of consideration.' **1937** Sandoz *Slogum* 291 **NE,** She was always back by dark, and married men got the go-by in a minute. **1956** McAtee *Some Dialect NC* 19. **1965–70** *DARE* (Qu. II5b, *When you don't want to have anything to do with a certain person because you don't like him, you might say, "I'd certainly like to give him the ________.")* 98 Infs, **scattered,** Go-by. [Of all Infs responding to the question, 64% were old; of those giving this response, 88% were old.]

go by and stop See **go by** v phr **1**

go by water v phr
To be a sailor.

1894 *DN* 1.331 **NJ,** *Go by water:* to follow the sea as a calling. (Coast.) **1899** (1912) Green *VA Folk-Speech* 198, A waterman is spoken of as one "who goes by water."

go-cart n

1 A child's walker; also fig.

1821 Weems *Letters* III.324 *(DAE),* You will help many a poor child by putting these little moral *'go-carts'* in his hands. **1876** Emerson *Letters & Social Aims* 3, The perception of matter is made the common-sense, and far cause. This was the cradle, this the go-cart, of the human child. **a1885** in 1934 Frear *Lowell & Abigail* 7 **MA,** My first recollection of you is you were standng in your "go cart" by the side of a chair on which you were playing. **1899** (1912) Green *VA Folk-Speech* 199, *Go-cart.* . . A small framework with casters or rollers, and without a bottom, in which children are taught to walk without danger of falling.

2 A handcart or pushcart.

a1870 Chipman *Notes on Bartlett* 171 *(DAE), Go-cart,* a hand-cart.—Essex Co. M[as]s. **1889** (1971) Farmer *Americanisms* 270, *Go-cart.* . . A hand-cart. **1929** (1954) Faulkner *Sound & Fury* 260 **MS,** "What do you want me to do," I says, "Buy an apron and a go-cart?" **1949** *PADS* 11.21 **CO,** Go-cart . . A small cart made with two wheels connected by an axle. Simpler and smaller than a go-devil . . usually used for carrying just a bit of grain.

3 A light, open, horse-drawn carriage.

1834 Simms *Guy Rivers* 2.309, Then came the compact, boxy, buggy, buttoned-up vehicle . . for which the unfertile character of our language, as yet, has failed to provide a fitting name—but which the backwoodsman of the west calls a go-cart. **1869** Twain *Innocents* 318, A rickety little go-cart hauled by a donkey not much bigger than a cat. **1966–67** *DARE* (Qu. N41a, *What kinds of horse-drawn vehicles are used around here, or used to be, to carry people?*) Inf **FL**6, Go-cart . . [one] seat, two wheels [Inf old]; (Qu. N41c, *Horse-drawn vehicles to carry light loads*) Inf **TN**1, Go-cart . . used by mail-carriers before cars [Inf old].

4 A stroller or baby buggy. *somewhat old-fash*

1902 Sears *Catalogue* 804, [Advt:] The body of this Go-Cart is made of the best quality of reeds. . . Closely woven cane seat, handsomely ornamented dash. . . This is one of the latest designs for 1902, and is a very handsome cart. **1960** *PADS* 34.50 **CO,** Go-cart 'baby buggy.' **1965–70** *DARE* (Qu. N43, *Vehicles for a small child—the kind it has to sit up in*) 211 Infs, **widespread,** Go-cart [Of all Infs responding to the question, 65% were old; of those giving this response, 89% were old.]; **SC**7, Baby go-cart; (Qu. N42, *Vehicles for a baby or small child—the kind it can lie down in*) 12 Infs, **chiefly PA, cIN,** Go-cart [8 of 12 Infs old]. **1970** Tarpley *Blinky* 107 **neTX,** A few informants above 60 call it [=vehicle used to push baby in] a go-cart. **1973** Allen *LAUM* 1.342 **NE, ND** (as of c1950), Go-cart. [2 infs.] **1983** *MJLF* 9.1.41 **ceKY,** *Go cart* . . a baby carriage in which the baby sits up.

5 A caboose.

1945 in 1953 Botkin–Harlow *Treas. Railroad Folkl.* 344, It is a caboose . . go-cart.

God n[1] Usu |gɑd|; also freq, esp in serious contexts |gɔd| Pronc-spp *Gawd, Gord;* for addit proncs and pronc-spp see quots

Std sense, var forms.

1853 Simms *Sword & Distaff* 139 **SC,** Gorrah Mighty bress you! How you do? **1887** Page *In Ole VA* 187 **eVA** [Black], He had not "teched a drap in Gord knows how long". **1891** *DN* 1.142 **cNY,** In 'God' [ɔ] is the reverential form, but [ɑ] occurs in oaths. **1893** Shands *MS Speech* 32, *Gawd* [gɔd]. Negro and illiterate white for *God.* **1901** *Century Illustr. Mag.* 62.906/2 **AR,** All ole Shed got am right here—de grabe uv he Ole Marster, Gord res' him! **1903** *DN* 2.292 **Cape Cod,** Before final [d] . . *o* was long [ɔ] in . . God. **1917** *DN* 4.393 **neOH,** I remember as a child that a connotation of reverence attacht to the pronunciation [gɔd], while [gɑd] suggested irreverence. **1922** Gonzales *Black Border* 263 [Gullah], Den, I gwine dey sho' ez Gawd lemme go. **1943** *LANE* Map 527, [Through New England proncs of the type [gɔd, gɒd] are most common. In serious use proncs of the type [gɑd] are also common in eastern New England; in oaths and exclamations this type is somewhat more widespread. Some infs who use the first type in serious contexts use the second in oaths and exclamations; the opposite distribution is very rare. Some rare types are [goəd, gʌd, gʊd, gæd].] **c1960** *Wilson Coll.* **csKY,** God is now always [gɑd]; some older people remember still older people's saying [gɔd]. **1967–69** *DARE* (Qu. NN27a, *Weakened substitutes for 'god': "My ______!"*) Infs **OH**18, **PA**66, Gawd; **IN**68, [gɑrd].

God adv Cf **God's, gracious**

Very—used as an intensifier.

1940 (1941) Bell *Swamp Water* 16 **Okefenokee GA,** "I bet he's been in that Okefenokee Swamp," Silas said slowly, accusingly. "He shore has," Bud Dorson agreed, "He God shore has." *Ibid* 40, I can still see that other fellow . . see him like it was last night, and he God shore needed killing.

go'd n[2] See **gourd**

God-a-massy intj [*OED God-a-mercy* a1440 →; "Obs."]

1952 Brown *NC Folkl.* 1.546, *God-a-massy* [ˌgɑd-ə-ˈmæsɪ]. . . A mild oath.

godaphro n

Among loggers: an imaginary monster.

1939 Tryon *Fearsome Critters* 39, *The Side-Hill Gouger.* . . there are some vigorous proponents of [the name] "Godaphro." . . Always a dweller in hilly country. He has to be, since his nigh legs are shorter than the off pair. . . Gougers must obviously travel counter-clockwise around the hillside, and in making their daily rounds for food they wear the characteristic, partly gouged-out paths so familiar to woodsmen.

goddam n [See quot 1945]

=ruddy duck.

1897 *Auk* 14.286 **LA,** *Ruddy Duck.*—The only name I have heard applied to this duck is God Damn, on account of its worthlessness. **1911** *Forest & Stream* 77.173 **LA,** *Erismatura jamaicensis.* . . God-Damn. **1916** *Times-Picayune* (New Orleans LA) 26 Mar mag sec 2, *Ruddy Duck.* . . God-damn. **1945** McAtee *Nomina Abitera* 32, Ruddy Duck. . . Goddam, Louisiana, Texas (various explanations of this term have been offered, of which the best seems to be that (of S. C. Arthur, Birds of Louisiana, 1931) to the effect that the ruddy in its brick-red summer plumage brought to mind the red coats of the British soldiers who were named "goddems" or "goddams," from their favorite expletive, which cognomen was passed on to this spruce, red-coated duck. . .)

go dead v phr

Of a person or animal: to die.

1896 *DN* 1.417 **NY,** *Go dead.* . . "Gone dead lately," recently deceased. **1907** *German Amer. Annals* 9.377 **sePA,** *Go dead.* . . Die. (Used of persons and animals.) "His horse went dead last night." **1909** *DN* 3.397 **nwAR,** *Go dead.* . . To die. "Her old man went dead on her and she had to take in washing." **1935** *AmSp* 10.167 **sePA,** He went dead (he died).

go-devil n

1 An evil spirit or a person made up to look like one.

1835 *Knickerbocker* April 273, [The figures drawn on the slate] would be led on by what they call in school-sports a go-devil, prancing about in high horns, and a spear on the end of his tail. **1950** *PADS* 14.32 **SC,** *Go-devil.* . . An evil spirit, supposed to roam the woods at night, uttering weird cries.

2 Any of various vehicles or farm implements on runners or wheels, as:

a A cultivator, esp one on runners; hence v *go-devil,* see quot 1945.

1852 Fleischmann *Wegweiser* 173 *(DA),* In Indiana und Illinois bedient man sich zum Zudecken der Maiskörner einer Art Hacke, welche unter dem Namen *Goe-Devil* bekannt ist. Dieselbe wird durch ein Pferd gezogen, ist leicht und kann mit einer Hand geführt werden. [=In Indiana and Illinois they used a kind of harrow, called a goe-devil, to cover the maize seeds. It is pulled by one horse, is light, and can be guided with one hand.] **1923** *DN* 5.208 **swMO,** *Go-devil.* . . An implement used in laying off several rows across a field at one time. **1945** *PADS* 3.10 **MO, NC,** *Go-devil.* . . A farm implement used in cultivating very young corn in a field that has been listed (deeply furrowed). It resembles a high sled with a seat on it. At the back of the sled is a disk on each side which throws a little dirt in to the corn. The verb means "to cultivate with this implement." **1947** Croy *Corn Country* 281, *Go-Devil:* A kind of riding plow. Was used when the corn was small. Very popular. **1949** *PADS* 11.21 **CO,** *Go-devil.* . . A knife-sled used for cultivation. **1954** Tolbert *Bigamy Jones* 122 **wTX** (as of 1870s), My cousin . . and I were put to running go-devils—which were rather crude sleds with weed-cutting knives attached to the runners—over the maize crops on the flats of our South Pasture. **1957** *Sat. Eve. Post Letters* **wTX** (as of c1930), They [=go-devils] were made of two runners about 10″ [sic] apart, . . a metal seat on top and a lever . . to raise and lower a set of discs for turning the soil on each side to the rear. A long, sharp knife was mounted on each side near the bottom of the runner on the outside. . . The go-devil straddled the cotton and the blades cut through the ridges on each side killing the weeds on top of the ridges. The discs behind were adjusted to throw fresh, moist soil from the ridges into the furrow around the base of the cotton plants. . . The go-devil was drawn usually by two mules. *Ibid* **eNM,** "Go-devil" for a small harrow. **1961** [see **2f** below]. **1965–70** *DARE* (Qu. L18, *Kinds of plows*) Infs **AR**56, **MO**39, **OK**27, **TX**42, 78, Go-devil; (Qu. L25, *The implement used to clean out weeds*) Inf **NM**13, Go-devil, go-devil cultivator; (Qu. L35) Inf **LA**8, Go-devil. **1968** *DARE* FW Addit **DE,** Go-devil . . a harrow with long teeth straight down for cutting roots on new-ground. It had a square frame.

b also *go-devil rake:* A large wheeled rake, usu drawn by horses, used for gathering hay. Cf **buck rake** n

1885 *Harper's New Mth. Mag.* June 14/2 **KS,** And the graceful 'go-devil' rake, travelling idly over the hay fields and gathering up the hay with all the ease of a lady's carpet-sweeper. **1893** *KS Univ. Qrly.* 1.139 **KS,** *Go-devil:* a kind of large rake used for drawing cocks of hay, several at a time, to the stack. It is pulled by two horses, each mounted by a boy. **1920** *DN* 5.81 **eWA,** *Go-devil.* A hay buck, an implement used to rake hay into a stack. **1940** Writers' Program *Guide OH* 87, The horse drawn hay fork and the hay loader and stacker, together with the hay tedder and the go-devil rake, lessened the amount of labor necessary in the hay-field. **1941** Writers' Program *Guide WY* 169, Stackers, go-devils, sweeps, and other hayfield equipment are for the most part constructed along the same lines whether in the ranching country of the Saratoga Valley or in Jackson Hole. **1949** *PADS* 11.21 **CO,** *Go-devil. . .* A bull-rake, a swivel-wheeled implement for hay harvest . . A sweep-rake. **1960** Bailey *Resp. to PADS 20* **KS,** A go-devil was to concentrate hay windrows into piles . . horse-drawn. **1961** [see **2f** below]. **1966–67** *DARE* (Qu. L16, *Machines used . . in handling hay*) Infs **KS**1, **WA**8, Go-devil; **CO**44, Go-devil was Kansas for sweep-rake.

c Any of various small cars designed to run on railroad tracks; esp a handcar.

1893 *KS Univ. Qrly.* 1.139 **KS,** Go-devil. . . A work wagon used in street railway construction. **1913** Beach *Iron Trail* 185 **AK,** Gordon had laid several hundred yards of light rails upon his grade, and on these he had mounted a device in the nature of a "go-devil" or skip, which he shunted back and forth by means of a donkey-engine and steel cable. **1918** *DN* 5.25 **nID,** *Go-devil. . .* A hand-car. General in northern Idaho, where the steep railroad grades make hand-car speeding good sport. **1966** *DARE* (Qu. N34, *An electric car that runs on tracks in a city*) Inf **WA**18, Go-devil. . . name of a particular line once used from here to Balleyhou. **1975** [see **2f** below].

d Any of various devices for dragging heavy loads; a sled, sledge, or stoneboat; esp, in logging, a pole drag, sled, or wheeled chassis used to support one end of a log while the other end drags on the ground. Cf **crotch** n[1] **B3**

1905 U.S. Forest Serv. *Bulletin* 61.36, *Dray. . .* A single sled used in dragging logs. One end of the log rests upon the sled. . . Syn[onyms]: bob, drag sled, go-devil. **1907** *DN* 3.244 **eME,** *Go-devil. . .* Same as *bob.* [*Ibid* 241, *Bob. . .* A drag for hauling logs on dry ground, made of two bent logs fastened together.] **1923** *DN* 5.208 **swMO,** *Go-devil. . .* A primitive form of sled made from the crotch or 'forks' of a tree. **1931** *Randolph Enterprise* (Elkins, W. Va.) 1 Jan. 1/1 *(DA),* We had to do that [=open the roads] ourselves with big sleds, bob-sleds and then sleighs, 'Yankee Jumpers' and 'Go Devils.' **1938** (1939) Holbrook *Holy Mackinaw* 48, A go-devil was nature's own sled, made from a forked birch with a crosspiece nailed midway of the V, and hauled by a pair of horses. **1940–41** Cassidy *WI Atlas* **cwWI,** *Go-devil. . .* In logging, a sled . . to which the front end of a log was chained, the back end dragging on the ground, to draw it out of the woods to the skidway. **1946** Gould *Yankee Storekeeper* 139 **ME,** A go-devil is a State of Maine vehicle—a single-horse sled with a pung body on it. It handles better in snow. **1948** *Salt Lake Tribune* 19 Jan. 13/1 *(DA),* This Hungry Behemoth Clears Snow . . It's a far cry from 'go-devils' and snow shovels. **1949** *PADS* 11.21 **CO,** *Go-devil. . .* Two wheels connected by an axle, which support the lashed ends of lumber while the other ends drag. . . One of several kinds of sleigh-like vehicles. **1950** *WELS (A low wooden platform used for hauling stones or heavy things out of the fields)* 1 Inf, **WI,** Go-devil. **1954** Jordan *Hell's Canyon* 149 **ID** (as of 1930s), The go-devil, a sled drawn by whatever horses were available, could not be had at once. **1965–70** *DARE* (Qu. L57, *A low wooden platform used for bringing stones or heavy things out of the fields*) Infs **AK**8, **IL**114, **MI**78, **MN**31, **MT**5, **WA**25, Go-devil; **CA**105, Go-devil—bobsled type thing in front, two wheels behind; (Qu. N40a, . . *Sleighs . . for hauling loads*) Inf **CT**13, Go-devil—small pung used in woods [for hauling logs]; **MN**19, Go-devil—for short trips, two runners; (Qu. N40c, . . *Sleighs for carrying other things*) Inf **AK**8, Go-devil—formerly used; **ID**5, Go-devil—just front half of bobsled. **1969** Sorden *Lumberjack Lingo* 48 **NEng, Gt Lakes,** *Go-devil*—A sled made from two natural crooks of maple or ironwood with timber bolted across, for hauling logs. The go-devil kept the end of the logs off the ground as they were dragged out of the woods. **1973** Allen *LAUM* 1.218 (as of c1950), *Go-devil,* found in former timber country of northern Minnesota, usually refers to a forked tree trunk upon which the end of a log rests when it is being dragged from the woods. One inf. describes a go-devil as having wheels. **1975** [see **2f** below]. **1981** *PADS* 67.26 **neMN,** *Dray* and *go-devil* [for *stoneboat*] have two occurrences each. . . The latter [is limited] to the eastern towns of Virginia . . and Biwabik.

e A child's coasting sled.

1907 *DN* 3.244 **eME,** *Go-devil. . .* Same as *bob.* [*Ibid* 241, *Bob. . .* Double runner, used for sliding down hill.] **1975** [see **2f** below].

f Various other vehicles and implements; see quots.

1937 Sandoz *Slogum* 315 **NE,** He . . could . . talk well about . . the construction of go-devils to skim the grasshoppers from the young stand [of corn]. Make the go-devils with just stuff from the old iron pile: a couple of wheels . . a piece of pipe twelve, fourteen feet long for the axle, with a plank trough for the water swung low to the ground and a back drop of old canvas to keep the hoppers from jumping over. Squirt a shot of coal oil on the water in the trough and just haul it over the field. **1949** *PADS* 11.21 **CO,** Go-devil . . Any self-propelled machine. . . A child's coaster car. **1958** McCulloch *Woods Words* 71 **Pacific NW,** *Go-devil. . .* A vehicle for which a better name is lacking. **1961** *AmSp* 36.268 **CO,** A rather confusing situation exists with regard to *go-devil* in Colorado. One Colorado informant even explains the word as a generic term for 'all kinds of contraptions.' Yet there are signs of settling in the various meanings the expression may have. It may, in eastern Colorado, refer to a cultivator, but several times it clearly means 'buck rake.' In central and western Colorado it is much more likely to refer to a V-shaped ditch cleaner. **1967** *DARE* (Qu. L57) Inf **OR**7, Go-devil—anything that goes. **1975** Gould *ME Lingo* 110, *Go-devil*—A word applied to many vehicles and contrivances used in Maine. A box-sleigh or pung body mounted forward on logging sleds to give a mite of comfort while teaming was a *go-devil. . .* The pole drag of the Indians—poles dragging like unattached thills behind a single horse—has been used for bringing game out of the woods, and is a *go-devil.* Early homemade farm tractors, often from parts of several automobiles, were called *go-devils,* sometimes doodlebugs. The pump-lever handcar used by railroad section men is a *go-devil.* Children make *go-devils* for sliding—a small seat erected on a barrel stave. Hence, about any device one may ride on or move a load with, but of some irregular sort.

3 In the petroleum industry: any of several devices that can be dropped down a well or pumped through a pipeline for various purposes; see quots.

1886 *St. Nicholas* Nov 48/1 *(DA),* A queer-looking, pointed piece of iron, called the 'go-devil,' is dropped down the well, and [strikes] . . a cap on the top of the torpedo. **1896** Redwood *Petroleum* 1.275, To explode the charge, an iron weight, known as a *go-devil,* was dropped into the well, and, striking the disc, exploded the cap and fired the torpedo. Now, however, a miniature torpedo, known as a *go-devil squib,* holding about a quart of nitroglycerine, . . is almost invariably employed. *Ibid* 2.473, To remove obstructions in the pipes . . an automatic rotary scraper is forced through . . The scraper is known as a 'go-devil.' **1903** *DN* 2.341, *Go-devil. . .* "A conical brush of steel wire furnished at the base, or rear end, with a leather valve in four sections and with steel wire guides. The 'go-devil' is pumped thro' [the pipe-line] with the oil, and travels at about 3 miles an hour." **1916** A.B. Thompson *Oil-Field Development* 548 *(DA),* The 'go-devil' is a tool with cutters that rotate when impelled forward to the pump after insertion in the pipe line. **1936** *Dly. Oklahoman* (Okla. City) 30 Aug. 8-B/1 *(DA),* The drift indicator can either be lowered into the hole on a steel line or can be dropped in a 'go-devil,' a steel-protective case with 'feelers' attached to slow the rapid movement of the instrument through the drill pipe to the bottom of the hole. **1951** *PADS* 15.74, Among tools and machinery [in the oil fields] there [is] . . [a] *go-devil,* a self-propelled device for cleaning a pipeline. **1966** *DARE* Tape **OK**29, [FW:] To test how straight the hole is . . what would they use on a rotary rig? [Inf:] All it is, there's a clock mechanism and you set this clock to go off and ever how many minutes you think it'll take it to fall through the drill pipe. It works a lot on the acid bottle theory. You just put it inside of a tube which is enclosed and if you drop it we call it a go-devil. It goes down on a go-devil.

4 A simple cableway.

1931 *Country Gentleman* April 24/1, Involuntarily the Westerner ejaculated, 'How'd you get acrost that river?' . . Sal answered more loudly, 'In the go-devil pa and Mr. Damson hev put in above the old ford.' **1944** Adams *Western Words* 65, *Go-devil*—A taut wire which stretches from the top of the bank of a stream to an anchorage in mid-stream and carries a traveling bucket for the water supply. **1967** *DARE* FW Addit **ID,** Go-devil. . . In the mountains of northern Idaho, this is applied to a special device for crossing rivers. It consists of a cable strung across the river and through a sheave-block at each side. A "chair" is suspended from the cable; by sitting in the chair and pulling on the upper cable one is pulled across the river.

5 A heavy splitting ax; also fig in phr *rain go-devils* to rain very hard.

1930 *DN* 6.87 **cWV,** *Go-devil*. . a rather heavy splitting axe used especially in preparing wood for the chemical or pulp mills. **1932** Dargan *Call Home* 2 **cwNC,** You won't [stay at home], less'n it's rainin' go-devils! **1937** Lutes *Home G.* 64 *(DA),* Old Man Covell came over to borrow a go-devil with which to split a stubborn log, and he and my father spent some time at the barn. **1939** *Hall Coll.* **wNC,** *Go-devil,* a hammer on one end and a kind of wedge on the other—to split logs with; a little sharper than a wedge, used like a wedge, only you strike with it. **1944** *PADS* 2.43 **NC, VA,** *Go-devil*. . . A heavy ax used to split logs. **1988** *DARE* File **NY,** Go-devil . . has a specific meaning in the Catskill Mountain region . . among woodsmen and farmers. . . It is . . a splitting maul, a sledge usually about six pounds head, with a flat face on one side of the head and a wedge on the opposite face.

6 A wedge used in felling a tree.

1976 *Yankee* Mar 24/1, [A go devil is] an iron wedge driven into the kerf or saw cut to make a tree lean away from the saw.

7 A kind of firework; see quots. Cf **nigger chaser**

1950 *PADS* 14.32 **SC,** *Go-devil*. . . A kind of fireworks. Coastal area. **1967** *DARE* (Qu. FF14, . . *Kinds of firecrackers*) Inf **AL**20, *Go-devils* . . don't explode, [they] run on the ground—same as nigger chaser.

8 A mole cricket *(Gryllotalpa hexadactyla).*

1953 Randolph–Wilson *Down in Holler* 248 **Ozarks,** Go-devil. . . The mole cricket *(Gryllotalpa borealis).*

9 =**hellgrammite 1.**

1966 *DARE* (Qu. P13, *What other ways of fishing do you have around here besides the ordinary hook and line? [Special kinds of bait, hooks, lures, nets, traps, spears, etc.?]*) Inf **GA**1, Hellgamite or go-devil; insect for catfish; (Qu. R3, *Whitish, worm-like creatures, found in ponds, that hatch into dobsonflies, and are commonly used for fish bait;* total Infs questioned, 75) Inf **GA**1, Hellgamite—go-devils.

10 Appar a **coot** n[1] **1,** prob *Fulica americana.*

1966 *DARE* (Qu. Q9, *The bird that looks like a small, dull-colored duck and is commonly found on ponds and lakes*) Inf **WA**18, Go-devil.

go-devil v See **go-devil n 2a**

go-devil rake See **go-devil n 2b**

godfather n Cf **godmother 2**

A guardian.

1968 Wilson *Folkl. Mammoth Cave Region* 86 **csKY,** [If a baby is] *bow-legged* . . he may have a bow-legged father or *godfather*—the local name for *guardian.* **1986** Pederson *LAGS Concordance,* 1 inf, **cMS,** Godfather—guardian; [1 inf, **neAR,** Godfather—in [the] old days agreed to look after [the] child.]

Godfrey n, intj For varr see quots [Euphem for *God*] **scattered, but chiefly NEng**

Used in var interjections and oaths; see quots.

1868 Nordhoff *Cape Cod* 16 **seMA,** Them thet's got shall hev, the Bible says, 'nd by Godfrey, them thet's got luck kin hev any thing else. **1904** Day *Kin o' Ktaadn* 32 **ME,** By Godfrey mighty, I'd set down and gnaw the string in two. **1904** *DN* 2.425 **Cape Cod MA** (as of a1857), *Godfrey!* . . An ejaculation. Also *godfrey mighty,* and *godfrey Lijah.* **1907** *DN* 3.188 **seNH,** *Godfrey mighty*. . . Softened form of God Almighty. **1909** *DN* 3.411 **nME,** *Godfrey*. . . Used as a mild oath in the phrase *by Godfrey.* **1914** *DN* 4.73 **ME, nNH,** *Godfrey dorman!* Innocuous oath, with faint echoes of far-past profanity. **1915** (1916) Johnson *Highways New Engl.* 269, One day an older brother and another feller got me down and tied me and sheared my hair all off. My godfrey! They didn't leave it an inch long. **1916** Lincoln *Mary-'Gusta* 313 **MA,** Oh, my godfreys! I'm all out of wind! **1929** *AmSp* 5.124 **ME,** [Emphatic and impatient exclamations:] Godfrey Dorman. **1942** Faulkner *Go Down* 14 **MS,** Gone away! I godfrey, he broke cover then! **1952** Brown *NC Folkl.* 1.546, *Godfry, by*. . . A mild oath. **1959** *VT Hist.* new ser 27.137, *By Godfrey Caesar!* . . Rare. *Godfreydoman!* . . Occasional. . . *Godfrey Mighty!* . . Rare. **1966–69** *DARE* (Qu. KK48) Infs **CT**21, **GA**15, By guess and by Godfrey; (Qu. NN27a, *Weakened substitutes for 'god': "My ______!"*) Infs **CT**22, **NH**5, By Godfrey; **RI**15, Godfrey; (Qu. NN28a, *Exclamations beginning with 'good': "Good ______!"*) Inf **CT**27, Godfrey nightis. **1968** *Territorial Enterprise & VA City News* (VA City NV) 15 Mar 3/3, But by Godfrey Virginia City has pluck. **1975** Gould *ME Lingo* 111, *Godfrey*—A favorite Maine term for the Almighty which is not considered offensive. . . *By Godfrey* and *Godfrey Mighty!* are the commonest ways to use *Godfrey*. . . A pleasant emphasis is often given to *Godfrey* by adding Jeezum! **1977** *Yankee* Jan 73 **csME,** "Gawdfrediamonds!" they're liable to say, "Come aboard!" **1979** *AmSp* 54.98 (as of c1910) **ME,** *Godfrey gommers*. . . (A mild oath).

go-dig n **CO** Cf **go-devil n 2a**

A type of cultivator.

1944 *Greeley* (Colo.) *D. Tribune* 30 Sep. 2/7 (*DA* at *bull* n.[1] 9 (13)), [For sale] Bull rake, 2 row go-dig, McD feed grinder. **1960** *PADS* 34.51 **CO,** Go-dig 'cultivator.' **1967** *DARE* File **cnCO,** *Go-dig*—A listed-row corn cultivator. 'Snake-killer' is said to be the Missouri name.

go divvies See **divvy n 2**

godly adv [*OED* 1530 →; "Now *rare*"]

Piously, devoutly.

1942 Hurston *Dust Tracks* 281 **FL** [Black], They became conscious of their sins. They were Godly sorry. But somehow, they could not believe.

godmother n

1 A midwife. Cf **granny woman**

1956 Ker *Vocab. W. TX* 319, One of the two younger and cultivated informants of Scurry county who responds with the modern term *nurse* also volunteers *God-mother.* **1960** *PADS* 34.52 **CO,** *Godmother* 'midwife' . . is an unmistakable response in both Fruita and Lake City, and is perhaps no more an oddity than granny or granny woman. **1961** Folk *Word Atlas N. LA* map 1212, *Woman who helps at childbirth* . . 3% [of 275 total infs responded] nurse [or] godmother. **1965–70** *DARE* (Qu. AA30, *An older woman who comes in* . . *to help when a baby is going to be born*) 11 Infs, **scattered, but esp Missip-Ohio Valleys,** Godmother. [9 of 11 Infs old] **1966** Dakin *Dial. Vocab. Ohio R. Valley* 2.433, Scattered speakers also say *godmother, midmother,* [etc., for *midwife*]. **1970** Tarpley *Blinky* 222 **neTX,** *Woman who helps at childbirth*— . . 2% [=4 infs] godmother. **1971** Wood *Vocab. Change* 37 **Sth,** Three other names in general though lesser use are *godmother, granny,* and *granny woman.* **1973** Gawthrop *Dial. Calumet* 74 **nwIN,** *Woman who helps at childbirth:* midwife 99 [infs], godmother 9, nurse 4.

2 See quot. Cf **godfather**

1986 Pederson *LAGS Concordance,* 1 inf, **cGA,** Godmother—guardian—takes care of children.

go-do n

1969 *DARE* (Qu. EE32, *A homemade merry-go-round*) Inf **PA**177, Go-do ['godo].

go do-do See **do-do, go**

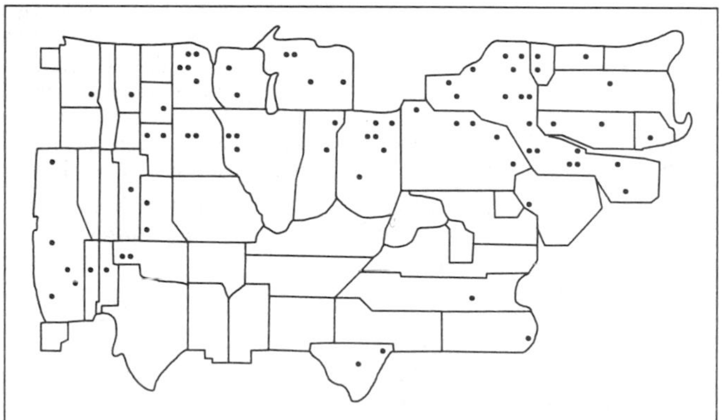

•go down v phr 1 (Qu. B13)

go down v phr

1 Of wind: to diminish, subside. [*OED* 1670 →] **chiefly Nth, West** See Map Cf **get down v phr 4**

1965–70 *DARE* (Qu. B13, *When the wind begins to decrease, you say it's ______*) 75 Infs, **chiefly Nth, West,** Going down. **1967** LeCompte

Word Atlas 97 **seLA,** After very hard blowing, the wind begins to . . go down. [1 of 21 infs]

2 To take to childbed; hence vbl n *going down.* Cf **get down** v phr **5**

1928 Peterkin *Scarlet Sister Mary* 74 **SC,** Her time to go down was not far off. *Ibid* 213, "Gwinen down don' worry me none 't all," Mary boasted. "I can birth a child easy as I can pop my finger."

3 in phr *go down sick with:* To contract, come down with (a disease). Cf **get down** v phr **6**

1968 *DARE* (Qu. BB44, *Words used around here about . . starting some sickness*) Inf **PA**90, Went down sick with.

go-down n

1 See quot.

1881 in 1882 *N&Q* 6th ser 5.65/1 **MT,** *Go down.*—A cutting in the bank of a stream for enabling animals to cross or to get to water.

2 A decline of health or spirits—used in phrr *on the go-down* in declining health; *the go-downs* a state of depression, the blues. Cf **go-backs**

1965 *Dict. Queen's English* 7 **NC,** *Go-down:* Sickly; not well. She's been on the go-down ever since she caught a cold. **1968** *DARE* (Qu. GG34b, *To feel depressed or in a gloomy mood*) Inf **VA**15, Got the go-downs. **1984** Wilder *You All Spoken Here* 207 **Sth,** On the go down, slowed back: In declining health; ain't gonna hold out or survive.

go down sick with See **go down** v phr **3**

god rock [Cf *EDD god-stone* (at *god* sb. 1. (15)) "a small, round, white stone, kept by children in the pocket as a treasure"]

1989 *DARE* File **seMA** (as of 1950s), God rock—kids used this term to refer to lumps of opaque white quartz. I guess because they were pure white, we thought they had some special place in god's system. When we threw rocks at each other, we felt it was a *sin* to use a "god rock." We were superstitious Catholics of an ethnic—Portuguese—background. We also felt it sacreligious [sic] to split or attempt to break open one of these white rocks.

God's adj Cf **God's amount, any; God's plenty** Cf *DJE God*

Used as an intensifier—usu in phr *God's thing.*

1928 Peterkin *Scarlet Sister Mary* 239 **SC,** Every God's thing he had bought to feed her and the children and himself for a whole week. **c1938** in 1970 Hyatt *Hoodoo* 2.1098 **cSC,** Write dat girl [sic] name down on a piece of papah. . . an' . . wrap it up . . an' bury it undah yore steps. An' she . . will come home. Yo don't do *a god's thing* to it atall. **1939** Griswold *Sea Is. Lady* 577 **sSC,** Dey gwine be cyaa'tin' off sugar an' meal an' tea an' coffee an' eb'ry Gawd t'ing fum pantry eb'ry bless ebenin'. **1950** *PADS* 14.31 **SC,** *Gawd's.* . . An illiterate use, mostly Gullah. "He ain't done a Gawd's thing." "I never ketch a Gawd swimp." **c1960** *Wilson Coll.* **csKY,** *Not a Gawd's thing*—a substitute for damned.

God's acre n Also *God's little acre*

A piece of farmland, the revenue from which is given to a church; see quot 1944.

1933 Caldwell *God's Little Acre* 38 **GA,** It might be on God's little acre. . . What would you do about that? You wouldn't dig nuggets when they were all going to the preacher and the church, would you? **1944** Howard *Walkin' Preacher* 271 **Ozarks,** As there were many tithers in the congregation there was always enough money in the treasury to pay all the church expenses for a year. Almost every family in that farming community had a God's Acre and the revenue from that acre, usually the highest-producing piece of ground on their place, went to the church.

God's amount, any n Also *any G. q., any God's immense, ~ quantity* Pronc-sp *any God's amint* Cf **God's plenty**

An indefinitely large amount.

1914 *DN* 4.73 **ME, nNH,** *God's amint, any,* or *Any God's immense.* . . "They's any God's amint . . o' woodchucks in them woods!" **1923** *DN* 5.200 **swMO,** We shore air a-havin' any God's amount o' rain this summer. **1943** *AmSp* 18.237 **seNY,** A white man, born in Ossining New York, in 1856 and college educated, used these expressions: *Any God's quantity,* also *Any G. q.,* n. phr., a great deal or a great many.

God's candle n Cf **desert candle, Our Lord's candle**

A **soapweed** (here: *Yucca elata*).

1940 Writers' Program *Guide NM* 14, *Yucca elata* . . has narrow flexible leaves and tall branched flower stocks, commonly called God's Candles.

God's country n Also *God's land, God's own country*

A region or place thought of as being especially favored by God.

1865 Kellogg *Life & Death* 118, I was willing to work hard, if I could only get out of that horrible den, into *God's country* once more. **1868** Goss *Soldier's Story* 171, In referring to the North, as distinguished from the South, it was often spoken of as "God's country." **1874** Taylor *World on Wheels* 163, They talked about "God's country," whither they were bound, till your heart ached to think how many of them would find "God's acre" before they reached the blessed North. **1908** *DN* 3.315 **eAL, wGA,** *God's country.* . . A name for one's own country, section, or state. "I'm glad to git back to God's country agin." Said particularly after a visit to some western state. **1920** Hunter *Trail Drivers TX* 179 (as of 1880), At last after many hardships and exciting experiences, we again enjoyed the comforts of "God's land," in the frontier town of Caldwell, Kansas. **1927** Foster *Tropical Tramp* 109, The Californians ran riot over the whole ship, telling the people of other states about the unsurpassable climate of "God's own country." **1946** Thompson *Amer. Daughter* 10, We worked hard and got this home, but we can work for another one, a real home this time, out in God's country! **1950** *WELS Suppl.* **swWI,** *God's country and the Indians'.* . . Name for out-of-the-way place. **c1960** *Wilson Coll.* **csKY,** *God's Country.* . . Some place pictured as much better than here and now, like the ancestral home of someone who lives on past memories. **1966** Barnes–Jensen *Dict. UT Slang* 19, *God's Country* . . a favorite region. "For me the Wasatch mountains are God's country." **1966–68** *DARE* (Qu. C33, . . *Joking names . . for an out-of-the-way place, or a very unimportant place*) Inf **NH**10, Out in God's country; **PA**110, Out of God's country. **1972** Hall *Sayings Old Smoky* 74, A man asked one of his kin where he lived. The latter replied, "I live in God's country." Asked to explain what he meant, he said, "I live where they worship 'In God We Trust,' " referring to New Jersey, where many former Smokies residents now live and work.

God's land See **God's country**

God's little acre See **God's acre**

God's off-ox n

=**Adam's off-ox 2.**

1848 in 1935 *AmSp* 10.42 **Nantucket MA,** *Poor as God's off ox.* Very poor. **1958** *VT Hist.* new ser 26.272, Lazier and slower than God's off ox. **1967** *DARE* (Qu. HH4, *Someone who has odd or peculiar ideas or notions*) Inf **MA**5, As odd as God's off-ox.

God's own country See **God's country**

God's plenty n [Cf *OEDS God's quantity* (at *God* sb. 16. c) 1911 →] Cf **God's amount, any**

An abundance; also fig.

1932 Stribling *Store* 471 **AL** [Black], Whut dat Alex Cady go'n' do to us tomah when She'f Mayhew come an' go go'n' be a Gawd's plenty. [=What that Alex Cady is going to do to us tomorrow when Sheriff Mayhew comes and goes is going to be a God's plenty.] **1949** Arnow *Hunter's Horn* 5 **KY,** Lord, I've already got a God's plenty fer supper with th possum an all. **1968** *DARE* (Qu. LL9a, . . *"We've got ______ of apples."*) Inf **IN**38, God's plenty.

God's thing See **God's**

God's time n Cf **sun time**

Formerly, time as told by the sun as opposed to standard time; later, standard time as opposed to daylight saving time.

1911 (1913) Johnson *Highways Gt. Lakes* 94, "So you carry standard time the same as the town fellers," commented the digger. "But sun time—God's time—is good enough for me." **1919** *Scientific Mth.* Nov 391, Many letters were written by farmers and farmers' wives to local papers protesting against the unholy interference [=the imposition of Daylight Saving Time] with God's time. **1942** *AmSp* 17.281 **PA,** In that . . summer [=1938] a bitter quarrel ensued in the local churches because the members who were farmers remained on Eastern Standard [Time], and would not consent to go to church on the 'devil's time' but insisted on the church's staying on 'God's time.' The corresponding Pennsylvania Dutch dialect terms were *Gottszeit* [gɔdsaɪd] and *Deifelszeit* [daɪflsdsaɪd]. **1945** *Sun* (Baltimore MD) 1 Oct 12/6 *(Hench Coll.),* At the office of the Western Union there were inquiries about "the correct time" and "is everybody now on God's time?" **c1960** *Wilson Coll.* **csKY,** *God's time.* . . Any time except railroad time or standard time; later, standard time as opposed to DST [=Daylight Saving Time]; I first heard the term used in World War I when time was moved up all over the nation; the new time was President Wilson's time; the previous time was God's. **1982** *Barrick Coll.* **csPA,** *God's time*—standard time as opposed to daylight saving time. **1986** Pederson *LAGS Concordance,* 1 inf, **cwFL,** God's time—not government's daylight saving time.

go Dutch (treat) See **Dutch** adv

God was a little boy, since adv phr

For a long time.

1959 *VT Hist.* new ser 27.137 **c,ceVT,** *Since God was a little boy. . .* A long time. Occasional.

go-easter n

1922 Rollins *Cowboy* 264, Punchers, when bound for the Eastern abattoirs . . provided themselves at the "general store" with "boughten" bags of carpet or of imitation leather, bags such as urban folk then employed. These new receptacles the punchers often termed *"go-easters."*

go-easy adj

1 Relaxed, easygoing. Cf **come easy, go easy**

1877 VT Dairymen's Assoc. *Report* 8.22, The many serious drawbacks which the 'go easy' dairymen of Vermont are compelled to encounter. **1967–69** *DARE* (Qu. KK46, . . *Expressions for taking things as they come and not worrying: "The whole family was sort of ______."*) Infs **MO**38, **NC**72, Go-easy; **AR**47, Go-easy type.

2 also used absol: See quots.

1970 *DARE* (Qu. HH10, *A very timid or cowardly person: "He's ______."*) Inf **TN**53, A go-easy. **1981** Pederson *LAGS Basic Materials,* 1 inf, **csTX,** *Jelly bean* was a 'go-easy kind of a fellow,' i.e., a sissy.

goed See **go** v **A6a**

goeduck See **geoduck**

goetta n |ˈgɛtə| Pronc-sp *get-ta* [Etym unknown] **Cincinnati OH area**

A dish similar to **scrapple,** composed chiefly of oatmeal and ground meat boiled together, cooled in a mold and then sliced and fried.

1983 DuSablon *Cincinnati Recipe Treas.* 152, Martha Finke Oehler of Covington, Kentucky claims that her ancestors "invented" goetta (pronounced get-ta) back around the turn of the century. *Ibid* 153, The goetta became popular and packages were transported across the Ohio River to Cincinnati markets where meat purveyors began selling their homemade versions in a German atmosphere. **1986** Valin *Life's Work* 37 **cnKY,** We drove to Newport to the Anchor Café and had eggs, goetta, and coffee in one of the spare wooden booths in the back room. **1987** *DARE* File, When I lived across the Ohio River from Cincinnati, I was introduced to a food I had never known before—goetta [ˈgɛtə]. It was kind of like oatmeal held together with a lot of lard. But people seemed to like it! It was eaten for breakfast.

gofer n See **gaufre**

gofer match n Also *gofer* [Pronc-sp for *go for;* cf *gofer* one who goes for (fetches) things for others] **esp West**

A paper match.

1965–70 *DARE* FW Addit **OK,** *Gofer matches*—book matches (strike one and you "go fer" another!); **TX**77, *Gofer matches* mean book matches, so called because they always go out, and you have to go fer more. **1967–70** *DARE* (Qu. F46) Inf **CA**11, Gofer matches—those in a book; **CA**205, Gofer matches; **OR**3, Paper matches . . gofers—it goes out and you go for another; **TN**26A, Gofer matches [laughter]. These are paper matches—you strike one and 'gofer' another one; **TX**5, Gofer matches—paperbook matches; **WA**21, Book matches . . gofer matches.

go-fetch-it n Also *go-fetch-'er* **esp GA**

=**goozle** n **1.**

c1940 *McDavid Coll.* **GA,** Go-fetch-'er = Adam's apple. **1968** *DARE* (Qu. X7, . . *Names for the throat*) Inf **GA**28, "Go-fetch-it" (same as goozle). **1986** Pederson *LAGS Concordance,* 1 inf, **cnGA,** Go fetcher—littler notch in the throat; 1 inf, **csGA,** Go fetcher—Adam's apple or goozle? 1 inf, **ceMS,** Go fetcher—goozle; 1 inf, **neTX,** Go fetchers—Adam's apple; 1 inf, **neGA,** Go fetch it; 1 inf, **csGA,** Go fetch it—Adam's apple; 1 inf, **seAL,** Go fetch it—Adam's apple, goozle; older term; [1 inf, **nwLA,** Goozle—gets food and carries it down, comes back].

go flummox See **flummox** adv

go for v phr [By ext from *go for* to pass for, serve as (someone or something)]

To be regarded as (of a particular nature).

1942 Hurston *Dust Tracks* 195 **FL,** Dat cracker quarters boss wears two pistols round his waist and goes for bad [=tough], but he won't break a breath with Big Sweet.

go forward v phr Cf **come forward**

1901 *DN* 2.140 **ceNY,** *Go forward. . .* Become converted.

go-from-me-come-to-me n

1956 Sorden–Ebert *Logger's Words* 16 **Gt Lakes,** *Go-from-me Come-to-me,* A pike pole.

gog v

1952 Brown *NC Folkl.* 1.546 **wNC,** *Gog. . .* To embarrass.

go galley-west See **galley-west**

go gay See **gay** adj **1**

go-get-'em n Also sp *go-git-'em*

Pep, energy.

1966–68 *DARE* (Qu. HH27b, *Of a very able and energetic person . . , "He's got lots of ______."*) Infs **FL**11, 20, **MO**36, **SD**8, Go-get-'em; **NC**30, Go-git-'em.

goggle n Also *wind goggle* [Prob var of *OED guggle* sb. 1. a "*Slang* and *dial.* The windpipe."] Cf **google**

1970 *DARE* (Qu. X7, *Other names for the throat*) Inf **NJ**67, Goggle; wind goggle.

goggle v[1]

1968 *DARE* (Qu. KK31, *To go about aimlessly looking for distraction: "He doesn't have anything to do, so he's just ______ around."*) Inf **IN**5, Goggling [ˈgɑgˌlɪŋ].

goggle v[2] See **guggle**

goggle-eye n

1 Any of var fishes with prominent eyes, as:

a also *goggle-eye(d) bass, ~ perch:* Any of several freshwater fishes of the family Centrarchidae; see below. **scattered, but chiefly Missip-Ohio Valleys** See Map

(1) A **rock bass** (here: *Ambloplites rupestris*).

1840 *Spirit of Times* 29 Aug 306/3 (Weingarten *Suppl. Notes*), *Goggle-eye* lights upon a red worm. **1882** U.S. Natl. Museum *Bulletin* 16.466, *A[mbloplites] rupestris. . . Goggle-Eye. . .* Head large. . . Eye very large. **1884** Goode *Fisheries U.S.* 1.406, *The Calico Bass—Pomoxys* [sic] *sparoides. . .* In the South, like *Ambloplites rupestris,* it becomes a "Goggle-eye" or "Goggle-eyed Perch." **1906** *DN* 3.138 **nwAR,** *Goggle-eyed perch. . .* A kind of perch with protruding eyes. **1929** Sale *Tree Named John* 66 **MS,** Dem's goggle-eyes, feller. **1932** Randolph *Ozark Mt. Folks* 144, Chuck full o' fish—mostly pearch an' goggle-eye! **1948** *Life* 5 Apr 58/2 **Ozarks,** *Fishing farm boy* stands under a willow tree and tries to catch goggle-eye bass. **1965–69** *DARE* (Qu. P1, . . *Freshwater fish . . that are good to eat*) 12 Infs, 11 **Lower Missip Valley, Ohio Valley,** Goggle-eye; **AR**22, Goggle-eye, rock bass—same; **LA**2, Goggle-eye—has a big mouth; **LA**12, Goggle-eye—a big red-eyed perch; **OK**52, Goggle-eye (big-mouthed perch); **IN**83, Goggle-eye bass; **LA**8, 44, Goggle-eye perch; **SC**32, Goggle-eyed bass; **OK**11, Goggle-eyed perch; **IN**7, **MS**73, Goggle-eyes; (Qu. P3, *Freshwater fish that are not good to eat*) Inf **NC**10, Goggle-eye perch. [*DARE* Ed: Some of these Infs may refer instead to **1a(2)** or **1a(3)** below.] **1967–68** *DARE* Tape **GA**20, Perch, most people call a goggle-eye; **LA**5, They have the goggle-eye which we call the goggle-eye perch (called rock bass in the Ozarks and warmouth in Florida); **LA**8, We catch . . goggle-eye perches. **1972** Sparano *Outdoors Encycl.* 368, *Rock Bass. Common Names . .* goggle eye, . . goggle-eye perch. **1983** Becker *Fishes WI* 852, *Rock bass. . .* Goggle eye. . . Dorsal region of head, back, and upper sides brown to olive. . . Eyes bright red to orange. **1988** Lincoln *Avenue* 184 **wNC** (as of c1940), The old black women . . came almost daily with cane poles and croker sacks to fish for the catfish and goggle-eyed perch hiding under the bank.

(2) A **warmouth** (here: *Lepomis gulosus*).

1854 Wailes *Rept. on Ag. & Geol. MS* 334, Calliurus gulosus. . . Goggle-eye. **1882** U.S. Natl. Museum *Bulletin* 16.467, *C[haenobryttus] antistius. . . Goggle Eye.* Body heavy, deep and thick. **1896** U.S. Natl. Museum *Bulletin* 47.992, *Goggle-eye. . .* Eastern United States from the Great Lakes to Carolina and Texas and west to Kansas and Iowa. Chiefly west or south of the Alleghanies; common in South Carolina. **1933** LA Dept. of Conserv. *Fishes* 342, The Warmouth Bass has come to bear many confusing popular names. These are: Warmouth, Goggle-eye [etc]. **1941** Writers' Program *Guide LA* 673, Jeems (or James) Bayou, an excellent fishing spot for . . warmouth bass (locally called goggle-eye). **1968** *DARE* (Qu. P1, . . *Freshwater fish . . that are good to eat)* Inf **LA**26, Goggle-eye [FW: =warmouth]; **LA**29, Goggle-eye [FW: From description, this is the warmouth bass.]. **1983** Becker *Fishes WI* 817, *Warmouth. Lepomis gulosus.* . . Goggle-eye. . . Body brown, . . ventral region of head and belly light brown. . . Iris red or reddish brown.

(3) =**crappie.**

1884 U.S. Natl. Museum *Bulletin* 27.461, *Pomoxys* [sic] *sparoides. . . Goggle-eye; Goggle-eye Perch.* . . This species reaches a length of one foot and is esteemed as a food fish. **1884** [see **1a(1)** above]. **1902** Jordan–Evermann *Amer. Fishes* 334, The crappie . . is . . a fish of wide distribution and has, in consequence, received many vernacular names. . . It is known as bridge perch, goggle-eye [etc]. **1906** NJ State Museum *Annual Rept. for 1905* 437, *Pomoxis sparoides.* . . Goggle Eyed Perch. . . Apparently an introduction from the Great Lakes and Mississippi valley region. **1933** LA Dept. of Conserv. *Fishes* 332, *The Sac-a-lait. Pomoxis annularis.* . . Crappie, Bachelor, . . Goggle-eye. **1947** Dalrymple *Panfish* 84, Here, my friend, are the various names by which you would address . . the Crappie, depending on where you happened to be at the moment: . . Goggle-Eye, Goggle-Eye Perch [etc]. **1983** Becker *Fishes WI* 857, *White Crappie.* . . Goggle-eye. . . Body and upper head dark green with many blue, green, and silvery reflections. . . Eyes yellow to green.

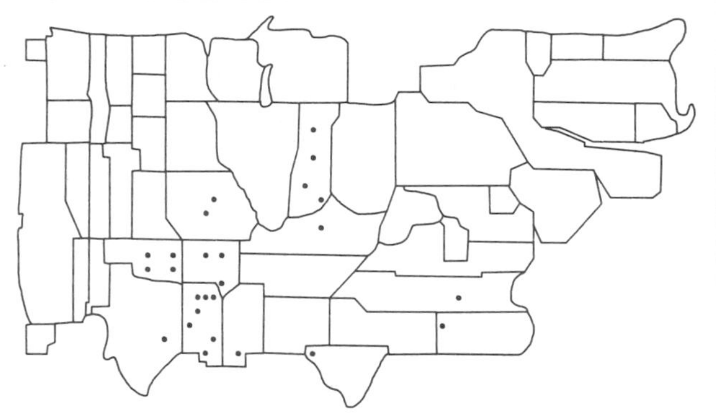

•goggle-eye 1a + varr (Qq. P1, P3)

b also *goggle-eye(d) jack, goggler:* Either of two saltwater fish: **(1)** also *goggle-eyed scad:* =**big-eyed scad.**

1873 in 1878 Smithsonian Inst. *Misc. Coll.* 14.2.25, *Trachurops crumenophthalmus.* . . Big-eyed scad; chicharro *(Cuba);* goggler; goggle-eyed Jack *(Bermudas).* Cape Cod to Florida. **1879** U.S. Natl. Museum *Bulletin* 14.41, *Big-eyed Scad; Goggle-eye.* Pelagic. **1889** *Century Dict.* 2564, *Goggle-eyed jack,* a name of the big-eyed scad, . . resembling the common scad of Europe, having goggle-eyes. . . Also called *goggler.* **1896** U.S. Natl. Museum *Bulletin* 47.911, *Goggler; Big-eyed Scad; Goggle-eye Jack.* . . The eye . . is very large. **1902** Jordan–Evermann *Amer. Fishes* 303, *T[rachurops] crumenophthalmus.* . . Its common names in American waters are goggler, big-eyed scad, and goggle-eyed jack. **1911** *Century Dict. Suppl., Goggle-eyed scad.* Same as goggle-eyed jack. **1973** Knight *Cook's Fish Guide* 381, Goggle-eye—*(f[resh]w[ater])* Bass, Rock or *(s[alt]w[ater])* Scad, Bigeye (nil food value) or Jack, Horse-eye (also nil food value).

(2) A **crevalle a** (here: *Caranx latus*).

1935 Caine *Game Fish* 90, *Caranx latus.* . . Goggle-eye Jack . . Goggler. **1946** LaMonte *N. Amer. Game Fishes* 37, *Horse-eye Jack. . . Names* . . Goggle-eye Jack. . . Large eye. **1973** [see **1b(1)** above].

2 A wood-nymph butterfly *(Cercyonis pegala)* with two fore-wing eyespots in a yellow patch.

1986 Scott *Butterflies N. Amer.* 240, *Cercyonis pegala.* Wood Nymph (Goggle Eye). . . The lower f[ore]w[ing] eyespot is bigger than the upper (sometimes the same size in males) in the west.

goggle-eye(d) bass See **goggle-eye 1a**

goggle-eye(d) jack See **goggle-eye 1b**

goggle-eye(d) perch See **goggle-eye 1a**

goggle-eyed scad See **goggle-eye 1b(1)**

gogglegoy n

=**hellgrammite 1.**

1901 Howard *Insect Book* 212 **RI,** *Corydalis cornuta.* . . Goggle goy. **1905** Kellogg *Amer. Insects* 226, The adult fly is most commonly called "hellgrammite." . . The following array of names . . are applied to the larva in Rhode Island alone: . . gogglegoy [etc].

goggle-nose n Also *google-nose* [See quot 1889]

=**surf scoter.**

1888 Trumbull *Names of Birds* 103, *Surf Scoter.* . . In Maine, at Winter Harbor, *Google-nose,* originally Goggle-nose, I presume. **1889** *Century Dict.* 2564 **ME,** *Goggle-nose.* . . The surf-scoter, a duck, . . *Œdemia perspicillita;* the spectacle-coot: so called from the pair of round black spots on the bill, resembling goggles. Also *google-nose.* **1909** Field Museum Nat. Hist. *Zool. Ser.* 9.345, *Surf Scoter. Local Names* . . Goggle-nose. . . Abundant on Lake Michigan in fall and winter, and in many of the interior waters of Wisconsin and Illinois until ice forms. **1925** (1928) Forbush *Birds MA* 1.277, *Oidemia perspicillata.* . . Gogglenose. **1955** Forbush–May *Birds* 86, *Surf Scoter.* . . Gogglenose.

goggler See **goggle-eye 1b**

go-git-'em See **go-get-'em**

goglin adj Cf **antigoglin**

1973 Allen *LAUM* 1.402 (as of c1950) **SD,** Goglin across: winding [1 inf].

gognocker n

1968 *DARE* (Qu. X7, . . *The throat)* Inf **VA**2, Gognocker ['gɑg,nɑkɚ].

gogo n [LaFr]

The buttocks.

1941 O'Donnell *Great Big Doorstep* 4 **sLA,** If he pinches your go-go, you haul off and push him in the bay. *Ibid* 143, I gotta take him [=a baby needing diapering] outside in the mosquitoes and get his lil go-go specked like a marsh-hen egg with the mosquito bites! **1945** Saxon *Gumbo Ya-Ya* 205 **LA,** If you ain't got no more sense than to sit your gogo on hot engine you ought to get burned good, yes.

go halvers See **halvers 1**

gohan n [Japanese] **HI**

Cooked rice.

1958 Hongo *Hey Pineapple* 15 **HI,** "What no gohan (rice)?" someone complained. **1972** Carr *Da Kine Talk* 91, Several varieties of sushi are made in Hawaii, all of them using gohan 'cooked rice' mixed with vinegar and sugar. *Ibid* 94, Japanese words . . heard in the everyday speech of Hawaii . . [include] gohan.

go holoholo See **holo**

go home See **home E**

goil See **girl** n

go in v phr

1 Of a meeting or church service: to begin. [Scots, Engl dial] Cf **go out 1, take in, take out**

1890 *DN* 1.59, *Go.* There are two peculiar expressions in Charleston, S.C., that I have never heard elsewhere. They say sometimes the *church goes in* at 11 o'clock and *goes out* at 12:30; more often they say the *church takes in* at 11 o'clock and *takes out* at 12:30. **1899** (1912) Green *VA Folk-Speech* 200, *Go in.* . . The time of the beginning of something. "School goes in at 9 o'clock." "Church goes in at 11." **1914** *DN* 4.152 **cME,** *Go in.* . . To begin, of a meeting. "School goes in at half past eight."

2 Of diseases or bodily conditions: to become more deeply seated.

1967 Jacobs *Rejoicing* 67 **cIN** (as of c1930), It was impossible to foresee what could arise to bring the whole roaring [=threshing] operation to a whining halt. It might be a runaway team, a man whose sweat "went in on him" and he became overheated, or a broken separator part. **1983** *MJLF* 9.1.41 **ceKY,** *Go in.* . . Informant 1 said if the bold hives "go in" they are usually fatal. **1986** *DARE* File **Madison WI,** Within the last five years I heard it said, with reference to the measles or the chicken pox, that if they "go in" they become more dangerous, even life-threatening. This notion struck me as very strange, and since I had never encountered it before, I asked the speaker what she meant. She said that when measles or such things "go in," the external rash or pustules actually disappear outwardly only to occur inwardly and that the person becomes much sicker.

3 To retire to winter quarters. Cf **go out 4**

1939 (1962) Thompson *Body & Britches* 295 **NY,** Ben Snyder used to recall the year when he "went-in" in late autumn. . . Several days' tramping from his base of supplies brought him to an ideal spot for winter quarters; but . . he discovered that he had left the nails at home. . . he used icicles for nails. They were holding staunchly when he "went-out" in the spring.

goina See **go** v **A4d**

go-in-and-out-the-window See **in-and-out-the-window**

going-home vbl n attrib Cf **home** adv **E**

Pertaining to a funeral or obituary.

1972 *DARE* File **ceTX,** *Going home card.* . . Decorated obituary notice and invitation to a Negro funeral. *Ibid,* Going home piece. . . Elaborate floral arrangement for a Negro funeral.

going-home-acrying n

A deserved punishment; a comeuppance.

1939 Coffin *Capt. Abby* 56 **ME** (as of c1860s), There's that young . . Sam going home crying again. . . I guess he got his going-home-a-crying at school today. His bladder must lie near that boy's eyes. **1975** Gould *ME Lingo* 111, *Goin'-home-acryin'*—From the way an unhappy child will run home to mummy in tears; a comeuppance. If a boy sarses another boy and gets his nose punched, that's his *goin'-home-acryin'.* . . It is not reserved for children; an older person who gets hoist on his own foolishness will get his *goin'-home-acryin'.*

going-in-and-out-the-window(s) See **in-and-out-the-window**

going jess(i)e See **jesse**

going of the moon vbl n Cf **growing moon**

The waning of the moon.

1970 *NC Folkl.* 18.66, If stakes are placed in the ground . . on the going of the moon, they will sink deeper.

going to bed adj phr Also *going to bad* **S Atl** See Map

In abundance, galore.

1965–70 *DARE* (Qu. LL9b, . . *All you need or more—for example, of clothes: "She's got clothes ______."*) Infs **SC**8, 21, 24, 44, 67, 69, **FL**2, 33, 48, 52, Going to bed; **SC**26, She have clothes sleeping, going to bed; **GA**28, **SC**40, Gone to bed; **SC**19, 34, 65, Going to bad; [**SC**32, 34, Going to wrack; **SC**31, Going to waste;] (Qu. U38a, . . *A great deal of money*) Infs **FL**48, **NC**85, Money going (*or* gone) to bed.

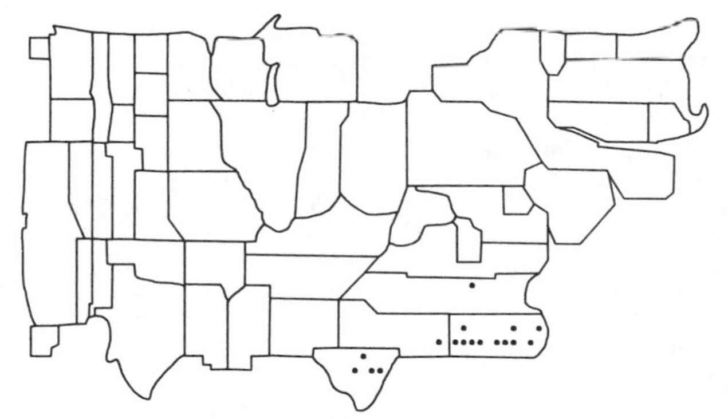

•going to bed + varr (Qq. LL9b, U38a)

going to Jerusalem See **Jerusalem, going to**

going to (the) mill See **go-to-mill**

go in halvers See **halvers 1**

Goins n Note: Both *Goins* and *Goin* are frequent surnames among mixed race people in the Mid Atl region; it is not always possible to determine from the quots which form is intended as the singular.

A member of a group of people of mixed race found esp in South Carolina.

1945 *Amer. Jrl. Sociol.* 51.35 **SC,** These outcastes, whom I call "mestizos," are designated by a wide variety of names, none of them flattering. . . In some localities they are given the most common surname in the group and are called . . "Goins." . . The probability is that the mestizos stem from the thirty-odd small . . Indian tribes which originally inhabited the coastal region of South Carolina. **1963** Berry *Almost White* 27, South Carolina abounds in groups who are "neither fish nor fowl." There are . . the Goins of Williamsburg, and the Turks of Sumter. *Ibid* 34, The surname Goins has a wide circulation, and in not a few places this is the term applied by outsiders to the entire community.

gointa See **go** v **A4d**

goiter See **German goiter**

go it Sal exclam

See quots.

1848 in 1935 *AmSp* 10.41 **Nantucket MA,** *Go it Sal.* . . Go ahead! **1965** *DARE* File (as of c1915), My grandmother, born in 1865 in the Salem, Massachusetts, area used the expression "Go it, Sal." If she knocked over, say, a bowl of apples, she'd let them fall and say, "Go it, Sal."

go jess(i)e See **jesse**

golardia See **gaillardia**

gold-and-green ball n Also *green-and-gold ball* **esp UT**

See quot 1987.

1968 *DARE* (Qu. FF4, *Names . . for different kinds of dancing parties*) Inf **UT**4, Gold-and-green ball . . a Latter-Day Saint dance held once a year to honor young people for service in the church; **UT**10, Green-and-gold ball. **1987** *DARE* File **nUT** (as of c1965), Gold-and-green balls were church (LDS)-sponsored dances usually held in the fall for young people—mostly teenagers; **AZ,** Gold-and-green balls are a tradition in the Mormon church; they are still held for the young people.

gold-and-silver plant n

Honesty (here: *Lunaria annua*).

1893 *Jrl. Amer. Folkl.* 6.138 **NJ,** *Lunaria biennis,* gold-and-silver plant.

gold aster See **golden aster 1**

goldback (fern) See **goldenback fern**

gold bass n

1 =**smallmouth bass.**

1820 Rafinesque *Ohio R. Fishes* 31, Streaked-Cheeks River-Bass. . . Vulgar names Yellow bass, Gold bass. **1946** LaMonte *N. Amer. Game Fishes* 134, *Small-mouth Black Bass. . . Names* . . Gold Bass.

2 A **yellow bass** (here: *Morone mississippiensis*).

1956 Harlan–Speaker *IA Fish* 120, *Roccus mississippiensis. . . Other Names* . . black-striped bass, gold bass. **1983** Becker *Fishes WI* 794, *Morone mississippiensis.* . . Gold bass. . . Overall, golden yellow in life.

gold beetle n

The dogbane leaf beetle *(Chrysochus auratus).*

c1930 Brown *Amer. Folkl. Insect Lore* 5, The little "gold beetles," found on the flowers of the spreading dogbane, were childhood "make-believe" jewels.

gold bird n

=**prothonotary warbler.**

1955 *Oriole* 20.12, *Protonotary Warbler.—Gold Bird* (from its largely yellow coloration).

gold blossom n *hist*

=**blossom rock.**

1846 Sage *Scenes Rocky Mts.* 334 (*AmSp* 43.86), The surface affords large quantities of 'gold blossom.' **1854** (1932) Bell *Log TX-CA Trail* 35.303, The hills are covered with white quartz that seems to have been melted. I am told that this is the gold blossom.

gold buttons n

1 A **fleabane** (here: *Erigeron compositus* var *discoideus*).

1953 Nelson *Plants Rocky Mt. Park* 165, *Gold buttons, Erigeron compositus discoideus* Gray, a variety without any ray flowers, is occasionally found growing with the species. **1959** Carleton *Index Herb. Plants* 53, *Gold buttons:* Erigeron discoides; Ranunculus acris fl. pl.

2 A **buttercup 1** (here: *Ranunculus acris*).

1959 [see **1** above].

gold carp See **golden carp**

gold chub n *obs*

A **shiner** (here: *Notropis chrysocephalus*).

1820 Rafinesque *Ohio R. Fishes* 48, *Luxilus chrysocephalus.* . . Vulgar names, Gold Chub, Shiner, Goldhead, &c. **1877** U.S. Natl. Museum *Bulletin* 9.26.

gold coast n [Orig in ref to an exclusive residential district in Chicago] **scattered, but esp Gt Lakes** See Map

A wealthy, exclusive residential area.

1902 *The Record* (Harvard) 18 March *(DAE)*, Out of the 'Yard'—How the Harvard students have gone to the 'Gold Coast.' **1920** Shackleton *Book of Chicago* 328, In that region there is so much of wealth . . that the name of the Gold Coast has been aptly given to it. **1944** *Sun* (Chicago IL) 30 Oct 7/2 *(Hench Coll.)*, Gold Coast residents paraded . . yesterday in support of Alexander J. Resa. **1948** *Chicago Tribune* (IL) 1 Aug sec I 12/3, The families of Russian personnel at the United Nations have converted a bourgeois chateau on the Long Island gold coast into a proletarian warren. **1954** *AmSp* 29.80 **neIL, seWI,** Newspaper words which refer to the city and its residents [include] . . *cave dwellers* (. . it is . . used to mean people living in penthouses and 'gold coast' areas). **1965–70** *DARE* (Qu. II24, . . *The part of a town where the well-off people live*) 30 Infs, **scattered, but esp Gt Lakes,** Gold coast; (Qu. C35, . . *Different parts of your town or city*) Infs **IL**137, 139, **WI**12, 47, Gold coast; **IL**50, Gold coast—rich apartment houses and homes on near North Side [of Chicago]; (Qu. II25, . . *The part of a town where . . special groups . . live*) Infs **CT**6, **DC**11, Gold coast; (Qu. C34, *Nicknames for nearby . . districts*) Inf **IL**99, Gold coast—high-rise area on the lake [*DARE* Ed: =Lake Michigan]. [25 of 33 total Infs female, 21 coll educ, 8 comm type 1] **1966–67** *DARE* Tape **FL**35, Well, the gold coast, they don't say too much about it up in around Jacksonville. When you leave there and get on down 'bout Coco, Cape Kennedy, they begin to call it, it gets a little golder 'til you reach Miami and then it just sparkles; **IL**15, She's out on the . . they call it the gold coast, out on Lake Shore Drive.

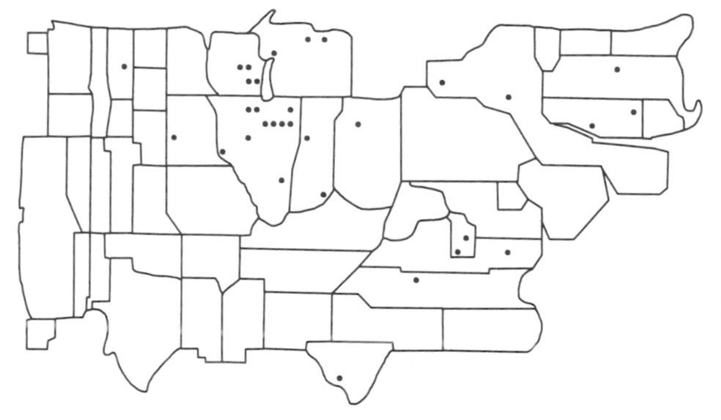

•gold coast (Qq. II24, C34, C35, II25)

gold coins n

A **partridge pea** (here: *Cassia fasciculata*).

1959 Carleton *Index Herb. Plants* 53, Gold coins: Cassia chamaecrista.

goldcrest n

1 =**golden-crowned kinglet.** [See quot 1895]

1889 *Century Dict.* 2565, *Goldcrest*. . . A golden-crested bird of the genus *Regulus*. . . That of the United States is *R[egulus] satrapa*. **1895** Minot *Land-Birds New Engl.* 52, *Satrapa*. . . *"Gold-crest."* . . Crown, with a yellow patch (inclosing in the male a scarlet one), bordered in front and on the sides by a continuous black line. **1917** (1923) *Birds Amer.* 3.220, *Golden-crowned Kinglet*. . . *Other Names*. . . Gold-crest. **1946** Hausman *Eastern Birds* 467, Goldcrest. . . The yellow crown, partially concealed by feathers, is seen only occasionally.

2 See **golden crest.**

goldcup n

1 A **buttercup 1.** [*OED* 1736 →]

1914 Georgia *Manual Weeds* 159, *Meadow Buttercup*. . . Goldcup. . . Flowers bright yellow, nearly an inch broad. **1935** (1943) Muenscher *Weeds* 241, *Ranunculus acris*. . . Gold cup. . . Pastures and meadows; chiefly on heavy moist soils. **1959** Carleton *Index Herb. Plants* 53, *Gold cup:* Ranunculus bulbosus.

2 A **cinquefoil** (here: *Potentilla gracilis*).

1953 Nelson *Plants Rocky Mt. Park* 93, *Gold cup* or *Northwest cinquefoil, Potentilla gracilis* Dougl., with bright yellow flowers, . . is frequent in meadows and fields below 9,000 feet.

goldcup oak See **golden-cup oak**

gold daisy n

A **goldenweed 1** (here: *Haplopappus spinulosus*).

1936 Whitehouse *TX Flowers* 161, *Iron Flower (Sideranthus spinulosus)*. . . The iron flowers are often called gold daisies.

gold dollars n

A **desert marigold** (here: *Baileya multiradiata*).

1957 Jaeger *N. Amer. Deserts* 274, *Gold Dollars*. . . *Baileya multiradiata*. Low woolly annual herb with yellow flowers set on long peduncles. . . A common and very showy roadside plant.

gold dust n *euphem* Cf **dust** n[1] **4**

1950 *WELS (Barnyard fertilizer used in the fields; joking or polite words)* 1 Inf, **ceWI,** Gold dust.

Gold Dust twins n pl [From the twin Black boys who appeared in advertisements for Gold Dust Washing Powder (c1900 →) to illustrate the slogan, "Let the Gold Dust twins do your work"]

1966–70 *DARE* (Qu. II3, . . *People are very friendly toward each other: "They're ______ ."*) Inf **MI**18, Gold Dust twins; **GA**53, Like the Gold Dust twins; **TN**53, Like two Gold Dust twins; **MI**101, Regular Gold Dust twins.

‡golded-up ppl adj

Gilded.

1937 (1977) Hurston *Their Eyes* 76 **csFL,** Didn't spit on his floor neither. Had that golded-up spitting pot right handy.

golden See **golden trout 4**

golden alexanders n Rarely *golden alexander*

1 A plant of the genus *Zizia*. Also called **golden parsnip, meadow parsnip.** For other names of *Z. aurea* see **cow parsnip 2, wild parsley**

1824 Bigelow *Florula Bostoniensis* 113, *Smyrnium aureum. Golden Alexanders*. . . About two feet high. . . Flowers orange yellow, in umbels of moderate size. **1848** Gray *Manual of Botany* 161, *Zizia*. . . *Golden Alexanders*. . . Smooth yellow-flowered perennials. **1892** IN Dept. Geol. & Nat. Resources *Rept. for 1891* 143, *Zizia aurea*. . . Golden Alexanders. **1910** Graves *Flowering Plants* 300 **CT,** Golden Alexanders. . . Low fields and wet meadows. **1940** Steyermark *Flora MO* 390, *Golden Alexanders (Zizia)*. . . Leaves light or dark green. **1952** Gleason *New Britton & Brown* 2.620, Golden Alexanders. . . Petals bright yellow. **1968** *DARE* (Qu. S20) Inf **PA**70, Golden alexander; (Qu. S26c, *Wildflowers that grow in woods*) Inf **PA**99, Golden alexander. **1982** Heat Moon *Blue Highways* 410 **IN,** I looped the city fast and came to Indiana 56, where corn, tobacco, and blue-sailor grew to the knee, and also wild carrot, fleabane, golden Alexander.

2 A **yellow pimpernel** (here: *Taenidia integerrima*).

1847 Wood *Class-Book* 288, *Z[izia] integerrima*. . . *Golden Alexanders*. . . Rocky woods, &c., N.Y. to Ohio and La. **1940** Clute *Amer. Plant Names* 104, *T[aenidia] integerrima*. Golden Alexanders. **1959** Carleton *Index Herb. Plants* 53, *Golden alexander:* Taenidia integerrima; Zizia aurea. **1968** Radford et al. *Manual Flora Carolinas* 775, *Golden Alexander*. . . On basic soils or outcrops, road banks and deciduous woods.

golden aster n

1 also *gold aster:* A plant of the genus *Chrysopsis*. Also called **goldeneye 2, golden star 2.** For other names of var spp see **flannelweed 2, ground gold, rosinweed, rosinwood**

1848 Gray *Manual of Botany* 215, *Chrysopsis*. . . *Golden Aster*. . . Disk and ray-flowers yellow. **1897** IN Dept. Geol. & Nat. Resources *Rept. for 1896* 688, *C[hrysopsis] villosa*. . . Golden Aster. . . Along the canal, between Ft. Harrison and Five-Mile Pond. **1911** NJ State Museum *Annual Rept. for 1910* 741, *Golden Aster*. . . In dry sands of the Pine Barrens. **1924** Hawkins *Trees & Shrubs* 91 **nwWY,** Golden asters, like street gamins, look quite uninteresting till one learns to like them. **1948** Stevens *KS Wild Flowers* 397, *Goldaster*. . . About 30 species of Chrysopsis native to North America, . . nearly all of them perennials noted for their hairiness and strong and deep taproots. **1961** Douglas *My Wilderness* 28 **CO,** I noticed a tiny gold aster *(Chrysopsis villosa)* with flakes of yellow in the snow. **1976** Bailey–Bailey *Hortus Third* 269, *Golden Aster*. . . Occasionally grown in border, wild garden, or rock garden.

2 A plant of the genus *Heterotheca*. Also called **camphor weed 2, telegraph weed.** For other names of var spp see **scurvy grass, silk grass, silver aster, silver grass**

1900 Lyons *Plant Names* 100, I[nula] graminifolia. . . Grass-leaved Golden-aster. **1936** Whitehouse *TX Flowers* 161, *Berlander's Golden Aster*. . . The heads are nearly an inch broad, the flowers all yellow. **1952** Gleason *New Britton & Brown* 3.412, *Heterotheca*. . . Golden Aster. . . About a half dozen species, native to S. U.S. **1964** Batson *Wild Flowers SC* 113, *Cottony Golden Aster*. . . Low perennial characterized by all-over cottonyness or cobwebbyness. **1976** Fleming *Wild Flowers FL* 47, *Heterotheca scabrella* . . , one of the more showy golden asters, is a yellow-flowered herb about 3 feet tall.

goldenback n

=**golden plover.**

1880 *Forest & Stream* 15.4, Golden plover. . . On Long Island and to the eastward it used to be known as the frost bird, . . but of late years it has generally been called the golden back. **1888** Trumbull *Names of Birds* 195, *American Golden Plover:* . . Golden-back. **1917** (1923) *Birds Amer.* 1.257, *Golden Plover*. . . *Other Names*. . . Golden-back. . . Upper parts conspicuously spotted with yellow. **1923** U.S. Dept. Ag. *Misc. Circular* 69, *Golden Plover*. . . *Vernacular Names*. . . *In local use*. . . Goldenback (Me.) **1955** MA Audubon Soc. *Bulletin* 39.444, *American Golden Plover*. . . Goldenback (Maine.)

goldenback fern n Also *goldback (fern)*

A gold fern *(Pityrogramma triangularis)* native to the western US, chiefly California. Also called **silverback fern**

1923 Davidson–Moxley *Flora S. CA* 23, *P[ityrogramma] triangularis*. . . Gold back Fern. Common in shaded places in the chaparral zone. **1959** Munz–Keck *CA Flora* 37, *Goldenback Fern*. . . Yellow-powdery beneath. **1961** Thomas *Flora Santa Cruz* 57 **cwCA,** Goldenback Fern. Shaded slopes in oak-madrone woods. **1976** Bailey–Bailey *Hortus Third* 882, *California g[old] f[ern], golden-back f[ern], goldback.* L[ea]v[e]s triangular, to 7 in. long and 6 in. wide, deep golden-yellow beneath, sometimes white.

golden banner n [Prob from the raceme of yellow flowers] **West**

=**false lupine 1.**

1953 Nelson *Plants Rocky Mt. Park* 99, *Golden banner,* or *golden pea, Thermopsis divaricarpa*. . . A very common plant . . with erect racemes of bright yellow flowers and three-foliate leaves. **1959** Carleton *Index Herb. Plants* 53, *Golden banner:* Thermopsis (v). **1967** *DARE* FW Addit **Denver CO,** Yellow pea, golden banner—*Thermopsis montana.* **1973** Hitchcock–Cronquist *Flora Pacific NW* 273, *Thermopsis*. . . Buck-bean; Golden-pea; Golden-banner. **1981** Pyle *Audubon Field Guide Butterflies* 759, Host plant [for *Erynnis persius*] is probably lupine *(Lupinus)* in East, definitely golden banner *(Thermopsis)* in West.

golden bass n

A **white bass** (here: *Roccus chrysops*).

1949 Caine *N. Amer. Sport Fish* 122, White bass. . . *Colloquial Names* . . Golden Bass.

golden beaver n

A Californian subsp of the beaver *(Castor canadensis subauratus).*

1921 Hall *Hdbk. Yosemite* 127 **cCA,** A day put in at a representative point, such as Snelling, would show the presence there of Mockingbirds, Texas Nighthawks, . . Fresno Pocket Gophers, Merced Kangaroo Rats, Golden Beavers, and other exclusively warm-belt types of animals. **1928** Anthony *N. Amer. Mammals* 331, *Golden Beaver*. . . A large Beaver similar in color to *frondator,* but darker. . . Found on the drainage of the Tuolumne and San Joaquin Rivers, California. **1939** Hamilton *Amer. Mammals* 298 **cCA,** Contrariwise, it is the lack of water which limits the spread of the Golden Beaver. This big semi-aquatic rodent is confined to the larger lowland streams of the San Joaquin–Sacramento basin of California.

golden bell n

=**forsythia.**

1900 Bailey *Cyclop. Horticult.* 2.603/1, *Oleàceæ*. Golden Bell. Highly ornamental, free-flowering shrubs. **1909** Doubleday *Amer. Flower Garden* 178, *Golden Bell*. . . Long, gracefully drooping branches of yellow flowers before the leaves. **1925** *Book of Rural Life* 2183, *Golden Bell*. . . Beautiful golden-yellow blossoms are one of the first pleasures of the springtime. **1950** *WELS* 1 Inf, **cWI,** Golden bell. **c1960** *Wilson Coll.* **csKY,** Forsythia—a shrub that is very common in the area, called golden bell, blooming willow, etc. **1967** *DARE* (Qu. S26a, . . *Roadside flowers*) Inf **IA**3, Golden bell. **1976** Olds Seed Co. *Seeds* 51, *Forsythia. (Golden Bell.)* One of the earliest shrubs to bloom.

golden bird n

=**Baltimore oriole.**

1946 Goodrich *Birds in KS* 313, Colloquial name . . bird, golden. . . Check-List . . oriole, Baltimore.

golden birthday n **esp WI**

See quots.

1981 *Capital Times* (Madison WI) 13 Mar 27/4, Today is his 13th birthday. Becoming 13 on the 13th also makes it Tom's "golden" birthday. **1988** *Capital Times* (Madison WI) 1 Nov 11/3, He even celebrated his golden birthday—he was 18 on Sept. 18—in bed. **1988** *DARE* File **Milwaukee WI,** Your golden birthday is the one on which your age and the date are the same. My brother celebrated his golden birthday on September 27 the year he was 27 years old. *Ibid* **IA, MN, sWI,** Your golden birthday is the birthday when your age equals the day of the month you were born on. *Ibid* **csWI, neWI,** Golden birthday.

golden bowl mariposa n Also *golden bowl*

A **mariposa lily:** usu *Calochortus concolor,* but also *C. clavatus.*

1923 in 1925 Jepson *Manual Plants CA* 235, *C[alochortus] concolor*. . . *Golden-bowl Mariposa*. . . Petals deep rich yellow tending toward orange. **1949** Moldenke *Amer. Wild Flowers* 320, In the *golden-bowl mariposa, C. concolor,* the 3 sepals are yellowish. **1959** Carleton *Index Herb. Plants* 53, *Golden bowl:* Calochortus clavatus. **1974** Munz *Flora S. CA* 923, *Goldenbowl Mariposa*. . . Dry slopes, 2000–7500 ft.

goldenbush n **SW**

1 =**goldenweed 1.**

1938 Van Dersal *Native Woody Plants* 53, *Aplopappus*. . . *Goldenbush*. . . A . . shrub; flowers September–October. **1941** Jaeger *Wildflowers* 263 **Desert SW,** *Linear-leaved Goldenbush*. . . *Fl[owers]:* yellow. . . Conspicuous in spring because of the numerous showy flower heads. **1960** Abrams *Flora Pacific States* 4.288, *Haplopappus cooperi*. . . Goldenbush. . . Common in rocky desert basins and mesas. **1967** Dodge *Roadside Wildflowers* 75, Slender goldenbush . . [is] usually much branched and rarely more than a foot high. The flowers resemble asters with many blossom heads.

2 A **rabbit brush** (here: *Chrysothamnus nauseosus*).

1947 (1976) Curtin *Healing Herbs* 57 **NM,** *Golden Bush.* Chrysothamnus graveolens. . . Nothing so completely characterizes the landscape as the silvery-green foliage and storm of yellow bloom. **1963** Craighead *Rocky Mt. Wildflowers* 202, *Chrysothamnus nauseosus*. . . Goldenbush . . is a conspicuous, bushy, goldenrod-like plant growing 2–3 ft. tall.

golden button n

1 pl: =**tansy** or its flowers.

1902 Earle *Old Time Gardens* 130, Tansy not only retains its scent for a long period, but the "golden buttons" retain their color. **1950** Gray–Fernald *Manual of Botany* 1518, *T[anacetum] vulgare* . . *Golden-buttons*. . . Roadsides, borders of fields, etc. **1961** Smith *MI Wildflowers* 423, *Golden-buttons*. . . Animals may be poisoned by this species, but because of the bitter taste they seldom eat it. **1976** Bailey–Bailey *Hortus Third* 1097.

2 A **milkwort** (here: prob *Polygala lutea*).

1968 *DARE* (Qu. S11, . . *Other names* . . *for* . . *bachelor's button*) Inf **VA**15, Golden button.

golden candlestick n

1 An **evening primrose a** (here: *Oenothera biennis*).

1898 *Jrl. Amer. Folkl.* 11.227 **KS,** *Oenothera biennis* . . golden candlestick.

2 =**forsythia.**

1956 McAtee *Some Dialect NC* 55, *Golden candlesticks*. . . sunshine bushes *(Forsythia).*

3 A **mullein.**

1966 *DARE* (Qu. S20, *A common weed that grows on open hillsides: It has velvety green leaves close to the ground, and a tall stalk with small yellow flowers on a spike at the top*) Inf **FL**27, Golden candlestick or ['mʌlɪn].

golden carp n Also *gold carp*

The common carp *(Cyprinus carpio).*

1949 Caine *N. Amer. Sport Fish* 154, Carp. . . *Colloquial names* . . Golden Carp. *Ibid* 155, There are three common varieties of carp: the most widely known is the . . gold carp which is fully scaled. **1975** Evanoff *Catch More Fish* 96, The carp *(Cyprinus carpio)* is also called . . golden carp [etc].

golden carpet n

1 A small prostrate plant *(Gilmania luteola)* native to Death Valley.

1941 Jaeger *Wildflowers* 44 **Desert SW,** *Golden Carpet. . . Fl[owers]* yellow. . . When the fruiting stage is reached, the leaves turn clear golden yellow and the stems turn up. **1944** Abrams *Flora Pacific States* 2.2, Golden Carpet. . . A local species of the Death Valley region, California.

2 =golden saxifrage.

1973 Hitchcock-Cronquist *Flora Pacific NW* 186, *Chrysoplenium. . .* Golden-carpet.

golden chinquapin See **chinquapin B3**

golden chipmunk n Also *golden-mantled chipmunk* [See quot 1928]

A **ground squirrel** n **b** (here: *Spermophilus lateralis*).

1928 Anthony *N. Amer. Mammals* 197, *Callospermophilus lateralis. . .* Golden Chipmunk; Golden-mantled Chipmunk. . . Shoulders washed more or less heavily with rusty yellowish to bright chestnut, this area . . forming a sort of mantle. **1935** Pratt *Manual Vertebrate Animals* 336, Golden chipmunks. . . *C. lateralis.* **1943** Gordon *W. Chipmunk* 8, These animals [of the genus *Spermophilus*] have been given many common names. . . Among these common names are big chipmunk, golden chipmunk [etc].

golden cholla n Cf **silver cholla**

A **prickly pear** (here: *Opuntia echinocarpa*).

1940 Benson *Cacti AZ* 42, "Golden cholla" [is] distinguished by its low, bushy habit and its bright golden spines. **1974** Munz *Flora S. CA* 316, *Golden cholla. . .* Golden spines 2–3 cm. long. . . Dry washes and mesas below 6000 ft.

golden clipper n

The American **egret** *(Casmerodus albus).*

1968 *DARE* (Qu. Q10, *Other water birds and marsh birds common around here*) Inf **GA**20, Golden clipper (nickname for common egret).

golden club n

1 An aquatic plant *(Orontium aquaticum)* with floating leaves and a club-shaped yellow spadix. Also called **bog torch 1, bull tongue 3, dog's dick, fireleaf, fire plant, floating arum, golden torch, neverwet, tawkin, tuckahoe, water dock**

1822 Eaton *Botany* 369, *Orontium. . . aquaticum* (golden club . .). Very plentiful in the west meadows, 2 miles from New-Haven, and in South Bay, Hudson. **1848** Gray *Manual of Botany* 448, *Golden-club. . .* Ponds, Massachusetts to Pennsylvania, near the coast. **1901** Lounsberry *S. Wild Flowers* 32, The golden club . . belongs to a monotypic genus, and little doubt as to its identity can enter the mind when its simple spadix is seen, crowned with small golden flowers. **1938** Matschat *Suwannee R.* 23 **GA,** The brown water . . where flat pads of water lilies floated and the golden club lifted its tall spears. **1959** [see 2 below]. **1968** *DARE* (Qu. S26b, *Wildflowers that grow in water or wet places*) Inf **GA**35, Golden club = neverwet, the common name. **1976** Bruce *How to Grow Wildflowers* 278, *Orontium aquaticum*—Golden-club. . . An aroid, but lacking the spathe, its naked yellow and white spadix [is] quite colorful in early spring.

2 =golden crest.

1959 Carleton *Index Herb. Plants* 53, *Golden club:* Orontium aquaticum; Lophiola aurea.

golden corydalis n

Std: any of var yellow-flowered spp of *Corydalis,* but usu *C. aurea* which is also called **Dutchman's breeches 2, golden smoke, scrambled eggs.**

golden crest n Also *golden crest-flower, goldcrest* [From the bright yellow perianth]

A woolly perennial plant *(Lophiola americana)* of bogs and wet pinelands. Also called **golden club 2**

1847 Wood *Class-Book* 540, *L[ophiola] Americana. . . Golden Crest-flower. . .* Corolla woolly and yellow within. . . Seeds white. **1911** NJ State Museum *Annual Rept. for 1910* 355, *Golden-crest. . .* From the downy, white clusters the little yellow flowers peep out like tiny stars. **1933** Small *Manual SE Flora* 358, *Gold-crest. . .* The golden perianths showing through glistening white wool, form a striking inflorescence. **1953** Greene-Blomquist *Flowers South* 20, *Gold-* or *Golden-Crest . .* is very conspicuous especially in the autumn sunshine. **1968** McPhee *Pine Barrens* 129 **cNJ,** Goldcrest grows here, too, and its nearest relative is in Australia. **1972** Brown *Wildflowers LA* 28, *Gold-crest. . .* Perennial herb 2 to 3 feet tall with elongate rootstalks. . . June to September.

golden croaker n

1 A **croaker** n[1] **1a(1)** (here: *Micropogon undulatus*).

1967 *DARE* Tape **TX**18, In early fall we catch a golden croaker . . a pound, three-quarters apiece. Their flesh is a little softer than most of our other fish. **1972** Sparano *Outdoors Encycl.* 386, *Atlantic Croaker. . . Common Names . .* golden croaker.

2 =roncador.

1946 LaMonte *N. Amer. Game Fishes* 82, *Spotfin Croaker. . .* Names . . Golden Croaker. **1960** Amer. Fisheries Soc. *List Fishes* 55, Croaker, golden—see croaker, spotfin.

golden-crowned kinglet n

Std: an American kinglet *(Regulus satrapa)* with a yellow, or yellow and orange, crown patch. Also called **flame-crest, goldcrest 1, kingbird, wood wren, yellowbird**

golden-crowned thrush n Also *golden-crown thrush* [See quot 1938]

=ovenbird.

1793 Morse *Amer. Universal Geog.* 1.190, Least Golden Crown Thrush—Turdus minimus, vertice aurio. **1810** Wilson *Amer. Ornith.* 2.88, Golden-Crowned Thrush. *Turdus Aurocapilla. . .* This is also a migratory species, arriving in Pennsylvania late in April. **1858** Baird *Birds* 260, *Golden-crowned Thrush. . .* The brownish orange of the crown is usually obscured by olivaceous tips to the feathers. **1910** Wayne *Birds SC* 172, *Golden-crowned Thrush. . .* In spring they are common by April 15, and the song, which is a loud chant, continues until the last bird has left. **1938** Oberholser *Bird Life LA* 550, Its trim plumage of olive green above with a brownish yellow crown and dark streaked white under parts so much resembles some species of thrushes that the bird is often called 'golden-crowned thrush', although it is not closely related to the thrushes. **1969** Longstreet *Birds FL* 137, Ovenbird. Other names: Golden-crowned Thrush.

golden cup n

=California poppy.

1959 Carleton *Index Herb. Plants* 53, *Golden cup:* Escholzia [sic] californica.

golden-cup oak n Also *goldcup oak* [See quot 1917] Cf **goldenleaf oak, golden oak 2a**

=canyon oak 1.

1869 (1911) Muir *First Summer* 345 **ceCA,** Here is about the upper limit of the dwarf form of the goldcup oak,—eight thousand feet above sea level. **1897** Sudworth *Arborescent Flora* 164 **CA,** *Quercus chrysolepis. . .* Golden-cup Oak. **1908** Britton *N. Amer. Trees* 311, It [=*Quercus chrysolepis*] is also called . . Golden cup oak. **1917** (1923) Rogers *Trees Worth Knowing* 64, The acorns [of *Quercus chrysolepis*] are large, and their thick, shallow saucers are covered with yellow fuzz. For this character, the tree is called the gold-cup oak. **1931** U.S. Dept. Ag. *Misc. Pub.* 101.24, *Canyon live oak . . ,* often called . . golden-cup oak, . . occurs in canyons and on ridges. **1948** *Desert Mag.* Feb. 8/1 *(DA),* The desert oak that I know best is the Canyon oak, Golden-Cup oak or Maul oak. **1961** Thomas *Flora Santa Cruz* 137 **cwCA,** Gold Cup Oak. Open woods, . . growing as a shrub or small tree in chaparral. **1979** Little *Checklist U.S. Trees* 228, Goldcup oak.

golden currant n

Either of two yellow-flowered **currants B1:** *Ribes aureum* or *R. odoratum.*

1847 Wood *Class-Book* 273, *R[ibes] aureum. . . Missouri, or Golden Currant. . .* A beautiful shrub. . . Flowers numerous, yellow, very fragrant. **1895** Gray-Bailey *Field Botany* 170, *Golden . . Currant. . .* Abundantly cult. for its spicy-scented bright-yellow flowers in early spring. **1910** Graves *Flowering Plants* 219 **CT,** *Ribes odoratum. . .* Golden Currant. . . Escaped from cultivation to roadsides and about old houses. . . Adventive from the West. **1928** Rosendahl-Butters *Trees MN* 145, *Ribes odoratum. . . Golden Currant. . . R. aureum* of many authors, . . not *R. aureum* Pursh. . . The far western *R. aureum* Pursh is a distinct species. **1939** Medsger *Edible Wild Plants* 16, The Golden Currant is a native shrub found from Minnesota to Texas west to Washington and California. **1973** Stephens *Woody Plants* 202, *Ribes odoratum. . .* Golden currant. . . The fruit is full of seeds but makes good jams and jellies and is sometimes used in pies.

golden daisy n

1 An **oxeye** (here: *Chrysanthemum leucanthemum*).

1876 Hobbs *Bot. Hdbk.* 43, Golden daisy, Ox eye daisy, Leucanthemum vulgare. **1889** *Century Dict.* 2566, *Golden daisy.* Same as *oxeye daisy.* **1900** Lyons *Plant Names* 98.

2 A cultivated **buttercup 1;** see quot.

1892 *Jrl. Amer. Folkl.* 5.91, *Ranunculus* (double garden buttercups), golden daisies. Richland Co[unty], O[hio].

3 A **bitterweed** (here: *Hymenoxys acaulis*).

1937 U.S. Forest Serv. *Range Plant Hdbk.* W6, Stemless actinea . . is known by a great variety of (and often misapplied) local names, such as . . golden-daisy.

golden dewdrop n

A shrub or small tree *(Duranta repens)* native to southern Florida and naturalized in Texas and Hawaii. Also called **pigeonberry, skyflower, yellow-hat tree**

1929 Neal *Honolulu Gardens* 272, *Golden dewdrop.* . . In some places duranta shrubs reach a height of ten feet. **1933** Small *Manual SE Flora* 1143, *Golden-dewdrop.* . . The accrescent calyx becomes golden-yellow. **1946** West–Arnold *Native Trees FL* 192, The . . golden dewdrop . . is native only in the Everglade Keys and the Florida Keys. **1960** Vines *Trees SW* 894, Golden Dewdrop . . is often cultivated for ornamental purposes. **1979** Little *Checklist U.S. Trees* 125, Golden dewdrop . . , a shrub often vinelike is recorded as sometimes a small tree to 20 ft (6 m) tall.

golden eagle n [*DCan* 1784 →]

A large brown eagle *(Aquila chrysaëtos).* Also called **black eagle 1, brown eagle 2, mountain eagle, ring-tailed eagle, royal eagle, war eagle**

1839 MA Zool. & Bot. Surv. *Fishes Reptiles* 262, The Golden Eagle, *Falco fulvus,* . . loves the wildness of desert and mountainous regions, where it neither seeks nor fears the presence of man. **1844** DeKay *Zool. NY* 2.4, The Golden Eagle is a rare species, a single pair appearing to monopolize a large district. **1884** Roe *Nature's Serial Story* 52 **seNY,** We have only two species of the genuine eagle in this country, the bald, or American, and the golden, or ring-tailed. **1916** Seton *Woodcraft Manual Girls* 305, The only other eagle found in the United States is the *Golden . . Eagle.* . . When full grown it is dark brown, with the basal half of tail more or less white. **1947** Cahalane *Mammals* 174, In California, trappers believe that the golden eagle is an important enemy [of the marten]. **1964** Phillips *Birds AZ* 24, Normally the Golden Eagle nests in a pothole of a cliff at an inaccessible height, and with a good view.

golden eardrops n [From the color and shape of the flowers]

A yellow-flowered plant *(Dicentra chrysantha)* native to California.

1911 Jepson *Flora CA* 179, *D[icentra] chrysantha.* . . Sometimes called "Golden Ear-drops." **1915** (1926) Armstrong–Thornber *Western Wild Flowers* 170, *Golden Eardrops* . . is exceedingly odd and beautiful. **1959** Munz–Keck *CA Flora* 202, *Golden Ear-Drops.* . . Frequent on burns and in disturbed places, dry slopes. **1976** Bailey–Bailey *Hortus Third* 380, *Golden-eardrops.* To 5 ft., . . fl[ower]s erect, in large panicled racemes, bright yellow.

golden eggs n

An **evening primrose b** (here: *Camissionia ovata*).

1911 Jepson *Flora CA* 282, *O[enothera] ovata.* . . *Golden Eggs.* . . Petals orbicular. . . Common in the Coast Range valleys. **1959** Carleton *Index Herb. Plants* 53, *Golden eggs:* Oenothera ovata. **1961** Thomas *Flora Santa Cruz* 251 **cwCA,** Golden Eggs. . . Young leaves . . make a passable substitute for lettuce, but according to one Italian resident of Boulder Creek, have a mild physic action. **1961** Peck *Manual OR* 545, *Golden Eggs.* . . Dry open ground, Umpqua Valley to Calif.

goldeneye n

1 also *golden-eye(d) duck;* Std: either of two ducks: *Bucephala clangula* or the related *B. islandica.* [*OED* 1678 →] Note: Both ducks are also known under the genus name *Glaucionetta.* Also called **pie duck, pied whistler, whistler, whistlewing.** For other names of *B. clangula* see **bluebill 5, brass-eye, brighteye, bronzehead, bullhead 2b, cobhead, cock dipper, copperhead** n[1] **2, cubhead, cur, fiddler duck 3, greathead, greenhead 4a(3), ice duck, ironhead, jingler, king diver, little redhead, merrywing, oyster duck, quandy, sizzle-britches, spirit duck, whiffler, whistle duck, widgeon, winter duck**

2 =**golden aster 1.**

1913 *Torreya* 13.251 **NY,** Many herbaceous plants cover the ground . . the "golden-eye," *Chrysopsis mariana* . . with large yellow flowers [etc]. **1924** *Amer. Botanist* 30.33 **West,** Clements gives "golden eye" for *Chrysopsis villosa.* **1953** Nelson *Plants Rocky Mt. Park* 168, *Golden-aster* or *golden eye.* . . The flowers resemble asters but have yellow rays. **1963** Craighead *Rocky Mt. Wildflowers* 201, *Chrysopsis villosa* . . Goldeneye . . is not sticky to the touch and this distinguishes it from Gumweed.

3 A **gilia** (here: *Gilia rigidula*).

1936 Whitehouse *TX Flowers* 105, *Golden Eye (Gilia rigidula),* differing markedly from the red gilia in the shape of the flowers, has a short, broadly flaring corolla with a conspicuous yellow center.

4 A plant of the genus *Viguiera.* **chiefly SW** For other names of var spp see **resin bush, rosinweed**

1937 U.S. Forest Serv. *Range Plant Hdbk.* W204, The species are usually called sunflowers, which name is best restricted to the true sunflowers (*Helianthus* spp.) . . Since *Viguiera* has no well-established common name, goldeneye, although never previously applied to this genus, is suggested as an appropriate common name. **1945** Benson–Darrow *Manual SW Trees* 349, *Viguiera. Goldeneye.* . . Herbs, suffrutescent plants, or small shrubs. **1960** Vines *Trees SW* 1011, *Parish Goldeneye* . . is also known as the Desert Sunflower. **1970** Correll *Plants TX* 1645, *Golden-eye.* . . Leaves usually opposite at least in the lower part of the plant. **1981** Pyle *Audubon Field Guide Butterflies* 590, Black or reddish-orange caterpillar has many white dots and black spines; feeds in groups on golden-eye (*Viguiera deltoidea* var. *parishii*) and sunflower *(Helianthus annuus).*

golden-eye(d) duck See **goldeneye 1**

golden-eyed grass n

A yellow-flowered **blue-eyed grass 1** (here: *Sisyrinchium californicum*).

1897 Parsons *Wild Flowers CA* 284, *S[isyrinchium] Californicum,* . . the "golden-eyed grass," with bright yellow flowers, is found in wet places all up and down the Coast. **1915** (1926) Armstrong–Thornber *Western Wild Flowers* 70, *Golden-eyed Grass.* . . This is very much like Blue-eyed Grass, but the flowers are bright yellow. **1949** Moldenke *Amer. Wild Flowers* 362, We can also boast of two yellow-flowered species—*S. brownei,* known only from . . southeastern Louisiana, and *S. californicum,* the *golden-eyed-grass,* of the California Sierra Nevada and Coast Ranges, extending northward into Oregon. **1961** Thomas *Flora Santa Cruz* 127 **cwCA,** Yellow-eyed Grass. . . Usually along or near the coast in boggy areas. **1976** Bailey–Bailey *Hortus Third* 1048.

goldeneyes n Cf **goldeneye 1**

=**ring-necked duck.**

1888 Trumbull *Names of Birds* 61, Mr. Long, in his American Wild Fowl Shooting, 1874, gives *Golden-eyes* as a "very common" name in the West. **1923** U.S. Dept. Ag. *Misc. Circular* 13.21, *Ring-necked duck.* . . Goldeneyes.

goldenfin n Also *golden(-finned) trout*

=**Dolly Varden 1.**

1965 *AK Sportsman* Nov 65 (Tabbert *Alaskan Engl.*), A particularly beautiful little freshwater Dolly, locally called "goldenfin," is found in the Copper River system as well as the Kenai Peninsula. **1978** *AK Fishing Guide* 69, *Salvelinus malma* . . is a highly variable fish in coloration and size. Some interior and Kenai Peninsula Dollies are locally called "golden-finned trout" or "golden trout" because of their high color.

golden fleece n **esp CA**

A **goldenweed 1** (here: *Haplopappus arborescens*).

1931 U.S. Dept. Ag. *Misc. Pub.* 101.156, *Goldenfleece* . . is a common evergreen shrub of California chaparral-covered foothills. **1938** Van Dersal *Native Woody Plants* 54, *Goldenfleece.* . . Grazing value nil. **1961** Thomas *Flora Santa Cruz* 347 **cwCA,** Golden Fleece. Chaparral from southern San Mateo County southward. **1974** Munz *Flora S. CA* 176, *Golden Fleece.* . . Dry foothills below 4000 ft.

golden-fronted woodpecker n Also *golden-front*

A **woodpecker** *(Centurus aurifrons)* native to Texas.

1917 (1923) *Birds Amer.* 2.161, *Golden-fronted Woodpecker. . . Other Name.*—Golden-front. . . Head, yellow; . . under parts, gray and light yellow. **1944** Hausman *Amer. Birds* 445, *Golden-fronted Woodpecker. . .* In Texas this Woodpecker is a common bird, nesting in the mesquites, oaks, and pecans, and in the vicinity of houses, in telegraph poles and bird boxes. **1957** Pough *Audubon W. Bird Guide* 161, *Golden-fronted Woodpecker. . .* North and east in Texas to Dallas and Corpus Christi and west to Eagle Pass. **1970** *DARE* (Qu. Q17, . . *Kinds of woodpeckers*) Inf **TX**84, Golden-fronted woodpecker.

golden garden spider See **golden spider**

golden girls n

A **morning brides** (here: *Chaenactis glabriuscula*).

1915 (1926) Armstrong–Thornber *Western Wild Flowers* 548, Golden Girls—*Chaenactis Fremontii. . .* They are a beautiful shade of clear bright yellow.

goldenglow n

A **coneflower 1** (here: *Rudbeckia laciniata*) or its double-flowered cultivars. Also called **green-headed coneflower, thimble flower, thimbleweed**

1900 Lyons *Plant Names* 326, *R[udbeckia] laciniata. . .* Double variety in cultivation, Golden-glow. *Plant* diuretic, tonic. **1910** Graves *Flowering Plants* 393 **CT,** Tall Cone-flower . . is often cultivated for ornament under the name of Golden Glow, and sometimes escapes to roadsides and waste ground. **1948** Stevens *KS Wild Flowers* 374, Cutleaf Coneflower. . . The double-flowered variety *hortensis,* the golden glow of our flower gardens, appearing spontaneously among individuals of the typical wild form, was propagated by cuttings and division of the rhizome and made available to the public about 1894. **1964** Campbell *Great Smoky Wildflowers* 40, Wild Golden-Glow . . flower[s] from July to September. **1968** Kellner *Aunt Serena* 80 **IN,** I led him to the old-fashioned double swing out by the Golden Glow bushes. **1968** *DARE* (Qu. S20) Inf **IN**48, Goldenglow; (Qu. S22) Infs **VA**34, **WV**2, Goldenglow; (Qu. S26a, . . *Roadside flowers*) Inf **MN**30, Goldenglow. **1971** *SC Market Bulletin* 18 Aug 8, "Susan's" [=the black-eyed Susan's] close cousins include the Brown-eyed Susan, Thin-leaved Coneflower, Green-headed Coneflower and Golden Glow.

golden grub n

The larva of a darkling beetle (*Tenebrio* spp, usu *T. molitor*); a mealworm.

1967 *DARE* (Qu. P6, *Other kinds of worms also used for bait*) Inf **SC**40, Golden grub. **1982** Sternberg *Fishing* 89, Mealworms, or *golden grubs,* are the larvae of darkling beetles. About 1 inch long, they vary from yellow to brown with darker heads.

golden hawkweed n

A **hawkweed** (here: *Hieracium praealtum*).

1895 U.S. Dept. Ag. *Farmers' Bulletin* 28.25, Golden hawkweed. . . Hieracium praealtum.

goldenhead n

A low desert shrub of the genus *Acamptopappus.*

1941 Jaeger *Wildflowers* 262 **Desert SW,** *Goldenhead. Acamptopappus sphaerocephalus. . . Fl[owers]:* pale yellow. . . In the ranges east of Death Valley and adjacent Nev. is found a goldenhead with bright yellow, radiate heads . . known as Shockley goldenhead, *A. Shockleyi.* During late April and in May almost every goldenhead bush has numbers of the . . cases of the goldenhead bagworm . . hanging from it. **1959** Munz–Keck *CA Flora* 1168, *Acamptopappus. . . Goldenhead.* Low much-branched desert shrubs with white bark. **1981** Benson–Darrow *Trees SW Deserts* 319, *Goldenhead. . .* Gravelly or sandy mesas and slopes.

goldenhead Indian tobacco n Cf **Indian tobacco**

A **bitterweed** (here: *Hymenoxys acaulis*).

1937 U.S. Forest Serv. *Range Plant Hdbk.* W6 **West,** Stemless actinea . . is known by a great variety of (and often misapplied) local names, such as . . golden-head Indian-tobacco.

golden heather See **gold heather**

golden hills n

A **brittlebush** (here: *Encelia farinosa*)

1915 (1926) Armstrong–Thornber *Western Wild Flowers* 526, *Golden Hills. . .* This grows on hillsides among the rocks and gives a golden hue which may be seen at a distance of seven or eight miles. **1931** U.S. Dept. Ag. *Misc. Pub.* 101.164, Golden hills . . is a bush 1 to 5 feet high, usually with a short trunk and a broad crown. **1949** Curtin *By the Prophet* 102 **SW,** *Encelia farinosa. . .* Golden Hills . . covers dry, rocky hillsides with a blanket of golden bloom.

golden honey plant n

A **crownbeard** (here: *Verbesina alternifolia*).

1959 Carleton *Index Herb. Plants* 53, *Golden-honey-plant:* Actinomeris alternifolia.

golden Jerusalem n

A **black-eyed Susan 2** (here: *Rudbeckia hirta*).

1892 *Jrl. Amer. Folkl.* 5.98 **NH,** *Rudbeckia hirta. . .* Golden Jerusalem. **1940** Clute *Amer. Plant Names* 86, *R[udbeckia] hirta. . .* Golden Jerusalem. **1959** Carleton *Index Herb. Plants* 54, *Golden Jerusalem:* Rudbeckia hirta.

golden lantern n

Either of two **mariposa lilies:** *Calochortus amabilis* or *M. pulchellus.*

1923 in 1925 Jepson *Manual Plants CA* 237, *C[alochortus] pulchellus. . . Golden Lantern. . .* Petals golden yellow, strongly arched or incurved. **1949** Moldenke *Amer. Wild Flowers* 320, Quite different in general appearance . . [is] the *goldenlantern, C. pulchellus.* **1959** Carleton *Index Herb. Plants* 54, *Golden lantern:* Calochortus amabilis.

goldenleaf chestnut n Also *goldenleafed chestnut, goldenleaved* ~

A **chinquapin B3** (here: *Castanopsis chrysophylla*).

1908 Sudworth *Forest Trees Pacific* 273, *Castanopsis chrysophylla. . .* Sometimes it is called "goldenleafed chestnut," in reference to the yellow under surface of the leaves. **1922** Sargent *Manual Trees* 234, Chinquapin. Golden-leaved Chestnut. **1979** Little *Checklist U.S. Trees* 78, *Giant chinkapin. . . Other common names . .* goldenleaf chestnut.

goldenleaf chinquapin See **chinquapin B3**

goldenleafed chestnut See **goldenleaf chestnut**

goldenleaf oak n Also *gold-leaf oak* [See quot 1910] Cf **golden-cup oak, golden oak 2a**

=canyon oak 1.

1908 Britton *N. Amer. Trees* 311, It [=*Quercus chrysolepis*] is also called California live oak, Canyon live oak, . . Golden leaf oak, . . and Maul oak. **1910** Jepson *Silva CA* 223, On account of the pollen-like powder on the under side of the younger leaves it [=*Quercus chrysolepis*] is famed as Gold-leaf Oak.

goldenleaved chestnut See **goldenleaf chestnut**

golden-mantled chipmunk See **golden chipmunk**

golden mullet n Also *golden redhorse,* ~ *sucker*

A **redhorse** (here: *Moxostoma erythrurum*).

1842 DeKay *Zool. NY* 4.201, *The Mullet Sucker . .* at Buffalo passes under the various names of . . *Golden Mullet,* and *Red Horse.* **1878** U.S. Natl. Museum *Bulletin* 12.124, *Golden Red Horse. . .* Great Lake Region, Upper Missouri and Ohio Valleys, and northward. **1929** OK Univ. Biol. Surv. *Pub.* 1.64, *Moxostoma erythrurum . .* Golden mullet; common redhorse. . . This mullet is obviously one of the commonest fishes in eastern Oklahoma and in Arkansas. **1956** Harlan–Speaker *IA Fish* 76, *Golden redhorse. . . Other Names*—golden mullet, golden sucker. *Ibid* 77, The color of the golden redhorse, as its name implies, is light yellow to deep gold. **1965** IL Nat. Hist. Surv. *Biol. Notes* 54.8, Golden redhorse. Generally distributed throughout the northern two-thirds of the state. **1983** Becker *Fishes WI* 657, *Golden Redhorse. . .* Other common names: golden mullet, . . golden sucker.

golden oak n

1 A **false foxglove** (here: *Aureolaria virginica*).

1830 Rafinesque *Med. Flora* 2.223, *Gerardia quercifolia. . . Golden Oak.* Specific of the Sioux for the bite of rattle snakes, used also for the tooth ache. **1876** Hobbs *Bot. Hdbk.* 36, False foxglove, Golden oak, Gerardia Quercifolia. **1900** Lyons *Plant Names* 132. **1959** Carleton *Index Herb. Plants* 54, *Golden oak:* Gerardia virginica.

2 Either of two oaks:

a =canyon oak 1. [See quot 1910] Cf **golden-cup oak, golden-leaf oak**

1910 Jepson *Silva CA* 223, On account of the pollen-like powder on the under side of the younger leaves it [=*Quercus chrysolepis*] is famed as Golden Oak. **1911** *Century Dict. Suppl.,* *Live oak. . . Cañon live-oak, Quercus chrysolepis,* an evergreen oak of the Pacific coast. . . Also called *golden oak, maul-oak,* and *Valparaiso oak.* **1921** Hall *Hdbk. Yosemite* 128 **ceCA,** The *Transition Zone* . . is characterized by the yellow pine, Douglas spruce, golden oak, black oak, and incense cedar.

b A **black oak** (here: *Quercus velutina*).

1916 Seton *Woodcraft Manual Girls* 283, *Black Oak, Golden Oak, or Quercitron. (Quercus velutina).* . . The outer bark is very rough, bumpy, and blackish; inner bark yellow. This yields a yellow dye called *quercitron.*

golden oriole n

=**Baltimore oriole.**

1844 DeKay *Zool. NY* 2.139, *The Golden Oriole. Icterus Baltimore.* . . Orange: head, neck, wings and tail black. **1882** Nash *2 Yrs. OR* 99 **OR,** Among them is sometimes seen the golden oriole (Icterus Bullockii) . . with his orange jacket and black cap. **1903** WI Nat. Hist. Soc. *Bulletin* 3.1–3.89, *Baltimore Oriole.* A common, or sometimes almost abundant summer resident, the "golden oriole" . . is known to everyone as one of our handsomest village birds. **1917** *Wilson Bulletin* 29.2.83, *Icterus galbula.* . . Golden oriole, Hickman, Ky. **1946** Hausman *Eastern Birds* 556, *Baltimore Oriole. . . Other Names* . . Golden Oriole.

golden owl n [See quot 1923]

=**barn owl 1.**

1898 Grinnell *Birds Pacific Slope* 23, *American Barn Owl.* . . It is popularly known as Golden Owl. **1917** (1923) *Birds Amer.* 2.98, *Barn Owl. . . Other Names.* . . Golden Owl. **1923** WV State Ornith. *Birds WV* 20, *Barn Owl.* . . Common Names: *Golden Owl.* [*Ibid* 21, The barn owls are the most beautiful owls we have. . . It is the wonderful color of the golden yellow plumage and the fine soft texture of the featers [sic] that are admirable.] **1946** Hausman *Eastern Birds* 351, Golden Owl. . . Its very light color is apparent in the gathering dusk.

golden parsnip n

A **golden alexanders 1** (here: *Zizia aptera*).

1933 Small *Manual SE Flora* 981, *Z[izia] cordata. . . Golden-parsnip.* . . Woods, thickets, and prairies.

golden pea n

=**false lupine 1.**

1915 (1926) Armstrong–Thornber *Western Wild Flowers* 246, *Golden Pea. Thermopsis montana* . . seems to me to be especially handsome in northern Arizona, but these plants are also beautiful in the Utah canyons. **1936** McDougall–Baggley *Plants of Yellowstone* 79 **nwWY,** *Goldenpea (Thermopsis montana)* is a stout herb with . . yellow flowers . . borne in a spike, . . quite showy. **1956** St. John *Flora SE WA* 233, *Golden Pea.* . . Pods 4–8 cm. long, . . straight, . . seeds . . bean-shaped, light brown. **1973** Hitchcock–Cronquist *Flora Pacific NW* 273, *Thermopsis.* . . Buck-bean; Golden-pea; Golden-banner.

goldenpert n

A small, usu yellow-flowered plant *(Gratiola aurea).*

1784 in 1785 Amer. Acad. Arts & Sci. *Memoirs* 1.403, *Veronica.* . . Goldenpert. **1821** Barton *Flora* 1.71, *Gratiola aurea.* Golden Pert. Golden-Flowered Hedge-Hyssop. **1900** Lyons *Plant Names* 177, *G[ratiola] aurea* . . is called also Goldenpert. **1919** (1923) House *Wild Flowers NY* 2.249, *Goldenpert.* . . Corolla . . bright yellow. . . Frequent on the sandy, coastal plain. **1940** Clute *Amer. Plant Names* 260. **1959** Carleton *Index Herb. Plants* 54, *Golden pert:* Gratiola aurea.

golden plover n [*OED* 1785 →]

Std: an American plover *(Pluvialis dominica).* Also called **black-breasted plover, bullhead 2a, field bird, field plover, frost-bird 1a, goldenback, goldenwing 3, gray plover 5, greenback 1, greenhead 4b(2), green plover, hillbird, Kankakee bar plover, lowland plover, muddy-breast, pale-belly, pasture bird, prairie bird, prairie pigeon, spotted plover, squealer, three-toed plover, toadhead, trout bird, turkeyback, whistling plover**

golden plume n

A **goldenrod 1** (here: *Solidago canadensis*).

1959 Carleton *Index Herb. Plants* 54, *Golden plume:* Solidago canadensis.

golden poppy See **gold poppy**

golden ragwort n

Std: any of var **ragworts,** but usu *Senecio aureus* which is also called **butterweed 2, cocash 3, coughweed 1, false valerian, fireweed d, liferoot, ragweed, snakeroot, squawweed, uncum, waxweed, wild valerian**

golden rain See **golden shower**

goldenrain tree n [See quot 1955]

A tree of the genus *Koelreuteria,* usu *K. paniculata* which is also called **gate tree, pride of India, varnish tree.**

1923 Amer. Joint Comm. Horticult. Nomenclature *Std. Plant Names* 256, *Koelreuteria.* Goldenrain-tree. *[K.] paniculata.* Goldenrain-tree. **1948** Stevens *KS Wild Flowers* 337, The golden-rain tree, *Koelreuteria paniculata,* often planted in parks and yards, . . has proved to be tolerant of drought and hot winds. It grows to be about 30 feet high, but begins blooming when much smaller. **1952** Blackburn *Trees* 174, Deciduous small tree with panicles of yellow flowers. *Koelreuteria paniculata* . . goldenrain-tree. **1955** *S. Folkl. Qrly.* 19.234, The *Golden Rain Tree.* . . According to the garden editor of the Florida *Times-Union,* the folk name is derived from the terminal panicles of many small flowers, which fall in a breeze like "golden rain." **1967–70** *DARE* (Qu. T16) Inf **IL**130, Goldenrain tree at New Harmony [from] Japan or China; **MO**7, Goldenrain tree. **1971** Kieran *Nat. Hist. NYC* 198, Indeed, there are many other introduced species doing so well in our area that it's quite possible they may "go native" in the long run. This would include the Golden-rain Tree or Pride-of-India *(Koelreuteria paniculata).*

golden redhorse See **golden mullet**

golden robin n

1 also *gold robin:* =**Baltimore oriole.**

1792 Belknap *Hist. NH* 3.165, Golden Robin or Gold Finch, *Oriolus baltimore?* **1808** Wilson *Amer. Ornith.* 1.23, *Oriolus Baltimorus. Baltimore Bird.* . . It is generally known, and, as usual, honored with a variety of names, such as Hang-nest, Hanging-bird, Golden Robin [etc]. **1839** MA Zool. & Bot. Surv. *Fishes Reptiles* 280 **MA,** *The Baltimore Oriole, Icterus Baltimore* . . is known by various names; children call it the gold-robin. **1872** Whittier *PA Pilgrim* 47, The gold-robin cried,/ A-swing upon his elm. **1899** Jewett *Queen's Twin* 167 **swME,** It was a bright cool evening in June, the golden robins sang in the elms. **1907** *DN* 3.188 **NH,** *Golden robin.* . . Baltimore oriole. **1956** MA Audubon Soc. *Bulletin* 40.130, *Baltimore Oriole.* . . Golden Robin (Rather general.) . . Gold Robin (Mass.) **1966–68** *DARE* (Qu. Q14) Inf **MI**65, Golden robin—Baltimore oriole; **NH**5, There's a golden robin, also called Baltimore oriole; **NY**10, Goldfinch—golden robin; **VT**10, Golden robin—same as oriole. **1978** Gromme *Birds WI* 219, Robin, Golden (Northern Oriole).

2 =**brown thrasher.**

1968 *DARE* (Qu. Q14, . . *Other names* . . *for* . . *brown thrasher*) Inf **NY**88, Golden robin.

goldenrod n

1 Std: a plant of the genus *Solidago,* or of a closely related genus such as *Euthamia* or *Petrodoria.* For other names of *Solidago* see **Aaron's rod 1, farewell-summer 2, flower of gold, yellowtop, yellowweed.** For other names of var spp of *Solidago* see **bellyache weed, dyer's weed, false goldenrod 1, golden plume, mountain tea, quobsque weed, silverrod, silverweed, white goldenrod, wallweed, wound weed**

2 A **goldenweed 1** (here: *Haplopappus parryi*).

1953 Nelson *Plants Rocky Mt. Park* 174, *Parry goldenrod Aplopappus parryi.* . . Foliage light green; rays pale yellow; heads about one-half inch high.

goldenrod bug n Also *goldenrod grub, ~ worm*

A larva of a fly of the genus *Eurosta.*

1968 *WI State Jrl.* (Madison) 8 Dec sec 3 8/4 **csWI,** With the fervor of squirrels hunting acorns, they gather goldenrod galls, and lay up the winter's stock of handy bait—goldenrod worms. **1968–69** *DARE* (Qu. P6) Inf **WI**17, Goldenrod bug—for ice fishing; **IL**32, Goldenrod worm—a light-colored worm [that] gets in goldenrod in the fall of the year. **1982** Sternberg *Fishing* 88, Goldenrod grubs are the larvae of goldenrod gall flies. The gallworm is whitish and about the size of a popcorn kernel.

goldenroot n

=**goldenseal 1.**

1971 Krochmal *Appalachia Med. Plants* 144, *Hydrastis canadensis. . . Common names* . . goldenroot.

golden saxifrage n

Std: a plant of the genus *Chrysoplenium.* Also called **golden carpet 2, water carpet.** For addit name of *C. americanum* see **branch lettuce**

goldenseal n

1 also *gold seal:* A perennial plant *(Hydrastis canadensis)* often gathered or grown for its medicinal root. [See quot 1965] Also called **eyebright 3, goldenroot, ground raspberry, ice root, Indiana dye, Indian dye, Indian paint, Indian plant, Indian turmeric, jaundice root, Ohio curcuma, orangeroot, sang-sign, seal herb, tonic root, turmeric root, yelloweye, yellow puccoon, yellowroot, yellowwort, yellow seal, wild curcuma**

1828 Rafinesque *Med. Flora* 1.251, *Hydrastis canadensis. . . Vulgar Names. .* Golden Seal, . . Indian paint, Eyebalm, &c. **1869** Porcher *Resources* 15, *Golden Seal. . .* It has a narcotic smell; used in this country as a tonic. **1911** (1916) Porter *Harvester* 415 **IN,** [This] plant . . has a string of names as long as a princess, but I call it goldenseal, because the roots are yellow. **1944** Howard *Walkin' Preacher* 82, Into the wagon we loaded . . a small sack of dried golden-seal roots which Ott said were being quoted at about three dollars a pound. **1944** Wellman *Bowl* 153 **KS,** After her own doctor give her up, it was. I used golden seal an' kingroot tea. She was up in five days. **1959** [see **3** below]. **1965** *Native Plants PA* 30, "Goldenseal" refers to the ¼ inch thick yellow underground stem with its seal-like scars where shoots of previous seasons emerged. **1966** *DARE* Wildfl QR Pl.87B Inf **AR**46, Goldenseal is the same as yellowroot; **OH**14, Goldenseal. **1968** *Foxfire* Summer 15 **nGA,** Golden seal has two divided green leaves topped by a whitish fuzzy flower in early spring. **1968–69** *DARE* (Qu. S26e, *Other wildflowers not yet mentioned)* Infs **KY**35, **WI**12, Goldenseal; (Qu. BB50d, *Favorite spring tonics around here)* Inf **MI**92, Goldenseal. **1970** *NC Folkl.* 18.21, Golden seal is good for sore eyes, according to the "yarb" doctors. **1976** Bailey–Bailey *Hortus Third* 579, *Goldenseal. . .* Vt. to Minn., s. to Ga., Ala., Ark.

2 A **false Solomon's seal** (here: *Smilacina racemosa*).

1894 *Jrl. Amer. Folkl.* 7.102, *Smilacina racemosa,* . . golden seal, Banner Elk, N.C. **1911** *Century Dict. Suppl., Goldenseal. . .* The false or wild spikenard, *Vagnera racemosa.* **1936** Winter *Plants NE* 9, Called . . Golden-seal or Zig-zag Solomon's Seal. *Smilacina racemosa.* **1940** Clute *Amer. Plant Names* 14, *S[milacina] racemosa. . .* Golden seal.

3 also *gold seal:* A **columbo** (here: *Frasera caroliniensis*).

1959 Carleton *Index Herb. Plants* 54, *Golden seal. . . Gold seal:* Frasera verticillata; Hydrastis canadensis.

golden shad n

Either of two related fish:

a also *gold shad:* A **skipjack** (here: *Alosa chrysochloris*).

1820 Rafinesque *Ohio R. Fishes* 39, *Pomolobus chrysochloris. . .* Greenish-yellow above, silvery beneath. . . Its vulgar names are Ohio Shad, Gold Shad, Green Herring, &c. **1877** U.S. Natl. Museum *Bulletin* 9.14, Clupea chrysochloris. Golden Shad. **1908** Forbes–Richardson *Fishes of IL* 48, *Pomolobus chrysochloris. . .* The golden shad . . is a beautiful symmetrical fish, shading from green to silvery, with rich golden reflections. . . It is not a common fish in Illinois. **1960** Amer. Fisheries Soc. *List Fishes* 69, Shad, golden—see herring, skipjack. **1983** Becker *Fishes WI* 265, *Alewife. . .* Other common names . . golden shad. *Ibid* 270, *Skipjack Herring. . .* Other common names . . golden shad.

b An **alewife** (here: *Alosa pseudoharengus*).

1946 LaMonte *N. Amer. Game Fishes* 150, *Alewife. Pomolobus pseudoharengus. . .* Golden Shad. . . Gray-green or blue-green on back and upper sides; silvery and sometimes very iridescent below. **1983** [see **a** above].

golden-shafted woodpecker See **goldenwing woodpecker**

golden shiner n

A fish *(Notemigonus chrysoleucas)* of the minnow family. Also called **bitterhead 2, bream B1, butterfish 2, dace, goldfish 2, gudgeon 1, roach, shiner, sunfish, windfish, young shad**

1882 U.S. Natl. Museum *Bulletin* 16.250, *Golden Shiner. . .* New England to Dakota and Texas; everywhere abundant in bayous and weedy ponds. **1896** *Ibid* 47.250. **1908** Forbes–Richardson *Fishes of IL* 127, The golden shiner is said to be an excellent pan-fish, if of sufficient size. **1947** Hubbs–Lagler *Fishes Gt. Lakes* 65, *Eastern Golden Shiner. . .* Ordinarily in ponds and sluggish streams. **1955** Carr–Goin *Guide Reptiles* 51, Southeastern Golden Shiner. . . A deep-bodied, laterally compressed, golden- and silvery-colored fish with a small, delicate mouth. **1971** Brown *Fishes MT* 79, The natural range of the golden shiner extends from southern Canada east of the Rockies south to the Gulf states. **1983** Becker *Fishes WI* 435, The golden shiner is a known host to the glochidial stage of the clam known as the floater, *Anodonta grandis.*

golden shower n Also *golden rain, golden shower tree*

An ornamental yellow-flowered tree *(Cassia fistula).* Also called **Midas tree**

1900 Lyons *Plant Names* 87, *C[assia] Fistula. . .* Cult. widely in tropical regions. Golden-shower tree. . . Tree highly ornamental. **1929** Neal *Honolulu Gardens* 142, One of the most beautiful flowering trees in Honolulu is the golden shower. **1953** Greene–Blomquist *Flowers South* 81, *Golden-shower. . .* In early spring, racemes a foot long of claw-like blossom, like a golden shower, hang gracefully from this small tree. **1967** *DARE* (Qu. T16) Inf **HI**11, Golden shower. **1976** Bailey–Bailey *Hortus Third* 228, *[Cassia] fistula. . .* Golden-rain. **1982** Perry–Hay *Field Guide Plants* 18, Golden shower . . golden rain. . . *Flowers:* clear yellow, 5 petals of unequal size, with thread-like curling stamens, fragrant, in pendent 30–45 cm . . sprays.

golden slipper n

1 A yellow **lady's slipper** (here: *Cypripedium calceolus* var *parviflorum* or *pubescens*). **esp Sth**

1903 Small *Flora SE U.S.* 311, *Cypripedium hirsutum. . .* In woods and on shaded banks. . . *Golden Slipper.* **1911** *Century Dict. Suppl., Golden-slipper. . .* The larger yellow lady's-slipper, *Cypripedium hirsutum.* **1949** Moldenke *Amer. Wild Flowers* 384, Also very well known are *C. parviflorum* and *C. calceolus* var. *pubescens,* . . with pale, or golden, yellow flowers and purple nectar guides. . . In the southern part of their range these lovely flowers are commonly called *goldenslippers.* **1950** Correll *Native Orchids* 24, *Cypripedium Calceolus* . . var. *pubescens. . . Common names* . . Golden Slipper. **1971** Krochmal *Appalachia Med. Plants* 106, *Cypripedium calceolus* . . var. *parviflorum. . .* Small golden slipper. . . It has large, sac-like yellow "slippers". **1976** Bailey–Bailey *Hortus Third* 356, *[Cypripedium] Calceolus. . .* Var. *parviflorum. . .* Small golden-slipper. . . Var. *pubescens. . .* Golden-slipper.

2 **=butter-and-eggs 1.**

1968 *DARE* (Qu. S11, . . *Other names . . for . . wild snapdragon)* Inf **OH**80, Golden slipper.

3 pl: See **golden slipper bird.**

golden slipper bird n Also *golden slippers* [See quot 1990] **=snowy egret.**

1936 *Auk* 53.347 **swFL,** *Egretta thula thula. Snowy Heron* (locally "Golden Slippers").—Particularly common, flocks of as many as fifteen encountered among mangroves of Shark River. About 100 individuals at roosting grounds. **1964** Will *Hist. Okeechobee* 94 **FL,** Golden slipper bird . . snowy egret. **1990** *Natl. Parks* May/June 47 **Everglades FL,** The snowy egret is an energetic hunter, . . occasionally stirring up the bottom with a flash of its yellow toes, which have earned it the nickname "golden slippers."

golden smoke n

A **golden corydalis** (here: *Corydalis aurea*).

1953 Nelson *Plants Rocky Mt. Park* 78, *Golden smoke . . Corydalis aurea. . .* A very attractive plant forming clumps of pale or bluish-green feathery foliage. **1967** Dodge *Roadside Wildflowers* 12, *Golden-smoke. . .* One of the first spring flowers, this low-growing perennial vies with the pussywillow in announcing arrival of a new growing season. **1973** Hitchcock–Cronquist *Flora Pacific NW* 145, Common over much of N[orth] Am[erica] . . g[olden] smoke.

golden spider n Also *golden garden spider*

Perh an orb weaver (*Araneus* spp).

1966–70 *DARE* (Qu. R28, . . *Kinds of spiders)* Infs **IL**135, **OH**74, Golden spider; **NM**6, Big golden spider . . a flycatcher type, builds a large web; **GA**65, Golden garden spider.

golden star n

1 usu pl: A yellow-flowered plant *(Bloomeria crocea)* native to California; also its blossom.

1897 Parsons *Wild Flowers CA* 154, *Golden Stars. . .* Just as the floral procession begins to slacken a little . . , the fields suddenly blossom out anew and twinkle with millions of the golden stars of the *Bloomeria.*

1915 (1926) Armstrong-Thornber *Western Wild Flowers* 22, In late spring the meadows around Pasadena and other places in the Coast Range are bright with pretty clusters of Golden Stars. **1949** Moldenke *Amer. Wild Flowers* 356, The *goldenstars* . . is a . . Californian plant with 30 to 50 orange-yellow flowers per cluster. **1959** Carleton *Index Herb. Plants* 54, *Golden star:* Bloomeria crocea (B. aurea); Chrysogonum virginianum; Chrysopsis mariana. **1976** Bailey-Bailey *Hortus Third* 167, *Golden-stars*. . . Fl[ower]s orange-yellow, striped with darker lines.

2 =**golden aster 1.**

1900 Lyons *Plant Names* 100, *C[hrysopsis] graminifolia*. . . Southeastern U.S. . . Golden-aster, Golden-star. **1940** Clute *Amer. Plant Names* 80, *C. mariana.* Golden Star. **1959** [see **1** above].

3 A low perennial plant *(Chrysogonum virginianum)* native from Pennsylvania to Florida and Louisiana. Also called **green-and-gold**

1949 Moldenke *Amer. Wild Flowers* 202, Natives of the coastal plain and Blue Ridge Mountains are partial to the brazen beauty of their *goldenstar.* **1953** Greene-Blomquist *Flowers South* 137, *Golden-Star* . . is a favorite with many lovers of wild flowers. **1959** [see **1** above]. **1965** *Native Plants PA* 52, Chrysogonum virginianum—Goldenstar. **1976** Bruce *How to Grow Wildflowers* 228, One of the first (if not the very first) of all composites to bloom is a creeping yellow daisy called "Goldenstar," *Chrysogonum virginianum.*

golden stripe n Also *golden-stripe terrapin*

A **red-bellied turtle** (here: *Chrysemys rubriventris*).

[**1952** Carr *Turtles* 272, During the latter part of the nineteenth century the immensely popular diamondback terrapin began to decline in abundance and to be increasingly replaced in many markets by red-bellied turtles of the Chesapeake Bay region. . . Today, . . this turtle may still be seen in the markets of Washington, Baltimore, and Philadelphia.] **1954** *Sun* (Baltimore MD) 7 Nov mag sec 9/3 **Chesapeake Bay,** It may come as a surprise to many to learn that the golden-stripe terrapin, that well-known competitor of the revered diamond-back for gastronomic honors, is quite abundant. *Ibid* 17/1, Snapper trappers catch hundreds of the golden stripes incidental to their labors. *Ibid* 17/2, At the other extreme are the cute and gentle golden stripes. Not only are their markings unusually beautiful, but they become excellent pets for children, learning to obey commands, and otherwise making themselves adaptable.

golden sucker See **golden mullet**

golden thread See **goldthread**

goldentop n

An introduced grass *(Lamarckia aurea).*

1911 *Century Dict. Suppl., Goldentop*. . . An ornamental grass, *Achyrodes aureum,* which grows in low tufts and bears elegant one-sided panicles. It has been introduced from the Mediterranean region into southern California, where it has become spontaneous. **1911** Jepson *Flora CA* 65, *L[amarckia] aurea. . . Golden-top*. . . Now abundant in the interior southern portions of the State. **1923** Abrams *Flora Pacific States* 1.196, Golden-top. . . Panicle dense, . . wide, shining, golden-yellow or purplish. **1959** Munz-Keck *CA Flora* 1495, *Golden-top*. . . Common weed in s. Calif. **1976** Bailey-Bailey *Hortus Third* 634, *Goldentop*. . . Sometimes cult. for ornament and escaped in Tex., Ariz., s. Calif.

golden torch n

=**golden club 1.**

1972 Brown *Wildflowers LA* 9, *Golden-torch. Orontium aquaticum*. . . Flowers tiny, sunken in a golden yellow apical portion of the spadix, the lower part is whitish. Scape erect in flower.

golden trout n [From the color]

1 A **trout** *(Salmo aquabonita)* native to California, but introduced into other parts of the West. [See quot 1904] Cf **4** below

1875 in 1909 Holder-Jordan *Fish Stories* 101 **CA,** So long ago as 1875, Mr. H. W. Henshaw noticed the *Salmo aquabonita* in the waters of the south fork of the Kern. He says. . . "The color is usually very bright, and for beauty this species takes rank with the foremost of its kind, and it has well been called the golden trout." **1883** in 1947 Sierra Club *Bulletin* 32.5.82 **CA,** We pushed on to Whitney Creek . . and we went farther up and stopped to fish. *Golden trout*—lovelier than gold fish, with red splashes on their sides—hundreds of them. **1896** U.S. Natl. Museum *Bulletin* 47.503, *Golden Trout of Mount Whitney*. . . Olive above; sides and belly light golden, always showing the dark cross shades of immature trout. **1904** *Salmon & Trout* 266, This fish has the most beautiful coloration of any of the salmon-trouts, and it is appropriately called the "golden trout," for a golden or orange tinge of different depths of color may be seen on all parts of the body, on the gill covers, and on the breast and anal fins. **1961** Douglas *My Wilderness* 36 **WY,** The golden trout of Wind River seemed more pretentious than any I had ever known; and they ran to two and two and a half pounds. **1963** Sigler-Miller *Fishes UT* 43, The golden trout is superficially similar to rainbow trout, but . . the deep orange color of the fins and belly are characteristic marks. **1968** *DARE* (Qu. P1, . . *Freshwater fish . . good to eat*) Inf **CA**45, Golden trout.

2 A char *(Salvelinus alpinus).* **nNEng**

1902 Jordan-Evermann *Amer. Fishes* 213 **NH,** *Salvelinus aureolus*. . . The golden trout of Sunapee Lake was not known to anglers until about twenty years ago and it was not described and named until 1888. **1904** *Salmon & Trout* 267, The popular name of this fish [=*Salmo aquabonita*], "golden trout," should not lead to confusion with the Sunapee Lake trout, which also has the common name of "golden trout"; the latter, fortunately, is a charr, and although a handsome fish, it does not have the mellow richness of color as is shown on the salmon-trout of Mt. Whitney. **1933** John G. Shedd Aquarium *Guide* 37, The Golden Trout of Lake Sunapee was originally found only in two or three lakes in New Hampshire and Maine, but its range has been considerably extended by the fish commissioners of those states. **1949** Caine *N. Amer. Sport Fish* 83, The golden trout . . prefers deep water and is usually caught trolling or still fishing at great depths. **1972** Sparano *Outdoors Encycl.* 355, Sunapee trout, Sunapee golden trout. . . *Salvelinus aureolus*. . . Found only in Sunapee Lake and in a few lakes and ponds in northern New England.

3 =**pikeperch.**

1927 Weed *Pike* 45 **NC,** *Stizostedion*. . . Golden Trout.

4 See **goldenfin.**

5 also *golden, gold trout:* A hybrid **trout** (*Salmo aquabonita* x *S. gairdneri*).

1968 *DARE* (Qu. P1, . . *Freshwater fish . . good to eat*) Inf **PA**168, Brown trout, gold trout, rainbow trout—also, recently crosses between these; **WV**8, Trout—golden and blue (both varieties were developed . . at the state hatchery in Petersburg); **WV**10, Trout—golden, rainbow, brown, brook. **1972** Sparano *Outdoors Encycl.* 357, Modern fish-breeding and stocking techniques have extended the range of the golden—or, rather, a golden-rainbow trout cross—to the Eastern states, including West Virginia and New Jersey.

golden warbler n

Any of several somewhat similar birds, as:

a Any of var warblers of the genus *Dendroica,* but usu a **yellow warbler** (here: *D. petechia*). [See quot 1911]

1872 Coues *Key to N. Amer. Birds* 97, *Golden Warbler*. . . Golden-yellow; back olive-yellow, . . wings and tail dusky, yellow-edged. **1889** *Century Dict.* 2566, *Golden warblers,* several species of the genus *Dendrœca,* which resemble the common summer warbler of the United States, *D. æstiva,* in being almost entirely of a bright-yellow color. **1895** Minot *Land-Birds New Engl.* 104, *Dendroica. . . aestiva. . . Golden Warbler.* In southern New England a very common summer resident. **1917** (1923) *Birds Amer.* 3.126, *Yellow Warbler. . . Other Names*. . . Golden Warbler. **1946** Hausman *Eastern Birds* 509, *Dendroica aestiva aestiva*. . . Golden Warbler. . . Our only entirely yellow bird. **1963** Gromme *Birds WI* 218.

b =**prothonotary warbler.**

1917 (1923) *Birds Amer.* 3.113, *Protonotary Warbler. . . Other Names.*—Golden Warbler. **1946** Hausman *Eastern Birds* 498, *Protonotaria citrea*. . . Golden Warbler. . . Male: Entire head, neck, and under parts rich (often an orange) yellow, paling on the abdomen. **1963** Gromme *Birds WI* 218.

c A western subspecies of the Wilson's warbler *(Wilsonia pusilla chryseola).*

1953 Jewett *Birds WA* 577, *Wilsonia pusilla chryseola*. . . Golden Warbler. . . Like the previous subspecies [=*Wilsonia pusilla pileolata*] but smaller and much brighter colored.

goldenwave n

A **tickseed,** usu *Coreopsis basalis* or *C. grandiflora.*

1923 Amer. Joint Comm. Horticult. Nomenclature *Std. Plant Names* 186, Goldenwave. *Coreopsis drummondi.* **1936** Whitehouse *TX Flowers* 178, *Golden Wave. Drummond's Coreopsis* . . is very abundant on sandy coastal prairies in April and May and is well known in cultivation. **1959** Carleton *Index Herb. Plants* 54, *Golden wave:* Coreopsis (v). **1961** Wills–Irwin *Flowers TX* 235, *Golden Wave. Coreopsis grandiflora. Ibid* 236, Long a favorite flower-garden subject . . , Golden-wave, . . is found as a wildflower in East Texas.

goldenweed n

1 A plant of the genus *Haplopappus.* Also called **golden-bush 1.** For other names of var spp see **burroweed 3, geyser daisy, gold daisy, golden fleece, goldenrod 2, iron plant, jimmy-weed, mock heather, pine bush, rabbitbrush, rheumatic plant, rosinweed, rubberweed, sawleaf daisy, turpentine bush, yellow aster, yellowbrush, yellow daisy**

1931 U.S. Dept. Ag. *Misc. Pub.* 101.156, *Goldenweeds.* . . Many of the species are worthless unless the range is overgrazed, overstocked, or both. **1961** Wills–Irwin *Flowers TX* 224, Saw-leaf Daisy, or Goldenweed, as it is sometimes called, is a drought-resistant plant. **1963** Craighead *Rocky Mt. Wildflowers* 214, This goldenweed [=*Haplopappus acaulis*] is a yellow-flowered composite that grows in dense patches. . . Yellow ray- and diskflowers form single heads ½–1 in. across. **1973** Hitchcock–Cronquist *Flora Pacific NW* 524, *Haplopappus.* . . Goldenweed. **1981** Benson–Darrow *Trees SW Deserts* 332, *Haplopappus cuneatus* . . *Wedgeleaf Golden Weed.* . . *Haplopappus linearifolius* . . *Narrowleaf Golden Weed.* . . The large, conspicuous flower heads make the species conspicuous in the desert landscape during the spring.

2 A similar plant *(Ericameria triantha).*

1960 Vines *Trees SW* 1006, *Three-flower Goldenweed.* . . Apparently known only from the Brewster County area of Texas.

goldenwing n

1 See **goldenwing woodpecker.**

2 See **golden-winged warbler.**

3 =**golden plover.**

1923 U.S. Dept. Ag. *Misc. Circular* 13.69, *Golden Plover. . . Vernacular Names. . . In local use.* . . Goldenwing (Miss.)

golden-winged warbler n Also *goldenwing*

A warbler *(Helminthophila chrysoptera)* with a conspicuous yellow wing patch. Also called **yellowbird**

1810 Wilson *Amer. Ornith.* 2.113, Golden-Winged Warbler, *Sylvia Chrysoptera* . . is another spring passenger thro the United States to the North. **1898** (1900) Davie *Nests N. Amer. Birds* 430, *Golden-winged Warbler.* . . Swampy lands that skirt small woods are its favorite resorts in Central Ohio. **1917** (1923) *Birds Amer.* 3.118, A hybrid may have either the song of the Golden-wing or the Blue-wing. . . The Golden-wing song is a sweet *zee-i-zee* or *zee-u-zwee* given three or four times and repeated many times when the bird . . bursts into joyous enthusiasm. **1936** Roberts *MN Birds* 2.195, Minnesota is on the northern limit of the range of the Golden-wing. **1955** Forbush–May *Birds* 413, The Golden-winged Warbler is a beautiful and graceful little bird. **1962** Imhof *AL Birds* 442, *Golden-winged Warbler.* . . Pearl gray above and white below with a *golden-yellow crown* and *wing bars* and a *black bill, throat,* and *cheeks.*

goldenwing woodpecker n For varr see quots

=**flicker** n² **1.**

1731 (1754) Catesby *Nat. Hist. Carolina* 1.18 **S Atl,** *The Gold-winged Wood-pecker* . . weighs five ounces. . . The beams of all the Wing Feathers are of a bright gold-colour. **1844** Giraud *Birds Long Is.* 181, *Golden-winged Woodpecker.* . . Under surface of wings and tail golden yellow. **1877** Burroughs *Birds & Poets* 118, Another marked April note . . is the call of the high-hole, or golden-shafted wood-pecker. **1891** Goss *Hist. Birds KS* 339, 'Flicker,' 'High-hole,' 'Yellow-hammer,' . . the Golden-wing is known by all these names. **1900** *Wilson Bulletin* 31.7, *Golden-shafted Woodpecker, Golden-wing,* . . *Golden-winged Woodpecker, Gold-wing Woodpecker, Golden-wing Woodpecker, Gold-winged Woodpecker.* In more or less frequent use. . . *Golden Woodpecker.* New York. **1956** MA Audubon Soc. *Bulletin* 40.82, Golden-wing Woodpecker (Maine, N.H. The shafts of the flight feathers and the underside of the wing are golden yellow.) **1969–70** *DARE* (Qu. Q17, . . *Kinds of woodpeckers*) Inf **MA67,** Golden-winged woodpecker; **TN53,** Golden woodpecker. **1969** Longstreet *Birds FL* 87, Flicker. Other names . . Golden-winged Woodpecker.

golden yarrow n

A **woolly daisy** (here: *Eriophyllum confertiflorum*) of dry areas in California and the Southwest.

1897 Parsons *Wild Flowers CA* 180, In early summer many a dry, rocky hill-slope is ablaze with the brilliant flowers of the golden yarrow. **1915** (1926) Armstrong–Thornber *Western Wild Flowers* 546, *Golden Yarrow* . . has small flowers, but it forms such large clumps that the effect of the golden-yellow clusters is handsome and very conspicuous. . . The leaves are more or less woolly. **1954** CA Div. Beaches & Parks *Pt. Lobos Wild Flowers* 33, *Eriophyllum confertiflorum.* Golden Yarrow. **1974** Munz *Flora S. CA* 163, *Golden Yarrow.* . . Perennial, somewhat woody at base to quite shrubby. . . Dry slopes and washes near the coast.

goldeye n Also *gold-eyed mooneye*

A **mooneye** (here: *Hiodon alosoides*).

1943 *Sat. Eve. Post* 1 May 25/1 **West,** Do the gold-eyes still bite the way they used to? **1946** LaMonte *N. Amer. Game Fishes* 102, *Hiodon alosoides.* . . Gold-eyed Mooneye. . . Ohio River northwest to Manitoba and Saskatchewan. **1956** Harlan–Speaker *IA Fish* 60, The goldeye is quite common in the Missouri River, occasional in some of its tributaries, and is taken rarely in its oxbow lakes. . . The eye . . is bright gold in color. **1966** *DARE* (Qu. P3, *Freshwater fish that are not good to eat*) Infs **MT3, ND9,** Goldeye. **1971** Brown *Fishes MT* 38, The goldeye . . will take natural and artificial bait and put up a good fight. . . Its flesh is soft and bony but palatable. **1983** Becker *Fishes WI* 283, There seems to be general agreement . . that smoked goldeye is a gourmet delicacy. This product, whether it comes from Canada or the border states, is known as "Winnipeg goldeye," and since 1930 the demand has regularly exceeded the supply.

gold-eyed grass n

A **star grass** (here: *Hypoxis* spp, esp *H. hirsuta*).

1959 Carleton *Index Herb. Plants* 54, *Gold-eyed-grass:* Hypnoxis [sic] hirsuta.

gold-eyed mooneye See **goldeye**

gold fields n [See quots 1911, 1915]

1 A plant of the genus *Baeria* or of the genus *Lasthenia.* **esp CA** For other names of *B. chrysostoma* see **fly-flower 1, scrambled eggs, sunshine**

1911 *Century Dict. Suppl., Gold-field* . . *pl,* In California, a plant of the composite genus *Baeria* and to some extent of the related genus *Lasthenia:* so named from the fact that these plants cover the ground with their yellow bloom. The species are low herbs, some of which endure saline or alkaline soil. **1915** *Nature & Sci.* 149 **sCA,** *Baeria chrysostoma* grows in such abundance that it is known as gold-fields. **1947** *Desert Mag.* April 12/3 *(DA),* April possibilities: staghorn cholla, hedgehog cactus . . gold fields . . and crownbeard. **1961** Thomas *Flora Santa Cruz* 368 **cwCA,** *Baeria.* . . Goldfields. . . Individual specimens are hard to place in one species or another. **1967** *DARE* (Qu. S26e) Inf **CA4,** Gold fields . . [a] desert flower in the daisy family. **1985** Dodge *Flowers SW Deserts* 86, *Goldfields. Lasthenia californica.* . . After winters of particularly heavy precipitation, these small close growing annuals with their sunflowerlike blossoms cover large patches of desert with a carpet of gold.

2 =**spring gold.**

1967 Gilkey–Dennis *Hdbk. NW Plants* 450, *Crocidium multicaule.* . . *Gold fields.* . . Heads . . golden-yellow. . . Moist open places, blossoming very early in the spring.

goldfinch n

1 A bird of the genus *Carduelis,* esp *C. tristis.* Also called **thistle bird, wild canary, yellowbird.** For other names of *C. tristis* see **alder bird, beet bird, corn-tossel bird, dandelion bird, flax bird, hemp bird, influenza sparrow, keehee, lettuce bird, salad bird, seed eater, shiner, summer yellowbird, swamp canary, thistle finch, tweet, twitter bird.** For other names of var spp see **pine siskin, tarweed canary**

[**1737** (1911) Brickell *Nat. Hist. NC* 196, The *Goldfinches.* There are a sort of Birds like these to be met with here, variegated with *Orange* and *Yellow* Feathers.] **1839** Audubon *Synopsis Birds* 116, Carduelis tristis. . . American Goldfinch. . . Male rich lemon-yellow, fading behind into yellowish-white; upper part of head, wings, and tail black. **1872** *Md. Laws* 664 *(DA),* It shall be unlawful . . to shoot or trap . . any of the following named birds: . . wren, pewit, goldfinch, . . [etc.] **1913** *Pacific Coast Avifauna* 9.76 **CA,** These goldfinches appear to be distributed everywhere through the lowlands of Fresno County. **c1960** *Wilson Coll.* **csKY,** *Goldfinch.* . . A bird known to nearly everybody in its summer dress but regularly called Wild Canary. **1961** Douglas *My Wilderness* 191 **MD,** The others were the goldfinches, which some call wild canaries. On warm days they drop in flight as if they were riding roller coasters, singing all the while, "Per-chik-o-ree." **1965–70** *DARE* (Qu. Q14) 250 Infs, **widespread,** Goldfinch; **CA**78, Greenback goldfinch, Lawrence goldfinch, willow goldfinch; **TX**84, Arkansas goldfinch.

2 =Baltimore oriole. NEast

1792 Belknap *Hist. NH* 3.165, Golden Robin or Gold Finch, *Oriolus baltimore?* **1832** Williamson *Hist. ME* 1.143, One has with us these three species: 1. the *Goldfinch* or *Golden Robin;* 2. the *Hang-bird;* and 3. the *Redwing Blackbird.* **1956** MA Audubon Soc. *Bulletin* 40.130, *Baltimore Oriole*. . . Goldfinch (N.H., Vt. About half of the plumage of the male is yellow to orange; however, the bird is not a finch nor does it resemble the birds of that family which are known as Goldfinches.) **1967** *DARE* (Qu. Q14) Inf **NY**10, Goldfinch: golden robin.

goldfish n

1 also *ocean goldfish:* **=garibaldi.**

1884 Goode *Fisheries U.S.* 1.276, On the California coast occurs . . the "Garibaldi". . . The names "Gold-fish" and "Red Perch" are also used, . . referring to its brilliant orange colorations. **1911** U.S. Bur. Census *Fisheries 1908* 310, *Goldfish*. . . The name is also applied to a California damsel-fish *(Hypsypops rubicundus).* **1939** Natl. Geogr. Soc. *Fishes* 230, These ocean goldfish, as they are known along the coast of southern California, . . are the most brilliant species to be seen . . off Santa Catalina Island. **1953** Roedel *Common Fishes CA* 115, *Garibaldi*. . . *Unauthorized Name:* Ocean goldfish.

2 =golden shiner.

1983 Becker *Fishes WI* 432, *Golden Shiner*. . . Other common names: . . goldfish.

goldflower n

Any of several **bitterweeds** of the genus *Hymenoxys;* see quots.

1941 Jaeger *Wildflowers* 298 **Desert SW,** Biennial Goldflower. *Hymenoxys biennis*. . . Bell Goldflower. *Hymenoxys chrysanthemoides excurrens*. . . *Fl[owers]:* yellow. **1960** Abrams *Flora Pacific States* 4.208, *Hymenoxys cooperi*. . . Cooper's Goldflower. . . *Hymenoxys lemmonii*. . . Lemmon's Goldflower. **1963** Craighead *Rocky Mt. Wildflowers* 221, *Hymenoxys grandiflora*. . . Alpine Goldflower. . . This plant, found above timberline, has large sunflower-like blossoms.

gold foxglove n

A **false foxglove** (here: *Aureolaria* spp).

1942 (1960) Robertson *Red Hills* 200 **SC,** Wild patches of blazing gold foxglove, . . and great gold beds of wild indigo and mustard.

gold-headed hornet n

=bald-faced hornet.

1966 *DARE* (Qu. R21) Inf **WA**30, Gold-headed hornet (white-faced).

gold heather n Also *golden heather*

A **beach heather,** usu *Hudsonia ericoides.*

1933 Small *Manual SE Flora* 881, *H[udsonia] ericoides*. . . Gold-heather. . . Especially in pinelands near the coast. **1948** Wherry *Wild Flower Guide* 67, *Woolly Gold-heather (Hudsonia tomentosa)*. . . Flowers small but numerous. . . A less woolly species, *H. ericoides,* known as *Gold-heather* . . , grows in Atlantic pinelands. **1950** Gray–Fernald *Manual of Botany* 1018, *H[udsonia] ericoides*. . . Golden-heather. **1971** GA Dept. Ag. *Farmers Market Bulletin* 25 Aug 8 **GA,** Hudsonia ericoides, commonly known as Poverty-weed, Beach-heather, Gold-heather, and Cloth-of-Gold are [sic] more likely to be found on the Georgia coast than its near relative Hudsonia tomentosa. The species native to our shore grows about 7 inches tall and its leaves are much greener than other Hudsonia plants.

gold-leaf oak See **goldenleaf oak**

goldplush n Also *goldplush pricklypear*

A **prickly pear** (here: *Opuntia microdasys*).

1942 Amer. Joint Comm. Horticult. Nomenclature *Std. Plant Names* 76/2, *[Opuntia] microdasys.* Goldplush P[ricklypear]. **1976** Bailey–Bailey *Hortus Third* 793, *[Opuntia] microdasys*. . . *Goldplush*. . . Areoles close-set, with many yellow glochids in a conspicuous tuft, rarely with a short yellow spine.

gold poppy n Also *golden poppy*

A plant of the genus *Eschscholtzia,* esp *E. californica.*

1902 Smith *Golden Poppy* 137, But the wild gold poppy is free. **1937** U.S. Forest Serv. *Range Plant Hdbk.* W76 (leaf 2), *Goldpoppies. Eschscholtzia* spp. The goldpoppies, a western North American genus of the poppy family. . . all . . resemble California-poppy in having . . orange or straw-colored petals. **1970** Correll *Plants TX* 662, *Eschscholtzia*. . . *California Poppy. Gold Poppy.* About a dozen species confined to western North America. **1973** Hitchcock–Cronquist *Flora Pacific NW* 143, *E[schscholtzia] californica*. . . Cal[ifornia] or gold poppy.

goldring n [See quot 1820]

A **crappie** (here: *Pomoxis annularis*).

1820 Rafinesque *Ohio R. Fishes* 33, *Pomoxis annularis*. . . Golden ring at the base of the tail. . . Vulgar names Gold-ring and Silver-perch. **1933** LA Dept. of Conserv. *Fishes* 333, *The sac-a-lait*. . . Names . . are as follows: . . Goggle-eye, Goldring [etc]. **1949** Caine *N. Amer. Sport Fish* 33, White . . crappie. . . *Colloquial Names*. . . Goldring.

gold robin See **golden robin 1**

gold seal See **goldenseal 1, 3**

gold shad See **golden shad a**

gold shell n [See quot 1889]

A **jingle shell** (here: *Anomia simplex*).

1881 Ingersoll *Oyster-Industry* 244, Gold-shell.—A species of *Anomia.* **1889** *Century Dict.* 2567, *Gold-shell*. . . *Anomia ephippium,* a bivalve mollusk, so called from one of its varieties having a golden luster. It is one of several species, all known as *clink-shells* and *jingle-shells*. . . Also called *silver-shell.*

goldsmith beetle n Also *goldsmith*

A beetle of the genus *Cotalpa,* usu *C. lanigera.*

1854 Emmons *Agriculture NY* 5.65, The common *horn beetle,* or the *goldsmith beetle,* which fly about in the evening in the months of June and July, may well represent this family. **1862** U.S. Patent Office *Annual Rept. for 1861: Ag.* 601 **sePA,** *Gymnetis nitida* . . [is] commonly called in this locality the "Goldsmith." **1868** *Amer. Naturalist* June 189 **NJ,** I have never found the Goldsmith in the fall. **1877** VT State Bd. Ag. *Report* 4.158, A somewhat larger golden bronze beetle, which is much less common, has been found in the larval state eating strawberry roots; but this beetle, *Cotalpa lanigera,* or goldsmith beetle, is not common enough to do much damage with us. **1926** Essig *Insects N. Amer.* 446, The *western goldsmith beetle, C[otalpa] tau* . . , is 20–26 mm. long, metallic yellowish. . . It often completely defoliates cottonwood trees. **1972** Swan–Papp *Insects* 436, The *Goldsmith Beetle, Cotalpa lanigera* . . , is similar in color, habits, and distribution [to *Pelidnota punctata*]. **1980** Milne–Milne *Audubon Field Guide Insects* 557, *Goldsmith Beetle (Cotalpa lanigera)*. . . This brilliantly colored beetle is [*DARE* Ed: Rather, it might have inspired] the celebrated "gold bug" of Edgar Allan Poe's short story.

gold star n

=spring gold.

1961 Peck *Manual OR* 828, *Crocidium*. . . Small slender annuals with mainly basal leaves and one to several simple stems; heads solitary. . . *C. multicaule*. . . *Gold-Star*. . . Wet banks, Columbia Gorge to eastern and southwestern Ore. and Calif.

goldthread n Also *golden thread*

1 also *gooldthread:* A plant of the genus *Coptis.* [See quots] **chiefly NEast** Also called **cankerroot 1.** For other names of *C. groenlandica* see **mouthroot, yellowroot**

1758 in 1923 House *Wild Flowers NY* 102, In the Memoirs of Bastram [sic for *Bartram*] and Marshall, . . John Ellis, the eminent naturalist, in a letter to Linnaeus, . . says: "Mr Colden of New York, has sent Dr Fothergill a new plant described by his daughter (Miss Jane Colden). It is called Fibraurea, gold thread." **1778** Carver *Travels N. Amer.* 513, *Gold thread.* This is a plant of the small vine kind, which grows in swampy places, and lies on the ground. The roots . . resemble a large entangled skain [sic] of thread of a fine bright gold colour. **1832** Williamson *Hist. ME* 1.124, *Golden-thread* derives its name from its roots, which are of a bright yellow colour, running in all directions like silken cords. **1855** *Harvard Mag.* 1.236 **MA,** A pretty and delicate little plant is the Goldthread, *Coptis trifolia,* so called from the bright golden color of its roots. **1913** Eaton *Barn Doors* 276 **MA,** The tiny jewels of gold-thread are the foreground for a vista of falling brook and emerald vale to the blue dome of the Taconics. **1955** *NY Folkl. Qrly.* 11.281 **NY,** A slightly astringent woodland plant called "gooldthread" by Grandad, came in very handily if any of the family suffered from sore mouth or gums. The roots were dug, dried, and chewed to cure sore mouth. If the gums were sore, the gooldthread was steeped and the tea rubbed on. **1960** Teale *Journey into Summer* 19 **VT,** Modest white flowers rose on slender stems above the . . three-lobed leaves. . . We . . revealed the roots. Against the black mold, each shone with metallic brilliance. It seemed plated with gold. Appropriately, the common name of this wildflower . . is goldthread. **1961** Douglas *My Wilderness* 226 **cNH,** The goldthread (so named for its long bright yellow rootstocks) shows delicate white petals. **1966–70** *DARE* (Qu. S26b, *Wildflowers that grow in water or wet places*) Inf **MA**78, Goldthread; (Qu. S26c, *Wildflowers that grow in woods*) Inf **NY**233, Goldthread; (Qu. S26e, *Other wildflowers*) Inf **MA**6, Goldthread; (Qu. BB50c, *Remedies for infections*) Inf **MA**79, Goldthread. **1966–68** *DARE* Wildfl QR Pl.60A Infs **MN**14, **NH**4, Goldthread. **1982** *Greenfield Recorder* (MA) 9 Jan sec A 4, Grandma told me to go where . . I knew the rather rare and delicate gold thread grew, dig up some of the roots and steep them and use it for a mouthwash.

2 also *goldthread vine:* **=dodder.**

1897 Parsons *Wild Flowers CA* 160, *Golden-thread. Cuscuta*. . . is indeed a beautiful sight, when it spreads its golden tangle over the chamisal, wild buckwheat, and other plants, often completely hiding them from view. **1912** Green *VA Folk-Speech* 270, *Love-vine*. . . Goldthread. **1935** (1943) Muenscher *Weeds* 374, *Cuscuta Gronovii*. . . *Goldthread vine*. . . Widespread and locally abundant throughout eastern North America. **1940** Clute *Amer. Plant Names* 167, Goldthread. *Cuscuta arvensis; Cuscuta Gronovii.* **1959** Carleton *Index Herb. Plants* 54, *Gold thread:* Coptis trifolia; Cuscuta (v).

goldtit n

=verdin.

1917 (1923) *Birds Amer.* 3.216, *Verdin*. . . *Other Names*.—Gold-Tit. . . Head, yellow. **1961** Ligon *NM Birds* 210, The dainty, spirited Verdin, formerly sometimes referred to as the Gold-tit, is resident in the arid lower Sonoran Life Zone of the southern part of the state.

gold tongue n [See quot 1953]

An **owl's clover** (here: *Orthocarpus luteus* or *O. tenuifolius*).

1953 Nelson *Plants Rocky Mt. Park* 143, *Gold-tongue*. . . *Orthocarpus luteus*. . . An erect plant . . with a dense spike of yellow flowers interspersed with green bracts. **1959** Carleton *Index Herb. Plants* 54, *Gold tongue:* Orthocarpus luteus. **1963** Craighead *Rocky Mt. Wildflowers* 173, *Orthocarpus tenuifolius*. . . Goldtongue. . . An erect annual plant. . . with dense spike of yellow flowers (often purple-tipped) at top, interspersed and partly hidden by purple-tipped bracts.

gold trout See **golden trout 5**

gold watch n

A **spatterdock** (here: *Nuphar luteum*).

1893 *Jrl. Amer. Folkl.* 6.136, *Nuphar advena,* gold watch. Mauch Chuck, Pa. (name perhaps not general there).

goldweed n

1 A **buttercup 1:** usu *Ranunculus arvensis,* but also *R. acris.*

1900 Lyons *Plant Names* 316, *R[anunculus] arvensis*. . . Gold-weed. **1911** *Century Dict. Suppl., Gold-weed*. . . The corn crowfoot, *Ranunculus arvensis.* **1959** Carleton *Index Herb. Plants* 54, *Gold-weed:* Ranunculus acris.

2 A **crownbeard** (here: *Verbesina encelioides*).

1940 Clute *Amer. Plant Names* 275, *Verbesina encelioides.* Goldweed. **1967** Dodge *Roadside Wildflowers* 85, *Goldweed.* An all-yellow, sunflower-like annual, . . the plants sometimes take over open fields creating spectacular mass displays like blankets of gold. . . *Verbesina encelioides.*

goldwing(ed) woodpecker See **goldenwing woodpecker**

goldwire n [See quots 1911, 1951] **CA**

A **St. John's wort** (here: *Hypericum concinnum*).

1911 Jepson *Flora CA* 263, *H[ypericum] concinnum*. . . *Gold-wire.* Stems wiry, numerous from the woody crown. **1951** Abrams *Flora Pacific States* 3.116, Gold Wire. . . Petals golden yellow, obovate. . . Dry ridges and slopes in the mountains. **1959** Munz–Keck *CA Flora* 192, *Gold Wire.* Bushy perennial with a woody crown and numerous wiry stems. **1976** Bailey–Bailey *Hortus Third* 584, *Goldwire*. . . Dry chaparral slopes, Sierra Nevada and n. Coast Ranges, Calif.

go-light See **go-sign**

golleroy n

1917 *DN* 4.412 **wNC,** *Golleroy*. . . The dottle of a pipe; also called *pipe-guts.*

golliwog n Also sp *gollywog* [From Golliwogg, a grotesque animated Black doll in the children's books of Bertha (d1912) and Florence (d1922) Upton; a doll resembling this character]

Used as an indefinite name for a nameless, indescribable, or imaginary thing or creature; or as an affectonate nickname.

1931 *AmSp* 6.259 **KS,** To the foregoing [list of indefinite names] . . might be added, perhaps, *sandflapper* . . , *gollywog* . . , and *optriculum.* I feel doubtful of their currency—though their reporters were trustworthy persons—since each was known to but one contributor. **1932** *Hench Coll.* **VA,** *Golliwog*—Heard orally: affectionate term for any small living thing, baby, etc. **1942** Berrey–Van den Bark *Amer. Slang* 120.79, *Imaginary creature* . . gollywog. **1953** Randolph–Wilson *Down in Holler* 248 **Ozarks,** *Gollywog*. . . A mythical monster, like a giant salamander. **1968** *DARE* (Qu. E20, *Soft rolls of dust that collect on the floor under beds or other furniture*) Inf **PA**131, Gollywogs.

gollop v Pronc-sp *gullop* [*OEDS* 1823 →; "*dial.* and *colloq.*"] Cf **gulp** v **1**

To gulp; to swallow greedily.

1834 *Life Andrew Jackson* 238, He look'd at me rite earnest, and arter gollopin tu or three mouthfuls of air, he held up his hands as if he thou't the day of judgment was come. **1859** Taliaferro *Fisher's R.* 90 **nwNC** (as of 1820s), They bought a whole bar'l uv salt herrin's; they cooked 'um, and she gulloped down the last one uv 'um. **1899** (1912) Green *VA Folk-Speech* 200, *Gollop*. . . To swallow greedily. "You golloped that down as if you liked it." **1943** *Sat. Eve. Post* 62/2 **LA,** Like I said, they golloped up the rabbit and Miz Swerts piled the bones in a napkin. **1965–70** *DARE* (Qu. DD17, *To drink a great deal, or too fast: "He doesn't just drink, he ________."*) Infs **LA**37, **SC**3, ['gɑləps]; **MD**25, ['gɑlɨps]; **MO**15, **NJ**16, (Just) ['gɑləps] it down; **OK**18, Just ['gɔləps] it down; **SC**43, Gollops; **OH**16, **PA**118, ['gʌləps]; **RI**6, ['gʌlɨps] it down; **MO**32, **TX**32, Gullops it down (*or* up); (Qu. H11a, *If somebody eats rapidly and noisily, you say he* ________) Inf **NJ**21, [Is] galloping his food [sic—FW sp]; **RI**1, Gullops his food; (Qu. H11b, *If he makes a noise with his food, he* ________) Inf **TX**58, Gullops.

gollop n Pronc-sp *gullop, gullup* Cf **gollop** v

A portion or amount; see quots.

1899 (1912) Green *VA Folk-Speech* 200, *Gollop*. . . A large morsel. **1932** *DN* 6.283 **swCT,** *Gullup.* A small quantity of liquid poured from a jug or bottle. "I put so many gullups of molasses in the cake." **1944** *PADS* 2.56 **nSC, MO,** *Gullup* ['gʌləp]. . . The amount of liquid—molasses—that can be poured from a jug or bottle before the container "gets air"? An onomatopoeic word? . . "I used three gullups of molasses in this cake." Rare. **1966–67** *DARE* (Qu. DD18, *A drink of liquor, or the amount of liquor taken in one swallow: "He took a good ________."*) Inf **OH**16, Gullop; (Qu. DD20, *A big drink: "He always takes ________."*; total Infs questioned, 75) Inf **AR**31, Gullop.

gollsocker n Cf **golly-whopper**

Something extraordinary of its kind.

1966 *DARE* (Qu. Y11, . . *A very hard blow*) Inf **SC**11, Gollsocker [ˌgɔl'sɑkə]. **1988** *DARE* File **WI** (as of c1940), That storm sure was a gollsocker ['gɑl'sɑkɚ]!

gollup See **gulp** v

gollybird n Cf **good god**

=ivory-billed woodpecker.

1945 McAtee *Nomina Abitera* 47, Ivory-billed woodpecker. . . One of them [=names], gollybird, is an additional semideified term.

golly-buster n Cf **buster 1, golly-whopper**

1912 *DN* 3.577 **wIN,** *Golly-buster*. . . A very large specimen. "Look at that fish: ain't it a golly-buster?"

gollylag v [By metath from **lollygag**]

1966 *DARE* (Qu. AA8, *When people make too much of a show of affection in a public place*) Inf **OK**18, Gollylaggin' around.

gollynipper See **gallinipper**

golly-whopper n Also *golly-wopper* **chiefly S Midl**

Something extraordinary of its kind.

1933 Williamson *Woods Colt* 16 **Ozarks,** The cat [=catfish] that is dyin' on the gravels is shore a golly-whopper. **1939** *AmSp* 14.90 **TN,** The fish which Sam caught was a golly whopper. **1941** *Jrl. Amer. Folkl.* 54.62 **TX,** *Golly whopper*. . . Cowboy lingo for a tall tale. **1941** Stuart *Men of Mts.* 37 **KY,** Everything purt nigh burnt up on this mountain last year. This year has been a golly-whopper on poor people. **1953** Randolph-Wilson *Down in Holler* 248 **Ozarks,** *Gollywhopper...* A wonder, a marvel. "I fixed me up a gollywhopper of a speech, an' learnt the whole thing by heart." **1954** *Harder Coll.* **cwTN,** *Gollywhopper...* A wonder, a marvel. **1966–68** *DARE* (Qu. R15b, .. *An extra-big mosquito*) Infs **WV**3, 12, Golly-whopper; (Qu. DD20, *A big drink: "He always takes ______."*) Inf **AR**31, A golly-whopper. **c1970** *Halpert Coll.* **wKY, nwTN.** **1972** Hall *Sayings Old Smoky* 143, Aunt Till said, 'Lordee me, if the world's as big yan way as it is yan way [toward the head of Cosby Creek], my God, it's a golly whopper!' **a1975** Lunsford *It Used to Be* 170 **sAppalachians,** A "gollywopper" means a big one.

golly-wobbled adj Also *golly-wop;* by metath, *wolly-gobble* Cf **galley-west, gollywobbles**

Askew, crooked.

1967–70 *DARE* (Qu. KK70, *Something that has got out of proper shape: "That house is all ______."*) Inf **CA**9, Golly-wobbled; **WA**28, Wolly-gobble; (Qu. MM2, *Suppose a little girl .. gets her dress on .. so that the back part is turned around, you could say, "Look, you've got your dress on ______."*) Inf **IL**126, Golly-wop.

gollywobbles n pl Cf **galleywobbles, gonnywobbles**

=**collywobbles 1, 2.**

1942 Berrey–Van den Bark *Amer. Slang* 130.2, *Gollywobbles ..* stomach-ache. **1967–69** *DARE* (Qu. BB5, *A general feeling of discomfort or illness*) Inf **MA**58, Gollywobbles; (Qu. BB19, .. *Looseness of the bowels*) Inf **IL**96, Gollywobbles; (Qu. BB28, .. *Imaginary diseases*) Infs **NY**34, 35, Gollywobbles; (Qu. GG34a, *To feel depressed or in a gloomy mood: "He has the ______ today."*) Infs **MI**108, **MA**58, Gollywobbles.

gollywog See **golliwog**

golly-wop See **golly-wobbled**

golly-wopper See **golly-whopper**

golly-wopper bird n Cf **golly-whopper,** *DS* CC17

An imaginary bird.

1954 Forbes *Rainbow* 68 **NEng,** I've heard a hundred stories of a peddler's tricks to one I've known of personally... I never saw cocoanuts sold for the eggs of the "Golly-wopper Bird" ("lady, all you do is set a goose on them—and will you be pleased when you actually see them hatch!")

gol-nation adv

=**tarnation** adv.

1904 Day *Kin o' Ktaadn* 46 **ME,** They was so gol-nation sure about that letter!

golombki See **golumpki**

golondrina n [AmSpan "swallow" (ornith)]

Any of several **spurges;** see quots.

[**1876** Hobbs *Bot. Hdbk.* 43, Gollindrinera, Euphorbia prostrata.] **1886** Havard *Flora W. & S. TX for 1885* 513, Small, prostrate herbs [=*Euphorbia albomarginata, E. stictospora, E. cinerascens*], common in Western Texas .. are known as Golondrina. **1951** Abrams *Flora Pacific States* 3.38, *Euphorbia polycarpa...* Golondrina.

go 'long v phr See **go along**

go-long n *among Black speakers*

An inevitable consequence, often undesirable, of a sequence of events—freq in phr *in the go-long.*

1937 (1977) Hurston *Their Eyes* 159 **csFL** [Black], Ah ruther be shot wid tacks than fuh you tuh act wid me lak you is right now. You got me in de go-long. **1938** *AmSp* 13.317 **NE** [Black], To be *caught in the go 'long* means to be an unfortunate victim of circumstances. **1942** Hurston in *Amer. Mercury* 55.223.92 **Harlem NYC** [Black], I was uptown when Joe Brown had you all in the go-long last night. Dat cop sure hates a pimp! All he needs to see is the pimp's salute, and he'll out with his night-stick and whip your head to the red. **1965** Bradford *Born with the Blues* 119 **NYC** (as of 1920) [Black], A lot of white southerners would join in the go-long [=would join Blacks in buying a Black singer's records] because they also like their blues and jazz served piping hot with that down-home beat. *Ibid* 123, She .. announced that .. "those two men sitting over there," would be included in the group. That got everybody in the go-long. From the loud hand-clapping, feet stomping and whistling applause, it seemed like the roof was caving in. **1980** *AmSp* 55.155 [Black], A friend of mine from Memphis, Tennessee, was telling me about some of her experiences in New York... She said that, when you call the police there, you know getting your own head "whupped" is just in the go-long. And I recently heard another woman in Memphis explain why she had not been paying visits, according to her custom. She said: "You know? My husband was in the hospital. He's out now, but I couldn't get around at all because I was in that hospital go-long." .. Many younger blacks are not familiar with the word, .. so it may be disappearing.

goloptious, goluptious See **galluptious**

golumpki n pl, but sg or pl in constr For prones and pronc-spp see **A** below [Cf Pol *gołąbki* pl of *golabek,* dimin of *gołąb* pigeon; cf also Ukrainian and Czech *hołub,* Yiddish *holep* in same sense] **chiefly NEast** *esp freq among speakers of Eastern European background* Note: In Slavic langs, *-i* forms are plural; in Engl, the plural-forming suff *-s* is occas added redundantly. While Amer Engl speakers distinguish between forms pronounced with initial /g/ and /h/, the distinction in the orig Slavic langs is essentially orthographic; therefore the var proncs and spp are treated together here.

A Forms.

|gə'lʌmpki, hə'lupki, kə'lʌmpki|; pronc-spp *golumski, golubtzi, halupcha, holupki, kolumpki;* for addit proncs and varr see quots.

1949 (1986) Leonard *Jewish Cookery* 199, *Galuptzi.* **1957** [see **B** below]. **1966–70** *DARE* (Qu. H45) Inf **MA**48, [kə'lʌmpki]; **PA**167, [hə'lupki]; **PA**221, Golumski; **SD**2, [hə'lupsɪ]; (Qu. H52) Inf **PA**134, Holupkas; **RI**5, ['glʌmpiz]; (Qu. H65) Inf **MD**8, [gə'lʌmpki]; **MA**1, Golumpki; **MA**48, 69, [kə'lʌmpki]; **PA**167, ['hlupkiz]; **PA**176, [hə'lupki]; **PA**225, Kolupkis; **PA**245 [hə'lupkiz]. **1987** [see **B** below]. **1989** *Valley Advocate* (Hatfield MA) 10 Apr 33/2, Another .. Polish dish is golombki. **1989** *WI State Jrl.* (Madison) 26 Apr sec C 8/3–4 **wPA,** The joys of Slovak cooking... holupki.

B Sense.

Stuffed cabbage leaves. [From the resemblance to a pigeon at rest] Cf **holishkes, pigs in blankets**

1949 (1986) Leonard *Jewish Cookery* 199, *Holishkes ..* also called .. *Galuptzi,* depending on locale. **1957** Showalter *Mennonite Cookbook* 145 **KS, OR,** Cabbage Bundles or Stuffed Cabbage Leaves—*Golubtzi.* **1966–70** *DARE* (Qu. H45, *Dishes made with meat .. that everybody around here would know, but that people in other places might not*) Inf **MA**48, Kolumpki—a Polish dish; **PA**167, Holupki; **PA**221, Golumski—a meat mixture rolled in cabbage leaves and baked in tomato sauce; **SD**2, Holupsi—like pigs in a blanket; (Qu. H52, *Dishes made with fresh cabbage*) Inf **PA**134, Holupkas—Polish, cabbage leaf with meat, etc, inside; also called pigs in the blanket; **RI**5, Glumpis—that's Polish—cabbage leaves and hamburg; (Qu. H65, *Foreign foods*) Inf **MD**8, Golumpki—ground meat and rice, wrapped in cabbage and cooked in tomato sauce—Polish; **MA**1, Golumpki; **MA**48, 69, Kolumpki; **PA**167, Holupkis—beef-and-rice-filled cabbage; **PA**176, Holupki—same as pig-in-a-basket; **PA**225, Kolupkis; **PA**245, Holupkis—cabbage and hamburg and rice. **1969** *DARE* Tape **PA**221, The golumpskis I make—that uses hamburg and rice and spices. You mix it up like .. a meat loaf. Then you take the outside of cabbage leaves .. put it [=the filling] in the center [of the leaves], roll them up .. in a big flat pan, cover it with tomato juice and vinegar, season it up, and it cooks maybe three, four hours. **1987** *DARE* File **Brooklyn NY** (as of 1940s), [hə'lʌpčəz]—cabbage stuffed with some kind of meat, some rice, some stuff. It's not a real special dish, but not an everyday dish either. You might have it for Shabbat [=Sabbath] or on holidays. [*Ibid,* We had what we kids called "stuffed cabbage"—cabbage rolled up with rice and chopped meat and onions and things. Now my mother and her sister—who by the way spoke more Yiddish than English—called it "holupcha"—something like that. But all the second generation Jewish kids used the English word]. **1989** *WI State Jrl.* (Madison) 26 Apr sec C 8/3–4 **wPA,** [At] the mother church of the American Carpatho-Russian Orthodox Greek Catholic Diocese... there's a wedding .. and this can mean only one thing: the joys of Slovak cooking... There are more variations on holupki than on themes by Paganini, but at its most basic this is the essence of eastern European cooking: meat, starch and cabbage in a zesty combination. **1989** *Valley Advocate* (Hatfield MA) 10 Apr 33/3, You can get take-out golombkis and pierogis by the half-dozen or more from Pulaski Hall and Chopin Restaurant. As Zajak informed us, "You're not getting a pizza."

goluses See **gallus** n

gom v, n See **gaum** v[1], n[1], n[2]

gombo See **gumbo**

gome v See **gaum** v[1]

gome n See **gaum** n[1]

gomicksing up vbl n Cf **gommick around**

Spoiling by over-elaboration; messing up.

1943 *Sun* (Baltimore MD) 19 Oct 16/5 *(Hench Coll.)*, On The Gomicksing Up Of Shad Fish With Red Wine And Oysters With Horse Radish.

gommick around v phr [Perh blend of **gammick** + **gaum** v[1]] Cf **gomicksing up, gormuck**

See quot.

1949 Hornsby *Lonesome Valley* 70 **eKY,** He gommicked the tobacco around in his mouth for a few seconds.

gommux n pl [Pronc-sp for *garments*]

1927 Kennedy *Gritny* 19 **sLA** [Black], Whah you bin paradin' today, droped-up in all yo' curuss clo'se an' gommux (garments)?

gompy n Cf *DS* Z3

1962 Atwood *Vocab. TX* 65, *Grandfather*. . . Miscellaneous nicknames recorded . . include: . . *Gompy.*

gomy See **gaumy** adj[2]

gon See **go** v **A4b**

gondola n

1 pronc-spp *gundalo(w), gunlow;* for addit varr see quots: A large, flat-bottomed river boat. [*OED* cites the var *gundalo* from 1697; cf **cupola, fistula** for similar phonetic changes]

1694 in 1868 NH *Prov. & State Papers* 2.147, Ordered . . that the said W. Furber keep attendance and a sufficient boat or gundaloe. **1723** *New-Engl. Courant* (Boston MA) 20–27 May 2/1, One Indian has likewise been lately kill'd by the English, who fir'd upon him from a Gondola going up a River at N. Yarmouth. **1859** (1968) Bartlett *Americanisms* 173, *Gondola*. . . A flat-bottomed boat or scow used in New England. . . In Pennsylvania and Maryland this word is spelled as well as pronounced *gundalo* or *gundelow*. **1886** *Harper's New Mth. Mag.* July 241/1, The "gondola"—pronounced by the natives gundolo, with accent on the first syllable—is an unwieldly sloop-rigged vessel still in use in the shallow waters of the New England coast. **1894** *Century Illustr. Mag.* 48.873, "Gundalow" was the name given to a large, rough flat-boat on the Potomac; it was to the lively imagination of the earliest boatmen a gondola, or, as they said it, a "gundalo." **1907** *DN* 3.244 **csME,** *Gundalow*. . . A flat boat or scow. **1909** *DN* 3.412 **cnME,** *Gundalow*. . . A flat-bottomed boat. **1966** *DARE* Tape **ME5,** A gunlow? . . It was a flat-bottomed boat and they poled it and they came in with the tide and then they go out with the tide. **1975** Gould *ME Lingo* 118, *Gundalow*—Pronounced gun-low. A river and harbor craft developed from a flat-bottomed, square-ended scow, propelled by sweeps or sails and sometimes poled. It evolved into a definite type of spoon-bowed, round-stern vessel decked completely over and capable of about thirty-five tons of cargo. It was used in sheltered waters to carry lumber and hay, mostly. The word is still heard when somebody compares an odd-looking mahogany job to a *gundalow*.

2 See quot.

1931 *AmSp* 7.79 **NE,** The dictionaries apparently have missed a use of *gondola* still current in Nebraska and possibly in other Western states. The gondola is a long wagon, deep in the middle and sloping up towards the ends. It is used for hauling where the roads permit. Where deep ruts have formed its use has to be given up, for the middle is only a foot and a half from the ground.

gondola hat n

A derby.

1967 Cerello *Dakota Co. MN* 63, My father's Sunday-go-meeting derby disappeared down hole number three [of an outhouse]. . . [He] would be expecting to wear his gondola hat to church on Sunday morning next.

gone adj

1 in phr *gone case:* A lost cause, hopeless case.

1735 in 1809 Edwards *Works* 7.466 **wMA,** When it is come to that [i.e., when backsliders no longer care about their convictions], it is commonly a gone case with persons as to those convictions. **1938** FWP *Guide MS* 116, [He] thought "it was a gone case" with him when Indians grabbed his bridle reins.

2 in combs *gone goose, ~ gosling, ~ beaver, ~ coon,* and varr: One who is past hope; a goner.

1830 *MA Spy & Worcester Co. Advt.* (Worcester MA) 7 July 4/1, You're a gone goose, friend. **1848** (1855) Ruxton *Life Far West* 55, He put his foot into a trap . . set by Mary Brand, . . the beauty of Memphis County. . . From that moment he was "gone beaver;" "he felt queer," he said, "all over, like a buffalo shot in the lights." **1859** *Unsworth's Burnt Cork Lyrics* 56, Well, as soon as the gal saw me, she caved right in. She was a gone coon. **1862** (1864) Browne *Artemus Ward Book* 159, The Browns giv theirselves up for gone coons. **1906** *DN* 3.138 **nwAR,** *Gone goslin.* **1907** *DN* 3.213 **nwAR, cCT,** *Gone coon.* **1908** *DN* 3.315 **eAL, wGA,** *Gone coon. . . Gone goslin.* **1912** Green *VA Folk-Speech* 200, *Gone-gosling*. . . A dead person. **1923** *DN* 5.235 **swWI,** *Gone coon, gone fawnskin, gone goose, gone gosling.* **1927** *AmSp* 2.355 **WV,** *Gone goose . . gone sucker.* **1944** *PADS* 2.56 **MO,** *Gone gosling*. . . A doomed person, animal, or thing. **1945** Thorp *Pardner* 69 **SW,** A cowboy without a horse was a gone gander for sure. **1946** *PADS* 6.15 **eNC** (as of 1900–10), *Gone gosling.* **1947** *PADS* 8.14 **sIN,** *Gone gosling. Ibid* 22 **cKY,** *Gone gosling.* **1948** Hurston *Seraph* 157 **FL,** If he don't . . he's a gone ginny. **1949** *PADS* 11.22 **CO,** *Gone gosling.* **1950** *PADS* 14.32 **SC,** *Gone gosling.* **1953** *PADS* 19.11 **sAppalachians,** He's a gone duck since Sal saw him with May. **1965–70** *DARE* (Qu. BB54, *When a sick person is past hope of recovery, you'd say he's [a] ______*) 11 Infs, **scattered,** Gone goose; **NY**42, **VA**46, Gone coon; **KY**70, **LA**14, Gone gosling; **VA**35, Gone dog; **MN**42, Gone duck; **TX**104, Gone goblin. **1966** Barnes–Jensen *Dict. UT Slang* 19, *Gone beaver* . . a lost man. . . *Gone gosling* . . a hopeless one.

3 Exhausted, faint, empty. Cf **gone in, goneness, gonesome, gone up**

1887 Freeman *Humble Romance* 84 **NEng,** I ain't sick, only kinder all gone with the warm weather. **1893** *KS Univ. Qrly.* 1.139, *Gone:* empty, weak, as 'I had such a gone feeling.' **1894** Twain *Pudd'nhead Wilson* 235 **seMO** [Black], I 'mos' flopped down on de groun', I felt so gone. **1899** (1912) Green *VA Folk-Speech* 200, *Gone*. . . Characterized by a sinking sensation, as if about to faint; weak and faint: as, a *gone* feeling. **1912** Dreiser *Financier* 688, Cowperwood . . experienced a peculiar sense of depression, a gone feeling which he did his best to conceal. **1941** *LANE* Map 482 *(Exhausted)* 1 inf, **RI,** I'm far gone. **1948** Young *Light* 25 **OH,** Willoughby . . had . . what Matild would have called a "gone" feeling in the pit of his concave stomach. **1967** *DARE* (Qu. BB6, *A sudden feeling of weakness, when sometimes the person loses consciousness*) Inf **MA**38, Feel all gone.

4 Intoxicated.

1929 *AmSp* 4.440, Expressions for "drunk" . . about gone, all gone, or gone. **1965–70** *DARE* (Qu. DD15, *A person who is thoroughly drunk*) Infs **CA**7, **CT**23, **LA**23, **PA**76, **SC**54, 69, **TN**50, **WA**30, Gone; (Qu. DD14) Infs **GA**82, **MI**101, **OR**14, **PA**19, 76, Half-gone; **TN**6, About gone; **GA**68, Pretty far gone.

5 also *gone by:* Ago.

1938 Rawlings *Yearling* 2 **nFL,** Ten year gone. **1956** *Living Wilderness* 19.50, I ain't never been through from Minnie's to Billy's but once 'bout 6 year gone. **1967** *DARE* (Qu. A17, *If it was 1960 and you were speaking of something that happened in 1950, you might say, "That was ten ______."*) Inf **TX**36, Years gone; **WA**17, [Years] gone by.

6 foll a unit of time: Last, previous.

1971 Cunningham *Syntactic Analysis Gullah* 75, C[reole:] I been doing that till July gone. E[nglish:] I did that until last July.

gone v See **go** v **A3b, 4b, 6b**

gone beaver See **gone** adj **2**

gone by adv See **gone** adj **5**

gone by (with) ppl adj See **go by** v phr **2**

gone case See **gone** adj **1**

gone coon (or goose, gosling) See **gone** adj **2**

gone in adj phr Cf **given out**

=**gone up.**

c1895 (1914) Norris *Vandover* 276 **San Francisco CA,** Too much whiskey! . . Put me to bed, will you, Bandy? I feel all gone in.

goneness n

A sinking feeling; faintness, exhaustion; also fig.

1848 *R.I. Words* (Bartlett MA.) *(DAE)*, *Goneness,* a peculiar feeling in the stomach. **1859** (1968) Bartlett *Americanisms* 174, *Goneness.* A peculiar sensation of weakness, or of great depression. A woman's word. **1879** *Atlantic Mth.* 43.90/2, *Goneness* . . might be accepted as good slang if it were in sufficiently common use. It is described as being a "woman's word;" but I have heard it from men. **1884** Nye *Baled Hay* 237, His mission seems to be mainly to make people feel a goneness in their exchequer. **1891** Cooke *Huckleberries* 342 **NEng,** I feel a goneness that I never had ketch hold o' me before. **1899** (1912) Green *VA Folk-Speech* 200, *Goneness*. . . A fainting or sinking sensation; faintness: as, a feeling of *goneness.* **1905** *DN* 3.10 **cCT,** *Goneness*. . . A weakness. **1907** *DN* 3.213 **nwAR,** *Goneness*. . . A weakness.

gonesome adj Cf Intro "Language Changes" III.1

1896 *DN* 1.417 **MI, NY,** *Gonesome:* hungry. "A gonesome feeling."

gone to bed See **going to bed**

gone to grass See **grass n 5b**

gone up adj phr

Finished, done for, exhausted.

1865 Kellogg *Life & Death* 98, We heard nothing from Richmond, although one of the guards told one of our boys, at this time, that it was *"a gone-up case,"* and that our armies were getting the better of them everywhere. **1868** Goss *Soldier's Story* 123, I thought we were "gone up;" but he merely stirred his fire. **1875** *Chicago Tribune* (IL) 3 Nov 1/7, The Huck men were hopeful, but the Hesingites felt themselves toward night clean gone-up. **1899** Garland *Prairie Folks* 84 **IA,** Land knows, I'm almost gone up; washin', an' milkin' six cows, and tendin' you, and cookin' f'r *him,* ought 'o be enough f'r one day! **1906** Johnson *Highways Missip. Valley* 257, We had such a storm that ever'one thought me 'n' my ole woman was gone up. **1966–67** *DARE* (Qu. KK20b, *Something that looks as if it might collapse any minute: "Our old washing machine is ______."*) Inf **GA**1, About gone up; **NY**9, It's gone up.

gone west See **go west**

goney See **gooney**

gonies See **gonnies**

gonk See **gunk 1**

gonna See **go v A4d**

gonnies n Also *gannies, ganny, gonies* [Euphem varr of *God;* cf **Guinea n³**] **chiefly Sth, S Midl** Cf **i prep**

In phr *I gonnies* and varr: By golly!—used as an exclam of surprise, annoyance, confirmation, etc.

1907 Wright *Shepherd* 285 **swMO, Ozarks,** I seed the blamdest [sic] sight las' night that ever was in these woods, I reckon. I gonies! Hit was a plumb wonder! **1916** *DN* 4.344 **seSC,** I ganny I got Indian blood in me. **1931** *PMLA* 46.1308 **sAppalachians,** "Cuss-words," expressions of surprise and intense expressions . . I (by) gonnies. **1937** (1963) Hyatt *Kiverlid* 66 **KY,** "I gonnies!" complained Calhoun, "hit's a plumb botherment about that boy gettin' my cart busted up." **1940** *Amer. Mercury* June 211/1 **Sth,** I knowed of a baby once larnt to smoke in the cradle. Ruther draw on a pipe than a tit. Aye gonnies, if that little 'un didn't grow up six feet two. **1952** Brown *NC Folkl.* 1.553, *Igonnies*. . . Mild oath. . . General. Old people. Rare. **1959** *VT Hist.* new ser 27.138, *I Gonnies!* . . Rare. **1965** TN Folk Lore Soc. *Bulletin* 31.102 **csKY,** Bywords were and are numerous. . . "Good granny," "By gum," "I gannies." **1969** *DARE* (Qu. NN32, *Exclamations like 'I swear' . . "I ______."*) Inf **GA**84, Ganny.

gonnywobbles n pl Cf **gollywobbles, mulligrubs**

=**collywobbles 1.**

1970 *DARE* (Qu. BB28, *Joking names that people make up for imaginary diseases: "He must have the ______."*) Inf **PA**234, Gonnywobbles and the rullygub.

gonter See **go v A4d**

gonus See **goonus**

gony See **gooney**

goo See **goop v¹**

goober n¹ [Of Afr origin; see quot 1949]

1 also *gauber, goob, goober nut, goobert, gooby, gouber, gub(b)er:* =**peanut. widespread, but chiefly SE, Lower Missip Valley, SW** See Map Cf **goober pea**

1834 *Cherokee Phoenix & Indians' Advocate* (New Echota GA) 24 May 3/4 [Black], But he so mean I frade of he,/ I guess he steal my goober. **1872** Schele de Vere *Americanisms* 400, It is not impossible that the word *Goober* or *Guber* may be connected with the geographical division of the country, as *Guber* is the name of a district in the Haussa (How-sa) country, where the nut abounds, and the Haussa language is in extensive use in trade. **1884** Smith *Bill Arp's Scrap Book* 72 **nwGA,** Moles eat the gubbers. **1900** Lyons *Plant Names* 42, *A[rachis] hypogaea*. . . Goober or Gouber (Negroes of southern States). **1903** *DN* 2.315 **seMO,** *Goober.* **1905** *DN* 3.81 **nwAR,** *Goober.* **1908** *DN* 3.315 **eAL, wGA,** *Goober.* **1919** *DN* 5.36 **KY, NC, VA,** *Goober.* **c1930** Swann *Lang. Circus Lot* 10, *Gooberts:* The one and only "peanut." **1946** *PADS* 5.23 **VA,** Goobers. **1946** [see **goober-grabber**]. **1949** Turner *Africanisms* 194, ['gubɑ] 'peanut' . . Kim[bundu (Angola)] [ŋgubɑ] 'peanut'; U[mbundu (Angola)] [oluŋgupɑ] 'peanut'; K[ongo] [ŋgubɑ] 'kidney' (used for peanut because of the resemblance between the kidney and the peanut). **1952** Brown *NC Folkl.* 1.546, *Goobies*. . . Peanuts; a child's word.—General. Somewhat rare now. **1957** *Sat. Eve. Post Letters* **sIN,** One of the women on the [mail] route came out and asked him "would he get her chilluns some gubbers?" **1965–70** *DARE* (Qu. I42) 381 Infs, **widespread, but chiefly SE, Lower Missip Valley, SW,** Goobers; 7 Infs, Goober nuts; **KY**5, Goobs; (Qu. H80) Infs **GA**1, 4, Goober candy; (Qu. H82a) Inf **GA**13, Goober candy.

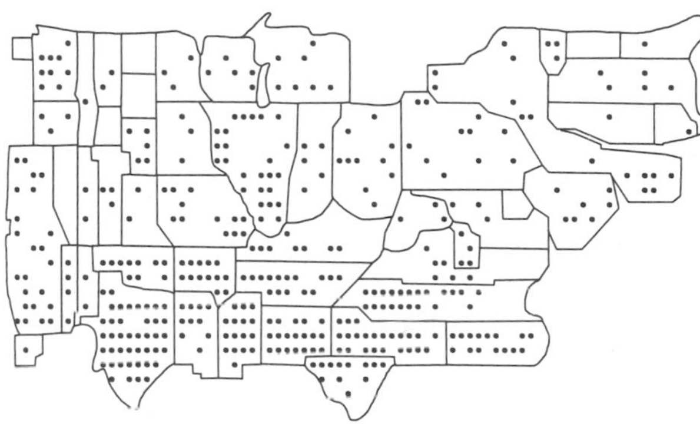

•goober n¹ 1 + varr (Qq. I42, H80, H82a)

2 =**hog peanut 1.**

1890 *AN&Q* 5.248, Besides the ordinary goober, or pinder . . there is a wild plant, not uncommon in the North as well as the South, the *Amphicarpaea monoica,* which is locally known as the goober in some districts of the Southern States.

3 A cultivated **potato** (here: *Solanum tuberosum*).

c1950 *McDavid Coll.* **neFL,** Goober—Irish potato. **1968–70** *DARE* (Qu. I9, *Other names [including nicknames] for potatoes*) Infs **CA**77, 113, **MI**113, Goobers.

4 =**goober-grabber;** here used esp of an inhabitant of North Carolina.

1865 Beaudry *Hist. Rec.* 339, Conscripts by the dozen. . . Some from Mississippi state and "Goobers" from Tar river [North Carolina]. **1872** Schele de Vere *Americanisms* 57 **NC,** During the late Civil War a conscript from the so-called "piney woods" of that State was apt to be nick-named a *Goober.* **1937** *Hall Coll.* **wNC,** *Goober*. . . Used some way in poking fun at the CCC boys who came from the 'goober country,' Georgia or Alabama.

5 The penis.

1954 *Harder Coll.* **cwTN,** Goober . . penis. **1980** *Children's Folkl. Newsl.* Spring 3 **seMN,** Eat my goober—Indicates disgust with or dislike of another . . ; homosexual imagery. **1988** *DARE* File (as of 1950s), I remember as quite a young child hearing the boys in the family which lived behind us refer laughingly to the penis as a "goober." I found their talk fascinating because it was so distinctive and so earthy, but my mother was disgusted by them and referred to them as "Okies." As I recall, these people actually had emigrated to central California from the northeastern part of Oklahoma, the Ozarks.

goober n² Cf **goomer**

1896 *DN* 1.417, *Goober:* a person who can enchant. Southern.

goober corn n [**goober n¹ 1**] *joc*

Corn that fails to form ears.

1942 *Hench Coll.* **cVA,** One thing [mentioned in a conversation about farming] was goober corn, which Dr. Macon said was corn that puts out no tassel. . . "If there's any corn grown, it's underground."

goober-digger See **goober-grabber**

gobered up adj phr Cf **goopy 1**

1966 *DARE* (Qu. Y40a, . . *Words referring to sticky stuff: "I've got to wash my hands. They're all ——."*) Inf **MT3**, Goobered up.

goober feather See **feather n B4**

goober-grabber n Also *goober-grubber;* for addit varr see quots Cf **goober n[1] 1, gruber**

One who digs peanuts; by ext, a poor countrified person—used as a nickname, esp for an inhabitant of Georgia.

1867 *Ball Players' Chron.* 27 June 6/2 *(DA),* As to playing for the 'championship bat of Georgia,' with a club outside of the State, we most respectfully decline—as that belongs to the so-called 'goober grabbers' alone. **1869** *Overland Mth.* 3.129/1 **SW**, A Georgian is popularly known in the South as a "Gouber-grabbler." **1880** *Harper's New Mth. Mag.* Feb 388/2, "I struck a kind of colony of gruber-grubbers from Georgia." "What are gruber-grubbers?" "Why, pea-nut diggers—worst lot you ever saw." **1895** *DN* 1.389 **TN**, *Goober:* peanut. So goober grubber = peanut digger. **1908** *DN* 3.316 **eAL, wGA**, *Goober-grabbler. . .* A Georgian. Sometimes used of any backwoodsman. **1936** *AmSp* 11.315 **Ozarks**, *Goober-grabbers. . .* People of southern Arkansas, as distinguished from the hillbilly. **1938** *AmSp* 13.5 **AR**, *Goober-digger. . .* Normally this word means a digger of peanuts. However, it has been extended into a general term of affection. **1946** McWilliams *S. CA Country* 172, Georgians are "crackers" and "gauber grubbers." **1966** *DARE* (Qu. HH1, . . *A rustic or countrified person*) Inf **GA11**, Goober-grabber.

gooberhead n

1970 *DARE* (Qq. N12, . . *Somebody who drives carelessly or not well; GG14, . . Someone who fusses or worries a lot, especially about little things;* HH3, *A dull and stupid person;* HH4, *Someone who has odd or peculiar ideas or notions*) Inf **TX98**, Gooberhead.

goober nut, goobert See **goober n[1] 1**

goober pea n Also sp *gouber pea;* pronc-sp *gooper ~* **[goober n[1] 1] chiefly S Midl** See Map

=peanut.

1833 *Louisville Pub. Advt.* 7 Nov. *(DA),* A few bags Gouber Pea, or Ground Pea [for sale]. **a1866** in 1960 Silber *Songs Civil War* 185, Lying in the shadow underneath the trees,/ Goodness how delicious, eating goober peas! **1872** Schele de Vere *Americanisms* 57, Far less valuable to the epicurean, but largely consumed by the masses, are the peanuts . . , known in North Carolina and the adjoining States as *Goober* peas. **1887** *Scribner's Mag.* 2.479 **AR**, I seen ye, myseff, feedin' up that innercent chile on gouber peas an' hog melts! **1919** *DN* 5.36 **KY, NC, VA**, *Goober (pea).* **1946** *PADS* 5.23 **VA**, *Goober peas.* **1958** *PADS* 29.11 **TN**, Goobers, goober peas: Peanuts. Social level suggested by the comment "used only by hired hands." **1965–70** *DARE* (Qu. I42, . . *Names or nicknames . . for peanuts*) 25 Infs, **chiefly S Midl**, Goober peas; **CT42**, Gooper peas—grandfather raised them in New Jersey; they look like a peanut but are round. **1983** *MJLF* 9.1.41 **ceKY**, *Goober peas . .* an "older" term for peanuts. **1986** Pederson *LAGS Concordance,* 34 infs, **chiefly TN**, Goober pea(s).

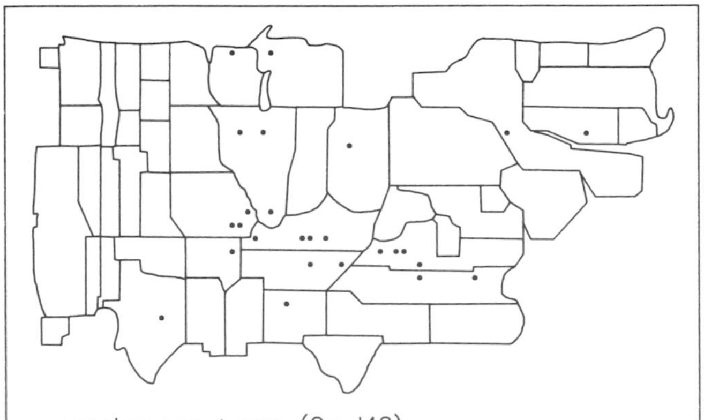

•goober pea I- var (Qu. I42)

goobie-sheepie v phr Cf **co-sheep(ie)** v phr

Come!—used to call sheep.

1972 *PADS* 58.18 **cwAL**, Calls to sheep. Most informants were not familiar with a call to sheep because the animal is not commonly raised in the area. However, . . one [informant] gave *goobie-sheepie.*

gooby See **goober n[1] 1**

goobyyan n [Pronc-sp]

=court bouillon.

1967 *DARE* (Qu. H45, *Dishes made with meat, fish, or poultry that everybody around here would know, but that people in other places might not*) Inf **TX37**, Goobyyan—fish.

gooch v [Perh blend of **geech + goose v 2**]

To poke or tickle; also fig.

1929 Wolfe *Look Homeward* 147 **NC**, "What're you laughin' at, son?" said Mary, gooching him roughly in the ribs, as he lay panting and prostrate. *Ibid* 254, He would burst into . . laughter, beyond all reason, with strange throat noises, tickling her roughly in the ribs. . . Often Eliza . . would slap at his hand angrily as he gooched her. **1950** *PADS* 14.32 **SC**, *Gooch. . .* Same as *geech.* Seems to be a blend of *goose . .* and *geech.* **1988** *DARE* File, I remember about 1960 a University acquaintance, a Pennsylvanian, very upset at having been embarrassed and abused in front of class, exclaiming of the professor's verbal jabs, "He gooched me! He *gooched* me!" The word struck all of us present as very funny, since we had never heard it before.

goochy adj **[gooch]** Cf **goosey 1**

Ticklish.

1944 *PADS* 2.34 **NC**, Goochy ['guči]. . . Goosey, ticklish. . . Common. **1950** *PADS* 14.32 **SC**, *Goochy. . .* Goosey. Same as *geechy.* Probably a blend of *goosey* and *geechy.*

good adj, adv

A Forms.

Compar, superl: usu *better, best;* also occas *gooder, goodest.*

1938 Rawlings *Yearling* 180 **nFL**, Foxes love corn gooder'n I do. **1949** in 1986 *DARE* File **seMI**, Gooder. . . A woman over forty used this in speaking to a little girl. "You've got gooder eyes." **1971** *Foxfire* Spring–Summer 102 **nGA**, Thrash'em old peas out—have th'goodest old time y'ever seen. **1985** *Commercial Appeal* (Memphis TN) 19 Mar **nwMS**, From Mrs. J. M. Stanford of Southaven: "Gooder'n snuff and not half as dusty."

B As adv.

1 foll by adj: Well.

1942 (1971) Campbell *Cloud-Walking* 27 **seKY**, She . . was just naturally good-behaved. **1949** Guthrie *Way West* 142 **CO** (as of 1847), Mercy can dance. Mercy's good turned. I declare, I never saw the beat of her! **1965** *DARE* FW Addit, That team's good broke = well broken; always said this way by horse trainers.

2 with expressions of extent: Fully, at least.

1943 Smiley *Gloss. New Paltz* **seNY**, I said . . "It must be 25 miles to the 'Bugger Hole'. " He replied, "Yes, it's good that."

goodadoon n Cf **bloodynoun**

A **bullfrog 1.**

1966 *DARE* (Qu. P22, . . *A very large frog*) Inf **SC9**, Goodadoon [ˌgʊdə'dun]—old name for [a] pond chicken—a frog sought for its legs.

good blood n [By analogy with *bad blood*]

Friendly feelings toward a person.

1953 Brewer *Word Brazos* 53 **seTX** (as of c1930), She 'speshly don' hab no good blood for anothuh sistuh in de chu'ch, what go by de name of Sistuh Susie. Dis de why she don' hab no good blood for Sistuh Susie: dey bof got gals, an' Sistuh Susie's gal done went an' tuck Sistuh Mariah's gal's beau an' marry 'im.

goodbye-summer See **farewell-summer 1**

good-bye taste n

=farewell 1.

1906 *DN* 3.138 **nwAR**, *Good-bye taste. . .* Aftertaste. "That medicine had a good-bye taste."

goodbye-to-spring See **farewell-to-spring**

good-bye wagon n

1969 *DARE* (Qu. N2, *The car used to carry a dead body for burial*) Inf **GA89**, Good-bye wagon.

good dark n Cf **dusk dark, first dark**

=full dark.

1929 Dobie *Vaquero* 91, A little after good dark they pulled out. **1931** *Scribner's Mag.* 90.625 **FL,** Long about good-dark he starts hisself a skeeter smudge. **1942** *Sat. Eve. Post* 22 Aug 40/1, It was just good dark when Sally finished the supper dishes. **1942** (1971) Campbell *Cloud-Walking* 73 **seKY,** The younguns climbed into bed before good dark. **1954** *Harder Coll.* **cwTN,** *Good dark* . . as dark as it will get to be. **c1960** *Wilson Coll.* **csKY,** *Good dark*. . . Real darkness rather than twilight or dusky dark. **1984** Wilder *You All Spoken Here* 61 **Sth,** Good dark: Dark as three feet up a bull's ass.

good daylight n Also *good day*

Broad daylight.

1942 (1971) Campbell *Cloud-Walking* 181 **seKY,** Way before good daylight the folks in the settlement were all astir. **1990** *DARE* File **Midl** (as of c1950), We started out before it was good day.

gooder, goodest See **good**

good fashion adv phr Also *in good fashion* **chiefly Sth, S Midl**

Thoroughly.

1922 Gonzales *Black Border* 304 **sSC, GA coasts** [Gullah glossary], *Good-fashi'n*—good fashion—well, thoroughly; as: "Uh lick da' gal good-fashi'n"—I gave that girl a thorough whipping. **1946** *PADS* 6.15 **eNC, VA,** *Good fashion*. . . Thoroughly. Used with threats. "I'll spank you good fashion." **1947** *PADS* 8.14 **IN,** *Good fashion.* **c1960** *Wilson Coll.* **csKY,** *Good fashion* . . thoroughly. **1965–66** *DARE* (Qu. LL27, . . *'Thoroughly'*) Inf **MS**49, Good fashion; **OK**48, In good fashion.

good feeling place n

1954 *Harder Coll.* **cwTN,** *Good feeling place*. . . A dip in the road.

good few n, adj [*OED* "*dial.* and *colloq.*"]

Quite a few; a good many.

1895 *DN* 1.371 **KY, NC, TN,** *A good few:* many. **1899** (1912) Green *VA Folk-Speech* 201, *Good-few*. . . An indefinite, but comparatively large, number. "There were a good-few people at church." **1942** Berrey–Van den Bark *Amer. Slang* 20.3, *Large amount; many* . . good few. **1974** Fink *Mountain Speech* 11 **NC, TN,** They's a good few apples this year.

Good-Friday bun n

1952 Dorson *Bloodstoppers* 116 **MI,** In some homes the Good Friday bun was hung on a string and left to dry up until the next Good Friday came around. A fresh bun was then hung out, and the old one grated and used to cure such diseases as members of the family might contract.

good god n

1 also *good god almighty, ~ bird, ~ woodpecker, good guard, good lord:* = **pileated woodpecker.** [Echoic] **Sth, S Midl**

1906 *DN* 3.138 **nwAR,** *Good God*. . . A large variety of woodpecker. **1913** *Auk* 30.496 **Okefenokee GA,** *Phloeotomus pileatus pileatus*. . . 'Good-God Woodpecker'. . . The birds are noisiest at sunrise, but their high-pitched, Flicker-like notes resound through the swamp at all times of the day. **1934** Vines *Green Thicket* 49 **cnAL,** You know, some folks call the purty things Indian hens, and some folks call 'em wood hens. But I call the noisy things Good-Gods. . . They say, *Good-God*. . . *Good-God*. . . *Good-God,* just like that. **1938** Matschat *Suwannee R.* 26 **sGA,** "Good-God" woodpeckers . . work with a continuous *r-r-r-rat-a-tat-tat-tat*. . . Local names [are] given them by the swampers to describe the individual sounds the birds make either in tapping their favorite trees, or calling in flight. . . Good-God is a hardwood tapper. **1945** McAtee *Nomina Abitera* 46, The most godified of our birds . . is none other than the pileated woodpecker. . . this bird's roll of godly titles . . is as follows: . . good God, good God bird, good God woodpecker. . . Various observers have said that the term Good God is in imitation of the bird's notes. Maybe it is, but to me the logcock repeats "cack, cack," or "puck, puck," with no touch of divinity about the performances. *Ibid* 47, The matter [of names] evidently is one of sounds[,] for other combinations of the basic syllables are used[,] as good guard [etc]. **1946** *Democrat* 12 Sep. 2/3 *(DA)* **swAL,** Yes, it's true that Kenneth killed a 'good god' for a squirrel. **1962** Parler *Folk Beliefs AR* 12.3975 **cnAR,** Seeing a "Good-God" is good luck. A Good-God is a rather rare species of a bird [Pileated woodpecker]. It is about the size of a crow and is colored exactly like a red-headed woodpecker. **1967–70** *DARE* (Qu. Q17, . . *Kinds of woodpeckers*) Inf **AR**56, Good god; (Qu. Q18, *Joking names and nicknames for woodpeckers*) Infs **KY**88, **VA**70, Good god; **TN**6, Good god almighty. **1968–69** *DARE* FW Addit **AR,** I'd ask daddy what that was making that noise and he'd say, "It's a good-god"; **Okefenokee GA,** Good-lord. Local name for pileated woodpecker.

2 =**redhead.**

1911 *Forest & Stream* 77.173, (Redhead) *Marila americana*. . . Good God, Menasha, Ark. **1945** McAtee *Nomina Abitera* 47, I heard the name Good God applied to the redhead duck in Arkansas, but fear that somewhere along the line there had been confusion with the pileated woodpecker in the cypress swamps of that country.

good god almighty, (or bird, woodpecker), good guard See **good god 1**

good grabs See **grabs, by**

good-handed adj

1969 *DARE* (Qu. U32, . . *A very generous person: "He's ______."*) Inf **RI**1, Good-handed.

good hickory See **hickory** n **B6**

good hokey See **hokey, by**

goodie See **goody 1**

‡goodles n pl [Prob blend of *gobs* + *oodles*]

1967 *DARE* (Qu. LL8a, *A large amount* . . : *"He's got ______ of time."*) Inf **TN**12, Goodles; (Qu. LL9a, *As much as you need or more* . . : *"We've got ______ of apples."*) Inf **TN**12, Goodles.

good lord See **good god 1**

good-luck bone n Cf **lucky bone**

A wishbone.

1967–68 *DARE* (Qu. K74, *A bone from the breast of a chicken, shaped like a horseshoe*) Infs **MD**24, **NJ**67, Good-luck bone. **1973** Allen *LAUM* 1.308 **Upper MW** (as of c1950), The fused clavicle or furcula of a fowl, broken apart by two persons to see which gets the longer part and hence his "wish," is known generally in the U[pper] M[idwest] by the spreading Northern term *wishbone*. . . *Good luck bone,* used in eastern South Dakota by an inf. of Vermont and Massachusetts parentage, may reflect the New Hampshire and Massachusetts variant, *lucky bone.*

good man n Also with *the* [*EDD the Good man* (at *goodman* sb. 7) "a child's name for God"] **Midl, esp S Midl** Cf **bad man 2**

God, Jesus; a representation of Jesus' face used as a charm.

1915 *DN* 4.183 **swVA,** *Good-man*. . . God. **1917** *DN* 4.412 **wNC,** *Good-man*. . . God; child's term. **1930** Shoemaker *1300 Words* 26 **cPA Mts** (as of c1900), *Good-man*—A charm sold by Gipsies, usually the face of Christ cut out of paper. **1937** (1963) Hyatt *Kiverlid* 87 **KY,** Some claimed them to be warnin's frum the Good Man. **1942** Warnick *Garrett Co. MD* 7 **nwMD** (as of 1900–1918), *Good man*. . . God. **1942** McAtee *Dial. Grant Co. IN* 29 (as of 1890s), *Good Man* . . God. **1952** Brown *NC Folkl.* 1.546, *Good man*. . . God; Jesus Christ. **1954** *Harder Coll.* **cwTN,** *Good man*. . . God. **c1960** *Wilson Coll.* **csKY,** *Good Man*. . . A child's word for God.

good measure n [Cf Luke 6:38] **esp Midl**

A full or generous portion of something bought.

1965–70 *DARE* (Qu. U15, . . *A little extra to make you feel that you're getting a good bargain, you call that ______*) 25 Infs, **chiefly Midl,** Good measure; (Qu. LL28, *Expressions meaning entirely full: "The box of apples was ______."*) Infs **CA**164, **KS**16, **MO**11, **NY**219, **TN**24, **VA**34, **WA**6, Good measure. [All Infs old or mid-aged]

good morning n

Any of several children's games; see quots.

1909 (1923) Bancroft *Games* 99, *Good Morning*. . . One player blinds his eyes. . . The teacher then silently points to some other player in class, who . . says, "Good morning, David!" (or whatever the child's name may be). The little guesser, if he has recognized the voice, responds with, "Good morning, Arthur!" (or other name). **1919** Elsom–Trilling *Social Games* 61, *Good-morning*. . . A circle is formed. . . An extra player runs around the outside . . and touches on the shoulder any one of the group. As soon as the runner does this he turns around and runs in the opposite direction. . . The one who has been tagged also immediately begins to run. . . When the two meet . . , they shake hands, and say, "Good morning!" as cordially & politely as circumstances will permit. Then each one continues . . , the object being to reach . . the vacant place. **1939** Harris *Purslane* 150 **cNC,** The first game was "good morning." Margie made Calvin get out of his corner to be her partner. He had joined the party in a sort of desperate hope that Milly might slip away and come. "Good mornin', good mornin', good mornin'," he went through the formula dully. "Can you make a cherry pie?" **1945** Boyd *Hdbk. Games* 84, *Good Morning*—The leader blinds the eyes of one player and silently designates another to say, "Good morning" to him. The blindfolded player tries to guess who spoke to him.

good-morning-spring n
=**spring beauty,** usu *Claytonia virginica.*
1892 *Jrl. Amer. Folkl.* 5.93, *Claytonia Virginica,* good-morning-spring. **1892** *Garden and Forest* 5.614/2, In some places the Claytonia, or Spring Beauty, is known as Good-morning-spring. **1900** Lyons *Plant Names* 106, *C. Caroliniana* . . and . . *C. Virginica* . . of the eastern U.S. are called . . Good-morning Spring. **1931** Clute *Common Plants* 139, Close in its [=*Erigenia bulbosa's*] wake come the spring beauties *(Claytonia Virginica),* just in time to make the name of good-morning-spring applicable. **1959** Carleton *Index Herb. Plants* 55, *Good-morning-spring:* Claytonia virginica.

goodness Agnes intj Also *goodness godness Agnes;* for addit varr see quots [Perh from *agnus dei*]
Used as an exclamation of surprise or pleasure.
1943 McAtee *Dial. Grant Co. IN Suppl. 2* 9 (as of 1890s), *Goodness godness agnes* . . not so mild imprecation; also an example of the articulated phrase. **1959** *VT Hist.* 27.123, For goodness-godness-Agnes! **1965–70** *DARE* (Qu. NN28b, *Exclamations beginning with 'goodness'*) Infs **CA**61, 160, **MI**67, **NY**146, Godness Agnes; **WA**6, 30, Gracious Agnes; **MI**112, Agnes; **IN**83, Godness Agnes Brown; [**NY**14, Gracious Agnus Dei;] **WA**28, Gracious Mable Agnes; **PA**223, Gracious meejus Agnes; **TX**5, Gracious Miss Agnes; (Qu. NN6a, *Exclamations of joy*) Inf **MI**67, Goodness Godness Agnes; (Qu. NN27a, *Weakened substitutes for 'god'*) Inf **NM**11, Goodness Agnes.

good night up here, but good morning down there, it's phr Cf *DS* W24a
c1960 *Wilson Coll.* **csKY,** It's "Good night" up here, but "Good morning" down there—A signal to a girl to tell her her slip is showing.

good old boy n [Expansion of *old boy;* see quot 1860] **chiefly Sth**
A man who embodies the traditional values of the White, rural South—also used ironically.
[**1860** Hundley *Social Relations S. States* 24, We remember travelling once on the Mississippi in company with an old gentleman from New-York, (it was in the autumn of '57)—a respectable member of the middle classes, intelligent and courteous, though somewhat of a cockney. He was quite a portly old gentleman . . a pretty fair specimen of what one might fitly call an Old Boy.] [**1898** Lloyd *Country Life* 135 **AL,** And then you can see some good old brother . . with his store bought clothes and his fried shirt on.] **1967** *DARE* File **SC,** *Good old boy*—just a regular sort of good fellow. **1976** *Harper's Mag.* Sept 18 **Sth,** This is the world of the Good Ole Boy, the country hick from down in the hollow, his innocent, God-fearing eyes scanning the world of corruption laid out before him at every crossroads grocery store, supermarket, and shopping center as he makes his way to the eternally damned metropolis his neighbors and friends reassure him he can save with the sword Calvin put in Christ's hand. **1976** Lynn-Vecsey *Loretta Lynn* 113 **eKY,** I was getting to be an old professional in lots of ways, handling them good old boys at the country fairs. You can picture 'em—husky boys in their bib overalls, boots still caked with manure. They may not have seen a woman in a dress since Christmas, and if you made your exit through the crowd, they'd show their appreciation by giving you a big old hug. **1976** *Time* 27 Sept 47, The core of the good ole boy's world is with his buddies, the comfortable, hyperhearty, all-male camaraderie, joshing and drinking and regaling one another with tales of assorted, exaggerated prowess. **1981** Pederson *LAGS Basic Materials* 1 inf, **ceAR,** He's a good old boy—mighty fine man (and) good-natured. **1984** Wilder *You All Spoken Here* 160 **Sth,** *Good ol' boy:* A rough and ready fun lover who can be counted on for most anything involving challenge and expression of virility. Many are identified by cowboy hats and boots, and by pick-up trucks equipped with CB radios, fishing rods, and fire-arms. **1988** *DARE* File **NC,** I am familiar with *good old boy* as an especially Southern term in the following senses: 1) A male—regardless of age—who is regarded as agreeable, worthy of approval, congenial. 2) A male—regardless of age—who is regarded as a scoundrel and hence viewed with contempt or occasionally with humor. This sense is thus ironical, essentially implying a *denial* of the qualities found in sense 1 above.

good place n Also with *the* Cf **bad place, good man**
Heaven.
1912 Green *VA Folk-Speech* 201, He is dead and gone to the good-place. **1942** Warnick *Garrett Co. MD* 8 **nwMD** (as of 1900–1918), *Good place* . . heaven. **1942** McAtee *Dial. Grant Co. IN* 29 (as of 1890s). **c1960** *Wilson Coll.* **csKY,** *Good place*. . . Heaven; a child's word. **1976** Ryland *Richmond Co. VA* 371, *Good-place*—heaven.

good religion n Cf **bad religion**
Genuine Christian conduct.
1953 Brewer *Word Brazos* 61 **seTX** (as of c1930), Hit tecks Good Religion for de great Gawd Awmighty to stan' up to you an' pilot you to de promus lan'.

goods exclam Also *goods on it* Cf *DS* V5b
=**dib** n^1 **2.**
1944 *AmSp* 19.38 **Philadelphia PA,** Goods (on it)! 'I claim a share.'

goody n
1 also sp *goodie:* A nutmeat; also fig. [Perh transf from *goody* a sweetmeat] **chiefly Sth, Midl** See Map
1859 Taliaferro *Fisher's R.* 213 **nwNC** (as of 1820s), Sam Lundy always added a few items of his own . . when he "sloped" to market; "wannit goody," "hick'ry-nut goody," and "haze-nut goody." **1893** Shands *MS Speech* 34, *Goody*. . . Used by all classes for the edible kernel of any kind of nut. **1905** *DN* 3.81 **nwAR,** The cake tasted like it had goodies in it. **1907** *German Amer. Annals* 9.377 **sePA,** Crack those nuts and pick out the goodies. **1929** *AmSp* 5.18 **Ozarks,** Them young-uns jes' set 'roun' a-pickin' out goodies all evenin'. **1941** Perry *Hold Autumn* 10 **TX,** A year in which the other man so exclusively got the goody and you got the hull. **1942** McAtee *Dial. Grant Co. IN* 29 (as of 1890s), *Goody.* **1953** *AmSp* 28.249 **csPA,** *Goody.* **1956** McAtee *Some Dialect NC* 19, *Goody.* **1965–70** *DARE* (Qu. I41, *The part of the nut that you eat*) 68 Infs, **chiefly Sth, Midl,** Goody. **1966** *Wilson Coll.* **csKY,** *Goodie*. . . Walnut kernel. [A] children's term. **1982** *Barrick Coll.* **csPA,** *Goody*—kernel; nut-meat. *Ibid, Goody picker*—pointed instrument for extracting nut-meats.

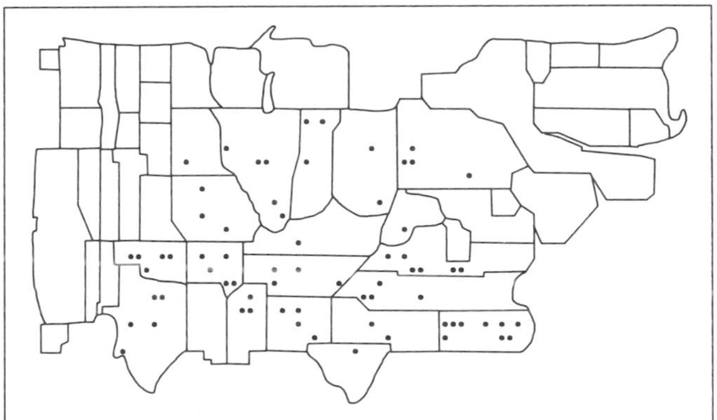
•goody 1 (Qu. I41)

2 The yolk of an egg.
1942 Warnick *Garrett Co. MD* 8 **nwMD** (as of 1900–1918), *Goody* . . the yolk of an egg. "Mother, this egg has two goodies in it." **1971** GA Dept. Ag. *Farmers Market Bulletin* 28 July 8, If I use a hypodermic needle to draw out some goody and insert strychnine in an egg, will it kill snakes if eaten?

3 The fish commonly called **spot** (here: *Leiostomus xanthurus*).
1873 in 1878 Smithsonian Inst. *Misc. Coll.* 14.2.27, *Liostomus obliquus*. . . Lafayette *(New York);* goody *(Cape May);* chub *(Norfolk).* **1884** Goode *Fisheries U.S.* 1.370, The Lafayette . . is known . . on the coast of New Jersey as the "Goody" and sometimes as the "Cape May Goody." **1894** *DN* 1.331 **NJ,** *Goodies:* a fish of peculiar delicacy, much eaten on the coast. The "spot fish" of Virginia. (Atlantic and Cape May.) **1933** LA Dept. of Conserv. *Fishes* 180, *The Spot*. . . Additional popular names for the species are Oldwife, Yellowtail and Goody. **1949** Brown *Amer. Cooks* 833 **VA,** Spots are sometimes called "goodies" and "old wives" in the interesting local nomenclature. **1973** Knight *Cook's Fish Guide* 381, Goody—Spot.

goody bone n
=**funny bone 1.**
1966 *DARE* (Qu. X33, *The place in the elbow that gives you a strange feeling if you hit it against something*) Inf **FL**33, Goody bone.

goody-bread n
=**crackling bread.**

1872 Schele de Vere *Americanisms* 459, Cracklings, a favorite toothsome dish of the Southern States, consisting of pieces of the rind of pork roasted, which are baked into the bread of negroes, and make one of their greatest luxuries, known as *goody-bread.*

goody up v phr
1967 *DARE* (Qu. JJ3a, *When a . . child makes a special effort to 'get in good' with the teacher in hopes of getting a better grade*) Inf **MA5**, Goodying up.

gooey n [Var of *hooey*]
1966–67 *DARE* (Qu. NN13, *When you think that the thing somebody has just said is silly or untrue: "Oh, that's a lot of ______."*) Infs **KS5**, **MS16**, Gooey.

gooey duck See **geoduck**

gooeyducking See **geoducking**

goof doctor n
One who practices **goofer** n.
1942 (1965) Parrish *Slave Songs* 33 **GA coast,** Mrs. A. S. Hilsman, who was born on a plantation at Fancy Bluff, tells me there was a witch or goof doctor among her father's Negroes, who had learned his magic in Africa.

goofer n, also attrib Also *gooffer, go(o)pher, gopheh, guffer* [Of Afr origin] **chiefly Sth** *chiefly among Black speakers* Cf **hoodoo n 1**
The practice of **conjure n 1;** a magic spell or something used to cast such a spell.
1880 Brown *My Southern Home* 79 **MO,** He took out of his pocket a bag made of the skin of the rattlesnake, and took from it some goopher, sprinkled it over the horseshoe, saying: "Dis is de stuff, Miss Marfa, dat's gwine to make you Mr. Scott's conqueror." **1893** Owen *Voodoo Tales* 149, Gopheh-duht [=dirt] mighty good ef yo' got de misery in de stummick. **1899** Chesnutt *Conjure Woman* 15 **csNC** [Black], She could wuk de mos' powerfulles' kin' er goopher,—could make people hab fits, er rheumatiz, er make 'em dcs dwinel [=dwindle] away en die. *Ibid* 16, W'en she got de goopher all ready . . she . . buried it under the root uv a red oak tree. **1914** *Jrl. Amer. Folkl.* 27.247 **SC,** "Gooffer" may be invoked against an opponent simply by pronouncing the word, or by adding a mark or cross-mark on the ground and spitting in or near it. **1926** Smith *Gullah* 32 **sSC, GA coasts,** There are curiously few survivals of native African words in Gullah. . . The commonest are the exclamation *ki* . . and *buckra*. . . To these may be added . . *guffer.* **1926** Puckett *Folk Beliefs S. Negro* 231, "Goofering is walking over a root-bag or goofer-bag. On the outside is goofer-root, then cloth, then more root, then another layer of cloth, and inside it is the goofer—strands from your hair, broken needles and graveyard dirt." One goofer-doctor dug up such a bag under a woman's step. **c1937** in 1983 Taft *Blues Lyric Poetry* 173, I'm going to poison you / Sprinkle gopher-dust : around your bed / Wake up some morning : find your own self dead. **c1938** in 1970 Hyatt *Hoodoo* 1.222 **csNC,** *Goofer dust* is dust right from the cemetery, but it's gittin' out from undah de footstone. . . Yo' tie it up an' yo' go tuh run—yo' cross runnin' watah and yo' bless it in de watah. . . Think about yo' dust. Den luck will come. . . Now when people talk of *putting de goofer on yo',* they do that to either run yo' or bring yo' undah dere control. *Ibid* 1.225 **cAR,** (What is *goofer dust*?) Well, *goofer*—dis stuff a *graveyard dirt,* red peppah an' black peppah. Ah call all that stuff—yo' kin git a snail an' powder him—all of 'em *goofer dust.* *Ibid* **seGA,** Yo' kin take a rattlesnake an' dry his haid up, pound it up, an' den yo' kin go to work an' use dat as *goofer dust.* Kill anybody. *Ibid* 1.226 **seLA,** At any time you use anyting from hoodoo—some call it hoodoo, some call it *goofer.* *Ibid* 1.227 **eMD,** A *hoodoo bag* . . contains a dust called *goofer dust,* and whatever they put it on they can conquer. . . They get these *goofer bags* from *root doctors* or *conjure doctors.* **1970** Anderson *TX Folk Med.* 31 **seTX,** The conjure ball [to keep off evil spirits] is made of thorns off of a locust tree, some wool or cotton from a mockingbird nest, and a piece of frog skin. Wrap all of this into a ball with goofer powder (the dust out of a dry tree in a cemetery.)

goofer v Also *goopher* **Sth** *chiefly among Black speakers*
To bewitch; to practice **conjure** n **1;** hence vbl n *goofering;* ppl adj *goofered.*
1899 Chesnutt *Conjure Woman* 11 **csNC** [Black], De truf er de matter is dat dis yer ole vimya'd is goophered . . —conju'd, bewitch'. *Ibid* 16, Mars Dugal, had hi'ed her ter goopher de grapevimes. **1923** in 1965 Bradford *Born with the Blues* 77 **Sth** [Black], I'll buy some poison,/ Goofer him now, 'cause he tried to quit me / And he didn't know how. **1926** Puckett *Folk Beliefs S. Negro* 215, Conjuration itself [is] known variously as "hoodooing," "goofering," "handicapping," or "tricking." *Ibid* 231, [The] goofer-doctor . . told the woman that her hair had been goofered. **c1938** in 1970 Hyatt *Hoodoo* 1.222 **csNC,** Lotta people say, "Well, *we'll goofer* sech an' sech a person because ah cares fo' dem"—'cause dey care fo' a person, prob'bly loves 'em an' wants dem tuh be around all de time. *Ibid* 1.224 **csNC,** (You *goofer them* you say. . . What do you mean by *goofer them?*). . . Well, yo'd be making them love yo'. **1941** Writers' Program SC *Folk Tales* 83, Grandma didn' b'liebe in nuthin lak goopherin ner conjurin ner nuthin. *Ibid* 97, Conjure is another name for hoodoo, voodoo, coocoo, and goofering.

goofer dirt, goofer doctor, goofer dust See **goofer** n

goofered See **goofer** v

goofer-fuzz n Cf **dust bunny**
1970 *DARE* FW Addit **NE,** *Goofer-fuzz* . . the rolls of dust that gather under beds, furniture, etc.

goofering See **goofer** v

goofer powder, goofer root See **goofer** n

go off v phr
To pass off, diminish.
1857 in 1983 *PADS* 70.35 **ce,sePA,** The snow went off rapidly but fortunately with much rain. **1876** in 1969 *PADS* 52.52 **seIL,** Before the snow goes off. **1932** Stong *State Fair* 251 **IA,** We'll see how I feel when we get there, Daddy. It's [=a stomach ache] kind of going off now, I think. **1983** *MJLF* 9.1.41 **ceKY,** *Going off* . . going down (a swelling).

gooffer See **goofer** n

go off to themselves See **go out to themselves**

goofies n Cf *DS* V5b
=**dib** n[1] **2.**
1905 *DN* 3.81 **nwAR,** *Goofies* [gufiz] *on.* . . The promise of. 'He's got goofies on the woolly [=cigar or cigarette stub].' . . Slang of Fayetteville boys.

goo-fish See **gou**

goofus bird n
=**filliloo bird.**
1935 *Sun* (Baltimore MD) 24 April 8/3 *(Hench Coll.)* **seMD,** Neighbours declare it is a dodo, a wampus or a goofus bird. William H. Collier, of the State Game Department, asserts it is a loon. . . The bird was discovered trying to fight six of the farmer's cows at once. **1939** Tryon *Fearsome Critters* 19, *The Filla-Ma-Loo Bird.* . . [Also] called the Goofus Bird. *Ibid,* [Low in intellectual curiosity, showing complete and consistent indifference as to where he's going. He prefers only to see where he's been; hence he always flies backwards.]

goofy n Cf **goofer** n
1965 *DARE* (Qu. C36, *Nicknames for special . . groups of people living around here;* total Infs questioned, 75) Inf **MS55**, Goofies—for Negroes.

google n [Perh blend of **goggle** n + **goozle** n **1**] **esp Sth, S Midl** Cf *DS* X7
Also in combs: =**goozle** n **1.**
1859 Taliaferro *Fisher's R.* 29 **nwNC,** Two things he was particularly fond of, and upon which he flourished whenever he could get them—turnip greens and "hog's gullicks," the "Adam's apple" of a hog's haslet, or the "google," as it is commonly called. **1897** *Boston Globe* 18 July 27/8 *(DA),* The word is 'google,' meaning Adam's apple, and is a Missouri provincialism. **1981** Pederson *LAGS Basic Materials (Neck, throat)* 1 inf, **neTN,** Google; 1 inf, **neTN,** Google—because it googles, makes a googling sound; 1 inf, **swMS,** Google—the part of your throat you swallow down; 2 infs, **nwGA, seMS,** Google—Adam's apple; 1 inf, **swAL,** Google, joogle—Adam's apple; 1 inf, **cnFL,** Google bone—Adam's apple; 1 inf, **cGA,** Your swallow and your google pipe; 1 inf, **csGA,** Google vein; [1 inf, **ceAL,** Googly bane in the neck].

googleberry n Cf **goober** n[1] **1**
=**peanut.**
1973 Allen *LAUM* 1.308 **MN** (as of c1950), A Minneapolis black inf. . . uses googleberries as a jocular synonym [for peanuts].

google bone See **google**

google-eye n
=**woodcock** (here: *Philohela minor*).

1968 *DARE* (Qu. Q7) Inf **WI**61, Woodcock. . . We call them google ['gugəl] eyes.

google-nose See **goggle-nose**

google pipe, google vein See **google**

googlum See **goozlum**

goo-gobs n pl Cf **gob** n^1 **2**
Lots; plenty.
1970 *DARE* (Qu. U38a, . . *"He's got ——— [of money]."*) Inf **MO**29, Goo-gobs; (Qu. LL8a, . . *"He's got ——— of time."*) Inf **MO**30, Goo-gobs; (Qu. LL9a, . . *"We've got ——— of apples."*) Inf **MS**88, Goo-gobs. [All Infs Black]

‡goohoopers n pl
=mulligrubs.
1968 *DARE* (Qu. GG34a, *To feel depressed or in a gloomy mood: "He has the ——— today."*) Inf **NY**108, Goo-hoopers.

gooie See **goop** v^1

‡gookoos n [Var of *boocoos* (at **beaucoup**)]
1968 *DARE* (Qu. U38a, *Words referring to a great deal of money: "He's got ——— [of money]."*) Inf **CA**59, Gookoos ['guˌkuz].

‡gookum n [*gook* sticky substance + *-um* as in *stickum*]
1966 *DARE* (Qu. T7, *The sticky stuff that comes out of pine trees*) Inf **WA**18, Gookum.

gool n^1 See **goal**

gool n^2 [Prob *EDD gowl* sb.[2] 1 (also sp *gool*) "A hollow passage, a defile between mountains; a gap, hole"; *SND gowl* n.[2] 2]
See quots.
1989 Mosher *Stranger* 3 **nVT** (as of 1952), When I was a boy growing up on the Kingdom gool, my father and my older brother Charlie couldn't say two words to each other without getting into an argument. *Ibid* 7, They . . went at it hammer and tongs over . . how obscure regional terms like "gore" and "gool" had evolved. Especially gool. Ever since I could remember, my father and Charlie had haggled fiercely over the derivation of this curious old Scottish word that had come down . . over the generations and designated the half-mile loop of washboard dirt road . . leading up the ridge . . into the gore. *Ibid* 209, Instead of continuing along the gool and crossing back over the river by way of the covered bridge, she headed up the twisty woods road into the gore. **1990** *DARE* File **sVT** (as of c1950), There was a road that circled the valley, going from Londonderry to another town, to another, and then back to Londonderry. When we took this road we said we were "going around the gool."

goold See **goal**

gooldthread See **goldthread 1**

goolie See **goalie**

goolie hole n Cf **goal, goalie 2**
In marble play: see quot.
1969 *DARE* (Qu. EE7, . . *Kinds of marble games*) Inf **KY**11, Goolie ['guli] hole—make three holes four feet apart; shoot marbles from hole to hole in a race. The second hole is purgatory ['pɛgəˌtoəri]; third hole is goolie hole.

gool-sticker, gool-sticking See **goal-sticker**

goolthrite n [Etym unknown]
See quot.
1914 *DN* 4.73 **ME, nNH,** *Goolthrite.* . . Any small, wizened, puckered object. She was all puckered up to a goolthrite, with the cold. *Ibid* 77, No bigger'n a . . goolthrite.

goom(b) See **gum** n^1, v^1

goomer v [Perh var of **goofer** n, but cf *DJE guma* the plant *Solanum nigrum,* used in root medicine] Cf **goober** n^2
To bewitch; hence n *goomer doctor.*
1947 (1964) Randolph *Ozark Superstitions* 265, These practitioners [of witchcraft] are variously known as witch masters, white witches, witch doctors, faith doctors, goomer doctors and conjure folks. **1953** Randolph–Wilson *Down in Holler* 248 **Ozarks,** Goomer . . . To bewitch.

goon n
1 A **coot** n^1 **1.** Cf **fool hen 5**
1966 *DARE* (Qu. Q9, *The bird that looks like a small, dull-colored duck and is commonly found on ponds and lakes*) Inf **NC**44, Goon.
2 A **bittern.** Cf **fool fowl**
1968 *DARE* (Qu. Q8, *A water bird that makes a booming sound before rain and often stands with its beak pointed almost straight up*) Inf **OH**67, Goon.

gooney n Also *goony, gon(e)y, gawny* [*EDD gawney* (varr *goney, gony, gooney*) "A fool . . a stupid awkward person"]
1 A stupid, awkward person. **scattered, but esp NEng**
1838 (1843) Haliburton *Clockmaker* (2d ser) 130 **CT,** If the feller has been such a ravin' destracted goney, I hope they will hang him. **1859** (1968) Bartlett *Americanisms* 174, *Goney* or *gony.* A great goose, a stupid fellow. New England. **1896** *DN* 1.418 **ME,** *Gooney:* foolish fellow, simpleton. "Don't be such a gooney." **1904** *DN* 2.425 **Cape Cod MA,** You great gooney, don't you know anything? **1909** *DN* 3.411 **nME,** You awkward gawny! **1945** Colcord *Sea Language* 88 **ME, Cape Cod, Long Island,** *Goney, gooney.* The sailor's name for an awkward sea bird found in southern latitudes. Alongshore a lubberly, though not necessarily a "lacking" person. **1948** Manfred *Chokecherry* 133 **nwIA,** Well, stop then, you goony, an' see what's the matter. **1950** *WELS (A dull and stupid person)* 1 Inf, **cwWI,** Drip, gooney, stupe, simple, nitwit. **1969** *DARE* File **neGA,** *Goon, goonie* . . stupid or crazy person . . used real often in this area.
2 Std: any of var seabirds, but esp the black-footed albatross *(Diomedea nigripes).*
3 The common **merganser** *(Mergus merganser).*
1923 U.S. Dept. Ag. *Misc. Circular* 13.4, *American Merganser. . . Vernacular Names. . . In local use. . .* Gony (N.Y.) **1982** Elman *Hunter's Field Guide* 226, *American Merganser . . Common & Regional Names . .* gony.
4 A stone, esp one of medium size; a cobble; transf, a knot or bump on the head. **esp PA, NY** Cf **doney** n^1 **1**
1949 *McDavid Coll.* **seNY,** *Goony:* a fist-sized rock or stone. **1950** *WELS Suppl.* 2 Infs, **upper NY, seWI,** *Goneys*—field stones. **1965–70** *DARE* (Qu. C25, . . *Stone . . size of a person's head . . smooth and hard*) Infs **IL**84, **PA**142, 146, **TN**33, 34, 35, Goney; **PA**72, 215, Gooney ['guni]; **PA**245, Gooney—round, but fist size; old-fashioned; (Qu. C22, *A piece of stone too big for one person to move easily*) Inf **NY**183, Gooney; (Qu. C24a, *A small piece of stone that you could easily throw*) Infs **PA**165, 176, Gooney; (Qu. X60, . . *A lump that comes up on your head when you get a sharp blow or knock*) Inf **PA**154, Gooney. **1986** *Barrick Coll.* **csPA,** *Gooney*—small stone found in fields.

goonger n
1957 *Sat. Eve. Post Letters* **nwMI,** The kids around here call especially big marbles 'goongers.' [Note: the "oo" is marked to indicate [ʊ] pronc.]

go on one's face See **face, run one's**

goonoo bird n
A **yellowlegs** (here: *Totanus flavipes*).
1932 Bennitt *Check-list* 30 **MO,** Lesser yellow-legs. . . Goonoo bird.

goonus n Also *gawnicus, gonus* [Facetious Latinizations of **gooney 1**]
A fool, dolt.
1842 *Dartmouth* IV.116 *(DAE),* A stupid fellow, a dolt, a boot-jack, an ignoramus, is here called a *gonus.* **1848** *Amherst Indicator* I.76 *(DAE),* Future gonuses will swear by his name. **1867** Lowell *Biglow* lviii **'Upcountry' MA,** *Gawnicus:* a dolt. **1959** *VT Hist.* ns 27.138, *Goonus. . .* A simpleton; a stupid person. Occasional.

goony See **gooney**

goop v^1, sometimes repeated Also *goo(ie)* **esp S Midl, Sth** Cf **co-ee, cope** v^2
Come!—used as a call to pigs.
1949 Kurath *Word Geog.* 44, The Carolinas have their own range of hog calls: *goop!, woop!,* and *piggoop!* . . These calls are heard from the Neuse River southward and westward to the Blue Ridge. **1966** Dakin *Dial. Vocab. Ohio R. Valley* 2.285, In addition to these most frequently used calls [to pigs] . . a large number of other variations and innovations are used by scattered individuals. Among them are: . . *gooie!* **1967** Faries *Word Geog. MO* 149, *Goop!*—1 [of c700 infs]. **1967–68** *DARE* (Qu. K84, *The call used around here to get the pigs in at feeding time*) Inf **SC**43, Goop; **AR**52, Goop, piggy; **GA**19, Oop goop goop pig pig. **1972** *PADS* 58.18 **cwAL,** Call to pigs. . . One informant gave *goo-piggy* (per-

haps a variant of Carolina and Georgia *goop* or *piggoop*). **1986** Pederson *LAGS Concordance* 1 inf, **cnFL,** Goop.

goop n **chiefly Inland Nth, N Midl, West** See Map
Any viscous, sticky substance or mixture.

1946 *AmSp* 21.74, *Goop.* 'Synthetic lava,' the mixture in an incendiary bomb, a rubbery compound or pyrogel of powdered magnesium, liquid asphalt, jellied gasoline, and other oils. . . The name goop arose from its sticky character. **1950** *Western Folkl.* 9.158 **nCA** [Mountaineering vocab], *Goop.* Any particularly inspired hash. **1958** McCulloch *Woods Words* 71 **Pacific NW,** *Goop*—a. Any dirty, sticky, smelly, messy stuff. b. Petroleum jelly used for starting slash fires. **1965–70** *DARE* (Qu. Y40b, *Other words referring to sticky stuff*) 38 Infs, **chiefly Inland Nth, N Midl, West,** Goop; (Qu. H37, . . *Words . . for gravy*) Infs **MT4, WA3,** Goop; (Qu. H64, *The sweet covering spread on top of a cake*) Inf **WY1,** Goop; (Qu. H82a) Inf **GA11,** Kool-aid goop; (Qu. BB35, *The yellowish stuff that comes out of a boil when the head breaks*) Inf **PA175,** Goop; (Qu. DD4, *Moisture in the mouth, colored brown by snuff or chewing tobacco*) Inf **CA56,** Goop. **1969** *DARE* Tape **CA117,** I was worried to death rather than I get toothpaste or hair goop on my hand. **1973** Allen *LAUM* 1.294 (as of c1950), *Goop* occurs twice in Nebraska [for the sweet liquid poured over pudding].

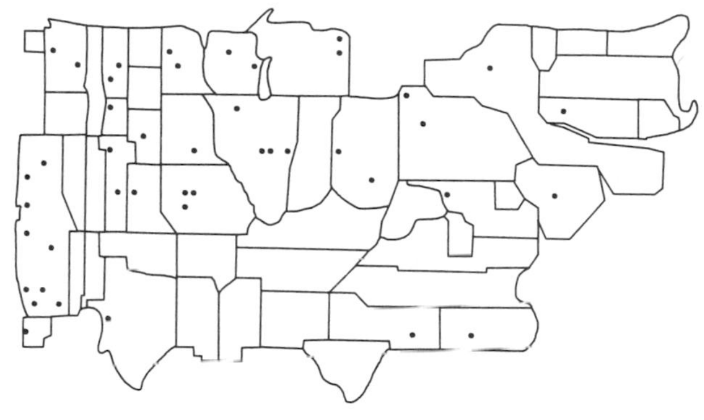

•goop n + var (Qq. Y40b, H37, H64, H82a, BB35, DD4)

goop v[2] Also with *up* **[goop n]**
To smear with something sticky; esp, to apply an oily or greasy preparation to the hair.

1965–70 *DARE* (Qu. KK38, . . *"I wish he wouldn't ______ his hair down so!"*) Infs **CA189, MS64, PA177, TX28,** Goop; (Qu. Y39, . . *"The children have been eating candy and they've got their faces all ______ ."*) Infs **AK1, CA189, CT11,** Gooped up; **OR6,** Gooped; (Qu. Y40a, . . *"I've got to wash my hands; they're all ______ ."*) Inf **NY199,** Gooped.

gooper pea See **goober pea**

goopher n, v See **goofer** n, v

goop up See **goop** v[2]

goopy adj

1 Sticky, smeared. **[goop n]**

1967–68 *DARE* (Qu. W36, . . *A woman who uses a lot of cosmetics*) Inf **PA170,** Goopy; (Qu. Y40a, . . *"I've got to wash my hands. They're all ______ ."*) Infs **AK1, CO39,** Goopy.

2 Tired; "under the weather."

1968–69 *DARE* (Qu. BB39, *On a day when you don't feel just right . . "I'll be all right tomorrow—I'm just feeling ______ today."*) Inf **IL47,** Goopy; (Qu. KK30, *Feeling slowed up or without energy: "I certainly feel ______ ."*) Inf **OH65,** Goopy.

3 Of the weather: unpleasant.

1969 *DARE* (Qu. B2, *If the weather is very unpleasant, you say it's a ______ day.*) Inf **IL47,** Goopy.

goose n

A Forms.

Pl: usu *geese;* also *gooses, geeses.*

1908 *DN* 3.316 **eAL, wGA,** *Gooses.* . . Geese. Fairly common. *Geeses* is sometimes heard.

B Senses.

1 =fulmar.

1904 Wheelock *Birds CA* 19, *Pacific Fulmar.—Fulmarus glacialis rodgersi.* . . Its common names are Goose [etc].

2 See quot.

1956 *AmSp* 31.183, American humor, noted for 'stretching' things, has not failed to exercise this proclivity in the folk nomenclature of birds. Although they are only eight to ten inches long, the phalaropes, shore birds that alight freely on open water, are called *geese* on Northeastern coasts and waters.

3 in phr *have a goose to pick:* **=crow to pick, have a.**

1967–69 *DARE* (Qu. KK14, *Something that people disagree about: "I have a ______ to pick with you."*) Infs **GA45, KY28, MO3,** Goose.

4 in phrr *lead a goose to water, bell a goose:* To do the simplest thing. **chiefly Sth, S Midl** Cf **bell a buzzard**

1965–70 *DARE* (Qu. JJ15a, *Sayings about a person who seems to you very stupid: "He hasn't sense enough to ______ ."*) 13 Infs, **chiefly Sth, S Midl,** Lead a goose to water; **FL31,** Bell a goose.

5 In children's games: see quot.

1967 *DARE* (Qu. EE14, *What do you call the place where the player who is 'it' has to wait and count while the others hide?*) Inf **MA8,** Goose; (Qu. EE15, *When he has caught the first of those that were hiding what does the player who is 'it' call out to the others?*) Inf **MA8,** Somebody's goose, one-two-three.

goose v

1 To repair boots by adding new leather; see quots. Cf **fox v 2**

1859 (1968) Bartlett *Americanisms* 175, *To Goose Boots.* To repair them by putting on a new front half way up, and a new bottom. **1897** Barrère–Leland *Slang* 1.397/2, *Goose.* . . (American), to enlarge or repair boots, by a process generally known as footing, *i.e.,* by putting in or adding pieces of leather.

2 rarely with *up:* To poke or tickle (someone) suddenly, esp in the buttocks, or to threaten to do so; to startle; to prod, spur; also fig.

1906 *DN* 3.138 **nwAR,** *Goose.* . . To create nervous excitement in a person by pointing a finger at him or by touching or tickling him and making a peculiar whistle. . . "They goosed him when he was drinking a cup of water, and he threw it in my face." **1908** *DN* 3.316 **eAL, wGA,** *Goose.* . . To punch or motion to punch (a person) with the finger, making at the same time a short smack or hiss. **1914** *DN* 4.163 **Pacific NW,** *Goose.* . . To startle, as by jumping or poking. **1915** *DN* 4.226 **wTX,** *Goose.* . . To tickle. **1931** Randolph *Ozarks* 253, W'y, he goosed them fish, o' course—jumpin' 'em, some calls it. Whenever'n th' river gits good an' muddy like, them 'ar linesides lays in the weeds, an' if you'all runs in 'twixt them an' deep water hit skeers hell out'n 'em, an' they most ginerly allus jumps right spang in th' boat. **1938** Farrell *No Star* 13 **Chicago IL** (as of 1914–15) Fag goosed him. Marty let out a yell as he jumped. **1948** Manfred *Chokecherry* 196 **nwIA,** Fats goosed him sharply, and Elof jumped. **1950** Stuart *Hie Hunters* 237 **KY,** "He was a hard man to take," Did said. "Sparkie had to goose 'im all the way here." **1952** Brown *NC Folkl.* 1.546, *Goose.* . . To make a person jump or flinch by thrusting him in the side (or elsewhere) with the finger or thumb, or to make a pretense of doing so. . . —General. **1967–68** *DARE* (Qu. Y6, . . *To put pressure on somebody to do something he ought to have done but hasn't*) Infs **IA22, MO26, PA93,** Goose him (a little bit); **PA134,** Goose him and make him get going; **LA2,** Goose him up. **1968** Adams *Western Words* 129, *Goose*—To spur a horse. **1975** Gould *ME Lingo* 112, *Goose*—Used in Maine as elsewhere for an intimacy of sorts, it has other meanings in the senses of sudden impetus, special persuasion and exhortation into activity. "Goose your engine and you'll back off that shoal." When a truck is stuck in the mud and everybody is ready to push, the cry will be "Now goose her!"—this means for the driver to rev the engine. A man who is reluctant to join a cause may be goosed by forthright persuasion. **1982** *Barrick Coll.* **csPA,** *Goose*—tickle by inserting finger or thumb between buttocks. **1982** Walker *Color Purple* 32 **GA** [Black], He say Harpo wasn't working hard like he should. Maybe little money goose his interest.

3 To depress the accelerator of (an engine, car, or other vehicle) suddenly; hence *goose up* to move a car forward a short distance from a stop.

1945 Hamann *Air Words* 27, *Goose'er, to.* To give her the gun; that is, to advance the throttle. **1948** Manfred *Chokecherry* 1 **nwIA,** The driver got in . . and began goosing the motor to start off again. **1954** *AmSp* 29.97 [Hot rod terms], Goose it! Give the engine full throttle. **1967–70** *DARE* FW Addit **CO29,** *Goose it*—Step on the accelerator; **KY,** *Goose up*—move further, push on. When someone stopped a car a little short of the place where the passenger wanted to get out, she said, "Goose up a little more." **1971** Tak *Truck Talk* 75, *Goose it:* to choke the engine, to feed it a richer fuel-to-air mixture. **1975** [see **2** above].

4 In railroading: to apply the brakes or throw the engine into reverse while it is moving.

1938 Beebe *High Iron* 221 [Railroad terms], *Goose, to:* To make an emergency stop. **1940** *RR Mag.* Apr 45, *Goose her*—Reverse locomotive or trolley car when she is underway.

5 See quot.

1958 *PADS* 29.11 **TN,** *Goose:* To weed, using geese. "We are going to goose strawberries."

goose and gander n

=**fox and geese 2.**

1967 *DARE* (Qu. EE33, *Other outdoor games*) Inf **CO**3, Goose and gander. A tag [game] in the snow. [There was] a big ring and a smaller ring inside it. [The two rings were connected] with prongs. [You] had to stay in the islands.

goose and the gander See **goosey goosey gander**

goose bean n Also *wild goose bean* [See quot 1978]

Any of several cultivars of the common bean *(Phaseolus vulgaris).*

1863 Burr *Field & Garden* 492, *Wild-Goose*. . . The ripe beans are pale cream-white, spotted with deep purplish-black (the cream-white gradually changing by age to cinnamon-brown). . . The variety has long been cultivated both in Europe and this country. **1966–69** *DARE* (Qu. I18, *The smaller beans that are white when they are dry*) Inf **MO**38, Goose beans; (Qu. I20, *Other kinds of beans that are grown around here*) Inf **NC**12, Gray goose beans; **CT**24, Wild goose beans. **1978** *Wanigan Catalog* 10, *Goose.* This variety deserves comment, primarily because it occurs so often and in so many areas. In general, each of the goose beans are different in color, size and growth. However, many have similar origins, i.e., the crop of wild geese shot in hunting. This is strange only at first thought. The bean goose of Europe is so named for its habit of feeding in bean fields. The knob on the upper mandible of geese is called a "bean". Also, the dry land feeding habit would suggest a dry crop, for a few hours at least! In addition to the many beans with goose in the name, there is turkey craw! These are all plausible origins. *Ibid* 21, *Wild Goose.* See *Goose.* This is the first bean seed having the Goose or Wild Goose name, acquired by Wanigan years ago. From a relative in Rhode Island, it matches early descriptions. **1985** *Seed Savers Exchange* Winter 99, *Bean . . dry . . pole . . Wild Goose*—round white bean with maroon spot. *Ibid* 121, *Snap . . bush . . Wild Goose . .* large black & white bean.

gooseberry n

1 Std: any of numerous plants of the genus *Ribes;* also the usu bristly or spiny fruit of such a plant. For other names of var spp see **dogberry e, straggle bush, wineberry** Cf **currant B1**

2 Any of several spp of **blueberry 1:** see quots. Cf **gander berry**

1739 (1946) Gronovius *Flora Virginica* 43, *Vaccinium* staminibus corolla longioribus. . . *Vitis Idaea* humilis, longiori & mucronato folio, floribus urceolatis racemosis, fructu robro majore. *Goose-Berrys.* [=*Vaccinium*—with stamens longer than the corolla. . . *Vitis Idaea*—low-growing, with rather longer, prickly leaf, urn-shaped flowers in clusters, biggish red fruit.] **1900** Lyons *Plant Names* 386, *V[accinium] arboreum*. . . Farkleberry, . . Gooseberry. . . *V. stamineum*. . . Deerberry, . . Goose-berry. **1911** *Century Dict. Suppl., Gooseberry*. . . The farkleberry, *Batodendron arboreum:* doubtless so called from its somewhat similar fruit. **1938** Van Dersal *Native Woody Plants* 280, *Vaccinium melanocarpum*. . . *Southern gooseberry*. . . A small shrub; . . fruit commonly produced in great quantities. **1953** Randolph–Wilson *Down in Holler* 247 **Ozarks,** The names . . *buck berry,* . . *goose berry,* and *he-huckleberry* are applied rather loosely to several species of *Vaccinium.* **1960** Vines *Trees SW* 816, *V[accinium] arboreum*. . . Vernacular names are Whortleberry, . . Gooseberry.

3 An unwanted third person. [*OED gooseberry* sb. 5 "A chaperon"; 1837 →]

1901 *DN* 2.141 **ME, Pacific,** *Gooseberry*. . . A person *de trop;* the third person who makes a "crowd."

4 pl; also *gooseberry pimples:* =**gooseflesh.**

1969 *DARE* (Qu. CC15, *When people say there are ghosts in a certain place, or when it gives you a creepy feeling to go near it*) Inf **IN**75, It gives me gooseberries; (Qu. X58, *When you are cold, and little points of skin begin to come on your arms and legs, you have* ______) Inf **GA**72, Gooseberry pimples.

‡**gooseberry grinder** n

1969 *DARE* (Qu. M21b, *Joking names for an outside toilet building*) Inf **CA**136, Gooseberry grinder.

gooseberry pimples See **gooseberry 4**

goosebill n [*OED* 1597 →]

A **cleavers** (here: *Galium aparine*).

1940 Clute *Amer. Plant Names* 259, *Galium aparine*. . . Goose-bill. **1959** Carleton *Index Herb. Plants* 55, *Goose bill:* Galium aparine.

goose bird n

1 =**Hudsonian godwit.** [See quot 1955]

1844 DeKay *Zool. NY* 2.253, *Limosa hudsonica*. . . In Boston it is called the *Goose-bird.* **1888** Trumbull *Names of Birds* 209, *Hudsonian Godwit*. . . In Massachusetts at Rowley, Salem, Boston markets, Provincetown, West Barnstable, and New Bedford, *Goose-bird.* **1917** (1923) *Birds Amer.* 1.240, *Hudsonian Godwit*. . . *Other Names*. . . Goose-bird; Black-tailed Godwit. **1946** Hausman *Eastern Birds* 290. **1955** *AmSp* 30.180, The name goosebird, applied to the Hudsonian godwit (N.H., Mass.), is said to refer to the fact that this bird, like the Canada goose, has a white rump.

2 =**willet.**

1956 MA Audubon Soc. *Bulletin* 40.18 **MA,** *Willet.* Goose Bird.

goose brant n

=**Hutchins's goose.**

1857 *Lawrence Republican* (KS) 2 July 1/3 **cwMO,** The plains also swarm with . . water fowl of every variety, the swan, goose brant, ducks, marmots. **1886** *Forest & Stream* 26.349/1, *Hutchin's Goose (Bernicla canadensis hutchinsi)*. . . is included by hunters with all the other small species under the general appellation of "brant" being further distinguished by the cognomen of "goose brant." **1888** Trumbull *Names of Birds* 4, Goose Brant. **1917** (1923) *Birds Amer.* 1.160, Hutchins's Goose . . is precisely like the Canada Goose in everything except size. . . Throughout its range it is variously known as Goose-brant, Little Canada Goose [etc]. **1923** U.S. Dept. Ag. *Misc. Circular* 13.36, *Hutchins Goose*. . . *Vernacular Names*. . . *In local use*. . . Goose brant (Ill.)

goose bumps n pl

1 rarely *goose lumps:* =**gooseflesh.** *somewhat more freq among younger speakers*

1867 Scott *Partisan Life* 407, And they all looked at Dr. Gog and laughed, he standing there forlorn and covered with goose-bumps. **1928** *Liberty* 11 Aug. 13/1 *(DA),* Chase these goose bumps from my skin. **1933** Miller *Lamb in His Bosom* 148 **GA,** She rubbed down the skin of her arms and legs where goose-bumps stood on every pore as though it were cold weather. **1941** Percy *Lanterns* 311 **nwMS,** I . . quaked on the edge of a tin bathtub . . which brought goose-bumps to the side away from the fireplace. **1946** *PADS* 6.15 **NC,** *Goosebumps*. . . Bumps on the human skin due to cold or fright. **1947** *PADS* 8.25 **wNY,** *Goose bumps:* Also *goose pimples.* **1949** *PADS* 11.22 **CO,** *Goose bumps.* **1950** *WELS* 8 Infs, **WI,** Goose bumps. **1954** *Harder Coll.* **cwTN,** *Goose bumps.* **1961** Salinger *Franny* 85 **NYC,** I'm goosebumps all over. . . By God, you inspire me. **1965–70** *DARE* (Qu. X58, *When you are cold, and little points of skin begin to come on your arms and legs, you have* ______) 311 Infs, **widespread,** Goose bumps; **CA**87, All over goose bumps; **AR**3, Goose bump; **MA**98, Goose lumps [Of all Infs responding to the question, 38% were young or mid-aged; of those giving these responses, 49% were young or mid-aged.]; (Qu. GG13b, *When something keeps bothering someone and makes him nervous, he may say: "It gives me the* ______.") Inf **IN**61, Goose bumps. **1968** *PADS* 49.16 **Upper MW** (as of c1950), Vocabularies sometimes change because a word from one dialect appears to have more prestige than that of another dialect. . . *Goose bumps,* appearing to be another Midland expression, seems to be replacing both *goose flesh* and *goose pimples.*

2 See quot.

1966 *DARE* (Qu. X59, . . *The small infected pimples that form usually on the face*) Inf **SC**19, Goose bumps.

goose-cap n [*OED goose-cap* sb. "?*Obs*. . . A booby, noodle, numskull, simpleton, fool"; 1589 →]

See quots.

1828 Webster *Amer. Dict., Goosecap*. . . A silly person. **1930** Shoemaker *1300 Words* 25 **cPA Mts** (as of c1900), *Goose cap*—A harum-scarum, unreliable girl.

goose down n

1 A light fall of snow. Cf **goosefeather 1**

1966 *DARE* (Qu. B39, *A very light fall of snow*) Inf **AL**1, Goose down.

2 See **down** n².

goose-drownder n Also *gosling-drownder, goose-strangler,* ~ (or *duck*)-*drencher, duck-drownder, chicken-~, hen-~* [*drownd* (at **drown 1**)] **chiefly Midl** See Map Cf **fish-drownder, frog-strangler**

A heavy rain, downpour.

1929 *AmSp* 5.180 **Ozarks,** *Goose-drownder*. . . A very heavy rain, a cloudburst. **1933** Williamson *Woods Colt* 73 **Ozarks,** A reg'lar old goose-drowneder [sic] of a rain, this un is. **1939** *AmSp* 14.90 **TN,** The rain was a goose drownder. **1944** *AmSp* 19.205 **cwIN,** *Goose-drownder.* **1950** *PADS* 14.32 **eSC,** *Goose drownder.* **1953** Randolph–Wilson *Down in Holler* 248 **Ozarks,** Oh Lord, send us rain! We don't want no *drizzle-drozzle,* Lord. We don't want no *gully-washer,* nor no *fence-lifter.* What we need is a regular old *goose-drownder,* Lord! **1954** *WELS Suppl.* **Milwaukee WI,** "Goose drownder" . . an unusually heavy rain. **1960** Criswell *Resp. to PADS 20* **Ozarks,** *(A heavy, continuous rain)* Hen-drownder. **1962** Atwood *Vocab. TX* 38, *Duck drencher.* **1965–70** *DARE* (Qu. B25, . . *Joking names* . . *for a very heavy rain*) 13 Infs, **chiefly N Midl,** Goose-drownder; **IL**81, **IN**29, Gosling-drownder; **IL**114, Goose-strangler; **OH**69, Goose-drencher; **KY**72, Goose-drownder, duck-drownder; **WV**4, 5, 8, Duck-drownder; **KY**28, Chicken-drownder; **KS**5, Hen-drownder; (Qu. B24, . . *A sudden, very heavy rain*) Infs **NE**9, **OH**36, 61, Goose-drownder. **1969** *Daily Progress* (Charlottesville, Va.) 22 Aug. 4/6 *(OEDS),* Other two-word names for a heavy rain . . are: bresh- or brush-mover, bridge-lifter, goose drownder, gully-washer, sand-packer, toad-strangler, and trash-mover. **1971** Bright *Word Geog. CA & NV* 113 **cwCA,** Gosling drownder—1 [inf]. **1983** *MJLF* 9.1.41 **ceKY,** *Goose drownder* . . a rain heavier than a *gulley washer.*

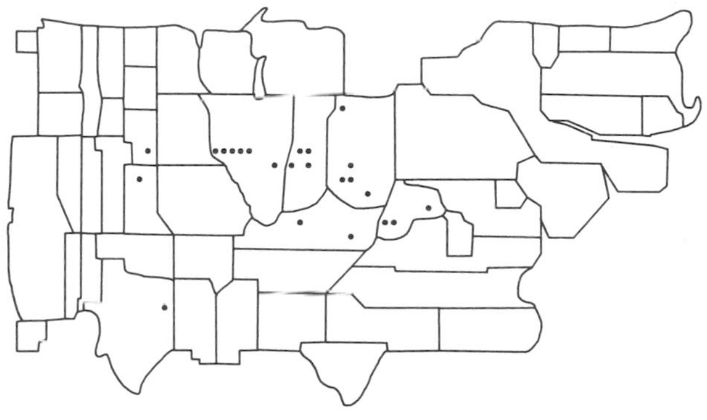

•goose-drownder + varr (Qq. B25, B24)

goose egg n

1 A knot or lump on the head as the result of a blow.

1953 Santee *Lost Pony Tracks* 61 **TX,** When you didn't mention how come that goose egg on yore head I figgered as much, myself. Shucks, ye're not the first boy that ol' pony has throwed. **1965–70** *DARE* (Qu. X60, *What do you call a lump that comes up on your head when you get a sharp blow or knock*) 240 Infs, **widespread,** Goose egg.

2 An illegitimate child.

1973 Allen *LAUM* 1.344 **cIA** (as of c1950), *Illegitimate child*. . . Other lively but rare Midland euphemisms [include] . . *goose egg* [given by one inf].

3 See quot. Cf *DS* M21a, b

1989 *DARE* File **neOH** (as of 1922), At the boy scout camp the outdoor toilet was called the "goose egg," from the shape of the hole in the seat.

goose eye n Cf **drake's eye, frogeye 3**

In moonshining: a large **bead** n **3.**

1968 *Foxfire* Fall-Winter 101 **nGA** [Stilling terms], *Goose Eye*—a good bead that holds a long time in the vial. **1974** Maurer–Pearl *KY Moonshine* 119, *Goose eye*. . . A perfect bead, indicating 100 proof.

goosefeather n

1 pl: Large, soft flakes of snow. Cf **goose down 1**

1965 Teale *Wandering Through Winter* 283 **VT,** It requires only six inches of the large, soft and soggy snow that is usually called "goose-feathers" to be equivalent to an inch of rainfall.

2 See **feather** n **B4.**

goose fever n

1968 *DARE* (Qu. BB28, *Joking names that people make up for imaginary diseases: "He must have the ______.*") Inf **WI**44, Goose fever.

goosefish n

A saltwater fish *(Lophius piscatorius).* Also called **allmouth 1, angler, bellows fish 3, devilfish 3, fishing frog, headfish 2, kettleman, molligut, monkfish, satchel mouth, sea devil, widegape**

1807 MA Hist. Soc. *Coll.* 2d ser 3.55, The sting-ray, the skaite, and the goose fish, or monk, or fishing frog, are common. **1842** DeKay *Zool. NY* 4.163, Its [=*Lophius piscatorius's*] monstrous form has given rise to many popular names, such as . . *Goose-fish, Monk-fish,* and various others. **1883** *Century Illustr. Mag.* 26.733/2, It was no mean triumph, for instance, to have reared those young flounders and goose-fish from eggs scooped up in the open sea. **1914** Steele *Storm* 50, I was as gloomy and dull as any goose-fish. **1933** John G. Shedd Aquarium *Guide* 162, It is impossible to mistake the Goosefish for any other fish. . . The body is soft and flabby and not favored for food in this country although it is of excellent flavor. **1970** *DARE* (Qu. P4) Inf **MS**81, Goosefish. **1982** Heat Moon *Blue Highways* 352 **ME,** Even more primordial is the monkfish, also called the "goosefish" and "angler fish."

goose flat See **goosetown**

gooseflesh n Also *gooseflesh bumps, goose meat* [From the resemblance to the skin of a plucked goose] *somewhat old-fash* Also called **duck bumps, gander ~, gooseberry 4, goose bumps 1, ~ pimples, gooseskin 1, hen flesh, hoar bumps** Cf **French knot**

Roughness of the skin caused by the erection of the hair bases due to cold or emotion; also fig.

1871 Lowell *Study Windows* 175, Irritating every pore of his vanity, like a dry northeast wind, to a gooseflesh of opposition and hostility. **1950** *WELS* 13 Infs, **WI,** Gooseflesh. **1954** *Harder Coll.* **cwTN,** *Gooseflesh*. . . An eerie feeling when something frightening occurs. " 'Em storms give me the goose flesh." **c1960** *Wilson Coll.* **csKY,** *Goose flesh*. . . Small bumps caused by being suddenly chilly. **1965–70** *DARE* (Qu. X58, *When you are cold, and little points of skin begin to come on your arms and legs, you have ______*) 105 Infs, **widespread,** Gooseflesh [Of all Infs responding to the question, 64% were old; of those giving this response, 79% were old.]; **AL**3, Gooseflesh bumps; **WV**2, Goose meat. **1968** [see **goose bumps 1**]. **1983** *MJLF* 9.1.41 **ceKY,** *Goose meat*. . . goose flesh.

goosefoot n

Std: a plant of the genus *Chenopodium.* Also called **lamb's quarters, pigweed, wild spinach.** For other names of var spp see **fat hen 2, hogweed 3, Jerusalem oak, Joseph's coat, Mexican tea, mutton-tops, notchweed, rag-jag, shoemaker's heels, soap plant, stinking motherwort, strawberry blite**

goosefoot maple n

1 =**striped maple.** [See quot 1901]

1884 Sargent *Forests of N. Amer.* 46, Striped Maple. Moose Wood. Goose-foot Maple. **1901** Lounsberry *S. Wild Flowers* 323, *A[cer] Pennsylvanicum*. . . Most often perhaps the mountaineers that "claim to know" the trees, call it the goosefoot maple, because its leaves which broaden towards the summit and divide into three well cut lobes suggest to them that bird's foot. **1931** Harned *Wild Flowers Alleghanies* 284, *Striped Maple*. . . Known also by the familiar names, Moose Wood . . and Goose-foot Maple. . . Easily identified by the leaves . . resembling the foot of a goose. **1952** Blackburn *Trees* 80, *A[cer] pennsylvanicum* (e N America) *Goose-foot maple.* **1967** Borland *Hill Country* 160 **nwCT,** Moosewood . . has two other common names, striped maple and goosefoot maple. . . The "goosefoot" designation comes from the shape of the leaves, which are three-pointed, shaped much like a goose's foot.

2 A **mountain maple** (here: *Acer spicatum*).

1971 Krochmal *Appalachia Med. Plants* 28, *Acer spicatum*. . . *Common Names:* Mountain maple, goosefoot maple. . . Leaves are thin, downy beneath, 3-lobed or sometimes 5-lobed, with coarse-toothed margins.

goose grass n

1 Any of var plants other than grasses, as:

a =**bedstraw,** esp *Galium aparine.* [*OED* 1530 →]

a1782 (1788) Jefferson *Notes VA* 57, I will confine myself to native plants. . . Clivers, or goose-grass. Galium spurium. **1833** Eaton *Botany* 152, *Galium. . . aparine* . . goose grass. . . Fruit hook-bristled. **1897** Parsons *Wild Flowers CA* 28, *Goose-grass. . . Galium Aparine*. . . A cold infusion of this little plant is used as a domestic remedy in cases of fever, where a cooling drink is desired. **1915** (1926) Armstrong-Thornber *Western Wild Flowers* 508, There are many kinds of Galium. . . The common name [is] Bed-straw. . . Other names are Goose-grass and Cleavers. **1940** Steyermark *Flora MO* 499, *Goose Grass*. . . Usually forming large tangled patches. **1965** GA Dept. Ag. *Farmers Market Bulletin* 2 Sept 8, Cleavers—goosegrass or bedstraw, common names for galium aparine, is a weak almost perennial herb that can't stand upright unless it is climbing on and supported by surrounding vegetation. **1975** Hamel-Chiltoskey *Cherokee Plants* 36, Goose-grass. . . Tea to move bowels.

b A **knotweed:** usu *Polygonum aviculare,* but also *P. erectum.*

1847 Darlington *Weeds & Plants* 281 *(DAE),* Bird Polygonum. Knot-grass. Goose-grass. Door-weed. **1876** Hobbs *Bot. Hdbk.* 45, Grass, Goose, Knot grass, Polygonum aviculare. **1897** *Jrl. Amer. Folkl.* 10.54, *Polygonum erectum,* . . goose grass, Sulphur Grove, Ohio. **1910** Graves *Flowering Plants* 160 **CT,** *Polygonum aviculare*. . . Goose . . Grass. . . The seeds are eaten by certain birds. . . *Polygonum erectum*. . . Goose Grass. Frequent. **1912** Blatchley *IN Weed Book* 67, *Polygonum aviculare*. . . Goose-grass. . . Very common, forming mats of spreading, wiry, jointed stems in yards and along pathways and roadsides where the ground is much trodden. **1974** (1977) Coon *Useful Plants* 212, *Polygonum aviculare* . . goose-grass. . . is just one of a number of *Polygonums* which grow very widely and are persistent weeds.

c also *goose tansy, goose weed:* A **silverweed** (here: *Potentilla anserina*). [*OED* c1387 →]

1847 Wood *Class-Book* 252, *P[otentilla] anserina*. Silver-weed. Goose-grass. **1876** Hobbs *Bot. Hdbk.* 45, Grass, Goose, Silverweed, Potentilla anserina. **1900** Lyons *Plant Names* 303, *P. Anserina*. . . Goose Tansy, Goose-grass. **1911** Jepson *Flora CA* 208, *Goose-grass*. . . Root bearing a tuft of leaves, stems and peduncles. . . Leaves white-silky beneath. **1948** Wherry *Wild Flower Guide* 78, *Silver-and-gold (P. anserina)*. . . Also known as . . *Goose-weed*. **1966** *DARE* (Qu. S26a, . . *Roadside flowers*) Inf **MI**31, Goose tansy. **1974** (1977) Coon *Useful Plants* 227, *Potentilla anserina* . . goose-grass, goose tansy. . . A weed spread everywhere in the country.

d Either of two bulrushes: *Scirpus americanus* or *S. robustus.* **esp LA**

1910 *Auk* 27.338 **seLA,** Every summer these flats are covered by a dense growth of . . "goose grass" *(Scirpus robustus)*. **1913** *Torreya* 13.228, *Scirpus robustus*. . . Goose grass (the rootstocks being eaten), Mississippi Delta, La. **1921** LA Dept. of Conserv. *Bulletin* 10.35, The ground has been turned by deer with their sharp hoofs to get the tender roots of . . the goose-grass (three-cornered grass or three-square). **1941** *Torreya* 41.46, *Scirpus americanus*. . . Goose grass, Mississippi Delta, La.

e An **arrowhead 1** (here: *Sagittaria teres*).

1913 *Torreya* 13.227, *Sagittaria teres*. . . Goose grass, Currituck Sound, N.C.

f An arrow grass of the genus *Triglochin,* esp *T. maritima.* **West**

1920 *Torreya* 20.18, *Triglochin maritima*. . . Goose grass, Lower Klamath Lake, Calif. **1963** Craighead *Rocky Mt. Wildflowers* 4, *Triglochin maritima*. . . Goosegrass. . . Saline, marshy areas. **1966** Barnes-Jensen *Dict. UT Slang* 20, *Goose grass* . . a local name for the Arrow-grass *(Triglochin maritima)*. **1970** Kirk *Wild Edible Plants W. U.S.* 159, *Triglochin maritima* . . Goosegrass. . . When roasted, the seeds were used by early western pioneers as a substitute for coffee.

g =**horsetail 1.**

1941 *Torreya* 41.45 **AK,** *Equisetum* spp.—Goose grass.

h =**dog fennel 1.**

1950 *WELS Suppl.* 1 Inf, **cwWI,** Goose grass. Another name for camomile, mayweed, or stink-weed, all of which I have heard for the bitter yellow daisy which flourishes in our home yard, an escapee from Grandma's herb garden.

2 Any of var grasses, as:

a A **bluegrass 1** (here: *Poa annua*).

1878 Killebrew *Grasses TN* 161, Annual speargrass—Goose grass *(Poa annua)* . . is a valuable grazing grass and sows itself. **1910** Graves *Flowering Plants* 72 **CT,** *Poa annua*. . . Low Spear Grass. Goose Grass. Common. Cultivated ground and waste places. **1945** Mathews *Talking Moon* 51, The goose grass is like a green velvet ceremonial rug.

b A grass of the genus *Eleusine,* esp *E. indica.* Also called **crabgrass 2, crowfoot 3, wire grass, yard grass.** For other names of *E. indica* see **dog grass 2, dogstail grass 2**

1889 Vasey *Ag. Grasses* 58 **SC,** *Eleusine Indica*. . . [I]n the lower and middle portions of that State the name of goose grass is generally applied. **1912** Baker *Book of Grasses* 166, *Goose-grass. . . Eleusine indica*. . . Cultivated grounds and waste places. **1935** (1943) Muenscher *Weeds* 154, Goose-grass. . . Widespread in the eastern United States; most common in the South. **1950** Gray-Fernald *Manual of Botany* 183, *Eleusine*. . . Goose-Grass. Yard-Grass. **1967** Braun *Monocotyledoneae* 133, *Goose Grass.* Easily recognized by the digitate arrangement of the wide (5mm) spikes. **1970** Kirk *Wild Edible Plants W. U.S.* 182, Goosegrass. . . The seeds may be gathered, cleaned, parched, and eaten whole, or ground into flour.

c =**Texas millet.**

1889 Vasey *Ag. Grasses* 25, *Panicum Texanum* (Texas Millet). . . In some localities it is known as . . goose grass, from its being supposed to have been introduced by wild geese.

d A **crowfoot 3** (here: *Dactyloctenium aegyptiacum*).

1894 Coulter *Botany W. TX* 534, *E[leusine] Aegyptiaca. . . Goose-grass*. . . Yards and cultivated land.

e =**alkali grass 2.**

1910 Graves *Flowering Plants* 75 **CT,** *Puccinellia angustata*. . . Goose Grass. . . *Puccinellia distans*. . . Goose Grass. Wet tidal sands and borders of salt marshes. **1911** *Century Dict. Suppl., Goose-grass*. . . The sea spear-grass, *Puccinellia maritima.* **1912** Baker *Book of Grasses* 217, *Goose-grass. Sea Spear-grass*. . . Salt marshes and sea beaches. . . Labrador to New Jersey, also on the Pacific Coast. **1950** Gray-Fernald *Manual of Botany* 108, *Puccinellia*. . . Alkali-Grass. Goose-Grass.

f =**barnyard grass.**

1913 *Torreya* 13.227, *Echinochloa crus-galli*. . . Goose grass, Grand Island, Illinois River.

goose green See **goosetown**

goose greens n

The seaside **plantain** *(Plantago maritima).*

1975 Gould *ME Lingo* 113, *Goose greens*—Also called *shore greens.* A short, smoothed-stemmed plant found along the Maine shore. Some would liefer have them than dandelions and *fiddleheads.*

goose ground n

1930 Shoemaker *1300 Words* 27 **cPA Mts** (as of c1900), *Goose-ground*—A common or market place.

goose hair n Also *geese hair*

Goose feathers or down; a bed or pillow filled with these.

1887 *Amer. Field* 27.62/3 **West,** When they want to ridicule a tender-foot . . they say "he wants a goose hair bed to sleep on;" when a cowboy is in luck he is described as having "a goose hair pillar" [=pillow]. **1897** Lewis *Wolfville* 117 **AZ,** Faro Nell puts another goose-ha'r piller onder him. **1926** Thorp *Tales Chuck Wagon* 7, Punchin' cows . . ain't like it is in a book I read . . where all the cute Waddie had ter do was ride slick fat horses, sleep on a geese-hair bed, set the boss' daughter en afterwards marry her. **1933** *AmSp* 8.1.31 **TX,** *Goose-hair.* Feather pillow or feather bed, the superlative luxury. **1940** *AmSp* 15.447 **eTN,** *Goose hair.* Feather bed. 'We'uns has slept on this goose hair fur twenty year.' **c1940** Eliason *Word Lists FL* 8 **wFL,** *Goosehair:* Goose feather. **1970** *DARE* (Qu. X40, *What other ways do you have of saying "I'm going to bed"?*) Inf **AR**56, Hit the goosehair.

goose hangs high, the phr Also *the goose honks high* [Perh because a goose hanging conspicuously in the larder is a sign of easy circumstances; the var with *honks* is prob a folk-etym]

All is well or prosperous.

1863 Converse *Old Cremona Songster* 26 *(DA),* Oh! you bet, your bogus dollars, Oh! you bet, the goose hangs high. **1894** *Congressional Record* 14 Feb 2185/2, If you believe there is a plethora of money, if you believe everything is lovely and the goose hangs high, go down to the soup houses in the city of New York. **1908** *DN* 3.316 **eAL, wGA,** *Goose hangs high, the.* Everything is in fine order. The goose honks high is not heard except sporadically among the well-informed. **1919** Kyne *Capt. Scraggs* 131 **CA,** Scraggsy, when all is lovely an' the goose honks high, it's our great American privilege to fight like bearcats if we feel that way about it. **1948** Bean *Yankee Auctioneer* 98 **wMA,** Those women think I'm a good guy—everything is lovely and the goose honks high. "Hangs" many people say, but "honks" is right. **1966** *DARE* (Qu. KK4, *When things turn out just right*) Inf **MS**14, [The] goose hangs high. **1984** Wilder *You All Spoken Here* 173 **Sth,** The goose hangs high: Everything is looking up.

goose hawk n
Perh =**goshawk 1.**
1969 *DARE* (Qu. Q4) Inf **KY**47, Goose hawk . . three feet wing-spread.

goose heaven n
See quots.
1903 (1965) Adams *Log Cowboy* 295 **West,** I'll bet my interest in goose heaven that I know what's the matter with him. **1914** *DN* 4.107 **KS,** *Goose heaven*. . . The abiding place of late lamented animal pets.

goose hill, goose hollow See **goosetown**

goose honks high, the See **goose hangs high, the**

goose hook See **goose poke**

goosel See **goozle n 1**

gooselock v, hence vbl n *gooselocking,* ppl adj *gooselocked* [See quot 1968] **esp AL** Cf **cowlick n 3, goosepicking, nitting, tagging**
To pick cotton ineptly so that part of the tuft is left in the boll.
1968 *DARE* FW Addit **AL,** [The Inf] says that he has been punished as a child for gooselocking. . . He was told that sometimes geese get into cotton fields and actually peck at the cotton, pulling it from the bolls and leaving a good bit of the fiber streaming from the boll. **1968–87** *DARE* File **neAL,** In cotton fields when you don't pick the cotton clean, you are said to be gooselocking; **Ozarks** (as of c1910), *Goose-lock:* To leave tiny bits of lint when picking cotton; **cnAL,** In the old days, a field of cotton poorly picked was said to be "gooselocked."

goose lumps See **goose bumps 1**

goose meat See **gooseflesh**

gooseneck clam n
Prob a **geoduck 1.**
1967 *DARE* (Qu. P18, . . *Kinds of shellfish*) Inf **CA**25, Gooseneck clam.

gooseneck hoe n Also *gooseneck* **esp S Midl**
See quot 1908.
1908 *DN* 3.316 **eAL, wGA,** *Goose-neck (hoe)*. . . A hoe with the connecting piece between the blade and the handle in the shape of a goose's neck. **1949** Hornsby *Lonesome Valley* 56 *(Hench Coll.)* **eKY,** He got out two gooseneck hoes and sharpened them. **c1960** *Wilson Coll.* **csKY,** *Gooseneck hoe*. . . One with a curving metal stem. **c1970** *Halpert Coll.* 26 **wKY, nwTN,** To pull a gooseneck = to hoe. "I've pulled a gooseneck for thirty year." **1976** Garber *Mountain-ese* 35 **Appalachians,** As soon as we could walk we wuz interduced to a gooseneck hoe. **1986** Pederson *LAGS Concordance,* 1 inf, **cnGA,** Gooseneck hoe—for shape of attachment to handle; 1 inf, **cwTN,** Gooseneck hoe—was used in the cotton field; 2 infs, **neAR,** Gooseneck hoe.

gooseneck squash n
A crookneck squash *(Cucurbita moscata).*
1950 *PADS* 14.32 **SC,** *Gooseneck squash*. . . The long, yellow, crooked-necked squash. **1954** *Harder Coll.* **cwTN,** Gooseneck squash.

goose nest n
A sinkhole.
1904 (1913) Johnson *Highways South* 148 **KY,** The region about the cave [=Mammoth Cave] is hilly; but instead of watercourses and ravines, there are numerous rounded, basinlike hollows known as sinkholes. Often the sink-holes are acres in extent. . . Their form and frequency has given the name of "Goose-nest land" to that part of Kentucky where they are most abundant. **1939** FWP *Guide KY* 294, This is a cave region and sinkholes—called "goose nests" by the natives—small caves and sinking streams are prevalent.

goose nibble See **goosetown**

goose owl n
An unidentified owl.
1966 *DARE* (Qu. Q2) Inf **GA**16, Goose owl.

goose pasture See **goosetown**

goose pen n **Pacific NW** Cf **barber chair**
A large hole burned in the base of a tree, esp a redwood; the tree itself.
1905 U.S. Forest Serv. *Bulletin* 61.38 [Logging terms], *Goosepen.* A large hole burned in a standing tree. (P[acific] C[oast] F[orest]). **1949** Powers *Redwood Country* 98, On the lower Klamath stood a hollow stump, thirty-eight feet in diameter, in which it is declared a packer in the 'seventies corralled his whole outfit of thirty-three pack mules. Lumbermen call these hollow redwoods 'goosepens.' **1958** McCulloch *Woods Words* 72 **Pacific NW,** *Goosepen*—In the redwoods, a large hole burned in the base of a big tree. **1984** *DARE* File **nCA,** I picked up the word *goose-pen tree* in California near Eureka on a trip to a redwood forest. The guide said when redwood trees had been hollowed out by fires the early settlers sometimes used them to shelter poultry . . sometimes for storage, even for dwellings.

goosepicking vbl n Cf **gooselock**
1968 *DARE* FW Addit **AL,** *Goosepicking* . . a term referring to . . a poor job of picking cotton. . . A cotton farmer in Florence AL is familiar with both *gooselocking* and *goosepicking,* but claims that the latter is more frequently used. He also mentioned two other terms for the same action: *tagging* and *nitting.* Where the fiber tuft is joined to the plant, there is a small, black speck which he calls the "nit" or the "tag." A good picker will take the entire fiber tuft from the boll, "nit" and all. Since the nit is the point of juncture between fiber and plant, careless pickers may frequently pull away the tuft, leaving the nit joined to the boll along with a good many strands of fiber. This is called *goosepicking.*

goose pimples n pl **widespread, but somewhat less freq Sth** See Map
=**gooseflesh.**
1889 *Century Dict.* 2576, *Goose-pimples*. . . The pimples of goose-flesh. **1914** *DN* 4.155 **Cape Cod MA,** *Goose-pimples*. . . Goose-flesh. ('Goose-flesh' is never used.) "Don't stay in bathing so long that you're all goose-pimples when you come out." **1947** *NYT Mag.* 2 Feb 18/4, The way it scraped in this maneuver makes goose-pimples on my spine even now. **1949** *PADS* 11.22 **CO,** *Goose pimples.* **1950** *WELS* 47 Infs, **WI,** Goose pimples. **c1960** *Wilson Coll.* **csKY,** *Goose pimples*. . . Small bumps caused by becoming suddenly chilled. **1965–70** *DARE* (Qu. X58, *When you are cold, and little points of skin begin to come on your arms and legs, you have _____*) 600 Infs, **widespread, but somewhat less freq Sth,** Goose pimples; (Qu. BB13, *Other words . . for chills and fever*) Inf **GA**23, Goose pimples; (Qu. GG12, *To have an inner feeling that something is about to happen*) Inf **CA**211, Goose pimples; (Qu. GG13b, *When something keeps bothering a person and makes him nervous, he may say: "It gives me the _____."*) Inf **VA**75, Goose pimples; (Qu. GG26, *A feeling of weakness from fear: "When she saw the dog coming at her she got _____."*) Inf **OH**57, Goose pimples; **NY**213, Goose pimples came out all over her; (Qu. II29b, . . *The unpleasant effect that person has on you: "He just _____."*) Infs **MI**103, **NY**102, Gives me goose pimples. **1968** [see **goose bumps 1**]. **1973** Allen *LAUM* 1.405 (as of c1950), A slight bristling of the hairs of the skin because of cold or fear is known as goose pimples to four out of five U[pper] M[idwest] infs. **1982** *Barrick Coll.* **csPA,** *Goose pimples*—horripilation.

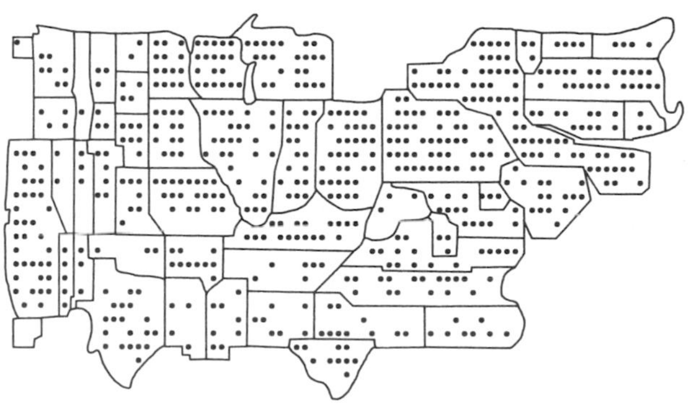

•goose pimples + varr (Qq. X58, BB13, GG12, GG13b, GG26, II29b)

goose plant n Cf **goose stickers**
Prob a **cleavers.**

1968 *DARE* (Qu. S14) Inf **PA**70, Goose plant—it sticks to your clothes.

goose plum n Cf **wild goose plum**

A **wild plum** (here: *Prunus americana*).

1897 Sudworth *Arborescent Flora* 237 **IN,** *Prunus americana. . . Common Names. . .* Goose Plum. **1913** Cather *O Pioneers* 29 **NE,** Stout as she was, she roamed the scrubby banks of Norway Creek looking for fox grapes and goose plums, like a wild creature in search of prey. **1940** Clute *Amer. Plant Names* 10, *P[runus] Americana. Wild Plum. . .* Goose-plum. **1950** Moore *Trees AR* 79, *American Plum. . .* Local Names . . Goose . . Plum. . . Fruits eaten and used for preserves locally. **1967–69** *DARE* (Qu. I46, *Other kinds of fruits that grow wild around here*) Infs **AL**34, **SC**46, 57, Goose plums; **KY**66, Red goose plums. **1976** Bailey–Bailey *Hortus Third* 918, *[Prunus] americana. . . Goose p[lum]. . .* Fr[uit] . . yellow or red, with a flattened stone. New Eng. to Man[itoba], S. to Fla. and New Mex.

goose poke n Also *goose hook, ~ yoke* **esp NEng** Cf **cow hook**

A yoke used to prevent a goose from slipping through a narrow opening.

1842 Kirkland *Forest Life* 1.120 **MI,** A "variety store," offering for sale every possible article of merchandise, from lace gloves to goose-yokes . . displayed its tempting sign. **1869** Murray *Adventures* 116 **eMA,** If I stumbled and fell, the confounded things would come like a goose-poke athwart my neck, pinning me down. **1878** (1977) Stowe *Poganuc People* 160 **CT,** Tim was whittling a goose-poke. **1933** *Hanley Disks* **swCT,** Goose-poke . . yoke for a goose. I saw what they called a goose-poke, put on the neck of a goose so he couldn't go under the fence. I'd seen cow hooks, but I'd never seen a goose hook.

goose pulling See **gander pulling**

gooser n [**goose** v 2]

1948 Hanna–Hanna *Lake Okeechobee* 343, The "gooser" was a cypress pole twelve to eighteen feet long on the end of which was a hook. This pole was thrust through the muck to find places where alligators had hidden.

goose-run n Also *duck-run*

1975 Gould *ME Lingo* 113, *Goosf* [sic]*-run*—Sometimes duck-run. A hunting hiatus incidental to other cruising. In the old days when so much of Maine's 'longshore business moved by boats, the arrival of the mail at an island might be delayed because the captain encountered a raft of birds he couldn't resist going after. In gunning season, passengers were sometimes forewarned that sea-ducks might delay arrival. Arriving late, a salesman might apologize by saying he was held up by a dam' *goose-run.* A lobsterman may say, as he leaves his harbor, "I may be late comin' in, if I make a goose-run." The term is transferred to almost any situation which gets delayed: "We meant to start out right after breakfast, but the women had to make some kind of a dam' goose-run, and we didn't get away 'til most noon."

gooses See **goose** n **A**

goose, set the v phr [*set* to put (a hen, etc) on eggs to hatch them]

1968 *DARE* (Qu. AA28, . . *Joking or sly expressions . . women use to say that another is going to have a baby*) Inf **MD**15, Somebody's set the goose.

goose-share n Also *goose's hare* [*OED* 1578 →]

A **cleavers** (here: *Galium aparine*).

1876 Hobbs *Bot. Hdbk.* 43, Gooses [sic] hare, Cleavers, Galium aparine. **1940** Clute *Amer. Plant Names* 259, *Galium aparine. . .* Goose-share. **1971** Krochmal *Appalachia Med. Plants* 126, *Galium aparine. . . Common Names* . . goose's hare.

gooseskin n

1 =**gooseflesh;** hence adj *goose-skinned.* [*OED* 1785 →]

1889 *Century Dict.* 2576, *Goose-skin. . .* Same as *goose-flesh.* **1926** Ferber *Show Boat* 100, Doc's knowledge of the gruesome history . . provided Magnolia with many a goose-skinned hour of delicious terror. **1950** *WELS* 1 Inf, **WI,** *Gooseskin.* **1967** LeCompte *Word Atlas* 386 **seLA,** Goose skin [1 inf out of 21].

2 See quot.

1912 Green *VA Folk-Speech* 201, *Goose-skin. . .* The wrinkled and colourless skin of the hands, caused by being long in water.

goose-skinned See **gooseskin 1**

goose stickers n Cf **goose plant**

Prob a **cleavers.**

1967 *DARE* (Qu. S13, *There's a common wild bush with bunches of round, prickly seeds; when they get dry they stick to your clothing—what are these called around here?*) Inf **MA**8, Goose stickers.

goose-strangler See **goose-drownder**

goose tang See **goose tongue**

goose tansy See **goose grass 1c**

goose teal n Cf **goose widgeon**

=**ruddy duck.**

1911 *Forest & Stream* 77.173, *Erismatura jamaicensis. . .* Goose-Teal, Galveston, Tex. **1955** *AmSp* 30.180, Why the ruddy duck is called *goose teal* (Texas), is a puzzle.

goose tongue n Pronc-sp *goose tang*

The seaside **plantain** *(Plantago maritima).*

1916 *Torreya* 16.239, *Plantago decipiens. . .* Goose-tongue, . . Matinicus I[slan]d, M[ain]e. **1925** Jepson *Manual Plants CA* 956, *P[lantago] maritima. . . Goose-tongue. . .* Ocean shore. **1940** White *Wild Geese* 205 **AK, WA** (as of 1890s), "Goose tang," enumerated Sally, depositing aboard a double handful of green, "the stuff Len told us about, lily-bulb rice, wild celery, Hudson Bay tea." **1943** Fernald–Kinsey *Edible Wild Plants E. N. Amer.* 341, *Seaside Plantain* is not very generally known as one of the most available summer vegetables, but on the New England coast, especially by the fishermen of eastern Maine, . . where the plant is regularly gathered under the name of *Goose-tongue,* it is extensively used. **1951** Graham *My Window* 47 **ME,** She is acquainted with a wide variety of edible plants. . . "Goose tongues is awful nice." **1966–68** *DARE* (Qu. I28a, *What kinds of things do you call 'greens' around here? Those that are eaten raw*) Inf **AK**3, Goose tongue; (Qu. I28b, *Kinds of greens that are cooked*) Inf **ME**12, Goose tongue. **1968** *DARE* Tape **AK**11, There's a green called goose tongue . . and when we cook pot roast we go down 'n' pluck this goose tongue, it grows just above high tide, . . cook it . . and pour the first water off an' then cook it again an' then chop it up again an' put melted butter in an' hard boiled eggs an' it's very much like spinach. . . a great deal of iron in it.

goose to pick, have a See **goose** n **B3**

goosetown n Also *goose flat, ~ hollow, ~ nibble;* for addit varr see quots **scattered, but esp N Cent, Upper MW**

Used as a nickname for a town or a section of a town, often a poor one.

1965–70 *DARE* (Qu. C35, . . *Different parts of your town or city*) Infs **IN**80, **MN**36, **OH**26, Goosetown; **AZ**1, Goose flat; **WI**57, Goose green; **GA**17, Goose holler; **IN**30, Goose nibble; (Qu. II25, . . *The part of a town where the poorer people, special groups, or foreign groups live*) Infs **IA**17, **IL**20, **IN**79, Goosetown; **IL**141, Goose nibble; **OH**95, Gooseville; (Qu. C34, . . *Nearby settlements, villages, or districts*) Inf **NY**37, Goose hill; **AR**55, Goose hollow; **IN**80, Goosetown. **1984** Santmyer *And Ladies* 18 **swOH,** They . . passed . . the square unadorned brick building that was the town's public school, and continued through the "goose pasture" where the Irish lived.

goose tracks n pl

=**hen scratching.**

1954 *Harder Coll.* **cwTN,** *Goose tracks* . . illegible handwriting. "I can't read this writin'; it 'us wrote a-layin' down. Like goose tracks; crooked as a blacksnake." **1968** *DARE* (Qu. JJ11, . . *Handwriting that's hard to read: "I can't make anything out of his ______."*) Inf **WI**5, Goose tracks.

goose up See **goose** v **2, 3**

gooseville See **goosetown**

goose weed n

1 =**saltbush.**

1940 Clute *Amer. Plant Names* 219, *Atriplex spp.* Goose-weeds. *Ibid* 252, *Atriplex confertifolia* . . goose-weed.

2 See **goose grass 1c.**

goose widgeon n **MA** Cf **goose teal**

=**ruddy duck.**

1888 Trumbull *Names of Birds* 111, "Ruddy" [=duck]. . . In the vicinity of Plymouth, Mass., *Goose Widgeon.* **1925** (1928) Forbush *Birds MA* 1.280, *Erismatura jamaicensis. . .* Other names . . goose widgeon. **1955** *AmSp* 30.182 **MA,** *Goose widgeon* . . for the ruddy duck seem[s] mysterious.

goosey adj Also sp *goosy*

1 Nervous, jumpy, ticklish. **scattered, but chiefly Sth, S Midl**

1906 *DN* 3.138 **nwAR,** *Goosy*. . . Used of a person who is susceptible to nervous excitement when a finger is pointed at him, or when he is hardly touched or tickled. "We can have some sport with him; he's goosy." **1908** *DN* 3.316 **eAL, wGA,** *Goosey*. . . Extremely nervous or ticklish: said of a person. When one motions to goose him, he jumps spasmodically. **1915** *DN* 4.226 **TX,** Goosey. **1917** *DN* 4.421 **IA, LA, eNC, PA,** *Goosey*. . . Said of a person who jumps when touched; who speaks aloud abruptly whatever is said to him; or who does impulsively whatever act is ordered of him. **1920** Hunter *Trail Drivers TX* 300, A "goosy" man is a man physically nervous. **1932** Farrell *Young Lonigan* 55 **Chicago IL,** Davy goosed Hennessey. Hennessey was goosey anyway, and he jumped. **1933** *AmSp* 8.1.31 **TX,** *Goosey*. Nervous, *touchy*. **1939** *AmSp* 14.90 **TN,** *Goosey*. . . Ticklish. **1939** *Hall Coll.* **wNC,** *Goosy*. . . Ticklish. "Are you goosy?" . . This expresssion seems to be current also in the Smokies. **1954** *Harder Coll.* **cwTN,** *Goosey*. **c1960** *Wilson Coll.* **csKY,** *Goosey*. **1964** Jackman–Long *OR Desert* 394 [App.], Goosey—nervous.

2 Foolish, stupid.

1919 *DN* 5.71 **CA,** *Goosey*, stupid. "Come, come, please do not be so goosey." **1967** *DARE* (Qu. HH9, *A very silly or light-headed person*) Inf **LA**6, Goofy? Goosey? [Inf uncertain]

3 Having **gooseflesh.**

1950 *WELS* (*When you are cold and little points of skin stick up on your arms and legs, you say you* ———) 2 Infs, **cWI,** Are goosey.

goosey goosey gander n Also *foxy goosey gander, goose and the gander*

=fox in the morning 1.

1952 Brown *NC Folkl.* 1.79, *Foxy Goosey Gander*. . . One side calls: "Foxy Goosey Gander!" The other answers: "'Way over yander." The first side calls: "How many geese have you?" The other replies: "More than you can manage," and they try to reach the base of their opponents without being caught. **1965** *DARE* FW Addit **swVA,** *Goosey goosey gander*. The game was played with one [person] on one side [and] a group on the other. Rhyme: Goosey goosey gander / Fox in the mander / You come here / and I go yonder. **1967–68** *DARE* (Qu. EE33, *Other outdoor games*) Infs **LA**8, **PA**163, Goosey goosey gander; [**NJ**18, "It" yells "goosey gander";] **VA**18, Goose and the gander . . played the same as fox in the morning: . . "Fox in the morning, how many men? More than you can handle." The fox would try to catch the geese; **MS**52, Foxy goosey gander—a tag game; (Qu. EE1, *What games do children play around here, in which they form a ring, and either sing or recite a rhyme?*) Inf **WI**47, Goosey goosey gander.

goosey night n Also sp *goosie night* **NJ** Cf **cabbage night**

The night before Halloween.

1977–78 Foster *Lexical Variation* 76 **NJ,** In Passaic County and adjacent portions of Bergen, Morris, and Essex, *Goosie Night* is the usual name [for the night before Halloween]. The origin of this name is also obscure. **1980** *MJLF* 6.21, When I was a child, the night before Halloween was always known as "mischief night" throughout New Jersey. . . In our household, though, the occasion was always called *goosey night*. **1984** *DARE* File **cnNJ,** *Goosey Night* is the night before Halloween.

goose yoke See **goose poke**

goosie night See **goosey night**

goosy See **goosey**

goot n Cf **galoot,** *coot*

1936 *AmSp* 11.275 **TN,** *Goot*. An insane person. 'Look at that goot.'

go out v phr

1 Of a meeting or church service: To let out, break up. [*EDD go* v. II. 3. (24) (b), but perh reinforced by Ger *geht aus*] Cf **go in 1**

1890 [see **go in 1**]. **1949** Kurath *Word Geog.* 79/1, Rare instances of *school goes out* [for *lets out*] have been noted on the Lehigh in Pennsylvania, where it clearly reflects the German idiom *geht aus*, but also in the city of Hudson on the Hudson River. **1967** Faries *Word Geog. MO* 119, *Goes out* . . occurs once each in the Missouri counties of Madison and Bollinger, a German settlement area.

2 in var phrr referring to social activities:

a *go out on the carpet;* Of a man: to visit women.

1896 *DN* 1.417 **PA,** *Go out on the carpet:* to call on ladies in the evening (used only of the male sex).

b *go out among them:* See quots.

1912 *DN* 3.577 **wIN,** *Go out among them*. . . To go to a social affair of some prominence. "Well, you're going out among them tonight, are you?" **1942** Warnick *Garrett Co. MD* 7 **nwMD** (as of 1900–1918), *Going out among 'em*, . . going visiting. **1950** *Western Folkl.* 9.117 **nwOR** [Logger speech], *Go out among 'em*. Equivalent of "do the town"; a logger who is "rigging up" to go to a dance is said to be "fixing up to go out among 'em tonight."

c *go out on company:* To go visiting.

1982 *DARE* File **cwWI,** In Baldwin WI when people go visiting they say they "went out on company": "Oh, last night we went out on company."

3 also *go out back, go outdoors, go outside:* To go to the privy; to relieve oneself.

1934 Carmer *Stars Fell on AL* 217, On the ninth morning . . that woman can't go out a bit [becomes constipated]. . . She'll be done stopped up tight. **1942** McAtee *Dial. Grant Co. IN Suppl. 1* 5 (as of 1890s), *Go out* . . go to the privy; "Teacher, may I ———?" **1948** *AmSp* 23.264 **Ozarks,** The hillbillies had no closets in their homes. . . When we wanted to be a bit more delicate, we would say we wanted to *go out*. This phrase really referred to the act of elimination, and we were likely to say, "He went out in his britches." **1954** *Harder Coll.* **cwTN,** *Go outdoors*. . . To relieve oneself. **c1960** *Wilson Coll.* **csKY,** *Go out*. . . To go to the privy or the bushes. Once innocent enough, it has fallen on evil days and is worse now than just plain "go to the restroom" or "gone to the privy." Even *Go out back* is a synonym. **1968** Kellner *Aunt Serena* 95 **sIN** (as of c1910), Making a trip to one of these buildings [=privies] was known as "going out" or "sitting down." Boys might say boldly, "I hafta go out." **1984** *Annals Internal Med.* 100.6.900 **cwAL,** Patients with modern plumbing continue to say *I have to go outside too much* . . instead of complaining of diarrhea.

4 To emerge from winter quarters.

1939 [see **go in 3**].

5 =go off.

1969 *DARE* FW Addit **MA**61, In the spring, when the ice is ready to go out [=to melt]. **1983** *MJLF* 9.1.41 **ceKY,** *Going out* . . going down (a swelling).

go out among them See **go out 2b**

go out back, go outdoors See **go out 3**

go out on company See **go out 2c**

go out on the carpet See **go out 2a**

go outside See **go out 3**

go out to themselves v phr Also *go off to themselves* **Appalachians**

Of newlyweds: to establish a separate residence.

1953 *PADS* 19.11 **sAppalachians,** *Go out to themselves*. . . Used in speaking of a newly wedded couple who plan to live in their own home instead of living with the bride's parents. "No, Max and Louizy aim to go out to themselves, so they won't scrouge us." **1956** McAtee *Some Dialect NC* 19, *Go out to themselves*. . . Said of newlyweds who start a new household. **c1960** *Wilson Coll.* **csKY,** *Go out (or off) to themselves*. . . Said of a young married couple who have moved to a house of their own rather than living with one set of parents.

go over the hill See **hill** n **5**

go over the road v phr

To go to jail.

1914 *DN* 4.111 **KS,** *Go over the road*. . . To be committed to the penitentiary. **1923** *DN* 5.208 **swMO,** *Go over the road*. . . To be sent to jail or prison.

goozem pipe See **goozle** n **1**

goozer n

1983 *Barrick Coll.* **csPA,** *Goozer*—crude sledge used for hand-dragging tan bark from the woods.

goozle n

1 also *goozlem;* for addit varr see quots; often in combs: The throat as a whole, or spec the gullet, windpipe, or Adam's apple.

[Varr of **guzzle 1**] **chiefly Sth, S Midl** See Map Cf **gizzle, goggle** n, **google, gorgle, gozzle** n

1883 (1971) Harris *Nights with Remus* 65 **GA** [Black], He ketch a whiff er de dram, en den he see it on de side-bode, en he step up en drap 'bout a tumbeler full some'rs down in de neighborhoods er de goozle. **1897** (1952) McGill *Narrative* 261 **ceSC,** Do let me go. I want to cut Tillman's d— goozle out. **1902** *DN* 2.235 **sIL,** *Goozle* [guzl̩]. . . The larynx. **1903** *DN* 2.315 **seMO,** I got up with a sore goozle this morning. **1906** *DN* 3.138 **nwAR,** *Goozle, gozzle, guzzle*. . . Throat. **1908** *DN* 3.317 **eAL, wGA,** *Goozle*. . . The throat, the neck. **1915** *DN* 4.184 **swVA,** *Goozle*. Variant of *guzzle*. **1917** *DN* 4.412 **wNC,** *Goozle*. **1927** *DN* 5.474 **Ozarks,** Wet yer goozle oncet with this hyar licker. **1938** Rawlings *Yearling* 275 **nFL,** If he [=a hog] didn't have no goozle, he couldn't squeal. **1939** Harris *Purslane* 119 **cNC,** John told them he had a sweet goosel where cider was concerned and couldn't use hard [=hard cider]. **c1940** Eliason *Word Lists FL* 8 **wFL,** *Goozle:* The trachea or windpipe. The term is used mostly in speaking of butchered animals. **1942** McAtee *Dial. Grant Co. IN* 30 (as of 1890s), *Goozlem* . . gullet. **1947** *True* 32.104 **New Orleans LA** [Black], They served real good cold beer in those days. . . It almost froze your goozle pipes. **1954** *Harder Coll.* **cwTN,** I heard tell o' windpipe. We allus call it goozle. **c1960** *Wilson Coll.* **csKY,** *Goozle(m)*. . . The neck or throat. **1965–70** *DARE* (Qu. X7, *Other names for the throat: "Some food got stuck in his ______."*) 109 Infs, **chiefly Sth, S Midl,** Goozle; **LA**8, **VA**73, Goozle pipe; **TX**86, Goozem pipe; **VA**13, Goozler. **c1970** Pederson *Dial. Surv. Rural GA (Throat)* 1 inf, **seGA,** ['gousəl]; 1 inf, **seGA,** ['gʊ·u·zl̩, 'go·ʊzl̩]. **1986** Pederson *LAGS Concordance* **Gulf Region** *(Neck; throat)* 456 infs, (A *or* your, etc) goozle; 28 infs, Goozle pipe [These resps are said by var infs to refer esp to the Adam's apple, windpipe, or gullet, or, less often, to the neck or throat in general; a few infs say it is used only of animals.]; 3 infs, Goozler; 2 infs, Gooze pipe—Adam's apple; 1 inf, Goozling pipe; 1 inf, Goozle bane; 1 inf, Goozle bane—lump part of throat; 1 inf, Goozle bone—Adam's apple, goozle vein, sugar bone; 1 inf, Goozle bone—where you swallow; 1 inf, Goozle vein. **1987** *DARE* File **nwAL,** Goozle [=Adam's apple].

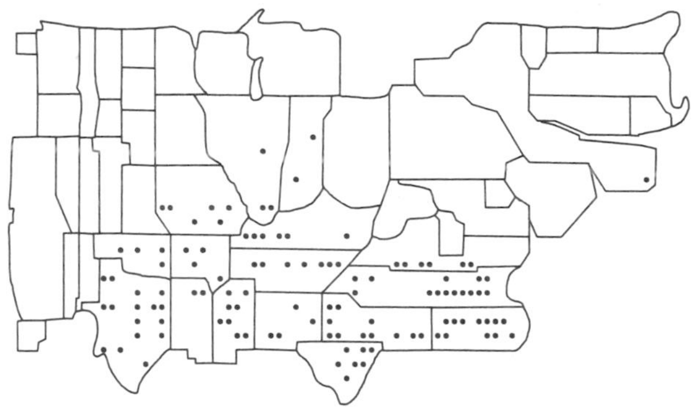

•goozle n 1 + varr (Qu. X7)

2 =**goozlum.**

1960 Wentworth-Flexner *Slang* 224, *Goozle*. . . Anything more or less of the consistency of thickened gravy.

3 A large amount. Cf **goodles**

1966 *DARE* (Qu. U38b, . . *"He made a ______ [of money]."*) Inf **SC**10, Goozle.

goozle v

1 To swallow, guzzle. Cf **gozzle** v

1969 *DARE* (Qu. DD17, *To drink a great deal, or too fast: "He doesn't just drink, he ______."*) Inf **GA**74, Goozles it. **1972** [see **2** below]. **1986** Pederson *LAGS Concordance,* 1 inf, **cnGA,** Goozle—meant to eat something; 1 inf, **cwMS,** Goozled, swallowed it.

2 See quot. Cf **gosling 1**

1972 Cooper *NC Mt. Folkl.* 93, *Goozle*—to speak hoarsely; to swallow rapidly.

goozlem, goozle pipe See **goozle** n **1**

goozler n

1 See quot. [Prob **goozle** v **1**; cf **guzzler** one who drinks to excess]

1952 Henderson *Home is Upriver* 157 **cwMS,** I be damn'—you see that old goozler [=an old man] come crawling out of that chimney?

2 See quot. [**goozle** v **2**]

1972 Cooper *NC Mt. Folkl.* 93, *Goozler*—a boy whose voice is changing.

3 See **goozle** n **1.**

goozling voice n Cf **goozle** v **2, gosling 1**

An adolescent boy's changing voice.

1986 Pederson *LAGS Concordance,* 1 inf, **cnMS,** Goozling voice—boy's voice changing.

goozlum n Also *googlum, goozlums* Cf **alamagoozlum, goozle** n **2**

A viscous food such as a sauce, gravy, or pudding; see quots.

1911 *DN* 3.544 **NE,** *Goozlum, googlum*. . . Used of syrup, molasses, etc., at table. "Pass the goozlum for these flapjacks." **1916** *DN* 4.275 **NE,** *Goozlums*. . . Cornstarch pudding. **1925** *AmSp* 1.137 **Pacific NW** [Logger talk], Gravy is "goozlum." **1950** *WELS Suppl.* **scWI,** "Pass the *goozlum*" to mean "pass the gravy" or any kind of sauce used on any kind of food. *Ibid* **scWI,** *Goozlum:* a thin custard sauce for puddings or fluffs—first heard it in Arizona about 1920. Used among miners there.

G.O.P. n [See quots]

Used as a nickname for a branch railway.

1905 *DN* 3.81 **nwAR,** *G.O.P.,* 'Get Out and Push.' 'Going out on the G.O.P. to-day?' Facetiously applied to a branch railway. **1966–68** *DARE* (Qu. N37, *Joking names for a branch railroad that is not very important or gives poor service*) Infs **PA**148, **TX**33, G.O.P.; [**MS**6, Get-Out-and-Push.]

gopheh See **goofer** n

gopher n[1]

1 A turtle, spec:

a also *gopher tortoise, ~ turtle:* A burrowing tortoise of the genus *Gopherus,* esp *G. polyphemus.* [Perh abbr for *magofer,* poss of AmInd origin] **esp FL, GA** See Map For other names of *G. polyphemus* see **cooter** n **3, Florida chicken, Georgia bacon, tunnel turtle;** for other names of other species see **desert turtle, Texas tortoise**

1791 Bartram *Travels* 182 **eGA,** Observed as we passed over the sandhills, the dens of the great land tortoise, called gopher. **1828** *Western Mth. Rev.* 1.591, In the pine barrens of Florida, Alabama and Mississippi, is found an animal, apparently of the tortoise class, commonly called the *gouffre*. It has a large and thick shell, and burrows to a great depth in the ground. It is of prodigious power and strength, and resembles in many respects the loggerhead turtle. **1884** Goode *Fisheries U.S.* 1.158, The three Gopher Tortoises of the South and West [are] [t]he Florida "Gopher," *Xerobates polyphemus* . . ; Agassiz's Gopher, *X. Agassizi,* . . found in Southern California and Arizona; and Berlandier's Tortoise, *X. Berlandieri,* . . Southern Texas. **1908** *DN* 3.316 **eAL, wGA,** *Gopher*. . . A burrowing tortoise, *Testudo Carolina,* common in the Southern States. **1927** Boston Soc. Nat. Hist. *Proc.* 38.7.313 **Okefenokee GA,** Gray Foxes. . . would seldom take to a tree, but sometimes seek refuge in a Gopher Turtle's burrow. **1956** Rayford *Whistlin' Woman* 40 **AL,** This gopher in Bayou la Batre is a highland, dry land tortoise, a tortoise, mind you! and he looks just like a turtle. Walks up on his legs, lifts his carapace away up in the air. **1965–70** *DARE* (Qu. P29, *Do you have 'gophers' around here? If yes, what other name do they have, or what other animal are they most like?*) 32 Infs, **esp FL, GA,** Gopher [=a kind of turtle or tortoise]; **FL**7, Turtle which digs a hole—hardshell gopher; **FL**16, Gophers—dryland turtles; **FL**17, Gophers—live in holes in highland, about 6–14 inches long—finest gumbo made from them; **FL**39, Gophers—soft-shell turtles; **FL**48, Gopher means "turtle" here; **GA**3, Land tortoise—gopher; **GA**5, Gopher—a land-living, hard-shelled turtle; **GA**65, Gopher—highland terrapin (he's eatable [sic]); **GA**77, Gopher is an underground turtle, over 12 inches in diameter, skull is dark brown; [they] live away from water, dig tunnels; in Tilton, Georgia, people call it a tunnel turtle; **GA**80, Turtles belonging to the terrapin family are called gopher around here; **MS**11, Gopher—those little form [sic] of turtles; **MS**16, Gopher—look like a tarrypin, only they are larger; **MS**72, Gopher—black but big like a streaked-headed turtle; (Qu. P24, *What kinds of turtles are found around here?*) 18 Infs, **chiefly S Atl,** Gopher; **FL**39, Soft-shell gopher; (Qu. A18, *Words or expressions used around here about a very slow person: "What's keeping him? He certainly is ______!"*) Inf **GA**7, Slow as a gopher; (Qu. H36, *Kinds of soup favored around here—any specialties?*) Inf **FL**17, ['gofə-gəmbo]; made from gophers—delicious; (Qu. H45) Inf **FL**17, Gopher gumbo; (Qu. H55, . . *Kinds of stew;* total Infs questioned, 75) Inf **FL**1,

Gopher stew. **1965–68** *DARE* Tape **FL**17, [They would] attach a gopher hook on the end of the [grape] vine. . . When a [gopher] hole was found, the vine would be pushed down into the hole. . . Now . . for the famous gopher gumbo; **GA**20, We got a land turtle, but we call that a gopher; **GA**48, We have that gopher here, too, but he lives in the ground; **GA**51, The gopher that makes them is . . something on the order of a soft-shelled turtle, only he's boxed in smaller than the turtle. **1988** *Nature Conserv. Mag.* 38.4.7, A species of the Florida sandhills, the . . gopher tortoise . . creates huge burrows some 30 feet deep that also shelter entire communities of other animal species.

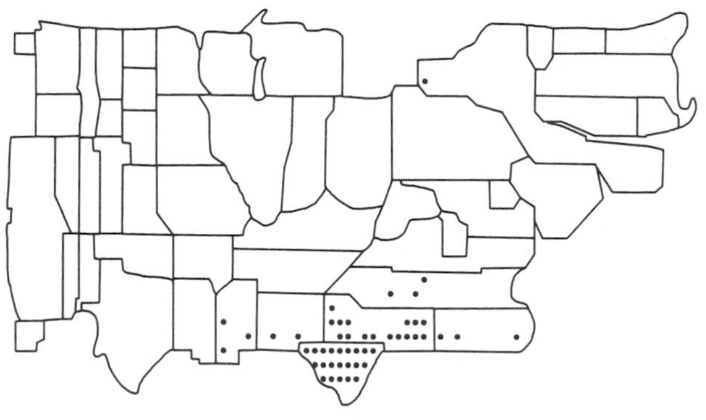

•gopher n[1] 1a + varr (Qq. P29, P24, A18, H36, H45, H55)

b A **diamondback terrapin** or similar turtle.

1966–70 *DARE* (Qu. P24, *What kinds of turtles are found around here?*) Inf **NC**63, Gopher; **NC**72, Gopher—terrapin; (Qu. P29, *Do you have 'gophers' around here? If yes, what other name do they have, or what other animal are they most like?*) Inf **FL**24, Diamondback terrapin; **NC**72, Gopher here is terrapin; **NJ**69, Gopher—he's like a terrapin (hard shell); **NY**101, Gopher—land tortoise.

2 Any of numerous burrowing rodents; see below. [Etym uncert, but see quot 1864 at **a** below]

a =pocket gopher. chiefly West, Missip Valley, Gulf States

1814 Brackenridge *Views of LA* 58, The *Gopher* . . lives under ground, in the prairies, and is also found east of the Mississippi. **1825** in 1974 *Fauna Americana* 153, *Mus bursarius. . . Mus saccatus. . . Geomys cinereus. . .* Vulgarly *Sand-rat, Goffer,* . . &c. **1834** Peck *Gaz. IL* 36, The *gophar* is a singular little animal, about the size of a squirrel. It burrows in the ground, is seldom seen, but its *works* make it known. **1864** (1873) Webster *Amer. Dict.* 580, *Gopher. . .* [Fr. *gaufre,* waffle, honeycomb . .]. An animal of several different species. The name was originally given by French settlers to many burrowing animals, from their honeycombing the earth. In Canada and Illinois, the name was given to a gray burrowing squirrel (*Spermaphilus* [sic] *Franklini*); west of the Mississippi to *S. Richardsonii;* and in Wisconsin to a striped squirrel. In Missouri, a common species is a pouched rat of a reddish or chestnut-brown color, with broad, mole-like fore feet, the *Geomys bursarius.* In Georgia, a snake *(Coluber couperi)* is called by the same name; and in Florida, a turtle (the *Testudo polyphemus*). **1888** *Ipswich* (Mass.) *Chronicle* 15 Sept. 2/4 *(DAE),* The true gopher is of a gray color and is about the size of a large rat. He has large pouches on each side of his mouth in which he carries dirt when making his burrows in the ground. His front teeth stand out most prominently in any of the great family of gnawers—rodents. His tail is short and looks very much like that of a rat. **1917** Anthony *Mammals Amer.* 266, The Pocket Gophers are the only rodents to which the term "gopher" can be accurately applied. . . This . . group of thick-set rodents . . receive their . . name . . from the . . cheek pouches opening outside the mouth. These are used as genuine pockets for carrying things of quite as much value to the Gopher as the contents of their pockets are to small boys. **1961** Jackson *Mammals WI* 184, *Geomys bursarius bursarius. . .* In Wisconsin generally called pocket gopher; sometimes simply gopher, though the term gopher in this state usually refers to the striped ground squirrel. **1965–70** *DARE* (Qu. P29, *Do you have 'gophers' around here? If yes, what other name do they have, or what other animal are they most like?*) 199 Infs, **chiefly West, Missip Valley, Gulf States,** Gopher; (Qu. P27) Infs **CA**153, **WA**6, Gopher. **1969** *DARE* Tape **CA**171, See, that's a gopher trap, and that's wire. **1980** Whitaker *Audubon Field Guide Mammals* 426, Gophers use their incisors to cut through earth and roots and to pry rocks loose; the crescent-clawed forefeet dig and shovel; and the hindfeet push back the earth accumulated under the animal's body.

b Any of var rodents of the family Sciuridae, as:

(1) =ground squirrel n b (here: *Spermophilus* spp). **chiefly N Cent, Upper MW, Rocky Mts**

1857 U.S. Patent Office *Annual Rept. for 1856: Ag.* 75, In Iowa, Wisconsin, and Northern Illinois, where this animal [=spotted prairie squirrel] is abundant and much complained of by farmers, it is universally called "gopher." **1864** [see **2a** above]. **1875** *Amer. Naturalist* 9.148, Naturalists . . have no English name for these animals [=*Spermophilus* spp]. But by the people who live among them they are universally called 'gophers'; and as this name will certainly stick in the vernacular for all time, we may as well accept it. **1889** (1971) Farmer *Americanisms* 279/1, *Spermophilus tridecemlineatus. . .* is also known as the *gopher.* **1928** Baylor Univ. Museum *Contrib.* 16.3, "Gopher" always refers to a burrowing animal; . . it is . . a striped ground squirrel in Indiana, and a gray ground squirrel in Wisconsin. **1961** [see **2a** above]. **1965–70** *DARE* (Qu. P29) 145 Infs, **chiefly N Cent, Upper MW, Rocky Mts,** Gopher; (Qu. P27) Inf **MT**3, Prairie squirrels—also called gopher. **1966** *DARE* Tape **MI**36, In the summertime . . I always got chipmunks and gophers [as pets]. **1970** *Western Folkl.* 29.169, The two most familiar terms [for *Spermophilus* spp] in the Upper Midwest are *gopher* and *ground squirrel.*

(2) =prairie dog. esp West

1848 Bartlett *Americanisms* 260, *Prairie-Dog. . .* Also called Gopher. **1872** Schele de Vere *Americanisms* 101, Another dweller on the prairie . . is the *Prairie-Dog* (Cynomys ludovicianus). . . In the West they are also known as *Gophers,* from the French *gaufre,* perhaps however through the English *to goffer,* to flute or crimp, because their countless holes honeycomb the soil in which they dig their villages. **1965–70** *DARE* (Qu. P29) Infs **KS**10, **MN**33, **MS**6, **TX**53, 62, 81, **UT**14, **VT**12, Gopher(s)—prairie dog(s); **NE**10, **UT**9, Gopher—prairie dog, mole; **CO**38, Gopher—prairie dog, groundhog; **NE**7, Gopher—ground squirrel, prairie dog; **VT**16, Gopher—a prairie dog; we don't have any here. **1975** Zwinger *Run River* 39 **UT**, The immaturity of the soil also shows in the pale tan rims of white-tailed prairie-dog holes which abound along the bank. Locally called "gophers," they stand picket-pin fashion on their haunches, stationed at the edges of their burrows, chirruping like birds.

(3) A **marmot,** esp a **woodchuck** (here: *Marmota monax*).

1888 *Ipswich* (Mass.) *Chronicle* 15 Sept. 2/4 *(DAE),* In some parts of the country a grey ground squirrel is called a gopher. In other parts a striped squirrel or prairie chipmunk is called by that name. In Kansas, Nebraska and many other parts of the West a small marmot, which is closely allied to the prairie dog, is called a gopher. **1965–70** *DARE* (Qu. P29) 51 Infs, **scattered, but esp NEast, Midl,** Gopher; 9 Infs, **scattered,** Gopher—(similar to) groundhog(s); **IN**58, 69, **RI**8, Gopher—woodchuck; **CT**2, **NY**134, **VT**16, Gopher—woodchuck, groundhog; **IL**144, Gopher—like a rat, also called groundhog; **NH**14, Gopher—similar to an overgrown mole, bigger than a rat; also called mud heavers; **NV**8, Gopher—called small groundhog by others; **PA**68, Gopher—larger than a mole, a burrowing animal; **VA**8, Some call groundhogs and woodchucks gophers, but real gophers live out West; (Qu. P31, . . *Names or nicknames . . for the groundhog*) Infs **CO**38, **NJ**10, **SC**21, Gopher.

(4) A **chipmunk** (here: *Tamias striatus*).

1887 *Forest & Stream* 28.248 **cNY,** When I was a boy, . . I heard a peculiar squeaking in the grass. . . The squeaking came from a gopher (squirrel) which was lying on its back kicking. . . The gopher scampered off and disappeared in the grass. **1888** [see **2b(3)** above]. **1904** *DN* 2.425 **Cape Cod MA,** *Gopher. . .* The chipmunk. **1939** *LANE* Map 229 **sNEng,** The following synonyms of *chipmunk* were offered . . *ground squirrel . . ,* and *gopher* [3 infs]. **1965–70** *DARE* (Qu. P29) 33 Infs, 28 **N Cent, W Midl,** Gopher; **IA**28, Gopher—a little one with two stripes down his back—also called ground squirrel or chipmunk; **IL**35, Gopher has stripes on its back and sides—also called chipmunk; **IL**44, Gopher—little striped animal, live [sic] in ground, a little bigger than a mouse; **IL**46, They call chipmunks gophers, but they're really not; **TN**22, **WI**32, Gopher—chipmunk.

(5) A **red squirrel** (here: *Tamiasciurus hudsonicus*).

1967 *DARE* (Qu. P29) Inf **WY**4, Gopher—ground squirrel; some call brown squirrels gophers.

c also *gopher mouse:* **A meadow mouse. chiefly N Cent, esp KY**

1872 Schele de Vere *Americanisms* 101, The term *gopher* has been applied to various animals . . [including] the little field-mouse of the

West. **1965–70** *DARE* (Qu. P29) Infs **IN**45, **KY**75, **WI**12, Gopher(s)—field mouse (*or* mice); **NY**2, **OH**41, 87, Gopher—mouse; **CA**97, Gopher—three different animals: vole [*DARE* Ed: = *Microtus* spp], mole, gopher; **KY**6, Gopher lives out in fields, eats onions—ground mice, some say; **KY**11, Gopher—also called gopher mouse; a field mouse, builds tunnels through the grass; **KY**23, Gopher—short-tailed fellow between a rat and a mouse; **KY**49, Gopher—ground mice; chubby, blunt, stubby tails and big eyes; **KY**82, Gopher—little bitty old small animal, sort of puts you in mind of a groundhog, but very much smaller; **NY**233, Gopher—vole or short-tailed meadow mouse; **NC**35, Gopher—ground mouse; **OH**20, Gopher—mole, vole, chipmunk.

d =mountain beaver.

1967 *DARE* (Qu. P29) Inf **WA**20, Gopher—mountain beaver, marmot; **WA**30, Gopher—mole, mountain beaver.

e =kangaroo rat.

1967 *DARE* (Qu. P29) Inf **CO**22, Some call kangaroo mice gophers.

f See **gopher rat 1.**

3 A mole (family Talpidae).

1965–70 *DARE* (Qu. P29) 47 Infs, 35 **Nth, N Midl, esp OH,** Gopher; **IL**132, Some call moles "gophers"; **NC**60, **PA**121, **WI**12, Gopher—mole; **MD**29, **VA**1, Gopher—ground mole; **WY**1, Call both of these [=ground squirrel and mole] gophers.

4 A shrew (family Soricidae).

1968 *DARE* (Qu. P29, *Do you have 'gophers' around here? If yes, what other name do they have, or what other animal are they most like?*) Inf **WI**12, Gopher—shrew.

5 A **camel cricket** (here: *Ceuthophilus* spp).

1905 Kellogg *Amer. Insects* 155, The genus Ceuthophilus includes the various species of stone, or camel, crickets found all over the country. . . The individuals of a species which live in the burrows of certain turtles in Florida are called "gophers."

6 A mole cricket (here: prob *Gryllotalpa hexadactyla*). **KY**

1969 *DARE* (Qu. P29, *Do you have 'gophers' around here? If yes, what other name do they have, or what other animal are they most like?*) Inf **KY**39, Gopher—an insect that flies; 1½–2 inches long, big as a finger; **KY**43, Gopher—1–2 inches long, much smaller than chipmunk, size of finger, an insect, bores in ground, is thick as finger; **KY**47, Gopher—insect 1½–2 inches long, looks like a newborn mouse with no hair.

7 See **gopher snake.**

8 See **gopher rockfish.**

9 See **gopher frog.**

10 also *gopher plow:* A kind of plow.

1854 *Spirit of Times* 4 Nov. 447/3 *(DAE),* Dad and me goes to the field, I . . a totin' the gopher plough on my back. *Ibid,* I hitched him onto the gopher, and away we went. **1868** U.S. Dept. Ag. *Rept. of Secy. for 1867* 424, Then there is the "scraper," the "half-shovel," "shovel," "gopher," and other peculiar forms of implements. **1894** *Congressional Record* 15 Mar 2995/1, The gopher is an iron plow. **1953** Randolph–Wilson *Down in Holler* 248 **Ozarks,** Gopher. . . A primitive plow. **1969** *DARE* (Qu. L18, *Kinds of plows*) Inf **KY**23, Gopher plow—laid off a furrow for corn.

11 also *gopher man;* Among loggers: one who digs; a tool or machine used esp in digging holes under logs so that chains can be passed around them.

1950 *Western Folkl.* 9.381 **neCA** [Lumberjack language], *Gopher.* A man who digs holes under the logs to enable the choker setter to put the chokers around them. **1958** McCulloch *Woods Words* 72 **Pacific NW,** *Gopher*. . . A digging tool used to scrape a hole under logs which were hauled by big wheels. This made it easier to pass a chain under the logs so they could be secured to the frame of the big wheels. . . A small power shovel. . . Gopher man. . . Powder man, particularly one who blew holes under logs for chokers. . . Man who dug a hole under logs which were to be hauled by big wheels.

gopher n^2 See **goofer** n

gopher v Also with *around*

1 To prospect or mine in a random or unsystematic manner; hence vbl n *gophering.* Cf **coyote v 1**

1889 *Century Dict.* 2577 **Pacific,** *Gopher*. . . To begin or carry on mining operations at haphazard, or on a small scale; mine without any reference to the possibility of future permanent development. Such mine-openings are frequently called *gopher-holes* and *coyote-holes.* **1905** (1909) Beach *Pardners* 22 **AK,** We cross-cut in three places, and never raised a colour, but we kept gophering around till March, in hopes. **1927** (1944) Russell *Trails Plowed Under* 129 **West,** This old boy is a prospector and goes gopherin' 'round the hills, hopin' he'll find something. **1954** in 1977 Randolph *Pissing in the Snow* 235 **Ozarks** (as of early 1900s), One time there was a bunch of Pukes lived over by Joplin. . . The boys didn't have nothing but picks and shovels in them days. . . They just gophered around in prospect holes, because there wasn't no powder to speak of. **1958** McCulloch *Woods Words* 72 **Pacific NW,** *Gophering*—Prospecting in the hills around camp on Sundays or other time off. **1966** *DARE* Tape **NM**15, Gophering is just going along a vein 'n' finding a likely place that might be some ore 'n' dig a hole there, and maybe you find some ore, maybe you don't. Go up the vein farther 'n' find another place. . . [FW:] You mean following a vein on the surface of the rock? [Inf:] Yes.

2 To wander around, potter about. Cf **coyote v 3**

1958 Latham *Meskin Hound* 190 **cTX,** Pa loved them old hills . . He'll be wanting to gopher around in them soon as he gets out [=of prison].

gopher apple n [See quots 1911, 1933] Cf **gopher plum 2**

An evergreen shrub *(Chrysobalanus oblongifolius)* native from South Carolina to Mississippi. Also called **deer-plum, gopher root, ground oak 2, ground plum 2**

1903 Small *Flora SE U.S.* 569, *Chrysobalanus oblongifolius*. . . A low shrub. . . Drupe ovoid to obovoid, 2.5–3.5 cm. long. . . *Gopher Apple.* **1911** *Century Dict. Suppl., Gopher-apple*. . . Same as *gopher-root:* so called from the often edible fruit, which, however, is a drupe and not like an apple. **1933** Small *Manual SE Flora* 645, *Gopher-apples*. . . The gopher—one of the large land turtles of Florida—is not the only animal that appreciates the fruits of these shrubs. **1939** FWP *Guide FL* 44, Coco-plums, sea-grapes, gopher apples, and sour oranges grow wild and are gathered throughout the year. **1953** Greene–Blomquist *Flowers South* 52, Gopher-apple . . *(Chrysobalanus oblongifolius)* is a relatively low plant . . growing in habitats similar to coco-plum. **1968** Radford et al. *Manual Flora Carolinas* 569, *C[hrysobalanus] oblongifolius*. . . *Gopher Apples.* Low shrub . . with an extensive underground stem system. **1982** *Naples Now* May 37 **swFL,** In the lesser developed areas of the scrub zone along Collier County and Naples beaches, the *gopher apple* may be found with its small, white fragrant flowers in compact clusters. The fruits are white with pink or purple blush, and its sweet and juicy pulp is consumed by gopher tortoises, small rodents, and birds.

gopher around See **gopher** v

gopherberry n

A **huckleberry 1:** usu *Gaylussacia dumosa,* but also *G. baccata.*

1901 *Torreya* 1.117 **GA,** *Gaylussacia dumosa*. . . Gopher-berry. Bulloch [County]. **1927** *Ibid* 27.36, *Gaylussacia Mosieri*. . . Hammocks, Coastal Plain, Florida to Louisiana.—Spring. This gopherberry [is] usually more or less closely associated with *Gaylussacia dumosa.* **1938** Van Dersal *Native Woody Plants* 336, Gopher berry *(Gaylussacia dumosa).* **1940** Clute *Amer. Plant Names* 41, *Gaylussacia dumosa*. . . Gopher-berry. *Ibid* 260, *Gaylussacia baccata.* Gopherberry. **1960** Vines *Trees SW* 813, *G[aylussacia] dumosa* var *hirtella*. . . Also known under the names of Gopherberry and Dwarf Huckleberry.

gopher case n Also *gopher scrape*

=groundhog case.

1908 *DN* 3.316 **c,sAL,** *Gopher case*. . . A hard case. **1954** *PADS* 21.28 **SC,** *Gopher scrape*. . . A case of necessity, where one has to do what would otherwise be considered improper. . . The phrase is supposed to be derived from the following story: A preacher was coming to dinner one Sunday after the sermon, and two small boys were sent out to dig a gopher out of his hole for the preacher's dinner. The digging was in progress when the preacher himself came along and reproved the boys for working on the Sabbath. The boys' answer was: "We've got to get this gopher out of here for the preacher's dinner."

gopher crane n [See quots]

=great blue heron.

1913 *Pacific Coast Avifauna* 9.21, *Ardea herodias herodias*. . . Known to nearly everyone as "Crane," . . "Gopher Crane." . . The farmers of this county [=Fresno] should do all in their power to afford protection to the Blue Heron, as it is one of the best gopher destroyers in existence. **1923** Dawson *Birds CA* 4.1891, As . . many of the customary water courses dry up, the Heron . . devotes himself to the extermination of mice, moles, and gophers, and even young ground squirrels. . . This species is known in the San Joaquin Valley as the Gopher Crane.

gopher frog n Also *gopher* [See quot 1906] **chiefly SE**

A stout-bodied, spotted frog *(Rana areolata)*. For other names of var subspp see **Hoosier frog 2, snake frog, white frog**

1893 *Science* 22.57 **FL,** [The burrows of the gopher. . . afford . . a domicile to a most interesting assemblage of animals. . . Another vertebrate also, a frog, here takes up its permanent abode and lives on terms of perfect friendship with the gopher.] *Ibid* 58, The gopher frog, *Rana areolata aesopus.* **1906** (1907) Dickerson *Frog Book* 194, The Gopher Frog. . . is squat and toad-like, having an unusually large head. [*Ibid* 195, Outside of the breeding season, it lives solitary in gopher-holes, hence its name. These so-called gopher-holes are the burrows of a Florida highland turtle.] **1927** Boston Soc. Nat. Hist. *Proc.* 38.7.355 **Okefenokee GA,** One July night . . we were searching for Gopher Frogs *(Rana aesopus).* **1928** Baylor Univ. Museum *Contrib.* 16.3, A "gopher" is . . a frog in some parts of Illinois. **1938** Matschat *Suwannee R.* 76 **seGA,** A few others, such as the gopher frog, apparently move in permanently. **1969** *DARE* Tape **GA**51, The big frog now that stays on the highland and near a gopher hole. . . That was the gopher frog now 'cause he'd always make his hidin' place near a place he could hide from you. **1979** Behler-King *Audubon Field Guide Reptiles* 368, The break in distribution in Louisiana, coupled with differences in coloration between the eastern and western populations, lead some authorities to consider the two . . different species: Crawfish Frog *(Rana areolata)* in the West with 2 subspecies; Gopher Frog *(Rana capito)* in the East with 3 subspecies.

gopher grass n Also *gopher weed* **esp GA**

A **wild indigo:** usu *Baptisia lanceolata,* but also *B. perfoliata.*

1893 *Jrl. Amer. Folkl.* 6.140 **GA,** *Baptisia lanceolata,* gopher-weed. **1927** Boston Soc. Nat. Hist. *Proc.* 38.7.214 **Okefenokee GA,** *Baptisia lanceolata* . . 'Gopher-grass'. **1933** Small *Manual SE Flora* 675, *B[aptisia] perfoliata.* . . Gopher-weed. **1969** *DARE* FW Addit **GA**51, *Gopher weed:* A low shrub with black pods and small leaves. **1970** Anderson *TX Folk Med.* 26, Diarrhea—Make a hot tea from gopher grass. Drink it as hot as you can stand it.

gopher hawk n

Either of two hawks: a **rough-legged hawk** (here: *Buteo regalis*) or **Swainson's hawk.**

1936 Roberts *MN Birds* 1.323, *Swainson's Hawk. . . Other names* . . Gopher Hawk. . . *Food.* Almost entirely gophers, mice, rabbits, grasshoppers, crickets, and locusts, rarely birds or poultry. Very beneficial. *Ibid* 329, The Ferruginous Rough-leg is the . . Gopher Hawk *par excellence,* and well deserves the name. The number of these pests destroyed by them is astonishing. **1946** Goodrich *Birds in KS* 315, Colloquial Name. . . Hawk, gopher. . . Common name. . . Rough-leg ferrugenous [sic].

gopher hole n

1 A **dugout 1;** see quot.

1880 Farrar *5 Years* 51 **MN,** There still exist in the State houses, nearly underground, covered with a roof of thatch, the whole not appearing more than a foot or two above the surface of the earth, and known as "Gopher-holes," which were the habitations of the earliest pioneers of settlement.

2 A small mine or mine opening; a shallow or haphazardly dug excavation. Cf **coyote n B2, gopher v 1**

1889 *Century Dict.* 2577, *Gopher.* . . In *mining,* to begin or carry on mining operations at haphazard, or on a small scale. . . Such mine-openings are frequently called *gopher-holes* and *coyote-holes.* [*Century* Ed: Pacific States] **1941** Writers' Program *Guide MO* 235, Piles of weathered rock and shallow, weed-grown depressions mark the shafts of abandoned "gopher hole" mines. **1943** Korson *Coal Dust* 4, Some farmers, however, overcame this fear and operated small mines variously called "country banks," "wagon mines," "dog holes," "gopher holes," or "father-and-son" mines.

3 In logging: see quot. Cf **gopher n[1] 11**

1958 McCulloch *Woods Words* 72 **Pacific NW,** *Gopher hole*—a. A hole shot under a log to run a choker under. b. Any hole *dug* for blasting powder, not poked with a bar, and not made for springing.

gophering See **gopher v 1**

gopherman See **gopher n[1] 10**

gopher mouse n

1 The Florida mouse *(Peromyscus floridanus).* [See quot 1980]

1957 Blair et al. *Vertebrates U.S.* 711, *Peromyscus floridanus.* . . Gopher mouse. . . Restricted to peninsular Florida, where it prefers scrub vegetation on sand. **1980** Whitaker *Audubon Field Guide Mammals* 478, The Florida or "Gopher" Mouse is almost exclusively a burrow dweller, most often using the burrows of the Gopher Tortoise . . or pocket gophers.

2 See **gopher n[1] 2c.**

gopher plant n

1 A **spurge** (here: *Euphorbia lathyris*). [Because it was thought to repel moles] **esp CA**

1900 Lyons *Plant Names* 157, *E[uphorbia] Lathyris.* . . Gopher plant. **1911** Jepson *Flora CA* 247, *Caper Spurge.* . . Also called "Gopher Plant." **1940** Clute *Amer. Plant Names* 223, *Euphorbia lathyrus.* . . Gopher-plant. **1961** Thomas *Flora Santa Cruz* 228 **cwCA,** Gopher Plant. Widely distributed along the margins of the Santa Cruz Mountains in most shaded situations, often along streams.

2 A **wild lettuce** (here: *Lactuca* spp).

1959 Carleton *Index Herb. Plants* 55, *Gopher-plant:* Lactuca (v); Silphium laciniatum.

3 A **rosinweed** (here: *Silphium laciniatum*).

1959 [see **2** above].

gopher plow See **gopher n[1] 10**

gopher plum n

1 =**Ogeechee lime.**

1884 Sargent *Forests of N. Amer.* 91, *Nyssa capitata. . . Gopher Plum.* . . A tree 9 to 18 meters in height. . . Large, acid fruit. **1897** Sudworth *Arborescent Flora* 311, *Nyssa ogeche. . . Common Names.* . . Gopher Plum (Fla.) **1908** Britton *N. Amer. Trees* 740, This [=*Nyssa ogeche*] is a round-headed tree, known also as . . Gopher plum. . . It is peculiar to the swamps of South Carolina, Georgia, and Florida.

2 =**coco plum.** Cf **gopher apple**

1897 Sudworth *Arborescent Flora* 236, *Chrysobalanus icaco. . . Common Names.* . . Gopher Plum (Fla.) **1903** Small *Flora SE U.S.* 570, *Chrysobalanus Icaco.* . . Gopher Plum. **1908** Britton *N. Amer. Trees* 483, *Chrysobalanus Icaco.* . . Also called the Gopher plum, this occurs along the coast in peninsular Florida. *Ibid* 484, The fruit is of the shape and size of a plum, insipidly sweet, but very variable as to size, color, and taste.

gopher rat n

1 also *gopher:* =**Norway rat.**

1965-70 *DARE* (Qu. P29, *Do you have 'gophers' around here? If yes, what other name do they have, or what other animal are they most like?*) Infs **TN**30, 42, 44, 56, 61, 65, Gopher—(large) rat; **AL**2, Gophers are rats—very destructive, dig holes in ground; **AL**10, Gopher—a big rat; gopher rat; **AL**28, Some call a rat a gopher—no true gopher—gopher rat; **AL**32, Rats—gopher rats; **MS**89, Gopher rat; **TN**46, Gopher—most like rats, ground rat; **TN**53, Gophers—field rats. [*DARE* Ed: Some Infs may refer instead to **gopher n[1] 2a.**] **1988** Lincoln *Avenue* 265 **wNC** (as of c1940) [Black], Hordes of big gopher rats from the dump roamed boldly through the cemetery, burrowing into the graves and even attacking the mourners on occasion.

2 =**woodchuck** (here: *Marmota monax*). Cf **gopher n[1] 2b(3)**

1969 *DARE* (Qu. P31, . . *Other names or nicknames . . for the groundhog*) Inf **TN**31, 36, Gopher rat.

gopher rockfish n Also *gopher*

Any of various **rockfish:** see quots.

1953 Roedel *Common Fishes CA* 133, *Gopher Rockfish. Sebastodes carnatus.* . . A species of moderate depths from the kelp beds outward and caught rather frequently. *Ibid* 134, *China Rockfish. Sebastodes nebulosus. . . Unauthorized Names* . . gopher. **1960** Amer. Fisheries Soc. *List Fishes* 37, Gopher rockfish. *Sebastodes carnatus.* **1973** Knight *Cook's Fish Guide* 382, Gopher—Rockfish, China [=*Sebastodes nebulosus*] or see Treefish [=*S. serriceps*].

gopher root n

=**gopher apple.**

1889 *Century Dict.* 2577/1, *Gopher-root.* . . A low rosaceous shrub, *Chrysobalanus oblongifolius,* with extensively creeping underground stems, found in the sandy pine-barrens of Florida, Georgia, and Alabama. **1900** Lyons *Plant Names* 99, *C[hrysobalanus] oblongifolius.* . . Florida to Alabama, Gopher-root.

gopher scrape See **gopher case**

gopher snake n Also *gopher*

1 =bull snake. chiefly West, esp CA, AZ See Map

1837 (1962) Williams *Territory FL* 68, The Bull Snake . . is sometimes called the Gopher snake. **1907** in 1974 Shaw–Campbell *Snakes West* 108, So often one sees the mangled remains along roadsides that it seems a wonder that there are any gopher snakes whatever left. **1928** Pope–Dickinson *Amphibians* 56 **WI,** *Bull Snake*. . . is also occasionally called the Yellow Gopher Snake. **1948** *Atlantic Mth.* Feb 88/1 **KY,** We acquired the hog-nosed viper and the gopher snake and the ringneck, and a dozen or more assorted reptiles. **1966–70** *DARE* (Qu. P25, . . *Kinds of snakes*) 39 Infs, 35 **CA,** Gopher snake; **CA**168, Gophers. **1970** *DARE* Tape **CA**212, [Inf:] However, if there's a little place to get in, the snakes will go through the wire and go in there [=into a birdhouse]. [FW:] What kind of snakes? [Inf:] Oh, little gopher snakes. **1974** Shaw–Campbell *Snakes West* 109, Few snakes range more widely over the American West, or for that matter, the entire United States, than the gopher snake. **1979** Behler–King *Audubon Field Guide Reptiles* 644, Gopher snake.

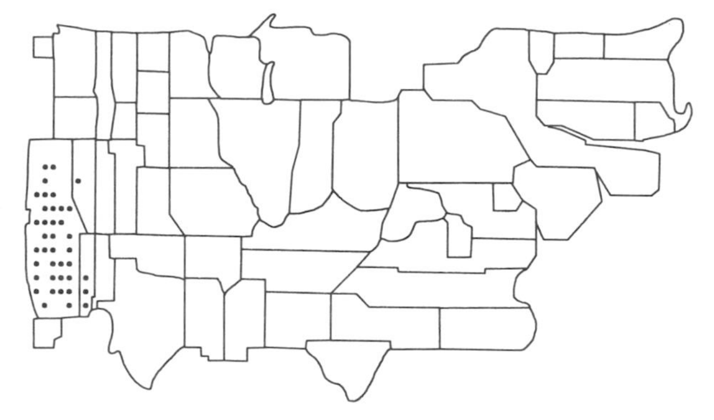

•gopher snake 1 + var (Qu. P25)

2 =indigo snake, esp *Drymarchon corais couperi* which is native to Florida and southeast Georgia. [See quot 1952]

1853 Baird–Girard *N. Amer. Reptiles* 165 (Index), Gopher Snake *(Georg[ia] Coup[eri])*. **1885** Kingsley *Std. Nat. Hist.* 3.367 **FL, GA,** *S[pilotes] couperi*. . . is known by the negroes as the indigo or gopher-snake. **1889** *Century Dict.* 2577, *Gopher*. . . A snake, *Spilotes couperi*. Also called *gopher-snake*. **1894** U.S. Natl. Museum *Proc.* 17.327, This snake, which is generally called "gopher snake" in south Florida, is not very common. **1952** Ditmars *N. Amer. Snakes* 100, The term Gopher Snake comes from the habit of this big reptile of commonly sheltering in burrows of the southern Gopher Tortoise. **1966** *DARE* (Qu. P25) Inf **FL**26, Gopher snake; **FL**27, Indigo snake or blacksnake [or] gopher snake; **FL**35, Gopher snake eats eggs, rats, snakes; **GA**7, Gopher snake.

3 =glossy snake. [Appar from the similarity of its coloration to **1** above]

1952 Ditmars *N. Amer. Snakes* 194, *The Genus Arizona*. . . Slender Gopher Snake, Sharp-nosed Gopher Snake. . . Southwestern Slender Gopher Snake, Faded Snake.

gopher tent n

1938 FWP *Guide MN* 304 (as of 1852), Women and children were crowded into a community tent, while the men slept in "gopher tents" whose sloping log sides were covered with grass.

gopher tortoise See **gopher** n[1] **1a**

gopher turtle See **gopher** n[1] **1a**

gopher vine n

An unidentified plant.

1911 (1913) Johnson *Highways Gt. Lakes* 326, Then the morning-glory vines and the pea vines and gopher vines and wild cucumber vines grow over them and so tangle the [corn] stalks together that dog gone if you can't almost take hold at one corner and shake the whole field!

gopher weed See **gopher grass**

gopherwood n

1 =yellowwood (here: *Cladrastis kentukea*).

1884 Sargent *Forests of N. Amer.* 57, *Cladrastis tinctoria*. . . *Yellow Wood. Yellow Ash. Gopher Wood*. . . Central Kentucky, . . middle Tennessee, . . east Tennessee to . . North Carolina. **1908** Britton *N. Amer. Trees* 553, It [=*Cladrastis kentukea*] is also called . . Gopher-wood. **1937** Thornburgh *Gt. Smoky Mts.* 28, "And this yellowwood," he adds, "is gopher wood. The old folks say that Noah's ark was made of it and I can't dispute it none." **1960** Vines *Trees SW* 528, Other vernacular names are Yellow-tree, . . Gopherwood, and Virgilia.

2 also *gopherwood tree:* A **stinking cedar** (here: *Torreya taxifolia*).

1962 Kurz–Godfrey *Trees N. FL* 2, *Torreya taxifolia*. . . Florida torreya; gopherwood-tree. **1967** Jahoda *Other FL* 69, Gopher wood trees. There's only one place in the world where they grow. That's here in Bristol. Some people call them Torrey trees. *Ibid* 70, Maybe, said Mr. Callaway, I'd already heard of gopher wood, or the Torrey tree.

go-poke n Cf **go-easter, go-'way bag**

A traveling bag or knapsack.

1952 Brown *NC Folkl.* 1.547, *Go-poke*. . . A traveling bag.—West. **1967** Williams *Greenbones* 233 **GA** (as of c1910), Before dawn he got up and, slipping his arms in the go-poke's straps, he left the place. **1972** Cooper *NC Mt. Folkl.* 92, *Go-poke*—a traveling bag.

go-quick n

=flowering spurge.

1898 *Jrl. Amer. Folkl.* 11.278, *Euphorbia corollata*, . . go-quick, Port Huron, Mich. . . Said to be the Indian name.

go-quick plant n [Perh from its laxative quality]

Rhubarb *(Rheum rhabarbarum)*.

1967 *DARE* FW Addit **CO**15, *Go-quick plant* . . name for rhubarb.

gorby n Also *gobby, gorby bird, gorley* ~ Also sp *gorbey, gorbie* [Prob Scots *gorbie*, dimin of *gorb* a greedy person or animal] **chiefly ME**

=Canada Jay.

1913 *DN* 4.2 **ME,** *Gobby*. . . The common Canadian jay. . . Used also in the Lake States and N.E. Canada. "That gobby flew away with a whole biscuit." **1956** MA Audubon Soc. *Bulletin* 40.84 **ME,** *Canada Jay*. . . Gorby . . Gorley Bird. **1961** *Jrl. Amer. Folkl.* 74.1 **nME,** The Canada Jay labors under the official name of *perisoreus canadensis canadensis* but it is more commonly called gorbey, moose-bird, meat-bird, grease-bird . . caribou bird . . woodsman's friend, or camp robber. **1966–68** *DARE* (Qu. Q16, . . *Jays . . around here*) Inf **ME**3, There is a gorby or moose-bird here (this is the Canada jay); **ME**8, Gorby or whiskey jack (common); **NH**14, Gorby or turd-bird or Canadian jay. **1975** Gould *ME Lingo* 113, *Gorby*—Also *gorbie* or *gorby-bird*. The handsome Canada jay. . . A deep woods relative of the blue jay, it seldom appears near villages, but is most friendly around woods *camps*. It'll come to take crumbs from one's hands in mere minutes. Woodsmen consider the *gorby* a lucky bird, as seamen do the albatross. In Maine legend they have led lost hunters back to *camp*.

gorch See **gorge** n[3]

Gord n[1] See **God**

gord n[2] See **goad**

gordolobo n Also *gordaldo, gordoloba* [Transf from or perh confused with Span *gordolobo* great mullein]

A **yarrow** (here: *Achillea millefolium*).

1896 *Jrl. Amer. Folkl.* 9.190 **CA,** *Achillea Millefolium* . . gordolobo. **1911** Henkel *Amer. Med. Leaves* 39, *Yarrow*. . . *Other common names*. . . Gordolobo. . . Very common along roadsides and in old fields, pastures, and meadows. **1940** Clute *Amer. Plant Names* 72, *A[chillea] millefolium*. . . Gordaldo. **1971** Krochmal *Appalachia Med. Plants* 30, Gordoloba. . . The herb is an aromatic with diaphoretic and emmenagogue activity.

gore n[1] [*OED gore* sb.[2] 1. b "A wedge-shaped strip of land on one side of an irregular field. . . Now only *dial*."] **chiefly NEng** Cf *DCan*

1 An irregular tract of land usu between larger, regularly surveyed areas; see quot 1988.

1679 in 1886 Braintree MA *Records* 19 **ceMA,** He shall have a small goere of land from the stile . . straight to the back side of the Shoole house and to the high way. **1733** in 1859 **RI** (Colony) *Records* 4.478, The gore of land (adjoining to Attleborough) in controversy between this colony and the Province of the Massachusetts Bay. **1773** *VA Gaz.* (Williamsburg) [Purdie–Dixon] 28 Oct 2/3 **ceVA,** Another Tract of

Land containing 148 Acres, within three or 400 Yards of the above, being only parted by a narrow Gore of *South Wales*. **1883** Twain *Life on Missip.* (Boston) 389, All along a line that's being surveyed, there's little dabs of land that they [=Californians] call 'gores,' that fall to the surveyor free gratis for nothing. **1887** G. W. Sears *Forest Runes p.vii (OED),* What New Englanders call a 'gore',—a triangular strip of land that gets left out somehow when the towns are surveyed. **1938** FWP *Guide NH* 338, He shrewdly refused any pay except 'a small gore of land'—which proved to be over 10,000 acres. **1966** FWP *Guide VT* 269, Travelers wanting to join the "251 Club"—individuals who visit all Vermont towns, cities, grants and gores—will have to visit Lewis either on horseback or afoot. **1975** Gould *ME Lingo* 114, *Gore*—A triangular or irregular area of land left over after surveyors have run their straight lines, and in Maine a word for certain townships thus shaped. . . Most original *gores* have been absorbed into adjacent townships, as Prout's *Gore* became a part of Freeport . . *Gore* is thus another of the Maine terms that mean *place.* **1988** *DARE* File **ME,** One of the reasons gores exist in New England is that King's Grant lands were each surveyed separately. The irregularly shaped pieces of land between them were called gores. Also because of surveying north-south lines on a spherical earth, not all the land can be divided into perfect squares. These (mainly triangular) correction pieces are called gores. Many occur along the Canadian border, where several towns have taken *gore* as part of their name, as Coburn Gore and Shelburne Gore.

2 also sp *ghor:* See quot.

1933 *AmSp* 8.1.83 **VT,** A *ghor* or *gore is any sharp valley or triangular pass through a mountain. A gore road* is a road built through such a valley or pass. The term is in common use in certain sections of southeastern Canada and in Vermont.

gore n² See **goad**

gore v

1 To annoy.

1970 *DARE* (Qu. II29b, . . *The unpleasant effect that person has on you: "He just _______."*) Inf **IL**141, Gores me.

2 ?To press.

1969 *DARE* Tape **NC**60, You git some black pepper an' put in both your hands an' you slip up behind him and just gore it in his eyes.

gore of blood n [*OED All in a* (or *one*) *gore of blood* (at *gore* sb.¹ 2. b) 1661 →; "Obs."]

A quantity of blood—often in phr *(in) a gore of blood* smeared with blood, bloody.

a1844 in 1935 *Filson Club Hist. Qrly.* 9.233 **ceKY,** The Indians killed him. . . She got away but went back that night and laid in her husband's bosom all in a gore of blood. **1899** (1912) Green *VA Folk-Speech* 201, *Gore.* . . Clotted blood; blood running in plenty. "He is all a gore of blood." **1914** *DN* 4.73 **ME, nNH,** *Gore o' blood.* . . A considerable quantity of blood. **1966** *DARE* FW Addit **AR**43, [From a tape recording of a ballad made in 1958:] Here I lie in a gore of blood.

gores shirt n [Var of **gauze shirt**] See Pronc Intro 3.I.23

1966 *DARE* (Qu. W15, *A shirt-length undergarment worn by women*) Inf **FL**2, Gores [goəz] shirt.

gorge n¹ **scattered, but chiefly NEast, Appalachians, Gt Lakes, SW** See Map

A usu steep-sided valley or ravine.

1777 in 1899 *VA Mag. Hist. & Biog.* 7.115, The trail went through a very narrow & deep gorge in the Mountain. **1836** Hall *Statistics* 39, There are few points on the river deserving the name of gorges. **1932** *DN* 6.221 **West,** *Gorge* . . [was] suited to the smaller ravines. *Ibid* 230, Although this word may be heard now and then, except, of course, in the plains country, it is used as a literary word. **1939** *LANE* Map 36 *(Ravine, notch), Gorge,* deep, narrow, with precipitous slopes. . . **scattered, but esp nNEng,** Gorge; 1 inf, **swCT,** It wouldn't be a gorge without it was very deep. **1946** Attwood *Length ME* 14, *Gorge*—A ravine with steep, rocky walls. **1965–70** *DARE* (Qu. C21, *A deep place cut in sloping ground by running water*) 111 Infs, **scattered, but esp NEast, Appalachians, Gt Lakes, SW,** Gorge; (Qu. C19, *What do you call low land running between hills*) 27 Infs, **scattered,** Gorge; (Qu. C15, *A place in mountains or high hills where you can get through without climbing over the top*) 17 Infs, **scattered,** Gorge; (Qu. C20, *What if it's broader or larger;* total Infs questioned, 75) Infs **NM**1, **OK**9, Gorge. **1968** *DARE* FW Addit **NY**97, *Gorge*—a narrow valley with steep sides and a fairly steep gradient. Mr. Kapfer refers to the area around Pixley falls on Lancingkill Creek as a gorge. **1970** *DARE* Tape **MA**92, An abutment down here at the gorge . . on the old toll road. **1971** Bright *Word Geog. CA & NV* 164, *Canyon* . . deeply cut valley or gully . . *gorge* [23% of infs]. *Ibid, Ravine* . . deep narrow valley of a small stream . . *gorge* [15% of infs].

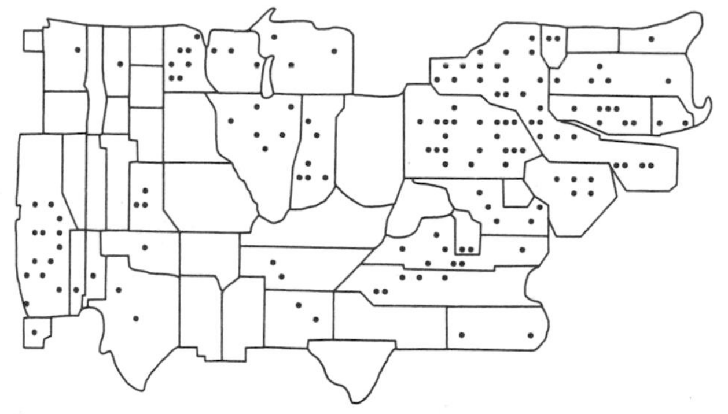

•gorge n¹ (Qq. C21, C19, C15, C20)

gorge n² Cf **gorgeous**

A large amount (of food); a surfeit.

1894 Riley *Armazindy* 49 **IN,** And jes *gorges* o' wild plums,/ Till a feller'd suck his thumbs / Clean up to his elbows! **1899** (1912) Green *VA Folk-Speech* 202, *Gorge* . . A heavy meal: as, to indulge in a gorge after long abstinence. "He has got his gorge." . . A disgust from too much of anything, "I've got a gorge and don't want any more now." **1929** *AmSp* 5.18 **Ozarks,** *Gorge.* . . A heavy meal, a large amount of food. "Jim shore did eat him a gorge o' thet 'ar ham-meat." **1954** *Harder Coll.* **cwTN,** *Gorge* . . a heavy meal; a large amount of food. **c1960** *Wilson Coll.* **csKY,** *Gorge* . . a heavy meal, maybe too heavy.

gorge n³ Also *gorge stick* Pronc-sp *gorch* [Perh var of *gord* (at **goad**)]

=**goad B.**

1965–70 *DARE* (Qu. K27) Infs **CA**193, **NY**65, 163, **PA**166, Gorge; **CA**136, Gorge stick; **MI**56, Gorch [gɔrč].

gorge daisy n

A **fleabane** (here: *Erigeron oreganus*).

1973 Hitchcock-Cronquist *Flora Pacific NW* 515, Gorge daisy. . . *E[rigeron] oreganus.*

gorgeous adj Cf **gorge** n²

Of food: rich, cloying.

1950 *PADS* 14.32, *Gorgeous.* . . Applied to articles of rich food, with which one's appetite is soon satisfied, and on which one is easily gorged. "Dat 'possum meat sho' is gorgeous." Negro usage of southeast Georgia. **c1960** *Wilson Coll.* **csKY,** *Gorgeous.* . . Rich, as applied to food.

gorge stick See **gorge** n³

gorgle n [Perh **goggle** n, infl by *gargle* v]

1967 *DARE* (Qu. X7, *Other names for the throat: "Some food got stuck in his _______."*) Inf **MA**2, Gorgle [goəgəl].

gork n

1903 *DN* 2.351 **neOH,** *Gork.* . . Bake stuff. The baker's product in general.

gorley bird See **gorby**

gorm v¹ See **gaum** v¹

gorm n¹ See **gaum** n¹

gorm v² See **gaum** v²

gorm n² See **gaum** n²

gormandize See **gaumandize**

gormed adj, adv [*EDD gorm;* perh rel to **gaum** v²] Cf **cussed gorm**

Damned—used as an intensifier.

1970 *DARE* FW Addit **MA**78, *Gormed fool:* "God-damned fool". . . Gormed mad.

gormey adj See **gaumy** adj²

gorming adj See **gauming** adj

gormity See **gorry mighty**

gormuck v [Perh blend of **gaum** v^1 **1** + *muck*] Cf **gommick around**

=**gaum** v^1 **1.**

1954 *PADS* 21.29 **SC,** *Gormuck*. . . To soil with grease, molasses or otherwise as the hands, face, clothing. This seems to be a blend of *gorm* and *mummock* . . both with approximately the same meaning. Charleston and coastal area.

‡**gormus** adj [Perh blend of *gormy* (at **gaumy** adj^1) + *enormous*]

1979 *DARE* File **OH** (as of c1920), Her mother . . used to use the term "gormus" for anything very large. Supposedly her mother . . used to say it to her too. As a "gormus mess" or a "gormus job."

gormy adj^1 See **gaumy** adj^1

gormy adj^2 See **gaumy** adj^2

gorn See **go** v **A4b, 7a**

go round one's fist to get to one's thumb See **elbow, go (all) around one's**

gorp v [Cf *gaup* to gulp or swallow greedily]

To eat noisily or greedily.

1913 *DN* 4.43, *Gorp*. . . To eat greedily. **1942** Berrey–Van den Bark *Amer. Slang* 94.12, *Eat greedily* . . gorp. **1969** *DARE* (Qu. H11b, *If he makes a noise with his food, he* ______) Inf **PA**186, Gorps.

gorping adj Cf *DS* MM13, 15

1949 *McDavid Coll.* **cNY,** *Gorping:* lying at an angle across the bed.

gorramity See **gorry mighty**

gorry n, intj [Euphem for *God;* cf *golly*] **chiefly NEng** Cf **i** prep

Used as an exclam of surprise—freq in phr *by gorry* pronc-spp *begorry, begorra.*

1854 (1969) Thoreau *Walden* 162 **MA,** Then, by gorry, your mind must be there. **1907** *DN* 3.188 **seNH,** *Gorry*. . . Used instead of the name of the deity as an imprecation. Not felt to be an Irish word. Very common. **1911** (1916) Porter *Harvester* 94, Begorry! The very idea! **1915** (1916) Johnson *Highways New Engl.* 195, I gorry! if he'd been a very little nigher he'd have got me! **1950** Moore *Candlemas Bay* 2 **ME,** Look at that depth recorder, by gorry. There's ten fathoms of water right here, and darn' if I ever knew that before. **1966–68** *DARE* (Qu. KK48, . . *"I just did it* ______*."*) Infs **ME**5, 16, **MA**6, 38, 56, **VT**16, By guess and by gorry; (Qu. NN27a, *Weakened substitutes for 'god'*) Infs, **ME**9, 16, 22, Gorry; **MA**37, **NH**5, By gorry; (Qu. NN30) Inf **IN**45, Jaysus begorra. **1979** Lewis *How to Talk Yankee* [14] **nNEng,** *Gorry!*. . . All true Yankees use this familiar expression. "I ice-fished Moosehead opening day, and *Gorry, wan't* it cold!"

gorry mighty intj Also *gor(ra)mity* [Euphems for *God almighty;* cf **gorry**]

1858 Hammett *Piney Woods Tavern* 254 **TX,** "Oh the Gorry Mighty! *Alligator! Alligator!* . . " **1894** *DN* 1.331 **NJ,** Gorramity [gɔrəmaiti]: for God Almighty. **1970** *DARE* FW Addit **MA**78, "God-A-mity", God-All-Mighty, or "Gormity."

gorsh n, intj Also *garsh* [Varr of *gosh* (euphem for *God*); see Pronc Intro 3.I.23]

1930s in 1944 *ADD* **eWV,** [gɑrš] garsh. **1940** in 1944 *ADD* **WV,** My gorsh! **1941** in 1944 *ADD,* My garsh! J. R. Williams cartoon 'Out Our Way.' **1942** in 1944 *ADD* **wPA,** [gɔːrš]. **1965–70** *DARE* (Qu. LL37, *To make a statement as strong as you can: "I could have wrung her neck, I was so* ______ *mad."*) Inf **MI**75, Garsh-awful; (Qu. NN20a, *Exclamations caused by sudden pain—a blow on the thumb*) Inf **MD**25, Oh, gorsh; (Qu. NN26a, *Weakened substitutes for 'hell': "Oh* ______*!"*) Inf **MD**25, Gorsh; **MD**26, Oh, garsh; (Qu. NN27a, *Weakened substitutes for 'god': "My* ______*!"*) Inf **MO**21, Gorsh; **WI**34, 55, My garsh; (Qu. NN27b, *Weakened substitutes for 'god': "For* ______ *sakes!"*) Infs **MI**13, **PA**167, **WI**34, Garsh; (Qu. NN30) Inf **PA**138, Garsh; **MD**25, Gee gorsh.

gos See **goss**

gosh all hemlock intj Also *gosh all fishhooks;* for addit varr see quots [Euphems for *gosh almighty* < *God almighty*] **esp NEng**

Used to express surprise or annoyance.

1857 *Lawrence* (Kan.) *Republican* 2 July 4 *(DAE),* 'Gosh all Potomac!' exclaimed our Yankee. **1864** (1868) Trowbridge *3 Scouts* 55, Gosh all hemlock! . . won't ye never stop twittin' a feller? **1887** (1895) Robinson *Uncle Lisha* 41 **wVT,** Oh, gosh all Connet'cutt! My eyes hain't god done smartin' yit! **1890** *DN* 1.73 **NH,** *Gosh all hemlock:* a mild or burlesque oath. **1892** *DN* 1.213 **NEng,** *Gosh all hemlock.* **1914** *DN* 4.73 **ME, nNH,** *Gosh all lightnin',* (or *all fish-hooks!*) Common ejaculations. **1942** McAtee *Dial. Grant Co. IN* 30 (as of 1890s), *Gosh-all-fish-hooks* . . mild oath. **1950** Stuart *Hie Hunters* 35 **eKY,** Gosh-old-hemlock, but he's up there. **1951** *PADS* 15.66 **NH,** *Gosh all hemlock*. . . Mild oath. **1959** *VT Hist.* new ser 27.138, Gosh all Fiddlesticks! . . Gosh all Filox! . . Gosh all Firelocks! . . Gosh all Frighty! . . Gosh all Fishhooks! . . Gosh all Hemlock! . . Gosh all Hemlocks and chew spruce gum! . . Gosh all Tarnation! . . Gosh all sufficiency! **1961** Sackett–Koch *KS Folkl.* 26, "Gosh-all-hemlocks, stranger," exclaimed the Kansas man . . "is it possible you hain't heard of it yet?" **1966** Barnes–Jensen *Dict. UT Slang* 20, Gosh all Friday is a mild expression of weariness, disappointment or disgust. *Ibid, Gosh all hemlock.* **1967** *DARE* FW Addit **cOR,** Gosh all fishhooks—an exclamation of wonder. **1969** *DARE* (Qu. NN20b) Inf **CT**36, Gosh all hemlock. **1983** *DARE* File **ceWI,** *Gosh all hemlock* . . an exclamation.

goshawk n Pronc-sp **esp PA, NY, NJ** *gosh-hawk*

1 A large short-winged hawk *(Accipiter gentilis).* **now chiefly Gt Lakes, PA** See Map Also called **blue darter 2, blue hawk 2, blue hen hawk 1, chicken hawk 1, dove hawk, gray hawk, hen hawk, partridge hawk**

[**1612** Smith *Map VA* 15, Hawkes there be of diuerse sorts as our Falconers called them. *Sparowhawkes,* . . *Goshawkes,* . . but they all pray most vpon fish.] **1709** (1967) Lawson *New Voyage* 143 **NC,** Goshawks are very plentiful in *Carolina.* **1893** Roosevelt *Wilderness Hunter* 121 **swMT,** I revenged myself for the miss by knocking a large blue goshawk out of the top of a blasted spruce. **1917** (1923) *Birds Amer.* 2.70/1, It is fortunate for the American hen that the Goshawk resides mostly north of the United States, migrating southward only in winter. **1932** Bennitt *Check-list* 22 **MO,** *Eastern goshawk*. . . Blue hawk; gosh-hawk. **1965–70** *DARE* (Qu. Q4, . . *Kinds of hawks* . . *around here*) 16 Infs, **esp PA,** Gosh-hawk; **CA**78, **CO**7, 47, **IA**3, **MI**36, **MN**18, Goshawk; **CA**41, ['goz] hawk; **NY**219, ['gɔz] hawk; **NC**48, Goshawk hawk.

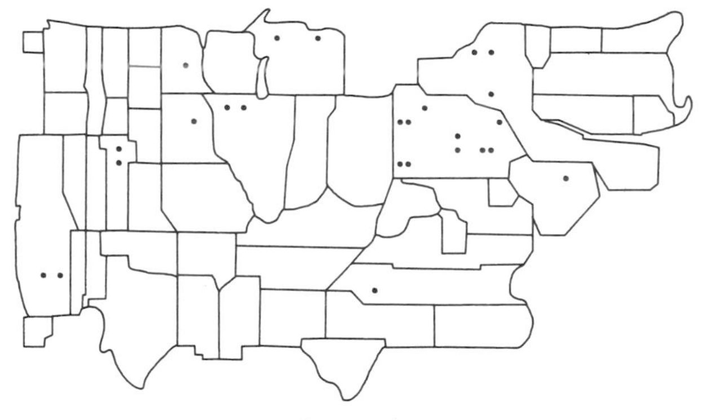

•goshawk 1 + varr (Qu. Q4)

2 =**marsh hawk.**

1913 *Auk* 30.504 **Okefenokee GA,** *Circus hudsonius*. . . We were told of a large, white-rumped hawk, which courses low over the prairies and islands, and feeds on snakes and frogs. It goes by the name of 'Gos-hawk.' **1955** *Oriole* 20.1.5 **GA,** *Marsh Hawk.—Goshawk* (that is goose hawk, a misnomer).

gosh-dinger n

=**dinger** n^1 **1.**

1912 *DN* 3.577 **wIN,** *Gosh-dinger*. . . An unusual specimen of any kind.

goshed adv *euphem*

1931 Hannum *Thursday April* 193 **wNC,** "This golderned thing," giving a sudden screw to his unaccustomed high collar, "is too goshed high to spit over!"

go-sheep-go n Also *go-sheepie-go, ~-sheepy-~, ~-sheep-run* **chiefly Midl, esp OH** See Map

=**run sheep run.**

1905 *DN* 3.81 **nwAR,** *Go, sheepy, go. . .* An out-door game played after dark. **1938** Burman *Blow for a Landing* 13 **Lower Missip Valley,** He passed a group of children playing 'Go, Sheepie, Go.' **1942** McAtee *Dial. Grant Co. IN* 30 (as of 1890s), *Go-sheep-go. . .* With us it was played by sides and only after dark. One side was the hunted, the other the hunters; the leader of the hunted side remained with their opponents, and by prearranged cries let his party known how near the other was. If and when the hunters got farther away from home base than the hunted, the shepherd called out go-sheep-go, and both sides rushed pell-mell for "home". The first reaching the base retained for his side the more desirable role of the hunted. **1957** *Sat. Eve. Post Letters* **swMO** (as of 1912–16), We also played Go Sheepie Go, Blackman, . . Kicks and Pinches. **1965–70** *DARE* (Qu. EE12, *Games in which one captain hides his team and the other team tries to find it*) 18 Infs, **chiefly N Midl, esp OH,** Go-sheep(ie) go; (Qu. EE4) Inf **IN**76, Go-sheep-run; (Qu. EE33, *Other outdoor games*) Inf **NY**145, Go-sheepie-go. **1966** *DARE* File **seIN,** *Go-sheepie-go.*

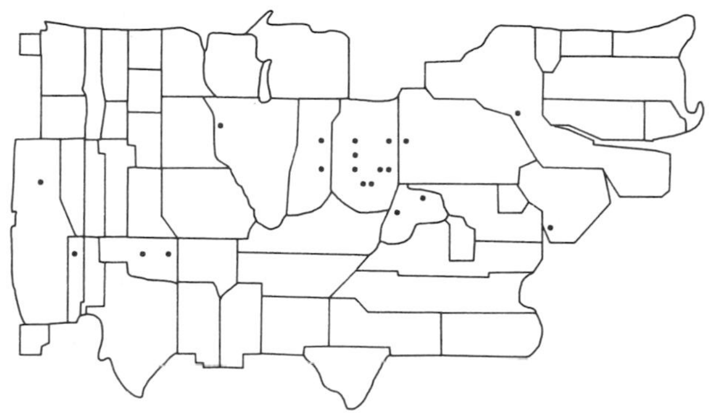

•go-sheep-go + varr (Qq. EE12, EE4, EE33)

gosh-hawk See **goshawk**

goship See **gossip**

go-sign n Also *go-away sign, go-(ahead) signal, go-light*
In phr *give one the go-sign:* to get rid of one, to give one the brush-off.

1950 *WELS (I'd like to give him the ——)* 1 Inf, **cWI,** Go sign. **1967–69** *DARE* (Qu. II5b, *When you don't want to have anything to do with a certain person . . , you might say, "I'd certainly like to give him the ——.")* Infs **IN**73, **MO**20, **WI**12, Go-sign; **LA**8, **MD**26, Go-ahead signal; **LA**16, Go-away sign; **TX**32, Go-signal; **GA**77, Go-light.

gosling n

1 pl; often with *the:* The voice change commonly undergone by adolescent boys; the period when this change occurs. **chiefly S Midl** Cf **gosling age**

1899 (1912) Green *VA Folk-Speech* 202, *Goslins. . .* When a boy's voice is changed, he is said to have the *goslins,* or to be in the *goslins.* **1933** *AmSp* 8.1.49 **Ozarks,** *Goslings. . .* The change of the masculine voice at puberty. A boy whose voice is changing is said to be *in th' goslin's.* [**1939** *Hench Coll.,* He's talking goslin's, he's talking goslin talk [=to talk with changing voice].] **1942** [see **gosling age**]. **1946** *PADS* 6.15 **swVA,** *Goslings. . .* The frequent break in an adolescent boy's voice. . . Common. **1948** Cain *Moth* 32 **Baltimore MD,** But even as I was talking to him my voice popped. And one of the bull fiddlers said: "That boy's got the goslins." **1954** *Harder Coll.* **cwTN,** *Got the goslin's . .* has a change in voice. **1983** *MJLF* 9.1.41 **ceKY,** *Goslins . .* the change of voice a boy experiences at puberty.

2 also *gosling flower, ~ weed:* An anemone, usu *Anemone patens.* [See quots 1911, 1937] **esp Upper Missip Valley**

1893 *Jrl. Amer. Folkl.* 6.136 **MN,** *Anemone patens,* var. *Nuttalliana . .* gosling. **1911** *Century Dict. Suppl., Gosling. . .* The American pasque-flower, *Pulsatilla hirsutissima:* so called from its dense, soft hairs. **1937** U.S. Forest Serv. *Range Plant Hdbk.* W159/2, The large downy-hairy buds suggest baby fowl to children who often call them goslings. **1950** *WELS Suppl.* **csWI,** Gosling flower. . . Pasque flower. "Gosling" because of downy covering. **1959** Carleton *Index Herb. Plants* 55, *Gosling:* Anemone pulsatilla (Pulsatilla vulgaris). *Gosling-weed:* Anemone (v). **1967–69** *DARE* (Qu. S23, *Pale blue flowers with downy leaves and cups that come up on open, stony hillsides in March or early April*) Infs **IL**27, 77, 85, 86, **MO**14, Gosling.

gosling age n Also *gosling patch* Cf **gosling 1, hog age**
The period when an adolescent boy's voice is changing.

1942 Berrey–Van den Bark *Amer. Slang* 116.1, *Gosling patch, goslings,* the period of adolescence in which a boy's voice is changing. **c1960** *Wilson Coll.* **csKY,** *Gosling age. . .* Adolescence, esp. referring to the uncertain voice of an adolescent boy.

gosling clam n
Prob =**soft-shell clam.**

1940 Brown *Amer. Cooks* 76 **CT,** Gosling clams, a little larger than your hand, are best in October and November, freshly dug out of soft sand when the tide is low.

gosling-drownder See **goose-drownder**

gosling flower See **gosling 2**

gosling grass n [*EDD* 1854 →]
=**cleavers.**

1900 Lyons *Plant Names* 167, *G[alium] aparine. . .* Cleavers. . . Gosling-grass. **1940** Clute *Amer. Plant Names* 52, *G[alium] aparine.* Cleavers . . gosling-grass.

gosling patch See **gosling age**

gosling weed See **gosling 2**

gosmore n [Perh var of *gossamer*]
=**cat's-ear 2.**

1900 Lyons *Plant Names* 198, *Hypochoeris. . .* Cat's-ear, Gosmore. **1935** (1943) Muenscher *Weeds* 503, *Hypochoeris radicata. . .* Gosmore. **1961** Peck *Manual OR* 852, *Hypochaeris* [sic] . . *radicata. . .* Gosmore. **1973** Hitchcock–Cronquist *Flora Pacific NW* 532, Gosmore—*H[ypochaeris] radicata.*

go snacks, go snooks, go snucks See **snack**

go south v phr

1 To lose; to be defeated, incapacitated.

1903 (1965) Adams *Log Cowboy* 186 **NM,** Before this game ends, I'll make old Quince curl his tail; I've got him going south now. **1914** *DN* 4.107 **KS,** *Go south. . .* To be baffled or beaten. **c1938** in 1970 Hyatt *Hoodoo* 2.1539 **Savannah GA,** If yo' got anybody dat chew [=you] hate an' yo' want 'em tuh die, yo' draw a coffin an' put dem in it an' six weeks aftah yo' draw dose coffins, if dey don't die, dey'll be so near dead, *dey'll go to de south* or go crazy or somepin.

2 To take a turn for the better.

1897 *KS Univ. Qrly.* (ser B) 6.88 **neKS,** *Going south:* taking a favorable turn.

3 See quot.

1982 *Barrick Coll.* **csPA,** *South, go*—steal, abscond with.

gospel bird n [See quots] *esp among Black speakers; joc* Cf **chicken-eater 2, chicken preacher**
A chicken.

1935 Hurston *Mules & Men* 32 **FL,** Come on, heart-string, and have some gospel-bird on me. **c1970** Pederson *Dial. Surv. Rural GA* **nwGA** [Black], Inf: "I fixed me a gospel bird." FW: "A what?" Inf: [With laughter] "A gospel bird. That's 'cause you always fix 'em for the preacher!" **1977** Dillard *Lexicon* 58, Like rural whites, the Blacks were likely to kill a chicken or two when the preacher came . . the prevalent Black name for the fowl: *gospel bird.*

gospel measure n [In allusion to Luke 6:38]
=**good measure.**

1916 *DN* 4.323 **KS,** *Gospel measure. . .* Good measure; more than is asked for or in strictness required. General. **1958** *DE Folkl. Bulletin* 1.32, *Gospel measure* (full to overflowing)—also Methodist measure. **1968–69** *DARE* (Qu. U15, . . *If the seller puts in a little extra to make you feel that you're getting a good bargain, you call that ——*) Inf **MD**17, Gospel measure; (Qu. LL28, . . *Entirely full: "The box of apples was ——.")* Infs **PA**207, **VA**31, Gospel measure. **1982** *Barrick Coll.* **csPA,** *Gospel measure*—full to overflowing.

gospel mill n Also *gospel shop joc*
A church.

1872 Twain *Roughing It* 331 **NV,** Are you the duck that runs the gospel-mill next door? **1909** *DN* 3.411 **nME,** *Gospel shop. . .* A church.

gospel sharp n Also *gospel shark,* ~ *shooter* **chiefly West**

A preacher; an unctuous person.

1872 Twain *Roughing It* 333, "What we want is a gospel-sharp. See?" "A what?" "Gospel-sharp. Parson." **1897** Lewis *Wolfville* 50 **AZ,** I've took the trouble to bring a gospel-sharp over from Tucson to do the marryin'. **1897** *Scribner's Mag.* 22.723/1 **cnPA,** Gospel sharks we know, and camp cooks, and honest Jew pedlers. **1900** *DN* 2.38 **KS, OH** [College words], *Gospel-shooter. . .* A preacher; used in contempt. *Ibid* **NJ,** *Gospel-shark. . .* A preacher, a goody-goody, or sanctimonious person. **1902** Morris *Stage Confidences* 224 **West,** The driver with the . . unlimited assurance of the Western hackman remarked genially: "Madame Elize, there's another gospel-sharp out on the edge of the town". **1920** Hunter *Trail Drivers TX* 257 **csTX** (as of 1870s), There is going to be some hell-fired racket here . . by fightin' Parson Potter . . a regular gospel shark. **1934** *AmSp* 9.26 [Prison parlance], *Gospel shark.* A preacher. **1942** *AmSp* 17.213 **West,** Jack contracted pneumonia, and someone brought the local 'gospel sharp' to his bedside.

gospel shoe n

1950 *PADS* 14.33 **SC,** *Gospel shoes. . .* Sunday shoes.

gospel shooter See **gospel sharp**

gospel shop See **gospel mill**

gospel whanger n Cf **Bible banger**

1909 *DN* 3.411 **nME,** *Gospel whanger. . .* A revivalist.

goss n Also sp *gos* [Etym uncert, but cf quot 1944]

Punishment—usu in phrr *give one* (or *get*) *goss.*

1840 *Daily Picayune* (New Orleans LA) 29 July 2/4, Six victims to report this morning . . offences trivial. . . Some of them got *gos,* and some got nothing. **1847** (1962) Robb *Squatter Life* 75 **West,** Gin him goss without sweeten'. **1851** Burke *Polly Peablossom* 170 **TN,** I say, . . are you gwine to leave afore I calls dad, for he'll jist give you goss in a minit, . . and we gals couldn't save your cussed ternal scalp if we wanted tu! **1899** (1912) Green *VA Folk-Speech* 202, *Goss. . .* An unnamed punishment. "If you do, he'll give you goss." **1906** Casey *Parson's Boys* 156 **sIL** (as of c1860), "Hooray, me brave boys," he shouted encouragingly, as he beheld the squirrel-studded tree top. "Give 'em goss!" Then with all a hunter's zest he took the gun and made quick exhibition of his skill as a marksman. **1944** *Hench Coll.* **seVA,** To give (a person) goss = to give a person a whipping. [He] said that this expression, used in his area, contains the regional pronunciation of *gorse,* and that "to give one gorse" means to whip a person with a gorse branch.

gossamer n Also *gossamer coat* *old-fash*

A lightweight raincoat.

1882 (1939) Mayne *Maud* 94 **swIL,** Will and I got to the hill and there, in gossamer, shawl, and under umbrella we sat till my feet were soaked. **1888** W.D. Howells in *Harper's New Mth. Mag.* 77.138/2, She saw the figure of a young man draped in a long India-rubber gossamer coat. *Ibid* 77.139/1, "Thanks, yes," said the young man, flinging off his gossamer. **1889** (1971) Farmer *Americanisms* 273, *Gossamer.* In the Eastern States a waterproof cloak. **1894** *Outing* 23.381/1, Be sure to have a mackintosh or gossamer with you. **1950** *WELS (A coat worn for protection against the rain)* 3 Infs, **WI,** Gossamer. [2 of the 3 Infs identify this as old fashioned.] **1967** *DARE* FW Addit **MI**47, Gossamer ['gɑzmɚ]—A raincoat.

gossan n [Corn dial; *OED* 1776 →] Cf **blossom rock, iron hat**

In mining: decomposed rock or vein material usu colored rusty-red as a result of the oxidation of pyrites; by ext, pay dirt.

1844 Lapham *Geogr. Descr. WI* 63, For about a depth of fifteen feet, the fissure was found to be filled with an iron ochreous substance named 'gossan,' and lumps of sulphuret and carbonate of copper mixed in it. **1860** Worcester *Dict.* 631, *Gossan. . . (Mining.)* An ochreous mineral substance; an imperfect iron ore. **1889** *Century Dict.* 2581, *Gossan. . .* This dark, rusty-brown material is the *gossan* of the Cornish miner, a term also in very common use in other mining regions. **1945** *CA Folkl. Qrly.* 4.319 **CO** [Mining terms], *Gossan:* "Blossom rock" (American). Ore near the surface which has been partially decomposed by the forces of erosion. I also heard it used in the more general sense of "pay dirt." **1953** Pough *Rocks & Minerals* 27, Like the rocks, the veins and their mineral-enriched borders are affected by exposure to . . air. . . A whole new group of ore minerals can form, or the surface exposure may be leached. . . Residual deposits of this sort are . . *gossans. . .* Any gold originally in the pyrite will be freed to remain in the gossan. **1968** Adams *Western Words* 130, *Gossan*—In mining, the outcrop of a lode, usually colored by the decomposition of iron. Picture ore of a very rich grade.

gossip n Pronc-sp *goship*

A Form.

1941 Writers' Program *Guide AL* 392, They go to town on Saturdays for a day of trading and what they call "goship" with their fellow-mountaineers.

B Sense.

A children's party game.

1923 Acker *400 Games* 273, *Gossip. . .* The leader whispers a sentence rapidly into the ear of his neighbor, who whispers what he *thought* he heard to *his* neighbor, and so on. **1966** *DARE* File **swIN,** *Gossip*—a type of children's party game. **1966** *DARE* Tape **AL**3, We talked about that game gossip. . . You start a sentence or verse. . . and then . . that person passes it to the next one. . . Then that person whispers what he hears. Finally it ends up over here, for the last one, but it's not anything like the original sentence that you started out of.

gossip fab n [*gossip* + *fab* abbr for *confab(ulation)*]

1966 *DARE* (Qu. KK12, . . *"They got together yesterday and had a real ______."*) Inf **MO**1, Gossip fab ['gɔsɪp ˌfæb].

goster(er), gostration See **gauster**

got See **get** v **A3, 4, B1**

got intj [Euphem for *God*]

1966–68 *DARE* (Qu. NN27a, *Weakened substitutes for 'god': "My ______!"*) Inf **LA**32, Got; **OK**27, Got (almighty); (Qu. NN25a, *Weakened substitutes for 'damn' or 'damned': "______ it all!"*) Inf **LA**32, Got dog.

gotch adj [Span *gacho* turned or bent downwards] **chiefly SW**

Drooping, askew—usu in combs *gotch-eared, gotch-eyed.*

1905 C. Driscoll *Girl of La Gloria* iii.21 *(OEDS)* **KS,** The *maveriquer* . . usually rode a gotch-eared Mexican pony. **1910** Porter *Strictly Business* 104 **AZ,** You are a concentrated, effete, unconditional, short-sleeved, gotch-eared Miss Sally Walker. **1941** Cleaveland *No Life* 67 **cwNM** (as of c1890), Bill Jones was seen riding down White Horse Cañon on his favorite cutting-horse, the sorrel with a gotch ear. **1954** Tolbert *Bigamy Jones* 3 **wTX,** He might have been all-around handsome if he hadn't been a kind of gotch-eyed man. He had yellow, narrow, almost crossed eyes, like the eyes of a loafer wolf. **1966–70** *DARE* (Qu. X26a, *If a person's eyes look in different directions, looking inward, he's ______*) Infs **OK**42, **TX**5, 33, Gotch-eyed; (Qu. X26b, *If a person's eyes look in different directions, looking outward, he's ______*) Infs **MI**123, **OK**42, 51, **TX**3, 37, Gotch-eyed. **1986** Pederson *LAGS Concordance,* 1 inf, **csTX,** Gotch-eared—a donkey with ear clipped.

go the big (or whole) figure See **figure B2**

go to bottom v phr

1916 Macy–Hussey *Nantucket Scrap Basket* 133 **MA,** Gone to Bottom—When a Nantucketer drops a thing, he is apt to speak of it as having gone to bottom.

go to business v phr **NEast, esp NY**

To go to work, to have a regular job.

1968 *DARE* FW Addit **NY**46, "Go to business" means to go to work. **1971** *Today Show Letters* **NY, ceMA,** Instead of asking, for example, "does your wife work" a person raised in New York would quite likely ask "does your wife go to business." My wife thinks this may be a Jewish turn-of-speech, since she says she's heard it in Brookline, Mass., where many Jewish people live. **1974** *DARE* File **NJ, NY, NEng,** *Go to business.* In contrast to 'go to work.'

go to glory See **glory** n[1] **B1**

go to grass See **grass** n **5**

go to Guinea See **Guinea** n[2]

go to Halifax See **Halifax 1**

go to haverty-grass See **haverty-grass, go to**

go-to-hell, I'll be exclam Rarely *I'll be go-to-helled*

An expression of surprise or annoyance.

1924 *DN* 5.269 **NY,** *Hell. . .* I'll be go to hell-ed. **1942** Whipple *Joshua* 8 **UT** (as of c1880), "I'll be go-to-hell!" shouted Brother Tuckett. **1942** Stegner *Mormon Country* 143 **UT,** I have not heard elsewhere the typical Mormon "I'll be go to hell." **1969** *DARE* (Qu. NN7, *Exclamations of surprise*) Infs **PA**230, **VT**16, I'll be go-to-hell; (Qu. NN25b, . . *"I'll be*

———!") Inf **VT**16, Go-to-hell. **1982** Heat Moon *Blue Highways* 96 **AL,** "Would anybody stop a black man if he wanted a drink in here?" "I'll be go to hell."

go to hell in a handbasket See **handbasket 2**

go-to-meeting adj, also used absol [Cf **Sunday-go-to-meeting**]

Usu of clothes: appropriate for a church service; best, most formal.

1790 Tyler *Contrast* 45, All my tunes [are] go to meeting tunes. **1804** Fessenden *Poems* 140 **NEng,** Each scrapes, huzzas, and kicks and bounces,/ Waves high her go-to-meeting cap. **1825** Neal *Brother Jonathan* 1.148 **CT,** His "go-to-meetin' " coat, as they call that, in America, which a farmer wears, on training days, and Sabbath days, had been . . of a strong, bright, claret colour. **1836** (1838) Haliburton *Clockmaker* (1st ser) 64, One of these blue-noses, with his go-to-meetin' clothes on. **1878** (1887) Cooke *Happy Dodd* 70, Why, Miss Rice she didn't never have more'n one caliker gown to her name, an' an old alipacky for a go-to-meeting'. **1887** *Lantern* (New Orleans LA) 5 Nov 3/1 (*AmSp* 25.33), 'I put on my best go-to-meetings.' **1899** (1912) Green *VA Folk-Speech* 202, *Go-to-meeting*. . . Proper to be worn to church; hence, best; applied to clothes: as, her *go-to-meeting clothes*. **1916** Lincoln *Mary-'Gusta* 15 **MA,** She was not, as usual, garbed in gingham, but was arrayed in her best go-to-meeting gown. **1942** Whipple *Joshua* 16 **UT** (as of c1860), Abijah, shaking hands, was certainly putting on his 'go-to-meeting' manner. **1950** *WELS* 1 Inf, **cWI,** Go-to-meeting clothes. **1965–70** *DARE* (Qu. W39) Infs **CA**15, **IA**22, **MS**6, **NE**1, **TN**24, **TX**40, **VA**69, **VT**3, Go-to-meeting clothes.

go-to-mill n Also *going to (the) mill,* occas *go-to-town* **chiefly IL, KY** Cf **Jerusalem**

A children's game played on paper: see quot 1970.

1905 *DN* 3.81 **nwAR,** *Go to mill*. . . The name of a children's game. **c1960** *Wilson Coll.* **csKY,** *Going to Mill,* an indoor game. **1965–70** *DARE* (Qu. EE39, . . *Games played on paper by two people*) Inf **IL**96, Go-to-mill; **IL**143, Go-to-town; **IN**30, Going to mill; **KY**7, Going to mill; Played with checks in a race to the bottom of the page. Guess right and get a check; wrong, get nothing, etc.; **KY**74, 77, Going to the mill. **1970** *DARE* Tape **KY**75, [FW:] You also mentioned another game called going to the mill. [Inf:] That was a pencil and paper game; which you would draw four lines . . and you'd divide 'em up in little square blocks. You would take an object . . that you could hold in your hand. You double your hands up and hold 'em behind your back and then turn around and the other one that was playing with you, he would guess which hand you were holding your object in. If he guessed it right he got a mark, a-going to the mill, that would be down the page. If he guessed it wrong, I got the mark and I got to go again. . . The first one that got his little squares all filled with cross marks, down and up, he was the winner.

go to mill v phr

1969 *DARE* (Qu. JJ15a, . . *"He hasn't sense enough to ———."*) Infs **KY**40, 41, Go to mill. [Both Infs suggest this is joc, old-fash.]

go to ride See **go** v **C9**

go to the bad v phr [*OED bad* sb. B. b. b 1864 →] **esp Sth**

To deteriorate morally or physically.

[**1904** *NY Eve. Jrl.* (NY) 25 Apr 10 *(Zwilling Coll.),* [In column "M'Graw's Talk to Tad":] That boy [=Christy Mathewson] is a 'pip' when he's right, but I think the cold weather put his whip [=pitching arm] to the bad that day.] **c1960** *Wilson Coll.* **csKY,** *Go to the bad*. . . Become slovenly, careless, even immoral. **1961** Cole *Idioms New Engl.* 36, To go to the bad. **1965–70** *DARE* (Qu. K9) Inf **GA**16, One tit went to the bad; (Qu. KK10, . . *Something failing*) Inf **NC**41, Went to the bad; (Qu. KK19, . . *Machine or appliance . . out of order*) Inf **CO**4, Went to the bad; **TX**75, Has gone to the bad; (Qu. KK20a, *Something that looks as if it might collapse*) Inf **GA**28, Going to the bad; (Qu. KK20b, *Something that looks as if it might collapse*) Infs **CO**4, **LA**25, Gone to the bad; (Qu. KK64, . . *"The neighborhood is sort of ———."*) Inf **VA**38, Gone to the bad; (Qu. Y35) Inf **TX**40, Gone to the bad. **1984** Wilder *You All Spoken Here* 167 **Sth,** Go to the bad: Spoil; something that can happen to country hams and even to children who were raised up right.

go-to-town See **go-to-mill**

go to walk See **go** v **C9**

Gotrocks n [*got* + *rocks* diamonds, money; perh with allusion to *Rockefeller*] Cf **Astorbilt 1**

Often treated as a surname: Used as a nickname for a rich, "high-society" person.

1965–70 *DARE* (Qu. II23, . . *People who are, or think they are, the best society of a community*) Infs **AL**37, **CA**110, **IL**97, 98, **NJ**16, **VT**12, **WV**1, Gotrocks; **MS**69, Mrs. Gotrocks; **GA**11, Gotrots [*DARE* Ed: prob FW error for *gotrocks*]; (Qu. U37, . . *Somebody who has plenty of money*) Infs **CA**36, **WA**6, Gotrocks; **MD**9, **WA**1, Mr. Gotrocks; (Qu. CC11) Inf **AZ**2, Mrs. Gotrocks; (Qu. GG19b, . . *A person . . feeling important or independent: "He seems to think he's ———."*) Inf **GA**89, Mr. Gotrocks. [11 of 15 Infs old]

gots See **get** v **B1a**

gotta See **get** v **B1a**

gotten See **get** v **A3, 4**

gou n Also *goo-fish, gou-fish* [Abbr for **gaspergou 1**] **LA** =**freshwater drum.**

[**1931** Read *LA French* 22, The aphetic forms *un gou, les gous* also occur.] **1967** *DARE* Tape **LA**5, You have the gou . . a scaly fish called gaspergou by people in Baton Rouge. **1967–68** *DARE* (Qu. P1, . . *Freshwater fish . . that are good to eat*) Infs **LA**3, 15, Gou; (Qu. P14, *If commercial fishing is done around here, what do the fishermen go out after?*) Infs **LA**14, 15, Gou. **1969** *DARE* File **LA,** Gaspergou . . the gou-fish . . the Freshwater Drum fish. **1983** *Reinecke Coll.* 5 **LA,** *Gaspergou* ['gæspə͵gu]. . . Freshwater Drum, or according to some, also the common sheephead. General in former sense among fishermen and seafood dealers. From La. Fr. "Casse-burgot" or barnacle-cracker, with same meaning. In . . north La., sometimes "goo-fish."

gouber See **goober** n[1] **1**

gouber-grabbler See **goober-grabber**

gouber pea See **goober pea**

gouch hook See **gancho 2**

goudy See **gowdy**

gou-fish See **gou**

gouge n

1 See quot.

1903 *DN* 2.298 **Cape Cod MA,** *Gouge*. . . A rough hole cut in cloth, etc.

2 also *gouger, gouge stick:* A goad. Cf **gouge** v **1, goad A, gorge** n[3]

1966–70 *DARE* (Qu. K27, *What do you call the sharp-pointed stick used to get oxen to move?*) Infs **AK**8, **IA**12, **MA**32, **OK**52, **VT**16, **WV**2, Gouge; **KY**84, Gouge stick; **IL**104, Gouger.

gouge v

1 To jab; to poke; hence *gouge up* to urge (an ox) with a goad. **esp Sth, S Midl**

1834 *Knickerbocker* 3.32 **wTN,** He gouged his old horse, who wriggled, shot forward, and curled it so rapidly, that all which remained visible of him was a dark streak. **c1960** *Wilson Coll.* **csKY,** *Gouge*. . . Stick or hurt with a pin. **1965–70** *DARE* (Qu. Y46a, . . *"He ——— a thorn into his hand."*) Infs **AR**47, **GA**38, **IN**30, **TX**76, **WA**18, Gouged; **WV**2, Gouged himself; (Qu. Y46b, . . *"She ——— herself with a needle."*) Infs **PA**205, **WV**2, Gouged; **GA**77, Gouged a needle into. **1968** *DARE* Tape **WV**2 (as of c1920), When he drove 'em [=plow oxen] he had a stick that was sharp on the end and they'd say, "Gouge 'em up, boy, push 'em along. . . gouge 'em up, punch 'em along, punch 'em up, cowpunchers, punch 'em along."

2 To lunge, dart.

1863 U.S. Congress *Congressional Globe* 37th Cong 3d Sess 28 Feb 1373/1 **MD,** If, like a pen of ill-managed cattle, one gouges one way, and one another, how are we to come together? **1943** Chase *Jack Tales* 124 **wNC,** So that night the old doctor and his wife were a-layin' in the bed upstairs, heard somethin' rattle against the side of the house, looked over at the window, saw a head rise up and gouge against it.

3 To gobble, gorge (oneself). [Perh by confusion with *gorge*]

1965–70 *DARE* (Qu. H11a) Inf **OH**89, Gouges it down; (Qu. H11b) Inf **OH**71, Gouges himself; (Qu. DD17) Inf **MI**49, Gouges it down.

gouger, gouge stick See **gouge** n **2**

gouge up See **gouge** v **3**

goujon n |gu'žõ| [Fr "gudgeon"] **Missip Valley, esp LA** =**flathead catfish 1.**

1882 U.S. Natl. Museum *Bulletin* 16.102, Mud Cat; Yellow Cat; Bashaw; Goujon. . . Rivers of the Mississippi Valley and Southern States. . . A fish of unprepossessing appearance, although much used as food. **1884** *Ibid* 27.491, *Leptops olivaris*. . . Mud Cat; . . Goujon. Ohio and Mississippi Valleys. **1908** Forbes–Richardson *Fishes of IL* 193, Goujon. . . This huge catfish . . is common in the Illinois and the Mississippi rivers, . . and less often referred to as the "cushawn," a corruption of the French *goujon*. **1933** LA Dept. of Conserv. *Fishes* 425, The Yellow Cat or Goujon . . has been known to reach a weight of 100 pounds and is highly regarded as food. **1966** LA Wild Life Comm. *Hunting Fishing Regulations 1967–68* np, Yellow Cat or Opelousas Cat or Goujon. 14 inches minimum length. **1968** *DARE* (Qu. P1) Inf **LA34**, Goujon [ˌguˈʒɔ̃] or mud cat—a large catfish with large head. **1968** *DARE* FW Addit **LA34**, "You remind me of a goujon—all mouth and no brains." Said of someone who talks too much. **1983** Becker *Fishes WI* 728, *Pylodictis olivaris*. . . Other common names . . goujon.

goun See **go** v **A4b**

gound See **gown** n

go under v phr **orig West**

To die.

1848 (1855) Ruxton *Life Far West* 14, Thar was old Sam Owins—him as got 'rubbed out' by the Spaniards at Sacramenty, or Chihuahuy, this hos doesn't know which, but he 'went under' any how. [Footnote to *rubbed out* and *went under*:] Killed, Died . . both terms adapted from the Indian figurative language. **1850** Garrard *Wah-to-yah* 25 **SW**, By his saddle, the fattest "cow" that had "gone under" that trip. **1888** *Daily Inter-Ocean* March (Farmer *Americanisms*), All solemnly vowed to see that the mine should be worked solely for the benefit of the girl whether Jim lived or had gone under. **1891** (1905) Ryan *Told in Hills* 330 **nwWA**, Denny took it, . . and when Denny went under, I took it. **1905** *DN* 3.10 **CT**, *Go under*. . . Perish. **1907** *DN* 3.213 **nwAR**, *Go under*. . . To perish. **1910** Mulford *Hopalong* 98, I'll fight until th' last man goes under! **c1960** *Wilson Coll.* **csKY**, *Go under*. . . Fail or die.

gounsh v, n [Cf PaGer *gaunsche* to swing]

To swing, bounce; a swing.

1872 Haldeman *PA Dutch* 59, *Gounsh*. . . As *to seesaw* implies reciprocal motion, so *to gounsh* is to move up and down, as upon the free end of an elastic board. . . Come, let us gounsh. **1939** Aurand *Quaint Idioms* 15 [PaGer], Gee, how we used to go out and *gounsh* (swing, as on the tree; a swing).

go up the flume See **flume, up the 1**

gourd n Pronc-sp *go'd*

1 The dried shell of a gourd, esp one used as:

a A bottle, jar.

1612 Smith *Map VA* 10 **eVA**, A sweete oyle, which they keep in goards to annoint their heads and ioints. **1705** Beverley *Hist. VA* 3.7, One of her Hands rests in her Necklace of Peak, and the other holds a Gourd, in which they put Water, or other liquid. **a1883** (1911) Bagby *VA Gentleman* 268 (as of 1850), That negro came forward with . . *a gourd full of soft soap*—this home-made greasy, villainous stuff. **1899** (1912) Green *VA Folk-Speech* 203, *Gourd*. . . A dried and cleaned gourd-shell prepared for use as a bottle, or dipper, or other purposes. **1953** *PADS* 19.13 **sAppalachians**, *Salt gourd*. . . A gourd kept near the stove in which salt is kept.

b also *gourd(-shell) dipper:* A dipper or cup; by ext, any dipper.

1843 (1916) Hall *New Purchase* 183, With tin cups and greasy gourds they ladled out broth till all was exhausted. **1850** Judd *Richard Edney* 406, The gourd-dipper,—how often had he dipped water with it, and held it by both hands to drink! **1868** *Harper's New Mth. Mag.* 36.542/1, [We] asked for a drink of water. We were plentifully supplied from a gourd-shell dipper. **1892** (1893) Botume *First Days* 51 **seSC** (as of 1864), The whiteness and cleanliness of table and piggins [=tubs or buckets], and occasionally a "gourd" or tin dipper. **1899** Chesnutt *Conjure Woman* 20 **csNC** [Black], She . . po'd [=poured] some out in a go'd fer Henry ter drink. **1899** [see **1a** above]. **1905** Cole *Early OR* 26, Old "Doc" came around with a bucket of water on one arm, in which there was a gourd. **1908** *DN* 3.316 **eAL**, *Gourd*. . . Dipper: often used of ordinary tin or metal dippers. **1939** *LANE* Map 133 *(Tin cup)* 1 inf, **CT**, 'Old-timers used to have a gourd'; 1 inf, **CT**, 'Old folks used a gourd'; 1 inf, **MA**, A gourd with a wooden handle. **1965–70** *DARE* (Qu. F28) Infs **FL**17, **KY**60, **TX**43, **VA**42, Gourd; **TX**99, Gourd dippers; **LA**2, Water gourd; (Qu. G2) Inf **GA**70, Gourd—there are people who won't drink out of anything else; **OK**3, Had tin cups at wells years ago and gourd dippers before that.

c also *gourd-box:* A martin house. Cf **gourd martin**

1731 (1754) Catesby *Nat. Hist. Carolina* 1.51, *Hirundo purpurea. The Purple Martin*. . . They breed like Pigeons . . in Gourds hung on Poles for them to build in. **1870** W. Baker *New Timothy* 183 *(DAE)*, Dozens of gourds hang also suspended from the tops of long and leaning poles, each gourd the home of a family of martins. **1898** Harris *Tales Home Folks* 151, No sign of life, save two bluebirds, the pioneers of spring, that were fighting around the martin gourds, preparing to take possession. **1899** (1912) Green *VA Folk-Speech* 203, *Gourd-boxes*. . . Boxes made of dry gourds, and put up on walls of houses or on posts for martins and other small birds to build their nests in. **1942** (1960) Robertson *Red Hills* 59 **SC**, There was a gourd tree for the purple martins, and beehives, and there was a well with an oak bucket. **1960** Hall *Smoky Mt. Folks* 63, As straight as a marten to his (her) gourd (nest). **1975** *Foxfire 3* 208 **nwGA**, People in years back put up martin houses to entice the martins to stay . . during the summer to chase off chicken hawks. . . The primary reason people erect purple martin gourds . . now is to keep flying insects away from their gardens.

d also *(nest-)egg gourd:* A nest egg.

c1960 *Wilson Coll.* **csKY**, *Gourd* for a nestegg [=an artificial egg] was common. **1986** Pederson *LAGS Concordance* **Gulf Region** *(If you want to make a hen start laying, what do you put in her nest to fool her?)* 13 infs, (Nest-)egg gourd(s); 2 infs, Gourds—used for nest-eggs; 1 inf, Little gourds; 1 inf, Nest-eggs were gourds.

2 also *gourdhead:* The head.

a1844 in 1935 *Filson Club Hist. Qrly.* 9.226 **neKY**, Jesse Yocum, before the battle of the . . Blue Licks would fall out with his father, tree him, and tell him, now to show his damned old gourd. . . Were both behind trees. **1891** (1935) Twain *Slovenly Peter* 32, He never got it through his gourd,/ That he was walking overboard. **c1960** *Wilson Coll.* **csKY**, *Gourd*. . . Humorous name for one's head or mouth. **1965–70** *DARE* (Qu. X28, *Joking words . . for a person's head*) Infs **FL**31, **GA**7, 9, 77, **HI**8, **IL**7, 12, **IN**26, **LA**2, **MI**123, **PA**72, **SC**29, Gourd; **GA**59, **SC**34, **TN**23, Gourdhead.

3 in phrr *saw* (or *cut*) *gourds:* To snore loudly. **Sth, S Midl** See Map

1890 *DN* 1.65 **KY**, *Gourds*. . . To "saw gourds" is to snore furiously. **1909** *DN* 3.366 **eAL, wGA,** *Saw gourds*. . . To snore. Facetious. **1912** *DN* 3.588 **wIN**, *Saw gourds*. **1915** *DN* 4.189 **swVA**, *Saw on (one's) gourds*. . . To snore. **1926** *DN* 5.402 **Ozarks**. **1950** *PADS* 13.9 **AL, GA,** *Saw gourds*. . . When the day's work is done . . he can draw his bobtail night shirt about him . . knowin' that while he sleeps and dreams and saws gourds, his worldly possessions are growin'. **1952** Brown *NC Folkl.* 1.547, *Gourds, to saw*. . . To snore while asleep.—General. **c1960** *Wilson Coll.* **csKY**, *Saw gourds*. . . Snore loudly. **1965–70** *DARE* (Qu. X45) 43 Infs, **chiefly Sth, S Midl,** Sawing gourds; **LA**12, **NC**11, Gourds; **KY**11, Sawing the gourds; **MS**16, Cutting gourds.

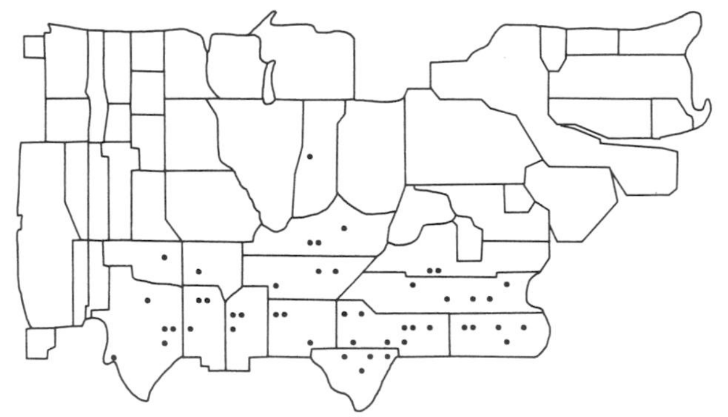

•gourd 3 + varr (Qu. X45)

gourd banjo n

A banjo made from a large gourd.

[**1960** Williams *Walk Egypt* 152, In the fall, too, children cut the largest and straightest-necked gourds for banjos.] **1980** *Foxfire 6* 54 **wNC**, Since Mr. Hodges is a concert violinist and violin maker, we were surprised to learn that his first musical instrument was a gourd banjo made for him when he was a small boy in the mountains of North Carolina by his grandfather. **1984** Gilmore *Ozark Baptizings* 50 **MO**, In Howell County two men furnished music played on a cornstalk fiddle and a gourd banjo.

gourd bird See **gourd martin**

gourd-box See **gourd 1c**

gourd bug n

A snout beetle (family Curculionidae).

1969 *DARE* FW Addit **neNC,** Gourd bug—insect with a long snout on it.

gourd calabash See **calabash gourd**

‡gourd cheese n

1966 *DARE* (Qu. H61, *Other kinds of homemade cheese;* total Infs questioned, 75) Inf **OK**51, Gourd cheese . . made by Italians—shaped like a gourd.

gourd corn See **gourdseed corn**

gourd dipper See **gourd 1b**

gourde n Also *gourde dollar* [LA Fr < Fr *(piastre) gourde* < Span *gordo* fat] **sLA**

A dollar.

c1867 Simmonds *Dict. Trade Products* 177/2, Gourde, a common name for the dollar. **1880** Cable *Grandissimes* 227 **LA,** Bras-Coupé . . in six months was the most valuable man ever bought for gourde dollars. [**1931** Read *LA French* 41, *Gourde*. . . In South Louisiana *gourde* "gourd," is used with the value of "dollar."] [**1984** Daigle *Dict. Cajun Lang.* 103, *Dollar*. . . gourde.]

gourd fiddle n Cf **gourd banjo**

A musical instrument made of a gourd and resembling a violin.

1858 Bennett *Chronology of NC* 102 (as of c1800), "Gourd fiddles" were then in vogue, "puncheon floors," and "corn-stalk bows!" **1941** Writers' Program *Guide AR* 325 (as of c1900), The bridal suite, when occupied, was serenaded by Negroes with gourd fiddles. **1945** FWP *Lay My Burden Down* 114 **LA** (as of 1860s), Some nigger women go back to the quarters and git the gourd fiddles and the clapping bones made outen beef ribs. [**1980** *Foxfire 6* 54 **cwNC,** His father and uncle had made gourd instruments. . . [He] remembered a photograph of them holding two such instruments, a fiddle and a banjo.]

gourdfish n

A **puffer** (here: *Arothron hispidus*).

1926 Pan-Pacific Research Inst. *Jrl.* 1.1.13 **HI,** Tetraodon hispidus. . . Oopuhue. Balloonfish; Gourd fish.

gourd gum n [**gourd 1** + **gum** n² **2**]

1906 *DN* 3.138 **nwAR,** *Gourd gum*. . . A hollow gourd larger than a pumpkin and used to contain meal, salt, or any similar commodity. Indian Territory.

gourd handles n pl Cf **long handles**

1965 *DARE* (Qu. W14, *Names for underwear, including joking names. Men's—long*) Inf **OK**1, Gourd handles.

gourdhead n

1 also sp *goardhead:* =**wood ibis.** [See quot 1955] **SE**

1911 *Forest & Stream* 77.174, *Mycteria americana.* Gourd Head, Gum Cove, La. In common use north to Missouri and Illinois. **1917** (1923) *Birds Amer.* 1.178, *Mycteria americana*. . . *Other Names*. . . Goard, or Gourd, Head. . . Bald head and neck. *Ibid* 179 **FL, sGA,** "Goard Head," . . and "Gannet" are the appellations given to these birds by many swamp-dwellers to whom the name Wood Ibis is unknown. **1917** *DN* 4.425 **LA,** *Flamant.* The wood ibis . . : also called *gourdhead.* **1932** Howell *FL Bird Life* 113, Wood Ibis. . . Gourdhead. **1946** Hausman *Eastern Birds* 113, *Wood Ibis*. . . Gourdhead or Goardhead. . . The head and neck bare, its skin dark and wrinkled. **1955** *Oriole* 20.1.3 **GA,** *Wood Ibis*. . . *Gourdhead* (from the shape of the bare head, including beak, the latter being the "neck" of the "gourd"). **1962** Imhof *AL Birds* 102, Gourdhead. . . This great white bird is almost as tall as the Great Blue Heron and is heavier.

2 =**whooping crane.**

1917 *Wilson Bulletin* 29.2.79, *Grus americana.*—Gourd head, . . Hickman, K[entuck]y.

3 See **gourd 2.**

gourdhead buffalo n Also *gourdseed buffalo* Cf **go-ahead n 2**

=**bigmouth buffalo.**

1902 Jordan–Evermann *Amer. Fishes* 39, In Louisiana, where they [=*Ictiobus cyprinellus*] are known as the gourdhead buffalo, they are of considerable commercial interest. **1933** LA Dept. of Conserv. *Fishes* 439, The Common Buffalofish . . has come to be known under many popular names . . enumerated here: Redmouth Buffalo . . Gourd Seed Buffalo . . Gourd Head Buffalo. **1983** Becker *Fishes WI* 615, *Ictiobus cyprinellus*. . . Other common names . . gourdseed buffalo, . . gourd-head buffalo.

gourd martin n Also *gourd bird* [**gourd 1c**] **Sth**

=**purple martin.**

1946 Hausman *Eastern Birds* 417, *Progne subis subis*. . . Gourd Martin. . . A common bird in the South, . . nesting in colonies, usually in martin houses or clusters of gourds set on high poles in the open. **1955** *Oriole* 20.10 **GA,** *Purple Martin*. . . *Gourd Martin* (from nesting in houses erected for it by man). **1962** Imhof *AL Birds* 369, Gourd Martin. [*Ibid* 370, The Purple Martin habitually nests in hollow gourds, which ordinarily are hung from a crossarm on a pole nine or more feet up from the ground.] **1966** *DARE* (Qu. Q14, . . *Other names . . for . . martin*) Inf **FL**16, Gourd bird. [There is] a saying 'Straight as a martin to his gourd.' **1969** Longstreet *Birds FL* 102, *Gourd Martin*. . . At one time they nested in hollow trees, but have adapted themselves so . . that they willingly use nesting boxes or gourds hung on poles.

gourdmouth See **gourdseed sucker**

gourdseed See **gourdseed corn**

gourdseed buffalo See **gourdhead buffalo**

gourdseed corn n Also *goardseed corn, gourdseed (maize), gourd corn* [See quot 1947] **chiefly Sth, S Midl**

A var of **Indian corn.**

1780 in 1930 Dunbar *Life* 73 **cLA,** Planted white Corn & goard Seed Corn. **1802** Drayton *View of SC* 137 **SC,** It consists of several varieties, of which the gourd and flint corn, are principally planted. The difference betwixt these kinds of corn, are, that the *gourd* is flowery, and wastes much in the grinding; whereas the *flint* is more hard and nourishing, and grinds more into grist. **1816** (1819) Thomas *Travels W. Country* 101 **IN,** The gourd seed corn is generally cultivated. . . The ears of this kind of corn are thick; and the grains so crowded as to be elongated like the seed of the gourd or calabash. **1826** in 1827 *Western Mth. Rev.* 1.313 **cLA,** Gourdseed maize as high as the waist. **1874** (1895) Eggleston *Circuit Rider* 14 **IN,** It was the long, yaller gourd-seed, and powerful easy to shuck. **1930** (1972) Cate *Our Todays* 209 **GA coast,** These negroes, they said, "would be provided with 3½ lbs. of pork or bacon and 10 qts. of gourd seed corn per week." **1947** St. Louis MO Bot. Garden *Annals* 34.15, The commonest name for these soft dents was 'Gourdseed,' since the flat kernels with a collapsed and more or less pointed tip resembled a pumpkin seed or gourd seed.

gourdseed sucker n Also *gourdmouth* **esp Missip Valley** Cf **pumpkinseed**

=**Missouri sucker.**

1878 U.S. Natl. Museum *Bulletin* 12.80 **TN,** *Cycleptus elongatus*. . . From the Cumberland at Nashville. This species is known as . . "Gourd-seed Sucker." **1887** Goode *Amer. Fishes* 436, The Black Horse . . , also called . . "Gourd-seed Sucker," . . is found in the river channels of the Ohio and Mississippi. **1889** *Century Dict.* 1422, *Cycleptus*. . . There is but one species, *C. elongatus,* . . common in the Mississippi valley, and popularly known as . . *gourd-mouth, gourdseed-sucker.* **1943** Eddy–Surber *N. Fishes* 108, Gourdseed Sucker. . . is highly esteemed as a food fish. **1983** Becker *Fishes WI* 611, *Blue Sucker*. . . Other common names . . gourdseed sucker.

gourd-shell dipper See **gourd 1b**

gourd snake n

An unidentified snake.

1968 *DARE* (Qu. P25) Inf **MO**16, Gourd snake. . . They're striped.

gourdy adj [See quot 1902]

Green; hence fig inexperienced, unsophisticated.

[**1902** Harben *Abner Daniel* 87, I'm as green as a gourd in business matters.] **1942** *AR Gaz.* (Little Rock) 3 May 5/2, "Gourdy"—green. **1953** Randolph–Wilson *Down in Holler* 249 **Ozarks,** *Gourdy*. . . Green, green as a gourd. . . Sometimes used figuratively, to mean countrified or unsophisticated. "Betty's a nice girl, but don't you think she's a little too gourdy for our crowd?" **1954** *Harder Coll.* **cwTN,** *Gourdy*. . . Green, green as a gourd.

gout n [*OED gout* sb.¹ 5 1503 →]

A lump of something semiliquid.

1899 (1912) Green *VA Folk-Speech* 203, *Gouts*. . . Lumps of clotted blood. "Gouts of blood." **1930** *AmSp* 6.98, *Gouts:* Mounds. "Under the trees gouts of snow lay like Indian mounds."

goutweed n

Std: a European umbelliferous plant *(Aegopodium podagraria)* naturalized in the U.S. Also called **bishop's weed 3, dwarf ash 3, goatsfoot, goatweed 1, snow-on-the-mountain**

gouty adj [*OED gouty* a. 3. b]

1899 (1912) Green *VA Folk-Speech* 203, *Gouty.* . . A thread full of knots, tangles, and kinks, is *gouty.*

gov See **governor**

government n Usu |'gʌvə(r)mənt|; in careful speech sometimes |'gʌvə(r)nmənt|; also |gʌvər'mɛnt, 'gʌvmənt, -mɪnt, 'gʌbmənt, 'gʌmmənt|; *old-fash* |'gɪvər,mənt|; for addit proncs see quots Pronc-spp *govrenment, gover-mint, gov'mint, guvment, guv'mer*

Std sense, var forms.

1905 *DN* 3.58 **eNE,** *Metathesis,* especially of *r,* is very frequent: . . *govrenment.* **1908** *DN* 3.280 **eAL, wGA,** Strong final accent is heard in many words of two or more syllables particularly those ending in . . *-ment:* . . [gəvɚ'mɛnt]. **1913** Kephart *Highlanders* 224 **sAppalachians,** In mountain dialect such words as . . government . . are accented on the last syllable, or drawled with equal stress throughout. **1933** *AmSp* 8.4.62 **Delmarva,** *Government* is [gʌvəmənt], [gʌvmənt], [gʌvɜmənt], [gʌvɜ̩rmənt], and [gʌvr̩nmənt]; and in these forms *-ment* may be [mɪnt]. **1933** [see **government cow**]. **1934** in 1944 *ADD* 262 **LA,** ['gʌ'bmənt]. Huey Long, radio. **1936** *AmSp* 11.156 **eTX,** *Government* [is] ['gʌvɚ,mɪnt], ['gʌvəmənt], and ['gʌ:vmənt]. *Ibid* 313 **Upstate NY,** In *government,* the first [n] may be dissimilated; in my records, the word appears 56 times with this [n] and 97 times without it; the word appears three times without [r], possibly by analogy with *governor.* **1940** Stuart *Trees of Heaven* 269 **KY,** I'm gittin tired of all this petticoat gover-mint you got us under. **1942** *AmSp* 17.151 **seNY,** Government—33 [infs use [ɚ]], 31 [infs use [ə]]. **1942** *Collier's* 12 Sept 15/1 **LA,** Miss Mildred was the guv'mer lady over at Benton. . . who worked for Uncle Sam himself. **1942** Hall *Smoky Mt. Speech* 41 **wNC, eTN,** The old pronunciation of *government* is said to have been ['gɪvɚ,mɛnt], which I heard only in jocular use. **1943** *LANE* Map 549, [Proncs of the type [gʌvmənt] and [gʌvəmənt] (sometimes in western New England also [gʌvɚmənt]) are about equally common throughout New England, and are often used interchangeably by the same informant. Proncs of the type [gʌvənmənt] (and, esp in western New England, [gʌvɚnmənt]) are considerably less common. Five infs gave proncs of the type [gʌmmənt] and three of [gʌbmənt]. For the last syllable [-mɪnt] is also occasionally found, esp in eastern and southeastern Massachusetts.] **1965–67** *DARE* (Qu. P35a) Inf **MN**2, Govemment; (Qu. X50) Inf **FL**22, ['gʌvɚmn̩t]; (Qu. AA21) Inf **ME**19, Guvermment. **1968** *DARE* Tape **AK**6, The US government ['gʌmmənt]. **1976** Garber *Mountain-ese* 36 **Appalachians,** *Guvment.* **1988** Pederson *LAGS Material,* [Proncs of *government* with retroflex *r* are disproportionately common among White infs, female infs, more educated and cultured infs, middle-class infs, and, though to a lesser extent, upper-class infs. Trisyllabic proncs in general show a similar though less striking bias (though sex is not a significant factor), while disyllabic proncs show the opposite bias. Proncs with syllabic *r* appear to be socially neutral.]

government beef n Also *government meat, governor's beef*

Also called **camp meat, county beef, farmer's beef, hemlock steak, mountain lamb, side-hill halibut, Uncle Sam's sheep, white-faced calf**

An illegally shot deer or its meat.

1967–69 *DARE* (Qu. P35a, *Names or nicknames for any deer shot illegally*) Inf **PA**180, Government beef; **MN**2, Government meat. **1976** *Green Bay Press-Gaz.* (WI) 31 Oct B/6 **WI** (as of 1920s), They made it the way many families did in those years. They lived off the land. They grew up eating deer, but everybody called it "government beef." **1982** *DARE* File **coastal ME,** Governor's beef: venison, usually shot out of season.

government cow n Also *government yearling* Cf **government beef**

1933 Rawlings *South Moon* 233 **nFL,** There were still immense areas that might be hunted during the open season. But it had seemed at first, with one section shut off by invisible lines, as though there were no other section worth hunting. The deer had come to be called "gov'mint cows" and "gov'mint yearlin's."

government house n [Perh alluding to toilets built under Work Projects Administration (1935–43)] Cf **courthouse 2, federal building**

1968–69 *DARE* (Qu. M21b, *Joking names for an outside toilet building*) Infs **IN**67, **OH**70, Government house.

government job n

Personal work done on company time.

1968 Adams *Western Words* 130, *Government job*—A logger's euphemism for a personal job that is done on company time. **1971** *Thompson Coll.* **MI, CA, GA** [Industry terms], Government job. . . A job done on company time for oneself or someone other than the company. [Thompson: heard in Detroit in the 1940s, Los Angeles in the 1960s, in Atlanta in 1971]

government meat See **government beef**

government socks n

See quots.

1923 *DN* 5.209 **swMO,** *Gover'ment socks.* . . The bare legs, i.e., no socks at all. **1953** Randolph-Wilson *Down in Holler* 249 **Ozarks,** *Government socks.* . . No socks at all. A farmer shows his bare foot and asks, "How do you like these here government socks we're all a-wearin' nowadays?"

government yearling See **government cow**

governor n Also *gov'ner, guv'nor;* abbrs *gov, guv*

1 A superior, boss. [*OED governor* sb. 7. a 1802 →]

1942 Berrey-Van den Bark *Amer. Slang* 388.4, *Principal or most important person; chief executive.* . . governor, guv, guv'nor. *Ibid* 624.24, *Circus manager.* . . governor. **1960** Wentworth-Flexner *Slang* 225, *Governor.* . . A superior; a manager or owner; one who governs. **1968** Adams *Western Words* 130, *Governor*—What the logger calls an employer, a superintendent, a manager, or a director.

2 One's father, grandfather, or husband. [*OED governor* sb. 7. b 1827 →]

1888 *TX Siftings* 25 Feb 11/2, A young man named Bartlett, who is widely known for his politeness and wit, never calls his father the "old man" or "governor," but always speaks of him as Bartlett *pére.*—Puck. **1912** Johnson, *Stover at Yale,* 223 (1960 Wentworth-Flexner *Slang*), An idea of the governor's [=speaker's father]. **1912** *Judge* 21 Dec np, [Cartoon:] *One on mother. The self-made man (emotionally)*—"There, children, that's the lil' old house where I first met your mother. I'm going to buy it and give it to her for a Christmas present." *Young hopeful*—"What's the joke, guv'nor?" **1941** *LANE* Map 371 *(Dad, pa)* 1 inf, **csME,** [gʌ˅vnə], used as a term of address. **1942** Berrey-Van den Bark *Amer. Slang* 446.11, *Father.* . . governor, guv, guv'nor. **1965–68** *DARE* (Qu. Z1, . . *Words* . . *for 'father' within the family*) Inf **PA**165, Governor; (Qu. Z3, . . *Words* . . *for 'grandfather'*) Inf **NJ**48, Gov; (Qu. AA23, *Joking names that a woman may use to refer to her husband*) Inf **PA**35, Governor. **1966** Dakin *Dial. Vocab. Ohio R. Valley* 2.419, The miscellaneous terms *the old man* (fairly common), *sire, (the) gov'ner,* and *pater* (only single instances of the last three) are all attested by informants as their actual usage.

3 See quot.

1983 *MJLF* 9.1.41 **ceKY,** *Governors* . . the testicles of livestock.

governor's beef See **government beef**

governor's gate n

1950 *PADS* 14.33 **SC,** *Governor's gate.* . . The gap left in a child's mouth where he has lost a front tooth. Also called *toll gate.*

governor's sauce n

1950 *WELS (Tasty or spicy side dishes served with meats)* 1 Inf, **WI,** Governor's sauce . . green tomato(es) with brown sugar.

govment, gov'mint See **government**

gov'ner See **governor**

govrenment See **government**

gow See **gowl**

go-wank n Also *go-wink* [Echoic] Cf **chewink** =**rufous-sided towhee** *(Pipilo erythropthalmus).*

1936 *Sun* (Baltimore MD) 17 Feb 7/2 *(Hench Coll.),* One side asserts it has seen "robins" hopping about in the snow; the opponents are scornful—they're not robins, but "go-wanks," or if that name fails to strike a responsive chord, they're towhees, . . chewinks, go-winks.

go 'way exclam Also *go 'way from here* Cf **get out** exclam
An expression of disbelief.
1922 Gonzales *Black Border* 160 [Gullah], "Ef uh 'tep 'puntop'um 'e gwine bite me." "Go 'way, man, snake ent gwine bite you w'en you hab muskick [=a musket] een you han'." **1942** McAtee *Dial. Grant Co. IN* 30 (as of 1890s), *Go 'way* . . exclamation of disbelief. **1965** *DARE* File **MS,** *Go 'way from here!* . . a typical response to unlikely or difficult to believe news. This is particularly common among the Negroes. **1968** *DARE* FW Addit **NY52,** *Go 'way* . . expression used when what somebody has said is silly or untrue.

go-'way bag n Also *go-'way sack* Cf **go-easter, go-poke**
A traveling bag or suitcase.
1917 *DN* 4.412 **wNC,** *Go-'way sack.* Satchel. Also *go-'way bag.* **1927** *AmSp* 2.355 **cwWV,** *Go-way bag* . . suit case. "He was carrying a go-way bag in his hand." **1967** Will *Dredgeman* 1 **FL,** Before you can say it twice, I'll have my little go-way bag packed.

go 'way from here See **go 'way**

go-'way sack See **go-'way bag**

gowdy n Also *goudy* [Perh *SND goudie* n[1] "A blow, a stroke"]
A beating, a hard time—usu in phrr *give one gowdy, catch gowdy.*
[**1851** Hall *College Words* 131 **VT,** The discomfited individual declares that they 'are all on a side,' and gives up, or 'rolls over' by giving his opponent 'gowdy.'] **1865** *Atlantic Mth.* 16.521, [Poem on the naval bombardment of Fort Henry:] It's a little cloudy,—/ Or rather, as one might say,/ *Smoky,* perhaps,—/. . . / But give 'em gowdy, give 'em gowdy,/ And it 'll soon clear away!/ Old Boss ain't to be balked.—/ All this, you know,/ Was only the way (or nearly so)/ The boys talked. **1899** Garland *Boy Life* 287 **nwIA,** "To-morrow—that's where we catch goudy," said Ben. "Oh, I don't know; it may rain," replied Lincoln. **1939** (1962) Thompson *Body & Britches* 503 **NY,** There is a phrase from Otsego County which uses a word that could be explained at Oxford: "If he doesn't do right, give him *gowdy.*"

gowel v [Pronc-sp for *gall*]
1950 Moore *Candlemas Bay* 44 **ME,** Ordinarily, it would have goweled Russ that another boat, even a picket boat, could move any faster than his.

go west v phr, hence ppl adj phr *gone west* Cf **go under**
To die.
1917 Dawson *Carry On* 78, Alive or "Gone West" I shall never be far from you. *Ibid* 85, So strange a havoc does this war work that, if I have to "Go West," I shall go *proudly.* **1918** *Lit. Digest* 26 Oct 55/1, One of your cigarets was smoked by a dying man. . . He praised your cigaret . . and quietly "went west." **1943** *LANE* Map 521 *(Kicked the bucket),* [9 infs gave the resp *went west;* two indicated that it was euphemistic rather than jocular.] **1960** Wentworth-Flexner *Slang* 226, Go west. . . To die. Orig. cowboy and Western use. Very common during W.W.I. **1970** *DARE* (Qu. BB56, *Joking expressions for dying*) Inf **VA52,** Go west; **TX6,** Went west.

go-wink See **go-wank**

gowk See **gawk** n

gowl n Also *gow* [PaGer *gaul* horse]
A horse. Note: Quot 1930 suggests that some speakers may use the word in var specialized senses; the two different forms probably represent proncs of different Infs.
1930 Shoemaker *1300 Words* 24 **cPA Mts** (as of c1900), *Gowl*—An entire horse or mare [sic]. *Ibid, Gow*—A gelding. **1935** *AmSp* 10.170 [English of PA Germans], *Gowl,* a horse. **1952** Brown *NC Folkl.* 1.547, *Gowl.* . . A horse.

gown n Usu |gaʊn|; (cf Pronc Intro 3.I.16); for varr see quot 1936 Pronc-spp, **esp NEng, Sth** *old-fash, geound, gound, gownd* (cf Intro "Language Changes" I.8)
Std sense, var forms.
1770 in 1967 *PADS* 48.39 **NC,** *Gound*—'gown.' **1781** *PA Jrl. & Weekly Advt.* (Philadelphia) 16 May 1/2, [In a list of vulgarisms more frequent in America than in England:] She has got a new gownd. **1815** Humphreys *Yankey in England* 105, *Gownd,* gown. **1867** Lowell *Biglow* xxx **'Upcountry' MA,** The Yankee, who omits the final *d* in many words, as do the Scotch, makes up for it by adding one in *geound.* **1899** (1912) Green *VA Folk-Speech* 203, *Gound.* . . Form of *gown.* **1923** (1946) Greer-Petrie *Angeline Doin' Society* 3 **csKY,** One of her *bleached* night gownds. **1936** *AmSp* 11.34 **eTX,** *Gown* [gjẽãʊ̃n], [gjẽæ̃ʊ̃n]; [gjɛ̃ãʊ̃n]; [gjɛ̃æ̃ʊ̃n]; [gjæ̃ãʊ̃n], [gjæ̃::ʊ̃n]; [gjĩãʊ̃n], [gjĩæ̃ʊ̃n].

gown v See **go** v **A7a**

gownd See **gown** n

Gown Man n
A folklore character; see quot.
1945 Saxon *Gumbo Ya-Ya* 77 **LA,** Another terror among the colored folk of New Orleans is the Gown Man. 'The Gown Man is tall and slim and wears a black cap and long black gown that reaches to the ground. He goes after the womens when they is alone. . . He has a long black automobile. . . He's a real mans, and not no ghost!' Not all the women agree. . . There are many who are certain he is a 'ghost.'

gown-tail n
See quots.
1951 *DE Folkl. Bulletin* 1.7/2, *Gown-tail* (probably a combination of "nightgown" and "shirt-tail"—as in "still in one's gown-tail," that is, not fully dressed yet). **1985** Ladwig *How to Talk Dirty* 30 **Ozarks,** She runs around in her gown-tail all mornin'. . . doesn't get dressed until noon.

gowrow n **Ozarks**
A fabulous monster.
1935 *Arcadian Life* June 18 **AR,** One member of the party . . took from his pocket a newspaper that told of William Miller's supposed experience with a gowrow of the goofus family in Searcy County thirty years ago. **1950** *AR Hist. Qrly.* 9.67, I have met elderly men in Missouri and Arkansas who publicly declared their belief that a few specimens of the gowrow may have survived into the present century. . . But whether these fellows were in earnest, I do not pretend to say.

gowster See **gauster**

go-yonders n pl Cf **down-yonders**
1967 *DARE* (Qu. BB19, *Joking names for looseness of the bowels*) Inf **TX20,** Go-yonders.

gozzle n
=**goozle n 1.**
1906 *DN* 2.138 **nwAR,** *Gozzle.* . . Throat. **1965-70** *DARE* (Qu. X7, *Other names for the throat: "Some food got stuck in his ______."*) 9 Infs, **scattered,** Gozzle; **MS73,** Gozzle pipe.

gozzle v [Var of *guzzle*] Cf **goozle v 1**
1966-68 *DARE* (Qu. DD17, . . *"He doesn't just drink, he ______."*) Infs **CA94, WV2,** Gozzles it (down); **GA1,** ['gɑzəlz].

grab v, hence vbl n *grabbing* **esp Sth, S Midl**
=**grabble v 2.** Note: Perh =**grabhook** v in some cases.
1954 *Harder Coll.* **cwTN,** *Grab* . . to catch fish . . "He's a-goin' to go grabbin' today." "He grabbed fish last night." **1965-70** *DARE* (Qu. P13, . . *Ways of fishing* . . *besides the ordinary hook and line*) Inf **MS25,** Grabbing or grabbling—search down in a stump for fish; **AR4,** Grabbing or grabbling; **AL38,** Grabbing—for red horse; **IN22, MS1,** 6, **NJ54, VA73,** Grabbing.

grab n
1 A fishing device consisting of several hooks fastened together with the points outward. Cf **grab** v
1946 in 1954 *Harder Coll.* **cwTN,** Mr. Grady Gooms and his boy caught about 50 pounds of fish with grabs down here at the creek below the cow lot, caught them in about 4 hours. **1954** [see **grabble** v **3**].
2 A device for catching crayfish; see quots.
1966 *DARE* (Qu. P13, . . *Ways of fishing* . . *besides the ordinary hook and line*) Inf **FL24,** Grabs—for catching crawfish—[the devices] grab it like a hand would. **1966** *DARE* Tape **FL24,** We do the same thing with the grabs. You have a grab nailed on your pole, an' you have . . a long string that runs up to the end of your pole that trips your grab.
3 See quot.
1939 *Hall Coll., Grabs*—paws. "The bear was hung on a laurel by the grabs."
4 A small general store, often a company store; among railroaders: a commissary car.
1934 (1940) Weseen *Dict. Amer. Slang* 80 [Loggers' and miners' slang], *Grab*—A company store. **1946** Nixon *Lower Piedmont* 138, Railroad section workers used to refer to a commissary rigged up in a moving car as "the grab." **1960** Wentworth-Flexner *Slang* 226, *Grab, the.* . . The main store or meeting place in a small town. *Dial. and archaic.* **1968**

DARE (Qu. U1a, *When you are going to a store or several stores to buy things, you say, "I'm going ______.")* Inf **GA**28, To the grab; (Qu. U1b, . . *If you're buying groceries*) Inf **GA**28, To the grab.

5 also *grab-all, grab-ass:* A stingy or greedy person. Cf **grabber 2**

1942 Berrey–Van den Bark *Amer. Slang* 400.1, *Selfish or greedy person*. . . Grab-all. **1954** *Harder Coll.* **cwTN,** *Grab-all* . . a stingy person. "He's an old grab all, takes ever'thing in sight, 'n' more too." . . *Grab-ass* . . a stingy person. **1968–69** *DARE* (Qu. U36b, . . *A person who saves in a mean way or is greedy in money matters: "She certainly is ______.")* Inf **NY**37, A grab-all; (Qu. U17, . . *A person who doesn't pay his bills*) Inf **TX**74, Grab, moocher.

6 See quot. Cf **catch n 1.**

1967 *DARE* (Qu. F11, *The thing you use to remove the lids . . from a wood-burning stove when it is hot*) Inf **TX**35, Grab.

grab-all See **grab n 5**

grab-and-gallop lunch counter See **grab-it-and-growl n**

grab-ass See **grab n 5**

grab baits (and run) See **grab dates (and run)**

grabber n

1 also *lunch grabber:* A hand. *joc*

1942 Berrey–Van den Bark *Amer. Slang* 121.54, *Hands* . . grabbers. **1950** *WELS (Joking or uncomplimentary names for the hands)* 3 Infs, **WI,** Grabbers; 1 Inf, **WI,** Lunch grabbers. **1969** *DARE* (Qu. X32) Inf **GA**84, Grabbers. **1970** Major *Dict. Afro-Amer. Slang* 61, *Grabbers:* the hands.

2 =grab n 5.

1942 Berrey–Van den Bark *Amer. Slang* 400.1, *Selfish or greedy person*. . . Grabber. **1965–70** *DARE* (Qu. U36a, . . *A person who saves in a mean way or is greedy in money matters: "He's an awful ______.")* Infs **IA**30, **NJ**14, **OH**6, **PA**242, **VA**106, Grabber; (Qu. U36b) Infs **CA**101, **CT**30, **MI**35, Grabber; (Qu. U17, . . *A person who doesn't pay his bills*) Inf **RI**15, Grabber. **1969** *DARE* Tape **MA**57, This [man] was what we call a grabber. He grabbed Orleans, and Eastham, and Harwich. . . He just took what he wanted.

3 A railroad conductor.

1931 *Writer's Digest* 11.41 [Railroad terms], *Grabber*—Conductor. **1936** (1947) Mencken *Amer. Lang.* 583, To [hoboes] a conductor is . . a grabber. **1939** FWP *ID Lore* 245, *Grabber*—conductor. **1945** Hubbard *Railroad Ave.* 345, *Grabber*—Conductor of a passenger train. (He grabs tickets).

4 See quot.

1967 *DARE* (Qu. C26, . . *Special kinds of stone or rock* . . *in this part of the state*) Inf **AL**14, *Grabbers* . . big round rock—some white, some grey, red.

grabbing See **grab v**

grabbing the apple See **grab the apple**

grabble v [*OED grabble* v. 1 "To feel or search with the hands, to grope about"; 1579–80 →]

1 also *gravel:* To dig, esp with the hands; to dig up (potatoes, or rarely peanuts) so as to leave the plant intact; hence n *grabbler.* **chiefly Sth, S Midl**

c1770 in 1833 Boucher *Glossary* 50 **MD,** Our man-boy, Jack, did, in his *new-ground patch / A runaway* a' *grabbling 'moodies* [=sweet potatoes] catch. **1869** [see **goober-grabber**]. **1884** *Anglia* 7.275 **Sth, S Midl** [Black], *To grabble 'mungs* = to dig among. **1888** Jones *Negro Myths* 122 **GA coast,** Buh Rabbit duh . . grabble onder de bottom er de pole, tel eh mek hole big nough, an den eh slip out. **1895** *DN* 1.389 **AR,** *Grabble:* in digging potatoes, to remove the large ones without disturbing the small. **1899** (1912) Green *VA Folk-Speech* 203, *Grabble*. . . To dig out of the ground with the hands. **1903** *DN* 2.315 **seMO,** I grabbled some new potatoes this morning. **1905** *DN* 3.81 **nwAR,** *Grabble potatoes*. . . To dig potatoes, taking only the largest. **1908** *DN* 3.316 **eAL, wGA,** I was grabbling potatoes with a table fork. *Ibid* 317, *Grabbler*. . . One who grabbles or digs with the fingers. **1909** *DN* 3.397 **nwAR,** *Grabble, gravel*. . . To take sweet or Irish potatoes from the ground before they are grown. **1914** *DN* 4.107 **KS,** *Gravel, v. t.* and *i.* To grabble (potatoes). **1917** *DN* 4.412 **IL, KS, wNC,** *Grabble*. . . To dig up a few of the best (potatoes) and smooth back the dirt. **1923** *DN* 5.209 **swMO,** *Grabble*. . . To remove potatoes or peanuts from a hill without disturbing the plant. **1927** *AmSp* 2.356 **wcWV,** *Grabble* . . to dig in a hill, take out a part of the contents, and smooth the dirt back over the remainder. "We had grabbled enough potatoes for dinner." **1944** *PADS* 2.9 **cAL, NC, VA,** *Grabble* ['græbl̩, 'grævl̩]. . . To take a few potatoes from the hill without disturbing the rest. **1946** *PADS* 6.15 **NC,** *Grabble*. . . To finish digging with the hands potatoes that have been turned up by a turning plow. **1953** Randolph–Wilson *Down in Holler* 249 **Ozarks,** *Grabble*. . . To get potatoes out of a hill without uprooting the plant. People in the Ozarks do not *dig* their potatoes until late in the season, but they often *grabble* a few little ones in June. **1954** *Harder Coll.* **cwTN,** *Grabble* . . dig (potatoes). **c1960** *Wilson Coll.* **csKY,** Gravel potatoes. . . To dig new potatoes out of the hill, usually with a table fork. Gravel seems to be more common [than grabble] for this idea. **1966–69** *DARE* Tape **SC**15, [FW:] What do they [=sea turtles] do with them hands? [Inf:] Got a hand, dey grabble dis hole, dey lay dem egg—big hole, and sit ready in it; **GA**51, [The turtles would] come out 'n' grabble a hole. Now that's somethin' interestin' to watch . . watch them dig their hole and lay their eggs. **1976** Garber *Mountain-ese* 36 **Appalachians,** We went to gravel new potatoes but they warn't big enough to cook. **1983** *MJLF* 9.1.41 **ceKY,** *Grabble* . . to dig more or less ripe potatoes out of the hill one at a time before the potatoes all get ripe.

2 also *grapple:* To fish with one's hands; to fish by hand for; hence vbl nouns *grabbling, grappling.* [Engl dial; cf *EDD grabble* v. 1, *grapple* v. 2, *OED grabble* v. 1 quots 1630, 1869] **Sth, S Midl** Cf **handfish, noodle, tickle**

1950 *PADS* 13.17 **TX,** *Grabble*. . . To catch fish with the hands. **1954** *PADS* 21.29 **SC,** *Grabble*. . . To grope underwater along the banks of a stream to catch fish. "To grabble for cats." **c1960** *Wilson Coll.* **csKY,** *Grabble*. . . To catch fish with the bare hands in drifts actual or made to form a place of refuge for the fish. **1965–70** *DARE* (Qu. P13, . . *Ways of fishing* . . *besides the ordinary hook and line*) Infs **AR**4, 56, **GA**76, **KY**86, **TX**42, Grabbling; **SC**34, Grabbling—feel under rocks at the shoals and catch fish; **IN**31, **NY**34, **VT**16, Grappling; **TX**68, Grappling—with hands. **1971** GA Dept. Ag. *Farmers Market Bulletin* 8 Sept 1/2, An old automobile tire can be used to catch fish. . . The Game and Fish Commission . . advised that catfish are prone to go into things such as this. . . [T]he person does grappling (or grabbing) the fish from the old tire with their hands. **1978** *Capital Times* (Madison WI) 7 Aug 25/1 **cMS,** Wrestling a 50-pound catfish is Tom Cleveland's idea of fun . . [he] takes to Mississippi lakes on weekends to "grabble" catfish out of their watery homes. **1981** *High Coll.* **ceKY** (as of c1930), *Grabble* . . used in the Gorge as part of the phrase, *grabbling for catfish,* meaning to pull catfish by hand from under rocks and from holes while they're nesting in June—an illegal practice. . . "*Grabbling for catfish* is against the law, and I wouldn't do it myself, but I wouldn't turn people in for it." **1984** Wilder *You All Spoken Here* 38 **Sth,** Grabble: Find by working the fingers, as in . . catching trout in mountain pools.

3 =grabhook v. [Engl dial; cf *EDD grabble* v. 3, *grapple* v. 3] Cf **grapple n**

1954 *Harder Coll.* **cwTN,** *Grabble* . . to fish by use of a grab or grapnel.

grabble n See **grapple**

grabbler See **grabble v 1**

grabbling See **grabble v 2**

grab, by See **grabs, by**

grab dates (and run) v phr Also *grab baits* (or *stakes*) *(and run)* Cf **date n**

In marble play: to take all the marbles and leave; also n *grab-baits-and-run* the act of so doing.

1934 *AmSp* 9.75 **ND,** *Grab-baits-and-run.* A contemptible act in which one grabs all the marbles and runs, as when the bell ending recess rings. **1942** Berrey–Van den Bark *Amer. Slang* 665.4, *Grab baits* or *dates (and run),* of a player . . to grab all the marbles in the ring and run. **1955** *PADS* 23.19 **cwTN,** *Grab baits (-stakes, -dates) (and run)*. . . To pick up all the marbles in the ring when something happens which indicates that the game will be stopped.

‡grab dinner n

1966 Peden *Land* 19 **cIN,** Before Mother got back we had a "grab" dinner, in which all leftovers were put on the table and everybody sat down. The rule was you had to take out and eat a serving of anything set in front of your plate, then you could pass it on to anyone you chose, not necessarily the person next to you.

‡grabenheimer n [Cf **grab n 5, wisenheimer**] **=grab n 5.**

1968 *DARE* (Qu. U36a, . . *A person who saves in a mean way or is greedy in money matters: "He's an awful ______.*") Inf **MD6**, Grabenheimer ['græbn̩ˌhaɪmɚ].

grab-fishing vbl n Cf **grab n 1, grabhook v**

?Catching fish with an unbaited hook.

1970 *DARE* (Qu. P13, . . *Ways of fishing . . besides the ordinary hook and line*) Inf **TN65**, Grab fishing—heavy pole, hook attached to it; **VA35**, Grab fishing. **1986** Pederson *LAGS Concordance*, 1 inf, **csTN**, Grab fishing—in spring when they are numerous.

grab-gutted adj

1902 *DN* 2.235 **sIL**, *Grab-gutted*. . . Greedy; selfish.

grabhook n

1 Perh a fishhook with multiple points.

1966 *DARE* Tape **GA3**, Take your two sections of grab hooks 'n' put 'em about 4 inches apart, and with a small pork rind or a small piece of fat meat, and hitch it on that two hooks.

2 A hand. *joc*

1946 McAtee *Dial. Grant Co. IN Suppl. 3* 5 (as of 1890s), *Grabhook* . . hand; "Keep your grabhooks off of me." **1966** *DARE* (Qu. X32, *Joking or uncomplimentary words for the hands—you might say, "Those are mine. You keep your ______ [out of them].*") Inf **GA13**, Grabhooks.

grabhook v, hence vbl n *grabhooking*

To catch fish by dragging one or more unbaited hooks through the water.

1902 U.S. Bur. Fisheries *Rept. for 1901* 27.276 **WV**, Some of them [=fish] were caught by what we call grab-hooking, which is to tie a number of hooks to a line and drag it through the water. **1976** Garber *Mountain-ese* 36 **Appalachians**, *Grab-hook* . . snare fish—We grab-hooked a mess uv fish down at the crick.

grab in v phr

To get busy.

1904 Day *Kin o' Ktaadn* 59 **ME**, Ase waited, let things work along to the right notch, an' then he grabbed in on *Absent-minded Heseki' Shaw* [=a poem]. **1914** *DN* 4.73 **ME, nNH**, Grab in! Get busy!

grab iron n

In railroading and logging: a steel handhold.

1940 Cottrell *Railroader* 127, *Grab iron*—Steel bar, used as a hand hold, required by I.C.C. regulations to be firmly attached to cars and engines as a safety measure. **1945** in 1953 Botkin–Harlow *Treas. Railroad Folkl.* 346, A curved grabiron which . . helped swing a know-how brakeman up the step of a moving string of cars. **1958** McCulloch *Woods Words* 73 **Pacific NW**, *Grab iron*—Any iron handle by which a man climbs on or hangs on to a piece of equipment.

grab it and growl v phr

1966 *DARE* (Qu. H8, *When you are having company for a meal and you want them to take their places at the table, you say ______*) Inf **GA13**, Grab it and growl.

grab-it-and-growl n Also *grab-and-gallop lunch counter*

A diner, lunch counter.

1935 Davis *Honey* 37 **OR**, She was running the kitchen and tending a grab-and-gallop lunch-counter for an average of forty men a day. **1966** *DARE* (Qu. D39, . . *A small eating place where the food is not especially good*) Inf **SD5**, Grab-it-'n'-growl.

grab onto v phr **chiefly Upper MW, N Cent** See Map

To appropriate, latch onto.

1965–70 *DARE* (Qu. V5b, *If you take something that nobody seems to own, you might say, "Before anybody else gets it, I'm going to ______ this.*") 18 Infs, **chiefly Upper MW, N Cent**, Grab onto.

grabs, by intj Also *by grab, good grabs* [Euphems for *by* (or *good*) *God*]

Used as an expression of surprise or annoyance.

1898 Harris *Tales Home Folks* 262 **GA**, We ain't dead, by grabs, and nowheres nigh it. **1906** *DN* 3.138 **nwAR**, *Grabs*. . . In the mild imprecation, "by grabs." "By grabs, he did it too." **1908** *DN* 3.317 **eAL, wGA**, *Grabs*. . . Used in minced oaths, as 'by grabs,' 'good grabs,' etc. **1959** *VT Hist.* new ser 27.139 **VT**, *By Grab!: interj.* Rare. **1971** Jennings *Cowboys* 171 **MT, WY** (as of 1877), By grab, if that ain't the ugliest damn child I ever laid eyes on in my whole gol-dang life!

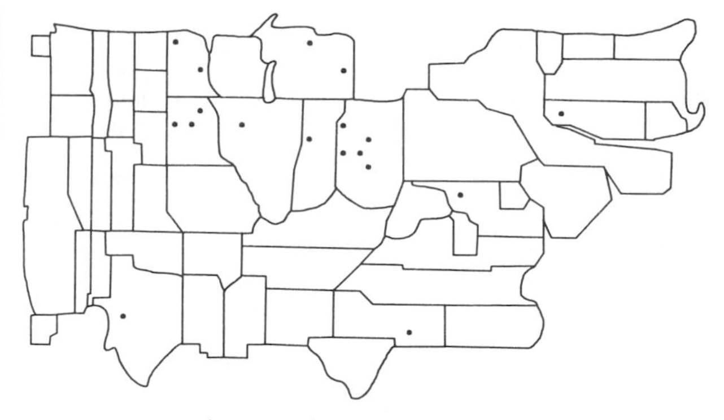

•grab onto (Qu. V5b)

grab stakes (and run) See **grab dates (and run)**

grab the apple v phr, hence vbl n *grabbing the apple* Also *grab the nubbin, ~ post* **[apple n 1] West**

To hang on to the horn of a saddle while riding.

1937 *DN* 6.619 **swTX**, When the bronco pitches . . [t]he cowboy violates the rules of the game if he catches hold of the pommel or any part of the saddle in order to stay on the pitching horse; and if he does so the spectators say he is *squeezing the biscuit, shaking hands with grandma, grabbing the nubbin,* or *reaching for the apple.* **1941** Writers' Program *Guide WY* 462, *Grabbin' the apple*—Grabbing the horn of the saddle to hang on. **1944** Adams *Western Words* 131, *Grabbin' the apple*—Catching the saddle horn while riding. *Ibid, Grabbin' the nubbin'* [sic]. . . *Grabbin' the post.* **1949** Emrich *Wild West Custom* 165 **West**, Among the cowboys, the expert horsemen bragged that they never . . *grabbed the apple,* holding on to the saddlehorn on a rough horse.

grab the bacon n Cf **duck on a rock**

1968 *DARE* (Qu. EE18, *Games in which the players set up a stone, a tin can, or something similar, and then try to knock it down*) Inf **AL42**, Grab the bacon.

grab the flag n

A children's sidewalk game.

1975 Ferretti *Gt. Amer. Book Sidewalk Games* 212, Another rough-house game is *Grab the Flag,* in which the flag is a white handkerchief stuck into a player's belt behind his back and left dangling. It is limited to two players but challengers can stand in line to play the winner. Like wrestlers, the two flag holders circle each other, arms extended, and try quick grabs at the handkerchiefs.

grab the nubbin (or post) See **grab the apple**

grabworm See **grubworm 1**

gracias exclam [Span] **scattered, but chiefly SW** See Map

Thank you.

1965–70 *DARE* (Qu. II39, *What other ways do you have of saying 'Thank you'?*) 40 Infs, **scattered, but chiefly SW,** (Muchas *or* mucho) gracias. **1990** *DARE* File **csWI**, "Here's the pole." "Gracias." [Speaker from Chicago]

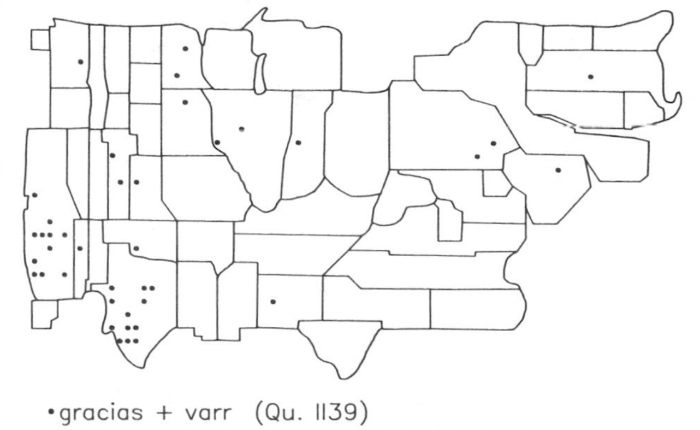

•gracias + varr (Qu. II39)

gracious adj
Very large, great.
1940 (1941) Bell *Swamp Water* 49 **Okefenokee GA,** I been thinking. They's one gracious heap of coon and otter in this here place. I could bring us some traps in here. *Ibid* 134, He may like to be snapped at every time he turns on his heels, but as fer me, I got a gracious sufficiency of it. **1986** Pederson *LAGS Concordance,* 1 inf, **cnFL,** A gracious lot—of plum trees.

grackle n Pronc-spp *cackle, crackle*
A Forms.
1965–70 *DARE* (Qu. Q11, . . *Kinds of blackbirds*) Infs **GA**35, **MI**104, **NC**36, **NH**14, **VT**4, **WI**12, Crackle; **VA**47, Gray crackle; **NY**83, Purple crackle; **NY**211, Purple cackle.
B Sense.
Std: a bird of the family Icteridae: see **boat-tailed grackle, Florida grackle, purple grackle.**

grade n
A road with a relatively even but usu steep gradient.
1867 Richardson *Beyond the Mississippi* 26 **cwMO** (as of 1857), On the hill above, where 'the Grade' was being cut fifteen or twenty feet deep, through abrupt bluffs. **1894** Robley *Hist. Bourbon Co.* 14 **seKS,** The military road from Fort Leavenworth was completed about 1843. The pike, or grade, like a railroad grade, was constructed across all river and creek bottoms. **1958** McCulloch *Woods Words* 73 **Pacific NW,** *Grade*. . . A hill. **1968** *DARE* Tape **CA**79, The road was turning icy. They decided to return home, rather than try climbing the Poway Grade; **CA**87, Down on Eagle Peak Grade, that's one of the grades that let out of the country here . . it's steep. **1979** *DARE* File **cwCA,** When teenagers in my hometown were learning to drive, a good test of their skill was to go over Wolfe Grade at night. The two-lane road was narrow, and it wound steeply up and then down the other side of a good-sized hill.

grade adj, also used absol [By ext from *grade* having an admixture of purebred blood]
Of a domestic animal: not purebred; hence, of uncertain or low quality.
1968–70 *DARE* (Qu. J1, . . *A dog of mixed breed*) Inf **MN**12, Grade—a non-registered cattle [FW: Inf also would use for a dog]; (Qu. K43, *A horse that was not intentionally bred, or bred by accident*) Inf **IL**125, Pasture bred; grade horse. **1984** Wilder *You All Spoken Here* 57 **Sth,** Pot licker, grade dog: A hunting dog without claim to registration papers.

grade door n Also *grade entry* [*grade* ground level]
See quots.
1950 *WELS Suppl.* 1 Inf, **scWI,** *Grade door:* Cellar door—"It's right even with the ground." **1984** *MJLF* 10.150 **cnWI,** *Grade entry.* A house door level with the ground, off to one side or in the back, used by the family when coming in from work. Keeps dirt out of the parlor, etc.

grader ditch n Also *grader furrow, grading ditch* **chiefly Sth, S Midl**
A ditch beside a graded road.
c1950 *Atlas Checklists* **MO,** Grader ditch. . . Ditch by the side of a graded road. *Ibid* **WI. 1965–70** *DARE* (Qu. N24, *A ditch along the side of a graded road*) Infs **AL**14, **KS**5, **MS**1, **MO**1, 2, 5, **WV**14, 16, 17, Grader ditch; **NC**21, Grader furrow; **FL**48, Grading ditch. **1967** *Smith Co. Pioneer* (Smith Center KS) 26 Oct 1/6, He dodged a cow . . and his car went into the right grader ditch. **1971** Wood *Vocab. Change* 53 **Sth,** *Grader ditch,* the second preference in Florida [after *ditch*] is chosen in about the same degree in Georgia, Arkansas, and Oklahoma.

grading house n Also *grading shed*
=strip house.
1967–70 *DARE* (Qu. M22, . . *Kinds of buildings . . on farms around here*) Inf **VA**7, Grading house—tobacco; **VA**49, Grading house; **TN**10, Grading shed—for tobacco; stripping tobacco is called "grading" here.

graduate v Usu |'græǰuet, 'græǰəwet|; for varr see quot 1942
Pronc-sp *gradjate*
Std sense, var forms.
1891 *PMLA* 6.167 **WV,** *Gradjate* and *sosation* [=association] are vulgarisms. **1942** Hall *Smoky Mt. Speech* 67 **eTN, wNC,** Graduate ['grædʒəeɪt]. . . *Graduate* was heard once as ['grædʒɪeɪt].

graff v [Var of *grasp*] Cf **grafty**
1922 Gonzales *Black Border* 257 **sSC, GA coasts** [Gullah], W'en e' graff at de rokkoon, please Gawd, de limb couldn' specify, en de limb bruk. [=When he grabbed at the raccoon, please God, the limb couldn't stand the strain and broke.]

graft n [By assoc with the horticultural process]
1954 Jordan *Hell's Canyon* 68 **ID,** Len called me to see a "graft." Sam was slipping the skin taken from a dead lamb onto a big twin whose mother was overburdened with two babies. Then Sam presented the changeling to the mother of the dead lamb.

‡graft widow n [Cf **grass widow 1**]
1967 *DARE* (Qu. AA26, *A divorced woman*) Inf **TN**15, Graft widow.

grafty adj Cf **graff**
Stingy, miserly.
1970 *DARE* (Qu. U36b, *Words . . to describe a person who saves in a mean way or is greedy in money matters: "She certainly is ______ ."*) Infs **FL**48, **MO**23, Grafty. [Both Infs Black]

graham bread n Also *graham flour bread* [Sylvester *Graham* (1794–1851) dietary reformer] **chiefly Nth, N Midl** See Map *somewhat old-fash* Cf **corn bread 1**
Bread made from whole wheat flour.
1834 *Sun* (NY NY) 20 Aug 2/3, The employer . . observed with astonishment that the mason had built about two feet of the wall with loaves of *Graham bread.* **1834** *Knickerbocker* 4.305, 'Hail' said I, 'thou pure, unadulterated substitute—*Graham bread!*' **1877** Ward *Story of Avis* 63 **ceMA,** Aunt Chloe held it to be impossible that any woman could make home happy without being able to make good Graham bread. **1941** *LANE* Map 281 *(Wheat bread)* 38 infs, **NEng,** Graham bread. **1955** Warren *Angels* 20 **cnOH,** Then Miss Idell cut it again, and said how at Oberlin they ate nothing but Graham bread and water. **1965–70** *DARE* (Qu. H18, . . *Special kinds of bread made now or in past years*) 42 Infs, **chiefly Nth, N Midl,** Graham bread; **CO**7, Graham flour bread; (Qu. H15, *Bread made with wheat flour*) 28 Infs, **chiefly Nth, N Midl,** Graham bread. [54 of 63 Infs old]

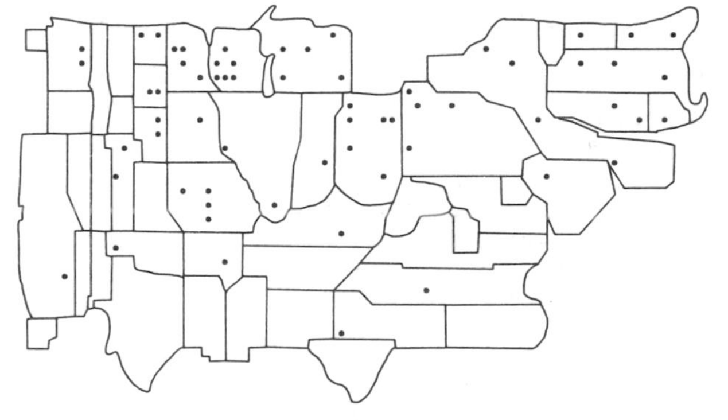

•graham bread + var (Qq. H18, H15)

grain n
1 A whit, a bit—used adverbially, often in phr *a little grain;* see quots. **now esp S Midl**
1858 Hammett *Piney Woods Tavern* 138 **seCT,** Planter's Hotel . . a leetle grain ahead of any house I ever stopped at, for good livin'. **1864** (1868) Trowbridge *3 Scouts* 24 **NEng,** Wal, to state it mild, I was a leetle grain disappinted. **1884** Baldwin *Yankee School-Teacher* 173 **VA** [Black], I wa'n't startled a grain. *Ibid* 176 [Black], An' wheder de Presb'terians b'lieve in hants or not don't matter a grain t' Jurdan an' me. **1901** Harben *Westerfelt* 287 **nGA,** Well, I don't know but I'm a leetle grain sorry. **1907** Wright *Shepherd* 76 **Ozarks,** 'Pears like you might o' been a grain warmer about hit. **1923** (1946) Greer–Petrie *Angeline Steppin'* 37 **csKY,** Hit may be the feller is a leetle grain foolish. **1939** *Hall Coll.* **eTN,** They (the bees) got so they wouldn't swell him nary a grain. *Ibid,* Hit looks a grain rainy tonight. **1955** Ritchie *Singing Family* 107 **seKY,** I could tell you're a Ritchie . . , but just which one was a-puzzling me a little grain.
2 A very small amount. **esp S Midl**
1950 *PADS* 14.33 **SC,** *Grain.* . . A drop of liquid. A fever patient begs for "just one grain of water to cool my parched mouth." **1952** Brown *NC Folkl.* 1.547, *Grain.* . . The least bit; a very small amount; generally of the abstract.
3 Courage, "grit."

1970 *DARE* (Qu. GG37, *Somebody who is very brave or courageous: "He's got plenty of______."*) Inf **SC**69, Grain.

4 See quot.

1969 Sorden *Lumberjack Lingo* 49 **NEng, Gt Lakes,** *Grain*—Beans.

grain v

1 To scrape, abrade. [By ext from *grain* to scrape a hide in tanning]

1845 Hooper *Advent. Simon Suggs* 197 **AL,** It took raal nice judgment to keep the infernal hook outen my meat; it grained the skin several times. **1857** Hammond *Wild N. Scenes* 330, Spalding's bullet had grazed its belly, raking off the hair and graining the skin. **1923** *DN* 5.209 **swMO,** *Grain*. . . To abraid [sic] slightly, as the skin in shaving. **1938** Stuart *Dark Hills* 101 **neKY,** The hard rocks that he had fallen on had grained and bruised the skin on his stomach.

2 rarely with *on:* To feed grain to (livestock). **esp Nth**

1852 (1971) Melville *Pierre* 30 **NEast,** No one grained his steeds, but himself. **1874** VT State Bd. Ag. *Rept. for 1873–74* 2.406, Older sheep should be grained the first of the season, after which they may do without till the first of March. **1913** *DN* 4.55 **ME,** *Grain*. . . To feed grain to (an animal). "Go, grain the cows, Jimmy." **1914** *DN* 4.152 **ME,** Butter has gone up now because we have to grain the cows. **1923** *DN* 5.209 **swMO. 1951** Porter *Ragged Roads* 26 **OK,** Job allowed his team would stand because he hadn't been grainin' 'em lately. **1969** *DARE* (Qu. K60, *When somebody is going to give the pigs food, he says, "I'm going to ______."*) Inf **MI**107, Grain 'em. **1970** *DARE* Tape **MI**116, We don't grain too awful heavy on 'em. . . We don't try to get a prime grade of beef. **1982** Brooks *Quicksand* 195 **swUT** (as of c1916), To *grain* the horses, *slop* the pigs, and *strip* the cows.

graine à voler n Also *graine à volet, ~ de volet* [See quot 1967] **LA**

=**water chinquapin** or its seed.

1921 LA Dept. of Conserv. *Bulletin* 10.58 **LA,** American lotus (*Nelumbo lutea:* known locally as "graine a voler"). [**1931** Read *LA French* 221, In the French language of Louisiana there are numerous descriptive terms that attest the quick wit and the ready imagination of Creole and Acadian . . *graines à volée*.] **1967** LeCompte *Word Atlas* 238 **seLA,** The seeds of the water lotus . . *Graine à volet* (flying seeds) are so named because they pop with great force from the ripe lotus seed pod. **1968** *DARE* FW Addit **LA**32, Graine de volet [ˌgræn də ˈvoʊˌleɪ]—Yonkapin, a kind of water lily. The French term is most common here.

grainery See **granary**

grainkind n Cf *DJE breadkind*

1950 *PADS* 14.33 **scSC,** *Grainkind*. . . Hominy or rice served as a cereal. "You ain't goin' to have no grainkind today?"

grain on See **grain** v **2**

grain room n **chiefly NEng** See Map

A storage place for grain; usu in a barn.

1931–33 *LANE Worksheets* **seCT,** Now people have a grain room. **1939** *LANE* Map 105 *(Granary; grain room; grain bin)* 50 infs, **throughout NEng,** Grain room. [Three infs said that it was in the barn; two Cape Cod infs that it was a separate building.] **1965–70** *DARE* (Qu. M6, *The place where grain is kept in a barn*) 15 Infs, **chiefly NEng,** Grain room; (Qu. M12, *What do you keep food for the cattle in over winter?*) Inf **NH**5, Grain room. **1989** Mosher *Stranger* 45 **nVT** (as of 1952), Beyond the woodshed were Mom's chicken house, a tool and machinery shed, a horse stable, a grain room, the milking parlor, and the milkhouse.

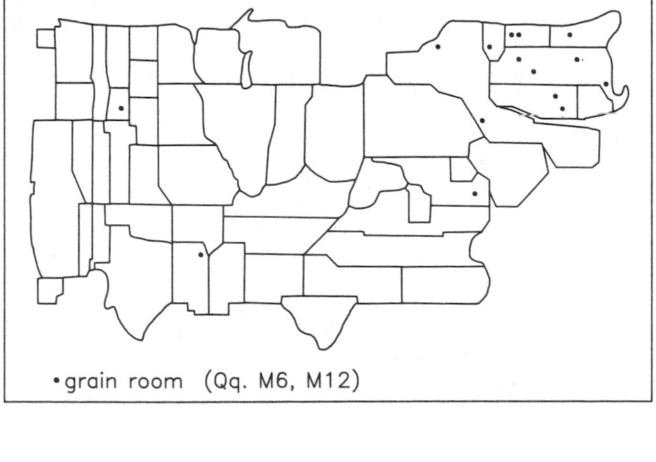

•grain room (Qq. M6, M12)

grains n pl

A fishing spear with two or more prongs.

1872 (1876) Knight *Amer. Mech. Dict.* 2.1007/1, *Grains*. . . A harpoon with several barbs. A five-pronged fish-spear. **1884** U.S. Natl. Museum *Bulletin* 27.865, *Fish-grains.* Two prongs with barbed ends. . . *Neptune eel-spear.* Galvanized iron, three flat prongs. . . *Dolphin-grains.* Three prongs, barbed; socket for handle. Length, with pole, 6 feet. **1966** *DARE* (Qu. P13, . . *Other ways of fishing . . besides the ordinary hook and line*) Inf **FL**24, Grains—spears.

grain tobacco n

Prob granulated tobacco.

[**1960** Heimann *Tobacco* 160, Green [=the maker of *Bull Durham*] did not press his leaf into twist or plug but shredded it. *Ibid* 176, The mighty *Bull Durham* . . [was] always a straight granulated Bright [tobacco].] **1966–70** *DARE* (Qu. DD1, . . *Different forms . . chewing tobacco come(s) in around here*) Inf **OK**25, Grain tobacco—large grains cut kind of stringy; **TX**104, Grain tobacco.

graip n [*OED "Sc.* and *north. dial."*] *arch*

1930 Shoemaker *1300 Words* 24 **cPA Mts** (as of c1900), *Graip*—A trident pitch fork.

g'raj See **garage**

galloch v, hence ppl adj *gralloched* Pronc-sp *grallock* [Scots dial]

To gut (a deer).

1897 *Outing* 29.440/1 **seLA,** We bore our gralloched game . . on double shoulder poles. **1930** Shoemaker *1300 Words* 26 **cPA Mts** (as of c1900), *Grallock*—To "gut", or disembowel a deer.

gram See **grandma** n **A4**

grama grass n Also *grama* [Span *grama* coarse grass] **West**

1 also sp *gramma (grass), gramme grass;* pronc-spp *grammer grass:* A grass of the genus *Bouteloua.* Also called **mesquite grass.** For other names of var spp see **black grama 1, buffalo grass e, chino grass, horseshoe grass, prairie oats, short grass, side-oats grama, six-weeks grama**

1828 (1933) Hulbert *Turquoise Trail* 194, Our mules have been recently much benefitted by the gramme grass, the best pasturage between the Atlantic and Pacific ocean. **1848** (1855) Ruxton *Life Far West* 103 **NM,** The bluffs near the . . river were covered with rich gramma grass. *Ibid* 152, The rich buffalo or *grama* grass was exchanged for a coarser species, on which the hard-worked animals soon grew poor and weak. **1859** (1965) Marcy *Prairie Traveler* 113, Several of the varieties of grass growing upon the slopes of the Rocky Mountains are of excellent quality; among these may be mentioned the Gramma and bunch grasses. **1897** Lummis *King of Broncos* 11 **NM,** The lathered "cow-ponies," . . were turned out to graze the scant tufts of grama. **1928** Barker *Buckaroo Ballads* 73 (Carlisle *Southwestern Dict.*), "Put herds o' cows on rollin' hills that's dark with *grammer grass.*" **1942** McAtee *Notes Thornton's Gloss.* [2], *Grama.* As this term is Spanish for grass, all its combinations with the latter word are tautologic. As a vernacular the term is now largely restricted to grasses of the genus *Bouteloua.* **1966–67** *DARE* (Qu. L9a, . . *Grass . . grown for hay*) Infs **CO**2, **KS**6, **ND**5, **NM**6, Grama grass; **OK**18, **TX**4, Grama; **CO**19, Native grama grass; (Qu. L9b, *Hay from other kinds of plants [not grass]*) Inf **NM**6, Grama grass; (Qu. S9, *Other kinds of grass that are hard to get rid of*) Inf **NM**2, Grama grass. **1966–67** *DARE* Tapes **KS**4, **SD**8, **TX**5, Grama grass. **1976** Bailey–Bailey *Hortus Third* 174, *Bouteloua*. . . Grama, gramma, grama grass, gramma g[rass].

2 often with modifier: = **muhly grass,** esp *Muhlenbergia porteri.* Cf **black grama 3**

1872 Bourke *Diary* 15 Dec **AZ,** Hills to-day well grassed with blue & white grama. **1889** *Century Dict.* 2594 **West,** *Grama-grass*. . . The name is also given to species of *Muhlenbergia,* common in the same region. **1941** *Torreya* 41.46, *Muhlenbergia porteri*. . . Bush grama, . . white grama, Tucson, Ariz.

gramammy See **grandma** n **A10**

gra-mary See **grandma** n **A13**

gramied See **gramy**

gramma See **grandma** n **A2**

gramma (grass) See **grama grass 1**

grammamma See **grandma** n **A5**

grammaw See **grandma** n **A3**

gramme(r) grass, See **grama grass 1**

grammom See **grandma** n **A6**

grammy See **grandma** n **A8**

gramp See **grandpa A6**

grampa See **grandpa A2**

grampaw See **grandpa A3**

grampel n [Prob var of *graupel*]
A snow pellet, somewhat like hail; see quots.
1966–67 *DARE* FW Addit **neWA,** *Grampel* ['græmpəl] . . round snow, neither hail nor ice nor sleet, but snow that falls over the Moscow Mountain range (Idaho and Washington); **swOR,** *Grampel* . . falls . . outside of Jacksonville. When it hits the earth it gives a little bounce, and then, melting, does a little wobbledy dance until it cannot be seen anymore.

gramper See **grandpa A2**

gramper worm n Cf **grampus 3**
1969 *DARE* (Qu. P6, . . *Worms . . used for bait*) Inf **GA**72, Gramper worm.

gramp-gramp See **grandpa A6**

gramps n
1 See **grandpa A7.**
2 See **grandma** n **A13.**

grampus n
1 arch spp *crampass, crampois, crampush:* Any of several cetaceans, but usu the widely distributed *Grampidelphis griseus* of northern seas which is also called **cowfish 2.**
1624 Smith *Genl. Hist. VA* 27, Of fish we were best acquainted with Sturgeon, Grampus, Porpus, Seales, *Stingraies.* **1635** in 1850 Dorchester Antiq. & Hist. Soc. *Coll.* 3.17, This day wee saw . . abundance of porpuyses, and likewise some crampushes as big as an oxe. **1670** (1937) Denton *Brief Descr.* 6 **seNY,** Upon the South-side of *Long*-Island in the Winter, lie store of Whales and Crampasses. **1709** (1967) Lawson *New Voyage* 158 **NC, SC,** Crampois is a large Fish, and by some accounted a young Whale; but it is not so. **1720** Neal *Hist. New Engl.* 1.84, They got down that Night into the Bottom of the *Bay,* where they discovered ten *Indians* about a dead *Grampus.* **1823** Cooper *Pioneers* 2.55 **cNY,** Whales and grampuses are to be seen, that are as long as one of them pine trees on yonder mountain. **1884** U.S. Natl. Museum *Bulletin* 27.633, The common Grampus, *Grampus griseus,* is not an infrequent visitor on the New England coast. **1903** *DN* 2.302 **Cape Cod MA,** Puffing like a grampus. **1950** *PADS* 14.33 **SC,** *Grampus.* . . The bottle-nosed dolphin.
2 **=vinegarone. esp FL**
1886 *Entomol. Amer.* 2.39, *T[helyphonus] giganteus* . . is found . . in the Southern States, where it is much feared by the people who call it . . Grampus. **1889** *Century Dict.* 2596 **FL,** *Grampus.* . . The whip-tailed scorpion, *Thelyphonus giganteus.* Also called *mule-killer, nigger-killer,* and in the West Indies *vinaigrier,* or vinegar-maker, from its acid secretion. **1913** Comstock *Spider Book* 19, *Mastigoproctus giganteus.* . . measures . . from four to five inches in length. . . In some parts of the South they bear the local name grampus, and are greatly feared on account of their supposed venomous powers. **1950** *PADS* 14.76 **FL,** *Grampus.* . . A large scorpion found under trash piles. **1966** *DARE* (Qu. R21, . . *Kinds of stinging insects around here*) Inf **FL**34, Grampus . . beetle claws in front and a stinger in back. **1967** Muma *Scorpions* 22, In Florida today, it [=*Mastigoproctus giganteus*] is known as the grampus or vinegaroon. **1980** Milne–Milne *Audubon Field Guide Insects* 932, *Giant Vinegorone*—"Grampus"—*(Mastigoproctus giganteus).* . . This formidable-looking whipscorpion is seldom encountered, because it hides by day and hunts in darkness.
3 also *water grampus:* **=hellgrammite 1.**
1889 *Century Dict.* 2596, *Grampus.* . . The dobson or hellgrammite: more fully called *water-grampus.* [*Century* Ed: Eastern U.S.] **1901** Howard *Insect Book* 212, In 1889 Professor W. W. Bailey, of Brown University, collected the names in use in Rhode Island alone for this insect. . . They are: Dobsons . . water grampus . . dragon and hell-diver. **1917** Kephart *Camping & Woodcraft* 2.411, One of the best natural baits for bass, when the water is clear, is that fierce-looking creature called hellgrammite, dobson, or grampus. **1948** *Field & Stream* July 42/2 *(DA),* Various stages of the dobson are known as . . water grampus . . and hell-divers.
4 Transf from **1** above:
a See quot. Cf *DS* CC17
1950 *PADS* 14.33 **SC,** *Grampus.* . . An imaginary sea monster. Used humorously. "To catch a grampus."
b See quot. [Cf *OED grampus* 1. c "A person given to puffing and blowing"]
1913 Beach *Iron Trail* 6 **AK,** My dear grampus, the mere love of luxury doesn't argue that a person is dishonest.
c A small locomotive; see quot.
1985 *DARE* File **seNY** (as of 1930s), In the evening of November 29, 1923, I watch[ed] the last train take the last trip down to Sterlington, N.Y. There were thirteen cars attached, leaving three at Sterling. Not until '36 did the other three was [sic] taken away by a small gasoline grampus.

grampy See **grandpa A8**

grams See **grandma** n **A4**

gramsey See **grandsire**

gramsey graybeard See **grandfather's beard 2**

gramy v, hence ppl adj *gramied* [Var of *grame* anger, vex; be vexed; *OED* →1526; *SND gram* v. →1928]
To vex, anger, bother.
1928 Chapman *Happy Mt.* 9 **seTN,** It gramys me to have it go naked. *Ibid* 16, It's the going on of things that gets a man all gramyed. *Ibid* 279, Burl Bracy . . was yet gramyed by the vapors of his drink. **1938** Matschat *Suwannee R.* 106 **neFL, seGA,** "It gramies me," she told her father. "Hearken to all the wonders in the world as set forth in this here book. . . All winter long I pine for 'em."

gran n
1 See **grandma** n **A9.**
2 See **grand.**

granary n |'gren(ə)ri, 'grænəri| Pronc-sp *grainery;* for addit varr see quots
Std sense, var forms.
1624 in 1915 VA House of Burgesses *Jrls.* 34 **eVA,** At his arrival heere he founde the Collony in all parts well stored with corne, and at *Charles Hundred* a granery well furnished by rentes. **1702** *Boston Rec.* 19 *(DAE),* The Grainary belonging to Mr. Arthur Mason butting on the Common or Training field. **1895** *DN* 1.397 **MA, CT, cNY, IA,** *Granary:* often pron. [grenərɪ]. **1899** (1912) Green *VA Folk-Speech* 203, *Grainery.* **1914** *DN* 4.107 **KS,** *Grainery.* **1916** *DN* 4.341 **seOH,** *Grainary.* **1921** *DN* 5.114 **CA,** *Granary* [grenərɪ]. **1923** *DN* 5.209 **swMO,** *Grainery.* **1937** *AmSp* 12.102 **eNE,** The word *granary* is nearly always pronounced *grainry,* and sometimes *grenery.* **1939** *LANE* Map 105 *(Granary; grain room; grain bin)* [*Granary* is fairly common **throughout NEng;** prones of the type [gren(ə)rɪ] are by far the more common; only 15 infs, 6 in the Boston area, reported prones of the type [grænərɪ].] **1950** *WELS Suppl.,* Granary ['grenrɪ]—never pronounced grănary except by teachers in the schoolroom; at home in their natural surrounding they use the *grain* sound too. **1965–70** *DARE* (Qu. M6, *The place where grain is kept in a barn*) 329 Infs, **widespread, but somewhat less freq Sth, NEng,** Grainery; 109 Infs, **widespread, but somewhat less freq Sth, NEng,** Granary; 15 Infs, **scattered,** Grainry; **IN**11, **MO**38, Grainery bin; **OK**1, Corn grainery, oats grainery; (Qu. M12, *What do you keep food for the cattle in over winter?*) 40 Infs, **chiefly Midl, West,** Grainery; **MI**78, **MO**16, 21, **NY**164, **PA**71, **TX**1, Granary; **MO**12, 18, Grainry; (Qu. M22, . . *Buildings . . on farms*) 38 Infs, **scattered, but esp MN,** Grainery; **IL**9, **MO**15, 19, **ND**3, **PA**75, 92, **WI**30, (Outside *or* wheat) granary; **IL**19, Grainery shed; **IL**38, Round steel grainery; **KY**72, Grainery ben; (Qu. M8, *The building where corn is kept*) 20 Infs, **scattered,** (Corn) grainery; **MO**32, **NC**63, **OH**41, Granary; **MO**10, 18, **NY**24, (Corn) grainry; (Qu. M1) Infs **AR**21, **CA**171, **CO**22, **MI**74, **MN**7, **ND**5, **NJ**35, Grainery; **MI**83, **OH**41, Granary; **DE**5, Grainry; (Qu. M7, *A separate building where grain is kept;* total Infs questioned, 75) 15 Infs, Grainery; **FL**7, **MS**66, Granary; (Qu. M4a; total Infs questioned, 75) Inf **OK**27, Grainery. **1976** Allen *LAUM* 3.276 (as of c1950), Although the rarity of /grænəri/ [as opposed to /grenəri/] in western New England might suggest an even lower frequency in the

U[pper] M[idwest], actually this form has slightly expanded, almost certainly through dictionary and school support. Its frequency in New England is only 6%; in the UM it is 12%, quite evenly distributed both socially and regionally.

gran'boy See **grandboy**

grancy See **grandsire**

grancy graybeard See **granddaddy graybeard 2**

grand n Pronc-sp *gran* **chiefly SC, GA** *esp among Black speakers*

A grandchild.

1922 Gonzales *Black Border* 304 **sSC, GA coasts** [Gullah glossary], *Gran'*—grand—grandchild, grandson, or anyone in such relationships of "grand". **1930** Woofter *Black Yeomanry* 209 **seSC,** It is rather unusual to find the old women living alone. There is usually a 'grand' who can be spared or a 'mudderless' who can be adopted. **1937** in 1972 *Amer. Slave* 2.107 **SC,** Aunt Hagar has grands settled all around her and she and the grands divide up the acreage which is planted in corn, sweet potatoes, cotton, and some highland rice. **1950** *PADS* 14.33 **SC,** *Grand.* . . A grandchild. Coastal Negro usage; also heard among up-country whites. **1966** *DARE* Tape **AL**24, I have three grands with me; **SC**10, [FW:] All these pictures on the wall is your children, eh? [Inf:] Yah. [FW:] How many you got? [Inf:] I got about ten, about fifteen head of gran' . . and one great-gran; **SC**16, This here ain't none of da gran'. . . I got 28 gran' . . and I got 53 great gran'; **SC**26, I take care of my gran'. [All Infs Black] **1966–67** *DARE* FW Addit **SC,** *Grand:* a grandchild. Occasional usage, esp among Blacks. **1971** Cunningham *Syntactic Analysis Gullah* 41, That's my great grand. **1983** Heath *Ways with Words* 69 **sNC, nSC,** [Black], It's her baby; she gotta be a woman, but dat's my gran [Heath: grandbaby], and it ain't gonna want for nut'n.

grandacoy See **grande écaille**

grandaddie, grandaddy See **granddaddy**

grandboy n Also *gran'boy* **chiefly Sth, S Midl**

A grandson.

1933 Miller *Lamb in His Bosom* 112 **GA,** She could not die in peace for fear that her boys and grandboys would be drug off to war. **1939** FWP *Guide NC* 98, A common usage among older people is "gran'boy" for grandson. **1965** *DARE* (Qu. Z7, . . *Words for any other relatives*) Inf **OK**7, Grandboy. **1966** *PADS* 46.26 **cnAR,** *Grandboy.* . . Grandson. **1966–68** *DARE* FW Addit **GA**31, I've got a four year old grandboy; **OK**50, Grandboy. **1984** Burns *Cold Sassy* 296 **nGA** (as of 1906), This here used to be my sewin' room. . . But I fixed it up for my grandboys, Horace and Ulysses.

granddad See **granddaddy 5**

granddad beard See **grandfather's beard 2**

granddaddy n Also sp *grandaddy, grandaddie*

1 A grandfather. **chiefly Sth, S Midl** See Map

1843 (1916) Hall *New Purchase* 113, "Agreed, grandaddie," responded Long Jake, "so here goes." **1884** *Anglia* 7.277 **Sth, S Midl** [Black], *To know de gran'daddy er a luckyman* = to know a luckyman's grandfather. **1929** Sale *Tree Named John* 5 **MS** [Black], Grandaddy's daddy wuz a Affiken kang. **1934** Stribling *Unfinished Cathedral* 186 **AL,** This boy's granddaddy married Susie. **1939** *Hall Coll.* **wNC,** *Granddaddy.* . . "My gran'daddy was raised right on Halls [sic] Top" (a mountain on the Tenn. side). **1962** Atwood *Vocab. TX* 65, *Grandfather.* . . Granddaddy. [8% of approx 270 infs gave this response.] **1965–70** *DARE* (Qu. Z3, . . *Words . . for 'grandfather'*) 189 Infs, **scattered, but chiefly Sth, S Midl,** Granddaddy. **1967–70** *DARE* Tape **TX**23, Somebody killed his granddaddy there; **TX**36, My granddaddy made it; **TX**40, Your granddaddy, after we married; **TX**46, There's a lot in there about their granddaddy; **TX**94, My granddaddy Hager. **1970** Tarpley *Blinky* 210 **neTX,** Usual term of affection for grandfather . . 9.0% [of 200 infs], Grand daddy. *Ibid* 211, Grand daddy is favored by the least educated and by informants under 50.

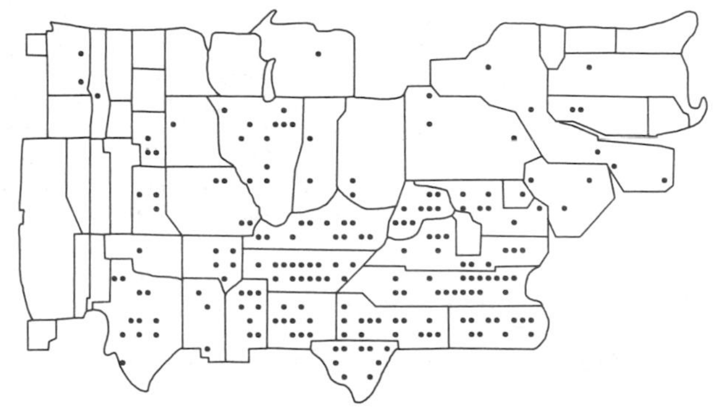

•granddaddy 1 (Qu. Z3)

2 also *granddad:* =**daddy longlegs 1.** [*OED* 1808 →] **chiefly Sth, S Midl** See Map Cf **granddaddy longlegs 1**

1899 Bergen *Animal Lore* 58 **nOH,** Gran'daddy, gran'daddy-long-legs,/ Tell me where my cows are or I'll kill you. **1908** Biol. Soc. DC *Proc.* 21.81 **TX,** Here they [=toads] . . feed largely on the long-legged monstrosities commonly known as "grand-daddies." **1931** *Jrl. Amer. Folkl.* 44.415 **LA,** When there are blue-balls (bubos), smear the swellings with mashed up granddaddies (daddy-long-legs) and it will bring them to a head. **1954** *Harder Coll.* **cwTN,** *Grandaddy* . . daddy-longlegs. **c1960** *Wilson Coll.* **csKY,** *Granddaddy.* . . The harvestman or daddy-longlegs. **1965–70** *DARE* (Qu. R28) 59 Infs, **chiefly Sth, S Midl,** Granddaddy (*or* -daddies); **NC**64, **TX**101, **WI**32, Granddad(s). **c1974** Jones *Ozark Hill Boy* 55 **AR** (as of c1930), The water was being strained through a cloth sack to remove the trash and other foreign matter including grand-daddys, scorpions, and an occasional frog.

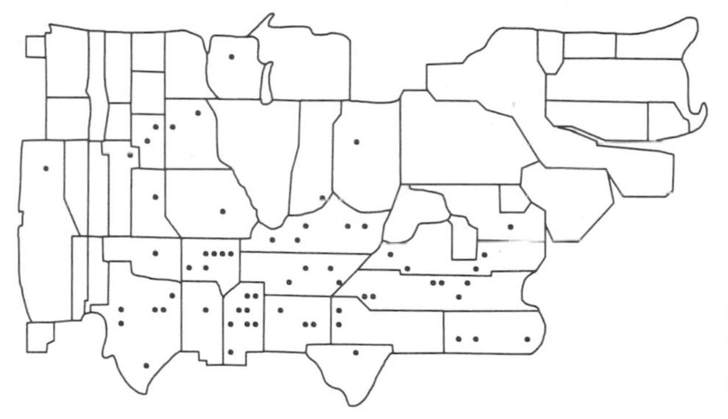

•granddaddy 2 + varr (Qu. R28)

3 =**praying mantis.**

1966–67 *DARE* (Qu. R9b, *An insect that holds up its front feet as if saying a prayer*) Infs **AL**35, **LA**10, Granddaddy; **SC**3, Granddaddies.

4 =**walkingstick.**

1969 *DARE* (Qu. R9a, *An insect from two to four inches long that lives in bushes and looks like a dead twig*) Inf **MO**39, Granddaddy—a smaller bug loosely resembling the devil horse.

5 also *granddad, grandfather frog:* A large frog such as a **bullfrog 1** or a **pig frog.**

1940–41 Cassidy *WI Atlas* **neWI,** Grandfather frog . . big green frog with deep voice (a bullfrog is brown). **1950** *WELS (Names or nicknames for a very large frog that makes a deep, loud sound)* 1 Inf, **ceWI,** Grandfather frog. **1966–69** *DARE* (Qu. P22, . . *A very large frog that makes a deep, loud sound*) Infs **CO**20, **FL**26, **GA**76, **IN**35, **KS**7, **MO**2, **NC**53, Granddaddy; **AL**28, Granddad.

6 also *grandpapa:* A large marble.

c1970 Wiersma *Marbles Terms* **seIA,** *Grand-daddies:* largest marbles; **MI** [Black], *Grandpapa.* . . The largest size marble.

granddaddy graybeard n

1 also *grandfather graybeard:* =**daddy longlegs 1.**

1872 MO State Entomol. *Annual Rept.* 17, An undetermined species of *Phalangium.* . . These animals are popularly called "Grand-Daddy-Long-Legs" in this country, but are also known as "Harvest-men" and "Grandfather-Gray-Beards," in some parts. **1899** Bergen *Animal Lore* 38, A grand-daddy gray-beard (daddy-long-legs) running over clothes means that you will soon have a new garment. *Boxford, Mass., and Cazenovia, N.Y.* *Ibid* 58 **wNY** (as of c1830), Grandfather graybeard,/ Tell me where my cows are or I'll kill you. **1923** *DN* 5.242 **KY,** *Gran'-daddy-gray-beard.* . . A kind of spider with elongated legs and feelers. **1937** Gardner *Folkl. Schoharie* 275 **ceNY,** When you don't know where the cows are, catch a grandfather graybeard and say to him: "Tell me where the cows are, or I'll kill you." **1967–68** *DARE* (Qu. R28) Infs **NY**22, 88, Grandfather graybeard.

2 also *granddad graybeard, grandfather ~, grandsir ~, grancy ~, gransy ~:* **=fringe tree. chiefly Gulf States, S Atl**

1908 *DN* 3.317 **eAL, wGA,** *Grandaddy-graybeard. . .* The fringe tree. Also called *grancy graybeard.* **1931** Clute *Common Plants* 88, Old man's whiskers . . may merely suggest an elderly gentleman, especially as *Chionanthus Virginica* is also known as grandfather graybeard. **1933** Small *Manual SE Flora* 1041, *Chionanthus. . .* Flowers . . in drooping festoon-like panicles. . . *Grandsir-graybeards.* **1945** *Clarke Co. Democrat* (Grove Hill AL) 29 Mar 2/1, Being out turkey hunting some spring afternoon with the air heavy with the scent of wild honey suckle . . and with the white of the granddaddy graybeards . . peeping out. *Ibid* 13 June 2/3, Every street in Grove Hill should be lined with gransy graybeards (fringe trees), redbuds, crape myrtles and mimosas. **1951** *PADS* 15.37 **TX,** *Chioanthus* [sic] *virginica. . .* Grand-daddy graybeard. **1960** Williams *Walk Egypt* 102 **GA,** There were a few perished-by-dust blooms in the undergrowth along the road, jasmine, wild verbena, Grancy Graybeard. **1966–69** *DARE* (Qu. S26c, *Wildflowers that grow in woods*) Inf **GA**89, Grancy graybeard; (Qu. S26e, *Other wildflowers*) Infs **SC**27, 32, 46, 57, Granddaddy graybeard. **1968** *DARE* FW Addit **LA**21, Grancy graybeard . . a fair-sized shrub (6 to 7 feet). Another name [is] *fringe tree.* Flowers hang in long white clusters like cord-strings; **LA**40, Granddaddy graybeard . . tree with lots of large feathery white blossoms; blooms early April. **1969** *SC Market Bulletin* 25 Sept 4, Grand dad grey beard in gallon pots, guaranteed to live and grow, $2 plus postage 25c. **1972** Brown *Wildflowers LA* 135, *Fringetree, Grancy-graybeard. . .* Flower cluster 5 to 10 inches long.

granddaddy longlegs n

1 also *granddaddy longleg, granddad longlegs, grandfather ~, grandpa ~, grandsir ~, granther ~:* **=daddy longlegs 1.**

1872 [see **grandaddy graybeard 1**]. **1875** Twain *Sketches New & Old* (Hartford) 130, The learned and aged Lord Grand-Daddy-Long-legs . . had been sitting, in deep study, with his slender limbs crossed. **1890** Howells *Boy's Town* 201 **OH,** You must not kill a granddaddy long-legs, or a lady-bug; it was bad luck. **1895** *DN* 1.397 **Gt Lakes,** *Grand daddy long legs:* the "daddy long legs" of Webster; more common than this shorter form. **1903** *DN* 2.298 **Cape Cod MA** (as of a1857), *Granther long legs. . .* Daddy long legs. **1907** *DN* 3.188 **seNH,** *Gran-daddy-long-legs. . .* An arachnid with a small suboval body and very long legs. "Don't kill that grandaddy-long-legs; he won't hurt you." **1926** Essig *Insects N. Amer.* 11, These long-legged creatures with small bodies are variously known as harvesters, . . grand-daddy-long-legs, . . and so forth. **1941** *LANE* Map 381, 2 infs, **ceCT,** Grandpa longlegs, a kind of spider. **1965–70** *DARE* (Qu. R28, . . *Kinds of spiders*) 115 Infs, **widespread,** Granddaddy longlegs; **ME**6, 24, **MD**15, 20, **MA**15, 66, **NY**231, Grandfather longlegs; **TX**78, Granddaddy long-leg; **ME**24, **MA**42, Grandpa (*or* grampa) longlegs; **NM**3, Granddad longlegs; **DE**4, Granddaddy longlegs spider; **NC**72, Grandsir longlegs; **AL**20, Granther longlegs.

2 =walkingstick.

1968 *DARE* (Qu. R9a, *An insect from two to four inches long that lives in bushes and looks like a dead twig*) Inf **IA**22, Granddaddy longlegs.

granddaddy's beard See **grandfather's beard 1**

granddaddy spider n Also *grandfather spider*

=daddy longlegs 1.

1967–69 *DARE* (Qu. R28, . . *Kinds of spiders*) Infs **CO**31, **MO**15, Granddaddy spider; **CT**31, Grandfather spider.

granddaddy's pipe n Cf **Indian pipe**

A **virgin's bower** (here: *Clematis ochroleuca*).

1966 *DARE* Wildfl QR Pl.74 Inf **CO**11, Granddaddy's pipe—Dutchman's pipe.

granddaddy's whiskers n Cf **gray-haired grandmother**

A **dandelion 1.**

1966 *DARE* (Qu. S11, . . *Other names . . for . . dandelion*) Inf **AR**10, Granddaddy's whiskers.

granddad graybeard See **granddaddy graybeard 2**

granddad longlegs See **granddaddy longlegs 1**

grand duke n

=great horned owl.

1930 Shoemaker *1300 Words* 26 **cPA Mts** (as of c1900), *Grand duke*—The hoot owl, or "great horned owl".

grande écaille n Also *grande (escaille), grand ecaille* Pronc-spp *grandacoy, grand-ecoy, grandykye, grundiquoit* [LaFr "big scale"] **chiefly Gulf States**

=tarpon.

1840 (1965) Moore *Map & Descr. TX* 36, Among these are red fish, grundiquoit, mullet, sea perch, sea trout, &c. **a1850** in 1882 *Amer. Naturalist* 16.387 **LA,** I could never have killed the grand ecaillé [sic], however, with the tackle I used, had I not been in a pirogue with a sure and steady arm at the paddle. **1882** U.S. Natl. Museum *Proc.* 5.246 **Gulf coast,** *Megalops atlanticus. . . Grande Ecaille; "Grandacoy." . .* It is said that several persons have been killed or injured when in small boats by the "Grande Ecaille" leaping into the boat. **1887** Goode *Amer. Fishes* 406, It [=the tarpon] is . . the "Grande-Ecaille," (Large-scale fish), or "Grandykye," as it is pronounced and sometimes spelled. **1902** Jordan–Evermann *Amer. Fishes* 85, Among other names by which the tarpon is known are . . grand ecaille, and silver king. [**1931** Read *LA French* 43, *Grande Ecaille. . .* The large scales of this noted game fish are responsible for the La.-Fr. name.] **1935** Caine *Game Fish* 134, *Tarpon. . . Synonyms:* Grande. Grande-écaille. Grandykye. **1946** *Times-Picayune* (New Orleans LA) 24 Mar sec 2 2/1, The grand-ecoy seems to be a fish, and a misspelled fish at that. **1973** Knight *Cook's Fish Guide* 382, Grande escaille—Tarpon. **1975** Evanoff *Catch More Fish* 217, Grande ecaille.

grandfather n Cf **granddaddy 2**

=daddy longlegs 1.

1899 Bergen *Animal Lore* 58 **cNY,** Grandfather gray,/ Tell me right away,/ Where the cows are / Or I'll kill you.

grandfather frog See **granddaddy 5**

grandfather graybeard n

1 See quot.

1967 *DARE* (Qu. R15b, . . *An extra-big mosquito*) Inf **NY**22, Grandfather graybeard.

2 See **granddaddy graybeard 1.**

3 See **granddaddy graybeard 2.**

grandfather longlegs See **granddaddy longlegs 1**

grandfather's beard n

1 also *granddaddy's beard:* **=fringe tree.** Cf **granddaddy graybeard 2**

1913 TX Acad. Sci. *Trans. for 1910–12* 12.87, *Chionanthus Virginiana . .* (Grandfather's Beard). Old Man's Beard. (Flowering Ash). Blooms in March. Rather common on hillsides and in sandy woods. **1966** *DARE* (Qu. S26c, *Wildflowers that grow in woods*) Inf **NC**10, Grandfather's beard; (Qu. S26e, *Other wildflowers*) Inf **FL**20, Granddaddy's beard. **1977** Kibler *Simms as Naturalist* 10 **SC,** The formal name of "old man's beard" is *Chionanthus virginica,* also called . . "Granddaddy's Beard."

2 also *gramsey graybeard, granddad beard, grandpa's ~:* A **virgin's bower** (here: *Clematis drummondii*). [See quot 1936] **TX**

1911 *Century Dict. Suppl., Grandpa's-beard. . .* In Texas, a species of virgin's-bower, *Clematis Drummondii:* so named from the fruiting panicle made showy by the feathery tails of the fruit. **1936** Whitehouse *TX Flowers* 28, The seeds mature in a few weeks, and soon the vine is covered with . . silky, feathery plumes, 2–4 in. long, which grow out from the seed cover. These plumes . . are responsible for many common names . . including grandfather's beard. **c1938** in 1970 Hyatt *Hoodoo* 2.1490 **seGA,** (*Ramsey graybeard.* What is that?) It grows a big long vine . . an' it's got . . little fine stickers all ovah it. (It's called Ramsey? Gramsey? What does Gramsey mean?) Well, ah-huh *dat Gramsey means dat it's great fo' whut ails yo'*—whut it is because it's a *Gramsey graybeard.* **1960** Vines *Trees SW* 266, Vernacular names for the plant are Texas Virgins-bower, . . Grandad Beard.

3 The tendrils of a **cat's-claw** (here: prob *Acacia* spp).

1915 *DN* 4.226 **wTX,** *Grandfather's beard. . .* The long bushy tendrils of the catclaw bush.

4 A **prairie smoke** (here: *Geum triflorum* var *ciliatum*).

1970 Kirk *Wild Edible Plants W. U.S.* 92, *Geum ciliatum . .* Grandfathers-beard. . . The plant is a finely glandular perennial, covered with soft hairs.

grandfather spider See **granddaddy spider**

grandfather's whiskers n Also *grampa whiskers* Cf **granddaddy's whiskers**

An anemone such as *Anemone patens.*

1966 *DARE* FW Addit **WI**34, Pasqueflower—also called grandfather's whiskers. **1968** *DARE* (Qu. S26a, . . *Roadside flowers*) Inf **WI**20, Grampa whiskers—four inches high, red with whiskers.

grand fir n

Std: a fir *(Abies grandis)* native from Canada to Montana and northwestern California. Also called **balsam fir, lowland fir, silver fir, stinking fir, white fir, yellow fir**

grandfolks n pl

Grandparents.

1890 *AN&Q* 5.6/2, I heard a man in New Jersey speak of his *grandfolks,* meaning *grandparents.* **1949** *McDavid Coll.* 1 inf, **cwNY,** *Grandfolks*—grandparents.

grand good adj phr

Very good.

1904 *DN* 2.425 **Cape Cod MA** (as of a1857), *Grand good.* . . Very good. 'We had a grand good time.'

‡grandied up adj phr

1966 *DARE* FW Addit **seWA,** All grandied up . . dressed sloppily.

grand list n

A list of property subject to taxation.

1966 *Yankee* Mar 104/1 **NEng,** "They are tax payers," Dan said. "On the grand list. They got their rights." **1969** *Yankee* June 82/1 **VT,** Avery's Gore . . has a Grand List of $438.16, no people, no roads, although there is a jeep track up to the fire watchtower on Gore Mountain. [*Ibid* 83, In the spring, she sends assessors out, and the List is drawn up. The tax rate is $3.00 on a 50% evaluation.]

grandma n Usu |ˈgræn(d)ˌmɑ, -mə| (last syll repr in *DARE* quots by sp *-ma*); also |ˈgræn(d)ˌmɑ, -ˌmɔ| (repr by *-maw*) For addit varr see **A** below

A Forms.

1 pronc-spp *gran(d)maw.* **chiefly Sth, Midl, West** See Map

1942 Faulkner *Go Down* 47 **MS,** The same thing made my pappy that made your grandmaw. **1965–70** *DARE* (Qu. Z4, . . *Words . . for 'grandmother'*) 195 Infs, **chiefly Sth, Midl, West,** Granmaw; 43 Infs, **scattered Sth, Midl, West,** Grandmaw; **CA**70, Great-grandmaw. **1970** Tarpley *Blinky* 208 **neTX,** Usual term of affection for Grandmother . . 44.5% [of 200 infs], Grandmaw.

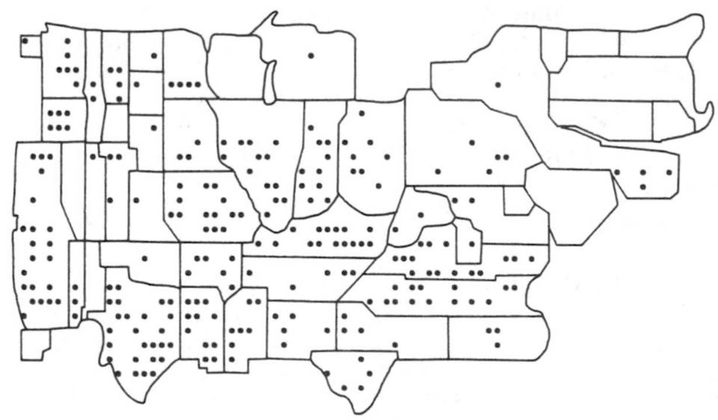

•grandma n A1 + varr (Qu. Z4)

2 pronc-sp *gramma.* **scattered, but chiefly Nth, N Midl, West** See Map

1922 Gonzales *Black Border* 304 **sSC, GA coasts** [Gullah glossary], *Gramma*—grandmother. **1928** Peterkin *Scarlet Sister Mary* 308 **sSC** [Gullah], E's you gramma, honey. **1948** Manfred *Chokecherry* 247 **nwIA,** Toots, she can go over to Gramp and Gramma Hansen. **1954** *Harder Coll.* **cwTN,** Gramma. **1962** Atwood *Vocab. TX* 65, *Grandmother* . . Gramma [was given by 7% of approx 270 infs]. **1965–70** *DARE* (Qu. Z4) 226 Infs, **scattered, but chiefly Nth, N Midl, West,** Gramma.

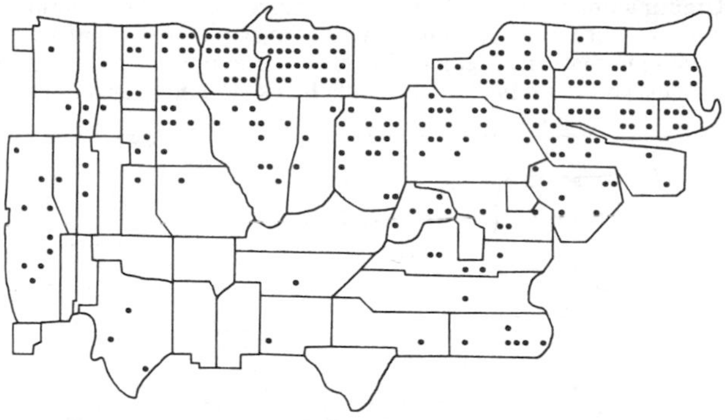

•grandma n A2 (Qu. Z4)

3 pronc-sp *grammaw.* **chiefly Midl; also Sth, West** See Map

1924 (1946) Greer–Petrie *Angeline Gits an Eyeful* 17 **csKY,** I've been a-studyin' about whut kind of grammaws they're a-gwine to make. **1965–70** *DARE* (Qu. Z4) 86 Infs, **chiefly Midl; also Sth, West,** Grammaw.

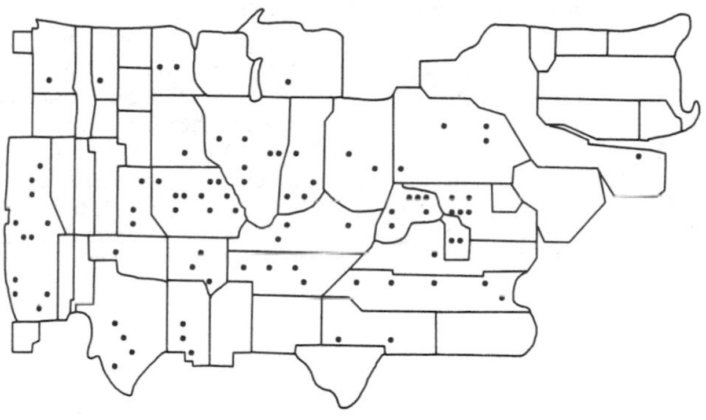

•grandma n A3 (Qu. Z4)

4 pronc-spp *gram(s).* **chiefly Nth, N Midl** See Map

1941 *LANE* Map 383 *(Grandma)* **esp nNEng,** Gram. **1957** Beck *Folkl. ME* 168, "Gram" [is the term] for grandmother. **1961** *Daily Mining Gaz.* (Houghton MI) 1 Aug sec 3 12/3, But, if one has a gramp or gram still residing in the Copper Country it might be appropriate to query him or her. **1962** Atwood *Vocab. TX* 65, Many private nicknames show up [for *grandmother*], most of them only once or twice each . . [including] Gram. **1965–70** *DARE* (Qu. Z4) 53 Infs, **chiefly Nth, N Midl,** Gram; **CA**1, 75, 138, **FL**33, **IA**4, **IL**29, 110, **NJ**3, **NY**121, **PA**126, Grams.

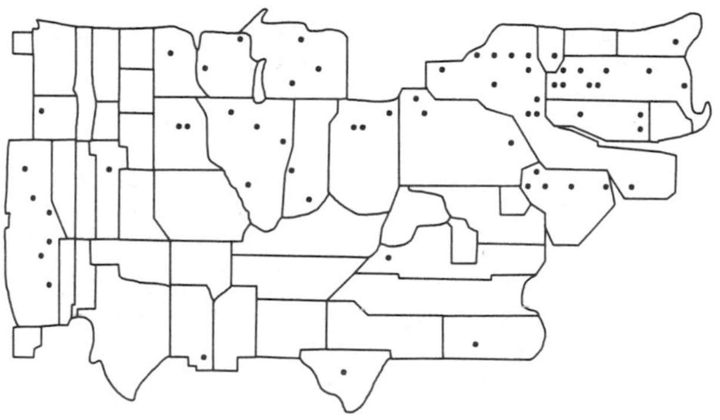

•grandma n A4 + var (Qu. Z4)

5 pronc-spp *grammamma, gran(d)mam(m)a, gran(d)mom-ma.* **chiefly Sth, S Midl** See Map *esp freq among Black speakers*

1942 [see **8** below]. **1965–70** *DARE* (Qu. Z4) 13 Infs, **chiefly Sth, S Midl,** Granmamma; 10 Infs, **chiefly Sth, S Midl,** Grandmamma; **AL**6,

Grammamma; **VA**46, 78, Grandmomma; **SC**29, 44, Granmomma; (Qu. W2) Inf **TN**53, Grandmamma's bonnet; (Qu. AA27) Inf **MS**84, It's grandmamma's time; grandmamma is here; (Qu. HH22c) Inf **SC**40, Rob his granmomma. [12 of 31 Infs Black, 18 young or mid-aged]

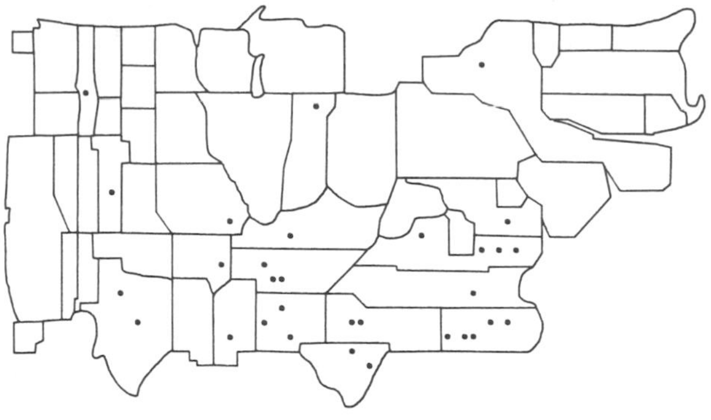

•grandma n A5 + varr (Qq. Z4, W2, AA27, HH22c)

6 pronc-spp *grammom, gran(d)mom, gran(d)ma('a)m, grandmahm, grandmum.* **chiefly C Atl** See Map

1862 *Atlantic Mth.* 9.790 **ceMA,** Your gran'ma'am put it there. **1907** *DN* 3.188 **NH,** *Grandma'am.* . . Grandmother. "Grandma'am knit my mittens." **1940** Richter *Trees* 10 **OH** (as of c1800), She . . said grand things that no one dared think of but she and her Granmam Powelly. **1941** *LANE* Map 383 *(Grandma)* **chiefly nNEng,** Grandmahm; **scattered nNEng,** Grandmum. **1942** [see **8** below]. **1965–70** *DARE* (Qu. Z4) Infs **CA**114, **MD**49, **MN**19, **NJ**23, 54, 55, **PA**29, 63, 96, 247, Grandmom; **DE**2, **MD**5, 36, 40, **NJ**51, **PA**170, Grammom; **MD**33, **NY**105, 135, **PA**237, Granmom; **PA**206, Grandmum.

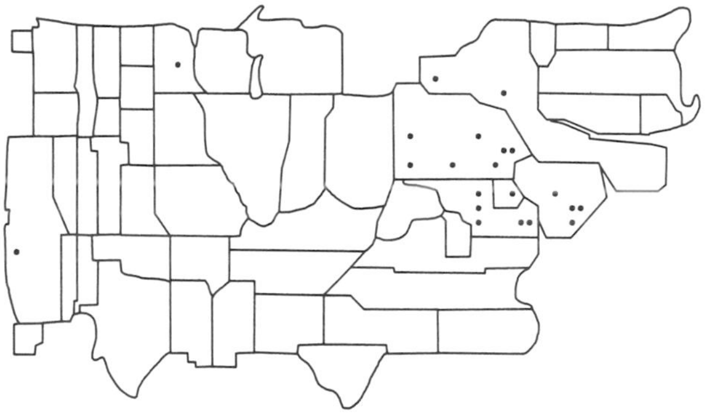

•grandma n A6 + varr (Qu. Z4)

7 pronc-spp *grannie, granny.* **widespread** Note: For senses associated with this form, see **granny** n

1815 Humphreys *Yankey in England* 105, *Granny,* grandmother. **1907** *DN* 3.188 **NH,** *Granny.* . . Grandmother. **1926** Roberts *Time of Man* 114 **cKY,** [A song] she learned offen her grannie. **1950** *PADS* 14.33 **SC,** *Granny.* . . A grandmother. **c1960** *Wilson Coll.* **csKY,** *Granny* . . formerly common for grandmother; now very rare. **1962** Atwood *Vocab. TX* 65, *Grandmother.* . . Granny [26% of approx 270 infs gave this response]. **1965–70** *DARE* (Qu. Z4, . . *Words . . for 'grandmother'*) 240 Infs, **widespread,** Granny; **CA**15, Old granny. **1970** Tarpley *Blinky* 208 **neTX,** Usual term of affection for Grandmother . . 14.5% [of 200 infs], Granny.

8 pronc-sp *grammy.* **chiefly Nth, N Midl** See Map

1914 *DN* 4.152 **ME,** *Grammy.* . . Grandmother. **1941** *LANE* Map 383 *(Grandma)* **chiefly nNEng,** Grammy. **1942** Berrey–Van den Bark *Amer. Slang* 446.4, *Grandmother.* . . Gammer, gammy, grammy, gran, gran(d)ma, gran(d)mama, gran(d)mammy, gran(d)mom, granny. **1965–70** *DARE* (Qu. Z4) 27 Infs, **scattered Nth, N Midl,** Grammy; **NY**209, Great-grammy.

9 pronc-sp *gran.*

1942 [see **8** above]. **1965–70** *DARE* (Qu. Z4) Infs **FL**28, **GA**57, **MD**17, 35, **MS**23, 70, **MA**25, 89, **NJ**3, **OH**50, **TN**12, **VA**78, 93, Gran.

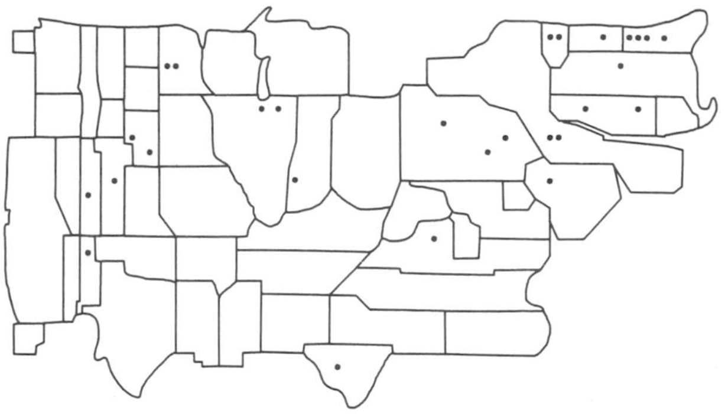

•grandma n A8 + var (Qu. Z4)

10 pronc-spp *gramammy, gran(d)mammy, gran'maamy.* **chiefly Sth, S Midl** Cf **mammy**

1922 Gonzales *Black Border* 304 **sSC, GA coasts** [Gullah glossary], *Gran'maamy*—grandmother. **1930** (1935) Porter *Flowering Judas* 68 **TX,** His own grand-mammy. **1934** Stribling *Unfinished Cathedral* 187 **AL,** He's named for his grandmammy's family. **1936** Reese *Worleys* 39 **MD** (as of 1865) [Black], An' heah, jis' undah de [cemetery] wall, is yo' granmammy. **1942** [see **8** above]. **1965** *DARE* FW Addit **MS** [Black], Granmammy. **1966–70** *DARE* (Qu. Z4) Infs **KY**11, 74, 86, **NY**96, Grandmammy; **NC**76, **VA**42, Granmammy; **AR**18, Gramammy.

11 pronc-spp *gran(d)mommy.*

1968–70 *DARE* (Qu. Z4) Infs **NC**86, **VA**73, Grandmommy; **NY**123, **WI**53, Granmommy.

12 with |-mæ|. **chiefly Mid Atl**

[**1955** *PADS* 23.37 **SC,** /æ/ in *pa, ma.*] **1965–70** *DARE* (Qu. Z4) Infs **IN**3, **MD**33, **NC**38, **SC**2, 4, 21, ['grænmæ]; **MD**35, **SC**11, 19, 24, ['græmæ]; **SC**10, [grʌmæ].

13 Other varr.

1847 in 1956 Eliason *Tarheel Talk* 311 **ne,ceNC,** *Grandma*—grandmar. **1922** Gonzales *Black Border* 304 **sSC, GA coasts** [Gullah glossary], *Grumma*—grandma. **1941** *LANE* Map 383 *(Grandma)* 1 inf, **csMA,** I'm more apt to say ['grænmɑr] in conversation; 1 inf, **seVT,** ['græᵊmər]; 1 inf, **cwMA,** [græmr]. **1942** [see **8** above]. **1965–70** *DARE* (Qu. Z4) Infs **GA**28, 57, Gaga; **GA**57, **PA**74, Gam; **GA**57, **WI**53, Gamma; **GA**57, **IL**28, Gammy; **GA**57, Gan-gan; **CA**138, **DC**11, Ganny; **NJ**13, G.g.; **OH**2, Gia; **PA**126, Gra-mary; **MI**72, Gramps; **CA**122, Grando; **NC**79, Granner; **SC**24, Grash; **KY**34, ['drænmɔ].

B Senses.

1 An old woman—used esp as a form of address.

1902 *DN* 2.235 **sIL,** *Granma.* . . Form of addressing any old woman. **1915** *DN* 4.226 **wTX,** *Grandma.* . . The polite form of address to all elderly ladies. **1942** Berrey–Van den Bark *Amer. Slang* 384.3, *Old woman.* . . Gammer, grandma. **c1960** *Wilson Coll.* **csKY,** *Grandma.* . . Also used to designate an elderly woman not related.

2 See quot.

1940 Writers' Program *Guide NV* 75, *Grandma.* . . Cowboy's term for the horn of the saddle.

3 A **freshwater clam.**

1941 Writers' Program *Guide AR* 207, Dredging the White River and its tributaries for fresh-water mussels used for button making affords farmers a part-time occupation. . . Payment, made by the ton, varies according to the type of shell, "grandmaws," "pocketbooks," and "cucumbers" bringing less than "elephant ears" and "niggerheads."

4 often *granny* (or *grannies*); Menstruation—often used in phrr to indicate the onset of a woman's menstrual period; see quots. Cf **grandmother troubles, granny chills, granny grunt 1**

1908 *DN* 3.317 **eAL, wGA,** *Granny.* . . Menses. . . Granny grunts. . . The menses. **1942** McAtee *Dial. Grant Co. IN Suppl. 1* 5 (as of 1890s), *Grannies* . . menses. **1948** *Word* 4.3.183, Female anthropomorphisms [for menstruation], particularly when phrased as relatives coming to visit, are numerous: *Grandma is here, Grandma has left . . Grandma's here from Red Creek.* **1954** *AmSp* 29.298 **FL, OK, TX,** Vernacular terms pertaining to menstruation. . . *Illness, inconvenience, or disability.* . . *got the grannies.* **1954** *Harder Coll.* **cwTN,** Grandma coming to see you. . . Menstruation has begun. **1965–70** *DARE* (Qu. AA27, . . *Menstruation*) Infs **MN**33, **OH**46, 47, Grandma came (to visit *or* today); **MI**75, Grandma comes visiting; **TX**74, Grandma's here; **MS**84, It's grandmamma's time; grandmamma is here; **GA**44, Grandmaw came to see me; **MO**29, Granmaw; **KY**44, **LA**2, Grannies; **CO**17, **IA**41, **MA**6, **OH**82, Granny; **GA**28, 67, (Old) granny's come; **CA**87, Granny's visiting; **TX**43, Gronnies [sic]. [15 of 19 Infs female] **1967** *DARE* FW Addit **MN,** *Granny*—a woman's period. Also called *granny chills.* **1971** Brunvand *Guide Folkl. UT* 37, Other commonly heard expressions are euphemistic references to sensitive subjects, like . . the term "Granny" for the menstrual period. **1978** *MJLF* 4.1.38 **cTX,** Euphemisms for menstruation—Some women personify the event: "Mother Nature," "Granny's coming."

5 See quots. Cf **granny hole 2**

1958 McCulloch *Woods Words* 73 **Pacific NW,** *Grandma*. . . The low gear on a truck. **1969** *AmSp* 44.205 [Trucker jargon], *Grandma* . . creeper gear [=lowest gear or combination of gears used for extra power].

6 See **grandmother 2.**

7 =**granny** n **3.**

1966 *DARE* (Qu. AA30, *An older woman who comes in . . to help when a baby is going to be born*) Inf **SD**2, The granma.

grandma v Also *granny* Also sp *grandmaw*

To steal timber; hence vbl nouns *grandmawing, grannying,* n *grandmawer:* see quot 1953.

1936 *AmSp* 11.315 **Ozarks,** *Grandmaw*. . . To steal timber. **1953** Randolph–Wilson *Down in Holler* 157, The Ozarker uses *grandmaw* as a verb, and it means to steal timber. In Howell County, Missouri, they say a young fellow accused of cutting ties on some rich man's property denied everything at first, but finally admitted that "*grandmaw* might have cut a few sticks over thar." Another explanation is that, asked where his firewood came from, a hillman answered "off'n grandmaw's place," meaning land belonging to some non-resident capitalist. Nancy Clemens identifies this with the common expression "grannying timber." In the *Missouri Conservationist* is an article entitled "Grandmawing Doesn't Pay," with the explanation that "here in the hills the act of cutting timber that doesn't belong to you is known as *grandmawing,* and the people who do such things are called *grandmawers.*"

grandma'am See **grandma** n **A6**

grandma bean n Also *granny*

A cultivar of the common bean (*Phaseolus* spp): see quots.

1970 *DARE* (Qu. I19, *Small white beans with a black spot where they were joined to the pod*) Inf **PA**234, Grammaw beans . . because they've been around so long. **1978** *Wanigan Catalog* 10, *Granny.* A size 2, fat, tan seed with a dark ring around the eye.

grandma gray n Also *old grandma gray*

A children's game.

1905 *DN* 3.82 **nwAR,** Gran'ma Gray, can I go play. . . The name of a girls' game. [**1969** Opie–Opie *Children's Games* 307 **Gt Brit,** Old Mother Grey. . . This game, which was highly popular in the nineteenth century, remains fairly general today among younger children. . . Usually one child is appointed 'Grandmother Grey' or 'Granny, Granny Grey' or 'Old Mother Grey,' and the other children gather around her chorusing. . . The children rush off, and play around, perhaps moving out of sight. . . Old Mother Grey runs after them, and whoever she catches becomes the next Mother.] **1970** *DARE* (Qu. EE33, . . *Outdoor games . . that children play now, or that were played in your childhood*) Inf **TX**104, Grandma Gray; **GA**90, Old granma gray.

grandmahm See **grandma** n **A6**

grandma hubbub See **grandmother humbum**

grandmam See **grandma** n **A6**

grandmam(m)a See **grandma** n **A5**

grandmamma's bonnet n Also *granny bonnet*

A sunbonnet.

1970 *DARE* (Qu. W2, . . *A cloth bonnet worn by women for protection from the sun*) Inf **TN**53, Grandmamma's bonnet—occasionally; **SC**70, Granny bonnet—no longer in use.

grandmammy See **grandma** n **A10**

grandmammy's nightcap n

A **dogtooth violet** (here: *Erythronium albidum*).

1897 *KS Univ. Qrly.* (ser B) 6.52, Easter-bells . . Granmammy's nightcaps . . (Erythronium albidum).

grandmar See **grandma** n **A13**

grandma's cap n Cf **Quaker bonnet**

A **lupine** (here: *Lupinus perennis*).

1966 *DARE* Wildfl QR Pl.106 Inf **WI**34A, Lupine . . grandmaw's cap.

grandma's darning needle n *arch*

A children's game.

1957 *Sat. Eve. Post Letters* **csIL,** Old witch and grandma's darning needle was played by my own grandmother when she was a child over one hundred years ago.

grandma's needles n Cf **beggar's needles**

=**beggar ticks 1.**

1967 *DARE* (Qu. S14, *Other prickly seeds, small and flat, with two prongs at one end, that cling to clothing*) Inf **SC**41, Grandma's needles—same as beggar lice.

grandmaw n See **grandma** n **A1**

grandmaw v See **grandma** v

grandmawer, grandmawing See **grandma** v

grandmom See **grandma** n **A6**

grandmomma See **grandma** n **A5**

grandmommy See **grandma** n **A11**

grandmother n

1 A **hedgenettle** (here: *Stachys bullata*).

1898 *Jrl. Amer. Folkl.* 11.277, *Stachys bullata* . . grandmother [Footnote: The flower looks like an old dame with a high cap.] . . San Mateo Co., Cal.

2 also *grandma:* A weak, timid, or cowardly man. *derog*

1940 (1942) Clark *Ox-Bow* 40 **NV** (as of 1885), Osgood was . . looking as if he were going to cry. . . Gil was behind us. He said to Osgood, "Shut up, gran'ma. Nobody expects you to go." **1969** *DARE* (Qu. HH11a, *Someone who is too particular or fussy . . a man*) Inf **NJ**57, Grandmother; **IN**61, Old grammaw.

3 in phrr *mean enough to kill his grandmother* (or *grandma*) and varr: Extremely mean, unkind.

1965–70 *DARE* (Qu. HH22c, *Talking about a very mean person, you might say, "He's mean enough to _______."*) 94 Infs, **scattered,** Rob (*or* arrest, beat, cheat, kill, shoot, steal from) his (own) grandmother; 21 Infs, **scattered,** Sell his (own) grandmother (down the river); **IL**7, **MN**38, **NY**105, **OH**61, **TX**10, **VA**5, Bite (*or* drown, fight, hurt, poison, skin) his grandmother; **CT**16, **IA**5, **KY**94, **MI**103, Screw (*or* starve, steal pennies from) his own grandmother; **IL**97, **MN**15, **NY**57, Steal his grandmother's eyeteeth (*or* last nickel, welfare check); **CA**145, Beat his grammaw; **AR**18, Beat up his granmaw; **MI**26, Cheat his own grammaw; **KY**10, Chop (*or* cut) his grandmother's head off; **AL**27, **AR**36, **NY**220, Hit his grandmother (with a shovel); **CA**1, Kill his grammaw downstairs; **MS**1, Kill his grandma; **SC**10, Kill he grammaw; **KS**18, Kill the grammaw; **PA**219, Not to give his grandmother a fair shake; **CA**66, Push his grandmother down the stairs; **WI**47, Rob his grandmother's grave; **SC**40, Rob his granmomma; **MN**36, Sell his grandmother to the glue works; **GA**77, Slap his grandmother down; **PA**35, Smack his grandma; **AZ**3, Steal the pennies off his own grandmother's eyes; **TX**28, Take the fillings out of his grandmother's teeth.

4 In marble play: a middle-sized marble. Cf **granddaddy 6**

c1970 Wiersma *Marbles Terms* **MI** [Black], *Grandmother*. . . A middle-sized marble, not the smallest or largest.

grandmother hooplescoople n Cf **old mother hobble-gobble**

1966 *Wilson Coll.* **csKY,** *Grandmother Hooplescoople* . . a children's game. "Grandmother Hooplescoople died last night." "How did she die?" "She died just so."—And you have to act it out.

grandmother humbum n Also *grandma hubbub*

=**old mother hobble-gobble.**

1953 Brewster *Amer. Nonsinging Games* 32, *Old Mother Hobble-Gobble* [Texas]—This game is known also as Grandmother Humbum, . . Mother McGee. **1967** *DARE* Tape **TX**40, We used to play one called, "Granmaw hubbub / sent me to you./ What to do?/ To beat two hammers / like I do!" And every one of 'em 'd be . . like they was beatin' hammers. Think they call that granmaw hubbub, and they'd go on two hands . . then go to their heads . . then they'd go to one foot, and then be about five or six by the time th' all get through.

grandmother's curl n
1968 *DARE* (Qu. E20, *Soft rolls of dust that collect on the floor under beds or other furniture*) Inf **PA**156, Grandmother's curls.

grandmother's darning needle n Cf **darning needle 2**
=**walkingstick.**
1969 *DARE* (Qu. R9a, *An insect from two to four inches long that lives in bushes and looks like a dead twig*) Inf **IL**30, Grandmother's darning needle.

grandmother's iron n *old-fash*
A sadiron.
1927 Sears *Catalogue* 970, Set of 3 Common Pattern 7-lb Sad-irons. . . Old style, commonly known as grandmother's irons, with a modern ventilated handle and smoothly polished bottoms.

grandmother's tea n Also *my grandmother doesn't like tea*
A children's game; see quots.
1945 Boyd *Hdbk. Games* 108, *My Grandmother Doesn't Like Tea*—One player who knows the game begins by saying, "My grandmother doesn't like tea but she likes coffee." The other players ask if she likes this or that. . . This continues until all the players have discovered that "grandmother" does not like anything the name of which contains the letter "t," but she does like everything the name of which contains double letters. **1966** *DARE* (Qu. EE33, . . *Outdoor games . . that children play now, or that were played in your childhood*) Inf **OK**31, Grandmother's tea—players are going to see grandmother, who can't have tea; in turn, players answer what they are going to bring her—food or drink, but none spelled with the letter "t"; if player can't answer, repeats, or gives an answer with the letter "t" (tomatoes, apricots, for example) he must pay a forfeit (sit on the floor, etc).

grandmother's thimble n
A **jack-in-the-pulpit.**
1968 *DARE* (Qu. S1, . . *Other names . . for the jack-in-the-pulpit*) Inf **KS**15, Grandmother's thimble.

grandmother stinks n Cf **stinking willie**
Perh a **trillium.**
1968 *DARE* (Qu. S26c, *Wildflowers that grow in woods*) Inf **NY**68, Grandmother stinks . . the leaves aren't too big; it don't grow up only about that high nohow [FW: about six inches].

grandmother troubles n
=**grandma** n **B4.**
1967 *DARE* (Qu. AA27, . . *Names . . for a woman's menstruation*) Inf **OH**31, Grandmother troubles.

grandmum See **grandma** n **A6**

grando See **grandma** n **A13**

grandpa n Usu |ˈgræn(d)ˌpɑ, -pa, -pə| (last syll represented in *DARE* quots by sp *-pa*); also |ˈgræn(d)ˌpɑ, -ˌpɔ| (repr by *-paw*) For addit varr see **A** below Cf **granther**
A Forms.
1 pronc-spp *gran(d)paw.* **chiefly Sth, S Midl** See Map
1960 Hall *Smoky Mt. Folks* 27, One of my grandpaws was part Black Dutch and part Irish. **1965–70** *DARE* (Qu. Z3, . . *Words . . for 'grandfather'*) 49 Infs, **chiefly Sth, S Midl,** Gran(d)paw. **1968** *DARE* Tape **AK**9, I stayed here with my granpaw [ˈgrænˌpɔ]. **1970** Tarpley *Blinky*

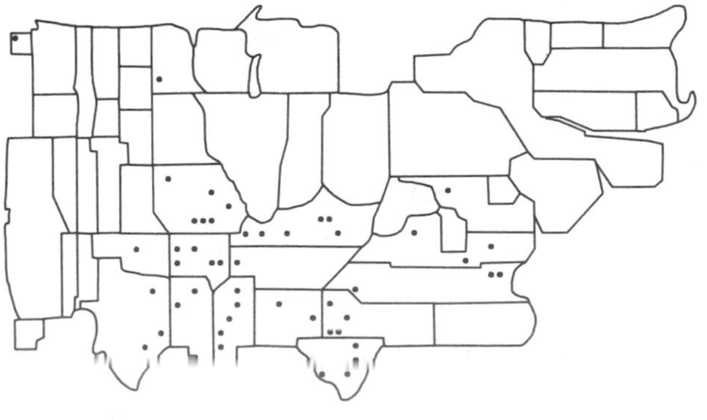
•grandpa A1 + var (Qu. Z3)

210 **neTX,** Usual term of affection for grandfather . . 48.5% [of 200 infs], Grandpaw. *Ibid* 211, The frequency of *grandpaw* diminishes as the informants grow younger and as community size grows larger.
2 pronc-spp *grampa, gramper.* **scattered, but chiefly Nth, N Midl, West** See Map
1894 in 1941 Warfel–Orians *Local-Color Stories* 742 **LA** [Black], How yer reckon I feels, mistus, when I looks at dem babies an' see how p'intedly dey favors dey gramper? **1934** Carmer *Stars Fell on AL* 177, Yes, grampa. **1941** *LANE* Map 381 *(Grandpa),* [Troncs of the types [græmpə, -pɑ, -pa, -pr] are very common throughout NEng.] **1954** *Harder Coll.* **cwTN,** Grampa. **1962** Atwood *Vocab. TX* 65, *Grandfather. . .* Grampa [5% of infs gave this response]. **1965–70** *DARE* (Qu. Z3, . . *Words . . for 'grandfather'*) 217 Infs, **scattered, but chiefly Nth, N Midl, West,** Grampa. **1967–69** *DARE* Tapes **AK**9, **IN**69, **TX**21, Grampa [ˈgræmpə].

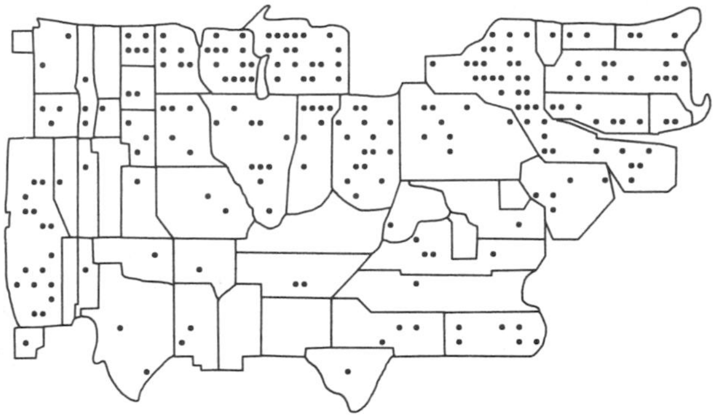
•grandpa A2 (Qu. Z3)

3 pronc-sp *grampaw.* **chiefly Midl; also Sth, West** See Map
1965–70 *DARE* (Qu. Z3, . . *Words . . people around here use for 'grandfather'*) 132 Infs, **chiefly Midl; also Sth, West,** Grampaw; (Qu. FF21a, *A joke that is so old it doesn't seem funny any more: "His jokes are all ______."*) Inf **IN**32, Grampaw jokes; (Qu. FF21b, . . *About old jokes people say*) Inf **IN**32, My grampaw fell out of the cradle laughing; (Qu. HH40) Infs **IL**143, **IN**49, Grampaw; (Qu. II10b) Inf **NY**234, Hey, grampaw. **1966** *DARE* Tape **FL**45, My friend . . here has told you about Nedley Turner, a relative of his grampaw's.

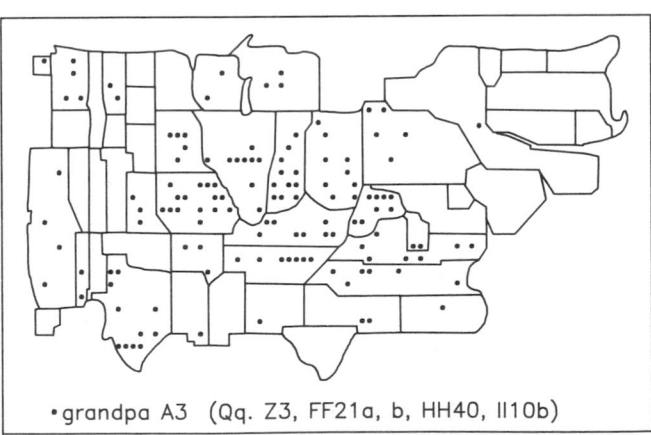

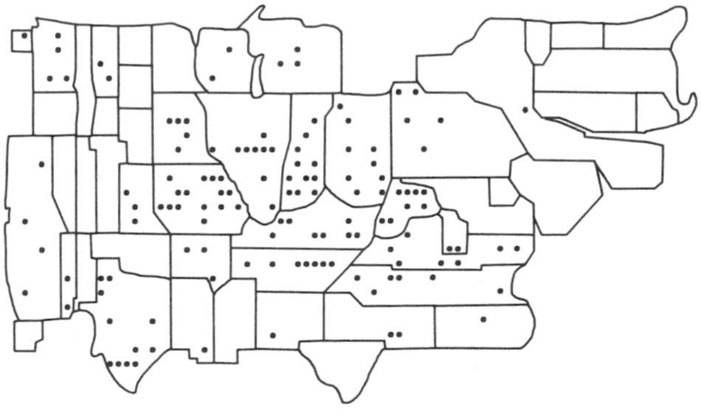
•grandpa A3 (Qq. Z3, FF21a, b, HH40, II10b)

4 also *gran(d)pap(py)* and varr. **scattered, but less freq N Atl, Pacific** See Map
1919 *DN* 5.39 **TN,** *Gran'-pappy. . .* Grand-father. "Before my pappy's er my gran'-pappy's time." **1934** Carmer *Stars Fell on AL* 183, An if'n yuh know what dat means, you'll git to bed right quick an' not try trickin' yo' great-gran'pappy no mo'. **1936** Reese *Worleys* 37 **MD** (as of 1865) [Black], Marse Mark Turnah's granpappy. **1938** Rawlings *Yearling* 92 **nFL,** Now Grandpappy, I kin see you settin' there on your stoop. **1939** *Hall Coll.* **wNC,** *Gran'pap. . .* Rather common colloquial for *grandfather.* "Eugene's gran'pap said *larn.*" **c1960** *Wilson Coll.* **csKY,** Grandpappy: Formerly used seriously; now largely comic. **1965–70** *DARE* (Qu. Z3) 25 Infs, **scattered, but less freq N Atl, Pacific,** Gran(d)pappy; 20 Infs, **scattered exc N Atl, Pacific,** Gran(d)pap; **IN**30, **MD**19, 21, 31,

PA94, 190, Grampap(py). **1982** *Barrick Coll.* **csPA,** *Grampap*—Grandfather.

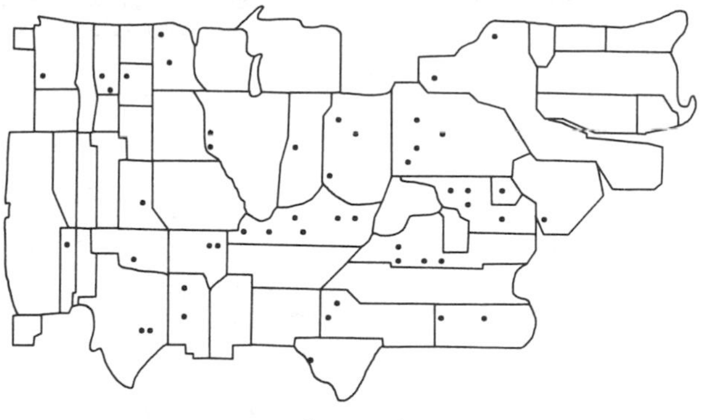

•grandpa A4 + varr (Qu. Z3)

5 also *gran(d)papa, grandpop(py),* and varr. **scattered, but chiefly C Atl, NY** See Map

1890 *Texas Siftings* 22 Nov. 10/1 *(OEDS),* 'Grandpop,' said he, 'did you know that there was flying fish?' **1899** Garland *Boy Life* 280 **nwIA,** But the dinner signal came . . through Gran'papa Stewart. **1931** in 1952 Crane *Letters* 10 Jan 363, Spinoza (Einstein's grandpop) furnishes plenty of discipline. **1965–70** *DARE* (Qu. Z3) 40 Infs, **scattered, but chiefly C Atl, NY,** Gran(d)pop; 12 Infs, **esp C Atl,** Grampop(py); **GA**57, **KY**80, 92, **NM**5, **PA**134, **TX**95, Grandpapa; **MS**15, **SC**7, Granpapa; **IL**28, **NY**123, Grandpoppy; **TX**51, Grampapa.

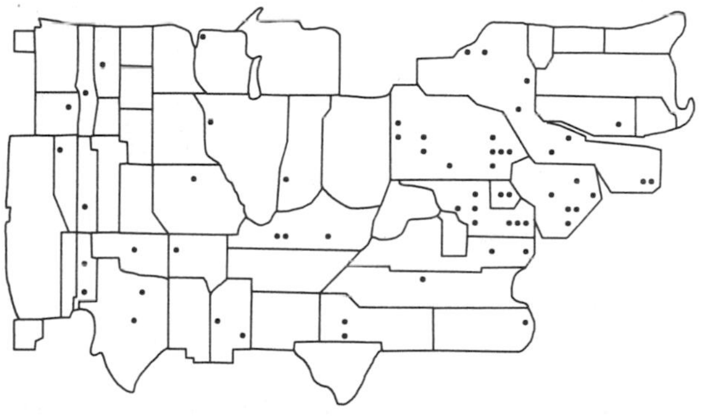

•grandpa A5 + varr (Qu. Z3)

6 abbr *gramp;* rarely *gramp-gramp.* **chiefly Nth, N Midl, esp NEng, Upstate NY** See Map

1941 *LANE* Map 381 *(Grandpa)* [Proncs of the type [græmp] are common **throughout NEng.**] **1944** *PADS* 2.25 **cwNC,** *Gramp. . .* Grandfather. **1948** Manfred *Chokecherry* 247 **nwIA,** Toots, she can go over to Gramp and Gramma Hansen. **1954** *Harder Coll.* **cwTN,** Gramp. **1960** Hall *Smoky Mt. Folks* 50, She was proud of the fact her "gramp" came to this country from across the waters about the time of the "Old War" (the Revolution). **1965–70** *DARE* (Qu. Z3, . . *Words . . people around here use for 'grandfather'*) 74 Infs, **chiefly Nth, N Midl, esp NEng, Upstate NY,** Gramp; **MA**42, Gramp-gramp.

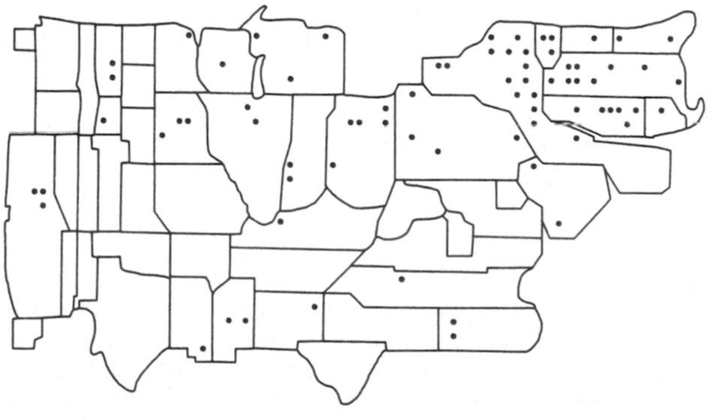

•grandpa A6 + var (Qu. Z3)

7 abbr *gramps.*

c1960 *Wilson Coll.* **csKY,** *Gramps. . .* Humorous name for grandfather; rare. **1962** Atwood *Vocab. TX* 65, *Grandfather. . .* Gramps [was given by 2.6% of approx 270 infs]. **1965–70** *DARE* (Qu. Z3) 84 Infs, **scattered,** Gramps.

8 also *grampy.* **esp NEast, N Cent**

1914 *DN* 4.152 **ME,** *Grampy. . .* Grandfather. **1941** *LANE* Map 381 *(Grandpa)* 51 infs, **chiefly ME,** Grampy. **1965–70** *DARE* (Qu. Z3) 11 Infs, **esp NEast, N Cent,** Grampy. **1989** *DARE* File **MA,** I didn't hear the term *grampy* used in Maine but when I was young [in the late 1950s] my parents and grandparents got together and decided that my brother and I should distinguish the sets of grandparents by calling my mother's parents Grandma and Grandpa, and my father's Grammy and Grampy, which we still do today.

9 also *grumpa, grumpuh, grumpy, grumps.*

1922 Gonzales *Black Border* 305 **sSC, GA coasts** [Gullah glossary], *Grum'pa, grum'puh*—grandpa, grandfather. **1970** *DARE* (Qu. Z3, . . *Words . . for 'grandfather'*) Inf **CO**47, Grumpy; **SC**66, Grumps.

10 with |-pæ|. **SC** Cf **grandma A12**

1966–67 *DARE* (Qu. Z3) Infs **SC**4, 19, 21, 24, 44, [grænpæ]; **SC**11, [græmpæ^{I}]; **SC**10, [grʌmpæ].

11 Other varr.

1941 *LANE* Map 381 *(Grandpa)* 1 inf, **nwVT,** [grɒmpiˑ]; 1 inf, **swVT,** [grɒmp]. **1966–70** *DARE* (Qu. Z3) Inf **CT**36, Granky; **MS**6, Grandy; **NY**250, Grandpan; **KY**34, [drænpæp].

B Senses.

1 An old man—also used as a term of address.

1942 Berrey–Van den Bark *Amer. Slang* 384.2, *Old man. . .* Gramp, grampy, gran(d)pappa, gran(d)pappy, grandpop. **1965–70** *DARE* (Qu. HH40, *Uncomplimentary words for an old man*) Infs **AL**60, **CA**117, **IL**46, 47, **NY**81, **OH**94, Grandpa; **NC**87, Grandpa (name); **IL**143, **IN**49, Grampaw; (Qu. HH11a, *Someone who is too particular or fussy —if it's a man*) Inf **OH**94, Old grandpa; (Qu. II10b, *Asking directions of somebody on the street when you don't know his name—what you'd say to a man*) Inf **NY**234, Hey grampaw.

2 In logging and railroading: a general supervisor or manager.

1968 Adams *Western Words* 131, *Grandpa*—What the logger calls the general superintendent. **1969** Sorden *Lumberjack Lingo* 49 **NEng, Gt Lakes,** *Grandpa*—A general superintendent. **1977** Adams *Lang. Railroader* 70, *Grandpa:* A general manager.

3 See quot.

1917 *DN* 4.421 **LA,** *Grandpa. . .* A bit of floating thistledown.

4 See quot.

1968 *DARE* (Qu. P21, *Small frogs that sing or chirp loudly in spring*) Inf **OH**60, Grampas.

5 A bull. *euphem* Cf *DS* K22, 23

1977 Jones *OR Folkl.* 101/2 (as of 1949), *Grandpa:* euphemism for bull.

grandpa house n

1938 FWP *Guide IA* 361, After the marriage [among the Hook and Eye Dutch] a small house is built behind the larger house of the young man's parents. This is called the "Grandpa House", because the parents move into it, giving the larger house to the newly-weds.

grandpa longlegs See **granddaddy longlegs 1**

grandpan See **grandpa A11**

grandpap See **grandpa A4**

grandpapa n

1 See **grandpa A5.**

2 See **granddaddy 6.**

grandpappy See **grandpa A4**

grandpa's beard See **grandfather's beard 2**

grandpa's specs n [Prob from the lenslike appearance of the seedpod]

An **honesty** (here: *Lunaria annua*).

1959 Carleton *Index Herb. Plants* 55, *Grandpa's specs:* lunaria annua (l. biennis).

grandpaw See **grandpa A1**

grandpa whiskers See **grandfather's whiskers**

grandpop(py) See **grandpa A5**

grand rascal n

A scoundrel; a mischievous child.

1929 *AmSp* 5.18 **Ozarks,** *Grand-rascal*. . . A cheat, a petty grafter. The noun and adjective are pronounced together as one word, with the accent on *grand*. **c1960** *Wilson Coll.* **csKY,** *Grand-rascal*. . . A cheat, a confidence man. **1966** *DARE* (Qu. Z16, *A small child who is rough, misbehaves, and doesn't obey, you'd call him a ______*) Inf **SC**10, Grand rascal—used about a boy; girls are "mischievous." **1984** Wilder *You All Spoken Here* 3 **Sth,** Grand rascal: A cheat; a scoundrel.

Grand River tuna n [*Grand River,* Michigan] *joc* Cf **Albany beef, family whitefish 2**

A **white sucker** (here: *Catostomus commersoni*).

1970 *DARE* (Qu. P3) Inf **MI**123, Grand River tuna—nickname for a sucker. [Also called] sewer bass. **1974** *DARE* File **swMI** (as of 1973), Grand River tuna. . . A sucker fish . . Humorous: Grand Rapids, Michigan.

grandsire n Also sp *gran(d)sir;* pronc-spp *gramsey, grancy, gransa, gransy* **chiefly NEng, S Midl**

A Forms.

1907 *DN* 3.188 **NH,** *Gran'sir*. . . Grandfather, grandsire. "Gran'sir was in the war of eighteen twelve." **1908** [see **granddaddy graybeard 2**]. **1913** Kephart *Highlanders* 291 **sAppalachians,** We will hear an aged man referred to as "old Grandsir' " So-and-So. **1924** Raine *Land of Saddle-Bags* 78 **Appalachians,** Then she dyes it [=yarn] . . and weaves it on the heavy loom that her grandsire made. *Ibid* 101, Grandsir (Grandsire) owns a big scope o' land. **1928** Chapman *Happy Mt.* 15 **seTN,** You're just like that time when you was a tinsey tad, and swallowed a cartridge out of your grandsir's sheriff gun. **c1938** [see **grandfather's beard 2**]. **1941** *LANE* Map 380 *(Grandfather)* 7 infs, **chiefly nNEng,** Grandsire. *Ibid* Map 381 *(Grandpa)* 14 infs, **chiefly nNEng,** Grandsir. **1945** [see **granddaddy graybeard 2**]. **1957** Beck *Folkl. ME* 168, "Gran'sir" [is the term] for grandfather. **1965–70** *DARE* (Qu. Z3) Inf **MA**5, Grandsir; **FL**17, Grandsire (plus last name). **1969** [see **B** below]. **1974** *AmSp* 49.62 **sME coast** (as of c1900), Grandsir, gran'sir . . Grandfather.

B Sense.

=daddy longlegs 1.

1969 *DARE* (Qu. R28, *What different kinds of spiders do you have around here?*) Inf **NC**72, Granddaddy longlegs, also called gransa ['grænsə].

grandsir graybeard See **granddaddy graybeard 2**

grandsir longlegs See **granddaddy longlegs 1**

grand'ther See **granther**

grandy See **grandpa A11**

grandykye See **grand écaille**

grange n **chiefly NEast** See Map

A cooperative association of farm families for the promotion of agricultural interests; a local unit of the association.

1868 in 1911 Commons *Doc. Hist. Amer. Industrial Soc.* 10.79, Every Grange is in intimate relation with its neighboring Granges, and these with the State Grange, and the State Granges are in unity with the National Grange. **1884** Cooper-Fenton *Amer. Politics* 1.218/1, So early as 1867 a secret society had been formed first in Washington, known as the Patrons of Husbandry, and it soon succeeded in forming subordinate lodges or granges in Illinois, Wisconsin, and other States. **1941** *Yankee* Dec. 25/1 *(DA),* Gossip and Apple Pie are only a small part of a Grange meeting. **1946** Holbrook *Lost Men* 215, Traveling often on something less than a shoestring, Kelley swept through the Middle West, dispensing charters for local granges to pay his expenses. **1965–70** *DARE* (Qu. FF22b, . . *Clubs and societies around here—for men*) 38 Infs, **chiefly NEast,** Grange; **NH**11, Grange club; **NJ**6, Grange lyric opera; (Qu. FF22a, . . *Clubs and societies around here—for women*) 20 Infs, **chiefly NEast,** Grange; **CT**23, Grange society; **IL**11, Grange circle; **MA**6, Grange number fifty-two; **NY**209, Women's auxiliary of the grange; **NJ**6, Grange lyric opera; **NJ**29, American grange; **OH**20, Women's grange; **OR**6, Grange home ec[onomics]; **PA**81, Grange ladies; (Qu. FF1, . . *A 'social' or 'sociable'*. . . *What kinds are there?*) Infs **NY**84, 105, **OH**72, **PA**165, **VT**12, Grange social; **NJ**20, Grange sociable; (Qu. FF2, . . *Kinds of parties . . around here*) Inf **MA**40, Grange meetings; (Qu. FF4, . . *Kinds of dancing parties*) Inf **NY**190, Grange dances; (Qu. FF16, . . *Local contests or celebrations*) Infs **CT**10, **ME**19, **MI**114, Grange fairs; **ME**19, **MA**58, Grange picnics; **RI**15, Grange harvest; (Qu. FF23, . . *Joking names . . for . . clubs or lodges*) Inf **CA**21, Grange.

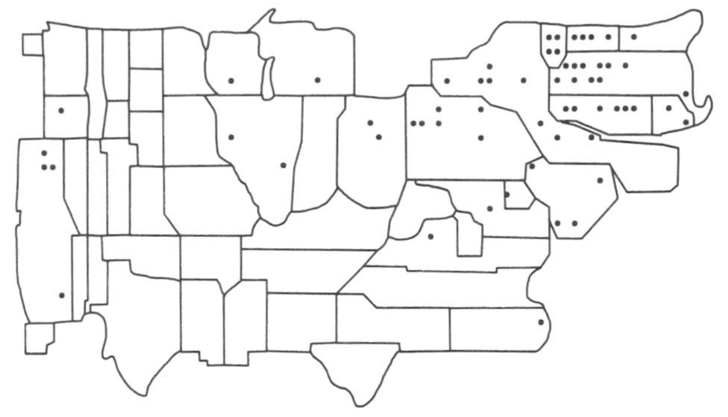

•grange + varr (Qq. FF22a, b, FF1, FF2, FF4, FF16, FF23)

granger n Also *granger farmer* Cf **nester**

A farmer.

1877 Burdette *Rise & Fall* 11 **seIA,** We have always pictured Adam as . . a puzzled looking granger who would sigh fifty times a day. **1887** Randall *Lady's Ranche Life* 121 **MT,** They call the farmers here "grangers," as distinct from ranchmen or stock-men, and it is a term of reproach—not quite that, either—but still the granger is held in low estimation by the stock-man. **1893** Roosevelt *Wilderness Hunter* 111 **swMT,** We hired a team and wagon from a "busted" granger, suspected of being a Mormon, who had failed . . in raising a crop. **1928** French *Ranchman NM* 40, We harvested our first potatoes, and Wilson and I were proud of them; but the cowboys looked askance and pronounced them only fit food for a 'granger'. **1931** *AmSp* 6.359 **Plains States,** The nester and the granger farmer fenced the lands and streams without which the cattleman could not survive. **1935** Sandoz *Jules* 22 **wNE** (as of 1880–1930), Only one more granger scalp if the Sioux broke out. *Ibid* 37, But you grangers'll never have no money.

granhaney See **granjeno**

granite n

In marble play: see quot.

1966–68 *DARE* (Qu. EE6a, . . *Kinds of marbles—the big one that's used to knock others out of the ring*) Inf **AL**26, Granite; (Qu. EE6d, *Special marbles*) Inf **IN**49, Granites.

granite orchard n

=marble orchard.

1968 *DARE* (Qu. BB61b, . . *Joking names for a cemetery*) Inf **NY**43, Granite orchard; tombstones used to be made of granite, not marble; hence the name.

granite toad n

A **treefrog** (here: *Hyla arenicolor*).

1947 Pickwell *Amphibians* 18, *Hyla arenicolor,* the . . Granite . . Toad. . . has a pattern of markings, sand colored as its specific name indicates, making it look much like the granite boulders to which it so frequently clings.

granjeno n Also *granhaney* [MexSpan] **esp TX**

A **hackberry** *(Celtis pallida)*. Also called **algeredo, corkscrew bush, thorny bill**

1895 *Jrl. Amer. Folkl.* 8.47, The *Granjeno* is a parasitic bush. **1925** TX Folkl. Soc. *Pub.* 4.36, *Granjeno* is a kind of thorny bush indigenous to the Southwest. Texans call it granhaney. . . Birds carry the seeds of the "granhaney" and sometimes an old fence . . will be almost lined with the bushes. **1937** Parks *Plants TX* 25, *Celtis pallida*. . . Granjeno. A bush-like shrub which is a honey plant and bears numerous berries in the fall which are collected for jellies and in many places sold under the name of algeredo. **1949** *Chi. Tribune* 20 Feb. 30/3 *(DA),* Cedar and mesquite alone are costing Texas ranchers 115 million dollars a year. Add the sage and cactus, . . persimmon, huisache, granjeno . . and prickly pear and the toll is terrific. **1967** *DARE* (Qu. T5, . . *Evergreens, other than pine, . . around here*) Inf **TX**22, Granjeno [ˌgrɑn'henjo].

granky See **grandpa A11**

granma('a)m See **grandma** n **A6**

gran'maamy See **grandma** n **A10**

granmam(m)a See **grandma** n **A5**

granmammy See **grandma** n **A10**

granmaw See **grandma** n **A1**

granmom See **grandma** n **A6**

granmomma See **grandma** n **A5**

granmommy See **grandma** n **A11**

granna bag n Also *granna sack* [Perh varr of **guano sack;** cf **guano A**] **MD** Cf **gunny sack**

See quots.

1957 Battaglia *Resp. to PADS 20* **eMD** (*A cloth container for grain*) Granna bag . . granna—coarse fiber. *Ibid* (*A large container made of rough, loosely woven light-brown cloth*) Granna bag. **1968** *DARE* (Qu. F19, *A cloth container for grain*) Inf **MD**35, Granna ['grænə] bag; (Qu. F20, *A cloth container for feed*) Inf **MD**19, Granna bag ['grænə ˌbeɪg], granna sack—old words; **MD**35, Granna bag; (Qu. F23, *A container made of rough, loosely-woven, brown cloth; commonly used for potatoes, etc*) Infs **MD**19, 35, Granna bag.

granner See **grandma** n **A13**

grannie See **grandma** n **A7**

granny n

1 See **grandma** n **A7.**

2 An old woman—also used as a term of address.

1899 (1912) Green *VA Folk-Speech* 203, *Granny*. . . An old woman. **1922** Gonzales *Black Border* 304 **sSC, GA coasts** [Gullah glossary], *Granny*—grandmother, but used for any old Negro woman, whether related or not. **1941** *LANE* Map 383, *Granny,* with or without a proper name, is used by three informants [in Connecticut] in referring to old women generally, especially to those of low station. **1956** *Hall Coll.* **eTN,** Ellis . . mentioned Granny Shields and Granny Perryman, but explained that they were not his grandmothers. "Everybody called 'em 'granny,'" he said. **1957** Beck *Folkl. ME* 168, "Granny" is the term for any elderly woman. **1967** *Daily Post–Athenian* (Athens TN) 15 Dec 7/2, Birthday greetings to . . Granny Loc Newton, who will be 77 years old Christmas Day.

3 also *granny midwife:* A midwife. **chiefly Sth, S Midl** See Map Cf **granny woman**

1794 in 1892 Washington *Writings* 13.18 **eVA,** An application was made to me by Kate at Muddy hole (through her husband, Will) to serve the negro women (as a Grany [sic]) on my estate. **1809** (1814) Weems *F. Marion* 20 **SC,** Among the Mohawks of Sparta, it was a constant practice, on the birth of a male infant, to set a military granny to examine him as a butcher would a veal for the market. **1814** in 1956 Eliason *Tarheel Talk* 274 **NC,** Paid Granny Judy. **1899** (1912) Green *VA Folk-Speech* 203, *Granny* . . a midwife. **1908** *DN* 3.317 **eAL, wGA,** *Granny* . . an accoucheuse, a midwife. **1945** Pickard–Buley *Midwest Pioneer* 32 (as of 1824), True, some of these local "grannies," as well as pioneer doctors, were very skillful at child delivery. **1946** *PADS* 5.24 **sAppalachians,** *Granny, granny-woman:* Midwife; common everywhere. **1949** [see **granny woman**]. **1950** *PADS* 14.33 **SC. c1960** *Wilson Coll.* **csKY,** *Granny*. . . A midwife or acting as one. **1965–70** *DARE* (Qu. AA30, *An older woman who comes in [or used to come in] to help when a baby is going to be born*) 62 Infs, **chiefly Sth, S Midl,** Granny; **CT**6, Old granny. **1968** *DARE* Tape **GA**67, If she had asked her [=a Black woman], "Auntie, are you a granny?" she would've said "Yes," because that's what they called the midwives. **1971** *Foxfire* Winter 247 **nGA,** In the state today there are about 85 granny midwives who are over 65 years of age, and there are only 196 total. They used to be up in the thousands.

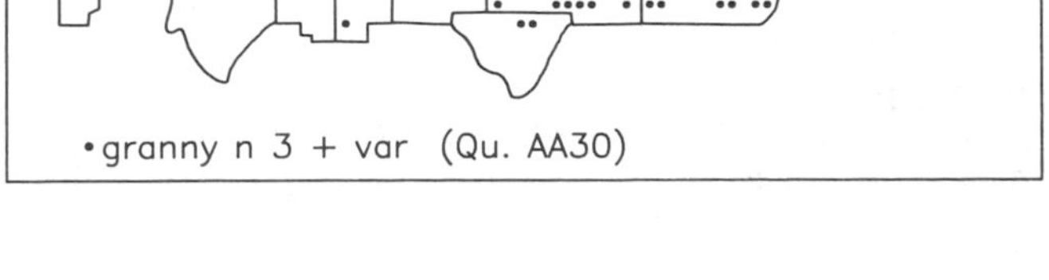

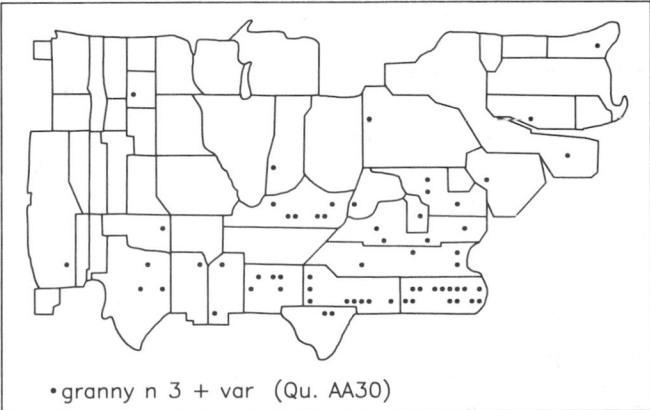

•granny n 3 + var (Qu. AA30)

4 A fussy, finicky old person. Cf **grandmother 2, granny grunt 2**

1842 (1844) Sealsfield *Life New World* (transl. Hebbe & Mackay) 205/1, The Creoles and French are, in this respect, careless, chattering, and barking grannies. **1907** *DN* 3.188 **NH,** *Granny*. . . A fussy person of either sex. "He's a terrible old granny." **1909** *DN* 3.411 **nME,** *Granny*. . . A fussy, officious, nervous man. **1923** *DN* 5.209 **swMO,** *Granny* . . a senile man or woman. **1930** Shoemaker *1300 Words* 25 **cPA Mts** (as of c1900), *Granny*—A womanish type of man. **1966–68** *DARE* (Qu. GG14, . . *Someone who fusses or worries a lot, especially about little things*) Inf **MN**2, Granny; **NJ**10, Granny; (Qu. HH11a, *Someone who is too particular or fussy—if it's a man*) Infs **CA**61, **CT**16, **SD**5, (Old, regular) granny; [(Qu. HH11b, *Someone who is too particular or fussy—if it's a woman*) Inf **VA**5, Worse than an old granny].

5 A grandfather.

1966–68 *DARE* (Qu. Z3, . . *Words . . for 'grandfather'*) Infs **LA**40, **SC**11, Granny.

6 See **granny knot 1.**

7 also pl; usu in phrr: Used as an exclamation of surprise, emphasis, annoyance, etc. **chiefly Sth, S Midl** Cf **gonnies**

1863 *Ladies' Repository* 23.482/2, "Repose, your granny," answered Addie, who, when vexed, never stopped for elegant phrases. **1875** (1876) Twain *Tom Sawyer* 25.193 **MO,** "Do they hop?" "Hop?—your granny! No." **1908** *DN* 3.317 **eAL, wGA,** *Granny, grannies*. . . A mild expletive. **1917** McCutcheon *Green Fancy* 256 **IN,** "Secret granny!" almost shouted O'Dowd. **1942** McAtee *Dial. Grant Co. IN Suppl. 1* 6 (as of 1890s), *Granny* . . rump, ass; "Aw yer ______", exclamation of disagreement or disbelief. **1952** Brown *NC Folkl.* 1.547, *Grannys alive*. . . A mild oath.—General. . . *Granny sakes*. . . A mild oath.—General. **1965–70** *DARE* (Qu. KK62) Inf **KY**16, My granny; (Qu. NN6b) Inf **SC**26, Good granny; (Qu. NN8b) Inf **NC**79, By granny; (Qu. NN28a) Inf **AR**41, Granny grief; **FL**28, Granny; **NM**6, Grannies alive; **SC**34, Grannies; (Qu. NN29a) Inf **GA**5, Granny; (Qu. NN32) Inf **MD**30, Grannies. **1975** Newell *If Nothin' Don't Happen* 25 **nwFL,** By grannies, you're a-goin' to anyhow.

8 also *old granny:* **=old-squaw.**

1888 Trumbull *Names of Birds* 89, Old Squaw. . . In New Jersey . . at Atlantic City and Somers Point, *Old Granny,* and *Granny* simply. **1917** (1923) *Birds Amer.* 1.141, *Old-squaw*. . . *Other Names*. . . Old Granny. **1923** U.S. Dept. Ag. *Misc. Circular* 13.24 **NJ,** *Clangula hyemalis*. . . *Vernacular Names*. . . *In local use*. . . Granny; . . old-granny. **1982** Elman *Hunter's Field Guide* 232, *Oldsquaw*. . . *Common & regional names* . . granny. *Ibid* 235, On the Atlantic Flyway, the "grannies" have traditionally supplemented scoters as winter targets for seagoing New Englanders.

9 See **grandma** n **B4.**

10 See **granny bar.**

11 also *granny gown, granny (Hubbard) dress:* See quot.

1965–70 *DARE* (Qu. W22, . . *A loose, full housedress that ties at the waist*) Infs **MA**6, **MI**51, **OK**9, 28, **WA**17, Granny; **GA**23, **OH**57, **OR**6, **WY**3, Granny dress; **CA**29, Granny gown; **GA**77, Granny Hubbard dress.

12 An unpopped kernel of popcorn; an **old maid.**

1968 *DARE* FW Addit **ID,** *Grannies* . . popcorn that doesn't pop.

13 See quot. Cf **granny wants a grunt**

1968 *DARE* (Qu. EE33, . . *Outdoor games . . that children play now, or that were played in your childhood*) Inf **OH**87, Granny; we used to say "Granny with her tinker tale / Went down into the wishing well." We sat in a circle and "granny" got in the middle.

14 pl; In marble play: a type of shot; see quot.

c1970 Wiersma *Marbles Terms, Grannies*—roll marble from the thumb placed against the index finger.

15 A mistake, error. [Cf **granny knot 1**]

1975 Gould *ME Lingo* 115, *Granny*. . . To make a *granny* is to pull a booboo; to do something *barse-ackwards*.

16 See **grandma bean.**

17 attrib; Of an eating utensil or knife: made of a single piece of metal with wooden facings on the handle.

1968 *Daily Republican Eagle* (Red Wing MN) 1 May 7/2, Finest Quality, Razor Sharp—Pure Stainless Steel—Granny Knife—7-inch length. [*DARE* Ed: It looks like a paring knife with the typical wooden handle.] **1985** *DARE* File **csMI,** A granny fork is made of a single piece of steel cut to the shape of a fork, with two wooden pieces fastened on the handle. Some are very plain and some fairly elaborate, with good wood and metal decoration.

granny v

1 also *granny-wife:* To perform the services of a midwife; to act as a midwife for; to assist in the delivery of (a child, or rarely, an animal); hence vbl nouns *grannying, granny-wifing.* **[granny n 3] chiefly Sth, S Midl**

1897 Stuart *Simpkinsville* 85 **AR,** She grannied yore mother when you was born. **1923** *DN* 5.209 **swMO,** *Granny*. . . To perform the duties of a midwife. **1931** Randolph *Ozarks* 83, *Granny* is often used as a verb, designating the actual delivery of the child. It is sometimes employed with reference to the lower animals, and I have heard a hillman speak of *grannyin'* a cow. **1939** *Hall Coll.* **eTN,** *Granny*. . . Of a grannywoman (midwife): To deliver a baby. "My mommy Nancy Hicks and Aunt Marg would granny the babies. Aunt Marg grannied me." **1942** (1971) Campbell *Cloud-Walking* 15 **seKY,** Mostly grannying didn't misput Sary no great sight. **1942** Hurston *Dust Tracks* 38 **FL** [Black], The man who grannied me was back next day to see how I was coming along. . . He remarked that I was a God-damned fine baby. **1947** *McDavid Coll.* **csGA,** I never would let no man granny no babies of mine. **1948** *Sat. Eve. Post* 221.26.16/2 **TN** [Black], She got her herbs . . And grannied for Poor Little Jesus! **1949** *AmSp* 24.109 **GA,** *Granny.* **1950** *PADS* 14.33 **SC,** *Granny.* **1960** Williams *Walk Egypt* 55 **GA,** She stayed out most of the time, yarbing [=gathering herbs] in the hills and granny-wifing.

2 See **grandma** v.

granny bar n Also *granny (tool)*

A crowbar.

1919 *DN* 5.56 **Pacific NW,** *Granny bar.* A huge crowbar used in quarries that takes several men to work. Probably because it is the grandmother of crowbars. **1942** Berrey–Van den Bark *Amer. Slang* 75.6, *Bar; prying tool* . . granny tool. *Ibid* 514.4, *Mining equipment* . . granny bar, *a large crowbar.* **1968** Adams *Western Words* 131, *Granny bar*. . . A logger's and miner's name for an enormous crowbar. **1969** *DARE* (Qu. L39, *An iron bar with a bent end, used for pulling nails, opening boxes, and so on*) Inf **NH**18, Granny.

granny bonnet See **grandmamma's bonnet**

granny cat n

=flathead catfish 1.

1902 Jordan–Evermann *Amer. Fishes* 32, In the South it [=the flathead catfish] is known as the "pieded cat," Opelousas cat, and mud cat, the last of these being also generally used in the North, where it is also called granny cat. **1927** *DN* 5.474 **Ozarks,** *Granny cat*. . . A small, square-nosed yellow catfish (*Pilodictis* [sic] *olivaris*). **1983** Becker *Fishes WI* 728, *Flathead Catfish—Pylodictis olivaris* . . flathead . . granny cat.

granny chills n pl Cf **granny grunt 1**

1967 *DARE* FW Addit **MN,** *Granny*—a woman's period. Also called *granny chills.*

granny doctor n Cf **granny woman**

A midwife; an obstetrician.

1917 *DN* 4.412 **wNC,** *Granny doctor.* Any obstetrician. **1966–70** *DARE* (Qu. AA30, *An older woman who comes in* . . *to help when a baby is going to be born*) Infs **KY**94, **SC**7, Granny doctor.

granny dress See **granny n 11**

granny frolic n Cf **granny n 3**

1984 Wilder *You All Spoken Here* 34 **Sth,** Granny frolic: A party of adult womenfolk to celebrate the birth of a grandchild.

granny gown See **granny n 11**

granny, granny, grunt See **granny wants a grunt**

granny grass n

Perh **=grama grass 1.**

1968 *DARE* (Qu. L8, *Hay that grows naturally in damp places*) Inf **IN**3, Granny grass; (Qu. S8, *A common kind of wild grass that grows in fields: it spreads by sending out long underground roots, and it's hard to get rid of*) Inf **IN**3, Granny grass.

granny graybeard n Also *granny's beard* Cf **granddaddy graybeard 2**

=fringe tree.

1967 *DARE* File **TX,** Granny graybeard, granny's beard—also called fringe tree.

granny grunt n

1 pl: See quot. Cf **grandma n B4**

1908 *DN* 3.317 **eAL, wGA,** *Granny grunts*. . . The stomach ache. . . The menses.

2 A fussy or querulous person. Cf **granny n 4**

1968 *DARE* (Qu. GG14, . . *Someone who fusses or worries a lot*) Inf **NJ**10, Granny grunt. **1986** *DARE* File **ceWI** (as of c1930), I remember hearing "granny grunt" often used when speaking about grumblers or malcontents, as, "He's such a granny grunt."

3 See quot.

1942 *Amer. Mercury* 55.223.85 **Harlem NYC** [Black], If you don't know what you talkin' 'bout, you better ask Granny Grunt. *Ibid* 223, *Granny Grunt*—a mythical character to whom most questions may be referred.

granny hatchet n

A **fence lizard 1** (here: *Sceloporus undulatus*).

1911 *DN* 3.538 **eKY,** Granny-hatchet. . . The gray lizard, *sceloporus undulatus.* **1940** (1978) Still *River of Earth* 57 **KY,** The guinea eggs hatched. The speckled fowls were as wild as partridges; they were as swift as granny hatchets. We rarely saw them.

granny hole n

1 =glory hole 1.

1968 *DARE* (Qu. D7, *A small space anywhere in a house where you can hide things or get them out of the way*) Inf **NY**123, Granny hole.

2 See quot. Cf **grandma n B5**

1984 *MJLF* 10.150, *Granny hole.* First gear [of a truck or tractor].

granny Hubbard dress See **granny n 11**

grannying vbl n

1 See **granny v 1.**

2 See **grandma** v.

granny knot n

1 also *granny, granny's knot:* An unreliable knot often mistakenly tied by greenhorns instead of a reef or square knot.

1853 (1949) Thoreau *Jrl.* 5.335, I had been all the while tying what is called a granny's knot. **1859** Shillaber *Knitting-Work* 170 **MA,** Another . . kept at home altogether, because the minister tied his handkerchief in a granny-knot. [**1909** *DN* 3.411 **ME,** *Granny-knot*. . . Two ends of a string tied together in one single knot.] **1912** Green *VA Folk-Speech* 203, *Granny's knot*. . . A knot that comes untied easily. **1945** Colcord *Sea Language* 88 **ME, Cape Cod, Long Island,** *Granny.* Shortened form of a granny's knot, a square-knot improperly tied so that it will slip. The mark of a landlubber. **1975** Gould *ME Lingo* 115, *Granny*—When the simple reef or square knot is improperly bent, it becomes a *granny.* This defeats the simplicity of undoing it.

2 also *granny pine:* See quot 1923. **[granny n 3]**

1923 *DN* 5.209 **swMO,** *Granny-knot*. . . A large pine knot that will burn all or most of a night and thus provide light by which a midwife may work. **1969** *DARE* FW Addit **KY**19, An anxious husband was caring for his pregnant wife. He kept a pine knot handy in case he'd have to go after the granny at night. When the time came, he said "time to fetch the granny pine." A joking phrase.

3 See quot.

1968 *DARE* (Qu. X3, *When a woman puts her hair up on her head in a bunch, you call this a* ______) Inf **VA**5, Granny knot.

granny midwife See **granny n 3**

granny-nipper n

1 =gallinipper 1a. [Prob by folk-etym]

1968 *DARE* (Qu. R15b, *An extra-big mosquito*) Inf **MD**36, Granny-nipper.

2 =**daddy longlegs 1.**

1968 *DARE* (Qu. R28, . . *Different kinds of spiders*) Inf **MD**36, Granny-nipper . . a daddy longlegs. Some people apply this term to a large mosquito, but it really refers to this spider.

granny off n

=**duck on a rock.**

1901 *DN* 2.141 **NY,** *Granny off.* . . The name of a game; same as duck on a rock.

granny pine See **granny knot 2**

‡granny pump n [Prob by metath and folk-etym]

1968 *DARE* FW Addit **csNC,** *Granny pumps* . . reported as a local variation of pomegranates by a school teacher.

granny rag n

1 See quot. Also called **chest bib**

1970 Anderson *TX Folk Med.* xvii, "Granny rag"—a flannel cloth smeared with suet or with lard, camphor, dry mustard, turpentine, or coal oil and some other "medicines" for good measure.

2 See quots. Cf **grandma** n **B4**

1957 *Sat. Eve. Post Letters* **cwNY,** *Granny rags* . . term for the home-made equivalent of Kotex. **1969** *DARE* FW Addit **MA**25, Granny rags . . pieces of cloth women and girls used years ago during menstruation.

3 A head scarf. Cf **babushka**

1966 *DARE* (Qu. W3, *A piece of cloth that a woman folds over her head and ties under her chin*) Inf **NC**36, Granny rag.

granny's beard See **granny graybeard**

‡granny's colt, ride v phr Cf **shanks' mare**

1969 *DARE* (Qu. Y24, . . *To walk, to go on foot: "I can't get a ride, so I'll just have to* ______ .") Inf **KY**28, Ride granny's colt [laughter]—old-fashioned.

granny scrape See **granny trouble**

granny's knot See **granny knot 1**

granny threads n

A **buttercup 1** (here: *Ranunculus repens*).

1900 Lyons *Plant Names* 316, *R[anunculus] repens.* . . Granny-threads. **1940** Clute *Amer. Plant Names* 229, *Ranunculus repens.* Granny-threads.

granny tool See **granny bar**

granny trouble n Also *granny scrape* [**granny** n **3**]

Childbirth.

1954 *PADS* 21.29 **SC,** *Granny scrape.* . . A birth in the family. "John is expecting a granny scrape at his house." *Granny* is rather generally used for a midwife. **1974** Fink *Mountain Speech* 11 **wNC, eTN,** *Granny-trouble* . . birth. "He had granny trouble at his house last night." **1976** Garber *Mountain-ese* 36 **Appalachians,** *Granny- trouble* . . childbirth—Ma is stayin' with Miz Brown, who is havin' granny trouble.

granny wants a grunt n Also *granny, granny, grunt* Cf **granny** n **13**

Any of var children's games; see quots.

1908 *DN* 3.317 **eAL, wGA,** *Granny, granny, grunt.* . . The name of a children's game. **1966–70** *DARE* (Qu. EE33, *Other outdoor games*) Infs **AL**3, **PA**35, **WV**7, 8, 14, Granny wants a grunt; **OK**42, Granny wants a grunt—not played much any more; one player is blindfolded and others grunt in turn; the blindfolded one has to guess who grunted; **PA**138, Granny wants a grunt—same as "who saw"; played with broom handles and a beat-up can; the handles are in a hole in the ground; hit the can away with the handle and players battle to get their handle back in the hole.

granny-wife, granny-wifing See **granny** v **1**

granny woman n **chiefly Sth, S Midl** See Map Cf **baby woman, granny doctor, midmother** Cf Intro "Language Changes" I.4

=**granny** n **3.**

1924 Raine *Land of Saddle-Bags* 226 **Appalachians,** Nursing, or midwifery, naturally falls to an occasional stalwart "granny-woman," or to a resolute widow, for experience is the only teacher. **c1940** Eliason *Word Lists FL* 8 **wFL,** *Granny woman:* A midwife. Obsolescent. **1943** Writers' Program NC *Bundle of Troubles* 37, Agin the granny woman got there they's folks on the porch and in the yard, a-waitin'. **1946** [see **granny** n **3**]. **1949** Kurath *Word Geog.* 48, The Midland shares the following expressions with the South: . . the folk word *granny* or *granny woman* . . for the midwife. **1950** *PADS* 14.33 **SC. 1953** Randolph–Wilson *Down in Holler* 157 **Ozarks,** A midwife is usually called a *granny-woman.* **1956** *Hall Coll.* **eTN,** I was a granny woman. I handled over two hundred babies. **c1960** *Wilson Coll.* **csKY. 1965–70** *DARE* (Qu. AA30, *An older woman who comes in [or used to come in] to help when a baby is going to be born*) 46 Infs, **chiefly Sth, S Midl,** Granny woman. **1972** Cooper *NC Mt. Folkl.* 92, *Granny woman*—a midwife.

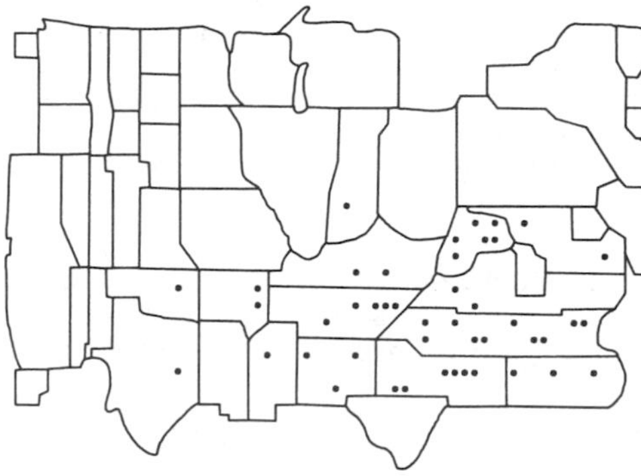

•granny woman (Qu. AA30)

granpap See **grandpa A4**

granpapa See **grandpa A5**

granpappy See **grandpa A4**

granpaw See **grandpa A1**

gransa, gransir, gransy See **grandsire**

gransy graybeard See **granddaddy graybeard 2**

granther n Also sp *grand'ther* [Var of *grandfather;* cf Engl dial *grandfer*] **chiefly NEng** *old-fash* Cf **grandpa**

1828 Cooper *Prairie* 1.153 **cNY,** Come, sit ye down beside me, lad; sit ye down, and tell me of what your grand'ther used to speak, when his mind dwelt on the wonders of the wilderness. **1867** Lowell *Biglow* 53 **'Upcountry' MA,** My gran'ther's rule was safer 'n 't is to crow:/ Don't never prophesy, —onless ye know. **1871** (1882) Stowe *Fireside Stories* 7 **MA,** He married Lois Peabody, that was cousin to your gran'ther then. **1895** *DN* 1.397 **NYC,** *Granther* . . frequently used by old people for grandfather. **1903** *DN* 2.298 **Cape Cod MA** (as of a1857), *Granther.* . . Grandfather. **1904** Day *Kin o' Ktaadn* 161 **ME,** My gran'ther was one o' the men. **1907** *DN* 3.188 **NH,** *Granther.* **1916** *DN* 4.334 **seMA,** *Gran'ther.* **1941** *LANE* Map 381 *(Grandpa)* 1 inf, **ceCT,** *Granther,* grandmother's term in referring to her grandfather; 1 inf, **seMA,** *Granther,* used by an aunt 'who would be about a hundred if she was alive'; 7 infs, **scattered NEng,** Granther. **1959** *VT Hist.* new ser 27.139, *Grandfather* [grăn'thûr] . . pronc. Obsolescent. **1967** *DARE* (Qu. Z3) Inf **MA**5, Granther ['grænθə], heard from old folks.

granther longlegs See **granddaddy longlegs 1**

grantogen See **garantogen**

grape n

Std: a plant of the genus *Vitis,* or its fruit. For other names of var spp see **bullace 2, catbird grape, desert grape, fox grape, frost grape, gulch grape, muscadine grape, mustang grape, panhandle grape, post-oak grape, riverbank grape, sand grape, sugar grape, summer grape, turkey grape, winter grape**

grape basket n **esp FL, GA**

See quot 1966–68.

1950 *WELS Suppl.* 2 Infs, **csWI,** Grape basket. **1956** Moody *Home Ranch* 97 **CO** (as of 1911), All the time Hazel had been talking to me, she'd been holding a little grape basket filled with milkweed silk. **1966–68** *DARE* (Qu. F17, *What peaches come in*) Inf **IN**41, Grape basket—long, oval; (Qu. F18, *The container grapes come in*) Inf **FL**1, Grape basket . . small, oblong, about a foot long; **FL**15, Grape basket . . wood, with handle, rounded ends; one foot long by 4–5 inches wide; **FL**30, Grape basket—made of thin wood; **GA**3, 10, 15, Grape basket.

grape geranium n

A begonia (here: *Begonia dregei*).

1913 (1980) Hardy *OH Schoolmistress* 109 (as of c1850), My aunt's greenhouse, built of brick and full of wonderful plants which I had never seen anywhere else, the "grape-geranium" (pink begonia), lemon verbena, an orange tree.

grape honeysuckle n [Prob because it tends to be a vine]

A **honeysuckle 2** (here: *Lonicera prolifera*).

1924 Deam *Shrubs IN* 299, *Lonicera prolifera. . . Grape Honeysuckle. . .* Its profusion of flowers and its long flowering period recommend this shrub for ornamental planting. **1940** Steyermark *Flora MO* 508, *Grape Honeysuckle. . .* Smooth bushy twining shrub. **1948** Stevens *KS Wild Flowers* 359, *Grape Honeysuckle. . .* A shrubby, twining vine 4–5 feet high. . . Berries yellow. **1960** Vines *Trees SW* 953, Grape Honeysuckle has been cultivated since 1840. **1976** Bailey–Bailey *Hortus Third* 681, *Grape h[oneysuckle]. . .* Summer. Ohio to Tenn. and Mo.

grape hyacinth n

Std: a plant of the genus *Muscari,* esp the common *M. botryoides.* For other names of var spp see **baby's breath 2a, bluebell 1c, bluebottle 2, graveyard hyacinth, feather hyacinth, sugar loaf**

grape pear n [Appar in ref to color, size, and shape of fruits] Cf **Indian pear**

A **serviceberry** (here: *Amelanchier obovalis*).

1900 Lyons *Plant Names* 27, *A[melanchier] Botrapium. . .* Grape Pear. **1940** Clute *Amer. Plant Names* 250, *Amelanchier Canadensis.* Grape pear.

grape picker n Cf **grape up**

One who curries favor.

1958 McCulloch *Woods Words* 73 **Pacific NW,** *Grape picker*—A man who shines up to the boss whenever possible. **1967** *DARE* (Qu. II20a, *A person who tries too hard to gain somebody else's favor*) Inf **WA**30, A grape picker—used in woods.

grape stake n Also *grape stick* **West, esp CA**

A long, slender usu roughhewn piece of wood orig used to support grapevines.

1967–69 *DARE* (Qu. L65, . . *Kinds of fences . . around here*) Inf **AZ**15, Grape-stake fence; **WA**27, Grape-stick fence—not two by two, handsplit. **1988** *DARE* File **sCA,** From as far back as the late 1940s, I remember the term *grape stake* as used in the combination *grape-stake fence* to mean a short (two to three foot high) decorative fence usually placed in the front yard and often used to set off a flower bed. The fence was made of roughhewn lumber, three to four inches thick. *Ibid* **sCA,** Grape stakes are made of redwood; they are about 5′ tall, 1¾″ by 1¾″, and split rather than sawn; they are usually used to make fences, the stakes being placed quite close together. *Ibid* **cwCA,** The man who has the recycling plant also collects old lumber; some of it is used to make grape stakes. *Ibid* **cwCA,** Grape stakes were originally used to stake grapes, and were roughhewn, being split from redwood. They are about 6′ long, 2″ wide, and more nearly triangular than rectangular, the shape depending on how they split off the log.

‡grape twist n [Sugg by grape tendrils]

A kink or snarl in one's hair.

1927 Kennedy *Gritny* 43 **sLA** [Black], Wid dem grape-twisses Dink got on 'is head, it'll take 'im all night to git thoo bat'lin wid 'um.

grape up v phr Also with *to* Cf **apple up, grape picker**

To curry favor with.

1967 *DARE* (Qu. II20b, *A person who tries too hard to gain somebody else's favor: "He's always trying to ______ the boss."*) Inf **OR**10, Grape up; **TX**19, Grape up to; [**WA**30, He's picking grapes and tramping down the bushes].

grapevine n

1 An intricate maneuver of the feet. [Transf from the dance step]

1921 Thorp *Songs Cowboys* 107 **West,** Den he [=a horse] bent en he twisted, en he bowed en he moaned, En done der grand grape-vine [in trying to throw a rider].

2 A grain cradle; see quot 1978.

1923 *DN* 5.209 **swMO,** *Grape vine. . .* A grain cradle with a peculiarly twisted snath. **1978** Massey *Bittersweet Country* 57 **Ozarks,** The cradle is a long-handled scythe with a built-on cradle consisting of four tapered fingers to catch the grain, and a thumb, the blade. Elvie's cradle, factory made and costing about five dollars, is called a "grapevine."

‡3 See quot. [Prob from the winding track] *joc*

1967 *DARE* (Qu. N37, . . *A branch railroad that is not very important or gives poor service*) Inf **IL**16, The Grapevine.

4 See quot.

1968 *DARE* File **cwNJ,** Grapevine—type of masonry: stones aren't plumb-level (straight), but zig and zag according to shape.

grapevine mesquite n Also *grapevine grass*

=**vine mesquite.**

1911 *Century Dict. Suppl., Mesquite. . . Vine-mesquite. . .* Sometimes called *grape-vine* mesquite or *grass.* **1937** U.S. Forest Serv. *Range Plant Hdbk.* G92, Vine-mesquite . . produces creeping stems, or stolons, . . sometimes 10 feet long. It is also known, especially in Texas, as grapevine-mesquite. **1939** Tharp *Vegetation TX* 45, Grapevine Mesquite *(Panicum obtusum). . .* is able to withstand considerable grazing which gives it local prestige among stockmen.

grapevine telephone n [Var of *grapevine telegraph*]

A means of circulating information by word of mouth.

1950 Stuart *Hie Hunters* 93 **eKY,** "All I haf to do is put the words yer pappy said about us on the grapevine telephone," Peg said, shaking his head and blowing a cloud of smoke. "It won't take long fer the news to git around."

grape-vineyard n [Redund; cf Intro "Language Changes" I.4]

1927 *AmSp* 3.9 **Ozarks,** Pleonasms like *tooth-dentist, sick-patient, grape-vineyard* and so on are in common use.

graping, go v phr

To play a game similar to **stealing grapes;** see quot.

1968 *DARE* Tape **DE**2, When I was young we used to play games, of course. We used to go graping. . . The fellows line up on one side and the girls line up on the other side, and the girl walks down one end and the boy down the other end, and he says to the girl, "Where you goin'?" And she says, "I'm goin' graping." And he says, "What are you gonna do if I come?" She says, "I'm gonna run!" Then she runs around both rows and tries to get back in place without him catching her. If he catches her, then she has to give him a kiss. Then the next one steps up and does likewise. Kissing games.

grapple v See **grabble** v 2

grapple n Also *grabble*

Any of var devices for snagging or hooking fish.

1872 *Maine Spl. Laws* 77 *(DA),* No person shall be allowed to take or catch any pickerel with spears, hooks or grapples, from Worthly pond. **1884** Knight *New Mech. Dict.* 421/1, *Grapple. . .* A tool with spring jaws which are closed by striking the fish. **1966–68** *DARE* (Qu. P13, . . *Ways of fishing . . besides the ordinary hook and line*) Inf **NY**92, Grapples—treble hooks; **MS**66, Grapple. **1989** *DARE* File **nwTN,** To fish by the use of a grab or grapnel. . . *Grabble* is the local pronunciation of *grapnel.*

grappling See **grabble** v 2

g'rarj See **garage**

grash See **grandma** n **A13**

grasp n

See quot.

1937 Thornburgh *Gt. Smoky Mts.* 30, "Take a grasp o' sourwood sprouts." . . "How much is a grasp?" I inquired. "Why a grasp is as much as ye can hold in your hand—the length of your grasp."

graspious adj

1984 Wilder *You All Spoken Here* 2 **Sth,** *Purse proud:* Stingy; grasping; graspious.

grass n

1 =**asparagus.** [Abbr for **sparrow grass:** see quots; *OED* 1747 →] **chiefly NEast, Pacific** See Map

1848 Bartlett *Americanisms* 163, *Grass.* A vulgar contraction of *sparrow-grass,* i.e. asparagus. Further than this the force of corruption can hardly go. **1895** *DN* 1.389, *Grass* (abbreviations for *sparrowgrass*): Asparagus. Common among grocers in N.Y. City. Also heard in Philadelphia, and Cambridge, Mass. **1909** *S. Atl. Qrly.* 8.38 **sSC coast**

[Gullah], *Asparagus,* that is to say, *sparrow-grass,* is cried in Charleston streets, *"Grass! fresh grass!",* as it is in the streets of *London.* **1950** *PADS* 14.33 **SC,** *Grass. . .* Asparagus. Shortened form of sparrowgrass. **1950** *WELS (Names or nicknames for asparagus)* 7 Infs, **WI,** Grass. **1965–70** *DARE* (Qu. I29, *Names or nicknames for asparagus*) 88 Infs, **chiefly NEast, Pacific,** Grass.

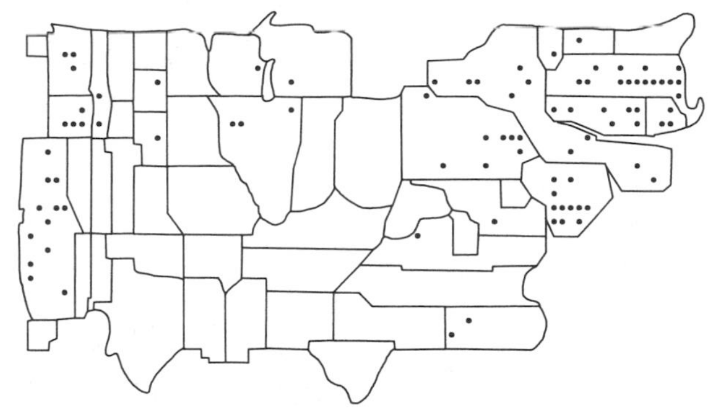

•grass n 1 (Qu. I29)

2 =eelgrass 1.

1948 Pearson *Sea Flavor* 117 **NEng,** Dead eelgrass is pulled to sea with the outgoing tides and is then brought back and cast on the beaches. Sometimes when a northeaster comes, it throws the windrows of dead grass high on the beach above the normal high-tide line. **1976** Warner *Beautiful Swimmers* 211 **Chesapeake Bay,** A fat roll of eelgrass rested snugly on the washboard. Marsh . . paused to inspect the grass. . . The grass was thin-stemmed—not at all fleshy in the manner of other "seaweeds".

3 The spring of the year. Cf **between hay and grass 2**

1778 *MD Jrl. & Baltimore Advt.* (MD) 24 March (1912 Thornton *Amer. Gloss.*), Strayed, a black Colt, three years old next grass. **1864** (1868) Trowbridge *Cudjo's Cave* 45 **TN,** He'll be nine year old next grass, I reckon. **1894** *DN* 1.331 **NJ,** *Grass:* spring of the year. "I'll move out o' here next grass." **1899** (1912) Green *VA Folk-Speech* 204, *Grass. . .* The grazing season; the spring. "A horse five years old last grass." **1931** *PMLA* 46.1305 **sAppalachians,** I aim to foal that mare, come grass (in the spring). **1950** *WELS Suppl.* **swWI,** I'll paint this wall, come next grass [=spring]. **1968** Adams *Western Words* 71, *Coming grass*—Approaching spring.

4 in phr *in the grass:* Choked with grass, overgrown with weeds. **chiefly Sth, S Midl**

1838 in 1925 Bassett *Southern Overseer* 111 **cnMS,** He will make Eighty five or Ninety Bales of cotton. He is somewhat in the grass, but promises with fair weather, which we now have, to be out in two weeks. **1889** Edwards *Runaways* 151 **GA,** An' there's Brother Spikes. He's er good han' fer weed out er church, ain't he? An' his cotton in the grass so bad that yer can't see hit from the road. **1945** *N. & Q.* Nov. 117/1 [sic *DA*—quot not found], He could easily remember the lengths to which an overseer or a Negro would go to avoid 'getting in the grass' (i.e., letting grass get a headstart in a cotton field). **1952** Brown *NC Folkl.* 1.547, *Grass, in the. . .* Of a crop: overcome by grass.—Granville county. **c1960** *Wilson Coll.* **csKY,** *In the grass. . .* Said of a crop that needs attention; a derogatory expression. **1984** Wilder *You All Spoken Here* 133 **Sth,** In the grass: A crop that needs weeding. Weeds often get a right good sling—a head start—if a farmer's hoe hands take sick or some other adversity develops.

5 in phr *go to grass:*

a also in extended phr *go to grass and eat hay* and varr; rarely *grow to grass:* Go to hell! Get lost! That's nonsense!—used with varying degrees of intensity. *euphem* Cf **Halifax 1**

1844 Stephens *High Life in NY* 1.55, Tell him to go to grass and eat bog hay till he's as fat as Nebuchadnezzar. **1872** (1973) Thompson *Major Jones's Courtship* 171, "But aint you gwine to be as good as your word, doctor?" ses she. "You jest go to grass," ses he; and that's the last we've seed of cousin Pete. **1890** *DN* 1.65 **KY, NEng,** Go to grass, and eat mullein! **1891** Maitland *Amer. Slang Dict.* 129, *Grass,* "gone to," dead. "Go to grass," said to a troublesome person, may be derived from "go to grace," which means, of course, "go to ______" somewhere else. **1907** *DN* 3.213 **cCT, nwAR.** **1908** *DN* 3.316 **eAL, wGA,** *Go to grass (an(d) eat mullen* [sic]). . . Used in disgust or impatience. **1922** *DN* 5.164 **AL, AR, CT, NE, NY,** *Go to grass. . .* To be off! Get out! Stop talking! "Oh you go to grass, I don't believe a word you say." **1927** *AmSp* 2.355 **WV,** *Go to grass.* **1939** *AmSp* 14.266 **IN,** Expressions indicative of contempt are . . 'Go to grass,' and 'Go to grass and eat hay.' **1943** McAtee *Dial. Grant Co. IN Suppl. 2* 9 (as of 1890s), *Go to grass. . .* A very mild, perhaps woman's version of "go to hell," usually preceded by, "Aw." **1946** *PADS* 6.15 **VA, NC.** **1947** *PADS* 8.19 **IA.** **1950** *PADS* 13.17 **cTX,** *Grass, to go to. . .* Often said to children, meaning for them to go away and amuse themselves. **1950** *WELS Suppl.* 1 Inf, **WI,** *Go to grass:* An expression when anything goes wrong. **1952** Brown *NC Folkl.* 1.547, *Grass, go to. . .* A friendly imprecation. "Oh, you go to grass. I don't believe he said it." **1965–70** *DARE* (Qu. NN26b, *Weakened substitutes for 'hell': "Go to ______!"*) 41 Infs, **scattered,** Grass; **IA**17, **OH**40, **PA**242, Grass and eat (clover) hay; (Qu. GG21a, *If you don't care what a person does, you might tell him*) Infs **IL**44, **NY**25, **WI**29, (You can) go to grass. **1986** *DARE* File **seWI** (as of 1940s), My mother always used to say "grow to grass," meaning go to hell, get out of here.

b To die; hence ppl adj phr *gone to grass.*

1858 Hammett *Piney Woods Tavern* 131, An old cow . . goin' to grass, nothin' but a bag of skin and bones. *Ibid,* Lookin' jest's if she was goin' to grass in rale [=real] good arnest [=earnest]. **1891** [see **5a** above].

grass v

1 To plant grass in.

1962 *Mt. Life* 38.1.17 **sAppalachians,** The mountain farmer . . "grasses" a field after he has "corned" it for a few years.

2 To throw to the ground; to bring down, defeat, kill. [*OED grass* v. 4 "To lay or stretch on the grass"]

1889 Nelson *50 Yrs.* 21 **West,** They all trotted up and sniffed at their dead companion. I lost no time in grassing another, and I believe I could have shot them all. *Ibid* 101, I killed and scalped my first Ute in one of these scrimmages. I had frequently grassed Indians before. **1942** Berrey–Van den Bark *Amer. Slang* 66.3, Grass, *to throw to the grass or ground. Ibid* 649.3, *Defeat* [in sports] . . grass, gravel. *Ibid* 702.16, *Knock down* [in boxing]. . . floor, flop, grass, gravel. **1944** Adams *Western Words* 67, *Grassed him*—Said when a horse has thrown his rider.

3 To have sexual intercourse with; to copulate, esp outdoors; hence vbl n *grassing.* [See **2** above]

1945 Webster *Town Meeting* 238 **eCT, RI,** Most of our sins are of lustful bodies. Not much is said about who is grassing who. **1954** McAtee *Dial. Grant Co. IN Suppl. 5* [2], *Grass:* . . to copulate, of humans. **1979** Lewis *How to Talk Yankee* [15] **ME,** *Grassin'. . .* Pursuit of the fleshly delights *al fresco.* "Janie, when are you and I goin' grassin'?" **1982–83** *DARE* File **ME coast,** Grassin': the activity of the male Mainiac in pursuit of the female; **FL,** The Black's definition of male pursuit (illicit): grassin'.

grass about the bows n

A beard, whiskers.

1945 Colcord *Sea Language* 89 **ME, Cape Cod, Long Island,** *Grass about the bows.* Alongshore, a facetious term for whiskers. **1975** Gould *ME Lingo* 115, *Grass about the bows*—A way to describe a man who has started to grow a beard. The term has been revived in some degree by the "hippy" look.

grass bag See **grass sack**

grass bass n

1 =crappie, usu *Pomoxis nigromaculatus.*

1879 U.S. Natl. Museum *Bulletin* 14.48, *Pomoxys nigromaculatus. . .* Grass Bass. [**1897** *Outing* 30.437/2 **Canada,** The calico, or grass bass, a showy, mottled fellow, sometimes a foot long, and a quick, jerky fighter.] **1911** U.S. Bur. Census *Fisheries 1908* 308, *Pomoxis sparoides. . .* In Lake Erie and in Ohio generally it is called "strawberry bass" or "grass bass." **1947** Dalrymple *Panfish* 84, Here, my friend, are the various names by which you would address that little gamester, the Crappie, depending on where you happened to be at the moment. . . Grass Bass. **1972** Sparano *Outdoors Encycl.* 361, *White Crappie* . . grass bass. . . *Pomoxis annularis. . . Black Crappie* . . grass bass. . . *Pomoxis nigromaculatus.* **1983** Becker *Fishes WI* 863, *Black Crappie. . .* Other common names . . grass bass.

2 A **black bass 1:** usu **largemouth bass,** but also **smallmouth bass** or **spotted bass.**

1883 *Century Illustr. Mag.* 26.376/2, [Black bass] have received names somewhat descriptive of their habitat, as . . moss, grass, and Oswego bass. **1902** Jordan–Evermann *Amer. Fishes* 358, This fish [=*Microp-*

terus salmoides] has received many vernacular names, among which may be mentioned . . grass bass. **1935** Caine *Game Fish* 7, *Small-mouthed Black Bass. . . Synonyms* . . Grass Bass. **1946** LaMonte *N. Amer. Game Fishes* 135, *Large-mouth Black Bass. . . Names* . . Grass Bass. . . Characteristically a fish of warm, sluggish, and muddy water, but often taken in the same waters with the Small-mouth. **1978** *Outdoor Life* Sept 56, Scientists call the large-mouth bass Micropterus salmoides. . . But there are many lesser-known names too. Some of them are . . grass bass, marsh bass [etc].

grass-bellied adj Also *grass-gut*

Of an animal: bloated; fig: well-supplied, flush.

1897 (1902) Moore *Songs & Stories* 186 **TN,** Their rule, es fur es I was able to see, was to hump up themselves on their grass-bellied ponies an' git up an' git. **1898** Wister *Lin McLean* 113 **WY,** I'm grass-bellied with spot-cash. **1948** Hurston *Seraph* 8 **wFL,** They were on the way to church that Sunday morning . . some even straddling grass-gut mules or in double wagons pulled by mules. **1966–68** *DARE* (Qu. K43) Inf **FL**7, Grass-gut—[of a] mule; (Qu. U37, . . *Expressions about somebody who has plenty of money*) Inf **CA**87, Grass-bellied with cash. **1967** Green *Horse Tradin'* 54 **TX,** We . . untied the mule, and backed her out on the ground. She was grass-bellied and fat. **1986** Pederson *LAGS Concordance* 1 inf, **cwFL,** A little grass-gut pony.

grassbelt See **grassplot**

grass-bird n [From the habitat] Cf **red grass-bird**

1 Either of two sparrows:

a also *gray grass-bird, grass bunting:* =**vesper sparrow.**

1784 Pennant *Arctic Zool.* 2.375, Grass Finch. . . Inhabits *New York.* Lays five eggs in *May,* in the grass. Called the *Grey Grass-bird.* **1839** Audubon *Synopsis Birds* 102, Grass or Bay-winged Bunting. . . Extremely abundant. **1844** DeKay *Zool. NY* 2.151, *Fringilla graminea. . .* This familiar sparrow, known in many parts of this State as the *Grass-bird* and *Grey Grass-bird,* is common in the Atlantic district during the whole year. . . The nest is placed on the ground. Feeds on insects and grass-seeds. **1878** U.S. Natl. Museum *Proc.* 1.415 **cCA,** *Pooecetes gramineus. . .* Western Grass Bunting.

b =**savannah sparrow.**

1962 Imhof *AL Birds* 543, *Savannah Sparrow. . . Other names* . . Grass Bird. . . The bird generally feeds in short grass and roosts in bad weather in tall grass.

2 Any of various sandpipers, as:

a =**pectoral sandpiper.**

1881 *Forest & Stream* 17.226/3 **Atlantic,** There is another beautiful plump little bird *(Tringa maculata)* well-known on our coast in summer and autumn under various cognomens, as . . "grass bird." **1888** Trumbull *Names of Birds* 175, *Pectoral Sandpiper. . .* At Pine Point, M[ain]e, Portsmouth, N.H., in Massachusetts . . *Grass-bird.* **1909** Field Museum Nat. Hist. *Zool. Ser.* 9.403, *Pectoral Sandpiper. . . Local names. . .* Grass Bird. . . Common in Illinois and Wisconsin during the migrations. **1925** (1928) Forbush *Birds MA* 1.408, The Pectoral Sandpiper, known to many Massachusetts gunners as the Grass-bird, is well named, for it is mainly a bird of grassy lands. **1944** Hausman *Amer. Birds* 514, Grass-bird—see Sandpiper, Baird's; see also Sandpiper, Pectoral. **1953** Jewett *Birds WA* 269, *Erolia melanotos. . .* Grassbird. **1956** MA Audubon Soc. *Bulletin* 40.18, *Solitary Sandpiper. . .* Grass Bird (Mass. As a visitant to temporary pools, it is seen among shallowly-flooded grass.) *Ibid* 19, *Pectoral Sandpiper. . .* Grass Bird (Maine, N.H., Mass. . . It delights in soppy, short grass.) . . *White-rumped Sandpiper. . .* Grass Bird (Mass. To some extent it shares the habitat of the Pectoral Sandpiper . .). *Baird's Sandpiper. . .* Grass Bird (Mass.) . . *Red-backed Sandpiper. . .* Grass Bird . . (Mass.)

b also *hill grass-bird:* The buff-breasted sandpiper *(Tryngites subruficollis).*

1886 [see **2c** below]. **1917** (1923) *Birds Amer.* 1.249, *Buff-breasted Sandpiper. . . Other Name.* Hill grass-bird. . . *Nest:* A depression in the ground, sparsely lined with grass and withered leaves. **1925** (1928) Forbush *Birds MA* 1.433, *Tryngites subruficollis* . . *Buff-breasted Sandpiper.* Other name: Hill Grass-bird. **1956** MA Audubon Soc. *Bulletin* 40.20, *Buff-breasted Sandpiper.* Grass Bird, Hill Grass Bird (Mass. It frequents fields such as those preferred by the Upland Plover.)

c =**white-rumped sandpiper.**

1886 *Forest & Stream* 27.287/1 **Cape Cod MA,** The "grass bird" is the . . pectoral sandpiper . . , though the name is also applied to one or two other less common species of small waders, among them the white-rumped sandpiper *(T[ringa] fuscicollis)* and the buff-breasted sandpiper *(Tryngites subruficollis).* **1956** [see **2a** above].

d Baird's sandpiper *(Erolia bairdi).*

1917 (1923) *Birds Amer.* 1.235, *Baird's Sandpiper. . . Other Name.* Grass-bird. . . It is found almost exclusively along the prairie sloughs and lagoons of the Middle West. **1932** Howell *FL Bird Life* 239, *Pisobia bairdi. . . Grass Bird. . .* Migrates chiefly through the Mississippi Valley, and irregularly on the Atlantic and Pacific coasts. **1932** Bennitt *Check-list* 31 **MO,** *Baird's sandpiper. . .* Grass bird. **1944** [see **2a** above]. **1956** [see **2a** above]. **1963** Gromme *Birds WI* 214, Grass Bird (Baird's Sandpiper).

e =**red-backed sandpiper.**

1956 [see **2a** above].

f =**solitary sandpiper.**

1956 [see **2a** above].

grass blade n [**blade 3**] **esp Sth, S Midl**

A tool for cutting weeds and other vegetation.

1966–69 *DARE* (Qu. L28, *Tools used in the past for cutting grain*) Inf **SC**7, Grass blade; (Qu. L37, *A hand tool used for cutting weeds and grass*) Infs **AL**2, **AR**15, **GA**22, 80, 84, **MS**72, **SC**32, Grass blade. **1968** *DARE* Tape **GA**22, [Inf:] We'd get in there then with a hand grass blade, you know, and cut that stuff [=crab grass]. . . [FW:] What was this grass blade—what did that look like? Was that a one-hand or a two-hand affair? [Inf:] Two-hand affair. Blade about that long on a kind of a crooked handle, and it got two handles on it, and you just swung it around. . . [FW:] I guess it's what we call a scythe up in Wisconsin. [Inf:] Yes.

grass bloom n

The healthy sleekness of an animal's coat due to its having eaten plenty of grass.

1967 Green *Horse Tradin'* 4 **TX,** I had let him [=a horse] out in a little pasture, and in a few days . . he had a little bit of grass bloom on him and was in nice shape to trade off.

grass boat n

A boat camouflaged with grass.

1970 *DARE* (Qu. O10, . . *Other kinds of boats* . . *used around here*) Inf **VA**47, Grass boats—a short boat with grass all around it; the grass is higher than the boat itself; used by market gunners [FW: =professional poachers of ducks and geese for the wild game market].

grass broom n Cf **brush broom** n[1]

1965–66 *DARE* (Qu. F36 . . *Kinds of brooms*) Inf **OK**15, Grass broom—used in yard; **SC**9, Grass broom—made of straw, for house sweeping.

grass bunting See **grass-bird 1a**

grass burr n Also sp *grass bur* **chiefly TX** See Map

=**burr grass** or its seed.

1942 Whipple *Joshua* 178 **UT** (as of c1860), Occasionally she would have to drop behind to pull out a grass-burr. **1965–70** *DARE* (Qu. S15) 23 Infs, **chiefly TX,** Grass burr(s); (Qu. S9) Inf **TX**104, Grass burrs; (Qu. S13) Inf **TX**3, Grass burrs; (Qu. S14) Infs **HI**4, **TX**33, 38, Grass burr(s). **1967** *DARE* Tape **TX**28, A cocklebur is much like a grass burr only it's bigger. **1970** Correll *Plants TX* 189, *Cenchrus incertus. . .* Grassbur, coast sandbur.

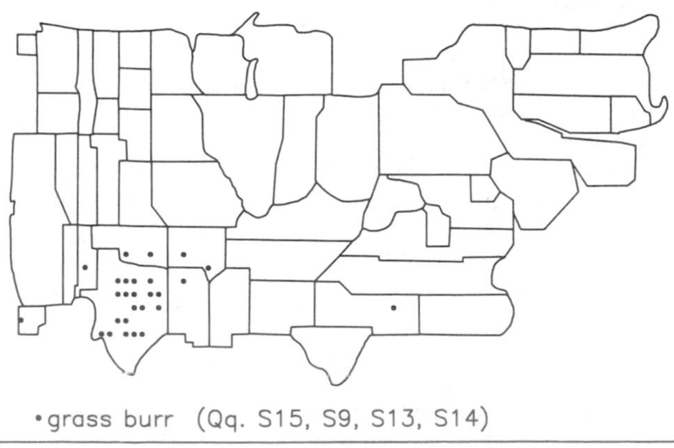

•grass burr (Qq. S15, S9, S13, S14)

grass cactus n [In ref to the leaves, which look like large blades of grass]
=**yucca.**

1932 Rydberg *Flora Prairies* 223, *Yucca*. . . Grass Cactus. **1936** Winter *Plants NE* 11, *Yucca*. . . Grass Cactus.

grass calf n

1967 *DARE* File **cwNY,** *Grass calf*—a calf not sold for veal, but kept to be raised to maturity.

grass chippie n Also *grass runner*, ~ *whistler*
The thirteen-lined **ground squirrel** n **b** *(Spermophilus tridecemlineatus).*

1961 Jackson *Mammals WI* 130, *Citellus tridecemlineatus tridecemlineatus*. . . *Vernacular names*. . . Grass chippie, grass runner, grass whistler. [*Ibid* 132, *Habitat.—Dry meadows, grassy fields*, . . *grassy fence rows.*]

grassee n

1907 *DN* 3.188 **NH,** *Grassee*. . . Artificial bank of earth covered with greensward. "There's a grassee now where the Judge Calef house stood."

grasser n **West** Cf **grass-bellied**
A beef animal fed predominantly on grass.

1881 *Chi. Times* 1 June *(DA)*, Several droves of Texas 'grassers' were among the fresh arrivals. **1911** Quick *Yellowstone Nights* 143, Top grassers, they was at last, in weight an' price. **1937** *AmSp* 12.103 **eNE,** *Grass-fat* cattle or *grassers* have acquired flesh and sleekness from eating grass only. **1948** *St. Paul* (Minn.) *Dispatch* 17 Sep. 42/1 *(DA)*, Medium grade short fed steers and heifers were taken at $27, with grassers at $22 **1968** Adams *Western Words* 131, *Grassers*—Grass-fed cattle.

grasset n [LaFr "fatty"] **LA**

1 also *joree-grasel:* =**rufous-sided towhee.**

1831 Audubon *Ornith. Biog.* 1.151, It is a plump bird, and becomes very fat in winter, in consequence of which it is named *Grasset* in Louisiana, where many are shot for the table by the French planters. **1844** DeKay *Zool. NY* 2.172, In Louisiana it [=*Pipilo erythrophthalmus*] is called, from its plumpness, *Grasset*, and is esteemed by epicures. **1917** *DN* 4.424 **LA,** The towhee . . also called . . *joree-grasel.* [**1931** Read *LA French* 43, *Grassel*, . . or its synonym *Grasset*, . . "fatty." The Towhee or Chewink *(Pipilo erythrophthalmus erythrophthalmus)*, which in winter becomes so fat that it was formerly shot for the table.]

2 =**wood thrush.**

1883 Nuttall Ornith. Club *Bulletin* 8.72, *Turdus mustelinus*. Its common names are: *Wood Thrush* [etc]. . . As for *Grasset* (Texas), I cannot explain it.

3 =**red-eyed vireo.**

1911 *Forest & Stream* 77.174, *Vireosylva olivacea.*—Grasset, La. **1917** *DN* 4.426 **LA,** *Grasset*. The red-eyed vireo (Vireosylva olvacea) [sic]: also called *green grasset.* **1921** LA Dept. of Conserv. *Bulletin* 10.119, In the fall. . . the vireo feeds on the seeds of magnolia and the bird becomes well flavored and fat, whence the Creole name of "grasset", applied also to the kingbird, or bee martin. **1929** Forbush *Birds MA* 3.183, *Red-eyed Vireo*. . . All through the South, wherever this tree [=magnolia] fruits, the vireos grow fat upon the seeds, and formerly in Louisiana many of them were killed for the table under the name of "grassets."

4 also *gros grasset:* A **kingbird** (here: *Tyrannus tyrannus*). Cf **black grasset**

1917 *DN* 4.427 **LA,** *Kingbird* (Tyrannus tyrannus). . . Gros grasset. **1921** LA Dept. of Conserv. *Bulletin* 10.115, The kingbird is the . . "gros grasset" of the Creoles. *Ibid* 119 [see **3** above].

grass-fat adj Cf **grass-bellied, grasser**
Of livestock: fed predominantly on grass.

1937 [see **grasser**]. **1966** *DARE* Tape **NM**13, They went from here up there as yearlings and they were kept up there until they were three and four old [sic] and then they were shipped . . as grass-fat beef.

grass finch n

1 =**vesper sparrow. chiefly Nth**

1785 Pennant *Arctic Zool.* 2.65, Grass Finch. . . Inhabits New York. . . Called the Gray Grass-Bird. **1858** Baird *Birds* 447, *Poocaetes gramineus*. . . *Grass Finch*. . . United States from the Atlantic to the Pacific. **1895** Minot *Land-Birds New Engl.* 209, The so-called Grass Finches, though they spend much of their time on the ground, often alight on the ridge-poles of barns, and on fences, or on telegraph-wires. **1910** KY Hist. Soc. *Register* 8.22, Grass Finch. A common summer resident. **1938** Oberholser *Bird Life LA* 657, *Eastern Vesper Sparrow*. . . 'Grass finch'. . . It lives chiefly on or near the ground. **1946** Goodrich *Birds in KS* 315, [Colloquial name] Finch, grass. [Common name, A.O.U. Check-List] Sparrow, western vesper. **1953** Jewett *Birds WA* 633, Western Grass Finch. . . [It] is a ground-loving species, and except when singing is found in the shelter of the sagebrush, bunch grass, or growing grain. **1963** Gromme *Birds WI* 214, Finch, Grass (Vesper Sparrow).

2 =**savannah sparrow.**

1962 Imhof *AL Birds* 543, *Savannah Sparrow*. . . *Other names*. . Grass Finch. . . It occurs on almost any grass field in sparse or tall cover, so long as it can feed on the ground.

grassflower n

1 A **blue-eyed grass 1** (here: *Sisyrinchium angustifolium*).

1894 *Jrl. Amer. Folkl.* 7.101 **ceMA,** *Sisyrinchium angustifolium* . . grass-flower. **1900** Lyons *Plant Names* 347, *S[isyrinchium] angustifolium*. . . Grass-flower. **1940** Clute *Amer. Plant Names* 148. **1966** *DARE* (Qu. S26e, *Other wildflowers*) Inf **WA**3, Grassflowers. **1966** *DARE* Wildfl QR Pl.28A, Inf **TX**44, Grassflower.

2 A **spring beauty:** usu *Claytonia virginica*, but also *C. caroliniana.*

1900 Lyons *Plant Names* 106, *C[laytonia] Caroliniana* . . and *C. Virginica* . . are called . . Grass-flower. **1940** Clute *Amer. Plant Names* 143, *C[laytonia] Virginica* . . grass-flower. **1959** Carleton *Index Herb. Plants* 55, *Grass-flower:* Claytonia virginica; Sisyrinchium angustifolium.

grass freight n Cf **corn freight, grass train**

1944 Adams *Western Words* 67, *Grass freight*—Goods shipped by bull team, called this because the motive power could eat their way to and from market. Grass freight was much slower, but much cheaper than freight hauled by mule teams.

grass frog n
Any of var frogs, as:

a Either of two somewhat similar frogs: a **leopard frog** (here: *Rana pipiens*) or the **pickerel frog.**

1967–70 *DARE* (Qu. P23) Inf **MI**112, Grass frogs; **OH**16, Grass frogs—green and spotted.

b also *green grass frog:* =**treefrog. esp Gt Lakes**

1950 *WELS (Small frogs that sing or chirp loudly in the spring)* 1 Inf, **csWI,** Grass frog. **1955** Carr–Goin *Guide Reptiles* 185, *Hyla ocularis* . . Little Grass Frog. . . Breeding voice a high, shrill, cricket-like chirp. . . Moist, grassy places. **1967–69** *DARE* (Qu. P21, *Small frogs that sing or chirp loudly in spring*) Infs **IL**32, **MI**101, **NE**1, **NY**6, 177, Grass frogs; **MI**105, **NY**71, Green grass frogs; **NY**191, **PA**35, Grass frogs; **OH**16, Grass frogs—green and spotted. **1979** Behler–King *Audubon Field Guide Reptiles* 410, *Little Grass Frog*. . . A true treefrog despite its small size and preference for perches within 1–2 feet . . of the ground.

grass gall n Cf **dew poison**

1912 Green *VA Folk-Speech* 204, *Grass-gall*. . . A sore between the toes of people who go barefooted in the summer, said to be caused by walking on the grass when it is covered with dew.

grass gopher n
A **ground squirrel** n **b** (here: *Spermophilus tridecemlineatus*).

1970 *Western Folkl.* 29.172, *Grass gopher* . . and *striped squirrel* are names for the thirteen-lined ground squirrel only.

grass, grow to See **grass** n **5a**

grass-gut See **grass-bellied**

grass hen n
A **bittern** (here: *Botaurus lentiginosus*).

1910 Wayne *Birds SC* 27, The Bittern [=*Botaurus lentiginosus*], which is locally known as "Indian Pullet," and "Grass Hen," is abundant during the winter months. **1953** *AmSp* 28.281 **SC,** Grass hen. American bittern.

grasshopper n

1 Std: an orthopterous insect of the families Acrididae, Gryllacrididae, Tettigoniidae, and Tetrigidae. For other names see **billy** n[1] **3, camel cricket, Canadian soldier 1, Carolina locust,**

chapulin 1, chew-tobacco 2, daddy longlegs 4, devil's hawk, devil's horse 3, Georgia hopper, Georgia thumper, graveyard hopper, gray dragon, grouse locust, hay jumper, hoghopper, hopgrasser, hopper 1, hoppergrass 1, hopping John 3, hopster, horse B5, Indian grasshopper, Jerusalem cricket, jumper, jumping Jack, katydid, locust, lubber grasshopper, luger, molasses hopper, Mormon cricket, pharoah bug, road-duster, spitter, spitting devil, spittle bug, spit tobacco, tobacco bug, tobacco chewer, tobacco spitter, toothpick grasshopper

2 also *grasshopper engine;* In railroading: see quots.

1853 Kennedy *Blackwater Chron.* 60 **WV,** Going off with a vehement, perpendicular movement, like one of the old grasshopper engines on the railroad, when under a great press of steam. **1916** *DN* 4.356 [Railroad terms], *Grasshopper...* An engine using the Walscheret [sic for *Walschaert*] valve gear. **1940** *RR Mag.* Apr 45, *Grasshopper*—Old-style locomotive with vertical boiler and vertical cylinders having a "walking-beam" arrangement that remotely suggested a grasshopper. **1953** Botkin-Harlow *Treas. Railroad Folkl.* 469, The earliest engines on the Baltimore and Ohio, the grasshoppers, burned coal, as did their successors, the crabs.

3 also *grasshopper plow, ~ stock:* Any of several types of plows, esp one used for breaking up sod. [Prob from the motion; see quot 1966-69] *old-fash*

1878 in 1937 Ruede *Sod-House* 229 **KS,** Such a time as we had, learning to get the grasshopper to go into the sod and remain there I hope never to have again. **1927** Sandburg *Amer. Songbag* 129 **KS,** With a Texas pony and a grasshopper plow. **1948** *AmSp* 23.73 **wNE** (as of 1880s), At that time a grasshopper plow was one with a narrow breaker bottom (perhaps upon occasion with a backset bottom) set very shallow, so it could be drawn by two or three scrawny ponies through the tough sod if they took it by fits and spurts. Later, in my childhood, *grasshopper plow* meant a light riding plow with either breaker or backset bottom, synonymous with *buggy plow,* if the latter was set very shallow. **1966-69** *DARE* (Qu. L18, .. *Plows used around here, at present and in the past*) Inf **AL**2, Grasshopper; **KY**43, Grasshopper plow—same as single plow, just cut the ground; it bounced in rocky ground and kicked so it was called a grasshopper plow; **SC**40, Single-plow grasshopper—a sweep used to finish up a planting operation; (Qu. L25, *The implement used to clean out weeds and loosen the earth between rows of corn*) Inf **KY**43, Grasshopper plow. **1967** *DARE* File **neCO,** *Grasshopper*—a sod-breaker plow. Old-fashioned. Found in the museum in Sterling, Colorado. Also called a 'jack rabbit'. **1986** Pederson *LAGS Concordance (Plow)* 1 inf, **cwFL,** Grasshopper stock; 1 inf, **cwFL,** Grasshopper stock—single stock plow; 1 inf, **ceTN,** Grasshoppers—single plows with iron feet.

grasshopper buggy n *old-fash*

A lightweight, single-seated buggy.

1935 Sandoz *Jules* 150 **wNE** (as of 1880-1930), That sky pilot, with his red beard cut like Christ's in the Sunday-school pictures, [was] preaching hell and damnation from the back of a grasshopper buggy. **1948** *AmSp* 23.73 **NE,** There was also .. a *grasshopper buggy* about the time of the grasshopper plow, 'a very light and precariously balanced one-seater, with or without top, and easily broken or upset.'

grasshopper engine See **grasshopper 2**

grasshopper frog n

The southern **spring peeper** *(Hyla crucifer bartramiana).*

1901 Fountain *Great Deserts* 63 **Okefenokee GA,** The grasshopper-frog .. is very abundant in the swamps. It is the smallest frog in the States, being only an inch and a half in length... It is grayish-green in colour, with some brown patches and light stripes on the body, and the legs barred with brown... They make a piping noise, quite unlike the ordinary croaking of a frog.

grasshopper hawk n [See quots]

1 A **sparrow hawk** (here: *Falco sparverius*).

1917 (1923) *Birds Amer.* 2.90, *Sparrow Hawk... Other Names...* Grasshopper Hawk. [*Ibid* 91, Grasshoppers, crickets, and other insects form its principal food during the warm months.] **1944** Hausman *Amer. Birds* 516, Hawk, Grasshopper—see Hawk, Sparrow. **1949** Swain *Insect Guide* 11, The species [of short-horned grasshoppers] occurring in large numbers in pasture and range lands are major items in the diets of the sparrowhawk, a bird .. more appropriately .. called the "grasshopper hawk," and by other hawks, including the Swainson's, marsh, and red-shouldered hawks, and by screech and barn owls. **1955** *Oriole* 20.1.6 **GA,** *Sparrow Hawk...* A .. name, based on food habits, is *Grasshopper Hawk.*

2 A **loggerhead shrike** (here: *Lanius ludovicianus migrans*).

1929 Forbush *Birds MA* 3.177, *Lanius ludovicianus migrans...* Grasshopper hawk. *Ibid* 179, The food of the Migrant Shrike consists very largely of .. the larger species of destructive insects, such as grasshoppers. **1932** Bennitt *Check-list* 51 **MO,** *Lanius ludovicianus migrans...* Grasshopper hawk. **1956** MA Audubon Soc. *Bulletin* 40.129, *Southern Shrike...* Grasshopper Hawk (Maine, Mass. From feeding upon those insects).

3 =**Swainson's hawk.**

1936 Roberts *MN Birds* 1.323, *Swainson's Hawk... Other names .. Grasshopper Hawk... Food.* Almost entirely gophers, mice, rabbits, grasshoppers, crickets, and locusts.

4 =**Mississippi kite.**

1955 *Oriole* 20.1.5 **GA,** *Mississippi Kite. Grasshopper Hawk* (from feeding on the insects named).

grasshopper mouse n [See quot 1980]

A mouse of the genus *Onychomys,* native to the western US. Also called **mole mouse, scorpion mouse**

1904 Hornaday *Amer. Nat. Hist.* 91/1 **West,** *The Grasshopper Mouse* [Footnote: *Onychomys leucogaster*], originally described by Audubon and Bachman as the *Missouri Mouse,* and often called the *Mole Mouse,* .. strongly resembles the white-footed mouse. **1908** U.S. Dept. Ag. *Farmers' Bulletin* 335.13, *Short-tailed grasshopper mouse. (Onychomys brevicaudus)...* The grasshopper mouse is common throughout the sagebrush valleys of the Great Basin Country. **1928** Anthony *N. Amer. Mammals* 340, The Grasshopper Mice are soft-furred, attractive rodents and little apt to be confused with any other Mice. **1938** FWP *Guide MN* 22, In addition to the common meadow mice, the observant may see the long-legged deer mouse, the rare grasshopper mouse, the tiny harvest mouse, or the queer stump-tailed bog lemming. **1940** *Jrl. Mammalogy* 21.177 **NV,** Grasshopper mice .. were taken at the burrows of antelope ground squirrels and kangaroo rats. **1957** Blair et al. *Vertebrates U.S.* 711, Grasshopper mice... Moderate- to small-sized mice, with short tails, small ears, and fairly long, very soft fur. **1980** Whitaker *Audubon Field Guide Mammals* 481, These mice .. feed heavily on grasshoppers... Grasshopper mice have several calls.

grasshopper plow See **grasshopper 3**

grasshopper sparrow n [See quots 1898, 1924]

A small sparrow (*Ammodramus savannarum* and races). Also called **grass sparrow e, ground sparrow 1f, harvest bird, quail sparrow, stink bird, yellow-winged sparrow**

1883 *Stoddart's Encycl. Americana* 1.530/1, The grasshopper sparrows *(Coturniculus passerinus, C. henslowi, C. lecontii).* **1898** (1900) Davie *Nests N. Amer. Birds* 371, *Grasshopper Sparrow...* Sometimes it will sing at short intervals for hours at a time a peculiar, monotonous song, which has been aptly compared to that of a grasshopper—hence its common name. **1924** Howell *Birds AL* 231, Although named grasshopper sparrow from its song, stomach examinations have shown this bird to merit the name also from its food habits, for grasshoppers constitute nearly one-fourth of its food. **1946** Kopman *Wild Acres* 60 **LA,** A great meadow... was the haunt of the grasshopper sparrow... The chirping, insect-like notes that give it its name were not hard to detect after a little acquaintance with the singer. **1949** *Nat. Hist.* 160, The nest of the grasshopper sparrow is rarely found, because it is cleverly concealed under a covering of grass. **1964** Phillips *Birds AZ* 193, An exceedingly handsome bird in the hand, the Grasshopper Sparrow as seen when flushed from its grassy haunts is an obscure grayish-brown streaky-backed sparrow with a short, thin tail. **1987** *Nature Conserv. News* 37.2.26 **RI,** Refuge for rare birds—including .. grasshopper sparrows.

grasshopper stock See **grasshopper 3**

grasshopper woodpecker n [See quots]

=**flicker** n^2 **1.**

1900 *Wilson Bulletin* 31.7, *Grasshopper Woodpecker.* Vermont. From its habit of frequenting open fields where grasshoppers *(Acrididae)* abound upon which it feeds. **1956** MA Audubon Soc. *Bulletin* 40.82, *Yellow-shafted flicker...* Grasshopper Woodpecker (Vt. From its feeding on grasshoppers.)

grassing See **grass** v **3**

grass lily n

=**Ithuriel's spear.**

1898 *Jrl. Amer. Folkl.* 11.281, *Brodiaea laxa* .. grass lilies.

grass line n Also *grass rope*

A rope made of organic fiber.

1841 (1973) Gurney *Journey* 69 **neNC,** A species of aloe is cultivated here, called the Bear's grass, the long spiked leaves of which consist of tough fibres. From these the Americans manufacture the "grass rope," which is quite as strong as that made of hemp, and is much used in this part of the country. **1907** White *AZ Nights* 245, They were good men, addicted to the grass-rope, the double circle, and the ox-bow stirrup. **1958** McCulloch *Woods Words* 73 **Pacific NW,** *Grass line*—A light line also more widely known as straw line or guinea line. **1967** *DARE* FW Addit **ND5,** Grass rope: hemp rope. **1968** Adams *Western Words* 132, *Grass line*—In steamboating, a Manila or other fiber rope, as distinguished from a wire cable. *Ibid, Grass rope*—A cowman's name for a rope of any fiber other than cotton; originally one made of bear grass, but now usually one made of sisal or Manila hemp.

grass mallard n

=mallard.

1943 Musgrove-Musgrove *Waterfowl IA* 19, Sportsmen commonly believe that there are several species of mallards found in our state, calling them . . grass mallards, cornfield mallards [etc]. . . Actually they are all one species.

grass moss n

A **pondweed** (here: *Potamogeton foliosus*).

1913 *Torreya* 13.226, *Potamogeton foliosus*. . . Grass moss, . . Menasha, Ark.

grassnut n

1 A **nut grass,** usu **chufa,** or its edible tuber. **Sth, S Midl**

1806 (1905) Clark *Orig. Jrls. Lewis & Clark Exped.* 5.73 **VA,** One [whistling squirrel] which I examoned [sic] had in his mouth two small bulbs of a species of grass, which resembles very much what is sometimes called the Grass Nut. **1835** Longstreet *GA Scenes* 201 **GA,** He was born in Nocatchey, and was raised upon nothing but grass-nuts and sweet potatoes; and just see what he's come to! He weighs nine hundred and fifty, dead weight. **1869** Porcher *Resources* 684 **Sth,** *Grass Nut (Cyperus repens.)* The nut or root of this is sweet, and is cultivated and sold in Charleston [SC] as an edible nut. **1968–70** *DARE* (Qu. I43, *What kinds of nuts grow wild around here?*) Inf **TN26,** Grassnuts—on a small plant; (Qu. S21, . . *Other weeds . . that are a trouble in gardens and fields*) Inf **TN52,** Grassnuts—trouble in gardens; a grass, not a weed. **1970** GA Dept. Ag. *Farmers Market Bulletin* 28 Oct 7/3, Chuffa grassnuts, 25¢ pkg.

2 Either of two **brodiaeas:** *Brodiaea laxa* or *B. pulchella;* also the edible corm of such a plant. **chiefly CA**

1877 Wright *Big Bonanza* 90 **swNV,** He war lookin' after mice, worms, bugs, grass-nuts, and sich like provender. **1897** Parsons *Wild Flowers CA* 262, This beautiful *Brodiaea (B. pulchella)* grows all over the hills in early spring. . . The little bulbs, eaten raw, are quite palatable, and are eagerly sought by the children, who call them "grass-nuts." **1898** *Jrl. Amer. Folkl.* 11.281 **CA,** *Brodiaea capitata* . . grass nuts. **1900** Smithwick *Evolution of a State* 179, California Indians . . gathered . . grass nuts, which constituted their staple food. **1915** (1926) Armstrong-Thornber *Western Wild Flowers* 16, *Grass Nuts*. . . *Brodiaea capitata* [=*pulchella*]. . . The little bulbs are edible and give the name of Grass Nuts. **1941** Jaeger *Wildflowers* 13 **Desert SW,** *Desert hyacinth. Brodiaea capitata pauciflora*. . . The small bulbs, being edible, served as a source of food both for the Indians and for the early white settlers, who called them "grass-nuts." **1949** Moldenke *Amer. Wild Flowers* 355, In the *grassnut* . . or *Ithuriels-spear, Triteleia laxa,* the funnel-form flowers are violet-purple in color. **1974** Munz *Flora S. CA* 1381, *B[rodiaea] laxa*. . . Grass Nut.

3 A **wild onion** (here: *Allium cernuum*).

1947 (1976) Curtin *Healing Herbs* 55, *Grassnut* . . Allium recurvatum. . . Its loose clusters of bluish pink flowers topping a slender stalk are a common sight in the lush grasslands of New Mexico. . . The bulbs may be eaten raw or cooked.

4 =peanut.

1976 Bailey-Bailey *Hortus Third* 96, *[Arachis] hypogaea*. . . *Grass nut*. . . Widely grown in trop. and warm temp. regions.

grassoline n [Blend of *grass* + *gasoline*] Cf **chip** n[1] **1**

Dried animal dung used as fuel.

1914 *DN* 4.107 **KS,** *Grassoline*. . . Cattle dung used as fuel. **1967** *Good Old Days* June 29/3 **KS,** The later settlers called them cow chips, or sometimes Grassoline.

grass onion n [Cf Norw *gresløk*]

A chive *(Allium schoenoprasum)*.

1950 *WELS (The small plants like onions with hollow green leaves that are cut up in salad)* 1 Inf, **cwWI,** Grass onion. [Inf of Norw background] **1950** *WELS Suppl.* 2 Infs, **WI,** Grass onion(s). **1965–70** *DARE* (Qu. I7) Infs **ME5, MI29, MO22, NC30,** 72, **UT3, WI53,** Grass onions.

grass pickerel n Cf **grass pike**

1 A **redfin pickerel:** usu *Esox americanus vermiculatus* which is also called **grass pike 1b, little pickerel, mud pickerel, pickerel, pike, slough pickerel.**

1927 Weed *Pike* 42, *Esox americanus*. . . Grass Pickerel; general, especially western. **1929** OK Univ. Biol. Surv. *Pub.* 1.97, *Esox vermiculatus* . . Grass Pickerel . . Red River system in Oklahoma. **1955** Zim-Shoemaker *Fishes* 64, *Grass Pickerel* (Barred Pickerel) is smaller and has cheeks and gill covers scaled—like the Eastern Pickerel [=*Esox niger*]. *Ibid* 155, Grass [Pickerel]: E[sox] americanus, F[reshwater]. **1956** Harlan-Speaker *IA Fish* 64, *Esox americanus vermiculatus*. . . The grass pickerel, as its name implies, prefers a vegetated habitat. . . The little grass pickerel prefers weedy areas, where it feeds extensively upon insects and their larvae and, especially, small fishes. **1968** *Living Museum* 30.4.29/1 **IL,** Grass pickerel. **1983** Becker *Fishes WI* 396, Grass pickerel are eaten by catfishes, sunfishes, yellow perch and by grass pickerel themselves.

2 =northern pike.

1927 Weed *Pike* 43 **IL,** *Esox lucius*. . . Grass Pickerel.

3 =chain pickerel.

1935 Caine *Game Fish* 22, *Pickerel—Esox reticulatus*. . . Grass Pickerel. **1946** LaMonte *N. Amer. Game Fishes* 128, *Eastern Pickerel—Esox niger*. . . Grass Pickerel.

grass pike n Cf **grass pickerel**

1 Any of several **pickerel** of the genus *Esox* as:

a =northern pike.

1884 U.S. Natl. Museum *Bulletin* 27.469, *Esox lucius*. . . *Grass Pike*. . . This is a well-known game fish and is very important commercially. **1927** Weed *Pike* 43, *Esox lucius*. . . Grass Pike; Western Pennsylvania (?). **1941** Writers' Program *Guide MI* xxvi, Game fish are defined as . . grass (great northern) pike or pickerel, muskellunge, and warmouth bass. **1946** LaMonte *N. Amer. Game Fishes* 126, *Northern Pike. Esox lucius*. . . *Names* . . Grass Pike. . . Sluggish streams and shallow, weedy places in lakes; also cold, clear, rocky waters. . . *Mud Pickerel. Esox vermiculatus*. . . *Names:* Grass Pike. This is a small pickerel, rarely running over 1′ and not ordinarily treated as a game fish. **1949** Caine *N. Amer. Sport Fish* 107, Northern pike. . . *Colloquial Names*. . . Grass pike.

b A **redfin pickerel,** usu *Esox americanus vermiculatus.*

1902 Jordan-Evermann *Amer. Fishes* 234, *Esox vermiculatus*. . . The grass pike occurs abundantly throughout the middle and upper Mississippi Valley and its streams tributary to Lakes Erie and Michigan. **1908** Forbes-Richardson *Fishes of IL* 206, *Esox vermiculatus*. . . Grass Pike. . . Color typically grassy to grayish green, with darker streaks, bars, and reticulations. **1933** LA Dept. of Conserv. *Fishes* 373, *Esox vermiculatus*. . . A miniature of the Common Pike of the north in its appearance and habits, our . . Grass Pike is a member of the True Pike family. **1946** [see **1a** above]. **1949** Caine *N. Amer. Sport Fish* 105, *Esox americanus*. . . is dusky green in color. . . It is also called . . grass pike. . . *Grass Pickerel. Esox vermiculatus*. . . The color is dark green. . . The common misnomer is grass pike. **1966** *Fishing World* 13.6.24, During years of scouting the Pennsylvania countryside, I have found. . . grass pike, a kind of pickerel that are dark green in color and seldom grow beyond the twelve-inch mark on a ruler. **1983** Becker *Fishes WI* 393, *Esox americanus vermiculatus*. . . Other common names . . grass pike.

c =chain pickerel.

1949 Caine *N. Amer. Sport Fish* 103, The largest of the true pickerels is the chain pickerel. . . *Colloquial Names* . . Grass Pike.

2 A **walleye** (here: *Stizostedion vitreum vitreum*).

1887 Goode *Amer. Fishes* 14, In the upper lakes . . *Stizostedion vitreum* is called the "Pike," with such local variations as . . "Grass Pike." **1927** Weed *Pike* 45, *Stizostedion*. . . Grass Pike; Great Lakes region. **1983** Becker *Fishes WI* 871, *Walleye. Stizostedion vitreum vitreum* . . Other common names . . grass pike.

grass pink n

1 An orchid of the genus *Calopogon* with a grasslike leaf and bearded pink flowers. Also called **rose-wings, swamp pink.** For other names of *C. barbatus* see **earrings**

1822 Eaton *Botany* 258, *Cymbidium . . pulchellum* . . grass pink. **1832** MA Hist. Soc. *Coll.* 2d ser 9.149 **cwVT,** [Cymbidium] pulchellum, Grass-pink. **1869** Fuller *Uncle John* 166, The first specimen we examined the next afternoon, was the *Calopōgon pulchellus,* or Grass Pink. **1901** Lounsberry *S. Wild Flowers* 90, Grass pink. . . is exquisitely bearded with gay colours which act as a lure, no doubt, to hungry insects. **1931** Harned *Wild Flowers Alleghanies* 141, Grass pink. . . persists in wearing its beard upside down. **1966** *DARE* Wildfl QR Pl.41A Inf **MI**57, Grass pink. **1968** *DARE* (Qu. S26b) Inf **GA**35, Grass pink; (Qu. S26c) Inf **PA**99, Grass pink orchid. **1968** *DARE* Tape **GA**30, We got about three or four different kinds of orchids. We got the green orchid, and . . what's that little pink one? . . the grass pink . . and the rose begonia. . . Them little orchids grows all over them prairies and side of the trails and everywhere out there. **1976** Fleming *Wild Flowers FL* 68, Grass pink blooms in early spring from Florida to North Carolina; look for it in acid meadows, swamps, and low pinelands along old roads.

2 =**rose pogonia.**

1894 *Harper's New Mth. Mag.* Mar 566, The sweet-pogonia or grass-pink of our sedgy swamps *(Pogonia ophioglossoides).*

3 The Deptford pink *(Dianthus armeria).*

1896 *Jrl. Amer. Folkl.* 9.182, *Dianthus Armeria* . . grass-pink, Paris, Me. **1911** *Century Dict. Suppl., Grass-pink.* . . The *Deptford* pink, *Dianthus Armeria.*

grassplot n Also *grassbelt, grass strip* **chiefly Atlantic** See Map

A grass-planted area by the side of a road or between paved roadways.

1965–70 *DARE* (Qu. N44, *In a town, the strip of grass and trees between the sidewalk and the curb*) 14 Infs, **chiefly Atlantic,** Grassplot; **CT**9, **ME**19, **MI**73, **NJ**8, **PA**55, Grass strip; (Qu. N17, . . *The separating area in the middle of a four-lane road*) Infs **GA**15, **MD**31, Grassplot; **PA**10, 204, Grass strip. **1971** Wood *Vocab. Change* 371 **Sth,** Grass plot [occurs rarely]. **1987** *Daily Hampshire Gaz.* (Northampton MA) 9 Dec 13/3, Place [old newspapers] at curbside or on the grassbelt where there is no curbing.

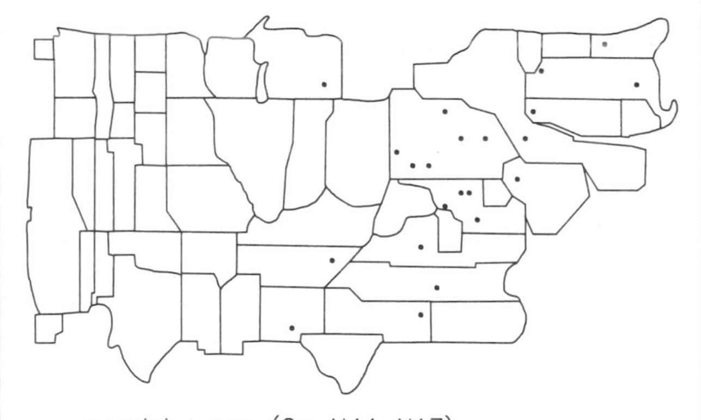

•grassplot + var (Qq. N44, N17)

grass plover n

1 =**upland plover.**

1844 Giraud *Birds Long Is.* 227, In Massachusetts, Rhode Island, New Jersey, and on the Shinnecock and Hempstead Plains, Long Island, it is common, where it is known by the name of . . "Grass . . Plover." **1876** *Forest & Stream* 7.149/1 **Long Is. NY,** Grass plover . . feed in the fields and uplands, always singly, never in flocks, and are very shy, wary birds, difficult to obtain. **1888** Trumbull *Names of Birds* 172, *Bartram's Sandpiper.* . . At New Bedford, Mass., Newport, R.I., and Stonington, Conn., and to some at Shinnecock Bay, L[ong] I[sland], *Grass Plover.* **1917** (1923) *Birds Amer.* 1.247, *Upland Plover. . . Other Names.* . . Grass Plover [etc]. **1932** Bennitt *Check-list* 29 **MO,** *Upland plover.* . . Bartramian sandpiper; . . grass plover. **1946** Hausman *Eastern Birds* 269, Grass Plover. . . *Habitat*—Meadows, fields, old pasture, often on hillsides. **1956** MA Audubon Soc. *Bulletin* 40.17, *Upland Plover.* . . Grass Plover (Maine, Vt., Mass., Conn., R.I.)

2 =**pectoral sandpiper.**

1956 MA Audubon Soc. *Bulletin* 40.19 **RI,** *Pectoral Sandpiper.* . . Grass Plover.

grass porgy n

A **porgy** (here: *Calamus arctifrons*) found in Florida waters.

1887 Goode *Amer. Fishes* 100, There are other species, . . such as . . "Grass Porgy" of Key West. **1902** Jordan–Evermann *Amer. Fishes* 440, The grass . . porgy . . is a small species. . . Colour, olivaceous. . . Though . . rarely exceeding a foot in length, it is nevertheless a good and important food-fish wherever found in sufficient numbers. **1933** John G. Shedd Aquarium *Guide* 111, *Grass Porgy.* A small porgy common in the eel grass on the Florida west coast. **1946** LaMonte *N. Amer. Game Fishes* 71, *Grass Porgy.* . . A very small fish. **1973** Knight *Cook's Fish Guide* 387.

grass rain n Also *grass shower* Cf **fodder shower**

1965–67 *DARE* (Qu. B23, . . *A light rain that doesn't last*) Inf **AR**55, Grass rain; (Qu. B24, . . *A sudden, very heavy rain*) Inf **MS**60, Grass shower.

grass relation n Cf **grass widow 1, graveyard widow**

A person related to another as a result of divorce and remarriage.

1942 (1960) Robertson *Red Hills* 51 **SC,** Our stepmother and our step-step-grandmother were sod relations of ours—not grass relations. We do not believe in divorce in South Carolina; it is against the law in South Carolina to seek divorce, so even until now we have never had a grass widower among our kinfolks.

grass rockfish n

A **rockfish** (here: *Sebastodes rastrelliger*).

1882 U.S. Natl. Museum *Bulletin* 16.671, *Grass Rock-fish.* Blackish green, with paler mottlings, the sides spotted with darker; belly pale greenish; . . the brightness of the olive and greenish shades is quite variable. . . Coast of California. **1884** Goode *Fisheries U.S.* 1.264, At San Francisco it is often called "Grass Rock-fish," perhaps from its color. **1898** U.S. Natl. Museum *Bulletin* 47.1819, *Grass Rock-fish.* **1953** Roedel *Common Fishes CA* 134, The grass rockfish has 22 or 23 short flat gill rakers nearly as high as wide. . . The grass rockfish [is usually found] close to rocky shores. **1960** Amer. Fisheries Soc. *List Fishes* 37, Grass rockfish. P[acific]. *Sebastodes rastrelliger.*

grass rope See **grass line**

grass runner See **grass chippie**

grass sack n Also *grass (-sack-)bag, sea grass sack* **chiefly C Atl, Lower Missip Valley, Ohio Valley** See Map Cf **coffee sack**

A **burlap bag** or other coarse-cloth bag.

1942 Footner *MD Main* 291, Saddles, "grass-bags," hats were thrown on the table. **1946** *PADS* 5.25 **VA,** *Grass sack, sea grass sack.* . . A large bag made of coarse canvas; on the Rappahannock and the Potomac. **1958** *PADS* 29.11 **TN,** *Grass sack.* **c1960** *Wilson Coll.* **csKY,** *Grass sack.* . . A sack or bag made of coarse fiber. This is the commonest name. **1963** Edwards *Gravel* 137 **eTN** (as of 1920s), Now and then the boys would piece together an old grass sack seine and make a raid on a few of the deepest holes along Davis Creek. **1964** *PADS* 42.17 **KY,** *Grass sack.* The commonest name for a coarse cloth bag. **1965–70** *DARE* (Qu. F23, *A container made of rough, loosely-woven, brown cloth; commonly used for potatoes, etc*) 26 Infs, **chiefly C Atl, Lower Missip**

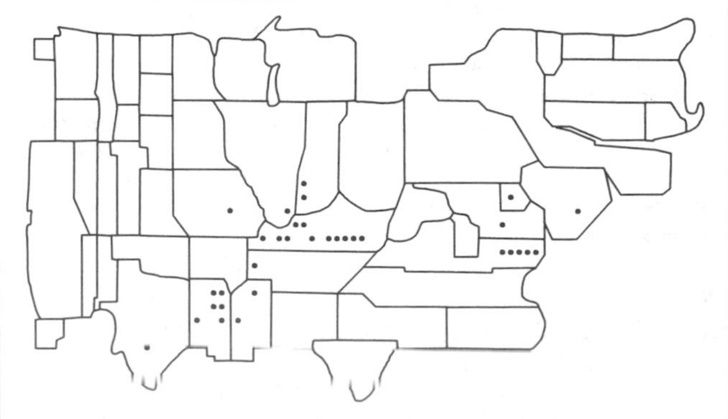

•grass sack + varr (Qq. F23, F19, F20)

Valley, Ohio Valley, Grass sack; **DE**3, **VA**76, Grass bag; **DE**3, One old man said grass-sack-bag; (Qu. F19, *A cloth container for grain*) Infs **KY**8, **LA**6, Grass sack; **MD**14, Grass bag; (Qu. F20, *A cloth container for feed*) Infs **IN**41, 52, **KY**5, **MS**18, 60, **TN**27, Grass sack. **1968** *DARE* FW Addit **DE**5, *Grass bag*—a burlap sack. **1983** Montell *Don't Go Up* 233 **csKY, cnTN,** Lumber company representatives at the destination removed the chaindogs and kept them for the pilot until his next trip. They were carried home in grass-sacks.

grass scythe n **esp NEast** Cf **grass blade**

A weed-cutting tool.

1787 (1925) Washington *Diaries* 3.243, Called on my return at French's where I had begun with grass Scythes (a cradle having been found not to answer). **1965–70** *DARE* (Qu. L35, *Hand tools used for cutting underbrush and digging out roots*) Infs **MA**68, **NY**70, Grass scythe; (Qu. L37, *A hand tool used for cutting weeds and grass*) Infs **CT**14, 26, **MA**68, **NJ**50, **NY**70, Grass scythe.

grass shower See **grass rain**

grass shrimp n Also called **glass shrimp**

A shrimp of the genus *Palaemonetes.*

1975 Evanoff *Catch More Fish* 161, The chum usually used here is the small grass shrimp. These tiny, translucent shrimp can be bought by the quart. . . [but] many weakfishermen try to catch their own shrimp in tidal bays and creeks. **1982** Sternberg *Fishing* 126, *Grass Shrimp.* Some species of grass shrimp live in fresh water; others are found only in salt water. *Ibid* 127, Grass shrimp are 1 to 2 inches long and have an almost glassy appearance. Saltwater types live in estuaries along the Atlantic and Gulf coasts. Freshwater species are most common in the southeastern United States. *Ibid* 130, Look for grass beds on shallow tidal flats. To catch grass shrimp, pull a fine-mesh seine through sparse vegetation near the shore. **1983** Fox *At the Sea's Edge* 214, The grass shrimp, *Palaemonetes,* and the brown shrimp, *Paneus,* live in vegetated areas, but start their life in shallow, muddy tidal creeks.

grass sling n

=grass blade.

1966 *DARE* (Qu. L37, *A hand tool used for cutting weeds and grass*) Inf **SC**12, Grass sling.

grass snake n

1 also *green grass snake:* A **green snake** (here: *Opheodrys* spp, usu *O. vernalis*).

1842 DeKay *Zool. NY* 3.40, *Coluber vernalis.* . . This innocent and beautiful species, known in this State as the *Green* or *Grass Snake,* has long been confounded with the *estivus* of the Southern States, from which it is readily distinguished by its inferior length and carinate scales. **1949** Dickinson *Lizards & Snakes WI* 28, *Smooth Green Snake — Opheodrys vernalis vernalis.* . . Often known as the grass snake due to its color, it is a beautiful little species sometimes attaining twenty inches in length. **1958** Conant *Reptiles & Amphibians* 152, The "green grass snake" [=*Opheodrys vernalis*]. **1974** Shaw–Campbell *Snakes West* 79, Among snakes closely allied to the racers, one of the prettiest . . is the smooth green snake *(Opheodrys vernalis),* sometimes called the grass snake because it is almost always found in meadow or grassy marsh. **1981** Vogt *Nat. Hist.* 132 **WI,** Green snakes or grass snakes, as they are often called, are found in mesic and wet prairie, oak savanna, bracken grassland, open areas in pine barrens, and grassy areas.

2 A **garter snake 1** (here: *Thamnophis sirtalis*).

1894 U.S. Natl. Museum *Proc.* 17.329, This beautiful snake [=*Thamnophis sirtalis*] called "Grass snake," or sometimes "Garter snake," is quite common in wet places in south Florida. . . The grass snake is ill-tempered and even a small one will bite ferociously. **1928** Pope–Dickinson *Amphibians* 69, *Common Garter Snake— Thamnophis sirtalis sirtalis.* . . Commonly but erroneously known as the Grass Snake. **c1940** Newman–Newman *Conserv. Notes* 5 **neLA,** Among the non-poisonous snakes we find the . . grass snake. **1981** Vogt *Nat. Hist.* 152 **WI,** *Thamnophis sirtalis.* . . The eastern garter snake, garden snake, or grass snake is a medium-sized slender snake.

3 =glass snake.

1938 Matschat *Suwannee R.* 263 **seGA,** "Grass snake," Pompano said, catching sight of the olive-green body, with a golden-bronze stripe down the side, and long tapering tail. "Horn snake," Cella corrected, with the swampers' name for it. "Lizard," said the Plant Woman. **1939** FWP *Guide FL* 29, Another lizard is the so-called 'grass' or 'glass' snake.

4 A **red-bellied snake** (here: *Storeria occipitomaculata*).

1974 Shaw–Campbell *Snakes West* 132, The red-bellied snake *(Storeria occipitomaculata)* is also called . . grass snake.

grass snipe n [See quot 1951]

=pectoral sandpiper.

1872 Coues *Key to N. Amer. Birds* 255, *Pectoral Sandpiper. . . Grass Snipe.* . . North America, abundant. **1888** Trumbull *Names of Birds* 176, *Pectoral Sandpiper.* . . At Pine Point, M[ain]e, Portsmouth, N.H., in Massachusetts . . , infrequently, *Grass Snipe.* **1907** Anderson *Birds IA* 217, The . . Grass Snipe . . is an abundant migrant in nearly all parts of the state. **1917** *DN* 4.426 **LA,** *Grass snipe.* **1928** Bailey *Birds NM* 272, The . . Grass Snipe . . is found in swamps and in meadows and flats with scattered cover. **1948** *Sat. Eve. Post* 16 Oct 54/4 **TX,** He is an expert on the feeding habits of the pectoral sandpiper, or grass snipe. **1951** Pough *Audubon Water Bird* 235, This bird [=*Erolia melanotos*] is well termed "grass snipe," as wet meadows, rain pools in grasslands, and even fairly dry, rough pastures are its favorite haunts. **1962** Imhof *AL Birds* 246, [The] Grass Snipe. . . is normally a little larger than the Spotted Sandpiper, but some individuals are as big as a snipe.

grass sparrow n Pronc-spp *grass spar(rer)* [From the habitat]

Any of var sparrows, as:

a =vesper sparrow.

1883 *Stoddart's Encycl. Americana* 1.530/1, The grass sparrows *(Poœcetes gramineus).* **1940** Todd *Birds W. PA* 709, Sparrow, Grass, *see* Sparrow, Eastern Vesper. **1946** Hausman *Eastern Birds* 600, *Eastern Vesper Sparrow. . . Other Names* . . Grass Sparrow. . . *Habitat*— Fields, dry meadows, scrubby pasture lands, cleared hillsides, weedy fence rows bordering fields.

b =field sparrow a.

1908 *DN* 3.317 **eAL, wGA,** *Grass-sparrow.* . . The common field sparrow. **1934** Vines *Green Thicket* 60 **cnAL,** He had a little old trunk nearly full of feathers and down from wild ducks and geese, and . . from tiny birds like the . . English spar (sparrow), grass spar, ground spar . . and other birds. **1962** Imhof *AL Birds* 559, *Field Sparrow.* . . Grass sparrow. . . It is the most common sparrow of broomsedge fields.

c =savannah sparrow.

1911 Howell *Birds AR* 62, *Savannah Sparrow.* . . This little grass sparrow is a common migrant in both spring and fall, and many remain in the State all winter. **1953** Jewett *Birds WA* 629, *Passerculus sandwichensis crassus.* . . Other names: Savannah Sparrow; . . Grass Sparrow. **1955** *Oriole* 20.1.13 **GA,** *Savannah Sparrow. Grass Sparrow* (from its habitat). . . *Bachman's Sparrow. Grass Sparrow. Ibid* 14 **GA,** *Swamp Sparrow. Grass Sparrow.* **1962** Imhof *AL Birds* 543, *Savannah Sparrow.* . . Grass Sparrow. . . The bird generally feeds in short grass and roosts in bad weather in tall grass, which makes partially-mowed fields or weedy fields next to pastures especially attractive.

d =pinewoods sparrow.

1926 *AmSp* 1.419 **Okefenokee GA,** Up flew a Grass Sparrer [Footnote: Pine-woods Sparrow]. **1955** [see **c** above].

e =grasshopper sparrow.

1955 Lowery *LA Birds* 485, The Grasshopper Sparrow. . . is the only one of the "grass sparrows" (that is, sparrows that are habitual denizens of dense stands of grass) with a plain breast.

f =swamp sparrow.

1955 [see **c** above].

grass spider n

Any of var spiders, usu of the genus *Agelenopsis,* that spin their webs on grass.

1890 *Century Dict.* 5830, *Grass spider,* one of many different spiders, as species of *Agalena,* which spin webs on the grass, such as may be seen spangled with dew in the morning in meadows. **1913** Comstock *Spider Book* 586, The grass spider is so-called because its webs are the most common webs found on grass. **1935** Pratt *Manual Invertebrate Animals* 493, *A[gelena] naevia.* . . Grass spider. . . Yellowish brown, or black in color, with gray or dark markings and spots on the abdomen and broad longitudinal stripes on the cephalothorax. **1966–69** *DARE* (Qu. R28, . . *Different kinds of spiders . . around here*) Infs **AR**52, **FL**4, **GA**11, 77, **OK**42, Grass spider. **1972** Kaston *How Know Spiders* 177, Genus *Agelenopsis.* Grass Spiders. . . The web . . is built on grass, on bushes, in stone fences, or in corners of buildings, and is firmly attached to the substratum. **1980** Milne–Milne *Audubon Field Guide Insects* 893, *Grass Spiders* (*Agelenopsis* spp.) . . The many different species can be distinguished only by a specialist.

grass sponge n Cf **glove sponge**

A commercial grade of sponge; also the sponge (usu *Hippiospongia* spp) itself; see quots.

1875 in 1884 Goode *Fisheries U.S.* 1.848, *Spongia graminea*. . . "This is one of the Grass Sponges of commerce." . . This species occurs at Key West, Florida. . . When living the color is black. **1881** Ingersoll *Oyster-Industry* 244, *Grass-sponge.*—An inferior grade of Florida commercial sponge, *Spongia cerebriformis.* (Florida Keys). **1898** (1910) Willoughby *Across Everglades* 93 **sFL,** The sponges that are marketable are the glove, sheep's wool, grass, and yellow. These vary somewhat among themselves in quality. **1901** Arnold *Sea-Beach* 104, Five species of commercial sponges are taken from Florida waters. They are graded by the trade in the order of their importance, as the "sheepswool," "yellow," "grass," "velvet," and "glove." **1935** Pratt *Manual Invertebrate Animals* 93, *H[ippiospongia] equina*. . . Horse sponge; . . grass sponge. . . Body massive, of coarse fibre and with extensive canal system. . . Much less valuable than [Hippiospongia lachne].

grass spur n Cf **grass burr**

=**burr grass** or its seed.

1908 *DN* 3.317 **eAL, wGA,** *Grass-spur*. . . Same as *sand-spur.* **1968** *DARE* (Qu. S15, . . *Weed seeds that cling to clothing*) Inf **GA**28, Grass spurs.

grass staggers n

1 Locoism.

1887 *Science* 9.32/1, A curious affection exists among the horses of north-western Texas known as 'grass-staggers.' It is caused by their eating the 'loco-weed,' and the affected animals are said to be 'locoed.' At first they lose flesh, and then become weak and staggering, and finally crazy. **1961** Adams *Old-Time Cowhand* 159, Speakin' of cattle bein' "locoed" meant the result of feedin' on the toxic loco week [sic]. An animal addicted to it would run about frantic and crazy, as though intoxicated. Such animals were said to be "weedy," or to have the "grass staggers".

2 Grass tetany.

1964 Kingsbury *Poisonous Plants U.S.* 504, The terms *grass tetany, grass staggers* . . have been applied to a syndrome in livestock which. . . is always associated with imbalance in the ionic components of blood serum—especially reduced magnesium levels—and generally with ingestion of lush forage or pasturage. **1967** *Merck Vet. Manual* 556, *Grass Tetany in Cattle and Sheep* (grass staggers). *Ibid* 557, In the most acute form of the disease, affected cows . . undergo severe paddling convulsions. . . In less severe cases, the cow . . walks with a stiff gait. . . The disease in sheep . . has the same clinical signs as the disease in cattle.

grass strip See **grassplot**

grass tetanus n [Folk-etym for *grass tetany*] Cf **grass staggers 2**

1969–70 *DARE* (Qu. K28, . . *Diseases that cows have*) Inf **TN**37, Grass tetanus; cattle die right off—a stomach disorder caused by eating grass and clover in April usually; **TN**58, Grass tetanus.

grass train n Cf **grass freight**

1944 Adams *Western Words* 67, *Grass train*—Ox trains of the early freighters, called this because oxen could live on grass, when horses and mules had to have grain.

grass whistler See **grass chippie**

grass widow n

1 A woman separated from her husband, either permanently or temporarily, for some reason other than death. *somewhat old-fash*

1845 Hooper *Advent. Simon Suggs* 183 **AL,** John Green's sister, (the grass widder, as lives with 'em,) she goes to her battlin bench. **1849** in 1956 Eliason *Tarheel Talk* 274 **NC,** Did the "grass widder" try to shine around our friend Daniel? **1899** (1912) Green *VA Folk-Speech* 204, *Grass-widow*. . . A woman temporarily separated from her husband, as while he is travelling or living at a distance on account of business. **1905** *DN* 3.10 **cCT,** *Grass widow*. . . A divorced woman. **1907** *DN* 3.213 **cCT, nwAR.** **1912** Thornton *Amer. Gloss.* 386, *Grass Widow*. . . "A grass widow" is an ambiguous term . . Mr. George Hempl of Ann Arbor, in April, 1893, examined a hundred students as to the use of the phrase. Nineteen understood it to mean a woman divorced; to thirty-seven it signified a woman divorced or informally separated from her husband, he being usually the deserting party. **1927** *AmSp* 2.355 **cwWV.** **1958** Humphrey *Home from the Hill* 276 **neTX,** Off up there in the big town where nobody knew her, all she would have to do was show her annulment paper (somewhat chewed) and be as sweet and sassy a young grass widow as you please. **1965–70** *DARE* (Qu. AA26, *A divorced woman*) 450 Infs, **widespread,** Grass widow. [Of all Infs responding to the question, 89% were mid-aged or old; of those giving this response, 97% were mid-aged or old.] **1975** Gainer *Witches* 10 **sAppalachians,** A woman who is separated from her husband but not divorced.

2 An unmarried mother. Cf **grass** v **3**

1899 (1912) Green *VA Folk-Speech* 204, *Grass-widow*. . . An unmarried woman who has had a child.

3 =**blue-eyed grass 1. chiefly AK, Pacific NW**

1938 (1958) Sharples *AK Wild Flowers* 140, *Sisyrinchium*. . . "Grass Widow". . . Southeastern Alaska. **1941** Writers' Program *Guide WA* 367, The stream banks are yellow and purple with buttercups . . and purple grasswidows. *Ibid* 401, Early in spring, slopes are carpeted with blue grasswidows. **1956** St. John *Flora SE WA* 96, *Sisyrinchium inflatum*. . . Grass Widow. **1961** Peck *Manual OR* 233, *S[isyrinchium] Douglasii*. . . Grass Widows. **1963** Craighead *Rocky Mt. Wildflowers* 35, *Grass-widows. Sisyrinchium inflatum*. . . Grass-widows appear soon after snow disappears. **1966** *DARE* (Qu. S26a, . . *Other wildflowers . . around here*) Inf **WA**6, Grass widows. **1966** *DARE* Wildfl QR Pl.28A Inf **WA**10, Grass widow. **1973** Hitchcock-Cronquist *Flora Pacific NW* 698, Grass-widows. . . *S[isyrinchium] inflatum*. . . *S. douglasii.*

grass widower n

See quot 1899.

1862 in 1912 Thornton *Amer. Gloss.* 1.386, David is a bachelor again, or rather a "grass-widower." **1899** (1912) Green *VA Folk-Speech* 204, *Grass-widower*. . . A man who, for any reason, is living apart from his wife. **1942** (1960) Robertson *Red Hills* 52 **SC,** It is against the law in South Carolina to seek divorce, so even until now we have never had a grass widower among our kinfolks.

grassworm n

The fall armyworm *(Spodoptera frugiperda).*

1814 in 1815 Lit. & Philos. Soc. NY *Trans.* 1.65, The ravages of the . . canker worm, palmer worm, grass worm, and rose bug, are incalculably injurious. **1856** U.S. Patent Office *Annual Rept. for 1855: Ag.* 83, The specimens [of the yellow caterpillar] observed . . appeared to be of solitary habits, not congregating together, like the cotton-caterpillar and grass-worm. **1882** (1903) Treat *Injurious Insects* 129, Still another insect, common in the Southern States, *(Laphrygma frugiperda)* . . has been called "Army Worm." Its proper name is "Southern Grass Worm," and it prefers grasses and weeds to cotton and other crops. **1889** *Century Dict.* 2604/3, *Grass-worm*. . . The fall army-worm. **1948** Wolfe *Farm Gloss.* 120, *Fall Army Worm*. . . Sometimes called "grass worms." . . Very destructive to grasses, grains, cotton, etc. in the South.

grass wrack n

1 =**eelgrass 1.** [*OED* 1776 →]

1822 Eaton *Botany* 520, Grasswrack, sea eel-grass. . . In bays and salt marshes. **1838** Audubon *Ornith. Biog.* 4.10, Its [=the canvasback duck's] subsistence . . is chiefly derived from the grass-wrack or Eelgrass, *Zostera marina.* **1868** (1870) Gray *Field Botany* 316, *Grass-Wrack* or *Eel-Grass* of salt water. . . Shallow bays of the ocean. **1900** Lyons *Plant Names* 404, *Z[ostera] marina* . . Grass-wrack. **1911** NJ State Museum *Annual Rept. for 1910* 166, *Zostera marina*. . . The long ribbon-like leaves are washed up on the shores of the bays and on the salt marshes in large masses, termed "grass-wrack" by the fishermen. **1933** Small *Manual SE Flora* 18, *Z[ostera] marina*. . . Grass-wrack. **1973** Hitchcock-Cronquist *Flora Pacific NW* 567, Grass wrack. . . *Zostera marina.*

2 A pondweed (here: *Potamogeton zosteriformis*).

1940 Clute *Amer. Plant Names* 153, *P[otamogeton] zosterifolius*. . . Grass wrack. **1959** Carleton *Index Herb. Plants* 55, *Grass-wrack:* Potomogeton [sic] Zosterifolius.

grass wren n

The short-billed **marsh wren** *(Cistothorus platensis).*

1917 (1923) *Birds Amer.* 3.195, *Short-billed Marsh Wren*. . . *Other Names*. . . Grass Wren. . . *Nest:* On or close to the ground, in a tussock of marsh grass. **1946** Hausman *Eastern Birds* 449, Grass Wren. . . One of the two smallest of our wrens . . , keeping itself well hidden in the tall meadow grass. **1978** Gromme *Birds WI* 221, Wren, Grass (Short-billed Marsh Wren).

grassy adj **chiefly C Atl** See Map Cf **bitter adj 1, garlicky, weedy**

Of milk: tainted.

1950 *WELS (Milk that has a taste from something the cow ate in the pasture)* 2 Infs, **WI,** Grassy; [1 Inf, Grass milk]. **1965–70** *DARE* (Qu.

K14) 20 Infs, **chiefly C Atl,** Grassy (milk); **MD**42, Garlic, grassy—depending on what she ate; **MO**11, Grassy taste; [**IL**87, **NJ**50, (Strong) grass; **PA**23, 158, Grass (flavored, milk); **MO**16, **PA**232, **SD**2, (Tastes, tastes of, smells like) grass].

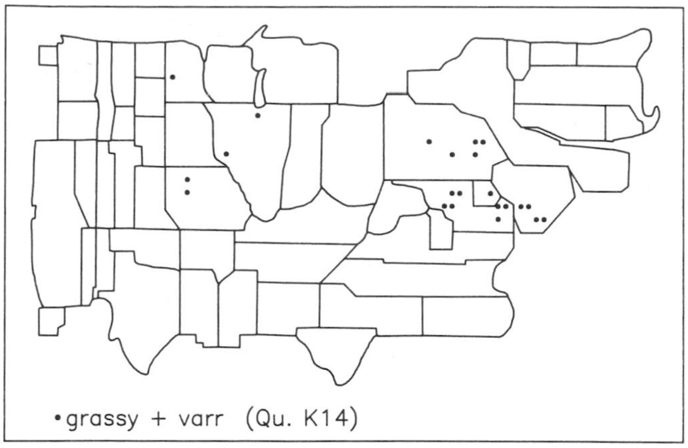

grated bread n
=**gritted bread.**
1944 *PADS* 2.19 **sAppalachians,** *Gritted bread*. . . Grated bread, made from the ears of corn half-hardened. **1986** Pederson *LAGS Concordance,* 1 inf, **cwTN,** *Grated bread*—made from young corn, hand grated.

graton n [LA Fr; see quot 1931] **sLA**
=**crackling 1.**
[**1931** Read *LA French* 43, *Gratons,* "cracklings," is a corruption of St.-Fr. *cretons*.] **1967** LeCompte *Word Atlas* 283 **seLA,** Hog scraps cut up and fried . . [15 of 21 infs] *gratons. Ibid* 295, Bread made of cornmeal and cracklings . . [1 inf] *graton* bread. **1986** Pederson *LAGS Concordance,* 1 inf, **New Orleans LA,** Graton.

gravedigger n
1 An armadillo (*Dasypus* spp). Cf **digger 5**
1966 *DARE* (Qu. P32, . . *Kinds of wild animals . . around here*) Inf **OK**52, Armadillo (also called "gravedigger" years ago).
2 =**opossum.**
1970 *DARE* (Qu. P31, . . *Names . . around here for the . . opossum*) Inf **TN**46, Gravedigger.

grave dirt See **graveyard dirt**

grave house n **KY**
A shelter erected over or near a grave.
1914 Furman *Sight* 35 **KY,** I can see her now, up thar on the hill-shoulder . . by Evy's grave-house. **1939** Writers' Program *Guide KY* 241, Many of them [=mountain cemeteries] have "grave houses"—rude log and clapboard shelters—that mountaineers customarily erect over and around the graves of their relatives. **1942** Clark *Kentucky* 196 **KY,** In earlier days when the body of a loved one . . was consigned to the earthly bosom of the hill country, a grave house was erected over the mound. These little houses protected the grave from both the elements and that fiendish ghoul, the "grave robber."

gravel n **esp S Midl** Cf Intro "Language Changes" II.7
Used as count noun rather than mass noun.
1937-38 in 1944 *ADD* **neKY,** Hens that perhaps didn't find any gravels for their craws . . well gravels or no gravels—Mom just . . crated them. . . The gravels fly and there are shouts of fighting men. [*DARE* Ed: from several unidentified stories by Jesse Stuart] **1939** *Hall Coll.* **wNC, eTN,** *Gravel*—These gravels are hard on yer feet. **1954** *Harder Coll.* **cwTN,** *Gravel*—He fell on them gravel. **1963** Edwards *Gravel* 41 **eTN,** Zack squinted his eyes and spat a sleuce of amber onto the limestone gravels at the edge of the road. **1986** Pederson *LAGS Concordance* **Gulf Region,** 1 inf, Cherty land has gravels in it; *(Designations of roads by size and material)* 5 infs, Gravels; 1 inf, Gravels on the road; 1 inf, It's made of gravels; 1 inf, Little gravels.

gravel v^1 **chiefly Sth, S Midl**
To annoy, distress, embarrass.
1871 Hay *Pike Co. Ballads* 22 **IL,** It gravels me like the devil to train / Along o' sich fools as you. **1919** Hough *Sagebrusher* 41 **MT,** "Feller's hopeless, that's what," complained Wid Gardner to himself. "It gravels me plenty." **1923** *DN* 5.209 **swMO,** *Gravel*. . . To embarrass, to humiliate. "Hit shore graveled me when she bawled me out." **1926** *DN* 5.398 **Ozarks,** Ab Lee's *blanny* shore did gravel th' school-marm. **1933** Williamson *Woods Colt* 115 **Ozarks,** Let's s'pose thar's a gal a-tormentin' of ye, an' it gravels ye, same as it would. **1952** Brown *NC Folkl.* 1.547. **1959** *VT Hist.* new ser 27.139 **neVT. c1960** *Wilson Coll.* **csKY. 1960** Carpenter *Tales Manchaca* 220 **cTX,** Hester was graveled at the idea of my sons finding me sick. **1966-69** *DARE* (Qu. Y2, *Other words for upsetting or disturbing somebody: "Losing all that money didn't seem to ______ him a bit."*) Inf **AL**3, Gravel; (Qu. GG9, *To suddenly embarrass somebody and throw him off balance: "When they told him what she had said about him, it certainly did ______ him."*) Infs **TN**43, **WV**16, Gravel. **1984** Doig *English Creek* 4 **nMT,** It gravels me every time I read a version of those times that makes it sound as if the Depression set in on the day Wall Street tripped over itself in 1929.

gravel v^2 See **grabble v 1**

gravel chickweed See **chickweed 1f**

gravel-flipper n Cf *bean-flipper* (at **bean-shooter**)
See quots.
1976 Garber *Mountain-ese* 36 **Appalachians,** *Gravel-flipper* . . slingshot—Jamie kilt a catbird with his new homade gravel flipper. **1984** Wilder *You All Spoken Here* 150 **Sth,** *Gravel flipper*. . . Beanshooter.

gravel-grass n
A **cleavers** (here: *Galium aparine*).
1900 Lyons *Plant Names* 167, *G[alium] Aparine*. . . Gravel-grass, Grip, Grip-grass. **1940** Clute *Amer. Plant Names* 223, *Galium aparine.* Gravel-grass.

gravel, hit the See **hit the grit 2**

gravel plant n [See quots 1873, 1911]
=**arbutus.**
1843 Torrey *Flora NY* 1.432, *Epigaea repens*. . . *Trailing Arbutus*. . . It is sold by the Shakers, under the name of *Gravel plant.* **c1873** in 1976 Miller *Shaker Herbs* 180, *Gravel Plant—Epigaea repens*. . . Gravel Weed. . . Ground Laurel. . . A superior remedy . . in gravel and all diseases of the urinary organs. **1901** Mohr *Plant Life AL* 656, The herb *(Epigaea repens),* known as "gravel plant," is used medicinally. **1911** Henkel *Amer. Med. Leaves* 18, *Epigaea repens*. . . Gravel plant is the name that is generally applied to it in the drug trade. **1959** Carleton *Index Herb. Plants* 55, *Gravel-plant:* Epigaea repens.

gravelroot n
1 A **joe-pye weed** (here: *Eupatorium purpureum*). [See quot 1869]
1869 Porcher *Resources* 453 **Sth,** Gravel Root *(Eupatorium purpureum)*. . . It is said to operate as a diuretic; and it is one of the popular remedies for calculus. **1889** *Century Dict.* 2608, *Gravelroot*. . . The joe-pye weed or trumpetweed . . , *Eupatorium purpureum*. . . Its root is used as a domestic remedy in various ailments of the urinary organs. **1899** Bergen *Animal Lore* 112 **WV,** *Eupatorium purpureum,* the Joe-Pye-weed, is called "gravelroot," and is evidently thought to be a remedy for calculi. **1910** Graves *Flowering Plants* 375 **CT,** Purple Boneset. . . Gravel-root. . . The root is valued for its medicinal properties and the leaves are also used. **1975** Hamel-Chiltoskey *Cherokee Plants* 41, Gravel root. . . *E[upatorium] purpurem* [sic]. Root is diuretic; for gout; . . roots used in decoction . . for difficult urination; . . tea for kidney trouble.
2 A **horse balm** (here: *Collinsonia canadensis*). [See quot 1869]
1869 Porcher *Resources* 486 **Sth,** Gravel Root . . *(Collinsonia Canadensis)*. . . The decoction is efficacious in catarrh of the bladder, . . gravel, dropsy, etc. **1892** (1974) Millspaugh *Amer. Med. Plants* 119, *Collinsonia canadensis*. . . *Com[mon] Names*. . . *Gravel-root*. . . Drs. A. French and Beers speak highly of it in pains of the bladder. **1959** Carleton *Index Herb. Plants* 56, *Gravel-root:* Collinsonia canadensis; Eupatorium purpureum.

gravelweed n
1 =**arbutus.** [See quot 1892]
c1873 in 1976 Miller *Shaker Herbs* 180, *Gravel Plant—Epigaea repens*. . . Gravel Weed. . . Ground Laurel. . . A superior remedy . . in gravel and all diseases of the urinary organs. **1876** Hobbs *Bot. Hdbk.* 48, Gravel weed, . . Epigaea repens. . . Diervilla Canadensis. . . Onosmodium Virginianum. **1892** (1974) Millspaugh *Amer. Med. Plants* 101, *Epigaea repens*. . . *Com[mon] Names*. . . *Gravel Plant*. . . It is stated

that in lithic acid gravel, and some forms of nephritis, cystitis and vesical catarrh, its use has often been of greater benefit than uva-ursi or buchu. **1943** Peattie *Great Smokies* 274, These white and pinkish waxy blooms, as delightful in their fragrance as they are humble in their growth ("gravelweed," the mountain people call the plant [=trailing arbutus]), always serve to mark a significant period in the chronicle of the year. **1975** Dwyer *Thangs* 37 **Sth, S Midl,** *Gravelweed*—Trailing Arbutus.

2 A **bush honeysuckle** (here: *Diervilla lonicera*).

1876 [see **1** above]. **1900** Lyons *Plant Names* 135, *D[iervilla] Diervilla*. . . Bush Honey-suckle, Gravel-weed. **1940** Clute *Amer. Plant Names* 54, *D[iervilla] lonicera*. . . Gravel-weed. *Ibid* 227, *Onosmodium virginianum*. . . Gravel-weed. *Ibid* 233, *Verbesina helianthoides*. . . Gravel-weed.

3 A **false gromwell** (here: *Onosmodium virginianum*).

1876 [see **1** above]. **1910** Graves *Flowering Plants* 330 **CT,** *Onosmodium virginianum*. . . Gravel-weed. . . The root and seeds are medicinal. **1940** [see **2** above].

4 A **crownbeard** (here: *Verbesina helianthoides*).

1940 [see **2** above].

grave rock n Also *grave slab* **chiefly Appalachians**

A gravestone or other grave marker.

1901 Harben *Westerfelt* 279 **nGA,** I'm goin' back to put a grave-rock over Jasper's remains. **1930** Shoemaker *1300 Words* 24 **cPA Mts** (as of c1900), *Grave-slab*—A headstone or wooden grave marker. **1932** Randolph *Ozark Mt. Folks* 108, The women who made them [=coverlets] have been silent dust for many years now, beneath the home-made "grave-rocks" in the buryin'-ground on the hill. **1960** Hall *Smoky Mt. Folks* 35 **wNC, eTN,** A few "grave-rocks" lay round about, but they could not be distinguished from ordinary stones of the field. **1976** Garber *Mountain-ese* 36 **Appalachians,** We put a new grave rock at Uncle Penn's grave in the buryin' ground.

gravestone n *joc*

1 also *headstone:* A tooth, esp a prominent one.

1909 *DN* 3.420 **Cape Cod MA,** *Grave stones*. . . Large prominent front teeth. **1950** *WELS (Large front teeth that stick out of the mouth)* 1 Inf, **WI,** Gravestones. **1965–70** *DARE* (Qu. X12) Infs **CT**1, **MS**45, **RI**1, Gravestones; (Qu. X13a, . . *Joking names . . for teeth*) Inf **NY**111, Headstones.

2 See quot.

1966 *DARE* (Qu. X13b, *Joking names for false teeth*) Inf **MS**23, Gravestones.

graveyard n

1950 *WELS Suppl.*, Graveyard: A descriptive name for a rather thick cluster of dead trees sticking up out of the water in the flowage. The illusion is almost perfect by moonlight. Very common in flowage country.

graveyard bird n

=**Carolina wren.**

1916 *Times-Picayune* (New Orleans LA) 30 Apr mag sec 5, *Carolina Wren*. . . Graveyard Bird.

graveyard cleaning See **graveyard working**

graveyard cough n

A severe cough, esp one associated with tuberculosis.

1873 Beadle *Undeveloped West* 33, I was shaken by an ominous graveyard cough. **1912** Green *VA Folk-Speech* 204, *Graveyard-cough*. . . A deep, hollow cough; meaning that the person with such a cough will soon die. **1952** Brown *NC Folkl.* 1.547, *Graveyard cough*. . . A cough indicative of death; a tuberculous cough. **1965–70** *DARE* (Qu. BB10, . . *Other names . . for tuberculosis*) Inf **NC**83, Graveyard cough; (Qu. BB11, . . *A deep cough that you can't seem to get rid of*) Infs **CA**97, **KY**24, **MS**15, Graveyard cough; (Qu. BB12, *The kind of cough that comes with bronchitis: "He has a ——— cough."*) Infs **LA**20, **MA**5, **NJ**39, **WV**2, Graveyard. **1972** Cooper *NC Mt. Folkl.* 92, *Graveyard cough*—a tubercular cough.

graveyard digging See **graveyard working**

graveyard dirt n Also *grave dirt* Cf **goofer** n

Soil taken from a grave for use in **hoodoo** n **1a.**

1884 *World* (NY NY) 12 Oct 12/3 **Philadelphia PA,** The clairvoyant assured the ignorant and superstitious woman that some person had taken grave dirt from Lebanon Cemetery, and flying down the chimney at midnight had deposited it in the cellar. **1926** [see **goofer** n]. **c1938** [see **goofer** n]. **1942** Kennedy *Palmetto Country* 168 **FL,** Graveyard dirt . . [is] often used by Negro rooming-house proprietors to get rid of non-paying guests. The mere threat of leaving a can of Graveyard Dirt under the window is usually sufficient. Anyone who digs the dirt personally must do the job at exactly twelve o'clock noon or midnight. Thirteen cents must be left on the grave to pay for the dirt, thus removing the dirt's curse from the digger. If he should later return and find the money gone, it is a good sign that the Spirits have found it acceptable—but woe to the digger who retrieves the money!

graveyard duster n [Perh from its use at funerals] Cf **jim swinger**

1984 Wilder *You All Spoken Here* 12 **Sth,** *Graveyard duster*—a split-tailed coat.

graveyard flower n

1 Prob =**cypress spurge.** Cf **graveyard weed**

1916 *DN* 4.345, *Graveyard flower.* A kind of shrubby plant, bearing a pinkish flower. . . Brunswick, Ga.

2 Frangipani *(Plumeria rubra).*

1967 *DARE* (Qu. S21, . . *Other weeds . . around here*) Inf **HI**2, Graveyard flower (frangipani) is the same as plumeria.

graveyard ground-pine See **graveyard weed**

graveyard hopper n

A **lubber grasshopper** (here: *Romalea microptera*).

1967 LeCompte *Word Atlas* 198 **seLA,** *Big black grasshoppers with red wings*. . . Graveyard hopper. [1 inf of 21]

graveyard hyacinth n

A **grape hyacinth** (here: *Muscari botryoides*).

1951 *PADS* 15.28 **TX,** *Muscari botryoides*. . . Graveyard hyacinth.

graveyard light n Cf **ghost light**

1968 *DARE* (Qu. CC16, *A small light that seems to dance or flicker over a marsh or swamp at night*) Inf **IN**38, Graveyard light.

graveyard moss See **graveyard weed**

graveyard onion n

A **wild onion** such as *Allium canadense.*

1966 *DARE* (Qu. I5, *The kind of onions that keep coming up without replanting year after year*) Inf **MS**73, Graveyard onions—these are wild but good to eat.

graveyard owl n

1 =**long-eared owl.** [See quot]

1955 Lowery *LA Birds* 322, *Long-eared Owl*. . . In some sections it is called the "graveyard owl" because of its fondness for the quietness of the cedars and other evergreens that characterize such places.

2 A **screech owl.** Cf **death owl**

1966 *DARE* (Qu. Q1, . . *The kind of owl that makes a shrill, trembling cry*) Inf **FL**16, Graveyard owl—screech owl.

graveyard sermon n

See quot.

1906 Johnson *Highways Missip. Valley* 131 **Ozarks,** The minister preached what the Ozarks folks call "a graveyard sermon." He worked on the feelings of his auditors cruelly, and made some of the women cry.

graveyard spurge See **graveyard weed**

graveyard stew n

Milk toast; by ext, any soft food, esp one served to the sick or dying.

1911 *DN* 3.544 **NE,** *Graveyard stew*. . . Bread and milk stew. "We had graveyard stew for the whole week." **1940** in 1944 *ADD* **nWV.** **1941** Writers' Program *Guide WY* 462, *Graveyard stew*—Milk toast. **1950** *WELS (Different kinds of stew)* 1 Inf, **WI,** Graveyard stew—toast soaked in hot milk. **1967–68** *DARE* (Qu. H23, . . *Hot cooked breakfast cereal*) Inf **MS**1, Graveyard stew; (Qu. H35, *When eggs are taken out of the shells and cooked in boiling water*) Inf **NJ**1, Graveyard stew—served to one who is ill; (Qu. H37, . . *Words . . for gravy*) Inf **IL**23, Graveyard stew; (QR, near Qu. H45) Inf **PA**159, Graveyard stew—toast and milk, what they feed before someone passes away. **1968** *DARE* FW Addit **LA**32, Graveyard stew—toasted bread with butter, warm milk, salt and pepper poured over it—milk toast in other places. Perhaps it's called this because it's what you eat when you're too sick to eat anything else. **1988** Fulghum *All I Really Need* 54 **OR,** Special praise for a side [order] of "Graveyard Stew," which is milk toast.

graveyard weed n Also *graveyard ground-pine, ~ moss, ~ spurge* [Because it is freq planted in cemeteries and is associated with cypress, a traditional symbol of mourning]

=cypress spurge.

1894 *Jrl. Amer. Folkl.* 7.98 **WV,** *Euphorbia Cyparissias* . . graveyard-weed. **1897** *Ibid* 10.143 **IN,** *Euphorbia Cyparissias* . . graveyard moss. **1935** (1943) Muenscher *Weeds* 321, *Euphorbia Cyparissias*. . . Graveyard-weed. **1940** Steyermark *Flora MO* 328, *Cypress Spurge, Graveyard Moss. . . Euphorbia Cyparissias*. . . Planted in cemeteries and sometimes established along roadsides and fields. **1959** Carleton *Index Herb. Plants* 56, *Graveyard-Ground-Pine:* Euphorbia cyparissias. **1964** Kingsbury *Poisonous Plants U.S.* 188, *Euphorbia cyparissias* . . cypress spurge, graveyard weed. . . This species, shown poisonous to cattle when contaminating hay in large amounts, produces scours, collapse, and death. **1968** *DARE* (Qu. S9, *Other kinds of grass that are hard to get rid of*) Inf **MN**36, Graveyard spurge.

graveyard widow n Cf **grass widow 1, sod widow**

See quots.

1954 *PADS* 21.38 **SC,** *Graveyard widow*. . . One whose husband is dead; not a grass widow. **1968** *DARE* (Qu. AA25, *A woman whose husband is dead*) Inf **GA**33, Graveyard widow.

graveyard working n Also *graveyard cleaning, ~ digging* **esp TX, AR**

A social gathering for the purpose of cleaning up a cemetery.

1940 Writers' Program *Guide TX* 375 **neTX,** In farming districts customs of the pioneer persist: "graveyard workings" (cemetery cleanups) are held regularly, all-day affairs at which lunch is spread outdoors. **1941** Writers' Program *Guide SC* 106, Less common occasions when neighbors get together are 'graveyard cleanings' and 'dumb suppers.' The former, more general in the Up Country, is an annual affair at country church cemeteries when, fortified by a huge picnic dinner, the church members with their friends gather to clean up the graveyard, dig up the weeds, and prop up the sagging tombstones. **1945** *New Yorker* 10 Mar 46 **TX,** The occasion was what was called 'a graveyard digging.' All the families that had kinfolks buried there went to the digging. They brought their dinners in baskets, tubs, or buckets, and everyone carried hoes, rakes, spades, shovels, or wire stretchers. **1959** Sanders *Echoes* 11 **swAR,** And until this day they meet on the first Saturday in June for a grave-yard working and dinner on the ground, with chicken-pie floating in butter and "tater" pies that have no equal. **1967** *DARE* (Qu. FF1, . . *A* . . *group meeting*) Inf **TX**33, Graveyard workings—members of a church clean graveyards about the first of the year; dinner too.

gravy n

1 A sweet sauce used as a topping; see quots. **chiefly NEast** Cf **dressing 1, dressing gravy**

1872 Schele de Vere *Americanisms* 481, *Gravy,* in New England used for any liquid accompanying certain dishes as, the *gravy* . . of a pudding. **1896** *DN* 1.418 **NH,** *Gravy:* pudding sauce. **1941** *LANE* Map 293 **scattered NEng,** [For 'a sweet sauce served with puddings,' 7 infs offered *gravy, sweet gravy,* or *sweetened gravy.*] **1967** *DARE* (Qu. H21, . . *The sweet stuff that's poured over [pan]cakes*) Inf **OH**8, Gravy; (Qu. H66a, *The sweet liquid that you pour over a pudding*) Inf **NY**226, Pudding gravy; **MA**5, Sweet gravy. **1971** Wood *Vocab. Change* 313 **FL,** [For 'a sweet liquid served with pudding,' 1 inf offered *gravy.*] **1978** *Greenfield Recorder* (MA) 20 May 8, Probably Maria made that old-time nutmeg or farmers pudding sauce that was so easy and so good. . . Many of the old-timers call it gravy instead of sauce. One Shutesbury man always called it "sweetened gravy."

2 in var phrr: Used as a mild oath or as an expression of surprise or annoyance. **scattered, but more freq Nth, N Midl, WV** See Map

1831 *Working-Man's Gaz.* (Woodstock VT) 19 Jan 130/1 **VT,** By gravy! I'll get up early to-morrow morning. **1851** (1969) Burke *Polly Peablossom* 108 **MO,** Good as wheat, by gravy! **1856** Kelly *Humors* 357 **VT,** Good gravy, but don't they? *Ibid* 360, By gravy, it was amazin' how the *brissels* flew. **1914** *DN* 4.73 **ME, nNH,** *Gravy! by,* Innocent ejaculation. **1959** *VT Hist.* 27.139, *By Gravy!* . . Rare. **1965–70** *DARE* (Qu. NN28a, *Exclamations beginning with 'good': "Good ______!"*) 92 Infs, **scattered, but more freq Nth, N Midl, WV,** Gravy; (Qu. NN8a, *Exclamations of annoyance or disgust: "Oh ______. I've lost my glasses again."*) Inf **VT**12, By gravy; (Qu. NN26a, *Weakened substitutes for 'hell': "Oh ______!"*) Inf **WA**3, Good gravy; (Qu. NN27a, *Weakened substitutes for 'god': "My ______!"*) Inf **WA**1, Good gravy; (Qu. NN28b, *Exclamations beginning with 'goodness': "Goodness ______!"*) Inf **VT**7, Gracious gravy; (Qu. NN29b) Inf **WA**33, Bowls of gravy; (Qu. NN30) Inf **VT**12, By gravy.

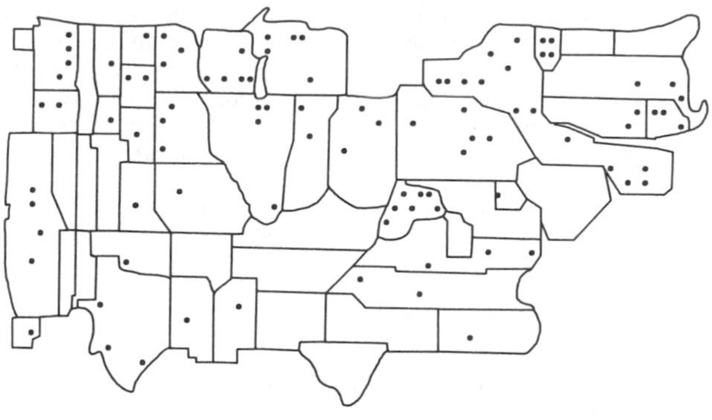

•gravy 2 + varr (Qq. NN28a, b, NN8a, NN26a, NN27a, NN29b, NN30)

‡gravy bowl n

1950 *WELS (Nicknames for a tobacco pipe)* 1 Inf, **WI,** Gravy bowl.

gravy sermon n Cf **graveyard sermon**

1939 FWP *Guide NJ* 630, Relays of preachers of varying sects followed one another with appeals to the emotions in "gravy" sermons, as they were termed.

gravy train preacher n Cf **gravy sermon**

See quot.

1953 Brewer *Word Brazos* 62 **eTX** [Black], De pastuh, Revun Preston, a gravy train preachuh, an' he allus tack de membuhship on some dark an' gloomy trip in his sermons.

gray n Also sp *grey*

1 A White person (but see also quot 1980); also adj, Caucasian. *among Black speakers*

1960 Wentworth-Flexner *Slang* 228/1, *Gray*. . . A white person. *Negro use.* **1963** *Freedomways* 3.57 **Harlem NYC** [Black], *Greys:* white folks. **1965** Brown *Manchild* 166 **Harlem NYC** [Black], I doubt that they're [sic] many, if any, gray people who could ever say "baby" to a Negro and make him feel that "me and this cat have got something going, something strong going." . . Somebody might say something like, "Man, what can anybody see in a gray chick, when colored chicks are so fine; they got so much soul." **1971** Roberts *Third Ear* np [Black], *Gray; gray boy* . . a white man. **1972** Kochman *Rappin'* 144 [Black], [Neutral names for White persons:] *Gray.* Implies the "dead" nature of white people in their physical appearance and actions. Black people equate the lack of pigmentation with lifelessness. Also, the actions of white people —especially the moderate unimpassioned behavior of middle-class whites—are seen by black people as lacking life. "Gray" implies all of this, and in this sense the label is slightly negative. **1972** Claerbaut *Black Jargon* 67, *Gray dude* . . a Caucasian male; white man. *Ibid* 66, *Gray broad* . . a Caucasian female; white girl. **1977** Smitherman *Talkin* 253 [Black], [Terms for Whites:] *Gray,* by now a fairly neutral term. **1980** Folb *Runnin' Down* 54 **Los Angeles CA** [Black], Many [Black teenagers] made no distinction between Chicanos and whites and often characterized them in terms usually identified with white people—*grey, honky, whitey.*

2 See **gray duck b.**

3 See **gray goose 1.**

4 See **gray squirrel 1.**

5 See **gray wolf 1.**

gray ash n

Either a **white ash** (here: *Fraxinus americana*) or the **green ash.**

1813 Muhlenberg *Catalogus Plantarum* 96 **VT,** *Fraxinus* . . *cinera* grey ash. **1843** Torrey *Flora NY* 2.126, *Fraxinus pubescens*. . . *Gray Ash*. . . Margins of rivulets, and in situations that are often overflowed. . . It is frequent in the adjoining parts of New Jersey. **1921** Deam *Trees IN* 268, *Fraxinus americana*. . . *White Ash. Gray Ash*. . . Twigs smooth, greenish gray and often covered with a bloom.

grayback n

1 Any of several birds, as:

a A **knot** (here: *Calidris canutus*).

1813 (1824) Wilson *Amer. Ornith.* 7.47, The common name of this species [=*Calidris canutus*] on our seacoast is the *Grey-back.* **1844** DeKay *Zool. NY* 2.244, From the middle of August until the beginning of October . . the red plumage beneath disappears, giving place to a white plumage spotted with dusky, ash-colored [sic] above; when it [=*Calidris canutus*] is called . . *Grey-back.* **1890** Warren *Birds PA* 84, The Robin-snipe or Gray-back, as the Knot *(Tringa canutus)* is called by hunters on the Atlantic coast of New Jersey, . . is a regular . . visitor. **1898** (1900) Davie *Nests N. Amer. Birds* 136, *Knot. . . Tringa canutus. . .* Red-breasted and Ash-colored Sandpiper and Gray-back are other names for it. **1925** (1928) Forbush *Birds MA* 1.402, *Calidris canutus. . . Knot. . .* Gray-back. **1944** Hausman *Amer. Birds* 514, Gray-back—see Duck, Scaup; see also Knot. **1969** Longstreet *Birds FL* 64, *Knot. . .* Grayback.

b as *upland grayback:* The buff-breasted sandpiper *(Tryngites subruficollis).*

1882 Godfrey *Is. Nantucket* 157 **seMA,** In the fall of 1881 large numbers of the upland gray-back, otherwise known as the brown-bird, made their appearance here on the marshes. **1956** MA Audubon Soc. *Bulletin* 40.20, *Buff-breasted Sandpiper. . .* Upland Grayback (Mass. The back in spring adults is brownish black, the feathers broadly edged with buff and tawny. All of the names indicate folk association of this species with the Upland Plover.)

c =dowitcher.

1888 Trumbull *Names of Birds* 161, *Red-breasted Snipe* [=*Limnodromus griseus*]. . . In New Jersey at Manasquan, Atlantic City, Somers Point, Cape May C.H., and Cape May City, in Virginia at Eastville, and Cobb's Island, Gray-back. **1910** Eaton *Birds NY* 1.305, The Dowitcher . . , also called . . Brown-back, Gray-back, . . often occurs in dense bunches over the bars and mud flats of Long Island. **1923** U.S. Dept. Ag. *Misc. Circular* 13.51, *Dowitcher (Limnodromus griseus)* . . grayback (N.J., Md., D.C., Va., N.C., Ind.) **1925** Bailey *Birds FL* 47, *Dowitcher . . Robin snipe, Grayback. . .* This is another one of the . . "shore birds" that migrate along our shore line, and remain only a short time to feed. **1970** *DARE* (Qu. Q10, *Other water birds and marsh birds common around here*) Inf **VA**52, Grayback—dowitcher.

d The **greater scaup** or the **lesser scaup. Cf dos gris**

1888 Trumbull *Names of Birds* 55 **neIL,** *Aythya marila nearctica. . .* Another title at Chicago is Gray-back. **1911** *Forest & Stream* 77.173, *Marila affinis. . .* Grayback . . Chef Menteur, La. **1917** (1923) *Birds Amer.* 1.135, *Scaup Duck. Marila marila. . . Other Names. . .* Gray-back. *Ibid* 136, *Lesser Scaup Duck. Marila affinis. . .* [Also has the] names of the Scaup Duck with or without qualifying terms. **1923** U.S. Dept. Ag. *Misc. Circular* 13.18, *Scaup Ducks* [=*Aythya affinis* and *A. marila*]. . . *Collective Vernacular Names. . . In local use. . .* Graybacks (Ill., La.) *Ibid* 20, *Lesser Scaup Duck. . . Vernacular Names. . . In local use. . .* Little grayback (Ala., La.) **1944** [see **1a** above]. **1962** Imhof *AL Birds* 149, *Greater Scaup. . . Other names . .* Grayback. **1967** *DARE* (Qu. Q5, . . *Kinds of wild ducks*) Inf **OR**13, Graybacks. **1982** Elman *Hunter's Field Guide* 206, *Greater Scaup (Aythya marila). Common & regional names . .* grayback. *Ibid* 209, *Lesser Scaup (Aythya affinis). Common & regional names . .* grayback.

e =spotted sandpiper.

1917 *Wilson Bulletin* 29.2.80, *Actitis macularia. . .* This and other small sandpipers are known as gray-backs . . at Beaufort, N.C.

f =sanderling. [See quot 1956]

1923 U.S. Dept. Ag. *Misc. Circular* 13.57 **MA,** *Sanderling. . . Vernacular Names. . . In local use. . .* Grayback. **1956** MA Audubon Soc. *Bulletin* 40.21, *Sanderling. . .* Gray-back (Mass. In winter plumage the birds are gray above with darker shaft streaks and paler feather margins.)

g =red-backed sandpiper.

1956 MA Audubon Soc. *Bulletin* 40.19 **MA,** *Red-backed Sandpiper. . .* Grayback.

h =English sparrow.

1956 MA Audubon Soc. *Bulletin* 40.130, *House Sparrow. . .* Grayback (Mass. The back is brownish rather than gray, except for the crown and rump of the adult male.)

2 An insect, as:

a A **louse** (here: *Pedicularis humanus*). **scattered, but esp W Midl, West** See Map

1862 in 1884 S. Hist. Soc. *Papers* 12.27, Graybacks have invaded our camp and are hard to repel. **1910** Johnson *Highways Rocky Mts.* 200, They'd divide their last mouthful with you—yes and divide their bed with you, and it made no difference whether there were graybacks in it or not. **1914** *DN* 4.73 **ME, nNH,** *Graybacks. . .* Body-lice. **1916** (1918) Lomax *Cowboy Songs* 160, The fleas and gray-backs worked on us, O boys, it was not slow,/ I'll tell you there's no worse hell on earth than the range of the buffalo. **1923** *DN* 5.209 **swMO,** *Gray back. . .* A body louse. **1926** Essig *Insects N. Amer.* 193 **West,** The *body louse, grayback* or *cootie, Pediculus corporis . .* is grayish in color. **1937** Sandoz *Slogum* 116 **NE** (as of 1900–20), In all the years Libby never let bugs of any kind get started. She could see a grayback a mile off. **1950** *WELS (Other names . . for body and head lice)* 4 Infs, **WI,** Grayback. **1964** Hargreaves–Foehl *Story of Logging* 59 **MI,** [Glossary:] *Grayback*—Lice or bedbugs. **1965–70** *DARE* (Qu. R25, *Joking names for a head louse, or body louse*) 37 Infs, **scattered, but esp W Midl, West,** Grayback.

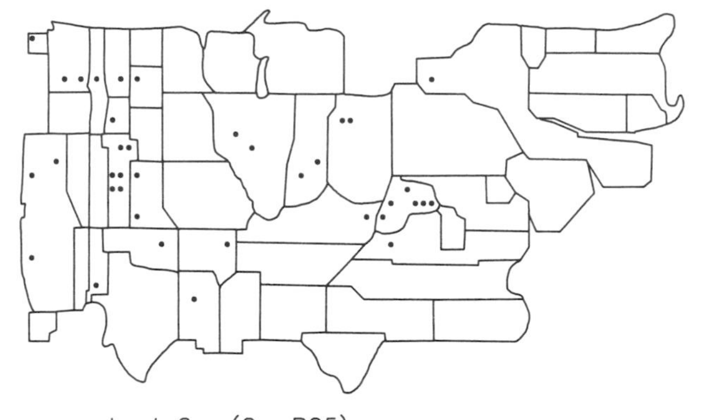

b The bedbug *(Cimex lectularius).*

1950 *WELS (Other names . . for bedbugs)* 1 Inf, **WI,** The men in the logging camps used to call them graybacks. **1964** [see **2a** above]. **1968** *DARE* (Qu. R24, . . *Other names . . for a bedbug*) Inf **IN**17, Grayback.

3 An aquatic animal; see below.

a =gray whale.

1888 Kingsley *Riverside Nat. Hist.* 5.197 **Pacific,** The gray whale has received many curious titles, such as "hard-head," "mussel-digger," "devil-fish," and "gray-back."

b also *grayback herring, ~ tullibee:* A **cisco** (here: *Coregonus artedii*).

1902 Jordan–Evermann *Amer. Fishes* 132, The lake herring *(Argyrosomus artedi)* has a large number of vernacular names . . in Lake Ontario . . grayback or grayback herring. **1972** Sparano *Outdoors Encycl.* 359, *Cisco . .* herring, lake herring . . grayback. . . *Coregonus artedii.* **1983** Becker *Fishes WI* 341, *Cisco or Lake Herring—Coregonus artedii . .* grayback tullibee.

c =round whitefish.

1946 LaMonte *N. Amer. Game Fishes* 122, *Prosopium quadrilaterale . . Names . .* Grayback.

d also *grayback turtle:* A young **map turtle** (here: *Graptemys pseudogeographica pseudogeographica* or *G. p. kohni*).

1958 Conant *Reptiles & Amphibians* 51, *Mississippi Map Turtle* [=*Graptemys pseudogeographica kohni*]. . . These and young of the False Map Turtle [=*G. p. pseudogeographica*], although they have brownish carapaces, are the "graybacks" of the pet trade. **1966** *DARE* (Qu. P24, . . *Kinds of turtles*) Inf **NC**10, Grayback. **1967** *DARE* Tape **LA**5, Now ya got another turtle about the same size as that [=the greenback turtle], what we call a grayback turtle. But right on the back of his shell he got little saws like . . [he hasn't] got a complete round hull like the streakyhead's got. **1972** Ernst–Barbour *Turtles* 121, Baby Mississippi map turtles often appear in the pet trade, where they are called graybacks.

4 =gray fox.

1982 Elman *Hunter's Field Guide* 352, *Gray Fox (Urocyon cinereoargenteus)*—Common & Regional Names: . . grayback.

5 A boulder. **Smoky Mountain area**

1937 Thornburgh *Gt. Smoky Mts.* 42, There is always the excitement of hopping the rocks, or rather boulders, which the mountain people affectionately have named "greybacks" or "mossbacks" according to their nature. **1950** *Scientific Mth.* July 32/1 **eTN, wNC,** Later he notices here and there [in the Great Smoky Mountains] rocky cliffs and crests . . , and the great boulders, or "graybacks," that are strewn over the mountainsides and choke each rushing torrent. **1956** *Hall Coll.* **NC,** *Grayback* . . rock. "Grayback—hit's real hard. Hit takes a good piece of steel to drill it." **1967** *DARE* (Qu. C26, . . *Special kinds of stone or rock . . in this part of the state*) Inf **TN**14, Grayback.

grayback herring, grayback tullibee See **grayback 3b**

grayback turtle See **grayback 3d**

grayback woodpecker n

=**black-backed woodpecker.**

1967 *DARE* (Qu. Q17, . . *Kinds of woodpeckers*) Inf **NY**10, Grayback woodpecker.

gray bass n

1 =**largemouth bass.**

1935 Caine *Game Fish* 3 **Sth,** *Large-mouthed Black Bass. . . Synonyms* . . Gray Bass.

2 A **white bass** (here: *Roccus chrysops*).

1949 Caine *N. Amer. Sport Fish* 122, White bass. . . *Colloquial Names* . . Gray Bass. **1975** Evanoff *Catch More Fish* 91, The white bass *(Roccus chrysops)* is also called . . gray bass.

3 =**freshwater drum.**

1972 Sparano *Outdoors Encycl.* 369, *Freshwater Drum. Common Names* . . gray bass.

graybeard n

1 A **virgin's bower:** usu *Clematis drummondii,* but also *C. vitalba.* Cf **grandfather's beard 2**

1900 Lyons *Plant Names* 107, *C[lematis] vitalba.* . . Gray-beard. **1936** Whitehouse *TX Flowers* 28, *Drummond's Virgin's Bower.* . . The seeds mature in a few weeks, and soon the vine is covered with iridescent masses of silky, feathery plumes. . . These plumes . . are responsible for many common names given to the vine, including . . gray beard. **1960** Vines *Trees SW* 266, Vernacular names for the plant [=*Clematis drummondii*] are Texas Virginsbower, Graybeard. *Ibid* 304, *Hydrangea quercifolia.* . . Vernacular names are Sevenbark, Gray Beard.

2 A **hydrangea 1** (here: *H. quercifolia*).

1903 Small *Flora SE U.S.* 506, *Hydrangea quercifolia.* . . Gray-beard. **1960** [see **1** above].

3 usu *graybeard tree:* =**fringe tree.** Cf **granddaddy graybeard 2, grandfather's beard 1**

1876 Hobbs *Bot. Hdbk.* 48, Gray beard tree, Fringe tree, Chionanthus Virginicus. **1911** *Century Dict. Suppl., Graybeard-tree.* . . The fringe-tree. **1960** Vines *Trees SW* 850, Vernacular names [for *Chionanthus virginicus*] are Flowering Ash . . and Graybeard-tree. **1969** *SC Market Bulletin* 11 Sept 4/5, Rhododendrons $1.50 ea.; Greybeards $1 ea.; Sarvis trees $1 ea. **1974** (1977) Coon *Useful Plants* 194, Graybeard tree. . . Long panicles of white flowers . . make it . . interesting . . to plant as an ornamental shrub.

graybeard moss See **gray moss**

graybeard tree See **graybeard 3**

gray birch n

Any of several grayish-barked birches, as:

a A small birch *(Betula populifolia)* native from Nova Scotia to Delaware. Also called **fire birch, old field ~, paper ~, pin ~, poverty ~, white ~, wire ~**

1851 (1856) Springer *Forest Life* 23, Of the Birch family there are several varieties, called the Black, Yellow, Red, Canoe, the Gray, and the Dwarf. **1884** Sargent *Forests of N. Amer.* 159, *Betula alba,* var. *populifolia. . . Gray Birch.* . . A small, short-lived tree of rapid growth, 6 to 9 meters in height, . . now generally springing up upon abandoned or burned land in eastern New England. **1897** Sudworth *Arborescent Flora* 139, *Betula populifolia. . . Common Names.* . . Gray Birch (Me., R.I., Mass.) *Ibid* 141, *Betula occidentalis. . . Common Names.* . . Gray Birch (Mont.) . . *Betula lutea. . . Common Names.* . . Gray Birch (Vt., R.I., Pa., Mich., Minn.) **1938** Van Dersal *Native Woody Plants* 325, Birch, Gray *(Betula lutea, Betula populifolia).* **1979** Little *Checklist U.S. Trees* 60, *Betula alleghaniensis. . . Yellow birch.* . . Gray birch. *Ibid* 63, *Betula populifolia.* . . Gray birch.

b =**yellow birch.**

1884 Sargent *Forests of N. Amer.* 161, *Betula lutea. . . Gray Birch.* . . One of the largest and most valuable deciduous trees of the northern New England and Canadian forests, often 21 to 29 meters in height. **1897** [see **a** above]. **1908** Rogers *Tree Book* 171, *Yellow Birch, Gray Birch.* . . The bark again gives the name to a large birch that grows here and there in the forests of the Northern States. The fringed and tattered outer bark, dingy gray with pearly lustre, and showing gleams of gold at every rent, is unlike the other birches. **1927** Keeler *Our Native Trees* 310, *Gray Birch.* . . On an old trunk, the bark . . is rather a silver gray with a yellow flush; and in extreme old age the surface is shaggy with light gray plates the size of a hand. **1950** Peattie *Nat. Hist. Trees* 170, Gray Birch. . . *Bark* of old trunks reddish brown or sometimes dull yellowish-brown, but on younger growth bright silvery gray or light orange, and lustrous. **1970** *DARE* (Qu. T16, . . *Kinds of trees [that] are 'special'*) Inf **MA**78, Gray birch. **1979** [see **a** above].

c =**western birch.**

1897 [see **a** above].

d A **paper birch** (here: *Betula papyrifera*).

1929 *Torreya* 29.150 **ME,** The Poplar was *"Popple,"* the American White Birch, the *"Gray Birch."*

gray bird n

Any of several birds with more or less gray plumage, as:

a =**sage thrasher.**

1872 *Amer. Naturalist* 6.396 **cnUT,** The mountain mocking-bird, familiarly known to the settlers as the "gray bird," is said to have similarly increased.

b =**vesper sparrow.**

1898 (1900) Davie *Nests N. Amer. Birds* 368, *Vesper Sparrow. Poocætes* [sic] *gramineus.* . . The Grass-Finch, Bay-winged Bunting, or "Gray Bird," as it is called, is an abundant species in Eastern United States. **1917** (1923) *Birds Amer.* 3.23, *Vesper Sparrow—Poœcetes gramineus gramineus.* . . Gray Bird. **1944** Hausman *Amer. Birds* 505, Bird, Gray—see Sparrow, Vesper.

c =**Ipswich sparrow.**

1929 Forbush *Birds MA* 3.48, *Passerculus princeps. . . Other names:* gray bird. . . *Adults in breeding plumage (sexes alike):* Above pale grayish or grayish-brown. **1946** Hausman *Eastern Birds* 589, *Ipswich Sparrow.* . . Gray Bird. . . In winter . . along the Atlantic coast . . as far south as Georgia.

d =**English sparrow.** Cf **grayback 1h**

1966–68 *DARE* (Qu. Q22, *Joking names or nicknames for the common sparrow*) Infs **CA**105, **MI**36, Gray bird.

gray bitch n Also *gray Nelly*

The female collared lizard *(Crotaphytus collaris).*

1928 Baylor Univ. Museum *Contrib.* 16.11 **TX,** In the Panhandle country of northwestern Texas, the female [of *Crotaphytus collaris*] is known as the *Gray Bitch* or *Gray Nelly.*

gray bob See **gray rabbit 1**

graybow n Cf **grayback 2a**

=**louse.**

1966 *DARE* (Qu. R25, *Joking names for a head louse, or body louse*) Inf **MS**47, Graybow.

gray brant n

1 =**white-fronted goose.**

1888 Trumbull *Names of Birds* 12, In a letter from Mr. A.B. Pearson, of San Diego, Cal., this species [=*Anser albifrons*] is referred to as the . . *Gray Brant.* **1911** *Forest & Stream* 77.173, *Blue Goose.* . . Gray Brant, Galveston, Tex. . . *White-fronted Goose.* . . Gray Brant, La. **1917** *DN* 4.430 **LA,** *White-fronted goose.* . . Gray Brant. **1923** U.S. Dept. Ag. *Misc. Circular* 13.34, *White-fronted Goose. . . Vernacular Names. . . In local use.* . . Gray brant (Minn., Iowa, La., B.C., Calif.) **1943** Musgrove-Musgrove *Waterfowl IA* 11, *White-fronted Goose.* . . Other names . . gray brant. . . Brownish-gray plumage. **1955** Forbush-May *Birds* 53, *White-fronted Goose. . . Other names* . . Gray Brant.

2 =**blue goose n 1.**

1911 [see **1** above]. **1917** *DN* 4.423 **LA,** *Blue goose.* . . Gray Brant. **1923** U.S. Dept. Ag. *Misc. Circular* 13.33, *Blue Goose. . . Vernacular Names. . . In local use.* . . Gray brant (La., Tex.) **1982** Elman *Hunter's Field Guide* 292, *Blue Goose. . . Common & regional names* . . gray brant.

3 One or more subspp of the **Canada goose;** see quots.

1923 U.S. Dept. Ag. *Misc. Circular* 13.36 **OR,** *Hutchins Goose... Vernacular Names... In local use...* Gray brant. **1953** Jewett *Birds WA* 105, *Lesser Canada Goose. Branta canadensis leucopareia...* Gray Brant... *Alaskan Cackling Goose. Branta hutchinsii minima...* Gray Brant.

gray cardinal n

=pyrrhuloxia.

1917 (1923) *Birds Amer.* 3.65, The Cardinal traits have been so noticeable that the bird [=*Cardinalis sinuatus*] has often been known as the Gray Cardinal. **1977** Bull–Farrand *Audubon Field Guide Birds* 611, Also called the "Gray Cardinal," it [=*Cardinalis sinuatus*] is similar to the Cardinal in most respects except that it is often found in flocks after the breeding season.

gray cloud n [From the color; see quot 1960] Cf **gray mule 1, silver cloud, white lightning**

See quots.

1956 *Hall Coll.* **wNC, eTN,** *Gray cloud*—moonshine liquor. "Give me some gray cloud." **1960** Hall *Smoky Mt. Folks* 65, "Popskull" is the name for low-grade moonshine, a term now being replaced by.. "gray cloud".. with reference to the "galvanize" (zinc) corroded from the steel still by the acid of the mash.

gray coot n Also *little gray coot, old gray coot*

An adult female or immature **scoter.**

1876 *Forest & Stream* 7.276/3 **CT,** *Pelionetta perspicilliata.* Female and young of the year: gray coot. **1888** Trumbull *Names of Birds* 104, The females and young males [of *Melanitta perspicillata*] are.. known.. *very generally* along our coast as *Gray Coot.* *Ibid* 107, The females and young [of *Melanitta americana*] (similar in appearance).. are very generally classed under.. *Gray Coot.* **1899** Howe–Sturtevant *Birds RI* 40, *Oidemia perspicillata...* Females are called *Gray Coot.* **1917** (1923) *Birds Amer.* 1.148, *Oidemia americana... Females..* Gray Coot. *Ibid* 151, *Oidemia perspicillata... Other Names...* Gray Coot. **1923** U.S. Dept. Ag. *Misc. Circular* 13.27, *Scoters... Collective Vernacular Names.. In local use...* Gray coots (the females and immature) (Me., Mass., R.I., Conn.) *Ibid* 28, *American Scoter... Vernacular Names... In local use...* Little gray coot (for the female and immature) (Mass.) *Ibid* 29, *White-winged Scoter...* Old gray coot (Long Id., N.Y.) **1946** Hausman *Eastern Birds* 167, *American Scoter...* Female and young: Brown Coot, Gray Coot, Smutty Coot.

gray cottontail See **gray rabbit 1**

gray crane n

=sandhill crane.

1955 *Oriole* 20.1.6 **GA,** *Sandhill Crane.*—Gray Crane.

gray crow n

Clark's **nutcracker** *(Nucifraga columbiana).*

1953 Jewett *Birds WA* 472, *Nucifraga columbiana...* Gray Crow.

gray dark n Cf **dusk dark**

1966 *DARE* (Qu. A5, *The time right after the sun goes out of sight, before it becomes all dark*) Inf **MS**45, Gray dark.

graydock n

A **balsamroot** (here: *Balsamorhiza sagittata*).

1937 U.S. Forest Serv. *Range Plant Hdbk.* W43, It [=*Balsamorhiza sagittata*] is also known simply as balsamroot and is locally called sunflower, graydock, and breadroot.

gray dragon n

A **lubber grasshopper** (here: *Dracotettix monstrosus*).

1980 Milne–Milne *Audubon Field Guide Insects* 420, "Gray Dragon"... Description... Ash gray. Head bulging. *Pronotal crest has 3 deep notches.* Wings short, flightless... These grasshoppers hop on roads, feeding on dead insects, including their own kind.

gray duck n

Any of several ducks (often the female or immature) with grayish plumage, as:

a also *gray wood duck:* **=wood duck.**

1792 Belknap *Hist. NH* 3.168, Grey Wood Duck, *Anas sponsa.* **1923** U.S. Dept. Ag. *Misc. Circular* 13.16 **MA,** *Wood Duck... Vernacular Names... In local use...* Gray duck (for the immature).

b also *gray:* **=gadwall.**

1834 Nuttall *Manual Ornith.* 2.383, *Gadwall,* or *Grey... Anas strepera.* **1898** (1900) Davie *Nests N. Amer. Birds* 79, The Gadwall, or Gray Duck,.. may be found nesting anywhere. **1909** Field Museum Nat. Hist. *Zool. Ser.* 9.322, *Gadwall... Local names:* Gray Duck... This species is common in Illinois and Wisconsin during the migrations. **1943** Musgrove–Musgrove *Waterfowl IA* 24, *Gadwall...* Other names: gray duck, gray... *Adult male*—The dullest-colored male of any species of surface-feeders... *Female*—mottled brown and gray. **1944** [see **c** below]. **1955** MA Audubon Soc. *Bulletin* 39.314, *Gadwall...* Gray Duck (General. There is a good deal of slaty gray in the plumage of the male; the female is more brownish and buffy. The term "gray duck" is often applied to specimens of various species for which the handler knows no definite name). **1968–69** *DARE* (Qu. Q5,.. *Kinds of wild ducks*) Infs **MI**107, **NJ**31, **WI**12, Gray duck; **MO**37, The little gray duck. **1982** Elman *Hunter's Field Guide* 147, *Gadwall... Common & regional names..* gray duck. *Ibid* 156, *Pintail...* Gray duck. *Ibid* 182, *American Widgeon...* Gray duck. *Ibid* 195, *Canvasback...* Gray duck.

c also *pied gray duck:* **=pintail.**

1844 Giraud *Birds Long Is.* 311, The young and females [of *Anas acuta*] are mistaken by many persons for a distinct species, which they call Gray Duck. **1888** Trumbull *Names of Birds* 37, From Bath [Maine] to the State of Connecticut the name *Gray Duck..* is usually given it [=*Anas acuta*]... I have heard this name popularly applied to the species.. on the Niagara..; in Connecticut, at Essex, Milford, and Stratford; at Bellport, Long Island; Washington, D.C.; and Alexandria, Va.; and very commonly in these localities, as elsewhere, to designate only the females, and the males in gray attire. *Ibid* 38, In Philadelphia, Baltimore, and St. Augustine, these young birds and females are also called Gray Duck. **1923** U.S. Dept. Ag. *Misc. Circular* 13.15, *Pintail... Vernacular Names... In general use...* Gray duck, sometimes meaning only the female and immature... *In local use...* Pied gray duck (Long Id., N.Y.) **1944** Hausman *Amer. Birds* 511, Duck, Gray—see Gadwall. Duck, Gray (female)—see Mallard; see also Pintail. *Ibid* 512, Duck, Pied Gray (female)—see Pintail. **1967** *DARE* (Qu. Q5,.. *Kinds of wild ducks*) Inf **IL**9, Gray duck. **1982** [see **b** above].

d **=mallard.**

1815 Lit. & Philos. Soc. NY *Trans.* 134, Anas boschas... The French, or gray duck, is much larger than the common. **1888** Trumbull *Names of Birds* 15, *Mallard...* The female (believed by many a distinct species) is known to marketmen and others at Detroit, to the "punters" of St. Clair Flats, at Point Pelee (near head of Lake Erie), West Barnstable, Mass., and in Atlantic Co., New Jersey, as *Gray Duck,* the name being used in like manner on the Niagara. **1917** (1923) *Birds Amer.* 1.114, *Mallard... Other Names...* Gray Duck (female). **1944** [see **c** above]. **1955** MA Audubon Soc. *Bulletin* 39.313, *Mallard.* Gray Duck... (Rather general. Sometimes means only the female, but often applies to the species. Gray is an indefinite term in the popular vocabulary. In the male Mallard the center of the back is brown, finely cross-waved with whitish: in the female the back feathers are dark brownish, edged with buffy.)

e **=baldpate 1.**

1911 *Forest & Stream* 77.172, *Widgeon or Baldpate...* Female called Gray Duck at Mud Lake, Ark. **1923** U.S. Dept. Ag. *Misc. Circular* 13.11, *Baldpate... Vernacular Names... In local use...* Gray duck (for the female, Mich., Ark., La., Tex.) **1955** *Oriole* 20.1.4 **GA,** American Widgeon... Gray Duck. **1982** [see **b** above].

f **=canvasback duck.**

1923 U.S. Dept. Ag. *Misc. Circular* 13.18 **LA,** *Canvasback... Vernacular Names... In local use...* Gray duck. **1982** [see **b** above].

g The American **scoter** *(Melanitta nigra).*

1955 MA Audubon Soc. *Bulletin* 39.377 **CT, MA, ME,** *American Scoter...* The female and young.. Gray Duck.

h **=European widgeon.**

1955 MA Audubon Soc. *Bulletin* 39.314, *European Widgeon.* Gray Duck (Maine. Strange species of this family are often dubbed "gray duck.")

gray-duck grass n Cf **duck grass 2**

A **pondweed** (here: *Potamogeton foliosus*).

1942 *Torreya* 42.157, *Potamogeton foliosus...* Gray-duck grass.. Louisiana.

gray-duck moss n

The common water nymph *(Najas guadalupensis).*

1926 *Torreya* 26.4, *Naias guadalupensis...* Gray duck moss, Mississippi Delta, La.

gray eagle n
An immature **bald eagle 1.**
1778 Carver *Travels N. Amer.* 466, There are only two sorts of eagles in these parts, the bald and the grey. **1813** (1824) Wilson *Amer. Ornith.* 7.17 **cwNY,** At the celebrated cataract of Niagara great numbers of these birds [=black or sea eagles], called there Gray Eagles, are continually seen . . in company with the Bald Eagles. **1874** Coues *Birds NW* 370, From the circumstance that several years (at least three) are required for the gaining of the perfect plumage, when the head and tail are entirely white, it follows that "Gray Eagles" . . are much the more frequently met with. **1917** (1923) *Birds Amer.* 2.80, Black Eagle; Gray Eagle; Washington Eagle. The . . three names refer to the immature Bald Eagle. **1955** MA Audubon Soc. *Bulletin* 39.442, *Bald Eagle. . .* For birds in immature plumage, which is grayish brown to blackish, often with white patches. . . Gray Eagle (Rather general.)

grayfish n
A **dogfish 1;** see quots.
1933 John G. Shedd Aquarium *Guide* 20, *Cynias canis . . Smooth Grayfish. . .* A small shark, abundant on the middle Atlantic coast. *Ibid* 21, *Squalus acanthias—Spiny Dogfish; Grayfish. . .* This abundant shark is . . packed in cans and sold as "Grayfish." **1960** Amer. Fisheries Soc. *List Fishes* 59, Grayfish—see dogfish. **1973** Knight *Cook's Fish Guide* 382, Grayfish—Dogfish, Smooth.

gray fox n
Std: a North American fox *(Urocyon cinereoargenteus)* with a black brush tip. Also called **colishé, cotton-white, desert gray fox, Dutch fox, grayback 4, southern fox, swamp ~, tree ~, wood ~**

gray frost n
A hard frost.
1940–41 Cassidy *WI Atlas,* 1 inf, **swWI,** Gray frost. Used more here than "white frost" [for a freeze]. **1970** *DARE* (Qu. B30, *A frost that kills plants is a* ______) Inf **CT**42, Gray frost.

gray ghost n Also *white ghost*
A **bonefish 1** (here: *Albula vulpes*).
1975 Evanoff *Catch More Fish* 216, The bonefish *(Albula vulpes)* is also known as the white ghost, gray ghost [etc].

gray goose n
1 often with adj; rarely *gray:* **=Canada goose.**
1637 (1972) Morton *New Engl. Canaan* 67 **MA,** Gray Geese . . are as bigg and bigger then the tame Geese of England, with black legges, black bills, heads, and necks black. **1796** Morse *Amer. Universal Geog.* 1.213, Great parti-coloured Brant or Grey Goose. *Anser branta, grisea maculata.* **1888** Trumbull *Names of Birds* 1, *Branta canadensis. . .* Big gray goose; common gray goose. *Ibid* 3, *Branta canadensis hutchinsii. . .* Small Gray Goose. **1898** Elliot *Wild Fowl N. Amer.* 47, *White-fronted Goose. . .* Gray Goose, Pied Brant. **1917** (1923) *Birds Amer.* 1.158, *Canada Goose—Branta canadensis canadensis. . .* Big Gray Goose. *Ibid* 161, Hutchins's Goose *(Branta canadensis hutchinsi)* is precisely like the Canada Goose in everything except size. . . Throughout its range it is variously known also as. . . Small Gray Goose, Little Gray Goose . . or Mud Goose. **1936** Roberts *MN Birds* 1.207, Common Canada Goose: *Branta canadensis canadensis. . . Gray Goose. Ibid* 210, Lesser Canada Goose: *Branta canadensis leucopareia. . . Lesser Gray Goose.* **1965–70** *DARE* (Qu. Q6, . . *Kinds of wild geese . . around here*) 16 Infs, **scattered,** Gray geese; **KY**5, Gray and white geese; **NY**97, Canadian goose [same as] Canadian grays. **1982** Elman *Hunter's Field Guide* 269, *Canada Goose . . Common & regional names . .* big gray goose.
2 =white-fronted goose. chiefly Pacific
1918 Grinnell *Game Birds CA* 219, The American White-fronted Goose. . . Its general gray tone of coloration has suggested the name Gray Goose in contradistinction to the white Snow Geese and black-headed Canada Geese and Brant. *Ibid* 221, The White-fronted Goose is one of the commonest geese on the market. "Gray geese" (under which term this species and perhaps also the Hutchins Goose is included) to the number of 19,419 were sold in the markets of San Francisco and Los Angeles in the season of 1895–96. **1923** U.S. Dept. Ag. *Misc. Circular* 13.34, *White-fronted Goose. . . Vernacular Names. . . In local use. . .* Gray goose (Ind., Tex., Alaska, Wash., Calif.) **1940** Gabrielson *Birds OR* 131, The Speckle Breast, or Gray Goose, is ardently sought by hunters of wild fowl. **1953** Jewett *Birds WA* 110, *Pacific White-fronted Goose. . .* Other names . . Gray Goose.

gray gopher n **chiefly Upper Missip Valley** Cf **gopher** n[1] **2b(1)**
A **ground squirrel** n **b** (here: *Spermophilus franklini*).
1857 U.S. Patent Office *Annual Rept. for 1856: Ag.* 79, The grey prairie-squirrel (grey-gopher, of Northern Illinois) exists throughout the prairie regions of Wisconsin, Illinois, Missouri, Iowa, and probably Minnesota. **1879** U.S. Natl. Museum *Bulletin* 14.15, *Spermophilus Franklini. . . Gray Gopher.*—Northern Illinois, northward to the Saskatchewan. **1899** Garland *Boy Life* 85 **nwIA** (as of c1870s), The prairie abounded at this time with two sorts of ground squirrel, which the settlers called "the striped gopher" and "the gray gopher." The striped gopher resembled a large chipmunk, and the gray gopher was apparently a squirrel that had taken to the fields. **1951** Martin *Amer. Wildlife & Plants* 250, The Franklin ground squirrel, also known as gray gopher, is a comparatively eastern species, its range extending from the Canadian prairies to Oklahoma and Illinois. **1967–69** *DARE* (Qu. P29) Infs **IA**4, 5, **IL**32, **MN**12, 16, 35, 42, **WI**22, Gray gopher. **1970** *Western Folkl.* 29.169, The term *gray gopher* has a heavy concentration in central and southwestern Minnesota; it also occurs twice in Mitchell County, Iowa, and sporadically in North Dakota. *Ibid* 172, *Gray gopher . .* refer[s] only to Franklin's ground squirrel.

gray grass-bird See **grass-bird 1a**

gray grosbeak n
=pyrrhuloxia.
1917 (1923) *Birds Amer.* 3.65, So far as known, the Gray Grosbeak eats practically no beneficial insect and damages no crop. **1928** Bailey *Birds NM* 672, Among the tornillos and mesquites of the Rio Grande Valley and the lower mesa near Mesilla Park, Professor Merrill found the Arizona Pyrrhuloxia or Gray Grosbeak most abundant. **1957** *AmSp* 32.185 **TX,** Mexican cardinal [is the term used for] Gray grosbeak.

gray grouper n
Either of two similar fish: **black grouper 1** or a **grouper 1a** (here: *Epinephelus striatus*).
1935 Caine *Game Fish* 71, *Black Grouper—Mycteroperca bonaci. . .* Gray Grouper. *Ibid* 72, *Epinephelus striatus. . .* Gray Grouper. **1946** LaMonte *N. Amer. Game Fishes* 49, *Black Grouper—Mycteroperca bonaci. . .* Gray Grouper. *Ibid* 53, *Epinephelus striatus. . . Names . .* Gray Grouper.

gray gull n
1 Usu the **herring gull,** but also the glaucous-winged gull *(Larus glaucescens)* or the **ring-billed gull.**
1792 Belknap *Hist. NH* 3.169, Grey Gull, *Larus fuscus?* **1806** (1965) Lewis–Clark *Hist. Lewis–Clark Exped.* 881 **Pacific NW,** The large Gray Gull, or white Larus. **1889** *Century Dict.* 2654, *Gray gull. (a)* The *Larus glaucescens* of the western coast of North America. *(b)* The young of the herring gull, *Larus argentatus,* and of sundry related species, when the plumage is mostly gray. [*Century* Ed: Eastern North America.] **1925** (1928) Forbush *Birds MA* 1.72, *Larus argentatus. . . Herring Gull. . .* Gray Gull. **1932** Bennitt *Check-list* 33 **MO,** *Herring gull. Larus argentatus . .* gray gull. . . *Ring-billed gull. Larus delawarensis. . .* Gray gull. **1956** MA Audubon Soc. *Bulletin* 40.22, *Great Black-Backed Gull. . .* Gray Gull (Mass. . . The immature.) *Ibid, Herring Gull. . .* Gray Gull (Maine, N.H., Mass. Birds in immature plumage are brownish gray with darker wing tips.)
2 A young **gull,** esp the immature **herring gull.**
1876 *Forest & Stream* 7.212/3 **eMA** (as of 1852), *L[arus] argentatus.* Adult, white; young, gray gull. *Ibid* 276/3 **NY,** *Larus.* All other varieties [except *L. marinus*]. Gull. (Young) grey gull. **1889** [see **1** above]. **1956** [see **1** above].

gray-haired grandmother n Cf **granddaddy's whiskers**
A **dandelion 1.**
1969 *DARE* (Qu. S11, . . *Other names . . for . . dandelion*) Inf **NY**205, When they go to seed and turn gray, they're called gray-haired grandmother.

gray hare See **gray rabbit**

gray hawk n Also *gray hen hawk*
=goshawk 1.
1955 MA Audubon Soc. *Bulletin* 39.441, *Goshawk. . .* Gray Hawk (Mass.); Gray Hen Hawk (Maine. Poultry remains were found in 116, or nearly half, of 243 stomachs examined by the U.S. Biological Survey. McAtee, 1935.) **1965–69** *DARE* (Qu. Q4, . . *Kinds of hawks*) Infs **IN**3, 80, **MO**37, **NJ**8, **ND**3, **OK**3, **TX**42, **WI**8, Gray hawk.

gray horse n

See quot.

1955 Ritchie *Singing Family* 218 **seKY,** He would take a big spoonful of molasses and let it run thick and slow over fresh-churned butter in a dish, then he'd take his fork and mix and stir, make Gray Horse to eat on his corn bread. Hot corn bread, or biscuits, either one it would go with fine.

gray jay n **esp Rocky Mts, Pacific NW**

=Canada jay.

1874 NY Acad. Sci. *Annals Lyceum Nat. Hist.* 10.7 **UT,** *Perisoreus Canadensis* . . var. *capitalis*. . . Gray Jay. Wahsatch mountains. **1917** (1923) *Birds Amer.* 2.227, The Gray Jay is found in the interior districts of northern California north through central Oregon and Washington to British Columbia. **1940** Gabrielson *Birds OR* 416, *Gray Jay: Perisoreus obscurus griseus* . . inhabits an area in Oregon roughly triangular in shape. **1953** Jewett *Birds WA* 456, At times the gray jay is the most silent, at others the noisiest bird in the woods. **1963** Murie *Birds Mt. McKinley* 66, *Gray Jay*. . . Their food consists chiefly of carrion, insects, and berries. **1966–68** *DARE* (Qu. Q16, . . *Kinds of jays*) Infs **CO**7, **ME**8, **MN**16, **WA**20, Gray jay. **1977** Udvardy *Audubon Field Guide Birds* 727, *Gray Jay*. . . *Dark gray above,* with narrow, light band across back; *light below*. . . Anyone who has camped in the mountains of the northern forests is familiar with this bird.

gray lapwing n

=black-bellied plover.

1844 Giraud *Birds Long Is.* 211, *Charadrius Helveticus*. . . Black-bellied Plover. . . Grey Lapwing. **1888** Trumbull *Names of Birds* 190, *Charadrius squatarola*. . . Black-bellied Plover. . . Swiss Sandpiper and Gray Sandpiper of Pennant, and Gray Lapwing of Swainson and Richardson.

grayleaf pine See **gray pine b**

grayling n

Std: a freshwater fish *(Thymallus arcticus)* of northern waters. Also called **garpin, poisson bleu, Rocky Mountain whitefish**

gray linnet n

1 **=pine siskin.**

1899 Howe–Sturtevant *Birds RI* 70, *Spinus pinus*. . . Gray Linnet. **1929** Forbush *Birds MA* 3.29, *Pine Siskin*. . . *Other names* . . gray linnet. **1946** Hausman *Eastern Birds* 583, Gray Linnet. . . Small bird. . . Flight bouncing, like a Goldfinch. **1955** Forbush–May *Birds* 497, Gray linnet.

2 **=purple finch,** usu the immature or female bird.

1917 (1923) *Birds Amer.* 3.5, *Carpodacus purpureus purpureus*. . . Gray Linnet (immature and female). **1946** Goodrich *Birds in KS* 317, Colloquial Name . . linnet, gray. . . Common name . . finch, eastern purple. **1956** MA Audubon Soc. *Bulletin* 40.254, *Purple Finch.* Gray Linnet (Mass. The female, which is olive grayish to olive brownish above.) **1978** Gromme *Birds WI* 218, Linnet, Gray (Purple Finch).

gray loon n

=red-throated loon.

1904 (1910) Wheelock *Birds CA* 32, It [=*Gavia stellata*] is the "gray loon" of the fishermen, and its long, wild cry . . is always a signal for the boats to seek shelter, for the storm will break and not "blow over." **1955** MA Audubon Soc. *Bulletin* 39.305 **ME,** *Red-throated Loon*. . . Gray Loon.

gray mallard n Cf **black mallard**

=mallard 1.

1888 Trumbull *Names of Birds* 16, In Baltimore, the female [of *Anas platyrhynchos*] is *Gray Mallard*. . . The name "gray mallard" is also commonly used . . at Washington, D.C., and Alexandria, Va., though generally in these localities to include the full-plumaged drake as well. **1917** (1923) *Birds Amer.* 1.114, *Mallard*. . . *Other Names*. . . Gray Mallard (female). **1923** U.S. Dept. Ag. *Misc. Circular* 13.8 **CA, DE, DC, MD, MA, KY, VA,** *Mallard*. . . *Vernacular Names*. . . *In local use*. . . Gray mallard. **1940** Todd *Birds W. PA* 707, Mallard, Gray, *see* Mallard, Common. **1955** MA Audubon Soc. *Bulletin* 39.313, *Mallard*. . . Gray Mallard. (Rather general. Sometimes means only the female, but often applies to the species. Gray is an indefinite term in the popular vocabulary.) **1966–70** *DARE* (Qu. Q6, . . *Kinds of wild ducks*) Inf **GA**25, Gray mallard, greenhead—same; **MI**2, Gray mallard; **VA**75, Gray mallard = mallard.

gray maple n

=silver maple.

c1960 *Wilson Coll.* **csKY,** The other common maple is the *gray maple* or *water maple (Acer saccharinum).* **1966–68** *DARE* (Qu. T14, . . *Kinds of maples*) Infs **CT**9, **ME**21, Gray maple.

gray-mare v, exclam

1957 *Sat. Eve. Post Letters* **wKY** (as of 1930s), If the school bell rang while we were playing [marbles] for "keeps" the first player to shout "gray-mare" could pocket all the marbles he could get his hands on. This practice was abused and "to gray-mare" soon became a synonym for "to swipe."

gray moccasin n

=water moccasin.

1940 Stong *Hawkeyes* 251 **IA,** I have seen and killed plenty of gray moccasins.

gray mockingbird n

=catbird 1.

1944 Hausman *Amer. Birds* 452, *Catbird—Dumatella carolinensis*. . . Gray Mockingbird.

gray moose n

1 The elk *(Cervus canadensis). old-fash*

1743 (1754) Catesby *Nat. Hist. Carolina* 2 [app] xxviii **NEng,** *Cervus Major Americanus.* The Stag of America. . . In *New England* it is known by the Name of the grey Moose. **1842** DeKay *Zool. NY* 1.119, It [=*Cervus canadensis*] has also, from the popular names applied to it, been confounded with the American Moose. . . It is called in various parts of the country . . *Grey Moose.* **1880** *Forest & Stream* 14.65/3, Wapiti, *Cervus canadensis.* Improperly called . . grey moose. **1930** Shoemaker *1300 Words* 26 **cPA Mts** (as of c1900), *Gray moose*—The Elk. (Cervus Canadensis).

2 The moose *(Alces alces).*

1784 Pennant *Arctic Zool.* 28, In most parts of *North America* they are called the Grey Moose. **1820** Eastburn–Sands *Yamoyden* 213 **seNY,** Now the gray moose may fearless fly. **1917** *Mammals of Amer.* 23 *(DA),* The gray moose was the first to recover himself.

gray moss n Also *graybeard moss*

A **Spanish moss** (here: *Tillandsia usneoides*).

1858 *Harper's New Mth. Mag.* 18.12/2 **swAL,** The tender green of the budding cypress contrasted strikingly with the graybeard moss that hung from every bough. **1908** *DN* 3.317 **eAL, wGA,** *Gray-moss*. . . Spanish moss. **1940** Clute *Amer. Plant Names* 150, *T[illandsia] usneoides* . . gray moss. **1959** Carleton *Index Herb. Plants* 56, *Gray-moss:* Tillandsia usneoides. **1967** *DARE* File **cnLA,** *Gray moss*—most frequent term here for Spanish moss.

gray mule n

1 Homemade liquor. Cf **gray cloud**

1965–68 *DARE* (Qu. DD21c, *Nicknames for whiskey, especially illegally made whiskey*) Infs **AZ**2, **WI**48, Gray mule; (Qu. DD31, *Joking names for homemade hard liquor;* total Infs questioned, 75) Inf **MS**60, Gray mule.

2 See quot.

1970 *DARE* (Qu. FF28, . . *Kinds of fireworks*) Inf **VA**75, Gray mule—ran around on the ground and whistled.

gray Nelly See **gray bitch**

gray oak n

1 A **red oak** (here: *Quercus rubra*).

1697 *Boston Rec.* 8 *(DA),* By Braintree road a heap of stones, . . from thence to another wallnut tree and so straight to a gray oak. **1784** in 1785 Amer. Acad. Arts & Sci. *Memoirs* 1.490, *Quercus*. . . The White Oak. The Red Oak. The Yellow Oak. The Grey Oak. The Black Oak. **1812** Michaux *Histoire des Arbres* 2.121, *Quercus ambigua*. . . Dans le district de Maine, dans le New-Hampshire, et sur la rive orientale du lac Champlain, dans l'Etat de Vermont. . . il est connu des habitans sous le nom de *Grey oak, Chêne gris*. . . Il a beaucoup d'analogie, par son feuillage, avec le vrai Chêne rouge . . , et par ses glands avec le *Quercus coccinea.* [=*Quercus ambigua*. . . In the area of Maine, in New Hampshire, and on the eastern shore of Lake Champlain, in the state of Vermont. . . it is known by the inhabitants under the name of *Grey Oak, Chêne gris*. . . It bears a strong resemblance to the true red oak in its leaves and to the *Quercus coccinea* in its acorns.] **1890** Newhall *Trees NEast Amer.* 122, The *Gray Oak* . . is . . sometimes found along the northeastern boundary of the States (as far as Lake Champlain) and northward. **1908** Britton *N. Amer. Trees* 290, *Gray Oak*. . . A tree very similar to the Red oak in its foliage and general appearance, but with acorns resembling those of the Scarlet oak. **1966–68** *DARE* (Qu. T10, . . *Kinds of oak trees*) Infs **DC**5, **LA**20, Gray oak. **1979** Little *Checklist U.S. Trees* 232, *Quercus grisea*. . . Gray oak. *Ibid* 240, *Quercus rubra*. . . *Other common names* . . gray oak.

2 An oak *(Quercus grisea)* native to Texas, New Mexico, and Arizona. Also called **live oak, mountain white oak, scrub oak, shin oak, switch oak, white oak**

1886 Havard *Flora W. & S. TX for 1885* 504, *Quercus grisea*. . . Gray Oak. . . The most abundant, I may say the characteristic, Oak of Western Texas. . . The cross-section is remarkable for the conspicuousness of its medullary rays, causing . . beautiful effects of silver-grain. **1931** U.S. Dept. Ag. *Misc. Pub.* 101.22, *Gray oak* . . , one of the commonest Southwestern live oaks, occurs both as a shrub and a tree. **1939** Tharp *Vegetation TX* 19 **wTX,** Practically all mesas and gentle slopes bear a more or less dense growth of grey oak. **1960** Vines *Trees SW* 168, Probably the most distinctive . . character of the foliage of Gray Oak . . is the fact that [it] is grayish green and tomentose, both above and below. **1979** [see **1** above].

3 A **live oak** (here: *Quercus turbinella*). [See quot 1937]

1910 Jepson *Silva CA* 218, *Quercus turbinella*. . . *Grey Oak.* Small rigid shrub; leaves pale on both surfaces. **1937** U.S. Forest Serv. *Range Plant Hdbk.* B125, Gray oak refers to the fact that the bark, leaves, and acorn cups of this species [=*Quercus turbinella*] frequently have a grayish hue.

gray owl n

1 =**great horned owl.** *obs*

1672 Josselyn *New-Englands Rarities* 12, The great *Gray Owl* with Ears, the little *Gray Owl,* and the *White Owl* which is not bigger than a *Thrush.*

2 also *little gray owl:* =**screech owl.**

1672 [see **1** above]. **1890** Warren *Birds PA* 154, *Megascops asio*. . . *Gray Owl*. . . This handsome little owl is the most common of all owls found in Pennsylvania. **1917** *Wilson Bulletin* 29.2.81, *Otus asio*. . . Little gray . . owl, Hickman, Ky. **1923** WV State Ornith. *Birds WV* 22, The screech owl is sometimes called . . gray owl. **1946** Hausman *Eastern Birds* 352, *Eastern Screech Owl*. . . *Other Names* . . Gray Owl. . . In gray phase: Upper parts brownish-gray delicately streaked with black and finely flecked with yellowish white. . . In the so-called red phase: Gray everywhere replaced by reddish brown. **1950** *WELS (Other kinds of owls)* 1 Inf, **WI,** Gray owl; 1 Inf, Gray owl—small with silvery gray coloring. **1966–69** *DARE* (Qu. Q2, . . *Kinds of owls*) Infs **ME**6, **MN**29, **OH**20, **PA**182, Gray owl; **MS**21, Little gray owl.

gray partridge n

1 =**Hungarian partridge 1.**

1927 Forbush *Birds MA* 2.12, *Perdix perdix perdix*. . . Gray partridge. **1936** Roberts *MN Birds* 1.407, The Gray Partridge is a hardy bird, adaptable if placed in suitable surroundings. **1953** Jewett *Birds WA* 219, The gray partridge bids fair to become the most successful game bird in eastern Washington. **1955** MA Audubon Soc. *Bulletin* 39.443 **CT,** *European Partridge.* Gray Partridge. **1977** Bull–Farrand *Audubon Field Guide Birds* 496, The Gray Partridge's high reproductive rate enables it to withstand hunting, predators, and cold snowy northern winters. **1982** Elman *Hunter's Field Guide* 43, The dog brings him a bird . . widely known as the gray partridge. . . He can see the soft, finely vermiculated gray covering its breast and belly. . . The flanks are gray, too.

2 =**ruffed grouse.**

1955 MA Audubon Soc. *Bulletin* 39.442, *Ruffed Grouse*. . . Gray Partridge (Maine. The species has red and gray color phases).

3 The chukar *(Alectoris chukar)*.

1982 Elman *Hunter's Field Guide* 37, *Chukar Partridge* . . *Common & regional names* . . gray partridge. [*Ibid* 39, Its [=the chukar's] upper body, wings, and breast are blue-gray.]

gray perch n

1 =**freshwater drum.**

1884 Goode *Fisheries U.S.* 1.370, *Haploidonotus grunniens*. . . In the Ohio River it is usually called "White Perch" or "Gray Perch," often simply "Perch." **1946** LaMonte *N. Amer. Game Fishes* 148, *Freshwater Drum*. . . Gray Perch.

2 Prob =**mademoiselle.**

1970 *DARE* (Qu. P2, . . *Kinds of saltwater fish* . . *[that] are good to eat)* Inf **VA**79, Gray perch.

gray pike n

1 also *gray pickerel, ~ pikeperch:* A **sauger** (here: *Stizostedion canadense*).

1842 DeKay *Zool. NY* 4.19, *The Gray Pike-perch*. . . General hue grayish. . . The first dorsal fin light-colored . . with a rounded or irregular blue-black spot on the membrane between each ray. **1884** Goode *Fisheries U.S.* 1.421, At all the fishing points between Ottawa City . . and the Huron fisheries, . . the greater part of the "Pickerel" are called "Gray Pickerel," and many say that they are totally different from the "Yellow" or "Blue" Pickerel. *Ibid* 424, The "Sauger," known also as the "Gray Pike," . . has its habitat . . in the Saint Lawrence River, Great Lake region, Upper Mississippi, and Upper Missouri Rivers, also in the Ohio. **1896** U.S. Natl. Museum *Bulletin* 47.1022, *Gray Pike*. . . Length 10 to 18 inches. **1908** Forbes–Richardson *Fishes of IL* 274, *Gray Pike*. . . A . . smaller fish . . seldom exceeding . . a weight of one to two pounds. **1949** Caine *N. Amer. Sport Fish* 117, *Sauger*. . . Frequently confused with the walleye, it is also known as . . Gray Pike, . . and Sand Pike. **1983** Becker *Fishes WI* 880, *Stizostedion canadense*. . . Other common names . . gray pikeperch, gray pickerel.

2 A **walleye** (here: *Stizostedion vitreum* and subspp).

1884 Goode *Fisheries U.S.* 1.422 **OH,** The "Gray," "Yellow," and "Blue" Pike grade into each other in this locality [=Sandusky Bay and vicinity] in such a manner that it is hard to draw the limiting line. Mr. Kumlien thinks that all of these represented as "Gray" and some "Blue" were *S[tizostedion] vitreum. Ibid* 423 **NY,** At Oswego this species [=*Stizostedion vitreum glaucum*] is called "Gray Pike," is quite common, and unusually silvery in appearance. **1890** *Century Dict.* 4484, *Gray pike.* Same as *blue-pike* [=*Stizostedion vitreum*]. **1935** Caine *Game Fish* 31, *Wall-eyed Pike*. . . *Synonyms* . . Gray Pike. **1957** Trautman *Fishes* 530, The intergrades between the Blue [Walleye] and the Yellow [Walleye], known as the "Gray Pike," were considered to be . . hybrids . . between the two species [=*Stizostedion vitreum glaucum* and *S. v. vitreum*]. **1983** Becker *Fishes WI* 871, *Stizostedion vitreum vitreum*. . . Other common names . . gray pike.

gray pikeperch See **gray pike 1**

gray pine n

A pine with gray-green foliage, as:

a =**jack pine.**

[**1810** Michaux *Histoire des Arbres* 1.49, Dans le District du Maine et à la Nouvelle-Ecosse, y est connue sous le nom de *Scrub Pine,* Pin chétif; et dans le Bas-Canada, sous celui de *grey Pine,* Pin gris. [=In the region of Maine and in Nova Scotia, there [it] is known under the name of Scrub Pine, *Pin chétif;* and in lower Canada under that of grey Pine, *Pin gris.*] *Ibid* 50, Les cônes sont le plus souvent réunis deux à deux; leur couleur cendrée ou gris paroît être l'origine du nom de Pin gris. [=Most often the cones are joined two by two; their ashy or gray color seems to be the origin of the name Gray pine.]] **1822** Eaton *Botany* 392, *[Pinus] banksiana* . . scrub pine, grey pine. . . Leaves short, rigid, divaricate. **1848** Gray *Manual of Botany* 439, *Gray,* or *Northern Scrub Pine.* . . Rocky banks, N. Maine and Michigan, thence northward. **1884** Sargent *Forests of N. Amer.* 201, *Gray Pine*. . . Wood . . largely used for fuel, railway ties, etc. **1899** Bergen *Animal Lore* 102 **VT,** *Pinus Banksiana,* the gray pine, is injurious to people, especially women. The ill effects are not removed by cutting down; the tree must be burnt. **1945** MI Ag. Exper. Sta. *Technical Bulletin* 201.13, Areas of gray pine or so-called Jack pine *(Pinus Banksiana)* occur in the interior. **1976** Bailey–Bailey *Hortus Third* 875, *Gray pine*. . . To 75 ft. or more, but usually smaller and sometimes shrubby. . . Nov[a] Sc[otia] to N.Y. and Minn.

b also *grayleaf pine:* =**digger pine.**

1897 Sudworth *Arborescent Flora* 18 **NV,** *Pinus monophylla*. . . Grey Pine. *Ibid* 23 **CA,** *Pinus sabiniana*. . . Gray-leaf Pine. **1908** Britton *N. Amer. Trees* 37, *Pinus sabiniana* . . , also called Gray pine, Bull pine, Grayleaf pine, . . occurs locally in the foothill region of western California. **1910** Jepson *Silva CA* 90, Gray Pine, Gray-leaf Pine, and Blue Pine are names which interpret the hue of the foliage. **1979** Little *Checklist U.S. Trees* 198, *Pinus sabiniana*. . . *Other common names* . . gray pine.

c A **piñon** (here: *Pinus monophylla*).

1897 [see **b** above]. **1908** Britton *N. Amer. Trees* 17, It [=*Pinus monophylla*] is also called . . Gray pine.

gray plover n

1 =**black-bellied plover.**

[**1624** Smith *Genl. Hist. VA* 171 **eVA,** Many sorts of Fowles, as . . the gray and greene Plouer, some wilde Ducks.] **1874** Coues *Birds NW* 449, *Black-bellied, Gray and Swiss Plover.* Beetle-head, Bull-head Plover, Oxeye, and a variety of other names. **1888** Trumbull *Names of Birds* 191, At Ash Point (near Rockland), Me., Seaford (Hempstead), L.I., and Barnegat, N.J., *Gray Plover* [=*Pluvialis squatarola*]. **1910** Eaton *Birds NY* 1.346, The . . Gray plover is well known to the gunners of the Long Island coast. **1955** MA Audubon Soc. *Bulletin* 39.445, *Black-bellied Plover.* . . Gray Plover (Maine. . . Adults are gray or grayish white, darker-streaked above, and the immature the same, almost all over.) **1969** Longstreet *Birds FL* 60, *Black-bellied Plover. Other names* . . Gray Plover. . . The upper parts are brownish-gray.

2 =upland plover.

1844 Giraud *Birds Long Is.* 227, In Massachusetts, Rhode Island, New Jersey, and on the Shinnecock and Hempstead Plains, Long Island, it [=*Bartramia longicauda*] is common, where it is known by the name of "Gray . . Plover." **1888** Trumbull *Names of Birds* 173 **Long Is. NY,** At Bellport, *Gray Plover* [=*Bartramia longicauda*]. **1956** MA Audubon Soc. *Bulletin* 40.17, *Upland Plover.* . . Gray Plover (Mass. There is a good deal of grayish brown, at least of feather-edging, in the plumage of the upper parts.)

3 A **knot** (here: *Calidris canutus*). [*SND* 1789 →]

1911 *Forest & Stream* 77.175, *Tringa canutus.*—Gray Plover (in autumn), Currituck Sound, N.C. **1917** *DN* 4.426 **LA,** *Gray plover.* The knot (Tringa canutus).

4 A **willet** (here: *Catotrophorus semipalmatus*).

1923 U.S. Dept. Ag. *Misc. Circular* 13.62 **CA,** *Western Willet. . . Vernacular Names. . . In local use.* . . Gray-plover. **1956** MA Audubon Soc. *Bulletin* 40.19 **ME,** *Willet.* . . Gray Plover.

5 =golden plover. [*EDD* 1885]

1923 U.S. Dept. Ag. *Misc. Circular* 13.69 **Long Is. NY, WA,** *Golden Plover. . . Vernacular Names. . . In local use.* . . Gray plover.

gray pond-hen n Cf **pond hen**

1 =pied-billed grebe.

1911 *Forest & Stream* 77.174, *Podilymbus podiceps.* Gray Pond Hen, Ponkapog, Mass. **1955** MA Audubon Soc. *Bulletin* 39.310 **MA,** *Pied-billed Grebe.* . . Gray Pond-hen.

2 =Florida gallinule.

1923 U.S. Dept. Ag. *Misc. Circular* 13.44 **MA,** *Florida Gallinule. . . Vernacular Names. . . In local use.* . . Gray pond-hen. **1925** (1928) Forbush *Birds MA* 1.366, *Gallinula chloropus chloropus.* . . Gray pond-hen. **1932** Bennitt *Check-list* 28 **MO,** *Florida gallinule.* . . Gray pond-hen.

gray rabbit n Also *gray hare*

1 also *gray cottontail, ~ bob:* A cottontail of the genus *Sylvilagus,* esp *S. floridanus.*

1842 DeKay *Zool. NY* 1.93, *The American Grey Rabbit. Lepus nanus.* . . Yellowish grey, varied with brown; . . in winter, the grey color predominates. **1882** *Amer. Naturalist* 16.856 **NJ,** It was not long before the man did make the acquaintance of our gray rabbit. **1917** Anthony *Mammals Amer.* 289/1, The Cottontail or Gray Rabbit, is a smaller animal than the Hare. **1935** Pratt *Manual Vertebrate Animals* 348, *S[ylvilagus] floridanus* . . gray rabbit; cottontail. **1961** Jackson *Mammals WI* 113, *Sylvilagus floridanus mearnsii. . . Vernacular names.* . . Gray rabbit. **1966–70** *DARE* (Qu. P30, *Do you have wild rabbits around here? What kinds?*) 61 Infs, **scattered, but esp Midl, Sth,** Gray rabbit; **MI**99, **TN**37, Gray cottontail; **MA**45, Common gray rabbit; **NY**207, Gray bob; **MA**6, Gray hare; **MO**9, Old gray rabbit. **1982** Elman *Hunter's Field Guide* 369, *Cottontail Rabbit (Sylvilagus)* Common & Regional Names: cooney, coney . . gray rabbit . . hotfoot.

2 =varying hare.

1947 Cahalane *Mammals* 583, *Varying Hare.* . . Other names for this graceful, fleet animal are white hare, gray hare, and gray rabbit. **1966** *DARE* (Qu. P30, *Do you have wild rabbits around here? What kinds?*) Inf **MA**6, Gray hare.

gray rat n

=Norway rat.

1792 Belknap *Hist. NH* 3.162, The *black rat (mus ______)* is a native, but it retires back into the country as the grey rat, which is imported in vessels from abroad, advances. The town of Hampton, though adjoining the sea, and one of the earliest settlements in New-Hampshire, had no grey rats till the year 1764, when an English mast ship was wrecked on the beech. This species of rat has advanced about thirty miles into the country. **1917** Anthony *Mammals Amer.* 222, House Rat. *Epimys norvegicus.* . . Gray Rat. . . The common Rat to be seen about cities. **1947** Cahalane *Mammals* 548, Many descriptive names are given to it: gray rat, . . Norway rat. **1961** Jackson *Mammals WI* 253, *Rattus norvegicus.* . . Gray rat.

gray rattlesnake n Also *gray rattler, little gray rattlesnake*

Prob **=massasauga.**

1846 in 1848 Emory *Notes Reconnoissance* 396 **KS,** A grey snake, marked with a row of blackish spots along the back . . is called the grey rattlesnake. **1968** *DARE* (Qu. P25, . . *Kinds of snakes*) Inf **NY**117, Gray rattler. **1974** Shaw–Campbell *Snakes West* 217, In the East the massasauga . . is called the swamp rattlesnake or sometimes the little gray rattlesnake.

gray runner n Cf **black racer 1**

A **racer,** prob *Coluber constrictor flaviventris.*

1967 *DARE* (Qu. P25, . . *Kinds of snakes*) Inf **TX**37, Gray runner.

gray saltbush n

=greasewood 2a.

1941 Writers' Program *Guide CO* 15, Gray saltbush, or chico-brush—better known as greasewood—grows in alkaline soil and in the shale beds of the lower foothills.

gray sandpiper n

=black-bellied plover.

1888 [see **gray lapwing**]. **1923** U.S. Dept. Ag. *Misc. Circular* 13.68, *Black-bellied Plover. . . Book Names.* . . Gray lapwing, gray sandpiper.

graysby n

A **grouper 1a** (here: *Petrometopon cruentatum*). Also called **coney** n[2] **c, red hind**

1933 John G. Shedd Aquarium *Guide* 98, *Petrometopon cruentatus*—Graysby; Coney. **1946** LaMonte *N. Amer. Game Fishes* 57, *Coney—Petrometopon cruentatus.* . . Red Hind, Graysby. **1960** Amer. Fisheries Soc. *List Fishes* 25, Graysby. . . *Petrometopon cruentatum.*

gray scoggin n Cf **scoggin**

=Louisiana heron.

1969 *DARE* FW Addit **NC,** Gray scoggin . . local name for Louisiana Heron. Bird of the Outer Bank. . . name given near the Pea Island Wildlife Refuge, NC.

grayslick See **slick**

gray snake n

=earth snake.

1937 Pope *Snakes Alive* 10, Unless you worked very hard you certainly would not get a specimen of the little gray snake that has been found in New Jersey only a few times. *Ibid* 206, *Gray Snake (Virginia).* **1958** Conant *Reptiles & Amphibians* 136, *Earth Snakes.* . . are small gray, brown, or reddish-brown snakes virtually devoid of any distinctive markings. . . The genus occurs only in the eastern United States, and a variety of names have been applied . . "gray snakes," "little brown snakes," etc.

gray snapper n **esp FL**

Either of two **snappers:** usu *Lutjanus griseus,* but also **schoolmaster.** For other names of *L. griseus* see **lawyer, mangrove snapper, Pensacola snapper, red snapper, spot snapper**

1775 (1962) Romans *Nat. Hist. FL* lii, The fish . . most commonly caught are such as seamen know by the following names, viz . . *red, grey and black snappers, dog snappers, . . mangrove snappers.* **1802** (1803) Ellicott *Jrl.* 255, Along the Florida Reef, and among the Keys, a great abundance and variety of fish may be taken: such as . . black, red, and gray snappers. **1879** U.S. Natl. Museum *Bulletin* 14.48, *Lutjanus caxis. . . Gray Snapper.* West Indian Fauna and Southern Atlantic States. **1902** Jordan–Evermann *Amer. Fishes* 408, At Key West . . it [=*Lutjanus griseus*] is called gray snapper. **1935** Caine *Game Fish* 123, *Lutjanus apodus.* . . Gray Snapper. *Ibid* 130, *Lutjanus griseus.* . . Gray Snapper. **1955** Carr–Goin *Guide Reptiles* 102 **FL,** Gray Snapper. . . A grayish or coppery, laterally compressed fish with a long dorsal fin and a tough mouth.

gray snipe n

1 =dowitcher.

1870 PA Laws *Laws Genl. Assembly* 50, No person shall kill, capture, [or] take . . any gray snipe. **1879** *Forest & Stream* 12.409/3, The red-breasted snipe . . is otherwise known as gray snipe, brownback and dowitcher. **1888** Trumbull *Names of Birds* 161, *Red-breasted Snipe* [=*Limnodromus griseus*]. . . Gray Snipe . . of Swainson and Richardson, 1831. **1918** Grinnell *Game Birds CA* 358, *Long-billed Dowitcher . . Other names* . . Gray Snipe (in winter). . . *Adults, both sexes, in fall and winter:* Top of head, hind neck, and back, quite uniform grayish brown, most of the feathers with obscurely darker shafts. **1923** U.S. Dept. Ag. *Misc. Circular* 13.51 **Long Is. NY, DE, MI, MN,** *Dowitcher. . . Vernacular Names. . . In local use. . .* Gray snipe. *Ibid* 52 **Long Is. NY,** *Knot. . . Vernacular Names. . . In local use. . .* Gray snipe. **1978** Gromme *Birds WI* 219, Snipe, Gray (Dowitcher).

2 A **knot** (here: *Calidris canutus*).

1903 Dawson *Birds OH* 504, *Knot. . . Robin Snipe; Gray Snipe. . .* Upper parts light gray, streaked centrally with black. **1923** [see **1** above]. **1953** Jewett *Birds WA* 267, *Calidris canutus rogersi. . .* Gray Snipe. . . On occasion, very abundant along the coast of Washington. **1956** MA Audubon Soc. *Bulletin* 40.18 **ME,** *American Knot. . .* Gray Snipe.

gray sole n

Usu the **winter flounder,** but also the **witch flounder.**

1960 Amer. Fisheries Soc. *List Fishes* 72, Sole, . . gray—see flounder, winter; flounder, witch. **1970** *DARE* (Qu. P2, . . *Kinds of saltwater fish . . good to eat*) Inf **MA**40, Gray sole; (Qu. P14) Inf **MA**40, Gray sole. **1973** Knight *Cook's Fish Guide* 391, Sole . . gray see Flounder, Winter.

gray squirrel n

1 also *gray;* Any of three squirrels: usu *Sciurus carolinensis,* native to the eastern half of the US, but also *S. arizonensis,* native to Arizona, and *S. griseus,* native to California. For other names of *S. carolinensis* see **cat squirrel 1, stump ear, timber squirrel;** for other names of *S. griseus* see **silver-gray squirrel**

[**1624** Smith *Genl. Hist. VA* 27, Their Squirrels some are neare as great as our smallest sort of wilde Rabbets, some blackish or blacke and white, but the most are gray.] **1674** Josselyn *Two Voyages* 86 **NEast,** There are three sorts, the mouse squirril, the gray squirril, and the flying-squirril. **1792** Belknap *Hist. NH* 3.162, Of *squirrels* we have four species. The *black (sciurus niger)* and the *grey (sciurus cinereus)* though distinguished by Linnæus, differ here only in colour; the former is very rare, the latter very common. This is the largest species of squirrels. **1879** U.S. Natl. Museum *Bulletin* 14.14, *Sciurus carolinensis. . . Gray Squirrel.* United States. . . *Sciurus fossor. . . California Gray Squirrel.* Pacific Slope. **1928** Anthony *N. Amer. Mammals* 251, *Sciurus carolinensis. . .* Gray Squirrel. . . *Upperparts.* Mixed gray and yellowish brown. *Ibid* 255, The Gray Squirrels of the *griseus* group are found in forested areas where conifers and oaks grow. *Ibid* 258, *Arizona Gray Squirrel. . .* General color of upperparts gray. **1967** *DARE* FW Addit **LA**5, [There is a] distinction between cat squirrel and gray squirrel. Gray squirrel is larger and lives in the swamps—its belly is sometimes an off-white color. **1982** Elman *Hunter's Field Guide* 397, Closely related to the eastern, or common, gray is the California, or western, gray *(S[ciurus] griseus),* whose range is restricted to the West Coast of the United States. . . Similar habitat is favored by the Arizona gray squirrel *(S. arizonensis),* which also looks like the eastern type, except for its yellowish belly.

2 A **ground squirrel** n **b:** usu *Spermophilus franklini* or *S. variegatus.*

1928 Anthony *N. Amer. Mammals* 193, *Rock Squirrel. Otospermophilus grammurus. . .* Gray Squirrel. . . *Upperparts.* Grizzled gray, brown and dusky, grayest on shoulders. **1968** *DARE* (Qu. P29) Infs **MN**12, 33, Gopher—gray squirrel. **1970** *Western Folkl.* 29.168, The expression *gray squirrel*—for the ground squirrel, not the tree-climbing animal—occurs in southeastern South Dakota and nearby Garfield County, Nebraska. *Ibid* 172, *Bushy tail, . . gray squirrel . .* refer only to Franklin's ground squirrel.

gray sucker n

A **white sucker** (here: *Catostomus commersoni*).

1974 WI Univ. *Fish Lake MI* 30, White Sucker—*Catostomus commersoni* . . grey sucker. **1983** Becker *Fishes WI* 682, White Sucker . . gray sucker.

gray teal n

=ruddy duck.

1917 (1923) *Birds Amer.* 1.152, Ruddy Duck—*Erismatura jamaicensis. . .* Gray Teal. **1925** (1928) Forbush *Birds MA* 1.280, *Erismatura jamaicensis*—Ruddy Duck. . . Gray Teal. **1944** Hausman *Amer. Birds* 528, Gray Teal—see Ruddy Duck.

gray thorn n

A **lotebush** (here: *Ziziphus obtusifolia*).

1941 *Torreya* 41.49 **AZ,** *Zizyphus* [sic] *lycioides. . .* Gray thorn. **1967** *DARE* FW Addit, *Gray thorn*—a thorn bush found in west Texas. **1981** Benson-Darrow *Trees SW Deserts* 147, *Ziziphus obtusifolia. . .* Gray Thorn.

gray trout n Cf **trout**

1 Either of two **weakfish:** usu *Cynoscion regalis,* but also *C. nebulosus.* **esp Mid Atl**

1870 O. Optic *Field & Forest* 254 *(DA),* I dreamed that I went a fishing with her, and that a big gray trout pulled her into the water. **1892** *Outing* 20.54 **Chesapeake Bay,** Some calls it the 'spotted squetauge [sic],' . . and others . . the 'gray trout.' **1935** Caine *Game Fish* 144, Weakfish—*Cynoscion regalis. . .* Spotted Weakfish—*Cynoscion nebulosus. . .* Gray Trout. **1946** LaMonte *N. Amer. Game Fishes* 75, Weakfish—*Cynoscion regalis. . .* Gray Trout. [*Ibid,* Spotted Weakfish—*Cynoscion nebulosus* . . any of the names used for the Weakfish.] **1966-70** *DARE* (Qu. P2, . . *Kinds of saltwater fish . . good to eat*) Infs **NC**12, 80, 82, **VA**79, Gray trout. **1984** *DARE* File **Chesapeake Bay** [Watermen's vocab], Gray trout.

2 A **lake trout** (here: *Salvelinus namaycush*).

1960 Amer. Fisheries Soc. *List Fishes* 74, Trout, . . grey—see trout, lake; weakfish. **1972** Sparano *Outdoors Encycl.* 356, Lake Trout . . gray trout. . . *Salvelinus namaycush.* **1974** WI Univ. *Fish Lake MI* 15, Lake Trout—*Salvelinus namaycush* . . grey trout. **1983** Becker *Fishes WI* 323, Lake Trout—*Salvelinus namaycush* . . gray trout, . . great gray trout.

gray twig n

A small tree *(Schoepfia chrysophylloides)* native to southern Florida. Also called **whitewood**

1946 West-Arnold *Native Trees FL* 193, The Gulf graytwig . . , a small tree with thin, pale bark, pale, unarmed branches, small, reddish flowers and fleshy, red fruits . . , occurs south of Lake Okeechobee. **1971** Craighead *Trees S. FL* 177, On the rim hammocks the important trees include live oak, . . gray twig, . . and randia.

gray violet n Cf **Confederate violet**

A **violet** (here: prob *Viola sororia*).

1969 *DARE* (Qu. S26c, *Wildflowers that grow in woods*) Inf **KY**24, Gray violet.

graywacker n

=flicker n² **1.**

1911 *Forest & Stream* 77.174, *Colaptes auratus. . .* Graywacker, eastern shore of Maryland.

gray wavey n Cf **wavey**

1 also sp *gray wavie:* **=white-fronted goose.**

1936 Roberts *MN Birds* 1.212, White-fronted Goose. . . Other names . . Gray Wavie. **1943** Musgrove-Musgrove *Waterfowl IA* 11, *White-fronted Goose. . .* Other names . . gray wavey. . . Brownish-gray plumage, lighter on the under parts where it is heavily blotched with black.

2 =blue goose n **1.**

1982 Elman *Hunter's Field Guide* 292, *Blue Goose. . . Common & regional names* . . gray wavey.

gray wavie See **gray wavey 1**

grayweed n

=wild buckwheat.

1930 OK Univ. Biol. Surv. *Pub.* 2.59, *Eriogonum alatum. . .* Winged Gray-weed. . . *Eriogonum annuum. . .* Annual Gray-weed. . . *Eriogonum jamesii. . .* James's Gray-weed. . . *Eriogonum lachnogynum.* . . Long-rooted Gray-weed. . . *Eriogonum longifolium. . .* Long-leaved Gray-weed. . . *Eriogonum tenellum. . .* Small Gray-weed.

gray whale n

A whale *(Rhachianectes glaucus)* of North Pacific waters. Also called **devilfish 2, grayback 3a, hardhead 3, mussel-digger, rip sack**

[**1860** *Merc. Marine Mag.* VII.213 *(OED),* The California Grey Whale.] **1879** U.S. Natl. Museum *Bulletin* 14.12, *Rhachianectes glaucus. . .* Gray Whale . . Pacific Ocean. **1888** Kingsley *Riverside Nat. Hist.* 5.197 **Pacific,** The gray whale has received many curious titles, such as "hard-head," "mussel-digger," "devil-fish," and "gray-back." **1928** Anthony *N. Amer. Mammals* 560, *Gray Whale. . . Rhachianectes* *glaucus*. . . In North America along Pacific coast. **1946** Dufresne *AK's Animals* 186, The Gray Whale [=*Rhachianectes glaucus*], sometimes called California Gray Whale, or Devilfish, is noted among whalers for the frenzied rushes it makes when harpooned, and for the mother's fierce guardianship of her young. **1957** Blair et al. *Vertebrates U.S.* 741, Gray whale. Size moderate; body length about 1070–1370 cm. General color blotched grayish black.

gray whistler n Cf **whistler**

=upland plover.

1956 MA Audubon Soc. *Bulletin* 40.17, *Upland Plover*. . . Gray Whistler (Mass. The song is a prolonged mellow whistle.)

gray whitewing n

The female and young of the **white-winged scoter.**

1888 Trumbull *Names of Birds* 98, *White-winged scoter*. . . In Massachusetts at Pigeon Cove and North Scituate . . *Black white-wing* for adult drake, and *Gray white-wing* for female and young; some gunners believing that these two plumages represent separate species. **1925** (1928) Forbush *Birds MA* 1.274, *White-winged Scoter. Other names* . . gray white-wing. **1946** Hausman *Eastern Birds* 165, Gray Whitewing. . . Female: A dull brown duck with two white patches on the side of the head and a white speculum. **1955** MA Audubon Soc. *Bulletin* 39.376, *White-winged Scoter*. . . Gray White-wing (Mass. The female and young, which are brownish, however, rather than gray.)

gray widgeon n

1 =gadwall.

1888 Trumbull *Names of Birds* 24 **GA,** *Gadwall*. . . Called also at Savannah *Gray Widgeon*. **1909** Field Museum Nat. Hist. *Zool. Ser.* 9.323 **IL, WI,** The Gadwall is known to gunners as Gray Widgeon and Creek Duck. **1923** U.S. Dept. Ag. *Misc. Circular* 13.10 **GA, WI,** *Gadwall. . . Vernacular Names. . . In local use.* . . Gray widgeon. *Ibid* 15 **CT, FL, MD,** *Pintail. . . Vernacular Names. . . In local use.* . . Gray widgeon. **1943** Musgrove–Musgrove *Waterfowl IA* 24, *Gadwall*. . . Other names . . gray widgeon. **1955** *Oriole* 20.1.3 **GA,** *Gadwall*. . . Gray widgeon. **1982** Elman *Hunter's Field Guide* 147, *Gadwall. . . Common & regional names* . . gray widgeon.

2 =pintail.

1888 Trumbull *Names of Birds* 38, In Philadelphia, Baltimore, and St. Augustine, these young birds and females [of *Anas acuta*] are also called Gray Duck, and in the latter locality *Gray Widgeon*. **1923** [see **1** above]. **1932** Howell *FL Bird Life* 137, *American Pintail. . . Other Names* . . Gray Widgeon. **1955** MA Audubon Soc. *Bulletin* 39.314 **CT,** *Pintail*. . . Gray Widgeon.

gray willow n

Any of several **willows,** but esp **prairie willow.**

1813 Muhlenberg *Catalogus Plantarum* 91 **PA,** Salix grisea—gray willow. **1848** Gray *Manual of Botany* 425, *S[alix] tristis. . . Dwarf Gray Willow. . . Leaves* . . grayish-woolly on both sides, the upper side becoming nearly smooth at maturity. **1860** Curtis *Cat. Plants NC* 75, *Gray Willow.* (S. tristis . .)—A shrub 1 or 2 feet high, very much branched, of a dull gray aspect on account of the young branches and leaves being covered with an ash-colored down or wool. **1865** IL State Ag. Soc. *Trans.* 5.753, *Salix alba*. . . The Society held a lengthy discussion upon the proper name for this tree, which is known as 'White Willow,' 'Gray Willow,' 'Timber Willow,' 'Powder Willow,' etc. **1920** *Torreya* 20.20, *Salix exigua*. . . Gray willow, Salt Lake Valley, Utah. **1924** Hawkins *Trees & Shrubs* 69 **WY,** *Wolf's Willow* (Salix Wolfii). . . In contrast with other willows and pines, it looks quite gray and is often called the Gray Willow. **1953** Strausbaugh–Core *Flora WV* 282, *S[alix] humilis* var. *microphylla* . . *dwarf gray willow*. A shrub usually less than 1 m. tall, the twigs brownish or grayish. . . *S[alix] cinerea* . . *gray willow* . . widely planted for . . showy catkins . . developed in early spring. **1968** *DARE* (Qu. T5, . . *Kinds of evergreens* . . *around here*) Inf **CA**105, Gray willow. **1976** Bailey–Bailey *Hortus Third* 996, *[Salix] humilis. . . Gray W[illow]*. . . N[ew]f[ound]l[an]d and s. Que[bec], s. to Fla., e. to N.Dak. and e. Tex.

gray wolf n

1 also *gray:* A large wolf *(Canis lupus)* of northern and western North America. Also called **buffalo wolf, loafer, lobo, timber wolf**

1805 (1814) Lewis–Clark *Hist. of the Exped.* 2.151, We caught in a trap a large gray wolf. **1843** (1940) Ferris *Rocky Mts.* 162 **NY,** During this jaunt, we killed a grey wolf which was fat, and made us a tolerable supper. **1886** *Outing* 9.102/1, 'See what a lot of coyotes, back there by the forest edge!' 'They don't like ter interrupt the grays at their feast.' **1923** Cook *50 Yrs.* 221, Indian spirits, in form of coyotes or big gray wolves, may sing serenades about his bones for years to come. **1935** Pratt *Manual Vertebrate Animals* 744, *Canis lupus*. . . Gray wolf. **1935** Sandoz *Jules* 159 **wNE** (as of 1880–1930), I said you was welcome and by damn you are, so long as you kill a gray now and then. **1958** Blasingame *Dakota Cowboy* 72 **SD,** The gray wolf, buffalo runner, timber wolf—name or color mattered little, for the animal was the same. **1980** Whitaker *Audubon Field Guide Mammals* 540, The Gray Wolf possesses various whines, yelps, growls, and barks—the usual one short, harsh, and uttered in a brief series; not all wolves are capable of barking.

2 =coyote n **B1.**

1937 Grinnell et al. *Fur-Bearing Mammals CA* 2.476, Because it is large for a coyote, has a heavy coat of fur and is gray in color, the mountain coyote [=*Canis latrans lestes*] is often known locally as gray wolf or timber wolf. *Ibid* 529, Many trappers . . recognize as "wolf" or "gray wolf" the large pale-colored race of coyote *(Canis latrans lestes).*

3 also *old gray wolf in the woodshed:* Any of var children's games; see quots. Cf **wolf**

1967–69 *DARE* (Qu. EE12, *Games in which one captain hides his team and the other team tries to find it*) Inf **OH**82, Gray wolf; **IL**29, Old gray wolf in the woodshed; (Qu. EE13a, *Games in which every player hides except one*) Inf **OH**11, Gray wolf; **IN**69, Gray wolf—one hides and everyone seeks him; (QR, near Qu. EE13a) Inf **MI**24, Gray wolf—an individual was doing the looking. **1983** *Holland Sentinel Weekender* (MI) 23 July sec B 6/3 (as of c1920), At recess the usual games of tag, Run Sheep Run, Fox and Geese, Gray Wolf, . . were played. **1987** *DARE* File **cwMI** (as of c1960), "Gray wolf" is a game much like hide-and-seek that we played at dusk. The person who was "it" stood on the front porch and chanted, "One o'clock, the wolf is near; two o'clock, the wolf is near," and so forth, up to, "Eleven o'clock, the wolf is coming; twelve o'clock, the wolf is here!" Then "it" would search for the others, who had hidden while he chanted. When he found someone, the two would race back to the porch.

gray wood duck See **gray duck a**

grease n Usu |gris|; also **esp coastal SC, GA, FL** |griəs|; for addit varr see quots

A Forms.

1893 [see **grease** v **A1**]. **c1960** [see **grease** v **A1**]. **1961** Kurath–McDavid *Pronc. Engl.* 105, Ingliding [iᶤ, iᵊ] is confined to the Low Country of South Carolina and coastal Georgia and Florida, where it occurs fairly regularly in checked position, as in *grease, bean.* **1981** Pederson *LAGS Basic Materials* **Gulf Region,** [For the noun *grease* there are 12 exx of ingliding proncs of the type [griɨs]; 3 exx of the type [griᵊs]; 2 exx of the type [griᵊz].]

B Senses.

1 See quots. Cf **axle-grease** n **1.**

1923 [see **eat the grease**]. **1932** *AmSp* 7.332 **MD** [Johns Hopkins jargon], *Grease*—butter.

2 in phr *as rich as grease:* Very wealthy. [Perh folk-etym for *Croesus*]

1960 *AmSp* 35.76 **IL,** He married the banker's daughter; they're as rich as grease.

3 See quot. Cf **greaser B1**

1971 Roberts *Third Ear* np [Black], *Grease* . . a black person.

4 See quot. Cf **grease** v **B3**

1975 *AmSp* 50.60 [Univ of AR slang], *Grease*. . . Meal, dinner—"Let's go to grease."

grease v

A Forms.

1 infin, pres: **chiefly Nth, West** |gris|; **chiefly Sth, Midl** |griz|; pronc-spp *greaze, grees.* Cf **blouse, greasy** adj **A**

1892 *DN* 1.239 **MO,** *Grease,* v. Pronounced in Kansas City [griz] as in the dictionaries. My family brought with them from western New York the sound of *s* instead of *z* in this word, and one very often hears this in Kansas City, but almost never in the surrounding country. [*DN* Eds: Is not *z* general in the South in the verb and the adjective *(greasy)?* . . In New England *s* is general in both.] **1893** Shands *MS Speech* 71, *Grease, greasy.* In *grease,* used as a verb, the *s* is given the sound of z; in the adjective *greasy* the same rule holds good. In the noun *grease,* however, *s* has its proper sound. **1896** *DN* 1.441, The North and the South present the two extremes [in the pronunciation of the verb *grease* and adjective *greasy*]: 88% [of the infs from the North used [gris] as opposed to [griz]] and 83% [used [grisi] as opposed to [grizi]] on the one hand, and 12% [of the infs from the South used [gris]] and 12% [used [grisi]] on the other. In the Midland Belt the figures are 42% and 34%; in the West, 56% and 45%. [*DARE* Ed: "South" here is equal to *DARE*'s **Sth, S Midl,** "Midland Belt" approx equals *DARE*'s **N Midl,** and "North" equals *DARE*'s **Nth.**] **1907** *DN* 3.189 **seNH,** *Grease,* v.t. . . Pronounced grees [gris]. **1939** *LANE* Map 188, [Proncs of the type [gris] prevail **throughout NEng;** 9 infs, 8 **CT,** give proncs of the type [griz]. One inf regards [gris] as older, [griz] as "proper."] **c1960** *Wilson Coll.* **csKY,** *Grease,* n. [gris], v. [griz]. **1966** *DARE* Tape **AL**14, We had to [griz] it off with a ol' oily rag. **1969** *DARE* (Qu. KK38, . . *"I wish he wouldn't ______ his hair down so!"*) Inf **MO**27, Greaze. **1972** [see **B3** below]. **1975** Gould *ME Lingo* 115, *Grease.* . . In Maine it is always pronounced like the country Greece. The southerly "greaze" is not heard. **1976** Allen *LAUM* 3.323 **Upper MW** (as of c1950), The voiced variant /griz/ of the . . verb *grease* is even less frequent than the form /grizi/. Only five Iowan Midland speakers have it . . and one Nebraskan. **1982** *Barrick Coll.* **csPA,** *Grease*—n. Pron. [gris]. v.t. pron. [griz].

2 past, past pple: usu |grist, grizd|; occas |grɛz|; pronc-sp *grez.*

1923 (1946) Greer-Petrie *Angeline Doin' Society* 22 **csKY,** I . . had grez 'em good. **1952** Brown *NC Folkl.* 1.548, *Grez* [grɛz]: *vb.* Past tense and past participle of *grease.* . . Illiterate.

B Senses.

1 See quot. [Cf *OED to melt one's grease* (at *grease* sb. d) "to exhaust one's strength by violent efforts"]

1930 Shoemaker *1300 Words* 27 **cPA Mts** (as of c1900), *Grease*—To exert or overtax oneself.

2 To flatter, fawn upon. [Engl dial]

1965-70 *DARE* (Qu. II20b, . . *"He's always trying to ______ the boss."*) Inf **NY**76, Grease; (Qu. JJ3a, . . *A special effort to 'get in good'*) Inf **PA**240, Grease; **MA**128, Greasing the teacher. [2 of 3 Infs Black]

3 To eat, esp voraciously; hence n *greaser. among Black speakers*

1970 Major *Dict. Afro-Amer. Slang* 61, *Grease* . . to eat. **1970** *DARE* (Qu. H9, *If somebody always eats a considerable amount of food, you say he's a ______.*) Inf **IL**139, Greaser ['grizɚ]. [Inf Black] **1971** Roberts *Third Ear* np [Black], *Grease.* . . To eat voraciously. **1972** *DARE* File **Chicago IL** [Black], *Grease* [griz]—to eat. **1972** Claerbaut *Black Jargon* 67, *Grease* . . to eat; dine: *Got to get back to the crib and grease.* . . *Greaser* . . one who is eating food.

grease a gimbler See **gimlet, grease a**

grease ant n **chiefly N Cent, Upper MW, CA** See Map

Usu the Pharaoh ant *(Monomorium pharaonis),* but sometimes the little black ant *(M. minimum).*

1965-70 *DARE* (Qu. R18) 37 Infs, **chiefly N Cent, Upper MW, CA,** Grease ant; Infs **IL**45, **IN**76, **NC**81, **OH**28, 37, Grease ant—(little) red ant; **NE**11, **OH**98, Grease ant—black ant; **CA**87, **IA**1, **IL**43, Grease ant—tiny. **1989** *DARE* File **csWI,** The crumbs . . that we left behind attracted a swarm of little red-brown ants. . . We put some ant killer out . . but they didn't go near it. We called an exterminator who said, "Yeah, those are grease ants. Actually, they're called pharaoh ants." *Ibid* **ceWI,** Grease ants are those awful, little reddish ones. They hang around the kitchen because they like greasy food; they ignore that syrupy ant killer because they don't like sweet food. We had one heck of a time getting rid of them!

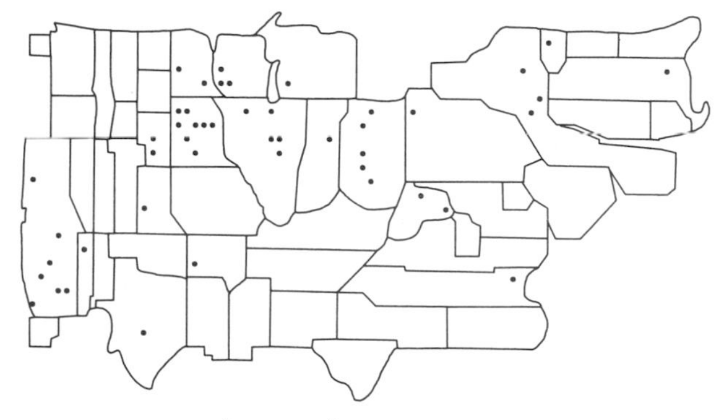

•grease ant (Qu. R18)

greaseball n

1 A person of foreign, esp Mediterranean, background. **esp NEast** *derog; usu considered offensive* Cf **greaser B1, 2**

1922 *DN* 5.147 **sePA** [College slang], *Grease ball*—a foreign cake-eater or bun duster. **1941** *LANE* Map 453 *(Italian)* 1 inf, **neMA,** Greaseball. **1964** *AmSp* 39.306 [Lingua Cosa Nostra], *Greaseball.* "A native-born Italian that don't talk English." **1965-70** *DARE* (Qu. HH28, . . *People of foreign background*) Infs **CA**81, 107, **MA**45, **NJ**1, **NY**12, 18, 32, 57, Greaseball—Greek; **NY**45, **PA**161, 230, **RI**4, **TX**95, Greaseball—Italian; **PA**193, Greaseball—Mexican.

2 also *greaseburner, greaseswabber:* A cook, esp a bad one.

1930 Irwin *Amer. Tramp* 91, *Grease ball.* . . a cook. **1934** Lomax-Lomax *Amer. Ballads* 559, Our grease-ball [Footnote: Cook] is a goddam dirty bum. **1941** Smiley *Hash House Lingo* 29, *Grease ball*—short order cook. **1942** Berrey-Van den Bark *Amer. Slang* 460.15 [Tramp and criminal], *Grease* . . *burner,* a poor cook. *Ibid* 511.8 [Logging], Camp cook. . . *greaseball, greaseburner. Ibid* 786.11 [Sea], Ship's cook. . . *grease burner. Ibid* 868.24 [Army], Cook. . . *greaseball, grease burner.* **1958** McCulloch *Woods Words* 73 **Pacific NW,** *Grease swabber*—A poor fry cook.

3 also *greaseburner;* Among railroad workers: see quots.

1920 *DN* 5.82 **Pacific NW,** *Grease burner.* The fireman on a locomotive which burns crude oil. **1942** Berrey-Van den Bark *Amer. Slang* 511.5 [Logging], *Grease burner,* a locomotive fireman. *Ibid* 771.27 [Railroad], Mechanic. . . *Greaseball.* **1946** in 1953 Botkin-Harlow *Treas. Railroad Folkl.* 351, A fireman will answer to his correct title, but you're asking for a dirty look if you call him greaseball.

grease bird n Cf **tallow bird**

=Canada jay.

1917 (1923) *Birds Amer.* 2.225, *Canada Jay.* . . Grease Bird. **1941** Writers' Program *Guide WY* 35, Unpopular for his insolence and thievery, the Canada jay, known also as Whiskey Jack, moose bird, meat hawk, and grease bird, is a native of the evergreen forests, where his whistlings, chucks, squalls, and screams are a familiar nuisance to still-hunters. **1946** Hausman *Eastern Birds* 419, *Canada Jay. Perisoreus canadensis canadensis.* . . Grease Bird. **1961** *Jrl. Amer. Folkl.* 74.1, The Canada Jay labors under the official name of *perisoreus canadensis canadensis* but it is more commonly called gorbey, moosebird, meat-bird, grease-bird . . or camp robber.

grease-bitch lamp See **grease lamp**

greasebrush n

1 See **greasewood 2b.**

2 See **greasebush 2.**

greaseburner See **greaseball 2, 3**

greasebush n Cf **greasewood**

1 =**greasewood 1.** Note: Some of these quots may refer instead to senses below.

1850 in 1852 U.S. Army Corps Topog. Engineers *Exped. Gt. Salt Lake* 235 **seWY,** The only vegetation, to-day, has been a little dwarf artemisia, grease-bush, . . and an occasional dwarf cedar on the bluffs. **1875** *N. Amer. Rev.* 120.5 **AZ,** The valleys [are covered] with grease-bush and sage. **1881** *Amer. Naturalist* 15.24 **CO,** Although the grease bushes, contrary to the rule of desert growths, are leafy, their abundant foliage is of precisely the same dull whitish color as the clay in which they grow.

2 also *greasebrush, greasethorn:* A plant of the genus *Forsellesia.*

1931 U.S. Dept. Ag. *Misc. Pub.* 101.97, *Greasebush (Forsellesia spinescens),* known also as greasebrush, is the best known and most widely distributed of the four species of Forsellesia (syn. Glossopetalon). **1938** Van Dersal *Native Woody Plants* 128, Dwarf greasebush. . . *Glossopetalon pungens.* . . Spiny greasebush. . . *Glossopetalon spinescens. Ibid* 337, Greasebush. . . Grease-thorn *(Forsellesia spinescens).* **1951** Abrams *Flora Pacific States* 3.55, *Glossopetalon nevadense.* . . Nevada Grease-bush. . . *Glossopetalon pungens.* . . Low Grease-bush. **1954** Harrington *Manual Plants CO* 365, *Greasebush.* Small, deciduous intricately branched shrubs; branches greenish, angled and more or less spinescent. **1960** Vines *Trees SW* 663, Texas Grease-bush is distinguished from the other species by the broad oblanceolate leaves with thickened margins and lack of stipules. **1970** Correll *Plants TX* 1000, *Grease-bush.* . . A small genus of 8 species in western United States.

3 A **buckbrush 3c** (here: *Ceanothus cuneatus*).

1937 U.S. Forest Serv. *Range Plant Hdbk.* B41, Wedgeleaf ceanothus, known locally as buckbrush . . and greasebush, is a rigid . . sometimes evergreen shrub.

4 =burrobrush 1.

1945 Wodehouse *Hayfever Plants* 149, *Hymenoclea* (Greasebushes). Of less importance in hayfever are the greasebushes, *H. Salsola* . . and *H. monogyra*. . . These are desert shrubs with narrow linear leaves, with flowers and inflorescences quite like those of the ragweeds.

greased chub n

A **stone roller** (here: *Campostoma anomalum*).

1908 Forbes–Richardson *Fishes of IL* 110, *Campostoma anomalum*. . . Stone-roller . . Greased Chub.

grease lamp n Also *grease-bitch lamp, grease light, greasy lamp* **chiefly S Midl** *old-fash*

=bitch n 1.

1933 *AmSp* 8.1.49 **Ozarks,** *Grease light*. . . A rude lamp, made by burning a rag wick in a *sasser* or clamshell filled with lard. Also called a *slut*. **1937** (1963) Hyatt *Kiverlid* 76 **KY,** They stink a sight wuss than a grease-bitch lamp or a taller slut. **1941** Smith *Going to God's Country* 28 **MO** (as of 1890), We used what was caled [sic] grease lights. We would take some old soft cloth or rags and twist them together and stand it up in a cup. Then we would put some kind of grease or lard and light the end. **1954** *Harder Coll.* **cwTN,** *Grease lamp*. **c1960** *Wilson Coll.* **csKY,** *Grease lamp*. . . A primitive lamp with lard as fuel. Now only a memory among very old people. **1968** *DARE* Tape **IN**3, I've heard my folks tell about the old grease lamps . . that they used. . . The old grease lamp, it was, seems as though they was a rag they put in the grease; **IN**30, I'll bet a lot of you younger ones don't even know what a grease lamp is. . . My sister does have one, and they were varied in shape. . . The one she had was more of . . an oblong, and it was . . five inches long and three inches across, and it was iron. It was just like a little iron box, and at one end it had a little . . bar across it. . . Then they would put one end of this long wick, it could just be a torn old rag string, . . and they would put one end of it down in their grease, then they would lay the other end of it upon this little bar, and they would light that end. . . These grease lamps, of course, they didn't do much more than to show you the way to walk around. **1983** *MJLF* 9.1.41 **ceKY,** *Greasy lamp* . . a grease lamp. **1986** Pederson *LAGS Concordance* **Gulf Region** *(A makeshift lamp)* 20 infs, Grease lamp; 6 infs, Grease light.

grease one's mouth v phr Cf **grease v B3**

1922 Gonzales *Black Border* 304 **sSC, GA coasts** [Gullah glossary], "Greese 'e mout'," to feed with fatness, as with bacon.

grease one's roots v phr

1957 *Sat. Eve. Post Letters* **OH,** "Now don't go greasing your roots" means "Don't be greedy." Early farmers buried fish along each hill of corn as fertilizer.

greaseplant See **greasewood 1**

grease pot n

=greasy spoon.

1968 *DARE* (Qu. D39, . . *A small eating place where the food is not especially good*) Inf **PA**136, Grease pot. **1969** *DARE* Tape **CT**36, Sometimes those places that look real expensive are no more expensive than some grease pots.

greaser n |'grisə(r), 'grizə(r)|

A Forms.

1906 [see **B1** below]. **1965–70** *DARE* (Qu. HH28) 47 Infs, **chiefly Inland Nth, N Midl, West, esp TX,** Greaser; 15 Infs, **chiefly West,** ['grizɚ]; (Qu. H9) Inf **IL**139, ['grizɚ]; (Qu. AA6b) Inf **VA**34, ['grizɚ]. **1968** *DARE* FW Addit **NY**52, ['grisɚ]. **1968** *DARE* File **New Orleans LA,** Greaser ['grizɚ]. **1986** [see **B1** below].

B Senses.

1 A Mexican or Mexican American. **scattered, but esp SW, CO** See Map *derog; usu considered offensive*

1836 in 1868 McCall *Letters Frontiers* 298, The terrific yells and shouts of the maddened Texans carried fear to the hearts of their enemy . . the defeated and disorganized *"Greasers"*. **1887** *Amer. Field* 27.61/2, Nor do I wish to defend the swarthy, loud oathed, heavily armed "greaser" of Mexico and the Texan ranges. **1906** *DN* 3.139 **nwAR,** *Greaser* [grizə] *land*. . . New Mexico or any other region where "greasers" (Mexicans) live. **1913** *DN* 3.60 **NM,** *Greaser,* a low class Mexican. **1929** *AmSp* 5.58 **NE,** A Mexican "hand" is called a "greaser." **1940** (1942) Clark *Ox-Bow* 20 **NV,** Nobody, no matter how genially, was calling his neighbor an old horse thief, or a greaser, or a card sharp, or a liar, or anything that had moral implications. **1949** *PADS* 11.22 **CO,** *Greaser*. . . A Mexican. **1965–70** *DARE* (Qu. HH28, . . *Nicknames . . for people of foreign background . . Mexican*) 62 Infs, **scattered, but esp SW, CO,** Greaser. **1970** Tarpley *Blinky* 258 **neTX,** *Nicknames for Mexican People*. . . 25% [of 200 infs] *greasers*. **1971** Bright *Word Geog. CA & NV* 194, *Mexican*. . . *Greaser* [used by 23% of 300 infs]. **1986** Pederson *LAGS Concordance* **Gulf Region,** 21 infs, **scattered, but esp TX,** Greaser(s); 1 inf, **csTX,** Mexican greaser. [7 infs remark that the term is insulting or derogatory; 15 of 21 different infs have prones of the type ['grizɚ]; 6 infs have prones of the type ['grisɚ].]

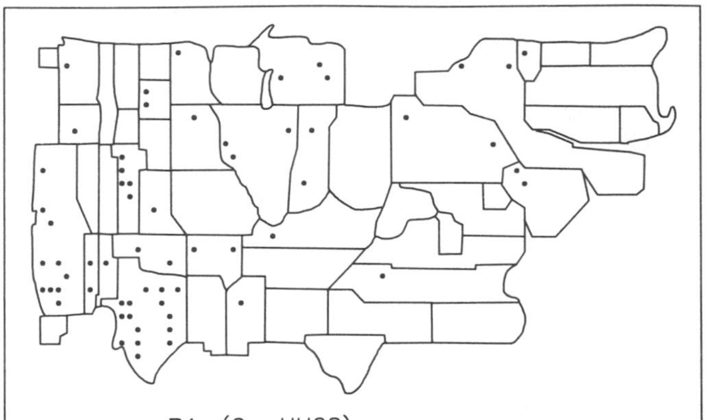

•greaser B1 (Qu. HH28)

2 A person of Mediterranean background. Cf **greaseball 1.**

1967–70 *DARE* (Qu. HH28, . . *Nicknames for people of foreign background*) Infs **MO**21, **MA**15, Greaser — Greek; **PA**94, Greaser — Italian.

3 =ruddy duck.

1888 Trumbull *Names of Birds* 112, At Havre de Grace, Md., Greaser, this being the commonest name here for the species [=*Oxyura jamaicensis*]. **1904** *Country Life* 5.254 **Chesapeake Bay MD,** In the past few years the diminutive "ruddy duck" known as "greaser" on the Flats, and below them as "coot," has deservedly come into great favor.

4 =cackling goose.

1923 U.S. Dept. Ag. *Misc. Circular* 13.37 **CA,** *Cackling Goose (Branta canadensis minima)* . . greaser. **1956** *AmSp* 31.180, The cackling goose . . is also dubbed *greaser;* this name has been recorded also for the ruddy duck (Md.), whether with the same significance is not known.

5 =yellow bullhead.

1908 Forbes–Richardson *Fishes of IL* 186, This fish [=*Ictalurus natalis*] is distinguished from the brown bullhead . . only by the more observant of our fishermen, some of whom call it "greaser." **1983** Becker *Fishes WI* 708, *Yellow Bullhead*. . . Other common names . . Mississippi bullhead, greaser.

6 A **cisco** (here: *Coregonus reighardi*).

1983 Becker *Fishes WI* 347, Shortnose Cisco. . . Other common names . . greaser (Lake Ontario).

7 A piece of salt pork used to oil a pan.

1923 [see **eat the greaser**]. **1939** [see **eat the greaser**].

8 See **grease v B3.**

greaser blackfish n

A cyprinid fish *(Orthodon microlepidotus)* native to California.

1957 Blair et al. *Vertebrates U.S.* 99, *Orthodon microlepidotus*. . . Greaser Blackfish. Kern River and Sacramento Basin; tributaries of Monterey and San Francisco Bays, California.

greaseroot See **greasewood 1**

grease spot n

Fig: a remnant; the smallest trace.

1829 in 1965 *AmSp* 40.129, I hit a man. . . dere was nothing left, Sept [sic] a little grease spot. **1841** in 1898 Griswold *Corresp.* 101, Aren't we horribly smashed up in this State? We haven't a grease-spot left — Assembly, Senate, Canal-Board, Appointments, all. **1908** *DN* 3.317 **ceAL, cwGA,** *Grease-spot*. . . Used facetiously in such expressions as 'to knock one into a grease-spot,' 'nothing left of him but a grease spot,' etc. **1911** Saunders *Col. Todhunter* 106 **MO,** There ain't goin' to be no more'n a grease-spot left of you if you keep on pesterin' old Mrs. Exall for her daughter. **c1960** *Wilson Coll.* **csKY,** *Grease spot*. . . A trace or evidence. "He didn't leave even a grease spot of that burglar." **1966**

Barnes-Jensen *Dict. UT Slang* 20, *Grease spot* . . trace. "He beat him so hard that he didn't leave a grease spot."

greaseswabber See **greaseball 2**

greasethorn See **greasebush 2**

greasetree See **greasewood 2h**

grease up v phr

Cheer up!—used in imper.

1967 *DARE* (Qu. GG27a, *To get somebody out of an unhappy mood, you might say to him, "Everything's going to be all right, so ______."*) Inf **OR**1, Grease up.

greaseweed n

1 The fourwing **saltbush** *(Atriplex canescens).*

1853 U.S. Army Corps Topog. Engineers *Rept. Sitgreaves* 34 **NM,** From El Paso, passing up the Rio Grande, along which stream the vegetation alters but little, the timber being principally . . the creosote plant, *(Larrea Mexicana,)* grease-weed, *(Obione canescens,)* . . and various specimens of artemisia and yucca.

2 A **lousewort** (here: *Pedicularis canadensis*).

1910 Graves *Flowering Plants* 357 **CT,** *Pedicularis canadensis.* . . Common Lousewort. . . Greaseweed.

greasewood n

1 also rarely *greaseplant, greaseroot:* Any of var sometimes resinous plants and shrubs of the West. Also called **greasebush 1** Note: These quots may refer specifically to senses below.

1838 in 1931 *Frontier* 11.285/2 **cWY,** Most of the country we have traveled since leaving Ft. Williams [=Fort Laramie] has been a sandy desert, bearing little but sedge and wormwood, flowers and grease wood. **1845** in 1906 Thwaites *Early W. Travels* 30.98 **ID,** Wild sage and grease wood [are] found in plenty. **1890** Custer *Following* 71 **KS,** The dull sage-brush, or grease-root, or the sparse buffalo-grass, were all that the sun spared from its scorching rays. **1891** (1958) Wister *Out West* 100, On the other side, a stretch of land, prickly-pears, grease plant, cans, here and there a cow's skull, would go down to the muddy, wrinkled river sliding quickly along, and barren bluffs beyond it. **1907** White *AZ Nights* 227, Tusky kep' the fire goin' and I rustled greasewood. **1927** Cather *Death Comes* 240 **NM,** Soon they left the wagon road and took a trail running straight south, through an empty greasewood country. **1968** *DARE* (Qu. T16) Inf **NV**8, Greasewood.

2 Spec:

a A more or less spiny shrub *(Sarcobatus vermiculatus)* native to much of the West. Also called **chico** **n**[1], **gray saltbush**

1847 J. Palmer *Rocky Mts.* 48 *(DAE),* Wild sage and grease wood [are] found in plenty. **1863** in 1876 MT Hist. Soc. *Contrib.* 1.178, Soil seems too sandy here for farming, and where it is not sand it is greasewood flats. **1894** Coulter *Botany W. TX* 365. **1906** Rydberg *Flora CO* 119, *Grease-wood.* . . In dry alkaline or saline soil from Neb. to Wash., Tex. and Calif. **1941** Writers' Program *Guide CO* 15, Gray saltbush, or chico-brush—[is] better known as greasewood. **1957** Jaeger *N. Amer. Deserts* 143, The true greasewood is a gray-green, succulent-leafed plant of saline moist soils, whereas the creosote bush is a brownish-green, thin-leafed plant of the lower, largely alkaline-free dry plains and mesas. **1967** *DARE* (Qu. T5, . . *Kinds of evergreens*) Infs **TX**10, 43, Greasewood. **1975** Zwinger *Run River* 98 **UT,** It is too alkaline for crops to grow in it; only greasewood bushes flourished. **1981** Benson-Darrow *Trees SW Deserts* 173, This [=*Sarcobatus vermiculatus*] is the true greasewood of the Great Basin, and it is not to be confused with the creosote bush to which the same common name sometimes is misapplied.

b also *greasebrush:* A **saltbush,** usu the fourwing **saltbush** *(Atriplex canescens).*

1846 in 1848 U.S. Congress *Serial Set* 517 Doc 41.434 **NM,** As there was no wood fit to burn, we were forced to use the grease brush; so the voyageurs call it on account of its burning with such a brilliant light. It is in truth the obione canescens. **1859** (1968) Bartlett *Americanisms* 179, *Grease wood.* (Obione canescens.) The chamizo of the Mexicans. **1872** Twain *Roughing It* 34 **West,** The sage-brush and its cousin the "grease-wood," which is so much like the sage-brush that the difference amounts to little. **1931** U.S. Dept. Ag. *Misc. Pub.* 101.34, *Fourwing saltbush (Atriplex canescens).* . . Other names in more or less common use are chamiza . . and (white) greasewood. **1937** U.S. Forest Serv. *Range Plant Hdbk.* B27, Other names sometimes applied to this well-known bush [=*Atriplex canescens*] include buckwheat shrub . . greasewood . . and wafer sagebrush. **1967** *DARE* Tape **OR**13, Yeah, [we have] lots of greasewood. . . It's kinda like a sagebrush, only different, kind of real green tops and black stalks. **1973** Hitchcock-Cronquist *Flora Pacific NW* 94, *Atriplex.* . . Greasewood.

c A **white sage** (here: *Salvia apiana*). **CA**

1894 *Jrl. Amer. Folkl.* 7.96 **sCA,** *Audibertia polystachya* . . greasewood. **1897** Parsons *Wild Flowers CA* 66, *Audibertia polystachya.* . . The plants cover extensive reaches of valley and hill-slopes, and are often called "greasewood." Certain it is that the white stems have a very greasy, gummy feel and a rank, aggressive odor. **1931** U.S. Dept. Ag. *Misc. Pub.* 101.141, *White sage (S[alvia] apiana . .)* known also as bee sage, greasewood, and white bee sage, is . . widespread. **1976** Bailey-Bailey *Hortus Third* 998, *S[alvia] apiana.* . . Greasewood.

d =**chamise 1. CA**

1897 Parsons *Wild Flowers CA* 60, Chamisal. Chamiso. Greasewood. *Adenostoma fasciculatum.* **1911** CA Ag. Exper. Sta. Berkeley *Bulletin* 217.993, Greasewood. Chamisal. Chamios [sic]. . . Eagerly visited by bees in Lake, Marin, Santa Barbara, and Ventura counties, and, no doubt, elsewhere. **1915** (1926) Armstrong-Thornber *Western Wild Flowers* 228, *Greasewood* . . is the most abundant and characteristic shrub of the higher Coast Ranges and Sierra Nevada Mountains. **1942** Hylander *Plant Life* 304, Greasewood or Chamise *(Adenostoma)* is another shrub of dry ridges and mesas of the California mountains; the . . leaves are sweet smelling and grouped in small clusters. **1976** Bailey-Bailey *Hortus Third* 26, *Greasewood.*

e =**pickleweed.**

1911 Jepson *Flora CA* 145, *S[pirostachys] occidentalis.* . . Kern Greasewood. . . Alkaline soil. **1960** Vines *Trees SW* 235, Pickleweed. *Allenrolfea occidentalis.* . . Also known by the vernacular names of Bush Pickleweed, Kern-greasewood, Iodine-bush.

f =**creosote bush. esp AZ**

1913 Wooton *Trees NM* 64, The name Greasewood is often mistakenly applied to a very different evergreen shrub, the Creosote Bush . . that grows on the mesas. **1920** Saunders *Useful Wild Plants* 202, An ill-smelling shrub of the Southwestern desert region [is] variously called Creosote bush, Greasewood (one of many Greasewoods, by the way) and, by its Spanish names, Gobernadora and Hediondilla. **1937** U.S. Forest Serv. *Range Plant Hdbk.* B67, Creosote, a shapely evergreen shrub, . . is known locally as gobernadora, greasewood, hediondilla, and numerous other common names referring to the strong, pungent odor or to the resinous properties of the plant. **1949** Curtin *By the Prophet* 62 **AZ,** On the Salt River Reservation members of the Women's Club call creosote "greasewood." **1973** *AZ Highways* 49.3.4, Waxy-leaved plants like the Creosote bush *(greasewood)* have a varnish-like, shiny coating which reflects heat. **1981** Benson-Darrow *Trees SW Deserts* 123, *Larrea tridentata.* . . In southern Arizona the commonly used name is "greasewood," applied to many plants. **1985** Dodge *Flowers SW Deserts* 76, Greasewood. . . Leaves . . are covered with a "varnish" which often glistens in the sunlight.

g A **bitterbrush 1** (here: *Purshia tridentata*).

1925 Jepson *Manual Plants CA* 504, *P[urshia] tridentata.* . . Antelope Brush. . . Also called Bitter-Brush, Greasewood (Lassen Co.) and Buckbrush (Modoc Co.)

h also *greasetree:* A **groundsel tree** (here: *Baccharis sarothroides*).

1931 U.S. Dept. Ag. *Misc. Pub.* 101.160, *Broom baccharis (B[accharis] sarothroides),* locally called greasewood and rosin brush, ranges from Lower California . . to southern California. **1960** Vines *Trees SW* 972, It [=*Baccharis sarothroides*] is also known under the vernacular names of Greasewood . . and Groundsel. **1969** *DARE* (Qu. T16) Inf **AZ**16, Greasetree.

i A **horsebrush 1** (here: *Tetradymia glabrata*).

1931 U.S. Dept. Ag. *Misc. Pub.* 101.176, Littleleaf horsebrush *(Tetradymia glabrata)* is a small-leaved, rather slender-branched shrub, known also as greasewood and spring rabbitbrush, . . ranging . . from Idaho to southeastern Oregon, California (east of the Sierras), and Utah.

j A **ceanothus:** either **snowbrush** or a **buckbrush 3c** (here: *Ceanothus cuneatus*).

1938 Van Dersal *Native Woody Plants* 337, Greasewood *(Adenostoma fasciculatum, Ceanothus velutinus, Covillea tridentata, Sarcobatus vermiculatus).* **1942** Stegner *Mormon Country* 122, There were dyeing vats for the coloring of cotton and wool cloth with home-made dyes like . . greasewood. **1967** Gilkey-Dennis *Hdbk. NW Plants* 254, *Ceanothus cuneatus.* . . *Greasewood. Buckbrush.* Shrub 1-4 m. tall, with stiff branches and branchlets. **1973** Stephens *Woody Plants* 374, *Ceanothus velutinus.* . . Sticky laurel, greasewood.

greasie See **greasy** n

greasy adj Cf Pronc Intro 3.I.15, **grease** v **A1**

A Forms. Note: While use of /s/ and /z/ shows regional patterning, analysis of *DARE* tapes also indicates that some Infs vary their use according to level of formality.

1 |'grisi|; pronc-sp *greecy*. **chiefly Nth, West** See Map

1896 [see **grease** v **A1**]. **1907** *DN* 3.189 **seNH,** *Greasy. . .* Pronounced greecy [grisi]. **1939** [see **A2** below]. **1961** Kurath–McDavid *Pronc. Engl.* 176, *Greasy. . .* Voiceless /s/ is nearly universal . . in New England and throughout the New England settlement area along the Great Lakes and in northern Pennsylvania. . . It predominates decisively . . in Eastern Pennsylvania . . but not in Philadelphia. **1965–70** *DARE* (Qu. D39, . . *A small eating place where the food is not especially good*) 219 Infs, **chiefly Nth, West,** Greasy ['grisi] spoon; 10 Infs, **chiefly Nth,** Greasy ['grisi] (bucket, kitchen, skillet, etc); **CT**9, Quick-and-greasy; (Qu. N22) 21 Infs, **chiefly Nth,** Greasy ['grisi].

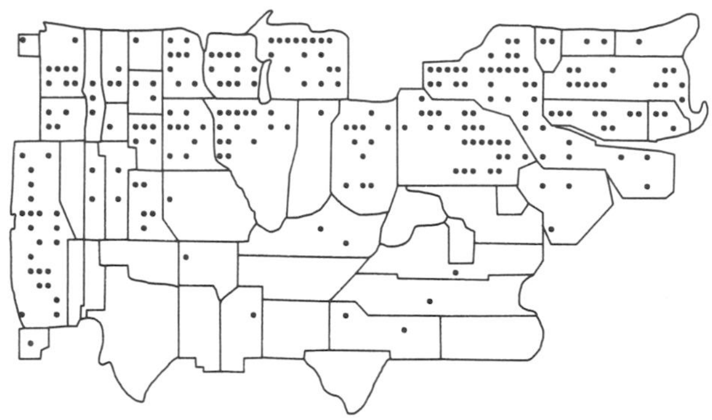

•greasy adj A1 + varr (Qq. D39, N22)

2 |'grizi|; pronc-sp *greazy*. **chiefly Sth, Midl** See Map

1896 [see **grease** v **A1**]. **1903** *DN* 2.315 **seMO,** *Greasy. . .* Pronounced greazy [grizi]. **1907** *DN* 3.231 **nwAR, seMO,** *Greasy. . .* Pronounced . . [grizi]. **1908** *DN* 3.317 **eAL, wGA,** *Greasy. . .* Universally pronounced [grizi]. **1939** *LANE* Map 188, [Proncs of the type ['grisɪ] prevail **throughout NEng;** 14 infs, 13 **MA, CT, RI,** offered proncs of the type ['grizɪ]. Two of these indicated that they did not use this form themselves and two that it was an acquired form; one inf commented that "[grizɪ] implies more greasiness than [grisɪ]."] **1961** Kurath–McDavid *Pronc. Engl.* 176, *Greasy. . .* Voiced /z/ . . is in universal use throughout the South and South Midland . . ; predominates decisively in Metropolitan New York . . and in New Jersey . . ; and . . is in exclusive use in southwestern and southcentral Pennsylvania and predominates in the southern two-thirds of Ohio. **1965–70** *DARE* (Qu. D39, . . *A small eating place where the food is not especially good*) 157 Infs, **chiefly Sth, Midl,** Greasy ['grizi] spoon; 10 Infs, **chiefly Sth, Midl,** Greasy ['grizi] (joint, kitchen, skillet, etc); (Qu. N22) Infs **CT**23, **IL**62, 66, **KY**6, **MD**20, **NJ**12, **OH**44, **PA**74, 235, **TN**11, Greasy ['grizi]; (Qu. I20) Infs **KY**28, **VA**2, Greasy ['grizi] beans; **KY**34, Greasy ['grizi] grits. **1967–70** *DARE* Tape **GA**30, You just pull them leaves off o' there and if your hands is not greasy [grizi], now it won't cut grease [gris]; **IN**3, **TX**40, 81, ['grizi]. **1973** *PADS* 60.59 **seNC,** *Greasy. . .* All of our informants used /z/. **1976** Allen *LAUM* 3.323 (as of c1950), In the U[pper] M[idwest], however, this voiced variant [=/grizi/] seems to be recessive, since it is not used by all Midland-type speakers. Except for three instances in Minnesota, most examples of [z] and [s̬] are in southern Iowa and eastern Nebraska.

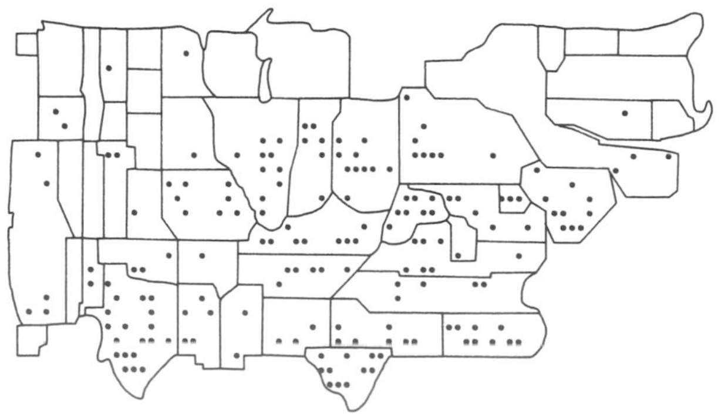

•greasy adj A2 + varr (Qq. D39, N22, I20)

B Sense.

Slippery, slick. **chiefly Nth, N Midl** See Map

1965–70 *DARE* (Qu. N22, *When a road that is surfaced with smooth pavement gets wet so that cars slip or skid on it, you say it's* ______) 31 Infs, **chiefly Nth, N Midl,** Greasy. **1971** WI Statist. Reporting Serv. *Report* 10 May, Just enough rain to keep fields greasy. **1972** *PADS* 58.24 **cwAL,** *The road is slippery. Slippery . .* and *slick . .* are most frequent. Three Negro informants gave *slippy* and one Negro informant gave *greasy.* **1973** Allen *LAUM* 1.399 **neIA, nMN** (as of c1950), The road was *slippery. . .* Two write-in instances of *greasy* occur. **1982** *Barrick Coll.* **csPA,** *Greasy . . slippery; oily.* "The road's a little greasy."

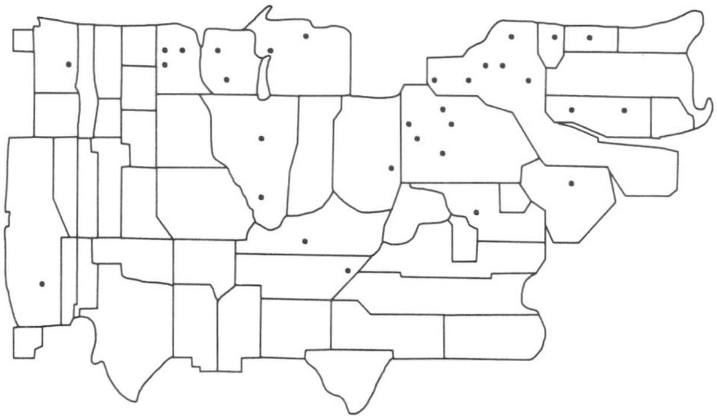

•greasy adj B (Qu. N22)

greasy n Also sp *greasie*

‡1 A rustic, "hick." Cf **greaser B1** and *DS* HH1

1967 LeCompte *Word Atlas* 257 **seLA,** Somebody from the country who doesn't know much . . Greasie. [1 of 21 infs]

‡2 =**boogerman 1.**

1970 *DARE* (Qu. EE41, *A hobgoblin that is used to threaten children and make them behave*) Inf **TN**46, Big-bad, green man, greasy.

3 See **greasy bean.**

greasy bacon n Cf **slippery mullein**

The moth **mullein** *(Verbascum blattaria).*

1940 Clute *Amer. Plant Names* 274, *Verbascum blattaria.* Greasy bacon.

greasy bean n Also *greasy (grits)* **esp S Midl**

A cultivated bean (*Phaseolus vulgaris* var).

1967–69 *DARE* (Qu. I20) Inf **KY**28, White stick beans—greasy ['grizi] beans; **VA**2, Greasy ['grizi] beans; **KY**34, Greasy ['grizi] grits or self-greasers. **1978** *Wanigan Catalog* 10, *Greasy*—P[ole bean]—The very fine velvet coat is absent from these round, green pods. . . White seed dries very late here [=Massachusetts]. *Greasy grits*—P[ole bean]—Similar seed size and color, but an earlier bearer than Greasy. Pods are longer, 5″, shiney [sic] green. **1985** *Seed Savers Exchange* Winter 69 **AR,** Bean/Pole/Snap: *Greasy . .* strong climber, . . pod has heavy strings but good flavor, been in Ozark Mountains since before Civil War. *Ibid* 129 **KY,** *Greasy, Brown Speckled . .* excel[lent] snapped or shelled dry . . *Greasy, White . .* same as Brown Speckled Greasy Bean except for seed color. *Ibid* 169 **NE,** *Greasy*—pods have a shiny surface giving it the name Greasy. *Ibid* 187 **OH,** All Greasies have strings. . . Greasy beans are a favorite of my Appalachian friends. *Ibid* 190 **OH,** *Greasy Grit, Blue . . Greasy Grit, White. Ibid* 228 **WV,** *Greasy, Brown Seeded . . Greasy, White.*

greasy corner n Also *greasy valley*

A poor settlement or neighborhood.

1966–68 *DARE* (Qu. C34, *Nicknames for nearby settlements, villages, or districts*) Inf **AR**39, Greasy valley; (Qu. C35, *Nicknames for the different parts of your town or city*) Inf **NC**48, Greasy corner (colored town); **NC**52, Greasy ['grizi] corner; (Qu. II25, *Names or nicknames for the part of a town where the poorer people . . live*) Inf **NC**52, Greasy ['grizi] corner—negroes and low whites.

greasy cutworm n [See quot 1926]
The larva of a phalaenid moth *(Agrotis ipsilon).*
1869 MO State Entomol. *Annual Rept.* 80, The Greasy Cut-Worm. . . In the *Prairie Farmer* for June 22, 1867, I described a large cut-worm under the name of the "Black cut-worm." I have since . . concluded to give it the above appellation. **1905** Kellogg *Amer. Insects* 402, The greasy cutworm . . is the larva of *Agrotis ypsilon.* **1926** Essig *Insects N. Amer.* 683, The greasy cutworm, *Agrotis ypsilon. . .* The caterpillars are dull brown to nearly black. . . The whole surface is shiny and greasy in appearance. **1967** *DARE* (Qu. R27) Inf **HI**14, Greasy cutworm. **1972** Swan–Papp *Insects* 277, Black Cutworm: *Agrotis ipsilon. . .* Sometimes called greasy cutworm.

greasy door n
See quots.
1972 Cooper *NC Mt. Folkl.* 92, *Greasy doors*—doors of a family who have recently slaughtered hogs. **1984** Wilder *You All Spoken Here* 146 **Sth,** *Greasy door family:* One that's just killed hogs.

greasy grits See **greasy bean**

greasy kitchen See **greasy spoon**

greasy lamp See **grease lamp**

greasy luck exclam [In ref to whalers' quest for oil] Also *greasy voyage* **chiefly sNEng coast**
Farewell, bon voyage!
1916 Macy–Hussey *Nantucket Scrap Basket* 133, "Greasy Luck"—To wish a whaleman greasy luck meant to wish him a good voyage, with plenty of oil; hence the Nantucketer uses it in well-wishes to his friends in any proposed venture. To say on parting, "Well, greasy luck to you!" is to say "bon voyage!" **1925** in 1938 Tripp *Flukes* 174 **seMA,** After wishing us "Greasy Luck," the sloop returned to the City. *Ibid* 183, The tug dropped the *Manta,* after giving us a salute of three loud blasts from the whistle, and a wish of a "Greasy Voyage," from her captain. **1945** Colcord *Sea Language* 89 **ME, Cape Cod, Long Island,** *Greasy luck.* The whaleman's farewell, used in whaling communities whenever one would say "Good luck!"

greasy-sack n attrib **West**
Of a ranching outfit or activity: having no chuck wagon; by ext, poor, second-rate.
1942 Berrey–Van den Bark *Amer. Slang* 913.13, *Cowboy "outfit." . . Greasy-sack outfit,* one which packs its commissary in a sack upon the back of a mule or pack-horse. **1944** Adams *Western Words* 68, *Greasy-sack outfit*—A small ranch outfit which carries its commissary pack in a sack on a mule in lieu of a chuck wagon. *Greasy-sack ride*—When a group of riders are sent, without a chuck wagon, to scour the rough country for cattle, they carry their food in small cotton bags, and these trips are called *greasy-sack* rides. **1965** *DARE* FW Addit **NM**13, Greasy-sack outfit . . a group of cowboys working without a chuck wagon—had to pack everything on horses in rawhide pack boxes.

greasy spoon n Also *greasy kitchen, ~ skillet;* for addit varr see quot 1965–70 Also called **grease pot**
A small, cheap restaurant that usually serves food of poor quality.
1925 *Writer's Monthly* June 486/2 *(OEDS), Greasy spoon,* a low-class restaurant. **1938** Hertzler *Horse & Buggy Dr.* 145 **KS,** Clarence began to take his nourishment at the Greasy Spoon, the well-known emporium specializing in home cooking, even though it were not so bad as all that. **1961** (1962) Griffin *Black Like Me* 97 **TX,** All the honors in the world cannot buy them a cup of coffee in the lowest greasy-spoon joint. **1965–70** *DARE* (Qu. D39, . . *A small eating place where the food is not especially good*) 370 Infs, **widespread,** Greasy spoon; **CO**47, Greasy bucket; **WI**23, Greasy house; **NY**52, Greasy Joe; **NM**1, **NY**210, **TX**27, Greasy kitchen; **SC**32, Greasy rag; **CA**156, **IL**102, **NY**88, Greasy skillet; **IL**27, Greasy thumb; **NJ**25, **NY**49, Greasy vest. **c1974** Jones *Ozark Hill Boy* 35 **AR** (as of c1930), The often heard expression of the "greasy spoon" café operator was—"I wouldn't feed anybody anything I wouldn't eat myself." **1990** *WI State Jrl.* (Madison) 29 Apr 3E, [Headline:] Greasy spoons can't spoil the fish.

greasy valley See **greasy corner**

greasy voyage See **greasy luck**

great adj, adv, n Usu |gre(ɪ)t|; also **chiefly Sth, S Midl, occas NEng** |grɛt| Pronc-spp *gred, gret(t)*
A Forms.
1797 in 1956 Eliason *Tarheel Talk* 311 **cnNC,** Gret. **1848** Lowell *Biglow* 144 **'Upcountry' MA,** Gret, *great.* **1861** Holmes *Venner* 2.175 **NEng,** Th' ol' Doctor, he's got a gre't cur'osity t' see ye. **1884** *Anglia* 7.258 **Sth, S Midl** [Black], Er gred big buster. **1899** (1912) Green *VA Folk-Speech* 206, *Gret. . .* For *great. Gret*-house. **1931** *AmSp* 6.167 **seVA,** The vowel [e] appears often without diphthongal character . . as in *make, great. . .* Sometimes the effect is that of [ɛ]. **1931** Faulkner *Sanctuary* 40 **MS,** The platform was deserted save for a negro with a broom. "Gret Gawd, white folks," he said. **1939** *LANE* Map 50–51, 1 inf, **ceVT,** [grɛt]. *Ibid* Map 102, 1 inf, **cMA,** [grɛ˘ət] beams; 2 infs, **eLong Is. NY,** [grɛt] beams. **1944** *PADS* 2.15 **neMS, NC, nSC, cTN, VA,** *Great* [grɛt] (at least when followed by *big*). **1949** Kurath *Word Geog.* 54 **cMA, eLong Is. NY,** *Great-beams* (pronounced *grett-beams*). **1976** Ryland *Richmond Co. VA* 371, *Gret*—great.
B As noun.
1 usu in neg constrs: A large amount, great deal. *arch*
1724 in 1900 Essex Inst. *Coll.* 36.337 **MA,** Mackey's Sloop Sunk at Boston & Spoild a great of our English Goods. **1861** Holmes *Venner* 2.186 **wMA,** The' was some things on the hoss, Squire, that the man he ketched said he didn' care no gre't abaout. **1884** Baldwin *Yankee School-Teacher* 125 **VA,** You know I don't think no gre't of doctors in general. *Ibid* 166, Wall, I didn't see him no gre't, but I knew I *could* 'thout takin' much trouble.
2 in phr *no great of:* No outstanding example of.
1865 (1889) Whitney *Gayworthys* 9 **ceMA,** She made "no great of a match." **1877** Jewett *Deephaven* 48 **ME,** She never was no great of a mouser. **1901** *Harper's Mth. Mag.* 104.47/1 **ME,** They've got a story up our way that poor Mis' Dennett ain't no gre't of a housekeeper. **1914** *DN* 4.77 **ME, nNH,** *No gret of a. . .* Not much of a. "He wa'n't no gret of a hand to wuk."
3 A great-grandchild. Cf **grand**
1955 Ritchie *Singing Family* 249 **seKY,** I growed up ignorant and mean; my offsprings was wuss; my grands is wusser, squandering their time drinking and shooting; and what my greats will be if something hain't done to stop the meanness of their maneuvers, God only knows!

great albacore n
=**bluefin 2.**
1896 U.S. Natl. Museum *Bulletin* 47.870, *Thunnus Thynnus. . .* Tunny. . . Great Albacore. **1946** LaMonte *N. Amer. Game Fishes* 22, *Bluefin Tuna. . .* Great Albacore.

great bat n [See quot 1955 *Oriole*]
=**chuck-will's-widow.**
1791 Bartram *Travels* 292, Caprimulgus lucifugus, the great bat, or chuck wills widow. **1917** (1923) *Birds Amer.* 2.166, *Chuck-Will's-Widow—Antrostomus carolinensis. . .* The Great Bat. **1946** Hausman *Eastern Birds* 370, *Chuck-Will's-Widow—Antrostomus carolinensis. . .* Great Bat, Bat Bird. **1955** *Oriole* 20.9, *Chuck-Wills-Widow. . . Great Bat* ("bat" from its nocturnal habits[)]; "great" to distinguish it from the Virginia bat (whippoorwill) and bullbat (nighthawk). **1955** *AmSp* 30.179 **GA, LA, VA,** The partially nocturnal activity . . is the significance of *bat-* cognomens of the chuck-will's-widow. . . *Great bat* . . has been recorded for it in Virginia, Georgia, and Louisiana.

great beam n, usu pl **esp NEng** Cf *DS* M3
=**high beam 1.**
1939 *LANE* Map 102 *(Loft; scaffold)* **scattered cMA, cNH, eLong Is. NY,** Great beam(s). **1949** Kurath *Word Geog.* 54, In Worcester County, Massachusetts, and in the Upper Connecticut Valley a platform right under the sloping sides of the roof is called the *high-beams,* less commonly the *great-beams* (pronounced *grett-beams*). *Great-beams* occurs also on the southeastern prong of Long Island. **1967** Faries *Word Geog. MO* 75 **MO,** To denote the space for hay in the upper part of a barn. . . There is one instance of . . *great-beams* [among 700 infs].

great black-backed gull n Also *blackback, black-backed gull*
Std: a large gull *(Larus marinus)* of the northeast Atlantic coast. Also called **black minister, cobb** n², **coffin-carrier, Daniel gull, dung-hunter, eagle gull, ghost bird 3, gray gull 2, minister, saddleback gull, turkey gull, winter gull**

great blue heron n Cf **great white heron 2**
Std: a large grayish-blue heron *(Ardea herodias)* common throughout much of the US. Also called **Benson's turkey, big crane, blue crane 1, blue herring** n², **Colorado turkey 2, crane 2, cranky** n, **cream-shitter, fish crane, forty-gallons-of-soup, frog-**

stabber 1, gander snipe, gopher crane, gum coat, han n[1], horse gannet, jim, John Henry, kelp heron, long Tom, lopann, major, old hand, poor Job, poor joe, preacher, red-shouldered heron, sandhill crane, shit-a-quart, shitepoke

great blue pike See **great pike**

great Carolina wren See **Carolina wren**

great day (in the morning) exclam Also *great dane;* for addit varr see quots [In ref to Judgment Day] **widespread, but chiefly Sth, Midl** See Map

Used as an exclam of surprise, annoyance, etc.

1914 *DN* 4.159 **cVA,** *Great dane a mawnin!* . . Goodness gracious (great-day-in-the-morning). Sometimes shortened to "great dane!" **1932** (1974) Caldwell *Tobacco Road* 100 **GA,** Just look at that shiny black paint! Great-day-in-the-morning! **1940** *Qrly. Jrl. Speech* 26.265 **VA,** A very common ejaculation of surprise is "Great day in the morning!" **1955** Stong *Blizzard* 58 **IA,** "Great day in the morning," said Abe—good clean words. **1959** McAtee *Oddments* 6 **cNC,** *Great Day, in the morning:* (i.e. early on Judgment Day), interj. of pleased surprise. **1965–70** *DARE* (Qu. NN29a, *Exclamations beginning with 'great': "Great ______!"*) 166 Infs, **widespread, but chiefly Sth, Midl,** Day in the morning; 75 Infs, **scattered, but chiefly Sth, Midl,** Day; **CA**1, **GA**84, **IN**61, **MN**42, **NC**52, **NY**157, **OH**21, 89, Days; **MN**34, **MS**1, Days in the morning; **MA**4, Dane [deɪn]; (Qu. NN6a) Infs **GA**1, 72, Great day in the morning; (Qu. NN7) Infs **MD**37, **VA**80, Great day (in the morning); (Qu. NN9a) Infs **KY**92, **NC**61, Great day; (Qu. NN20b) Inf **PA**35, Great day; (Qu. NN21a) Inf **MS**86, Great day; (Qu. NN30) Inf **MO**11, Great day. **1968** *DARE* FW Addit **NC,** Great day, he was a big fella! **1972** Cooper *NC Mt. Folkl.* 91, Great day in the morning!

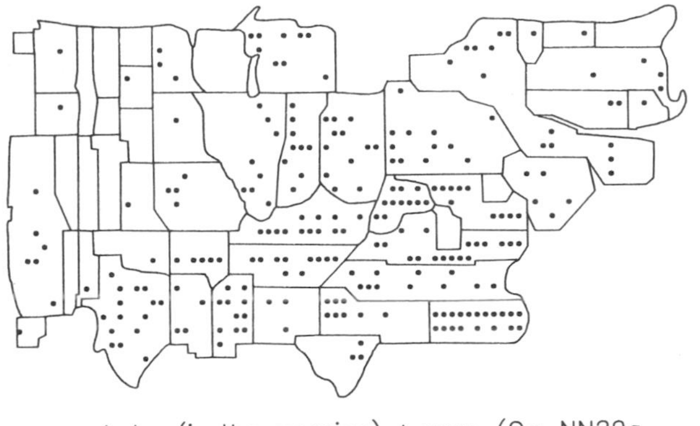

•great day (in the morning) + varr (Qq. NN29a, NN6a, NN7, NN9a, NN20b, NN21a, NN30)

great divide See **divide 2**

great doin's See **doing 4**

greater scaup n

Std: a **scaup** (here: *Aythya marila*). Also called **big winnebago, blackhead 1, blackjack 1a, blackneck a, bluebill, broadbill 1, bullhead 2c, bullneck 1, canvasback bluebill, coldshin, dogs, dos gris, floating fowl, flock duck, grayback 1d, greenhead 4a(2), laker, mussel duck, nun, oyster scaup, polridge, quinder, raft duck, sea duck, shuffler, troop fowl, widgeon, winter duck**

great-footed hawk n Also *great-footed falcon*

=duck hawk.

1814 Wilson *Amer. Ornith.* 9.120, Great-Footed Hawk. *Falco Peregrinus* . . was described as darting with the rapidity of an arrow on the ducks when on the wing, and striking them down. **1844** Giraud *Birds Long Is.* 15, The Great-footed Hawk is said to inhabit the North American continent, from one extremity to the other—as well as the continent of Europe. **1895** Minot *Land-Birds New Engl.* 362, *Great-footed Hawk.* Very rare in Massachusetts, though known to have bred on Mount Tom, near Springfield. **1917** (1923) *Birds Amer.* 2.87, *Duck Hawk. . . Other Names. . .* Great-footed Hawk. **1953** Jewett *Birds WA* 185, *Falco peregrinus anatum. . .* Great-footed Falcon; Duck Hawk.

great fork-tail(ed) cat See **forktail catfish 1**

great gar n

The **alligator gar** or the **longnose gar.**

1896 U.S. Natl. Museum *Bulletin* 47.111, *Lepisosteus tristoechus. . . Alligator Gar; Great Gar. . .* A huge, muscular, voracious fish, useless as food, remarkable for its armature of enameled scales. **1973** Knight *Cook's Fish Guide* 381, Gar . . great—Alligator; Longnose.

‡great gingo exclam

1916 *DN* 4.342 **seOH,** *Great Gingo!* An ejaculation.

great god n Also *great god woodpecker* Cf **good god 1, lord god**

=pileated woodpecker.

1917 (1923) *Birds Amer.* 2.154, *Pileated Woodpecker. . . Other Names. . .* Great God Woodpecker. **1930** OK Univ. Biol. Surv. *Pub.* 2.138, *Pileated Woodpecker. . .* In McCurtain and Choctaw counties it is often referred to as a great god, good god, or lord god. **1945** McAtee *Nomina Abitera* 46, This bird's [=the pileated woodpecker's] roll of godly titles . . is as follows: . . great God (North Carolina), great God woodpecker . . (Georgia, Louisiana). **1951** *AmSp* 26.93 **AL, MS, NC, OK,** Pileated woodpecker. . . *great god.*

great gray owl n

A large owl *(Strix nebulosa)* native to the northern United States. Also called **spruce owl**

1832 Nuttall *Manual Ornith.* 1.128, *Great Grey . . Owl. . .* This is the largest American species known. **1895** Minot *Land-Birds New Engl.* 344, The Great Gray Owls exceed in size all other American species and stand no less than two feet high. **1927** Forbush *Birds MA* 2.208, The Great Gray Owl frequents the woods, and often watches for its prey from a tall tree. **1966–69** *DARE* (Qu. Q2, . . *Kinds of owls*) Infs **CA**115, **MI**2, 42, 53, Great gray owl. **1977** Bull–Farrand *Audubon Field Guide Birds* 678, *Great Gray Owl. . .* A huge, dusky gray, earless owl of the north woods with large facial disks and distinctive black chin spot.

great guns exclam For varr see quots *euphem* **widespread, but more freq Nth, N Midl** See Map

Used as an expression of surprise, annoyance, etc.

1875 Landon *Eli Perkins* 181, "Great guns!" interrupted the South Carolinian. **1885** Twain *Huck. Finn* 106 **MO,** Great guns! is *he* her uncle? **1908** *DN* 3.317 **eAL, wGA,** *Great guns.* **1917** *DN* 4.393 **neOH,** *Great guns and little gunner!* . . Not frequent. **1942** McAtee *Dial. Grant Co. IN* 31 (as of 1890s), *Great guns* . . exclamation of surprise or consternation. **1956** McAtee *Some Dialect NC* 20, *Great Guns!* **1959** *VT Hist.* new ser 27.139, *Great Guns!* . . Occasional. *Great guns and little fishes!* . . Rare. **1965–70** *DARE* (Qu. NN29a, *Exclamations beginning with 'great': "Great ______!"*) 255 Infs, **widespread, but more freq Nth, N Midl,** Guns; **ID**5, **MS**73, **TX**20, Guns and little fishes; **KY**72, Guns in the morning; **VA**34, Guns alive; (Qu. NN8a) Inf **NM**9, Great guns; (Qu. NN30) Inf **CA**110, Great guns. **1966** Barnes–Jensen *Dict. UT Slang* 20, *Great Guns* . . an exclamation of consternation. "Great guns, what can we do to get out of this swamp?" **1983–85** *DARE* File **GA,** Great guns and little pistols: it voices astonishment in Georgia; **ceWI,** Great guns and little fishes!

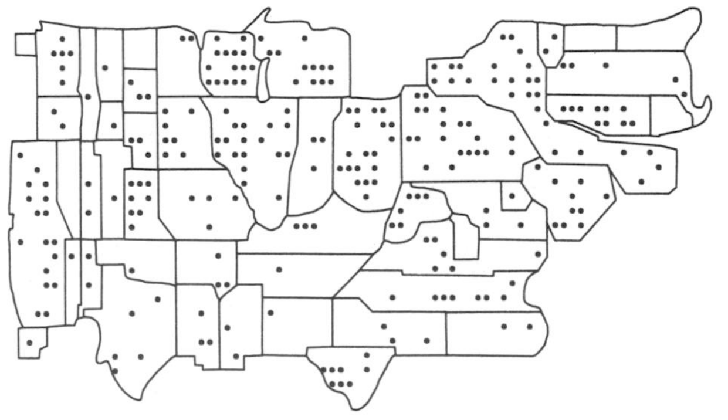

•great guns + varr (Qq. NN29a, NN8a, NN30)

great han See **han n[1]**

greathead n [See quot 1844]

=goldeneye 1.

1844 Giraud *Birds Long Is.* 334 **seNY,** *Golden-Eye. . .* By some it is called "Great Head," from its beautiful, rich, and thickly-crested head. **1888** Trumbull *Names of Birds* 79, *Golden-eye. . .* At Seaford (Hempstead), L[ong] I[sland], *Great-head.* **1898** (1900) Davie *Nests N. Amer.*

Birds 88, The American Golden-eye, . . or "Great-Head," . . has a large round white spot before the eye. **1925** (1928) Forbush *Birds MA* 1.246, *Glaucionetta clangula americana*. . . Great-head. **1955** MA Audubon Soc. *Bulletin* 39.316, *American Goldeneye*. . . Great-head (Mass. The head is puffy with feathers.)

great horned owl n [See quot 1938]

A large owl *(Bubo virginianus)* with prominent ear tufts. Also called **cat owl, chicken owl, cuckatoo owl, gray owl 1, higguhrihee, hoo-owl, hoot owl 1, horned owl, king owl, panther owl, skunk owl, tugadoo, Virginia owl**

1812 Wilson *Amer. Ornith.* 6.54, The priests, or conjurers, among some of our Indian nations, have taken advantage of the reverential horror for this bird, and have adopted the *Great Horned Owl* . . as the symbol . . of their office. **1844** DeKay *Zool. NY* 2.24, *The Great Horned Owl* . . is one of the largest of our Owls, and its aspect and dismal tones struck terror into the breasts of our early colonists. **1895** U.S. Dept. Ag. *Yearbook for 1894* 229, One or other of the races of the large and handsome *great horned owl* is found throughout the United States where suitable timber exists for its habitation. **1917** (1923) *Birds Amer.* 2.114, Persons often confuse . . the Great Horned Owl and the Barred Owl, though there is a marked difference between the hoots of these two birds. **1938** Oberholser *Bird Life LA* 334, *Bubo virginianus virginianus* . . may be distinguished from the Barred Owl by the two very prominent so-called ear tufts, from which its name 'Great Horned Owl' has arisen. **1966–70** *DARE* (Qu. Q2, . . *Kinds of owls*) 35 Infs, **scattered,** Great horned owl. **1977** Bull–Farrand *Audubon Field Guide Birds* 677, The Great Horned Owl preys on a wide variety of creatures including grouse and rabbits as well as beetles, lizards, and frogs.

great horned toads exclam For varr see quots

=**great guns.**

1959 *VT Hist.* new ser 27.139, *Great horned toads!* . . Rare. **1966–68** *DARE* (Qu. NN29a, *Exclamations beginning with 'great': "Great ______!"*) Infs **WA**1, 28, Horn toads; **MI**67, Flying horn toads; **PA**94, Horny toads.

great horn spoon, by the See **horn spoon 2**

great house n **esp VA**

=**big house 1.**

1633 in 1867 NH *Prov. & State Papers* 31.77, *In the Great House.* 3 ruggs and 2 pentadoes. **1773** (1957) Fithian *Jrl. & Letters* 32 **ceVA,** I have to myself in the Evening, a neat Chamber, a large Fire, Books, . . and my Liberty . . to sit over at the great House with Mr. & Mrs. Carter. **1849** *S. Lit. Messenger* 15.71/2 **VA** [Black], I can get one of the children to carry them up to the great house. **1899** (1912) Green *VA Folk-Speech* 205, *Great-house*. . . A house of the better class; generally the master's distinguished from the negroes' houses. **1939** FWP *These are Our Lives* 29 **VA,** De Yankees broke in de smokehouse, brought big middlin's o' meat in de great-house, and throwed 'em on de fire whole. **1976** Ryland *Richmond Co. VA* 371, *Great-house*—planter's house or mansion.

great I-am See **I-am**

Great Lake(s) pike n

=**northern pike.**

1884 Goode *Fisheries U.S.* 1.462, It [=*Esox lucius*] is sometimes known as the "Great Lake Pike." **1902** Jordan–Evermann *Amer. Fishes* 236, *Great Lakes Pike* . . is found from New York and the Ohio River northward. **1911** *Century Dict. Suppl., Pike*. . . *Great Lakes pike,* the common pike. **1946** LaMonte *N. Amer. Game Fishes* 126, *Esox lucius*. . . *Names* . . Great Lakes Pike.

Great Lake(s) trout n

=**lake trout.**

1882 U.S. Natl. Museum *Bulletin* 16.317, *S[alvelinus] namaycush*. . . *Great Lake Trout*. . . Great Lake region and lakes of Northern New York, New Hampshire, and Maine, to Montana and northward. **1904** *Salmon & Trout* 286, This charr . . is, in addition to the name of Great Lake trout, called Mackinaw trout in the region of the Great Lakes. **1911** U.S. Bur. Census *Fisheries 1908* 317, *Trout*.—A common name given to . . the genus *Cristivomer* or Great Lakes trout. **1933** John G. Shedd Aquarium *Guide* 38, The Great Lake Trout differs from the Charrs in that the spots on the body are gray instead of red. **1946** LaMonte *N. Amer. Game Fishes* 115, *Lake Trout*. . . *Names:* Great Lake Trout [etc]. **1983** Becker *Fishes WI* 323, Great Lakes trout.

great laurel n

A **rosebay** (here: *Rhododendron maximum*).

1784 in 1785 Amer. Acad. Arts & Sci. *Memoirs* 1.442, *Great Laurel. Wintergreen*. . . The Indians are said to have made small dishes, spoons, and other utensils, out of the roots. They are sometimes employed by people in the country for similar purposes. **1848** Gray *Manual of Botany* 269, *R[hododendron] maximum*. . . Great Laurel. **1898** Sudworth *Forest Trees* 102 **MA, MN, NH, NJ, NY, NC, PA, RI,** *Rhododendron maximum*. . . Great Laurel. **1950** Peattie *Nat. Hist. Trees* 517, *Rhododendron maximum*. . . Great Laurel. **1976** Bailey–Bailey *Hortus Third* 959, *Rhododendron* . . *maximum*. . . Great Laurel, Rosebay.

great long adj phr **chiefly S Midl**

Very long.

1912 Green *VA Folk-Speech* 205, *Great long*. . . Very long: "The foot-bridge was made over the creek with two great long logs." **1942** McAtee *Dial. Grant Co. IN* 31 (as of 1890s), *Great* . . very; "a great long log". Slang. **1953** *Hall Coll.* **wNC,** So he set there and told a great long story about what he done trapping and how many bears he killed in one season. **1956** McAtee *Some Dialect NC* 20. **1969** *DARE* FW Addit **ceNC,** A great long arm.

great norther(n) See **great northern bean**

great northern See **great northern pike 1**

great northern bean n Also *great norther,* ~ *northern(er),* ~ *northern white bean* **scattered, but esp Sth, Midl** Also called **forty-four, navy bean, poster**

A white dry bean (*Phaseolus vulgaris* cultivar).

1954 *Harder Coll.* **cwTN,** Beans that are white when they dry; also known as *great northerners, navy beans, forty-fours, posters.* **1965–70** *DARE* (Qu. I18, *The smaller beans that are white when they are dry*) 32 Infs, **scattered, but esp Sth, Midl,** Great northern beans; **AR**51, **FL**37, **GA**23, Great northerns; (Qu. I20, *Other kinds of beans* . . *around here*) Infs **CO**3, **FL**31, **GA**79, **IL**26, **KY**37, **NY**28, **VA**40, Great northern beans; **OK**49, Great northern white beans; **AR**55, **MI**88, Great northerns; **TN**20, Great northers. **1976** Olds Seed Co. *Seeds* 6, *Olds' Field Beans*. . . *Great Northern*. . . It will cook in two-thirds the time required for navy beans and has a much better flavor. **1982** Gurney Seed & Nursery *Spring Catalog* 6, *Soup Beans*. . . *Great Northern*. . . A large white bean excellent for baking and cooking. Makes great Boston baked beans. **1986** *Seed Savers Exchange* Harvest Ed. 180 **ND** (as of late 1880s), The tried-and-true [Oscar H.] Will introductions [included] . . the Great Northern bean, a gift from Hidatsa Indian Son-of-Star.

great northern diver n **chiefly N Atl, esp NY**

The common **loon** *(Gavia immer).*

1814 Wilson *Amer. Ornith.* 9.84 **N and C Atl,** Great Northern Diver, or Loon: *Colymbus glacialis* . . is said to be restless before a storm. **1844** Giraud *Birds Long Is.* 378 **seNY,** The Great Northern Diver or Loon, as it is termed by the gunners, seldom associates in flocks. **1857** Hammond *Wild N. Scenes* 142 **nNY,** We passed through these [=ponds], in which there were several loons, or great northern divers, quietly floating. **1869** Murray *Adventures* 101 **nNY,** The agile bird,—well named the Great Northern Diver,—ever on the alert, had gone under with the flash. **1898** (1900) Davie *Nests N. Amer. Birds* 6, The present species is known as the Great Northern Diver. **1917** (1923) *Birds Amer.* 1.12, Loon—*Gavia immer*. . . Great Northern Diver. **1968** *DARE* FW Addit **ceNY,** The great northern diver is the loon.

great northerner See **great northern bean**

great northern pike n

1 also *great northern (pickerel):* =**northern pike.**

1856 *Spirit of Times* 29 Nov 209/2, This great and noble pike—superior in whiteness, firmness, and delicacy of flesh to the yet larger mascalonge—has recently . . received a new and more distinctive name—*Borealis,* or northern. . . In the great northern pike, the lower jaw is nearly straight. **1927** Weed *Pike* 43, *Esox lucius*. . . Great Northern Pickerel; northern North America. . . Great Northern Pike; Wisconsin. **1943** Eddy–Surber *N. Fishes* 168, In Minnesota and parts of Wisconsin the northern pike is often called "pickerel" or "great northern pike." **1956** Harlan–Speaker *IA Fish* 64, *Esox lucius* . . *Other Names*—Common pike, great northern pike. **1972** Sparano *Outdoors Encycl.* 367, *Northern Pike. Common Names* . . great northern. **1978** *AK Fishing Guide* 77, *Great Northern Pike*. . . *Esox lucius* is the only member of its family found in Alaska—the pickerel and muskellunge are absent.

1983 Becker *Fishes WI* 398, *Esox lucius. . .* Other common names: great northern pike, . . great northern pickerel.

2 =muskellunge, usu *Esox masquinongy immaculatus.*

1896 U.S. Natl. Museum *Bulletin* 47.630, *Lucius masquinongy immaculatus. . . Great Northern Pike. . .* Body unspotted, or with vague, dark cross shades. . . Lakes and rivers of Wisconsin and Minnesota, locally abundant. **1902** Jordan–Evermann *Amer. Fishes* 240, *Great Northern Pike. Esox immaculatus. . .* This muskallunge is known only from Eagle Lake and other small lakes in northern Wisconsin and Minnesota. **1911** *Century Dict. Suppl., Pike. . . Great northern pike,* a maskalonge, *Lucius masquinongy immaculatus,* found in lakes and rivers of Wisconsin and Minnesota. **1927** Weed *Pike* 43, *Esox immaculatus. . .* Great Northern Pike; northwestern Wisconsin.

great northern white bean See **great northern bean**

great pike n Also *great blue pike*

=muskellunge.

1890 *Century Dict.* 4484, *Great pike,* the maskalonge, *Esox nobilior.* **1902** Jordan–Evermann *Amer. Fishes* 238, The muskallunge . . is known by many different common names. . . Among those which deserve mention are . . maskinongy and great pike. **1927** Weed *Pike* 44, *Esox masquinongy. . .* Great Pike; general. **1949** Caine *N. Amer. Sport Fish* 98, Muskellunge. . . *Colloquial Names . .* Great Pike. **1972** Sparano *Outdoors Encycl.* 366, *Muskellunge. Common Names . .* great pike. **1973** Knight *Cook's Fish Guide* 386, Pike . . great blue see Muskellunge.

great ragweed See **giant ragweed**

great snakes exclam For varr see quots

=great guns.

1862 *Harper's New Mth. Mag.* 25.568/1 **KY,** Why, great snakes and aligators [sic]! **1916** Porter *Just David* 233 **NH,** "Great snakes!" muttered Perry Larson, reaching out his hand and gingerly picking up one of the gold-pieces. **1965–70** *DARE* (Qu. NN29a, *Exclamations beginning with 'great': "Great ______!"*) Infs **CA**3, 39, **FL**18, **MN**1, **PA**161, **WV**10, Snakes; **CA**209, Snake [FW sugg]. **1966** Barnes–Jensen *Dict. UT Slang* 21, *Great snakes!:* an ejaculatory expression. "Great snakes! It's gold ore."

greatspoon n, hence n *greatspoonful*

A tablespoon.

1884 Barber *Diary* 37 **nwMA,** Made them presents. 2 great spoons & 6 tea do. **1914** *DN* 4.73 **ME, nNH,** *Gret-spoonful.* A table-spoonful.

great-tailed grackle n

Std: a **grackle B** *(Quicalus mexicanus)* native to the Southwest. Also called **fan-tailed grackle, jackdaw 1, Texas grackle** Note: this bird was formerly considered one with the **boat-tailed grackle** *(Quicalus major)* under the name *Cassidix mexicanus.*

great white crane n

1 =whooping crane.

1898 (1900) Davie *Nests N. Amer. Birds* 120, The Great White or Whooping Crane is confined to the interior of North America. **1917** (1923) *Birds Amer.* 1.198, *Whooping Crane—Grus americana. . .* Great White Crane. **1932** Howell *FL Bird Life* 196, *Grus americana. . .* Great White Crane. **1955** *Oriole* 20.6, *Whooping Crane. . .* Great White Crane. **1955** [see **2** below].

2 =great white heron 1.

1946 Hausman *Eastern Birds* 99, *Great White Heron—Ardea occidentalis. . .* Great White Crane. **1955** Forbush–May *Birds* 27, *Great White Heron—Ardea occidentalis. . .* Great White Crane. *Ibid* 155, *Whooping Crane—Grus americana. . .* Great White Crane.

great white heron n

1 A white subsp *(Ardea herodias occidentalis)* of the **great blue heron,** native to Florida. Also called **arsenicker, Florida heron, great white crane 2, white crane**

1835 Audubon *Ornith. Biog.* 3.542 **sFL,** The Great White Heron. *Ardea occidentalis . .* is . . remarkable . . for the pure white of its plumage at every period of its life. **1872** Coues *Key to N. Amer. Birds* 267, *Great White Heron. . .* Color entirely pure white. **1898** (1900) Davie *Nests N. Amer. Birds* 113, *Great White Heron. . .* This Heron nests usually in large colonies, and in company with the Great Blue Heron. **1917** (1923) *Birds Amer.* 1.184/2, I have always found the Great White Heron extremely shy and difficult to approach. **1954** Sprunt *FL Bird Life* 23, *Great White Heron. . .* Much of its range is now included in the Everglades National Park, which insures its future welfare. **1977** Bull–Farrand *Audubon Field Guide Birds* 478, *"Great White Heron" (Ardea herodias occidentalis). . .* Until recently, the "Great White Heron" was considered a distinct species. But both dark and white young have been found in a single nest, and it is now treated as a white phase of the Great Blue Heron that occurs only in Florida and the Caribbean region.

2 also *great white river heron:* The American **egret** *(Casmerodius albus).*

1791 Bartram *Travels* 185, A[rdea] immaculata, the great white river heron. **1834** Nuttall *Manual Ornith.* 2.47, Great White Heron. . . *Ardea egretta.* **1844** DeKay *Zool. NY* 2.220, The Great White Heron. . . *Ardea Leuce.* **1917** (1923) *Birds Amer.* 1.186, *Egret —Herodias egretta. . .* Great White Heron. **1957** Pough *Audubon W. Bird Guide* 42, *Egret. . . Casmerodius albus. . .* Great White Heron. **1977** Bull–Farrand *Audubon Field Guide Birds* 406, *Casmerodius albus. . .* Formerly known as the . . "Great White Heron," its official name in North America is now Great Egret.

greaze See **grease** v **A1**

greazer See **greaser**

greazy See **greasy** adj **A2**

grebe n

Std: a diving water bird of the genus *Podiceps* or of the genus *Podilymbus:* see **horned grebe, pied-billed grebe, red-necked grebe.**

gred See **great**

gredge n [Pronc-sp for *grudge*] Cf **judge**

1913 Kephart *Highlanders* 171 **sAppalachians,** Hit's jest somebody who has a gredge agin the blockader. **1921** Haswell *Daughter Ozarks* 44 (as of 1880s), Maybeso [=perhaps] some on [=of] 'em had old scores and gredges of their own.

‡greeble v

1950 *WELS Suppl.* **WI,** Greebling [griblɪŋ]—going about whining, looking for sympathy. "She's forever greebling."

greecy See **greasy** adj **A1**

greed n

A **duckweed 1** (here: *Lemna minor*).

1959 Carleton *Index Herb. Plants* 56, Greed: Lemna minor.

‡greedy dog n

1969 *DARE* (Qu. H42, *. . [A sandwich] in a much larger, longer bun, that's a meal in itself*) Inf **GA**79, Greedy dog [laughter].

greedygut(s) n

1 A glutton. [*OED* 1550 →]

1899 (1912) Green *VA Folk-Speech* 205, *Greedy gut. . .* A glutton; a belly-god. **1942** Berrey–Van den Bark *Amer. Slang* 425.2, *Voracious eater; glutton . .* greedy gut *or* guts. **1946** *Western Folkl.* 5.241 **OR,** Don't be a Greedy-gut. **1969** Kantor *MO Bittersweet* 17, Don't you get to be such an old greedy-gut. I got the green beans on already. **1970** *DARE* (Qu. H9) Inf **MO**29, Greedygut.

2 A miser or tightwad. **esp S Midl**

1899 (1912) Green *VA Folk-Speech* 205, *Greedy gut. . .* A greedy person . . also, a covetous person. **1942** Berrey–Van den Bark *Amer. Slang* 400.1, *Selfish or greedy person . .* greedy-gut(s). **1954** *Harder Coll.* **cwTN,** *Greedy-gut . .* same as *grab-all.* **1965–70** *DARE* (Qu. U33, *. . A stingy person*) Infs **GA**77, **VA**31, Greedygut; (Qu. U36a, *. . A person who saves in a mean way or is greedy in money matters*) Infs **GA**77, **KY**85, **MI**108, **TN**65, Greedygut; **SC**34, Greedyguts.

Greek n Cf **brass ankle, Goins, Guinea** n[1] **2**

A member of a mixed-race group living esp in coastal South Carolina.

1945 *Amer. Jrl. Sociol.* 51.35 **SC,** People . . who do not fit into the biracial caste system. . . These outcastes, whom I call "mestizos," are designated by a wide variety of names, none of them flattering. . . they are called "Greeks," [etc]. **1946** *Social Forces* 439 **SC,** Brass Ankles and allied groups of South Carolina . . are located mainly on the coastal plain area of the State. . . Nicknames are "Greeks," . . or simply "those Yellow People." **1963** Berry *Almost White* 36, Sometimes these outcasts are thought to be descendants of certain well known nationalities, and are named accordingly. For instance, we have . . the Greeks in South Carolina, and the Portuguese in Tennessee.

Greek fire n [*Greek fire* any of several flammable mixtures]

1967–68 *DARE* (Qu. FF28, . . *Kinds of fireworks*) Inf **NY**42, Greek fire; (Qu. HH30) Inf **NJ**48, Greek fire.

Greek valerian n [*OED* 1578 →]

A **Jacob's ladder:** usu *Polemonium caeruleum amygdalinum* in western US and *P. reptans* in eastern US.

1822 Eaton *Botany* 397, *Polemonium reptans,* greek valerian. **1847** Wood *Class-Book* 440, *P[olemonium] reptans* American Greek Valerian. . . *P[olemonium] coeruleum.* . . Greek Valerian. **1915** (1926) Armstrong–Thornber *Western Wild Flowers* 384, Jacob's Ladder—*Polemonium occidentale (P. caeruleum).* . . The common name comes from the shape of the leaf and it is also called Greek Valerian. **1937** U.S. Forest Serv. *Range Plant Hdbk.* W152, The cultivated Greek-valerian *(P[olemonium] caeruleum)* is a member of this genus, and the name Greek-valerian is sometimes given to other species. **1950** *WELS Suppl.* 1 Inf, **csWI,** Greek valerian was a bluebell to us. **1963** Craighead *Rocky Mt. Wildflowers* 152, Sky Pilot *Polemonium viscosum.* . . Greek Valerian. **1968** *DARE* (Qu. S26b, *Wildflowers that grow in water or wet places*) Inf **PA**99, Greek valerian.

green adj

1 also used absol; Of a crab: see quot 1976. Cf **comer 2, peeler**

1961 *W3, Green . . of a crab:* not quite ready to shed. **1976** Warner *Beautiful Swimmers* 27 **Chesapeake Bay,** Some will be "white sign" crabs, also known as "snots" or "greens," which have about two weeks or less to moult. *Ibid* 214, Marsh dropped the pesky little green into a bushel basket near him under the washboard. **1984** *DARE* File **Chesapeake Bay,** White rim, green peeler, green crab, white line crab.

2 Of milk: tainted. Cf **bitter** adj **1, grassy**

1965–70 *DARE* (Qu. K14, *Milk that has a taste from something the cow ate in the pasture*) Infs **IN**2, **MN**28, **TX**27, Green; **NJ**35, Green—tastes like grass.

green n

1 An area of grassland, esp in the center of a town or village; a public square. **chiefly N Atl** Cf **common** n **2**

1649 in 1901 Portsmouth RI *Early Rec.* 44, To Veiw the prison & remove it . . and place it sum wheare upon the greene. **1732** *SC Gaz.* (Charleston) 12 Feb [4]/2, Stolen or stray'd, from off the Green in Charlestown, a Week before Christmas last, a blackish Horse. **1899** (1912) Green *VA Folk-Speech* 205, *Green.* . . A piece of grass-land in a village or town reserved by the community for ornamental purposes. "Courthouse Green." "College Green." **1906** Churchill *Coniston* 3 **NH,** Jack descended from his work on the steeple to perceive the ungainly figure of Jethro Bass coming toward him across the green. **1931–33** *LANE Worksheets* **nwCT,** Green . . public square. "It used to be the green before it was fenced." **1966** *DARE* FW Addit **SC,** *Green*—the town square. Open land on both sides of the street—deeded to the town for civic purposes. **1967** *Times Herald Rec.* (Middletown NY) 15 Aug 4/1, Punch was served on the church green. **1968** *Amherst Rec.* (MA) 27 Nov 4, The annual custom of installing a monomental [sic] creche on the public green this holiday upcoming will again be honored in the observance.

2 also *green strip:* A grass-covered median strip; the grassy area between curb and sidewalk.

1965–70 *DARE* (Qu. N17, . . *The separating area in the middle of a four-lane road*) Infs **MA**15, **NY**80, Green; **MD**18, **WI**12, Green strip; (Qu. N44, *In a town, the strip of grass and trees between the sidewalk and the curb*) Infs **MA**15, **OH**6, 90, Green; **CA**114, **NY**32, Green strip.

3 pl; in phr *for greens:* See quot. [Prob in ref to *greens* leafy vegetables, given as payment in kind]

1953 Randolph–Wilson *Down in Holler* 249 **Ozarks,** *Greens.* . . Something extra, without serious purpose or significance. "Them folks didn't have no money, but me an' Jim warn't doin' nothin' nohow, so we holp 'em out just for greens"—without any payment, that is.

green v

1 also with *on, out:* To tease; to make a fool of. **S Midl**

1887 Eggleston *Graysons* 206 **sIN,** Somebody's been a-greenin' on you, Jake. **1923** *DN* 5.209 **swMO,** *Green.* . . To annoy with practical jokes. "The boys was all a-greenin' him about 'is gal." **1949** Webber *Backwoods Teacher* 137 **Ozarks,** First he thought they was jist greenin' him, and then when he seen they wasn't he was still mad. **1952** Brown *NC Folkl.* 1.547, *Green (out).* . . To outwit; to make a fool of.

2 usu with *out:* To outwit (in a transaction); to swindle. **sAppalachians**

1913 Kephart *Highlanders* 294 **sAppalachians,** "Sim greened him out bodaciously" (to green out or sap is to outwit in trade). **1917** *DN* 4.413 **wNC,** *Green out.* . . To swindle. **1926** Roberts *Time of Man* 171 **cKY,** Nohow Shine greened Tom outen a good shotgun. **1931** *PMLA* 46.1305 **Appalachians,** Buck greened-out (outwitted) that Ashley feller in the trade.

3 also vbl n *greening:* See quot 1933. Cf **fiddlehead** v

1933 *AmSp* 8.1.49 **nwAR, swMO,** *Green.* . . To gather green plants for food. *Maw she done went a-greenin' this mornin'.* **1966** *DARE* FW Addit **ME**15, Greenin' . . picking greens. **1975** Gould *ME Lingo* 116, *Greening*—Going *greening* is to gather dandelions, *fiddleheads, goose greens* for table.

green alder n

1 An alder: either *Alnus crispa* or *A. serrulata.* Note: The latter is often included in *A. rugosa.*

1869 *Amer. Naturalist* 3.408 **MT,** Green Alder . . has a range similar to that of the western birch. **1891** Jesup *Plants Hanover NH* 38, A. viridis, DC. (Green or Mountain Alder.) Banks of Conn. river, Hanover, etc. **1933** Small *Manual SE Flora* 418, *A. rugosa.* . . *Green-alder.* . . Various provinces, except Blue Ridge to Adirondacks, Fla. to Tex., Minn., and Me. *Ibid* 419, *A. Alnobetula.* . . *Green-alder.* . . Blue Ridge and more northern provinces, N.C. and Tenn. to Man[itoba], N.Y., and Lab[rador]. **1953** Strausbaugh–Core *Flora WV* 296, *A. crispa.* . . *Green alder.* . . A shrub to 3 m. high. **1972** Viereck–Little *AK Trees* 140, *American Green Alder (Alnus crispa . .).* Other names: green alder. . . *Leaves* . . above shiny yellow green and hairless, beneath pale green. **1974** (1977) Coon *Useful Plants* 76, Green, speckled, or black alder . . is a good dye plant, the roots giving a brown dye, the leaves a yellow-green, and the bark a yellow-brown.

2 A **dogwood 1** (here: *Cornus rugosa*).

1940 Clute *Amer. Plant Names* 256, *Cornus circinata* . . green alder.

green amaranth n **now esp West**

An **amaranth:** either *Amaranthus hybridus* or *A. retroflexus.*

1857 Gray *Manual of Botany* 368, *A[maranthus] hybridus.* . . *Green Amaranth.* . . Waste places and gardens; common. **1900** Lyons *Plant Names* 27, *A[maranthus] hybridus.* . . Green or Red Amaranth (varieties). **1923** in 1925 Jepson *Manual Plants CA* 334, *A[maranthus] hybridus.* . . Green Amaranth. **1936** Winter *Plants NE* 195, *A[maranthus] retroflexus.* . . Green Amaranth. . . Plants turn red in the fall or are reddish in the western part of the state. **1956** St. John *Flora SE WA* 132, *Amaranthus retroflexus.* . . *Green Amaranth.* . . A native weed in waste ground. **1968** Barkley *Plants KS* 135, Amaranthus retroflexus. . . Green Amaranth. **1973** Hitchcock–Cronquist *Flora Pacific NW* 102, Green a[maranth]. . . *A[maranthus] retroflexus.* **1976** Bailey–Bailey *Hortus Third* 65, *[Amaranthus] hybridus.* . . *Green a[maranth].* . . Common tall weed . . spikes green. L[ea]v[e]s and seeds are edible. . . *[Amaranthus] retroflexus.* . . *Green a[maranth].* . . Fl[ower]s green.

green-and-gold n

=**golden star 3.**

1964 Batson *Wild Flowers SC* 119, *Green and Gold: Chrysogonum virginianum.* . . Early spring. Pennsylvania to Florida. **1975** Duncan–Foote *Wildflowers SE* 210, *Green-and-gold.* . . An excellent ornamental for open, sunny borders.

green-and-gold ball See **gold-and-green ball**

green-apple quickstep n Also *green-apple trot, ~ two-step;* for addit varr see quots *joc* Cf **apple blossom two-step, crab apple two-step**

Diarrhea.

1950 *WELS (Diarrhea or looseness of the bowels)* 2 Infs, **WI,** Green-apple two-step; 1 Inf, Green-apple quickstep; 1 Inf, Green-apple disease. **1965–70** *DARE* (Qu. BB19) Infs **CA**49, **IN**28, **MI**55, **NJ**21, **PA**202, **VA**30, **VT**12, **WV**12, Green-apple quickstep; **CA**49, 59, **IA**47, **NE**2, **NY**1, **OH**15, 34, Green-apple two-step; **NJ**2, **SC**2, Green-apple trot; **KS**2, Green-apple dirties; **PA**126, Green-apple disease; **GA**11, Green-apple walk; [**VA**101, Green-apple bellyache;] (Qu. BB28) Inf **IL**35, Green-apple two-step. **1985** *NC Folkl. Jrl.* 33.38 **wNC** (as of c1920), Sometimes we ate them too early and got the "green apple trots" as the result of our impatience. **1987** *DARE* File, [Letter from an 82-year-old woman:] I didn't go to church this morning did get partly dressed, but had the green apple two step, was keeping the bathroom busy, didn't want to take a chance.

green ash n [See quot 1846]

An American ash *(Fraxinus pennsylvanica).* Also called **bastard ash 1, black ash 2, blue ash 2, brown ash 2, gray ash, piss ash, prairie ash, red ash, river ash, swamp ash, water ash, white ash, yellow ash**

[**1810** Michaux *Histoire des Arbres* 1.34, F[raxinus] concolor. *Green ash* (Frêne vert), nom donné par moi à cette espèce, qui n'en a aucun dans les pays où elle croît. [=(Green ash), name given by me to this species, which has none [=no name] in the region where it grows.]] **1846** Browne *Trees* 398, It [=*Fraxinus pennsylvanica*] is easily recognized by the brilliant green colour of its young leaves; and by its leaves being nearly of the same colour on both surfaces. From this uniformity, which is rarely observed in the foliage of trees, . . Michaux gave this tree the popular name of the "Green Ash." **1897** Sudworth *Arborescent Flora* 329, *Fraxinus lanceolata. . . Common Names.* Green Ash (Mass., R.I., Conn., N.Y., N.J., Pa., Del., N.C., S.C., Ala., Miss., La., Tex., Mo., Ill., Kans., Nebr., Mich., Minn., S. Dak., Ohio, Ont., Iowa.) **1945** Wodehouse *Hayfever Plants* 124, Green ash . . is a small tree seldom more than 60 feet high with ashy gray branchlets marked by pale lenticels. **1962** Kurz-Godfrey *Trees N. FL* 279, The green ash becomes a large tree and has a single trunk which is buttressed when growing where inundated for long periods. **1969** *DARE* (Qu. T16) Inf **IL**44, Green ash.

greenass See **greenhead 6**

greenback n

1 =**golden plover. esp NEast**

1844 DeKay *Zool. NY* 2.213, *The Golden Plover. . .* They are frequently also called *Greenbacks.* **1876** *Forest & Stream* 7.149/2 **Long Is. NY,** The green-back or golden plover comes next. . . These green-backed plovers go in flocks, sometimes as many as two hundred and fifty together. **1880** *Ibid* 15.4/2, Golden plover. . . On the New Jersey and Delaware coasts it is termed the green-back. **1888** Trumbull *Names of Birds* 195, American Golden Plover *[Charadrius dominicus].* . . At Provincetown, Mass., and Moriches, L.I., Green-back. **1927** Forbush *Birds MA* 1.462, *Pluvialis dominica dominica. . .* Golden Plover. . . Green-back. **1955** MA Audubon Soc. *Bulletin* 39.444, American Golden Plover. . . Green-back, Green-head (Mass.)

2 See **green-backed goldfinch.**

3 also *greenback frog, green-backed bullfrog:* A frog such as a **bullfrog 1.**

1889 *Century Dict.* 2617, *Greenback. . .* A frog. [*Century* Ed: Anglers' slang.] **1932** Wright *Life-Hist. Frogs* 384, *Rana heckscheri. . . Common Names.* Greenback. **1967-70** *DARE* (Qu. P21, *Small frogs that sing or chirp loudly in spring*) Infs **CT**2, **NY**233, Greenback; **NJ**53, Greenback frogs; **NJ**1, Green-backed bullfrog.

4 also *greenback herring:* A **cisco** (here: *Coregonus artedii*).

1902 Jordan-Evermann *Amer. Fishes* 132, Greenback . . or greenback herring. . . These different names are simply the fisherman's way of distinguishing individual variations in colour, sex, age or time of run. . . Usually the fishermen claim . . greenbacks and bluebacks run in the late fall, and are regarded, very naturally, as a better fish than the graybacks.

5 also *greenback turtle:* A **cooter** n **1.**

1967 *DARE* Tape **LA**5, [Inf:] What we call a streaky-head is a greenback turtle. Got kind of red stripes on his neck. . . [FW:] How big do they get? [Inf:] 'Bout the size of the top of a eight-quart water bucket. [FW:] 'Bout 14 inches? [Inf:] Uh huh. . . That's usually a greenback, greenback turtle.

6 See **greenback trout.**

green-backed bullfrog See **greenback 3**

green-backed goldfinch n Also *greenback* [See quot 1964]

A **goldfinch 1** (here: *Carduelis psaltria hesperophilus*) native to the Pacific coast and the southwestern US.

1898 (1900) Davie *Nests N. Amer. Birds* 362, *Spinus psaltria* . . is also called the Arkansaw [sic] Green-backed . . Goldfinch. **1913** *Pacific Coast Avifauna* 9.76 **cCA,** *Green-backed Goldfinch. . .* When the country was given over largely to grain ranches, . . this goldfinch found conditions much more to its liking. **1917** (1923) *Birds Amer.* 3.15, *Astragalinus psaltria psaltria. . .* Arkansas Greenback. *Ibid* 16, A slightly variant form . . is known as the Green-backed Goldfinch. **1928** Bailey *Birds NM* 704, The center of abundance of the Green-backed Goldfinch is in California. *Ibid* 705, In California the Green-back has apparently decreased in numbers with the cultivation of the land. **1940** Gabrielson *Birds OR* 548, The Green-backed Goldfinch much resembles the Willow Goldfinch in flight and notes. **1964** Phillips *Birds AZ* 188, Except for the Springerville region, all Arizona birds are currently referred to *S[pinus] p[saltria] hesperophilus* . . , green above, and therefore formerly known as the Green-backed Goldfinch.

green-backed trout See **greenback trout**

greenback frog See **greenback 3**

greenback herring See **greenback 4**

greenback mackerel n Also *green mackerel*

=**Pacific mackerel.**

1939 Natl. Geogr. Soc. *Fishes* 224, *Pneumatophorus diego. . .* On the Pacific coast where it is called greenback mackerel, . . it occurs from Prince William Sound, Alaska, southward to California. **1946** La-Monte *N. Amer. Game Fishes* 19, *Pneumatophorus japonicus. . .* Greenback Mackerel. . . Back dark, metallic green. **1953** Roedel *Common Fishes CA* 84, *Pacific Mackerel. . . Unauthorized Names:* Blue mackerel, green mackerel. **1973** Knight *Cook's Fish Guide* 384, Mackerel . . green.

greenback shower n Also *greenback wedding, greenie shower*

A shower or wedding at which money is given as a gift.

1965-70 *DARE* (Qu. FF3) Inf **MA**6, Greenback shower—give money for bride; **MA**82, Greenback shower—money tree given to recipients, common in Massachusetts for anniversaries especially; **NY**10, Greenback showers—money as gift (greenie showers). **1980** *DARE* File **swME,** [On a wedding invitation:] Greenback Wedding.

greenback trout n Also *greenback, green-backed trout*

Usu a **cutthroat trout** (here: *Salmo clarki stomias*), but also the extinct emerald trout *(S. smaragdus).*

1904 *Salmon & Trout* 211, The Green-back trout,—*Salmo clarkii stomias.* **1911** *Century Dict. Suppl., Greenback. . . Salmo stomias,* the trout of the Arkansas river. *Ibid, Trout. . . Green-backed trout, Salmo clarkii stomias,* of the head-waters of the Arkansas and South Platte rivers. **1935** Pratt *Manual Invertebrate Animals* 45, *T[rutta] stomias. . .* Green-back. Similar to *T. clarki;* body deep green above; spots mostly back of the anal fin: head waters of the Arkansas and South Platte. *Ibid* 47, *T. smaragda. . .* Greenback. Form slender; scales 124; color green above: Pyramid Lake region, Nevada.

greenback turtle See **greenback 5**

greenback wedding See **greenback shower**

green ball n

The fruit of the **Osage orange.**

1989 *Mid-Amer. Rev.* 9.1.131 **sIL,** Another *bois d'arc* zips through the brown-leafed limbs of hickories on the hillside. . . Grapefruit-sized with green warty skin, we call them by the nickname Green Balls.

green bass n

The **largemouth bass, smallmouth bass,** or **spotted bass.**

1820 *Western Rev.* 2.54 **nwKY,** Ohio Red-eye. *Aplocentrus calliops. . .* It lives in the lower parts of the Ohio, in Green river, &c. Vulgar names Red-eyes, Bride pearch, Batchelor's pearch, Green bass. **1882** U.S. Natl. Museum *Bulletin* 16.484, *M[icropterus] salmoides. . .* Green Bass. **1887** Goode *Amer. Fishes* 56, "Marsh Bass," . . "Green Bass," . . are other names applied to one or both species [=*Micropterus salmoides, M. dolomieu*]. **1935** Caine *Game Fish* 3, Large-Mouthed Black Bass *Micropterus salmoides. . .* Green Bass. *Ibid* 7, Small-Mouthed Black Bass *Micropterus dolomieu. . .* Green Bass. **1983** Becker *Fishes WI* 801, *Smallmouth Bass. . .* Other common names . . green bass. . . Back and head brown, or yellow-brown, or olive to green. *Ibid* 809, *Largemouth Bass. . .* Other common names . . green bass. . . Back and head dark green to light green.

Green Bay fly n [*Green Bay,* Wisconsin] **chiefly WI, neMI** Cf **bay fly, lake fly**

=**mayfly.**

1876 WI State Hist. Soc. *Coll.* 7.267, Everybody has heard of the Green Bay flies. . . In the height and heat of summer, the waters at the head of the bay . . become coated with a green scum. . . There appears in it myriads of a kind of sack . . and we perceive a living insect within struggling to escape. **1950** *WELS* 12 Infs, **WI,** Green Bay fly. **1966-69** *DARE* (Qu. R1, *A large winged insect that hatches in summer in great numbers around lakes or rivers, crowds around lights, lives only a day or so, and is good fish bait*) Infs **AL**25, **CT**6, **MI**14, 27, **MS**16, **WI**8, 37, 61,

71, 77, Green Bay fly. **1983** *Isthmus* (Madison WI) 18 Mar 14/3, On the U.S. Government pier,/ foreigners thick / as the Green Bay flies.

green bean n **widespread, but less freq NEng, Sth** See Map and Map Section Cf **snap bean, string bean**

A cultivated bean *(Phaseolus vulgaris)* eaten in the pod.

1847 (1852) Crowen *Amer. Cookery* 183 **NY,** *Green Beans.*—Cut the bud and stem end off, and take the strings from the side of stringed beans; cut them in inch lengths, . . then put them into a stew-pan of hot water. **1896** *Daily News Cook Book* 281 **IN,** Green Beans, Maitre d'Hôtel Dressing. *Ibid* 428 **NY,** Green Beans on Toast—String one quart of fresh, tender beans [etc]. **1942** Rawlings *Cross Creek* 214 **nFL,** Even string beans, which here we call green beans or wax beans according to color, now seem insipid to me. **1946** *PADS* 5.24 **VA,** *Green-beans*. . . String beans; west of the Blue Ridge. **1949** Kurath *Word Geog.* 73, Three terms for string beans are current over large areas: *string beans* north of the Potomac, *snap beans* south of it, and *green-beans* in the West Midland from the upper Ohio to the Carolinas. . . *Green-beans* dominates the mountains of North Carolina and all of West Virginia, and it is still common on the upper Ohio and its tributaries. On the eastern flank it is yielding ground. . . There are relics of *green-beans* in central Pennsylvania. The term survives also in the Catskills. **1951** *AmSp* 26.252, West Midland: *green beans* (string beans). . . For none of these words is it necessary to assume Midland or Southern origins when we find them in Upstate New York. *Green beans* is found in the Hudson Valley. **1954** *Harder Coll.* **cwTN,** *Green beans*. . . String beans. **1965–70** *DARE* (Qu. I14, *Kinds of beans that you eat in the pod before they're dry*) 570 Infs, **widespread, but less freq NEng, Sth,** Green beans; **NY**106, Italian green beans; **NC**55, Tennessee green bean; (Qu. I20) 17 Infs, **scattered,** Green beans; **IA**30, Italian green beans. **1966** Dakin *Dial. Vocab. Ohio R. Valley* 2.371, The West Midland term *green-beans* is the usual regional term in the Ohio Valley. **1971** Wood *Vocab. Change* 41 **Sth, S Midl,** *String beans, snap beans,* and *green beans* are the chief terms, with *snap beans* and *string beans* alternating in preference everywhere but in Tennessee and Oklahoma; there *green beans* is the more frequent choice over *string beans.*

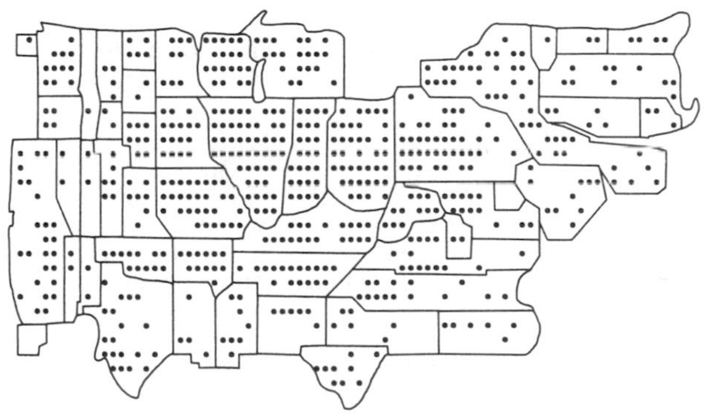

•green bean + varr (Qq. I14, I20)

green bird n

=**indigo bunting.**

1890 Warren *Birds PA* 248, *Passerina cyanea*. . . Indigo Bunting; Green-bird; Indigo-bird.

green bittern n

=**green heron.**

1813 (1824) Wilson *Amer. Ornith.* 7.103, When alarmed, the Green Bittern rises with a hollow guttural scream. **1917** (1923) *Birds Amer.* 1.192, *Green Heron—Butorides virescens virescens*. . . Green Bittern. **1925** (1928) Forbush *Birds MA* 1.334, *Butorides virescens virescens*. . . *Green Heron*. . . Green Bittern. **1946** Hausman *Eastern Birds* 107, *Eastern Green Heron*. . . Green Bittern.

greenbottle fly n

1 also *greenbottle:* A blowfly of the family Calliphoridae, usu *Phaenicia sericata* or *Lucilia illustris,* usu having a metallic blue-green abdomen. Cf **bluebottle fly, green fly 1**

1901 Howard *Insect Book* 164, Another well known flesh-fly is *Lucilia caesar,* generally known as the green-bottle fly, which is sometimes driven into houses on the approach of a storm. **1905** Kellogg *Amer. Insects* 344, The commonest bluebottle- or greenbottle-fly is *Lucilia caesar,* which lays its eggs in cow-dung as well as on flesh, and which often comes into houses, particularly before rain. **1911** *Century Dict. Suppl., Fly*[2]. . . *Green-bottle fly,* any green sarcophagid fly of the genus *Lucilia* or some closely allied genus. Also *green-bottle.* **1938** Brimley *Insects NC* 372, *Lucilia* . . Green-bottle Flies. **1966–70** *DARE* (Qu. R13, *Flies that come to meat or fruit*) Infs **DC**11, **NC**16, **NY**34, Green-bottle fly. **1980** Milne–Milne *Audubon Field Guide Insects* 686, The Green Bottle Fly [=*Phaenicia sericata*] is . . often found near slaughter-houses and garbage cans. The similar Caesar Green Bottle Fly (*Lucilia illustris,* formerly known as *L. caesar*) . . is common in the West.

2 also *greenbottle prairie fly:* A **horsefly 1** (here: prob *Tabanus atratus*). Cf **greenhead 2**

1838 Flagg *Far West* 2.107, My horse . . [was] severely troubled by that terrible insect, so notorious all over the West, the large green-bottle prairie fly, called the *"green-head."* **1960** Williams *Walk Egypt* 149 **GA,** The mule stamped; greenbottle flies were pestering the life out of it.

greenbrier n Also sp *greenbriar* [See quot 1943]

A plant of the genus *Smilax.* Also called **bamboo, ~ brier, ~ vine, bramboo brier, bullgrip, carrion flower 1, catbrier, cat's-paw 6, dead-man's bryony, devil's clothesline, hell-rope, horse brier, sarsaparilla, sawbrier, squirrel brier, wild sarsaparilla.** For other names of var spp see **bindweed 2, biscuit-leaves, blaspheme vine, bread-and-butter 1, bullbrier, Christmas-berry 5, China brier, Chinaroot 1, coral greenbrier, devil greenbrier, devil's hopvine, dog brier, false sarsaparilla 2, ground brier, hagbrier, hellfetter, hungry vine, Indian brier, Jackson brier, Jacob's ladder, niggerhead, red bamboo, sow brier, stretchberry, wait-a-bit, wild asparagus, wild bamboo, wild spinach**

c1785 S. Pears *Narrative* (MS) 4 *(DA),* We had not anything to live on . . except . . greenbrier berreys. **1832** MA Hist. Soc. *Coll.* 2d ser 9.156 **cwVT,** Smilax rotundifolia, Green briar. **1899** (1912) Green *VA Folk-Speech* 206, *Greenbriar*. . . A greenish-yellow climbing plant with prickly stem and thick leaves. **1937** Thornburgh *Gt. Smoky Mts.* 22, A few of the more common vines you may encounter . . are . . Dutchman's pipe . . and greenbrier, which is also called saw brier, cat brier and bamboo brier. **1943** Shimer *Plant Names* 19, The same plant is called Cat briar for its sharp stout prickles, and Green briar because of its bright green bark. **1950** Stuart *Hie Hunters* 10 **eKY,** The little fox path where greenbriers lapped over to stick their legs. **1969** *DARE* FW Addit **ceNC,** *Catbrier.* Tree common on Hatteras Island. Also called 'smilax.' (Local name is greenbrier.) **1976** Bailey–Bailey *Hortus Third* 1050, *Smilax* L. *Greenbrier, catbrier*. . . Sometimes prickly.

green bristle(grass) See **green foxtail**

green broke adj phr Also *green broken* Cf **cowboy-broke**

Of a horse: newly or not fully trained for use; see quot 1989.

1967 Green *Horse Tradin'* 258 **TX,** I guessed I could say they were green-broke, although that usually just meant a pair of horses that hadn't been worked much. **1968** Adams *Western Words* 133, *Green-broke*—Said of a horse ridden only a time or two and then turned out for the winter. **1969** *SC Market Bulletin* 9 Jan 4, Gelding horse 2½ years old, green broke. **1970** GA Dept. Ag. *Farmers Market Bulletin* 5 Aug, Buckskin stallion, very gentle, $650; two yr. old Appaloosa colt, green broken, subject to registration. **1989** *DARE* File **WI,** If a horse is green broke it means he has had someone on his back. He may know "whoa" and how to turn, but he isn't finished: his head isn't set properly, he isn't accustomed to aids of hands, legs, or voice with any finesse; he might still jump, buck, or spook.

greenbug n

1 A grain- and grass-infesting aphid *(Schizaphis graminum).* **West**

1910 Johnson *Highways Rocky Mts.* 44, Another time we had the green bug. Eighty acres of wheat and oats that I'd put in never yielded a grain of anything. **1925** *Book of Rural Life* 2458, The spots where the green bugs are killing the wheat . . should be plowed under or burned. **1926** Essig *Insects N. Amer.* 248, *The green bug, Toxoptera graminum* . ., is a medium sized, pale green species with darker green longitudinal stripes and black-tipped cornicles. . . New Mexico is the only Western State where the aphis is noted as being a serious pest. **1934** *Sun* (Baltimore MD) 24 Mar 17/1, Some notice was taken of reports from Wichita, Kan., that wheat fields adjacent were infested with green bugs. **1966–68** *DARE* (Qu. R26, . . *The small greenish lice that come on plants*) Infs

CO22, **KS**20, **OK**18, 25, Greenbug. **1972** Swan-Papp *Insects* 154, *Greenbug. . . Range:* Throughout North America, first recorded in the U.S. (Virginia) in 1882; most destructive in wheat-growing areas of the West.

2 A tree cricket (here: *Oecanthus fultoni*).

1955 Richardson *House on Nauset Marsh* 125 **MA,** My young friend . . asked me one evening what the sound was. I said it was a field cricket. "Are you sure?" he asked. "I have an idea it is a green bug." . . The green bug's song is rather low, and all on the same note. This newly found cousin of the singers in the field I now know is called the "green tree cricket."

green bunch(ing) onion See **bunch onion**

‡green calabash, cut the v phr

1926 Smith *Gullah* 35 **sSC, GA coasts,** *To cut de green calabash,* to exaggerate, to draw the long bow (calabash is a gourd).

green chop v phr

To cut a field crop for immediate use as livestock feed; hence n *green chopper* a machine that cuts such a crop.

1965 *Bee* (Phillips WI) 19 Aug [9/3], Much second cutting in the south is too short for hay and is being green-chopped to bring on a better third crop. **1968** WI Statist. Reporting Serv. *Report* 3 Sept, Most third crop hay being green chopped or pastured. **1968** *DARE* Tape **WI**17, A green chopper is the [machine] that goes out in the field and chops it [=a crop such as sudan grass or sorghum] there. **1968** *DARE* FW Addit **MD,** To green chop. . . To cut field crop (of almost any edible kind) to be fed immediately, while still fresh and green, to the cattle. **1969** WI Statist. Reporting Serv. *Report* 12 May, A Wood County farmer has started to green-chop already. **1984** *MJLF* 10.151 **cnWI,** *Green chop.* To machine chop young oats and grass into moveable feeder wagons, to provide a high protein supplement, especially for milking cows in summer pastures.

green chop n Cf **chop** n[1] **1**

A field crop which has been chopped to be fed fresh to livestock.

1967 *DARE* (Qu. L10, *After hay has been cut, then it grows back and you cut it again, you'd call that* ______) Inf **CA**1, Green chop. **1968** *DARE* Tape **WI**17, You have to cut down some of the other crops you might have planted to feed the cows in place of hay in case it had been killed, like sudan grass or sorghum, sudan cross. You feed them green chop or else feed them in the barn.

green chopper See **green chop** v phr

green cod n

1 =pollack. N Atl coast

1882 U.S. Natl. Museum *Bulletin* 16.806, *G[adus] virens. . .* Pollack; Coal-fish; Green Cod. **1902** Jordan-Evermann *Amer. Fishes* 509, The common pollack, coal-fish, or green cod, . . is common on both coasts of the Atlantic. **1939** Natl. Geogr. Soc. *Fishes* 40, The pollock, also called green cod, or coalfish, . . is not taken in commercial quantities south of New Jersey. **1972** Sparano *Outdoors Encycl.* 383, *Pollock. . .* Boston bluefish, green cod, coalfish.

2 A **lingcod** (here: *Ophiodon elongatus*). **Pacific coast**

1889 *Century Dict.* 2617, *Green-cod. . .* A Californian fish of the family *Chiridae, Ophiodon elongatus,* sometimes attaining a length of 3 or 4 feet, and highly ranked as a food-fish. **1953** Roedel *Common Fishes CA* 139, *Lingcod. . .* Not a true cod. . . Northwestern Alaska south . . at least to San Martin Island. . . A market fish of moderate importance. . . *Unauthorized Names* . . green cod, cultus.

green corn n

1 Corn plants while growing or when cut green for fodder.

1645 *Springfield Rec.* I.181 *(DA),* Divers that keep teames on the other side of ye River . . have much damnified other men by theyr Cattell, in eating the greene corne. **1966** *DARE* Tape **NH**5, Now . . we don't cut by hand anymore. We got . . a corn harvester that cut it and bound it, and then . . we could handle a bundle of green corn without gettin' rocks 'n' dirt into the ensilage. . . [With] the later ones [=harvesters], as we use them now, the ensilage is cut . . into silage, right out in the field. **1967-69** *DARE* (Qu. L9b, *Hay from other kinds of plants [not grass]*) Inf **TX**63, Green corn; **AL**20, Green corn—in silos.

2 Corn in the milky stage before complete maturity, esp **sweet corn** as prepared for human consumption. **scattered, but esp eNEng, Gt Lakes, sCA** See Map

1697 in 1930 *MD Hist. Mag.* 15.116 **cnMD,** [An Indian] comes on the Back of his Plantation gathers his Green Corn cutts up his Corn stalks [etc.] **1745** (1899) MacSparran *Letter Book* 35 **RI,** Molly Browne went home in the afternoon, after eating some green Corn. **1810** (1817) Bradbury *Travels* 114, *Sweet corn,* is corn gathered before it is ripe, and dried in the sun: it is called by the Americans *green corn,* or *corn in the milk.* **1856** in 1862 Colt *Went to KS* 73 **NY,** Feasted on green corn, beans, pease, and cucumbers. **1887** Parloa *Miss Parloa's Kitchen Companion* 518, *Green Corn in Cream.*—Husk the corn, and boil it for ten minutes. Cool it a little, Draw a sharp knife down each row of kernels [etc.] **1941** *LANE* Map 261, [133 infs, **scattered, but more freq eNEng,** offered *green corn* in the sense of sweet corn, or accepted it as a suggested response; 32 infs, **scattered,** used *green corn* to refer to "young or unripe corn of any variety, whether intended for human consumption or not."] **c1960** *Wilson Coll.* **csKY,** *Green corn. . .* Roasting ears. **1965-70** *DARE* (Qu. I33, . . *Ears of corn that are just right for eating*) 54 Infs, **chiefly Nth, West,** Green corn; (Qu. I34, *If you don't have sweet corn, you can always eat young* ______) Infs **IL**31, **ME**16, **MI**113, 116, **MA**55, **OH**15, Green corn; (Qu. P35b, *Illegal methods of shooting deer*) Inf **FL**48, Baiting with green corn. **1971** Bright *Word Geog. CA & NV* 184, *Sweet corn* served on the cob . . *green corn* [33 of 300 infs].

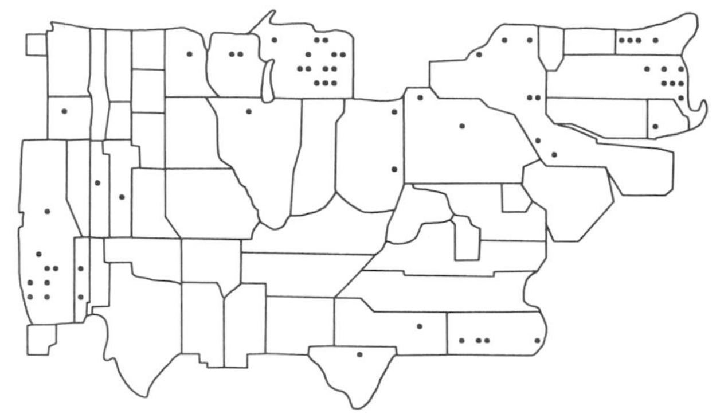

•green corn 2 + var (Qq. I33, I34, P35b)

3 usu attrib: An annual Indian celebration near the time of the corn harvest; the dance and song performed at such a celebration.

1725 in 1916 Mereness *Travels* 134 **Sth,** I have given Orders to them to meet me at the Great dance here (called the Green Corn dance). **1800** (1821) Asbury *Jrl.* 2.389, The gentry had made a dinner at a small distance from the town: a kind of green corn feast, with a roasted animal, cooked and eaten out of doors, under a booth. **1899** Cushman *Hist. Choctaw* 20, Mordecai . . asserted that in their Green Corn Dances he had heard them often utter in graceful tones, the word Yavoyaha! Yavoyaha! **1907** Hodge *Hdbk. Amer. Indians* 1.460/2, New fire was made in the Green-corn ceremony of the Creeks. **1941** Daniels *Tar Heels* 245 **NC,** Most of them [=Indians] are Baptists or Methodists now, but the Methodists and Baptists move in the Green Corn Dance still at harvest time in appreciation to gods whose dance they remember even if their names are forgotten by some of the dancers. **1950** *PADS* 14.76 **FL,** *Green corn, the:* . . The June meeting of the Indians, when the corn is "in the milk." Participants "sing [*PADS* Ed: or dance] the green corn." **1965-70** *DARE* (Qu. FF16) Inf **IN**13, Green corn dances—old-fashioned; **OK**9, Creek Indians have green corn dances.

green cypress trout n Cf **cypress trout**

=bowfin.

1967 *DARE* Tape **LA**5, Around here . . is what we call a choupique. . . they have so many names for 'em; they call it green cypress trout, choupique, and grunnels. **1973** *DARE* FW Addit **LA,** Along the fringe of French Louisiana, in the Baton Rouge-St. Francisville area . . English speakers call it [=the bowfin] green cypress trout.

green darner n

A **darning needle 1** (here: *Anax junius*).

1929 Needham-Heywood *Hdbk. Dragonflies* 7, The big green darner . . is a handsomely colored insect. Its robust olive-green body has neat trimmings of blue and brown. *Ibid* 128, *Anax. . .* The Green Darners. **1954** Borror-DeLong *Intro. Insects* 113, The green darner, . . a common and widely distributed species that occurs about ponds, has a greenish thorax and a bluish abdomen, and a targetlike mark on the upper part of the face. **1967** *PA Game News* Aug 19, Darting over Pennsylvania's hills, streams, and ponds in summer is the

Green Darner, one of the largest and most fascinating insects of our state. **1968** *AmSp* 43.53 **KS,** Answers written in for 'dragonfly' . . included *green darner.* **1980** Milne–Milne *Audubon Field Guide Insects* 364, The Green Darner is one of the fastest and biggest of the common dragonflies.

green dock n

A **dock** n[1] (here: *Rumex conglomeratus*).

1848 Gray *Manual of Botany* 393, *R[umex] conglomeratus*. . . Smaller Green Dock. **1911** Jepson *Flora CA* 135, *Green Dock*. . . Abundant in lowlands about San Francisco Bay and southward to Southern California. **1945** Wodehouse *Hayfever Plants* 201, Green dock *(R. conglomeratus).* **1966** *DARE* Wildfl QR Inf **CO**7, Green dock . . on wastelands. The poor man's orchid. **1976** Bailey–Bailey *Hortus Third* 988, *R. conglomeratus*. . . Green Dock.

green dragon n [See quots 1901, 1953]

A **jack-in-the-pulpit** (here: *Arisaema dracontium*). Also called **dragon arum, dragonhead 4, dragonroot 1, dragon's tail, dragon turnip, green jack, Indian turnip, pepper turnip**

1822 Eaton *Botany* 182 **nwMA,** *Arum . . dracontium* . . green dragon. **1861** Wood *Class-Book* 668, *A[risaema] Dracontium*. . . *Green Dragon*. . . Less common in New England than the former species [=*A. triphyllum*]. . . Fruit a bunch of red berries. **1901** Lounsberry *S. Wild Flowers* 34, *Green Dragon*. . . The leaves which are grotesquely formed are said to kindle a vivid imagination into seeing the claws and foot of a dragon, while "fiercely acrid" has been the term applied to the corms' juices. **1939** *Natl. Geogr. Mag.* 76.220/1, Color in this charming ground cover is provided by blue and yellow violets . . Jacob's-ladder, the mottled jack-in-the-pulpit and green dragon. **1953** Greene–Blomquist *Flowers South* 3, The green-dragon . . [is] so-called in allusion to its long, attenuate spathe resembling the tail of a reptile. **1966** *DARE* (Qu. S1, . . *Other names . . for the jack-in-the-pulpit*) Inf **MS**38, Green dragon. **1974** (1977) Coon *Useful Plants* 65, *Arisaema dracontium*—Green dragon, dragon root.

green eelgrass n [Appar from a resemblance to **eelgrass**]

A **buttercup 1** (here: *Ranunculus aquatilis*).

1900 Lyons *Plant Names* 59, *B[atrachium] trichophyllum*. . . Green Eel-grass. **1910** Graves *Flowering Plants* 185 **CT,** Common White Water Crowfoot. Water Milfoil. Green Eel Grass. . . Ponds and slow streams. **1911** *Century Dict. Suppl., Eel-grass*. . . *Green eel-grass,* the white water-crowfoot, *Batrachium trichophyllum.*

greener n

A greenhorn.

1877 in 1921 Thorp *Songs Cowboys* 157 **NM,** When he meets a greener he ain't afraid to rig,/ Stands him on a chuck-box and makes him dance a jig. **1920** Hunter *Trail Drivers TX* 125 (as of 1881), We had one "greener" with us on this trip and we never missed a chance to play a prank on him. **1923** *DN* 5.209 **swMO,** *Greener*. . . A newcomer, a tenderfoot, one unfamiliar with the work in which he is engaged. **1966–70** *DARE* (Qu. HH15, *A very inexperienced person, one who is just learning how to do a new thing*) Infs **OH**95, **SC**19, Greener. **1971** Jennings *Cowboys* 103 **MT, WY** (as of 1877), The boys lounged on their saddles. . . All sat with a certain cocky ease in the way most comfortable to himself. Only a greener thinks there's just one way to sit in a saddle.

green-eyes n [See quots 1955, 1975]

A plant of the genus *Berlandiera.* For addit name of var sp see **Florida dandelion**

1933 Small *Manual SE Flora* 1415, *Berlandiera*. . . Green-eyes. **1955** *S. Folkl. Qrly.* 19.233, *Green Eyes* . . is so called because the center of the flower is green, circled with eight to twelve petals or ray flowers. **1970** Correll *Plants TX* 1623, *Berlandiera*. . . Green-eyes. **1975** Duncan–Foote *Wildflowers SE* 208, Green-eyes. . . When in bud the disc flowers are green, thus the common name. **1976** Fleming *Wild Flowers FL* 58, *Green Eyes* . . is a perennial.

green family n

A children's game; see quot.

1966 *DARE* (Qu. EE33) Inf **OK**31, Green family—all players except the leader go into another room and return, one by one, as they are called. One or two players other than the leader know what is happening and go in first; the others should not know what is going on. The players with the leader are the green family; as the others come in, one at a time, the green family mocks whatever they do or say until the player catches on, then he joins the green family and another comes in.

green farmer n

1965 *DARE* FW Addit **OH,** Green farmer . . one who raises no stock, only crops.

green finch n

=**Texas sparrow.**

1872 Coues *Key to N. Amer. Birds* 153, *Green Finch*. . . Valley of the Rio Grande, and probably of the Gila, and southward. **1889** *Century Dict.* 1890, The . . greenfinch is *E[mbernagra] rufovirgata,* a common species in the lower Rio Grande valley. **1917** (1923) *Birds Amer.* 3.57, Green Finch. . . There is nothing very noticeable about the . . bird. . . Its plain olive and brown colors do not attract attention. **1944** Hausman *Amer. Birds* 513, Finch, Green—see Sparrow, Texas.

green fingers n pl [By analogy with *green thumb*] **chiefly S Midl** Cf **green hand 2**

Fig: a striking ability to make plants thrive.

1944 *Sun* (Baltimore MD) 2 June 10/3 *(Hench Coll.)* **MD,** All the green thumbs and green fingers in the world would get them nowhere unless they fed the plants and worked the soil. **1944** *PADS* 2.37 **TN,** "She has green thumbs" means: everything she plants grows well and flourishes. . . In Wilson Co., Tenn., *green fingers* means the same thing. **1945** *Richmond Times-Dispatch* (VA) 19 Mar 18, [Advt:] Nowadays, everybody has green fingers. . . so you're all invited. **1953** Randolph–Wilson *Down in Holler* 249 **Ozarks,** *Green fingers*. . . The ability to grow vegetables and flowering plants. A woman whose garden always flourishes is said to have *green fingers* or *growin' fingers.* **1954** *Harder Coll.* **cwTN,** *Green fingers* . . the ability to grow plants.

greenfish n

1 =**bluefish 1.** [See quot 1743]

1743 (1754) Catesby *Nat. Hist. Carolina* 2.14, *Saltatrix.* Skipjack. . . When just taken [they] are green on the Back, which in *Virginia* has given them the Name of *Green Fish.* **1842** DeKay *Zool. NY* 4.131, The *Blue-fish,* or, as it is sometimes called, the *Horse Mackerel, Greenfish* in Virginia, and *Skip-jack* in Carolina, is a common inhabitant of our waters from May until late in the autumn. **1939** Natl. Geogr. Soc. *Fishes* 86, It is evident, then, that the bluefish gets its name from its color. Small fish are called "tailors" in some localities, and the names "snapping mackerel" and "greenfish" are heard. **1946** LaMonte *N. Amer. Game Fishes* 42, *Bluefish—Pomatomus saltatrix*. . . Greenfish. **1973** Knight *Cook's Fish Guide* 382, Greenfish—Bluefish or see Opaleye.

2 =**opaleye.** [See quot 1939]

1898 U.S. Natl. Museum *Bulletin* 47.1382, *Girella nigricans*. . . Green-fish. **1933** John G. Shedd Aquarium *Guide* 112, The Greenfish [=*Girella nigricans*] is a fair food fish. It grows to be about a foot long and is abundant on rocky shores of southern California. **1939** Natl. Geogr. Soc. *Fishes* 248, *Opaleye or Greenfish*. . . The opaleye is light or dark green, the shade depending on light conditions. . . The greenfish depends on its great activity to escape its enemies. **1953** Roedel *Common Fishes CA* 118, *Opaleye*. . . *Unauthorized Names:* Black perch, . . button perch, blue bass, greenfish. **1973** [see **1** above].

3 usu *Alaska greenfish:* A **greenling** (here: *Hexagrammos octogrammus*). [See quot 1884]

1884 U.S. Natl. Museum *Bulletin* 27.392 **AK,** A marked peculiarity of *H[exagrammos] ordinatus,* which is very common at Unalashka, is its green flesh, from which it has derived the name "green-fish;" the green color disappears in the process of cooking, and the flesh is excellent. **1902** Jordan–Evermann *Amer. Fishes* 501, *H. octogrammus,* the Alaska green-fish, occurs among the Aleutian Islands and westward to Kamchatka. **1928** Pan-Pacific Research Inst. *Jrl.* 3.3.13 **OR, WA,** *Octogrammus octogrammus*. . . Alaska greenfish. **1946** Dufresne *AK's Animals* 285, The Atka-fish . . belongs to the same general family . . [as] the strange Alaska greenfish . . the flesh of which is sometimes grass green, sometimes even livid blue in color.

green-flowered milkweed See **green milkweed**

green fly n

1 A blowfly of the family Calliphoridae. **scattered, but chiefly Sth, S Midl, SW** See Map Cf **greenbottle fly 1**

1805 (1904) Lewis *Orig. Jrls. Lewis & Clark Exped.* 2.319 **VA,** The eye knats have disappeared. [T]he green or blowing flies are still in swarms. **1851** *S. Lit. Messenger* 17.351/2 **ceVA** [Black], Indians carred [sic] wallet of beef on one side, canteen of water on 'tother; green flies follow 'em 'bout in great swarms. **1945** Mathews *Talking Moon* 195 **OK,** Green flies buzzed about the place where I had dressed some quail. **1954** *Harder Coll.* **cwTN,** Fly . . blow fly, green fly. **1965–70** *DARE* (Qu.

R13, *Flies that come to meat or fruit*) 168 Infs, **scattered, but chiefly Sth, S Midl, SW,** Green fly; (Qu. R12, . . *Other kinds of flies*) 49 Infs, **chiefly Sth, S Midl,** Green fly. **1976** Warner *Beautiful Swimmers* 121, The cool air off the water allows one to "walk marsh" without stirring up the gnats, green flies and hungry mosquitoes that make this an excruciating exercise in summer.

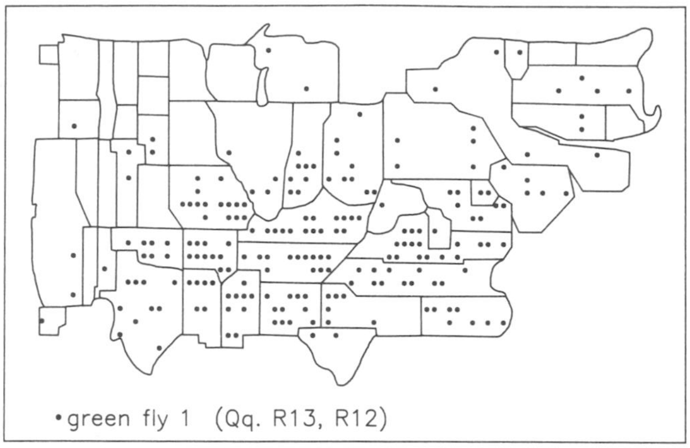

2 =mayfly. Cf **Green Bay fly**

1969–70 *DARE* (Qu. R4, *A large winged insect that hatches in summer in great numbers around lakes or rivers, crowds around lights, lives only a day or so, and is good fish bait*) Infs **IL**69, 78, 86, **TN**31, 34, Green fly; **OK**58, Big green fly.

3 A midge (here: prob *Tanytarsus* spp) of the family Chironomidae.

1968–69 *DARE* (Qu. R10, *Very small flies that don't sting, often seen hovering in large groups or bunches outdoors in summer*) Infs **KY**60, **LA**23, **VA**2, Green fly.

green-fly orchid n [From the shape and color of the flowers]

A **tree orchid** (here: *Epidendrum conopseum*).

1933 Small *Manual SE Flora* 391, *Epidendrum conopseum*. . . Green-fly orchid. **1953** Greene–Blomquist *Flowers South* 23, Green-Fly Orchid *(Epidendrum conopseum)*—This is the most frequent and widely distributed epiphytic orchid in the southeastern states. **1972** Brown *Wildflowers LA* 36, Green-fly Orchid. . . This is the only native, epiphytic orchid thus far found in Louisiana. **1976** Fleming *Wild Flowers FL* 42, Green-fly orchid is the most common epiphytic orchid in Florida found north of the range of the Florida butterfly orchid.

green foxtail n Also *green bristle(grass)*

A **foxtail 1** (here: *Setaria viridis*).

1843 Torrey *Flora NY* 2.430, *Pennisetum viride*. . . Green Foxtail. Bottle-grass. . . Cultivated grounds; frequent. **1878** Killebrew *Grasses TN* 218, *Setaria Viridis*, Beauv.—(Green Foxtail). **1906** Rydberg *Flora CO* 22, *Chaetochloa viridis*. . . *Setaria viridis*. . . Green Foxtail. **1932** in 1957 Old Farmer's Almanac *Sampler* 289, Green foxtail. **1933** Small *Manual SE Flora* 85, *C[haetochloa] viridis*. . . Green-foxtail. **1939** FWP *Guide KS* 11, Also ubiquitous, but of little or no grazing value, are tumble grass, green bristle, and love grasses. **1970** U.S. Ag. Research Serv. *Selected Weeds* 85, *Green foxtail, green bristle-grass*. . . One of the most serious and widespread grass weeds of cultivated soils and waste places.

green frog n

Any of var frogs, as:

a also *greenie*: **=treefrog.**

[**1709** (1967) Lawson *New Voyage* 137 **NC,** The small green Frogs get upon Trees, and make a Noise.] **1737** (1911) Brickell *Nat. Hist. NC* 140, The *Green Frog,* so called from it's [sic] Colour, it is one of the smallest sort I ever met with; these climb up Trees, and sing or make a noise much like the *Grass-hopper,* but much louder. **1950** *WELS (Small frogs that sing or chirp loudly in the spring)* 6 Infs, **WI,** Green frog; *(Names for the treefrog)* 1 Inf, Green frog. **1965–70** *DARE* (Qu. P21) 60 Infs, **widespread exc NEng,** Green frogs; **PA**245, Greenies; (Qu. P23) Infs **MO**7, **OH**60, Green frog. **1966** Dakin *Dial. Vocab. Ohio R. Valley* 2.387, A bewildering list of names appear to be used for the small frogs whose shrill peeping announces the coming of spring in late March or April. . . Only *(spring) peeper* which appears in scattered records from Ohio . . , Indiana . . , and north-central Kentucky . . , and *green frog,* which has the same distribution . . approach being regional terms.

b A **bullfrog 1,** usu *Rana clamitans.*

1827 Williams *View W. FL* 29, The shad-frog, speckled, and green frogs, are confined usually to the water. **1891** in 1895 IL State Lab. Nat. Hist. Urbana *Bulletin* 3.327, *Rana clamitans*. . . *Green Frog*. . . Color above green or brown posteriorly, with obscure black spots of irregular size. . . This is a large species more closely resembling the bull frog than any other. **1906** (1907) Dickerson *Frog Book* 140, We hear in the distance what must be the low croaking of a green frog, but . . find it is made by a downy woodpecker drumming on a resonant sycamore. **1928** Baylor Univ. Museum *Contrib.* 16.6.10, Green Frog *(Rana clamitans)*. . . This frog is much smaller than the true Bullfrog (*Rana catesbiana* Shaw). **1968–70** *DARE* (Qu. P22, *Names or nicknames for a very large frog that makes a deep, loud sound*) Inf **OK**1, Big old green frog; **IL**115, **NY**97, **PA**70, Green frog. **1982** Sternberg *Fishing* 112, Green frogs are popular among fishermen in the eastern half of the country. They are normally found in marshlands but may live along streams. *Ibid* 113, Green frogs grow to 3½ inches. Ridges extend from the eye two-thirds of the way down the back. . . Color varies from pale green to brown. **1985** Clark *From Mailbox* 46 **ME,** The tadpoles of green frogs . . may take several years to reach the "frog" stage.

green gar n Also *green garfish* [See quot 1906]

A **needlefish** (here: *Strongylura* spp).

1743 (1754) Catesby *Nat. Hist. Carolina* 2.30, *Acus maxima, squammosa, viridis.* The green Gar-Fish. **1906** NJ State Museum *Annual Rept. for 1905* 204, Genus *Tylosurus* Cocco. The Green Gars. . . *Tylosurus marinus*. . . Green Gar. . . A good food-fish, but avoided usually on account of the greenish color of the bones and flesh, especially by the ignorant, who regard it as poisonous. **1969** *DARE* FW Addit **ceNC,** Green gar—a fish.

green gentian n

Any of var plants of the genus *Frasera,* but usu the western spp such as *F. speciosa.* Also called **columbo, deer's ears, elkweed, monument plant.** For other names of var spp, see **deer-tongue 3, feltwort 2**

1936 McDougall–Baggley *Plants of Yellowstone* 101, *Greengentian (Frasera speciosa)*.—The stems of this plant are 2 to 5 feet high and very leafy. **1957** Roberts–Nelson *Wildflowers CO* 65, *Green Gentian*. . . blooms in late July or August and occurs throughout the montane zone. **1961** Douglas *My Wilderness* 17 **CO,** Green gentian or elk weed *(Swertia radicata)* with broad basal leaves every other year shows a stalk of creamy white flowers several feet high. **1970** Kirk *Wild Edible Plants W. U.S.* 70, Green Gentian . . is found mostly above 5000 feet in . . open areas throughout the West. **1976** Bailey–Bailey *Hortus Third* 485, *Frasera*. . . *Green gentian*. . . Sometimes transplanted from the wild.

green grass n

=bluegrass 1, usu *Poa pratensis.*

1837 Darlington *Flora Cestrica* 75, *P[oa] pratensis*. . . Meadow Poa. *Vulgo*—Spear grass. Green grass. **1859** (1880) Darlington *Amer. Weeds* 383, *P[oa] pratensis*. . . This species varies considerably. . . In our best soils, the radical leaves are very long and luxuriant,—when it is known by the name of "Green Grass." **1911** *Century Dict. Suppl.* **PA,** *Grass*. . . *Green grass,* the Kentucky blue-grass, *Poa pratensis.* **1937** U.S. Forest Serv. *Range Plant Hdbk.* G95, The bluegrasses are often called speargrasses, and sometimes also pinegrasses and greengrasses.

green grasset See **grasset 3**

green grass frog See **grass frog b**

green grass snake See **grass snake 1**

green gravel n Also *sweet gravel* [Engl dial]

A children's singing game; see quot 1883.

1883 Newell *Games & Songs* 71, *Green gravel.* A girl sits in the ring, and turns her head gravely as a messenger advances, while the rest sing to a pleasing air. **1888** *Amer. Anthropologist* 1.244, *Sweet Gravel*. . . Sweet Gravel, sweet Gravel,/ Your true love is dead;/ He wrote you a letter / To turn back your head. One in the ring turns her head over her shoulder. Then the lines are sung again and another turns likewise. This continues until all have turned. **1940** *Qrly. Jrl. Speech* 26.266 **VA,** Other names of games are. . . "Green Gravel." **1941** Writers' Program *Guide SC* 106, Such singing games as 'Green Gravel' and 'Here We Dance, Looby Loo,' are played on every schoolground and even by adults at country parties. **1946** TN Folk Lore Soc. *Bulletin* 12.1.20, Other singing games were "Green Gravel," . . and such. **1957** *Sat. Eve. Post Letters* **cwPA** (as of c1900), We little girls liked very much [to play] "All around the Mulberry Bush" and "Green Gravel," I think principally because we liked the song[s] which went with them. **1965** *DARE* FW Addit **sIN** (as of 1900–40) Green gravel was played in southern Indiana.

green hand n

1 An inexperienced person; a greenhorn. **chiefly Sth, S Midl** See Map

1808 in 1853 U.S. Congress *Debates & Proc.* 10th Cong 2d Sess 13 Dec 850/2 **NY,** We are all embarked in the same ship, and must sink or swim together; and although I am but a green hand, and before the mast, I will do all in my power to keep the vessel from going down. **1850** Garrard *Wah-to-yah* 23, But, finding myself a "green hand", at least not an adept, in the mysteries of prairie butchering, I mounted *Paint.* **1851** *Alta Californian* 30 July *(DAE),* The price of labor, says the Sacramento Union, is rapidly advancing throughout the mining districts, and there is a great demand even for 'green hands.' **1885** Twain *Huck. Finn* 135 **MO,** Tell them pap was behind, coming along with a trading-scow, and was a green hand at the business. **1894** (1899) Ford *Peter Stirling* 100 **NY,** He's such a green hand that we ought to be able to down him. **1965–70** *DARE* (Qu. HH15, *A very inexperienced person, one who is just learning how to do a new thing*) 23 Infs, **chiefly Sth, S Midl,** Green hand. **1981** *KS Qrly.* 13.2.67, *Green hand*. . a new employee on the ranch or an inexperienced person.

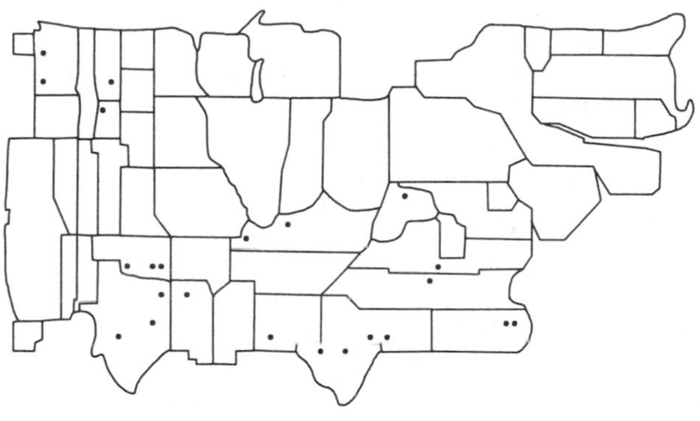

•green hand 1 (Qu. HH15)

2 =**green fingers.** Cf **growing hand**

1944 *PADS* 2.37 **VA, NC,** "She has green thumbs" means: everything she plants grows well and flourishes. . . In Va. and some places in N.C. a *green hand* means the same thing. **1952** Brown *NC Folkl.* 1.547 **cnNC,** *Green hand, to have a.* . . To have the knack of growing fruits and vegetables.

greenhead n

1 A **striped bass** (here: *Roccus saxatilis*).

1815 Lit. & Philos. Soc. NY *Trans.* 1.503, The largest rock-fish, that is, those that weigh from twenty-five pounds to sixty pounds, are called *green heads.* **1884** Goode *Fisheries U.S.* 1.425, *The Striped Bass*. . [is] sometimes known in New England by the names 'Greenhead' and 'Squid-hound.' **1935** Caine *Game Fish* 44 **Sth,** Greenhead. **1941** O'Donnell *Great Big Doorstep* 5 **sLA,** 'Hurry up!' Topal yelled across the water. 'The greenheads are biting like ole hell!' **1972** Sparano *Outdoors Encycl.* 380, *Striped Bass. . . Common Names*. . greenhead. . . Coloration is dark-green to almost black on the back. **1975** Evanoff *Catch More Fish* 202, The striped bass *(Roccus saxatilis)* is also called . . greenhead.

2 as *creeping greenhead:* Clustered bluet *(Oldenlandia uniflora).*

1822 Eaton *Botany* 299, *Hedyotis*. . *glomerata* (creeping greenhead . .). Damp or wet. **1861** Wood *Class-Book* 403, *O[ldenlandia] glomerata. . . Creeping green-head.* . . A plant varying in size . . , found in swamps, &c., N.Y. to La. **1940** Clute *Amer. Plant Names* 53, *O. uniflora. Clustered bluets.* Creeping greenhead.

3 also *greenhead fly, green-headed (black) fly:* Any of several, often green-eyed, biting flies of the family Tabanidae. **widespread, but esp Atlantic** Cf **greenbottle fly 2**

1837 Wetmore *Gaz. MO* 65, In the early settlement of the country, the value of the prairies was underrated by a knowledge of the mischievous power vested in the greenheads, or prairie fly. **1838** Flagg *Far West* 2.107 **IL,** My horse . . [was] severely troubled by that terrible insect, so notorious all over the West, the large green-bottle prairie fly, called the *"green-head."* **1894** *DN* 1.331 **NJ,** *Green head:* a fly common in the coast district. **1905** Kellogg *Amer. Insects* 328, Nearly 200 species of horse-flies are known in North America. The large bluish-black and brownish-black ones . . belong to the genera Tabanus and Therioplectes; the smaller "greenheads" with banded wings and brilliantly colored eyes and black or brown and yellow bodies mostly belong to the genus Chrysops. **1906** Lincoln *Mr. Pratt* 96 **seMA,** As for the livestock, that was seven thousand hop-toads, twenty million sand fleas, and green-heads and mosquitoes forever and ever, amen. **1930** Stoney–Shelby *Black Genesis* 48 **seSC,** She fix Br' Hoss he long-hair tail so he can smack he haunch, an' kill a whole fambly o' green-head fly to once. **1965–70** *DARE* (Qu. R12) 42 Infs, **scattered, but esp Atlantic,** Green-headed fly; 13 Infs, **scattered, but esp Atlantic,** Greenhead fly; **AR**41, **CO**37, **CT**15, 17, **MA**72, **NC**60, **NJ**59, **OK**46, Greenheads; (Qu. R13) Inf **DE**4, Greenhead fly; **DC**2, Green-headed black fly; **NY**240, Green-headed fly. **1968** *DARE* Tape **LA**31, When they [=flies] come is whenever the marsh dries up. . . Greenhead flies, and deer fly and . . big ol' black horse fly and . . little horn flies.

4 Any of var birds, as:

a A duck:

(1) also *greenhead duck, ~ mallard:* =**mallard,** usu the male. **esp Sth, West**

1852 Stansbury *Expedition* 322 **UT,** *Anas boschas,* L.—Mallard; Green-head. . . Found throughout the United States, California, Oregon, and fur countries. **1887** *Amer. Field* 27.50/3 **IL, WI,** The resounding "quack! quack!" of the sturdy old green heads and their near relations. **1888** *Century Illustr. Mag.* 37.296/1 **FL,** One day he succeeded in snaring a green-head duck. **1918** Grinnell *Game Birds CA* 92, *Mallard. . . Other names*—Greenhead. . . *Adult male:* Head and neck brilliant metallic green. **1937** Sandoz *Slogum* 203 **NE,** On his fish pond swam two mallard ducks, greenheads, making soft, friendly talkings to each other in the warm sun. **1958** Humphrey *Home from the Hill* 46 **TX,** By the necks hung . . duck decoys: greenhead mallards. **1965–70** *DARE* (Qu. Q5, . . *Kinds of wild ducks*) 14 Infs, **esp Sth, West,** Greenhead; **OK**23, Greenhead duck; **IN**42, **SC**40, Greenhead mallard. **1975** Newell *If Nothin' Don't Happen* 36 **nwFL,** She had to admit that a big old canvasback drake were mighty fine and would stack up pretty dern well with them greenheads she was always a-braggin' about. **1982** Elman *Hunter's Field Guide* 150, *Mallard (Anas platyrhynchos)*—Common & Regional Names: greenhead. *Ibid* 205, *Greater Scaup (Aythua marila)*—Common & Regional Names: . . greenhead.

(2) also *greenhead broadbill:* Usu the **greater scaup,** but also the **lesser scaup.** Cf **broadbill 1**

1888 Trumbull *Names of Birds* 55 **MD,** Crisfield duckers frequently, however, distinguish the greater scaup [=*Aythya marila*] as *Green-Head.* **1917** (1923) *Birds Amer.* 1.135, *Scaup Duck. . . Other Names.* . . Green-head. . . *Adult Male: Entire head, neck and fore parts of body black with green and bluish reflections.* [*Ibid* 136, *Lesser Scaup Duck.* . . Black Jack . . and names of the Scaup Duck with or without qualifying terms.] **1923** U.S. Dept. Ag. *Misc. Circular* 13.19, *Greater Scaup Duck. . . Vernacular Names. . . In local use.* . . Greenhead (Md.) . . *Lesser Scaup Duck.* . . Greenhead broadbill (Long Id., N.Y.) **1925** (1928) Forbush *Birds MA* 1.237, *Marila marila. . . Other names* . . green-head. **1982** [see **4a(1)** above].

(3) =**goldeneye 1.**

1943 Musgrove–Musgrove *Waterfowl IA* 56, *American Goldeneye.* . . Other names . . greenhead. . . *Adult male*—Head iridescent green with white spot on each side at base of black bill.

b A plover:

(1) =**black-bellied plover.**

1877 Bartlett *Americanisms* 777, *Bottle-head.* . . The black-bellied plover; also called 'beetle-head' and 'green head.'

(2) =**golden plover. esp MA**

1887 *Forest & Stream* 28.84/2 **MA,** In Nantucket the golden plover . . is generally called greenhead. **1888** Trumbull *Names of Birds* 195, *American Golden Plover.* . . At West Barnstable and New Bedford (Mass.), and Newport, R.I., *Green-head.* **1925** (1928) Forbush *Birds MA* 1.462, *Golden Plover. Other names* . . green-head. **1955** MA Audubon Soc. *Bulletin* 39.444 **MA,** *American Golden Plover.* . . Greenhead.

c The common **loon** *(Gavia immer).*

1917 (1923) *Birds Amer.* 1.12, *Loon. Gavia immer. . . Other Names.* . . Greenhead. . . *Adults in summer:* Head and neck all around, glossy purplish-black with greenish reflections. **1946** Hausman *Eastern Birds* 62, *Common Loon. . . Other Names* . . Greenhead.

5 A frog:

a A **bullfrog 1,** usu *Rana clamitans.*

1899 Bergen *Animal Lore* 61, Folk-names of Animals [include] . . Green-heads, large frogs, *Rana clamata.* **1966** Dakin *Dial. Vocab. Ohio R. Valley* 2.387, *Bullfrog. . . Green frog* and *green head* are attested several times, but it is plain that these are general terms. **1967–70** *DARE* (Qu. P22, *Names or nicknames for a very large frog that makes a deep, loud sound*) Infs **IL**135, **MO**38, Greenhead.

b A **treefrog.**

1967 *DARE* (Qu. P21, *Small frogs that sing or chirp loudly in spring*) Inf **MO**5, Greenheads.

6 also *greenass:* **=green hand 1.**

1942 Berrey–Van den Bark *Amer. Slang* 456, *(Inexperienced person; novice.)* . . green . . hand, green head. **1966–68** *DARE* (Qu. HH15, *A very inexperienced person, one who is just learning how to do a new thing*) Inf **IN**1, Greenass; **CA**81, Green head. **1986** Pederson *LAGS Concordance (A rustic)* 1 inf, **cnLA,** Greenhead—don't know nothing about nothing.

greenhead broadbill See **greenhead 4a(2)**

greenhead duck See **greenhead 4a(1)**

green-headed black fly See **greenhead 3**

green-headed coneflower n

=goldenglow.

1900 Lyons *Plant Names* 326, *R[udbeckia] laciniata. . .* Green-headed Cone-flower. . . *Plant* diuretic, tonic. **1912** Blatchley *IN Weed Book* 172, Green-headed cone-flower . . disk oblong-cylindric, greenish-yellow, and the rays . . bright yellow. **1931** Harned *Wild Flowers Alleghanies* 573, *Green-headed Cone-flower. . .* is cultivated and known under the familiar name Golden-Glow. **1971** GA Dept. Ag. *Farmers Market Bulletin* 18 Aug 8/1, "Susan's" close cousins include the Browneyed Susan, Thin-leaved Cornflower [sic], Green-headed Cornflower [sic] and Golden Glow. **1973** Hitchcock–Cronquist *Flora Pacific NW* 544, Green-headed coneflower. . . *R[udbeckia] laciniata.*

green-headed fly See **greenhead 3**

green-headed widgeon n

=baldpate 1.

1888 Trumbull *Names of Birds* 20, *Anas Americana. . .* Baldpate. . . Green-headed widgeon. **1925** (1928) Forbush *Birds MA* 1.205, *Mareca americana. . . Baldpate. . .* Green-headed widgeon. **1943** Musgrove–Musgrove *Waterfowl IA* 26, Green-headed widgeon. . . *Adult male*—Head light gray finely speckled with black, with a rich, greenish iridescent patch running from eye to nape of neck. **1947** *Sun* (Baltimore MD) 24 Jan 12/3 *(Hench Coll.),* Baldpate. . . Also known as . . green-headed widgeon. **1982** Elman *Hunter's Field Guide* 182, *American Widgeon* (*Anas americana,* also classified as *Mareca americana*)—Common & Regional Names: baldpate . . green-headed widgeon . . poacher.

greenhead fly See **greenhead 3**

greenhead mallard See **greenhead 4a(1)**

green heron n Also *little green heron*

A small dark heron *(Butorides striatus).* Also called **cap-cap 1, chalk-line, chucklehead 2, cow-cow 1, crabcatcher, cream-shitter, fly-up-the-creek 1, green bittern, Indian hen, Indian pullet, kelly fisher, little crane, minnow fisher, mudhen, mudpoke, poke, rain crow, shitepoke, skeow**

1785 Pennant *Arctic Zool.* 2.447, *Green Heron. . .* Inhabits from *New York* to *South Carolina.* **1855** *Knickerbocker* 46.222 **seNJ,** Night-herons, snowy-herons, green-herons, and little-herons construct their nests so closely together that four or five hundred of them may be counted upon twenty or thirty cedars. **1883** *Century Illustr. Mag.* 26.653/1 **Cape Cod MA,** Among the most common birds [is] . . the green heron. **1917** (1923) *Birds Amer.* 1.192, *Butorides virescens virescens. . .* Little Green Heron. . . Though a comparatively small Heron, the Green Heron is perhaps the best known member of his family in this country. **1967–70** *DARE* (Qu. Q10, . . *Water birds and marsh birds*) Infs **CT**29, **GA**20, **IA**20, **MN**18, **PA**162, **TN**11, 34, Green heron; **CT**5, **MA**5, 78, Little green heron. **1977** Udvardy *Audubon Field Guide Birds* 460, Green Herons are rather solitary, which is unusual for herons.

greenhouse n

1 A root cellar. Cf *DNE*

1966 *DARE* (Qu. M19, *A place for keeping carrots, turnips, potatoes, and so on over the winter*) Inf **ME**1, Greenhouse—built into bank with logs, years ago.

2 See quot.

1968 *DARE* (Qu. M21a, *An outside toilet building*) Inf **OH**87, Greenhouse.

greenhouse frog n

A small frog *(Eleutherodactylus planirostris)* widespread in Florida.

1955 Carr–Goin *Guide Reptiles* 191, Greenhouse Frog. . . A small, active, brownish frog an inch or less in length. **1958** Conant *Reptiles & Amphibians* 261, *Greenhouse Frog. . .* Usually to be found in gardens, greenhouses, hardwood hammocks, and in small stream valleys. **1979** Behler–King *Audubon Field Guide Reptiles* 419, *Greenhouse Frog. . .* On humid nights it is frequently seen foraging on lawns. It can be brought out and encouraged to call by sprinkling.

green ibis n

=glossy ibis 1.

1917 (1923) *Birds Amer.* 1.177, Glossy Ibis—*Plegadis autumnalis. . .* Green Ibis. **1932** Bennitt *Check-list* 16 **MO,** Eastern glossy ibis. *Plegadis falcinellus* . . green ibis (young). **1944** Hausman *Amer. Birds* 115, Eastern Glossy Ibis. . . Green Ibis.

green ice n

=rubber ice.

1965–70 *DARE* (Qu. B35, *Ice that will bend when you step on it, but not break*) Infs **IN**68, **MO**18, **OH**17, Green ice.

greenie See **green frog a**

greenie shower See **greenback shower**

greening See **green** v **3**

greenings n pl

The leafy tops of vegetables; vegetables.

1940–41 Cassidy *WI Atlas* **seWI,** Greenings . . the green tops of spring onions. **1950** *WELS (Any general word . . for garden vegetables)* 1 Inf, **WI,** Greenings. **1981** *PADS* 67.36 **neMN,** *Greens. . . Greens* is the choice of 12 of 13 Mesabi respondents. Other Range terms are *(beet) tops* . . [2 infs], *beet leaves* . . [1 inf], and *greenings* . . [1 inf].

green jack n

=green dragon.

1951 *PADS* 15.27 **TX,** *Muricauda dracontium. . .* Green jack.

green jacket n

A **dragonfly** (here: *Erythemis simplicicollis*).

1929 Needham–Heywood *Hdbk. Dragonflies* 246, Green Jacket. . . A clear winged species of medium size, having a body of bright green when young. . . A vigilant, if somewhat sedentary species.

green lampblack n Cf *DS* HH14, **white lampblack**

A nonexistent item used as the basis of a practical joke.

1938 FWP *Guide CT* 274, Apprentice boys were sent from shop to shop in search of 'stirrup oil,' 'limbering oils,' and 'green lampblack.'

greenleg n

=stilt sandpiper.

1923 U.S. Dept. Ag. *Misc. Circular* 13.52, *Stilt Sandpiper. . . Vernacular Names. . . In local use. . .* Greenleg (Long Id., N.Y.) **1946** Hausman *Eastern Birds* 285, Stilt Sandpiper *Micropalama himantopus.* . . Greenleg. . . *Field Marks. . .* The very long greenish legs. **1951** Pough *Audubon Water Bird* 331, Greenleg. *See* Stilt sandpiper. **1955** Forbush–May *Birds* 201, Stilt Sandpiper—*Micropalama himantopus. . .* Green-leg.

green-legged crane n

A **bittern** (here: *Botaurus lentiginosus*).

1890 Warren *Birds PA* 55, The Bittern or "Green-legged Crane," as this wader is called by many sportsmen, is readily distinguished from other birds of the family by its brownish-yellow plumage, greenish-colored legs, and large size.

green-legged peep n

=least sandpiper.

1923 U.S. Dept. Ag. *Misc. Circular* 13.55, *Least Sandpiper. . .* Green-legged peep. **1936** Roberts *MN Birds* 1.509, *Green-legged Peep. . . Field Marks.*—Smallest of the Sandpipers; . . legs olive-green. **1946** Hausman *Eastern Birds* 281, Green-legged Peep. . . A very common migrant along the Atlantic coast, less so in the interior. **1955** Forbush–May *Birds* 198.

greenlet n [See quots 1917, 1946]
=**vireo.**

1831 Richardson *Fauna Boreali-Amer.* 2.233, *Vireo olivaceus* . . Red-eyed Greenlet. *Ibid* 235, *Vireo Bartramii* . . Bartram's Greenlet. *Ibid* 237, *Vireo longirostris* . . Long-billed Greenlet. **1871** Burroughs *Wake-Robin* 20, The ornithologist will direct you where to look for the greenlets. **1903** Dawson *Birds OH* 1.294, The plumage of this modest "Greenlet" boasts only enough green to enable its owner to lose itself easily in the foliage of the upper branches. **1917** (1923) *Birds Amer.* 3.102, Vireos are sometimes called Greenlets; the Latin word *Vireo* means 'I am green.' **1946** Hausman *Eastern Birds* 481, Our vireos are small, olive-grayish-backed birds (greenish in strong light; hence the name greenlets) with plain, unmarked whitish or yellowish underparts. **1978** Gromme *Birds WI* 215, Greenlet, Bell's (Bell's Vireo).

green light(, red light) See **red light, green light**

green lily n
A liliaceous plant *(Schoenocaulon drummondii)* native to Texas.

1961 Wills–Irwin *Flowers TX* 93, Abundant along highways and on hillsides in South Central and Trans-Pecos Texas . . is the Green-lily. From among the . . leaves there arise the scape, . . bristling with tiny green-yellow flowers. **1970** Correll *Plants TX* 384, *Schoenocaulon drummondii*. . . Green lily.

greenling n
A fish of the Pacific family Hexagrammidae, esp of the genus *Hexagrammos,* but also including the Atka **mackerel** *(Pleurogrammus monopterygius).* Also called **ling cod, rock cod, rock trout.** For other names of var spp of *Hexagrammos* see **greenfish 3, kelp cod, kelpfish, red rock trout, rockfish, sea trout.** For other names of the Atka **mackerel** see **horse mackerel 7, sea bass, Spanish mackerel, striped fish, yellowfish.** For other names of *Oxylebius pictus* see **convict** n

1898 U.S. Natl. Museum *Bulletin* 47.1863, Hexagrammidae. *(The Greenlings).* . . Carnivorous fishes, mostly of large size, living in kelp and about rocks in the North Pacific; some of them highly valued as food. **1902** Jordan–Evermann *Amer. Fishes* 501, The genus *Hexagrammos,* which contains the true greenlings or rock trouts, differs from *Pleurogrammus* chiefly in having the dorsal fin deeply notched or divided. **1929** Pan-Pacific Research Inst. *Jrl.* 4.4.9 **sCA,** *Hexagrammidae.* The Greenlings. **1938** *Natl. Geogr. Mag.* 74.479, Often incorrectly called Rock Trout, greenlings *(Chiropsis decagrammus . .)* are valued as filets on the Pacific coast. Anglers seek them around rocky headlands. **1953** Roedel *Common Fishes CA* 142, *Hexagrammos decagrammus*. . . In the Pacific Northwest "greenling" prevails and that name is now reported entering California. It is far more appropriate [than "seatrout"], as the fish is not remotely related to the trouts. **1955** U.S. Arctic Info. Center *Gloss.* 6, *Atka mackerel*. . . Sometimes incorrectly called 'greenling' or 'Atka fish.' **1973** Knight *Cook's Fish Guide* 382, Greenling.

green lizard n
1 A chameleon of the genus *Anolis,* usu *A. carolinensis.* **Sth**

1709 (1967) Lawson *New Voyage* 136 **NC,** Green Lizards are very harmless and beautiful, having a little Bladder under their Throat, which they fill with Wind, and evacuate the same at Pleasure. **1743** (1754) Catesby *Nat. Hist. Carolina* 2.65, *Lacertus viridis Carolinensis.* The Green Lizard of Carolina. . . They frequent Houses, are familiar and harmless, and are suffered with Impunity to sport and catch Flies on Tables and Windows. **1821** in 1830 Royall *Letters AL* 139, The Camelion is also a native of this place. . . They are called the "Green Lizard," by the inhabitants. **1881** *Amer. Naturalist* 15.96, The green lizard *(Anolis principalis)* of the Southern United States is sometimes called the American chameleon, but it is not related to the chameleon of the Old World. **1908** Biol. Soc. DC *Proc.* 21.71 **cnTX,** *Anolis carolinensis*. . . *Green Lizard*. . . In the spring of 1899 I collected two specimens about eight miles south of Waco. **1928** Baylor Univ. Museum *Contrib.* 16.10 **TX,** *Anolis carolinensis* . . is called *Chameleon* by the white inhabitants of eastern Texas and Louisiana. It is also known as the *Green Lizard* [and] *Pink-throated Green Lizard.* **1930** *Copeia* 4.154 **swGA,** Green lizard; 'Chameleon'. . . One of the residents said that when this lizard distends its pink throat, they speak of its 'taking out its pocketbook.'

2 as *big green lizard:* The collared lizard *(Crotaphytus collaris).*

1928 Baylor Univ. Museum *Contrib.* 16.10 **TX,** *Crotaphytus collaris*. . . In the granite country of west central Texas it is the *Big Green Lizard* or *Ring-necked lizard.*

green locust n
A **black locust** (here: *Robinia pseudoacacia*).

1832 Browne *Sylva* 298, There are said to be several varieties of the locust [=*Robinia pseudoacacia*] growing in the United States; those trees are reputed the best whose heart is red; the next in esteem are those with a greenish-yellow heart; and the least valuable are those with a white heart. From this variety in the color of the wood, which probably arises from a difference of soil, are derived the names of *Red, Green* and *White Locust.* **1897** Sudworth *Arborescent Flora* 258 **TN,** *Robinia pseudacacia*. . . *Locust*. . . Green Locust. **1950** Moore *Trees AR* 85, *Black Locust*. . . Local Names . . Green Locust. . . *Wood* . . brown or rarely light greenish brown with pale yellow sapwood. **1960** Vines *Trees SW* 566, *Black Locust*. . . Other vernacular names are White Locust. . . Green Locust.

green mackerel See **greenback mackerel**

green maple n
1 Prob **vine maple.**

1844 Lee–Frost *10 Yrs. OR* 7.81, The whole of the north-west coast is exceedingly mountainous and rugged, with dense forests of fir, hemlock, spruce, . . and a species of maple, called green-maple, or 'devil wood,' remarkable for its toughness.

2 =**striped maple.**

1975 Hamel–Chiltoskey *Cherokee Plants* 44, Green maple. . . *Acer pennsylvanicum.*

green milkweed n Also *green-flowered milkweed*
Any of several **milkweeds** (*Asclepias* spp) formerly included in the genus *Acerates,* but esp *Asclepias viridiflora.*

1829 Eaton *Botany* 90, *[Acerates] viridiflora*. . . Green milkweed. . . No little horn in the nectaries. **1848** Gray *Manual of Botany* 369, *Acerates*. . . Green Milkweed. Nearly as in Asclepias. . . *A. viridiflora*. . . Green-flowered Milkweed. *Ibid* 370, *A. longifolia*. . . Long-leaved Green Milkweed. **1892** Coulter *Botany W. TX* 267, *Green Milkweed*. . . Greenish flowers in compact many-flowered umbels. **1936** Whitehouse *TX Flowers* 100, In the green-flowered milkweed, purple hoods are attached to the crown and hang over the pollen-sacs. **1968** Barkley *Plants KS* 275, Asclepias engelmannia. . . Asclepias hirtella. . . Asclepias lanuginosa. . . Asclepias stenophylla. . . Green milkweed. **1972** Brown *Wildflowers LA* 145, *Green-flowered Milkweed. Asclepias viridiflora*. . . Also Texas, Arkansas, and Mississippi. April to August.

green mist n
A **boneset 1** (here: *Eupatorium capillifolium*).

1941 Walker *Lookout* 53 **TN,** Green mist . . is a lovely late flower, whose branches and foliage are as beautiful as its tiny flowers.

green molly n
A **summer cypress** (here: *Kochia americana*).

1960 Vines *Trees SW* 242, Greenmolly Summer-cypress—*Kochia americana.* **1974** Munz *Flora S. CA* 366, *K[ochia] americana*. . . Green-Molly.

green mullet n
A **redhorse;** see quots.

1878 U.S. Natl. Museum *Bulletin* 12.131, *Myxostoma Thalassinum*. . . Green Mullet. **1902** Jordan–Evermann *Amer. Fishes* 61 **nwNC,** Green mullet *(M[oxostoma] thalassinum),* Yadkin River.

green on See **green** v **1**

green onion n
1 also *greentail onion, green-top:* Usu a **scallion,** but also a young **onion;** see quots. **chiefly west of Appalachians** See Map and Map Section Cf **potato onion, rareripe, set onion, shallot, spring onion, winter onion**

1847 (1852) Crowen *Amer. Cookery* 189 **NY,** *Shalots, or Green Onions.*—Take off the outer skin or leaf; cut off all but about an inch or two of the green part, and lay them in cold water for an hour, then take them from the water on to a plate, and serve with salt. **1941** *LANE* Map 258, The map shows the terms *scallion, . . rareripe, . . spring onion, green* ~ . . , denoting either a shallot . . or a variety of the onion . . , usually characterized by a small bulb and a long fleshy stem and eaten raw. . . 4 infs, **ME, MA,** Green onion. **1950** *WELS (The kind of onions that are served raw early in the year)* 36 Infs, **WI,** Green onions; 1 Inf, Early green onions; 1 Inf, Little green onions. **1965–70** *DARE* (Qu. I6) 406 Infs, **chiefly west of Appalachians,** Green onions; **IL**41, Green-tops; **TX**27, Little green onions; **VT**16, Greentail onions; (Qu. I5, *The kind of onions that keep coming up without replanting year after year)* 14 Infs, **scattered,** Green onions; (Qu. I28a, *What kinds of things do you call 'greens' around here? Those that are eaten raw)* Infs **CA**94, 107, **IN**48, **KY**22, **LA**40, **MN**6, Green onions; (Qu. I28b, *Kinds of greens that are cooked)* Inf **LA**40, Green onions. **1966** Dakin *Dial. Vocab. Ohio R. Valley* 2.367, *Green onion, spring onion,* and *young onion* seem most often to mean the onions which are planted in the spring and grow singly. The rather complete description from informant 253 B suggests what may be a rather general distinction in usage. This speaker says that one sets out a *potato onion* or *multiplier* which makes *young onions* or *scallions* "quick—earlier than *green onions.*" They grow in bunches. *Green onions* grow singly. . . The most widely distributed term is *green onion.* **1971** Wood *Vocab. Change* 42 **Sth,** The usual name of edible onions that appear in the spring is *green onions* everywhere but in Georgia; there *spring onions* has a somewhat greater preference.

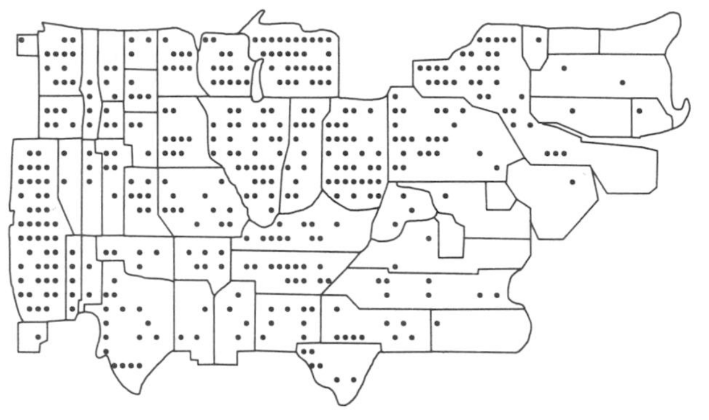
•green onion 1 + varr (Qq. I6, I5, I28a, b)

2 A chive *(Allium schoenoprasum).*

1950 *WELS (The small plants like onions with hollow green leaves that are cut up in salad)* 2 Infs, **WI,** Green onion. **1966–70** *DARE* (Qu. I7) 11 Infs, **scattered,** Green onions; **CA**170, Little green onions.

green osier n Also sp *green ozier* Cf **red osier**

A **dogwood 1,** usu *Cornus alternifolia* or *C. rugosa.*

1876 Hobbs *Bot. Hdbk.* 48, Green ozier. . . Green Osier, Cornus circinata [=*C. rugosa*]. **1896** *Jrl. Amer. Folkl.* 9.189, *Cornus alternifolia,* . . green osier, Paris, M[ain]e. **1897** Sudworth *Arborescent Flora* 310 **VT,** *Cornus alternifolia.* . . Green Osier. **1911** *Century Dict. Suppl., Osier. . . Green osier.* . . Either the round-leaved dogwood, *Cornus circinata,* or the alternate-leaved dogwood, *C. alternifolia,* the twigs of which are green. **1940** Clute *Amer. Plant Names* 97, *C[ornus] alternifolia.* . . Green-osier. *Ibid* 257, *Cornus florida.* . . Green osier. **1950** Gray-Fernald *Manual of Botany* 1108, *C. alternifolia. . . Green Osier.* Shrub or small tree up to 8 m. high, the *branches* . . of recent years *greenish.*

green out v phr[1] See **green** v **1, 2**

green out v phr[2] See **green up** v phr

green ozier See **green osier**

green parrot('s) feather n

A **water milfoil** (here: *Myriophyllum pinnatum*).

1968 Barkley *Plants KS* 255, Myriophyllum pinnatum. . . Water Milfoil. Green Parrot Feather. **1970** Correll *Plants TX* 1138, *Myriophyllum pinnatum* . . Green parrot's-feather.

green pea n

1 =**garden pea. chiefly Nth** Cf **English pea**

[1630 Higginson *Nevv Englands Plantation* sig B3[r] **MA,** Our Gouernour hath store of greene Pease growing in his Garden as good as euer I eat in *England*.] **1766** in 1860 *Essex Inst. Coll.* 52.79 **MA,** Dined on . . Roast Lamb Green pease & tarts. **1805** in 1899 McClure *Diary* 121 **MA,** Today 11th dined on green peas. **1860** Emerson *Conduct* 202 **MA,** It is strange that superior persons should not feel that they have some better resistance against cholera, than avoiding green peas and salads. **1950** *WELS (Kinds of peas grown in your neighborhood)* 6 Infs, **WI,** Green pea(s). **1954** [see **garden pea**]. **1961** Folk *Word Atlas N. LA* Map 1017, Small green peas grown in spring gardens—English peas 87% [of 275 infs]; green peas 9%; others [=sweet peas, early peas, snap peas] 4%. **1966–68** *DARE* (Qu. H49, *Dishes made by boiling potatoes with other foods)* Inf **AL**38, Young potatoes and green peas; (Qu. I14, *Kinds of beans that you eat in the pod before they're dry)* Infs **NC**52, **WA**27, Green peas; (Qu. I28b, *Kinds of greens that are cooked)* Inf **WA**18, Green peas. **1989** *DARE* File **NYC** (as of early 1950s), Unlike most kids, I was always fond of eating raw vegetables, especially green peas (with the stress on *green*), the kind that you had to remove from their canoe-like shell. In our house, peas always meant green peas.

2 A greenhorn. Cf **green hand 1.**

1942 Berrey–Van den Bark *Amer. Slang* 456.1 *(Inexperienced person; novice.)* . . green pea. **1944** Adams *Western Words* 68, *Green pea* . . a tenderfoot. **1990** *DARE* File **seSC,** Green pea—rookie, newcomer.

green pepper n

1 A sweet pepper (*Capsicum annuum* Grossum Group). **widespread exc SE, Lower Missip Valley** See Map and Map Section Cf **bell pepper, mango**

1847 (1852) Crowen *Amer. Cookery* 389 **NY,** *Green Peppers.*—These are pickled the same as cucumbers. It is best to slit one seam, and take out the seeds or core, that they may be less strong. . . The best peppers for pickling are those thick skinned and green; they may be stuffed with white onions, green beans sliced, horseradish, and mustard seed, the same as melon mangoes. **1945** *Chicago Daily News* (IL) 29 May 9/2, Combine . . one teaspoon finely chopped green pepper . . and one-fourth teaspoon prepared mustard. **1965–70** *DARE* (Qu. I22d, . . *Kinds of peppers—large sweet)* 213 Infs, **widespread exc SE, Lower Missip Valley,** Green peppers; **CT**21, **MN**34, Sweet green peppers; **OR**13, Big green peppers; (Qu. I22c, . . *Peppers—small sweet)* 32 Infs, **chiefly Nth, N Midl, West,** Green peppers.

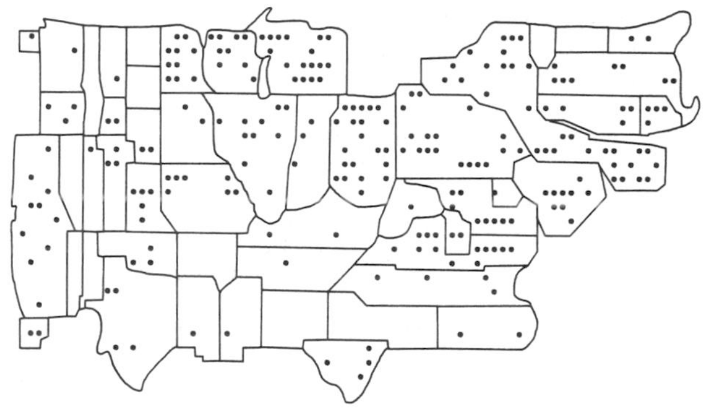
•green pepper 1 + varr (Qq. 122c, d)

2 A hot pepper *(Capsicum annuum).* **scattered, but esp Nth, N Midl** See Map

1834 Pike *Prose Sketches* 96 **cnNM,** The sala, or long hall, . . garnished with . . huge strings . . of red and green pepper. **1885** *Harper's New*

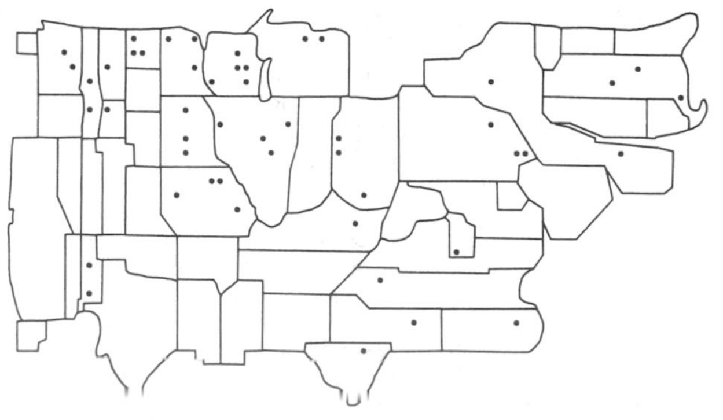
•green pepper 2 + var (Qq. 122a, b)

Mth. Mag. 70.825/2 **NM,** The train wandered on for twenty miles or so through sprouting fields of Indian corn and green peppers. **1965–70** *DARE* (Qu. I22b, . . *Kinds of peppers—large hot*) 33 Infs, **esp Nth, N Midl,** Green peppers; **FL**8, **SC**3, Hot green peppers; (Qu. I22a, . . *Peppers—small hot*) 18 Infs, **esp Nth, N Midl,** Green peppers; **IL**60, Hot green peppers.

green perch n

1 =black bass 1.

1887 Goode *Amer. Fishes* 56, The Small-mouth shares with the Large-mouth . . the names. . . "Marsh Bass," . . "Green Bass," . . "Green Perch." **1890** *Century Dict.* 4387, *Green perch,* the large-mouthed black-bass. **1935** Caine *Game Fish* 3 **Sth,** *Large-Mouthed Black Bass. . . Synonyms* . . Green Perch. *Ibid* 7, *Small-Mouthed Black Bass. . .* Green Perch. *Ibid* 9, *Spotted Small-Mouthed Black Bass.* . . Green Perch.

2 =opaleye.

1953 Roedel *Common Fishes CA* 118, *Opaleye. . . Color:* Greenish blue, becoming paler below. . . *Unauthorized Names* . . green perch. **1955** Zim-Shoemaker *Fishes* 117, *Opaleye,* also called Green Perch or Catalina Perch, is the only common member of a Pacific family and a favorite sports fish for surf casters. **1960** Amer. Fisheries Soc. *List Fishes* 63, Perch . . green—see opaleye; perch, yellow. **1973** Knight *Cook's Fish Guide* 386, Perch . . green—yellow or see Opaleye.

3 =green sunfish 1.

1956 Harlan-Speaker *IA Fish* 131, *Green Sunfish—Lepomis cyanellus. . .* Other Names—Rubber tail, green perch, sunfish, sand bass. **1983** Becker *Fishes WI* 822, *Green Sunfish—Lepomis cyanellus. . .* Other common names: green perch . . rubbertail, sand bass.

4 =yellow perch.

1960 [see **2** above]. **1973** [see **2** above].

green pike n

1 A **walleye** (here: *Stizostedion vitreum*).

1877 U.S. Natl. Museum *Bulletin* 10.46, *Stizostethium vitreum. . .* Wall eyed Pike. . . Glass Eye. . . Horn fish. . . Green Pike. . . Yellow Pike. **1887** Goode *Amer. Fishes* 14 **Gt Lakes,** In the upper lakes . . *Stizostedion vitreum* is called the "Pike," with such local variations as . . "Green Pike." **1902** Jordan-Evermann *Amer. Fishes* 361, Elsewhere it [=*Stizostedion vitreum*] is called . . green pike. **1935** Caine *Game Fish* 31. **1946** LaMonte *N. Amer. Game Fishes* 130. **1983** Becker *Fishes WI* 871, *Walleye. Stizostedion vitreum vitreum. . .* Other common names . . green pike.

2 =chain pickerel.

1882 U.S. Natl. Museum *Bulletin* 16.353, *E[sox] reticulatus. . . Green Pike. . .* Color green of varying shades. . . Not found west of the Alleghanies. **1896** *Ibid* 47.627, *Lucius reticulatus. . .* Green Pike. **1935** Caine *Game Fish* 22, *Pickerel—Esox reticulatus. . .* Green Pike. **1946** LaMonte *N. Amer. Game Fishes* 128, *Eastern Pickerel—Esox niger. . .* Green Pike. **1973** Knight *Cook's Fish Guide* 386, Pike . . green see Pickerel, Chain.

green plover n

=golden plover.

1624 Smith *Genl. Hist. VA* 171 **eVA,** Many sorts of Fowles, as . . the gray and greene Plouer, some wilde Ducks. **1743** (1754) Catesby *Nat. Hist. Carolina* 2 [app] xxxvi, European Water-Fowls which I have observed to be also Inhabitants of America, which tho' they abide the Winter in Carolina, most of them retire North in the Spring to breed. . . The Turn-stone. The Green Plover. The Grey Plover. [*DARE* Ed: Catesby was mistaken in equating the European with the American golden plover.] **1886** *Forest & Stream* 27.343/1 **Cape Cod MA,** I am sure that nearly all of the gunners of Orleans, Chatham and other towns along the Cape call the golden plover the "green plover." **1888** Trumbull *Names of Birds* 195, *American Golden Plover. . .* At Portsmouth, N.H., and in Massachusetts at Salem and Chatham, *Green Plover.* **1917** (1923) *Birds Amer.* 1.257, Golden Plover—*Charadrius dominicus dominicus. . .* Green Plover. **1955** MA Audubon Soc. *Bulletin* 39.444, *American Golden Plover. . .* Green Plover (Maine, Mass. The yellow spotting on dark ground seems to be the basis of these names.)

green pop n [See quot 1911] **LA**

A female or young **painted bunting** (here: *Passerina ciris*).

1911 *Forest & Stream* 77.174, *Passerina ciris. . .* Female, Green pop . . Chef Menteur, La. . . Pop is merely the English fonetic [sic] spelling of the French name "pape" (pope) by which these birds are known to irreverent Louisianians. **1916** *Times-Picayune* (New Orleans LA) 23 Apr mag sec 5/5, *Painted Bunting. . .* Female and young only: Pape Vert; Green "Pop." . . The female has a simple dress of greenish-gray.

green racer n

1 =blue racer 1.

1869 *Amer. Naturalist* 3.124 **cwMT,** *Green Racer* (*Boscanion vetustus* B. and G., or *B. flaviventris?*). I saw one dead specimen of this snake along Hell Gate River. **1900** U.S. Natl. Museum *Annual Rept. for 1898* 794, The *Zamenis constrictor* is the "black snake" of the East and the "blue" and "green racer" of the West. **1928** Ortenburger *Whip Snakes* 175, *Coluber constrictor flaviventris. . .* Green Racer. *Ibid* 213, *Coluber constrictor mormon. . .* Green Racer, Blue Racer. **1928** Pope-Dickinson *Amphibians* 53, *Blue Racer—Coluber constrictor flaviventris. . .* Other common names include Yellow-bellied Racer and Green Racer. **1952** Ditmars *N. Amer. Snakes* 94, *Green Racer* . . *Coluber constrictor flaviventris. . . Coloration:* Bluish green, pale or dark olive. **1967** *DARE* (Qu. P25) Inf **CO**20, Green racer—will fight a pickup [=truck].

2 A **whip snake** (here: *Masticophis taeniatus*).

1928 Baylor Univ. Museum *Contrib.* 16.15 **TX,** This variety of Coachwhip Snake [=*Masticophis flagellum flavigularis*] has many common names . . specimens from the Rio Grande country whose dorsal coloration is greenish are *Green Racers.* **1957** Wright-Wright *Hdbk. Snakes* 1.464 **csTX,** Green racer. . . *Masticophis taeniatus schotti.*

green rattlesnake n Also *green rattler* [See quot 1974]

A **rattlesnake** (here: *Crotalus lepidus, C. molossus*) native to the Southwest.

1928 Baylor Univ. Museum *Contrib.* 16.5, Green Rattlesnake *(Crotalus lepidus . .).* **1952** Ditmars *N. Amer. Snakes* 260, Green Rattlesnake, *Crotalus lepidus lepidus.* **1958** Conant *Reptiles & Amphibians* 194, (Northern) Black-Tailed Rattlesnake—*Crotalus molossus molossus. . .* The "green rattler" of the central Texas uplands and westward. **1974** Shaw-Campbell *Snakes West* 224, A common name for this snake [=*Crotalus lepidus*] is "green rattlesnake," because it is often green in base color.

green sandpiper n

=solitary sandpiper.

1785 Latham *Genl. Synopsis Birds* 3.1.170, *Green S[andpiper]. . .* Tringa ochropus. . . Is found also in *America.* This has a musky kind of smell. **1890** *Century Dict.* 5331, Green sandpipers belong to the genus *Rhyacophilus,* as . . *R. solitarius* of America. **1898** (1900) Davie *Nests N. Amer. Birds* 145, Solitary Sandpiper. *Totanus solitarius. . .* The Solitary Tattler, or the American Green Sandpiper, is found throughout . . North America. **1917** (1923) *Birds Amer.* 1.245, Solitary Sandpiper—*Helodromas solitarius solitarius. . .* Green Sandpiper; American Green Sandpiper. **1946** Hausman *Eastern Birds* 271, Eastern Solitary Sandpiper *Tringa solitaria solitaria. . .* Green Sandpiper.

green sauce n **[sauce]** *old-fash*

=garden sauce.

1867 Lowell *Biglow* xlvi **'Upcountry' MA,** *"Green sauce"* for *vegetables. . .* Our rustic pronunciation *sahce* . . may be the older one. **1872** Schele de Vere *Americanisms* 397 **Sth,** *Green Sauce* for vegetables. **1940** Brown *Amer. Cooks* 814 **VT,** "Green sass" (that is, dandelion greens, turnip tops, cabbage, etc.) is invariably cooked with it [=salt pork]. **1941** *LANE* Map 253 *(Garden vegetables)* 1 inf, **csRI,** Green sauce. **1945** Saxon *Gumbo Ya-Ya* 30 **LA,** Earlier counterparts of present-day hawkers were the Green Sass Men, no longer in existence.

green saucers n

A **four o'clock 1** (here: *Mirabilis comata*).

1941 Jaeger *Wildflowers* 62 **Desert SW,** *Green saucers. Allionia comata. . .* Called "green saucers" because of the greenish, wide-flaring flowers.

greens, for See **green** n **3**

greensides willow n

=heartleaf willow.

1931 U.S. Dept. Ag. *Misc. Pub.* 101.16, Five important essentially shrubby western willows are . . Idaho willow . . ; Barclay willow . . ; greensides willow *(S[alix] monochroma)* of the Northwest (reaching southeast to Colorado), with thin, relatively broad leaves. **1937** U.S. Forest Serv. *Range Plant Hdbk.* B141, The greensides willow of the Northwest . . rates as an outstanding browse willow in that section. **1938** Van Dersal *Native Woody Plants* 361, Willow, greensides *(Salix monochroma).*

green smelt n

A **silversides** of the family Atherinidae such as *Menidia menidia.*

1884 Goode *Fisheries U.S.* 1.456, In general appearance they [=Atherinidae] resemble the smelt, and at various places are called "Sand Smelts" and "Green Smelts." They may be readily distinguished from the true smelt by the absence of the adipose second dorsal fin. . . The most important species on the Atlantic side is the Green Smelt of the Connecticut coast, *Menidia notata.* **1911** U.S. Bur. Census *Fisheries 1908* 316, *Silversides (Atherinidae).*—A small food fish, found along the Atlantic and Pacific coasts. Different species are known as "sand smelt," . . "green smelt."

green snake n [See quot 1778] **scattered, but chiefly Sth, S Midl, NEng** See Map

Either of two similar colubrid snakes: *Opheodrys aestivus* or *O. vernalis.* For other names of *O. aestivus* see **doctor snake, grass snake 1, green tree snake, green whip snake, summer snake, vine snake.** For other names of *O. vernalis* see **grass snake 1**

1709 (1967) Lawson *New Voyage* 137 **NC,** Green-Snakes are very small, tho' pretty. **1778** Carver *Travels N. Amer.* 486, The *Green Snake* is about a foot and half long, and in colour so near to grass and herbs, that it cannot be discovered as it lies on the ground. **1891** in 1895 IL State Lab. Nat. Hist. Urbana *Bulletin* 3.282, *Cyclophis vernalis.* . . Green Snake. . . *Phyllophilophis aestivus.* . . Green Snake. **1930** *Copeia* 2.30 **OK,** Rough green-snake. Common in low grass, and bushes at the edge of wooded pastures. **c1940** Newman–Murphy *Conserv. Notes* 5 **neLA,** There are . . varied reptiles in the parish. . . Among the non-poisonous snakes we find the . . green snake. **1949** Palmer *Nat. Hist.* 464, Keeled green snake also known as "rough" or "Southern green snake." **1965–70** *DARE* (Qu. P25) 142 Infs, **chiefly Sth, S Midl, NEng,** Green snake. **1974** Shaw–Campbell *Snakes West* 79, The smooth green snake is a slender snake; like the racers, its scales are smooth, regular, with the luster of fine satin. *Ibid* 82, Larger than its smooth-scaled generic cousin, the adult rough green snake *(Opheodrys aestivus)* is from two to nearly four feet long. **1979** Behler–King *Audubon Field Guide Reptiles* 639, *Rough Green Snake.* . . A graceful, mild-tempered tree-dweller. *Ibid* 640, *Smooth Green Snake.* . . A capable climber, but is largely terrestrial.

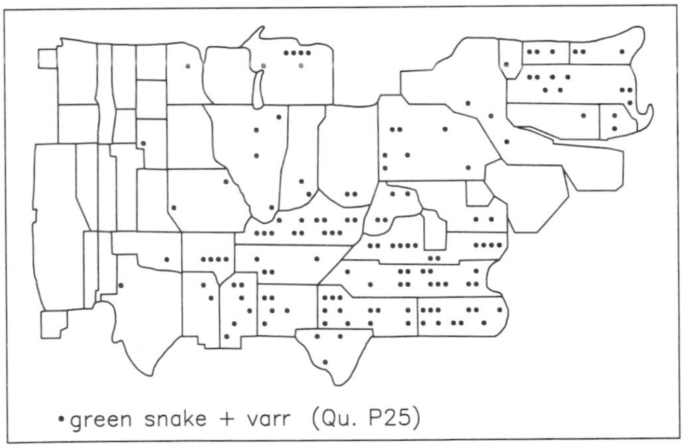

green strip See **green n 2**

green sunfish n

1 A freshwater fish *(Lepomis cyanellus).* Also called **blackeye sunfish, blue bass, bluefish 3, blue sunfish 1, bream B3, green perch 3, logfish, perch, redeye, rubbertail, sand bass, sunfish, wood bass**

1896 U.S. Natl. Museum *Bulletin* 47.996, *Apomotis cyanellus.* . . *Green Sunfish.* . . Color variable, the prevailing shade green with a strong brassy luster on sides, which becomes nearly yellow below. **1929** OK Univ. Biol. Surv. *Pub.* 1.106 **AR, OK,** Green sunfish. . . Specimens from different localities often have a distinctive appearance. **1933** John G. Shedd Aquarium *Guide* 91, The Green Sunfish is the commonest member of the family in the Mississippi Valley and Great Lake region. **1946** LaMonte *N. Amer. Game Fishes* 138, Green Sunfish—*Lepomis cyanellus.* **1971** Brown *Fishes MT* 158, Because of its small size, the green sunfish has little value either for sport or food. It does strike eagerly at most baits. **1983** Becker *Fishes WI* 823, Green sunfish nests are seldom located in water deeper than 35 cm.

2 Either of two related fish: **bluegill 1** or **longear sunfish.**

1933 LA Dept. of Conserv. *Fishes* 349, *The Long-eared Sunfish or Blackears—Xenotis megalotis.* . . The Long-ear has now many common names. . . Small Green Sunfish, Sun Perch. Many of these it will be noticed it shares in common with other species. **1949** Caine *N. Amer. Sport Fish* 38, *Bluegill—Lepomis macrochirus.* . . Colloquial Names. . . Green Sunfish.

greentail n

1 also *greentail bunker, green-tailed shad:* A **menhaden** (here: *Brevoortia tyrannus*). **esp NJ**

1884 Goode *Fisheries U.S.* 1.569, The Menhaden has at least thirty popular names, most of them limited in their use within narrow geographical boundaries. . . In Delaware Bay, the Potomac, and the Chesapeake, we meet with the "Alewife," . . and "Green-tail." **1890** *Century Dict.* 3707, *Menhaden.* . . Popular names . . *moss bunker* . . *green-tailed shad.* **1894** *DN* 1.332 **sNJ,** *Menhaden:* called . . "green tails" . . in Cape May County. **1943** *Sun* (Baltimore MD) 14 Oct 22/7 *(Hench Coll.),* Menhaden, commonly known as bugfish, greentails, bugheads, mossbunkers, alewives, oldwives and ellwives. **1945** Beck *Jersey Genesis* 147 **NJ,** We've called 'em [=menhaden] mossybunkers, greentails, and Sam Days, too. **1968** *DARE* (Qu. P4) Inf **NJ**16, Greentail bunker.

2 Prob the green shrimp *(Peneus setiferus).*

1956 Rayford *Whistlin' Woman* 145 **AL,** There are two kinds of shrimp: the greentail and the brownie. The greentail is the big one.

3 See **green-tailed towhee.**

4 See **greeny 2.**

greentail bunker See **greentail 1**

green-tailed bunting, green-tailed finch See **green-tailed towhee**

green-tailed shad See **greentail 1**

green-tailed towhee n Also *greentail, green-tailed bunting, ~ finch*

A small **towhee** *(Pipilo chlorurus)* native to the West. Also called **red-top**

1872 Coues *Key to N. Amer. Birds* 153, *Green-tailed . . Finch.* Above dull olive-green, brighter on the wings and tail. **1898** (1900) Davie *Nests N. Amer. Birds* 398, *Green-tailed Towhee.* . . Called the . . Green-tailed Bunting, . . it is a characteristic bird of the eastern slope of the Sierra Nevada. **1904** (1910) Wheelock *Birds CA* 251, In the higher Sierra Nevada, where the solitaire and leucosticte form the mountain chorus, look for the Green-tailed Towhee. *Ibid* 253, The Green-tail uses his bill more and his heels less in procuring his food than do others of his kind. **1917** (1923) *Birds Amer.* 3.62, Green-Tailed Towhee—*Oreospiza chlorura.* . . Green-tailed Bunting. **1961** Ligon *NM Birds* 281, While some Green-tailed Towhees [=*Chlorura chlorura*] may be observed in winter . . they are confined in summer . . to brushy . . mountain valleys and canyons. **1977** Udvardy *Audubon Field Guide Birds* 600, *Green-tailed Towhee.* . . This shy bird hops and scratches for food under low cover, flicking its tail and erecting its rufous cap into a crest.

greentail onion See **green onion 1.**

green to green adj phr

1975 Gould *ME Lingo* 116, *Green to green*—This means everything's fine; clear sailing. It comes from the rules of navigation and the helmsman's jingle: Green to green and red to red,/ Perfect safety, go ahead, etc. Reference is to port and starboard lamps, and meeting a vessel at sea: "If things look green to green, we'll go to the fair tomorrow."

greenthread n

A plant of the genus *Thelesperma.* For other names of var spp see **Navajo tea, nippleweed, wild tea**

1954 Harrington *Manual Plants CO* 600, *Thelesperma.* . . *Greenthread.* . . Leaves . . usually finely pinnately parted or divided into linear or narrower divisions. **1970** Kirk *Wild Edible Plants W. U.S.* 135, *Thelesperma* . . Greenthread. . . An excellent tea may be made by boiling the dried flowers and young leaves for several minutes. **1976** Dodge *Roadside Wildflowers* 86, *Colorado greenthread.* . . Hopi Indians . . obtained from the plants a reddish-brown dye. **1990** *Plants SW* (Catalog) 39, *Thelesperma ambiguus* . . *Greenthread.* Closely related to Cota . . , this lovely, bushy wildflower also makes a fine-tasting tea.

green-top See **green onion 1**

green tree snake n

A **green snake** (here: *Opheodrys aestivus*).

1928 Baylor Univ. Museum *Contrib.* 16.14, This [=*Opheodrys aestivus*] is a climbing snake. . . It is commonly known as the *Green Tree Snake* or *Vine Snake.*

green trout n chiefly **Sth**

The **largemouth bass, smallmouth bass,** or **spotted bass.**

1853 Hammett *Stray Yankee in TX* 65, I found but little difficulty in obtaining a supply of green trout and other kinds of river fish. **1933** LA Dept. of Conserv. *Fishes* 314, The Large-Mouthed Black Bass or "Green Trout." **1935** Caine *Game Fish* 3, Large-Mouthed Black Bass—*Micropterus salmoides.* . . Green Trout. *Ibid* 7, Small-Mouthed Black Bass—*Micropterus dolomieu.* . . Green Trout. **1966** *DARE* Tape **MS**73, A six-pound bass, black bass, or green trout as we call 'em. **1966–69** *DARE* (Qu. P1) Infs **LA**44, **MS**73, **NC**63, Green trout. **1967** LeCompte *Word Atlas* 212 **seLA,** *Edible fresh water fish.* . . green trout [5 of 21 infs]. **1978** *Outdoor Life* Sept 56, Scientists call the large-mouth bass Micropterus salmoides. . . But there are many lesser-known names too. . . Some of them are slough bass, green trout [etc]. **1983** Becker *Fishes WI* 809, *Largemouth Bass.* . . Other common names . . green trout.

green up v phr Also *green out*

To become green; to put forth new growth.

1933 Williamson *Woods Colt* 5 **Ozarks,** The trees have only just begun to green up. **1942** Perry *Texas* 240, It was getting on toward spring. The mesquites were beginning to "green up." **c1950** *McDavid Coll.,* How fast the country can green up after a rain. **1958** McCulloch *Woods Words* 74 **Pacific NW,** *Greening up*—Said of a cutover area in which vegetation is starting to grow after a heavy fire. **1975** Gould *ME Lingo* 116, Trees leaving out in the spring are said to be *greenin',* or *greenin' out.*

greenup n

Spring.

1941 Writers' Program *Guide WV* 41, 'Greenup' time would find them [=early settlers] eagerly looking for fresh green food. **1971** Dwyer *Dict. for Yankees* 26 **Sth, S Midl,** *Greenup*—Springtime, i.e., "It's comin' greenup." **1985** Clark *From Mailbox* 42 **ME,** There's a period of time between the melting snows and ice-out and the green-up when there's a sense of transition. Time to view the lawns and gardens . . and prepare for another season of growth.

green violet n

A plant of the genus *Hybanthus,* esp *H. concolor.*

1900 Lyons *Plant Names* 124, *Cubelium.* . . Green Violet. . . Herb with inconspicuous flowers. **1910** Shreve *MD Plant Life* 458, *Cubelium concolor.* . . Green Violet. . . In moist forests. **1931** Harned *Wild Flowers Alleghanies* 326, *Green Violet* . . is a perennial, leafy stemmed herb with alternate leaves, slightly downy, 1 to 2 ft. high. **1946** Tatnall *Flora DE* 179, *Green Violet.* . . Infrequent, but locally abundant. **1968** Barkley *Plants KS* 240, Hybanthus concolor. . . Green Violet. Rich woods. . . Hybanthus linearis. . . Green Violet. Dry prairies and plains. **1970** Correll *Plants TX* 1078, *Hybanthus.* . . Green Violet.

green vivian n

=**blue cohosh 1.**

1933 Small *Manual SE Flora* 545, *C[aulophyllum] thalictroides.* . . Blue-cohosh. . . Green-vivian.

green wasp n

A **mud dauber** (here: *Chalybion californicum*).

1969 *DARE* (Qu. R20, *Wasps that build their nests of mud*) Inf **MI**93, Yellow jacket—small; round paper nest. Green wasp—larger.

green water See **greeny 2**

green whip snake n Cf **whip snake**

A **green snake** (here: *Opheodrys aestivus*).

1928 Pope–Dickinson *Amphibians* 52, This snake [=*Opheodrys aestivus*] also may be known as the Green Whip Snake and Keeled Green Snake.

green widow n Cf **grass widow 1**

1969 *DARE* (Qu. AA26, *A divorced woman*) Inf **CA**154, Green widow.

green-winged teal n Also *greenwing (teal)*

A small, dark duck *(Anas crecca).* Also called **butterball 3, congo** n[1] **5, lake teal, mud teal, partridge duck, redhead teal, redhead widgeon, sarcelle, spring teal, water partridge, winter teal**

1637 (1972) Morton *New Engl. Canaan* 68, Teales, there are of two sorts greene winged, and blew winged. **1792** Belknap *Hist. NH* 3.168, Green Winged Teal, *Anas* ———. **1883** *Century Illustr. Mag.* 4.925/2, The little pools and creeks, which are sure to be found in extensive snipe marshes, furnish food for the blue and green winged teal. **1917** *DN* 4.426 **LA,** *Green-winged teal* (Nettion carolinensis) Sarcelle; Sarcelle d'hiver; Congo. **c1960** *Wilson Coll.* **csKY,** Green-winged Teal . . is rare in the area and is known to few except hunters. **1965–70** *DARE* (Qu. Q5) 17 Infs, **scattered,** Greenwing teal; **IA**3, 22, **ME**8, **MI**36, 53, **MN**18, **RI**4, **WI**32, Green-winged teal. **1982** Elman *Hunter's Field Guide* 178, *Green-winged Teal (Anas crecca carolinensis)* Common & Regional Names: greenwing . . butterball . . breakfast duck.

greeny n

1 A naive or inexperienced person; a greenhorn; a simpleton.

1848 Judson *Mysteries NY* 3.58 **NYC,** The gambler answered by taking a box . . , which Circle opened, and found to contain a large number of impressions from locks. "Anybody could know that these was took by a greeny," said Old Jack, looking at them contemptuously. **1863** in 1922 *Outlook* 130.257/1 **DC,** I asked one of the guards where people landed when they passed through that side door. His reply was, "Why, greeny, that goes to the President's room." **1896** Harris *Sister Jane* 188 **GA,** I called on the squire for to ax him if it's lawful for a country chap to jine in with these town play-actors. . . I did n't know but there was some sort of a trap set in it for to catch greenies. **1899** (1912) Green *VA Folk-Speech* 206, *Greeny.* . . A greenhorn; a simpleton. **1910** Johnson *Highways Rocky Mts.* 12, Hundreds of wolves would gather around, and I tell you their howling was a peculiar music. It was enough to make a greeny's hair stand on end. **1965–70** *DARE* (Qu. HH15, *A very inexperienced person, one who is just learning how to do a new thing*) Infs **LA**46, **MD**26, 31, **MN**36, **MS**45, 88, **NY**211, **PA**66, 114, 175, Greeny; (Qu. HH3, *A dull and stupid person*) Inf **VA**25, Greeny.

2 also *greentail, green water:* A patch of rough or choppy water. Cf **cat's-paw 7**

1968–70 *DARE* (Qu. O12, *A disturbance caused by wind which seems to run and spread quickly along the surface of water*) Inf **DE**4, Greentail—it only covers a half acre or an acre; **MD**36, Greeny—because it turns the water green; (Qu. O15) Inf **VA**84, Green water (very rough).

3 A children's tag game; see quot.

1916 *DN* 4.269 **New Orleans LA,** *Greeny.* . . A game like tag, in which the person touching something green is immune from being tagged.

4 In marble play: see quot.

c1970 Wiersma *Marbles Terms, Greeny* . . a very prized marble that is cloudy green in color. They usually come in various sizes, but never larger than a half-pint. In some marble-playing circles it is referred to as a "snotty."

grees See **grease** v **A1**

greeting n *joc*

A summons or subpoena.

1969–70 *DARE* (Qu. V8a, *What do you call a paper ordering somebody to appear in court?*) Inf **GA**72, Greetings from the judge; (Qu. V8b) Inf **TX**98, Well, I got my greeting.

gregory n

Often with a qualifier: A **demoiselle 1** (here: *Eupomacentrus* spp).

1898 U.S. Natl. Museum *Bulletin* 47.1555, *Eupomacentrus Leucostictus.* . . Beau Gregory. *Ibid* 1556, [Footnote:] In the younger individuals the white dots are much more distinct, and this may have induced the fishermen to give them the name of Beau Gregory. **1933** John G. Shedd Aquarium *Guide* 139, *Eupomacentrus fuscus*—Brown Gregory. . . *Eupomacentrus leucostictus*—Beau Gregory. . . The Gregorys are little demoiselles of the West Indies and Florida coast. They are even more plentiful than the Sergeant Majors around the wharfs at Key West.

greisle See **greissel**

greislich see **greisslich**

greissel v Also sp *greisle* [PaGer; cf Ger *Es gruselt mir* it gives me the creeps] **PaGer area**

To disgust, sicken, irritate.

1939 Aurand *Quaint Idioms* 15, Such talk at the table *greisles* (sickens) me. **1968** *Helen Adolf Festschrift* 35, *Greissel*—This verb, derived from Pennsylvania German *greissle,* is used in the sense of 'nauseate,' 'sicken,' 'turn one's stomach'; for example, "It greissels me just to look at him." **1968** *DARE* (Qu. II29b) Inf **PA**151, Greissels ['graɪsəlz] = Rubs me the wrong way. **1987** *Jrl. Engl. Ling.* 20.170 **ePA,** *Greissel* 'to make sick, to nauseate'. [7 of 100 infs indicated that they use this term; only one of them was under 56 years of age.]

greisslich adj Also sp *greislich* [PaGer; cf Ger *gruselig* creepy, gruesome; *grässlich* horrible, frightful] **PaGer area** Cf **greissel**
Having or producing a feeling of horror, disgust, or nausea.

1872 Haldeman *PA Dutch* 57 [English influenced by German], "It makes me greisslich to see an animal killed" (makes me shudder and revolt with disgust—turns my stomach). A strong word without an English equivalent. **1939** Aurand *Quaint Idioms* 15, There were so many people killed and hurt—it was *greislich* (horrible).

greist See **grist**

grenouille n [Fr] **LA** Cf **green frog a**
A frog or **toad;** see quots.

[**1931** Read *LA French* 43, *Grenouille*. . . Any small green frog—not the bullfrog. . . Many Acadians pronounce *grenouille* as if it were written *grounouille.*] **1967** LeCompte *Word Atlas* 208 **seLA,** *Dry-land animal that hops/supposed to cause warts* . . [1 of 21 infs] grenouille. *Ibid* 209, *Frogs that chirp after rain* . . [15 of 21 infs] grenouille.

gret See **great**

gretch See **krex**

grett See **great**

grevious See **grievous**

grex See **krex**

grey See **gray**

greyslick See **slick**

grez See **grease** v **A2**

grice See **grist**

griddle n

1 =**cap** n[1] **2a.** [From its use as a cooking surface] **chiefly NEast, esp Upstate NY, VT** See Map

1894 Frederic *Marsena* 192 **nNY,** "The Perkinses asked me why you didn't get the butcher to cut up the pig," I remarked at last, rubbing my hands together over the hot stove griddles. **1965–70** *DARE* (Qu. F10, *If you are familiar with wood-burning stoves—what do you call the round flat pieces that you take out to put in the wood?*) 41 Infs, **chiefly NEast, esp Upstate NY, VT,** Griddle; **MI**68, **NY**1, 11, 68, **VT**8, Stove griddle; (Qu. F11, *The thing you use to remove the lids* . . *from a wood-burning stove*) 10 Infs, **chiefly NEast,** Griddle lifter; **NY**109, Griddle holder. **1966** *DARE* Tape **NH**6, [FW:] Back to the griddles you were talking about before, now they're the same thing as stove lids? [Inf:] Yes.

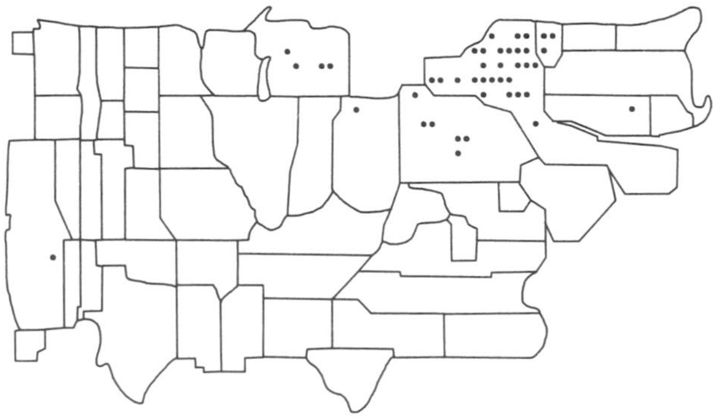

•griddle 1 + varr (Qq. F10, F11)

2 See **griddle cake 1.**

griddle bread See **griddle cake 2**

griddle cake n

1 also *(hot-cake) griddle:* A pancake. **widespread, but chiefly Nth, N Midl** See Map

1810 in 1956 Eliason *Tarheel Talk* 275 **NC,** At breakfast. . . your little Brothers snatch up all the Griddle Cakes they can reach. **1842** Kirkland *Forest Life* 2.106 **MI,** My woman wants to set some griddles, and she took a notion she must have risin' to put in 'em. **1859** *Harper's New Mth. Mag.* 18.486/2 **NEng,** Do take some more of the griddles, will thee? **1902** (1904) Rowe *Maid of Bar Harbor* 66 **ME,** He hastily devoured the smoking griddle-cakes upon his plate. **1946** *PADS* 5.24 **VA,** *Griddle cake* . . A pancake . . among cultured people, rare. **1949** Kurath *Word Geog.* 69, *Griddle cake* is characteristic of Eastern New England as far west as the Connecticut Valley; it is used to some extent also in Metropolitan New York, the Hudson Valley, East Jersey, and parts of Pennsylvania. **1958** Humphrey *Home from the Hill* 153 **neTX,** The hunters sat in the kitchen without speaking while griddlecakes sputtered on the stovelids. **1965–70** *DARE* (Qu. H20b, . . *Pancakes*) 234 Infs, **widespread, but chiefly Nth, N Midl,** Griddle cake; **AR**47, **CT**24, **NY**67, Griddles; **AK**8, Hot-cake griddle [in conv]. **1971** Bright *Word Geog. CA & NV* 177, *Pancakes* . . *griddle cakes* [30 of 300 infs].

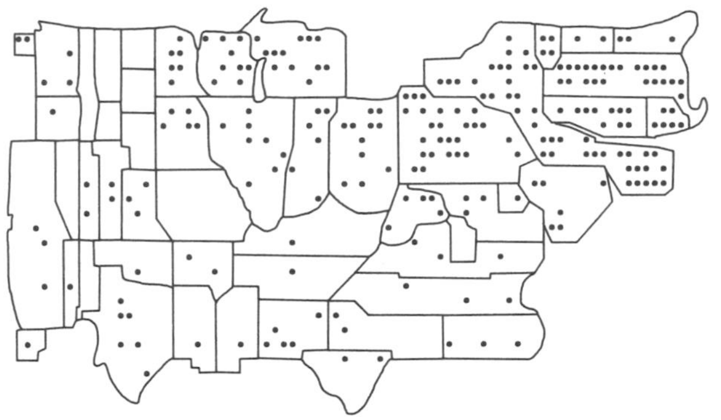

•griddle cake 1 + varr (Qu. H20b)

2 also *griddle bread:* A pancake or bread made with cornmeal.

1847 (1852) Crowen *Amer. Cookery* 437 **NY,** *Indian Griddle Cakes.*—One quart of milk, one pint of corn meal, four well beaten eggs, four tablespoonfuls of flour, and one teaspoonful of salt, beat it well together, and bake on a griddle or in a pan. **1917** WI Farmers' Inst. *Women's Bulletin No. 10* 67, Fifty-fifty Corn Meal Griddle Cakes. **1966–69** *DARE* (Qu. H14, *Bread that's made with cornmeal*) Infs **FL**37, **PA**128, **RI**14, **SC**22, Griddle cake(s); (Qu. H25, . . *Names* . . *for fried cornmeal*) Infs **DC**4, **NC**10, Griddle cakes. **1972** *PADS* 58.20 **cwAL,** *Corn griddle cake.* Southern and South Midland *hoe cake* (19) [of 27 infs] and *corn dodger* (2) are most frequent, but *corn cakes, griddle cake,* and *griddle bread* also occur. **1986** Pederson *LAGS Concordance,* 1 inf, **eTN,** Griddle bread—made with cornmeal; 1 inf, **neAR,** Griddle bread—made with rough ground corn; 1 inf, **csGA,** Griddle cakes—cornmeal batter fried in a skillet; 1 inf, **csGA,** Griddle cakes—of cornmeal.

gridiron n [Perh for **andiron**]

1966–67 *DARE* (Qu. D32, *The metal stands in a fireplace that the logs are laid on*) Infs **OR**13, **PA**60, Gridiron(s); [**MO**1, That isn't the grids, is it?].

gridiron-tailed lizard n Also *gridiron-tail* [See quot 1947]
A lizard *(Callisaurus draconoides)* native to the Southwest. Also called **zebra-tailed lizard**

1893 in 1900 U.S. Natl. Museum *Annual Rept. for 1898* 274, Dr. Merriam gives the following description of . . *Callisaurus draconoides ventralis:* "The gridiron-tailed lizard is the most characteristic reptile of the Lower Sonoran deserts." **1911** *Century Dict. Suppl., Gridiron-tail*. . . A small iguanoid lizard, *Callisaurus ventralis,* from the desert regions of southern Utah: named from the dark bars on its tail. **1935** Pratt *Manual Vertebrate Animals* 184, *Callisaurus*. . . Gridiron-tailed lizard. **1947** Pickwell *Amphibians* 28, The Gridiron-tailed Lizard is unmistakable . . the striking markings are the four or more black bands which cross the tail. . . These markings give the name "gridiron-tailed."

grievous adj Also *gr(i)evious, grievyous* [Cf Intro "Language Changes" I.8] Cf **blasphemious, heinous, mischievious**
Std sense, var forms.

1683 in 1852 PA Prov. Council *Minutes* 1.87, The Grand Jury being called Over, went forth to find the Bill against Charles Pickering, and returned and found ye Bill as being a Heynous and Grevious Crime. **1837** Sherwood *Gaz. GA* 70, Provincialisms. . . *Grievyous,* grievous. **1911** *DN* 3.549 **NE,** Analogical modification of suffix occurs frequently in . . *grievious.* **1920** Hunter *Trail Drivers TX* 13 (as of 1917), In the death of these two members our Association has suffered a grevious loss. **1920s** in 1944 *ADD* **cNY,** ['grɪviəs]. Not uncommon.

griffe n Also *griffane, griffin* Also sp *griff* [LaFr < AmSpan *grifo* the offspring of a White and a Black < Span *grifo,* of hair: kinky] **esp LA** *old-fash*

The offspring of a mulatto and a Black person; a mulatto.

1840 *Daily Picayune* (New Orleans LA) 2 Aug 2/6, $25 Reward will be given for the slave Harry, . . a dark griffe, heavy built. *Ibid* 23 Sept 2/6, $10 Reward will be given for the apprehension and delivery to the undersigned of the girl Lucy who ran away. . . Lucy is a *griffane.* **1849** Lyell *Second Visit* 2.59 **AL,** The auctioneer began to describe him as a fine griff (which means three parts black), twenty-four years old, and having many superior qualities. **1859** (1968) Bartlett *Americanisms* 180, *Griffin, Griffe.* This word, like the French *griffone,* is constantly used in Louisiana, both in conversation and in print, for a mulatto, particularly the woman. **1889** *Jrl. Amer. Folkl.* 2.229 **KY, TN,** A certain man is described as having a "griff complexion." He belonged to a colored regiment, but the particular shade intended I am unable to say. **1894** Chopin *Bayou Folk* 289 **LA,** It was Madame herself who led the pretty, tiny little "griffe" girl to her mother. [**1931** Read *LA French* 44, *Griffe. . .* The offspring of a negro and a mulatress, of obscure origin; perhaps a backformation from Fr. *griffon,* 'griffin.']

grig n[1] **esp NEast**

A cricket—used in similes as an example of liveliness and high spirits. Note: It is possible that the meaning "cricket" is a deduction from the use in similes; see *OED grig* sb.[1] 4, 5.

1939 (1962) Thompson *Body & Britches* 495 **NY,** [Proverbs:] Merry as a wedding bell, as a grig (cricket). **1950** Moore *Candlemas Bay* 195 **ME,** There was the youngest sister, the pretty one, who flitted about like a grig and chattered like a magpie. **1989** *DARE* File **eMA** (as of c1910), 'Merry as a grig'—yes, I've known that since childhood. It means a cricket, with pleasant associations, like "cricket on the hearth."

grig n[2] [Prob var of **gig** n[2] **1**]

A fish spear; also vbl n *grigging* fishing with such a spear.

1822 in 1904 Thwaites *Early W. Travels* 10.234 **OH,** Two men . . began fishing . . striking the fish with a gig, or grig, like a dung-prong, with barbed points. **1969** *DARE* (Qu. P13, . . *Other ways of fishing . . besides the ordinary hook and line*) Inf **MO**39, Grigging.

grigri See **gris-gris** n

grillade n [Fr] **Fr settlement areas, esp LA**

A meat dish; see quots.

1939 (1959) Ramsey-Smith *Jazzmen* 122 **New Orleans LA,** There was a ready market for charcoal, which was used in little tin furnaces for preparing many of the Creole delicacies such as *bouillabaisse, grillades,* and gumbo. **1966** *Time* 21 Oct 80/2 **New Orleans LA,** Grillades and grits—peppers pounded into a veal round, then cooked in a creole gravy. **1966** *DARE* Tape **ME**1, Grillade? That's where they'd slice pork and fry it, see? Fried pork. They used to call 'er grillade ['grɪˌɑd] French, that is. Yah, they used to eat a lot of that. **1968** *DARE* (Qu. H45, *Dishes made with meat . . that everybody around here would know, but that people in other places might not*) Inf **LA**33, Grillade—marinated meat fried. **1983** *Reinecke Coll.* 5 **LA,** *Grillades*—thin veal rounds cut into scallops and cooked in covered cast-iron skillets over a slow fire in brown, almost black roux gravy.

grill cake n [Perh by syncope]

=griddle cake 1.

1969 *DARE* (Qu. H20b, . . *Pancakes*) Inf **OH**88, Grill cakes. **1977-78** Foster *Lexical Variation* 35 **NJ,** Mercer and Burlington are the only counties in which *griddle cake* is common; northern Mercer has the variant *grill cake.*

grim n, hence adj *grim(m)y* [Varr of *grime, grimy*]

1914 *DN* 4.108 **KS,** *Grim* [grɪm]. . . Grime. Also *grimy.* **1969** *DARE* Tape **MA**22, He was trying to get settled up there in the parsonage and he was kinda grimmy ['grɪmi].

grinder n

1 See quot. [Prob from the sound it makes] Cf **clunker 2, croaker** n[1] **2**

1904 *DN* 2.397 **nePA,** *Grinder. . .* Colloquial name for a frog.

2 =freshwater drum.

1956 Harlan-Speaker *IA Fish* 159, The freshwater drum has a . . number of local names. . . It is called . . croaker, . . grinder. . . It feeds extensively . . on small fresh-water mussels, crayfish, snails. **1983** Becker *Fishes WI* 957, *Freshwater Drum. . .* Other common names . . grinder, . . bubbler, gaspergou.

3 also *guinea* (or *hero, Italian, submarine*) *grinder:* **=submarine sandwich. chiefly NEng** See Map and Map Section Cf **hero**

1954 (1955) *W2 Addenda* cxii, *Grinder. . .* A large sandwich made of two slabs of bread cut lengthwise from the loaf and containing ham, salami, or other meat, usually cheese, and pickle, tomato and lettuce, or other appetizers. **1955** *Sat. Eve. Post* 1 Jan 17/1 **seCT,** One would suppose that submarines would be called submarines in New London, Connecticut, where the Navy has a submarine base. Up there they are called grinders. This might be due to the workout one's teeth get while consuming a grinder. **1964** De Vries *Reuben* 332 **CT,** He had two beers and a thing called a meatball grinder, which some failure of the faculty of disgust enabled him to eat. It seemed to consist of two, or possibly three, boiled golfballs obscenely lurking in a loaf of bread longitudinally sawn. **1965-70** *DARE* (Qu. H42, *The kind [of sandwich] in a much larger, longer bun, that's a meal in itself*) 38 Infs, **chiefly NEng,** Grinder; **NH**2, **VT**16, Italian grinder; **CT**33, Hero grinder, submarine grinder; (Qu. H41, . . *Kinds of roll or bun sandwiches*) Inf **NY**84, Grinder; (Qu. H65, *Foreign foods*) Inf **NH**2, Grinders—Italian. **1966** *PMLA* 89.2.11, *Grinder. . .* sandwich, so called in upstate New York. **1967** *DARE* FW Addit **sCA,** Grinder—a large sandwich; **nwMA,** Grinder—a submarine sandwich. **1971** *Today Show Letters* **CT, NY** (as of c1955), I was driving thru New York state and Connecticut and met for the first time these long overstuffed sandwiches called *grinders* at roadside stands; **sePA,** In this area a *grinder* is a hoagie that has been heated in an oven. **1988** *DARE* File **Madison WI,** Until recently there was a pizzeria in town called "Iven's Greek Pizza" which featured "Iven's Grinders"; **Des Moines IA,** A family-owned take-out place that made hot submarine sandwiches had a specialty they advertised as a "Guinea grinder." I didn't know what "guinea" was, but I assumed it meant that the sandwich had some kind of chicken in it. It's only now that I've learned it meant an "Italian grinder."

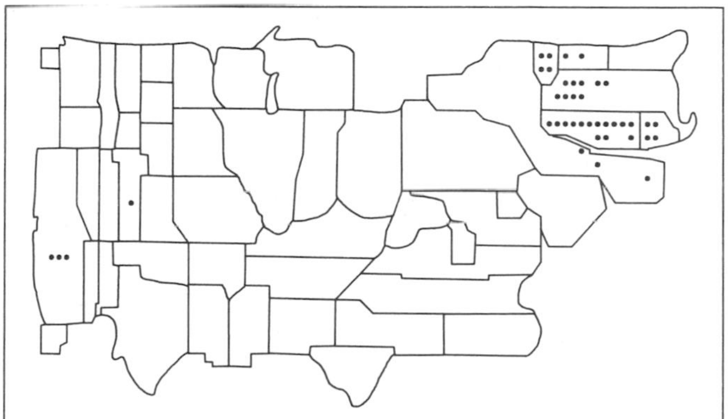

grinding n

1903 *DN* 2.315 **seMO,** *Grinding. . .* Grist. 'The boy went to mill and had to wait till dark before he got his grinding.'

grinding coffee vbl n

Jumping rope in a particular way; see quot 1974.

1946 TN Folk Lore Soc. *Bulletin* 12.1.18, Rope jumping . . offered a chance for the exhibition of individual skill in endurance, speed, and special stunts through . . "Grinding Coffee." **1961** *Western Folkl.* 20.180, *Grinding coffee*—One girl jumping, another girl jumping around her like an old box-type coffee grinder. **1974** Skolnik *Jump Rope* 62, *Grinding coffee:* This game is named for an old-fashioned coffee grinder in which the grinding wheel revolves around a central core. One jumper jumps in place, and a second player jumps around her in a tight circle.

grinding gravel vbl n *joc*

Snoring.

1950 *WELS (Humorous words and expressions about snoring)* 1 Inf, **ceWI,** Grinding gravel. **1968** *DARE* (Qu. X45) Inf **WI**50, Grinding gravel.

grinding rock See **grind rock**

grindins exclam [Prob pronc-sp for *grindings*]
In marble play: see quot.
1901 *DN* 2.141 **swMA,** *Grindins* [graɪndɪnz]. . . A boy pirate sometimes swooped down on a game of marbles and saying "grindins!" seized and carried off all the marbles.

grindle n[1] Pronc-spp *grinnel(l), grinner;* rarely *gringska* [Transf from Ger *Gründel* a fish such as *Gobius niger*] **chiefly lower Missip Valley, eTX** See Map
=**bowfin.**
1709 (1967) Lawson *New Voyage* 163 **NC, SC,** Grindals are a long scaled Fish with small Eyes; and frequent Ponds, Lakes, and slow-running Creeks and Swamps. **1851** *De Bow's Rev.* 11.56 **LA,** *Fishes. . . Shore Pique,* or Grinnell. **1882** U.S. Natl. Museum *Bulletin* 16.94, *A[mia] calva. . .* Mud-fish; Dog-fish; Bow-fin; Grindle; "John A. Grindle"; Lawyer. **1908** Forbes–Richardson *Fishes of IL* 39, The usual local name of this species is "dogfish" in the Great Lake region and the upper Mississippi Valley. It is known eastward and southward oftener as "bowfin," or "grindle," the latter becoming "grinnel" in southern Illinois. **1933** LA Dept. of Conserv. *Fishes* 383, In Louisiana it [=*Amia calva*] is known throughout the southern part of the State as . . Chupique [sic] . . while in the northern part of the State it is often called the Grindle. **1937** in 1977 *Amer. Slave Suppl. 1* 1.43 **AL,** We wud karch trout, gar, Jack, gringska, an' carp. **1953** Randolph–Wilson *Down in Holler* 250 **Ozarks,** *Grinnel. . .* A long, slender fish taken in several Arkansas lakes. It is the dogfish or bowfin, also known as *grindle (Amia calva).* **1965–70** *DARE* (Qu. P3, *Freshwater fish that are not good to eat)* 32 Infs, **chiefly Lower Missip Valley, eTX,** Grindle; **IL**81, **OK**23, Grinnel; **LA**10, Grinner; (Qu. P1, . . *Freshwater fish . . that are good to eat)* Infs **GA**25, **LA**8, 15, **MS**1, **OK**52, Grindle; (Qu. P14) Inf **MS**1, Grindle. **1965–68** *DARE* Tape **GA**20, Mudfish, he's known as a ['grɪnl], bowfin; **GA**35, We have bream, boarmouths, catfish, [grɪnl]; **LA**5, Choupique. . . Well, it has so many names . . , we call it green cypress trout, choupique, an' ['grɛˑnəlz]; **LA**8, We catch gar, an' German carp, an' goggle-eyed perches, an' ['grʌnəlz]. **1983** Becker *Fishes WI* 251, *Bowfin. . .* Dogfish . . grindle, . . grinnel. **1990** *DARE* File **cwMS,** The word "grinner" is in common usage here (especially among Blacks) to refer to . . the bowfin.

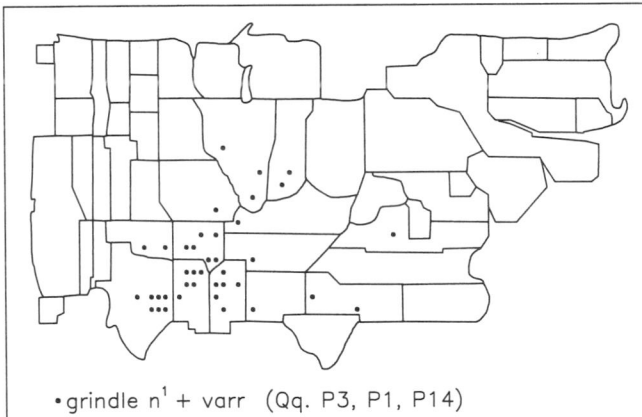

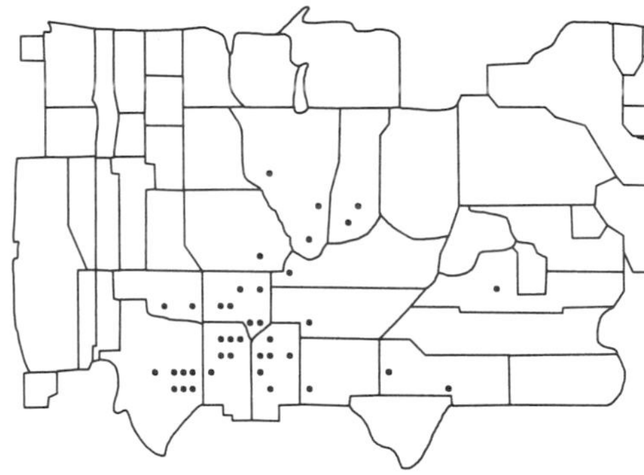
•grindle n[1] + varr (Qq. P3, P1, P14)

‡**grindle** n[2] [Prob for *brindle*] Cf Intro "Language Changes" IV.4
See quot.
1970 *DARE* (Qu. K37, . . *A horse of mixed colors)* Inf **VA**70, Grindle.

grindlestone n [Engl dial; cf *EDD*] *relic*
A grindstone.
1899 (1912) Green *VA Folk-Speech* 206, *Grindlestone. . .* Grindstone. **1939** *LANE* Map 160 *(Grindstone)* 1 inf, **seNH,** Grindle stone—very old; 1 inf, **seNH,** Grindle stone—father's term.

grind one's own bait v phr **eNEng** Cf **kill one's own snakes**
See quots.
1909 *DN* 3.420 **Cape Cod MA,** *Grind one's own bait. . .* A figure taken from fishermen's language. To do as one pleases. "It's a tight squeeze to weather that point but after that we can grind our own bait." **1922** *DN* 5.165 **ME.** **1945** Colcord *Sea Language* 28 **ME, Cape Cod, Long Island,** "Grind your own bait" (be independent; or, in some connections, "Do your own dirty work"). **1975** Gould *ME Lingo* 3, *Bait. . .* To grind your own *bait* is to do your own work.

grind organ n
A hand-turned barrel organ.
1901 *DN* 2.141 **ePA,** *Grind organ. . .* Hand organ. **1909** *DN* 3.397 **nwAR,** *Grind organ. . .* A hand organ.

grind rock n Also *grinding rock* **chiefly Sth, S Midl** See Map
A grindstone.
1895 *DN* 1.374 **eTN,** *Grind-rock* = grind-stone. **1913** Kephart *Highlanders* 371 **sAppalachians,** A mountaineer. . . sharpens tools on a grindin'-rock. **1946** *PADS* 5.24 **VA,** *Grindrock:* Grindstone; rare. **1954** *Harder Coll.* **cwTN,** *Grindrock.* **c1960** *Wilson Coll.* **csKY,** *Grindrock* was formerly more common than grindstone. Also called grinding rock. **1965–70** *DARE* (Qu. L38, *What do you use around here to sharpen tools in the field?)* 25 Infs, **scattered, but esp Sth, S Midl,** Grind rock; **AL**55, **GA**60, **LA**10, **SC**7, 12, 43, Grinding rock. [26 of 31 Infs old] **1970** *Foxfire* Spring-Summer 88 **nGA,** I wish I did have a good sharp knife. Used t'have a good grind rock put up there on th'crib shed, an'Eulis'd hold th'knives an' I'd turn th'grind rock. **1970** Tarpley *Blinky* 135 **neTX,** *Grind rock . .* usually defined as large wheels mounted on a wooden frame and turned by hand or by a foot pedal—[is] used chiefly by informants over 50. **1974** Fink *Mountain Speech* 11 **wNC, eTN,** *Grinding rock.* **1986** Pederson *LAGS Concordance,* 121 infs, **Gulf Region,** Grind rock(s); 114 infs, **Gulf Region,** Grinding rock(s).

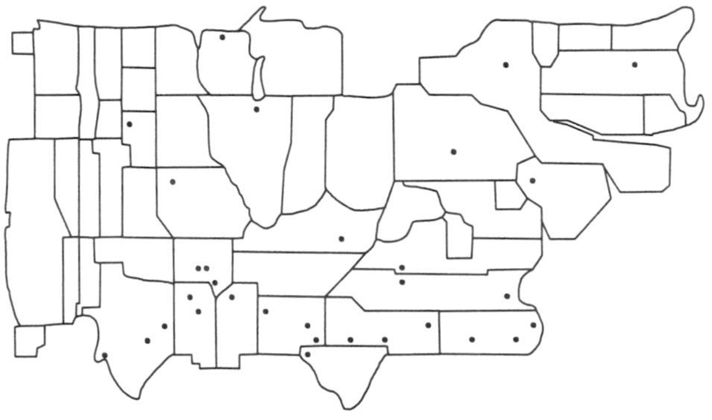
•grind rock + var (Qu. L38)

grind salt v phr Pronc-spp *grin(e) salt* *Gullah*
To circle around.
1888 Jones *Negro Myths* 15 **GA coast,** De fish done dead. . . Buh Tukrey Buzzud, wah bin a grine salt way up in de element, scent um, an down eh come. **1922** Gonzales *Black Border* 304 **sSC, GA coasts** [Gullah glossary], *Grin' salt*—"grinding salt," said of a hawk or vulture circling aloft.

grind smoke v phr Cf **smoke-grinder,** *DS* NN12a, b
See quots.
1946 *PADS* 6.16 **swVA,** *Grinding smoke. . .* An evasive answer given a child who inquisitively asks what one is doing. **1966–68** *DARE* (Qu. NN12b, *Things that people say to put off a child when he asks, "What are you making?")* Inf **NM**11, Wind-diddler to grind smoke; **VA**11, Wimmydiddle to grind smoke; **WV**12, Whimpadiddle to grind smoke with.

grindstone n Usu |graɪn(d) ston|; also **esp NEng,** |grɪn stən, -stʌn| Pronc-spp *grin'st'n, grinstone, grinstun*
A Forms.
1858 Stearns *Practical Guide Pronc.* lxv, Sound the *i* long, and *not* short, in the following words: . . grindstone. **1894** *Century Illustr. Mag.* 48.872 **nNY,** The real sound of grindstone here is "grin'st'n'." **1897** *KS Univ. Qrly.* (ser B) 6.53 **KS,** *Grinstone:* grindstone. **1939** *LANE* Map 160 *(Grindstone)* **throughout NEng, but esp ME, NH, VT,** [grɪn ston, -stɔn, -stən]; 2 infs, **nwCT, sME,** [grɪnstən]; 1 inf, **sME,** [graɪn stʌˑn]. . . Pronunciations of the type of [grɪn~] are regarded as older or old-fashioned though still in use by . . [16 infs]. Pronunciations of the type of [-stən] or [-stʌn] are regarded as older though still in use by . . [3 infs]. **1987** Stegner *Crossing* 172, The foot-powered grindstone, which he liked to call a grinstun in the Vermont fashion, stood like a paleolithic bicycle in the middle of the floor.
B Sense.
See quot.
1967 *DARE* (Qu. X13a, . . *Joking names . . for teeth)* Inf **TX**13, Grindstones.

grine salt See **grind salt**

grin-go-foot n Also *laugh and go foot* Cf **foot n C5b**
A children's game; see quot 1968.
1905 *DN* 3.86 **nwAR,** *Laugh and go foot. . .* The name of a game. **1968** *DARE* FW Addit **VA**16, *Grin-go-foot:* Players divide into two opposing lines. Each are given answers and questions, one line answers and the other questions. One player asks a question and the opposite reads his answer. They must do this three times in a row without laughing or go to the foot of the line.

gringska, grinnel(l), grinner See **grindle** n[1]

grinnie n Also sp *grinny*
1 A **chipmunk** (here: *Tamias striatus*). **chiefly N Midl, esp wPA**
1949 Kurath *Word Geog.* 36, *Grinnie . .* for the chipmunk, from the valley of the Allegheny to Wheeling. **1966** Dakin *Dial. Vocab. Ohio R. Valley* 2.400, *Tamias striatus. . .* Several instances of the Pittsburgh localism *grinnie* are attested not far from the National Road in Ohio and [græʊnɪ] (*grinnie,* or a blend of this name and "ground" of *ground squirrel*?) appears on the upper Ohio opposite Wheeling. **1967** Faries *Word Geog. MO* 110, *Chipmunk. . .* The North Midland terms, *ground hackie, chickery,* and *grinnie,* seem to be rarely used in Missouri. **1968** *DARE* (Qu. P27, . . *Kinds of squirrels*) Infs **OH**72, **PA**75, Grinnie. **1970** *Western Folkl.* 29.167, The term *grinnie* is used in the western midland from the Alleghenies to Wheeling, West Virginia . . what is the animal named by these terms? . . In the eastern United States there is only one candidate, the eastern chipmunk, or *Tamias striatus.* **1971** Wood *Vocab. Change* 13, Regional words . . which presumably originated in Pennsylvania or in states still further north [are]. . . pitch pine, . . grinnie. *Ibid* 35, *Chipmunk . .* [there are] a few scattered instances of *grinnie* in Tennessee and north Georgia. **1982** McCool *Sam McCool's Pittsburghese* 13 **PA,** Grinny: a small wild animal common in Pennsylvania; also known as a chipmunk. **1987** *DARE* File **wPA,** Grinnie is the common word for a chipmunk.
2 A **ground squirrel n b. esp IA**
1928 *AmSp* 4.130 **cnNE,** Ground squirrels are "grinnies." **1968** *DARE* (Qu. P27, . . *Kinds of squirrels*) Inf **IA**34, Grinnie. **1970** *Western Folkl.* 29.168, Ground squirrels. . . *Grinnie,* an Ohio Valley term in the eastern United States, is found in the vicinity of Oskaloosa, Iowa, being used by both informants in Mahaska County; it pops up once again in Monana County, Iowa, on the Missouri River. **1973** Allen *LAUM* 1.322 (as of c1950), *Grinnie . .* has been carried westward with the same general transference of meaning. It occurs three times in Iowa [for *ground squirrel*]. **1986** *DARE* File, Grinnie—a ground squirrel—so-called in the area of Iowa-Missouri, in recent past and still current.
3 =**fox squirrel.**
1967 *DARE* (Qr, near Qu. P27, . . *Kinds of squirrels*) Inf **PA**27, Red fox—also known as grinnies.

grin salt See **grind salt**

‡grinsheep n
1906 *DN* 3.139 **nwAR,** *Grinsheep. . .* A person who grins sheepishly.

grin'st'n, grinstone, grinstun See **grindstone**

grip n
1 =**catch n 3.** [Cf *EDD grip* sb.[4] 12 "A sharp pain, esp. in the bowels; *gen.* in *pl.*"]
1967 *DARE* (Qu. BB3c, *A sudden pain that comes in the side*) Inf **TX**10, Grip.
2 also *gripgrass:* A **cleavers** (here: *Galium aparine*).
1900 [see **gravel-grass**]. **1940** Clute *Amer. Plant Names* 52, *G[alium] aparine.* Cleavers . . grip, grip-grass.

grisette n [Fr < *gris* gray]
A **death cap:** usu *Amanita vaginata,* but also *A. inaurata* or *A. calyptrata.*
1972 Miller *Mushrooms* 28, *Amanita vaginata. . .* "Grisette." **1981** Lincoff *Audubon Field Guide Mushrooms* 550, The Grisette [=*Amanita vaginata*] has many different color forms. . . Although some people do eat the Grisette, not enough is known about its edibility to recommend it. **1987** McKnight-McKnight *Mushrooms* 218, *Amanita calyptrata. . .* Hooded Grisette. *Ibid* 226, *Amanita inaurata. . .* Gilded Grisette.

gris-gris n |'griˌgri| Also sp *grigri* [Fr creole, ult of Afr orig] **chiefly LA**
1 =**hoodoo n 1c.**
1763 LePage du Pratz *Hist. LA* 2.255, They [=Black people] are very superstitious, and are much attached to their prejudices, and little toys which they call *gris, gris.* **1882** (1883) Buel *Mysteries of Cities* 532 **LA,** We shall make a grigri charm to hold him fast. **1916** *DN* 4.269 **csLA,** *Gris gris. . .* A magic formula to bring bad luck to an opponent in a game. **[1931** Read *LA French* 122, *Gris-gris. . .* An object worn as a protective charm against evil, or used, on the other hand, for the purpose of inflicting injury. . . Among the *gris-gris* that protect against evil or bring good luck a favorite was, and is, a dime with a hole in it, which is often worn about the ankle.] **1945** Saxon *Gumbo Ya-Ya* 196 **LA,** If you go out on picnic and she is rain hard, go out in yard and make cross with two sticks and put some salt on top that cross. That sure stop rain! That what us Cajuns call *gris-gris.* **1946** Tallant *Voodoo* 90 **New Orleans LA,** The *gris-gris* sold by Marie II included small bags to be worn for protection or for good luck. These were bits of cloth into which were placed such articles as bits of bone, colored pebbles, goofer dust—dirt from a graveyard—some salt and some ground red pepper. **1967** LeCompte *Word Atlas* 394 **seLA,** A magic formula or talisman [20 of 21 infs:] *gris-gris.* **1983** *Reinecke Coll.* 5 **LA,** *Gris-gris*—['griˌgri] . . a spell, a magic object related to voodoo. . . A little black coffin is a real bad grisgris.
2 =**hoodoo n 1a.**
1967 LeCompte *Word Atlas* 393 **seLA,** A Negro religion of sorcery and the person who practices this religion—[1 of 21 infs:] *gris-gris.* **1983** *Reinecke Coll.* 5 **LA,** She can do grisgris and will put a grisgris on you.

gris-gris v [**gris-gris n**] **chiefly LA**
=**hoodoo v 1.**
1923 *DN* 5.243 **LA,** *Gris-gris. . .* To make a spell, usually by waiving [sic] the hands over someone. **1934** (1943) *W2, Grigri. . .* To bewitch. . . *Southern U.S.* **1967** LeCompte *Word Atlas* 395 **seLA,** To make a spell, usually by the waving of hands [17 of 21 infs:] *gris-gris.*

Grishtkind'l See **Kriss Kringle**

grist n Pronc-spp **esp Appalachians** *grice, greist, gryste*
A Forms.
1859 Taliaferro *Fisher's R.* 139 **nwNC,** I . . carried many a "grice" to William Easley's tub-mill. **1913** Kephart *Highlanders* 133 **sAppalachians,** Red grains of corn being harder than white ones, it is a humurous [sic] saying in the mountains that "a red grain in the gryste . . will stop the mill." **1956** McAtee *Some Dialect NC* 20, *Greist:* . . Grist with a long "i." "Doodle-bug, doodle-bug; come out of your hole and get your greist of corn." **1983** *DARE* File **NC,** The *grice* pronunciation is genuine in . . part of North Carolina.
B Sense.
A large number or quantity. [By ext from *grist* a quantity of grain ground at one time]
1832 Paulding *Westward Ho* 1.77 **Ohio Valley,** There has been a mighty grist of rain lately up above. **1845** Thompson *Pineville* 174 **GA,** There was a whole grist of 'em all follerin' right after the fust ones. **1848** Cooper *Oak-Openings* 1.49 **NY,** "There's an onaccountable grist on 'em"—Gershom was never very particular in his figures of speech, usually terming anything in quantities a "grist;" and meaning in the present instance . . a number not to be counted. **1881** Greene *Cape Cod Folks* 295, "Grists on 'em, this year!" he said. "Heaps!" Aunt Patty responded, readily. **1896** *Harper's New Mth. Mag.* 93.345 **MO,** Dunlap is a long sight richer than any of the others, and owns a whole grist of niggers. **1933** *Sun* (Baltimore MD) 17 Jul 6/1 *(Hench Coll.),* He fought with a gusto and style which always commanded a hearing for his ideas and, *ipso facto,* a grist of angry replies. **1966-68** *DARE* (Qu. LL8b, . . *A large number—for example, of cousins: "She has a whole ______ of cousins."*) Infs **ID**1, **MI**75, **NY**22, Grist. **1974** *AmSp* 49.62 **ME,** *Grist. . .* Multitude. "There was grists of folks there."

grit v, hence ppl adj *gritted,* vbl n *gritting* [Var of *grate* v, prob infl by **grits 1b**] **chiefly S Midl** Cf **dough stage, gritted bread**
To grate ripe but not yet hardened corn into coarse meal; to prepare (corn) in such a way.
1848 (1932) Robinson *Jrl. Santa Fe* 28 **MO,** Their [=the Indian women of New Mexico's] manner of grinding corn is . . worthy of notice. . . and I think preferable to gritting, which is frequently practised in the west. **1897** Barton *Truth about Trouble* 15 **seKY,** To eat bread with a crust less hard and a texture less coarsely grained than gritted corn pone. *Ibid* 79, We 've ben grittin' ever sence roastin' years got good. But they kin grind now, I reckon. **1903** *DN* 2.315 **seMO,** *Grit. . .* To grate; prepare grits. This is done on a piece of perforated tin, resembling a large

nutmeg-grater. **1941** Smith *Going to God's Country* 19 **MO** (as of 1890), But as soon as the rosten ears was hard enoughf to grit my father made a grater and then we had plenty of corn bread. **1948** Dick *Dixie Frontier* 289, When the kernels grew more mature and hard, the ears were rubbed over the rough side of a piece of tin studded with nail holes. This was called 'gritting' (grating) and made the sweetest corn meal imaginable. **1952** Brown *NC Folkl.* 1.548 **cwNC,** *Grit. . .* To grate (corn on a *gritter*). **1983** *MJLF* 9.1.42 **ceKY.** **1986** Pederson *LAGS Concordance,* 1 inf, **ceTN,** To grit the corn—make meal from ear of corn; 1 inf, **neTN,** You grit the meal; 1 inf, **nwAR,** They used a gritter to grit corn.

grit n[1] Also *grits* Cf *DS* HH1

A rustic; see quots.

1968 *DARE* FW Addit **neNY,** Grit—a backwoods person. "Somebody who has to have their weather pumped into them." Rare. **1983** *DARE* File **NC,** Grit—a nickname for a rustic or countrified person. **1984** Wilder *You All Spoken Here* 160 **Sth,** *Grit, grits:* Hillbilly, mountain boomer, cracker, po' bukra. . . Courses in Southern literature at Clemson University, Clemson, South Carolina, are called by students "grit lit."

grit n[2] [Prob for *brit* a young herring]

1957 Beck *Folkl. ME* 126, These latter [=herring], commonly called "grits," were placed in the "kitchen" [of the lobster pot] in a little net bag called a "purse."

grit bread See **gritted bread**

grit-corn See **grits 1b**

gritchel n [Blend of *grip* + *satchel*] **Sth, S Midl**

A piece of hand luggage.

1917 in 1944 *ADD* **WV,** *Gritchel. . .* A traveling bag. **1927** *AmSp* 2.356 **cwWV,** *Gritchel . .* a traveling bag. "Let me carry your gritchel for you." **1940** *Qrly. Jrl. Speech* 26.265 **VA,** *Suitcases* may be "gritchels." **1941** in 1944 *ADD* **NC,** *Gritchel . .* = combined grip & satchel. Reported used. **1984** Wilder *You All Spoken Here* 28 **Sth,** *Gritchel:* A valise.

grit-corn See **grits 1**

grit, hit the See **hit the grit**

gritny See **grundniss**

grits n pl [*OED grit* sb.[2] "Now only *pl.* and *dial.* . . 2. Oats that have been husked but not ground (or only coarsely); coarse oatmeal"; 1579 →]

1a Coarse particles of grain, separated from husks and germ.

1883 *Harper's New Mth. Mag.* 67.462/1 **eNEng,** All the fancy grits and groats in the market did not meet his demand. **1884** Knight *New Mech. Dict.* 1.426, *Grits. (Milling.)* Cracked fragments of wheat smaller than *groats.* An incident to the *High Milling* process. **1888** New Sydenham Soc. *Lexicon* np, *Grits. . .* In America, fine hominy is called grits, and wheat prepared in the same way is likewise so designated. **1896** (c1973) Farmer *Orig. Cook Book* 86 **MA,** From corn is made corn meal . . ; from wheat, wheaten or white flour, Wheatena, Wheatlet, Wheat Grits, Pettijohns, etc. **1896** *Godey's Mag.* Feb. 207/1 *(OEDS),* When Mr. Dives turns from his recondite menu to nibble at wheaten grits and graham bread. **1986** Pederson *LAGS Concordance,* 1 inf, **cLA,** Grits—from barley and oats, not corn; 1 inf, **ceTN,** Grits—not made from corn but from rice.

b freq *hominy grits,* also *grit-corn;* Esp: grated or coarsely ground hulled corn, or occas whole kernels of **hominy B1;** the dish made by boiling or otherwise preparing any of these. **chiefly Sth, S Midl, esp S Atl, Gulf States** See Map Cf **grit** v

a1816 (1848) Hawkins *Sketch* 78 **GA** (as of 1798-99), He eats two or three spoonfulls of boiled grits. **1877** Henderson *Practical Cooking* 71, When the milk is salted and boiling, stir in the hominy grits, and boil for twenty minutes. **1887** [see **hominy B2**]. **1903** *DN* 2.315 **seMO,** *Grit-corn* or *grits. . .* Corn grated from the cob while soft. Used for making bread. The corn must be more ripe than for 'roastin-ears.' **1907** *DN* 3.231 **nwAR, seMO,** *Grits. . .* Corn grated from the corn when soft. . . Also applied to a kind of cracked corn or hominy. **1908** *DN* 3.317 **eAL, wGA,** *Grits. . .* Cracked Indian corn. **1933** Rawlings *South Moon* 4 **nFL,** They handed plates to their mother, which she filled with thc stew, with soft-cooked grits and white flour biscuits. **1942** Rawlings *Cross Creek Cookery* 72 **FL,** Grits are the Deep South member of the hominy family. What the North knows as hominy, we call "big hominy." . . Grits are hominy dried and ground fine. . . We use them in place of potatoes. Never as cereal. For the benefit of Northern cooks, they may be found in many grocery stores, packaged, and labeled "Hominy Grits." These are coarser than Southern grits. **1948** Dick *Dixie Frontier* 249 **Sth,** By means of a crude homemade sifter the coarse material, called grits, was separated from the fine and then boiled for hominy. **1965–70** *DARE* (Qu. H23, *Hot cooked breakfast cereal*) 138 Infs, **chiefly Sth, S Midl,** Grits; 17 Infs, **chiefly Sth, S Midl,** Hominy grits; **DC**1, Hominy grits—some people have strong ideas about whether ground or whole better; **MS**79, Hot grits; **NY**70, Hominy grit [sic]—we got this in Florida; **SC**43, Hominy—cooked; grits when raw—old-fashioned; (Qu. H24, . . *Boiled cornmeal*) 14 Infs, **scattered,** Grits; **AR**55, Hominy grits—coarser than cornmeal used for bread; **MD**37, Hominy grits [Inf distinguishes them from cornmeal]; **MO**3, Would that be hominy grits? **NJ**1, Hominy grits—whole kernel yellow corn and wood ashes boiled to remove hulls and remainder is boiled for hominy grits; **VA**1, Hominy grits; (Qu. H14, *Bread . . made with cornmeal*) Inf **CT**2, Grits—down South; **MO**3, Hominy grits; (Qu. H25, . . *Fried cornmeal*) Inf **LA**3, Fried grits; **TN**5, Grits; (Qu. H43) Inf **MO**21, Some call it [=cornmeal] grits; (Qu. H45, *Dishes . . that everyone around here would know*) Infs **FL**3, **VA**9, Grits; (Qu. H50) Infs **NC**60, 63, Grits; (Qu. BB50c) Inf **SC**70, Grits poultice; (Qu. HH20c, . . *"He isn't worth ______ ."*) Infs **FL**36, **GA**19, 30, Salt that goes in his grits. **1968** *DARE* FW Addit **GA**33, "Lyed hominy" or "hominy grits"—big grain hominy, made with potash lye; breakfast cereal variety is just called "grits." **1979** *New Yorker* 5 Mar 96 **swAL,** We go to breakfast place: grits and eggs. **1986** Pederson *LAGS Concordance* **Gulf Region,** [The resp *grits* is widespread; most of the infs for whom comments were recorded described it as "ground." 72 infs offered the compounds *hominy* (or *homily*) *grits;* of these, 27 described them as "ground" or said they are the same as grits, 3 said they were coarser than grits, and six indicated that they consist of whole kernels.]

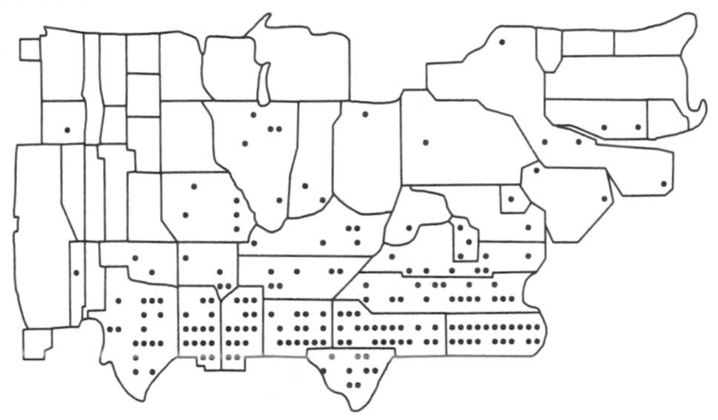

•grits 1b + varr (Qq. H23, H24, H14, H25, H43, H45, H50, BB50c, HH20c)

2 See **grit** n[1].

gritsmill n [Perh infl by *gristmill*] **Sth**

A mill for grinding **grits 1.**

1939 McGuire *FL Cracker Dial.* 176, *Grits mill. . .* Grist mill. **c1950** *McDavid Coll.* **ceSC,** A rock dam and a small grits mill house. **1969** *SC Market Bulletin* 11 Sept 2/4, *Want . .* small grits mill in running condition. **1986** Pederson *LAGS Concordance,* 5 infs, **AL, FL, GA, MS,** Gritsmill—gristmill; 1 inf, **cGA,** Gritsmill—it ground the grits.

gritted See **grit** v

gritted bread n Also *gritters, grit(ting) bread, gritty ~* [**grit** v] **chiefly S Midl**

Corn bread, usu made from grated cornmeal.

1886 *Harper's New Mth. Mag.* 73.59/2 **seKY,** Over this [punched] tin the ears are rubbed, producing a coarse meal, of which "gritted bread" is made. **1903** *DN* 2.315 **seMO,** *Grit-bread. . .* Bread made from grit corn, or grits. Grit-bread is very common and is really delicious. **1913** Kephart *Highlanders* 291 **sAppalachians,** The ears [of corn] are grated into a soft meal and baked into delectable pones called gritted-bread. **1930** *VA Qrly. Rev.* 6.243 **S Midl,** Bread made from milky grain continues to be called gritted bread. **1944** *PADS* 2.19 **sAppalachians,** *Gritted bread.* **1952** Brown *NC Folkl.* 1.548 **cwNC,** *Gritted bread. . . Gritty bread.* **1969** *DARE* (Qu. H14, *Bread that's made with cornmeal*) Inf **KY**40, Grit bread, gritted bread. **1981** Howell *Surv. Folklife* 104 **swVA,** Gritted bread could be made late in the summer when the meal from last year's harvest might be running low. That recipe replaced meal with grated corn which was past the roasting ear stage, but still milky. **1983** *MJLF* 9.1.42 **ceKY** (as of 1956), *Gritted bread* . . bread made from meal that has been gritted. . . *Gritters* . . gritted bread. . . *Gritting bread* . . gritted bread. **1986** Pederson *LAGS Concordance,* 1 inf, **neTN,** Gritted bread—scalded corn bread.

gritter n [**grit v**] **chiefly S Midl**

A grater, esp one for grating corn into meal.

1877 Bartlett *Americanisms* 265, Some carried the *gritter* in their haversacks, others had it slung to their belts. **1888** *Congressional Record* 1 May 19.4.3587/2 **KY,** The "gritter" is a piece of cast-away tin or sheet-iron, through which holes have been punched with a nail, so as to throw out the surface on one side and make it rough. In its use it is what we would call a grater. **1944** *PADS* 2.19 **sAppalachians. 1952** Brown *NC Folkl.* 1.548 **cwNC,** *Gritter.* . . A perforated piece of tin (about 8 x 24 inches) used to grate green corn on to make *gritted bread.* **1955** *PADS* 23.50 **eKY. 1960** Hall *Smoky Mt. Folks* 44, Bread trays and gritters are made by hand. Ears of fresh or dried corn rubbed on the gritters make good cereal grits or meal for gritted bread. **1968** *DARE* FW Addit **swVA. 1986** Pederson *LAGS Concordance,* 1 inf, **cnAR,** Gritter—they used to grit corn; 1 inf, **cnMS,** Gritter—grit [=grate] a mess of corn with that; 1 inf, **cTX,** Gritter—a pan or lid punched with little holes.

gritters See **gritted bread**

gritting See **grit v**

gritting bread, gritty bread See **gritted bread**

grizzly bear n

Std: A large powerful bear *(Ursus arctos)* native to western North America. Also called **silvertip.** For other names of *U. a. horribilis* see **roachback;** for other names of *U. a. middendorffi* see **Kodiak bear**

grizzly bear cactus n Also *grizzly bear*

A **prickly pear** (here: *Opuntia erinacea* var *ursina*).

1925 Jepson *Manual Plants CA* 656, *O[puntia] ursina. . . Grizzly Bear Cactus.* . . Copious flexible bristle-like ashy-gray spines 3 to 8 in. long. **1940** Benson *Cacti AZ* 51, *Grizzly bear cactus.* Low-growing prickly pear forming clumps a foot or more in diameter and from less than 1 foot up to 3 feet high. **1947** *Desert Mag.* May 28/3 *(DA),* Visitors in May and June will find a good display of . . beavertail and grizzly bear cactus. **1959** Munz–Keck *CA Flora* 314, *O[puntia] erinacea. . .* Var. *ursina. . . Grizzly Bear Cactus.* . . Spines . . flexible and threadlike, strongly reflexed, almost matted. **1976** Bailey–Bailey *Hortus Third* 792/1 **nwAZ, seCA, sNV,** *Grizzly-bear cactus, grizzly-bear.*

groaner n **esp ME** Cf *DNE*

A whistling buoy or foghorn.

1903 *Century Illustr. Mag.* 66.538/1 **ME,** 'These here plaguy bell-b'ys an' groaners is a ter'ble ole nuisance, you!' exclaimed Cap'n Roundturn. **1941** Eliot *Dry Salvages* 5 **MA,** *Groaner:* a whistling buoy. **1947** White *Hdbk. Sailing* 236, Effective at night in fog or low visibility, whistling buoys do not sound like a whistle but like a groan, and are called "groaners" by seafaring men. **1966** *DARE* (Qu. O14b, . . *Kinds of buoys)* Inf **ME**10, Groaner—makes a groaning sound. **1975** Gould *ME Lingo* 116, *Groaner*—A foghorn with a prolonged moan and only one tone. A two-toned horn, listed on charts as a diaphone, is called a grunter.

grocer's mix(ed) See **grocery mix**

grocery n

1 also *grocery store:* A **confectionary 1;** a speakeasy. *old-fash*

1806 *Balance* (Hudson NY) 28 Jan 31/1, A writer in the Albany Gazette, states, that there are *one hundred and seventy-four* licensed Grocery Stores . . in the city of Albany. **1818** Fearon *Sketches* 28 **NYC,** Both wholesale and retail wine and spirit sellers are grocers: their establishments are called grocery stores. **1825** (1832) Pickering *Inquiries* 31, Almost all the roads leading to a town in America are full of houses on their sides, called "taverns," or "liquor," "beer and cake," or "grocery," stores. **1858** Hammett *Piney Woods Tavern* 227 **TX,** Mr. Jarboe was aroused from his reverie on the closing of the grocery. **1903** *DN* 2.315 **seMO,** *Grocery.* . . The most common name for a saloon or dramshop. **1911** *DN* 3.538 **eKY,** *Grocer.* . . A small hut where the "rat" . . sells illicit whiskey. **1923** *DN* 5.240 **swWI,** *Grocery.* . . A grocery store where liquor was sold, for which very often no license was paid.

2 pl: Eating; food to eat; see quot.

1986 Pederson *LAGS Concordance (Food)* 1 inf, **swGA,** He [=a crawfish]'d be pretty good groceries; 1 inf, **swGA,** Buttermilk was some kind of good groceries.

3 in phrr *lose* (or *blow*) *one's groceries:* To vomit. Cf *lose one's cookies* at **cookie** n[1] **3,** *DS* BB17, 18

1986 Pederson *LAGS Concordance (Vomit . . crude and jocular terms)* 1 inf, **cLA,** Blow his groceries; 1 inf, **swGA,** Lose his groceries—crude term. **1989** *DARE* File **nwAR,** My colleague and I are both a couple of "Ozark boys." We say "you lose your groceries" to mean you vomit. I mean, really vomit [laughter].

grocery mix n Also *grocer's mix, grocery mix candy* **esp KY, TN**

An inexpensive candy mixture; hence adj phrr *grocery mixed, grocer's mixed.*

1965–70 *DARE* (Qu. H82a, *Cheap candies sold especially for schoolchildren)* Inf **KY**44, Grocery mix; (Qu. H82b, *Kinds of cheap candy that used to be sold years ago)* Infs **GA**19, **KY**15, 44, **TN**13, Grocery mix(ed); **KY**25, **TN**11, 13, 14A, Grocer's mix(ed). **1986** Pederson *LAGS Concordance,* 1 Inf, **eTN,** Grocery-mix candy, a sack of (jellied hard candy).

grocery store See **grocery 1**

grog n [Cf *OED grog* sb. 1. b "A social gathering at which grog is drunk."] Cf **gam** n[1]

1967 *DARE* (Qu. O21, *When men out in . . boats get together for a visit . . that's called a* ______) Inf **MN**2, Grog—drink liquor, on Lake Superior or smaller northern Minnesota lakes; groups of fishermen.

grogshop n [*grogshop* a disreputable drinking place]

1975 Gould *ME Lingo* 117, A *grog*-shop is seldom a tavern in Maine, but means the state liquor store.

grommet n Pronc-sp *grummet*

A small particle; a little bit.

1941 *LANE* Map 417 *(A little bit)* 1 inf, **neMA,** [grʌ›mɪt]. 'An old Marbleheader would say *just a grummet* for a very small portion.' **1966** *DARE* FW Addit **MA**6, *Grommets*—small particles left in pan in which salt pork has been rendered. "Pick up the grommets, add milk, and thicken for milk gravy."

gromwell n

Std: a plant of the genus *Lithospermum.* Also called **Indian paint, puccoon.** For other names of var spp see **cat's tooth 2, dyeroot puccoon, Indian bouquet, Indian puccoon, lady's keys, lemon weed, orange puccoon, paint plant, pigeon-weed, railroad puccoon, redroot, stone weed, yellow puccoon**

gronnut See **groundnut**

groom n [Var of *goom* (at **gum** n[1], v[1])]

1904 *DN* 2.397 **NY,** *Grooms* . . gums, of the mouth.

groomsman n Also *usher groomsman* **widespread exc NEast, West** See Map Cf **waiter**

A male attendant upon a bridegroom.

1851 (1927) Rodman *Diary* 305 **MA,** Edmund officiated last ev'g as groomsman to Charles Randall who was married to Sarah Perry. **1899** (1912) Green *VA Folk-Speech* 207, *Groomsman.* . . One who acts as attendant on a bridegroom at his marriage. **1960** *PADS* 34.58 **CO,** Groomsman 'best man'. . . These expressions are more typical of older folk speech than of other types. **1965–70** *DARE* (Qu. AA17, . . *Other*

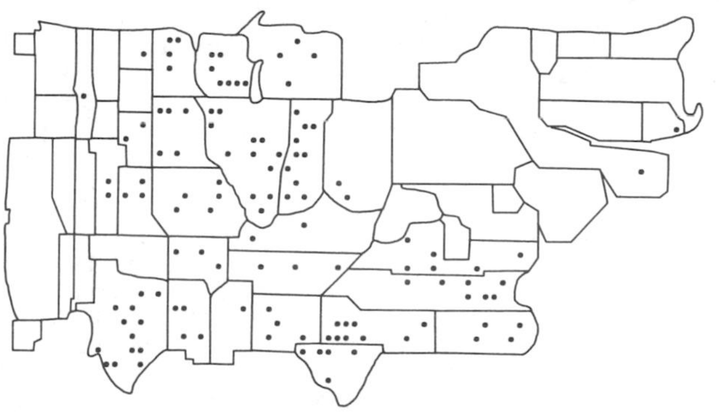

•groomsman + varr (Qu. AA17)

people beside the bride and groom . . in a wedding party) 120 Infs, **widespread exc NEast, West,** Groomsman (*or* groomsmen); **GA**18, Usher groomsmen—same as ushers. **1966** *Clinton Herald* (IA) 13 Aug 3/4, The bride's brother . . was best man. His groomsmen were Darrell Liedtke . . and Richard Maher. **1968** *Catskill Mt. News* (Margaretville NY) 4 July 9/5, Ushers and groomsmen were Sinclair Armstrong . . and Jerry Joern. **1969** *Weakley Co. Press* (Martin TN) 2 Oct 3/2, Jackie Green, brother of the groom, served as best man. Groomsman was Glen Frazier and ushers were Mike Snider and Donnie Green. **1972** *PADS* 57.43 **seOH,** *Groomsman.* Surprisingly, . . [1 inf] gave this Southern form. The other informants used the general term *best man.*

grooper, groper See **grouper 1a**

gropie n Cf **crappie, grubby 2**

1975 Gould *ME Lingo* 117, *Gropie*—The sculpin, mostly along the York County shore.

grosbeak n

Std: any of several birds of the family Fringillidae, as **cardinal 1, evening grosbeak, pine grosbeak, purple finch, pyrrhuloxia,** or **rose-breasted grosbeak.** See also **gray grosbeak, purple grosbeak, summer grosbeak.** For other names of the blue grosbeak *(Guiraca caerulea)* see **big indigo, blue pop 2, blue ricebird, king eveque, wheat bird**

gros-bec n |ˈgro(ʊ),bɛk, ˌgroˈbɛk| [Fr "thick beak"] **chiefly LA**

=**night heron.**

[**1835** Audubon *Ornith. Biog.* 3.275, *The Night Heron.* . . In Lower Louisiana the Creoles call it *"Gros-bec."*] **1841** *S. Lit. Messenger* 7.77/1 **swLA,** The king-bird of the prairie is the Grosbec. **1911** *Forest & Stream* 77.174 **LA,** *Nycticorax nycticorax naevius.* Gros Bec. . . Used throughout lower Louisiana and applied to *Nystanassa* [sic] *violacea* also. **1916** *Times-Picayune* (New Orleans LA) 2 Apr mag sec 5, *Black-crowned Night Heron.* . . Gros-bec. . . *Yellow-crowned Night Heron.* . . Gros-bec. **1917** *Wilson Bulletin* 29.2.78, *Nycticorax nycticorax* . . winter gros-bec. . . Marksville, La. **1941** O'Donnell *Great Big Doorstep* 225, Papa was after grosbec. Every tree had a nest with young grosbec. **1962** Imhof *AL Birds* 98, *Yellow-crowned Night Heron—Nyctanassa violacea.* . . Gros-bec. **1966** LA Wild Life Comm. *Hunting Fishing Regulations 1967–68* 8, *Grosbec* (Night Heron)—It is against Federal and State laws to kill Grosbecs or any other kind of Herons, Egrets or Cranes at any time. **1967** LeCompte *Word Atlas* 207 **seLA,** The black crowned night heron/has thick, heavy bill . . *Gros bec* is a literal translation of "big beak". **1967–68** *DARE* (Qu. Q8) Inf **LA**20, Gros-bec [ˌgroˈbɛk]; (Qu. Q10) Infs **LA**10, 15, 26, 44, Gros-bec [ˈgro(ʊ),bɛk]. **1983** *Reinecke Coll.* 5 **LA,** *Grosbec* [ˈgrobɛk] . . night heron.

gros grasset See **grasset 4**

gross bump n [**bump n 1**] Cf *DS* X59

1912 Green *VA Folk-Speech* 207, *Gross-bumps.* . . Small pimples on the face of young people.

grotto n Cf **cave n 1,** *DS* M19

1976 Garber *Mountain-ese* 36 **Appalachians,** *Grotto* . . outside pantry. We put enough canned beans in the grotto to last us all winter.

grouch n Also *grouch(i)es*

A mood of depression, annoyance, or irritation—often in phrr *have* (or *get*) *a grouch on* and varr.

c1895 (1914) Norris *Vandover* 183 **San Francisco CA,** Beale sent me to court the other morning to get the judge's signature. He had a grouch on, and wanted to put me off. You ought to have heard me jolly him. **1896** *DN* 1.418 **cNY, seMI,** *Grouch:* "To go on a grouch," to become a little out of sorts. Also, "To get on (or have) a grouch." **1900** Willard *Itinerant Policeman* 160, They began to get a grouch on against the gay-cats that kep' comin' to their camps. **1903** *Harper's Bazaar* Oct 947, No woman who comes down to her breakfast table with what her son frankly calls a 'grouch on,' is grouchy to herself alone. **1905** *DN* 3.61 **NE,** *Grouch.* . . Sullen or gloomy fit. "Don't get a grouch." **1909** *DN* 3.397 **nwAR,** *Grouch.* . . A fit of ill humor; a dislike. **1914** Adams *Clarion* 335, "Something's biting the old geezer," he informed Hal and Ellis. "Seems to have a grouch." **1965–70** *DARE* (Qu. BB28, *Joking names . . for imaginary diseases: "He must have the ______."*) Inf **AL**1, Grouches; (Qu. GG34a, *To feel depressed or in a gloomy mood; "He has the ______ today."*) Infs **MA**24, **NY**235, **OH**70, 74, **TX**64, Grouch; **AR**22, Grouches; **GA**72, Grouchies; **WA**18, He has a grouch on; (Qu. GG39, *Somebody who seems to be looking for reasons to be angry: "He's a ______."*) Infs **CO**21, **WI**20, He has (*or* he's got) a grouch on.

grouch-box n [**box n 5a**]

An irritable or grouchy person.

c1960 *Wilson Coll.* **csKY,** *Grouch box*—A scolder, a belly-acher. **1966–69** *DARE* (Qu. GG16, . . *Finding fault . . complaining: "You just can't please him—he's always ______."*) Inf **NC**82, Old grouch-box; (Qu. GG38, *Somebody who is usually mean and bad tempered: "He's an awful ______."*) Infs **GA**3, 82, Grouch-box.

grouch(i)es See **grouch**

grouch-pot n Also *grouch-pod* [Cf **pot**]

=**grouch-box.**

1968 *DARE* (Qu. GG39, *Somebody who seems to be looking for reasons to be angry: "He's a ______."*) Inf **OH**45, Grouch-pot. **1988–89** *DARE* File **AZ, AR, OK,** (as of c1920), My grandmother always referred to a grouchy person as an "awful grouch-pod"; **CA** (as of c1950), Grouchpod. . . I'd feel better about verifying with my grandmother just how that word got into her vocabulary.

ground n

1 in var combs: A piece of land that will sustain a crop; a field.

[**1622** Mourt's Relation *Iournall Plimoth* 7, We went and found more Corne ground, but not of this yeare.] **1778** Hutchins *Topographical Descr.* 4 **Ohio Valley,** The lands which lie upon the *Ohio* . . also consist of rich intervals and very fine farming grounds. **1859** (1968) Bartlett *Americanisms* 181, *Grounds.* "Tobacco grounds," . . "corn grounds," are terms applied to lands in Virginia. **1886** Smith *Hist. KY* 367 (as of 1775–1800), Uncle Ben . . plowed the corn-ground. **1902** *DN* 2.235 **swIL,** *Ground.* . . Soil; as 'This patch is good ground.' **1907** *DN* 3.223 **nwAR.** **1940** *AmSp* 15.30, The tendency in Virginia to use *ground* where *land* would be preferred in many other parts of America has . . perhaps been overemphasized. It appears that in the following terms they are used interchangeably: . . *corn ground, corn land.* **1949** *AmSp* 24.107 **cnGA,** *Corn-ground.* . . Cornfield. **1950** *WELS (A piece of land with a hay crop planted on it)* 1 Inf, **cwWI,** Hay ground. **1966–69** *DARE* (Qu. L7) Infs **IL**108, **IA**36, 39, **ME**9, **NM**10, **PA**218, **UT**4, Hay ground; (Qu. L24) Inf **WI**42, Hay ground.

2 Soil; dirt. [*OED ground* sb. 16. a a1300 →; cf also Ger *Grund* ground, soil] Cf **ground cellar**

1806 (1970) Webster *Compendious Dict.* 136/1, *Ground* . . soil. **1935** *AmSp* 10.171 **sePA,** *Ground.* Regularly used instead of soil, earth, or dirt. 'Before I plant grass I want to get a man to bring me a load of ground.' **1965–70** *DARE* (Qu. C30, . . *Loose, dark soil*) Infs **DE**1, **IL**126, **OH**31, **SD**2, Black ground; **OH**76, **SD**2, Rich ground; **CO**18, Bottom ground; **ME**1, Dark ground; **PA**162, Ground; **NJ**39, Mucky ground; **PA**242, Woods ground; **OH**69, Black ellum ground; (Qu. C31, . . *Heavy, sticky soil*) Inf **KY**16, Limestone ground; **MO**21, Mucky ground; **NJ**67, Clay ground. **1968** *Helen Adolf Festschrift* 37 **cePA,** Ground (Pennsylvania German *Grund*) is used regularly instead of soil, earth, or dirt; for example, "Where shall I put the load of ground?" **1987** *Jrl. Engl. Ling.* 20.2.170 **ePA,** *Ground* 'dirt, soil'. . . The recessive nature of *ground* is suggested by the fact that only four informants are less than 40 and three of them are Mennonites or Brethren.

ground apple n

1 An **Indian breadroot** (here: *Psoralea esculenta*). *obs* Cf **pomme de terre**

1823 James *Acct. of Exped.* 1.206 **NE,** They often bear a heavy staff of wood, sharpened to a broad edge at one end for the purpose of digging up the *Nu-ga-re,* or ground apple, called by the French *Pomme blanche.* **1841** Kennedy *Texas* 1.107, Primroses, violets, and the delicate flower of the ground-apple, are common embellishments of the soil.

2 A **potato** (here: *Solanum tuberosum*).

1967–68 *DARE* (Qu. I9, . . *Potatoes*) Infs **CT**2, **DE**3, **NJ**1, Ground apples.

ground artichoke n

=**Jerusalem artichoke.**

1932 Rydberg *Flora Prairies* 839, *Helianthus.* . . Ground artichoke. **1940** Clute *Amer. Plant Names* 260, *Helianthus tuberosus.* Ground artichoke. **1950** Jr. League Charleston *Receipts* 274 **SC,** People ain' fuh know groun' artichoke good fuh mek pickle; 'stead dey gib um tuh de pig! [*DARE* Ed: Precedes recipes for whole artichoke pickle and chopped artichoke pickle, both made with Jerusalem artichokes.] **1968** *DARE* (Qu. I4, . . *Vegetables . . less commonly grown around here*) Infs **LA**20, 33, Ground artichoke.

ground bait n

=earthworm.

1966 Dakin *Dial. Vocab. Ohio R. Valley* 394, *Fish(ing) bait* is fairly common beside the usual *red-worm* in southern Kentucky. This term (sometimes *ground bait* or simply *bait*) also has rare scattered use in Ohio and Illinois within the *fish worm/fishing worm* areas.

ground bass n

A **rock bass** (here: *Paralabrax nebulifer*).

1953 Roedel *Common Fishes CA* 74, *Paralabrax nebulifer*. . . A desirable sport species. . . *Unauthorized Names:* Ground bass.

ground bee n Also *ground honey bee, ground-nesting bee*

A bee, such as those of the family Andrenidae, which nests in the ground.

1965–70 *DARE* (Qu. R21, . . *Kinds of stinging insects*) 12 Infs, **scattered,** Ground bee; **TX**1, Ground honey bee; **NY**113, Ground-nesting bee.

groundberry n

1 A **wintergreen,** usu *Gaultheria procumbens.*

1828 Rafinesque *Med. Flora* 1.202, *Gautiera* [sic] *Repens*. . . *Vulgar Names*. . . Groundberry. **c1873** De Vere *MS. Notes* 368 *(DAE),* In central parts of Nebraska [there are] groundberries, [the] size of [a] plum, grow[in]g on a vine w[ith] leaves like [a] fern. **1900** Lyons *Plant Names* 169, *Gaultheria procumbens*. . . Ground-berry. **1930** Sievers *Amer. Med. Plants* 63, *Wintergreen—Gaultheria procumbens* . . groundberry. **1967** *DARE* (Qu. I44, . . *Kinds of berries*) Inf **MI**44, Groundberries.

2 =partridgeberry. *obs*

1867 De Voe *Market Asst.* 392 **NEast,** *Tallow-berries,* or *ground-berries.*—These small red berries are found growing on a small, tender vine resting on the ground, in the cleared woods; and when eaten, they have a sort of sweetish, tallowy taste, but rather pleasant.

3 A blackberry such as *Rubus hispidus;* see quots.

1940 Steyermark *Flora MO* 265, Deam's Groundberry. . . *R[ubus] Deamii. Ibid* 268, Prickly Groundberry . . *Rubus missouricus.* **1953** Strausbaugh-Core *Flora WV* 508, *R[ubus] inobvius*. . . *hispidus*. . . *vagulus*. . . *vegrandis*. . . *Huttonii*. . . *orbicularis*. . . *davisiorum*. . . *zaplutus*. . . Groundberry.

4 A **ground-cherry;** see quot.

1968 Barkley *Plants KS* 305, Physalis angulata. . . Cutleaf Groundberry. . . Physalis missouriensis. . . Missouri Groundberry. . . Physalis pubescens. . . Downy Ground Berry. . . Physalis pumila. . . Prairie Ground Berry. . . Physalis virginiana. . . Virginia Ground Berry.

ground birch n

A **scrub birch** or similar birch.

1955 U.S. Arctic Info. Center *Gloss.* 36, *Ground birch.* Any shrub or tree of the birch family having a prostrate, creeping habit. **1972** Viereck-Little *AK Trees* 130, *Resin Birch (Betula glandulosa)*. . . Other names . . ground birch.

ground bird n [From the habitat] Cf **ground sparrow**

Any of var sparrows, as:

a =field sparrow a. esp MA

1789 in 1941 Howay *Voyages Columbia* 63 **MA,** In the woods we find several sorts of woodpickers, Robbins, . . long tailed thrush[,] ground birds, tomtits. **1829** in 1832 Bryant *Poems* 168 **cwMA,** Columbines, in purple drest,/ Nod o'er the ground bird's hidden nest. **1858** Holmes *Autocrat* 128 **ceMA,** The ground-bird builds her nest where the beetle had his hole. **1884** Roe *Nature's Serial Story* 206, One of these little sober-coated creatures that Thoreau well calls a "ground-bird" would fly to the top of a plum-tree and trill out a song. **1917** (1923) *Birds Amer.* 3.43, *Spizella pusilla pusilla*. . . Ground Bird. [*Ibid* 44, This Sparrow's habits of running along the ground and skulking through the brush are characteristics which aid in its identification.] **1944** [see **b** below]. **1956** MA Audubon Soc. *Bulletin* 40.254, *Savannah Sparrow.* Ground Bird (Mass.) *Ibid* 255, *Field Sparrow*. . . Ground Bird (Maine). . . *Song Sparrow*. . . Ground Bird (Mass.)

b also *brown ground bird:* **=song sparrow.**

1823 in 1832 Bryant *Poems* 42 **cwMA,** And the brown ground bird, in thy glen,/ Still chirps as merrily as then. **1898** (1900) Davie *Nests N. Amer. Birds* 390, *Song Sparrow*. . . So great is the diversity [of the eggs] in their coloration and size that they generally serve to represent the eggs of several different species of "ground-birds" in the small boy's collection. **1914** Eaton *Birds NY* 2.317, Mr Ralph Paddock . . has a photograph of a Song sparrow's nest in a hollow apple tree. . . This bird, however, is the common "ground bird" or "brown ground bird" of the school boy, and 90 per cent of their nests are placed upon the ground. **1929** Forbush *Birds MA* 3.92, *Melospiza melodia melodia*. . . Ground-bird. **1944** Hausman *Amer. Birds* 515, *Ground-bird*—see Sparrow, Field; see also Sparrow, Vesper; also Sparrow, Song; also Sparrow, Savannah. **1946** Goodrich *Birds in KS* 313, Bird, ground—sparrow, eastern song. **1956** [see **a** above].

c =vesper sparrow.

1889 *Century Dict.* 2637 **NEng,** *Ground-sparrow*. . . A ground-bird; one of several small grayish and spotted or streaked sparrows which nest on and usually keep near the ground, as the savanna-sparrow and the grass-finch, bay-winged bunting, or vesper-bird. **1910** KY Hist. Soc. *Register* 8.22, *Pooecetes gramineus*. . . Grass Finch. . . Although eminently a "ground bird," whenever one of them experiences the musical impulse he flies to the top of the nearest high tree. **1938** Oberholser *Bird Life LA* 657, *Eastern Vesper Sparrow*. . . Other names for this bird are . . 'grass finch', or 'ground bird', which, of course, refer to its habits. **1944** [see **b** above]. **1955** Forbush-May *Birds* 516, *Eastern Vesper Sparrow*. . . *Other names* . . Ground-bird.

d =savannah sparrow.

1889 [see **c** above]. **1929** Forbush *Birds MA* 3.53, *Savannah Sparrow.* Other names . . *ground-bird.* [*Ibid* 55, It feeds, nests and sings on the ground, but it is by no means entirely terrestrial.] **1932** Bennitt *Check-list* 62 **MO,** *Passerculus sandwichensis savanna*. . . Ground bird. **1944** [see **b** above]. **1956** [see **a** above].

groundbreak See **groundslide**

ground brier n

A **greenbrier** (here: *Smilax pumila*).

1960 Vines *Trees SW* 72, *Smilax pumila*. . . Vernacular names are . . Brier-vine, Ground-brier, and Wild Sarsaparilla. It differs from most greenbriers by its . . prostrate habit.

‡ground bunny n

A **chipmunk** (here: *Tamias striatus*).

1966 Dakin *Dial. Vocab. Ohio R. Valley* 2.400, *Tamias striatus*. . . A Nelson County, Kentuckian says *ground bunnies.*

ground cedar n

1 A **juniper** (here: *Juniperus communis* or *J. horizontalis*).

1854 Hammond *Hills* 39 **NY,** This opening contained . . a clump of what my guide termed ground-cedar. This shrub grows from a single stem, as large perhaps as a man's arm, from which branches spread out along upon, or a few inches from, the ground, to a distance of from six to ten feet, so that one of these shrubs will extend over a circle from ten to twenty feet in diameter. . . A fawn . . had been hid away by its dam beneath the ground-cedar. **1916** *Torreya* 16.236, *Juniperus horizontalis*. . . Ground . . cedar, Matinicus Id., Me. **1927** Keeler *Our Native Trees* 492, *Juniperus communis*. . . The common Juniper or Ground Cedar is a most interesting plant. **1960** Vines *Trees SW* 37, *Common Juniper—Juniperus communis*. . . Vernacular names are Horse Savin. . . Ground Cedar . . and Gin Juniper. **1968** *DARE* (Qu. T5, . . *Kinds of evergreens, other than pine*) Inf **WI**12, Ground cedar, ground juniper.

2 A **club moss:** usu *Lycopodium complanatum* or *L. tristachyum.* [*DCan* 1832 →; see quot 1942] **chiefly NEast, Pacific NW, AK**

1900 Lyons *Plant Names* 233, *L[ycopodium] complanatum*. . . Ground Cedar. **1923** Abrams *Flora Pacific States* 1.44, *Lycopodium complanatum*. . . Ground-cedar. . . Horizontal stems prostrate and wide-creeping. **1942** Hylander *Plant Life* 125, Ground Cedar . . is a fern-relative with overlapping scale-like leaves which resemble those of the Cedars. **1950** Gray-Fernald *Manual of Botany* 15, *L. complanatum*. . . Ground-Cedar. . . *L. tristachyum*. . . Ground-Cedar. **1951** Graham *My Window* 46, Ground cedar or club moss. **1968** Radford et al. *Manual Flora Carolinas* 6, *L. tristachyum*. . . *Ground-Cedar*. . . Dry, sandy woods and rocky slopes; chiefly mts. **1974** Welsh *Anderson's Flora AK* 5, *Ground Cedar.* Stems perennial, . . producing erect, freely branched aerial stems 6–25 (30) cm tall.

3 =beach heather.

1900 Lyons *Plant Names* 194, *H[udsonia] tomentosa*. . . Ground Cedar. **1940** Clute *Amer. Plant Names* 134, *H[udsonia] tomentosa* . . ground cedar. **1951** Hough *Singing in Morning* 39 **Martha's Vineyard MA,** Dried beach heather—also known popularly as . . ground cedar.

ground cellar n [Cf PaGer *Grundkeller* ground cellar] **esp PA** Cf **dirt cellar**
=root cellar.
1965–70 *DARE* (Qu. M19, *A place for keeping carrots . . and so on over the winter*) Infs **NY**66, **OH**58, 81, **PA**51, 56, 141, 153, 158, 242, Ground cellar.

ground centaury n
1 A **milkwort** (here: *Polygala nuttallii*).
1876 Hobbs *Bot. Hdbk.* 49, Ground centaury, Polygala Nuttallii. **1900** Lyons *Plant Names* 164, *F[rasera] Carolinensis. . .* Ground Centaury. . . *Fresh root* emeto-cathartic. *Ibid* 298, *P[olygala] Nuttallii. . .* Ground Centaury.
2 A **columbo** (here: *Frasera carolinensis*).
1900 [see **1** above]. **1940** Clute *Amer. Plant Names* 223, *Frasera Carolinensis.* Ground centaury, Indian lettuce, meadow pride.

ground chaparral n
A **wild buckwheat** (here: *Eriogonum jamesii*).
1937 U.S. Forest Serv. *Range Plant Hdbk.* W70, James eriogonum *(E. jamesii),* known locally as antelope sage, ground chaparral, ground eriogonum, and redroot, ranges from Kansas and Colorado to Arizona, Texas, and south into northern Mexico.

ground cheepie See **ground chippy 1**

ground-cherry n
A plant of the genus *Physalis.* Also called **cherry tomato, Chinese lantern 1, globe apple, husk-tomato, Jerusalem cherry, strawberry tomato, wild cherry, winter ~.** For other names of var spp see **balloon weed, cowslip vine, garden huckleberry 2, groundberry 4, ground tomato, hog plum 4, jamberry, Japanese lantern, little tomato, paper hearts, poha, tomatillo, wild tomato, yellow henbane**
1807 Scott *Geog. MD & DE* 26, Common and white plantain, thorowax, . . ground cherries, pursley and yams. **1859** (1968) Bartlett *Americanisms* 181, *Ground Cherry. (Physalis.)* A wild fruit lately introduced into our gardens and markets. Sometimes called Winter Cherry. **1893** *Harper's New Mth. Mag.* May 939 **CO,** There were . . plums, quinces, grapes, and ground-cherries. **1906** *DN* 3.139 **nwAR,** *Ground-cherry. . .* A wild trailing plant. **1913** Cather *O Pioneers* 29 **NE,** She made a yellow jam of the insipid ground-cherries that grew on the prairie. **1965–70** *DARE* (Qu. H63, *Kinds of desserts*) Inf **IN**66, Ground-cherry pie; (Qu. I4, . . *Vegetables . . less commonly grown around here*) Inf **WA**1, Ground-cherry—a semi-sweet fruit; (Qu. I44, . . *Berries [that] grow wild*) Infs **NE**2, **ND**3, **PA**88, **VA**24, Ground-cherries; (Qu. I46, . . *Fruits that grow wild*) Infs **IA**19, 47, **NC**44, **UT**8, **WI**72, Ground-cherries; **ID**1, **WI**13, Ground-cherry; (Qu. I53, . . *Fruits grown around here*) Infs **IN**67, **IA**2, Ground-cherries; (Qu. S4) Inf **NJ**3, Ground-cherry; (Qu. S21, . . *Weeds . . that are a trouble in gardens and fields*) Inf **NJ**58, Ground-cherry; **KY**40, Wild ground-cherry. **1966** *DARE* Tape **OK**31, Ground-cherries . . have a kind of . . husk around 'em, only it would be kind of like grass only . . thick. We'd peel that off, an' the cherries'd . . have a kind of a funny taste.

ground chipmunk n
A **chipmunk** (here: *Eutamias* spp).
1968 *DARE* (Qu. P27, . . *Kinds of squirrels*) Inf **CA**83, Ground chipmunk.

ground chippy n
1 pronc-sp *ground cheepie:* **=song sparrow. esp PA** Cf **chipping sparrow**
1890 Warren *Birds PA* 242, *Melospiza fasciata. . . Song Sparrow; Ground Chippy. . .* The nest . . is built on the ground or in a low bush. **1900** *Congressional Record* 30 Apr 33.6.4872/2 **nePA,** The ground chippy darted under the fences and had its nest in the tall grass. **1968** *DARE* (Qu. Q22, *Joking names or nicknames for the common sparrow*) Inf **PA**168, Ground cheepie.
2 =rufous-sided towhee.
1956 MA Audubon Soc. *Bulletin* 40.254 **CT,** *Towhee. . .* Ground Chippy. . . That is, ground sparrow. . . Its black and cinnamon coloration suggests that of the Robin.

ground chuck n [**chuck** n[2]; *DCan* "Obs."]
A **woodchuck** (here: *Marmota monax*).
1967 *DARE* (Qu. P31, . . *Names or nicknames . . for the groundhog*) Inf **NJ**3, Ground chuck. **1989** *DARE* File **csWI,** That ground chuck in the garden really makes a lot of noise sometimes. I heard him last night—he must have seen the neighbor's cat.

ground cone n [See quots 1961, 1987]
A parasitic plant of the genus *Boschniakia,* native chiefly to the Pacific Northwest and Alaska. Also called **squirrel's grandfather.** For other names of var spp see **poque**
1960 Abrams *Flora Pacific States* 4.10, *Boschniakia hookeri. . .* Vancouver or Small Ground Cone. . . *Boschniakia strobilacea. . .* California Ground Cone. **1961** Peck *Manual OR* 735, *Boschniakia. . .* The fruiting plant usually very thick and cone-like. . . Ground-cone. **1973** Hitchcock–Cronquist *Flora Pacific NW* 444, *Boschniakia. . .* Ground-cone. **1974** Welsh *Anderson's Flora AK* 302, *Boschniakia rossica . . Ground-cone. . .* Most commonly found on the roots of *Betula, Vaccinium, Picea, Salix,* and *Chamaedaphne.* **1987** Hughes–Blackwell *Wildflowers SE AK* 50, Ground-cone. . . The pine cone-like stem is crowded with yellowish, purplish or brownish, scale-like leaves.

ground creeper n Cf **creeper 1**
A **bindweed 1.**
1969 *DARE* (Qu. S5, . . *Names . . for the wild morning glory*) Inf **IN**76, Ground creeper.

ground cricket n
Prob a field cricket such as *Gryllus pennsylvanicus.*
1946 Waters *Colorado* 95, Ground crickets that migrate into towns like locusts and eat the very clothes in the house. **1968** *DARE* (Qu. R4, *A large winged insect that hatches in summer in great numbers around lakes or rivers, crowds around lights, lives only a day or so, and is good fish bait*) Inf **GA**35, Ground cricket.

ground cuckoo n
=roadrunner.
1869 *Amer. Naturalist* 3.477, I obtained . . a ground Cuckoo *(Geococcyx Californianus).* **1873** *Ibid* 7.324, The Ground Cuckoo . . [is] noted for its swift-footedness, inhabiting the Southwestern Territories and California, and abundant in Southern Arizona. **1897** *Oölogist* 14.79 **TX,** In Texas this bird [=the roadrunner] is almost universally known as the Chaparal [sic] Bird or Mexican Peafowl; sometimes it is called the Ground Cuckoo, Snake Killer and Paisano. **1936** McKenna *Black Range* 225, The roadrunner, or chaparral cock . . is known . . [as] the 'ground cuckoo,' because he cannot fly high or far. **1940** Writers' Program *Guide TX* 28, The road runner or ground cuckoo, also locally called the chaparral bird, "Texas bird of paradise," and *paisano,* found over the entire middle and western parts of the State, is the clown of the highways. **1969** *DARE* FW Addit **NM,** Ground cuckoo . . also called roadrunner, chaparral cock, chaparral hen, and snake killer. **1977** Udvardy *Audubon Field Guide Birds* 797, Roadrunners are ground cuckoos.

ground daisy n Cf **Easter daisy**
A low-growing western plant *(Townsendia scapigera)* with daisylike flower heads.
1941 Jaeger *Wildflowers* 270 **Desert SW,** *Ground-daisy. Townsendia scapigera. . .* The plants are generally wedged between small stones and lie flat, close to the surface of the ground. **1960** Abrams *Flora Pacific States* 4.308, Ground-daisy. . . Rocky ridges in the pinyon-juniper forest. . . California to Nevada.

ground dog See **ground puppy 1a, b, c**

ground dove n [*DJE* 1679 →]
A small grayish dove *(Columbina passerina)* native to the southern US. Also called **little dove, mourning dove, tobacco dove**
1731 (1754) Catesby *Nat. Hist. Carolina* 1.26, The Ground-Dove. . . They sometimes approach so far North as *Carolina,* and visit the lower parts of the Country near the Sea. **1832** Nuttall *Manual Ornith.* 1.636, The Ground Dove is an inhabitant of all the states of the Union south of Virginia. . . They feed on various seeds and berries, particularly on those of the tooth-ache tree. **1888** *Century Illustr. Mag.* 36.702/2, The ground or moaning dove is scarcely larger than a sparrow. **1917** (1923) *Birds Amer.* 2.50, Ground Dove—*Chaemepelia passerina terrestris.* **1938** Rawlings *Yearling* 170 **nFL,** He was able to make out a track, pointed and dainty as the mark of a ground-dove. **1946** Hausman *Eastern Birds* 344, Eastern Ground Dove *Columbigallina passerina passerina.* **1977** Udvardy *Audubon Field Guide Birds* 509, The Ground Dove flies incredibly fast, with its short wings beating rapidly, almost like those of a quail.

grounded exclam Cf **anti-come-back**
=**pigtail** exclam.
1968 *DARE* (Qu. EE23b, *In the game of andy-over . . if you fail to get the ball over the building and it rolls back . . you call out*) Inf **IN**32, Grounded.

grounder minnow n
A **troutperch** (here: *Percopsis omiscomaycus*).
1983 Becker *Fishes WI* 741, *Trout-Perch. . .* Other common names: grounder minnow.

grounders and fliers n Also *grounders* [Varr of **flies and grounders**]
=**scrub.**
1967 *DARE* (Qu. EE11, *Bat-and-ball games for just a few players*) Infs **PA**11, 22, Grounders; **NY**28, Grounders and fliers.

ground festoon See **festoon pine 2**

ground fir n Cf **fir club moss**
A **club moss** such as *Lycopodium alpinum, L. clavatum,* or *L. sabinaefolium.*
1889 *Century Dict.* 2636, *L[ycopodium] clavatum . .* is also called . . *ground-fir.* **1900** Lyons *Plant Names* 233, *L. sabinaefolium . .* Ground Fir. **1950** Gray-Fernald *Manual of Botany* 14, *L. sabinaefolium. . .* Ground-Fir. *Ibid* 15, *L. alpinum. . .* Ground-Fir. **1974** Welsh *Anderson's Flora AK* 3, *Lycopodium alpinum. . . Ground Fir. . .* Meadows in tundras and heathlands, and in woods. **1987** Hughes-Blackwell *Wildflowers SE AK* 111, Alpine Club Moss, ground fir *(Lycopodium alpinum . .)* up to 6″ tall.

ground frog n **esp S Midl**
A **toad.**
1966 Dakin *Dial. Vocab. Ohio R. Valley* 2.391, *Ground frog* has some use in the Mountains [of eastern Kentucky] but is attested nowhere else. **1967** *DARE* (Qu. P23, . . *Animal similar to the frog that lives away from water*) Inf **SC**53, Ground frog. **1970** *McDavid Coll.* **cnGA,** *Ground frog:* a toad. **1986** Pederson *LAGS Concordance,* 3 infs, **neAL, cnGA, nwLA,** Ground frog(s).

ground gold n Also *ground goldflower*
A **golden aster 1** (here: *Chrysopsis falcata*).
1940 Clute *Amer. Plant Names* 80, *C[hrysopsis] falcata.* Ground Goldflower. **1959** Carleton *Index Herb. Plants* 56, Ground Gold: Chrysopsis falcata.

ground goldenrod n
A **goldenrod 1** (here: *Solidago mollis*).
1930 OK Univ. Biol. Surv. *Pub.* 2.87, *Solidago mollis. . .* Velvety or Ground Goldenrod. **1936** Winter *Plants NE* 146, Ground Goldenrod. . . Found throughout the state, most frequent westward. **1940** Clute *Amer. Plant Names* 88.

ground goldflower See **ground gold**

ground gopher n
1 A **ground squirrel** n **b** (here: *Spermophilus* spp). Cf **gopher** n[1] **2b(1)**
1969 *DARE* (Qu. P29, *Do you have 'gophers' around here? If yes, what other name do they have, or what other animal are they most like?*) Inf **IL**54, Ground gopher. **1970** *Western Folkl.* 29.172, The terms [for *Geomys, Spermophilus,* and *Tamias striatus*] that are used ambiguously are . . *gopher, ground gopher. Ibid* 173, Ground gopher [=] Richardson's Ground Squirrel . . Franklin's Ground Squirrel.
2 A **chipmunk** (here: *Tamias striatus*). Cf **gopher** n[1] **2b(4)**
1969 *DARE* (Qu. P29) Inf **NY**198, Ground gopher. **1970** [see **1** above].
3 =**pocket gopher.** Cf **gopher** n[1] **2a**
1970 [see **1** above].

ground hackee n Also *ground hackey, ~ hackie, ~ hikey;* rarely *fence hackee* **esp csPA** Cf **fence mouse, hackee**
A **chipmunk** (here: *Tamias striatus*).
1949 Kurath *Word Geog.* 74, In the Philadelphia area (on the Delaware, the lower Susquehanna, and the Juniata) an older expression, *ground hackie,* is being replaced by *chipmunk.* **1967** Faries *Word Geog. MO* 110, *Chipmunk. . .* The North Midland terms, *ground hackie . . grinnie,* seem to be rarely used in Missouri. *Ibid* 143, Ground hackie. . . 3 [infs]. **1967-68** *DARE* (Qu. P27, . . *Kinds of squirrels*) Infs **MD**32, **PA**38, Ground hackee; **PA**29, Fence hackee—about 3 in. long, belongs to chipmunk family. **1970** *Western Folkl.* 29.167, Two relics [for *chipmunk*] are *ground hackie* around Philadelphia and *chickery* to the south and east of Philadelphia. **1982** *Barrick Coll.* **csPA,** *Ground hackey*—chipmunk. . . Also *ground hikey.* **1984** *DARE* File **csPA,** Ground hackies—chipmunks.

ground hemlock n Also *creeping hemlock*
A **yew** (here: *Taxus canadensis*).
1832 Williamson *Hist. ME* 1.116 **ME,** *Low* or *Ground hemlock* is a shrub which branches upon the ground, bears berries, transparent, pleasant to the taste, large as currants, and of amber colour. **1853** (1864) Thoreau *ME Woods* 107, I . . found that the ground-hemlock, or American yew, was the prevailing under-shrub. **1894** *Jrl. Amer. Folkl.* 7.100 **WV,** *Taxus canadensis. . .* creeping hemlock. **1904** Waller *Wood-carver* 7 **NEng,** The Pent Road . . trailed its grass-grown, rocky length . . through acres of sweet fern and ground-hemlock. **1931** Clute *Common Plants* 69, *Taxus canadensis . .* we usually call ground hemlock after a more noticeable evergreen, being unfamiliar with the European yew-tree. **1966-67** *DARE* (Qu. T5, . . *Kinds of evergreens, other than pine*) Infs **MI**2, 53, Ground hemlock; (Qu. T16, *What kinds of trees are 'special' around here?*) Inf **NC**36, Ground hemlock. **1976** Bailey-Bailey *Hortus Third* 1098, Ground hemlock.

ground hikey See **ground hackee**

groundhog n
1 also *groundpig:* A **marmot,** usu the eastern **woodchuck** *(Marmota monax).* [Perh calque from Du *aertoercken* arch var of *aardvarken* literally "earth pig"] **widespread, but esp Midl** See Map Cf **woodchuck**
[**1655** Donck *Beschryvinge* 38 **NY,** Daer zijn ooch *Aertoercken, . . Trommelslaghers,* en verscheyde andere soorten die wy niet kennen ofte gesien hebben. [=There are also *groundhogs, . . drummers,* and various other kinds which we have not known or seen.]] **1742** (1849) Darlington *Mem. John Bartram* 148, The *Monac,* or groundhog . . will be as tame as a cat (for I gave one to Sir Hans Sloane, who was much delighted with it). **1755** in 1963 Franklin *Papers* 6.85 **sePA,** I imagine it to be the same that in New England is called a *Woodchuck. . .* Having never seen one of them before, I immediately took some Notes towards a Description of it, to show our Friend Bartram, who tells me it is what we here call a *Ground Hog.* **1825** in 1974 *Fauna Americana* 158, *Arctomys monax. . . Wood-chuck,* in Maryland. *Ground-hog,* in Pennsylvania. **1859** Colton *Mt. Scenery* 101 **NC,** Then there is the ground-hog. As his name indicates, he burrows in the ground, and, like the prairie dog, builds a perfect city. He is about as large as a medium-sized opossum, and has similar hair. His color is a sort of dark gray. **1930** Shoemaker *1300 Words* 26 **cPA Mts** (as of c1900), *Ground-hog*—The common name of the Woodchuck in the West Branch valley, called Woodchuck further North. **1954** *Harder Coll.* **cwTN,** *Groundhog. . .* Woodchuck. **c1960** *Wilson Coll.* **csKY,** *Groundhog* is the only name for the animal in the area, except for an occasional extra—*whistle pig.* **1965-70** *DARE* (Qu. P31, . . *Other names . . for the groundhog*) 408 Infs, **widespread, but esp Midl,** Groundhog; **KY**11, Groundpig; **OH**33, Grundswine [sic]; (Qu. P29) 67 Infs, **esp Midl,** Groundhog; **NV**8, Small groundhog. **1966-70** *DARE* Tape **AL**1, We used to eat all kinds of old varmints and things. . . We used to eat possums, . . coons, and groundhogs; **VA**62, We have groundhogs; they dig holes in the fields. **1980** Whitaker *Audubon Field Guide Mammals* 385, Groundhog. . . It emerges in early spring (according to legend, on

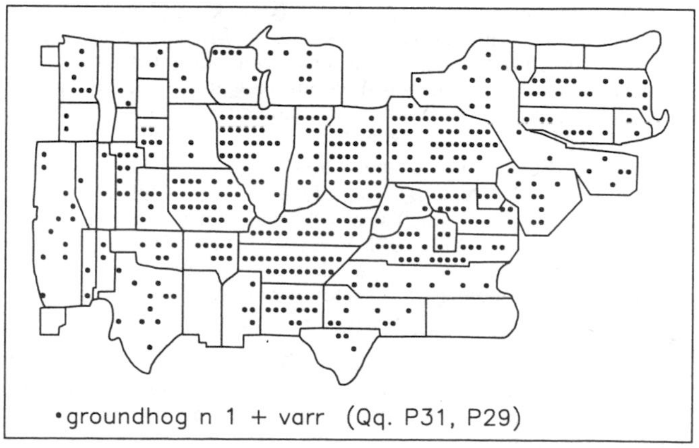

•groundhog n 1 + varr (Qq. P31, P29)

February 2, "Groundhog Day," but much later in northern parts of its range).

2 A **chipmunk** (here: *Tamias striatus*). Cf **ground hackee**

1968 *DARE* Tape **IN**30, Groundhog. . . We also call 'em chipmunks . . funny little rodent.

3 A **woodpecker.** Cf **woodchuck**

1966–69 *DARE* (Qu. Q18, *Joking names and nicknames for woodpeckers*) Infs **CO**31, **IN**58, **MI**27, **PA**163, Groundhog.

4 An unidentified plant. Cf **hogweed**

c1938 in 1970 Hyatt *Hoodoo* 1.300 **seNC,** He [=a root doctor] showed me the *groundhog,* the *sow* and the *boar,* that's a 'erb that grows.

5 In railroading: see quots.

1932 *RR Mag.* Oct 368, *Groundhog*—Brakeman. **1940** *RR Mag.* 45, *Groundhog*—Brakeman; also switch engine. **1976** Gould *Blackie's RR Hdbk.* 2, *Chief Maintenance Engineer:* . . Ground Hog. **1977** Adams *Lang. Railroader* 72, *Groundhog:* A brakeman. A yardmaster. A switch engine.

6 also *groundhog furnace, ~ still, hog (still);* In moonshining: a still set in or on the ground with the furnace surrounding it. **sAppalachians** Cf **hog B10a**

1968 *Foxfire* 2.3.53 **nGA,** *Diagram A* illustrates an interesting variation on furnace design which was once fairly popular. Called the "groundhog" or "hog" still, it was unique in that the still sat directly on the ground, and the furnace of mud, clay and rocks was built up around it with the flue at the back. *Ibid* 95, Those who use them say that the groundhog stills are much hotter than the other varieties, and thus make better stills. **1969** *DARE* Tape **GA**72, First thing is, dig out a level place, level it up and build you a furnace. . . of late days we build 'em out of concrete blocks . . and brick. . . A long furnace with an openin' at one end, and your still sits in the other end, is called a groundhog furnace; **NC**54, You can build a groundhog furnace. . . you dig a hole out in the ground . . an' you put a piece of iron across it to set your still on. **1974** Dabney *Mountain Spirits* xxi **sAppalachians,** Groundhog: This still, sometimes called a "hog," is usually found dug into the side of a hill or bank and is usually a huge metal cylinder with a wooden top and bottom.

7 also *groundhog liquor, ~ whiskey;* By ext: homemade liquor or moonshine. **sAppalachians**

1883 (1972) McDowell *Dialect Tales* 157 **eTN,** I'd have as good shoes as you, Jane Oscar, 'f my man wuz in the ground-hog whiskey business. *Ibid* 158, Speaking o' ground-hog, who'll have a drink? **1968** *DARE* (Qu. DD28b, . . *Fermented drinks . . made at home*) Inf **GA**30, Groundhog liquor—made with yeast and wheat bran. **1974** Dabney *Mountain Spirits* 229 **sAppalachians,** We decided we'd make some ground hog likker, and we had two big ground hogs. We paid so much a gallon for this feller to run it. **1986** Pederson *LAGS Concordance,* 1 inf, **nGA,** Groundhog—moonshine; 1 inf, **nAL,** Groundhog whiskey.

8 See **groundhog thrasher.**

9 A pork sausage. [With pun on *ground* (past pple of *grind*) + **hog B3a]**

1911 *DN* 3.544 **NE,** *Groundhog. . .* Sausage. "Give us that there groundhog." **1967** *DARE* (Qu. H40, *A small sausage*) Inf **OR**3, Groundhog [laughter]. **1982** *Barrick Coll.* **csPA,** *Ground hog*—humorous: *sausage.*

groundhog v

1 To store away; hence vbl n *groundhogging.* Cf **ground squirrel** v phr

1939 *Hall Coll.* **wNC,** *Ground-hog. . .* To pocket money during a poker game; i.e., to take money out of the game. . . "In a poker game a man will have so much money, maybe a dollar, and stick half a dollar in his pocket—that's what they call groun'-hoggin'." The speaker . . explained the semantics of the term as follows: *Ground* referred to putting something in a hole; *hog* meant trying to get everything.

2 with *it:* See quots. Cf **poor hog**

1939 *Hall Coll.* **eTN, wNC,** *Ground-hog*—To have difficulty in gaining a livelihood; to live on small means. "A man that groundhogs it is a man that can't help hisself." **1972** Hall *Sayings Old Smoky* 76, *Groundhog. . .* "I'm just havin' to groundhog it". . . Explained . . as meaning that he had to get along on the poorest rations.

groundhog case n **chiefly Sth, S Midl**

A situation in which one has no choice; a case of "do or die."

1885 Siringo *TX Cowboy* 125, Dangerous to cross. But the wagons being over made it a ground hog case. **1893** Shands *MS Speech* 34, *Ground-hog case. . .* It means *the last resort, the ultimatum;* as, "Do you suppose that he will succeed this time?" "He has to, it is a ground-hog case with him." **1897** *KS Univ. Qrly.* (ser B) 6.88. **1903** *DN* 2.315 **seMO,** *Ground-hog case. . .* A situation without an alternative. 'I work because I have to. It's a ground-hog case with me—work or starve.' **1907** *DN* 3.231 **nwAR.** **1908** *DN* 3.317 **eAL, wGA,** *Groun(d)-hog case. . .* An extreme case, no other alternative. "It was a ground hog case with him." **1927** *AmSp* 2.356 **cwWV,** *Ground hog case* . . something that has to be settled immediately. "But this is a ground hog case." **1928** French *Ranchman NM* 176, It was what the boys called a 'groundhog case'—either show up with your witnesses or lose the land. **1942** McAtee *Dial. Grant Co. IN* 31 **AL, MO** (as of 1890s). **c1960** *Wilson Coll.* **csKY.**

groundhog furnace See **groundhog** n **6**

groundhogging See **groundhog** v **1**

groundhog it See **groundhog** v **2**

groundhog kiln n Cf **groundhog** n **6**

Prob a low, horizontal kiln.

1969 *DARE* Tape **NC**74, We take the pottery as it comes off the wheel. . . an' then you put it in what we call a groundhog kiln. . . That type of salt glaze is done in the groundhog kiln.

groundhog liquor See **groundhog** n **7**

groundhog mill See **groundhog sawmill**

ground hog-plantain n Also *ground hog-mustard*

=self-heal.

1973 *Foxfire 2* 84 **nGA,** Ground Hog Plaintain *(Prunella vulgaris). . .* Mrs. Ethel Corn said, "It looks sort of like rabbit plantain, only the leaves are darker green and bunch up more." . . Mrs. Norton said, "There is a wild ground hog mustard, they call it, and it grows little and low on the ground, and it's got a round leaf, It has a bloom comes up, it's a purple flower. . . Just cook it with your wild mustard or anything."

groundhog salad n

A **saxifrage** (here: *Saxifraga micranthidifolia*).

1899 *Plant World* 2.198 **PA,** *Groundhog Salad, Deer Tongue* for *Saxifraga erosa* Pursh. Used as a salad by the country people. The shape of the leaves might suggest the second name.

groundhog sawmill n Also *groundhog mill*

See quot 1986.

1941 Writers' Program *Guide OK* 38, The market for this lumber . . was good, and others began to operate in the same field with small "groundhog" mills that could easily be moved from place to place. *Ibid* 94, After the first small "groundhog" sawmills were set up, boxing-board shacks became common. **1986** Pederson *LAGS Concordance,* 1 inf, **AR,** Groundhog sawmill—a small country sawmill.

groundhog's ear n

Appar a **wild lettuce** (*Lactuca* spp) or similar plant; see quot.

1967 *DARE* Tape **KY**34, [FW:] Do people still go out and gather greens in the spring? [Inf:] Yeah, they pick salad. . . they pick old field lettuce and . . groundhog's ear.

groundhog's forehead n

=arbutus.

1975 Hamel–Chiltoskey *Cherokee Plants* 23, Ground hog's forehead. . . *Epigaea repens.*

groundhog squirrel n

Prob a **ground squirrel** n **b** (here: *Spermophilus* spp). Cf **groundhog** n **2**

1967 *DARE* (Qu. P27, . . *Kinds of squirrels*) Inf **TX**13, Groundhog squirrel.

groundhog still See **groundhog** n **6**

groundhog thrasher n Also *groundhog;* for addit varr see quots **esp S Midl** *old-fash*

A simple, usu horse-powered, threshing machine.

1903 *DN* 2.315 **seMO,** *Ground-hog. . .* A small thrashing-machine without separator. Formerly very commonly used. **1949** *AmSp* 24.109 **GA,** *Ground-hog thrasher. . .* Old-fashioned, horse-drawn threshing machine. **1956** *Sun* (Baltimore MD) 2 Mar 16/4 *(Hench Coll.),* [Caption:] This "Groundhog" thresher, circa 1840, is one of the historical farm implements on display at the University of Maryland's agricultural exhibit. **1965–70** *DARE* (Qu. L32a, *In early days, how was the grain separated from the straw?*) Inf **KY**76, Groundhog thrasher—horse-powered thrashing machine; **OH**95, Groundhog; **NC**54, Groundhog frasher [sic]; **TN**62, Groundhog thresher; **GA**72, Groundhog thrasher—was mule-powered. **1986** Pederson *LAGS Concordance,* 1 inf, **cnTN,** Groundhog thrasher—mules walk in circles.

groundhog whiskey See **groundhog** n 7

ground holly n

1 A **wintergreen** (here: *Gaultheria procumbens*).

1828 Rafinesque *Med. Flora* 1.202, *Gautiera* [sic] *Repens... Vulgar Names...* Ground holly. **1892** (1974) Millspaugh *Amer. Med. Plants* 102, *Gaultheria procumbens... Com. Names...* Ground holly... This well-known perennial, spicy-aromatic evergreen grows, in its upright height, from 3 to 5 inches. *Ibid* 104, *Chimaphila umbellata... Com. Names...* Ground holly... This small.. evergreen perennial, springs from a long.. creeping.. root,.. giving off numerous fine rootlets, and sending up many branches. **1931** Bell *Cape Cod Color* 101 **seMA,** The wintergreen berry grows under many an alias; checker-berry, box-berry, tea-berry, spice-berry, ground-holly, and partridge-berry. **1971** Krochmal *Appalachia Med. Plants* 128, *Gaultheria procumbens..* ground holly.

2 A **pipsissewa** (here: *Chimaphila umbellata*).

1869 Porcher *Resources* 415 **Sth,** *Ground Holly, (Chimaphila umbellata)..* may be used extemporaneously among troops for its combined tonic and diuretic properties, associated with astringency. Its uses consequently are obvious in the convalescence from fevers. **1876** Hobbs *Bot. Hdbk.* 49, Ground holly,.. Chimaphilla [sic] umbellata. **1892** [see **1** above]. **1930** Sievers *Amer. Med. Plants* 45, *Pipsissewa...* Other common names.. ground holly. **1974** (1977) Coon *Useful Plants* 217, Ground holly.. has also been used to give its pleasing taste to root beer.

3 A **bearberry 2** (here: *Arctostaphylos uva-ursi*).

1940 Clute *Amer. Plant Names* 38, *A[rctostaphylos] uva-ursa* [sic]. *Bear-berry...* Ground-holly. **1959** Carleton *Index Herb. Plants* 57, *Ground-holly:* Arctostaphyllos uva-ursa [sic]; Chimaphila (v).

ground honey bee See **ground bee**

ground honeysuckle n

A **bird's-foot trefoil** (here: *Lotus corniculatus*).

1900 Lyons *Plant Names* 230, *L[otus] corniculatus...* Ground Honeysuckle. **1914** Georgia *Manual Weeds* 237, *Lotus corniculatus...* Ground Honeysuckle. **1933** Small *Manual SE Flora* 687. **1940** Steyermark *Flora MO* 298, Ground Honeysuckle... *L[otus] americanus.* **1959** Carleton *Index Herb. Plants* 57.

ground hornet n Also *ground wasp* Cf **digger wasp**

A wasp, esp one of the families Pompilidae, Scoliidae, and Sphecidae, which nests in the ground or at ground level.

1822 Hawley *Jrl.* 94 **swNY,** A nest of ground hornets, concealed under the log-way. **1880** Allan-Olney *New Virginians* 1.98 **VA,** There is a small ground-wasp, like the English wasp in shape and colour; and a very large ground-wasp, whose sting is very vicious. **1966-69** *DARE* (Qu. R20, *Wasps that build their nests of mud*) Inf **ID**5, Ground hornets (come out of holes in the ground); **WI**37, Ground wasp (similar to the yellow jacket, but not striped and not as colorful); (Qu. R21,.. *Kinds of stinging insects*) Infs **NH**14, **OH**37, **PA**29, **WA**30, Ground hornet; **IL**37, **NC**24, Ground wasp.

grounding vbl n

1940 Writers' Program *Guide NM* 113, *Grounding*—Cowboy term for letting bridle reins touch ground; horse then stands without tying.

ground itch n **chiefly Sth, S Midl** Cf **dew poison**

A skin rash or infection, esp of the feet.

1778 (1827) Thacher *Military Jrl.* 146 **MA,** A considerable number of men.. were infected with the *ground itch,* generated by laying on the ground. **1857** Stone *Life Howland* 81 **RI,** My first effort at improvement was to eradicate the last stages of the Scotch distemper, the ground itch. **1945** Pickard-Buley *Midwest Pioneer* 80 **IL, IN, OH** (as of c1880), Poison ivy would cause no trouble throughout the entire year if one in early spring would but eat a small portion of its leaves or roots, and immunity from ground itch could be obtained by tying around the ankle a white woolen cord. **1947** *PADS* 8.19 **NC, VA.** **1956** McAtee *Some Dialect NC* 20. **c1960** *Wilson Coll.* **csKY.** **1965-70** *DARE* (Qu. BB25,.. *Common skin diseases*) Infs **SC**40, 44, Ground itch; **FL**51, Ground itch—comes between your toes and they split; **LA**2, Ground itch—children that go barefooted in the barn lot have this; **SC**19, Ground itch—get it from the dew; **SC**24, Ground itch—from going barefooted, caused by a little worm. **1970** *NC Folkl.* 18.24, For ground itch, use clean white sand in the tobacco curing barn, walk over it and then go to the pump and run water into porch sink, and then stand in the cold water. **1986** Pederson *LAGS Concordance,* 36 Infs, **chiefly GA,** Ground itch. [*DARE* Ed: Elicited in conversation rather than in response to a specific question]

ground ivy n

1 Std: a creeping perennial *(Glecoma hederacea)* widely naturalized in North America. Also called **cat's-foot 1, cat's-paw 1, cattail 2g, creeping Charlie 2, creeping Jennie 4, field balm 1, Gill-over-the-ground, hen and chickens 1, Jack-over-the-ground, Lizzie-run-in-the-hedge, Robin-runaway, roving Charley, runaway-Jack, runaway-Nell, trailing Charley, wild snakeroot**

2 Any of several other, usu trailing, plants, as:

a A **wintergreen** (here: *Gaultheria procumbens*). Cf **ground holly 1**

1804 A. F. M. Willich *Domestic Encycl.* III.150/2 *(OEDS),* It is called Canadian Gaultheria, or Mountain Tea, Grouse- berry, Deer-berry, Ground-ivy. **1828** Rafinesque *Med. Flora* 202, *Gautiera* [sic] *Repens... Vulgar Names...* Ground ivy. **1971** Krochmal *Appalachia Med. Plants* 128, *Gaultheria procumbens..* ground ivy.

b =**arbutus.**

1854 Wailes *Rept. on Ag. & Geol. MS* 346, *Plants, Useful, Medicinal, and Ornamental...* Ground Ivy. Epigaea repens.

c A **marsh marigold** (here: *Caltha palustris*).

1869 Porcher *Resources* 17 **Sth,** *Marsh Marygold* [sic]; *Colt Foot; Ground Ivy, (Caltha palustris...).* The flower buds are pickled for use as a substitute for capers. The juice of the fresh roots is acrid and caustic... A syrup prepared from this plant is a popular remedy for coughs.

d A **maypop** (here: *Passiflora incarnata*).

1959 Carleton *Index Herb. Plants* 57, *Ground-ivy..* Passiflora incarnata. **1975** Dwyer *Thangs* 37 **Sth, S Midl,** *Ground ivy*—Passion flower.

e A common weedy plant *(Modiola caroliniana)* of the mallow family.

1964 Kingsbury *Poisonous Plants U.S.* 182, *Modiola caroliniana..* Ground ivy... Waste, low ground, Virginia to Florida, to Texas and California... *Poisonous Characteristics...* Circumstantial cases of incoordination and prostration in goats, sheep, and cattle.

f Appar =**poison ivy.**

1970 Tarpley *Blinky* 66 **neTX,** *A poisonous vine that makes the skin break out..* ground ivy.

ground juniper n [*DCan* 1793 →] Cf **ground cedar 1**

A **juniper** (here: *Juniperus communis* or *J. horizontalis*).

1943 Fernald-Kinsey *Edible Wild Plants E. N. Amer.* 81, Ground-Juniper, *Juniperus communis... Uses:* fruit (as a pleasant nibble). **1950** Peattie *Nat. Hist. Trees* 77, *Common Juniper.. Other Names:* Dwarf, or Ground, Juniper. **1955** U.S. Arctic Info. Center *Gloss.* 37, *Ground juniper.* The creeping juniper. **1961** Douglas *My Wilderness* 111 **MN,** Next.. was a patch of ground juniper in prostrate form, only a few feet high and fashioned into a circular clump. **1968** *DARE* (Qu. T5, *What kinds of evergreens, other than pine, do you have around here?*) Inf **WI**12, Ground cedar, ground juniper. **1976** Bailey-Bailey *Hortus Third* 616, *[Juniperus communis]* Var. *depressa... Ground j[uniper]...* Lab. to B.C., s. to N.Y. and Mont.

ground keeper n Cf **evergreen onion, everlasting ~, multiplier**

An onion (here: *Allium cepa* Aggregatum Group).

1967 *DARE* (Qu. I5,.. *Onions that keep coming up without replanting year after year*) Inf **ID**5, Ground keepers.

ground laurel n

=**arbutus.**

1814 Bigelow *Florula Bostoniensis* 164, *Epigæa repens...* Ground laurel. **1848** in 1850 Cooper *Rural Hours* 41 **cNY,** Near the summit of the hill we found a bunch of fresh ground laurel. **1869** Porcher *Resources* 417 **Sth,** *Ground Laurel..* has been freely used for some years in diseases of the urinary organs and of the pelvic viscera generally. **1897** Creevey *Flowers* 332 *(DAE),* Trailing Arbutus. Ground Laurel. Mayflower... A universal favorite and a candidate for honorable mention as our national flower. **1911** Henkel *Amer. Med. Leaves* 18, *Epigaea repens...* Ground laurel... This shrubby little plant spreads out on the ground in sandy soil, being found especially under evergreen trees from Florida to Michigan and northward. **1959** Carleton *Index Herb. Plants* 57, *Ground-laurel:* Epigaea repens.

ground lemon n [See quot 1930] Cf **citron 1**

A **mayapple** (here: *Podophyllum peltatum*).

1830 Rafinesque *Med. Flora* 2.59, *Podophyllum montanum. . . Fr[uit]* . . Ground Lemons. . . Berry oblong, yellowish. *Ibid* 60, The fruit is only ripe late in summer, and is edible, tasting somewhat like the Papaw. **1900** Lyons *Plant Names* 296, *P[odophyllum] peltatum. . .* Ground Lemon. **1930** Sievers *Amer. Med. Plants* 41, *Mayapple. . . Other common names. . .* Ground lemon. . . The fruit . . is about 2 inches in length, lemon shaped, green at first, then yellow. **1933** Small *Manual SE Flora* 544, *Ground-lemon. . .* The rootstock is used in medicine. The fruit is edible. **1971** Krochmal *Appalachia Med. Plants* 198, Ground lemon.

ground lily n

A **trillium** (here: *Trillium cernuum, T. erectum,* or *T. grandifolium*).

1830 Rafinesque *Med. Flora* 2.96, *Trillium latifolium. . .* Ground Lily. **1876** Hobbs *Bot. Hdbk.* 49, Ground lily, Bethroot, Trillium pendulum. **1900** Lyons *Plant Names* 378, *T[rillium] cernuum.* . . Ground Lily. **1940** Clute *Amer. Plant Names* 14, *T[rillium] cernuum* . . ground lily. . . *T. grandiflorum* . . ground lily. **1970** *NC Folkl.* 18.16, Trillium (birthroot such as wood lily or ground lily) was effective as cough syrup. **1971** Krochmal *Appalachia Med. Plants* 256, *Trillium Erectum* . . ground lily.

ground lizard n

1 A **salamander** of the genus *Ambystoma. obs*

1851 *De Bow's Rev.* 11.53, **LA,** There is an animal living under logs, being smooth skinned, slimy and blue, and white color, resembling lizards in shape, and known here as the *ground lizard* or *ground puppy.* They are reputed to be poisonous.

2 also *ground skink:* A skink *(Scincella lateralis)* native chiefly to the southeastern US.

1890 *Century Dict.* 5673, Common skinks in the United States are the blue-tailed . . and the ground-skink. **1891** in 1895 IL State Lab. Nat. Hist. Urbana *Bulletin* 3.259, *Oligosoma laterale. . . Ground Lizard.* . . Southern Illinois; not common. . . Frequents wooded regions and is found under rocks and among leaves. **1930** *Copeia* 3.28 **OK,** Ground lizard. Fairly common and easily collected from under rocks, and in all habitats where snakes and lizards are found. *Ibid* 4.154 **swGA,** Ground lizard. Noted quite commonly on the ground among dead leaves in oak and pine woods. **1930** OK Univ. Biol. Surv. *Pub.* 2.233 **OK,** Ground lizard. . . Eastern two-thirds of state. **1958** Conant *Reptiles & Amphibians* 97, *Ground Skink. . .* A small, smooth, golden-brown to blackish-brown lizard with a *dark* dorsolateral stripe. **1979** Behler–King *Audubon Field Guide Reptiles* 578, *Ground Skink. . .* New Jersey south through Florida, west to c. Texas, north to Nebraska and Missouri.

ground maple n

=alumroot 1.

1828 Rafinesque *Med. Flora* 1.241, *Heuchera acerifolia. . .* Ground Maple. **1876** Hobbs *Bot. Hdbk.* 49, Ground maple. . . Heuchera acerifolia. **1900** Lyons *Plant Names* 189, The names American Sanicle and Ground Maple apply especially to . . *H[euchera] villosa* . . , Virginia to Tennessee. **1940** Clute *Amer. Plant Names* 224, *Heuchera villosa.* Ground maple.

ground master n

A **barrel cactus** (here: *Echinocactus texensis*).

1959 Carleton *Index Herb. Plants* 57, *Ground master:* Homalocephala texensis (Echinocactus texensis).

ground mole n Pronc-spp *grummole, gru'mole* **scattered, but esp SC** Cf **ground-mole rat**

A mole (family Talpidae).

1819 Thomas *Travels W. Country* 212 **IN,** The *Ground Mole* of this country is nearly as large as the common rat. It is very injurious in gardens. It moves along at the depth of two or three inches under ground, raising a considerable ridge. **1836** Simms *Mellichampe* 1.142 **SC,** He'd be through you like a ground mole, though in much shorter time. **1843** (1971) Mathews *Writings* 141 **NYC,** If this ain't the best-built thing you've ever known, call me a ground-mole. **1922** Gonzales *Black Border* 305 **sSC, GA coasts** [Gullah glossary], *Grummole, Gru'mole*—ground-mole, ground-moles. **1927** Boston Soc. Nat. Hist. *Proc.* 265 **Okefenokee GA,** *Scalopus aquaticus australis. . .* Florida Mole. . . This species is generally spoken of as 'Ground Mole' by residents of the region. **1930** Stoney–Shelby *Black Genesis* 49 **seSC,** An' Br' Grummole (Ground Mole) mek he house in de earth. **1961** Jackson *Mammals WI* 61, *Scalopus aquaticus machrinus. . .* Prairie Mole. . . In Wisconsin, commonly called the mole. Other names include . . garden mole, ground mole. **1966–70** *DARE* (Qu. P32, *What other kinds of wild animals do you have around here?*) 15 Infs, 11 **SC,** Ground mole; (Qu. P29, *Do you have 'gophers' around here? If yes, what other name do they have, or what other animal are they most like?*) 13 Infs, 7 **OH, PA,** Ground mole. [*DARE* Ed: The OH and PA Infs may refer instead to **ground-mole rat.**] **1983** *MJLF* 9.1.42 **ceKY,** *Ground mole* . . a mole.

ground-mole rat n Also *ground-mole mouse* Cf **ground mole**

A **shrew** such as *Cryptotis parva, Blarina brevicauda,* or *B. carolinensis.*

[**1917** Anthony *Mammals Amer.* 310, The Short-tailed Shrew . . resembles the Common Mole, for which animal it is often mistaken.] **1927** Boston Soc. Nat. Hist. *Proc.* 38.7.269 **Okefenokee GA,** Shrews in the Okefinokee are generally spoken of as . . 'Ground-mole Rats' (Chesser's Island). . . probably employed for *Blarina brevicauda carolinensis* as well as for *Cryptotis parva parva,* [the name] . . may be applied more especially to the latter species, since it appears to be the one more often met with. **1961** Jackson *Mammals WI* 42, *Blarina brevicauda brevicauda. . . Vernacular names. . .* Ground mole rat. *Ibid* 56, *Cryptotis parva harlani. . . Vernacular names. . .* Ground mole-mouse.

ground moss n

1 A **haircap moss** (here: *Polytrichum juniperinum*).

1876 Hobbs *Bot. Hdbk.* 49, Ground moss, Hair cap moss, Polytrichum juniperum [sic]. **1900** Lyons *Plant Names* 194, *H[udsonia] tomentosa. . .* Ground Moss. *Ibid* 301, *P[olytrichum] juniperinum.* . . Ground Moss.

2 A **beach heather** (here: *Hudsonia tomentosa*).

1900 [see **1** above]. **1940** Clute *Amer. Plant Names* 134, *H[udsonia] tomentosa* . . ground-moss. **1959** Carleton *Index Herb. Plants* 57, *Ground-moss:* Cyperus strigosus; Hudsonia tomentosa.

3 A **nut grass** (here: *Cyperus strigosus*).

1940 Clute *Amer. Plant Names* 156, *C[yperus] strigosus* . . ground-moss. **1959** [see **2** above].

ground mouse n

=meadow mouse.

1792 Belknap *Hist. NH* 3.153, Ground mouse *(Sorex murinus.)* Field mouse *(Sorex araneus.)* **1839** Buel *Farmer's Companion* 99, Moles or ground-mice cannot penetrate and find a shelter. **1857** U.S. Patent Office *Annual Rept. for 1856: Ag.* 84, Where several species [of meadow mice] are found in one locality, they are commonly considered by farmers as one animal, known under various names, as . . "Ground Mice," [etc]. **1883** *Harper's New Mth. Mag.* 67.462/2 **eNEng,** A storm of expletives that must have startled the ground-mice and the birds. **1966–69** *DARE* (Qu. P29) Inf **KY**6, Lives out in fields, eats onions—ground mice, some say; **KY**49, Ground mice—chubby, [with] blunt, stubby tails and big eyes—most common name is ground mice; **NC**35, Ground mouse; (Qu. P32) Inf **MD**20, Ground mouse.

ground-nesting bee See **ground bee**

groundnut n Usu |'graʊn(d),nʌt|; also **chiefly SC** |'graʊnət, 'grʌnət, 'gronət| Pronc-spp *gronnut, grounet, grunnot, grunnut*

A Forms.

1922 Gonzales *Black Border* 305 **sSC, GA coasts** [Gullah glossary], *Grunnot, Grunnut*—groundnut, groundnuts, peanuts. **1950** *PADS* 14.33 **SC,** *Gronnut, grounet* ['grʌnət, 'graʊnət] *cake.* **1965–70** *DARE* (Qu. I42, . . *Names or nicknames . . for peanuts*) 12 Infs, **esp C and S Atl,** Groundnuts; **SC**9, 19, 26, 43, ['graʊnəts]; **SC**4, ['graʊnɨ˺ts]; **SC**11, ['graʊn,nʌts]; **SC**67, ['gronət]; **SC**70, ['grʌnət]; (Qu. H80) Inf **SC**70, ['grʌnət] candy; (Qu. H82b) Inf **SC**67, ['gronət].

B Senses.

1 A plant of the genus *Apios.* **esp NEng** For other names of the common *A. americana* see **Dakota potato, ground pea 2, hog peanut 3, Indian bean, Indian potato, Micmac potato, pig potato, potato bean, potato pea, rabbit vine, trailing pea, traveler's-delight, white apple, wild bean, wild wisteria**

1602 Brereton *Discouerie VA* 7, Also . . , are great store of Ground nuts, fortie together on a string, some of them as bigge as hennes egges; they grow not two inches under ground. **1703** in 1878 Southampton NY *Records* 3.373, The Trustees . . grant liberty to . . [Indians of Shinnecock] . . to dig ground nuts. **1792** Belknap *Hist. NH* 3.123, There are two species of *Ground-nuts. . .* The other *(glicine apios)* is a vine, which twines itself about bushes, and bears a blossom and fruit resembling a pea. The roots are much used for food by the Indians, and are indeed very palatable. **1832** MA Hist. Soc. *Coll.* 2d ser 9.150 **cwVT,** [Glycine] apios, Groundnut. **1854** (1969) Thoreau *Walden* 257 **MA,** Digging one day for fish-worms I discovered the ground-nut . . on its string, the potato of the aborigines. **1891** Coulter *Botany W. TX* 87, *Ground-nut. . .* Flowers brown-purple or chocolate-color, violet-scented. **1920** Saunders *Useful Wild Plants* 3, The Groundnut is really no nut at all but a starchy tuber, which, when cooked, tastes somewhat like a white potato. **1966–69** *DARE* (Qu. S26a, . . *Roadside flowers*) Inf **ME**7, Groundnut; (Qu. S26d, *Wildflowers that grow in meadows*) Inf **RI**15, Groundnut. **1974** (1977) Coon *Useful Plants* 165, Ground nut. . . The nuts dug in the fall are edible uncooked. . . Diabetics can use these as a medicinally safe substitute for ordinary potatoes. **1976** Bailey–Bailey *Hortus Third* 1252, Groundnut: *Apios americana, Arachis hypogaea, Panax trifolius.*

2 =peanut. chiefly Sth

1770 Royal Soc. London *Philos. Trans. for 1769* 59.379, They . . are the produce of a plant . . much cultivated, in the Southern colonies, . . where they are called ground nuts, or ground pease. **1792** Imlay *Western Terr.* 212, The Carolina ground-nut grows low down on the Mississippi. **1811** *Ag. Museum* 1.233 **sePA,** From the kernel of the ground nut I have obtained an oil perfectly sweet. **1853** Simms *Sword & Distaff* 493 **SC,** Tom gave the party a rice pudding. . . [and] raisins, ground-nuts (*peanuts* or *pindars,*) and black walnuts. **1872** Schele de Vere *Americanisms* 401, The *Groundnut* (Arachis hypogaea) . . has the strange habit of burying its pods underground after flowering in order to ripen its nuts. **1901** Mohr *Plant Life AL* 69, Cultural plant formations . . [include] patches of . . ground nuts *(Arachis hypogaea).* **1936** Smith–Sass *Carolina Rice* 72 **SC coast** (as of 1850s), At this they were able to get Charleston prices for corn or rice, for chickens and eggs, honey, peas, ground-nuts, or whatever else they might produce. **1965–70** [see **A** above].

3 =Jerusalem artichoke. *obs*

1792 Belknap *Hist. NH* 3.123, There are two species of *Ground-nuts.* One *(helianthus tuberosus)* bears a yellow blossom, resembling the sunflower.

4 A **ginseng B1** (here: *Panax trifolius*).

1822 Eaton *Botany* 371, *[Panax] trifolia* (dwarf ground-nut . .). Root round-tuberous, and very deep in the earth in proportion to the size of the plant. **1896** *Jrl. Amer. Folkl.* 9.189 **ME,** *Aralia trifolia* . . ground nut. **1916** Keeler *Early Wildflowers* 162, A sweet, nut-like tuber, about half an inch in diameter, lies deep in the earth. . . This tuber is edible, and there is a tradition that the early settlers of this country used it for food, whence the name Ground-nut. **1943** Fernald–Kinsey *Edible Wild Plants E. N. Amer.* 284, *Groundnut, Panax trifolium. . .* The globular, bulb-like root . . when boiled a few minutes in salted water . . becomes very palatable, either as a hot vegetable or eaten cold like salted nuts. **1961** Smith *MI Wildflowers* 249, Dwarf Ginseng, Ground-Nut—*Panax trifolius.* **1976** [see **B1** above].

5 A **nut grass** (here: *Cyperus esculentus*).

1830 Rafinesque *Med. Flora* 2.215, *C[yperus] esculentus,* or Ground Nuts. Roots edible, sudorific, diuretic, useful after fevers. **1933** *Torreya* 33.82, *Cyperus esculentus. . .* Ground nut. **1940** Clute *Amer. Plant Names* 222, *E[rigenia] bulbosa. . .* Harbinger-of-Spring. *Ibid* 256, *Claytonia Virginica.* Ground-nut. *Ibid* 257, *Cyperus esculenta.* Ground nut.

6 =brodiaea.

1920 *Torreya* 20.19 **Los Angeles CA,** *Brodiaea* sp. . . *Wild onion, ground-nut.*

7 =spring beauty.

1932 Rydberg *Flora Prairies* 312, *Claytonia. . .* Spring Beauty, Ground-nut. **1940** [see **B5** above]. **1963** Craighead *Rocky Mt. Wildflowers* 45, SpringBeauty [sic]—*Claytonia lanceolata. . .* Other names: Groundnut. **1974** Angier *Field Guide Edible Plants* 212.

8 =harbinger-of-spring.

1940 [see **B5** above].

9 A **tick trefoil** (here: *Desmodium rotundifolium*).

1966 *DARE* Wildfl QR Pl.110, Inf **OH**14, Groundnut.

ground oak n

1 Any of var scrubby oaks, such as **chinquapin oak 2.** *obs*

1766 (1942) Bartram *Diary of a Journey* 44/1, Bay and water-oak, then ground-oak, chamaerops, then pine-land. **1797** in 1802 Priest *Travels U.S.A.* 12, Ground oak is bushy, and . . bears a small acorn of a very superior flavour, which is the chief food of the deer, and sheep. **1838** Wilson *Foresters* 85 **cePA** (as of 1804), Ground oak. . . This species of dwarf oak produces great quantities of acorns. . . It grows to a height of about five feet . . and affords good shelter for the deer and bear.

2 =gopher apple.

1903 Small *Flora SE U.S.* 570, *Chrysobalanus oblongifolius. . .* Ground Oak. **1953** Greene–Blomquist *Flowers South* 52, Gopher-apple or ground oak *(Chrysobalanus oblongifolius)* is a relatively low plant with underground stems, growing in habitats similar to coco-plum. **1966** Grimm *Recognizing Native Shrubs* 144, Deer-Plum *Chrysobalanus oblongifolius. . .* Also called Gopher-apple or Ground-oak.

ground owl n

=burrowing owl.

1892 *Auk* 9.1 **FL,** At this point I spent a day collecting birds, and . . chanced to meet a 'cracker' who . . said that he could take me to a place where there were "plenty of ground Owls." **1907** Anderson *Birds IA* 269, An old Winnebago Indian . . told me . . that the "little ground owls" used to live in a prairie-dog town in the northwest corner of Woodbury county, Iowa. **1911** Wright *Barbara Worth* 138 **CO,** Always there were the same deep nights with . . the weird, quavering call of the ground owl. **1919** in 1953 Botkin–Harlow *Treas. Railroad Folkl.* 123, There remained only the graveyard, the station agent, . . and the undisturbed prairie dogs and ground owls. **1948** *Chicago Daily Tribune* (IL) 30 May mag sec 14, The ground owl burrows into the earth to make its home. It lies on its back to scratch out its tunnel, emerging to shake off the waste dirt. **1965–70** *DARE* (Qu. Q2, . . *Kinds of owls*) 13 Infs, **chiefly West,** Ground owl.

ground pea n

1 =peanut. chiefly S Atl See Map

1770 Royal Soc. London *Philos. Trans. for 1769* 59.380, They . . are the produce of a plant . . much cultivated, in the Southern colonies, and in our American sugar islands, where they are called ground nuts, or ground pease. **1789** Morse *Amer. Geog.* 414, Ground peas . . are eaten raw or roasted, and taste much like a hazlenut. **1890** *AN&Q* 5.234, *Ground-pea* is also a very common and certainly a much better name than the meaningless one now used. **1892** *Jrl. Amer. Folkl.* 5.95 **KY,** *Arachis hypogæa,* . . groundpeas. **1899** (1912) Green *VA Folk-Speech* 208. **1903** *DN* 2.315 **seMO,** *Ground-peas. . .* Peanuts; goobers. **1905** *DN* 3.82 **nwAR,** 'I didn't raise any groun' peas this year.' Rare. **1908** *DN* 3.317 **eAL, wGA,** *Groun(d)-pea. . .* The peanut, goober, pinder. All four words are used, but perhaps *goober* is the favorite. **1946** *PADS* 5.24 **VA. 1965–70** *DARE* (Qu. I42) 49 Infs, **chiefly S Atl,** Ground peas. **1966** *Greenville Advocate* (AL) 3 Nov 2/1, In Greenville, the peanut might be *goober, ground pea* or *pender* [sic]. **1971** Wood *Vocab. Change* 42, *Peanuts. . . Ground peas* and *ground nuts* do not occur west of the Mississippi. **1972** *PADS* 58.21 **cwAL,** *Goobers.* Southern *goobers* (26) [of 27 infs] is in general use, but it is usually considered a humorous term. *Ground peas* (7) and South Carolina-Georgia *groundnuts* (1) and *pinders* (2) occur as alternate responses. **1986** Pederson *LAGS Concordance,* 104 infs, **chiefly AL, GA,** Ground peas.

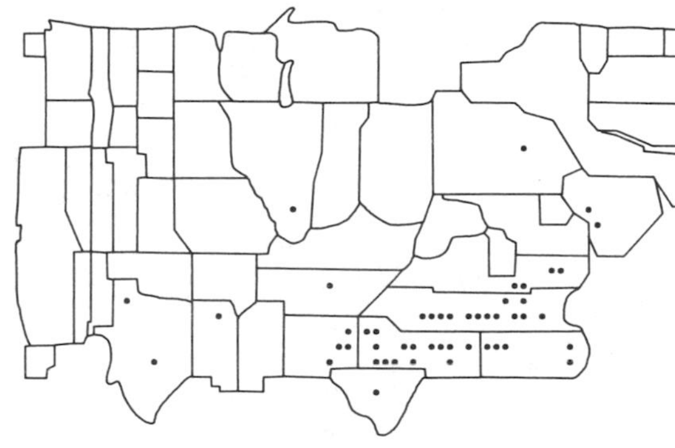

•ground pea 1 (Qu. I42)

2 A **groundnut B1** (here: *Apios americana*).

1823 James *Acct. of Exped.* 1.218, The squaws . . are often necessitated to dig the Pomme de terre . . and to scratch the ground-pea. This vegetable is produced on the roots of the *Apios tuberosa.* **1893** *Jrl. Amer. Folkl.* 6.140 **NEast,** *Apios tuberosa,* ground-pea. **1940** Clute *Amer. Plant Names* 117, *A[pios] tuberosa* . . ground-pea. **1959** Carleton *Index Herb. Plants* 57, *Ground pea:* Apios tuberosa.

ground phlox n
=moss pink.

1938 Madison *Wild Flowers OH* 84, *Ground Phlox or Moss Pink. Phlox subulata*. . . Plant low. Apr-June. Dry, sandy or rocky soil. **1968** *DARE* (Qu. S26a, . . *Roadside flowers*) Inf **IN**28, Ground phlox—same as sweet William.

groundpig See **groundhog n 1**

ground pike n
A **sauger** (here: *Stizostedion canadense*).

1884 Goode *Fisheries U.S.* 1.424, The "Sauger," known also as the . . "Ground Pike," . . has its habitat . . in the Saint Lawrence River, Great Lake region, Upper Mississippi, and Upper Missouri Rivers, also in the Ohio. **1911** U.S. Bur. Census *Fisheries 1908* 313/2, "Gray pike," . . "ground pike," . . are names for the sauger *(Stizostedion canadense)*. **1946** LaMonte *N. Amer. Game Fishes* 131, Ground Pike. **1983** Becker *Fishes WI* 880, *Sauger*. . . Other common names . . ground pike.

ground pilot n Cf **rattlesnake pilot**
=copperhead snake 1.

1967 *DARE* FW Addit **seAR,** Ground pilot [ˌgraʊn 'paɪlət]—local name for copperhead.

ground pine n
1 A **St. John's wort** (here: *Hypericum gentianoides*).

1762 Gronovius *Flora Virginica* 47, *Sarothra*. . . Ground-pine. **1830** Rafinesque *Med. Flora* 2.261, *Sarothra gentianoides*. . . Groundbroom, groundpine. **1900** Lyons *Plant Names* 334, *S[arothra] gentianoides*. . . Ground Pine. **1940** Clute *Amer. Plant Names* 133, *H[ypericum] gentianoides* . . ground pine. **1959** Carleton *Index Herb. Plants* 57, *Ground-pine* . . Hypericum gentianoides; Lycopodium.

2 =club moss. [See quot 1952]

1822 Eaton *Botany* 344, *[Lycopodium] complanatum* (ground pine . .). Woods. **1830** Rafinesque *Med. Flora* 2.240, *Lycopodium*, L. *Ground pine*. . . They kill lice and insects, dye various colors, mend bad wines. **1892** (1974) Millspaugh *Amer. Med. Plants* 180, *Lycopodium clavatum*. . . *Ground pine*. . . This evergreen perennial extends to a length of 30 feet or more. **1941** Walker *Lookout* 56 **TN,** Beautiful lycopodiums, or ground pines, whose spores are so inflammable that they have long been . . used for making fireworks, especially in producing artificial lightning, congregate under . . hemlocks. **1952** Strausbaugh-Core *Flora WV* 6, *L[ycopodium] obscurum* . . *groundpine*. . . The plants strikingly resemble miniature pine trees. **1966-69** *DARE* (Qu. T5, . . *Kinds of evergreens, other than pine*) Infs **NJ**21, **NY**165, Ground pine; (Qu. T16, *What kinds of trees are 'special' around here?*) Infs **NC**36, **PA**6, Ground pine; (Qu. T17, . . *Kinds of pine trees*) **RI**10, Ground pine. **1968** McPhee *Pine Barrens* 46 **cNJ,** Shiploads of holly, laurel, mistletoe, ground pine, . . and boughs of pitch pine were sent to New York for sale as Christmas decorations.

ground pink n
1 A **moss pink** (here: *Phlox subulata*).

1837 Darlington *Flora Cestrica* 129, *P[hlox] subulata*. . . Ground Pink. . . When in full bloom, the hills, at a distance, appear as if covered with a sheet of flame. **1848** Gray *Manual of Botany* 345, *Ground . . Pink*. . . Corolla pink-purple or rose-color (rarely white). **1901** Lounsberry *S. Wild Flowers* 442, Ground . . pink. . . Range extends from Florida to the southern part of New York. **1916** Keeler *Early Wildflowers* 191, *Ground-pink*. . . The depressed stems with their little sharp-pointed leaves make dense mats of moss-like foliage. **1942** Hylander *Plant Life* 442, Ground Pink, a densely tufted plant, forms a matted growth on bare sandy slopes from New England southward. **1959** Carleton *Index Herb. Plants* 57, *Ground-pink:* Linanthus dianthiflorus (Gilia dianthoides); Phlox subulata.

2 A **gilia** (here: *Linanthus dianthiflorus*) native to California.

1897 Parsons *Wild Flowers CA* 216, Ground-Pink. . . *Gilia dianthoides*. **1915** (1926) Armstrong-Thornber *Western Wild Flowers* 390, Ground Pink. . . *Linanthus dianthiflorus*. **1959** Munz-Keck *CA Flora* 511. **1976** Bailey-Bailey *Hortus Third* 666.

ground plum n [See quots]
1 Any of several, chiefly western, **milk vetches,** but esp *Astragalus crassicarpus;* also the fruit of such a plant. For other names of *A. crassicarpus* see **buffalo bean, buffalo pea 1, Indian pea, pomme de terre, prairie apple, sheep pod**

1857 Gray *Manual of Botany* 97, *Ground Plum*. . . Dry soil, on the Mississippi River, . . and westward and southward. . . The unripe fruits . . are edible, and are eaten, raw or cooked, by travellers. **1871** *Amer. Naturalist* 5.213 **CO,** These [=pods] . . assume a fine purple tinge, which gives them the appearance of grapes or plums, hence the plant is commonly called Ground Plum. **1936** IL Nat. Hist. Surv. *Wildflowers* 169, The Ground Plum . . is sometimes found . . in this state. . . The unripe fruits resemble green Plums and . . are frequently collected by prairie dogs for their winter store. **1948** Stevens *KS Wild Flowers* 297, The ground-plum milk-vetch neither lifts its fruits above nor buries them in the ground but spreads them over the surface to ripen where they become purple on the upper surface exposed to the sun while remaining greenish below. **1970** Correll *Plants TX* 845, *Astragalus crassicarpus*. . . Ground Plum. *Ibid* 846, *Astragalus gypsodes*. . . Gyp Ground Plum. **1976** Bailey-Bailey *Hortus Third* 126, *[Astragalus] crassicarpus*. . . *Ground plum*. . . Minn. to Tex.

2 =gopher apple.

1960 Vines *Trees SW* 421, *Gopher-apple*. . . Also known under the vernacular names of Ground-oak or Ground-plum.

ground puppy n Cf **mud puppy**
1 Any of var **salamanders** (order Caudata), as:
a also *ground dog:* **=hellbender 1.**

1826 *Amer. Jrl. Science* 11.278, Hell-bender. Mud-devil. Ground-puppy. Tweeg. Young Alligator. Vulgo. **1890** *Century Dict.* 3709, *Menopoma* . . are popularly known by the names of *hell-bender*, . . *ground puppy*. **c1938** in 1970 Hyatt *Hoodoo* 1.358 **ceVA,** I was sick one day and the next day I were well. I went on until I had it every change of the moon. I throwed up a groun' dog [Hyatt: ground puppy = mud puppy = hellbender = salamander] that's as big as your finger, it has spots on it.

b also *ground dog, ~ pup:* A **salamander** of the genus *Ambystoma*. **chiefly Sth**

1851 [see **ground lizard 1**]. **1854** Wailes *Rept. on Ag. & Geol. MS* 328, Salamandra salmonea. S. fasciata. S. bilineata. S. fusca. S. porphyritica. Ground puppy. **1872** Schele de Vere *Americanisms* 388, Others [=salamanders] are indifferently called . . *Ground-Puppies*. **1891** *Jrl. Amer. Folkl.* 4.151, "Ground-pup" or "ground-dog" . . the common spotted salamander. **1899** (1912) Green *VA Folk-Speech* 208, *Ground-puppy*. . . A small animal said to live under the ground, and bark when disturbed. **1926** TX Folkl. Soc. *Pub.* 5.62 **Sth,** Ground . . puppies are land salamanders. . . If you kill a ground puppy and dry its body and powder it and then place it in a small bag and conceal the bag under the doorstep of a house, the first person who crosses the threshold will receive into his veins the rejuvenated body of the ground puppy. **1928** Baylor Univ. Museum *Contrib.* 16.7 **TX,** *Ground-puppy*. . . *Ground-dog*. In Texas, these . . names refer to three species of land salamanders. . . *Ambystoma maculatum*, . . *A. opacum*, . . and . . *A. texanum*. **c1940** Newman-Murphy *Conserv. Notes* 5 **neLA,** There are . . varied reptiles in the parish. . . ground puppies.

c also *ground dog:* A **water dog** (here: *Necturus maculosus*).

1899 Bergen *Animal Lore* 62 **ceMD,** Ground-dog or ground-puppy or puppy, salamander, *Necturus maculatus*.

d The slimy **salamander** *(Plethodon glutinosus)*.

1930 *Copeia* 4.153 **swGA,** *Plethodon glutinosus* . . Slimy salamander. . . This and other salamanders of the region are called 'ground puppies.' One of the boys helping me said: 'If one of these ground puppies pops his teeth at you three times you'll die.' **1934** Vines *Green Thicket* 68 **cnAL,** From the groundpuppy on up to me and you, everything that's alive and moves helps Him run this place that way.

2 See quot.

1946-47 *McDavid Coll.*, 2 infs, **ce,seGA,** Ground puppy—type of burrowing bee(?), not the same as yellow jacket.

3 A **mole cricket** such as *Scapteriscus vicinus*.

1968 *DARE* (Qu. R4) Inf **GA**20, Ground puppy. **1969** *DARE* FW Addit **seGA,** Ground puppy—a mole cricket (a cricket-like insect 1½ inches long, light brown, [that] has feet like a mole, burrows at roots of garden plants; [it] eats the roots and kills the plants, and perforates the ground; [it makes] good fish bait).

ground raspberry n [See quots 1828, 1892]
=goldenseal 1.

1828 Rafinesque *Med. Flora* 1.251, *Hydrastis canadensis*. . . Ground Raspberry. [*Ibid* 252, The fruit ripens in May, and is very much like a Raspberry of a bright red color; but scarcely edible.] **1892** (1974)

Millspaugh *Amer. Med. Plants* 9, *Ground-raspberry*. . . This low perennial herb . . grows from 6 to 10 inches high, its leaves and fruit much resembling those of the raspberry. **1940** Clute *Amer. Plant Names* 3, *Golden Seal*. . . Ground raspberry. **1959** Carleton *Index Herb. Plants* 57. **1971** GA Dept. Ag. *Farmers Market Bulletin* 15 Sept 8/1, Goldenseal is often known as Orange-root or Ground-raspberry according to the part of the country you are from. **1974** (1977) Coon *Useful Plants* 220, Ground raspberry. . . A low-growing, small-flowered perennial plant of rich woodlands.

ground rat n

A **pocket gopher** (here: *Geomys pinetis*). Cf **gopher rat 1**

1791 Bartram *Travels* 7 **seGA,** There is a large ground-rat, more than twice the size of the common Norway rat. In the night time, it throws out the earth, forming little mounds, or hillocks. **1958** Harper *Travels William Bartram* 338, [In reference to quot 1791 above] The "hillocks of fresh earth, thrown up in great numbers in the night," [citation from Bartram, page 18] were doubtless not the mounds in front of the Gopher Turtles' burrows . . (which rarely have a fresh appearance), but the heaps of soil pushed out on the surface from the excavations of the Georgia Pocket Gopher *(Geomys pinetis pinetis)*. . . This note [from page 18], and the one on page 7 concerning a "ground-rat," are apparently the first references to *Geomys* in Georgia or anywhere else in the country. **1970** *DARE* (Qu. P29, *Do you have 'gophers' around here? If yes, what other name do they have, or what other animal are they most like?*) Inf **TN46**, Ground rat.

ground rattler n

1 See **ground rattlesnake 1.**

2 An **earthworm.**

1967 Williams *Greenbones* 170 **GA** (as of c1910), The trail broadened, and the horse broke out upon an upland pasture filled with sheep-skull rocks and little mounds of dirt thrown up by the fishing worms called ground rattlers.

ground rattlesnake n

1 also *ground rattler:* The pygmy **rattlesnake** *(Sistrurus miliarius)* of the southeastern US.

1709 (1967) Lawson *New Voyage* 129 **SE,** The Ground Rattle-Snake, wrong nam'd because it has nothing like rattles. **1791** Bartram *Travels* 274 **SE,** The bastard rattle snake, by some called ground rattle snake, is a dangerous little creature, their bite is certainly mortal if present medical relief is not administered. **1827** Williams *View W. FL* 28, There is a little ground rattlesnake, that escapes the fires in his burrow, he is very diminutive . . but his bite is very poisonous. **1854** Wailes *Rept. on Ag. & Geol. MS* 329, Crotalophorus milarius [sic]. Ground Rattlesnake. **1866** *Beadle's Monthly* 1.569/2 **Sth,** There is a smaller variety, called the ground-rattlesnake. This is seldom more than two feet in length. **1908** Biol. Soc. DC *Proc.* 21.78 **TX,** *Ground Rattlesnake*. . . while we were camped on the North Bosque River, Gooch found . . this pretty little rattlesnake under an old newspaper lying in the middle of our camp. **1928** Baylor Univ. Museum *Contrib.* 16.19, *Sistrurus miliarius*. . . This is the *Ground Rattlesnake* of eastern Texas from Texarkana south to Houston. **1965–70** *DARE* (Qu. P25, . . *Kinds of snakes . . around here*) 38 Infs, **chiefly S Atl, Gulf States,** Ground rattler; **FL26, TX12**, Ground rattlesnake; **GA80**, Old-field ground rattler. **1969** *DARE* Tape **GA48**, We have the rattlesnakes, then we have those little ol' rattlesnakes, ground rattlers we call 'em, 'bout eighteen inches; **GA51**, We got the li'l bitty rattler . . called the ground rattler. **1979** Behler–King *Audubon Field Guide Reptiles* 698, [*Sistrurus miliarius* is] called "ground rattler" in parts of range. The tiny rattle makes a buzzing sound audible only for a few feet. Usually encountered in the summer.

2 Any of var other snakes; see quot.

1928 Baylor Univ. Museum *Contrib.* 16.6, *Ground Rattlesnake*. The small species of rattlesnakes of the genus *Sistrurus* which have small rattles . . are the serpents most commonly known by this name. However, the same name is also applied to many snakes which are not in any way related to rattlesnakes. Many snakes when angered or nervous through fright will vibrate their tails among dead leaves, in this way producing, on a smaller scale, the rattling of the . . [rattlesnake's] little "bell." *Ibid* 19, *Sistrurus catenatus edwardsii*. . . Edward's Massasauga is known as *Ground Rattlesnake* in the Panhandle country and in the coast region (Victoria, Matagorda, Nueces, etc. counties) of southwestern Texas.

ground robin n

1 =**rufous-sided towhee.** [See quots 1844, 1890] **chiefly NEast**

1794 Amer. Philos. Soc. *Trans.* 4.110, This bird was the chewink, or ground-robin. **1844** DeKay *Zool. NY* 2.172, *The Chewink* . . is familiarly known in this State (where it breeds) under the name of . . *Ground Robin*, from its seldom attempting to fly high. **1861** OH Laws *Genl. & Local Acts* 125, It shall be unlawful for any person . . to catch, kill or injure . . any . . chewing [sic] or ground robin. **1890** Warren *Birds PA* 244, *Pipilo erythrophthalmus*. . . From its terrestrial habits and conspicuous chestnut-colored sides, has arisen the name of Ground Robin, which, although much less appropriate than any of those previously mentioned, is, nevertheless, the one by which it is best known in eastern Pennsylvania. **1895** Minot *Land-Birds New Engl.* 234, *Pipilo . . erythrophthalmus*. . . "Ground Robin." **1929** Forbush *Birds MA* 3.107, *Pipilo erythrophthalmus*. . . Ground robin. **1950** *WELS (Different kinds of robins or birds like robins)* 1 Inf, **ceWI**, Ground robin. **1956** MA Audubon Soc. *Bulletin* 40.254, *Towhee*. . . Ground Robin (General. Its black and cinnamon coloration suggests that of the Robin.) **1967** Borland *Hill Country* 128 **nwCT,** The towhees are also called chewinks and ground robins. **1969** *DARE* (Qu. Q14) Inf **MA21**, Towhee, same as ground robin.

2 =**wood thrush 1.**

1808 Wilson *Amer. Ornith.* 1.29, *Turdus melodus* [sic]. Wood thrush. . . is called by some the wood robin, by others the ground robin. **1844** Giraud *Birds Long Is.* 88 **NY,** The Wood Thrush or Ground Robin arrives on Long Island in the latter part of April, or early in May, according to the progress of vegetation. **1969–70** *DARE* (Qu. Q14, . . *Other names . . for . . thrush*) Infs **MA21**, 78, Ground robin.

groundsel tree n Also *groundsel (bush)*

A plant of the genus *Baccharis,* esp *B. halimifolia.* Also called **cotton bush, hightide bush, kinks-bush, marsh elder, saltwater bush, sea myrtle.** For other names of the chiefly Atlantic and Gulf coastal *B. halimifolia* see **consumption weed 2, lavender, lowbush merkle, mangle, manglier, mangrove, marsh laurel, pencil tree, saltbush, sand myrtle, sea sage, silverling, silver sage, water bush, water gall.** For other names of var spp see **chaparral broom, coyote brush, desert bloom, desert broom 1, false everlasting, false willow, greasewood 2h, Indian broom, mule fat, oil willow, Roosevelt weed, rosin bush, seep willow, squaw waterweed, water motie, water willow, yerba de pasmo**

1741 *Complete Fam.-Piece* II.412 *(DA),* You have also the black Hellebore now in Flower with the Spurge Laurel, Virginian Groundsel Tree. **1848** Gray *Manual of Botany* 216, *Baccharis*. . . Groundsel-Tree. . . *B. halimifolia*. . . Sea Groundsel-Tree. **1899** (1912) Green *VA Folk-Speech* 208, *Groundsell*. . . A plant. Used as a domestic remedy. **1900** Lyons *Plant Names* 56, *Baccharis*. . . Groundsel. . . *B. halimifolia*. . . Groundsel tree, Groundsel bush. **1970** Correll *Plants TX* 1558, *Baccharis*. . . Groundsel-tree. **1976** Bruce *How to Grow Wildflowers* 220, Another excellent seashore shrub, one of the commonest yet most distinct, is *Baccharis halimifolia,* Groundsel Bush. **1977** Kibler *Simms as Naturalist* 2 **SC,** *Baccharis halimifolia,* called locally "saltwater-myrtle," "silverling," or "groundsel." **1978** Whipple *Vintage Nantucket* 238 **MA,** At the edge of the outer beach was another tree, the groundsel, also growing in low clumps along the ground.

ground silo n

1966 *DARE* (Qu. M12, *What do you keep food for the cattle in over winter?*) Inf **ND3**, Ground silo—a pit dug in earth.

ground skink See **ground lizard 2**

ground sleuth v phr, hence vbl n, ppl adj *ground sleuthing,* n *ground sleuther* Cf **ground swat**

1968 *DARE* FW Addit **swNV,** *Ground sleuthing*—shooting a game bird while it is on the ground or on water. Considered very poor sportsmanship and hated by people who consider themselves real hunters. A person who does this is a "meat hunter" in contrast to a hunter. A person who ground sleuths is a ground sleuther or, more commonly, a ground sleuthing son-of-a-bitch. One ground sleuths and one never talks of *a* ground sleuth.

ground slide n[1] See **slide**

groundslide n[2] Also *groundbreak*

1966–70 *DARE* (Qu. C16, *When a mass of earth and rock comes loose from a high place and rushes down, you call it a ______*) Inf **MS72**, Groundbreak; **VA42**, Groundslide.

groundsmoke n

A low-growing plant of the genus *Gayophytum,* having many tiny white flowers. Also called **baby's breath 2c**

1942 Amer. Joint Comm. Horticult. Nomenclature *Std. Plant Names* 271, *Gayophytum.* Groundsmoke. **1953** Nelson *Plants Rocky Mt. Park* 110, Babysbreath or groundsmoke.—A . . plant with . . tiny white flowers which turn to red as they wither. **1973** Hitchcock–Cronquist *Flora Pacific NW* 308, Groundsmoke; Gayophytum.

ground snake n Cf **speckled ground snake**

Any of several snakes, as:

a A **worm snake** (here: *Carphophis amoenus*).

1885 Kingsley *Std. Nat. Hist.* 3.362, The genus *Carphophis* is very generally distributed; in the United States, the species *amoena* . . as the thunder, ground, or worm-snake, is most familiar. **1891** in 1895 IL State Lab. Nat. Hist. Urbana *Bulletin* 309, *Carphophis amoenus.* . . *Ground Snake.* . . Reaches a length of about 12 inches, with the tail 1.50. **1909** Biol. Soc. DC *Proc.* 22.134, *Carphophiops* [sic] amoenus. . . Ground Snake. Taken each year rather commonly under logs in woods. **c1960** *Wilson Coll.* **csKY,** *Ground snake*—A very small (lead-pencil size) harmless wood snake. **1966–70** *DARE* (Qu. P25, . . *Kinds of snakes*) Infs **GA**72, **KY**11, 47, **NC**44, **VA**38, Ground snake; **NC**36, Brown (*or* mottled *or* spotted) ground snake. **1968** *DARE* Tape **NC**53, Comin' on to the post office, he seen a little ol' ground snake. He caught the little ol' feller an' put it in his pocket an' . . bought an envelope and mailed it to Aunt Jane.

b A **red-bellied snake** (here: *Storeria occipitomaculata*).

1928 Pope–Dickinson *Amphibians* 64, This little snake [=*Storeria occipitomaculata*] is also known as the Brown Snake, Ground Snake . . and by other local names. **1974** Shaw–Campbell *Snakes West* 132, The red-bellied snake *(Storeria occipitomaculata)* is also called Storer's snake . . ground snake . . grass snake, and perhaps a few other names as well.

c =**earth snake.**

1930 *Copeia* 3.36 **OK,** *Potamophis striatulus* . . Ground snake. Occasionally found from March 4 until late fall in heavily wooded areas, under sandstone and limestone rocks. **1937** Pope *Snakes Alive* 194, *Ground Snake (Potamophis).* . . Virginia to northern Florida; westward to central Texas, Oklahoma, and Missouri. **1951** Conant *Reptiles OH* 94, *Virginia valeriae valeriae* . . *Ground Snake* . . A small snake which may attain a length of about a foot. **1958** Conant *Reptiles & Amphibians* 136, *Earth Snakes* . . are small gray, brown, or reddish-brown snakes virtually devoid of any distinctive markings. . . The genus occurs only in the eastern United States, and a variety of names have been applied . . "ground snakes," "little brown snakes," etc.

d A small burrowing snake *(Sonora semiannulata)* native chiefly to the southwestern US.

1937 Pope *Snakes Alive* 111, Ground snakes are able literally to swim in, as well as crawl on, sand. *Ibid* 218, Western Ground Snakes *(Sonora).* **1947** Pickwell *Amphibians* 50 **Pacific,** *Sonora semiannulata linearis,* the Striped Ground Snake, has a reddish or vermilion band extending from the back of the head to the tip of the tail. . . *Sonora semiannulata isozona,* the Vermilion Ground Snake, may or may not have crossbands. **1957** Blair et al. *Vertebrates U.S.* 348, Genus *Sonora.* . . Ground snakes. Small, secretive, burrowing snakes with a pattern of bands. **1974** Shaw–Campbell *Snakes West* 152, An extremely large adult western ground snake *(Sonora semiannulata)* is a foot and a half long; a small one is only eight inches long. **1979** Behler–King *Audubon Field Guide Reptiles* 653, *Ground Snake.* . . 8–19″. . . Tiny glossy snake; grayish, brownish, or reddish with great variation in back pattern.

e =**sharp-tailed snake.**

1952 Ditmars *N. Amer. Snakes* 210 **Pacific,** *Pacific Ground Snake* . . *Contia tenuis.* . . Small, maximum length not much over 12 inches. . . Brown above, with a reddish-brown band on each side.

ground-soaker See **sod-soaker**

ground spar See **ground sparrow b**

ground sparrow n [From the habitat] Cf **ground bird**

Any of various sparrows, as:

a =**vesper sparrow.**

1858 *Atlantic Mth.* Oct 594/2 **NEng,** In several localities, these two species [=the song sparrow and vesper bird] are distinguished by the names of Bush-Sparrow and Ground-Sparrow, from their supposed different habits of placing their nests, one in a bush, and the other on the ground. **1874** Taylor *World on Wheels* 249 **cnNY,** The ground-sparrows build in its margins. **1882** VT State Bd. Ag. *Report* 7.67, The blue bird, cat bird, wren and ground sparrows are acknowledged to be beneficial. **1895** Minot *Land-Birds New Engl.* 207, Three common birds . . [are] frequently confused by the ignorant or inexperienced, namely, the Savannah Finch, the Bay-winged Bunting, and the Song Sparrow. . . These streaked species, as well as their ground-nesting relations, are often indiscriminately called "Ground Sparrows". . . One may often hear it said that "the Ground Sparrow sings charmingly"; but whether this refers to the Field, Song, or Bay-winged Sparrow, it is impossible to say, though doubts are lessened if the bird is described as streaked beneath. **1932** Bennitt *Check-list* 63 **MO,** *Eastern vesper sparrow.* . . Ground sparrow. **1940** Todd *Birds W. PA* 709, Sparrow, Ground, *see* Sparrow, Mississippi Song and Eastern Vesper. **1965–70** *DARE* (Qu. Q21, *Different kinds of sparrows around here*) 63 Infs, **scattered east of Rocky Mts,** Ground sparrow. [*DARE* Ed: Some of these Infs may refer instead to senses below.]

b also *ground spar:* =**savannah sparrow.**

1889 *Century Dict.* 2637 **NEng,** *Ground-sparrow.* . . A ground-bird; one of several small grayish and spotted or streaked sparrows which nest on and usually keep near the ground, as the savanna-sparrow and the grass-finch, bay-winged bunting, or vesper-bird. **1895** (1907) Wright *Birdcraft* 147, *Savanna Sparrow.* . . It is essentially a ground Sparrow (which is one of its local names); for, in addition to building on the ground, it limits its flight to low bushes. **1934** Vines *Green Thicket* 60 **cnAL,** He had a little old trunk nearly full of feathers and down from wild ducks and geese, and . . from tiny birds like the . . English spar (sparrow), grass spar, ground spar . . and other birds. **1944** Hausman *Amer. Birds* 526, Sparrow, Ground—see Sparrow, Field; see also Sparrow, Savannah; also Sparrow, Song. **1946** Kopman *Wild Acres* 96 **Gulf coast,** Savanna sparrows, the "ground sparrows" of boy hunters . . , were common enough in the short grass or on . . what had been kitchen garden patches of the preceding summer. **1956** MA Audubon Soc. *Bulletin* 40.254, *Savannah Sparrow.* . . Ground Sparrow (Maine, Mass.). *Grasshopper Sparrow.* Ground Sparrow (Mass.) *Ibid* 255, *Field Sparrow.* . . Ground Sparrow (Maine, Mass., R.I.) . . *Song Sparrow.* . . Ground Sparrow (Maine, Mass.)

c =**song sparrow.**

1895 [see **a** above]. **1917** (1923) *Birds Amer.* 3.50, *Song Sparrow.* . . *Other Names.* . . Ground Sparrow. **1944** Walker *Winter Wheat* 300 **MT,** Ground sparrows dart up from the stubble. **1956** [see **b** above].

d =**field sparrow a.**

1895 [see **a** above]. **1899** Howe–Sturtevant *Birds RI* 73, *Spizella pusilla.* . . *Field Sparrow. Ground Sparrow.* A common summer resident. **1917** (1923) *Birds Amer.* 3.43, *Field Sparrow.* . . *Other Names.* . . Ground Sparrow. **1946** Goodrich *Birds in KS* 319, Colloquial Name . . sparrow, . . ground. . . Common name, A.O.U. Check-List . . sparrow, eastern song [and] sparrow, field. **1956** [see **b** above]. **1963** Gromme *Birds WI* 217, Ground Sparrow (Field Sparrow).

e =**swamp sparrow.**

1955 *Oriole* 20.1.14 **GA,** Swamp Sparrow. . . Ground Sparrow.

f =**grasshopper sparrow.**

1956 [see **b** above].

ground spider n

Any of var ground-inhabiting spiders, esp of the families Lycosidae and Salticidae.

1867 *Amer. Naturalist* 1.410 **TX,** Some of the ground spiders carry their eggs in a sack attached to the tip of their abdomen. **1881** *Ibid* 15.396 **DC,** I had at last before me the so-long looked for home of a certain ground spider or Lycosa. **1911** *Century Dict. Suppl., Ground-spider.* . . Any ground-inhabiting spider, especially any member of the families *Lycosidae* and *Attidae.* **1967–70** *DARE* (Qu. R28, . . *Kinds of spiders*) Infs **GA**65, **TN**11, **TX**11, Ground spider; **VA**38, Low ground spider.

ground squirrel n

Any of var usu burrowing rodents, as:

a The eastern **chipmunk** *(Tamias striatus).* [See quot 1709] **chiefly Midl, Sth**

1688 in 1844 Force *Tracts* 3.12.36 **VA,** The third is the Ground-Squirrel, I never saw any of this sort, . . and have had them thus described to me, to be little bigger than a Mouse finely spotted like a young Fawn. **1709** (1967) Lawson *New Voyage* 130 **NC,** Ground Squirrels are so call'd, because they never delight in running up Trees, and leaping from Tree to Tree. **1791** Bartram *Travels* 284 **S Atl,** The ground squirrel, or little striped squirrel of Pennsylvania and the northern regions, is never seen here, and very rarely in the mountains northwest of these territories. **1907** *DN* 3.189 **NH,** *Ground-squirrel.* . . Chipmunk. **1917** *DN*

4.431 **IL, KY, LA,** *Ground squirrel.* The chipmunk (Tamias striatus): also called *striped squirrel.* **1939** *LANE* Map 229 **sNEng,** The following synonyms of *chipmunk* were offered . . *ground squirrel* [3 infs] . . , and *gopher* [3 infs]. **1949** Kurath *Word Geog.* 15, *Ground squirrel* is shared by the Midland and the South as an old folk term, but *chipmunk* has largely replaced it in Eastern Pennsylvania and has spread to Maryland and the lower Shenandoah. **1950** *WELS (Names and nicknames for the chipmunk)* 13 Infs, **WI,** Ground squirrel. **1954** *Harder Coll.* **cwTN,** Ground squirrel. . . Chipmunk. **1961** Folk *Word Atlas N. LA* 153, Kurath says that *ground squirrel* is the Southern and South Midland term. The map shows that *ground squirrel* is predominant but *chipmunk* is crowding it out. **1965–70** *DARE* (Qu. P27, . . *Kinds of squirrels*) 94 Infs, **chiefly Midl, Sth,** Ground squirrel; (Qu. P29, *Do you have 'gophers' around here? If yes, what other name do they have, or what other animal are they most like?*) 34 Infs, **chiefly Midl,** Ground squirrel; (Qu. P32, . . *Other kinds of wild animals*) Infs **AL**28, **NC**36, Ground squirrel. [*DARE* Ed: Some of these Infs may refer instead to **b** below.] **1966** Dakin *Dial. Vocab. Ohio R. Valley* 2.398, In Kentucky and Illinois (and undoubtedly in Indiana although only a few scattered field records include this item) the regular name for this small terrestrial squirrel is *ground squirrel. . . Chipmunk* and *ground squirrel* are scattered throughout the state [=Ohio] with about equal frequency. **c1970** *McDavid Coll.* **ceSC,** We saw the little ground squirrel of brown color with white streaks along its body. **1982** Ginns *Snowbird Gravy* 51 **nwNC,** The ground squirrels then would bury chestnuts. They call 'em chipmunks; we call 'em ground squirrels.

b A squirrel of the genus *Spermophilus* or *Ammospermophilus.* [See quot 1917] **chiefly West, Upper MW** Also called **gopher n[1] 2b(1), picket pin, rock squirrel.** For other names of *Spermophilus* see **desert rock-squirrel, digger 4, earth squirrel, flickertail 2, gray squirrel 2, grinnie 2, ground gopher 1, prairie squirrel, squinny.** For other names of var spp of *Spermophilus* see **copperhead n[1] 4, federation squirrel, fence mouse, flag squirrel, golden chipmunk, grass chippie, grass gopher, gray gopher, Minnesota gopher, mound gopher, parka squirrel, pocket gopher, scrub gopher, sod runner, spotted ground squirrel, striped gopher, striped squirrel, tiger squirrel, whistlesneak, yellow gopher, yellowhead.** For other names of *Ammospermophilus* see **antelope ground squirrel**

1852 Stansbury *Expedition* 160 **UT,** A single ground-squirrel was seen; but how he got here, and where he obtained water to sustain life, is somewhat of a mystery. **1879** U.S. Natl. Museum *Bulletin* 14.15, *Spermophilus grammurus. . . California Ground Squirrel.* Western Texas and New Mexico west to Sierra Nevada Mountains. . . *Spermophilus Harrisi. . . Harris' Ground Squirrel.* The Great Interior Basin and Lower California. **1899** Garland *Boy Life* 85 **nwIA** (as of c1870s), The prairie abounded . . with two sorts of ground squirrel, which the settlers called "the striped gopher" and "the gray gopher." The striped gopher resembled a large chipmunk, and the gray gopher was apparently a squirrel that had taken to the fields. **1917** Anthony *Mammals Amer.* 179, Ground Squirrels are found in the greatest numbers on the great plains of the West. Because of the scarcity of trees they have doubtless lost their tree-climbing propensities, and they prefer to dig deep tunnels underground, in which they fix up very cozy quarters. **1965–70** *DARE* (Qu. P27, . . *Kinds of squirrels*) 107 Infs, **chiefly West,** Ground squirrel; **CA**130, Golden-mantle ground squirrel, red ground squirrel; **CA**12, Desert ground squirrel; **CO**12, Gray ground squirrel; (Qu. P29, *Do you have 'gophers' around here? If yes, what other name do they have, or what other animal are they most like?*) 56 Infs, **chiefly West, Upper MW,** Ground squirrel; **MT**4, Columbia ground squirrel; (Qu. P32, . . *Other . . wild animals*) Inf **CA**114, Ground squirrel. [*DARE* Ed: Some of these Infs may refer instead to **a** above.] **1966–67** *DARE* Tape **IL**15, My younger brother and I used to have a lot of fun catching ground squirrels; **MI**2, We have what we call a ground squirrel that didn't used to be here. **1970** *Western Folkl.* 29.169, The two most familiar terms [for *Spermophilus* spp] in the upper Midwest are *gopher* and *ground squirrel;* the former is used by 50 percent and the latter by 44 percent of the informants. **1973** Gawthrop *Dial. Calumet* 76 **MI,** *Small squirrel-like animal that runs along the ground:* chipmunk 100 [infs], ground squirrel 29. **1980** Whitaker *Audubon Field Guide Mammals* 371, Unlike chipmunks, most ground squirrels *(Spermophilus, Ammospermophilus)* have no stripes at all, but when they do, none are on the head. All are burrowers, nearly all hibernate, and many are colonial.

c =prairie dog. Cf **prairie squirrel**

1965 *DARE* (Qu. P31) Inf **OK**11, Prairie dog—ground squirrel.

ground squirrel v phr, hence vbl n *ground squirreling,* ppl adj phr *ground-squirreled up* Cf **groundhog v 1**

To hide away, conceal.

1939 *Hall Coll.* **eTN, wNC,** *Ground-squirrel*—To hide, to keep a secret from a buddy, to pocket money in a poker game. . . "Rattin' on the other man, keepin' a secret from your buddy, hiding something that you don't want somebody else to know about." . . "Ground-squirrelin' on a buddy—that means slippin' money out of a pot you win and hidin' it; that is, taking money out of the game." **1967** *DARE* (Qu. Y47, *To hide something away for future use: "I know he's got it ______ somewhere."*) Inf **TN**13, Ground-squirreled up.

ground squirrel pea n [See quot 1830]

=twinleaf.

1830 Rafinesque *Med. Flora* 2.11, *Jeffersonia bartoni. Names.* Common Twinleaf. *Vulgar* . . Ground Squirrel Pea. [*Ibid* 12, The squirrels eat the seeds.] **1876** Hobbs *Bot. Hdbk.* 49, Ground squirrel pea, Twin leaf root, Jeffersonia diphylla. **1900** Lyons *Plant Names* 207, *J[effersonia] diphylla. . .* Ontario to Virginia and west to Wisconsin. . . Ground-squirrel Pea. **1930** Sievers *Amer. Med. Plants* 58, *Twinleaf. . . Other common names* . . ground-squirrel pea. **1971** Krochmal *Appalachia Med. Plants* 146, Ground squirrel pea. . . The rhizomes and roots have been used to treat chronic rheumatism, dropsy, spasms, and as a gargle.

ground swallow n

=bank swallow 1.

a1782 (1788) Jefferson *Notes VA* 77, Ground swallow. Hirundo riparia. **1956** MA Audubon Soc. *Bulletin* 40.84 **VT,** *Bank Swallow. . .* Ground Swallow. **1966** *DARE* (Qu. Q20, . . *Kinds of swallows*) Inf **ME**20, Ground swallow.

ground swamp robin n **esp NEng** Cf **swamp robin**

=hermit thrush 1.

1883 Nuttall Ornith. Club *Bulletin* 8.73 **ME,** *Turdus "pallasi". . .* Nearly all the names of this shy and solitary bird refer to its habit of haunting for the most part the undergrowth of secluded and damp woods. . . *Ground Swamp Robin.* **1898** (1900) Davie *Nests N. Amer. Birds* 502, The Hermit Thrush or "Ground Swamp Robin," . . is common in the northern portions of New England in summer, and in Maine, where it is abundant, it begins to breed during the last week of May. **1956** MA Audubon Soc. *Bulletin* 40.128, *Hermit Thrush. . .* Ground Swamp Robin.

ground swat v phr, hence n *ground swatter* Cf **ground sleuth**

See quot 1971.

1968 *DARE* FW Addit, In Pennsylvania, one who ground sleuths is a ground swatter. **1971** *DARE* File **cwWI,** *Ground swat:* To shoot a bird on the ground. **1989** *Ibid* **ceNY, NEng** (as of 1970s), He wasn't a real partridge hunter, he was always ground swatting birds.

ground sweet n

=arbutus.

1898 *Jrl. Amer. Folkl.* 11.273 **Philadelphia PA,** *Epigaea repens* . . ground sweet.

groundswine See **groundhog n 1**

ground tea n

A **wintergreen** (here: *Gaultheria procumbens*).

1959 Carleton *Index Herb. Plants* 57, *Ground-tea:* Gaultheria procumbens.

ground thrush n

=brown thrasher.

1917 (1923) *Birds Amer.* 3.179, *Brown Thrasher—Toxostoma rufum. . .* Ground Thrush. **1967** *DARE* (Qu. Q14) Inf **VA**7, Ground thrush.

ground tomato n

A **ground cherry** (here: *Physalis neomexicana*).

1947 Curtin *Healing Herbs* 188, *Ground Tomato—Physalis neomexicana. . .* This plant is a common inhabitant of desert washes, mesas and stony hillsides throughout New Mexico.

ground vine n

=twinflower.

1830 Rafinesque *Med. Flora* 2.239, *Linneusia borealis. . . Ground vine.* Bitterish subastringent, diuretic. **1900** Lyons *Plant Names* 227, *L[innaea] borealis. . .* Ground-vine. **1906** Rydberg *Flora CO* 323, *Lin-*

naea. . . Ground-vine. **1940** Clute *Amer. Plant Names* 54, *L[innaea] borealis var Americana. . .* Ground-vine.

ground warbler n

A warbler which frequents the ground, esp the **yellowthroat** or the **mourning warbler.**

1839 Audubon *Synopsis Birds* 63, *Trichas. . . Ground-Warbler. Ibid* 64, Trichas Macgillivrayi. . . Macgillivray's Ground-Warbler. . . Trichas Philadelphia. . . Mourning Ground-Warbler. *Ibid* 65, Trichas Marilandica. . . Maryland Ground-Warbler. [*DARE* Ed: Birds given by Audubon as members of the genus *Trichas* are now included in the genera *Oporornis* and *Geothlypis.*] **1844** Giraud *Birds Long Is.* 64, *Trichas marylandica. . . Maryland Ground Warbler. . .* It inhabits low, swampy grounds, passing its time among the small bushes and briars. . . It . . builds its nest on the ground among the briars. *Ibid* 65, *Trichas philadelphia. . .* Mourning Ground Warbler. **1868** *Amer. Naturalist* 2.176, The Maryland Yellow-throat . . belongs to the Ground Warblers, so named because they show a marked preference for the ground, seldom ascending to the tops of the trees. **1895** Minot *Land-Birds New Engl.* 84, *Maryland "Yellow-throat." Black-masked Ground Warbler.* A common summer resident throughout New England. . . The nest is usually placed on the ground. **1917** (1923) *Birds Amer.* 3.157, *Oporornis philadelphia. . .* Black-throated Ground Warbler; . . Mourning Ground Warbler. *Ibid* 159, *Geothlypis trichas trichas. . .* Black-masked Ground Warbler; Ground Warbler. *Ibid* 161, The Yellow-throat . . frequently alights on the ground, where he also places his deep cup-shaped nest, and hence his somewhat misleading popular name of "Ground Warbler," which would be fairly accurate if it were applied to the Oven-bird or the Water-Thrushes. **1946** Hausman *Eastern Birds* 535, *Mourning Warbler. . . Other Names . .* Black-throated Ground Warbler, Mourning Ground Warbler. **1955** Forbush-May *Birds* 451, *Maryland Yellow-throat. . . Other names:* Yellow-throat; Ground Warbler.

ground wasp See **ground hornet**

ground woodpecker n

=**flicker** n² **1.**

1955 *Oriole* 20.1.9 **GA,** *Yellow-shafted Flicker. . . Ground Woodpecker* (seen on the ground more than are other woodpeckers).

groundworm n

1 =**earthworm.** [*OED* 1599 →]

1946 *PADS* 5.24 **VA,** *Ground worm. . .* An earthworm; on the Eastern Shore and on the shore of the Middle Neck. **1949** Kurath *Word Geog.* 46, West of . . [Chesapeake] Bay we find certain local expressions . . *ground worm* . . for the earthworm on the Middle Neck and the Eastern Shore. *Ibid* 74, *Ground worm* is found on the Eastern Shore of Virginia and the points of land between the Rappahannock and the James. **1965-70** *DARE* (Qu. P5, . . *The common worm used as bait*) 9 Infs, **scattered,** Groundworm; (Qu. P6, *Other kinds of worms also used for bait*) 9 Infs, **scattered,** Groundworm. [*DARE* Ed: Some of these Infs may refer instead to **2** below]. **1966** Dakin *Dial. Vocab. Ohio R. Valley* 2.394 **KY,** *Ground worm* . . [is] attested once. **1967** Faries *Word Geog. MO* 151, *South and North Midland Expressions* . . ground worm 1 [occurrence]. **1970** Greatman *Dial. Atlas MD* 301, *Southern* [terms] . . Receding . . ground worm. **1972** *PADS* 58.22 **cwAL,** *Earthworm. . . groundworm* (1) [inf]. **1977-78** Foster *Lexical Variation* 66 **cNJ,** *Fish worm . . ground worm* . . and *huckleberry worm* . . were also attested, mostly among older informants.

2 A cutworm (family Noctuidae) or similar larva injurious to plants.

1708 in 1886 NC *Colonial Rec.* 1.682 **MD,** The Planters having suffered . . [from] lack of Plants, the Fly, the ground worme the house wormes. **1772** in 1919 *MD Hist. Mag.* 14.273 **MD,** Our crop . . will all stand if the ground worme will let it. **1844** (1969) Emerson *Essays 2d Ser.* 277 **eMA,** A society for the protection of ground-worms, slugs, and mosquitos was to be incorporated without delay. **1966-69** *DARE* (Qu. R27, . . *Caterpillars or similar worms*) Infs **CA**171, **UT**6, Groundworm. **1969** Herndon *Wm. Tatham Tobacco* 475 **VA** (as of c1800), [Glossary:] Ground-Worm. More commonly known today as the "cutworm."

grounet See **groundnut**

group n¹ [Prob for *roup*]

1966-68 *DARE* (Qu. K78, *What diseases do chickens commonly get around here?*) Infs **CA**31, 63, **GA**3, Group.

group n² Similarly, adj *groupy* [Pronc-sp for *croup*] Cf Pronc Intro 3.I.15

1968-70 *DARE* (Qu. BB12, *The kind of cough that comes with bronchitis*) Inf **LA**37, Group; **CA**188, Groupy.

grouper n

1 Any of various fish of the family Serranidae, as:

a also *grooper, groper, gruper:* A fish of the genus *Epinephelus.* [Port *garoupa,* Span *garopa*] For other names of var spp see **black grouper 2, gray grouper, hamlet, hapuu 2, jewfish, red grouper, red hind, rockfish, rock hind, spotted grouper, warsaw, white grouper, yellow-finned grouper**

[**1687** Blome *Present State* 250 **West Indies,** Here is a great plenty of excellent Fish; as, the *Groper.*] **1775** (1962) Romans *Nat. Hist. FL* app 7, At this place there is vast abundance and variety of fish, . . particularly *groopers* are in great plenty. **1842** DeKay *Zool. NY* 4.23, This beautiful fish [=*Epinephelus morio*], which is not unusual in our markets in June and July, where it sells from six to twelve cents per pound, is called by the fishermen, *Groper. . .* It is a southern species, and is brought hither from the reefs of Florida. **1897** *Outing* 29.331/2 **FL,** The grouper, or "gruper," or "garoupha," . . is capable of entering with great spirit into a chowder. **1911** U.S. Bur. Census *Fisheries 1908* 310, Grouper *(Epinephelus).*—A food fish found off the south Atlantic coast and in the Gulf. The different species . . vary in size greatly. . . The name "grouper" is also applied to the rock cod of southern California and to the tripletail of the St. Johns River [Florida]. **1946** LaMonte *N. Amer. Game Fishes* 45, *Spotted Jewfish—Promicrops itaiara. . .* Grouper. *Ibid* 53, *Nassau Grouper—Epinephelus striatus. . .* Grouper. *Ibid* 56, *Red Hind—Epinephelus guttatus. . .* Grouper. **1966-70** *DARE* (Qu. P2, . . *Saltwater fish . . good to eat*) Infs **FL**4, 7, 13, 39, **SC**21, 63, **TN**65, Grouper(s); (Qu. P14) Infs **FL**17, 39, **SC**63, Grouper(s). [*DARE* Ed: Some of these Infs may refer instead to **1b** below.] **1966** *DARE* Tape **FL**14, You make a stew, but you don't put your fish in until your potatoes and all is cooked for maybe a couple hours and then you put your fish in and let your fish cook and then you got a grouper chowder. **1975** Evanoff *Catch More Fish* 106, The groupers are another large family, such as the red, black, yellow, and Nassau groupers. They also run big in size, with some members such as the Warsaw grouper and Jewfish.

b A fish of the genus *Mycteroperca.* Also called **rockfish.** For other names of var spp see **black grouper 1, black rockfish 2, gag, gray grouper, jewfish, red grouper, scamp, spotted grouper, tiger grouper, warsaw, yellow-finned grouper**

1882 U.S. Natl. Museum *Proc.* 5.273, *Trisotropis stomias. . . Black grouper. . . Trisotropis falcatus. . . Scamp. . .* is one of the best food-fishes, more delicate than the other "Groupers." **1933** John G. Shedd Aquarium *Guide* 100, The flesh of this handsome grouper [=*Mycteroperca venenosa*] is sometimes poisonous. . . The Black Grouper [=*M. bonaci*] attains a weight of fifty pounds. **1966** *Fishing World* 13.6.47, Suddenly the sea was boiling alive with . . even the much-sought-after "scamp" or broom-tailed grouper, favorite food fish of the Alabama reefs. **1973** Knight *Cook's Fish Guide* 382/1, Grouper . . Broadtail [=*Mycteroperca xenarcha*].

2 A **rockfish** of the genus *Sebastodes,* esp *S. paucispinis.*

1884 Goode *Fisheries U.S.* 1.262, These fishes are universally known by the names of Rockfish and Rockcod. . . In the southern part of California, the name "Garrupa" or "Grouper" is in common use, especially for the olivaceous species. **1928** Pan-Pacific Research Inst. *Jrl.* 3.13, The rock-cods. . . *Sebastodes paucispinis. . .* Bocaccio; grouper. **1953** Roedel *Common Fishes CA* 121, *Bocaccio—Sebastodes paucispinis. . .* Unauthorized Names: Grouper, salmon grouper. **1968** *DARE* (Qu. P2, . . *Saltwater fish*) Inf **CA**65, Grouper.

3 =**tripletail.**

1884 Goode *Fisheries U.S.* 1.444 **FL,** The "Triple-tail" of the New York market, *Lobotes surinamensis,* [is] known . . to the fishermen of St. John's River as the "Grouper." **1911** [see **1a** above].

groupy See **group**

grouseberry n

1 A **wintergreen** (here: *Gaultheria procumbens*).

1804 A. F. M. Willich *Domestic Encycl.* III.150/2 *(OEDS),* It is called Canadian Gaultheria, or Mountain Tea, Grouse-berry, Deer-berry, Ground-ivy. **1828** Rafinesque *Med. Flora* 1.202, *Gautiera* [sic] *Repens. . . Vulgar Names. . .* Grouse-berry. **1900** Lyons *Plant Names* 169, *Gaultheria procumbens. . .* Grouse-berry. **1911** Henkel *Amer.*

Med. Leaves 19. **1930** Sievers *Amer. Med. Plants* 63. **1971** Krochmal *Appalachia Med. Plants* 128.

2 A **huckleberry 1** (here: *Gaylussacia dumosa*).

1899 *Plant World* 2.199, *Grouseberry* for *Gaylussacia dumosa.*

3 also *grouse whortleberry:* A **blueberry 1:** usu *Vaccinium scoparium,* rarely *V. caespitosum.* **chiefly NW**

1932 Rydberg *Flora Prairies* 618, *V[accinium] scoparium. . . Grouseberry.* Mountain sides: B.C.—Calif.—Colo.—S.D.—Al[ber]ta. **1948** Baumann *Old Man Crow's Boy* 221 **ID,** The canyon itself was heavily grown with raspberries and grouse berries. **1952** Davis *Flora ID* 533, *V[accinium] scoparium. . . Grouse-berry.* Shrub 1–3 dm tall, . . fruit 2–4 mm in diameter, bright red. **1953** Nelson *Plants Rocky Mt. Park* 118, *Red grouseberry* or *grouse whortleberry, Vaccinium scoparium* . . green, angled stem, smaller leaves, and small red berries. . . *Dwarf grouseberry* or *dwarf blueberry, Vaccinium caespitosum* . . may be distinguished from the above by its round . . branches and its more spreading habit. The berries are blue. **1973** Stephens *Woody Plants* 432, *Vaccinium scoparium. . .* Grouseberry. . . Small birds are seen frequenting the shrubs during fruiting time. **1973** Hitchcock-Cronquist *Flora Pacific NW* 349, Grouseberry. . . *V[accinium] scoparium.*

4 =**highbush cranberry.**

1976 Bailey-Bailey *Hortus Third* 1155, *Viburnum . . trilobum. . .* Grouseberry.

‡groused ppl adj [Prob from *grouse* to complain]

1969 *DARE* (Qu. GG34b, *To feel depressed or in a gloomy mood: "She's feeling ____ today."*) Inf **TX**74, Groused.

grouse flower n

A **kittentails** (here: *Synthyris reniformis*).

1934 Haskin *Wild Flowers Pacific Coast* 323, *Grouse Flower. Synthyris rotundifolia. . .* I prefer . . [the] name . . of grouse-flower. The name is particularly fitting, for just when the "blue," or sooty grouse are filling the woods with their "hooting," these flowers are at their best. . . The first precocious grouse-flowers blossom upon sunny banks, and sheltered southern slopes.

grouse hawk n Cf **partridge hawk**

Prob =**goshawk 1.**

1969 *DARE* (Qu. Q4, . . *Kinds of hawks*) Inf **MA**15, Grouse hawk.

grouse locust n [See quot 1949]

A pygmy **grasshopper 1** of the family Tetrigidae.

1852 Harris *Treatise on Insects* 163, The habits of the grouse-locusts are . . the same as those of other locusts. **1905** Kellogg *Amer. Insects* 148, As all the grouse-locusts are dark-colored and . . choose for habitat the dark ground along streams and ponds, or swampy meadows, they are infrequently seen except by persistent students. **1926** Essig *Insects N. Amer.* 70, Grouse or Pygmy Locusts . . are the smallest of the locusts. **1949** Swain *Insect Guide* 12, These insects are often called "grouse locusts," and when at rest they do resemble sitting birds in body outline. **1980** Milne-Milne *Audubon Field Guide Insects* 416, Pygmy grasshoppers . . are also called grouse locusts.

grouse whortleberry See **grouseberry 3**

grouty adj **esp NEng**

Surly, sullen, ill-tempered; hence n pl *the grouties* bad feelings.

1836 in 1894 Lowell *Letters* 1.11 **MA,** Been quite "grouty" all the vacation, "black as Erebus." **1859** (1968) Bartlett *Americanisms* 182, Cross, ill-natured. Northern. **1871** (1882) Stowe *Fireside Stories* 128 **MA,** Old Black Hoss was awfully grouty about Miry's refusin' Tom Beacon. **1893** *KS Univ. Qrly.* 1.139 **KS,** *Grouty:* pouty, cross. **1895** *DN* 1.389 **neMA,** *Grouty:* surly or sulky. **1899** (1912) Green *VA Folk-Speech* 208, *Grouty. . .* Sulky; surly; cross. **1909** *DN* 3.412 **nME,** *Grouty. . .* Surly, sullen. "He's as grouty as a bear." **1941** *LANE* Map 472 *(Angry)* 1 inf, **cwVT,** *Grouty,* 'a degree less than mad.' **1959** *VT Hist.* new ser 27.139 **c,ceVT,** *Grouty. . .* Irritable. **1969** *DARE* (Qu. BB5, *A general feeling of discomfort or illness*) Inf **GA**72, We got the grouties.

grove meeting See **camp meeting**

grow v

Std senses, var forms.

1 past: usu *grew;* also **scattered, but chiefly Sth, S Midl** (See Map) *esp freq among speakers with little formal educ, growed;* occas *grown* (pronc-sp *growen*); rarely *grow.* Cf **-ed 2**

1851 Hooper *Widow Rugby's Husband* 45 **AL,** When I growed up, I thort it would be the devil to find a woman that'd be willing to take me, ugly as I was. **1867** Lowell *Biglow* xxvi **'Upcountry' MA,** Of weak preterites the Yankee retains *growed, blowed.* **1884** *Anglia* 7.252 [Black], [Grow:] *Past.* growed . . grown. **1893** *DN* 1.277 **wCT,** *Grow*—growed. **1893** Shands *MS Speech* 34, *Growed. . .* Negro for *grew.* **1899** Chesnutt *Conjure Woman* 13 **csNC** [Black], De vimes [=vines] growed. **1903** *DN* 2.293 **Cape Cod MA** (as of a1857), There is a tendency to make strong verbs weak. Thus the following . . *growed.* **1930** *VA Qrly. Rev.* 6.248 **S Midl,** Questioned whether he grew the corn, . . a sequestered old-timer replied, "O no, the cawn growed itself. I planted it." **1953** Atwood *Survey of Verb Forms* 15, The preterite *growed* . . occurs in very scattered fashion in s. and w. N. Eng., while in the northeast it shows considerable frequency. **1965–70** *DARE* (Qu. OO23a, . . *"During the summer he ____ [two inches]."*) 866 Infs, **widespread,** Grew; 129 Infs, **scattered, but chiefly Sth, SMidl,** Growed [Of all Infs responding to the question, 27% were gs educ or less; of those giving this response, 58% were gs educ or less.]; **AR**51, **NY**75, **NC**49, Outgrowed his clothes (*or* them); **FL**36, **MO**17, **NC**35, **NY**20, Grown; **NC**47, **SC**10, Grow; **MO**34, Growen; **SC**26, Done grow; (Qu. OO35a, . . *"The plants really ____."*) 180 Infs, **widespread,** Grew; 26 Infs, **esp Sth, S Midl,** Growed; **KY**62, **ME**19, Growed good; **IN**35, Growed fast; **TN**4, Growed fine; **GA**38, Growed off good; **OK**18, Growed well; (Qu. II21) Inf **RI**15, He just growed; (Qu. OO37a, . . *"The first time my wool socks were washed they ____."*) Inf **NY**68, Growed darn small. **1965–70** *DARE* Tape **FL**43, It growed into a . . bigger business at the time; **GA**25, After I growed older and I got large enough to go to work; **SC**3, The hair growed . . that long; **VA**38, Then . . the plant growed.

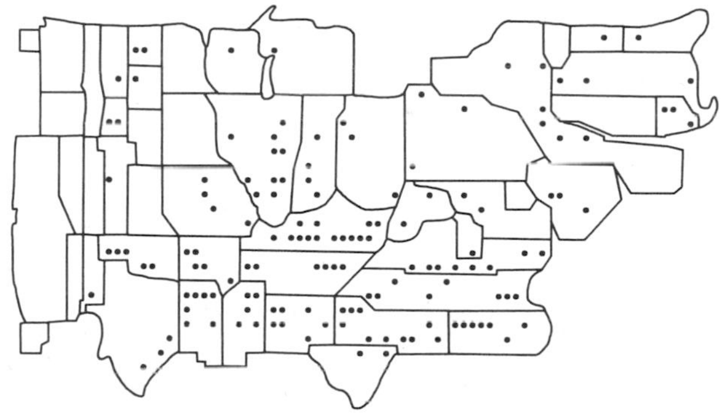

•growed + varr (at grow 1) (Qq. OO23a, OO35a, II21, OO37a)

2 past pple, ppl adj: usu *grown;* also **scattered, but chiefly Sth, S Midl** (See Map on p. 830) *esp freq among speakers with little formal educ, growed;* **scattered, but chiefly Nth, N Midl** (See Map on p. 830), *grew;* rarely *grow, growned.*

1871 Eggleston *Hoosier Schoolmaster* 83 **sIN,** I think that tree must a-growed in the night. **1899** (1967) Chesnutt *Wife of Youth* 12, De w'ite folks 'prenticed him ter my marster . . 'tel he wuz growed up. **1934** *WV Review* Dec 79, *Growed* for *grew* and *grown.* **1938** Rawlings *Yearling* 301 **nFL,** You've done a growed man's work today. **1962** *Mt. Life* 38.1.17 **sAppalachians,** Past participles used as direct adjectives are often given *-en* or *-ed* endings: . . *a growned man.* **1965–70** *DARE* (Qu. OO23b, . . *"You wouldn't think a child could have ____ [so fast]."*) 834 Infs, **widespread,** Grown; 146 Infs, **scattered, but chiefly Sth, S Midl,** Growed [Of all Infs responding to the question, 28% were gs educ or less; of those giving this response, 61% were gs educ or less.]; 40 Infs, **chiefly Nth, N Midl,** Grew [37 of 40 Infs hs educ or less]; **SC**10, 26, **SD**1, **TN**47, Grow [3 of 4 Infs Black]; (Qu. OO35b, . . *"Nothing has ever ____ there."*) 26 Infs, **esp Midl, Sth,** Growed; 9 Infs, **scattered,** Grew; **GA**17, 19, 28, **TN**13, Growed good; **KY**28, Growed well; **MN**12, Grew very good; **OR**3, Grew on it; (Qu. K55, *A pig that doesn't grow well and is not worth keeping*) Inf **NY**27, Growed all in front; (Qu. Z17, *To take care of or bring up a child: "All her children were ____ [on the farm]."*) Inf **MO**19, Growed up. **1966–70** *DARE* Tape **AL**24, He lived around here until he get growned; **CA**120, There was an old mine there so it was pretty well grew up with brush; **GA**35, He's growed a foot an' a half, maybe two foot; **PA**17, The pine trees had growed up; **VA**43, Like it ought to be growed.

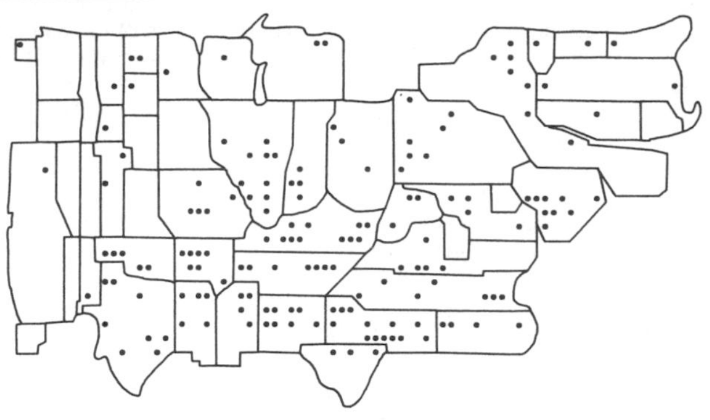

•growed + varr (at grow 2) (Qq. 0023b, 0035b, K55, Z17)

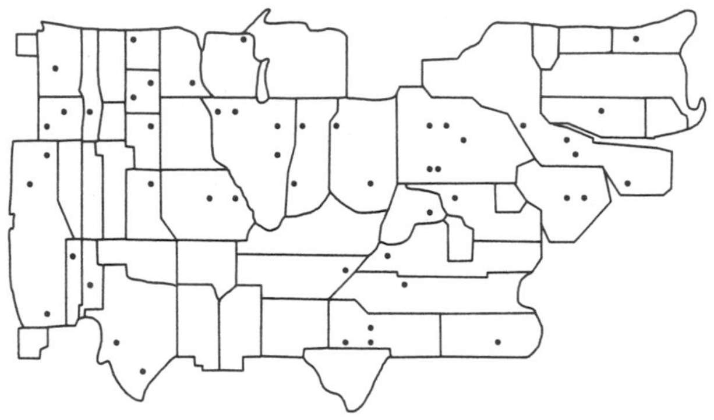

•grew + varr (at grow 2) (Qq. 0023b, 0035b)

‡growing cheese n
1967 Schilla *Prairies* 102 **ND** (as of c1880–1900), The mother made cottage cheese and some other types that seem to be nameless. One was called a "growing cheese." If some were removed from a dish, the hole would be filled up in a short time.

growing day See **growing weather**

growing hand n Cf **green hand 2**
An exceptional ability to make plants thrive; a "green thumb."
1930 Stoney–Shelby *Black Genesis* 45 **seSC,** She got a growin' han'. What she put dat han' to will tek root, an' grow good. **1940** Writers' Program *Guide MD* 8, A 'growing hand' is the gift of a person who succeeds in making sickly plants thrive. **1982** Heat Moon *Blue Highways* 390 **csMD,** The front yards of our houses are made from oyster shells. Throw down a bucket of shells, a bucket of dirt, and presto-chango, a yard! Don't need a growing hand here.

growing moon n Also *growing (side) of the moon* **esp Sth, S Midl** Cf **dark of the moon**
The waxing moon.
c1938 in 1970 Hyatt *Hoodoo* 1.357 **swTN** [Black], A growin' moon is fo' prospects an' when de moon's 'bout on de waste away, dat's de time den dat yo' fo' not a good success, yo' understan'. **1967** *DARE* (Qu. L26, *Sayings about corn and other important crops around here—when to put it in, how fast it should grow, etc.;* total Infs questioned, 75) Inf **GA**7, Plant cane on a growing moon. **1970** *NC Folkl.* 18.66, If stakes are placed in the ground on the growing of the moon, they will rise. **1975** Dwyer *Thangs* 26 **Sth, S Midl,** Do not nail shingles, or boards on the growing side of the moon or the ends will darken and curl and go crooked. **1982** Brooks *Quicksand* 197 **swUT** (as of c1916), She did talk to me . . of some of our folkways . . practices in planting the plants that mature underground during the dark of the moon, those whose fruit is above ground in the light of the moon, or during the growing moon. **1986** Pederson *LAGS Concordance,* 1 inf, **eFL,** Growing moon—sign of the moon; 1 inf, **seAL,** Growing of the moon—not a good time to plant; 1 inf, **eTN,** Growing of the moon—the time to lay rail fence.

growing shower n Cf **growing weather**
1968 *DARE* (Qu. B23, . . *A light rain that doesn't last*) Inf **VA**1, Growing shower—just makes gardens grow.

growing side of the moon See **growing moon**

growing weather n Also *growing day* Cf **growing shower**
See quot 1899.
1899 (1912) Green *VA Folk-Speech* 208, *Growing-weather*. . . Weather with the proper warmth and moisture to make crops grow; alternate rain and sunshine. **1903** *DN* 2.315 **seMO,** *Growing weather*. . . Weather suitable for growth of vegetation. **1966–69** *DARE* (Qu. B4, *A day when the air is very still, moist, and warm—it's ______*) Inf **IN**54, Growing weather; **MS**48, Growing day—farm term. **1976** Ryland *Richmond Co. VA* 371, *Growing weather*—the right combination of rain and sun for crops.

growler n[1]
1 =largemouth bass.
1829 Cuvier–Valenciennes *Histoire Naturelle* 3.41, Le Growler salmoïde. *(Grystes salmoides. . .)* Tel est le *growler* de New-York, dont nous devons la connaissance à M. Milbert, mais qui n'a point été décrit par M. Mitchill. Ce nom de *growler,* qui signifie *grogneur,* vient peut-être de quelque bruit qu'il fait entendre comme les sciènes ou les trigles, mais nous n'avons à cet égard aucun renseignement positif. *Grystes* en est l'équivalent grec. [=The salmon-like Growler. *(Grystes salmoides. . .)* This is the *growler* of New York, the knowledge of which we owe to Mr. Milbert, but which has not at all been described by Mr. Mitchill. The name of *growler,* which means *grogneur,* comes perhaps from some noise which it makes like the drums or the grunts, but we have no positive information in regard to this. *Grystes* is the Greek equivalent.] **1842** DeKay *Zool. NY* 4.26, *The Growler. Grystes salmoides*. . . In Carolina, it . . is considered an excellent food, and passes under the name of *Trout.* **1856** *Porter's Spirit of Times* 25 Oct 129/2, There was not, never had been, and never could be a salmon within a thousand miles of the Kentucky River, and . . the fish so called by the people of that State is either the pike-perch . . or another analogous fish, sometimes called the growler, the *Gristes Salmoeides* of authors. **1880** *Lib. Universal Knowledge* 2.281, The growler, *grystes salmonus,* is the white salmon of the southern states. **1933** LA Dept. of Conserv. *Fishes* 313, None of our other fresh water fishes has been given so many popular names. . . They are . . as follows: Large-mouthed Black Bass; . . Growler [etc]. **1935** Caine *Game Fish* 3, Large-Mouthed Black Bass—*Micropterus salmoides*. . . Growler.
2 A fish of the family Sciaenidae, such as the **freshwater drum** or a **croaker** n[1] **1a(1)** (here: *Micropogon undulatus*). [See quot 1835] Cf **grumbler 2, grunter 2**
1835 Audubon *Ornith. Biog.* 3.199, The usual length of this fish, which on the Ohio is called the White Perch, and in the State of New York the Growler, is from fifteen to twenty inches. One of the most remarkable habits of this fish is that from which it has received the name of Growler. When poised in the water, close to the bottom of a boat, it emits a rough croaking noise, somewhat resembling a groan. **1976** Warner *Beautiful Swimmers* 129 **eMD,** If there are no roe shad, they may choose . . "growlers," as croakers are called. **1984** *DARE* File **Chesapeake Bay** [Watermen's vocab], Croaker, grumbler, growler, hardhead, pinhead, kingbilly, roundhead.
3 =grunt n 1. [See quot]
1889 *Century Dict.* 2643, *Grunt*. . . A fish of the family *Hæmulonidæ* . . so called from the noise they make when hauled out of the water. Also called *pig-fish* and *growler* for the same reason.

growler n[2] [Etym unknown]
1 A pail or similar container in which beer is fetched from a tavern—usu in phr *rush the growler* and varr, to fetch, buy, or drink beer. **chiefly Nth, N Midl** *old-fash*
1888 *NY Herald* (NY) 29 July 15/1 **NYC,** One evil of which the inspectors took particular notice was that of the employment . . of boys and girls . . to fetch beer for them, or in other words "to rush the growler." **1890** Palmer *Stories* 70 **swOH,** President Thorner . . was one of the first to help put down his share of the growler's contents. **1890** *DN* 1.61 **OH,** *To rush or work the growler:* to buy beer in a growler. **1905** *N.Y. Ev. Post* 5 Oct. 9 *(DAE),* Lynch, going to the roof, found the men 'rushing the growler' very noisily. **1920** Lewis *Main Street* 391, He made for her a picture of his work in a large tailor shop in Minneapolis: the steam and heat, . . men who "rushed growlers of beer." **1943** Writers' Program MT *Copper Camp* 9 **swMT,** One crew from the Moonlight Mine daily climbed two hundred and fifty feet . . to have a fresh "growler" for the lunch period. **1950** *WELS* (*Common containers for liquor)* 1 Inf, **seWI,** Growler—a beer pail. **1954** Armstrong *Satchmo* 88 **LA** (as of c1920), She would have killed her if it had not been for Black Benny and some of the boys who gambled and rushed the growler

around Liberty and Perdido. **1968** *DARE* FW Addit **PA**88, *Rush the growler:* to go to the saloon to get a bucket of beer. Old. **1968** *DARE* File **RI**, *Rushing the growler:* a growler is a bucket with a handle. Women used to go out to the saloon to get beer in a pail to take home. **1982** *NY Times* (NY) 23 Feb sec B 2/2 **neNJ** (as of c1930), Mayor Dunn, whose father worked at the plant for 41 years, has childhood memories of earning nickels by "rushing the growler," a job as common for a boy in Elizabeth as delivering newspapers was in other towns. He said German workers lowered covered beer bails, called "growlers," out the windows of the factory on ropes to the boys, who would rush them over to Grampp's tavern to be filled.

2 By ext: see quots.

1975 *AmSp* 50.60 **AR** (as of c1970), *Growler* . . Toilet. **1989** *DARE* File **RI** (as of c1900), *Growler*—the pot in a commode, a slop pail.

grow off v phr **chiefly Sth, S Midl**

To grow; to grow up.

1924 Raine *Land of Saddle-Bags* 99 **sAppalachians,** If you give your pigs a good start they'll *grow off.* **1939** *Sat. Eve. Post* 25 Nov 58/2 **nFL,** They [=roosters] growed off big and fine. **1939** *AmSp* 14.90 **eTN,** *Grow off.* An expression meaning to grow up. 'Your family has growed off fast.' **1942** (1971) Campbell *Cloud-Walking* 57 **seKY,** He . . studied how maybe he could trade his pig for cash money, when it growed off big. **c1960** *Wilson Coll.* **csKY,** *Grow off:* To grow well or rapidly. **1967–68** *DARE* Tape **GA**69, Our Georgia nurseries found that the summers were hot and often dry and that our seedlings did not grow off as well; **TX**8, [FW:] Do they [=cattle] make pretty good weight? [Inf:] Yes, they grow off real fast for the first six months. **1968** *DARE* (Qu. OO35a, *Talking about vegetables thriving: "Last year we fertilized the garden, and the plants really ______.")* Inf **GA**38, Growed off good.

grow out v phr Also *grow up*

To raise, bring up.

1966–67 *DARE* Tape **AR**55, [After I married,] I grew up three nice boys, and they got big enough to he'p in the store; **NC**6, Now when we used to grow out our own little ones, when we'd buy them day old and grow 'em into pullets, we . . had a little bit of trouble with cannibalism then, but we don't have any trouble with it now.

grow to grass See **grass n 5a**

grow up See **grow out**

grub n

1 A root or stump, usu one remaining in the ground after clearing; underbrush; scrub.

1788 (1925) Washington *Diaries* 3.336 **VA,** The Women . . were employed in taking up the Persimon grubs in No. 7. **a1816** (1848) Hawkins *Sketch* 50, On the hill sides and their tops, hickory grub and grape vines. **1872** (1876) Knight *Amer. Mech. Dict.* 1027, *Grubber*. . . A machine or tool to pull *grubs;* that is, stumps and roots of bushes, saplings, and small trees. **1882** Hough *Elements of Forestry* 52 **MN, WI,** In *"grub-prairies,"* in the Northwestern States, the soil is full of the roots of trees and bushes . . that have been killed back to the roots by annual fires. **1899** Garland *Boy Life* 382 **nwIA** (as of c1870s), The stove was a big square box into which some public-spirited soul rolled huge red oak "grubs." **1905** *DN* 3.82 **nwAR,** *Grub*. . . Root, sprout. 'I've been getting grubs out of this field all day long.' Common. **1954** *Harder Coll.* **cwTN,** *Grub-land:* Land which has been cleared, but now needs sprouts and small bushes taken out. **1958** McCulloch *Woods Words* 74 **Pacific NW,** *Grub*. . . Hardwood sprout growth, as grub oak, grub maple, etc. **1968** *DARE* (Qu. L36, . . *When you dig out roots and underbrush to make a new field*) Inf **MN**16, Rake out the grub.

2 also *grub pin, ~ stake:* See quot 1956.

1844 in 1927 *PA Mag. Hist. & Biog.* 51.73 **swNY,** After examining it [=a lodged raft], found that by cutting the grub plank in two we might get it off. **1881** Burroughs *Pepacton* 35 **ePA, wNJ,** Some parts of the framework of the raft they call "grubs." **1933** Sheffer *True Tales* 96 **nwPA,** The first thing in rafting boards:—lay down three planks . . with three holes bored in each plank. . . Grubs are stood up through these holes. These grubs are about three feet long or longer and have a knot on one end. . . We put the plank over the grubs and then we were ready to draw it up and wedge it. **1945** *NY Folkl. Qrly.* 1.226 **wPA, cwNY,** If the grubs squeaked a great deal as the long raft went over rough water on riffles, that was a good sign. **1956** Sorden–Ebert *Logger's Words* 17 **Gt Lakes,** *Grub,* A pin usually made out of the root of an elm or an iron-wood tree. Used for fastening lumber in a crib when lumber was sent down the river to market. **1969** Sorden *Lumberjack Lingo* 50 **NEng, Gt Lakes,** *Grub pin*—A thirty-inch pin used for fastening in a crib lumber being sent down the river to market. . . *Grub stake*—A wooden stake on a lumber raft that, with one or two others, confines the load.

3 A type of **earmark;** see quot; hence v *grub* to mark in such a way.

1936 Adams *Cowboy Lingo* 132, The 'grub' was a cruel ear-mark made by cutting the entire ear off smoothly with the head. A man who 'grubbed' was looked upon with suspicion, as it was resorted to by rustlers to destroy original ear-marks. **1941** Dobie *Longhorns* 212 **TX,** The Blocker earmark was grub the left ear—the ear cut off almost to the root—and two under-bits out of the right ear.

grub ax n Also *grubbing ax* **esp Nth** See Map Cf **grubbing hoe 1, grub hoe**

A **mattock** or similar tool.

1643 in 1916 MA (Colony) Probate Court (Essex Co.) *Records* 1.30, I give vnto him my grug [sic] axe. **1731** in 1924 *MD Hist. Mag.* 19.289 **cMD,** To Mr Wm Hunt. . . 1 Dozn Grubing axes. **1872** (1876) Knight *Amer. Mech. Dict.* 1027/2, *Grubbing-axe.* An implement having a curved bit presented at right angles to the helve, like an adze; and another bit presented in the line of the helve, like an axe. A *mattock.* **1908** *DN* 3.317 **eAL, wGA,** *Grub-ax*. . . A worn out or dull ax used to grub stumps, etc. **1950** *WELS (Hand tools used for cutting underbrush)* 2 Infs, **WI,** Grub ax. **1965–70** *DARE* (Qu. L35) 17 Infs, **esp Nth,** Grub ax; **FL**12, **NC**52, **PA**230, **SC**9, Grubbing ax.

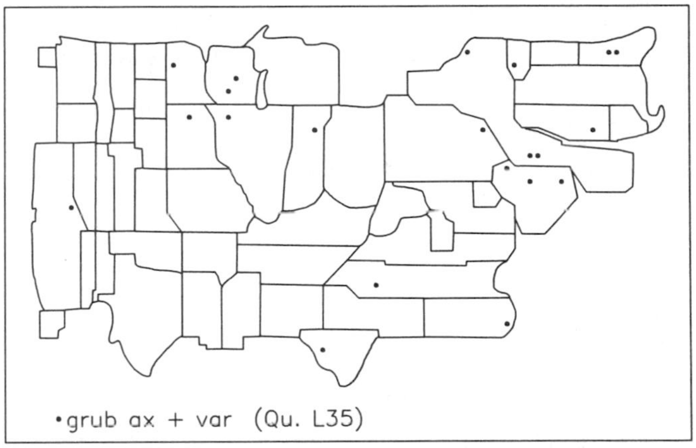

grubber n

A **bonefish 1** (here: *Albula vulpes*).

1887 Goode *Amer. Fishes* 410, *Albula vulpes* . . is usually called the "Lady-fish;" . . the "Bone-fish," or "Grubber." **1935** Caine *Game Fish* 50, *Bonefish*. . . *Synonyms*. . . Grubber. [*Ibid* 51, Bonefish feed on muddy flats in shallow water, on crustaceans and mollusks.] **1973** Knight *Cook's Fish Guide* 382, Grubber—Bonefish.

grubbing ax See **grub ax**

grubbing hoe n

1 A heavy hoe or **mattock. widespread exc Nth** See Map on p. 832 and Map Section

1727 in 1923 *MD Hist. Mag.* 18.226 **cMD,** 6 Grubbing hoes. **1815** in 1956 Eliason *Tarheel Talk* 275 **NC,** *Grublin* [sic] *hoe.* **1829** Flint *George Mason* 29 **MS,** The red-bird, springing away from the briar copse, which he began to disturb with his grubbing-hoe. **1849** in 1956 Eliason *Tarheel Talk* 311 **cnNC,** Groubing [sic] hoe. **1908** *DN* 3.317 **eAL, wGA,** *Grubbin(g)-hoe*. . . A mattock. **1954** *Harder Coll.* **cwTN,** *Grubbing-hoe:* A tool used for digging out stumps and for cutting underbrush; the tool has a pointed side for loosening the soil, and a cutting side for chopping roots. **1960** Criswell *Resp. to PADS 20* **Ozarks,** *Grubbing hoe:* A heavy hoe like a mattock except that it did not have the cutting projectile that the mattock has on the back side; used for grubbing out sprouts and for heavy garden work. **1965–70** *DARE* (Qu. L35, *Hand tools used for cutting underbrush and digging out roots*) 195 Infs, **widespread exc Nth,** Grubbing hoe; (Qu. L36, . . *When you dig out roots and underbrush to make a new field*) Inf **AR**40, Use dynamite and grubbing hoe; (Qu. L37, *A hand tool used for cutting weeds and grass*) Infs **DC**2, **MS**28, **OK**14, Grubbing hoe. **1983** *MJLF* 9.1.42 **ceKY,** *Grubbing hoe.*

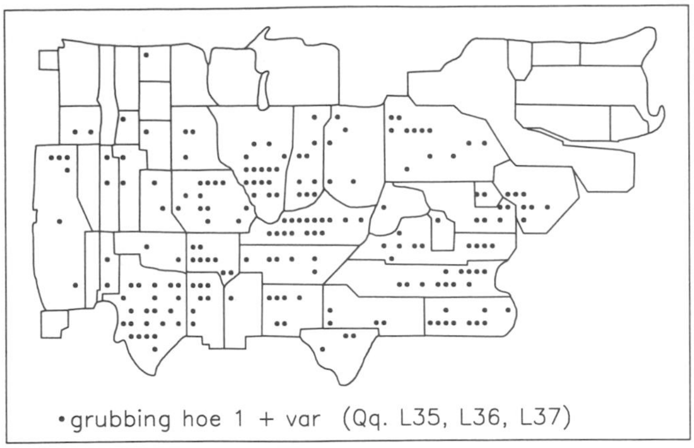

2 Fig: a buck tooth.

1912 Green *VA Folk-Speech* 208, *Grubbing-hoes. . .* The front teeth standing out from the jaws. **1966** *DARE* (Qu. X12, . . *Large front teeth that stick out of the mouth*) Infs **NC**24, 82, Grubbing hoes.

grubbing worm See **grubworm 1**

grubby n

1 also *grubley:* A **toadfish** (here: *Opsanus tau*). *obs*

1859 (1968) Bartlett *Americanisms* 182, *Grubby.* See *Toad-Fish. Ibid* 481, *Toad-fish. (Batrachus variegatus.)* This repulsive creature, and fisherman's pest, is called also . . "Grubley" on the coast of New England.

2 A **sculpin:** usu *Myoxocephalus aeneus,* but also *M. octodecemspinosus.* **Atlantic, esp N Atl**

1873 in 1878 Smithsonian Inst. *Misc. Coll.* 14.2.22, *Cottus octodecimspinosus* [sic]. . . Grubby. Nova Scotia to Cape Hatteras. **1882** U.S. Natl. Museum *Bulletin* 16.702, *C[ottus] æneus. . . Grubby. . .* Coast of Southern New England and New York; our smallest species; common in seaweeds near shore. **1887** Goode *Amer. Fishes* 301, On our Atlantic coast are found several species . . generally known by the name of "Sculpin," and also by such titles as "Grubby." **1892** *DN* 1.210 **neMA,** *Grubby:* the sculpin. Salem. **1911** U.S. Bur. Census *Fisheries 1908* 315, Several species of sculpin are found on the Atlantic and Pacific coasts. . . Those on the Atlantic are called "grubby" . . etc. **1933** John G. Shedd Aquarium *Guide* 130, *Acanthocottus æneus. . .* The Grubby is the common sculpin of New England and New York. **1960** Amer. Fisheries Soc. *List Fishes* 40, Grubby. *Myoxocephalus aeneus.*

gruber n Also *gruby* [*goober,* perh infl by *grub* v] Cf **goober** n[1] **1, grundniss**

=**peanut.**

1916 *DN* 4.338 **PA,** *Grubies* [grubiz]. . . Peanuts. Also *grubers.* **1950** *WELS (Other names or nicknames for peanuts)* 3 Infs, **WI,** Grubers. **1968** *DARE* (Qu. I42) Inf **MN**42, ['grubɚ].

gruber-grubber See **goober-grabber**

grub hoe n **chiefly Nth** See Map and Map Section

=**grubbing hoe 1.**

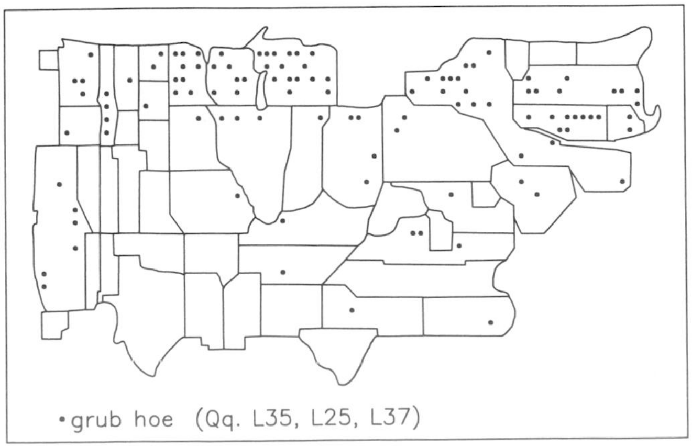

1814 in 1956 Eliason *Tarheel Talk* 275 **NC,** *Grub hoes.* **1899** Garland *Boy Life* 17 **nwIA** (as of c1870s), Both stumbled over nail-kegs and grub-hoes. **1909** *DN* 3.412 **nME,** *Grubhoe. . .* A heavy hoe used for cutting up roots. **1935** [see **grub line**]. **1947** *PADS* 8.19 **IA, NC,** *Grubbing hoe:* Always *grubhoe.* **1950** *WELS (Hand tools used for cutting underbrush)* 12 Infs, **WI,** Grub hoe. **1965–70** *DARE* (Qu. L35) 106 Infs, **chiefly Nth,** Grub hoe; **MN**40, Grub hoes; [**NY**164, Grub hole;] (Qu. L25, *The implement used to clean out weeds and loosen the earth between rows of corn*) Inf **MA**101, Grub hoe; (Qu. L37, *A hand tool used for cutting weeds and grass*) Infs **CA**63, 195, 208, Grub hoe. **1969** Sorden *Lumberjack Lingo* 50 **NEng, Gt Lakes,** *Grub hoe*—A heavy handled hoe used in place of a shovel in fire fighting and in leveling roads.

grub hyson n [*grub* root + Chinese *hyson* a type of green tea]

Sassafras tea.

1942 (1974) Masterson *AR Folkl.* 188 (as of 1876), S.— . . Will you have coffey for supper? T.—Yes, sir. S.—I'll be hanged if you do, tho', we don't have nothin' that way here, but Grub Hyson, and I reckon it's mighty good with sweetnin'. [Footnote to *Grub Hyson:*] Tea brewed from sassafras roots; sassafras tea is a common beverage in parts of Arkansas, where bunches of dried sassafras root are sold by grocers. **1953** Randolph-Wilson *Down in Holler* 250 **Ozarks,** Grub hyson. . . Sassafras tea. **1978** *AP Letters* **swIL** (as of 1820), If we could get some of those biscuits and some coffee made of burnt crusts or parched meal on Sunday mornings, we enjoyed it as a great treat. Genuine coffee, sweetened with sugar, being altogether out of the question, although we had plenty of honey to eat and to use in sweetening our "grub-hyson," which we used pretty freely.

grubley See **grubby 1**

grub line n **West**

=**chuck line;** hence n *grub liner* or *grub (line) rider* one who frequents such places, adj phr *on the grub line* looking for free meals.

1912 Raine *Brand Blotters* 27 **AZ,** He was no booze-fighting grubliner. **1915** *DN* 4.244 **MT,** *On the grub line. . .* Descriptive of one who always stays for meals. "Stone's [sic] never worked and were always on the grub line." **1920** *Outing* 76.201/1 **WY,** All "Grub riders" (cowpunchers out of a job) have always been sure of a meal and a place to sleep at his ranch or any of his camps. **1935** Sandoz *Jules* 242 **wNE** (as of 1880–1930), With a few days' help from some of the more regular grub-line riders, free boarders, Mary wielded the axe, the spade, and the grub hoe against the bushes and trees. **1941** Train *Story* 303 **West,** Cowboys hired for the season saddle up and "ride the grub line" from ranch to ranch, looking for another job. **1959** Martin *Gunbarrel* 279 **WY,** Like giving my grub-liner friends a handout when they stop in at all hours.

grub pin See **grub 2**

grub rider See **grub line**

grubroot n

1 See quot. Cf **bloodroot**

1876 Burroughs *Winter Sunshine* 25 **cwMD,** Bloodroot they [=Black women] generally call "grubroot."

2 =**blazing star 2.**

1940 Clute *Amer. Plant Names* 220, *Chamaelirium luteum.* Grubroot. **1971** Krochmal *Appalachia Med. Plants* 82, *Chamaelirium luteum* . . grub root.

grubs n pl [Prob abbr for **mulligrubs**]

1966 *DARE* (Qu. GG34a, *To feel depressed or in a gloomy mood: "He has the ______ today."*) Inf **CA**2, Grubs.

grub stake See **grub 2**

grubworm n

1 also *grabworm, grubbing worm, grumworm:* An insect larva, esp that of a beetle; also fig. **widespread exc NEast, Pacific** See Map

1807 Irving *Salmagundi* 1.156 **NY,** Giblet was as arrant a grub-worm as ever crawled. **1846** Thorpe *Mysteries* 66 **sMissip Valley,** The choice pecan-nut is neglected for that immense "grub-worm" that rolls down the decayed stump, too large to crawl. **1862** U.S. Patent Office *Annual Rept. for 1861: Ag.* 598, *Lamellicornia* . . in their larva state . . are most commonly known as the *"grub-worm."* **1908** *DN* 3.317 **eAL, wGA,** *Grub-worm. . .* The larva of a beetle, the grub. **1949** *PADS* 11.7 **wTX,** *Grub-worm. . .* A grub; a larval worm found in old wood. **1950** *WELS (The whitish worm that hatches into a dragonfly and is often used for fish* *bait)* 3 Infs, **WI,** Grubworms. **1954** *Harder Coll.* **cwTN,** *Grub worm.* **1958** McCulloch *Woods Words* 74 **Pacific NW,** *Grub worm*—A wood borer, especially a big one in dead timber (sometimes ½ inch in diameter and 2 inches long). **c1960** *Wilson Coll.* **csKY,** *Grubworm:* A grub of certain kinds of beetles, often used for fish bait. **1962** Atwood *Vocab. TX* 58, In any case, several other worms are mentioned as usable for fish bait: *catawba worms, grubworms, . . tomato worms,* and so on. **1965–70** *DARE* (Qu. P6, *Other kinds of worms also used for bait*) 205 Infs, **widespread exc NEast, Pacific,** Grubworm; **AR**4, Grabworm; **AR**46, Grumworm; **NC**87, Grubbing worm—2 inches long, big as the end of a man's little finger, white; (Qu. P5, *What do you call the common worm used as bait?*) 17 Infs, 9 **OK,** Grubworm; **NC**80, Grubbing worm. **1966** *PADS* 45.14 **cnKY,** *Grubworm. . .* The larva of the Green June Beetle. It damages tobacco seedlings by uprooting them. **1966** *Fishing World* 13.6.57 **PA,** Certain cold-weather baits are found in easy, accessible places. . . It is advisable to pry into some of these spots: Grub worms . . can be taken by the dozens from the galls or round balls of goldenrod.

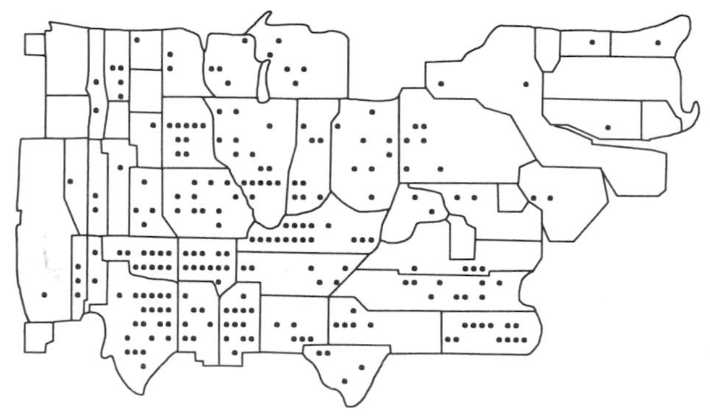

•grubworm 1 + varr (Qq. P6, P5)

2 See quot.

1990 *DARE* File **wNC** (as of c1910), *Grubworm* was the term I learned in earliest childhood for the penis. As an adult I recognized its euphemistic character. But as a young child, it was mostly used with caution—almost as taboo as *penis* (which was not used at all).

gruby See **gruber**

grudgin n Also sp *grudjin* [Var of *gurgeons* coarse meal; cf *EDD grudgings* sb. pl. "*Obsol.* . . 1. Coarse wheaten meal"]

1 Coarse whole wheat flour.

1966 *DARE* (Qu. H15, *Bread made with wheat flour*) Inf **SC**26, Grudgin [grʌǰɪn] bread—it's dark, the flour before you get white flour. **1967** *DARE* FW Addit **SC,** *Grudgin* ['grʌǰɪn]: The first unrefined flour—not fully milled. Dark.

2 Transf: see quot.

1984 Wilder *You All Spoken Here* 88 **Sth,** *Grudjin's* [sic]: Biscuit made of lard, cornmeal, and hop leaven.

grulla adj, often used absol Also *grullo* Pronc-spp *gruller, gruya(y), gruyer* [MexSpan *grullo* (masc), *grulla* (fem) rose gray, dark gray] **chiefly SW, esp TX**

Of a horse or occas mule: dark in color; see quots.

1866 *Wilkes' Spirit of Times* 28 Apr 130/3 **cTX,** We had little pot-gutted duns, with manes like buffalo; we had "gruyays," or crane color. **1892** *DN* 1.190 **TX,** *Grúllo . .* smoke-colored, "clay bank," of isabel color, in speaking of horses. **1903** (1965) Adams *Log Cowboy* 14 **West,** It was my good fortune that morning to get a good mount of horses,—three sorrels, two grays, . . and a *grulla.* **1925** (1926) James *Drifting Cowboy* 210 **West,** He was a big powerful 'gruller' horse, tall and rawboned and all muscle. **1929** Dobie *Vaquero* 4 **TX,** The horse Father gave me was a *grulla* (mouse colored) dun paint. **1931** *Lariat* April 4 (Bentley *Spanish Terms*), He had never roped much of anything except catclaw bushes and the . . tail of his gruya mule. **1948** *Eaton's Ranch* Spring 4 **WY** *(Hench Coll.),* Awaiting a call to the saddle sheds, the blacks, whites . . pintos, gruyers. **1949** *Sat. Eve. Post* 9 Apr 43/1 **NM,** The horse he was on was a dull gray-brown color that I couldn't put a name to then, but which I later learned to call *grullo.* **1965–70** *DARE* (Qu. K37, . . *A horse of mixed colors*) Inf **CO**38, ['grulə], ['grulo]—not really blue or brown, blackish, dark brown; **TX**6, ['grujə]; (Qu. K38, *A horse of a dirty white color*) Inf **TX**11, ['grijə]; **TX**22, ['grujə]; **TX**29, ['grujo]; (Qu. K39, . . *Names . . for horses according to their colors*) Inf **CA**11, ['grujɚ]—mouse-colored; **CA**87, ['gruljə]—a blue horse with a black stripe on his back; **NM**13, ['grujə]; **TX**4, 6, Grulla. **1967** *DARE* Tape **TX**46, He was a ['grujɚ] roan, . . kind of a bluish roan, gruyer they call it.

grum adj *old-fash*

Grim, surly, sullen.

1771 in 1887 Franklin *Complete Wks.* 1.69, And, lastly (my brother still grum and sullen), I gave them a piece of eight to drink, and took my leave. **1827** Cooper *Red Rover* 1.76, A voice from behind, that was quite as dogmatical, though a little less grum, than that of the loquacious boatswain. **1874** (1895) Eggleston *Circuit Rider* 304 **sOH** (as of early 19th cent), Pinkey was grum. He didn't like to be neglected, if he was a highwayman. **1899** (1912) Green *VA Folk-Speech* 209, *Grum. . .* Morose; surly; sullen; glum. **1901** Harben *Westerfelt* 262 **nGA,** Why are you so devilish grum? *Ibid* 282, He thinks I've got a fresh dose o' religion. I didn't let 'im know no better, an' he wus grum all the way home. **1950** *PADS* 14.33 **SC,** *Grum and chuff. . .* Sulky in demeanor and surly in speech; morose and forbidding.

grumbler n

1 =**sea robin.**

1889 *Century Dict.* 2642, *Grumbler. . .* A fish of the family *Triglidæ;* a gurnard: so called from its making a grumbling noise while struggling to disengage itself from the hook.

2 A **croaker** n[1] **1a(1)** (here: *Micropogon undulatus*). Cf **growler** n[1] **2**

1984 *DARE* File **Chesapeake Bay** [Watermen's vocab], Croaker, grumbler, growler, hardhead, pinhead, kingbilly, roundhead.

grumblesome adj Cf **-some**

See quots.

1950 *PADS* 14.33 **SC,** *Grumblesome. . .* Irritable, complaining, given to *grumbling.* **1954** *Harder Coll.* **cwTN,** *Grumblesome:* Irritable, complaining.

grumma See **grandma n A13**

grummet v [Perh for **grum it;* cf **grum**]

1909 *DN* 3.412 **nME,** *Grummet. . .* To sulk.

grummet n See **grommet**

grum(m)ole See **ground mole**

grumpa, grumps, grumpuh, grumpy See **grandpa A9**

grumworm See **grubworm 1**

grundiquoit See **grande écaille**

grundniss n Pronc-spp *gritny, gruntny* [PaGer]

=**peanut.**

1967–68 *DARE* (Qu. I42, . . *Names or nicknames . . for peanuts*) Inf **NJ**2, Gruntnies—from Pennsylvania Dutch; **PA**143, Gritnies ['grɪtniz]; **PA**159, Grundniss ['gruntnɪs].

grunion n Also sp *grunyon* [Cf Span *gruñon* grumbler]

A **silversides** (here: *Leuresthes tenuis*) of the California coast.

1917 *Overland Monthly* 70.529/1, Of all the peculiar fish of which the southern coast of California boasts, the Grunyon is the most peculiar, on account of its phenomenal manner of spawning. **1919** *Fish Bulletin* (Calif. Fish & Game Commission) 15 July 3 *(OEDS),* At Long Beach no name other than 'grunion' is ever heard, although one gleans from scientific works such names as 'silver-sides' and 'little-smelt'. **1953** Roedel *Common Fishes CA* 78, California Grunion—*Leuresthes tenuis. . .* Because of its remarkable spawning habits, it is of great interest to amateur fishermen, who catch large numbers on the beaches during the open months of the spawning season. **1955** Zim–Shoemaker *Fishes* 82, California grunion is a larger and better known relative of the silverside. **1967–70** *DARE* (Qu. P2, . . *Kinds of saltwater fish*) Infs **CA**25, 45, 80, 191, Grunion; (Qu. P13, . . *Other ways of fishing*) Infs **CA**36, 45, 52, 75, 80, Grunion run; **CA**83, Grunion hunting. **1968** *DARE* Tape **CA**104, [FW:] Do you have grunion up here? [Inf:] Well, they do up there in Penzion. Maybe these are grunion that come in on the beach, I don't know. They have different names for 'em; **CA**105, There's grunion . . come in the streams . . up in Trinidad, around . . Crescent City. **1983** Becker *Fishes WI* 767, Most silversides are small fishes. They include the well-known California grunion, a spectacular fish which during high tide is thrown up onto the beach sands to spawn.

grunnot, grunnut See **ground nut**

grunt v

1 To complain or grumble; hence vbl n *grunting* complaining, adj *grunty* irritable, grouchy.

1744 (1907) Hamilton *Itinerarium* 244 **cnMD,** I went and paid a visit to the parson and his wife, who were both complaining, or grunting (as the country phrase is). **1892** Smith *Farm & Fireside* 151 **GA,** A man who ain't . . gets on the piazza, tired and grunty. **1899** (1912) Green *VA Folk-Speech* 209, *Grunt*. . . To complain. "There needn't be any grunting as it must be done." **1915** *DN* 4.226 **wTX,** *Grunt*. . . To complain. **1954** *Harder Coll.* **cwTN,** *Grunt*—to be fussy, quarrelsome because of feeling unwell. **c1960** *Wilson Coll.* **csKY,** *Grunt:* To complain. *Grunty:* Complaining, able to complain. **1969** *DARE* (Qu. GG16, *Words for . . complaining: "You just can't please him—he's always ———.")* Inf **NY**220, Grunting.

2 also with *around:* To be ill or ailing.

1893 Shands *MS Speech* 34, *Gruntin*. . . Negro and illiterate white for *unwell,* but *not dangerously sick;* as, "Mr. Jones is still gruntin this morning"; i.e. Mr. Jones is still somewhat ill. **c1960** *Wilson Coll.* **csKY,** *Grunt*—To . . be ailing, often too obviously. **1960** Criswell *Resp. to PADS 20* **Ozarks,** *Grunt around, to*—To be ailing, unwell, but not ill enough to take to bed. "She's not exactly sick, but she's been gruntin' around for weeks." Formerly very common. **1967** *DARE* (Qu. BB41, *Not seriously ill, but sick enough to be in bed: "He's been ——— for a week.")* Inf **MI**47, Grunting around.

3 also with *out, up:* See quots.

1926 (1949) McQueen–Mizell *Hist. Okefenokee* 61 **seGA,** Another method [of hunting alligators] is to go to some lake or prairie where it is known the alligators stay, and "grunt" them up, by making a calling sound similar to the grunt of the alligator. **1941** Faherty *Big Old Sun* 33 **FL** *(Hench Coll.),* Hunting in the 'Glades is the best thing to do. Grunting out gators in the water holes in the saw grass, and punching them out of their caves in the canals, and blowing out their eyes with your shotgun. **1984** Wilder *You All Spoken Here* 150 **Sth,** *Grunt:* Attract alligators by imitating their calls.

4 To draw worms to the surface by causing the subsoil to vibrate, esp by rasping a planted stake; hence vbl n *grunting,* n *grunter.* Cf **fiddle v 2, grunt worm**

1971 [see **fiddle** v 2]. **1982** Sternberg *Fishing* 56, In southern states, collectors draw grunt worms to the surface by a unique method called *fiddling* or *grunting*. . . Hundreds of worms may be picked up during a single fiddling operation. *Ibid* 59, Fiddling, or grunting, is a technique used in the South for collecting grunt worms. Rub an axe or piece of steel across the top of a board driven into the ground. The vibrations draw grunt worms to the surface. **1989** *Nat. Hist.* Aug 10 **nFL,** Worm grunting is an effective and profitable means of gathering earth-worms for fish bait. The worm grunter drives a wooden stake into the ground and rasps against it with a notched stick or a coil spring from an old car. Earthworms quickly emerge from the ground and wriggle across the surface away from the source of vibration. . . about 700 people pay thirty dollars annually for permits to grunt for worms in the Apalachicola National Forest. . . The worms appear to respond to just about any kind of vibration in the soil. . . A woman . . reported that worms surfaced around a power mower she had left running in the yard, and that another time they popped up around the feet of her daughters who were practicing their cheerleading routines in the yard.

grunt n

1 also *gruntfish, grunts:* A fish of the family Pomadasyidae, esp of the genus *Haemulon.* [See quot 1884; *DJE* 1679 →] Also called **growler** n[1] **3, grunter** n[1] **3, pigfish.** For other names of var genera and spp see **black grunt 2, croaker** n[1] **1b, flannelmouth 1, French grunt, humpback grunt, mango croaker, margaret grunt, margatefish, open-mouthed grunt, pompon, porkfish, redmouth, ronco, sargo, Spanish grunt, squirrelfish, striped grunt, sailor's choice, tomtate, white grunt, yellow grunt, yellow-striped grunt**

1772 in 1924 Phillips *Notes B. Romans* 123 **FL,** It Abounds here in fish of all kinds, . . Principally . . Spanish Mackerel, Grunts Black and Red Drum, . . besides prawns and Many others too Tedious to Mention. **1814** in 1815 Lit. & Philos. Soc. NY *Trans.* 406, *Speckled Grunts. (Labrus fulvo-maculatus)*. . . Length five inches; depth one inch and a half. Caught in the bay of New York. [*DARE* Ed: *Labrus fulvo-maculatus* is now *Orthopristes chrysopterus.*] **1861** Acad. Nat. Sci. Philadelphia *Proc.* 32, *Haemulon arcuatum*. . . "Grunts." **1884** Goode *Fisheries U.S.* 1.398, From their habit of uttering a loud, rather melodious sound when taken from the water they have acquired the name of "Grunt" and "Pig-fish." **1911** U.S. Bur. Census *Fisheries 1908* 310, *Grunt.* The name of several small *Hæmulidæ* quite common off the south Atlantic and Gulf coasts, and sometimes found on the California coast. . . They make a peculiar grunting noise when taken from the water. **1933** John G. Shedd Aquarium *Guide* 106, It is said that a school of grunts playing around the bottom of an anchored boat on a still . . night will make enough noise to awaken the sleeping crew. **1941** Faherty *Big Old Sun* 49 **sFL,** She emptied the soapy water . . into a pail, put into it a skilletful of pale little boiled grunt fish and scraps of mullet and grits and bread, and grease. . . tipped the pail . . into the trough and onto the pigs. **1973** Knight *Cook's Fish Guide* 382, Grunt . . g[oo]d to ex[cellent].

2 also *grunts:* **=drum 1.** Cf **grunter** n[1] **2b**

1814 in 1815 Lit. & Philos. Soc. NY *Trans.* 405, *Grunts. (Labrus grunniens.)* . . This fish is called by fishermen, *young sheep's head,* and young drum, from its resemblance to those creatures. The common name is given on account of a grunting noise he is supposed sometimes to make. *Ibid* 417, *Middle Grunts (Bodianus costatus.)* . . Teeth, in the throat, above and below. [*DARE* Ed: *Labrus grunniens* and *Bodianus costatus* are now *Micropogon undulatus* and *Pogonias cromis* respectively.] **1842** DeKay *Zool. NY* 4.82, The Banded Drum, *Pogonias fasciatus,* . . has the various popular names, such as Grunter, Young Drum, Grunts, and Young Sheepshead. **1854** Wailes *Rept. on Ag. & Geol. MS* 333, Micropogon undulatus. . . Croaker, or grunt.

3 An ill-tempered, grouchy person; a dullard. *derog* Cf **granny grunt 2**

1968–69 *DARE* (Qu. GG38, *Somebody who is usually mean and bad tempered: "He's an awful ———.")* Inf **CA**158, Grunt; (Qu. HH3, *A dull and stupid person)* Inf **PA**93, Grunt.

4 A dessert pudding or dumpling made with fruit. **chiefly NEng** Cf **apple grunt, slump**

1896 *DN* 1.411 **cnNY,** *Apple-grunt:* a kind of apple dumpling. **1918** *DN* 5.25 **nOR,** *Huckleberry grunt*. . . Huckleberry dumpling. General in northern Oregon. **1939** Wolcott *Yankee Cook Book* 363, *Grunt.* Cape Cod name for a steamed berry pudding. **1947** Bowles–Towle *New Engl. Cooking* 178, The word grunt in Massachusetts and particularly on Cape Cod was another name for dumpling. Both the grunts and the slumps were transition desserts, halfway between the boiled and baked puddings but simpler to make. **1963** Haywood *Yankee Dict.* 86 **NEng,** *Huckleberry grunt*—An old fashioned Cape Cod dessert. . . some hold it to be descriptive of the satisfied guttural uttered by a hungry man who has eaten well. **1982** *Chr. Sci. Monitor* (Boston MA) 24 June 16, The "Slump" and the "Grunt" are dumpling desserts. **1989** *WI State Jrl.* (Madison) 9 Aug sec D 1/2, I found myself driven to make a blueberry grunt . . just to see if my creation, as the cookbook promised, would make a grunting sound as it steamed on top of the stove. . . You simmer a layer of fruit . . in a skillet, then add a layer of biscuit dough. As the biscuit steams, it's supposed to grunt or sigh.

5 Pork or bacon.

1934 (1940) Weseen *Dict. Amer. Slang* 80 [Logging and mining slang], *Grunt*. . . Pork in any form. **1968** Adams *Western Words* 134, *Grunt*—A logger's term for pork or bacon. **1970** *DARE* (Qu. H38, . . *Words for bacon)* Inf **MO**22, Grunt.

6 also *grunt, pig, grunt:* A children's game; see quots.

1905 *DN* 3.82 **nwAR,** *Grunt*. . . The name of a young people's game. **1975** Ferretti *Gt. Amer. Book Sidewalk Games* 164, Lots are fine for such games as *Blind Man's Bluff*. . . A 1930s suburban New York version called *Grunt, Pig, Grunt* also involves a blindfolded player ("It") surrounded by the other players grouped in a circle. The blindfolded player gropes around the circle, finally pointing his finger at one player and commanding, "Grunt, Pig, Grunt!" The person pointed at has to squeal and grunt and snort like a pig . . and "It" tries to guess his name. If he guesses correctly, the person named is blindfolded and goes through the same process.

7 See quot.

1968 *DARE* (Qu. K54, . . *The smallest pig in a litter)* Inf **IN**19, Grunt or runt.

8 pl: See quot. Cf **grunt** v 2

1970 *DARE* (Qu. BB5, *A general feeling of discomfort or illness that isn't any one place in particular)* Inf **TX**105, Grunts.

grunt around See **grunt** v 2

grunt box n

1966 *DARE* (Qu. M21b, . . *An outside toilet building)* Inf **NH**5, Grunt box [laughter].

grunter n[1]

1 A **sea robin,** usu of the genus *Prionotus.* [See quot 1839] Cf **grumbler 1, pigfish**

1807 in 1846 MA Hist. Soc. *Coll.* 2d ser 3.56 **seMA,** The grunter . . when it is taken out of the water . . makes a noise like the grunting of a hog, and soon dies. **1839** MA Zool. & Bot. Surv. *Fishes Reptiles* 12 **seMA,** Prionotus. . . P. *strigatus. . . Sea Robin. Gurnard. Grunter. . .* This species . . is frequently taken in the vicinity of Holmes Hole . . but is not used. *Ibid* 14, P. *carolinus. . . The Web-fingered Grunter. Ibid* 15, Both these species are called *"grunter,"* from the peculiar noise made by them. **1842** DeKay *Zool. NY* 4.46, This species [=*Prionotus evolans*] is not uncommon, and is known under the various popular names of *Grunter, Gurnard, Sea Robin,* and *Flying Fish.* **1884** Goode *Fisheries U.S.* 1.256, Among the fish that may be classed as edible . . is the Sea-Robin, Grunter, or Gurnard. **1969** *DARE* (Qu. P4, *Saltwater fish that are not good to eat*) Inf **RI**17, Grunters.

2 A **drum 1,** as:

a also *grunting perch:* =**freshwater drum.** [See quot 1820] Cf **growler** n[1] **2, grunt** n **2**

1820 Rafinesque *Ohio R. Fishes* 24, *Aplodinotis grunniens. . .* The vulgar names of this fish are . . grunting-perch, bubbling-fish, bubbler. . . A remarkable peculiarity of this fish consists in the strange grunting noise, which it produces. . . It is intermediate between the dumb grunt of a hog and the single croaking noise of the bull frog. **1957** Trautman *Fishes* 607 **OH,** Before 1932, the much prized Drum of southern Ohio was known by several names, including Grunter, . . White or Gray Perch, and Buffalofish. **1972** Sparano *Outdoors Encycl.* 369, *Freshwater Drum* . . grunter. **1983** Becker *Fishes WI* 957, *Freshwater Drum. . .* Other common names . . grunter, . . grunting perch.

b A **croaker** n[1] **1a(1),** esp *Micropogon undulatus.* [See quot 1947] Cf **growler** n[1] **2, grumbler 1, grunt** n **2**

1842 DeKay *Zool. NY* 4.82, The Banded Drum, *Pogonias fasciatus,* . . has the various popular names, such as Grunter, Young Drum, Grunts, and Young Sheepshead. **1947** Caine *Salt Water* 17, Croakers derive their name from the croaking sound they produce either below or above the water. They are also known as . . grunter. **1973** Knight *Cook's Fish Guide* 383, Grunter—croaker.

3 =**grunt** n **1.**

1898 U.S. Natl. Museum *Bulletin* 47.1289, *Haemulidae. (The Grunters.)* . . Carnivorous fishes of the warm seas, most of them valued as food. **1905** NJ State Museum *Annual Rept. for 1904* 317, *Haemulidae.* The Grunters. . . Several species recorded from our shores.

4 =**pig frog.**

1966 LA Wild Life Comm. *Hunting Fishing Regulations 1967–68* 6, Southern Bullfrogs (Rana grylio), also called lagoon frogs or grunters. **1967** *LA Conservationist* 19.7–8.9/1 **LA,** There are two species of frogs in Louisiana of significant sport and commercial value. These are the bullfrog and the pig frog or grunter. . . The smaller pig frog is confined generally to southern portions of the State.

5 A two-toned foghorn.

1975 [see **groaner**].

grunter n[2] See **grunt** v **4**

gruntfish n

1 See **grunt** n **1.**

2 also *grunt sculpin:* A **sculpin** (here: *Rhamphocottus richardsoni*).

1960 Amer. Fisheries Soc. *List Fishes* 40, Grunt sculpin. *Rhamphocottus richardsoni. Ibid* 59, Gruntfish—see sculpin, grunt.

grunt, granny, granny See **granny wants a grunt**

grunting See **grunt** v **1, 4**

grunting list, be on the v phr [**grunt** v **1, 2**]

1954 *Harder Coll.* **cwTN,** *Grunting list, be on the*—To be quarrelsome because of not feeling well. "I am on the grunting list. Been feeling bad for about a week."

grunting perch See **grunter** n[1] **2a**

gruntny See **grundniss**

grunt out See **grunt** v **3**

grunt, pig, grunt See **grunt** n **6**

grunts See **grunt** n **1, 2**

grunt sculpin See **gruntfish 2**

grunt up See **grunt** v **3**

grunt worm n [**grunt** v **4**]

See quot.

1982 Sternberg *Fishing* 56, The grunt worm is the general name for several kinds of worms that are collected by fiddling. They average 6 inches in length. Color varies from pink to gray or brown. *Ibid* 59, In southeastern states, anglers gather grunt worms in pine-studded woodlands with acid soil.

grunty See **grunt** v **1**

grunyon See **grunion**

gruper See **grouper 1a**

grutch v [Var of *grudge* begrudge] Cf Pronc Intro 3.I.15

1899 (1912) Green *VA Folk-Speech* 209, *Grutch. . .* To give or permit with reluctance; grant or submit to unwillingly; begrudge. **1909** *S. Atl. Qrly.* 8.39 **sSC coast** [Gullah], Yo' ent grutch me sumphm fo' tas'e me mout'? [=You don't grudge me something to put a taste in my mouth?]

gruya(y), gruyer See **grulla**

gryste See **grist**

guaco n [AmSpan]

=**Rocky Mountain bee plant.**

1844 Gregg *Commerce* 1.278 **NM,** This kind of crockery . . is often fancifully painted with colored earths and the juice of a plant called *guaco,* which brightens by burning. **1947** Curtin *Healing Herbs* 93 **NM,** Guaco. Stink Weed. *Cleome serrulata Pursh.* Rocky Mountain Bee Plant. Caper Family. *Capparidaceæ.* The familiar *guaco* that fringes so many roadsides with its white and orchid pattern, contains a large supply of nectar—hence its name of bee plant.

guajilla, guajillo See **huajillo**

guano n Usu |'gwɑno|; also **chiefly GA, SC** |gju'ænə(r)|; also |gwɑnə|; for addit varr see quots Pronc-spp *guana(s), guanner* Cf Intro "Language Changes" IV.1.c

A Forms. For addit pronc evidence see quots at **B** below

1903 *DN* 2.291 **Cape Cod MA** (as of a1857), *Guano* was [gju'ænə]. **1912** Green *VA Folk-Speech* 209, *Guan'ner. . .* For *guano,* the manure. **1940** [see **guano sack**]. **1965–70** *DARE* (Qu. F19) Inf **PA**203, [gwænə] sack; **VA**62, [gwɑnə] sack; (Qu. F20) Infs **VA**83, 94, [gwɑnə] sack; (Qu. F23) Inf **NJ**15, [gwænə] sack; **NJ**21, [gwɑnɛ] sack; **VA**30, [gwanə] sack; **VA**104, [gwɑnə] bag; (Qu. L17) Inf **AL**47, ['gɑno]; **GA**68, [jo'ænə]; **NC**80, [go'ænə]; **SC**30, [gju'ænə]. **1966–67** *DARE* Tape **AL**1 [Black], [gju'ænə]; **AL**33, [gu<'æ̃·nɚ]; **GA**1, Some called it guano [gju'ænə]. **c1970** [see **guano sack**]. **1981** Pederson *LAGS Basic Materials* **chiefly GA,** [A total of 31 Georgia infs, 3 northern Florida infs and 3 eastern Alabama infs gave pronunciations for *guano.* Most proncs were of the type [gju'ænə(r)]; 7 proncs were of the type [gju'ɑnə]; 1 inf, **swGA,** [gə̆wænə̆]; 1 inf, **swGA,** [gwa·ᵋ'ænə̆]; 1 inf, **swGA,** [dʒɪ<'æ>nə]; 1 inf, **csGA,** [dʒʊʉ'æ<nə̆].]

B Sense.

Fertilizer. **chiefly S Atl**

1844 *Dial* 4.498 **ceMA,** Agricultural chemistry . . offering, by means of a teaspoonful of artificial guano, to turn a sandbank into corn. **1884** U.S. Natl. Museum *Bulletin* 27.1151, Guano manufactured from salt fish, and bones, waste that has been removed in preparing boneless fish for the market. In 1882 there were 3000 tons of this waste; it had a market value of $12.00 per ton. **1930** *DN* 6.81 **cSC,** *Guano. . .* Commercial fertilizer, universally pronounced [gjuænə]. **c1937** in 1972 *Amer. Slave* 2.130 **SC,** Good people come up again and flourish in de green fields of Eden. Bad people no come up. Deir bodies and bones just make phosphate guano, 'round de roots of de ever bloomin' tree of life. **1938** in 1989 *Encycl. S. Culture* 36, [Photo of billboard:] Dixie Guano Co. Mfrs. of High Grade Fertilizers[,] Laurinburg, N.C. **1966** *DARE* FW Addit **SC,** *Guano* [gju'ænə], a generic name for commercial fertilizer. **1967** *DARE* (Qu. L17, . . *Names . . for manure*) Inf **SC**30, Guano—any bought fertilizer. **1981** Pederson *LAGS Basic Materials,* 4 infs, **wGA,** Guano distributor; 3 infs, **GA,** Guano—fertilizer [Two infs indicate that this is an old term.]; 1 inf, **GA,** A sack of guano; 1 inf, **GA,** Guano comes in a crocus sack.

guano sack n Also *guano bag;* for addit varr see quots **chiefly C and S Atl** Cf **burlap bag, granna bag, gunny sack, tow sack**

Orig a bag in which guano was sold; hence any large cloth bag.

1856 *Porter's Spirit of Times* 4 Oct 81/3, The State Inspector of Guano in Maryland . . [urges] farmers to destroy or erase the marks on guano bags after emptying them. **1940** *Qrly. Jrl. Speech* 26.265 **VA,** A *burlap bag* may be a . . "guanas," "gauna" [sic] or "guano bag." **1946** *PADS* 5.25 **VA,** *Guano sack . . :* A large bag made of coarse canvas; in the northern Piedmont. **1949** Kurath *Word Geog.* 57, *Guano sack* is common in Maryland, both east and west of the Bay, and in the Shenandoah Valley. **1956** McAtee *Some Dialect NC* 20, *Guano sack* . . a large bag of coarse material. **1965–70** *DARE* (Qu. F19, *A cloth container for grain*) Infs **PA**203, **VA**62, Guano sack; (Qu. F20, *A cloth container for feed*) Infs **VA**83, 94, Guano sack; (Qu. F23, *A container made of rough, loosely woven, brown cloth*) Infs **NJ**15, 21, **VA**30, 83, 94, Guano sack; **VA**42, 104, Guano bag; **NJ**17, Guano. **1966** Dakin *Dial. Vocab. Ohio R. Valley* 2.139, Burlap sack. . . 2 infs, **OH,** Guano bag/sack. **1966** *DARE* Tape **AL**1 [Black], They had guano [gju'ænə] sacks. . . And the sacks was made out of white cloth. And Mama would take these sacks and boil 'em out and that's what we had for sheets and pillowcases. **c1970** Pederson *Dial. Surv. Rural GA* 1 inf, **seGA,** We used to say *guano* [gjʉu'ˀænɚ] or *croker sack;* 1 inf, **seGA,** Guano [gjʊu'ænə] sack. **1971** Wood *Vocab. Change* 51, *Guano sack* has its chief occurrences in Georgia, Florida, and Alabama. **1986** Pederson *LAGS Concordance* **AL, FL, GA,** 17 infs, Guano sack(s); 1 inf, Guano sack, saved, washed and made clothes of [them]; 1 inf, Guano sacks, used for towels, sheets, and underwear; 1 inf, Guano.

guard n, v Usu |gɑ(r)d|; also **esp Mid and S Atl** |gjɑ(r)d| Pronc-spp *geard, g(h)yard, gyaa'd* Cf Pronc Intro 3.I.16

A Forms.

1867 Lowell *Biglow* xxx **NEng,** Some delicate mouths . . are careful to observe . . *ge-ard* for *guard.* **1899** Chesnutt *Conjure Woman* 89 **csNC** [Black], He walked right pas' de gyard at de do' [=door]. **1899** (1912) Green *VA Folk-Speech* 209, *Guard.* . . Always pronounced with the *g* hard, *geard.* **1917** in 1944 *ADD* **swVA,** Ghyarded. **1922** Gonzales *Black Border* 305 **sSC, GA coasts** [Gullah glossary], *Gyaa'd* . . guard, guards, guarded, guarding. **1950** *PADS* 14.34 **SC,** *Gyard.* . . Dialect pronunciation of . . guard. . . A survival of an eighteenth-century pronunciation which is still heard in the coastal area, especially in Charleston, but only sporadically in the remainder of the state. **1968** *DARE* FW Addit **csNC,** *Guard* pronounced [gjɑrd].

B As noun.

1 See **horse guard.**

2 =**fireguard.**

1884 Aldridge *Ranch Notes* 14 **cKS** (as of 1877), After the ploughing and mowing were done, we proceeded to burn the guard. **1935** Sandoz *Jules* 181 **wNE** (as of 1880–1930), The Panhandle was spotted with the black path of prairie fires. Old-timers advised ploughed guards, with a burned strip between. A rancher near Alliance, on the Burlington, let his guard fire get away.

3 See quot.

c1938 in 1970 Hyatt *Hoodoo* 2.1136 **seGA,** Yo' goes right back to de woman's house an' yo' git dis woman's *guards* [Hyatt: menstrual cloth]. Yo' take dat *guard* an' yo' boil it.

guardeen See **guardian**

guardfish n [Appar folk-etym for **garfish**]

A **needlefish** (here: *Strongylura raphidoma*).

1709 (1967) Lawson *New Voyage* 160 **NC, SC,** The white Guard-Fish is shaped almost like a Pike, but slenderer. **1802** in 1917 Essex Inst. *Coll.* 53.207, [The fish which are caught] are chiefly Dolphin, Parrot fish, guard fish, and some others whose names I know not. **1896** U.S. Natl. Museum *Bulletin* 47.715, *Tylosurus raphidoma.* . . *Guardfish.* . . Jaws unusually short, stiff, strong, rapidly tapering forward; large teeth of jaws very strong, knife-shaped.

guard fly See **horse guard**

guardian n Usu |'gɑ(r)dɪən|; also *among speakers with little formal educ, old-fash* |g(j)ɑ(r)'din|; for addit varr see quots Pronc-spp *gahdeen, gardien, g(e)ardeen, guardeen, gyardeen, gyarjean, gyarjun* Note: The proncs [gɑ(r)'din] are prob a survival of earlier *gardein,* current from the 15th–18th cents; cf *OED* at *guardian.*

Std sense, var forms.

1761 in 1892 *DN* 1.213 **eMA,** *Guardeen.* **1829** Kirkham *Engl. Grammar* 195, [Improper:] guar deen [pronounced:] gyar je an. **1833** Neal *Down-Easters* 1.97 **NEng,** Have a gardeen 'pynted for *you* as soon as I git ashore. **1839** in 1956 Eliason *Tarheel Talk* 311 **nw,cwNC,** *Guardian*—guardeen. **1858** Stearns *Practical Guide Pronc.* xxxviii, Say . . guar'di an (gar'-) *[not]* gyar'jun *[nor]* gar dēen'. **1874** (1895) Eggleston *Circuit Rider* 48 **sIN,** I've got a right to choose a gardeen. **1887** (1967) Harris *Free Joe* 6 **GA** [Black], Marse John Evans is my gyardeen. **1893** Shands *MS Speech* 34, *Gyardeen* [gjɑ'din]. Illiterate white for *guardian.* . . *Gadeen* [gɑdîn] is used in Kentucky. **1897** Lummis *King of Broncos* 162 **NM,** Yo' need a guar*deen.* **1899** (1912) Green *VA Folk-Speech* 191, *Gardien.* . . A guardian; pronounced *geardeen.* Guardeen. **1905** *DN* 3.62 **NE,** *Guardēen.* **1908** *DN* 3.317 **eAL, wGA,** *Guardēen.* **1909** *DN* 3.396 **nwAR,** *Gahdeen, gyardeen.* *Ibid* 411 **cnME,** *Gardēen.* **1912** *DN* 3.576 **wIN,** *Gardeen.* **1915** *DN* 4.183 **swVA,** *Gardeen.* **1941** *LANE* Map 391 *(Guardian),* [Proncs of the type [ˌgɑ(r)'din] are widespread throughout New England, though somewhat more common towards the north. Occas, esp towards the south, there are forms with stress on the first syll or with level stress. 6 infs in the Narraganset Bay area offer proncs of the type ['gadʒn̩].] **1951** VA Univ. *Univ. Studies* 5.116, The next feature which is charted . . is the medial [-dʒ-] in *guardian*—[gɑrdʒən] or [gɑrdʒənt] (to avoid confusion, the "Virginia" [gj-] is not entered on the map). Although this pronunciation occurs at a few points around Narragansett Bay, it is otherwise characteristic only of Eastern Virginia—elsewhere in the East the almost universal popular pronunciation is [ˌgɑr'din]. The ['gɑrdʒən] type. . . is almost exclusively an uneducated pronunciation. . . At various points on the fringes of the ['gɑrdʒən] area (particularly in North Carolina), this form is blended with the more usual American [ˌgɑr'din] to produce [ˌgɑr'dʒin]. How this in turn is transmuted into [ˌgar'dzin] defies conjecture. [*DARE* Ed: In the map legend these proncs appear as ['gɑədʒən(t)], [ˌgɑə'dʒin], and [ˌgɑə'dzin].] **c1960** *Wilson Coll.* **csKY,** *Guardian,* among the elderly, is /ˌgɑr'din/ or /ˌgjɑr'din/. **1975** *DARE* File **cnMA** (as of c1915), Two words I remember children pronouncing strangely were *guardian* and *siren.* Most of them said ['gɑdin] and ['saɪrin]. **1976** Allen *LAUM* 3.288 **Upper MW** (as of c1950), More than one-fifth of all U[pper] M[idwest] infs. offer a pronunciation with a heavily stressed final syllable, as in /ˌgɑr'din/ or, more rarely . . /'gɑr'din/. . . A marked social contrast appears in the distribution of infs. who have the /'din/ form. Three-fourths of them are the older and less well educated speakers in Type I, and the remaining one-fourth are in Type II [=mid-aged with approx hs educ]. No college-trained speaker has it. **1981** Pederson *LAGS Basic Materials* **Gulf Region,** [For *guardian,* proncs of the types [ˌgɑ(r)'din], less often ['gɑ(r)ˌdin], are found throughout the Gulf Region, but most frequently in Arkansas and Mississippi. Seven infs used proncs of the type ['gɑ(r)dn̩]; two of the type ['gɑdžn̩].]

guard the sheep n

=**sic-a-nine-ten.**

1896 *DN* 1.418, *Guard the sheep:* the game of *sic-a-nine-ten.*

guayacan n [MexSpan] **TX**

=**Texas porliera.**

1891 Coulter *Botany W. TX* 50, *Guiacum angustifolium.* . . A straggling shrub (on bluffs) or a small tree (in valleys) with very smooth branches and leaves. . . Called "guayacan," and of considerable repute in various diseases. **1892** *DN* 1.190 **TX,** *Guayacán:* lignum vitæ (*Guiacum angustifolium,* Engelm). A medicinal plant used by Mexicans. *Ibid* 248, *Guyacán.* . . The root is used as a substitute for soap. **1941** *Torreya* 41.49 **TX,** *Porlieria angustifolia.* . . Guayacan. **1967** *DARE* (Qu. T16) Inf **TX**22, Guayacan. **1967** *DARE* Tape **TX**29, We have made soap from guayacan. . . Pick the root and just . . scrape the root; then the easiest way to do this is just form it into a sort of little pad or ball. It makes a nice lather. . . Just wet it, it lathers. **1970** Correll *Plants TX* 902, *Porlieria angustifolia.* . . Guayacan, Soap-bush.

guayule n

A western plant of the genus *Parthenium,* usu the rubber-producing *P. argentatum.* Also called **false ragweed 2** For other names of var spp see **feverfew 3, horsebrush 4, Indian mugwort, mariola, ragweed, rubber plant, sage, Santa Maria, wild wormwood**

[**1906** *Bul. Imper. Inst.* IV.114 *(DA),* The Guayule rubber of Mexico.] **1913** Wooton *Trees NM* 145, This little plant [=*Parthenium incanum*] is a near relative of the guayule . . found in Western Texas and northern Chihuahua. **1918** Visher *Geog. SD* 69, Two decades ago, for example, it was not anticipated that thc guayule shrub would give to desert lands where it grows a value which it now does because it became profitable to extract the rubber which it was found to contain. **1940** Writers' Program *Guide TX* 616, The guayule (Mexican rubber plant) once supplied an industry here. **1960** Vines *Trees SW* 1017, *Parthenium* *incanum* . . is sometimes called Guayule in error, but the name should apply more properly to *P. argentatum.* **1970** Correll *Plants TX* 1626, *Parthenium argentatum*. . . Guayule. **1981** Benson-Darrow *Trees SW Deserts* 297, *Parthenium. Guayule*. . . Shrubs or herbs; herbage gray with dense hair. *Ibid* 298, Guayule . . *Parthenium argentatum*. . . during the First and Second World Wars . . was cultivated at many points, first near Continental, near Tucson, Arizona.

gub(b)er See **goober** n[1] **1**

gubbin See **gobbin**

gubious See **dubious A1**

gudgeon n

1 also *gungeon:* Any of several fish of the family Cyprinidae, but esp the **golden shiner;** also a **killifish.**

[**1709** (1967) Lawson *New Voyage* 162 **NC,** The same Gudgeons as in *Europe* are found in *America.*] **1722** *New-Engl. Courant* (Boston MA) 2 Apr 1/1 **ME,** We hear there is no catching Fish at Winter-Harbour without baiting the Hook with a *Gudgeon.* **1814** in 1815 Lit. & Philos. Soc. NY *Trans.* 439, *New-York Gudgeon (Esox flavulus)*. . . A pretty little fish, of five or six inches long, and an inch and a quarter deep. [*DARE* Ed: *Esox flavulus* is now *Fundulus majalis.*] **1842** DeKay *Zool. NY* 4.394, *The Niagara Gudgeon. Gobio cataractæ*. . . Body elongated and rounded. . . Back deep gray . . and becoming silvery on the belly. Length five inches. [*DARE* Ed: *Gobio cataractae* is now *Rhinichthys cataractae.*] **1888** *Outing* 12.392, I have eaten everything from a fried gudgeon to a boiled sucker! **1906** NJ State Museum *Annual Rept. for 1905* 127, Genus *Hybognathus*. . . The Gudgeons. *Hybognathus nuchalis regius*. . . Gudgeon. Silvery Minnow. *Ibid* 128, It [=*Hybognathus nuchalis*] is less common in the Delaware than *Notropis hudsonius amarus,* with which it is found associated and for which it may be easily mistaken. Few anglers are able to distinguish between the two species, and frequently they are called "gudgeon" alike. *Ibid* 135, *Brama crysoleucas* [=*Notemigonus chrysoleucas*]. . . Gudgeon. *Ibid* 141, *Notropis hudsonius amarus*. . . Gudgeon. **1938** FWP *U.S. One* 170 **MD,** Beneath the structure is one of the best gudgeon fishing spots in the State. Anglers . . come by the hundreds to cast their lines for the tiny fish that make such a succulent meal. **1946** LaMonte *N. Amer. Game Fishes* 158, *Golden Shiner—Notemigonus crysoleucas*. . . Gudgeon. *Ibid* 166, *Burbot—Lota maculosa*. . . Gudgeon. **1968** *DARE* (Qu. P2, . . *Saltwater fish . . good to eat*) Inf **MD**5, Gungeons [gʌnǰɪnz]—4 inches long, thin, light scales; rub off scales with sand and fry. **1983** Becker *Fishes WI* 432, *Golden Shiner—Notemigonus crysoleucas* . . gudgeon. *Ibid* 747, *Burbot—Lota lota* . . gudgeon.

2 =**burbot.**

1946 [see **1** above]. **1973** Knight *Cook's Fish Guide* 382, Gudgeon—Burbot or Shiner, Golden. **1983** [see **1** above].

3 =**mottled sculpin.**

1983 Becker *Fishes WI* 969, Mottled Sculpin—*Cottus bairdi*. . . Other common names: sculpin . . gudgeon.

guégué See **guigui**

guernsey n Usu |'gɝnzi|; rarely |ǰɝnzi| Cf **gansey**

A Form. [Perh infl by *jersey*]

1967 *DARE* FW Addit **TN**17, Guernsey pronounced ['ǰɝnzɪ].

B Sense.

A man's underwear top. [Prob by ext from *guernsey* a knitted shirt or sweater]

1936 *McDavid Coll.* **NC,** A pair of guernseys ['gæənzɪz]: an undershirt vest of the old-fashioned type. **1966** *DARE* (Qu. W14, *Names for underwear*) Inf **NC**14, Guernsey—the top part of men's long johns.

guero See **huero**

guess coming, have another v phr For varr see quots **scattered, but esp Inland Nth**

To be wrong or mistaken—used as a strong expression of disagreement.

1942 Berrey-Van den Bark *Amer. Slang* 170.5, *Be wrong; mistaken*. . . have another guess coming. **1946** McAtee *Dial. Grant Co. IN Suppl. 3* 6 (as of 1890s), *Guess coming . . you've got another,* saying, meaning you're mistaken. **1965-70** *DARE* (Qu. KK59, *To have a mistaken idea, or to be quite wrong about something: "If he thinks she'll help him, he's ______.*") 40 Infs, **scattered, but esp Inland Nth,** Got (*or* has) another guess (coming); **MN**6, Got a guess coming; **NM**6, Got another guess a-coming. **1966** Barnes-Jensen *Dict. UT Slang* 46, *You've got another guess coming:* saying, you are mistaken.

guessies n Also *guessing, guess game*

A guessing game played with marbles; see quots.

1957 *Sat. Eve. Post Letters* **WI,** Guess game: a game in which a player guesses how many marbles an opponent is holding; he has to give the opponent the difference between the guess and the number of marbles held. **c1970** Wiersma *Marbles Terms* (as of 1960), *Guessies*—Hold marbles in fist. If opponent guesses how many, he wins all. **1976** *WI Acad. Rev.* Mar 10/1 (as of 1920s), In some games, marbles were used as objects of exchange and not for their intrinsic qualities. *Guessing* was such a game, and it was played by only two people. A player put his hand into his marble bag . . or marble box . . and drew out one to five mibs in a closed fist. The opponent then guessed how many were concealed in the fist. If he guessed correctly, he claimed the lot; if the player misguessed, he paid the difference in marbles and took his turn at confounding his opponent.

guess stick n Also *guessing stick* Cf **gyp stick**

=**cheat stick.**

1934 *Oregonian* (Portland OR) 18 Nov mag sec 7/1 [Foresters' lingo], *Guessing stick.* A Biltmore stick used in estimating diameter and heights of trees. **1958** McCulloch *Woods Words* 75 **Pacific NW,** *Guessing stick*—A cruiser's stick marked to give the number of logs in a tree, and the diameter of trees. **1969** Sorden *Lumberjack Lingo* 50 **NEng, Gt Lakes,** *Guess stick*—A stick used by a cruiser to ascertain the number of logs in a tree and to read the diameter of trees.

guffer n[1] [Cf **duffer,** *gaffer*]

A fellow.

1950 Moore *Candlemas Bay* 98 **ME,** Poor old guffer, she thought, moving between the cupboard and the stove. **1966** *DARE* (Qu. II10a, *Asking directions of somebody on the street when you don't know his name—what you'd say to a boy: "Say, ______, where's the post office?"*) Inf **ME**13, Young guffer.

guffer n[2] See **goofer** n

guffin n [Cf *OED guffin* "A stupid, clumsy person"]

1899 (1912) Green *VA Folk-Speech* 209, *Guffins*. . . Very large feet. "Look what guffins he's got."

guggle v Also *goggle* [Echoic; cf **gurgle** v **1**]

To drink greedily; to guzzle.

1948 Manfred *Chokecherry* 63 **nwIA,** He lifted the jug onto the crook of his elbow and tipped it up and guggled awhile. **1966-67** *DARE* (Qu. DD17, *To drink a great deal, or too fast: "He doesn't just drink, he ______."*) Inf **SC**26, ['gɔgl]; **TN**14, Goggles it down; **TN**16, Guggles it down.

‡guggler bird n

Appar a **bittern.**

1970 *DARE* (Qu. Q8, *A water bird that makes a booming sound before rain and often stands with its beak pointed almost straight up*) Inf **MI**120, Guggler bird.

guh See **go** v **A4b**

guiaskuitus See **gyascutus**

guichy See **geechee**

guiding rod n Also *guide, (water) guider*

=**dowsing rod.**

1967-70 *DARE* (Qu. CC13a, . . *A forked stick that's used to show where there's water underground*) Inf **LA**12, Guide; **SC**32, Guider, water guider [made of] peach wood or hickory; **GA**9, Guiding rod.

guigui n Also *gigi, guégué* [Etym unknown] **LA** Cf **habitant**

See quots.

1916 *DN* 4.269 **csLA,** *Guégué* [ge ge]. . . Derogatory term for the conservative French element. **1923** *DN* 5.243 **LA,** *Gi-gi* [gi gi]. . . Term of contempt for a Creole, especially from the country, or for an Italian. [**1931** Read *LA French* 44, *Guigui*. . . An old *habitant* of New Orleans.] **1968** *DARE* (Qu. HH28, *Names . . for people of foreign background: French*) Inf **LA**20, Guigui ['gi'gi]. **1983** *Reinecke Coll.* 6 **LA,** *Guegue*—['ge͵ge] an unreconstructed New Orleans French person, one who has not taken to American ways. Seems Fr. but etymology uncertain. Obsolescent. . . Also ['gigi]. [**1984** Daigle *Dict. Cajun Lang.* 2.79, *Guigui*. . . Country bumpkin, a rustic, an ignorant person.]

Guin See **Guinea** n[1] **3**

guine See **go** v **A4a**

Guinea n[1], also attrib Also sp *Ginee, Ginn(e)y, Guiney, Guinie, Guinny*

1 also *Guinea negro:* A Black person, orig one from the Guinea region of the West African coast.

1748 in 1952 *AmSp* 27.283 **SC,** Run-Away, a likely well-made Guiney Negro Man, named Toney. **1789** (1918) Low *Politician Outwitted* 384 **NYC,** He talks as crooked as a Guinea niger [sic]. **1823** Cooper *Pioneers* 2.153 **cNY,** But damn the bit of manners has the fellow any more than if he was one of them Guineas, down in the kitchen there. **1856** Cartwright *Autobiog.* 192 **KY** (as of 1818), If he don't get his soul converted, God will damn him as quick as he would a Guinea negro! **1923** *DN* 5.243 **LA,** *Guinea blue.* The color of negroes' blue dresses or aprons: an old trade name. **1928** Peterkin *Scarlet Sister Mary* 164 **seSC** [Black], You got so you act like a don'-care, triflin Dinka nigger; or a puny, sickly no-manners Guinea. **c1937** in 1972 *Amer. Slave* 2.252 **SC,** I come from de Guinea family of niggers, and dat is de reason I is so small and black. De Guinea nigger don't know nothin', 'cept hard work, and for him to be so he can keep up wid bigger folks, he has to turn 'round fas'. **1960** Carpenter *Tales Manchaca* 173 **cTX** [Black] (as of c1885), "I'se a Guinea Nigra," she often said haughtily. **1965** *DARE* Tape **TX**35, In slavery times they was about three different grades of slaves. They was the ones that came from central Africa and they were kinda dumb. . . But now they got a lot of slaves out of the South Sea Islands and they were part Arabian and they were a little brown nigger and they . . called 'em Guinea niggers and they could just learn most anything. **1969** *DARE* (Qu. HH28, *Names . . for people of foreign background: Negro*) Inf **NY**156, Guinea. **1990** *DARE* File **eMA,** One of my students from an affluent Boston suburb says that *guinea* is the only term she heard as a kid . . [for] Blacks and dark-skinned Portuguese.

2 also *Guinea Negro;* pl *Guineamen:* A member of a distinct mixed-race group living esp in Maryland, Virginia, and West Virginia; see quots. Cf **brass ankle, issue, Jackson White**

1899 in 1946 Washington Acad. Sci. *Jrl.* 36.1 **nWV,** The mixed bloods of that county are called "Guineas" under the mistaken notion that they are Guinea Negroes. **1940** Writers' Program *Guide VA* 142 **seVA,** At the eastern point of Gloucester County live a people, known as Guineamen, whose backgrounds are lost to history. These fisherfolk and truckers speak with a Middle English accent, but there is nothing in dress or mannerism to indicate their origin. Women wear sunbonnets and put on shoes only when they attend the Church of God, a Holy Roller sect. **1946** *Social Forces* 24.442 **nwMD, WV,** *Guineas of West Virginia and Maryland. . .* "Guinea" said to be an epithet applied to anything of foreign or unknown origin. Other names applied locally are "West Hill" Indians, Maileys, "Cecil" Indians, "G. and B." Indians, and "Guinea niggers." **1947** *AmSp* 22.83 **nwMD, WV,** A rather hesitant effort by a mixed-blood group to find a name . . more distinctive . . than a generalized family name which might also be found among Negroes and whites is reflected in the terms *Our People* (which the *Guineas* use of themselves, together with the name *Maleys*) and *Melungeons.* **1953** *Sun* (Baltimore MD) 25 Oct mag sec 30/5 *(Hench Coll.),* Along its shores are the aloof We-Sorts who claim descent from the Indians, the descendants of the Hessians, the Virginia Guineamen, the lately arrived Amish, and the isolated families of Dorchester county. **1963** Berry *Almost White* 19, West Virginia is the home of . . [a] hybrid people known as Guineas. They are especially concentrated in Taylor and Barbour counties, though they are found also . . in the northeast corner of the state.

3 also lower case; also *Guin(zo):* A person of southern European, esp Italian, ancestry; a person of similar appearance. **chiefly NEast** See Map *derog*

1896 *DN* 1.418 **c,seNY,** *Guinea:* an Italian. **1904** Number 1500 *Life in Sing Sing* 249, *Ginny.* An Italian. **1923** Watts *Luther Nichols* 29 **OH,** Luther had been pricked to a certain curiosity about these "ginneys" . . because he had been taken for one of them. . . nobody else . . could . . be taken for a "ginny." **1929** *AmSp* 4.372, *Guinie . . dago.* **1931** *Collier's* 10 Jan 10/3 **NYC,** I have a lot of very good friends among the Italians, and I never speak of them as wops, or guineas, or dagoes or grease balls. **1934** (1947) O'Hara *Appointment* 49, Tony Marascho, who up to that time had been known only as a tough little guinny, was matched to fight a preliminary bout. **1941** *LANE* Map 453 *(Italian)* 8 infs, **chiefly eMA,** Guinea; 1 inf, **ceMA,** Guinea-wop; 1 inf, **seCT,** Wops are from northern Italy, Guineas from southern Italy; 5 infs, **chiefly eMA,** Guinea [=Portuguese]; 3 infs, **MA,** Guinea [=any foreigner]; 1 inf, **ceMA,** Guinea [=Greek]. **1967** [illegible] 151, Guinea boats, by Maine definition, are a type of long, narrow vessels with pole masts held together with dirt and some paint, manned chiefly by nondescript crews of Portuguese and Italian fishermen from Boston and thereabouts. **1965–70** *DARE* (Qu. HH28, *Names . . for people of foreign background*) 67 Infs, **chiefly NEast,** Guinea—Italian; **FL**4, Guinea—Jew; **MA**68, Guinea—Greek; **RI**11, Guinea—Portuguese; **AL**25, Guin—Italian; **PA**94, Guinzo—Italian; (Qu. C35, *Nicknames for the different parts of your town or city*) Inf **NY**36, Guinea Town; (Qu. H42) Inf **NJ**1, Guinea sandwich; (Qu. DD7, . . *Names for cigars*) Inf **MA**15, Guinea stinker; **NY**55, Guinea stinker, a long and twisted Italian cigar; (Qu. DD27, . . *Nicknames . . for wine*) Inf **CT**10, Guinea red; (Qu. DD28b, . . *Fermented drinks . . made at home*) Inf **MA**123, Guinea wine, large Italian population makes dago or guinea wine; (Qu. HH18, . . *Insignificant or low-grade people*) Inf **MA**28, Guinea—low-class Italian person; (Qu. II25, . . *The part of a town where the poorer people . . live*) Inf **MA**71, Guinea Town. **1969** Gordone *No Place* 51 **NYC** [Black], One thing I gotta give you Ginees credit for. Sho' know how to stick together. **1975** *DARE* File **nNJ,** *Guinea-wop . .* a nickname for Italians.

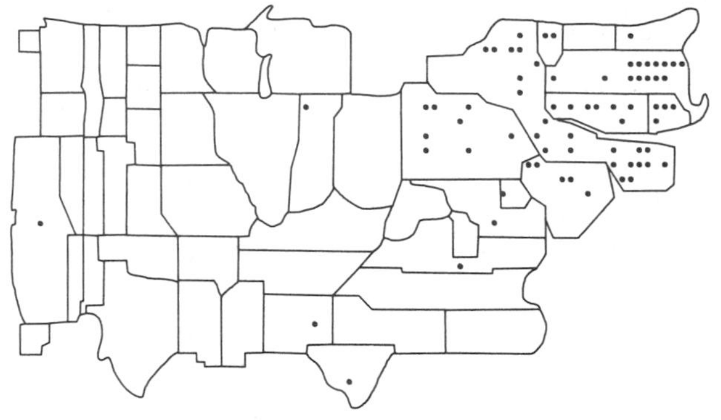

•Guinea n[1] 3 + varr (Qq. HH28, C35, H42, DD7, DD27, DD28b, HH18, II25)

4 lower case: A guy, fellow.

1902 *Bulletin* (San Francisco CA) 31 Jan 7 *(Zwilling Coll.),* [In cartoon "Clever Jack Root Meets George Gardner To-night":] The wise guinea from Chicago is "on" Root. **1914** Jackson *Criminal Slang* 39, *Guinea. . .* General usage. In the sense of a man it is synonymous with "gazabo," "gink," "mark." **1931** Faulkner *Sanctuary* 303 **MS,** "You'd better get your lawyer," the judge said. "All right," Popeye said. He turned and spoke generally into the room: "Any of you ginneys want a one-day job?" **1968** *DARE* (Qu. HH40, *Uncomplimentary words for an old man*) Inf **NV**7, Guinea.

5 lower case: Usu a guinea fowl *(Numida meleagris),* but also a chicken *(Gallus gallus)* with similar dark-speckled plumage. **widespread exc NEast, Pacific** See Map Also called **guinea chicken, guinea hen 1** Cf **guinea goose, guinea keet 1**

1925 *Book of Rural Life* 4.2477/2, White guineas are also found quite widely distributed, and are probably sports from the Pearl variety. **1965–70** *DARE* (Qu. K76, . . *Other kinds of poultry . . raised around here*) 304 Infs, **widespread exc NEast, Pacific,** Guinea(s); **NM**3, White guinea; green guinea or speckled guinea—size of a chicken; they fly, hide nests well; maybe a little smaller, but plumper than a chicken; **SC**23, Guinea—like a big quail, but flecks and white speckles; also a white guinea; ate tobacco worms.

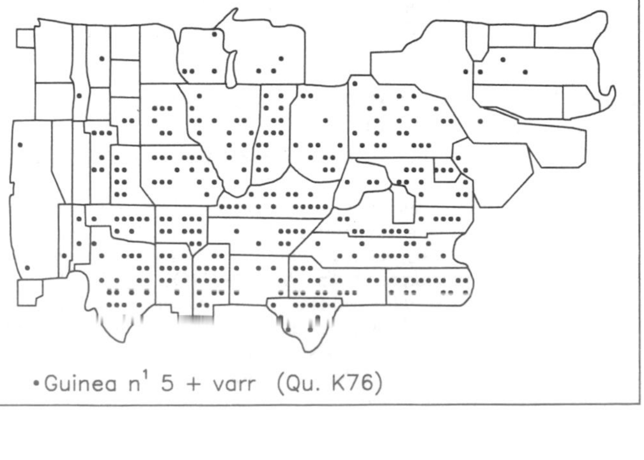

•Guinea n[1] 5 + varr (Qu. K76)

Guinea n[2] Also *Ginny Gall* [Perh in ref to *Guinea* region in West Africa] **esp Sth**

Hell; a far distant place—usu in phr *go to Guinea.*

1834 Smith *Letters Jack Downing* 151, I've wished the Bank to Guinea more than fifty times. **1908** *DN* 3.317 **eAL, wGA,** *Guinea. . .* Ballyhack. **1935** Hurston *Mules & Men* 150 **FL,** You'd pass slap thru hell proper. Jus' a bouncin' and a jumpin' and go clear to Ginny Gall, and dat's four miles south of West Hell. *Ibid* 190, Ah'm from down in Ginny-Gall where they eat cow-belly, skin and all. **1952** Brown *NC Folkl.* 1.548, *Guinea, go to. . .* A mild imprecation. Probably a euphemism for *go to gehenna.* **1965–70** *DARE* (Qu. NN26b, *Weakened substitutes for 'hell': "Go to ______!"*) Infs **LA**12, **NC**79, 82, **PA**242, **VA**75, 99, Guinea.

Guinea n[3] [Euphem for *God;* cf *EDD guiny* "An expletive"] Cf **gonnies, i prep**

See quots.

1938 *AmSp* 13.6 **seAR,** *Guinea. . .* This is an expression of the 'Old South' according to incomplete evidence. 'I guinea! That horse can run.' **1967** *DARE* (Qu. NN32, *Exclamations like 'I swear' or 'I vow': "I ______."*) Inf **NJ**2, Swear to Guinea.

guinea chicken n

=**Guinea** n[1] **5.**

1896 Read *Jucklins* 33 **nAL,** She looked exactly like a little guinea chicken. **1967–69** *DARE* (Qu. K76, . . *Kinds of poultry*) Infs **CA**97, **GA**22, **MO**12, **PA**158, 166, 226, Guinea chicken(s).

guinea corn n

1 A **sorghum** (here: *Sorghum bicolor,* usu Cernuum Group, but also Caffrorum Group). Cf **guinea grass 2**

1671 in 1897 SC Hist. Soc. *Coll.* 5.333 **SC,** Guiney Corne growes very well here. **1709** (1967) Lawson *New Voyage* 82 **NC,** *Guinea* Corn, which thrives well here, serves for [feeding hogs and poultry]. **1743** (1754) Catesby *Nat. Hist. Carolina* 2 [app] xviii, *Milium Indicum.* Bunched Guinea Corn. But little of this grain is propagated, and that chiefly by *Negroes,* who make Bread of it, and boil it in like Manner of Firmety. Its chief Use is for feeding Fowls. . . It was at first introduced from *Africa* by the *Negroes.* **1822** (1972) Deane *New Engl. Farmer* 180/1, Guinea Corn, or *Holcus Sorghum. . .* This plant is cultivated in South Carolina, and yields from sixty to eighty bushels of seed to an acre. . . The seed is used for feeding poultry, and sometimes . . boiled and eaten with milk, and is said to be equal to rice. **1835** Shirreff *Tour N. Amer.* 249, [In Illinois] I observed a few plants of Guinea corn, which its cultivators said answered as a substitute for coffee, but none of them seemed to have given it a trial. **1869** Porcher *Resources* 648 **Sth,** *Guinea corn, Indian millet, or doura corn, (Holcus sorghum.)* . . has been for a long time cultivated with great success on the plantations in the Carolinas and Georgia, and it grows throughout the Southern States. The seed [sic] are produced in great abundance—they are pounded and eaten by the negroes, and are fed to poultry. **1900** Lyons *Plant Names* 352, *S[orghum] vulgare. . .* Var. *cernuum* . . is Guinea Corn; var. *Durra* is . . in U.S. called Guinea Corn, Coffee Corn . . (used as a substitute for coffee). **1959** Carleton *Index Herb. Plants* 57, *Guinea-corn:* Holcus sorghum (Andropogon vulgare).

2 A **panic grass** such as *Panicum miliaceum* or *P. maximum. obs* Cf **guinea grass 1**

1775 (1962) Romans *Nat. Hist. FL* 84, They cultivate for bread all the species and varieties of the *Zea,* likewise two varieties of that species of *Panicum* vulgarly called guinea corn. **1797** Imlay *Western Terr.* 242, Panic; panicum, or guinea corn; differs from maiz in being more difficult to be reduced into food, and being of too hot a nature for brutes, especially poultry, who will become blind by eating it often.

3 =**Indian corn.**

1892 *Jrl. Amer. Folkl.* 5.105 **OH,** *Zea mays,* a species of pop-corn, with variegated ears; guinea-corn. . . Because speckled like a guinea-fowl.

guinea cypress n

A **St. John's wort** (here: *Hypericum fasciculatum*).

1941 *Torreya* 41.49, *Hypericum fasciculatum. . .* Guinea cypress, Bassenger, Fla.

guinea duck n [From the black-and-white speckled plumage; cf **Guinea** n[1] **5**]

The common **loon** *(Gavia immer).*

1917 (1923) *Birds Amer.* 1.12, Loon *Gavia immer. . .* Guinea Duck. **1946** Hausman *Eastern Birds* 62, Common Loon *Gavia immer immer. . .* Guinea Duck. **1951** Pough *Audubon Water Bird* 331, Guinea duck. *See* Common loon.

guinea goose n

A guinea fowl *(Numida meleagris).*

1968 *DARE* (Qu. K76, . . *Other kinds of poultry*) Inf **MD**20, Guinea geese—blue with white dots, or white—size of chicken.

guinea grass n

1 A **panic grass** (here: *Panicum maximum*). Cf **guinea corn 2**

1785 (1925) Washington *Diaries* 2.360, Sowed the Guinea grass seed sent me. **1855** Amer. Inst. NYC *Annual Rept. for 1854* 623, About the year 1755, also, Mr. Henry Laurens, of Charleston, imported from remote parts of the globe, . . olives, capers, limes, ginger, Guinea-grass. **1872** Schele de Vere *Americanisms* 408, *Guinea-Grass* (Panicum maximum) has only lately made its way into the United States, having been imported from the West Indies, where it has long been cultivated mainly to furnish fodder for horses. **1901** Mohr *Plant Life AL* 135, Cattail millet, Hungarian grass, and the so-called Johnson grass . . furnish green forage and hay crops throughout the summer; to which, near the coast, can be added . . the genuine Guinea grass *(Panicum jumentorum).* **1937** U.S. Forest Serv. *Range Plant Hdbk.* G89, Under irrigation, in the warmer parts of the Southwest and California, Guinea grass [=*Panicum maximum*] probably would be a valuable forage crop, as six to eight cuttings a year of excellent hay can be made. **1950** Hitchcock–Chase *Manual Grasses* 695, *Guinea grass. . .* Southern Florida, and southern Texas. . . Much of the green feed cut for forage is this species. **1976** Bailey–Bailey *Hortus Third* 816, *[Panicum] maximum. . .* Guinea grass.

2 also *false guinea grass:* =**Johnson grass.**

1887 Beal *Grasses N. Amer.* 1.172, *S[orghum] halapense . . Johnson Grass. . .* It has sometimes been called *Guinea grass,* though this name has more generally been applied to another, *Panicum jumentorum.* **1889** Vasey *Ag. Grasses* 36, *Sorghum halepense* [sic] (Johnson Grass; Mean's Grass) . . has been called. . . Alabama Guinea Grass. **1895** Gray–Bailey *Field Botany* 469, *Sorghum Halapense. . . Johnson Grass. Guinea Grass* (erroneously). **1914** Georgia *Manual Weeds* 22, *Johnson-grass. . .* False Guinea-grass. **1935** (1943) Muenscher *Weeds* 157, False Guinea-grass. . . Perennial, reproducing by seeds and extensive rootstocks. **1968** *DARE* (Qu. S8, *A common kind of wild grass that grows in fields: it spreads by sending out long underground roots, and it's hard to get rid of*) Inf **LA**15, Guinea grass.

3 A **lady's thumb** (here: *Polygonum persicaria*).

1966 *DARE* Wildfl QR Pl.47B Inf **TX**34, Guinea grass.

guinea grinder See **grinder 3**

guinea hen n

1 =**Guinea** n[1] **5. chiefly Nth, West** See Map

1806 (1970) Webster *Compendious Dict.* 137, *Guineahen* . . a fowl of the gallinaceous kind from Africa. **1819** Dana *Geog. Sketches* 53, The *Praira Hen. . .* in shape is more like the guinea hen. **1883** (1885) Allen *New Amer. Farm Book* 494, The Guinea hen . . is beautifully and uniformly speckled but occasionally . . white on the breast. **1912** Nicholson *Hoosier Chron.* 259 **IN,** The roasting of the guinea hen would require thirty minutes the waiter warned them. **1965–70** *DARE* (Qu. K76) 96 Infs, **chiefly Nth, West,** Guinea hen(s); **CT**14, Guinea hens—speckled chickens; they make a lot of noise when a hawk comes around; **MN**12, Guinea hens—a speckled hen with a short tail and a small neck

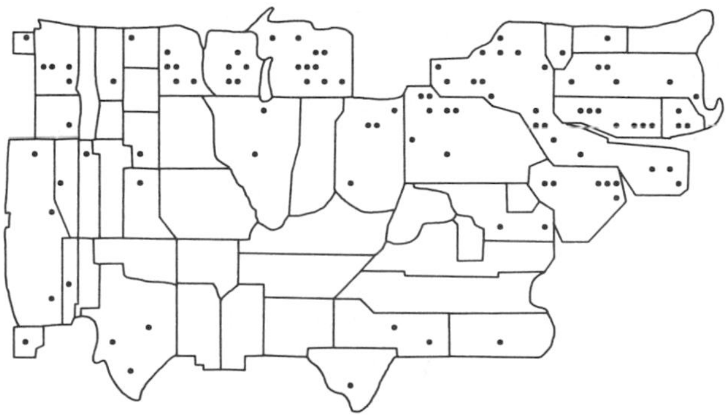

•guinea hen 1 (Qu. K76)

and head; **MA**51, Guinea hens—speckled black and white like a small turkey; tail turns down rather than up; **NE**11, Guinea hens—some rub them for good luck; they say they'll keep the coyote away; **NY**79, Guinea hens—short, plump, red head, gray and white feathers; shouts something like "buckwheat."

2 See **water guinea.**

guinea hornet See **guinea wasp**

guinea keet n Also *keet*

1 also sp *(guinea) keat:* A guinea fowl *(Numida meleagris).* [See quot 1859] **esp C Atl** Cf **guinea hen 1**

1859 (1968) Bartlett *Americanisms* 184, *Guinea-keet,* or simply *Keet.* A name given in some localities to the Guinea fowl, and probably derived from its cry. **1894** *Outing* 276/1 **VA,** The Guinea keets, warned by strange instinct, have left their haunts in the box wood. **1899** Bergen *Animal Lore* 61, Keets, young Guinea fowls. *Chestertown, Md.* **1899** (1912) Green *VA Folk-Speech* 210, *Guinea-keet...* A guinea fowl. **1924** U.S. Dept. Ag. *Farmers' Bulletin* 1377.9, In some markets guineas are called "keets" or "guinea keets." **1940** Writers' Program *Guide MD* 8, Contributions made by Negroes to Maryland vernacular are highly vivid and colorful. For instance,.. the domestic guinea-fowl is a 'guinea keat,' or merely a 'keat.' **1966** *DARE* (Qu. K76,.. *Other kinds of poultry)* Inf **DC**5, Guinea keet, keets. **1986** Pederson *LAGS Concordance (Fowl)* 1 inf, **csGA,** A keet—a small guinea.

2 The American **coot** n[1] **1** *(Fulica americana).* [Cf **Guinea** n[1] **1**] Cf **water guinea**

1966–68 *DARE* (Qu. Q7, *Names and nicknames for other kinds of game birds around here)* Inf **DC**8, Guinea keet ['gɪnɪˌkit]; **IN**19, **MO**3, Keet; (Qu. Q9, *The bird that looks like a small, dull-colored duck and is commonly found on ponds and lakes)* Infs **IN**19, **MO**3, Keet [kit].

guinea melon n Also *guinea muskmelon, ~ watermelon*

A melon (here: either *Citrullus lanatus* or *Cucumis melo*); see quots.

1709 (1967) Lawson *New Voyage* 83 **NC,** Of Musk-Melons we have very large and good, and several Sorts, as the Golden, Green, Guinea, and Orange. **1908** *DN* 3.317 **eAL, wGA,** *Guinea (water-)melon...* A small worthless melon that grows voluntarily in cultivated fields. **1966** *DARE* (Qu. I26,.. *Kinds of melons)* Inf **SC**3, Guinea melons.

Guineamen See **Guinea** n[1] **2**

guinea muskmelon See **guinea melon**

Guinea negro See **Guinea** n[1] **1, 2**

guinea pea n

The seed of the **crab's eye.**

1889 Larcom *New Engl. Girlhood* 95 **neMA,** I wonder what has become of those many, many little red "guinea-peas" we had to play with! It never seemed as if they really belonged to the vegetable world, notwithstanding their name.

guinea perch n

=**Rio Grande perch.**

1946 Stilwell *Hunting in TX* 112, He's called a guinea perch because his coloring is bluish black with white specks, a lot like a guinea fowl's... The guinea perch is native to the Rio Grande country... He's a fine scrapper and a ready striker and is fine eating. **1967** *DARE* (Qu. P1,.. *Freshwater fish.. good to eat)* Inf **TX**19, Guinea perch—Rio Grande perch.

guinea sapsucker See **guinea woodpecker 2**

guinea seed n

A grain of paradise *(Aframomum melequeta).*

c1938 in 1970 Hyatt *Hoodoo* 2.1354 **seLA,** Now, yo' take a seed dat dey call a guinea seed. It's a little bit of red seed. Yo' take dat.. lemon, red vinegah an' guinea seed, an' yo' take hot stuff [Hyatt: pepper sauce] an' yo' put into dat lemon.

guinea snake n

Prob a **kingsnake** (here: *Lampropeltis* spp).

1966 *DARE* (Qu. P25,.. *Kinds of snakes)* Inf **MS**47, Guinea snake.

guinea squash n [**Guinea** n[1] **1**] **chiefly SC**

An eggplant *(Solanum melongena* var *esculentum).*

1847 Rutledge *Carolina Housewife* 101, To fry guinea squash, or egg-plant. **1895** Gray–Bailey *Field Botany* 314, *S[olanum] Melongena... Eggplant, Aubergine, Guinea Squash.* Cult. for the large oblong or ovate violet-colored or white esculent fruit. **1930** *DN* 6.81 **cSC,** *Guinea Squash...* Egg plant. Both terms are used, though Guinea Squash is the more common. **1950** *PADS* 14.33 **SC,** *Guinea squash...* The eggplant. **1966** *DARE* FW Addit **SC,** Guinea squash: eggplant. **1966–67** *DARE* (Qu. I4,.. *Vegetables.. less commonly grown)* Infs **SC**4, 9, 11, 21, 26, 38, 43, Guinea squash; (Qu. I23,.. *Kinds of squash)* Inf **SC**4, Guinea squash. **1980** *Des Moines Register* (IA) 16 Nov mag sec 20/3, Eggplant has several names, too. It is aubergine and bunjal and mad apple and—to people who don't care how they talk—it's guinea squash.

guinea squat n For varr see quots **esp AL, FL, GA**

A children's game; see quot 1966.

1908 *DN* 3.317 **eAL, wGA,** *Guinea, guinea, squat...* A children's game. **1965–70** *DARE* (Qu. EE1, *What games do children play around here, in which they form a ring, and either sing or recite a rhyme?)* Infs **AL**6, 10, 15, 20, **FL**8, 26, **NY**120, Guinea squat; **FL**18, **GA**3, Guinea guinea (all) squat. **1966** *DARE* Tape **AL**6, [FW:] Did you ever play guinea squat? [Aux Inf:] Little guinea pigs, big guinea all squat down. They all join hands and march around and when they say "all squat down," they all squat down. [Inf:] The last one that squats is fined. [Aux Inf:] Well, ring around the rosy is just about the same thing as big guinea little guinea all squat.

guinea turnip n

A **jack-in-the-pulpit.**

1968 *DARE* (Qu. S1,.. *Other names.. for the jack-in-the-pulpit)* Inf **CT**2, Guinea turnip.

guinea wasp n Also *guinea hornet* **chiefly S Atl, Gulf States** See Map

=**yellow jacket.**

1966–70 *DARE* (Qu. R21,.. *Other kinds of stinging insects)* 24 Infs, **chiefly S Atl, Gulf States,** Guinea wasp; **GA**13, Guinea hornet. **1968** *DARE* FW Addit **LA**31, Guinea wasp—a small yellow-marked wasp; the same one which is called yellow jacket further south. **1986** Pederson *LAGS Concordance,* 58 infs, **Gulf Region,** Guinea wasp.

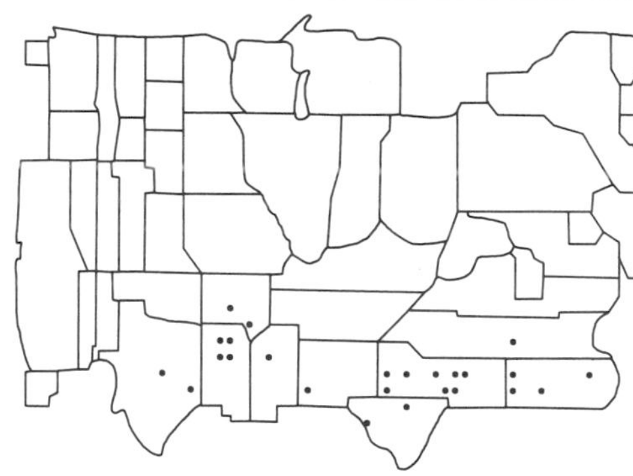

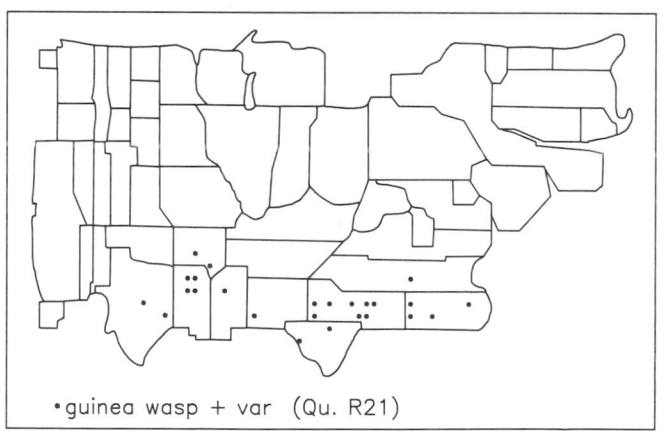

•guinea wasp + var (Qu. R21)

guinea watermelon See **guinea melon**

guinea woodpecker n [From the black-and-white plumage; cf **Guinea** n[1] **5**] Cf **little guinea woodpecker, nigger guinea**

1 also *big guinea woodpecker:* =**hairy woodpecker.**

1899 Bergen *Animal Lore* 61 **nOH,** Guinea woodpecker, family *Picidæ.* **1917** (1923) *Birds Amer.* 2.140, *Hairy Woodpecker—Dryobates villosus villosus...* Guinea Woodpecker. **1930** OK Univ. Biol. Surv. *Pub.* 2.1.118, *Dryobates villosus villosus...* Hairy Woodpecker... Local names: Speckled woodpecker,.. guinea woodpecker. **1932** Howell *FL Bird Life* 310, *Southern Hairy Woodpecker: Dryobates villosus...* Big Guinea Woodpecker. **1955** Forbush–May *Birds* 302, *Southern Hairy Woodpecker... Other name:* Big Guinea Woodpecker... Breeds in South Atlantic and Gulf States.

2 also *guinea sapsucker:* =**red-bellied woodpecker.**

1920 Shirling *Birds Kansas City MO* 105, The Red-bellied or Guinea Woodpecker is fairly common in the deeper woods of the Park during summer. **1932** Howell *FL Bird Life* 307, *Red-bellied Woodpecker... Other Names..* Guinea Sapsucker. **1955** Forbush–May *Birds* 297, *Red-bellied Woodpecker...* Guinea Sapsucker... About size of Hairy Woodpecker; black and white *barred back* and wings and *gray under parts..;* 'red belly' not usually visible.

Guiney, Guinie, Guinny See **Guinea** n[1]

Guinzo See **Guinea** n[1] **3**

guisache See **huisache**

guitar n Usu |gɪˈtɑr, gɪˈtɑ(r)|; also **chiefly Sth, S Midl, esp Appalachians** |ˈgɪtɑr, ˈgitɑr|; for addit varr see quots Pronc-spp *geetar, git-ar, gittar, gitter* Cf Intro "Language Changes" IV.2
Std sense, var forms.

1897 *KS Univ. Qrly.* (ser B) 6.88 **neKS,** *Git-ar:* guitar. **1928** *AmSp* 3.407 **Ozarks,** The hillman usually places a strong emphasis upon the first syllable of . . *guitar.* **1934** Carmer *Stars Fell on AL* 44, Monkey's brother is his *guit*ar picker. **1942** Hall *Smoky Mt. Speech* 56 **eTN, wNC,** *Guitar* is still prevailingly [ˈgɪˌtaɚ]. **1942** *New Yorker* 5 Dec 52/1 **TX** [Black], I always carry a gitter in my truck. **1943** *Time* 4 Oct 49/1, All over the country were the Appalachian accents of the geetar. **c1960** *Wilson Coll.* **csKY,** Guitar is often [ˈgɪtˌtɑr]. **1961** *Mt. Life* Spring 18 **sAppalachians,** You better take a coat along with you, Alan, and something to cover your gittar if it rains. **1966–67** *DARE* FW Addit **cwNC,** *Guitar* pronounced [ˈgɪtɑr, ˈgitɑr]. **1975** Newell *If Nothin' Don't Happen* 27 **nwFL,** He had a old gittar and when he felt real good he used to sing a Indian song.

gulch n

1 A small, steep-sided valley; a ravine or gully. **scattered, but esp CA** See Map

1859 (1942) Patterson *Travel Diary* 195 **CO,** It is thought that all the gulch streams will dry up by the first of august. **1860** (1936) Hawley *Diary* 19.341 **WI,** We camped half way up the gulch [in Colorado]. **1860** (1937) Lewis *Diary Pike's Peak* 14.213 **PA,** Travelled up gulch, crossing a brook very often with muddy and steep banks. **1905** *DN* 3.11 **CT,** *Gulch.* . . A deep ravine. **1910** Hart *Vigilante Girl* 325 *(DAE)* **CA,** Here the original prospectors had found a rich gulch on the very edge of the desert. **1923** Cook *50 Yrs.* 75 **OK,** Suddenly we came to a gulch about fifteen feet deep. **1925** [see **3** below]. **1950** *AmSp* 25.166 **CO,** A 'gulch' is wider and deeper than a 'gully,' which, in turn, is deeper than a 'draw.' **1958** McCulloch *Woods Words* 75 **Pacific NW,** *Gulch.* . . A small steep-sided valley. **1965–70** *DARE* (Qu. C21, *A deep place cut in sloping ground by running water*) 37 Infs, **scattered, but esp CA,** Gulch; (Qu. C1) Inf **CA**137, Gulch; **CO**35, Gulch—dry sometimes. **1968** Adams *Western Words* 135, *Gulch*—A ravine, canyon, or gully; the deep and narrow bed of an intermittent stream. **1968** *DARE* Tape **CA**100, An' I was workin' on one side of the gulch.

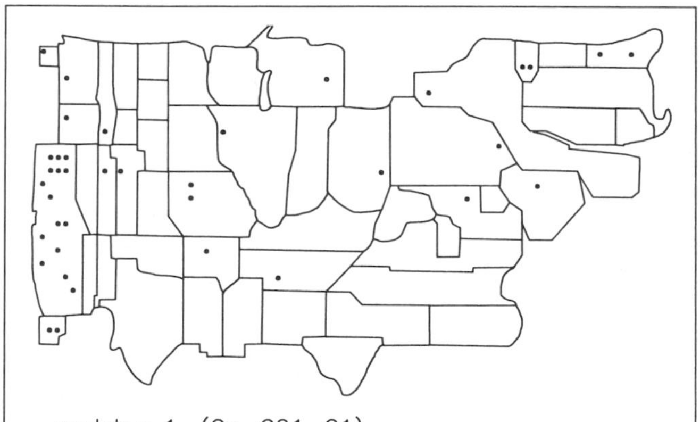

•gulch n 1 (Qq. C21, C1)

2 See quots. Cf **gap** n[1] **1, gully 1, 3, notch**

1946 Attwood *Length ME* 14 [Geographical terms], *Gulch*—A valley or notch. **1965–70** *DARE* (Qu. C15, *A place in mountains or high hills where you can get through without climbing over the top*) Infs **IN**29, **LA**15, **NE**5, **NJ**8, **OR**13, **UT**3, **WA**2, Gulch; (Qu. C19, . . *Low land running between hills*) Infs **CA**137, **CO**35, Gulch.

3 Used as the last element in place-names; by ext, used in derisive nicknames for places.

1872 Twain *Curious Dream* 45 **NV,** The post route from Indian Gulch . . changed partly to the old Mormon trail. **1925** Stuart *40 Yrs.* 2.83 **neMT** (as of 1868), A party of Piegans appeared at Confederate gulch, drove off all the horses and fired a parting shot at some miners working in a gulch just below town. **1942** Berrey–Van den Bark *Amer. Slang* 51.5, *Broadway, N.Y.C.* . . Beer Gulch . . Gin Gulch. **1965–70** *DARE* (Qu. C33, . . *Joking names* . . *for an out-of-the-way place, or a very unimportant place*) Inf **CO**47, Neighbor's Gulch; (Qu. C34, *Nicknames for nearby settlements, villages, or districts*) Inf **NM**11, Calvert's Gulch; **MN**2, Gully Gulch; **CA**195, Hangman's Gulch; **CA**211, Hungry Gulch; (Qu. C35, *Nicknames for the different parts of your town or city*) Inf **KS**19, Goat's Gulch; **ID**4, Poverty Gulch; (Qu. D39, . . *Nicknames* . . *for a small eating place where the food is not especially good*) Inf **CA**82, Ptomaine Gulch; **OR**1, Ulcer Gulch. **1970** *DARE* Tape **CA**186, Christian Brothers was over on a place we call Gower Gulch at Gower and Sunset.

gulch v Also with *down* [Engl, Scots dial; cf *EDD*]
See quots.

1848 Bartlett *Americanisms* 167, *To gulch.* To swallow voraciously. . . In low language this word is still heard in New England. **1968** *DARE* (Qu. H11a, *If somebody eats rapidly and noisily, you say he* ———) Inf **MN**23, Gulches it down.

gulch grape n Cf **arroyo grape**
Any of three **grapes:** *Vitis acerifolia, V. arizonica,* or *V. treleasei.*

1938 Van Dersal *Native Woody Plants* 290, *Vitis treleasei.* . . *Gulch grape.* . . A vine or shrub; much branched; scarcely climbing. *Ibid* 337, Grape, . . Gulch *(Vitis longii, Vitis treleasei).* **1970** Correll *Plants TX* 1019, *Vitis arizonica.* . . *Canyon grape, gulch grape.* . . Grapes . . black and sometimes with a thin bloom, the skin thin, the pulp juicy and sweet.

gulf n

1 =**gulch** n **1. scattered, but esp NY**

1787 in 1940 *AmSp* 15.267 **VA,** Thence West Twenty seven degrees South 700 poles to the Gulf at New River. **1817** in 1918 IN Hist. Soc. *Pub.* 328 **NY,** We then went up the creek through the weeds and bushes and over some bad gulfs until we were fatigued. **1839** Kirkland *New Home* 276 **NY,** I own two hundred and seventy-odd acres jist round there; and that 'ere gulf is part on't. **1895** *DN* 1.397 **NY,** *Gulf:* a small gorge or ravine, usually narrow and having steep sides. **1901** *DN* 2.141 **ceNY,** *Gulf.* . . A creek with steep wooded banks. *Ibid* **cNY,** A creek with steep banks wooded and more or less rocky, the bed being somewhat difficult of access. **1946** Attwood *Length ME* 14 [Geographical terms], *Gulf.* . . A deep chasm in the earth's surface. **1975** *DARE* File **cwNY,** *Gulf* is still commonly used in Ripley, New York. So common that when I mentioned it a few years ago my hostess said she never thought of it as a gulch. It had always been the gulf.

2 See quot. Cf **hole** n **2**

1969 *DARE* (Qu. C19, . . *Low land running between hills*) Inf **TN**37, Gulf—a gulf is a valley, more or less circular, usually found in a wild, wooded area. To get in and out of a gulf one must climb the mountain—there is no natural exit.

gulf bird n
The red phalarope *(Phalaropus fulicarius).*

1917 (1923) *Birds Amer.* 1.217/1, Red phalarope. . . Gulf-bird. . . migrates along both coasts of United States. **1946** Hausman *Eastern Birds* 296, *Red Phalarope.* . . *Other Names* . . Gulf Bird. **1956** MA Audubon Soc. *Bulletin* 40.21, *Red Phalarope.* . . Gulf Bird (Mass. Of the Gulf of St. Lawrence.)

gulf cloud n Also *gulf coast rock* [In ref to the *Gulf* of Mexico] **TX**

1965–70 *DARE* (Qu. B8, *When clouds come and go all day, you say it's* ———) Inf **TX**1, Gulf clouds—floating past; **TX**11, Gulf clouds; (Qu. B10, . . *Long trailing clouds high in the sky*) Inf **TX**56, Gulf clouds; (Qu. B11, . . *Other kinds of clouds*) Inf **TX**13, Gulf clouds—come from south, no rain; **TX**43, Gulf clouds—fast-moving, low, thin; in the morning; **TX**54, Gulf clouds—just in the morning; **TX**35, Gulf clouds; **TX**100, Gulf coast rocks—low, fast-moving clouds in waves.

gulf trout n
A **weakfish** (here: *Cynoscion nebulosus*).

1967 *DARE* (Qu. P2, . . *Saltwater fish* . . *good to eat*) Inf **TX**14, Gulf trout.

gulfweed n [*Gulf* of Mexico + *weed*]
A floating seaweed of the genus *Sargassum,* usu *S. bacciferum.*

1674 Josselyn *Two Voyages* 40, We met with abundance of Sea-weeds called Gulf-weed coming out of the Bay of *Mexico.* **1726** in 1887 Franklin *Complete Wks.* 1.123, We took up several branches of gulf-weed (with which the sea is spread all over, from the Western Isles to the coast of America). **1871** *Harper's New Mth. Mag.* July 188/2 **sFL,** The gulf-weed derives its nourishment directly from the sea. **1901** Arnold

Sea-Beach 34, The gulfweed lives . . a pelagic life and adapts itself to the conditions of the floating state. **1942** Hylander *Plant Life* 43, Gulfweed *(Sargassum)* looks like a small flowering plant instead of a species of Brown Algae; the main "stem" has flattened leaf-like outgrowths and special berry-like air bladders which serve to keep the seaweed afloat. **1949** Palmer *Nat. Hist.* 46, *Gulfweed. Sargassum filipendula*. . . This species grows attached to shells and stones in relatively quiet water from low-tide level to 100 ft. deep. **1989** *DARE* File **swFL,** Sometimes an onshore wind brings in so much gulfweed that the fishing boats can hardly get out through it.

gull n

Std: a bird of the family Laridae: see **Franklin's gull, glaucous gull, gray gull 2, great black-backed gull, herring gull, kittiwake, laughing gull, little black-headed gull, old lighthouse shitter, ring-billed gull, Sabine's gull, sea pigeon, shitass, spitting-ass, square-tail gull, surf gull, tern, white-headed gull**

gull-billed tern n

Std: a pigeon-sized **tern** *(Gelochelidon nilotica)* with a stout black bill. Also called **marsh tern, striker**

gull chaser See **gull hunter**

gulley jumper See **gully jumper**

gull grass n

=**bedstraw.**

1900 Lyons *Plant Names* 167, *Galium*. . . Gull-grass.

gull hunter n Also *gull chaser, ~ teaser* [See quot 1917]

Usu a **jaeger,** rarely a **tern.**

[**1831** Richardson *Fauna Boreali-Amer.* 429, The Pomarine Jager or Gull-hunter is not uncommon. . . It retires from the north in the winter, and makes its first appearance at Hudson's Bay in May, coming in from seaward.] **1884** U.S. Bur. Fisheries *Rept. for 1882* 324, *Gull-chasers* (Genus *Stercorarius*). *Ibid* 327, The jaeger rarely attacks the larger species of gulls, though I have seen the common gull . . fiercely chased by a jaeger when the gull was flying away with food in its beak. **1889** *Century Dict.* 2655, *Gull-teaser*. . . A bird that teases gulls, as a tern or jaeger. Also called *gull-chaser*. **1898** (1900) Davie *Nests N. Amer. Birds* 25, Another of the falcon-like sea fowls [=the pomarine jaeger], commonly called Gull Hunter by the fishermen. **1903** Dawson *Birds OH* 2.543, Pomarine Jaeger. . . *Stercorarius pomarinus*. . . Gull-Hunter. **1917** (1923) *Birds Amer.* 1.33, *Pomarine Jaeger*. . . *Other Names.—* Gull Hunter. *Ibid* 36/1, *Long-tailed Jaeger*. . . *Other Names* . . Gull-teaser. . . Like the other members of the genus, this Jaeger is a persistent and merciless robber of the smaller Gulls, swooping down on them and forcing them to disgorge fish or mollusks they have taken, and capturing the food as it falls. **1925** (1928) Forbush *Birds MA* 1.52, *Stercorarius pomarinus*. . . Gull chaser. *Ibid* 55, *Stercorarius parasiticus*. . . Gull chaser. **1946** Hausman *Eastern Birds* 300, Pomarine Jaeger *Stercorarius pomarinus*. . . Gull Hunter, Gull Chaser. **1956** MA Audubon Soc. *Bulletin* 40.21 **ME, MA,** *Pomarine Jaeger*. Gull-chaser (. . Jaegers harass gulls until they disgorge food, which the jaeger then seizes in the air.) . . *Parasitic Jaeger*. Gull-chaser . . *Long-tailed Jaeger*. Gull-chaser.

gullick n Also sp *gullock, gulluck* [Pronc varr of *gullet;* cf Intro "Language Changes" IV.4 and *EDD gullock* "To swallow greedily"] Cf **gullikin stick**

1859 Taliaferro *Fisher's R.* 29 **nwNC,** He was particularly fond of . . turnip greens and "hog's gullicks." **1899** (1912) Green *VA Folk-Speech* 210, *Gulluck*. . . Gullet; the throat. Gullock. **1952** Brown *NC Folkl.* 1.548, *Gullick* ['gʌlɪk]. . . *Gullet*. . . Illiterate.

gullie n [Prob **gull** + dimin *-ie*]

=**tern.**

1951 Pough *Audubon Water Bird* 332, Gullie. *See* Tern.

gullikin stick n [Pronc-sp for **gulleting;* cf **gullick**]

1956 Rayford *Whistlin' Woman* 215 **AL,** On snapper boats, we use a gullikin stick. Looks like a forked broom handle. You use it to take the hook out of a snapper's throat when he swallows the bait too deep.

gullock See **gullick**

gullop v[1] See **gollop** v

gullop v[2] See **gulp** v **1**

gullop n See **gollop** n

gull teaser See **gull hunter**

gulluck See **gullick**

gullup v See **gulp** v **1**

gullup n See **gollop** n

gully n

1 See quot. [By ext from std sense] **chiefly NEast** See Map Cf **gulch** n **2**

1965–70 *DARE* (Qu. C15, *A place in mountains or high hills where you can get through without climbing over the top*) 13 Infs, **chiefly NEast,** Gully.

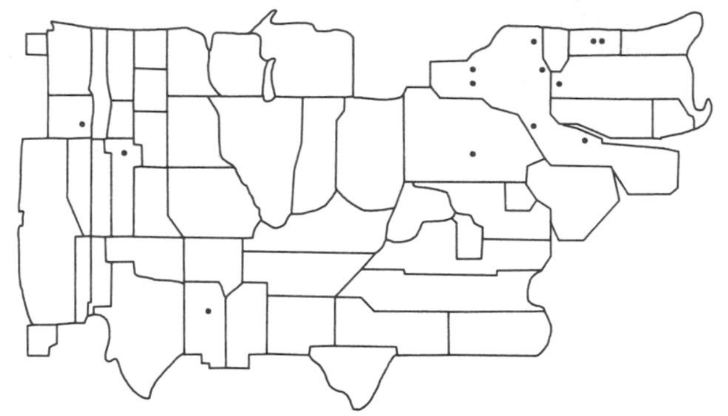

•gully 1 (Qu. C15)

2 See quot. **chiefly NEast, N Cent** See Map

1965–70 *DARE* (Qu. N30, . . *A sudden short dip in a road*) 23 Infs, **chiefly NEast, N Cent,** Gully. [19 of 23 Infs old]

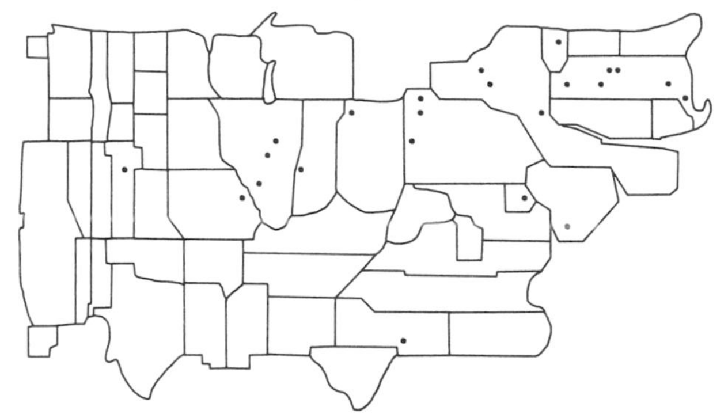

•gully 2 (Qu. N30)

3 See quots. [*EDD gully* sb.[2] 1 "a narrow brook or stream"] **esp Gulf States** Cf **gulch** n **2**

1966–68 *DARE* (Qu. C1, . . *A small stream of water not big enough to be a river*) Infs **AL**1, **FL**35, **LA**27, Gully. **1968** *DARE* Tape **GA**30, There was a little ol' creek, what we call a gully, that run out from the swamp. **1986** Pederson *LAGS Concordance (Creek)* 5 infs, **Gulf Region,** Gully (*or* gullies).

4 also *gully spout:* =**eaves trough. scattered, but esp Gulf States**

1965–70 *DARE* (Qu. D28, *What hangs below the edge of the roof to carry off rain-water?*) Infs **AL**25, **GA**17, **MS**85, Gully; (Qu. D29, *The pipe that takes the collected rain-water down to the ground or to a storage tank*) Infs **FL**26, **IL**15, **NY**210, Gully; **MS**79, Gully [FW sugg]; **DC**11, Gully spout. **1986** Pederson *LAGS Concordance (Eaves trough)* 23 infs, **Gulf Region,** Gully (*or* gullies).

5 The gullet. [Cf *EDD gully* sb.[2] 5]

1969 *DARE* (Qu. X7, *Other names for the throat: "Some food got stuck in his ______."*) Infs **MA**59, **NY**210, Gully.

6 See **gully washer.**

gully bird See **gully martin**

gully buster, gully cutter See **gully washer**

gully dirt n **Sth, S Midl**

Fig: something worthless or contemptible.

1966–70 *DARE* (Qu. HH18, *Very insignificant or low-grade people*) Inf **VA**42, Gully dirt; (Qu. HH20c, *Of an idle, worthless person you might say, "He isn't worth ______."*) Inf **TN**53, Gully dirt; **GA**77, Sorry as gully dirt. **1984** Wilder *You All Spoken Here* 9 **Sth,** He's an empty sack: He's triflin'; no 'count; ain't worth gully dirt. **1986** Pederson *LAGS Concordance (Common, of people)* 1 inf, **seAL,** Common as gully dirt—grandmother's expression. **1989** *DARE* File **cnNC,** Anybody who fails to fit conventional norms or follow the Protestant work ethic is usually said to be "sorry as gully dirt" in some areas here.

gullygut n [*OED* →1694]

1937 *AmSp* 12.231 **NJ,** The obsolete noun *gully-gut* (a glutton) . . is still heard among negroes.

gully jumper n Also sp *gulley jumper*

1 A farmer; a rustic.

1939 *AmSp* 14.90 **eTN,** *Gully jumper.* Farmer. 'We're just poor gully jumpers.' **1951** *Courier-Jrl.* (Louisville KY) 22 Feb sec 2 **GA,** [Column by Allan Trout:] What we call ridge runners and apple knockers in Kentucky are called gulley jumpers and clod hoppers down here in Georgia. **1967** *DARE* (Qu. HH1, *Names and nicknames for a rustic or countrified person*) Inf **TN**1, Gully jumper.

2 A two-wheeled cart.

1966 *PADS* 46.26 **cnAR,** *Gully jumper*. . . A two-wheel cart. **1968** *DARE* (Qu. N41a, . . *Kinds of horse-drawn vehicles*) Inf **NC**55, Gully jumper—for 1 horse, 2 wheels.

3 A train; see quots. *joc*

1942 Berrey–Van den Bark *Amer. Slang* 774.1, *Train*. . . gully jumper. **1967** *DARE* (Qu. N37, . . *A branch railroad that is not very important or gives poor service*) Inf **TX**38, Gully jumper.

gully keeper n Cf **goalie 2**

Prob a var of the children's game prisoner's base.

1875 (1876) Twain *Tom Sawyer* 217, They had an exhausting good time playing "hi-spy", and "gully-keeper" with a crowd of their school-mates. **1970** *DARE* (Qu. EE33, . . *Outdoor games*) Inf **VA**75, Gully keeper—one in the gully, other ran across, gully keeper tried to tag one who would replace him in the gully.

gully maker See **gully washer**

gully martin n Also *gully bird* [See quot 1955]

=rough-winged swallow.

1924 Howell *Birds AL* 268, *Rough-winged Swallow* . . *Gully Martin*. . . The nests are placed in holes in cut banks, or in crevices in stone walls or cliffs. **1946** Hausman *Eastern Birds* 414, Rough-Winged Swallow *Stelgidopteryx ruficollis serripennis*. . . Gully Martin. **1955** Forbush-May *Birds* 327, Rough-Winged Swallow. . . Gully Martin. **1955** *Oriole* 20.10, Rough-Winged Swallow.—Gully Martin (it often nests in burrows in banks). **1962** Imhof *AL Birds* 364, Rough-winged Swallow—*Stelgidopteryx ruficollis*. . . Gully Martin. . . Gully Bird. . . The nest is usually in a burrow in an exposed bank, but the Rough-winged Swallow uses almost any other reasonable substitute. **1970** *DARE* (Qu. Q20, . . *Kinds of swallows and birds like them*) Inf **VA**43, Gully martin.

gullynapper See **gallinipper**

gully pour See **gully washer**

gully spout See **gully 4**

gully washer n Also *gully, gully buster, ~ cutter, ~ maker, ~ pour, ~ whopper* **widespread exc NEng, less freq Inland Nth, Pacific** See Map

A very heavy rain or the runoff it occasions.

1903 Fox *Little Shepherd* 59 **seKY,** Send us, not a gentle sizzle-sozzle, but a sod-soaker, O Lord, a gully-washer. **1912** Green *VA Folk-Speech* 210, *Gully-washer*. . . A heavy rain that washes gullys in the ground. **1923** *DN* 5.209 **swMO,** *Gully washer*. . . A heavy fall of rain. **1937** Sandoz *Slogum* 89 **NE,** They came home in a gullywasher that fell so fast it barely soaked an inch of the dry earth. But it tore the roads into long, man-deep washouts. **1949** *PADS* 11.22 **CO,** *Gully washer*. **1950** *WELS Suppl.* **csWI,** [Radio:] La Crosse had 2.01 inches of rain—a real gully washer. **1951** *AmSp* 26.74 **sIL,** *Gully-washer*. A graphic term that suggests the damage done to the hill-dweller's land by a heavy rain. **1952** Brown *NC Folkl.* 1.548, *Gully-washer*. **1954** *PADS* 21.29 **SC,** *Gully buster*. . . A heavy downpour of rain. Northern and eastern region. **1958** McCulloch *Woods Words* 75 **Pacific NW,** *Gully-washer*. **1965–70** *DARE* (Qu. B25, . . *Joking names . . for a very heavy rain*) 216 Infs, **widespread exc NEng, less freq Inland Nth, Pacific,** Gully washer; **MS**11, Gully pour; **NC**31, Trash mover and gully washer; (Qu. B27, *A sudden rush of water coming from heavy rain*) 100 Infs, **chiefly Midl, Sth,** Gully washer; **MS**32, **MO**22, Gully; **OH**45, 50, Gully maker; **NC**20, Gully cutter; (Qu. B24, . . *A sudden, very heavy rain*) 18 Infs, **scattered, but esp Midl, Sth, SW,** Gully washer; **OH**50, Gully maker; (Qu. B26, *When it's raining very heavily, you say, "It's raining ______."*) Infs **IN**3, **IA**36, Gully washer. **1965** *DARE* File **neGA,** Gully whopper. **1975** Zwinger *Run River* 110 **UT,** The dugway . . is still visible, beveled into the shale cliff, . . a narrow shelf that must have rutted deeper with every gully washer. **1984** *DARE* File **ID,** Gully washer.

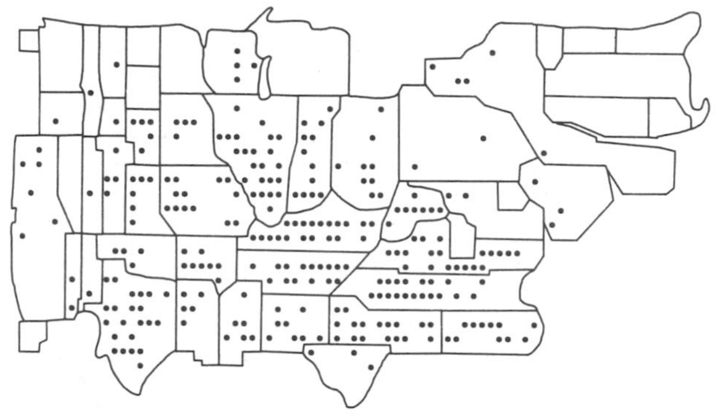

•gully washer + varr (Qq. B25, B27, B24, B26)

gulp v

1 pronc-spp *gullop, gullup:* To belch; hence n *gulp* a belch. Cf **gollop** v, Intro "Language Changes" I.8

1894 *DN* 1.341 **wCT,** *Gullop:* to belch. **1903** *DN* 2.298 **Cape Cod MA** (as of a1857), *Gulp*. . . Pronounced gullup. To belch. . . A belch.

2 also with *up:* To vomit copiously.

1966–68 *DARE* (Qu. BB18, *To vomit a great deal at once*) Inf **WA**18, Gulp; **IL**4, **NY**107, Gulp (it) up.

gulp n See **gulp v 1**

gulp up See **gulp v 2**

gulver's root n Also *gulver (root)*

=culver's root 1.

1869 Porcher *Resources* 712, Gulver's root. **1938–57** *Hall Coll.* **wNC, eTN,** Gulver root. It was used as a tonic and laxative. . . Gulver . . a kind of plant used in the treatment of liver and stomach ailments. . . Gulver . . old plant name. Dig the roots and make a tea. . . Gulver . . they used hit for some kind of fever.

gum n^1, v^1 Pronc-spp **chiefly Nth** *goom(b)* (See Map), also *gawm* [The form *goom* is the expected reflex of OE *gôma* inside of the mouth, and survives in Engl dial.]

Std senses, var forms.

1907 *DN* 3.188 **seNH,** My gooms are all red. **1907** *DN* 3.244 **eME,** *Goomb*. . . *Goom* with adventitious *b*. **1910** *DN* 3.442 **cwNY,** My

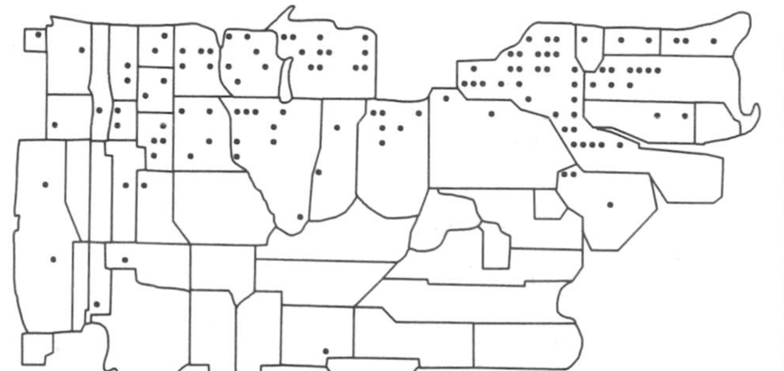

•goom + var (at <u>gum</u> n^1, v^1) (Qq. X11, DD3b)

gooms are sore. **1923** *DN* 5.208 **swMO,** *Goom.* **1932** Randolph *Ozark Mt. Folks* 39, She had that 'ar bridle onto me, with a big iron bit a-cuttin' up my gooms somethin' turrible! **1940** *AmSp* 15.49 **sAppalachians,** The sound . . [ʌ] is replaced by [u] in *gums:* gooms. **1950** *WELS Suppl.,* "Yep, I'm a-goomin' it now." Old-fashioned. **1953** Randolph–Wilson *Down in Holler* 250 **Ozarks,** *Gum: v.t.* . . Sometimes pronounced *goom.* **1959** *VT Hist.* new ser 27.139, *Gum* [gum]. . . Common among uneducated persons. **1965–70** *DARE* (Qu. X11, *What do you call the flesh that the teeth are set in*) 942 Infs, **widespread,** Gum(s); 118 Infs, **chiefly Nth, N Midl,** Gooms; NY69, 233, Goom; NY61, VA24, Gawms [gɔmz]; (Qu. DD3b, *How do people take snuff around here?*) Inf NY70, Rub it on their gooms. **1966** *DARE* Tape **MI**19, His lip and front of the goom was repaired when he was two weeks old.

gum n^2

1 See **gum tree.**

2 also attrib: A section of a hollow log or tree trunk.

1817 Bradbury *Travels* 286 **seIL,** Hollow trees were . . cut across in different lengths, and used by the first settlers as tubs to hold grain, &c. Any portion so cut off is called a gum, a name probably arising from the almost exclusive application of the gum tree to these purposes. **a1864** Gesner *Coal, Petrol.,* etc. (1865) 33 *(OED),* When the soil is not deep, a circular excavation is made down to the rock bed, and a hollow log, or 'gum', as it is called, is placed in it on one end. **1879** *Harper's New Mth. Mag.* Sept 508/2 **GA,** The gravel [was washed] . . by running it through sluice-boxes and splint baskets into a "gum rocker," which was nothing but a split and hollowed out log a dozen or so feet in length. **1899** (1912) Green *VA Folk-Speech* 210, *Gum.* . . A section of a hollow log or tree. **1917** *DN* 4.413 **seKY, wNC,** *Gum.* . . A hollow log. **1933** *AmSp* 8.1.49 **Ozarks,** *Gum crib.* . . A cradle made from a section cut out of a hollow log.

3 Any of var containers, implements, devices, etc, made (or orig made) from **2** above, spec:

a A box, barrel, or cask.

1767 in 1941 Woodward *Ploughs & Politicks* 297 **seNJ,** They [=potatoes] are kept over in Gums or boxes putt in the Chimney corner packed in Dry Sand. **1843** *Amer. Pioneer* 2.450 **ceOH** (as of c1800), Gums are hollow trees cut off with puncheons pinned on, or fitted in one end, to answer in the place of barrels. **1851** Hooper *Widow Rugby's Husband* 42 **AL,** A dozen fowls clustered on top of the *ash-gum.* **1891** *PMLA* 6.168 **WV,** *Beegum* was at first the body of the gum tree hollowed out and used for bees. A larger section, hollowed out in the same way, is used for a grain receptacle and is called a *gum.* **c1902** Clapin *New Dict. Amer.* 217, *Gum.* . . Originally . . the hollow trunks of gum-trees, and now extended . . to any casks or firkins for domestic use. **1917** *DN* 4.413 **seKY, wNC,** *Gum.* . . Barrel. "I'm goin' to put my ashes into that gum." **1923** *DN* 5.233 **swWI,** *Ash-gum.* . . A piece of a tree, generally of the trunk, hollowed out to collect ashes for soap. A barrel thus employed is often so called. When water is poured upon the ashes, the receptacle becomes a *lye-gum.* **1968** *DARE* Tape **GA**22, [FW:] And then [after cooking cane syrup down to sugar] you'd put it in some special kind of container? [Inf:] Yes sir. . . A gum or a . . hollow cypress. **1986** Pederson *LAGS Concordance (Keg)* 1 inf, **nwFL,** Gum—cut off one end of a hollow log and box the other end.

b A beehive. **chiefly Appalachians** See Map Cf **bee gum 1a, b**

1869 U.S. Dept. Ag. *Rept. of Secy. for 1868* 274, In the southern States the favorite form of the hive is the "gum." This consists of a hollow log, generally a portion of a cypress stump, about two feet in length and a foot in diameter; upon the top of the hollow is placed a board, and at the bottom is cut a small notch for the entrance of the bees. **1895** *DN* 1.372 **seKY, eTN, wNC,** *Gum:* bee-hive. "Folks is goin' into church to-day like bees into a gum." **1902** *DN* 2.236 **sIL,** *Gum.* . . A bee-hive. **1904** (1913) Johnson *Highways South* 103 **nGA,** The hives in which the bees were domiciled were spoken of as "gums." Usually they were simply oblong, upright boxes of home manufacture; but in earlier times sections of hollow black-gum trees served the purpose—hence the name. **1907** *DN* 3.223 **nwAR, sIL,** *Gum.* . . A beehive. **1933** *AmSp* 8.1.49 **Ozarks,** *Gum.* . . An old-fashioned beehive made of a section cut from a hollow log. **1965–70** *DARE* (Qu. R19a, *The place where bees live and store their honey—tame bees*) 11 Infs, **chiefly Appalachians,** Gum. [9 of 11 Infs old] **1969** *SC Market Bulletin* 11 Sept 3/5, *10 Stand* of bees, all in A-I root [=A.I. Root Co.] new patent gums, all with extra supers. **1969–70** *DARE* Tape **GA**48, [A storm] blew 'em [=bees] off the shed in their gum. . . it's a cypress tree, generally, ol' hollow cypress tree; **VA**43, He cut the bee tree and hived his bees in his old homemade gum. That was just . . a gum, just four twelve-inch planks nailed together. **1973** *Foxfire 2* 32 **sAppalachians,** In the early days of beekeeping, the hives were nothing more than twenty-four to thirty-inch long sections of hollow black gum trees—a fact that has caused even modern hives in the mountains today to be called "gums," "beegums," or "plank gums." **1986** Pederson *LAGS Concordance,* 1 inf, **nwGA,** Gum—beehive.

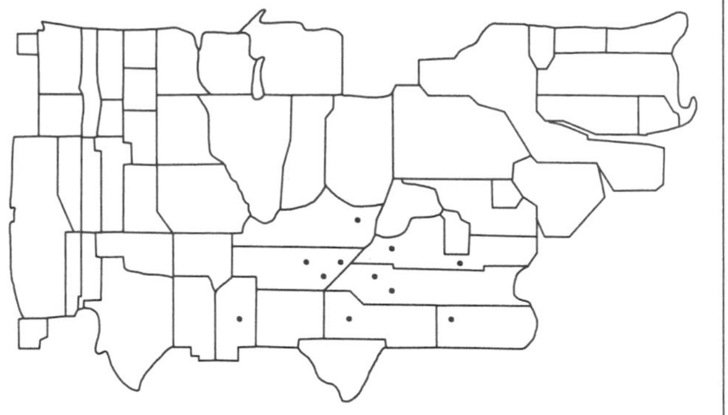

•gum n^2 3b (Qu. R19a)

c also *hare gum, rabbit gum:* A trap for small animals, usu rabbits; hence v *gum* to catch animals with such a trap. **esp sAppalachians, Ozarks**

a1883 (1911) Bagby *VA Gentleman* 48, Set gums for "Mollie-cotton-tails," mash-traps and deadfalls for minks. **1899** (1912) Green *VA Folk-Speech* 210, *Gum.* . . A section of a hollow log or tree . . used . . to make . . a trap for catching rabbits; "old-hare gum." **1923** *DN* 5.218 **Ozarks,** *Rabbit gum.* . . A box or a length of hollow log used in capturing rabbits and other small game alive. **1933** *AmSp* 8.1.49 **Ozarks,** *Gum.* . . A wooden rabbit trap. **1938** Caldwell *Southways* 39 **GA,** These here is plump rabbits I gummed in my own cotton patch. **1950** Peattie *Nat. Hist. Trees* 499, Usually the decay attacks the heartwood [of *Nyssa sylvatica*] first, so that hollow trees are common. When the country folk in the South find such a tree, they cut it down and saw it into . . sections. . . Longer sections are often arranged as traps for rabbits and laid in the woods; the hunter calls these rabbit-gums. **1966** *Daily Progress* (Charlottesville VA) 1 June 28/1 (as of 1910), I can think of nothing that compares with setting and attending rabbit traps . . or "gums." **1967** *DARE* File **ceVA,** *Hare gum*—a hollow gum-tree trunk made into a box to trap rabbits and possums. Old-fashioned.

d often attrib: A curbing or edging for a well or spring. **esp Appalachians**

1899 (1912) Green *VA Folk-Speech* 210, *Gum.* . . A section of a hollow log or tree . . used to form a well-kearb. **1901** Harben *Westerfelt* 13 **nGA,** She used to . . set in the shady holler at the gum spring, whar yore pa went to water his hoss. **1906** *DN* 3.139 **nwAR,** *Gum-spring, gum-well.* . . A spring (or well) walled in with the hollow trunk of a sweet-gum tree. **1941** Stuart *Men of Mts.* 257 **neKY,** Rister stood at the well-gum. **1956** McAtee *Some Dialect NC* 20, *Gum* . . the original sense seems to have been "a section of a hollow tree," and in this way as curbing gave many a spring the name of Gum Spring. **c1960** *Wilson Coll.* **csKY,** *Gum*—a hollow log used to enclose a spring.

4 also *gum turpentine:* Liquid crude turpentine, pine resin. Cf **dip** n^1 **4**

1884 Sargent *Forests of N. Amer.* 517 **SE,** The following grades of turpentine are recognized in the trade: "Virgin dip", or "Soft white gum turpentine." **1941** *AmSp* 16.236 **GA,** When the gum is collected in the cup it is then removed to barrels and the barrels are taken to a still. **c1960** *Wilson Coll.* **csKY,** Gum—the term often applied to pine tar. **1966–68** *DARE* Tape **FL**6, [FW:] Is that when the gum runs? [Inf:] Yes, it runs in the summer. . . In the fall you take that that has clung to the tree . . and distill it and get what they can out of it. Of course, you don't get as much out of it as you do the gum . . the runny gum; **GA**7, We call it [=pine resin] tar, or gum, or turpentine. 'Course, it's not turpentine until it distills; **GA**22, I chipped the boxes and let the gum run out in the box and then I dipped it out in a bucket.

5 **=gumbo 6a.**

1966–68 *DARE* (Qu. C31, . . *Heavy, sticky soil*) Infs **AL**1, **LA**20, Gum; **MS**45, Gum bottom.

6 See **gum band.**

7 See **gum boot.**

gum v^2 See **gum** n^2 **3c**

gum v[3], hence ppl adj *gummed,* pronc-sp *gum* [Orig in phr *dad gum,* by metath from *God damn*] **chiefly Sth, S Midl** Cf **dad** n[2]

To damn—usu in euphem phrr *dad-gum (it).*

1905 *DN* 3.76 **nwAR,** *Dad gum* . . for 'God damn.' **1912** Raine *Brand Blotters* 62 **West,** Dad gum it. **1965–70** *DARE* (Qu. NN25b, *Weakened substitutes for 'damn' or 'damned': "Well, I'll be ——!"*) 31 Infs, **chiefly Sth, S Midl,** Dad-gummed; **CA**136, Gummed; (Qu. NN8b, . . *"This jar won't come open, —— it."*) 13 Infs, **scattered Sth, S Midl,** Dad-gum; (Qu. HH31) Inf **LA**17, Dad-gum foreigner; (Qu. LL37, . . *"I was so —— mad."*) Infs **AL**5, **TX**92, 98, Dad-gum(med); (Qu. NN9a, *Exclamations showing great annoyance: "——. The electric power is off again."*) Inf **MA**52, Dad-gum it.

guma n[1] [Etym unknown]

1899 (1912) Green *VA Folk-Speech* 210, *Guma*. . . Seminal fluid.

guma n[2] Cf *DJE*

Prob a **nightshade** (*Solanum* spp).

1970 *DARE* (Qu. I53, *Other fruits grown around here*) Inf **LA**3, Guma berries—wonderful for making jelly—about the size of a small fingernail; red when ripe.

gumball machine n Also *gumball*

=**bubblegum machine.**

1966–68 *DARE* (Qu. N4, *A police vehicle with a red, blue, or yellow flashing light on top*) Inf **MI**97, Gumball; **WI**18, Gumball machine. **1966** *DARE* File **cwWI,** Gumball machine—the red flashing light on top of a police car. **1981** *Ibid,* I knew *gumball machine* meaning a police car in Michigan.

gumball tree n

=**sycamore.**

1961 Folk *Word Atlas N. LA* map 205, Sycamore tree—sycamore . . button ball . . others—button wood . . gum ball tree.

gum band n Pronc-sp *gumban* Also *gum (link), gummy band* [Ger *Gummiband*] **chiefly PA** See Map

A rubber band.

1959 *VT Hist.* 27.139, *Bum* [sic] *bands*. . . Rubber bands. Occasional. Older people. **1965–70** *DARE* (Qu. F49, *What do you call this? [Show rubber band]*) 12 Infs, **PA,** Gum band; **PA**176, Gum; **OH**61, Gum link; **CA**59, Gummy band. **1970–89** *DARE* File **swPA, swME, seMN** (as of c1960), Gum band—rubber band; **Pittsburgh PA,** A secretary might stop at the five 'n' ten for a box of gum bands. **1972** *Atlanta Letters* **PA,** When I asked for a gumband they [=Georgians] had no idea I was asking for a rubberband. **1982** McCool *Sam McCool's Pittsburghese* 13 **PA,** *Gumbans:* pieces of soft elastic rubber, occasionally used to keep trouser cuffs out of bicycle chains, or papers from flying around in your brief case. "Where are the gumbans and paper clips?" **1983** *Barrick Coll.* **csPA,** *Gum band*—rubber band. Formerly common, now rare.

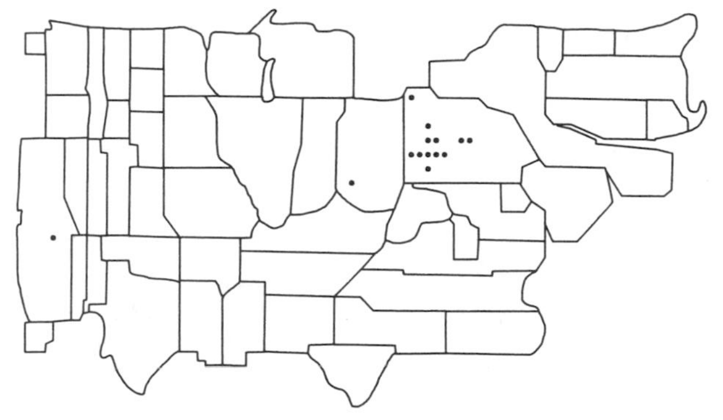

•gum band + varr (Qu. F49)

gumbee n Also *gumboe*

In marble play: see quot.

1966–68 *DARE* (Qu. EE6b, *Small marbles or marbles in general*) Inf **OH**87, Gumbees; (Qu. EE6c, *Cheap marbles*) Inf **WA**1, Gumbees; **OK**52, Gumboes.

gumberoo n

An imaginary animal; see quots.

1910 Cox *Fearsome Creatures* 11 **Pacific NW,** In size the beast corresponds closely to a black bear. . . [but] the gumberoo is almost hairless. . . The body is smooth, tough, and shiny and bears not even a wrinkle. . . A whole horse may be eaten at one sitting, distending the gumberoo out of all proportions. . . Whatever strikes the beast bounds off with the same force. . . A rock or peavey thrown at the creature bounds back at whoever threw it, and a bullet shot against its hide is sure to strike the hunter between the eyes. **1939** Tryon *Fearsome Critters* 21, *The Gumberoo*. . . Paul Bunyan['s] . . description . . : "A pot-bellied body, almost exactly like the bunkhouse stove, even to the umbilical damper . . a pair of long, powerful, monkey-like forearms, and a little round head and no neck. . . He's got three bowed rear legs, each with a clawed foot clutching an iron ball, the same as an iron stove. . . For real travel he's got eight pairs of strong, springy legs set around his middle."

gumberry n

1 also *gumberry tree:* A **tupelo** such as **black gum 1,** or its fruit.

1709 (1967) Lawson *New Voyage* 121 **NC,** Neither is it [=the flesh of the bear] good, when he feeds on Gum-berries. **1894** *Harper's New Mth. Mag.* Aug 339/1 **ceNJ,** The quiet waterways have the peculiar Southern color, which some attribute . . to contact with the roots of the gumberry-trees. **1913** Eaton *Barn Doors & Byways* 198 *(DA),* Many bears are killed in the swamp, . . when the leaves are off the trees and the little blue gum-berries, which the bears love, are ripe. **1968** *DARE* (Qu. T13) Inf NC49, Gumberry.

2 =**stretchberry.**

1951 *PADS* 15.29 **TX,** *Smilax bona-nox*. . . Stretch-berry; gum-berry.

gumberry tree See **gumberry 1**

gumbo n Also *gombo* [LaFr, of African origin; see quot 1949 at **1** below]

1 Okra *(Abelmoschus esculentus).*

1859 (1968) Bartlett *Americanisms* 173, *Gombo,* or *Gumbo*. . . The Southern name for what is called, at the North, Okra. **1868** (1870) Gray *Field Botany* 74, *H[ibiscus] esculentus,* Okra or Gumbo. **1879** Bishop *4 Months* 205 **New Orleans LA,** The mild-eyed Louisiana Indian woman with her sack of gumbo spread out before her. **1905** W.R. Beattie *Okra* 5 *(DA),* Okra, or gumbo, as it is commonly called. **1925** *Book of Rural Life* 4.2481/1, *Gumbo,* another name for the *okra,* a garden plant of warm climates, cultivated for its edible seed pods. **1949** Turner *Africanisms* 194 **sSC, GA coasts** [Gullah], [Words used in conversation:] ['gʌmbo] 'okra'—T[shiluba], tʃiŋgɔmbɔ 'okra'; U[mbundu], otʃiŋgɔmbo 'okra'. **1976** Bailey–Bailey *Hortus Third* 781, Okra is the large, green, erect pod of *Abelmoschus esculentus,* and is also known as gumbo. From these pods is made the well-known gumbo soup of the South, where the plant is more extensively grown than in the North. **1986** Pederson *LAGS Concordance,* 1 inf, **eLA,** Gumbos—some call okra this.

2 also *gumbo soup:* A thick soup or stew of vegetables, meat, or seafood. **chiefly Gulf States, esp LA, but becoming widely recognized elsewhere** See Map

1805 in 1843 *Amer. Pioneer* 2.233 **New Orleans LA,** Shrimps are much eaten here; also a dish called *gumbo.* This last is made of every eatable substance, and especially of those shrimps which can be caught at any time. **1832** Hall *Legends West* 130 **seLA,** His aunt . . resolutely refused, through life, to eat *gumbo*-soup. **1835** Audubon *Ornith. Biog.* 3.199, To me *"Ecrevisses,"* whether of fresh or salt water, stripped of their coats, and blended into a soup or a "gombo," have always been most welcome. **1851** Hall *Manhattaner* 10 **New Orleans LA,** Those [men] fresh from the gombo soup, and the ham, . . rushing back again. **1853** (1982) Lea *Domestic Cookery* 33, *Gumbo Soup.* Take two pounds fresh beef; put this in a dinner-pot, with two gallons of water; . . throw in a quarter of a peck of ocra [sic], . . and about a quart of ripe tomatoes. **1905** *DN* 3.82 **nwAR,** *Gumbo*. . . A thick soup made of okra, chicken, tomatoes, and onions. **1914** *DN* 4.163 **NW,** *Gumbo*. . . A soup of meat, vegetables, and rice. **1927** Kennedy *Gritny* 23 **sLA** [Black], Lemme fix you a plate o' gumbo. **1965** Little *Autobiog. Malcolm X* 96 **NYC** (as of 1943), Bill sold plates of his spicy, delicious Creole dishes—gumbo, jambalaya. **1965–70** *DARE* (Qu. H36, *Kinds of soup favored around here*) 28 Infs, **chiefly Gulf States, esp LA,** Gumbo; **AL**21, **CA**91, 107, **LA**11, **TN**49, Chicken gumbo; **LA**11, **TX**15, 17, Shrimp gumbo; **LA**43, **MS**17, Seafood gumbo; **TX**17, Crab gumbo; **FL**17, Gopher gumbo; **LA**11, Okra gumbo; (Qu. H45, *Dishes made with meat, fish, or poultry that everybody around here would know, but that people in other places might not*) Infs **AL**21, **MS**2, 23, **NC**72, **SC**4, Gumbo; **OH**42, Chicken gumbo; **OK**53, Chicken pie gumbo; **FL**17, Gopher gumbo; NC72, Gumbo soup; **IL**22, Shrimp gumbo; **LA**11, Wild duck gumbo; (Qu.

H43, *Foods made from parts of the head and inner organs of an animal*) Inf **LA**24, Gumbo; (Qu. H50, *Dishes made with beans, peas, or corn that everybody around here knows, but people in other places might not*) Inf **TX**99, Gumbo; **SC**67, Okra gumbo, tomato gumbo; **LA**11, Vegetable gumbo; (Qu. H65, *Foreign foods favored by people around here*) Inf **AL**6, Gumbo. **1988** *DARE* File **csWI,** [Menu:] Creole gumbo.

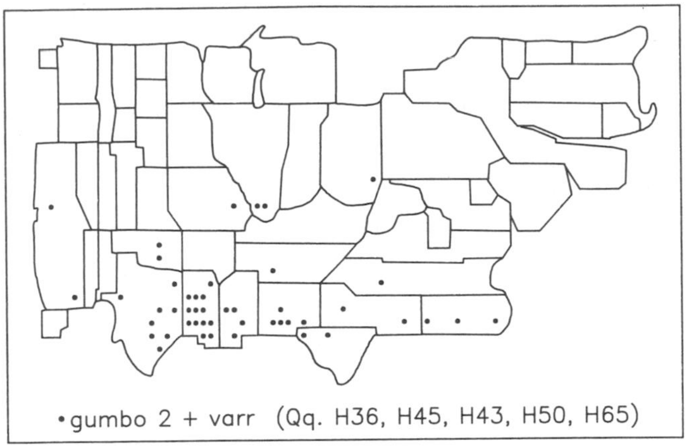

3 Prob =**gumbo filé 2.** *obs* Cf **gumbo zab 1**

1845 in 1912 Thornton *Amer. Gloss.* 1.403, At St. Peter's [Ill.] there is a large commerce carried on between the whites and redskins, for beads and whiskey, in exchange for skins and *gumbo.*

4 also attrib: A dialect or creolized form of French, esp one spoken by Creoles and Blacks in Louisiana; a speaker of this language.

1834 in 1835 Hoffman *Winter in West* (NY) 2.11 **swWI,** The seats, rising like the pit of a theatre, were so adjusted as to separate the audience into three divisions: the officers with their families furnished one, the soldiers another, and "gumboes," Indians, and a negro servant or two made up the third. **1838** Flagg *Far West* 2.36 **ceMO,** A spirited colloquy ensued in the *patois* of these old hamlets—a species of *gumbo-French,* which a genuine native of *La Belle France* would probably manage to unravel quite as well as a Northern Yankee. **1839** Hoffman *Wild Scenes* 2.113 **nwOH,** I saw at once it was an old gumbo hunter, and knowing what a guileless set they are I felt instantly at ease. [*DARE* Ed: The narrator is referring to a white hunter who speaks a patois of French and an Indian language.] **1883** Sala *Amer. Revisited* 2.65 **New Orleans LA,** The coloured people . . gabble a wondrous salmagundi of a patois, made up of French, Spanish, and indigenous African, which is known as "Gumbo." **1888** *Harper's New Mth. Mag.* 76.749/2 **sLA,** You're the only Creole in this crowd. . . talk *gumbo* to her. **1928** Saxon *Fabulous New Orleans* 271 **LA,** Then, too, there is the "gumbo" French—that means simply French incorrectly spoken—a sort of patois. **1931** Read *LA French* 122, *Gombo. . .* the negro-French patois. **1947** *Sat. Eve. Post* 17 May 103/2 **seLA,** She saw the old gumbo Negro in his ragged overalls. **1986** Pederson *LAGS Concordance,* 1 inf, **eLA,** That damn Gumbo—of informant's creole.

5 A Black person—also used as a nickname. [Perh by ext from **4** above]

1858 *N.Y. Tribune* 13 April 3/3 *(DA),* Gumbo [a Negro] was considerably astonished. **1860** Hundley *Social Relations S. States* 63, The Southern Gentleman . . would rather stand in the shoes . . of the laziest and most ignorant gumbo whose back was ever made to bleed under the overseer's lash . . than to become . . the *slave of public opinion.*

6a Thick, sticky mud; hence a type of dark fine-grained soil that becomes very sticky when wet. **chiefly Missip Valley, West** See Map Cf **black wax**

1892 *KS Univ. Qrly.* 1.97 **KS,** *Gumbo:* a peculiar, putty-like dark soil. **1894** *Century Illustr. Mag.* Jan 453/1, Do you know what gumbo is? Well, it is the clay of northern Wyoming. When wet it is the blackest, stickiest, most India-rubber-like mud that exists on earth. **1925** *Book of Rural Life* 1.193/1, Very fine-grained bottom-land clay soil . . is a rich, black, waxy soil, usually poorly drained and difficult to work. It is often called "gumbo." **1947** Croy *Corn Country* 55, The reason a town near the geographical center was chosen was because of the difficulties of travel; ox teams, gumbo, washouts. *Ibid* 281, *Gumbo:* The stickiest mud there ever was. **1948** *Time* 52.24.78/1 **cwCA,** Rain turned Tanforan's racing strip into thick, black gumbo. **1950** *AmSp* 25.230 **ceMS,** *Gumbo land.* Rich, black soil that looks like heavy, black grease when wet. **1958** Blasingame *Dakota Cowboy* 29, It was a badland butte which stuck up out of a gumbo flat. **1960** Teale *Journey into Summer* 238, In Illinois we plowed through gumbo mud almost hub deep. **1965–70** *DARE* (Qu. C31, . . *Heavy, sticky soil*) 178 Infs, **chiefly Missip Valley, West,** Gumbo; **IA**30, **NC**23, Black gumbo; **AR**55, **MS**18, Gumbo mud; **LA**27, Gumbo land; (Qu. C30, . . *Loose, dark soil*) Infs **FL**21, **IA**8, **IL**93, Gumbo; **MS**86, Buckshot gumbo—a dark soil that is very sticky. **1986** Pederson *LAGS Concordance* **chiefly Lower Missip Valley, TX,** [154 infs, Gumbo, black gumbo, gumbo clay, gumbo land, etc.]

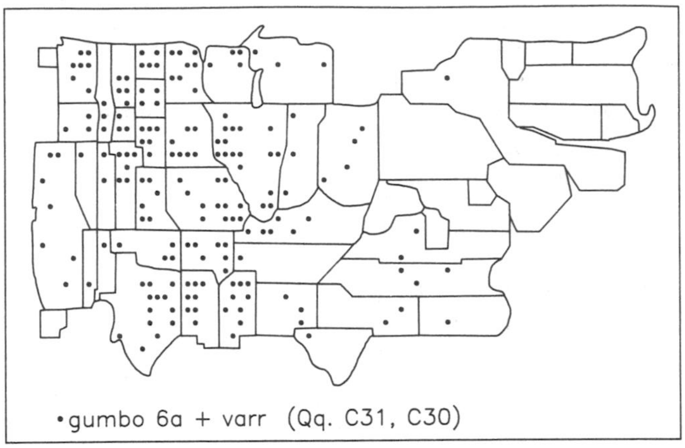

b A hard, impervious layer of clay subsoil; any hard or unworkable soil. **chiefly west of Missip R, Sth** Cf **hardpan 1**

1881 *Chicago Times* (IL) 16 Apr 13/1 **NE,** Such a thing as hard-pan, bed rock near the surface or gumbo is not found here. [*DARE* Ed: This quot may refer instead to sense **6a** above.] **1892** *DN* 1.236 **KS, MO, OK,** *Gumbo* . . a hard, tough soil underlying the good soil. *Gumbo* can scarcely be plowed through at all, and is called a sure sign of poor soil. I have heard it also called *hard-pan.* **1895** NE Ag. Exper. Sta. *Bulletin No. 43* 107, The "gumbo" subsoil to a greater extent than any other found in this state, prevents the moisture from penetrating deeply into the soil. **1905** *DN* 3.82 **nwAR,** *Gumbo. . .* Hard, tough, and unproductive soil. **1944** *PADS* 2.57 **MO, GA, LA, TX,** *Gumbo. . .* A tough, hard clay soil. **1952** *Argosy* (NY) June 25/2 **LA,** Deep-laid with forest humus, the alluvial soil over thoroughbred yellow gumbo grows all manner of wild food for animals. **1989** *DARE* File, According to a member of the Illinois State Geological Survey, farmers in general tend to apply "gumbo" to any type of soil that they find difficult to work and not just the heavy, sticky, dark-colored stuff with which the word is most commonly associated.

gumboat See **gunboat 1**

gumboe See **gumbee**

gumbo filé n **chiefly LA**

1 A **gumbo 2,** usu one made with **filé** n **1.** **Cf gumbo zab 2**

1823 in 1868 McCall *Letters Frontiers* 121 **nwFL,** In a few minutes the door opened, and black François entered with a tureen of *gombo filé,* a special favorite in the South. **1850** [see **gumbo zab 2**]. **1880** Hearn *Creole Sketches* (1924) 103 *(DA),* Gombo Filé . . is made exactly like the other, but with pulverized okra instead of fresh green okra. **1894** Chopin *Bayou Folk* 92 **cwLA,** 'Tite Reine came to serve them with the gumbo-filé that she had come out of the field to cook at noon. **1931** Read *LA French* 122, *Gombo. . .* now applied . . to other kinds of gumbo thickened with a powder prepared from sassafras leaves. This powder goes by the name of *filé* . . hence *gombo filé.* **1934** *AmSp* 9.79 **nLA,** One student used *gumbo filé* . . in his school composition. To many of . . [his classmates] *gumbo filé,* a thick soup or stew, or the seasoning thereof, seemed unusual in a composition, though the seasoning was on sale in north Louisiana grocery stores. **1967** LeCompte *Word Atlas* 299 **seLA,** *A brown soup of chicken, shrimp, etc., thickened with file. . .* gumbo filé [9 of 21 infs]. . . *gombo filé* [4 infs].

2 =**filé** n **1.**

1877 Bartlett *Americanisms* 210 **LA,** *Gumbo feelay,* sassafras leaves dried and powdered. **1934** [see **1** above]. **1942** Harlow *Trees E. U.S.* 191 **LA,** The Choctaw Indians of Louisiana powdered the leaves [of the sassafras] (then called "gumbo filet," "gumbo file," or "gumbo zab") and used them for flavoring and giving a ropy consistency to soup. **1967**

LeCompte *Word Atlas* 327 **seLA,** *Powder made from the dried leaves of the sassafras tree. . .* gumbo *filé* [1 of 21 infs]. **1986** Pederson *LAGS Concordance,* 1 inf, **seLA,** Gumbo file—powdered sassafras leaves for gumbo; 1 inf, **seMS,** Sassafras makes gumbo file.

3 =sassafras.

1897 Sudworth *Arborescent Flora* 202, *Sassafras sassafras. . . Common Names. . .* Gumbo file (La. negro dialect). **1960** Vines *Trees SW* 298, Sassafras has been cultivated since 1630. . . Other commonly used vernacular names are Ague-tree, Cinnamon-wood, . . and Gumbo-file.

gumbo-gwackum See **gumbo-whackum**

gumbo lily n

1 A **stickleaf** (here: *Mentzelia decapetala*). Cf **gunebo lily**

1938 FWP *Guide ND* 177, In June the large, white, open flowers of the low-growing gumbo lily, also known as the cowboy lily . . appear in the otherwise barren soil at the foot of the buttes. **1949** Moldenke *Amer. Wild Flowers* 33, Best known and perhaps handsomest of the group is the . . *gumbolily.* **1959** Carleton *Index Herb. Plants* 57.

2 also *gumbo primrose:* An **evening primrose a** (here: *Oenothera caespitosa*). [Perh **gumbo 6a**]

1950 Stevens *ND Plants* 215, *Oenothera caespitosa. . .* It is of course not a lily, but the name "gumbo lily" is commonly used in this area. **1963** Craighead *Rocky Mt. Wildflowers* 121, Morning Primrose, Gumbo Primrose.

gumbo limbo n [*gumbo* assoc with *gum* resin + *limbo* of uncert origin; but perh var of *gum elemi*] **FL**

The West Indian birch *(Bursera simaruba).* Also called **gum elemi 1**

1837 (1962) Williams *Territory FL* 26 **swFL,** The Indians. . . make bird-lime from the juice of the Gum Elemi, which they call Gumbo-limbo. *Ibid* 98 **FL,** Gum Elemi.—Called by the inhabitants Gumbo-limbo, is a large spreading tree, with a smooth brown bark. **1846** Browne *Trees* 189, Gumbo-limbo . . is an evergreen tree, attaining a height of fifty or sixty feet, with a trunk from three to five feet in diameter. **1890** Field *Bright Skies* 70 **FL,** Perhaps some old savage . . has been punished for his cruelty by being turned into that gumbo-limbo tree. **1897** Sudworth *Arborescent Flora* 269, *Bursera simaruba. . .* Gumbo Limbo. . . Gum Elemi. . . West Indian Birch. **1939** FWP *Guide FL* 346, In this jungle, and elsewhere on southern Merritt Island where the land has not been cleared, are found trees growing more than 200 miles north of their native habitat on the Florida Keys. . . among others, ironwood, gumbo limbo, soapberry. **1961** Douglas *My Wilderness* 148 **Everglades FL,** One was the gumbo limbo, whose copper-colored bark peels in papery shreds like a birch and whose wood is so light that it is used to make the horses on merry-go-rounds. **1967** Will *Dredgeman* 68 **FL,** Here and there could be seen a gumbo limbo. . . In tropical countries saplings of gumbo limbo are used for fences, for they take root and are known as "growing posts." **1979** Little *Checklist U.S. Trees* 67, *Bursera simaruba* . . gumbo-limbo . . gum elemi.

gum boot n Also *gum (rubber) somewhat old-fash* Cf **gumshoe**

A rubber boot or overshoe.

1850 (1930) Christman *One Man's Gold* 119, I put on my long gum boots and waded through the water. **1872** Schele de Vere *Americanisms* 420 **Philadelphia PA,** [This] has led to an utter confusion, in many minds, between the terms *gum* and *rubber. . .* "She was cleaning her gums upon the mat"—meaning her India-Rubber shoes. **1939** Aurand *Quaint Idioms* 24 [PaGer], I ain't got wet feet; I have on my *gums* (rubbers, overshoes, or boots). **1948** *Hoosier Folkl. Bulletin* 7.1.12 **cnWV,** Shoes, slippers, old gum boots. **1960** Criswell *Resp. to PADS 20* **Ozarks,** *Gum boots. . .* Rubber boots. Frequent old expression which is still in use though not so frequent as formerly. **c1960** *Wilson Coll.* **csKY,** *Gumboots. . .* Rubberboots. **1969** *DARE* Tape NC65, When I was a boy, in the wintertime we'd have a hard rain . . a hard, hard rain, and the next morning you'd have to wade or wear your gum boots. **1979** Lewis *How to Talk Yankee* [29] **nNEng,** Bizarre attire: "You can't imagine what *rigs* they wear down in the city. I see one feller with a long black cloak, gum rubbers, a coonskin hat—and ear rings!"

gumbo primrose See **gumbo lily 2**

gumbo road n [**gumbo 6a**]

A dirt road that becomes sticky when wet.

1941 Koenigsberg *King News* 35 **San Antonio TX** (as of 1888), Half a mile along Alazan Creek and another mile and a half of gumbo road brought me to the Marshall Street School. **1966–70** *DARE* (Qu. N27a, . . *Kinds of unpaved roads*) Infs **MI40, MS88, ND2,** Gumbo road. **1986** Pederson *LAGS Concordance,* 1 inf, **eLA,** Gumbo roads—sticky, mud, sometimes impassable.

gumbo soup See **gumbo 2**

gum-bow n

c1960 *Wilson Coll.* **csKY,** *Gum-bow. . .* A slingshot, probably because of the use of rubber strings for the power.

gumbo-whackum n Also *gumbo-gwackum* [See quot]

A **lignumvitae** (here: either *Guaiacum officinale* or *G. sanctum*).

1964 *PADS* 42.18 **csKY,** *Gumbo-whackum* (or *gumbo-gwackum*). The local pronunciation of *gum guaiacum,* the resinous sap of two tropical trees—*Guaiacum officinale* and *G. sanctum,* formerly used by many people in cough syrups and still kept in stock by at least one drugstore in the region.

gumbo-ya-ya n

See quots.

1941 Writers' Program *Guide LA* 689, *Gumbo-ya-ya. . .* A gathering of women at which there is much chatter and gossip. **1945** Saxon *Gumbo Ya-Ya* v **LA,** *Gumbo Ya-Ya*—*'Everybody talks at once'*—is a phrase often heard in the Bayou Country of Louisiana. This *Gumbo Ya-Ya* is a book of the living folklore of Louisiana. *Ibid* 173, Elderly Creole ladies were fond of gathering at each other's houses to spend the day. All the gossip would be exchanged. . . Such a gathering of women was known, scornfully, as a *gumbo ya-ya.*

gumbo zab n Also *gumbo zhebe* [Appar Creole Fr pronc-sp for *gombo des herbes*] Cf **zydeco**

1 =filé n 1.

1942 Harlow *Trees E. U.S.* 191 **LA,** The Choctaw Indians of Louisiana powdered the leaves [of the sassafras] (then called . . "gumbo zab") and used them for flavoring and giving a ropy consistency to soup. **1986** Pederson *LAGS Concordance,* 1 inf, **New Orleans LA,** Gumbo 'zhe'be—a German cultural relic [*DARE* Ed: meaning uncertain].

2 =gumbo filé 1.

1850 Emerson *Rept. Trees & Shrubs* 321, In the southwestern states, the dried leaves [of the sassafras] are much used as an ingredient in soups. . . [which] gives them a ropy consistence, and a peculiar flavor. . . To such soups are given the names *gombo filé* and *gombo zab.*

gum buckthorn, gum bumelia See **gum elastic**

gum coat n

=great blue heron.

1956 *AmSp* 30.184, The great blue heron has . . names alluding to its appearance in flight . . : *gum coat* (Cape May, N.J.) because the flying bird suggests a raincoat flapping in the wind.

gum cottonwood n

A **tupelo gum** (here: *Nyssa aquatica*).

1940 Clute *Amer. Plant Names* 265, *Nyssa aquatica. . .* Gum cottonwood.

gumdrop n attrib

1 Shaped like a gumdrop; see quots.

1938 FWP *Guide MN* 347 **neMN,** Numerous little farmhouses in this valley have pole-anchored birchbark or shake-shingle roofs, rounded or "gumdrop" canvas-covered haystacks, "toothpicked" to the ground with pegs like a circus tent. **1944** Nute *Lake Superior* 193, "Gumdrop" piles of hay.

2 Sissy; see quot.

1902 Wilson *Spenders* 344, Think of a husky, two-fisted boy like him lettin' himself be called by a measly little gum-drop name like Percival.

gumdrop tree n [In ref to the berries]

A **lotebush** (here: *Ziziphus obtusifolia*).

1953 Little *Native Trees U.S.* 300, *Ziziphus obtusifolia* . . lotebush . . gumdrop-tree. **1970** Correll *Plants TX* 1013, *Ziziphus obtusifolia. . .* Lotebush, gumdrop tree.

gum elastic n Also *gum buckthorn, ~ bumelia* [See quot 1884]

A plant of the genus *Bumelia:* usu *B. lanuginosa,* but also **southern buckthorn.** For other names of *B. lanuginosa* see **black haw 2, chittamwood 2, coma, false buckthorn, hen-wood, mountain buckthorn, mountain gum, Noah's ark, slow bush, stifftwig gum, woollybucket bumelia, woolly buckthorn**

1884 Sargent *Forests of N. Amer.* 102, *Bumelia lanuginosa. . . Gum*

Elastic. Shittim wood. . . A clear, very viscid gum exuded from the freshly-cut wood is sometimes used domestically. **1897** Sudworth *Arborescent Flora* 319, *Bumelia lanuginosa*. . . *Common Names*. . . Gum Elastic. **1933** Small *Manual SE Flora* 1034, *B[umelia] lanuginosa*. . . *Gum-elastic*. . . Fla. to Tex., Kans., Ill. and Ga. . . The yellow or light-brown heartwood is close-grained, but rather soft. **1946** Reeves–Bain *Flora TX* 117, *B[umelia] lanuginosa*. . . (Gum Elastic) Bush or tree, usually 2–several m. tall. **1960** Vines *Trees SW* 833, *Bumelia lanuginosa*. . . Gum Elastic, Gum Bumelia. *Ibid* 834, *Bumelia lycioides*. . . Gum Elastic. . . *Bumelia monticola*. . . Vernacular names used are Gum-elastic . . and Gum-buckthorn. Some botanists have listed Brazos Bumelia [=*B. monticola*] under. . . *B. lanuginosa*. **1967** *DARE* (Qu. T16, *What kinds of trees are 'special' around here?*) Inf **TX**13, Gum elastic. **1979** Little *Checklist U.S. Trees* 65, *Bumelia lanuginosa* . . *gum bumelia* . . gum elastic.

gum elemi n

1 =**gumbo limbo;** also the exudate of such a plant.

c1729 in 1754 Catesby *Nat. Hist. Carolina* 1.30/1, The Gum-elimy Tree. . . This Tree produces a large quantity of Gum, of a brown colour, and of the Consistence of Turpentine. **1775** (1962) Romans *Nat. Hist. FL* 153, *Gum elemi* is a resin fit for many medicinal uses, and the product of a species of *Pistachia* [sic], very common in the southern and south-eastern parts of *Florida*. **1837** [see **gumbo limbo**]. **1884** Sargent *Forests of N. Amer.* 33, *Bursera gummifera*. . . Gum Elemi. Gumbo Limbo. West Indian Birch. **1933** Small *Manual SE Flora* 764, *E[laphrium] Simaruba*. . . *Gum-elemi*. . . It is the only deciduous-leaved tropical tree among its evergreen associates. **1979** Little *Checklist U.S. Trees* 67, *Gumbo-limbo*. . . *Other common names* . . gum-elemi. . . S. Fla. incl. Fla. Keys, n. near coasts to C. Fla.

2 A **torchwood** (here: *Amyris elemifera*). *obs*

1806 Shecut *Flora Carolinæensis* 1.146, *A[myris] Elemifera*, Gum Elemi, or Gum Lemon Shrub, is a native of Carolina. . . it grows to the height of about six feet.

gumfudgit, stick like v phr

1983 *DARE* File **ceWI**, [It] sticks like gumfudgit = [it] sticks tight.

gum game n [Cf quot 1859] Cf **come** v **C2**

A trick, dodge, or scheme—often in phr *come the gum game over (someone)*, to deceive or trick (someone).

1840 in 1941 *Amer. Lost Plays* 14.118, I've come the gum game over you. **1859** (1968) Bartlett *Americanisms* 185, *Gum game*. A trick, a dodge. Opossums and raccoons, when pursued, will fly for refuge to the Sweet Gum tree, in preference to any other. This tree is very tall, slim, smooth, and void of branches except a tuft at the top, which is a place of security for any animal expert enough to reach it. As they are hunted in the night, they are, of course, beyond the reach of the hunter's penetrating eye at the great height of the gum tree. This is called "coming the *gum game*" over the hunter. **1871** Eggleston *Hoosier Schoolmaster* 118 **sIN**, You don't come no gum games over me with your saft sodder. **1872** Schele de Vere *Americanisms* 209, This is what the Western man calls coming the *gum-game*, and he applies the phrase with great shrewdness and force to any case in daily life in which he thinks he sees a desire to overreach him by concealment. **1910** *DN* 3.442 **cwNY**, *Gum-game*. . . A trick; a scheme to deceive. "You can't work any gum-game on me." **1942** Berrey–Van den Bark *Amer. Slang* 491.3 [Underworld lingo], Swindling activity or trick; confidence game. . . *gum game*.

‡gum-gooley n

1966 *DARE* (Qu. K50, *Joking nicknames for mules*) Inf **AR**21, Gum-gooley.

gum-grease n Cf **grease** v **B2**

Sweet talk, friendly persuasion.

1960 Williams *Walk Egypt* 64 **GA**, First they tried to pet her with words. . . Gum-grease didn't work, so they tried tongue-whip.

gum leaves See **gum plant 3**

gum lemon shrub n [Appar from the scent and lemon-like fruit] *obs* Cf **gumbo limbo**

=**gum elemi 2.**

1806 [see **gum elemi 2**].

gum link See **gum band**

gummed See **gum** v³

gummer n

1 See quots.

1931 *AmSp* 6.359 **West** [Sheep ranching lingo], Given plenty of salt and good grass and water, even a "gummer," or an old sheep without teeth, will take on sufficient flesh for the fall market. **1940** Writers' Program *Guide NV* 78, Instead of granny as the mark of age, *gummer* is the label for the old ewes—those without teeth.

‡2 pl: See quot.

1967 *DARE* (Qu. X13b, *Joking names for false teeth*) Inf **LA**11, Gummers.

gum moss n [Prob **gum** n² **1**]

Prob a **Spanish moss** such as *Tillandsia usneoides*.

1945 Saxon *Gumbo Ya-Ya* 526 **LA**, For bad blood, a handful of gum moss. . . Steep and take every morning.

gummy adj [Cf Ger *Gummi* rubber] **esp PA** Cf **bending ice, rubber ice**

Of ice: rubbery, flexible.

1968–69 *DARE* (Qu. B33b, *Talking about the first thin ice that forms over the surface of a pond or pool*) Inf **PA**164, It's gummy; (Qu. B35, *Ice that will bend when you step on it, but not break*) Inf **PA**197, Gummy; **PA**176, Gummy ice.

gummy intj Also *by gummy* [Cf *gum* euphem for *God*]

Used as a mild oath; see quots.

1845 Judd *Margaret* 139 **swME**, "Gummy!" retorted the woman. "He has been a talkin' about me, and a runnin' of me down." **1872** Schele de Vere *Americanisms* 607, *Gum*, by, and *Gummy*, are . . euphemistic oaths, mainly heard in the New England States. **1904** (1916) Porter *Freckles* 57 **cnIN**, I'll be having a book about all the birds . . Yes, by gummy!

gummy band See **gum band**

gump n¹

1 also *gump-head, gumpy:* A stupid, foolish, or awkward person; hence adj *gump-headed.* [Engl, Scots, Ir dial] *old-fash*

1722 *New-Engl. Courant* (Boston MA) 8 Jan 1/1 **ceMA**, We have such a poor[,] careless, lazy, gump-headed . . Post-Master, as is not to be found in the whole *Lunar World*. **1825** Neal *Brother Jonathan* 2.42 **swME**, He's . . sort of a naiteral too, I guess; rather a gump, hey? **1848** Bartlett *Americanisms* 167, *Gump*. A foolish person; a dolt. **1892** *DN* 1.236 **cwMO**, *Gump(y)*. Both *gumpy* and *gump* are heard; = stupid dunce, awkward creature. **1893** Shands *MS Speech* 71, *Gump* . . an idiot, a senseless person. . . In Mississippi *gumpy* is sometimes heard for *gump*. **1898** Westcott *Harum* 216 **Upstate NY**, "You needn't make me out more of a gump 'n I was," protested Mrs. Bixbee. **1902** (1904) Rowe *Maid of Bar Harbor* 182 **ME**, "Wa'al, you gump! you've been an' done it now," cried the girl with a burst of derisive laughter. **1905** *DN* 3.62 **NE**, *Gump*. . . A silly. *Ibid* 82 **nwAR**, He's the biggest gump I ever saw. **1906** *DN* 3.139 **nwAR**, Its [sic] a pity he's such an old gumpy. **1908** *DN* 3.317 **eAL, wGA**, *Gump*. **1915** *DN* 4.199, *Gump*. **1916** *DN* 4.275 **NE, PA, KS**, *Gump*, or *gump-head*. **1919** *DN* 5.66 **NM**, *Gump*. **1950** *PADS* 14.34 **SC**, *Gump*. **1968–69** *DARE* (Qu. HH3, *A dull and stupid person*) Inf **KY**26, Gump; (Qu. HH21, *A very awkward, clumsy person*) Inf **OH**41, Gump.

2 =**black-bellied plover.**

1917 (1923) *Birds Amer.* 1.256, *Black-Bellied Plover—Squatarola squatarola*. . . Gump. **1927** Forbush *Birds MA* 1.459, *Squatarola squatarola*. . . *American Black-bellied Plover*. . . Gump. **1955** MA Audubon Soc. *Bulletin* 39.445, *Black-Bellied Plover*. . . Gump (Mass. The immature, hence unwary.) **1956** *AmSp* 31.300, Epithets of similar meaning [="simpleton"] are not rarely bestowed upon shore birds. Consider: *Fool plover* . . *foolish curlew* . . *foolish godwit* . . *gump* (black-bellied plover, bird of the year, Mass.); and *simpleton*.

gump n² [Prob var of *gunk*]

1968 *DARE* (Qu. Y40b, . . *Words referring to sticky stuff: "I've got to wash my hands. They're all covered with ______."*) Inf **OH**48, Gump.

gump-head(ed) See **gump** n¹ **1**

gum pike n

A **walleye** (here: *Stizostedion vitreum vitreum*).

1983 Becker *Fishes WI* 871, *Walleye*. . . Other common names . . gum pike.

gum plant n

1 A plant of the genus *Grindelia*. [See quot 1916] Also called **arnica B2c, August flower, gumweed 1, resinweed, rosinweed,**

sticky-heads, tarweed. For other names of *G. squarrosa* see **curlycup gumweed**

1886 Havard *Flora W. & S. TX for 1885* 522, *Grindelia squarrosa* . . (Gum Plant.) Common on prairies west of the Pecos, and . . useful in bronchial affections and as a topical application in poisoning by *Rhus toxicodendron.* **1898** *Jrl. Amer. Folkl.* 11.229, *Grindelia . . robusta. . . Grindelia squarrosa* . . gum plant. **1916** Parsons *Wild Flowers CA* 180, The grindelias are especially characteristic of the region west of the Mississippi River, and are all known as "gum-plants" . . owing to the balsamic exudation which is found mostly upon the flower-heads. **1930** OK Univ. Biol. Surv. *Pub.* 2.1.85, *Grindelia lanceolata. . .* Narrow-leaved Gum-plant. . . *Grindelia squarrosa. . .* Broad-leaved Gum-plant. **1949** Moldenke *Amer. Wild Flowers* 210, Related to these are the *gumplants* or *tarweeds, Grindelia,* of which we have some 17 kinds. **1970** Kirk *Wild Edible Plants W. U.S.* 136, *Grindelia* species . . Gum Plant, Gumweed. . . The dried or green leaves make a pleasing tea. **1974** (1977) Coon *Useful Plants* 109, *Grindelia (various species)*—Gum plant.

2 A **comfrey** (here: *Symphytum officinale*).

c1873 in 1976 Miller *Shaker Herbs* 160, Comfrey—*Symphytum officinale*—Gum Plant. **1876** Hobbs *Bot. Hdbk.* 50, Gum plant, Comfrey, Symphytum officinale. **1930** Sievers *Amer. Med. Plants* 24, Comfrey—*Symphytum officinale* . . gum plant. **1940** Clute *Amer. Plant Names* 68, *S[ymphytum] officinale* . . gum plant. **1974** (1977) Coon *Useful Plants* 80.

3 also *gum leaves:* A **yerba santa** (here: *Eriodictyon californicum*). **CA**

1900 Lyons *Plant Names* 149, *E[riodictyon] Californicum. . .* Gum plant. . . Expectorant; masks bitterness of quinine. **1902** (1974) Chestnut *Plants Indians* 381, *Eriodictyon californicum. . .* grows profusely on dry, bushy hillsides throughout Mendocino County, and is known under the names . . gum leaves, tarweed [etc]. . . The leaf is the only part used. As a cure for colds and for asthma it is considered a specific by the native whites and Indians. . . It is also smoked and chewed like tobacco. **1920** Saunders *Useful Wild Plants* 198, Yerba Santa. . . An American common name for the plant—Consumptive's Weed—indicates one of its popular uses. . . It . . is a shrubby plant, . . with dark green, resinous leaves. . . Others [=names] are Mountain Balm, Gum Leaves.

4 A **rosinweed:** either *Silphium laciniatum* or *S. terebinthinaceum.*

1940 Clute *Amer. Plant Names* 87, *Rosin-weed. . . S[ilphium] laciniatum. . .* Gum-plant. . . *S. terebinthinaceum. . .* Gum-plant.

gum poplar n

=**balsam poplar.**

1968 *DARE* (Qu. T12, *The kind of poplar tree that has sticky, sweet-smelling buds*) Inf **PA**165, Gum poplar.

‡gumps n Cf *grumps* (at **grandpa A9**)

1969 *DARE* (Qu. Z3, . . *Words . . for 'grandfather'*) Inf **IL**36, Gumps—in our family [gʌmps].

gumpshun See **gumption**

gump stump See **up a stump**

gum succory n

Std: a naturalized weed *(Chondrilla juncea).* Also called **devil's grass 2, hog bite, naked weed, skeletonweed, stickweed**

gumption n Also sp *gumpshun, gumtion* [Scots, Ir, Engl dial]

1 Common sense, good judgment. **scattered, but esp Sth, S Midl**

1815 Humphreys *Yankey in England* 105, *Gumtion,* sense, understanding, intellect. **1899** (1912) Green *VA Folk-Speech* 210, *Gumption. . .* Acuteness of practical understanding; clear, practical common sense; quick perception of the right thing to do under unusual circumstances. **1906** *DN* 3.139 **nwAR,** *Gumption. . .* Common sense, good sense. "If he'd had more gumption, he wouldn't have stuck to it the way he did." **1908** *DN* 3.318 **eAL, wGA. 1909** *DN* 3.412 **nME. 1941** Writers' Program *Guide IN* 118, This promised land turned out to be a land of plenty and, as George Ade once said, 'The pioneer had gumption enough to unpack once he had arrived.' **1947** *PADS* 8.22 **KY, NC, VA,** *Gumption:* Common sense only. **1950** *PADS* 13.17 **cTX,** *Gumption. . .* We used the word to mean common sense. *Ibid* 14.34 **SC. c1960** *Wilson Coll.* **csKY,** *Gumption. . .* Horse sense, common sense. **1966** Barnes–Jensen *Dict. UT Slang* 21. **1968** Kellner *Aunt Serena* 57 **cIN** (as of c1920), If you had the gumption of a goat you'd have dumped her in the crick. **1969** *DARE* FW Addit **KY**50, *Gumption*—common sense. "He ain't got no gumption"; that is, he's stupid. Common. **1972** *Atlanta Letters* **nwGA,** *Gumpson* [sic]—Brains, Sence [sic].

2 Ambition, initiative; tenacity.

1862 (1864) Browne *Artemus Ward Book* 213 **ME,** I like . . your enterprise, gumpshun &c. **1905** *DN* 3.62 **NE,** *Gumption. . .* Energy, initiative. **1946** *PADS* 6.16 **eNC,** *Gumption. . .* Courage, enterprise, initiative. . . Common. [*PADS* Ed: The more common meaning elsewhere in the state is, perhaps, common sense.] **1947** *PADS* 8.19 **IA, NC, VA,** *Gumption:* Courage, enterprise, initiative. *Ibid* 25 **wNY, NC, VA,** *Gumption* suggests not only enterprise and initiative but also ambition: "If you had any gumption, you'd get to work and do it." **1948** Manfred *Chokecherry* 56 **nwIA,** An' come back showin' me you still got some git an' gumption t'yuh besides all that fop readin' an' educatin' you're doin' to yerself. **1950** *PADS* 14.34 **SC,** *Gumption. . .* Energy. **1950** *WELS (Energetic person who gets things done: "He's got lots of ——.")* 4 Infs, **WI,** Gumption; *(A very lively, active person: "He's got lots of ——.")* 3 Infs, **WI,** Gumption. **1965–70** *DARE* (Qu. HH27b, *Of a very able and energetic person . . , "He's got lots of ——."*) 57 Infs, **scattered,** Gumption; (Qu. KK8, *Other words for succeeding, especially in spite of difficulty: "He had a hard time, but at last he ——."*) Inf **KY**16, Had the gumption; (Qu. LL18, *To do no work at all . . "She hasn't ——."*) Inf **IL**59, Got the gumption. **1984** Wilder *You All Spoken Here* 164 **Sth,** *Gumption:* True grit; . . git-up-an'-go.

3 Courage; nerve.

1904 *DN* 2.425 **Cape Cod MA** (as of a1857), *Gumption. . .* Courage. **1946** [see **2** above]. **1947** [see **2** above]. **1948** *Time* 1 Mar 15/3, In 1848, an intrepid band of ladies, full of git & gumption, descended on Seneca Falls, N.Y., to declare a rebellion. **1950** *WELS (Brave or courageous: "He's got lots of ——.")* 3 Infs, **WI,** Gumption; *(When a person does something unexpectedly bold or forward: "Well, she certainly has a lot of ——.")* 1 Inf, **WI,** Gumption; *(Energetic person)* 1 Inf, **WI,** Gumption also means "courage, nerve." **1965–70** *DARE* (Qu. GG37, *Somebody who is very brave or courageous:* "He's got plenty of ——.") 33 Infs, **scattered,** Gumption; (Qu. GG5, *When someone does something unexpectedly bold or forward . . "Well, she certainly has a lot of ——."*) 16 Infs, **scattered,** Gumption. **1989** *DARE* File **MI, OH, WI** (as of 1920 →), He quit; he didn't have the gumption to stick to the job.

gumption up v phr [**gumption 3**]

To muster, bring forth.

1943 *AN&Q* 3.7/2 **NEng** (as of c1925), All the smiles I could gumption up [*AN&Q* Ed: *Gumption* as a noun is well-known. This use as a verb is not, however, common.]

gumptious adj

1 Proud, conceited. [Scots, Ir, Engl dial]

1877 Bartlett *Americanisms* 271, *Gumptious.* [Said of] One who has a good opinion of himself; a "knowing one." **1899** (1912) Green *VA Folk-Speech* 210, *Gumptious. . .* Supercillious [sic]; conceitedly proud.

2 See quot. [**gumption 1**]

1899 (1912) Green *VA Folk-Speech* 210, *Gumptious. . .* Having quick preception [sic] and sound judgment.

3 Ambitious, energetic, aggressive. [**gumption 2**]

1942 Berrey–Van den Bark *Amer. Slang* 240.9, Enterprising; energetic. . . *gumptious. Ibid* 273.3, Ambitious. . . *gumptious.* **1970** *DARE* (Qu. KK28, *Feeling ambitious and eager to work*) Inf **CA**177, Gumptious. **c1970** *DARE* File **ceIA,** *Gumption. . .* If the meaning of this is "aggressiveness," I have been familiar with it since my . . childhood. [Also] adj. *gumptious.* I would label it as colloquial rather than common.

4 Splendid, fine, excellent. Cf **humgumptious**

1916 *DN* 4.275 **NE,** *Gumptious* . . = *scrumptious* [=fine, elegant]. "We had a gumptious time." **1942** Berrey–Van den Bark *Amer. Slang* 29.4, Excellent; first-rate. . . *gumptious.*

gumpy adj [**gump** n[1] **1**]

1949 in 1986 *DARE* File **Detroit MI,** *Gumpy*—a disparaging adjective to describe anything. "Of all the gumpy ideas!"

gumpy n See **gump** n[1] **1**

gum rubber See **gum boot**

gum session n [Cf *beat one's gums* to talk excessively]

1970 *DARE* (Qu. Y12a, *A fight between two people, mostly with words*) Inf **NY**249, Gum session.

gumshoe n *somewhat old-fash*
=gum boot.
1863 Davis *Young Parson* 12, A little boy who wore his father's gum shoes in dry weather. **1886** Bates *Old Salem* 54 **MA,** My rubbers, too, instead of being of the shiny, blue-lined sort so dear to childish souls, were literally what Miss Lucy called "gumshoes," being made of pure rubber spread while hot over a last. **1913** Johnson *Highways St. Lawrence to VA* 328, Will had on these here gum shoes to keep from slippin'. **1959** *VT Hist.* new ser 27.139, *Gum shoes. . .* Overshoes; galoshes. Occasional. Older people. **1969** Sorden *Lumberjack Lingo* 51 **NEng, Gt Lakes,** *Gum shoes*—Rubbers worn by lumberjacks when working in the woods.

gumshot n Cf **gum-bow**
1984 Wilder *You All Spoken Here* 150 **Sth,** *Gumshot:* Slingshot.

gum-spring See **gum** n² **3d**

gumstickum n
1901 Harben *Westerfelt* 172 **nGA,** A short figure returned from the bushes with a bucket of tar. . . "Heer's yore gumstickum."

gum stump See **up a stump**

gumsuck v, hence vbl n *gumsucking* Also *gumsuck around old-fash*
To kiss.
c1873 [De Vere] *MS Notes* 420 *(DA), Gumsucking* = kiss[in]g in Ky. and Tenn.; coupled with *neck-sawing.* **1877** Bartlett *Americanisms* 271, *Gum-sucking,* a disgusting word, applied to the tendency of lovers, young ones especially, to carry their innocent endearments to an excess that displeases a third party. A friend informs me that he first heard it at Princeton College, in 1854, and thinks it may be a Jersey word. **1941** Stuart *Men of Mts.* 252 **neKY,** He kissed her right there before me. . . God, it made me sick as a horse. It's all right when *you're* loving a woman. . . But when you see somebody else gumsuck around. . . It's a sickening thing. **1942** McAtee *Dial. Grant Co. IN* 31 (as of 1890s), *Gum-sucking* . . kissing. **1949** *AmSp* 24.109 **ceGA,** *Gum-sucking.* . . Kissing.

gumsucking n [**gum** n² **1**]
1872 Schele de Vere *Americanisms* 420, The resinous gum exuding from these trees [=black gum and sour gum] and the Juniper is much used for chewing in North Carolina, Virginia, and the Western States, where *gumsuckings* are quite a festive occasion for the votaries of that amusement.

gum sugar n
In maple sugar production: see quot.
1938 FWP *Guide MN* 345, *Cusson.* . . Today the homes of one or two settlers and a CCC camp are its only signs of civilization. In the spring the Indians in this section erect temporary shelters resembling wigwams, in which they live while making maple sugar. . . The Indians call the molded sugar "cake sugars"; the "gum sugar" is put into other containers.

gumswizzled adj Cf **hornswoggle** v **3**
1911 *DN* 3.544 **NE,** *Gumswizzled, I'll be* . . expressing annoyance, or surprise. "You never went? Well, I'll be gumswizzled!" **1916** *DN* 4.272 **NE,** *Bumswizzled.* . . Used in "I'll be bumswizzled." [In Pa., *gumswizzled.*]

gumtion See **gumption**

gum tree n Also *gum*
1 =tupelo.
1676 in 1677 Royal Soc. London *Philos. Trans. for 1676* 11.628 **VA,** There is likewise black *Walnut* . . *Gum-tree, Locust* . . with several others. **1739** (1946) Gronovius *Flora Virginica* 121, *Nyssa pedunculis unifloris.* . . Black-berry-bearing-gum. **1843** Thompson *Major Jones' Courtship* 18 **GA,** "What pretty grapes on that tree!" ses Miss Mary, lookin up half-way to the top of the grate big gum that stood rite over the water. **1860** Curtis *Cat. Plants NC* 62, *Black Gum.* . . Common in swamps and shallow ponds of the Lower and Middle Districts, often called . . *Gum Tree.* **1908** Rogers *Tree Book* 277, The name "gum tree" is also applied to our tupelos, and to certain species of Eucalyptus. **1921** Deam *Trees IN* 259, *Nyssa sylvatica. . . Gum.* *Ibid* 261, The uses of gum are many. The quality of not splitting makes many uses for it. **1950** Moore *Trees AR* 102, *Blackgum.* . . Local Names . . Gum Tree. . . A source of a substantial part of the spring honey crop. **1965–70** *DARE* (Qu. T15, . . *Kinds of swamp trees*) 15 Infs, **chiefly Sth, Midl,** Gum tree; (Qu. T13) Inf **MS**21, Gum; **MA**15, Gum tree; (Qu. T5, . . *Kinds of evergreens, other than pine*) Inf **FL**32, Gum. [*DARE* Ed: Some of these Infs may refer instead to **2** below.] **1966** *DARE* Tape **AR**32, It was all . . surrounded with . . a great forest of the gum trees. **1968** Radford et al. *Manual Flora Carolinas* 789, *Nyssa* L. *Gum.* . . Fruit a drupe.
2 =sweet gum. [See quot 1872]
1700 in 1924 *MD Hist. Mag.* 19.347 **cnMD,** Timber Proof, 200 acres Sur. the 22d of decembr 1672 for George Wells in delph Creek at a marked gum. **1851** *De Bow's Rev.* 11.45 **LA,** Pre-eminent among the forest trees stands the *gum.* . . The sweet gum . . logs soon sob when on the ground, and thereby are nearly indestructible by fire. . . The gum which exudes is masticated by the slaves, and often by the whites. This gum is also frequently collected, and combined with tallow and wax, to make a healing unguent or salve. **1851** (1878) Aime *Plantation Diary* 147 **LA,** Cut down three hundred and sixty large gum trees. **1872** Schele de Vere *Americanisms* 204, A rich store of honey is often found in hollow trees, among which the bee seems to prefer the *gum-trees* (Liquidambar styræiflua [sic]), which grow to a large size both in swamps and in dry woods. It has its name from the fact that the bark, if wounded in summer, distils a fluid gum or resin in very small quantity, which has an agreeable fragrance, and is often chewed at the South. **1897** Sudworth *Arborescent Flora* 205, *Liquidambar styraciflua. . . Common Names.* . . Gum (Va.). Gum Tree (S.C., La.) **c1940** Newman–Murphy *Conserv. Notes* 6 **neLA,** The gum tree grows to great height, averaging about three feet at the base, diminishing but little until it gets near its first limbs. The lumber, of a lovely reddish color, is extensively used in the manufacture of furniture. **1950** Peattie *Nat. Hist. Trees* 310, Country folk refer to it [=*Liquidambar styraciflua*] simply as Gum tree, and to furniture salesmen the wood is plain Gum. **1966** *DARE* (Qu. T14) Inf **FL**34, Gum. **1974** Morton *Folk Remedies* 91, *Gum Tree. . . Liquidambar styraciflua.* . . Leaves . . are chewed and the juice swallowed to relieve sorethroat and also to overcome "loose stomach" (diarrhea). . . The gum of the tree is chewed as a masticatory and will stop diarrhea.
3 A tree of the genus *Eucalyptus.* [*AND* 1789 →] **CA**
1876 Hobbs *Bot. Hdbk.* 50, Gum tree, Eucalyptus robusta. **1908** CA Ag. Exper. Sta. Berkeley *Bulletin 196* 110, The following two species will produce more wood than any of the others on any good land. . . *Eucalyptus globulus,* and *viminalis,* [are] the two most rapid growing gums we have in this country. **1908** [see **1** above]. **1942** Hylander *Plant Life* 394, Introduced into California some forty years ago, and . . now commonly seen throughout the southern and central parts of the state, . . over forty thousand acres of Gums were planted in the hope that they would serve as timber trees. **1959** Munz–Keck *CA Flora* 963, *Eucalyptus. . . Gum Tree.* . . Many are grown in Calif. and some occasionally establish themselves outside of cult[ivation]. **1968** *DARE* (Qu. T5, . . *Kinds of evergreens, other than pine*) Inf **CA**65, Gum. **1976** Bailey–Bailey *Hortus Third* 449, *Eucalyptus. . . Gum tree.* . . In the warmer regions of the U.S. the largest number have been introduced into Calif., where they now form part of the natural scene.

gum turpentine See **gum** n² **4**

gum wax n Cf **chewing wax**
The exudate of a plant such as **sweet gum** or **Jersey pine,** esp when chewed; hence also chewing gum.
1900 Lyons *Plant Names* 227, *L[iquidambar] Styraciflua. . . Balsamic exudate* . . Gum-wax. **1903** *DN* 2.336 **seMO,** *Wax* or *gum wax.* . . Chewing gum. **1907** *DN* 3.238 **nwAR, seMO,** *(Gum)-wax.* . . Chewing gum. **1943** Weslager *DE Forgotten Folk* 160, Pine Wax or Gum Wax . . *Scientific Name—Pinus virginiana* (N)[,] *Use*—Chewed by children for enjoyment. [**1946** *PADS* 6.29 **eNC** (as of 1900–10), *Sweet gum; sweet gum wax.* . . The fragrant resin of the sweet gum, used for chewing gum. . . Common.] **1968** *DARE* (Qu. T7, *The sticky stuff that comes out of pine trees*) Inf **MO**4, Gum wax. **1970** *DARE* FW Addit **KY**75, *Gum wax*—The sap of the gum tree used like chewing gum.

gumweed n
1 =gum plant 1. [See quot 1937]
1911 *Century Dict. Suppl., Gum-weed.* . . 1. The gum-plant, *Grindelia.* . . 2. A weed of the Great Plains, *Lygodesmia juncea,* of the *Cichoriaceæ.* It is a rigid, branching, skeleton-like plant with most of the leaves very small or reduced to scales. **1936** Winter *Plants NE* 143, *Grindelia.* . . Gum weed. **1937** U.S. Forest Serv. *Range Plant Hdbk.* W86, *Gumweeds. Grindelia* spp. . . Particularly well represented in the United States west of the Mississippi. . . The resinous character of many species has given rise to the common names, gumweeds [etc]; the flower heads

usually exude the most of this medicinal resin. **1948** Stevens *KS Wild Flowers* 346, *Grindelia lanceolata*—Narrowleaf Gumweed. . . *Grindelia squarrosa*. . . Curlycup Gumweed. **1967** Gilkey-Dennis *Hdbk. NW Plants* 430, *Grindelia nana*. . . *Small gum-weed*. . . Heads . . sticky, appearing varnished. . . *Grindelia integrifolia*. . . *Common gumweed*. **1976** Bailey-Bailey *Hortus Third* 526, *Grindelia*. . . *Gumweed*. . . On poor land.

2 A **tarweed** (here: *Madia gracilis*). [See quot 1954] **esp CA**

1911 Jepson *Flora CA* 440, *M[adia] dissitiflora*. . . *Gum-weed*. . . Stream banks, open bushy places or wooded slopes in the mountains. **1954** CA Div. Beaches & Parks *Pt. Lobos Wild Flowers* 23 **cwCA,** *Gum-weed (Madia dissitiflora)*. . . A heavily scented, viscid secretion from the herbage glands is responsible for the common name of this wildflower. **1959** Munz-Keck *CA Flora* 1116, *M[adia] gracilis*. . . Gumweed. **1973** Hitchcock-Cronquist *Flora Pacific NW* 538, Often along roadsides. . . Gum-weed. . . *M[adia] gracilis.*

3 A **skeletonweed** (here: *Lygodesmia juncea*).

1911 [see **1** above]. [**1939** Medsger *Edible Wild Plants* 232, The Skeleton Weed is . . often infested with small round galls which contain much gum. According to M. R. Gilmore, this plant was used by the Indians of the Missouri River valley for producing chewing gum. He says: "The stems were gathered and cut into pieces to cause the juice to exude. When this hardened, it was collected and used for chewing."]

gum-well See **gum** n^2 **3d**

gumwood n

Esp **sweet gum,** but also **black gum 1;** also the wood of such a tree or of a **gum tree 3.**

1709 (1967) Lawson *New Voyage* 217 **NC,** The [Indian] Women . . make Bowls, Dishes, and Spoons, of Gum-wood, and the Tulip-Tree. [*DARE* Ed: This quot most likely refers to *Nyssa sylvatica*, once known as "bowl gum."] **1762** Gronovius *Flora Virginica* 151 **eVA,** *Liquidambar foliis palmato-angulatis*. . . Nostratibus Gumwood. **1876** Hobbs *Bot. Hdbk.* 51, Gum wood, the wood of Eucalyptus. **1950** Peattie *Nat. Hist. Trees* 310, To furniture salesmen the wood [of *Liquidambar styraciflua*] is plain Gum, or Gum wood, which is confusingly ambiguous, since many trees are called so. **1960** Vines *Trees SW* 325/2, American Sweetgum—*Liquidambar styraciflua*. . . Vernacular names are White Gum. . . Gum-wood . . and Star-leaf Gum.

gun n

1 See **gunning stick.**

2 in phr *my guns:* Used as a mild oath; see quot. Cf **great guns**

1966 *DARE* (Qu. NN27a, *Weakened substitutes for 'god': "My ______!"*) Inf **SD**1, Guns.

gun v^1

In logging:

a See quots; hence vbl n *gunning*. Cf **gunning stick**

1905 U.S. Forest Serv. *Bulletin* 61.39 [Logging terms], *Gun*. . . To aim a tree in felling it. In the case of very large, brittle trees, such as redwood, a sighting device (gunning stick) is used. **1956** Sorden-Ebert *Logger's Words* 17 **Gt Lakes,** *Gunned* [sic]. . . To direct the fall of a tree. **1958** McCulloch *Woods Words* 75 **Pacific NW,** *Gunning*—Using a sight gun to look out the line of fall of a tree. Also called sighting.

b Of a log or pole: to slip out of place or position; also, to cause a log to fall out of place; see quots.

1939 FWP *ID Lore* 244, [The foreman] put him to work sky-hooking (top-loading) with me, but seeing he was a stubble-jumper (greenhorn), the school mom (forked pole used in loading) gunned (turned) and got me. **1942** Berrey-Van den Bark *Amer. Slang* 512.14 [Logging terms], Gun, *of a log, to slip up endwise in a boom.* **1956** Sorden-Ebert *Logger's Words* 17 **Gt Lakes,** *Gunned*. . . Failed to get a log on a car or a sleigh, so that one end rests on the ground resembling the barrel of a cannon.

gun v^2 See **give A2a, 3a**

gun-barrel house n **esp GA** Cf **gunshot house**

=**shotgun house.**

1971 *Thompson Coll.* **AL, GA,** *Gun-barrel house* . . shotgun house. Both terms known in Birmingham 1920's, Pike Co GA 1971. **1986** Pederson *LAGS Concordance,* 3 infs, **GA,** Gun-barrel house.

gunboat n

1 also, by assim, *gumboat:* A large foot or shoe. [From the size and shape] *joc* Cf **canal boat**

1870 Macrae *Americans* 1.68 **NYC,** Most of the people wear rubbers over their boots—gunboats as they sometimes call them from their size. **1872** Schele de Vere *Americanisms* 343, It was reserved for the soldiers of the late Civil War to bestow the name of *gunboats* upon the contract shoes furnished them, which were apt to be as clumsy and awkward as gunboats appear to sailors. **1919** *DN* 5.69 **NM,** *Gunboats,* the feet. "Keep your gunboats out of my way." **1950** *WELS (Big feet)* 14 Infs, **WI,** Gunboats. **1950** *WELS Suppl.* 3 Infs, **WI,** *Gunboats*—large or heavy shoes. **1956** McAtee *Some Dialect NC* 21, *Gunboats* . . shoes, especially large ones, facetious. **c1960** *Wilson Coll.* **csKY,** *Gunboats*. . . Shoes, esp. big ones. **1965-70** *DARE* (Qu. X38, *Joking names for unusually big or clumsy feet*) 78 Infs, **scattered,** Gunboats; **CA**170, **PA**49, Gumboats; (Qu. W11, *Men's low, rough work shoes*) Inf **MA**79, Gunboats; (Qu. W42b, . . *Nicknames for men's square-toed shoes*) Inf **NC**82, Gunboats. **c1970** *Halpert Coll.* 27 **wKY, nwTN,** His gunboats are number twelve = big shoes.

2 In railroading: see quots.

1940 *RR Mag.* Apr 45, *Gunboat*—Large steel car. **1942** Berrey-Van den Bark *Amer. Slang* 774.8 [Railroad lingo], *Gunboat, steel boy,* a steel freight car. **1960** Wentworth-Flexner *Slang* 235, *Gunboat*. . . An iron coal car; a railroad gondola. *Railroad use.*

3 pl: A game; see quot. Cf **battleship**

1968 *DARE* (Qu. EE39, . . *Games played on paper by two people*) Inf **NY**67, Gunboats.

gunbright n [See quots 1918, 1929]

A **horsetail 1:** usu *Equisetum hyemale,* but also *E. arvense.*

1876 Hobbs *Bot. Hdbk.* 51, Gunbright, Scouring rush, Equisetum hyemale. **1898** *Jrl. Amer. Folkl.* 11.283, *Equisetum hiemale* [sic] . . gun bright, Oxford Co., Me. **1900** Lyons *Plant Names* 147, *E[quisetum] hyemale*. . . Gun-bright. **1918** Farrow *Dict. Military Terms, Gunbright,* Dutch rush *(equisetum hyemale)* much used in scouring gun barrels. **1929** *Torreya* 29.149 **ME,** The curious Equisetum arvense might not attract every child's attention, but it did mine, and its universal name was *"Gunbright"* because it was used to brighten the metal parts of guns, as well as pewter. Not until many years later did I know it as *"Scouring Rush."* **1950** FWP *Guide ID* 63, Less lovely but more widely distributed in Idaho is the scouring-brush, one of the commonest of the large horsetails. . . Known variously as scrub-grass, . . gun-bright [etc].

gundalo(w) See **gondola 1**

gundinga n

1949 *AmSp* 24.109 **neFL,** *Gundinga* [gən'dɪŋə]. . . A kind of pudding, or sausage, made from hog haslet (liver, lights, and heart).

gunebo lily n [See quot 1896] Cf **gumbo lily 1**

A **stickleaf** (here: *Mentzelia decapetala*).

1896 *Jrl. Amer. Folkl.* 9.188 **ND,** *Mentzelia ornata*. . . Gunebo lily, . . Grown in Gunebo Hills. **1900** Lyons *Plant Names* 245, *M[entzelia] decapetala*. . . Gunebo Lily. **1911** *Century Dict. Suppl., Lily*. . . *Gunebo lily, Mentzelia decapetala* . . native of the Great Plains.

gun fence n *old-fash* Cf *DS* L61, 62

See quots.

1889 *Century Dict.* 2179, *Gun fence,* a fence built of rails, with one end resting upon the ground, the other supported by two crossed stakes. **1933** *Hanley Disks* **NH,** *Gun fence*. . . A zigzag rail fence. Some call it a gun fence. . . but we've forgot that now, we don't use it.

gun fever n Cf **buck fever 1**

1970 *DARE* (Qu. P36, *When a hunter sees a deer or other game animal and gets so excited he can't shoot, he has ______*) Inf **PA**242, Gun fever.

gungeon See **gudgeon 1**

gun greaser n

=**red-throated loon.**

1955 MA Audubon Soc. *Bulletin* 39.309, *Red-Throated Loon*. . . Gun-greaser (New England. Perhaps the fat was used as a preservative of firearms.)

gunja n, also attrib Pronc-spp *gunjer, gunjuh, gunjur* [See quot 1949] **chiefly S Atl** *esp freq among Gullah speakers*

Gingerbread; a ginger or molasses cake or cookie.

1836 Simms *Mellichampe* 2.192 **seSC** [Black], "Take piece of gunja—he berry good, Mass Booram—my wife make 'em." The negro broke his molasses-cake evenly between himself and the soldier. **1922** Gonzales

Black Border 305 **sSC, GA coasts** [Gullah glossary], *Gunjuh*—the scalloped molasses cakes sold in Southern country stores and commissaries. **1930** Woofter *Black Yeomanry* 54 **seSC** [Gullah], *Gunjuh:* ginger or molasses cookies. **1930** [see **horse cake**]. **1939** Harris *Purslane* 3 **neNC,** The supper dishes washed, the milk set to clabber, a pan of gunjers [Footnote: Molasses cookies] made for tomorrow. **1949** Turner *Africanisms* 193 [Gullah], ['gɑnǰɑ ('kɑnǰɑ)] 'gingerbread' [<] H[ausa], [sɑkɑndzɑbir] 'ginger'. **1950** *PADS* 14.34 **SC,** *Gunjer* ['gʌnǰə]. . . 1. Gingerbread. 2. A huge ginger cracker formerly sold in country stores. . . *Gunjer pone.* . . A pone of gingerbread. **1950** [see **horse cake**]. **1984** Wilder *You All Spoken Here* 84 **Sth,** *Gunjers:* Ginger or molasses cookies.

gunk n

1 also *gonk:* A dull, stupid person. [Cf *EDD, SND gunk* a dunce or blockhead, but perh an independent development]

1966–67 *DARE* (Qu. HH3, *A dull and stupid person*) Inf **GA**13, Gonk; (Qu. HH16, *Uncomplimentary words . . to show that you don't think much of a person: ". . He's a______.*") Inf **GA**13, Gonk; **AR**55, Gunk.

‡**2** with *the:* See quot. [Prob *gunk* dirty or sticky residue]

1968 *DARE* (Qu. BB28, *Joking names that people make up for imaginary diseases: "He must have the ______."*) Inf **NY**80, Gunk.

gunlow See **gondola 1**

gunmouth snapper n

The blackfin **snapper** *(Lutjanus buccanella).*

1960 Amer. Fisheries Soc. *List Fishes* 71, Snapper . . gunmouth—see snapper, blackfin.

gunna See **go** v **A4d**

gunneled out adj phr [*gunnel* var of *gunwale*]

1949 *AmSp* 24.109 **cnGA,** *Gunneled out.* . . Projecting, as of a boy's pockets.

gunnerfitz, gunnerfitzich See **wunnerfitz**

gunnie sack See **gunny sack** n

gunning See **gun** v[1] **a**

gunning stick n Also *gun(stick)*

In logging: a sighting device; see quots.

1905 [see **gun** v[1] **a**]. **1958** McCulloch *Woods Words* 75 **Pacific NW,** *Gun.* . . A frame of long sticks used for sighting the direction of fall and the angle of the undercut, when falling big trees. **1959** *AmSp* 34.78 **nCA** [Logger lingo], *Gunstick, gunning stick.* . . Two sticks attached by a hinge, used to determine the direction of the fall of a tree.

gunny bag(ging) See **gunny sack** n

gunny-bag season n [Cf **gunny sack** n]

A period of time when hunting is illegal and game is concealed in a bag.

1966 *DARE* (Qu. P35a) Inf **MT**4, Gunny-bag season—when hunting season is closed.

gunny sack n Also *gunny bag,* ~ *poke* Also sp *gunnie sack;* pronc-spp *gurney sack* (cf Intro "Language Changes" I.8), *ginnie sack;* for addit varr see quots **chiefly west of Appalachians** See Map and Map Section Cf **bran sack, croker sack, guano sack** =**burlap bag;** also *gunny sacking,* ~ *bagging* a strong, coarse sacking fabric.

1820 *Columbian Centinel. Amer. Federalist* (Boston MA) 1 Jan 3/5 **Boston MA,** [Advt:] *At Auction. . . Borax, Ginger,* Gunny Bags, &c. **1856** Olmsted *Journey Slave States* 630, A curtain or screen, of gunny-bagging, was hung across the doorway. **1862** in 1943 *Pacific NW Qrly.* 34.42 **Pacific NW,** To look at the claims on the hill. They are on the *rim rock* & prospect very fine, as much as a dollar to the gunny sack. **1903** (1965) Adams *Log Cowboy* 220 **West,** If you've got any gunny sacks or old tarpaulins, bring them. **1905** *DN* 3.82 **nwAR,** *Gunny sack.* . . A bag made of tow. 'This gunny sack's full of bran.' Common. **1909** Porter *Options* 148, His outward vesture appeared to be kind of gunny-sacking cut and made into a garment that would have made the fortune of a London tailor. **1914** *DN* 4.108 **KS,** *Gurney.* . . Gunny. "Gurney sacks to put potatoes in." **1927** in 1944 *ADD* **WV,** Gunnie sack = Crocus bag. **1940** *Qrly. Jrl. Speech* 26.265 **VA,** A *burlap bag* may be a "gunny sack." **1965–70** *DARE* (Qu. F23, *A container made of rough, loosely woven, brown cloth; commonly used for potatoes, etc*) 270 Infs, **widespread, but less freq Atlantic,** Gunny sack; **CA**138, **IL**31, **IN**48, **WI**58, 66, Gunny bag; **WI**58, Gunny poke; (Qu. F19, *A cloth container for grain*) 52 Infs, **chiefly west of Appalachians,** Gunny sack; **UT**3, Gunny bag; (Qu. F20, *A cloth container for feed*) 43 Infs, **chiefly west of Appalachians,** Gunny sack; (Qu. F21, *A cloth or paper container that you buy flour in*) Inf **IL**45, Gunny sack; (Qu. W41, . . *Expressions . . for someone whose clothes never look right or who always dresses carelessly*) Inf **WA**30, Fits like a gunny sack tied in the middle. **1966** *DARE* FW Addit **FL**1, *Ginnie sack* . . burlap sack. **1968–69** *DARE* Tape **AZ**11, For a cooling system . . Father made shelves outside and put gunny sacks down them; **CA**90, They put a gunny sack, or a burlap sack around them; **CA**100, Just then a man came along with a gunny sack full; **TX**18, I've gone out there in two or three hour time catch a gunny sack full of golden croakers. **1973** Allen *LAUM* 1.210 **Upper MW** (as of c1950), *Gunny sack* prevails throughout the U[pper] M[idwest].

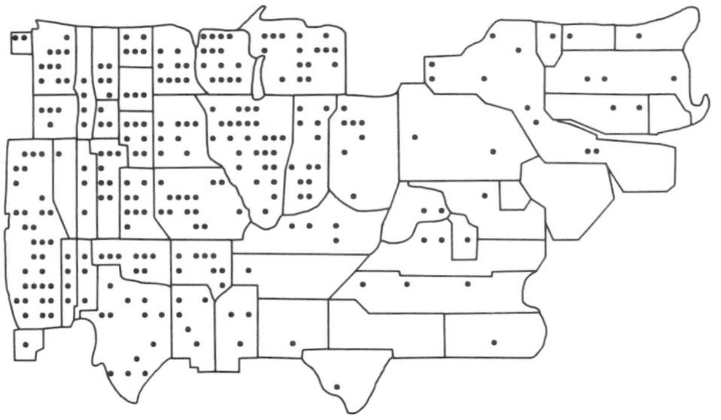

•gunny sack n + varr (Qq. F23, F19, F20, F21, W41)

gunny sack adj Also *gunny sacked* Cf **haywire** adj **1**

Of little value or substance; damaged, misused.

1927 *DN* 5.449 [Underworld jargon], *Gunny sack charge.* . . To be arrested on the charge of being a "suspicious person." **1942** *AmSp* 17.103 [Truck driver lingo], *Gunnysacked.* Badly abused (of a truck). **1950** *Western Folkl.* 9.381 **neCA** [Lumberjack language], *Gunnysack.* Does not amount to much. Used of persons and things. **1958** McCulloch *Woods Words* 75 **Pacific NW,** *Gunny sack show*—A poor operation; haywire. *Gunny sacked*—Broken or fouled up. **1971** Tak *Truck Talk* 79, *Gunny sack job:* a badly used, dilapidated truck.

gunny sacking See **gunny sack** n

gunpoint wedding See **gunshot wedding**

gunshoot n

A gun battle.

1939 Griswold *Sea Is. Lady* 131 **SC** (as of c1865) [Gullah], Yankee been comin' an' goin' sense de gunshoot to Bay P'int. *Ibid* 182, "De gunshoot to Bay P'int," that cataclysmic hour from which all island time was now reckoned.

gunshot house n [Prob by metath from **shotgun house;** cf Intro "Language Changes" I.1] Cf **gun-barrel house**

1967 LeCompte *Word Atlas* 117 **seLA,** *A long house one room wide, of two or three rooms. . .* gun-shot house. [1 of 21 infs] **1986** Pederson *LAGS Concordance (A house having three or more rooms arranged in a line)* 3 infs, **Gulf Region,** Gunshot house; 1 inf, **Atlanta GA,** The little gunshot houses.

gunshot wedding n Also *gunpoint wedding* [Prob by metath from *shotgun wedding*]

1968–70 *DARE* (Qu. AA20, *A marriage that takes place because a baby is on the way*) Infs **CT**1, 6, **IA**41, **MA**69, **NJ**9, **NC**82, **VA**41, Gunshot wedding; **RI**1, Gunshot [wedding]; **MD**41, Gunpoint wedding. [8 of 9 Infs old; 8 of 9 Infs female]

gunstick n

1 A ramrod.

1709 (1967) Lawson *New Voyage* 107 **NC, SC,** Arrow-Wood . . is used, by the *Indians,* for Arrows and Gun-Sticks. **1899** (1912) Green *VA Folk-Speech* 210, *Gunstick.* . . A ramrod; generally a long and big one, used for cleaning a gun. **1934** (1943) *W2, Gunstick.* . . A ramrod. *Rare.* **c1950** *Hall Coll.* **eTN, wNC,** *Gun-stick.* . . A ramrod.

2 See **gunning stick.**

gunter n [In ref to Engl mathematician Edmund *Gunter* (1581–1626)] *arch*

In var phrr indicating accuracy, exactitude, certainty: See quots.

1751 RI (Colony) Laws Statutes *Acts & Resolves* 22, No Rum, Molasses, Wine . . or any other Liquid . . sold by Measure in Casks, shall be gagued [sic] in any other Way . . but according to the most . . exact Mathematical Rule, commonly called, Gauging by *Gunter.* **1854** Stephens *High Life in NY* 101 **CT,** If I don't du everything according to gunter, he'll be . . fussing about like an old hen. **a1859** *NY Tribune* [nd] (Bartlett *Americanisms*), A respected citizen of Detroit . . has published a letter entirely exonerating General Cass from the charge of having defrauded his association in the land speculations. He is positive that all was done *according to Gunter.* **1909** *DN* 3.377 **eAL, wGA,** *Sure as gunter. . .* Very surely.

gunter worm n

=**earthworm.**

1949 *AmSp* 24.109 **nwSC,** Gunter worm. . . Earthworm.

gunwad n

Either the **piping plover** or the **least sandpiper.**

1923 U.S. Dept. Ag. *Misc. Circular* 55 **VA,** Least Sandpiper *(Pisobia minutilla).* . . In local use . . gunwad. *Ibid* 70, Piping Plover *(Charadrius melodus).* . . In local use . . gunwad, little plover. **1956** *AmSp* 31.184 **VA,** *Gunwad*—Piping plover . . Least sandpiper.

gun-wadding n Also *gun-wadding bread* Cf *DS* H13, **wasp's nest**

Bread, esp that with insubstantial texture.

1942 Berrey–Van den Bark *Amer. Slang* 926.3 [Western terms], Gunwaddin' bread, wasp nest, *light bread.* **1946** *AmSp* 21.33 **ceTX** [College slang], *Gun-wadding. . .* Bread. . . not use[d] . . as an adjective. **1958** *PADS* 29.11 **nw,cwTN,** *Gun wadding* (. . light bread, store bread, wasp nest): A disparaging term for bread.

gunwood n

The black **walnut** *(Juglans nigra).*

1950 Moore *Trees AR* 26, *Black Walnut (Juglans nigra . .).* Local Names: Walnut, American Walnut, Gunwood. . . *Uses* Furniture, . . gun stocks, . . and ornamentals. The nuts are a valuable product.

guope v [Var of **cope** v[2]]

Come!—used to call horses from pasture.

1956 Ker *Vocab. W. TX* 203, Call to horses in the pasture. . . *goupe* or *goupe* plus name. [7 of 67 infs]

guppy-gobbler n [In ref to eating fish on Friday] *joc* Cf *DS* CC4, **mackerel snapper**

A Catholic.

1964 *PADS* 42.34 **Chicago IL,** The Catholic . . *guppy-gobbler. . .* given playfully by [a Catholic] Irish[man]. **1983** Allen *Lang. Ethnic Conflict* 53, *Catholics* (generic terms) . . fish-eater . . also guppy-gobbler.

gurgeon stopper n [*gurgeon* prob var of *gurjun* a balsam tree]

A **stopper** (here: *Eugenia foetida*).

1884 Sargent *Forests of N. Amer.* 88, *Eugenia buxifolia. . .* Gurgeon Stopper. **1897** Sudworth *Arborescent Flora* 305, *Eugenia buxifolia. . .* Gurgeon Stopper. **1946** West–Arnold *Native Trees FL* 154, *Gurgeon Stopper. . .* occurs from Cape Canaveral on the east coast and the Caloosahatchee River on the west coast southward. **1979** Little *Checklist U.S. Trees* 128, *Eugenia foetida* . . boxleaf stopper . . gurgeon stopper.

gurgle v

1 also with *down:* To eat noisily; to drink, guzzle. [*OED gurgle* v. 3 "To *gurgle down:* to swallow with a gurgle." 1825; cf **guggle**]

1942 Berrey–Van den Bark *Amer. Slang* 92.13, *[To] drink. . .* gurgle. **1966–70** *DARE* (Qu. H11b, *If . . [somebody] makes a noise with his food, he* ______) Infs **MI**34, **NY**12, **VA**72, Gurgles; (Qu. DD17, *To drink a great deal, or too fast: "He doesn't just drink, he* ______*."*) Infs **AR**47, **NC**87, **OK**52, **TX**74, Gurgles (it down).

2 To gargle. [*OED gurgle* v. 1 *"Obs."*] *arch*

1913 *DN* 4.4 **swME,** *Gurgle. . .* To gargle. **1934** (1943) *W2, Gurgle. . .* To gargle. *Obs.*

gurgle n

Liquor; a gulp or swallow of liquor.

1942 Berrey–Van den Bark *Amer. Slang* 99.1, *Liquor. . .* gurgle. **1966–69** *DARE* (Qu. DD18, *A drink of liquor, or the amount of liquor taken in one swallow: "He took a good* ______*."*) Infs **CA**158, **WA**11, Gurgle.

gurgle down See **gurgle** v **1**

gurky adj [Echoic; cf *OEDS gurk* v. "To belch"]

1986 *DARE* File **swWI** (as of c1950), *Gurky*—squeamish; reported by an elementary school teacher.

gurnet n [Etym unknown]

An ocean inlet or cove—often used in place names; see quots.

1890 *DN* 1.11 **swME, seMA,** The word "gurnet," as heard at Brunswick, Me., used of a small inlet from the ocean, and the use of the same word as a proper name ("The Gurnet" at Plymouth, Mass.) **1946** Attwood *Length ME* 14 [Geographical terms], *Gurnet*—The meaning of this term is not clear from its various applications: The Gurnet, a two mile long cove between Orr Island and Sebascodegan Island . . [;] Simons Gurnet, a narrow passage south of Buttermilk Point . . ; Prince Gurnet, a narrow passage south of Prince Point . . ; and Gurnets Nose, . . an unidentified place name in York Deeds. **1975** Gould *ME Lingo* 119, *Gurnet*—A word of unknown origin, it means a thoroughfare in salt water. Older Mainers pronounced it *GURN-n't,* accenting the first syllable, but today it is usually *gur-NETT. The Gurnet* connects Harpswell Sound with the Atlantic Ocean, and adjacent land in both Brunswick and Harpswell is called *The Gurnet.*

gurney n [See quot 1965] *old-fash*

An ambulance.

1965 Tamony *Americanisms* **San Francisco CA** (as of c1912), San Francisco's. . . emergency hospital ambulances were called *gurneys. Ibid,* As the San Francisco police patrol wagon developed . . to a sided-and-roofed vehicle in the 1890's, with its entrance at the rear, and as the ambulance gift of Mr. Fair's daughters in 1894–1895 trotted to calls, it may be assumed that these vehicles were nicknamed after the rear-entrance Gurney Cab, then also a novelty. **1967** *DARE* (Qu. N1, . . *An ambulance*) Inf **CA**15, Gurney. [*DARE* Ed: Inf **CA**15 is author of quot 1965.]

gurney sack See **gunny sack** n

gurnipper See **gallinipper**

gurried up See **gurry** n **2**

‡**gurrump** n [Echoic]

A **bullfrog 1.**

1968 *DARE* (Qu. P22, . . *A very large frog that makes a deep, loud sound*) Inf **NY**66, Gurrump [gɚˈrʌmp].

gurry n [*SND goor* n. 4 "Slimy matter scraped from fish; fish refuse. . . Also *gouries* . . and *goorie*"]

1 Fishing offal.

1838 MA Ag. Surv. *Rept. for 1837* 101, Animal Manures. . . Fish. Fish oil. Gurry and blubber. **1859** (1968) Bartlett *Americanisms* 186, *Gurry.* The slime and blood of fish. A fisherman's word. **1882** *Harper's New Mth. Mag.* Sept 593/1 **eNEng,** It do look as if you had been wading through gurry, or cutting fish bate, or something. **1905** Wasson *Green Shay* 55 **NEng,** I came out aboard of ye to-night a-purpose to see what about them gurry-pens you was telling was stove up so bad here a spell ago. **1940** White *Wild Geese* 79 **NW** (as of 1890s), It did not seem credible that a grown man should never have seen a deep-sea gurry rig. **1968** *DARE* (Qu. O2, . . *An old, clumsy boat*) Inf **AK**1, Gurry wagon—for a fishing boat—disparaging or affectionate; (Qu. BB25, . . *Common skin diseases*) Inf **AK**1, Gurry sores—fishermen get gurry sores on their wrists from handling fish. **1975** Gould *ME Lingo* 119, *Gurrybutt*—A bowl, pail, tub, etc., used as a receptacle for clam and lobster shells at table. **1990** *DARE* File **sME coast** (as of c1970), They just throw the gurry overboard as they clean the fish. Makes a slimy mess.

2 By ext: dirt; clutter; also adj phr *gurried up* dirty; messy.

1942 ME Univ. *Studies* 56.63, Whaling and fishing . . terms were . . often used in a figurative sense. . . The slimy mess of scales and guts from cleaning fish was called *gurry* [Footnote: Fig[urative meaning] Disgusting, thick dirt]. **1949** *Harper's Mag.* July 54/1 **NYC,** The children finally dropped off to sleep, spread amid the gurry on the back seat, like dolls thrown any which way on a rumpled bed. **1975** Gould *ME Lingo* 119, To be "all *gurried* up" is to be in a mess, whether from fish gurry or something else.

3 Fig: rubbish, nonsense.

1937 *Sun* (Baltimore MD) 2 Jan 6/5 *(Hench Coll.),* Mr. Kent struck a new note with his reference to "this kind of gurry." A distinct shiver went over those readers who follow Mr. Mencken, and sure enough!—the very next day . . Mr. Mencken made an attack upon "the lamentably non-constructive Frank R. Kent."

gush n, v Pronc-sp *gursh* Cf Intro "Language Changes" I.8

A Forms.

1930s in 1944 *ADD* **eWV,** *Gush.* . . Gursh [gɝš], v. **1942** Hall *Smoky Mt. Speech* 41 **eTN, wNC,** The occasional employment of [ɝ] for [ʌ] in *bus, fuss, gush* suggests hypercorrection for such forms as [bʌst] *burst,* etc.

B As noun.

1 An abundance, a large quantity. *arch*

1849 *Knickerbocker* 34.407/2, Shese a powerfull big boat, and kin tote a gush of pork. **1859** (1968) Bartlett *Americanisms* 186, *Gush.* A great abundance. A Texan would say, "We have got a gush of peaches in our neck of the woods." **1889** (1971) Farmer *Americanisms* 282, *Gush.*—A large quantity; abundance; e.g., a *gush* of cattle, fruit, etc.

2 Nonsense, lies.

1887 in 1950 *AmSp* 25.33 **New Orleans LA,** About Gogan gettin' dat gun from Weideman is all gush. **1965** *DARE* (Qu. NN13, *When you think that the thing somebody has just said is silly or untrue: "Oh, that's a lot of ______.")* Inf **MS**30, Gush.

3 See quot.

1968 *DARE* (Qu. X9, . . *A person's mouth . . "I wish he'd shut his ______.")* Inf **PA**162, Gush [gʌš], trap.

4 also *gusher;* Of wind: a gust; also v *gush* to gust, adj *gushy* gusty. [Engl dial] **scattered, but esp Sth, TX** See Map

1965–70 *DARE* (Qu. B14, *When the wind is blowing unevenly, sometimes strong and sometimes weak, you say it's ______*) 12 Infs, **esp Sth, TX,** Blowing in gushes; **GA**19, **LA**11, **SC**20, 26, 29, Coming in gushes; **AL**48, **NY**3, 70, **OH**31, 69, **PA**176, **SC**1, Gushy; **LA**24, **NH**14, **OK**4, Gushing; **MO**1, **TN**24, Gushes; **AZ**7, Blowing in gushers; **GA**22, In gushes. **1986** Pederson *LAGS Concordance,* 1 inf, **neMS,** Gushy—gusting, blowing sporadically; 1 inf, **seMS,** Gushy; 1 inf, **cFL,** Gushes—gusts of wind.

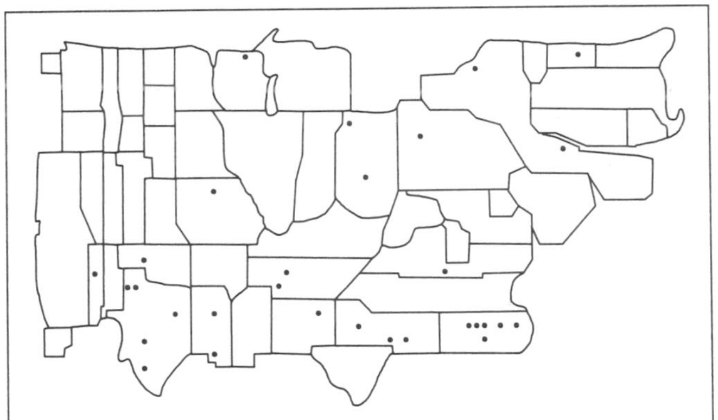

•gush B4 + varr (Qu. B14)

gusher n

1 A heavy rain.

1961 Folk *Word Atlas N. LA* map 0105, A very hard rain that comes suddenly and does not last very long. . . *gusher.* [1 of 275 infs] **1965–69** *DARE* (Qu. B25, . . *A very heavy rain . . "It's a regular ______.")* Infs **AR**52, **MO**2, 17, **OH**39, 66, 71, **OK**4, **TX**2, 62, Gusher; (Qu. B24, . . *A sudden, very heavy rain)* Inf **OH**81, Gusher. [8 of 10 Infs old] **1966** Dakin *Dial. Vocab. Ohio R. Valley* 2.21, *Gusher.* [2 of 246 infs]

‡2 See quot.

1966 *DARE* (Qu. DD18, *A drink of liquor, or the amount of liquor taken in one swallow: "He took a good ______.")* Inf **MS**1, Gusher.

3 See **gush B4.**

gush-foot n

1970 *DARE* (Qu. X38, . . *Unusually big or clumsy feet)* Inf **MO**29, Gush-foot.

gushy See **gush B4**

guspachy See **gazpacho**

gusset, bust a v phr Also *bust one's gusset* [*gusset* a piece of fabric sewn into a garment to make it roomier] Cf **bust a gut**

1 To exert great effort.

1968 *DARE* (Qu. A22, . . *'To start working hard': "She had only ten minutes to clean the room, but she ______ [and had it done in no time].")* Inf **NJ**39, Bust her gusset.

2 also *split a gusset:* To break out laughing; to laugh very hard.

1950 *WELS (To laugh very hard: "I thought he would ______.")* 1 Inf, **WI,** Bust a gusset; 1 Inf, Split a gusset. **1966–69** *DARE* (Qu. GG30, *To suddenly break out laughing: "When he told her that, she just ______.")* Inf **WA**28, Bust a gusset [laughter]; (Qu. GG31) Infs **AL**6, **LA**23, **NJ**30, **NY**25, **PA**223, Bust a gusset; **CA**61, **CT**3, Split a gusset.

3 See quot.

1950 *WELS (When a person becomes over-excited, and loses control: "I thought he was going to ______!")* 1 Inf, **WI,** Bust a gusset.

Gussie n

In var intj phrr: See quots.

1966 *DARE* Tape **TX**46, One night she went out t' the thicket and the Rangers surrounded her. Boy, she did talk to 'em, by Gussie! "Come up on a decent woman out like that," [she] said, "y'ain't got no manners!" **1984** *DARE* File **csPA,** I recall hearing "Dear Gussie!" as an exasperated exclamation in Cumberland Co., Pa., during the late 1940s or early 1950s. *Ibid* **NEng,** Gussie Pete!—used as an interjection.

gussy adj [Cf *gussy up* to dress up, embellish]

1970 *DARE* (Qu. HH35, *A woman who puts on a lot of airs: "She's too ______ for me.")* Inf **OH**95, Highfalutin, gussy ['gʌsi].

gust n esp C Atl Cf **thunder-gust**

A thunderstorm, heavy rain.

1772 in 1919 *MD Hist. Mag.* 14.280 **cnMD,** We have some Apearance of a gust now at 5 a Clock. **1805** Parkinson *Tour* 1.45 **neVA,** Those hasty showers in the summer. . . are called *gusts.* A small cloud appears first, and very quickly gathers and blackens the sky. The wind begins to blow, with thunder and lightning. **1896** *DN* 1.418 **nwMD,** *Gust:* storm, shower. "It's so hot I believe we'll get a gust." **1907** *German Amer. Annals* 9.378 **sePA,** *Gust.* Thunder-storm. "I was kept at home by a gust." **1950** *WELS (A strong wind accompanied by rain)* 1 Inf, **WI,** Gust. **1951** *DE Folkl. Bulletin* 1.4/2, *Gust* (thunder-storm). **1966–68** *DARE* (Qu. B22, *Rain accompanied by thunder and lightning)* Infs **MD**26, **PA**29, Gust; (Qu. B24, . . *A sudden, very heavy rain)* Infs **AR**19, **IN**33, **KS**7, Gust. **1968** *DARE* FW Addit **PA**169, *Gust*—a thunderstorm. **1982** *Barrick Coll.* **csPA,** *Gust*—thunderstorm; usu. *thunder-gust.*

gust v [**gust** n]

To storm.

1939 *AmSp* 14.43 **PA,** 'It's going to gust' in Pennsylvania is nothing but a Kentucky 'downpour' or a South Carolina 'pourdown' or even a Rhode Island 'tempest.'

gut n

1 A stream, channel, or pool, esp in a tidewater area—often used in place names. **esp Delmarva** Cf **gutter** n[1] **2**

1636 in 1940 *AmSp* 15.269 **VA,** Beginning at a small gutt that runneth into the woods at the west end of the Clift of Westover. **1785** (1925) Washington *Diaries* 2.396 **eVA,** A channel through the bed of the River in a strait direction . . would be preferable to that through the Gut. **1813** in 1940 *AmSp* 15.269 **VA,** Thence to Potocam River crossing the uper [sic] end of a gut or pond. **1872** Schele de Vere *Americanisms* 97, The *Gut* is a local offshoot of the Susquehanna. . . in the Southern States *[gut]* is used to designate the outlet of a lake or river. **1899** (1912) Green *VA Folk-Speech* 211, *Gut.* . . A small waterway through a marsh. **1927** Adams *Congaree* 113 **Sth** [Black], *Gut:* a natural drain in the swamps, during the rainy season full of water. Every gut has a name, often known only to the Negroes. **1946** Attwood *Length ME* 14 [Geographical terms], *Gut*—A narrow passage in tidewater. Herring Gut. . . Or in a lake, Elliott Gut. **1946** *PADS* 6.16 **eNC** (as of 1900–10), *Gut.* . . A shallow, narrow, winding arm of a creek in a salt-water region. . . Common. **1968–70** *DARE* (Qu. C1, . . *A small stream of water not big enough to be a river)* Inf **DE**4, Gut—smaller than a crick; **MD**15, Gut—narrow stream through marsh where creek stops; Adeline Gut, Mill's Gut; **MD**36, Gut—much narrower than a creek; Sandy Creek Gut; **VA**47, Gut—salt water, runs up in fresh water but still called a gut, usually tidal; Andrews Gut; (Qu. C14, *A stretch of still water going off to the side from a river or lake)* Inf **DE**1, Gut—one local one is Emma's Gut; **VA**105, Guts—meaning a backwater; (Qu. C35) Inf **MD**32, Ben's

Gut—a ravine in Elkton [MD] with water running in it, divides the town [*DARE* Ed: This response may instead belong with sense **2** below]. **1970** *DARE* Tape **VA47**, They would make for tough . . sailing through these marshes because just a maze of guts and creeks . . and real sharp turns. **1970** *DARE* FW Addit **VA51**, "Taylor's Gut"—a low place where tidal water collects in high tide. Drains in during high tide and out through a drain during low tide. **1976** [see **hole** n **1b**]. **1982** Heat Moon *Blue Highways* 392 **Chesapeake Bay,** To the west, we could see across the entanglings of guts and coves and marsh grass, the far gray line of water.

2 A narrow passageway, esp a ravine or narrow valley. Cf **gutter** n[1] **3**

1640 in 1940 *AmSp* 15.269 **VA,** By the maine branch side to the Eastward of a little Gutt or Vally. **1860** in 1940 *AmSp* 15.269 **VA,** To 2 dogwoodes on the ridge at the head of a steep Gut. **1939** *LANE* Map 36 *(Ravine, notch)* 1 inf, **neMA,** Gut, deep and narrow. **1958** McCulloch *Woods Words* 75 **Pacific NW,** *Gut*—A narrow passage-way.

3 See quot. [Cf *EDD gut* sb.[1] 5 "A glutton"]

1968 *DARE* (Qu. H9, *If somebody always eats a considerable amount of food, you say he's a ______*) Inf **PA66**, Gut.

gut v See **get** v **A3, 4**

gut-breaker n Cf *DS* EE29

=**belly-flop 2.**

1916 *DN* 4.305 **eMA,** *Gut-breaker. . . = belly-whopper,* a flat dive.

gutbucket n

1 A pail or bucket; see quots.

1939 (1959) Ramsey-Smith *Jazzmen* 12 **New Orleans LA,** From barrel-houses and honkey-tonks came many of the descriptive words which were applied to the music played in them; such as . . "gutbucket," referring originally to the bucket which caught drippings or "gutterings" from the barrels, later to the unrestrained brand of music that was played by small bands in the dives. **1942** Berrey-Van den Bark *Amer. Slang* 84.13, *Chamber pot* . . gut bucket. **1959** *Jazz Rev.* 2.2.12/3 (as of c1920) [Black], You could only hear the blues and real jazz in the gutbucket cabarets where the lower class went. The term 'gutbucket' came from the chitterlings bucket. Chitterlings are the guts of a hog and the practice used to be to take a bucket to the slaughter house and get a bucket of guts. **1960** Wentworth-Flexner *Slang* 236 (as of c1890-1900), *Gutbucket*. . . A pail used to carry beer, food, or water. *c1890, used by Southern chain gangs and laborers, usu. Negro.* . . A bucket or other container hung in a conspicuous place or passed around in a crowd in order to solicit or collect contributions of money for beer or food. *A practice of itinerant musicians, c1900; usu. used in the South, esp. Mississippi river towns such as New Orleans.*

2 See quot.

1975 Gould *ME Lingo* 119, *Gut bucket*—A bait boat. Hence, any untidy craft, and a home, shop, baithouse, shed that needs a housecleaning.

gut burglar See **gut robber**

gut chain See **gut wrapper**

gut-hammer n Cf **gut-horn**

Esp among loggers: a dinner or wake-up bell; see quots.

1927 *DN* 5.449 [Underworld jargon], *Gut-hammer*. . . The dinner gong at a construction camp. **1934** (1940) Weseen *Dict. Amer. Slang* 80 [Among loggers and miners], *Gut hammer*—A triangular piece of iron on which a camp cook beats the signal for meal time. **1949** Peattie *Cascades* 149 **Pacific NW** [Logger talk], The gut-hammer would ding-dong the men out of their blankets at five. **1950** *WELS Suppl.* **cwWI,** *Gut-hammer*—A triangle used for dinner bell in lumber camp. **1956** Sorden-Ebert *Logger's Words* 17 **Gt Lakes. 1958** McCulloch *Woods Words* 75 **Pacific NW,** *Gut hammer*—A short piece of iron used to pound an old saw, an iron triangle, a truck brake drum, or other chunk of metal to make a loud noise indicating when grub is on the table. Also used to waken men in some camps. **1964** Hargreaves-Foehl *Story of Logging* 59 **MI.**

gut-hook n Also *gut-lancer, ~-wrench* **West**

A spur.

1936 Adams *Cowboy Lingo* 36, Naturally they [=spurs] received a full share of slang names, such as . . 'gut hooks.' **1940** Writers' Program *Guide NV* 76, The buckaroo's spurs are referred to as *steel, gads, hooks, gut lancers,* or *chihuahuas.* **1942** Whipple *Joshua* 334 **UT** (as of c1860), His ankles jingled with spurs—guthooks, the boys called them. **1968** Adams *Western Words* 137, *Gut wrenches*—A cowboy's name for his spurs. **1988** *DARE* File [Unidentified newspaper clipping], At the Fiesta de Los Vaqueros you'll hear words like gut hooks—spurs.

gut-horn n Cf **gut-hammer**

Among loggers: =**dinner horn.**

1958 McCulloch *Woods Words* 76 **Pacific NW,** *Gut horn*—In the old days, a long tin horn blown by the cook's helper to call a logging crew to eat; especially used when hot grub was carried out to the job. **1969** Sorden *Lumberjack Lingo* 46, *Gabriel*—A tin horn about three feet long used to call lumberjacks to meals. Same as dinner horn, gut horn.

gut-lancer See **gut-hook**

gutling adj [Cf *EDD gutling* ppl. adj. (at *guttle* v. 1. (2). (b)) "greedy, gluttonous."]

1969 *African Lang. Rev.* 8.45 [Gullah], Greedy . . ['gʌtlɪn].

gut pucker n Cf *DS* X34

1950 *WELS (The navel)* 1 Inf, **cwWI,** Gut pucker.

gut robber n Also *gut burglar* Cf **belly robber**

Esp among loggers: a cook, esp an inferior one.

1925 *AmSp* 1.137 **Pacific NW** [Logger talk], For each grade of cook they have a name full of meaning. "Gut-burglar," "stomach-robber," "stewbum," "sizzler," . . and "star chief." **1930** Williams *Logger-Talk* 18 **Pacific NW,** *Gut-robber:* An inferior or overly economical cook. **1956** Sorden-Ebert *Logger's Words* 17 **Gt Lakes,** *Gut-robber.* **1958** McCulloch *Woods Words* 76 **Pacific NW,** *Gut robber.* **1965** *DARE* FW Addit **nwCA** [Mining terms], *Gut robber*—mining camp cook. **1966** *DARE* Tape **MI10**, When you got into the cook camp part of a large [lumber] camp organization, it seemed to be kind of inevitable that a poor cook would be a "gut robber." **1967** *DARE* (Qu. D39) Inf **WA21**, Gut robber.

gut-rot n [By metath from *rotgut*]

1967 *DARE* (Qu. DD21b, . . *Bad liquor*) Inf **NY7**, Gut-rot.

guts n pl

1 See quot. [Abbr for *(a)spareguts* or similar var] Cf **asparagus A**

1969 *DARE* (Qu. I29, *Names or nicknames for asparagus*) Inf **CA111**, Guts.

2 in phr *keep one's guts:* To keep a secret, be discreet. [By analogy with *spill one's guts* to tell all]

1927 *Ruppenthal Coll.* **KS,** *To be unable to keep one's guts*—to disclose freely matters that should be kept secret or shared with the very discreet only. "One of the boys gave the thing away. He ain't able to keep his guts."

guts, feathers, and all n Cf *hair and hide* (at **hair** n **C3**), **hide and tallow,** *DS* LL25

Everything.

1958 McCulloch *Woods Words* 76 **Pacific NW,** *Guts, feathers and all*—The whole works.

gut-shrunk adj

1936 Adams *Cowboy Lingo* 153, When he [=the cowboy] expressed himself as being hungry, he was apt to use such phrases as being 'gut-shrunk.'

gut-sprung adj

Having a hernia or similar condition.

1947 Adams *Banner* 289 **NY,** Medicaments. Cure anything. Books to read. All tastes. Dandy shirts. . . Trusses for the gut-sprung. Good licker for the downhearted.

gutter n[1]

1 also *gutter pipe, ~ spout(er):* =**eaves trough. widespread, but somewhat less freq Inland Nth, N Midl** See Map on p. 856 and Map Section

1641 in 1857 New Haven (Colony) *Records* 55 **csCT,** If there be . . gutters to be laid. **1724** in 1925 Colonial Soc. MA *Pub.* 16.513 **ceMA,** [Voted], That Mr Flynt . . be desired to procure Spouts and Gutters . . for the North side of the Old College. **1839** Longfellow *Hyperion* 2.136 **ME,** Then the whole scene changed; and he thought himself a monk's-head on a gutter-spout. **1895** Remington *Pony Tracks* 77, The doorways and the gutter-pipes and the corral fences are festooned with the beef left to dry in the sun. **1949** Kurath *Word Geog.* 53, *Gutters* is in regular use on all social levels . . in the Southern area, . . in the Hudson Valley, Long Island, and nearly all of New Jersey, and . . in Eastern New

England. In southwestern Connecticut and in Philadelphia and vicinity *gutters* is now very common, but older regional expressions are still used by many. **1965–70** *DARE* (Qu. D28, *What hangs below the edge of the roof to carry off rain-water?*) 526 Infs, **widespread, but somewhat less freq Inland Nth, N Midl,** Gutter(s); 13 Infs, **scattered exc Sth, S Midl,** Rain gutter(s); **KY**45, **MA**8, **NY**69, 107, **TN**23, **VA**13, Gutter pipe(s); **CA**36, **NJ**22, **UT**3, Storm gutter(s); **CA**156, Drain gutter; **NJ**56, Hanging gutter; **DC**12, Gutter spouter; (Qu. D29, *The pipe that takes the collected rain-water down to the ground or to a storage tank*) 49 Infs, **scattered, but less freq Inland Nth, N Midl,** Gutter (pipe); **IL**5, **SC**66, Gutter spout; **CA**182, Rain gutter. **1967** Faries *Word Geog. MO* 73, The devices to carry off rain from the roof. . . *gutter spouts* [not common]. **1971** *AmSp* 46.170 **Chicago IL,** 'Suspended, or built-in, horizontal open-piping for draining rain from a roof' . . *gutters* [32 of 37 infs]. **1973** *AmSp* 48.55 **Upper MW,** *Gutters,* the trade term employed by carpenters, roofers, and their suppliers, has made deep inroads upon Northern *eavestrough.*

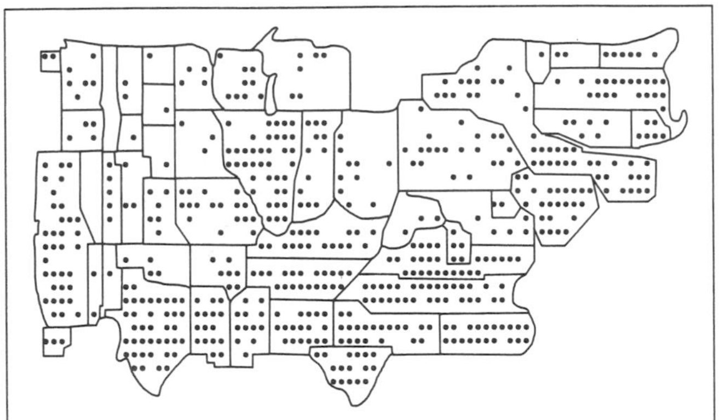

•gutter n[1] 1 + varr (Qq. D28, D29)

2 =gut n 1. [Cf *OED gutter* sb.[1] 1 "A watercourse . . a small brook or channel. . . *Obs.*" *EDD* →1889] **esp NEng, S Atl**

1656 in 1940 *AmSp* 15.269 **VA,** Running by gutter swampe unto the place of the Indian stone. **1675** in 1893 Providence RI Rec. Comm. *Early Rec.* 4.39 **RI,** On ye East sid [sic] of a little gutter on ye south side of a swompe. **1813** in 1940 *AmSp* 15.269 **VA,** To two beeches on the bank of a Gutter. **a1862** (1865) Thoreau *Cape Cod* 32 **seMA,** We crossed a brook . . called Jeremiah's Gutter. **1966** *DARE* (Qu. C1, . . *A small stream of water not big enough to be a river*) Inf **GA**11, Gutter—saltwater; backs up to a creek. **1983** Neuffer-Neuffer *Correct Mispronc.* 121 **seSC,** Mellisham Gutter. . . A gutter is a narrow saltwater drain that interlaces the marshes, usually dry at low tide. **1986** Pederson *LAGS Concordance (Small freshwater stream)* 2 infs, **GA, LA,** Gutter.

3 =gut n 2.

1966–70 *DARE* (Qu. C19, . . *Low land running between hills*) Inf **GA**77, Gutter, holler; (Qu. C21) Inf **MA**6, Gorge; Rattlesnake Gutter; **MA**100, Gutter; the Great Gutter—used to be where the courthouse now stands; Sandy Gutter. **1977** *Greenfield Recorder* (MA) 10 Dec 8, It began to get a little dusk there on the road up through the Gutter, and it was so quiet we could hear a tree snap in the frosty air. **1978** *Ibid* 25 Nov, My brother-in-law was going down Rattlesnake Gutter in Leverett, when a full grown wildcat crossed the road leisurely in front of him.

4 A channel cut by water.

1939 *LANE* Map 37 *(Gully, washout),* A channel cut by a stream of water in a field or across a road. . . 7 infs, **esp sNEng,** Gutter; [2 infs, **sNEng,** [gʌrə]]. **1954** *DE Folkl. Bulletin* 1.16/1, Gutter (gully eroded in a field). **1968–69** *DARE* (Qu. C21, *A deep place cut in sloping ground by running water*) Inf **GA**77, Gutter hole—the water guttered it out; **NY**80, Gutter, washout. **1986** Pederson *LAGS Concordance (Channel cut by erosion in road or field)* 7 infs, **Gulf Region,** Gutter.

5 The street. **NYC**

1981 *DARE* File **Brooklyn NYC** (as of c1950), One of my partners . . , who grew up in Brooklyn, tells me that in his childhood the street was called the "gutter." **1988** *Ibid* **Bronx NYC** (as of early 1950s), *Gutter* was commonly used for *street* especially by mothers when admonishing their children: "Don't run out in the gutter," or "Don't play in the gutter." *Ibid* **Bronx NYC.**

gutter n[2] Cf **gut-breaker,** *DS* EE29
=belly-flop 2.

1960 Wentworth-Flexner *Slang* 236, *[Gut]ter.* . . In diving, an attempted dive in which the diver falls prone on the water instead of going in head foremost; a belly-whacker. *Dial.* **1972** *DARE* File **Philadelphia PA,** *Gutter*—a dive in which the body is flat and the belly hits the water.

guttering n Pronc-sp *guttern* **chiefly S Midl** See Map
=eaves trough.

1956 Ker *Vocab. W. TX* 98, Troughs to take water off roof. . . guttering [1 of 67 infs], guttern [1 inf]. **1965–70** *DARE* (Qu. D28, *What hangs below the edge of the roof to carry off rain-water?*) 19 Infs, **chiefly S Midl,** Guttering; (Qu. D29, *The pipe that takes the collected rain-water down to the ground or to a storage tank*) Infs **MO**10, **VA**18, Guttering. **1970** Tarpley *Blinky* 76 **neTX,** *Troughs to take the water off the roof.* . . Other [=infrequent] responses . . guttering[,] guttern.

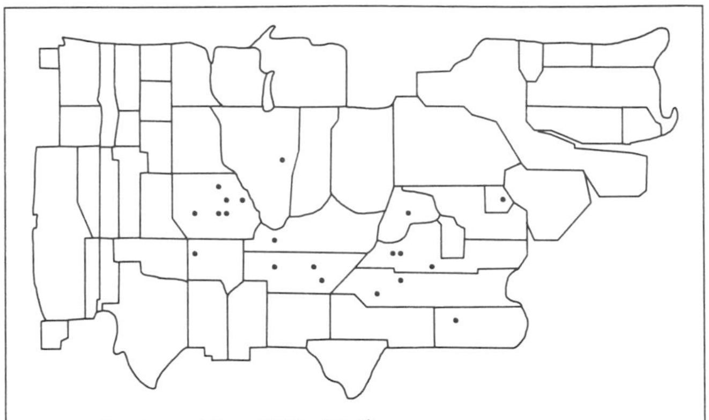

•guttering (Qq. D28, D29)

gutterman n Cf **swamper**
In logging: see quot 1969.

1902 U.S. Forest Serv. *Bulletin* 34.35 **NY,** The men cutting off the limbs are called "guttermen;" those driving the teams "skidders." **1905** *Ibid* 61.50 [Logging terms], *Gutterman.* . . [same as] Swamper. **1967** *DARE* Tape **NY**26, [FW:] What do they call the different men who work in the woods? [Inf:] For horses, they had the gutterman. He picked up the brush and got the logs all ready to hook onto, y'know. . . And I 'magine that he was the man that . . hooked the chain, or hooked the cable, whatever you use. **1969** Sorden *Lumberjack Lingo* 51 **NEng, Gt Lakes,** *Gutter man*—A man who cuts the limbs off a tree after felling, or cuts out a skidding road. Same as swamper, trimmer.

guttern See **guttering**

gutter pipe See **gutter** n[1] **1**

gutter road n
In logging: see quot 1969.

1905 U.S. Forest Serv. *Bulletin* 61.39 [Logging terms], *Gutter road.* The path followed in skidding logs. . . Syn[onyms]: drag road, runway, skidding trail, snaking trail. **1969** Sorden *Lumberjack Lingo* 51 **NEng, Gt Lakes,** *Gutter road*—A road for dragging logs from woods to skidway.

guttersnipe n

1 =Wilson's snipe.

1874 NY Acad. Sci. *Annals Lyceum Nat. Hist.* 10.383 **IL,** *G[allinago] gallinaria.* . . Common Snipe; Gutter Snipe. **1917** (1923) *Birds Amer.* 1.227, Wilson's Snipe—*Gallinago delicata.* . . Gutter Snipe. **1923** U.S. Dept. Ag. *Misc. Circular* 13.50 **IL,** Wilson Snipe . . *Gallinago gallinago delicata* . . In local use . . guttersnipe. *Ibid* 64 **ID,** Spotted Sandpiper *(Actitis macularia).* . . In local use . . gutter-snipe. **1932** Bennitt *Check-list* 29 **MO,** *Wilson's snipe. Capella delicata* . . gutter-snipe.

2 =spotted sandpiper.

1923 [see **1** above].

guttersnipe v, hence n *guttersniper,* vbl n *guttersniping*

1950 *WELS (Expressions meaning to pick up cigarette ends that have been thrown away)* 3 Infs, **WI,** Guttersniping; 2 Infs, Guttersnipe; 1 Inf, Guttersniper.

gutter spout(er) See **gutter** n[1] **1**

gutter trough n Cf **eaves trough**
See quots.

1969 *DARE* (Qu. D28, *What hangs below the edge of the roof to carry off rain-water?*) Inf **CA**107, Gutter troughs. **1973** Allen *LAUM* 1.178 **SD** (as of c1950), The channel at the edge of a roof to catch rainwater. . . gutter troughs [inf uncertain].

gutter washer n Cf **gully washer**

1969 *DARE* (Qu. B25, . . *Joking names . . for a very heavy rain*) Infs **GA**77, **IN**69, Gutter washer.

guttle v, hence n *guttler* [*OED* 1654 →]

See quots.

1899 (1912) Green *VA Folk-Speech* 211, *Guttler*. . . A greedy or gluttonous eater; a gormandizer. **1952** Brown *NC Folkl.* 1.548, *Guttle*. . . To swallow liquid noisily and avidly.

gutty adj [Scots, nEngl dial; cf *SND gutty* (at *guttie* adj. I. 2) "Fond of good eating, greedy, gluttonous"]

1950 *WELS (Words and expressions about greedy people: "She certainly is ———.")* 1 Inf, **seWI,** Plenty gutty. Common.

gutwagon n

1 A vehicle used to transport newly-delivered ewes and their lambs.

1950 Reeves *Man from SD* 216 **SD,** This year I put the herder on the tractor in the morning, and as fast as lambs came he loaded them under the tent on the "gutwagon." When he had six ewes and their lambs in the gutwagon, he came home to the barn. **1978** Doig *This House* 162 **MT** (as of c1955), Then a sledge with half a dozen of the jug pens atop it and pulled by a team of horses would begin to shuttle—the *gutwagon,* named for the placenta and accompanying muss from the newly-delivered ewes. . . As the gutwagon was unloaded, Dad or one of his helpers would tip each ewe onto her rump.

2a A hearse. Cf **meat wagon**

1949 Emrich *Wild West Custom* 72, An old-fashioned, windowed hearse, or "gut wagon," upon which tourists clamber macabrely to be photographed.

b in var phrr; Perh by ext: see quots.

1966–68 *DARE* (Qu. HH22c, *Talking about a very mean person . . "He's mean enough to ———."*) Inf **IA**45, Scare the buzzards off a gutwagon; (Qu. NN23, *Exclamations when people smell a very bad odor*) Inf **OK**42, That would stink a dog off a gutwagon. **1968** *Foxfire* Fall-Winter 25 **nGA,** If something has a strong, unpleasant scent, some say "It smells like a buzzard on a gut wagon."

3 Among loggers: see quot.

1958 McCulloch *Woods Words* 76 **Pacific NW,** *Gut wagon*—The camp supply wagon.

gut wrapper n Also *gut chain* **chiefly Pacific NW**

In logging: see quots.

1950 *Western Folkl.* 9.381 **neCA** [Lumberjack language], *Gut wrapper*. A chain or cable that is placed around a half-loaded truck to secure the load better. **1956** *AmSp* 31.150 **nwCA** [Logger lingo], *Gut wrapper*. . . A piece of chain or cable within a load of logs used to hold together an individual tier. **1958** McCulloch *Woods Words* 75 **Pacific NW,** *Gut chain*—A chain used when loading logs to pull the wing logs closer together, making a better saddle for the log on top. . . *Gut wrapper*—Same as gut chain. **1962** *AmSp* 37.269 **sCA** [Language of traffic policemen], *Gut-wrapper*. . . The main binding chain encircling a truck load of logs. **1967** *DARE* FW Addit **cOR,** *Gut wrapper*—A steel cable with a hook on one end and 10 feet of chain on the other; it ties on to the log to haul it.

gut-wrench See **gut-hook**

guv v See **give A2d, 3d**

guv n See **governor**

guv'mer See **government**

guv'nor See **governor**

guy n [Engl dial; cf *EDD guy* sb.[2] "A disguised form of the word 'God,' used in petty oaths."]

Used as a mild oath—also in phr *guyhang it.*

c1815 in 1847 Paulding–Paulding *Amer. Comedies* 46 **seNY,** But don't you know, guyhang it, if there be two of anything, one can swear for the other. **1838** *Knickerbocker* 12.297 **seNY,** 'Guy!' said he, in a tone which seemed hardly to realize the truth, 'I b'lieve I'm upsot!' **c1845** in 1847 Paulding–Paulding *Amer. Comedies* 140 **seNY,** Guy, he's as careful as a city mosquito in the autumn. **1949** in 1986 *DARE* File **swMI,** Guy! this bike stops fast. **1968** *DARE* (Qu. NN8a, *Exclamations of annoyance or disgust: "Oh ———. I've lost my glasses again."*) Inf **CA**80, Guy—young people say this.

guy v, hence ppl adj *guying* [*guy* to deride as if an effigy of Guy Fawkes] **scattered, but more freq Sth, S Midl** *somewhat old-fash*

To tease, kid, josh.

1869 Twain *Innocents* 278, Happy the Roman street-boy who ate his peanuts and guyed the gladiators from the dizzy gallery. **1897** Lummis *King of Broncos* 241 **NM,** I have seen friendly eyes turn misty on a sudden, when he "guyed" himself about it [=his poor marksmanship]. **1916** Lincoln *Mary-'Gusta* 131 **MA,** After the way I guyed you when I first came in! **1935** Sandoz *Jules* 81 **wNE** (as of 1880–1930), The Ainsworth *Journal* was running a matrimonial column, begun as a joke, but soon clothing itself in seriousness. The apparently guying surface was discounted by men who needed a cook. **1939** *Hall Coll.* **eTN, wNC,** *Guy*. . . To tease or rib. "These boys are always a-hollerin' and guyin' me about diggin' groundhogs." . . "They guy me about it." **1944** *PADS* 2.29 **KY, nwNC,** *Guy*. . . To tease. . . Common. **1950** *WELS* 1 Inf, **swWI,** Kidded him or guyed him. **1954** *Harder Coll.* **cwTN. 1960** Criswell *Resp. to PADS 20* **Ozarks,** *Guy*. . . Goes back over fifty years and still frequent. "Aw, quit guyin' him; you keep on and he'll quit the job." **c1960** *Wilson Coll.* **csKY. 1966–68** *DARE* (Qu. GG3, *To tease*) Inf **GA**1, Guying; **TX**40, Guy [FW: used by Inf in conv]; (Qu. KK36, *Talking about a person who is easily fooled: "It's easy to ———."*) Inf **LA**40, Guy him [FW: used by Inf in conv]. **1966–68** *DARE* FW Addit **TN**24, He was guying us about eating popcorn; **neWA,** I'm not guying you. **1969** *DARE* Tape **CA**158, People used to guy him about having to stay up to keep ahead of his students.

guyanosa See **gyanousa**

guyanther n

=**gyascutus.**

1950 *WELS (Imaginary wild animals that people tell stories about)* 1 Inf, **cWI,** Wampus cats, swamp auger, silver cats, guyanthers.

guyascutus, guyaskutus, guyasticutus See **gyascutus**

guyhang it See **guy** n

guying See **guy** v

-guys suff **HI** Cf **and them, them**

Used to form the plural of nouns; also used with names to refer to other people associated with the one named.

1972 Carr *Da Kine Talk* 132 **HI,** "We goin' meet Jane-guys at the movie." Heard in . . nonstandard speech . . , *-guys* is a kind of suffix with the meaning extended to include both female and male persons, that is, 'Jane and her pals'. **1981** *Pidgin To Da Max, -Dem*. . . You can add this word on when you want to describe a whole bunch of people and you don't want to name them all. Also *-guys, -folks.* **1983** *AmSp* 58.69 **HI,** In Hawaiian Creole. . . *Guys* is simply the plural morpheme, replacing older *them* or *dem*. . . *Guys* was first used only with animate nouns, e.g. *horse guys* = 'horses', but since 1920 or so has been used with inanimate nouns as well: *house guys* = 'houses'.

guy-scoot-er-sky, guy skootas See **gyascutus**

guzzle n

1 also *guzzler:* =**goozle** n **1.** [Engl, Scots dial] *somewhat old-fash*

1906 *DN* 3.138 **nwAR,** *Boozle, gozzle, guzzle*. . . Throat. **1943** Writers' Program NC *Bundle of Troubles* 29, Mr. Bullfrog swell up his neck, and he turn green around the guzzle. *Ibid* 106, He is skinny and runty, and he got a big Adam apple in his guzzle what bob up and down when he talk. **1950** *WELS (The throat)* 2 Infs, **cWI,** Guzzle. **1965–70** *DARE* (Qu. X7) 13 Infs, **esp Sth, S Midl,** Guzzle; **CO**20, **IA**4, **IN**32, **MA**15, **MO**2, **NY**10, Guzzler. **1986** Pederson *LAGS Concordance (Neck, throat)* 3 infs, **GA, LA,** Guzzle.

2 A swig, gulp. [Cf *OED guzzle* sb. 2 "Drink, liquor"; *EDD guzzle* sb.[2] 5 "Food, esp. drink; ale, small beer"]

1942 Berrey–Van den Bark *Amer. Slang* 102.2, *Drink of liquor*. . . guzzle. **1966–70** *DARE* (Qu. DD18, *A drink of liquor, or the amount of liquor taken in one swallow: "He took a good ———."*) Infs **AR**22, **CA**117, **CT**42, **GA**44, **MA**19, **MS**1, **MO**26, **NY**223, Guzzle; [(Qu. C35, *Nicknames for the different parts of [a] . . town or city*) Inf **MA**78, The Guzzle—where there used to be many "liquor joints."]

3 See quot. [Engl dial; cf *EDD guzzle* sb.[1] 1 "A drain, gutter, a narrow ditch."]

1986 Hendrickson *Amer. Talk* 41 **seMA,** *Guzzle,* for a small channel between two sandbars of a stream through a marsh, comes from Cape Cod.

4 See quot.

1954 *Harder Coll.* **cwTN,** *Guzzle. . .* A rain.

guzzle hole n [Prob **guzzle 3** + **hole** n **1b**]

See quot 1975.

1908 Wasson *Home from Sea* 94 **ME,** I kep' off and followed a fisherman clean up into this 'ere little guzzle-hole. **1975** Gould *ME Lingo* 119, *Guzzle hole*—A basin or inlet with some kind of population, thus better than an *eel rut* and larger than a *gunkhole.*

guzzler See **guzzle 1**

guzzle-water n [Cf **guzzle 2**]

1968 *DARE* (Qu. DD21a, . . *Words . . for any kind of liquor*) Inf **AK**8, Guzzle-water [FW: used by Inf in conv].

‡guzzy-wootchit n Cf **widget**

1967 *DARE* (Qu. NN12b, *Things that people say to put off a child when he asks, "What are you making?"*) Inf **WA**28, A guzzy-wootchit ['gʌzi,wʊčɪt].

gwa(i)n See **go** v **A4a**

gweduck See **geoduck**

gwi' See **go** v **A4a**

gwinder See **gwinter** n

gwine See **go** v **A4a**

gwinen See **go** v **A5**

gwinen down See **go down** v phr **2**

gwinter v See **go** v **A4d**

gwinter n Also sp *gwinder*

=**gyascutus.**

1920 Hunter *Trail Drivers TX* 483 (as of c1887), The boys then started in telling him [=a greenhorn] about the narrow escapes they had had from "gwinders," a very vicious animal with one short leg in front and one behind, so they could circle around a mountain and catch a man and tear him all to pieces. **1945** Mencken *Amer. Lang. Suppl. 1* 245, One of the characteristic inventions of pre-Civil War days was the *guyascutus,* an imaginary animal that still survives in American folklore. . . In those early days various other variations of the name were recorded, *e.g., guyanosa, gyascutus, guyastacutus, . . sidehill gouger . . prock, gwinter* and *cute-cuss* or *cuter-cuss,* and the habits of the bearer were described differently by different authorities. **1965** *DARE* FW Addit **cwMS,** *Gwinter*—Mythical animal of the Yazoo Valley, something like a goat with two legs on one side longer, for easier grazing on hillsides.

gwyne See **go** v **A4a**

gyaa'd See **guard**

gyaa'd'n, gyaden See **garden**

gyanousa n Also sp *guyanosa*

=**gyascutus.**

1846 *Knickerbocker* 28.37, *The Gyanousa,* from the disputed territory of Penobscot; a monster of gigantic proportions. He vegetates on the tops of trees, and gets his living on the tallest branches of the poplar. *Ibid* 38, Ladies and gentlemen! leave the house immediately! Save yourselves! *The Gyanousa am loose!* **1853** *Harper's New Mth. Mag.* 7.709/1, The lecturer dwelt at some length upon. . . the ravenous nature of the *Guyanosa,* and his enormous strength.

gyap See **gap** n^1 **2**

gyar See **gar** n

gyarb See **garb** n^1, v

Gyarbro n [Appar reinterpretation and var of **garbroth** in phr *mean as garbroth*]

The devil.

1930 *Herald–Advt.* (Huntington WV) 30 Nov sec 3 6/6 **KY, WV,** If a mountaineer speaks of a man being "as mean as the old Gyarbro himself," he means that the man is the reincarnation or the "Old Scratch" himself.

gyar-broth See **garbroth**

gyard See **guard**

gyardeen See **guardian**

gyarden, gyardin See **garden**

gyarjean, gyarjun See **guardian**

gyarp See **gape**

gyascutus n Also *giasticutus, girasticutus, guiaskuitus, guyas(ti)cutus, guyaskutus;* for addit varr see quots Cf **guyanther, gwinter, gyanousa**

An imaginary creature; see quots.

1846 *OR Spectator* (Oregon City) 15 Oct 1/2, The Guiaskuitus is not only remarkable for his ferocious appearance, but for the terrible tones of his voice. **1855** *Pioneer & Democrat* (Olympia WA) 22 June 2/3 **cwWA,** Whither shall the democracy flee? The Guyascutis *am* loose! **1869** *Overland Mth.* 3.130 **TX,** When one of the fellows is a "gyascutus," and the other is a "kiamuck," you may look for some rare sport. **1897** Stuart *Simpkinsville* 57 **AR,** Holdin' me up . . for all Simpkinsville to laugh at—same ez ef I was some sort o' guyaskutus! **1911** Saunders *Col. Todhunter* 132, Blamed if you wouldn't ha' thought I was the original roarin' ring-tailed guyasticutus of Calaveras County, suh, and the only one in captivity. **1930** *DN* 6.81 **cSC,** *Guy Skootas.* A mythical creature, used to frighten children and ignorant negroes. Less common than it was ten years ago. **1934** Stribling *Unfinished Cathedral* 62 **AL,** He's the high grand guyescutis of his association. **1949** *Sun* (Baltimore MD) 28 July 14/1 *(Hench Coll.)* **MD,** [It] made its appearance in Frederick county in 1902. This particular species [of snallygaster] was classified as the crosswise *Gyascutus.* It was said to have caused a serious flood by falling asleep while lying across Carroll Creek. There is brief notice of its return in 1909. In this latter instance it seems to have taken the form of a headless calf, whose presence was reported by several "reliable witnesses." **1950** *PADS* 14.34 **SC,** *Guyascutus. . .* An imaginary monster. **1952** Brown *NC Folkl.* 1.703 (as of 1921), In Wilkes county, foreigners, those from beyond the county line, are told of the guy-scooter-sky, the wonderful native steer with hind legs several inches longer than forelegs, thus admirably adapted to mountain climbing. **1953** Randolph–Wilson *Down in Holler* 247 **Ozarks,** *Giasticutus. . .* A legendary bird of prey, with a wingspread of fifty feet and a habit of carrying off full-grown cattle. **1967–68** *DARE* (Qu. CC17, *Imaginary animals or monsters that people . . tell tales about—especially to tease greenhorns*) Inf **MI**44, Girasticutus [ˌǰaɪˌræstəˈkjutəs]—something of horror; no specifics; **IN**38, [ˈǰɑjəstəˌkjutəs]—a hillside animal [whose] legs on one side are shorter than on the other. It can't run on level ground.

gyirl See **girl** n

gympson weed See **jimson weed**

gyp n^1 Also sp *gip, jip* [Prob abbr for *gypsy*] **chiefly Sth, S Midl**

A female dog, bitch.

1878 C. Hallock *Amer. Club List & Sportsman's Gloss.* p. v *(OEDS), Gyp,* the young female pup. **1895** *Outing* 27.75/2 **neNC,** One of the pack—a long-limbed gyp named Queen came out of the swamp all covered with black pitch-like mud. **1926** *AmSp* 1.416 **Okefenokee GA,** The ol' gip, when she finds pups, 'll be hongry, an' range these woods, diggin' turtle aigs. **1933** *AmSp* 8.1.49 **Ozarks,** *Gyp. . .* A female foxhound. The word *bitch* is considered vulgar, and is seldom used in mixed company. **1946** *PADS* 6.16 **swVA** (as of 1942), *Gyp. . .* A female dog. **1965** *McDavid Coll.* **cw,csOK,** Gyp—bitch. **1967–68** *DARE* FW Addit **LA**5, Gyp—female dog [FW: Common term among lower-class whites; competed with *bitch* among plantation whites]; **LA**26, They showed a gyp having some puppies. **1968** *DARE* (Qu. J2, . . *Joking or uncomplimentary words . . for dogs*) Inf **GA**23, Gyp—a she-dog; **NC**53, Gyp—a girl dog; **PA**163, Gyp. **1975** Newell *If Nothin' Don't Happen* 153 **nwFL,** Melody was a young hound gyp hardly a year old and she'd just whelped eight pups. **1976** Garber *Mountain-ese* 34 **Appalachians,** *Gip.* **1982** *Barrick Coll.* **csPA,** *Jip*—female dog; *bitch* is used only as a technical term by breeders.

gyp n^2, often attrib Also sp *gip, jip* [Abbr for *gypsum*] **West**

1 Gypsum; soil or rock containing gypsum.

1916 *DN* 4.324 **KS,** *Gyp. . .* Gypsum. **1920** Hunter *Trail Drivers TX* 62 (as of c1888), That day while drifting along up the Pecos River I went ahead to hunt a watering place and when I rode up on a gyp hill overlooking the herd I saw six or seven men in a bunch. **1942** Whipple *Joshua* 326 **UT** (as of c1860), There was the red clay, the gyp of the canal walls always softening. And there was the silt continually thwarting him. **1964** Wallace *Frontier Life* 12 **OK** (as of 1893–1906), This same gyp rock that made the water so unsavory for drinking and so unsatisfactory for doing the laundry did bring some pleasure to the artistically inclined people of the community. Many of the women carved from this alabaster-like rock. **1966–69** *DARE* (Qu. C26, . . *Special kinds of stone . . in this part of the state*) Infs **NM**1, **OK**18, **TX**54, 71, Gyp rock; **IA**30, Gypsun [sic] or gyp; **TX**45, Gyp. **1968** *DARE* Tape **KS**12, We have the gyp hills to the west which are very unique. **1982** Brooks *Quicksand* 273 **swUT** (as of c1923), "Where have you spent the summer?" "Working in the dining room at the gyp mine out on the desert."

2 attrib; Of water: containing gypsum, hence unpalatable; also used absol. Cf **gyppy**

1902 (1944) Biggers *From Cattle Range* 30/1 **wTX,** The water in the Clear Fork . . was "gyp" and wholly unfit to drink. **1909** *Pioneer Days SW* 314 **TX,** We all started up the river to the water, and when we got there it was alkali or jip. **1920** Hunter *Trail Drivers TX* 331 (as of 1871), Things of interest or disinterest . . were many stampedes, sleepless nights, gyp water and poor chuck [=food]. **1939** in 1984 Lambert–Franks *Voices* 14 **OK,** Gosh, it was hot out in that bald prairie. We had to drink hot gyp [*Voices:* gypsum] water, and we wasn't able to buy ice. **1941** Smith *Going to God's Country* 44 **MO** (as of 1890), One of our mules drank so much of that gip water that he took the collic [sic] and died. **1971** Adams *Cowman* 160, After drinking some gyp water, one cowhand observed, "That gyp water's so mean it'd run uphill and wouldn't stay in a jug."

‡gyp n³

Pine resin.

1965 *DARE* (Qu. T7, *The sticky stuff that comes out of pine trees*) Inf **OK**11, Gyp.

gyp v¹ [By ext from *gyp* to cheat]

1 To play hookey.

1967 *DARE* (Qu. JJ6, *To stay away from school without an excuse*) Inf **CA**14, Gyp.

2 vbl n *gypping:* Cheating on a test.

1966–69 *DARE* (Qu. JJ7, *Words or expressions for cheating in school examinations*) Infs **NH**10, **NY**43, **RI**4, 17, Gypping. [All Infs old]

gyp v², hence vbl n *gypping*

To sicken (someone) with **gyp** n² **2.**

1935 *Cattleman* 21.11.6 **cwTX,** Mention was made of cowboys getting "gypped." . . Most of the creeks and rivers are heavily impregnated with gypsum, or other alkaline salts. . . Taken in moderate quantities, and if fairly cool, the water causes no ill effects, but if drunk in large quantities during the summer months when it is tepid, . . the effect is similar to that suffered by the small boy who has eaten too freely of green apples, only worse—much worse. No matter how old the old timer, or how much of it he has drunk in the past, he is never immune from gypping.

gyp corn See **Egyptian corn 2**

gype n [Scots, Ir dial; cf *EDD gype* v. and sb. 3]

1930 Shoemaker *1300 Words* 24 **cPA Mts** (as of c1900), *Gype*—A silly easily fooled person.

gyp grama n [**gyp** n² **1**]

A **grama grass 1** (here: *Bouteloua breviseta*).

[**1912** Wooton–Standley *Grasses NM* 103, There is one . . species of Grama, *Bouteloua breviseta,* . . that occurs only on gypsum soils in New Mexico, so far as our observation goes. . . It is not valuable as forage except for the fact that it will grow on such soils and is a degree better than nothing, a consideration which is sometimes of importance in areas of considerable extent.] **1970** Correll *Plants TX* 246, *Bouteloua breviseta. . . Gyp grama. . .* Locally abundant in areas of gypsum sands at the leeward sides of gypsum lake-beds, summer-fall; also s. N.M.

gyp grass See **Egyptian grass 2**

gypo See **gyppo** n

gypping vbl n¹ See **gyp** v²

gypping vbl n² See **gyp** v¹ **2**

gyppo n Also sp *gippo, gypo* [Perh from *gypsy,* infl by *gyp* to cheat] **chiefly NW, Pacific**

Esp in logging:

a A pieceworker; hence v *gyppo* to work by the piece. Cf **bushel C**

1927 *DN* 5.449 [Underworld jargon], *Gyppo. . .* A piece worker. "A gyppo's a goddam skunk what's too goddam mean to join a union." **1939** FWP *ID Lore* 244 [Lumberjack jargon], In the St. Maries area and elsewhere: . . *Put her in the gippo notch*—to labor very hard. **1950** *Western Folkl.* 9.381 **neCA** [Lumberjack language], *Gyppo.* A man who does piecework instead of by the day or hour; that is, a man who gets paid for what he does and not for the amount of time he puts in. **1976** Maclean *River Runs Through* 107 **wMT** (as of 1927), To gyppo . . was to be paid by the number of thousands of board feet you cut a day. Naturally, you chose to gyppo only if you thought you could beat wages and the men who worked for wages. *Ibid* 113, Jesus . . you're no gyppo. Any time a guy's not sawing he's not making money.

b often attrib: A small contractor or operation; a job done by contract; hence v *gyppo* to work by contract.

1930 Williams *Logger-Talk* 24 **Pacific NW,** *Gypo:* Originally applied to the piece-work system instituted by the logging operators; since, it has come to be quite generally applied to small concerns in the contemptuous phrase *gypo outfit.* **1938** (1939) Holbrook *Holy Mackinaw* 261, *Gyppo.* Any sort of contract work. **1941** Writers' Program *Guide WA* 75, "Gyppo outfits" . . usually offer little more than subsistence. **1941** *AmSp* 16.233 [Timberland terminology], *Gyppo.* A small-time logging contractor, usually contracting to saw fell trees into logs. **1950** *Western Folkl.* 9.118 **nwOR** [Logger speech], *Gyppo outfit.* A small sawmill or logging outfit working small lots of timber which could not be profitably handled by larger operators. **1956** *Western Folkl.* 15.203 [Loggers' lingo], *Gyppo*—a small contract logger or small operator. . . Gyppo as used today is widely accepted and universally accredited, and does not denote that a gyppo is a gyp. **1958** McCulloch *Woods Words* 76 **Pacific NW,** *Gypo* (or *gyppo*). . . A small logger. . . Almost any woods job done on contract. . . To log by contract. **1977** Jones *OR Folkl.* 101/2, *Gyppo:* small contract logger.

gyppo v See **gyppo** n **a, b**

gyppy adj Also sp *gippy* [**gyp** n² **2**]

Of water: tainted with gypsum.

1961 Adams *Old-Time Cowhand* 213 **West,** The old-time cowhand quenched his thirst with the first water he came across, no matter what the kind. It might be clear or muddy, cool or warm, or alkalied and gyppy. **1966** *DARE* Tape **NM**13, Most of the water . . was so darn badly alkaline, and gyppy, that it was almost impossible to cut the grease off those darn plates. **1967** Green *Horse Tradin'* 160 **TX,** I will tell you now that water wasn't very good—it was a little salty, a little gippy, and a little sulphury—but if you was dry enough and tough enough you could drink it. **1987** *DARE* File **OK,** I have been looking over some county histories. . . I have seen words there that you might have like: *gyppy*—[of] well water full of gypsum.

gypsieweed See **gypsyweed**

gyp stick n

In logging: **=cheat stick.**

1958 McCulloch *Woods Words* 76 **Pacific NW,** *Gyp stick*—Same as cheat stick. **1959** *VT Hist.* new ser 27.139 **c,ceVT,** *Gyp stick. . .* In logging, a log scale. Common among loggers. **1969** Sorden *Lumberjack Lingo* 51 **NEng, Gt Lakes,** *Gyp stick*—A cheat stick or guess stick. A stick used to measure board feet of lumber.

gypsum pink n

A **baby's breath 1** (here: *Gypsophila paniculata*).

1940 Clute *Amer. Plant Names* 62, *G[ypsophila] paniculata. . .* Gypsum pink.

gypsum weed n [Appar folk-etym for *jimson*] Cf **gypsyweed 3**

=jimson weed.

c1937 in 1972 *Amer. Slave* 2.146 **SC,** Git the gipsy (gypsum) weed. Beat 'em up for [intestinal] worm. Give 'em when the moon change. **1959** Carleton *Index Herb. Plants* 57, *Gypsum-weed:* Datura stramonium.

gypsy flower n Also *gipsy flower, gypsy plant*

A **hound's-tongue 1** (here: *Cynoglossum officinale*).

1900 Lyons *Plant Names* 129, *C[ynoglossum] officinale. . .* Gypsy-flower. **1912** Blatchley *IN Weed Book* 113, Gipsy Flower. . . A vile ill-smelling weed common in dry soil along roadways, in shady pastures and waste places. **1949** Moldenke *Amer. Wild Flowers* 258, In the *gypsyflower* . . the 1½- to 3-foot stems are very leafy to the top and the large . . branches of flowers are reddish purple or, rarely, white. **1974** Peden *Speak to Earth* 82 **cIN,** Hound's tongue grows two feet tall. . . The five-petaled flower is a poke-juice red. At that late point in its growing season the stalk held both flower and seed pod and looked unkempt, which is probably why the herbalist calls it gypsy plant.

gypsy fowl n Also *gipsy face*

See quot 1930.

1930 Shoemaker *1300 Words* 24 **cPA Mts** (as of c1900), *Gipsy face*—A famous strain of old English game fowls popular in central Pennsylvania. Their faces were a peculiar shade of red like sumac. **1940** Richter *Trees* 154 **OH** (as of c1800), You couldn't pen up humans in different coops like they did Gypsyfowl back in Pennsylvania.

gypsy in the parlor n Cf **nigger in the woodpile**

1968 *DARE* (Qu. BB27, *When somebody pretends to be sick [often to get out of doing something] . . he's* ______) Inf **KS**13, A gypsy in the parlor.

gypsy plant n

1 See **gypsyweed 1.**

2 See **gypsy flower.**

gypsy tea n

1968 *DARE* (Qu. H70, *When people bring baked dishes, salads, and so forth to a meeting-place and share them together, that's a* ______) Inf **OH**41, Gypsy tea—[used] more in the South.

gypsyweed n Also *gipsyweed, gypsieweed*

1 also *gypsy plant:* =**bugleweed.**

1830 Rafinesque *Med. Flora* 26. *Lycopus Virginicus. . .* Gypsie Weed. **1876** Hobbs *Bot. Hdbk.* 51, Gypsie weed, Bugle weed, Lycopus Virginicus. **1900** Lyons *Plant Names* 233, *L[ycopus] Virginicus. . .* Gypsieweed. **1930** Sievers *Amer. Med. Plants* 17, *Bugleweed—Lycopus virginicus . .* gypsyweed. **1959** Carleton *Index Herb. Plants* 57, *Gypsy-plant:* Lycopus (v). **1971** Krochmal *Appalachia Med. Plants* 166, *Lycopus Virginicus . .* gypsyweed.

2 A **speedwell** (here: *Veronica officinalis*).

1894 *Jrl. Amer. Folkl.* 7.96 **WV,** *Veronica officinalis . .* gypsy-weed. **1940** Clute *Amer. Plant Names* 33, *V[eronica] officinalis. . .* Gipsy weed. **1959** Carleton *Index Herb. Plants* 57, *Gypsy-weed:* Datura stramonium; . . Veronica officinalis. **1976** Bailey–Bailey *Hortus Third* 1151, *[Veronica] officinalis. . . Gypsyweed. . .* Fl[ower]s in dense, many-fl[owere]d racemes . . , corolla pale blue. . . Eur., Asia, N. Amer.

3 =**jimson weed.** [Appar folk-etym for *jimson*] Cf **gypsum weed**

c1937 [see **gypsum weed**]. **1959** [see **2** above].

gy(u)rl See **girl** n

H

h' See **have** v[1] **A1c**

ha v[1] See **have** v[1] **A1a, c**

ha' v[2] See **have** v[2]

haa'bis' See **harvest**

haa'd See **hard** adj

haa'kee See **harky**

haa(l)f See **half** n

haan See **hain't** v

haa'ness See **harness**

haant See **haunt**

haat n[1] See **heart** n[1]

h'aa't' n[2] See **hearth A4**

hab See **have** v[1] **A1a**

haberty-grass (or habidygrass), go to See **haverty-grass, go to**

habitant n Pronc-spp *habitan, habitaw* [Fr "inhabitant, settler"; *DCan* 1789 →]

A yeoman farmer of French origin; by ext, a person of French origin, esp one who is poor or lower-class.

1856 Olmsted *Journey Slave States* 682 **LA,** A hamlet of cottages, occupied by Acadians, or what the planters call *habitans,* poor white, French Creoles. **1859** (1968) Bartlett *Americanisms* 186 **LA,** *Habitan*. . . A term applied to what, in English, is called a yeoman; i.e. a small country proprietor. **1872** Schele de Vere *Americanisms* 104 **LA,** The *voyageur,* when grown old, is apt to settle down into a *habitant* or *habitan,* as the humbler among the French settlers are still called in Canada and Louisiana. . . The term is, however, fast disappearing from Louisiana, and even in Canada it is rarely heard outside of the purely French districts on the St. Lawrence. **1950** *WELS (Names and nicknames for people of foreign background: French)* 1 Inf, **cwWI,** Habitaws. **1958** McCulloch *Woods Words* 79 **Pacific NW,** *Habitant*—A French-Canadian logger. **1966** *DARE* (Qu. HH18, . . *Low-grade people*) Inf **MI**10, ['hæbətɑː], a native, but a low type. **1967** LeCompte *Word Atlas* 171 **seLA,** Farmer who works on shares . . *habitant.* [1 of 21 infs] [**1984** Daigle *Dict. Cajun Lang.* 2.79 **LA,** *Habitant*. . . Farmer.]

habited ppl adj [*OED habited* ppl. a. 3 *"Obs."*]

Familiarized, accustomed.

1782 Paine *Letter Raynal* 60 **PA,** A *Mind* habited to actions of meanness and injustice, commits them without reflection, or with a very partial one. **1942** (1971) Campbell *Cloud-Walking* 10 **seKY,** I don't misdoubt them women will turn out right common and good after they get habited to the pioneering ways of mountain folks. **1960** Williams *Walk Egypt* 270 **GA,** The old folks'll come back—they habited to it—but the young ones will get used to store-bought meal or bread.

habits on, have one's v phr [*habit* an addiction]

1970 *DARE* (Qu. GG34a, *To feel depressed or in a gloomy mood*) Inf **TN**53, He has his habits on; (Qu. HH25, . . *Never has anything to say*) Inf **MO**29, He's got his habits on. [Both Infs Black]

habs See **have** v[1] **A1a**

habutus See **arbutus**

hachel See **hatchel** n **1**

hacienda n [Span] **chiefly SW**

1 The central compound, particularly the main house, of a ranch or estate.

1810 Pike *Expeditions* 256 **NM,** The Hacienda of Pattos was a square enclosure of about three hundred feet, the building being one story high. **1876** Harte *Gabriel Conroy* 232 **CA,** Viewed from the Mission towers, it [=the fog] broke a cold gray sea against the corral of the *hacienda* and half hid the walls of the *hacienda* itself. **1894** *Overland Mth.* (2d ser) 24.90/1 **AZ,** There were evidences of a recent Mexican occupation, with the ruins of towns[,] missions, presidios, haciendas, and ranches. **1940** Writers' Program *Guide NM* 114, *Hacienda*. . . A ranch house. **1956** Ker *Vocab. W. TX* 109, The main ranch house. . . *Hacienda* is current in only three counties, Randell, Terry, and Young. **1962** Atwood *Vocab. TX* 44 **TX,** *Hacienda* . . meaning the central establishment of a ranch, usually a very luxurious one, is concentrated in Southwest Texas, with West Texas also showing a few occurrences. **1986** *Amer. Architectural Roots* 92, Some towns evolved from *haciendas,* which were more common in California than in New Mexico or Texas. The *haciendas* often consisted of the main house . . surrounded by the houses of the *peones* (laborers) and *vaqueros* (cowboys) and often a church and a school.

2 A ranch or estate, usu an extensive one.

1825 in 1924 Austin *Papers* 1.1016 **TX,** He sends you the Notes of my Hacienda and the notes of Gates Tract. **1892** *DN* 1.190 **TX,** *Haciénda:* a large farm or plantation. **1910** Hart *Vigilante Girl* 153 **nCA,** As an *hacienda* in Spanish America is closely analogous to an English manor, so is the building occupied as a residence by the *hacendado* a close correlative to that of the lord of an English manor. **1962** Atwood *Vocab. TX* 125, *Hacienda.* A large or fine or important ranch or estate.

3 In mining: see quots.

1881 Raymond *Gloss. Mining* 46, *Hacienda*. . . In mining it is usually applied to the offices, principal buildings, and works for reducing the ores. **1968** Adams *Western Words* 137, *Hacienda*. . . In mining, a smelter.

hack v[1]

1 To cut with a **hack** n[1] **2a;** hence vbl n *hacking.*

1856 Olmsted *Journey Slave States* 340 **NC,** After the first hacking, the trees are again scarified. *Ibid* 341, These hackings being made three or four times a month. **1859** Perry *Turpentine Farming* 77, When chipping is commenced on the faces, it is called 'hacking boxes'; it should be named 'hacking pines.' *Ibid* 78, Hacking is to strike with the tool, and it requires a slight stoop to cut the right quantity, and do it well. **1872** (1876) Knight *Amer. Mech. Dict.* 2.1046/1, Pine trees are *hacked* for turpentine.

2 also *hack off, hell-hack:* To embarrass, annoy, or disconcert. [Prob < *hack* chop, but cf *EDD hake* v. 4 "To tease, worry, importune" also *hock* v.[2] "To jeer"] **chiefly Sth, S Midl** Cf **hack** n[1] **1, hacked** ppl adj[1], **hawk** v[2]

1908 *DN* 3.318 **eAL, wGA,** *Hack*. . . To guy, confuse by guying, rattle. "We tried to hack the pitcher." Chiefly heard in the pp. in the sense 'chagrined, rattled.' **1917** *DN* 4.413 **NC, KY,** *Hack*. . . To annoy; nettle. "That joke hacks Steve to this day." **1952** Brown *NC Folkl.* 1.548, *Hack*. . . To embarrass, to tease. . . Somewhat rare. **1965** *DARE* FW Addit **MS,** Hacks me, or hacks me off: This means that something or someone disgusts someone to a very great degree. **1966–70** *DARE* (Qu. GG9, *To suddenly embarrass somebody*) Inf **LA**17, Hack—recent; **TN**24, Hack—slangy; (Qu. GG13a, . . *Something keeps bothering a person*) Infs **LA**17, **TX**74, Hacks; (Qu. Y7, . . *To be mean . . or to annoy another*) Inf **SC**19, Hell-hacking [FW sugg]; **SC**24, Hell-hacking [FW sugg], hacking; **SC**40, Hacking [FW sugg]. **c1970** *Halpert Coll.* **wKY, nwTN,** *Hack*—That hacked him = embarrassed. **1974** Fink *Mountain Speech* 12 **wNC, eTN,** *Hack* . . to annoy, embarrass.

3 often in neg constrs: To tolerate, put up with (someone or something); to manage (a situation); to succeed. Cf **cut** v **11**

1916 *DN* 4.275 **NE,** *Hacking her. . .* An expression of greeting, like "How are you?" used frequently to start a conversation. "Well, how are you hacking her?" **1953** Randolph-Wilson *Down in Holler* 250 **Ozarks,** *Hack. . .* To achieve, to accomplish something. "I cain't quite hack it" is an admission that some specific task is beyond the speaker's ability. **1955** *Antioch Rev.* 15.379 **OH,** One thing I don't hack is a man stealing. **1968–69** *DARE* (Qu. II29a, . . *Dislike . . "I don't know why, but I just can't ______ him."*) Infs **CA**169, **IA**32, **PA**167, Hack. **1971** Landy *Underground Dict.* 95, *Hack. . .* Cope with; tolerate; stand—eg. *I can't hack my job.* **1972** *Newsweek* 7 Aug 18/2 **MO,** I had proved to the world during my four years in the Senate . . that I can hack it. **1974** Lurie *War Tates* 331 **NY,** It's a nice compromise for types like me who haven't been able to hack it spiritually. **1976** Flexner *America Talking* 369, *Hack it,* to be able to stand up to opposition, criticism, etc., an updating of *to cut it, to cut the mustard . .* meaning to come up to expectations, to succeed. *Hack it* became truly well known when President Nixon used it in his March 4, 1971, news conference, saying that General Creighton Abrams had reported to him that the South Vietnamese could "hack it." **1987** *DARE* File **WI,** [Men meeting:] "Hi, how're y' doin'?" "Oh—, I'm hackin' it."

4 with *around, off:* To loaf, lounge, or idle. [Cf *EDD hake* v. 1 "To wander about aimlessly and idly; to loiter or lounge."]

1923 *DN* 5.209 **swMO,** *To hack around . .* to ramble around. **1967–68** *DARE* (Qu. KK31, *To go about aimlessly looking for distraction: "He doesn't have anything to do, so he's just ______ around."*) Inf **CT**9, Hacking—son and friends use it; **MA**1, Hacking off. **1979** *Wall St. Jrl.* (NY NY) 28 Feb 1/1 **MD,** She recalls fondly the times in Potomac when she always had someone to talk to, go to the movies with, or just "hack around" with at a nearby shopping mall, wandering among the shops and munching junk food.

5 To enter fighting cocks in a **hack** n^{1} **5;** hence vbl n *hackfighting.*

1950 *Grit & Steel* 52.8.2, Hacked two before derby and won both, then won six in derby, making eight straight. **1979** *DARE* File **seKS,** Hackfighting. This is just two people, each with a rooster of nearly equal weight, getting together to fight their birds. It is the most informal way of fighting chickens. . . In a hack, the matching is usually done by the owners of the roosters.

hack n^{1} [*hack* a cutting instrument, or mark made by such an instrument]

1 in var phrr: A state of embarrassment, confusion, or defeat. Cf **hack** v^{1} **2, hacked** ppl adj^{1}

1835 Longstreet *GA Scenes* 27 **GA,** You cut such high shines, that I thought I'd like to back you out; and I've done it. Gentleman, you see I've brought him to a hack. **1855** Haliburton *Nature* 2.41 **NEng,** Oh, warn't she brought to a hack! She had a great mind to order me out, but then that word 'proposal' . . sounded so nice to the ear. **1884** Lanier *Poems* 170 **GA,** Them figgers is got me under the hack. **1899** (1912) Green *VA Folk-Speech* 211, A person is said to be "under *hack*" when he is controlled and ordered by another. "She has her husband under hack." **1930** *DN* 6.81 **cSC,** *Hack, on the. . .* Embarrassed. **1950** *PADS* 14.34 **SC,** *Hack. . .* to render ill at ease. . . As a noun; "to get, or keep a person under hack." **1952** Brown *NC Folkl.* 1.548 **cNC,** *Hack, to put (one) under . .* To hack [=to embarrass, to tease].

2 In turpentine production: see below. **chiefly S Atl** Cf **box** n **1**

a A tool for cutting into the sapwood of pine trees.

1872 (1876) Knight *Amer. Mech. Dict.* 2.1046/1, The turpentine hack is a tool with a curved or angular edge to cut channels through the bark and albernum in an oblique direction, so as to lead the resin towards a *boxing* cut in the tree, or to a cup suspended to catch the drip. **1904** *DN* 2.395, In the turpentine industry . . "The chipper stands in front of the box and with his hack removes a strip of bark and sapwood three-quarters of an inch wide just above the exposed surface." **1952** Early Amer. Industries Assoc. *Chronicle* 5.27, [Illustration:] Hacks used in bleeding the long-leafed pine. **1968–70** *DARE* Tape **GA**22, You go and cut a streak on each side every week with a hack; **GA**23, You chip it with a chip, with a hack.

b The cut made in the trunk of a pine tree.

1856 Olmsted *Journey Slave States* 342 **NC,** The turpentine flows from the most recent hack.

3 In logging: see quot.

1969 Sorden *Lumberjack Lingo* 52 **NEng, Gt Lakes,** *Hack. . .* A mark stamped on a log to denote ownership.

4 A type of **earmark;** see quot.

1968 Adams *Western Words* 137, *Hack*—An earmark made with a short split about half the length of the split or slash.

5 also *hackfight;* In cockfighting: an independent match arranged between owners, often prior to a **main.** Cf **tournament**

1937 *NY Herald Tribune* (NY) 6 June sec 2 1/2, Tournaments, hacks and mains are being fought weekly in many parts of New York State, some of the mains being battled to a finish for wagers as high as $10,000 a side. **1939** FWP *Guide FL* 455, The *Deer Island Pit . .* [is] a barnlike structure with a seating capacity of more than 1,000, the scene of great activity and excitement during the cock-fighting season. . . Known as 'mains,' 'hacks,' or 'meetings,' the fights are not advertised by press or radio, but for several months before the tournament trade papers carry half-page announcements of the event. **1945** *Feathered Warrior* 44.6.10 **NY,** Most of the cocks turned down by McNerney as not suitable for his use, were later fought at local hacks by the breeders. **1958** *NY Herald Tribune* (NY) 20 July 3/2 (as of 1948), Besides the sixteen fights in the derby, there were several "hacks," independent fights arranged by the owners. **1976** Haley *Roots* 484, Hackfights were for those who were able to fight only one or two or three usually second- or third-rate birds.

hack n^{2} [Abbr for *hackney* a horse or vehicle for hire; *OED* 1704 →]

1 also *hack wagon:* Any of var light horse-drawn vehicles, often one for hire.

1795 *Boston Gaz. & Weekly Republican Jrl.* (MA) 28 Dec 3/1, There is but little safety for the ladies and children [in the streets of Boston], but in the *Hacks.* **1802** in 1851 U.S. Congress *Debates & Proc.* 7th Cong 1st Sess 1066, In Baltimore there are a great number of hacks, which are not owned by the rich. . . Do the poor of Baltimore ride about in hacks? The very circumstance of the existence of so great a number of hacks proves the carriage tax not to be oppressive. **1872** Howells *Wedding Journey* 55 **NY,** 'We must have a carriage,' he added . . hailing an empty hack. **1903** *DN* 2.315 **seMO,** *Hack. . .* Stage. Also any two-seated vehicle. **1907** *DN* 3.231 **nwAR, seMO,** *Hack.* **1923** *DN* 5.209 **swMO,** *Hack. . .* A light spring wagon. **c1960** *Wilson Coll.* **csKY,** *Hack*—A topless buggy. **1960** Bailey *Resp. to PADS 20* **KS,** A hack was a passenger vehicle drawn by one or two horses. As late as 1910 they were used to transport Santa Fe and MK and T [=Missouri, Kansas, and Texas] passengers to and from stations. **1965–70** *DARE* (Qu. N41a, . . *Horse-drawn vehicles . . to carry people*) 164 Infs, **widespread,** Hack; **NJ**22, Hack wagon; **IN**58, Kid hack—a horse drawn school bus [Of all Infs responding to the question, 68% were old; of those giving these responses, 84% were old]; (Qu. N41c, *Horse-drawn vehicles to carry light loads*) 20 Infs, **scattered exc Atlantic,** Hack; **TX**42, Delivery hack [18 of 21 Infs old]; (Qu. L42, . . *What kind of thing do you call a 'rig'?*) Inf **GA**74, Hack, a buggy for two; **TN**7, Hack, a higher standard of living than a wagon; (QR, near Qu. N2) Inf **WI**72, Hack—a funeral buggy which carried people, not the body. **1967–69** *DARE* Tape **TN**31, When we went to Gallatin, they was a whole hack pulled by the horses and we'd get on at the post office; **TX**47, I drove a mail hack for a man, or a gig, what you like; **TX**69A, Mail hack; **VA**12, They were hauled in a hack, which was a conveyance that was pulled by two horses and had three rows of seats in it.

2 Transf:

a An omnibus or taxicab.

1938 *AmSp* 13.307 [Among bus drivers], *Hack.* A designation for any bus. **1942** Berrey-Van den Bark *Amer. Slang* 766.5, *Taxicab . .* hack. **1986** Chapman *New Dict. Amer. Slang* 189, *Hack . . fr early 1900s* A taxicab. **1987** *DARE* File **NYC** (as of 1953), I remember my father going down to the Motor Vehicle Bureau to pick up his hack [=taxicab] license.

b A hearse.

1950 *WELS (Car in which a dead body is taken to be buried)* 1 Inf, **WI,** Glass-covered hack. **1968–69** *DARE* (Qu. N2) Infs **CA**114, **KY**17, **MA**19, **VT**16, **WI**61, Hack; **IL**71, Hack—in the days of horse-drawn vehicles; **LA**29, Hack—a horse-drawn vehicle.

c An ambulance.

1969 *DARE* (Qu. N1, . . *Names for an ambulance*) Inf **KY**17, Hack.

d An old or dilapidated vehicle or boat.

1950 *WELS (Nicknames for an old broken-down car)* 3 Infs, **WI,** Hack. **1965–70** *DARE* (Qu. N5) 10 Infs, **scattered exc Sth,** Hack; **MI**93, **OH**10, **WA**1, Old hack; (Qu. O2, *Nicknames . . for an old, clumsy boat*) Inf **MN**16, Old hack.

e also *hack sleigh:* A sleigh.

1937 Mitchell *Horse & Buggy* 86 **NEng,** The hack sleighs—hacks with their wheels removed and runners substituted—were apt to be top-heavy. **1966** *DARE* (Qu. N40b, . . *Sleighs for carrying people*) Inf **MI**36, Hack—enclosed, two sets of runners.

f A caboose. Cf **buggy** n[1] **1**

1916 *DN* 4.356, *Hack*. . . A freight caboose. **1922** *DN* 5.181, *Hack*. . . A caboose. Railroad usage. **1932** *RR Mag.* Oct 368, *Hack, Hay wagon, Hearse*—Caboose. **1945** Beebe *Highball* 207, Probably there is more warmth of homeliness and sentiment about a hack at the end of a string of high cars, a little self-contained world of animation and reality as it diminishes down the tracks behind a hustling symbol freight, than exists for any other of a railroad's tangible properties. **1958** McCulloch *Woods Words* 79 **Pacific NW,** *Hack* . . The caboose on a log train.

hack v[2] Also *hack around, hack it*

To drive or ride in a **hack** n[2]; hence vbl n *hacking.*

1879 *Philadelphia Times* May 8 *(Century Dict.),* Are we more content to depend on street cars and walking, with the occasional alternative of hacking at six times the money? **1923** *DN* 5.209 **swMO,** *To hack around* . . to drive about in a hack. **1942** Berrey-Van den Bark *Amer. Slang* 767.2, To travel by bus . . hack (it). *Ibid* 767.3, To drive a bus or taxicab . . hack. **1958** *Sat. Eve. Post Letters* **sIN** (as of 1910–20), We're going to "hack it" (ride in a hack).

hack n[3] [Cf *EDD hack* sb.[2] 19 "A wooden grating or fence set across a stream to catch fish."]

1967 *DARE* (Qu. P13, . . *Ways of fishing . . besides . . hook and line*) Inf **SC**40, Hack—built inside the trap; keeps the fish from going back out; usually have one or two.

hack v[3] [*hack* a rack, frame or place for drying]

1 also with *up:* To place in an ordered pile for drying; hence ppl adj *hacked.*

1872 (1876) Knight *Amer. Mech. Dict.* 2.1046/1, They [=bricks] are sun-dried or *hacked.* **1899** (1912) Green *VA Folk-Speech* 211, Newly split rails are *hacked up* to dry. Piled by crossing the ends, the other end lying far apart. (2) To pile up newly made bricks to dry.

2 as vbl n *hacking:* Framing up tobacco for market. Cf **burden** v, **hack** n[6]

1967 Key *Tobacco Vocab.* **MD,** "You basket it up and get it on the market." Hacking = basket[ing] it = burden[ing] it down.

hack n[4] [Perh var of **hawk** n **3**] *chiefly among Black speakers*

1 A guard, esp one in a jail or prison.

1914 Jackson *Criminal Slang* 41, *Hack*. . . A night watchman; a night policeman or marshal. Most usually it signifies the watchman of a building. **1946** (1972) Mezzrow-Wolfe *Really Blues* 333, *Hack:* keeper in a jail. **1952** Himes *Cast the First Stone* 295 **FL** [Black], Those wolves down there [=in prison] would try to rape you right in front of the hacks. **1965** Brown *Manchild* 239 **NY** [Black], The guards—the hacks, as they called them—were hillbillies. . . A Negro who was too suave had a hell of a hard time to go. The hacks were always kicking his ass for no good reason. **1970** Major *Dict. Afro-Amer. Slang* 63, *Hack* . . a prison guard.

2 A white person.

1934 *AmSp* 9.26 [Prison talk among Blacks], *Hack.* A white person. **1942** Berrey-Van den Bark *Amer. Slang* 385.2, *White person*. . . hack. *Ibid* 460.5 [Tramp and criminal slang], Hack . . *a white person.* **1970** Major *Dict. Afro-Amer. Slang* 63, *Hack* . . a white person.

hack n[5]

1 also *hack tree:* A **hackberry,** usu *Celtis occidentalis.*

1897 Sudworth *Arborescent Flora* 185, *Celtis occidentalis*. . . Hack Tree (Minn.) **1940** Clute *Amer. Plant Names* 255, *Celtis occidentalis*. . . Hack tree. **1952** Taylor *Plants Colonial Days* 46 **VA,** *Celtis occidentalis*. . . Other common names are nettle tree, . . hack tree. **1968–69** *DARE* (Qu. T13, . . *Names . . for . . hackberry*) Inf **IN**45, Hack; **MO**32, Hack tree.

2 =**tamarack.**

1966 *DARE* (Qu. T5, . . *Kinds of evergreens*) Inf **ME**21, Hack—sheds leaves. **1975** Gould *ME Lingo* 121, *Hack*—Maine contraction of *hackmatack* when cut for pulpwood and lumber. In the Maritimes *hack* is called juniper. Westerly, *hack* is the tamarack. . . *Hackmatack* lumber resists weather and makes good porch floors. In Maine shipbuilding lore, there is frequent mention of *hackmatack* knees. The main root of the *hack* grows at right angles to the trunk, and woodsmen dug out this natural joint, or bracket, to sell to shipyards, where it was used as a support for deck timbers.

hack n[6] Cf **hack** v[3] **2**

=**burden** n **B2.**

1939 *Sun* (Baltimore MD) 12 Apr 13/5 *(Hench Coll.),* The new method . . for handling Maryland's tobacco is designed to save packing in hogsheads before sale, as the "hacks" or "burdens" will . . be packed in hogsheads in the auction room. **1966** *DARE* Tape **DC**5, [FW:] Tobacco basket is the whole thing all bound up, with the frame at each end? [Inf:] Yes sir, when you get 'em up like that, we call it a hack of tobacco, or a burden. . . When it's laid up just like that, we call it a burden or a hack.

hack n[7] [Perh < **hack** v[1] **2**]

1962 *Jrl. Amer. Folkl.* 75.313 **cNC** [Black], Local synonyms for the [evil] spell[s] are "curse," . . and "hoodoo." Other less common terms are "wuwu," "hack," and "underworlded."

hack v[4] Also *hack up* [Cf *EDD howk* int. "An exclamation used to attract the attention of horses running loose in a field."] **esp S Atl, Gulf States**

1966–68 *DARE* (Qu. K36b, . . *To make a horse go backwards*) Infs **FL**32, 34, **GA**22, **SC**40, 63, Hack; **LA**22, [hæ:k]; **LA**39, **SC**63, Hack up. **1986** Pederson *LAGS Concordance (Horse . . to back them)* 1 inf, **seLA,** Hack.

hackamatack See **hackmatack 1a**

hackamore n [Span *jáquima*] **chiefly West**

A bridle or halter; see quots 1929, 1968.

1850 Ryan *Personal Advent.* 1.152 **CA,** He overtook me, mounted on a well saddled horse, and leading another by the *hackamore.* **1887** *Scribner's Mag.* 2.508 **West,** *Hackamore,* [a] bridle made of horse-hair. **1920** *DN* 5.82 **eOR,** *Hackamore*. . . A bridle. **1929** *AmSp* 5.62 **NE,** The rider may use a "hackamore," a rope halter fashioned like an ordinary leather halter but having knots which fit over the horse's nostrils, to "break" a horse to "ride" before he is used to the bridle. The "hackamore," sometimes called a "stockamore," has knots fitting close to the nostrils and really punishes a "bronc" to submission. **1941** Writers' Program *Guide WY* 462, *Hackamore*—A halter of rawhide, braided and snug-fitting. **1944** Adams *Western Words* 71, *Hackamore*. . . usually an ordinary halter having reins instead of a leading rope. More commonly a headpiece something like a bridle with a bosal in place of a bit, and a browband about three inches wide that can be slid down the cheeks to cover the horse's eyes, but it has a throat latch. **1961** Folk *Word Atlas N. LA* Map 706, Rope device on horse's head—used to control a wild horse or to lead him—*hackamore* [given by 26% of 275 infs]. **1962** Atwood *Vocab. TX* 52, For various devices, formerly made of rope, used to control an unruly horse, the prevalent word is *hackamore* . . which is most common in the old ranch country. This hardly occurs in the states to the east of Texas, but is apparently known in New Mexico. **1964** O'Hare *Ling. Geog. E. MT* 145, A rope halter—*hackamore.*

hack around v phr[1] See **hack** v[1] **4**

hack around v phr[2] See **hack** v[2]

hackberry n

A plant of the genus *Celtis;* also its fruit. Also called **clickel tree, hack** n[5] **1, hackleberry, hackyberry, hashberry, nettle tree, palo blanco** For other names of var spp see **beaverwood 2, cumaro, dog cherry, false elm, granjeno, hagberry, hedge-berry, hen-turd tree, hog berry 1, hoop ash 2, hornbeam 5, huckberry, huckleberry 3, juniper tree, lotus tree, minny-berry, nettleberry, nigger-pill, one-berry, pompion-berry, rim ash, sugarberry, sugar hackberry, sugar nut, wild orange**

1779 in 1903 Summers *Hist. SW VA* 700, Marking a Poplar and two Hackberry trees with initials of our names. **1818** in 1824 Knight *Letters* 87 **KY,** As you range the woods, the eye is delighted with the novelty of strange trees; among others, the hackberry, whose berries are not distasteful. **1833** (1847) Lundy *Life & Travels* 51 **TX,** The hackberry, persimmon and mulberry are abundant. **1854** (1874) Glisan *Jrl. Army Life* 132 **NM,** For nearly a fortnight subsequent to her escape she subsisted upon hackberries. **1929** Sale *Tree Named John* 10 **MS,** A hackberry buds first of all, but its bark is too rough. **1935** Sandoz *Jules* 27 **wNE** (as of 1880–1930), That evening Jules rode into the Sioux broken circle of tipis set among the hackberry and box elders at the foot of Indian Hill. **1965–70** *DARE* (Qu. T13, . . *Names . . for . . trees*) 205 Infs, **widespread, but esp west of Appalachians exc West,** Hackberry; **GA**65, Hackberry bush—it'd make a tree; (Qu. T16, . . *Kinds of trees . . "special" around here*) 12 Infs, **esp Cent, Plains States,** Hackberry; (Qu. I44, *What kinds of berries grow wild around here?*) Infs **LA**14, **TN**4, **TX**28, 42, Hackberries; **TX**40, Hackberries—not good to eat; (Qu. I46, *Other kinds of fruits that grow wild around here*) Inf **IN**30, Hackberries; **PA**242, Hackberry—same as sugarberry; (Qu. T11, . . *Kinds of elms*), Inf **IL**44, Hackberry; (Qu. DD3b, *How do people take snuff around here?*) Inf **TX**101, On a twig from hackberry. **1966** *DARE* Tape **AL**13, We'd go out in the woods and pick hackberries and eat them.

hacked ppl adj^1 Also *hacked off* [**hack** v^1 **2**] **chiefly Sth, S Midl** Cf **croker sack, hacked to the**

Embarrassed, annoyed, cowed, flustered.

1892 Harris *Uncle Remus & Friends* 349 **GA** [Black], When you once git 'em hacked dey er hacked fer good; dey des give right up en roll der eyes. **1903** *DN* 2.351 **seGA,** *Hacked*. . . Unwilling to speak one's mind; not free to act. 'Never since I was born have I seen a crowd of people so hacked. You're afraid even to talk.' **1905** *DN* 3.82 **nwAR,** *Hack* . . To embarrass. "He was hacked." **1936** *AmSp* 11.368 **nLA,** *Hacked*. . . Annoyed; confused; as 'John was hacked when I told him his horse was gone.' **1959** Lomax *Rainbow Sign* 81 **AL** [Black], We was *both* embarrassed. When he got off the train, he just didn't have nerves enough to come out to where we lived in the country. And I was so hacked that I was scared to tell Mama and Papa which day he was comin on. **c1960** *Wilson Coll.* **csKY,** *Hack*. . . To embarrass. Hacked adj. **c1965** *DARE* File **neGA,** His date stood him up and he was really hacked about it. (Recent) **1970** *DARE* FW Addit **ceTX,** *Hacked off,* annoyed, peeved. **1973** *Patrick Coll.* **cAL** (as of c1946), Hacked. . . Embarrassed, put out, made to feel sheepish.

hacked ppl adj^2 See **hack** v^3 **1**

hacked off See **hacked** ppl adj^1

hackee n Also sp *hackie, hacky* Cf **ground hackee**

A **chipmunk** (here: *Tamias striatus*).

1838 in 1849 Audubon–Bachman *Quadrupeds* 1.75, The *Tamias striatus* differs . . widely from our American Chipping Squirrel or Hackee. **1842** DeKay *Zool. NY* 1.63, This common species [=*Tamias striatus*] is well known under the various popular names of *Hacky,* . . *Chipmunk.* **1872** Schele de Vere *Americanisms* 52, In some of the Eastern States the familiar name of the playful little creature, unknown in England, is *Hackee.* **1889** *Century Dict.* 2675, *Hackee*. . . [*Century* Ed: Imitative of the animal's cry.] The common chipmunk . . *Tamias striatus.* **1928** Anthony *N. Amer. Mammals* 241, Eastern Chipmunk.—*Tamias striatus* . . Names.—Chipmunk; . . Chipping Squirrel; Hackee. **1961** Jackson *Mammals WI* 142, *Vernacular names.* In Wisconsin most commonly called chipmunk. Other names of general application include . . hackie.

hackel See **jacal**

hacker n [**hack** v^1 **1**]

In turpentine production:

a One who uses a **hack** n^1 **2a.** Cf **chipper 1**

1856 Olmsted *Journey Slave States* 342 **NC,** The hackers are wholly employed in scarifying the trees.

b =**hack** n^1 **2a.**

1896 *Pop. Sci. Mth.* 48.469 **Sth,** There are two kinds of hackers—the open and the closed hacker. . . [The former] has an open, strong knife with curved edge, and the other a closed knife blade, fastened to a long iron handle. A heavy weight is attached at the end in order to give momentum to the blows. **1896** Mohr–Roth *Timber Pines* 69 **S Atl, AL, MS,** The removal of the bark and of the outermost layers of the wood—the "chipping" or "hacking"—is done with a peculiar tool, the "hacker".

hackfight See **hack** n^1 **4**

hackfighting See **hack** v^1 **5**

hackie n^1 [**hack** n^2]

A cabdriver.

1926 Finerty *Criminalese* 28, *Hackie*—A taxi or horse cab driver. **1946** (1972) Mezzrow–Wolfe *Really Blues* 99, Weaving . . like an expert hackie in heavy traffic. **1949** (1961) Partridge *Underworld Dict.* 316, *Hackie.* A taximan . . applied, ca. 1902, to 'a *hack*ney-cab driver.' **1949** *NY Times* (NY) 24 July 1/2, One thousand cab drivers of this city [=Newark NJ] who, like 'hackies' everywhere, have a sharp eye. **1950** *Reader's Digest* June 103 **NY,** I've been a New York hackie for almost 30 years now, mostly on the night shift. I *like* driving a cab.

hackie n^2 See **hackee**

hacking vbl n^1 See **hack** v^1 **1**

hacking vbl n^2 See **hack** v^2

hacking vbl n^3 See **hack** v^3 **2**

hacking n

1975 Gainer *Witches* 11 **sAppalachians,** *Hackin'* . . the underbrush. "He's workin' in the hackin'."

hacking and hammering vbl n [*EDD hack and hammer* "To hum and haw; to hesitate or stammer in speech." (at *hack* v.^{1} 27)] Cf **back and fill 2**

Vacillating, equivocating.

1975 Gould *ME Lingo* 1, A politician who won't state his position, but talks around it, is *backing and filling*. . . but a farmer might also call this hackin' and hammerin', deriving from short, ineffective strokes with a tool.

hacking stick n [Prob *hack* to cause short, dry coughs]

1969 *DARE* (Qu. DD6b, *Nicknames for cigarettes*) Inf **PA**214, Hacking stick.

hack it See **hack** v^2

hack knife n Cf **tomahawk knife**

1967 Key *Tobacco Vocab.* **TN,** Hack knife, A tomahawk-shaped knife used to harvest tobacco.

hackleback n

1 also *hackleback sturgeon:* =**shovelnose sturgeon.** [See quot 1956]

1956 Harlan–Speaker *IA Fish* 48, The color of the hackleback [=*Scaphirhynchus platorynchus*] is buff or olive-drab above and light beneath. The body is completely armored with heavy plates. **1968** *DARE* (Qu. P1, . . *Freshwater fish . . good to eat*) Infs **IN**51, **MN**21, Hackleback. **1968** *WI Conserv. Bulletin* May/June 14, The gar are sometimes mistaken for the hackleback or shovelnose sturgeon. **1971** *WI State Jrl.* (Madison) 29 Aug sec 4 5/1, Between the four of us we caught one small walleye, . . and a hackleback sturgeon, also known as a sand sturgeon. **1983** Becker *Fishes WI* 227, *Shovelnose Sturgeon—Scaphirhynchus platorynchus* . . Other common names: hackleback, . . flathead sturgeon.

2 A **heelsplitter** (here: *Lasmigona complanata*).

1911 *Century Dict. Suppl., Hatchet-back*. . . Also called *hackle-back.* **1979** *WI Week-End* Apr 6, Hacklebacks were the most valuable during the decades of the pearl button industry.

hackleback sturgeon See **hackleback 1**

Hacklebarney n [Cf *SND Hecklebirnie* n. 1 "A euphemism for Hell." Cf **ballyhack** n]

See quots.

1950 *AmSp* 25.71 **DE,** In Sussex County, Delaware . . there is a crossroads which formerly went by the name [ˌhæklɪˈbarnɪ]—a name of derision and insult. . . In New Castle County, Delaware, a community which, for the past seventy years or so, has been called *Kiamensi* was formerly known as [ˌhækl̩ˈbɝnɪ]. [**1960** *VT Hist.* 28.136, *Hackly Barney.* To go Hackly Barney. (To be lost.)] **1982** Heat Moon *Blue Highways* 206 **MO,** Missourians sometimes speak of a place called Hacklebarney: a non-existent town you try to get to that is forever just around the next curve or just over the next hill, a town you believe in but never get to.

hackleberry n

A **hackberry.**

1965–70 *DARE* (Qu. T13, . . *Names . . for . . trees*) 8 Infs, **scattered,** Hackleberry.

hackled ppl adj [Engl dial; see *EDD hackle* v.^{2} 2. (1) "*Hackled* . . peevish, cross-grained, angry"; but cf **hacked** ppl adj^1]

Confused, angry.

1937 (1977) Hurston *Their Eyes* 85 **csFL** [Black], Got her so hackled she'd make the wrong change for stamps.

hackled up See **hackle up**

hacklehead n Cf **hackleback 1**

Perh a **burfish.**

1968 *DARE* (Qu. P4, *Saltwater fish . . not good to eat*) Inf **NY**47, Spiny fish such as hacklehead.

hackles, through the prep phr [*hackle* a comb-like instrument used in processing flax or hemp] Cf **flint mill, go through the**

1970 *DARE* (Qu. CC12b, . . *If a person has a lot of bad luck . . "He's been* ______.") Inf **VA**71, Through the hackles.

hackle up v phr, hence vbl n *hackling up,* ppl adj *hackled up* [*hackles* erectile hairs on a dog's neck and back which, when erect, indicate anger]

To become angry.

1935 Davis *Honey* 129 **OR,** He was high-tempered and overbearing, partly because of his wealth and partly because most of his timber-cutting was against the law and he could keep people from asking questions about it by hackling up and yelling at them. **1970** *Thompson Coll.* **cnAL** (as of 1920s), Hackle up—become angry. He got all hackled up when they told him.

hackling adj [Engl dial; see *EDD*]

1968 *DARE* (Qu. BB12, . . *Cough that comes with bronchitis: "He has a* ______ *cough."*) Inf **NH**14, Hacking, hackling ['hækəlɪŋ].

hackling up See **hackle up**

hackmatack n

1 Any of several conifers as:

a also *hackamatack, hackmatac, hackmetack, hacmack, hacmatac(k), hakma(n)tak:* **=tamarack 1;** also the wood of such a tree. **chiefly Nth, esp NEng**

1792 Belknap *Hist. NH* 3.33 **NH,** On some mountains we find a shrubbery of hemlock and spruce, whose branches are knit together so as to be impenetrable. The snow lodges on their tops, and a cavity is formed underneath. These are called by the Indians, Hakmantaks. **1804** Fessenden *Poems* 26 **NH,** Miss Tabitha Towzer is fair, . . Like a hakmatak slender and spare. [Footnote to *hakmatak:* The Indian name for the Pinus Canadensis.] **1824** Bigelow *Florula Bostoniensis* 360, *Red Larch. Hacmatack.* . . A fine tree, differing remarkably from the Pines. **1876** Hobbs *Bot. Hdbk.* 51, Hackmatac, . . Hackmetack, Tamarack, Larix Americana. **1900** Lyons *Plant Names* 215, *L. laricina.* . . Hackmatack (Hackmetack, Hacmatac, Hacmack). **1950** *WELS (Name for tamarack)* 2 Infs, **WI,** Hackmatack; 1 Inf, Hackamatack. **1951** Teale *North with Spring* 218 **NC,** An American plant hunter . . may return with juglans, kinnikinnic, hackmatack, missey-moosey, daffydowndilly, hurr-burr or robin-runs-away. **1961** Douglas *My Wilderness* 280 **cnME,** Here and there was a larch or hackmatack whose roots were used in the old days as knees in building ships and as tree nails or wooden pegs. **1966** *York Co. Coast Star* (Kennebunk ME) 28 Apr 3/5, Usually framing here was done in oak, hackmatack (popular types) or hard pine, and very rarely in elm and rock maple. **1966–69** *DARE* (Qu. T5) Infs **ME**5, 12, 24, Hackmatack; (Qu. T13) Infs **ME**8, **MA**6, 13, 25, **NH**10, 14, Hackmatack; **MA**42, Called hackmatack in New England; needles off in wintertime, back in summer; roots of hackmatack are ship knees; used to make hull of boats; (Qu. T15) Infs **ME**5, 8, Hackmatack. **1967** Borland *Hill Country* 331 **nwCT,** The larch is also called the tamarack, sometimes known as hackmatack. **1973** Hitchcock–Cronquist *Flora Pacific NW* 61, Hackmatack. . . *L[arix] occidentalis.*

b A **juniper** (here: *Juniperus communis*).

1892 *Jrl. Amer. Folkl.* 5.103, *Juniperus communis,* hackmatack. Ipswich, Mass. **1930** U.S. Dept. Ag. *Misc. Pub.* 77.25, *Juniperus communis.* . . *Other common names.* . . Hackmatack. **1960** Vines *Trees SW* 37, Vernacular names are . . Hackmatack, . . and Gin Juniper. **1971** Krochmal *Appalachia Med. Plants* 152, Hackmatack. . . A small evergreen shrub or tree 12 to 30 feet in height. **1974** (1977) Coon *Useful Plants* 125.

c =lodgepole pine.

1896 *Garden and Forest* 9.263/1, *Hackmatack* (Larix Americana).—A corruption (an anagram, really) of tacamahac, an early name in Massachusetts for the same tree. The name has been transferred to several other conifers, such as Thuya [sic] occidentalis, Pinus contorta, P. Murrayana and Juniperus communis.

d A **white cedar** (here: *Thuja occidentalis*).

1896 [see **1c** above].

2 A **spirea.**

1931–33 *LANE Worksheets* **swCT,** Hackmatack, hard hack, a bad bush; grows in pasture.

3 =sassafras.

1969 *DARE* (QR, near Qu. T13) Inf **CT**31, Hackamatack is really sassafras, also called sassy-ass.

4 =balsam poplar.

1971 Krochmal *Appalachia Med. Plants* 206, *Populus balsamifera.* . . *Common Names:* Balsam poplar, . . hackmatack. **1979** Little *Checklist U.S. Trees* 205, *Balsam poplar.* . . *Other common names* . . hackmatack, cottonwood.

hackmetack See **hackmatack 1a**

hackney n Also *hackney horse* [*hackney* a riding horse] Cf **coach horse**

A bob-tailed horse.

1950 *WELS (A horse with his tail cut short)* 2 Infs, **WI,** Hackney. **1966–69** *DARE* (Qu. K41) Infs **NC**36, **NY**160, Hackney; **CO**22, Hackney horse—cut clear up on bone.

hack off See **hack** v[1] **2, 4**

hack on v phr

1966 *DARE* (Qu. Y19, *To begin to go away from a place*) Inf **SC**10, Hack [hæk] on.

hack out v phr Also *hack over* Cf **hash over, hatch v 1**

1967 *DARE* (Qu. JJ36, *To work out a plan . . "Mary knows more about that, you and she can* ______ *together."*) Inf **WA**22, Hack it out; **IL**45, Hack it over.

hack sleigh See **hack** n[2] **2e**

hack tree See **hack** n[5] **1**

hack up v phr[1] See **hack** v[3] **1**

hack up v phr[2] See **hack** v[4]

hack wagon See **hack** n[2] **1**

hacky n See **hackee**

‡**hacky** adj [Perh from *hack* indifferent or ordinary; perh infl by *tacky*]

1969 *DARE* (Qu. W41, . . *Someone whose clothes never look right or who always dresses carelessly*) Inf **CA**165, Hacky.

hackyberry n

A **hackberry.**

1965–70 *DARE* (Qu. T13, . . *Names . . for . . trees*) 10 Infs, **chiefly S Midl,** Hackyberry.

hacmack, hacmatac(k) See **hackmatack 1a**

had See **hard** adj

hadder See **have** v[1] **A3b**

haddick See **haddock**

had die See **fad die**

haddo n Also *haddoh* [Nisqualli *huddoh*]

=humpback salmon.

1882 U.S. Natl. Museum *Bulletin* 16.305, *O[ncorhynchus] gorbuscha.* . . *Haddo.* . . Pacific coast and rivers . . from Oregon northward. **1887** Goode *Amer. Fishes* 480, *Oncorhynchus gorbuscha* . . is known . . on Puget Sound as the "Haddoh." **1902** Jordan–Evermann *Amer. Fishes* 150, Among other names applied to this species are haddo [etc]. **1949** Caine *N. Amer. Sport Fish* 54, *Humpback salmon.* . . This species is also known as . . Haddo.

haddock n Pronc-sp *haddick*

A fish *(Melanogrammus aeglefinus)* of the Atlantic seaboard. Also called **dickie** n[1], **skulljoe**

1616 Smith *Descr. New Engl.* 29, [There were] Haddock, Cole, Cusk, or small Ling [etc]. **1789** Morse *Amer. Geog.* 205, Around the shores of Rhode Island . . are cod, . . haddock, &c. **1896** Jewett *Pointed Firs* 189 **eME,** Goin' to have this 'ere haddock an' some o' my good baked potatoes. **1904** Day *Kin o' Ktaadn* 187 **ME,** Cod an' pollock, hake an' haddock, gaff 'em in an' pile her full. **1929** *AmSp* 5.130 **ME,** The pronunciations . . "haddick" or "haddick fish" for haddock . . were common. **1965–70** *DARE* (Qu. P2, *What kinds of saltwater fish . . are good to eat?*) 23 Infs **chiefly NEng,** Haddock; (Qu. P14, . . *Commercial fishing . . what . . the fishermen go out after*) 15 Infs, **chiefly NEng,** Haddock.

haddock gull n

=kittiwake.

1946 Hausman *Eastern Birds* 318, Atlantic Kittiwake *Rissa tridactyla tridactyla* . . Other Names—Snow Gull, . . Haddock Gull.

haddoh See **haddo**

hade See **head** n

had-to See **have-to**

haet See **hate** n

ha'f, hafe, haff n See **half** n

haf v See **have** v **A1a**

haf n See **hearth A3**

haffen adj, n [*haff* pronc-sp for *half* + *-en* var of **on** of]
See quots.
1884 Murfree *TN Mts.* 46, Let him treat haffen the country ez he done me, ef he wants ter. **1886** Amer. Philol. Assoc. *Trans.* 17.39, *Haffen* for half, which Craddock [=Murfree] uses so much, as a "haffen pone of bread," has been criticised as not used in East Tennessee.

haffers n pl [Prob var of Engl or Scots dial *halver/halfer* a half]
1954 *PADS* 21.29 **cnSC,** *Haffers*. . . Lights [=lungs] of a slaughtered hog. . . Mostly Negro usage.

haf(f)ter, haffuh, hafta, hafto See **have** v[1] **A1b**

hag n

1 also *hag spirit:* A witch; the evil spirit of a dead person, sometimes supposed to cause nighmares. [*OED hag* sb. 1 1552 →] **esp SE** *esp among Black speakers*
1894 *Jrl. Amer. Folkl.* 7.66, Beliefs of Southern Negroes Concerning Hags. *Ibid* 67, Two distinct hag theories are developed. . . The first . . is the theory of the skinless body. . . The other is the theory of the hag spirit. **1910** Hart *Vigilante Girl* 310 **nCA,** According to the testimony, she had been a party to an elaborate system of espionage, by which all sorts of charms had been administered to the millionaire without his knowledge. He had been ceaselessly shadowed; voodoo hags had been secreted in his apartments. **1919** *Jrl. Amer. Folkl.* 32.363 **sSC coast** [Gullah], One ol' conjure-man tol' her if she would pay him ten dollars, he'd ketch the ol' hag for her. He wait outside de do' one night; and when de ol' hag drap her skin on de do'step, he got an' put salt an' pepper on her. When de ol' hag comes out to put on she skin, it would bu'n her. **1937** in 1970 Hyatt *Hoodoo* 1.158 **seVA** (as of c1886), They used to say it was something they called *The Old Hag*. . . Used to ride folks. And this old man used to come to this other man's house and *ride him like a horse*. **c1938** in *Ibid* 1.135 **ceGA,** De hag is a ha'nt, a spirit. Dere's two of 'um (two kinds of hags). One of 'um is comin' so you can't sleep in de night—dat's ha'nts, dat's a ha'nt (spirit of a dead person). An' another one is a hag—a hag is a living person; dey've becomes a hag, dey deals with de devil. **1941** Writers' Program SC *Folk Tales* 89, The hag is a woman who changes herself into all sorts of shapes for the purpose of bringing evil upon people. *Ibid* 91 **sSC coast** [Gullah], De say hag sperit can go troo de keyhole of de do' en ef dey lak you de goes in en sucks yer blood troo yer nose. **1949** Turner *Africanisms* 275 **SC** [Gullah], When the hag will ride you, you'll groan. *Ibid* 277, Then he catch the hag. And when he catch the hag, he didn't see the hag.

2 An old man—used as a joc or opprobrious nickname. [*W3* "Obs."]
1967–68 *DARE* (Qu. AA23, *Joking names . . husband*) Inf **TN**27A, Old hag; (Qu. HH40, *Uncomplimentary words for an old man*) Inf **AL**8, Old hag—for a man as well as a woman.

3 See **hagfish 1.**

4 See **hagdon.**

hag v[1], hence vbl n *hagging* Also with *on* [Engl dial; cf *EDD hag(g)* v.[1] 1] Cf **egg** v[1]
To provoke, annoy, or incite; to complain.
1806 (1970) Webster *Compendious Dict.* 137, *Hag* . . to fatigue, tire, harass, torment. **1967–70** *DARE* (Qu. Y7, *When one person never misses a chance to be mean to . . or to annoy another*) Inf **TX**11, Hagging; (Qu. GG16, *Words for finding fault, or complaining*) Inf **MO**23, Hagging; (Qu. Y5, *Words meaning to urge somebody to do something he shouldn't*) Inf **KY**75, Hagged him on.

hag v[2], hence vbl n *hagging* [**hag n 1**] Cf **hagride**
To cast spells; to cast a spell on, bring misfortune to.
c1938 in 1970 Hyatt *Hoodoo* 1.138 **cSC,** Dey went tuh work after he [=a **hag** n **1**] come out of his skin, in order to ketch him so dey would know whether it was de man who was *haggin'* de people. **1941** Writers' Program SC *Folk Tales* 90 **sSC coast** [Gullah], Ef you is marry wid a hag, she gits up en slips out'n she skin an' hide it under de stairsteps. . . Ef she gone haggin, she sho lef' it, en if you salts it, she kaint git back in. *Ibid* 96, Gone right to place where he wuz to hag dat night!

hagaloo bird n
=**Wilson's snipe.**
1923 U.S. Dept. Ag. *Misc. Circular* 13.50, Common snipe *(Gallinago gallinago). . . In local use.*— . . hagaloo bird (Mich.)

Hagar's children See **Aunt Hagar's children**

hagberry n **esp Sth, S Midl**
A **hackberry,** usu *Celtis occidentalis.*
1822 Eaton *Botany* 227, *Celtis crassifolia* . . (hag-berry, hoop-ash.) **1937** *Torreya* 37.96, *Celtis occidentalis*. . . Hagberry . . Kentucky and Virginia. **1966–70** *DARE* (Qu. T13, . . *Other names . . for . . hackberry*) Infs **AR**55, **GA**91, **LA**8, 22, 26, **SC**3, **TX**68, Hagberry.

hag-boat n [*OED* 1700–1867; "Origin unknown"]
1966 *DARE* (Qu. O2, . . *An old, clumsy boat*) Inf **MS**11, Hag-boat.

hag bridle n [From the appearance, similar to a bridle, as if the sleeper had been *hag-ridden;* cf **hagride**] Cf **witches' stirrups**
See quots.
1909 *S. Atl. Qrly.* 8.47 **sSC coast** [Gullah], *The trickle* of slaver which often runs from the mouth-corners in troubled and uneasy sleep, is a *hag-bridle.* **1919** *Jrl. Amer. Folkl.* 32.363 **sSC coast** [Gullah], Because she was thin, she said the ol' hag used to ride her every night. . . In the mornin', when she woke, she would have ol' hag bridle each side her mouth. (Perhaps she was drulin'.)

hagbrier n
A **greenbrier** (here: *Smilax hispida*).
1903 Small *Flora SE U.S.* 282, *Smilax hispida*. . . Hagbrier. **1960** Vines *Trees SW* 74, *Bristly Greenbrier—Smilax hispida* . . Vernacular names are Hagbrier . . Wild Sarsaparilla.

hagdon n Also *hag, hagdel, hagden, hagdul, haglet, haglin* [*DNE* 1670 →] **NEng**
Usu a **shearwater,** esp *Puffinus gravis,* but also the **fulmar.**
1832 Williamson *Hist. ME* 1.150, The *Hagdel,* of a dark brown colour, about as large as a Murr, though its feathers are longer. **1889** *Century Dict.* 2679, *Hagdel*. . . Same as *hagden*. . . *Hagden, hagdon*. . . Hagdens sometimes gather in flocks of thousands, . . Also *hag.* [*Century* Ed: Local, New Eng.] **1905** Wasson *Green Shay* 59 **NEng,** "Some of them big shays are dretful able boats though, and no mistake. You can't never drownd one of 'em, no more 'n a can-buoy." "Drownd one, no! They're right up atop of every sea same's so many hagdons." [Footnote:] A species of gull. **1925** (1928) Forbush *Birds MA* 1.141, In summer on the banks of Newfoundland and New England, . . there the "hags" are almost certain to be found. **1931–33** *LANE Worksheets* **neMA,** In the garney there'd be hagdon, smoked halibut, tongues and sounds. **1933** *AmSp* 8.3.77 **ME,** *Hagduls* or *hagdens* are jaegers or skua gulls that rob smaller species of their catch. **1955** MA Audubon Soc. *Bulletin* 39.310, *Sooty Shearwater.* Black Hag (Mass. Hag traces to hagdown, a term used in Great Britain, derivation unknown, but when reduced to this meaningful monosyllable the significance is probably derogatory); Black Hagden (Maine); Black Hagdon (Maine; Mass; RI. . .); Black Haglet (Mass. Latter term means the little hag; it is a shortening of hagdown, but probably has a meaning of its own—the usual sense in our language.); Hag (Maine); Hagdon (northeast). *Manx Shearwater.* Black Hagdon (Maine . .). *Greater Shearwater.* Common Hagden (Maine); Gray Hag, Gray Haglet (Mass.); Hag (Maine, Mass.); Hagdon (Maine, Mass., R.I.); Haglet, White Haglet (Mass.) **1959** *Names* 7.112, Hag, alone, is applied to the sooty shearwater (Nfd., Me., N.Y.), greater shearwater (Nfd., Labr., Northeastern Banks, Me., Mass.), and fulmar (Me.). The sooty shearwater is further known as black haglet (Mass.) and the greater shearwater as: gray haglet, haglet, and white haglet (Mass.) and haglin (N.B., Me.)

hagfish n

1 also *hag:* A fish of the family Myxinidae. [*OED* 1611 →] For other names of *Myxine glutinosa* see **sleepmarken, slime eel, slime-fish, sucker.** For other names of *Polistotrema stouti* see **lamperina**
1873 in 1878 Smithsonian Inst. *Misc. Coll.* 14.2.36, *Myxine glutinosa* . . Hag-fish; . . slime-fish. **1882** U.S. Natl. Museum *Bulletin* 16.5, *Myxine glutinosa* . . Hag-fish; Borer. **1896** *Ibid* 47.7, *Myxine Glutinosa* . . Hagfish; Borer. *Ibid* 6, It is thought that the hags [=*Polistotrema stouti*] enter the fishes after they are caught. **1928** Pan-Pacific Research Inst. *Jrl.* 3.10, *Polistotrema stouti* . . California hagfish.—*Po-*

listotrema deani . . Alaska hagfish. **1955** Zim–Shoemaker *Fishes* 19, Hagfishes or Slime Eels, blind and slimy, are common marine pests.

2 See quot. **[hag n 1]**

1950 *PADS* 14.34 **SC,** *Hagfish*. . . Stale fish peddled on the streets which, when eaten, cause ptomaine poisoning, are alleged by the peddlers to have been caught in the night by witches or *hags* flying over the river and plunging like seagulls on their prey, and thus to have been impregnated with a malevolent essence. Negro usage.

‡hagger v [By rhotacism from *haggle*]

1970 *DARE* (Qu. U12, *If you . . argued with the person selling it till you made him lower the price*) Inf **TX**76, Haggered over the price.

hagging vbl n¹ See **hag** v¹

hagging vbl n² See **hag** v²

haggle v [*OED haggle* v. I. 1 1599 →]

To chop roughly; to hack.

1899 (1912) Green *VA Folk-Speech* 212, *Haggle*. . . Cut or chop in an unskillful manner; mangle in cutting. **1941** Writers' Program *Guide AR* 4, He built a dogtrot cabin, haggled the timber off a hillside, and plowed furrows around the stumps. **1950** Moore *Candlemas Bay* 271 **ME,** Jen . . sat at the kitchen table, haggling open the pea pods with her thumbnail.

haggle n [Cf *EDD hag* sb.⁶ 7 "A clearing or cutting down of timber; a cutting in a wood"]

1966 *DARE* FW Addit **nME,** *Haggle*, a place where evergreens had been blown down and younger trees were growing up. Very difficult to get through.

haggly adj [*EDD haggly* rough, unevenly cut (at *haggle* v. 1)]

1939 *Hall Coll.* **wNC, eTN,** *Haggly* . . Rough, covered with rocks(?)

hag-hollering n Cf **fowl-crow**

1908 *S. Atl. Qrly.* 7.342 **sSC coast** [Gullah], [Divisions of "the negro's day" *(ibid.)* include] *can'le-lightin', night-time, platt-eye prowl,* and *hag-hollerin'*. [Footnote:] Presumably midnight, when graves give up their dead and the spirits of the damned howl abroad . . and hags oppress their unhappy victims: hags are witches.

haglet, haglin See **hagdon**

hag on See **hag** v¹

hagride v [**hag** v²] **esp SE** *esp among Black speakers*

To harrass, torment, esp during sleep; to cause nightmares or nightmare-like experiences; hence n *hagrider* one who causes such torment; ppl adj *hagridden* affected by such torment.

1909 *S. Atl. Qrly.* 8.47 **sSC coast** [Gullah], *To have nightmare* [sic] is *to be hag-ridden.* **[1937** see **hag n 1.]** **c1938** in 1970 Hyatt *Hoodoo* 1.143 **seVA,** An old lady . . use to go out every night *witch-riding*. . . So while she was gone her husband came home and saw . . [her] skin on the floor . . and he recognized the ring on it. . . So he found out that she was a *hag-rider*. **1941** Writers' Program SC *Folk Tales* 89 **sSC coast,** The ordinary person may call the experience of being hag-ridden a nightmare, but the more primitive, whose diet is more indigestible and irregular, are certain of the presence of hags. [*Ibid* 91 [Gullah], When hag rides you, you mek noise same lak er little shiverin' owl. You can't wake up en you won't wake up twell somebody tech you. You calls dat de hag ridin you.] **1970** Hyatt *Hoodoo* 1.135, The . . witch, the old man's *living person* sold to the devil—who hag-rides and casts spells and cures—is also called a *witch-hag.*

hag's needle n Cf **beggar's needles**

A **beggar ticks 1.**

1970 *DARE* (Qu. S15) Inf **SC**67, Hag's needle—black seed, half inch long, flat, spurs on end.

hag spirit See **hag n 1**

hahd See **hard** adj

hah-dee-dah-dah n

1939 (1962) Thompson *Body & Britches* 61 **NY,** In the middle of a group of glacial cones called *hah-dee-dah-dahs*—and who will explain that word?—he could kindle a fire whose smoke was screened from Indian eyes by the lofty cones.

hahf See **half** n

hahnd See **hand**

hahngry See **hungry**

hahnsome, hahnsum See **handsome**

hahr See **hire**

haht See **heart** n¹

haid See **head** n

hail n¹ [*W3 "archaic"*]

A hailstorm.

1788 in 1853 Jefferson *Writings* 2.458 **VA,** A very considerable portion of this country has been desolated by a hail. **1954** *Harder Coll.* **cwTN,** It come a hail Monday morning and it was thick and stones the size of large marbles. **1966** *DARE* Tape **NC**8, More than likely there will come one or two or maybe three hails during the run of the summer.

hail n² Also *hailing* [*SND hale* II. n. "A haul (esp. of fish), the hauling in of nets;" 1888 →] Cf **fare** n, **get n 1**

A catch of fish; see quots.

1930 *AmSp* 5.388 **NEng coast,** Station WHDH . . broadcasts daily market reports, hails, and bits of gossip or news from vessel to vessel and from shore to the grounds. *Ibid* 390, *Hail*. . . The total number of pounds of fish which a vessel may *have* in her hold at the time a declaration is made; daily *hails* are sent in by most company-owned boats each day by radio. **1942** Berrey–Van den Bark *Amer. Slang* 797.1, *Hail,* the total weight of fish carried by a vessel. **1972** *Petersburg Press* (AK) 25 May 1/5, *Halibut Hailings* May 18 Seabound 9,000 / Sandra L 39,000 / Johnny L 28,000 / Keku Connie 9,500. **1975** Gould *ME Lingo* 121, *Hail* is also the term for the estimated get of a fishing vessel, the approximate tonnage being brought into port; the skipper will radio his *hail* in the hold, average size of the fish, and estimated time of arrival at dockside.

hail n³ [*hail* v to call or shout; naut usage] Cf **hail from**

1 The home port of a vessel.

1905 Wasson *Green Shay* 13 **NEng,** It's got so bad now'days I feel kind of shamefaced like, to put the hail of 'Kentle's Harbor' on the stern of my little hooker, there. **1975** Gould *ME Lingo* 121, *Hail*—The name of a vessel's home port, from which she *hails.* The *hail* is properly painted or carved on the stern or transom along with the name, thus: *Miss Gussie —Portland.*

2 By ext: an address.

1968 Coatsworth *ME Memories* 155, When she told us how her brother had once carved his name and address on the claw of a lobster which he was sending to market, she said, "He cut his hail on its claw, and within a week or two he had a letter from a man in New Haven."

3 A telephone call.

1945 Colcord *Sea Language* 92 **ME, Cape Cod, Long Island,** Alongshore, *[hail]* may mean to call up by telephone: "Give me a hail when you're ready to start."

hail-back See **hail-over 2**

hail Columbia n, freq cap Also *hail Columbus,* ~ (or *hale*) *Columby;* occas *hail Columbia happy land* [From the title of the patriotic song *Hail Columbia* by Joseph Hopkinson, 1798]

A punishment or scolding; the dickens; hell—usu in phrr *catch* (or *get, raise*) *hail Columbia, give one hail Columbia.*

1854 *Oregon Weekly Times* Sept. 9 (1912 Thornton *Amer. Gloss.*), The note in which he says we gave him Hale Columby. **1867** Lowell *Biglow* 18 **'Upcountry' MA,** People's impulsiver down here than wut our folks to home be,/ An' kin' o' go it 'ith a resh in raisin' Hail Columby. **1907** *DN* 3.189 **seNH,** *Hail Columbia*. . . A sound scolding. "He give him hail Columbia." **1908** *DN* 3.315 **eAL, wGA,** *Give one hail Columbia, Happy Land*. . . To punish, beat, berate. *Happy Land* is sometimes omitted. *Ibid* 318, *Hail Columbia, (Happy Land)*. . . Used to express a severe drubbing literal or figurative. "We caught Hail Columbia, Happy Land!" **1910** *DN* 3.442 **cwNY,** *Hail Columbia*. . . A severe punishment or scolding. **1946** *New Yorker* 25 May 25/3 **NY,** I got Hail Columbia from Father for that escapade. **1950** *WELS (If someone gives you a very severe scolding: "I certainly got ——— for that!")* 1 Inf, **WI,** Hail Columbia; *(Weakened substitutes for "hell": "What the ———!")* 1 Inf, **ceWI,** Hail Columbia. **1968–70** *DARE* (Qu. Y4, *Other words for a very uncomplimentary remark*) Inf **TX**95, Give him hail Columbia; **MO**9, Hail Columbus. **1969** *DARE* Tape **CA**172B, That night the army—I guess it was a sergeant, probably; it coulda been a captain—was giving their men hail Columbia for not following their orders.

hailey-over See **haily-over**

hail from v phr
See quots 1848, 1942.
1839 (1840) Simms *Border Beagles* 2.59, Few tradesmen were known in the southern country, who did not "hail from" New England or New York. **1848** Bartlett *Americanisms* 168, *To hail from*. . . A phrase probably originating with seamen or boatmen, and meaning to come from, to belong to; as, 'He hails from Kentucky,' i.e. he is a native of Kentucky. **1872** Schele de Vere *Americanisms* 343, Even the manner of speaking to vessels at sea, by hailing aloud or through a speaking-trumpet, has been transferred to land usage, and a man is familiarly said to *hail from* his native State, or a stranger is accosted with the words, "Well, sir, and where did you hail from last?" **1907** *DN* 3.213 **nwAR, cCT,** *Hail from* . . . To come from. **1910** *DN* 3.442 **cwNY,** *Hail from*. . . To come from (as a place of residence). **1911** (1916) Porter *Harvester* 333 **IN,** "Where do you hail from?" "Well not from the direction of hail," laughed the Girl. "I lived in Chicago." **1942** ME Univ. *Studies* 56.8, After the ship is launched . . she is enrolled at the custom house of a port of entry. . . She is said to *hail from* that port, the name of which is painted, along with her own, on her stern. **1945** Colcord *Sea Language* 92 **ME, Cape Cod, Long Island,** A ship hails from her port of registry. A landsman is often said to hail from a place, though not necessarily his birthplace.

hailing n[1] Cf **gam** n[1]
1967 *DARE* (Qu. O21, *When men in seagoing boats get together for a visit and a cup of hot coffee, that's called a* ______) Inf **CA**31, Hailing.

hailing n[2] See **hail** n[2]

hail-o n
1 See quot.
1970 *DARE* (Qu. EE12, *Games in which one captain hides his team and the other team tries to find it*) Inf **CA**174, Hail-o.
2 See **hail-over.**

hail out v phr
To be ruined by a hailstorm.
1978 Doig *This House* 183 **MT** (as of c1955), They hailed out up across the Marias. Pounded the damned wheat flat to the ground.

hail-over n, exclam Also *hail-over-the-house, hell-over-(the-)housetop, hail-o, hell-o, ell-over* [Perh from Scots *hail* + *over;* cf *SND hail* v.[2] "To score a goal;" *hail* n. 3 II. 1 "The cry of 'Hail' raised when a goal, etc., is scored."] **S Atl, Gulf States** See Map and Map Section Cf **haily-over**
1 =Antony-over.
1897 (1952) McGill *Narrative* 30 **ceSC,** In playing "Hail Over" the house the girls dashed around to the other side equal to the boys. **1908** *DN* 3.318 **eAL, wGA,** *Hail-over*. . . A game. . . The cry *'hail over!'* is called by the side throwing the ball to give warning. **1939** Harris *Purslane* 134 **cNC,** I use to try to keep them window lights in, but that pa'cel o' younguns chunked rocks so bad a-playin' hail-over I give up. **1952** Brown *NC Folkl.* 1.36 **cNC,** Players are in two equal (or nearly equal) groups on opposite sides of a building. The group which has the ball calls "Anti-over" and the other side responds, "Let it come!" (or they call, "Hail Over" and the response is "Hail-over"). **1965–70** *DARE* (Qu. EE22, . . *Game in which they throw a ball over a building . . to a player on the other side*) 29 Infs, **S Atl, Gulf States,** Hail-over; **LA**2, Hail-over ['heɪˌloʊvɚ]; **LA**12, 15, Hail-over ['heɪˌloʊvə]; **FL**48, Hail-over [he'lovə]; **NC**72, Hail-over-the-house; **GA**18, 19, 33, Hail-o ['heˌlo]; **MS**6, **TX**35, Hail-o; **GA**3, Hell-over-the-housetop; **FL**26, Hell-o; **GA**8, Ell-over [ɛl ovə]; (Qu. EE23a, . . *What do you call out when you throw the ball?*) 29 Infs, **S Atl, Gulf States,** Hail-over; **GA**18, 19, 33, Hail-o ['heˌlo]; **LA**12, Hail-o ['heɪˌloʊ]; **TX**35, Hail-o; **GA**3, Hell-over-house-top; **FL**26, Hell-o; **GA**8, Ell-over [ɛl ovə]. **1966** *DARE* Tape **FL**8, [FW:] And how about this, the game you mentioned, talking about throwing the ball over the roof. [Inf:] That was hail-over. And one would be on one side of the house and one on the other side and you had to keep throwing until you were able to throw the ball completely over to the other side. And then if it, if the player on the other side let the ball bounce one time and he caught it, why then he exchanged sides. Why, I don't know.
2 also *hail-back:* **=pigtail** exclam.
1966 *DARE* (Qu. EE23b, . . *If you fail to get the ball over the building and it rolls back, what do you call out?*) Infs **FL**6, 8, Hail-over; **FL**10, Hail-back.

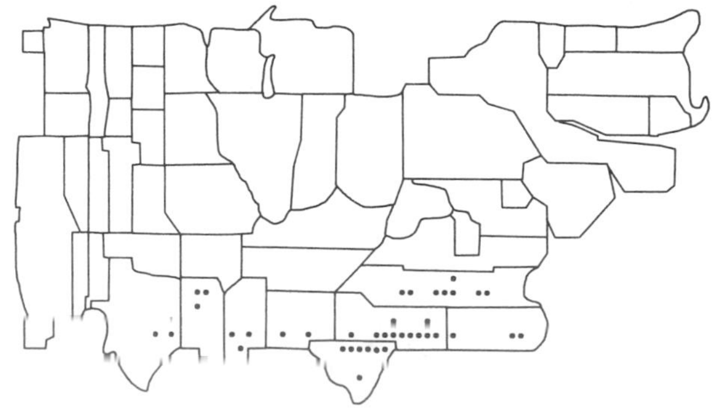
•hail-over + varr (Qq. EE22, EE23a, b)

hailweed See **hellweed 1**

haily adj
1896 *DN* 1.418 **KY, NH,** *Haily:* wild, reckless. "A haily crowd."

haily exclam See **haily-over**

haily-baily(-over) See **haily-over**

haily-come-back exclam
In the game **haily-over: =pigtail** exclam.
1968 *DARE* (Qu. EE23b, . . *If you fail to get the ball over the building and it rolls back, what do you call out?*) Inf **NH**15, Haily-come-back.

haily-over n, exclam Also *haily, haily-baily(-over), haily-haily-over, haily-over-the-house* Also sp *hailey-over, haley-over* [Cf **hail-over**] **esp NEast, OH** See Map and Map Section Cf **handy-over**
=Antony-over.
1883 Newell *Games & Songs* 181 **CT,** *Haley-Over.* **1894** *DN* 1.341 **wCT,** *Haily over* . . a game among the schoolboys, in which they choose sides and the parties get on opposite sides of a building. A ball is thrown over; if one of the opposite side makes a fair catch when it comes over, he is entitled to run round and throw it at any one of the other party, who if hit must change sides. **1904** *Youth's Companion* 14 Apr 188/1, Under the schoolhouse wall / I sat and heard them call— / "Ha-a—ley over!"/ And then on the other side / The childish voices cried,/ "Under!" **1909** *DN* 3.412 **nME,** *Hailey over*. . . A children's game of ball . . : The players choose sides and take positions on opposite sides of a barn. One player throws the ball over the barn, crying out, *hailey over.* Some one of the opposing players tries to catch it, and then tags one of his opponents with the ball. The player tagged has to change sides. The side wins which gains all of the players. **1933** *Hanley Disks* **Rockland ME,** Haley-over. **1950** *WELS Suppl.* 1 Inf, **WI,** My husband, who is from Aurora, Maine, called the game haily-baily and added over as a cry in the game; 1 Inf, **ceWI,** Haily-over = anty-I-over. **1965–70** *DARE* (Qu. EE22, . . *Game in which they throw a ball over a building . . to a player on the other side*) 11 Infs, **esp NEast,** Haily-over; **ME**11, 23, ['hæli]-over; **SC**3, ['hɛlɪ oʊvɚ]; **OH**15, Haily-haily-over; (Qu. EE23a, . . *What do you call out when you throw the ball?*) 11 Infs, **esp NEast,** Haily-over; **PA**11, ['hæli]-over; **SC**3, ['hɛlɪ oʊvɚ]; **NC**72, Haily-over-the-house; **OH**8, Haily.

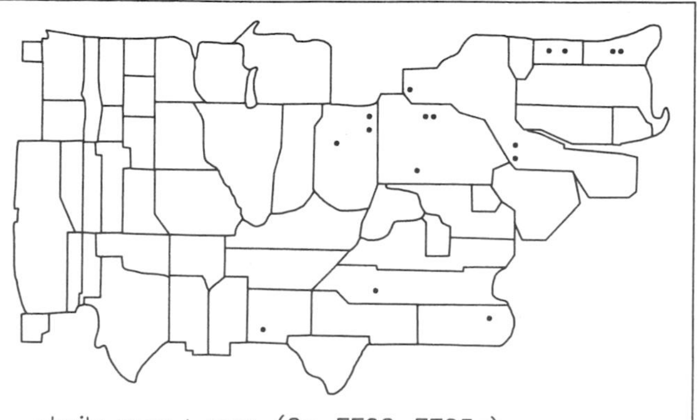
•haily-over + varr (Qq. EE22, EE23a)

haina interrog exclam Cf **huh not**
=ainna.

1986 *DARE* File **nePA,** Putting *haina* on the end of a statement makes the statement a question. It doesn't matter who you're talking to, or when the thing happened. "You're going dancing Friday night, haina?" means "Are you going dancing Friday night?" "He did that last night, haina?" means "Did he do that last night?"

haincty See **hincty** adj

haint See **haunt**

hain't v Also sp *haan, han't, hante, hent* [Contr of *has not, have not* (Engl dial; cf *EDD have* v. I. 1. ii); used also for *am not, are not, is not*] **chiefly NEast, Sth, S Midl, esp Appalachians** Cf **ain't** v[1], **be C**

1 Has not, have not.

1815 Humphreys *Yankey in England* 105, *Han't* . . have not. **1843** (1846) Haliburton *Attaché* (1st ser) 2.210 **NEng,** I hante see'd a hoss equal to her a'most. **1843** (1916) Hall *New Purchase* 331 **cIN,** You'r all servunts of the people and hain't the right no how to give away their edicashion money without thar consent. **1844** Thompson *Major Jones's Courtship* 31 **GA,** Men what haint got no edecation wont stand no sort of chance with 'em. **1856** Olmsted *Journey Slave States* 558 **AL** [Black], I haan been used to sich treatem. Dey haan got but one servant for all dis hall. **1885** Twain *Huck. Finn* 41 **MO,** I hain't got only a dollar. **1886** *S. Bivouac* 4.348 **sAppalachians,** You-uns hain't got the wuth [=worth] of yer quarter [=a 25 cent coin] yit. **1893** Shands *MS Speech* 34, *Hain't* [hent]. Used by illiterate whites to mean: *is not, are not, am not, has not,* and *have not.* **1895** *DN* 1.376 **eTN,** *Haint.* **1898** Westcott *Harum* 8 **cNY,** I hain't no pressin' use fer another hoss. **1901** Harben *Westerfelt* 2 **nGA,** Leastwise, I hain't seed narry one to beat it. **1907** *DN* 3.213 **nwAR, cCT,** *Haint.* **1908** *DN* 3.318 **eAL, wGA,** *Hain't.* **1923** *DN* 5.209 **swMO,** *Haint.* **1939** FWP *These are Our Lives* 19 **ceNC** [Black], I can't tell you 'bout her, 'cause I hain't heard from her in three years. **1966** *PADS* 46.26 **cnAR** (as of 1952), *Hain't.* **1966–68** *DARE* Tape **FL**37, I hain't been; **VA**27, You hain't [tried it]? Well, you ought to try it. **1968** *DARE* FW Addit **NY**68, *Hain't*—contraction for haven't, have not. "You hain't got much storage room." [FW: This contraction is not used for *is not, are not.*]

2 Am not, are not, is not.

1887 (1895) Robinson *Uncle Lisha* 153 **wVT,** They don't ketch fish, an' consequentially they hain't fishers. **1892** *DN* 1.210 **NEng,** *Hain't.* . . I hain't very well. **1893** [see **1** above]. **1904** *DN* 2.423 **Cape Cod MA** (as of a1857), *Ah hain* [hẽ] *gunty* (I'm not going to). **1908** Fox *Lonesome Pine* 11 **KY,** Hit hain't! **1909** *DN* 3.412 **nME,** *Haint.* . . Are not. **1930** Shoemaker *1300 Words* 29 **cPA Mts** (as of c1900), *Haint*—Aint, am not. **c1960** *Wilson Coll.* **csKY,** *Hain't* for have not, has not, is not, am not, are not, rather common in some places. **1965–70** *DARE* (Qu. EE15) Infs **IN**30, **IN**39, All hain't hid; (Qu. HH4) Inf **FL**7, Hain't all there; (Qu. LL14) Inf **SC**44, Hain't [=isn't] ary a one; **KY**34, Hain't none left; (Qu. LL17) Inf **KY**33, They hain't no more. **1966** *PADS* 46.26 **cnAR** (as of 1952), *Hain't.* **1966–69** *DARE* FW Addit **eKY, c, cwNC,** *Hain't* = ain't. **1967** *DARE* Tape **TN**15, [FW:] Is that one of the violins you made . . yourself? [Inf:] No, no, it hain't. **1984** Wilder *You All Spoken Here* 169 **Sth,** *Hent:* Isn't. **1987** *DARE* File, Hain't = are not [rare]. Heard in oral usage, Newville, Pa. "They hain't supposed to be finished till Thanksgiving."

hain'ting-ain'ting ppl adj [From the use of non-std forms **hain't** and **ain't**]

Uneducated, rustic.

[**1939** in 1944 *ADD* **FL,** He speaks with a hain't, 'tain't, & a tutter [=t'other].] **1951** West *Witch Diggers* 308 **IN** (as of 1900s), The newcomers, blown up in her mind to the size of dukes and duchesses, when she called on them nothing more than some hain'ting-ain'ting couple with a farm heired off an old childless uncle.

hainty See **haunty**

hair n Usu |hɛr, hɛə|; also |hɑ(r), hær, hæə, her, heə|; for other varr see **A** below Pronc-spp *har(r), hawr, heyar, hyah, hya'r* Cf Pronc Intro 3.I.1.b, 3.II.26

A Pronc varr.

1823 *Natl. Intelligencer* (DC) 1 May (*DN* 4.47) **MS,** *Harr.* . . That substance which covers the skin of quadrupeds. **1872** Burnham *Memoirs U.S. Secret Service* 207 **NY,** You've got me where the ha'r is short! **a1883** (1911) Bagby *VA Gentleman* 56, If he is a tidewater man . . instead of saying the "har" of the head, he says "heyar." **1887** Page *In Ole VA* 46 [Black], Wid her hyah mos' straight as white folks. **1893** Shands *MS Speech* 35, *Har* [hɑ]. Negro for *hair.* **1905** Culbertson *Banjo Talks* 124 **SE** [Black], Gemman wid long gray hya'r. **1927** Shewmake *Engl. Pronc. VA* 33, [In] *hair* . . Virginians usually employ the sound of *a* as in *man,* which may be represented by *æ*. . . *hae-uh.* **1931** *AmSp* 6.161 **VA,** Hair . . [hɛː]. **1942** Hall *Smoky Mt. Speech* 24, [æ] occurs in . . hair. *Ibid* 25, A tendency to use a centralized and raised [æ] was noticed in *air, hair* . . [hæ̈·ɚ]. . . The vowel [also] often tends to be retracted, as in . . [hɛ̈ɚ]. **1950** Hubbell *Pronc. NYC* 75, /ɛə̆/. The diphthong in . . *hair* ordinarily begins at a point somewhat lower than the position of the [ɛ] in *pet* and then glides to a mid-central position. **c1960** *Wilson Coll.* **csKY,** *Hair* [hɑr], among very old. **1967** Fetterman *Stinking Creek* 142 **seKY,** If you are a real good Christian you are not supposed to cut your hawr and wear this makeup. **1968** Kellner *Aunt Serena* 148 **cIN** (as of 1920s), Her sister went and cut his hair (she called it "harr"). **1968** *DARE* FW Addit **csMD,** [hær]. **c1970** Pederson *Dial. Surv. Rural GA* **seGA,** [*Hair* is most frequently pronounced [hɛɚ, hɛə]; also frequent are [heɚ, heə]; infrequent pronunciations are [hæɚ, hæə, heɪjə, hɪə] and [eɚ, eə].]

B Gram forms.

1 Used as a count noun rather than a mass noun in reference to the hair of the head. [This was once common in Engl (see *OED hair* sb. I. 1. b), but US use prob reflects infl of Ger, Fr, and other European langs in which this is common.]

1965–70 *DARE* (Qu. X4a, . . *Of somebody's hair getting gray, you might say, "His _____ is/are getting gray."*) 13 Infs, **scattered, but somewhat more freq Nth, N Midl,** Hairs are; **IL**77, **NJ**53, **TX**4, **SC**44, Hairs is; **MI**95, He's getting gray hairs; **IL**105, Some old people still say hairs; **LA**37, Daddy says hairs; **NY**23, Frenchman, Canuck, says hairs; **PA**162, Many people say hairs; (Qu. X4b, . . *"I have to wash my [hair/hairs]."*) 15 Infs, **chiefly Inland Nth,** Hairs. [**1968** *DARE* FW Addit **csLA,** The barber said, "Now, Sir, you comb 'em the way you want 'em and tell me how you like it."] **1983** *Reinecke Coll.* **LA,** Hairs [hæz] used rather than "hair" by rural French background persons. "Comb your hairs, sugar." La. French plural "Peigne tes cheveux."

2 Used as a collective singular with plural concord. [Prob from Ger dial loss of noun plural ending with retention of plural verb and pronoun] **chiefly German settlement areas, esp PaGer**

1935 *AmSp* 10.165 **PaGer,** I had my hair cut yesterday, but the barber cut them too short. **1950** *WELS Suppl.* 4 Infs, **WI,** Hair are. **1966–68** *DARE* (Qu. X4a, . . *Of somebody's hair getting gray, you might say, "His _____ is/are getting gray."*) Infs **GA**9, **MO**21, 25, **PA**142, Hair are. **1971** *Today Show Letters* **sePA,** I just washed my hair and can't do a thing with them. **1986** *DARE* File **sePA** (as of 1949), In the Pennsylvania Dutch section near Reading, Pa., the word hair (referring to the hair on one's head) is used as if it were plural, as, "My hair *are* dirty, so I shall wash *them* tonight."

C Senses.

1 also *corn hair, silk hair:* A corn silk—also used collectively. Cf **beard B2**

1967–69 *DARE* (Qu. I31) Inf **MN**6, Hair; **CT**39, Silk hair. **1973** Allen *LAUM* 1.313 **cwND** (as of c1950), *Silk* (on the ear of corn). . . hair. **1989** Pederson *LAGS Tech. Index* 193 **Gulf Region,** *Corn silk* . . corn hair (2 [infs]) . . hair (31) . . hairs (2) . . silk hair (1).

2 usu neg; also in phrr *hair (n)or hide* and varr: A sign or trace of someone or something. [Inversion of std *hide nor hair;* cf *OED hide* sb.[1] 1. b 1330 →] **chiefly Sth, S Midl** See Map Cf **head** n **D1**

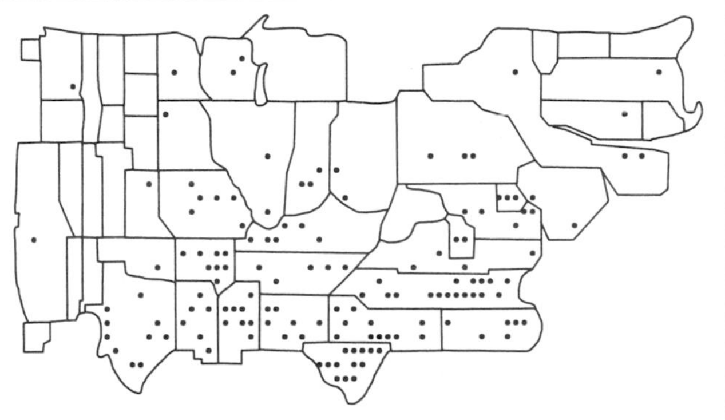

•hair n C2 + varr (Qu. LL29)

1837 Smith *Col. Crockett's Exploits* 31 **S Midl,** They examined it all over, and could find neither hair nor hide of my bullet. **1896** Harris *Sister Jane* 310 **GA,** Mandy hain't seed nuther ha'r nor hide of Sandy. **1908** *DN* 3.318 **eAL, wGA,** I haven't seen hair nor hide of it. **1922** *DN* 5.165 **AL, NE,** *Hair (n)or hide*. . . Used in negative expressions. "I haven't seen hair nor hide of it." **1927** *AmSp* 2.356 **WV,** *Hair nor hide of it* . . no knowledge of the matter. "I have not seen hair nor hide of that saddle." **1941** Heydrick–Thompson *Americans All* 274 **PA,** They ain't goin' to lay eyes on yo' father, hair nor hide of him. **1946** *PADS* 6.38 **cwVA,** I hain't seen hair nor hide of him. **1955** Adams *Grandfather* 79 **NY** (as of 1830s), I never set eye on hair nor hide of them again. **1959** Sanders *Echoes* 9 **swAR,** No one has heard hair nor hide of him since. **1965–70** *DARE* (Qu. LL29, *Any sign or trace: "He left last week, and nobody's seen ——— of him since."*) 108 Infs, **chiefly Sth, S Midl,** Hair nor hide; 18 Infs, **chiefly Sth, S Midl,** Hair or hide; 12 Infs, **chiefly Sth, S Midl,** A hair; NY241, WI61, Nary a hair; **FL**36, Hair, hide, nor hoof; **MA**28, Hair or head; **TN**6, Hair nor toenails.

3 in phr *hair and hide* and varr: The totality, the entirety; totally, entirely. Cf **hide and hair** adv phr

1955 Funk *Heavens to Betsy* 164, *Hair and hide (horns and tallow)*—The whole works; every part; the entirety. The first part, hair and hide, has long been used in the same sense. **1969** *DARE* (Qu. LL25, *Expressions meaning entirely, completely: "He sold out the whole place, ———."*) Inf **PA**177, Hair, hide, and all.

4 in phrr *to a gnat's* (or *frog's, cock's*) *hair* and var: To the last detail, accurately. [Expansions of std *to a hair*]

1940 White *Wild Geese* 189 **NW** (as of 1890s), He's got to drop his tree to a gnat's hair, or all his other calculations are no good at all. **1954** *Harder Coll.* **cwTN,** To the last hair on a gnat's ass, to the last detail, said of something planned or executed very carefully. **1966–69** *DARE* (Qu. KK50, . . *To the last detail*) Infs **KY**60, **TN**26, Down to a gnat's hair; **AR**31, **GA**9, To a frog's hair; **GA**1, To a cock's hair.

5 in var phrr indicating strong denial: See quot.

1966–70 *DARE* (Qu. KK55a, *To deny something very firmly: "No, not by a ———."*) Inf **AZ**1, Hair of my chinny-chin-chin; **CA**117, Hair on your fanny; **ID**5, **IN**45, Not by the hair on my (*or* of your) chinny-chin-chin; **IL**4, Not by the hair on my neck; **MS**80, Not on your hair; **TX**5, Frog hair.

6 in phrr *keep one's hair on* (or *down*): To remain calm.

1885 Harte *By Shore & Sedge* 212 **CA,** 'Keep yer hair on!' remonstrated the old man with dark intelligence. **1955** Funk *Heavens to Betsy* 88, *To keep one's hair on*—To restrain one's temper; to remain calm and serene, unruffled despite provocation. . . it could have reflected the Indian raids. . . Settlers and wagoners who could remain unexcited in the face of any such raid were the most likely to be able to fight off a threatening horde and thus to retain their scalps. This is, of course, conjecture. **1968–70** *DARE* (Qu. GG23a, *If you speak sharply to someone to make him be patient, you say, "Now just keep your ———."*) Infs **MA**100, **NY**66, **TN**30, Hair on; **GA**84, Hair down.

7 in phrr *all hair by the nose, hair in* (or *on*) *the nose:* Angry, quarrelsome, touchy. [Cf *OED a hair in one's neck* (at *hair* sb. 8. f) "a cause of trouble or inconvenience"]

1924 *DN* 5.287 **Cape Cod MA,** When one gets angry he is 'all hair by the nose'. **1960** Criswell *Resp. to PADS 20* **Ozarks,** *Hair in the nose*—Used of a high-handed quarrelsome person, always "Old hair in the nose." **1967** *DARE* (Qu. GG8, *When a person is very easily offended: "Be careful what you say to him, he's ———."*) Inf **IL**11, Hair on the nose.

8 in phr *have a hair crossed:* To be touchy, sensitive, or defensive.

1968 *DARE* (Qu. GG39, *Somebody who seems to be looking for reasons to be angry*) Inf **CA**83, He's got a hair crossed.

9 in phr *pound hair* and varr: To drive a team of horses or mules; hence n *hair pounder* a teamster. [See quot 1975]

1927 *AmSp* 2.356 **WV,** *Hair, to pound* . . to drive a team. "The boys have been pounding hair on the West Fork for a month." **1930** *DN* 6.86 **cWV,** *Beating hair,* driving a team of horses. **1934** *Hanley Disks* **csME,** That's just an up-river expression: "What are you doing?" "Well, I'm hair-pounding for so-and-so." . . In the western part, they'd call it mule-skinning. **1938** (1939) Holbrook *Holy Mackinaw* 261 [Logging], *Hair-pounder.* A horse teamster. **1958** McCulloch *Woods Words* 79 **Pacific NW,** *Hair pounder*—A teamster, mule skinner, or in the old days, an ox driver. **1972** *Yesterday* Mar–Apr 25 [Logging], A good "hair pounder" could command his horses to tug with anything from five pounds pull to full power, and from five seconds to five minutes. **1975** Gould *ME Lingo* 122, *Hair pounder*—From the slapping of reins on flanks, the woodsman's term for a teamster.

10 in phr *come through with all hairs lying flat:* See quot.

1934 Smiley *Gloss. New Paltz* **seNY,** "He came through with all hairs laying flat." Means he came through unscathed.

11 in phr *set the hair:*

a See quot; hence vbl n *setting the hair.*

1936 Adams *Cowboy Lingo* 102, It would be a long time before the rider . . could ride him on duty without first riding him long enough to take the kinks out of his back which the cowboy spoke of as . . 'settin' the hair.' **1944** Adams *Western Words* 140, *Set the hair*—To ride a horse long enough to take the meanness out of him.

b See quot.

1984 Wilder *You All Spoken Here* 165 **Sth,** *That will set the hair:* That will anger, surprise, frighten, or give one pause. The expression comes from butchering hogs in family farm operations. After being killed, the hogs are scalded in water heated to 135–140 degrees, depending on heft of the animal. This sets the hair—stands it on end—making it easier for one to scrape it from the carcass.

12 in phr *hair in the butter:* See quots.

1944 Adams *Western Words* 71, *Hair in the butter* . . a delicate situation. **1980** *Houston Chron.* (TX) 11 Nov sec 3, In East Texas, as an expression of suspicion of some statement or event, it is often said "There's a hair in the butter."

13 in phr *have hair on;* Of jokes: to be old, worn-out, out-of-date. Cf **hairy 1**

1966–68 *DARE* (Qu. FF21a, *A joke that is so old it doesn't seem funny any more*) Infs **AR**3, **NC**33, Got hair on them; **NJ**27, So old it has hair on it; **WA**1, So old they got hair on; **CA**117, They got hair growing on them; (Qu. FF21b, *Or about old jokes people say: "The first time I heard that one* . . *———."*) Inf **NY**38, It had hair on its teeth. [5 of 6 Infs old] **1987** *DARE* File **NYC** (as of c1950), I remember my father saying "That joke has hair on it" when some television comic like Milton Berle would drag out some old chestnut.

hair adj

1936 *AmSp* 11.368 **nLA,** *Hair*. . . Expert at something; determined; as, 'He is hair on catching a mess of fish.'

hair v

See quot 1895.

1895 *Std. Dict. Engl. Lang.* (Funk) 810/1, Hair. . . To produce hair-like fibers: said of maple-sirup when boiled so low as to string out when dripped from a spoon. **1906** Gregory *Woman's Cookbook* 335, Boil one cupful of granulated sugar with one-quarter cupful of water until it "hairs." **1913** *DN* 4.4 **ME,** *Hair*. . . To grow thick and ropy in cooking until it draws out like a hair. Used of syrup, frosting, etc. "Boil it till it hairs."

hair and hide See **hair** n **C3**

hair apple n [Perh for *haw apple* (at **apple haw**)]

The fruit of a **hawthorn.**

1896 *DN* 1.418, *Hair apple:* haw. . . Parker Co., Tex.

hair ball n **S Midl**

A ball of hair formed naturally in an animal's stomach, or artificially by a person, and used for magic or witchcraft.

1885 Twain *Huck. Finn* 27 **MO,** Miss Watson's nigger, Jim, had a hair-ball as big as your fist, which had been took out of the fourth stomach of an ox, and he used to do magic with it. **1914** *Jrl. Amer. Folkl.* 27.328 **KY,** The picture of the victim crudely scrawled upon a tree . . by a witch who wishes to work the black art, does not mean much unless the witch-ball or hair-ball is used. A small bunch of hair from a horse or cow is rolled between the two hands into a small round ball, and this ball is used as a bullet. In whatever part the ball hits the picture, in the corresponding part of the victim a wound is inflicted. **1935** Hyatt *Folk-Lore Adams Co. IL* 467, "A cow licks her hair and that hair goes down in the left side of the pouch and that forms a ball, and if you have one of those in your hand you can bewitch anyone." *German.* **c1938** in 1970 Hyatt *Hoodoo* 1.544 **seLA,** Now, dere's a *hairball*—dat's concernin' a lady, misfortune between yo' an' her. Now, yo' kin wear dis *hairball* tuh keep in contact with her an' yo' kin wear it dat chew may nevah git in contact with her no mo'. . . Well, it's hair dat's from ole dead people, yo' know, befo' it's event'lly decayed. . . Put in in a thimble or somethin' round that chew may put it in a ball. **1947** (1964) Randolph *Ozark Superstitions* 271, "Hair ball"—just a little bunch of black hair mixed with beeswax and rolled into a hard pellet. The old woman tossed this thing at the persons whom she wished to eliminate, and they fell dead a few hours later. **1965** Hyatt *Folk-Lore Adams Co. IL* 797, "They went out to find the cow and found it dead. It had been shot in the thigh with a hair-ball. . . You see, a witch always uses a silver bullet or a hair-ball to kill anything." . . German. **1970** TN Folk Lore Soc. *Bulletin* 36.4, She was referring to the hair or conjure balls thrown at intended victims to bring sickness or death.

hairbell n

1 See **harebell 1.**

2 A **mariposa lily** (here: *Calochortus albus*). [Prob from the hairy petals]

1897 Parsons *Wild Flowers CA* 54, *Calochortus albus*. . . Wherever they grow, these flowers win instant and enthusiastic recognition; and they have received a variety of common names in different localities, being known as . . "hairbell [etc]." **1898** *Jrl. Amer. Folkl.* 11.281 **CA,** *Calochortus albus*, . . hairbell. **1915** (1926) Armstrong–Thornber *Western Wild Flowers* 58, These plants grow on shady banks in the Coast Ranges and have several pretty common names, such as . . the misleading name Hairbell, which causes this flower to be confused with . . Campanula.

hair bird See **hair sparrow**

hair brand n Cf **cold brand**

A temporary mark used to identify cattle; hence v phr *hair brand,* to make such a mark; vbl n *hair branding* the process of making such a mark.

1936 Adams *Cowboy Lingo* 130, A 'hair brand' was one whereby the branding iron was held against the animal just long enough to burn the hair, not the hide. The hair grew out, effacing the signs of the brand, and the rustler could then put his own brand on the animal. **1940** Writers' Program *Guide NM* 114, *Hair branding*—Brand made by burning only hair. A temporary brand used on trail herds. **1941** Writers' Program *Guide WY* 462, *Hair brand* . . a temporary brand made by burning or picking out the hair. If skillfully done, it looks like an old brand. **1977** Watts *Dict. Old West* 156, *Hair branding*—Cold branding. . . Used for trail-branding or by cow-thieves. A not uncommon trick was to hair-brand a calf with the owner's brand . . when this hair brand grew out, the animal would be rebranded by the thief.

haircap moss n Also *haircap, hairy-cap, hair moss* [See quot 1947]

A moss of the genus *Polytrichum*. For other names see **bear moss, bear's bed 1, bird wheat, ground moss 1, pigeon wheat, robin's rye, rum-sucker**

1822 Eaton *Botany* 403, *Polytrichum . . juniperinum* (hair-cap moss.) . . In dry woods, &c. **1848** Gray *Manual of Botany* 659, *Polytrichum, L. Hair-Cap Moss.* Calyptra densely hairy. **1890** *Century Dict.* 3869, *Hair-moss.* Same as *haircap-moss.* **1907** Marshall *Mosses* 248, Hairy-Cap Mosses. *Ibid* 252, Ohio Hairy-cap, *Polytrichum Ohiense.* **1947** Grout–Howe *Mosses & Liverworts* 39, *Polytrichum. The Hair-Cap Mosses.* . . The hairy cap that gives this genus of mosses its name is composed of long hairs growing from a little scale-like body, the calyptra proper, at the top of the capsule. The Hair-Caps . . are subject to great extremes of moisture and dryness.

hair chaps See **hair pants**

hair chimney n Cf **cat-and-clay, stick-and-clay chimney**

1954 *Harder Coll.* **cwTN,** *Hair chimney,* a chimney made of hog hair, mud, boards, and gravel.

hair cinch n

See quot 1968.

1873 Miller *Modocs* 177 **CA,** At length the leader set his spurs in the broad hair-sinch . . and rode down to the water's edge. **1953** *Western Folkl.* 12.185, One old-time ranchman . . forbade the use of hair cinches, since they would "cause cinch sores." **1968** Adams *Western Words* 138, *Hair cinch*—A saddle cinch made of horsehair.

haired up adj phr Also *hared out, har(r)ed up* [Cf **hackle up**] **NEng**

Angry, upset, anxious.

1914 *DN* 4.73 **ME, nNH,** *Haired,* or *harred (up).* . . Angry, vexed. (Harrowed?) **1929** *AmSp* 5.127 **ME,** "All haired up" (excited and angry). **1941** *LANE* Map 472, **chiefly NH, ME,** 'Angry, enraged' . . *hared up;* 1 inf, **swME,** *Hared out.* *Ibid* Map 476–477, **chiefly ME, NH, eMA,** When a person is waiting in nervous suspense for an expected event, when he is 'on tenderhooks' with excitement . . *hared up.* **1946** in 1957 Old Farmer's Almanac *Sampler* 237 **NEng,** Joel wasn't one to get "haired up" over anything. **1948** Bean *Yankee Auctioneer* 74 **wMA,** It was a sorry-looking sight, but nothing to get haired-up over. **1968** *DARE* (Qu. GG40, . . *Violently angry*) Inf **CT**3, Really haired up. **1974** *AmSp* 49.62 **swME** (as of c1900), *Haired-up.* . . Distraught, excited. **1975** Gould *ME Lingo* 122, *Haired up*—Angry, upset.

hair fern n

A **maidenhair fern** (here: *Adiantum pedatum*).

1900 Lyons *Plant Names* 15, *A[diantum] pedatum* . . Hair Fern. **1911** *Century Dict. Suppl., Hair-fern.* . . The American maidenhair, *Adiantum pedatum.* **1971** Krochmal *Appalachia Med. Plants* 36, *Adiantum Pedatum* . . American maidenhair, hair fern, . . sweet fern.

hair goat n [Abbr for *mohair + goat*]

1970 *DARE* Tape **TX**81, Angora goats, or what we call hair goats, raised locally.

hairgrass n

1 Any of various grasses, as:

a An annual grass of the genus *Aira.*

1790 in 1793 Amer. Philos. Soc. *Trans.* 3.160 **sePA,** *Aira,* Hairgrass. **1832** MA Hist. Soc. *Coll.* 2d ser 9.146 **cwVT,** *Aira flexuosa,* Hair grass. **1876** Hobbs *Bot. Hdbk.* 141, *Aira* . . Hair grass. **1912** Baker *Book of Grasses* 132, Silvery Hair-grass [=*Aira caryophyllea*] is a tiny annual that has become only locally abundant since its accidental introduction from Europe. **1950** Hitchcock–Chase *Manual Grasses* 298, *Aira caryophyllea* . . Silver hairgrass. **1974** Munz *Flora S. CA* 943, *Aira* . . Hairgrass.

b also *hairygrass:* A **bentgrass 1** (here esp *Agrostis hiemalis,* but also *A. scabra*).

1850 U.S. Patent Office *Annual Rept for 1849: Ag.* 157 **MS,** *Trichodium laxiflorum,* hair-grass, also springs up. **1891** Jesup *Plants Hanover NH* 53, *A[grostis] scabra* . . Hair-Grass. **1936** Winter *Plants NE* 33, *A[grostis] hyemalis* . . Hairy-grass. **1940** Gates *Flora KS* 121, *Agrostis hyemalis* . . Hairgrass. **1946** Tatnall *Flora DE* 30, *A[grostis] hyemalis* . . Hair Grass. **1952** Strausbaugh–Core *Flora WV* 114, *A[grostis] hyemalis* . . Hairgrass.

c A **muhly grass** (here esp *Muhlenbergia capillaris*).

1857 Gray *Manual of Botany* 546, *M[uhlenbergia] capillaris.* . . *Hair-Grass.* . . The awns . . are about 1′ long. **1912** Baker *Book of Grasses* 108, Long-awned Hair-grass. *Muhlenbergia capillaris.* **1933** Small *Manual SE Flora* 98, *Muhlenbergia* . . Hair-grasses. *Ibid* 99, *M. capillaris* . . Hair-grass. **1946** Tatnall *Flora DE* 32, *M[uhlenbergia] capillaris* . . Hair Grass. **1950** Gray–Fernald *Manual of Botany* 172, *M[uhlenbergia] capillaris.* . . *Hairgrass.* . . Awn 5–15 mm. long. . . *M. expansa.* . . *Hairgrass.* . . Awn only 1–4 mm. long.

d An annual or perennial grass of the genus *Deschampsia.*

1889 Vasey *Ag. Grasses* 107, *Deschampsia cæspitosa* (Hair Grass). This is an exceedingly varied species, having a wide distribution in this and other countries. **1912** Baker *Book of Grasses* 136, By the dry paths of early summer delicate panicles of Wavy Hair-grass [=*Deschampsia flexuosa*] rises. . . Tufted Hair-grass *(Deschampsia caespitosa)* prefers the moister soil of lake shores and river banks. **1937** U.S. Forest Serv. *Range Plant Hdbk.* G49, About five species of hairgrass [=*Deschampsia* spp] are recognized . . as occurring in the western United States. **1952** Strausbaugh–Core *Flora WV* 120, *D[eschampsia]* . . *flexuosa* . . Hairgrass. **1974** Munz *Flora S. CA* 961, *Deschampsia* . . Hairgrass.

e A **needlegrass** (here: *Stipa columbiana*).

1937 U.S. Forest Serv. *Range Plant Hdbk.* G115, Subalpine needlegrass [=*Stipa columbiana*], also called . . hairgrass, is one of the fine-leaved, slender-stemmed needlegrasses.

f See **hairgrass dropseed.**

2 A **spikerush** (here: *Eleocharis acicularis*).

1976 Bailey–Bailey *Hortus Third* 420, *Eleocharis* . . *acicularis* . . Hair Grass.

hairgrass dropseed n Also *hairgrass*

A **dropseed 3** (here: *Sporobolus airoides*).

1923 in 1957 Old Farmer's Almanac *Sampler* 289, Hair-grass dropseed. **1930** OK Univ. Biol. Surv. *Pub.* 2.53, *Sporobolus airoides* . . Hair-grass Dropseed. **1936** Winter *Plants NE* 33, *S[porobolus] airoides* . . Hair-grass. **1937** U.S. Forest Serv. *Range Plant Hdbk.* G109, Alkali sacaton [=*Sporobolus airoides*], also known as . . hairgrass dropseed, is a robust, perennial grass. **1961** Peck *Manual OR* 129, *S[porobolus] airoides* . . Hair-grass Dropseed.

hair in the butter See **hair** n **C12**

hair in the nose See **hair** n **C7**

‡hairlash n

A close contest.

1967 *DARE* (Qu. KK54, *Just about equal, very close: "They were both fast runners and it was ——— all the way."*) Inf **TX**31, A hairlash.

hair moss See **haircap moss**

hair nor hide See **hair** n **C2**

hair on the nose See **hair** n **C7**

hair or hide See **hair** n **C2**

hair pants n pl Also *hair chaps* **West** Cf **woolies**

=**chaps** made of hide from which the hair has not been removed.

1907 Mulford *Bar-20* 187 **West,** "Yu runt, I'm a better man than yu even if yu do wear hair pants," referring to Hopalong's chaps. **1933** White *Dog Days* 203 **CA,** The chaparejos also were strictly utilitarian and were worn only in thick cover. In this Southern country the shaggy "hair pants" were unknown simply because their water and snow-shedding properties were unnecessary. **1937** Sandoz *Slogum* 291 **NE** (as of 1900–1920), The little Sunday rodeos where the young fellows in secondhand hair pants showed off the powers of their long legs to scratch anything that walked on four feet and burned grass. **1980** *AZ Highways* Feb 7, In the north country, where the weather was said to get so cold that milk cows gave icicles, cowboys wore "hair pants," angora chaps made from the fur of rabbit or goat and worn with the hair side out. **1981** *KS Qrly.* 13.2.67, *Hair chaps*. . . Old-style leather chaps made from Angora goat skins with the fleece intact and facing out.

hairpin v, hence vbl n *hair-pinning* [From the forked shape of a *hairpin*]

To mount (a horse).

1927 *AmSp* 3.168 **SW,** To mount a horse is to "hairpin" . . him. **1929** *AmSp* 5.64 **NE,** Mounting the horse is sometimes called "hair-pinning 'im." **1944** Adams *Western Words* 71, *Hairpin*—To mount a horse. **1959** Robertson *Ram* 296, The truly colorful words of the old West were first used around the corral and the campfire, and the synthetic ones were given birth to by a typewriter, and so we tried to avoid the popular magazine jargon such as using "ankled" for walked, and "hair-pinning" for mounting.

hair plant n Cf **hairweed**

Prob a **dodder.**

1945 Saxon *Gumbo Ya-Ya* 170 **LA,** Other things used for cure and prevention of illness included hair plant.

hair plow n [Perh folk-etym of *harra plow* (<*harrow plow*); cf Pronc Intro 3.I.12d]

1969 *DARE* (Qu. L20, *The implement used in a field after it's been plowed to break up the lumps*) Inf **CA**117, Hair plow, because it looks like a comb, with teeth.

hair pounder See **hair** n **C9**

hairs See **hair** n **B5**

hair, set the See **hair** n **B19**

hair snake n Also *hairworm*

=**horsehair snake.**

1890 Howells *Boy's Town* 201 **OH,** No one had ever seen it happen, but every one knew that if you put long horsehairs into a puddle of water and let them stay, they would turn into hair-snakes. **1911** *Century Dict. Suppl., Hair-snake*. . . Also known as *hairworm* and *horsehair-snake*, from the popular superstition that it is a hair that has metamorphosed into a worm. **1925** in 1966 Goldstein–Byington *Two Penny Ballads* 160 **PA,** If you put a horsehair on top of the water trough at night, it will turn into a hare [sic] snake. **1931–33** *LANE Worksheets* **csCT,** Hair snake . . A long gray-white worm. **1950** *WELS (Kinds of snakes found in your neighborhood)* 1 Inf, **csWI,** Hair snake. **1954** *Harder Coll.* **cwTN,** *Hair snake*—snake supposed to grow from a hair that has remained in the water for nine days. **1967–69** *DARE* (Qu. P25, . . *Snakes . . around here*) Inf **OH**16, Hair snake, some kind of worm I guess; (Qu. R14, *Small worm-like things [seen in rain barrels or standing water] that hatch into mosquitoes*) Inf **IN**58, Hair snakes; don't know if they are mosquitoes when they hatch.

hair sparrow n Also *hair bird, hairy sparrow*

A **chipping sparrow** (here: *Spizella passerina*).

1853 in 1884 Thoreau *Summer* 227, If I wish for a horse-hair for my compass sights, I must go to the stable; but the hair-bird, with her sharp eyes, goes to the road. **1886** Burroughs *Signs & Seasons* 75 **NY,** A correspondent writes me that . . he also found a "chippie" (called also "hair bird") suspended from a branch by a horse-hair, beneath a partly-constructed nest. **1936** Roberts *MN Birds* 2.412, *Eastern Chipping Sparrow: Spizella passerina passerina . . Other names:* Hair Bird. **1946** Goodrich *Birds in KS* 319, Hair sparrow. **1955** MA Audubon Soc. *Bulletin* 39.255, *Chipping Sparrow*. . . Hair Bird (General); Hair Sparrow (Mass. It uses animal hair to line its nest.) **1967** *DARE* (Qu. Q21, . . *Kinds of sparrows*) Inf **MA**5, Hair sparrow, chipping sparrow, used horsehair to make nests; **GA**38, Hairy sparrow. **1983** *Greenfield Recorder* (MA) 21 May [Hemenway column] (as of 1920), At my home there was an old, sweet-smelling white syringa, in which, every year, a little "hair bird" (chipping sparrow) built its nest. The nest always blew down in winter, so we had a chance to marvel at the way they wove those hairs (probably gathered from where the barbed wire had snagged the cow tails) with only their bills and tiny little feet. When hair was scarce in later years they used more tiny rootlets or a little dew berry vine.

‡hairspring n [Perh for *handspring*]

1968 *DARE* FW Addit **ME**4, Hairspring—A childhood acrobatic trick—you jump forward, land on your hands, and turn over.

hairt See **heart** n[1]

hair tobacco n Cf **nigger-hair**

1896 *DN* 1.418 **ceTX,** *Hair tobacco:* fine-cut tobacco.

‡hair topper n [*topper* a cover, perh infl by *toupée*]

1970 *DARE* (Qu. X1a, . . *False hair, worn by men*) Inf **NJ**63, Hair topper.

hair twister n **West**

=**spinner;** see quots.

1953 *Western Folkl.* 12.181, [Map shows that during the height of the cattle period a hand-held rope or yarn spinner was known in **eOR** and **wID** as a hair twister.] **1981** *KS Qrly.* 13.2.67, *Hair twister* . . a device used for twisting horsehair into cords that were twisted into macardies. . . Nevada ranchers and buckaroos make their own.

hairweed n [Prob from the long hair-like stems]

=**dodder.**

1900 Lyons *Plant Names* 126, *Cuscuta . . Epilinum* . . Hair-weed. **1911** *Century Dict. Suppl., Hailweed*. . . Dodder, especially the thyme-dodder or the flax-dodder. Also *hairweed.* **1914** Georgia *Manual Weeds* 324, *Clover Dodder—Cuscuta Epithymum* . . Hairweed. **1935** (1943) Muenscher *Weeds* 372, *Cuscuta Epilinum* . . Hairweed.

hair wig n [Redund; cf Intro "Language Changes" I.4]

See quots.

1954 *Harder Coll.* **cwTN,** Hair wig, false hair. **1970** *DARE* (Qu. X1a, . . *False hair, worn by men*) Inf **FL**48, Hair wig, ain't many men around here wears 'em; (Qu. X1b, *False hair worn by women*) Inf **FL**48, Hair wig.

hairworm n

1 See **hair snake.**

‡2 A mosquito larva; see quot. Cf **hair snake**

1969 *DARE* (Qu. R14, *Small worm-like things . . that hatch into mosquitoes*) Inf **NY**183, Hairworm.

hairy adj [Prob from the assoc of long hair with old age; perh infl by *hoary*] Cf **hair** n **C13**

Of jokes: old, out-of-date.

1960 Wentworth–Flexner *Slang* 239, *Hairy* . . Old, already known, passé; usu. said of a joke or story. **1966–69** *DARE* (Qu. FF21a, *A joke that is so old it doesn't seem funny any more*) Infs **CT**23, **IL**96, **KY**70, **OH**47, **SC**5, Hairy.

hairy back n

=**gizzard shad.**

1943 Eddy–Surber *N. Fishes* 72, *Gizzard Shad* . . Hairy Back. **1983** Becker *Fishes WI* 273, *Gizzard Shad—Dorosoma cepedianum* . . Other common names: eastern gizzard shad, . . hickory shad . . hairy back.

hairybell See **harebell 1**

hairy-bind n [Prob from the twining strands]

=**dodder.**

1900 Lyons *Plant Names* 126, *Cuscuta . . Epilinum* . . Hairy-bind.

hairy-cap See **haircap moss**

hairy caterpillar n Also *hairy horse, ~ worm*

A caterpillar such as a **woolly bear.**

1913 in 1927 Forbush *Birds MA* 259, This woodpecker is quite destructive to hairy caterpillars, and feeds its young on noxious larvae of many species. **1966–70** *DARE* (Qu. R27, . . *Caterpillars or similar worms*) Infs **CO**31, **IL**26, **NC**36, **PA**58, Hairy caterpillar; **TX**12, Black hairy worm; **NY**59, Hairy horse; **MS**86, Hairy worm.

hairy crown n Also *hairy-crowned fisherman, hairy-crowned teal* Cf **hairy head**

Either of two **mergansers:** *Mergus serrator* or *Lophodytes cucullatus.*

1888 Trumbull *Names of Birds* 69, *Merganser Serrator. . .* In a notice of the Ducks and Shooting of the Chesapeake, by Dr. J. T. Sharpless, Cabinet of Nat. Hist., Vol. III., 1833, the present species is referred to as *Hairy-Crown,* a name reminding us of that similar one, Hairy-head, belonging to Hooded Merganser. **1923** U.S. Dept. Ag. *Misc. Circular* 13.6, *Red-breasted Merganser (Mergus serrator). . . In local use. . .* hairycrown, hairy-crowned fisherman (Md.) *Ibid* 7, *Hooded Merganser (Lophodytes cucullatus.) . . In local use. . .* hairycrown (Mass., Md., N.C., Miss., La.); . . hairy-crowned teal (N.C.) **1931** Read *LA French* 8, In the United States a common local name for this small duck [=*Lophodytes cucullatus*] is . . *Hairy-Crown.* **1938** Oberholser *Bird Life LA* 146, *Red-Breasted Merganser—Mergus serrator serrator. . .* The Red-breasted Merganser . . is often called, 'sawbill' or 'hairycrown'. **1982** Elman *Hunter's Field Guide* 230, *Red-breasted Merganser (Mergus serrator)* Common & Regional Names: fish duck, . . hairycrown, . . sea robin.

hairydick n Also sp *Harry dick, Harry Dick* **chiefly SE**

1 A bull calf or yearling, usu one unbranded or otherwise unmarked; a **maverick.** [Cf quot 1896 at **Harry Dick 1;** perh because its unmarked condition makes it different from the norm]

1912 Green *VA Folk-Speech* 217, *Harry-Dick. . .* A half grown bull. **1930** Stoney–Shelby *Black Genesis* 64 **seSC,** De boy would tek mo' int'res' in ridin' billy-goat, an' brokin'-in harry-dick bull calf, dan tendin' to de business dat he Pa is tryin' to teach him. *Ibid* xxi, Among unusual Gullah words and phrases are. . . Harry-dick—an adolescent bull. **1934** *AmSp* 9.236 **FL,** *Hairydick* is, he says, the Florida cattleman's equivalent of the western 'maverick.' He doubts whether the word ever appeared in print. **1942** Kennedy *Palmetto Country* 223 **FL, sGA, sAL,** Most likely candidates for rustling are unbranded calves and cattle, called 'mavericks' in the West, but, for 150 years more or less, known as 'hairydicks' in the Palmetto Country. **1944** Adams *Western Words* 71, *Hairy-dick*—Unbranded animal, especially a calf. **1950** *PADS* 14.36 **SC,** *Harry dick. . .* 1. Baby beef. Harry dick has the flavor neither of veal nor of full grown beef, and is less desirable than either. The Florida cattleman's term for a maverick is hairydick, whence probably our phrase. 2. A castrated beef of about yearling age. **1954** McAtee *Suppl. to Nomina Abitera* [1] **FL,** [Place name:] *Hairy Dick Prairie,* Florida Everglades.

2 By ext: an adolescent male.

1950 *PADS* 14.36 **SC,** *Harry dick. . .* An adolescent boy.

hairygrass See **hairgrass 1b**

hairy head n Also *hairy-headed duck, harrow-head* **chiefly C and S Atl**

=**hairy crown.**

1814 Wilson *Amer. Ornith.* 8.79, *Hooded merganser. Mergus cucullatus* . . on the [Atlantic] sea coast is usually called the *Hairy head.* **1888** Trumbull *Names of Birds* 74, *Lophodytes cucullatus. . .* at Somers Point, Cape May C.H., and Cape May City, and at Eastville, Va., Wilmington, N.C., and St. Augustine, Fla., *Hairy-Head.* **1923** U.S. Dept. Ag. *Misc. Circular* 13.6, *Red-breasted Merganser (Mergus serrator). . . In local use. . .* hairyhead (N.C., Fla.) *Ibid* 7, *Hooded Merganser (Lophodytes cucullatus.) . . In local use. . .* hairyhead (Mass. to Fla., Ky.; most common name in Middle Atlantic States). **1931** Read *LA French* 8, In the United States a common local name for this small duck [=*Lophodytes cucullatus*] is *Hairy-Head.* **1932** Howell *FL Bird Life* 160, *Red-Breasted Merganser: Mergus serrator* . . Other Names: Sawbill; . . Hairyhead. *Ibid* 158, *Hooded Merganser: Lophodytes cucullatus* . . Other Names: Hooded Sheldrake; . . Hairyhead. **1951** *AmSp* 26.91, *Harrow-head*—a twist from 'hairy-head' (in allusion to the ample crest)—has been heard in Maryland. **1954** Sprunt *FL Bird Life* 86, *Hooded Merganser: Lophodytes cucullatus. . .* Local Names: Hairy-head. *Ibid* 88, *Red-Breasted Merganser: Mergus serrator serrator. . .* Local Names: . . Hairy-head. **1968–70** *DARE* (Qu. Q5, . . *Wild ducks*) Infs **GA**20, **VA**47, Hairy-headed duck. **1969** Longstreet *Birds FL* 37, *Red-Breasted Merganser—Other names: . .* Hairyhead.

hairy horse See **hairy caterpillar**

hairy sparrow See **hair sparrow**

hairy woodpecker n **chiefly Nth, N Midl** See Map

A common woodpecker (*Dendrocopos villosus* and subspp). Also called **chib-chab, guinea woodpecker 1, pique bois, sapsucker, spotted sapsucker, spotted woodpecker, white-breasted woodpecker, wood-knocker**

1731 (1754) Catesby *Nat. Hist. Carolina* 1.19, *Picus medius quasi villosus. The Hairy Wood-pecker.* Weighs two ounces. **1808** Wilson *Amer. Ornith.* 1.150 **PA,** [The] *Hairy Woodpecker* . . is another of our resident birds, . . a haunter of orchards, and borer of apple-trees, an eager hunter of insects. **1884** *Century Illustr. Mag.* 29.221/2 **seNY,** As it [=a hole] was nearly two inches in diameter, it could not have been the work of the downy, but must have been that of the hairy, or else the yellow-bellied woodpecker. **1945** *Natl. Geogr. Mag.* 87.731, Larger Double of the Downy Is the Hairy Woodpecker. **1950** *WELS (Kinds of woodpeckers)* 9 Infs, **WI,** Hairy woodpecker. **1955** Lowery *LA Birds* 352, *Hairy Woodpecker. . .* I have no idea how this woodpecker acquired its name, for it certainly does not possess a single hair on its body. **1965–70** *DARE* (Qu. Q17) 86 Infs, **chiefly Nth, N Midl,** Hairy woodpeckers; **NY**22, Great hairy woodpecker; (Qu. Q18) Inf **GA**18, Hairy woodpecker; (Qu. Q23) Inf **IN**69, Hairy woodpecker.

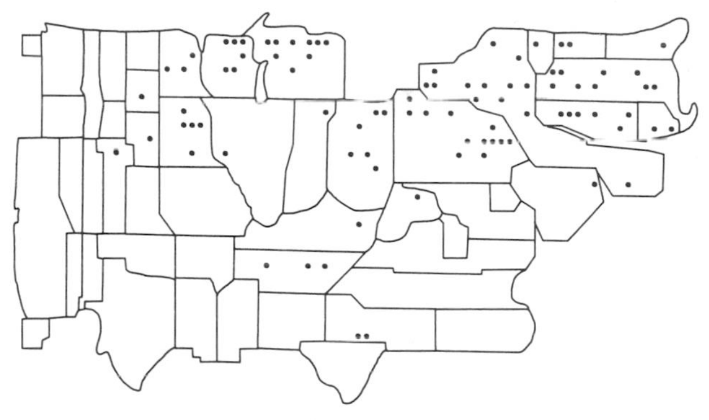

•hairy woodpecker + var (Qq. Q17, Q18, Q23)

hairy worm See **hairy caterpillar**

haish exclam [Cf Scots, Engl dial *hait* a call to urge animals on]

1907 *DN* 3.244 **eME,** *Haish. . .* Whoa! Used to horses. "Whoa, haish!"

hais-law n [Etym unknown] Cf **heal-all**

An unidentified plant.

1940 (1941) Bell *Swamp Water* 46 **Okefenokee GA,** When he woke, Keefer was bent over the pot, slowly and deliberately stirring a tea of hais-law.

haist See **hoist**

hait n See **hate** n

hait adj See **height**

haitch n [Var of *hitch*]

=**hitching weight.**

1976 *DARE* File **sIN** (as of c1910), A delivery man (grocery, ice, milk, etc.) throwing out a hitching weight, attached either to the horse's halter, or out the back of the delivery wagon, might be heard saying to his helper: "Throw out the haitch [heɪč]."

haith See **height**

Haiti n

1 also sp *Hayti,* pronc-sp *Het-eye:* A section of a town where Black people live.

1857 *Knickerbocker* 50.428 **swPA,** 'Hayti' is the name given to that part of our town where 'pussons ob color' reside. **1951** Swetnam *Pittsylvania Country* 182 **PA,** Both Uniontown and Pittsburgh had sizable colored sections dubbed "Hayti." The word was often spelled, and is still pronounced at Uniontown, as "Het-eye," but Pittsburgh's Hayti has long been swallowed up in its growing Hill district. **1970** *DARE* (Qu. C35, *Nicknames for the different parts of your town or city*) Inf **VA64**, Haiti ['he'taɪ], settlements for Black people; (Qu. II25, . . *Nicknames for the part of town where the poorer people, special groups . . live*) Inf **VA68**, Haiti ['he'taɪ], colored section.

2 See quot. [Folk-etym for *Hades*]

1950 *WELS (Words for hell)* 1 Inf, **WI**, Haiti.

hake n

1 Std: A fish of the genus *Merluccius;* in the United States:

a *M. bilineatus* of the Atlantic. Also called **frostfish 4, goatfish 2, poor John, silver hake, stockfish, white hake, whiting**

b *M. productus* of the Pacific. Also called **horse mackerel 5, merluccio**

2 A fish of the genus *Urophycis.* For other names of var spp see **ling, mud hake, old English hake, red hake, squirrel hake, thimble-eyed ling, white hake**

1814 in 1815 Lit. & Philos. Soc. NY *Trans.* 1.372, *Codling (Gadus longipes.)* . . This is the *hake* of the New-York fishermen. **1842** DeKay *Zool. NY* 4.292, It [=*Urophycis chuss*] is called indiscriminately *Hake* and *Codling* by our fishermen. **1887** Goode *Amer. Fishes* 360, Owing to their great similarity, *Phycis chuss* and *P. tenuis,* are usually known indifferently by the name "Hake." **1902** Jordan–Evermann *Amer. Fishes* 518, *Genus Urophycis.* . . The Codlings, or Hakes. **1939** Natl. Geogr. Soc. *Fishes* 51, The total catch of "hake" for New England . . for 1935 was 26,541,000 pounds. **1960** Amer. Fisheries Soc. *List Fishes* 22, Gulf hake . . *Urophycis cirratus.* . . Carolina hake . . *Urophycis earlii.* . . Southern hake . . *Urophycis floridanus.* . . Spotted hake . . *Urophycis regius* [etc].

3 A cod-like fish *(Phycis chesteri).*

1879 U.S. Natl. Museum *Bulletin* 14.30, *Phycis Chesteri.* . . Long-finned Hake. **1960** Amer. Fisheries Soc. *List Fishes* 22, Longfin hake . . *Phycis chesteri.*

4 A **kingfish** (here: *Menticirrhus saxatilis*). **esp NJ**

1859 (1968) Bartlett *Americanisms* 186, *Hake.* The New Jersey name for the King-Fish. **1873** in 1878 Smithsonian Inst. *Misc. Coll.* 14.2.27, *Menticirrus* [sic] *nebulosus.* . . Hake *(New Jersey).* **1887** Goode *Amer. Fishes* 123, The King-fish, *Menticirrus* [sic] *nebulosus,* also known as the "Hake" on the coast of New Jersey and Delaware. **1906** NJ State Museum *Annual Rept. for 1905* 336, *Menticirrhus saxatilis.* . . King Fish. Hake. Barb.

hakemouth n [See quot 1978] **ME**

1 also *hakemouth head:* A type of opening to a lobster trap.

1966 *DARE* Tape **ME17**, [Inf:] Some [trap heads] have hakemouth, some have funnel hoop. [FW:] What's the difference? [Inf:] Well, a funnel hoop is five inches and a hakemouth is six. You can get a bigger lobster with a hakemouth. . . Hakemouth is in the bedroom [=inner chamber] of all traps anyhow. **1978** Merriam *Illustr. Lobstering* 43 **ME,** *Hake Mouth Head*—A head on the lobster trap which is knitted to have a narrow opening into the parlor [=inner chamber] which makes it more difficult for the lobster to get out. It is named hake mouth head because it resembles the mouth of a hake.

2 By ext: used as a nickname for a lobsterman who employs a trap with such an opening.

1975 Gould *ME Lingo* 122, *Hakemouth*—Instead of shaping their trap heads in a circle . . some lobstermen prefer a flattened shape that suggests the mouth of a hake. More than one lobsterman given to this has been nicknamed *Hakemouth.*

hakemouth head See **hakemouth 1**

hakma(n)tak See **hackmatack 1a**

haky See **harky**

hala n **HI**

A **screw pine** *(Pandanus tectorius).*

1929 Neal *Honolulu Gardens* 20, Formerly perhaps the plant most useful to the Hawaiians was the hala [=*Pandanus tectorius*]. **1933** Bryan *Hawaiian Nature* 65, The Hawaiians ate the sweet tender part of the wedgeshaped segments of the hala fruit *(Pandanus tectorius).* **1955** Day *HI People* 296, Thatching of pili grass, or sometimes of hala, sugar cane, or ti leaves, was tied in bundles and lashed to battens. **1965** Krauss–Alexander *Grove Farm* 43 **HI,** He showed little Samuel how to gather hala seed pods from an enormous, gnarled tree in the yard to burn in the new Franklin stove. **1967** *DARE* (Qu. S26e, . . *Wildflowers*) Inf **HI4**, Hala root—the lowest point before it reaches the ground is a good laxative.

hale n Usu |'hɑle|; also |'hɑli| [Haw] **HI**

A building, esp a house—freq in compounds; see quots.

1934 Frear *Lowell & Abigail* 269 **HI** (as of 1880s), Royalty returned from a trip around the world with a planned innovation for the miniature kingdom—a real palace of concrete to replace the hip-roofed wooden *Hale* of former kings. **1938** Reinecke *Hawaiian Loanwords* 9, *Hale.* . . A house. . . *Hale kukae* . . or *kukae hale;* . . A privy. Also called "the *hale*" . . [and] *hale liilii.* . . *Hale pupule.* . . [*Hale* and *pupule,* crazy.] The Territorial Hospital for the Insane. **1954–60** Hance et al. *Hawaiian Sugar* 2, *Hale* ['hɑle] house. **1967** *DARE* (Qu. M9, *The part of a barn where horses are kept*) Inf **HI3**, Hale lio; (Qu. M10, . . *Where cows are kept*) Inf **HI3**, Hale pipi; (Qu. M21a, *An outside toilet building*) Inf **HI14**, Hale lii [ˌhɑle 'liʔi] = small house; (Qu. V11, . . *Joking names . . for a jail*) Inf **HI6**, Halepaahao = house, close, lock up. **1969** *DARE* File **Honolulu HI,** ['hɑli] house, home. Used in titles rather than speech, for instance the city hall here is called Honolulu Hale. **1972** Carr *Da Kine Talk* 86 **HI,** *Hawaiian Words Commonly Heard In Hawaii's English.* . . *Hale.* House, building. **1984** Sunset *HI Guide* 85, *Hale*—house.

hale-bind See **hell-bind**

hale columby See **hail columbia**

haley-over See **haily-over**

half n, v, adj, adv Usu |hæf|; also **NEng** |hɑf, haf|; **widespread Sth** |hæᴵf|; for addit varr see **A** below Pronc-spp *haa(l)f, ha'f, hafe, haff, hahf, harf* Cf Pronc Intro 3.I.7, 3.II.5 Cf **hapa**

A Forms.

1853 Simms *Sword & Distaff* 510 **SC,** Hafe man, hafe horse, and two parts alligator. **1861** Holmes *Venner* 1.52 **wMA,** 'T 's the same cretur that haäf ēat up Eben Squires's little Jo. *Ibid* 2.188, Ha'n't ēat b't haälf his feed. **1862** (1864) Browne *Artemus Ward Book* 41, My naburs is mourn harf crazy. **1887** *Scribner's Mag.* 2.475/2 **AR** [Black], 'Twar a year'n haff ole, jest. *Ibid* 479/2, I'm blamed my skin . . if I ever spent dollar'n haff on the chile. **1916** *Scribner's Mag.* Mar 358/2 **Sth** [Black], She holp herse'f ter a plate o' baddy-bread an' harf uv a fried roe-herrin'. **1930** *AmSp* 5.341 **nwNH,** In . . *half* . . the sound may be farther back, but it gives the effect of [æ]. *Ibid* 345 **PA, OK,** [æ] tense in . . *half.* *Ibid* 348 **neMA,** [ɑ] in . . *half;* **csME,** [a] in . . *half.* *Ibid* 350 **swTX,** [æ], long and tense, in *half.* *Ibid* 354 **seSC,** [æ] [ɑ]. The vowel approaches [a] in . . *half.* **1941** Heydrick–Thompson *Americans All* 211 **Sth** [Black], 'T ain't mo' 'n a mile an' a ha'f by de shawt cut. **1942** *AmSp* 17.33 **seNY,** [In the word *half,* 50 speakers used [æ], 8 used [a].] **1942** Hall *Smoky Mt. Speech* 23, *Half* [hæef, hɛef]. **1943** in 1944 *ADD* **Portland ME,** |hɑf| hahf. **c1960** *Wilson Coll.* **csKY,** *Half* /hæɪf/. **1961** Kurath–McDavid *Pronc. Engl.* 104, Before the voiceless fricatives of . . *half* [etc], upgliding [æᶦ] is widespread in the South, except in the Low Country of South Carolina and on the coast of Georgia and Florida. It is most common in North Carolina but occurs also frequently in Tidewater Virginia. . . In New England . . *half* [has] the vowel of *car.* *Ibid* 113, In . . areas that have the free /ɑ ~ a/ it occurs regularly in *car.* . . In Eastern New England it appears also in *half.* **1970** *DARE* (Qu. L55) Inf **KY77**, Half [heɪf] a load.

B As noun.

1 in var combs used in telling time:

a *half* (+ *hour*): Thirty minutes before the hour named. [Cf Du *half een,* Ger *halb eins,* literally "half one," i.e., 12:30] **prob formerly more widespread, now esp in Ger settlement areas**

1832 (1919) Irving *Jrls.* 3.117 **NY,** Waggons set off at half-two o'clock. **1950** *WELS* 1 Inf, **csWI,** Half two [said by those of Swiss descent]; 1 Inf, **csWI,** German immigrant[s say] half two. **1968** *DARE* (Qu. A7) Inf **MI76**, Half eleven, in Sebewaing, a German district twenty-six miles from here. **1987** *DARE* File **sePA, WI,** *Half two* meaning 1:30 was commonly heard in the Pennsylvania Dutch country as recently as ten years ago, and is still heard in parts of Wisconsin. I have not heard it, however, in the German settlement areas of Ohio.

b *half after* (+ *hour*): Thirty minutes after the hour named. **formerly more widespread**

1800 (1907) Thornton *Diary* 207 **PA,** Went to bed about ½ after nine. **1906** Lovett *Old Boston Boys* 9, I remember a weather-beaten driver of one of these omnibuses, who, upon being asked the time of starting upon the trips, invariably droned out, "Quarter a'ter, half a'ter, quarter to, and *at,*" the last word causing me much perplexity until it was explained that it meant "on the even hour." **1907** *DN* 3.220 **nwAR, sIL,** *After.* . . Often in phrases like "half after ten." **1939** *LANE* Map 80 **VT, NH, ME,** The expression *half after seven* is regarded as older [than *half past seven*] though still in use by [17 infs]. **1952** Brown *NC Folkl.* 1.548, *Half after, ten* (etc.) *minutes till.* . . A term used in expressing time. "It's ten minutes till half after twelve." That is: 12:20.—Rare. **1959** *VT Hist.* new ser 27.139, *Half after.* . . Half past. Obsolescent. **c1960** *Wilson Coll.* **csKY,** *Half after ten* . . Past is about equally common. **1965–70** *DARE* (Qu. A7) Infs **CA**87, **MO**14, 21, **NY**107, 123, **OH**78, **VA**13, 28, 36, Half after ten. **1975** Allen *LAUM* 2.68 (as of c1950), *[Half] after* . . survives in the UM with only one inf., . . Duluth, Minnesota . . Two Minnesota auxiliary infs. report having heard it in their communities, one terming it a "smart-alecky Yankee expression."

c *half past* (+ *hour*):

(1) Thirty minutes after the hour named. **widespread** *somewhat old-fash*

1832 (1919) Irving *Jrls.* 3.117, Went out half-past two to West's. **1950** *WELS* 50 Infs, **WI,** Half past one. **1951** Johnson *Resp. to PADS 20* **DE,** Half past one. **c1960** [see **1b** above]. **1965–70** *DARE* (Qu. A7) 307 Infs, **widespread,** Half past ten; **MO**18, **NY**1, 69, 222, **PA**67, Half past. [Of all Infs responding to the question, 70% were old; of those giving these responses, 82% were old.] **1971** Bright *Word Geog. CA & NV* 140, *Seven-thirty* 83% G[eneral] C[al.]–N[evada distribution]. *Half past seven* 48% G.C.–N. Seven indicated they had used this term as children but now considered it old-fashioned. **1975** Allen *LAUM* 2.68 (as of c1950), *Half past* is itself declining in face of competition from the newer compound with *-thirty* following the hour term.

(2) Fig: used in var phrr to indicate that a person's underwear is showing; see quot. Cf **half-mast 1**

1968–70 *DARE* (Qu. W24a, . . *To warn a woman slyly that her slip is showing*) Inf **RI**15, It's half-past noon; **AK**1, It's half-past two; (Qu. W24c, . . *To warn a man that his trouser-fly is open*) Inf **MA**79, Looks like half-past three.

2 in var combs used to refer to one's spouse, esp one's wife: See quots.

1942 Berrey–Van den Bark *Amer. Slang* 446.15, *Wife.* . . better half *or* fraction. **1965–70** *DARE* (Qu. AA22, *Joking names that a man may use to refer to his wife*) 407 Infs, **widespread,** Better half; 9 Infs, **scattered,** Other half; **IL**25, **TX**95, Lesser half; **OK**18, **OR**4, Worse half; **NY**232, Best half; **IL**11, Bitter half; **DC**8, Small half; **MO**27, Worst half; (Qu. AA23, *Joking names that a woman may use to refer to her husband*) 120 Infs, **widespread,** Better half; **HI**6, **NY**198, **PA**247, **RI**15, Other half; **CO**42, **NY**109, **WA**17, Bitter half; **IL**7, 75, Lesser half; **CA**127, **NJ**64, Worst half; **CA**59, Bigger half.

3 in phr *and a half:* Used as an intensifier; see quots.

1832 Paulding *Westward Ho* 2.7 **KY,** Bushfield, too, was here in all his glory, and was not only a whole team, but a team and a half, good measure, as he affirmed. **1867** Lowell *Biglow* lviii **'Upcountry' MA,** *First-rate and a half.* **1897** *KS Univ. Qrly.* (ser B) 6.53 **KS,** *Half:* an intensive word, in such expressions as, a 'man and a half.' **c1960** *Wilson Coll.* **csKY,** *And a half* . . a facetious remark about some obstreperous person: "That Jimmy is a boy and a half." **1968–70** *DARE* (Qu. Y11) Inf **IL**140, Lick and a half; (Qu. DD15) Inf **NH**14, Had a skinful and a half.

4 In railroading: see quots.

1940 Cottrell *Railroader* 128, *Half*—Two weeks (period). **1945** Hubbard *Railroad Ave.* 346, *Half*—Period of two weeks. **1969** *AmSp* 44.257 [Railroad terms], *Half*—Length of time for one pay period, usually two weeks.

5 pl: See **halves.**

C As verb.

To halve, divide equally. [*half* n; Scots and Engl dial; cf *SND, EDD*] **scattered, but esp SC**

1965–70 *DARE* (Qu. II8, *When one person wants to share or divide something with another, he might say, "Let's ______ [on that].")* 14 Infs, **scattered, but esp SC,** Half it; **SC**3, Half [hæɪf], split into two parts; **SC**11, Half; **SC**26, Half [hæf] it up; **SC**32, Half that.

half-a-cape See **half-house**

half acre exclam [Cf *EDD half* adj. 6 (1)]

1895 *DN* 1.397 **cNY,** *Half acre:* when the score of one side in a game is half that of the other, a common remark of encouragement is "a *half acre* raises good corn if it's hoed well"; often merely the phrase *half acre* is used alone.

half after See **half** n **B1b**

halfance n Also *halfings* [Cf *OED halvans*] **Sth**

=**halvers.**

c1937 in 1970 Yetman *Voices* 143 **TX,** It wasn't long till he moved into Tyler and left my paw running the farm on a halfance with him and the nigger workers. **1970** *DARE* (Qu. II8, *When one person wants to share or divide something with another*) Inf **VA**43, Go halfin's ['haɪfɪnz]. **c1971** *Thompson Coll.* **cnAL, cwGA,** Boys "went in halfance" with one another. Those "in halfance with" one yelled, e.g. "halfance on thim peanuts," and one gave. To "go halfance" on something or with someone: to pay half the cost. B[irming]ham AL 1920's; Pike Co GA 1971.

half-and-half n

Something that is or appears to be a mixture of two elements, as:

a A person of mixed blood; a half-breed.

1828 Cooper *Prairie* 1.38, The half-and-halfs, that one meets in these distant districts, are altogether more barbarous than the real savage. **1967–70** *DARE* (Qu. HH29a, . . *People of mixed blood—part Indian*) Infs **CA**56, **CT**39, **LA**20, **MD**26, Half-and-half; (Qu. HH29b, . . *Part Negro*) Infs **FL**52, **MD**26, **MO**21, **TX**27, Half-and-half.

b A person with the characteristics of both a man and a woman; also adj *half-and-half* having such characteristics.

1935 *Amer. Mercury* 35.229 [Carnival talk], *Half-and-half:* hermaphrodite. **1944** *PADS* 2.43 **VA** [Black], *Half-and-half.* . . A hermaphrodite; hermaphroditic. "De say he half-and-half." . . Generally used by Negroes. **1946** Dadswell *Hey There Sucker* 100, *Half and half,* a side-show performer who claims to be half woman, half man. **1967** *DARE* (Qu. HH38, *A womanish man*) Inf **PA**19, Half-and-half.

c A variety of lima bean *(Phaseolus lunatus).* Cf **ham gravy pea**

1978 *Wanigan Catalog* 10, A butter lima, having nearly equal parts white and maroon. From Tennessee.

d See **half bread.**

e In var other applications; see quots.

1893 Shands *MS Speech* 34, *Half and half* . . This expression is used in England to mean a mixture of equal parts of two kinds of liquor or of half liquor and half water, but I have never heard of its being used for a mixture of half molasses and half coffee anywhere else than among the illiterate whites of the backwood districts of Mississippi. **1928** *AmSp* 4.128 **NE,** The more well-to-do would perhaps build a "half and half," a house half in the ground and half out, or part "soddy" and part "frame" or wood. **1949** *PADS* 11.7 **wTX** (as of c1920), *Half and half.* . . Cotton with half seed and half lint by weight. **1950** *WELS (Joking names for mules)* 1 Inf, **ceWI,** Half and halfs. [*DARE* Ed: The mule is a cross between a horse and an ass.] **1966** *DARE* FW Addit **WA,** *Half and half,* drink made of half beer, half tomato juice. **1967–68** *DARE* (Qu. FF4, . . *Kinds of dancing parties*) Inf **OH**48, Half-and-half—half square dance, half round dance. **1967** *DARE* File **NYC,** *Half-and-half,* a ham and (Swiss) cheese sandwich.

half-and-half adj See **half-and-half b**

half a quarter n **Lower Missip Valley**

As a unit of measure: an eighth of a mile.

1902 *DN* 2.236 **sIL,** *Half a quarter.* . . A furlong. The latter never used. **1903** *DN* 2.315 **seMO,** *Half a quarter.* . . One-eighth of a mile. A rather common unit of measure. 'He lives half a quarter from here.' **1907** *DN* 3.231 **nwAR,** *Half a quarter.* . . One-eighth of a mile. **1955** Faulkner *Big Woods* 175 **MS,** I seen him, about half a quarter up the river, swimming. **1967** *DARE* (Qu. MM6, *Other words meaning 'very close' or 'only a short distance away'*) Inf **MO**11, Half a quarter.

half-a-shirt n Also *half shirt* [See quot 1956] **SC**

=**red-headed woodpecker.**

1949 Sprunt–Chamberlain *SC Bird Life* 333, *Red-headed Woodpecker.* . . *Melanerpes erythrocephalus erythrocephalus.* . . *Local Names:* Half-a-shirt. **1950** *PADS* 14.35 **SC,** *Half-a-shirt.* . . The red-headed woodpecker. **1956** *AmSp* 31.184, The redheaded woodpecker, with its lower back and rump (as well as matching parts of the wings) white, is called *shirttail* throughout the Southeast, as well as *shirttailer* (Del.), *half shirt* (S.C.) and *white shirt* (S.C., Ga.) **1966** *DARE* (Qu. Q17, . . *Kinds of woodpeckers*) Inf **SC**19, Half-a-shirt.

‡half-ass v [**half-assed** adj]

To do something in a careless or haphazard fashion.

1968 *DARE* (Qu. KK63, *To do a clumsy or hurried job of repairing something: "It will never last—he just ______."*) Inf **IN**31, Half-assed it.

half-assed adj, also used absol Also *half-ass* **scattered, but more freq Nth**

Careless, inadequate, incompetent, mediocre.

1932 *AmSp* 7.333 **MD** [College use], *Half-assed*—mediocre; insignificant. **1942** McAtee *Dial. Grant Co. IN Suppl. 1* 6 (as of 1890s), *Half-assed,* adj., imperfect, unsatisfactory; "That's a ______ way of doing it." **1956** Ker *Vocab. W. TX* 337, The local preacher; an unprofessional, part-time, lay preacher: . . Half-ass preacher [1 inf]. **1959** Mailer *Advt. for Myself* 399 **NYC,** He spent years hobnobbing with gentlemanly shits and half-ass operators. **1965–70** *DARE* (Qu. KK63, . . *A clumsy or hurried job*) 16 Infs, **scattered, but more freq Nth,** Half-ass(ed) job; **CA**72, Half-assed; (Qu. N12) Inf **WI**34, Half-assed driver; (Qu. N37) Inf **MA**9, Half-ass railroad; (Qu. W29) Infs **NY**89, **TX**89, Half-assed job; (Qu. W41) Inf **NY**219, Half-assed dresser; (Qu. BB39) Inf **MA**6, Half-assed; (Qu. CC7) Inf **PA**199, Half-assed Methodist, half-assed Episcopalian; (Qu. CC10) Infs **LA**14, **MA**6, **NC**72, **TX**51, Half-ass(ed) preacher; **IL**114, Half-ass; (Qu. LL2) Inf **VT**12, Half-assed.

half-assed adv

Carelessly, haphazardly.

1967–69 *DARE* (Qu. W29, . . *Things that are sewn carelessly*) Inf **OR**10, Done half-assed; **WI**12, Put together half-assed; (Qu. KK48, . . *"I didn't have anything to go by, so I just did it ______."*) Inf **WI**55, Half-assed; (Qu. KK49, . . *"I'm not going to give the place a real cleaning, I'll just ______."*) Infs **NY**217, **WI**77, Do it half-assed.

half-assed backwards adj, adv [Cf **half-assed, ass-backwards**]

Backward, awkward; clumsily, badly.

1969 *DARE* (Qu. KK63, *To do a clumsy or hurried job of repairing something*) Inf **CA**166, Did it half-assed backwards; (Qu. MM3, . . *"This is the front, you've got the whole thing turned ______."*) Inf **CA**166, Half-assed backwards. **1978** *DARE* File **neNJ,** I was never very good at building model planes: no matter how I put the parts together, they always turned out half-assed backwards.

half-ball n Cf **half-rubber**

A game played with half of a rubber ball; the ball itself.

1967 *DARE* (Qu. EE33, . . *Outdoor games*) Inf **MA**33, Half-ball—a pimple ball cut in half. You would skim the ball toward the batter. The distance he hit it would determine whether or not it was a single, double, etc. **1975** Ferretti *Gt. Amer. Book Sidewalk Games* 191, In parts of Pennsylvania, this game [**=egg ball**] is called *Half Ball.* **1977** *Durham Morning Herald* (NC) 24 Oct np, They don't play stickball in Philadelphia. They play a game called halfball using half a rubber ball.

half bed n

See quots.

1950 *PADS* 14.35 **SC,** *Half-bed*. . . A single bed. **c1960** *Wilson Coll.* **csKY,** *Half bed,* a narrow bed. Also called single bed.

halfbill n [Var of *halfbeak*]

A **balao.**

1889 *Century Dict.* 2686, *Halfbill*. . . A fish of the genus *Hemiramphus;* . . a halfbeak. **1976** Warner *Beautiful Swimmers* 225 **Chesapeake Bay MD,** The little half bills, or balaos as they are called in the tropics, gave off the bright silver sheen that makes them prized in their adult form for swordfish bait in deep sea sport fishing. *Ibid,* Between the extremes of the pipefishes' creaky motion and the eels' squirming were the gars and half bills, which flapped more or less as you might expect from a fish out of water.

half-bit n attrib [*half-bit* a piece of cut money of small value]

1969 *DARE* (Qu. LL2, *Other words meaning too small to be worth much: "I don't want that ______ potato."*) Inf **NC**61, Half-bit.

half blood n, also attrib

1 An animal with one purebred and one scrub parent.

1815 *Niles' Natl. Reg.* 8.320/2, Yeaned from 28 common ewes, . . *forty-three lambs,* (half bloods). **1874** VT State Bd. Ag. *Report* 2.365, Mr. Chester Lamberton sold a pair of half-blood steers in July. **1973** Allen *LAUM* 1.243 **cnIA** (as of c1950), *Mongrel* . . half-blood. **1980** *Des Moines Register* (IA) 16 Nov picture sec 20/1, If you overhear a group of Iowans talking about half-blood . . hold your fire. They are honorable, cool-tempered men whose work happens to be the marketing of wool, and they are talking about breeding lines and grades of fleece.

2 The offspring of parents of different races, esp a child of Native American and Caucasian parentage; hence adj *half-blooded.*

1824 Blane *Excursion* 408 **NY,** As the white men occasionally form a very intimate acquaintance with the Squaws, a race of what the Americans call half-bloods is the consequence. **1830** (1892) McCall *Jrl.* 12.185 **NY,** He is a half Blood St. Regis, with a half Blood Menomonie wife. **1835** Parker *Trip to TX* 112, I confess it gave me unpleasant feelings to see half a dozen of *half-bloods* running about the house. **1923** Cook *50 Yrs.* 194 **SD,** Baptiste Garnier, a half-blood Sioux Indian whose father was of French descent. **1965–70** *DARE* (Qu. HH29a, . . *People of mixed blood—part Indian*) Infs **PA**75, **VA**41, Half-blood; **TX**95, Half-blooded; (Qu. HH29b, . . *Part Negro*) Inf **OK**1, Half-blood.

half bread n Also *half-and-half*

1967 *DARE* (Qu. H18, . . *Special kinds of bread made now or in past years around here*) Inf **TX**1, Half bread—flour, meal, made like corn bread; **TX**4, Half-and-half: cowboy breads cooked over a campfire, tallow for shortening.

half-breed n

A small **siscowet.**

1983 Becker *Fishes WI* 330, *Siscowet*. . . Other common names: . . half-breed. *Ibid* 331, The so-called half-breed is considered by fishermen to be a result of a cross between the lean lake trout and the fat siscowet. Khan and Qadri (1970) found no significant difference in the morphometry of half-breeds and siscowets. . . This suggests that half-breeds may reasonably be considered to be small siscowets.

half-breed adj

See quot.

1922 Rollins *Cowboy* 148, If the bar in the horse's mouth humped up in the middle like a narrow croquet wicket for two or two and a half inches in height, and within this hump, or port, were a "roller," that is a vertical wheel with a broad and corrugated rim, and there were added no other attachment save possibly a curb chain, the bit was "half-breed."

half-breed weed n [From the yellow leaves]

A **marsh elder** (here: *Iva xanthifolia*).

1940 Clute *Amer. Plant Names* 262, *Iva xanthifolia.* Half-breed weed.

half-brindle-to-buck adj phr Pronc-sp *half brinnel to buck*

See quots.

1952 Brown *NC Folkl.* 1.549, *Half-brindle-to-buck*. . . Of uncertain pedigree or ancestry. "That bull is half-brindle-to-buck." **a1975** Lunsford *It Used to Be* 165 **sAppalachians,** The term "half brinnel to buck" is speaking of a yearling or a calf, or a cow. You'd ask what stock it is and if it's a kind of a mixed breed, they'd say "It's half brinnel to buck."

half-brother n

1914 *DN* 4.108 **KS,** *Half-brother*. . . Cousin where the fathers are brothers.

half caille n

=hermit thrush 1.

1916 *Times-Picayune* (New Orleans LA) 30 Apr mag sec 5/8, *Hermit thrush* (Hylocichla guttata pallasii). Little Caille, Caille Petite, Half Caille.

half-circle n

In marble play: see quot.

1967 *DARE* (Qu. EE7, . . *Kinds of marble games*) Inf **CO**3, Half-circle; four players lag for first, second, etc; from the starting line they shoot taw to a half circle of marbles to knock them out; played for keeps.

half-cocked See **cocked**

half-crock n Cf **steelie**

In marble play: see quot.

c1970 Wiersma *Marble Terms* **swMI,** *Half-crock;* steel marbles that were one half the size of a large crock. Often the word was used to include all steelies.

half-crop n Cf **crop** n **B1, figure seven**

A type of **earmark.**

1915 *DN* 4.185 **swVA,** A cutting of the ear (of hogs, sheep, cattle) for identification,—of various kinds: *halfcrop,* the tip cut half off. **1936** Adams *Cowboy Lingo* 131, The 'upper half-crop' or 'over half-crop' was made by splitting the ear from the tip, midway about halfway back toward the head and cutting off the upper half; the 'under half-crop' was the same cut on the lower side of the ear. **1967** *DARE* (Qu. K18, *What kind of mark is used around here to identify a cow?*) Inf **LA**2, Lower half-crop, upper half-crop.

half-cropper See **cropper 1**

half-cut adj

1 Crude, uncultivated.

1843 (1916) Hall *New Purchase* 467 **IN,** All the shot-guns and horse-pistols were sought and fixed . . since there were half-cut backwoodsmen enough, and some degenerate natives to use them. **1894** *Century Illustr. Mag.* 48.868 **NY,** "Half-cut" is a folk-word heard in New York city. . . The phrase is sometimes, "half-cut quality"—people whose social position is the irksome one of looking down on nearly everybody, except those who look down on them. . . "Half-cut quality" is only "bob-tailed quality."

2 See **cut** ppl adj **1.**

half-cut n

1968 *DARE* (Qu. X5, . . *Kinds of men's haircuts*) Inf **NC**49, Half-cut, thin on the edges, thick on top; **VA**9, Half-cut.

half deck n [Prob from the shape]

A **slipper shell** (here: *Crepidula fornicata*).

1881 Ingersoll *Oyster-Industry* 245, *Half-deck.*—The slipper limpet, *Crepidula fornicata.*

half dugout n [*half* + **dugout 1**] **esp OK**

A dwelling built partially under the ground.

1889 *Century Dict.* 1793, *Half dugouts* are partly excavated and partly built of logs. [This] kind is frequently used in Montana for dwellings. **1943** Hamner *Short Grass* 6 **OK,** Later half dugouts were made, several feet in the ground, several feet built above, this upper part being made of sod or logs and having full-size windows. **1951** Porter *Ragged Roads* 84 **OK** (as of 1930s), I found her one day, shingling the roof of her half-dugout with tin cans. **1966** *DARE* Tape **OK**30, We also had a half dugout there. . . You dig a hole in the ground about four feet or five, and then you build up the sides another two or three feet and cover it. And that way it is half underground and half above ground. But of course you have to go down in steps to get into it.

halfer See **half hand 2**

halfers See **halvers**

half farmer n **PA** Cf **farm for (the) half**

=**cropper 1.**

1967 Key *Tobacco Vocab.* **PA,** *Half farmer,* a farmer who shares his crop with the landowner half and half. **1967** *DARE* (Qu. L3, *A man who lives on the farm and does the work, but divides the expenses and profits with the owner*) Infs **PA**23, 29, Half farmer.

half-field n

1966 *DARE* (Qu. EE11, *Bat-and-ball games for just a few players*) Inf **SC**7, Half-field.

half-ham v, hence vbl n *half-hamming;* rarely v *half-hammon* [Cf *EDD half-hammer* (at *half* adj. 6) "the game of hop, skip, and a jump;" also *hammer* v.[1] 9 "To walk . . in . . a noisy, clumsy way"]

1 To move with a hop, skip, and a jump; see quots; hence n *half-hammer* a hopping or jumping motion.

1906 Casey *Parson's Boys* 105 **sIL** (as of c1860), They went back to the house "half-hammon" [sic] and bolted breakfast, hardly stopping to chew. **1907** Cockrum *Pioneer IN* 343 (as of c1800), Jumping was much indulged in, stand and go—three jumps or half hamen [sic], a hop, a skip and a jump. **1940** in 1953 Randolph–Wilson *Down in Holler* 250 **swMO,** To say that children go *half-hammin'* to school means that they use a kind of triple step, "a hop, a skip, an' jump." **1942** *Ibid* 250 **swMO,** You take a running start with both feet but land on the right one. Then cross the left foot behind the right ankle and jump again, landing on the left foot, with feet still crossed. Then make a third jump from the left foot and land on both. If you have made twenty feet in the three jumps, making them all as nearly as possible in one continuous movement, you are good. And this is what is meant to *half-hammon* down the street. **1967** Green *Horse Tradin'* 132 **swTX,** She [=a mare] never crow-hopped with me or hit the ground crooked or made any kind of half-hammer motion. . . Well, this will make her cross her legs and do the half hammer.

2 By ext: see quot.

1954 *Harder Coll.* **cwTN,** *Half-ham.* . . To go around doing something ain't got no business doing.

3 as vbl n: See quot.

1968 Adams *Western Words* 138, *Half hamming*—A manner of riding in which the rider sits on one side, on one thigh, one spur being hooked solidly in the cinch.

half hand n

1 A person who does, or is allotted, half the amount of work expected of an able-bodied adult. **esp SC** *hist*

1856 Olmsted *Journey Slave States* 433 **SC, GA,** The children beginning as 'quarter-hands,' advancing to 'half-hands,' and then to 'three-quarter hands;' and finally, when mature, and able-bodied, . . to 'full hands.' As they decline in strength, from age, sickness, or other cause, they retrograde in the scale, and proportionately less labor is required of them. **1865** *S.C. Statutes at Large 1860–66* 38 *(DAE),* After the words 'servant in husbandry' may be inserted, if it be required, the words 'to be rated as (full hand . . half hand, . . ') as the case may be. **1936** Smith–Sass *Carolina Rice* 70 (as of 1850s), The young negroes were called 'half-hands' and were allotted a half-task; those still younger, and yet too old to be kept as nurses to the babies were 'quarter-hands.' **1937** Heyward *Madagascar* 38 **SC** (as of 1800s), Half hands were placed two in a half acre, and when it was possible their tasks adjoined those of their parents. **1949** Turner *Africanisms* 283 **seSC** (as of a1860) [Gullah], They have three class: whole hand, and three-quarter, and half hand. . . [The] whole hand have to do two task . . for day's work. . . The three-quarter hand must do one of those whole task and a half. . . The half hand shall do one of those whole task.

2 also *halfer, half man:* =**cropper 1. Sth**

1967 *DARE* (Qu. L3, *A man who lives on the farm and does the work, but divides the expenses and profits with the owner*) Infs **LA**8, 10, 14; **NC**49, Half man; **TX**38, Half hand. **1970** Major *Dict. Afro-Amer. Slang* 63, *Halfers:* (1890–1900's) Southern Negro sharecroppers.

half-high adj Cf **high** adj **B4**

1966–70 *DARE* (Qu. DD14, *When a person is partly drunk, "He's ______."*) Infs **MS**43, **NC**87, **TN**53, **VA**61, 68, 69, Half-high. [4 of 6 Infs Black]

half-high blueberry n Also *half-high huckleberry*

A **blueberry 1** (here: *Vaccinium vacillans*).

1891 Jesup *Plants Hanover NH* 25, V. vacillans. . . Half-high Blueberry. **1907** *DN* 3.189 **seNH,** *Half-high blueberry.* . . A blueberry growing on a bush about two feet high and maturing in August. **1966** *DARE* (Qu. I44, *What kinds of berries grow wild around here?*) Inf **ME**5, Half-high huckleberries.

half horse, half alligator n, also attrib *hist* Cf **alligator horse, ring-tailed roarer**

A swaggering, pugnacious frontiersman, esp a riverboatman.

[**1809** Irving *Hist. NY* 2.85, It is for similar reasons . . that the back-wood-men of Kentucky are styled half man, half horse and half alligator, by the settlers on the Mississippi.] **1817** Paulding *Letters from South* 89 **VA,** The great western road, which is travelled by the west country wagoners—some of whom, you know, are "half horse, half alligator;" others "part earthquake, and a little of the steam-boat." **1835** Parker *Trip to TX* 93, The half-horse and half-alligator race are no longer to be found. **1841** H. Playfair *Papers* I.32 *(DAE),* 'Half-horse, half-alligator,' with a 'streak of the snap-turtle,' is the usual appellation of those amphibious men who spend their lives on the banks, and as boatmen on the waters of the Mississippi. **1865** Crockett *Life* 218, I was very genteel and quiet, and so I suppose I disappointed some of them, who expected to see a half horse half alligator sort of fellow. *Ibid* 277, There are some first-rate men there, of the real half horse half alligator breed. **1948** Dick *Dixie Frontier* 241 **Sth** (as of a1860), More than once a "half-horse and half-alligator" possessed accurate information on politics and government.

half-house n Also *half-a-cape*

See quots.

1937 FWP *Guide MA* 81, The 'half-a-cape [=Cape Cod],' a plain dwelling with a chimney at one end, derived its name from the fact that its owner always hoped the day would come when he could add the other half and convert his cottage into a proper house with a central chimney. **1962** Williams–Williams *Old Amer. Houses* 159 **NEng,** *Half-house:* half of a central-chimney house (including the chimney), built with the idea of later adding a like section the other side of the chimney. **1966** *York Co. Coast Star* (Kennebunk ME) 28 Apr 8/3, Half-house for rent. Desirable Kennebunkport location.

halfies See **halvsies**

half in and half out n

1940–41 Cassidy *WI Atlas* **swWI,** *Half in and half out,* a boys' game, a running chase through the woods, also called "hunko."

halfings See **halfance**

half in two adv phr, adj phr [Redund; cf *EDD half in two* (at *half* 9. (4))] **chiefly Sth, S Midl**

In half, in two pieces; nearly in two pieces.

1899 (1912) Green *VA Folk-Speech* 213, *Half in two. . .* Almost in two pieces. "That rope is half-in-two." **1935** Hurston *Mules & Men* 93 **FL,** Break your hoe-cake half in two. Half on the plate, half in the dinner bucket. **1950** *WELS Suppl.,* 2 Infs, *Half in two*—in half: I'll cut it half in two; 1 Inf, I cut the bread loaf half in two. **1960** Criswell *Resp. to PADS 20* **Ozarks,** *Half in two:* in halves. A very frequent expression after a verb of action from long ago but still used. Almost the only way to say this. "Well, if you cut that stick half in two you can use it." **1972** *Atlanta Letters,* People from Georgia use the worse [sic] language of all. They murder the American language[,] cut words half into [sic]. **1973** *DARE* File **cAL** (as of c1946), *Half in two:* in half; **TX, Sth,** It was cut half in two. **1973** *Patrick Coll.* **Sth,** *Half in two . .* in half. Cut this string half in two. **1975** Newell *If Nothin' Don't Happen* 82 **nwFL,** I've seen one of them big sharks cut a tarpon half-in-two as clean as if you'd sawed him with a crosscut saw. **1976** Ryland *Richmond Co. VA* 371, *Half in two*—"He cut the log half in two."

half-leg deep adj phr Also *half-leg high* **chiefly Sth, S Midl**

Approximately knee-deep or knee-high; see also quots 1752, 1946.

1752 (1901) Hempstead *Diary* 599 **seCT,** A great Snow knee Deep . . Last night & ys morning half Leg Deep & more. **1832** Kennedy *Swallow Barn* 2.13 **VA,** The snow was lying about half-leg deep all over the fields. **1852** in 1927 Jones *FL Plantation Rec.* 65, I have a Little Corn half Leg high. **1899** (1912) Green *VA Folk-Speech* 213, "Half-leg deep." Water reaching halfway up the leg. **1903** *DN* 2.315 **seMO,** *Half-leg high. . .* Knee high. 'My corn is half-leg high.' **1946** *PADS* 6.16 **ceNC,** *Half-leg high. . .* Half the distance from the sole of the foot to the knee. Used by farmers in speaking of the height of plants. Common.

half-live fence n Cf **live fence**

c1960 *Wilson Coll.* **csKY,** *Half-live fence,* made by chopping half down some saplings and brush around a small area like a plantbed, and then bending them over in line to make a temporary fence; frequently the fence kept on growing.

half man n

1 also *half-a-man:* See quots. [Cf *SND halfman* (at *half* II. 1. (14) (b)) "a half bottle (of spirits)"]

1939 *AmSp* 14.90 **eTN,** *Half man. . .* A half pint of whiskey. 'A half man laid him out.' **1988** Lincoln *Avenue* 63 **wNC** (as of c1940) [Black], On weekdays most people just wanted half-a-man to get them through the day. *Ibid* 64, If you want a man, or half-a-man, then pay your $3, or your $1.50, and get your whiskey.

2 See **half hand 2.**

half-mast n **chiefly Nth**

1 Fig: often in phrr; used to indicate that a person's underwear is showing; see quots.

1950 *WELS (Expressions or sly words of warning for: a woman's slip showing)* 1 Inf, **csWI,** Half-mast. **1967–70** *DARE* (Qu. W24a, . . *To warn a woman slyly that her slip is showing*) Inf **NC61,** Half-mast; (Qu. W24c, . . *To warn a man that his trouser-fly is open*) Infs **MA9, NJ63,** Flag's at half-mast; **VT16,** At half-mast; **OH20,** Half-mast; **NY105,** You're at half-mast.

2 in phr *at half-mast:* Poorly, unwell.

1968 *DARE* (Qu. BB39, . . *When you don't feel just right, though not actually sick*) Inf **IA47,** At half-mast.

half-moon n

1 also *half-moon house:* An outhouse, a privy. [From the half-moon freq cut in the door] *joc, euphem*

1950 *WELS (Joking names, an outside toilet building)* 1 Inf, **seWI,** Half-moon. **1966–68** *DARE* (Qu. M21b, *Joking names for an outside toilet building)* Infs **NJ2,** 40, **OH27,** Half-moon; **OH90, WI65,** Half-moon house; [**NJ6,** One with the half-moon.]

2 A clear marble with a semicircular internal design.

[**1958** *PADS* 29.34 **KY,** [In marble play:] *Half moon. . .* "A half moon appeared in a genuine agate if hit hard enough".] **1968** *DARE* (Qu. EE6d, *Special marbles*) Inf **NC53,** Half-moon, same as cat-eye. **c1970** Wiersma *Marbles Terms* **csMI,** *Half moon*—transparent marble with crescent design in the center.

3 See **half-moon pie.**

half-moon eye n [See quot 1982]

=**white-winged scoter.**

1925 (1928) Forbush *Birds MA* 1.274, *Oidemia deglandi . . White-winged Scoter. . .* Half-Moon-Eye. **1955** Forbush–May *Birds* 85. **1982** Elman *Hunter's Field Guide* 251, *White-winged Scoter (Melanitta fusca)* Common & Regional Names: coot, . . halfmoon-eye, . . tar bucket. . . The eye itself is peculiar—pale bluish gray or almost white. A narrow white border encircles it, and a short white streak curves back and up from the bottom of the border to form a stubby half-moon.

half-moon house See **half-moon 1**

half-moon pie n Also *half-moon* [From the shape] **esp S Midl**

See quots.

1940 Yoder *Rosanna* 46 **PA,** Half-moon pies . . are made of dried apples. . . The dried apples are spread on one half of this circular pie crust and the other half is brought over the apples and pinched tight at the edges, making a pie the form of a half circle or half moon. **1950** Klees *PA Dutch* 416, That variation of the snitz pie, the Amish half-moon, is the perfect pie for "preachings" or the lunch boxes the youngsters carry to school. **1952** Tracy *Coast Cookery* 171 **NC,** Fried or halfmoon pies are also made from cooked dried peaches or apples, mashed and sweetened. One half of a circle of uncooked pastry is covered with the fruit pulp. The other half is folded over the fruit and the edges pressed together with the fingers or fork. The pie is fried in fat about 1 inch deep, in a heavy skillet until brown on both sides. It is best served hot. **1957** *Sat. Eve. Post Letters* **MO, TN,** In Arkansas a favorite dessert was little fried pies with dried fruit or applesauce filling. Two friends of mine, one from Missouri and one from Tennessee, always call them half-moon pies (they are made in that shape). **1960** Criswell *Resp. to PADS 20* **Ozarks** (as of 1910), *Half-moon pie:* a pie in the shape of a half-circle. This was always a fried apple or fried apricot pie. **1966–67** *DARE* (Qu. H28, *Different shapes or types of doughnuts*) Inf **OH8,** Half-moon, or horn; (Qu. H31, *Other foods made with dough and cooked in deep fat*) Inf **GA1,** Half-moon pie, a fried pie or turnover. **1969** *DARE* Tape **GA74,** There would be . . four or five earthware jug of sulfured peaches or apples. You burnt sulfur some way or 'nother . . and use acid; put on top o' those cooked apples and that would keep it from spoiling. So we'd have those apples for our pies, the half-moon pies.

half-near adv

1968 *DARE* (Qu. LL30, *Words and expressions meaning 'nearly' or 'almost'*) Inf **MN42,** Half-near.

half-over n

1908 *DN* 3.318 **eAL, wGA,** *Half-over. . .* A game somewhat similar to leap-frog. The player who is down tucks his head low, and the other players leap over him from the side. The leader institutes various pranks, such as a slap, a kick, a pinch, or combinations of these, and if any player fails to follow the lead he is down.

half past See **half n B1c**

half past kissing time n Also *half past kissing time and time to kiss again*

See quots.

1910 *DN* 3.442 **cwNY,** *Half past kissing time. . .* Facetious reply to the question: "What time is it?" Sometimes the expression *time to kiss again* is added. **1928** *Ruppenthal Coll.* **KS,** Half past kissing time and time to kiss again: From an old play or game of youths—a jocular response to inquiry as to what time it is. **1942** McAtee *Dial. Grant Co. IN* 32 (as of 1890s). **1950** *WELS (What time is this [=1:30]?)* 1 Inf, **WI,** Half past kissing time.

half-pick n

1969 *DARE* File **GA,** [Heard from a farmer:] *Half-pick*—sharing half-and-half between the grower and the picker. "We got strawberries on the half-pick," = we picked them and gave the grower half of what we picked.

half-pint n

In marble play: see quots.

1967 *DARE* Tape **IA27,** Half the size of a boulder makes a half-pint.

c1970 Wiersma *Marble Terms* **seIA,** *Half-pint,* a playing marble next size larger than common size; **swMI,** *Half-pint,* a marble half the size of a boulder.

half pounder n

=**rainbow trout.**

1953 Roedel *Common Fishes CA* 43, *Steelhead Rainbow Trout—Salmo gairdneri* . . Unauthorized Names: Salmon trout, half pounder, . . hardhead.

half-renter n

=**cropper 1.**

1969 *DARE* (Qu. L3, *A man who lives on the farm and does the work, but divides the expenses and profits with the owner*) Inf **TX**83, Half-renter.

half-rigged saddle n

1961 Adams *Old-Time Cowhand* 109, The "half-rigged" saddle's one with a triangle of leather tacked on for a seat.

half-round square n

A nonexistent item serving as the basis for a practical joke.

1960 Bailey *Resp. to PADS 20* **KS** *(A 'left-handed monkey wrench')* Half-round square. **c1960** *Wilson Coll.* **csKY,** *Half-round square.* . . A mythical object that a yokel or greenhorn is sometimes sent to borrow or find. **1967–68** *DARE* (Qu. HH14, *Ways of teasing a beginner or inexperienced person—for example, by sending him for a 'left-handed monkey wrench': "Go get me ______."*) Infs **AR**51, **CA**101, **VA**5, **WI**66, [A] half-round square.

half-rubber n Cf **half-ball GA, SC**

A game played with half of a rubber ball; see quot 1982.

1966 *DARE* FW Addit **SC**21, *Half-rubber*—Cut a solid rubber ball in half. The pitcher sails it to a batter who tries to hit it with a broom stick. **1970** *DARE* (Qu. EE11, *Bat-and-ball games for just a few players*) Inf **SC**69, Half-rubber; use a sponge ball and broom handle, have three or four cats [=boys]; catcher, pitcher, hitter. **1982** *DARE* File **ceGA** (as of 1937–41), *Half-rubber*. . . A bat-and-ball game using a broomstick bat and a half-rubber . . ball. Thrown sidearm, flat side down, the half-rubber tends to "float" but veers in ways hard to meet with the slender bat. At least three players are needed: pitcher, batter, catcher (fielders optional); they rotate after an agreed number of outs resulting from missed swings or from hits caught in flight. . . I have never seen the word in print, have not heard the word nor encountered the game anywhere but in Savannah.

half-runner n

1 See **half-runner bean.**

2 An unidentified berry.

1970 *DARE* (Qu. I44, *What kinds of berries grow wild around here?*) Inf **AR**56, Half-runners.

half-runner bean n Also *half-runner (white), half-white runner, white half-runner (bean)* [From its climbing less high than a *runner bean*] **chiefly sAppalachians** See Map

A rambling legume *(Phaseolus vulgaris).*

1965–70 *DARE* (Qu. I20) 15 Infs, **esp sAppalachians,** Half-runners; 11 Infs, **esp sAppalachians, KY,** Half-runner beans; **GA**81, **KY**28, **TN**20, White half-runner beans; **NC**37, White half-runners; (Qu. I14) Inf **NC**55, Half-white runner bean; (Qu. I18) Inf **SC**57, Half-runner beans; **AL**34, White half-runner beans; **AR**39, White half-runners. **1970** GA Dept. Ag. *Farmers Market Bulletin* 12 Aug 5, Tested Oct. beans, white & speckled running butter peas, Halfrunner beans. **1978** *Wanigan Catalog* 10, *Half Runner White*—A rambling plant, to 4′ on twine. Pods are rough, thin, round, 6″. Bears white size 2 pea beans. Late.

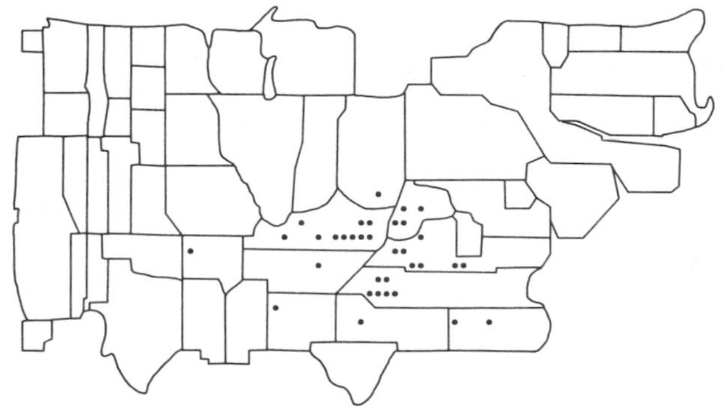

•half-runner bean + varr (Qq. I20, I14, I18)

half-sense n

A minimum of intelligence or common sense.

1937 *Hall Coll.* **wNC, eTN,** Half-sense . . "She didn't have more than half-sense nohow." (She didn't have good sense; used of a mentally deficient person.) **1942** Warnick *Garrett Co. MD* 8 **nwMD** (as of 1900–18). **1942** McAtee *Dial. Grant Co. IN* 32 (as of 1890s). **c1960** *Wilson Coll.* **csKY** *Half sense,* Usually an understatement for good sense: "If he had half sense, he wouldn't do that."

half-share farmer n Also *half-share man, half-sharer*

=**cropper 1.**

1967 LeCompte *Word Atlas* 171 **seLA,** *Half-share farmer:* Farmer who works on shares. [1 of 21 infs] **1970** *DARE* (Qu. L3, *A man who lives on the farm and does the work, but divides the expenses and profits with the owner*) Inf **VA**40, Half-share man; **VA**70, Half-sharer.

half shirt See **half-a-shirt**

halfsies See **halvsies**

half-sizer n

=**half-pint.**

c1970 Wiersma *Marbles Terms* **swMI,** *Half-sizer,* a marble of any color, half the size of a boulder.

half-skirt See **skirt**

half-sled n

1 A sledge.

1952 Brown *NC Folkl.* 1.549 **wNC,** *Half-sled.* . . A sled for hauling logs. **1967** *DARE* (Qu. L57, *A low wooden platform used for bringing stones or heavy things out of the fields*) Inf **TN**14, Half-sled, runners and bed.

2 in phrr *like a half-sled on ice* (or *in a snowstorm*): In an uncontrolled or unmanageable manner.

1873 Beadle *Undeveloped West* 743 **UT, NV,** First one side getting ahead and then the other . . as we used to say on the Wabash, 'like a half sled on ice'. **1893** Owen *Voodoo Tales* 272 **MO,** Granny told them candidly that they were 'kyarin' on lak er half-sled in er snow-stawm.'

half-smoke n Also *half-smoker* **chiefly sNJ**

1968 *DARE* (Qu. H40, *A small sausage that is put into a long roll or bun to make a sandwich*) Infs **NJ**15, 18, 21, 32, 40, 53, **PA**88, Half-smoke; **NJ**21, Half-smoker, just enough [smoke] to flavor. **1987** *DARE* File **DC,** A half-smoke is larger and spicier than a hot dog, but it's also served in a long bun. There are carts on the street corners in Washington, and also in Philadelphia, where they are sold.

half-strainer n Also *half-way strainer* [Cf *EDD half-strain* "mongrel," *half-strained gentry* " 'shabby-genteel' persons"] **Sth** *old-fash*

A social climber.

1887 Page *In Ole VA* 147, "He's a half-strainer," said the woman, with sudden anger. "How he gwine help it?" **1896** *DN* 1.418, *Half-way strainer:* one who tries to live above one's true station. Southern (thought to be from N. C.) **1909** *Atlantic Mth.* July 136/2 **Sth,** I shall avail myself of the words furnished us by our Negroes, who are so wisely discerning in social matters. . . The "half-strainer" . . is born to prove that a little breeding is a dangerous thing. It is the half-strainer everywhere who does the most violence to the mother tongue. **1944** *PADS* 2.43 **sVA, cNC,** *Half-strainer.* . . One who puts on airs, tries to associate with his superiors; a word of decided contempt. . . Obsolescent. **1946** *PADS* 6.16 **swVA** (as of 1890s), *Half-strainer* . . A social climber.

half-stripe adj [*stripe* sort, type]

Half-breed.

1935 Davis *Honey* 65 **OR,** Zack Wall said shucks, those half-stripe Siwashes could stand cold that a white man would stiffen out an die in.

half-sweep n [**sweep**]

1967 *DARE* (Qu. L18, *Kinds of plows used around here*) Inf **TX**32, Half-sweep, called twist and shovel.

halfto See **have** v[1] **A1b**

half-vining bean n
=**half-runner bean.**
1968 *DARE* (Qu. I20, *Other kinds of beans*) Inf **IN**7, Half-vining beans.

half-way strainer See **half-strainer**

half-white runner See **half-runner bean**

halibut n Usu |'hæləbət|; for varr see quots Pronc-spp *haulibut, holibut;* folk-etym *haul-a-boat*
A Forms.
1792 Belknap *Hist. NH* 3.177, The *Holibut* is the largest fish which is taken for food. **1814** in 1815 Lit. & Philos. Soc. NY *Trans.* 386, *Holibut. (Pleuronectes hippoglossus).* This very large and excellent fish is brought plentifully to New-York alive, in the spring. **1884** Goode *Fisheries U.S.* 1.191, Halibut. . . In. . . New England . . "Haul-a-boat," which our fishermen have frequently assured me was the proper name, referring to the size and strength of the fish. **1969–70** *DARE* (Qu. P14) Inf **MA**7, ['hælɪbɪt]; **MA**40, [hælɪbət]; **MA**97, [hɔlɪbət]. **1975** Gould *ME Lingo* 123, *Halibut*—Entered here only to give the correct Maine pronunciation. Give it the long haul—*haulibut.* Never as in Prince Hal.
B Senses.
1 Std: a **flounder B** of the genus *Hippoglossus.*
2 =**Monterey halibut. sCA**
1884 Goode *Fisheries U.S.* 1.182, This fish (*Paralichthys maculosus* Girard) . . is known as the Halibut, Bastard Halibut, and Monterey Halibut. South of San Francisco, where the true Halibut is not found, the larger individuals, which really greatly resemble the Halibut, are known by that name. **1946** LaMonte *N. Amer. Game Fishes* 98, *California Halibut. . . Names:* Halibut, . . Alabato. **1953** Roedel *Common Fishes CA* 55, *California Halibut. . .* Central California south into the Gulf of California. . . Heaviest local catches have been made in the Santa Barbara area in recent years. One of the most desirable sport species in Southern California. **1967–70** *DARE* (Qu. P2, *[In saltwater areas] What kinds of saltwater fish caught around here are good to eat?*) 10 Infs, **sCA,** Halibut; (Qu. P14, *If commercial fishing is done around here, what do the fishermen go out after?*) Infs **CA**25, 52, 65, 168, 191, Halibut.

Halifax n Also *Halifat* [Orig in ref to Halifax, Yorkshire (cf *OEDS Halifax* 1630 →), later in ref to Halifax, Nova Scotia] Cf **haverty-grass**
1 Hell—often in phr *go to Halifax.*
1807 in 1852 U.S. Congress *Debates & Proc.* 10th Cong 1st Sess 11 Dec 1169 **VA,** The victor, as if in contempt, had thrown the worthless thing [=a U.S. Navy warship] back upon our hands, instead of sending it where he wished it had gone, to Halifax, or to the bottom. **1882** *Congressional Record* 13 July 6015/1 **KY,** He told them . . that he had no further use for them, and they could go home, ashore, or to Halifax. **1895** *DN* 1.382 **NJ,** *Halifax.* Mr. Skillman thinks that the common enough expression, "Go to Halifax!" is a survival from Revolutionary times, and meant originally "You are a Tory; go where you belong!" This, because he has heard "Go to Nova Scotia!" in the same way. **1906** Casey *Parson's Boys* 173 **sIL** (as of c1860), I'll jist be diddle-de-diddle-de-daggon if I don't wish the dern corn wuz in Halifax and him with it! **1922** *DN* 5.165 **NJ, NH,** *Halifax, go to* . . Go where you belong. **1948** Funk *Hog on Ice* 192, *Go to Halifax!* Most people regard this as a polite euphemism, probably American, for the blunter request, go to hell! . . [I]n the sixteenth century the people of [Halifax, in northern England] had become so harassed by thievery that they had instituted what became known as "Halifax Law." This provided "that whosoever doth commit any felony . . he is forthwith beheaded upon one of the next market days." . . not so much a euphemism for "go to hell," as a substitute with equal force. **1965–70** *DARE* (Qu. NN26b, *Weakened substitutes for 'hell': "Go to ——!"*) 28 Infs, **scattered,** Halifax; (Qu. V2b, . . *"I wouldn't trust him ——."*) Inf **AR**47, To Halifax; (Qu. CC9, . . *Words . . for hell*) Infs **MI**33, 72, **MO**19, **NY**36, **RI**15, Halifax; **MS**45, Halifat ['hælɪ,fæt]; **WV**4, Halifat; (Qu. GG21b, . . *"Go ahead—I don't give a ——."*) Inf **MS**39, Hoot in Halifax; (Qu. HH20b, . . *"He doesn't amount to ——."*) Inf **NY**232, Hoop in Halifax; (Qu. HH20c, . . *"He isn't worth ——."*) Infs **MI**72, **RI**15, Powder (and shot) to blow him to Halifax; **OK**9, Two hoots in Halifax; (Qu. KK17, . . *"It isn't worth ——."*) Inf **MS**39, Hoot in Halifax; (Qu. NN11, . . *Ways of saying 'good-bye'*) Inf **MI**63, Be seein' you in Halifax. **1979** *DARE* File **cnMA** (as of c1915), When I was a child a very discreet way of "swearing" was to say "Go to Halifax." No one could object, for people frequently went to Halifax, sailed from Boston in a boat.
2 See quot.
1903 *DN* 2.298 **Cape Cod MA** (as of a1857), *Halifax. . .* In expression 'go way to Halifax,' to go out of the way, or an unnecessarily long distance.

halishkes See **holishkes**

hall n[1] See **hallway 2**

hall n[2] Also *hall berry* [*haw* + excr *l*]
The fruit of a **hawthorn.**
1908 *DN* 3.318 **eAL, wGA,** *Hall. . .* A berry-like fruit, the haw. Red halls and yellow halls are common in the South. **1968** *DARE* (Qu. I46, . . *Fruits that grow wild around here*) Inf **MD**24, Hall [hɔl] berry.

hallabaloo See **hullabaloo**

hall bedroom n Also *hall room* **chiefly NYC**
A small bedroom, sometimes formed by partitioning off part of a hallway; see quots; hence v *hall room* to live in such a room.
1738 in 1914 NH *Prov. & State Papers* 32.280, Samuel Brewster shall Have . . ye Hall Bed Room. **1859** *Ladies' Repository* 19.466/2 **NYC,** The little hall-room is just large enough for the boys to sleep in. **1886** James *Bostonians* (Amer. ed.) 186 **NYC,** One of his rooms was directly above the street-door of the house; such a dormitory, when it is so exiguous, is called in the nomenclature of New York a "hall bedroom." **1902** (1906) Porter *4 Million* 48 **NYC,** If you survived Mrs. Parker's scorn, you were taken to look at Mr. Skidder's large hall room. *Ibid* 141, The restaurant was next door to the old red brick [sic] in which she hall-roomed. **1903** *Harper's Mth. Mag.* July 213/2 **NYC,** The lonely who sit in the cheerless solitude of hall bedrooms. **1922** Bennett *Lilian* 76, Lilian had the tiny mean bed-room on the second floor over the hall; in New York it would have been termed hall-bedroom. **1966** *DARE* (Qu. D15a, *Other rooms in your house;* total Infs questioned, 75) Inf **AR**38, Hall room, hall turned into a bedroom.

hall berry See **hall** n[2]

hallelujah n Also sp *halleluyah;* pronc-sp *hallelulya* Usu |,hælə'lujə; ,hælə'lɪujə|; for varr, see **A** below
A Forms.
1924 *DN* 5.269, *Halleluyah.* **c1960** *Wilson Coll* **csKY,** *Hallelujah* is often in songs /,hælɪ'lujə/. **1966** *Ibid* **csKY,** *Hallelujah* [,hælə'luyər]. **1967–70** *DARE* (Qu. NN6a) Inf **AR**47, [,hælɪ'lulja]; **CA**127, Hallelulya; **VA**50, ['hælə,lujɚ].
B Senses.
1 Hell. *euphem*
1950 *WELS (Weakened substitutes for "hell": "Oh ——!")* 2 Infs, **WI,** Hallelujah. **1966–69** *DARE* (Qu. NN26a) Infs **AR**41, **MI**63, 67, **RI**3, Hallelujah; (QR, near Qu. FF18) Inf **VA**75, Raised hallelujah.
2 also attrib: See quot.
1966–70 *DARE* (Qu. FF17, *Words meaning that people had a very good or enjoyable time*) Inf **GA**8, Hallelujah time; (Qu. FF18, . . *About a noisy or boisterous celebration or party*) Inf **MD**35, Did have a hallelujah.

‡hallelujah v [Prob from the emotion and movement associated with the singing and shouting of *hallelujah*]
To leap or move violently about.
1961 Adams *Old-Time Cowhand* 296, It took a man with whiskers to curry the kinks out of some of them broncs when they warped their backbones and hallelujahed all over the lot.

hallelulya(h) See **hallelujah**

halligatawkin n
A type of apple; see quot.
1977 *DARE* File **ceIA,** Halligatawkin—A special eating apple, similar to pears when cooked, and delicious in pies. It was favored by settlers in Boone Co., Iowa (1850's–1860's) who passed it on to neighbors and later comers. In 1910–15 a nonagenarian of a pioneer Boone County family said the sweet-flavored apple was given the name by the Indians of the locality. It was in use up into the first quarter of the 20th century.

hallow v, n[1] See **holler** v, n[1]

hallow n[2], adj See **hollow** n[1], adj

hall rack n **esp NEast, OH** *old-fash*
=**hall tree.**

1965–70 *DARE* (Qu. E1, *A piece of furniture that stands against the wall, and you hang clothes in/on it:*) 17 Infs, **esp NEast, OH,** Hall rack. [16 Infs old]

hall room See **hall bedroom**

hall tree n **scattered, but esp NCent, MO** See Map Cf **hat tree**

A clothes tree, hat rack, or hallstand.

1891 *Harper's New Mth. Mag.* June 79/1 **TN,** One could distinguish a hall sofa, long and hard, covered with tattered black hair-cloth, and . . the hall tree, whereon Rhodes's hat swung in its place. **1900** Peake *Darlingtons* 79, She . . walked back to the sitting-room, stopping to touch up her hair before the glass in the hall-tree. **1950** *WELS (Place where you hang clothes)* 1 Inf, **WI,** Hall tree, common; 1 Inf, Hall tree. **1954** Steinbeck *Sweet Thursday* 111 **CA,** He busted two windows and run off with the deer-antler halltree. **1965–70** *DARE* (Qu. E1, *A piece of furniture that stands against the wall, and you hang clothes in/on it:*) 71 Infs, **scattered, but esp NCent, MO,** Hall tree. **1970** *DARE* FW Addit **KY**85, Hall-tree, an elaborate piece of furniture for hanging coats, hats, umbrellas, etc. It has hooks, a mirror, baskets for umbrellas, and a seat with storage space inside. Old-fashioned. **1978** *DARE* File **NEng,** I have often been struck in visiting old houses in New England how few built-in storage places our ancestors had, how few closets. Both chests of drawers and chests with lids took care of many articles of clothing—not to mention hat trees or hall trees (I have heard both terms in New England) where visitors and family alike hung up their outdoor clothes.

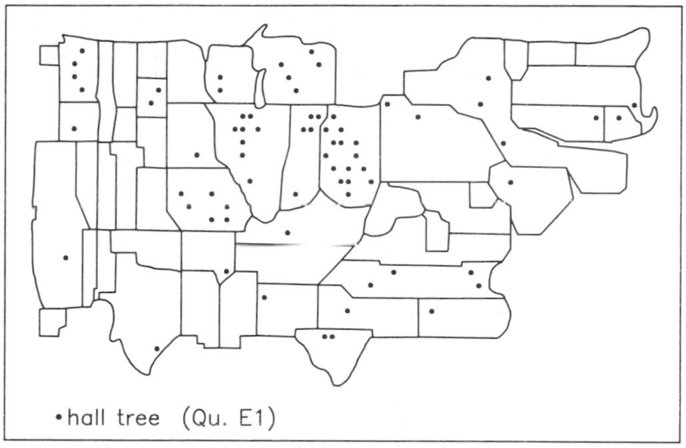

hallway n **esp TN**

1 A space between two buildings.

1939 *Hall Coll.* **wNC, eTN,** They come a big rain and washed the old foot-bridge plumb into the hallway between the barns.

2 also *hall:* A central aisle or open space in a barn.

1965–68 *DARE* (Qu. M4a, . . *The spaces or sections between the joists in a barn*) Inf **MS**58, Hallway; (Qu. M9, *The part of a barn where horses are kept*) Inf **TN**1, Hallway; (Qu. M10, *The part of the barn where cows are kept*) Inf **TN**24, Hall, a big wide part for bad weather. **1986** Pederson *LAGS Concordance (Barn)* 1 inf, **nwTN,** Hallway—through middle; 1 inf, **swTN,** Hallway—in middle of barn; *(Building for storing corn)* 1 inf, **cwAR,** Barn was a straight building with hallway; *(Shelter for horses)* 1 inf, **cTX,** Hallway—in barn; stalls on sides; *(Place where cows penned for milking)* 2 infs, **cwTN, nwGA,** Hallway—in barn; 1 inf, **cwTN,** In a hallway or in a stall.

halter broke ppl adj phr [*halter broken* accustomed to the halter]

Fig: submissive, lacking in spirit.

1910 *Sat. Eve. Post* 27 Aug 50/1 **NM, TX,** The law-abiding then term him an outlaw, and he in turn describes the law-abiding as 'halter-broke.' **1916** 'Bower' *Phantom Herd* 29 *(DAE),* We're all plumb halter-broke and so tame. **1969** *DARE* (Qu. AA15b, *What joking ways do you have around here of saying that a man is getting married*) Inf **GA**89, Got halter-broke.

halter-carrier n

1912 *DN* 3.577 **wIN,** *Halter-carrier.* . . An imposter. In the early days if a horse escaped and followed a trail back, the people who lived along the way boarded the owner free of charge until he had found the horse. Men who wanted to return to Kentucky or Ohio made their way easily, therefore, by carrying a bridle or halter as if they were looking for a horse.

halt's maul v phr [Ger] **WI**

Be quiet! Shut up!

1950 *WELS (A command to stop talking: not so polite)* 2 Infs, **WI,** Halt's maul; *(When you want people to stop talking for a moment so that you can hear something)* 1 Inf, **WI,** Halt's maul. **1968** *DARE* (Qu. X10b, *To tell a person to stop talking—not very politely*) Inf **WI**13, Halt's maul [hals mal]; **WI**50, Halt's maul [haʊs maʊ]. **1987** *DARE* File **seWI** (as of 1950), *Halt's maul*—be quiet, shut up. Frequently heard in the Racine area and used and understood even by those of non-German background.

halulu adj [Haw *halulu* to roar, thunder]

1967 *DARE* (Qu. GG7, *Words meaning annoyed or upset: "Though we were only ten minutes late, she was all ______.*") Inf **HI**13, Halulu; (Qu. GG26, *A feeling of weakness from fear: "When she saw the dog coming at her she got ______.*") Inf **HI**13, Halulu.

halum-scalum adj [Prob by lambdacism from *harum-scarum*]

Easy going, happy-go-lucky.

1966 *DARE* (Qu. KK46, . . *Expressions for taking things as they come and not worrying: "The whole family was sort of ______.*") Inf **GA**7, Halum-scalum ['heləm-skeləm].

halushky n pl Also *haluski, halusky* [Slovak *halušky*]

Dumplings; broad noodles; see quots.

c1965 Randle *Cookbooks* (Ask Neighbor) 1.22 **OH,** *Halushky* (Slovak) . . potatoes . . salt . . egg . . flour. Mix. . . Drop dough . . into boiling water. . . Add drained halushky [to sauteed onions]. Serve with thick sour cream or cottage cheese. *Ibid* 24, *Haluski Skapustu (Dumpling & cabbage).* . . Fry [cabbage in butter.] Now take the wide noodles [=haluski]. . . Put into the fried cabbage. *Ibid* 26, *Haluski with cabbage.* **1989** *WI State Jrl.* (Madison) 26 Apr sec C 8/3–4 **wPA,** [At] the mother church of the American Carpatho-Russian Orthodox Greek Catholic Diocese. . . there's a wedding . . and this can mean only one thing: the joys of Slovak cooking. . . *Halusky (noodles and cabbage).*

halvers n pl Also sp *halfers, hav(v)ers* [Cf *EDD halver*] **scattered, but esp Sth, S Midl**

1 Half shares; hence exclam *halvers* used to claim a half share in something.

1872 Schele de Vere *Americanisms* 484, *Halves,* in Pennsylvania corrupted into *havvers,* is an exclamation heard by the person who happens to witness the finding of a valuable object, in order to claim half of the treasure-trove. **1899** (1912) Green *VA Folk-Speech* 218, *Havvers.* . . Claiming half of what another finds. **1932** Faulkner *Light in August* 394 **MS,** *Byron Bunch, that weeded another man's laidby crop, without any halvers.* **1966** *DARE* (Qu. II8, *When one person wants to share or divide something with another*) Inf **NM**6, Halvers, boners.

2 In phrr:

a *go (in) halvers:* To agree to share equally.

1897 *KS Univ. Qrly.* (ser B) 6.53, *Havers* . . in 'to go havers with one', to share with. **1902** *DN* 2.235 **sIL,** *Go Havers.* **1906** *DN* 3.139 **nwAR,** *Halvers.* . . go halvers. **1908** *DN* 3.318 **eAL, wGA,** *Ha(l)vers.* . . 'go halvers.' **1915** *DN* 4.183 **swVA,** *Go halvers.* . . To share equally. **1925** Cather *Professor's House* 20 **NE,** All right. I'll go halvers. Easy come, easy go. **1936** Morehouse *Rain on Just* 117 **NC,** Things might have been better if her mammy had gone havvers on saw milling with Garley Brock instead of blowing all she had so devil-may-care. **1954** *Harder Coll.* **cwTN,** *Go in halvers.* **c1960** *Wilson Coll.* **csKY,** *Go halvers.* **1965–70** *DARE* (Qu. II8, *When one person wants to share or divide something with another*) 26 Infs, **scattered, but esp Sth, S Midl,** Go halvers; **OH**40, **PA**151, 167, **TX**4, Go halfers; **GA**77, Go halvers in this; (Qu. II9, *If several people have to contribute in order to pay for something*) Inf **KY**19, Go halvers.

b *on (the) halvers:* In partnership; with an agreement to share profits. Cf **halves 1**

1939 Faulkner *Wild Palms* 255 **MS,** He was in partnership now with his host, hunting alligators on shares, on the halvers he called it. **1957** in 1958 Brewer *Dog Ghosts* 69 **TX** [Black], Husban' done died 'long time ago, an' what let out de li'l' spot of lan' her husban' done lef' her on halvers to whosomevuh wanna crop on hit. **1959** Lomax *Rainbow Sign* 92 **AL** [Black], Mama, she went on farmin a small farm on the halvers, and she had to tend Papa like he was a baby.

c *by halvers:* Incompletely.

1867 Twain *Jumping Frog* 37, No man can say he ever see him do any thing by halvers.

halves n pl Also sp *halfs*

1 in phrr *on (the) halves, to (the) halves* and varr: For a half share of the produce or profit.

1644 in 1904 Manwaring *Digest CT Probate* 1.13, To Susana and Johana Wattson . . one Black hefer that John Gray hath tto the Haffes ffor ffouer yers. **1733** (1876) Byrd *Journey to Eden* 6 **VA,** [We] rode up the River 6 Miles . . where Master Hogan was Tenant upon Halves. *Ibid* 33, [We] came to the Plantation of Joshua Nicholson, where Daniel Taylor lives for Halves. **1789** *Thomas' MA Spy or Worcester Gaz.* (MA) 19 Mar 4/4, To be let, on the halves, . . A *Good* Farm. **1833** Neal *Down-Easters* 1.45 **NEng,** [He] lives by . . preachin' at the halves, or maybe for his board an' hoss-keep a' sabba-days. . . in partnership for what's taken up arter the sarmon's over. **1853** *Putnam's Mag.* 1.533, I've tended bar, worked farms to halves, been twice to the South seas. **1867** Lowell *Biglow* xlvii **'Upcountry' MA,** *To the halves* still survives among us [=Americans], though apparently obsolete in England. It means either to let or to hire a piece of land, receiving half the profit in money or in kind. **1895** Brown *Meadow-Grass* 141 **NEng,** Here they let Kelup carry on the farm at the halves. **1904** Waller *Wood-carver* 86 **VT,** Uncle Shim has let out four acres to cut to halves. **1950** *PADS* 13.18 **cTX,** Farmers spoke of *renting on the halves* when the rental agreement called for renter and owner to share equally. **1950** *WELS (A man who lives on a farm and does the work, sharing expenses and profits with the owner)* 1 Inf, **WI,** Farms on halves; 1 Inf, Working farm on halves; 1 Inf, Worker on halves. **1967–70** *DARE* (Qu. L3) [Inf **LA**22, Working on half;] **NY**27, On halfs, **TX**78, Working it on halves; **NY**176, Sharing on halves.

2 in phr *on the halves:* Piecemeal, divided up. [Cf **halvers 2c** and *by halves* inadequately]

1909 in 1914 Stewart *Letters* 15 **WY,** My parents died . . and left six of us to shift for ourselves. Our people offered to take one here and there . . but we refused to be raised on the halves . . so arranged to stay at Grandmother's and keep together.

halvsies n pl Also *half(s)ies, halvies;* rarely sg *halvsy* **=halvers.**

1956 *AmSp* 31.37, Halvsies on the candy bar! **1957** *Sat. Eve. Post Letters* **swMA** (as of 1925), If two boys both saw a valuable item on the ground, but one picked it up first, the second could claim part ownership by saying "halfsies." **1967–70** *DARE* (Qu. II8, *When one person wants to share or divide something with another*) Inf **PA**165, Go halvies; **NY**35, Halvies; **MA**1, Go halvsies; **LA**23, Go halvsy; **NY**239, Go halfies.

ham n[1] [From the resemblance to a *ham*]

1 A hand.

[**1919** Kyne *Capt. Scraggs* 107 **CA,** I had a bunch o' red whiskers an' a pair o' fists like two picnic hams.] **1950** *WELS (Joking or uncomplimentary words for the hands)* 7 Infs, **WI,** Hams. **1954** *Harder Coll.* **cwTN,** *Hams,* uncomplimentary name for hands. **1960** Bailey *Resp. to PADS 20* **KS,** Big hams. **1966–69** *DARE* (Qu. X32) Infs **AZ**10, **CA**107, **GA**89, **MO**1, 5, **NY**123, 152, Hams.

2 also *ham hock:* A foot.

1965–70 *DARE* (Qu. X38, *Joking names for unusually big or clumsy feet*) Infs **MS**10, **WI**13, Hams; **PA**234, Ham hocks.

ham n[2] [Cf *EDD haulm* sb. 5 "The husk of corn or of peas, beans, &c."]

A pod; see quots.

1930 Stoney–Shelby *Black Genesis* 32 **seSC,** God come in dat end o' de garden, an' notice a soun' like somebody trowin' out a lot o' cow-pease hams (pods) on a plank floor. **1966–67** *DARE* (Qu. I10, *The outside covering of green peas that you break open to get the peas out*) Inf **SC**22, Ham, an old name; **SC**43, Pea hams.

ham and egger n [See quot 1960]

See quots.

1932 *AmSp* 7.333 **MD** [Johns Hopkins Univ. slang], *Ham & egger*—a person who is below par; a "second rater". **1960** Wentworth–Flexner *Slang* 240, *Ham and egger*. . . An average person . . one as common as ham and eggs. **1967** *DARE* File **cnNY,** *Ham and eggers*—guys that try to bluff you.

hambeer n [Var of **ambeer 2,** perh infl by folk-etym *ham + beer*]

1965–70 *DARE* (Qu. DD4, *Moisture in the mouth, colored brown by snuff or chewing tobacco*) Infs **KY**47, **OK**1, **VA**46, Hambeer ['hæmbiɚ].

hambleman n [Ger *Hampelmann* a puppet on a string; by ext, an awkward person]

1950 *WELS Suppl.* **seWI,** Hambleman—a sort of weakish person, but lacking ability to make the most of his talents.

hambone n

1 The knee or thigh. Cf **hog bone**

1908 in 1965 London *Letters* 275 **cwCA,** I have to get down on my ham-bones [=knees] and beg forgiveness. **1942** (1965) Parrish *Slave Songs* 114 **GA coast,** In that position he is able to lift his "ham bone" [=thigh] a little higher and do a rather more complicated bit of patting. **1966** *DARE* (Qu. X36, *Joking names for the knees;* total Infs questioned, 75) Inf **FL**15, Hambones.

2 The penis.

1927 in 1983 Taft *Blues Lyric Poetry* 19, [Song title: *Ham Bone Blues*] I got to go to Cincinnati / Just to have my hambone [=penis] boiled / Womens in Alabama / Going to let my hambone spoil. **1977** Dillard *Lexicon* 33, Other Black terms for the penis include . . *Hambone,* very frequent in the older Blues.

3 A body-slapping play routine with accompanying rhymes; also n *hamboner,* vbl n *hamboning.* Note: While the verb *hambone* undoubtedly exists, *DARE* has no citations for it.

1949 (1972) Funk & Wagnalls *Dict. Folkl.* 477, *Ham Bone*—An American Negro hand-patting rhythm accompanied by a rimed chant. . . [which] begin[s] with such phrases as: "Ham bone, ham bone pat 'em on the shoulder". . . or "Ham bone, ham bone, where you been?" **1972** Jones–Hawes *Step it Down* 34 **eGA** [Black], "Hambone" probably refers to the part of the anatomy most involved in playing this hand jive game. **1980** *DARE* File, *Ham-boning* . . a rhythmic movement of the hands from the chest to the thighs in which the ham-boner continuously slaps his hands to his chest and thigh to create something of a tune. . . It is a mountain tradition and is known to practically all mountain people, especially in Eastern Kentucky and Tennessee.

4 In marble play: see quot.

1957 *Sat. Eve. Post Letters* **cwKY** (as of 1930s), *Hambone*—Once a player had made the circuit [in the game Roly-holy], he was rewarded with the privilege of taking a "hambone" during the next round. That is, he could (only once) when he needed it, move his marble the length from his elbow to his fingertip.

hambone v [Perh *ham bone* a bone with little meat on it]

To live very frugally.

1942 Perry *Texas* 63, Nineteen years ago, "hamboning" along on almost no money at all, a candy salesman sank a well that brought in the West Texas fields.

hamboner, hamboning See **hambone** n 3

hamburg n

1 also *hamburg steak:* Ground beef; a cooked patty of ground beef. [*Hamburg* Germany] **chiefly NEast, C Atl, OH, MI** See Map Cf **frankfurt**

1884 *Boston Eve. Jrl.* (MA) 16 Feb 2/3 **cwCA,** To make tamales we take a chicken and boil it. When it is cold we cut it up as they do meat to make Hamburg steak. **1903** A. Boss *Meat on Farm* 34 *(DAE),* Lean beaf [sic] from the round makes the choicest Hamburg. . . Hamburg steak is not stuffed into casings, but left in bulk and made into patties for frying. **1935** *AmSp* 10.159 **NE,** Hamburgs 5c. **1945** *Progressive* 7 May 11/2, In the East, culinary tradition records that "hamburg" was first heard of about the turn of the century, and I can remember "going to the store" for it about that time. **c1965** Randle *Cookbooks* (Ask Neighbor) 57 **OH,**

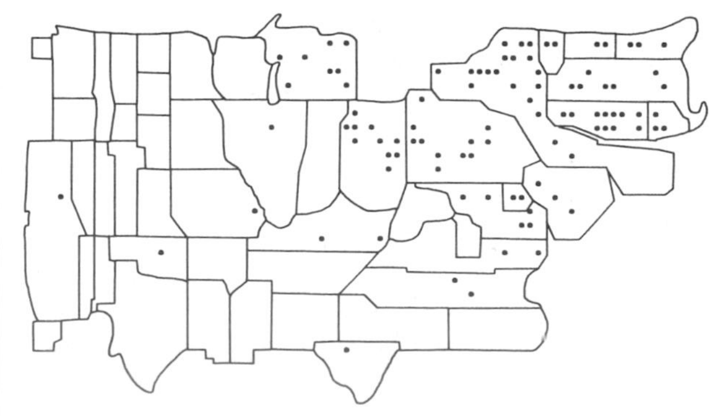

•hamburg 1 + varr (Qq. H41, D39, H18)

Dad's prize winning parsley hamburgs. **1965–70** *DARE* (Qu. H41, . . *Roll or bun sandwiches favored around here*) 95 Infs, **chiefly NEast, C Atl, OH, MI,** Hamburg; **NY**209, **PA**234, Hamburg sandwich; (Qu. D39) Infs **MI**28, 68, 75, **NY**209, 220, Hamburg joint; (Qu. H18) Inf **MI**94, Hamburg buns; (Qu. H52) Inf **RI**5, Glumpies . . cabbage leaves and hamburg; (Qu. H65) Inf **PA**245, Hamburg and rice. **1968** *DARE* File **cNY,** Hamburg, cheeseburg, fishburg [sandwich list on a wall menu]; **cNY,** Hamburg, = hamburger; **seDE,** Hamburg steak = large fried patty of ground beef. **1969** *DARE* Tape **PA**221, Hamburg and rice and spices.

2 See quot.

c1970 Wiersma *Marbles Terms* **swMI** (as of c1963), *Hamburg* . . any brown-coloured marble. Eg. I've got a bag full of hamburgs.

hame n

1a One of a pair of curved bars fitted into the collar of a harness to which the traces are attached. Note: Some *DARE* Infs may be confusing the hames with other parts of a work harness. [*OED* 1303 →]

1899 (1912) Green *VA Folk-Speech* 213, *Hames*. . . Pieces of wood on the collar of the horse on which the traces are fixed. **1904** *DN* 2.425 **Cape Cod MA** (as of a1857), *Hames*. . . The frame around a horse's collar to which the traces are attached. **1930** Omwake *Conestoga Teams* 45 **PA,** Whenever one wagoner helped another in distress on those rough or slippery roads, he received as a reward the hame bells of the hapless one. **1930** Shoemaker *1300 Words* 30 **cPA Mts** (as of c1900), *Hame-bells*—Bells on the hames of horse collars, used principally in the lumber woods, to notify the axe men of proximity of the horses and their drivers. **1962** Faulkner *Reivers* 84 **MS,** Standing hitched to a tree just off the road (canal) were two mules in plow gear—that is, in bridles and collars and hames, the trace chains looped over the hames and the plowlines coiled into neat hanks and hanging from the hames also. **1965–70** *DARE* (Qu. L49) 63 Infs, **scattered,** Hame(s); **CA**208, Hames—tugs are anchored to these; **CT**2, Hames—traces hook to them; **CT**17, Hames—go over collar; **FL**15, Hames—in collar, iron pieces; **IL**134, The collar is fastened to the hames, which are fastened to the traces; **MD**29, Hames—go around the collar; **MD**34, Traces goes from hames to singletree; **MD**48, Hames—go around collar, traces run from hames to singletree; **MA**25, Hame—fits on collar, fastened on other end to tugs; **MO**11, Actually, the tugs were fastened to the hames and the hames fit around the collar; **MO**27, Hame, traces—he's heard both of these used; **NC**80, The traces hooks into the hames; **NY**224, Hames go on the collar, tugs go on the hames; **NY**233, Hames—goes on collar to fasten tugs to; **WA**20, Hame—goes on collar, tugs [go] from hame to load; **LA**7, Gear hames; **IL**78, Collar hames; **OK**20, Hanes or hames [Inf doubtful]; **CO**47, Hanes [sic]; (Qu. L51, *The leathers or ropes that a driver holds to guide a horse*) Inf **MD**24, Hames; (Qu. L53b, *The band that goes under a horse's middle to hold a saddle on . . if it's a part of a work harness*) Inf **TX**57, Hames—leather strip on wood collar of harness.

‡b See quot.

1967 *DARE* (Qu. L44, *On a buggy, two long pieces of wood stick out in front and the horse goes between them*) Inf **AR**47, Buggy hames—different from collar hames.

2 in combs *hame string, ~ strap:* See **hame string.**

3 attrib: Shaped like a **hame 1a.**

1968 *DARE* (Qu. X37, . . *People's legs if they're noticeably bent, or uneven, or not right*) Inf **DE**2, Hame legs, bowed; **MD**31, Hame leg, leg with noticeably large calf relative to ankle.

4 See quot.

1972 Claerbaut *Black Jargon* 67, *Hame*. . . a job; vocation.

hamed-jawed adj [Cf **hame 3**]

=ham-jawed.

1968 *DARE* (Qu. X6, *If a person's lower jaw sticks out prominently, you say he's* ______) Inf **WV**2, Hamed [heımd]-jawed.

hame-head n, hence adj *hame-headed* [**hame 1a**] Cf **hammer-headed 2**

See quots.

1937 *DN* 6.618 **swTX,** A *hame-headed* horse is stupid. **1984** Weaver *TX Crude* 37, A *hame-head* is a dunce.

hame strap See **hame string 1**

hame string n

1 also *hame strap:* One of the two straps used to attach the **hames** to the collar of a draft horse or mule. Note: A few of the *DARE* Infs appear to have confused the hame strings with other parts of a work harness.

1856 Davis *Farm Bk.* 66 *(DA),* Bring in 11 plow lines single & 1 hame string. **1929** Faulkner *Sound & Fury* 264 **MS,** I'll take a hame string to you. *Ibid* 287, Haggling over a twenty cent hame string. **1950** *PADS* 14.35 **SC,** *Hamestrap*. . . A leather strap with a buckle on one end, used to strap the hames together permanently at the top. *Hamestring*. . . A leathern thong about three feet long with a large knot on one end, used to tie the hames together at the lower ends. The hamestring is tied and untied each time the gear is put on and taken off an animal. **c1960** *Wilson Coll.* **csKY,** *Hamestring*—The tanned or rawhide cord that ties the hames together across the collar of a plow horse. **1965–70** *DARE* (Qu. L49, *Leathers or ropes, fastened to the collar, that a horse or mule pulls by*) 48 Infs, **scattered, but more freq Sth, S Midl,** Hame string(s); **CA**145, Hame strings [Inf corrected resp to "reins and tugs"]; **GA**17, Hame strings—on a plow it's a line; **GA**77, A top hame string and a bottom hame string; **IA**31, Hame strings—from one hame to another, on the collar, holds collar on; **MN**2, Hame strings—a part of the bridle that hitches to the wagon [this response was suggested by the FW]; **MS**81, Hame strings [resp suggested by FW; Inf corrected resp to "gear"]; **NC**31, Hame strings—tie collar on horse, traces are fastened to hames; **NJ**44, Hame strings or hame straps—hames go around collar; **SC**4, Hame strings—the lacing for the hames to keep them properly adjusted; **SC**19, Hame strings—to adjust the fit of the two hames in the collar; **SC**23, Hame strings—used to adjust fit of the hame; **SC**26, Hame strings—for adjusting the fit of the hames; **TN**7, Hame strings—fastened to hames, not collar; **TN**14, Hame strings—tie hames on with these; **TN**56, There are hame strings to tie hames and chains fasten to hames; **TX**32, Hame strings—in collar; **VA**40, Hame strings—they hold hames to collar; **CA**99, 138, **GA**80, **IL**66, **NJ**44, **NY**93, Hame strap(s); **MO**18, The hame strap hooks the harness around the collar on his neck, the tug hitches onto it; (Qu. L53b, *The band that goes under a horse's middle to hold a saddle on . . if it's a part of a work harness*) Inf **FL**37, Girt, hame string; **NY**62, Hame strap.

2 Transf: see quot.

1949 *AmSp* 24.109 **ceGA,** *Hamestrings*. . . Large earthworms.

hamestrung adj

1958 *AmSp* 33.270 **eWA,** *Hamestrung*. . . Of a horse, having strained a ligament in one of his quarters. . . [as opposed to] *Hamstrung*. . . having had the main tendon of a hind leg severed.

ham gravy n [From the color] Cf **hambeer**

=ambeer 2.

1966 *DARE* (Qu. DD4, *Moisture in the mouth, colored brown by snuff or chewing tobacco*) Inf **SC**19, Ham gravy.

ham gravy pea n Also *ham gravy bean* Cf **half-and-half c**

A cultivated bean (var *Phaseolus vulgaris*), perh similar to **Jacob's cattle.**

1941 *McDavid Coll.* **nwSC,** This reminded me of *ham gravy peas,* which I ate once with an informant. . . I think I've heard them called *ham gravy beans*. . . [They are] prolate spheroids, with one end red and the other white.

ham hock See **ham** n[1] **2**

‡ham in v phr [Prob infl by *butt in*]

1967 *DARE* (Qu. II22, *Expressions to tell somebody to . . mind his own business*) Inf **MN**2, Don't ham in.

ham-jawed adj

1968 *DARE* (Qu. X6, *If a person's lower jaw sticks out prominently, you say he's* ______.) Inf **VA**24, Ham-jawed.

hamleg n [Perh from the presumed fleshiness of the legs of an inactive person]

1954 *Harder Coll.* **cwTN,** *Hamleg,* a lazy person.

hamlet n [Etym unknown, but cf *DJE*] **FL**

A **grouper 1a** (here: *Epinephelus striatus*).

1876 U.S. Natl. Museum *Bulletin* 5.57, *Epinephelus striatus*. . . The young fish are called Hamlets; but, after reaching a length of eighteen or twenty inches, are known as Groupers. **1896** *Ibid* 47.1157, *Hamlet*. . . West Indies, Key West to Brazil; very common; a well-marked species and a food-fish of importance. **1933** John G. Shedd Aquarium *Guide* 98, *Nassau Grouper; Hamlet*. . . can be immediately identified by the square blotch of jet black on the base of the tail and by the ring of tiny black dots around each eye. **1946** LaMonte *N. Amer. Game Fishes* 53, Hamlet. . . Most frequently found on the Florida Keys outside the belt of coral and sea fans.

ham-meat n [Cf Intro "Language Changes" I.4] **S Midl** Cf **hog meat**

Ham; occas bacon.

1916 *DN* 4.294 **sAppalachians,** *Ham-meat.* **1924** Raine *Land of Saddle-Bags* 105 **Appalachians,** This desire for exactness has given such expressions as . . ham-meat. *Ibid* 211, Usually he slaughters a hog or two for his "meat." This, salted and sometimes smoked, provides the necessary supply of bacon, "ham-meat" and lard. **1927** *DN* 5.469 **Appalachians,** *Ham-meat.* . . Bacon. **1930** *VA Qrly. Rev.* 6.248 **S Midl,** There are the analogous compounds . . ham meat, [etc]. **1933** Williamson *Woods Colt* 218 **Ozarks,** No trackin' ham-meat, no linin' a bee tree, no nothin'. **1938** Stuart *Dark Hills* 329 **KY,** Here is cold ham meat. **1946** *AmSp* 21.97 **sIL,** *Ham-meat,* ham. **c1960** *Wilson Coll.* **csKY,** *Ham-meat,* tautology, very common in the area. **1972** Cooper *NC Mt. Folkl.* 92, *Ham-meat*—pork ham.

hammer n Usu |hæmə(r)|; also |'hamə(r), 'hɑrmər| Pronc-spp *harmar, hommer*

A Forms.

1818 in 1824 Knight *Letters* 107 **KY,** Some words are . . by the lower classes in society, pronounced very uncouthly, as . . hommer. **1899** (1912) Green *VA Folk-Speech* 229, *Hommer.* . . A hammer. **1917** *DN* 4.393 **neOH,** *Hammer* [hamɚ, hamə]. . . Used by a native of R. I. who migrated 1830. . . [Vt. harmar.] **1934** (1943) *W2* 1193/1, *Hommer.* . . Dial. var. of *Hammer.* **1959** *VT Hist.* new ser 27.140, *Hammer* ['hɑrmɚ] . . pronc. Occasional. Rural areas.

B Sense.

A woman. *among Black speakers* Cf **nail**

1969 *Current Slang* 4.2.7 **IA** [Black], *Hammer* . . A girl. **1970** *Ibid* 5.2.8 [Black], *Hammer* . . A pretty girl. **1970** *DARE* (Qu. HH34, *General words around here for a woman*) Inf **PA**236, Hammer. [Inf Black] **1970** Major *Dict. Afro-Amer. Slang* 63, *Hammer:* beautiful Afro-American girl. **1972** Claerbaut *Black Jargon* 51, A *hammer* is a female.

hammer-and-square-boy n

1967 *DARE* (Qu. HH15, *A very inexperienced person, one who is just learning how to do a new thing*) Inf **MO**3, Hammer-and-square boy (carpentry).

hammer bird See **hammerhead 6**

hammered-down ppl adj

Stunted; wretched; worthless.

1919 Kyne *Capt. Scraggs* 248 **nCA,** Now, I notice that the king is a miserable, skimpy, sawed-off, and hammered-down old cove. **1942** Berrey–Van den Bark *Amer. Slang* 39.10, *Short; low.* . . Hammered-down. **1968–69** *DARE* (Qu. HH18, *Very insignificant or low-grade people*) Inf **CT**3, Hammered-down; (Qu. HH20c, *Of an idle, worthless person*) Inf **MI**26, Knock-kneed, hammered-down son-of-a-bitch.

hammered hell n

1970 *DARE* (Qu. BB38, *When a person doesn't look healthy, or looks as if he hadn't been well for some time, you'd say, "He looks ______."*) Inf **VA**42, Like hammered hell.

hammered woodpecker See **hammerhead 6**

hammerhandle n

A **pike** such as the **redfin pickerel:** see quots.

1949 Caine *N. Amer. Sport Fish* 105, It [=barred pickerel *(Esox americanus)*] is found from Maine to Florida and Alabama, east of the Allegheny Mountains. It is also called bulldog pickerel, grass pike and hammerhandle. **1973** *DARE* File **Upper Missip Valley,** Small pike are known as hammerhandles or snakes, the first indicating metaphorically the size and shape of a yearling pike, the second indicating shape and a value judgement besides.

hammer handles (and pitchforks), rain v phr Cf **pitchforks and hammer handles, rain**

1968–69 *DARE* (Qu. B26, *When it's raining very heavily, you say, "It's raining ______."*) Inf **OH**61, Hammer handles; **MA**15, Hammer handles and pitchforks.

hammerhead n [From the hardness or shape]

1 A stupid, annoying, or unattractive person. [*OED hammer-head* "A blockhead." 1532 →]

1935 *AmSp* 10.52, Epithets disparaging mentality . . You hammerheads. **1937** (1959) Weidman *I Can Get It* 166 **NY,** The best way out is for one of the three to be a hammerhead. **1941** *Life* 27 Jan 78 **Detroit MI,** Since a number of boys do not meet with subdeb approval, they are lumped together under such terms as . . *meatballs, hammerheads.* **1947** R. Taylor *Bar Nothing Ranch* (1949) xvi. 151 *(OEDS),* The meanest old hammerheads under her tutelage became as cooing doves. **1969** *DARE* (Qu. NN9b, *Exclamations showing great annoyance: "He's run off with my hammer again, ______!"*) Inf **NY**183, That hammerhead. **1975** *AmSp* 50.60 **AR**(as of c1970), *Hammerhead* . . One who is stubborn, obstinate.

2 A head, esp one thought to resemble the head of a hammer. Cf **hammerheaded 1**

1933 *N. Amer. Rev.* 236.428/1 **CA,** Billy's own horse was a stringy cayuse with a *hammer head,* but he nearly always won the first prizes at the stock trials. Billy could rope a steer, take a double half-hitch about the horn [of the saddle] with his riata and dismount, and his horse would play the steer as an angler plays a fish, keeping a tight rope until the steer was down or beaten. **1967** *DARE* (Qu. X28, *Joking words . . for a person's head*) Infs **IL**7, **MD**29, Hammerhead.

3 A horse or mule, esp one considered inferior. Cf **hammerheaded 2**

1941 Writers' Program *Guide UT* 103, The accepted theory is that the Indian horses were descended from animals that escaped from early Spanish explorers. The breed degenerated, producing "hammerheads" and "broomtails," but occasionally, in the wild herds, there is a throwback with the build, spirit, speed, and bearing of the pure-blood Arabian. **1944** Adams *Western Words* 72, *Hammerhead*—An unintelligent horse. **1970** *DARE* (Qu. K50, *Joking nicknames for mules*) Infs **VA**38, 43, Hammerhead.

4 See quot.

1968 *DARE* (Qu. FF14, . . *Kinds of firecrackers*) Inf **MD**8, Hammerheads. [FW: Now outlawed but Inf remembers these]

5 See **hammerhead sucker.**

6 also *hammer bird, hammered woodpecker:* A **woodpecker** such as the **flicker** n^2 **1.** [From its use of its head]

1950 *WELS (Different kinds of wood-peckers)* 2 Infs, **WI,** Hammerhead; *(Nicknames for wood-peckers)* 1 Inf, Hammerhead. **1956** MA Audubon Soc. *Bulletin* 40.82, *Yellow-shafted Flicker.* . . Hammerhead (Mass. Appropriate name for any woodpecker.) **1965–70** *DARE* (Qu. Q18, *Joking names and nicknames for woodpeckers*) 18 Infs, **chiefly Nth, Midl,** Hammerhead; **OH**70, Hammer bird; (Qu. Q17, . . *Woodpeckers . . around here*) Infs **IL**32, **LA**10, **MS**6, **MT**4, **PA**235, Hammerhead; **KY**72, Hammered woodpecker.

7 also *hammerheaded borer:* =**flatheaded borer.** [From the shape of its head]

1905 Kellogg *Amer. Insects* 266, The whole larva *[Rhagium lineatum]* . . is thus a footless whitish tadpole-like grub, expressively known as a flat-headed or hammer-headed borer. **1909** Smith *Insect Friends* 60, In the larval stage these [=*Buprestidae*] are known as flat-headed borers or "hammerheads."

hammerhead catfish n

Prob a **flathead catfish 1.**

1968 *DARE* (Qu. P1 . . *Freshwater fish . . good to eat*) Inf **TX**52, Hammerhead catfish.

hammerheaded adj

1 Of a horse: having a head shaped like a hammer; see quot 1976. [**hammerhead 2**]

1905 *DN* 3.82 **nwAR,** *Hammer-headed* . . Having a long head and a straight neck. 'Just see that hammer-headed horse.' **1927** *AmSp* 2.356 **WV,** *Hammer-headed horse* . . a horse with a head shaped like a hammer. "Pap came home with an old hammer-headed horse." **1951** Faulkner *Requiem* 27 **MS,** Pettigrew was grooming his ugly hammer-headed . . horse. **1976** Brown *Gloss. Faulkner* 98, *Hammer-headed. . . horse* . . a horse with a bony ridge between the ears and, supposedly, a low mentality.

2 Stubborn, obstinate. [**hammerhead 3**]

1954 *Harder Coll.* **cwTN,** *Hammer-headed,* hard-headed. **1970** *DARE* (Qu. GG18, *Other words meaning obstinate*) Inf **PA**242, Hammerheaded.

hammerheaded borer See **hammerhead 8**

hammerhead sucker n Also *hammerhead* [See quot 1889]

=**hog sucker.**

1882 U.S. Natl. Museum *Bulletin* 16.130, *Hog Sucker;* . . *Hammerhead.* . . Head flattened above, transversely concave between the orbits. **1884** Goode *Fisheries U.S.* 1.615, The Stone-roller or Hammer-head Sucker, *Catostomus nigricans,* abounds in most waters from the Great Lakes southward. **1889** *Century Dict.* 2698, *Hammerhead.* . . A catostomine fish, *Hypentelium nigricans,* having a peculiarly shaped head, which is flat above and transversely concave between the eyes, while the snout is abruptly turned down. **1968** *DARE* (Qu. P3, *Fresh-water fish that are not good to eat*) Inf **PA**136, Hammerheads—look like suckers. **1983** Becker *Fishes WI* 678, *Hypentelium nigricans.* . . Hammerhead sucker.

hammerjawed adj [From the shape]

1966–69 *DARE* (Qu. X6, *If a person's lower jaw sticks out prominently, you say he's ______.*) Infs **KY**28, **SD**3, **WA**9, Hammer-jawed.

hammerlock n

=cedar waxwing.

1962 Imhof *AL Birds* 417, *Cedar Waxwing. . . Other Names:* Seal, Cedar Bird, Hammerlock.

hammerman n

See quot.

1934 *AmSp* 9.288 **PA** [Black], *Hammerman.* . . Generally: anyone with more authority than the speaker; specifically: a professor.

hammer mill n **esp Sth**

A feed mill utilizing small, rapidly revolving hammers.

1950 Faulkner *Stories* 47 **MS,** [He] slipped and caught his leg in the hammer mill this afternoon. **1967–69** *DARE* Tape **NC**68, We get maybe five different kind of clay [for pottery] an' dry 'em, run 'em through hammer mills, same as a feed mill; **TX**32, He had a hammer mill and he would hammer several bushels of corn and then feed it to the cattle in the winter. **1969** *SC Market Bulletin* 11 Sept 2/4, *Want*—Tractor post hole digger, small hammer mill in running condition, small grits mill in running condition. **1986** Pederson *LAGS Concordance Gulf Region,* 1 inf, A lot of them got to using a hammer mill; metal hammer mill—now gristmill; 1 inf, Hammer mill—for grinding corn; 1 inf, Hammer mills—formerly used to thrash wheat.

hammock See **hummock**

hammock bird n [See quot 1946] Cf **hangnest**

=Baltimore oriole.

1917 (1923) *Birds Amer.* 2.258, *Baltimore Oriole. . . Other Names. . .* Hammock-bird. **1946** Hausman *Eastern Birds* 556, Hammock Bird. . . Long, purse-like, gray, pendant nests . . dangling from . . branches. **1963** Gromme *Birds WI* 217.

hammock land See **hummock 2c**

hammock maple n [*hammock* var of **hummock 2**]

=Florida maple.

1979 Little *Checklist U.S. Trees* 39, *Florida maple. . . Other common names* . . hammock maple.

hammock snake n [*hammock* var of **hummock 2**]

Perh a **rat snake.**

1966 *DARE* (Qu. P25, . . *Kinds of snakes . . around here*) Inf **NC**1, Hammock snake.

hammock soil See **hummock 2c**

hammocksweet n Also *hammocksweet azalea* [*hammock* var of **hummock 2**]

A **swamp azalea** (here: *Rhododendron serrulatum*).

1960 Vines *Trees SW* 829, Hammock-sweet Azalea. *Rhododendron serrulatum.* **1976** Bruce *How to Grow Wildflowers* 111, The Swamp Azalea . . has two close relatives which . . are glossy-leaved, late-flowering whites with small, fragrant blossoms. These are . . Texas or Oklahoma Azalea, and *R. serrulatum,* the Florida Swamp Azalea or Hammocksweet.

hammock wren n [*hammock* var of **hummock 2**]

Perh a **Carolina wren.**

1933 Rawlings *South Moon* 33 **nFL,** A gal no bigger'n a hammock wren, standin' there a-claimin' a hull pertater field. [**1969** Longstreet *Birds FL* 114, The Carolina wren. . . lives chiefly in swamps, river bottoms, and dense hammock thickets.]

hamper n

1 A basket, usu of standardized capacity, used for storage, transport, or packing as:

a also *bushel hamper, hamper basket:* A basket for the handling of fruits, vegetables, or grains. **chiefly Sth, S Midl** See Map

[**1806** (1970) Webster *Compendious Dict.* 138/2, *Hamper.* . . a covered basket used for carriage.] **1899** (1912) Green *VA Folk-Speech* 213, *Hamper.* . . A basket with handles on the edge, made of white-oak splits, holding about a bushel and used for handling corn in the ear. **1908** *DN* 3.318 **eAL, wGA,** *Hamper basket.* . . A hamper, a large open basket made of white-oak splits for holding cotton, corn, etc. Also called *cotton-basket. Hamper* alone is very rare. **1965–70** *DARE* (Qu. F17, *What peaches come in—different kinds*) 33 Infs, **chiefly Sth, S Midl,** Hamper; 9 Infs, **chiefly Sth, S Midl,** Bushel hampers; **LA**31, Bushel hamper, vegetables come in this; (Qu. F18, *The container grapes come in*) Inf **FL**17, Hamper; (Qu. F19, *A cloth container for grain*) Inf **LA**11, Hamper, like a bushel basket covered with cloth, made of wood; (Qu. LL9a, *As much as you need or more—for example, of apples: "We've got ______ of apples."*) Inf **LA**11, Hampers. **1968** *DARE* FW Addit **LA**40, *Hamper*—holds a bushel. [FW illustr: taller and narrower than a bushel basket]

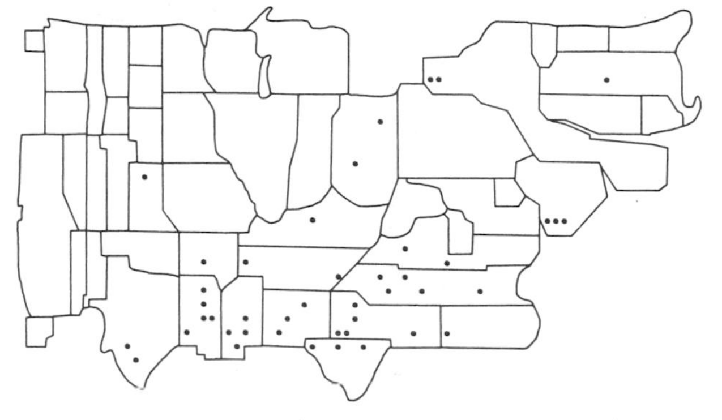

•hamper 1a + var (Qq. F17, F18, F19, LL9a)

b A basket for the handling of oysters or fish.

1889 *Century Dict.* 2699/1, *Hamper.* . . A two-bushel basket for oysters. [*Cent:* New York, U.S.]. . . A measure for fish holding about a bushel. [*Cent:* Virginia, U.S.] **1931–33** *LANE Worksheets* **swCT,** *Hamper,* a large oyster basket. A hamper would hold a bushel and a peck.

2 See quot.

1968 *DARE* (Qu. F44, *What do you call a container for coal to use in a stove*) Inf **AK**8, Hamper, for delivering coal by the ton.

hamper basket See **hamper 1a**

Hampton (boat) n [Prob *Hampton* New Hampshire] **chiefly ME**

A dory-type sailboat usu used for fishing or lobstering.

1835 Audubon *Ornith. Biog.* 2.522 **NEng,** For every couple of these hardy tars, a Hampton boat is provided. **1880** *Harper's New Mth. Mag.* Aug 350/2 **ME Islands,** The Hampton boat—a modified pink-stern, with shoulder-of-mutton-sails on its small masts—was the 'abler,' that is to say, better qualified to stand the exigencies of all sorts of weather. **1947** Coffin *Yankee Coast* 163 **ME,** It is the Hampton boat, the reach-boat, the backbone of the profession of lobstering, which is the boat that now most means Maine. **1957** Beck *Folkl. ME* 128, To facilitate hauling these fish aboard the boats were designed to "roll down" easily, but with increasing stability. . . At York and the Isles of Shoals the boat that filled the bill was the Hampton boat, a two-masted dory type. **1968** *DARE* (Qu. O9, . . *Kinds of sailboats*) Inf **MD**34, Hampton, a classboat, built according to size and style, regulations required for type.

ham-sam adv [*EDD ham-sam* "in confusion or disorder"]

1959 *VT Hist.* 27.140 **neVT,** *Ham-sam.* . . In disorder. Rare.

ham-scram n [Cf *EDD hamstram* "Difficulty"]

A difficult situation.

1948 Hurston *Seraph* 70 **FL,** That means I'm in the ham-scram and got to hustle like hell to get a house up for him to be born in.

Ham's grandson n [*Ham* son of Noah and traditionally regarded as the ancestor of Black people; cf Genesis 9:18–25]

1970 *DARE* (Qu. HH28, *Names and nicknames around here for people of foreign backgrounds: Negroes*) Inf **NC**87, Ham's grandson.

han n[1] Also *great han* Cf **old hand**

=great blue heron.

1955 MA Audubon Soc. *Bulletin* 39.312, *Great Blue Heron. . .* Great Han, Han (Maine. This would appear to be a dialectal pronunciation of "heron.")

han' n[2] See **hand**

hana n, v |hɑnɑ| [Haw] **HI**

1 Work, labor; to work, to make.

1951 *AmSp* 26.22 **HI,** Other common Hawaiian words are . . *hana* (labor, work; to make). **1954–60** Hance et al. *Hawaiian Sugar* 2, *Hana* /'hɑnɑ/ To work. **1967** Reinecke-Tsuzaki *Hawaiian Loanwords* 94 (as of 1938), *Hana* . . To work; to labor. . . F[requent]. **1972** Carr *Da Kine Talk* 86, *Hawaiian Words Commonly Heard in Hawaii's English. . . Hana.* Work, activity. **1984** Sunset *HI Guide* 85, *Hana*—work.

2 in varr combs: See quots.

1954–60 Hance et al. *Hawaiian Sugar* 2, *Hana hou* /'hɑnɑ 'ho/ Repeat, do it again. *Hana pa* . . Bind together, closely tie. *Hanawai* . . To irrigate. *Ibid* 9, Irrigator *Hanawai-man.* **1967** Reinecke-Tsuzaki *Hawaiian Loanwords* 94 (as of 1938), *Hana. . .* "Used in a most extensive sense of to cause and to act," esp. in compound words. . . *Hanahemo* . . To loosen or untie. *Hanahou* . . Encore! A term used principally to cheer singers and *hula* dancers. . . *Hanamake* . . To kill; to cause the death of. *Hanapaa* . . 1. To fasten. . . 2. To tighten. . . *Hanawai* . . 1. To irrigate. . . 2. Irrigation. **1981** *Pidgin To Da Max, Hana hou. . .* Do it again. Instant replay. One mo' time. **1984** Sunset *HI Guide* 85, *Hana hou*—encore.

hanahana n, v, adj [Haw] **HI**

See quots.

1967 Reinecke-Tsuzaki *Hawaiian Loanwords* 94 (as of 1938), *Hanahana* . . v., n., adj. . . 1. To labor. 2. Labor; hard work. . . 3. Warm, as a hot day. . . 4. Heated, as with exercise. . . V[ery] F[requent] in first two senses. **1972** Carr *Da Kine Talk* 113 **HI,** *Hanahana man* (pidgin Hawaiian + English). A laborer on a plantation. *Hanahana* is the reduplicated form of the Hawaiian noun *hana* 'labor' or 'activity'.

hanahill n Also *hannahill(s)*

=black sea bass 1.

1814 in 1815 Lit. & Philos. Soc. NY *Trans.* 1.416 **NY,** *Sea Basse. (Perca varia.)* . . *Black harry, hannahills,* and *blue-fish,* are some of the names by which he [=sea bass] is known. **1842** DeKay *Zool. NY* 4.25, *Sea Bass* . . is sometimes called *Blue-fish, Black Harry, Hannahills,* and *Black Bass.* **1884** Goode *Fisheries U.S.* 1.407 **C Atl,** In the Middle States the Sea Bass is called "Black Will," "Black Harry," and "Hannahills." **1889** (1971) Farmer *Americanisms* 287, *Hannahill (Centropristes nigricans).*—The black sea-bass; black harry is another popular name for this fish. **1946** LaMonte *N. Amer. Game Fishes* 48, Sea Bass *Centropristes striatus* . . Names: Blackfish, . . Hanahill, . . Rock Bass.

hanai n, adj [Haw] **HI**

See quots.

1967 Reinecke-Tsuzaki *Hawaiian Loanwords* 94 (as of 1938), *Hanai;* /hānai/; adj., n. 1. Pertaining to the "*hanai* system" of the Hawaiians, i.e., the informal adoption or fostering of young children by relatives or friends. 2. A child so adopted. 3. Foster parent, as in the phrases "*hanai* papa" and "*hanai* mama." **1972** Carr *Da Kine Talk* 113, *Hānai child* (Hawaiian + English). 'Foster child', often not legally adopted. The Hawaiian *hānai* means 'foster child'.

hanau v Also *hanau hapai* [Haw] **HI** Cf **hapai** adj

To give birth.

1967 *DARE* (Qu. K10, *Words used about a cow that is going to have a calf*) Inf **HI**3, Hanau hapai [hɑnau hɑ'paɪ] = giving birth; (Qu. K11, *When a cow has a calf, you say that she* ______.) Inf **HI**3, Hanau; (Qu. K45, *When a mare has had a young horse*) Inf **HI**3, Hanau.

hanch n [*OED* "Obs."]

A haunch.

1893 Shands *MS Speech* 6, The [æ] sound is given . . to the vowel in . . *haunch.* **1922** Gonzales *Black Border* 34 **sSC, GA coasts** [Gullah], 'E done eat de hog' two hanch. *Ibid* 306 [Gullah glossary], *Hanch*—haunch, haunches, hind quarters. **1941** *Sat. Eve. Post* 5 Apr 116/1 **OH,** He finely gets hisself into a stanch nobody'd ever seen on a ball field before, kinda squattin' down on his hanches.

hanchker See **handkerchief**

hand n Usu |hænd|; also |hand, hæənd| Pronc-spp *hahnd, han'*

A Forms.

1864 Sargent *Peculiar* 110 **VA,** The fak is, I'm in fur a hahnd at euchre. **1899** Chesnutt *Conjure Woman* 18 **csNC** [Black], One er [=of] de fiel' han's died. **1922** Gonzales *Black Border* 306 **sSC, GA coasts** [Gullah glossary], *Han'*—hand, hands. **1941** *AmSp* 16.5 **eTX** [Black], Before *m, n,* the sound is sometimes lengthened, sometimes diphthongized to [æə]: *dam, hand.* **1942** *AmSp* 17.34 **seNY,** *Hand* [11 infs used [æ]; 7 infs [a]; no infs [ɑ]]. **1953** Brewer *Word Brazos* 12 **eTX** [Black], So dey don' relish no chu'ch servus on a Sunday night for de han's. De han's sing so long some Sunday nights till dey keep de boss-mens wake an' dey cain't go to sleep dey se'f.

B Senses.

1 A laborer, esp a farm worker. **scattered, but chiefly Sth, S Midl, TX** See Map Note: The comb *hired hand* is widespread and not regional. Cf **wages hand**

1639 in 1885 *Archives of MD* 3.86, That Good labouring hands be pressed to Supply the places of such planters as shall be pressed upon the Service. **1737** (1899) Parkman *Diary* 42 **MA,** About 18 or 20 hands husked out all my Corn. **1853** in 1917 Twain *Letters* 1.26, On Monday the hands are paid off in sparkling gold. **1907** *DN* 3.223 **sIL, nwAR,** *Hand. . .* A person in service. **1950** *WELS (What do you call people who work in these places?)* 21 Infs, **WI,** Mill hand; 4 Infs, Factory hand; 1 Inf, Shop hand; 1 Inf, Plant hand. **1959** *VT Hist.* 27.140, *A good hand. . .* A good worker. **1963** Owens *Look to River* 8 **TX,** "I come up this way looking for me a job." He looked at Basil. "You wouldn't be needing a hand, would you?" **1965–70** *DARE* (Qu. L1, *A man who is employed to help with work on a farm*) 62 Infs, **chiefly Sth, S Midl, TX,** Hand. **1969** *DARE* Tape **CA**113, In the northern part of the State—the first railroads—the Irish and the Chinese were the first section hands on the railroads, but later on . . the Mexican has been takin' over most all those jobs. **1975** Gould *ME Lingo* 123, *Hand*—A workman.

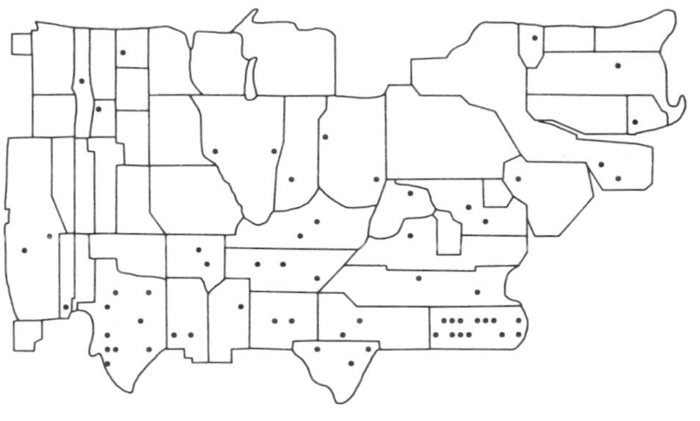

•hand B1 (Qu. L1)

2 One who is skilled at or inclined to engage in a particular activity.

1914 *DN* 4.74 **ME, nNH,** *Hand to, a gret* [sic]. . . A person greatly addicted to anything. "A gret hand to drink tea." **1916** Lincoln *Mary-'Gusta* 105 **MA,** I never was any hand to write letters. **1937** *Hall Coll.* **cwNC,** She's an awful hand to fish. **1938** Matschat *Suwannee R.* 119 **nFL, sGA,** Manthy was a master hand for smartin' up. **1939** *Hall Coll.* **eTN, wNC,** I reckon I'm a poor hand to judge. *Ibid,* He was no hand to hunt. **1949** *Ibid,* Jack is an old hand to coon-hunt. **1950** *WELS (He's an awful* ______*)* 1 Inf, **swWI,** Hand to tag along; *(Woman who sews carelessly)* 1 Inf, **seWI,** She's no hand with a needle. **1968** *DARE* FW Addit **NY**73, A great hand = one who does something habitually or frequently . . "He [=a cat] was a great hand to jump out at you." **1971** *Foxfire* Spring-Summer 102 **nGA,** I'm not a good hand t'set up till all hours.

3 By ext: one with a particular fondness; a fancier.

1856 Whitcher *Bedott Papers* 71 **NY,** Melissy never eats 'em nother—she ain't no pickle hand. **1904** *DN* 2.397 **NYC,** *Hand. . .* "He's no great hand for potato," he does not care for potato. **1967** *DARE* FW Addit **nNY,** We never was any hand for cheese—we don't eat cheese.

4 also *lucky hand:* An amulet or good luck charm. **chiefly Sth, S Midl** *among Black speakers*

1931 *Jrl. Amer. Folkl.* 44.369 **LA** [Black], It was my business to assist wherever possible, such as . . undressing and handling patients, writing out formulas as they were dictated, and finally making "hands." **1934** (1943) *W2* 1132/2, *Hand*. . . Among American negroes, a charm or prepared amulet, esp. one in red flannel. **c1938** in 1970 Hyatt *Hoodoo* 1.192 **csNC,** (Hyatt: This is the *lucky hand* you say—and how is that made?) It [is] made with peppah an' salt an' a penny or a dime. . . Yes, an' sew it up in a piece of red flannel. An' dere's a string left to it an' when yo' git ready to—fo' anything to happen in yore favor, you hold it by de string lak dat an' talk to it. . . (Hyatt: You ask questions of it?) Yeah. An' hit goes certain ways, an' whatevah it says, yo' do. *Ibid* 5.4273 **seNC** [Black], A woman, she loved a man, an'a, you know, de man kina rule huh an' she couldn't rule 'im so good. So she went an' git a *hand* to make 'im do as she said do. **1939** FWP *Guide TN* 139 **wTN** [Black], Cunjur doctors will sell you "hands" or "tobies" enabling you to detect witches and ward off their spells. **1945** FWP *Lay My Burden Down* 29 **TN** (as of c1870) [Black], Little pinch o' pepper,/ Little bunch o' wool. . . / Wrop it in a rag and tie it with hair,/ Two from a hoss and one from a mare. . . That's how the niggers say Old Bab Russ used to make the . . hands he made for the young bucks and wenches. **1947** (1964) Randolph *Ozark Superstitions* 170 [Black], Charms. . . little cloth bags containing feathers, hair, blood, graveyard dirt, salt, and sometimes human bones. . . They are called *charms, conjures, hands, jacks* or *jujus*. **1962** *Jrl. Amer. Folkl.* 75.314 **NC,** Local names for amulets are "mojo," "monjo," "lucky hand," "hand," . . and "jomo." These are all made by the conjurer and may consist of one or more of the following materials or some unknown substance wrapped in a little black, brown, or green cloth bag: roots, rats, lizards, snakes, . . red dirt, steel wool, gray clay, and pumpkin seeds. **1970** *DARE* (Qu. CC14, . . *One person supposedly casts a spell over another*) Inf **TN**53, Hand-giver. [Inf Black]

5 in phr *by hand:* On foot. [Cf *by hand* without the use of machines; perh also infl by the use of the hand in hithchiking]

1968–69 *DARE* (Qu. Y24, *Expressions meaning to walk, to go on foot: "I can't get a ride, so I'll just have to ______."*) Inf **CT**22, Go by hand [FW: laughter]; **IN**18, Go by hand; **NY**93, Go down by hand—one old fellow said this.

hand v, hence vbl n *handing* [Appar by convergence of *hand* a bunch of tobacco leaves and *hand* to pass] Cf **hand up**

To pass (tobacco leaves) in bunches to the person who ties them on sticks for drying; hence n *handing* a bunch of leaves so passed; n *hander.*

1941 Writers' Program *Guide SC* 367, Even the tiniest child can 'hand' tobacco—pass it on, several leaves at a time, to an elder who strings it on a stick. **1965** Tyler *Tin Can Tree* 92 **NC,** Joan . . handed her the next bunch of tobacco leaves. . . Beside her stood three other women—two handing to Mrs. Hall, who was the fastest tobacco-tier in the county, and the other helping Joan do the handing to Missouri. *Ibid* 93, She was having trouble finding a full handing of leaves. *Ibid* 102, "I got the answer," Mrs. Hall's first hander called. . . She kept on handing as she spoke, thrusting precisely neat bunches at Mrs. Hall with lightning speed. **1967** Key *Tobacco Vocab.* **GA, NC,** Handers—those who bunch up a few leaves of freshly cut tobacco and hand them to the person who attaches them with string to the stick.

hand-a-running See **hand running 2**

handbag n

1 A woman's bag used for carrying money and personal effects. *somewhat old-fash*

1866 (1881) Whitney *Leslie Goldthwaite* 25 **MA,** Their hand-bags were hung up. **1907** Sears *Catalogue* 1094/3, Ladies *Hand Bag* in fine walrus grain leather . . fitted with leather coin purse, leather card case, fancy ornamented gold finished powder box, mirror, and memorandum book. **1913** *Vanity Fair* Dec 79/2, Fashion decrees a hand bag of velvet. **1941** *LANE* Map 368, *Pocket book, bag* and *hand bag,* [denote] a larger receptacle used to contain paper money as well as other articles. Several informants state that the *purse* is carried inside the *pocket book* or *hand bag*. . . *Purse* may also be used as an equivalent of *hand bag.* **1965–70** *DARE* (Qu. U30, *What do you keep money in when you carry it around with you?*) 113 Infs, **widespread,** Handbag. [Of all Infs responding to the question, 66% were old; of those giving this response, 88% were old.] **1971** Bright *Word Geog. CA & NV* 161, *Handbag* was described as large by 17 [informants]; 6 used it as a general term, 4 as synonymous with *purse,* and 2 considered it old-fashioned.

2 A paper bag.

1966–68 *DARE* (Qu. F22a, *A smaller paper container for bringing groceries home from the store*) Infs **ME**2, **VA**9, Handbag.

3 in phr *in a handbag:* =**handbasket 2.**

1987–89 *DARE* File **NYC** (as of 1969), To go to hell in a handbag meant that one was surely on the road to perdition; **cTN** (as of 1940), We used either *go to hell in a handbasket* or *go to hell in a handbag.*

handbasket n

1 See quot 1899. Cf **handle basket**

1714 (1882) S. Sewall *Diary* 3.23 **MA,** A committee brought in something about Piscataqua. Govr said he would give his head in a Hand-Basket as soon as he would pass it. **1806** (1970) Webster *Compendious Dict.* 138/2, *Handbasket*. . . a small basket for the hand. **1899** (1912) Green *VA Folk-Speech* 214, *Handbasket*. . . A small basket that with its contents can be handled with one hand. **1968–69** *DARE* (Qu. F17, *What peaches come in*) Inf **MI**95, Hand basket, just a few; **SC**19, Hand basket [FW illustr: a small rectangular basket with a handle going over the top widthwise].

2 in adv phr *in a handbasket:* Quickly, surely, easily—usu in phr *go to hell in a handbasket.*

[**1914** *DN* 4.107 **KS,** *Go to heaven in a handbasket*. . . To have a sinecure.] **1923** *DN* 5.238 **swWI,** *Go to heaven in a hand basket*. . . To do something easily. "Why, he'd want to go to heaven in a hand basket!" **1955** *AmSp* 30.234, *Hand basket.* Taken literally, this term has little meaning, and the only use of it that I know is in the saying, *going to hell in a hand basket,* that is, surely and speedily. **1966** *DARE* FW Addit **neWA,** As a result of the Informant's dancing, her father warned her that she was going to hell in a hand basket. **1968** *Burlington Co. Herald* (Mount Holly NJ) 8 Aug 5B/5, It's the one or two bad apples in the lot that spoil things and make it seem as if the younger generation is "going to hell in a handbasket." **1969** *DARE* (Qu. GG21a, *If you don't care what a person does, you might tell him:*) Inf **MA**58, You can go to hell in a handbasket. **1985** Rattray *Advent. Dimon* 255 **Long Is. NY,** I'd heard old men say that the country was going to hell in a handbasket, that it wasn't what it was set up to be, a nation of independent farmers and fishermen, like the Roman Republic.

handbook n [Prob blend of **handbag** and *pocketbook*]

1966 *DARE* (Qu. U30, *What . . you keep money in when you carry it around with you*) Inf **NC**16, Handbook.

handbow n

1966 *DARE* (Qu. EE9b, *If children jump forward, land on the hands, and turn over*) Inf **GA**3, Handbow.

hand broom n **chiefly S Midl, Mid Atl** See Map

A whisk broom.

1965–70 *DARE* (Qu. F35, *A small broom that you hold in one hand*) 14 Infs, **chiefly S Midl, Mid Atl, esp KY,** Hand broom; (Qu. F36, *Other kinds of brooms*) Infs **CA**94, **GA**19, **IN**73, **KY**5, **MO**19, **SC**42, **VT**16, Hand broom; **KY**74, Hand household broom.

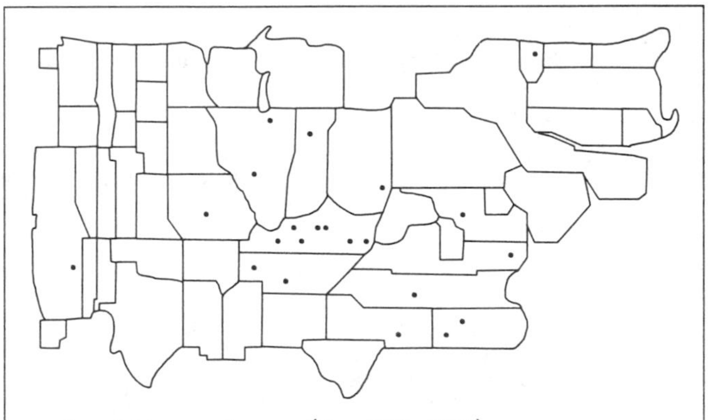

•hand broom + var (Qq. F35, F36)

hand cheese n [Calque of **handkäse**] **chiefly German settlement areas, esp WI**

A cheese molded with the hands.

1890 *Harper's New Mth. Mag.* July 231/1 **TX,** Her balls of hand-cheese, strewed with caraway seeds, are white and appetizing. **1941** *Language* 17.332 **WI,** *Hand cheese* 1 [inf]: *o*[ldest group] . . says the local Germans use this (because the cheese is molded in cupped hands.) **1950** *WELS (Different kinds of home-made cheese)* 5 Infs, **WI,** Hand cheese; 1 Inf, Hand cheese, old-fashioned; 1 Inf, Hand cheese, made of curd, but made by hand in round balls and wrapped and buried in the ground for a while. **1950** *WELS Suppl.* **ceWI,** Hand cheese—a form of cottage cheese shaped into balls by hand then put away for days or weeks to ripen. After it had acquired a certain strong flavor and a yellowish hue it was ready. **1968** *DARE* (Qu. H60, *The lumpy white cheese that is made from sour milk*) Inf **MN**37, Hand cheese, worked in the hands till it formed a loose cake, then aged. **1972** *Yesterday* 1.2.39 **WI,** Perhaps some "hand" cheese would also be curing to add its equally pungent scent to the already heavy air.

hand-dog n Cf **andog**

1877 Bartlett *Americanisms* 274, *Hand-Dog.* A fire dog; an andiron. New England.

hand-down n [Var of *hand-me-down*]

Something (esp clothes) passed on from one person or group to another.

1900 *DN* 2.40 **LA,** *Hand-down*. . . Any book or other article of student property transferred from one generation of students to another, generally as a gift. **1929** *WV Review* Oct 9, These words have been hand-downs from the past. . . This . . is an argument in favor of the hand-down theory. **1965–70** *DARE* (Qu. U3, *A . . garment that is passed on from one person to another*) 36 Infs, **scattered,** Hand-down.

hander See **hand** v

handfish v, hence vbl n *handfishing* **esp MO** Cf **grabble** v **2, hog C8, snag**

See quots.

1966–69 *DARE* (Qu. P13, . . *Ways of fishing . . besides . . hook and line*) Inf **IA**45, Handfish—stick hands in fishes' gills and pull them out on hot days; **MO**2, 15, **PA**35, Handfishing; **MO**3, Handfishing—done when catfish are spawning; two persons involved, one stops one hole of [fish] nest under rock [while] the other reaches in other hole; the fish generally bite the hand but if you don't withdraw it the bite is not painful; you really get some nice channel cat that way—illegal; [**AR**42, Catch [hogfish] with hand; **NY**198, Hands]. **1989** *DARE* File **neMO,** Handfishing is a way of catching fish. . . You go down to the river . . and look for a hole—that's a pocket or hole that cuts back in under the bank. The hole might be up to an arm's length deep. And what you want is for a catfish say, to be lying in that hole, waiting. You just reach in with your hand and grab whatever's in the hole. You hope to grab it by the mouth, but anyway you grab it. Then you haul it out and try to throw it all the way onto the bank as quick as you can because some of these fish are quite large. That's handfishing.

hand-fried adj Cf **home fried potatoes, pan-fried**

1969 *DARE* (Qu. H47, . . *Fried potatoes*) Inf **NY**162, Hand-fried, cut up, sliced thin, cooked raw in fat or oil.

handful of minutes n

See quot.

1953 *PADS* 19.11 **sAppalachians,** *Handful of minutes*. . . Denoting smallness. "She ain't no bigger than a handful of minutes, but she can whip us."

hand game n

1969 *DARE* (Qu. EE7, . . *Marble games*) Inf **KY**17A, The hand game, a series of holes; you started by putting your thumb in the hole and making a sweep with your hand. You could shoot to the next hole from the edge of the sweep.

hand going adv phr **sAppalachians**

=hand running 1.

1890 *DN* 1.65 **KY,** *Hand running.* As in Bartlett. *Hand going* (negro, *hand gwine*) means the same thing. **1911** *DN* 3.538 **eKY,** *Hand-going*. . . In succession . . "He was there two days hand-going." **1940** (1968) Haun *Hawk's Done Gone* 118 **eTN,** Meady got scared . . and blowed the fox horn. She blowed it long and loud. Three times hand-going she blowed it. **1944** *PADS* 2.19 **sAppalachians,** *Hand-goin'*. . . One after another. Same as *hand-runnin'*. "Mace's Jim sot up with [=courted] Nance's Liz two nights hand-goin'."

hand horse n **Delmarva**

=near horse.

1949 Kurath *Word Geog.* 46, The Eastern Shore of Maryland and southern Delaware. . . Here we find *hand horse* for the near-horse. **1968** *DARE* (Qu. K32b, *The horse on the left side in plowing or hauling*) Infs **MD**13, 38, Hand horse.

handily adv **sAppalachians** Cf **kindly**

See quot 1952.

1913 Kephart *Highlanders* 297 **sAppalachians,** You cain't handily blame her. **1928** Chapman *Happy Mt.* 31 **seTN,** But, Dena, you can't handily blame a man when things get all mazed in his head. **1952** Brown *NC Folkl.* 1.549, *Handily*. . . Rightly, justly. "You can't handily get rid of him."

handing See **hand** v

handing-over n, exclam [Prob var of **handy-over**]

=Antony-over.

1970 *DARE* (Qu. EE22, . . *Game in which they throw a ball over a building . . to a player on the other side*) Inf **VA**69B, Handing-over; (Qu. EE23a, . . *What do you call out when you throw the ball?*) Inf **VA**69B, Handing-over.

handiron n[1] [Folk-etym for **andiron;** *OED handiron* "obs. form of *Andiron*" → 1793] **chiefly Atlantic**

1649 in 1916 MA (Colony) Probate Court (Essex Co.) *Records* 1.99, One paire Hande Irons. **c1783** in 1941 Woodward *Ploughs & Politicks* 408 **NJ,** Hand Irons Fire shovel & Tongs. **1790** in 1956 Eliason *Tarheel Talk* 306 **NC,** Handirons. **1891** *DN* 1.167 **cNY,** [H] is excrescent in *'handiron'* < *andiron* by folk-etymology. **1946** *PADS* 5.25 **VA,** *Handirons* . . Iron utensils used to support the wood in a fireplace. **1949** Kurath *Word Geog.* 51, In the *andirons* area the common folk not infrequently say *hand irons,* especially (1) in an area extending from Delaware Bay to the Rappahannock in Virginia and (2) in the northern counties of Pennsylvania. **1962** *AmSp* 37.173 **eNC,** In the total absence of *dog irons, dogs,* and *firedogs* in Ocracoke usage, we may consider *andirons,* which together with one instance of *handirons* takes their place, a true folk word in Ocracoke usage. **1965–70** *DARE* (Qu. D32, *The metal stands in a fireplace that the logs are laid on*) Infs **DE**1, 3, **IA**43, **KY**85, **MA**17, **NJ**3, 67, **NY**24, 200, **OH**98, **PA**134, **VA**4, 47, 75, **VT**16, Handirons. **1981** Pederson *LAGS Basic Materials,* 9 infs, **Gulf Region,** Handiron(s).

hand iron n[2]

A flatiron.

1965–70 *DARE* (Qu. F29, *Different kinds of irons—not electric*) 20 Infs, **scattered,** Hand irons. **1967** LeCompte *Word Atlas* 134 **seLA,** *Device / not electric / to smooth clothes after washing*—hand iron [3 of 21 infs].

hand-it-over n [Prob var of **handy-over**]

=Antony-over A.

1968 *DARE* (Qu. EE22, . . *Game in which they throw a ball over a building . . to a player on the other side*) Inf **KS**7, Hand-it-over.

handkäse n [Ger]

=hand cheese.

1948 *AmSp* 23.107 **swIL,** A small, homemade cheese is called locally [=in a German settlement area] a *handkäse. Handkäse* is a hard cheese, round in shape. **1950** *WELS (Different kinds of home-made cheese)* 1 Inf, **seWI,** Hand cheese, Handkäse.

handkerchief n Usu |'hæŋkə(r)čɪf, -čif|; also |'hænkərčif, 'hæŋkəčə, 'hænčə(r)| Pronc-spp *hanchker, hanke(r)cher, hansker, hengkitchuh;* for addit pronc and sp varr see **A** below

A Forms.

1795 Dearborn *Columbian Grammar* 136, *List of Improprieties,* Hankicher for Handkerchief. **1823** Cooper *Pioneers* 1.220 **cNY,** It would be as easy to stop a hurricane with a Barcelony hankerchy. **1826** Royall *Sketches* 58 **WV,** They pronounce . . handkerchief *hancorchy,* (emphasis on the second syllable). **1843** (1916) Hall *New Purchase* 431 **IN,** They jumped down to pick up Polly Logrul's "bag as had her handkichif in!" **1844** Thompson *Major Jones's Courtship* 36 **GA,** They had to put ther hankerchers to ther faces to hide the tears. **1859** (1968) Bartlett *Americanisms* xxvii, *Hankecher* [for] handkerchief. **1861** Holmes *Venner* 1.120 **wMA,** Scent your pocket-handkerchers. **1872** Schele de Vere *Americanisms* 485, *Handkercher* . . There can be no doubt that the word was, in the 17th century, written by good authors exactly as it was pronounced, and thus imported from England into Virginia, where it has maintained itself unchanged to the present day. In Pennsylvania, *hankitcher* is quoted by Dr. Elwyn, and *hangcatcher* by S. S. Haldeman. **1889** *MLN* 4.206 **TN,** *Handkercher* is a form of the word *handkerchief* which is sometimes heard. . . The negroes contract it still further, as . . han'kcher. **1899** Catherwood *Queen of Swamp* 36 **OH,** John can't go anywhere unless she ties his neck han'ketcher for him. **1899** (1912) Green *VA Folk-Speech* 215, *Hankercher*. . . A handkerchief. **1902** *DN* 2.236 **sIL,** *Handkerchief* [hænkə-čif]. . . Pronounced with n not *ŋ*.

1907 *DN* 3.223 **nwAR,** *Handkerchief.* . . Pronounced [hænkəčɪf.] **1908** *DN* 3.318 **eAL, wGA,** *Handk(er)cher.* . . Handkerchief. . . Also pronounced [hænktəšif] [sic]. **1916** *Scribner's Mag.* 59.358/1 **Sth** [Black], De men an' de gells a-stuffin' dey pocket-hanchkers in dey moufs. **1922** Gonzales *Black Border* 153 **sSC, GA coasts** [Gullah], Tie de aig' een yo' hengkitchuh. **1927** *DN* 5.470 **Appalachians,** *Handkerchief*—hankersher. **1930** *DN* 6.81 **cSC,** *Hankcherkuf.* The usual pronunciation of handkerchief. **c1938** in 1970 Hyatt *Hoodoo* 2.971 **seGA,** Git chew a pocket hans'cuff. *Ibid* 1130 **seGA,** All dat she gotta do is tuh buy a nickel plain han'chief. **1952** Brown *NC Folkl.* 1.549, *Hancher* ['hænčə, -ɚ] . . *Handkerchief.*—Illiterate. **1953** Brewer *Word Brazos* 21 **eTX** [Black], She teck out her hankershuf an' staa't to cryin'. **1955** Ritchie *Singing Family* 90 **seKY,** He'd take his hankcher and wipe off his face. **c1960** *Wilson Coll.* **csKY,** *Handkerchief* /hæŋkə·čə/, rarely. **1969** Emmons *Deep Rivers* 35 **eTX** [Black], Me and my sisters give him our hanchikifs. **1982** Walker *Color Purple* 29 **GA** [Black], She sit down and start to fan herself with a hansker. It sure is hot, she say. **1985** *Esquire* Aug 111, The large, white "twenty-five-cent hanskers" her grandfather had used.

B Sense.

The game of drop-the-handkerchief. **esp KY, TN**

1946 TN Folk Lore Soc. *Bulletin* Mar 18, A game not so active and one affording a chance for the love-lorn to bestow slight attention was "Handkerchief." **1967–70** *DARE* (Qu. EE1, . . *Games . . children play around here, in which they form a ring, and either sing or recite a rhyme*) Infs **KY**40, 41, 50, 74, **LA**11, **TN**62, 66, Handkerchief.

handkerchief head n *among Black speakers*

1 An **Uncle Tom.** [See quot 1959] Cf **head rag**

1942 *Amer. Mercury* 55.223.95 [Harlem slang], Handkerchief-head—sycophant type of Negro; also an *Uncle Tom.* **1944** Myrdal *Amer. Dilemma* 774 **Sth** [Among urban Blacks], They can afford to take it out on their leaders by defaming them for their "kowtowing," . . and "Uncle Tomming"; by calling them "handkerchief heads" and "hats in hand." **1950** Lomax *Mr. Jelly Roll* 233 **LA,** This corny old handkerchief-head would assert that Count Basie did not know piano. **1956** Longstreet *Real Jazz* 147, A *handkerchief-head* is an old-fashioned Negro who doesn't know his rights. **1959** Tallman *Dict. Amer. Folkl.* 139, *"Handkerchief heads"*—A term of insult to what the modern Negro calls the "take it easy boys." They are the ones willing to accept compromise on segregation or who will accept white restrictions without protest. The reference is to the bandannas worn by the old mammies and thus symbolizes the Negro of slavery days. **1960** Williams *Walk Egypt* 84 **GA,** They said this to farm kin whom they had left five or ten years ago, scoffing at them for "handkerchief-head niggers" and "kissingfoots." **1972** Claerbaut *Black Jargon* 67, *Handkerchief head.* . . A black male who is a traitor to his race. **1976** Flexner *America Talking* 45, One's *conk* . . or processed hair was often covered with a protective *do-rag,* which is why Black militants of the 1960s called subservient Blacks handkerchief heads.

2 See quots.

1970 Major *Dict. Afro-Amer. Slang* 64, *Handkerchief head* . . (1940's) one who wears a rag on his head to preserve his expensively processed hair-do. **1972** Claerbaut *Black Jargon* 67, *Handkerchief head.* . . A black male who has a processed hairstyle with a head scarf covering it.

handle n, v[1] Usu |hændəl|; freq |hænl| Pronc-spp *hanl, han'le, hannle*

A Forms.

1878 *Appletons' Jrl.* 5.413 **PA,** The Pennsylvanian . . says *cannle,* and *hannle,* and *bunnle,* for *candle,* and *handle,* and *bundle.* **1891** *DN* 1.166 **cNY,** [hænl]. **1902** *DN* 2.236 **sIL,** [hænl]. . . Handle, as ax-hanl. **1910** *DN* 3.456 **KY,** *Handle* (han'le), *v.* **1942** Hall *Smoky Mt. Speech* 87, [d] after [n] is in most cases not sounded before [l] . . as in . . handle. **c1960** *Wilson Coll.* **csKY,** *Handle* /hænl̩/, nearly always.

B As noun.

1 also *pen handle, wooden handle:* The shaft of a **dip pen.** **scattered exc SE** See Map Cf **staff**

[**1902** Sears *Catalogue* 267, Straight Handled Penholder.] **1965–70** *DARE* (Qu. JJ10b, *Parts of an ink pen*) 66 Infs, **scattered exc SE,** Handle; **CA**27, **MI**55, **MO**38, **NY**103, **PA**97, 124, 126, **SC**2, **WI**5, Pen handle; **MA**53, Wooden handle.

2 The nose. [*OED handle* sb. 1639 →]

1950 *WELS (Common or joking words for the nose)* 5 Infs, **WI,** Handle. **1965–70** *DARE* (Qu. X14, *Joking words for the nose*) Infs **AR**51, **GA**1, **IN**32, **MN**39, **NY**205, **VA**102, **WA**18, Handle; **UT**7, Handle on his face; (Qu. X15, . . *Kinds of noses*) Inf **MD**21, Handle.

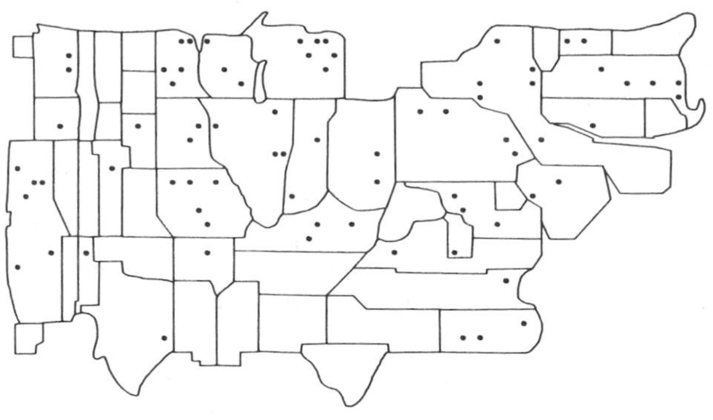

•handle n, v[1] B1 + varr (Qu. JJ10b)

3 A title or epithet used with a name. **now esp Sth, S Midl**

1858 Hammett *Piney Woods Tavern* 106, We hadn't got hauled out inter the stream [=gulf stream] afore the rest on us got a handle fixed to his axe, and it was "Petersham"; and most a grand name it was; it was named after his coat. **1870** (1935) Duval *Advent. Big Foot* 236 **TX,** I would rather be called "Big-Foot Wallace" than "Lying Wallace". . . Such handles to my name would not be agreeable. **1875** Holland *Sevenoaks* 8 **N Atl,** My name is Butterworth, I tell you, and it's got a handle to it. **1916** Lincoln *Mary-'Gusta* 219 **MA,** A handle's all right on a jug or a sasspan, but don't seem as if 'twas necessary to take hold of a friend's name by. **1946** *AmSp* 21.33 **TX** [College slang], *Handle.* . . A title, such as 'fish' or 'mister,' used before a name. **1966–67** *DARE* FW Addit **SC,** "You put a handle to my name?"—means that he should call the speaker (Negro) *Uncle* Ben, not just Ben. *Ibid* **SC,** Auntie. Title applied to older Negroes, also without the name if you didn't know it. You were supposed to put a handle to all elderly people. *Ibid* **AR,** *Handle*—"Mr." or "Mrs." (and perhaps "Dr." and "Miss") before a name. "They got two white men on that ballot, they didn't put no handle in front of *their* names, but that damn Nigger they put *Mrs.* Ollie Davis."

C As verb.

1 To castrate. *euphem*

1949 *AmSp* 24.109 **eSC,** *Handle.* . . To castrate. **1968** *DARE* (Qu. K70, *Words used around here for castrating an animal*) Inf **MD**34, Handle, in the old days, today castrate.

‡2 See quot.

1969 *DARE* (Qu. K10, *Words used about a cow that is going to have a calf*) Inf **NY**189, Handling; heavy with calf.

handle v[2] [Ger *handeln* to dicker or haggle]

1968 *DARE* (Qu. U12, *If you were buying something and you argued with the person selling it till you made him lower the price, you might say, "I ________."*) Inf **WI**48, Handled.

hand leap n

1966–69 *DARE* (Qu. EE9b, *If children jump forward, land on the hands, and turn over*) Inf **MO**20, Hand leap.

handlebars n pl Cf **long handles**

1967 *DARE* (Qu. W14, *Names for underwear, including joking names. Men's—long*) Inf **IA**13, Handlebars; **NE**3, Long handlebars.

handle basket n **SC**

=handbasket 1.

1966–68 *DARE* (Qu. F17, *What peaches come in*) Inf **SC**3, Handle basket—½ bushel [FW illustr: a small basket with a woven, rectangular body and a wooden handle across the width]; **SC**19, 43, 46, 51, Handle basket. **1967** *DARE* Tape **SC**38, It [=a peach basket] has a handle, it's a woven basket more or less out of wide pieces. . . Just call it a handle basket.

handles See **long handles**

handle to a hen's nest See **hen's nest 2**

hand-mammy n

A midwife.

1970 *DARE* (Qu. AA30, *An older woman who comes in . . to help when a baby is going to be born*) Inf **TN**46, Hand-mammy was said by my great-grandmother.

hand man n [Redund **hand** n **B1** + *man*]

1969 *DARE* (Qu. L1, *A man who is employed to help with work on a farm*) Inf **VT**16, Hand man.

hand-me-down adj, n **chiefly N Midl, West** *somewhat old-fash*

Ready-made; a ready-made piece of clothing.

1882 Peck *Peck's Sunshine* 213, A hand bill for a Chicago hand-me-down clothing store. **1893** *KS Univ. Qrly.* 1.139 **KS,** *Hand-me-down:* ready-made, as, a hand-me-down suit of clothes. **1896** (1898) Ade *Artie* 170 **Chicago IL,** They'll be workin' for some Reub that come into town wearin' hand-me-downs. **1926** Finerty *Criminalese* 30, *Hand-me-downs*—Ready-made clothing. **1951** Johnson *Resp. to PADS 20* **DE,** *(A dress not made at home—one you buy:)* Hand-me-down. **1960** Bailey *Resp. to PADS 20* **KS,** Hand-me-down. **1965–70** *DARE* (Qu. U2, *What do you call a piece of clothing not made at home—one that you buy?*) 20 Infs, **chiefly N Midl, West,** Hand-me-down. [16 of 20 Infs old, 18 of 20 Infs male]

hand-over exclam [Prob var of **handy-over**]

=**Antony-over.**

1966 *DARE* Tape **AL**1, The one that has the ball holler "hand-over," then you throw it over there. **1970** *DARE* (Qu. EE23a, *In the game of andy-over . . what . . you call out when you throw the ball*) Inf **VA**69, Hand-over.

hand pie n

1967 *DARE* (Qu. H63, . . *Desserts*) Inf **KY**34, Hand pie, made of dried apples.

hand pocket n [Perh blend of **handbag 1** + *pocketbook*]

See quots.

1958 *PADS* 29.11 **TN,** *Handpocket,* A bag, handbag. **c1960** *Wilson Coll.* **csKY,** *Hand pocket,* Handbag, reticule.

hand purse n

Perh a coin purse.

1968 *DARE* (Qu. U30, *What . . you keep money in when you carry it around with you*) Inf **NC**50, Hand purse.

hand rag n Cf **facecloth**

See quots.

1939 *LANE* Map 141 **csCT,** Hand rag, for washing children's faces. **1968** *DARE* Tape **IN**18, Wipe 'im [=a catfish] off good with a rough rag, like a hand rag, inside and out.

hand-rite See **handwrite**

handrock n Cf **handstone**

1949 *AmSp* 24.109 **neSC,** *Hand-rock.* . . Whetstone. **1981** Pederson *LAGS Basic Materials (A portable sharpening stone for sharpening a scythe)* 1 inf, **nwMS,** Hand rock [hæ·énd ra·k].

hand-roomance n, exclam Cf **clearance(s), roundance**

In marble play: room or space for one's hands; a call to claim same.

1868 *Jasper* (Texas) *News-Boy* 11 Jan. 4 *(DA),* 'Hand-roomance!' shouts the boy at his game of marbles. **1883** (1971) Harris *Nights with Remus* 67 **GA,** Ef you'll des gimme han'-roomance en come one at a time, de tussle'll las' longer. [Footnote:] Southern readers will recognize this [Vents yo' uppance!] and han'-roomance as terms used by negroes in playing marbles,—a favorite game on the plantations Sunday afternoons. These terms were curt and expressive enough to gain currency among whites. **1892** Harris *Uncle Remus & Friends* 306 **GA,** I got ter have all de han' roomance what I kin git.

hand rubber n

1968 *DARE* (Qu. F49, . . *A rubber band*) Inf **GA**17, Hand rubber.

hand running adv phr [Cf *EDD* (at *hand* 1. (79))]

1 Consecutively, in succession; continuously. **widespread, but more freq Sth, S Midl**

1859 (1968) Bartlett *Americanisms* 187, *Hand running.* Consecutively: as, "He can hit the bull's eye at fifty paces ten times hand running." **1890** *DN* 1.65 **KY,** *Handrunning.* As in Bartlett. **1893** Owen *Voodoo Tales* 13 **MO** [Black], Dey bin mad hand-runnin' sence dat. **1898** Lloyd *Country Life* 16 **AL,** I could sleep a whole entire week hand runnin. **1899** (1912) Green *VA Folk-Speech* 214, *Hand running.* . . In immediate succession; without break; consecutively: as, "He went five days hand-running." **1902** *DN* 2.236 **sIL. 1906** *DN* 3.119 **sIN. 1907** *DN* 3.223 **nwAR, sIL. 1908** *DN* 3.318 **eAL, wGA. 1913** *DN* 4.4 **csME. 1929** Sale *Tree Named John* 20 **MS** [Black], She had good dreams about that baby for the last three Friday nights "han' runnin'." **1932** Smiley *Gloss. New Paltz* **seNY,** I heard Mrs. Vredenburg use the expression "mop two days hand running". **1944** *PADS* 2.43 **GA, LA, NC, SC, TN, VA,** *Hand-running.* . . Continuously. "I been setting up two nights hand-running." **1950** *WELS (One right after the other, in succession)* 5 Infs, **WI,** Hand running. **1965** Garrison *What's in a Word* 45, When a player received a number of good cards in a single deal, he spoke of getting them "in the run of a hand." This implied quick succession, so *hand running* came to designate any group of things which follow one another rapidly or consecutively. **1965–70** *DARE* (Qu. KK33, *Other ways of saying 'in succession'*) 23 Infs, **scattered but more freq Missip Valley, West,** Hand running. **1973** *Patrick Coll.* **Sth.**

2 as *hand-a-running:* See quot.

1945 Colcord *Sea Language* 93, *Hand-a-running* . . Fast and easily. . . Alongshore, hand-a-running means in succession.

handsault n Also *hand somersault* [Blend of **handspring** + *somersault*]

=**handspring a.**

1969 *DARE* (Qu. EE9b, *If children jump forward, land on the hands, and turn over*) Inf **MO**32, Handsault, hand somersault.

handshaker n [From the custom of shaking the hands of nearby worshippers as part of the service] Cf **Methodist handshake**

See quot.

1967 *DARE* (Qu. CC4, . . *Nicknames . . for various religions or religious groups*) Inf **OH**31, Handshakers = Methodists.

hand shark n Cf **moose sled**

1975 Gould *ME Lingo* 124, *Hand shark*—A farmer's utility hand sled. Used about as a *moose sled* in the woods, it replaced the summertime wheelbarrow. *Moose sleds* often had wooden runners, but *hand sharks* were generally ironed.

hand shoe n Also, by analogy, *hand sock* [Prob Ger *Handschuh* glove]

A glove or mitten.

1930 *RR Man's Mag.* June 470, Hand shoes—Gloves. **1958** McCulloch *Woods Words* 79 **Pacific NW,** *Hand shoes*—Gloves. . . *Hand sox*—Gloves or mittens. **1976** Gould *Blackie's RR Hdbk.* 16, *Hand shoes:* Mitten or gloves.

hands-in-the-pocket weather n

1986 Hendrickson *Amer. Talk* 161, Colorful Pennsylvania Dutch idioms include *hands-in-the-pocket weather* for very cold weather.

handsled n Also *handsleigh* **chiefly Nth, esp NEng**

A light vehicle on runners, not drawn by animals, as:

a One used for hauling or carrying; also v *handsled* to haul on such a sled.

1746 in 1889 NH Hist. Soc. *Coll.* 9.141, Went to mill with a hand sled. **1832** NH Hist. Soc. *Coll.* 3.190 (as of 1760s), When neither oxen or horses could be conveniently used, a ready substitute was found by the athletic husbandman in his hand-sled. **1841** Powers *Hist. Sketches* 70 **NEng** (as of c1770), They prepared a rude hand sleigh. . . The flat and wide side was the bottom of the runner, and it was bent up forward. **1877** VT State Bd. Ag. *Report* 4.92, Provided with a handsled, the boy would first roll on to it the back log. **1934** *Hanley Disks* **neME,** They'd handsled it (wood) out on wide-runner handsleds. **1939** (1962) Thompson *Body & Britches* 158 **NY,** You ought to trade that horse off for a handsled; you could draw it a great deal easier. **1943** *LANE* Map 573–574, *Hand sled* is used of 'coasting sleds' as well as of handdrawn 'work sleds'. **1965** *DARE* Tape **MA**92, [FW:] How did you get them [=large stones] out? [Inf:] Well, some of them on a handsled when there's little snow on the woods, and some of them with tackle blocks as they call it. **1968–69** *DARE* (Qu. N40a, . . *Sleighs . . for hauling loads*) Inf **PA**163, Handsled; (Qu. N40c, . . *Sleighs for carrying . . things*) Inf **NY**92, Handsleigh, small, used for hauling wood; **NY**127, Handsleigh; (Qu. N42, *Vehicles for a baby or small child*) Inf **NY**88, Handsleigh, in wintertime.

b One used by children for coasting on snow.

1842 *Lowell Offering* 2.116 **MA,** Then commenced the delightful sport of sliding down hill, seated on a hand-sled—the boys in the front part, and the girls on the hinder part. **1923** *Outing* Jan 152/3, Farther along, the land takes the form of a hog's-back, an ideal place for the toboggan and the hand-sleigh. **1943** [see **a** above]. **1950** *WELS (Names for different kinds of sleighs)* 2 Infs, **WI,** Handsled; 1 Inf, Handsled, for children **1950** *WELS Suppl.* 1 Inf, **swWI,** *Handsleigh;* a child's sled; 1 Inf, **csWI,** *Handsled;* used by children **1966–69** *DARE* (Qu. EE24a, *When there's snow, children go down the hill on a ______*) Infs **NH**5, **NY**75, 113, Handsled; **ID**1, **NY**88, 199, Handsleigh; **NY**92, Handsleigh, small, used by kids.

handsled v See **handsled** n **a**

handsleigh See **handsled** n

hand's length exclam Cf **hand-roomance**

In marble play: see quots.

1934 *AmSp* 9.75 **csND,** *Hand's length.* The cry entitles one to move his shooter a hand's length nearer to the marbles before shooting. **1942** Berrey–Van den Bark *Amer. Slang* 665.6, *Hand's length.* . . A call for permission to move the "shooter" a given distance from the "target" when it is too close to shoot. **1955** *PADS* 23.19 *Hand's length* . . A call that allows the shooter to move his marble or taw away from the defensive marble in order to allow greater freedom of movement. **c1970** Wiersma *Marbles Terms* **csMI,** *Hand's length*—A call entitling a player to move his marble a hand's length closer to the target marble.

hand sock See **hand shoe**

handsome adv, adj Pronc-spp *hahnsome, ha(h)nsum, harnsome*

A Forms.

1815 Humphreys *Yankey in England* 105 **NEng,** *Hansum,* handsome. **1854** Stephens *High Life in NY* 226, A holding in two tremendous harnsome black horses that stood hitched to the carriage. **1858** Holmes *Autocrat* 297, *Eighteen hundred;*—it came and found / The Deacon's Masterpiece strong and sound./ Eighteen hundred increased by ten; —/ "Hahnsum kerridge" they called it then. **1861** Holmes *Venner* 1.167 **wMA,** Very hahnsome supper,—very hahnsome. . . there's meat and cakes and pies and pickles enough on that table to spread a hahnsome cōlation.

B As adv.

Handsomely.

1913 Kephart *Highlanders* 121 **sAppalachians,** The big fellers that makes lots of money out o' stillin', and lives in luxury, ought to pay handsome for it. **1939** Coffin *Capt. Abby* 48 **ME** (as of c1860s), The older children had spread out handsome, for certain. In the year 1840, Jacob's old eyes saw four big mansions already around his modest house on the hill.

handsome Harry n

A **meadow beauty** (here: *Rhexia virginica*).

1893 *Jrl. Amer. Folkl.* 6.142, *Rhexia Virginica,* handsome Harry. Hanover, Mass. **1896** *Ibid* 9.188, *Rhexia Virginica* . . handsome Harry, Eastern Mass. **1933** Small *Manual SE Flora* 927, *Handsome-Harry.* . . Sandy swamps and damp meadows. **1974** (1977) Coon *Useful Plants* 186, Handsome Harry. . . has pretty purple flowers and leaves of a sweetish acid taste which may be eaten by man.

handsome husband n Cf **old maid**

1966–69 *DARE* (Qu. H71, *Words for the last piece of food left on a plate*) Inf **MA**38, Handsome husband; [**MD**50, If you take the last piece, you'll get a handsome husband; **MA**10, Get a handsome husband if you take the last piece; **MA**65, If a girl gets the last piece you say she's going to have a handsome husband]. [All Infs female, old]

hand somersault See **handsault**

handspan n Cf **handstand 1**

1969 *DARE* (Qu. EE9b, *If children jump forward, land on the hands, and turn over*) Inf **GA**72, Handspan.

handspring n Note: It is not always possible to determine to which sense some of the following quots apply.

Any of var tumbling feats in which the body turns end over end, as:

a also *flying handspring, handspring jump:* One in which the body starts upright, flips first to the hands, and then quickly to the feet. **widespread, but less freq S Atl**

1872 Twain *Roughing It* 63, He would actually throw one handspring after another. **1895** *Nation* 19 Dec 437/3 **NY,** Children . . throwing handsprings. **1943** *LANE* Map 578, A different kind of turn, in which the hands but not the head touch the ground, is called a *handspring.* **c1960** *Wilson Coll.* **csKY,** *Handspring*—A somersault without touching the head to the ground or floor. **1965–70** *DARE* (Qu. EE9b, *If children jump forward, land on the hands, and turn over*) 583 Infs, **widespread, but less freq S Atl,** Handspring; **DE**7, Flying handspring; **SC**26, Handspring jump.

b A somersault.

1893 Farmer–Henley *Slang* 3.260, *Handsprings. To chuck handsprings* . . (common).—To turn somersaults. **1943** *LANE* Map 578 **ceMA,** *[Handspring] = somersault,* different from a [cartwheel]. **1966–68** *DARE* (Qu. EE9a, *The children's trick of turning over rapidly straight forward close to the ground*) Infs **AR**24, 28, **NJ**8, Handspring. **1973** Allen *LAUM* 1.392 (as of c1950), [For *somersault*] *Handspring,* offered by five Minnesotans who insist upon this meaning for the word.

c A cartwheel.

1943 *LANE* Map 578 **seMA,** *[Handspring]* thought to be the same as cartwheel. **1950** *WELS (The children's trick of turning over rapidly sideways)* 13 Infs, **WI,** Handspring; 1 Inf, We sometimes say handspring instead of cartwheel. **1965–70** *DARE* (Qu. EE9c, . . *If children spread their arms and turn over sideways*) Infs **IN**61, **KY**11, **MI**34, 44, **NH**17, **NY**52, 75, **OH**89, **TN**24, Handspring; **MD**20, Side handspring.

handspring jump See **handspring a**

hand stack n

A small stack or pile of hay or grain.

1902 *DN* 2.236 **sIL,** *Handstack.* . . Small stack of grain or hay, which, owing to error in building the main stack, must be placed in a small stack by itself. **1949** Kurath *Word Geog.* 54, Other terms for the haycock . . *hand stack,* scattered in Pennsylvania. **c1950** *Atlas Checklists* **neIL, WI,** Handstacks. Small piles of hay in the fields. **1967–69** *DARE* (Qu. L12, . . *Small piles of hay standing in the field*) Infs **AL**31, **IL**77, 83, **NY**140, **PA**232, Hand stacks. **1971** Wood *Vocab. Change* 43 **Sth,** As for hay, the small piles in the field are . . *hand stacks.* **1973** Gawthrop *Dial. Calumet* 78 **nwIN.** **1973** Allen *LAUM* 1.186 (as of c1950), [Haycock]—the Pennsylvania *handstack,* reported five times in South Dakota, twice in Iowa, and once each in North Dakota and Nebraska.

handstand n

1 =**handspring a.**

1965–70 *DARE* (Qu. EE9b, *If children jump forward, land on the hands, and turn over*) Infs **LA**23, **MO**14, **MA**82, 100, **NC**47, **OH**46, 77, **PA**23, Handstand; **TX**104, Front handstand.

2 =**handspring c.**

1969 *DARE* (Qu. EE9c, . . *If children spread their arms and turn over sideways*) Inf **NY**211, Handstand.

handstick n

See quot 1950.

1946 Wilson *Fidelity Folks* 204 **swKY,** We could lift at the end of a handstick until our eyes bulged. **1950** *PADS* 14.35 **SC,** *Handstick,* A stout pole, six to eight feet long, used in carrying heavy timber. The *handstick* is placed under the timber forward of the middle and one man lifts on either side. The tail end is then carried by one man who *tails* the burden. Two handsticks may also be used with four bearers. **c1960** *Wilson Coll.* **csKY,** *Handstick,* A strong stick, usually of hickory, used in lifting logs at a log-rolling. Called also handspike.

handstone n Cf **handrock**

A small whetstone.

1950 *WELS* 1 Inf, **cWI,** To sharpen tools in the field a handstone is used. **1966–69** *DARE* (Qu. L38, *What . . you use around here to sharpen tools in the field*) Infs **AK**4, **CA**111, 117, 161, **MI**38, **WI**42, Handstone.

hand's turn n

1 See quot.

1899 (1912) Green *VA Folk-Speech* 214, *Hand's-turn.* . . A helping hand; assistance.

2 A stroke of work—usu in neg constrs. Cf **turn a hand**

1901 *DN* 2.141 **nNY,** *Hand's turn.* . . "Hadn't done a hand's-turn"—not a thing. **1912** Green *VA Folk-Speech* 214, *Hand's-turn.* . . A piece of work of any kind. "She can't do a hand's-turn at anything." **1968** *DARE* (Qu. LL18, *To do no work at all, not even make any effort: "She hasn't ______ all day."*) Inf **IN**38, Done a hand's turn.

3 in phr *at every hand's turn:* See quot.

1899 (1912) Green *VA Folk-Speech* 214, *Hand's-turn.* . . At every hand's turn: often; frequently. "He has to be waited on at every hand's turn."

hand turn n

1 =handspring a.

1968–69 *DARE* (Qu. EE9b, *If children jump forward, land on the hands, and turn over*) Infs **CT**23, **IN**35, **WV**1, Hand turn.

2 =handspring c.

1969 *DARE* (Qu. EE9c, . . *If children spread their arms and turn over sideways*) Inf **KY**25, Handturn.

hand up v phr [*hand* a bunch of tobacco leaves]

To tie tobacco leaves into a bunch.

1966 *DARE* Tape **FL**26A, With shade tobacco you hand it up. . . You . . take a stick 'n slide the tobacco together on a string 'n take a string 'n wrap it around the head of it 'n that's called a hand. . . about 35 leaves.

handwrite n Also sp *hand-rite* **chiefly Sth, S Midl**

Handwriting.

1836 (1861) Tucker *Partisan Leader* 16 **VA,** He has got a paper in the captain's hand-write to show him the way. **1843** (1916) Hall *New Purchase* 405 **IN,** Clarinse made Polly's step-son bring excusis on paper in hand-rite! **1859** (1968) Bartlett *Americanisms* 187, *Handwrite,* for handwriting, a common barbarism at the South; as "I can't read his *handwrite.*" **1871** Eggleston *Hoosier Schoolmaster* 188 **IN,** Ralph opened the thumb-paper note, written on a page torn from an old copy-book, in Bud's "hand-write." **1893** Shands *MS Speech* 34, *Hand-write* . . for handwriting. . . I think it is especially common among the illiterate whites of Mississippi, who very rarely indeed use the correct form. **1907** *DN* 3.231 **nwAR, seMO,** *Handwrite.* **1908** *DN* 3.318 **eAL, wGA,** *Handwrite.* **1909** in 1917 Twain *Letters* 2.830, I most vividly see your hand-write on a square blue envelop. **1914** *DN* 4.108 **KS,** *Handwrite.* **1969** *DARE* (Qu. JJ11, *Joking names for handwriting that's hard to read*) Inf **TX**75, Handwrite [FW: Inf suggests as common among uneducated].

handy adv [Engl dial; cf *EDD*]

1 Easily, readily.

1931–33 *LANE Worksheets* **eMA,** I might say, dinner's served, but that don't come handy to a New Englander. **1949** Arnow *Hunter's Horn* 281 **KY,** I couldn't handy take all th youngens outside at onct: after bean inside so long they'd start a runnen ever whichway. **1952** Brown *NC Folkl.* 1.549, *Handy*^{1}. . . Easily, quickly, readily. "I'll come as soon as I handy can." . . Old people, Rare.

2 Justly, rightly.

1939 (1962) Thompson *Body & Britches* 305 **NY,** I sorta wanted to keep it, too, but I couldn't refuse it very handy. **1952** Brown *NC Folkl.* 1.549, *Handy*^{2}. . . Rightly, justly. "You just can't handy blame him for not telling you the truth."

3 Well, properly.

1943 Writers' Program NC *Bundle of Troubles* 71, Your dress don't fit atall handy, leastways looks to me like it don't.

4 ?At that time; see quot.

1967 *DARE* Tape **MA**5, They used to leave them [=baked beans] in the oven and have them for Sunday dinner . . and then they wouldn't have to make any preparation handy.

5 with *onto:* **=nigh onto.** Cf **handy to, hard** adv **2**

1943 *LANE* Map 714 1 inf, **eME,** [Equivalents of the adverb in the sentence *It is almost midnight*] Handy onto.

handy-Andy n

=Antony-over A.

1967–70 *DARE* (Qu. EE22, . . *The game in which they throw a ball over a building* . . *to the player on the other side*) Infs **IL**5, 126, **IN**10, Handy-Andy.

handy by See **handy to**

handy-dandy n

1 See quot.

1968 *DARE* (Qu. L28, *Tools used in the past for cutting grain*) Inf **GA**17, Handy-dandy.

2 =hogo n^2.

1973 [see **hogo** n^2].

handy-handy-over, handy-I-over See **handy-over**

handy-iron n Cf **Andy-iron, handiron** n^1

1967 *DARE* (Qu. D32, *The metal stands in a fireplace that the logs are laid on*) Inf **TX**26, Handy-iron [hændi aɪrn].

handy onto See **handy 5**

handy-over n, exclam Also *handy-handy-over, handy-I-over* [Varr of **Andy-over**] **chiefly Missip-Ohio Valleys, Inland Sth** See Map

=Antony-over.

1965–70 *DARE* (Qu. EE22, . . *The game in which they throw a ball over a building* . . *to the player on the other side*) 19 Infs, **chiefly Missip-Ohio Valleys, Inland Sth,** Handy-over; **PA**71, Handy-handy-over; **IA**29, Handy-I-over; (Qu. EE23a, *In the game of andy-over* . . *what* . . *you call out when you throw the ball*) 19 Infs, **chiefly Missip-Ohio Valleys, Inland Sth,** Handy-over; **IA**29, Handy-I-over.

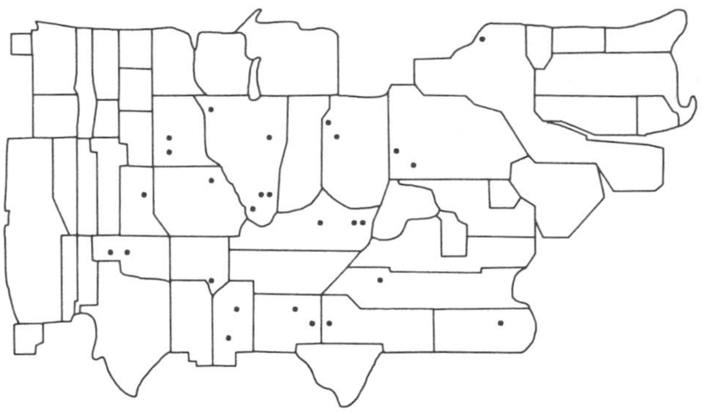

•handy-over + varr (Qq. EE22, EE23a)

handy-spandy n [Var of *handy-dandy;* cf *OED handy-dandy* sb. 1. a quot 1847–78]

1968 *DARE* (Qu. EE3, *Games in which you hide an object and then look for it*) Inf **NJ**30, Handy-spandy, hide it in the hand, guess which hand.

handy to prep phr, adv phr Also *handy by* Cf **handy 5, hard** adj **B2**

Near; nearby.

1893 (1904) French *Stories W. Town* 136, It is customary in the Lossing Building to say, "We are so handy to the cars." **1966–70** *DARE* (Qu. MM6, *Other words meaning 'very close' or 'only a short distance' away: "The house is ______ the park."*) Infs **MI**118, **MA**40, **NY**94, Handy to; **ME**1, Quite handy to; **NH**16, **PA**130, Handy by. **1967** *DARE* Tape **MA**105, The president of the historical society was handy by. **1974** *AmSp* 49.62 **swME** (as of c1900), *Handy-by* . . Nearby.

hang v

A Forms.

1 pres: usu *hang;* also *heng, hing.* Note: The forms *hing* and *heng* are Scots, nEngl dial for *hang* in all senses except "to execute by hanging"; the past is regularly *hang,* past pple *hung.* For more on hist and distribution of forms, see *OED.*

1861 Holmes *Venner* 2.189 **wMA,** I sh'd like t' hev them things wal enough to heng up 'n the stable. **1893** *DN* 1.277 **wCT,** Hang (pron. [hɛŋ]). **1916** Howells *Leatherwood God* 10 **OH,** Long, glossy, jet-black hair hengun down back of his ears. **1922** Gonzales *Black Border* 306 **sSC, GA coasts** [Gullah glossary], *Heng*—hang, hangs, hanged, hung, hanging. **1928** *AmSp* 4.132 **cnNE,** Retch up and hing the 'glim' (the lantern) so's I can bed the horses. **1952** *AmSp* 27.188 **WA,** Words like *hang* and *catch* are regularly pronounced 'heng' and 'ketch.'

2 past: usu *hung;* also, esp with ref to death by hanging, *hanged;* also *esp among Black speakers, hang* (cf Pronc Intro 3.I.22); infreq *hankt, heng, hing, hunkt.*

1836 (1838) Haliburton *Clockmaker* (1st ser) 183 **NEng** [Black], Massa Jim Munroe he hang himself. **1884** *Anglia* 7.252 **SE,** *Pres.* hang—*Past.* hankt, hunkt. **1922** [see **A1** above]. **1950** *WELS* (*He ______ his coat on my hook*) 2 Infs, **WI,** Hanged; 1 Inf, Hung. **1952** Brown *NC Folkl.* 1.550, *Hing.* . . Past tense of hang. **1965–70** *DARE* (Qu. OO8b, . . *He ______ [himself];* not asked in early QRs) 741 Infs, **widespread,** Hung; 208 Infs, **widespread,** Hanged; **MS**80, **MO**1, **SC**10, 26, **VA**70, Hang [4 Infs responding *hang* were Black]; (Qu. OO8c, *He ______ his coat on my hook;* total Infs questioned, 75) 71 Infs, **widespread,** Hung; **FL**28, **OK**6, Hanged, hung; **FL**31, Hang. **1978** *Capital Times* (Madison WI) 15 Aug 2/5, That patient . . later hung herself and died.

3 past pple: usu *hung,* also, esp with ref to death by hanging, *hanged;* infreq *hang, heng.*

c1885 in 1981 Woodward *Mary Chesnut's Civil War* 823 **SC,** This *Herald* announces that Jeff Davis will be hung at once—not so much for treason as for his assassination of Lincoln. **1899** (1912) Green *VA Folk-Speech* 236, *Hung. . .* For *hanged.* "The murderer was hung yesterday." **1916** Lincoln *Mary-'Gusta* 5 **MA,** The knot is supposed to be under your chin, not under your ear as if you were going to be hung. **1922** [see **A1** above]. **1950** *WELS (It has ——— there for two days)* 2 Infs, **WI,** Hanged; 1 Inf, Hung. **1953** Atwood *Survey of Verb Forms* 16, "The murderer was (hanged)." The form *hung* /hʌŋ/ predominates in all areas and among all types. In N. Eng. about one fourth of the informants give the form *hanged* /hæŋd/, more often than not alongside *hung.* There is no clear distinction between the age groups, but *hanged* is slightly more common in the educated types (IIIA and IIIB) than in Types I [=older, poorly educated] and II [=middle-aged, better educated]. Of the cultured informants, nine use only *hanged,* six others use both *hanged* and *hung.* In the M[iddle Atlantic States] *hanged* is used by about one sixth of the Type I informants and by about one third each of the Type II and the cultured informants. In the S[outh Atlantic States] *hanged* is rare (10 occurrences) in Type I and is used by a little less than one third of the Type II and the cultured informants. **1965–70** *DARE* (Qu. OO8a, *Talking about hanging a criminal: "Before the electric chair came in, a murderer would be ———";* not asked in early QRs) 628 Infs, **widespread,** Hung; **CA**200, Hung by the neck til dead; **MI**97, Hung by the rope; 330 Infs, **widespread,** Hanged; **HI**6, **SC**10, Hang up by his neck; (Qu. OO8d, *It has ——— there for two days;* total Infs questioned, 75) 72 Infs, **widespread,** Hung; **GA**1, 7, Hanged.

B Senses.

1 To catch or stick; hence ppl adj *hung* caught, stuck, delayed; also fig.

1840 (1847) Longstreet *GA Scenes* 17, Jake hung his toe in a crack of the floor, and nearly fell. **1859** (1968) Bartlett *Americanisms* 188, *To hang.* To stick fast, come to a standstill; as, the jury *hung.* **1899** (1912) Green *VA Folk-Speech* 215, *Hang. . .* To get fast; catch. . . "Tom hung a big fish but he got away." **1947** Natl. Coal Assoc. *Gloss.* 12, *Hung shot*—A charge in a blast hole which has failed to explode immediately on detonation. **1958** McCulloch *Woods Words* 91 **Pacific NW,** *Hung tree*—In falling timber, a tree which has become jammed against another as it starts to fall to the ground; difficult and often dangerous to release. **1960** Carpenter *Tales Manchaca* 107 **cTX** (as of c1915), My sister Portervine has a pomegranate hung in her mouth and she's fair choking to death. **1966** *DARE* (Qu. P12, *When the fish takes the bait with a quick pull;* total Infs questioned, 75) Inf **FL**7, Got hung good; **MS**72, Hung. **1966–68** *DARE* FW Addit **GA**25, I was fishing on Billy's Lake one day and I hung a great big fish; **cwNC,** Hung—To have the fishing line stuck on trash, logs, rocks, etc. "My line is hung"; **cwNC,** *Hung. . .* To fall in love. "I'm hung"; **ceVA,** "She hung on me." [Inf is referring to his pump action shotgun which had jammed] **1968** *DARE* (Qu. AA28, . . *Joking . . expressions . . to say that another is going to have a baby? "She['s] ———.")* Inf **NY**80, Hung. **1976** Ryland *Richmond Co. VA* 372, *Hang*—catch; "I hung my foot in the rung of the chair." **1981** Harper–Presley *Okefinokee* 40 (as of a1952), Meanwhile the hound had crawled into a very small hollow and got stuck or "hung."

2 often reflexive; also with *up:* To marry. **scattered, but esp C Atl, Ohio Valley** See Map *joc*

1941 *LANE* Map 408 *(Married)* 1 inf, **cCT,** He hung himself. **1965–70** *DARE* (Qu. AA15b, . . *A man is getting married . . "He ———.")* Infs

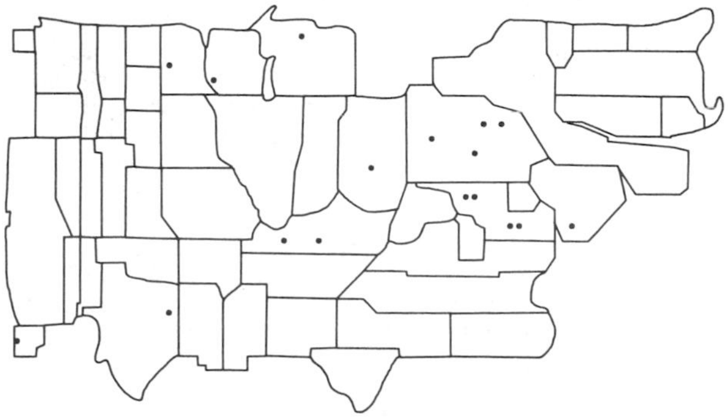

•hang v B2 + varr (Qq. AA15a, b, AA4a)

HI6, **KY**11, **MD**13, 15, 28, **MN**42, **NJ**33, **OH**31, **PA**167, Hung himself; **KY**74, **PA**243, Hanged himself; **PA**42, Got hung; **MD**21, Hung hisself; (Qu. AA4a, . . *A man who is very eager to get married? "He's ———.")* Inf **PA**243, Ready to hang himself; **HI**6, Wants to hang himself; (Qu. AA15a, . . *Joking ways . . of saying that people got married? "They ———.")* Inf **KY**74, Hanged themselves; **MI**19, Are getting hung; **PA**110, Hung themselves; **TX**40, Got hung up; **WI**44, Got hung.

3 See quot.

1968 *DARE* File **ceVA,** *Hang nets,* construct or make fish nets.

C Phrases.

1 in phr *hang and drain:* See quot. [From the process of drying clothes, utensils, etc]

1901 *DN* 2.141 **cNY,** *Hang and drain. . .* Said of an unfinished piece of work; also, in deliberative bodies, of business discussed at unnecessary length. "That motion seems to hang and drain a long time."

2 in phr *hang in:* See quot.

1970 *DARE* (Qu. X43b, *If you sleep later than usual one day on purpose, you'd say, "I ———.")* Inf **FL**51, Hung in.

3 in phr *hang it on one's back* and varr: See quot.

1968–69 *DARE* (Qu. W40, . . *A woman who overdresses or who spends too much on clothes)* Inf **IL**51, Hangs it all on her back; **IA**46, She hangs it on her back; **WI**50, Every cent she earns she hangs on her back.

4 in phr *hang one's lip* and varr: See quots.

1950 *WELS (Somebody who is usually in a bad temper: "She's always ———.")* 1 Inf, **ceWI,** Hanging her lip. **1966–69** *DARE* (Qu. GG35a, *To sulk or pout)* Infs **NY**166, **WA**6, Hang your lip; **CO**3, Hang your lower lip; (Qu. GG35b, *Of a person who acts annoyed or disappointed)* Inf **OH**33, Letting her lip hang down.

5 in phr *hang to the rigging:* See quot.

1966 *DARE* (Qu. GG23c, . . *Expressions [to tell someone to be patient])* Inf **ME**15, Hang to the riggin'.

hang n See **hangman**

hang and drain See **hang** v **C1**

hangaround(er) n Cf **hanger-on**

An idler; a loafer.

1938 (1939) Nash *I'm a Stranger* 240, The hang-arounders' cheerful chirrups. **1950** Lomax *Mr. Jelly Roll* 57 **LA,** The absolute favorite of all the hangarounders in the Garden District. **1967–68** *DARE* (Qu. Y28, *A person who loiters about with nothing to do)* Infs **IA**32, **MN**2, (A) hang-around.

hangback adj

Shy.

1987 Childress *Out of the Ozarks* 60, Matt must have been all of twelve when I first saw him . . a hangback little stringbean who took a while to get acquainted.

hangbird n [From the pendent nest] **esp NEng** Cf **little hangbird**

=Baltimore oriole.

1789 Morse *Amer. Geog.* 59, Upwards of one hundred and thirty American *Birds* have been enumerated . . Hangbird. **1831** (1876) Adams *Memoirs J.Q. Adams* 8.426 **MA,** The oriole of Baltimore is the fiery hang-bird. **1845** Judd *Margaret* 29 **NEng,** She's as bad as a hang-bird that steals my yarn on the grass. **1872** Schele de Vere *Americanisms* 374, The *Oriole . .* is also known as . . *Hangbird* from its peculiar nest. **1907** *DN* 3.189 **seNH,** *Hang-bird. . .* Less common name of the Baltimore oriole than *golden robin.* "Hang-birds hang their nests from elm trees." **1956** MA Audubon Soc. *Bulletin* 40.130, *Baltimore Oriole. . .* Hangbird (N.H., Mass.)

hang by one's eyelashes See **eyelids, hang by one's 2**

hang-downs n pl

1970 *DARE* (Qu. GG34a, *To feel depressed or in a gloomy mood: "He has the ——— today.")* Inf **VA**101, Hang-downs.

hang 'em See **hangman**

hanger n

1 In tobacco farming.

a See quot.

1948 *AmSp* 23.309 **WI** [Tobacco terms], *Hanger* is one layer of tobacco as it is hung.

b See quot. Cf *hander* (at **hand** v)

1966 *PADS* 45.15 **cnKY,** *Hanger. . .* One who hangs sticks of tobacco on the rails of the tobacco barn. . . "The hangers have to climb up in the framework."

2 A woman's breast. Cf **hang-heavy**

1968 *DARE* (Qu. X31, *Other words . . for a woman's breasts*) Inf **IN**9, Hangers.

3 See **hanger-on.**

4 See quot.

1970 *DARE* File **NEng, esp MA,** *Hanger. . .* A bract of linden . . or the winged seeds of maple or ash.

hanger-on n Also *hanger* **chiefly Nth, N Midl**

An idler; a loafer.

1950 *WELS (To go around aimlessly, loiter: . . "He's just a _______.")* 1 Inf, **cWI,** Hanger-on. **1965–70** *DARE* (Qu. Y28, *A person who loiters about with nothing to do*) 15 Infs, **chiefly Nth, N Midl,** Hanger-on; **KS**12, Hanger.

hang-heavy n

1967 *DARE* FW Addit **LA**11, *Hang-heavies,* breasts.

hang in v phr See **hang** v **C2**

hang-in n

c1950 *Hall Coll.* **eTN, wNC,** *Hang-in, stand-in . .* "Pull," influence. "He got a hang-in with a big man."

hanging See **hangman**

hanging bird n [From the pendent nests]

1 An oriole, usu the **Baltimore oriole.**

1778 in 1789 Anburey *Travels* 2.198 **MA,** The most remarkable are the Fire-bird, Hanging-bird, Blue-bird and Humming-bird. **1808** Wilson *Amer. Ornith.* 1.23, Baltimore Oriole . . is generally known, and, as usual, honored with a variety of names, such as Hang-nest, Hanging-bird. **1969** *DARE* (Qu. Q14) Inf **KY**11, Hanging bird, orioles, because they build hanging nests.

2 Either of two vireos: the **red-eyed vireo** or the **white-eyed vireo.**

1924 Howell *Birds AL* 275, The red-eyed vireo, known to many as "hanging bird," is one of the most common . . of our summer birds. *Ibid* 279, Hanging Bird: *Vireo griseus.* **1932** Howell *FL Bird Life* 375, White-eyed Vireo. . . Other Name: Hanging Bird. **1956** MA Audubon Soc. *Bulletin* 40.129, *White-eyed Vireo.* Hanging Bird (Mass. The nest is suspended in the fork of a twig.) **1962** Imhof *AL Birds* 430, *Red-eyed Vireo. . . Other Name:* Hanging Bird. . . The nest is a well-woven, dainty cup suspended . . in a hardwood.

hanging game See **hangman**

hanging moss n

=Spanish moss.

1891 *Century Dict.* 6338, This species *[Tillandsia usneoides]* bears two-ranked awl-shaped recurved leaves, and small solitary green flowers, and is variously known as *Florida moss, hanging-moss,* etc. **1900** Lyons *Plant Names* 372, *T[illandsia] usneoides . .* Hanging Moss. **1940** Clute *Amer. Plant Names* 150, *T[illandsia] usneoides.* Spanish Moss. Long moss, . . vegetable hair, hanging moss.

hang it on one's back See **hang** v **C3**

hangman n Also *hang, hang 'em, hanging (game), hang the butcher* (or *Chinaman*), *hangman's noose, hangsman* **wide-spread, but less freq Sth, S Midl** See Map

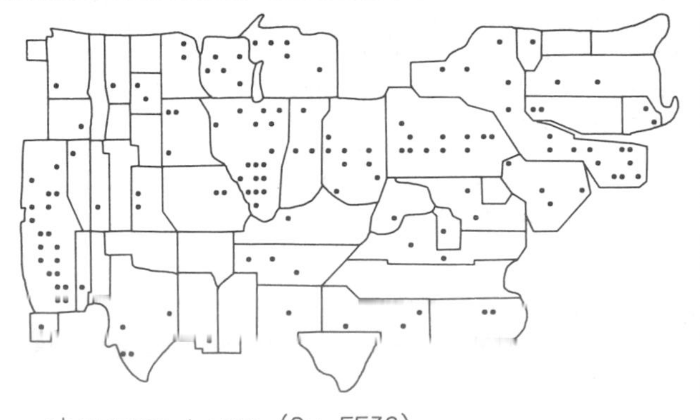

•hangman + varr (Qu. EE39)

A word game in which a player tries to guess a word one letter at a time that another has chosen, one part of a hanged man being drawn for each wrong guess until the player either guesses the word correctly or is hanged.

1899 Champlin–Bostwick *Young Folks' Games* 403, *Hanging game, the,* a game played by two persons, one of whom puts on paper a row of dots, one for each letter of a familiar proverb, while the other tries to guess the proverb. **1950** *WELS (Games played on paper or a blackboard by two people)* 8 Infs, **WI,** Hangman; 2 Infs, Hanging. **1953** Brewster *Amer. Nonsinging Games* 132 **NJ,** *Hang the Butcher.* **1965–70** *DARE* (Qu. EE39, . . *Games played on paper by two people*) 122 Infs, **wide-spread, but less freq Sth, S Midl,** Hangman; **IL**135, **IN**30, **PA**4, **RI**15, Hang; **IL**30, 98, 100, **PA**126, Hang the butcher; **IL**116, Hangman's noose; **KS**15, Hang 'em; **MT**1, Hang the Chinaman; **OK**10, Hangsman.

hangnest n [From the pendent nest] Cf **hammock bird, hang-nest bird, little hangnest**

Either of two orioles: esp the **Baltimore oriole,** but also the **orchard oriole.**

1796 Morse *Amer. Universal Geog.* 1.209, Baltimore Bird, or Hang Nest Oriolus Baltimore. **1844** Giraud *Birds Long Is.* 143, *Baltimore Hang-nest. . .* From the singular manner in which it constructs its nest, which is suspended from the limb of a tree, it is known by the name of "Hang-nest." *Ibid* 144, *Icterus spurius. . .* Orchard Hang-nest. **1874** Coues *Birds NW* 192, *Icterus spurius. . .* Orchard Oriole; Chestnut Hangnest. . . *Icterus Baltimore. . .* Baltimore Oriole; . . Hangnest. **1917** (1923) *Birds Amer.* 2.256, *Orchard Oriole. . . Other Names. . .* Orchard Hang-nest. *Ibid* 258, *Baltimore Oriole. . . Other Names. . .* Hang-nest. **1949** Sprunt–Chamberlain *SC Bird Life* 498, Well made and strongly attached, [the nest] often withstands winter storms and is a conspicuous object in a leafless tree. This type of architecture is responsible for the local name of "hang-nest" in some localities.

hangnest bird n Cf **hanging bird 2, hangnest**

Either the **red-eyed vireo** or the **white-eyed vireo.**

1925 Bailey *Birds FL* 118, *Red-eyed Vireo. . .* Hang nest bird. *Ibid* 120, *White-eyed Vireo. . .* Hang nest bird.

hang-on n [Var of *hanger-on* a parasite]

1966–68 *DARE* (Qu. II18, *Someone who joins himself on to you and your group without being asked and won't leave*) Infs **CA**101, **DC**3, **IN**32, Hang-on.

hang one's lip See **hang** v **C4**

‡hang-out n Cf **hanger-on**

1970 *DARE* (Qu. Y28, *A person who loiters about with nothing to do*) Inf **MA**127, Hang-out.

hangsman See **hangman**

hang the butcher (or Chinaman) See **hangman**

hang the moon v phr **chiefly S Midl**

To be very important; to be exceptionally able or talented—usu in phr *think one hung the moon* to have an extremely high opinion of someone.

1953 Randolph–Wilson *Down in Holler* 250 **Ozarks,** Hang the moon. . . To be very powerful or important. "Lucy thinks that fool boy of hern is God's own cousin! She thinks he hung the moon!" **1954** *Harder Coll.* **cwTN,** Hang the moon. . . Thank [=think] they know it all. **c1960** *Wilson Coll.* **csKY,** *Hang the moon. . .* Be a VIP, esp. to one's followers. **1976** Lynn–Vecsey *Loretta Lynn* 94 **eKY,** There were even rumors about me and Ernest Tubb, and he's like a father to me. As far as I'm concerned, Ernest Tubb hung the moon. **1979** *DARE* File **ceAL,** This hyperbole has been familiar to me since childhood in Talladega, Ala (1907–) always in past tense form in such a sentence as "He thinks she hung the moon" meaning he thinks she is superlative, he allows no derogatory opinion of her. It means she reaches the unattainable. **1979** *NADS Letters* **TX, OK,** Used only in the past tense. . . "Mary Sue thinks Billy Bob hung the moon," that is, she admires him so much she thinks he is the one who put the moon in the sky. *Ibid* **AR,** We say "He thinks so-and-so hung the moon" in Benton Co, Arkansas, and I believe I have also heard it from as far north as Springfield, Missouri. **1980** *DSNA Letters* **cnAL,** About twenty years ago an educated Southern woman, . . telling me how much her son admired me, said, "Joe believes that you hang [sic] the moon." I took this metaphor to mean that I did wonderful, though difficult, things for people.

hang the white flag up See **flag** n² 2

hang to the rigging See **hang** v **C5**

Hangtown fry n [From *Hangtown,* early name for Placerville, California] **CA, WA**

A dish consisting of eggs and oysters.

1949 Brown *Amer. Cooks* 46 **CA,** Hangtown fry . . scrambled eggs with oysters. This dish was popularized in Hangtown, a mining camp, where in boom days eggs were almost worth their weight in gold dust. **1952** Tracy *Coast Cookery* 255 **WA,** *Hangtown Fry* . . oysters . . eggs. **1964** Amer. Heritage *Cookbook* 538, According to some Californians, Hangtown Fry was created in 1849. A miner from Shirttail Bend hailed into Hangtown with a poke full of nuggets, plunked his fortune down on the counter of Cary House, and said he wanted the finest, most expensive meal they had. When he was told that oysters and eggs were the most expensive items on the menu . . he told the cook to put them together and serve the food. **1979** *DARE* File **cwCA,** [Restaurant menu:] Sea Foods. . . Hangtown Fry. . . $4.75. **1979** *NY Times* (NY) 29 Oct 9/5, One of the most memorable of food names is the West Coast specialty called Hangtown fry.

hang up v phr

1 also in phrr *hang up one's boots* (or *fiddle*) and varr: To quit work, retire; to die.

1830 Smith *Life & Writings of Downing* 90 (We.) [sic *DA*—quot not found], You'll have to hang up your fiddle till another year. **1845** in 1956 Eliason *Tarheel Talk* 276 **neNC,** Made 2 hauls & hung up [Eliason: for the fishing season]. **1893** Shands *MS Speech* 64, *Time to hang up.* Used by all classes for *time to quit work.* **1895** *DN* 1.372 **eTN,** *Hang up:* quit work. A mower, when rain was coming on: "I reckon we'll have to hang up for all day." **1942** Berrey-Van den Bark *Amer. Slang* 117.11, *Die.* . . hang up, hang up one's harness or tack, hang up one's hat. **1968** Adams *Western Words* 140, *Hang up his rope*—A cowboy's expression meaning *to quit one's job* or *to quit the calling.* Also said of someone too old to work with cattle any longer. *Ibid* 157, *Hung up his saddle*—A reference to death. **1968** *Current Slang* 2.2.28 **Los Angeles CA** [Black student slang], *Hang up.* . . To stop doing what you have been doing. **1970** *DARE* Tape **TN**51, Most of my life was spent in the city in a white woman's kitchen, an' I got sick an' tired o' that. I was so glad when time come for me to hang up I didn't know what to do. **c1970** *DARE* File **West,** [Unidentified newspaper clipping:] When a man dies he has hung up his saddle, blown out his lamp. **1975** Gould *ME Lingo* 125, *Hang up your boots*—To die, or, less deperately [sic], to come to the end of your working days.

2 To break a trip, usu for the night. *arch*

1854 U.S. Congress *Congressional Globe* 33rd Cong 1st Sess 24 Jan app 31.108/2 **KY,** In the language of the Kentucky boatman, . . When I came to that point I "was befogged, and hung up for the night." **1874** (1895) Eggleston *Circuit Rider* 142 **IN,** You mout git a place about a mile furder on whar you could hang up for the night. **1897** *KS Univ. Qrly.* (ser B) 6.53, *Hang up:* to put up over night. **1912** Thornton *Amer. Gloss.* 417, *Hang up.* To lie by; not to proceed.

3 To record (a debt) for later payment; to charge (a purchase). [From the practice of hanging notes of debt on the wall of a tavern or shop]

1873 Twain-Warner *Gilded Age* 131, The Colonel . . muttered something to the bar-keeper about "hanging it up." **1891** Maitland *Amer. Slang Dict.* 136, *Hang it up,* to obtain credit. Equivalent to "put it on the slate" or on the ice. **1942** Berrey-Van den Bark *Amer. Slang* 468.3, Hang up . . *to buy on credit.* **1968-69** *DARE* (Qu. U11, *If you buy something but don't pay cash for it, you might say, "I ______.")* Infs **NY**66, 87, 207, 209, Hung it up; **MA**58, Hung up.

4 To raise up, lift.

1942 in 1944 *ADD* 275 **swPA,** She hangs up 5 fingers.

5 See **hang** v **B2.**

hang up one's boots (or fiddle) See **hang up 1**

hankecher See **handkerchief**

hanker v

1 also with *about, after:* To hang about or around, usu with the hope of some benefit.

1832 Trollope *Domestic Manners* 67 **NY,** The good woman told us that she had overslept herself, and that the cow had come and gone again, "not liking, I expect, to hanker about by herself for nothing, poor thing." **1894** Twain *Tom Sawyer Abroad* 17 **MO,** There's plenty of boys that will come hankering and groveling around you when you've got an apple. **1899** (1912) Green *VA Folk-Speech* 215, *Hanker.* . . To linger with expectation; hang about: as, an animal *hankering* about a gate with the expectation of getting in. **1931** *AmSp* 7.90 **eKY,** *Hanker,* to hang around after. "You orter have more spunk than to hanker ater somebody who doesn't want you."

‡2 To disturb.

1969 *DARE* (Qu. Y2, *Other words for upsetting or disturbing somebody: "Losing all that money didn't seem to ______ him a bit."*) Inf **IN**79, Hanker.

hankercher, hankerchy See **handkerchief**

hankering n

A suspicion or premonition.

1940 (1968) Haun *Hawk's Done Gone* 65 **eTN,** Enzor must have got a hankering some way, because when his horse come along Enzor wasn't on it. **1969** *DARE* (Qu. GG12, *To have an inner feeling that something is about to happen*) Inf **CA**169, Hankering.

hankicher See **handkerchief**

hankt See **hang** v **A2**

hankty See **hincty** adj

hanky n, adj Cf **arnchy**

1967 *DARE* (Qu. HH35, *A woman who puts on a lot of airs: "She's too ______ for me."*) Inf **MO**8, Hanky [hæŋki]; (Qu. II7, *Somebody who doesn't seem to 'fit in' or to get along very well, you might say about him, "He's kind of a ______."*) Inf **MO**8, Hanky.

hanl, han'le See **handle** n, v[1]

Hannah n Usu |hænə|; also |hænɚ; hænɪ| Pronc-spp *Hanner, Hanny* Cf Pronc Intro 3.I.12.b

A Forms.

1871 Eggleston *Hoosier Schoolmaster* 72 **IN,** Hanner's got a bad cold this morning. **1915** in 1944 *ADD* **swVA,** -|ɪ|. Hanny. **1933** *AmSp* 8.1.25 **eKY, swVA,** Some words ending in "a" add "r". . . *Hannah* [is] *Hanner.* **1942** Hall *Smoky Mt. Speech* 77, The tendency . . to develop [ə] into [ɚ] is manifest also in words spelled with *-a, -ah,* especially . . *Hannah* (family and place-name) . . ['hænɚ].

B Senses.

Used in var phrr: See quots.

1889 (1971) Farmer *Americanisms* 287, *That's what's the matter with Hannah.*—A street catch-phrase with no especial meaning. For a time it rounded off every statement of fact or expression of opinion amongst the vulgar. **1891** Maitland *Amer. Slang Dict.* 137, *Hannah,* "that's what's the matter with" . . an expression used to corroborate an asseveration, expressive of certainty. **1907** *DN* 3.186 **seNH,** *Dead as Hannah Emerson.* . . Entirely dead. **1924** *DN* 5.269, *Hannah:* so help me ______. **1941** *LANE* Map 473 *(Mad as a wet hen)* 1 inf, **cnMA,** [mæd əz hænə] (Hannah?) [Inf indicated amusement] **1960** *DE Folkl. Bulletin* 1.36, So help me Hannah! (a mild oath). **1966-69** *DARE* (Qu. A16, *A very long period of time: "I haven't seen him ______."*) Inf **NJ**20, Since Hannah was a rag doll; (Qu. A24, *Speaking of someone who has always been the same way: "He's been hot-tempered from ______."*) Inf **NH**5, Ever since Hannah died; (Qu. HH20b, *Of an idle, worthless person you might say, "He doesn't amount to ______."*) Inf **MA**55, Hannah's cooked pies; (Qu. NN29c, *Exclamations beginning with 'holy': "Holy ______!"*) Infs **MN**15, **WV**12, Hannah; (Qu. NN32, *Exclamations like 'I swear' or 'I vow': "I ______."*) Inf **AK**8, So help me Hannah.

Hannah Cook n [Perh folk-etym for *hand or cook;* see quot 1975] **chiefly NEng**

In var phrr signifying unimportance or insignificance, often of persons; see quots.

1895 Brown *Meadow-Grass* 147 **NEng,** Now there's plenty of folks that wouldn't care a Hannah Cook about such old truck. **1907** *DN* 3.189 **seNH,** "Don't amount to a Hannah Cook," i.e. is of no account. **1924** *DN* 5.287 **Cape Cod MA,** A shiftless type of person is said not to 'amount to Hannah Cook.' Hannah Cook was an old character that existed on the end of the Cape for many years, and tho long since dead her name has lived on in the above phrase, common in every household on the end of the Cape. **1927** *AmSp* 3.135 **ME coast,** A shiftless person was "easy as old Tilly" or "did not amount to a Hannah Cook." **1942** ME Univ. *Studies* 56.11, A thing of no value was said not to be worth *a Hannah cook.* **1959** *VT Hist.* new ser 27.140, *Hannah Cook.* . . A name used to denote something worthless. Not worth a *Hannah Cook.* Common. **1966-69** *DARE* (Qu. HH20b, *Of an idle, worthless person you might say, "He doesn't amount to ______."*) Infs **MA**5, 6, 71, Hannah Cook; **NH**17, Hannah Cook [laughter]—my grandmother said this. **1966**

DARE FW Addit **NH**5, Time doesn't amount to Hannah Cook. **1968** Moody *Horse* 166 **nwKS** (as of c1920), I doubt me that . . you'll see any rise in the cattle market that amounts to a Hannah Cook. **1975** Gould *ME Lingo* 125, "Doesn't amount to a *Hannah Cook*" is a saying common in Maine and on Cape Cod. . . It comes from seafaring and has to do with signing on as a member of a ship's crew. . . A man who signed on as a hand or cook didn't have status as one or the other and could be worked in the galley or before the mast as the captain wished. The hand or cook was nondescript, got smaller wages, and became the Hannah Cook of the adage.

hannahill(s) See **hanahill**

Hanner See **Hannah**

hanner-on-the-rock n Cf **Hannah A**

An unidentified edible green.

1961 *Mt. Life* Spring 57 **Appalachians,** In almost any old field can be found wild lettuce, pepper grass, sheep's tongue, poke, hanner-on-the-rock, creasies, crow's foot, and a hundred others.

hannie-i-over n [Var of *Annie-i-over* (at **anti-i-over**)]

=**Antony-over A.**

1968 *DARE* (Qu. EE22, . . *The game in which they throw a ball over a building . . to a player on the other side*) Inf **OH**70, Hannie-i-over.

hannle See **handle** n, v[1]

Hanny See **Hannah**

hanover n

1 =**rutabaga.** [See quot 1948] **esp WV, VA, MD**

1942 Warnick *Garrett Co. MD* 8 (as of 1900-18), *Hanover* . . rutabaga. "How come, I can't find hanover in the seed catalog?" **1948** Mencken *Amer. Lang. Suppl. 2* 161 **MD,** *Hanover,* a rutabaga. . . Possibly from Hanover county, Pennsylvania. **1968–70** *DARE* (Qu. I3, *What do you call the large yellowish root vegetable, similar to a turnip, with a strong taste?*) Infs **MD**21, **VA**13, **WV**1, 3, 4, 13, 14, Hanover; (Qu. I4, *What vegetables are less commonly grown around here?*) Inf **WV**3, Hanover; (Qu. I28b, *Kinds of greens that are cooked*) Inf **VA**46, Hanover; **NC**81, Hanover salad. **1968** *DARE* FW Addit **VA**15, ['hɪno,vɚz]—rutabaga.

2 See quot. [*Hannover,* town in northern Germany and English royal house; as a euphem for *Hell* cf *EDD*] Cf **Halifax 1**

1968 *DARE* (Qu. NN26b, *Weakened substitutes for 'hell': "Go to _______!"*) Inf **NJ**53, Hanover.

hansker See **handkerchief**

hansum See **handsome**

hanswurst n [Ger "buffoon, clown," lit "Jack Sausage," the name of a stock comic character]

See quots.

1942 Berrey–Van den Bark *Amer. Slang* 385.9, *German.* . . Hans Wurst. **1975** *Studies in Honor of Kasten* 29 **swIL,** *Hanswurst* [< *Hans Wurst*]—Idiot.

han't v[1] See **hain't** v

ha'n't v[2] See **have** v[1] **A2**

hant n, v[3] See **haunt**

hant bleach n [*hant* (at **haunt B1**); cf *as pale as if he had seen a ghost*]

A pallor.

1940 (1968) Haun *Hawk's Done Gone* 45 **eTN,** His skin, it was white as a strawberry blossom. Some folks said he looked like he had the hant bleach.

hante See **hain't**

hantle n [Scots and nEngl dial "a handful; a large quantity or number"; cf *OED, EDD*] **chiefly sAppalachians**

1 with *full:* A handful; a small number.

1936 *AmSp* 11.275 **eTN,** *Hantle full.* Small crowd. 'There was only a hantle full at the meeting.'

2 A large number, a crowd.

1928 Chapman *Happy Mt.* 63 **seTN,** The inside of the schoolhouse was scarcely to be seen for the hantle of people. **1938** Matschat *Suwannee R.* 127 **nFL, sGA,** A "hantle" of men sprawled in comfort beneath the giant water oaks. **1940** *AmSp* 15.46 **KY, eTN, Ozarks,** Hantle, a great many.

hantle full See **hantle 1**

hantny-over-the-house n, exclam Also *hantny* [Varr of **Antony-over**]

1967 *DARE* (Qu. EE22, . . *The game in which they throw a ball over a building . . to a player on the other side*) Inf **TX**40, Hantny-over-the-house [hæntnɪ]; (Qu. EE23a, *In the game . . what do you call out when you throw the ball?*) Inf **TX**40, Hantny. **1967** *DARE* Tape **TX**40, We threw the ball over the house and there'd be some on one side an' some on the other. . . That was hantny-over-the-house. . . Seemed like one side'd holler "hantny" and the other would say "over the house," and it'd just come over, an' if they caught it, why, they'd come around with it.

hant's breath n [*hant* (at **haunt B1**)]

See quots.

1954 *PADS* 21.30 **seSC,** *Hant's breath.* . . A current of warm air felt out of doors in the evening, especially when riding on horseback or in a buggy. This is supposed also to be the *hant* itself, warm because from the lower regions. **1988** *DARE* File **eKY** (as of 1980), *Hant's breath*—An ill smelling current of air.

hanty See **haunty**

haole n, also attrib |haʊli; haʊle| Pronc-spp *haore, houri, howrie* [Haw "foreigner"] **HI**

One who is not a Hawaiian of Polynesian ancestry, esp a Caucasian.

1826 Ellis *Narrative HI* 236, We had escaped only because we were *haore,* foreigners. No Hawaiian . . would have done so with impunity. **1834** in 1934 Frear *Lowell & Abigail* 90 **HI,** A large number of natives gazed, wondered and admired while the "Houri" [Frear: *Haole* (Foreigner)] was eating with their own kinsmen. **1844** Jarves *Scenes Sandwich Is.* 104 **HI,** One brings vegetables, another fish . . in short, any thing and every thing which they suppose the *haole,* (foreigner,) to want. **1866** in 1966 Twain *Letters HI* 202, To the natives all whites are haoles—how-ries—that is, strangers, or, more properly, foreigners. **1951** *AmSp* 26.19 **HI,** One seldom hears the word *white man* in Hawaii. He is a 'haole,' a foreigner; and this term has come to mean anyone of European stock. *Haole* is used often as an adjective as well as a noun. **1967** Reinecke–Tsuzaki *Hawaiian Loanwords* 94, *Haole.* . . Originally, a foreigner. . . A white person of the dominant social and economic group in Hawaii. **1967** *DARE* (Qu. X57, *A person with light-colored hair and skin*) Inf **HI**9, A haole ['haʊle˜]; (Qu. HH2, *Names and nicknames for a citified person*) Inf **HI**13, A haole = [one who has] false-seeming sophistication; (Qu. HH28, *Names . . for people of foreign backgrounds*) Inf **HI**1, Haole = Caucasian, formerly meant foreigner; **HI**6, Haole, Caucasian, any white person regardless of language; **HI**13, Haole, Caucasian; (Qu. HH35, *A woman who puts on a lot of airs*) Inf **HI**13, She acts like a haole; (Qu. II23, *Joking names for the people who are, or think they are, the best society of a community*) Inf **HI**13, Rich haoles. **1969** *DARE* File **HI,** Haole ['hɑʊli], a Caucasian, white person, also used as adj, e.g., He had a haole girl with him. **1980** Bushnell *Water of Kane* 88 **HI,** But what will happen when, having harvested my crop of cane, I take it to a haole man's mill to be made into sugar?

haole koa n Also *koa haole* [Haw *haole* foreign + *koa,* the largest Hawaiian forest tree *(Acacia koa)*] **HI**

A **lead tree** (here: *Leucaena glauca*).

1929 Neal *Honolulu Gardens* 133, *False koa . . koa haole, . . (Leucaena glauca . .) . .* The false koa is a common roadside shrub that here and there becomes a small tree. **1929** Pope *Plants HI* 111, Koa Haole [=*Leucaena glauca*] is found quite generally distributed throughout the lowlands of the Hawaiian Islands. . . The Hawaiian name, Koa Haole, meaning foreign koa, has reference to its likeness to the native koa [=*Acacia koa*]. *Ibid* 282, Haole koa. **1954–60** Hance et al. *Hawaiian Sugar* 2, Haole koa. . . False koa, *Leucaena glauca.* **1967** *DARE* (Qu. S21, . . *Weeds . . that are a trouble in gardens and fields*) Inf **HI**2, Haole koa ['haole 'koɐ] = white-man's koa—timber tree—when horses eat it they lose hair from tail, but if silaged, it is not harmful. **1967** Reinecke–Tsuzaki *Hawaiian Loanwords* 94, *Haole . .* Foreign, in the Hawaiian names of several introduced plants, such as *koa haole,* or *haole koa. . .* V[ery] F[requent].

haolified adj [**haole**] **HI** *derog*

Having the manners or traits of a **haole.**

1951 *AmSp* 26.19 **HI,** Such a barbarism as *haolefied,* implying affected or snobbish imitation of non-native ways, is heard. **1967** Reinecke–Tsuzaki *Hawaiian Loanwords* 94, *Haolefied. . .* To be or act like the *haoles* in manners and habits of thought; used somewhat in a derogatory sense, as of one who wishes to be thought superior to his ethnic group or class. V[ery] F[requent].

haore See **haole**

haour See **hour**

haouse See **house**

hap n [Scots dial; cf *SND hap* n[1] 2] **chiefly PA**
=comforter 1.

1907 *German Amer. Annals* 9.378 **sePA,** *Hap...* A wadded covering for a bed; a comfort. **1916** *DN* 4.338 **PA,** *Hap...* A bed 'comforter.' "There are two blankets and a hap on the bed." **1930** Shoemaker *1300 Words* 28 **cPA Mts** (as of c1900), *Hap*—Bed covering of woolen material. **1949** Kurath *Word Geog.* 61, In the mountains of central Pennsylvania *hap,* one of the few Scotch-Irish words, is in common use beside *comfort.* **1953** *AmSp* 28.249 **csPA,** *Hap...* A bedquilt. In general use. **1968** *DARE* (Qu. E16, *A padded covering used on a bed, mostly for warmth*) Inf **PA**163, Hap. **1978** *DARE* File **nwPA,** Hap—a comforter. **1982** McCool *Sam McCool's Pittsburghese* 15 **PA,** Hap: a comforter or quilt, as in "I need my hap to take a nap."

hapa n [See quot 1972 at **1** below] **HI**

1 A part; also adj, half; adv, partly.

1934 Frear *Lowell & Abigail* 267 **HI** (as of 1880s), Dodd's bus, *hapa ha* (twenty-five cents) the round trip to town. [*DARE* Ed: *hā* a fourth, hence *hapahā* a fourth part (of a dollar).] **1954–60** Hance et al. *Hawaiian Sugar* 2, Hapa.. ['hɑpɑ] A small part, half. **1967** *DARE* (Qu. L55, *If the wagon was only partly full*) Inf **HI**3, Hapa; (Qu. U23, .. *A 25-cent piece*) Inf **HI**4A, Hapa haa; (Qu. U24, .. *A 50-cent piece*) Inf **HI**4A, Hapa lua. [*DARE* Ed: *lua* second; hence *hapalua* a second part (of a dollar).] **1967** Reinecke-Tsuzaki *Hawaiian Loanwords* 94, *Hapa...* A part of a thing... F[requent]. **1972** Carr *Da Kine Talk* 114 **HI,** Hapa is the English word *half,* assimilated phonologically into the Hawaiian language, the /f/ replaced by /p/ and the final vowel added.

2 also in phr *hapa haole;* also attrib: A person of partly Caucasian extraction, esp Hawaiian-Caucasian. Cf **haole**

1919 Kyne *Capt. Scraggs* 137 **CA,** But them two *hapahaole* kids o' yourn, Gib... neither black nor white—too good for the natives an' not good enough for the whites. **1951** *AmSp* 26.20 **HI,** A *hapa haole* is 'part white,' one of mixed blood. **1955** Day *HI People* 35, The mingling of the races began as soon as Cook's ships dropped anchor, and caused a new and increasing element in the islands—the *hapa-haole,* or those of mixed blood. **1967** Reinecke-Tsuzaki *Hawaiian Loanwords* 94, *Hapa...* A person of mixed blood; a half-breed... F[requent]... *Hapa haole...* A person of part *haole* blood or of mixed Hawaiian and *haole* (or, more loosely, Caucasian) blood; sometimes restricted to persons of only one-half (known) *haole* blood. **1967** *DARE* (Qu. HH29a, *Names.. for people of mixed blood*) Inf **HI**1, Hapa haole, half white + half Hawaiian, Japanese, Chinese, etc; **HI**6, Hapa haole, half white, half Hawaiian; **HI**13, Hapa haole, half Caucasian. **1972** Carr *Da Kine Talk* 114 **HI,** *Hapa haole...* A part-white person or a person of part-Caucasian extraction.

3 in phr *hapa pake:* A person of partly Chinese ancestry, esp Hawaiian-Chinese. Cf **pake**

1967 *DARE* (Qu. HH29a, *Names.. for people of mixed blood*) Inf **HI**6, Hapa pake, half Hawaiian, half Chinese. **1967** Reinecke-Tsuzaki *Hawaiian Loanwords* 95, *Hapa pake...* A person of part Chinese blood or of mixed Hawaiian and Chinese blood; sometimes restricted to persons of half Hawaiian and half Chinese descent.

hapa haole See **hapa 2**

hapai v [Haw] **HI**

To carry, lift, take, deliver.

1954–60 Hance et al. *Hawaiian Sugar* 2, Hapai.. ['hɑ 'paɪ] To lift, carry, bear. **1967** Reinecke-Tsuzaki *Hawaiian Loanwords* 95, *Hapai...* To take; to deliver... To lift; to carry... As a command: Raise it! Lift! Heave! Carry it!.. V[ery] F[requent]. **1969** *DARE* File **HI,** Hapai [hɑp'hɑɪ], as verb = to carry. **1972** Carr *Da Kine Talk* 86 **HI,** *Hawaiian Words Commonly Heard in Hawaii's English.* .. *Hāpai...* To carry, lift.

hapai adj [**hapai** v] **HI**

Pregnant.

1951 *AmSp* 26.21 **HI,** Some localisms are handy euphemisms: *hapai* (pregnant). **1954–60** Hance et al. *Hawaiian Sugar* 2, Hapai.. ['hɑ'paɪ].. pregnant. **1967** *DARE* (Qu. K10, *Words used about a cow that is going to have a calf*) Inf **HI**2, Hapai, for humans too; (Qu. AA28, .. *Joking or sly expressions.. women use to say that another is going to have a baby*) Inf **HI**1, Hapai ['hɑp'haɪ], used generally as a euphemism by Haoles too. **1967** Reinecke-Tsuzaki *Hawaiian Loanwords* 95, *Hapai...* Carrying young, i.e. pregnant. V[ery] F[requent]. **1969** *DARE* File **HI,** Hapai [hɑp'hɑɪ], as adj = pregnant. "You almost *never* hear 'Is she pregnant?' around here—*hapai* is always used." **1972** McCormick *Vocab. HI* 74, *Hapai..* pregnant. **1972** Carr *Da Kine Talk* 86 **HI,** *Hawaiian Words Commonly Heard in Hawaii's English.* .. *Hāpai...* pregnant.

hapa pake See **hapa 3**

‡haphazard v

1969 *DARE* (Qu. KK63, *To do a clumsy or hurried job of repairing something: "It will never last—he just ______."*) Inf **GA**72, Haphazard it up.

happen v Pronc-spp *happin, hap(p)'m, happ'n;* for *happened,* pronc-sp *happent*

A Forms.

1884 [see **B3** below]. **1908** *DN* 3.282 **eAL, wGA,** *n* has become vocalic *m* after *p*.. as in.. hap-m. **1922** Gonzales *Black Border* 306 **sSC, GA coasts** [Gullah glossary], *Happ'n*—happen, happens, happened, happening. **1923** [see **B2** below]. **1927** Shewmake *Engl. Pronc. VA* 33, *Happen..* often become[s].. *happ'm.* **1931** *AmSp* 6.347, The following are examples of what may be called Regressive Assimilation. A final *n* is assimilated to a preceding labial.. ribbm.. happm [in the central western region of the US].

B Senses.

1 To become.

1942 (1971) Campbell *Cloud-Walking* 6 **seKY,** It happened darker and Sary got shivery from the night air as the mist crept up from the hollers.

2 with *to:* To meet with, suffer, or have (an accident or injury). [Cf *EDD happen* v[1] 2] **chiefly S Midl**

1824 in 1956 Eliason *Tarheel Talk* 145 **NC,** I arrived safte at home and hapened to know accidents.. I have hapened to Some misforchunes. **1903** *DN* 2.315 **seMO,** *Happened to* (an accident)... Suffered an accident. **1907** *DN* 3.231 **nwAR, seMO,** *Happen to* (an accident).. To suffer an accident. **1908** *DN* 3.318 **eAL, wGA,** *Happen to an accident...* To suffer an accident. **1923** *DN* 5.209 **swMO,** *Happen...* To suffer, as an accident. "Bill happened (usually happent) to a right bad hurt." **1941** *Sat. Eve. Post* 25 Oct 35/3 **AL** [Black], An' does you try any fumadiddles, you is right away gwine happen to a catastrophe. **1953** Randolph-Wilson *Down in Holler* 168 **Ozarks,** Instead of saying that "Joe *had* a bad accident" or "*suffered* a bad accident".. the Ozarker says, "Joe *happened to* a bad accident t'other night." **1960** Criswell *Resp. to PADS 20* **Ozarks,** *Happen to:* Incur, meet with. Extremely common from long ago. "He happened to a bad accident over at the mill."

3 with *up with:* See quot.

1884 *Anglia* 7.276 **Sth, S Midl** [Black], *To happin up wid* = to meet by accident.

happenchance n, v [Cf *EDD* (at *happen* v[1] 6. (1)), *OEDS* (at *happenstance*)]

A chance or accidental occurrence; the possibility of such an occurrence; hence v *happenchance* to come by chance or accident.

1911 *DN* 3.544 **NE,** *Happenchance...* Happening, circumstance. Used facetiously. **1941** *Sat. Eve. Post* 22 Mar 24/3 **Sth,** Even if by happen-chance a hailstorm didn't come along and ruin the crop, there was always something to fight. **1953** Randolph-Wilson *Down in Holler* 250 **Ozarks,** Happen-chance... An accident, a coincidence. **1962** Faulkner *Reivers* 64 **MS,** Just in case some meddling busybody is hanging around just on the happen-chance. *Ibid* 66, We done gone through too much to have somebody happen-chance by and snap it shut because they thought I forgot to.

happenly so adv

1918 *DN* 5.20 **NC,** *Happenly so,* by chance. "*Happenly so,* my friend was a girl."

happen-so n **chiefly Sth, S Midl**

A chance occurrence.

1908 *DN* 3.318 **eAL, wGA,** Happen-so... An accidental occurrence. "It was just a happen-so." **1938** Rawlings *Yearling* 310 **neFL,** Gittin' that buck was pure happen-so. **1942** McAtee *Dial. Grant Co. IN* 32 **IN, AL, MD** (as of 1890s). **1942** Faulkner *Go Down* 346 **MS,** "Luck," the third said. "Chance. Happen-so." **1952** Brown *NC Folkl.* 1.549 **cnNC,** *Happen-so...* A coincidence; a thing that merely happened without pre-arrangement or intention. **1953** Randolph–Wilson *Down in Holler* 250 **Ozarks,** Happen-so. . . An accident, a fluke. **c1960** *Wilson Coll.* **csKY.** **1963** Edwards *Gravel* 146 **eTN** (as of 1920s), That's how the Duffer happened to be along. The whole thing was a sort of happen-so. **1986** *DARE* File **ceMD** (as of 1949), Did you do it on purpose or was it just a happen-so?

happen-so v

1954 *Harder Coll.* **cwTN,** *Happen-so:* To come about by chance. "It happen-so I got to go."

happent See **happen**

happen to See **happen 2**

happen up with See **happen 3**

happin, happ'm, happ'n See **happen**

happy adj

1 Overcome with religious enthusiasm—freq in phr *get happy.* **chiefly Sth, S Midl** *esp freq among Black speakers*

1851 Burke *Polly Peablossom* 84 **GA,** He . . looked on as quietly as if his master was *happy* at a camp-meeting. **1884** Baldwin *Yankee School-Teacher* 111 **VA,** Here and there, amid the swaying throng, were women who had "got happy;" who, in fact, appeared oblivious of every earthly surrounding. **1896** Harris *Sister Jane* 150 **GA,** We'd find two hours ample time for to git happy in—ample time. **1923** *DN* 5.209 **swMO,** *Happy*. . . Overcome with religious excitement to the extent of hysteria. **c1936** in 1972 *Amer. Slave* 7.2.58 **MS,** Old Daddy Young was 'bout de bes' preacher us ever had. . . Old Daddy could sho' make 'em shout an' roll. Us have to hol' some of 'em dey'd git so happy. **1938** FWP *Guide DE* 514, When everybody finally "gets happy" enough to suit the preacher he has six or eight good voices take up an old-time spiritual. **1942** McAtee *Dial. Grant Co. IN* 28 (as of 1890s), *Get happy*. . . experience religious conversion. **1959** Lomax *Rainbow Sign* 22 **AL** [Black], Every time I sings my solo . . the folks get happy and just shout all over the church. **1960** Criswell *Resp. to PADS 20* **Ozarks,** *Happy*—Filled with religious fervor. Frequent term years ago, still used less commonly. "They tell me old Jim got happy over at the church Sunday night." **1970** Abrahams *Positively Black* ix [Black], Everybody 'round heah is talkin' 'bout 'ligion, gittin' happy and shoutin'. **1977** Smitherman *Talkin* 72 [Black], Church folk refer to spirit possession and mystical, religious ecstacy as *gittin happy.*

2 also *happy drunk:* Drunk, usu slightly so. **chiefly Nth, N Midl** See Map

1835 Mahony *6 Months* 58 **MA,** Mr. M. was a little happy when he said it. **1950** *WELS (A drinker who is just beginning to show the effects of liquor: "He's _____.")* 2 Infs, **WI,** Happy. **1965–70** *DARE* (Qu. DD13, *When a drinker is just beginning to show the effects of the liquor, you say he's _____*) 16 Infs, **chiefly Nth, N Midl,** Happy; 10 Infs, **chiefly Nth, N Midl,** Feeling (*or* getting) happy; **MD**29, Beginning to feel happy; **RI**1, Get happy; **OH**61, Happy drunk; **NY**111, Just getting happy; (Qu. DD14, *When a person is partly drunk, "He's _____."*) 12 Infs, **chiefly Nth, N Midl,** Happy; **NJ**35, **WY**5, Getting happy; **IA**11, Feeling happy; **MI**76, Pretty happy; (Qu. DD15, *A person who is thoroughly drunk*) **TX**33, Happy drunk.

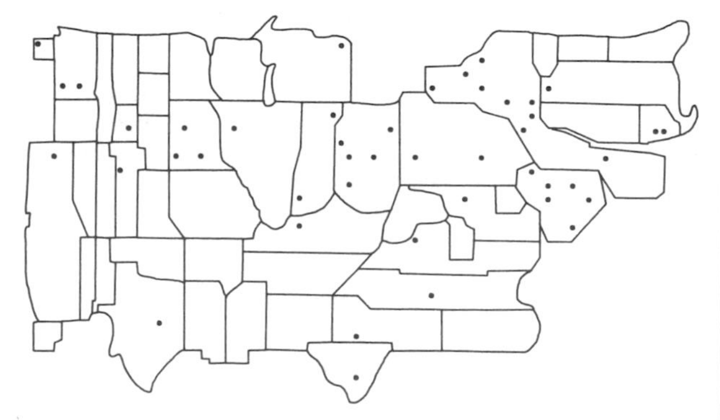

•happy adj 2 + varr (Qq. DD13, DD14, DD15)

3 also used absol: Used in var phrr as a mild oath, see quot. **Mid and S Atl**

1966–69 *DARE* (Qu. GG21b, *If you don't care what a person does, you might say, "Go ahead—I don't give a _____."*) Infs **GA**3, 7, 9, **NC**37, Happy; **VA**11, Happy damn; **GA**77, Happy hooligan; **NC**1, Happy hoot.

4 See quot. [Prob by ext from *-happy* in *slap-happy* and similar combs]

1970 *DARE* (Qu. X6, *If a person's lower jaw sticks out prominently . . he's _____*) Inf **PA**237, Chin-happy.

happy n

1 A toy or plaything. Cf **pretty**

1924 Raine *Land of Saddle-Bags* 105 **sAppalachians,** I want to buy a *pretty* for my baby-child. I told her she should have her *happy.* **1934** (1943) *W2, Happy*. . . A toy. Local, U.S.

2 Entertainment; enjoyment.

1942 (1971) Campbell *Cloud-Walking* 28 **seKY,** He told a heap of tales and riddles and give tother men folks their happy while they worked. *Ibid* 204, The Little Teacher left them have their happy just looking and handling the pretties.

happy drunk See **happy** adj **2**

Happy Hooligan n [Prob after the character in the comic strip of that name (1900–1932)]

1 A powerful firecracker.

1950 Kimbrough *Innocents* 2 **IN,** I had helped my cousin, Charles Robbins, put a Happy Hooligan giant firecracker in the path our tutor took. *Ibid* 4, We didn't believe a Happy Hooligan could have killed anyone, just put him out of commission for a while. **1968** *DARE* (Qu. FF14, . . *Kinds of firecrackers*) Inf **NY**57, Happy hooligans, very powerful.

2 See quot.

1968 *DARE* (Qu. X21a, . . *To describe people according to their eyes . . if they stick out*) Inf **NY**40, Happy hooligan.

3 See **happy** adj **3.**

happy is the miller See **miller**

happy Jack n

1 See quot. Cf **bitch 1**

1968 Adams *Western Words* 140, *Happy jack*—A cowman's term for a crude lamp made from a tin can in which a candle burns.

2 See **hopping John 1.**

happy John See **hopping John 1**

happy pappy n **Appalachians**

See quots.

1969 *DARE* FW Addit **seKY,** *Happy-pappies*—joking term for men employed in government-sponsored anti-poverty projects. *Ibid* **ce,seKY,** *Happy-pappies*—men on welfare who do busy-work on roads or just draw money. **1976** Garber *Mountain-ese* 38 **Appalachians,** *Happy-pappy* . . man on dole.

happy wagon n

1950 *WELS (The car or wagon that takes arrested people to the police station or to jail)* 1 Inf, **Milwaukee WI,** Happy wagon.

happy water n

Liquor.

1950 *WELS (Names and nicknames for liquor in general)* 1 Inf, **cWI,** Happy water. **1968** *DARE* (Qu. DD21c, *Nicknames for whiskey, especially illegally made whiskey*) Inf **SC**64, Happy water.

Hapsburg jaw n Also *Hapsburg (chin)* [From the protruding jaw characteristic of the Hapsburg dynasty]

1966–68 *DARE* (Qu. X6, *If a person's lower jaw sticks out prominently*) Inf **CA**43, Hapsburg jaw, of a long jaw; **MS**37, Hapsburg jaw; **IL**50, Hapsburg; **CA**15, Hapsburg chin.

hapuu n [Haw]

1 A tree fern of the genus *Cibotium.*

1929 Neal *Honolulu Gardens* 4, *Cibotium,* hapuu. **1930** Degener *Ferns of HI* 30, The pith of the *hapuu* trunk is rich in starch. **1933** Bryan *Hawaiian Nature* 123, Tree ferns [=*Cibotium* spp] form a large and attractive part of the flora . . of the Hawaiian forest. . . There are three species. . . The other two species [=*C. chamissoi; C. glaucum*] . . are called *hapu* [sic] by the Hawaiians. **1965** Neal *Gardens HI* 10, The hapu'u [=*Cibotium splendens*] is one of the commonest tree ferns in

Hawaii, where it is native and is cultivated in many gardens. **1967** *DARE* (Qu. S11) Inf **HI4**, Hapuu, root or stump of tree fern; stays damp—grow maidenhair ferns.

2 usu dim *hapuupuu,* referring to the young stage: A **sea bass** (here: *Epinephelus quernus*).

1926 Pan-Pacific Research Inst. *Jrl.* 1.1.9, *Epinephelus quernus . .* Hapu'upu'u. **1960** Gosline-Brock *Hawaiian Fishes* 157, *Epinephelus quernus* (Hapu'upu'u). **1967** *Honolulu Star-Bulletin* (HI) 31 May F1/4, Hapuupuu—Sea Bass. **1967** *DARE* (Qu. P2, . . *Kinds of salt-water fish . . good to eat*) Inf **HI4**, Hapuu = butterfish.

har n[1] See **hair** n

har n[2] See **harrow**

haracan See **hurricane**

harbinger-of-spring n [See quot 1916]

A small, white-flowered plant *(Erigenia bulbosa).* Also called **groundnut B8, pepper-and-salt, turkeyfoot, turkey pea**

1857 Gray *Manual of Botany* 159, *Harbinger-of-Spring. . . E. bulbosa . .* Western New York and Penn., to Wisconsin, Kentucky, &c. **1892** IN Dept. Geol. & Nat. Resources *Rept. for 1891* 143, *Erigenia bulbosa. . .* Harbinger of Spring. **1916** Keeler *Early Wildflowers* 167, *Harbinger-of-Spring. . .* is one of the earliest to bloom as well as the smallest and most delicate of our early visitors. **1931** Fassett *Spring Flora* 117 **WI**, *Harbinger-of-Spring. . .* Milwaukee, Racine and Kenosha Counties. **1968** *DARE* (QR p128) Inf **PA**99, Erigenia bulbosa = harbinger-of-spring = pepper and salt. **1976** Bailey-Bailey *Hortus Third* 437, *Harbinger-of-spring. . .* Among the first plants to bloom in spring.

harbis See **harvest**

harbor See **arbor**

harbor goose n

Any of var phalaropes but esp *Lobipes lobatus, Phalaropus fulicarius, Steganopus tricolor.*

1956 MA Audubon Soc. *Bulletin* 40.21, *Red phalarope. . .* Harbor Goose . . (Maine. "Goose" facetious for a small water bird; it is sometimes seen in harbors.) . . *Wilson's Phalarope. . .* Harbor Goose (Maine). . . *Northern Phalarope. . .* Harbor Goose . . (Maine.)

harbor gull n

Either of two gulls:

a =**herring gull.**

1917 (1923) *Birds Amer.* 1.42, *Herring Gull. . . Other Names. . .* Harbor Gull. **1944** Hausman *Amer. Birds* 516, Gull, Harbor—see Gull, Glaucous; see also Gull, Herring. **1956** MA Audubon Soc. *Bulletin* 40.22, Harbor Gull, Herring Gull (Maine, Mass.)

b =**glaucous gull.**

1944 [see **a** above]. **1946** Hausman *Eastern Birds* 309, *Glaucous Gull. . . Other Names . .* Great Harbor Gull, Harbor Gull.

c The glaucous-winged gull *(Larus glaucescens).*

1923 Dawson *Birds CA* 3.1366, Glaucous-winged Gull. . . Harbor Gull. [*Ibid* 1367, Retires in winter to open harbors. . . Common winter resident south along the coast to San Diego.] **1953** Jewett *Birds WA* 292, *Glaucous-winged Gull. . .* Harbor Gull. [*Ibid* 293, The glaucous-winged gull . . is a familiar sight through the winter months about the docks and wharves of Seattle and other coastal cities.]

harbor porpoise n

Std: a cetacean *(Phocaena phocaena)* found in both Atlantic and Pacific coastal waters. Also called **herring hog, puffing pig, snuffing pig**

harbour See **arbor**

hard adj Pronc-spp *haa'd, ha(h)d* Cf Pronc Intro 3.III.1

A Forms.

1891 Page *Elsket* 126 **VA** [Black], He got had foolishness logicated in he haid. **1893** Owen *Voodoo Tales* 82 **MO** [Black], Hit wuz er hahd (hard) un! **1922** Gonzales *Black Border* 260 **sSC, GA coasts** [Gullah], De bottom uh yo' foot haa'd same lukkuh [=like a] alligettuh' back. **1953** Brewer *Word Brazos* 14 **TX** [Black], He hab a job . . gittin' de haa'd-haa'ted sinnuh man to settle on de chu'ch. *Ibid* 40 [Black], Looks lack hits kinda ha'ad for me to get up ma faith tonight.

B Senses.

1 Harsh, uncomplimentary.

1872 Twain *Roughing It* 229 **West,** He called Ollendorff all manner of hard names—said he never saw such a lurid fool as he was. **1968** *DARE* FW Addit **IA**30, "Nurses had a hard name in those days," i.e., immoral.

2 Tired, exhausted.

1941 *LANE* Map 459 *(Emaciated, peaked)* 3 infs, **cCT, wMA,** Hard. *Ibid* Map 482 *(Exhausted)* 1 inf, **swMA,** He looks hard, i.e. overworked or dissipated.

3 Angry.

1963 Owens *Look to River* 53 **TX,** You ain't got no call to feel hard at me, Cannie.

4 prec infin: Able only with difficulty. Cf **bad** adj **B4, easy** adj **3**

1968 *Foxfire* Fall-Winter 24 **neGA, swNC,** "Hard," indicating, "It's hard for me to . . ," as in, "I'm awful hard to remember names."

5 Good, excellent. Cf **bad** adj **B6**

1960 Wentworth-Flexner *Slang* 243, *Hard. . .* Excellent; fine. *Jive use.* **1970** Major *Dict. Afro-Amer. Slang* 64, *Hard:* (1930's-40's) like the word "bad," for black people "hard" has a positive connotation, *terribly* good.

6 in phr *'ass why hard:* See quots. [For *that's why (it's) hard*] **HI**

1972 Carr *Da Kine Talk* 133 **HI,** *Hard, 'Ass why hard! . .* "I miss da bus and mus' walk from down Mo'ili'ili—'ass why ha:d!" . . The popular Hawaiianism is heard everywhere. . . It is roughly equivalent to "Too bad!" "It's terrible!" **1981** *Pidgin To Da Max* np, *Ass why hard* (ass why *hahd*) Life is tough, yeah?

hard adv

1 Very much; extremely; intensely.

1850 (1914) Kingsley *Diary* 97 **CA,** Mr. Hopkins is hard sick. **1862** G. K. Wilder *Diary* (MS.), 28 Feb. *(DAE),* I fear he will be hard sick. **1907** Porter *Trimmed Lamp* 13, He isn't a millionaire so hard that you could notice it, anyhow. **1942** Faulkner *Go Down* 119 **MS,** Because they were not married very hard. **1966** *S. Folkl. Qrly.* 30.256 **AR,** Grandpa, if you actually don't care too hard, why don't we go out coonhuntin' tonight?

2 with *onto:* =**nigh onto.** Cf **handy 5**

1943 *LANE* Map 714 *(Almost),* In the sentence *It is almost midnight. . .* 1 inf, **ceME,** Hard onto.

hard n

1950 *PADS* 14.36 **SC,** *Hard. . .* Dry land; a careenage. "On the hard," on dry land or sound gravel beach. "To put a boat on the hard," to haul out of the water for painting, calking, repair, or winter storage.

hard v See **hire**

‡hardback n [Prob by analogy with *greenback*]

1966 *DARE* (Qu. U27, *Names for a silver dollar*) Inf **NC**3, Hardback.

hard-backed cooter n Also *hard-shell cooter* **sGA, nFL** Cf **hard-shell turtle**

A **cooter** n **1,** such as *Chrysemys floridana.*

1934 *Natl. Geogr. Mag.* 65.612 **Okefenokee GA,** The Florida terrapin, known in the local vernacular as the "hard-backed cooter," is the species most frequently seen basking on logs projecting above the water. **1938** Matschat *Suwannee R.* 75 **sGA,** The terrapin of Okefenokee. . . The "hard-backed cooter," as the swampers call it, is often seen sunning itself on logs above the water. **1942** Rawlings *Cross Creek* 226 **nFL,** We are partial to the hard-shell cooter and I can never be in too big a hurry on my way to town to stop the car and get out and capture one. **1952** Carr *Turtles* 301, The local esteem for the "Suwannee chicken" is . . by no means unjustified, although in my judgment the disparity in flavor between this and the other hard-shelled cooters is not so great as the Suwannee River people would have one believe.

hardback turtle See **hard-shell turtle**

hard-bargain hickory nut n [Because it is difficult to crack and yields little]

The fruit of a **hard-shell hickory.**

1969 *DARE* (Qu. I43, . . *Kinds of nuts . . wild*) Inf **MO**20, Hard-shell hickory nut, called hard-bargain hickory nut by my grandmother.

hard-bark hickory n

A **mockernut hickory** (here: *Carya tomentosa*).

1897 Sudworth *Arborescent Flora* 114 **IL,** *Hicoria alba . .* Mockernut (Hickory). . . Common Names. . . Hardbark Hickory. **1960** Vines *Trees SW* 131, *Mockernut Hickory—Carya tomentosa. . .* Vernacular names are Whiteheart Hickory, . . Hardbark Hickory.

hard-bill blackbird n
An unidentified bird.
1967 *DARE* (Qu. Q11, . . *Kinds of blackbirds*) Inf **AL**17, Hard-bill blackbird.

hardblow n [By metath from *blowhard;* cf Intro "Language Changes" I.1]
A braggart.
1966 *Wilson Coll.* **csKY,** *Hard-blow* . . blowhard.

hard-boiled adj Cf **boiled shirt**
Of clothing: stiff, rigid; esp in phr *hard-boiled hat* a derby.
1903 (1965) Adams *Log Cowboy* 127, That fellow in front of the drug store over there, with the hard-boiled hat on. **1906** *DN* 3.139 **nwAR,** *Hard-boiled hat*. . . A derby hat. **1907** White *AZ Nights* 321, He sifted in wearin' one of those hard-boiled hats. **1919** Lewis *Free Air* 86, To Claire, traveling men were merely commercial persons in hard-boiled suits. **1968** Adams *Western Words* 140, *Hard-boiled hat*—A cowboy's name for a derby.

hardboot n [See quot 1951] **esp KY**
A person interested in horses; spec, a horse breeder.
1939 FWP *Guide KY* 154, Latonia [race track] has been dubbed "Death Valley" by some Kentucky "hard boots" (chronic backers of Kentucky horses) because they believe the best horses are beaten there. **1951** *PADS* 16.34, *Hardboot*. . . A horse breeder from the Kentucky hills or from Tennessee; so called because in the old days his boots hardened from the mud and water through which they had traveled. . . An old-time, experienced breeder. **1956** Betts *Across the Board* 316 *(DAS)*, *Hardboot*—A bantering or derisive term for a Kentucky horseman; it stems from envy, the hardboot being shrewder than horsemen in other parts of the country. **1957** McMeekin *Old KY Country* 135, If you take a tour of any of these establishments [=horse breeding farms] you will . . fall into conversation with some knowledgeable "hard boots" who will acquaint you with various facts.

hardbound adj [Engl dial; cf *EDD*] *old-fash*
Constipated.
1889 *Century Dict.* 2717, *Hard-bound*. . . Constipated: said of the bowels. [*Century* Ed: Colloq.] **1966–70** *DARE* (Qu. BB21, . . *Words for being constipated*) Infs **MA**4, **NJ**64, **OH**89, **TN**34, **WA**18, Hard-bound. [All Infs old]

hard bowels n Cf **hardbound**
1967–70 *DARE* (Qu. BB21, . . *Words for being constipated*) Infs **KY**81, **LA**8, **TX**36, Hard bowels.

hard bread n
=**hardtack 1a** or **b.**
1781 in 1903 Putnam *Memoirs* 187 **MA,** The major is gone to the commissary to obtain some hard bread if possible. **1857** Chandless *Visit to Salt Lake* 11 **neKS,** What we call rolls, in America are ycleped biscuits, and biscuits in their turn hard bread. **1867** Higginson *Harvard Mem. Biog.* 2.9, He has divided his last cake of hard-bread, and compelled me to take it. **1905** Cole *Early OR* 12 **nCA,** Having no more salt "junk" or hard bread left, we applied for a breakfast. **1926** Ashley *Yankee Whaler* 132, *Hard Bread:* Thick square biscuit, made very hard in order to resist dampness and deterioration. *Hardtack:* Another name for the above.

hard by prep phr, adv phr [Cf *EDD hard by* (at *hard* adv. 2)] Cf *handy by* (at **handy to**)
Near; nearby.
1951 Johnson *Resp. to PADS 20* **DE** *(Something that is close: "The farm is ______ the school.") Hard by*—old fashioned. **1960** Bailey *Resp. to PADS 20* **KS,** *Hard by* the school. **1966–70** *DARE* (Qu. MM5, . . *A house that's not far away: "The house is over______."*) Inf NY59, Hard by; (Qu. MM6, . . *'Very close' or 'only a short distance' away: "The house is ______ the park."*) Infs **IL**135, **NY**59, **NC**33, **VA**21, Hard by.

hard chance n
A difficult time.
1957 Beck *Folkl. ME* 167, A man in trouble is having a "hard chance".

hard clam See **hard-shell clam 1**

Hard-core Baptist See **hard-shell 2**

hard corn n Cf **soft corn**
A var of **Indian corn,** perh **flint corn.**
1968–69 *DARE* (Qu. I34, *If you don't have sweet corn, you can always eat young ______*) Infs **IL**52, **LA**20, Hard corn.

hard crab See **hard-shell crab**

hard craw n
A disease of chickens and turkeys, characterized by an impacted crop.
1966 *DARE* (Qu. K78, . . *Diseases . . chickens commonly get*) Inf **SC**23, Hard craw.

hard dollar n [Perh from Span *peso duro* hard peso, the Spanish or Spanish American "silver dollar"]
A silver dollar.
1780 *NJ Gaz.* (Trenton) 22 Nov 3/2, Whoever will take up said mare and deliver her . . shall have Three hard Dollars reward. **1788** Gordon *Hist. U.S.A.* 3.331 **NY,** He was told that the trees would in a little time be worth . . many thousand hard dollars. **1789** *KY Gaz.* 4 July 1/2, Ten acres of the above to be cleared by contract, for which payment will be made in hard dollars. **1830** (1877) Breck *Recollections* 186 **Boston MA,** They put down the item *Faculty* in my father's tax-bill at eleven hundred and twenty-five hard dollars for one year. **1842** *S. Lit. Messenger* 8.406/1 **St. Louis MO,** After receiving a quantum of hard dollars . . we bade adieu to the lively town. **1909** Porter *Roads of Destiny* 156 **TX,** I'd blow de express car and make hard dollars where you guys gets wind. **c1938** in 1970 Hyatt *Hoodoo* 2.1034 **neSC,** Yo' take yo' three silver—*hard dollahs*. **1967–68** *DARE* (Qu. U27, *Names for a silver dollar*) Infs NJ3, 8, 9, 14, Hard dollar. **1973** *DARE* File **cAL** (as of c1946), Silver dollar: Hard dollar, case dollar, bo (bow?) dollar.

hard down adj phr **Sth, S Midl**
1 Tough, adamant.
1851 Hooper *Widow Rugby's Husband* 22 **AL,** You are reether hard down on your Union friends. **1962** *Hall Coll.* **ceTN,** He was hard down on lawlessness.
2 in phr *hard down knucks:* Having the knuckles firmly on the ground. Cf **knucks**
1980 *NADS Letters* **cnAL,** "Hard down knucks",—which means that the one about to shoot [his marble] must keep his shooting fist on the ground (not raised a bit for some advantage).
3 Real, true.
1938 *AmSp* 13.6 **seAR,** *Hard-down*. . . Pure; unadulterated. 'That's just hard-down meanness.'

hard down adv phr [**hard down** adj phr 3] **chiefly Sth**
Really, truly, genuinely.
1959 Lomax *Rainbow Sign* 113 **AL** [Black], I get more kick out of the old songs. . . I don't even hard down try to learn the new ones. **1960** (1962) Lee *Mockingbird* 32 **AL,** He's a mean one, a hard-down mean one. **1968** *DARE* (Qu. HH3, *A dull and stupid person*) Inf **GA**19, Hard down dumb. **1970** Tarpley *Blinky* 246 **neTX,** *A lazy, unambitious person in the community* . . hard down lazy.

hard dressing See **hard sauce**

hard elm n
Prob **white elm.**
1968 *DARE* (Qu. T11, . . *Kinds of elm trees*) Inf **WI**68, Hard elm.

hardest, by the adv phr
1935 Hurston *Mules & Men* 164 **nFL** [Black], So they tied de cow up short to a tree and de ole man got on by de hardest [Footnote: With great difficulty], and de boy passed a rope under her belly and tied his papa on.

hard-faced bird n
A **woodpecker.**
1950 *Western Folkl.* 9.118 **nwOR** [Logger speech], *Hard-faced bird.* A woodpecker: also used in referring to a high climber.

hard-favored adj [Engl dial; cf *EDD* at *hard* adj. 1. (17)] **Sth, S Midl** Cf **favor B2**
Coarse-featured; unattractive.
1806 (1970) Webster *Compendious Dict.* 139/1, *Hardfavored*. . . having coarse features, rough. **1835** Longstreet *GA Scenes* 16, She hadn't seen *me* then, or she never could have loved such a hard favoured man as you are. **1899** (1912) Green *VA Folk-Speech* 216, *Hard-favoured*. . . Having coarse features; harsh countenance[d]; ugly. **1927** *AmSp* 2.356 **WV,** *Hard-favored* . . presenting a poor appearance. "There were many hard-favored men at the first day of court." **1946** TN

Folk Lore Soc. *Bulletin* 12.4.4, I knowed when she got old and hard-favored he'd start runnin' round with some young hussy. **1984** Wilder *You All Spoken Here* 52 **Sth,** *Hard-favored:* [Having a] . . face to stop a clock.

hard fodder n

1914 *DN* 4.74 **ME, nNH,** *Hard fodder.* Bad luck.

hard fry n

1968 *DARE* (Qu. H45, *Dishes made with meat, fish, or poultry*) Inf **MD**8, Hard fries, crab fried in batter, shell and all.

hard grass n

=orchard grass.

1876 Hobbs *Bot. Hdbk.* 45, Grass, Hard, . . Dactylis glomerata. **1945** Wodehouse *Hayfever Plants* 43, Orchard grass . . , also called cocksfoot, dew or hard grass, is a tall perennial with flat leaves and spreading panicles.

hardhack n

1 Any of several **spireas,** but esp *Spiraea tomentosa.* **chiefly NEng**

1814 Bigelow *Florula Bostoniensis* 120 **MA,** *Spiræa tomentosa. . . Downy Spiræa. Hardhack. . .* A very common shrub in pastures and low grounds. **1822** Eaton *Botany* 478, *Spiraea salicifolia* . . (meadow-sweet, willow hard-hack.) . . *Spiraea tomentosa* . . (steeple-bush, purple hard-hack, meadow-sweet.) . . *Spiraea opulifolia* (nine-bark, snowball hardhack.) . . *Spiraea hypericifolia* . . (john's wort hardhack.) **1845** Judd *Margaret* 216 **NEng,** She made a nose-gay . . of mountain laurel leaves, red cedar with blueberries, and a bunch of the white hard-hack, a cream-like flower, innerly blushing. **1887** Freeman *Humble Romance* 135 **NEng,** The blackberry vines climbing over the stone walls on either side, and the meadow-sweet and hardhack bushes were powdered thickly with dust, and had gray leaves instead of green. **1915** (1926) Armstrong–Thornber *Western Wild Flowers* 230, *Hardhack, Steeple-bush. Spiraea Douglasii. . .* Wash., Oreg., Cal. **1931–33** *LANE Worksheets* **swCT,** Hackmitack, hard hack, a bad bush; grows in pasture. **1947** *Sat. Review* 31 May 15/2 **NH,** The hill pastures . . are in season apt to be full of spiraea tomentosa, alias hardhack, alias steeple bush. **1966–69** *DARE* (Qu. S26a, . . *Wildflowers . . roadside flowers*) Inf **NY**195, Hardhack; **MA**67, Hardhack, same as steeplebush, a pink shrubby plant found in pastures; (Qu. S26d, *Wildflowers that grow in meadows*) Inf **RI**15, Hardhack, same as steeplebush; (Qu. T13, . . *Names . . for . . trees*) Inf **MI**14, Have heard the term hardhack but I don't know if we have it around here; (Qu. T15, . . *Swamp trees*) Inf **MI**14, Hardhack; (Qu. T16, . . *Kinds of trees [that] are 'special'*) Inf **NY**71, Hardhack = good deer cover, a little lower than pigeon brush. **1966** *DARE* Wildfl QR Pl.93A, 94A, Inf **NH**4, Either steeplebush or hardhack.

2 =horse balm.

1876 Hobbs *Bot. Hdbk.* 51, Hardhack, Stone root, Collinsonia Canadensis. **1900** Lyons *Plant Names* 111, *C. Canadensis. . .* Hard-hack. **1940** Clute *Amer. Plant Names* 256, *Collinsonia Canadensis.* Hardhack. **1959** Carleton *Index Herb. Plants* 58, Hardhack: Collinsonia canadensis; Potentilla fruticosa; Spiraea tomentosa. **1974** (1977) Coon *Useful Plants* 156.

3 also *hardhock:* A **hop hornbeam** (here: *Ostrya virginiana*).

1894 *Jrl. Amer. Folkl.* 7.99, *Ostrya Virginica* [sic], . . hardhack, Franconia, N. H. **1897** Sudworth *Arborescent Flora* 147, *Ostrya virginiana. . . Common Names. . .* Hardhack (Vt.) **1940** Clute *Amer. Plant Names* 162, *O. Virginiana. . .* Hard-hack. **1960** Vines *Trees SW* 145, Vernacular names are Ironwood, . . Hardhock.

4 A **cinquefoil** (here: *Potentilla fruticosa*).

1896 *Jrl. Amer. Folkl.* 9.187, *Potentilla fruticosa,* . . hardhack, Stockbridge, Mass. **1910** Graves *Flowering Plants* 233 **CT,** Hardhack. Goshen Hardhack. Shrubby Cinquefoil. **1937** U.S. Forest Serv. *Range Plant Hdbk.* B70, Shrubby cinquefoil . . is also known locally as . . hardhack. **1959** [see **2** above]. **1976** Bailey–Bailey *Hortus Third* 905, *[Potentilla] fruticosa. . .* Golden hardhack.

hardhead n

1 Used as an epithet for various peoples or groups: see quot. [*hardhead* an obstinate or shrewd person]

1966–69 *DARE* (Qu. HH28, *Names and nicknames . . for people of foreign background*) Infs **MN**33, **PA**227, Hardheads—Germans; **NY**92, Hardhead—Dutchman; **PA**199, Hardheads—English; (Qu. CC4, . . *Nicknames . . for various religions or religious groups*) Inf **TN**13, Hardheads, Primitive Baptists.

2 Any of several fishes, as:

a also *hardhead shad:* A **menhaden** (here: *Brevoortia tyrannus*). **NEast, esp NEng**

1792 Belknap *Hist. NH* 3.180, *Hard Head, Clupea* dura. **1812** (1914) Bentley *Diary* 4.124 **eMA,** The true Herring . . very distinct from the species common on our coast, called Alewive & Hardhead. **1814** in 1815 Lit. & Philos. Soc. NY *Trans.* 1.453, *Bony-fish, Hard-heads, or Marsbankers, of New York. (Clupea menhaden.)* About fourteen inches long. **1838** MA Ag. Surv. *Report* 58, The Munhaden, Alewives, or Hardheads, as they are called, come to the shores in the early part of the season. **1848** Bartlett *Americanisms* 171, *Hardhead.* A fish of the herring species; the menhaden; so called in the State of Maine. **1887** Goode *Amer. Fishes* 385 **MA,** About Cape Ann, "Pogy" is partially replaced by "Hard-head" or "Hard-head Shad." **1889** (1971) Farmer *Americanisms* 288, *Hard head.*—The popular name in Maine for the *menhaden* or *bonyfish.* **1889** *Century Dict.* 2718, *Hardhead* . . The menhaden, *Brevoortia tyrannus. . .* [*Century* Ed: New Eng.] **1905** NJ State Museum *Annual Rept. for 1904* 103, *Brevoortia tyrannus* . . Menhaden. . . Hard Head.

b =rainbow trout. West

1882 U.S. Natl. Museum *Bulletin* 16.313 **nCA,** *S[almo] gairdneri* . . Steel-head; Hard-head; Salmon Trout. **1904** *Salmon & Trout* 165, The steelhead . . on the west coast is known as . . hardhead. **1946** LaMonte *N. Amer. Game Fishes* 110. **1953** Roedel *Common Fishes CA* 43, *Steelhead Rainbow Trout. . . Unauthorized Names* . . hardhead. **1975** Evanoff *Catch More Fish* 79, The steelhead . . is actually a rainbow trout. . . They are also called . . hardheads.

c also *hardhead halfbeak:* A halfbeak (here: *Chriodorus atherinoides*).

1896 U.S. Natl. Museum *Bulletin* 47.719, *Chriodorus atherinoides. . . Hardhead. . .* Bones of top of head smooth, hard, and translucent. . . Florida Keys. . . A handsome little fish, and an excellent pan-fish. **1911** *Century Dict. Suppl., Hardhead. . .* The name is also applied to many other fishes having hard heads: as in America to *Chriodorus atherinoides* of the family *Hemiramphidæ.* **1960** Amer. Fisheries Soc. *List Fishes* 20, Hardhead halfbeak. . . *Chriodorus atherinoides.*

d A **croaker** n[1] **1a(1)** (here: *Micropogon undulatus*). **chiefly Delmarva**

1907 Smith *Fishes NC* 318, *Micropogon undulatus* (Linnæus). "Croaker"; "Crocus"; "Hard-head". **1935** Caine *Game Fish* 61, *Croaker. . . Synonyms* . . Hardhead. **1946** LaMonte *N. Amer. Game Fishes* 83, Hardhead. . . Cape Cod, Massachusetts to Texas. **1947** *Times-Herald* (Wash., D.C.) 9 May D-3/1 *(DA),* While there are thousands upon thousands of hardheads in the Chesapeake Bay country at present it's just not the proper time for the anglers. **1957** Battaglia *Resp. to PADS 20* **eMD,** Hardhead. **1965–70** *DARE* (Qu. P2, . . *Kinds of saltwater fish . . good to eat*) 10 Infs, **chiefly Delmarva,** Hardhead; **DC**2, Hardheads; (Qu. P14, . . *Commercial fishing*) Inf **MD**42, Hardhead, same as croaker; most people say hardhead; they used to be plentiful but no longer are; **DE**1, Hardheads; old-fashioned. **1968** *DARE* Tape **DE**3, We used to have a lot of croakers, we called 'em hardheads. **1976** Warner *Beautiful Swimmers* 223 **Chesapeake Bay,** Find a silvery little fish with a gasping mouth right under its nose and you could almost be sure it was a hardhead or croaker.

e also *hardhead cat:* **=sea catfish. LA, TX**

1933 LA Dept. of Conserv. *Fishes* 253, *Galeichthys felis. . .* The Hardhead shares with the Gaff-topsail the strange breeding habit in which the male carries the eggs around in his mouth until hatching. **1965–70** *DARE* (Qu. P2) Inf **LA**22, 44, Hardhead cat; (Qu. P3) **TX**101, Hardhead; (Qu. P4) **LA**37, Hardhead cat; **TX**19, Saltwater catfish—also called hardhead and rustler; **TX**88, 101, Hardhead; (Qu. P7) **TX**88, Hardhead; (Qu. P14) **LA**44, Hardhead cat. **1970** Anderson *TX Folk Med.* 58, Punctures—Apply the slime from the body of a "hard head" catfish. This is a small salt water catfish that has a poisonous fin on it. The slime is believed to protect the fish in case of contact with each other. *Nueces.*

f A cyprinid fish *(Mylopharodon conocephalus)* native to California.

1957 Blair et al. *Vertebrates U.S.* 105, *Mylopharodon conocephalus. . .* Hardhead. Sacramento and San Joaquin River systems and Russian River, California. **1960** Amer. Fisheries Soc. *List Fishes* 14, Hardhead. . . *Mylopharodon conocephalus.*

g A **killifish** (here: *Fundulus diaphanus*).

1968 *DARE* (Qu. P3) Inf **NY**71, River hardhead; (Qu. P7) Inf **NY**71,

Hardhead, dark brown along back, then has a black stripe, then he's butter yellow further down. **1983** Becker *Fishes WI* 755, *Banded Killifish. . .* Other common names . . hardhead.

3 =gray whale.

1884 Goode *Fisheries U.S.* 1.31, The California Gray Whale. . . Called by whalemen 'Devil-fish,' 'Hard Head,' 'Gray Back.' **1889** *Century Dict.* 2718, *Hardhead* . . The California gray whale, *Rhachianectes glaucus:* so called by whalers because it has a habit of butting boats.

4 A saltwater sponge.

1879 Hyatt *Commercial Sponges* 17, Canals of the first class connect with the main trunks on the surface, and . . are formed by the coalescence of other trunk tubes in the interior. [Footnote:] In the Hard-head, these main trunks are also formed upon the exterior as canals, and can be seen in all stages of formation. **1883** *Fisheries Exhib. Catal.* (ed. 4) 160 *(OED),* The principal varieties . . are known as sheep-wool, white reef, abaco velvet, dark reef, boat, hardhead, grass, yellow and glove. **1884** Goode *Fisheries U.S.* 1.845, [American commercial sponges include] Glove Sponge . . and Yellow and Hard Head, both under the name of *(Spongia agaricina),* subspecies *corlosia.*

5 Any of several birds, as:

a also *hard-headed broadbill, ~ dipper:* **=ruddy duck.**

1888 Trumbull *Names of Birds* 110, *Ruddy Duck. . .* At Stonington, Conn., *Hard-headed Broad-bill. Ibid* 111, In Massachusetts at Falmouth and Martha's Vineyard, in Connecticut at Stonington, East Haddam, mouth of Connecticut River, Wilmington, N.C., and Savannah, Ga., Hard-head. **1889** *Century Dict.* 2718, *Hardhead* . . The ruddy duck, *Erismatura rubida,* more fully called *hard-headed dipper.* **1927** Forbush *Birds MA* 1.280, *Erismatúra jamaicénsis (Gmelin).* Ruddy Duck. . . Hard-head; . . Hard-headed broad-bill. **1954** Sprunt *FL Bird Life* 85, *Ruddy Duck. . . Local Names* . . Hardhead.

b A **woodpecker.**

1967 *DARE* (Qu. Q18, . . *Woodpeckers*) Inf **MA4**, Hardhead.

6 Any of several plants, as:

a usu pl: A **knapweed:** usu *Centaurea nigra,* but also *C. jacea.* [*OED* 1794–1861]

1889 *Century Dict.* 2718, *Hardhead* . . The knapweed, *Centaurea nigra:* so called from its resemblance to the loggerhead, a ball of iron on a long handle. **1903** Porter *Flora PA* 342, *Centaurea nigra. . .* Hardheads. **1910** Graves *Flowering Plants* 407 **CT,** Hardheads. Knapweed. . . Roadsides and waste ground. **1935** (1943) Muenscher *Weeds* 467, *Centaurea Jacea. . .* Hard-heads. . . North central states and the Pacific Northwest. **1973** Hitchcock-Cronquist *Flora Pacific NW* 499, Hardheads. . . *C[entaurea] nigra.*

b =yellow-eyed grass.

1927 Boston Soc. Nat. Hist. *Proc.* 38.245 **Okefenokee GA,** There are . . widespreading ranks of yellow 'hardhead' *(Xyris).* **1949** *Emory Univ. Qrly.* 5.116 **Okefenokee GA,** Dotted here and there over the prairies are floating masses of vegetation without trees but covered with moss and herbaceous plants such as "Hard-heads". **1966** *DARE* Wildfl QR Pl.2B Inf **NC28**, Hardheads.

c A **staggerbush** (here: *Lyonia ferruginea*). **Okefenokee GA**

1927 Boston Soc. Nat. Hist. *Proc.* 38.220 **Okefenokee GA,** *Shrubs. . . Xolisma ferruginea* . . Hardhead. **1943** Amer. Philos. Soc. *Trans.* 33.211/1 **neFL, seGA,** Ledum Andromeda: probably staggerbush, "poor grub," or "hardhead" *(Lyonia ferruginea).*

d A **pipewort** (here: *Eriocaulon decangulare*).

1972 Brown *Wildflowers LA* 11, *Hard-heads, Pipewort. Eriocaulon decangulare. . .* Whitish compact, dense head, consisting of tiny flowers and bracts.

7 A rounded rock or stone; see quots. **chiefly Gt Lakes** See Map and Map Section

1820 in 1821 *Amer. Jrl. Science* 3.57 **VT,** The ore bed . . is covered by a stratum of sand, about two feet thick, containing innumerable round, quartzose stones of various sizes, called by the inhabitants of the town, *hardheads.* **1928** *AmSp* 3.408, "Hardhead" . . has also a colloquial use, referring to the small, dark, rounded rocks which we call "niggerheads" when we find them in our Nebraska pastures. **1940–41** Cassidy *WI Atlas* **seWI,** Hardhead, a large stone the greatest part of which is below ground surface. **1950** *WELS (Stones of particular size, shape, color, etc.)* 6 Infs, **WI,** Hardhead; 1 Inf, Hardheads—usually weathered granite, round . . , the size of a human head; 1 Inf, Hardhead, a field stone; 1 Inf, Hardheads—granite rocks rounded by glacial action, diameter a few inches to a few feet; 1 Inf, Hardheads—various sizes which seem to come to the surface in tilled ground; *(A piece of stone that one person could move but not throw)* 1 Inf, **WI,** Hardhead. **1959** *VT Hist.* new ser 27.140, *Hardhead. . .* A round, smooth stone about the size of a football. **1965–70** *DARE* (Qu. C25, . . *Kinds of stone* . . *[size of a person's head], smooth and hard*) 32 Infs, **chiefly Gt Lakes,** Hardhead; **MI76**, Hardhead stone; (Qu. C22, *A piece of stone too big for one person to move easily*) Inf **WI50**, Hardhead; (Qu. C26, . . *Kinds of stone or rock*) Inf **MI2**, Hardhead, smooth, hard to crack, can be any size; **NY142**, Hardheads.

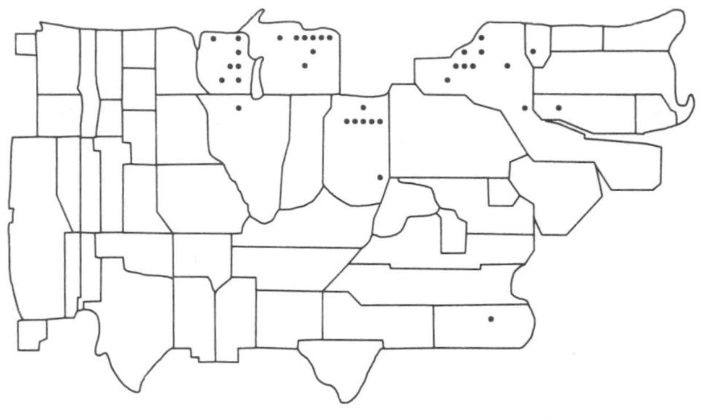

•hardhead 7 + var (Qq. C25, C22, C26)

8 A mule.

1950 *WELS (Joking names for mules)* 1 Inf, Hardhead. **1966–69** *DARE* (Qu. K50) Infs **KY6, SC23, TN10**, Hardhead.

hardhead cat See **hardhead 2e**

hard-headed broadbill (or dipper) See **hardhead 5a**

hardheaded match See **hard match**

hardhead halfbeak See **hardhead 2c**

hardhead lettuce n

A head lettuce; see quot.

1970 *DARE* (Qu. I4, . . *Vegetables* . . *less commonly grown*) Inf **SC66**, Hardhead lettuce.

hardhead shad See **hardhead 2a**

hard hearing adj phr [From *hard of hearing*]

1965–70 *DARE* (Qu. X19a, *When a person's hearing is not very good, you say he's ______*) 16 Infs, **scattered,** Hard hearing; (Qu. X19b, . . *If a person's hearing is very bad, you say he's ______*) Infs **MO35, NY70**, Hard hearing; **MO16**, Very hard hearing.

hard hickory See **hard-shell hickory**

hardhock See **hardhack 3**

hard-iron n

A **saltbush** (here: *Atriplex patula*).

1900 Lyons *Plant Names* 54, *A[triplex] hastata* [*DARE* Ed: now called *A. patula*]. . . Hard-iron. *Plant* sometimes used as a pot herb.

hard keeper n Cf **easy keep(er)**

An animal or person requiring a lot of food or care to maintain good condition; a heavy eater.

1950 *WELS (If somebody always eats a great deal)* 1 Inf, **cWI,** Hard keeper. **1966–69** *DARE* (Qu. K15, *A thin, bony, or poor-looking cow*) Inf **MO11**, Hard keeper; (Qu. K44, *A bony or poor-looking horse*) Infs **CO4, CT2, PA218**, Hard keeper; [**ID3**, Hard-kept].

hard knot n [*knot* a mass or lump]

1 See quot.

1976 Ryland *Richmond Co. VA* 372, *Hardknot:* hate—almost never used, carefully avoided.

2 A person not to be trifled with; a "tough character."

1981 Mebane *Mary* 165 **cnNC,** Across the aisle from me was Flora, a very black woman who looked like a "hard knot." She was short and skinny, and she looked as though she drank a lot.

hard land n

1 Rough, rocky land.

1827 Mrs. Hall *Letters* 106 *(DA),* The country which we passed through to-day is of the same character as the rest of the New England States that we have seen, 'hard land,' as some people call it, I suppose in ridicule, as it is neither more nor less than good, honest rocks and stones.

2 In mining; see quot. Cf **hard rock**

1929 *AmSp* 5.146 **CO,** *Hard land* . . miner's slang for hard rock.

3 Rich, fertile land.

1928 *AmSp* 4.126 **cnNE,** The better farming land regions of the sandhills are "hard" or "table" lands. **1935** Sandoz *Jules* 19 **wNE** (as of 1880–1930), There, close enough to the river for game and wood, on the hard land that must be black and fertile.

hard liver n *esp freq among Black speakers*

Cirrhosis of the liver.

1966–70 *DARE* (Qu. DD24, . . *Diseases that come from continual drinking*) Infs **FL**48, **NC**85, **SC**26, 69, Hard liver. [All Infs Black]

hardly adv

A Syntax.

1 Used with redundant negative; see quots. **chiefly Sth, S Midl**

1865 in 1983 *PADS* 70.37 **ce,sePA,** We had not hardly swallowed our breakfast when the order came. **1939** *Hall Coll.* **cwNC,** We didn't know hardly what to think; **ceTN,** Not hardly that far, I don't guess. **1954** *Harder Coll.* **cwTN,** *Hardly* (always with the negative): "We won't hardly get done." **c1960** *Wilson Coll.* **csKY,** *Hardly* is more often *not hardly.* **1966–68** *DARE* (Qu. H74b) Inf **CA**107, It won't hardly run out of the pot; (Qu. Y23) Inf **SC**19, Couldn't hardly budge; **MO**16, Couldn't hardly git up; (Qu. AA4b) Inf **OH**6, Can't hardly wait; (Qu. GG11) Infs **FL**10, 14, **NC**82, Can't hardly wait; (Qu. KK55c) Inf **LA**32, I don't hardly believe. **1966** *DARE* Tape **FL**19, They used to be so bad . . you couldn't go inside of a store or restaurant an' sit down an' eat for the mosquitoes. . . But since they have mosquito control you don't hardly ever see 'em or feel a mosquito.

2 Spec; in phr *not hardly:* Used to express emphatic denial.

1947 *AmSp* 22.122 **OH,** *Not hardly.* A negative expression. Another way of saying 'no' or 'not.' **1965–70** *DARE* (Qu. NN4, . . *Ways of answering 'no'*) 34 Infs, **scattered, but esp Sth, S Midl,** Not hardly.

B Sense.

Vigorously, strenuously; with difficulty. [Overcorrection from *hard;* cf Intro "Language Changes" II.12]

a1853 (1890) Cutler *Life & Times* 84 **neCT,** The loss of this hardly-earned money was a serious dissappointment to me. **1920s** in 1944 *ADD* **cNY,** We have worked hardly. **1942** *Ibid* **WV,** It's been a hardly contested game. **1943** *Time* 1 Mar 56/3 **WA,** Airmen sadly agreed that probably no other man in aviation could be so hardly spared.

hardly able fever n *joc*

The "illness" of feeling lackadaisical.

1904 (1913) Johnson *Highways South* 248 **WV,** "When the sun is so hot this time of year," said he, "it gives you the spring fever—the 'hardly able' fever."

hard maple n **chiefly Nth, N Midl** Cf **soft maple**

Any of var **maples,** but esp **sugar maple** (here: *Acer saccharum*).

1778 Carver *Travels N. Amer.* 496, The *Maple.* Of this tree there are two sorts, the hard and the soft. **1832** Browne *Sylva* 108 **NEast,** This species, the most interesting of American maples, is called *Rock Maple, Hard Maple* and *Sugar Maple.* **1897** Sudworth *Arborescent Flora* 284, *Acer saccharum. . .* Sugar Maple. . . *Common Names. . .* Hard Maple. *Ibid* 285, *Acer saccharum nigrum. . . Common Names. . .* Hard Maple (Minn.) *Ibid* 286, *Acer saccharum grandidentatum. . . Common Names. . .* Hard Maple (Utah). **1916** Seton *Woodcraft Manual Girls* 290, *Sugar Maple, Rock Maple, or Hard Maple (Acer saccharum).* A large, splendid forest tree, 80 to 120 feet high. . . Its sap produces the famous maple sugar. **1949** Kurath *Word Geog.* 75, *Hard maple* in Western New England and the entire New England settlement area in New York State, Pennsylvania, and Ohio. **c1960** *Wilson Coll.* **csKY,** *Hard maple* . . The sugar maple *(Acer saccharum).* **1965** Teale *Wandering Through Winter* 292 **VT,** But it is from the hard or rock maple, the true sugar maple, *Acer saccharum,* that the yield is sweetest and the flavor best. **1965–70** *DARE* (Qu. T3, *The tree that produces syrup and sugar*) 113 Infs, **chiefly Nth, N Midl,** Hard maple; (Qu. T14, . . *Kinds of maples*) 300 Infs, **chiefly Nth, N Midl,** Hard maple; (Qu. T16) 11 Infs, **chiefly Nth, N Midl,** Hard maple; (Qu. T15, . . *Kinds of swamp trees*) Inf **RI**15, Hard maple. **1971** Wood *Vocab. Change* 34 **Sth,** One tree with sweet sap is almost always called a *sugar maple. . .* The second choice in Louisiana is *hard maple* which is also known in all other states but Alabama and Oklahoma.

hard match n Also *hardheaded match*

1970 *DARE* (Qu. F46, . . *The kind of matches you can strike anywhere*) Inf **FL**49, Hard matches—a rat can strike them and set your house on fire; **NJ**69, Hardheaded matches. [Both Infs Black]

hard-mouth n

=**chiselmouth.**

1882 U.S. Natl. Museum *Proc.* 5.91 **OR,** *Acrochilus alutaceus. . .* Hard mouth. **1889** *Century Dict.* 2718, *Hardmouth. . .* It reaches a length of about a foot. . . [*Century* Ed: Columbia river, U.S.] **1896** U.S. Natl. Museum *Bulletin* 47.208, *Hard-mouth. . .* Upper jaw . . covered with a fleshy lip, inside of which is a . . cartilaginous plate . . ; lower lip covered with a firm cartilaginous plate.

hardness n **chiefly Appalachians** Cf **hard** adj **B3**

Ill will; resentment.

1838 Walker in 1940 Drury *Pioneers Spokanes* 100 **ME,** We had an interesting, and, I think, a happy session, not withstanding all the hardness that has existed among us. **1895** *DN* 1.372 **TN, NC, eKY,** *Hardness:* ill feeling. "There's a right smart of hardness between them two boys." **1917** *DN* 4.413 **wNC, KY,** *Hardness. . .* Ill feeling. "Likely to git up right smart o' hardness between 'em." **1927** *AmSp* 2.356 **WV,** *Hardness* . . ill feeling. "There has been a hardness between those families for a long time." **1944** *PADS* 2.34 **cnNC, sVA,** *Hardness* . . Breach of concord. "There ought not to be no hardness between neighbors." **1954** *Harder Coll.* **cwTN,** Hardness . . ill feeling. **1984** Wilder *You All Spoken Here* 14 **Sth,** *Hardness:* Bad feelings between people; bad blood between families.

hardnose n

1 in phrr *have a* (or *get the*) *hardnose:* To become angry or irritated.

1939 *AmSp* 14.262 **IN,** One who is irritable or angry . . 'has a hard nose.' **1946** *AmSp* 21.33 **ceTX** [College slang], *Hard nose. . .* 'I got the hard nose.' . . Peeved or angry. 'I am getting the hard nose on this machine.'

2 An angry, mean, or rude person.

1958 McCulloch *Woods Words* 80 **Pacific NW,** *Hard-nose*—A tough man, any mean, ornery cuss. **1962** *AmSp* 37.269 **sCA** [Traffic policeman slang], *Hardnose. . .* A vindictive, abusive, offensively driving motorist. **1970** *DARE* (Qu. AA6b, . . *A man who is fond of being with women and tries to attract their attention—if he's rude or not respectful*) Inf **CA**187, Hardnose.

hardnose turtle n

Either a **snapping turtle** (here: *Chelydra serpentina*) or a **hard-shell turtle.**

1968 *DARE* (Qu. P24) Inf **PA**168, Hardnose turtle, same as snapper or hard-shell turtle.

hard oak n Cf **iron oak, rock oak**

An unidentified oak or oaks (*Quercus* spp).

1965–70 *DARE* (Qu. T10, . . *Kinds of oak trees*) 38 Infs, **chiefly Nth, N Midl, Inland Sth,** Hard oak; (Qu. T16) Inf **OH**97, Hard oak.

hardock n [Cf *OED hardock* "app. . . *hoar* + *dock*"]

1 A **burdock 1** (here: *Arctium lappa*).

1876 Hobbs *Bot. Hdbk.* 51, Hardock, Burdock, Arctium lappa. **1914** Georgia *Manual Weeds* 508, *Great Burdock. . .* Hardock. **1959** Carleton *Index Herb. Plants* 58, *Hardock:* Arctium Lappa.

2 =**horse balm.**

1940 Clute *Amer. Plant Names* 256, *Collinsonia Canadensis. . .* Hardock.

hard oil n

1 Lubricating grease.

1960 Criswell *Resp. to PADS 20* **Ozarks,** *Hard oil*—More or less solid lubricating substances which will not flow, like, for instance, axle grease. A very frequent term, especially among farmers.

2 Transf: see quots. Cf **axle-grease** n **1**

1942 Berrey–Van den Bark *Amer. Slang* 91.18, *Butter. . .* Hard oil. **1970** Major *Dict. Afro-Amer. Slang* 64, *Hard-oil:* (1940's) lard or oleomargarine.

hard onto See **hard** adv **2**

hard oyster n Cf **soft oyster**

1881 Ingersoll *Oyster-Industry* 245, *Hard-oyster.*—The northern "native" oyster. (Staten Island sound.)

hard packed adj phr
=**hardbound.**

1967 *DARE* (Qu. BB21, . . *Words for being constipated*) Inf **SC**32, Hard packed.

hardpan n

1 A hard, compacted soil or subsoil. **chiefly Nth, N Midl, West** Cf **caliche 1**

a1817 (1821) Dwight *Travels* 1.374 **MA,** The stratum . . immediately under the soil . . is what is here called *hard pan,* a very stiff loam, so closely combined, as wholly to prevent the water from passing through it. **1879** *Scribner's Mth.* Dec 243/1 **seNY,** Passing out of the clay and hard pan, we came into the gravel. **1894** *DN* 1.341 **wCT, MA,** *Hard-pan:* mixture of clay and subsoil ("yellow dirt") underlying the upper soil in certain situations throughout the region. When this is reached in digging the work is much harder. **1908** Johnson *Highways Pacific Coast* 139 **sCA,** Most of the land in the neighborhood was only fit for grazing, and close under the surface lay "hardpan"—a soft sandstone. **1928** *Ruppenthal Coll.* **KS,** *Hardpan*—Soil not easily plowed, esp. slightly below the surface. One of the queries of early settlers on the plains was whether or not the subsoil that lay below the depth of ordinary plowing was hardpan, difficult to plow, and not taking or retaining water. **1937** Sandoz *Slogum* 40 **NE** (as of 1900–20), It was she who guided the bucking breaker bottom through the hardpan sod. **1965–70** *DARE* (Qu. C31, . . *Heavy, sticky soil*) Infs **CA**6, **CT**10, **GA**31, **IL**11, **NY**75, 233, **OH**81, **SD**8, **WI**12, Hardpan; (QR, near Qu. C30) Inf **IL**113, Hardpan, water doesn't get through. **1966–70** *DARE* FW Addit **OK**42, Hardpan or alkali spots—hard spots in a field where nothing will grow; **seOR,** Hardpan—heavy alkali ground that won't grow anything; **cNY,** The hardpan is up [to] the second rail in the fence—nothing can grow there (literally, hard clay that lets no water through: hardpan). **1968** *DARE* Tape **UT**3A, We just dug down onto the hardpan and laid railroad ties on top of that. . . It's dirt that's pressed together into a rock-type form. **1981** *KS Qrly.* 13.2.67, *Hardpan.* . . a hardened layer of compacted clays and soils almost impenetrable that lies below the thin, rough Nevada topsoil; sometimes known as *calichi* (which more properly is the crust of soil.)

2 Fig: fundamental or harsh reality; hence *come* (or *get*) *down to hardpan* and varr, to face up to reality, become realistic. [See quot 1861] *arch*

1852 in 1968 Hawthorne *N. Hawthorne* 1.444, You are the only one who breaks through the hard-pan. **1861** Holmes *Venner* 1.168 **NEng,** Mr. Silas Peckham had gone a little deeper than he meant, and come upon the "hard pan," as the well-diggers call it, of the Colonel's character. **1875** Stowe *We & Neighbors* 289 **NYC,** Mr. Selby . . had a genuine interest in . . coming to the real "hard-pan" on which our social fabric is founded. **1883** *Boston Journal* 11 Nov. *(DA),* The City Council is making rapid progress toward the hard pan of disgrace when a first-class hotel keeper refuses to trust its members. **1883** *Century Illustr. Mag.* 26.285/2, It didn't appear to get down to hard-pan or to take a firm grip on life. **1893** Frederic *Copperhead* 84 **nNY,** If you come down to hard-pan, it ain't none o' my business.

3 Fig: a financial low point.

1870 (1878) Medbery *Wall St.* 212, Hard pan is soon reached, and both old world and new are full of hard-pan capitalists. **1889** (1971) Farmer *Americanisms* 288, When prices are at *hard pan,* it means that they are at the lowest point. **1902** Day *Pine Tree Ballads* 123 **ME,** But a mortgage can tucker the likliest man / And Ozy he found himself flat on hard pan. **1928** *Ruppenthal Coll.* **KS,** *Hardpan*—[A situation in which one is] without money or means.

4 attrib: Basic, fundamental; conservative.

1870 [see **3** above]. **1896** Frederic *Damnation* 53 **NY,** He's all wool an' a yard wide when it comes to right-down hard-pan religion.

hard peach n **chiefly Sth** Cf **hard stone**
=**clingstone.**

1949 *AmSp* 24.105 **S Atl,** This word list . . does not include . . terms widely distributed though comparatively infrequent, such as *hard peach* for the *clingstone peach.* **c1950** *Atlas Checklists* **MN,** Hard peach . . peach whose meat sticks to seed. **c1960** *Wilson Coll.* **csKY,** *Hard peach.* . . The clingstone variety. **c1970** Pederson *Dial. Surv. Rural GA* **seGA** *(What do you call a peach whose meat sticks to the seed?)* 2 Infs, Hard peach. **1970** *DARE* (Qu. I52, *The kind of a peach where the hard center is tight to the flesh*) Inf **SC**70, Hard peach. **1971** Wood *Vocab. Change* 302 **Sth,** 29 [infs,] Hard peach.

hard pine n [From the relative hardness of the wood] Cf **soft pine**

1 A **longleaf pine** (here: *Pinus palustris*). **Sth**

1884 Sargent *Forests of N. Amer.* 202, *Pinus palustris.* . . Long-leaved Pine. Southern Pine. Georgia Pine. Yellow Pine. Hard Pine. **1897** Sudworth *Arborescent Flora* 30 **AL, MS, LA,** *Pinus palustris.* . . Hard Pine. **1916** Seton *Woodcraft Manual Girls* 267, *Long-leaved Pine, Georgia Pine, Southern Pine, Yellow Pine, or Hard Pine (Pinus palustris).* A fine tree, up to 100 feet high; . . it supplies much of our lumber now; and most of our turpentine, tar, and rosin. **1960** Vines *Trees SW* 26, Longleaf Pine. . . Vernacular names are . . Hard Pine [etc]. . . The wood is very desirable because of its strength and durability. **1979** Little *Checklist U.S. Trees* 195, *Pinus palustris. . . Other common names* . . hard pine.

2 Either of two chiefly northern pines: **Norway pine** or a **pitch pine** (here: *Pinus rigida*).

1890 *Boston Journal* 3 Nov. *(advt.) (DAE),* A valuable tract of hard-pine timber-land. **1897** *Jrl. Amer. Folkl.* 10.144, *Pinus resinosa* . . Norway pine, hard pine, Oxford County, Me. **1897** Sudworth *Arborescent Flora* 19 **WI,** *Pinus resinosa.* . . Hard Pine. *Ibid* 27 **MA,** *Pinus rigida.* . . Hard Pine. **1965–70** *DARE* (Qu. T17) 13 Infs, **NEng, Missip-Ohio Valleys,** Hard pine. **1966** *DARE* Tape **ME**25, A large boat . . [will] have heavy stuff—Oregon fir or hard pine.

3 Any of several other **pines;** see quot.

1908 Rogers *Tree Book* 21, "Hard pine" is a carpenter's term applied to pines whose wood is heavy, close and resinous. It includes everything but soft pine among the staple lumber pines. The "hard pines" are *P[inus] palustris, P. taeda, P. echinata* and *P. heterophylla* in the South; *P. ponderosa,* and *P. ponderosa,* var. *Jeffreyi,* in the West, and *P. resinosa* in the East and North.

hard pushed adj phr [*EDD hard-pushed* (at *hard* adj. 1. (45)) "hard put to it"] **esp NEng** *old-fash* Cf **hard run**

Hard pressed; subjected to pressure of one kind or another, usu financial.

1834 Greene *Perils of Pearl St.* 123 **NYC,** At the end of six months we began to be hard pushed. Our credit, however, was still fair. **1848** Bartlett *Americanisms* 171, *Hard pushed.* To be hard pressed; to be in a difficulty; and especially, as a mercantile phrase, to be hard pressed for money; to be short of cash. **1875** Holland *Sevenoaks* 291 **NEng,** When a feller comes to think of a lot o' woman as is so hard pushed that they hanker arter Mike Conlin, it fetches me. **1895** Jewett *Life of Nancy* 175 **eMA,** I'm dreadful hard pushed losin' of your mother. **1896** *Harper's New Mth. Mag.* 93.345/2 **MO,** Poor old Uncle Silas—why, it's pitiful, him trying to curry favor that way—so hard pushed and poor. **1905** *DN* 3.11 **cCT,** *Hard pushed.* . . Hard pressed. **1906** Freeman *Debtor* 41 **NEng,** Well, I'm willin to allow that I am not as hard pushed as you are. **1907** Mulford *Bar-20* 215 **West,** "They've got our bronchs," replied Mr. Connors in an injured tone. . . "Mebby they was hard pushed an' wanted fresh cayuses," he said. "A whole lot of people get hard pushed in this country." **1969** *DARE* (Qu. U40, *Somebody who is temporarily out of money: You might say, "At this moment he's ________."*) Inf **MA**40, Hard pushed for money. [Inf old]

Hard-rind Baptist See **hard-shell 2**

hard road n Also *hard-surface road* **chiefly Midl, esp IL** See Map Cf **hard-top**

A paved road.

1946 Stuart *Tales Plum Grove* 62 **seKY,** Pa had been laid off the section, but he got a job pouring concrete in Greenup. They were putting in the first hard road in the county. **1953** Botkin–Harlow *Treas. Railroad Folkl.* 261 **nwNC** (as of 1920s), For now the coming of the "hard road" aroused the same hopes which had once been pinned to the iron horse. **1956** Ker *Vocab. W. TX* 84, Cement road; paved road—[6 infs] hard road. **c1960** *Wilson Coll.* **csKY,** *Hard road:* One paved with bituminous substance or cement. *Hard-surface road* is more common in usage. **1965–70** *DARE* (Qu. N23, . . *Kinds of paved roads around here*) 19 Infs, 13 **IL,** Hard road; **NJ**22, Hard road means concrete as opposed to blacktop; (Qu. N16a, . . *Highway with two lanes on each side and a separation down the middle*) Infs **IL**78, **TN**36, Hard road; (Qu. N21, *Roads that are surfaced with smooth black pavement*) Infs **IL**5, **PA**154, **VA**27, Hard road. **1967–70** *DARE* File **sIL,** Hard road—paved road; **IL,** Hard road, asphalt or concrete road, heard in Illinois by Oklahoman. **1969** *DARE* Tape **IL**78, I have appeared several different times before legislative committees . . our legislature had the whole hearing locally, particularly [relating to] hard roads. . . It was designating the hard road system for Illinois. . . They designate the highways. **1971** Wood *Vocab. Change* 52 **Sth,** [For roads paved with concrete] *hard road* and *hard surface road* have scattered occurrences; in Arkansas, however, *hard road* is an important term. **1973** Allen *LAUM* 1.238 (as of c1950), [Cement road]—The single instance of *hard road* in eastern Iowa reflects its popularity in Illinois. . . [Checklist:] Iowa and Nebraska report 22 choices [from 484 respondents] of *hard road.* **1982** Heat Moon *Blue Highways* 29 **cTN,** With these hard roads now, everybody gets out of the hollers to shop or work. Don't stay up in here anymore. This tar road under my shoes done my business in.

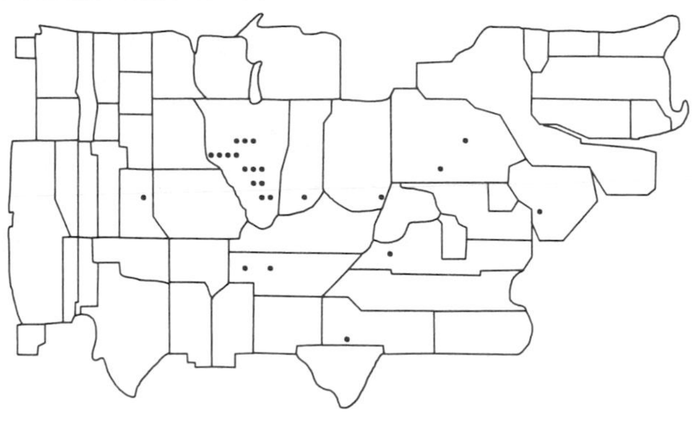

•hard road (Qq. N23, N16a, N21)

hard-rock n

A massive igneous or metamorphic rock formation; hence n *hardrocker* a miner of such formations. **West, esp Rocky Mts**

1923 Sinclair *Parowan Bonanza* 48 **NV,** Tommy's an old, hard-rock man. **1926** *AmSp* 2.87, The old *hardrock* miners (now nearly extinct) were either *single jackers* or *double jackers.* **1939** FWP *Guide MT* 414, *Hardrocker*—Quartz miner; miner who digs ore out of rock. **1943** Howard *Montana* 41, These officials were mostly easterners, pilgrims and tenderfeet; the "hill rats" and "hardrockers" didn't take to them, and the feeling was mutual. **1960** Amer. Geol. Inst. *Suppl. Gloss.* 29/1, *Hard rock*. . . Loosely used to distinguish igneous and metamorphic from sedimentary rock. **1966** Barnes–Jensen *Dict. UT Slang* 22, *Hard rock* . . a type of miner who works in quartz or other hard rock. **1967** *DARE* (Qu. F46, . . *The kind of matches you can strike anywhere*) Inf **CO**47, Hard-rock—most of [the] miners used [them] to light carbide lamps. **1968** Thrush *Dict. of Mining* 528, *Hard-rock miner.* A workman competent to mine in hard rock. Usually used to indicate an expert miner as compared with one fit only to mine in soft rocks. **1977** Jones *OR Folkl.* 37 (as of early 1900s), Miners call other miners that are good at the trade "Hardrock." If he is a particularly good miner and they believe in him, they call him "Hardrock" because hardrock rings like steel, a true quality character. A soft ring is false, therefore, you don't want to set foundations or timbers on it.

Hard-rock Baptist See **hard-shell 2**

hardrocker See **hard-rock**

hardrock maple n Cf **hard maple**

A **sugar maple** (here: *Acer saccharum*); also its wood.

1968 *State & Columbia Rec.* (SC) 5 May sec E 8, New early American round solid hardrock Maple drop leaf dinette table. **1968–69** *DARE* (Qu. T14, . . *Kinds of maples*) Infs **MD**9, **PA**216, Hardrock maple.

hard row of stumps (or to hoe) See **row**

hard run adj phr

=**hard pushed.**

1791 (1927) Maclay *Jrl.* 354 **Philadelphia PA,** He is your enemy. He said you will be hard run, and mentioned Smilie as being your competitor. **1822** (1898) Fowler *Jrl.* 22 June 163 **NY,** We Have left them all be Hind, and Will be Hard Run for meat. **1834** U.S. Congress *Reg. of Debates* 23rd Cong 1st Sess 10 Mar 10.1.848 **MA,** Men . . who, to use the mercantile phrase, are "hard run" to make ends meet. **1845** *NY Tribune* (NY) 1 Nov 2/2 **NYC,** We knew the Tammany party were hard run; but we did not know it was reduced to the necessity of stealing the principles of Nativism. **1848** Bartlett *Americanisms* 172, *Hard run.* To be hard pressed; and especially to be in want of money. **1892** *DN* 1.230 **KY,** *Hard-run.* To be *hard run* is to lack money and the comforts of life. **1899** (1912) Green *VA Folk-Speech* 216, *Hard-run.* . . Hard pressed; ill provided; needy; without resources. **1905** *DN* 3.82 **nwAR,** *Hard run.* . . In need of money. 'I've been hard run this month.' **c1960** *Wilson Coll.* **csKY,** *Hard-run.* . . Needy.

hard run of stumps See **run** n

hard salve n

A healing ointment; see quots.

1965 Needham–Mussey *Country Things* 137 **sVT,** For the hard salve he would send me out to collect white-pine pitch. **1972** *Yesterday* 1.1.41, A sure-cure for chapped hands, a cut on the hoof of an ox, or an aching tooth was a generous dab of hard salve. To make it, boil down resin, mutton tallow, white pine pitch, and buds from the Balm of Gilead tree. Form into a stick and it's ready to apply. **1975** *Mt. Eagle* (Whitesburg KY) 26 June sec B 3, The buds [of Balm of Gilead], along with a quantity of pine rosin and mutton tallow were boiled down into a thick concoction, strained, and then poured out into small crocks or containers where it congealed and became what was known as "hard salve."

hard sauce n Also *hard dressing* **chiefly Nth, N Midl** See Map Cf **dressing 1**

A dessert sauce; see quots.

1896 (c1973) Farmer *Orig. Cook Book* 335, *Harvard Pudding*. . . serve with warm apple sauce and Hard Sauce. **1932** (1946) Hibben *Amer. Regional Cookery* 257 **VA,** *Hard Sauce* . . butter . . powdered sugar . . Jamaica rum . . cream. . . Serve with plum pudding, apple cake, or with fruit dumplings. *Ibid* 258 **MA,** *Hard Sauce* . . butter . . powdered sugar . . nutmeg or . . vanilla. **1941** *LANE* Map 293, A sweet sauce served with puddings. . . 4 infs, Hard sauce, of butter and sugar. **1956** Ker *Vocab. W. TX* 263, *Hard sauce,* made of confectioners' sugar, butter and flavoring, although not a liquid, is the response of . . [1 inf] of Lynn county. **1965–70** *DARE* (Qu. H66a, *The sweet liquid that you pour over a pudding*) 25 Infs, **chiefly Nth, N Midl,** Hard sauce; **NE**8, Hard dressing.

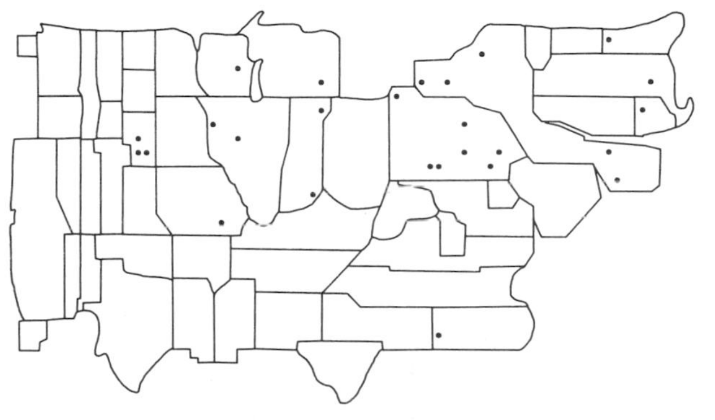

•hard sauce + var (Qu. H66a)

hardscrabble n

1 A difficult struggle; a scramble.

1812 *Salem Gaz.* (MA) 29 May 2/3 **PA,** [Title:] Presidential Hard Scrabble! **1854** (1919) Hale *Letters* 7 **Boston MA,** By a well-organised hard-scrabble, Luc. and I get the breakfast things washed by nine o'clock. **1960** Williams *Walk Egypt* 299 **GA,** Traveling these times is a hard-scrabble, and you ain't never been off before.

2 attrib: Involving a difficult struggle, esp to gain a livelihood—often used in names and nicknames for places; hence absol *hardscrabble* used as a name or nickname for a place; n *hardscrabbler.*

1804 (1905) Lewis *Orig. Jrls. Lewis & Clark Exped.* 7.38 **MO,** Got on our way at hard Scrable Perarie. **1851** (1976) Melville *Moby-Dick* 318, It was my cheerful duty to attend upon him while taking that hard-scrabble scramble upon the dead whale's back. **1888** *Congressional Record* 1 May 19.4.3589/1 **OH,** For the farmer, in those days, there was mighty bad sledding on the road to Hard Scrabble. **1914** Adams *Clarion* 8 **NY,** "Here's trouble," remarked a man at the front. "Allus comes with a Hardscrabbler." "What's a Hardscrabbler?" queried the well-dressed man. "Feller from the Hardscrabble Settlement over on Corsica Lake." **1917** *DN* 4.393 **neOH,** *Hardscrabble*. . . Hamlet in Medina Co. . . Place name in N. Eng. also. **1946** Partridge–Bettmann *As We Were* 173

NEast, Many a farmer who had barely been able to eke a living from a hard-scrabble hillside came into a prosperous business of "taking in" summer boarders. **1965–70** *DARE* (Qu. C34, *Nicknames for nearby settlements, villages, or districts*) Infs **AL**6, **IL**102, **PA**192, Hardscrabble; **CT**7, Hardscrabble, some of the smaller towns; **IL**3, Hardscrabble, particularly in mining areas; **IL**38, Call Streator Hardscrabble now as a nickname, but it was named that before they changed it; **NY**1, Hardscrabble, real name; (Qu. C33, . . *Joking names . . for an out-of-the-way place, or a very unimportant place*) Inf **PA**192, Hardscrabble, a place where the land is poor and won't sustain crops; (Qu. C34) Inf **MA**100, Shall-I-go-naked—a neighborhood—hardscrabble kind of place; (Qu. C35, *Nicknames for the different parts of your town or city*) Inf **NY**72, Hardscrabble, for a valley; **NY**206, Hardscrabble, stony area near Bloomingburg; **CA**125, Hardscrabble Alley, actually a name of the alley, a very rough road. **1972** *Science* new ser 176.4037.891/1 **AL, TN,** The reservoir would back up along the creek and inundate 125 small, hardscrabble farms.

3 as *New England hardscrabble:* A type of bread pudding. Cf **brewis**

1939 Wolcott *Yankee Cook Book* 187, *Brown Bread Brewis* . . hard crusts from brown bread . . salt and cold water. . . simmer. Add a small piece of butter and a little cream or rich milk. . . New England Hard-Scrabble is another name for this dish.

4 =headcheese 1. [Prob punning allusion to **scrapple**]

1960 Criswell *Resp. to PADS 20* **Ozarks,** *Hardscrabble*—A term used years ago for scrapple, a dish made of hog's head, often also called head cheese.

hardscrabbler See **hardscrabble 2**

hardseed See **hardstone**

hard-shell adj Also *hard-shelled*

1 Conservative, straitlaced; unyielding, hardhearted; hence n *hard-shell* a person with these characteristics.

1858 Taylor *N. Travel* 256 **PA,** Oh, you hard-shelled, unplastic insulated Englishmen! **1858** *S. Cultivator* 16.187/2 **GA,** We have, however, one or two specimens in our eye of the genus, *hard shell,* who still do as their *daddies* did. **1873** W. Mathews *Getting On in World* 153 *(DA),* There is no man so 'hard-shelled' that his soul cannot be reached by kindness. **1900** *Congressional Record* 17 Jan 33.1.916/2 **IL,** The old hard-shell Presbyterian of the old school took occasion in his remarks . . to say that the Lord had ordered everything. **1901** *World's Work* June 798/1 **Sth,** Now the schoolmaster and the manufacturer are fast getting the better of these "hard-shell" types of men. **1902** *Munsey's Mag.* 27.599/2, Some of the old hardshells muttered about the roundhouse that it was rather tempting Providence to start out two opposing fast trains with engines numbered respectively nine and thirty six. **1916** Lincoln *Mary-'Gusta* 107 **MA,** She's got inside my vest, somehow or 'nother, and I did think I was consider'ble of a hard-shell. **1916** Wilson *Somewhere* 135 **ID,** A grouchy old hardshell with white hair and whiskers whirling about his head. **1938** *Rocky Mt. News* (Denver) 30 April 8/4 *(DA),* There is a real chance to get some worthwhile decisions from our Supreme Court since our President UN-packed that old hard-shelled outfit. **1948** *Time* 9 Feb 17/2, Almost everybody except hardshell pacifists agreed that the U.S. must be stronger than before World War II. **c1960** *Wilson Coll.* **csKY,** *Hardshell.* . . Strict, unyielding, fundamenistic [sic] in point of view. Also thick-skinned. **1969** *DARE* (Qu. CC4, . . *Nicknames . . for various religions or religious groups*) Inf **NC**61, Hard-shell Methodists.

2 in combs *hard-shell(ed) Baptist* and varr, also n *hard-shell* a member of the Primitive Baptist Church; a strict and rigid Baptist; hence adj **hard-shell** pertaining to this church. **chiefly Sth, S Midl** See Map

1838 in 1914 *SW Hist. Qrly.* 17.54 **TX,** Was introduced to Daddy Spraggins, a Hardshell Baptist preacher. **1842** Buckingham *Slave States* 1.197 **GA,** The Baptists are of the order called here "Hardshelled Baptists," a phrase . . which was given to them, as I understand, from their being so impenetrable to all influences of a benevolent kind, and so hostile to all the auxiliary aids of missions . . and other charitable and philanthropic associations. **1903** *DN* 2.316 **seMO,** *Hardshell Babtiss* [sic]. . . A sect of Baptists. General Baptists. **1905** *DN* 3.11 **cCT,** *Hardshelled Baptist.* . . Baptist of the strait-laced order. **1906** *DN* 3.139 **nwAR,** *Hard Shell doctrine.* . . The tenets of the so-called Hardshell Baptists. "I believe in footwashing, saving your seed potatoes, and paying your honest debts. This is the Hardshell doctrine." **1907** *DN* 3.231 **nwAR,** *Hardshell Baptis'.* . . General Baptist; one of a sect of Baptists. **1908** *DN* 3.319 **eAL, wGA,** *Hardshell.* . . A Primitive Baptist. **1946** *PADS* 6.16 **eNC** (as of 1900–10), *Hardshell.* . . A Primitive Baptist. . . Now rare. **1950** *WELS (Nicknames for different religions)* 2 Infs, **WI,** Hard-shell Baptist. **1954** *Harder Coll.* **cwTN,** *Hard shells.* . . Nickname for members of the Primitive Baptist Church. **1965–70** *DARE* (Qu. CC4, . . *Nicknames . . for various religions or religious groups*) 92 Infs, **chiefly Sth, S Midl,** Hard-shell(ed) Baptists; 12 Infs, **chiefly Sth, S Midl,** Hard-shell(s); **LA**11, **TX**101, Hard-shell Babtist [sic]; **VA**54, Hard-core Baptists; **NC**72, Hard-rind Baptists; **WV**12, Hard-rock Baptists; **KY**91, Hard-side Baptists; (Qu. CC10, . . *An unprofessional, part-time lay preacher*) Inf **AL**10, Hard-shell Baptist. **1968** *DARE* Tape **IN**7, He was the son of a hard-shell Baptist preacher by the name of George W. Brock. They were from Kentucky; **LA**28, They sing those old hard-shell songs and no music. **1983** *MJLF* 9.1.42 **ceKY,** *Hardshells* . . Primitive Baptists.

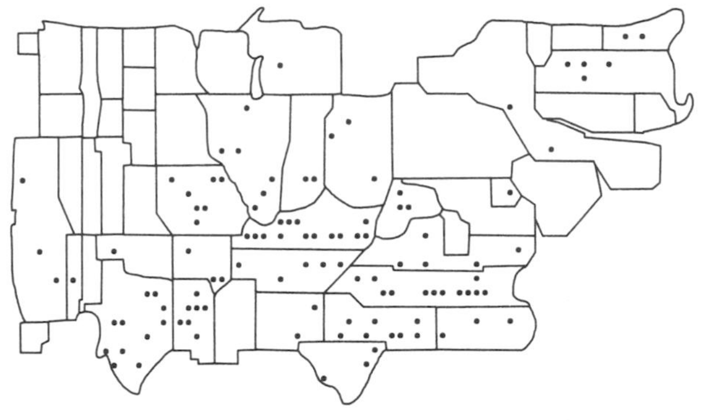

•hard-shell adj 2 + varr (Qq. CC4, CC10)

hard-shell n

1 See **hard-shell** adj **1.**

2 See **hard-shell** adj **2.**

3 See **hard-shell clam 1.**

4 See **hard-shell beetle.**

hard shellback See **hard-shell turtle**

hard-shell Baptist See **hard-shell** adj **2**

hard-shell beetle n Also *hard-shell (bug), hard-shelled beetle, ~ bug*

A beetle, here esp a **June beetle.**

1865 IL Dept. Ag. *Trans.* 5.408, *Coleoptera.* This order consists of the various species of beetles, or, as they are sometimes called, "hard-shelled bugs." **1967–70** *DARE* (Qu. R5, *A big brown beetle that comes out in large numbers in spring and early summer, and flies with a buzzing sound*) Inf **IN**14, Hard-shell bug; **OR**3, Hard-shell; (Qu. R30, . . *Beetles*) Infs **KS**1, 5, Hard-shelled beetle; **IL**126, Hard-shell beetle; **AZ**2, Hard-shelled bugs; **MI**67, Hard-shells.

hard-shell clam n Also *hard-shelled clam*

1 also *hard clam, hard-shell:* **=quahog. Atlantic**

1782 Crèvecoeur *Letters* 135 **Nantucket MA,** The shores of this island abound with the soft-shelled, the hard-shelled, and the great sea clams. **1818** *Amer. Monthly Mag. & Crit. Rev.* 2.296/2 **NY,** The hard shell clam . . is cooked by roasting, or frying, or is made into soup. **1855** *Knickerbocker* 46.222 **NJ,** In the sounds, 'hard-shell' clam-catchers, fishermen, and oyster-men steadily ply their different callings. **1883** U.S. Natl. Museum *Bulletin* 27.233, *Venus mercenaria* . . is the 'quahaug,' or 'round clam,' sometimes known as the 'hard clam.' **1939** *LANE* Map 235, 7 infs, **CT, RI, MA,** Hardshell clam; 5 infs, **CT, RI, MA,** Hard clam; 2 infs **seCT, ceMA,** Hardshelled clam; 1 inf, **seCT,** Hardshell. **1939** Wolcott *Yankee Cook Book* 26 **RI,** The best chowder is from equal portions of both soft- and hard-shell clams. **1949** Kurath *Word Geog.* 27 **Long Island Sound,** *Round clam* or *hard clam* . . the large sea clam which has retained its Indian name *quahog* or *cohog* from Narragansett Bay eastward. **1968–70** *DARE* (Qu. P18, . . *Kinds of shellfish*) Infs **MD**36, **MA**55, Hard-shell clam; **NY**47, **VA**47, Hard clams.

2 A **littleneck** (here: usu *Protothaca staminea,* but also *P. laciniata*). **Pacific**

1883 U.S. Natl. Museum *Bulletin* 27.240, *Tapes staminea* . . known as the . . 'Hard-Shelled Clam', is abundant on the whole Californian coast. *Ibid* 241, *Tapes laciniata* . . and . . *T. staminea*. . . Both . . sold as "Little-Neck" or "Hard-Shell" clams. **1901** Arnold *Sea-Beach* 451, *T[apes] staminea* . . is sold in the San Francisco markets as the "hard-shell clam." **1952** Morris *Field Guide Shells* 47, *Protothaca staminea*. . . The valves are quite thick—the bivalve is known locally as the "hard-shelled clam."

hard-shell cooter See **hard-backed cooter**

hard-shell crab n Also *hard crab*

A crab—esp a blue crab—which has not recently molted.

1889 *Century Dict.* 2719, *Hard-shell*. . . Specifically applied . . to the common edible crab, *Callinectes hastatus,* when its shell is grown hard. **1905** U.S. Bur. Fisheries *Rept. for 1904* 419, There are six stages of a crab's life, commonly classified as follows: First, the "hard crab," or one in its natural condition. **1965** McClane *McClane's Std. Fishing Encycl.* 121, *Blue Crab*. . . Also known as the hardshell or softshell crab. **1966** *DARE* Tape **NC**1, That's the hard crab I'm talking about. . . I'm talking about the blue crab, that's what I'm talking about, but the soft crab they just fry them. **1968–70** *DARE* (Qu. P18, . . *Kinds of shellfish*) Infs **MD**15, **NJ**67, 69, **NY**132, Hard-shell crab; **MD**34, Hard crab; (Qu. P19) Inf **PA**168, Hard-shell crab. **1970** *DARE* Tape **VA**47, Just the regular hard crab. . . The soft crabs . . you can find anytime in different places.

hard-shelled See **hard-shell** adj **1**

hard-shelled Baptist See **hard-shell** adj **2**

hard-shelled beetle, hard-shelled bug See **hard-shell beetle**

hard-shelled clam See **hard-shell clam**

hard-shelled hickory See **hard-shell hickory**

hard-shelled possum n

An armadillo (*Dasypus* spp).

1968 *DARE* FW Addit **LA,** Now the Cajuns classify them [=armadillos] as hard-shelled possums.

hard-shelled (road) turtle See **hard-shell turtle**

hard-shell hickory n Also *hard(-shelled) hickory*

A **pignut** (here: *Carya glabra*).

1796 in 1916 Hawkins *Letters* 17 **GA,** After entering the savanna ¼ of a mile, enter a grove of dwarf hard shelled hickory trees. **1897** Sudworth *Arborescent Flora* 115 **WV,** *Hicoria glabra* . . Pignut (Hickory) . . Hard Shell. **1908** Britton *N. Amer. Trees* 237, It [=*Carya glabra*] is also called Pignut, . . Hardshell, . . and White hickory. **1940** Clute *Amer. Plant Names* 254, *Carya glabra* . . hard hickory. **1969** *DARE* (Qu. I43) Inf **MO**20, Hard-shell hickory nut.

hard-shell inland turtle See **hard-shell turtle**

hard-shell squash n

Prob a winter squash.

1967–68 *DARE* (Qu. I23) Inf **AZ**8, Hard-shell squash; **VA**7, Hard-shell squash—pear shaped.

hard-shell turtle n Also *hard shellback, hard-shell inland turtle, hard-shelled (road) turtle, hardback turtle* **chiefly N Cent, Cent, Gulf States** See Map Cf **hard-backed cooter, softshell turtle**

A turtle of the family Emydidae, esp of the genus *Chrysemys*.

c1940 Newman–Murphy *Conserv. Notes* 5 **neLA,** There are . . varied reptiles in the parish. . . Among the varieties of turtles are . . smooth hard shell. **1942** Rawlings *Cross Creek Cookery* 126 **nFL,** We have five varieties of turtle in Florida—the rather scarce sea turtle, the hard-shell inland turtle, the alligator cooter, or turtle, the soft-shell cooter, and the so-called "gopher". . . The alligator turtle is close kin to the hard-shell turtle. **c1960** *Wilson Coll.* **csKY,** *Hard-shell turtle*. . . One of the rather common species found in the area. **1965–70** *DARE* (Qu. P24, . . *Kinds of turtles*) 137 Infs, **chiefly N Cent, Cent, Gulf States,** Hard-shell turtle; **GA**9, 14, **IN**27, **MO**8, **OH**78, **OR**4, Hardback turtle; **CO**20, Hard-shelled road turtle; **MO**5, Hard-shelled turtle; **NY**103, Hard shellback.

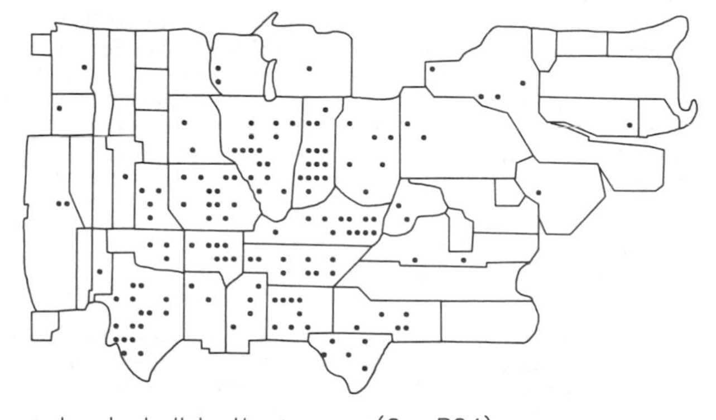

•hard-shell turtle + varr (Qu. P24)

Hard-side Baptist See **hard-shell 2**

hard sledding See **sledding**

hardstone n Also *hardseed* Cf **hard peach**

=**clingstone.**

1941 *LANE* Map 267 1 inf, **seNH,** *Hard-stone*. **1968** *DARE* (Qu. I52, *The kind of a peach where the hard center is tight to the flesh*) Inf **NY**58, Hardstone; **VA**7, Hardseed.

hard-surface road See **hard road**

hardtack n

1 Any of various types of bread; see below. Note: It is not always possible to determine to which sense some of the following quots apply.

a A saltless hard or crisp flat biscuit that remains edible for a long time.

1836 *Knickerbocker* 8.203 **NEast,** When I was the size of that monkey there, who knows how to do nothing but gnaw hard tack. **1862** Winthrop *John Brent* 119, He was putting a large share of earnestness in his manner of holding cups and distributing hard-tack. **1864** in 1926 Harte *Sketches* 138 **CA,** After a fortnight's roasting, turn out the hard-tack, invulnerable to all softening influences for evermore. **1868** *Putnam's Mag.* Aug 164/2 **FL,** Some luckless wight stationed thereabout, munching his pork and hard-tack, had named it the Parker House. **1955** U.S. Arctic Info. Center *Gloss.* 38, *Hardtack* . . A kind of saltless biscuit, baked in flattish, round, or square pieces, which is often a staple of diet of travelers and explorers in arctic and subarctic North America. Also called 'pilot bread,' 'sea biscuit.' **1964** Amer. Heritage *Cookbook* 52, Hardtack, not bread, was the lot of the mountain man . . (sometimes called sea bread or ship's biscuit or pilot bread but always a dehydrated mixture of flour and water which, though never tempting, would stay edible for months). **1966–69** *DARE* (Qu. H18, . . *Kinds of bread*) Inf **MI**34, Hardtack, Finnish; **MI**94, Hardtack, same as rye crisp; **MN**6, Hardtack, made flat like rye crisp now, in a ring with a hole in the middle, hung up to dry after it was baked, made from dark flour; **MN**16, Hardtack; **MN**17, Hardtack—mother made it with rye bread dough, rolled out when it started to raise to a thin cake, baked in the oven bottom, very crisp; (Qu. H65, *Foreign foods*) Inf **MI**94, Hardtack with soft cheese.

b A biscuit; see quots.

1915 *DN* 4.244 **MT,** *Hardtack*. . . Biscuit (not applying to ship's biscuit). "These hot days I get tired of hardtack." **1967–69** *DARE* (Qu. H19, . . *Biscuit*) Inf **IL**37, Hardtack, biscuits without baking powder, old-fashioned; **NE**5, Hardtack; **PA**66, Hardtack, made by hand or dropped off by spoon.

c Corn bread.

1939 *AmSp* 14.90 **eTN,** *Hard tack and sow belly.* Corn bread and meat. 'We eat hard tack and sow belly three times a day.' **1950** *WELS (Names for bread made with corn meal)* 1 Inf, **WI,** Hardtack. **1966** *DARE* (Qu. H22, . . *Food dipped in batter and fried in deep fat*) Inf **MS**2, Hardtacks, fried corn bread; dip leftover bread in batter and fry.

d Stale bread.

1932 *AmSp* 7.168 **NE** [Pioneer talk], "Hardtack" often referred to stale bread rather than to an especially hard baked biscuit. **1958** McCulloch *Woods Words* 80 **Pacific NW,** *Hardtack*. . . Very, very stale bread.

e in phrr *hardtack outfit* (or *show*): See quots.

1938 (1939) Holbrook *Holy Mackinaw* 261 [Logging], *Hardtack outfit*. A concern that sets a poor table. It derives from the hard and cheap Swedish bread. **1958** McCulloch *Woods Words* 80 **Pacific NW,** *Hardtack show*—A camp with a poor cookhouse, poor grub.

2 Transf: see quot. *arch*

1895 *DN* 1.397 **cNY,** *Hard tack:* silver money, especially dollars.

3 Transf: a type of hard candy; a piece of such candy. **chiefly Nth, N Midl**

1935 *Jrl. Abnormal Psych.* 363 [Prison jargon], *Hard tacks*—commissary candy. **1965–70** *DARE* (Qu. H82a, *Cheap candies sold especially for schoolchildren*) Infs **IL**15, **IN**66, **NV**7, **OH**31, 65, 66, **PA**134, **UT**4, Hardtack; **OH**48, Hardtack, it's real hard candy; (Qu. H82b, . . *Cheap candy that used to be sold years ago*) Infs **NY**80, **PA**134, **WV**8, 17, Hardtack; **NY**210, Hardtack, like a very hard caramel; **OR**3, Hardtack, sugar boiled in water, pulled, and cut in lumps; **UT**8, Hardtacks; (Qu. H80, *Kinds of candy often made at home*) Inf **OH**80, Hardtack; **PA**167, Hardtack chips.

4 =hardpan 1.

1966 *DARE* (Qu. C31, . . *Heavy, sticky soil*) Inf **WA**3, Hardtack.

5 =ruddy duck.

1888 Trumbull *Names of Birds* 113, *[Ruddy Duck]* On the Ogeechee River, Ga., *Hard-tack.* **1889** *Century Dict.* 2718, *Hardhead. . . 6.* The ruddy duck. . . Also *hardtack.*

6 =mountain mahogany, esp *Cercocarpus montanus.*

1911 Jepson *Flora CA* 205, *C[ercocarpus] parvifolius. . . Hard Tack.* Spreading shrub 5 to 8 ft. high. **1931** U.S. Dept. Ag. *Misc. Pub.* 101.43, *Mountain-mahoganies. . .* Numerous other . . local names for these shrubs include . . hard-tack, sweetbrush, and tallow bush. **1938** Van Dersal *Native Woody Plants* 338, Hardtack *(Cercocarpus betuloides).*

hardtack outfit (or show) See **hardtack 1e**

hardtail n

1 also *hardtail(ed) jack, hardtail runner:* A **crevalle a** (here: *Caranx crysos*). Also called **dollarfish 5, horse crevalle, horse mackerel 4, jack** n, **jack crevalle, jackfish, jurel, runner, running jack, skipjack, tide runner, yellowjack, yellow mackerel**

1884 Goode *Fisheries U.S.* 1.324 **FL**, *Caranx pisquetus. . .* Known about Pensacola as the "Jurel," "Cojinua," and "Hard-tail". **1896** U.S. Natl. Museum *Bulletin* 47.921, *Caranx crysos. . .* Hard Tail. **1911** U.S. Bur. Census *Fisheries 1908* 311/2, *Jurel (Caranx chrysos).*—A food fish found along the Atlantic and Gulf coasts. It is known about Pensacola as "jurel" and "hardtail;" along the Florida coast as "jack-fish" and "skipjack;" in South Carolina as the "horse crevallé;" at Fort Macon as the "horse-mackerel;" and about New York and on the coast of New Jersey as the "yellow mackerel." They measure from 12 to 18 inches in length, and are caught in seines. **1933** John G. Shedd Aquarium *Guide* 82, *Paratractus crysos*—Hard-tail. **1935** Caine *Game Fish* 48, Blue Runner—*Caranx crysos. . . Synonyms:* Cojinua, . . Hardtail, Hard-tail Runner, Hard-tailed Jack. **1946** LaMonte *N. Amer. Game Fishes* 34, Blue Runner *Caranx crysos. . .* Names: Hardtailed Jack, . . Hardtail. **1960** Amer. Fisheries Soc. *List Fishes* 60, Hardtail—see runner, blue. **1973** Knight *Cook's Fish Guide* 383/1, Jack . . hardtail see Runner, Blue.

2 An **amberjack 2** (here: *Seriola dumerili*).

1907 NJ State Museum *Annual Rept. for 1906* 167, *Seriola lalandi* Valenciennes. Hard Tail. About Sea Isle City.

3 A chub of the genus *Gila.* Cf **bonytail**

1911 *Century Dict. Suppl., Gila. . .* A genus of cyprinoid fishes or chubs, found in the Gila river in Arizona, known as *hardtails. . . G. elegans* is the common species.

4 A mule. [See quots 1930, 1931] **chiefly Sth, S Midl, West**

[**1917** Empey *Over the Top* 294, *"Hard tails."* Mules.] **1930** Irwin *Amer. Tramp* 95, *Hard Tail.*—A mule, so called since the buttocks or "tail" of the animal is hard to make an impression upon with a whip or goad. **1931** 'D. Stiff' *Milk & Honey Route* 207 *(OEDS), Hard tails,* mules, usually old ones. So named because they show little response to the skinner's whip. Young mules are shave-tails. **1936** *AmSp* 11.275 **TN,** *Hard-tail.* Mule. 'See him plow the hard-tail.' **1939** FWP *Guide TN* 275, It ain't nothing to see a man come in and trade in a tractor and a three-year-old Buick and $100 down on a span of hard-tails. **1939** McGuire *FL Cracker Dial.* 176, *Hard-tail. . .* Mule. **1941** Nixon *Possum Trot* 89 **neAL,** Steel mules are invading the cotton fields of Dixie and displacing the "hard-tail," or "jar-head," variety. **1949** *PADS* 11.22 **CO,** *Hardtail. . .* A mule. **1950** *WELS (Joking names for mules)* 1 Inf, **csWI,** Hardtail. **c1960** *Wilson Coll.* **csKY,** *Hardtail. . .* Humorous name for mule. **1965–70** *DARE* (Qu. K50, *Joking nicknames for mules*) 30 Infs, **chiefly Sth, S Midl, West,** Hardtail(s). **1966** *PADS* 46.26 **neAR,** *Hard tail. . .* Mule.—"I was driving an old pair of hard tails." **1968** Adams *Western Words* 140, *Hardtail*—A cowboy's and logger's name for a mule.

5 See quot.

1969 *DARE* (Qu. K78, . . *Diseases . . chickens commonly get*) Inf **NC**76, Hardtail—baby chicks' bowels stop up.

hardtail(ed) jack See **hardtail 1**

hardtail runner See **hardtail 1**

hard timer n Cf **hardtack 1c**

1928 *Ruppenthal Coll.* **KS,** *Hard timer*—(Army) corn bread.

hard times n

1 A cheap fabric of poor quality; see quot 1891. *arch*

1844 in 1863 Goode *Outposts of Zion* 182 **wAR,** At Conference he appeared in character, with 'hard-times' coat and striped blanket, looking quite as much like a missionary as any of us. **1891** Welch *Recoll. Buffalo* 354 **cwNY** (as of 1830–40), A kind of goods were manufactured . . for men's clothing, adapted for and called "Hard Times," a mixed cloth, of black and white or grey and black, spun and woven of coarse, loose thread, presenting the appearance of heavy wool mixtures, which was really nothing but a sort of cotton shoddy, and sold for twenty-five cents per yard. **1894** (1934) Robinson *Danvis Folks* 76 **VT,** The shelves bore the same rolls of calicoes, ginghams, jeans, hard-times, and cotton.

2 in phr *hard times party* and varr: A party to which one wears worn or seedy clothes.

1923 *Outing* Apr 6/3 **WA,** Well, Sparks, you might just as well hang up the rest of that shirt somewhere; it's draped over your shoulders like a costume for a hard-times social. **1948** *Aurora* (Ill.) *Beacon-News* 7 Nov. 21/6 *(DA),* This yearly dance has the aura of hard times parties as the guests come attired in blue jeans, slacks and sweaters. **1950** *WELS Suppl. (Kinds of dancing parties)* 1 Inf, **WI,** Hard time dance. **1965–70** *DARE* (Qu. FF2, . . *Kinds of parties*) Infs **CA**202, **IL**26, **MI**108, **PA**29, **WI**47, 49, 61, Hard times party; **AL**10, Hard times party, also tacky party; **CT**6, Hard times party, still done, dress in old clothes, eat down-to-earth food; **IN**10, Hard times party, same as hobo party; (Qu. FF4, . . *Kinds of dancing parties*) Inf **NY**228, Hard times dance.

hard-top n Also *hard-top road*

=hard road.

c1950 *Atlas Checklists* **MA,** Hard top . . road paved with concrete. **1956** Ker *Vocab. W. TX* 84, Cement road; paved road—[2 infs] hard top. **1960** Teale *Journey into Summer* 7 **NH,** A side road, first hardtop, then gravel, then dirt, then, at last, little more than wheeltracks leading on, had carried us to the upper reaches of the tumbling stream. **c1960** *Wilson Coll.* **csKY,** *Hardtop road . .* One paved with tar or concrete rather than a mere graveled road; a tar road is most often meant. **1966** Dakin *Dial. Vocab. Ohio R. Valley* 2.214, [In eastern Kentucky and southeastern Ohio] the term *hard-surface(d) road, hard-top road* is more common [than *hard road.*] **1966–67** *DARE* Tape **AR**55, Now most all our roads are paved. . . They use some concrete but mostly asphalt—hard-top, they call it. They measure about two or three inches, an' it holds up pretty good; **NC**23, My property starts at that little swamp ridge down there and goes up here to this hard-top road. **1970** *DARE* (Qu. N21, *Roads that are surfaced with . . black pavement*) Inf **MO**23, Hard-top.

hard-turned adj

Difficult; hard to approach.

1949 Arnow *Hunter's Horn* 117 **KY,** [The rooms] looked too fine to live in. He wondered if the doctor who lived in such a place wouldn't be a hard-turned man to deal with, but when he came, an old man with a shock of white hair, Nunn liked him at once.

hardware n

Hard liquor.

1839 *Spirit of Times* 1 June 153/3, He prepared to swallow his fifth invoice of "hardware." **1852** *Knickerbocker* 39.105, He was reckless and 'extravagant;' that is, he spent all his money for 'hardware.' **1920** *NY Eve. Jrl.* (NY) 14 Apr 10 *(Zwilling Coll.),* [In cartoon:] Oh Cyril—oo-hoo—Got any hardware on the hip? **1960** Wentworth–Flexner *Slang* 244, *Hardware. . .* Whisky; hard liquor. *Since c1850; still a little dial. use.* **1967** *DARE* (Qu. DD21a, *General words . . for any kind of liquor*) Inf **NY**2, Hardware.

hardware disease n Also *cow hardware, hardware (stomach)*
scattered, but esp Gt Lakes

See quot 1967.

1965–70 *DARE* (Qu. K28, . . *Chief diseases that cows have*) Infs **KS**5, **MI**19, 23, 49, **MS**53, **OH**30, **PA**33, 193, **WI**77, Hardware; **IA**8, **VA**24, Hardware disease; **FL**7, **MI**47, Hardware stomach, [**MI**10, Disease from hardware]; **MA**37, Cow hardware. **1967** *Merck Vet. Manual* 137, *Traumatic reticuloperitonitis* (Traumatic gastritis, "Hardware" disease)

—A disease of cattle resulting from perforation of the reticulum, and sometimes the rumen, by a sharp object. . . most common in mature dairy cattle and in beef cattle less than 3 years of age.

hardwood n
=he-huckleberry 1.
1927 Boston Soc. Nat. Hist. *Proc.* 38.7.213 **Okefenokee GA,** *Cyrilla racemiflora* 'Hardwood.' **1934** *Natl. Geogr. Mag.* 65.603 **Okefenokee GA,** Here the "hardwood" makes a showy display when its tiny flowers burst forth into white masses during the warm May days.

hardwood bush n
=sugar bush.
1966 *DARE* (Qu. T4, *The place where these [=syrup producing] trees grow together and sap is gathered*) Inf **MI**36, Hardwood bush.

hardwood gravy n
1966 *DARE* Tape **MI**10, [In lumber camps] they had a mixture of scorched grease and flour and water they called hardwood gravy.

hardwood lily n
Perh a **wood lily.**
1966 *DARE* (Qu. S26c, *Wildflowers that grow in woods*) Inf **MI**2, Hardwood lily.

hardwood maple n
A **hard maple.**
1966 *DARE* (Qu. T14) Inf **MI**26, Hardwood maple.

hare n Pronc-spp *hyah, hyar* Cf Pronc Intro 3.I.16
Std sense, var forms.
1890 *DN* 1.68 **KY,** *Hare.* Called "rabbit," except in negro-songs. "Ole hyar, what you doin' dyar?" They never say "ole hare." **1891** Page *Elsket* 134 **VA** [Black], Jes like a ole hyah in a trap.

hare and hound(s) n Infreq *hare and the hound, hound and hare* **chiefly Nth, N Midl** Cf **fox and hounds**
Any of var children's games; see quots.
1889 *Century Dict.* 2719, *Hare and hounds.* . . An outdoor game modeled after the hunting of hares with hounds. Two players known as hares start off on a long run or ride, scattering behind them small pieces of paper called the scent; the other, known as the hounds, following the trail so marked, try to catch the hares before they reach home again. **1891** *Jrl. Amer. Folkl.* 4.223 **Brooklyn NYC,** *Hare and hounds.* Two equal sides are chosen, and each player is provided with a piece of chalk. The "hares" are given three minutes' start, and on their way . . they must make a straight mark . . upon the pavement. The "hounds" who follow them must cross the chalk marks made by the "hares." The chase is continued until the "hares" are caught. **1899** Champlin–Bostwick *Young Folks' Games* 404, *Hare and Hounds,* or *Paper Chase,* a running game played by any number of persons. **1932** *Hanley Disks* **cnMA,** *Hound and Hare*—A children's game. We'd divide up in pairs. One would be the hound and one the hare. The hound would chase the hare through the woods, . . with or without a paper trail. **1950** *WELS (Games played in the snow)* 1 Inf, **WI,** Hare and hounds; 1 Inf, Hare and hounds—players tracking down the "hare" in the snow. **1965** *DARE* File **Boston MA** (as of 1895–1905), Hare and hounds. **1967–70** *DARE* (Qu. EE3, *Games in which you hide an object and then look for it*) Inf **CA**114, Hare and hound; (Qu. EE12, *Games in which one captain hides his team and the other team tries to find it*) Inf **CA**97, Hare and hounds; **IL**47, Hare and hounds [corr to] run sheep run; **NJ**43, Hare and hound; (Qu. EE16, *Hiding games that start with a special, elaborate method of sending the players out to hide*) Inf **PA**245, Hare and hounds; (Qu. EE33, *Other outdoor games*) Inf **PA**49, Hare and the hound.

harebell n
1 also *hairbell, hairybell:* A **bellflower** of the genus *Campanula.* [*OED* 1765 →] **chiefly Nth** Also called **bluebell 1a, bluebells-of-Scotland 1.** For other names of var spp see **cup-and-saucer 1a, flax bellflower, heath-bell, highbelia, lady's thimble, Scotch bellflower, Scotch bluebell, throatwort**
1822 Eaton *Botany* 216, *Campanula rotundifolia* . . (flax bell-flower, hair-bell.) **1838** Flagg *Far West* 2.28 **MO,** The blue dewy harebell; the pale oxlip; the flowering *arbute* . . lie sprinkled. **1840** MA Zool. & Bot. Surv. *Herb. Plants & Quadrupeds* 109, *C[ampanula] rotundifolia.* . . Hair Bell, or Scotch Bell. A beautiful and slender plant. **1857** (1864) Thoreau *ME Woods* 277, Splendid large harebells nodded over the edge and in the clefts of the cliff. **1885** *Harper's New Mth. Mag.* July 192/1 **MT,** The gayly colored wild flowers—yellow sunflowers, daisies, blue harebells—mingle their bright hues. **1944** Nute *Lake Superior* 293, Near them, but out on the shore ledges in clefts and crannies, bloom the still more fragile and much smaller harebells. **1966–69** *DARE* (Qu. S26d, *Wildflowers that grow in meadows*) Inf **MI**31, Hairybells; (Qu. S26a, *Roadside flowers*) Inf **CA**126, Harebell; (Qu. S26c, *Wildflowers that grow in woods*) Infs **MI**42, **NY**21, Harebells. **1979** *Blair & Ketchum's Country Jrl.* Sept 63 **nNEng,** Harebell or Bluebell.
2 =blue toadflax.
1951 *PADS* 15.40 **TX,** *Linaria texana.*—Harebell.

hared out, hared up See **haired up**

hare gum See **gum** n² **3c**

harelip n See **harelip sucker**

harelip v
To disfigure, destroy—used in var fig phrr suggesting dire consequences; see quots.
1960 Criswell *Resp. to PADS 20* **Ozarks,** *To harelip the government:* A phrase used to express dire consequences, used in the negative most often, but not always. Very frequent in earlier days and probably still used. "Well, I don't think it will harelip the government even if you don't get all this work done by sundown." **1970** *Thompson Coll.* **cnAL** (as of 1920s), *Hare-lip hell.* . . To show great determination regardless of consequences. "I'm gonna do it if it hare-lips hell." *Ibid* **Detroit MI** (as of 1946–60), *Hare-lip hell* . . *[used by] Southerners.* **1980** *Houston Chron.* (TX) 9 June sec 3, Waco . . [has] an expression of dogged determination: "I'll do it if it harelips every mule in Texas!" **1984** Weaver *TX Crude* 2, *If it harelips the governor.* . . No matter what the cost. Equals "come hell or high water" and implies an implacable determination. . . "I know she's married . . but I'm gonna bed her if it harelips the governor." **1985** Ladwig *How to Talk Dirty* 38 **Ozarks,** By golly, I'm going to do it even if it harelips all the hogs in Texas.

harelip sucker n Also *harelip*
A catostomid fish *(Lagochila lacera)* with a mouth that resembles a harelip. Also called **may sucker, pea-lip sucker, rabbit-mouth sucker, split-mouth sucker**
1877 Acad. Nat. Sci. Philadelphia *Proc.* 281 **GA, TN, AL,** The commonest and most valued species of sucker found in that region . . is everywhere known by the name of "Hare-lip Sucker." **1896** Jordan–Evermann *Check List Fishes* 243, *Lagochila lacera* . . Hare-lip Sucker; Cut-lips; Split-mouth Sucker; May Sucker. **1957** Trautman *Fishes* 265, The Harelip [=*Lagochila lacera*], with its small, specialized mouth and closely bound gill-covers must have been particularly susceptible to asphyxiation through impacting about the gills by colloidal clays.

hare's lettuce n [*OED* 1597 →]
A **sowthistle** (here: *Sonchus oleraceus*).
1900 Lyons *Plant Names* 351, *S[onchus] oleraceus.* . . Hare's Lettuce. . . *Leaves* bitter, used as a pot herb. **1959** Carleton *Index Herb. Plants* 58, *Hare's-lettuce:* Sonchus oleraceus. **1967** *DARE* Wildfl QR Inf **TX**44, Sow-thistle, hare's lettuce, *lechuguilla.*

hare's lip n
A **lady's slipper** (here: *Cypripedium acaule*).
1950 Correll *Native Orchids* 20, *Cypripedium acaule.* . . Hare's Lip.

hare's tail n
1 also *hare's-tail grass, hare tail:* A **cotton grass 1,** usu *Eriophorum viridicarinatum.* [From the soft 'tassels']
1900 Lyons *Plant Names* 149, *E[riophorum] vaginatum.* . . Hare's-tail. **1910** Graves *Flowering Plants* 89 **CT,** *Eriophorum callitrix.* . . Hare's Tail. **1933** Small *Manual SE Flora* 167, *E. viridicarinatum.* . . Hare-tail. **1949** Moldenke *Amer. Wild Flowers* 374, *E. viridicarinatum,* the *haretail* or *tassel cottongrass,* with bright white tassels. **1959** Carleton *Index Herb. Plants* 58, *Hare's tail:* Eriophorum callitrix. **1968** Hultén *Flora AK* 204, *Eriophorum vaginatum* subsp. *vaginatum.* Hare's-Tail Grass. Tufted, forming tussocks.
2 also *hare's-tail grass:* An introduced and somewhat naturalized grass *(Lagurus ovatus).* Also called **rabbit-tail grass**
1889 *Century Dict.* 2603, *Grass.* . . *Hare's-tail grass.* . . The dense, oblong, woolly panicles bear a resemblance to a hare's tail. **1923** in 1925 Jepson *Manual Plants CA* 120, *L[agurus] ovatus* L. *Hare's-tail Grass.* . . Cult. for ornament and sparingly escaped. **1959** Munz–Keck *CA Flora* 1525, *L. ovatus.* . . Hare's Tail. . . Occasionally natur., especially in Bay Region and about Monterey. **1976** Bailey–Bailey *Hortus Third* 634, *Hare's-tail, hare's-tail grass.* . . N.J., N.C., Calif.

hare's-tail grass See **hare's tail 1, 2**

hare tail See **hare's tail 1**

hare tangle n
1966 *DARE* (Qu. C28, *A place where underbrush, weeds, vines and small trees grow together so that it's nearly impossible to get through*) Inf **ME**9, Hare tangle.

harf n^{1} See **hearth A3**

harf n^{2} See **half** n

haricane See **hurricane**

hark v^{1} Cf **harky**

1a To listen, pay attention. [*W3* "archaic"]
1858 Hammett *Piney Woods Tavern* 269 **TX,** Open on it [=begin the story], Doctor; Uncle Billy's a harkin'. **1887** (1967) Harris *Free Joe* 185 **GA,** Lordy, jess hark ter the creetur! **1959** *VT Hist.* new ser 27.140, *Harking*. . . Listening in over a party-line. Rare. **1975** Gould *ME Lingo* 126, *Hark*. . . To listen: "Nobody harks to me."

b imper; also in phr *hark ye,* pronc-sp *harkee:* Listen! Be quiet!
1827 Cooper *Red Rover* 3.235, Hark ye, Harry, for your sake, I will deal generously by the rogue. **1847** Paulding–Paulding *Amer. Comedies* 28, And harkee, admiral—d'ye see this inimitable tie? **1864** (1868) Trowbridge *3 Scouts* 12, Now, hark ye. **1891** (1967) Freeman *New Engl. Nun* 139, Hark, there she is, singin'. **1907** *DN* 3.245 **eME,** *Hark*. . . Keep quiet, to children, who are making a noise. **1913** *DN* 4.54 **sNY,** *Hark*. . . Hush! Be quiet. It is used especially in silencing noisy children; as, "William, hark!" **1950** *WELS (When you want people to stop talking for a moment so you can hear something)* 3 Infs, **WI,** Hark; 1 Inf, My mother says hark. **1951** West *Witch Diggers* 75 **IN** (as of c1900), "Hark, what's that I hear?" . . The word "hark" was unusual too; it announced something out of the ordinary. **1953** Randolph–Wilson *Down in Holler* 20, **Ozarks,** The Ozarker's . . "Harkee now!" must have been "Hark ye" originally. **1959** *VT Hist.* new ser 27.140, *Hark*. . . A command to be quiet. Old Fashioned. Rare. **1965–70** *DARE* (Qu. NN19, *When you want people to stop talking for a moment so that you can listen for something*) 20 Infs, **Nth, esp NEast,** Hark; (Qu. NN12a, . . *To put a child off when he asks too many questions*) Inf **NY**2, Hark, like shut up; (QR, near Qu. X18) Inf **MA**55, Hark [hɑk], also used in telling children to listen; old-fashioned. [20 of 22 Infs old]

c in imper phr *hark your noise:* Be quiet!
1946 in 1986 *DARE* File **seMI,** *Hark:* A woman in her early thirties used this in addressing her child who was making some noise. "Hark your noise!" **1950** *WELS (A command to stop talking: not so polite)* 1 Inf, **cWI,** Hark your noise. **1971** *Down East* Nov 24 **ME,** No dictionary, so far as I know, defines *hark* or *hark your noise* as we use it in Maine, meaning, "be quiet!" **1975** Gould *ME Lingo* 126, *Hark*—Means to be quiet; children are told to "Hark your noise!"

2 with *after:* To follow.
1899 Tarkington *Gentleman* 109 **IN,** Men were running around a corner of the court-house, and the women and children were harking after.

hark v^{2} [Perh var of *hack* or **hawk** v^{2}] Cf **harp** v
To cough.
1967–68 *DARE* (Qu. BB11, *Speaking of a deep cough that you can't seem to get rid of: "Listen to him ______.")* Inf **MD**30, Hark and spit [hɑrk]; **TX**26, Hark. **1984** *Annals Internal Med.* 100.6.900 **cwAL,** *Hark (he harked up phlegm),* means to cough or clear the throat and is, I believe, a variation of *hawk,* which means the same and is imitative of the sound of this act.

hark after See **hark** v^{1} **2**

harkee See **hark** v^{1} **1b**

harken on v phr [*EDD* (at *hearken* v. 8) "to encourage, urge on, incite"]
1970 *DARE* (Qu. Y5, . . *To urge somebody to do something he shouldn't: "Johnny wouldn't have tried that if the other boys hadn't ______.")* Inf **VA**47, Harkened him on it.

harker n^{1}
1914 *DN* 4.74 **ME, nNH,** *Harker*. . . A fine, strong person or thing.

harker n^{2} [Transf from *harker* a listener]
1941 *LANE* Map 486, 1 inf, **csNH,** [hɑ˃·kə], older term for *ear.*

hark from the tomb n, adv phr
Something severe, esp a scolding or admonition; with great severity; at full tilt.
1851 (1969) Burke *Polly Peablossom* 71 **Sth,** Parson James, he was up on er log er preachin', an' er goin' it "hark from the tomb!" **1858** in 1986 *This State of Wonders* 7 **cIA,** Old Man Wells pitched into your father the other Sunday and gave his doctrines hark from the tombs. **1885** Twain *Huck. Finn* 225, Then Susan *she* waltzed in; and . . she did give Hare-lip hark from the tomb! **1889** Twain *CT Yankee* 109, A newspaper has its faults, and plenty of them, but no matter, it's hark from the tomb for a dead nation. . . You can't resurrect a dead nation without it. **c1960** *Wilson Coll.* **csKY,** *Hark-from-the-tomb* . . A severe scolding[:] "He sure give me a hark-from-the-tomb."

harking See **hark** v^{1} **1**

harky v Also *haa'kee, haky* [By ext from *hark ye* (at **hark** v^{1} **1b**)]
Hear, give heed.
1888 Jones *Negro Myths* 30 **GA coast,** Buh Wolf, him haky ter um. *Ibid* 168, *Haky, Harky,* hearken to, heed. **1922** Gonzales *Black Border* 283 **sSC, GA coasts** [Gullah], One who holds a warning as of small account will often say in response to an admonitory "haa'kee!" "Yaas, bubbuh, uh haa'kee, but uh yent yeddy"—literally, I hearken but I don't hear, while actually meaning I hear but I don't heed.

hark ye See **hark** v^{1} **1b**

hark your noise See **hark** v^{1} **1c**

Harlan's hawk n Also *Harlan hawk, Harlan's buzzard*
Std: a dark-colored subsp *(Buteo borealis harlani)* of the **red-tailed hawk.** Also called **black hawk 2, black warrior 1, chicken hawk 1, hen hawk, pi-ank**

Harlem oil n
A medicine containing kerosene or petroleum.
1887 Crew *Petroleum* 127, Petroleum is also the chief ingredient of a still popular medicine known as "Harlem Oil." **1969** *DARE* Tape **MI**103, Harlem oil for anybody that got sick, had a sore throat. It . . really was, I think, unrefined kerosene. [You] put a drop on a spoon of sugar. . . That was a real curse when I was a kid.

harlequin n
1 See **harlequin duck.**
2 See **harlequin quail.**
3 See **harlequin snake.**

harlequin cabbage bug n Also *cabbage bug, harlequin bug* [See quots 1872, 1889]
A brightly marked **stink bug** *(Murgantia histrionica)* which is a pest on cabbage and other crucifers. Also called **Abe Lincoln bug, calico-back 2, firebug 2, terrapin bug, Texas cabbage bug, third-party bug**
1872 MO State Entomol. *Annual Rept. for 1871* 35, *The Harlequin Cabbage-Bug.—Strachia [Murgantia] histrionica*. . . has of late years been gradually traveling toward us from the more southern States, and has already made its presence . . manifest in some of our southern counties, and in Kansas. . . so called from the gay theatrical harlequin-like manner in which the black and orange-yellow colors are arranged upon its body. **1889** *Century Dict.* 746, *Cabbage-bug*. . . The *Murgantia histrionica,* more fully called *harlequin cabbage-bug,* from its brilliant markings. **1892** Kellogg *Common Insects KS* 57, *Harlequin cabbage bug*. . . *(Murgantia histrionica)*. . . It is said that half a dozen adult insects will kill a cabbage in one day. **1926** Essig *Insects N. Amer.* 340, The harlequin cabbage bug, *Murgantia histrionica.* **1946** *Progress* March 11/2 *(DA),* It is quick and certain death to leaf hoppers, Lygus bugs, chinch bugs, squash bugs[,] cabbage caterpillars, the harlequin bug, the fireworm (on cranberries), and cattle lice. **1949** *AmSp* 24.109 **cnGA,** *Harlequin bugs* ['hɑːə·lɪkɪn]. . . A destructive species of insects, preying on cabbage leaves. **1980** Milne–Milne *Audubon Field Guide Insects* 486, *Harlequin Cabbage Bug*. . . Causes white and yellow blotches on the foliage of infested plants, ruining their commercial value.

harlequin caterpillar n
The larva of the milkweed **tiger moth** *(Euchaetias egle).*
1980 Milne–Milne *Audubon Field Guide Insects* 788, *Euchaetias egle*. . . The colorful black, white, and orange caterpillar is often called the "Harlequin Caterpillar."

harlequin duck n Also *harlequin*

A colorful water bird *(Histrionicus histrionicus).* Also called **glacier duck, lady lord, lord and lady, lord bird, mountain duck, painted duck, rock duck, sea mouse, sea pigeon, squeaker, squealer**

1814 Wilson *Amer. Ornith.* 8.139 **NEng coast,** The Harlequin Duck, so called from the singularity of its markings. **1875** *Amer. Naturalist* 9.76 **MT,** Dr. F. V. Hayden brought us from the mountains a pair of harlequin ducks *(Histrionicus torquatus).* **1882** Godfrey *Is. Nantucket* 243, Rarer species . . summer duck, red-head duck, harlequin, scoter. **1884** *Harper's New Mth. Mag.* Apr 706/2 **WA,** Harlequin- ducks of the gayest plumage . . also abound. **1917** (1923) *Birds Amer.* 1.143, Harlequin duck *Histrionicus histrionicus* . . Northern North America. **1946** Hausman *Eastern Birds* 161, The Harlequin [=*Histrionicus histrionicus*], not a very common duck, is frequently found in flocks of Golden-eyes. **1968** *DARE* (Qu. Q5, . . *Kinds of wild ducks*) Inf **AK**1, Harlequin.

harlequin quail n Also *harlequin* [Appar from the markings]

The Mearns quail *(Cyrtonyx montezumae),* native to the Southwest. Also called **crazy quail, fool quail, Massena quail, Montezuma quail, painted quail, partridge, squat quail**

1889 *Century Dict.* 1434, *Cyrtonyx.* . . the harlequin quails. **1961** Ligon *NM Birds* 98, When in danger, the Harlequin Quail rely for protection on inaction. . . No other Quail of the Southwest has such altitudinal range variation as the Harlequin. **1982** Elman *Hunter's Field Guide* 102, The harlequin, or Mearns, quail . . has a small range. . . But since it is legal game in Arizona . . , the harlequin merits description.

harlequin snake n Also *harlequin* [From the variegated colors]

=**coral snake 1a.**

1831 Audubon *Ornith. Biog.* 1.278, *The Harlequin Snake* . . is rather rare in the United States, where I have seen it only in the south. **1885** Holder *Marvels Animal Life* 131, The coloring of the harlequin . . is exceedingly rich. **1908** Biol. Soc. DC *Proc.* 21.77 **TX,** *Harlequin Snake.* This handsome snake is not uncommon. **1921** *Outing* Aug 219/2, The coral snake (known also as the harlequin snake) ranges from South Carolina southwestward to Texas. **1953** Schmidt *N. Amer. Amphibians* 223, *Micrurus fulvius fulvius.* . . *Common name.*—Coral snake, harlequin snake.

harlequin squash n

A **turban squash.**

1969 *DARE* (Qu. I23, . . *Kinds of squash*) Inf **MI**108, Harlequin squash, called turban or Mexican, has a large orange bottom.

harm adj [Perh abbr for *harmful* or attrib use of *harm* n injury]

Harsh; unkind.

1889 (1971) Farmer *Americanisms* 289, In Georgia *harm* is used in the sense of unkind; thus unkind words would be *harm* words, and in speaking well of a person it might be said that "he never did a harm thing to anyone." **1928** Peterkin *Scarlet Sister Mary* 264 **SC,** I hate to say a harm word, but dat 'oman ain' decent to come in a church. **1984** Wilder *You All Spoken Here* 46 **Sth,** *Harm words:* Words used in bad-mouthin'.

harmar See **hammer**

harmonate v Cf Intro "Language Changes" III.1

1968 *DARE* (Qu. II1a, *If two people don't get along well together, you'd say, "They don't ______."*) Inf **AK**8, Harmonate.

harmonica n Also *harmonia, harmonic(um), harmoniky, harmonister*

A Forms.

1916 *DN* 4.347 **TX, PA,** *Harmonicum.* . . Harmonica. **1966–69** *DARE* (Qu. FF7, *A small musical instrument that you blow on, and move from side to side in your mouth*) Inf **FL**23, Harmonic; **GA**77, Harmonister [hɑ'mʌnɨstə]; **WV**7, Harmoniky [ˌhɑɚ'mɑ·nəkɪ]. **1973** Allen *LAUM* 1.207 (as of c1950), For the small wind instrument the literary and commercial term, *harmonica,* has a quite uniform distribution throughout the U[pper] M[idwest] [although it is not the main term used]. *Ibid* **cSD,** Harmonia [1 inf].

B Sense.

A Jew's harp.

1967 *DARE* (Qu. FF8, . . *Small instrument that you hold between the teeth and pluck on*) Infs **AR**47, **MO**12, Harmonica.

harness n Also *harny* Pronc-sp *haa'ness, horness* See Pronc Intro 3.I.1.c

A Forms.

1922 Gonzales *Black Border* 305 **sSC, GA coasts** [Gullah glossary], *Haa'ness*—harness. **1930** *DN* 6.88 **cnWV,** *Harny,* shortened form of harness. **1976** Garber *Mountain-ese* 43 **Appalachians,** *Horness* . . harness—Put the horness on the ole mare and hitch her to the bull-tongue plow.

B Senses.

1 Clothing, esp a uniform. Cf **trotting harness**

1853 Simms *Sword & Distaff* 374 **SC,** He proceeded, with the help of Tom and Pomp, to put himself in harness. **1899** (1912) Green *VA Folk-Speech* 217, *Harness.* . . Clothing; dress; garments. **a1910** in 1917 Twain *What is Man* 225, At the Metropolitan in New York they sit in a glare, and wear their showiest harness. **1914** Jackson *Criminal Slang* 42, *Harness.* General currency. A uniform. **1931** *Writer's Digest* 11.42 [Railroad terms], *Harness*—Passenger conductor's uniform. **1943** *AmSp* 18.166 [Railroad terms], *Harness.* Dress uniform of a passenger conductor, blue tail-coat. **1966–68** *DARE* (Qu. W39, *Joking ways of referring to a person's best clothes*) Inf **MD**49, Sunday harness; (Qu. W43, . . *Joking words . . for clothes*) Infs **CO**47, **WA**18, Harness.

2 Suspenders.

1941 *LANE* Map 363 *(Suspenders)* 1 inf, **cCT,** I call it my [harnə˞s]. **1950** *WELS (What . . a man wear[s] over his shoulders to hold up his trousers)* 1 Inf, **swWI,** Harness.

harness cask n [Etym uncert; cf quots 1859, 1957] **chiefly NEng** *obs*

A cask or tub with a tight-fitting cover used primarily on shipboard for storing or soaking salt meat.

1840 (1841) Dana *2 Yrs.* 362, Before any of the beef is put into the harness-cask, the steward comes up, and picks it all over, and takes out the best pieces. **1859** (1968) Bartlett *Americanisms* 190, *Harness-cask.* A conical cask bound with iron hoops, from which salt meat is served out at sea. The cask is usually painted green and the hoops black; the resemblance of the latter to the black leathern straps of harness, has probably given rise to the name. **1904** *DN* 2.426 **Cape Cod MA** (as of a1857), *Harness cask.* . . A wooden barrel with a close fitting cover for salt meat, etc. **1905** (1906) Low *Some Recoll.* 19 **NYC** (as of 1840s), I also enjoyed cutting a piece of raw salt pork from the harness cask at ten o'clock at night, and walking the deck with a hard navy biscuit and the pork. **1957** Beck *Folkl. ME* 194, On many American vessels a barrel of salt beef was taken out of the storeroom each week and dumped into a large chest . . called the "harness cask." . . The term [sic] harness cask and salt horse were largely derived from the fact that this chest was secured to the deck by means of four horseshoes spiked to its sides. **1975** Gould *ME Lingo* 126, *Harness cask*—An oaken tub with brass hoops used for overnight soaking or freshening of salted meats. Both mariners and woodsmen always maintained most of the meat they got was "salt-horse," so the word *harness* is apt.

harnessed, get oneself v phr Also *get one in the harness* Cf **double harness**

To get married; to cause one to get married.

1903 (1965) Adams *Log Cowboy* 81 **TX,** Now a girl can't show her true colors . . but get her in the harness once, and then she'll show you the white of her eyes, balk, and possibly kick over the wagon tongue. **1968–69** *DARE* (Qu. AA15a, . . *Joking ways . . of saying people got married*) Inf **NY**37, Got harnessed; (Qu. AA15b, . . *Joking ways . . of saying that a man is getting married*) Inf **NC**72, Got himself harnessed.

harness-head tub n Cf **cannikin 1, harness cask**

1904 *DN* 2.426 **Cape Cod MA** (as of a1857), *Harness head tub.* . . A wooden firkin-shaped pail with wooden handle and close fitting cover, used for sugar, crackers, etc. In some parts of the country it is called a *canny pail,* or *can pail.*

harness weight n

=**hitching weight.**

1967 *DARE* Tape **TX**9, An iron weight. . . We called it a bridle weight, a harness weight. . . You kept it in the floor of the buggy or surrey. . . You'd lift it out and attach it to the bridle and then put the weight on the ground.

harnsome See **handsome**

harnswaggle See **hornswoggle**

harnt See **haunt**

harny See **harness**

harp n

1 A harmonica. **chiefly Sth, S Midl** See Map Cf **French harp 1, mouth harp**

1887 *Scribner's Mag.* 2.481 **AR,** He caught Bulah's hand just in time to prevent harp and handkerchief going into the Black River. **1896** *DN* 1.418 **wFL,** *Harp:* mouth organ. **1905** *DN* 3.82 **nwAR. 1908** *DN* 3.319 **eAL, wGA. 1916** *DN* 4.347 **TX. 1938** Stuart *Dark Hills* 262 **neKY,** We got the Potter boys over with the banjo, fiddle, harp and guitar. **1942** Thomas *Blue Ridge Country* 320, He puts a harp in his mouth and plays it. **1965–70** *DARE* (Qu. FF7, *A small musical instrument that you blow on, and move from side to side in your mouth*) 107 Infs, **chiefly Sth, S Midl,** Harp. **1972** *PADS* 58.16 **cwAL,** *Harmonica.* Southern *harp* (14 [infs]) is more frequent than South Midland *french harp* (10 [infs]) and the general term *harmonica* (3 [infs], educated usage); *harp* was used by all Negro informants.

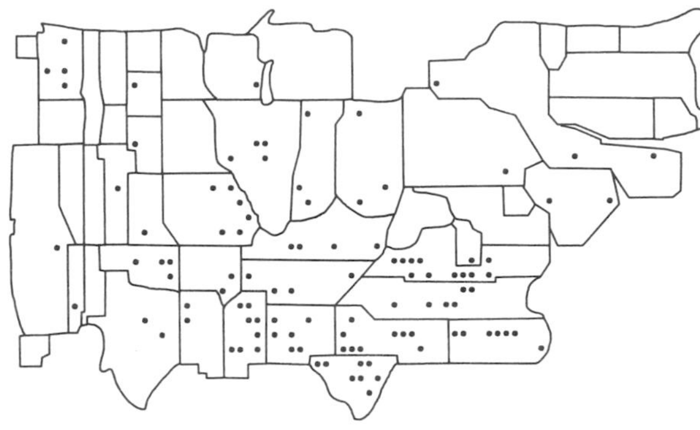
•harp n 1 (Qu. FF7)

2 A Jew's harp.

1941 *LANE* Map 413 **chiefly ME,** [*Harp* . . is given by 27 infs for "a bent tongue set in a lyre-shaped metal frame, held against the teeth and sounded by striking with the finger."] **1967–70** *DARE* (Qu. FF8, . . *Small instrument that you hold between your teeth and pluck on*) Infs **CA**207, **MO**15, **MA**33, Harp.

3 A person of Irish birth or descent. [From the harp as an emblem of Ireland] **chiefly NEast** *often derog*

1904 Number 1500 *Life in Sing Sing* 249/1 **NY,** *Harp.* An Irishman. **1914** Jackson *Criminal Slang* 43, *Harp.* . . General currency. An Irishman; used principally to designate the raw type. **1922** *DN* 5.181 **nID** [Miners' speech], *Harp.* . . An Irishman. miners in northern Idaho. **1924** Marks *Plastic Age* 169 **NEng,** "He's a harp," said a brother scornfully. "At any rate, he's a Catholic." **1930** Irwin *Amer. Tramp* 96, *Harp.* . . An Irishman, more especially an ignorant or stupid one. **1936** Dos Passos *Big Money* 75 **NYC,** The foreman was a big loudmouthed harp. **1941** *LANE* Map 454 *(Nicknames for an Irishman)* **scattered, but esp MA,** Harp. **1965–70** *DARE* (Qu. HH28, . . *Nicknames* . . *for people of foreign background: Irish*) 15 Infs, **chiefly NEast,** Harp; (Qu. CC4, . . *Nicknames* . . *for various religions or religious groups*) Infs **MD**49, **NJ**19, Harps—Irish (Roman) Catholics; [**NY**80, **PA**49, 90, 175, 202, Harps—Catholics]. **1968** Adams *Western Words* 141, *Harp*—What the logger calls an Irishman. **1969** *DARE* Tape **PA**225, I don't know what they [=Protestants] call us [=Catholics]—harps or something. [Inf is of Irish descent.]

4 also attrib: Any of several collections of hymn tunes written with **shape notes.** [Abbr for **sacred harp**] Cf **fasola**

1930 *Chr. Sci. Monitor* (Boston MA) 2 June 3/4 **TN, NC,** They sing from a collection of psalm and hymn tunes called the New Harp of Columbia, hence the name for the meetings, "Harp Singings." **1933** Jackson *White Spirituals* 94, B. F. White and E. J. King produced the first edition of the *Sacred Harp* in Hamilton, Harris County, Georgia, in 1844. . . Its title was a favorite. The number of song books appearing in the first half of the nineteenth century with the word "Harp" in their titles is amazing, and there were several "Sacred Harps" among them. **1960** Hall *Smoky Mt. Folks* 61, *Harp singin':* a community of church singing in which a *Sacred Harp* song book is used. (The Sacred Harp is a collection of psalm and hymn tunes with the music written with shape notes.) **1967** *DARE* Tape **TX**49A, He's an old harp singer, too, you oughta hear him sing an old harp song.

harp v Cf **hark** v²

To cough; to hack.

1968–69 *DARE* (Qu. BB11, *Speaking of a deep cough that you can't seem to get rid of: "Listen to him ______.*") Infs **IN**75, **IA**27, Harp.

harpoon n

1 The penis.

1960 Criswell *Resp. to PADS 20* **Ozarks,** *Harpoon.* . . The male sexual organ. Very frequent[ly] used among men in speaking of the sexual act, still used. "I'd shore like to throw the harpoon in her."

2 See quot. [Abbr for *harpoon-fork*]

1950 *WELS (Forks used in farm work)* 1 Inf, **cwWI,** Harpoon or grapple to unload hay from wagon to mow.

harpoon v [Transf from *harpoon* to capture with a harpoon]

To pursue and catch (a mate).

1851 (1976) Melville *Moby-Dick* 391, The gentleman had originally harpooned the lady. **1968** *DARE* (Qu. AA5, *If a woman seems to be going after one certain man that she wants to marry: "She's ______ him."*) Inf **NY**76, Out to harpoon.

harpooning vbl n

1969 *DARE* (Qu. II27, . . *A very sharp scolding*) Inf **CA**169, Harpooning.

harr See **hair** n

harred up See **haired up**

harrer See **harrow**

harricane See **hurricane**

harrier n Also *harrier hawk*

=**marsh hawk.**

1858 Baird *Birds* 38, *Circus hudsonius.* . . *The Harrier—The Marsh Hawk* . . well known as one of the most common hawks inhabiting the States of the Atlantic, . . is equally abundant on the coasts of the Pacific. **1874** Coues *Birds NW* 331, It often courses very low over the ground, and rather swiftly, turning, passing and repassing, "quartering" the ground like a well-broken dog. This is the habit that has given it the name of "Harrier." **1883** *Cassell's Nat. Hist.* III. 270 *(OED),* They retain the facial ruff of the Harriers, and hence the name of Harrier-Hawk. **1917** (1923) *Birds Amer.* 2.65, *Marsh hawk, Circus hudsonius.* . . Slowly and steadily with a gliding flight the Harrier quarters back and forth across the fields. **1968** *DARE* (Qu. Q4, . . *Kinds of hawks*) Infs **PA**155, **WI**58, Harrier hawk.

Harris's sparrow n

Std: a North American sparrow *(Zonotrichia quaerula).* Also called **black-cape sparrow, blackhood, mourning sparrow**

harrow n, v Usu |ˈhæro, -ə, ˈhɛro, -ə|; also freq |ˈhɑro, -ə|; for addit varr see quots See also Pronc Intro 3.I.2.a, 3.I.12.d Pronc-spp *har, harrer, harruh, harry, horry*

Std senses, var forms.

1890 *DN* 1.71 **LA,** *Harrow* . . with *a* as in father. **1908** *DN* 3.319 **eAL, wGA,** *Harrow.* . . Pronounced [ˈhɑrə]. **1914** *DN* 4.103 **cKS,** The sound [ɑ] occurs in . . *harrow.* **1922** Gonzales *Black Border* 306 **sSC, GA coasts** [Gullah glossary], *Harruh*—harrow. **1923** *DN* 5.209 **swMO,** *Har'.* . . Harrow. **1936** *AmSp* 11.243 **eTX,** Harrow *Plantation-Type* [ˈhærə], *Hill-Type* [ˈhærə], [hæ˄ɚ], *Negro* [hæ:ə]. **1938** FWP *Guide DE* 500, A sparrow is a *sporry* in some spots, a harrow a *horry.* **1939** *LANE* Map 167, [*Harrow* is usually pronounced [ˈhæro(u), hærə], also [hɑrə], infrequently [ˈhɛroʊ].] **1940** Writers' Program *Guide MD* 378, Women wear old-time slat bonnets as they "horry" the corn. **1942** Warnick *Garrett Co. MD* 1 (as of 1900–1918), Words ending in "row" were often pronounced "ry" as in borry, furry, harry. **1942** Hall *Smoky Mt. Speech* 25, *Arrow, harrow* . . *wheelbarrow.* Usage of [ɑ] and [æ] appears to be about evenly divided in these words. [Footnote:] Local informants say, however, that [ɑ] is much more frequent than [æ]. **c1960** *Wilson Coll.* **csKY,** *Harrow.* . . Often it is /ˈhɑrə/ or /ˈhɑrr̩/ among older people. **1967–69** *DARE* Tape **CT**2, Harrow [ˈhæəro]; **GA**77, [hæɚ]; **TX**5, [hæro]; **TX**8, [hɛrə, hɛəɚ]. **1968** *DARE* (Qu. L20, *The implement used in a field after it's been plowed to break up the lumps*) Inf **NJ**10, Cut harrer. **1976** Allen *LAUM* 3.33 (as of c1950), As is true in the East neither *harrow* . . nor . . *barrel* has the high incidence of [ɑ] found in *wheelbarrow.* In both words the low-front [æ] seems to have a Northern weighting, in contrast with Midland strength in [ɛ].

harrow drag See **drag harrow**

harrow-head See **hairy head**

harruh, harry See **harrow**

harrycane See **hurricane**

Harry Dick n

1 The devil. [Cf Engl dial *Old* (or *Lord*) *Harry* the devil]

[**1896** *DN* 1.418 **Everglades FL,** *Harry dick:* pop. etym. for *heretic.*] **1950** *PADS* 14.36 **SC,** *Harry Dick. . .* The devil. "The old Harry Dick."

2 See **hairydick.**

harrykin See **hurricane**

harry wicket n [Echoic] **NEng**

=**flicker** n² **1.**

1887 *Forest & Stream* 28.248, *Colaptes auratus. . .* Harry Wicket. N[ew] H[ampshire]. **1914** *DN* 4.154 **NH,** *Harry wicket. . .* A golden-winged woodpecker. **1927** Forbush *Birds MA* 2.292, *Colaptes auratus luteus. . .* Harrywicket. **1956** MA Audubon Soc. *Bulletin* 40.82, *Yellow-shafted Flicker. . .* Harry-wicket (N.H., Mass., Conn., Sonic.)

harsee n [Etym unknown]

=**saguaro.**

1974 (1977) Coon *Useful Plants* 83, *Cereus giganteus*—Suwarrow, harsee.

harsh n [Ger *Hirsch*]

1930 Shoemaker *1300 Words* 31 **cPA Mts** (as of c1900), *Harsh*—A deer.

harslet See **haslet**

‡**hart** n [Var of *hod,* perh by hypercorrection]

1970 *DARE* (Qu. F44, . . *A container for coal*) Inf **DC**12, [ko·l hɑrt]—shaped like a bucket with a spout on it.

hartshorn See **hartshorn plant**

hartshorn bush n

=**royal fern.**

1876 Hobbs *Bot. Hdbk.* 51, Harts horn bush, Buckhorn brake, Osmunda regalis. **1900** Lyons *Plant Names* 270, *Osmunda regalis. . .* Hartshorn bush. . . tonic, astringent, demulcent.

hartshorn plant n Also *hartshorn*

A **pasqueflower** (here: *Anemone patens,* usu *A. p.* var *wolfgangiana* also known as *A. nuttalliana*).

1893 *Jrl. Amer. Folkl.* 6.136, *Anemone patens,* var. *Nuttalliana.* . . hartshorn plant, headache plant. . . Minnesota. **1900** Lyons *Plant Names* 311, *Pulsatilla hirsutissima. . .* Hartshorn plant, Headache plant. **1937** U.S. Forest Serv. *Range Plant Hdbk.* W159, Although pasqueflower is the common name most widely used, such other appellations as . . hartshorn, . . have . . designated this species. **1950** Gray-Fernald *Manual of Botany* 663, *Hartshorn-plant. . .* Prairies and exposed slopes. **1970** Correll *Plants TX* 649, *Anemone patens* L. var. *Wolfgangiana* (Bess.) Koch. . . Hartshorn-plant. **1976** Bailey-Bailey *Hortus Third* 76, *[Anemone] Nuttalliana. . .* Hartshorn plant.

hart's tongue n [From the shape of the fronds]

1 Std: a widely distributed fern *(Phyllitis scolopendrium).* Also called **lamb's tongue, seaweed fern, snake fern**

2 A **strap fern** (here: *Campyloneurum phyllitidis*).

1868 (1870) Gray *Field Botany* 363, *P[olypodium] Phyllitidis, Harts-tongue,* of Tropical America.

harve v [Cf *EDD harve* v. "To harrow"; but perh abbr for *harvest*]

1968 *DARE* (Qu. L10, *After hay has been cut, then it grows back and you cut it again*) Inf **GA**52, Of soybeans: cut it and harve it in.

harve, gang See **gang harve**

harvest n, v Pronc-spp *haa'bis', harbis, harves'* Cf Pronc Intro 3.I.17, 3.I.22

A Forms.

1922 Gonzales *Black Border* 305 **sSC, GA coasts** [Gullah glossary], *Haa'bis'*—harvest. **1946** *AmSp* 21.271 **neKY,** *Harvesses.* This pl. of harvest is a 'correct' analogical formation from the mispronounced *harves'.* **1954** *PADS* 21.30 **SC,** *Harbis home.*

B As noun.

Attrib: in var combs referring to a celebration held during or at the conclusion of the harvest. **chiefly Nth, N Midl** Cf **harvest home 2**

1824 Doddridge *Notes Indian Wars* 169 **WV, wPA** (as of 1763-83), At house raisings, log rollings and harvest parties every one was expected to do his duty faithfully. **1845** *Knickerbocker* 26.410 **PA,** One nice Dutch landlady . . was very handsomely dressed, to attend a 'harvest-meeting;' a meeting for prayer and thanksgiving. **1950** *WELS Suppl.* **ceWI,** *Harvest supper*—A church supper held in October. **1965-70** *DARE* (Qu. FF16, . . *Local . . celebrations*) 19 Infs, **chiefly Nth, N Midl,** Harvest festival; 16 Infs, **chiefly Nth, N Midl, esp PA,** Harvest fair; **CT**12, **MA**5, 14, Harvest supper; **PA**122, Harvest dances; **PA**104, Harvest days; **GA**70, Harvest sale; **PA**54, Harvest service; [**RI**15, Grange harvest;] (Qu. FF1, . . *Group meeting called a 'social'*) Infs **MI**9, **MN**33, Harvest festival; **MI**108, **NY**121, Harvest supper; (Qu. FF2, . . *Kinds of parties*) Inf **SC**69, Harvest parties.

harvest bee See **harvest fly**

harvestbells n

A **gentian** (here: *Gentiana saponaria*).

1900 Lyons *Plant Names* 171, *G[entiana] Saponaria. . .* Soapwort Gentian, . . Harvestbells. **1949** Moldenke *Amer. Wild Flowers* 227, *D[asystephana] saponaria,* known also as . . *harvestbells,* lives in swamps and wet places . . , blooming from August to October.

harvest bird n

Either the **dickcissel** or the **grasshopper sparrow.**

1951 *AmSp* 26.277, When men are in the harvest fields they see birds unnoticed at other times and have named a few of them from the season, as *harvest bird* (grasshopper sparrow and dickcissel, Kans.)

harvest brodiaea n

A **brodiaea** (here: usu *Brodiaea coronaria,* but also *B. elegans*).

1897 Parsons *Wild Flowers CA* 318, In the latter part of May and early in June, just as the grain is mellowing in the fields, the dry grasses of our hill-slopes and roadsides begin to reveal the beautiful blossoms of the "harvest Brodiaea." **1915** (1926) Armstrong-Thornber *Western Wild Flowers* 18, *Harvest Brodiaea. . .* At the time of the hay harvest, these handsome flowers, which look like clusters of little blue lilies, begin to appear. **1934** Haskin *Wild Flowers Pacific Coast* 9, *Harvest Brodiaea. . .* In late June and July when the hillsides are turning brown from the drought. **1961** Thomas *Flora Santa Cruz* 126 **cwCA,** *B[rodiaea] elegans. . .* Harvest Brodiaea. . . *B. coronaria. . .* Harvest Brodiaea. **1976** Bailey-Bailey *Hortus Third* 181.

harvest bug n

1 =**harvest mite.** [*OED* 1768-74 →]

1889 *Century Dict.* 2731, *Harvest-bug. . .* Same as *harvest-tick.* **1967-68** *DARE* (Qu. R11, *A very tiny fly that you can hardly see, but that stings*) Inf **SC**46, Harvest bug; **DE**1, Harvest bugs, little tiny things that look like a strand of hair; they come in July when the wheat is ripe; (Qu. R12, . . *Kinds of flies*) Inf **MD**20, Harvest bug, a crawling insect, gets on ripening wheat.

2 See **harvest fly.**

harvest cluster-lily See **harvest lily**

harvester n

1 See **harvestman 1.**

2 A small, chiefly orange-and-brown butterfly *(Feniseca tarquinius).* Also called **wanderer**

1902 Holland *Butterfly Book* 251, But one species of the genus is known. . . *Feniseca tarquinius. . .* The Harvester. **1905** Kellogg *Amer. Insects* 444, The harvester . . is a common species all through the eastern states west to the Mississippi River. **1981** Pyle *Audubon Field Guide Butterflies* 402, No other North American butterfly looks or behaves like the Harvester.

harvester ant n Also *harvesting ant* Cf **cutting ant**

Any of several spp of ants of the genera *Pogonomyrmex* and *Pheidole* which gather and store up seed. Also called **agricultural ant**

1882 (1970) Romanes *Animal Intelligence* 102, The harvesting or agricultural ants of Texas. **1926** Essig *Insects N. Amer.* 860, *The Texan harvester or agricultural ant, Pogonomyrmex barbatus . .* is the largest and most powerful harvester. **1940** Teale *Insects* 89, In some species of harvester ants, the larger soldier insects have the job of "nut crackers" for the colony. They crush the shells of the seeds with large jaws. **1950**

WELS 1 Inf, **cwWI,** Harvester ant. **1954** Borror–DeLong *Intro. Insects* 728, The ants in the genera *Pogonomyrmex* and *Pheidole* are often called harvester ants or agricultural ants; they feed on seeds, and store seeds in their nests. **1967** *DARE* (Qu. R18, . . *Kinds of ants*) Inf **WY**1, Harvester ant, not in immediate area, [but in] lower elevations.

harvest fish n [See quot 1814]

A **butterfish 1** (here: *Peprilus alepidotus, P. paru, Poronotus triacanthus*).

1814 in 1815 Lit. & Philos. Soc. NY *Trans.* 1.366 **NY,** *Harvest fish. (Stromateus longipinnus)*. . . So called by some of the fishermen, because he visits the coast about the season of harvest. **1842** DeKay *Zool. NY* 4.136, *The Long-finned Harvest-fish. Rhombus longipinnis*. . . Its present ascertained geographical range is from South-Carolina to the coast of New-York. *Ibid* 4.137, *The Short-finned Harvest-fish. Rhombus triacanthus* . . is equally remarkable for . . its excellence as an article of food. **1887** Goode *Amer. Fishes* 221, The "Butter-fish" of Massachusetts and New York, *Stromateus triacanthus,* sometimes known in New Jersey as the "Harvest-fish." **1897** Amer. Museum Nat. Hist. NY *Bulletin* 9.363-4, *Rhombus triacanthus*. . . *Harvest-fish* . . is found in Gravesend Bay from April to November. . . *Rhombus paru*. . . *Harvest-fish.* **1906** NJ State Museum *Annual Rept. for 1905* 270, *Poronotus triacanthus*. . . Butter Fish. Harvest Fish. Dollar Fish. **1939** Natl. Geogr. Soc. *Fishes* 68, Other local names [for *Poronotus triacanthus*] are harvestfish (a name more widely used for *Peprilus alepidotus*), shiner, and skipjack. **1955** Zim–Shoemaker *Fishes* 92, *Harvestfish* [=*Peprilus* spp] live more to the south than Butterfish and are not as important as food fish. . . The California Pompano [=*Palometa simillima*] (not a true pompano) is a common Pacific harvestfish. **1960** Amer. Fisheries Soc. *List Fishes* 45, Southern harvestfish . . *Peprilus alepidotus* . . Northern harvestfish . . *Peprilus paru.*

harvest flow n Also *harvest water* **S Atl**

In rice cultivation: the final flooding of the field.

1859 *Harper's New Mth. Mag.* Nov 728/2 **S Atl,** To the long flow there succeeds the fourth and last, or the harvest flow . . which is kept on until the rice is fully headed. **1867** *Harper's Weekly* 5 Jan 6/1 **seGA,** This flooding is kept up with the changes of the tide—being careful not to stretch the rice too much—till the time arrives for harvest-water, which is the last flooding. **1922** Gonzales *Black Border* 305 **sSC, GA coasts** [Gullah glossary], *Haa'bis'-flow*—harvest-flow, or last irrigation of the ricefields preceding the harvest. **1936** Smith–Sass *Carolina Rice* 28 **SC coast** (as of 1850s), When the ears were about to form, the last flow called the "harvest-flow" was put on to assist the ears in filling. The harvest-flow lasted from forty to fifty days, according to the maturing of the rice. The water was kept up to the "bead"—this being the top of the hollow joint in the barrel, where the ear was being formed. **1937** Heyward *Madagascar* 38 **csSC,** Should there be little or no rain, and should the crop begin to go backward, the time for putting on the "harvest-flow" would be advanced. This last irrigating was done solely to benefit the rice, for it was too late for the water to have any effect upon the grass.

harvest fly n Also rarely *harvest bee,* ~ *bug* **chiefly Nth**

=**cicada.**

1854 Emmons *Agriculture NY* 5.149, The *Homoptera* are divided into three families: 1. The *Harvest-flies,* called in systematic arrangement *Cicadidæ,* or *cicadians.* **1870** MO State Entomol. *Annual Rept.* 131, Reminding one of the mode of escape of our Harvest-flies *(Cicadæ).* **1878** Taylor *Between the Gates* 234 **IL,** From the great cathedral clock, to the mantel-shelf affair that ticks like a harvest-fly. **1881** *Harper's New Mth. Mag.* Dec 75/1 **NH,** Even the cicada, or drumming harvest fly, . . is his [=the sand-hornet's] very common victim. **1905** Kellogg *Amer. Insects* 167, The cicada that is most familiar, and on hand every summer . . is the large . . harvest-fly, *Cicada tibicen.* **1926** Essig *Insects N. Amer.* 200, The cicadas or harvest-flies are medium to large insects. **1967–70** *DARE* (Qu. R7, *Insects that sit in trees or bushes in hot weather and make a sharp, buzzing sound*) Infs **MA**15, **NJ**3, 12, Harvest fly; **NY**93, Harvest bee; **PA**231, Harvest bug; (Qu. R8, . . *Creatures that make a clicking or shrilling or chirping kind of sound*) Inf **NJ**66, Harvest fly.

harvest gnat n

=**harvest mite.**

1970 *DARE* (Qu. R11, *A very tiny fly that you can hardly see, but that stings*) Inf **VA**82, Harvest gnat.

harvest hawk n

=**sharp-shinned hawk.**

1951 *AmSp* 26.277, When men are in the harvest fields they see birds unnoticed at other times and have named a few of them from the season, as . . *harvest hawk* (sharp-shinned hawk, Colo.)

harvest home n

1 The conclusion of the harvest; see quot.

1954 *PADS* 21.30 **SC,** *Harbis home*. . . The time when the harvest has been gathered into the barn or otherwise under shelter.

2 A celebration held in connection with harvest time.

1831 Peck *Guide for Emigrants* 156, Whoever has passed down the Ohio in a November moon-light night, has heard the . . songs and shouts of merriment from the Kentucky side. It is the real harvest home of the slaves. **1851** in 1983 *PADS* 70.37 **ce,sePA,** Cloudy younger part of the family with Jonathon went to Harvest home at Centreville. **1939** FWP *Guide NJ* 132, Harvest home suppers are a standby of many rural churches throughout the State. **1951** Johnson *Resp. to PADS 20* **DE** *(Local holidays)* Harvest homes. **1967–68** *DARE* (Qu. FF16, . . *Local contests or celebrations*) Inf **PA**59, Harvest homes, gift to church and it is distributed; **OH**77, Harvest home festival, it's a fair; (Qu. FF1, . . *Group meeting*) Inf **NJ**51, Harvest home—big dinner, people bring food, dancing, at harvest time.

harvesting ant See **harvester ant**

harvest-lice n pl [Because the seeds appear at harvest time and stick like lice to clothing]

The fruits of agrimony (*Agrimonia* spp), **beggar ticks 1,** or **cleavers;** also the plants themselves.

c1873 in 1976 Miller *Shaker Herbs* 163, *Bidens frondosa*. . . Harvest Lice. *Ibid* 182, Harvest-Lice. *Bidens connata.* **1876** Hobbs *Bot. Hdbk.* 150, Bidens connata, . . Harvest lice. **1889** (1971) Farmer *Americanisms* 289, *Harvest lice* is a misnomer; the term is applied to the adhesive seeds of plants of the *Bidens* species. **1900** Lyons *Plant Names* 19, *Agrimonia*. . . Harvest-lice. *Ibid* 63, *B[idens] frondosa*. . . Harvest-lice. **1940** Clute *Amer. Plant Names* 5, *A[grimonia] Eupatoria*. . . Harvest-lice. *Ibid* 52, *G[alium] aparine*. . . Harvest-lice. **1976** Bailey–Bailey *Hortus Third* 41, *Agrimonia*. . . Harvest-lice.

harvest lily n Also *harvest cluster-lily*

A **brodiaea:** either **harvest brodiaea** or **Ithuriel's spear.**

1934 Haskin *Wild Flowers Pacific Coast* 9, *Harvest Cluster-Lily*. . . In late June and July when the hillsides are turning brown from the drought, the harvest lilies begin to appear. **1967** *DARE* FW Addit **swOR,** Harvest lily, brodiaea laxa.

harvest louse n Also *hay louse*

=**harvest mite.**

1889 *Century Dict.* 2731, *Harvest-louse*. . . Same as *harvest-tick.* **1968** *DARE* (Qu. R12, . . *Kinds of flies*) Inf **MD**26, Harvest lice or hay lice, in July, a short season for these small lice.

harvestman n

1 also *harvester, harvest spider:* =**daddy-long-legs 1.** [See quot 1980]

1864 (1873) Webster *Amer. Dict.* 499/3, *Father-long-legs*. . . A species of spider of the family *Phalangidæ;* . . called also *harvest-man, shepherd-spider,* and *daddy-long-legs.* [Webster: *U.S.*] **1869** *Amer. Naturalist* 3.46, A Harvest-man or Daddy-long-legs, allied to, but lower than the spiders. **1872** MO State Entomol. *Annual Rept.* 17, These animals are popularly called "Grand-Daddy-Long-Legs" in this country, but are also known as "Harvest-men" and "Grandfather-Gray-Beards." **1901** Howard *Insect Book* 94, The term "daddy-long-legs" in this country is applied exclusively to the so-called harvest spiders of the family Phalangiidæ. **1926** Essig *Insects N. Amer.* 11, The Phalangida . . are variously known as harvesters, harvestmen, harvest spiders, . . and so forth. **1967** *DARE* (Qu. R28, . . *Kinds of spiders*) Inf **OH**37, Harvestman, also called granddaddy longlegs. **1980** Milne–Milne *Audubon Field Guide Insects* 920, They are also called harvestmen, because the first species to be described were seen in fall at harvest time.

2 See quot. Cf **arab** n **B3, huckster**

1968 *DARE* (Qu. U6, *Someone who sells vegetables or other articles from a wagon or truck, going from house to house*) Inf **NC**50, Harvestman.

harvest mite n [In ref to their being esp troublesome to people harvesting grain and forage crops]

A predacious larval mite of the family Trombiculidae. Also called **chigger 1, harvest bug 1, harvest gnat, harvest louse, harvest tick, jigger, redbug, red louse, red mite**

1873 *Amer. Naturalist* 7.17, *The American Harvest mite (Leptus Americanus?. .)* . . is barely visible with the naked eye, moves readily and is found more frequently upon children than upon adults. **1874** MO State Entomol. *Annual Rept.* 122. *"Jiggers"* or *Harvest-mites: Leptus irritans,* . . and *L. Americanus.* **1915** U.S. Dept. Ag. *Farmers' Bulletin* 671.2 **Sth, Cent,** Soon after the harvest mite burrows under the human skin a small red spot appears. **1954** Borror–DeLong *Intro. Insects* 789, The majority of the harvest mites (also called chiggers or redbugs) which attack man belong to the family Trombiculidæ. **1967** *Merck Vet. Manual* 1183, *Chiggers* (*Trombicula alfreddugesi:* Red bugs, Harvest mites).

harvest mouse n

A small, dull-colored field mouse (*Reithrodontomys* spp) chiefly distinguished by grooved upper incisors.

1867 *Amer. Naturalist* 1.398, The little Harvest-mouse of the Southern States *(Reithrodon humilis).* **1938** FWP *Guide MN* 22, In addition to the common meadow mice, the observant may see the long-legged deer mouse, the rare grasshopper mouse, the tiny harvest mouse. **1950** *WELS* 1 Inf, **seWI,** Harvest mouse. **1980** Whitaker *Audubon Field Guide Mammals* 461, The tiny harvest mice *(Reithrodontomys)* . . live mainly in open grassy areas.

harvest pike n

A **needlefish** (here: *Strongylura* spp, esp *S. marina*).

1906 NJ State Museum *Annual Rept. for 1905* 204, *Tylosurus marinus.* . . Harvest Pike. . . A good food-fish, but avoided usually on account of the greenish color of the bones and flesh, especially by the ignorant, who regard it as poisonous. **1946** LaMonte *N. Amer. Game Fishes* 18, *Strongylura.* . . Harvest Pike.

harvest root n *obs*

=**butterfly weed 1.**

1830 *Huntingdon* (Pa.) *Courier* 15 Sep. 4/5 *(DA),* Harvest Root or Butterfly Wort, (Asclepias Tuberosa.)

harvest spider See **harvestman 1**

harvest tick n

=**harvest mite.**

1889 *Century Dict.* 2731, *Harvest-tick.* . . One of several different mites or acarids which are abundant and troublesome late in the summer and in autumn. They attach themselves like ticks to the skin.

harvest trout n

=**cutthroat trout.**

1972 Sparano *Outdoors Encycl.* 356, *Cutthroat Trout. Common Names* . . Harvest trout.

harvest water See **harvest flow**

harvey (bag) n

1989 *DARE* File, The act of lifting a person (from behind) by the belt, belt buckles, top of the underwear, the seat of the pants. . . 2 infs, **swIL, swCA,** Harvey; 2 infs, **cUT,** Harvey bag; 1 inf, **cUT,** Harvey bag—I associate this with a bag of toys, called a *harvey bag,* given to children who participated in a radio program called "Hotel Balderdash."

hase See **make haste**

hasenpfeffer n Also, by folk-etym, *hoss and peffer, horse and pepper;* abbrs *hoss(y)* [See quot 1952] **chiefly ePA** See Map

A card game; see quot 1974.

1913 *Official Rules of Card Games* 242, *Hasenpfeffer.* **1940** Wood–Goddard *Complete Games* 142, *Card games* . . *The Euchre Group* . . *Hasenpfeffer.* **1944** *Sat. Eve. Post* 25 Nov 27/1, Here, listed according to how widely they are known, are the card games America plays today: . . hasenpfeffer [approx 44th in the list]. **1952** Culbertson *Card Games* 209, *Hasenpfeffer*—Like the parent game, this variant of Euchre was probably invented by the Pennsylvania Dutch. It may have been named after the rabbit dish hasenpfeffer, or more likely, after the German expression *Hase im Pfeffer,* used like the American "in a pickle," for the player to whom the joker is dealt is apt to find it not an unmixed blessing. **1967–70** *DARE* (Qu. DD35, . . *Card games*) Infs **PA**25, 36, 48, 55, 83, 245, Hasenpfeffer; **PA**19, [hɔsn̩fefɚ]; **PA**29, [hɑsɪnpɛfɚ]; **PA**63, [hɑsn̩pɛfɚ]; **PA**139, [hɑsn̩fefɚ]; **PA**153, [hɑsipɛfɚ]; **PA**243, [ˈhɔsənfɛfɚ]; **PA**36, Hoss and peffer—called hossy; **PA**42, Hoss [hɔs]. **1967** *DARE* Tape **PA**22, And then they play hasenpfeffer. **1974** Gibson *Hoyle* 139, *Hasenpfeffer:* A cross between *Euchre* . . and *Five Hundred* . . played with a twenty-five-card pack, aces down to nines, with joker included as highest trump or "best bower". **1987** *NY Times*

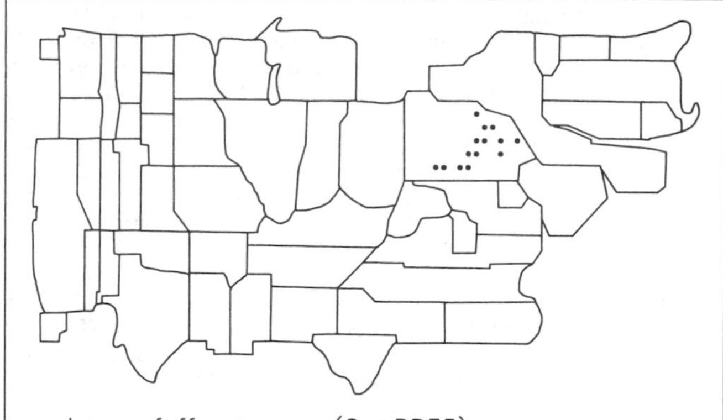

•hasenpfeffer + varr (Qu. DD35)

(NY) 27 Sept 29/3 **cnVT,** The first fiddle contest . . grew out of the club's regular games of horse and pepper, a game similar to bridge.

hash n

1 See quots. **Sth, S Midl** See Map

1954 *Harder Coll.* **cwTN,** *Hash* . . Meat food made from the head of a butchered hog. **1965–70** *DARE* (Qu. H43, *Foods made from parts of the head and inner organs of an animal*) Infs **SC**51, 56, **TN**30, **VA**39, Hash; **GA**4, **SC**11, Hog-head hash; **FL**26, **GA**88, Liver hash; **SC**51, Barbecue hash; **SC**38, Hog liver hash; **VA**48, Liver and light hash.

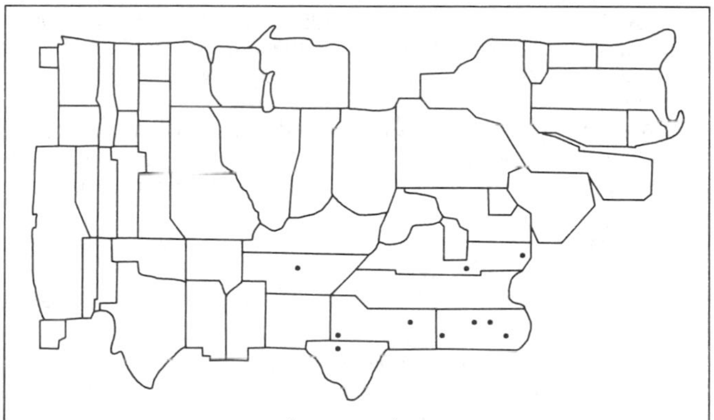

•hash n 1 + varr (Qu. H43)

2 also *pig hash:* Nonsense; gossip; hogwash.

1927 *AmSp* 2.276 **CA** [Stanford Univ slang], *Hash*—gossip. **1967–69** *DARE* (Qu. NN13, . . *Silly or untrue: "Oh, that's a lot of________."*) Infs **GA**72, **NE**3, Hash; **TX**32, Pig hash.

3 See **hash browns.**

hash adj [Pronc-sp for *harsh*] **esp NEng** Cf **mash** n

1818 Fessenden *Ladies Monitor* 172 **NEng,** A list of some provincial words and phrases, which ought to be avoided: . . *hash* for harsh. **1875** Holland *Sevenoaks* 36 **N Atl,** Has anybody spoke ha'sh to ye? **1891** *DN* 1.163 **cNY,** [hæš] < harsh. **1896** *DN* 1.418 **CT, NY,** *Hash:* for *harsh.* **1899** (1912) Green *VA Folk-Speech* 217, *Hash.* . . A variant of *harsh.* **1909** *DN* 3.412 **nME,** *Harsh* [hæš]. . . Sharp-tempered. *Ibid* 420 **Cape Cod MA,** *Hash.* Harsh. **1914** *DN* 4.74 **ME, nNH,** *Ha'sh* [ˈhɑɛš]. . . Harsh, hard. **1926** *DN* 5.383 **NEng,** *Hash* for harsh.

hashan See **hessian**

‡hashberry n

A **hackberry.**

1970 *DARE* (Qu. T13, . . *Trees*) Inf **VA**73, Hashberry [ˈhɛɪšbɚɪ].

hash-brown potatoes n pl Also *hash browns;* for addit varr see quots Cf **American fried potatoes 1, home fried potatoes**

Chopped or shredded potatoes packed together and fried on both sides.

1887 Parloa *Miss Parloa's Kitchen Companion* 501 **NEast,** *Hashed and Browned Potatoes.* . . Use . . cold boiled potatoes, cut into cubes, . . butter, . . flour, . . salt, . . pepper, and . . stock. . . When the mixture becomes browned, fold it like an omelet, and turn out on a hot dish. **1896** (c1973) Farmer *Orig. Cook Book* 285, *Hashed Brown Pota-*

toes. . . Mix potatoes thoroughly with fat; cook three minutes, stirring constantly; let stand to brown underneath. **1917** WI Farmers' Inst. *Women's Bulletin No. 10* 52, *Hashed Brown Potatoes.* Chop potatoes until fine . . season with onion juice, salt and pepper, and turn into a well greased frying pan; add one-fourth cupful of milk and cook without stirring for ten minutes. Fold and roll like an omelet on a hot platter when ready to serve. **1950** *WELS (Kinds of fried potatoes)* 2 Infs, **WI,** Hash brown; 1 Inf, Cottage-fried or hash-brown—diced, boiled or baked potatoes browned in bacon fat or other shortening; 1 Inf, Hash brown—cut up and fried in butter or bacon fat; 1 Inf, Hash-browned-potatoes, chopped and browned; 1 Inf, Hashed brown—chopped fine and fried. **1965–70** *DARE* (Qu. H47, *Kinds of fried potatoes*) 189 Infs, **widespread,** Hash-brown (potatoes); 43 Infs, **scattered exc NEast,** Hash browns; 31 Infs, **scattered,** Hash-browned; 26 Infs, **scattered,** Hashed-brown; 16 Infs, **scattered,** Hashed-browned; **IN**60, Hashed browns; **MN**30, Brown hashed potatoes.

hash-browns See **hash-brown potatoes**

hasher n

1 A waiter or waitress. [*hash* a lunch counter or cafeteria meal] **scattered, but esp NW**

1916 *Editor* 43.6.297/2 **MT, WY,** Hasher, meaning waitress. **1918** *DN* 5.25 **NW,** *Hasher.* . . A waiter in a restaurant; usually a woman. **1927** *AmSp* 2.276 **CA** [Stanford Univ slang], *Hasher*—table waiter. **1930** *Amer. Mercury* Nov 345/2, A man who ran a swell eating-house . . was going to give them jobs as hashers. **1940** Cottrell *Railroader* 128, *Hasher*—A waitress—the word is used by many other groups. **1943** *AmSp* 18.308 **eTX, wLA** [Café terms], *Hasher.* A boy or man who waits on customers. **1950** *WELS (Joking names for waiters or waitresses in restaurants)* 4 Infs, **WI,** Hasher. **1958** McCulloch *Woods Words* 81 **Pacific NW,** *Hasher*—A waitress. **1961** *AmSp* 36.271 **NW** [Truck drivers' language], At a *truck stop* . . the *hasher* serves your *diesel* or *Joe* or *Java.*

2 A cook. [*hash* a dish of chopped food, often leftovers]

1950 *WELS (Joking or nicknames for a cook)* 1 Inf, **seWI,** Hasher. **1968** Adams *Western Words* 141, *Hasher*—A logger's name for the cook.

3 A Chinese person. [Perh from Chinese dishes consisting of many and finely chopped ingredients]

1967 *DARE* (Qu. HH28, . . *People of foreign background: Chinese*) Inf **MI**47, Hashers.

hash fries n pl Also *hash fried potatoes*

1 =**hash browns.**

1967–69 *DARE* (Qu. H47, *Kinds of fried potatoes*) Inf **NY**209, Hash fried; **NY**35, Hash fries.

2 See quot.

1950 *WELS (Kinds of fried potatoes)* 1 Inf, **csWI,** Hash fried, fried with leftover meat.

hash over v phr

To reheat (food).

1931–33 *LANE Worksheets* **csCT,** Hash it over, warm it over.

hash up v phr [Perh var of *hatch up* infl by *hash out* or *hash over*]

1969 *DARE* (Qu. JJ36, *To work out a plan . . "Mary knows more about that, you and she can ______ together."*) Inf **MA**48, Hash it up.

haslet n Usu |hæslɪt|; for addit varr see quots Also sp *harslet, hasslet* **formerly more widespread, now esp Sth** See Map

Usu the edible viscera and occas other parts of an animal; a dish made from the viscera.

1806 (1970) Webster *Compendious Dict.* 139/2, *Harslet.* . . the heart, liver, lights, &c. of a hog. **1847** (1852) Crowen *Amer. Cookery* 104 **NY,** *To make a dish of the Harslet.*—Having boiled the heart, liver, &c. [of a roasting pig], . . chop them small, add a good bit of butter . . , season high with pepper and salt, dredge in a large teaspoonful of flour, stir it and let it simmer gently until it is hot, then serve in a side dish with the pig. *Ibid* 127, *Sheep Harslet Hashed.*—When you cut up the sheep, take the heart, liver, and lights, wash them in cold water, then boil them tender [etc]. **1899** (1912) Green *VA Folk-Speech* 217, *Harslet.* . . The heart, liver, and lights of hogs, sheep, beeves. **1903** *DN* 2.298 **Cape Cod MA** (as of 1850s), *Haslet.* . . Liver, lights, and tongue of a killed pig. **1908** *DN* 3.319 **eAL, wGA,** *Haslet.* . . 1. The windpipe of an animal. 2. The liver and lights of a slaughtered pig. **1914** *DN* 4.74 **ME, nNH,** *Haslet,* or *harslet.* **1933–34** *Hanley Disks* **ceMA,** In pigs they call the haslet the heart and lungs. *Ibid* **csMA,** *Haslet* [hɑtslɪt], just the heart itself. **1939** *LANE* Map 209, The *haslet* . . may include the heart, liver and lights . . the heart, liver and kidney . . the heart and liver . . or the liver and lights . . or it may denote only the liver . . or the lights. . . One informant uses *haslet* of 'the wind pipe and the swallow pipe' . . [and] another says the haslet is the pluck chopped up and cooked. Three informants apply the term to the membrane which covers the heart. **1940** Harris *Folk Plays* 49 **NC,** And you take this here and fill it up with haslet-hash. **1949** Kurath *Word Geog.* 21, *Harslet* . . for the edible inner organs of a pig is largely confined to coastal New England—eastern Massachusetts, New Hampshire, and Maine *Ibid* 38, *Hasslet* . . is the usual Southern folk term for the edible inner organs of a pig. It is in regular use on Delamarvia and from the Potomac southward to Georgia. In Maryland west of the Bay it survives only in the two southernmost counties of St. Marys and Charles. It has not entered the Shenandoah Valley but has been carried westward into the corridor that leads to the Cumberland Gap. **1949** *AmSp* 24.109 **cSC,** *Haslet pudding.* . . Liver pudding, a kind of pudding (usually stuffed as a sausage) prepared from the liver, lights, and heart of a hog. **1965–70** *DARE* (Qu. H43, *Foods made from parts of the head and inner organs of an animal*) Infs **GA**24, 62, **MS**79, **SC**19, 51, **TX**1, Haslet ['hæslɪt, -ɛt]; **TN**52, Haslet ['hæzlɛt]; **SC**43, Harslet [hɑ·slɪt]; **MA**40, Haslet ['hæsløt]—used for cooking—heart and lungs, but not a dish; **NC**88, Haslet ['hæslɪt]—liver and lungs; **SC**7, Haslet—a hog's liver, the lights go along with the liver, a separate organ; **SC**22, Haslet ['hæslɪt]—kidneys, lights (lungs); **VA**42, Haslet ['hæslɨt]—kidneys, lights, melts, swaller, liver, and sweetbread; (Qu. HH30) Inf **GA**44, Scotch liver haslet. **1984** Wilder *You All Spoken Here* 89 **Sth,** *Haslet:* A hearty stew consisting mainly of the edible viscera of the hog—heart, liver, lights—and made more savory by liberal application of red pepper, sage, and onions. **1990** Pederson *LAGS Regional Matrix* 102 **Gulf Region,** *[Edible "insides" of a pig or calf:]* Haslet [occurs 100 times, scattered, but esp freq in MS, AL, FL].

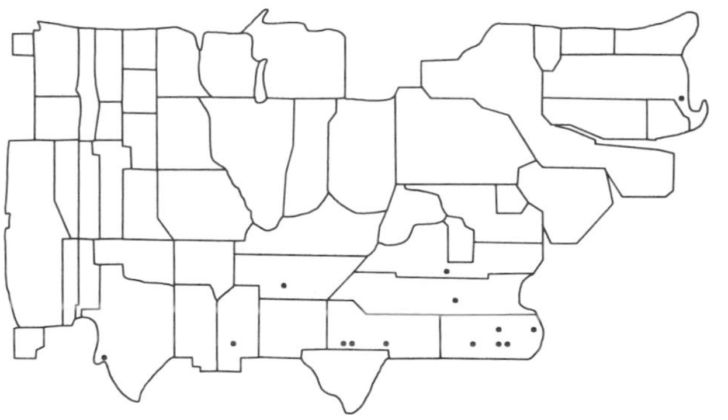

•haslet + varr (Qq. H43, HH30)

has-no-harra n [Etym unknown]

See quots.

1931 *Jrl. Amer. Folkl.* 44.412 **LA,** Has-no-harra: Jasmine lotion. Brings luck to gamblers. **1945** Saxon *Gumbo Ya-Ya* 546 **LA,** *Perfumes to bring luck to gamblers.* . . 'Has-no-harra' (jasmine lotion).

hassayampa n Also *hassayamper* [From the Hassayampa River] **AZ**

1 Orig an Arizona gold-rusher; an old-timer, esp one given to exaggeration; later, a liar; also vbl n *hassayamping* telling a lie, making a preposterous claim.

1901 *Out West Mag.* July 54 **AZ,** Is it not about time to leave these Hassayampings and fakes to the Vacant Tourist? *Ibid* 55, Even Bancroft "had fun" with these Hassayamper myths. **1906** *Ibid* Feb 73, It is not the stranger who has made Arizona what she is today, but the "Hassayamper"—the man who came in his youth and lost none of his faith and enthusiasm with the graying of his hair. [**1935** Barnes *AZ Place-Names* 200, Originally spelled "Assamp" in old mining notices. Later, "Hassamp" or "Hasiamp." . . "Was first called 'Haviamp.' " . . "According to a Yuma Indian employed by me, this name 'Hasayamp' means 'water that is hidden' or 'water that is in a dry bed.' " . . "You've heard about the wondrous stream / They call the Hassayamp./ They say it turns a truthful guy / into a lying scamp."] **1940** Writers' Program *Guide AZ* 162, The Arizona term "Hassayampa," which means somebody very old and out-of-date, or a liar, or both, was originally coined to apply to the territory's first gold rushers. **1959**

Tallman *Dict. Amer. Folkl.* 142, *Hassayampers*—A western expression for a liar. There was a popular legend that anyone who drank of the Hassayampa River in Arizona would never again tell the truth.

2 in phr *to cross the Hassayampa River:* See quot.

1927 *Ruppenthal Coll., To cross the Hassayampa River:* to become unable to tell the truth. From an address given by the president of the American Bar Association.

hassle v Also sp *hassel* [Perh from the noise; cf *EDD hassle* "To hack at; to cut with a blunt knife and with a sawing motion."] **chiefly SE**

To pant or breathe noisily; hence (vbl) n *hass(e)ling* panting, labored breathing.

1928 in 1944 *ADD* **Sth** [Black], *Hassle, hassel. . .* 'The dog is hasslin'.' **1933** Rawlings *South Moon* 27 **nFL,** Listen to me hasslin'. **1935** Hurston *Mules & Men* 218 **FL,** Lil dog run and set down in front of 'im and went to hasslin' [Footnote: Panting] and says, "Me too." **1940** *Sat. Eve. Post* 23 Nov 10/1 **sGA,** Ben felt Trouble [=a dog] move in the boat, then heard his breath hasseling in his busy nostrils. **1952** Brown *NC Folkl.* 1.549, *Hassel, hassle* ['hæsl̩]. . . To pant, to be out of breath and breathe heavily. **1960** Williams *Walk Egypt* 22 **GA,** His face was lavender, his breath hasseled like a sick dog's. *Ibid* 195, Together they . . listened to her mother's harsh hasseling slack off. **1967** *DARE* FW Addit **seAR,** *Hassling* ['hæslɪn], panting in hot weather, said of a dog. **1975** Newell *If Nothin' Don't Happen* 240 **nwFL,** Her breathin' got shorter and shorter all the time. After while she couldn't walk six steps without hasslin' so loud you could hear her in the next room and we all knowed we wouldn't have her long. **1984** *Annals Internal Med.* 100.6.900 **cwAL,** Patients with dyspnea hassle like a dog.

hasslet See **haslet**

hassling See **hassle**

hassock n Also *hussick* [*OED* 986 →; *EDD hassock* sb. "Also *hassick . . hussick . . hussock*"] **esp NEng** Cf **hummock 1, 2**

A tuft of coarse grass, usu growing in a boggy place; a small clump of trees in a swamp.

1843 in 1892 Whittier *Prose Works* 1.321 **neMA,** I was stumbling over the rough hassocks and sinking knee-deep in the black mire. **1871** (1872) Nichols *Fireside Science* 111 **MA,** After digging out the hassocks [from a bog] and burning them, the patch was turned over with a spade. **1939** *LANE* Map 30 *(Swamp; bog)* 1 inf, **seMA,** [bɔ˞gz] = [hæsɪks]; 1 inf, **seNH,** Bog, 'a hassock of grass in a swamp.' *Ibid* Map 38 **eNEng,** The word hummock, denoting a small lump in a meadow, pasture, swamp or field, was offered by thirty-eight informants. . . The word *hassock,* synonymous with *hummock,* was offered by three informants (. . [hæsɪk], . . [hæsə˞k], . . [hʌ˞sɪk]). **1968** *DARE* (Qu. T1, . . *A bunch of trees growing together in open country, especially on a hill*) Inf **NJ**39, Hussick ['hʌsɪk]—in a swamp.

haste v Also with *along, up* *old-fash*

To hurry; to hasten.

1868 *Atlantic Mth.* 22.252, I look and long, then haste me home. **1942** (1971) Campbell *Cloud-Walking* 149 **seKY,** Iffen Lize didn't haste along. **c1960** *Wilson Coll.* **csKY,** *Haste* (or *haste up*). . . To hurry; often used in a command to workers.

haste up See **haste**

hasty consumption n

=**galloping consumption.**

1968 *DARE* (Qu. BB10, . . *Tuberculosis*) Inf **OH**63, Hasty consumption.

hasty pudding n [From the dish's quick preparation]

1 Cornmeal mush. **chiefly NEng** Cf **corn mush, gap-and-swallow**

1714 (1879) S. Sewall *Diary* 2.436 **MA,** Sat awhile in the wigwam . . eat roste Alewife and very good Hasty Pudding. **1775** in 1974 Winslow *Amer. Broadside* 141 **NEng,** And there we see the men and boys / As thick as hasty pudding. **1831** in 1957 Old Farmer's Almanac *Sampler* 73 **NH,** The rich, golden corn makes the best *hasty pudding.* **1891** (1967) Freeman *New Engl. Nun* 219, Nicholas . . got a bowl out of a rude closet; it was nearly full of cold hasty-pudding. **1949** Kurath *Word Geog.* 17, Hasty-pudding . . is the well-known New England term for mush made of corn meal. West of the Hudson hasty-pudding is very rare. **1952** Tracy *Coast Cookery* 105 **MA,** *Hasty pudding*—Today called cornmeal mush. Also known as Stir-About Pudding. It was served also with meat and gravy, or as a dessert, with maple syrup, and was the main dish for breakfast, dinner, or supper. **1965–70** *DARE* (Qu. H24, . . *Boiled cornmeal*) 12 Infs, **NEng,** Hasty pudding; (Qu. H25, *Fried cornmeal*) Inf **MA**98, Hasty pudding; (Qu. H63, *Kinds of desserts*) Inf **CT**39, Hasty pudding, meal, hot water and salt and sugar. **1966** *DARE* Tape **NH**6, The hasty pudding made from . . cornmeal mush was made . . much more often . . than we have it now. **1973** Allen *LAUM* 1.301 (as of c1950), Kurath's description of *hasty pudding* as rare west of the Hudson is apt for the U[pper] M[idwest], where two of the five occurrences are actually the recalled usage of parents with eastern background.

2 Fig: a quick or unwise decision.

1984 Burns *Cold Sassy* 160 **nGA** (as of 1906), When I left this mornin', I seen him settin' on that big rock in Miss Mattie Lou's rose garden. Repentin' of his hasty puddin', I don't doubt.

hat n Pronc-sp *yat*

A Form.

1909 *S. Atl. Qrly.* 8.44 **sSC coast** [Gullah], An' e' tief de buckra buttah an' pit um een 'e yat [=And he stole the white man's butter and put it in his hat].

B Senses.

1 also *weather hat:* See quot. [Cf *EDD hat-sheaf* or *shav* (at *hat* sb.[1]) "The covering sheaf of a corn-stook"]

1968 *DARE* (Qu. L31, . . *The top bundle of a shock*) Inf **MN**15, Hat; **NJ**53, Weather hat.

2 in var phrr used as an exclam of surprise, etc: See quots.

1924 *DN* 5.269, *Hat:* great ______ (Penn.) . . holy ______s (surp[rise]). **1968–70** *DARE* (Qu. NN27a, *Weakened substitutions for 'God': "My ______!"*) Inf **TN**46, Hat; (Qu. NN29c, *Exclamations beginning with 'holy'*) Inf **NY**42, Hat.

3 in var phrr referring to strong coffee: See quot.

1965–70 *DARE* (Qu. H74a, . . *Words for coffee . . very strong*) Inf **RI**5, Knock your hat off; **NY**49, Raise your hat; **WI**24, Take the hat off your head; **WA**13, Tip your hat; **AR**38, Will take your hat off.

hat v

1 See **high-hat** v.

2 See **hat up.**

hatajo See **atajo**

hat ball n **chiefly S Midl**

A children's game; see quot 1953.

1832 Kennedy *Swallow Barn* 2.37 **VA,** It [=a boy's cap] finds hard service at hat-ball where . . it is popular for its pliability. **1883** Eggleston *Hoosier Schoolboy* 49 **sIN,** I am going to show the boys how to play hat-ball. **1905** *DN* 3.82 **nwAR,** *Hat-ball. . .* The name of a children's out-door game. **1946** Wilson *Fidelity Folks* 145 **sKY,** In Hat Ball we "nailed to the cross" the loser, that is, the one who got the most forfeits or "pigs." . . The boy, often a little fellow like me who could not throw well and had thus acquired many pigs, was stood against a sapling while all the boys took turns throwing a ball at him. **1953** Brewster *Amer. Nonsinging Games* 84 **IL,** *Hat Ball. . .* Players put their caps in a circle on the ground, then stand in a ring around them. The player who has previously been counted out as "It" drops a ball into the cap of one of the others. All the players except the latter start running. He must run to his cap, take out the ball, and try to hit someone with it. **1954** *Harder Coll.* **cwTN,** *Hatball. . .* A children's game in which a ball is placed in a hat, and players try to grab the ball and hit "it" with it.

hatch n[1]

1 also *hatch hole:* =**hay chute.**

1965–70 *DARE* (Qu. M5, . . *Hole for throwing hay down below*) 29 Infs, **scattered,** Hatch; **KY**68, **TX**26, Hatch hole; **FL**15, Hatches.

2 A jail—also in phrr *clap* (or *lay*) *under hatches* to incarcerate. [Abbr for **booby hatch**]

1914 Jackson *Criminal Slang* 43, *Hatch. . .* General usage. A calaboose; a prison; police station; a jail. Derived from the nautical term "booby-hatch." **1945** Colcord *Sea Language* 95 **ME, Cape Cod, Long Is,** In coastal dialect . . to clap or lay under hatches is an old term for put in prison. **1967** *DARE* (Qu. V11, . . *Joking names . . for a . . jail*) Inf **PA**48, Hatch.

hatch v Also *hatch out* *joc* Cf **hatching jacket**

To give birth; to give birth to; to carry an unborn child; to be born.

1929 *AmSp* 4.348 **NC,** One man, when I told him I was from North Carolina, exclaimed, "Well, I'm a son of a ghost! I was hatched out in that state myself." **1965–70** *DARE* (Qu. AA28, . . *Expressions . . women use to say that another is going to have a baby*) 9 Infs **scattered,** About ready to hatch; **FL**26, **KY**11, 36, Going to hatch; **OH**71, **SC**29, About to hatch; **TX**62, Gonna hatch; **CA**117, Gonna hatch one out; **MI**19, Ready to hatch; **GA**89, **NC**36, Hatching; **NY**7, Hatching out.

hatch n^2 [Var of *hutch* a coop or cage, prob infl by *hatch* v]

1966 *DARE* (Qu. M16, *The small shelter for a hen that can be moved about from place to place*) Inf **MT**4, Chicken hatch.

hatchel n Pronc-sp *hetchel*

1 also sp *hachel:* A comb-like instrument for cleaning flax, hemp, etc. **chiefly NEast**

1722 in 1875 Temple–Sheldon *Hist. Northfield* 160 **MA,** To making 36 hatchel teeth 0 3 0. **1761** in 1947 *AmSp* 22.1.2.37 **CT,** 1 *hachel* retornd. **1869** Stowe *Oldtown Folks* 530 **MA,** She don' know no more 'bout religion than an' [sic] old hetchel. **1891** *DN* 1.128 **cNY,** [hɛčl̩] 'hatchel'. **1900** Shelton *Salt-Box House* 143 **CT,** Mops were made of corn-husks bound to a handle, the husks having been drawn through a hetchel which shredded them. **1931–33** *LANE Worksheets* **swCT,** Grandmother used to cord [sic] and spin wool; she used a hetchel [hɛtʃl̩]. **1934** *Hanley Disks* **cwCT,** You probably know what the old fashioned hatchels are. . . There are some sharp teeth probably five inches long—as sharp as needles—made of steel. **1939** (1962) Thompson *Body & Britches* 496 **NY,** [Proverb:] Rougher than a hetchel (hatchel, used in dressing flax). **1967** *DARE* File **ceNY,** *Hatchel,* for cleaning broomcorn.

2 See quot. Cf **hatchel v 2**

1969 *DARE* (Qu. GG38, *Somebody who is usually mean and bad tempered*) Inf **VT**12, Ornery old hetchel ['hɛčəl].

hatchel v Pronc-sp *hetchel* [**hatchel n**]

1 To use a **hatchel n 1;** hence ppl adj *hetcheled* separated into strands.

1940–41 Cassidy *WI Atlas* 1 inf, **cWI,** *Hetcheled-like* (said in describing how broom-splints looked). **1949** *PADS* 11.61 [Hemp terms], *Hatchel.* . . to clean hemp with this comb or brush. **1950** (1965) Richter *Town* 254 **OH,** I'd be hatchelling and carding wool.

2 To bother, annoy; to call to account; hence n *hetcheling* a scolding. Cf **flax v 1a**

1800 *Aurora Genl. Advt.* (Philadelphia PA) 20 Oct 2/4 **sePA,** They have harrowed the feelings of the people by *gag bill, stamp-acts,* and land taxes, and hatchelled them with prosecutions, fines, and imprisonments, in order to break up and destroy the spirit of liberty. **1890** *Jrl. Amer. Folkl.* 3.311 **nOH,** *Hetcheling.*—A "blowing up," or scolding. "I'll give you a hetcheling." . . from the *heckling* of flax. **1895** *DN* 1.382 **NJ,** *Hetchel:* to tease, to call to account. Metaphor from the days of the domestic flax industry. **1834** Davis *Letters Downing* 288 **NY,** If the Senate hetchels a chap for bad conduct with the doors closed . . it would be jist as bad for him as if they did so with open doors. **1959** *VT Hist.* new ser 27.142, *Hetchel.* . . To bother; to annoy. (From hatchel). Occasional. **1969** *DARE* (QR, near Qu. II27) Inf **NY**206A, A woman who nags her husband; she hetchels ['hɛčəlz] him—a weaving term.

3 with *up:* To cobble up; see quots.

1950 *WELS Suppl.* **cwWI,** We hetcheled up some wood for the stove. **1965** *DARE* File **csWI** (as of c1950), *Hetchel up*—to improvise hastily; to put (something) together in a hurry, or to find (something) to more or less suit an immediate need. To hetchel up an excuse; to hetchel up a group of people for some activity.

hatcher n Also *hatch(ing) hen*

A setting hen.

1960 *PADS* 34.59 **CO,** Hatching hen 'setting hen'. **1961** Folk *Word Atlas N. LA* 166, 89% of the [275] informants call the *setting hen* a *setting . . hen.* The remaining 11% provided quite a variety of names . . [including] *hatching hen.* **1965–70** *DARE* (Qu. K72, *When the hen stops laying and begins to sit on the eggs to hatch them, she's a* ———) Infs **IN**35, **NJ**3, **NY**88, 220, **OH**80, **PA**141, Hatcher; **NJ**3, **NY**196, **PA**10, Hatching hen; **NY**72, Hatch hen. **1966** Dakin *Dial. Vocab. Ohio R. Valley* 2.255, A *setting hen* is regularly called by that name. . . The terms *broody hen* . . as well as *hatching hen* . . are all used. [*Hatching hen* is] offered only once. **1973** Allen *LAUM* 1.255 (as of c1950) **IA,** Hatching hen [1 inf].

hatchet n Pronc-spp *Gullah, hatchi(t)ch*

A Forms.

1888 Jones *Negro Myths* 20 **GA coast** [Gullah], Eh hab eh dog fuh tree de coon, an eh hatchich fuh chop down de tree. **1922** Gonzales *Black Border* 306 **sSC, GA coasts** [Gullah glossary], *Hatchitch*—hatchet, hatchets. **1930** Stoney–Shelby *Black Genesis* 34 **seSC,** God reach down in he belt an' pull out a little gol' hatchitch an' fling at dem.

B Senses.

1 See quot.

1949 *AmSp* 24.109 **ceSC,** *Hatchet.* . . An uneducated, part-time, lay preacher, generally rather poor.

2 See quot.

1969 *DARE* (Qu. AA22, *Joking names that a man may use to refer to his wife*) Inf **PA**177, Hatchet.

3 attrib in var combs: See below.

a *hatchet face:* A long, narrow face, often with sharp features; a person with such a face; hence adj *hatchet-faced.* **chiefly Nth, Midl**

1806 (1970) Webster *Compendious Dict.* 139/2, *Hatchetface.* . . an ugly or very ill-formed face. **1824** Irving *Tales of a Traveller* 1.12 **NY,** A thin, hatchet-faced gentleman, with projecting eyes like a lobster. **1898** Lloyd *Country Life* 31 **AL,** The teacher was a tall young man, with hump shoulders and a pale, hatchet face. **1899** (1912) Green *VA Folk-Speech* 218, *Hatchet-faced.* . . A thin face, lean and furrowed by deep lines. **1903** *DN* 2.298 **Cape Cod MA** (as of a1857), *Hatchet-face.* . . A person with a long, narrow face. **1912** *DN* 3.577 **wIN,** *Hatchet-faced.* . . Sharp-faced. **1927** *AmSp* 2.356 **WV,** *Hatchet-faced* . . sharp-featured. "Did you ever see such a hatchet-faced woman?" **1950** *WELS (Joking or uncomplimentary terms for a person's face)* 1 Inf, **ceWI,** Hatchet face; *(If a person's lower jaw sticks out)* 1 Inf, **seWI,** Hatchet-faced, occas. **1965–70** *DARE* (Qu. X29, *Joking or uncomplimentary words for a person's face*) Infs **IN**18, **MI**110, **MT**3, **NC**62, **WA**24, Hatchet face; **IL**30, **KY**84, **PA**74, Hatchet-faced.

b *hatchet leg:* A crooked or misshapen leg; hence adj *hatchet-legged.*

1970 *DARE* (Qu. X37, . . *People's legs . . noticeably bent, or uneven, or not right*) Inf **VA**46, Hatchet legs; **DC**13, Hatchet-legged. [Both Infs Black]

c *hatchet blow:* See quot. Cf **where the Indian shot you**

1969 *DARE* (Qu. X34, . . *Nicknames for the navel*) Inf **PA**227, Hatchet blow.

hatchetback n

A **heelsplitter** (here: *Lasmigona complanata*).

1911 *Century Dict. Suppl.* np, *Hatchet-back.* . . A large river-mussel, *Symphynota complanata.* **1935** Pratt *Manual Invertebrate Animals* 655, *L[asmigona] complanata.* . . Hatchet back.

hatchet blow See **hatchet B3c**

hatchet face, hatchet-faced See **hatchet B3a**

hatchet leg, hatchet-legged See **hatchet B3b**

hatch hen See **hatcher**

hatch hole See **hatch n^1 1**

hatchich See **hatchet**

hatching dress See **hatching jacket**

hatching hen See **hatcher**

hatching jacket n Also *hatching dress, jacket* [**hatch v**] **chiefly Inland Nth, N Midl** *joc*

A maternity blouse or dress.

1965–70 *DARE* (Qu. AA28, . . *Expressions . . women use to say that another is going to have a baby*) 24 Infs, **chiefly Inland Nth, N Midl,** Wearing the hatching jacket; **WI**63, Get out the hatching jacket; **MO**3, Wearing a hatching jacket; **KY**80, Got on a hatching dress; **SD**8, Wearing the jacket. **1967** Cerello *Dakota Co. MN* 62, *Hatching jacket.* . . She's been wearing a hatching jacket for eight weeks now. . . Women nowadays have no sense; they shouldn't be out and around wearing shorts and a hatching jacket.

hatchitch See **hatchet**

hatch out See **hatch v**

hatchway n Also *hatchway door* **chiefly NEast, OH** See Map Cf **cellarway**

=**bulkhead 1.**

1901 *DN* 2.141 **c,eNY,** *Hatchway*. . . Outside cellarway. **1965–70** *DARE* (Qu. D20, . . *A sloping outside cellar door*) 60 Infs, **chiefly NEast, OH,** Hatchway; **NY**75, Hatchway doors.

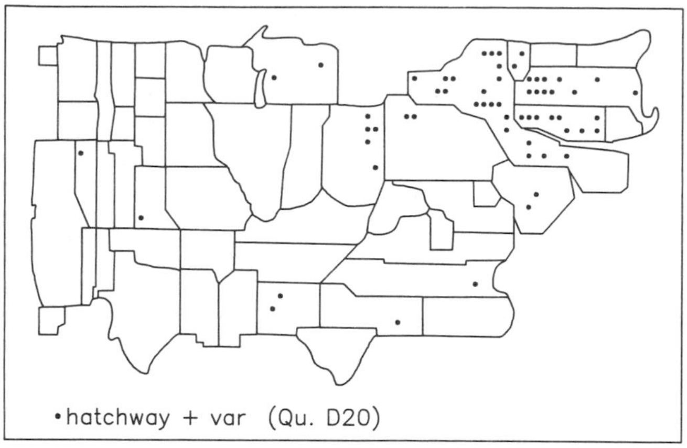

hate v **KY, TN, Ozarks**

To regret; to mourn, feel sorry about.

1927 *DN* 5.474 **Ozarks,** *Hate*. . . This word is often used in the sense of regret. A mountain man, on hearing of his mother's death, said: "Oh my Gawd, I hate that!" **1937–41** *Hall Coll.* **eTN,** You'll hate you said it; [He] said he wouldn't hate to die; I sure did hate that I didn't get to see you. **1954** *Harder Coll.* **cwTN** (as of 1945), He hated so bad because he didn [sic] see you; I sure did hate his being sick. **c1960** *Wilson Coll.* **csKY,** *Hate*—To regret. "I hate it because I didn't get to see Uncle George."

hate n Also sp *haet, hait* [Scots dial; cf *OED hate, haet* sb.[2]]

A whit, a jot, the smallest thing; a thing—freq in phr *not to give a hate* not to give a damn. **chiefly Appalachians, Ohio Valley**

1826 Royall *Sketches* 58 **WV,** But their favorite word of all, is *hate*, by which they mean the word thing; for instance, *nothing*, "not a hate—not wann hate will ye's do." **1843** (1916) Hall *New Purchase* 147 **cIN,** The Ingins . . never did us harm, no, not a *hait—(little bit)*. **1895** *DN* 1.389 **PA, KY, OH,** *Hate:* in phrase "didn't get a hate" = didn't get a thing (meaning *anything*). **1914** *DN* 4.108 **KS,** *Hait*. . . Jot; iota. [Scottish.] **1929** *WV Review* Oct 9/3, *Hate* . . has been generally used as an equivalent for *a thing*. . . It was once heard most in such expressions as *I don't care a hate* or *I didn't have a hate to do*. It was also used in such expressions as *I couldn't turn a hate*, meaning *could not turn a wheel* or *make a move*, and in *I don't give a hate*, an expression of indifference. **1930** Shoemaker *1300 Words* 28 **cPA Mts** (as of c1900), *Hait*—"I don't give a hait", a matter of no consequence. **1956** Settle *Beulah Land* 252 **WV,** They hain't a hate nobody can do. **1968** *DARE* (Qu. KK42a, *Expressions about a person who does something very easily*) Inf **VA**25, That wouldn't be a hate for him; old-fashioned. **1971** Dwyer *Dict. for Yankees* 27 **Sth, S Midl,** *Hate, haet, hait*—A bit, small amount.

hateful adj **chiefly Sth, S Midl**

Stubborn; obstinate.

1954 *Harder Coll.* **cwTN,** *Hateful*. . . Stubborn. **1957** Battaglia *Resp. to PADS 20* **eMD,** Stubborn: "She's just being hateful now." **1965–70** *DARE* (Qu. GG18, *Other words meaning 'obstinate'*) Infs **FL**14, **GA**23, **KY**30, 40, 41, **MO**3, 8, **MA**14, **NC**37, Hateful.

hateful n [Absol use of *hateful*] **Ozarks, sAppalachians**

An obnoxious or vexatious person or creature.

1913 Kephart *Highlanders* 283 **sAppalachians,** "Them bugs—the little old hatefuls!" **1933** Williamson *Woods Colt* 18 **Ozarks,** A houn' dog with the wrong color to his nose, an' a hateful from town with the wrong kind of a face. **1953** Randolph–Wilson *Down in Holler* 52 **Ozarks,** Them Pea Ridge folks is all *hatefuls*. **1954** *Harder Coll.* **cwTN,** A old hateful.

hate out v phr, hence vbl n *hating out*

To drive away by hostility.

1824 Doddridge *Notes Indian Wars* 168, The punishment for idleness, lying, dishonesty, and ill fame generally was that of "Hating the offender out." **1872** Schele de Vere *Americanisms* 190 **West,** Characteristic of those early days, and still occurring in many parts of the West, is the *hating out*. **1941** Writers' Program *Guide WV* 42, Violators of common rights were 'hated out' of the neighborhood. **1948** Dick *Dixie Frontier* 263 **KY, TN** (as of c1830), So hot did public disapproval wax that he felt it more comfortable to leave the country. In such a case he was said to have been "hated out."

hater See **have** v[1] **A3b**

hath See **hearth A2**

hat holder See **hat rack 2**

hating out See **hate out**

hat it up See **hat up**

hat peg See **hat rack 2**

hatpin plant n

A **bead lily** (here: *Clintonia borealis*).

1949 Moldenke *Amer. Wild Flowers* 333, *Clintonia borealis*. . . The flowers are followed by long-stalked bright blue berries which have given the plant its popular name of *hatpinplant*.

hatpins n [See quot 1949]

=**pipewort;** also its flower stalks.

1933 Small *Manual SE Flora* 257, *Eriocaulon*. . . Hat-pins. **1937** *Torreya* 37.96, *Eriocaulon* spp.—Hatpins, eastern North Carolina. **1949** Moldenke *Amer. Wild Flowers* 304, In many of our North American species [of *Eriocaulon*] the white-topped flower stalks resemble old-fashioned hatpins. . . The "hatpins" are 1 to 3 feet tall. **1975** Duncan–Foote *Wildflowers SE* 240, Hatpins. *Eriocaulon decangulare*.

hat rack n

1 Fig: a scrawny animal or person. **scattered but esp NY**

1935 *AmSp* 10.271 **NE,** *Hatrack*. An old, thin cow, a *nellie* or *canner*. **1944** *PADS* 2.57 **cnMO,** *Hatrack:* . . An old ((emaciated?)) cow. **1950** *WELS (A bony or poor looking horse)* 2 Infs, **WI,** Hat rack. **1965–70** *DARE* (Qu. K15, *A thin, bony, or poor-looking cow*) Infs **GA**11, **IL**4, **MI**101, **NY**79, 189, **NC**63, **OH**22, **SC**40, **VA**46, Hat rack; (Qu. K8, *Joking terms for milking a cow*) Inf **IL**104, Milk the old hat rack; (Qu. K44, *A bony or poor-looking horse*) Infs **CT**36, **LA**31, **NJ**29, **NY**2, 66, 79, 189, 224, Hat rack; (Qu. X49, . . *A person who is very thin*) Inf **NY**2, Hat rack.

2 also *hat holder*, ~ *peg:* A person's head. *joc*

1942 Berrey–Van den Bark *Amer. Slang* 121.56, *Head* . . hat peg or rack. **1963** *Freedomways* 3.50 **NYC** [Black], If you spent half as much time tryin' to put something *inside* that wothless [sic] hat-rack as you did havin' your brains fryed. **1965–70** *DARE* (Qu. X28, *Joking words . . for a person's head*) 48 Infs, **scattered,** Hat rack; **PA**182, Hat holder.

hatses See **-es** suff[1] **2**

hat squash n

Prob a **turban squash.**

1971 GA Dept. Ag. *Farmers Market Bulletin* 10 Nov 8, I have grown what is called hat squash. . . [Y]our squash is probably the variety known as Turk's Turban.

hatter See **have** v[1] **A3b**

hat time n Cf **hat up**

See quots.

1972 Kochman *Rappin'* 214 [Black], The players all started heading for the door, stating, "Peace," "Later," "Hat Time," "I'm in the wind," etc. **1972** Shafer *Dict. Prison Slang* 20 **TX,** Hat time—quitting time in the field; when the captain takes off his hat and waves it.

hat to See **have** v[1] **A3b**

hat tree n **chiefly NEast**

=**hall tree.**

1819 *Mass. Res.* 18 June, p.m. 87 *(DA)*, (Ernst), Bryant, Nathaniel, for two hat trees. **1853** (1864) Thoreau *ME Woods* 90, Used for ornamental hat-trees, together with deers' horns, in front entries. **1875** Stowe *We & Neighbors* 87 **NYC,** She snatched from the hat-tree a shawl. **1883** *Century Illustr. Mag.* 26.644/1 **Cape Cod MA,** A people . . who hang Calcutta hats upon their hat-trees. **1966–67** *DARE* (Qu. E1, *A piece of furniture that stands against the wall, and you hang clothes . . on it*) Infs **MI**9, **MO**11, **MA**34, Hat tree.

hattuh See **have** v[1] **A1b**

hat up v phr Also *hat (it up)* *chiefly among Black speakers* Cf **hat time**

To leave or depart, often hurriedly; to run.

1968 *DARE* FW Addit **PA**66, *Hat up*—leave town. [Inf Black] **1969–70** *DARE* (Qu. Y18, *To leave in a hurry: "Before they find this out, we'd better______!"*) Inf **IL**48, Hat; (Qu. Y20, *To run fast*) Inf **PA**241, Hat up. **1971** Landy *Underground Dict.* 99, *Hat it up* . . (B[lack]) Leave; depart. **1971** Roberts *Third Ear* np [Black], *Hat up!* an imperative urging one to leave. **1972** Claerbaut *Black Jargon* 50, *Hat up*—means to leave, alluding obviously to putting on one's hat and coat.

hat vine n

A wild **morning glory** (*Ipomaea* spp).

1970 *DARE* (Qu. S5, . . *Wild morning glory*) Inf **VA**43, Hat vine.

hau n |hau| **HI**

A tropical **hibiscus** (here: *H. tiliaceus*).

1839 in 1934 Frear *Lowell & Abigail* 138 **HI,** Took our luncheon under some hau trees. **1844** Jarves *Scenes Sandwich Is.* 117, Groves of dark-leaved *hau.* **1866** in 1966 Twain *Letters HI* 99, Large tracts were covered with large hau (how) bushes, whose sheltering foliage is so thick as to be almost impervious to rain. **1929** Neal *Honolulu Gardens* 196, In former times, the hau [=*Hibiscus tiliaceus*] was a useful tree to the Hawaiians. **1930** Degener *Ferns of HI* 213, The *hau* is usually a small tree producing numerous, long, spreading branches which readily strike root upon touching the ground. . . The *hau,* because of its usefulness, was held in . . high regard. **1955** Day *HI People* 295, It was necessary to renew the soil with fertilizers, which included rotted hau leaves, weed mulch, and burned bones. **1965** Krauss–Alexander *Grove Farm* 23 **HI,** George and . . Edward, trussed "Smut" fore and aft to a stick with strips of hau bark. [**1971** Pukui–Elbert *Hawaiian Dict., Hau.* . . A lowland tree *(Hibiscus tiliaceus),* found in many warm countries, some spreading horizontally over the ground forming impenetrable thickets, and some trained on trellises. The leaves are rounded and heart-shaped, the flowers cup-shaped, with five large petals that change through the day from yellow to dull-red.]

haul v

1 also with *about, (a)round, off;* Of wind or clouds: to change direction; to shift. **chiefly N and C Atl**

1840 (1841) Dana *2 Yrs.* 369, The wind hauled to the southward. **1858** Taylor *N. Travel* 265, The morning looked . . threatening, but the clouds gradually hauled off to the eastward. **1864** Lowell *Fireside Travels* 123 **ME,** The wind also is hauling round to the right quarter. **1945** Colcord *Sea Language* 96 **ME, Cape Cod, Long Island,** Of the wind, to haul, or haul round, is to change clockwise; to veer. **1968–70** *DARE* (Qu. B15, *When the wind suddenly begins to blow in a different direction, you say it ______*) Infs **MD**43, 49, **VA**44, Hauled about; **MD**43, **NJ**39, Hauled; **NJ**20, Hauls around; **AK**2, Haul about. **1975** Gould *ME Lingo* 127, A wind that hauls around usually brings good weather.

2 In logging: see quots.

1958 McCulloch *Woods Words* 81 **Pacific NW,** *Hauled*—Broke free; said of a log jam which has been dynamited or otherwise loosened. **1975** Gould *ME Lingo* 126, A log jam *hauls* when it is broken and begins to move.

3 See quot. [*OED haul* v. 1. c "*Obs.*"]

1937 *AmSp* 12.232 **NJ,** Negroes use *haul* in the obsolete sense of 'to pester': 'Woman, quit haulin' me.'

4 To pull up.

1872 Schele de Vere *Americanisms* 486, *Haul,* to, weeds is common in many States instead of to pull up weeds. **c1902** Clapin *New Dict. Amer.* 222, *Haul.* A New Jerseyism used in sense of to pull up, as "to haul weeds."

haul-a-boat See **halibut**

haul about (or around) See **haul 1**

haul ass v phr Also *haul buggy, ~ tail, ~ one's freight;* for addit varr see quots

1 To leave; to depart, esp hurriedly; to travel rapidly. **chiefly Sth** Cf **drag** v **4, drag ass, pull foot, pull one's freight**

1928 McKay *Home to Harlem* 47, "Come on, let's haul bottom away from here to Harlem." **1938** Stuart *Dark Hills* 113 **KY,** That pinhead . . got sore and hauled his freight this morning. **1938** *AmSp* 13.307 [Lingo of bus drivers], *Haulin' the mail.* . . When he covers a good many miles in exceptionally good time and makes up time he has been 'haulin' the mail.' **1940** (1941) Bell *Swamp Water* 8 **Okefenokee GA,** They's *one* buck deer in these here woods that's got a cold-out night of hauling tail ahead of him. **1954** *AmSp* 29.97 **sCA** [Hot rod terms], *Haul ass.* . . To travel at a high velocity. **1954** *PADS* 21.30 **SC,** *Haul buggy.* . . To go away, to go home, to leave, especially in flight or in haste. Not necessarily in a buggy. **1965** Bradford *Born with the Blues* 156 **Sth** (as of 1921) [Black], I hauled pork home in 129th Street and got my gun and hurried back with blood in my eyes. **1965–70** *DARE* (Qu. Y18, *To leave in a hurry: " . . We'd better ______!"*) Infs **SC**26, **TX**9, Haul ass; **SC**21, **TX**9, Haul freight; **GA**44, Haul buggy; **AL**8, Haul it; **SC**70, Haul pork, haul tail; (Qu. Y19, *To begin to go away from a place*) Inf **MI**32, Haul ass; **NJ**18, Haul tail; (Qu. Y20, *To run fast*) Infs **FL**10, **SC**26, Haul buggy; **GA**54, Haul ass; **AL**8, Haul it; **SC**26, Haulin' ass, haulin' tail; **LA**25, Hauling it; **VA**69, Hauling pork; **GA**3, Hauling special. **1970** Major *Dict. Afro-Amer. Slang* 64, *Haul ass:* to run; go. **1978** *DARE* File **OR,** We're really haulin' ass! **1984** Wilder *You All Spoken Here* 68 **Sth,** *Haul buggy.* . . Leave hurriedly.

2 To increase one's output of energy or effort.

1966–67 *DARE* (Qu. JJ26, *If somebody has been doing poor work or not enough, the boss might say, "If he wants to keep his job he'd better ______."*) Infs **MI**32, **OR**1, Haul ass; **OR**1, Haul logs.

haulback n

See quots.

1905 U.S. Forest Serv. *Bulletin* 61.39 **Pacific,** *Haul back.* A small wire rope, traveling between the donkey engine and a pulley set near the logs to be dragged, used to return the cable. **1941** *AmSp* 16.233, *Haulback.* A smaller cable used to haul the heavy main cable back to the cut logs.

‡haul horse n [Prob var of *haw horse* (at **haw** n)]

1967 *DARE* (Qu. K32b, *The horse on the left side in plowing or hauling*) Inf **MO**38, Haul horse.

haulibut See **halibut**

hauling, haul it See **haul 4**

haul loose v phr [Perh blend of *haul off* + *let loose*]

See quots.

1968 *DARE* FW Addit **TN**26, *To haul loose.* This expression . . usually precedes some act of violence or threat of violence. . . "Just haul loose and get mad." . . It seems to imply a release of repressed emotion or desire. You wouldn't "haul loose and shut the door" but you might very well "haul loose and slam the door." . . Used in northwest Arkansas and southwest Missouri as well as northwest Tennessee. **1969** *DARE* File **cIA,** *Haul loose*—get busy and get some specific job done. "I'm going to haul loose and scrub the floors." Denotes extreme ambition. Never in context of violence.

haul off See **haul 1**

haul one's ashes See **ashes 2**

haul one's freight See **haul ass**

haul out v phr

To leave, depart.

1866 in 1932 *NE Hist.* 13.156, Hauled out before sunrise and corralled at the Springs by 9 o'clock. **1903** McFaul *Ike Glidden* 282 **ME,** The train hauled out while the officer was taking him into custody. **1968** *DARE* (Qu. Y19, *To begin to go away from a place*) Inf **AK**1, Haul out.

haul round See **haul 1**

haul seine n **Delmarva**

A large fishing net; see quot 1884; also vbl n *haul seining* fishing with such a net.

1884 Knight *New Mech. Dict.* 447/1, *Haul Seine.* . . A long net depending from a cork line and leaded at its lower depending edge, used to sweep large areas of water. **1943** Weslager *DE Forgotten Folk* 185, The larger nets made by the fisherman are used for dragging across the channel of a river or one of the small inlets of the bay. They are called "haul seines" or "drag nets." One end is fastened to the shore, or held by the fisherman's assistant. The fisherman then takes the loose end in his hands and wades into the water. He proceeds until the net is played out and then returns to the shore, his steps forming a semi-circle. The two men then pull the net ashore with the catch. **1965–70** *DARE* (Qu. P13, . . *Ways of fishing . . besides the ordinary hook and line*) Infs **DE**3, 4, **VA**55, 75, Haul seine; **MD**15, Haul seine [hɔl sen]—a net hauled from both ends, fish caught between; **MD**32, Haul seine—a big net, drag it through the river, one man on each side, haul in fish; **MD**36, Haul seine—one end hooked to shore, you haul other end around; (Qu. P15, . . *Fishing . . from a slowly moving boat*) Inf **VA**46, Haul seining ['hɔ,seɪnɨn]; (Qu. O10, . . *Kinds of boats*) Inf **VA**79, Haul seine boats.

haul tail See **haul ass**

hauna v, exclam [Haw *hauna* unpleasant odor, as of spoiling fish or meat] **HI**

See quots.

1967 *DARE* (Qu. NN23, *Exclamations when people smell a very bad odor*) Inf **HI**13, Hauna ['haʊnɑ]. **1981** *Pidgin To Da Max* **HI,** *Hauna* (HOW nah) Stink. Whew, Chahlie! Hauna yo' breath! You no mo' Listerine?

haunched adj [Perh infl by *hunched* ppl adj] Cf **hunker** v **1a**

1968 *DARE* Tape **AK**11, I could still see the old squaws sitting haunched on the floor with their blankets.

haunt n, v, hence ppl adj *haunted* Usu |hɔnt, hɑnt|; also **chiefly Sth, S Midl** |hæ(ɪ)nt, he(ɪ)nt|; for addit varr see quots Pronc-spp *ha(a)nt, haint, harnt, hunt* Cf **haunty**

A Forms.

1840 Haliburton *Clockmaker* (3d ser) 94 **NEng,** It fairly harnted me. **1843** Winnemore & Reps *Cudjo's Wild Hunt* (song) 3 *(OEDS),* It am de hunt ob Cudjo dat nigger so bold. **1890** *DN* 1.65 **KY,** *Hants* [hænts]. **1892** *DN* 1.239 **cwMO,** *Haunt.* Pronounced by the natives . . [hænt]. **1893** Shands *MS Speech* 35, *Hant* [hænt]. . . used by the negroes of Mississippi both as a noun and as a verb. **1885** Twain *Huck. Finn* 79 **MO,** A man that warn't buried was more likely to go a-ha'nting around. **1901** *DN* 2.141 **cNY, NYC,** *Haunt,* pron. [hænt]. **1908** *DN* 3.318 **eAL, wGA,** *Hant.* **1909** *DN* 3.398 **nwAR,** *Hant.* **1910** *DN* 3.458 **FL, GA,** *Hants.* **1922** Gonzales *Black Border* 305 **sSC, GA coasts** [Gullah glossary], *Haant*—haunt, haunts; apparition; ghost, ghosts. **1960** (1962) Lee *Mockingbird* 28 **AL,** "A hain't lives there," he said cordially, pointing to the Radley house. **c1960** *Wilson Coll.* **csKY,** /hæɪnt/. . . Sometimes it is /hent/. **1961** Kurath–McDavid *Pronc. Engl.* 161, *Haunted.* . . The /ɔ/ of *law* predominates . . from the Connecticut Valley westward to the Great Lakes, in Metropolitan New York and vicinity, and in all of Pennsylvania except the south-central and southwestern sections. . . In Massachusetts and on Narragansett Bay, /a/ is now all but universal. . . In the South and the South Midland *haunted* regularly has the /æ/ of *bag* in folk speech and predominantly so in the speech of the middle group. . . Elsewhere this variant is confined to folk speech . . or entirely avoided; only in northeastern New England does it have wider currency. . . *haunted,* with the vowel /e/ of *eight,* occurs in parts of the Carolinas, in Georgia, and in West Virginia. **1965–70** *DARE* (Qu. CC15, *When people say there are ghosts in a certain place . . "They say that the old house is _______."*) 852 Infs, **widespread,** Haunted; 88 Infs, **chiefly Sth, S Midl,** Hanted; **IL**47, **KY**59, **NJ**39, **NY**69, **NC**72, **OH**44, **OK**51, **PA**70, Hanted—old-fashioned; **NY**202, **PA**115, Hanted—jocular; **AR**12, ['hæntɪd] used by Blacks; **TX**95, 101, ['hæntɪd, 'hændɪd]—used by less educated; **VA**5, ['hæəntɪd], mountain expression; 30 Infs, **chiefly Sth, S Midl,** Hainted; **AR**39, **LA**2, Hainted ['he(ɪ)ntɪd]—old-fashioned; **FL**51, She says ['hɒnɪd], most people say ['henɪd]; **IL**118, ['hentəd]—used by uneducated people; **NJ**39, Hainted ['hentəd]—old; **TX**15, ['hentəd]—darky talk. **1968** *DARE* Tape **NC**54, I had to come back down by what they call the hainted holler. **1970** Tarpley *Blinky* 281 **neTX,** [20% of infs used *haints* or *hants* . . 2.5% *haunts.*] *Hant* or *haint* increases in usage with the age groups above 40 and is typically heard among the least educated and in rural communities. . . *haints* or *hants* has greater occurrence than *ghost* in the lowest educational category, while *haunts* is never heard from this group. **1973** *PADS* 60.52 **seNC,** It is my impression that the spread of /ɔ/ [in *haunted*] has considerably accelerated in the South since the [1940s]. . . The responses of our informants bear this out. Only one said /æ/ only; one said both /æ/ and /ɔ/, while the rest [=10 Infs] said /ɔ/ only.

B As noun.

A ghost or spirit. **chiefly Sth, S Midl** *esp freq among Black speakers*

1843 [see **A** above]. **1869** Stowe *Oldtown Folks* 80 **MA,** But this 'ere's a regular *haunt,* . . they'd seen a figger of a man. **1884** *Anglia* 7.263 **Sth, S Midl** [Black], *To b'leeve in ha'nts* = to believe in ghosts. **1890** *DN* 1.65 **KY,** There's hants in this here house. **1908** *DN* 3.318 **eAL, wGA,** *Hant.* . . A ghost, a spirit. **1909** *DN* 3.398 **nwAR,** *Hant.* . . I never seed a hant myself, but my aunt did. **1913** Kephart *Highlanders* 91 **sAppalachians,** I'd believe he's a hant if 't wasn't for his tracks. **1914** *DN* 4.159 **VA,** *Hants* [hænts]. . . The hants an' evils 'll getcha! **1943** Writers' Program NC *Bundle of Troubles* 52, I never knowed the difference between a hant and a ghost until I spent the night at Pickey Bailey's. A hant is female and a ghost is male. **1950** *PADS* 14.35 **SC,** *Ha'nt.* . . A spirit, supernatural being, whose main object is to frighten people. A ghost is supposed to be the spirit of some dead person, but the *ha'nt* has ordinarily no such association. . . Dogs may be misled at night by a *ha'nt.* **1950** *WELS (Names for ghosts and supernatural creatures)* 3 Infs, **WI,** Haunts; 1 Inf, **ceWI,** Hants. **1965–70** *DARE* (Qu. EE41, *A hobgoblin that is used to threaten children and make them behave*) 15 Infs, **chiefly Sth, Inland Sth,** Hants; **IN**5, Hants [hæɪnts]; **NJ**68, Southern expression [is] hants; **DC**2, Darkies said hants [hænts]; (Qu. CC17, *Imaginary animals or monsters*) Infs **KY**85, **NC**41, **SC**32, 54, **VA**26, 41, Hants; **CT**42, **TN**6, 13, **VA**106, Hants [hænts]; **TN**53, Haunts or hants; **KY**76, Haunts; **OK**55, Haints; (Qu. CC15) Inf **CA**87, Got haints [hents]; **FL**6, The hants'll getcha; **GA**18, It has [hents] in it—colored people; **LA**14, When I was a child, the Negroes would speak of hants [hænts]; **VA**54, Got hants [hænts]; (Qu. CC16) Inf **VA**41, Hant; **TN**53, Hant heaven or haven; (Qu. W36) Inf **AL**36, Look like a haint [hent]; (Qu. X47) Inf **SC**34, Tired as a hant; (Qu. OO28a) Inf **KY**30, Ran like a hant. **1976** Lynn–Vecsey *Loretta Lynn* 31 **eKY,** Doolittle says I'm crazy to believe in "haints"—that's our word for ghosts.

C As ppl adj.

Accustomed, habituated.

1903 *DN* 2.316 **seMO,** My cattle have got haunted to the place. **1923** *DN* 5.209 **swMO,** *Hant.* . . To haunt, to become accustomed to or to become habituated to a certain place. Thus, hogs fed continually at one place, 'git hanted thar.' **1934** (1943) *W2, Haunted.* . . Wonted. *Obs. exc. Dial.*

haunt bird n

=**nighthawk.**

1959 *Names* 7.113, Other birds are locally deemed as creatures of ill omen. . . Haunt bird in various parts of the South . . is the nighthawk.

haunted See **haunt**

haunty adj Also *hainty, hanty;* for addit varr see quots [**haunt**] **Sth, S Midl** *among Black speakers*

Haunted.

1965–70 *DARE* (Qu. CC15, *When people say there are ghosts in a certain place . . "They say that the old house is _______."*) Inf **FL**48, A hanty ['hænɪ] house; **LA**8, Hainty ['heɪntɪ]; **MO**23, Haunty ['hʌntɪ], hainty ['henti]; **OK**13, Haunty ['hɔnti]; **TN**53, Haunty ['hʌni] or ['heni]. [All Infs old] **c1970** Pederson *Dial. Surv. Rural GA (An old dilapidated house that evil spirits might live in. Little children are afraid to go into a _______.)* 6 Infs, **seGA,** [hæ̃ntɪ, hæ̃ə̃ntɪ haʊs, hæ̃·nɪ, heɪntɪ ha·ʊs, heɪnɪ, hɑ·ntɪ hæʊs]. [All infs old, Black] **1988** Lincoln *Avenue* 190 **wNC** (as of c1940) [Black], Anybody wanting to talk to him about some ol' run-down plantation with . . a ha'nty-looking ol' house on it would have to catch him another time.

haupia n [Haw] **HI**

A coconut pudding.

1955 Day *HI People* 310, *Haupia:* pudding of coconut milk. **1967** Reinecke–Tsuzaki *Hawaiian Loanwords* 95 (as of 1930s), *Haupia* [hau'pia]. . . Originally, arrowroot and coconut pudding; now, a white (or gray) pudding made of cornstarch and coconut cream. F[requent]. **1967** *DARE* (Qu. H63, *Kinds of desserts*) Infs **HI**1, Haupia [ˌhaʊ'pi-e] = fresh coconut milk, sweetened, jellied in a small cube or block, very common; **HI**6, Haupia [ˌhaʊ'pi-e], originally of arrowroot, now of coconut, a kind of pudding; **HI**9, Haupia = coconut pudding. **1972** Carr *Da Kine Talk* 86 **HI,** *Hawaiian Words Commonly Heard in Hawaii's English. . . Haupia.* Coconut cream pudding formerly thickened with arrowroot and now with cornstarch.

hausfrau n Pronc-sp *housefrow* [Ger] *occas derog*

A housewife.

1919 Mencken *Amer. Lang.* 88, The new immigrants now contributed . . *hausfrau.* **1942** Berrey–Van den Bark *Amer. Slang* 446.15, *Wife.* . . hausfrau, housefrow. **1943** *MLJ* 27.488, *Hausfrau* . . Housewife. Well known to Americans for at least two generations. It is a naturalized word, although used as a pejorative. American women fighting for their rights in the latter years of the nineteenth century referred to the German woman, whose only interests were supposed to be *"Kinder, Küche, und Kirche,"* as a *"mere Hausfrau."* **1947** Lewis *Kingsblood* 8 **eMN,** She was a graduate of Sweet Briar College in Virginia. . . But she said, "I'm no highbrow. At heart, I'm a Hausfrau." **1948** *AmSp* 23.108 **swIL.** **1968–70** *DARE* (Qu. AA15c, . . *Joking ways . . of saying that a woman is getting married*) Inf **NY**66, Is a hausfrau; (Qu. HH34, . . *A woman*) Inf **MI**113, Hausfrau.

havalena See **jabalina**

havance n[1] Also *havins* [*have* to possess] Cf **halfance**
In marble play: see quot.
1899 (1912) Green *VA Folk-Speech* 218, *Havance*. . . When boys keep the marbles they win at play, it is playing for *havance* or *keeps*. . . *Havins*. . . Havings. A game of marbles where . . each boy keeps all he knocks out.

havance n[2] [Aphetic form of *behave; SND havin(g)s* "Behaviour, deportment, (good) manners"; *EDD havance* "*Obs*. . . Manners, behaviour."]
1899 (1912) Green *VA Folk-Speech* 218, *Havance*. . . Good manners. Behaviour. "Have havance"—behave yourself.

have v[1]
A Pronc varr.
1a *have:* usu |hæv|; rarely |hev|; for addit varr see quots; pronc-spp *a, ha, haf, hev, of; freq among Black speakers, hab(s)* (cf Pronc Intro 3.I.17).
1823 Cooper *Pioneers* 1.243 **cNY** [Black], Hab anoder shot. **1848** Lowell *Biglow* 105 **'Upcountry' MA,** To hev it said you're some gret shakes. **1856** Olmsted *Journey Slave States* 558 **AL** [Black], Dey ought to hab two at de least. **1866** (1881) Whitney *Leslie Goldthwaite* 61 **NEng,** I guess I hev been! **1887** *Scribner's Mag.* 2.474 **AR** [Black], De boat tied up fur ter hab de b'iler fixed. **1895** Brown *Meadow-Grass* 118 **NEng,** I dunno's I ought to ha' stirred up rye 'n' Injun. **1899** (1912) Green *VA Folk-Speech* 211, *Hab*. . . A variant of *have*. **1913** *DN* 4.54 **sNY,** *Have* [hev]. **1919** *DN* 5.38 **OK** [Some "broken English" of the Cherokee Indians], *Haf,* v. Have. **1922** Gonzales *Black Border* 146 **sSC, GA coasts** [Gullah], Uh hab house en groun'. *Ibid* 155, Him hab comb. *Ibid* 305 [Glossary], *Hab*—have, has, had, having. **1929** *AmSp* 4.314, In the auxiliaries *have* is often reduced to *a* (mod. ə) at an early date, e.g. "shee little thought to *a* bin mother of such a dafter," Sa. 1692 [=*Records of Salem Witchcraft*, 1692. Roxbury, 1864]. **1930** Stoney–Shelby *Black Genesis* 27 **seSC,** When dark come an' I knock off, I habs to chop wood, an' fetch water. **1938** Rawlings *Yearling* 84 **nFL,** I'd love to of seed him. **1938** Matschat *Suwannee R.* 88 **nFL, sGA,** Can I hev the smellin' water ye got in yer sack? **1953** Brewer *Word Brazos* 40 **c,sTX** (as of c1890) [Black], Dey hab a lots of signs. **1954** *Harder Coll.* **cwTN,** *Have* . . [hæɪf]. **1967** *DARE* FW Addit **nwLA,** Customer to waitress: "We've been going up to the Gourmet [=a rival cafe]." Waitress: "I know you have [hæɪjəv]." This emphatic pronunciation is heard chiefly in slightly artificial situations when intonation contours are exaggerated, as on the phone, joking with someone you are not intimate friends with, etc.

b in phr *have to:* pronc-spp *hafta, hafto, haf(f)ter, haffuh, halfto, hatter, hattuh.*
1884 *Anglia* 7.240 **SE,** *Hatter* (have to), *hadder* (had to). **1890** *DN* 1.61 **swOH,** *Have:* pronounced *haf* in such a phrase as "I haf to have it." (I am conscious of a tendency to slip into this pronunciation. Probably acquired in my boyhood in Philadelphia. J.M.H.) [*DN* Ed: Also common in New England, and due to partial assimilation to the following unvoiced consonant in any careless pronunciation. So, too, "had to" may become "hat to." "Hafter" for "have to" is also reported.] **1893** Shands *MS Speech* 35, *Hattuh* [hætə]. Negro for *have to,* in the sense of being under obligation to do. **1894** Riley *Armazindy* 8 **IN,** This-here part the story I / Allus haf to hurry by. **1909** *DN* 3.397 **nwAR,** *Hafter*. . . Have to. **1913** Kephart *Highlanders* 36 **sAppalachians,** When I move, all I haffter do is put out the fire and call the dog. *Ibid* 79, That's whar they hafter come to feed. **1922** Gonzales *Black Border* 143 **sSC, GA coasts** [Gullah], Now uh haffuh tek me two foot en' walk! *Ibid* 306 [Glossary], *Haffuh*—have to, had to. **1937** (1977) Hurston *Their Eyes* 46, It's uh sorta long trip—specially if Ah hafter lead one on de way back. **1950** Stuart *Hie Hunters* 26 **eKY,** That's why I haf to be keerful. **1954** *Harder Coll.* **cwTN,** You will halfto learn her. **1960** (1962) Lee *Mockingbird* 128 **AL,** That doesn't mean you hafta talk that way when you know better.

c with modal: pronc-spp *a, er, h', ha, of.*
1658 (1882) Southold NY *Town Rec.* 1.472, Beefe and pork . . would a bin as good as beaver to him. **1777** in 1911 *MD Hist. Mag.* 6.144, You would not a thought of Billy Ogg's house. **1861** Holmes *Venner* 1.177 **wMA,** The ol' Doctor, he'd h' ker'd [=carried] 'em threugh. **1871** (1882) Stowe *Fireside Stories* 137 **NEng,** It was so still you might a heard a pin drop. **1889** Edwards *Runaways* 19 **GA,** Ef I cood pick'd de ve'y fish I wanted fur ter mek dat chowd'r, hit 'u'd er been dis same cat. **1908** *DN* 3.285 **eAL, wGA,** *A*. . . Commonly heard as a reduced form of have, as, 'would a.' **1913** Wharton *Custom of Country* 87 **NY,** I guess if Mrs. Van Degen looked like a rose she'd 'a worn a rose. **1916** Lardner *You Know Me Al* 124, I could of had her. **1916** Howells *Leatherwood God* 86 **OH,** I might ha' thought he had thrown a spell on 'em. **1924** Raine *Land of Saddle-Bags* 83 **Appalachians,** I reckon thar must ha' been forty or nigh about. **1927** *AmSp* 3.4 **Ozarks,** *Could have* and *might have* are sometimes pronounced in three syllables, something like *could-a-of* and *might-a-of,* but *would have* is usually contracted to *would-a*. **1936** (1947) Mencken *Amer. Lang.* 443, Sometimes . . *[have]* is confused ignorantly with a distinct *of,* as in "she would of drove" and "I would of gave." More often it is shaded to a sort of particle attached to the verb as an inflection, as in "He woulda tole you," "Who coulda took it?" **1955** Faulkner *Big Woods* 176 **MS,** I would 'a' had to holler. **1965** *DARE* (Qu. CC12b, . . *If a person has a lot of bad luck . . "He ______."*) Inf **OK**7, Must not a been paying his preacher.

2 *has:* usu |hæz|; pronc-sp *hez;* neg usu |'hæzn̩t|; occas |'hædn̩| (cf Pronc Intro 3.I.17); pronc-sp *ha'n't.*
1837 Smith *Col. Crockett's Exploits* 31 **S Midl,** There is no snakes if it ha'n't followed the very track of the other. **1848** Lowell *Biglow* 92 **'Upcountry' MA,** An' ez the North hez took to brustlin'. **1861** Holmes *Venner* 2.182 **wMA,** The one th't hez a fair right to the whole concern! **1954** *PADS* 21.18 **SC,** Careless speech may also be responsible for . . *hasn't* . . [hædn̩]. **1974** Fink *Mountain Speech* 12 **wNC, eTN,** *Hez* . . *has.*

3a *had:* pronc-sp *hed;* neg usu |'hædn̩t|; also rarely |hænt|.
1848 Lowell *Biglow* 104 **'Upcountry' MA,** The clymit seems to me jest like a teapot made o' pewter Our Prudence hed, thet would n't pour . . to suit her. **1893** Shands *MS Speech* 36, *Hed* [hɛd]. Frequently used by negroes for *had*. **1913** Kephart *Highlanders* 93 **sAppalachians,** I wish t' we *hed* roasted the temper outen them trap-springs. **1934** (1970) Wilson *Backwoods Amer.* 69 **Ozarks,** Then there may be unlooked-for internal vowel alterations, like *hed* for *had*. **1959** *VT Hist.* new ser 27.139, Hadn't [hænt]. . . pronc. Rare.

b in phr *had to:* pronc-spp *hadder, hat(t)er, hat to.*
1883 Harris *Nights with Remus* 188 **GA** [Black], He hatter hug a tree fer ter keep fum drappin' on de groun'. **1884** [see **A1b** above]. **1890** [see **A1b** above]. **1899** Chesnutt *Conjure Woman* 21 **csNC** [Black], W'en de sap begin [=began] ter rise . . he ha' ter come en see her ag'in.

B Gram forms.
1 infin: usu *have;* infreq *had.*
1884 *Anglia* 7.251 **Sth** [Black], The simple imperfect is often insufficient for the requirements of Negro emphasis; hence it frequently inserts the auxiliary did; he *did* had some peace. **1937** (1977) Hurston *Their Eyes* 209 **csFL** [Black], Naw, mah husband didn't had nothin' but hisself. **1967** Green *Horse Tradin'* 75 **TX,** She was a good mare that a trader would have to had made some belittling remark about.

2 pres (exc 3rd pers sg): usu *have;* also *has.*
1781 *PA Jrl. & Weekly Advt.* (Philadelphia) 16 May 1/3, Disagreement of the number, giving a verb singular to a nominative plural, . . as, after all the *stories* that *has* been told, all the *reasons* that *has* been given. **1798** (1922) Manning *Key of Libberty* 10 **MA,** Grate panes has bin taken. **1867** Lowell *Biglow* 10 **'Upcountry' MA,** An' ther' 's gret changes hez took place. **1913** Kephart *Highlanders* 77 **sAppalachians,** You'll spy, to-morrow, whar several trees has been wind-throwed and busted to kindlin'. **1949** Guthrie *Way West* 308, Others has been through. **1953** Atwood *Survey of Verb Forms* 26, Only two white informants, both in Md., give the form [I] *has* . . and three Negro informants (Va. and N.C.) use this form. **1966–69** *DARE* Tape **AL**24, I has a grandson; **CA**63, Many restaurants has the lima bean soup here; **MO**1, Some of 'em has their laundry. . . some has carpet on the floor; **SD**8, The research men has really perfected some serums. **1968** *Budget* (Sugarcreek OH) 18 July 10/6 **IA,** Some oats has been combined. **1972** *Foxfire Book* 22 **nGA,** My hands never has been nothin', but boys they's done lots'a hard work.

3 pres 3rd pers sg: usu *has;* also *had, have(s).*
1884 Baldwin *Yankee School-Teacher* 45 **VA,** Here she hab got a lob-letter from Mas'r Percy. **1901** *DN* 2.182 **KY** [Black], *Has* hab. **1922** Gonzales *Black Border* 179 **sSC, GA coasts** [Gullah], Da' nigguh sho' hab uh hebby appetite. *Ibid* 305 [see **A1a** above]. **1935** *AmSp* 10.167 [PaGer], This month he had told me repeatedly that he will write her (he has told). **1952** Brown *NC Folkl.* 1.549, *Haves*. . . Present tense third person singular of *have*. . . Illiterate. **1966** *DARE* Tape **AL**24, She just have a part-time job. **1968** *Sat. Eve. Post* 15 June 29/2 **AL,** He hadn't [=hasn't] got enough brains in his whole head to try a chicken thief in Chilton County. [*DARE* Ed: Cf **A2** above; this may be a pronc-sp.]

4 past: usu *had;* also

a *have.*

1922 [see **A1a, b** above].

b in contrary-to-fact subjunctive without conditional *if, has.* Cf **be B5c(1)**

1960 Williams *Walk Egypt* 26 **GA,** I'd do it myself, I has the time. But I ain't.

5 past perfect; usu *had* + past pple; also *have* + past pple.

1908 *German Amer. Annals* 10.38 **sePA,** "Last night after I have done my work." . . Pa. Ger. uses the compound with *hŏwă* in this way.

6 aux omitted: See quots. Cf **be B8b**

1872 (1973) Thompson *Major Jones's Courtship* 44, I do blieve I'd had them grapes if I'd had to dig the tree up by the roots. *Ibid* 109, If you could jest seen her as she was dressed then, . . you couldn't help but envy my luck. **1899** Chesnutt *Conjure Woman* 49 **csNC** [Black], He had a big skyar [=scar] on his lef' leg, des lack [=just like] it be'n skunt [=skinned]. **1981** *PADS* 67.47 **Mesabi Iron Range MN,** *I been,* common with other Minnesota informants . . , is frequently recorded for the Mesabi informants.

C Sense.

See quots. [Infl by Ger *haben*] **German settlement areas**

1916 *DN* 4.338 **PA,** *Have*. . . Used for *be,* as to *have* homesick, or to *have* the shrink (to be shrunken). Cf. German, *Er hat Heimweh.* **1933** Smiley *Gloss. New Paltz* **seNY,** Their [sic] is one that is not of age. . . She has 2 years and five months. **1935** *AmSp* 10.167 **sePA,** He has great homesick. **1968** *Helen Adolf Festschrift* 39 **cePA,** Let us consider . . syntax, an area in which the influence of the Pennsylvania German dialect on the English is also immediately apparent; for instance: . . "*It has* (Pennsylvania German *es hot*) people like that."

D In var phrr.

1 *have a catch:* See quots.

1981 *DARE* File **NJ,** *To have a catch:* To play catch. **1986** Hendrickson *Amer. Talk* 63, Native New York kids still *have a catch* (whereas other American youngsters *play catch*). **1988** *DARE* File **NYC** (as of 1953), In asking a friend if he wanted to play catch one would always say something like "You wanna have a catch?" This idiomatic use of *have* was not, however, extended to other games. One didn't say "You wanna have a stickball?" but rather "How 'bout a game a stickball?"

2 *have a lot to do:* See quot.

1960 Criswell *Resp. to PADS 20* **Ozarks,** *To have a lot to do:* To have little right to (say something). Very frequent some time ago and still used. "You've got a lot to do laughing at me when you happened to the same accident yourself last year."

3 *have it:*

a also with *around, out, up and down:* To argue, quarrel, or fight.

1884 *Anglia* 7.269 **Sth, S Midl** [Black], *To have it up en' down* = to quarrel. **1893** Shands *MS Speech* 35, *Have it*. . . Used by all classes for *to fight* or *quarrel;* as, "He and his wife had it up and down all day long"; "They talked until their patience gave out and then they had it." The phrase *up and down* is very frequently joined to this expression, and seems to imply that the fight or quarrel was a thorough and complete one. **1914** *DN* 4.108 **KS,** *Have it*. . . To dispute. "They were just having it over politics." **1923** *DN* 5.209 **swMO,** *Have it up and down*. . . To argue heatedly. **1942** McAtee *Dial. Grant Co. IN* 32 (as of 1890s), *Have it up and down* . . argue heatedly. **1943** Chase *Jack Tales* 75 **wNC,** Jack jumped down off the ladder right on top of him. They had it around awhile, till fin'ly Jack tumbled him. **c1960** *Wilson Coll.* **csKY,** *Have it up and down*. . . Argue heatedly. **1965–70** *DARE* (Qu. EE21b, . . *"For a while those fellows really ________."*) 16 Infs, **scattered,** Had it (out); **IA**32, Had it out against each other; **TX**68, Were having it out; (Qu. Y12a, *A fight between two people, mostly with words*) Infs **TN**38, **WI**34, Had it out; (Qu. KK13, *Other words for arguing*) Infs **CT**8, **HI**6, Having it out. **1966** Barnes–Jensen *Dict. UT Slang* 22, *Having it up and down* . . arguing vehemently. "They were shouting and having it up and down, I'll tell you."

b also *have got it:* To suffer pain. [Infl by Ger *haben*]

1882 (1971) Gibbons *PA Dutch* 391, "How are you, Chrissly?" . . "Oh! I've got it so in the back." **1907** *German Amer. Annals* 9.378 **sePA,** *Have it.* To suffer, be ill; always with part affected. "She had it in the head very bad."

have v² Pronc-spp *a, er, ha', of, 've* [Prob by analogy with std *could have seen, should have gone, might have walked,* etc, where *have* is freq reduced to [ə] (pronc-spp *coulda, shoulda, mighta*)] **widespread, but chiefly Sth, S Midl**

Following *had:* Used redundantly in counter-factual constrs.

1798 (1922) Manning *Key of Libberty* 46 **MA,** If the Swinnish Multitude had a behaved so they would soone have had the adultrious Hambleton after them. **1834** *Life Andrew Jackson* 248 **TN,** Now, I'm of the opinion, gineral that if you had've let the Bank alone all wou'd've bin prosperous. **1853** Simms *Sword & Distaff* 369 **SC,** Ef the dream hadn't ha' come true, I'd ha' hardly eaten to-day. **1884** *Anglia* 7.258 **Sth, S Midl** [Black], Ef I had er seed him! **1906** *DN* 3.139 **nwAR,** *Had a, had of*. . . Had. Used with perfect participle to form a pluperfect tense. "If I *had of* forgotten, I'd a been ashamed of myself." "If I'd a known it, I'd a gone." **1908** *DN* 3.285 **eAL, wGA,** *A*. . . Commonly heard as a reduced form of *have,* as . . 'had a,' etc. **1916** Lardner *You Know Me Al* 123, If I had of thought at the time I would of knew. *Ibid* 128, If he had not of been nasty. **1928** *Ruppenthal Coll.* **KS,** If it had a been as he thought, we would a been in danger. **1930** Faulkner *As I Lay Dying* 32 **MS,** If He'd a aimed for man to be always a-moving and going somewheres else, wouldn't He a put him longways on his belly, like a snake? **1950** *WELS* (*"If they hadn't ________, I wouldn't have bought them."*) 1 Inf, **cwWI,** A-fit. **1965–70** *DARE* (Qu. Y5, . . *Johnny wouldn't have tried that if the other boys hadn't ________*) Inf **NY**70, A tempted him; **KY**28, 42, A begged him (into it); **MO**16, A talked him into it; (Qu. OO38b, . . *"I wouldn't have bought them [=shoes] if they hadn't ________ [just right]."*) Infs **AR**41, **MS**57, **MO**34, 37, 38, 39, **TN**13, 'A fit; **KY**77, 'A fit good; **VA**42, 'A fitted. **1970** *DARE* File **NE, OK,** If I had 've known it.

have v³ |hev| [Aphet form of *behave*]

1884 *Anglia* 7.266 **Sth, S Midl** [Black], *To 'have yo'se'f* = to behave yourself. **1893** *Harper's New Mth. Mag.* 86.975/1 **Sth** [Black], Now come 'long home wid me an' 'have yourself. [**1916** *DN* 4.291 **sAppalachians,** The prefix *be-* is often dropped, as in "Ole Miss (Mrs.) Watts *witched* three cows last night." "He *friended me* when I's (I was) in trouble."] **1954** *Harder Coll.* **cwTN,** *Have* [hev]—A harsh command for someone to be quiet or to stop creating a disturbance: "If ye ain't 'have yeself, I'm a-goin' take ye out and jist ware ye out."

have v⁴ [Cf *SND hae* v. B5 "To put, bring, take, convey, send"]

To give; to lend.

1966 *DARE* (Qu. U16, *I need five dollars before Saturday, will you ________ it to me?*) Inf **SC**21, Have.

have adj [By reanalysis of *behave* as *be* + *have*]

Well behaved.

1954 *Harder Coll.* **cwTN,** *Have*—well-behaved. "I'm being have now. . . He's been a-being have all morning."

have a catch See **have** v¹ **D1**

have a down on See **down** n¹ **E1**

have a feeling in one's bones See **feel in one's bones**

have a goose to pick See **goose** n **B3**

have a housecleaning See **housecleaning, have a**

have a lot to do See **have** v¹ **D2**

have got it See **have** v¹ **D3b**

'haveishness See **'havishness**

have it See **have** v¹ **D3**

have it around (or out, up and down) See **have** v¹ **D3a**

have no flies on one See **fly** n² **4**

have off v phr¹ **Sth, S Midl**

To take off, remove.

1906 *DN* 3.139 **nwAR,** *Have off*. . . Take off, remove, doff. "Have off your hat and coat." Common. **1908** *DN* 3.319 **eAL, wGA,** *Have off*. . . To remove, take off (coat, hat, shawl, or the like). "Have off your things an' set a while." **1937** (1963) Hyatt *Kiverlid* 14 **KY,** Set down, Nancy, have off your shawl. **1946** *PADS* 6.17 **eNC,** *Have off*. . . To take off (one's coat, hat, etc.). "Have off your things and stay a while." . . Common.

have off v phr² [Perh infl by *haul off*]

To act belligerently.

1942 Hurston *Dust Tracks* 234 **FL** (as of 1900s), Then when she do git wake she'll have off and ast you, 'Nigger, what you wake me up for?'

have one in the hopper See **hopper 5**

have one's Dutch up See **Dutch** n **4**

have one('s) foot in the road See **foot** n **C5f**

have one's foot on the rail See **foot** n **C5g**

have one's habits on See **habits on, have one's**

have over v phr

1936 *AmSp* 11.368 **nLA,** *To have over.* To reprimand; to complain at; to castigate; as, 'When my old man gets in, I am going to have him over.'

havers See **halvers**

haversack n

The American avocet.

1951 *AmSp* 26.91, Variations in pronunciation seem to be the major source of folk etymology. Among . . bird names are: . . *Haversack* (S. Dak.) . . for the avocet.

haverty-grass, go to v phr Also *go to haberty-grass, ~ habidy-grass* [Varr of *Havre de Grace* town in Maryland; perh infl by *go to grass* go to hell, die] Cf **Halifax 1**

To go to hell, go to the devil.

1895 *DN* 1.382 **NJ,** "Go to Halifax!" . . (and also, "Go to Haverty-grass (Havre-de-grace),["] which he cannot explain historically. Can any one account for this, or for "go to grass," which suggests a connection?) **1927** *Ruppenthal Coll.* **KS, PA,** *Go to habidygrass*—a mild imprecation—probably Havre de Grace, Md., where troops embarked for Europe when driven out of America. "If he does not like that, he can go to Habidygrass." **1967** *DARE* (Qu. NN26b, . . *"Go to ______!"*) Inf **PA**46, Haberty-grass.

hav-e-ry brav-e-ry n Cf **heartleaf**

An unidentified plant.

c1938 in 1970 Hyatt *Hoodoo* 1.240 **neVA,** There's a weed that grows called *devil's wishbone* and another one called *hav-e-ry brav-e-ry.* It has a leaf on it as tall as your finger, it's a little leaf that sticks up right on the end in the shape of a heart. There's only one leaf.

haves See **have** v[1] **B3**

have something on one's hip See **hip** n[1] **1**

have the hookworm See **hookworm 2**

have-to n, also attrib Also *had-to, have-to-be*

Something one is forced by social or other pressure to accept.

1936 Morehouse *Rain on Just* 319 **NC,** All my druthers and my have-tos are bedded well together. **1965–70** *DARE* (Qu. AA20, *A marriage that takes place because a baby is on the way*) 59 Infs, **scattered, but less freq West,** (Case of) have-to; 20 Infs, **scattered, but esp Midl,** Have-to case (*or* affair, marriage, situation, wedding); **GA**10, Have-to-be marriage; **DE**5, **MN**19, **SC**3, 40, (Case of) had-to; (Qu. BB20, *Joking names . . for overactive kidneys*) Inf **TN**12, Case of have-to. **1968** *DARE* Tape **MI**96, They could go from our school to any of the colleges without an examination. . . Most of the students go to college. . . We just thought that was a have-to. We got through there and we just had to go on.

have you ever seen a lady See **did you ever see a lassie**

havins See **havance** n[1]

'havishness n Also sp *'haveishness* [Aphet forms of **behavishness**]

Misbehavior.

1883 (1971) Harris *Nights with Remus* 102 **nGA,** Dey wuz times . . w'en de creeturs 'ud segashuate tergedder des like dey aint had no fallin' out. Dem wuz de times w'en ole Brer Rabbit 'ud 'ten' [=pretend] lak he gwine quit he 'havishness, en dey'd all go 'roun' des lak dey b'long ter de same fambly connexion. *Ibid* 399, Now, den, I bin a-beggin' un you fer ter quit yo' 'haveishness des long ez I'm a-gwinter.

havvers See **halvers**

haw v Cf **gee** v[1] **1**

To turn left (or, less freq, to turn right, go faster, stop, or back up)—usu used as a command to a draft animal; to give this command, say "haw" to; hence vbl n *hawing;* n *haw* the command "haw."

1843 (1916) Hall *New Purchase* 102 **IN,** Accordingly the fellow [=a horse], after performing wonders on the journey . . in hawing and gee-ing, and in pulling right dead ahead up one side a mountain . . &c. *Ibid* 202, The whole intended field . . was resounding with all kinds of cries, noises, and echoes, such as shouts—orders . . gees and haws. **1843** *Knickerbocker* 21.494, He admonishes them with his goad, and ejaculates, *'Haw!'* **1846** *Ibid* 27.119 **NEng,** The plough-boy has hardly energy to cry out . . 'Gee-haw, there! I tell you to haw, now!' **1861** IL Dept. Ag. *Trans.* 4.99 **IL,** Thirteen teams . . were required to plow lands of about fifteen rods in length, and "haw" about. On the third furrow, all rested. **1899** (1912) Green *VA Folk-Speech* 218, *Haw.* . . Word used by driver to his oxen to make them turn to the left. **1908** Fox *Lonesome Pine* 19 **KY,** Git up—Whoa—Haw—Gee, Gee! **1914** *DN* 4.74 **ME, nNH,** *Haw.* . . Turn to the left (oxen). **1922** Gonzales *Black Border* 193 **sSC, GA coasts** [Gullah], Old Pickett . . submitted to the indignity of being "gee'd" and "haw'd". **1923** *DN* 5.210 **swMO,** *Haw,* A word of direction to a team meaning "Turn to the left." **1950** *WELS (Command to make horses turn to left)* 38 Infs, **WI,** Haw; *(. . To right)* 7 Infs, **WI,** Haw. **1954** *Harder Coll.* **cwTN,** *Haw:* "C'mere haw," an order to oxen to turn left. **1965–70** *DARE* (Qu. K35b, . . *To make the horses or mules turn left;* total Infs questioned, 75) 46 Infs, Haw; (Qu. K34, . . *To make the horses stop*) Infs **CA**99, **OH**90, Haw; **NC**87, Haw haw; (Qu. K35a, . . *To make the horses or mules turn right;* total Infs questioned, 75) Infs **MS**60, **OK**33, Haw; (Qu. K36a, . . *To make a horse go faster*) Infs **IL**41, 69, Haw; (Qu. K36b, . . *To make a horse go backwards*) Infs **NJ**67, **TX**94, Haw; (Qu. K81, *To make a cow stand still*) Inf **LA**39, Haw. **1972** Jones–Hawes *Step it Down* 208 **eGA** [Black], I hawed to the mule but the mule wouldn't haw this morning. **1973** Allen *LAUM* 1.261 (as of c1950), No significant regional patterns appear in the data for directional calls to draft animals, typically *haw* to the left and *gee* to the right. But the decline in the use of such animals is reflected in the uncertainty of 26 scattered infs. as to which word means right and which means left, and is even more sharply indicated in the complete semantic reversal accepted by the 4 infs. who insist that *gee* is equivalent to "Go left" and by the 6 reported as believing that *haw* means "Go right."

haw n

1 See **haw horse.**

2 See **haw** v.

Hawaiian ash n

The Shamel ash *(Fraxinus uhdei).*

1965 Neal *Gardens HI* 675, *Fraxinus uhdei.* . . A Mexican tree is called Hawaiian ash in Hawaii, where it is proving to be one of the most successful trees for reforestation.

Hawaiian buttercup n Also *Hawaii buttercup*

A native **buttercup 1** (here: *Ranunculus hawaiiensis*).

1930 Degener *Ferns of HI* 156, The Hawaii buttercup, *R[anunculus] hawaiiensis* . . is limited to the Island of Hawaii and to the eastern part of the Island of Maui. . . It is an erect, coarsely hairy herb, two to four feet high. **1967** *DARE* (Qu. S21, . . *Weeds . . that are a trouble in gardens and fields*) Inf **HI**2, Hawaiian buttercup, used for leis.

Hawaiian huckleberry n

=**ohelo.**

1896 *Pop. Sci. Mth.* 48.757, On the island of Hawaii are great thickets of the *ohelo,* or Hawaiian huckleberry *(Vaccinium reticulatum).*

Hawaiian time n *joc* or *derog* Cf **Alaska time, Indian time, Jewish time**

A flexible system of time; a disregard for punctuality.

1974 *DARE* File **HI,** *Hawaiian time:* [Used of one who is] somewhat late. Anywhere from five minutes to five hours after the appointed time. **1988** *DARE* File **HI,** Hawaiian time? Yeah, sure. Hawaiian time. Any country you're in—Filipino time, Indian time, Hawaiian time. It means elastic time, rubber time.

Hawaii buttercup See **Hawaiian buttercup**

haw apple See **apple haw**

hawbuck n Also *hawbucker* [Engl dial; cf *EDD*]

An awkward or unmannerly person; hence v *hawbuck* to behave like such a person.

1896 *DN* 1.418 **NJ,** *Hawbuck* (n.): a tomboy. (v.) To act boisterously. **1930** Shoemaker *1300 Words* 28 **cPA Mts** (as of c1900), *Hawbucker*—An ignorant country fellow. **1934** (1943) *W2, Hawbuck . . n. . .* A bumpkin; a lout.—*v.i.* To act like a hawbuck. *Both Dial.*

haw-eater n [*haw* the fruit of a **hawthorn**]

See quots.

1904 in 1944 *ADD* **WV.** **1939** *Ibid* **nWV,** *Haw-eater. . .* [n.]. A West Virginian. In ref. to his eating the black haw. **1944** *ADD, Haw-eater. . .* A mountaineer.

hawfinch n

Any of var American grosbeaks, but esp the **evening grosbeak.**

1889 *Century Dict.* 2742, *Hawfinch*. . . The name is extended to sundry related American grosbeaks, as the evening grosbeak, *Hesperiphona vespertina,* the rose-breasted grosbeak, *Zamelodia* or *Habia ludoviciana,* etc. **1917** (1923) *Birds Amer.* 3.2, *Evening Grosbeak—Hesperiphona vespertina vespertina*. . . Other Names. . . American Hawfinch. **1946** Hausman *Eastern Birds* 577, *Eastern Evening Grosbeak—Hesperiphona vespertina* . . Other Names—American Hawfinch.

hawg See **hog**

haw-haw See **hee-haw**

haw hissy See **hissy**

haw horse n Also *haw, haw-side horse* **scattered, but esp IN, IL, OH** Cf **gee horse**

=**near horse.**

1950 *WELS (The horse on the driver's left)* 5 Infs, **WI,** Haw; 1 Inf, Gee horse or haw horse. I'm not sure . . which is left and which is right. **1962** Atwood *Vocab. TX* 55, *Haw (horse)* . . usually means the left-hand horse—*gee (horse)* . . the one on the right. **1965–70** *DARE* (Qu. K32b, *The horse on the left side in plowing or hauling*) 59 Infs, **scattered, but esp IN, IL, OH,** Haw (horse); **CT**29, **IL**87, **MS**19, **NC**36, Haw-side horse; (Qu. K32a, . . *The horse on the driver's right hand*) Infs **AZ**10, **IL**7, 9, **IN**27, 72, **NY**107, 142, **PA**232, Haw horse. [For discussion of confusion of terms for right- and left-hand horses see note at **near horse.**] **1973** Allen *LAUM* 1.268 (as of c1950), The horse on the left side of a team. . . The guidance term *haw* has been carried into the expression *haw horse* in Iowa and Nebraska.

hawing See **haw** v

hawk n

1 also with *the;* also *Hawkins:* The wind, esp that of winter; cold weather; winter. **chiefly Chicago IL** *chiefly among Black speakers*

1946 (1972) Mezzrow–Wolfe *Really Blues* 333 **IL,** Hawk: *winter.* Hawk's out with his axe: *it's freezing weather.* **1958** Hughes–Bontemps *Negro Folkl.* 484, *Hawkins:* The wind, wintertime, cold weather, ice, snow. In February, Hawkins talks. **1966** *Lou Rawls "Live"* (Phonodisc) **Chicago IL,** In the wintertime when it's very, very cold . . when it's around ten above zero and it's about twelve inches of snow outside, and the hawk, I'm speakin' of the almighty hawk, Mr. Wind, when he blows down the street around 35, 40 miles an hour it's just like a giant razorblade blowin' down the street, and all the clothes in the world can't help you. **1970** *DARE* (Qu. B18, . . *Kinds of wind*) Infs **IL**137, Hawk [hɔwk]; **IL**139, The hawk [hɔk]. [Both Infs Black, both from Chicago IL] **1972** Claerbaut *Black Jargon* 68, *Hawk*. . . the wind: *The hawk is strong tonight.* **1972** *DARE* File **Chicago IL** [Black], *The hawk*—cold weather, esp with strong cold winds. The hawk is coming. **1977** Smitherman *Talkin* 67 [Black], *Ashy* refers to the whitish coloration of black skin due to exposure to the *Hawk* (cold and wind). **1981** *DARE* File, The hawk—nickname for a cold wind. In the late 30's there was a great trumpet-player, Erskine Hawkins, with a big band; he was called the "20th Century Gabriel"—he was said to blow a "cold blast." **1989** *Capital Times* (Madison WI) 13 Dec 15/1 **Chicago IL,** Wait until the Hawk arrives, I warned, the howling arctic wind that rips through town in January and February.

2 A **dragonfly.** Cf **arrow hawk, mosquito ~**

1968 *DARE* (Qu. R2, . . *Names* . . *for the dragonfly*) Inf **SC**57, Hawk.

3 also *chicken hawk:* See quots. Cf **hack** n^4 **1**

1936 *AmSp* 11.122 [Narcotics argot], *Hawks.* Guards in Federal prisons. **1942** Berrey–Van den Bark *Amer. Slang* 460.18, *Detective*. . . hawk. *Ibid* 460.19, *Guard; watchman*. . . hawk. **1968–70** *DARE* (Qu. V10a, . . *Joking names* . . *for a sheriff*) Inf **NC**87, Hawk; (Qu. V10b, . . *Joking names for a marshal*) Inf **OH**81, Chicken hawk. [Both Infs old, male]

hawk v^1 [From the attributes of the *hawk*]

1 To capture, pounce upon; hence vbl n *hawking.*

1806 (1970) Webster *Compendious Dict.* 140/1, *Hawk*. . . catch. **1909** Ware *Passing Engl.* 151, *Hawking (Amer.).* Pouncing. Derived from the action of birds of prey crashing on their quarry. **1942** Berrey–Van den Bark *Amer. Slang* 367.9, *Hawk,* to pounce upon.

2 To watch closely; to keep under surveillance.

1886 *Lantern* 6 Oct 2/3 (*AmSp* 25.34) **New Orleans LA,** And to keep solid home he hawks the baby. **1971** Roberts *Third Ear* np [Black], *Hawk*. . . to watch closely (often pronounced "hack"). **1979** *Capital Times* (Madison WI) 30 Jan 1/5, If they were in a special class, they'd be hawked to keep working all the time.

3 =**hack** v^1 **2. esp Mid Atl**

1928 *Ruppenthal Coll.* **KS,** *To hawk*—to jeer with intent to provoke. **1935** Sheppard *Cabins* 168 **nwNC,** They just hawked hell out of me with their everlasting talk. **1944** *PADS* 2.43 **NC, VA,** *Hawk* [hɔk]. . . To exasperate, to chagrin, to "get the best of." . . "Hit sho hawked ole Rafe when his young wife run off with that boarder at his house." **1946** *PADS* 6.16, *Hack*. . . To discomfit, to daunt, to faze. ((*Hawk,* Southern dialect, has the same meaning.)) **1952** Brown *NC Folkl.* 1.549, *Hawk*. . . To annoy; to tease; to embarrass.

4 See quot.

1971 Roberts *Third Ear* np [Black], *Hawk*. . . to walk rapidly; to pursue closely.

hawk v^2 Also sp *hock* [*OED* 1583 →] **scattered, but esp NEast, S Midl**

To cough, clear the throat; also with *up:* to cough (up phlegm); also fig.

1806 (1970) Webster *Compendious Dict.* 140/1, *Hawk* . . to force up phlegm. **1871** (1882) Stowe *Fireside Stories* 27 **NEng,** Just because I believe Ruth Sullivan, I'm not going to believe, right and left, all the stories in Cotton Mather, and all that anybody can hawk up to tell. Not I. **1899** (1912) Green *VA Folk-Speech* 218, *Hawk*. . . To cough voluntarily for the expectoration of phlegm. **1929** Wolfe *Look Homeward* 175 **NC,** He passed on, hocking into the gutter a slimy gob of phlegm. **1930** Shoemaker *1300 Words* 31 **cPA Mts** (as of c1900), *Hawk*—To expectorate. **1938** Farrell *No Star* 412 **Chicago IL** (as of 1914–15), Danny hawked to get saliva in his mouth. **1951** Styron *Lie Down* 362 **Sth,** He hocked something up, spat it out the window. **1965–70** *DARE* (Qu. BB11, *Speaking of a deep cough* . . *"Listen to him ______."*) Infs **LA**14, **MI**114, **MA**27, **NJ**21, 35, **NY**2, 7, 24, Hawk; (Qu. BB12, *The kind of cough that comes with bronchitis*) Inf **ME**9, Hawking; (Qu. DD4) Inf **NY**10, ['hɑk ə 'lʌŋɚ]—when they seem to spit up a lung. **1984** Wilder *You All Spoken Here* 190 **Sth,** *Hawk*. . . To hawk . . means to clear one's throat with a harsh palatal sound.

hawk and chickens n

=**chickamy chickamy craney crow.**

1883 Newell *Games & Songs* 155 **NEng, Sth,** *Hawk and Chickens.* A hen with her brood. A child represents the "Old Buzzard," about whom the rest circle. The hen addresses the latter: "Chickany, chickany, crany, crow." . . In the Southern States a witch takes the place of the bird of prey and the rhyme is, "Chickamy, chickamy, crany, crow." **1953** Brewster *Amer. Nonsinging Games* 71, *Chickamy Chickamy Craney Crow.* This familiar game is known by many names: Old Dame . . Hawk and Chickens.

hawkbill n [From the shape]

1 also *hawkbeak, hawk's beak:* A nose, esp one hooked or sharp; hence adj *hawk-billed* having such a nose. **chiefly Sth, S Midl**

1954 *Harder Coll.* **cwTN,** *Hawkbill* . . Nose. **1965–70** *DARE* (Qu. X15, . . *Kinds of noses*) Infs **NC**76, **TN**23, 65, Hawkbill; **KY**40, **MS**16, **VA**24, Hawkbill nose; **FL**31, **MI**47, Hawkbeak; **MD**17, Hawk's beak; **NC**36, Hawk-billed—sharp; **TX**32, Hawk-billed.

2 A pocketknife with a hooked blade.

1966–69 *DARE* (Qu. F39, *A large pocket knife with blades that fold in and out*) Infs **KY**28, **SC**9, Hawkbill. [Drawings in QRs show knife with a curved blade.] **1969** *DARE* FW Addit **KY**39, *Hawkbill knife*—a knife with a curved or hooked tip—usually a pocketknife.

3 See **hookbill 1.**

hawk-billed See **hawkbill 1**

hawk-bird n [Redund; cf Intro "Language Changes" I.4]

1940 *Sat. Eve. Post* 30 Mar 62/3 **eKY,** Go like a hawk bird flying.

hawkbit n

1 Std: A plant of the genus *Leontodon.* For other names of var spp see **fall dandelion**

2 A **hawkweed,** esp *Hieracium venosum.*

1876 Hobbs *Bot. Hdbk.* 51, Hawk bit, Hawkweed, Hieracium venosum. **1900** Lyons *Plant Names* 191, *H. aurantiacum*. . . Orange or Tawny . . Hawkbit. *Ibid* 192, *H. venosum*. . . Veiny-leaved . . Hawkbit. **1940** Clute *Amer. Plant Names* 70, *H. venosum*. . . Hawkbit. **1959** Carleton *Index Herb. Plants* 58, *Hawk-bit:* Taraxacum officinale . . ; Hieracium (v).

3 A **dandelion 1** (here: *Taraxacum officinale*).
1959 [see **2** above].

hawk-caller n [Prob from the sound]
1952 Brown *NC Folkl.* 1.234, [Folk-toys:] *Blate* (Bleat?) or *Hawk-caller.*—This consisted of a split stick with a leaf tongue.

hawker n Also rarely *hawkster* **chiefly Nth, N Midl** Cf **arab** n **B3**
A street vendor or itinerant peddler.
1683 (1911) Mather *Diary* 1.65 **MA,** There is an old *Hawker,* who will fill this Countrey with devout and useful Books, if I will direct him. **1721** *Mass. H. Rep. Jrnl.* III.144 *(DAE),* A Committee, to prepare some Addition to the Act against Hawkers, Peddlers, &c. **1815** (1874) Adams *Memoirs J.Q. Adams* 3.165, I found the hawkers had got to it. **1865** in 1882 MI Laws *Genl. Statutes* 1.375, Every person who shall be found traveling and trading . . contrary to the terms of any license that may have been granted to him as a hawker or peddler, shall for each offense forfeit . . one hundred dollars. **1950** *WELS (Someone who sells small articles on a street corner or from house to house)* 5 Infs, **WI,** Hawker; 1 Inf, Hawkster—old-fashioned. **1965–70** *DARE* (Qu. U5, *Someone who sells small articles on a street corner*) 63 Infs, **chiefly Nth, N Midl,** Hawker; **CT**15, Curb-hawker; (Qu. U6, *Someone who sells vegetables or other articles from a wagon or truck, going from house to house*) 15 Infs, **chiefly Nth, Midl,** Hawker; (Qu. U7, *A man who goes from town to town selling things*) Inf **MI**24, Hawker.

hawkey See **hockey** n[1] **2**

hawkeye n
1 See quot. Cf **cat's-eye 1**
1969 *DARE* (Qu. EE6d, *Special marbles*) Inf **CA**133, Hawkeyes.
2 See quot.
1969 *DARE* (Qu. K42, *A horse that is rough, wild, or dangerous*) Inf **NY**189, Hawkeye ['hɔkaɪ].
3 Appar a **black-eyed pea** or similar legume.
1950 *WELS (Small white beans with a black spot where they were joined to the pod)* 1 Inf, **seWI,** Hawkeyes.

hawk-eyed adj
1960 Bailey *Resp. to PADS 20* **KS,** *Hawk-eyed:* Pop-eyed, bug-eyed, banjo-eyed.

hawking See **hawk** v[1] **1**

Hawkins See **hawk** n **1**

hawk-jawed adj
1966 *DARE* (Qu. X6, *If a person's lower jaw sticks out prominently*) Inf **WA**33, Hawk-jawed.

hawk-nosed salmon See **hook-billed salmon**

hawk owl n
1 also *owl hawk:* An owl *(Surnia ulula)* which looks and hunts somewhat like a hawk. Also called **day owl 1**
1812 Wilson *Amer. Ornith.* 6.64, *Hawk Owl. Strix Hudsonia. . . This* is another inhabitant of both continents . . a connecting link between the Hawk and Owl tribes. **1872** Coues *Key to N. Amer. Birds* 205, *Surnia Dumeril.* Hawk Owl. Day Owl. **1880** *Harper's New Mth. Mag.* 61.670/1, I am very glad indeed that you have the hawk-owl. **1909** Field Museum Nat. Hist. *Zool. Ser.* 9.499, *American Hawk Owl. . .* south in winter to northern borders of United States and casually as far as Illinois and New England. **1917** (1923) *Birds Amer.* 2.117, *Surnia ulula caparoch. . .* the Hawk Owl is a winter visitor to our Northern States from the Arctic regions. . . not only is its appearance Hawk-like but its manner of hunting is similar, in some respects, to that of the Hawks. **1950** *WELS (Kinds of owls)* 1 Inf, **cWI,** Hawk owl—medium size, long tail feathers like a hawk. **1963** Murie *Birds Mt. McKinley* 57 **AK,** The handsome hawk-owl, about 15 inches long, has a sharply defined black and white facial pattern. **1965–70** *DARE* (Qu. Q2, . . *Kinds of owls*) Infs **IL**7, **KY**72, **MI**2, 36, **NY**80, 87, **OH**87, **OK**25, Hawk owl; **MN**2, Owl hawk; (Qu. Q1, . . *Owl that makes a shrill, trembling cry*) Inf **VT**16, Hawk owl.
2 =**short-eared owl.**
1889 *Century Dict.* 2743, *Hawk-owl. . .* The short-eared owl, *Strix brachyotus.*
3 A snowy owl (here: *Nyctea nyctea*).
1889 *Century Dict.* 2743, *Hawk-owl. . .* The harfang or great snowy owl, *Nyctea nivea.*

hawk's beak See **hawkbill 1**

hawk's-eye n
1 =**golden plover.**
1888 Trumbull *Names of Birds* 195 (as of 1750), *Charadrius dominicus. . .* Hawk's Eye. **1917** (1923) *Birds Amer.* 1.257, *Charadrius dominicus dominicus. . .* Hawk's eye. **1923** [see **2** below].
2 Either the **least sandpiper** or the **semipalmated sandpiper.**
1923 U.S. Dept. Ag. *Misc. Circular* 13.57, *Semipalmated Sandpiper (Ereunetes pusillus) . . In local use. . .* hawk's-eye (Mass.) *Ibid* 13.69, *Golden Plover (Charadrius dominicus) . .* hawk's eye. **1925** (1928) Forbush *Birds MA* 1.419 **NEng,** *Ereunêtes pusillus. . .* Semipalmated Sandpiper. . . Hawk's eye; oxeye. **1955** *AmSp* 30.182, In 1750 George Edwards wrote of the golden plover, 'I suppose when it is living it has a bright shining eye, because. . . the English settled in Hudson's Bay call it the Hawk's Eye.' In Massachusetts, at a much later time, the same name has been applied to the least and semipalmated sandpipers. **1956** MA Audubon Soc. *Bulletin* 40.20, *Semipalmated Sandpiper. . .* Hawk's-eye (Mass. From its obviously keen sight.)

hawk's mouth n Cf **hawk** n **1**
1985 *DARE* File **ME,** Hawk's mouth: in Maine this describes a light sky with a sullen horizon above a black sea. It is considered a sure sign of bad weather.

hawkster See **hawker**

hawk stone n
1967 *DARE* (Qu. C25, . . *Kinds of stone . . about so big [Show size of a person's head], smooth and hard*) Inf **AL**27, Hawk stones—a rock about that size, flinty; they'd say the hawks sharpened their bills on them.

hawk-tailed gull n
=**Sabine's gull.**
1917 (1923) *Birds Amer.* 1.53, *Sabine's Gull—Xema sabini . .* Hawk-tailed Gull. **1946** Hausman *Eastern Birds* 319, *Sabine's Gull Xema sabini. . .* Other Names—Fork-tailed Gull, Hawk-tailed Gull.

hawk up See **hawk** v[2]

hawkweed n
Std: a plant of the genus *Hieracium.* Also called **devil's paintbrush 1, hawkbit 2.** For other names of var spp see **devil's weed 2c, Flora's paintbrush 1, golden hawkweed, high dandelion, king devil, leopard's tongue, mouse-ear, orange hawkweed, poor Robin's plantain, possum-ear, rattlesnake weed, snake plantain, veinleaf, woollyweed, yellow devil**

hawky n[1] See **hockey** n[1] **2**

hawky n[2] See **hockey** n[2], **v**

hawky adj See **hockey** adj

hawngry See **hungry**

hawnker See **honker** n[1] **1**

hawn' owl See **horned owl**

hawnyock See **hunyak 3**

hawps n [*EDD hawps* "A tall, awkward person"]
1930 Shoemaker *1300 Words* 31 **cPA Mts** (as of c1900), *Hawps*—A tall awkward girl.

hawr See **hair** n

hawse See **horse**

haw-side horse See **haw horse**

hawss See **horse**

hawthorn n
Std: a plant of the genus *Crataegus.* Also called **alisier, hair apple, hall** n[2], **hog apple 2, red haw, scarlet haw, thorn, thorn apple, thorn plum, white thorn.** For other names of var spp see **apple haw, black haw 3, cockspur 1, cockspur thorn, hedge thorn, hog haw, mayapple, may hawthorn, newcastle thorn, parsley hawthorn, pear hawthorn, pine thorn, pin thorn, pommette bleue, river hawthorn, senellier, sugar haw, summer haw, tree haw, turkey hawthorn, Washington thorn, yellow hawthorn**

hay v
See quots.
1911 *DN* 3.544 **NE,** *Hay. . .* To feed hay. "Go and hay the stock." **1950** *WELS Suppl.* **seWI,** *Hay:* To give hay to. "Go hay the horses."

hayback n
=**hayseed 1.**
1941 *LANE* Map 450 **seMA, swVT,** Terms, largely derogatory and jocular, applied to a person who lives in the country—specifically to an old farmer who seldom visits the village or city. . . *Hayback.*

haybag n, also attrib [*OEDS* 1851] *derog*
A woman, esp a slovenly one; a female hobo or camp follower.
1877 in 1924 NYC Pub. Lib. *Bulletin* 28.793 **MT,** I asked a passing corporal the way to the haybag quarters. He was a married man and he lived in haybag row. [Footnote:] A Haybag is a married or single white woman who does laundry sews and make [sic] bread, cakes and all kinds of goodies for the soldiers to buy at all times. They was then furnished quarters and fuel by the government free. **1919** *DN* 5.41, *Hay bag.* A woman hobo. **1927** *DN* 5.449 [Underworld jargon], *Hay bag.* . . A female hobo. **1931** Runyon *Guys* 171 **NYC,** She is nothing but an old haybag, and generally ginned up. **1939** Abbott-Smith *We Pointed Them* 143 **MT,** A woman they called Big Ox, who was one of those old haybags that used to follow the buffalo camps. **1944** (1967) McNichols *Crazy Weather* 114 **SW,** Again he would start to rave out of all reason, cursing Fate for dealing him "three dirty deuces from the bottom of the deck": a Mexican hay bag for a wife, a life in exile, and a thirst for hard liquor. **1967-69** *DARE* (Qu. HH34, *General words . . for a woman*) Inf **CO**47, Old haybag; (Qu. HH36, *A careless, slovenly woman*) Inf **GA**72, Haybag.

hay baler n [From its being fed bales of hay] Cf **hayburner 5b, c**
A horse or cow.
1950 *WELS (Joking terms for milking a cow)* 1 Inf, **seWI,** Squeeze the haybalers. **1958** *AmSp* 33.270 **eWA,** *Hay baler.* . . horse. **1967** *DARE* (QR, near Qu. K55) Inf **CO**4, Haybalers, poor cattle.

hay-baling ppl adj Also *hay-burning* Cf **hayburner 5**
See quot 1949.
1940 Faulkner *Hamlet* 310 **TX,** Hup, you broom-tailed hay-burning sidewinders. **1949** *PADS* 11.22 **CO,** *Hay-baling.* . . An adjective of vague abuse, usually with *bastard.*

hay barber n Also *hay john*
One who works on a farm or ranch during the summer and as a miner during the winter.
1943 Korson *Coal Dust* 5 **Midl,** Full-time miners naturally resented them and expressed their distrust by calling them "winter diggers," "wheats," "corncrackers," "hay johns," "pumpkin rollers," "clodhoppers," "greenies," "scissorbills," and "sagers." **1949** Emrich *Wild West Custom* 164 **UT** (as of c1880), Many of these greenhorns actually were farmers, cowboys, or lumberjacks who worked in the fields and on ranches during the summer and supplemented their wages by work in the mines in winter. . . In Utah, the miners called them . . *hay barbers.*

hay barge See **header barge**

hay barrack n [Folk-etym for Du *hooiberg* haystack] **chiefly NEast, C Atl** Cf **haycap**
A **barrack** or other structure for storing or protecting hay.
1797 (1893) Hiltzheimer *Extracts Diary* 6 Jan 13 **Philadelphia PA,** Thomas Shoemaker and I measured at the hay barrack, below the house, where the water left a mark, and found it had been five feet four inches. **1831** Sherburne *Memoirs* 293 **seNH,** We proceeded about fifteen miles that night, and slept in a hay barrack. **1848** Bartlett *Americanisms* 173, *Hay barrack.* (Dutch, *Hooi-berg,* a hay-rick.) A straw-thatched roof, supported by four posts, capable of being raised or lowered at pleasure, under which hay is kept. A term peculiar to New York State. **1949** *Amer. Photography* Feb 116/2 **NEng,** The crannies in the hay barracks beneath the conical roof are a favorite haunt for . . hibernations. **1965-70** *DARE* (Qu. M1, . . *Special kinds of barns*) Inf **DC**5, Hay barrack [bæ·k]; **NJ**1, Hay barrack—four corner poles, pole sides added, roof raised as needed on pegs; (QR, near Qu. L14), Inf **NY**79, Hay barracks—four sticks on side, very high; (Qu. M3, *The place inside a barn for storing hay*) Inf **DC**2, Hay barrack—building in the center of a hay-growing area, has a drive-through center, long and very high (as barn), load from wagon to sides.

hay bed n
=**hayrack 1.**
1966-70 *DARE* (Qu. L13, *The kind of wagon used for carrying hay*) Infs **AL**43, **VA**95, Hay bed; **MS**40, Wagon with a hay bed.

hay-bells n
=**bellwort.**
1933 Small *Manual SE Flora* 299, *Uvularia.* . . Hay-bells.

haybird n
=**pectoral sandpiper.**
1888 Trumbull *Names of Birds* 176, In New Jersey . . at Pleasantville (Atlantic Co.), Atlantic City, and Cape May City, *Hay-bird.* **1917** (1923) *Birds Amer.* 1.233, *Pectoral Sandpiper—Pisobia maculata . . Other Names.* . . Hay-bird. **1923** U.S. Dept. Ag. *Misc. Circular* 13.54, *Pectoral Sandpiper (Pisobia maculata) . . In local use.* . . haybird (N.J.)

hay bottom n
1 See quot.
1958 *AmSp* 33.270 **eWA,** *Hay bottom.* . . A place where hay has been, or is customarily, stacked.
2 See quot. Cf **bottom n 5**
1958 *AmSp* 33.270 **eWA,** *Hay bottom.* . . The last couple of feet of a hay stack.

hay break See **break** n[1] **8**

hay buck n
1 also *hay bucker:* =**buck rake** n.
1920 *DN* 5.82 **eWA,** *Hay buck.* . . An implement used to rake hay into a stack. **1967-68** *DARE* (Qu. L16, *Machines used . . in handling hay*) Inf **KS**15, Hay buck—has long teeth, picks up the hay and puts it in piles; **MN**4, Hay bucker—loader type of stacker used with loose hay.
2 See **buck** n[2] **3.**

hay bucker See **hay buck 1**

hayburner n
1 A stove which burns hay as fuel. **chiefly Plains States** Cf **hay-tie**
1878 *State Jrl.* (Lincoln NE) 5 Oct 4/4 (*AmSp* 15.338), The coming stove is Wood's Patent Hay Burner, for which a Diploma was given at the [Nebraska] State Fair. . . The farmers are jubilant . . as the money saved for fuel would in five years pay for, or stock a farm. **1935** Sandoz *Jules* 391 **wNE** (as of c1915), The usual January thaw . . did not come this year. Old hay burners were dug up and smoked the tinted walls. **1940** *AmSp* 15.338 **NE,** *Hay burners* have been used by settlers recently in the western Nebraska sandhills. . . The hay is twisted into big ropes and fed into the stove. **1947** Croy *Corn Country* 86 **Upper MW,** An extra stove. This was a hayburner. . . But no hay-burning stoves now; only Grandpa remembers them. **1948** *NE Hist.* 29.96 (as of 1866-1900), In some parts of Nebraska, Kansas, western Oklahoma, and other prairie states a stove was sometimes fitted out as a "hayburner."
2 An old or primitive locomotive; a cheap automobile.
1916 *DN* 4.356 [Railroad terms], *Hay-burner.* . . An old type diamond stack wood burning locomotive. **1921** *DN* 5.114 **CA,** *Hay-burner.* . . A cheap automobile. **1940** Cottrell *Railroader* 128, *Hay burner*—An old and inefficient engine.
3 A pipe or cigar. Cf **barn burner 1**
1921 *DN* 5.114 **CA,** *Hay-burner.* . . A smoking-pipe. **1942** Berrey-Van den Bark *Amer. Slang* 111.11, *Pipe.* . . hay-burner. **1950** *WELS (Nicknames for a tobacco pipe)* 2 Infs, **WI,** Hayburner. **1968** *DARE* (Qu. DD6a, . . *Nicknames for cigars*) Inf **IN**22, Hayburner.
4 A lantern or torch.
1931 *Writer's Digest* 11.42 [Railroad terms], *Hay-Burner*—Hand oil lantern. **1938** Beebe *High Iron* 221 [Railroad terms], *Hay Burner:* Inspection torch. **1964** Clarkson *Tumult* 364 **WV** [Loggers' words], *Hayburner.* . . A kerosene lantern. **1970** *Current Slang* 5.1.8, *Hayburner.* . . A kerosene burning trainmen's lantern. (No longer is [sic] use, but still referred to by older trainmen.)
5 A hay-eating animal, esp a horse or mule. *often joc* or *derog* Cf **hay baler**
1917 *DN* 4.420 **SC, seLA,** *Hay burner.* . . A mule. **1921** *DN* 5.114 **CA,** *Hay-burner.* . . A horse. **1929** *Ruppenthal Coll.* **KS,** *Hayburners:* Army mules. **1930** Williams *Logger-Talk* 24 **Pacific NW,** *Hay-burner:* A horse. **1939** *AmSp* 14.90 **eTN,** *Hay burner.* A mule. **1940** O'Hara *Pal Joey* 74, Before the hay-burners stop running at Hialeah. **1962** Wyld *Low Bridge* 23 **cNY** (as of 1800s), Mules, in Erie [Canal] parlance, said one informant, were "long-eared robins." Steam packet men later called them "hayburners." **1965-70** *DARE* (Qu. K50, *Joking nicknames for mules*) 28 Infs, **scattered, but esp Sth,** Hayburner; (Qu. K15, *A thin,*

bony, or poor-looking cow) Infs **IN**35, **NY**189, Hayburner; (Qu. K44, *A bony or poor-looking horse*) Inf **NY**219, Hayburner; (QR, near Qu. K50) Inf **IA**1, Hayburner—for any animal that eats a lot and doesn't get fat. **1966** *DARE* Tape **MI**10, A horse was a hayburner. **1968** Adams *Western Words* 141, *Hay burner*—A cowboy's name for a horse, usually one kept and fed hay and grain instead of being turned out to pasture. Also, a horse of little value.

hay-burning See **hay-baling**

haycap n **chiefly Nth, esp NEng** Cf **Dutch cap, hay barrack**

A covering for a haystack (and occas other crops); less freq the haystack itself.

1853 (1864) Thoreau *ME Woods* 88, The white hay-caps, drawn over small stacks of beans or corn in the fields on account of the rain, were a novel sight to me. **1855** *Chi. W. Times* 19 July 4/6 *(DA),* This loss may be saved by simply being provided with a supply of hay caps. These can be made by pieces of common sheeting. **1873** in 1874 VT State Bd. Ag. *Rept. for 1873–74* 2.187, He cures his grass . . the day it is cut, and puts it up in medium- sized cocks for the night, covering each with a "hay cap." **1939** *LANE* Map 104, In southeastern Mass. the square or oblong stack may have a roof sliding on four corner posts, which is called a *Dutch cap* . . or a *hay cap*. . . These terms are presumably applied also to the stack together with the roof. **1951** *AmSp* 26.251 **Upstate NY,** There are examples . . of . . such localized terms as . . *hay cap* (haystack). **1966** *DARE* (Qu. L11, *What . . you do to hay in the field after it's cut*) Inf **ME**5, Heap it up and put haycaps on it. **1971** Wood *Vocab. Change* 43 **Sth,** A large pile of hay outside is ordinarily a *haystack*. . . *Hay cap* occur[s] in one-twentieth or less of the choices.

hay carriage n **esp MD**

1968 *DARE* (Qu. L13, *The kind of wagon used for carrying hay*) Infs **DC**8, **MD**29, 31, 48, Hay carriage; **MD**20, Hay carriage wagon.

hay chute n **widespread, but chiefly Nth, N Midl** See Map Cf **alley** n[1] **5, hay hole 1**

See quot 1950.

1950 *WELS (The hole [in a barn loft] for throwing hay down below)* 50 Infs, **WI,** Hay chute. **1960** Bailey *Resp. to PADS 20* **KS,** *Hay chute.* **1960** Criswell *Resp. to PADS 20* **Ozarks,** *Hay chute.* **c1960** *Wilson Coll.* **csKY,** *Haychute.* Not widely used. **1965–70** *DARE* (Qu. M5, . . *The hole for throwing hay down below*) 208 Infs, **widespread, but chiefly Nth, N Midl,** Hay chute.

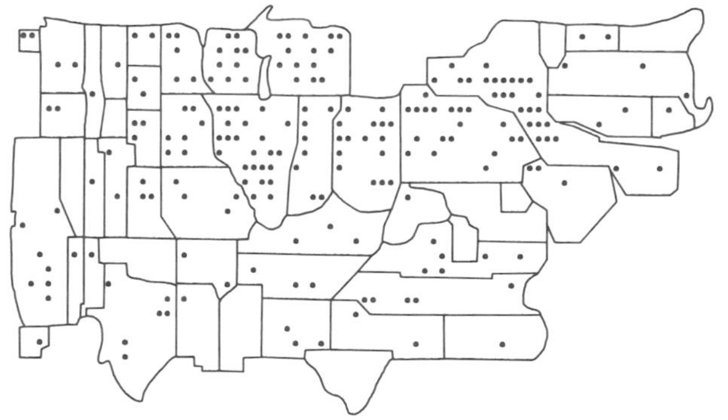

•hay chute (Qu. M5)

haycock n

1 See **cock** n[2].

2 See **haystack 3.**

haycock v Cf **haystack 1**

1968 *DARE* (Qu. O15, . . *Different kinds of waves . . referring to how the water acts*) Inf **NJ**16, Haycocking [=making a] short, choppy wave.

hay corral n **chiefly Rocky Mts, West**

See quot 1931.

1856 in 1929 Jaeger *Diary Fort Yuma* 216 **seCA,** Hauled some poles also for the hay corral. **1872** Twain *Roughing It* 220 **NV,** The crowd rushed in a body to the hay-corral and began to tumble down the huge stacks of baled hay and roll the bales up on the high ground. **1931** *AmSp* 7.121 **eID,** A *hay corral* is a fenced enclosure to keep stock away from stacked hay. **1935** Davis *Honey* 33 **sOR,** Put 'em in the hay-corral yonder, hey? **1961** *AmSp* 36.269 **CO,** *Hay corral.* **1967** *DARE* FW Addit **sID,** A *hay corral* is built around stacks to keep cattle away from them. This practice is also common in Montana and cattle areas of the Dakotas.

hay crate n

=**hayrack 1.**

1970 *DARE* (Qu. L13, *The kind of wagon used for carrying hay*) Inf **VA**70, Hay crate, special rack with high sides to put on a wagon to carry more hay.

haydagay n [Cf *OED hay-de-guy* (at *hay* sb.[4] 2) →1694; "*Obs.*"]

1930 Shoemaker *1300 Words* 28 **cPA Mts** (as of c1900), *Haydagay*—A mountain dance to a lively tune in triple measu[r]e.

hay derrick See **derrick** n

hay doodle n

1 See **doodle** n **1.**

2 In marble play: see quot.

1963 *KY Folkl. Rec.* 9.3.62, *Small pinch of dirt on which a marble is sometimes elevated:* Haydoodle.

hay farm n

1983 *MJLF* 9.1.42 **ceKY,** *Hay farm* . . a meadow.

hayfield drink n Also *haying water*

=**switchel.**

1953 Piercy *Shaker Cook Book* 37 **OH** (as of 1823–89), Shaker haying water or switchel . . sugar, or . . maple syrup . . molasses . . ginger . . water. **1967** *DARE* Tape **MA**6, We always called it [=a mixture of ginger, molasses, hot water and milk] hayfield drink . . always used it in the hayfield.

hayfield lobsterman n

One who is both farmer and fisherman by season.

1975 Gould *ME Lingo* 62, *Cow yard tar*—One of many Maine-isms for a saltwater farmer. A fisherman who grows a good garden or a farmer who goes clamming. "Hayfield lobsterman" and "straw sailor" are similar terms.

hayfield wasp n

=**sweat bee.**

1969 *DARE* (Qu. R21, . . *Stinging insects*) Inf **WI**77, Hayfield wasp—same as sweat bee.

hay flat n Also *flat* **PA**

A flat-bed wagon for carrying baled hay.

1967–70 *DARE* (Qu. L13, . . *Wagon used for carrying hay*) Infs **PA**33, 137, 242, Hay flat; **PA**23, Farm wagon or hay flat; the old ones had a rack, new ones just are flat; **PA**13, Flat—with baled hay.

hay fly n

Perh a **harvest mite.**

1970 *DARE* (Qu. R11, *A very tiny fly that you can hardly see, but that stings*) Inf **TX**104, Hay fly.

hay frame n **chiefly Sth, S Midl** See Map

=**hayrack 1.**

1833 (1930) Sewall *Diary* 152/1 **ME,** Making hay frame. **c1960** *Wilson Coll.* **csKY,** *Hay frame*—A frame on a farm wagon arranged to hold a large load of hay. **1965–70** *DARE* (Qu. L13, *The kind of wagon*

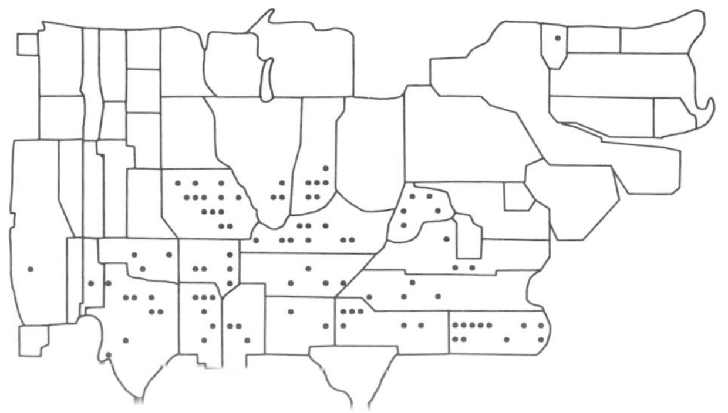

•hay frame + varr (Qu. L13)

used for carrying hay) 87 Infs, **chiefly Sth, S Midl,** Hay frame; **GA**1, **MO**16, **NM**3, Wagon with a hay frame (on it); **MS**4, Hay frame on wagon; **MO**21, Hay frame wagon; **OK**16, Just an ordinary wagon with a rack (=hay frame) on it; **AR**18, Road wagon with a hay frame.

hay gate n

Perh a wooden frame resembling a gate on which hay is loaded and dragged along the ground.

1970 *DARE* (Qu. L13, *The kind of wagon used for carrying hay*) Inf **KY**84, Hay gate—drug it on the ground; 6–8 feet by 10–12 feet; old-fashioned.

hay grazer n

Appar grass grown for hay.

1966 *DARE* (Qu. L9a, . . *Kinds of grass . . grown for hay*) Inf **OK**43, Hay grazer. **1969** *SC Market Bulletin* 9 Jan 2, Good sericea and hay-grazer hay, cut and baled.

hay heap See **heap** n **2**

hay hill n

1938 (1939) Holbrook *Holy Mackinaw* 261 [Loggers' dictionary], *Hay hill.* A hill on a road on which hay, or dirt, has been sprinkled to act as a brake on sleigh runners.

hay hole n

1 =**hay chute. chiefly Nth, Midl, esp PA** See Map

1950 *WELS (The hole for throwing hay down below)* 2 Infs, **WI,** Hay hole. **1954** *Harder Coll.* **cwTN,** *Hay hole*—The hole in the floor of a barn loft for throwing hay down below. **1965–70** *DARE* (Qu. M5, . . *The hole for throwing hay down below*) 82 Infs, **chiefly Nth, Midl, esp PA,** Hay hole. **1969** *DARE* Tape **CT**38, You just had pitchforks and rakes, and that's how you got it in when you had to have some men with backbone, too, to throw it up into that hay hole.

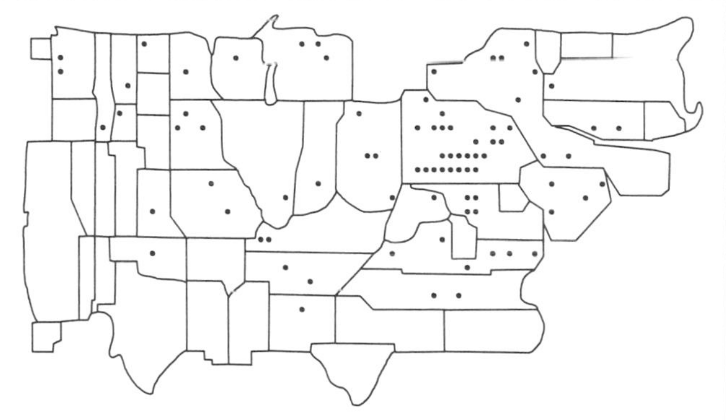

•hay hole 1 (Qu. M5)

2 See quot. Cf **hay pole 1**

1954 *Harder Coll.* **cwTN,** *Hay hole*—A hole dug in the ground in which the hay pole is anchored.

hayilage See **haylage**

haying horse n

1946 Gould *Yankee Storekeeper* 137 **ME,** A few steeds of doubtful value. . . are known as haying horses, because they can rake hay all right, but can't stand the heavy work of winter.

haying water See **hayfield drink**

hay john See **hay barber**

hay jumper n

A **grasshopper 1.**

1950 *WELS (Grasshopper)* 1 Inf, **seWI,** Hay jumper.

hay kicker n

1 =**hayseed 1.**

1967 *DARE* (Qu. HH1, *Names and nicknames for a rustic or countrified person*) Inf **PA**11, Hay kicker.

2 See **kicker.**

hay ladder n Also *ladder wagon* **esp N Midl** See Map

=**hayrack 1.**

1968–70 *DARE* (Qu. L13, *The kind of wagon used for carrying hay . . special wagon or frame put on ordinary wagon*) Infs **IL**134, **IN**67, **PA**163, 191, Hay ladder; **PA**207, Hay ladder—frame placed on a wagon; **PA**235, Hay ladder—20 feet long, stanchion in front and back, y-wheels, ladder in back and front; **WV**10, Hay ladder—frame that fits inside wagon; **PA**147, Ladder wagon; **OH**81, Ladder wagon—flat, eight by fourteen feet long; **OH**95, Wagon with hay ladders; **PA**153, Ladder wagon—had a rack, now a flat bed; (Qu. N41b, *Horse-drawn vehicles to carry heavy loads*) Inf **MD**29, Wood ladder wagon—ladder built onto it, used for hauling wood.

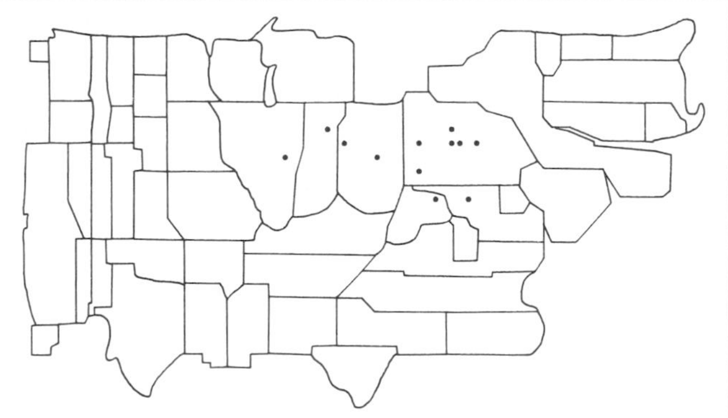

•hay ladder + varr (Qq. L13, N41b)

haylage n Also *hayilage* [Blend of *hay* + *silage*]

Alfalfa or hay which has been chopped, fermented, partially dried and stored.

1967 WI Statist. Reporting Serv. *Report* 29 Aug 2, Cows have picked up some on milk from 2nd crop haylage. **1968** *Sauk Centre Herald* (MN) 4 July 7/6, The area is perhaps in the midst of making a good amount of haylage. Haylage is referred to low moisture alfalfa grass silage put up at about 40–60% moisture range. **1968** *Courier-Freeman* (Potsdam NY) 28 Mar 16, 18 x 50 silo half-full hayilage. **1968** *DARE* FW Addit **NY,** Haylage and grass silage—entries in Boonville Fair; Haylage—chopped hay for storing in a silo; seen on posters near Kinderhook. **1968** *DARE* Tape **NY**73, Now they put a lot of hay in it . . green hay, haylage, they call it. **1984** *MJLF* 10.151 **cnWI,** *Haylage*. . . Green, chopped hay, partially dried and stored in a silo.

hayloft See **loft**

hay louse See **harvest louse**

haymaker n

1 =**hayseed 1.**

1847 *Lit. World* 6 Mar 106/1, "Pull, pull, you lubberly *hay makers!*" cries the boat-header. **1941** *LANE* Map 450 *(A Rustic)* 1 inf, **nwVT,** *Haymaker,* rare. **1950** *WELS (A city person's names and nicknames for a country person)* 1 Inf, **cwWI,** Haymaker.

2 A **cicada.** Cf **harvest fly**

1966 *DARE* (Qu. R7, *Insects that sit in trees or bushes in hot weather and make a sharp, buzzing sound*) Inf **MA**6, Haymaker.

3 =**praying mantis.**

1968 *AmSp* 43.53 **KS,** Praying mantis . . haymaker.

haymaker's mushroom Also *haymaker mushroom*

A mushroom *(Psathyrella foenisecii)* common in lawns and pastures.

1942 Hylander *Plant Life* 56, Also brown-spored is the edible . . Haymaker's Mushroom common in early summer on lawns and other grassy places. **1985** Weber–Smith *Field Guide S. Mushrooms* 229, The haymaker's mushroom . . usually has a . . rounded, zoned cap, and its spores are distinctly ornamented. **1987** McKnight–McKnight *Mushrooms* 282, *Haymaker Mushroom*. . . Although this is reportedly edible, we do *not recommend* it.

hay mound, haymow, hay mown See **mow**

hay needle n

A seed of **needle and thread.**

1950 Stevens *ND Plants* 72, *Needle-and-thread*. . . The sharp grains mature in early July. They penetrate tissues of mouths of animals and cause injury. . . They are commonly called "hay needles".

hay-over n, exclam [Var of **hail-over**]
=Antony-over.
1966–67 *DARE* (Qu. EE22, . . *The game in which they throw a ball over a building . . to a player on the other side*) Inf **FL**22, Hay-over; (Qu. EE23a, . . *What do you call out when you throw the ball?*) Inf **NC**41, Hay-over.

hay plover n **VA**
=pectoral sandpiper.
1917 *Wilson Bulletin* 29.2.79, *Pisobia maculata.*—Hay plover, Wallops Id., Va. **1923** U.S. Dept. Ag. *Misc. Circular* 13.54, *Pectoral Sandpiper (Pisobia maculata) . . In local use. . .* hay-plover (Va.) **1970** *DARE* (Qu. Q10, . . *Water birds and marsh birds*) Inf **VA**47, Hay plover.

hay pole n
1 A pole or stick around which hay or straw is stacked.
1801 in 1812 Philadelphia *Ordinances* 175, Said inspector shall. . . [have] made a suitable allowance for any undue moisture of the hay or straw, haypole, mud or dirt. **1803** in 1977 Whiting *Early Amer. Proverbs* 203/1 [Yankee phrases], As tall as a hay pole her size. **1954** *Harder Coll.* **cwTN,** *Hay pole*—A stick of wood ten to twelve feet long with limbs cut off a few inches from the trunk, around which hay is stacked. **1967** *Amer. Agric. & Rural New Yorker* Mar 76, Hay poles were three or more long poles coming to a peak at the top, used in stacking hay or straw.
2 A pole for carrying hay; see quots.
1967 *Amer. Agric. & Rural New Yorker* Mar 76 **NJ,** Hay poles. . . two spruce poles about twelve feet long. . . On swampy land too soft to drive a horse and wagon, these poles were put under large heaps of hay, and with a man at each end in a short time a good load of hay could be carried to dry ground. **1967** *DARE* (Qu. L16, *Machines used . . in handling hay*) Inf **NJ**1, Hay pole—for carrying out of marsh or meadow. **1985** *NC Folkl. Jrl.* 33.53 **wNC** (as of c1920), After the hay was in windrows, it was shocked by hand with pitchforks in piles about as big as two men could carry on a set of haypoles. These were made of carefully selected, straight saplings about four inches in diameter. They were peeled and scraped to remove all knots and splinters, sharpened on the ends and seasoned to make them light and springy.

hay pounder n
=hayseed 1.
1941 *LANE* Map 450 **cVT,** Derogatory and jocular [terms for] . . a person who lives in the country. . . Hay pounder.

hayrack n, also attrib
1 A wagon frame for hauling hay or other loads; a wagon with such a frame. **widespread, but chiefly Nth, N Midl, West** See Map Also called **hay bed, hay crate, hay frame, hay ladder, hayrick 1, hayrig, header barge, rack**
1872 (1876) Knight *Amer. Mech. Dict.* 1082/2, *Hay-rack. . .* A frame mounted on the running-gears of a wagon, and used in hauling hay, straw, sheaves, etc. **1902** (1969) Sears *Catalogue* 715, *The Acme Combination Grain, Hay and Stock Rack. . .* Warranted to carry 4,500 pounds. A rear end stock gate and a rear hay standard are furnished with each rack. . . Made in 14 and 16-foot lengths. **1950** *WELS (The kind of wagon used for carrying hay)* 37 Infs, **WI,** Hayrack; 7 Infs, Wagon with hayrack; 2 Infs, Hayrack, old-fashioned; 1 Inf, Hayrack, or rack wagon; 1 Inf, Hayrack wagon; *(Tools and machines used for different steps in handling hay)* 7 Infs, Hayrack. **1958** *AmSp* 33.270 **eWA,** *Hay rack. . .* A wagon with one high rack and one low, used for loading and hauling hay. **1965–70** *DARE* (Qu. L13, *The kind of wagon used for carrying hay*) 267 Infs, **widespread, but chiefly Nth, N Midl, West,** Hayrack; **OK**10, Farm wagon with hayrack on it; **NY**224, Lumber wagon with hayrack; **OK**43, Wagon with hayrack on it; (Qu. N40a, . . *Kinds of sleighs . . for hauling loads*) Inf **PA**199, Hayrack sleigh; (Qu. N40c, . . *Kinds of sleighs for carrying*) Inf **WA**12, Hayrack on bobsled; (Qu. N41a, . . *Horse-drawn vehicles . . to carry people*) Inf **ME**15, Hayrack—to carry heavy loads; for hayride; **MN**5, Hayrack—to carry light loads; (Qu. N41b, . . *To carry heavy loads*) Infs **CO**3, 20, **ME**10, 15, **MA**74, **NE**3, Hayrack; (Qu. N41c, . . *To carry light loads*) Infs **MI**105, **MN**5, Hayrack; **WA**12, Hayrack on bobsled. **1966** *DARE* Tape **OK**18, Still hauled the bundles in hay racks and teams. **1967** *Smith Co. Pioneer* (Smith Center KS) 26 Oct 4/2, The group enjoyed a hayrack ride to the Harold Shockley home where they had a wiener [sic] roast. **1983** *MJLF* 9.1.42 **ceKY,** *Hay rack . .* a framework extension on a wagon to permit carrying larger quantities of hay.

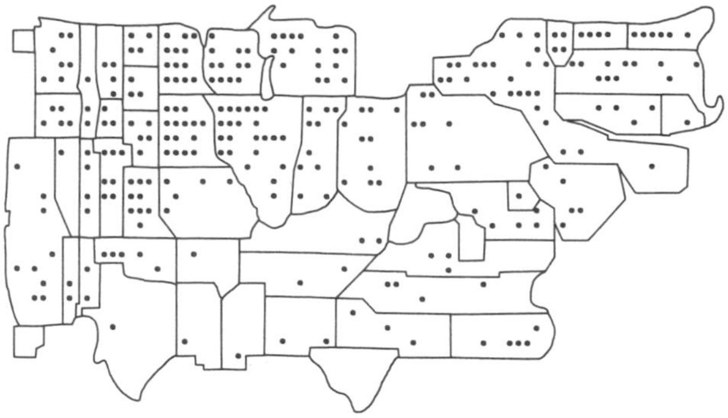

•hayrack 1 + varr (Qq. L13, N40a, c, N41a, b, c)

2 An openwork frame, either freestanding or attached to a barn wall, used to dispense hay to animals. **chiefly Sth, S Midl**
1854 (1923) Holmes *Tempest & Sunshine* 6 **KY,** Scattered about the yard . . were corn cribs, hay racks, pig troughs, carts. **1887** Eggleston *Graysons* 191 **cIL,** The deputy sheriff and then his prisoner had to climb over a hay-rack and thence down to the ground. **1938** Faulkner *Unvanquished* 82 **MS,** Ringo jumped down from the hayrack onto his [=a horse's] head. **1940** *Collier's* 6 July 27/1 **LA,** Uncle Henry saw that Ringo had placed the proper amount of corn in the long troughs, had the hayrack filled and the pump running. **1958** *AmSp* 33.270 **eWA,** *Hay rack. . .* A heavy rack with stanchions into which hay is piled in a feed lot. **c1960** *Wilson Coll.* **csKY,** *Hayrack. . .* A place to put hay for one animal. **1965–70** *DARE* (Qu. M5) Infs **AL**11, **KY**34, 35, 86, Hayrack [FW illustr in two QRs: hayrack is attached to wall beneath hay chute]; (Qu. M6, *The place where grain is kept in a barn*) Inf **AL**2, Hayrack; (Qu. M22, . . *Kinds of buildings*) Inf **AR**55, Hayrack. **1976** Brown *Gloss. Faulkner, Hayrack . .* a container built onto a stable wall, making a *V* with the wall at the bottom of the rack. It is made of widely spaced slats, so that hay put into the rack can be pulled out between them. **1989** *DARE* File **c,cnIN,** My friend used the term *hay rack* to refer to a free-standing structure that has slats in it and you put hay in the top for feeding animals.
3 Appar a **loft.**
1966–68 *DARE* (Qu. M3, *The place inside a barn for storing hay*) Inf **MO**8, Hayrack—that's the loft; **GA**45, Hayrack, hayloft; **AL**7, Hayrack; (Qu. M12, *What do you keep food for the cattle in over winter*) Inf **OH**60, Hayrack.
4 also *rack:* A haystack. [Prob var of *hayrick* (at **rick**)]
1966–70 *DARE* (Qu. L14, *A large pile of hay stored outdoors*) Infs **FL**4, **LA**12, **MS**81, **OH**58, Hayrack; **AL**55, Rack.
5 A thin, gaunt animal. Cf **frame 1, rack of bones**
1967–68 *DARE* (Qu. K44, *A bony or poor-looking horse*) Infs **NJ**45, **SC**43, Hayrack; (Qu. K15, *A thin, bony, or poor-looking cow*) Inf **SC**43, Hayrack.
6 also *hay wagon:* **=walkingstick.**
1968–70 *DARE* (Qu. R9a, *An insect . . that lives in bushes and looks like a dead twig*) Inf **MN**12, Hayracks; **VA**73, Hay wagon.

hayrick n Also *rick* [Prob *hayrick* haystack infl by **hayrack 1, 2,** and, for sense **1, hayrig**]
1 =hayrack 1.
1908 Lincoln *Cy Whittaker* 86 **MA,** The Bayport contingent went over in a big hayrick on runners and the moonlight ride was jolly enough. **1960** Bailey *Resp. to PADS 20* **KS,** [Referring to a wagon for carrying hay] Both hayrack and hayrick were used. **1961** *AmSp* 36.268 **CO,** *(Hay)rick* refers to . . (once) a hay wagon. **1965–70** *DARE* (Qu. L13, *The kind of wagon used for carrying hay*) 18 Infs, **scattered,** Hayrick; (Qu. N41b, *Horse-drawn vehicles to carry heavy loads*) Infs **CT**5, **NM**5, Hayrick.
2 =hayrack 2.
1961 *AmSp* 36.268, In Colorado, *(hay)rick* refers to a . . *Y*-shaped rack through which cattle can feed even with fairly deep snow on the ground.

hayrig n Also *hayrigging* **chiefly NEast** See Map
Equipment for handling hay; spec, a **hayrack 1.**
1852 MI State Ag. Soc. *Trans. for 1851* 3.30 [Best] hay rigging. **a1862** (1865) Thoreau *Cape Cod* 3 **MA,** We met several hay-riggings and

farm-wagons . . each loaded with three large, rough deal boxes. **1865** (1889) Whitney *Gayworthys* 60 **NEng,** Gabriel . . stood high up on the loaded hay-rigging. **1896** *Advance* 31.414/1, Two great farm-wagons, provided with those wide, projecting frames, technically known as hay-rigs. **1965–70** *DARE* (Qu. L13, *The kind of wagon used for carrying hay*) 18 Infs, **chiefly NEast,** Hayrigging; **NC**68, **NJ**29, **NY**107, Hayrig; **CT**2, Wagon with a hayrigging ['he rɪgən] on it; (Qu. L42, . . *What kind of thing do you call a 'rig'?*) Infs **NJ**10, 29, **RI**17, Hayrig; **CT**9, Hayrig—hay equipment; **NJ**6, Hayrig—derived from hayrick; **NY**93, Hayrig—on a wagon for hay; **NY**123, Hayrig—an oblong wagon with racks out at the sides; **NY**233, Hayrig—a wagon; **TN**10, Hayrig-baler—tractor behind baler, wagon behind tractor; **NC**68, Hayrig—special wagon for hay; (Qu. N41b, *Horse-drawn vehicles to carry heavy loads*) Inf **NY**111, Hayrig.

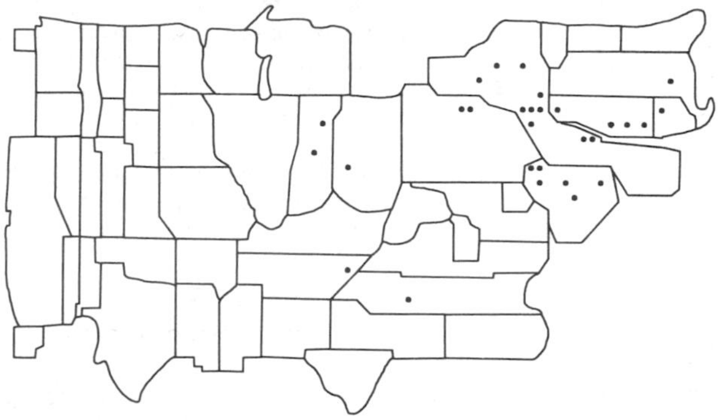

•hayrig + varr (Qq. L13, L42, N41b)

hay rotter n

1968 *DARE* (Qu. B25, . . *Joking names . . for a very heavy rain*) Inf **VA**13, Hay rotter.

hayrow n [Cf *OED harrow, haro* int., *SND harro* a call for help, a cry of alarm or of encouragement] Cf **I spy**

1901 *DN* 2.141 **nwPA,** *Hayrow*. . . The name of a game like I-spy, in which, after the blinder has counted, he says "hayrow" three times, then seeks the hiders.

hayseed n, also attrib

1 also *hayseeder:* A rustic; an unsophisticated person. **widespread, but more freq Nth, N Midl**

[**1840** (1841) Dana *2 Yrs.* 42, His boat's crew were a pretty raw set, just out of the bush, and, as the sailor's phrase is, 'hadn't got the hayseed out of their hair.'] **1851** (1976) Melville *Moby-Dick* 34 **NEng,** Ah, poor Hay-Seed! how bitterly will burst those straps in the first howling gale. **1891** Welch *Recoll. Buffalo* 368 (as of 1830–40), These young swells scorned the waiting for the afterpiece, or farce, as vulgar; only the thing for "hay-seeders" or common people to do. **1892** (1925) Walsh *Lit. Curiosities* 453, *Hay-seeds* (that is to say, rustics), in the language of American politics, a nickname for farmers or their representatives and delegates. In State legislatures "the hay-seed delegation" is a term applied collectively to the representatives of the rural constituencies. **1909** *DN* 3.412 **nME,** *Hayseeder.* **1916** *DN* 4.347 **TX** (as of 1896), *Hayseeder.* **1919** *DN* 5.65 **NM,** *Hay-seed,* a rough, uncouth fellow. **1922** *DN* 5.165 **ME,** *Hayseeder.* **1934** *AmSp* 9.80 **NE,** As a name for an imaginary small town located in the 'sticks'. . . Hayseed Center. **1937** *DN* 6.618 **swTX,** His lingo is at first likely to bewilder the greenhorn or hayseed, as the tenderfoot is impartially called. **1950** *WELS (A city person's names and nicknames for a country person)* 30 Infs, **WI,** Hayseed. **1965–70** *DARE* (Qu. HH1, *Names and nicknames for a rustic or countrified person*) 216 Infs, **widespread, but more freq Nth, N Midl,** Hayseed; **NY**75, Old hayseed; **NJ**4, 61, **PA**175, Hayseeder; (Qu. L1, *A man who is employed to help with work on a farm*) Inf **MN**2, Hayseed; (Qu. HH3, *A dull and stupid person*) Inf **NY**35, Hayseed; (Qu. HH16) Inf **KS**5, Hayseed; (Qu. W41, . . *Someone . . who . . dresses carelessly*) Inf **PA**220, Looks like a hayseed; (Qu. FF16, *Local contests or celebrations*) Inf **ME**11, Hayseed ball. **1971** Wood *Vocab. Change* 38 **Sth,** A rustic. . . *Backwoodsman . . hayseed . .* and *yokel* are known throughout the region. **1973** Allen *LAUM* 1.348 **Upper MW** (as of c1950), The most common term [for a rustic] in the U[pper] M[idwest] is *hayseed,* which, though found in all five states, seems to exhibit slight Northern preference.

2 See quot.

1969 *DARE* (Qu. FF21a, *A joke that is so old it doesn't seem funny any more: "His jokes are all ———."*) Inf **NY**205, Hayseeds.

hayseeder See **hayseed 1**

hayshaker n

1 also *hayshagger:* =**hayseed 1. chiefly Nth**

1940–41 Cassidy *WI Atlas* 1 Inf, **seWI,** *Hayshaker,* a farmer. **1942** Berrey–Van den Bark *Amer. Slang* 391.3, Rustic; bumpkin. . . *hayshaker.* **1950** *WELS (A city person's names and nicknames for a country person)* 6 Infs, **WI,** Hayshaker. **1966–68** *DARE* (Qu. HH1) Infs **MA**6, **MT**3, **PA**114, **VT**4, Hayshaker; **WI**27, Hayshagger. **1971** Jennings *Cowboys* 44 **MT, WY** (as of 1877), You may be a bunch of pea-picking hay-shakers, but I want *my* horses' tails kept thin and short. Only farmers and dudes lets them grow way long. **1973** Allen *LAUM* 1.350 **Upper MW** (as of c1950), A rustic. . . *hay shaker.* [14 infs]

2 See quot.

1945 Hubbard *Railroad Ave.* 366, Railroaders' derisive term for cowboy . . *hay shaker.*

hayshant, hayshun See **hessian**

hay sled n **esp Plains States**

See quots.

1967 *DARE* (Qu. L13, *The kind of wagon used for carrying hay*) Inf **NE**10, Hay sled; (Qu. L16, *Machines used . . in handling hay*) Inf **NE**2, Hay sled—for moving stacks in the winter; (Qu. N40a, . . *Kinds of sleighs . . for hauling loads*) Infs **CO**33, **NE**3, Hay sled; (Qu. N40c) Inf **NE**10, Hay sled. **1968** Adams *Western Words* 142, *Hay sled*—A large sled used to collect hay from the shocks for hauling to the stack; used in conjunction with a derrick or stacker.

hay slide n

1954 *Harder Coll.* **cwTN,** *Hay slide*—A sled on which hay is moved from one part of a field to another.

haystack n

1 A dome-shaped wave; see quots 1969, 1988. Cf **haycock** v

1942 Rich *We Took to Woods* 313 **cwME,** Me, I adore the White Water Crowd. . . They talk about haystacks when they mean swells. **1969** *DARE* (Qu. O15, . . *Different kinds of waves*) Inf **MA**26, Haystack—the wind coming from all directions; get them during thunderstorms. **1979** McPhee *Giving Good Weight* 170 **ME,** I underestimated the haystacks. They are about as ponderous as, for this loaded canoe, they can safely be. I look steeply down at Moody in the bottoms of the troughs. **1988** *DARE* File **nWI,** In whitewater canoeing, a haystack is a rounded mound of water from six inches to several feet high. It is caused by a submerged boulder that forces the water up and over it. The size and shape of the haystack are dependent on the volume and velocity of the water as well as the shape of the boulder. *Ibid* **nwMA,** My parents learned whitewater canoeing from the AMC [=Appalachian Mountain Club] and my family went on quite a few of their trips. Haystacks were one river feature to be watched out for. They are stationary, dome-shaped upwellings of water caused by the topography of the riverbed.

2 See quot.

1969 *DARE* (Qu. C17, . . *A small, rounded hill*) Inf **CT**29, Haystack.

3 also *haycock:* A hairdo; see quot.

1967–69 *DARE* (Qu. X3, *When a woman puts her hair up on her head in a bunch*) Infs **MO**37, **OH**74, **PA**76, **TN**1, Haystack; **KS**6, Haycock.

4 See quot.

1969 *DARE* (Qu. H82b, *Kinds of cheap candy that used to be sold years ago*) Inf **OH**75, Chocolate haystacks; **IL**37, Coconut haystacks—little mounds of coconut held together with heavy syrup of some kind.

5 in phrr indicating untidiness or disorder: See quot.

1968 *DARE* (Qu. E22, *If a house is untidy and everything is upset . . "It looks like ———."*) Inf **CA**54, Haystack; (Qu. W41, . . *Someone . . who . . dresses carelessly*) Inf **GA**59, Looks like a haystack.

6 See quot. *euphem*

1950 *WELS (Humorous substitutions for stronger exclamations: "Why the son of a ———.")* 1 Inf, **cnWI,** Haystack.

7 pl; In the game of jacks: one or more nesting jacks; hence exclam *haystacks.*

1975 Ferretti *Gt. Amer. Book Sidewalk Games* 101, "Easies" also permits the separation of "kissies" . . and "haystacks" (one jack nestling inside another). Upon calling "kissies," or "haystacks," the player can pick up the touching jacks and drop them again before beginning her pickups. **1989** *DARE* File **csWI** (as of c1972), My friends and I played jacks as often as possible. Sometimes two or more jacks landed on top of each other; we called this phenomenon "haystacks" or "piggyback."

haystack agreement n

1928 *Ruppenthal Coll.* **KS,** *Haystack agreement*—A secret understanding. "We want everything open and above board; no haystack agreements for us."

haystack kid n

1967 *DARE* (Qu. Z11b, *Nicknames and joking words for a child of unwed parents*) Inf **MO5**, Haystack kid.

haystack weed n

A **pokeweed** (here: *Phytolacca americana*).

1897 *Jrl. Amer. Folkl.* 10.54, *Phytolacca decandra*. . . Haystack weed, Conn.

hay sweep n

=**buck rake** n.

1884 Knight *New Mech. Dict.* 449/2, *Hay sweep*. . . A form of rake for gathering hay, either from the windrow or the cock, to the place where it is to be stacked or ricked. **1929** *AmSp* 5.56 **NE,** The "hay sweep" for "stacking" the hay into great stacks. **1967** *DARE* (Qu. L16, *Machines used . . in handling hay*) Inf **NE8**, Hay sweep.

hay tedder See **tedder**

Hayti See **Haiti 1**

hay-tie n Cf **hayburner 1**

Twisted hay used as fuel; a stove which burns such fuel.

1947 Croy *Corn Country* 86 **Upper MW,** In the early days, when a blizzard came upon them, the pioneers put up an extra stove. This was a hayburner; it had two cylinders. Hay was twisted by a machine and stuffed into the cylinders where a spring pushed it forward into the fire. The people loved their hay stoves and affectionately called them "hay-ties." **1952** FWP *Guide SD* 338 (as of 1880), Twisted hay, known as "haytie", was used as fuel during the winter.

hay wagon See **hayrack 6**

hayweed n

Scotch broom *(Cytisus scoparius).*

1974 (1977) Coon *Useful Plants* 166, *Cytisus scoparius* . . hay-weed. . . It is especially happy in dry, sandy, and salt-air areas and it has a good and seemingly great value as a plant for sloping ground.

hay widow n

=**grass widow 1.**

1931–33 *LANE Worksheets* **cVT,** Hay widow, them are the kind whose husbands ain't dead yet.

haywire adj

1 Inadequately equipped, inefficient, makeshift. [From the use of hay-baling wire for makeshift repairs] **chiefly Nth**

1905 U.S. Forest Serv. *Bulletin* 61.39 **Gt Lakes, NEng,** *Hay wire outfit.* A contemptuous term for loggers with poor logging equipment. **1927** *DN* 5.449 [Underworld jargon], *Hay wire outfit*. . . One at which the workers are furnished with poor living facilities. **1942** Rich *We Took to Woods* 295 **cwME,** Anything that is held together with haywire is a haywire rig. Broadening the scope of the term, so is any makeshift expedient whatsoever. If you run out of cornstarch and have to thicken a chocolate pudding with flour, that's a haywire rig. **1950** in 1953 Botkin–Harlow *Treas. Railroad Folkl.* 274, A rawhide railroad was a road that depended on cheap substitutes or extreme economies, just as a haywire outfit was one that had inadequate equipment. **1966–67** *DARE* (Qu. N37, *Joking names for a branch railroad that is not very important or gives poor service*) Infs **MI20**, 27, Haywire line; **MI11**, Haywire; **MI56**, Haywire road. **1966** *DARE* Tape **MI10**, Almost universally, even up to the present day, an inefficient company or a logger has been called a just plain haywire outfit. **1984** *MJLF* 10.151 **cnWI,** *Haywire outfit*. . . A farm or outfit where things are not properly repaired, but "just wired together".

2 See quot. [By ext from std sense 'broken, out of order']

1966 *DARE* (Qu. H46, *When meat begins to go bad, so that you can't eat it, you say it's* ______.) Inf **MT3**, Haywire.

haywire v

To repair; see quots.

1928 *AmSp* 4.128 **ncNE,** To "hay wire" anything is to mend or repair it. **1967** *DARE* (Qu. KK63, *To do a clumsy or hurried job of repairing something*) Inf **ID5**, Haywired it.

hay wood n

1954 *Harder Coll.* **cwTN,** *Hay wood*—Pieces of quartered wood about three and one-half feet long and six to eight inches around, placed around a hay pole so that the air will circulate through the stack to facilitate curing.

hazarae n Also sp *chazzerai, hazzerai* [Yiddish *khazeray* junk, trash]

See quots.

1969 Gordone *No Place* 67 **NYC,** [Black speaker talking about a set of drums:] All of a sudden I done gone deaf an' blin'. Now, git this hazarae out'a here. **1975** (1982) Ludlum *Road to Gandolfo* 45, "The ambassador said you were adamant. A trial or a lot of hazzerai." "Hazzerai?" "It means trouble. It's Jewish." **1982** Rosten *Hooray for Yiddish* 178, *Khazeray* means awful food, cheap merchandise, obscenity . . contemptible reading. . . "crap." **1988** *DARE* File **NYC** (as of 1960), The word *chazzerai* (with *ch* pronounced as in the Scots *loch*) was used (as I remember it) most commonly among Jewish families of Eastern European background when referring to various kinds of disapproved comestibles such as candy, pizza or cheap hamburgers. A child discovered with a predilection for White Castle Hamburgers (16¢ a piece) might be admonished, "Whaddye eatin that chazzerai for, it'll just make you sick."

haze v, hence vbl n *hazing* Also with *in* **West**

To urge, direct, or control the movement of (an animal); hence n *hazer.*

1890 D'Oyle *Notches* 68 *(DAE),* Bill 'hazed' 'em again, and they ran up and stood about opposite to me, and I got two. **1897** Hough *Cowboy* 90, Two other men, sometimes known in these days of modern ranching as "hazers," now mount and ride up with their quirts in hand ready to drive on the horse that is to be broken. **1923** Sinclair *Parowan Bonanza* 9 **NV,** Hazing burros over the trail is going to be hot work, from now on until fall. **1928** *AmSp* 4.130 **cnNE,** Three or four "hazers" plant themselves about to "haze" or "fence" the "broncs," keep them from running into a fence or into the crowd. **1938** Faulkner *Unvanquished* 165 **MS,** All right, boys. Rope them [=mules] together and haze them out of there. **1941** Writers' Program *Guide WY* 462, *Haze*—To ride at the side of an obstreperous broncho in an effort to keep the horse from running into a fence or some obstruction. Term used in breaking horses. *Hazer*—An assistant to keep horses from the fences. **1961** Adams *Old-Time Cowhand* 248, On the out trip each man tried to save his hoss in order to have 'im in good shape for the actual hazin' of the cattle from the brush and canyons. **1967** *DARE* Tape **TX25**, You have a hazer to help you. He's just another boy on a horse and he keeps the steer in line for you and keeps the steer from . . fading out from you, where you have a good jump at him. **1978** Doig *This House* 40 **MT,** The hill broncs which would be hazed in somewhere . . were not scruffy little mustangs.

haze n [Perh for *Hades*]

1968 *DARE* (Qu. NN26b, *Weakened substitutes for 'hell': "Go to* ______*!"*) Inf **VA29**, Haze.

haze in See **haze** v

hazel alder n

An alder, either *Alnus rugosa* or *A. serrulata.* Note: The latter is often included in the former.

1924 Deam *Shrubs IN* 74, *Alnus rugosa*. . . *Hazel Alder*. . . Maine to Minnesota, south to Florida and Texas. **1930** Sievers *Amer. Med. Plants* 33, Hazel alder is found in swamps and along the marshy banks of streams. **1942** Tehon *Fieldbook IL Shrubs* 68, *Alnus rugosa*. . . The Hazel Alder . . is an erect shrub, usually 12 or 14 feet high but often in its larger growth somewhat treelike. **1971** Krochmal *Appalachia Med. Plants* 42, *Alnus serrulata*. . . Hazel alder. **1979** Little *Checklist U.S. Trees* 49, *Alnus rugosa*. . . *Other common names* . . hazel alder. . . *Alnus serrulata*. . . Hazel alder.

hazel pine n Also *hazel wood*

=**sweet gum** or its wood.

1938 Brown *Trees NEast U.S.* 261, *Liquidambar styraciflua*. . . The brown heartwood is sold as 'satin walnut' . . , the sapwood frequently as 'hazel pine.' **1940** Clute *Amer. Plant Names* 263, *Liquidambar styraciflua*. . . Hazel-wood.

hazel snout n

1952 Brown *NC Folkl.* 1.549, *Hazel-snout*. . . A turned-up nose. . . Rare.

hazel splitter n

1 A **razorback hog.** Cf **elm peeler 1, hickory grubber**

1865 in 1868 IL Dept. Ag. *Trans. for 1865–66* 6.334, They belong to a class . . who prefer the active, energetic "hazel splitters" to the lazy Berkshire. **1868** IA State Ag. Soc. *Rept. for 1867* 13.91, The original hazel splitter is most generally used to breed on. **1929** *AmSp* 5.18 **Ozarks,** *Hazel splitter. . .* A wild, lean range hog, a razor-back.

2 Transf: see quot.

c1970 *DARE* File **Ozarks** (as of c1910), Girls with a bad reputation were hellcats or hazel splitters.

hazel wood See **hazel pine**

hazelwort n

A **wild ginger 1** (here: *Asarum canadense*).

1940 Clute *Amer. Plant Names* 137, *A[sarum] Canadense. . .* Hazel-wort. **1959** Carleton *Index Herb. Plants* 59, *Hazel-wort:* Asarum canadense.

‡hazely adj [Perh *hazy* infl by *hazily*]

1968 *DARE* (Qu. B11, . . *Kinds of clouds*) Inf **NC**49, Hazely ['heɪzli], in the fall when it starts to get cool, the sky is gray, no sun.

hazenut n **esp KY**

A hazelnut.

1923 *DN* 5.210 **swMO,** *Haze-nut. . .* Hazel nut. **1967–70** *DARE* (Qu. I43, . . *Kinds of nuts . . wild*) Infs **KY**34, 40, 42, 81, 85, Hazenuts.

hazer See **haze** v

hazing See **haze** v

hazzerai See **hazarae**

he pron Pronc-spp *e, ee, eh, hee* Note: While the contracted form *'e* for *he* is common in StdE in unstressed position, it is the usual form in Gullah in both stressed and unstressed positions. Cf **heself, him** pron

1 Used redundantly with a noun subject. [*OED* c1000 →; cf *EDD he* II. 2] Cf **it,** Intro "Language Changes" II.4

1637 (1972) Morton *New Engl. Canaan* 46, The subtile Sachem hee playd the tragedian. **1836** (1838) Haliburton *Clockmaker* (1st ser) 183 **NEng** [Black], Massa Jim Munroe he hang himself. **1859** Taliaferro *Fisher's R.* 188 **nwNC** (as of 1820s) [Black], Cain he kill his brudder Abel wid a great big club. **1861** Holmes *Venner* 1.177 **wMA,** The ol' Doctor, he'd h' ker'd 'em threugh. **1883** Harris *Nights with Remus* 97 **eGA** [Black], Brer Wolf, he tuck atter'm. **1893** Shands *MS Speech* 35, *He. . .* The almost universal use of the third person pronoun after names by illiterate whites of Mississippi should be noted. They . . nearly always [say] "John he" or "Susan she" did it. **1916** Howells *Leatherwood God* 69 **OH,** Dylks he told them to let him alone. **1934** Carmer *Stars Fell on AL* 177, Den de knee-high man he set in his house. **1975** Allen *LAUM* 2.82 **nwND** (as of c1950), My dad he hauled buffalo bones.

2 His. *among Blacks, esp Gullah speakers*

1823 Cooper *Pioneers* 1.56 **cNY** [Black], "Had he a pack and an ax?" "No sir, only he rifle." **1829** Tenney *Female Quixotism* 2.40 **Philadelphia PA** [Black], Pose he want sumbody wass he sirt, cook he vittles, make he bed. **1853** Simms *Sword & Distaff* 217 **SC** [Black], De Copp'ral will ease he limbs yonder. **1888** Jones *Negro Myths* 3 **seGA** [Gullah], Eh yent crack eh teet to Buh Rabbit. [=He didn't crack his teeth, i.e., say a word to, Brother Rabbit.] **1891** Page *Elsket* 127 **VA** [Black], Den he kine o' let he feathers down. **1925** *DN* 5.356 **seGA, swSC** [Black], Ah done wrap he feet an he han wid cotton. [ɑ dɒn rɛp i fit n i hɛn wɪd kɑ-n]. **1927** Adams *Congaree* 2 **cSC** [Black], He knock on de door wid he hat in he han'. **1934** Carmer *Stars Fell on AL* 293 [Black], In he country . . there is nothing to harm him. **1940** Crum *Gullah* 104 **SC,** I nebber see a buckra teck so long to say e prays [=prayers]. **1942** Rawlings *Cross Creek* 363 **nFL** [Black], Mr. Jackson done left he wife to her devices. **1966** *DARE* (Qu. HH7b) Inf **SC**10, He lab he mouth; (Qu. HH10) Inf **SC**10, Scared of he shadow; (Qu. HH22c) Inf **SC**10, Kill he grammaw; (Qu. JJ15b, . . *"He doesn't know ______."*) Inf **SC**10, He asshole from he elbow; (Qu. JJ27, *"He had no idea that she was up to anything, but I put ______."*) Inf **SC**10, Advisement in he head; (Qu. JJ44) Inf **SC**10, Keep he tongue tied. [Inf is a Gullah speaker.]

3 Him. [Cf *EDD he* II. 4] Note: While *he* occurs as a hypercorrection for *him* in non-stdE in compound objects (as in *I saw he and his wife*), its occurrence as a simple object appears to be restricted to Black speech. Cf **him** pron **B5**

1934 Stribling *Unfinished Cathedral* 152 **AL** [Black], Chris' let de chillun ob dis worl' crucify He.

4 She; her. [Cf *EDD he* II. 3] *esp among Gullah speakers*

1853 Simms *Sword & Distaff* 196 **SC** [Black], Miss Ebleigh! *He's* a bressed (blessed) woman, for sartin. . . He's a mos' 'spectable pusson, is dat Mrs. Ebleigh. **1888** Jones *Negro Myths* 84 **GA** [Gullah], De po gal . . hide eh feelin but eh berry onsaterfy een eh mine. [=The poor girl hid her feelings but she was very unsatisfied in her mind.] **1909** *S. Atl. Qrly.* 8.49 **seSC,** [In Gullah] The feminine form is [used] . . much less than masculine or neuter; a child, a girl, is almost invariably referred to as he . . *him: "Me tell Jane 'e mus'n't do so; but him will do."* **1919** *DN* 5.38 **OK** [Cherokee Indians], *He.* With such pronouns as *her, him* and *his,* is used indiscriminately, without regard to gender. . . An old Cherokee, replying to . . an inquiry as to the health of his wife, said: "He some better, now, him stand up in bed an' eat coffee." **1922** Gonzales *Black Border* 95 **sSC, GA coasts** [Gullah], Uh gwine tek dis t'ing to da' 'ooman house en' t'row one spell 'puntop 'um fuh mek'um pit 'e min' puntop some dem toddah man en' lemme 'lone. [=I am going to take this thing to the woman's house and throw a spell upon her to make her put her mind on some of those other men and let me alone.] **1928** Peterkin *Scarlet Sister Mary* 112 **SC** [Gullah], Dat blue hen sho made me sweat befo I could put em an' all e chillen in dat basket. You wouldn' believe it to see how quiet e is now. **1951** *AmSp* 26.26, In the pidgin of Hawaii. . . *He* is the pronoun for all genders.

5 It; they. [Cf *EDD he* II. 4] *esp among Gullah speakers*

1838 (1852) Gilman *S. Matron* 211 **SC** [Black], Here blood . . but he an't too much. **1914** *DN* 4.159 **cVA,** *He. . .* It. "Wheah's thu shuvva (shovel)?" "Heah he!" (here it is). **1919** *DN* 5.31 **OK,** In the . . English of the Cherokees . . the pronouns are used indiscriminately, without regard to sex or case. . . *That* is often used for *the,* or *those,* . . "that hills, he's steep." *Ibid* 38, "That day, he's hot." **1922** Gonzales *Black Border* 278 **sSC, eGA coasts** [Gullah glossary], " 'E," a contraction of he . . (but used also for it). . . If winter comes, " 'e freeze," and in summer weather " 'e hot." **1925** *DN* 5.357 **eGA** [Gullah], He pump e [=a pitcher] full. **1926** Smith *Gullah* 36 **SC,** 'E yent matter 'bout de road, so long as 'e kah yo to de right place. **1928** Peterkin *Scarlet Sister Mary* 124 **SC** [Gullah], If e don' work, den I'll quit makin' love-charms for de rest o' my life. **1987** *AmSp* 62.23 **SC** [Gullah], Based on their use of the five different variants [used for *it*] (*hit, ee, he,* and *it* in subject position and *hit, ee, um,* and *it* in object position) . . , Nichols divided the speakers into two groups.

6 See quots. [Cf *EDD he* II. 6] *arch*

1878 *Appletons' Jrl.* 5.416 **NJ,** The old-time people in portions of [New Jersey] . . show a deference to persons of station or worth, or to strangers, by speaking to them in the third person. Instead of saying, "How do *you* do?" in inquiring after your health, they will say, "How does *he* do?" or perhaps will use your name, and say to you, "How does Mr. Brown do?" And such persons are particular to demand of their children that they shall say *he* and *she* in addressing their father and mother. . . It is, however, an ominous fact that this usage is fast disappearing. **c1902** Clapin *New Dict. Amer.* 223 **MA, CT, NJ,** The 3d person is used instead of the 2d by bashful, ignorant people. In talking with you, they will say: "Will he take a chair?"

he n Also sp *hee*

1 freq attrib: A male. [*OED* c1300 →] *freq euphem* Cf **boar, buck** n[1] **1, 2**

1806 (1905) Clark *Orig. Jrls. Lewis & Clark Exped.* 5.36, Two bears . . one of them an old hee was in fine order. **1834** *Life Andrew Jackson* 3, He'd git . . a heeboddys [=he-biddy's] tale stuck in a straw hat for a ginerals fether. **1843** (1916) Hall *New Purchase* 165 **IN,** She denominated the chanticleer—chickbidde—or, he-bidde—or, old-rooster. **1895** *Outing* 26.434/2, I'd . . yell the core out of my Adam's apple, for one wild mill with a game old he coon. **1899** (1912) Green *VA Folk-Speech* 219, *He. . .* A male animal, a bird, beast, or fish of the male sex: as, a *he*-goat. **c1937** in 1972 *Amer. Slave* 2.16 **SC,** Every he thing from a he king down to a bunty rooster gits 'cited 'bout she things. **1938** Matschat *Suwannee R.* 63 **GA,** Truly there was nothing he-uns of any age enjoyed more than showin' off afore a womern. **1939** *LANE* Map 190, The euphemisms used when a direct reference to the bull is avoided . . *(the) he, . . he cow, ~ ox, ~ animal, ~ critter.* *Ibid* Map 200 **swRI,** *He-sheep.* *Ibid* Map 206 **ceCT,** A boar is a ['hi ˌwʌ^n]. **1950** *WELS (Words used by women or in mixed company for a bull)* 2 Infs, **WI,** He-cow. **1965–70** *DARE* (Qu. K22, *Words used for a bull*) Infs **NC**36, **NM**6, **OH**66, **PA**246, He-cow; **NC**30, He-brute; (Qu. K23, *Words used by women or in mixed company for a bull*) Infs **FL**7, **MD**24,

NY230, **OR**1, **PA**141, **TX**54, He-cow; **NC**30, He-brute; **MS**63, He-oxen; (Qu. K52, *A male pig kept for breeding*) Inf **KY**32, He; **SC**7, He-hog. **1970** Tarpley *Blinky* 160 **neTX,** *Male horse* . . he-horse. *Ibid* 166, *Male cow (euphemism)* . . he-cow. **1973** Allen *LAUM* 1.244 (as of c1950), Bull. . . he animal [1 inf, **MN**] . . he cow [1 inf, **IA**]. **1983** *MJLF* 9.1.42 **ceKY,** *He* . . a euphemism for bull. **1984** *DARE* File **Chesapeake Bay** [Watermen's vocab], He-crabs. **1986** Pederson *LAGS Concordance* **Gulf Region** *(Boar)* 4 infs, He-hog; 1 inf, He-hog—euphemism.

2 attrib; Transf: see quot 1958.

1851 Hooper *Widow Rugby's Husband* 64 **AL,** A class of individuals who . . described themselves as "*he* fellows, hard to head." **1942** Berrey-Van den Bark *Amer. Slang* 109.5, *He stein* . . a large beer mug. **1950** *WELS Suppl.* **MA, NH,** *He-dishes*—Pots and pans, utensils. Usually used in the context of washing them. Familiar to several generations of Yankees, in contrast with *she-dishes* (glass, china, silverware). **1958** McCulloch *Woods Words* 82 **Pacific NW,** *He*—Anything extra big, stout, strong, as a he log, a he truck, etc. **1968** *DARE* (Qu. F46, . . *Matches you can strike anywhere*) Inf **NY**111, He-matches. **1970** Tarpley *Blinky* 54 **neTX,** *Very heavy rain that doesn't last long* . . he-rain.

3 with *one:* Anyone or anything large, difficult to manage, or important; see quots.

1904 Day *Kin o' Ktaadn* 181 **ME,** After about a month the Gen'ral had to go out an' say to the old head He One,—Now, Chief, . . you better take your men an' go home. **1941** *Nature Mag.* 34.137, An extra large worm—an old "he-one." **1943** *AmSp* 18.238 **seNY,** *A he one* or *An old he one* . . one large of its kind. **1949** *PADS* 11.22 **CO,** *He-one*. . . A big tough one, hard to handle—a person or a thing. **1969** *DARE* (Qu. R15b, . . *An extra-big mosquito*) Inf **MA**58, Old he-one.

4 A men's toilet. Cf **buck** n[1] **2h**

1969 *DARE* (Qu. F37, *Names for an indoor toilet*) Inf **NY**213, A he and a she.

hea See **here A1**

heab See **hebe**

heaben, heabm, heabun See **heaven**

heaby See **hebby**

head n Usu |hɛd|; also **esp Sth, S Midl** |hed| Pronc-spp *hade, haid*

A Forms.

1770 in 1947 *AmSp* 22.38 **CT,** 2 hads & plooks [=plucks, inner organs]. **1893** Owen *Voodoo Tales* 176 **MO** [Black], Yo' look lak er ooman strong in de haid. **1893** Shands *MS Speech* 34, *Hade* [hed]. Negro for *head.* **1941** Heydrick-Thompson *Americans All* 215 **Sth** [Black], Dey kin be powahful contra'y when sets dey hai'd to it. **c1960** *Wilson Coll.* **csKY,** *Head* /hed/ among older people occasionally. **1967** *DARE* (Qu. HH5) Inf **SC**44, Tetched in the haid.

B Senses.

1 The hair on the head—often in phrr *comb* (or *wash*) *one's* (or *the*) *head.* [*OED* 13 . . →] **scattered, but esp Midl, Sth**

1795 Murdock *Triumphs* 30 **Philadelphia PA,** If I don't comb his head with a three-legged stool, there is no snakes in Ireland. **1899** (1912) Green *VA Folk-Speech* 122, *Comb*. . . Instead of combing the *hair* they always *comb the head.* **1902** *DN* 2.231 **sIL,** *Comb*. . . The expression is always 'comb the head,' never 'the hair.' **1915** *DN* 4.225 **wTX,** *Comb one's head.* **1942** McAtee *Dial. Grant Co. IN* 19 (as of 1890s), *Comb the head.* **1950** *WELS (Joking terms for getting your hair cut)* 1 Inf, **WI,** Have my head trimmed. **1960** Criswell *Resp. to PADS 20* **Ozarks,** *Head* for hair, as in "Comb your head." Very common at one time; perhaps still so. **c1960** *Wilson Coll.* **csKY,** *Wash the head*—Wash the hair; very common. **1965-70** *DARE* (Qu. X4b, . . *"On Saturday I have to wash my ______."*) 69 Infs, **scattered, but esp Midl, Sth,** Head [Of all Infs responding to the question, 30% were comm type 5, 64% were old, 31% were coll educ, 55% male; of those giving this response, 51% were comm type 5, 75% were old, 13% coll educ, 55% male.]; (Qu. X4a, . . *Speaking of somebody's hair getting grey*) Infs **LA**40, **PA**239, **SC**55, **VA**73, Head (is) getting gray; **LA**8, Head (is) turning white; **AR**55, Head's getting frosty; **TN**13, Head's turnin' silvery. **1982** *Barrick Coll.* **csPA,** *Head—hair.* "I gotta comb my head now."

2 The mouth—usu in phrr referring to speech. Cf **face n 1**

1849 *Neal's Sat. Gaz.* (Phila.) 17 Feb. 1/1 *(OEDS),* But don't you open yer head about it to no other indiwiddiwal. **1856** Holmes *Lena Rivers* 399 **NEng,** "Shut up your head," roared John Jr. **1877** Twain *Rambling Notes* 2.587 **NEng,** The meek mouth began to open. "Shet your head!" shouted the old mariner. **1884** *Anglia* 7.261 **Sth, S Midl** [Black], *Not ter put nuthin' in yo' head* = to eat nothing. **1898** Deland *Old Chester* 307 **PA,** He "hardly opened his head for the whole twenty-one miles." **1956** Gipson *Old Yeller* 1 **TX,** When he [=a dog] opened his head, the sound he let out came closer to being a yell than a bark. **c1960** *Wilson Coll.* **csKY,** *Head*—Humorous for mouth; "Shut your head and keep it shut." **1966-68** *DARE* (Qu. HH7b, *Someone who talks too much or too loud: "He's always ______."*) Infs **NM**12, **WV**4, Shooting off his head; **LA**3, Running his head; **IL**11, Running off at the head; (Qu. JJ22, *To express your opinion*) Inf **WV**1, Shot my head off.

3 An individual—used as a unit in enumerating persons, esp children. **chiefly Sth, S Midl**

1895 *DN* 1.389 **seMD,** *Head:* "A man has six or eight head of children." **1949** Turner *Africanisms* 289 **seSC** [Gullah], Five hundred head of man from all about—Virginia, Georgia, and every which and way. **1950** *PADS* 14.36 **SC,** *Head*. . . In numbering, applied to persons as well as animals. "Six head of chillun." **1954** *DE Folkl. Bulletin* 1.16/1, Ten head of children. **1966-70** *DARE* Tape **FL**50, They's 'bout eight head of us children; **GA**22, They raised fourteen head o' children on Billy's Island; **SC**10, I got about fifteen head of grand [=grandchildren]. . . and nine head of children of my own. **1968** *DARE* File **csNC,** *Head*—used as a measure for cats, and very often, children; e.g. "that man has a heap of children but I don't care if he has thirty head." **1968** *DARE* FW Addit **GA**25, "They was five head o' tourists here this evening and they was six head o' us here in the house;" **GA**33, I have heard "head" used for people; "eight head o' young 'uns"; **LA**15, Yes, I read about that, where they [=the police] picked up three head of 'em [=people.] **1976** Ryland *Richmond Co. VA* 372, *Head*—people; "How many head for lunch?"

4 Life—esp in phrr *bet one's head (on it)* and varr. [*OED* a1000 →] **esp Sth, S Midl**

1965-70 *DARE* (Qu. JJ20, *If you felt very sure about something, and wanted to show it: "I'm so sure, I'd ______ it."*) 10 Infs, **esp Sth, S Midl,** Bet my head (on); **LA**35, Bet my head on a block; (Qu. KK55b, *To deny something very firmly* . . *"Not on your ______."*) Inf **MS**21, Head.

5 Simple reasoning or intuition.

1969-70 *DARE* (Qu. KK48, *When you work something out as you go, without having a plan or pattern to follow: "I didn't have anything to go by, so I just did it ______."*) Inf **VA**69, By head; **KY**40, By my head; **KY**28, By my own head; **NC**76, Through my head.

6 Assistance; a helping hand.

1945 Saxon *Gumbo Ya-Ya* 376 **LA,** *Gimme a head* means to ask for aid in lifting a heavy load.

7 Of tobacco:

a A hand or small bundle.

1839 (1969) Briggs *Advent. Franco* 1.254, The boatswain . . bet his silver call, chain and all, against a head of tobacco. **1865** IL Dept. Ag. *Trans. for 1863* 5.668 **KY,** Others . . tie them in bands of six or eight leaves . . so as to form a head of one and a half to two inches in length. **1940** *AmSp* 15.134 [Tobacco market], *Hands or heads.* A number of leaves tied in a bunch. **1967** Key *Tobacco Vocab.,* Heads.

b See quot.

1966 *DARE* (Qu. DD1, . . *Forms* . . *chewing tobacco come[s] in*) Inf **ME**22, Head, same as plug.

8 See quot.

1916 *DN* 4.269 **seLA,** *Head*. . . The river end of a street.

9 =**hummock 2. chiefly FL, GA** Cf **bay** n[3] **2**

1954 *Living Wilderness* 19.50.4 **Okefenokee GA,** "Heads" or "houses," so-called because they house game. These are the real "quivering earth." They are large and small floating islands, formed by peat rising to the surface, on which small vegetation begins. **1964** Will *Hist. Okeechobee* 80 **FL** (as of 1922), Also there were small "heads" or hammocks of magnolia, bay and myrtle elevated a foot or more above the water. **1965** Will *Okeechobee Boats* 13 **FL,** As fur as he could see thar weren't nothing but wet prairie with here and yonder in the fur distance, a trifling hammock, a cypress head or a clump of cabbage trees. **1966** *DARE* Tape **FL**39, A cypress head is . . a section of cypress growing in a swampland. **1966** *DARE* (Qu. C7, . . *Land that usually has some standing water with trees or bushes growing in it*) Inf **FL**15, Bay head; **FL**37, Cypress heads—if cypress trees grow in it; (Qu. T1, . . *A bunch of trees growing together in open country, especially on a hill*) Inf **FL**09, Cypress head—wet ground; pond in middle. **1972** *DARE* FW Addit **nwFL,** Cypress head: A bay is about the same. **1975** Newell *If Nothin' Don't Happen* 118 **nwFL,** A cypress head is just a little old island of cypress timber settin' out in the flat piney woods or the marsh and might be only a acre or two in size.

10 The opening of a lobster trap; the net covering the opening. **ME**

1957 Beck *Folkl. ME* 126, Some [lobster pots] had two openings or "heads" at opposite ends, others one "head". . . The heads were "knitted" of tarred twine and the small end was kept open by a round withe of spruce. **1966** *DARE* Tape **ME**17, It's [=a lobster trap is] about three foot long and it's got two heads in one end and a bedroom head in the other. **1978** Merriam *Illustr. Lobstering* 45 **ME,** *Head*—A funnel-shaped net that is attached to the openings in the trap and also is found between the parlor and the kitchen. The head allows the lobsters to enter the trap. Heads are usually knitted by the lobsterman himself.

11 =copperhead snake 1.

1953 Randolph–Wilson *Down in Holler* 251 **Ozarks,** *Head*. . . A copperhead snake *(Agkistrodon mokasen)*. "Some feller up on Crane Creek stepped on a head this mornin'. They say his leg's swole up big as a stove-pipe."

C Combs.

1 Used to refer to types of persons, as: see below. *usu derog*

a An unpleasant or dull-witted person. Cf **coconut head, cottonhead 2, doughhead, gourd~ 3, lunk~, pin~, rattle~**

1894 Twain *Pudd'nhead Wilson* 26 **seMO,** "The man ain't in his right mind." . . "Well, he's a lummox, anyway." . . "Perfect jackass—yes, and it ain't going too far to say his is a pudd'nhead." **1960** Wentworth–Flexner *Slang* 630, *-head* refers to one's intelligence, usually in a derogatory sense and often by describing figuratively the head's size or shape *(dumb-head, pea-head)*. **1965–70** *DARE* (Qu. HH8, *A person who likes to brag*) Inf **PA**130, Braghead; **NY**119, Prickhead; (Qu. HH9, *A very silly or light-headed person*) Inf **NY**42, Bubblehead; **CT**28, Bughead; **OK**51, Dumbhead; **NY**123, Lighthead; **NC**82, Nuthead; (Qu. HH13, . . *A person . . not very alert or . . aware of things*) Inf **NY**92, Dullhead; (Qu. HH16, *Uncomplimentary words . . used when you want to show that you don't think much of a person: "Don't invite him. He's a ______ ."*) Inf **MA**11, Thickhead.

b A person whose race or ethnic background is different from the speaker's. Cf **buddhahead, burrhead** n[1] **1, coconut head, fish ~ 2**

1966–69 *DARE* (Qu. HH28, *Names and nicknames. . . Negro*) Inf **GA**89, Nappyheads—nigger children; **MS**30, Jughead; (Qu. HH28, . . *Irish*) Inf **PA**227, Whiskeyhead; (QR, near Qu. HH28) Inf **CA**81, Gighead [sic], onionhead, potatohead—Whites, called by Negroes [Inf Black]. **1966** *DARE* FW Addit **cSC,** Pepperhead—a Negro. [Inf is white] **1986** Pederson *LAGS Concordance* **Gulf Region** *(Negro)* 1 inf, Lint head—wife's father uses; 1 inf, Kinky head; 1 inf, Nubbin head.

c A heavy drinker. **chiefly Sth, S Midl** See Map

1955 S. Whitmore *Solo* 247 *(OEDS)*, The juiceheads . . got so fractured [i.e., drunk] that they wouldn't show up for a date. **1965–70** *DARE* (Qu. DD12, . . *A person who drinks steadily or a great deal*) Infs **AL**31, **FL**35, **GA**74, **NY**249, **NC**72, **SC**26, 58, 69, Liquorhead; **DC**12, **FL**48, **KY**34, **LA**11, **NY**249, **PA**94, Winehead; **DC**12, **KY**49, **LA**3, **MA**71, **SC**69, Whiskeyhead; **AL**62, **DC**12, Juicehead; **TN**50, Hoochhead; **MO**24, Jickhead; **LA**2, Rumhead; **KY**70, Slophead; **PA**94, Sophead; **KY**11, Sothead; **TX**26, Tonichead. [8 of 23 Infs Black] **1986** Pederson *LAGS Concordance* **Gulf Region** *(A drunk)* 2 infs, Booze head; 2 infs, Lush head. [This question was asked chiefly in urban areas.]

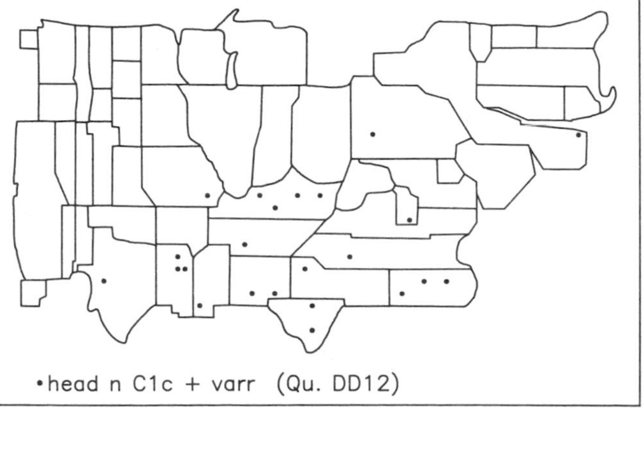

•head n C1c + varr (Qu. DD12)

2 Used to refer to the effects of prolonged overuse of alcohol: see quot.

1965–70 *DARE* (Qu. DD24, . . *Diseases that come from continual drinking*) Infs **IN**13, **MS**68, **NC**40, **PA**188, Whiskeyhead; (Qu. DD22, . . *Delirium tremens*) Inf **KY**35 Hophead.

D Phrases.

1 in phrr *head nor hair* (or *heels, hide, tail*) and varr: A vestige or trace; see quots. [Varr of *hide (n)or hair*]

1856 Cary *Married Not Mated* 186, I have n't seen head nor heels of him for the last three days. **1966–70** *DARE* (Qu. LL29, *Any sign or trace: "He left last week, and nobody's seen ______ of him since."*) Inf **GA**80, Head nor hair (*or* tail); **GA**11, Head nor hide; **NY**89, Head nor tails; **FL**52, Head or tail; **LA**20, Head or tail of where he is; **VA**42, Head, hoof and hide.

2 in phr *make one's head save one's heels:* See quot c1968.

1946 *PADS* 6.38 **cwVA,** Make your *head* save your heels. **1947** *PADS* 8.26 **wNY** (as of 1928). **c1968** *DARE* File **ceIA,** *Make your head save your heels*—Advice to use your brain.

3 in phr *on (top of) one's head:* Anxious.

1966–68 *DARE* (Qu. GG11, *To be quite anxious about something . . "He's ______ ."*) Inf **VA**24, On his head; **FL**35, On top of his head; [**GA**1, Standing on his head.]

4 in phr *have (something) running out of one's head:* See quot. [Var of *to have (something) coming out of one's ears*]

1967 *DARE* (Qu. LL9b, *All you need or more—for example, of clothes: "She's got clothes ______ ."*) Inf **SC**45, Running out of her head.

5 in phr *put over one's head:* ?To endure; to put behind one.

1944 *PADS* 2.34 **wNC,** *Head, to put over* (one's). . . "The worst day and night I ever put over my head" (heavy rain and high wind).

6 in phr *hold one's head:* See **hold** v **C1c.**

head adj [Cf *EDD head* II. 18 "Chief . . best, most excelling"; *OED headest* (at *head* sb. 63. c) "=chiefest. *Obs. rare.*"]
Best; most able; hence superl *headest* most advantageous.

1895 *DN* 1.372 **eTN, wNC,** *Head* . . best, chief. "That's the head trick I ever see." **1939** in 1972 Hall *Sayings Old Smoky* 79 **ceTN,** *Head*. . . Most droll, most entertaining, ablest. "He was the head feller that I ever saw." **1944** *PADS* 2.57 **MO,** *Headest start*. . . An advantage. A term commonly used by school children. "It's no fair: you had the headest start." **1956** *Hall Coll.* **eTN,** Used of a comic character: "He's the head feller you've ever seen in your life."

head v

1 To intercept, turn (someone or something) aside.

1707 in 1884 Lancaster MA *Early Rec.* 165, We have sent about thirty men to waylay them or head them if they can. **1791** Bartram *Travels* 223, If any one strolled from the rest at too great a distance, the dog would spring up, head the horse and bring him back to the company. **1849** Parkman *CA & OR Trail* 67, The Captain was roaring to us to head her. **1872** (1973) Thompson *Major Jones's Courtship* 277, The horsemen tuck the road to the woods, to try to head him, and them on foot was climbin the fences . . all hollerin to Sam to stop. **1884** *Century Illustr. Mag.* 27.509/2, Sheridan had headed Lee's army. **1954** *Harder Coll.* **cwTN,** 'E could'n head a calf in lane wi' them old bow-legs o' hisn. **1969** *DARE* Tape **GA**51, It [=a fire] got into the Okefenoke swamp. . . It was beyond control. Uncle Sam's army couldn't a' headed it.

2 To outwit; to get the better of.

1851 Hooper *Widow Rugby's Husband* 64 **AL,** A class of individuals who . . described themselves as "*he* fellows, hard to head." **1888** Jones *Negro Myths* 90 **GA coast** [Gullah], Wen de ole man mek up eh mine eh couldnt fine out wuh day een de barrel, . . eh mek answer: "Mossa, hoona done head de ole coon dis time." [=When the old man made up his mind that he couldn't find out what was in the barrel, . . he answered: "Master, you have got the better of the old coon this time."] *Ibid* 96, Eh tek a smart somebody fuh head Buh Rabbit.

headache n

1 See **headache post.**

2 A poppy (here: *Papaver argemone*). [Thought by some to cause headaches]

1956 St. John *Flora SE WA* 160, *Papaver Argemone* . . Headache.

headache exclam **chiefly West**

Used as a warning to beware of falling or low-hanging objects.

1944 *AmSp* 19.231 **NW** [Shipyard terms], *Headache*. . . a warning to look up and beware of objects moving overhead. A term easier to use than 'Heads Up!' **1949** *AmSp* 24.33 [Language of oil fields], In rig building the cry *headache* is a signal to run when something falls, if one wants to avoid a real headache. **1961** *PADS* 36.28 **West** [Heavy construction jargon], *Headache*. . . A warning cry used to alert workers on a lower level to danger from above; employed when an object has been accidentally dropped or before deliberately throwing material to the ground. **1967** *TX Observer* (Austin) 7 July 2/3, The cry of "headache!" means somebody has dropped a wrench, or a steel cable or bolt is coming down, or other iron is falling, and all hands duck and run with a sidelong upward glance. **1968** Adams *Western Words* 142, *Headache!* A logger's warning to duck or to beware a heavy load overhead.

headache ball n Also *headache pill*

See quots.

1942 *AmSp* 17.280 **Philadelphia PA** [Navy Yard], *Headache pill*. A heavy steel ball that hangs from the crane cable to keep it taut. **1961** *PADS* 36.28 **West** [Heavy construction jargon], *Headache ball*. . . A heavy metal ball or other weight fastened to the end of the hoist line of a crane to cause the line to run off the drum when the brake is released.

headache dock n

=**curled dock.**

1959 *Western Folkl.* 18.333 **VA** [Black], To draw proud flesh, take "headache dock" (a great big leaf), beat it, make a poultice and it will draw out flesh from the sores.

headache flower n

1 See **headache plant.**

2 A **rhododendron.**

1966 *DARE* (Qu. S26e) Inf **SC**27, Wild azalea, also headache flower.

3 A **trillium.**

1968 *DARE* (Qu. S2, . . *The flower that comes up in the woods early in spring, with three white petals that turn pink as the flower grows older*) Inf NY94, Headache flowers.

headache pill See **headache ball**

headache plant n Also *headache flower* [From its use against headaches]

A **pasqueflower,** usu *Anemone patens.*

1893 *Jrl. Amer. Folkl.* 6.136, *Anemone patens,* var. *Nuttalliana,* headache plant. **1931** Clute *Common Plants* 124, Headache-plant *(Anemone pulsatilla).* **1937** U.S. Forest Serv. *Range Plant Hdbk.* W159, Although pasqueflower is the common name . . , such other appellations as . . headache-plant . . have variously designated this species. **1950** *WELS (Pale blue flowers with downy leaves and petals that bloom on hillsides in March or early April)* 1 Inf, **WI**, Headache flower. **1959** Carleton *Index Herb. Plants* 59, *Headache plant:* Anemone pulsatilla.

headache post n Also *headache (rack)* Cf **headache** exclam

A structure designed to protect workers from a falling or shifting weight.

1887 Crew *Petroleum* 179 [Oil drilling terms], As its name indicates, the headache post is designed to save the driller a headache, or perhaps his life in case the wrist-pin should break, or the pitman fly off of it, while drilling, thus causing the derrick end of the walking beam to drop under the great weight of the suspended drilling tools, and endangering the safety of all within reach. **1903** *DN* 2.341 **wNY, wPA, WV** [Oil well language], *Headache-post*. . . A pillar inside the derrick which supports the end of the walking-beam when disconnected. Also called the *life-preserver.* **1949** *AmSp* 24.33 [Oil field language], There are two explanations for the origin of the term *headache post*. . . The driller leaned on it when his drilling worries gave him the headache. Probably a better explanation is that its purpose is to save the driller's skull if the walking beam should pull loose from the pitman or crank. The term has been transferred in the shortened form *headache* to any protecting structure which supports weight, such as in the frame on the cab of a truck which protects the top of the cab from heavy loads. **1969** *AmSp* 44.205 [Trucker's talk], *Headache rack.* **1971** Tak *Truck Talk* 81, *Headache rack:* the heavy meshwork grill on the rear of a cab that protects it from damage from a load that may shift forward in the event of a sudden stop or accident. **1982** *Barrick Coll.* **csPA** (as of 1970s), *Headache rack*—iron frame mounted behind the cab in long-distance trucks, for fastening tie chains, etc.

headache stick n

In moonshining: the pipe that conducts the hot vapors into the **doubler 5b** or **thump barrel.**

1968 *Foxfire* Fall-Winter 49 **nGA,** *Still Parts And Tools. . . Headache Stick*—the long thump rod. **1974** Dabney *Mountain Spirits* xxii [Corn whiskey glossary], *Headache stick:* the long vapor line pipe that goes down into the thumper keg.

headache weed n

1 Prob **chinchweed** or **lemonscent.** [From its use against headaches]

1875 *Amer. Naturalist* 9.145 **sUT,** A plant . . probably a Pectis, . . its foliage so strongly charged with an aromatic oil that it is extracted by a rough process of distilling for domestic use, the plant receiving the popular name of "head-ache weed."

2 A **virgin's bower** (here: *Clematis viorna*).

1940 Clute *Amer. Plant Names* 2, *Clematis viorna*. . . Headache weed.

3 Perh a **rue anemone.**

1966 *DARE* (Qu. S3, *A flower like a large violet with a yellow center and small ragged leaves*) Inf **FL**7, Headache weed.

headache whiskey n Cf *DS* DD21c, **busthead 1, popskull**

1968 *Foxfire* Fall-Winter 101 **nGA,** Names given moonshine include . . headache whiskey.

head and ears See **head over ears**

head and footer n Also *leader and footer*

A children's game; see quots.

1891 *Jrl. Amer. Folkl.* 4.227 **Brooklyn NYC,** *Head and footer*. . . The one who is "it" stands at the cross line with his feet parallel to that line, and stoops over, and the leader, who is always first, places his hands upon his back, and jumps over him. The others follow in turn, and a fresh line is drawn across the course at the point touched by the one who makes the shortest jump. . . If one of the players cannot follow the leader, he becomes "it." **1901** *DN* 2.141 **csNY,** *Head-and-footer*. . . The name of a game somewhat like leap-frog. **1937** (1947) Bancroft *Games* 151, Leapfrog with one back. . . *Leader and footer.* One player is chosen to be "back," and he chooses a leader, generally the poorest jumper, and a "footer"—the best jumper. A starting . . line is drawn on the ground. . . The . . players line up . . with the leader at the head and the footer at the rear. . . The footer dictates the way in which the back is to be cleared. . . he may . . require . . a hop and skip. . . Any player failing in the feat becomes back.

head and head adj phr Also *head to head* [By analogy with *neck and neck*]

1966–67 *DARE* (Qu. KK54, *Just about equal, very close: "They were both fast runners and it was ______ all the way."*) Infs **GA**5, **MI**69, NJ3, **NY**18A, Head and head; **NJ**68, **NY**109, 241, Head to head.

head and heel n Cf **header 4, heel** v^2

See quot 1936; hence v phr *head and heel* to rope a calf in such a way.

1936 McCarthy *Lang. Mosshorn* np **MT** [Rodeo terms], *Head 'n Heel.* The event where one roper catches the steer by the front feet and another roper lassos the hind feet and both putting the animal down against time. **1976** Sublette Co. Artist Guild *More Tales* 310 **WY** (as of c1900), I have seen eight ropers at a branding. It didn't make any difference if a calf was a month old or a yearlin', it was head and heeled. Nobody did any wrestlin'.

head betony n

A **lousewort** (here: *Pedicularis canadensis*).

1795 Winterbotham *Amer. U.S.* 3.398, Among the native and uncultivated plants of New-England, the following have been employed for medicinal purposes: . . Head Betony, Betonica officinalis, Horse-mint, spearmint [etc]. **1900** Lyons *Plant Names* 278, *P[edicularis] Canadensis*. . . head betony. **1930** OK Univ. Biol. Surv. *Pub.* 2.2.80, *Pedicularis canadensis*. . . Head betony. **1940** Clute *Amer. Plant Names* 29.

head boat n [See quot 1979] Cf **drift boat**

A boat for hire used for sport fishing; a **party boat.**

1968 *Harrington Jrl.* (DE) 17 May 6/4, There is a fishing pier in the bay, and deep sea fishing "head boats" may be taken at nearby Lewes. **1975** Evanoff *Catch More Fish* 103 **FL,** Bottom fishing is often done from party boats (also called "head boats" and "drift boats" in many areas). They sail from. . . ports along the . . coasts, and charge a few dollars for a day's fishing. **1979** *DARE* File **ceDE,** These [boats] are called 'head boats' because they charge per person or 'by the head' for a day's trip fishing.

head-buster n Also *head-splitter*
=**busthead 1.**

1966–70 *DARE* (Qu. DD21b, . . *Bad liquor*) Infs **NC**87, **SC**26, 32, Head-buster; **NC**7, Head-splitter.

headcheese n

1 also *heads cheese:* The meat of the head (and sometimes feet and inner organs) usu of a pig, boiled, chopped, and then molded into the shape of a cheese or sometimes prepared as a sausage; see quots. [Cf Du *hoofdkaas*] **chiefly Nth, Midl, West** See Map and Map Section Also called **head meat, ~ pudding, ~ sausage, ~ souse, hedge cheese, hog-head hash, ~ pudding, ~ souse, hog's head cheese**

1841 *S. Lit. Messenger* 7.39/2 **Sth,** The animal . . may be traced in the stewed chine and souse, the head-cheese and sausages. **1848** Bartlett *Americanisms* 173, *Head-cheese.* The ears and feet of swine cut up fine, and, after being boiled, pressed into the form of a cheese. **1906** Gregory *Woman's Cookbook* 131, *Head Cheese.* Take the head, ears and feet of a pig after being cleaned thoroughly. Boil them till tender in water that is salted. When done chop very fine and season with salt, pepper and sage. Put into molds until cold. **1941** *LANE* Map 305 **chiefly wNEng,** Head cheese is made of the fleshy parts of a hog's head (mainly the jowls or cheeks), which are boiled, chopped up fine or ground, heated again, and then permitted to cool in cakes or stuffed into a pig's stomach. . . Souse may be made into head cheese. **1948** *Sat. Eve. Post* 14 Aug 94/4 **ePA,** They see nothing wrong with calling something "head cheese" or "hog maw," and any outlander who can overcome a slight shuddering repugnance to taste them will wonder why he never even heard of such dishes before. **1950** *WELS (Meat from the head and inner organs of an animal cut up and pressed into a mold)* 51 Infs, **WI,** Headcheese; *(Kinds of sausage)* 3 Infs, **WI,** Headcheese sausage. **1965–70** *DARE* (Qu. H43, *Foods made from parts of the head and inner organs of an animal*) 530 Infs, **chiefly Nth, Midl, West,** Headcheese; **NH**6, **RI**3, 14, Heads cheese; (Qu. H61, . . *Kinds of homemade cheese;* total Infs questioned, 75) Inf **OK**21, Headcheese; (Qu. H65, *Foreign foods*) Inf **KS**7, Headcheese. **1966** Dakin *Dial. Vocab. Ohio R. Valley* 2.337, *Head cheese* is the usual name everywhere north of the Ohio, and appears to be a term which originated in the North Midland. **1970** Major *Dict. Afro-Amer. Slang* 65, *Headcheese:* various cheap grades of pork meat prepared and sold as lunch meat. **1973** Allen *LAUM* 1.288 (as of c1950), *Head cheese. . .* is common both on the east coast and in the U[pper] M[idwest].

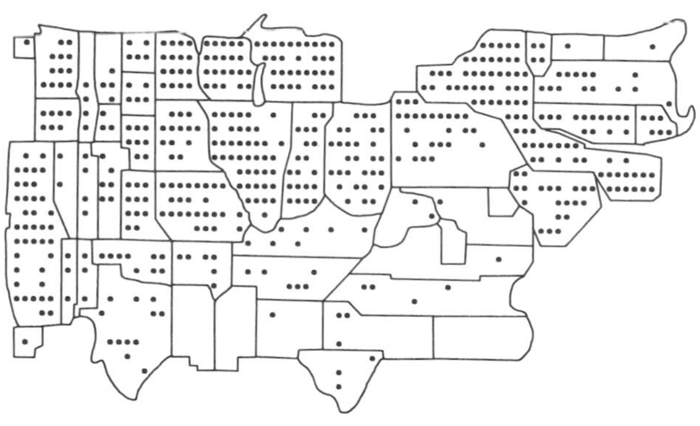

•headcheese 1 + var (Qq. H43, H61, H65)

2 Smegma. Cf **duck butter 1, gnat butter**

1942 McAtee *Dial. Grant Co. IN Suppl. 1* 6 (as of 1890s), *Headcheese* . . cheesy matter collecting under the prepuce behind the glans of the penis. **1981** *DARE* File **ME,** In Maine, what I [from central west Tennessee] call *duck butter* is [called] *head cheese,* which seems to me more appropriate than *d.b.*

headcloth n [*OED* a1000 →; cf also Ger *Kopftuch*] **esp Sth; also Ger settlement areas** Cf **babushka, head handkerchief, head rag, head wrap**

A piece of cloth worn as a head covering; a kerchief.

1747 in 1912 Augusta Co. VA *Chronicles* 1.529, They were . . robbed of . . women's head cloths, . . a curb and a snaffle, a rifle gun (double tricked). **1942** Faulkner *Go Down* 100 **MS,** In the same clean white headcloth and aprons which he first remembered. **1950** *WELS (A square cloth that women fold and tie over their heads)* 1 Inf, **Milwaukee WI,** Headcloth. [*DARE* Ed: Inf is German.] **1966–70** *DARE* (Qu. W3, *A piece of cloth that a woman folds over her head and ties under her chin*) Infs **PA**142, **SC**10, 70, Headcloth.

head-down bird n
=**white-breasted nuthatch.**

1933 *Amer. Midland Naturalist* 14.525 **csKY,** *White-breasted nuthatch: Sitta carolinensis carolinensis. . .* The quaint bob-tailed, blue-gray, white-breasted nut-hatch, or "head-down bird," as it is called from its odd habit of walking straight down the side of a tree trunk, is one of the pleasantly familiar birds of the cave region.

headen See **heading**

header n, also attrib

1 A reaper which cuts off the heads of grain. **chiefly West, esp CA** See Map

1865 IL Dept. Ag. *Trans. for 1862* 5.234 **IL,** We are aware of the claim . . that grain may be cut by the Header and safely stacked after it. **1875** in 1877 Phillips *Letters CA* 41, Wheat, in all these valleys, is mostly cut by the "header" machines, thus leaving the straw in the field. **1879** *Scribner's Mth.* Nov 134/2 **KS,** The plentiful reaping-machines. . . the header, which clips off only the tips of the stems. **1882** Nash *2 Yrs. OR* 65, The "header" is a huge construction ten feet wide. Revolving frames in front bend the wheat to the knives, where it is cut and delivered in an endless stream into a great header-wagon, driven alongside the cutting-machine. **1937** Sandoz *Slogum* 306 **NE** (as of 1900–20), Here the flames . . ran, swift and low, through the header stubble and into the close-leafed corn. **1965–70** *DARE* (Qu. L28, *Tools used in the past for cutting grain*) 14 Infs, **chiefly West,** Header; (Qu. L29, *Machines now used for cutting grain*) 10 Infs, **chiefly West,** Header; (Qu. L32a, *In early days, how was the grain separated from the straw?*) Inf **CA**79, The header just took off the top; (Qu. L33, *How . . the grain [is] separated from the straw*) Infs **CA**181, **CT**24, **TX**89, Header; **CT**14, The header thrashes it. **1966** *Good Old Days* Apr 2 **nwTX,** The wheat was cut with headers, pulled by six horses. **1966–67** *DARE* Tape **MI**49, A header would be pulled with around six horses an' then have another team of horses an' a wagon an' it'd head this grain and elevate it right up into the wagon; **OK**18, Later on, why, they got to heading wheat with a header; **OR**2, A header is a great big . . sickle that goes back and forth t' cut the heads off of the grain.

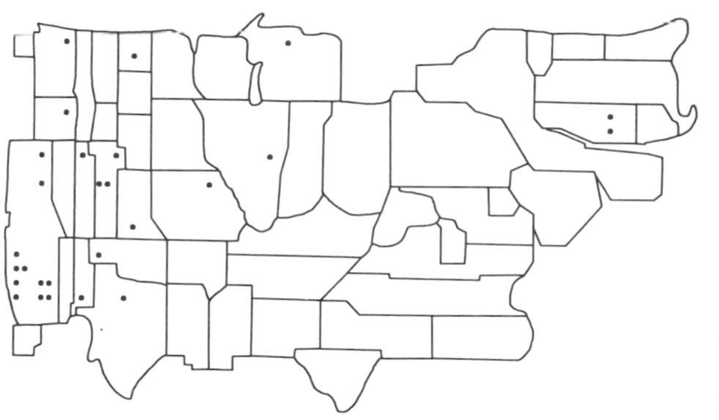

•header 1 (Qq. L28, L29, L32a, L33)

2 See **header barge.**

3 A headfirst fall; a dive—freq in phr *take a header.* **scattered, but esp NEast, Upper Missip Valley**

1912 Paine *Mark Twain* 2.767 (as of 1884), They were curious things, those old high-wheel machines. You were perched away up in the air, with the feeling that you were likely at any moment to strike a pebble or something that would fling you forward with damaging results. . . The word "header" seems to have grown out of that early bicycling period. Perhaps Mark Twain invented it. **1928** *AmSp* 3.408, To take a "header" is to fall headforemost, headfirst, or headlong. **1950** *WELS (A fall: "He slipped on the steps and took quite a ______.")* 2 Infs, **WI,** Header; *(Of a person who is standing up and falls over flat)* 1 Inf, **WI,** Took a header. **1954** Armstrong *Satchmo* 132 **LA,** The policeman slipped, lost his balance and took a header into the mud. **1965–70** *DARE* (Qu. Y1, . . *"He slipped on the steps and took quite a ______."*) 28 Infs, **scattered, but esp NEast, Upper Missip Valley,** Header; (Qu. EE25,

When a child picks up his sled . . runs with it, and then throws himself down on it, that's a ______) Inf **MO**1, Header.

4 In roping contests: see quots. Cf **head and heel, heel** v²

1967 *DARE* Tape **TX**25, A header is the guy that ropes the head of the steers, and then you have a heeler, well, all he does is heel the steer. . . Well, he ropes the hind legs of the steer, then they stretch the steer out, flat, and then the header dismounts from his horse an' runs down there and ties a square knot below the hocks of the steer. **1968** Adams *Western Words* 143, *Header*—In roping, a member of a two-man roping team who ropes the steer by the head. The header has two loops; if he misses with both, the team retires with no time. **1985** Ehrlich *Solace* 93 **WY,** Header and heeler come out of the box at the same time, steer between them, but the header acts first: he ropes the horns of the steer, dallies up, turns off, and tries to position the steer for the heeler who's been tagging behind this duo.

header barge n Also *barge, header, ~ bed, ~ box, ~ wagon* **chiefly West**

A wagon frame resembling a **hayrack 1** used for collecting grain; a wagon with such a frame.

1882 [See **header 1**]. **1914** *DN* 4.108 **KS,** *Header-barge*. . . Header wagon. *Header-box*. . . A box on wagon wheels to convey grain from the header to the stack. **1926** *K.C.* (Mo.) *Star* 11 June *(DA)*, They are the harvesters who plan to be in the heart of the wheat belt when the first header barge and the first binder take to the field to harvest the huge crop. **1944** Wellman *Bowl* 183 **KS,** Til . . borrowed a header-barge, a curious contraption of the plains country, something akin to a hayrack but with one high side and the other low, the latter to accommodate the elevator of the heading machine. . . When one barge was filled, the other took its place with the header. **1965–70** *DARE* (Qu. L13, . . *Wagon used for carrying hay*) Infs **CA**28, 116, 193, Header bed; **CA**23, Header bed or header, loaded on the low side; a special frame put on any running gear; **CA**79, Header wagon—one high side, one low side; (Qu. L28, *Tools used in the past for cutting grain*) Inf **CO**19, Header barge—elevator went up and put grain in the barge, a big, wide hayrack; **NM**13, The header blew the grain and straw into a header barge pulled behind. **1966** *DARE* Tape **OK**18, There was always two header barges. . . They were built out o' slats. . . One side was low. . . This side probably would be two foot high and then run from two up to four feet and this elevator would . . ride on this low side and run the wheat in here. **1966** *Good Old Days* Apr 2 **nwTX,** There were several wagons with barges on them, instead of a regular wagon bed. They were built high on one side and low on the side where the grain fell in from the header.

headest See **head** adj

head-feed n

Prob a var of field corn.

1966 *DARE* (Qu. L21, . . *Kinds of grain*) Inf **OK**43, Head-feed, a maize. **1966** *DARE* Tape **OK**43, They [=the farmers around here] raise a little head-feed maize.

head fire n

The apex of an advancing forest or prairie fire; see quot 1968.

1898 *S. Dakotan* 1.130/2 **SD,** A scorching headfire broke through the marsh with flame and smoke. **1946** Thompson *Amer. Daughter* 48 **ND,** Jumping the firebreak, the headfire went within half a mile of our hayfield. . . They fought the side fires until late in the evening. **1954** Tolbert *Bigamy Jones* 37 **wTX** (as of 1870s), But that don't explain why it was such an unnatural sort of burn, . . all head fire and no side fires. An the head fire traveled through all them grasslands to our hiding place. **1967** *Goliad Advance-Guard* (TX) 13 Apr 3/7, A head fire, one that has the wind behind it. **1968** McPhee *Pine Barrens* 108 **cNJ,** A forest fire moves in a V, like the wake of a ship. The point of the V is called the head fire.

headfish n

1 =**mola.** [See quot 1898]

1842 DeKay *Zool. NY* 4.332, The Great Sun-fish, or Head-fish, is not unfrequently captured along the coast. **1882** U.S. Natl. Museum *Bulletin* 16.865, *Sun-fish; Head-fish; Mola*. . . It reaches a weight of almost 500 pounds. **1898** *Ibid* 47.1752, *Molidae. . . The Head-Fishes*. . . Fishes of the open seas, apparently composed of a huge head to which small fins are attached. **1906** NJ State Museum *Annual Rept. for 1905* 308, The Head Fishes. . . The flesh is not used as food as it is coarse and tough. *Ibid* 425, The Anglers. *Lophius piscatorius* . . Bellows Fish. . . Head Fish. **1933** LA Dept. of Conserv. *Fishes* 254, The Puffers . . are evidently closely related . . to the huge, remarkable and profoundly dissimilar Headfishes. **1960** Amer. Fisheries Soc. *List Fishes* 60, Headfish—see sunfish, ocean; mola, sharptail.

2 =**goosefish.**

1906 [see **1** above].

head fly n Cf **ear fly, face fly, nose fly**

1967–70 *DARE* (Qu. R12, . . *Kinds of flies . . that fly around animals*) Infs **KY**84, **MO**3, **NY**75, 233, **VA**26, Head fly.

head handkerchief n Also *headkerchief* **chiefly Sth** *esp freq among Black speakers*

=**headcloth.**

1852 Eastman *Aunt Phillis's Cabin* 252 **VA,** She [=a Black woman] has on a head-handkerchief and apron white as snow. **1887** *Princeton Rev.* 4.363 **New Orleans LA,** Those who had ante-emancipation costumes of flowered mousseline-de-laine gowns, black-silk aprons, and real bandanna head-kerchiefs, put them on for volunteer service in the dressing-room. **1893** Owen *Voodoo Tales* 10 **MO,** I'll buy you [=a Black woman] a head-handkerchief with my own money. **1898** Harris *Tales Home Folks* 409 **GA,** On her [=a Black woman's] face there was a frown, and her "head-han'k'cher," which usually sat straight back from her forehead, had an upward tilt that gave her a warlike appearance. **1908** *DN* 3.319 **eAL, wGA,** *Head-hank(er)cher*. . . A head-rag. **1912** Green *VA Folk-Speech* 219, *Head-handkerchief*. . . A handkerchief of cotton, of red, blue, green and yellow checks that the negro women used to wear tied around their head. **1928** Peterkin *Scarlet Sister Mary* 23 **SC** [Black], Wid earrings a-danglin an' a head-kerchief makin' em look like a grown 'oman. **1942** Faulkner *Go Down* 70 **MS,** The hand rose . . and touched the back of her headkerchief. **1968** *DARE* (Qu. W3, *A piece of cloth that a woman folds over her head and ties under her chin*) Inf **VA**16, Head handkerchief.

head hog cheese See **hog's head cheese**

head in v phr

1 In railroading: see quot 1945.

1945 Hubbard *Railroad Ave.* 346, *Head in*—Take a sidetrack when meeting an opposing train. **1951** in 1953 Botkin–Harlow *Treas. Railroad Folkl.* 327, When I tell him to head in, he says run around and back in!

2 Fig: To back down or yield in an argument.

1949 (1961) Partridge *Underworld Dict.* 324, *Head in*. . . to withdraw from an argument, to keep—or become—quiet. . . 'From the railroads, where a train "heads in" when it pulls into a side track, off the main line.' **1979** *DARE* File **West,** My grandmother regularly used *to head in* meaning to yield in an argument or confrontation. She would say such things as: "Well, he certainly knew where and when to head in—I was hopping mad, but I didn't get a chance to say anything." Or, "At that time I saw I was wrong and knew I'd have to head in."

3 in phrr *show* (or *tell*) *someone where to head in:* To severely scold or reprimand.

1945 Colcord *Sea Language* 97 **ME, Cape Cod, Long Island,** "I told him where to head in at," i.e., put him in his place. **1966–67** *DARE* (Qu. JJ25, *To show somebody that you're the boss*) Inf **MS**15, Showed him where to head in; (Qu. JJ35b, *When you have lost patience and are just about ready to tell somebody what you think of him*) Inf **OH**15, Tell him where to head in. **1975** Gould *ME Lingo* 128, "I told him where to head in!" means some exceptionally good advice was imparted. **1979** *DARE* File **West,** When he said that, I showed him where he could head in.

heading n Pronc-sp *headen*

1 A pillow or bolster; cloth or other material used to support the head. **Sth, S Midl**

1853 Hammett *Stray Yankee in TX* 92, A bed was prepared . . of blankets and counterpanes, with anything and everything stuck under the end for "heading." **1878** Bishop *Voyage Paper Canoe* 236 **SC,** A roll of homespun for a pillow, which the women called *"heading."* They often said, "Let me give you some heading for your bed." **1903** *DN* 2.316 **seMO,** *Heading*. . . Pillow, bolster, etc. 'If you haven't heading enough I'll get you another pillow.' **1910** *DN* 3.458 **FL, GA,** *Headen*. . . Pillow. **1923** *DN* 5.210 **swMO,** *Headin'*. **1927** *DN* 5.474 **Ozarks,** *Heading*. . . Pillow. "Corncobs is all right in their place, but they shore make a mighty sorry headin'." **1946** *PADS* 6.17 **eNC** (as of 1900–10), *Heading*. . . A pillow.

2 See quot.

1954 *Harder Coll.* **cwTN,** *Heading*—A stack of peanut plants, piled in the field to dry.

headingest adj Cf **-est 1b, head** adj

1952 Brown *NC Folkl.* 1.549 **wNC,** *Headingest. . .* Most unusual or striking.

head in the hat n

A children's game: see quot.

c1974 Jones *Ozark Hill Boy* 6 **AR** (as of c1910), The favorite games were—"Double Cat", "Fox and Hounds", "Anti-over", "Wrap Jack", "Follow the Leader", "Head in the Hat", . . and many other games requiring little or no equipment.

headish adj [*OED* "Obs. rare."]

1908 *DN* 3.319 **eAL, wGA,** *Headish. . .* Headstrong. "He's a little headish."

head joint n

A nonexistent item used as the basis of a practical joke.

1968 *DARE* (Qu. HH14, *Ways of teasing a beginner or inexperienced person—for example, by sending him for a 'left-handed monkey wrench': "Go get me ______."*) Inf **GA**23, A bucket full of head joints—bricklaying.

headkerchief See **head handkerchief**

head knock n, often cap *among Black speakers* Cf **knocker**

See quot 1970.

1946 (1972) Mezzrow-Wolfe *Really Blues* 333 **NYC** [Black], *Head Knock:* God. **1958** Hughes-Bontemps *Negro Folkl.* 484 **NYC,** *Head knock:* The deity. When the head knocks [sic] calls, you got to go. **1970** Major *Dict. Afro-Amer. Slang* 65, *Head Knock:* (1930's-40's) God, the Lord, or Jesus.

head-knocker n

1 See quots.

1965 *DARE* (Qu. BB52, . . *Joking words . . for a dentist*) Inf **MS**60, Head-knocker. **1986** Pederson *LAGS Concordance* (*Policeman;* this question was asked chiefly in urban areas) 1 inf, **Memphis TN,** Head knocker.

2 See **knocker.**

headland n

1 See quot 1896.

1637 in 1894 Watertown MA *Records* 26 Feb 3, There shalbe two Rod of hadland lying next to every mans particular meddow. **1896** *DN* 1.420 **cnNJ,** Such strips at the end of the field, on which the team is turned in ploughing the other sections, are called *headlands.* **1899** (1912) Green *VA Folk-Speech* 219, *Headland. . .* The part of the field close to the fence, ploughed parallel to the fence, and at right-angles to the other furrows; where the plough teams turn; headrow.

2 See quots.

1968 *DARE* (Qu. N27a) Inf **LA**26, Headlands—roads through fields of cane; also called field roads.

headlight n

1 A light-skinned Black person; a **high yellow.**

[**1925** Hunter *Trail Drivers TX* 334, A very black negro is characterized as a "headlight to a snowstorm."] **1934** *AmSp* 9.26 [Prison jargon], *Head light.* A light-skinned negro. **1970** Major *Dict. Afro-Amer. Slang* 65, *Headlight:* a light-complexioned Afro-American girl.

2 A woman's breast. Cf **cat's-head 1**

1960 Wentworth-Flexner *Slang* 249, *Headlights. . .* Prominent, well shaped female breasts. Usu in the admiring "look at those headlights." c1940. **1965-70** *DARE* (Qu. X31, . . *A woman's breasts*) 10 Infs, **scattered,** Headlights; **DE**3, Big headlights; **PA**237, Set of headlights. **1970** Major *Dict. Afro-Amer. Slang* 65, *Headlight(s)* . . any woman's breasts. **1980** Folb *Runnin' Down* 141 **Los Angeles CA** [Black], There are a number of vernacular terms that refer to a woman's breasts as big, tasty, touchable, and formidable—*grapes, apples, . . headlights.*

3 in pl: Eyeglasses.

1942 Berrey-Van den Bark *Amer. Slang* 137.6, Headlights . . *colored spectacles.* **1968** *DARE* (Qu. X23, . . *Joking words . . for eyeglasses*) Infs **VA**13, **WV**3, Headlights.

‡**4** See quot.

1967 *DARE* (Qu. H32, . . *Rolls and pastries*) Inf **NY**28, Headlights, chocolate outside, cream inside.

5 See **headlight oil.**

headlighting vbl n **chiefly TX, nMI** See Map Cf **jacking, shining**

Hunting deer by dazzling them with a car's headlights.

1965-70 *DARE* (Qu. P35b, *Illegal methods of shooting deer*) 27 Infs, **chiefly TX, nMI,** Headlighting; [**AR**55, Using a headlight; **LA**20, With a headlight; **TX**31, Headlight; **OH**58, Headlights; **TX**62, Headlights of a car].

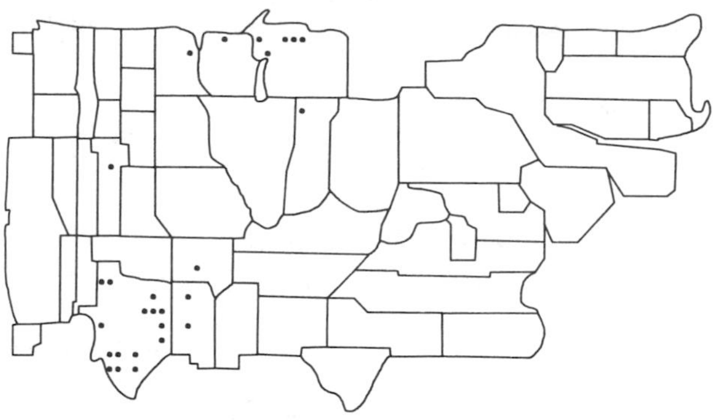

•headlighting (Qu. P35b)

headlight oil n Also *headlight*

See quots.

1887 Crew *Petroleum* 263, An oil with a fire-test of 150° and "water-white" in color, known in the trade as "head-light," is now much in demand. **1911** *Century Dict. Suppl., Headlight oil,* an illuminating oil distilled from petroleum, colorless and of 150° F. fire-test, fit for use in the headlight lamps of locomotives. **1940** *Qrly. Jrl. Speech* 26.264 **swVA,** In Wise County *kerosene* may be called "headlight." **1968** *DARE* (Qu. F45, . . *Fuel that's used in an ordinary lamp*) Inf **DE**3, Headlight oil—I saw a sign over in Jersey that said that.

head line n

=**taw line.**

1966 *DARE* (Qu. EE8, *The line toward which the players roll their marbles before beginning a game, to determine the order of shooting*) Inf **SC**26, Head line.

headlock n Also *headstall* **esp Sth**

A stanchion.

1968-70 *DARE* (Qu. M11, *What . . you put the cow's head through when she stands in the barn*) Infs **FL**1, **GA**39, **MS**21, Headlock; **GA**72, **VA**75, Headstall.

headmark n **chiefly Sth, S Midl** Cf **foot** n **C5b**

A mark of recognition given to a student for being at the head of the class, often in spelling; see quots.

1904 Darrow *Farmington* 47 **PA,** In their efforts to make us study, they resorted to every sort of means—headmarks, presents, praise. **1905** *DN* 3.82 **nwAR,** *Head-mark. . .* Highest mark in a public school class. The holder stands at the head of the class one day and then 'goes foot' to try to work his way up again. 'Wouldn't I like to get a head-mark and go foot.' **1908** *DN* 3.319 **eAL, wGA,** *Head-mark. . .* A reward for staying at the head of a class for a specified length of time. **1946** *PADS* 6.17 **eNC** (as of 1900-10), *Head-mark. . .* A merit mark for being at the head of a class in spelling at the end of the day. **1946** Wilson *Fidelity Folks* 136 **swTN,** We also had headmarks, that is, the one standing at the head at the end of the lesson was given a mark of merit. **1947** Croy *Corn Country* 281 **IA,** *Head-Mark:* At school, children spelled standing up in line. When a scholar missed a word, the one standing next in line had a chance at it. If he spelled it correctly, he got to move up a notch. The pupil standing at the head, when the lesson was over, got a "head-mark." The person who got the most head-marks, during the eight months' term, was the best speller and was given a prize. **1954** *Harder Coll.* **cwTN,** *Head-mark*—A merit-mark for being at the head of a class in spelling at the end of the day. **c1960** *Wilson Coll.* **csKY,** *Headmark*—A merit given to the child standing at the head of the spelling line at the end of the lesson; he got the mark and then went foot to try to work his way up again. Often choice rewards were given for the most headmarks in a given year. **1988** *DARE* File **wNC,** In a public school in Burke Co., I received the prize for winning the most headmarks in a year (1915-16) in the spelling class.

head meat n

=**headcheese 1.**

1949 *AmSp* 24.109 **cSC,** *Head meat. . .* Hog-head cheese, a kind of meat, often stuffed as a sausage, prepared from the head of a hog. **1950** *WELS (Meat from the head and inner organs of an animal cut up and pressed into a mold)* 1 Inf, **swWI,** Head meat. **1965–70** *DARE* (Qu. H43, *Foods made from parts of the head and inner organs of an animal*) Infs **IL**63, **IN**23, **OH**66, 70, 89, **PA**136, 143, 186, **MO**21, Head meat. **1971** Wood *Vocab. Change* 44 **Sth,** Meat from the hog's head and jowls . . pressed into a loaf. . . Among the volunteered words *head meat* comes from the largest number of states. *Ibid* 313, [91 infs from AL, AR, GA, OK, and TN offered the term *head meat.*] **1973** Allen *LAUM* 1.288 **Upper MW** (as of c1950), *Head cheese. . .* Several terms . . appear on the checklist . . as voluntary write-ins of the respondents. Most common is *head-meat,* with Midland orientation.

head mogul See **high mogul**

head nor hair (or heels, hide, tail) See **head** n **D1**

head of prep [Aphet form of *ahead of*] See Intro "Language Changes" I.7

1966–70 *DARE* (Qu. MM9, . . *"We stood in line and John was ______ me."*) Infs **MA**128, **WA**3, Head of.

head of the herd n Also *head of the flock* *euphem*

A bull.

1931–33 *LANE Worksheets* **cMA,** Head of the herd . . euphem for bull. **1950** *WELS (Words used for bull)* 5 Infs, **WI,** Head of the herd. **1966–70** *DARE* (Qu. K22, *Words used for a bull*) Infs **VA**43, **WA**18, Head of the herd; **WA**18, Head of the flock; (Qu. K23, *Words used by women or in mixed company for a bull*) Inf **MA**58, Head of the herd. **1973** Allen *LAUM* 1.244 **SD** (as of c1950), *Bull. . .* head of the herd. [1 inf]

head on n Cf **king**

A children's game; see quot.

1901 *DN* 2.141 **neNY,** *Head on. . .* The name of a game like king . . played on ice.

head over ears adv phr Also *(over) head and ears*

Deeply or completely.

1822 in 1917 Adams *Writings J.Q. Adams* 7.284 **DC,** George is plunged head over ears in the *Fortunes of Nigel.* **1824** Irving *Hist. NY* 107, Nor did they stop until they had buried themselves, head and ears, in the marshes on the other side. **1840** Haliburton *Clockmaker* (3d ser) 23, I felt I was on the edge of a wharf, and only one step more was over head and ears chewallop in the water. **1843** (1916) Hall *New Purchase* 390 **IN,** Although John was never *over head and ears* in love, he yet was always *falling* into it. **1846** (1927) Hone *Diary* 2.777 **NY,** I am head over ears in the election. **1954** *Harder Coll.* **cwTN,** *Head 'n' ears*—completely. To cover up head 'n' ears. Occasional.

head over teakettle adv phr Also *head over (tin) kettle, ~ tin-cup(s)* Cf **ass-over-teakettle**

Head over heels.

1940 Richter *Trees* 25 **OH,** Some turned head over tincup till it made a body dizzy to watch. **1960** Rockwell *Adventures* 127, I slipped on a patch of ice and tumbled down head over tin kettle. **1968** Abbey *Desert Solitaire* 33 **seUT,** To my amazement the stone flies true (as if guided by a Higher Power) and knocks the cottontail head over tincups. **1974** *AmSp* 49.62 **swME** (as of c1900), *Head over kittle. . .* Head over heels—"He fell head over kittle." **1979** *NYT Article Letters* **Tunbridge VT,** A common expression here for "head over heels" is "head over tea kettle."

headpiece n

1 The head; fig: understanding or intellect.

1671 in 1896 *Some Corresp. of the New Engl. Co.* 42 **seMA,** I have used my best skill & hedpes to discover anything that might tend to the hurt of o[u]r nation. **1806** (1970) Webster *Compendious Dict.* 140, *Head-piece . .* understanding. **1881** Twain *Prince & Pauper* 116, I believe thee, whether thy small head-piece be sound or cracked, my boy. **1914** Furman *Sight* 45 **KY,** I . . had such faculty in my head-piece that I were able to manage and contrive and bring to pass. **1928** *AmSp* 3.408, "Headpiece" may refer both to the head and one's mental ability. **1967** *DARE* (Qu. X28, *Joking words . . for a person's head*) Inf **MI**67, Head-piece.

2 A covering for the head, esp a hat or kerchief. *old-fash*

1910 Hart *Vigilante Girl* 378 **nCA,** The few men who in their hurry had forgotten to remove their headpieces blushed, took them off, looked around uneasily, and finally hung them on the floor. **1967–69** *DARE* (Qu. W3, *A piece of cloth that a woman folds over her head and ties under her chin*) Infs **KY**24, **LA**8, **MI**93, **OR**13, **TX**40, Headpiece; (Qu. W2, . . *A cloth bonnet*) Inf **AL**26, Headpiece; not in use. [5 of 6 Infs old]

3 A hairpiece. *old-fash*

1965–70 *DARE* (Qu. X1a, . . *False hair, worn by men*) 9 Infs, **scattered,** Headpiece; (Qu. X1b, . . *By women*) Infs **LA**20, **NJ**3, 18, **NY**65, **OH**4, **VA**60, Headpiece. [12 of 14 Infs old]

head pudding n Also *hog's head pudding* Cf **pudding**

=**headcheese 1.**

1966 Dakin *Dial. Vocab. Ohio R. Valley* 2.339, *Souse. . .* A number of miscellaneous terms . . appear scattered throughout the Valley. Among them are: *head sausage . . (hog's) head pudding.* **1968** *DARE* (Qu. H43, *Foods made from parts of the head and inner organs of an animal*) Inf **OH**81, Head pudding. **1972** *Press* (Pittsburgh PA) 15 Oct 10/1, "Scrapple" in this state becomes "head pudding" in southern Ohio and Kentucky.

head rag n **chiefly Sth, S Midl** See Map Cf **do-rag**

=**headcloth.**

1908 *DN* 3.319 **eAL, wGA,** *Head-rag. . .* A kerchief, a cloth (usually brilliantly colored) formerly widely used by negro women for covering the head. **1929** Sale *Tree Named John* 5 **MS,** Her [=a Black woman's] head, always covered with a "haid-rag" of white cloth or a bright colored bandanna worn like a turban, was well poised on her shoulders. **1936** (1951) Faulkner *Absalom* 215 **MS,** The old woman who must be more than seventy now . . had no white hair under that headrag. **1942** Hurston *Dust Tracks* 128 **FL** [Black], She . . shook her head so vigorously that her head rag wagged. **1960** Williams *Walk Egypt* 286 **GA,** She [=a Black woman] leaped to put on an old hat over a clean head-rag. **1965–70** *DARE* (Qu. W3, *A piece of cloth that a woman folds over her head and ties under her chin*) 25 Infs, **chiefly Sth, S Midl,** Head rag; (Qu. W2, . . *A cloth bonnet worn by women for protection from the sun*) Inf **OK**57, Head rag. [7 of 25 total Infs Black] **1966** *Good Old Days* 2.10.13 **MD** (as of c1910), A quick look . . revealed [the Gypsy] men and women dressed almost alike. Red polka-dot shirts and head rags, and gold ear rings. **1968** *DARE* FW Addit **TN**27, *Headrag* = scarf. **1982** Walker *Color Purple* 41 **GA** [Black], A new dress won't help none with my notty [sic] head and dusty headrag.

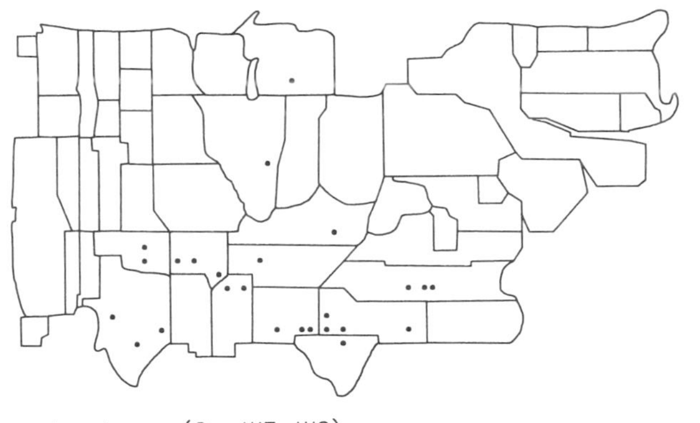

•head rag (Qq. W3, W2)

headrest n Also *headrest piece* Cf **tidy**

An antimacassar.

1967–69 *DARE* (Qu. E10, *Knitted or crocheted pieces placed on the back and arms of a chair for decoration and cleanliness*) Infs **IL**68, **LA**11, **MD**28, **MO**5, 14, 15, Headrests; **CA**134, Headrest pieces.

head rise n [*head* a mass of water in motion] Cf **headwater**

A flash flood.

1944 Wellman *Bowl* 99 **KS,** The Cimarron was a river of head rises, and a head rise differs markedly from even the fiercest flood of an ordinary stream. The sluggish rivulet, which was the Cimarron ordinarily, might be creeping among its sand bars on the floorlike level of orange sand, when a sudden incredible roar would come, and down the bed would sweep insanely a solid, tossing wall of water—ten feet high or more from foot of wave to lip, and level from bank to bank, carrying on its crest foam and debris almost with express-train speed, and rushing by with a violence that rocked the shores. **1966–68** *DARE* (Qu. B21, *A sudden rush of water coming from heavy rain*) Infs **OK**21, **TX**51, Head rise.

headrock n Cf **graverock**

1954 *Harder Coll.* **cwTN,** *Head rock*—Tombstone. Many graves are still marked with sand rocks.

head sausage n

=**headcheese 1.**

1950 *WELS (Kinds of sausage)* 1 Inf, **WI,** Head sausage. **1966** Dakin *Dial. Vocab. Ohio R. Valley* 2.339, *Souse*... A number of miscellaneous terms.. appear scattered throughout the Valley. Among them.. *head sausage.* **1967–69** *DARE* (Qu. H43, *Foods made from parts of the head and inner organs of an animal*) Infs **IL**13, **MO**21, **WI**53, Head sausage; **TX**62, Head sausage—boil it, season with salt and pepper, stuff it into entrails, boil it again. **1967** Faries *Word Geog. MO* 124, A list of terms [for *headcheese*] suggested by informants but occurring only occasionally.. *head souse*.. *head sausage.* **1973** Allen *LAUM* 1.289 **ND** (as of c1950), Head sausage. [1 inf]

heads cheese See **headcheese 1**

headset adj

Obstinate, headstrong.

1986 Pederson *LAGS Concordance,* 1 inf, **cwTN,** You're the most head-set person that God-Almighty ever tangled a gut in.

headshrinker n

A **woodpecker.**

1970 *DARE* (Qu. Q18, *Joking names.. for woodpeckers*) Inf **PA**247, Headshrinkers.

head souse n Cf **souse**

=**headcheese 1.**

1704 (1935) Knight *Jrl.* 35 **CT,** My guide said it smelt strong of head sause [sic]. **1956** Ker *Vocab. W. TX* 275, *Head souse.* [1 inf] **1967** Faries *Word Geog. MO* 124, Terms [for *headcheese*] suggested by informants.. *head souse.* **1968–70** *DARE* (Qu. H43, *Foods made from parts of the head and inner organs of an animal*) Infs **IL**94, **IN**27, **KY**62, 85, Head souse. **1982** Ginns *Snowbird Gravy* 36 **nwNC,** They used all the parts of the hog—all of them. Out of the head they made head-souse, which was cooked, and you'd put vinegar over it and let it set for several days.

head-splitter See **head-buster**

head square n

=**headcloth.**

1950 *WELS (A square cloth that women fold and tie over their heads)* 1 Inf, **cwWI,** Head square.

headstall See **headlock**

head stick n

A board set up at the head of a grave.

c1938 in 1970 Hyatt *Hoodoo* 2.1292 **Charleston SC,** Anybody you know buried, you dig 'em up... Den you come away from dere an' you bring de *head stick* and de *foot stick* [Hyatt: wooden footboard of grave]... You put de *head stick*.. to de right,.. and de *foot stick* to de left.

head-swimming n Cf **swimmy-headed**

See quots.

1917 *DN* 4.413 **wNC,** *Head-swimmin'*... Vertigo. **1927** *AmSp* 2.356 **WV,** *Head-swimming*.. dizziness. "I have had head-swimming all week."

head to head See **head and head**

head up adv phr, adj phr Also *with one's head up* Cf **tail**

Often in combs; Fig: in a lively, impetuous, or determined manner; eager, cocky.

1854 in 1953 Lincoln *Coll. Wks.* 2.227 **IL,** Harris will be with you, head up and tail up, for Nebraska. You must have some one to make an anti-Nebraska speech. **1859** (1968) Bartlett *Americanisms* 524, Head and tail up, like chicken-cocks in laying-time. **1912** *DN* 3.578 **wIN,** *Head up and tail over the dashboard*... In a lively, spirited manner. "Ever since election day he has been going around with his head up and tail over the dashboard [*DARE* Ed: i.e., of a horsedrawn carriage]." **1923** *DN* 5.239 **swWI,** *Head up and tail a-rising*... With great rapidity and temper. (Transferred from a steer or a bull.) "And there he come, head up an' tail a-risin'!" **1959** *VT Hist.* new ser 27.141, *Go head up*... To go rapidly... *Go head up and tail a-risin'*... Go with some sprightliness.

headwater n Cf **head rise**

Floodwater; see quots.

1968–69 *DARE* (Qu. B27, *A sudden rush of water coming from heavy rain*) Inf **IN**35, Headwater; **KY**20, Headwater—water coming down a swollen branch or creek; (Qu. C9, *Water from a river that comes up and covers low land when the river is high*) Inf **IN**35, Headwater. **1970** *DARE* Tape **TN**44, Headwater is water that's comin' offa the mountains and it can't get to the river fast enough so it spreads out an' floods an area.

head wrap n

=**headcloth.**

1896 *Godey's Lady's Book* Feb 202/1, Fastening.. a sombre head-wrap over her soft black hair, she rustled quickly through the hall. **1967** *DARE* (Qu. W3, *A piece of cloth that a woman folds over her head and ties under her chin*) Inf **TX**35, Head wrap.

heah See **here A1**

heahoftah See **hereafter**

heaht See **heart** n[1]

heal See **heel** v[1]

heal-all n

1 A **fringed orchid** (here: *Habenaria orbiculata*).

1807 (1969) Pursh *Jrl. Bot. Excursion* 28 **nePA,** Orchis bifolia... This plant is called here Allheal or Healall, & used by the people in fresh wounds, where it is found the most healing thing they would wish to have. **1830** Rafinesque *Med. Flora* 2.248, *O[rchis] orbiculata* and *macrophylla,* vulnerary leaves, called *Healall.* **1900** Lyons *Plant Names* 181, *H[abenaria] orbiculata*.. called Heal-all. **1950** Correll *Native Orchids* 93, Heal-all... Perhaps it is the most "timid" of our Habenarias. **1976** Bailey–Bailey *Hortus Third* 534, *Heal-all*... Early summer—early autumn.

2 =**self-heal.**

1822 Eaton *Botany* 410, *Prunella*... *pensylvanica* [sic]... Heal-all, self-heal. **1832** MA Hist. Soc. *Coll.* 2d ser 9.154 **cwVT,** Prunella pennsylvanica, Heal-all. **1837** Darlington *Flora Cestrica* 352, *P[runella] vulgaris*... Heal-all... Its reputation, as a medicinal plant, is quite obsolete. **1899** Bergen *Animal Lore* 112 **cnOH,** Heal-all (*Brunella* [sic] *vulgaris*) is said to be useful as a remedy for diarrhœa and dysentery. **1931** Harned *Wild Flowers Alleghanies* 426, It was also used in the healing of wounds of all kinds, whence the name "Heal-all" doubtless originated. **1966–67** *DARE* Wildfl QR Pl.187 Inf **SC**41, Heal-all; **WA**10, Heal-all, although I don't know that anybody calls it by that name. Also self-heal. **1967–69** *DARE* (Qu. S26a,.. *Wildflowers*) Inf **MA**5, Heal-all; (Qu. S26d,.. *Wildflowers.. in meadows*) Inf **NJ**58, Self-heal or heal-all (more common). **1973** Hitchcock–Cronquist *Flora Pacific NW* 406.

3 =**figwort 1,** esp *Scrophularia marilandica.*

1830 Rafinesque *Med. Flora* 2.262, *Scrophularia*... *Heal-all*... Deemed good for all kind [sic] of sores in men and cattle, cures the scab of dogs and swine. **1876** Hobbs *Bot. Hdbk.* 51, Healall, Prunella vulgaris... Scrophularia Marilandica... Collinsonia Canadensis. **1906** Rydberg *Flora CO* 305, *Scrophularia*... Fig-wort, Heal-all. **1914** Georgia *Manual Weeds* 380, Heal-all... The knotted roots of this plant have long been reputed a cure.. and are salable in the drug-market. **1930** OK Univ. Biol. Surv. *Pub.* 2.80, *Scrophularia marilandica*... Heal-all. **1959** Carleton *Index Herb. Plants* 59, *Heal all:* Clintonia borealis; Collinsonia canadensis; Prunella vulgaris (P. incisa); Scrophularia (v); Sedum rhodiola (Rhodiola rosea).

4 =**horse balm.**

1828 Rafinesque *Med. Flora* 1.111, *Collinsonia canadensis*... *Vulgar Names*.. Heal-all. *Ibid* 113, It is one of the plants called *Heal-all,* in the United States, because they cure sores and wounds. **1847** Griffith *Med. Botany* 514, It [=*Collinsonia*].. is taken in the form of an infusion for headache, colic, indigestion, &c., and hence has received the common name of Heal-all. **1900** Lyons *Plant Names* 111, *C[ollinsonia] Canadensis*... Heal-all... *Root* diuretic, diaphoretic, expectorant. *Leaves* vulnerary. **1959** [see **3** above]. **1971** Krochmal *Appalachia Med. Plants* 100, Heal-all... Roots are used as a sedative and antispasmodic, diuretic, astringent, and tonic.

5 A **bead lily** (here: *Clintonia borealis*).

1900 Lyons *Plant Names* 108, *C[lintonia] borealis*... Heal-all. **1940** Clute *Amer. Plant Names* 11, *C. borealis*... Heal-all. **1959** [see **3** above].

6 =roseroot. [*OED* 1853 →]

1889 *Century Dict.* 2753, *Heal-all*. . . A plant supposed to possess great healing virtues, especially *Prunella vulgaris*. . . Among the other plants sometimes called by this name are *Collinsonia Canadensis*, . . *Rhodiola rosea*, . . and *Scrophularia nodosa*. **1900** Lyons *Plant Names* 340, *S[edum] roseum* [sic]. . . Heal-all. **1940** Clute *Amer. Plant Names* 230, *Sedum roseum* [sic]. Heal-all. **1959** [see **3** above].

healing balsam n

=Fraser fir.

1897 Sudworth *Arborescent Flora* 50, *Abies fraseri*. . . *Common names*. . . Healing Balsam.

healing herb n

1 =comfrey.

c1873 in 1976 Miller *Shaker Herbs* 160, *Symphytum officinale*. . . Healing Herb. . . Useful in diarrhea, dysentery, coughs, leucorrhea, and female debility. **1876** Hobbs *Bot. Hdbk.* 51, Healing herb, Comfrey, Symphytum officinalis [sic]. **1903** Small *Flora SE U.S.* 1001, *Comfrey*. Healing-herb. **1930** Sievers *Amer. Med. Plants* 24, Healing herb. . . Dug in autumn or in early spring. **1974** (1977) Coon *Useful Plants* 80, Healing herb. . . Long known as having many medicinal values.

2 A **plantain** (here: *Plantago media*).

1900 Lyons *Plant Names* 295, *P. media*. . . Healing-herb. **1940** Clute *Amer. Plant Names* 110, *P. media*. . . Healing-herb. **1959** Carleton *Index Herb. Plants* 59, *Healing-herb:* Plantago media; Symphytum oficinale [sic].

healing tape n

1970 *DARE* (QR, near Qu. BB50c) Inf **FL**49, Band-Aids are called healing tape.

heal stick n

A nonexistent item used as the basis of a practical joke.

1968 *DARE* (Qu. HH14, *Ways of teasing a beginner or inexperienced person—for example, by sending him for a 'left-handed monkey wrench': "Go get me ______.'"*) Inf **NY**48, A heal stick.

healt See **hold** v **A2a**

healy-healy-over exclam [Prob var of **haily-over**]

=Antony-over B.

1950 *WELS (In the game . . [in which you throw a ball over a building] what do you shout when you throw the ball?)* 1 Inf, **WI**, Healy-healy-over.

he-animal See **he** n **1**

heap n

1 A large number, great deal. **chiefly Sth, S Midl**

1810 (1912) Bell *Journey to OH* 39 **MA**, There is another family here, with several little children—They say there has been a *heap* of people moving this fall. **1818** in 1824 Knight *Letters* 107 **KY**, Some words are used, even by genteel people . . in a new sense; and . . pronounced very uncouthly, as . . heap of times. **1827** (1939) Sherwood *Gaz. GA* 139, *Whole heap*, for many, several, much, large congregation. **1836** in 1956 Eliason *Tarheel Talk* 276 **NC**, I would not be in their places for a heap. **1902** *DN* 2.236 **sIL**. **1903** *DN* 2.316 **seMO**, *Heap*. . . 'There were a heap of people at the fair on Thursday.' **1903** *DN* 2.316 **seMO**. **1905** *DN* 3.11 **cCT**. **1908** *DN* 3.319 **eAL**, **wGA**. **1943** *LANE* Map 416 *(A lot of fun)*, The map shows the expressions *a lot of fun, lots ~, loads ~, a heap ~, heaps ~* [etc]. [*Heaps* is scattered throughout **NEng**, esp **nNEng**; *a heap* occurs much less freq.] **1963** Owens *Look to River* 42 **TX**, It took him a heap o' years to learn all he knows—a heap o' years and a heap o' wandering. **1965** *DARE* File **MS**, *Heap*—a great quantity or a lot of something. Common. **1966** *DARE* Tape **GA**1, A heap of folks call it breakin' corn. **1979** *AmSp* 54.98 **swME** (as of 1899–1910), *Heap*. . . (Large amount, great deal) "She makes a heap of him."

2 also *hay heap:* A haystack, esp a small or loose one; a sheaf; a bundle or pile of sheaves. **esp nAppalachians, CT** See Map

1931 *AmSp* 7.19 **swPA**, *Hay heaps*. Hay cocks. **1939** *LANE* Map 104 *(Hay stack; cock)*, 1 inf, **swCT**, 40 to 60 heaps make a load; 1 inf, **cwCT**, I use *heap*, my uncle says *cock;* 1 inf, **cwCT**, *Cocks* are shaped, *heaps* are just flung together; 1 inf, **cnCT**, Stack, 5 to 8 ton; heap, 3 or 4 forkful; 1 inf, **nwCT**, *Tumble*, a loose heap; 1 inf, **nNH**, *Heap* more common than *bunch* or *tumble*. **1949** Kurath *Word Geog.* 54, Other terms for the haycock, more local in character, are: *heap* (1) in parts of New England and (2) in the Pennsylvania German area (cf. Pennsylvania German *Haufe*). **1965–70** *DARE* (Qu. L12, . . *The small piles of hay standing in the field*) 11 Infs, **chiefly sPA, nMD**, Heaps; **MD**20, **PA**3, 6, Hay heaps; **CT**6, **NJ**3, Heaps of hay; **ME**5, Heap of hay; (Qu. L14, *A large pile of hay stored outdoors*) Inf **VA**49, Heap of hay; (Qu. L30a, *When grain is cut it is . . tied up in ______*) Inf **CT**17, Heaps; (Qu. L30b, . . *These sheaves . . are set together in piles called ______*) Infs **GA**77, **NJ**3, Heaps. **1971** Wood *Vocab. Change* 43 **Sth**, Hay, the small piles in the field. . . *heaps* [is given by 43 infs]. **1973** Allen *LAUM* 1.186 **IA** (as of c1950), *Haycock* (in the field). . . heap. [1 inf] **1986** Pederson *LAGS Concordance* **Gulf Region** *(Cock)* 15 infs, Heap(s); 1 inf, Heaps of hay; 1 inf, Heaps or shocks; 1 inf, Wind heaps; *(Shock)* 7 infs, Heap(s); 1 inf, Stalk heap; *(Sheaf)* 3 infs, Heap(s); *(Haystack)* 1 inf, Heap.

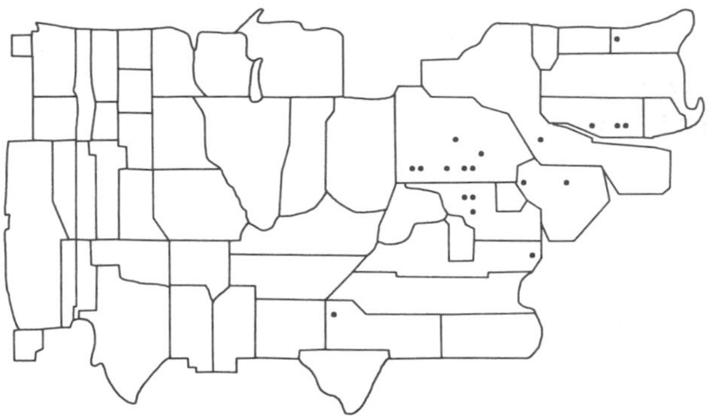

•heap n 2 + varr (Qq. L12, L14, L30a, b)

3 in adv constrs: Very much; a lot; see below.

a usu as *a heap* or *heaps:* See quots. **chiefly Sth, S Midl**

1848 in 1893 Farmer–Henley *Slang* 3.289/2, He pronounced himself a heap better. **1871** Eggleston *Hoosier Schoolmaster* 164 **sIN**, "That air woman," said the weak-eyed girl, "used to holler a heap." **1884** *Anglia* 7.261 **Sth, S Midl** [Black], *To be heap better'n* = to be much better than. **1887** (1967) Harris *Free Joe* 129 **GA**, I'd a heap druther see you fillin' them slays an' a-fixin' up for to weave your pappy some shirts. **1889** *MLN* 4.206 **TN**, I am a heap better today. **1893** Shands *MS Speech* 36, I like him a heap. **1906** *DN* 3.140 **nwAR**, *Heap(s)*. . . Great deal, much. . . "I like him heaps better than I did." **1933** Rawlings *South Moon* 17 **nFL**, A heap neater'n I figgered you'd git it! **1939** *Hall Coll.* **ceTN**, I'd say nigher two hundred would come a heap closer. **1946** *PADS* 6.17 **eNC** (as of 1900–10), *Heap*. . . Much; very much. "He's a heap larger than I am." "I'd a heap ruther not go." **1963** Owens *Look to River* 11 **TX**, It's a heap better here'n in the bottoms. **1968** *DARE* Tape **VA**27, You could cross over these here mountains and make it a heap nearter [sic] to walk or ride a-horseback.

b in phr *a heap sight:* See quots. **chiefly S Midl**

1871 Eggleston *Hoosier Schoolmaster* 15 **sIN**, Pluck . . goes for a heap sight more'n sinnoo with boys. **1895** *DN* 1.372 **eTN**, *Heap sight:* good deal or much. "I'd a heap sight rather stay than go." **1909** *DN* 3.398 **nwAR**, Small pox is a heap sight worse than measles. **1918** *DN* 5.20 **NC**, *Heap sight more*. **1942** McAtee *Dial. Grant Co. IN* 33 (as of 1890s), *Heap sight* . . a good deal or by a good deal, "I'd a' heap sight ruther go than stay". **c1960** *Wilson Coll.* **csKY**, *Heap sight*—sort of adverbial idea. Much. "I'd a heap sight rather go than stay here."

4 in adv phr *all of a heap* and varr:

a Into a state of amazement or stupefaction—usu in phr *strike (one) all of a heap*. Cf **all of a**

1756 in 1968 Laurens *Papers* 2.269 **Charleston SC**, The advice of War Struck our planters all of a heap. **1790** (1927) Maclay *Jrl.* 173 **PA**, I feel so struck of an heap, I can make no remark on the matter. **1836** (1838) Haliburton *Clockmaker* (1st ser) 183 **NEng**, I thought he'd a fainted too, he was so struck up all of a heap. **1844** Stephens *High Life in NY* 1.250 **CT**, He felt all struck up of a heap. **1914** *DN* 4.80 **ME, nNH**, When they heerd the ole man was dead, they was *struck all in a heap*. **1950** (1965) Richter *Town* 47 **OH**, Now her own sister, Genny, held back as if struck all of a heap to think she would soon be kin to the Morrisons. **1968** *DARE* (QR p 266) Inf **WI**29, That just hit me all of a heap, kind of took my breath away.

b Suddenly.

1981 De Vries *Sauce* 27 **IN**, It just came to me, all of a heap, as Mommy used to say.

heap v, hence ppl adj *heaped* [**heap** n **2**] Also *heap up*

To arrange (hay) into stacks or piles.

1939 *LANE* Map 104, 1 inf, **swCT,** Some say *cock* and *cocked up,* but it's *heap* and *heaped up* round here; 1 inf, **swCT,** If it's heaped it's ready to pitch; 2 infs, **cwCT,** Heap up. **1966–68** *DARE* (Qu. L11, *What do you do to hay in the field after it's cut?*) Infs **CT**6, 17, Heap it; **ME**5, Heap it up and put hay caps on.

heaped See **heap** v

heap of bones n Also *bone heap*

1968–69 *DARE* (Qu. K44, *A bony or poor-looking horse*) Infs **NJ**10, 25, **PA**116, 193, Heap of bones; **PA**116, Bone heap; (Qu. K15, *A thin, bony, or poor-looking cow*) Inf **NJ**25, Heap of bones.

heap row n **esp Sth**

A windrow; a line along which something is piled; see quots.

a1857 in 1969 Turner *Cotton Planter's Manual* 90 **ceAL,** The manure is hauled out on the land in carts. . . A row is selected, fifteen feet from the fence or beginning. This is the heap row. Fifteen feet from the end of this row, the first heap, or half the load is deposited; it is raked out by removing the hind gate of the body. **1949** *AmSp* 24.109 **cSC, seGA,** *Heap row*. . . Windrow. **1968** *DARE* (Qu. L11, *What do you do to hay in the field after it's cut?*) Inf **GA**33, Roll it up into heap rows. **1981** Pederson *LAGS Basic Materials,* 1 inf, **cwMS,** Heap row—a long pile of fodder tied in bundles; 1 inf, **cnLA,** Heap row—where fodder lay in the field; [2 infs, **neAL,** Heap row—a hay cock.]

heaps See **heap** n **3a**

heap sight, a See **heap** n **3b**

heap up See **heap** v

hear v

A Pronc and gram varr.

1 pres: usu |hiə(r), hɪə(r)|; also:

a |hjɪə(r), hjɝ, hjɛə(r)| (cf Pronc Intro 3.I.1.a, 3.I.23); pronc-spp *hyeah, hy(e)ar, hyere.* **chiefly Sth, S Midl**

1875 *Scribner's Mth.* 10.240 **GA,** Don't you hyar / Somebody holl'in'? **1893** Owen *Voodoo Tales* 178 **MO** [Black], Do yo' hyeah me? **1898** *Congregationalist & Herald* 13 Oct 484/1, I kin hyeah it. **1923** *DN* 5.212 **swMO,** I'm keen t' hyear how th' 'lection went. **1931** Hannum *Thursday April* 8 **wNC,** Efn yo're sot on eatin' yore life out over one puny man, then I won't have nary bit more truck with you, hyere? **1941** *AmSp* 16.4 **eTX** [Black], *Hear* . . [hjɛə]. **1942** Hall *Smoky Mt. Speech* 16 **eTN, wNC,** The vowel in *hear* . . is often preceded by a palatal glide, and such variations as . . [hjɪɚ], [hjɛɚ], [hjɝ] . . are current. **1968–70** *DARE* (Qu. NN5, *Other ways of saying 'Do you understand?': "You take hold of it this way, ———?"*) Infs **SC**59, 65, [hjɪə].

b pronc-spp *year, yeddy, yerre, yerry.* [Cf *EDD year, yer(r)* (at *hear* v. I. 1. (8), (9), (10)) and *DJE yerry*] *chiefly Gullah*

1853 Simms *Sword & Distaff* 446 **SC** [Black], Yerry wha' I say, and feel youse'f 'strong 'fore de time for de fight come on. **1887** [see **A2d** below]. **1908** *S. Atl. Qrly.* 7.341 **sSC coast** [Gullah], Yez yerre yondah senkah yerre yuh. [=Ears hear yonder same as they hear here.] **1922** Gonzales *Black Border* 339 **sSC, GA coast** [Gullah glossary], *Yeddy, yerry*—hear, hears. **1930** Woofter *Black Yeomanry* 48 **seSC** [Gullah], 'E yeddy Buh Rahbit duh come wid de cyaat. [=He hears Brother Rabbit coming with the cart.]

2 past, past pple: usu |hɝd, hɜd|; also:

a |hiə(r)d|; pronc-spp *heer(e)d, heared.*

1789 Webster *Dissertations Engl. Lang.* 126, In the fashionable world, *heard* is pronounced *herd* or *hurd.* This was almost unknown in America till the commencement of the late war. *Ibid* 128, Analogy requires that we should retain our former practice; for we may as well change *feared* . . into *ferd* . . as to change *heard* into *herd.* **1815** Humphreys *Yankey in England* 105, *Heerd,* heard. **1836** (1955) *Crockett Almanacks* 54 **wTN,** The feller . . was never heered on arterwards. **1884** *Anglia* 7.270 **Sth, S Midl** [Black], *I done heered* = I have heard. **1893** *DN* 1.277 **wCT,** *Heared* . . [hiɚd]. **1902** *DN* 2.236 **sIL,** [hiɚd]. **1906** *DN* 3.119 **sIN,** I ain't heerd about it yet. **1914** *DN* 4.74 **ME, nNH,** *Heerd.* Heard. **1923** *DN* 5.210 **swMO,** *Heerd*. . . Heard. **1927** *AmSp* 3.3 **Ozarks,** [Past and past pple of *hear:*] Heerd. **1962** *Mt. Life* 38.1.17 **Appalachians,** The past and past participle of . . *hear* [become] *heared.* **1967–68** *DARE* Tape **AR**43, I know some of you [hiɚd] that answer; **LA**7 [Black], And he had nevah [hiəd] that name; **VA**9, And Mama said they [hiɚd] a great roar. **1970** *DARE* File **ceTX,** [hiɚd]—common pronc. **1975** Allen *LAUM* 2.20 **NE, SD** (as of c1950), *Heared* /hird/. [3 infs]

b |hiərn, h(j)ɝn|; pronc-spp *hearn, heern, hyearn.* [Cf *EDD heern* (at *hear* v. I. 3. (11))] **chiefly Sth, S Midl**

1795 Dearborn *Columbian Grammar* 136, *List of Improprieties*. . . *Hearn* for Heard. **1840** (1847) Longstreet *GA Scenes* 192, I've always hearn it was wonderful in hives and measly ailments. **1843** (1916) Hall *New Purchase* 119 **sIN,** Neighbour Bushwack . . would like to hear if any body . . has heern or seed a stray critter of hissin. **1893** Shands *MS Speech* 36, *Hearn*. . . Illiterate white for *heard.* **1899** (1912) Green *VA Folk-Speech* 220, *Hearn*. . . For *heard.* **1902** *DN* 2.236 **sIL,** [hiɚn, hɝn]. **1923** *DN* 5.210 **swMO,** *Hyearn*. . . Heard. **1927** *AmSp* 3.3 **Ozarks,** [Past and past pple of *hear:*] Heern. **1952** Brown *NC Folkl.* 1.553, *Hyearn* [hjɝn]. . . Past tense and past participle of *hear.*—General. **1959** *VT Hist.* new ser 27.141, Heard [hɝn] tell. . . Occasional. Rural areas. **1989** Pederson *LAGS Tech. Index* 48–9 **Gulf Region,** [Pronunciations of the past participle of *hear* include those of the type [hɛən, hɪrn, h(j)ɪən].]

c |hjɝd, hjiə(r)d| and varr; pronc-spp *hyeahd, hyear(e)d, hyurd.* Cf Pronc Intro 3.I.1.a, 3.I.16, 3.I.23 **Sth, S Midl, esp Appalachians**

1886 *S. Bivouac* 4.348 **sAppalachians,** He'd never tuck no pay fer nothin' ter eat in his life, an' he'd hyeard his father say he'd never tuck none. **1893** Shands *MS Speech* 36, [hjiəd]. . . Negro and illiterate white for heard. **1923** *DN* 5.211 **swMO,** *Hyeard*. . . Heard. **1929** Sale *Tree Named John* 52 **MS,** Ain'chu hyeahd 'nough 'bout him? **1944** *PADS* 2.29 **eKY, nwNC,** *Heard* [hjɪrd, hjɛrd]. . . Common. **1952** Brown *NC Folkl.* 1.553, *Hyeard* [hjɝd]. . . *Heard.*—General. **1956** Settle *Beulah Land* 110 **WV** (as of 1754–74), Y'ain't niver seed nuthin or hyeared nuthin. **c1960** *Wilson Coll.* **csKY,** *Heard* /hjɛrd/ or /hjird/ is still common among people of all ages. **1969** *DARE* Tape **GA**51, I've [hjɛɚd] people say they knowed their way to the swamp. **1976** Garber *Mountain-ese* 45 **Appalachians,** I hyurd the sound uv a gunshot. **1989** Pederson *LAGS Tech. Index* 48 **Gulf Region,** [Pronunciations of the past of *hear* include those of the type [hjɪəd, hjɪrd, hjɝd]. *Ibid* 49, [Pronunciations of the past participle of *hear* include those of the type [hjɪəd, hjɪr(ɨ)d, hjɜəd, hjɛrd, hjɝd].]

d pronc-spp *yeard(y), year, yerre.* [Cf *EDD yeard, yerd, yih'n* and varr (at *hear* v. I. 2, 3)] **chiefly S Atl** *esp freq among Black speakers*

1883 (1971) Harris *Nights with Remus* 99 **eGA** [Black], De news you bring, I yeard las' year. **1887** (1967) Harris *Free Joe* 10 **cGA** [Black], All of a sudden I year sumpin at de do'—scratch, scratch. I tuck'n tu'n [=took and turned] de meat over, en make out I aint year it [=I hadn't heard it]. **1892** (1969) Christensen *Afro-Amer. Folk Lore* 4 **eSC** [Black], But I was gwine to tell you 'bout my ol' gran'daddy. I ofting yeardy him tell how 'e was bring ober from Arfrica in a ship when 'e was a boy. **1908** *S. Atl. Qrly.* 7.340 **sSC coast** [Gullah], Me yerre um. [=I heard him/them.] **1966** *DARE* FW Addit **AR**43, [Tape recording of 1958:] You yeard me sing that.

B Senses.

1 with *to:* To consent to; to heed, listen to—usu in neg constrs. [Scots, Engl dial] *somewhat old-fash*

1798 (1922) Manning *Key of Libberty* 53 **MA,** But not being heard to . . some countyes ware so follish as to stop the Corts of Justis by force. **1833** in 1918 *MD Hist. Mag.* 13.379 **cCT,** I made a move to depart—but they would not hear to that. **1869** Stowe *Oldtown Folks* 243 **NEng,** She has her own ways and doings, and she won't hear to reason. **1895** *DN* 1.389 **CT, MA,** *Hear to:* give heed to. **1899** (1912) Green *VA Folk-Speech* 220, *Hear to*. . . To permit; to receive favorably; to give consent; mostly used in the negative: as, "He would not hear to it." **1909** *DN* 3.398 **nwAR,** *Hear to*. . . Agree to. "He wouldn't hear to any such arrangement." **1915** Poole *Harbor* 202 **NYC,** When I tried at last to turn our talk to . . our affairs at home, at first she would not hear to it. **1917** *DN* 4.393 **OH,** *Hear to*. . . Consent to. "He wouldn't hear to it." General. **1923** (1946) Greer-Petrie *Angeline Doin' Society* 17 **csKY,** Betty wouldn't hear to it. **1927** *AmSp* 2.357 **cwWV,** *Hear to* . . to consent to. "He wouldn't hear to that." **1951** Porter *Ragged Roads* 105 **wOK** [Black], She wouldn't heah to me a-choppin' down dat tree. **1954** *Harder Coll.* **cwTN,** Hear to—consent to. **1968** Kellner *Aunt Serena* 135 **sIN** (as of c1920), I had counted on selling seeds to my Grandmother and Grandfather and all my aunts, uncles, cousins . . but Aunt Serena said . . A person oughtn't to *ever* ask kinfolks for money-favors, and she wouldn't hear to it.

2 To understand; to assent; to heed—used as a tag question; see below. **chiefly Sth, S Midl**

a used with simple interrogatory force: See quots.

1893 Owen *Voodoo Tales* 178 **MO** [Black], Go out in de woods an' 'fresh yo'se'f 'fo' yo' staht. Go 'long! Do yo' hyeah me? Is yo' gwine? **1931** [see **A1a** above]. **1966–68** *DARE* (Qu. NN5, . . *Ways of saying 'Do you understand?': "You take hold of it this way, ______?"*) Infs **MO**3, **NC**55, Do you hear (me)? **AL**3, 6, 16, **SC**59, 65, Hear? **1986** Pederson *LAGS Concordance,* 1 inf, **cLA,** You hear?—do you hear? 1 inf, **ceAR,** Hear?—do you understand? 1 inf, **seGA,** That's a darn good job, hear—you understand; 1 inf, Hear?—Do you hear?

b used with imperative force and the expectation of compliance: See quots.

1856 Holmes *Lena Rivers* 72 **KY** [Black], Knock Lion out dat kittle; does you har [sic]? **1970** *DARE* File **cnGA,** "You clean your room now, hear?" meant that I had better do it, and do it well. **1986** Pederson *LAGS Concordance,* 1 inf, **seGA,** You do, hear?—You do that now!

c used in formulaic invitations: See quots. Cf **come back (again)**

1968 *Sat. Eve. Post* 15 June 61/1 **AL,** We'll see yawl, heah? [Speaker is George Wallace.] **1970** *DARE* (Qu. NN11, *Informal ways of saying 'good-bye' to people you know quite well*) Inf **VA**85, Y'all come back, you heah. **1976** Ryland *Richmond Co. VA* 372, Come see us, hear? **1984** Wilder *You All Spoken Here* 104 **Sth, S Midl,** Y'all come to see us, heah: A way to end an exchange of small talk and possible involvement or commitment; euphemism for "Good-bye. . . I'll see you later," or for "Here's my bus." **1986** Pederson *LAGS Concordance* **AL, GA** *(Come again!)* 1 inf, You hear? 1 inf, Be sure and come back, you hear? 1 inf, Y'all come back now, hear?—facetious.

3 in phrr *hear one's ears (think):* See quots.

1967 *DARE* (QR, near Qu. NN18b) Inf **AL**30, [To tell a child to be still:] Sit down, I can't hear my ears think. **1976** Ryland *Richmond Co. VA* 372, So much noise you couldn't hear your ears.

heared See **hear A2a**

hearf See **hearth A3**

hearing n

1 in phr *lay a hearing on:* To abuse verbally; to lay a curse on. [*SND hearin(g)* vbl. n. 2 "A scolding, 'lecture,' 'talking to' "]

1931 Hurston in *Jrl. Amer. Folkl.* 44.405 **FL** [Black], She did tell Aunt Judy and it is said she laid a hearing on Mr. Horace. . . Before he could reach home, it was discovered that he was defecating through his mouth and nose. **1935** Hurston *Mules & Men* 107 **FL** [Black], Well, if you cussed 'im an' he didn't do nothin' tuh you, de nex' time he make me mad Ah'm goin' tuh lay uh hearin' on him.

2 A letter; a reply. [Cf *OED hearing* vbl. sb. 5 "report, rumour, news. *dial.*"]

1943 in 1944 *ADD* **AR,** I thought sure she'd git a hearin' from that nurses' outfit today. **1970** *DARE* Tape **WV**14, You get a hearin' instead of a letter; that's an old, old mountain expression. . . You had a hearin' from John.

hearn See **hear A2b**

hear one's ears (think) See **hear B3**

hearse n Usu |hɝs, hɜs|; for addit varr see quots Pronc-spp *hearst, hurrus, hurst* Cf Intro "Language Changes" I.8

A Forms.

1893 Shands *MS Speech* 38, *Hurrus* ['hʌrəs]. Illiterate white for *hearse.* **1908** *DN* 3.283 **eAL, wGA,** *s* becomes *š* . . sometimes in [hɝš] (hearse). **1917** in 1944 *ADD* **cwWV,** Hearst. **1959** *VT Hist.* new ser 27.141, *Hearse* [hʌs] . . Common. Rural areas. **1968–70** *DARE* (Qu. N2, *The car used to carry a dead body for burial*) Inf **IA**30, Hearse [hɝs, hɝst]; **IN**56, **UT**15, Hearse [hɝst]; **VA**59, Hearse [hɝs], hearst; (Qu. N1, . . *Ambulance*) 145 Infs, **chiefly Sth, S Midl, Hearse; IA**30, Hearst. **1976** Garber *Mountain-ese* 44 **Appalachians,** They hauled him to the burryin' ground in a long black hurst. **1978** *DARE* File **cCA,** [Sign with picture:] John H. Carley constructed the first automobile hearst in Angels Camp from a Reo touring car.

B Senses.

1 An ambulance. **scattered, but chiefly Sth, S Midl** See Map

1942 Berrey–Van den Bark *Amer. Slang* 531.2, Ambulance. . . *a hearse.* **1965–70** *DARE* (Qu. N1, . . *Ambulance*) 145 Infs, **scattered, but chiefly Sth, S Midl,** Hearse; **IA**30, Hearst.

2 A large automobile; see quots.

1938 *AmSp* 13.315 [Language of garages and gas stations], *Hearse.* A high large old 'crate,' similar in appearance to a hearse. **1986** Pederson

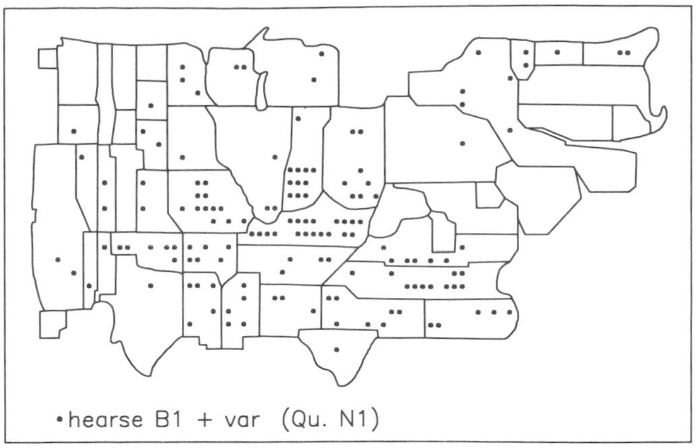

LAGS Concordance (*Large and pretentious sedans;* this question was asked chiefly in urban areas) 4 infs, 3 **FL,** Hearse. [3 of 4 infs Black]

3 A caboose. Cf **ape wagon**

1931 *Writer's Digest* 11.42 [Railroad terms], *Hearse*—Caboose. **1946** in 1953 Botkin–Harlow *Treas. Railroad Folkl.* 350, If you ever have occasion to locate the caboose on a freight train, don't ask the ORC (conductor) to show you the way to the . . hearse.

heart n[1] Pronc-spp *haat, haht, hairt, heaht*

A Forms.

1885 Cable *Dr. Sevier* 171 **New Orleans LA** (as of 1850s–60s) [Black], Hairt to hairt sur; sperit to sperit. **1893** Owen *Voodoo Tales* 175 **MO** [Black], May hit bring 'im 'is haht's *de*sire. **1901** *DN* 2.182 **KY** [Black], *Heart*—heaht. **1909** *S. Atl. Qrly.* 8.47 [Gullah], Lay down yo' mammy haa't. **1922** Gonzales *Black Border* 305 **sSC, GA coasts** [Gullah glossary], *H'aa't*—heart, hearts. **1942** *Sat. Eve. Post* 3 Oct 68 [Gullah], Oh, my haa't is full of sorrer.

B Senses.

1 The central portion of a seed or fruit, spec:

a The germ of a kernel of corn.

1946 McAtee *Dial. Grant Co. IN Suppl. 3* 6 (as of 1890s), *Heart* . . embryo of a corn kernel (Ohio). **1968–69** *DARE* Tape **KY**13, A lot of [corn] mills, they take that heart. They call it a hominy heart; **IN**32, [The corn] has to be washed over and over . . but once having removed all the hearts and the shells, why, then we cook it. [Both Infs old, comm type 4 or 5]

b The kernel of a seed or nut.

c1960 *Wilson Coll.* **csKY,** *Heart.* . . The kernel of a seed. **1966** *DARE* (Qu. I41, *The part of the nut that you eat*) Inf **SC**26, Heart. **1986** Pederson *LAGS Concordance* **Gulf Region** *(Seed of a peach)* 4 infs, Heart—inside seed; 2 infs, Heart—inside (the) stone.

c The hard, inedible center of a piece of fruit. **esp Sth** Cf **kernel, pit, stone**

1968 *DARE* (Qu. I48, *The hard center of a cherry*) Inf **NC**50, **VA**7, Heart; (Qu. I49, . . *The hard center of a plum*) Inf **NC**50, Heart. **c1970** Pederson *Dial. Surv. Rural GA (The hard thing in the middle of a cherry)* 3 infs, **seGA,** Heart. [All infs Black] **1971** *AmSp* 46.180 **Chicago IL,** Cherry heart. [1 inf] **1971** Wood *Vocab. Change* 43 **Sth,** *Heart* and *kernel,* are least prevalent in either sense [=the seed of a cherry (20 infs, *heart*) or of a peach (13 infs, *heart*)]. **1973** Allen *LAUM* 1.305 **MN** (as of c1950), *Seed* (of a cherry). . . heart. [1 inf] **1986** Pederson *LAGS Concordance* **Gulf Region** *(Seed of a cherry)* 13 infs, Heart; 1 inf, Heart of it; *(Seed of a peach)* 3 infs, Heart.

2 A part of a fish trap; see quots.

1918 *DN* 5.16 **seMA,** *Heart.* . . Applied to *one-half* of the heart-shaped portion of a fish-trap. The two parts together form a heart-shaped net, but being separable for ease in handling they are called "the hearts." **1967–68** *DARE* Tape **MI**54, They [=fish] go up the lead and come into the hearts and they'd . . circle around in the hearts and then they'd go back and go through the tunnel into the pot; **NC**58, Close to the pocket was called the heart. It was a net . . half-heart shaped; **WI**75, The hearts . . 're crooked . . they're wider at the mouth . . the fish swim into 'em . . and then the hole is kinda crossways-like and they have quite a time finding their way when they git in there.

3 See quot. [Cf *OED dear heart* (at *heart* sb. 14. b) "a boon companion. *Obs.*"]

1970 *DARE* (Qu. II1, . . *A close friend* . . *"He's my ______."*) Inf **MS**88, Heart.

4 in phr *in (good) heart;* Of land: fertile. [Engl dial; cf *EDD heart* 8]

1774 (1900) Fithian *Jrl.* 1.140 **VA,** Their method of farming is slovenly, without any regard to continue their Land in heart, for future Crops. **1804** Roberts *PA Farmer* 101 **sePA,** If the land is in good heart, sow three bushels per acre. **1874** VT State Bd. Ag. *Rept. for 1873–74* 2.214 **nNY,** He said by feeding the straw to young cattle he got manure enough to keep his land in heart. **1899** (1912) Green *VA Folk-Speech* 220, *Heart.* . . Condition; said of ground. "My land is now in very good heart."

heart n² See **hearth A4.**

heart bird n

=ruddy turnstone.

[**1811** Wilson *Amer. Ornith.* 4.76, In this country the Magpie was first taken notice of . . on Hudson's bay, where the Indians used sometimes to bring it in, and gave it the name of *Heart-bird,* for what reason is uncertain.] **1844** DeKay *Zool. NY* 2.216, *The Turnstone* . . is known among our *gunners* . . under the names of *Brant-bird, Heart-bird, Horsefoot Snipe* and *Beach-bird.* **1888** Trumbull *Names of Birds* 186, *Arenaria interpres.* . . Heart-bird. **1889** *Century Dict.* 2757, *Heart-bird.* . . [*Century* Ed: Prob. so called from the large black area on the breast.] The turnstone, *Strepsilas interpres:* a gunners' name.

heartburn v [*OED heart-burn* v. *"Obs.",* but *heart-burning* sb. →1874]

To be affected with jealousy or discontent; hence n *heartburning* jealousy, resentment.

1824 Irving *Hist. NY* 146 **seNY,** It was a breaking forth of the grudge and heartburning that had existed between those two eminent burghers. **1899** (1912) Green *VA Folk-Speech* 220, *Heartburning.* . . Discontent; especially, envy or jealousy; enmity. **1939** FWP *Guide TN* 134, Of a jealous lover . . "Oh, he's heart-burning the worst kind over that little gal."

heartease See **heartsease 1**

hear tell v phr

1 To hear, learn by word of mouth. [*OED hear tell* (at *hear* v. 3. c) 1297 →; "still in dialectal or colloquial . . use"] **chiefly Sth, S Midl**

1834 in 1944 *ADD* 283/2, The tarnelest racket you ever hear tell on. **1843** (1916) Hall *New Purchase* 177 **IN,** Jerry Simpson *had* laughed when he heard tell of it!! **1867** Lowell *Biglow* 19 **MA,** I *hev* hearn tell o' wingëd words. **1899** (1912) Green *VA Folk-Speech* 220, *Hear tell.* . . To hear about something. "So I've heard tell." **1907** *DN* 3.189 **neNH,** *Hear tell.* . . To be informed, to hear. **1910** *DN* 3.443 **cwNY,** Did you ever hear tell of such a thing? **1915** *DN* 4.226 **wTX,** *Hearn tell of.* . . "I've hearn tell of sech." **1927** *AmSp* 3.11 **Ozarks,** He's th' dangdest fool I ever heerd tell on. *Ibid* 139 **ME,** "Hearn tell," or "heerd." **1956** McAtee *Some Dialect NC* 22, *Hear tell of* . . hear, learn of by words of mouth. **1959** *VT Hist.* new ser 27.141, *Heard* . . *tell.* . . Occasional. Rural areas. **1963** Owens *Look to River* 71 **TX,** I ain't never seen nobody on the chain gang—just heard tell of it. **1966** Barnes–Jensen *Dict. UT Slang* 22, *Hear tell of* . . hear, learn by word of mouth. "I never heard tell of such a thing." **1967–68** *DARE* Tape **SC**32, Back then you never did hear tell of a queen [of May Day celebrations]; **SC**57, I've heard tell of 'em [=pilot snakes]. **1974** Fink *Mountain Speech* 12 **wNC, eTN,** Did ye ever hear tell o' sich? **1976** Garber *Mountain-ese* 39 **Appalachians,** *Hear-tell* . . learn, hear. I hear-tell as how Clyde ain't gonna take his wife back this time. **1984** Wilder *You All Spoken Here* 163 **Sth,** *Hear tell:* Understand, as "I hear tell that she don't keep her ankles crossed."

2 with *of:* To tolerate; consider.

1941 in 1944 *ADD* **nWV,** You probably wouldn't hear tell of that. **1968** *DARE* FW Addit **IA**30, My father wouldn't hear tell of nursing for me.

hearth n

A Forms.

Usu |hɑ(r)θ|; also:

1 |hɝθ, hɜθ|; pronc-spp *herth, hurth, hyearth.* *somewhat old-fash; esp freq among speakers with little formal educ*

1893 Shands *MS Speech* 38, *Hurth* [hɝθ]. Illiterate white pronunciation of *hearth.* **1903** *DN* 2.290 **Cape Cod MA,** *Hurth* for *hearth,* as in *earth, dearth.* **1908** *DN* 3.319 **eAL, wGA,** *Hearth.* . . Pronounced [hɝθ]. **1910** *DN* 3.443 **cwNY,** *Hearth.* . . Pronounced *herth* [hɝθ]. **1941** *LANE* Map 329 *(Hearth),* Pronunciations of the type of [ha·θ] [which are widespread throughout New England] are described as natural or more common by [4 infs] . . and as older or old-fashioned though still in use by [9 infs]. (The label 'older' applied to this pron. may simply mean that it is less familiar.) Pronunciations of the type of [hɜ·θ] [which are widespread throughout New England] are described as more common by [2 infs] . . and as older or old-fashioned though still in use by [23 infs]. *Ibid,* 1 inf, **wCT,** 'I guess I was brought up to say [hɚθ], but the old folks called it [hɑrθ]; 1 inf, **wMA,** [hɜ·θ] 'more correct because in old times it was actually made out of [ɜ·θ]. [Other pronunciations including those of the types [hæ·θ, hɝ·θ] are scattered throughout New England; those of the type [hɤ·θ] are found especially in **ME.**] **1953** Kenyon–Knott *Pronc. Dict.* 198, *Hearth* hɑrθ; E[ast] S[outh] hɑ:θ . . *Poetic* hɝθ, hɜθ *is still occas. heard.* **1953** Randolph–Wilson *Down in Holler* 32 **Ozarks,** Many Ozarkers rhyme hearth with *worth,* and one often hears something like *hyearth.* **1961** Kurath–McDavid *Pronc. Engl.* 143, *Hearth* with the vowel /ɜ/ of *thirty* . . is characteristic . . of the North and North Midland, and . . of the Lower South, areas where it predominates decisively in folk speech and is rather common among the middle group, except in urbanized areas. In the Upper South it occurs only in coastal communities. Relics of /hɜθ/ survive in cultivated speech along the coast of South Carolina and in western Pennsylvania. **1965–70** *DARE* (Qu. D31, *In front of a fireplace* . . *stonework on the floor*) 150 Infs, **widespread,** Herth [Of all Infs responding to the question, 71% were old, 28% gs educ or less; of those giving this response, 81% were old, 45% gs educ or less.]; (Qu. F12) Infs **IL**134, **MO**9, **MT**5, **NC**25, Herth. **1973** Allen *LAUM* 3.280 **Upper MW** (as of c1950), *Hearth.* . . Two-thirds of the U[pper] M[idwest] infs. have /hɑrθ/; one-third have a retroflex vowel in [hɚθ]. . . a marked social contrast appears in the UM, where the former pronunciation is closely related to the degree of schooling. . . The form [hɚθ] . . is considered old-fashioned [by several infs]. . . /hɛrθ/ . . [is] used by two rural informants in . . southern Iowa. **1975** Gould *ME Lingo* 138, *Hurth*—A hearth. Maine masons use *hurth* and harth about fifty-fifty not only for that part of an open fireplace, but for the little shelf on a stove. People who are not masons seem to run toward harth. **1981** Pederson *LAGS Basic Materials* **Gulf Region,** [Pronunciations of the type [hɝθ] occur frequently.]

2 |hæθ|; pronc-sp *hath.* **esp Sth, S Midl**

1837 Sherwood *Gaz. GA* 70, *Hath,* for hearth. **1844** Thompson *Major Jones's Courtship* 13 **GA,** She sot on one side of the fire-place, and I sot on tother, so I could spit on the hath. **1859** (1968) Bartlett *Americanisms* xxvii, [Words incorrectly pronounced:] Hath for hearth, S[outh]. **1894** *Century Illustr. Mag.* 48.873, I find "daythe" for dearth in early colonial letters, and "haythe" for height in Vaughan's journal of 1684, but I nowhere find the Hoosier "hath" for hearth. **1908** *DN* 3.319 **eAL, wGA,** *Hearth* . . [hæθ]. **1936** *AmSp* 11.23 **eTX** [Black], Occasionally . . [hæ:θ] [is] . . heard for *hearth.* **1952** Brown *NC Folkl.* 1.549, *Hath* [hæ:θ, hæɪθ]. . . *Hearth.* **1941** [see **1** above]. **1961** Kurath–McDavid *Pronc. Engl.* 143, /hæθ/ . . is largely confined to the folk speech of the South, although a few instances occur in southern New Jersey and in the New England settlement area. . . /hæθ/ occurs only in areas that have /æ/ in *care, stairs,* etc. **1967–68** *DARE* (Qu. D31, *In front of a fireplace* . . *stonework on the floor*) Inf **GA**46, Old people say [hæθ]; (Qu. F12) Inf **MO**12, [In] the old-fashioned stoves it was called a [hæθ]. **1981** Pederson *LAGS Basic Materials* **Gulf Region,** [Pronunciations of the type [hæθ] occur rarely.]

3 |hæf, hɑrf, hɝf|; pronc-spp *ha(r)f, hearf.* Cf Pronc Intro 3.I.17 *esp freq among Black speakers*

1901 *DN* 2.180 **neKY** [Black], [Hearth:] *hearf* . . *harf.* **1941** *AmSp* 16.13 **eTX** [Black], [θ] > [f] in *both, breath, hearth.* **1968–70** *DARE* (Qu. D31, *In front of a fireplace* . . *stonework on the floor*) Inf **NC**50, Some people called it [hæf]; (Qu. F12) Inf **VA**53, [haəf]. **1976** Allen *LAUM* 3.325 **nwNE** (as of c1950), *Hearth.* . . One . . inf. . . has the lisped variant /hɚf/. **1981** Pederson *LAGS Basic Materials* **Gulf Region,** [Pronunciations of the type [hɑɚf, hɝf] occur infrequently, among both Blacks and Whites.]

4 |hɑrt, hɝt|; pronc-spp *h'aa't', heart.* Cf Pronc Intro 3.I.17 **esp Sth, S Midl**

1922 Gonzales *Black Border* 305 **sSC, GA coasts** [Gullah glossary], *H'aa't'*—hearth, hearths. **1942** Faulkner *Dollar Cotton* 268, What was left of the body had fallen into the heart embers. **1950** *WELS Suppl.* **csWI,** *Hearth* pronounced [hɑɚt]. **1966–70** *DARE* (Qu. D31, *In front of a fireplace* . . *stonework on the floor*) Infs **GA**91, 92, Heart rock; **GA**4, [fɑɪəhɝt]; **MO**12, Heart [hɑɚt]; **WI**12, Heart [hɑɚt] stone. **1981**

Pederson *LAGS Basic Materials* **Gulf Region,** [Pronunciations of the type [hɑɚt, hæ·ɛt, hɜɪt] occur rarely.]

B Senses.

1 also *stove hearth:* See quot 1891. *somewhat old-fash*

1890 *Century Dict.* 5974 **NEng,** *Stove-hearth. . .* The horizontal shelf or ledge which in some stoves lies outside and in front of the grate containing the fuel. **1895** Brown *Meadow-Grass* 134 **NEng,** She drew up before the shining stove, and put her feet on the hearth. **1902** (1969) Sears *Catalogue* 826/3, *Acme Cottage Heater. . .* This stove is trimmed with a fancy highly polished *nickel plated* foot rail flush with hearth. **1941** *LANE* Map 329, Another meaning of *hearth,* more familiar to some New Englanders, is 'the projecting part of the fire box of an iron stove'. . . *Stove hearth* always has this meaning. **1965–70** *DARE* (Qu. F12, *The flat metal piece below a wood-burning stove, to catch the ashes*) 19 Infs, **scattered,** Hearth; **IL**134, **MO**9, **NC**25, Herth; **NY**72, Stove hearth; [**MT**5, Ash pan sets in the herth]. [21 of 24 Infs old] **1973** Allen *LAUM* 1.161 **Upper MW** (as of c1950), Although most U[pper] M[idwest] infs accepted *hearth* as the name for the floor of a fireplace, more than one-fourth considered it primarily or exclusively as the designation of a projecting shelf on either a kitchen stove or a base-burner.

2 A fireplace.

1972 *Atlanta Letters* **cwGA,** My grandmother always called the fireplace "the hearth." **1973** Allen *LAUM* 1.161 **SD** (as of c1950), *Hearth* is almost synonymous with *fireplace.* [1 inf]

‡3 The mantel above a fireplace.

1968–69 *DARE* (Qu. D36, . . *The shelf over the fireplace*) Inf **CA**125, Hearth; **MO**35, The shelf or the hearth.

hearth broom n **chiefly Sth, S Midl** See Map

A broom for sweeping a hearth.

1851 *Harper's New Mth. Mag.* 2.672/2, In my opinion she would storm a town, single-handed, with a hearth-broom, and carry it. **1881** Tourgée *Royal Gentleman & Zouri* 489 **sVA,** He . . carefully brushed the ashes from it with the hearth-broom. **1893** Owen *Voodoo Tales* 6 **MO,** The place of vegetables was taken by . . hearth-brooms, socks, mittens. **1908** *DN* 3.319 **eAL, wGA,** *Hearth-broom. . .* A small broom used only about the open fireplace. Sometimes called *parlor-broom.* **1912** Green *VA Folk-Speech* 220, *Hearth-broom. . .* A small, short handled broom used for sweeping the hearth before wood fires. **1938** Rawlings *Yearling* 49 **nFL,** Ma Forrester flailed at them [=dogs] with a hearthbroom. **1950** *WELS (Kinds of brooms)* 1 Inf, **cWI,** Hearth broom. **1965–70** *DARE* (Qu. F36) 43 Infs, **chiefly Sth, S Midl,** Hearth (broom); **KY**48, Herth broom; (Qu. F35, *A small broom that you hold in one hand*) Infs **CT**9, **FL**8, **GA**13, **MS**13, 48, **NC**14, 16, **TN**11, Hearth broom. [43 of 52 Infs old]

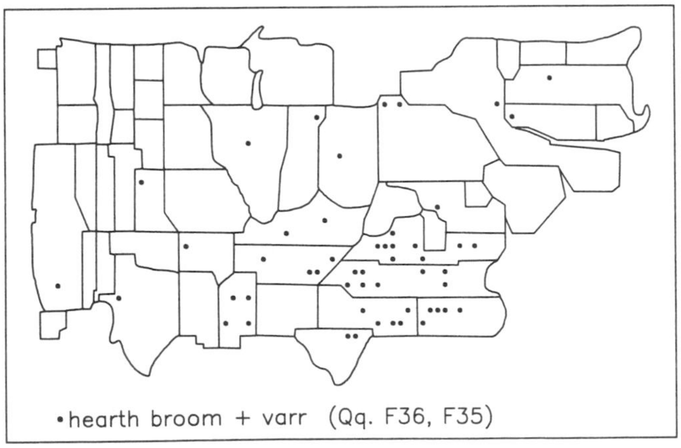

•hearth broom + varr (Qq. F36, F35)

hearth brush n **esp NEng**

=hearth broom.

1775 in 1877 Essex Inst. *Coll.* 13.186 **eMA,** 5 Chairs red covered with Callicoe, 1 Hearth Brush, 1 Family Picture. **1967–70** *DARE* (Qu. F36, . . *Kinds of brooms*) Infs **CT**5, **MA**5, 98, Hearth brush.

hearth cricket n [*OED* 1789]

A house cricket *(Acheta domestica).*

1967 *DARE* (Qu. R8, . . *Creatures that make a clicking or shrilling or chirping kind of sound*) Inf **SC**46, Hearth crickets—light-colored.

hearth dog n

=andiron.

1941 *LANE* Map 329 **cCT,** [hɚθ dɒgz], andirons.

hearth rock n **chiefly Appalachians**

=hearthstone.

1917 in 1944 *ADD* **sWV,** Hath rock. **1926** Roberts *Time of Man* 379 **KY,** Ellen was sitting in her stiff little chair across the hearth rocks. **1931** *AmSp* 7.93 **eKY,** *Hath-rock,* a stone forming a hearth. "Sary baked her corn-pone on the hath-rock." **c1960** *Wilson Coll.* **csKY,** *Hearth rock*—Heard occasionally among very old people; the hearth was often made of native stone. **1961** *Mt. Life* 37.1.6 **sAppalachians,** In a few words, however, *r* is omitted . . *gooey* (gory), *fust, hathrock* (hearthrock). **1966** *DARE* (Qu. D31, *In front of a fireplace . . stonework on the floor*) Infs **GA**91, 92, Heart rock; **WA**14, Herth rock. **1971** *Foxfire* Spring–Summer 74 **nGA,** They killed him and buried him under th' hearth rock.

hearthstone n **scattered, but chiefly Nth, N Midl** See Map

A stone or stones forming a hearth; also fig.

1823 in 1847 Emerson *Poems* 58 **MA,** I go to seek my own hearthstone. **1941** *LANE* Map 329, 13 Infs, **sNEng,** Hearthstone. **1950** *WELS (The stone work on the floor in front of a fireplace)* 2 Infs, **WI,** Hearthstone. **1965–70** *DARE* (Qu. D31) 37 Infs, **scattered, but chiefly Nth, N Midl,** Hearthstone; **WI**12, Heart stone. **1980** *Greenfield Recorder* (MA) 8 Nov, The hearth stone in the old "cellar kitchen" of the Hemenway house in North Leverett, is smooth-surfaced, but not quite all flat.

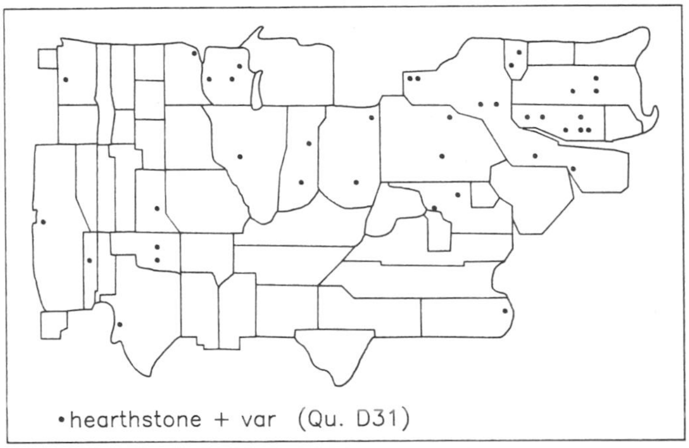

•hearthstone + var (Qu. D31)

heartleaf n

1 A **floating heart 1** (prob *Nymphoides cordata*).

1854 (1969) Thoreau *Walden* 194 **MA,** A few small heart-leaves and potamogetons.

2 **=hepatica.**

1889 *Jrl. Amer. Folkl.* 2.99 **wNC,** Liverwort is known by the appropriate name of "heart leaf," and the peculiar shape of its leaves has suggested their use as a love philter.

3 also pl: **=wild ginger** (here: either *Asarum* spp or *Hexastylis* spp). **Sth** Note: Some authors include the latter genus in the former.

1894 *Jrl. Amer. Folkl.* 7.97, *Asarum arifolium* . . heart-leaves, Ga. *Asarum Virginicum* . . heart-leaves, Banner Elk, N.C. **1907** *Ibid* 20.249 **NC,** Hart [sic] leaves and bark from root of red alder are good to regulate the bowels. **1908** *DN* 3.319 **eAL, wGA,** *Heart-leaf. . .* A plant, the wild ginger. **1924** *Torreya* 24.79, "Heart-leaf" seems to be the universal common name for any species of *Hexastylis* in Georgia and Alabama, if not throughout the South, but like many other southern plant names, it does not seem to have found its way into books written by northern botanists. **1960** Williams *Walk Egypt* 11 **GA,** He drank it. It tasted of heart leaf, and a month later they were married. **1964** Batson *Wild Flowers SC* 40, *Wild ginger, heart leaf: Hexastylis arifolia. . .* Common in hardwood forests. Early spring. Virginia to Florida. **1968** Haun *Hawk's Done Gone* 314 **TN,** He would come down here and play with me, taking me to hunt heart leaves and sang and black gum. **1969** *DARE* (Qu. S26b, *Wildflowers that grow in water or wet places*) Inf **GA**80, Heartleaf; the flower looks like a little jug.

4 pl: A **false lily of the valley** (here: *Maianthemum canadense*)

1940 Clute *Amer. Plant Names* 226, *Maianthemum Canadense.* Heart-leaves.

5 An **arrowhead 1** (here: *Sagittaria latifolia*).

1966 *DARE* Wildfl QR Pl.1 Inf **NC**28, Heartleaf.

heartleaf lily n

A **false lily of the valley** (here: *Maianthemum canadense*).

1948 Wherry *Wild Flower Guide* 21, *Heartleaf-lily (Maianthemum canadense)*. . . Leaves few, heart-shaped.

heartleaf solomon's-plume n

A **false lily of the valley** (here: *Maianthemum canadense*).

1949 Moldenke *Amer. Wild Flowers* 333, *Heartleaf solomonsplume, Maianthemum canadense*. . . grows only 2 to 6 inches tall, but usually forms dense carpets.

heartleaf willow n

Std: a shrubby **willow** *(Salix rigida)* with cordate leaves. Also called **diamond willow, dune willow, greensides willow, rock willow**

heart lesson n

See quots.

1932 Randolph *Ozark Mt. Folks* 24, Thar was some as would make reg'lar speeches, too—we called them kind o' speeches heart-lessons, 'cause they l'arnt 'em by heart. **1942** McAtee *Dial. Grant Co. IN* 77 (as of 1890s), *Heart lessons* . . those memorized or learned "by heart." **1956** McAtee *Some Dialect NC* 22, *Heart lessons.*

heart liverleaf n Also *heart liverwort*

=**hepatica.**

1829 Eaton *Botany* 241, *Hepatica. . . acutiloba* . . heart-liverleaf. . . Grows in woods, preferring the north side of hills and mountains. **1893** *Jrl. Amer. Folkl.* 6.136 **NY,** *Hepatica triloba*. . . Heart liverwort. **1900** Lyons *Plant Names* 187, *H[epatica] acuta*. . . Canada to Georgia, west to Minnesota. . . Heart Liver-leaf. . . *H[epatica] hepatica*. . . N. America, south to Florida and Missouri. . . Heart Liverwort. **1901** Lounsberry *S. Wild Flowers* 179, *Heart Liver-Leaf*. . . *Hepatica acuta*. . . It can be distinguished by its pointed leaf-lobes. **1971** Krochmal *Appalachia Med. Plants* 140, *Hepatica acutiloba*. . . heart liverleaf.

heart-mad adj [Cf *OED heart-angry, heart-burdened, heart-happy* (at *heart* sb. 55. c)]

Very angry.

c1938 in 1970 Hyatt *Hoodoo* 1.58 **seNC,** This woman [Hyatt: who] had the son didn't want fer her child . . to marry this woman's daughter. But anyhow, they went on together an' courtin' an' got married. An' this woman was *heart-mad* about it.

heart-nut n [See quot 1937]

A **ratany** (here: *Krameria glandulosa*).

1931 U.S. Dept. Ag. *Misc. Pub.* 101.82, *Range ratany* . . , locally known as heart-nut, is a low, densely, and diffusely branched shrub. **1937** U.S. Forest Serv. *Range Plant Hdbk.* B88, Range ratany, also called. . . heart-nut on account of its somewhat heart-shaped fruits, . . is . . 1 to 2 feet high.

hear to See **hear B1**

heart of palm n **esp FL**

The edible bud of a **cabbage palm.**

1938 Matschat *Suwannee R.* 211 **nFL, sGA,** The early settlers called this palm the cabbage because of the tender heart, which they ate as a vegetable. This is the salad served today as "hearts of palm." **1939** FWP *Guide FL* 479, The swamp cabbage is the bud of the cabbage palm, a delicacy long relished in Florida. . . Uncooked it appears on hotel menus as hearts of palm, often at $1 a portion. **1942** Kennedy *Palmetto Country* 4 **FL, sAL, sGA,** Swamp cabbage. . . the buds are then canned and shipped to appear on America's ultra-swank menus as "Heart-of-Palm Salad."

heart pea n

A **balloon vine** (here: *Cardiospermum halicacabum*).

1900 Lyons *Plant Names* 81, *C. Halicacabum*. . . Heart Pea. **1933** Small *Manual SE Flora* 827, *Heart-pea*. . . The root is medicinal. **1976** Bailey–Bailey *Hortus Third* 221, *[C.] Halicacabum*. . . *Heart pea*. . . Woody per[ennial], to 10 ft.

heart pine n [From its distinctive red-orange heartwood]

=**longleaf pine** or its resinous heart wood.

1897 Sudworth *Arborescent Flora* 31, *Pinus palustris*. . . Southern Heart Pine (general). . . Heart Pine (N.C. and South Atlantic region). . . Georgia Heart Pine (general). **1905** Chesnutt *Col.'s Dream* 20 **GA,** Heart-pine and live-oak, mused the colonel, like other things Southern, live long and die hard. **1933** Rawlings *South Moon* 14 **nFL,** Old man Wilson said, watching Lantry at a pile of cypress slats ready for the fencing, "I favors a split-rail fence. Good heart pine." **1936** Smith–Sass *Carolina Rice* 14 **SC coast** (as of 1850s), Some . . mansions . . were of cypress or heart-pine upon high brick foundations or basements. **1941** Writers' Program *Guide SC* 73, Many of the houses built long before the War between the States are still in good condition. Timber was so abundant that the 'sap wood' was often discarded, only the inner or 'heart wood' being used. Houses built of 'heart pine' will stand almost indefinitely. **1960** Vines *Trees SW* 26, Longleaf Pine. . . Vernacular names are . . Heart Pine, Turpentine Pine, and Florida Pine. **c1970** *DARE* File **AL,** *Heart pine* . . after pine rots, the red heart remains full of pitch—it is a rose color like a rooster's comb. **1970** *DARE* (Qu. T8, *Joints of pine wood that burn easily and make good fuel*) Infs **AR**56, **VA**47, 105, Heart pine. **1971** Krochmal *Appalachia Med. Plants* 192, *Pinus palustris*. . . *Common Names:* Longleaf pine, . . heart pine. . . A valuable source of turpentine, pine oil, tar, pitch, and rosin. **1986** Pederson *LAGS Concordance* **Gulf Region** *(Lightwood)* 3 infs, Heart pine; *(Common trees)* 1 inf, Longleaf heart pine; 1 inf, Yellow heart pine trees.

hearts-a-bustin'-with-love n For varr see quots [See quots] **chiefly sAppalachians**

A **burning bush 1** (here: *Euonymus americanus*).

1937 Thornburgh *Gt. Smoky Mts.* 25, One of the showiest shrubs in the Great Smokies [is] the evonymous [sic], wahoo or spindlebush . . especially lovely in October when its seed-pod bursts open displaying orange-colored seed in its glowing red heart. It has many descriptive local names—swamp willow, strawberry bush, catspaw, jewel-box, but most descriptive of all is the name given by a mountain man of, "Hearts-bust-in'-with-love." **1941** Walker *Lookout* 59 **TN,** A wild strawberry shrub . . becomes very ornamental . . when its crimson red seed capsule bursts and exposes a cluster of orange-scarlet seeds inside. . . The sentimental people of the mountain refer to it as "heart a-bustin' with love." **1943** Peattie *Great Smokies* 284, By the end of September many a wild plant is ripening its fruits. Of these, the strawberry bush, called "hearts a-bustin' with love" by some of our mountain people, dangles its rich glossy crimson fruits from frosty-pink husks and becomes a favorite with many who discover it. **1951** *PADS* 15.16, *Euonymus americanus*. . . Hearts-bustin-with-love, Pinhook, Tennessee; the longest plant name I have heard in folk use; Miss Davison caught it as "hearts-a-bustin-with-love" (also in Tennessee) which is still longer. **1964** Batson *Wild Flowers SC* 72, *Strawberry bush, Hearts-bursting-with-love:* Euonymus americanus. **1964** Campbell *Great Smoky Wildflowers* 78, *Hearts-a-bustin'.* **c1970** *DARE* File **nAL,** Hearts-a-bustin'-(with-love). **1971** in 1983 Johnson *I Declare* 135, Prickly pods of euonymus . . will pop open to expose scarlet seeds and give meaning to its Georgia highlands name, "hearts-a-bustin'." **1981** *DARE* File **cwMA,** *Euonymus atropurpureus* is called (on account of its seeds) *hearts are breaking* and *hearts are bursting with love* (depending on your point of view). **1984** Wilder *You All Spoken Here* 176 **Sth,** Heart's a-bustin': Swamp dogwood; strawberry bush; spindle bush; arrowwood.

heart's angel n

A **blue curls 1** (here: *Trichostema dichotomum*).

1898 *Jrl. Amer. Folkl.* 11.277, *Trichostema dichotomum* . . heart's angel, Oxford Co., Me.

heart's-delight n

A **sand verbena** (here: *Abronia fragrans*).

1961 Wills–Irwin *Flowers TX* 106, One of the most beautiful Texas plants . . is the Sand-verbena. . . Also known as Heart's-delight, this species has been introduced as a garden plant, especially in South Texas.

heart's-ear n

A **lady's thumb** (here: *Polygonum persicaria*).

1900 Lyons *Plant Names* 300, *P[olygonum] Persicaria*. . . Heart's-ear.

heartsease n

1 also *heartease:* Any of several **violets,** but esp *Viola tricolor.*

1778 Carver *Travels N. Amer.* 520 **MI, WI, MN,** Heart's Ease, Lilies red and yellow, Pond Lilies, Cowslips. **1866** (1881) Whitney *Leslie Goldthwaite* 2 **NEng,** A garden heart's-ease,—that flower of many names. **1884** Roe *Nature's Serial Story* 255, "You must let Johnnie show you her garden, and especially her pansies." "Heart's-ease is another name for the flower, I believe." **1916** Parsons *Wild Flowers CA* 31, *Mountain Heart's-Ease. Viola Beckwithii. Ibid* 52, *Viola ocel-*

lata. . . This dainty little heart's-ease has nothing of the . . self-assertive look of our yellow pansy. **1938** Damon *Grandma* 81 **CT,** All through Grandma's garden stood old-fashioned flowering shrubs. . . There was love-in-a-mist, bleeding heart, and heart's-ease, too (ease from angina or love, I wondered, and used to eat the blooms to see; but as I had neither affliction I felt unsure of my conclusions). **1941** Walker *Lookout* 46 **TN,** Among this class of flowers is heartsease, or field pansy, birdfoot violet, and harebell. . . or bluebell. **1966** *DARE* (Qu. S26e, . . *Wildflowers*) Inf **FL**20, Heartease, small pansies. **1985** Clark *From Mailbox* 54 **ME,** The Johnny-jump-ups are blooming in every corner. . . Also known as ladies' delights, heartease and wild pansy, these hardy violas resemble miniature pansies.

2 Any of several **knotweeds,** but esp *Polygonum persicaria.* **chiefly Nth**

1784 in 1785 Amer. Acad. Arts & Sci. *Memoirs* 1.440 **PA,** *Heartsease. Spotted Arsmart.* The leaves have a dark spot on their upper surface, in form of a crescent. **1832** Williamson *Hist. ME* 1.124, *Hearts-ease* resembles arsmart in appearance, except that it has a large reddish heart-formed spot on its leaf. **c1873** in 1976 Miller *Shaker Herbs* 182 **NY,** *Heart's Ease, Polygonum persicaria* Ladies' Thumb. Spotted Knot Weed. Said to be useful in asthma, colds, and fevers. Useful as a diuretic. **1899** Bergen *Animal Lore* 115 **cnOH,** A common smartweed *(Polygonum Persicaria)* with heart-shaped markings on the leaves is called heart's-ease, and is supposed to be useful in diseases of the heart. **1965** Needham–Mussey *Country Things* 139 **sVT,** Smartweed grows wild around here, and looks so much like heartsease that you can scarcely tell them apart unless you handle the smartweed or get it in your eyes. **1966** *DARE* File **neCO,** Heart's ease—knotweed. **1968** *DARE* FW Addit **NY**93, Heart's ease ['hɑɚt‚siz] or smartweed. **1970** *NC Folkl.* 18.41, To keep an erring husband make tea of heartsease blossoms.

3 **=self-heal.**

1897 *Jrl. Amer. Folkl.* 10.53, *Brunella vulgaris* . . hearts' ease, Cambridge, Mass. **1898** *Ibid* 11.277 **MA,** *Brunella vulgaris*. . . heartsease. [Footnote:] Thought to cure diseases of the heart.

4 A **wild ginger** (here: prob *Hexastylis arifolia*).

1960 Williams *Walk Egypt* 253 **GA,** We found heartsease. Zadie gave me the jugs to eat. She held out a thin palm. . . Great heart-shaped leaves lay there, and one of two tiny brown "jugs" that were the flower of the plant, sweet and gingery to the taste.

heartseed n [See quot 1953]

A plant of the genus *Cardiospermum* such as **balloon vine.**

1847 Wood *Class-Book* 215, *C[ardiospermum] Haliacăbum* [sic]. *Heart-seed. Balloon-vine*. . . Native on the Missouri and its branches. . . Naturalized in the W. States. **1895** Gray–Bailey *Field Botany* 109, *Heartseed*. . . Wild in S.W. States, and cult. for the inflated pods. **1900** Lyons *Plant Names* 81, *C[ardiospérmum] Halicácabum*. . . South America and cult. in gardens. Balloon-vine, Heart-seed. **1953** Greene–Blomquist *Flowers South* 70, *Heart-Seed* . . a translation of the generic name *Cardiospermum* given to these herbaceous or woody vines in allusion to their black seeds with a white spot fancied to be heart-shaped. **1976** Bailey–Bailey *Hortus Third* 221, *Cardiospermum* L. Heartseed, balloon vine.

heart snakeroot n [Cf quot 1743]

A **wild ginger,** usu *Asarum canadense,* but also *Hexastylis arifolia.*

1743 (1754) Catesby *Nat. Hist. Carolina* 2.41/1, The *Indians* . . have likewise some Roots, which they pretend will effect the Cure [of a rattlesnake bite], particularly a kind of *Assarum,* commonly called *Heart-Snake-root.* **1828** Rafinesque *Med. Flora* 1.70, *Asarum canadense*. . . Heart Snakeroot. **1930** Sievers *Amer. Med. Plants* 19, *Canada Wildginger, Asarum canadense* . . heart snakeroot. **1971** Krochmal *Appalachia Med. Plants* 66, *Asarum canadense*. . . heart snakeroot. **1974** Morton *Folk Remedies* 73, *Heart Snakeroot*. . . *Hexastylis arifolia. . . South Carolina (Current use):* Commonly employed as a folk remedy. "Tea" . . usually taken for colds or just because people regard it as "good for you."

hearts on a chain n

=coral vine 3.

1965 Neal *Gardens HI* 329, *Hearts on a Chain. Antigonon leptopus*. . . A sun-loving vine.

heart-spot knotweed n Also *heartspot* [From the heart-shaped spot on the leaf] *obs* Cf **heartweed**

A **lady's thumb** (here: *Polygonum persicaria*).

1822 Eaton *Botany* 401, *Polygonum* . . *persicaria* . . heart-spot knotweed. **1840** MA Zool. & Bot. Surv. *Herb. Plants & Quadrupeds* 101, *P[olygonum] persicaria* . . Heartspot.

heart twister n [See quot 1976]

A **hedgehog cactus 3** (here: *Echinocereus triglochidiatus* var *melanacanthus*).

1959 Carleton *Index Herb. Plants* 59, *Heart twister:* Echinocereus coccineus. **1967** Dodge *Roadside Wildflowers* 45, The yellow-green fruits are edible but are believed by Navajo Indians to cause internal pains, hence the name "heart twister." . . *Echinocereus triglochidiatus* variety *melanacanthus.*

heartweed n [From the heart-shaped spot on the leaf]

1 A **lady's thumb** (here: *Polygonum persicaria*).

1894 *Jrl. Amer. Folkl.* 7.97 **ME,** *Polygonum Persicaria,* heart-weed. **1931** Clute *Common Plants* 127, The heartweed *(Polygonum persicaria),* which has heart-shaped markings on the leaves. **1966** *DARE* Wildfl QR Pl.47A Inf **NC**28, Heartweed; Pl.47B Inf **NC**28, Heartweed—the devil cut his wife's heart out and wiped the knife on the leaf. **1969** *DARE* (Qu. S21, . . *Weeds*) Inf **NJ**56, Heartweed.

2 A **water pepper** (here: *Polygonum hydropiper*).

c1873 in 1976 Miller *Shaker Herbs* 251, *Water Pepper. Polygonum hydropiper.* Smart Weed. Arsmart. Heartweed. . . The leaves are marked with a brownish spot.

heat v

A Forms.

Past, past pple: usu *heated,* also:

1 *het.* [*OED* c1400 →] *chiefly among speakers with little formal education* For addit exx of the past pple see **het up**

1805 (1904) White *Jrl.* 22 **MA,** We het water and got out lye all the forenoon. **1848** Lowell *Biglow* 144 **'Upcountry' MA,** Het, heated. **1890** *DN* 1.71 **LA, NEng,** *Het:* heated. **1899** (1912) Green *VA Folk-Speech* 223, *Het*. . . Past tense of *heat.* **1907** *DN* 3.206 **nwAR, seMA.** **1908** *DN* 3.320 **eAL, wGA.** **1915** *DN* 4.226 **wTX.** **1923** *DN* 5.210 **swMO.** **1934** *WV Review* Dec 78, [Archaic forms still in use in West Virginia include] *het.* **1953** Atwood *Survey of Verb Forms* 16, The past participle (adjective) form *het* /hɛt/ . . is quite common in n.e.N. Eng., where about one fourth of the informants offer it. . . Elsewhere in the Eastern States only a sprinkling of informants use *het* . . with no geographical concentration. **1965–70** *DARE* (Qu. OO5a, . . *"Our house was ______ [with a stove].'*) 137 Infs, **widespread,** Het; **AR**55, Het up; (Qu. OO5b, . . *"Years ago they ______ [the house] with a stove."*) 133 Infs, **widespread,** Het [Of all Infs responding to Qq. OO5a, b, 29% were gs educ or less; of those giving this response, 55% were gs educ or less.]; (Qu. H68, *When food remains over from one meal and you heat it again . . "She got out Sunday's roast and ______ [it]."*) Inf **MO**2, Het; **IL**5, **MO**6, **MA**5, **NC**60, Het it up; **GA**24, 81, **IL**113, **IN**52, **NY**42, Het up (*or* over). **1976** Garber *Mountain-ese* 40 **Appalachians,** We jist het the coffee in the pot. **1983** Beyle *How Talk Cape Cod* 32, As Gifford said, "Once they's [=stones used in a clambake] het up, the goodness is gone. The life is out of them."

2 *heat.* **esp Sth, S Midl**

1965–70 *DARE* (Qu. OO5a, . . *"Our house was ______ [with a stove].'*) Infs **GA**5, **MO**8, **MS**63, **SC**26, **TN**34, **WI**23, Heat; (Qu. OO5b, . . *"Years ago they ______ [the house] with a stove."*) Infs **MO**8, 39, **SC**26, **TN**34, **MS**69, Heat.

B Sense.

See quot. Cf **heat** n

1947 *PADS* 8.19 **IA, VA, NC,** *Heat:* To break out with heat.

heat n **Sth, S Midl** See Map

A heat rash, prickly heat.

1899 (1912) Green *VA Folk-Speech* 221, *Heat*. . . An itching eruption on the skin, generally in hot weather. **1946** *PADS* 6.17 **eNC** (as of 1900–10), *Heat*. . . Children's summer rash. **1954** *Harder Coll.* **cwTN,** *Heat*—Summer rash. **1956** McAtee *Some Dialect NC* 22, *Heat:* . . prickly-heat, an inflammation of the skin in hot weather. **c1960** *Wilson Coll.* **csKY,** *Heat* (or *prickly heat*)—A rash, a "breaking out." **1965–70** *DARE* (Qu. BB25, . . *Common skin diseases*) 13 Infs, **Sth, S Midl,** Heat. **1976** Ryland *Richmond Co. VA* 372, *Heat*—heat-rash

heat-a-piece See **heater piece**

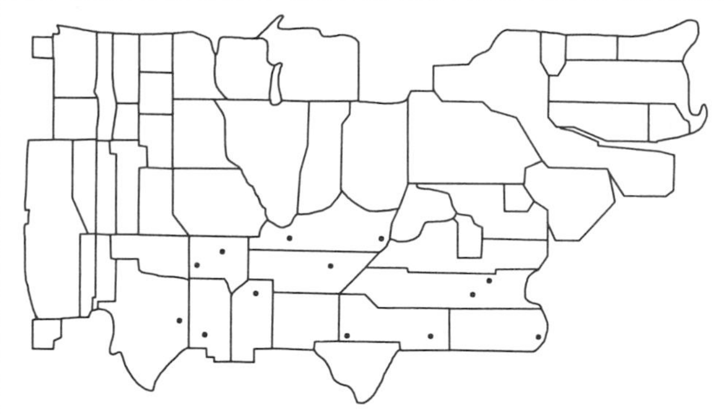

•heat n (Qu. BB25)

heat bug n Also *heat beetle*
=**cicada.**

1968–69 *DARE* (Qu. R7, *Insects that sit in trees or bushes in hot weather and make a sharp, buzzing sound*) Infs **IL**45, **MO**36, **NY**214, Heat bug; (Qu. R8, . . *Creatures that make a clicking or shrilling or chirping kind of sound*) Inf **MA**122, Heat bugs; (Qu. R30) Inf **PA**225, Heat beetle.

heater piece n Pronc-sp *heat-a-piece* [*heater* a triangular piece of iron heated on a stove and inserted in a hollow flatiron] **chiefly NEng Cf flatiron b**

A small triangular plot of land.

1859 (1968) Bartlett *Americanisms* 193 **NEng,** *Heater piece.* A gore or triangular piece of land, so called, probably, from a flat iron, the form of which it resembles. **1863** (1864) Mitchell *My Farm* 243 **CT,** Waal—kinder like to have a little 'heater' piece; the boys, you see, hoc it out in odd spells. **1884** Jewett *Mate of Daylight* 209 **ME,** I could n't help thinking of Joe's mansion, that he and his father hauled down to the heater piece in the fork of the roads. **1897** *KS Univ. Qrly.* (ser B) 6.53 **KS,** *Heat-a-piece:* an untilled corner between fields. **1903** *DN* 2.298 **Cape Cod MA** (as of a1857), *Heater piece.* . . A triangular strip of land, shaped like a heater. **1963** Haywood *Yankee Dict.* 78, *Heater piece*—The corner made by two streets or roads that intersect at an acute angle, so called because its outline resembles that of a flatiron. **1969** *DARE* (Qu. L6a, . . *A piece of land under cultivation—less than an acre*) Inf **CT**29, Heater piece—old-fashioned. **1975** Gould *ME Lingo* 128, A *heater piece* is . . a triangular plot of land; specifically, the grassy place at a road intersection left untraveled by wagons that always cut the corners.

heath n Usu |hiθ|; also **ME** |heθ|

1 A flat tract of land that is bare or covered with low shrubs and bushes. [*OED* a1000 →] **chiefly sME**

1792 Belknap *Hist. NH* 3.44, A large area, called the plain. It is a dry heath, composed of rocks covered with moss, and bearing the appearance of a pasture, in the beginning of the winter season. **1939** *LANE* Map 30, *Heath* . . grown with cranberries, blueberries or heather; 10 infs, **seME,** [heɨθ]. **1946** Attwood *Length ME* 14, *Heath*—a raised bog. An open level tract of land covered with coarse herbage. The usual pronunciation is as if spelled "hath" with long "a." **1966** *DARE* (Qu. C6, . . *Land that's often wet, and has grass and weeds growing on it*) Inf **ME**10, Heath [heɪθ]; (Qu. C28, *A place where underbrush, weeds, vines and small trees grow together so that it's nearly impossible to get through*) Inf **ME**5, Heath [heɪθ]—a tough place; (Qu. I44, . . *Berries [that] grow wild*) Inf **ME**23, Heath [heɪθ] cranberries.

2 Any of var low-growing plants generally found on a **heath 1** as:

a Std: Any of var plants of the family Ericaceæ, esp of the genera *Erica* and *Calluna.*

b A **crowberry 1** (here: *Empetrum nigrum*).

1824 Latham *Gen. Hist. Birds* 10.261, Their [=brent geese's] food chiefly consists of plants, such as the small bistort, and black-berried heath. . . [Footnote:] Empetrum nigrum. **1900** Lyons *Plant Names* 145, *Empetrum nigrum* . . Heath, Black-berried Heath. *Ibid* 194, *Hudsonia tomentosa* . . Heath. **1916** *Torreya* 16.238, *Empetrum nigrum* . . heath, Matinicus Id., Me. **1942** *Ibid* 42.162, *Empetrum nigrum* . . Black-berried heath.

c A **beach heather** (here: *Hudsonia tomentosa*). Cf **barren heath, false heather 1**

1896 *Jrl. Amer. Folkl.* 9.182, *Hudsonia tomentosa* . . heath, . . Wellfleet, Mass. **1900** [see **2b** above].

d also *heath bush:* Any of var other plants; see quot.

1939 *LANE* Map 30 1 inf, **csME,** *Bog,* open or wooded, grown with *heaths* [heɨθs]. Heaths include the heather family, bog moss, orchids and spruce; 1 inf, **seME,** *Heath,* grown with low bushes, the so-called ['he˘ɨθ] bushes.

heath apple n

The berry of the **hobblebush.**

1940 Brown *Amer. Cooks* 332 **ME,** The mooseberry or heath apple, a berry produced on a single stalk like a mulberry, planted, scientists say, by the migratory birds on the low promontories extending into the Atlantic at Lubec and Jonesport.

heath aster n

An aster: usu *Aster ericoides,* but also *A. pilosus.*

1900 Lyons *Plant Names* 52, *Aster ericoides* . . White Heath-aster. **1914** Georgia *Manual Weeds* 433, Heath Aster *(Aster ericoides).* **1940** Clute *Amer. Plant Names* 76, *Aster ericoides.* White Heath-aster. **1951** Voss-Eifert *IL Wild Flowers* 235, The heath aster [=*Aster pilosus*] arranges its small white flowers along secondary stems.

heath-bell n Also *heatherbells*

A **harebell 1** (here: *Campanula rotundifolia*).

1900 Lyons *Plant Names* 77, *C[ampanula] rotundifolia.* . . Heath-bell. **1920** *Torreya* 20.25, *Campanula rotundifolia* L.—Blue or heatherbells, Traverse City, Mich.

heathberry n

A **serviceberry.**

1869 U.S. Dept. Ag. *Rept. of Secy. for 1868* 178 **AK,** Small fruits are there in the greatest profusion. Among them may be noted . . service or heath-berries.

heath bush See **heath 2d**

heath cock See **heath hen 1**

heathen n Usu |'hiðən|; also **S Midl** |'hiðərn| Pronc-sp *heathern* Cf Intro "Language Changes" I.8

Std sense, var form.

1926 *DN* 5.400 **Ozarks,** *Heathern.* . . Heathen, non-religious person or persons. **1942** Hall *Smoky Mt. Speech* 70 **wNC, eTN,** There has been a tendency in old Smokies speech to develop [ə] into [ɚ], especially before *n.* . . *heathen* ['hiðɚn]. **1953** Randolph-Wilson *Down in Holler* 28 **Ozarks,** Heathen is nearly always pronounced *heathern.* **c1960** *Wilson Coll.* **csKY,** *Heathen* (more often *heathern*). **1976** Garber *Mountain-ese* 39 **Appalachians,** *Heathern.*

heathen Chinee n, also attrib Also *heathen Chinese* [From the poem "Plain Language from Truthful James" by Bret Harte; see quot 1870] *old-fash*

A Chinese person, esp one regarded as devious and cunning.

1870 in 1886 Harte *Complete Poetical Wks.* 129 **CA,** For ways that are dark / And for tricks that are vain,/ The heathen Chinee is peculiar. *Ibid* 130, "We are ruined by Chinese cheap labor,"—/ And he went for that heathen Chinee. **1872** Schele de Vere *Americanisms* 155, The *Heathen Chinee,* as he will, no doubt, be called for many a year to come, . . has only so lately appeared on our shores, that Chinese terms can hardly be said to have found their way yet into our speech. **1889** (1971) Farmer *Americanisms* 293, The picture there [=in Bret Harte's poem] drawn of the *Heathen Chinee* . . took and still retains the public fancy to such a degree that, without doubt, the nickname is now as permanent a one as Brother Jonathan or John Bull. **1890** *Congressional Record* 7 June 21.6.5791/2 **PA,** This bill . . has something of a Heathen Chinee flavor about it and . . it is framed with "intent to deceive." **1968** *DARE* (Qu. HH28, . . *Chinese*) Inf **CT**10, Heathen Chinese.

heather n

1 Any of var ericaceous plants, as:

a =**mountain heather.**

1898 *Jrl. Amer. Folkl.* 11.273, *Bryanthus* (sp.), Alpine heather, Cal.—*Bryanthus empetriformis,* . . heather . . Wash. **1915** (1926) Armstrong-Thornber *Western Wild Flowers* 350, There are only a few kinds of Phyllodoce, . . often called Heather, but we have no native Heather. **1934** Haskin *Wild Flowers Pacific Coast* 265, *Red Heather. Phyllodoce empetriformis. Ibid* 267, Cream-Colored Heather. *Phyllodoce glanduliflora.* **1963** Craighead *Rocky Mt. Wildflowers* 142, *Mountain Heath—Phyllodoce empetriformis.* . . *Other names:* Heather. **1966** [see **1c** below].

b A **beach heather** (here: *Hudsonia ericoides*).

1911 NJ State Museum *Annual Rept. for 1910* 561, This [=*Hudsonia ericoides*] is the "Heather" of the Pine Barrens.

c =mountain heather.

1931 U.S. Dept. Ag. *Misc. Pub.* 101.126, Cassiope is a group of 8 or 10 . . heathlike shrubs. . . The species are frequently called . . moss-heathers, and white (or pink) heather. **1961** Douglas *My Wilderness* 226 **nNH,** Alpine saxifrage and the cassiope or heather show tiny white flowers. **1966** Heller *Wild Flowers AK* 62, Heather . . *Cassiope tetragona* . . *Cassiope stellariana* . . *Phyllodoce glanduliflora.*

2 See quot.

1966–67 *DARE* (Qu. S11, . . *Bluets*) Inf **AR**41, Heather ['hi:θɚ] flowers; (Qu. S23, *Pale blue flowers with downy leaves and cups that come up on open, stony hillsides in March or early April*) Inf **MN**2, Heather or laurel weed.

heather v [Var of *hither;* cf *EDD hither* 2 "To the left."] Cf **near horse**

1966 *DARE* File **seNC,** As a command to horses *heather* means to turn to the left. *Gee* means turn to the right.

heatherbells See **heath-bell**

heathern See **heathen**

heath hawk n

=marsh hawk.

1966 *DARE* (Qu. Q4, . . *Kinds of hawks*) Inf **ME**6, Heath [heɪθ] hawk, a swamp hawk.

heath hen n

1 also *heath cock;* pronc-spp *hethen, heth'n:* An extinct subsp of the **prairie chicken** *(Tympanuchus cupido cupido).*

1634 Wood *New Engl. Prospect* 29 **NEng,** Pheasons bee very rare, but Heathcockes, and Partridges be common. . . the flesh of the Heath-cockes is red. **1648** in 1852 MA Hist. Soc. *Coll.* 4th ser 1.202 **MA,** The Turkies, Partridge, Heath-hens and their young ones tracing passe,/ The woods and meadowes. **1781** Peters *Genl. Hist. CT* 255, The feathered tribe in Connecticut are . . heath-hens, blackbirds. **1870** MA Genl. Court *Acts & Resolves* 224, Whoever . . takes or kills any of the birds called pinnated grouse, or heath hens . . shall forfeit for every such bird twenty-five dollars. **1888** Trumbull *Names of Birds* 136, *Tympanuchus americanus.* . . Other old names are *Barren hen, Heath cock,* and *Pinnated heath cock.* **1930** Shoemaker *1300 Words* 30 **cPA Mts** (as of c1900), *Heath-cock*—The pinnated grouse, (Tympanuchus Americanus), now extinct in Pennsylvania. **1953** *AmSp* 28.279, The Eastern race of pinnated grouse, called *heath hen* (now extinct), was a denizen of the pine barrens of New Jersey and the scrub-oak plains of Long Island (N.Y.), and was found in southern New England, including Cape Cod and Martha's Vineyard (Mass.) The name prevailed in all these localities but was sometimes shortened, particularly on Martha's Vineyard, to *hethen* or *heth'n.*

2 =spruce grouse.

1888 Trumbull *Names of Birds* 141 **ME,** The Ruffed-grouse . . at Jonesport, . . is Partridge simply, and the present species [=*Canachites canadensis*] *heath-hen.* **1923** U.S. Dept. Ag. *Farmers' Bulletin* 1375.17 **IL,** *No open season:* . . heath hen. **1927** Forbush *Birds MA* 2.23, *Canachites canadensis canace.* . . Heath hen. **1946** Hausman *Eastern Birds* 209. **1953** [see **3** below]. **1955** Forbush–May *Birds* 133, *Canada Spruce Grouse. . . Other names* . . Heath Hen.

3 =bittern.

1953 *AmSp* 28.279, *Heath hen.* . . The spruce grouse has acquired this title in Maine and by some devious transfer, the American bittern also, in New York.

heath-hen plum n

A **partridgeberry** (here: *Mitchella repens*).

1811 Wilson *Amer. Ornith.* 3.109, A favourite article of their [=pinnated grouses'] diet, is the *heath-hen plum,* or partridge-berry. **1937** *Torreya* 37.100, *Mitchella repens.* . . Heath-hen plum, Long I[slan]d, N.Y.

‡heating n

In tobacco cultivation: see quot.

1967 Key *Tobacco Vocab.* **TN,** *Heating* [=house burn—darkening of the curing leaf due to excess moisture in the barn].

heating-out n

A severe scolding or heated discussion.

1969 *DARE* (Qu. II27, . . *A very sharp scolding*) Inf **KY**26, Heating-out. **1980** *NADS Letters* **KY,** Heating-out . . refers to a heated discussion between two people.

heavalled up adj phr [By metathesis of *upheaval*] Cf **heaval, up in a**

1950 *WELS (Confused, mixed up: "The things in the drawer are all ______.")* 1 Inf, **WI,** Heavalled up.

heaval, up in a adj phr [By metathesis of *in an upheaval*] Cf **heavalled up**

Out of order; mixed up.

1988 *DARE* File, A friend of my mother's, who grew up near Springfield, Missouri, used to say facetiously that things were "all up in a heaval." She might be referring to her house after a party, to plans that had to be changed because of unforeseen events, or anything that was not as it should be. She had heard this from someone in Missouri.

heave v

A Forms.

1 pres: usu *heave:* rarely *hive.* [Scots, Engl dial *hive;* cf *SND; EDD* (at *heave*)]

1971 *Foxfire* Spring–Summer 76 **nGA,** He got a'hold a'that rock and he begin t'hive and hive, and directly he pulled it up.

2 past, past ppl: usu *heaved;* also *somewhat old-fash, hove;* rarely *heave, hev, hoved, huff.*

1770 *Boston News-Letter* (MA) 15 Feb 2/2 **swME,** The Ice which is computed to be 40 Feet thick, hove one upon the Top of another. **1788** (1925) Washington *Diaries* 3.406 **VA,** Land was also sowed with Buck Wheat, for the experiment of its falling with the frost and by laying on the Wht. during the Winter keeping it warm and from being hove out of the grd. **1815** *Niles' Natl. Reg.* 9.201/1 **PA,** The outer ends of the floats had settled down about a foot by the thaw; but this hove them up something worse than they were at first. **1836** (1955) *Crockett Almanacks* 42 **wTN,** I hauled out a five dollar note, and hove it down. **1862** (1864) Browne *Artemus Ward Book* 173 **NEng,** "Heave two [=to]!" I hear him holler again, and stickin my head out of the cabin winder, *I hev.* **1884** *Anglia* 7.252 [Black], *Heave—Past.* huff, heave. **1899** (1912) Green *VA Folk-Speech* 233, *Hove.* . . Past tense and past participle of *heave.* **1923** *DN* 5.211 **swMO,** *Hove.* . . Heaved. **1931–33** *LANE Worksheets* **CT,** Hove up . . vomited. **1955** Ritchie *Singing Family* 51 **seKY,** [The geese] made that filly so nervous-wild that she hove up on her hind legs and come down and then kicked up on the front ones. **1965–70** [see **B1** below]. **1968** *Filson Club Hist. Qrly.* 158 **swKY** (as of 1800s–1920s), Sometimes the verb carried the regular past tense ending, being written *hoved up.*

B Senses.

1 To throw, cast, hurl; also fig. **chiefly Nth, West** See Map

1806 (1970) Webster *Compendious Dict.* 140/2, *Heave.* . . cast. **1904** *DN* 2.426 **Cape Cod MA,** *Heave.* . . To throw. 'If you don't want it, heave it out the window.' **1943** *LANE* Map 667, Several informants say *He threw a stone,* but *He heaved (hove)* . . *a rock.* [4 infs *heaved;* 6 infs *hove*] **1965–70** *DARE* (Qu. Y10, . . *"The dog came at him, so he picked up a stone and ______ it at him."*) 77 Infs, **chiefly Nth, West,** Heaved; **NY**86, Heave; **ME**16, 22, Hove; (Qu. C24b, . . *He took a stone . . and ______ it.*) 32 Infs, **chiefly Nth, West,** Heaved; **CT**32, **MA**17, **NJ**2, Throw, heave; **ME**16, 22, **NH**14, Hove; **NY**230, Heave, toss; (Qu. KK63, . . *A clumsy . . job of repairing something: "It will never last—he just ______."*) Inf **MA**56, Hove it together.

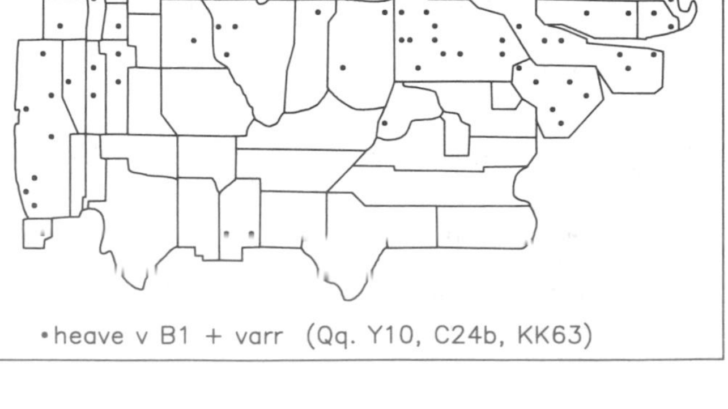

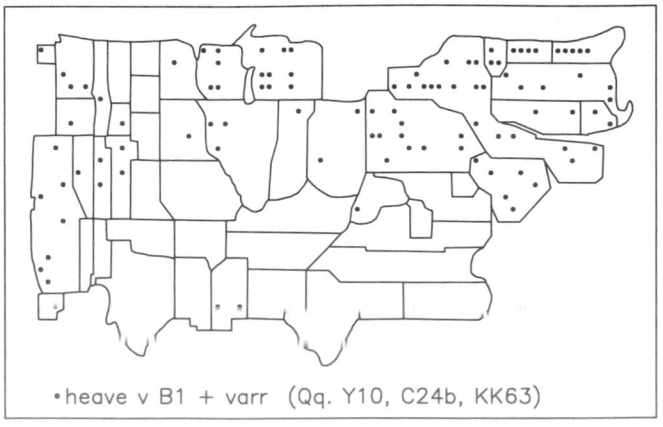

•heave v B1 + varr (Qq. Y10, C24b, KK63)

2 with *to;* Fig: to hurry; to exert oneself energetically; hence n *heave to* energy.

1967–68 *DARE* (Qu. A20, *Joking ways of telling somebody to hurry*) Inf **NY**63, Heave to; (Qu. KK28, *Feeling ambitious and eager to work*) Inf **WI**34, Got the old heave to; (Qu. KK29, *To start working very hard*) Inf **NY**2, Heaves to it.

3 with *down;* To careen (a ship); hence ppl adj phr *hove down;* also fig. [*OED heave down* (at *heave* v. 20. b) 1745 →]

1938 Tripp *Flukes* [x], At one wharf was a ship "hove down," as the sailors say, that is, by means of a heavy block attached at the lower mainmast head; . . the vessel was hove over on her beam ends until the length of her keel was exposed. **1942** Berrey–Van den Bark *Amer. Slang* 796.5, Heave down a ship, *to careen a ship.* **1985** Rattray *Advent. Dimon* 246 **Long Is. NY** (as of c1900), She's living down there by Bellyache Swamp, hovedown in bed half the time and up playing Mrs. Hopkins the other half.

heave n See **heaves**

heave a project v phr

To cast a spell; also fig.

1908 *Atlantic Mth.* 101.242/1 **sME,** There's a woman alive right here to this Cove . . that can turn to and heave a project full better'n what ever Aunt Polly Belknap could! **1975** Gould *ME Lingo* 129, *Heave a project*—Occasionally heard in the sense of cast a spell, but not with any suggestion of witchcraft: "She *hove* me a *project* and I can't get her off my mind!" To make an impression on somebody.

heaven n Usu |'hɛvən|; also, *esp freq among Black speakers,* |'hɛbm̩, 'hɛbn̩| Cf Pronc Intro 3.I.17 Pronc-spp **chiefly Sth, S Midl** *esp among Black speakers, heaben, heabm, heabun, heavm, he(a)vun, heb(b)en, heb-m, heving* (cf **-ing**), *hiven*

A Forms.

1837 Sherwood *Gaz. GA* 70, *Heavun,* for heaven. **1853** Simms *Sword & Distaff* 376 **SC** [Black], You mustn't tink for raise up you arm to de heabens. **1862** (1864) Browne *Artemus Ward Book* 87, Allowin the free air of hevun to blow. *Ibid* 176, I should move heving & arth. **1884** *Anglia* 7.256 **Sth, S Midl** [Black], Yea, Fader in hebben! **1893** Shands *MS Speech* 36, *Heben* [hɛbn]. Negro for *heaven.* **1896** Harris *Sister Jane* 133 **GA** [Black], Gabe Bowden done dead an' gone ter heav'm. **1908** *DN* 3.282 **eAL, wGA,** *n* has become vocalic *m* after *p* or *b,* as in . . heb-m. **1922** *DN* 5.135 **cWest,** *Hevings* for *heavens.* . . heard only when the word is used as an interjection. **1931** *AmSp* 6.347 **cWest,** Heavm, heabm. **1934** *WV Review* Dec 79, *Hiven.* . . may still be heard once in a while in West Virginia. **1938** Matschat *Suwannee R.* 233 **nFL, sGA** [Black], Br'er Rabbit was so mad he went straight up to hebben an' stood befo' de Lawd. **1953** Randolph–Wilson *Down in Holler* 26 **Ozarks,** I once knew a jimson-weed preacher . . who . . pronounced heaven as if it were spelled *heving.* **1953** Brewer *Word Brazos* 40 **c,sTX** (as of c1890) [Black], Unkuh Ebun seent anothuh star shoot crost de heabuns. **c1960** *Wilson Coll.* **csKY,** *Heaven* is sometimes /hɛbm̩/.

B Sense.

Usu in comb: see quot. Cf **nigger heaven, peanut heaven**

1967–70 *DARE* (Qu. D40, . . *The upper balcony in a theater*) Infs **NY**67, **OH**42, Heaven; **MN**2, Lovers' heaven; [**MI**91, Nearly heaven;] **TX**5, Neckers' heaven; **IL**9, 31, **MI**69, Seventh heaven; **OH**11, Something heaven. **1990** *DARE* File **ceIA** (as of c1975), Those of us who worked on plays in the old theatre called the upper level of seating "heaven." Since we rarely had a full house, friends and crew would sit there for free.

heavenly crown See **feather crown**

heavenly days intj Cf *DS* NN8a, 9a, 26a, 29a

Used as an expression of joy or surprise.

1924 *DN* 5.269, *Heavenly:*—days (surp[rise]). *Ibid* 285 **seNE.** **1942** McAtee *Dial. Grant Co. IN* 33 (as of 1890s), Heavenly days. **1959** *VT Hist.* 27.141, *Heavenly days!* . . Common. **1966** Barnes–Jensen *Dict. UT Slang* 22, *Heavenly days!* . . expression of joy. **1968** *DARE* Tape **IL**28, I wouldn't live in a city. . . Heavenly days where would you go for what and why.

heavens to Betsy intj Also sp *heavens to Betsey* [Etym unknown]

Used as an expression of joy, surprise or annoyance.

1891 Cooke *Huckleberries* 173 **NEng,** "Heavens to Betsey!" gasped Josiah. "That old feller?" **1914** *DN* 4.74 **ME, nNH,** *Heavens to Betsy!* Common exclamation among women. **1955** Funk *Heavens to Betsy* 11, Possibly the phrase [=*Heavens to Betsy*] was known in Revolutionary War days, but I doubt it. Nor do I think . . that it pertained in any way to the maker of the first American flag, Betsy Ross. It is much more likely to have been derived in some way from the frontierman's rifle or gun which, for unknown reason, he always fondly called Betsy. . . I am reluctantly forced to resort to . . "Source unknown." **1959** *VT Hist.* 27.141, *Heaven to Betsy!* . . Occasional. **1966–68** *DARE* (Qu. NN6a, *Exclamations of joy*) Inf **WA**3, Heavens to Betsy; (Qu. NN7, *Exclamations of surprise*) Infs **MD**37, **SC**5, Heavens to Betsy; (Qu. NN8a, *Exclamations of annoyance or disgust*) Inf **MN**26, Heavens to Betsy; (Qu. NN9a, *Exclamations showing great annoyance*) Infs **ME**12, **MN**26, Heavens to Betsy; (QR, near Qu. NN27) Inf **CA**87, Heavens to Betsy. **1976** Garber *Mountain-ese* 39 **Appalachians,** *Heavens-to-Betsy* . . Oh my. Heavens to Betsy, the old cow is in the rosneer [=roasting ear] patch again.

heaven tree n Also *heavenward tree*

=**tree of heaven.**

1900 Lyons *Plant Names* 20, *A[ilanthus] glandulosa.* . . Heavenward tree. **1960** Vines *Trees SW* 600, *Ailanthus . . altissima.* . . Vernacular names for the tree are . . Heavenward-tree [etc]. **1969** *DARE* (Qu. T16, *What kinds of trees are 'special' around here?*) Inf **WV**17, Heaven tree—ailanthus.

heaver n [In ref to its *heaving,* as a result of **heaves**]

1968–69 *DARE* (Qu. K48, *When a horse is short of breath*) Infs **KY**6, **NY**102, A heaver.

heaves n pl Freq with *the* Rarely *heave* **widespread, but more freq NEast, N Cent, C Atl** See Map Cf **bellows C**

Shortness of breath, esp equine emphysema.

1793 *Thomas' MA Spy or Worcester Gaz.* (MA) 8 Aug 1/1, If an old maiden chances to have the *heaves,* 'tis . . dignified with a polypus upon the heart. **1836** (1838) Haliburton *Clockmaker* (1st ser) 174 **NEng,** I am proper tired; I blow like a horse that's got the heaves. **1906** *Harper's Mth. Mag.* 113.341/2 **West,** It gives me [=Buffalo Bill's horse] the heaves just to think of it. **1965–70** *DARE* (Qu. K48, *When a horse is short of breath*) 238 Infs, **widespread, but less freq Sth,** (Got *or* has) (the) heaves; **CT**39, **DC**5, **IL**5, **MI**27, **VA**46, (Got the) heave; (Qu. **K**47, . . *Diseases . . [of] horses or mules*) 200 Infs, **widespread, but more freq NEast, N Cent, C Atl,** Heaves; **AR**9, 33, Dry heaves; (Qu. K28, . . *Diseases . . cows*) Inf **NJ**45, Heaves. **1969** Sorden *Lumberjack Lingo* 55 **NEng, Gt Lakes,** *Heaves*—A lung disease of horses that prevented proper breathing. **1984** *MJLF* 10.151 **cnWI,** *Heaves.* A lung disease common among horses and aggravated by hot, humid weather and dusty hay.

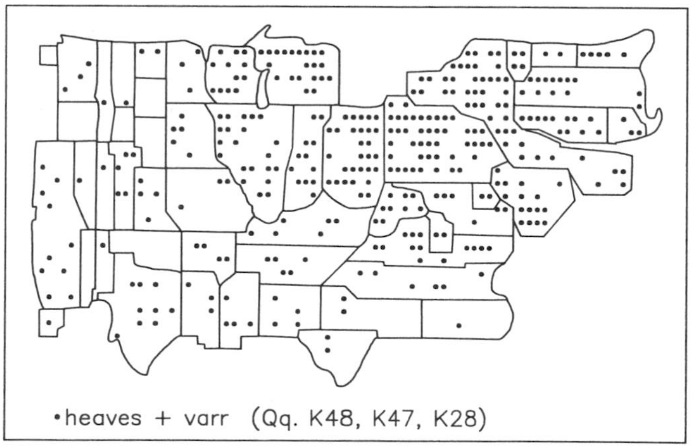

heave to See **heave** v **B2**

heave up Jonah See **Jonah**

heavey See **heavy**

heavm, heavun See **heaven**

heavy adj |'hivi, -ɪ| Pronc-sp *heavey* **chiefly Nth, Midl** See Map and Map Section

Short-winded; afflicted with the **heaves.**

1864 (1873) Webster *Amer. Dict.* 616/3, *Heavy.* . . Having the heaves; as a *heavy* horse. **1950** *WELS* (*A horse that is short on breath*) 20 Infs, **WI,** Heavey. **1958** McCulloch *Woods Words* 83 **Pacific NW,** *Heavey*

—A man or an animal with "asthma" or any wind difficulty. **c1960** *Wilson Coll.* **csKY,** *Heavy* [hivɪ]—Said of a horse out of breath; afflicted with heaves. **1965–70** *DARE* (Qu. K48, *When a horse is short of breath, you say it's ____*) 116 Infs, **chiefly Nth, Midl,** Heavy; **OH**35, Heavy devil; **PA**21, Heavy horse; (Qu. K47, . . *Diseases . . [of] horses or mules*) Inf **WI**6, Heavy; **AR**51, Heavy horse; (Qu. K44, *A bony or poor-looking horse*) Inf **NY**2, Heavy [hivi]; (QR, near Qu. X55b) Inf **IA**8, Heavy [hivi]—windbroken; an old, shrewd horsetrader, would, if he suspected a horse was heavy, suddenly poke him in the ribs; if the horse then farted, it was proof he was heavy. Thus the saying "fart like a heavy horse." **1969** Sorden *Lumberjack Lingo* 55 **NEng, Gt Lakes,** *Heavy*—Describes a man or beast with the heaves, asthma, or generally any breathing difficulty.

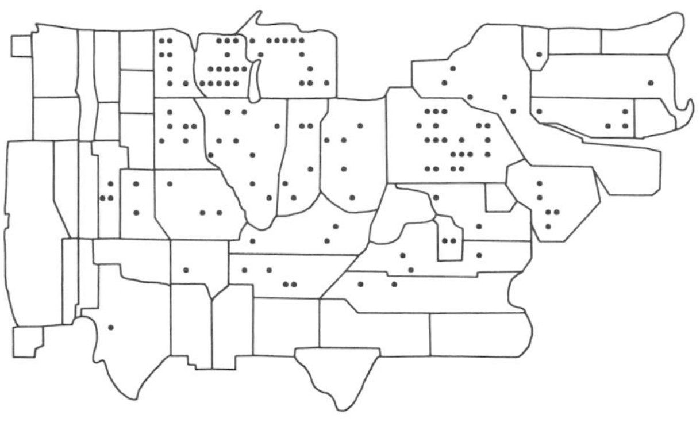

•heavy + varr (Qq. K48, K44, K47)

heavy-heavy-high-over n
=**Antony-over A.**

1967 *DARE* (Qu. EE22, . . *The game in which they throw a ball over a building . . to a player on the other side*) Inf **PA**35, Heavy-heavy-high-over.

heavy, heavy, what hangs over n
The game of *forfeits* (at **forfeit** n).

[1899 [see **forfeit** n].] **1968** *DARE* (QR, near Qu. EE3) Inf **PA**167, Heavy, heavy, what hangs over—something is held over a blindfolded person's head; he guesses [what it is]; (Qu. EE4, *Games in which one player's eyes are bandaged and he has to catch the others and guess who they are*) Inf **PA**112, Heavy, heavy, what hangs over.

heavy pine See **heavy-wooded pine**

heavy-tailed duck n Also *heavy-tailed coot*
=**ruddy duck.**

1830 *Cabinet Nat. Hist.* 1.41/2, As early as the first and second week in October, the smaller Ducks, as the Buffel-head, . . and the Ruddy, or Heavy-tailed Duck, *(A. rubidus,)* &c., begin to show themselves in the upper part of the bay [=Chesapeake Bay]. **1888** Trumbull *Names of Birds* 112, [Ruddy duck] referred to . . as *heavy-tailed duck.* **1917** (1923) *Birds Amer.* 1.152, *Ruddy Duck. . . Other Names. . .* Heavy-tailed coot.

heavy-wooded pine n Also *heavy pine*
=**ponderosa pine.**

1836 P. & C. Lawson *Agriculturalist's Manual* 354 *(OEDS),* Pinus ponderosa—Heavy Wooded Pine. . . Introduced by Mr. Douglas from the west coast of North America in 1828. **1858** Warder *Hedges* 250 **NW,** *Pinus ponderosa,* or Heavy-wooded Pine, has leaves from nine inches to a foot long. **1892** Apgar *Trees Nth. U.S.* 174, *Western Yellow or Heavy-wooded Pine. . .* A large Pacific coast species, 100 to 300 ft. high. **1897** Sudworth *Arborescent Flora* 20 **CA,** *Pinus ponderosa. . .* Heavy Pine. **1923** Dallimore–Jackson *Coniferae* 437 **WA, OR, nCA,** *Pinus ponderosa. . .* Heavy Pine; Heavy-wooded Pine. **1976** Yepson *Trees* 268, *Pine, ponderosa . .* heavy pine, heavy-wooded pine.

he-balsam n [See quot 1943] Cf **he n 3, she-balsam**
Either **black spruce 1** or **red spruce.**

1860 Curtis *Cat. Plants NC* 27, *Black Spruce.* (A. nigra, Poir.) . . Called *He Balsam.* **1883** Hale *Woods NC* 48, And it is, I believe, what is most commonly and absurdly called *He Balsam.* **1917** *DN* 4.413 **wNC,** *He-balsam. . .* Black spruce. **1937** Thornburgh *Gt. Smoky Mts.* 28, My mountain guide calls the red spruce "he balsam" and the Fraser fir is "she-balsam." **1943** Peattie *Great Smokies* 161, In the trunks of the fir under the bark, there are often big rosin blisters filled with a clear liquid (the balsam of commerce) which the mountain folk have whimsically compared to milk. So they named this the "she-balsam." Thinking perhaps that it needed a mate, and finding the spruce tree, which is devoid of "milk," commonly accompanying it, they named it the "he-balsam"! **1976** Bailey–Bailey *Hortus Third* 871, *[Picea] rubens. . . Red s[pruce], he balsam. . .* Important timber tree and main source of spruce gum.

hebben See **heaven**

hebby adj Also sp *heaby* [Varr of *heavy;* cf Pronc Intro 3.I.17] *among Black speakers*

1888 Jones *Negro Myths* 118 **GA coast,** De King . . gen um de gal, an dem bin hab er hebby [=consequential] weddin. **1908** *S. Atl. Qrly.* 7.346 **sSC coast** [Gullah], *Hebby rain duh falls* [=falls or fell]. **1922** Gonzales *Black Border* 306 **sSC, GA coasts** [Gullah glossary], *Hebby*—heavy, great; as: "uh hebby cumplain' "—a great outcry. **1936** Reese *Worleys* 18 **MD** (as of 1865) [Black], She heaby enough wid care an' sorrow.

hebe n, also cap Also sp *heab, heeb* [Abbrs for *Hebrew*] **scattered, but esp NEast** See Map *derog*
A Jew.

1932 Farrell *Young Lonigan* 148 **Chicago IL,** He shoulduh been a nigger or a hebe instead of Irish. **1946** (1972) Mezzrow–Wolfe *Really Blues* 333, Heeb: *Jewish person.* **1950** *WELS (People of foreign background: Jewish)* 3 Infs, **WI,** Hebe. **1951** Green–Laurie *Show Biz* 569, *Hebe comic*—Jewish comedian. **1953** *AmSp* 28.116 **Pacific** (as of 1940s) [Carnival Talk], *Hebe. . .* A Jew. **1956** Ker *Vocab. W. TX* 368, Jew (nicknames) . . *Hebes* [1 inf]. **1964** *PADS* 42.34 **Chicago IL** [Abusive terms for a Jew], *Hebrew* and *Hebe* were found among all social groups except the Jews themselves. **1965–70** *DARE* (Qu. HH28, . . *People of foreign background*) 26 Infs, **scattered, but esp NEast,** Hebe; (Qu. CC4, . . *Nicknames . . religious groups*) Inf **MO**26, **NJ**19, **VA**85, Hebes. **1967** *Current Slang* 2.2.17 [Air Force Academy], *Heab* (Heeb). . . A Jewish person. **1972** *Natl. Observer* 27 May 17/4, They [="polack jokes"] will be followed close upon their heels by miserly Hebes, and cheating kikes.

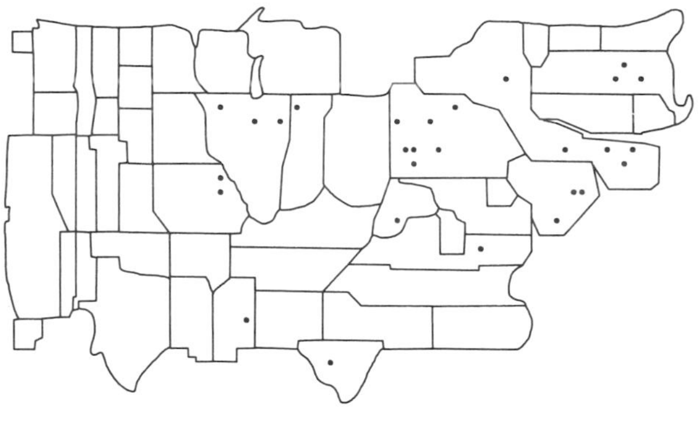

•hebe (Qq. HH28, CC4)

heben, heb-m See **heaven**

he-biddy, he-brute See **he n 1**

Hec See **Hector 1**

hechs See **hex n 1**

hechsed See **hex v**

Heck See **Hector 1**

hecker n [Etym uncert; cf PaGer *hecke* bushes, undergrowth] **PaGer area** Cf **Hector 3**
A rustic; rural backcountry.

1904 *DN* 2.397 **sNJ,** *Hecker. . .* A rustic, a countryman, a "buckwheat." **1967–69** *DARE* (Qu. C33, . . *An out-of-the-way place*) Inf **PA**40, [hɛkɚ]; in the sticks or in the backwoods; definitely Dutch; (Qu. HH1, . . *A rustic or countrified person*) Inf **PA**48, Country hecker, **NJ**20, Hecker. **1982** *Smithsonian Letters* cet A, In Tamaqua, a farmer was a hecker. There is in German a "hecker" who, as a farmer, engaged in animal breeding and brooding.

heck-how n

A **poison hemlock** (here: *Conium maculatum*).

1900 Lyons *Plant Names* 113, *C[onium] maculatum*. . . Heck-how. **1904** Henkel *Weeds Used in Med.* 39, Poison Hemlock—*Conium maculatum* . . heck-how. **1930** Sievers *Amer. Med. Plants* 46, Poison Hemlock—*Conium maculatum* . . heck-how.

he-clam n [See quot]

A clam worm *(Nereis virens).*

1889 *Century Dict.* 2767/1 **ME,** *He-clam*. . . A kind of sea-worm, as species of *Nereis;* a clam-worm, as *N. virens,* believed by fishermen to be the male of the long clam, *Mya arenaria.*

he-coon, he-cow, he-crab, he-critter See **he** n **1**

hectic adj

Of weather: see quot.

1968–70 *DARE* (Qu. B2, *If the weather is very unpleasant*) Inf **TX**104, Hectic; (Qu. B8, *When clouds come and go all day*) Inf **MO**36, Hectic day; (Qu. B14, *When the wind is blowing unevenly*) Inf **MN**29, Hectic.

Hector n

1 also abbr *Hec(k);* in phr *since Hector was a pup* and varr: For a long time; a long time ago.

[**1828** Cooper *Prairie* 1.102, The dam of Hector . . was then a pup, and apt to open on the game the moment she struck the scent.] **1912** *DN* 3.589 **wIN,** *Since Hec was a pup*. . . For a long time. **1914** *DN* 4.112 **KS,** *Since Heck was a pup.* **1915** *DN* 4.190 **swVA,** *Since Hec was a pup*. . . For a long time. **1923** *DN* 5.221 **swMO,** *Since Heck was a pup.* **1926** *AmSp* 2.45 **IN** [Animal Comparisons], Since Hec (Hector) was a pup. **1927** *AmSp* 2.364 **WV,** We have lived here since Heck was a purp. **1943** *AmSp* 18.237 **seNY,** *Since Hector was a pup.* **1959** *VT Hist.* 27.141, *Since Hector was a pup*. . . Common. **c1960** *Wilson Coll.* **csKY,** Since Heck (or Hector) was a pup. **1965–70** *DARE* (Qu. A16, *A very long period of time: "I haven't seen him ______."*) 31 Infs, **scattered,** Since Hec(tor) was a pup; (Qu. FF21b, . . *Old* . . *"The first time I heard that one I ______."*) 11 Infs, **scattered,** (Was when) Hec(tor) was a pup(py); (Qu. A24, *Speaking of someone who has always been the same way: "He's been hot-tempered from ______."*) 10 Infs, **scattered,** (Ever) since Hec(tor) was a pup. **1967** *DARE* FW Addit **cnLA,** *Since Heck was a pup*—That's how long you haven't seen somebody. **1972** Cooper *NC Mt. Folkl.* 95, *Since Heck was a pup*—a long while ago. **1976** Garber *Mountain-ese* 82 **Appalachians,** That's not a new road, it's been there ever since heck wuz a pup.

2 in var compar and intj phrr: See quots. [Perh euphem for *hell*]

1904 Day *Kin o' Ktaadn* 85 **ME,** Oh, mother's full o' hector 'bout I'm goin' to be a sport,/ Jest because I'm on the jury and a-goin' down to court. **1908** *DN* 3.304 **eAL, wGA,** *Dead as Hector*. . . Entirely dead. Very common. **1966–68** *DARE* (Qu. GG40, . . *Violently angry*) Infs **SC**21, 24, Mad as (old) Hector; (Qu. HH22b, . . *A very mean person* . . *"He's meaner than ______."*) Inf **MD**37, Hector; (Qu. NN26a, *Weakened substitutes for 'Hell': "Oh ______!"*) Inf **MI**67, Hector.

3 See quot. Cf **hecker**

1968 *DARE* (Qu. HH1, . . *A rustic or countrified person*) Inf **PA**118, Hector from the farm.

he-cup See **hiccup**

hed See **have** v[1] **A3a**

hedeondillo, hedeundilla See **hediondilla**

hedge n Also *hedge plant, hedgerow, hedge tree* [See quots 1950, 1976] **chiefly N Cent, Cent** See Map

=Osage orange.

1897 Sudworth *Arborescent Flora* 190, *Toxylon pomiferum*. . . *Common Names*. . . Hedge (Ill.) Hedge Plant (Iowa, Nebr.) **1930** OK Univ. Biol. Surv. *Pub.* 2.59, *Maclura pomifera*. . . Hedge-tree. **1936** (1972) Ise *Sod & Stubble* 71 **KS,** Early in April Henry and Rosie set out a quarter of a mile of hedge, and a large patch of wild plums. **1940** Clute *Amer. Plant Names* 164, *Osage-orange*. . . Hedge plant. *Ibid* 264, *Maclura pomifera*. . . Hedge. **1941** Writers' Program *Guide AR* 314, *Bois d'arc,* known variously as . . hedge, applewood, or rabbit hedge, is highly prized by makers of archery equipment. **1950** Moore *Trees AR* 67, *Osage-orange*. . . Local Names . . Hedge. . . *Uses.* Extensively for hedges. **1965–70** *DARE* (Qu. T13) 26 Infs, **esp N Cent, Cent,** Hedge; 11 Infs, **esp N Cent, Cent,** Hedge tree; **IL**30, Hedgerow; (Qu. T16) Infs **OK**18, 42, 52, Hedge tree(s). **1976** Yepson *Trees* 262, Hedge plant. . . The Osage orange bears formidable spines and can be grown into an impenetrable hedge. **1979** Little *Checklist U.S. Trees* 165, Hedge.

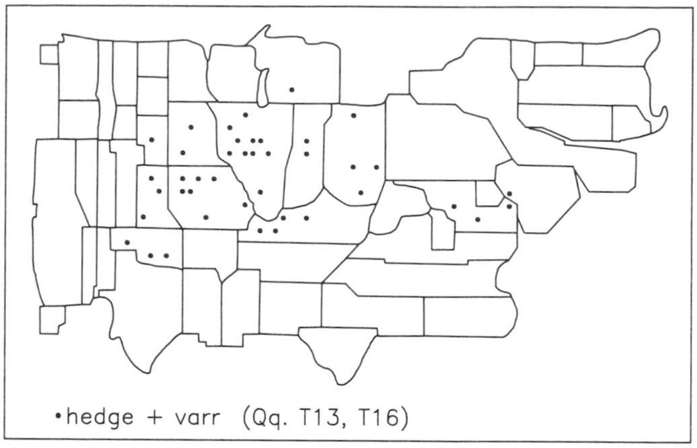

hedge apple n [See quot 1953] **chiefly W Midl** See Map Cf **hedge orange**

=Osage orange.

1929 Bell *Some Contrib. KS Vocab.* 178, The large round fruit of the tree is called *hedge-balls* or *hedge-apples.* **1940** Steyermark *Flora MO* 151, *Hedge Apple (Maclura pomifera* . . *).* Planted frequently as a hedge or windbreak in prairie or open country. **1953** Strausbaugh–Core *Flora WV* 312, *Osageorange*. . . Widely planted . . for hedges (. . hence the common name, hedgeapple). **1965–70** *DARE* (Qu. T13, . . *Osage orange*) 88 Infs, **chiefly Midl, esp OH, IN, IL, KY,** Hedge apple; (Qu. I46, . . *Fruits that grow wild*) Infs **IN**63, **MD**19, Hedge apple(s); (Qu. L65) Inf **IL**59, Hedge apple fence; (Qu. T15, . . *Swamp trees*) Inf **TN**52, Hedge apple tree. **1987** *Columbus Dispatch* (OH) 18 Oct sec A 16, I asked readers whether hedge apples, which grow on Osage orange trees, actually repel bugs.

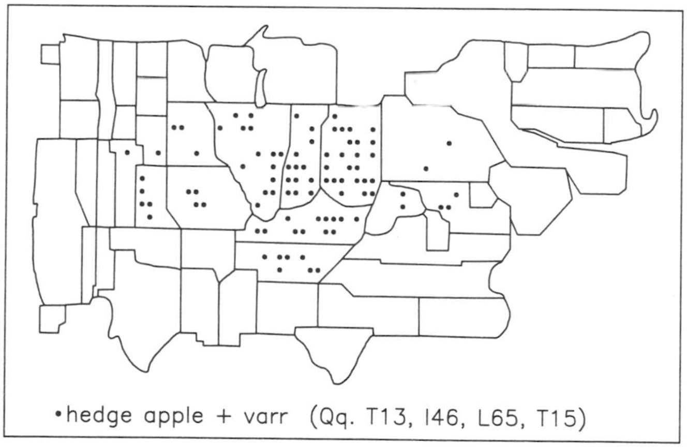

hedge ball n **IL, KS, KY**

=Osage orange.

1929 [see **hedge apple**]. **1961** in 1970 *DARE* File **ceKS,** Hedgeball—fruit of osage orange. **1967–70** *DARE* (Qu. T13, . . *Osage orange*) Infs **IL**7, 110, **KY**49, 75, Hedge ball. **1970** *DARE* Tape **IL**114, Well, a hedge fence was a hedge set so often; they'd just plant those little hedge balls . . get those little seeds and plant them, and they come up and you have a hedge fence . . about four feet high. **c1970** *DARE* File (as of c1890), In my youth in Kansas people always said hedge balls, never hedge-apple, for the fruit of the osage orange. **1980** Koch *Folkl. KS* 382, To kill bugs, put a hedge ball in the basement.

hedge-berry n

A **hackberry** (here: *Celtis occidentalis*).

1940 Clute *Amer. Plant Names* 164, *C[eltis] occidentalis*. . . Hedge-berry.

hedge bindweed n

1 A plant *(Calystegia sepium)* of the family Convolvulaceae.

Also called **bellbind, bindweed 1, devil vine, hedge glorybind, hellweed 3, Kentucky hunter, lady's-nightcap, morning glory, pea vine, Rutland beauty, wild potato, woodbind, woodbine**

1900 Lyons *Plant Names* 115, *Convolvulus* [=*Calystegia*] *Sepium*. . . Hedge Bindweed. **1910** Graves *Flowering Plants* 325 **CT,** *Convolvulus sepium*. . . Hedge Bindweed. **1970** Correll *Plants TX* 1246, *Calystegia*. . . Hedge-bindweed.

2 **=climbing false buckwheat.**

1910 Graves *Flowering Plants* 163 **CT,** *Polygonum scandens*. . . Hedge Bindweed.

3 A **bindweed 1.**

1966 *DARE* FW Addit **CO**7, *Convolvulus arvensis* . . hedge bindweed. **1970** *DARE* (Qu. S5, . . *Wild morning glory*) Inf **MA**78, Hedge bindweed.

hedge bird n

=loggerhead shrike.

1926 *DN* 5.400 **Ozarks,** *Hedge-bird*. . . The Southern shrike or butcherbird.

hedge cheese n

1 **=headcheese 1.**

1941 *LANE* Map 305 *(Head Cheese; Souse)*, [14 infs, **w,sNEng**] Hedge cheese. **1967** Faries *Word Geog. MO* 124, Terms suggested by informants but occurring only occasionally . . *head's (hedge) cheese.* **1973** Allen *LAUM* 1.288 (as of c1950), One South Dakotan has the variant *hedge cheese.*

‡**2** See quot.

1941 *LANE* Map 299 *(Cottage cheese)* 1 inf, **csRI,** *Hedge ch[eese]*, from lobbered milk.

hedge cornbind n

=climbing false buckwheat.

1948 Stevens *KS Wild Flowers* 142, *Polygonum scandens*—Hedge Cornbind.

hedge glorybind n

=hedge bindweed 1.

1948 Stevens *KS Wild Flowers* 158, *Convolvulus sepium*—Hedge Glorybind.

hedge grass n **esp NEng**

=timothy.

1931–33 *LANE Worksheets* **cVT,** Hedge grass . . same as timothy grass. **1966–68** *DARE* (Qu. L9a, . . *Kinds of grasses . . grown for hay*) Infs **ME**14, **NH**14, Hedge grass; **ME**5, Timothy or hedge grass.

hedgehog n

1 **=porcupine.** [See quot 1947] **chiefly NY, NEng**

1605 Rosier *Virginia* (1887) 159 *(DA)*, Beasts: Reine-Deere, Stagges, Fallow-Deere, Beares, Wolues, Beauer, Otter, Hare, Cony, Hedge-Hoggs. **1736** (1977) Gyles *Memoirs* 26 **swME,** Our *Hedge-Hog* . . is about the bigness of a Hog of six Months old, his Back and Sides and Tail are full of sharp Quills. **1832** Williamson *Hist. ME* 1.138, The *Porcupine*, or Hedgehog, or more scientifically, the *Urchin* [Footnote: Hystrix Dorsata], is a quadruped, slow in motion, of a gray colour. **1897** *Oölogist* 14.33, But these observers (?) belong to that class who call . . a Porcupine a hedgehog:—their opinion amounts to nothing. **1904** Day *Kin o' Ktaadn* 144 **ME,** 'T would make raw hedge-hog taste all right. **1928** Anthony *N. Amer. Mammals* 465, *Erethizon dorsatum*. . . Names.—Porcupine; Hedgehog (a misnomer, for the true Hedgehog is an insectivore). **1930** Shoemaker *1300 Words* 30 **cPA Mts** (as of c1900), *Hedge hog*—The common name of the Canada porcupine in Northern Pennsylvania. **1947** Cahalane *Mammals* 571, Because the North American porcupine has quills something like those of the Old World hedgehog, it is frequently called a hedgehog. **1965–70** *DARE* (Qu. P31, . . *Porcupine*) 37 Infs, **chiefly NY, NEng,** Hedgehog.

2 A **woodchuck.** **chiefly NEast, C Atl**

1950 *WELS (Groundhog)* 1 Inf, **cwWI,** Hedgehog. **1965–70** *DARE* (Qu. P31, . . *Groundhog*) 19 Infs, **chiefly NEast, C Atl,** Hedgehog.

3 See **hedgehog caterpillar.**

4 See **hedgehog coneflower.**

5 A **buttercup 1** (here: *Ranunculus arvensis*).

1959 Carleton *Index Herb. Plants* 59, Hedgehog: . . *Ranunculus arvensis.*

6 See quot.

1919 *DN* 5.64 **CA,** *Hedge-hog,* a greedy, underhanded person.

hedgehog cactus n Also *hedgehog*

1 also *hedgehog thistle:* **=barrel cactus.**

1876 Hobbs *Bot. Hdbk.* 52, Hedge hog cactus, *Echinocactus Texensis.* **1925** Jepson *Manual Plants CA* 658, *Echinocactus*. . . Hedgehog Cactus. **1959** Carleton *Index Herb. Plants* 59, Hedgehog-thistle: *Echinocactus* (v). **1967** *DARE* (Qu. S26e, . . *Wildflowers*) Inf **CA**4, Hedgehog cactus. **1968** Abbey *Desert Solitaire* 24 **seUT,** The most beautiful individual flower, most people would agree, is that of the cacti: the prickly pear, the hedgehog, the fishhook. **1970** [see **2** below]. **1982** *NY Times* (NY) 3 Jan sec 10 17/2 **AZ,** Clusters of hedgehog cactus, and prickly pear with names like clockface and cows-tongue, have wedged roots into the rock.

2 also *hedgehog thistle:* A **prickly pear.**

1900 Lyons *Plant Names* 266, *O[puntia] Opuntia*. . . Devil's-tongue, Hedgehog Thistle. **1940** Clute *Amer. Plant Names* 227, *Opuntia vulgaris*. . . Hedgehog-thistle. **1941** Jaeger *Wildflowers* 162, *Hedgehog Cactus*. . . *Opuntia erinacea*. . . Long, shaggy, flexible brown or white spines. **1957** Jaeger *N. Amer. Deserts* 141, On the mountain sides and in rocky canyons grow . . hedgehog cactus . . and a number of low-growing nipple cacti.

3 A cactus of the genus *Echinocereus.* Also called **pitaya.** For other names of var spp see **heart-twister, hen and chickens 1c, lace cactus, merry-widow cactus, mound cactus, purple torch, rainbow cactus, spinemound, strawberry cactus, Texas golden rainbow, torch cactus**

1915 (1926) Armstrong–Thornber *Western Wild Flowers* 306, *Hedgehog Cactus. Echinocereus polyacanthus*. . . This forms a clump of several stems, each about the size and shape of a cucumber, and armed with bunches of long, stiff spines. **1933** *Torreya* 33.61, The *Hedgehog Cactus* (*Echinocereus engelmanii* [sic]) is a most abundant desert succulent and is everywhere easily distinguished by its cucumberesque stems, all cruelly armed with varicolored spines and its great open chalices of rose-purple loveliness filled with golden stamens. **1940** Benson *Cacti AZ* 83, *Echinocereus* (Hedgehog Cactus). **1947** *So. Sierran* May 4/2 *(DA)*, The yellow Encelia, the apricot Mallow and magenta Hedgehog cactus also captured our interest. **1970** Correll *Plants TX* 1095, *Echinocereus*. . . Hedgehog Cactus. *Ibid* 1103, *Ferocactus setispinus*. . . Hedgehog cactus. **1971** Dodge *100 Desert Wildflowers* 49, Not only are there many species of *Echinocereus,* popularly called the "hedgehog cactuses," but there are also several varieties of *Echinocereus triglochidiatus*. . . When blossoming in May and June these clustering "hedgehogs" create a spectacular display. **1973** *AZ Highways* Mar 12, The word Hedgehog is used universally in describing several species of. . . *Echinocereus*. . . In many cases the clumps or clusters of stems suggest a litter of hedgehogs rather than single specimens. **1974** Munz *Flora S. CA* 311, *Echinocereus engelmannii*. . . Hedgehog Cactus. **1985** Dodge *Flowers SW Deserts* 128, *Echinocereus.* Hedgehog Cactus. . . Growing in open clumps with stems resembling spine-covered cucumbers standing on end, the hedgehog is the first cactus to blossom in the spring.

hedgehog caterpillar n Also *hedgehog* [See quots] Cf **woolly bear**

The larva of a **tiger moth** (here: *Isia isabella*).

1872 MO State Entomol. *Annual Rept.* 143, *The Isabella Tiger Moth—Arctia Isabella*. . . The larva of this insect is very common with us and is familiarly known by the name of the Hedge-hog Caterpillar. . . It feeds . . after passing the winter . . rolled up like a hedge-hog. **1898** Lugger *Butterflies* 131, *Pyrrharctia isabella*. . . This is the well-known caterpillar frequently called the "Hedge-Hog," from the habit of rolling itself into a ball when alarmed. **1905** Kellogg *Amer. Insects* 412, The woolliest woolly bear is the larva, sometimes called "hedgehog," of the Isabella tiger-moth. . . "Hedgehogs" killed by muscadine [=fungus disease] are found stiffly attached to their food plants. **1926** Essig *Insects N. Amer.* 676, The densely hairy larvae . . are known as hedgehog caterpillars, because of the habit of rolling into a ball when disturbed or when hibernating. **1970** *DARE* (Qu. R27, . . *Caterpillars or similar worms*) Inf **VA**43, Hedgehog; it stings, is on corn.

hedgehog coneflower n Also *hedgehog* [See quot 1930]

A **purple coneflower** (here: *Echinacea angustifolia* and esp *E. purpurea*).

1889 *Century Dict.* 1179, *Cone-flower. . . Purple* or *hedgehog cone-flower,* the nearly allied [to the *Rudbeckia*] *Echinacea purpurea* and *E. angustifolia,* of the prairies of the western United States. **1900** Lyons *Plant Names* 69, *Brauneria purpurea. . .* Hedgehog Cone-flower. **1930** Sievers *Amer. Med. Plants* 27, *Echinacea angustifolia. . .* Other common names.—Hedgehog-coneflower, . . niggerhead (in Kansas). . . This herb grows . . sending up a rather stout, bristly haired stem bearing thick hairy leaves. **1940** Clute *Amer. Plant Names* 78, *Brauneria purpurea.* Purple Cone-flower. Hedgehog cone-flower. **1959** Carleton *Index Herb. Plants* 59, Hedgehog coneflower: *Echinacea purpurea.* **1971** Krochmal *Appalachia Med. Plants* 112, *Echinacea purpurea . .* hedgehog. **1974** (1977) Coon *Useful Plants* 107, *Echinacea purpurea . .* hedgehog.

hedgehog grass n

1 =**burr grass.**

1790 in 1793 Amer. Philos. Soc. *Trans.* 3.182, *Cenchrus,* Hedge-hog-grass. echinatus. **1822** Eaton *Botany* 228, *Cenchrus echinatus* (hedge-hog grass . .). **1894** *Jrl. Amer. Folkl.* 7.104, *Cenchrus tribuloides* . . hedgehog-grass, West Va.—hedgehog-grass or bear-grass, Iowa. **1912** Baker *Book of Grasses* 83, Hedgehog-grass. *Cenchrus carolinianus.* **1920** U.S. Natl. Museum *Contrib. Herbarium* 22.50, In the United States they [=*Cenchrus* spp] are commonly called sandburs. Other names are burgrass, sand spur, hedgehog grass, and devil's burs. **1973** Hitchcock-Cronquist *Flora Pacific NW* 632, *Cenchrus. . .* Burgrass; Hedgehog-grass.

2 A **bottlebrush 1** (here: *Hystrix patula*).

1832 MA Hist. Soc. *Coll.* 2d ser 9.149 **cwVT,** [Elymus] hystrix, Hedge-hog grass.

hedgehog oak n

A **tanbark oak** (here: *Lithocarpus densiflorus* var *echinoides*).

1938 Van Dersal *Native Woody Plants* 338, Hedgehog oak *(Lithocarpus densiflora).*

hedgehog ray n Also *hedgehog skate* [See quot 1906]

A **skate** (here: *Raja erinacea*).

1825 *Amer. Jrl. Science* 9.290, The Hedgehog-Ray—a species of Fish taken occasionally near New-York, in the Atlantic Ocean, and now, as is believed, for the first time described. **1842** DeKay *Zool. NY* 4.372, The Hedge-hog Ray, *Raia erinaceus, . .* was taken off the coast of New Jersey, in seven fathoms of water. **1906** NJ State Museum *Annual Rept. for 1905* 70, *Raja erinacea. . .* Hedge Hog Ray. . . Skin slimy, scaleless, beset with prickles in spots or patches. **1908** NJ State Museum *Annual Rept. for 1907* 128, *Raja erinacea . .* Hedge Hog Skate.

hedgehog thistle See **hedgehog cactus 1, 2**

hedge mustard n

1 Std: a plant of the genus *Sisymbrium,* esp *S. officinale.* Also called **tumble mustard.** For other names of var spp see **Jim Hill mustard 2, Lucifer-matches, tansy mustard, tumbling mustard, tumbleweed**

2 =**wallflower** (here: *Erysimum* spp).

1889 *Century Dict.* 2769, *Hedge-mustard. . . 1.* A plant of the genus *Sisymbrium,* especially *S. officinale. . . 2.* Less correctly, a plant of the genus *Erysimum.* **1959** Carleton *Index Herb. Plants* 59, *Hedge-mustard . .* Erysimum (v); . . Sisymbrium officinale.

3 A **pennycress** (here: *Thlaspi arvense*).

1974 (1977) Coon *Useful Plants* 124, *Thlaspi arvensee* [sic]—Penny-cress, hedge mustard and other local names.

hedgenettle n

Std: a plant of the genus *Stachys.* For other names of var spp see **Chinese artichoke, dead nettle 3, grandmother 1, Japanese artichoke, knotroot, mouse-ear, pink mint**

hedge orange n **esp KY, OH** Cf **hedge apple**

=**Osage orange.**

1965-70 *DARE* (Qu. T13, . . *Osage orange*) Infs **CA**36, **KY**65, 72, 80, 86, **OH**4, 41, 64, **PA**1, **NJ**21, Hedge orange; (Qu. EE33, . . *Outdoor games*) Inf **KY**66, Hockey—with balls from hedge oranges. [All Infs old]

hedgepig n Cf **whistlepig**

=**hedgehog 1.**

1968 *DARE* (Qu. P31, . . *Porcupine*) Inf **NY**92, Hedgepigs, hedgehogs.

hedge pink n

=**bouncing Bet 1.**

1900 Lyons *Plant Names* 334, *S[aponaria] officinalis. . .* Hedge Pink. **1910** Graves *Flowering Plants* 180 **CT,** Hedge Pink. . . Often occurs with double flowers. **1912** Blatchley *IN Weed Book* 79, Bouncing Bet. Soapwort. Hedge Pink. **1933** Small *Manual SE Flora* 505, *Hedge-pink. . .* A rapid-spreading and persistent weed.

hedge plant See **hedge**

hedgerow See **hedge**

hedge sparrow n

=**song sparrow.**

1674 Josselyn *Two Voyages* 100 **NEng,** Other sorts of Birds there are, as . . the Dunneck or hedge-*Sparrow* who is starke naked in his winter nest. **1917** (1923) *Birds Amer.* 3.50, Song Sparrow *Melospiza melodia. . .* Hedge Sparrow. **1946** Goodrich *Birds in KS* 319, Colloquial Name . . hedge sparrow—Common name . . eastern song sparrow.

hedge thorn n

Any of var **hawthorns;** see quots.

1897 Sudworth *Arborescent Flora* 219 **MT,** *Crataegus coccinea. . . Common Names. . .* Hedge Thorn. **1900** Lyons *Plant Names* 121, *C[rataegus] Oxyacantha. . .* Hedge-thorn. . . *C. cordata. . .* American Hedge-thorn. **1933** Small *Manual SE Flora* 644, *C[rataegus] phaenopyrum. . .* Hedge-thorn.

hedge tree See **hedge**

hediondilla n Also *hedionda, hideondo;* for addit varr see quots [Span *hediondo* literally "stinker"; MexSpan dimin *hediondillo, -a;* see quot 1973] **Desert SW**

=**creosote bush.**

1848 Emory *Notes Reconnoissance* 52 **cNM,** The iodeodonda is a new plant, very offensive to the smell, and, when crushed, resembling kreosote. [**1853** U.S. Army Corps Topog. Engineers *Rept. Sitgreaves* 39 **Desert SW,** Ascending a sandy aroyo, there was to be seen occasionally a . . hediondea, or stinking weed of the Mexicans.] **1878** Hinton *Arizona* 347 *(DA),* The hedeundilla is the bush or shrub which covers the as yet dry valleys and high mesas of Arizona to such an extent as to be met with at every step. **1897** Parsons *Wild Flowers CA* 191, *Hideondo. . .* Ill-smelling, resinous shrubs. **1904** Wooton *Native Ornamental Plants N.M.* 32 *(DA),* Hediondilla *(Covillea tridentata) . .* is an evergreen shrub of the mesas which would make an excellent low hedge plant. [**1912** Lumholtz *New Trails* 223, The Mexicans for the same reason call it by the uncomplimentary name *hediondia.*] **1932** AZ Ag. Exper. Sta. *Bulletin* 141.24, These include creosote bush or hedeondillo, gray thorn or desert buckthorn, . . and mimosas. **1960** Vines *Trees SW* 574, *Larrea tridentata. . .* Vernacular names are . . Hediondilla, . . Hedionda. **1971** Dodge *100 Desert Wildflowers* 40, Following rains its foliage gives off a musty, resinous odor, suggestive of creosote, stimulating the . . name *hediondilla* (little stinker). **1981** Benson-Darrow *Trees SW Deserts* 123, The abundance of the species and the odor have led to application of such local names as hedionilla or "little bad smeller."

hee pron See **he** pron

hee n See **he** n

heeb See **hebe**

heebie n [Cf **heebie-jeebies 1**]

A spell or hex.

1969 *DARE* (Qu. CC14, *Words or expressions . . Where one person supposedly casts a spell over another*) Inf **CA**169, Put the heebie on.

heebie-jeebies n [Coined c1923 by Amer cartoonist Billy Debeck]

1 usu prec by *the;* also *eebie-jeebies, heebies, hibbie-jibbies, hibbies, high bijeebees;* for addit varr see quots:

=**all-overs 1, 2.**

1923 *Chicago Herald & Examiner* (IL) 26 Oct sports sec 1, ["Barney Google" cartoon:] You dumb ox—why don't you get that stupid look offa your pan—you gimme the heeby jeebys. **1924** *Cosmopolitan* Oct 114/2 **NYC,** That discovery gave my new found friend the hibby jibbys. **1945** Street *Gauntlet* 88 **TX** (as of 1920s), This unhappy maiden plunking the last string always gives me the heebie-jeebies. **c1960** *Wilson Coll.* **csKY,** *Heebie-jeebies. . .* Excessive and, sometimes, unwarranted nervousness. Very modern word. **1965-70** *DARE* (Qu. GG13b, *When something keeps bothering a person and makes him nervous, he may say: "It gives me the ______.")* 155 Infs, **widespread,** Heebie-jeebies; **KY**73, **OH**22, Hibbie-jibbies; **CA**169, **MS**63, Hibbies; **KY**70, Hibbie-jeebies;

TX51, Hibbies-jibbies; (Qu. BB28, . . *Imaginary diseases*) 41 Infs, **scattered, but esp N Midl,** Heebie-jeebies; **NM**12, Heebies; (Qu. GG34a, *To feel depressed or in a gloomy mood: "He has the ______ today."*) 12 Infs, **scattered,** Heebie-jeebies; **MA**14, High bijeebees; (Qu. P36, *When a hunter sees a deer . . and gets so excited he can't shoot, he has ______*) Infs **IN**35, **MA**80, Heebie-jeebies; (Qu. BB5, . . *General feeling of discomfort or illness*) Infs **AR**18, **GA**44, **HI**1, **MS**15, **NC**82, Heebie-jeebies; **AR**27, Heebie-jeebers; (Qu. BB7, *A feeling that lasts for a short while, with difficult breathing and heart beating fast*) Inf **GA**72, The heebie-jeebies; (Qu. GG7, . . *Annoyed or upset: "Though we were only ten minutes late, she was all ______."*) Inf **NJ**16, Heebie-jeebies; (Qu. GG11, . . *Quite anxious about something . . "The letter hasn't come and he's ______."*) Inf **NJ**16, Got the heebie-jeebies; (Qu. II29b, . . *The unpleasant effect that person has on you: "He just ______."*) Inf **DC**3, Gives me the eebie-jeebies ['i:bi'ǰibiz].

‡2 The hiccups.

1968 *DARE* (Qu. X54, . . *A spell of going 'hic' . . he's got the ______*) Inf **WI**33, Heebie-jeebies.

3 also *heebies:* Delirium tremens.

1926 Maines & Grant *Wise-Crack Dict.* 9/2 *(OEDS),* Heebie-jeebies, alcoholic shimmy. **1966–69** *DARE* (Qu. DD22, . . *Delirium tremens*) 11 Infs, **scattered,** Heebie-jeebies; **MI**103, Heebies.

4 **=heaves.**

1968 *DARE* (Qu. K48, *When a horse is short of breath, you say it's ______*) Inf **MD**3, Got heebie-jeebies.

heebies See **heebie-jeebies 1, 3**

heeckack See **heekack**

hee-cup See **hiccup**

heedance n Cf Intro "Language Changes" III.1

Heed, notice.

1931 *AmSp* 6.267 **KY,** Ole Uncle Abner never tuck no heedance of the gret new Stranger.

heegan See **hegan**

hee-haw n Also *haw-haw, ee-aw* [Echoic]

A donkey or mule.

1938 *Sun* (Baltimore MD) 17 Sept 4/3, Races are also on tomorrow . . including . . a "hee-haw" handicap open only to mules. **1942** Berrey–Van den Bark *Amer. Slang* 120.21, *Donkey*. . . hee-haw. **1950** *WELS (Joking names for mules)* 3 Infs, **WI,** Hee-haws. **1967–68** *DARE* (Qu. K50) Infs **NJ**16, **NY**2, **WI**52, Hee-haw; **IN**30, Ee-aws ['i 'ɔz]; **NJ**16, Haw-haw [laughter].

heekack n Also *heeckack, heekyak, hick-hack* [Etym uncert; but perh **he** n 2 + **cack** v²] Cf **hootenkack**

An argument, quarrel, or controversy.

1986 *Independent* (Ashland KY) 20 July 39, The word as I spell it . . is heekyak, meaning quarrel or continuing controversy. . . Or, as the consensus went . . heeckack. But . . the Huntington Herald-Dispatch . . spelled it hick-hack. **1986** *DARE* File **neKY,** *Heekack*—a noisy argument with everyone talking at the same time. Applied to both political and family disagreements. "I left because they got into a big heekack." Everyone in this part of the country has heard it and I've heard people use it for many, many years.

heekaw See **hiccup**

heekyak See **heekack**

heel v¹ Also sp *heal* [Transf from naut use]

To fall; to lean or incline.

1836 (1838) Haliburton *Clockmaker* (1st ser) 183 **NEng,** She gave a lurch ahead, then healed over and sunk right down in another faintin fit. **1912** Green *VA Folk-Speech* 221, *Heel*. . . To lean over like a boat by the force of the wind. **1975** Gould *ME Lingo* 129, *Heel*—To tip or slant; at sea a vessel *heels* from the pressure of the wind. . . Both *heel* and list are used in Maine for anything aslant, from a toppling shed to a person in his cups.

heel v², hence vbl n *heeling,* n *heeler* **West**

To rope or throw (an animal) by the hind legs.

1887 *Scribner's Mag.* 2.508 **West,** *Heel,* to lariat an animal by the hind leg. **1903** (1965) Adams *Log Cowboy* 94 **NM,** As he threw his horse back to check the cow, I rode to his assistance, my rope in hand, and as the cow turned ends, I heeled her. **1933** *AmSp* 8.1.28 **nTX,** *Heel.* To throw by catching the heels. **1936** McCarthy *Lang. Mosshorn* np **MT** [Rodeo term], *Heelin'.* The art of catching a critter by its hind feet. **1941** Writers' Program *Guide WY* 462, *Heel*. . . To rope cattle by the hind feet. **1967** *DARE* Tape **AZ4,** The other man's got ta' heel 'im 'n stretch him out 'n tie 'im; **TX**25, [see **header 4**]. [*DARE* Ed: in rodeo team roping] **1968** Adams *Western Words* 144, *Heeler*—In rodeo, a member of a two-man roping team who ropes second and tries to catch one or both feet of a steer after his partner has already roped the head.

heel burner n

=foot burner.

1967 *DARE* (Qu. L18, *Kinds of plows*) Inf **TX**5, Heel burner.

heeler See **heel** v²

heel fly n **chiefly West, esp SW** See Map Cf **bomb fly**

A warble fly (*Hypodermata bovis* or *H. lineata*); also fig.

1878 in 1937 Ruede *Sod-House* 224 **KS,** The "heel flies" troubled the cattle very much the last few days, and they tore loose and ran off; today I greased their heels, which seemed to relieve them. **1901** Howard *Insect Book* 156, Early in the spring the flies appear and are immediately attracted to cattle, laying their eggs upon the legs, especially just above the hoof, which explains the southwestern name "heel fly." **1905** Kellogg *Amer. Insects* 338, The bot-flies, warble-flies, or heel-flies of cattle [=*Hypoderma bovis* & *H. lineata*] . . also have their eggs swallowed. **1905** *DN* 3.82 **nwAR,** *Heel-fly*. . . Primarily, a fly injurious to the heels of cattle; secondarily, a man injurious to his fellows. 'Mr. Warlick refused, calling his progressive brethren a set of heel-flies.' Rare. **1913** (1979) Barnes *Western Grazing* 323, *Heel flies* (Hypoderma bovis—H. Lineata).—These flies do an immense amount of damage to cattle, both domestic and range, every year. They are also locally known as "bot" flies and "warble flies." . . The supposition is that the heel flies sting animals on the heels or hind legs. **1956** Gipson *Old Yeller* 24 **TX,** There went the frightened, snorting cattle, stampeding through the trees with their tails in the air like it was heel-fly time. **1964** Jackman–Long *OR Desert* 96, When separating cattle, a poor hand on an ill-mannered horse can be like a heel fly in a rodero. **1965–70** *DARE* (Qu. R12) 41 Infs, **chiefly West; also S Midl,** Heel fly. **1968** Adams *Western Words* 144, *Heel fly*—A small fly which stings cattle in the tender part of the heel, driving them frantically to water or bog holes to escape the torment.

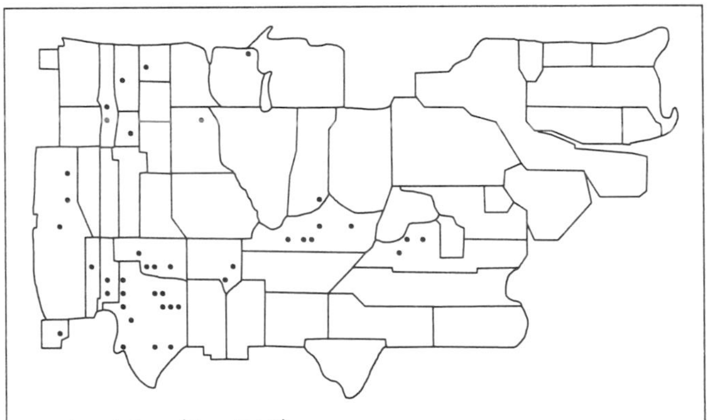

•heel fly (Qu. R12)

heeling See **heel** v²

heel-licker n

=ass-licker 1.

1960 Bailey *Resp. to PADS 20* **KS,** *Heel licker*—Refers to acting like a teacher's pet. **1965–70** *DARE* (Qu. II20a, *A person who tries too hard to gain somebody else's favor*) 9 Infs, **scattered,** Heel-licker. [8 of 9 Infs old]

heel plate n **scattered, but chiefly Nth, Midl**

A metal plate fixed to the heel of a boot or shoe to prevent wear or slipping.

1895 *Montgomery Ward Catal.* 526/1 *(OEDS),* Star heel plates, for preventing boots and shoes from wearing off at the heels. **1950** *WELS (Heavy pieces of metal under the soles of boots to keep them from slipping)* 2 Infs, **WI,** Heel plates. **1959** *Sears, Roebuck Catal.* Spring & Summer 565/1 *(OEDS),* Home shoe repair outfit, includes . . 6 pairs of heel plates. **1965–70** *DARE* (Qu. W12b, *Metal pieces under . . shoes*) 29 Infs, **chiefly Nth, Midl,** Heel plates; (Qu. W12a, *Heavy pieces of metal fastened under the soles of boots*) 14 Infs, **chiefly Midl,** Heel plates.

heel pot n Cf **pot**

In marble play: see quot.

c1970 Wiersma *Marbles Terms* **neIL** (as of 1928), *Heel pot*. . . In this game you dug out with your heel a series of random grooves and holes in the square to make the marbles more difficult to hit.

heelsplitter n [From the sharp shell] Cf **pink heelsplitter**

A **freshwater clam** of the genus *Lasmigona*. For other names of *L. complanata* see **hackleback 2, hatchetback, pancake**

1979 *WI Week-End* Apr 6, Do you know what a white heelsplitter is? How about . . a fat mucket? These are the names of some of the fresh water clams which. . . were harvested for their shells. **1982** U.S. Fish & Wildlife Serv. *Fresh-Water Mussels* 38, White Heelsplitter. . . *(Lasmigona complanata)*. *Ibid* 40, Creek Heelsplitter. . . *(Lasmigona compressa)*.

heels, throw up one's v phr Also *puke up one's heels, vomit up one's heels* Cf **toenails, vomit up one's; toes, throw up one's**

1965–70 *DARE* (Qu. BB18, *To vomit a great deal at once*) Infs **MA**6, **MO**27, Puked (*or* threw) up his heels; **CA**30, **IN**30, **NE**2, **OH**43, **OR**6, Throw (*or* throwing *or* vomit) up your heels.

heel string n

The Achilles tendon.

c1938 in 1970 Hyatt *Hoodoo* 1.54 **MD,** There was a lady, who said that she was out late one night, and a *student doctor* stole her and carried her into the hospital and put her upon the table and cut her heel string. **1943** *Time* 13 Sept 24/1 **GA,** Four convicts have used safety razor blades to cut their "heel strings" (the Achilles' tendon) and thus crippled themselves to escape the work and beatings.

heel-taps n

A **woodpecker.**

1899 Edwards *Defense* 216 **GA,** I feel sorry fer 'im—settin' back dere, 'way out en de wet swamp, so col' an' lonesome, an' de owls des er-hollerin' an' de heel-taps er-hammerin' up en de dead trees.

heely-heely-over See **hilly-over**

heer(e)d See **hear A2a**

heern See **hear A2b**

hees See **his**

heety-hoty tree n Cf *DJE iitiuoti*

An unidentified tree.

1970 *DARE* (Qu. S17) Inf **NC**80, Heety-hoty ['hiti,hoti] tree.

hegan n Also sp *heegan*

See quots.

1916 *DN* 4.324 **KS,** *Hegan, heegan*. . . A Bohemian. **1928** *Ruppenthal Coll.* **KS,** *Hegan, heegan*—A Czech or Bohemian. Perhaps a corruption of Bohemian. Used as far back as 1878 in central Kansas after the Czech immigration of 1875–76.

he-goat, he-hog See **he n 1**

he-hoing vbl n [Prob from *heave ho*]

1969 *DARE* (Qu. BB17, . . *Vomiting*) Inf **IN**54, He-hoing.

he-huckleberry n

1 A small graceful tree *(Cyrilla racemiflora)* native to the Coastal Plain from southeastern Virginia to southeastern Texas. Also called **black titi 2, fireweed k, hardwood, honeysuckle 5g, ironwood, leatherwood, red titi, swamp ironweed, titi, white titi**

1860 Curtis *Cat. Plants NC* 105, *He Huckleberry*. (Cyrilla racemiflora, Walt.)—This is an absurd name, but I have never heard any other. **1897** Sudworth *Arborescent Flora* 277, *Common Names*. . . He Huckleberry (N.C., S.C.) **1940** Clute *Amer. Plant Names* 126, *C[yrilla] racemiflora*. . . He-huckleberry. **1960** Vines *Trees SW* 643, Vernacular names are Black Titi . . and He-huckleberry. **1976** Bruce *How to Grow Wildflowers* 149, *Gray's Manual of Botany* (which lists its common names as He-huckleberry and Black Ti-ti as well as those already given) says the following about the plant: "Autumnal foliage scarlet or orange, gorgeous when mingled with the bright yellow fruit."

2 A **blueberry 1.** [**he n 2 + huckleberry 2**]

1927 *DN* 5.472 **Ozarks,** *He-huckleberry*. . . A variety of huckleberry, the fruit of which is twice the size of the ordinary kind. **1953** Randolph-Wilson *Down in Holler* 247 **Ozarks,** The names *buck berry, hog berry*, . . and *he-huckleberry* are applied rather loosely to several species of *Vaccinium*.

3 =**maleberry.**

1940 Clute *Amer. Plant Names* 226, *Lyonia ligustrina*. He-huckleberry. **1968** *DARE* (Qu. I44) Inf **NC**55, He-huckleberry—on high bushes near the branches; a little darker; look polished. **1976** Bailey-Bailey *Hortus Third* 690, *He huckleberry*. . . Deciduous shrub to 12 ft., but often less.

4 A "he-man." Cf **2** above

1933 Williamson *Woods Colt* 17 **Ozarks,** This whelp must figger he's a reg'lar old he-huckleberry, the way he butts into ever'thing.

heifer n

1a also *she-heifer:* A woman or girl. *usu disparaging* or *joc*

1835 Longstreet *GA Scenes* 115, He rushed into the kitchen in a fury. "You infernal heifer!" said he to aunt Clary. **1858** Hammett *Piney Woods Tavern* 112, There was a young heifer, and not a bad lookin' one either, jumped right at me, and got her arms round me . . and begged me to save her. **1872** Twain *Roughing It* 28 **KS,** When people comes along which is my equals, I reckon I'm a pretty sociable heifer after all. [*DARE* Ed: The speaker is a woman.] **1931** Randolph *Ozarks* 79, To call a hill woman a *heifer* is to call her a meddlesome gossip. **1942** McAtee *Dial. Grant Co. IN* 33 (as of 1890s), *Heifer* . . a term of disapproval when applied to a woman; "the old heifer." **1958** McCulloch *Woods Words* 84 **Pacific NW,** *Heifer*—A fresh young gal. **1965–70** *DARE* (Qu. HH34, . . *Words . . for a woman, not necessarily uncomplimentary*) Infs **ID**1, **MN**38, **MA**35, Heifer; **FL**7, Prissy heifer, she-heifer; (Qu. AA22, *Joking names . . wife: "I have to go down and pick up my______.")* Inf **IL**41, Heifer; (Qu. GG36a, *The kind of person who is always poking into other people's affairs: "She's an awful______.")* Inf **OK**6, Nosy old heifer. **1974** Fink *Mountain Speech* 12 **wNC, eTN,** *Heifer* . . derogatory term for a woman. **1976** Lynn-Vecsey *Loretta Lynn* 112 **eKY,** At first, he wouldn't let me wear any makeup on stage. . . But makeup couldn't stop this heifer from being clumsy.

b Spec: a woman of questionable morals. *esp freq among Black speakers*

1942 Berrey-Van den Bark *Amer. Slang* 507.4, *Brothel*. . . heifer barn *or* den. **1960** Bailey *Resp. to PADS 20* **KS,** *Heifer*—In our neighborhood a heifer was a hefty girl, usually a farm girl, and quite often one who proudly wiggled her fanny. **1965–70** *DARE* (Qu. HH37, *An immoral woman*) Infs **CA**158, **IL**126, **SC**40, 68, 69, **VA**69, Heifer; (Qu. AA7b, . . *A woman who is very fond of men and is always trying to know more—if she's not respectable about it*) Infs **KY**94, **SC**40, Heifer. [4 of 7 Infs Black] **1973** *Black World* 22.3.62/2 **NYC** [Black], That heifer that been trying to get next to my man Lucky since the year one. **1982** Walker *Color Purple* 40 **GA** [Black], He talk bout a strumpet in short skirts, smoking cigarettes, drinking gin. Singing for money and taking other women mens. Talk about slut, hussy, heifer and streetcleaner.

2 See quot.

1982 *Smithsonian Letters* **cnWV,** *Heifer*—a mischievous person, i.e. a child.

heifer dust n

1 See **dust** n[1] **4.**

2 Nonsense. [Euphem for *bullshit*]

1942 Berrey-Van den Bark *Amer. Slang* 151.2, *Nonsense*. . . heifer dust. **1950** *WELS (When you think that the thing somebody has just said is silly or untrue: "Oh that's a lot of______!")* 1 Inf, **ceWI,** Heifer dust. **1985** Ladwig *How to Talk Dirty* 40 **Ozarks,** Heifer-dust is what girls say when they mean bullshit.

3 =**dust** n[1] **3.**

1935 Davis *Honey* 77 **OR,** He took out his tobacco and spilled about a handful on the floor trying to hit a cigarette paper with it. . . "Roll me one of these things while I rake up this heifer dust I spilt." **1948** Manfred *Chokecherry* 41 **nwIA,** Me, I chew snoose. Heifer dust. Never no fear a fire. **1969** Sorden *Lumberjack Lingo* 55 **NEng, Gt Lakes,** *Heifer dust*—Snuff.

4 See quot.

1982 *Smithsonian Letters* **cnWV,** Heifer dust — a loved one. (A term of affection.)

heifered up adj phr

See quots.

1941 *LANE* Map 476–477 *(Excited, all nerved up)* 1 inf, **sME,** Heifered [hɛfəd] up. **1966–69** *DARE* (Qu. GG7, *Words meaning annoyed or upset)* Inf **CT**37, Heifered up—real old; **ME**9, Heifered up [laughter].

heifer egg n
1950 *WELS Suppl.* **cwWI,** *Heifer eggs*—Said humorously of small pullet eggs.

height n Usu |haɪt|; also |haɪ(t)θ|, rarely |heθ| Pronc-spp *hait(h), heighth, hi(gh)th* [Forms with [-θ] represent the original pronc, gradually superseded in std use by Scots, nEngl dial forms with [-t]. Forms with [-tθ] prob reflect infl of *width* [witθ].] Cf **drought**

A Forms.
1805 in 1956 Eliason *Tarheel Talk* 125 **NC,** Their was a terable uproar amongst the Baptists . . they have never got to such a hith with you as what they have bin hear. **1806** (1970) Webster *Compendious Dict.* 143, *Highth. . .* highness, altitude, elevation. **1817** (1930) Sewall *Diary* 21 **ME,** He carried me on a heighth of land called Mount Araratt. **1886** *S. Bivouac* 4.343 **sAppalachians,** Heighth (. . height). **1894** *Century Illustr. Mag.* 48.873, One not only hears "haith" but also "hait" for height in the Adirondacks. **1896** *DN* 1.418, **CT, eMA, cNY,** *Heighth* [haɪtθ]: still used for *height.* **1899** (1912) Green *VA Folk-Speech* 224, *Highth. . .* A form of height. **1908** *DN* 3.319 **eAL, wGA,** *Heighth. . .* Usually pronounced [haɪtθ]. **1909** *DN* 3.398 **nwAR,** *Heighth.* **1914** *DN* 4.108 **KS,** *Heighth.* **1917** *DN* 4.394 **neOH,** *Highth* [haɪtθ]. . . Height. **1959** *VT Hist.* 27.141, *Height* [haɪθ] . . pronc. Occasional. Also [heθ]. . . Obsolete. **1967** *DARE* Tape **AZ2,** The stalk will reach a [haɪθ] of two to four feet. **1968** *DARE* FW Addit **NY96,** *Height* [haɪtθ]. **1987** *DARE* File **nwMA,** *Height*—To say [haɪtθ] comes naturally to me and I'm sure my family pronounced the word with *th* at the end. My husband, from Catskill, New York, pronounces the *th* but without the stop before it [haɪθ].

B Sense.
See quot. [Engl dial; cf *EDD*]
1952 Brown *NC Folkl.* 1.550, *Height. . .* The greater quantity. "I cut the height of my wheat last week."

height social n
1906 *DN* 3.140 **nwAR,** *Height social. . .* A party to which one pays an admission fee proportioned to one's height.

heinie n^1
1 also *heine, hiney:* A person of German ancestry. **chiefly NEast, West** See Map
1904 Number 1500 *Life in Sing Sing* 249/1, *Hiney.* A German. **1931** 'D. Stiff' *Milk & Honey Route* iii.38 *(OEDS),* Germans of all kinds are 'Dutchmen', 'squareheads' or 'Heines'. **1942** Berrey-Van den Bark *Amer. Slang* 385.9, *German. . .* Heinie. **1950** *WELS (People of foreign background: German)* 5 Infs, **WI,** Heinie. **1965-70** *DARE* (Qu. HH28) 41 Infs, **chiefly NEast, West,** Heinie; **NY43,** Heine keplatz.

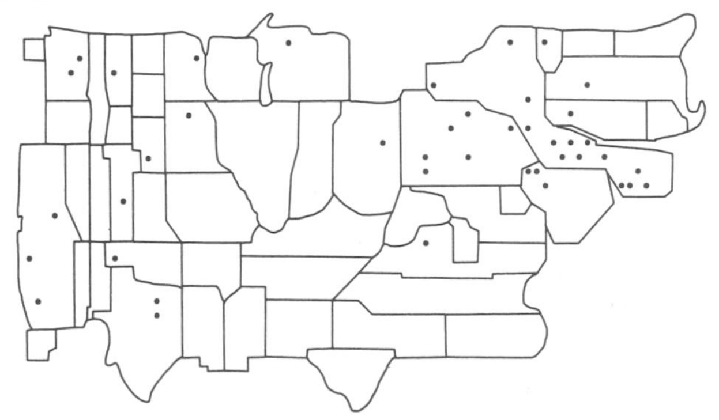

•heinie n^1 1 + var (Qu. HH28)

2 also *hiney:* A very short haircut. **esp MN, WI**
1950 *WELS (Men's haircuts)* 13 Infs, **WI,** Heinie. **1967-69** *DARE* (Qu. X5) Infs **CA128, MN2,** 18, **WI50,** 66, Heinie; **IL47,** Heinie—same as a crew cut; **MN16,** Heinie—a short haircut; **MN28,** Heinie—really close. **1985** Keillor *Lake Wobegon* 120 **MN,** He had a heinie and a fat face and was "after" me at school. **1989** *WI State Jrl.* (Madison) 11 June sec G 1/1, As a boy, what I got for the summer was what some these days call a "butch" or a "buzz." My father called it a "hiney," a name I believe is related to the relatively hairless part of the anatomy also known as the "hind end." *Ibid* 20 June sec C 1/1, The callers were certain the haircut name comes from "heinie," a derogative term for German soldiers. . . Elmer Cox remembers hearing the term back in the 1920s. W. Richard Steffen of Stevens Point noted that . . "The German soldiers usually wore their hair short. . . Thus, any short haircut in the '20s and '30s frequently was called a 'Heinie' because the wearer resembled a German soldier." **1989** Gores *Wolf Time* 210 **MN,** His sparse hair, chopped short in the World War II cut known as a heinie, stood up off his head exactly like hog bristles.

3 =**heinz dog.**
1966 *DARE* (Qu. J1, . . *A dog of mixed breed*) Inf **GA11,** Heinie.

heinie n^2 See **hiney**

heinous adj Also *henious, hyenous* Cf **grievous**
Std sense, var forms.
1908 *DN* 3.322 **eAL, wGA,** *Hyenous* [haɪ'inəs]. . . A variant of *heinous,* probably by association with *hyena.* Rare. **1920s** in 1944 *ADD* **cNY,** ['hiniəs] henious. Not uncommon. A bookword.

heinz dog n Also *heinz, heinz fifty-seven dog;* for addit varr see quots [See quot 1956] Cf **duke's mixture 2**
A dog of mixed or indeterminate breed; a mutt.
1950 *WELS (A dog of mixed breed)* 1 Inf, **WI,** Heinz (57 varieties); 1 Inf, Heinz dog—57 varieties; 1 Inf, Heinz's 59 different varieties. **1956** McAtee *Some Dialect NC* 56, *Heinz dog. . .* A mongrel; in allusion to the advertising by the Heinz Company of 57 varieties. **1965-70** *DARE* (Qu. J1, . . *A dog of mixed breed*) 29 Infs, **scattered,** Heinz (fifty-seven) dog; 9 Infs, **scattered,** Heinz fifty-seven variety (*or* varieties) dog; **ME19,** Heinz forty-seven variety dog; **MO27,** Heinz's dog; **MO11,** Heinzee hound; [**CA166, IA33,** 41, **WI65,** Fifty-seven varieties dog; **NY69,** Fifty-seven variety dog;] (Qu. J2, . . *Joking or uncomplimentary words . . for dogs*) 33 Infs, **scattered,** Heinz (fifty-seven) dog; 10 Infs, **scattered,**Heinz mixture (*or* variety); **MI91,** Heinz fifty-seven varieties dog; **OH43,** Heinz terrier; **RI15,** Heinz's sixty-seven dog; **MO11,** Heinzee hound; [**TX87,** Fifty-seven dog; **CA166,** Fifty-seven varieties dog]. **1971** Wood *Vocab. Change* 45 **Sth,** A dog of mixed and uncertain breed. . . *heinz.* [Offered by 24 of approx 1000 infs] **1973** Gawthrop *Dial. Calumet* 71 **nwIN,** Worthless dog . . *heinz,* 8 [of 125 infs].

heir v Eye-dial sp *air* [*OED* c1330 →] **chiefly S Midl**
To become an heir to; to inherit.
1806 (1970) Webster *Compendious Dict.* 141/2, *Heir. . .* to inherit, take by descent. **1899** (1912) Green *VA Folk-Speech* 221, *Heir. . .* To inherit. He heired that land from his mother. **1909** *DN* 3.398 **nwAR. 1923** *DN* 5.210 **swMO. 1928** *Ruppenthal Coll.* **KS,** *Heir*—to inherit; to fall heir to. "These here children heired this here land." **1942** (1971) Campbell *Cloud-Walking* 27 **seKY,** Nelt had heired a passel of land on Laurel Mountain from his grandpap. **1951** *New Yorker* 10 Feb 36/1 **TN** [Black], Mr. Thad and Mr. Will had bought Munsie her house, and Crecie had heired hers from her second husband. **1956** *DE Folkl. Bulletin* 1.24/2. **1958** Randolph *Sticks* 97 **Ozarks,** His close kinfolks had all died off, but there was four cousins left, expecting to heir the old man's money. **1968** *DARE* File **nwLA** [Black], *Heir*—to inherit. **1968** Kellner *Aunt Serena* 103 **cIN** (as of c1920), Her aunt had died . . and Miz Lewis heired all she had. **1977** Miles *Ozark Dict.* 1, *Aired*—Inherited. "He aired the house from his mama." **1983** *MJLF* 9.1.43 **ceKY. 1984** Burns *Cold Sassy* 265 **nGA,** (as of 1906), She was likely to get more out of Grandpa than Mama could stand—and heir more, too.

heirloom bread n
1970 *DARE* (Qu. H18, . . *Special kinds of bread*) Inf **PA234,** Heirloom bread—brown bread with cinnamon and nuts.

heish See **hush** v

heist See **hoist**

heisted See **hoist C2**

heister n [Prob from **hoist**]
1970 *DARE* (Qu. W1c, . . *Joking names . . for an umbrella*) Inf **SC70,** ['haɪstə].

he-juniper n Cf **he-huckleberry**
=**box huckleberry.**
1922 *Torreya* 22.18 **WV,** Some patches [of *Gaylussacia brachycera*] do not bear, or at least very little, and are called by the negroes "he junipers."

he-kicking ppl adj phr Cf **he** n **2**
1944 *PADS* 2.44 **NC, VA,** *He-kicking. . .* Alive, fresh. "Fish ain't no good unless you put them in the pan he-kicking."

hel See **hold** v **A2a**

helch n [Euphem for *hell*]

1968 *DARE* (Qu. NN26c, *Weakened substitutes for 'hell': "What the ______!"*) Inf **VA24**, Helch [laughter].

hele v Also with *on* [Haw] **HI**

See quots.

1938 Reinecke *Hawaiian Loanwords* 11, *Hele* ['he:le]. . . To walk; to go. **1940** Von Tempski *Paradise* 236 **HI**, Kamanawa shouted "*Hele*—go!" and Daddy plunged in. **1972** Carr *Da Kine Talk* 114 **HI**, *Hele on!* (Hawaiian + English) 'Come on!' **1981** *Pidgin To Da Max* np **HI**, *Hele on*. . . To get moving.

Helen n Also *Helena* [Euphems for *hell*]

In var combs: See quots.

1924 *DN* 5.269, *Helen Maria* . . hell. **1966–69** *DARE* (Qu. CC9, . . *Words or expressions for hell: "That man is headed straight for ______."*) Inf **MS45**, Helena; (Qu. NN26a, *Weakened substitutes for 'hell': "Oh ______!"*) Inf **TX4**, Oh Helen Blazes; **TX67**, Helena; (Qu. NN26b, *Weakened substitutes for 'hell': "Go to ______!"*) Inf **MO3**, Helena Montana. **1988** *DARE* File, *Helen Maria* ['helənmə'raıə] was a favorite oath of Charles Gates Dawes (Vice President from 1925–29) in the 1920s.

hele on See **hele**

helg(r)amite See **hellgrammite**

helicopter n Pronc-sp *heliocopter*

1 A dragonfly. Cf **airplane n 1**

1965–69 *DARE* (Qu. R2) Infs **IN62**, **MS25**, **PA68**, Helicopter(s). **1970** Tarpley *Blinky* 172 **neTX**, *Insect with a double set of transparent wings, seen flying over water*. . . Helicopters. **1973** Allen *LAUM* 1.318 **Upper MW** (as of c1950), The students . . volunteered equivalents for *dragonfly* as . . *helicopter*.

2 See quots. [From the shape; perh also a trade name]

1968–70 *DARE* (Qu. FF28, . . *Kinds of fireworks*) Infs **LA35**, 46, Helicopters; **VA54**, Heliocopters. **1988** *DARE* File **csWI**, Helicopters are a kind of "buzz bomb"; they go up and shoot out.

heliotrope n

1 Std: a plant of the genus *Heliotropium*. For other names of var spp see **baby morning-glory, bindweed 4, devil's-weed 4, false morning-glory, tie-vine, whiteweed**

2 often with qualifier: =**valerian**.

1896 *Jrl. Amer. Folkl.* 9.190, *Valeriana officinalis*, . . hardy heliotrope, summer heliotrope, Sulphur Grove, Ohio. Garden heliotrope, Middleborough, Mass., Northern Ohio. **1938** (1958) Sharples *AK Wild Flowers* 149, *Valeriana*. . . "Wild Heliotrope." **1940** Clute *Amer. Plant Names* 106, *Common Valerian*. . . Summer heliotrope, hardy heliotrope. **1956** St. John *Flora SE WA* 398, *Valeriana sitchensis*. . . *Heliotrope*. . . The plant has a sour odor. **1959** Carleton *Index Herb. Plants* 60, *Heliotrope:* Heliotropium (v); Valeriana (v). **1973** Hitchcock–Cronquist *Flora Pacific NW* 455, M[oun]t[ain] heliotrope. . . *V[aleriana] sitchensis*.

helitywhoop See **hellity-split**

hell n

1 A dense thicket, often of rhododendron or laurel. **esp sAppalachians** [In ref to its thorny, nearly impassable habit, but cf also *OED hele* sb. "Obs. exc. dial. . . A hiding-place. . . Cover"; cf also *EDD hell* sb. 4 "*Obsol.* A dark place in the woods"]

1883 Zeigler–Grosscup *Heart of Alleghanies* 139 **wNC**, Nature has. . . planted in vast tracts impenetrable tangles of the rhododendron and kalmia. These tangles are locally called "Hells," with a proper noun possessive in remembrance of poor unfortunates lost in their mazes. **1913** Kephart *Highlanders* 301 **sAppalachians**, A "hell" or "slick" or "woolly-head" or "yaller patch" is a thicket of laurel or rhododendron, impassable save where the bears have bored out trails. **1937** Thornburgh *Gt. Smoky Mts.* 27, The knife-like ridges are often covered with the Catawba rhododendron . . , and lower ridges with laurel and leucothoe, often so dense that they are locally called "Slicks" and "Hells." **1947** Coffin *Yankee Coast* 199 **eME**, We had walked one whole day and part of a night, through bogs and gullies, through junipers and blackberry hells. **c1950** *Hall Coll.* **wNC, eTN**, *Hell*. . . An impenetrable tangle of rhododendron, mountain laurel, briar, etc., as in Huggins' Hell . . and Jeffry's Hell. **1984** Wilder *You All Spoken Here* 178 **Sth**, Laurel slick, Laurel hell: Southern Appalachian mountainsides dominated by native rhododendron.

2 See quots. *esp freq among Black speakers*

1934 *AmSp* 9.288 **PA** [Black student slang], *A hell* (also *a fair hell*). Anyone who excels at something. **1960** Wentworth–Flexner *Slang* 252, *Hell*. . . A person who excels. *Some Negro and jive talker use*. **1970** Major *Dict. Afro-Amer. Slang* 65, *Hell:* . . an impressive person.

3 in phrr *I'll be go-to-hell(ed):* See **go-to-hell, I'll be.**

4 in phr *hell and half of Georgia* and varr: Everywhere, a large area; see quots.

1959 *VT Hist.* new ser 27.141, *All over Hell and part of Groton*. . . Everywhere. var: All over Hell and half of Winhall; All over Hell and part of York state. Common. **1984** Wilder *You All Spoken Here* 72 **Sth**, *All over hell and half of Georgia:* A considerable area, especially if you're a-lookin' for somebody.

5 in phrr *like* (or *quicker than*) *hell beating tanbark, like hell on stilts* and varr: Very fast, at full speed; energetically. Cf **devil n B3**

1863 Fremantle *3 Months* 43 **eTX**, We descended the hills at a terrific pace—or, as Mr Sargent expressed it, *"Going like h—ll a-beating tan bark."* **1889** (1971) Farmer *Americanisms* 293, Rapidity of motion . . "quicker than *hell* a beatin' tan bark." **[1902** White *Blazed Trail* 192 **nMI**, Old Morrison he's as busy as hell beatin' tan-bark.] **1906** *DN* 3.145 **nwAR**, *Like hell beating tanbark*. . . With energy or speed. "He drove along like hell beating tanbark." **1909** *DN* 3.398 **nwAR**, *Hell on stilts, like*. . . Very rapidly. **1912** *DN* 3.582 **wIN**, *Like hell for Texas*. . . In a hurry; very swiftly. "When he jumped onto the brush the rabbit went out through the stubble like hell for Texas." **1927** *AmSp* 2.362 **wcWV**, He started for home quicker'n hell beating tanbark.

6 with *for* or *on:* Concerned with, insistent on. Cf **for B4c**

1850 U.S. Congress *Congressional Globe* 31st Cong 1st Sess 31 Jan app 19.1.91/1, Mammy has always been *hell on dignity*. **1851** Burke *Polly Peablossom* 71 **MS**, The wimmin folks 'bout where I lives, is h–ll fur new fashions. **1951** in 1977 Randolph *Pissing in the Snow* 215 **swMO** (as of c1935), The people that live on Horse Creek are all hell for politeness, because they don't want to hurt nobody's feelings.

7 in phr *till hell wouldn't have it* and varr: Aplenty, in abundance, galore. **esp NW**

1935 Davis *Honey* 122 **OR**, You might have to cut a few logs, but it's a good grade and grass till hell wouldn't sneeze at it. **1939** FWP *ID Lore* 242, *Till hell wouldn't have it*. **1967** *DARE* (Qu. LL9b, . . *All you need or more—for example, of clothes: "She's got clothes ______."*) Infs **WA28**, 30, Till hell wouldn't have it; **NE11**, Till heck wouldn't have it. **1990** *DARE* File **csWI**, The garden did really well this year; we've got tomatoes till hell won't have it.

8 in phr *hell with the hide off:* Trouble, problems.

1961 Adams *Old-Time Cowhand* 325, He'd soon be givin' the town hell with the hide off, doin' his best to uphold the cowhand's rep'tation for bein' wild and woolly.

9 in phr *come hell or high living:* See quot. [Var of *come hell or high water*]

1968 *DARE* FW Addit **NY92**, *Come hell or high living:* no matter what happens.

hellabal(l)oo See **hullabaloo**

hellacious adj Cf **bodacious**

Extreme or remarkable with respect to a particular (usu negative) quality.

1934 *AmSp* 9.289 **PA** [Black student slang], *Hellacious*. Outstanding. **1943** *Sat. Eve. Post* 216.17.20/3 **TX**, A sample of Johnston dialogue runs, "We saw this little old airfield the Japs were using, so we gave it a strictly hellacious pasting." **1966** *DARE* (Qu. HH22a, *A mean or disagreeable person;* total Infs questioned, 75) Inf **FL7**, Hellacious [hel'eıšəs]. **1975** *AmSp* 50.61 **AR** (as of c1970), *Hellacious* . . Fantastic, terrific, or tremendous: "We had a hellacious time at the Rink Saturday." **1986** Pederson *LAGS Concordance*, 1 inf, **nwAR**, Hellacious—dreadful, terrible; 1 inf, **seFL**, Hellacious tides; 1 inf, **seTX**, A hellacious noise.

hell a-hooting See **hell's a-popping**

hell all Friday intj [Perh euphem for *God Almighty*]

Used to express objection or disgust.

1966 Barnes–Jensen *Dict. UT Slang* 22, *Hell all Friday* . . remonstrance, disgust.

hell and half of Georgia See **hell 4**

hell a-popping, hell a-whooping See **hell's a-popping**

hellbender n

1 also *hellbinder:* A large aquatic salamander *(Cryptobranchus alleganiensis).* Also called **alligator** n[1] **B1, devil dog 2, ground puppy, land pike, lizard, mud devil, mud puppy, tweeg, water dog, water puppy**

1812 Barton *A Memoir concerning an animal of the class of reptilia, or amphibia, which is known, in the United-States, by the names of Alligator and Hell-bender* [title]. **1842** DeKay *Zool. NY* 3.89, The Allegany Hell-bender . . feeds on worms, crayfish, fishes, and aquatic reptiles. **1893** Leland *Memoirs* II.179 *(DAE),* That extraordinary fish lizard . . known as the hell-bender from its extreme ugliness. **1926** TX Folkl. Soc. *Pub.* 5.63, At Boiling Spring, Missouri, a negro fisherman very gravely told my friend . . that the animal is called "hellbender" because it is one of the creatures that inhabit the infernal regions. **1948** *Sat. Eve. Post* 4 Dec 10/2 **SC,** It was like a gigantic hellbender. **1968** *DARE* Tape **NC**55, [FW:] What are spring lizards? [Inf:] They're a salamander that lives in a branch. . . They're black and they get about six inches long—the biggest ones. [FW:] Is there a kind of big one . . ? [Inf:] Water dog or mud puppy? Yeah; its real name is hellbinder ['hɛlbaɪndɚ]. **1979** Behler–King *Audubon Field Guide Reptiles* 269, *Hellbender. . .* Range: Sw. New York to n. Alabama and Georgia. Separate populations in Missouri and in Susquehanna River (New York and Pennsylvania). **1988** *DARE* File **cnOH** (as of 1920), We boy-scouts caught salamanders in the creeks near Akron and called them hellbenders. They were sluggish, black, as much as a foot long, and, though harmless, thought to be poisonous. Some called them mud-puppies.

2 Among loggers: see quot.

1968 Adams *Western Words* 145, *Hell bender*—A logger's term for a log.

hell-bent and crooked See **hell-west and crooked**

hell-bent for breakfast See **hell-for-breakfast**

hell-bent for election adv phr [Var of *hell-bent* adv]

1 also *like hell bent for election:* In a hurried, excited, or reckless manner. Cf **hell-for-leather** adv, **hell-for-breakfast**

1905 (1906) Green *At the Actors' Boarding House* 134 **ID,** The critter got away in the down timber an' went, hell bent fur 'lection, down acrost the little bench below here, an' up the creek. **1909** *DN* 3.398 **nwAR,** *Hell bent for election, like. . .* Very rapidly. **1913** *DN* 4.4 **ME,** Recklessly. . . *hell bent for election.* **1927** *Ruppenthal Coll.* **KS,** *Hell-bent for election*—furiously; . . fast in speed. **1960** Criswell *Resp. to PADS 20* **Ozarks,** *Hell-bent for election.* **1966** Barnes–Jensen *Dict. UT Slang* 22, *Hell bent for election* . . in a great hurry. **1968** *DARE* (Qu. Y20, *To run fast: "You should have seen him ______!"*) Inf **AK**8, Go hell-bent for election. **1984** Wilder *You All Spoken Here* 68 **Sth,** Hell bent for election. . . When one moved in a hurry. **1985** Rattray *Advent. Dimon* 162 **Long Is. NY,** I could see men and boys headed for the beach hell bent for election in front. I'd be too late.

2 also *hell-bent for Sunday, hell-for-election:* In all directions, helter-skelter.

1960 Bailey *Resp. to PADS 20* **KS,** *(In all directions)* Hell-bent for Sunday. **1968–70** *DARE* (Qu. MM12a, . . *'In all directions' . . "He shot into a flock of birds and they went ______."*) Inf **GA**31, Hell-bent for election; (Qu. MM12b, . . *'In all directions' . . "When she was out on the dance floor, she broke her beads and they went ______."*) Inf **PA**234, Hell-bent for election; **IA**23, Hell-for-election.

hell-bent for election adj phr [Var of *hell-bent* adj]

Reckless; determined.

1927 *Ruppenthal Coll.* **KS,** *Hell-bent for election* . . reckless. **1959** *VT Hist.* new ser 27.142, *Hell-bent for election. . .* Dogged; determined. **1966** *DARE* FW Addit **NH**12, *Hell-bent for 'lection*—fast, furious. **1976** Garber *Mountain-ese* 39 **Appalachians,** *Hell-bent-for-election*—in a determined mood—There wuz no stoppin' Clancy, he was shore hell-bent-fer-election.

hell-bent for leather See **hell-for-leather**

hell-bent for Sunday See **hell-bent for election** adv phr **2**

hell-bind n Also *hale-bind*

=**dodder.**

1900 Lyons *Plant Names* 126, *Cuscuta . . Epilinum. . .* Hale-, Hell-, . . bind. **1914** Georgia *Manual Weeds* 324, *Clover Dodder—Cuscuta Epithymum. . .* Hellbind.

hellbinder See **hellbender 1**

hell-borer n Cf **hell-diver 1**

=**pied-billed grebe.**

1959 *Names* 7.111, The pied-billed grebe has the more facetious sobriquet of hell-borer in Illinois.

hell-buster n

Something extremely difficult or arduous.

1949 Guthrie *Way West* 29, Is it such a hell-buster of a trip?

hell-cart n [Cf *OED hell-cart* "an early nick-name for a hackney carriage" 1630–1654 (at *hell* sb. 12)]

1949 *PADS* 11.22 **CO,** *Hell-cart. . .* A two-wheeled cart, a go-devil.

hellcat n **chiefly Sth, S Midl**

1 A spiteful or malicious person, esp a woman; a reckless, impertinent, or vexatious person.

1899 (1912) Green *VA Folk-Speech* 222, *Hellcat. . .* A devil-may-care person. "Hell-cat Billy Jones." **1903** *DN* 2.298 **seMA,** *Hell cat. . .* A witch (a person). **1906** *DN* 3.119 **sIN,** *Hell cat. . .* One who pesters or annoys. "That kid 's a regular hell cat." *Ibid* 140 **nwAR. 1908** *DN* 3.319 **eAL, wGA,** *Hell-cat. . .* A mean, spiteful person. **1909** *DN* 3.398 **nwAR,** *Hell-cat. . .* A person who causes a great deal of trouble. **1927** *AmSp* 2.357 **cwWV,** *Hell cat* . . a trouble maker, usually used in reference to an elderly person. **1942** McAtee *Dial. Grant Co. IN* 33 (as of 1890s). **1954** *Harder Coll.* **cwTN,** *Hellcat. . .* A vicious person, esp a woman. **1960** Criswell *Resp. to PADS 20* **Ozarks,** *Hellcat. . .* A fiery, malicious woman. **1965–70** *DARE* (Qu. Z16, *A small child who is rough, misbehaves, and doesn't obey*) Infs **LA**20, **ME**21, (Little) hellcat; (Qu. GG38, *Somebody who is usually mean and bad tempered*) Inf **VA**4, Hellcat—a mean or bad tempered woman; (Qu. HH11b, *Someone who is too particular or fussy—if it's a woman*) Infs **LA**40, **MS**56, Hellcat; (Qu. HH34y, *Disrespectful words . . for a woman;* total Infs questioned, 75) Inf **OK**18, Old hellcat [laughter]; (Qu. II36b, . . *Somebody who talks back or gives rude answers*) Inf **CA**147, Hellcat. **1973** *DARE* File **Ozarks** (as of c1910), Girls with a bad reputation were hellcats or hazel splitters. **1976** Garber *Mountain-ese* 40 **Appalachians,** *Hell-cat* . . lewd person—Llewellen shore married a hell-cat, they's no way on earth to handle her.

2 A skittish or ill-tempered animal; see quots.

1912 *DN* 3.578 **wIN,** *Hell-cat. . .* A skittish animal, especially a horse. **1968** *DARE* (Qu. K16, *A cow with a bad temper*) Inf **GA**17, Hellcat.

3 See quot.

1965–70 *DARE* (Qu. CC8, *Other names for the devil*) Infs **MS**62A, **TN**53, Hellcat.

hell-devil n

=**hellgrammite.**

1889 in 1901 Howard *Insect Book* 212, The names in use in Rhode Island . . for this insect [=*Corydalus cornutus*] . . are: Dobsons, . . hell devils [etc]. **1911** *Century Dict. Suppl., Hell-devil* . . The hellgrammite-fly or its larva.

hell-diver n

1 A **grebe** (here: esp *Colymbus auritus*). Cf **hell-borer**

1839 *Knickerbocker* 14.344 **seNY,** He could live under water like that notable species of wild duck, commonly called the Hell-diver. **1888** Trumbull *Names of Birds* 82, The Grebes, particularly the Pied-billed Grebe, *Podilymbus podiceps,* that lively little nuisance, familiar to us all, under one or more of the following titles: Hen-bill, . . Hell-diver, . . Dipper. **1917** (1923) *Birds Amer.* 1.5, Horned Grebes [=*Colymbus auritus*] are commonly known as "Hell-divers" . . because of their facility in disappearing and the mystery as to where they go. *Ibid* 7, *Pied-billed Grebe—Podilymbus podiceps. . .* "Hell-diver," by the way, is another name applied to Grebes as well as to Loons. *Ibid* 12, Loon—*Gavia immer . . Other Names. . .* Hell-diver. **1950** *WELS (Water and marsh birds)* 2 Infs, **WI,** Hell-diver—grebe; *(The bird that looks like a small dull-colored duck)* 1 Inf, **WI,** Horned grebe—hell-diver. **1955** [see **2** below]. **1959** *Names* 7.111, Some of the diving birds submerge so long and reappear in so unexpected and distant a quarter that salty observers may remark that they have been to hell. So hell-diver is the vernacular, and it is applied to all of the grebes, practically throughout their ranges. **1969** *DARE* FW Addit **eNC,** *Hell diver:* Local name for grebe.

2 =**bufflehead 2.**

1888 Trumbull *Names of Birds* 82, *Buffle-head. . .* "Devil-diver" and "Hell-diver" have also appeared in print once or twice as aliases of this bird . . ; I have never heard either of them used by a gunner for any bird but a grebe, and I think they have probably been credited to the present species inadvertently. **1917** (1923) *Birds Amer.* 1.140, *Buffle-head—Charitonetta albeola .. Other Names...* Hell-diver. **1923** U.S. Dept. Ag. *Misc. Circular* 13.23, *Bufflehead (Charitonetta albeola)...* hell-diver (Mass., Md., Miss.) **1951** [see **3** below]. **1955** MA Audubon Soc. *Bulletin* 39.316, *Buffle-head...* Hell-diver (Maine, Mass. Facetious exaggeration of its diving abilities. A name more often applied to the loons and grebes.) **1959** *Names* 7.111, Other hell-divers include the common loon (rather generally), bufflehead (N.B., N.S., Me., Mass., Md., Ohio, Miss., Iowa), .. hooded merganser (Wis.), .. common guillemot (Me.), coot (rather generally).

3 A loon (here: esp *Gavia immer*).

1917 [see **1** above]. **1950** *WELS (Other names for "loon")* 4 Infs, **WI,** Hell-diver. **1951** Pough *Audubon Water Bird* 332, Hell-diver... Loons, Grebes, Bufflehead. **1955** MA Audubon Soc. *Bulletin* 39.309, *Common Loon...* Hell-diver (Rather general. This name refers to the bird's almost supernatural diving powers.) **1955** *Oriole* 20.1, *Common Loon.*—Diver, Hell-diver. **1962** Imhof *AL Birds* 59, Expert swimmers and divers, they [=loons] usually prefer to escape danger by diving rather than by taking flight, and this characteristic plus their ability to stay under water for a long period of time has earned them the name "hell-diver." **1965–70** *DARE* (Qu. Q10) 48 Infs, **chiefly Inland Nth,** Hell-diver.

4 **=hooded merganser.**

1923 U.S. Dept. Ag. *Misc. Circular* 13.7, [Hooded merganser] *Vernacular Names... In local use...* Hell-diver (Me., Wis., La.) **1959** [see **2** above].

5 A **coot** n[1] **1,** prob *Fulica americana.*

1950 *WELS (The bird that looks like a small dull-colored duck and is commonly found on ponds and lakes)* 12 Infs, **WI,** Hell-diver. **1959** [see **2** above]. **1965–70** *DARE* (Qu. Q9) 47 Infs, **scattered,** Hell-diver; (Qu. Q5) 13 Infs, **Nth,** Hell-diver. **1968** *DARE* FW Addit **NY**71A, *Hell-diver:* A coot.

6 The black guillemot *(Cepphus grylle).*

1956 MA Audubon Soc. *Bulletin* 40.80, *Black Guillemot...* Hell-diver (Maine. With unusual, perhaps supernatural, diving ability.) **1959** [see **2** above].

7 Appar a **chicken hawk 1.**

1966 *DARE* (Qu. Q4, .. *Kinds of hawks)* Inf **OK**18, Hell-diver: they're death on little chickens.

8 **=hellgrammite 1.**

1889 in 1901 Howard *Insect Book* 212, Names in use in Rhode Island .. for this insect [=*Corydalus cornuta*] .. arc: Dobsons, crawlers, .. hell-diver [etc]. **1948** *Field & Stream* July 42/2 (*DA* at *conniption bug*), Various stages of the dobson are known as .. hell-divers.

hell-driver n [Var of **hell-diver**]

1 **=pied-billed grebe.**

1897 *Oölogist* 14.50 **MI,** Shot Pied-bill Grebe, Hell Driver for short, which I sneaked on and shot before it recognized my presence.

2 **=hellgrammite 1.**

1889 *Century Dict.* 2779 **cNC,** *Hell-driver...* The dobson or hellgrammite.

helleborine n

Std: a plant of the genus *Epipactis.* For other names of *E. gigantea* see **chatterbox, false lady's slipper, stream orchid**

hellety split See **hellity-split**

hell-fer-sartain See **hell-for-certain** n

hell-fer-sartin See **hell-for-certain** n, adj

hellfetter n [From its prickly, entangling stems]

A **greenbrier** (here: *Smilax hispida*).

1933 Small *Manual SE Flora* 312, *S[milax] hispida ..* Hellfetter. **1960** Vines *Trees SW* 74, *Bristly Greenbrier—Smilax hispida...* Vernacular names are .. Hellfetter, and Wild Sarsaparilla. **1970** Correll *Plants TX* 412, *Smilax hispida...* Hellfetter. **1973** Stephens *Woody Plants* 22, *Smilax hispida...* Bristly greenbrier, smilax .. hellfetter.

hellfire n **chiefly Sth, S Midl** *somewhat old-fash*

1 Hell—often used as an intj or oath.

1924 *DN* 5.269, *Hell ..* hellfire. **1932** (1974) Caldwell *Tobacco Road* 3 **GA,** She's going to hell-fire when she dies, sure as day comes. **1965–70** *DARE* (Qu. CC9, *Other words or expressions for hell: "That man is headed straight for ______.")* Infs **FL**18, **MD**30, **NC**87, **OH**15, **PA**133, **SC**3, 46, **TX**4, **VA**31, 42, Hellfire; (Qu. NN8a, *Exclamations of annoyance or disgust: "Oh ______. I've lost my glasses again.")* Inf **MS**69, Hellfire; (Qu. NN9a, *Exclamations showing great annoyance)* Inf **GA**73, Hellfire; (Qu. NN9b) Inf **MS**21, Hellfire; (Qu. NN20b, *Exclamations caused by sudden pain)* Inf **GA**31, Hellfire; (Qu. NN21a) Inf **KY**6, Hellfire; (Qu. NN21b) Inf **GA**19, Hellfire; (Qu. NN26a, *Weakened substitutes for 'hell': "Oh ______!")* Inf **TX**104, Hellfire. [14 of 17 Infs old; 12 of 17 Infs comm type 5]

2 A cheap or low-grade whiskey. Cf *DS* DD21b, c

1863 Gilmore *S. Friends* 61 **Sth,** 'Taint right to give even nigs sech hell-fire as they sell round har. **1909** Wason *Happy Hawkins* 163 *(DAE),* Get me a drink of hell-fire!

hell-fired adj, adv Also superl *hell-firedest*

=all-fired.

1833 Neal *Down-Easters* 1.79 **NEng,** See what a hell-fired noise it makes! **1929** *AmSp* 5.119 **ME,** A man who had done something dishonest was .. a "hell-fired cuss." **1941** *Hall Coll.* **swNC,** It was the hell-firedest wreck I've ever seen. **1942** *Esquire* 18.1.51/3 **neKY,** The Pratts were hell-fired mad at Ceif. **1982** Ginns *Snowbird Gravy* 191 **nwNC,** "Well, I hunted in the hell-fired branch for three hell-fired rocks." (That was his by-word, hell-fired.)

hell-for-breakfast adv Also *hell-bent for breakfast* **chiefly West** Cf **hell-for-leather** adv, **hell-bent for election** adv phr **1, hell-to-breakfast, from**

Very fast, at top speed.

1930 Dobie *Coronado* 104 **csTX,** I was going lickety-split, hell-bent for breakfast, trying to head off a gotch-eared brown stallion and his bunch. **1943** *Reader's Digest* Dec 115/2, The cruiser Juneau and all the cans [=destroyers] went snorting out, hell-for-breakfast after the sub, throwing out depth charges. **1945** Thorp *Pardner* 50 **SW,** In the movies you sometimes see a man supposedly cutting cattle out of the herd, running his horse hell-for-breakfast through the herd, scattering the cattle in all directions, which shows that that cowboy, or his director, knew nothing about the handling of cattle. **1966** Barnes–Jensen *Dict. UT Slang* 23, *Hell for breakfast...* "He went hell for breakfast after that hobbled horse."

hell-for-certain n Pronc-sp *hell-fer-sartain, ~ -sartin*

See quot c1960.

1931 *PMLA* 46.1311, Bizarre .. place names .. *Harlon Co., Ky.* Hell-fer-Sartain. **1955** Roberts *S. from Hell-fer-Sartin* 2 **seKY,** Ten miles down .. is the mouth of Hell-for-Certain ("Hell-fer-Sartin") Creek. **c1960** *Wilson Coll.* **csKY,** *Hell-fer-sartin ..* a nickname for some out-of-the-way or run-down place... a seedy place.

hell-for-certain adj Pronc-sp *hell-fer-sartin* Cf **hell-bent for election** adj phr

1976 Garber *Mountain-ese* 40 **Appalachians,** *Hell-fer-sartin ..* determined—Kenny has sich a hell-fer-sartin way they's no use to argy with him.

hell-for-election See **hell-bent for election** adv phr **2**

hell-for-leather adv Also *hell-bent for leather* [Engl dial; cf *EDD* (at *hell* sb. 1. (9))] **scattered, but esp West** Cf **hell-bent for election** adv phr **1**

At top speed, in great haste.

1919 *DN* 5.76 **wMA,** *Hell bent for leather* is the expression to which I am most used. **1939** (1973) FWP *Guide MT* 414, *Hell-for-leather*—In great haste. "Ridin' hell-for-leather" suggests very hard use of leather (i.e., whip). **1939** in 1984 Lambert–Franks *Voices* 46 **OK,** Many a time I've seen a bunch of bandits come riding hell-for-leather past the camp, the Regulars (the soldiers) pounding along right behind. **1940** (1942) Clark *Ox-Bow* 81 **NV,** I saw that kid Greene, from down to Drew's, come by here hell-for-leather half an hour ago. **1950** *WELS (To run very fast, especially running away from something)* 1 Inf, **seWI,** Run hell-for-leather. **1954** Forbes *Rainbow* 181 **NEng,** "He's coming so Hell-for-leather," says Jude, "he may shoot right by us." **1968** Adams *Western Words* 145, *Hell-for-leather.* **1988** *DARE* File, My Dad, who grew up in Idaho, uses the term "hell-for-leather"; I was surprised when his cousin, who is from Nebraska, said he knew it as "hell-for-election."

hell-for-leather adj Cf **hell-bent for election** adj phr

Fast-moving, rip-roaring.

1942 Perry *Texas* 21, We Texans have a short past .. but it has been a turbulent, rip-snorting, hell-for-leather past.

hellfull n [*OED hellful* "As many as hell could hold"; 1637–1884]

1969 *DARE* File **cVT,** *Hellfull*—a large amount, a potful.

hellfull adj

Extremely full, chock-full.

1931 Faulkner *Sanctuary* 304 **MS,** The privilege of having his place hell-full of folks not spending a cent.

hell fuzzy intj Also *hell's fuzzy*

See quots.

1953 Randolph–Wilson *Down in Holler* 251 **Ozarks,** *Hell's fuzzy.* . . An exclamation comparable to *hell's bells!* or *hell's delight!* both of which are common in the Ozarks. **1966** *DARE* (Qu. NN9a, *Exclamations showing great annoyance: "______. The electric power is off again."*) Inf **MS**16, Hell fuzzy.

hellgrammite n Also *hel(l)gamite, hel(l)gramite, hellgermite*

1 Usu the larva, but also the adult, of the **dobsonfly.** For other names of the larva see **algamite, alligator** n^1 **B3, amly, bogart** n^1, **clipper 2, conniption bug, crawler** n^1 **6, crock** n^4, **devil scratcher, dobsonfly, dragon B2, flip-flap 2, gator flea, gogglegoy, grampus 3, hell-devil, hell-diver 8, hell-driver 2, hojack, snake-doctor**

1866 *Wilkes' Spirit of Times* 14 July 315/3, There is another bait for bass called *kill devil* a—sort of indescribable Barnum-what-is-it thing. . . An old friend of mine denominated them "hell gramites." **1884** Kingsley *Std. Nat. Hist.* 2.156, They [=*Corydalus cornutus*] are much sought after as fish-bait . . and they are called by fishermen "crawlers," "dobsons," and sometimes, we hope rarely, "hellgrammites." **1940** Teale *Insects* 154, The underwater larvae of the Dobson flies are the familiar bass bait, hellgrammites. **1949** Swain *Insect Guide* 71, Newly hatched dobsonfly larvae, commonly called "hellgrammites," drop directly into the water or crawl to it from the egg mass. **1950** *WELS Suppl.* 1 Inf, **cwWI,** Hellgrammite: used here more than crawler. I hear Dobsonfly used by the conservation people. **1965–70** *DARE* (Qu. P6) 37 Infs, **scattered,** Hellgrammite; 12 Infs, **scattered,** Hellgamite; **NJ**8, **WV**8, Hellgermite; (Qu. P13) Infs **NY**71, **PA**168, Hellgrammite; **GA**1, Hellgamite; (Qu. R3; total Infs questioned, 75) Infs **MS**53, **NM**6, 13, **OK**11, Hellgrammite; **GA**1, ['hɛlžəmaɪt; 'hɛljəmaɪt]. **1982** Sternberg *Fishing* 85, Hellgrammites, or dobsonfly larvae, live in rocky streams and in some large lakes. They have a tough, brown body and protruding jaws that can inflict a painful bite. Some species grow to 3 inches in length.

2 Any of var insects, larvae, worms, or other small creatures used as fish bait; see quots.

1950 *WELS Suppl.* 1 Inf, **csWI,** Helgamites/helgramites: Dragonfly larvae used as fish-bait. First pronunciation most common; with [r] less frequent. *Ibid,* Helgramites: Oversized earthworms, used as fish bait. **1965–70** *DARE* (Qu. P18, . . *Shellfish*) Inf **OH**77, Hellgamites; (Qu. P19, . . *Small, freshwater crayfish*) Infs **NJ**65, **NY**84, Hellgamites; **CT**10, Hellgrammite; (Qu. R4, *A large winged insect that hatches in summer in great numbers around lakes or rivers, crowds around lights, lives only a day or so, and is good fish bait*) Infs **CT**29, **IN**45, **NY**211, **PA**155, **WY**1, Hellgrammite; (Qu. R14, *Small worm-like things . . that hatch into mosquitoes*) Inf **MA**42, Hellgamites—I think they're called this; (Qu. R21, . . *Stinging insects*) Inf **TX**84, Hellgrammite, looks like a scorpion; (Qu. R23b, *Blood-sucking creatures—in water*) Inf **PA**242, Hellgamites.

hellgrammite fly n

The adult **dobsonfly.**

1873 MO State Entomol. *Annual Rept.* 142, *The hellgrammite fly—Corydalus cornutus* (Linn.). (Ord. *Neuroptera,* Fam. *Sialidae.*) *Ibid* 145, The body of the Hellgrammite Fly is soft, and were the jaws of the male horny, and armed with teeth, in securing the female they would injure her. **1889** *Century Dict.* 2780, *Hellgrammite-fly.* . . The adult *Corydalus cornutus.*

hell-hack See **hack** v^1 **2**

hell-hen n Cf **hell-borer**

=**pied-billed grebe.**

1959 *Names* 7.111, The pied-billed grebe is termed hell-hen, locally in South Carolina.

hellhole n [Cf *EDD hellhole* "a dark nook supposed to be haunted" (at *hell* sb. 1. (10) (b))] Cf **hidey-hole**

See quots.

1967–69 *DARE* (Qu. D7, *A small space anywhere in a house where you can hide things or get them out of the way*) Infs **MI**68, **PA**179, Hellhole. **1988** *DARE* File **swID,** My grandparents had a small storage room in their basement that was full of boxes, wrapping paper, ribbons, etc, that they called "the hellhole."

hellian See **hellion**

‡hell-in-me-mad adj

1966 *DARE* (Qu. GG40, . . *Violently angry*) Inf **MS**71, Hell-in-me-mad.

hellinyear n [Var of **ellenyard**]

1940 Writers' Program *Guide MD* 8 [Black], The constellation Orion among old-fashioned Negroes is known as 'hellinyear.'

hellion n Usu |'hɛljən|; infreq |'hɛljɚn| (cf Pronc Intro 3.I.23); for addit varr see **A** below Also sp *hellian, hellyon* [Prob varr of Scots and Engl dial *hallion, hallian, hallyon* "idler, rascal" infl by *hell;* cf *EDD, SND*]

A Forms.

1857 *Jrl. of Discourses* 5.135/2, We are going to dig a cache . . and put all the whining men and women into it. . . We want to be released from such poor hellyons. **1896** Harris *Sister Jane* 136 **GA,** Ef dey ever wuz a hellian he wuz one! **1927** Kennedy *Gritny* 69 **sLA** [Black], Y'all *sho* goin' see how Lizzie goin' 'zamine de nasty Hellians, once she got her two han's on 'um. **1965–70** *DARE* (Qu. Z16) Inf **NH**11, ['hɪljən]; **NY**144, ['hɛljɚn]; **OH**4, ['hiliən]; (Qu. JJ1a, . . *A schoolteacher—a woman*) Inf **WA**1, Old hellion ['hɪliɚn]; (Qu. NN24, *Humorous substitutes for stronger exclamations: "Why the son of a ______!"*) Inf **MA**30, Hellion.

B Sense. [Transf from *hellion* a rambunctious or troublesome person]

See quot.

1966–68 *DARE* (Qu. K16, *A cow with a bad temper*) Infs **FL**7, 27, 32, Old hellion; (Qu. K42, *A horse that is rough, wild, or dangerous*) Inf **PA**174, Hellion.

hellity-split adv Also *helitywhoop, hellity-hoop, hellity-larrup* Also sp *hellety split* [Var of *lickety-split* infl by *hell*] Cf **hell-to-split** adv

At full speed; hell-bent.

1867 *Territorial Enterprise* (VA City NV) 1 Jan 1/4 **ceCA,** The firemen in returning to house their hose carts came "hellety split." **1895** (1969) Crane *Red Badge* 95, There's a batt'ry comin' helitywhoop down th' road. **1935** Davis *Honey* 284 **OR,** The dogs cocked their tails and went whooping across it hellity-split. **1940** *Sat. Eve. Post* 212.45.80/3, Riding hellity-larrup toward McKelty's. **1959** *VT Hist.* new ser 27.142, *Go hellity-hoop.* . . To go fast. Occasional. Older people.

hello intj

1 Used to express surprise; see quots. Cf *DS* NN7

1917 *DN* 4.393 **neOH, PA, KY,** *Hello.* . . indicating surprise. **c1950** *Hall Coll.* **wNC, eTN,** *Hello.* . . This is an interjection used to express surprise . . frequently employed in such instances in the Smokies. . . "Hello, what's this!"

2 also *hello Mary:* Used as mild oath; see quot. [Euphems for *hell, hail Mary*]

1966–69 *DARE* (Qu. NN26a, *Weakened substitutes for 'hell': "Oh ______!"*) Infs **GA**77, **NM**9, **TN**14, Hello; **AL**27, Hello Mary; (Qu. NN26c, *Weakened substitutes for 'hell': "What the ______!"*) Inf **IN**45, Hello.

hell-o See **hail-over**

hell-of-a-baloo See **hullabaloo**

hello Mary See **hello** intj **2**

hell on wheels n Also *hell upon wheels*

Anything regarded as a formidable or impressive example of its kind.

1843 *Quincy* (Ill.) *Herald* 10 March 1/4 *(DA), Hell-upon-Wheels!* now if that ain't the most appropriate name for that craft [i.e., a steam-boat named *Heliopolis*], you may blow me. **1927** James *Cow Country* 119, He ain't in your string, and besides, he's sure hell on wheels when it comes to bucking. **1951** *PADS* 15.55 **cn,neIN,** *Hell on wheels.* . . The ultimate. "He thinks he's hell on wheels." **1967–69** *DARE* (Qu. KK41, *Something that is very difficult to do: "I managed to get through with it, but it was ______."*) Inf **AL**8, Hell on wheels. **1986** Chapman *New*

Dict. Amer. Slang 204, *Hell on wheels*. . . A very impressive, nasty, violent, etc, situation or event: *That party sure was hell on wheels / This house is going to be hell on wheels in six months*—Lawrence Sanders.

hell-over-(the-)housetop See **hail-over**

hell-pepper n

Prob a **water pepper.**

1937 (1963) Hyatt *Kiverlid* 37 **KY,** Burn my neck with a poultice o' hell-pepper roots.

‡**hell-pick** v [Cf *raise hell, pick a fight*]

?To look for trouble.

1969 *DARE* (Qu. KK60, *Having nothing in particular to do: "I'd just as soon go with you this afternoon—I'm ______ anyway."*) Inf **GA**72, Hell-pickin'.

hellpuke n

A shady or disreputable person.

1941 Fisher *Illusion* 26 **ID,** He's up guarding our mine against all the hellpukes and thieves coming in.

hell-pumper n

A **bittern** (here: *Botaurus lentiginosus*).

1959 *Names* 7.112 **IA,** The American bittern . . utters calls . . likened to the sounds made by an old-fashioned wooden pump. . . To some these utterances have seemed of lower-world relationships, and, accordingly, they have denominated the bittern as hell-pumper.

hellpup n [Var of *hellhound*]

See quot 1960.

1903 Fox *Little Shepherd* 263 **KY,** I've got one word to say to you, you hell-pup.

hell ripper n

1975 Gould *ME Lingo* 130, *Hell ripper*—A real hurricane that rips hell out of everything.

hell room n Cf **houseroom**

A space in Hell—usu in phr *not worth hell room.*

1899 (1912) Green *VA Folk-Speech* 36, Not worth hell-room. **1927** *AmSp* 3.139 **eME,** They discussed a new invention, often dismissing it with the statement "I would not give it hellroom." **1927** *Ruppenthal Coll.* **KS,** *Not worth hell room.* Worthless, as not worth space in hell. **1952** Brown *NC Folkl.* 1.423, Not worth hell room. **1960** Bailey *Resp. to PADS 20* **KS,** *("It's not worth ______.")* Hell room. **1963** Haywood *Yankee Dict.* 78 **NEng,** *Hell room*—When one holds a fellow mortal in very low esteem, the opinion is frequently expressed by the statement, "I wouldn't give him hell room." **1966–69** *DARE* (Qu. HH20c, . . *An idle, worthless person . . "He isn't worth ______."*) Infs **CA**36, **NJ**54, Hell room; **MS**71, Hell room in Georgia.

hellroot See **hellweed**

hell-rope n Cf **devil's clothesline**

A **greenbrier.**

1913 *Torreya* 1.229, *Smilax* spp.—Called by the very appropriate name hell-ropes in Arkansas.

hell's a-popping phr Also *hell a-popping,* ~ *a-hooting,* ~ *a-whooping, hell's a-busting* Cf **a** prep[1] **5**

Used to indicate great intensity, forcefulness, or turmoil; see quots.

1935 Sandoz *Jules* 177 **wNE** (as of 1880–1930), Steal his stock the minute his back was turned! He would find the rustlers, and when he did there would be hell a-popping. **1950** *WELS (To run very fast, especially running away from something)* 1 Inf, **WI,** Like hell a-popping. **1956** Ker *Vocab. W. TX* 61, *"Blowin' like hell," "hell's a bustin'," "hell's a poppin',"* and *"tater wagon's rollin'"* are all picturesque expressions [referring to a thunderstorm]. . . As a folk idiom the expression "hell's a poppin'" antedates, of course, the musical comedy thus entitled [*DARE* Ed: *Hellzapoppin'*, 1938, by Ole Olsen and Chic Johnson]. **1968** *DARE* (Qu. MM12a, . . *'In all directions' . . "He shot into a flock of birds and they went ______."*) Inf **NH**14, Hell a-whooping. **1972** Cooper *NC Mt. Folkl.* 93, *Hell a-hooting*—trouble starting; . . serious quarrels or fights in progress.

hell's banjer intj [Var of **banjo**] **sAppalachians**

Used as an oath; see quots.

1913 Kephart *Highlanders* 171 **sAppalachians,** Hell's banjer! they don't go prodjectin' around looking for stills. They set at home . . til some feller comes and informs. **1928** Chapman *Happy Mt.* 48 **seTN,** Don't seem to be damaged any. But Hell's banjer, efn I ain't lost my folding knife! **1936** *WV Review* Aug 346, Some of our expressions do smack of a desire to be humorous. . . Of this kind [is] . . Hell's banjer (banjo).

hell's bells and little fishes intj Also *hell's bells and panther tracks* [Varr of *hell's bells*] Cf **hell's fire,** *DS* NN8a, b

Used as an expression of vexation or disappointment.

1919 Kyne *Capt. Scraggs* 4 **CA,** Hell's bells an' panther tracks! **1959** *VT Hist.* 27.142 **neVT,** *Hell's bells and panther tracks!* . . Rare. Essex. *Hell's bells and little fishes, Iron spoons and wooden dishes!* . . Rare.

hell's bottom See **hell's hollow**

hell's fire intj Also *hell's fire and little fishes*

Usu used as an expression of annoyance or disgust; also occas used as an expression of joy.

1903 (1965) Adams *Log Cowboy* 108 **West,** We . . patiently awaited a response. It did not come. . . "Hell's fire and little fishes!" said Joe Stallings, as we clambered into our saddles to return. **1965–68** *DARE* (Qu. NN6a, *Exclamations of joy*) Inf **IN**42, Hell's fire; (Qu. NN8a, *Exclamations of annoyance or disgust: "Oh ______. I've lost my glasses again."*) Inf **CT**8, Hell's fire; (Qu. NN9a, *Exclamations showing great annoyance: "______. The electric power is off again."*) Inf **NE**11, Hell's fire; (Qu. NN26a, *Weakened substitutes for 'hell': "Oh ______!"*) Inf **FL**18, Hell's fire. **1983** *Lutz Coll.* **neNJ** (as of c1920), An expression of annoyance or disgust. . . One of my friends says her mother's phrase was "Hell's fire!" used rather as my own mother might have said, "For Heaven's sake!" . . for example, "Hell's fire! what now?" or, "Hell's fire, what's up?"

hell's fuzzy See **hell fuzzy**

hell's half-acre n Cf **devil's half-acre**

1 A small, remote, disreputable, or otherwise undesirable place; a low-class barroom or dive.

1874 McCoy *Cattle Trade* 141, The keepers of those "hell's half acres" [=dance halls] find some pretext arising from "business jealousies" or other causes, to suddenly become belligerent. **1942** Berrey–Van den Bark *Amer. Slang* 47.4, *Slum district*. . . hell's (half) acre. **1960** Carpenter *Tales Manchaca* 8 **cTX,** So on September 14, 1851, my parents were married in Webberville, which was also known as "Hell's Half Acre." **1966–69** *DARE* (Qu. C33, . . *Joking names . . for an out-of-the-way place, or a very unimportant place*) Infs **CT**29, **IN**42, **MD**42, **NM**1, **PA**72, Hell's half-acre; **IA**22, Way out there in hell's half-acre [FW: used by Inf in conv]; (Qu. C34, *Nicknames for nearby settlements, villages, or districts*) Infs **NJ**31, **NY**23, Hell's half-acre; (Qu. C35, *Nicknames for the different parts of your town or city*) Inf **IA**46, Hell's half-acre. **1985** *WI State Jrl.* (Madison) 8 Dec 1/5, South Madison became a kind of ethnic melting pot, with a relatively high percentage of families with low incomes, poor housing and a crime rate that caused some people to start calling it "Hell's half-acre."

2 in phrr *all over* (or *around*) *hell's half-acre:* Everywhere, all over the place; somewhere.

1931 *AmSp* 6.435, All over hell's half acre. **1950** *WELS (To do something in an unnecessarily roundabout way: "I don't know why he had to go ______ to do that.")* 2 Infs, **WI,** All over hell's half-acre. **1967–69** *DARE* (Qu. KK52) Inf **OH**16, 'Round hell's half-acre; (Qu. MM11, *When you're trying to find something—you don't know where it is—you might say, "I must have left it ______."*) Inf **NY**163, All over hell's half-acre, somewheres. **1967** *DARE* File **swWA,** *All over hell's half-acre*—all over the place.

hell's hollow n Also *hell's bottom, hell's point*

A remote, disreputable, or undesirable place.

1954 *Harder Coll.* **cwTN,** *Hell's holler*. . . Symbolic place-name: a bad, unpleasant, godforsaken place; an out-of-the-way, forbidding place. "Whar'd 'ey all come from?" "Come from tother side o' Hell's Holler." **1966–69** *DARE* (Qu. C33, . . *Joking names . . for an out-of-the-way place, or a very unimportant place*) Inf **DC**8, Hell's bottom—three miles from here; bad land and rough people; (Qu. C34, *Nicknames for nearby settlements, villages, or districts*) Inf **MA**47, Hell's hollow—where the family drank a great deal; (Qu. C35, *Nicknames for the different parts of your town or city*) Inf **MD**15, Hell's point—the dock area. [**1970** *DARE* Tape **CA**201, They'd mine all up and down the Merced River, and in the gulches too . . and Hell's Hollow, Sherlock, Whitlock, and a bunch of those canyons.]

hell-snorter n *joc*

1967 *DARE* (Qu. B17, *A destructive wind that blows straight*) Inf **IA**8, Hell-snorter.

hell's peekhole, by intj

Used as an oath.

1944 *AmSp* 19.244, Picturesque oaths . . *by hell's peekhole.*

hell's point See **hell's hollow**

hell stick n Cf *DS* F46

A match; see quots.

1900 *DN* 2.40 **NEast, OH** [Student lingo], *Hell-sticks*. . . Matches. **1944** Adams *Western Words* 75, *Hell stick*—What the cowman sometimes called the sulphur match so common on the range in the early days, because when struck it really gave him a "whiff of hell."

hell-thrashing rats adv phr

=hell-for-leather adv.

1989 *DARE* File **Upstate NY,** *Hell-thrashing rats* means "speeding," "as fast as possible," "damn fast!" Railroad workers use it. You'd say of someone coming out of a tunnel, "He came up out of there hell-thrashing rats." That means the guy was really speeding. You don't say "like" with it at all—it's faster than that. You use it outside of railroad work too, like if you're trying to finish something by tomorrow, you'd be going hell-thrashing rats.

hell-to-breakfast, from adv phr Less freq *from hell to bush* (or *Harlem*); for addit varr see quots **chiefly Nth, West** Cf **hell-for-breakfast**

1 Helter-skelter; in all directions.

1942 Berrey–Van den Bark *Amer. Slang* 44.7, *Everywhere* . . from hell to breakfast. **1966–68** *DARE* (Qu. MM12a, . . *"He shot into a flock of birds and they went _______."*) Infs **TX**5, **WY**4, Scattered from hell-to-breakfast; **NY**92, Scattered from hell to Harlem; (Qu. MM12b, . . *"She broke her beads and they went _______."*) Infs **ID**4, **OR**10, (Flying) from hell-to-breakfast. **1975** Gould *ME Lingo* 130, *Hell to breakfast*—One of numerous Maine terms for the general surroundings in all directions. "All over hell's kitchen" is another.

2 Thoroughly, decisively, violently.

1928 Asbury *Gangs* 345, Policemen . . clubbed the Gophers . . from hell to breakfast. **1942** Berrey–Van den Bark *Amer. Slang* 24.19, *Completely; utterly; thoroughly* . . from . . hell to breakfast. **1946** White *Autobiog.* 159 **KS**, God-damning me from hell to breakfast. **1959** Robertson *Ram* 51 **ID** (as of c1875), I helped run the sons-of-bitches out of Missouri, and I cheered when a lot of the bastards were massacred. . . I fought 'em from hell to bush.

3 For a considerable distance or long time.

1939 (1962) Thompson *Body & Britches* 499 **NY,** All the way from hell to breakfast; or, hell to Harlem. **1959** *VT Hist.* new ser 27.141, *From Hell to breakfast*. . . A long distance. . . Also, to Hell and breakfast. Occasional. **1967** *DARE* (Qu. A24, *Speaking of someone who has always been the same way: "He's been hot-tempered from _______."*) Inf **CO**47, Hell-to-breakfast. **1972** *NYT Article Letters* **ME,** Do people besides us Down-Easters "go from Hell to Hackony"? **1985** Ladwig *How to Talk Dirty* 12 **Ozarks,** It went on from hell to breakfast.

hell to pay and no pitch hot n Also *devil to pay and no pitch hot* [Var of *devil to pay (and no pitch hot)*; cf *OED* note at *devil* 22. j]

A predicament, critical situation, or perplexing foul-up.

1927 *AmSp* 3.136 **eME,** "Hell to pay and no pitch hot," originally referring to a leak in a boat when no oakum and hot pitch could be had. **1929** *AmSp* 4.378 [Nautical terms], Hell to pay and no pitch hot . . a perplexing situation, and especially a piece of work demanding immediate attention, but for which no adequate facilities are at hand. **1958** Randolph *Sticks* 88 **Ozarks,** It looked like there was hell to pay everywhere, and no pitch hot. **1959** *VT Hist.* new ser 27.141, *Hell to pay and no pitch hot!* . . Rare. **1963** Haywood *Yankee Dict.* 78 **NEng,** *Hell to pay and no pitch hot*—Sometimes it is "the devil to pay and no pitch hot." **1975** Gould *ME Lingo* 130, *Hell to pay and no pitch hot* means . . an unenviable situation; a *jeezley* foul-up. [**1976** *Harper's Weekly* 65.18, To express disgust over someone's procrastination or his not getting a task completed on time my grandfather would snort "All of hell to pave and no pitch hot."]

hell-to-set See **hell-to-split adj**

hell-to-split adv Also *hell-to-toot* Cf **hellity-split**

Very fast, energetic; hell-bent

1871 Hay *Jim Bludso* 19 **cnIN,** Hell-to-split over the prairie / Went team, Little Breeches and all. *Ibid* 21, Hell-to-split over the prairie!/ I was almost froze with skeer. **1917** *DN* 4.393 **neOH** (as of c1890), *Hell to toot*. . . Recklessly fast. . . "They [horse-thieves] went by here hell to toot." **1946** *PADS* 6.38 **eNC** (as of c1900), *Hell to split for Boston.* (In great haste.)

hell-to-split adj Also *hell-to-set*

Very fast, energetic.

1907 Porter *Heart of West* 150 **TX,** He's an early starter and a hell-to-split driver. **1958** Blasingame *Dakota Cowboy* 168, Then, without any urging from my girl-leg spurs, he . . bounced into stiff-legged, hell-to-set bucking, zig-zagging as he went.

hell-to-toot See **hell-to-split** adv

helltown n

A run-down or disreputable place.

1966–70 *DARE* (Qu. C34) Infs **CA**204, **IN**58, Helltown; (Qu. II25, . . *The part of a town where the poorer people, special groups, or foreign groups live*) Infs **MI**33, **VA**31, Helltown.

hellum See **helm**

hellup See **help** v **A1c,** n

hell upon wheels See **hell on wheels**

hell-vine n

1 =trumpet creeper.

1924 Deam *Shrubs IN* 289, This vine [=*Campsis radicans*] in the Wabash bottoms where it is a menace to the farmers, is known as "hell-vine."

2 A **wild morning glory.**

1968 *DARE* (Qu. S5, *Other names around here for the wild morning glory*) Inf **IN**41, Hell-vine.

hellweed n Also *hellroot*

1 also *hailweed:* **=dodder.**

1900 Lyons *Plant Names* 126, *Cuscuta* . . *Epilinum*. . . Hell-weed, Hail-weed. **1911** [see **hairweed**]. **1931** Clute *Common Plants* 85, Of the plants known as hell-weeds or hell-roots, we may mention the lesser broom-rape *(Orobanche minor),* the clover dodder *(Cuscuta epithymum),* the buttercup *(Ranunculus arvensis)* also known as devil's claw, the flax dodder *(Cuscuta epilinum),* which also bears the inelegant name of devil's guts, and the hedge bindweed *(Convolvulus sepium),* otherwise the devil's vine.

2 A **buttercup 1** (here: *Ranunculus arvensis*).

1900 Lyons *Plant Names* 316, *R[anunculus] arvensis*. . . Hell-weed. **1931** [see **1** above].

3 =hedge bindweed 1.

1931 [see **1** above].

4 A **broomrape 1** (here: *Orobanche minor*).

1900 Lyons *Plant Names* 268, *O[robanche] minor*. . . Hell-root. **1901** Lounsberry *S. Wild Flowers* 470, *O[robanche] minor,* clover broom-rape, . . or more viciously known as hellroot. **1931** [see **1** above].

hell-west and crooked adv phr Also *hell-western crooked(y), hell-bent and crooked* Cf **high, west, and crooked**

=galley-west.

1898 Canfield *Maid of Frontier* 100 **TX,** Break 'em with a snaffle, an' they bolt hellwestern crooked. **1907** White *AZ Nights* 38, Now all this knocked me hell-west and crooked, and I said so, but I couldn't get a word out of Gentleman Tim. All the answer I could get was just little laughs. **1914** *DN* 4.74 **nNH, ME,** *Hell-bent an' crooked*. . . In a swift, disorderly, excited manner. "He lit out fer hum, hell-bent an' crooked." **1941** *AmSp* 16.23 **sIN,** *Hell-west and crooked.* **1950** *WELS* 1 Inf, **WI,** Hell-west and crooked. **1951** West *Witch Diggers* 306 **IN,** You've been knocked hell west and crooked already or I miss my guess. **1962** *Mt. Life* 38.4.12 **sAppalachians,** Shet up yer big mouth before I knock ye hell-western crookedy! **1966–69** *DARE* (Qu. MM12a, . . *'In all directions'* . . *"He shot into a flock of birds and they went _______."*) Infs **MA**61, **NY**163, 219, **SD**5, **VT**12, Hell-west and crooked; (Qu. MM12b, . . *'In all directions'* . . *"When she was out on the dance floor, she broke her beads and they went _______."*) Infs **NH**14, **VT**12, Hell-west and crooked.

hell wind n

1929 *AmSp* 5.56 **NE,** When the wind velocity is unusually great, the rancher experiences a "twister," or "tornado" ("hell winds"), which generally fills the air with blinding and cutting sand, a "sand storm."

hell with the hide off See **hell 8**

hellyon See **hellion**

helm n Pronc-spp *hel(l)um* Cf Intro "Language Changes" I.8 and Pronc Intro 3.I.23 Cf **elm**

A Forms.

1818 *Thomas' MA Spy or Worcester Gaz.* (MA) 4 Mar 3/2, We also freely admit . . the claims he urges . . in favour of Capt. C.'s being placed at the *helum* of state. **1848** Lowell *Biglow* 144 **'Upcountry' MA,** Hellum, *helm.* **1872** Twain *Roughing It* 447, He took one more to "put him on an even keel so that he would mind his hellum and not miss stays and go about, every time he came up in the wind." **1899** (1912) Green *VA Folk-Speech* 222, Hellum. . . For *helm.* **1907** *DN* 3.245 **eME,** *Hellum.* . . Helm. **1908** *DN* 3.282 **eAL, wGA,** Hel(u)m. **1912** Thornton *Amer. Gloss.* 288, A mode of pronunciation common in New England. . . "hellum" for helm.

B Sense. [*OED helm* sb.[2] 3 "A handle, helve. *Obs.*"]

1939 *Hench Coll.* **VA,** Two fellow-teachers, both Virginians, said today that their customary name for an ax-handle is "ax helm." They added that they might consider "ax helve" more correct but that it was not their natural word.

helmet n Pronc-spp *helment, hemlet* Cf Intro "Language Changes" I.1, 8

Std sense, var forms.

1905 *DN* 3.58 **NE,** *Hemlet.* **1916** *DN* 4.275 **NE,** *Helment.* . . Helmet. Used by schoolchildren. "Holding up their large helments to protect them." **1943** in 1944 *ADD* **WV,** Spelt *helment* in 5 of 35 MSS. written from dictation, the wd. being pron. ['hɛlmɪt], -[ɛt].

helmetflower n [See quot 1915]

=**skullcap.**

1876 Hobbs *Bot. Hdbk.* 52, Helmet flower, Scull [sic] cap, Scutellaria lateriflora. **1915** (1926) Armstrong–Thornber *Western Wild Flowers* 446, There are many kinds of Scutellaria. . . The curious helmet-shaped calyx . . suggests the common names, Skullcap and Helmet-flower. **1949** Moldenke *Amer. Wild Flowers* 298, Almost 30 kinds of *skullcap* or *helmetflower, Scutellaria,* grow wild in North America. **1971** Krochmal *Appalachia Med. Plants* 232, *Scutellaria lateriflora. . . Common Names:* . . helmet flower.

helmetpod n [See quot 1830]

=**twinleaf.**

1830 Rafinesque *Med. Flora* 2.11, Helmetpod. . . Pod coriaceus, covered with a lid like a helmet. **1876** Hobbs *Bot. Hdbk.* 52, Helmet pod, Twin leaf root, Jeffersonia diphylla. **1930** Sievers *Amer. Med. Plants* 58, *Twinleaf. . . Other common names.* . . Helmet pod. **1971** Krochmal *Appalachia Med. Plants* 146, Helmet pod. . . In large doses it is an emetic.

helmet quail n [From the crest]

Either **California quail 1** or **Gambel's quail.**

1884 Coues *Key to N. Amer. Birds* (ed. 2) 591 *(DAE), Lophortyx.* . . Helmet Quail. . . Two elegant species in the U.S. **1889** *Century Dict.* 2781, *Helmet-quail.* . . A quail of the genus *Lophortyx,* having an elegant recurved crest like that of a helmet. There are two species in the United States, *L. californicus* [sic], the common valley-quail of California, and *L. gambeli,* which abounds in Arizona. **1898** (1900) Davie *Nests N. Amer. Birds* 166, It [=*Lophortyx californica*] is known also by the name of Helmet Quail. **1917** (1923) *Birds Amer.* 2.8, *California Quail—Lophortyx californica. . . Other Names.*—Valley Quail; . . Helmet Quail. **1918** Grinnell *Game Birds CA* 514, *Valley Quail—Lophortyx californica—Other Names*—Valley Partridge . . Helmet Quail.

help v

A Forms. Cf Pronc Intro 3.II.27 with ref to assimilation of /l/

1 infin, pres exc 3rd pers sg: usu |hɛlp|; also:

a |ho(l)p|; pronc-spp *holp(e), hope.* [Engl dial, by analogy with strong past and past ppl forms; cf *EDD help* I. 1. (4), (5) and **A2, 3** below] **chiefly Sth, S Midl**

c1770 in 1933 *DN* 6.328 **VA,** *Holp* for *help.* **1789** Webster *Dissertations Engl. Lang.* 384 **VA,** *Holpe* or *holp.* . . pronounced *hope.* "Shall I hope you, Sir." **1823** *Natl. Intelligencer* (DC) 1 May [Western dialect], *Hope.* . . To help. **1827** (1939) Sherwood *Gaz. GA* 139, *Holpe,* for help. **1837** *Ibid* 70, *Hope,* help.—The obsolete verb *holp* was in use 200 years ago. **1883** Amer. Philol. Assoc. *Trans.* 14.49 **Sth,** From this [=*holp* as past and past participle] they even form an infinitive *to holp (hope),* instead of *to help.* **1889** Edwards *Runaways* 23 **GA** [Black], O Lord, Mass' Craffud, come holp me tu'n dis buck loos'. **1893** Shands *MS Speech* 37, *Hope* [hop]. Negroes use this pronunciation of *holp,* which they employ for *help* and *helped.* **1901** *Century Illustr. Mag.* 62.903/2 **wTN** [Black], But I cain't hope hit. **1902** *DN* 2.236 **sIL,** *Holp.* . . Help, present or preterit. **1917** *DN* 4.413 **wNC, KY, SC,** *Holp.* . . "I axed him to holp me out." . . Pronounced [hop] by the younger generation. **1931** Randolph *Ozarks* 20, Paw he snuck in one day . . an' tried for t' holp out. **1953** Goodwin *It's Good* 135 **sIL** [Black], "Hope me git Big Chick onto this pallet," she grunted. **1969** *DARE* FW Addit **NC,** Help—[holp]. **1970** *DARE* FW Addit **neTX,** Help—[hop], old-fashioned. **1984** *Annals Internal Med.* 100.6.900 **cwAL,** *Hope me* means help me. **1984** Burns *Cold Sassy* 79 **nGA** (as of 1906), Lemme holp you up, Will.

b |hɛ(ə)p|; pronc-sp *hep.* **chiefly Sth, S Midl**

1884 *Anglia* 7.277 **Sth, S Midl** [Black], *To he'p yo' long pow'ful* = to be of great assistance to you. **1899** (1912) Green *VA Folk-Speech* 222, *Hep.* . . For *help.* "I can't hep it." **1901** *DN* 2.141 **sNY,** *Hep.* **1908** *DN* 3.281 **eAL, wGA,** *Hep.* **1914** *DN* 4.108 **KS,** *Hep.* **1927** *DN* 5.470 **Appalachians,** *Help*—he'p. **1940** in 1944 *ADD* **Sth,** [hɛəp]. Common. **1944** *PADS* 2.15 **AL, VA, NC,** *Help* [hɛp]. **1955** *DE Folkl. Bulletin* 1.20, Hep (help). **1966–70** *DARE* Tapes **FL9, SC34, TN51,** [hɛp]. **1967** *DARE* FW Addit **TN10,** Let me help [hɛp] you with that. **1968** *DARE* (Qu. L5, *When a farmer gets help on a job from his neighbors in return for his help on their farms later on, you call it* ________) Inf **NC54,** I'll hep my neighbor. **1976** Allen *LAUM* 3.315 **IA** (as of c1950), [hɛp] [3 infs]. **1984** Burns *Cold Sassy* 35 **nGA** (as of 1906), Hep me not to beg You to spare her.

c |'hɛləp|; pronc-sp *hellup.*

1970 *DARE* (Qu. NN26b) Inf **PA234,** Hellup ['hɛləp] me up again.

d |hɛɯp|; for addit varr see quot.

1976 Allen *LAUM* 3.315 **Upper MW** (as of c1950), [hɛɯp] [4 infs]; [hɛɤp] [1 inf]; [hɛʉ˃p] [1 inf].

2 past: usu |hɛlpt|; also:

a |ho(l)p|; pronc-spp *holp(e), hop(e).* [Engl dial strong past tense forms; cf *EDD help* I. 2. (4), (6)] **chiefly Sth, S Midl**

1816 Pickering *Vocab.* 105 **VA,** *Holpe* or *holp.* (*Pret.* and *part. pass.* of *help.*) **1840** (1847) Longstreet *GA Scenes* 192, None of 'em holp her at all. **1883** (1971) Harris *Nights with Remus* 30 **GA** [Black], De house. . . had rooms fer all de creeturs w'at went inter cahoots en hope make it. **1890** *DN* 1.68 **KY,** *Holp* [holp]: for *helped.* "He holp me out of the scrape." **1893** [see **A2b** below]. **1895** *DN* 1.376 **TN, KY, NC,** *Holp* (pron., generally [hop]) = helped. **1899** (1912) Green *VA Folk-Speech* 230, *Hope.* . . Past tense of *help;* holp. **1902** *DN* 2.236 **sIL,** *Holp.* **1905** *DN* 3.82 **nwAR,** *Hope.* . . 'He hope me out.' **1907** *DN* 3.232 **nwAR, seMO,** *Holp.* **1910** *DN* 3.456 **KY,** He holp me with my work. **1915** *DN* 4.184 **swVA,** *Hope.* **1923** *DN* 5.210 **swMO,** Past tense . . *Holp.* **1946** *AmSp* 21.97 **sIL,** The Elizabethan strong preterite *holp* . . is not uncommon. **1950** *PADS* 14.38 **SC,** *Holp* [hop]. **1950** *WELS (Assisted)* 4 Infs, **WI,** Holp. [1 Inf called this "occasional," 1 called it "common."] **1954** *Harder Coll.* **cwTN,** *Help.* . . hop. **1965** *Dict. Queen's English* 8 **NC,** I hope him with his farm work. **1966–69** *DARE* FW Addit **GA, KY, LA, NC,** *Holp, hope* [hop]. **1985** *DARE* File **eNC,** I was reared on a farm in eastern North Carolina and had a grandfather born in 1844. . . Grandfather always used *holp* as the past tense of *help!* (help, holp, holpen).

b |ho(l)pt, hopəd|; pronc-spp *holp(e)d, holpt, hop(e)d, hopt* [Double past, with weak past tense added to existing strong form; cf *EDD help* I. 2. (5) and **-ed suff 3**] **chiefly Sth, S Midl**

1775 in 1906 Litchfield *Diary* 325 **MA,** I holpd git wood. **1816** Pickering *Vocab.* 105 **VA,** *Holpe* or *holp.* (*Pret.* and *part. pass.* of *Help.*) . . is still used in Virginia; where . . it is corrupted into *holped. . . "Will you be holped (or holpe) to any thing."* **1847** Hurd *Grammatical Corrector* 41 **Sth,** Hoped, for *helped;* as, "Who hoped you to get it?" **1890** *DN* 1.71 **LA,** *Ho'p'd:* helped (pret. and p.p.) **1893** Shands *MS Speech* 37, *Hope* [hop]. Negroes use this pronunciation of *holp,* which they employ for *help* and *helped;* sometimes, however, they form a past tense *holped* [hopeḍ] [sic] from the present *holp.* **1908** *DN* 3.321 **eAL, wGA,** *Ho(l)p(t).* **1923** *DN* 5.210 **swMO,** Past tense . . *Holped.* **1936** *AmSp* 11.275 **TN,** *Holpt* (or *Hoped*). Helped. 'She hoped me piece my quilt.' **1939** *Hall Coll.* **eTN,** "I ho'ped a party run his generation . . back not long ago." [=I helped a man trace his family back, etc.] **1948** *AmSp* 23.305 **Ozarks,** It just holped me up to hear him. (A woman after a telephone conversation with her son in California.) **1950** *WELS (Assisted)* 2 Infs, **WI,** Hoped; 7 Infs, Holped. [1 Inf said that *holped* is used among Germans.] **1954** *Harder Coll.* **cwTN,** *Help. . .* hoped, hop. **1972** Cooper *NC Mt. Folkl.* 93, *Holp, holped*—helped. **1985** *Amer. Jrl. Med.* Feb 183 **eTN,** That Motrin tablet ain't holped me.

c pronc-sp *holpen.* [By analogy with strong past ppl form; cf *EDD help* I. 2. (9) and **3c** below] *arch*

1828 Webster *Amer. Dict.* np, *Holpen,* the antiquated *pret. . . help.* **1899** (1912) Green *VA Folk-Speech* 228, Holpen, the past tense and past participle of *help.* **1927** *AmSp* 2.357 **WV,** He holpen me over the creek. **1965** *DARE* File **c,cwVA** (as of 1920), *Holp, holpen*—used as past tense of help.

d |hɛpt|; pronc-sp *hep(p)ed.* **chiefly Sth, S Midl**

1894 Riley *Armazindy* 5 **IN,** *She'd* ben to school / At *New Thessaly,* i gum!—/ Fool before, but that hepped *some.* **1923** *DN* 5.210 **swMO,** *He'p. . .* To help. Past tense, *He'pped.* **1939** *Hall Coll.* **eTN,** I he'ped take his bones to Gatlinburg. **1950** *WELS (Assisted)* 9 Infs, **WI,** Hepped. [3 of 9 Infs called it "old-fashioned," 2 called it "rare."] **1969** *DARE* Tape **KY**16A, I had to build it all but he hepped [hɛpt] a little. **1988** *DARE* File **seGA** (as of 1968), He hepped [hɛpt] me out, yes he did.

3 past pple: usu |hɛlpt|; also:

a |ho(l)p|; pronc-spp *holp(e), hop(e).* [Engl dial; cf *EDD help* I. 3. (5), (8)] **chiefly Sth, S Midl**

1816 [see **A2b** above]. **1828** (1970) Webster *Amer. Dict.* np, *Holp, holpen,* the antiquated *pret.* and *pp.* of *help.* **1891** Johnston *Primes & Neighbors* 252 **GA,** It's too late for it to be holp. **1893** Shands *MS Speech* 37, *Hope* [hop]. Negroes use this pronunciation of *holp,* which they employ for *help* and *helped;* sometimes, however, they form a past tense *holped* [hopt] from the present *holp.* In this word the negroes preserve the vowel *o* of the past tense of the A.-S. strong verb *helpan,* but on this strong stem they sometimes form a weak past and past participle, as mentioned above. *Holp* is used also in Louisiana. Bartlett says the word *holp* is heard in Virginia and New England, and in Virginia *holped* also is used. **1903** *DN* 2.317 **seMO,** *Holp. . .* Helped. 'I'm sorry but it can't be holp.' **1907** *DN* 3.232 **nwAR, seMO,** *Holp.* **1908** *DN* 3.321 **eAL, wGA,** *Hope, pret.* and *pp.* of *help.* **1942** Faulkner *Go Down* 148 **MS,** "Dat ar cant help you." "Hit done awready hope me," he said. **c1942** *Harder Coll.* **cwTN,** [hop]. . . [Letter:] It sure have hope my nerves. **1954** *Ibid* **cwTN,** *Help. . .* [past participle] hep, hop. **1957** *Sat. Eve. Post Letters* **LA,** *Hope* for helped. It can't be hope. **1962** *Mt. Life* 38.1.16 **sAppalachians,** Verbs which retain either the strong preterites of Middle English or variant preterites of the English dialects . . *Past Participle*—holp. **1972** [see **A2b** above].

b |ho(l)pt|; pronc-spp *holped, hop(e)d.* [Double past pple, with weak form added to existing strong form; cf *EDD help* I. 3. (6), (9)] **chiefly Sth, S Midl** *old-fash*

1816 [see **A2b** above]. **1848** Bartlett *Americanisms* 181, *Hoped.* Used among the illiterate in North Carolina as the past part. of *to help. . .* 'It can't be hoped.' **1889** Edwards *Runaways* 26 **GA** [Black], It can't be holped. **1890** [see **A2b** above]. **1893** [see **A3a** above]. **1933** Rawlings *South Moon* 319 **nFL,** Ary one would of holped him. **1972** [see **A2b** above].

c pronc-sp *holpen.* [Engl dial; cf *EDD help* I. 3. (7)] *old-fash*

1806 (1970) Webster *Compendious Dict.* 144, *Holpen . . ob[solete].* **1828** [see **A3a** above]. **1899** [see **A2c** above]. **1952** Brown *NC Folkl.* 1.552, *Holpen. . .* Past participle of *help.* This was the normal form of the past participle in Anglo-Saxon and was very common in Middle English. . . West. Illiterate. Rare. **1955** Ritchie *Singing Family* 66 **seKY,** She even let us drink a little bit of the elderberry wine that I had holpen her make. **1985** [see **A2a** above].

d |hɛp(t), he^{ɯ}pt|; pronc-spp *hep, hep(p)ed.*

1954 *Harder Coll.* **cwTN,** *Help. . .* [past participle] hep, hop. **1956** Ker *Vocab. W. TX* 423, *Helped . .* [past participle] hepped . . heped . . hep. **1966** *DARE* Tape **FL**34, [hɛpt]. **1981** Pederson *LAGS Basic Materials* **Gulf Region,** Helped [freq instances of [hɛpt, hɛ^{ə}pt, hɛ^{ɯ}pt]].

B Senses.

1 with *up:* To encourage, cheer up; hence ppl adj phr *holp up* (pronc-spp *hope(d) up*) encouraged, cheered up. [Cf *EDD help* II. 1. (4)] **Sth, S Midl**

1883 Amer. Philol. Assoc. *Trans.* 14.49 **Sth,** "Considerably *holp* up" is a phrase often heard. **1886** *S. Bivouac* 4.350 **sAppalachians,** Holp up (encouraged). **1896** Harris *Sister Jane* 310 **GA,** We shorely tell 'em, an' they'll be might'ly holp up—might'ly holp up. **1903** *DN* 2.317 **seMO,** *Holp up. . .* Encouraged. 'He is mightily holp up since he got well.' **1942** (1971) Campbell *Cloud-Walking* 251 **seKY,** Nelt was mighty holp up to have Sary 'pear to be mending in health. **1948** [see **A2b** above]. **1960** Criswell *Resp. to PADS 20* **Ozarks,** *Hoped up*—encouraged. "I'm all hoped up over the new preacher. I think he will revive our church." **1966** *DARE* (Qu. GG19a, *When you can see from the way a person acts that he's feeling important or independent: "He surely is ______ these days."*) Inf **MS**45, Highly hope up.

2 ppl adjs *holp, hope:* Served; see quots.

1907 *DN* 3.221 **eAL, wGA,** At table, "I'm mighty well hope, I thank you." **c1960** *Wilson Coll.* **csKY,** *I'm well holp . .* in response to "Have some."

help n Usu |hɛlp|; also **chiefly Sth, S Midl** |hɛp|; infreq |hɛləp| Cf Pronc Intro 3.I.23, 3.II.27 Pronc-spp *hellup, hep* Similarly, n *helper,* pronc-sp *hepper*

A Forms. Cf **helm**

1890 *DN* 1.68 **KY,** *Help.* "I have no help". . . Often pronounced *he'p.* **1908** *DN* 3.320 **eAL, wGA,** *Hep, v.* and *n.* Help. Very common. **1940** Stuart *Trees of Heaven* 56 **eKY,** No wonder Pa can't hire hep. **1967–70** [see **B** below]. **1968–69** *DARE* (Qu. L5, *When a farmer gets help on a job from his neighbors in return for his help on their farms later on, you call it ______*) Inf **MD**20, Help for help [hɛp fɚ hɛp]; (Qu. HH15) Inf **GA**72, Hepper. **1984** Burns *Cold Sassy* 22 **nGA** (as of 1906), The day Camp walked into the store and asked for a job, Grandpa took one look and said he didn't need no hep right now.

B Sense.

Used as an emphatic intj; see quot. [Euphem for *hell*]

1967–70 *DARE* (Qu. NN21a, *Exclamations caused by sudden pain—a pinched finger*) Inf **OH**57, Help; (Qu. NN26a, *Weakened substitutes for 'hell': "Oh ______!"*) Infs **CA**166, **IA**41, **IL**119, **KS**8, **LA**17, Help; **NY**105, Hellup; **TX**35, Hep; (Qu. NN26b, *Weakened substitutes for 'hell': "Go to ______!"*) Inf **PA**234, Hellup ['hɛləp] me up again.

help Andy v phr

1927 *AmSp* 2.357 **WV,** *Help Andy . .* to do nothing. "What are you doing today? Oh, I'm just helping Andy."

helper See **help** n

help for help n Also *help for help back*

=**back help.**

1968–69 *DARE* (Qu. L5, *When a farmer gets help on a job from his neighbors in return for his help on their farms later on*) Infs **MD**20, 29, Help for help; **PA**204, **WV**7, Help for help back.

helpkeeper n

See quot.

1936 *NY Times* (NY) 30 Nov 23 **RI,** Explaining that the speech of the residents is very similar to that of their forefathers, Professor Hibbit said that they often referred to . . "helpkeeper" for "housekeeper."

helpmate v [*helpmate* n]

To help, assist.

1931 *AmSp* 6.267 **KY,** She'll never be *helpmated* by him no more.

help my time intj

1969 *DARE* (Qu. NN7, *Exclamations of surprise: "They're getting married next week? Well, ______."*) Inf **TN**39, I'll swear! Good grief! My soul and body! Help my time!

helpsome adj [Engl dial; cf *EDD helpsome* "Ready and willing to help"; cf Intro "Language Changes" III.1]

Helpful.

1942 (1971) Campbell *Cloud-Walking* 38 **seKY,** It would be more helpsome to you to go along with your ownselves. *Ibid* 269, He aimed to get a pile of learning in the level country and then fetch it back amongst the mountain folks and be sight how helpsome.

help tag n

A children's game; see quot.

1968 *DARE* (Qu. EE33, . . *Outdoor games . . that children play*) Inf **PA**163, Help tag—the caught kids help the one who is "it." [**1969** Opie–Opie *Children's Games* 89 **Gt Brit,** 'Help Chase' . . those who are touched by the chaser help him to chase the rest. . . Eventually all are had and the time comes to start again. The first one had in the last game is hee [="it"] in the next.]

help the poor exclam **sMI**

1971 *DARE* File **Detroit MI,** *Help the poor!*—Expression used on Halloween by children instead of "trick or treat." **1988** *Detroit Free Press* (MI) 3 Nov sec D 16/1, My brothers and I spent most of Halloween evening doing the soft shoe for small change in smoky neighborhood beer gardens instead of going door-to-door asking poor neighbors to "help the poor!" **1988** *NADS Letters* **seMI,** "Help the poor" is used by Detroit-area children when they go begging on Halloween. My mother and father (aged 70 and 69 . .) report that the term was current when they were growing up in . . the city. . . My parents . . tell me that usage is now split between "help the poor" and "trick or treat." *Ibid* **csMI,** Several students in class knew the term [=*Help the poor*]. They were all from Detroit and surrounding suburbs. However, none use it. It appears to be *last used among their parents,* i.e., 40–60 year olds. It seems to be associated with the term *"begging"* which some of the students still use, that is, they go out "begging" on Halloween, but when they knock on the door, they say "trick or treat" instead of "help the poor."

help up See **help** v **B1**

helt v See **hold** v **A2a, 3a**

helt n See **hold** n **2**

heltrot See **eltrot**

helum See **helm**

hem v Usu |hɛm|; also |hæm|

A Form.

1942 Hall *Smoky Mt. Speech* 19 **eTN, wNC,** Hem . . One of the dogs [hæmd] the bear in.

B Senses.

1 often with *up:* To corner, surround, catch; also fig. **chiefly Sth, S Midl**

1939 *Hall Coll.* **wNC,** One of the little dogs hemmed the bear and turned him away from Uncle Steve. **1941** Writers' Program *Guide AR* 60, Unfortunately, a mule generally becomes most evil-eyed and active when you try to hem him up so you can slip the bridle on. **1942** Hurston *Dust Tracks* 138 **FL,** It's a swell job if you can get it. . . I told my husband to do all he can, and he thinks he's got it hemmed up for you. **1951** Faulkner *Requiem* 278 **MS,** He can walk in there and hem some of them up and even catch them if he's careful about not never turning his back on the ones he aint hemmed up. **1960** Hall *Smoky Mt. Folks* 66, In a "bear race" the dogs try to catch up with the bear and corner it against a tree or a cliff. They try to "hem the bear," as the mountaineer says. **1982** Ginns *Snowbird Gravy* 105 **nwNC,** They say you can hem a jackrabbit, and a lot of them'll just fall dead. Half of 'em or more, right in the field where they was hemmed, fall down and go to kicking and dying because they was hemmed up. Heart failed 'em, they say.

2 in phr *hem a pig* and varr: See quots. [Cf **B1** above]

1968–70 *DARE* (Qu. X37, . . *People's legs if they're noticeably bent, or uneven, or not right*) Inf **GA**23, They couldn't hem up a hog in a ditch with a sack between their legs; **TX**98, He couldn't hem up a pig in a rail fence. **1985** *Commercial Appeal* (Memphis TN) 2 Apr sec D 12/4, Of a bowlegged person: "He couldn't hem a pig in a one-foot ditch."

hemdurgan n

=rosefish.

1839 MA Zool. & Bot. Surv. *Fishes Reptiles* 26, *S[ebastes] Norvegicus.* Cuv. *The Norway Haddock.* . . By our fishermen it is known by the names of *"Rosefish," "Hemdurgan," and "Snapper."* **1884** Goode *Fisheries U.S.* 1.260, The Rose-fish, *Sebastes marinus,* is . . also known as . . 'Hemdurgan.' **1902** Jordan–Evermann *Amer. Fishes* 495, The only important species of the family on our Atlantic Coast is . . known as the . . hemdurgan, bream or John Dory.

hem-haw v Also with *around* [Var of *hem and haw*] Cf **hum and haw**

1954 *Harder Coll.* **cwTN,** *Hem-haw* . . to speak hesitatingly; to avoid giving a clear answer. "That old candydate hemmed-hawed 'round, never come to nothing." **1966–70** *DARE* (Qu. A11, *When somebody takes too long about coming to a decision . . "I wish he'd quit ______."*) Infs **AR**56, **IN**1, **MS**2, **TX**71, Hem-hawing (around); (Qu. II31, *In an argument between two people, when one of them claims too much and the other shows him up: "He saw that he was wrong, so he started to ______."*) Inf **CO**17, Hem-haw; (Qu. JJ45, *When someone avoids giving a definite answer: "We tried to pin him down, but he just kept ______."*) Infs **GA**80, **PA**208, Hem-hawing.

hemlet See **helmet**

hemlock n

1 Std: any of var often large plants of the family Apiaceae.

2 also *hemlock fir,* ~ *spruce (fir),* ~ *spruce pine;* pronc-sp *himlock:* A tree of the genus *Tsuga.* For other names of var spp see **spruce, spruce pine, tanbark tree, weeping spruce**

1662 Evelyn *Silva* (1729) 119 *(DA),* The Hemlock-tree (as they call it in New-England) is a kind of Spruce. **1739** (1946) Gronovius *Flora Virginica* 153, Hemlok Spruce-Firr. **1832** MA Hist. Soc. *Coll.* 2d ser 9.153 **cwVT,** [Pinus] canadensis, *(Pursh.)*—Hemlock. **1897** Sudworth *Arborescent Flora* 42, Hemlock. . . Hemlock Spruce. *Ibid* 44, *Tsuga caroliniana.* . . Hemlock (N.C., S.C.) *Ibid* 45, *Tsuga mertensiana.* . . Hemlock Spruce (Cal.) . . Hemlock (Oreg., Idaho, Wash.) **1903** Small *Flora SE U.S.* 30, *Tsuga Canadensis.* . . Hemlock. . . *Tsuga Caroliniana.* . . Hemlock. Crag Hemlock. Carolina Hemlock. **1907** *DN* 3.179 **NH,** *Himlock.* . . Hemlock. Pronunciation of older generation. **1965–70** *DARE* (Qu. T5) 289 Infs, **chiefly Nth,** Hemlock; **MD**30, Hemlock spruce; (Qu. T17) 18 Infs, **chiefly east of Missip R,** Hemlock; (Qu. T16) 10 Infs, **chiefly NEast,** Hemlock; (Qu. T15) 8 Infs, **chiefly NEast,** Hemlock. **1971** Krochmal *Appalachia Med. Plants* 258, *Tsuga Canadensis.* . . Common Names: Eastern hemlock, Canada hemlock, hemlock, hemlock fir, hemlock spruce, hemlock spruce pine, . . weeping spruce.

3 **=fetterbush 3.**

1860 Curtis *Cat. Plants NC* 96, *Dog Laurel.* (Leucothoe Catesbæi, Gray.)—Found only in the Mountains where it is also called *Hemlock,* growing on the cool margins of streams. **1894** *Jrl. Amer. Folkl.* 7.93 **NC,** *Leucothoe,* sp., hemlock. **1913** Kephart *Highlanders* 295 **sAppalachians,** What the mountaineers call hemlock is the shrub leucothoe.

hemlock bug n

A bedbug (Cimicidae).

1969 *DARE* (Qu. R24) Inf **VT**13, Hemlock bug.

hemlock fir See **hemlock 2**

hemlock pink n

Perh **=moss pink.**

1969 *SC Market Bulletin* 9 Jan 4, Hemlock pink.

hemlock special n

A train used primarily for transporting logs; see quots.

1967 *DARE* (Qu. N37, . . *A branch railroad that is not very important or gives poor service*) Inf **MI**47, Hemlock special—mainly for hauling sawlogs, and some passengers. **1969** Sorden *Lumberjack Lingo* 55 **NEng, Gt Lakes,** *Hemlock special*—A long train of sleighs loaded with logs being pulled by a steam hauler.

hemlock spruce, hemlock spruce fir, hemlock spruce pine See **hemlock 2**

hemlock steak n

=government beef.

1969 *DARE* (Qu. P35a, . . *Any deer shot illegally*) Inf **WI**78, Hemlock steak—deer meat, they fed on hemlock.

hemlock trout n

An unidentified fish.

1930 Shoemaker *1300 Words* 28 **cPA Mts** (as of c1900), *Hemlock trout*—The small native black trout with silver sides, now almost extinct in Pennsylvania streams.

hemlock warbler n

The Blackburnian warbler *(Dendroica fusca).*

1812 Wilson *Amer. Ornith.* 5.114, Hemlock Warbler. *Sylvia Parus.* . . This is another nondescript, first met with in the Great Pine swamp, Pennsylvania. **1895** Minot *Land-Birds New Engl.* 113, *Blackburnian Warbler. Hemlock Warbler.* . . Mr. Maynard thought that the "Blackburnians" built in the highest branches of the spruces and hemlocks, and such is very probably their custom. **1917** (1923) *Birds Amer.* 3.137, Hemlock Warbler. . . Wonder and delight . . are inspired by the appearance of this gaudy little sprite of the deep forest. **1963** Gromme *Birds WI* 218/2, Warbler, . . Hemlock (Blackburnian Warbler).

hemo v [Haw] **HI**

To loosen, remove, separate; hence adjs *hemo* and (by analogy with Engl ppl adjs) *hemoed* loosened, separate; see quot 1938.

1938 Reinecke *Hawaiian Loanwords* 11, *Hemo* ['he:mo, 'hɛmo]. . . A blanket word of the greatest variety of meaning. . . The primary meaning includes any type of loosening or removal: *hemo* (open) the door, *hemo* (tear out) a sheet of paper, *hemo* (cross out) a silent letter, *hemo* (take off) a shirt, etc. . . To bear young; to bear a child. . . To be separate. . . Loose; opened; separate; *hemo*-ed in any sense. (In this sense, *hemo*-ed is more commonly used.) **1954–60** Hance et al. *Hawaiian Sugar* 2, *Hemo* ['hemo]—loose, separate, to be loosened or separated. **1968** *Jrl. Engl. Ling.* 2.80 **HI** [Haw loan words], *Hemo*. . . To loosen, unfasten, separate, open, remove . . [;] Loose, loosened, unfastened, separate, separated, open, opened, removed. **1981** *Pidgin To Da Max* np **HI,** *Hemo*. . . To take off or remove. "Hemo yo' shoes when you eenside da house!" Hemo skin = Peeling.

hemp n, also attrib

1 also *hemp bag, ~ sack:* **=burlap bag.** *old-fash*

1965–70 *DARE* (Qu. F23, *A container made of rough, loosely-woven, brown cloth; commonly used for potatoes, etc*) 10 Infs, **scattered east of Missip R exc NEng,** Hemp (sack *or* bag); (Qu. F16, *The container apples come in;* total Infs questioned, 75) Inf **GA**10, Hemp sack; (Qu. F19, *A cloth container for grain*) Inf **MI**68, Hemp sack; (Qu. F20, *A cloth container for feed*) Inf **VA**9, Hemp sack. [All Infs old] **1966** Dakin *Dial. Vocab. Ohio R. Valley* 2.140, *Hemp sack, jute sack/bag.* These are quite rare.

2 in combs *hemp fever, ~ party, ~ stretching:* A hanging or lynching; similarly, v phr *pull hemp* to be hanged. **esp West** *old-fash*

1892 *Dispatch* (Columbus, O.) 6 Dec. *(DA),* If the incendiarist is found, a hemp party may result. **1921** Haswell *Daughter Ozarks* 162 (as of 1880s), Ye've got to git, and git immediate, and keep a'gittin', or ye'll pull hemp shore's hell. **1934** (1940) Weseen *Dict. Amer. Slang* 99 [Westerners' slang], *Hemp fever*—Hanging. **1949** *AmSp* 24.262 **West** (as of c1850s), Hanging has been called by various names: *hemp stretching, ridin' under a cottonwood limb, midair-dance, lynching bee, necktie social.*

hemp bag See **hemp 1**

hemp bird n

=goldfinch 1.

1858 *Atlantic Mth.* 2.595/2, The American Goldfinch, or Hemp-bird, *(Fringilla tristis,)* [is] one of the most interesting and delicate of the feathered tribe. **1956** MA Audubon Soc. *Bulletin* 40.254, *Goldfinch*. . . Hemp Bird (Mass.)

hemp dogbane n [See quot 1948] **chiefly West**

An **Indian hemp** (here: *Apocynum cannabinum*).

1936 McDougall-Baggley *Plants of Yellowstone* 101, *Hemp dogbane* . . has smaller, greenish-white flowers. **1937** U.S. Forest Serv. *Range Plant Hdbk.* W17, The bark fiber of both spreading dogbane and hemp dogbane . . provided the principal cordage for the western aborigines. **1948** Stevens *KS Wild Flowers* 17, *Hemp Dogbane*. . . Bast fibers of this plant, like those of the hemp, . . useful for making cordage, rope, etc. **1973** Hitchcock-Cronquist *Flora Pacific NW* 362, In most of US and much of Can[ada] . . hemp d[ogbane].

hemp fever See **hemp 2**

hempine n [Prob blend of *hemlock* + *pine*]

=hemlock 2.

1939 *Hall Coll.* **wNC,** The dogs . . treed up a big hem-pine. **1967** *Ibid* **eTN,** They was plenty of hempine [in the Devils Courthouse], big trees, 3 or 4 foot through. **1970** *Foxfire* Spring-Summer 32 **nGA,** And they run that thing . . and treed it up a big hem pine, an' I run that coon all night that night.

hemp nettle n

Std: a plant of the genus *Galeopsis.* For other names of *G. tetrahit* see **dead nettle 2, dog nettle 1, ironweed, stinging nettle, wild hemp**

hemp party See **hemp 2**

hemprape n

The hemp **broomrape 1** (here: *Orobanche ramosa*).

[**1911** *Century Dict. Suppl., Broom-rape*. . . *Hemp broom-rape, Orobanche ramosa,* an Old World species, in Kentucky now an annoying parasite on the roots of hemp and tobacco.] **1966** *PADS* 45.15 **cnKY,** Hemprape . . = *broomrape*. . . "Hemprape gets on the roots of the plants."

hemp sack See **hemp 1**

hemp stretching See **hemp 2**

hemp tree n [Perh from some resemblance of the leaf to that of hemp]

=chaste tree.

1900 Lyons *Plant Names* 395, *Vitex Agnus-castus*. . . Hemp-tree. **1960** Vines *Trees SW* 898, *Lilac Chaste-tree—Vitex agnus-castus*. . . Vernacular names are Monk's Pepper-tree, Wild Pepper, . . Hemp-tree, . . Chaste Lamb-tree. **1970** Correll *Plants TX* 1340, *Vitex Agnus-castus*. . . Hemp-tree. **1976** Bailey-Bailey *Hortus Third* 1161. **1979** Little *Checklist U.S. Trees* 294, *Vitex agnus-castus* . . common chastetree (hemptree, monks-peppertree, Indian-spice) is a shrub or sometimes small tree to 16 ft (5 m) high widely planted in se. U.S.

hempvine See **climbing hempweed**

hempweed n

A **boneset 1;** see quots.

1790 in 1793 Amer. Philos. Soc. *Trans.* 3.176 **sePA,** Eupatorium, Hempweed. **1822** Eaton *Botany* 276, *Eupatorium hyssopifolium,* hyssop-thoroughwort, hempweed. **1843** Torrey *Flora NY* 2.517, *Eupatorium hyssopifolium*. . . Hyssop-leaved Hempweed. . . *Eupatorium album*. . . White-headed Hempweed. . . *Eupatorium resinosum*. . . Resinous Hempweed. **1940** Clute *Amer. Plant Names* 259, *Eupatorium purpureum*. . . Hemp-weed. **1971** Krochmal *Appalachia Med. Plants* 120, *Eupatorium purpureum*. . . *Common Names* . . hempweed. **1974** (1977) Coon *Useful Plants* 108, Hempweed. . . Among herbalists it is claimed to be of value as a diuretic and tonic.

hem up See **hem** v **B1**

hen n[1] Usu |hɛn|; also |hɪn|; rarely |hen|; for addit varr see **A1** below Cf Pronc Intro 3.I.4.a Pronc-sp *hin*

A Forms.

1 Pronc varr.

1907 *DN* 3.190 **seNH,** *Hin*. . . Hen. Older generation. **1939** in 1944 *ADD* **Midwest,** Hin. **1941** *AmSp* 16.5 **eTX** [Black], *Hen* . . [ɛ] becomes [ĭ]. **1941** *LANE* Map 473 *(Wet hen),* [**widespread throughout NEng** [hɛn, he^{ə}n]; 6 infs, **MA, VT,** [he(ə)n]; 1 inf, **seME,** [hæ^{ə}n]; 3 infs, **eMA, seNH,** [hɪn].] **1942** Hall *Smoky Mt. Speech* 19 **eTN, wNC,** [ɛ] is often raised to or toward [ɪ] . . hen.

2 used attrib in combs where possessive often occurs: See quots. [Cf *OED hen-egg* "in mod. Eng. *hen's egg* is more commonly used"] **chiefly Sth, S Midl** Cf **bird** n **A2**

1837 Sherwood *Gaz. GA* 70, *Hen-aig,* for hen's egg. **a1883** (1911) Bagby *VA Gentleman* 51, He selects, with unerring accuracy, a piece of the poorest "hennest" grass-land in his native county. **1890** *DN* 1.68 **KY,** *Hen nest* [hɛnnɛst]: for *hen's nest.* **1905** *DN* 3.82 **nwAR,** *Hen-nest*. . . Hens' nest. 'There ought to be some eggs in that hen-nest.' **1908** *DN* 3.320 **eAL, wGA,** *Hen-nest*. . . Hen's nest. **1949** *PADS* 11.7 **wTX** (as of c1911), *Hen egg*. . . A hen's egg. Common. **c1960** *Wilson Coll.* **csKY,** *Hen egg* is the regular form; hen's egg sounds strange. **1967–70** *DARE* (Qu. M16) Infs **KY**23, **MS**81, **NC**48, **TX**22, Hen nest; **LA**7, Hen nest—a boxlike affair up off the ground built together with others in a row; (Qu. X60, . . *A lump that comes up on your head when you get a sharp blow or knock*) Infs **AL**36, **LA**31, **TX**54, Hen egg; (Qu. HH14, . . *A 'left-handed monkey wrench': "Go get me ______.")* Inf **MD**31, Some hen teeth. **1969** *SC Market Bulletin* 11 Sept 3/4, 12 hole galv. steel hen nests, good condition, $5 per set.

B Senses.

1 See **hen clam 1.**

2 usu pl; also *hen violet:* A **Canadian wood violet** or similar violet. Cf **rooster**

1893 *Bot. Gaz.* 18.423, *Viola Canadensis,* hens. Ferrisburgh, Vt. **1900** Lyons *Plant Names* 394, *V[iola] Canadensis*. . . Canada Violet, American Sweet Violet, June-flower, Hens. **1959** Carleton *Index Herb. Plants* 60, *Hens:* Viola canadensis. **1969** *DARE* (Qu. S11, . . *Violet*) Inf **KY**28, Hen violets—a crook in the stem; **MO**37, Hen and rooster—purple ones are roosters.

3 **=prairie chicken.**

1899 Garland *Boy Life* 363 **nwIA** (as of c1870s), "I kill no more hens and cats," he said, meaning prairie chickens and rabbits.

4 also *hen trigger:* **=ruffed grouse.**

1966–68 *DARE* (Qu. Q7, . . *Game birds*) Inf **ME**22, Hen; **NH**14, Partridge—hen trigger or hen or just bird.

5 in phrr *a hen on (the nest):* An urgent, important, or secret plan or project in the making.

1878 in 1927 *Pacific NW Qrly.* 18.192 **cwWI,** Keep cool, boys, there's a hen on. **1887** Kirkland *Zury* 537 **IL,** *Hen on. . .* Something of importance hatching out. **1896** (1898) Ade *Artie* 104 **Chicago IL,** Artie spoke abruptly. "Miller," said he, "I got a hen on." "What is it?" "It's like this. Would you dally with politics if you thought you stood to win out a good thing?" **1916** Lincoln *Mary-'Gusta* 155 **MA,** Mr. Keith and me are tryin' to do a little stroke of business together. We've got a hen on as the feller said. *Ibid* 159, "We've got a hen on . . " he declared. "When it's time for the critter to come off the nest you'll see what's been hatched same as the rest of us." **1946** *CA Folkl. Qrly.* 5.231 **wOR,** *She's got a hen on.* She is hatching up some scheme. **1949** *Western Folkl.* 8.105 **CA,** *To have a hen on the nest*—To have a project that is taking shape. **1960** Criswell *Resp. to PADS 20* **Ozarks,** *To have a hen on*—To have an urgent project on hand. Rather common in older days, perhaps rare now. "Jim couldn't come along with us, he's got a hen on."

6 in adj or adv phr *like a hen on a hot griddle* and varr: Agitated, anxious; in an agitated or nervous manner. [Engl dial; cf *EDD* (at *hen* sb.[1] 3. (4)), *SND* (at *hen* n.[1] 2. (3))]

1899 (1912) Green *VA Folk-Speech* 34, Like a hen on a hot griddle. **1946** *PADS* 6.41 **swVA,** *To run around like a hen on a hot griddle.* (To busy oneself with trifles.) **1958** *VT Hist.* 26.274, To act (bob around) like a hen on a hot griddle. . . As jumpy as a hen on a hot brick. **1966–68** *DARE* (Qu. GG11, *To be quite anxious about something*) Inf **FL**33, Like a hen on a hot hoe; [**VA**31, She's a hen on a hot griddle—a woman who is spluttering—extremely agitated].

7 in phr *beat a hen a-rootin'* and varr: To be highly unusual or noteworthy; to be very exasperating.

1939 in 1972 Hall *Sayings Old Smoky* 83 **swNC,** That beats a hen a-rootin'. **1944** *PADS* 2.57 **nMO,** *To beat hens a-rastlin'. . .* To be most unusual. **1966–68** *DARE* (Qu. GG22b, *When you have come to the end of your patience, you might say*) Inf **TN**26, Don't that beat a hen a-flyin'; **NC**37, [That] beats a hen a-rootin'. **1984** Wilder *You All Spoken Here* 52 **Sth,** *That beats hens a-pacin':* Observation made of a sexy woman's gait, manner, or dress.

hen n[2] [Euphem for *hell*]

Used as a mild oath; see quots.

1907 *DN* 3.189 **seNH,** In the mild oath, *by Hen.* "By Hen, feed her out." **1924** *DN* 5.269 **cnNY,** *Hen:* oh —, by — [expressing] surp[rise], vex[ation]. **1959** *VT Hist.* new ser 27.142, *By hen!* . . Occasional. **1969** *DARE* (Qu. NN26a, *Weakened substitutes for 'hell': "Oh ______!"*) Inf **MI**103, Hen.

hen and biddies n **GA**

1 also *hens and biddies:* A **pitcher plant.** Cf **hen and chickens**

1966–68 *DARE* (QR, near Qu. S1) Inf **GA**35, Hen and biddies—old-fashioned for pitcher plant; (Qu. S11) Inf **GA**7, Hens and biddies; (Qu. S26b) Inf **GA**20, Hen and biddies . . flower from pitcher plant. Baby chickens used to be called biddies. **1980** *DARE* File **Okefenokee GA,** [Park guide:] Pitcher plants—some call 'em hens and biddies.

2 See quot.

1969 *DARE* (Qu. Z8, *General word for your own immediate family group*) Inf **GA**72, The hen and biddies.

hen and chickens n

1 also *hen(s) and chick(en)s:* Any of var plants, such as the English daisy *(Bellis perennis),* **ground ivy 1,** or *Echeveria* spp, which have numerous offsets, runners, or clustered flowers, but in the US esp:

a Any of several succulent plants of the family Crassulaceae, as:

(1) A **houseleek 1** (here: *Sempervivum tectorum*).

1892 *Jrl. Amer. Folkl.* 5.96 **nOH,** *Sempervivum tectorum,* hen and chickens. **1910** Graves *Flowering Plants* 215 **CT,** Houseleek. Hen-and-chickens. . . Long persistent and spreading from former cultivation. **1950** Gray-Fernald *Manual of Botany* 734, *Hens-and-chickens.*—Leaves of the dense basal and lateral rosettes (on short thick offsets) ovate. **1967** *DARE* (Qu. S26e) Inf **NY**12, Hen and chickens, cactus-like. **1974** (1977) Coon *Useful Plants* 121, The "hen and chickens" comes from the way in which the plant sends out little plants from a central mother, the mother dying after blooming. [**1976** Bailey-Bailey *Hortus Third* 1032, One houseleek, *S. tectorum,* is an old-fashioned plant about houses and in borders, prized for its durable rosettes and the progeny of smaller ones.]

(2) A **live-forever:** here either *Dudleya cymosa* or **bluff lettuce. chiefly CA**

1897 Parsons *Wild Flowers CA* 142, *Cotyledon Californicum. . .* Owing to their habit of producing a circle of young plants around the parent, they are commonly called "hen-and-chickens." **1915** (1926) Armstrong-Thornber *Western Wild Flowers* 194, *Hen-and-Chickens. Dudleya Nevadensis. . .* Other smaller rosettes form a circle around it [=a large rosette], hence its nice little common name. **1954** CA Div. Beaches & Parks *Pt. Lobos Wildflowers* 19, *Dudleya farinosa. . .* Bluff Lettuce, stone-crop, hen-and-chickens are all frequently-used common names.

(3) A **stonecrop** such as *Sedum rosea.*

1938 (1958) Sharples *AK Wild Flowers* 121, *Sedum Rhodiola. . .* "Hen and Chickens." Cluster of stems 4–10 inches high, rising from one crown, erect and unbranched. **1950** Stevens *ND Plants* 163, *Orpine Family. . .* Here belong hen-and-chickens and species of *Sedum* often grown in rock gardens. **1967** *DARE* (Qu. S26e) Inf **MA**5, Hens and chickens—sedum. **1989** *DARE* File **csWI, cIA,** Hens and chicks are little cabbage-shaped succulents that grow in rock gardens; **csWI,** This year my rock garden will be planted with several hen and chicks, or sedums, which a neighbor gave me.

b also *hen and chickens pea:* A **wild indigo** (here: *Baptisia leucophaea*).

1936 Whitehouse *TX Flowers* 53, *Large-Bracted False Indigo (Baptisia bracteata)* is sometimes called hen-and-chickens pea from the growth habit of the plant. **1951** *PADS* 15.34 **TX,** *Baptisia bracteata. . .* Hen-and-chickens.

c A **hedgehog cactus 3** (here: *Echinocactus triglochidiatus* var *mojavensis*).

1942 Whipple *Joshua* 189 **UT** (as of c1860), The old hen-and-chickens, the beaver-tail, clumps of tall cactus like vicious shocks of wheat, yellow spines flung like blobs of sunlight on the gray desert floor. **1959** Carleton *Index Herb. Plants* 60, *Hen-and-chickens:* Bellis perennis; Echinocereus mojavensis; Nepeta hederacea (Glecoma); Sempervivum (v).

d A **Venus's looking-glass** (here: *Triodanis perfoliata*).

1961 Wills-Irwin *Flowers TX* 219, Venus' Looking-glass, or Hen-and-chickens, as it is sometimes called, grows in fields and open woods.

e also *hen and chicken:* =**butter-and-eggs 1.**

1966–69 *DARE* (Qu. S11) Inf **MA**25, Hens and chickens—wild snapdragon [FW: Inf heard]; **MI**17, Hen and chicken [FW: Inf uncertain]; (Qu. S26b) Inf **MI**67, Hen and chickens; (Qu. S26d) Inf **NJ**21, Hens and chickens.

f Appar a **bluet 2.**

1970 *DARE* (Qu. S26e) Inf **KY**89, Hens and chickens—tiny blue flowers that come up before Easter.

g A **pincushion cactus** (here: *Mammillaria aggregata*).

1967 Dodge *Roadside Wildflowers* 46, *Arizona pincushion. . .* Although it usually grows as a single stem, it sometimes appears in small clusters, leading to the name hen-and-chickens.

2 =**chickamy chickamy craney crow.**

[**1894** A.B. Gomme *Trad. Games Eng. Scotl. & Irel.* I. 201 *(OEDS),* Hen and Chicken. . . The game is played in the usual manner of 'Fox and Goose' games. One is chosen to be the Hen, and one to be the Fox. The rest are the Chickens.] **1953** Brewster *Amer. Nonsinging Games* 71, Hen and chickens. . . One player is the hawk, another is the hen, and the rest are chickens. . . the hawk makes a dash for one of the chickens. . . The hen stretches out her arms . . to ward off the hawk's attacks. Each chicken caught must drop out of the game; the last to be caught becomes hawk for the next game played. **1968** *DARE* (Qu. EE33, . . *Outdoor games . . that children play*) Inf **GA**58, Hen and chickens.

hen and chickens pea See **hen and chickens 1b**

hen and chicks See **hen and chickens 1**

hen apple See **hen berry**

Henary See **Henry**

henbait See **henbit 1**

hen berry n Also *hen apple joc* Cf **hen fruit**

An egg.

1939 *AmSp* 14.90 **eTN,** *Hen apples.* Eggs. 'I eat scrambled hen apples for breakfast.' **c1960** *Wilson Coll.* **csKY,** *Hen apples. . .* Humorous name for eggs. **1960** Criswell *Resp. to PADS 20* **Ozarks,** *Hen berries*. . . Once used humorously for eggs. **1966** *DARE* (Qu. H33, *Joking names for eggs;* total Infs questioned, 75) Infs **OK**19, 21, Hen berries; **MS**1, Hen apples.

henbill n

1 A **coot** n[1] **1** (here: *Fulica americana*).

1844 DeKay *Zool. NY* 2.273, This bird [=*Fulica americana*], which has also received the popular names of *Mud-hen, White-bill* and *Hen-bill,* is found in this State from the latter part of March to the middle of November. **1844** Giraud *Birds Long Is.* 200, The Coot [=*Fulica americana*] . . is sufficiently frequent to be known to the gunners, by whom the more familiar appellation of "Mud Hen"—or, in some sections of the Island, as at Egg Harbor, "White" or "Henbill," is applied. **1888** [see **2** below]. **1917** (1923) *Birds Amer.* 1.214, *Coot—Fulica americana*. . . *Other Names.*—American Coot; . . Hen-bill; . . Pull-doo.

2 also *hen-billed diver:* A **grebe,** esp the **pied-billed grebe.**

1888 Trumbull *Names of Birds* 82, The Grebes, particularly the Pied-billed Grebe, *Podilymbus podiceps,* that lively little nuisance, familiar to us all, under one or more of the following titles: Hen-bill, . . Hell-diver. *Ibid* 118, *Fulica Americana* . . *Coot:* . . known . . at Egg Harbor, N.J. as . . *Hen-bill.* **1889** *Century Dict.* 2792, *Henbill*. . . The hen-billed diver, or Carolina grebe or dabchick, *Podilymbus podiceps.*

hen bird n

=**pileated woodpecker.**

1955 *AmSp* 30.181, Of bird names given for size, consider . . *hen bird* (the same species [=pileated woodpecker], Tenn.)

henbit n

1 also pronc-sp *henbait:* =**dead nettle 1,** esp *Lamium amplexicaule.*

1813 Muhlenberg *Catalogus Plantarum* 55, *Lamium* Archangel . . , henbit. **1894** *Jrl. Amer. Folkl.* 7.96 **IA,** *Lamium amplexicaule* . . henbit. **1913** *Torreya* 13.240, *Lamium amplexicaule.* Henbit. Occasionally found in waste places. **1932** Rydberg *Flora Prairies* 687, *Lamium* . . Dead nettle, Henbit. **1968** *Sussex Countian* (Georgetown DE) 23 May 8/3, Several annual weeds such as German moss, henbit, chickweed, and crabgrass can be controlled chemically. **1968–69** *DARE* (Qu. S21, *What other weeds do you have around here that are a trouble in gardens and fields?*) Inf **PA**88, Henbait; (Qu. S26a, . . *Roadside flowers*) Inf **TN**39, Henbit. **1974** (1977) Coon *Useful Plants* 158, *Lamium amplexicaule*—Hen-bit, dead nettle, white archangel. A naturalized weed throughout the country, it is a plant which may be boiled and eaten, but is otherwise not notably useful.

2 A **speedwell** (here: *Veronica hederifolia*).

1900 Lyons *Plant Names* 391, *Veronica hederæfolia*. . . Ivy-leaved Speedwell, . . Small Henbit. **1940** Clute *Amer. Plant Names* 33, *Veronica hederæfolia.* Ivy-leaved Speedwell . . small henbit. **1959** Carleton *Index Herb. Plants* 60, *Hen Bit:* . . Veronica hederæfolia.

hen-cackle n Also *hen-cackling*

1968–70 *DARE* (Qu. KK12, *A meeting where there's a lot of talking: "They got together yesterday and had a real ______."*) Inf **MO**22, Hen-cackling; **UT**6, Hen-cackle—if it's women.

‡**henchies is walking** n Cf **handkerchief A**

The game drop-the-handkerchief.

1970 *DARE* (Qu. EE1, . . *Games . . children play . . in which they form a ring, and either sing or recite a rhyme*) Inf **FL**48, Henchies is walking [FW: the same as drop-the-handkerchief].

hen clam n [From the belief that they are only female]

1 also *hen:* A **surf clam** (here: *Spisula solidissima* or *S. polynyma*) of the Atlantic coast. **chiefly NEng, esp ME**

1802 MA Hist. Soc. *Coll.* 1st ser 8.192 **seMA,** The sea clam, which is at present called the *hen,* the quahaug having lost that appellation, is bivalve . . and oval. **a1862** (1865) Thoreau *Cape Cod* 78, Our host told us that the sea-clam, or hen, was not easily obtained. **1877** Bartlett *Americanisms* 784, *Hen-Clam.* The Broad Sea-clam. (*Macta* [sic] *gigantea.*) Common on the shores of New England. **1884** U.S. Natl. Museum *Bulletin* 27.231, *Spisula solidissima* . . is known commonly as the "sea," "surf," or "hen" clam. **1884** (1885) Kingsley *Std. Nat. Hist.* 1.278, *Mactra solidissima* and the closely allied *M. ovalis* are known along our northern coasts as hen-clam, sea-clam, and surf-clam. **1913** *DN* 4.4 **ME,** *Hen clam*. . . The sea clam. Biddeford. **1939** *LANE* Map 235, 6 infs, 5 in **ME,** Hen clam. [Two infs label the term old-fashioned.] **1949** *Sat. Eve. Post* 25 June 52/4 **swME,** He went after herring with a deep net, dragged for hen clams and harpooned tuna. **1981** Rehder *Audubon Field Guide Seashells* 753, *Atlantic Surf Clam*. . . This shell is called . . in Maine the Hen Clam.

2 =**pismo clam.**

1879 U.S. Natl. Museum *Bulletin* 14.256, "Hen clam" *(Pachyderma crassatelloides . .).* California. **1884** Goode *Fisheries U.S.* 1.708, Aboriginal money was made from the valves of the ponderous Hen Clam of southern California (*Pachydesma* [=*Pachyderma*] *crassatelloides*). . . This money was called *"hawok,"* and took the shape of perforated disks which could be strung as beads.

henclaw grass n [Prob from the configuration of spikes] Cf **cocksfoot grass**

Appar a **crabgrass 1.**

1968 *DARE* (Qu. S8) Inf **IN**30, Henclaw grass.

hen coop n **esp Nth** See Map Cf **chicken coop 1** Note: *hen coop,* meaning a small, often portable, cage or enclosure for poultry, is widely scattered throughout the US.

=**hennery a.**

1939 *LANE* Map 112, *Hen coop* . . is used by some of our informants [chiefly in **seNH, neMA, ME**] also for a small *hen house* provided with roosts. **1966** Dakin *Dial. Vocab. Ohio R. Valley* 2.258, Some speakers say *chicken coop* (occasionally *hen coop*) for a structure of any size and purpose . . the equivalent of the *chicken house* or *hen house* of other speakers. **1966–69** *DARE* (Qu. M17, *A building where chickens or hens are kept*) 11 Infs, **esp Nth,** Hen coop; (Qu. II21, . . *"The way he behaves, you'd think he was ______."*) Inf **MA**61, Brought up in a hen coop. **1973** Allen *LAUM* 1.256 **MN, IA** (as of c1950), *Hen coop = hen house.* [2 infs]

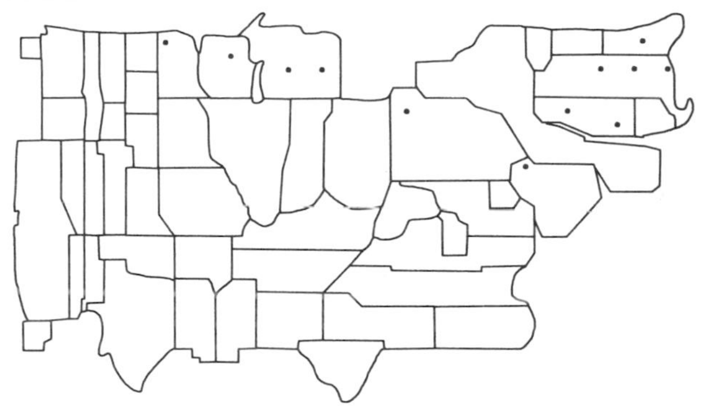

•hen coop + var (Qq. M17, II21)

hen curlew n [See quot 1955]

=**long-billed curlew.**

1889 *Century Dict.* 2793 **MA,** *Hen-curlew*. . . The long-billed curlew, *Numenius longirostris.* **1946** Goodrich *Birds in KS* 314, Colloquial Name. . . Curlew, hen. . . Common name. . . Curlew, long-billed. **1955** MA Audubon Soc. *Bulletin* 39.446, *Long-billed Curlew*. . . Hen Curlew . . (Mass. From its speckled brown color and its large size.)

hendance See **hinder** v

hender See **hinder** v

hendersome See **hindersome**

Henderson-wood n

A **yaupon** (here: *Ilex cassine*).

1913 *Torreya* 13.232, *Ilex cassine* L.—Henderson wood, Okefenoke [sic] Swamp[,] Charlton Co., Ga. **1933** Small *Manual SE Flora* 816, *I[lex] Cassine* L. . . Dahoon. Yaupon. Cassena. Henderson-wood. **1960** Vines *Trees SW* 650, *Ilex cassine*. . . Vernacular names are Christmas-berry, Yaupon, and Henderson-wood. **1979** Little *Checklist U.S. Trees* 148, *Ilex cassine* L. . . *Other common names* . . Henderson-wood.

hendrance See **hinder** v

hen-drownder See **goose drownder**

henduh See **hinder** v

hen-dung tree See **hen-turd tree**

hen-eater n

1969 *DARE* (Qu. HH28, . . *People of foreign background: French*) Inf MA30, Hen-eaters.

hen egg n

1 See **hen** n[1] **A2.**

2 See **hen's egg.**

Henery See **Henry**

hen-fat See **fat hen 2**

hen fest n [Cf *hen party*]

A women's gathering or party.

1942 Berrey-Van den Bark *Amer. Slang* 94.7, *Henfest,* a dinner for women. *Ibid* 365.3, *Women's party. . .* henfest. **1968** *DARE* (Qu. KK12, *A meeting where there's a lot of talking: "They got together yesterday and had a real ______."*) Inf **MN**42, Hen fest—of women; bull session—of men.

henfire n [Euphem for *hellfire;* cf **hen** n[2]]

1967-69 *DARE* (Qu. KK55c, . . *Expressions of strong denial*) Inf **GA**77, Henfire no; (Qu. NN26c, *Weakened substitutes for 'hell': "What the ______!"*) Inf **SC**34, Henfire.

henflesh n [Engl dial; cf *EDD* (at *hen* sb.[1] 1. (19))]

=gooseflesh.

1950 *WELS (When you are cold and little points of skin stick up on your arms and legs, you say you have ______)* 1 Inf, **cnWI,** Henflesh.

hen flew endways See **in flew endways**

hen food n

=hen fruit.

1950 *WELS (Joking names for eggs)* 1 Inf, **swWI,** Hen food. Common. **1965** *DARE* (Qu. H33, *Joking names for eggs;* total Infs questioned, 75) Inf **MS**60, Hen food.

hen fruit n Cf **cackleberry, hen berry**

Eggs; an egg.

1854 *Harper's New Mth. Mag.* Jan 280/2, A young lady is said to have asked a gentleman at the table of a hotel "down East" to pass her the "hen fruit." She pointed to a plate of eggs. **1900** *DN* 2.15 [Student lingo], Eggs are *hen-fruit,* as often outside of college. **1907** *DN* 3.231 **nwAR, seMO,** *Hen-fruit. . .* Eggs. Used seriously by many country people. **1908** *DN* 3.319 **eAL, wGA,** *Hen-fruit. . .* Eggs. **1915** *DN* 4.226 **wTX,** *Hen fruit. . .* Eggs:—facetious, but common. **1930** Williams *Logger-Talk* 25 **Pacific NW. 1950** *WELS (Joking names for eggs)* 47 Infs, **WI,** Hen fruit. **1954** *Harder Coll.* **cwTN,** *Hen fruit. . .* A joking name for an egg. **1960** Criswell *Resp. to PADS 20* **Ozarks,** *Hen fruit* and *cackleberries* are both rather old terms, used mostly by men. **c1960** *Wilson Coll.* **csKY,** *Hen fruit. . .* An egg or more than one. **1965-70** *DARE* (Qu. H33; total Infs questioned, 75) 24 Infs, Hen fruit. **1969** Sorden *Lumberjack Lingo* 55 **NEng, Gt Lakes. 1976** Garber *Mountain-ese* 40 **Appalachians,** *Hen-fruit . .* eggs—My family likes plenty uv fresh hen fruit fer breakfast.

heng See **hang** v **A1, 2, 3**

hengkitchuh See **handkerchief**

hen harrier n **NEast**

=marsh hawk.

1844 DeKay *Zool. NY* 2.20, The *Marsh Hawk,* or *Hen Harrier,* is common over this continent. . . It . . occasionally makes a dash at the poultry yard. **1845** Judd *Margaret* 146 **eNEng,** A hen-harrier bore in his talons a chicken to his young. **1955** MA Audubon Soc. *Bulletin* 39.442, *Marsh Hawk. . .* Hen Harrier (Vt., Mass.)

hen hawk n Cf **chicken hawk 1**

Any of var hawks which prey (or are thought to prey) upon poultry, esp the **red-tailed hawk** and the **red-shouldered hawk;** see quots.

1792 Belknap *Hist. NH* 3.165, Hen Hawk, *Falco sparverius?* **1844** DeKay *Zool. NY* 2.14, It [=the duck hawk] is . . known under the various popular names of *Hen Hawk, Chicken Hawk* and *Pigeon Hawk.* **1895** Minot *Land-Birds New Engl.* 375, *Buteo. . . borealis. . .* "Hen Hawk." *Ibid* 376, *B[uteo] lineatus. . .* "Hen Hawk." **1899** (1912) Green *VA Folk-Speech* 222, *Hen-hawk. . .* A hawk that preys on fowls. **1925** Bailey *Birds FL* 69, *Harlan Hawk. . .* Hen hawk, Chicken hawk. *Ibid, Red-tailed Hawk. . .* Hen hawk, Fantail, Chicken hawk. **1940** Faulkner *Hamlet* 612 **MS,** The horse . . come helling back up that lane like a scared hen-hawk. **1946** Hausman *Eastern Birds* 183, *Eastern Goshawk. . . Other Names . .* Hen Hawk. **1955** MA Audubon Soc. *Bulletin* 39.441, *Cooper's Hawk. . .* Hen Hawk (General. Remains of domestic fowls were found in 60 of the 754 stomachs examined.) . . *Red-shouldered Hawk. . .* Hen Hawk (General. Less applicable to this species than to the Red-tail. Remains of chickens were found in only 8 of 391 stomachs.) . . *Broad-winged Hawk.* Hen Hawk. (Mass. The Broad-wing seldom takes poultry, and none was found in 111 stomachs.) **1955** *Oriole* 20.6 **GA,** *Pigeon Hawk—Hen Hawk* (the bird is too small to be much of an enemy to poultry). **1965-70** *DARE* (Qu. Q4) 59 Infs, **chiefly NEast,** Hen hawk; **NH**6, Hen hawk—red-shouldered, red-tailed; **VT**13, Red-tail hen hawk.

hen-headed adj Also *hen-minded* [Cf *EDD hen-headed* (at *hen* sb.[1] 1. (23))]

Brainless, capricious.

1892 Howells *Quality of Mercy* 6, She was really one of those hen-minded women, who . . are made up of only one aim at a time, and of manifold anxieties at all times. **1912** *DN* 3.578 **wIN,** *Hen-headed. . .* Brainless. "That hen-headed cuss can't do anything you tell him." **1938** Bill *Astrophel* 76, Elizabeth, always short of money . . , railed against the required outlay like a hen-headed housewife over a coal bill, but she finally gave her approval. **1942** Berrey-Van den Bark *Amer. Slang* 151.9, *Foolish; silly; witless. . .* hen-headed. *Ibid* 212.4, *Flighty; capricious. . .* hen-headed.

hen-house way n Cf **cock of the roost**

Fig: see quot.

1986 Pederson *LAGS Concordance,* 1 inf, **neTX,** He has hen-house ways—things must be his way.

‡hen-husband n Cf *henpecked*

Prob **=hen-hussy 3.**

1960 Williams *Walk Egypt* 208 **GA** [Black], Mr. Wick sho ain't no hen-husband. Mostest mens flaps and squawks round.

hen-hussy n Also *hen-huzzy* [Cf *EDD hen-hussey* (at *hen* sb.[1] 1. (28))]

1 See quot. *arch*

1899 (1912) Green *VA Folk-Speech* 222, *Hen-huzzy. . .* A woman who looks after fowls.

2 Transf: see quot.

1969 *DARE* (Qu. GG36a, *The kind of person who is always poking into other people's affairs: "She's an awful ______."*) Inf **VT**12, Hen-huzzy.

3 pronc-sp *hennessy:* See quots.

1890 *DN* 1.74 **seMA,** *Hen-hussy . .* a man who concerns himself overmuch with household matters or housekeeping. . . Also . . *hennessy,* the second syllable evidently slurred in pronunciation. Explained as a man who meddles with women's affairs. **1892** *DN* 1.216 **sCT, swMA,** *Hen-hussy.* **1934** (1943) *W2, Henhussy. . .* A man who busies himself with womanish affairs, esp. about the house. **1942** Berrey-Van den Bark *Amer. Slang* 405.2, *Effeminate man. . .* hen-hussy.

4 See quot.

1967 *DARE* (Qu. AA7b, . . *A woman who is very fond of men and is always trying to know more—if she's not respectable about it*) Inf **IA**8, A hen-hussy.

henious See **heinous**

hen-minded See **hen-headed**

hen mite n

=harvest mite.

1968 *DARE* (Qu. R22) Inf **MI**96, Hen mites.

henna interrog exclam [Pronc-sp for **ainna**]

1986 *DARE* File **cPA,** "Henna" . . is, in fact, a complete sentence, a question really. . . Is it not so? Ain't it so? Ain't it? Henna? I think it's rather unique, henna?

hennery n |ˈhɛn(ə)ri|

An enclosure for poultry, spec:

a A hen house. **chiefly NEast** See Map *old-fash*

1850 Judd *Richard Edney* 378 **swME,** There were so many persons to see the hennery. **1860** Hundley *Social Relations S. States* 341 **Nth,** Each family of negroes has a house or cabin of its own, generally with sufficient garden-ground, piggery, hennery, and so forth. **1939** *LANE*

Map 111 *(Hen house)* **scattered NEng,** [hɛn(ə)rɪ]. **1960** Bailey *Resp. to PADS 20* **KS,** Chicken house, hennery. **1966–69** *DARE* (Qu. M17, *A building where chickens or hens are kept*) 11 Infs, **chiefly NEast,** Hennery. [10 of 11 Infs old] **1973** Allen *LAUM* 1.255 **sMN** (as of c1950), N[orth] E[astern] *hennery* . . survives in this same inf.'s [=an inf of New York and New Jersey parentage] speech as well as in that of two other Minnesotans.

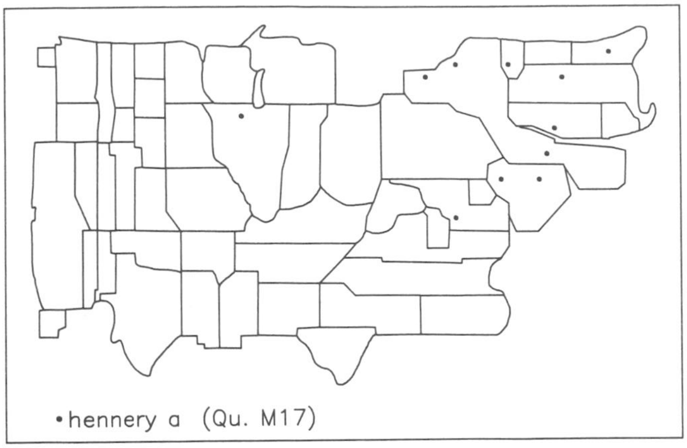

b A portable shelter. Cf **hen pen b**

1969 *DARE* (Qu. M16, *The small shelter for a hen that can be moved about from place to place*) Inf **CA**111, Hennery.

hennessy See **hen-hussy 3**

hen nest n

1 See **hen's nest 1.**

2 See **hen** n[1] **A2.**

henny adj, also used absol [Cf *SND hennie, henny* timid, cowardly (at *hen* v. 1)]

Fussy, petty, finicky.

1950 *WELS (Someone who worries a lot, or who worries about little things)* 1 Inf, **seWI,** Henny; *(Somebody who is very particular or fussy: Women)* 3 Infs, **WI,** Henny; *(A person who is always finding fault about unimportant things)* 1 Inf, **cWI,** Henny.

hen of the woods n [See quot 1980] Cf **hickory chicken**

An edible mushroom *(Grifola frondosa).*

1942 Hylander *Plant Life* 64, *Polyporus* includes many common species. One, more edible than the others, is known as Hen of the Woods. *Ibid* 640, Hen of the Woods—Polyporus frondosus. **1980** Marteka *Mushrooms* 161, *Hen of the Woods*. . . To the imaginative eye, a clump of the fungus looks like a setting hen that has just fluffed its feathers after being disturbed on the nest . . ; thus, the mushroom's common name. The fluffed feathers are actually smoky gray to brown mushroom caps that grow at the tips of short white-stems. . . The caps grow so close together that the short stems aren't visible to an observer standing over a mushroom clump. **1981** Lincoff *Audubon Field Guide Mushrooms* 463, Hen of the Woods. *Grifola frondosa*. . . On ground at base of oak and other deciduous trees, and some conifers; also on stumps. . . This choice edible is often hard to differentiate from the fallen leaves that are usually around it. **1987** McKnight–McKnight *Mushrooms* 128, *Hen-of-the-Woods. Grifola frondosus*. . . Edible and highly prized, but tends to be tough in age.

henpeck n

1 A small or unimportant place.

1967–70 *DARE* (Qu. C33, . . *An out-of-the-way place, or a very small or unimportant place*) Inf **OH**17, Henpeck; (Qu. C34, *Nicknames for nearby settlements, villages, or districts*) Inf **NY**230, Henpeck; **OH**17, Henpeck [FW: used by Inf in conv].

2 also pl: =**hen scratching.**

1968 *DARE* (Qu. JJ11, . . *Handwriting that's hard to read: "I can't make anything out of his ______."*) Infs **NY**70, **WI**34, Henpeck(s).

hen pen n [Engl dial, cf *EDD hen pen* (at *hen* sb.[1] 1. (37))] **esp NEng**

An enclosure for poultry, spec:

a =**hennery a.** Cf **hen coop**

1939 *LANE* Map 111 *(Hen house)* **esp seNH, neME,** Hen pen. **1965** Gould *You Should Start* 14 **swME,** These birds [=ruffed grouse and woodcock] can't be hatched and nurtured in a hen-pen. **1966** *DARE* (Qu. M17, *A building where chickens or hens are kept*) Inf **ME**24, Hen pen.

b =**hennery b.**

1966–70 *DARE* (Qu. M16, *The small shelter for a hen that can be moved about from place to place*) Infs **ME**24, **MS**81, **NH**16, Hen pen.

hen pepper n

=**shepherd's purse.**

1920 *Torreya* 20.21, *Bursa bursa-pastoris*. . . Hen pepper, pepperweed, Marion, Ind. **1933** Small *Manual SE Flora* 554, *B. Bursa-pastoris*. . . Hen-pepper. **1967** *Wilson Coll.* **csKY,** *Hen pepper*. . . Peppergrass. A species of rather "hot" mustard that grows wild everywhere in the area. **1968** *DARE* Tape **IN**32, One thing that I've always done is to be able to hunt my own greens in the spring. . . I get mountain sprouts, sour dock, wild beets, shawny, crow foot, deer tongue, hen pepper, and oh so many others.

hen plant n

Either of two **plantains:** *Plantago lanceolata* or *P. major.*

1889 *Century Dict.* 2794, *Hen-plant*. . . The rib-grass, *Plantago lanceolata;* also, the door-yard plantain, *P. major.* **1900** Lyons *Plant Names* 294. **1959** Carleton *Index Herb. Plants* 60, *Hen-plant:* Plantago lanceolata. **1973** *Foxfire 2* 85 **nGA,** Broadleaf plantain *(Platago major)* . . hen plant.

henroost n

=**hennery a. chiefly NEng**

1806 (1970) Webster *Compendious Dict.* 142, *Henroost*. . . a house or place where poultry rest. **1883** (1971) Harris *Nights with Remus* 273 **GA** [Black], Ef youder s'arch de country fum hen-roost to river-bank, you won't fine a no mo' kuser [=curiouser] man dan Brer Rabbit. **1939** *LANE* Map 111 *(Hen house)* **esp CT, RI,** Hen roost. **1968** *DARE* (Qu. M17, *A building where chickens or hens are kept*) Inf **CT**14, Hen roost—with a yard; **NY**68, Hen roost—old-fashioned.

Henry n Usu |'hɛnri|; also |'hɪnri, 'hɛnəri| Pronc-spp *Henary, Henery*

A Forms.

1905 *DN* 3.58 **NE,** Henary. **1922** in 1944 *ADD* **cwUS,** Henery. Dial. or jocular. **1942** Hall *Smoky Mt. Speech* 19 **eTN, wNC,** Words, in which [ɛ] is often raised to or toward [ɪ] . . Henry. **1954** Forbes *Rainbow* 143 **VT,** Yet next moment he was . . begging Jude to call him Henry—that was how he pronounced the name (he had a nasty, quick, slick way of talking). Of course Jude really called him "Henery," for so all country people said it. **1989** *DARE* File **cwMA,** The pronunciation ['hɛnɚi] is heard occasionally as a child's pronunciation and as a nickname or teasing variant of ['hɛnri].

B Senses.

1 also *old* (or *tin*) *Henry:* An automobile, esp a Ford. [In ref to *Henry* Ford]

1928 *Ruppenthal Coll.* **KS** (as of 1921), *Henry*. . . an automobile made by Henry Ford. He tried to crank up his Henry. **1928** *WI News* 18 Oct 22 *(Zwilling Coll.),* ["Outdoor Sports" cartoon:] Standing by your dead Henry as the John Law of traffic spills a lot of guff about your tin steed. **1934** (1940) Weseen *Dict. Amer. Slang* 349, *Henry*—A Ford automobile. **1966–68** *DARE* (Qu. N5, *Nicknames for an automobile, especially an old or broken-down car*) Infs **TN**18, 24, (Old) Henry; **VA**22, Old Henry—for a Ford [laughter]; **MI**2, Tin Henry.

2 Used as a mild oath; see quot. [Euphem for *hell,* with pun on *O. Henry* (William Sydney Porter)] Cf **hen** n[1] **B5**

1924 *DN* 5.269 **NY** [Exclamations], *Henry:* O. [Henry].

hens and biddies See **hen and biddies 1**

hens and chick(en)s See **hen and chickens 1**

hens and roosters n Cf **chicken fight 1, hen** n[1] **B2, rooster**

A **Canadian wood violet** or similar violet.

1969 *DARE* (Qu. S11) Inf **MO**15, Hens and roosters.

hen scratch n

1 See **hen scratching.**

2 also *hen's grass:* A short distance.

1898 Lloyd *Country Life* 64 **AL,** Good Lord, only forgive me for runnin away and walkin my fool legs off this time, and I'll never git a henscratch from home agin, so help me. **1950** *WELS Suppl.* **WI,** *Hen's grass*—a very short distance. "I've never been a hen's grass from my dooryard." Common.

hen scratching n Also *hen scratch;* for addit varr see quots [Cf *EDD hen's-toes* "bad writing" (at *hen* sb.[1] 1. (51))] Also called **chicken scratch 1, ~ tracks, crow tracks, dog tracks, duck ~, goose ~, henpeck 2, hen tracks, pig scratching, rabbit tracks, turkey scratching**

Handwriting that is difficult to read.

1899 (1912) Green *VA Folk-Speech* 222, *Henscratches*. . . A bad hand-writing. "His writing looks like henscratches." **1942** Warnick *Garrett Co. MD* 8 **nwMD** (as of 1900–18), *Hen-scratching* . . poor hand-writing. **1950** *WELS (Handwriting, especially if it is hard to read)* 25 Infs, **WI,** Hen scratching; 1 Inf, Hen scratches. **1952** Brown *NC Folkl.* 1.550, *Hen scratches.* **c1960** *Wilson Coll.* **csKY,** *Hen-scratching*. . . Humorous name for poor penmanship. **1965–70** *DARE* (Qu. JJ11 . . *"I can't make anything out of his ______."*) 192 Infs, **widespread,** Hen scratching; 41 Infs, **scattered,** Hen scratch(es); **OK**48, **TX**54, Hen scratchings; **TN**12, **VA**31, Hen scribbling; **OK**51, Hen-scratch writing; (Qu. JJ12) Inf **CT**21, Hen scratching.

hen's egg n Also *hen egg*

=**goose egg 1.**

1967–70 *DARE* (Qu. X60, . . *A lump that comes up on your head when you get a sharp blow or knock*) Infs **CA**134, **NY**103, 219, **PA**234, **TX**29, Hen's egg; **AL**36, **LA**31, **TX**54, Hen egg.

hen's grass See **hen scratch 2**

hen skin n **chiefly West**

1 also attrib: A thin comforter or quilt, often stuffed with feathers.

1902 *Out West Mag.* 16.620 **NM,** Why don't you burn these henskins and get you a decent bed? **1908** (1966) Thorp *Songs Cowboys* 312, *Hen-skin bedding.* Bed cover stuffed with feathers. **1920** Hunter *Trail Drivers TX* 62 **TX** (as of 1882), The contents of the trunk were one apple-horn saddle, a pair of chaps, a Colt's 45, one sugan, a hen-skin blanket, and a change of dirty clothes. **1936** Adams *Cowboy Lingo* 36, The cowboy's bed was made of blankets and . . 'soogans,' which were heavy comforts often made from the patches of pants, coats and over-coats. If these latter were stuffed with feathers, they were called 'hen-skins.' **1947** Price *Trails* 49 **neMT,** I didn't have much of a bed, just a few hen-skins and an old sougan.

2 A small or inferior saddle. Cf **chicken saddle**

1942 Berrey–Van den Bark *Amer. Slang* 75.9, *Hen skin,* an inferior saddle. **1961** Adams *Old-Time Cowhand* 106, What he [=the cowman] called them little Eastern saddles that he held in such contempt. Such saddles as the Easterner rode on some city bridle path . . "chicken saddles," "henskins."

3 also pl; Among loggers: lightweight underwear; see quots.

1957 *Perrin Coll.* **cwWA,** *Hen skins*—Summer underwear in the logging camps. **1958** McCulloch *Woods Words* 84 **Pacific NW,** *Hen-skin*. . . Light underwear. **1967** *DARE* (Qu. W14, . . *Underwear . . men's—short*) Inf **WA**20, Hen skins. **1977** *WI State Jrl.* (Madison) 16 Jan sec 5 5/4 [Logger lingo], *Hen skins*—Light summer under-wear.

4 Among loggers: see quot.

1958 McCulloch *Woods Words* 84 **Pacific NW,** *Henskin*. . . Thin soled shoes not stout enough to take calks [=spikes].

hen's nest n

1 also *hen nest:* See quot.

1967–70 *DARE* (Qu. M16, *The small shelter for a hen that can be moved about from place to place*) Infs **KY**23, **MS**81, **NC**48, **TX**22, Hen nest; **LA**7, Hen nest—a boxlike affair up off the ground built together with others in a row; **NJ**3, Hen's nest.

2 in phrr *handle* (or *buckle*) *to a hen's nest:* See quot.

1969 *DARE* (Qu. NN12b, *Things that people say to put off a child when he asks, "What are you making?"*) Inf **RI**1, A handle to a hen's nest; **NY**191, Buckle to a hen's nest.

hen snipe n

A phalarope.

1923 U.S. Dept. Ag. *Misc. Circular* 13.47, *Boreal Phalaropes* . . hen snipe (Long Id., N.Y.)

hen stable n Also *chicken stable* [Cf Ger *Hühnerstall* hen house]

=**hennery a.**

1968 *DARE* (Qu. M17, *A building where chickens or hens are kept*) Inf **MI**78, Hen stable—old-fashioned, used by German settlers. **1973** Allen *LAUM* 1.255 (as of c1950), U[pper] M[idwest] terms not reported in New England are *"A" coop, chicken barn, chicken shed, chicken stable.*

hen's tail n Cf **chicken butt, rooster's ass**

1969 *DARE* (Qu. X34, . . *Names and nicknames for the navel*) Inf **KY**28, Hen's tail.

hens' toes n

A **ladies' tresses** (here: *Spiranthes cernua*).

1897 *Jrl. Amer. Folkl.* 10.144, *Spiranthes cernua* . . hens' toes, Paris, M[ain]e.

hen's tooth n

1 pl; also *hen teeth:* Something imaginary or nonsensical. [Cf *scarce as hen's teeth*]

1942 Berrey–Van den Bark *Amer. Slang* 151.2, Nonsense. . . *hen's teeth.* **1968** *DARE* (Qu. HH14, *Ways of teasing a beginner or inexperienced person—for example, by sending him for a 'left-handed monkey wrench': "Go get me ______."*) Inf **MD**31, Some hen teeth; **VA**33, Hen's teeth.

2 in phr *clean as a hen's tooth:* See quot. [Error for or ironic var of *clean as a hound's tooth*]

1969 *DARE* (Qu. KK1b, *Words meaning 'in the very best condition': "His farm is ______."*) Inf **TX**70, Clean as a hen's tooth.

hen's tracks See **hen tracks**

hent See **hain't** v

hen teeth See **hen's tooth 1**

hen tracks n pl Also *hen's tracks* *somewhat old-fash*

=**hen scratching.**

1928 Andrews *Recollections* 48 **swNH,** He wrote with a quill pen and used a great deal of ink, making regular hen's tracks. **1950** *WELS (Joking names for handwriting, especially if it is hard to read)* 5 Infs, **WI,** Hen tracks; 1 Inf, Hen's tracks. **1951** *PADS* 15.66 **NH,** *Hen-tracks*. . . Poor hand writing. **1954** *Harder Coll.* **cwTN,** *Hen-tracks.* **1960** Criswell *Resp. to PADS 20* **Ozarks,** *Hen tracks.* **c1960** *Wilson Coll.* **csKY,** *Hen tracks*. . . Poor penmanship. **1965–70** *DARE* (Qu. JJ11, . . *"I can't make anything out of his ______."*) 41 Infs, **scattered, but more freq Nth, N Midl,** Hen tracks; **MA**6, 68, **VT**8, Hen's tracks. [35 of 44 Infs old]

hen trigger See **hen** n[1] **B4**

hen-turd tree n Also *hen-dung tree* [Perh from the "warts" on the bark]

A **hackberry** (here: *Celtis laevigata*).

1913 *Torreya* 13.229, *Celtis mississippiensis*. . . Hen-turd tree, Church's Island, N.C. [**1960** Vines *Trees SW* 204, *Celtis laevigata*. . . *Bark.* Pale gray, thin, smooth or cracked, with prominent warty excrescences.] **1984** Wilder *You All Spoken Here* 151 **Sth,** Slick as a button on a shithouse door: Slick as bark on a hen turd tree. **1986** Pederson *LAGS Concordance,* 1 inf, **sMS,** Hen-dung trees.

hen-us n [Pronc-sp for *henhouse*] Cf **cuppen**

1899 (1912) Green *VA Folk-Speech* 222, *Hen-us*. . . A house fitted up for hens, with nests to lay in, "pearches" [sic] for them to roost on.

hen violet See **hen** n[1] **B2**

hen-wallow-jostle n Pronc-sp *hen-waller-jostle*

See quots.

1921 *DN* 5.118 **KY,** *Hen-waller-jostle*. . . When anything is done in a lively manner, it is done like a "hen-waller (wallow)-jostle"; that is, as a hen lies in the sun, in the dust, and vigorously shakes herself. **1984** Wilder *You All Spoken Here* 52 **Sth,** *Hen waller jostle:* A lively move-ment in place, starting from the bottom and moving up. From the way a hen shakes all over in a dust bath.

hen wire n, freq attrib **NEng** Cf **hog wire**

A type of wire mesh; see quot.

1968–69 *DARE* (Qu. L63, *Kinds of fences made with wire*) Infs **MA**55, **RI**15, Hen wire fence; **CT**14, Hen wire fence—2-inch mesh; **MA**40,

Hen fence—same as chicken fence, henyard fence—made of hen wire; [MA68, Hen fence [FW: used by Inf in conv];] **MA**74, Hen wire fence—had bigger openings; chicken wire—had smaller openings.

hen-wood n

A **gum elastic** (here: *Bumelia lanuginosa*).

1953 Randolph–Wilson *Down in Holler* 251 **Ozarks,** *Hen-wood*. . . The chittamwood *(Bumelia lanuginosa),* also called *yellow-wood* or *smoke tree.* Many old folks insist that Noah used this wood to build the Ark. **1954** *Harder Coll.* **cwTN,** Hen-wood. . . *Bumelia lanuginesa* [sic].

hen wrangler n

A chore boy on a farm or ranch; also adj *hen-wrangling* having the duties of a chore boy.

1944 Adams *Western Words* 75, *Hen wrangler*—A name given a chore boy when one is employed upon a ranch. **1971** Jennings *Cowboys* 52 **MT, WY** (as of 1877), And what you going to do with ten little bitty hen-wrangling younkers [=youngsters]?

he-one See **he** n **3**

he-ox See **he** n **1**

hep v See **help** v **A1b, 3d**

hep n See **help** n

hepatica n Also *capatica, patica* **chiefly NEast, N Midl, Gt Lakes** See Map

A plant of the genus *Hepatica.* For other names see **blue mayflower, Easter flower 3, heartleaf 2, heart liverleaf, kidneywort, liverleaf, liver moss, liverweed, liverwort, mayflower, mouse-ears, pass blummies, red coon-root, spring beauty, squirrel cups, windflower**

1818 (1826) MA Hist. Soc. *Coll.* 2d ser 8.168 **nwMA,** Among our herbaceous wild plants, the first that appear are the delicate claytonia, the graceful three-lobed hepatica [etc]. **1867** Beecher *Norwood* 20 **seNY,** Snow-drops and crocuses were in bloom, as also hepaticas. **1905** Wiggin *Rose o' the River* 112 **ME,** Under the shade of the pines the white stars of the hepatica glistened. **1938** Madison *Wild Flowers OH* 28, *Hepatica. Hepatica triloba.* Blue, lavendar [sic], or white. **1965–70** *DARE* (Qu. S23) 18 Infs, 17 **NEast, Gt Lakes,** Hepatica(s); **ME**8, Spring hepatica; (Qu. S26c) 19 Infs, **NEast, N Midl, Gt Lakes,** Hepatica(s); (Qu. S2) 9 Infs, **NEast, Gt Lakes,** Hepatica; (Qu. S3) Inf **IL**37, Hepatica; **NY**142, Capatica; **OH**33, Patica; (Qu. S4) Infs **NY**126, **WI**52, Hepatica; (Qu. S11) Inf **IL**4, Hepatica; (Qu. S26a) Infs **IA**3, **NY**232, Hepatica; (Qu. S26d) Inf **NY**233, Hepatica; (Qu. S26e) Infs **DC**2, **IL**47, **MI**96, **NY**103, 106, Hepatica; **MI**116, Blue hepatica.

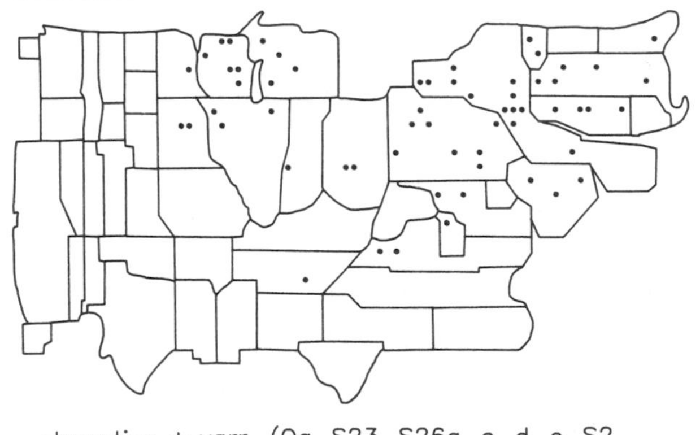

•hepatica + varr (Qq. S23, S26a, c, d, e, S2, S3, S4, S11)

hepazootis See **epizootic 2**

heped v See **help** v **A2d, 3d**

hepizootic See **epizootic 1**

hepped v See **help** v **A2d, 3d**

hepper See **help** n

her pron Usu |hɝ, hɜ|, weakly stressed |ɝ, ɜ|; also |hʌ|; for varr see **A** below Pronc-spp *'er, (h)uh;* similarly *huz* (for *hers*) Cf **he** pron **4, she**

A Forms.

1923 *DN* 5.243 **LA,** *Huh.* Pronunciation of *her,* more marked than the common Southern slurring. *Huz.* Pronunciation of *hers.* **1927** Shewmake *Engl. Pronc. VA,* In some parts of the South *her* is pronounced in a way that closely approaches *huh*. . . Thus, *Tell her to come* might be represented in dialect by *Telluh to come.* **1929** Wolfe *Look Homeward* 136 **NC** [Black], *You* go see *huh.* **1931** *AmSp* 6.171 **seVA,** [stampɪn hʌ fʊt] [=stomping her foot]. **1942** Hall *Smoky Mt. Speech* 41, **eTN, wNC,** *Her* [hʌɚ]. **1954** [see **B2** below]. **1970** *DARE* (Qu. AA15c) Inf **TN**46, Shore got her [hə] something.

B Senses.

1 Herself—used as indirect object. **scattered, but less freq NEast** Cf **him** pron **B1**

1906 *DN* 3.140 **nwAR,** *Him, her*. . . Common for *himself* and *herself.* "He organized him a band of traders." **1926** Roberts *Time of Man* 138 **cKY,** Miss Cassie, she bought her a mare. **1965–70** *DARE* (Qu. AA15c) 56 Infs, **scattered, but less freq NEast,** Got her a man; 14 Infs, **chiefly Sth, S Midl,** Got her a husband (*or* boss, bread-earner, breadwinner, job cooking, liability, mate, meal ticket); **GA**3, **SC**42, Found (*or* finally got) her a husband; **AR**15, **TN**1, Hooked (*or* finally caught) her a man; **TN**15, Has got her a home; **TN**46, Shore got her something; (Qu. AA4b, . . *A woman who is very eager to get married? "She's ______."*) Infs **KY**80, **TX**12, Hunting her a man (*or* husband); **KY**19, **SC**58, Out (*or* trying) to get her a man. **1987** Jones–Wheeler *Laughter* 142 **Appalachians,** She went over to the fireboard, got her down some medicine and dosed him with it.

2 It—used as impersonal object after a verb. **scattered, but esp West, Upper Missip Valley** See Map Cf **him** pron **B4, hit her up**

1903 [see **hit her up**]. **1916** *DN* 4.275 **NE,** An expression of greeting, like "How are you?" used frequently to start a conversation. "Well, how are you hacking her?" **1923** (1946) Greer–Petrie *Angeline Steppin'* 39 **csKY,** As pretty as that hat was, the feller a-settin' behind me had the asshorance to ax me to *take hit off*. . . I shore told him, *'I'd not do her.'* **1954** *Harder Coll.* **cwTN,** He high tailed 'er outa here when 'at old man got atter'im wi'old shot gun. **1960** Criswell *Resp. to PADS 20* **Ozarks,** *Her*. . . It. Usually used in reference to a difficult or embarrassing action, in the negative. . . "Well, he wanted me to take that old talky Jones woman to town with me today, and I just told him I couldn't do her." "He asked me to tell a lie for him, and I said I just couldn't do her." **1965–70** *DARE* (Qu. FF18, . . *A noisy or boisterous celebration or party: "They certainly ______ last night."*) 17 Infs, **scattered, but esp NW, Upper MW,** Whooped her up; **PA**59, Hit her off; **WY**5, Hooped her up; **NC**53, Let her blow; **WI**34, Let her rip; (Qu. A20, . . *Telling somebody to hurry*) Inf **OR**2, Shake her up; (Qu. A21) Inf **TX**100, Slow her down; (Qu. X45, . . *Snoring*) Inf **MO**35, Knocking her off; **NY**96, Whooping her up; (Qu. Y20, *To run fast*) Inf **NY**68, Leg her; (Qu. Y24, . . *To walk, to go on foot*) Inf **MO**5, Foot her; **IL**143, Hoof her; (Qu. BB11, . . *A deep cough . . "Listen to him ______."*) Inf **NY**96, Whoop her up; (Qu. CC11) Inf **WI**24, Hit her high; **PA**185, Really lived her up; (Qu. EE21b, . . *Fighting very actively*) Inf **OR**13, Mixed her up; (Qu. KK8, . . *Succeeding*) Inf **OK**18, Got her under control; (Qu. KK29, *To start working very hard*) Inf **MO**1, Gets her; **WI**77, Givin' her hell; **CA**145, Got her in gear; (Qu. KK43) Inf **OK**6, Got her whipped now; (Qu. KK47, *Something . . left undecided or unfinished*) Inf **MN**15, Let her lay; **CA**145, Let her slide; (Qu. KK49, *When you don't have the time*

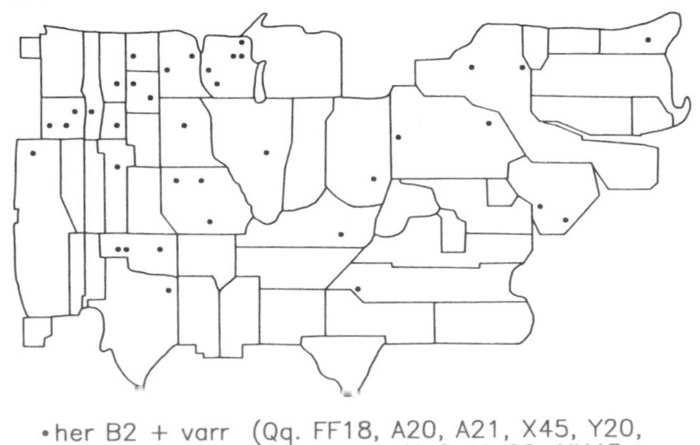

•her B2 + varr (Qq. FF18, A20, A21, X45, Y20, Y24, BB11, CC11, EE21b, KK8, KK29, KK43, KK47, KK49, KK63)

or ambition to do something thoroughly) Inf **CA**145, Dung her out; **MT**5, Touch her up; (Qu. KK63, *To do a clumsy or hurried job of repairing something)* Inf **KY**16, Blotched her up. [34 of 37 Infs comm type 4 or 5; 28 of 37 Infs male] **1978** Massey *Bittersweet Country* 82 **Ozarks,** They [=mules] got the instinct to know where home is. If he'd left them alone, they'd made her in that day, too.

herald-of-summer n

A **farewell-to-spring** (here: *Clarkia amoena*).

1916 Parsons *Wild Flowers CA* 246, Godetia. . . Herald of Summer. . . In early summer the rosy flowers . . make bright masses of color along dry banks and hill-slopes. **1934** Haskin *Wild Flowers Pacific Coast* 227, *Godetia amoena*. . . is distinguished by the specific appelation [sic] of herald-of-summer. In this latitude it distinctly deserves that name, for I invariably find the first seasonal blooms within a day or two of the summer solstice.

heraus mit 'em exclam Also *raus mit ('em);* for addit varr see quots [Ger *heraus* (or colloq *'raus*) *mit* away with, out with + personal pron; Ger *ihm, ihnen* sometimes understood as Engl *'im* him, or *'em* them]

Get out! Away with you (*or* that)! rarely adj; fig: incapacitated; done for.

1905 Hobart *Get Next* 97 **cnMD,** When I cut loose with the observation that men were all in at 40 and *raus mittim* at 60 I kept several exceptions up my sleeve. **1919** Kyne *Capt. Scraggs* 16, "That [sic] for them rotten eggs, you miser," he growled. "Heraus mit 'em!" Captain Scraggs fled. **1919** Mencken *Amer. Lang.* 89, *'Rous mit 'im* (from *heraus mit ihm*). These phrases . . are familiar to practically all Americans, no matter how complete their ignorance of correct German. **1934** Stone *Studien* 59, *'Rous mit 'im*. . . This phrase is one to be found only in the spoken language. **1967–69** *DARE* (Qu. NN22a, *Expressions used to drive away people or animals)* Inf **IN**58, Raus mit 'em ['raʊs,mɪtəm]; (Qu. NN22b, *Expressions used to drive away children)* Inf **NY**132, Raus mit 'em ['rɔs,mɪddɪm]; **PA**11, Raus mit dich ['rɔs,šmedɪk]; (Qu. NN22c, *Expressions used to drive away a dog)* Inf **MI**63, Raus mit ['raʊs,mɪt]; **MN**12, Aus mit du, verdapte [sic] hund. **1988** *DARE* File **nUT** (as of c1960), When I was a child my father sometimes used the expression "heraus mit Ihnen" to shoo away a stray dog or a bothersome child. To me it clearly meant 'scram' or 'beat it' but wasn't as harsh because he used it, I think, a little self-consciously, a little tongue-in-cheek. **1990** *Ibid* **nwOH** (as of 1929), *'Raus mit 'em* is usually a command, but it can also be an undirected exclamation of rejection equivalent to "Away with that!" or "Throw the bum out!"

herb n, v Usu |(h)ɝb|; for varr see **A** below

A Forms. [Cf *EDD herb* sb. and v. 1]

1 |jɝb|; pronc-spp *ye(a)rb, yurb.* **chiefly Sth, S Midl**

1807 Irving *Salmagundi* 1.166 **NY,** The whole catalogue of *yerb* teas was at her finger's ends, from formidable wormwood down to gentle *balm.* **1837** Sherwood *Gaz. GA* 72, *Yearb,* for herb. **1872** Schele de Vere *Americanisms* 395 **NY,** Then we had an Erie Railroad 'splendid breakfast:' bean-coffee, *yerb*-tea, leather-steak, and rain-water milk. *Ibid* 488, *Herb*. . . generally pronounced *yerb* or *yarb* by the multitude. **1884** Smith *Bill Arp's Scrap Book* 73 **GA,** We have a plenty of peas and potatoes and other garden yerbs. **1899** (1912) Green *VA Folk-Speech* 494, *Yerb*. . . A form of herb. **1909** *DN* 3.390 **eAL, wGA,** *Yerb*. . . Herb. Sometimes *yarb.* **1911** *DN* 3.540 **eKY,** *Yerb*. . . Herb. **1915** [see **A2** below]. **1924** Raine *Land of Saddle-Bags* 130 **Appalachians,** The only medicines we-uns has is yerbs. **1952** Brown *NC Folkl.* 1.609, *Yarb, yerb.* **c1960** [see **A2** below]. **1972** *Atlanta Letters* **nwGA,** Yurbs—herbs.

2 |(j)ɑrb|; pronc-spp *(y)arb.* **now chiefly Sth, S Midl, formerly also NEng**

1818 Fessenden *Ladies Monitor* 171 **VT,** *Arbs* for herbs. **1821** Cooper *Spy* 1.69 **NY,** "I doctor'd him mostly with yarbs," said the housekeeper. **1843** (1916) Hall *New Purchase* 54 **IN,** Tisn't nun of your spice-wood or yarb stuff, but the rele gineine *store* tea. **1872** Schele de Vere *Americanisms* 394, *Yarb* very generally for herb . . *yarb-tea* . . especially in the New England States. **1893** Shands *MS Speech* 68, *Yarb*. . . Negro for *herb.* **1899** (1912) Green *VA Folk-Speech* 493, *Yarb*. . . A form of *herb.* **1899** Chesnutt *Conjure Woman* 76 **csNC** [Black], Some roots en [=and] yarbs. **1903** *DN* 2.298 **seMA** (as of a1857), *Herb*. . . Pronounced *arb.* Pl. *arbs,* medicinal herbs especially. *Ibid* 337 **seMO,** *Yarb*. . . The old-fashioned pronunciation of herb. **1909** [see **A1** above]. **1915** *DN* 4.193 **swVA,** *Yarb, yerb.* Variants of *herb.* **1924** Raine *Land of Saddle-Bags* 187 **Appalachians,** She was a "yarb-doctor." **1929** in 1944 *ADD* **eME,** Roots & yarbs. **1930** Shoemaker *1300 Words* 69 **cPA Mts** (as of c1900), *Yarbs*—Garden herbs. **1933** Williamson *Woods Colt* 114 **Ozarks,** She's a yarb doctor, an' she knows a heap about signs, an' all them things. **1959** *VT Hist.* new ser 27.167 **neVT,** *Yarb*. . . An herb. Rare. **c1960** *Wilson Coll.* **csKY,** *Herb* . . sometimes among the elderly /jɝb/ or /jɑrb/. **1972** *Atlanta Letters* **cGA,** My grandmother was a firm believer in her arb (herb) tea. She pronounced it arb. **1985** *DARE* File **KY,** *Yarb:* in Kentucky, a medicinal herb.

B As noun.

1 esp in phr *big herb:* An important person; something especially good.

1905 Wasson *Green Shay* 11 **NEng,** Cunnin' enough, ain't ye, Mister? You jest cal'late you're a consid'ble big herb, now don't ye, though! *Ibid* 128, Folks that have been called the biggest herbs [Footnote: Important men] up there to the meetin' house afore this have been known to rob them that was cast away in wracks around here out of their last dollar. **1942** Warnick *Garrett Co. MD* 8 **nwMD** (as of 1900–18), *Herb* . . anything especially good was said to be a "pretty good herb." **1975** Gould *ME Lingo* 131, *Herb, a big*—A big wheel, an important man, a VIP. And not exactly in jest; *a big Herb* will really be somebody.

2 also pl: Marijuana; a marijuana cigarette. *among Black speakers*

1970 Abrahams *Deep Down* 266 [Black], *Herbs*—Marijuana. Probably descriptive of common properties of feel, smell, and texture. **1971** Roberts *Third Ear* np [Black], *Herb* . . (pronounced "erb" with exaggerated emphasis) a marijuana cigarette. **1972** Claerbaut *Black Jargon* 68, *Herb* . . marijuana. **1980** Folb *Runnin' Down* 242 **Los Angeles CA** [Black], *Herb(s)*—Marijuana. **1986** Chapman *New Dict. Amer. Slang* 205, *So you get fines to pay and you've lost your herbs*—Wall Street Journal.

C As verb.

Also with *it:* To hunt for and gather herbs; hence vbl n *herbing.* [Engl dial; cf *EDD herb* sb. and v. 7 "To gather herbs. . . *Yarbing*. . . the gathering of herbs."]

1884 *Harper's New Mth. Mag.* 69.788/1 **NEng,** Been herbin' again? **1941** *Time* 9 June 86, North Carolina has a "yarbing" industry (from mountain lingo for "herb"). . . Middlemen . . are the "yarb house" operators. . . After World War I, imports kept "yarbing" prices down. **1943** Writers' Program NC *Bundle of Troubles* 191, We farmed a little in the cove, hunted most all winter, and yarbed it spring and fall. I still believe they's no better medicine for a body than good yarbs. **1960** Williams *Walk Egypt* 55 **GA,** She stayed out most of the time, yarbing in the hills and granny-wifing. *Ibid* 296, Remember when I used to go yarbing with you? **1984** Wilder *You All Spoken Here* 131 **Sth,** *Yarbing:* Hunting for and digging ginseng and other herbs in mountain areas.

herba impia n [See quot 1848]

=cotton rose 2.

1848 Gray *Manual of Botany* 238, *F[ilago] Germanica*. . . *Herba Impia*. . . Stem . . producing a capitate cluster of woolly heads, from which rise one or more branches, each terminated by a similar head, and continued in the same manner:—hence the common name applied to it by the old botanists, as if the offspring were undutifully exalting themselves above the parent. **1933** Small *Manual SE Flora* 1404. **1946** Tatnall *Flora DE* 266. **1950** Gray–Fernald *Manual of Botany* 1449, *Herba Impia*. . . Dry fields, local, s. N.Y. to O[hio], W.Va. and Ga. June–Oct.

herbbane n [See quot 1889]

A **broomrape 1.**

1889 *Century Dict.* 2799, *Herb-bane*. . . The broom-rape, *Orobanche major:* probably so called from its injurious effect upon the herbs on the roots of which it is parasitic. **1900** Lyons *Plant Names* 268, *O[robanche] minor*. . . Herb-bane. **1901** Lounsberry *S. Wild Flowers* 470, *O[robanche] minor,* clover broom-rape, herb-bane.

herb cellar n Cf **cellar** n^1 **B1**

1968 *DARE* (Qu. M19, *A place for keeping carrots, turnips, potatoes, and so on over the winter)* Inf **MO**4, Herb cellar.

herb Christopher n

=baneberry 1.

1795 Winterbotham *Amer. U.S.* 3.395, Other poisonous plants, are . . the Water Elder, . . the Herb Christopher, . . the Stinking Snakeweed [etc]. **1832** Williamson *Hist. ME* 1.124, *Herb Christopher,* two and a half feet high, has berries poisonous. **1892** (1974) Millspaugh *Amer. Med. Plants* 10, *Actaea alba.* White Baneberry. . . Com[mon] Names. . . American herb christopher. **1900** Lyons *Plant Names* 14, *A[ctaea] alba.* . . Herb Christopher. . . *A[ctaea] rubra.* . . Herb Christopher. **1940** Clute *Amer. Plant Names* 1, *A. alba.* . . Herb-Christopher. . . *A. rubra.* . . Herb-Christopher. **1968** *Foxfire* Summer 47, The white baneberry (Actaea). . . is also called "herb-Christopher," and the ground up roots are used to poultice snakebite.

herbe au coeur n

=**banana waterlily.**

1942 *Torreya* 42.160, *Castalia flava.* . . Herbe au coeur, Louisiana.

herbing See **herb C**

herbish adj Cf **bitter** adj **1**

Of milk: having the flavor of plants which cows have grazed on.

1950 *WELS (Milk that has a taste from something the cow ate in the pasture)* 1 Inf, **cWI,** Herbish taste. **1967–69** *DARE* (Qu. K14, . . *"That milk is ______."*) Inf **NY**34, Herbish; **NY**43, Herbish [FW: Inf has heard]; **NY**198, Herbish [FW sugg; Inf queries]; **WI**52, Herbish.

herb it See **herb C**

herb of Gilead See **balm of Gilead 1**

herb Robert n

Std: a **cranesbill 1** (here: *Geranium robertianum*). Also called **mountain geranium, musk geranium, red robin, wild geranium**

herbster n

An herb doctor.

1968 *DARE* FW Addit **neIL,** *Herbster* ['hɝbstə]—If you were sick you couldn't get the town herbster—in the winter when there was 12 ft. of snow.

herb trinity n

=**trillium.**

1949 Moldenke *Amer. Wild Flowers* 338, Because of this very conspicuous arrangement of all their organs in 3's or multiples thereof, these plants are often known as *three-leaved nightshades, herbtrinity,* or *trinitylilies.*

Hercules'-club n

1 A prickly, sometimes shrubby, tree *(Aralia spinosa)* native to the eastern US. Also called **angelica tree 1, devil's club 1, devil's walkingstick 2, monkey tree, prickly ash, prickly elder, pick tree, pigeon tree, pigeon weed, sea ash, shotbush, spikenard tree, tear-blanket, toothache tree, white root, wild orange**

1859 (1880) Darlington *Amer. Weeds* 156, *A[ralia] spinosa.* . . *Prickly Aralia.* Angelica Tree. Hercules' Club. **1868** IL State Ag. Soc. *Trans. for 1865–66* 6.390, We buy the Pawpaw under the name of *Anona glabra,* and our native Hercules club comes back in its company. **1910** Graves *Flowering Plants* 296 **CT,** Angelica Tree. Hercules' Club. Devil's Walking-stick. **1931** Harned *Wild Flowers Alleghanies* 338, *Hercules' Club.* . . A shrub or very low tree with thick stem, and spines or prickles on the branches and petioles. **1950** [see **2** below]. **1976** Bruce *How to Grow Wildflowers* 270, *Aralia spinosa.* . . is interesting even in winter by reason of its persistent fruit (on which birds feed for most of the season) and its large, clublike thorny shoots. I know of few thornier plants—even the petiole of the leaf bears spines. The common names Hercules' Club, Devil's Cane, and Prickly-ash allude to this characteristic. **1979** Little *Checklist U.S. Trees* 55, *Aralia spinosa.* . . *Other common names*—Hercules-club. *Ibid* 298, *Zanthoxylum clava-herculis.* . . Hercules-club, from the spiny branches. *Ibid* 299, *Zanthoxylum coriaceum.* . . Hercules-club. . . *Zanthoxylum hirsutum.* . . Hercules-club.

2 Any of several **prickly ashes** of the genus *Zanthoxylum,* often *Z. clava-herculis:* see quots.

1876 Hobbs *Bot. Hdbk.* 53, Hercules' club, Yellow prickly ash, Xanthoxylon [sic] clava Herculis. Hercules' club, prickly elder, Aralia spinosa. **1908** Britton *N. Amer. Trees* 571, *Xanthoxylum coriaceum.* . . Also called Hercules' Club, this is a spiny shrub or small tree growing in southern peninsular Florida and the adjacent Keys. **1941** Walker *Lookout* 60 **TN,** Hercules club. . . is covered with slightly curved spines which prick the hiker's hand when he grasps it for support. **1944** AL Geol. Surv. *Bulletin* 53.141, *X[anthoxylum] Clava-Herculis.* . . Called prickly ash, Hercules club [etc]. **1950** Peattie *Nat. Hist. Trees* 427, *Zanthoxylum americanum.* . . Hercules'-club. Spitberry. *Ibid* 493, Hercules'-Club. *Aralia spinosa.* **1979** [see **1** above].

Hercules'-club gourd n Also *Hercules'-club* [From its often elongated shape]

=**bottle gourd.**

1976 Bailey–Bailey *Hortus Third* 633, *[Lagenaria] longissima;* a hort. name sometimes used for the form of *L. siceraria* known as *Hercules' club.* . . *[L.] siceraria.* . . Includes the *dipper,* . . *Hercules'-club,* . . and *trumpet gourds.*

Hercules' parsnip n

A **cow parsnip 1** (here: *Heracleum lanatum*).

1953 Nelson *Plants Rocky Mt. Park* 112, *Hercules parsnip.* . . A stout plant three to six feet high. **1963** Craighead *Rocky Mt. Wildflowers* 126, *Cow-Parsnip. Heracleum lanatum.* . . *Other names* . . Hercules-parsnip.

herd v, hence vbl n *herding*

See quots.

1896 *DN* 1.418 **cNY,** *Herding:* taking care of children. **1968** *DARE* (Qu. Z13, *If a mother has to leave her baby for a little while, she might ask a neighbor, "While I'm gone, will you ______ the baby for me?"*) Inf **CA**87, Herd.

herder n

In railroading: see quots.

1930 *RR Man's Mag.* 470 [Railroad terms], *Herder*—A man who couples engines on and takes them off on the arrival and departure of trains. **1970** *Current Slang* 5.1.8 [Railroad terms], *Herder.* . . A railroad employee who guides trains and engines to and from the main track, and through yards. **1976** Gould *Blackie's RR Hdbk.* 1, *Switchman (who couples and uncouples engines at Terminals):* Herder.

herd(ge) grass See **herd's-grass 1**

herdic n Also sp *herdick* [In ref to Amer inventor Peter *Herdic* 1824-88] **esp eMA** *old-fash*

A small horse-drawn vehicle; see quots.

1882 Hudson *Scamper through Amer.* 74 **DC,** Taking a herdick (small one-horse 'bus named after the inventor) we drove to the White House at the further end of Pennsylvania Avenue. **1897** Barrère–Leland *Slang* 1.433/2 **Chicago IL,** *Herdic* . . a carriage for public conveyance, something like a small omnibus. . . They are now common in most American cities. **1900** *Congressional Record* 12 Feb 33.2.1729/1, The old herdic coaches are now charging a full 5-cent fare. **1944** Holton *Yankees Were Like This* 96 **Cape Cod MA** (as of c1890), Yet even the horsecars weren't as thrilling as the herdic, which we took when we had to get across the city in the quickest possible time. **1948** *NE Hist.* 29.16 **seNE** (as of c1880), Lincoln's local transit was by means of a "herdic" (carry-all). **1962** Morison *One Boy's Boston* 29 **ceMA** (as of 1890s), The herdic . . , peculiar to Boston, was a miniature omnibus on two wheels, in which four big or six small passengers, entering from the rear, could sit facing each other. . . a ride in one over the cobblestones of downtown Boston jolted the very teeth out of you. **1966–69** *DARE* (Qu. N41a, . . *Horse-drawn vehicles . . used . . to carry people*) Inf **MA**13, Herdic ['hɜ:dɪk]; (Qu. N41c, *Horse-drawn vehicles to carry light loads*) Inf **MA**42, Herdic ['hɝdɪk]—bought in Canada, an all-around wagon. **1979** *DARE* File **cnMA** (as of c1885), I have heard my father's sister tell of being taken to . . Sunday school in a herdic as a child. It was a horse-drawn vehicle, small, which came to one's door, like a taxi.

herding See **herd**

herd's-grass n

1 also *herd grass;* pronc-spp *herdge grass, herge ~, hurge ~:* =**timothy. chiefly NEng**

1747 in 1887 Franklin *Complete Wks.* 2.81 **sePA,** I sowed near thirty acres with red clover and herd-grass. **1751** in 1934 Eliot *Field Husbandry* 61 **CT,** *Herd-Grass* (known in Pennsylvania by the Name of *Timothy-Grass*). . . It is said that Herd-Grass was first found in a swamp in Piscataqua [New Hampshire]. **1774** in 1850 Adams *Works* 2.326 **ceMA,** Shall I try to introduce fowl-meadow, and herds-grass into the meadows? **1889** Vasey *Ag. Grasses* 44, *Phleum pratense* (Herd's Grass [of New England and New York]). **1903** *DN* 2.298 **seMA,** *Herd's grass.* . . Pronounced herdge grass. **1904** Day *Kin o' Ktaadn* 8 **ME,** No longer did the drooping herd's-grass stalks fringe the mows with odorous lambrequins. **1922** (1926) Cady *Rhymes VT* 204, The hurge grass takes another week. **1965–70** *DARE* (Qu. L9a) 13 Infs, **chiefly NEng,** Herd's-grass; **ME**5, **TN**26, 62, Herge [hɝǰ] grass; (Qu. L8) Inf **CT**32, Herd's-grass; **NH**5, Herge [hɝǰ] grass; (Qu. L9b) Inf **GA**72, Herd's-grass. **1966** *DARE* Tape **ME**8, I wondered what the names of the grasses were. I knew one or two of 'em like herd's-grass and witchgrass. **1969** *DARE* FW Addit **NJ,** *Herd grass:* grass with little fuzzy top on an eight-inch stalk; grows wild. **1976** Bailey–Bailey *Hortus Third* 860, *Phleum . . pratense. . .* Herd's grass.

2 A **bentgrass 1** (here: either *Agrostis alba* or *A. tenuis*).

1856 Olmsted *Journey Slave States* 41 **eVA,** Herd's-grass (red-top of New York), sometimes taking the place of the clover, or being grown with it for hay. **1861** Wood *Class-Book* 774, *A[grostis] vulgaris* [=*Agrostis tenuis*]. . . Red Top. . . Herd's Grass of the S. States. **1889** Vasey *Ag. Grasses* 46 **PA,** *Agrostis vulgaris . .* Herd's Grass. **1930** OK Univ. Biol. Surv. *Pub.* 2.49, *Agrostis alba. . .* Red-top. Herd's-grass.

herd sire See **sire**

here adv, adj, exclam, pron Usu |hɪr, hɪə|; for varr see **A** below

A Forms.

1 pronc-spp *hea(h).*

1858 Hammett *Piney Woods Tavern* 27 **TX** [Black], Why look hea, ole mossa [=master]. **1891** Page *Elsket* 121 [Black], I tell dese folks up heah dee don't know nuthin' 'bout rail quality. **1914** *DN* 4.158 **cVA** (as of c1901), Ah means *aiah* [=air] like this heah. **1934** Carmer *Stars Fell on AL* 182, Come heah, Miss B'ar. **1954** *Harder Coll.* **cwTN,** *Heah. . .* Call to dogs: "Heah, puppy, heah, heah." **1965** *Dict. Queen's English* 7 **NC,** *Heah* (he-ah): Here. *Heah* is the campsite. **1973** *Black World* 22.8.61 [Black], Yo ole man in heah?

2 |hjɛ(ə), hjɝ, hjir, hjɑr, hjɪə, hjo| (cf Pronc Intro 3.I.1.a, 3.I.23); pronc-spp *hyah, hyar(e), hyer(e), hye(a)h, hyur, hyo;* for addit troncs and spp see quots. [Cf *OED hyer* (at *here* adv.)] **chiefly Sth, S Midl**

1856 Simms *Eutaw* 429 **SC,** Hyar's a boy that reads. **1891** *PMLA* 6.163 **WV,** The negro pronunciation of *here* is [hjɑɚ]. Among the white population . . both [jɪɚ] and [jɑɚ] are common. *Ibid* 166, *Here* [hjiɚ] . . the *h* frequently becomes silent, or rather a mere breathing [jiɚ]. **1893** Owen *Voodoo Tales* 80 **MO** [Black], She comed in hyeah. **1899** Garland *Boy Life* 163 **nwIA** (as of c1870s), Hyare, young feller. **1903** *DN* 2.316 **seMO,** *Here. . .* Pronounced hyer [hjir] with weak h, for yer [jɝ]. **1908** Fox *Lonesome Pine* 12 **KY,** "Where is he?" "Hyeh he is!" **1913** Kephart *Highlanders* 36 **sAppalachians,** This is good, strong land, or it wouldn't hold up all the rocks there is around hyur. **1917** *DN* 4.393 **neOH,** *Here. . .* Used in command to a dog. . . ['hjɪ,ə] . . with slight accent on the last. The form [hjæær] was used for a too vicious or inobedient attack by the dog. **1923** *DN* 5.211 **swMO,** *Hyar.* **1924** Raine *Land of Saddle-Bags* 80 **Appalachians,** We couldn't ha' brung them in hyer, noway. *Ibid* 130, We can't git a doctor up hyar less'n three days. **1926** *AmSp* 1.413 **seGA,** I wuz a-standin' right hyere. **1928** *Ruppenthal Coll.* **KS,** Settlers who came from eastern Ohio along the West Virginia border brought with them a pronunciation of "here" that was substantially "hyur", sometimes "hyere." **1941** Heydrick–Thompson *Americans All* 211 **Sth** [Black], Dey jes' sont me down hyeah to fin' you. **1942** Faulkner *Go Down* 139 **MS,** Whut's Ah doin hyar? **1953** Randolph–Wilson *Down in Holler* 15 **Ozarks,** Many old timers pronounce here as if it were spelled *hyar;* others make it sound more like hyur, to rhyme with burr. **1960** Criswell *Resp. to PADS 20* **Ozarks,** [hjɛə]. **c1960** *Wilson Coll.* **csKY,** *Here* is sometimes [hjɑr]; often [hjɝ] or [ə'hjɛr]. *Ibid, Here!* Call to dog. [hjɛə]. **1965–70** *DARE* (Qu. J7, . . *Call to a dog to make it come;* total Infs questioned, 75) 14 Infs, Hyuh; **MS**1, 2, **OK**43, Hyuh (puppy *or* pup); (Qu. K36b, *What do you say to make a horse go backwards?*) Inf **KY**35, Hyeah back; (Qu. K80, *The call . . to get the cows in from the pasture*) Inf **WY**5, Hyo-boss; (Qu. K84, *The call . . to get the pigs in at feeding time*) Inf **KY**23, Hyo-pig [hjo]; **OK**10, Hyah piggy, hyah piggy. **1967** *DARE* FW Addit **seAR,** [hjɪ̃ə̃]—common local pronunciation of *here,* nasalized; [hjɛː], old-fashioned.

3 |jɪr, jɑr, jir|; pronc-spp *yer(e), y(e)ur, yuh, yeer, year, yeah;* for addit troncs and spp see quots. [Cf *EDD yere* (at *here* adv.)] **chiefly Sth, S Midl** *esp freq among Black speakers*

1837 Sherwood *Gaz. GA* 72, *Year,* for here;—come right *year,* for come here. **1847** (1962) Robb *Squatter Life* 94 **MO,** I . . am the furst white man ever seed in these yeur diggins. **1851** (1969) Burke *Polly Peablossom* 108 **MO,** I heerd tha wur gettin' it fixed up yur in St. Louis. **1853** Simms *Sword & Distaff* 217 **SC** [Black], Yer's de place for you. **1859** (1965) Marcy *Prairie Traveler* 212, Governor of these yeer United States. **1864** (1868) Trowbridge *3 Scouts* 16, This yer's what I found. **1867** *Harper's New Mth. Mag.* 34.274/2 **swMO,** This yere is Colonel N_______, who wants ter know yer. **1887** *Scribner's Mag.* 2.475 **AR** [Black], Yeah's de twurn, Mist' Griffin! **1888** Jones *Negro Myths* 85 **GA coast** [Gullah], Befo eh bring you yuh. **1891** [see **A2** above]. **1893** Shands *MS Speech* 69, *Yur* [jə-ə]. A pronunciation of *here* sometimes used by negroes. **1899** (1967) Chesnutt *Wife of Youth* 12 [Black], Go way f'm yere. **1899** (1912) Green *VA Folk-Speech* 494, *Yer. . .* A form of *here.* **1903** *DN* 2.316 **seMO,** *Here. . .* Pronounced hyer [hjir] with weak h, for yer [jɝ]. **1906** *DN* 3.165 **nwAR,** *Yere. . .* Here. **1922** Gonzales *Black Border* 340 **sSC, GA coasts** [Gullah glossary], *Yuh*—here. **1929** (1951) Faulkner *Sartoris* 270 **MS** [Black], Yere dey is, Cunnel.

4 |ɛr, ær, iə, ɪə|; for addit troncs see quots; pronc-spp *are, ere.* Cf **C** below

1834 Smith *Letters Jack Downing* 130, This ere sickness of the President. **1837** Sherwood *Gaz. GA* 71, *This year,* or *this 'ere,* for this. **1843** (1916) Hall *New Purchase* 116 **IN,** The closest of any other chap, young or old, in these 'are diggins. **1875** Holland *Sevenoaks* 34 **N Atl,** This 'ere breathin' is worse nor an old swamp. **1887** in 1953 Botkin–Harlow *Treas. Railroad Folkl.* 105, You 'n' me's got a pertickler spite agin this 'ere railroad. **1943** *LANE* Map 624, [**chiefly ME, eVT, eMA,** [iə], [ɪə]; 5 infs, **swME, sNH, eMA** [æə]; 1 inf, **nME** [ɪᵊr]; 1 inf, **nME** [ɪɚ]; 1 inf, **cNH** [ɪər].] **c1960** *Wilson Coll.* **csKY,** *Here* in *this here,* a very common expression, is often [ɛr] or [ær].

5 following |t|: |čɪr, čir|. [See quot 1942] **Sth, S Midl**

1916 in 1944 *ADD* **seOH,** [aučir], out cheer = out here. **1939–44** in 1944 *ADD* **nWV,** In such phrases as *get here, out here, right here, wait here, eat here,* [ʃ] or [ʃj] very commonly replaces [h]. 'I believe I'll eat here this evenin' ' [ə 'bliv əl 'it'ʃir ðɪs 'ivnɪn]. 'Right here' ['raɪt'ʃir]. 'Wait here for us' ['wet'ʃir fr̩ 'ʌs]. **1942** Hall *Smoky Mt. Speech* 96 **eTN, wNC,** [t] is combined with a following palatal glide [j] by partial assimilation to form the voiceless affricate [tʃ]. . . In the Expression *right here* ['raɪtʃɪɚ], [t] + [(h)j] become [tʃ]. **1968** *DARE* FW Addit **eMD,** *Here*—in "out here" [jɪr] or [čɪr].

B As adv.

1 in phr *here's at you:* Used to express assent or resolution. *arch*

1835 Longstreet *GA Scenes* 27, But as I bantered you, if you say an even swap, here's at you. **1859** Taliaferro *Fisher's R.* 89 **nwNC** (as of 1820s), But here's at you, as you look like you'd die ef you don't hear it. **1884** Harris *Mingo* 49 **cGA,** There was a little pause. . . Then the response came,—"Here's at you!"

2 in phr *here too, Pete:* See quot.

1928 *Ruppenthal Coll.* **KS,** *Here too, Pete*—phrase of approbation, approval, agreement; "I am mighty tired." "Here too, Pete." . . The rough secular equivalent of the religious "amen," but more especially in willingness or consent.

C As adj, pron.

In phrr *this* (or *these*) *here:* Used for emphasis in indicating a thing near at hand, or a person or thing under discussion; see quots. [*OED here* adv. 1. d "*dialectally* or *vulgarly* appended to *this, these,* when used adjectivally"; cf also *EDD these* II. 2., 4, *this* II. 7. (4)] **chiefly Sth, S Midl** Cf **there**

1795 Dearborn *Columbian Grammar* 139, *List of Improprieties. . .* This here for This. **1837** Sherwood *Gaz. GA* 71, *This year,* or *this 'ere,* for this. **1843** (1916) Hall *New Purchase* 174 **IN,** He [=God] made these here woods. **1887** (1967) Harris *Free Joe* 110 **GA,** Thish yer Mister Hightower you er talkin' about is got a mighty bad case of measles. **1899** (1912) Green *VA Folk-Speech* 444, *This-here. . .* This; near at hand. **1907** *DN* 3.202 **seNH,** This 'ere rake wo'n't answer. *Ibid* 227 **nwAR,** *This here. . .* This; this thing at hand. **1922** Gonzales *Black Border* 61 **sSC, GA coasts** [Gullah], Dishyuh t'ing hol' mo'n uh pint. *Ibid* 297 [Gullah glossary], *Deseyuh*—these here. **1942** McAtee *Dial. Grant Co. IN* 33 **AL, sIL, MD** (as of 1890s), This here Jim Bosley, do you know him? **1958** Humphrey *Home from the Hill* 17 **neTX,** No coffin's going into this here grave. **1966** *DARE* (Qu. KK46, . . *Expressions for taking things as they come and not worrying*) Inf **MS**49, Wear this here world like a loose garment—used by Negroes. **1966** *DARE* Tape **AR**41, The water flowed through and hit this-here . . wheel. **1967** *DARE* FW Addit **neIL,** "This here would have been the big city." "They sure got these here [=chickens] cold."

hereafter adv, n Also *herearter, hereatter, heahoftah, yerarter* Cf **after A, here A**

A Forms.

1884 *Anglia* 7.254 **Sth, S Midl** [Black], *Yerarter* (hereafter). *Ibid* 266 **Sth, S Midl** [Black], *De big Herearter* = le Grand Peut-Être. **1901** *DN* 2.182 **neKY** [Black], *Hereafter*—heahoftah. **1940** Stuart *Trees of*

Heaven 220 **neKY,** She's allus on my bones about the hereatter. I want to live while I live.

B As noun.

1 See quot.

1942 McAtee *Dial. Grant Co. IN* 33 (as of 1890s), *Hereafter* . . dessert; "Is there any ______?"

2 See quot.

1927 *Ruppenthal Coll.* **KS,** *Hereafter* . . consequences. I never figured there would be any hereafter about it.

hereaway adv Also *hereaways* [Engl, Scots dial] *arch*

See quot 1899.

1793 (1892) Lindley *Exped. Detroit* 17.586 **PA,** We had to dine with us a religious Dunker and his wife, settlers hereaway, with whom we had fellowship. **1826** Cooper *Last of Mohicans* 2.3 **nNY,** I remember to have fout the Maquas hereaways, in the first war in which I ever drew blood. **1866** Whittier *Prose Works* 61 **MA,** What the people hereaway are to look for from the Massachusetts jurisdiction. **1899** (1912) Green *VA Folk-Speech* 223, *Hereaway*. . . Hereabouts; in this neighbourhood, or in this direction.

here come fifty men to work n

A children's game; see quot.

1950 *WELS (Outdoor games)* 1 Inf, **cWI,** *Here Come Fifty Men To Work*—What's your occupation?—opponents act it out, and the others guess. If they guess right, they try to catch their opponents.

here comes a duke n Also *here come three dukes a-roving;* for addit varr see quots [Cf *EDD duke* sb.[1]]

A children's singing game; see quots.

1883 Newell *Games & Songs* 47 **ceMA,** *Here Comes a Duke*. . . A company of little girls sit in a row. A little girl from the middle of the room goes dancing up to the first one in the row, singing, "Here comes a duke a-roving,/ . . will you come out,/ To join us in our dancing?" . . These two now retire, singing together. . . They join hands and call out the next one in the row; thus the play goes on until the last is selected, when they form a ring, dance, and sing. **1901** *DN* 2.142 **nOH,** *Here come three dukes a-roving*. . . The name of a game. **1957** *Sat. Eve. Post Letters* **sIN** (as of c1910), There was a game that we played outdoors, with a sung accompaniment, entitled "Here Come Three Dukes A-riding." It was a stately, deliberate choosing-game, employing archaic and unusual words and motions, as well as outmoded concepts. *Ibid* **sNJ** (as of c1915), Girls here used to play a number of singing games. . . I remember "Oh dear Doctor!" and "Here Comes a Duke A-riding." *Ibid* **csPA,** When I was a child . . we played singing games with these names: "Here Comes a King A-courting." **c1970** *DARE* FW Addit **eVA,** *Here comes a duke*—The players divide into two groups. A player from one side approaches the other. The rhymes are gone through. The chosen one then goes to the other side. The game is repeated till all are chosen; old-fashioned.

here comes the bluebird n Also *bluebird, bluebirds and yellowbirds*

A children's singing game; see quots.

1883 Newell *Games & Songs* 118 **swOH,** *Blue-birds and Yellow-birds*. A ring of girls with their hands clasped and lifted. A girl, called (according to the color of her dress) blue-bird, . . yellow-bird, etc., enters, and passes into the ring under an arch formed by a pair of lifted hands, singing. . . ["]Here comes a blue-bird through the window["]. . . After the dance the chosen partner leads, named, as before, according to the color of her costume. **1940** *Handy Play Party Book* 36, *Blue Bird*. . . A single circle. . . During the singing of the verse, the girls go in and out of the circle under the upraised arms of the players, stopping in front of a chosen partner. **1957** *Sat. Eve. Post Letters* **Chicago IL** (as of c1900), Girls' singing ring games, always played in a circle. "Here Comes the Bluebird."

here come three dukes a-roving See **here comes a duke**

hereford adj [*Hereford* a breed of white-faced cattle] Cf **bald-faced shirt**

White; hence n *hereford* something that is white; something having a white front.

1893 Farmer–Henley *Slang* 3.305/1, *Hereford*, adj. (American cowboy). White. **1889** Barrère–Leland *Slang* 1.433, *Hereford* (American cowboy), white. A white shirt he calls a *Hereford* shirt because Hereford cattle have white faces. Similarly calls anything *Hereford* that is white; for example, *Hereford* dishes and *Hereford* hats. Carrying this fancy still further, a "white" man is known as a *Hereford* man.—*Philadelphia Press*. **1952** Peattie *Black Hills* 183, Cattle barons in dinner jackets—nicknamed "Herefords." **1961** Adams *Old-Time Cowhand* 78, The city man's dress suit with no front in the vest and jes' a little windbreak down the back. . . He [=the cowhand] called 'em Herefords because of the white front.

here I come n

A children's game: = **lemonade station.**

[**1950** *WELS Suppl.* **WI,** "Here I come." "Where from?" "What's your trade?" "Lemonade." "Go to work and show me some." Side one then acts out some activity. If side two guesses, then it is their turn.] **1957** *Sat. Eve. Post Letters* **csMN** (as of c1900), *Here I come*—There are two sides, one of which has a secret. Both sides come up to a line facing each other. The side with the secret sings out: "Here I come!" The answer: "Where from?" "Pudden Mountain." "Give us some ______." Then they pantomime their idea. When the others guess the idea, there is a wild rush back to the goal. If caught before they reach the goal, they become prisoners and are taken out of the game. The side having the most prisoners wins.

here lately adv phr

1960 Criswell *Resp. to PADS 20* **Ozarks,** *Here lately*. . . recently. "Here lately he has been dressin' up a little on Sunday." Still common.

here's at you See **here B1**

here too, Pete See **here B2**

herewith n [By analogy with *wherewith(al)*]

1967 *DARE* (Qu. U19a, *Words used . . for money in general: "He's certainly got the ______."*) Inf **TX**1, Herewith.

herge grass See **herd's-grass 1**

‡herher n Cf *DS* E20

See quot.

1982 *DARE* File **cnMA** (as of c1915), [ˈhɝˈhɝz]—dust rolls under furniture.

herman crab n [For *hermit crab*] Cf **herman thrasher**

1975 Newell *If Nothin' Don't Happen* 84 **nwFL,** Some feller told me to dig one of them herman crabs out of a conch shell and use him for bonefish bait. I found me one of them red rascals and put a chunk of him on a hook and cast it out.

herman thrasher n Also *herman thrush* [See quot 1955] **GA**

=**hermit thrush 1.**

1951 *AmSp* 26.91, Among other instances in bird names are: . . *Herman thrasher* (Ga.) for the hermit thrush. **1955** *Oriole* 20.11 **GA,** *Hermit Thrush*.—*Herman Thrush* (through mishearing of the first term).

hermit n

1 See **hermit thrush 1.**

2 =**Swainson's thrush.**

1967 *DARE* (Qu. Q14) Inf **CO**7, Swainson's brown hermit.

3 See **hermit warbler.**

4 A kind of cookie; see quot 1988. **esp NEng** Cf **filled cookie**

1896 (c1973) Farmer *Orig. Cook Book* 407, Hermits [=a butter cookie with raisins and spices]. **1947** Bowles–Towle *New Engl. Cooking* 213, *Mincemeat Hermits* [contain spices and mincemeat. Dropped by spoonfuls on cookie sheet]. *Ibid* 214, *Aunt Hat's Old-Fashioned Soft Hermits* [=spice cookies with raisins baked ½ inch thick on cookie sheet and cut into squares]. **1957** *Sat. Eve. Post Letters* **seMA** (as of c1904), Dark cookies were hermits and light ones sugars. **1963** Pilgrim Soc. Plymouth MA *Notes* 13.4, "When I was a boy there used to be a cookie jar in the closet at the end of this hall. I would be allowed to put my hand right in—" "Suppose you go and do it now," said his hostess. And there he found the cookie jar, with the same sort of hermits in it. **1979** Flagg *Cape Cod Cooking* 238, *Hermits*—There is a legend that Hermits originated in Harwich. Although I have been unable to track down the story, many old cook books contain recipes for "Harwich Hermits." **1988** *DARE* File **swME** (as of 1981), Hermits are soft, chewy, raisin and date cookies. Hermits from the bakery are baked in sheets with ground raisins and dates in a layer between two thin layers of dough. They are about ½″ thick, cut in about 3″ x 5″ rectangles. Homemade hermits have the raisins and dates mixed in and are lumpy cookies.

hermit bird See **hermit thrush**

hermit sandpiper n
=solitary sandpiper.
1946 Hausman *Eastern Birds* 271, *Eastern Solitary Sandpiper—Tringa solitaria solitaria. . .* Hermit Sandpiper.

hermit thrush n
1 also *hermit (bird), hermit woodthrush:* A thrush *(Catharus guttatus)* with a spotted breast and a reddish tail. Also called **apple bird 2, bell bird 2, ground swamp robin, half caille, herman thrasher, little caille, lonesome bird, nightingale, swamp angel, swamp robin, swamp sparrow, swamp thrush, trotter, witch, woodchuck, wood thrush**
1812 Wilson *Amer. Ornith.* 5.95, The Hermit Thrush is rarely seen in Pennsylvania. **1895** *Outing* 26.69/2 **coastal ME,** A hermit-thrush . . flew off with a querulous *pay* as if he wished me to recompense him for my invasion. **1914** Eaton *Birds NY* 2.528, The Hermit makes its nest on the ground or in the low branches of some thick tree. **1942** (1960) Robertson *Red Hills* 178 **SC,** She heard the hidden song of the hermit thrush. **1944** in 1948 *Pacific Discovery* Mar-Apr 17/1 **San Francisco CA,** A hermit thrush savored the grape-sized fruit of the persimmon tree. **1948** *Green Bay Press-Gaz.* (WI) 30 June 4/2 **nMI,** In a lonely, shaded spot in the woods we heard the hermit sound out its sweet flutelike notes. **1950** *WELS (Other names for birds)* 1 Inf, **WI,** Hermit thrush; 1 Inf, Hermit bird; 1 Inf, Hermit. **1965-70** *DARE* (Qu. Q14) 14 Infs, **chiefly NEast,** Hermit thrush; **MA**67, Hermit woodthrush.
2 A **wood thrush** (here: *Hylocichla mustelina*).
1890 Warren *Birds PA* 324, *Turdus mustelinusa. . . Wood Thrush; Wood Robin. . .* The Wood Robin, the name by which the Wood Thrush is best known in many localities in Pennsylvania (some term it Hermit Thrush), is a common inhabitant of woods.

hermit warbler n Also *hermit* [See quot 1944]
A yellow-headed warbler *(Dendroica occidentalis)* native to the western United States.
1839 Audubon *Ornith. Biog.* 5.55, Hermit Warbler. *Sylvia Occidentalis.* **1917** (1923) *Birds Amer.* 3.146, The yellow head, black throat, and white breast and belly of the Hermit Warbler are so characteristic that it can hardly be confused with any other bird within its range. **1944** Hausman *Amer. Birds* 416, The Hermit Warbler, deriving its name from its eremetical [sic] habits of keeping itself well within the recesses of the great forests of the northern mountains, is a shy species. **1964** Phillips *Birds AZ* 153, Two distinct song types are heard; one of them is wheezy and full of *z*'s, as is characteristic of the whole group of black-throated dendroicas, through the Hermit.

hermit woodthrush See **hermit thrush 1**

herm up v phr [Cf *SND herm* "To grumble, to be peevish or fretful" (at *harm* n., v. II. 1)] **ME**
Of weather: see quot 1975.
1903 Wasson *Cap'n Simeon's Store* 37 **sME,** She'll turn to and herm up all of a smudge to loo'ard jes' though we was in for a brush sure. **1927** *AmSp* 3.136 **eME,** When the weather was cloudy or overcast, the old folks would say it is "herming up for a storm." **1975** Gould *ME Lingo* 131, *Herm up*—To cloud up and become overcast.

hern pron [Engl dial; prob *her/hern* by analogy with *my/mine*] **chiefly Sth, S Midl, NEng** *old-fash* Cf **hisn**
Hers.
1815 Humphreys *Yankey in England* 105, *Her'n,* her own, hers. **1851** Hooper *Widow Rugby's Husband* 88 **AL,** That bonnet o' hern. **1891** Johnston *Primes & Neighbors* 270 **GA,** She hain't got over her'n yit. **1894** Frederic *Marsena* 45 **nNY,** Did you ever notice them eyes o'hern. **1899** (1912) Green *VA Folk-Speech* 223, *Hern. . .* Hers. **1907** *DN* 3.245 **eME,** *Hern.* **1908** *DN* 3.320 **eAL, wGA,** *Hern.* **1909** *DN* 3.412 **nME,** *Hern.* **1923** (1946) Greer-Petrie *Angeline Steppin'* 31 **csKY,** Them six pigs of hern. **1926** *DN* 5.378, *Her'n.* **1934** *WV Review* Dec 79 **WV,** We still hear this form of the possessive in our *hisn, theirn* and *yourn,* as well as in *hern* and *ourn.* **1952** Brown *NC Folkl.* 1.550, *Hern.* **1960** Criswell *Resp. to PADS 20* **Ozarks,** *Hern. . .* Hers. Extremely common up until the last twenty years, but now not too often used. **1965** *Dict. Queen's English* 7 **NC,** *Hern:* Hers. That is *hern.* **1975** Allen *LAUM* 2.55 (as of c1950), In the U[pper] M[idwest] the *-n* forms [=*hisn, hern, theirn*] survive largely as remembered or locally heard. They are clearly nonstandard relics. **1983** *MJLF* 9.1.43 **ceKY,** *Hern.*

hern n See **heron**

hero n Also *hero sandwich* [Etym uncert, but cf quots 1971 and 1984] **scattered, but esp NYC** See Map and Map Section Cf **Cuban sandwich, grinder 3, hoagie**
=submarine sandwich.
1955 *Sat. Eve. Post* 227.27.16/2 **NYC,** When he got back to Brooklyn, the first thing he asked for was an Italian hero sandwich. . . two inches thick and eighteen inches long. **1958** in 1962 *Western Folkl.* 21.31 **Los Angeles CA,** Italian hero sandwich—an overly large sandwich most often constructed upon a foundation of Italian bread and salami. **1963** Scherf *Diplomat* 65, They have hot and cold heros next door. **1965-70** *DARE* (Qu. H42, *The kind [of sandwich] in a much larger, longer bun, that's a meal in itself*) 59 Infs, **scattered, but chiefly NEast, esp NYC,** Hero; **NY**57, Hero sandwich; **MA**83, Hero and heroine—a little one cut in quarters; (Qu. H41, . . *Kinds of roll or bun sandwiches*) Inf **MA**122, Hero. **1967** *Times Herald Rec.* (Middletown NY) 15 Aug 42/6, [Classified advt:] *Pizza-Hero-Bar* Modern equipped, all-year business. **1971** Morris-Morris *Dict. of Word & Phrase Origins* 3.132 **NYC,** *Hero* is the name given in the New York area to the kind of sandwich known in other parts of the country variously as "grinder," "poor boy," "submarine," and "hoagie." It consists of a small loaf of French bread, sliced lengthwise and containing a variety of meats, seasonings, and usually lettuce. The best explanation for the *hero* name is that one has to be something of a hero to work his way through one. **1972** *NYT Article Letters* **ceMO,** One of my favorite local variations is the different names for the same sandwich: Philadelphia—Hoagie or Hogie; Boston—Sub or submarine; St. Louis—Heroes; New Orleans—Poor Boy or Po' Boy. **1976** *Yankee* Oct 156, And the name changed—They [=grinders] became "Poor Boys" in Ohio, "Heroes" in New York City, "Hoagies" in the mid-Atlantic states. **1984** *AmSp* 59.375, Greek restaurants nowadays are serving a sandwich called a *gyro,* consisting of meat, tomatoes, onions, and sauce, on pita bread. . . Is it possible that *gyro* is the origin of the *hero* sandwich? . . Could it be that New York deli owners interpreted Greek *gyro* sandwich in the 1950s in terms of their own meats and breads, and the unfamiliar palatal fricative was transformed into an American [h], *gyro* thus subsumed by folk etymology to the familiar word *hero?*

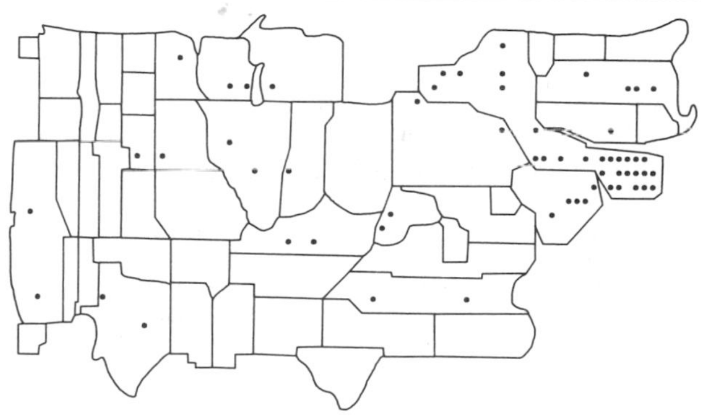

•hero + varr (Qq. H42, H41)

Herod all handsaws intj
Used as a mild oath.
1937 Crane *Let Me Show You VT* 33, Her great uncle used "Herod all handsaws!" as his device to delude the Almighty; for obviously this, like "Gosh all fish-hooks!" and many others common to Vermont are mere euphemisms for "God Almighty." **1959** *VT Hist.* new ser 27.142, *Herod all handsaws!* . . Rare.

hero grinder See **grinder 3**

heron n Also *hern* [Pronc-spp for *herring*] Cf **herring** n[2]
1873 Harte *Mrs. Skaggs* 170 **CA,** Thar's whiskey. And crackers. And red herons. And cheese. **1943** Weslager *DE Forgotten Folk* 171, Tie a hern [herring] on the bottom of your foot next to the skin. Leave it on until the fish dries up. Then the fever will go. This cure is awful good for tyford [sic] fever. **1989** *DARE* File **eMA** (as of 1967), The pronunciation [hɛrən] is so common for the fish that when . . [a friend] told me about a stream called [hɛrən rʌn] I thought she was talking about a bird. . . It turned out to be *Herring Run.*

heron blanc n [Fr "white heron"]
=snowy egret.

1917 *DN* 4.426 **LA,** *Heron blanc.* The snowy egret (Egretta candidissima): also called *little white crane.*

heron fly n Cf **herring fly**

1931–33 *LANE Worksheets* **seMA,** Heron flies ['hırən,flaız]. . . A type of fly. . . shedding wings and becoming pissmires.

heron gull n [Prob pronc-sp for **herring gull**]

1969 *DARE* (Qu. Q10) Inf **RI**17, Heron gull.

hero sandwich See **hero**

herricane See **hurricane**

herrin' chucker See **herring choker 1**

herring n[1] Cf **heron**

1 Std: any of numerous fish of the family Clupeidae.

2 =**cisco,** esp *Coregonus artedi.* **Gt Lakes**

1902 Jordan–Evermann *Amer. Fishes* 132, The lake herring has a large number of vernacular names. The most widely used are lake herring, or merely herring. **1905** U.S. Bur. Fisheries *Rept. for 1904* 687 **MI,** Herring are very plentiful in the Saginaw Bay. **1933** John G. Shedd Aquarium *Guide* 39, *Leucichthys artedi* . . erroneously called "Herring" in the Great Lake [sic] region, is very closely allied to the Common Whitefish. **1939** Berolzheimer *U.S. Cookbook* 442, Herring is the most abundant food fish in the Great Lakes. **1965–70** *DARE* (Qu. P14) 17 Infs, **Gt Lakes,** Herring; (Qu. P1) 11 Infs, **Gt Lakes,** Herring. [*DARE* Ed: An additional 18 Infs at Qu. P14 and 4 Infs at Qu. P1 referred to sense **1** above.] **1966** *DARE* Tape **MI**21, They call 'em bluefin, but all they are is a big overgrown herring. They don't even look like a real bluefin. . . They're a different specie [sic] altogether. **1976** *DARE* File **Isle Royale MI,** Most of the catch was herring. **1983** Becker *Fishes WI* 341, *Coregonus artedi*. . . Herring.

3 Either of two fishes of the Pacific coast:

a =**queenfish.**

1946 LaMonte *N. Amer. Game Fishes* 74, *Seriphus politus*. . . *Names:* White Croaker, Herring. . . A schooling fish. Shallow water near sandy shores. **1953** Roedel *Common Fishes CA* 94, *Seriphus politus*. . . *Unauthorized Names:* Herring [etc].

b =**little roncador.**

1946 LaMonte *N. Amer. Game Fishes* 82, *Genyonemus lineatus*. . . *Names:* . . Herring. . . Schools with the Queenfish and others. **1953** Roedel *Common Fishes CA* 100, *Genyonemus lineatus*. . . *Unauthorized Names:* . . herring.

herring n[2] [For *heron;* cf Intro "Language Changes" II.12] Cf **heron**

1953 Randolph–Wilson *Down in Holler* 26 **Ozarks,** A stately lady near Cotter, Arkansas, spoke at great length about the *herrings* she had seen on White River; it was some time before I realized she meant herons, the birds which most Ozarkers mistakenly call cranes. **1966–67** *DARE* (Qu. Q10, *Other water birds and marsh birds common around here*) Infs **MI**36, Blue herring [FW: heron]; **NY**32, Blue herring. **1989** *DARE* File **scWI,** Canoeing on the Fox River this summer near my condo at Waterford, I've seen a lot of herrings—usu blue herrings—, but other ones, too. There was even a green herring in the condo complex's fountain one day.

herring bird n

A phalarope.

1917 *Wilson Bulletin* 29.2.79 **ME coast,** *Lobipes lobatus.*—Herring bird. **1923** U.S. Dept. Ag. *Misc. Circular* 13.47 **ME,** *Boreal Phalaropes* . . herring-birds.

herringbone n attrib Cf **curdled sky, mackerel sky**

Of clouds: patterned like the skeleton of a herring; of sky: having such clouds.

1950 *WELS (Kinds of clouds)* 1 Inf, **seWI,** Herringbone [cloud]—little dark cloud like the bones of a herring; 1 Inf, **cWI,** Herringbone sky. **1966–70** *DARE* (Qu. B11) Infs **OH**51, **WV**12, Herringbone; **TN**52, Herringbone [FW: Inf heard parents use this term.]; **HI**1, Herringbone sky; **MI**17, Herringbone sky—we haven't heard anybody else say it, but we say it.

herringbone fence n esp **NEng** Cf **buck fence**

A type of rail fence; see quot 1909.

1869 U.S. Dept. Ag. *Rept. of Secy. for 1868* 258 **csWI,** This form of thorn fence is similar to the old time "herring-bone" rail and stake fence, and the name "herring-bone hedge" would not be inappropriate. **1909** *DN* 3.412 **nME,** *Herring bone fence*. . . A fence built of rails of which one end rests in the fork of crossed stakes and the other end on the ground. **1939** *LANE* Map 117 *(Rail fence)* 5 infs, **cCT, sRI, cME,** Herringbone [fence]. **1949** Kurath *Word Geog.* 55, Other types of fences . . built of rails: . . the *herring-bone fence* = *stake-and-rider fence* = *buck fence* (Eastern Pennsylvania) = *rip-gut fence,* in which the rails are supported by crossed stakes. **1968** *DARE* (Qu. L62, *A fence made of split logs*) Inf **CT**17, Herringbone fence—a type of rail fence.

herring choker n

1 pronc-sp *herrin' chucker:* A person from the Canadian Maritime Provinces; a French Canadian. **NEng**

1914 *DN* 4.74 **nNH, ME,** *Herrin'-choker*. . . A Prince Edward's Islander, or native of any of the Provinces "down east." **1931–33** *LANE Worksheets* **ceMA,** *Herrin' chuckers* . . Nova Scotians. **1954** Forbes *Rainbow* 185 **NEng,** They came from everywhere and from nowhere—Frenchies from Canada, Herringchokers and Bluenoses from down East. **1968–69** *DARE* (Qu. HH28) Infs **MA**68, **NH**14, Herring chokers—Nova Scotians; **MA**55, Herring chokers—French Canadians. **1975** Gould *ME Lingo* 131, *Herring-choker*—Specifically, a New Brunswicker, but loosely construed in old Maine usage to any native of the Maritime Provinces. The saying was that the people ate so many herring they couldn't take their shirts off because of the bones sticking from their shoulders.

2 also *herring destroyer,* ~ *snapper:* A Scandinavian. **esp wGt Lakes**

1930 Williams *Logger-Talk* 15 **Pacific NW,** *Herring-choker:* A Scandinavian. **1950** *WELS (Names and nicknames for people of foreign background)* 3 Infs, **WI,** Herring choker—Norwegian; 1 Inf, Herring choker, herring destroyer—Scandinavians; 1 Inf, Herring snapper—Swedish. **1950** *WELS Suppl.* **WI,** *Herring chokers*—Derogatory for Norwegian immigrants from the northern fishing villages of Norway. Used by inlanders and [in] southern towns. **1964** *PADS* 42.39 **Chicago IL,** *Herring choker, herring destroyer,* and *Norski* were restricted to Norwegians. **1968** *DARE* (Qu. HH28) Inf **MN**35, Herring chokers—Norwegians, Swedes.

herring chopper n Cf **chopper 6**

=**bluefish 1.**

1894 *Youth's Companion* 68.562/4 **seMA,** Sometimes it would happen that, in pursuit of food, a great dull-blue "herring chopper" would work inshore.

herring destroyer See **herring choker 2**

herring fly n

A house fly *(Musca domestica).*

1909 *DN* 3.420 **seMA,** *Herring flies*. . . House flies in herring time, attracted to the house by the fish.

herring frog n

Appar a **spring peeper.**

1951 Johnson *Resp. to PADS 20* **DE,** Herring frogs. **1968** *DARE* (Qu. P21) Inf **MD**32, Herring ['hɛrɨn] frog—heard in the spring of the year in swampy places.

herring gull n [See quot 1904]

A large, light-colored gull *(Larus argentatus).* Also called **dago gull, gray gull 1, harbor gull a, lake gull, sea gull, white gull, winter gull**

1828 NY Acad. Sci. *Annals Lyceum Nat. Hist.* 2.361, *Herring Gull,* . . *Larus argenteus*. . . Inhabits both continents: not uncommon near New-York and Philadelphia. **1857** (1864) Thoreau *ME Woods* 206, The Indian said that *Caucomgomoc* meant Big-gull Lake, (i.e. Herring-gull, I suppose,) *gomoc* meaning lake. **1883** U.S. Natl. Museum *Bulletin* 27.168, *Larus argentatus*. . . Herring Gull. **1904** Wheelock *Birds CA* 38, Its name of Herring Gull is probably derived from its habit of following a school of herring, and gorging itself upon them as it flies. **1917** *DN* 4.426 **LA,** *Herring gull* (Laurus [sic] argentatus). Gœlan. **1965–70** *DARE* (Qu. Q10) 12 Infs, **scattered, but esp Atlantic, Gt Lakes,** Herring gull. **1968** *Cook Co. News–Herald* (Grand Marais MN) 9 May 2/6, [He] found a dead, banded herring gull at the mouth of Cross River.

‡herring-head n

1966 *DARE* (Qu. HH20b, *Of an idle, worthless person you might say, "He doesn't amount to* ______.*"*) Inf **SC**10, A herring-head.

herring hog n

=**harbor porpoise.**

1825 in 1974 *Fauna Americana* 285, *Herring-Hog*. . . Head ventricose; forehead elevated; snout very pointed, and abruptly separated from the forehead; colour of the body, white. Inhabit the seas of Canada, coast of New England, Long Island, &c. **1879** U.S. Natl. Museum *Bulletin* 14.11, *Phocæna brachycion*. . . *The Snuffing Pig* or *Herring Hog*.—Atlantic Coast. **1884** *Ibid* 27.640, Herring Hog. Atlantic coast of the United States. This is one of the commonest species, frequenting the harbors and ascending the rivers. **1928** Anthony *N. Amer. Mammals* 571, *Herring Hog*.—*Phocoena phocoena*. . . Found on both coasts, ascends rivers.

herring salmon n Also *herring whitefish*

A fish of the genus *Coregonus* such as *C. artedi.*

1836 Richardson *Fauna Boreali-Amer.* 3.180, The Herring salmon forms its [=the namaycush's] principal food in Lake Huron. **1879** U.S. Natl. Museum *Bulletin* 14.57, *Argyrosomus Artedi*. . . *Herring Whitefish*.—Great Lakes, etc. **1911** *Century Dict. Suppl., Herring-salmon*. . . A whitefish, *Argyrosomus artedi,* found in the Great Lakes. It is neither a herring nor a salmon.

herring snapper See **herring choker 2**

herring whitefish See **herring salmon**

herrschel See **herschel**

Herr Schmidt n Also *Herr Schultz*

A type of polka; see quot 1954.

1950 *WELS (Steps and figures in dancing)* 2 Infs, **WI,** Herr Schmidt—old-fashioned. **1954** Piper-Piper *175 Folk Dances* 20, *Herr Schmidt* [polka]. . . P[ar]tn[er]s facing, h[an]ds joined. **1968** *DARE* (Qu. FF5a) Inf **MI**76, Herr Schultz.

herschel n Also sp *herrschel*

An abrupt change in the weather; a storm.

1950 Klees *PA Dutch* 282, *Herschel,* introduced by the almanacs, is a noun used in Lebanon and Lancaster counties to denote a sharp change in the weather. Herschel is the name once proposed for the planet Uranus in honor of its discoverer, Sir William Herschel. Though the Pennsylvania Dutch call Uranus by its proper name they have bestowed the old name for the planet on the sort of weather they expect Uranus to bring. **1978** *DARE* File **sePA,** *Herrschel*—a storm.

‡hershel v

1950 *PADS* 14.36 **SC,** *Hershel*. . . To call coaxingly, as a dog.

herth See **hearth A1**

he's See **his**

heself pron Pronc-sp *hese'f* **chiefly SC** *among Black speakers* Cf **'eself, hisself**

Himself; rarely, herself.

1853 Simms *Sword & Distaff* 75 **SC,** You see nudder t'ing, Toby—de hoss tak' out and gone! He nebber tak' out hese'f. *Ibid* 450, Dis dah wedding time, when ebb'ry body, wha' aint git marry hese'f, kin hab he fun. **1887** Page *In Ole VA* 454 [Black], He al'ays handled heself to he raisin' [=according to his upbringing]. **1927** Adams *Congaree* 37 **cSC** [Black], Kill him if he try to 'fend he-self. **1934** Carmer *Stars Fell on AL* 181 [Black], Brer Rabbit fling out de bag o' goobers an' jump out heself. **1949** Turner *Africanisms* 276 **sSC coast** [Gullah], [dɑt ol ledɪ ɪz go fəm hyɛ, bɪkɒz hil tɛk hɪsɛf bɑk.] [=That old lady has gone from here, because she'll take herself back (i.e., because this is her habit).] **1966** *DARE* (Qu. Y29a) Inf **SC**10, He beat heself about; (Qu. AA15b) Inf **SC**10, He tie up heself in knot; (Qu. BB57) Inf **SC**10, Kill (*or* choke) heself; **SC**27, Kill heself—Negro; (Qu. HH8) Inf **SC**10, Toots by heself. **1987** Jones-Jackson *When Roots Die* 117 **sSC coast** [Gullah], Rabbit drank up heself [=got up his nerve].

hesh See **hush** v

he-sheep See **he** n **1**

hesitate v

?To cause to slow down.

1965 in 1983 Johnson *I Declare* 52 **nwFL,** If you have a tendency toward misery in your arm, "it'll hesitate you when you go to iron 'em dry." (That is, it'll hesitate you unless you're "even-handed" and spell the hurtin' arm by ironing with the other.)

‡hesitated up adj phr

1916 *DN* 4.275 **NE,** *Hesitated up*. . . Excited. "He is all hesitated up."

hessian n Pronc-spp *hashan, hayshant, hayshun, hussian* **chiefly Sth, S Midl, NEng**

A troublesome, unpleasant, or boorish person, esp a woman; an unruly or mischievous child.

1906 *DN* 3.140 **nwAR,** *Hessian*. . . Scoundrel. "You old Hessian, you [jə]." Not used by the younger generation. **1907** *DN* 3.245 **eME,** *Hessian*. . . Term of reproach. "You old Hessian, you!" "You stop that, you little Hessian." **1908** *DN* 3.320 **eAL, wGA,** *Hessian*. . . Still commonly used as a term of opprobrium. **1914** *DN* 4.74 **ME, nNH,** *Hussian*. . . A troublesome, mischievous child, as in young *Hussian.* **1930** Shoemaker *1300 Words* 29 **cPA Mts** (as of c1900), *Hessian*—"A regular Hessian", a loud-mouthed overbearing person; "old Hessian". **1936** *AmSp* 11.315 **Ozarks,** *Hessian*. . . A term of reproach, usually applied to a vicious or meddlesome old woman. It has no connection to nationality. **1942** *AmSp* 17.130 **IN,** *An old Hashan [Hessian?]* (usually applied to a virago). **1943** *AmSp* 18.72 **sIN,** 'Hessian' . . 'Hayshun'. . . is applied to anyone who is rough, uncouth, boorish, or . . whose moral character is of the lowest. It appears to be used chiefly of women (with the second meaning), though I have occasionally heard it applied to men. **1944** *PADS* 2.29 **eKY, NC,** *Hayshant*. . . A rascal; an annoying child. "Get out of this kitchen and leave them pies alone, you little hayshant." **1968** *DARE* (Qu. GG14, . . *Someone who fusses or worries a lot, especially about little things*) Inf **VA**11, Old hessian. **1984** Wilder *You All Spoken Here* 79 **Sth,** *Hessian; hayshant:* An epithet usually reserved for a disobedient or defiant child; a throw-back to the Revolutionary War in America when hired Hessians fought for the Crown. My mother used to say, with some frequency, "I'll slap you windin', you little Hessian you."

het v See **heat** v **A1**

het adj See **het up**

hetch See **hitch** n **2**

hetchel n See **hatchel** n **1**

hetchel v See **hatchel** v

hetcheled See **hatchel** v **1**

hetcheling See **hatchel** v **2**

hetchel up See **hatchel** v **3**

Het-eye See **Haiti 1**

hethen See **heath hen 1**

hether adv, adj See **hither** adv, adj

hether exclam [Perh var of *hither;* cf **hither horse**] Cf **haw** v

Used as a command to a horse to turn left.

1894 *DN* 1.331 **eNJ,** *Hether* equivalent to *peddy whoa* [=go to the left]. **1946** *PADS* 6.17 **eNC,** *Hether*. . . Command to a horse to turn to the left.

heth'n See **heath hen 1**

het up adj phr Also rarely *het* **[heat** v **A1]** *somewhat old-fash*

Angry, upset, excited.

1862 in 1867 Lowell *Biglow* 60 **MA,** Don't you get het: they thought the thing was planned;/ They'll cool off when they come to understand. **1909** *DN* 3.398 **nwAR,** *Het*. . . "He got putty het up by the argument." **1911** (1916) Porter *Harvester* 286 **IN,** You will become wrought up, and 'het up,' as Granny Moreland says, which will make you very ill. **1923** *DN* 5.210 **swMO,** *Het up* = angry. **1926** *DN* 5.387 **ME,** *Het-up*. . . Angry. "He was all het-up." Obsol[ete]. **1941** *LANE* Map 472 *(Angry), Het up*. . . also used to mean 'excited, all nerved up'. **1950** *PADS* 14.36 **SC,** *Het*. . . Heated; angry; excited. Usually with *up.* **1960** Criswell *Resp. to PADS 20* **Ozarks,** Riled up, het up (older people), hot, stirred up, mad. **c1960** *Wilson Coll.* **csKY,** *Het up*. . . Excited, angry, enthusiastic, or in some other nervous condition. **1965–70** *DARE* (Qu. GG4, *Stirred up, angry*) 32 Infs, **scattered,** (All *or* real) het up; (Qu. GG7, . . *Annoyed or upset*) 27 Infs, **chiefly Nth, N Midl,** Het up; (Qu. A21, *When someone is in too much of a hurry . . "Now just slow down! Don't ________."*) Inf **NC**62, Get all het up; (Qu. GG8, *When a person is very easily offended*) Inf **CT**28, Het up; (Qu. GG11, *To be quite anxious about something*) Infs **CA**192, **VA**33, (All) het up; (Qu. GG27b, *To get somebody out of an unhappy mood . . "Don't ________."*) Inf **NY**22, Get all het up; (Qu. GG40, *Words or expressions meaning violently angry*) Infs **CA**158, **CT**42, **NY**93, **WA**13, (All) het up; (QR, near Qu. OO5b) Inf **SC**11, So and so was all het up—was mad. [49 of 67 Infs old; 17 of 67 Infs mid-aged] **1986** Pederson *LAGS Concordance (Angry)* 3 infs, **Gulf Region,** (All) het up.

heush See **hush** v

hev v[1] See **have** v[1] **A1a**

hev v[2] See **heave** v **A2**

heving See **heaven**

hevun See **heaven**

hewgag n Also sp *hugag*

1 A type of horn; see quots 1928, 1955. Cf **gewgaw**

1850 *California Courier* (San Francisco) 6 Sept. 2/3 *(OEDS)*, Beat the hong-gong; sound the hew-gag! **1855** *Burlington Daily Free Press* (VT) 8 June 2/1 **VT,** The T.I.N. Horn-et Band, with Sackbut, Psaltery, Dulcimer and Shawm, Tanglang, Locofodeon and Hugag, marched next. **1928** Ritchie *Forty-Niners* 249 **CA,** The most bellows-lunged Clamper [=member of **E Clampus Vitus**] appears with an eight foot tin horn—the "hewgag." On this he sounds three mighty blasts which can be heard away down the canyon. **1955** Lewis *High Sierra* 249 **CA,** Members [of **E Clampus Vitus**] were summoned . . the signal being ear-splitting blasts from a ten-foot-long horn called the "hewgag."

2 An imaginary animal; see quots. Cf **hodag** n[2]

1910 Cox *Fearsome Creatures* 9 [Logger talk], The hugag is a huge animal of the Lake States. . . In size the hugag may be compared to the moose, and in form it somewhat resembles that animal. Very noticeable . . are its jointless legs, which compel the animal to remain on its feet, and its long upper lip, which prevents it from grazing. **1939** Tryon *Fearsome Critters* 29 [Logger talk], The legs lack knee, fetlock, or hock joints so the Hugag can't lie down. Has to sleep standing. Usually braces its splayed feet and leans against a tree to take a nap.

hex v, hence ppl adjs *hexed, behexed, hechsed,* vbl n *hexing* [PaGer *hexe,* Ger *hexen*] **widespread, but less freq S Midl** See Map Cf **conjure** v, **ferhex**

To bewitch, cast a spell on; to practice witchcraft.

1830 Watson *Annals Philadelphia* 232, A decent storekeeper once got him to hex for his wife, who had conceited that an old Mrs. Wiggand had bewitched her and made her to swallow a piece of linseywoolsey. **1929** *Ruppenthal Coll.* **KS,** *Hex* . . to bewitch; to place a spell upon. . . A family in York county, Pennsylvania, believed that it was, in Pennsylvania Dutch dialect "hexed." . . A powwow doctor went to the house of a hexer (sorcerer) to get a tuft of his hair to bury in the earth as a cure for the family's ills. Words relating to hexing . . were brought to central Kansas by colonies from Pennsylvania. **1930** Shoemaker *1300 Words* 30 **cPA Mts** (as of c1900), *Hechsed*—Bewitched, or under a spell. **1939** Aurand *Quaint Idioms* 15 [PaGer], She is hechsed ("hexed;" bewitched). **1950** Klees *PA Dutch* 281, *Hex,* the noun for *witch* or verb for *to bewitch,* is in common usage. **1950** *WELS (Expressions . . for one person casting a "spell" over another)* 8 Infs, **WI,** Hex; 5 Infs, Hexed; 1 Inf, Hexing—used in this community only among Germans; 1 Inf, Behexed—when anything you do goes wrong, you're 'behexed'; *(A place where there are ghosts: "They say that old house is ______.")* 1 Inf, **WI,** Hexed. [9 of 16 Infs of Ger ancestry] **1954** *DE Folkl. Bulletin* 1.15, Granny Hessy . . hexed a man to death. According to "old heads," the man stole one of Granny Hessy's piglets. **1965–70** *DARE* (Qu. CC14) 200 Infs, **widespread, but less freq S Midl,** Hex; (Qu. CC12b, . . *If a person has a lot of bad luck you might say, "He's been ______."*) 10 Infs, **scattered, exc Sth, S Midl,** Hexed; (Qu. BB51b, . . *'Magical' cures for corns or warts*) Inf **PA**49, Hex them off; (Qu. CC15) Inf **WA**18, Hexed.

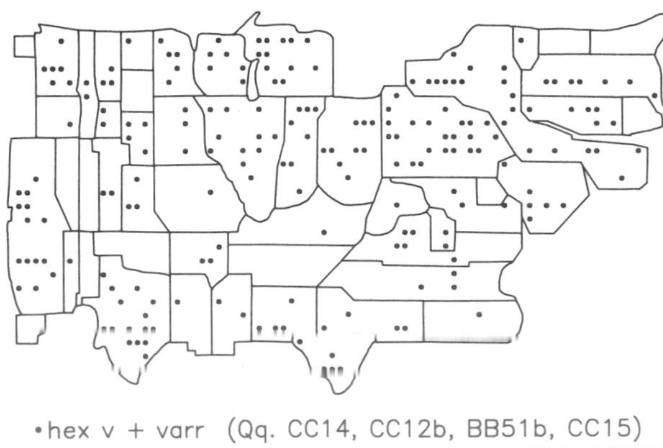

•hex v + varr (Qq. CC14, CC12b, BB51b, CC15)

hex n

1 also attrib; also sp *hechs;* also *hexer, hex-woman:* A witch; a mean or witch-like person, esp a woman. [PaGer < Ger *Hexe* a witch] **esp PaGer area**

1894 (1895) Hoover *Enemies* 113 **sePA,** Say, Galsch, you old hex, . . don't you go and make our cows give bloody milk. **1907** *German Amer. Annals* 9.378 **sePA,** *Hex.* Witch, or a general term of reproach; hag. "The old hex is always meddling around." **1929** [see **hex** v]. **1930** Shoemaker *1300 Words* 28 **cPA Mts** (as of c1900), *Hechs*—A witch, or spell-casting old woman. **1935** *AmSp* 10.170 **sePA,** *Hex,* a witch . . [is] well established in the English of this region. . . 'the hex trial at Lancaster.' **1940** Writers' Program *Guide PA* 4, In the Pennsylvania Dutch sections . . the visitor will meet with . . a wealth of native folklore, and occasionally with a body of dark and gloomy superstition such as that which centers about the 'Hex-woman.' **1950** [see **hex** v]. **1950** *WELS (Uncomplimentary names for a woman)* 1 Inf, **seWI,** Hex. **1950** *WELS Suppl.* **WI,** *Hex.* . . Used by children for someone not liked, most often referring to women. *Ibid, Hex*—A malignant witch, as opposed to more benign words *witch* or *wizard. Ibid, Hex.* . . A mean woman. **1968** *DARE* (Qu. CC14, . . *Expressions used . . where one person supposedly casts a spell over another*) Infs **MN**35, **NY**59, Hexer; (Qu. HH40, *Uncomplimentary words for an old man*) Inf **NY**43, Old hex.

2 also attrib: A magic spell or curse—often in phrr *put a* (or *the*) *hex on* and varr. [Cf **hex** v]

1909 *Sat. Eve. Post* 181.29.7/1 **NY,** "Old pal," agreed J. Rufus, "the hex is sure on me." **1925** in 1966 Goldstein–Byington *Two Penny Ballads* 156 **PA,** Putting "the hex" on an individual was a common threat heard in Pennsylvania thirty-five years ago. **1939** Aurand *Quaint Idioms* 31 [PaGer], Don't let the women put a hex (spell . .) on you. **1950** *WELS (Expressions for one person casting a "spell" over another)* 1 Inf, **WI,** A hex; 1 Inf, **WI,** Someone put a hex on another. **c1960** *Wilson Coll.* **csKY,** *Hex.* . . A spell cast over someone. **1965–70** *DARE* (Qu. CC14) 26 Infs, **scattered,** Put a (*or* the) hex on; **AL**39, **AR**12, 37, **MI**118, Put a hex (over). **1970** *NC Folkl.* 18.48, To outwit witches, paint objects, such as barns, red as a "hex sign."

hexed See **hex** v

hexer See **hex** n **1**

hexerei n [Ger] **PaGer area**

Witchcraft, magic.

1871 Leland *Breitmann Ballads* 281 **Philadelphia PA,** *Hexerei*—Witchery, sorcery. **1929** Aurand *Acct. Witch Murder Trial* 30 (*DA* at *hex* n), White men brought 'hexerei' to the hills where it blended with the Indian 'powwow.' **1942** Weygandt *Plenty* 48 **PaGer area,** A share of it [=folk medicine] came from "Indian doctors," who are responsible as well for some of our hexerei. **1950** Klees *PA Dutch* 304, This is pure hexerei—black magic or witchcraft.

hexing See **hex** v

hex-woman See **hex** n **1**

hex yeast n [Cf **hex** n, v] Cf **spook yeast**

A type of yeast; see quots.

1950 *WELS (Kinds of yeast)* 1 Inf, **cwWI,** Hex yeast—used by Germans and New Englanders. **1950** *WELS Suppl.* **ceWI,** *Hex yeast*—continuous yeast; used to describe the continuous kind like the old time buckwheat cake variety—used by Germans and Swiss. **1967–68** *DARE* (Qu. H17, . . *Kinds [of yeast]*) Inf **PA**29, Hex yeast—Dutchmen's use; **WI**5, Hex yeast—used to make buckwheat pancakes, old term.

hey exclam

1 also in combs: Used as a greeting. **chiefly Sth, Lower Missip Valley** See Map

1901 *DN* 2.142 **seNY,** *Hey wat.* . . Hello. **1930** *DN* 6.81 **cSC,** *Hey,* the usual informal greeting between social equals. . . probably fairly general in the south. **1944** *PADS* 2.9 **AL, VA, NC,** *Hey.* . . The common term of familiar salutation of children and young people in most of the South; *hello* seems to them either semiformal or archaic. On many Northern and Western campuses the term is *hi.* **1956** McAtee *Some Dialect NC* 22, *Hey:* . . informal greeting. **1960** (1962) Lee *Mockingbird* 156 **AL,** "Tell him hey for me, won't you?" . . "I'll tell him you said hey." **1965–70** *DARE* (Qu. NN10a, *Expressions . . used when you meet somebody you know quite well*) 60 Infs, **chiefly Sth, Lower Missip Valley,** Hey; 9 Infs, **chiefly Sth,** Hey there; **DC**11, **FL**52, **IL**115, **TN**46, Hey baby (*or* broz, buddy, chile, man); **IL**119, **SC**8, Hey, how you (doing); **NC**52, Hey (name), how are you; **SC**21, Hey-hey; **SC**34, Hey, how're you; **OH**103, Hey, what's happening; (Qu. II12, *Talking about meeting somebody on the street and speaking only a few words with him: "We just ________.")* Infs **FL**18, **NY**238, Said hey (ya); (Qu. NN10b, *Greetings used when you meet somebody you do not know well)* Infs **GA**72, **PA**66, **VA**85, Hey (there). **1966** Barnes–Jensen *Dict. UT Slang* 23, *Hey there* . . words of greeting. **1971** *Today Show Letters* **Sth,** In the North, what is hi to us, is hey in a Southerner's vocabulary. **1979** *McCalls* 106.7.129 **New Orleans LA,** Say 'hey' to Dixie.

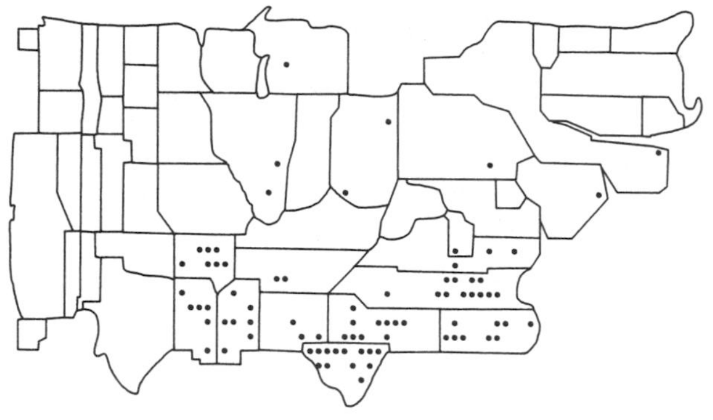

•hey exclam 1 + varr (Qq. NN10a, b, II12)

2 Used as a call to animals; see quot. **scattered, but less freq Nth, Atlantic, West** See Map

1965–70 *DARE* (Qu. NN22d, *Expressions used to drive away animals other than dogs)* 91 Infs, **scattered, but less freq Nth, Atlantic, West,** Hey; **MO**15, **WI**66, Hey there; **LA**2, Hey, cow.

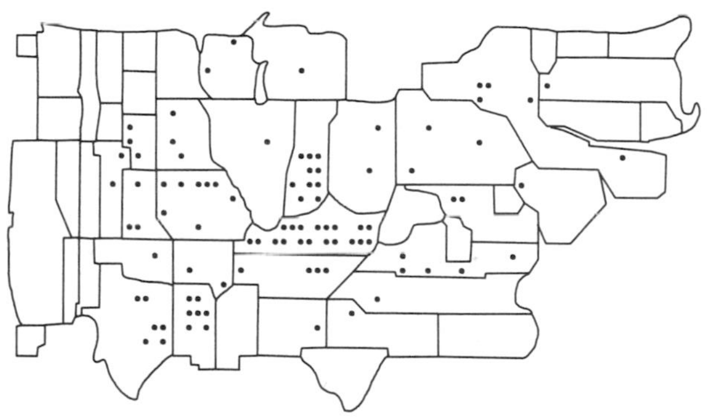

•hey exclam 2 + varr (Qu. NN22d)

hey interrog exclam Cf **eh** interrog exclam

1 =ainna.

1825 Neal *Brother Jonathan* 2.42 **swME,** He's . . sort of a naiteral too, I guess; rather a gump, hey? **1871** Eggleston *Hoosier Schoolmaster* 91 **IN,** But when people is a-bein' robbed it's well to look out. Hey? **1899** (1977) Norris *McTeague* 223 **CA,** Well, it's a go then, hey? **1935** Davis *Honey* 33 **sOR,** Put 'em in the hay-corral yonder, hey? **1940** Faulkner *Hamlet* 72 **MS,** Want that horse shod, hey? Good, good: save the hoof and save all. **1966** *DARE* (Qu. NN3, *Words and expressions meaning 'Don't you agree?': "She's a nice-looking woman, ________?" or "We ought to come back here again, ________?")* Infs **MI**33, **WA**16, Hey?

2 What did you say? **scattered, but esp NEast** See Map *old-fash*

1942 Berrey–Van den Bark *Amer. Slang* 172.6, *What?.* Come again; hey?, how? **1943** *LANE* Map 594 *(What did you say?)* **scattered NEng,** [he(ɪ), hẽ, hɛɪ]. **c1960** *Wilson Coll.* **csKY,** *Hey?*—Asking over. **1965–70** *DARE* (Qu. X18, . . *When one person doesn't quite hear what another person said, what does he say?)* 22 Infs, **scattered, but esp NEast,** Hey? **MI**65, Hey what say? [20 of 23 Infs old]

hey v [Cf *EDD hey* "to cry 'hey' " (at *heigh* int. and v. 4)]

1907 *DN* 3.245 **eME,** *Hey.* . . To attract one's attention by using the interjection "hey!" "Who are you heying?"

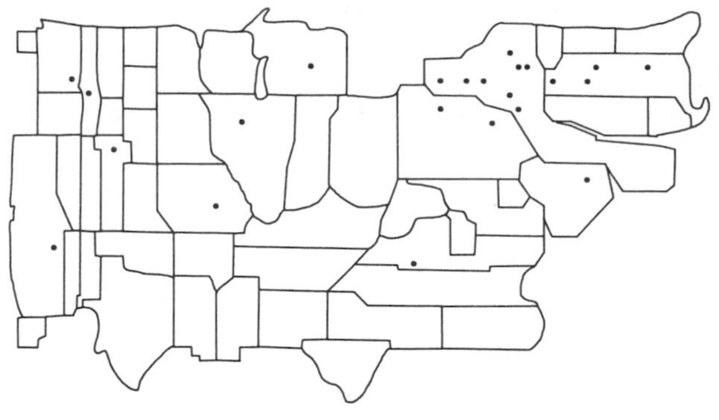

•hey interrog exclam 2 + var (Qu. X18)

heyar See **hair** n

hez See **have** v[1] **A2**

hi See **hie**

hiacapooka n Also *hiacapookum(s)*

An imaginary disease.

1908 *DN* 3.320 **eAL, wGA,** *Hiacapooka* [haɪækɑ'pʊkɑ]. . . An unnameable or indescribable disease, general debility. "I've got the hiacapooka, I reckon." Also *hiacapookum(s).*

hiah See **hi-ya**

Hiawatha's chicken n

=robin.

a1950 in 1982 *Barrick Coll.* **csPA,** Hiawatha's chickens—*robins.*

hibbie-jibbies, hibbies See **heebie-jeebies 1**

hibiscus n

Std: A malvaceous plant of the genus *Hibiscus.* Also called **marshmallow, rose mallow.** For other names of var spp see **Confederate rose, China rose, flower-of-an-hour, hau, okra, paleface, rose-of-sharon, sea-hollyhock, swamp mallow, swamp rose, swamp rose-mallow, sweating weed**

hi-boy See **highboy**

hi-bye-fly adj

Of inferior quality, cheap, inexpensive.

1970 *DARE* Tape **TN**46, That casket, girl, I know looked like about four hundred dollars. It wasn't just no lil' hi-bye-fly stuff, you know.

hicatee n Also *hicatee terrapin, (highland) hickity* [*DJE* 1698–1873] **NC**

=spotted turtle.

1942 *Amer. Midland Naturalist* 28.294 **eNC,** *Kinosternon subrubrum.* Mud-turtle; "hickity." . . *Clemmys guttata.* Spotted turtle; "highland hickity." **1966–68** *DARE* (Qu. P24, *What kinds of turtles are found around here?)* Inf **NC**27, Hicatee ['hɪkədi]; **NC**80, Hicatee ['hɪkɨti] terrapin; **NC**82, Hicatee ['hɪkɪti].

hiccup n Usu |'hɪkəp|; also *esp freq among speakers with little formal educ* |'hikəp|; occas *esp among old speakers and coll educ speakers* |'hɪkəf, -əf| (sp-pronc based on sp *hiccough*); for addit varr, see quot 1965–70 Also sp *hiccough, hickup* Pronc-spp *he(e)-cup, hickoff;* rarely *heekaw* Also abbr *hick*

Std sense, var forms.

1806 (1970) Webster *Compendious Dict.* 143, *Hickup,* n. a convulsed motion of the stomach. **1883** (1971) Harris *Nights with Remus* 156 **GA** [Black], 'E is bin-a tek wit' da *he*cup. **1923** *DN* 5.210 **swMO,** *Hee-cup.* **1930s** in 1944 *ADD* **neWV,** *Hiccup.* . . *heecup* ['hikʌp]. **1942** *Sat. Eve. Post* 10 Oct 103/2 [Black], It'll give you the heekaws. **1950** *WELS* 8 Infs, **WI,** He-cup(s); 1 Inf, Hickoff; 1 Inf, Hickoff—by those wishing to appear correct. **1960** Bailey *Resp. to PADS 20* **KS,** Hickoff. **c1960** *Wilson Coll.* **csKY,** *Hiccough* is always hickup in pronunciation. **1965–70** *DARE* (Qu. X54) 153 Infs, **widespread,** He-cup(s); 33 Infs, **scattered,** Hickoff(s); **FL**8, **KY**50, 84, **IL**88, **NY**221, ['hɪkɔfs]; **KY**70, ['hɪkɔfs]—correct; **KY**52, 65, **NC**14, ['hɪkəfs]; **IN**3, **PA**70, ['hɪkɑ(u)fs]; **MI**96, Hickoff—the proper name; **NY**136, Hickoff—some old timers say this; **OK**47, It's really hickoff; **TX**9, Hickoff [FW: Inf gave the impression that he thinks *hickoff* is proper but *hiccup* is more common.]; **IN**53, ['hɪkɔvz]; **GA**15, 72, **MN**29, **NE**10, (The) hicks. [Of all Infs responding to the question, 64% were old, 26% gs educ, 31% coll educ; of those giving the responses *he-cup(s)*, 47% were gs educ; of those giving the responses *hickoff(s)*, 85% were old, 50% coll educ.] **1983** *MJLF* 9.1.43 **ceKY,** *Hee cups* . . hiccough.

hice See **hoist**

hick n¹ [Perh var of *heck*]

1967 *DARE* (Qu. GG21b, *If you don't care what a person does, you might say, "Go ahead—I don't give a ______.")* Inf **MA**5, Hick.

hick n² See **hickory** n

hick n³ See **hickey** n²

hick n⁴ See **hiccup**

hicker n¹ Also *hickle* Cf **nicker, whicker**

1970 *DARE* (Qu. K40, . . *Sound that a horse makes*) Inf **VA**46, Hickle ['hɪkʊl], hicker ['hɪkɚ].

hicker n² See **hickory** n

hicker-nut tree See **hickory nut 1**

hicket n [*OED hicket* sb. 1544–1684; *"Obs."; EDD hicket* v. "To hiccup"] *?relic*

1969 *DARE* (Qu. X54, . . *A spell of going 'hic' . . he's got the ______*) Inf **MI**107, Hicket.

hickey n¹ Also sp *hickie*

1 A tool, fitting, or fixture; see quots.

1919 *DN* 5.56 **NW,** *Hickie*. . . A piece of pipe with a T large enough to slip over another pipe. Used to bend pipe. **1927** (1930) *WNID, Hickey*. . . *a* A device for bending a conduit, consisting of an iron pipe used as a handle fitted at one end with a tee. . . *b* A small fitting used in wiring for electric lights[;] a fixture piped for gas. **1956** Sorden–Ebert *Logger's Words* 18 **Gt Lakes,** *Hickey,* Stick used for tightening brakes on a logging train. **1961** Labbe–Goe *Railroads* 258 **Pacific NW,** *Hickey:* A metal handle used by the brakemen in setting up the hand brakes.

2a also *hinkie* (cf Intro "Language Changes" I.8), *hickey-doodle, ~-jigger, hickum skivver:* **=doohickey 1.**

1913 *DN* 4.58 **cnSC,** *Hickey*. . . Thing. . . "Hand me that hickey." **1931** *AmSp* 6.258 **NE, KS,** Hickey, hinkie. **1943** in 1944 *ADD* **cnWV,** [hɪ'ki]. **1965** *DARE* File **swPA** (as of 1920s), *Hickey*—Thingamajig; everything, no matter what, if you couldn't think of the name of it immediately, was called a hickey or a thingamajig. **1968** *DARE* (Qu. F11, *The thing you use to remove the lids . . from a wood-burning stove*) Inf **GA**17, Little iron hickey, I guess; (Qu. NN12a, . . *To put a child off when he asks too many questions: "What's that for?"*) Inf **PA**133, Hickey-jigger; (Qu. NN12b, . . *To put off a child when he asks, "What are you making?"*) Inf **PA**134, Hickey for hootenanny; **PA**223, Hickum skivver; **WV**8, Hickey-doodle. **1970** *DARE* FW Addit **AL,** *Hickey*—A reference to any object whose name can not be immediately recalled—common.

b Prob by ext: see quot.

1990 *DARE* File **seSC,** *Hickey*—what someone calls you when they don't know your name: "Hey, hickey!"

3 also *hickey board, hick(y) horse:* A seesaw. **esp eNC**

1935 in 1944 *ADD* **ceNC,** [hɪ'ki]. **1946** *PADS* 6.17 **seNC** (as of 1900–10), *Hickey*. . . A seesaw. . . Common among rural children. **1949** Kurath *Word Geog.* 59 **ceNC,** *Hicky-horse, hick horse* between Albemarle Sound and the lower Neuse. **1966–68** *DARE* (Qu. EE31) Infs **NC**1, 82, Hickey board. **1967** Faries *Word Geog. MO* 84, *Hicky-horse* . . occur[s] sporadically . . [in] Missouri.

4 A small token, something of little value; see quots. Cf **hicky** adj²

1940 *Sat. Eve. Post* 15 June 38/2 **LA,** There was a violent distaste for the fraction-of-a-cent tokens, disks of aluminum with a hole in the center. These were variously called "Chinese money," "hickeys," "monkey money" and "agony money." **1970** *DARE* (Qu. DD35, . . *Favorite card games . . around here*) Inf **MT**3, Hickey gambling—In earlier days, 30 years ago, gamble for hickeys, trade checks; [it] was legal then; [**IL**135, Hickey;] (Qu. EE6c, *Cheap marbles*) Inf **TN**46, Hickeys.

hickey n² Also *hinkey* (cf Intro "Language Changes" I.8), *hicky, hick*

A blemish or mark on the skin, spec:

a A pimple, boil, or carbuncle. **scattered, but less freq NEng, S Atl**

1918 *DN* 5.25 **NW,** *Hickey*. . . A pimple on the face; limited to this. **1937** *Ten-Story Love Mag.* May 2 (Advt.) *(OEDS),* Hickies spoil everything. I know. I had 'em until I began eating Fleischmann's yeast. **1946** *PADS* 6.17 **swVA,** *Hickey*. . . A small festered spot on the skin of a person. **1956** McAtee *Some Dialect NC* 22, *Hickey:* . . pimple. **1960** Bailey *Resp. to PADS 20* **KS,** In my youth a "hickey" was just one thing, a skin eruption from a pus formation or a blackhead. **1965–70** *DARE* (Qu. X59, . . *Small infected pimples . . on the face*) 114 Infs, **scattered, but less freq NEng, S Atl,** Hickeys; **AR**3, **NC**6, (Little) hickey(s); **IL**114, **IN**3, 9, 19, Hinkeys [Of all Infs responding to the question, 25% were mid-aged, 32% coll educ; of those giving these responses, 38% were mid-aged, 45% coll educ.]; (Qu. BB24, . . *A rash that comes out suddenly . . "He's got some kind of ______ all over his chest."*) Inf **CA**15, Blackheads and hickeys; (Qu. BB25, . . *Common skin diseases*) Inf **IA**3, Hicks; (Qu. BB33a, . . *A swelling under the skin, bigger than a pimple, that comes to a head*) Infs **CA**15, 106, **DC**11, **IL**97, **MD**9, **PA**133, **UT**3, Hickey; (Qu. BB33b, . . *A swelling under the skin—if it is very big or serious*) Infs **AL**4, **DC**11, **MS**45, **OK**58, **TX**92, Hickey. **1982** *Barrick Coll.* **csPA,** Hickey—*pimple, boil.* **1986** Pederson *LAGS Concordance,* 1 inf, **csGA,** A hickey—pimple.

b A bruise or bump resulting from a sharp blow. **chiefly Sth, S Midl** See Map and Map Section *esp freq among Black speakers*

1923 *The Confessions of a Bank Burglar* (Partridge *Underworld Dict.*), They knew something was wrong when they saw the two beautiful "hickeys" that I had. **1965–70** *DARE* (Qu. X60, . . *A lump that comes up on your head when you get a sharp blow or knock*) 41 Infs, **chiefly Sth, S Midl,** Hickey; **VA**46, Hick; (Qu. X20, . . *A black eye*) Inf **LA**15, Hickey. [10 of 42 total Infs young, 21 Black] **c1970** *Halpert Coll.* **wKY, nwTN,** *Hinkey*—same as *hickey.* "That fall should make a hickey come up on your forehead." **1977** *NY Times* (NY) 6 July 29 **NYC,** We just hit him in the arms so he gets hickeys. **1986** Pederson *LAGS Concordance,* 1 inf, **seLA,** A hickey—egg-like swelling, not a passion mark.

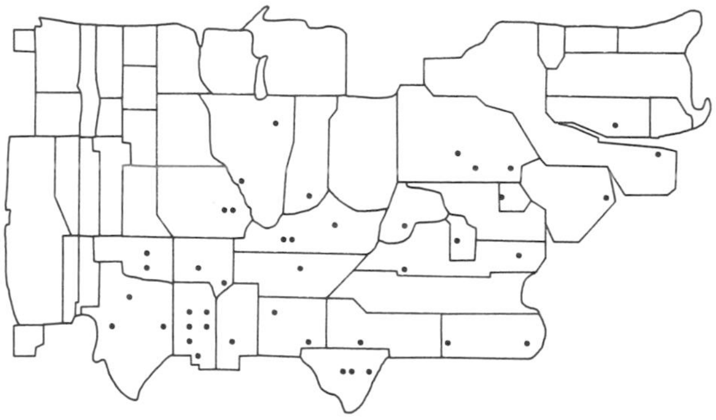

•hickey n² b + var (Qq. X60, X20)

c A "passion mark"; see quots. **widespread exc Sth** See Map

1942 Berrey–Van den Bark *Amer. Slang* 355.4, *Hicky* . . a red mark caused by sucking or biting. **1960** Criswell *Resp. to PADS 20* **Ozarks,** *Hickey*—Refers to mark on skin made by sucking hard. **1965–70** *DARE* (Qu. X39, *A mark on the skin where somebody has sucked it hard and brought the blood to the surface*) 234 Infs, **widespread exc Sth,** Hickey; **OR**10, Hinkey. [Of all Infs responding to the question, 15% were young; of those giving these responses, 25% were young.] **1970** *DARE* FW Addit **AL,** *Hickey*—Also among young people, it refers to a passion mark or bruise on the neck brought by sucking on the skin and drawing the blood to the surface—common. **1973** Piercy *Small Changes* 8 **wNY,** "And hickeys," Dolores whispered, . . because when Beth had been seeing Jim on the sly she had used to worry that her father would see the marks on her neck. **1986** Pederson *LAGS Concordance,* 1 inf, **nwFL,** Giving her a little hickey—biting girl on neck.

‡hickey n³

1968 *DARE* (Qu. BB10, . . *Names or nicknames . . for tuberculosis*) Inf **NY**79, The hickey.

hickey n⁴ See **hickory** n

hickey adj See **hicky** adj¹

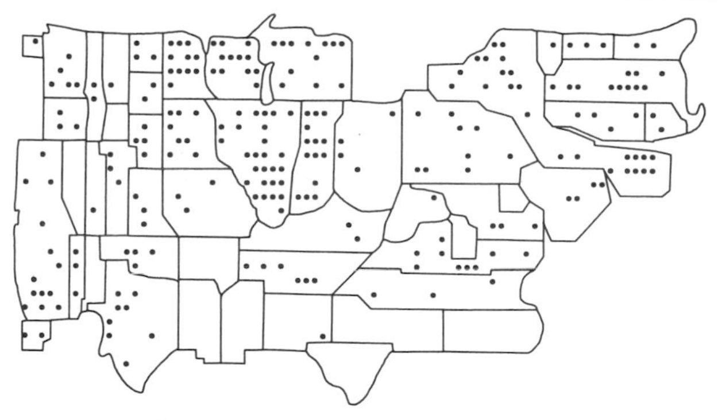

•hickey n^2 c + var (Qu. X39)

hickey board See **hickey** n^1 **3**

hickey-doodle, hickey-jigger See **hickey** n^1 **2**

hick-hack See **heekack**

hick horse See **hickey** n^1 **3**

hickie See **hickey** n^1

hickish See **hicky** adj^1

hickity See **hicatee**

hickle v [PaGer < Ger dial *hikele*]
To limp, hobble.

1907 *German Amer. Annals* 9.378 **se, cePA,** *Hickle.* (Rare.)—To hop; go lame. "I had to hickle along on one foot." **1968** *DARE* (Qu. BB1, *When a person has been injured so that when he walks he steps more heavily on one foot than the other: "He ______."*) Inf **PA**150, Is hickling ['hɪklɪŋ] along.

hickle n^1 See **hicker** n^1

hickle n^2 Cf **hickle** v

1907 *German Amer. Annals* 9.378 **se, cePA,** *Hickle* . . the name for "hopscotch."

hickledy-pickledy adv [Var of *higgledy-piggledy; see EDD*]

1967 *DARE* (Qu. MM12b, . . *'In all directions'* . . *"When she was out on the dance floor, she broke her beads and they went ______."*) Inf **ID**5, Hickledy-pickledy.

hick-nut tree See **hickory nut 1**

hickoff See **hiccup**

hickok plum n [See **coco plum**] *obs*
=coco plum.

1837 (1962) Williams *Territory FL* 19, The ovino, custard apple, hickok, and huesco plumbs are abundant, on the east bank of Indian River. *Ibid* 33, Here are several cocoanut trees in bearing, orange, lime, papayer, hawey, and hickok plum.

hickory n, also attrib Usu |'hɪk(ə)ri, -ɪ|; in combs, as *hickory nut, ~ shad,* also |'hɪkə(r)|; abbr |hɪk|; for addit varr see quots Pronc-spp *hick(er), hickey, hickor, hickry*

A Forms.

1891 *PMLA* 6.3.175 **TN,** The word *hickory* is pronounced *hick'ry,* and in connection with *nut* it forms *hicker-nut*—sometimes pronounced almost as one syllable, *hick-nut.* **1901** *DN* 2.182 **neKY,** *Hickory*—hick'ry. **1906** *DN* 3.119 **sIN,** *Hickory.* . . Regularly pronounced ['hɪkrɪ]. **1917** *DN* 4.394 **OH, KY, CT,** *Hickernut.* **1923** *DN* 5.210 **swMO,** *Hicker nut.* **1954** *Harder Coll.* **cwTN,** Hickory /hɪkər/ nuts. **1960** Criswell *Resp. to PADS 20* **Ozarks,** *Hickory,* . . pron. *hickry. Ibid,* Hickory nuts (always called hicker nuts). **c1960** *Wilson Coll.* **csKY,** *Hickory nut.* . . /'hɪkəˌnʌt/ or /'hɪkrɪˌnʌt/ common. **1963** Watkins-Watkins *Yesterday Hills* 47 **cnGA,** We . . et walnuts and hickornuts. **1965–70** *DARE* (Qu. T16) Infs **IL**69, **IN**19, **MD**18, 22, 24, 34, 49, **MI**116, **NC**52, 81, **OH**16, 25, **OK**46, **PA**216, **TX**99, **VA**96, ['hɪkri]; **DE**5, **GA**28, **KY**9, **LA**7, 15, **MD**15, **MS**60, ['hɪkrɪ]; **CT**13, **MS**86, **SC**67, **WV**21, ['hɪkɚi]; **FL**49, ['hɪkə nət]; **KY**9, ['hɪkɪ]; **NY**148, ['hikɚi]; **TX**106, **VA**57, ['hɪknət]; (Qu. I37) Inf **OH**95, Hickory ['hɪkri] jack; (Qu. I43) Inf **FL**27, Field ['hɪkrinəts]; (Qu. P3) Inf **FL**1, Hick shad; (Qu. T15) Inf **GA**18 ['hɪkɚɪ]; **LA**3 ['hɪkrɪ]. **1971** Green *Village Horse Doctor* 155 **cwTX** (as of 1940s), His head was shaped about as round as a hicker nut.

B Senses.

1 Std: any of var trees of the genus *Carya;* also the fruit of such a tree: Also called **hickory nut 1.** For other names of var spp see **bitternut 1, hard-bargain hickory nut, hard-shell hickory, ironball hickory, mockernut hickory, nutmeg hickory, pecan, pignut, red hickory, sand hickory, shagbark hickory, shellbark hickory, smoothbark hickory, soft-shelled hickory, water hickory**

2 A stick or switch, often of some wood other than hickory; spec:

a also *hickory frail, ~ limb, ~ stick, ~ switch, ~ towel, ~ withe:* A slender flexible stick used esp to punish children. **chiefly Sth, S Midl** Cf **hickory** v

1734 in 1894 *Documents Colonial & Post-Revol. Hist. NJ* 11.359, Several Indians had seiz'd a Boy . . whom they stript and whipt with Hickery Switches. **1834** Caruthers *Kentuckian* 1.30, I gin him a wink, as much as to let him know that if ever I caught him on my trail, I would wipe him down with a hickory towel. **1855** Simms *Forayers* 119 **SC,** I thought of giving him a wipe with a hickory towel more than once. **1902** *DN* 2.236 **sIL,** *Hickry.* . . Generic name for rod of chastisement. **1906** *DN* 3.124 **neAR,** *Apple hick'ry.* . . Apple switch. "The teacher made me go out and cut an apple hickry." **1908** *DN* 3.320 **eAL, wGA,** *Hick(o)ry.* . . "I'll get a peach-tree hickry after you." **1915** *DN* 4.184 **swVA,** *Hickory.* . . switch. **1929** *AmSp* 5.18 **Ozarks,** The hillman frequently cuts his *hickory* from an ash or dogwood tree. **1936** *AmSp* 11.315 **Ozarks,** Sassafras allus makes th' best hick'ry, if ye kin git it. **1950** *PADS* 14.36 **SC,** *Hickory.* . . Any kind of switch, hickory or otherwise. **1956** Ker *Vocab. W. TX* 409, Switch (for punishing children) . . hickory limb. **1968** *DARE* (Qu. EE41) Inf **NY**75, I'll take a hickory stick to you. **1970** *DARE* Tape **IL**114, A hickory withe. . . It's a branch off a hickory tree . . you put it across the fireplace and dry it out. **1970** *DARE* FW Addit **csVA,** *Hickory frail*—A hickory switch used for whipping. **1983** *MJLF* 9.43 **ceKY,** *Hickory* . . a switch for whipping children, of any kind of wood. . . *Hickory withe.*

b A walking stick, cane. *obs*

1748 in 1904 Thwaites *Early W. Travels* 1.39 **sePA,** The French had very hard heads & your Country afforded nothing but Sticks & Hickerys which was not sufficient to break them. **1798** (1851) U.S. Congress *Debates & Proc.* 5th Cong Sess 7.1049, Griswold immediately struck Lyon . . with the little end of the cane, or hickory, aforesaid. **1833** S. Smith *Major Downing* 185 *(DA),* The Gineral pulled his own chair up to the other side of the table and laid his hickory and hat down before him. **1857** *Harper's New Mth. Mag.* Aug 15.422/1 **cwMS,** Tom . . placed under his arm the gold-headed *hickory,* which was . . his staff of office.

c also *hickory stick:* A sharp-pointed stick, usu with an attached lash, used to drive oxen, horses, or mules. **chiefly Sth, S Midl**

1899 Chesnutt *Conjure Woman* 106 **NC** [Black], Eve'y time I cuts a mule wid a hick'ry, 'pears ter me mos' lackly I's cuttin' some er my own relations. **1949** Kurath *Word Geog.* 56, Many of the older country folk still remember the ox goad, a stout pointed stick with a lash. There are many different terms for it . . hickory in the western part of the Carolinas. **1951** *AmSp* 26.252 **Upstate NY,** *Hickory* (ox whip). **1956** Ker *Vocab. W. TX* 409, *Hickory*—ox goad. . . reported chiefly by older informants. **1966** *DARE* (Qu. K27, . . *The sharp-pointed stick used to get oxen to move*) Inf **DC**8, Hickory stick. **1967** Faries *Word Geog. MO* 127, *Hickory* . . is the predominant expression in Missouri to denote a stout, pointed stick with a lash used in driving oxen, a practice still remembered by most of the informants. **1967** *PADS* 47.7 **wNC, nw, cnSC,** Hickory 'goad.' **1983** *MJLF* 9.43 **ceKY,** *Hickory* . . a pointed stick of any kind of wood used as a goad for oxen.

3 also *hickory (limb) oil, hickory tea;* By ext from **2a:** a whipping. **chiefly S Midl** Cf **peach-tree tea**

1827 *Amer. Sentinel* (Georgetown, Ky.) 21 April 3/2 *(DA),* Hickory oil is the grand restorative. **1905** *DN* 3.82 **nwAR,** *Hickory tea.* . . Whipping. 'You'd better watch out, or you'll get a dose of hickory tea.' **1906** *DN* 3.140 **nwAR,** *Hick'ry.* . . whipping. "That boy needs a good hick'ry." **1908** *DN* 3.320 **eAL, wGA,** *Hick(o)ry oil.* **1939** *AmSp* 14.267 **IN,** An obstreperous youngster is likely to be dosed with 'peach tree tea,' 'hickory tea,' or 'strap oil.' **1940** *AmSp* 15.215 **wFL,** My mother never gave me any *hickory tea,* 'whipping,' . . But she talked a lot about giving me *hickory-oil. Peachtree-oil,* though, was what she enjoyed giving me most. **1953** Randolph *Down in Holler* 251 **Ozarks,** *Hickory-limb oil.* . . A whipping. Country schoolteachers speak casually of administering "a dose of hickory-limb oil" to an unruly pupil. The term *peach-tree tea* is used with the same meaning. **c1970** *Halpert Coll.* **wKY, nwTN,** The schoolteacher feeds hickory tea to the bad boys—whips them.

4 attrib:

a Flexible, yielding. Cf **hickory bender**

1872 Schele de Vere *Americanisms* 58, The strong *hickory*. . . possessing great toughness, combined with unusual flexibility . . the name of the plant is constantly transferred to persons or objects notable for either. . . a *hickory armchair,* if not actually made of the wood, is a chair of more than usually yielding material. **1973** Allen *LAUM* 1.157 **IA** (as of c1950), "What do you call the ice that forms on a pond the first cold night?" . . hickory ice. [1 inf]

b Fig: flexible or lax in adherence to doctrine or principle. Cf **huckleberry 7**

1824 Singleton *Letters* 15 *(DA),* There are at present various species of this sect [i.e., Quakers]; the starch primitives in faith and practice; and the hickory, or half-blooded by intermarriages with the world's people. **1872** Schele de Vere *Americanisms* 58, A *Hickory Catholic* . . is free from bigotry and asceticism. *Ibid* 283, Secret military imprisonment of suspected sympathizers with the South, a measure silently deprecated but passively consented to by the *Hickory Unionists* of the Border States, a large and influential class of men. **1912** Thornton *Amer. Gloss.* 1.433, *Hickory Mormons.* Those who are half-hearted. **1931** *AmSp* 7.120, [Footnote:] A *Hickory Mormon* was a half-hearted Mormon, sometimes the child of Mormon parents, but not a thorough-going *Saint* himself. **1940** *Sat. Eve. Post* 30 Mar 37/4 **sePA,** He is "under the ban," and referred to by the neighbors as a "hickory Amish" because of some infraction not publicly mentioned, but most likely that of going to a movie.

5 also *hickory cane, ~ shirting, ~ stripe:* A heavy twilled cotton fabric, often with blue stripes, used to make work clothes—usu in combs *hickory shirt, ~ trousers* etc. [Etym uncert; cf quots 1872, c1960]

1831 *N.Y. Tribune* 31 Dec. *(DAE),* The ball was extracted [from his lungs] a few days ago, along with a piece of hickory shirting which was used for packing. **1851** Ryan *Personal Advent.* 2.8 **CA,** A little man, in a "hickory shirt," . . darted out from some dark corner. **1857** *Jrl. of Discourses* 4.205 **UT,** Get some good hickory cloth, or some buckskins, and let the sisters make dresses and garments that cannot be easily torn. **1872** Schele de Vere *Americanisms* 58, A kind of shirts made of heavy twilled cotton, generally with a narrow blue stripe, which are much worn by hard-working men, are called *hickory shirts,* from their strength. . . *Hickory* trousers owe their name to the same good quality. **1885** *Century Illustr. Mag.* 29.834/1 **wWA,** In their blue shirts and hickory trousers they [=Indians] had nothing of the look of the savage about them, save their long hair. **1892** Harte *Col. Starbottle* 113, He was warming his hands and placidly ignoring his gaunt arms in their thinly-clad "hickory" sleeves. **1923** *DN* 5.235 **swWI,** *Hickory shirt*. . . A work shirt made of crossbarred cotton cloth, which is called hickory shirtin'. **1925** Stuart *40 Yrs.* 1.66 **CA** (as of c1851), His pay for this would be one hickory cotton shirt which cost seventy-five cents. **1927** *AmSp* 2.357 **WV,** *Hickory shirt.* **1927** (1970) Sears *Catalogue* 166, Standard Hickory—Especially durable. Strong, heavyweight hickory shirting. . . Suitable, too, for men's . . overalls. . . Indigo blue with white stripes. **1942** Perry *Texas* 102, My great-uncle woke up running, hickory night shirt flying. **1944** Clark *Pills* 208 **Sth** (as of 1865–1915), Underneath jeans britches and hickory-striped shirts for most of the year were the red flannels. **1944** *PADS* 2.27 **cwOH, cwNC,** Hickory shirt. **1950** *PADS* 14.37 **SC,** *Hickory shirt.* **1950** *WELS* 1 Inf, **WI,** Hickory stripe [=material used to make overalls]. **c1960** *Wilson Coll.* **csKY,** *Hickory shirt*. . . A shirt made of heavy cotton material, maybe originally at Hickory, North Carolina. Sometimes called *hickory cane.*

6 in phr *good hickory:* A rapid gait. **chiefly S Midl**

1839 Willis *A l'abri* 135 **NY,** You're going a good hickory, Mister! **1903** *DN* 2.316 **seMO,** *Hickory*. . . Gait, a good hickory, a rapid gait. 'He made a good hickory for home;' that is, he made good time. **1906** *DN* 3.119 **sIN,** *Hickory*. . . Rapid, fast. "He run a good hickry." **1907** *DN* 3.231 **nwAR, seMO.** **1914** *DN* 4.108 **KS,** *Hickory*. . . Rapid gait; clip; as, riding a good hickory. **1915** *DN* 4.184 **swVA.** **1923** *DN* 5.210 **swMO,** *Hick'ry*. . . Speed. "He pulled out at a right good hick'ry." **1960** Criswell *Resp. to PADS 20* **Ozarks,** *Hickory*. . . Speed. Rather common some years ago and probably still used to some extent yet. "He come down that road at a right good hickory (hickry) when old man Horne set the dog on him." **c1970** *Halpert Coll.* 53 **wKY,** Came down the road a pretty good hickory = at high speed.

7 See quot. [Prob by analogy with *chestnut*]

1968 *DARE* (Qu. K39, . . *Names* . . *for horses according to their colors*) Inf **IA**45, Hickory.

8 See quot.

1931–33 *LANE Worksheets* **csCT,** *Hickory* . . nickname for cottage cheese.

9 in var phrr: See quots. *euphem*

1912 *DN* 3.590 **wIN,** *Son of a hickory*. . . A euphemism for *son of a bitch.* **1924** *DN* 5.260, Substitutes for "hell". . . "oh heck," "oh hicky," "oh hickory." *Ibid* 270, [Exclamations:] *Hickory:* by ——— (surp[rise] or vex[ation]). **1933** Williamson *Woods Colt* 111 **Ozarks,** There he jumps up an' runs like all hick'ry.

10 =sagebrush.

1931 *AmSp* 7.120 **eID,** Sagebrush is known locally as *hickory.*

hickory v Also *hickory limb, ~ whip* **[hickory n B2a]**

To whip soundly.

1854 Haliburton *Americans at Home* 122 **KY,** You won't hick'ry your wife much more, ole hoss! **1871** U.S. Congress *Congressional Globe* 42nd Cong 1st Sess 4 Apr pt 2 app 293/2 **nwSC,** They threatened me that if I ever came back they would take me out and hickory-whip me. **1890** *Voice* 21 Aug. *(DAE),* If he renewed the traffic in spirits they would hickory-whip him. **1934** Vines *Green Thicket* 119 **cnAL,** The merchant had tried to hickory-whip *Lattie.* **1954** *Harder Coll.* **cwTN,** I'll hickry-limb ye, iffen ye do 'at jist one more time.

hickory adj

Of weather: see quot.

1918 *DN* 5.16 **seMA,** *Hickory*. . . Rough, tempestuous. "It looks a little too hickory to haul the trap this morning."

hickory bender n [Cf **hickory n B4a, bender 1**]

=rubber ice. Cf **tiddly-bender**

1950 *WELS (Soft ice that will bend when you step on it but will not break)* 1 Inf, **WI,** Hickory bender. **1969** *DARE* (Qu. B35) Inf **TN**31, Hickory bender.

hickory cane n See **hickory n B5**

hickory chicken n Also *hickory jack* **esp S Midl** Cf **dryland fish 1, fried-chicken mushroom, hen of the woods**

An edible mushroom such as *Laetiporus sulphureus;* see quots.

1966–70 *DARE* (Qu. I37, *Small plants shaped like an umbrella that grow in woods and fields—which are safe to eat*) Inf **KY**17, Hickory chickens—type of edible mushroom, old-fashioned; **OH**95, Hickory ['hɪkri] jack—a mushroom—grows on bark of hickory tree; **VA**42, Hickory chicken—morel; (Qu. S19, *Mushrooms that grow out like brackets from the sides of trees*) Infs **OH**33, 38, Hickory jacks; **MS**38, Hickory chicken. **1983** *MJLF* 9.43 **ceKY,** Hickory chicken . . a mushroom.

hickory devil See **hickory horned devil**

hickory elm n

A **rock elm** (here: *Ulmus thomasii*).

1884 Sargent *Forests of N. Amer.* 123, *Ulmus racemosa*. . . Hickory Elm. **1927** Keeler *Our Native Trees* 244, It [=*Ulmus thomasii*] is sometimes called the Hickory Elm. **1950** Peattie *Nat. Hist. Trees* 246, *Cork Elm—Ulmus Thomasii* . . —Other Names: Rock, Hickory, Corkbark, or Cliff Elm. **1960** Vines *Trees SW* 214, It [=rock elm] is also known under the names of Cork Elm, . . Hickory Elm . . Wahoo Elm. **1969** *DARE* (Qu. T11 . . *Different kinds of elm trees*) Inf **IN**67, Hickory elm.

hickory frail n See **hickory n B2a**

hickory grubber n Cf **hazel splitter 1**

A razorback hog.

1919 *DN* 5.34 **KY,** *Hick'ry grubber*. . . Slang for a "razor back" hog. Knott Co.

hickoryhead n Cf **hardhead 5a**

=ruddy duck.

1888 Trumbull *Names of Birds* 112, *Erismatura rubida*. . . At Manasquan, N.J., Hickory-Head. **1917** (1923) *Birds Amer.* 1.152, *Ruddy Duck—Erismatura jamaicensis* . . Other Names.—Dumpling Duck; . . Hickoryhead. **1944** Hausman *Amer. Birds* 517, Hickory-head . . Ruddy Duck.

hickory horned devil n Also *hickory (horn) devil, horned hickory devil* [See quots 1938, 1980]

The larva of the **royal walnut moth.**

1818 Kirby-Spence *Intro. Entomology* 2.238, This caterpillar is called in Virginia the hickory-horned devil. **1891** *Century Dict.* 6813, *Walnut-moth...* Any moth whose larva feeds on walnut, as the regal walnut-moth, *Citheronia regalis,* whose larva is known as the *hickory horned devil.* **1909** *Country Life* 16.652/3, The caterpillars emerged on the 27th of July, and bore the characteristic markings which are responsible for their common name "Hickory Horn-devil." **1912** *Country Life* 15 Jun 31, [Photo caption:] Regalis caterpillar, commonly called the horned hickory devil. **1938** Brimley *Insects NC* 266, The larva is known as the "hickory devil" or "simmon bull" and feeds on cotton, hickory, sweet gum, walnut, pecan, persimmon, sourwood, Paulownia. **1968** *DARE* (Qu. R27, .. *Kinds of caterpillars or similar worms*) Inf **IN**38, Hickory horned devil. **1980** Milne-Milne *Audubon Field Guide Insects* 773, This moth's [=*Citheronia regalis*] caterpillar is called the "Hickory Horned Devil" because of its black-tipped orange horns.

hickory jack n

1 See **hickory chicken.**

2 See **hickory shad.**

hickory limb n See **hickory** n **B2a**

hickory limb v phr See **hickory** v

hickory limb oil See **hickory** n **B3**

hickory nut n

1 also *hick(er)-nut tree, hickory-nut ~:* =**hickory** n **B1.**

1950 *WELS (Nut-bearing trees in your neighborhood)* 12 Infs, **WI,** Hickory nut; 1 Inf, Wild hickory nut. **c1960** *Wilson Coll.* **csKY,** Hickory nut... The nut or the tree. **1965-70** *DARE* (Qu. T16) 22 Infs, **scattered,** Hickory-nut tree; **TX**106, **VA**57, Hick-nut tree. **1984** Burns *Cold Sassy* 14 **neGA** (as of 1906), I was just fixing to quit weeding and rest a spell under the big hickernut tree.

2 A freshwater mussel *(Obovaria olivaria).*

1982 U.S. Fish & Wildlife Serv. *Fresh-Water Mussels* 1, *Hickorynut .. Obovaria olivaria ..* Shell yellow or brown with green or brown rays; moderately to very heavy.

3 A fossil of the genus *Pentremites.*

1939 FWP *Guide KY* 25, Fossils of the decorative Pentremites, the so-called fossil "hickory nut," are found in abundance in some of the limestones in the Pennyrile.

hickory-nut tree See **hickory nut 1**

hickory oak n

=**canyon oak 1.**

1897 Sudworth *Arborescent Flora* 164, *Quercus chrysolepis...* Hickory Oak (Kern Co., Cal.) **1908** Britton *N. Amer. Trees* 311, It [=*Quercus chrysolepis*] is also called California live oak, Canyon live oak, .. Hickory oak. **1923** in 1925 Jepson *Manual Plants CA* 275, Hickory Oak... furnishes the most valuable wood amongst our species, being strong, tough and close-grained.

hickory oil See **hickory** n **B3**

hickory pine n

1 =**bristlecone pine. esp CA**

1897 Sudworth *Arborescent Flora* 18, *Pinus aristata...* Common Names. Hickory Pine (Cal. lit.) **1923** in 1925 Jepson *Manual Plants CA* 47, Hickory Pine. Trees 25 to 55 feet high; .. young bark milky white. **1948** *Pacific Discovery* Nov-Dec 18/1, They are the limber pine .. ; the hickory pine *(P. aristata)* of the high desert ranges north of the Mohave Desert. **1960** Vines *Trees SW* 20, The genus name *Pinus* is the classical Latin name, and the species name, *aristata,* refers to the bristles on the cones. Other vernacular names are Foxtail Pine and Hickory Pine. **1979** Little *Checklist U.S. Trees* 188, *Bristlecone pine... Other common names ..* hickory pine. *Ibid* 196, *Table Mountain pine... Other common names*—hickory pine.

2 =**Table Mountain pine.**

1884 Sargent *Forests of N. Amer.* 199, *Pinus pungens...* Table-mountain Pine. Hickory Pine. **1901** Lounsberry *S. Wild Flowers* 3, Hickory Pine... Another of the tree's points of beauty is its cones which... project the sharpest and stoutest spines of the South Atlantic species. **1979** [see **1** above].

hickory poplar n **chiefly C and Mid Atl**

=**tulip tree.**

1893 *Jrl. Amer. Folkl.* 6.136 **WV,** *Liriodendron tulipifera,* white, yellow, or hickory poplar. **1897** Sudworth *Arborescent Flora* 198, *Liriodendron tulipifera ..* Tulip-tree... *Common Names...* Hickory Poplar (Va., N. C., W. Va.) **1910** Graves *Flowering Plants* 194 **CT,** *Liriodendron Tulipifera ..* Hickory Poplar. **1960** Vines *Trees SW* 280, *Tulip-tree—Liriodendron tulipifera...* Other vernacular names in use are Yellow-poplar, .. and Hickory-poplar. **1968** *DARE* (Qu. T12, *The kind of poplar tree that has sticky, sweet-smelling buds*) Infs **MD**29, **PA**132, Hickory poplar; (Qu. T13, .. *Other names .. for .. poplar*) Inf **VA**24, Hickory poplar; (Qu. T16) Inf **MD**26, Hickory poplar, wood near heart is yellow, white outside.

hickory quaker n

=**canvasback duck.**

1923 U.S. Dept. Ag. *Misc. Circular* 13.18, *Canvasback (Aristonetta valisineria)... In local use...* hickory-quaker (Md.)

hickory shad n Also *hickory jack, ~ shit, hicks, hick shad* [Etym uncert, but see quot 1887] **chiefly Sth, S Midl**

A **herring** n[1] **1:** especially *Alosa mediocris* but also **gizzard shad 1, 2.** For other names of *A. mediocris* see **fall herring, forerunner 1, freshwater tailor, herring** n[1] **1, mattowacca, shad, shad herring, shadine, tailor herring, tailor shad**

a1816 (1848) Hawkins *Sketch* 53 **GA** (as of c1799), The fish taken here are, the hickory shad, rock, trout, perch. **1884** Goode *Fisheries U.S.* 1.608, The name "Hickory" Shad... is used in the Chesapeake and in the Albemarle regions, and on the Ogeechee, Savannah, and Altamaha Rivers, where it is familiarly called "Hicks." **1887** Goode *Amer. Fishes* 405, The derivation of the name "Hickory" Shad cannot easily be traced. It may be that the word "Hickory" is used in a derogatory sense, but a more reasonable explanation is that it refers to the striped markings on the fish, which resemble those upon the coarse cotton fabric known in the South as "Hickory," and frequently used by the fishermen. **1896** U.S. Natl. Museum *Bulletin* 47.416, *Dorosoma cepedianum ..* Gizzard Shad; Hickory Shad. *Ibid* 425, *Pomolobus mediocris ..* Hickory Shad. **1899** (1912) Green *VA Folk-Speech* 223, *Hickory-shad ..* Same as *gizzard-shad.* **1903** NY State Museum & Sci. Serv. *Bulletin* 60.198, The name hickory shad is applied to this species [=*Pomolobus Mediocris*] from the Chesapeake bay region southward, and in some Georgia rivers this is abbreviated to hicks. **1911** U.S. Bur. Census *Fisheries 1908* 312, It is called 'hickory shad' and 'hicks,' particularly in the South. **1933** LA Dept. of Conserv. *Fishes* 215, The Gizzard Shad [*Dorosoma cepedianum*] has been given many names in Louisiana, chief among them being Hickory Shad (a name which belongs to another fish). **1947** Dalrymple *Panfish* 341, Then suddenly a big buck Shad of four or five pounds, or a small Alewife or Hickory Shad, will break away, dart out and smack the lure. **1954** *Harder Coll.* **cwTN,** *Hickory shad ..* a type of non-edible fish. **1960** Criswell *Resp. to PADS 20* **Ozarks,** Non-edible fish: carp, gar, hog sucker, most smaller regular suckers (too many bones), hickory shad. **1965-70** *DARE* (Qu. P3, .. *Freshwater fish that are not good to eat*) Infs **GA**89, **IL**69, 77, 84, 132, **IN**83, **MS**21, **MO**38, 24, **SC**3, Hickory shad(s); **FL**1, Hick shad; **KY**72, Hickory shit [laughter]—same as hickory shad; (Qu. P1, .. *Freshwater fish .. that are good to eat*) Inf **MS**21, Hickory shad; (Qu. P2, .. *Kinds of saltwater fish .. good to eat*) Inf **NC**15, Hickory shad; (Qu. P7, .. *Small fish used as bait*) Inf **OK**25, Hickory [hɪkrɪ] shad; (Qu. P14, .. *What do the fishermen go out after?*) Inf **SC**43, Hickory shad. **1984** *DARE* File **Chesapeake Bay** [Watermen's vocab], Hickory shad .. hickory jack.

hickory shirt(ing) n See **hickory** n **B5**

hickory shit See **hickory shad**

hickory stick n

1 See **hickory** n **B2a, c.**

2 A pole bean.

1969 *DARE* (Qu. I20, .. *Kinds of beans .. grown around here*) Inf **KY**28, Hickory sticks, a pole bean.

hickory stripe See **hickory** n **B5**

hickory switch See **hickory** n **B2a**

hickory tea See **hickory** n **B3**

hickory towel See **hickory** n **B2a**

hickory trousers See **hickory** n **B5**

hickory whetstone n

Appar a type of whetstone that is believed to be made of petrified hickory wood.

1954 *Harder Coll.* **cwTN,** *Whetstone...* A stone used to sharpen tools; distinguished from *whetrock ..* by being made from petrified hickory wood; hence sometimes called hickory whetstone. "Put a hickory log in water for years and it turns to a whetstone."

hickory whip See **hickory** v

hickory withe See **hickory** n **B2a**

hickry See **hickory** n

hicks See **hickory shad**

hick shad See **hickory shad**

hickum skivver See **hickey** n^1 **2**

hickup See **hiccup**

hickwall n [Engl dial; cf *EDD*]

=flicker n^2 **1.**

1956 MA Audubon Soc. *Bulletin* 40.82, Hickwall (Conn. A name transferred from the Green Woodpecker, the most similar European species; in British folk use, it traces back to Anglo-Saxon terms referring to the "laughing" notes of the bird.)

hicky n See **hickey** n^2

hicky adj^1 Also *hickey, hickish* [*hick* an unsophisticated or countrified person]

Rustic, countrified.

1942 Berrey–Van den Bark *Amer. Slang* 147.6, Boorish; rustic . . *hickish, hicky.* **1966** *DARE* FW Addit **OK,** *Hicky*—Apparently from "hick"; rustic, countrified—the *hicky* way of saying it. **1967–69** *DARE* (Qu. HH1, . . *A rustic or countrified person*) Inf **MA**73, Old, hickish; **WI**76, Hickish. **1968** Kellner *Aunt Serena* 80 **cIN** (as of c1920), His contemptuous look passed from my gingham pinafore to my bare feet. "Hickiest place I ever been in my life." **1981** *Courier-Jrl.* (Louisville KY) 22 Mar mag sec 43/1, Everything I want is right here on this hill. Some people hear us talk about life here and think of it as dull, hicky, limited, but it isn't. It's always challenging. **1986** *NYT Mag.* 29 June 16/2 **OK,** He had made it out of Muldrow, Okla., . . out of Billy Phillips's station where he pumped gas after school and on weekends, out of a life that was, he complained, "just plain hickey." **1986** Chapman *New Dict. Amer. Slang* 206, This man is from some hicky farm in Shit Creek, Georgia—Eldridge Cleaver.

hicky adj^2 Cf **hickey** n^1 **4**

1969 *DARE* (Qu. LL2, . . *Too small to be worth much: "I don't want that little ______ potato."*) Inf **GA**72, Hicky.

hicky horse See **hickey** n^1 **3**

hicky-my-funker n Also *ben-hicky-my-funker*

1944 *PADS* 2.17 **sAppalachians,** Ben-hicky-my-funker. . . A term of disparagement. "He's a pyore ben-hicky-my-funker." Also hicky-my-funker.

hi cock the oriole n [Folk-etym for *high cockalorum;* cf *OED cockalorum* sb. 3; cf Intro "Language Changes" I.6, 13] Cf **Johnny-on-the-pony**

A children's game; see quot.

1981 *DARE* File **csWI** (as of c1940–1950), *Hi cock the oriole*—A game in which the first player of one team bends at the waist and holds on to a tree trunk or pole. A second player from that team then grabs the first player around the waist, and each additional player grabs the waist of the one in front to form a human chain. When the entire first team is so situated, players of the second team, one at a time, run and leap on the backs of the first team attempting to cause the first team to founder.

hictamus n Cf *DS* BB28

1950 *WELS (Joking or fantastic names for imaginary diseases)* 1 Inf, **WI,** Hictamus.

hiddened See **hide** v

hidden-flower n

=forget-me-not 1f.

1957 *Plateau* 30.33 **AZ,** *Cryptanthas,* sometimes known as hidden-flower, were associated with the Cacti.

hide n^1 See **hide-and-seek A**

hide n^2

1 also *bones and hide, dry-hide, hide and hair:* A thin or poor-looking horse or cow. Cf **dry hides on the bone**

1954 *Harder Coll.* **cwTN,** *Dry-hide. . .* A bony or poor-looking horse or mule. "An old dry hide." **1966–69** *DARE* (Qu. K15, *A thin, bony, or poor-looking cow*) Inf **CA**124, Hides; **IL**93, **IN**44, Old hide(s); **FL**7, Bones and hide; **TX**11, Hide 'n hair; (Qu. K44, *A bony or poor-looking horse*) Inf **IN**44, An old dry-hide.

2 See quots. [*EDD hide* sb.^{1} 4 *"Obs."; SND hide* n.^{2} 2]

1967 *DARE* (Qu. HH34, . . *Words . . for a woman, not necessarily uncomplimentary*) Inf **TX**37, Hide. **1971** *Today Show Letters* **cAR** (as of 1930), Hide—A girl in a beer joint frequented by servicemen. **1972** Shafer *Dict. Prison Slang* **TX,** *Hide*—a girl (1950s). **1984** Weaver *TX Crude* 114, *A hide.* A woman, usually a very old one. A crone. A hag.

3 in phr *mean as one's hide would hold one* and var: Extremely mean. [Cf *hidebound* miserly; *W3 "obs"*]

1968–69 *DARE* (Qu. HH22b, . . *A very mean person, . . "He's meaner than ______."*) Inf **GA**19, His hide would hold him; **GA**77, He's as mean as his hide will hold him—old-fashioned.

4 in phr *get under one's hide:* To irritate, annoy, frighten someone. [Var of *get under one's skin*]

1966–69 *DARE* (Qu. GG24, . . *To frighten: "Now don't let those fellows ______ you."*) Inf **NY**92, Get under your hide; (Qu. II29b, . . *The unpleasant effect . . [a] person has on you: "He just ______."*) Infs **CA**154, **KS**15, **SD**5, Gets under my hide.

5 in phrr *no hide off one's back, nothing off of one's hide:* See quots. [Cf *no skin off one's nose*]

1965–70 *DARE* (Qu. GG21a, *If you don't care what a person does, you might tell him, "You can go ahead and do it ______."*) Inf **OK**48, Nothing off of my hide; (Qu. KK26, *Something that makes no difference at all to you: "He can think what he likes, it ______ me."*) Inf **IL**116, Is no hide off my back.

6 in phrr *hide won't hold shucks* (or *hay, shavings*): Used as a threat; see quots.

1923 *DN* 5.238 **swWI,** Lick him so his hide won't hold shavings, won't hold hay. **c1960** *Wilson Coll.* **csKY,** *Hide won't hold shucks*—threat to children.

7a in phrr *let the tail go with the hide, let the hide go with the tallow* and varr: See quots.

1916 *DN* 4.325 **KS, NE,** *Let the tail go with the hide. . .* To ignore little matters in the presence of greater; to neglect details when larger matters are lost. Also *let the hide go with the tallow.* "After he lost his case, he paid little attention to excessive costs, as he just let the tail go with the hide." "If he beats me out of the land, he can have the crop too; I'll let the hide go with the tallow." **1923** *DN* 5.240 **swWI,** *Tail goes with the hide.* In the days before fixed prices, a clothing merchant, asked to include a pair of suspenders with a suit of clothes just purchased, hesitated at first, and then acquiesced, saying, "Oh well, take 'em; tail goes with the hide." The figure is from selling a slaughtered beef. **1927** *AmSp* 2.359 **WV,** *Let the tail go with the hide . .* to dispose of the details with the larger questions. "It doesn't matter who draws up the deed; let the tail go with the hide." **1975** Gould *ME Lingo* 285, *Tail goes with the hide. . .* The expression comes from the slaughter house, where the hide was the butcher's fee. In short, it doesn't matter much one way or the other. The expression is used today in almost any situation where gain and profit are dubious, and the consequences not likely to make or break.

b See quot.

1916 *DN* 4.342 **KS,** *Tail go with the hide.* To risk everything.

hide v

Std sense, var forms. Past pple and ppl adj: usu *hidden;* often *hid;* rarely *hide, hiddened*

1893 *DN* 1.277 **wCT,** *Hide*—[past pple is] hid. **1903** *DN* 2.293 **Cape Cod MA** (as of a1857), The same form for the past and past participle. . . hide—hid. **1940** Faulkner *Hamlet* 400 **MS,** There was somebody hid in that ditch, he thought. **1950** *WELS (To hide something away for future use: "He's got it ______ somewhere.")* 16 Infs, **WI,** Hidden (away); 9 Infs, Hid (away). **1957** Battaglia *Resp. to PADS 20* **eMD,** He's got it hid somewhere. **1960** Criswell *Resp. to PADS 20* **Ozarks,** Hid, hidden away. **1965–70** *DARE* (Qu. Y47, . . *"I know he's got it ______ somewhere."*) 347 Infs, **widespread,** Hidden (away, around) [Of all Infs responding to the question, 32% were coll educ; of those giving responses with *hidden,* 42% were coll educ]; 243 Infs, **widespread,** Hid (away) [and var phrr: see *DS*] [Of all Infs responding to the question, 24% were gs educ, 29% comm type 5; of those giving responses with *hid,* 37% were gs educ, 39% comm type 5]; **SC**26, Hide; (Qu. MM11, . . *Trying to find something . . "I must have left it ______."*) Infs **IN**80, **VA**50, Hid; (Qu. Y48) Infs **KY**79, **MS**16, Hid. **1967–69** *DARE* Tape **CA**155, They found a lot of silver lamps and things that were hid underneath the floor; **IN**17, The Hoosier schoolmaster's supposed to have hid when they were going to tar and feather him; **LA**11, They hide their eyes while the switch is being hiddened.

hide-and-coop n Also rarely *hide-and-coot* [Cf *EDD hide* v.[2] II. 1. (8)] **chiefly NEast** Cf **coop** n[3]

=hide-and-seek A.

1850 Judd *Richard Edney* 128 **ME,** As if religion were a game of hide and coop. **1891** (1967) Freeman *New Engl. Nun* 83 **seMA,** Come out-doors an' play hide an' coot wis me, Polly. **1904** *DN* 2.418 **nwAR, eIA, seNH,** *Hide and Coop.* **1906** Johnson *Highways Missip. Valley* 99 **TN** (as of 1833) [Black], "I was about ten years ole, I reckon," said Uncle Henry, "and I was out playin' hide and coop wid a parcel er white boys." **1907** *DN* 3.190 **seNH,** *Hide and coop. . .* Hide and seek. The latter is a book expression. Coop is the warning cry of the player who is "it." **1909** *N&Q* 120.371/1 **NY,** *Hide-and-coop.* This variant of the hiding game was familiar to American children long before 1850. . . In "hide-and-coop" each called from his secret place a faint, long-drawn "c-o-o-p," in a way to mislead the seeker as much as possible. **1910** *DN* 3.443 **cwNY,** *Hide and coop.* **1917** *DN* 4.394 **neOH,** "Hide and seek" . . was always hide and coop ['haɪdn 'kup]. **1957** *Sat. Eve. Post Letters* **swMI,** We played 'hide and coop.' My husband lived about seven miles from me and he called it 'hide and seek.' **1966–69** *DARE* (Qu. EE13a, *Games in which every player hides except one, and that one must try to find the others*) Inf **ME**5, Hide-and-coop—hiders hollered 'coop' to seeker too—player hollered 'coop' when he found a hider and both ran for starting place; **MA**5, Hide-and-coop; **MA**42, Hide-and-coop—when players were hidden, they would holler 'coo', then player who was "it" would go to find them. **1978** *DARE* File **cMA** (as of c1918), As a child I remember being amused at older people saying ['haɪdn̩ˌkup].

hide-and-go-peep, hide-and-go(-to)-seek See **hide-and-seek**

hide-and-go-whoop See **hide-and-whoop**

hide and hair n See **hide** n[2] **1**

hide and hair adv phr [Cf *hide (n)or hair; EDD hide and hair* "the whole" (at *hide* sb.[1] 2)] Cf *hair and hide* (at **hair** n **C3**), **head** n **D1, hide and tallow**

See quots.

1934 (1940) Weseen *Dict. Amer. Slang* 349, *Hide and hair*—Entirely; completely. **1968** *DARE* (Qu. Y48, *To look in every possible place for something you've mislaid . . "I've ______."*) Inf **PA**148, Hunted hide and hair.

hide-and-hoop, hide-and-hoot See **hide-and-whoop**

hide-and-hunt See **hide-and-seek A**

hide-and-look n

Perh **=hide-and-seek A.**

1933 *Hanley Disks* **seMA,** *Hide-and-look*—A children's game. "Yes, hide and look. . . You don't hide and never expect to find him, you know."

hide-and-seek n Also freq *hide-and-go-seek;* for other varr see below

A Std sense (the children's hiding game), var forms. Usu *hide-and-seek;* also **widespread** *hide(-and)-go-seek;* **Sth, S Midl** *hiding(-seek);* **PA** *hidey(-go-seek);* also *hide, hide-and-go-peep, hide(-and-go-to)-seek, hide-and-hunt*

1724 in 1900 Essex Inst. *Coll.* 36.333 **ceMA,** At night was at Madm Brownes Playing hide & Goe Seek. **1821** Cooper *Spy* 2.280 **cNY,** Since when . . we have been playing hide-and-go-peep with the ships. **1908** *DN* 3.320 **eAL, wGA,** *Hidin(g). . .* Hide-and-seek. "Le's play hiding." **1925** Fitzgerald *Gatsby* 98, At first I thought it was another party, a wild rout that had resolved itself into "hide-and-go-seek." **1950** *WELS* 32 Infs, **WI,** Hide-and-seek; 20 Infs, **WI,** Hide-and-go-seek. **1952** Brown *NC Folkl.* 1.37, *Hide and seek. . .* 'Hide and Hunt.' . . Reported from Stanly county [csNC]. **1965–70** *DARE* (Qu. EE13a, *Games in which every player hides except one, and that one must try to find the others*) 627 Infs, **widespread,** Hide-and-seek; 339 Infs, **widespread,** Hide(-and)-go-seek; **AR**52, **FL**26, **GA**68, 86, **LA**8, **TX**13, Hiding(-seek); **PA**16, 36, **TX**38, Hide(-and-go-to)-seek; **PA**16, 134, 162, Hidey(-go-seek); **GA**58, Hide. **1970** *DARE* Tape **KY**80, We used to play hidin' a lot. . . Somebody would hide their eyes and then the others would go hide, and [he would] try to find 'em, and then if you could beat him back to the base, you'd be home free, and he couldn't catch you, but if he caught you, and then you'd have to be "it."

B Senses. [Transf from std sense above]

1 also *hide-go-seek:* Hide-the-thimble or a similar game.

1899 Champlin–Bostwick *Young Folks' Games* 442/2, Another game sometimes called Hide and Seek, is called in this book *Hide the Handkerchief.* [*Ibid* 410/1, *Hide the Handkerchief*. . often called "Hide the Thimble."] **1965–70** *DARE* (Qu. EE3, *Games in which you hide an object and then look for it*) 57 Infs, **scattered,** Hide-and-seek; 15 Infs, **scattered,** Hide(-and)-go-seek. **1970** *AmSp* 45.206, As late as the middle of the nineteenth century . . the name *hide-and-seek* was used for a game in which a hidden object was sought by the players. In the third and fourth quarters of the century it also became applied to the now familiar game in which players hide from a seeker or a team of seekers.

2 also *hide-seek-and-go:* The game **run sheep run.**

1965–70 *DARE* (Qu. EE12, *Games in which one captain hides his team and the other team tries to find it*) 24 Infs, **scattered,** Hide-and-seek; 10 Infs, **scattered,** Hide-and-go-seek; **VA**1, Hide-seek-and-go.

3 Any of var other children's games: see quots.

1950 *WELS Suppl.* **WI,** *Hide-and-seek*—Played somewhat like "I'll draw the frying pan." Someone would say, "Draw a sammy [=semi] circle and dot it with a dot." Then someone would draw a complete circle. If "it" could guess who had drawn the circle, then that person would be "it." **1965–70** *DARE* (Qu. EE1, . . *Games . . children play . . in which they form a ring, and either sing or recite a rhyme*) Inf **TX**26, Hide-and-go-seek; (Qu. EE2, *Games that have one extra player—when a signal is given, the players change places, and the extra one tries to get a place*) Inf **FL**22, Hide-and-seek; (Qu. EE4, *Games in which one player's eyes are bandaged and he has to catch the others and guess who they are*) Infs **GA**23, **IL**30, **NJ**19, **OK**55, 58, **OR**3, **PA**74, 239, Hide-and-seek.

hide-and-spy n

1 **=hide-and-seek A.** [Perh var of **hy spy** n]

1965–70 *DARE* (Qu. EE13a, *Games in which every player hides except one, and that one must try to find the others*) Infs **DC**12, **IL**30, **MD**15, 20, **MS**60, **NY**59, **WA**22, Hide-and-spy.

2 The game hide-the-thimble. Cf **hide-and-seek B1, hy spy n 2**

1968 *DARE* (Qu. EE3, *Games in which you hide an object and then look for it*) Inf **MD**15, Hide-and-spy.

hide and tallow n Also *hide, hoofs, and taller* [Orig in ref to all usable parts of an animal]

Everything.

1927 *AmSp* 3.136 **ME,** A badly cheated one [=person] had lost "hide, hoofs and taller." **1943** McAtee *Dial. Grant Co. IN Suppl. 2* 9 (as of 1890s), *Hide and tallow. . .* All; "He took the whole business, hide and tallow." **c1960** *Wilson Coll.* **csKY,** *Hide and tallow. . .* A humorous expression for everything, all.

hide-and-whoop n Also *hide-and-go-whoop, hide-and-hoop, hide-and-hoot, hidey-(w)hoop* [Cf *EDD* hide v.[2] II. 1. (9)] Cf **whoop, whoop-and-hide**

=hide-and-seek A.

1890 Howells *Boy's Town* 84 **swOH,** With the races came the other plays which involved running, like hide-and-go-whoop. **1892** *DN* 1.236 **NEng,** In New England the game . . is variously called *I spy, hi spy, hi spry* (Cape Cod), *hide and (go) seek, hide and whoop.* **1918** Lincoln *Shavings* 49 **eMA,** Four of 'em . . had been playin' hide and hoot amongst my paint pots. **1933** *Hanley Disks* **seMA,** *Hide and hoop* ['haɪd ən 'hup]—Hide and seek. "They'll hide and then you have to go and find them and then they holler." **1940** *McDavid Coll.* **GA,** ['haˑ·ɨdn,hʉˑ·p] for hide-n-seek. **1942** Hurston *Dust Tracks* 28 **ceFL** [Black], On moonlight nights . . the village children . . would be playing hide and whoop, chick-mah-chick, hide and seek, and other boisterous games in our yard. **1957** *Sat. Eve. Post Letters* **swIN,** *Hidey-hoop.* In the after years I learned the game was Hide-and-go-seek. I still prefer Hidey-hoop. **c1960** *Wilson Coll.* **csKY,** Hide-and-Whoop. . . Also Hidey Whoop. **1966–70** *DARE* (Qu. EE13a, *Games in which every player hides except one, and that one must try to find the others*) **FL**2, Hide-and-hoop; **MA**100, Hide-and-whoop.

hideaway n Also *hideout*

A small place to hide things; transf, a pocket.

1966–70 *DARE* (Qu. D7, *A small space anywhere in a house where you can hide things or get them out of the way*) Infs **MI**111, **NJ**17, **NY**95, 210, **NC**5, **PA**235, **SC**22, Hideaway; **VA**69, Hideout ['hadaʊt]; (Qu. D8, *The small room next to the kitchen . . where dishes and sometimes foods are kept*) Inf **CA**111, Hideaway. **1970** Major *Dict. Afro-Amer. Slang* 65, *Hideaways:* (1940's) one's pockets.

hide-behind n

1 also *high-behind, nigh-behind:* An imaginary creature or ghost; see quots.

1918 *DN* 5.25 **NW,** *High-behind, splinter cat. . .* Fabulous creatures, capable of amazing feats, that infest the sage brush when the cow-punchers hump about their fires. **1939** Tryon *Fearsome Critters* 23 [Logger talk], *The Hidebehind*—A highly dangerous animal, but, owing to its intense aversion to the odor of alcohol, never known to attack an inebriate. . . standing about six feet and walking erect. . . The short, well-muscled forelegs are equipped with grizzly-like claws. Its food is chiefly intestines. Leaping from its hiding-place with a demoniacal laugh, it swiftly disembowels its victim with one swipe. . . The beast can go seven years without eating. **1951** Randolph *We Always Lie* 47 **Ozarks,** The famous high-behind, a lizard as big as a bull. . . lies in wait for human beings on the trails at night. . . Some people call it the "hide-behind," because it always hides behind some object. **1953** Randolph *Down in Holler* 252 **Ozarks,** *High-behind. . .* A mythical lizard as big as a bull, a bloodthirsty enemy to all mankind. The names *nigh-behind* and *hide-behind* refer to the same legendary beast. **1983** Glimm *Flatlanders* 171 **cnPA,** Now, you know about the hide-behind because the Seneca Indians were just terrified of them. The Indians always walked single file through the woods because their paths were so narrow. Nobody wanted to be the last one in line because of the hide-behind. . . He'd hear a twig break, a bush rustle, and he would whirl around. Just then the hide-behind would dart behind a rock or a tree. . . The hide-behind is so fast that no one can ever turn his head fast enough to see it.

2 In logging: see quot.

1958 McCulloch *Woods Words* 85 **Pacific NW,** *Hidebehind*—Anything used as a shelter during blasting operations.

hide crop n

The hides taken from cattle that have died in one season.

1929 Dobie *Vaquero* 24 **swTX,** The cow people of the lower country came to speak of the "skinning season" as naturally as they spoke of the "branding season." A settler short on a corn crop could count on a "hide crop." The cow outfits of summer became the "skinning outfits" of winter. In the disastrous "die-up" of 1872–1873, for instance, Jim Miller's outfit on the Nueces skinned 4000 dead cattle.

hide-go-seek See **hide-and-seek A, B1**

hideho See **hidey-hole**

hide, hoofs, and taller See **hide and tallow**

hide-nasty n Also *hide-nesty* **cVA** Cf **glory hole 1,** *DS* D7

1942 *Hench Coll.* **cVA,** *Hide-nasty*—A closet or other place, often a loft, where all sorts of things are stored away. **1943** *Ibid,* A glory-hole (place to hide things like a closet) is called a hide-nasty or hide-nesty. **1950** *Ibid,* A place in a house to hide things in (like a closet) is called by some people a hide-nasty.

hide nor tallow n Also *hide nor light* [Cf *hide nor hair*] Cf **hide and tallow**

1967–68 *DARE* (Qu. LL29, *Any sign or trace: "He left last week, and nobody's seen ——— of him since."*) Inf **AR**47, Hide nor tallow ['tælɚ]; [**LA**35, Hide or low;] **NJ**35, Hide nor light.

hideondo See **hediondilla**

hideout n

1 A children's game; see quot.

1968 *DARE* (Qu. EE3, *Games in which you hide an object and then look for it*) Inf **GA**23, Hide-out.

2 in combs *Nellie's hideout, Roosevelt ~:* An outdoor toilet, outhouse. Cf **F.D.R., Roosevelt**

1967–68 *DARE* (Qu. M21b, *Joking names for an outside toilet building*) Inf **UT**7, Roosevelt hideout; **WY**4, Nellie's hideout; White House; goin' to see the President's [=Roosevelt's] wife.

3 See **hideaway.**

hide-raiser n

1972 *Atlanta Letters* 21 **nwGA,** When I use the term "hide raiser", I mean something that scares me. Have you ever had "goose bumps" when you're afraid?—This means the same thing

hide-seek See **hide-and-seek A**

hide-seek-and-go See **hide-and-seek B2**

hides, to the adv phr

To the bone; completely.

1969 *DARE* (Qu. LL26b, . . *'Entirely' . . "He's Irish ———."*) Inf **KY**36, To the hides [laughter].

hide the button See **button B2c**

hide the switch See **switch** n

hide won't hold hay (or shavings, shucks) See **hide** n^2 **6**

hidey(-go-seek) See **hide-and-seek A**

hidey-hole n Also *hideho, hidey-place, hiding-hole* Also sp *hidie-hole* [Cf *SND hidie-hole* (at *hidie* adj., n. I. 1); *EDD hidy-hole* (at *hidy* adj.)]

A hiding place, retreat or refuge; a small place to put or hide things away.

1851 (1852) Stowe *Uncle Tom's Cabin* 1.298 **swOH,** The more drawers and closets there were, the more hiding-holes could Dinah make. **1939** (1962) Thompson *Body & Britches* 197 **NY,** At one time, the entire jaw of a whale used to stand on the principal street . . ; it is said that a favorite way for a naughty child to escape its mother's vengeance was to slip into this hidie-hole. **1947** Guthrie *Big Sky* 195 **West,** Summers could go back in his mind and see the gentler country in Missouri State . . rich in soil turned and the corn rising higher than a boy's head, making a hidey-hole for him. **1950** *WELS (Small space . . where you can hide things or get them out of the way)* 1 Inf, **WI,** Hidey-hole. **1967–68** *DARE* (Qu. C33, . . *Joking names . . for an out-of-the-way place, or a very unimportant place*) Inf **OH**87, Hidey-hole [FW: Inf queries]; (Qu. D7) Inf **GA**46, Hidey-hole [FW: laughter]; **OH**61, Hidey-hole [FW: used by Inf in conv]; **TN**4, Hidey-place; (QR, near Qu. EE13a) Inf **GA**58, *Hidey-hole*—A small place you can fit yourself into. **1967–70** *DARE* FW Addit **csPA,** *Hidey-hole*—any place to hide something; **IL**118, *Hidey-hole*—a sanctuary. **1969** *AmSp* 44.17 **Pacific NW** [Painter jargon], *Hideho. . .* A place to hide from the boss; a place to loaf, sleep, play cards, or gamble while on the job. **1977** Miles *Ozark Dict.* 4, *Hidey-hole*—A storm cellar. "Quick, Chlorine, git to the Hidey-hole. . . it's a-blowin' turrible." **1986** Chapman *New Dict. Amer. Slang* 206, *Hidey hole. . .* "Conceal themselves in one of the hidey hole apartments of their proliferating step-parents"—Village Voice. **1988** *WI State Jrl.* (Madison) 8 Feb sec 3 1/1, I had a vague idea of constructing another hidey-hole for the cats. A cave, sort of, in the hay and chaff laying [sic] all over the mow.

hidey-hoop See **hide-and-whoop**

hidey-place See **hidey-hole**

hidey-whoop See **hide-and-whoop**

hidie-hole See **hidey-hole**

hiding n See **hide-and-seek A**

hiding vbl n See **hide** v^2

hiding-hole See **hidey-hole**

hiding-seek See **hide-and-seek A**

hiding sheep n Cf **hide-and-seek B2**

=run sheep run.

1967 *DARE* (Qu. EE12, *Games in which one captain hides his team and the other team tries to find it*) Inf **MO**2, Hiding sheep; (Qu. EE16, *Hiding games that start with a special, elaborate method of sending the players out to hide*) Inf **MO**2, Hiding sheep.

hid-jus n [Pronc-sp for *hideous*]

1984 Burns *Cold Sassy* 37 **nGA** (as of 1906), They's a old woman in Mr. Blakeslee's cheer. Go away, woman! She's hid-jus, Willy—face all puckered like them doll heads made out'n dried apples.

hidy exclam Also *hidy-do, hidy-doody* [Prob var of *howdy,* with [aː] rather than [aʊ] (cf Pronc Intro 3.II.14); but cf quot 1962] **chiefly S Midl, TX** See Map

Used as an expression of greeting.

1960 (1962) Lee *Mockingbird* 245 **AL,** Hidy do, Mr. Arthur. *Ibid* 272, There's just some kind of men you have to shoot before you can say hidy to 'em. **1961** Folk *Word Atlas N. LA* map 1314, Hidy. **1962** Atwood *Vocab. TX* 101, *Hidy* (*hi + howdy*). **1965–70** *DARE* (Qu. NN10a, *Expressions . . used when you meet somebody you know quite well*) 24 Infs, **chiefly S Midl,** Hidy; **CA**14, Hidy-doody; **LA**8, Hidy-do; (Qu. NN10b, *Greetings used when you meet somebody you do not know well*)

Infs **AR**41, **MS**69, Hidy-do. [23 of 28 Infs were comm type 4 or 5] **1967** Fetterman *Stinking Creek* 137 **seKY,** He greeted the bereaved: "Hidy, Mrs. Sizemore." **1971** Green *Village Horse Doctor* 111 **cwTX** (as of 1940s), After a few "Hidy's" and light conversation, I told Buck that I needed to get back to Fort Stockton. **1973** Allen *LAUM* 1.387 **SD** (as of c1950), *How are you?* (to an intimate friend). . . hidy do. [1 inf]

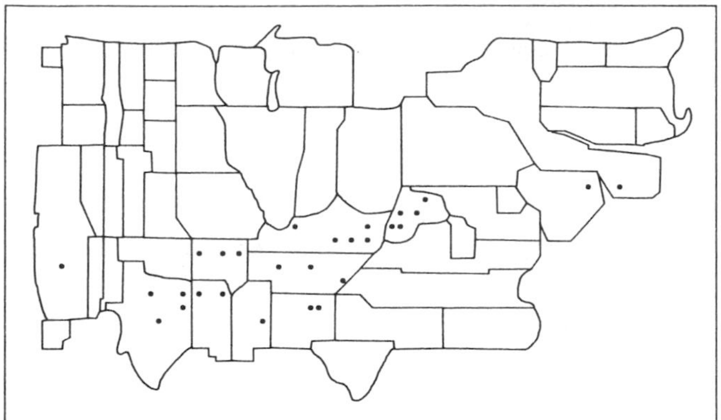

•hidy exclam + varr (Qq. NN10a, b)

hidy v [**hidy** exclam]

To exchange greetings.

1970 *DARE* (Qu. II12, . . *Meeting somebody on the street and speaking only a few words with him: "We just ________."*) Inf **TX**95, Hidied a little bit.

hidy-do(ody) See **hidy** exclam

hidy-tidy See **highty-tighty**

hie v Also *hi*

Used as a call or command to various animals: see quots. [Cf *EDD hie* int. and v.[1]] Cf *DS* K80

1892 *DN* 1.237 **cwMO,** Perhaps the usual cry in driving stock, especially cows, is *hi there.* **1949** Kurath *Word Geog.* 19 **NEng,** The call *hoist!* . . or *hie!* . . to a cow that is being milked, which barely survive[s] in New England today, may simply have been lost earlier in the New England settlements beyond the Hudson. *Ibid* 64, Calls to Cows during Milking. . . *Hoist!* . . and the shortened *hie!* [have survived] in New England (now rare) and in southernmost New Jersey. **1966–70** *DARE* (Qu. J9b, *To tell a dog to stand without moving*) Inf **LA**10, For bird dogs they say hie way ['haɪ'weɪ]; (Qu. K36a, *What do you say to make a horse go faster?*) Infs **CA**90, 211, **NM**6, Hi; (Qu. K79, *How do you call the chickens to you at feeding time?*) Inf **MA**58, Hi hi hi; (Qu. K82, . . *Call* . . *to get horses in from the pasture*) Inf **MI**23, Hi boy; (Qu. K83, *To call a calf to you at feeding time*) Inf **NY**187, Hi bossie; (Qu. NN22d, *Expressions used to drive away animals*) 11 Infs, **scattered, but esp Sth, S Midl,** Hi (boss, there *or* on); **1967** Faries *Word Geog. MO* 92, *Calls to cows during milking. . . hie* . . of New England origin. . . seems characteristic of the German settlements in Missouri. **1973** Allen *LAUM* 1.243 **MN, IA, NE** (as of c1950), Call to summon dog. . . hie (+ name). [3 infs] *Ibid* 1.258, Both infs. in Rolla, North Dakota, next to the Canadian border use *hi hi hi. Ibid* 1.259 **ND, SD,** Calls to cows. . . hi, hi boss. [2 infs]

hi'ed See **hire**

hierba de cristo See **calico bush 3**

hierba dulce n

A **bee brush:** either *Aloysia lycioides* or *Lippia graveolens.*

1960 Vines *Trees SW* 888, Vernacular names are Bee-brush, . . Hierba Dulce [etc]. *Ibid* 889, *Lippia graveolens* . . is also known under the vernacular name of Hierba Dulce. **1970** Correll *Plants TX* 1331, *Lippia graveolens.* . . Hierba dulce.

‡hieronymous n [Perh < Gk *hieron osteon* sacrum]

1969 *AmSp* 44.238, Seventy years ago in southern and central Indiana, *hieronymus* was a euphemism for the posterior or crotch. I sometimes heard my grandmother (1880–1967) use it, usually in disparaging remarks about the length of other women's dresses: "Her dress was so short you could pret' near see her hieronymus." . . From an informant who remembers the word from 1910 and later, I have this sample sentence: "There's room for three of us here if you can scoot your hieronymus over a little bit."

hie spy See **hy spy**

hifalute v [Back-formation from *highfalutin*]

To talk in a bombastic, pompous manner.

1904 Day *Kin o' Ktaadn* 198 **ME,** I ain't much stuck on actress gals, they hifalute too much. **1942** Berrey–Van den Bark *Amer. Slang* 190.2, *Be bombastic; grandiloquent.* . . highfalute . . talk highfaluten.

hifer v Cf **hyper**

To linger, loiter.

1848 Bartlett *Americanisms* 176, *To Hifer.* To loiter. Used in North Pennsylvania. **1955** Adams *Grandfather* 248 **NY** (as of 1830s), Medad Pomeroy must still have his beetle-ring and who is to ply the metal if I hifer here listening to thy silly whoobub?

higdom n [Etym unknown]

See quots.

1940 Brown *Amer. Cooks* 593 **NY,** *Higdom* . . green tomatoes, . . onions, . . cabbage, . . green peppers, all chopped fine. Put in preserving kettle, with . . water and vinegar. . . boil. Then put in a stone jar . . and cover with hot vinegar. **1969** *DARE* (Qu. H57, *Tasty or spicy side-dishes served with meats*) Inf **NY**169, ['higdɛm]; **PA**217, ['hɪgdəm]—a chopped pickle and ketchup.

higear(y) See **high-gear**

higgle v, hence vbl n *higgling* Also *higgle-haggle* [*OED higgle* v. 1 1633 →; *EDD higgle* v. 1 "In dial. use in Sc. Irel. and Eng."] Note: *higgle* seems to have been replaced by *haggle* in contemp use.

To bargain in a tedious or petty manner, haggle; to quibble.

1806 (1970) Webster *Compendious Dict.* 143, *Higgle.* . . to bargain hard, haggle. **1848** Bartlett *Americanisms* 176, *To Higgle.* To chaffer; to be penurious in a bargain. **1855** (1968) Whitman *Leaves of Grass* 22, The purchaser higgles about the odd cent. **1899** (1912) Green *VA Folk-Speech* 224, *Higgle*—see haggle. *Ibid, Higgling.* . . Close bargaining; chaffer. **1942** Berrey–Van den Bark *Amer. Slang* 348.5, *Higgle-haggle* . . to dispute pettily, quibble.

higguhri-hee n For var see quot 1949 [Echoic] *Gullah*

An owl.

1922 Gonzales *Black Border* 306 **sSC, GA coasts** [Gullah glossary], *Higguhri-hee*—the great horned owl. **1949** Turner *Africanisms* 237, The following are a few of the many onomatopoetic expressions heard in Gullah. . . ['higə'hi] 'owl'.

high adj Usu |haɪ, hɑɪ|; also **esp Sth** |ha:, haə|; **VA** |hʌɪ|; **NC** |hɔɪ| Pronc-spp *hoi(gh), hoy*

A Forms.

1927 Shewmake *Engl. Pronc. VA* 24, The second of the two distinctive and yet largely neglected sounds in the speech of Eastern Virginians is that of *i* in such words as *bright, like,* and *price.* The standard sound of this diphthong is approximately that of *a* as in *father* plus that of *i* as in *pin;* the dialectal sound is approximately that of *u* as in *hut* plus that of *i* in *pin.* The standard sound may be indicated by *(ai)* or *(ah-i);* the dialectal by *(uh-i).* **1941** Daniels *Tar Heels* 28 **eNC,** He says "hoi toide" for high tide and knows it. **1941** *LANE* Map 306 *(Spoiled),* 1 inf, **cwMA,** [haɪ]; 1 inf, **ceMA** [hɑ˂:ɛ]. **1942** *AmSp* 17.149 **NYC, seNY,** High . . 16 infs [aɪ]; 3 infs [ɑɪ]. **1950** Hubbell *Pronc. NYC* 66, In cultivated metropolitan speech, the diphthong in *high, ride, white* begins at an advanced low-central position. Its gliding movement is upward and forward to a height lower than that of the end-point of /eɪ/. The quality of the first element may vary somewhat from speaker to speaker and from utterance to utterance; it may be advanced a little and raised; it may be retracted as far as the [ɑ] of *pot;* and it may be shifted slightly toward mid-central position. **1965** *Dict. Queen's English* 2 **NC,** *Hoigh* (for high) (pronounced as hoy): There was a hoigh wind over the ocean. **1968–70** *DARE* (Qu. P23) Inf **NC**49, Highland ['hɑ·læn] frog; (Qu. BB50d) Inf **FL**49, Highland ['halænd]. **1969** *DARE* FW Addit **ceNC,** "High tide on the sound side" = [hɔɪ tɔɪd an ðə sɔn sɔɪd]. **c1970** Pederson *Dial. Surv. Rural GA* 1 inf, **seGA,** High land ['ha·ə 'læn] terrapin. **1987** *DARE* File **seGA** (as of c1970), *High* was often pronounced [ha:] or [haə].

B Senses.

1 Of tobacco: excessive in moisture content—usu in phrr *high case, high order.* Cf **case** n[1] **2**

1640 in 1883 *Archives of MD* 1.98, Bad tobacco shall be judged ground leafes Second Crops leafs notably brused . . fro[s]t bitten . . in the house sooty wett or in too high Case. **1850** U.S. Patent Office *Annual Rept. for*

1849: Ag. 322 **cwMD,** Tobacco should not be too moist, or *"high"* as it is termed, when put in the stalk-bulks, or it will get warm, the leaves stick to the stalk, get a bad smell, and change color; besides, if left too long it will rot. **1863** in 1865 IL State Ag. Soc. *Trans. for 1861–64* 5.669 **neKY,** Care must be taken that the tobacco does not imbibe too much moisture, or get too high in case before it is bulked. **1948** *AmSp* 23.309 **WI** [Tobacco terms], *In high case* is too wet to take down; high case is usually from too much rain or from the tobacco having hung too long. **1966** *PADS* 45.15 **cnKY,** *High case*. . . An excessive degree of moisture in the curing tobacco leaf. . . "High case is when it's too moist." **1967** Key *Tobacco Vocab.* 52 **GA,** In too high order; **MD,** Bulking tobacco down in too high order. . . it sweats. . . we call it 'heating'; **NC,** High order—wet; **TN,** Too high case will black it—it bruises.

2 in compar phr *as high as:* As many as, as much as, as long as.

1939 *Hall Coll.* **wNC,** *High*. . . "I've saw as high as twenty drunk the same day." **1952** Brown *NC Folkl.* 1.550, *High, as — as*. . . As many as. "I've killed as high as twenty squirrels a day."—General. Old people. **c1960** *Wilson Coll.* **csKY,** *As high as* . . meaning as many as or some good-sized number. "He's killed as high as ten squirrels in one morning." **1966–69** *DARE* Tape **IN**68, They have employed as high as twelve hundred; **ME**17, You can use 'em [=foam fishing floats] year in, year out. We've used some high as six years; **MI**65, I have caught as high as ninety-seven muskrats in one night; **NC**65, I've seen high as ten, twelve [vessels] down here in Inlet Channel. **1984** Wilder *You All Spoken Here* 72 **Sth,** We raised as high as a bale a acre.

3 See quot.

1950 *WELS Suppl.* **cwWI,** *High*—greatly favored. "Angel cake is high for birthdays and weddings."

4a Inebriated, tipsy.

1838 Kettell *Yankee Notions* 188, The world is indebted to them [=Cold Water Tee-totallers] for the discovery of the method of . . getting high on cold water. **1892** *Nation* 55.66/3, I was told, that Governor and legislators would get high on whiskey illegally sold on the evening of the very day when they had passed a stringent amendment to the [Maine] law. **1899** (1912) Green *VA Folk-Speech* 224, *High*. . . Excited with drink. **1965–70** *DARE* (Qu. DD13, *When a drinker is just beginning to show the effects of the liquor . . he's* ______) 118 Infs, **scattered,** Getting (*or* beginning to get, etc) high; 103 Infs, **scattered,** (Little) high; 14 Infs, **scattered,** Feeling (kinda) high; 4 Infs, Flying (*or* good and, kind of, half-) high; (Qu. DD14, *When a person is partly drunk, "He's* ______.") 72 Infs, **scattered, but more freq Sth, S Midl,** (Little) high; 13 Infs, **scattered,** Feeling (*or* getting, etc) high; 11 Infs, **esp Sth, S Midl,** Very (*or* pretty, rather, slightly, half-) high; [Of all Infs responding to Qq. DD13 and DD14, 11% and 10% respectively were young; in each case 6% were Black; of those giving these responses, 22% and 27% respectively were young; 15% and 24% respectively were Black.]; (Qu. DD15, *A person who is thoroughly drunk*) 6 Infs, **scattered,** (Really *or* floating) high.

b in var compar phrr:

(1) *high as a kite.*

1939 *AmSp* 14.90 **eTN,** *High as a kite*. . . Completely drunk. 'He's high as a kite.' **1950** *WELS (A person who is very drunk)* 1 Inf, **WI,** High as a kite; 1 Inf, Higher than a kite. **1960** Criswell *Resp. to PADS 20* **Ozarks,** *High as a kite*. . . Almost always used of a person who is very drunk. Very frequent. **1965–70** *DARE* (Qu. DD15) 11 Infs, **scattered,** High as (*or* higher than) a kite; (Qu. DD13) Inf **AL**6, High as a kite; (Qu. DD14) Infs **GA**44, **IL**135, **MI**80, **MS**6, High as (*or* higher 'n) a kite. **1976** Garber *Mountain-ese* 41 **Appalachians,** *High-as-a-kite* . . inebriated.

(2) in phrr *high as* (or *higher than*) *a Georgia pine.* **chiefly Sth, S Midl**

1937 *Writer* 50.239 **neOH** [Black], *High as a Georgia pine*—the state of being happily intoxicated; being very drunk. **1938** *AmSp* 13.317 **NE** [Black], Higher than a Georgia pine. **1950** *WELS (A person who is very drunk)* 1 Inf, **WI,** High as a Georgia pine. **1962** *Mt. Life* Winter 11 **sAppalachians,** The impetuous one . . "swigs" at the bottle for some time . . but having reached the half-way place he is soon "as high as a Georgy pine." **1968–70** *DARE* (Qu. DD14, *When a person is partly drunk, "He's* ______.") Inf **DC**12, High as a Georgia pine; **IL**135, Higher 'n a Georgia pine; (Qu. DD15, *A person who is thoroughly drunk*) Infs **GA**72, **VA**6, 39, High as (a) Georgia pine; **VA**12, High as a Georgia pine—yes, that's an old one [FW sugg]. **1972** *Atlanta Letters* **seGA,** *High as a Georgia pine*—Drunk. **1976** Garber *Mountain-ese* 41 **Appalachians,** *High as a Georgia pine* . . drunk. **1984** Wilder *You All Spoken Here* 165 **Sth,** *High as a Georgia pine:* Intoxicated.

(3) in phrr *high for* (or *high up to*) *picking cotton:* See quots. *obs*

1818 Weems *Drunkard's Looking Glass* 4, The patient goes by a variety of nicknames . . such as *boozy* . . *tipsy* . . *high up to picking cotton* (Georgia.) **1829** *Maysville Eagle* 8 April (*DA* at *cotton),* I have been . . most too 'high for picking cotton.'

(4) in var other phrr: See quots.

1858 Hammett *Piney Woods Tavern* 155, He kept on goin', tell he got as high as ninety. **1942** Berrey–Van den Bark *Amer. Slang* 106.7, *Drunk*. . . high as . . the sky,—a steeple. **1969–70** *DARE* (Qu. DD15) Inf **GA**72, High as a cat's back, high as a fiddler's fist; **SC**68, High as Lindbergh.

5 in phrr *(as) high as a cat's back:*

a also *higher than a cat's back:* Very high; in an intense manner, to an extreme degree.

1833 Smith *Life Jack Downing* 200 (Taylor–Whiting *Dict. Amer. Proverbs*), Cutting up capers as high as a cat's back. *Ibid* 231, Make you jump higher than a cat's back. **1848** in 1935 *AmSp* 10.42 **Nantucket MA,** 'Dust as high as a cat's back.' Quite a row. **1894** in 1950 *PADS* 13.13 **AL,** The Lucas generation got their dander up as high as a cat's back. **1903** (1965) Adams *Log Cowboy* 269 **West,** The dealer has lowered the limit from a hundred to fifty, for old Paul is playing them as high as a cat's back. **1912** *DN* 3.578 **wIN,** *High as a cat's back*. . . Very high. **1942** Berrey–Van den Bark *Amer. Slang* 39.7, *Tall; high*. . . higher than a cat's back. **1984** Wilder *You All Spoken Here* 72 **Sth,** *As high as a cat's back:* 'Way up.

b also *high as the hair on a cat's back:* Expensive. **scattered, but esp freq Sth, S Midl**

1906 *DN* 3.140 **nwAR,** *High as a cat's back*. . . Very high-priced. "Yes, apples are high as a cat's back." Used by tradespeople. **1927** *Ruppenthal Coll.* **KS,** *High as a cat's back*—very high, esp. as to price, cost, etc. **1934** Smiley *Gloss. New Paltz* **seNY,** *High as a cat's back*—Speaking of the price of maple syrup: "Syrup is going to be as high as a cat's back." **1960** Criswell *Resp. to PADS 20* **Ozarks,** *High as a cat's back*. . . Very high. One of the commonest phrases of comparison, still common. Probably more often used in price comparisons than elsewhere, "This bacon is high as a cat's back." **1965–68** *DARE* FW Addit **OK,** *High as a cat's back*—expensive. "Twelve-gauge shells are high as a cat's back anymore;" **LA,** *High as a cat's back*—very expensive. **1971** *Today Show Letters* **TX,** That store is as high as the hair on a cat['s] back.

6 in phr *high as quinine:* Very expensive.

1952 *DE Folkl. Bulletin* 1.11/2, "High as quinine!"—said of something very expensive.

7 in phr *how is that for high?:* What do you think of that?—often used ironically. [See quot 1872 Schele de Vere] *old-fash*

1872 Schele de Vere *Americanisms* 326, The phrase, "How is that for *high?*" [is] borrowed from a low game, known as Old Sledge, where the *high* depends, not on the card itself, but on the adversary's hand. Hence the phrase means, What kind of an attempt is that at a great achievement? It is of Western origin, having made its appearance in some of the Northwestern journals, but has spread . . all over the Union. . . A familiar nursery-rhyme . . : "Mary had a little lamb,/ It jumped up to the sky,/ And when it landed on its feet,/ Cried: *How is that for high?*" **1872** Twain *Roughing It* 334 **NV,** He was always nifty himself, and so you bet you his funeral ain't going to be no slouch—solid silver door-plate on his coffin, six plumes on the hearse, and a nigger on the box in a biled shirt and a plug hat—how's that for high? **1873** Bailey *Life in Danbury* 64 **swCT,** Occasionally some one fell down, and his neighbors stepped on him and walked over him, and facetiously enquired, "How was that for high?" **1907** *DN* 3.191 **seNH,** *How's that for high?* . . Can you beat that? Originally a card players' term? **1909** *DN* 3.420 **Cape Cod MA** (as of a1857), How's that for *high,* meaning what do you think of that?

8 in phr *off the high end:* See quot. [Prob infl by *off the deep end*]

1966 *DARE* (Qu. HH6, *Someone who is out of his mind*) Inf **MS**45, Off the high end.

9 In **hoodoo n 1a:** powerful, efficacious.

c1938 in 1970 Hyatt *Hoodoo* 1.284 **MD** [Black], I have a fellah, he told another boy an' myself—we always knowed 'im being *very high* [Hyatt: a *high man* = *cunjureman*]—he could do anything he wanted to do. *Ibid* 1.711 **ceGA,** Dat's one of de highest luck things dat ah evah used, an' ah'm goin' on 50 yeahs in it. *Ibid* 2.1422 **Jacksonville FL,** Yo' kin git any kind of a egg and write a person's name on it . . an' at a certain hour of de night, de high hour at twelve o'clock, yo' go to de do' [*Hyatt:* door] an' throw dat egg right upon de facin' . . an' tell it, "You must go—you must git out and go." *Ibid* 2.1484 **seGA,** It conquers anything dat will come inside of dat house in de way of, yo' know, line of devilments—dat's why it's called de *High John de Conquer.* Well, hit beats de *Low John de Conquer.*

10 superl:

a Eldest, tallest. Cf **least** adj

1936 Morehouse *Rain on Just* 36 **NC,** Dolly, the highest girl at home . . had cared for young uns almost ever since she could lug her own bucket.

b in phr *to the highest:* Enormously, extremely.

1972 *Atlanta Letters* **cnGA,** I enjoyed the dinner to the "high-est."

high adv

1 Very, especially.

1955 Ritchie *Singing Family* 62 **seKY,** It was a high good day we had for going. The sun was shining and it was right warm and windy.

2 In ref to the seasoning of food: heavily.

1847 [see **haslet**]. **1966** *DARE* Tape **SC**15, We . . salt it [=crab meat] just like you want it salted, high or low.

high n

1 See quot. Cf **high** adj **B4, high lonesome**

1893 *KS Univ. Qrly.* 1.139 **KS,** *High:* a spree, as, 'He's off on a high.'

2 pl: =**high beam 2.**

1966–70 *DARE* (Qu. N10, . . *The bright and dim lights on a car*) Infs **CT**7, **FL**4, **MA**2, **PA**40, 104, 110, 121, **SC**45, **VA**78, Highs (and lows).

high alps n pl Cf **tetons**

1968 *DARE* (Qu. X31, . . *A woman's breasts*) Inf **MD**17, High alps.

high-Andy-over, high-Antony See **high-over**

high as a cat's back See **high** adj **B5**

high as a Georgia pine See **high** adj **B4b**

high as a kite See **high** adj **B4a**

high as quinine See **high** adj **B6**

high as the hair on a cat's back See **high** adj **B5b**

high-back n

1 See quot.

1931–33 *LANE Worksheets* **cRI,** *High Back.* . . A kind of sleigh.

2 pl: A type of overalls; see quot.

[**1927** (1970) Sears *Catalogue* 389, *High Back Apron Overalls.* . . the *solid* high back style which is both higher and broader than the ordinary kind.] **1954** *Harder Coll.* **cwTN,** *High-backs.* . . A type of overalls: galluses do not button in back.

3 In the children's game **jump-for-down:** see quot.

1957 *Sat. Eve. Post Letters* **cwWA** (as of c1900), Having vaulted[,] the leader bent his back and took his place beside the man 'down' [=bent over]. The next man vaulted over both of them and then joined them. If there were more than four or five playing it is obvious that the last to make the try had a lot of backs to clear. Usually he called on the second or third man 'down' to give him a 'high' back. Sometimes the 'high' back, at the last instant, in a spirit of playfullness, dropped his back and the contestant, charging at full speed, missed his hold and plummetted sprawling into the dirt.

highback carpsucker See **highfin carpsucker**

highback whitefish See **humpback whitefish b**

highball n [See quots 1930, 1938 at **1a**]

1a Esp in railroading: a signal to proceed at full speed; "the go-ahead."

1897 *Chi. Record* 1 Mar. 6/1 *(DA),* 'Milk trains' . . have 'rights' over the rails and get nothing but 'high balls.' **1913** *DN* 4.11 **MN** [Railroad terms], *High-ball.* . . Signal, or order (to go). . . "The conductor gave the engineer the high-ball to go ahead." **1923** *DN* 5.243 **LA,** *High-ball.* . . A railway signal to go at full speed. **1927** *Ruppenthal Coll.* **KS,** *To give one the highball*—(Railroad argot and general) to indicate that one shall or may go, start, run, play, move, etc. "They gave us the highball and we started." **1930** *RR Man's Mag.* 470, *Highball*—Signal waved by the hand or by lamp in a high, wide semiarc, the meaning of which is to get out of town at full speed ahead. **1938** Beebe *High Iron* 221 [Railroad terms], *Highball:* Signal for a clear track, deriving from the first train signals which were in the form of painted metal globes hoisted to the crossarm of a tall pole when trains were to proceed. **1952** Brown *NC Folkl.* 1.550, *High-ball.* **1956** Sorden–Ebert *Logger's Words* 18 **Gt Lakes,** *Highball,* A command to go ahead. **1967** *DARE* Tape **ID6,** The engineer couldn't move except on signal from the conductor like when they got the orders—what they call the high ball, the proceed signal, they'd start moving.

b Fig:

(1) in phr *strike a highball:* To go as fast as possible.

1920 Hunter *Trail Drivers TX* 354, Mr. Butler and I told them [=cowboys] . . to strike a high ball to town.

(2) The brush-off or cold shoulder—usu in phr *give one the highball*

1952 Brown *NC Folkl.* 1.550, *High-ball.* . . A girl's refusal to go with a man, or to accept a drink. **1965–70** *DARE* (Qu. II5b, *When you don't want to have anything to do with a certain person because you don't like him, you might say, "I'd certainly like to give him the ______."*) 9 Infs, **scattered,** Highball; (Qu. AA11, *If a man asks a girl to marry him and she refuses*) Infs **SC**19, 24, 34, **TX**35, Give (*or* gave) him the highball; (Qu. AA12, *If a man loses interest in a girl and stops seeing her*) Inf **SC**19, Gave her the highball. **a1975** Lunsford *It Used to Be* 170 **sAppalachians,** She send[s] a little note that she has other company, or she wants to make other arrangements, and this means she gives you the "highball."

2 also attrib: A fast train.

1930 *RR Man's Mag.* June 470, *Highball artist*—A locomotive engineer who is noted for fast running. **1934** (1940) Weseen *Dict. Amer. Slang* 71, *Highball* . . a fast freight. **1938** Beebe *High Iron* 221 [Railroad terms], *Highball artist:* Locomotive engineer noted for speedy running. **1967–68** *DARE* (Qu. N35, *A fast train that goes from one big city to another without stopping at all the stations*) Infs **MO**9, **NH**14, Highball; [(Qu. N37, . . *A branch railroad that is not very important or gives poor service*) Inf **MN**10, The highball [*DARE* Ed: Perh facetious, perh mistaken]].

3 attrib; rarely used absol: Involving fast, uninterrupted activity or all-out effort.

1920 Hunter *Trail Drivers TX* 68, We had a high ball trail from there on. **1927** *DN* 5.449 [Underworld jargon], *Highball camp.* . . A camp in which the straw boss speeds up work by methods which to the worker are unethical. **1930** Williams *Logger-Talk* 25 **Pacific NW,** *High-ball:* Fast; used generally as a descriptive adjective, as *high-ball outfit, high-ball engineer.* **1934** (1940) Weseen *Dict. Amer. Slang* 80 [Loggers and Miners], *Highball outfit*—A large or first-class business, especially in lumbering. **1950** *Western Folkl.* 9.118 **nwOR** [Logger speech], *Highball.* All out effort; full speed. **1958** McCulloch *Woods Words* 85 **Pacific NW,** *Highball*—A fast moving logging outfit. **1966** *DARE* Tape **SD**4A, They also have what they call a highball drift down there, drifts that they want driven in a hurry.

highball v [See **highball** n **1a**]

1 Esp in railroading: to give a signal to proceed; by ext, to beckon.

1912 *RR Man's Mag.* 17.493/2, The con high-balled, and the manifest freight / Pulled out on the stem behind the mail. **1927** *DN* 5.449 [Underworld jargon], *Highball.* . . To signal for a train to move. **1935** Hurston *Mules & Men* 187 **FL,** Big Sweet was high balling me to come over to the skin game. **1970** *Current Slang* 5.1.8 [Jargon of railroad employees], *Highball.* . . To give such a signal [=a go ahead signal].—I highballed the streamliner.

2 also with *it:* To leave—esp in a hurry; to go at top speed, to speed up operations; hence n *highballer.* Cf **ball the jack 1**

1912 *RR Man's Mag.* 17.493/2, She whistled twice and high-balled out,/ They were off—down the Gila Monster Route. **1917** *DN* 4.413 **wNC,** *High-ball.* . . To decamp. "I'll make him high-ball out o' here." **1941** *AmSp* 16.233 [Logger talk], *High ball.* To speed up operations. A 'high ball' camp is a hurry up affair. **1943** in 1953 Botkin–Harlow *Treas. Railroad Folkl.* 296, When a train highballed out of the station, the engineer was on his own, a man who rode destiny and twisted her tail. **1945** Hubbard *Railroad Ave.* 346, Verb *highball* or phrase *'ball the jack* means to make a fast run. **1950** *WELS (To run very fast, especially running away from something)* 1 Inf, **cnWI,** Highballing. **1950** *Western Folkl.* 9.381 **neCA** [Lumberjack language], *Highball it.* To work at full speed. **1967–68** *DARE* (Qu. Y18, *To leave in a hurry: "Before they find this out, we'd better ______!"*) Inf **VA**24, Highball it; (Qu. Y20, *To run fast: "You should have seen him ______!"*) Inf **SC**29, Highball. **1969** *DARE* (Qu. HH27a, *A very able and energetic person who gets things done*) Inf **CA**128, A highballer—in the railroad they highball a train through. **1971** Tak *Truck Talk* 82, *Highball it:* to drive a tractor-trailer at or near its top speed.

3 In railroading: see quot 1970.

1942 Berrey–Van den Bark *Amer. Slang* 781.10, *Highball the switch* . . not to slow down for the brakeman to close the switch, leaving this to a switchman. **1970** *Current Slang* 5.1.8 [Jargon of railroad employees], *Highball*. . . To pass by, leave undone.—Highball the work at Marysville.—Highball the switch. (Don't bother to operate it.)

highballer, highball it See **highball v 2**

high banker n

Among loggers: appar a proud or overbearing person.

1903 White in *McClure's Mag.* 20.577/2 **MI,** "Come on Jimmy," "Don't be a high banker." **1908** White *Riverman* 10 **nMI,** Are you going to let that old high-banker walk all over you?

highbarkalorum n [An imitation of *high cockalorum,* suggesting importance, with play on *bark* of trees (often used medicinally) and simulating medical Latin]

1967 *DARE* Tape **TX1,** They had this old doctor. . . and they asked him, "You make two kinds o' medicine outta pecan bark. . . What do yer call it?" [The doctor answered:] "Highbarkalorum [ˌhaɪbɑɚkəˈloɚəm] 'n lowbarkahighrum [ˌlobɑɚkəˈhaɪrəm]." . . high-barkalorum, yer cut it up here 'n yer strip it down. Ah think that is fo' dropsy.

high beam n

1 usu pl: A hayloft. **chiefly NEng** Cf **great beam,** *DS* M3

1939 *LANE* Map 102 *(Loft; scaffold),* **chiefly cMA, nNEng,** High beam(s). **1949** Kurath *Word Geog.* 22 **eNEng,** *High-beams, great-beams* . . for the loft of a barn (mostly in the upper Connecticut Valley and in Worcester County, Massachusetts). *Ibid* 54, A platform right under the sloping sides of the roof is called the *high-beams*. . . The hay is said to be *on the high-beams* or *in the high-beams.* **1967** Faries *Word Geog. MO* 75, To denote the space for hay in the upper part of a barn. . . There is one instance of *high-beams.* [1 of 700 infs]

2 The bright, long-range light of an automobile headlight. **widespread, but less freq Sth, W Midl** See Map Cf **country light, low beam**

1939 *Daily Progress* (Charlottesville VA) 19 Aug 4/1, The invention is described . . as "a 'sealed beam,' which at once provides . . increased range and breadth of light with stronger intensity through its high, or 'country,' beam and reduction of glare with increased illumination of the right side of the road with its low or 'traffic' beam." **1950** *WELS (The bright lights on a car)* 4 Infs, **WI,** High beam. **1957** Battaglia *Resp. to PADS 20* **eMD,** *(Other words for the bright and dim lights on a car)* High beam, dimmers. **1965–70** *DARE* (Qu. N10, *What other words are used around here for the bright and dim lights on a car?*) 122 Infs, **widespread, but less freq Sth, W Midl,** High beam(s); 24 Infs **scattered,** High (beam) and low beam; **CO47, MA19, NH1, 5, NY76, 111, PA204,** High (beams) and low beams; **NJ1, WA11,** High beam, low beam; **MI85, VT7,** Low beam (and) high beam; **TX54,** High-low beams; **UT3,** High versus low beams.

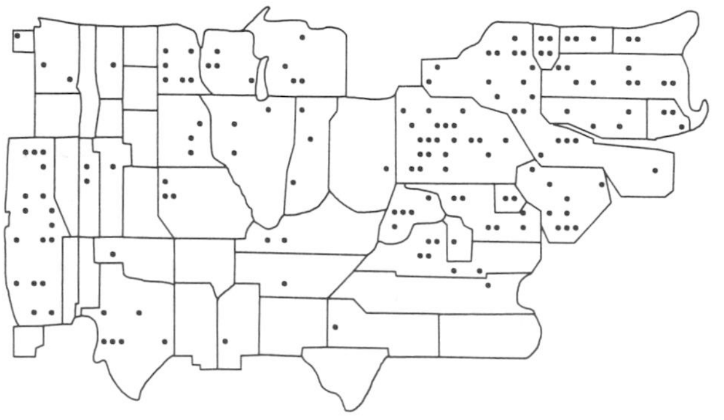
•high beam 2 + varr (Qu. N10)

high-behind See **hide-behind 1**

high behind, got See **got high behind**

highbelia n [Folk-etym; see quot 1843] Cf **lowbelia**

A tall **lobelia,** such as **cardinal flower,** *Lobelia siphilitica,* or *L. spicata.*

1843 Torrey *Flora NY* 1.424, *Lobelia syphilitica*. . . Being much taller and more robust than the *L. inflata,* which is frequently used in domestic practice under the name of *Low belia,* it was supposed as a matter of course by those better acquainted with its near affinity to the latter, than with its etymology, that it must be *High belia!* **1859** (1968) Bartlett *Americanisms* 257, The other species *[Lobelia cardinalis],* which towers high above its humble relative, is accordingly dubbed *High-belia.* **1892** (1974) Millspaugh *Amer. Med. Plants* 98, *Lobelia syphilitica*. . . In some localities it is called *high belia,* in unconscious pun upon its lowlier but more frequently-used companion, L. inflata, or *low belia,* as they term it. **1894** *Jrl. Amer. Folkl.* 7.93, *Lobelia syphilitica,* . . high belia. . . Somewhat general among herb-collectors. **1941** *Torreya* 41.52, *Lobelia cardinalis* . . Highbelia. **1950** Gray–Fernald *Manual of Botany* 1356, *L[obelia] spicata* . . "Highbelia".

high bijeebees See **heebie-jeebies 1**

high blood n [Cf *DBE*]

1 High blood pressure. **chiefly Sth, S Midl** Cf **low blood**

1952 Giles *40 Acres* 163 **csKY,** He had the high blood, Mama Tooney said proudly. "When his blood gits up," she sighed, "he ain't good fer nothin'. Jist plumb gives out. He ortent to ever do a day's work in the sun." **1954** *Harder Coll.* **cwTN,** *High blood*. . . High blood pressure. "He had high blood." **1959** *Hall Coll.* **eTN,** *High blood*. . . High blood pressure. **1967** *DARE* FW Addit **ceTN,** *High blood*—high blood pressure. Many of the farm women around Maryville [TN] complain of high blood; **swVA,** An old lady of Big Stone Gap who stopped to sit on our tail gate to rest her "high blood." **1967–70** *DARE* (Qu. BB49, . . *Kinds of diseases* . . *common around here, or used to be common)* Infs **MS80, MO9, TN16,** High blood; (Qu. DD24, . . *Diseases that come from continual drinking)* Infs **MO24, TN53,** High (or low) blood. **1971** Cunningham *Syntactic Analysis Gullah* 30 **seSC,** They come for find out I was growing up having *high blood.* You having that *high blood,* you have to be real particular. **1987** *DARE* File **ceAL,** Black patients at Tuskegee Institute use *high blood* for *high blood pressure;* **seWI,** My Black patients at Mt. Sinai Hospital in Milwaukee use *high blood* to mean 'high blood pressure' and *low blood* to mean 'anemia.' **1986** Pederson *LAGS Concordance* **Gulf Region,** 9 infs, High blood.

2 High blood-sugar level; diabetes.

1966 *DARE* (Qu. BB48, *When a person has too much sugar in his blood and may have to take insulin for it, you'd say he has* ______.) Inf **NC33,** High blood.

high blueberry See **highbush blueberry**

high-bob n

1918 *DN* 5.18 **NC,** *High-bob* . . a high chair.

high box dip n [**box n 1**]

1859 Perry *Turpentine Farming* 148, Solid box turpentine is called high box dip, but how high the box must be to merit the appellation has not yet been explained.

highboy n Also sp *hi-boy* [Orig trademark, now more widely used]

A spraying machine used in the cultivation, esp of tobacco plants; see quot 1966 *PADS.*

1966 *PADS* 45.15 **cnKY,** *Highboy*. . . A spraying machine designed to move through tobacco fields without damaging the plants. Brand name. . . "A Highboy looks like it's on stilts." **1966** *Lexington Herald & Leader* (KY) 27 Aug 16/4, *Hahn Hi-boys*—$650 up. 3 to choose from. Ready to spray and drop tobacco sticks. See at Link's tobacco warehouse. **1967** Key *Tobacco Vocab.* 121 **NC,** Highboy—a machine used to spray with; **TN,** Highboy—Not widely used—a few in the area are rented out; **MO,** Highboy. **1968** *DARE* Tape **IN42,** The next forward step we made for modernization was we bought a highboy sprayer; . . you didn't have to use a hoe and hoe the weeds out of corn.

high-bred n, adj Also sp *hybred* [Folk-etym for *hybrid*]

1896 *DN* 1.418 **wNY,** *High-bred:* pop. etym. for *hybrid.* **1940–41** Cassidy *WI Atlas* 1 inf, **swWI,** [ˈhɑɪbrɛd]—for 'hybrid' corn. **1967** *PMLA* 82.3.18 **swWI** (as of 1940), The farmers universally pronounced the word "hybred" and I wondered whether this was merely due to the substitution of the vowel [ɛ] for [ɪ], or whether folk-etymology was involved. I had my answer in a store one spring morning when a farmer, buying his seed corn, remarked, "You know, I tried that hybred last year, and it did so good that I won't plant anymore of the low-bred!" **1972** *NYT Article Letters* **swIA,** In the 1940's I had a friend in Red Oak, Iowa, who owned farms in Montgomery and Adams Counties in that section of southwest Iowa. The tenants on his farms consistently and carefully called hybrid corn "high-bred" corn. **1987** *DARE* File **swCA,** We tried one of the high-breds, only we didn't like the flavor.

high-brow v Cf **high-hat** v, **high-top** v

1965–68 *DARE* (Qu. II6, *If you meet somebody who used to be a friend, and he pretends not to know you: "When I met him on the street he ______.")* Infs **UT**3, 6, High-browed me.

high-brown adj **chiefly Sth** Cf **high yellow**

Of a Black person: having light-brown skin; hence n *high brown* this skin color, a person of this skin color; also fig.

1927 Sandburg *Amer. Songbag* 29, Then come all you rounders, an' all you high-browns too. **1932** Faulkner *Light in August* 66 **MS,** It was said that some masked men had scared her into quitting because she was what is known as a high brown and it was known that there were two or three men in the town who would object to her doing whatever it was which she considered contrary to God and nature. **1933** in 1983 Taft *Blues Lyric Poetry* 238 [Black], Up in Harlem: every Saturday night / When the high browns get together: it's just too tight / They all congregates there: in an all night strut. **1938** *AmSp* 13.314 [Black], *High brown.* (Original meaning) Just the right shade, neither too dark nor too light. (New meaning) Anything that is high class or up to date. *Step aside, coal car, and let a high brown pass.* Reply to someone who has been outwitted. **1962** Faulkner *Reivers* 164 **MS,** Right there in the kitchen where I set it. . . That gold-tooth high-brown seen it. **1965–70** *DARE* (Qu. HH28, *Names . . for people of foreign background: . . Negro*) Inf **MS**73, High-brown; (Qu. HH29b, *Names for people of mixed blood—part Negro*) Infs **MS**56, **NY**241, High-brown; **SC**11, High-brown [FW sugg]. **1970** *Thompson Coll.* **Birmingham AL** (as of 1920s), *High brown*—The color, not definitely specified, of some Negroes, especially high-brown gals. **1986** Pederson *LAGS Concordance* **Gulf Region,** 2 infs, High brown; 1 inf, High browns—high yellow.

highbush blueberry n Also *high blueberry* Cf **half-high blueberry, lowbush blueberry**

Any of var spp of **blueberry 1,** but usu *Vaccinium corymbosum* which is also called **deerberry a, highbush huckleberry 2, huckleberry 2, swamp blueberry, whortleberry.**

1891 Jesup *Plants Hanover NH* 25, V[accinium] corymbosum, L. (High or Swamp Blueberry.) Ripens later; abundant and variable. **1900** Lyons *Plant Names* 386, *V[accinium] corymbosum. . .* High-bush Blueberry. **1913** Eaton *Barn Doors* 179 **MA,** Over east of the North Reading road, toward Danvers, there used to be a swamp into which we youngsters penetrated for a mile or so, finding high-bush blueberries, hornpout pools and wet feet. **1913** *Torreya* 13.28 **NY,** The high-bush blueberry *(Vaccinium corymbosum)* . . is the most striking both in flower and fruit. **1945** Pearson *Country Flavor* 31 **NH,** There is an area of high-bush blueberries, which mean juicy pies in late July. **1950** Gray–Fernald *Manual of Botany* 1134, *V. corymbosum. . .* Highbush-B[lueberry]. . . *V. atrococcum. . .* Black Highbush-B[lueberry]. **1960** Vines *Trees SW* 820, *Vaccinium corymbosum. . .* Vernacular names are Whortleberry . . and Northern High-bush Blueberry. The fruit has commercial value but flavor varies from mediocre to good. *Ibid* 827, *Arkansas High-bush Blueberry. Vaccinium arkansanum. . .* is also known by the name of Black High-bush Blueberry. **1967** *DARE* (Qu. T15, *What kinds of swamp trees do you have?*) Inf **MA**5, Highbush blueberry. **1987** *DARE* File **nwMA, swNH,** The best place to look for highbush blueberries is around the edges of ponds or lakes and in wet areas in power line cuts. In many places the bushes grow higher than I can reach.

highbush cranberry n Also *high cranberry* [See quot 1843]

A **viburnum** (here: *Viburnum trilobum*). Also called **arrowwood a, cramp bark, cranberry tree, dog elder, grouseberry 4, mooseberry, moosewood viburnum, pimbina, pincushion tree, squashberry, squawbush, summerberry, water elder, wild guelder-rose**

1805 (1905) Clark *Orig. Jrls. Lewis & Clark Exped.* 3.169 **csWA,** They gave us High bush cramburies. **c1805** R. Putnam *Memoirs* 19 *(DAE),* We had northing to eat Sence morning, but Beech buds and a few high Cramberries. **1843** Torrey *Flora NY* 1.307, *Viburnum opulus. . . Bush Cranberry,* or *High Cranberry. . .* The acid fruit is sometimes used as a substitute for cranberries. **1876** Hobbs *Bot. Hdbk.* 27, Cramp bark, High cranberry, Viburnum opulus. **1910** Graves *Flowering Plants* 368 **CT,** *Viburnum Opulus* . . var. *americanum. . .* High-bush Cranberry. . . Swamps and wet ground. . . The fruit is edible. **1949** *Mo. Bot. Garden Bul.* April 92 *(DA),* Some desirable shrubs which need very little care are Mento barberry . . , highbush cranberry [etc]. **1960** Teale *Journey into Summer* 10, A cranberry tree spread its broad, three-pointed leaves. This north-country viburnum . . is variously known as the squaw bush, the water elder, the high-bush cranberry and the pincushion tree. **1967–69** *DARE* (Qu. I44, *What kinds of berries grow wild around here?*) Infs **MI**53, **NH**14, **NY**97, 218, High-bush cranberries. **1976** Bruce *How to Grow Wildflowers* 134, A final American viburnum, one probably more familiar to readers from the northern part of the country than to others: *V. trilobum,* the "High-bush Cranberry."

highbush gallberry n

=**gallberry.**

1927 Boston Soc. Nat. Hist. *Proc.* 38.7.288 **Okefenokee GA,** Ben Chesser speaks of 'high-bush gallberries' *(Ilex coriacea)* as a favorite food of the Bear.

highbush huckleberry n Cf **lowbush huckleberry**

1 A **huckleberry 1** (here: *Gaylussacia baccata*).

1889 *Century Dict.* 2909, *G[aylussacia] resinosa* is the common high-bush huckleberry or black huckleberry of the markets. **1903** Porter *Flora PA* 241, *Gaylussacia resinosa. . .* High-bush huckleberry. **1942** Tehon *Fieldbook IL Shrubs* 229, Highbush Huckleberry . . is an erect or ascending shrub up to 4 feet tall but commonly 1½ to 2½ feet high. **1960** Vines *Trees SW* 815, *Gaylussacia baccata. . .* Also known as the High-bush Huckleberry and Black Snap.

2 Any of var spp of **blueberry 1,** but usu **highbush blueberry.**

1927 Boston Soc. Nat. Hist. *Proc.* 38.239, 'High-bush huckleberries' . . constitute an intermediate growth between the trees and the lower shrubs. *Ibid* 240, *Shrubs. . . Vaccinium corymbosum* 'High-bush huckleberry.' **1934** *Natl. Geogr. Mag.* 65.603/2 **Okefenokee GA,** At this season, also, one may go a-berrying by boat and pluck appetizing "high-bush huckleberries" where they overhang the water. **1940** Steyermark *Flora MO* 404, High-bush huckleberry *(Vaccinium stamineum). Ibid* 405, High-bush huckleberry *(Vaccinium melanocarpum).* **1966–68** *DARE* (Qu. I44, *What kinds of berries grow wild around here?*) Inf **CT**17, Highbush huckleberries; **ME**5, Huckleberries—highbush and lowbush; **SC**7, Highbush huckleberries. [*DARE* Ed: These Infs may refer instead to **1** above.]

highbush laurel n

=**sweetleaf.**

1860 Curtis *Cat. Plants NC* 65, Symplocos tinctoria. . . *High Bush Laurel. . .* In poor soils it is only a shrub 2 to 6 feet high; but in those which are fertile, as on the borders of swamps, it becomes a small tree. . . The leaves, which are 3 to 5 inches long, are sweet to the taste but rather dry, and greedily eaten by cattle and deer in Winter.

high-button-shoe-boy n

1950 *PADS* 14.74 **FL,** *High-button-shoe-boy. . .* A person from West Florida. Suwannee backwoods expression.

high cake n

See quot 1950.

1937 Gardner *Folkl. Schoharie* 3 **ceNY,** I succeeded in allaying suspicions to the extent that I was sometimes treated to "high cake." **1950** Klees *PA Dutch* 425, The angel-foods and sponge cakes and the "high cakes," as the layer cakes are called, . . differ very little from these cakes elsewhere.

high calf n

1969 *DARE* (Qu. K22, . . *A bull*) Inf **TN**30, High calf [hɑɪ kæf].

high case See **high** adj **B1**

high center n, v

A raised area or obstruction in the middle of a roadway; to become or cause to become hung up on such an obstruction.

1950 *Western Folkl.* 9.381 **neCA** [Lumberjack language], *High center.* Refers usually to a tractor being hung up on a rock or a stump. **1954** Jordan *Hell's Canyon* 39 **cwID,** It was a heady feeling again to ride in an automobile, even at five miles an hour, over high-centers and around hairpin turns. **1987** *DARE* File **swID,** In the spring, dirt roads often get muddy and rutted, causing the center of the road to be much higher than the tracks. It's easy to high center a car on the raised middle part, especially if a rock sticks up. "He high centered and put a hole in his floor pan." **1987** *DARE* File **cnUT,** It is easy to high center a car in the mountains. Cars are built too low to clear large rocks or high places in a dirt road which can catch a car's frame so that the wheels lose their traction. Once a car is high centered, it usually takes a tow truck to free it.

high check rein n attrib

1975 Gould *ME Lingo* 131, *High check rein*—It was considered stylish to drive a horse that held his head high, and the *check rein* was that part of the harness that kept him from lowering his head. To carry the check rein high was a *ritchbitch* practice simple farmers did not affect. *High check reins* were uppity. Hence, any ostentatious display or snobbish comportment is *high check rein* stuff.

high climber n **chiefly Pacific NW** Cf **high rigger, high-lead**

In logging: the person who tops, limbs, and often rigs, the **spar tree** for use in cable logging.

1925 *AmSp* 1.137 **Pacific NW** [Logger talk], The greatest of all woods heroes, "the high-rigger." "High-climber," he is often called. He is the bully brave boy with heart of oak and muscles of steel, who "tops the spars." **1938** (1939) Holbrook *Holy Mackinaw* 261, *High climber, or high rigger*. . . The man who tops and prepares a high-lead tree for logging. **1942** *AmSp* 17.222 **ME, Gt Lakes, Pacific NW** [Logger's lingo], *High climber*. . . Since his is the most dangerous job in the industry, he is permitted to be the only prima donna in the woods. **1946** Peattie *Pacific Coast* 242, The high-climber . . dug his spurs into the treacherous bark, hitched his steel rope about the tree, and wriggled his way up. . . he carried axe and saw dangling from his belt. . . Inching his way up to a dizzy height, he made the undercut and then sawed his way through till the top began to tremble, then sway; and finally, with a roar of cracking fibers, it crashed to earth. **1958** McCulloch *Woods Words* 85 **Pacific NW,** *High climber*—A logger who climbs and tops a tree getting it ready for rigging; in some camps he also rigs the tree.

high clover, be in v phr Also *walk in high clover* [Blend of *high cotton* + *in (the) clover* prosperous]

=**high cotton 1.**

1944 *AmSp* 19.154 **Sth,** *To walk* (or *be*) *in high clover* . . to be well off, to be happy, successful.

high cockalavitch n [Var of *high cockalorum*]

1968 *DARE* (Qu. HH17, *A person who tries to appear important, or who tries to lay down the law in his community: "He'd like to be the ——— around here."*) Inf **NY**199, High cockalavitch.

high collar n [From *high collar* an item of dress associated with especially correct behavior] Cf **high-collared rooster**

A person of prominence or high standing in a community.

1926 in 1983 Truman *Dear Bess* 326 **MO,** He told me about a former saloonkeeper of his town who was such a good citizen and ran such a clean place that all the high collars and "the ribbon ladies" (Thomas called them that) looked on him with favor.

high-collared rooster n

1906 *DN* 3.140 **nwAR,** *High-collared rooster*. . . A well-dressed gentleman. "We don't want no high-collared roosters to represent us in the legislature."

high cotton n

1 in phr *be in high cotton* and varr: To live well, prosper; to be in good spirits, feel important. [From the prosperity brought by a thriving cotton crop] **chiefly Sth, S Midl, TX** Cf **tall cotton, low cotton**

1942 Perry *Texas* 136, We frequently, if less delicately, refer to times of great prosperity as those in which we were defecating "in high cotton." **1949** *PADS* 11.7 **wTX** (as of c1920), *High (tall) cotton, in the*. . . Doing well. "He had trouble at first, but now he's in the high cotton." **1950** *PADS* 14.79 **FL,** *Livin' in high cotton.* Suwannee backwoods simile for lush living. **1952** Brown *NC Folkl.* 1.550, *High cotton, to be (walk) in*. . . To be prosperous; in good social standing.—General. **1960** Wentworth–Flexner *Slang* 468, *Shit in high cotton*. . . To live more prosperously, pleasantly, or luxuriously than one has formerly; to be enjoying the results of good fortune, success, or prosperity; to eat high off the hog. **1966–69** *DARE* (Qu. BB47, *Feeling in the best of health and spirits: "I'm feeling ———!"*) Inf **OR**1, In high cotton; (Qu. GG19a, . . *A person . . feeling important or independent: "He surely is ——— these days."*) Inf **GA**28, Shitting in high cotton [laughter]; **GA**77, Flying in high cotton; (QR, near Qu. GG34b) Inf **AL**6, [Feeling] in high cotton—when things are going well. **1967** *DARE* Tape **TX**49, Molly got her first pair of new shoes. Why, she thought she was in high cotton, and I did too. **1967** *DARE* FW Addit **c,swAR,** *In high cotton, shittin' in high cotton*—Living high, enjoying good fortune. The first is the polite, mixed-company form, reported to me by a woman in Magnolia. The second is the form used by men among themselves—I remembered it from my Arkansas Tech days, used by a man from Benton, Saline County; **LA**4, If you had a stove with a reservoir, you were in high cotton. **1980** *Capital Times* (Madison WI) 28 Jan 17/1 **LA,** Diane Ladnier . . is in high cotton just now. . . "I'm being paid a fortune. The money's so good hell wouldn't have it" [she said]. **1986** Pederson *LAGS Concordance,* 1 inf, **csAL,** Travel in high cotton—rich man, Blacks' term.

2 By ext: see quot.

1967 *DARE* (Qu. U19a, *Words used around here for money in general: "He's certainly got the ———."*) Inf **TX**33, High cotton.

3 A short cotton dress—also in phr *be* (or *walk*) *in high cotton* to wear such a dress. Cf **cotton 4**

1944 *AmSp* 19.154 **NC,** *High cotton*. . . The short cotton dress that a child had outgrown—it had become high cotton. **1952** Brown *NC Folkl.* 1.550, *High cotton, to be (walk) in*. . . To be wearing a short cotton dress.—Guilford county.

high cranberry See **highbush cranberry**

high cream n Cf **high yellow**

A Black person with an esp light complexion.

1934 Stribling *Unfinished Cathedral* 99 **AL,** The girl, too, whom he had taken for a white girl, now stood before him for what she was, a high cream, and was therefore not entitled to the courtesy.

high-daddy adj

Slick, deceptive; grand, dandy.

1898 Smith *Caleb West* 21 **NEast,** Now don't try any of your high-daddy tricks on me. **1904** *NY Tribune* (NY) 22 Oct 1/6, The Democratic press is trying to get up a regular high-daddy time over it. **1968** *DARE* (Qu. NN7, *Exclamations of surprise: "They're getting married next week? Well, ———."*) Inf **NY**43, That's high-daddy—it pleases and surprises me.

high daddy n

In railroading: see quot 1976.

1932 *RR Mag.* Oct 368, *High-daddy* or *Hi-daddy*—Flying switch in which cars are cut off behind the engine and switch is thrown after engine has passed. **1938** Beebe *High Iron* 221 [Railroad terms], *High daddy:* Flying switch. **1976** Gould *Blackie's RR Hdbk.* 10, A switching movement in which car or cars are uncoupled from engine and switch is lined between the cars and engine so that car or cars will roll into auxiliary track on their own momentum: . . *High Daddy.*

high dandelion n

A **hawkweed** (here: *Hieracium canadense*).

1900 Lyons *Plant Names* 191, *H. Canadense*. . . High Dandelion. **1940** Clute *Amer. Plant Names* 70, *H[ieracium] Canadense*. . . High dandelion.

high-deck v Cf **cold-deck v 2**

1958 McCulloch *Woods Words* 85 **Pacific NW,** *High deck*—To cold deck logs by skidder into small piles parallel to the railroad track, ready for loading on cars.

high dick, put on the v phr [Cf **dicty** adj, n; cf also *OED dick* sb.[4] "slang . . 'Fine language, long words' "; *OED up to dick* "up to the proper standards, excellent, 'proper' " (at *dick* sb.[5])]

1970 *DARE* (Qu. W38, *When a man dresses himself up in his best clothes . . he's ———*) Inf **VA**45A, Putting on the high dick—extravagantly dressed. [FW: used by Inf in conv]

high diver n

Perh a **pied-billed grebe.**

1970 *DARE* (Qu. Q9, *The bird . . like a small, dull-colored duck . . commonly found on ponds and lakes*) Inf **KY**88, High diver—goes under water.

high droppers See **eye-drops**

high dutch adv phr [Cf **high dutcher**]

?In a showy or extreme manner.

1830 Watson *Annals Philadelphia* 242 **PA,** Skating "High Dutch," and being able to cut the letters of his own name at one flourish, constituted the Doctor's fame as a *skater.* **1857** in 1983 *PADS* 70.38 **ce,sePA,** Little Neshaminy [Creek] has been cutting up high Dutch again [flooding].

high dutcher n [Cf quot 1889] *hist* Cf **high dutch**

A type of ice skate; see quot 1872.

1837 *Knickerbocker* 9.289 **NY,** Give me a satisfactory pair of *high-dutchers,* curled fantastically over the toe of my boots, the straps nicely adjusted, the line of steel ringing and thrilling along my sole, the Delaware or Fair-Mount dam for my theatre, and I can enact more wonders. **1872** Schele de Vere *Americanisms* 608, *High Dutchers,* a cant term for skates, the blade of which is curled up high in front.

high-ended adj

?Cocky, overconfident.

1963 *Mt. Life* 39.2.51 **sAppalachians,** The middle-aged mountain man is likely to be harsh in his evaluation of the youth just rising to maturity. . . "Look at 'im! High-ended as popcorn, I do reckon."

high end, off the See **high** adj **B8**

higher than a cat's back See **high** adj **B5a**

higher than a Georgia pine See **high** adj **B4b**

high-farkin' adj [Perh var of *highfalutin* but cf **forked 3**]

1937 Sandoz *Slogum* 70 **NE** (as of 1900–20), What was that high-farkin' Annette going around thundered up like a saloon keeper's flossie for if she couldn't keep a knot-head like the sheriff off a them?

high feather, in See **feather** n **B6**

high fence n Cf **low fence**

Something difficult or complex.

1967 Will *Dredgeman* 121 **FL,** Jim decided that his health couldn't stand such mental strain. . . Thad summed it up right neatly, "Jim jist had too low an eye for a right tolerably high fence."

high fi See **high five 3**

highfin carpsucker n Also *highback carpsucker, high-finned ~, highfin (sucker)* [See quot 1957]

A carpsucker (here: *Carpiodes velifer*).

1956 Harlan–Speaker *IA Fish* 75, *Highback Carpsucker. . . Other Names*—Highfin. . . The highfin can be readily recognized [sic] from the northern carpsucker by the length of the anterior, or first rays, in the dorsal fin. **1957** Trautman *Fishes* 241 **OH,** *Highfin Carpsucker. . .* Anterior dorsal rays of large young and adults, when unbroken, longest of any species of carpsuckers; they are usually longer than the dorsal base. *Ibid* 243, The largest population of Highfins occurred in the moderately deep waters of the Ohio River and the lower halves of its largest tributaries. **1967** Cross *Hdbk. Fishes KS* 180, The high-finned carpsucker is almost extirpated in Kansas. **1983** Becker *Fishes WI* 638, *Highfin Carpsucker. . .* Other common names: highfin, . . highfin sucker. . .Of all carpsuckers, the highfin has the most restricted range.

high five n

1 A card game; see quot 1974. Cf **cinch** n[1] **3**

1893 *Outing* 22.426/1, The gentlemen betook themselves to a shady spot on the beach to play "High Five" or some such wicked game. **1913** *Official Rules of Card Games* 154, *High-Five* (Double Pedro). . . Four players. . . Beginning with eldest hand, each player may bid for the privilege of naming the trump suit. . . Each player must bid higher than preceding bids or pass. . . Highest bidder names trump suit. **1938** Asbury *Sucker's Progress* 323 (as of 1875), [Footnote:] At first the Nevadans used the room principally as a place in which to play Cinch, a variation of All-Fours which was also known as Double Pedro or High Five, but after a few years it was devoted almost entirely to Poker. **1960** Criswell *Resp. to PADS 20* **Ozarks** *(Card games)* A few people played high-five. **1967–70** *DARE* (Qu. DD35, . . *Favorite card games*) Infs **KS**5, **KY**59, **MO**3, 24, **MA**15, **OR**10, **TX**1, High five. **1968** *DARE* Tape **CA**5, We used to have a regular card club . . I played two, three times a week. . . I think we played high five mostly. **1974** Gibson *Hoyle* 65, "High five" . . this game is actually an elaboration of *Auction Pitch* . . including features of *Pedro,* with additional features that characterize it as a game in its own right. It is a four-player game . . the trump suit includes the five of the other suit of the same color.

2 See quot.

1966 *DARE* (Qu. EE5, *Games where you try to make a jackknife stick in the ground*) Inf **NC**2, High five.

3 also *high fi:* A jail. [See quots]

1968 *DARE* (Qu. V11, . . *Joking names . . for a county or city jail*) Inf **TX**51, High five—the floor of the courthouse where the jail is. **1970** Tarpley *Blinky* 271 **neTX,** *High five* (sometimes called *high fi* by folk analogy) originally referred to the jail on the fifth floor of a county court house, but the term has been extended to include the jail on any of the upper floors of a municipal building.

highflier See **highflyer**

high-flies n pl

In marble play: see quot.

c1970 Wiersma *Marbles Terms, Hi-flies:. . .* Practice of throwing marble up in the air first, then letting it fall. Believed to be a foul.

highflyer n Also sp *highflier*

1 also *high-fly:* An extravagant or ostentatious person; a lively, spirited person; a hussy, immoral woman. [*OED* 1663 →]

1914 *DN* 4.74 **ME, nNH,** *High-fly. . .* A lively, spirited person, usually a woman. **1930** Shoemaker *1300 Words* 29 **cPA Mts** (as of c1900), *High flyer*—A showy, fashionable person. **1941** Smith *Going to God's Country* 118 **OK,** You old bachelors had beter think before you get maried to some of these young high fliers and blonds. **1950** *WELS (An immoral woman)* 1 Inf, **cwWI,** Highflyer. **1951** West *Witch Diggers* 43 **IN,** Dandie Conboy orders a coffin, baby size, blue satin lining, German-silver handles. . . May get out there and find he plans to use the thing for a collar box. The boy's a high-flyer, and for all I know that may be his latest conceit. **1966–69** *DARE* (Qu. U37, . . *Somebody who has plenty of money*) Inf **NC**61, Highflyer; (Qu. W40, . . *A woman who overdresses or who spends too much on clothes*) Inf **NE**3, Highflyer; (Qu. Y29a, *To 'go out' a great deal, not to stay at home much: "She's always ______."*) Inf **CA**107, A highflyer; (QR, near Qu. HH34) Inf **AR**39, Highflyer—disrespectful term; (Qu. HH37, *An immoral woman*) Inf **OH**8, Highflyer; (Qu. II23, . . *People who are, or think they are, the best society of a community: The ______*) Infs **IA**38, **NJ**10, **TX**9, Highflyers; **MS**21, Highflyer. **1976** Garber *Mountain-ese* 41 **Appalachians,** *Highflyer* . . big time spender. "He was shore a high flyer, as long as his inheritence lasted."

2 See quot.

1930 Shoemaker *1300 Words* 29 **cPA Mts** (as of c1900), *High flyer.* . . A pigeon released on a long string, used to attract the wild pigeons to the nets.

high-flying vbl n Cf **highflyer 1**

See quot 1942.

1875 Holland *Sevenoaks* 292 **N Atl,** I have to . . promise to raise the divil wid her whiniver she gits a fit o' high flyin'. **1942** Berrey–Van den Bark *Amer. Slang* 313.1, *Dissoluteness; dissipation. . .* high flying. *Ibid* 375.1, *Extravagance. . .* High flying.

high fog n **chiefly wCA** Cf **tule fog**

Thin fog that tends to remain suspended above the ground; see quots; also used facetiously.

1935 *Sun* (Baltimore MD) 14 Feb 26/1 *(Hench Coll.),* When it rains out in Hollywood, as it did on five successive days recently, the patriotic Californians refer to the downpour as a "high fog." **1939** *LANE* Map 96 *(Fog),* 1 inf, **csRI,** A high fog; 1 inf, **csRI,** [haɪ fɔg] one that burns off. **1939** *Sun* (Baltimore MD) 23 May 10/3 *(Hench Coll.),* The "high" fog which is one of the region's [=San Francisco's] peculiarities. . . They drift in from the Pacific, sometimes not touching the ground—the so-called "high" fogs—but hanging two or three hundred feet above the surface, and continuing to hang for amazing lengths of time. **1967–69** *DARE* (QR, near Qu. B19) Inf **CA**35, High fog—a high overcast—may stay six weeks; (Qu. B21, *When fine drops of moisture are falling*) Inf **CA**107, A high fog. **1987** *DARE* File **cwCA,** Along the coast near San Francisco there is an upwelling of very cold water. When air that is supersaturated goes over this cold water, it condenses, causing fog to drift over the land; it's often a light fog that burns off quickly as it goes inland where it's warmer. This is a high fog, that allows good visibility at ground level, very different from a dense, low-lying tule fog.

highfoot it v phr [Perh by analogy with *hotfoot it*]

1967 *DARE* (Qu. Y24, . . *To walk, to go on foot: "I can't get a ride, so I'll just have to ______."*) Inf **LA**12, Highfoot it.

high for picking cotton See **high** adj **B4c**

high-gear n Also *higear(y)* [Folk-etym]

Hegari: a **sorghum** (here: *Sorghum bicolor*) of the Caffrorum Group grown in the southwestern United States.

1942 Amer. Joint Comm. Horticult. Nomenclature *Std. Plant Names* 101, *Cereals (sorghum). . .* Hegari. *Dwarf Hegari; Higear; Higeary; Higrain Wheat.* **1960** Criswell *Resp. to PADS 20* **Ozarks,** In late years . . a number of the newer canes like highgear, Sudan grass, etc. for silos have come in. **1966–69** *DARE* (Qu. L21, *What kinds of grain are grown around here—anything special?;* total Infs questioned, 75) Infs **NM**3, **OK**18, High-gear; **OK**27, High-gear—similar to a maize; (Qu. L9b, *Hay from other kinds of plants [not grass]*) Inf **TX**63, High-gear (milo). **1970** *DARE* File, High-gear (corn). . . Folk-etym[ological] form used in Texas panhandle. It grows about 6 ft. high, one crop per year. **1986** Pederson *LAGS Concordance,* 1 inf, **cnTX,** High gear—type of hay to mow and bale; 1 inf, **ceTX,** Bundle of high gear—a fodder.

high geranium n Also *hygeranium* [Folk-etym var of *hydrangea;* cf *EDD*] Cf **highbelia**

A **hydrangea 1** (here: *H. arborescens*).

1940 Clute *Amer. Plant Names* 59, *H[ydrangea] arborescens. Wild Hydrangea. . .* high geranium. **1976** Ryland *Richmond Co. VA* 372, Hygeraniums—hydrangeas. [**1986** Pederson *LAGS Concordance,* 1 inf, **swGA,** Hydrangea ['ha·ɛdʒəˌreᵻniᵛə].]

highgolla flips See **higulcion flips**

high-grade v

1 To steal high-grade ore; by ext, to steal; hence vbl n *high-grading,* n *high-grader* a thief. **chiefly West**

1904 *Sun* (NY NY) 14 Aug 2.1/1, One of the pests of gold mining in Colorado is the high grader, which is a polite term for the ore thief. . . The term high grader comes from the fact that they steal only high grade ore. **1904** *Alliance News* (S.F.) Oct. 8/3 *(DA),* Many miners. . . make snug little fortunes, and then, as a rule, they 'blow them in,' and continue to work and to 'high grade.' *Ibid (DA),* Throughout this camp are men known to rumor as 'high graders,' in other words ore stealers. **1910** Johnson *Highways Rocky Mts.* 136 **West,** There was lots of high-grading going on—that is, there were fellows stealing high-grade ore. They'd go down abandoned workings and hike around through into a mine where the ore was valuable. **1914** *DN* 4.163 **NW,** *High grader. . .* Among miners, one who works in, or steals, high grade metals. **1941** Writers' Program *Guide UT* 415, Wealth pouring out of the hills started an epidemic of "high-grading," which forced some of the mines to shut down. Miners sneaked rich ore out of the mines in their lunch buckets, up their noses, in special pockets in their overalls, and once a whole carload of exceedingly rich ore disappeared from the railroad station. **1960** Wentworth-Flexner *Slang* 256, *Highgrade. . .* To steal something. . . [Highgrade]r. . . One who appropriates another's property; a thief. **1968** *DARE* (Qu. V6, . . *Words . . for a thief—any kind of thief*) Inf **CA**62, *High grader*—steals gold ore; extra rich dabs will go out with them in lunch buckets, pockets, clothing—an accepted crime. **1976** Gould *Blackie's RR Hdbk.* 13, *High grade:* To steal.

2 See quot. [Cf *upgrade*]

1981 *KS Qrly.* 13.2.68, *High grade. . .* To put discarded, used, or obsolete materials to a new or improved use.

high grade n **[high-grade v 1]**

1942 Berrey-Van den Bark *Amer. Slang* 490.2, *A theft. . .* Highgrade.

high-grader, high-grading See **high-grade v 1**

high-grass constable n

A rural law officer.

1908 McGaffey *Sorrows* 188, I'll have you know that I am only nicked by the best cops on Broadway, and not by any high-grass constable. **1968** Adams *Western Words* 147, *High-grass constable*—A cowboy's name for a rural law officer.

high-ground willow oak n

=**bluejack 1.**

1894 Coulter *Botany W. TX* 417, *Q[uercus] cinerea. . . High-ground willow-oak. . .* Sandy barrens, extending from the Gulf States to the valley of the Brazos. **1898** Sudworth *Forest Trees* 176, *Quercus brevifolia [Q. incana]. .* High-ground Willow Oak (S.C.) **1960** Vines *Trees SW* 178, *Quercus incana . .* High-ground Willow Oak. **1976** Bailey-Bailey *Hortus Third* 934, *Quercus incana . .* High-ground Willow Oak.

high-happy adj

?Inebriated.

1945 Thorp *Pardner* 40 **SW,** When the railroad was being built past Langtry, a high-happy cowboy caught a coolie track laborer by the cue, and hooked the cue over the horn of his saddle.

high-hat n

1 also *high-hatter:* A self-important, stuck-up, or citified person; hence adjs *high-hat, ~-hatted, ~-hatting, ~-hatty* snobbish, conceited, haughty; adv *high-hat* snobbishly.

1922 *DN* 5.147 **sePA,** *High hatty*—conceited, aloof, exclusive. **1923** *NY Times* (NY) 9 Sept 7.2/1, *High hat:* Swelled head. **1924** in 1952 Crane *Letters* 171 **OH,** It's become fashionable for the high-hatted uptowners now to buy Matisse's paintings. **1924** Marks *Plastic Age* 149 [College lingo] Christmas Cove's a nice place; not so high-hat as Bar Harbor, but still it's a nice place. **1942** Berrey-Van den Bark *Amer. Slang* 402.3, *Snob . .* high-hatter. **1950** *WELS (A woman who puts on a lot of airs: "She certainly is ______.")* 10 Infs, **WI,** High-hat; 1 Inf, A high-hat; *(A person . . feeling important or independent)* 3 Infs, **WI,** High-hat; 1 Inf, High-hatted; 1 Inf, [He's beginning to] go high-hat; *(Someone who has a very high opinion of himself)* 3 Infs, **WI,** High-hat; *(People who are [or who think they are] the best society of a community)* 3 Infs, **WI,** High-hat(s); 1 Inf, High-hatters; *(People who try to appear important or influential)* 1 Inf, High-hat; 1 Inf, Acting high-hat; *(Somebody who . . pretends not to know you: "When I met him on the street, he ______.")* 1 Inf, Appeared very high-hat. **c1960** *Wilson Coll.* **csKY,** *High-hat*—Arrogant, self-important. **1965-70** *DARE* (Qu. HH35, . . *"She's too ______ for me."*) 97 infs, **chiefly Nth, N Midl,** High-hat; 9 Infs, **Nth, N Midl,** High-hatted; **CA**158, High-hatty; **NC**9, High-hatting; **IL**61, **VA**42, High-hatter; (Qu. GG19a, . . *"He seems to think he's ______."*) 30 Infs, **Nth, N Midl,** High-hat; **DC**3A, **TX**95, High-hatted; **DE**1, Acting high-hat; [**VA**80, Has the high-hat;] (Qu. II23) 21 Infs, **scattered, but more freq Nth, N Midl,** High-hats; **AR**3, **NY**43, 219, **OR**3, **WA**1, High-hatters; **NY**70, They're high-hatted; (Qu. HH2, . . *A citified person*) Infs **AR**3, **TN**15, High-hat; **GA**74, **TX**36, High-hatter; (Qu. HH4, *Someone who has odd or peculiar ideas or notions*) Inf **NY**200, High-hat; (Qu. HH11b, *Someone who is too particular or fussy—if it's a woman*) Inf **WY**1, A high-hat; **CA**158, High-hatty; (Qu. HH41) Inf **MS**49, High-hat; (Qu. II6) Infs **CA**147, **NH**10, He'd gone high-hat; **MD**33, Was high-hat; **NY**206, He's high-hat; (Qu. II24, . . *The part of town where the well-off people live*) Inf **FL**8, High-hat section.

2 in phrr *give one* (or *make, put on*) *the* (or *a*) *high-hat:* To give one the brush-off; to assume a superior attitude.

1923 *WI News* (Milwaukee) 5 Mar 6 *(Zwilling Coll.),* ["Indoor Sports" cartoon:] There's that swelled up pitcher talkin' to the boss. Yeah—don't he put on the high hat though. **1950** *WELS (If you meet somebody who used to be a good friend, and he pretends not to know you: "When I met him on the street, he ______.")* 1 Inf, **WI,** Gave me the high-hat. **1965-70** *DARE* (Qu. II6, . . *"When I met him on the street he ______."*) Inf **GA**77, **MI**10, **NY**145, **SC**44, **VA**50, Gave me the high-hat; **FL**14, **ME**16, **OK**9, Give me the high-hat; **GA**72, Made a high-hat; **NY**219, Put on the high-hat.

high-hat adj, adv See **high-hat n 1**

high-hat v, hence vbl n *high-hatting* Also *hat*

To ignore or snub (someone); to assume a superior attitude.

1924 *Cosmopolitan* Apr 68/1 **NYC,** "Why high hat me?" he complains. "I'm harmless and I may be able to do you a lot of good." **1928** *Ruppenthal Coll.* **KS,** *High hat*—to act haughtily; to ignore others; to pass by without greeting or with coldness. "Other times men may high hat people but when running for office they know everbody [sic] and greet all." **1938** Matschat *Suwannee R.* 233 **nFL, sGA** [Black], Ah'm tired of de way she hats us pore folks. *Ibid,* Sis Coontie am a law-abidin' 'oman, an' never done no high-hattin' nohow. **1947** *Chicago Tribune* (IL) 16 Nov comics sec 5, I haven't noticed him doing any high-hatting. *Ibid,* Now I guess Wallet won't go around high-hattin' us because he's got a new car! **1950** *WELS (If you meet somebody who used to be a good friend, and he pretends not to know you: "When I met him on the street, he ______.")* 14 Infs, **WI,** High-hatted me; *(A person . . feeling important or independent)* 1 Inf, High-hatting; 1 Inf, [He's beginning to] high-hat. **1960** Criswell *Resp. to PADS 20* **Ozarks** *(Country person's names for a city person)* City people were said to be stuck up, high steppers, snooty; they high-hatted country people. **1965-70** *DARE* (Qu. II6) 174 Infs, **widespread,** High-hatted (me); **NC**82, **SC**59, High-hat me; **FL**19, Is high-hatting me; (Qu. Y22, *To move around in a way to make people take notice of you: "Look at him ______."*) Inf **MN**10, High-hatting; (Qu. GG19a, *"He surely is ______ these days."*) Infs **MN**3, **OH**16, **WA**25, High-hatting (us).

high-hatted See **high-hat n 1**

high-hatter See **high-hat n 1**

high-hatting vbl n See **high-hat v**

high-hatting adj See **high-hat n 1**

high-hatty See **high-hat n 1**

high-head n

An important person; a conceited or pretentious person.

a1874 in 1949 *PADS* 11.32 **ME,** Another fellow gazed on her—/ A swanking, brainless high-head. **1954** *Harder Coll.* **cwTN,** *High-head*—Someone important.

high-headed adj, also used absol

Of a person: haughty, proud; important, self-important; hence adv *high-headed* in a haughty or self-important manner.

1837 *S. Lit. Messenger* 3.86/2 **NC,** It may suit my neighbor . . to have one of them high-headed Roanoke planters to come here with his family, and spend his money. . . But, for my part, I would rather they would stay at home. **1887** (1895) Robinson *Uncle Lisha* 11 **wVT,** We can't expeck to be all on us suited . . an' them 'at is mus' try an' not kerry 'emselves too high-headed. **1909** Wason *Happy Hawkins* 10, You always was the most obstinate, high-headed, bull-intellected thin-skin 'at ever drew down top wages fer punchin' cows. **1935** Davis *Honey* 48 **OR,** You didn't always come out of it nearly as high-headed as you went in. **1953** Randolph *Down in Holler* 252 **Ozarks,** *High-headed*. . . Proud, arrogant, spirited. Usually refers to horses, occasionally to human beings. **1954** *Harder Coll.* **cwTN,** *High-headed* . . of people: important. **c1960** *Wilson Coll.* **csKY,** High-headed—Self-important, too much so. **1966–70** *DARE* (Qu. GG19a, . . *A person . . feeling important or independent*) Infs **KY**85, **MI**9, **NY**70, **TX**26, **VA**69, High-headed; (Qu. HH35, *A woman who puts on a lot of airs: "She's too ______ for me."*) Infs **AK**8, **KY**85, **PA**206, **TX**51, High-headed; (Qu. II23, *People who are, or think they are, the best society of a community: The ______*) Inf **PA**206, High-headed.

high heal-all n
=**lousewort.**

1822 Eaton *Botany* 381, *Pedicularis . . gladiata* . . high heal-all. **1900** Lyons *Plant Names* 278, *P[edicularis] Canadensis* . . High Heal-all.

high-heeled adj
Haughty, arrogant, disdainful.

1903 Fox *Little Shepherd* 46 **KY,** The people lived in big houses of stone and brick . . and rode . . in shiny covered wagons, with two "niggers" on a high seat in front and one little "nigger" behind to open gates, and were proud and very high-heeled indeed. *Ibid* 380, That's why I hate you . . fer worryin' him an bein' so high-heeled that you was willin' to let him mighty nigh bust his heart about somethin' that wasn't his fault. **1912** Raine *Brand Blotters* 190 **AZ,** A joke's a joke, girl. That's twice hand-runnin' I get a call-down. You're mighty high-heeled to-day, 'pears like.

high-heeled shoes n pl
In phrr *have on one's high-heeled shoes* (or *slippers*) and varr: To be haughty, "stuck-up"; to be unrestrained, powerful.

1859 (1968) Bartlett *Americanisms* 195, *High-heeled shoes.* To say of a woman that she "has on her *high-heeled shoes*" is to intimate that she sets herself up as a person of more consequence than others allow her to be. . . that she is "stuck up." New England. **1861** in 1986 Messer *Civil War Letters* 8 **VT,** You tel the Dr that I am afraid he is geting on his high healed shoes (in regard to his price for board) and I am afraid that I shall have to come out their and talk to him a little. **1864** (1868) Trowbridge *3 Scouts* 27 **TN,** I ain't goin' to see him turned out into the woods a night like this, jest 'cause my wife's got on her high-heeled shoes, not by a long chalk! **1905** *DN* 3.11 **cCT,** *High-heeled shoes*. . . Pride. **1936** in 1953 Botkin–Harlow *Treas. Railroad Folkl.* 50, We were whittling that lost time away to nothing, and Mr. Casey was still in high spirits. As we left Durant, he stood up and hollered to me over the boiler head. He said: 'Oh, Sim! The old girl's got her high-heeled slippers on to-night. We ought to pass Way on time.'

high-heeled time n Also *high-heel (good) time*
An exciting or enjoyable time.

1898 Lloyd *Country Life* 249 **AL,** And it did look to me like of all the places in a discovered world for a youngster to go and have a high heel good time that was the mainest place. **1942** Hurston *Dust Tracks* 181 **FL** [Black], Dick, the lovable, the irresponsible, was having a high-heel time up and down the east coast of the United States. *Ibid* 271, All dressed to kill and gone out for a high-heel time. **1966** *DARE* (Qu. FF17, *Words meaning that people had a very good or enjoyable time: "We all had a ______ last night."*) Inf **AL**5, High-heeled time. **1968** Adams *Western Words* 147, *High-heeled time*—A common description of the cowboy's idea of a good time with fun and frolic.

high henry [Perh in ref to Amer railroad folk hero John *Henry*]

1934 Hurston *Jonah's Gourd Vine* 167 **S Atl** [Black], "Where you bound fuh?" John asked. "Tuh ketch me uh high henry." "Whuss dat?" "Uh railroad train, man, where you been all yo' days you don't know de name of uh train?"

high-hill rattler See **highland rattler**

high-holer n [Folk-etym varr of *hickwall;* see *OED high-hole*]
1 also *high-hold(er), high-hole:* Any of var **woodpeckers,** but usu **flicker** n^2 **1.**

1808 Wilson *Amer. Ornith.* 1.53, [The Gold-winged woodpecker] has numerous provincial appellations in the different states of the Union, such as "High-hole," from the situation of its nest. **1844** Giraud *Birds Long Is.* 181, *Picus auratus . . Golden-winged Woodpecker* . . This handsome bird is well known by a variety of names, such as "High-hold," "Wake-up," and "Flicker;" by some it is called "English wood-pecker." **1858** Baird *Birds* 118, *Colaptes Auratus* . . Flicker; Yellow Shafted Woodpecker; High Holder. **1895** Minot *Land-Birds New Engl.* 324, *Colaptes Auratus. . . "High-hole."* . . They [=the nests consisting always of a hole] are usually made more than six feet from the ground, and more often in a trunk than in a limb. **1913** Johnson *Highways St. Lawrence to VA* 50 **seNY,** Do you see those dead trees up there on that slope? There used to be lots of highholes in them. A highhole is a bird with a big, long mouth. It's like a woodpecker, only larger. They're good to eat. **1928** *Ruppenthal Coll.* 8 **KS,** *High hole* . . A kind of woodpecker; the *yellow hammer* or *flicker,* mottled black and gray with a small red tuft on the head. **1950** *WELS (Joking names for woodpeckers)* 3 Infs, **WI,** Highholer; 1 Inf, Flicker = highholer; 2 Infs, Highhole(s). **1956** MA Audubon Soc. *Bulletin* 40.82, High-holder, High-hole (Mass., Conn. In the United States, such terms are assumed to refer to the Flicker's choice of a lofty location for its nest—it is often low, however. But to philologists these names are adapted from those of the Green Woodpecker. British folk names "High-hoe" and "High-hole" are traced back to Anglo-Saxon words, referring to the "laughing" notes of that bird.) **1965–70** *DARE* (Qu. Q17, . . *Kinds of woodpeckers*) Infs **MI**53, **NY**69, 71, 73, **WI**50, High-holer; **IL**32, **MI**65, **NY**107, **OH**67, High-holder; **MA**21, **NY**73, 165, 191, High-hole; (Qu. Q18, *Joking names and nicknames for woodpeckers*) Infs **CA**78, **NJ**43, **NY**52, 155, High-hole; **OH**16, **PA**234, High-holder; **PA**223, High-holer; (Qu. Q14) Inf **VT**10, High-hole, wake-up (a speckled bird with a red spot on the back of the head—sort of a woodpecker).

2 in phr *high-holer's nest:* See quot. Cf **hurrah's nest 1**

1968 *DARE* (Qu. E22, *If a house is untidy and everything is upset, you might say, "It's a ______!"*) Inf **PA**119, High-holler's [sic] nest—a high-holler is a kind of bird.

high-hole swallow n
A swallow.

1968 *DARE* (Qu. Q20, . . *Kinds of swallows*) Inf **NY**83, High-hole swallow.

high hook n Cf **highline** n **5**
Among anglers: see quot 1848.

1848 in 1935 *DN* 6.453 **RI,** *High Hook,* the one who catches the largest or the greatest quantity of fish. **1894** *Outing* 24.259/2 **IL,** F. was high hook with a five and a-half pounder. **1899** (1900) Van Dyke *Fisherman's Luck* 109 **NYC,** When we came together . . to compare notes . . and make up the fish-stories for the year, Beekman was almost always "high hook." We expected, as a matter of course, to hear that he had taken the most and the largest fish. **1939** Chamberlain *Nantucket* 11 **MA,** Mr. James Wood . . is the oldest man on the island . . and "high hook" of Nantucket, a distinction coming from his feat of making the largest single catch of codfish on local record.

high hosey n Cf **hosey, hot pepper**

1988 *DARE* File **ceMA,** *High hosey* was the name for the high-speed version of rope jumping.

high iron n
In railroading:

a See quot 1945. Cf **highline** n **4**

1930 *RR Man's Mag.* 470, *High iron*—The main line or the high speed track of a system of main tracks. **1940** in 1953 Botkin–Harlow *Treas. Railroad Folkl.* 407, An alternate crossing of the Blue Ridge forking from the high iron [or main line of the Louisville & Nashville] at Etowah, Tennessee, . . is the famous "Hook and Eye" Division. **1945** Hubbard *Railroad Ave.* 346, *High iron*—Main line or high-speed track (which is laid with heavier rail than that used on unimportant branches or spurs). **1958** *Daily Progress* (Charlottesville VA) 26 Aug 11/1, The last steam passenger train on the "high iron"—the main lines—chugged into memory in July.

b also *high-iron dog:* See quots.

1976 Gould *Blackie's RR Hdbk.* 6, *Passenger train* . . High Iron—Stream Liner. *Ibid, Train (on Main Line):* High Iron. **1977** Adams *Lang. Railroader* 78, *High-iron dog:* A passenger train.

high-jack v
To steal or acquire illegally or by cheating, spec:

a as vbl n *high-jacking:* See quot. **esp NEast** Cf **highlight, jack** v

1967–69 *DARE* (Qu. P35b, *Illegal methods of shooting deer*) Infs **CT**22, **NJ**8, 10, **NY**20, 205, **PA**83, High-jacking.

b To claim, appropriate; see quot.

1968 *DARE* (Qu. V5b, *If you take something that nobody seems to own, you might say, "Before anybody else gets it, I'm going to ——— this."*) Inf **CA**62, High-jack.

c To cheat, treat dishonestly.

1965–67 *DARE* (Qu. U10, *If something costs a great deal, or more than you think it's worth, you might say, "That's ———."*; total Infs questioned, 75) Infs **AR**30, **FL**22, High-jacking (you); **OK**31, I got high-jacked; (Qu. LL23, *Cheated, treated dishonestly: "These apples are wormy, I think you got ———."*) Inf **DC**1, High-jacked.

high-jack n

1 A marble game.

1969 *DARE* (Qu. EE7, . . *Kinds of marble games*) Inf **NC**72, High-jack.

2 See **jack** n.

high-jacker n

1968 *DARE* (Qu. HH19, *Other words or nicknames for a tramp*) Inf **AK**8, High-jacker—always traveling, can't trust him.

high-jacking See **high-jack v a**

‡high-jeetis n

1970 *DARE* (Qu. BB28, . . *Imaginary diseases*) Inf **IL**135, High-jeetis [ˈhɑijitɨs].

high jinks n pl, but sg in const

1 =**high-muck-a-muck 2.**

1969 *DARE* (Qu. HH17, *A person who tries to appear important, or who tries to lay down the law in his community: "He'd like to be the ——— around here."*) Inf **GA**84, High jinks.

2 See quot.

1969 *DARE* (Qu. V11, . . *Joking names* . . *for a county or city jail*) Inf **AZ**16, High jinks.

high John the Conqueror See **conquer John**

high-kaflutin adj Also *high-kaflootinary, high-konflukin, hiki-fallootin* [Varr of *highfalutin* + infixed **ker-**]

1912 *DN* 3.578 **wIN,** *Hiki-fallootin*. . . Unnecessarily high or formal. **1941** Stuart *Men of Mts.* 39 **neKY,** I'm a man of mountain ways and I can't git high-kaflutin' and go back on what I was raised on. **1965–66** *DARE* FW Addit **MS,** *High-kaflootinary*—I've heard this only a few times by Negroes in north Mississippi. **1967–70** *DARE* (Qu. HH35, *A woman who puts on a lot of airs: "She's too ——— for me."*) Infs **IN**60, **NM**4, **NY**232, High-kaflutin; **TN**6, [ˌhakəˈflutɪn]; **MI**101, High-konflukin.

high keys, be on one's v phr Also *get on one's high keys*

1899 (1912) Green *VA Folk-Speech* 224, *High-keys*. . . A person is said to be on his *high-keys* when he is loud in voice, and boisterous in action. "There's no telling what he'll do when he gets on his high-keys."

high kicker n

A "fast" or dissolute person.

1897 *KS Univ. Qrly.* (ser B) 6.88, *High kicker:* fast person.—General [usage in US]. **1923** *DN* 5.238 **swWI,** *High kicker*. . . An expression of derogation. The figure is borrowed from horsemanship. The term *high stepper* has no derogatory connotation. **1942** Berrey–Van den Bark *Amer. Slang* 438.1, *Dissolute person*. . . high-kicker.

high knuckle adj phr Cf **knuckle down**

In marble play: with the knuckles raised from the ground.

1976 *WI Acad. Rev.* June 20/1 (as of 1920s), Our favorite "shooters" developed a fine roughness from constantly colliding with other marbles and the texture aided in "high knuckle" shooting.

high-konflukin See **high-kaflutin**

highland adj **chiefly S Atl**

Of reptiles, amphibians, and some mammals: living away from water; upland. Cf **dry-land frog, dry-land moccasin, dry-land turtle**

1846 [see **highland moccasin**]. **1889** [see **highland moccasin**]. **1952** [see **hicatee**]. **1965–70** [see **highland moccasin**]. **1965–70** [see **highland terrapin 1**]. **1966–69** [see **highland rattler**]. **1966–70** [see **hill rabbit**]. **1968** [see **highland frog**].

highland cooter See **highland terrapin 1**

highland cranberry n

A **mountain cranberry** (here: *Vaccinium vitis-idaea*).

1916 *Torreya* 16.239, *Vaccinium vitis-idaea*. . . High land cranberry, Matinicus I[sland], M[ain]e. **1966** *DARE* (Qu. I44, *What kinds of berries grow wild around here?*) Inf **ME**23, Highland cranberries.

highlander See **highland plover**

highland frog n Cf **dry-land frog**

A **toad.**

1968 *DARE* (Qu. P23, . . *The animal similar to the frog that lives away from water*) Inf **GA**65, Toad-frog—the highland frog; **NC**49, Highland frog. **1986** Pederson *LAGS Concordance (Toad)* 1 inf, **csMS,** Highland frogs.

highland gopher See **highland terrapin 1**

highland hard maple See **highland maple**

highland hickety See **hicatee**

highland live oak See **highland oak**

highland maple n Also *highland hard maple*

A **hard maple.**

1966 *DARE* (Qu. T14, *What different kinds of maples do you have around here?*) Inf **NC**13, Highland maple [as opposed to "swamp maple"]. **1986** Pederson *LAGS Concordance,* 1 inf, **csTN,** Highland hard maple.

highland moccasin n **chiefly SE** See Map

A **copperhead snake 1** (here: *Agkistrodon contortrix contortrix* or *A. contortrix mokeson*).

1842 Holbrook *N. Amer. Herpetology* 3.45 **TN,** The Trigonocephalus atro-fuscus . . [is] called in Tennessee Highland Moccassin. **1846** (1973) Porter *Quarter Race* 93 **MS,** I'd rather fight the biggest bar in the swamp . . than come in contact with a big rusty highland moccasin or rattlesnake. **1890** *Century Dict.* 3809, The same or a very similar snake found on dry land, the so-called *high-land moccasin, A[ncistrodon] atrofuscus,* known in the southern United States as the *cottonmouth,* and much dreaded. **1892** Johnston *Mr. Fortner's* 151 **GA,** There were a great big full-grown high-land moccasin quiled [=coiled] up on the baby's breast. **1928** Bradford *Ol' Man Adam* 6 **cwTN** [Black], Eve see a great big highland moccasin crawlin' long twarg her. **1952** Ditmars *N. Amer. Snakes* 63, Northern Copperhead Snake, . . Highland Moccasin . . *Agkistrodon mokasen cupreus*. *Ibid* 85, Copperhead Snake, . . Highland Moccasin, . . *Agkistrodon mokasen mokasen*. **1958** Conant *Reptiles & Amphibians* 185, The Copperhead *[Agkistrodon contortrix mokeson]* has many aliases—"chunkhead," "highland moccasin," "pilot," "adder," etc. **1965–70** *DARE* (Qu. P25, . . *Kinds of snakes*) 15 Infs, **chiefly SE,** Highland moccasin. **1971** GA Dept. Ag. *Farmers Market Bulletin* 20 Oct 1, Are black snakes, solid black, no markings, poisonous? Do they eat other snakes? . . I've had one in my house and now have one in my yard plus a highland moccasin. **1986** Pederson *LAGS Concordance,* 6 infs, **AL, LA, MS,** Highland moccasin(s).

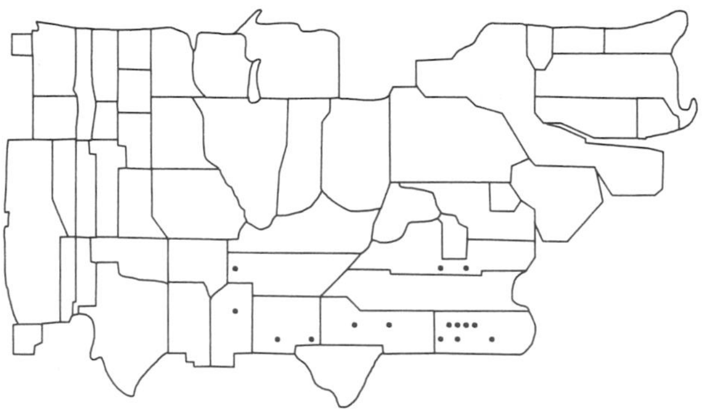

•highland moccasin (Qu. P25)

highland myrtle n

=**mountain laurel** (here: *Kalmia* spp).

1970 *DARE* (Qu. BB50d, *Favorite spring tonics*) Inf **FL**49, Highland-myrtle tea. **1986** Pederson *LAGS Concordance (Mountain laurel)* 1 inf, **csMS,** Highland myrtle.

highland oak n Also *highland live oak*

A **live oak** (here: *Quercus wislizeni*).

1897 Sudworth *Arborescent Flora* 165 **CA,** *Quercus wislizeni*. . . Highland Live Oak. **1898** Sudworth *Forest Trees* 56, *Quercus wislizeni*. . . Highland Oak. **1908** Rogers *Tree Book* 210, The *Highland Oak* . . is a large tree on the elevated foothills back from the coast in California. **1945** Wodehouse *Hayfever Plants* 80, The . . highland live oak . . is . . native of the interior of California. **1979** Little *Checklist U.S. Trees* 245, *Quercus wislizeni*. . . *Other common names*—highland live oak.

highland plover n Also *highlander* **NEng**

=**upland plover.**

1888 Trumbull *Names of Birds* 172, *Bartramia longicauda*. . . At Bath and Portland, Me., *Highland plover*. **1923** U.S. Dept. Ag. *Misc. Circular* 13.64, *Upland Plover (Bartramia longicauda)*. . . *In local use*. . . highland plover (Me.) **1925** (1928) Forbush *Birds MA* 1.447. **1956** MA Audubon Soc. *Bulletin* 40.17, *Upland Plover*. . . Highlander (Mass.); Highland Plover (Maine).

highland potato n

1 =**Ithuriel's spear.**

1902 (1974) Chestnut *Plants Indians* 327 **CA,** *Triteleia laxa*. . . The most abundant and widespread of all the Indian potatoes. . . It grows in fields, especially on the hills, and is known as the "highland potato."

2 See quot.

1967 *DARE* (Qu. I23, . . *Kinds of squash*) Inf **LA**2, Highland potatoes are a lot like sweet potatoes in use, but they are related to [the] squash.

highland rabbit See **hill rabbit**

highland rattler n Also *high-hill rattler* Cf **highland moccasin**

A rattlesnake, perh of the genus *Sistrurus*.

[**1846** (1973) Porter *Quarter Race* 93 **MS,** I'd rather fight the biggest bar in the swamp . . than come in contact with a big rusty highland moccasin or rattlesnake.] **1966–69** *DARE* (Qu. P25, *What kinds of snakes are found around here?*) Inf **GA**77, Highland rattler (poisonous)—smaller than a mountain rattler; **SC**19, High-hill rattler.

highlands n

A wealthier or more prestigious neighborhood located on high ground.

1966–68 *DARE* (Qu. C35, *Nicknames for the different parts of your town or city*) Inf **ME**16, The highlands; **MA**5, Highlands—for the better part in mill towns, mill owners live there; (Qu. II24, . . *The part of a town where the well-off people live*) Infs **ME**9, **WI**47, The highlands; **MA**5, Highlands—in a mill town where the owners and nabobs live.

highland spruce n

A **white spruce.**

1968 *DARE* (Qu. T5, . . *Kinds of evergreens, other than pine*) Inf **MN**19, White or highland spruce; **MN**29, White spruce or highland spruce.

highland terrapin n

1 also *highland cooter, ~ gopher, ~ turtle*: =**gopher** n[1] **1. chiefly Gulf States, S Atl**

1851 *De Bow's Rev.* 11.53 **LA,** *Turtles* are found in great numbers. . . I have not met with any *high land* terrapins. **1965–70** *DARE* (Qu. P24, . . *Kinds of turtles*) Infs **FL**17, 48, **VA**70, Highland turtle; **FL**4, **GA**77, **SC**63, Highland terrapin; (Qu. P29, *Do you have 'gophers' around here? . . What other name do they have?*) Inf **FL**32, Highland turtle; **FL**35, Highland turtle—burrows in the ground; **GA**28, Like a turtle—he's a highland cooter, ain't he? **SC**63, Highland cooter—rare. **c1970** Pederson *Dial. Surv. Rural GA* 1 inf, **seGA,** High land terrapin. **1986** Pederson *LAGS Concordance* **Gulf Region,** 13 infs, Highland turtle(s); 9 infs, Highland terrapin(s); 1 inf, Highland gopher.

2 See quot.

1966 *DARE* (Qu. HH1, . . *A rustic or countrified person*) Inf **MS**73, Highland terrapin.

highland ti-ti n

Perh a **staggerbush.**

1933 Rawlings *South Moon* 47 **FL,** She went a short way into the scrub and cut boughs of highland ti-ti for a new yardbroom.

highland turtle See **highland terrapin 1**

high laurel n Cf **low laurel**

=**calico bush 1.**

1941 *LANE* Map 249 *(Mountain laurel)* 8 Infs, **RI, seMA,** High laurel.

high-lead n, often attrib |ˈhaɪ ˈlid| **chiefly NW** Cf **highline n 1**

In logging: see quot 1958.

1933 *Natl. Geogr. Mag.* 63.152/1 **WA,** A straight Douglas fir makes an ideal spar tree for high-lead logging, and an expert woodsman climbs to the desired height and chops off the upper part of the trunk. To this tall pole, firmly rooted in the ground, cables and hoisting tackle are attached. **1940** Writers' Program *Oregon* 357, At certain locations are towering spar-trees from which "high lead" lines swing huge logs across hills and canyons for miles, and drop them beside the road. **1946** Peattie *Pacific Coast* 242, Someone thought up the idea of the high lead, by which the end of the log could be lifted above the tangle of obstacles in its path as it was dragged from the ministrations of the hook tender. **1958** McCulloch *Woods Words* 85 **Pacific NW,** *High lead*—The widely used system of logging using a spar tree which carries the main line and haulback cables through blocks high above the ground. Developed from rigging used on masts aboard ship, and improved from the tree rigged Lidgerwood skidder. The high lead was a great advance of the low lead, or ground lead method which it replaced, because in the latter the logs were merely dragged on the ground and hung up on every rock and stump. **1967** *DARE* FW Addit **cOR,** *High lead loggers*—Everything is skidded in on cables, above ground. **1967** *DARE* Tape **WA**24, Then in 1918, they started in on the high leads [ˈhaɪ ˈlidz]. **1969** Sorden *Lumberjack Lingo* 56 **NEng, Gt Lakes,** *Highlead*—Modern-type power logging where logs are yarded by means of a block hung on spar tree or steel tower or pole, used very little in lake states. Generally a western term.

high life n Also sp *hi-life* [Prob from its stimulating effect on the heart rate; cf **high-lifed**]

Carbon disulfide when used as a fumigant or stimulant; also fig; hence v phr *high life* to treat with carbon disulphide.

1906 *DN* 3.140 **nwAR,** *High life*. . . Bi-sulphide of carbon. "Give me a dime's worth of high life." **1925** *Nation* 18 Nov 561/2 **cwWA,** Several of the bucking horses were doctored up, too, with High Life, to make them buck. High Life is a liquid and is usually put in the mane. **1946** *Harder Coll.* **cwTN,** *Hi-life*. . . An aphrodisiac; something that makes one move faster. "A snail could keep up with him walking. He needs some Hi-Life on him." **1947** *Democrat* 14 Aug. 6/2 *(DA)*, Fumigate corn with carbon bisulphide (high life) about two weeks after it is put into the crib. **1951** Giles *Harbin's Ridge* 169 **eKY,** When Zeb Barnes' coon hounds were high-lifed, we were there, and we knew who'd thought of that, too. But he managed to get Silas blamed for that. **1954** McAtee *Dial. Grant Co. IN Suppl. 5* [2], *High-life*: . . Carbon bisulphide as put into the fundament of a horse to make it "buck" at a rodeo. **1963** Edwards *Gravel* 107 **eTN** (as of 1920s), The horse shied, snorted, then jumped and broke into a wild run. The doctor was hard put to stay on his back. It was as if the horse had been shot full of "high-life," and he plunged forward down the entire length of the ridge road. **1969** *DARE* (Qu. JJ26, *If somebody has been doing poor work or not enough, the boss might say*) Inf **CA**161, Give him a touch of high life—the acid they use to burn a bronco with before he goes into the ring to buck.

high-lifed adj Also *high-life, high-lived*

Esp of animals: high-spirited, lively.

1861 IL State Ag. Soc. *Trans.* 4.376, A long narrow-headed, high-lifed, brainless animal should be quietly handled. **1902** A. D. McFaul *Ike Glidden* ix.70 *(OEDS)*, Ike told him . . to always drive on the bit, because the colt was a high-life fellow. **1913** London *Valley of Moon* III.xxi *(DAE)*, 'She's used to spurs,' Billy called after. 'Spanish broke, so don't check her quick. . . She's high-life, you know.' **1941** *LANE* Map 461 *(Lively, Spry)*, 1 inf, **ceMA,** High-lifed. **1947** Hervey *Amer. Trotter* 37, He was not a horse of kind disposition but very high-lived, always requiring a strong hand to control him, and in especial very cross to strangers. **1950** Stuart *Hie Hunters* 188 **eKY,** They're high-lifed mules. **1969** *DARE* Tape **CT**38, We had livery horses that you couldn't rent because we had to send drivers with 'em because they're a little bit high-lifed horses.

high-lift v [Cf *lift, hijack* to steal]

1969 *DARE* (Qu. V4, *Other words for stealing something valuable—for example, a watch: "Yesterday somebody ______ my watch."*) Inf **MA**26, High-lifted.

highlight v, hence vbl n *highlighting* Cf **high-jack v 1, jack v**

To hunt deer illegally at night by shining a bright light that causes the deer to stand immobile.

1967 *DARE* (Qu. P35b, *Illegal methods of shooting deer*) Inf **MA**34, Highlighting—headlights from a car are used to attract. **1987** *DARE*

File **NEast,** The wardens fly around looking for lights so if you are going to highlight deer you put a light in a field where you aren't going to be.

highline n

1 In logging: a heavy cable strung high above the ground and used esp to haul logs out of the woods. **chiefly West** Cf **high-lead**

1925 *AmSp* 1.137 **Pacific NW** [Logger talk], Nowadays the ground-lead system is going out of use, and logs are generally hauled in on a "high-line." **1931** *AmSp* 7.49 **Sth, SW** [Lumberjack lingo], A "high line," which is of one-inch steel, extends, often one-half mile, to either end of the "set." On this line is run an inverted steel "bicycle" to which the logs are attached and drawn to the railroad. **1941** Writers' Program *Guide WA* 554, The great cable is then suspended between the two spar trees, near the tops. Upon this aerial, or highline, is a huge block that acts as a trolley for the several cables suspended from it and the logs, or trees, being hauled to the pole deck. **1958** McCulloch *Woods Words* 85 **Pacific NW,** *High line*. . . A name sometimes used to mean high lead, log tramway, or skyline.

2 A road or trail high on a mountainside; see also quot 1958. **West**

1880 *Harper's New Mth. Mag.* 60.556/2 **CO,** These Colorado railroad builders . . propose carrying the Colorado Central . . over the "high line" by which we came. **1944** Walker *Winter Wheat* 302 **MT,** Bailey says up on the high line they've lost half their winter wheat crop; they're going to have to reseed to spring. **1958** McCulloch *Woods Words* 85 **Pacific NW,** *High line*. . . The upper of two logging roads in the mountains. **1961** Adams *Old-Time Cowhand* 176 **West,** When he [=the average cowhand] did fall from grace and stampede to the wild bunch it wasn't long till he was jes' two jumps ahead of a sheriff. And once he started ridin' the high lines, he couldn't quit. . . He was sometimes forced to ride over trails that'd make a mountain goat nervous and in a country so rough an ordinary man couldn't find his saddle seat with a forked stick.

3 A high-voltage electric transmission line.

1942 Berrey–Van den Bark *Amer. Slang* 804.5, *High line,* the electric lead of primaries transmitting current from the source to various towns on the circuit. **1950** *WELS Suppl.* 4 Infs, **WI,** *Highline*—high voltage electric lines. **1967–68** *DARE* Tape **TX**9, Umbrella ribs became unprofitable because when a kite got tangled in the high lines, which they were building then, why, it shorted out—blew out the transformers; **WI**26, Our tailing pile got pretty close to high line and some kid come down—went up on that tailing pile . . grabbed a hold o' the high line—just burned him to a crisp; **WI**60, This happened about way back in the era before the high lines were scattered all over the country . . and all of these small utilities had their own generating stations.

4 In railroading: see quots. Cf **high iron a**

1942 Berrey–Van den Bark *Amer. Slang* 775.1, *Railroad*. . . high iron, highline, main, main drag, main iron, *a main or trunk line.* **1977** Adams *Lang. Railroader* 78, *Highline:* The main track.

5 also *highliner:* In fishing: see quots 1889, 1945; by ext, the best or highest achiever of a group. Cf **high hook**

1856 C. Nordhoff *Whaling & Fishing* xviii.354 *(OEDS),* Several had at different times been 'high line' from Harwich. **1889** Munroe *Dorymates* 21 *n. (DAE), High-line,* the man who catches the most fish on a trip, or the vessel that brings in the heaviest fare of the season. **1913** London *Valley of Moon* II.XV *(DA),* She was among the high line weavers when the jute mills closed down. **1914** Steele *Storm* 56 **Cape Cod MA,** On the grounds he was a great "killer," an unmerciful "driver," and for three years running now the "high liner" of the Old Harbor fleet. **1945** Colcord *Sea Language* 100, **ME, Cape Cod, Long Island,** *High line.* A Banks-fisherman's term for the boat that brings back the best fare; used figuratively in shore speech for excellence in general. **1947** *Chicago Tribune* (IL) 2 Nov 10, [In the comic strip "John West":] Such luck, on the heels of these record hauls was maddening! We'd have been the "high liners[”]" of the fleet! **1954** *AK Sportsman* June 15/1 **AK,** Peter has long since become a successful fisherman, one of the highliners, but there was a time when he ran the gamut of trouble.

highline v Cf **highline** n **5**

In fishing: see quot.

1951 Ryan *Maggie Murphy* 93 **AK,** The fishermen of Port Alexander were a hardy, weather beaten breed of deep sea mariners who enjoyed a prominence in the village only in proportion to their reputation for "fishing tough." To win respect in this community, a fisherman had to show supreme disregard for foul weather and consistently "highline," or outearn, his fellow skippers.

highliner n

1 See quots. [Cf **highline n 4**]

1930 *RR Man's Mag.* 470, *Highliner*—Main line fast passenger [train]. **1956** *Sun* (Baltimore MD) 29 Feb 4/2, The brakeman of the halted train reportedly ran back with a red flag to warn of the stalled train—but apparently his signal was unseen by the high-liner engineer.

2 See **highline n 5.**

high-lived See **high-lifed**

high living, come hell or See **hell 9**

highlone adv, v [*OED high-lone* adv. 1597–1760; *"Obs."*]

Alone, without assistance or support; to walk without assistance or support.

1760 in 1889 Washington *Writings* 2.155 **neVA,** Mulatto Jack return'd home with the Mares he was sent for; but so poor were they, and so much abus'd had they been . . that they were scarce able to highlone, much less to assist in the business of the plantations. **1899** (1912) Green *VA Folk-Speech* 224, *Highlone*. . . Alone, without help. **1917** *DN* 4.385 **KY,** *Highlone*. . . To walk without the support of the nurse: said of a baby. Ky.—H.G. Shearin. **1961** *W3, Highlone . . dial: alone* <the baby has just learned to stand ~>.

high lonesome n

1 A drinking spree or binge, esp one indulged in alone.

1897 *KS Univ. Qrly.* (ser B) 6.53, *High lonesome:* a 'glorious' drunk or spree: as, He goes off on a high lonesome occasionally. **1915** *DN* 4.184 **swVA,** *High-lonesome*. . . Debauch; spree. **1917** *DN* 4.380 **KS,** *High lonesome,* a drunken spree. **1928** *Ruppenthal Coll.* **KS,** *High lonesome*—A drunken spree, without companions. He went on a high lonesome—he drank heavily alone. **1941** *AmSp* 16.312 **NE** (as of c1891), Mrs. Hic Heiman ordered Lafe Brown not to give her husband liquor, but he did and Hic got on a "high lonesome." **1942** *Sun* (Baltimore MD) 17 Nov 14/2 *(Hench Coll.),* Jane always knows when Bill is primed for a high lonesome. He starts a quarrel with her, so he'll have an excuse to drown his sorrows. **1960** Criswell *Resp. to PADS 20* **Ozarks,** *High lonesome*. . . A drunken spree. Pretty common among men even to this day. **1970** *DARE* (Qu. DD16, *To have a drinking bout and get drunk is to go on a* _______) Inf **TX**89, High lonesome.

2 in phr *hit the high lonesome:* See quot.

1939 FWP *ID Lore* 241, *Hit the high lonesome*—to depart, usually in haste; or to set out for an unknown destination.

high-low n

1 also *high-low chair:* A high chair; see quot.

1960 Criswell *Resp. to PADS 20* **Ozarks,** *High-low*. . . A high chair. . . the term high-low chair was common forty years ago. This chair was used for a baby at the table and for a woman at the weaving loom.

2 =**Antony-over A.**

1968 *DARE* (Qu. EE22, . . *The game in which they throw a ball over a building . . to a player on the other side*) Inf **MO**25, High-low.

high-low chair See **high-low 1**

high-low-jack n Also *high-low-jack and* (*a* or *the*) *game* [See quot 1974; cf *EDD*] Cf **cinch** n[1] **3**

A card game; see quots 1952, 1974.

1843 (1973) Porter *Big Bear AR* 16, [They] laughed at my calling the principal game in Arkansaw poker, and high-low-jack. **1844** Featherstonhaugh *Excursion Slave States* 136/1 **Lower Missip Valley,** I was kept awake by his sitting up with Rector and continuing to play at high, low, jack, and the game. **1938** FWP *Guide DE* 411, Between duties the members of the [Coast Guard station] crew sit around reading, talking, or playing "high-low-jack-and-the-game" (pitch) with a worn deck of cards. **1952** Culbertson *Card Games* 229, The original All Fours was known in America . . as Seven-Up, Old Sledge, High-low-Jack. . . All Fours presently gave way to a more elaborate offspring, Pitch, which probably developed in the New England states. **1960** Bailey *Resp. to PADS 20* **KS** *(Card games played a good deal in your neighborhood)* High-low-jack. **1960** Criswell *Resp. to PADS 20* **Ozarks** *(Expressions, generally used, that come from card games)* High-low-jack and the game. **1966–69** *DARE* (Qu. DD35, . . *Favorite card games*) Infs **MD**34, **MA**6, 11, **NH**2, **NY**213, **RI**8, **SD**2, High-low-jack; **CT**6, **DC**8, High-low-jack and (a) game; **MN**42, High-low jack and the game. **1974** Gibson *Hoyle* 111, *High low jack:* A once common name for *Pitch* . . and similar games in which high, low, and jack of trumps represent three of the points. Also called *High, Low, Jack and Game,* to include the fourth point.

high-low-sheepie n
The game blindman's buff.
1967 *DARE* (Qu. EE4, *Games in which one player's eyes are bandaged and he has to catch the others and guess who they are*) Inf **PA**7, High-low-sheepie.

high man n Cf **high** adj **B9, hoodoo** n **1a**
1970 Hyatt *Hoodoo* 1.240, *High man* is the usual term [for a hoodoo doctor] on the Eastern Shore of Maryland.

high-mass n
A **bee brush** (here: *Lippia wrightii*).
1960 Vines *Trees SW* 886, *High-mass*. . . Western shrub to 6 ft, slender-branched, hairy, aromatic. . . *Lippia wrightii.*

high-minded adj [*OED* *high-minded* a. 1 c1503–1865; *"arch."*] **esp Sth, S Midl**
Proud, haughty, touchy.
1818 (1930) Sewall *Diary* 42 **ME,** I have heard it remarked that the people in general are a haughty, high-minded, as well as dissipated people. **1966–70** *DARE* (Qu. GG8, *When a person is very easily offended: "Be careful what you say to him, he's ———."*) Inf **NC**33, High-minded; (Qu. GG19a, . . *A person . . feeling important or independent*) Infs **FL**52, **LA**8, **MO**23, **SC**26, High-minded; (Qu. HH11b, *Someone who is too particular or fussy—if it's a woman*) Inf **MO**15, High-minded; (Qu. HH35, *A woman who puts on a lot of airs: "She's too ——— for me."*) Infs **AL**16, **MD**31, **OH**33, **TX**86, **WI**22, High-minded; **MA**15, High-minded with herself; (Qu. HH41, *Someone who has a very high opinion of himself;* total Infs questioned, 75) Inf **MS**71, High-minded; (Qu. II23, . . *People who are, or think they are, the best society of a community*) Inf **FL**1, High-minded [*DARE* Ed: Inf may intend this as a noun]. [6 of 14 Infs Black]

high mogul n Also *head mogul*
=**high-muck-a-muck 2.**
1906 *DN* 3.140 **nwAR,** *High mogul*—Chief officer or representative. **1950** *WELS (A person . . feeling important or independent)* 1 Inf, **WI,** Play high mogul. **1950** *WELS Suppl.* **WI** (as of c1920), *Head mogul*—The leader or instigator for action in a community. Sometimes used in a derogatory manner for someone who is rich. **1965–70** *DARE* (Qu. GG19b, . . *A person . . feeling important or independent: "He seems to think he's ———."*) Inf **VT**12, The high mogul; (Qu. HH17, *A person who tries to appear important, or who tries to lay down the law in his community: "He'd like to be the ——— around here."*) Infs **AR**12, **CA**174, **IA**9, **MI**92, **NE**9, **OH**49, **TX**65, High mogul; (Qu. II23, . . *People who are, or think they are, the best society of a community*) Infs **CO**7, 27, High moguls.

high-muck-a-muck n Also *high-muckety-muck, high-muck(y)-muck, high-you(-muck-a-muck);* for addit varr see quots **scattered, but esp Nth, N Midl** Cf **muck-a-muck**
1 as *hi(y)u* (or *hiou*) *muckamuck:* Good food; an abundance of food. [Chinook Jargon *hiu* plenty + *muckamuck* food]
1853 *Oregonian* (Portland) 20 Aug. 2/6 *(advt.) (DA),* Thomas Pritchard, General Store: *Hiou Muckamuck* of all kinds, but *Halo Lum* [=no rum]. **1946** Peattie *Pacific Coast* 235, *Hiu muckamuck* (lots of food) meant steady crews. **1950** *Western Folkl.* 9.118 **nwOR** (as of 1892) [Logger talk], *Hiyu muckamuck.* Good food . . ; a big shot.
2 A person of real or imagined authority; hence occas adj *high-muck-a-muck* haughty, pretentious. [Prob by folk-etym from **1**] Cf **high mogul**
1856 *Democratic State Jrl.* (Sacramento CA) 1 Nov 3/1, The professors —the high "Muck-a-Mucks"—tried fusion, and produced confusion. **1866** in 1966 Twain *Letters HI* 32, Not if I was High-You-Muck-a-Muck and King of Wawhoo. **1905** *DN* 3.62 **NE,** *High mucky-muck.* . . Person in authority, or prominence. "He was high mucky-muck in the show." **1906** *DN* 3.140 **nwAR,** *High muck.* . . Chief officer or representative. "He's the high muck of the concern." **1908** *DN* 3.320 **eAL, wGA,** *High-muck(-a-muck).* . . Chief officer, boss, manager, leader. **1919** *DN* 5.72 **NM,** *Monkey-monk, high* . . an aristocrat. "They are the high monkey-monks of the town, so be careful what you say." **1947** *PADS* 8.19 **IA,** *High mucky muck.* **1950** *WELS (The top person in charge of a group of workmen)* 1 Inf, **WI,** High-mucky-muck; [1 Inf, Big mucky-muck;] *(Joking names for . . the best society of a community)* 1 Inf, **WI,** High-mucky-mucks. **1951** Johnson *Resp. to PADS 20* **DE,** *(A person who tries to appear important or who tries to lay down the law in his community: "He thinks he's ———." "He wants to be ———.")* High-muckety-muck. **c1960** *Wilson Coll.* **csKY,** *High-muck (or muck-ity)-muck.* . . An important person, a "big boy." Humorous. **1965–70** *DARE* (Qu. II23, . . *People who are, or think they are, the best society of a community*) 10 Infs, **chiefly Nth,** High-mucky-mucks; **IN**49, **MO**2, **NJ**18, **PA**114, **SC**21, High-muckety-mucks; **MD**30, **SC**11, High-muck-a-mucks; **MS**71, High-monkey-monks; **OH**8, High-mucky-moguls; **TX**9, High-mocha-marines; (Qu. HH17, *A person who tries to appear important, or who tries to lay down the law in his community*) 10 Infs, **chiefly Nth,** High-mucky-muck; **GA**67, **PA**242, **TX**4, High-muckety-muck; **MI**44, **NY**123, High-monkey-monk; **CA**169, High-mucky; **NV**7, High-you; (Qu. HH35, *A woman who puts on a lot of airs: "She's too ——— for me."*) Inf **DE**7, High-muckety-muck; **HI**6, High-mucka-mucka; (Qu. II24) Inf **IA**22, High-muckety-mucks; **RI**6, Where the high-munk-a-mugs live; (Qu. U37, . . *Somebody who has plenty of money*) Inf **MI**108, High-mucky-mucks; (Qu. V10a, . . *Joking names . . for a sheriff*) Inf **OR**6, High-mucky-muck. **1966–68** *DARE* Tape **GA**11, All of the high muckety-mucks all around came; **NJ**15A, Some of the high-mucky-mucks around town here, they bankrupt him, they didn't pay for their cars.

high near adv phr
1968 *DARE* (Qu. LL30, . . *'Nearly' or 'almost': "He fell off the ladder and ——— [broke his neck]."*) Inf **VA**34, High near.

high nine n
1966–69 *DARE* (Qu. DD35, . . *Favorite card games*) Infs **AR**22, **KY**87, High nine; **KY**84, High nine—similar to pitch, but both nines used.

high-nose n Cf **high-head**
Arrogance; hence *the high-nose* a slight or snub.
1942 Berrey–Van den Bark *Amer. Slang* 301.2, Arrogance . . *high nose.* *Ibid* 352.1, Slight; snub . . *the high-nose.* *Ibid* 352.2, Slight; snub . . *give the high-nose.*

high-nosed adj Cf **high-headed 1**
Snobbish, pretentious.
1942 Whipple *Joshua* 282 **UT** (as of c1860), Clory, watching the faces about her, sincere, devoted, only a few like Marianne Snow's too high-nosed for simple folk. **1942** Berrey–Van den Bark *Amer. Slang* 301.6, Arrogant; haughty . . high-nosed. **1967** *DARE* (Qu. HH35, *A woman who puts on a lot of airs: "She's too ——— for me."*) Inf **HI**6, High-nosed. **1984** Wilder *You All Spoken Here* 12 **Sth,** She carries herself proud; she thinks a-right smart of herself—*High-nosed.*

high on oneself adj phr
Conceited, stuck-up.
1965–68 *DARE* (Qu. GG19a, . . *A person . . feeling important or independent: "He surely is ——— these days."*) Inf **KS**13, High on himself; (Qu. HH8, *A person who likes to brag*) Infs **OK**1, 45, **TX**4, (Sure) high on him-(or his-)self; (Qu. HH41, *Someone who has a very high opinion of himself;* total Infs questioned, 75) Infs **OK**45, 51, High on him-(*or* her-)self.

high on the hog adj phr [By ext from std sense *high on the hog* richly, luxuriously, in ref to eating the more desirable loin meat rather than the **side meat** or **belly-bacon**]
1968–70 *DARE* (Qu. GG19a, . . *A person . . feeling important or independent: "He surely is ——— these days."*) Inf **MA**128, High on the hog today.

high order See **high** adj **B1**

high-o-see exclam Cf **calf-rope,** *DS* EE20
=**uncle.**
1987 *DARE* File **ceMA,** *(When two boys are fighting, and the one who is losing wants to stop, he calls out, "———.")* High-o-see.

high-over n, exclam Also *high-Andy-over, ~-Antony, hytry over*
=**Antony-over.**
1899 (1912) Green *VA Folk-Speech* 67, "High Antony." A game of ball played by two parties of boys on opposite sides of a house, over which the ball is thrown. **1940** *Qrly. Jrl. Speech* 26.266 **VA,** One children's game is called "Antony over" or . . "hytry over." **1950** *WELS (In the game . . what . . you say or call out when you throw the ball)* 1 Inf, **cWI,** High-over. **1967–68** *DARE* (Qu. EE22, . . *The game in which they throw a ball over a building . . to a player on the other side*) Inf **NC**41, High-over; **VA**9, High-Andy-over; (Qu. EE23a, . . *What do you call out when you throw the ball?*) Inf **PA**35, High-over; **VA**9, High-Andy-over.

high-penny-over n
=**Antony-over A.**

1942 Warnick *Garrett Co. MD* 8 **nwMD** (as of 1900–18), *High-penny-over*. . . Antony-over, the game.

high pennyroyal n
=**dittany.**
1900 Lyons *Plant Names* 125, *C[unila] origanoides*. . . High pennyroyal. **1940** Clute *Amer. Plant Names* 221, *Cunila origanoides*. . . High pennyroyal.

high-pitch n
=**Antony-over A.**
1970 *DARE* (Qu. EE22, . . *The game in which they throw a ball over a building . . to a player on the other side*) Inf **VA**65, High-pitch [hapɪč].

‡high place n
Prob =**facing bench.**
1968 *DARE* (Qu. CC5, *Names for seats in a church, especially near the front*) Inf **PA**126, Sitting in the high places—in Friends' Meeting—the place up front.

highpockets n pl, but sg in constr
A tall, lanky person—also used as a nickname for such a person.
1912 *DN* 3.578 **wIN,** *High-pocket(s)*. . . A long-legged, lank man. "See what a high-pockets he is, anyhow." **1934** in 1946 Chandler *Finger Man* 16, It's your money, highpockets. **1958** McCulloch *Woods Words* 85 **Pacific NW,** *High pockets*—A tall man. **1968** *DARE* (Qu. V10a) Inf **GA**23, Highpockets—the sheriff is a tall man. **1976** Garber *Mountain-ese* 41 **Appalachians,** *High-pockets* . . leggy person. "Say there high-pockets, how's the weather up there?" **1985** Ehrlich *Solace* 2 **WY,** They call him "Highpockets," because he's so long-legged.

high-poler See **high roller 1**

high-posted adj
Of a room: having a high ceiling; of a person: tall.
1907 *DN* 3.190 **seNH,** *High-posted*. . . Tall. "She's terrible high-posted." **1965** *DARE* File **MA** (as of 1953), *High-posted* . . of a room, having a high . . ceiling. "The room is high-posted."

high-power adj
Unrefined, vulgar, rowdy.
1935 Davis *Honey* 155 **OR,** One [song] was "Old Mother Kelly's Got a Pimple on Her Belly," and it was too high-power to be possible [to sing for a woman]. The other was in the aggregate almost as bad, but it did have spots that weren't too rowdy.

high power n
A high-power rifle.
1937 *Hall Coll.* **eTN,** *High power*—A term for a gun; a 30-30 rifle, much used in bear hunting. "Ah'd like to shoot that crane with my high-power." **1960** Hall *Smoky Mt. Folks* 35, Uncle Dave chuckled at his memory of old Quill Rose riding his jack, with his "high-power" on his arm. *Ibid* 61, *High power:* a high-power gun.

high-prime v [Cf *OED prime* v.² 2 "to domineer"]
To prance, swagger.
1883 (1971) Harris *Nights with Remus* 101 **GA** [Black], [A boy has charged Uncle Remus with snoring. Remus replies indignantly:] Man can't lean hisse'f 'pun his 'membunce, 'ceppin' dey's some un fer ter come high-primin' 'roun' en 'lowin' dat he done gone ter sleep. *Ibid* 113, W'iles he think youer off some'rs a-snifflin' en a-feelin' bad, yer you is a-high-primin' 'roun' des lak you done had mo' supper dan de King er Philanders.

high private n
A person of slight rank among those with no rank.
1863 *Harper's New Mth. Mag.* May 860/1, One of the high privates . . found himself . . in a situation demanding a reconnaisance [sic]. **1869** Browne *Adventures* 280 **AZ,** There was a California volunteer in our party, holding the position of high-private. **c1928** *Ruppenthal Coll.* **KS,** *High private in the rear ranks*—One who is not prominent or a leader in any matter; one of the average as contrasted to the leaders or officials. "I don't want a nomination for office in this fight for a principle, but am satisfied to be a high private in the rear ranks."

high riding vbl n Cf **highline n 2**
Escaping quickly.
1944 Adams *Western Words* 60 **West,** *Fixin' for high ridin'*—Preparing to leave the country in a hurry. . . Also said of one doing something which will get him into trouble.

high rigger n chiefly **NW**
In logging: the person who rigs (and also often tops and limbs) the **spar tree** for use in cable logging.
1925 [see **high climber**]. **1938** [see **high climber**]. **1941** Writers' Program *Guide WA* 554, A "high-rigger" climbs to the top of the tree to be felled, by looping his belt around the trunk and driving his spurs into the heavy bark, and then descends, stripping the tall, straight trunk of its branches as he goes. **1942** *AmSp* 17.222 **ME, Gt Lakes, Pacific NW** [Loggers' lingo], *High rigger.* The *high climber* during the latter phase of his operation. **1956** *Perrin Coll.* **cwWA,** *High rigger*—The men who climb trees to cut off the top and to install heavy rigging blocks necessary for transporting logs in a "high lead" system. Also called "high climber." **1958** McCulloch *Woods Words* 85 **Pacific NW,** *High rigger*. . . A logger who tops trees and rigs them with guys, blocks, and lines, getting ready to yard logs. . . In some camps the high rigger rigs only, after the climber has topped the tree. **1966** *DARE* Tape **MT**4, They'd take the limbs off t'approximately 200 feet down to a 15- or 18-inch top. The fellow that did that work they called him the high rigger.

high roller n
1 also *high-poler:* A high-bucking horse. **chiefly West**
1936 Adams *Cowboy Lingo* 98, A 'high-roller' was a horse that leaped high into the air when bucking, also called a 'high-poler.' **1936** McCarthy *Lang. Mosshorn* np **West** [Rodeo term], *High Roller.* A horse that leaps high in the air when bucking. **1941** Writers' Program *Guide WY* 462, *High roller*—A high bucker.
2 See quot.
1940 Writers' Program *Guide NV* 78, During shearing season common terms . . [include] *high roller,* a shearer who works fast but poorly.

high salty n
A ranch foreman.
1945 Thorp *Pardner* 111 **NM,** Singling out Allen as high salty of our outfit, she said sharply. "Have you had any education?" **1961** Adams *Old-Time Cowhand* 64 **West,** The foreman of a good ranch . . was knowed by such titles as . . "high salty."

highs and splits n pl
In marble play: see quot.
c1970 Wiersma *Marbles Terms, Highs and splits*—how a kiss [=a tie or draw] is resolved[.] (Both marbles are thrown into the air and divided in mid-air by the coned point of one's hands and arms.[)]

‡high sassereier n
1968 *DARE* (Qu. II23, . . *People who are, or think they are, the best society of a community*) Inf **NC**82, He's the high sassereier [ˌsæsɚˈɑɪɚ].

high sheriff n [*OED High Sheriff* (at *high* a. and sb.² A. IV. 20) the supreme or highest ranking sheriff; 1662] **chiefly Sth, S Midl**
A sheriff or marshal—usu used as a joc or derog nickname.
c1938 in 1970 Hyatt *Hoodoo* 1.76 **cwFL** [Black], "Well, de high sheriff in dis town is gon'a git killed to-morrow." . . "Well, de high sheriff went out to make [an] arrest, an' when he went out to make arrest on one brother, . . the other brother shot him." **c1960** *Wilson Coll.* **csKY,** *High sheriff*. . . Often used derogatorily for sheriff. **1965–70** *DARE* (Qu. V10a, . . *Joking names* . . *for a sheriff*) 81 Infs, **chiefly Sth, S Midl,** High sheriff; **TX**9, Mr. high sheriff; (Qu. V10b, . . *Joking names for a marshal*) Inf **WI**62, High sheriff; (Qu. HH17, *A person who tries to appear important, or who tries to lay down the law in his community: "He'd like to be the ______ around here."*) Inf **GA**84, High sheriff. **1983** *MJLF* 9.1.43 **ceKY, TN** (as of 1956), *High sheriff* . . the elected sheriff, as opposed to a deputy sheriff.

high shots n pl, but sg in attrib use Also *high shot backins, high shot liquor* Cf **backings, first shot**
In whiskey distilling: see quots 1968, 1974.
1968 *Foxfire* Fall–Winter 101 **nGA** [Stilling terms], *High Shots*—pure, untempered, unproofed whiskey. At times it is as strong as 200 proof. **1969** *DARE* Tape **GA**72, It'll only take about ½ gallon of water to proof down what we call high shot liquor. . . When it comes out condensed at the end of your condenser . . then it is hot shots or high shots. . . These backins that are barely dead, they are what we call the high shot backins, and the alcoholic content of 'em is very high. **1974** Dabney *Mountain Spirits* 20 **sAppalachians,** He was used to homemade corn of 120 proof and higher—and what he liked particularly were the "high shots" that even he admitted would "take your breath away." **1974** Maurer–Pearl *KY Moonshine* 119, *High shots*. . . Very high-proof liquor which must be cut with water or backings to 100 proof.

high-side v Cf **high sign 2**

1967 Cleaver *Soul* 27 [Black], They walking in fours and kicking in doors . . drinking wine and committing crime, shooting and looting; high-siding and low-riding. [Footnote to *high-siding*:] Cutting up. Having fun at the expense of another.

high sign n, v [By ext from *high sign* a signal]

1 The identifying mark (through gesture, special clothing, or the like) of membership in a group; to display the mark or sign of such membership.

1980 Folb *Runnin' Down* 80 [Black], I'z Watts gang. Three finger high sign. Each gang, you know, he dress different. . . They walk around frontin', high signin' their gang. *Ibid* 242, *High sign.* . . Special colors, sign, or greeting that designate group or gang affiliation.

2 Something showy or ostentatious; to show off, outdo, or upstage.

1980 Folb *Runnin' Down* 12 [Black], My expressed interest in the vernacular seemed to promote involvement and moved teenagers to "high sign" (show off) their knowledge of . . the vernacular. *Ibid* 109, Terms like to *style,* to *front off* . . to *high sign* . . all of which mean to show off or upstage others. *Ibid* 115, Da's what they do in their cars. . . Some jus' high sign. Cadillacs da's all it is—a high sign. You don' hafta make d'car look good by you doin' extra curriculin' things, 'cause it's *there.*

high social n

A big party; an elaborate or formal kind of entertaining.

1927 in 1983 Truman *Dear Bess* 330 **MO,** I hope you had a good time at Helen's luncheon. She seems to be doing the high social right. **1967** *DARE* (Qu. FF1, *Do you have around here a kind of group meeting called a 'social' or 'sociable'? What kinds are there? [What goes on?]*) Inf **MN**2, Nothing that would include [the] whole community except the high social, where [the] whole town gathered, a few years ago, everybody brought some food, a big party, no booze.

high-sprung adj See **sprung** adj

high spy See **hy spy** n

highstericky See **hystericky**

highsteries See **highstrikes**

highstick v

Among loggers: see quot.

1958 McCulloch *Woods Words* 85 **Pacific NW,** *Highsticked*—Slapped on the face by a stick which flies up when one end is stepped on.

high strawberry n

A **cinquefoil** (here: *Potentilla norvegica*).

1898 *Jrl. Amer. Folkl.* 11.226, *Potentilla Norvegica,* . . high strawberry, Androscoggin Co., Me.

highstrikes n pl, but sg in constr Also *highsteries, hysterikes* [Varr of *hysterics,* perh by folk-etym; cf *OEDS highstrikes "jocular colloq.,* orig. *dial.* or *vulgar";* 1838] Cf **hystericky**

Hysterics; wild or uncontrollable behavior—often in phr *give one the highstrikes.*

1835 in 1956 Eliason *Tarheel Talk* 71 **NC,** Last night I drank a glass, filled it up again and *challenged* the general (a young man). . . but he backed out. . . Now dont you think such is enough to give me the *high strikes.* **1858** Hammett *Piney Woods Tavern* 141, They'd been at their high strikes, and was putty [=pretty] well up in the picters [=pictures, i.e., they were fairly intoxicated]. The empty bottles was layin' around putty thick, and the company ginrally was a howlin' out French songs. **1871** (1882) Stowe *Fireside Stories* 147, Then Quassia she haw-hawed louder. Says she, "It's hy-sterikes, Miss Cinthy; that's all it is." **1894** Twain *Tom Sawyer Abroad* 20 **MO,** It just give the poor old man the high strikes. It made him sick to listen to Tom. **1912** Green *VA Folk-Speech* 224, *Highsteries.* . . For *hysterics.* **1930** Shoemaker *1300 Words* 30 **cPA Mts** (as of c1900), *High-strikes*—Hysteria, or nervous disorders. **1954** *PADS* 21.30 **c,cwSC,** *High strikes.* . . Hysterics. . . Only in such a phrase as "Isn't that enough to give you the high strikes?" **1971** *Today Show Letters* **cIL,** Another relative noted for originality always said *high strikes* for hysterics.

hightantrabogus n [Pseudo Latin; cf *EDD tantarabobus* "A name for the devil; a bogie"] Cf **tantibogus**

1892 *DN* 1.210 **NEng,** *Hightantrabogus* . . a noisy good time; as in "raisin' hightantrabogus."

high temper n Cf **high-tempered**

1966–69 *DARE* (Qu. GG5, *When someone does something unexpectedly bold or forward, you might say: "Well, she certainly has . . ______.")* Inf **OK**18, A high temper; (Qu. GG8, *When a person is very easily offended: "Be careful what you say to him, he's ______.")* Inf **NC**69, Got a high temper; (Qu. GG41, *To lose patience easily: "You never did see such a ______.")* Inf **SC**10, High temper.

high-tempered adj **[high temper] chiefly Sth, S Midl**

Touchy, irritable, impatient.

1941 *LANE* Map 470 *(Touchy, quick-tempered),* 1 inf, **neRI,** ['haɪ 'tɛmpəd]. **1956** Ker *Vocab. W. TX* 352, Easily offended . . high-tempered. **1965–70** *DARE* (Qu. GG41, *To lose patience easily: "You never did see such a ______ person.")* 11 Infs, **chiefly Sth, S Midl,** High-tempered; (Qu. GG8, *When a person is very easily offended: "Be careful what you say to him, he's ______.")* Infs **AR**47, **GA**7, **KY**84, **LA**2, 11, **MO**18, **TX**98, High-tempered; (Qu. GG38, *Somebody who is usually mean and bad tempered)* Infs **MO**8, **VA**24, (He's) high-tempered; **AR**47, **IN**73, High-tempered fellow (*or* guy); (Qu. GG40, *Words or expressions meaning violently angry)* Infs **AL**40, **GA**67, High-tempered; (Qu. HH11b, *Someone who is too particular or fussy—if it's a woman)* Inf **MO**9, High-tempered. **1966** Dakin *Dial. Vocab. Ohio R. Valley* 2.468, [Meaning] a person who is easily offended . . *high-tempered* is more frequent among the older speakers. **1968–70** *DARE* Tape **CT**10, They were full of mischief and my father was somewhat high-tempered. . . and he'd chase them outa the store; **TN**48, People said she was beautiful and very high-tempered; when I was young I was high-tempered too, but now I don't think I'm high-tempered. **1984** Wilder *You All Spoken Here* 14 **Sth,** *High-tempered:* Has a short fuse.

high-test adj, usu used absol **chiefly east of Missip R** See Map and Map Section Cf **ethyl**

Of gasoline: high in octane.

1934 (1943) *W2* 1178/3, *High-test.* . . said of gasoline. **1965–70** *DARE* (Qu. N15b, *Gas stations . . usually have two kinds of gasoline: A more expensive kind that's called ______)* 458 Infs, **chiefly east of Missip R,** High-test; **MD**20, High-test gas.

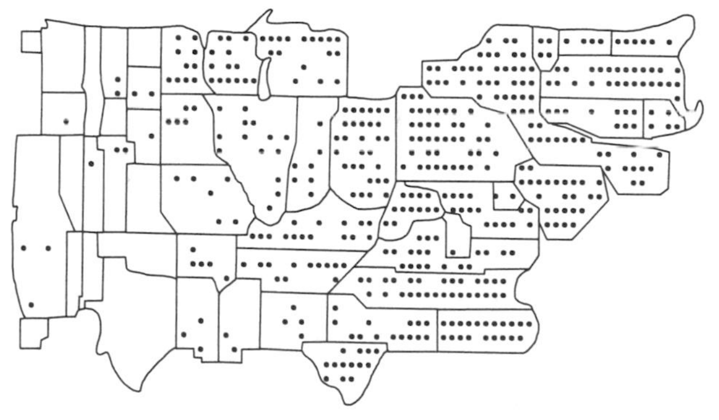
•high-test + var (Qu. N15b)

highth See **height**

high-tide bush n Cf **high-water shrub**

=groundsel tree.

1926 *Torreya* 26.6, *Baccharis* spp. . . The two plants [=*Baccharis* spp and *Iva* spp] are confused under other appellations also, as . . high-tide bush. **1937** *Torreya* 37.101, *Baccharis* spp. . . There is an excusable tendency to confuse *Baccharis* and *Iva* in the application of local names and the terms, marsh elder and hightide bush, according to Clarence Cottam, are so confused on the New York coast. **1940** Clute *Amer. Plant Names* 253, *Baccharis halimifolia.* . . High tide bush.

high-tide hen n

=clapper rail.

1951 *AmSp* 26.278, Connecting bird movements with those of the tide . . *high-tide hen* (clapper rail, G[eorgi]a).

high tilt n Cf **high beam 2**

1968 *DARE* (Qu. N10, *What other words are used around here for the bright and dim lights on a car?)* Inf **PA**74, High tilt.

high time n
=**fast time 2.**
1931 [see **fast time 2**].

high-time adj
High-class, superior, of high social status.
1937 (1977) Hurston *Their Eyes* 169 **csFL** [Black], He don't know you'se useter uh more high time crowd than dat. *Ibid* 219, Mah Janie is uh high time woman and useter things. . . Ah got her outa big fine house.

hight-l'arnt adj [Cf *EDD high-learned* "scholarly, well-educated" (at *high* adj. 1. (26)); prob var of *highly learned*]
1884 *Anglia* 7.276 **SE** [Black], Hight-l'arnt talk = learned talk.

‡high toe nail n
1969 *DARE* FW Addit **cnMA**, Keep a stiff upper lip and a high toe nail [FW: perh folk-etym for *Keep a stiff upper lip and a high-toned air*].

high-tone n Also *high-toner*
A dignified or prominent person; a pretentious or snobbish person.
1865 *Natl. Anti-Slavery Std.* 23 Sept 1/5 **TN**, The 'high-tones,' as the Western soldier calls the 'chivalry,' make many asseverations of . . loyalty. **1876** Bornemann *Madame Jane Junk* 66 *(DA), (Title),* Meeting with Hightoners. **1942** Berrey–Van den Bark *Amer. Slang* 402.3, *Snob* . . high-toner. **1966–69** *DARE* (Qu. II23, . . *People who are, or think they are, the best society of a community: The* ______) Infs **CA**97, **WA**6, High-tones; **MT**2, High-toners.

high-tone v
1966 *DARE* (Qu. II6, *If you meet somebody who used to be a friend, and he pretends not to know you: "When I met him on the street he* ______.") Inf **OK**51, High-toned me.

high-toner See **high-tone** n

hightop n
1967 *DARE* (Qu. X5, . . *Kinds of men's haircuts*) Inf **TX**40, Hightop.

high-top v Cf **high-hat** v
1967 *DARE* (Qu. II6, *If you meet somebody who used to be a friend, and he pretends not to know you: "When I met him on the street he* ______.") Inf **TX**13, High-topped me.

highty adj
1912 Green *VA Folk-Speech* 225, *Highty*. . . For *high*.

highty-flighty adj Cf **hoity-toity**
1966 *DARE* (Qu. HH35, *A woman who puts on a lot of airs: "She's too* ______ *for me."*) Inf **AR**3, Highty-flighty.

highty-tighty adj Also sp *hidy-tidy, hity-tity* [Varr of **hoity-toity;** cf *OED hoity-toity* "The sense seems in later times to have gradually been influenced by *high, height,* and their family; this becomes explicit in the spelling *Highty-tighty*"] Cf Pronc Intro 3.I.11
=**hoity-toity;** rarely v *highty-tighty* to make much of.
1840 *Spirit of Times* 18 July 229/3 **OH**, As for them *highty tighty* sort of tunes he sung, why they arnt no more tu be compared tu the good old-fashioned ones. **1872** Schele de Vere *Americanisms* 488, *Hity-tity,* as the English *hoity-toity* is more frequently sounded and written in America, is here also used as a verb. "She expects to be hitied[sic]-titied, that is, to be made much of." **1905** *DN* 3.57 **eNE**, For [oɪ], [aɪ] is very common . . [haɪtɪ taɪtɪ] (hoity toity). **1966–68** *DARE* (Qu. GG19a, *When you can see from the way a person acts that he's feeling important or independent: "He surely is* ______ *these days."*) Inf **OH**61, Hidy-tidy; (Qu. HH35, *A woman who puts on a lot of airs: "She's too* ______ *for me."*) Inf **MT**2, Highty-tighty; **NY**93, Highty-tighty [ˌhaɪtɪ ˈtaɪtɪ].

high up to picking-cotton See **high** adj **B4c**

‡high-upum-boofum n
1968 *DARE* (Qu. CC17, *Imaginary animals or monsters*) Inf **IN**38, High-upum-boofum—just generally dangerous.

high walkers n pl Cf **tom walkers**
Stilts.
1969 *DARE* (Qu. EE33, *Long wooden poles with a footpiece that children walk around on to make them tall*) Inf **TN**37, High walkers.

high-water adj
Of an article of clothing or a haircut: unusually or unfashionably short—often in phr *high-water pants;* hence n pl *high waters.*
1856 (1928) Twain *Advent. Snodgrass* 9 **seIA**, Then some soldiers with bob-tailed tin coats on (high water coats we used to call 'em in Keokuk) come in, then some gals (with high water dresses on). **1902** (1903) Lorimer *Letters* 6 **Chicago**, High-water-pants boys, who take their college education and make some fellow's business hum with it. **1928** *Ruppenthal Coll.* **KS**, *High water pants*—pants so short as to expose the ankles, or . . the leg yet higher toward the knee, as if intended to be kept out of reach of water in wading a stream, especially when at high water. **1942** Berrey–Van den Bark *Amer. Slang* 87.27, *High-water pants* . . trousers shorter than the fashion. *Ibid* 512.12 [Logging terms], *High-water pants,* trousers rolled up halfway to the knees. **1947** *Prairie Schooner* 21.142 **nwNE** (as of c1910), His hair was clipped far above his ears in a highwater cut, as we called it, his knobby head showing blue around the back. **1950** *WELS (Trousers rolled up or cut off below the knee)* 8 Infs, **WI**, High-water pants; 3 Infs, High waters. **1958** McCulloch *Woods Words* 85 **Pacific NW**, *High water pants*—Pants stagged off below the knees to allow the greatest freedom when working on logs in the water. [**1960** Criswell *Resp. to PADS 20* **Ozarks,** *Cut high water,* . . Used of breeches which are too short. "Your breeches are sure cuttin' high water. Ain't they your little brother's?" Once common; prob no longer so.] **c1960** *Wilson Coll.* **csKY**, *High-water pants* or *high waters*. . . A boy's pants after they have shrunk or he has grown, or both, so that they seem to have been cut in time of high water. Locally there is a saying to such a boy: "Whyn't you throw a party for your shoetops and invite your pants?" **1975** Gould *ME Lingo* 132, *High-water* pants have legs that are too short. **1986** Pederson *LAGS Concordance* (*Lower than knee-length shorts;* this question was asked chiefly in urban areas) 6 infs, **Gulf Region**, High waters; [1 inf, **seLA**, High tides—loose-fitting pants, not ankle-length].

high water n
1 also pl: A jump-rope maneuver in which the rope is turned some distance above the ground or is gradually raised; hence adv phr *high water* with the rope raised.
1953 Brewster *Amer. Nonsinging Games* 118 **IN**, *Jumping the Rope*. . . Frequently a good jumper, desirous of demonstrating her skill, will ask those holding the rope to turn "high water" or "hot pepper." To do the former means to turn the rope in such a way that on its downward path it clears the ground by three or four inches, the jumper thus being forced to jump higher than ordinarily. **1956** *Western Folkl.* 15.47 **TX**, In "High Waters" the two rope throwers throw the rope in complete turns in the air about a foot or two above the ground while the jumper jumps. The rope is not allowed to touch the ground as the jumper is jumping. **1957** *Sat. Eve. Post Letters* **neKS** (as of c1900), *High water*—A rope game in which two girls gently swung the rope back and forth, beginning at ground level and gradually raising the rope. Players jumped back and forth over the rope and were eliminated as they "missed." **1961** *Western Folkl.* 20.180, *High waters*—Turning the rope so that it does not touch the ground. *Ibid* 185 **csGA**, [Jump-rope verse:] When it rains the Mississippi River / Gets higher, higher, higher, and higher. *(Raise the rope—high waters.)* **1966** *DARE* Tape **AL**6, [Inf:] I know one [=a jump-rope game] about the rope. . . You hold it high and you call it water, high water. [FW:] And you'd raise it higher. [Inf:] Each time. **1976** Knapp–Knapp *One Potato* 120, A jumper in Texas defiantly replies, "H-e-l-p!" She spells slowly because each letter means something: with *h,* she demands "high waters" or "hot peppers." **1987** *DARE* File **nwMA** (as of 1965), When someone said "high water" while jumping rope, it was a signal to the rope turners to keep the rope higher (off the ground), making the jumper jump higher.
2 A full bladder.
1948 Manfred *Chokecherry* 207 **nwIA**, "Bo, I got high water. How about you?" "Man, you hit it. My teeth are floating."

high-water v
To reach the flood stage.
1926 Ferber *Show Boat* 12 **Missip Valley**, She [=the Mississippi] won't high-water this year till June.

high-water grass n
=**cordgrass** (here: *Spartina patens*).
1950 Gray–Fernald *Manual of Botany* 180, *S[partina] patens* . . High-water grass.

high-water pants, high waters See **high-water** adj

high-water shrub n
=**marsh elder.**
1814 Bigelow *Florula Bostoniensis* 204, *Iva frutescens*. . . *High Water Shrub*. . . A fleshy shrub, about the borders of salt marshes. **1848** Gray

Manual of Botany 220, *Iva*. . . Highwater-shrub. **1892** Coulter *Botany W. TX* 208, *Iva*. . . Highwater-shrub. **1895** U.S. Dept. Ag. *Farmers' Bulletin* 28.26, Marsh elder, high-water shrub. Iva xanthifolia. **1933** Small *Manual SE Flora* 1298, *I[va] frutescens*. . . High-water-shrub. **1960** Vines *Trees SW* 998, *Iva frutescens*. . . Vernacular names are High Water Shrub . . and False Jesuit Bark.

highway n **widespread, but less freq N Cent, NEast, C Atl** See Map Cf **route**

Used in referring to a specific numbered or lettered main road. Note: As a generic term for a main road, *highway* is not regional; cf *DS* N16a.

1965–70 *DARE* (Qu. N18, *How do you speak of roads that have numbers or letters? For example, if someone asked directions . . , you might say, "Take ______."*) 273 Infs, **widespread, but less freq N Cent, NEast, C Atl,** Highway ([number]); 18 Infs, **scattered, but esp TX,** Highway + [number] [compass direction]; 10 Infs, **scattered,** Highway number [number]; 12 Infs, **scattered,** State (*or* federal, U.S., interstate) highway ([number]); **MO**13, 34, **OK**1, 18, **TN**24, [Number] highway ([compass direction]); **CA**138, Highway 229-W—said as "W"; **MI**40, Highway U.S. [number] [compass direction]; **MO**37, [Letter] highway. **1968** *Green River Star* (WY) 25 Jan 1/6, However, the highway commission did not place Highway 530 on a reconstruction schedule at this time. **1968** *State* (Columbia SC) 2 May sec B 10, [He] was killed Tuesday night when his car hit a tree on U.S. Highway 15, 3 miles south of McColl. **1978** *WI Week-End* 16 Aug 8/3, Highways 10 and 53 also go through town.

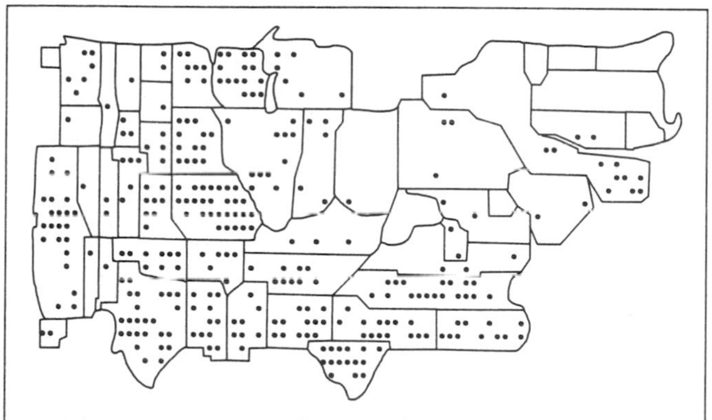

•highway n + varr (Qu. N18)

highway v Also with *it*

To hitchhike.

1967 Fetterman *Stinking Creek* 158 **MS,** "We highwayed it up here from Mississippi," says Mrs. Gordon. "We put four of the kids in foster homes and just put out our thumbs." **1967** *DARE* FW Addit **TX**5, *Highway*—To hitchhike.

highway light n Cf **country light**

=**high beam 2.**

1967–70 *DARE* (Qu. N10, . . *The bright and dim lights on a car*) Infs **MO**26, **PA**247, Highway lights; **MO**29, Street lights and highway lights.

highway patrol n

See quot 1975.

1965–68 *DARE* (Qu. N33, *A man whose job is to take care of roads in a certain locality*) Infs **KS**1, **IL**78, 87, **ME**22, **NH**10, **VT**7, **WI**57, Highway patrol(man). **1975** Gould *ME Lingo* 132, *Highway patrol*—In Maine, this does not mean the state constabulary as it does in other places. In Maine it is the road repair gang, seen moving very slowly except when going home to dinner.

high, west, and crooked adv Cf **galley-west, east and west**

In every direction, every which way.

1965 *DARE* File **swMI,** *High, west, and crooked*—every which way. **1968** *DARE* (Qu. MM12a, . . *'In all directions'* . . *"He shot into a flock of birds and they went ______."*) Inf **MN**15, High, west, and crooked.

high wheel n Also *high-wheel cart*

In logging: see quot.

1958 McCulloch *Woods Words* 85 **Pacific NW,** *High wheel*—A cart with large wheels used in the pine country to *haul* logs. Called also high wheel cart. Not to be confused with big wheels which were used to *skid* logs.

high-wheel artist See **highwheeler 1b**

high-wheel cart See **high wheel**

highwheeler n

1 In railroading:

a A type of passenger engine; a fast passenger train.

1930 *RR Man's Mag.* 470, *High-wheeler*—Passenger locomotive; a fast passenger train. **1977** Adams *Lang. Railroader* **78,** *High-wheeler:* A locomotive with very large driving wheels for greater speed. A fast passenger train.

b also *high-wheel artist:* A locomotive engineer known for running an engine at high speed. Cf **highball n 2**

1930 *RR Man's Mag.* 470, *High-wheeler* . . a highball artist. **1967** *DARE* Tape **ID**9, Of course someone who likes to run fast is known as a high-wheel artist. The old passenger locomotives did have high wheels—big drivers on them. Some of them were as large as 82 inches. And they were capable of very high speeds well over 100 miles per hour. A person who did run a locomotive at high speed was known as a high-wheel artist, generally speaking.

2 In logging: one who works with the **big wheels.**

1958 McCulloch *Woods Words* 86 **Pacific NW,** *Highwheelers*—The loggers behind the big wheels.

highwheeling vbl n

1976 Gould *Blackie's RR Hdbk.* 4, *Running an engine at high speed*. . . High Wheeling.

high, wide, and handsome adj phr, adv phr

Grandiloquent, stylish, successful; in a grandiloquent, confident, or successful manner.

1907 White *AZ Nights* 35, Tim could talk high, wide, and handsome when he set out to. **1927** *Ruppenthal Coll.* **KS,** *High, wide and handsome*—very pleasant; very satisfactory. "Everything goes high, wide and handsome." **c1960** *Wilson Coll.* **csKY,** *High, wide, and handsome*. . . stylish in looks or dress or conduct; acting in this way. **1966** Barnes–Jensen *Dict. UT Slang* 23, *High, wide and handsome*. . . in a most grandiloquent manner. "He entered the parade ground high, wide and handsome." **1969** *DARE* (Qu. GG19a, . . *A person* . . *feeling important or independent: "He surely is ______ these days."*) Inf **MA**14, High, wide, and handsome. **c1970** *Halpert Coll.* 52 **wKY, nwTN,** *Riding high, wide, and handsome*—everything going successfully, going smoothly. Talking high, wide, and handsome is "spreading it on" too thickly. **1976** Maclean *River Runs Through* 116 **wMT** (as of 1927), At first I felt kind of sorry for her because she was so well known in camp and was so much talked about, but she was riding "High, Wide, and Handsome."

high windows n, exclam Also *hold high windows*

A children's ring game; a call in this game; see quots.

1909 (1923) Bancroft *Games* 104, *High windows*. . . All of the players but one join hands in a circle. The odd player in the center . . hits one of the players . . or tags him. . . Both players then run out of the circle, it being the object of the player who was tagged to catch the odd player before he can run three times around the outside of the ring. As the runner completes his third time around, the players in the circle cry "High Windows!" and raise their clasped hands to let both of the players inside. **1954** *Harder Coll.* **cwTN,** *Hold high winders*. . . A ring game: "Holdgie [=hold your] hands high, let others go under."

high-windy n [*windy* verbose, bombastic]

1967 *DARE* (Qu. II35, *A person who is disliked because he seems to think he knows everything*) Inf **TN**15, High-windy [*DARE* Ed: Inf may intend this as an adj].

high words n pl

Words used in a charm or incantation; see quot.

1964 Smith *PA Germans* 147, "They said I was welcome but the dog was hard and nipped at everybody. I took my little granddaughter in the yard and up came the dog hard at me. I said the words (in the dialect) ending with the high words, and the dog turned and went quietly away. I can turn any dog with the words." It is reported that any number of people in the Brushy Fork area are able to say words that will stop running dogs and hold them still. Various informants have recounted how dogs have been turned from chasing a rabbit. . . Spells on dogs were broken by several rituals. . . place a key in the dog's mouth and . . turn it three times and each time say the high words.

high yellow n Pronc-spp *high yalla(h), ~ yaller, ~ yella, ~ yelluh* **scattered, but chiefly C and S Atl, Gulf States** See Map Cf **ash-faced, cocoa, yellow, high brown**

A light-skinned Black person; a person of mixed race; the skin color of such a person.

1923 Dos Passos *Streets of Night* 133 **SD,** Ought to see them high yallers down there if you're stuck on girls. **1926** in 1983 Taft *Blues Lyric Poetry* 43 [Black], Some screaming high yellow: I scream black or brown / For high yellow may mistreat you: but black won't turn you down. **1943** Ottley *New World* 177 [Black], There are a scattering of organizations whose memberships consist entirely of fair-skinned or mulatto types, and where the blackball is rigorously employed against any crasher whose coloring is deeper than high yaller. **1945** Saxon *Gumbo Ya-Ya* 13 **LA,** All them sailors wanted a brownie. High yellows fared poorly then. **1948** Mencken *Amer. Lang. Suppl. 2* 270, *High yallah,* a light mulatto. **1950** *WELS (People of mixed blood: part Negro)* 1 Inf, **WI,** High yaller—mostly white. **1951** Johnson *Resp. to PADS 20* **DE** *(Nicknames for people of foreign background: Creole)* High yellow. **1957** Battaglia *Resp. to PADS 20* **eMD** *(Names and nicknames for people of foreign background: Creole)* High yellow. **1965–70** *DARE* (Qu. HH29b, *Names for people of mixed blood—part Negro*) 110 Infs, **scattered, but chiefly C and S Atl, Gulf States,** High yellow; **CT**9, **MS**71, High yalla; **FL**52, High yella; (Qu. HH28, *Names . . for people of foreign background: . . Creole*) Infs **AL**10, 16, **CA**15, **IL**138, **LA**46, **WA**20, **WV**21, High yellow; (Qu. HH29a, *Names . . for people of mixed blood—part Indian*) Inf **GA**53, High yellow—everybody that's mixed if there's any white; **MS**64, High yellow. **1970** Major *Dict. Afro-Amer. Slang* 66, *High yaller (yella):* light-skinned Afro-American, especially female. **1977** Smitherman *Talkin* 252 [Black], *High-yellow,* pronounced in soul talk as *yelluh;* refers to very light-skinned blacks.

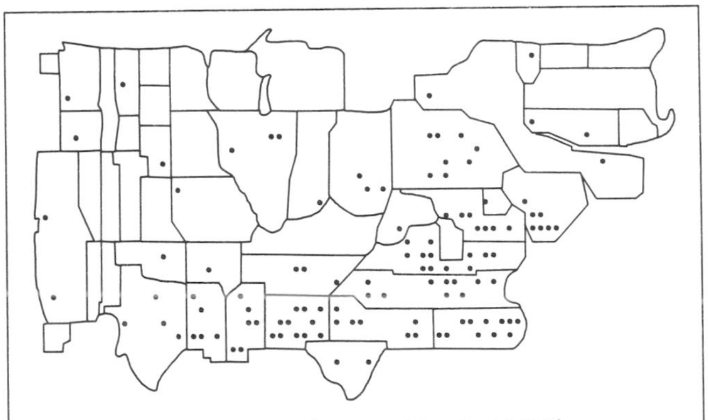

•high yellow + varr (Qq. HH29a, b, HH28)

high-yi See **hi-yi** exclam[2]

high-you(-muck-a-muck) See **high-muck-a-muck**

‡high zeke n Cf *DS* II23

1930 Shoemaker *1300 Words* 28 **cPA Mts** (as of c1900), *High zeke*—A member of the local aristocracy.

higulcion flips n Also *highgolla flips* [Pseudo-medical]

An imaginary disease.

1869 *Overland Mth.* 3.130 **TX,** As for diseases. . . [I]n Texas they have the "higulcion flips," which is what the French would call a sort of *maladie sans maladie;* about equivalent, perhaps, to our "conniption fits". **1970** *DARE* (Qu. BB28, . . *Imaginary diseases*) Inf **TN**48, Highgolla flips [haɪgɑləflɪps].

hike v

1a also refl; often with *out,* less freq with *it* or *off;* also *hike 'em, hikem, hiker, hiket:* To hurry, hasten to do something; to depart quickly, start out—freq used in imper. [*EDD hike* v. 12 "To move suddenly or hastily; to go away"] Note: Forms ending in *-em, -er, -et* may be *hike* plus reduced pronoun. Cf **hyper**

1887 Kirkland *Zury* 537 **IL,** *Hike out. . .* To go away, clear out, depart. **1895** *DN* 1.397 **PA,** *Hike. . .* to hasten. **1902** *DN* 2.236 **sIL,** *Hike. . .* Specifically, to go in haste seeking information: to hasten to learn the truth or details of a report; to hasten to forestall any one, or to take advantage of circumstances. But the expression, 'Hike yourself off,' is used to an intruder, or to hasten one on an errand. **1903** *DN* 2.316 **seMO,** *Hike* or *hike out. . .* To start out. (Facetious.) **1905** *DN* 3.62 **NE,** *Hike. . .* Hurry. "Hike yourself up town." **1907** *German Amer. Annals* 9.378 **sePA,** *Hike.* (Slang.) Get away quickly; usually with "out." "Hike out of here now, right quick!" **1908** *DN* 3.320 **eAL, wGA,** *Hike (out). . .* To start out, hasten away. **1909** *DN* 3.398 **nwAR,** *Hike. . .* To move rapidly. "Hike for the pike." "We went a-hikin' for home." **1912** *DN* 3.567 **cNY,** *Hike. . .* "Hike along there." **1923** *DN* 5.210 **swMO,** *Hiker. . .* "He shore did hiker!" Also *Hiket.* "Hiket out o' hyar, now." **1923** (1946) Greer-Petrie *Angeline Steppin'* 42 **csKY,** He told Desdimony to 'Hike 'em and be quick about hit, fur he couldn't promise how long his stren'th would hold out.' **1930s** in 1944 *ADD* **eWV,** 'Hikem out of there.' Said to one or more persons. **1965–70** *DARE* (Qu. A19, *Other ways of saying "I'll have to hurry": "I'm late, I'll have to ______."*) Inf **MI**100, Hike; (Qu. Y18, *To leave in a hurry: "Before they find this out, we'd better ______!"*) Infs **IL**85, **MS**30, **OH**16, **TX**9, Hike (it *or* 'em); (Qu. Y19, *To begin to go away from a place: "It's about time for me to ______."*) Infs **IL**82, **MS**30, Hike (for home); (Qu. Y20, *To run fast: "You should have seen him ______!"*) Infs **IL**77, 78, **KY**94, **OH**16, **RI**15, Hike.

b Spec: used as a command to sled dogs; see quots.

1945 *AK Sportsman* June 20 **AK,** The expression, "Mush," is never used at Nulato. The Indians usually say "Hike!" or just "All right!" **1976** in 1981 Tabbert *Alaskan Engl.* 316, *"Hike!"*—A command [to sled dogs] to go forward. **1979** *Fairbanks Daily News-Miner* (AK) 10 Mar sec B 3 (Tabbert *Alaskan Engl.*), Dog mushing terms. . . the word "hike" is pretty widespread as a command to get the dogs going and keep them going.

c See quots.

1967 *DARE* (Qu. NN22b, *Expressions used to drive away children*) Inf **CA**1, Hike; (Qu. NN22d, *Expressions used to drive away animals other than dogs*) Infs **NE**1, 3, Hike.

2 To climb; to climb a pole; hence n *hiker.*

1940 Cottrell *Railroader* 129, *Hiker*—A lineman who "hikes sticks" rather than, prosaically, climbs poles. **1942** Berrey-Van den Bark *Amer. Slang* 512.14, *Hike . .* to climb a pole. **1960** Wentworth-Flexner *Slang* 257, *Hike. . .* To climb or work on an electric wire or telephone pole. . . *Lineman use since c1925.* **1968** Adams *Western Words* 147, *Hike*—A logger's term meaning *to climb a pole.*

3 in phr *hike a ride:* To hitchhike.

1948 Manfred *Chokecherry* 227 **nwIA,** Elof wondered if Young Domeny Hillich would make some comment about the sin of his having hiked a ride on Sunday.

4 To skip school.

1940–41 Cassidy *WI Atlas* 1 Inf **swWI,** [haɪkt].

5 To chase or throw (a ball). [*EDD hike* v. 3 "To throw; to throw up"] *arch*

1895 *DN* 1.397, *Hike. . .* 1. of balls, to chase. . . 2. of balls, to throw up in the air. "Hike it up."

6 See quot 1901.

1901 *DN* 2.142 **nNY,** *Hike. . .* Carry, lug. . . "He hiked the basket off home." **1973** Allen *LAUM* 1.394 **MN, IA, ND, NE** (as of c1950), [In context] I *lugged* that heavy suitcase down to the station. . . *Hike* appears sporadically. [6 infs]

7 To hide, save; see quots.

1960 Wentworth-Flexner *Slang* 257, *Hike. . .* To save, put away, store away. *Not common.* **1970** Major *Dict. Afro-Amer. Slang* 66, *Hike:* (1940's) to hide a valuable object.

8 To steal, swipe, swindle. [*EDD hike* v. 7 "To snatch away; to run off with anything, not necessarily with a felonious intention"]

1911 *Century Dict. Suppl., Hike. . .* To snatch away; run off with. **1951** *NY Times* (NY) 15 June 14/7, They're in such a hurry to hike someone out of some money. **1966–68** *DARE* (Qu. V4, *Other words for stealing something valuable—for example, a watch: "Yesterday somebody ______ my watch."*) Infs **MD**25, **ME**21, Hiked.

hike n Also *hikey* *usu derog* Cf **Ikey**

An Italian immigrant.

1896 *NY Herald* (NY) 13 Jan 3/4 **cePA,** The average Pennsylvanian contemptuously refers to these immigrants as "Hikes" and "Hunks." The "Hikes" are Italians and Sicilians. **1898** *Century Illustr. Mag* 55.811 **cPA,** The Italians are termed "Hikes." **1967** *DARE* (Qu. HH28, *Names and nicknames around here for people of foreign background: Italians*) Inf **PA**11, Hikeys [hɑɪkiz].

hike a ride See **hike** v **3**

hike 'em See **hike** v **1a**

hike, hit the See **hit the hike**

hike it, hikem, hike off, hike out See **hike** v **1a**

hiker n

1 See **hike** v **2.**

2 In logging: see quot.

1956 Sorden-Ebert *Logger's Words* 18 **Gt Lakes,** *Hiker,* A lumberjack who has quit the job. Same as spiker.

3 See quot.

1911 *Century Dict. Suppl., Hiker*. . . An over-drawn [=too tight] bridle-check. [*Century* Ed: Local, southern U.S.]

hiker v See **hike** v **1a**

hikers' gentian n Cf **explorer's gentian**

A **gentian** (here: *Gentiana simplex*).

1959 Munz-Keck *CA Flora* 443, *G. simplex. . . Hikers' gentian. . .* Meadws [sic], 4000-9500 ft.

hikes n, exclam Also *hikes-up* [*hike* to raise, lift]

In marble play: a method of shooting; also used as a call to claim permission to use such a method; see quot.

1963 *KY Folkl. Rec.* 9.3 64, The act of lifting the shooter to a shooting position above the ground: *hikes . . hikes-up. Ibid* 66, To ask for permission to elevate shooting hand with shooter to a position on top of the free hand: *hikes.*

hikes, hit the See **hit the hike**

hikes-up See **hikes**

hiket See **hike** v **1a**

hikey See **hike** n

hikiee n [Haw] **HI**

A couch or sleeping platform.

1938 Reinecke *Hawaiian Loanwords* 11, *Hikie'e* ['hi:ki'eʔe] ['hi:ki'e:]. . . A raised platform for sleeping. . . A sleeping couch. **1951** *AmSp* 26.23 **HI,** *Hikiee* (an elevated sleeping platform). **1967** *DARE* (Qu. E9, *A piece of upholstered furniture*) Inf **HI**1, Hikiee ['hɪkɪˌe:]—a very large couch for several people to loll on. **1972** Carr *Da Kine Talk* 87 **HI,** *Hawaiian Words Commonly Heard in Hawaii's English. . . Hikie'e.* Large Hawaiian couch. **1984** Sunset *HI Guide* 85, *Hikie'e*—large couch.

hiki-fallootin See **high-kaflutin**

hiki no phr [Haw; see quot 1938] **HI**

Used as an expression of affirmation; see quots.

1938 Reinecke *Hawaiian Loanwords* 11, *Hiki no* ['hi:ki 'no:]. . . [*Hiki,* to be able to do a thing, and *no,* truly, indeed.] 1. Satisfactory; O.K. . . 2. I understand. **1951** *AmSp* 26.21 **HI,** *Hiki no* (it's possible; 'can do').

hilahila adj, n, v [Haw] **HI**

1 Ashamed, shy; shame; to be ashamed.

1938 Reinecke *Hawaiian Loanwords* 12, *Hilahila.* . . Ashamed; bashful; flustered through bashfulness. **1951** *AmSp* 26.23 **HI,** *Hilahila* (ashamed). **1954-60** Hance et al. *Hawaiian Sugar* 2, *Hilahila* ['hila'hila]—To be ashamed, shame. **1972** Carr *Da Kine Talk* 87, Hawaiian Words Commonly Heard in Hawaii's English. . . *Hilahila.* Bashful, shy, ashamed.

2 as n; also *pua-hilahila:* A **sensitive plant.** Cf **be-shame' bush, shame plant**

1954-60 Hance et al. *Hawaiian Sugar* 2, *Hilahila* ['hila'hila]—Sensitive plant, *Mimosa pudica.* **1965** Neal *Gardens HI* 412, Sensitive plant, pua-hilahila. *Mimosa pudica.* . . A low, branching, perennial herb or somewhat woody plant that spreads 2 or 3 feet over the ground on roadsides is from tropical America, whence it has migrated to all tropical countries.

hild See **hold** v **A2b**

hi-life See **high life** n

hill n

1a A small mound of earth in which several seeds or seedlings are planted, or which is raised around growing plants; by ext, a cluster of plants, usu planted in such a hill. **chiefly Sth**

a1676 in 1679 Royal Soc. London *Philos. Trans.* 1066 **NEng,** Where the Ground is bad or worn out, the Indians used to put two or three of the forementioned Fishes, under or adjacent to each Corn-hill. **1748** (1754) Catesby *Nat. Hist. Carolina* xvi **SE,** After the [Indian] Corn is come up some small Height, there are drop'd into every Hill two or three Beans. **1775** (1962) Romans *Nat. Hist. FL* 120, A man ought to go through the field, and pull up those plants that look least promising leaving only three plants in each hill. **a1817** (1821) Dwight *Travels* 1.108 **NEng,** The earth is raised to the height of from four to six inches, around the corn, and is denominated a hill; whence every planting is called a *hill of corn.* **1856** Simms *Charlemont* 27, They walk as if perpetually in the faith that their corn-rows and potatoe-hills were between their legs. **1899** (1912) Green *VA Folk-Speech* 225, *Hill.* . . A little mound raised about a cluster of cultivated plants: as, a hill of corn or potatoes. **1967** Key *Tobacco Vocab.* 122, **NC,** [Tobacco was planted in hills] before transplanter came into use; **KY,** Hill; **MD, GA, TN,** Hill; **MO,** "A hill of tobacco." **1975** Logan *Land Remembers* 24 **swWI** (as of c1920), Each time a little tripper on the planter hit one of the knots [stretched the length of the field], . . several kernels of corn dropped in a cluster, which we called a hill. The hills were aligned so that the corn rows ran both lengthwise and crosswise. **1976** Ryland *Richmond Co. VA* 372, *Hill*—mound, as for cucumbers, corn, etc.

b in phr *on the hill;* Of tobacco: in the field, unharvested.

1944 *PADS* 2.66 **sVA,** Tobacco . . "on the hill" (in the field).

2 usu in comb *potato hill:* A mound of dirt or straw in which potatoes or other root crops are kept over the winter. **chiefly Sth** See Map Cf **bank n[1] 1, kiln**

1843 (1973) Porter *Big Bear AR* 22, Them ar "Indian mounds" ar tater hills. **1888** *Harper's New Mth. Mag.* 76.705/1 **GA,** When Jones watched his potato hill, his smoke-house was sure to be entered. **1912** Green *VA Folk-Speech* 331, *Potato-hill.* . . Sweet potatoes are put in a pile, covered with pine-tags, and then with earth, to keep in winter. **1926** Roberts *Time of Man* 286 **cKY,** They had better save the potatoes now while there were turnips in plenty, for three to feed all winter would lower the potato hill fast. **1965-70** *DARE* (Qu. M19, *A place for keeping carrots, turnips, potatoes, and so on over the winter*) 35 Infs **chiefly Sth,** (Potato, turnip, *or* carrot) hill; **DC**2, Hill of dirt. **1967** *DARE* Tape **NC**41, [Inf:] Then you had a big potato hill, they called 'em. [FW:] What's a potato hill? [Inf:] Well, you'd dig out a place in the ground, line it all with straw. That's where you put your sweet potatoes. [FW:] Over the winter? [Inf:] Yeah. [FW:] It didn't rot or anything? [Inf:] Oh, no. **1986** Pederson *LAGS Concordance (Where did you store your potatoes . . in the winter?)* 23 infs, 19 **AL, GA,** (Potato) hill. [*DARE* Ed: Usu described as a round hole covered with straw or cornstalks, and dirt.]

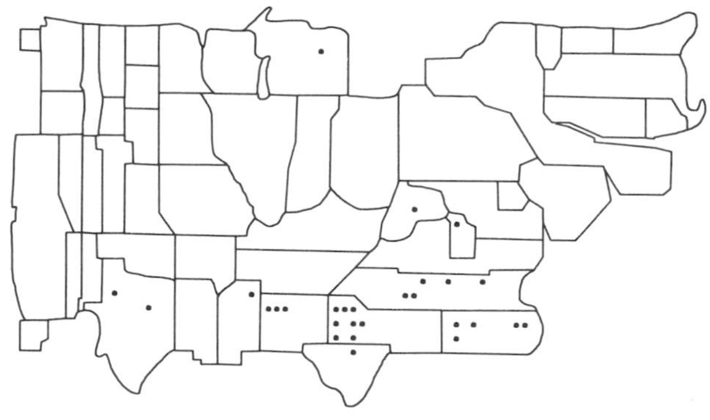

•hill n 2 + varr (Qu. M19)

3 An area of solid ground in a swampy or tidal region; see quots. [*EDD hill* sb.[1] 5] **esp SC** Cf **house B2**

1950 *PADS* 14.37 **SC,** *Hill.* . . Land above water, not covered by high tides, or by freshets in a river. Coastal area. **1954** *PADS* 21.30 **SC,** *Hill.* . . Solid ground, as opposed to swamp. When timbers are moved out of the swamp they are said to be on the hill when they reach solid ground. **1967-68** *DARE* FW Addit **SC**19, *Hill*—an "island" in the swamp; **GA**31, Hill—The bank of wherever you're fishing.

4 in phr *no hill for a stepper:* No obstacle for a competent person. [*OED hill* sb. 2 "*fig.* . . something not easily mounted or overcome."]

1949 *PADS* 11.14 **wTX** (as of c1920), *That's no hill for a stepper.* (That's not too hard a task for a good worker.) Occasional. **1984** Wilder *You All Spoken Here* 146 **Sth,** *That ain't no hill for a stepper:* It's no problem for one who knows his business.

5 in phr *go over the hill:* To get married. Cf **fool's hill** quot 1966

1967 *DARE* (Qu. AA15a, . . *Joking ways . . of saying that people got married? "They ———."*) Inf **MO**14, Went over the hill; (Qu. AA15b, . . *Joking ways . . of saying that a man is getting married*) Inf **MO**11, Another good Indian gone over the hill.

6 also *marble hill, still hill:* See quot. Cf **boot hill, marble orchard**

1965–70 *DARE* (Qu. BB61b, . . *Joking names for a cemetery*) Infs **IA**11, **KS**13, **NE**8, 10, **NJ**2, 56, **NY**2, (Out *or* up) on the hill; **CO**33, **MN**2, **WI**12, The hill; **CA**140, **MD**17, Still (*or* marble) hill.

hill v Also with *up*

1 To form small mounds of earth around plants or in preparation for planting; to heap earth around (plants) with a hoe or plow; to heap (earth) around plants; hence vbl n *hilling.* [Cf **hill** n **1a**] Cf **dirt** v **1**

1796 in 1851 Adams *Works* 3.416 **ceMA,** To-day ploughing for hilling among the corn. **1813** Taylor *Arator* 267 **VA,** How often he had passed over the land . . in fallowing, hilling, cutting off hills, planting, replantings. **1884** *Anglia* 7.278 **SE,** To hill up de corn = to put the finishing touches to. **1933** Rawlings *South Moon* 31 **nFL,** Sweet potatoes had been hilled and the hills knocked down again for digging. **1938** Rawlings *Yearling* 88 **nFL,** He had hitched old Cæsar to the plow and plowed over the sugar-cane and hilled it up. **1948** *AmSp* 23.308 **csWI** [Tobacco terms], The [tobacco] plants must be *hilled up* carefully by hand, since tobacco cannot be planted in even rows. **1950** *WELS (When you cover celery to keep it white)* 2 Infs, **WI,** Hilling. **1959** *VT Hist.* 27.142, *Hill. . .* To hoe. Occasional. **1968** *DARE* Tape **IN**14, We have always raised tobacco. . . my grandfather . . would go into the field or patch, whatever he was gonna set, an' make hills for it, ta set every plant in. Then later on we got ta makin' rows. . . We would have to hoe it probably two or three times—hill it up they called it. **1975** Logan *Land Remembers* 25 **swWI** (as of c1920), As the planter moved slowly, slowly down the row, it made a little furrow, water squirted down, a [tobacco] plant was inserted into the furrow, and then the machine hilled soil up around the stem of the plant.

2 also with *out:* To cover (fruits or vegetables) with earth or straw for winter storage; to protect such crops by covering them. Cf **bank** v **2, hill** n **2**

1899 (1912) Green *VA Folk-Speech* 225, *Hill. . .* To form small hills or heaps of earth around; "To hill up potatoes." **1956** McAtee *Some Dialect NC* 22, *Hill up. . .* to cover vegetables or fruits with straw and earth for winter storage. **c1960** *Wilson Coll.* **csKY,** *Hill up. . .* To cover up vegetables with a mound of earth to protect them for winter. **1968–70** *DARE* (Qu. M19, *A place for keeping carrots, turnips, potatoes, and so on over the winter*) Inf **AR**15, Hilling potatoes—pile in bank; **AR**56, Hill them out; **MO**17, We'd hill 'em up with dirt.

hillberry n

1 A **wintergreen** (here: *Gaultheria procumbens*). [See quot 1828]

1828 Rafinesque *Med. Flora* 1.202 *Gautiera repens. . . Vulgar names*—Partridge-berry, . . Hillberry, Box-berry, Chequer-berry, &c. *Ibid* 1.203, *Locality*—On hills and mountains, in shady woods, Pine woods, rocky and sandy soils. **1876** Hobbs *Bot. Hdbk.* 53, Hillberry, Checkerberry, Gaultheria procumbens. **1911** Henkel *Amer. Med. Leaves* 19, Hillberry. . . Globular, somewhat flattened berries . . ripen in autumn and remain on the plant, sometimes until spring. **1930** Sievers *Amer. Med. Plants* 63. **1971** Krochmal *Appalachia Med. Plants* 128, Hillberry . . is primarily a source of true wintergreen oil.

2 A cranberry produced by an immature cranberry bog; see quot.

1969 *DARE* Tape **MA**102, [Inf:] And then three years later you pick a crop. [FW:] The vines don't bear before then? [Inf:] About that. There'll be somethin' they called hillberries, which means there're just a few, but the bog doesn't vine over in less than three years.

hillbilly n

1 also rarely *hill William;* also sp *hill billie:* A countrified or rustic person; an ignorant or uncouth person. **widespread, but esp freq S Midl**

1900 *NY Eve. Jrl.* (NY) 23 Apr 2/5 **AL,** In short, a Hill-Billie is a free and untrammelled white citizen of Alabama, who lives in the hills, has no means to speak of, dresses as he can, talks as he pleases, drinks whiskey when he gets it, and fires off his revolver as the fancy takes him. **1904** *DN* 2.418 **nwAR,** *Hill Billy. . .* Uncouth countryman, particularly from the hills. "You one-gallused Hill Billies, behave yourselves." **1908** *DN* 3.320 **eAL, wGA,** *Hill-billy. . .* "Come listen to me, you lazy hill-billies." **1917** *DN* 4.413 **KS, KY, LA, wNC,** *Hill-billy.* **1922** *DN* 5.189 [Black], *Hill Billy.* A poor white. **1923** *DN* 5.210 **swMO,** *Hill billy.* **1941** *Hall Coll.* **eTN,** *Hillbilly. . .* People who live back in the hills; . . "I've got an old hill-billy up here—got him to spend all his money on the piccolo [=nickelodeon]"; **wNC,** *Hillbilly. . .* Used occasionally of mountain people of low-class or uneducated types . . "She's no hillbilly," said of a person known for her fine qualities. **c1960** *Wilson Coll.* **csKY,** *Hillbilly. . .* A derogatory term, not for a person who lives among the hills, but for a greenhorn, yokel, ignoramus. **1965–70** *DARE* (Qu. HH1, *Names and nicknames for a rustic or countrified person*) 271 Infs, **widespread, but esp freq S Midl,** Hillbilly; **MI**78, Hill William; (Qu. C33, . . *An out-of-the-way place, or a very unimportant place*) Inf **NY**39, Hillbilly town; (Qu. C36, . . *Special communities or groups of people;* total Infs questioned, 75) Inf **OK**18, Hillbillies—in the hills [to the] north; a few are there now; (Qu. D39, . . *A small eating place where the food is not especially good*) Inf **OH**81, Hillbilly place; (Qu. H18, . . *Special kinds of bread*) Inf **AL**30, Hillbilly bread—any kind of homemade bread; **CA**77, Hillbilly bread—a brand name; (Qu. FF16, . . *Local contests or celebrations*) Inf **TN**20, Hillbilly homecoming; (Qu. HH18, *Very insignificant or low-grade people*) Infs **CA**8, **MD**2, **MI**13, 26, **NY**190, **OH**84, Hillbillies; (Qu. HH28) Inf **OH**70, Hillbilly; (Qu. HH36, *A careless, slovenly woman*) Inf **MD**33, Hillbilly; (Qu. II21, *When somebody behaves unpleasantly or without manners: "The way he behaves, you'd think he was ———."*) Inf **DC**8, A hillbilly; (Qu. II25, . . *The part of a town where the poorer people, special groups, or foreign groups live*) Infs **MD**2, **OH**16, Hillbilly heights (*or* section). **1970** *DARE* Tape **IL**137, This family down the street, they're hillbillies and I think it's the only house of hillbillies here in the neighborhood. . . you know those hillbillies play country music. **1989** *NY Times* (NY) 13 Dec 31/1 **cnMD,** Protestants who came of Appalachian stock were called "hillbillies," and the term connoted ignorance, poverty, vile habits and, in general, low-lifers perfectly at home in the pigpen. These, of course, were my [=Russell Baker's] people, and they were considered singularly loathsome when they flocked to Baltimore for war jobs in the 1940's.

2 A wealthy or prominent person. *facetious* Cf *hilltopper* (at **hilltop**)

1967 *DARE* (Qu. II23, . . *The best society of a community*) Inf **CA**8, Hillbillies; (Qu. II24) Inf **AL**37, Hillbillies—with the idea that they live on the hill, or in a good section.

3 See quot.

1951 Johnson *Resp. to PADS 20* **DE** *(Any kind of bad liquor)* Hill-billy.

4 A cottontail (here: *Sylvilagus floridanus*). Cf **hill rabbit**

1966 *DARE* (Qu. P30, *Do you have wild rabbits around here? What kinds?*) Inf **AL**2, Hillbillies; **AL**38, Hillbillies (brown; cottontail); **MS**6, Cottontails, dodger, hillbillies, sailor [are the] same.

hillbilly adj

Rustic, countrified.

1982 Ginns *Snowbird Gravy* 116 **nwNC,** They changed [the name] Pick-Breeches to Mountain Dale. And what happened, why they changed it to Mountain Dale, the times changed, and it got to be a little bigger living. They thought that sounded a little better. Pick-Breeches was too hillbilly.

hillbird n [See quot 1955]

A **golden plover** or an **upland plover.**

1888 Trumbull *Names of Birds* 172, *Bartramia longicauda* . . in Maynard's Birds of Eastern Massachusetts, *Hill Bird.* **1917** (1923) *Birds Amer.* 1.247, *Upland Plover—Bartramia longicauda. . .* Hill-bird. **1923** U.S. Dept. Ag. *Misc. Circular* 13.64, *Upland Plover (Bartramia longicauda). . . In local use* . . hill-bird (Mass.) **1955** MA Audubon Soc. *Bulletin* 39.444, American Golden Plover. . . Hill Bird (Mass. [It resorts to grasslands more than do its relatives, except the Killdeer]).

hill dill n **esp MA** Cf **huck chuck**

A children's running game; see quots.

1909 (1923) Bancroft *Games* 105, *Hill dill*—Two parallel boundary lines are drawn from thirty to fifty feet apart; or the game is often played between the curbings of a street, which serves as boundaries. One player is chosen to be It, and stands in the center. The other players stand in two equal parties beyond the boundary lines, one party on each side. The center player calls out, "Hill dill! come over the hill!" the other players then exchange goals, and as they run across the open space the one in the center tries to tag them. Any who are tagged assist him thereafter in tagging the others. **1943** *LANE* Map 585, 1 inf, **ceMA,** The game of hill dill. **1957** *Sat. Eve. Post Letters,* **ceMA,** "Hill-Dill"—Not sure about this one either, but the words "Hill Dill come over the hill / Or else I'll catch you standing still" were used. These games were played in Hingham, Mass. in the 1880's. . . I think it was something like this. . . It was played in a restricted area with boundary lines on ends and sides. The boy who was "it" stood in the center and called out the words as given. The other boys stood on the line at one end and started for the line at the other end as soon as the call was ended. The boy who was "it" had to tag or catch one boy before he reached the opposite line. The boy who was caught then became "it" and so on. *Ibid* **ceMA,** There were many running games such as—Hill Dill. . . The boys all lined up against the fence. The "it" boy made the call. All the boys ran to the other fence. A boy tagged became another "it." So back and forth till all were caught. *Ibid* **ceMA,** Hill dill—played at recess by the whole school (male) who divided into two groups with two chosen leaders. One group [was] stationed half way between two goals. . . At a signal the other group tried to cross over to the other goal without being touched by those on the field. It was a rough, tough game. **1969** *DARE* (Qu. EE33, . . *Outdoor games*) Inf **MA**73, Hill dill.

hill grass-bird See **grass-bird 2b**

hill hawk n

1930 Shoemaker *1300 Words* 29 **cPA Mts** (as of c1900), *Hill-hawk*—A shiftless resident of the rough foot hills.

hill-hooter n Cf **hooter 2**

=great horned owl.

1930 Shoemaker *1300 Words* 31 **cPA Mts** (as of c1900), Hill-hooter—The grand duke, or great horned owl.

hillie n

In marble play: see quot 1963.

1963 *KY Folkl. Rec.* 9.3.62, Small pinch of dirt on which a marble is sometimes elevated: *hillie.* **1968** *DARE* (Qu. EE7) Inf **SC**65, Hillie—a tee; put marbles up on a small pile of dirt.

hilliken n Also sp *hilligen, hillikin* [Cf *SND hillikin* "a small rounded hill" (at *hill* n. I. (4))] **OH**

A rural or rustic person.

1916 *Ohio State Jrl.* 19 Nov mag sec 1 *(Ruppenthal Coll.),* For a second time in recent years, the legal interests of the state of Ohio will be prosecuted and defendant [sic] by a "hillikin" from Jackson County. **1940** Writers' Program *Guide OH* 483 (as of 1840), During the [Harrison-Van Buren presidential] campaign a newspaper editorial characterized General William Henry Harrison as a hard-drinking, log-cabin 'hilliken' unfit for the presidency. Ohio resented this attempt to discredit her candidate. **1966** Dakin *Dial. Vocab. Ohio R. Valley* 2.452, *Hilliken, hilligen* [=a rustic] is common along the Ohio from Athens County to Lawrence County. A single instance in Champaign County, Ohio, is the only other appearance. **1970** *DARE* (Qu. HH28) Inf **OH**95, ['hɪləkənz]—from the South.

hilling See **hill** v **1**

hilling hoe n [**hill** v **1**] **esp Mid Atl**

A type of hoe used to **hill** plants or to work newly broken ground.

1639 in 1883 *Archives of MD* 1.80, A hilling hoe. **1786** in 1956 Eliason *Tarheel Talk* 276 **NC,** 1 hilling hoe. **1800** in 1969 Herndon *Wm. Tatham Tobacco* 12 **VA,** The *narrow* or *hilling* hoe follows the operation of the sprouting hoe. It is generally from six to eight inches wide, and ten or twelve in the length of the blade . . the blade is thin, and by means of a moveable wedge which is driven into the eye of the hoe, it can be set more or less *digging* (as it is termed). **1946** *PADS* 6.17 **eNC** (as of 1900–10), *Hilling hoe.* . . A hoe used for working newly broken stumpy ground. Wider and shorter than a grubbing hoe. **c1960** *Wilson Coll.* **csKY,** *Hilling hoe.* . . A garden or farm hoe, quite wide, for making tobacco, cabbage, or tomato hills. **1970** *DARE* Tape **VA**38, We grow bright leaf tobacco in this section. . . We first sow the seed in bed and we use canvas over it for it to come up and then we transplant it to the field and then, the yearly thing, we weed it with a hilling hoe by hand, and from that the crop grows and then we harvest it.

hillins n pl [*EDD hilling* sb. (1) "bed-covering, a coverlet, bed-clothes" (at *hill* sb.[2] 1)]

1936 *AmSp* 11.191 **swWY,** *Hillins.* Bedding or bed-clothing. 'Have you enough hillins to keep you warm?'

hill oak n

1 =blue oak 2.

1908 Britton *N. Amer. Trees* 323, This [=California Rock Oak—*Quercus douglasii*] is one of the most beautiful of the California oaks. It is also called Mountain white oak, . . Hill oak, and Blue oak.

2 =Texas oak.

1960 Vines *Trees SW* 192, Texas Oak. . . Common on the dry uplands of central and west Texas. . . Also known under the names of . . Hill Oak, Spotted Oak, Red Oak.

hill-of-snow See **hills-of-snow**

hill onion n Cf **ramp**

See quots.

1966 Dakin *Dial. Vocab. Ohio R. Valley* 2.366, The names *potato onion* (apparently from the cluster of new bulbs which grow around the set—several informants say *hill onion*), . . *winter onion* all clearly refer to the latter type [="spring onions"]. **1968–70** *DARE* (Qu. I5, *The kind of onions that keep coming up without replanting year after year*) Infs **IN**12, **KY**71, **WV**8, Hill onions; (Qu. I6, *The kind of onions that come up fresh early in the year, and you eat them raw*) Infs **VA**40, **WV**8, Hill onion(s).

hill out See **hill** v **2**

hill partridge n Also *hill snipe*

=woodcock.

1923 U.S. Dept. Ag. *Misc. Circular* 13.49, *American Woodcock (Rubicola minor). . . In local use.*— . . hill-partridge (Ala.) **1932** Howell *FL Bird Life* 225, *American Woodcock: Philohela minor* . . Other Names: Wood Snipe; Bog-sucker; Hill Partridge. **1955** *Oriole* 1.7, *American Woodcock. . . Hill Snipe* (especially in the fall, this bird frequents uplands). **1955** Forbush-May *Birds* 178, *American Woodcock—Philohela minor* . . Other Names: Little Whistler; . . Hill Partridge; Wood Snipe. **1962** Imhof *AL Birds* 231, *American Woodcock—Philohela minor.* . . Other Names: Hill Partridge . . Timber Doodle.

hill pine n

=longleaf pine.

1953 Little *Native Trees U.S.* 195, *Pinus palustris . . longleaf pine* . . Other common names . . hill pine . . heart pine. **1967–68** *DARE* (Qu. T17) Infs **AR**51, **GA**20, **LA**18, Hill pine.

hill rabbit n Also *highland rabbit* Cf **hillbilly 4**

A wild rabbit; see quots.

1966–70 *DARE* (Qu. P30, *Do you have wild rabbits around here? What kinds?*) 8 Infs, **chiefly Sth,** Hill rabbit; **NC**85, Highland rabbit—brown, with a white tail [as opposed to "swamp rabbit"]; **SC**26, Highland rabbit [as opposed to "swamp rabbit"]. **1969** *DARE* Tape **GA**51, Then we got the bright bright red colored like, white tailed that lives on the hill. We got a swamp rabbit and a hill rabbit.

hill rat n

1939 (1973) FWP *Guide MT* 414, *Hill rat*—Prospector.

hill robin n Also *Japanese hill robin* **HI**

The red-billed leiothrix *(Leiothrix lutea).*

1967 *DARE* (Qu. Q14) Inf **HI**14, Hill robin. **1972** Berger *Hawaiian Birdlife* 211, Known in the cagebird trade as the Pekin Nightingale and Japanese Hill Robin, the Red-billed Leiothrix is not native to either area. . . The Leiothrix was imported to Hawaii as a cage bird as early as 1911, and . . probably escaped and became established before 1918.

hill-rooter n

c1960 *Wilson Coll.* **csKY,** Hill-rooter. . . A lean long-nosed, bony hog, usually one half wild.

hillside n attrib **chiefly Sth, S Midl** Cf **long green**

Of tobacco: homegrown.

1927 *AmSp* 2.357 **WV,** *Hillside navy* . . a twist of home-cured tobacco. "Can you chew hillside navy? No, it is too strong." **1943** Writers' Program NC *Bundle of Troubles* 132, Dick Wilson's a lean and lennegy feller what always has a twist of hillside navy in his jeans and a good-size hunk of the same in his guzzle. **c1960** *Wilson Coll.* **csKY,** *Hillside tobacco.* . . Home-grown rather than store-bought chewing or smoking tobacco. Also called long green. **1960** Heimann *Tobacco* 90, Those who passed on through the port cities could obtain or grow "hillside navy" so much better than the manufactured product of Germany or Holland that there was no point in buying factory twist. **1968–69** *DARE* (Qu. DD1, . . *Different forms [of] . . chewing tobacco*) Inf **GA**72, Hillside navy—home grown; **MD**15, Hillside Ned—homemade tobacco plug, long twisted cylinder, about 2 inches in diameter.

hillside horse n Cf **hither horse, near horse**

1970 *DARE* (Qu. K32b, *The horse on the left side in plowing or hauling*) Inf **VA**105, Hillside horse.

hillside plow n Also *hillside turner, ~ turning plow* **chiefly Appalachians, sOH** See Map Cf **turning plow**

A type of plow designed for use on hillsides; see quot 1954.

1827 U.S. Congress *Serial Set* 149 Doc 27.9, [Improvement] in the hill-side, double nosed, cast iron plough [patented April] 12 [by] John Shepherd. **1924** Raine *Land of Saddle-Bags* 228 **Appalachians,** There is a very large acreage where even the turning plow cannot be used. A makeshift, called a "hillside turner," is widely used, and the simple "bull-tongue" or shovel plow (occasionally the "double-shovel") does what plowing is possible. **1954** *Harder Coll.* **cwTN,** *Hillside plow* . . a plow with a reversible plowshare which enables plowing on hillsides. **1957** Battaglia *Resp. to PADS 20* **eMD,** Hillside plow. **1966** *Cynthiana Democrat* (KY) 28 Apr 6/7, *Public Auction* . . crow bar; hill side plow; 2 cord wood saws. **1966–69** *DARE* (Qu. L18, *Kinds of plows*) 30 Infs, **chiefly Appalachians, sOH,** Hillside plow; **GA**72, **NC**48, Hillside turner (for one or two horses); **KY**16, **NC**30, Hillside turning plow; **PA**163, Hillside horse plow; **NC**33, One-horse hillside plow. **1968** *DARE* Tape **OH**58, A hillside plow is a plow that when you go round the side of a hill and you get out to the end you turn it round and turn the mowboard [=moldboard] over and the point, they're combined together, and you hook it and start right back again. **1976** Garber *Mountain-ese* 41 **Appalachians,** *Hill-side-plow* . . mountain plow—His land is so steep that he's obliged to use a hillside-plow.

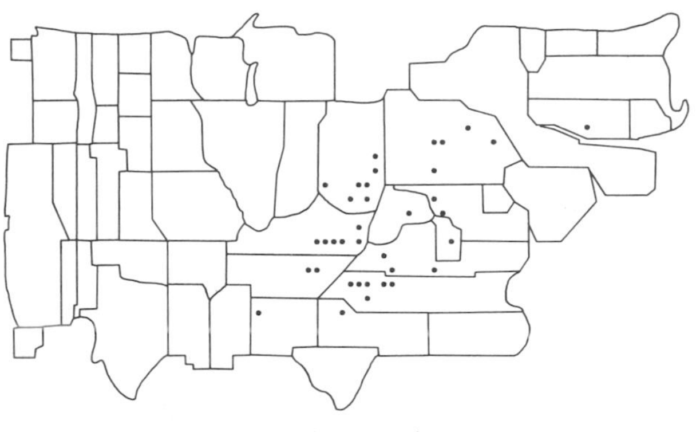

•hillside plow + varr (Qu. L18)

hillside show n

In logging: see quot.

1958 McCulloch *Woods Words* 86 **Pacific NW,** *Hillside show*—A logging operation requiring the use of an incline or a switchback, in the days of railroad logging.

hillside tobacco See **hillside navy**

hillside turner (or turning plow) See **hillside plow**

hill snipe See **hill partridge**

hills-of-snow n Also *hill-of-snow* [From the clusters of white flowers]

A **hydrangea** (here: *Hydrangea arborescens*).

1940 Clute *Amer. Plant Names* 59, *H[ydrangea] arborescens*. . . Hills-of-snow. **1960** Vines *Trees SW* 306, *H. arborescens*. . . Vernacular names are Hill-of-Snow, Mountain Hydrangea. **1976** Bailey–Bailey *Hortus Third* 578, Hills-of-snow.

hilltop n

The more affluent or prestigious section of a town or city; hence *hilltopper* a wealthy or prominent person.

1950 *WELS (People who are [or think they are] the best society of a community)* 2 Infs, **WI,** Hilltoppers. **1967–70** *DARE* (Qu. C35, *Nicknames for the different parts of your town or city*) Inf **OH**99, The bottoms; the hilltop; (Qu. II24, . . *The part of a town where the well-off people live*) Inf **CA**14, Hilltop; **CT**9, Hilltoppers—rich people.

hill up See **hill** v

hill William See **hillbilly** n **1**

hilly adj

Difficult, obscure.

1942 Berrey–Van den Bark *Amer. Slang* 172.5, *Hard to understand; obscure; deep*. . . hilly. *Ibid* 256.12, *Difficult*. . . hilly. **1976** Garber *Mountain-ese* 41 **Appalachians,** *Hilly* . . difficult to do—That's the most hilly task I've had to do fer some time.

hilly-over n, exclam Also *heely-heely-over, hilly-holley-over* [Prob varr of **haily-over**]

=Antony-over.

1950 *WELS Suppl.* 1 Inf, **seWI,** North Fond du Lac children played anty-over, but 8 miles out, at Edam, they played hilly-holley-over. **1967–69** *DARE* (Qu. EE22, *What do you call the game in which they throw a ball over a building?*) Inf **CT**37, Hilly-over; **NY**12, Heely-heely-over ['hili 'hili]; (Qu. EE23a, *In the game of andy-over* . . *what do you call out when you throw the ball?*) Inf **NY**12, Heely-heely-over.

hilo grass n [*Hilo* city on island of Hawaii] **HI**

An introduced **bullgrass 1** (here: *Paspalum conjugatum*).

1929 Pope *Plants HI* 27, *Hilo Grass. Paspalum conjugatum*. . . reached these islands about 1840, first appearing in the district of Hilo. . . In a very short time it spread to all of the islands of the group and became generally known as "Hilo Grass." **1965** Neal *Gardens HI* 73, *Hilo grass*. . . This perennial grass is a weed in many lawns in Hawaii.

hilt v See **hold** v **A2c, 3a**

hilt n See **hold** n **2**

hilter-skilter adv [Var of *helter-skelter;* cf *SND hilter-skilter* I. adv. "in rapid succession, confusedly, pell-mell. . . obs."]

1969 *DARE* (Qu. MM13, *The table was nice and straight until he came along and knocked it* ______.) Inf **RI**6, Hilter-skilter.

him pron Pronc-spp *em, im, um* [Cf *EDD im, em, um* "Dial. forms" (at *him* pron. 1)]

A Forms.

1875 Holland *Sevenoaks* 38 **N Atl,** I'd do more fur 'im nor fur any livin' live man. **1888** Jones *Negro Myths* 7 **GA coast,** Buh Wolf no question um no mo. **1899** Garland *Boy Life* 159 **nwIA** (as of c1870s), I'll tell 'im that. **1922** Gonzales *Black Border* 273 **sSC, GA coasts** [Gullah], Dat boy Joe run'way en' gone to de upcountry jis' 'cause I lick'um. [=That boy Joe ran away and went to the upcountry just because I licked [=whipped] him.] **1925** in 1953 Botkin–Harlow *Treas. Railroad Folkl.* 227, When they pulled me off muh meat [=opponent], I had 'im bloody as a hawg. **1928** Peterkin *Scarlet Sister Mary* 84 **sSC** [Gullah], You say July begged you to marry em? **1949** Turner *Africanisms* 227 [Gullah], [hɪm, əm] 'him'. **1958** Humphrey *Home from the Hill* 51 **neTX,** 'At's my ole whomper-jawed Rip hound! Lissen to im go! **1966** *DARE* Tape **AL**3, That ol' colored man we fixed up had a . . saddle house, where we kept our saddles, . . and we put 'im a bed in there. **1971** Cunningham *Syntactic Analysis Gullah* 116, *Em* 'him, her, it, them'.

B Senses.

1 Himself—used as indirect object. [Cf *OED him* II. 4. a 1605] **chiefly Sth, S Midl** Cf **her B1**

1906 *DN* 3.140 **nwAR,** *Him*. . . Common for *himself*. . . "He organized him a band of traders." "He aims to hunt him a cook this fall." **1960** Criswell *Resp. to PADS 20* **Ozarks,** *Him*. . . "Next spring Clabe'll draw him the richest piece of cornland you ever laid eyes on." **1965–70** *DARE* (Qu. AA15b, . . *A man is getting married*) 21 Infs, **chiefly Sth, S Midl,** Got him a cook (*or* ball and chain, housekeeper, jewlacky, old lady, wife, etc); **IL**102, Found him a housekeeper; **NC**49, Started him a family; **KY**65, **OR**13, Took him a Pardner (*or* wife); (Qu. AA4a, . . *A man who is very eager to get married*) Inf **SC**26, Hunting him a wife; **SC**58, Out to get him a woman. **1967–69** *DARE* Tape **AR**47, He's gonna . . build him a frozen fruit plant; **KY**16A, He [was] a huntin' him a woman. **1987** Jones–Wheeler *Laughter* 138 **Appalachians,** Old Steamer worked him out 35 cents and got him one of them old, brown, round, hairy coconuts and carried that mule egg home like some family jewel. . . Old Steamer started counting the days. . . he knowed just any day now that mule egg was going to pop open and there was going to be him a nice little brown, fluffy, long-eared baby mule.

2 Herself—used as an indirect object. *Gullah*

1928 Peterkin *Scarlet Sister Mary* 122 **SC** [Gullah], Why, Cinder's de very one what come here last month and got a love-charm to catch em a beau.

3 Her—used as an object. *Gullah*

1892 [see **B6** below]. **1922** Gonzales *Black Border* 147 **sSC, GA coasts** [Gullah], Ef uh tek uh nyung gal fuh wife, wuh ent know nutt'n', uh kin bruk'um fuh suit, same lukkuh oxin bruk fuh pull plow. [=If I take a young girl for a wife, who doesn't know anything, I can break her to suit, just as oxen are broken to pull a plow.] *Ibid* 336 [Gullah glossary], *Um*—him, her, it, them. **1926** Smith *Gullah* 26 **SC**, Similarly *'um* stands for all objective case forms of the third person pronoun: *'e tief 'um* (steals or stole it or them); *'e lick 'um* (of wife, child, or mule); *'e bu'n 'um; uh done 'um; uh shoot 'um.* **1928** Peterkin *Scarlet Sister Mary* 123 **SC** [Gullah], I'd like to kill Cinder [=a woman], Daddy—kill em dead. *Ibid* 233, Doll is spoiled. You done too much for em, Cousin. . . It don' pay to let a woman run over you. **1971** [see **A** above].

4 It—used as an object. [Cf *EDD him* pron. II. 4] **chiefly Sth, S Midl** *esp freq among Black speakers*

1829 Tenney *Female Quixotism* 1.120 **Philadelphia PA** [Black], But what debil put him in your head . . to . . go in de grobe [=grove]? **1909** *S. Atl. Qrly.* 8.44 **sSC coast** [Gullah], An' e' tief de buckra buttah an' pit um een 'e yat [=And he stole the white man's butter and put it in his hat]. **1922** Gonzales *Black Border* 151 **sSC, GA coasts** [Gullah], "You got any bakin'?" "Yes." "Wuh kind'uh bakin?" "Side meat and shoulder meat." "Hummuch fuh him?" **1926** [see **3** above]. **1940–41** Cassidy *WI Atlas* 1 inf **swWI,** Informant frequently used *he* or *him* in reference to inanimate objects, for example mushroom, stone, tree: "Cut him down," "Root him out," etc. **1942** in 1953 Botkin–Harlow *Treas. Railroad Folkl.* 57, The credit belongs to an old lady who kept pounding me on the back and urging: "Please make him [=the train] go, mister!" **1944** *PADS* 2.44 **NC, VA,** *Him* . . It. "I ain't never eat a better apple than him [the June pippin]." **1966–68** *DARE* Tape **MD**45, He [=crab pot] 's about twenty by twenty square inches, and you bait 'im with fish and put 'im overboard. That's what they make a living around here with now . . crabpottin'; **SC**10 [Gullah], [Inf:] Yeah . . got television. . . [FW:] You watch 'im much? . . [Inf:] No, I don watch 'im much. **1971** [see **A** above]. **1987** Jones-Jackson *When Roots Die* 127 **sSC coast** [Gullah], By and by, the li bird what see em all happen, e sit on the fence and sing de de daddy where e find Sister's bone. [=By and by, the little bird that saw it all happen sat on the fence and sang to the daddy where he would find Sister's bones.]

5 He. [Cf *EDD him* pron. II. 3] *esp freq among Black speakers* Note: While *him* occurs for *he* in non-stdE in compound subjs, in comparisons after *than* and *as,* or in the predicate after forms of *be,* its occurrence as a simple subj appears to be restricted to Black speech.

1888 Jones *Negro Myths* 20 **GA coasts,** Buh Tukrey Buzzud, him yent [=didn't] hab no sense no how. **1909** *S. Atl. Qrly.* 8.44 **sSC coast** [Gullah], Ebrybuddy bemean um so 'im leff de settlement. [=Everybody vilified him so he left the settlement.] *Ibid,* 'Im gone buckra house, an' 'im say [=He went to a white man's house, and he said]. **1922** Gonzales *Black Border* 306 **sSC, GA coasts** [Gullah glossary], *Him*—he, she, it. **1926** Smith *Gullah* 26 **sSC, GA coasts** [Black], Him soon will. **1977** Dillard *Lexicon* 151 [Black], Him been dead.

6 She. *esp Gullah*

1892 (1969) Christensen *Afro-Amer. Folk Lore* 33, Bimeby de eldes' daughter mek de same complaint dat de smoke do um so bad 'e can't stan' it nohow; and presently him fall down too. **1909** *S. Atl. Qrly.* 8.49 [Gullah], Me tell Jane 'e mus'n't do so; but him will do. *Ibid* **sSC coast** [Gullah], Write me a lettah to muh wife; tell 'im say him gotter sen' me dem shut 'e promuss [=Write a letter for me to my wife; tell her that she's got to send me those shirts she promised]. **1919** *DN* 5.38 **OK** [Cherokee Indians], *He.* With such pronouns as *her, him* and *his,* is used indiscriminately, without regard to gender. . . An old Cherokee, replying . . to an inquiry as to the health of his wife, said: "He some better, now, him stand up in bed an' eat coffee." **1922** Gonzales *Black Border* 306 **sSC, GA coasts** [Gullah glossary], *Him*—he, she, it.

7 His, hers, its. *Gullah*

1922 Gonzales *Black Border* 306 **sSC, GA coasts** [Gullah glossary], *Him* . . his, her's [sic], its.

him adj Also *him's, im* [Cf *EDD hims* poss. pron.] *chiefly Gullah*

His, her, its.

1853 Simms *Sword & Distaff* 76 **SC**, Da's de t'ing;—but I tell you, Toby, John Sylvester nebber guine le' Joe Bossick put he dirty, poor buckrah paw 'pon him shoulder agen! **1883** (1971) Harris *Nights with Remus* 255 **GA** [Black], One tam dere bin one ole Affiky ooman, 'e call 'im name Coomba. **1888** Jones *Negro Myths* 20 **GA coast,** Buh Pattridge whistle fuh him chillum. **1908** *S. Atl. Qrly.* 7.342 **sSC coast** [Gullah], Dem kill one cow an' git de mores' pa't of 'im libbah fuh brile. [=They kill a cow and get the biggest part of her (or its) liver to broil.] **1909** *Ibid* 8.44 **sSC coast** [Gullah], De buttah melt; eh ron een 'e yeye an' 'im yez. [=The butter melted; it ran in his eyes and his ears.] *Ibid,* Ol' Mis' Preston lib een Fujinny; him daughteh lib two mile away. [=Old Mrs. Preston lived in Virginia; her daughter lived two miles away.] **c1937** in 1972 *Amer. Slave* 2.105 **SC**, He might send for Dr. Madden, him's son-in-law, as how he was.

hime See **hymn**

himlock See **hemlock 2**

hi'most adj [By ellipsis from *hindmost*]

1899 (1912) Green *VA Folk-Speech* 225, *Hi'most.* . . The last of a row of several. Hindermost.

him's See **him** adj

hin n See **hen** n[1]

hin' prep See **hind** prep

hinahina n [Haw *hina* fall over] **HI**

1 =**Spanish moss.**

1965 Neal *Gardens HI* 170, In Hawaii, it [=*Tillandsia usneoides*] is sometimes seen around houses and in gardens, suspended from baskets, and is known as hinahina, or as "Mr. Dole" because its slender, gray flexible, hanging stems and leaves resemble the beard of the "grand old man of Hawaii." [**1971** Pukui–Elbert *Hawaiian Dict.* 66, *Hinahina.* . . Florida moss *(Tillandsia usneoides),* an air plant, growing on tree branches and hanging baskets, forming masses of gray, threadlike stems and leaves. It is often substituted for the heliotrope . . as the flower of Kahoolawe, and so called.]

2 also *hinahina grass:* A Hawaiian grass; see quot.

1987 *DARE* File **HI,** Hinahina grass is common. It has broad leaves, kind of soft. Hinahina is a grass.

hinchy See **hincty** n

hincty adj Also sp *hinkty;* pronc-spp *hankty, haincty*

1 Snobbish, stuck-up, pretentious; contentious, unpleasant. *chiefly among Black speakers* Cf **dicty** adj

1926 (1949) Handy *Treas. Blues* 144, We'll I am hinkty and I'm low down too. **1946** (1972) Mezzrow–Wolfe *Really Blues* 72, It wasn't like the joint went broke for being so hincty. Even the smallest party couldn't get out of there without dropping at least two grand for the night. **1958** Hughes–Bontemps *Negro Folkl.* 484, *Hincty:* Same as dicty [=high hat, snooty]. *Muriel is a hincty hussy.* **1970** *DARE* (Qu. HH35, *A woman who puts on a lot of airs: "She's too ——— for me."*) Inf **SC**68, Hincty ['hɪŋktɪ] [laughter]. **1977** *DARE* File **cSC,** *Hincty,* Stuck-up. **1977** Smitherman *Talkin* 68 [Black], *Saddity* is applied to uppity-acting blacks who put on airs; *haincty* to those who are contentious and unpleasant-acting. **1980** Folb *Runnin' Down* 47 **Los Angeles CA** [Black], For ghetto teenagers in particular, a Tom is anyone who puts on airs, who acts *hincty, seddity,* or *uppity,* no matter whether a middle-class or a ghetto person. **1986** Chapman *New Dict. Amer. Slang* 208, *Like you do a hankty heifer in the bed and make her like it*—Village Voice.

2 also *hinky:* Suspicious.

1934 *AmSp* 9.26 [Prison jargon], *Hinkty.* Suspicious. **1960** Wentworth–Flexner *Slang* 258, *Hinkty*[,] *hincty.* . . Suspicious. **1980** *Birmingham News* (AL) 13 Sept 1/4, The woman, he said, tried to cash a bogus $4,500 check, but tellers tried to stall her while police rushed to the scene. "She got hinky and left," the investigator said. **1986** Chapman *New Dict. Amer. Slang* 208, *Something hinky is going down*—The Renegades (TV program).

hincty n Also *hinchy, hinkty* [**hincty** adj] *chiefly among Black speakers*

1 A snobbish, pompous or overbearing person; a prominent or important person.

1970 *DARE* (Qu. II23, *Joking names for the people who are, or think they are, the best society of a community: The* ———) Inf **SC**68, Hincty. **1970** Major *Dict. Afro-Amer. Slang* 66, *Hinkty:* (1930's–40's) a snobbish or pompous person. **1984** Wilder *You All Spoken Here* 171 **Sth,** *Hincty, hinchy:* Sporty patrons of sporting houses—white, overbearing, pompous, some wearing pearl-buttoned spats with revolvers to match.

2 See quot. Cf **honky 1**

1960 Wentworth-Flexner *Slang* 258, *Hinkty*[,] *hincty*. . . A white person.

hind prep Pronc-spp *hin', hine* [Aphet varr of *behind*] Cf Pronc Intro 3.I.22

1922 Gonzales *Black Border* 306 **sSC, GA coasts** [Gullah glossary], *Hin'*[,] *Hine* . . behind. **1943** *LANE* Map 723 *(Behind)* 2 infs, **neMA, swME,** Hind. **1954** *Harder Coll.* **cwTN,** *Hind*—behind. "She keeps the broom 'hind the door." **1958** *PADS* 29.6 **cwTN,** Behind. . . Pronunciation *hine* [haɪn]. **1960** Criswell *Resp. to PADS 20* **Ozarks,** Hind. Fairly often used in earlier times and probably still occasional. "Don't be a hidin 'hind that house; come on out."

hind n Also *hind part(s)* *esp freq among Black speakers* Cf **hind end 1**

The buttocks.

1967–70 *DARE* (Qu. X35, . . *The part of the body that you sit on*) Infs **LA**8, **PA**239, Hind parts; **TX**106, Hind part; **NC**88, Hind pots [sic; FW: heard in conv]; **CO**7, [haɪn]; **FL**48, Hind; **SC**26, Gave her his hind to kiss. [6 of 7 Infs Black] **1986** Pederson *LAGS Concordance*, 1 inf, **cnAL,** If you don't straighten up, boy, I'm going [to] tan your hind part all [to] pieces. [Inf White]

hinda See **hindu** exclam

hind-back-forward See **hind-foremost**

hind end n Pronc-spp *hin' en(d), hine end* [*SND hin(t)-end* "the hindquarters, posterior" (at *hint* I. adj. (4))] Cf **hinder** n, **hind** n, **hindside** n

1 The buttocks, rump. **scattered, but less freq Atlantic** See Map

1915–25 in 1944 *ADD* **cNY,** Common. 'I'll kick your hin' en' (['haɪn 'ɛn]).' **1942** McAtee *Dial. Grant Co. IN Suppl. 1* 6, *Hind-end* . . buttocks. **1950** *WELS* 1 Inf, **cWI,** Hind end. **1954** *Harder Coll.* **cwTN,** "I'm a-gonna kick 'is old hin' end plumb up atween 'is shoulder blades iffen 'e don't stop a-messin' 'round 'ere." **1960** Criswell *Resp. to PADS 20* **Ozarks,** Butt; back end (more polite); hind end (pron. hine end). **c1960** *Wilson Coll.* **csKY,** *Hind end*. . . The buttocks, with an obscene twist. **1965–70** *DARE* (Qu. X35, . . *The part of the body that you sit on*) 41 Infs, **scattered, but less freq Atlantic,** Hind end; (Qu. K73, . . *The rump of a cooked chicken*) Infs **CA**72, **MO**36, Hind end; (Qu. Y21, *To move about slowly and without energy*) Inf **WI**34, Dragged his hind end; (Qu. JJ20) Inf **WI**34, Bet my hind end on it; (Qu. JJ21) Inf **WI**34, Bet your hind end I am; (Qu. KK29, *To start working very hard*) Inf **NY**184, Got his hind end in high gear; (Qu. LL37) Inf **WA**20, My hind end is getting red. **1968** *DARE* Tape **IN**45, I guess you've wondered why dogs go around smelling of each others' hind ends. **1986** Pederson *LAGS Concordance*, 1 inf, **neTN,** Move your hind end over a hair; 1 inf, **nwMS,** They would have tore my hind end up (=spanked).

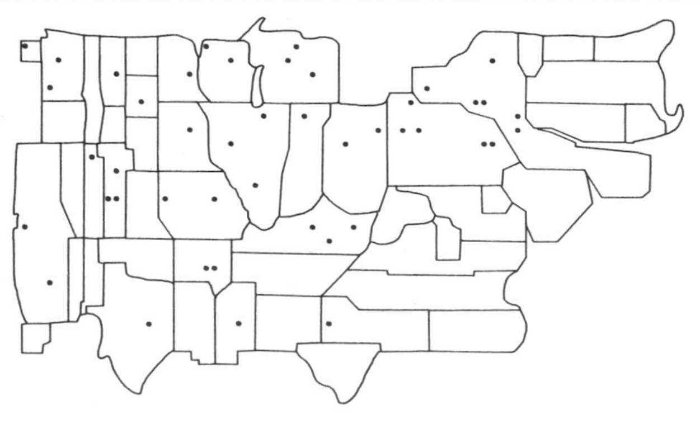

•hind end 1 + varr (Qq. X35, K73, Y21, JJ20, JJ21, KK29, LL37)

2 in phr *on the hind end of nothing:* See quot. Cf **hindside of nowhere**

1927 *AmSp* 3.134 **eME,** The New England contempt of lack of industry expressed itself in such locutions as "always on the hind end of nothing."

hind-end-foremost adv For varr see quots Cf **hind-foremost, hind-part-before**

=**backside-to.**

1934 (1943) *W2, Hind-end-foremost.* With the hind part before; in reversed order. Dial., U.S. **1950** *WELS* 1 Inf, **cwWI,** Hind-end-first; 1 Inf, **ceWI,** Hind-end-to. **c1960** *Wilson Coll.* **csKY,** *Hind-end-foremost* . . Turned around. **1966–69** *DARE* (Qu. MM2, . . *"You've got your dress on ______."*) Infs **MA**5, **PA**8, 150, Hind-end-foremost; **MA**24, **NY**220, **SD**5, Hind-end-to; **OH**72, **VT**16, Hind-end-first; **MI**68, Hind-foot-foremost; **MO**38, Hind-end-before; (Qu. MM3, . . *"This is the front, you've got the whole thing turned ______."*) Infs **MI**76, **WA**20, Hind-end-to.

hind end shack See **hind shack**

hinder v Usu |'hɪndər|; also **chiefly Sth, S Midl, NEng** |hɛndə(r)| Pronc-spp *hender, henduh* Similarly, n *hindrance* Pronc-spp *hendance, hendrance*

Std sense, var forms.

1837 Sherwood *Gaz. GA* 70, *Hender*, for hinder. **1867** Lowell *Biglow* xxvii **NEng,** The New-Englander . . changes the *i* into *e* in *red* for *rid, tell* for *till, hender* for *hinder*. **1871** Eggleston *Hoosier Schoolmaster* 102 **sIN,** You can't hender it. **1890** *DN* 1.68 **KY,** *Hender* [hɛndə]: hinder. "You can't hender me." [*DN* Ed: Also in New England.] *Ibid* 71 **LA,** *Hender.* **1893** Shands *MS Speech* 36, *Hender* [hɛndə]. This is always used by negroes for *hinder*. **1899** (1912) Green *VA Folk-Speech* 222, *Hender.* **1907** in 1944 *ADD* **nwAR, seMO,** Hendrance. **1908** *DN* 3.319 **eAL, wGA,** *Hendance*. . . Hindrance. *Hender*. . . To hinder. **1909** *DN* 3.398 **nwAR,** *Hender.* **1922** (1926) Cady *Rhymes VT* 73, Every man that comes along / . . Unless his woman henders,/ He hefts each piece and buys the one / That has the reddest tag on. **1922** Gonzales *Black Border* 306 **sSC, GA coasts** [Gullah glossary], *Henduh* —hinder, hinders, hindered, hindering. **1923** *DN* 5.210 **swMO,** *Hender.* **c1960** *Wilson Coll.* **csKY,** *Hinder* is often *hender*.

hinder adj [*OED hinder* a.[1] "does not differ in sense from *hind*, but is more frequently used." c1290 →] *arch*

Situated last or in the rear; hind.

1606 in 1624 Smith *Genl. Hist. VA* 27, The Beaver is as big as an ordinary water dog, but his legs exceeding short. His forefeete like a dogs, his hinder feet like a Swans. **1843** (1916) Hall *New Purchase* 143 **IN,** And such a hanging of dish-cloths and milk-strainers on the "yaller buttins" of the hinder man!

hinder n |'haɪndər| Also *hindey* [*EDD hinder* sb.[2] 4] **chiefly Nth, N Midl** *somewhat old-fash* Cf **hind end 1**

The buttocks.

1920s in 1944 *ADD* **cNY,** [haɪndr]. **1930** Shoemaker *1300 Words* 30 **cPA Mts** (as of c1900), *Hinder*—The human fundament. **1935** Sandoz *Jules* 399 **wNE** (as of 1880–1930), "Ach, if our eyes were meant to see that far ahead we would n't need our padded hinders to fall on," Mary tried to comfort. **1950** *WELS* 13 Infs, **WI,** Hinder. **1965–70** *DARE* (Qu. X35, . . *The part of the body that you sit on*) 12 Infs, **chiefly Nth, N Midl,** Hinder; **WI**76, ['haɪndɚ]; **IL**26, Hindey. [11 of 14 Infs old] **1966** *DARE* FW Addit **MA** (as of c1880), Face as red as a baby's hinder. **1987** *DARE* File **MN,** [Radio:] It could poke the horse in the hinder ['hɑɪndɚ].

‡hinder prep [Prob **hind** prep + *er* (at **of** prep)]

1969 *DARE* (Qu. MM8, *A bad housekeeper sweeps the dirt either under the rug or ______ the door*) Inf **MA**58, Hinder—old-fashion.

hindersome adj Pronc-sp *hendersome* [**hinder** v + **-some**] See Intro "Language Changes" III.1

1899 (1912) Green *VA Folk-Speech* 222, *Hendersome*. . . In the way; obstructive. "He is more hendersome than anything else." **1934** (1943) *W2, Hindersome*. . . Likely to hinder. Now Dial. **1984** Wilder *You All Spoken Here* 156 **Sth,** *Hindersome:* In the way.

hindey See **hinder** n

hind foot v phr

To tie the hind feet of; see quot.

1967 *DARE* Tape **TX**24, We had to trim 'em [=mules] up. . . Did it in a pen. . . we had to rope 'em and hind foot 'em and throw 'em.

hind-foremost adv Also *hind-back-forward, hind-forward(s)* Cf **hind-part-before**

=**backside-to.**

1899 (1912) Green *VA Folk-Speech* 225, *Hind-foremost*. . . Hind part before. Opposite to what it ought to be. "Everything has been going hindforemost today." **1957** Battaglia *Resp. to PADS 20* **eMD** *(With the* *back part forward: "She had her dress on _______."*) Hind-forward. **1966–68** *DARE* (Qu. MM2, . . *"You've got your dress on _______."*) Infs **GA**11, **PA**4, 25, 28, 55, **SC**39, Hind-foremost; **IN**45, Hind-back-forward; **PA**175, Hind-forwards.

hind-heal n

1 A **Jerusalem oak** (here: *Chenopodium botrys*).

1900 Lyons *Plant Names* 95, *C[henopodium] botrys* . . Hind-heal. *Ibid* 364, *T[anacetum] vulgare* . . Hind-heal.

2 =tansy.

1900 [see **1** above]. **1971** Krochmal *Appalachia Med. Plants* 246, *Tanacetum vulgare* . . Common Names: . . hind heal, parsley fern, scented fern.

hind hook See **hind shack**

hind leg, hold one's v phr [Prob in ref to holding up a horse's leg to restrain it] *joc*

To act as one's best man.

1849 in 1956 Eliason *Tarheel Talk* 276 **NC,** I have just returned from a small wedding of one of my cousins. . . I had the honor of holding his hind leg.

hind man See **hind shack**

hindoo See **hindu** exclam

hind part See **hind** n

hind-part-before adv For varr see quots **chiefly Sth, S Midl** See Map and Map Section Cf **hindside-before** adv, **hindside-to =backside-to.**

1943 Writers' Program NC *Bundle of Troubles* 25, You turns my heart hind part before, Miss Muskrat, [said Mr. Bullfrog] and it's tickin' like a love clock. **1951** Johnson *Resp. to PADS 20* **DE** *(With the back part forward: "She had her dress on _______.")* Hind-part-before. **1960** Criswell *Resp. to PADS 20* **Ozarks,** *Hind-part-before.* **c1960** *Wilson Coll.* **csKY,** *Hind-part-before.* . . With the rear part turned forward; hind-foremost. **1965–70** *DARE* (Qu. MM2, . . *"You've got your dress on _______."*) 172 Infs, **chiefly Sth, S Midl,** Hind-part-before; **MS**57, **SC**31, **TX**32, **VA**69, Hind-part-in-front; **CA**102, 114, **IL**92, 96, Hind-part-to; **NC**84, **SC**67, **VA**54, Hind-part-first; **FL**18, Hind-partly-fore; **MS**1, Hind-part-forward; **NC**61, Hind-part-backwards; **TN**46, Hind-part-fore; **TX**12, Hind-part-foremost; **TX**36, Hind-parts-before; **VA**21, Hind-part-tofore; (Qu. MM3, . . *"This is the front, you've got the whole thing turned _______."*) 11 Infs, **Sth, S Midl,** Hind-part-before; **DC**3, Hind-part-fore.

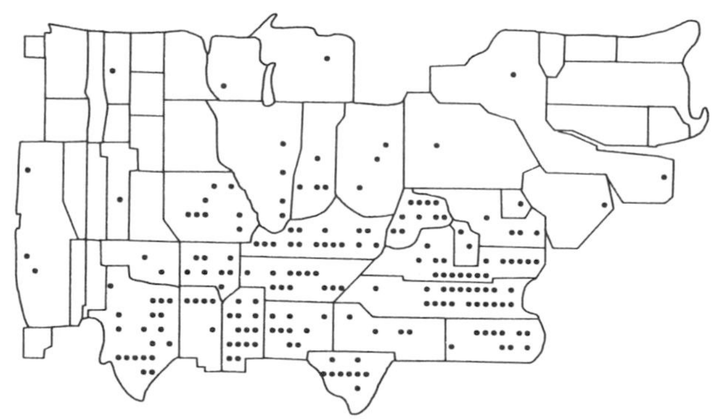

•hind-part-before + varr (Qq. MM2, MM3)

hindrance See **hinder** v

hind shack n Also *hind end shack, hind hook, ~ man*

In railroading: the rear brakeman.

1900 in 1953 Botkin–Harlow *Treas. Railroad Folkl.* 314, The hind 'shack' was freezing a hot hub. . . this was translated to mean that . . the rear brakeman was cooling off a journal. **1940** Cottrell *Railroader* 129, *Hind shack*—Rear brakeman. Protects the rear of a train. **1940** *RR Mag.* Apr 46, *Hind hook*—Rear freight brakeman. **1943** *AmSp* 18.166 [Railroad terms], *Hind shack, hind hook.* Rear brakeman. **1945** in 1953 Botkin–Harlow *Treas. Railroad Folkl.* 341, I'll never forget the day the hind man kept signaling for more whistling. **1958** McCulloch *Woods Words* 86 **Pacific NW,** *Hind end shack*—The read [sic] end brakeman on a train crew. **1969** *AmSp* 44.250 [Language of railroading], On a freight crew, the brakeman who rides in the engine is called the *head man,* and the one who rides in the caboose, the *hind man.*

hindside prep Also with *of old-fash*

Behind.

1903 *DN* 2.298 **Cape Cod MA** (as of a1857), *Hindside*. . . Behind. The broom is hindside the door. **1943** *LANE* Map 723 *(Behind)* 3 infs, **swME, cnCT,** Hindside. **1950** *WELS* 1 Inf, **seWI,** Hindside. [FW sugg; Inf has heard] **1966** Dakin *Dial. Vocab. Ohio R. Valley* 2.51, An informant in the southern Indiana hills remembers that "old timers" said *hindside (of).*

hindside n Cf **hind end 1**

The buttocks.

1942 Berrey–Van den Bark *Amer. Slang* 121.71, *Posteriors*. . . hindside. **1942** *New Yorker* 10 Oct 33 **sME,** What's she doing out in this rain, shoving along the beach on her hindside? **1960** Bailey *Resp. to PADS 20* **KS,** Hindside. **1966** *DARE* (Qu. X35, . . *The part of the body that you sit on*) Infs **SC**2, **WA**33, Hindside.

hindside-backways adv Also *hindside-backward, hind-side-ways* Cf **backways, hind-part-before**

=backside-to.

1967–68 *DARE* (Qu. MM2, . . *"You've got your dress on _______."*) Inf **NY**30, Hindside-backward, hindside-backways; **PA**118, Hind-side-ways.

hindside-before adv For varr see quots [Cf *SND hin'side afore* "back to front," *hint-side foremost* "Backwards" (at *hint* adj. I. (8)); *EDD hin'side afore* (at *hind* adj. 2. (10))] **widespread, but less freq Sth, S Midl** See Map and Map Section *old-fash* Cf **ass-side-before, hind-part-before**

=backside-to—also rarely in phr *get out of bed hindside-before:* see quot 1939.

1913 Kephart *Highlanders* 102 **sAppalachians,** I wish t' my legs growed hind-side-fust. **1929** in 1944 *ADD* **neNY,** Your dress is on hindside fore. **1939** *AmSp* 14.262 **swIN,** One who is irritable or angry 'got up on the wrong side of the bed,' 'got out of bed hindside before'. **1944** *PADS* 2.25 **cwNC,** *Hindside first*. . . Backwards. "You've put that neck-yoke hindside first." **1950** *PADS* 13.18 **cTX,** *Hindside first*. . . The expression among the uneducated was *hindside foremost.* **1950** *WELS* 7 Infs, **WI,** Hindside-before; 3 Infs, Hindside-fore; 1 Inf, Hindside-foremost; 1 Inf, Hindside-on. **1954** *Harder Coll.* **cwTN,** *Hindside-front*. . . Backwards. **1960** Criswell *Resp. to PADS 20* **Ozarks,** Hindside-before. **1965–70** *DARE* (Qu. MM2, . . *"You've got your dress on _______."*) 79 Infs, **scattered, but esp Nth, N Midl, West,** Hindside-before; 18 Infs, **Nth, N Midl,** Hindside-fore; 11 Infs, **esp NEast,** Hindside-foremost; **CA**61, **IL**75, **MA**18, **SD**8, **WI**71, Hindside-forward; **CA**39, **IL**17, **NY**126, Hindside-first; **IA**15, 34, **MO**11, Hindside-front; **CA**138, **NJ**11, Hindside; **AZ**1, Hindside-in-front; **NY**209, Hindside-before-most; **SC**45, Hindside-out; **TN**20, Hindside-and-front; **VA**24, Hind-side-afore; **VA**31, Hindsight [FW: sic]; (Qu. MM3, . . *"This is the front, you've got the whole thing turned _______."*) 34 Infs, **scattered,** Hind-side-before; **HI**1, **IL**5, **ME**12, 19, **NY**30, 37, **RI**1, **TX**10, Hindside-fore(most); **IN**61, Hindsides-before; **NJ**64, Hindside-forward; **TX**33, Hindside-out [Of all Infs responding to these questions, 63% were old; of those giving these responses, 83% were old].

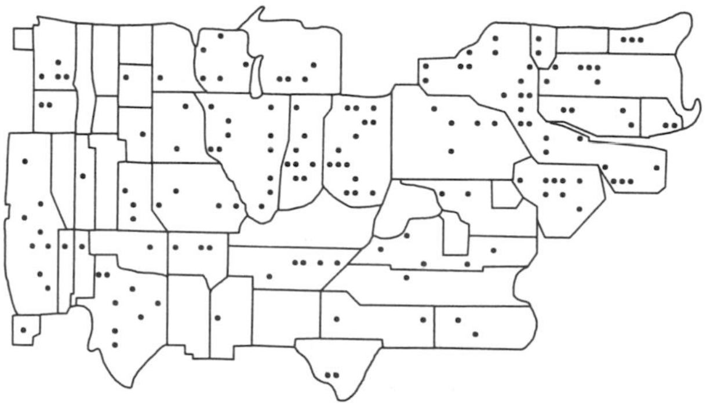

•hindside-before adv + varr (Qq. MM2, MM3)

hindside-before adj Also *hindside-fore* [Cf **hindside-before** adv]
Backward; confused.
1929 (1951) Faulkner *Sartoris* 270 **MS,** Negro in a hind-side-before collar. **1933** *Hanley Disks* **seMA,** That's the way he was—hindsight-fore [sic] and everything.

hindside of See **hindside** prep

hindside of nowhere n *joc* Cf **backside of nowhere, hind end 2**
=end of nowhere(s).
1978 *AP Letters* **neGA** (as of c1900), There are some [words] that are still used by old-timers, such as: . . He came from the hind side of nowhere.

hindside-to adv Also *hindside-to-forward, hindside-to-the-fore, hind-to, hind-way-to* **chiefly Nth, N Midl** Cf **hindside-before** adv
=backside-to.
1920s in 1944 *ADD* **NY,** Hind side to. **1935** Davis *Honey* 86 **OR,** Uncle Preston's fit of early-day firmness had got turned hind side to overnight. **1943** *LANE* Map 723, 1 inf, **neMA,** [Hindside-to] = 're-versed'. **1950** *WELS* 1 Inf, **seWI,** Hind-to. **1965–70** *DARE* (Qu. MM2, . . *"You've got your dress on ________.")* 48 Infs, **chiefly Nth, N Midl,** Hindside-to; **MI**117, Hind-way-to; **TX**5, Hindside-to-the-fore; **WA**28, Hindside-to-forward; (Qu. MM3, . . *"This is the front, you've got the whole thing turned ________.")* Infs **AK**5, **CA**164, **MA**40, **NH**1, **NJ**39, **NY**130, 234, **OH**80, Hindside-to; **MI**117, Hind-way-to. **1975** Gould *ME Lingo* 132, *Hind side to*—Back to the front, in reverse. The Maine euphemism for this is *barse-ackwards.* **1979** *AmSp* 54.98 **swME** (as of 1899–1910), *Hind-side to. . .* (Backwards) "He got out of bed hind-side to."

hind-sideways See **hindside-backways**

hindsights n pl
1 in phrr *knock the hindsights out* (or *off*) and varr: To deal a heavy blow to, defeat, kill; to outdo, surpass. [See quot 1950; prob also euphem for **hindside** n] **chiefly S Midl**
1834 Caruthers *Kentuckian* 1.21, As sure as you saw the fire at the muzzle of his gun, so sure he knocked the creter's hind sights out. **1836** *Quarter Race Ky.* (1846) 18 *(DAE),* Oh! my Grapevine! tear the hind sights off him! **1848** (1855) Ruxton *Life Far West* 15 **Rocky Mts,** Old St. Vrain could knock the hind-sight [sic] off him though, when it came to shootin. **1850** Garrard *Wah-to-yah* 279 **West,** They backed their ears preparatory to kicking the hindsights off the first man that struck them. **1871** Eggleston *Hoosier Schoolmaster* 87 **sIN,** That's ile from a black dog. . . it'll knock the hind sights off of any rheumatiz you ever see. **1892** *DN* 1.232 **KY,** To whip one thoroughly . . to "knock one's hind-sights off." **1950** *PADS* 14.37 **SC,** *Hind sights. . .* In the expression "to knock the hind sights out of . . " to deal a destructive blow to a person or thing, to knock to pieces. Probably refers originally to the *hind sights* of a gun. **c1960** *Wilson Coll.* **csKY,** *"Knock his hindsights out". . .* Heavy blow on the head.
2 See quot.
1953 Randolph–Wilson *Down in Holler* 252 **Ozarks,** *Hind-sights. . .* The Old Testament. . . a backwoods preacher [in Missouri] . . announced, "I'll take my text from the hind-sights this mornin'."

hind-to See **hindside-to**

hindu n See **honda**

hindu exclam Also *hinda, hindoo* [Prob varr of *hinder* accidental interference with the ball in a game such as handball or squash]
See quots.
1981 *Verbatim Letters* **NYC,** One interesting term that came out of that game (Chinese handball) was cried out as, "Hinda" or "Hindu." I would suspect that this is a corruption of the word "hinder" and was used if the ball accidentally hit some object. Today the term is "Do-over." **1987** *DARE* File **NYC** (as of 1960), In the games of Chinese handball, box ball, or king and queen, "hindoo" was called out if the ball went out of play owing to some type of interference.

hindward adj [*OED hindward* a. 1797; "rare"] Cf **hinder** adj
1899 (1912) Green *VA Folk-Speech* 223, *Hindward. . .* Posterior, in the rear.

hind-way-to See **hindside-to**

hindwheels of destruction n Also *hindwheels of bad luck*
Fig: see quots.
1959 McAtee *Oddments* 4 **cNC,** *Hindwheels of destruction, looks like the . .* in bad order, indeed. Simile. Used in the same way as "looks like degradation." **1965** Barbour *Proverbs IL* 197, To look like the hind-wheels of bad luck. **1972** Hall *Sayings Old Smoky* 56 **cwNC,** The hind wheels of destruction started to hell to aggravate the devil to death.

hindwise adv Cf **hind-part-before**
1968 *DARE* (Qu. MM3, *When someone does something the wrong way round you might tell him: "This is the front, you've got the whole thing turned ________.")* Inf **OH**72, Hindwise.

hine See **hind** prep

hine end, hin' en(d) See **hind end**

hiney n[1] See **heinie** n[1] **1, 2**

hiney n[2] Also sp *heinie, hinie* [Perh **hind** n [haɪn] + *-y*]
The buttocks.
1965–70 *DARE* (Qu. X35, . . *The part of the body you sit on)* 37 Infs, **scattered,** Hiney. **1975** *Studies in Honor of Kasten* 30 **swIL,** *Heinie . .* child's rump. **1980** *Wall St. Jrl.* (NY NY) 14 July 13 **NC, TN,** "Does this look like fun?" Mr. De Lozier says, "I'd have my heinie off this mountain if I had my druthers." **1982** *Barrick Coll.* **csPA,** *Hinie . .* rear end; buttocks. "I seen his little hinie." *Ibid, Hiney*—ass, posterior.

hing See **hang A1, 2**

hinge n [Cf *EDD hinge* sb. 3 "*pl. Fig.* Joints."]
A joint of a human body.
1942 Berrey–Van den Bark *Amer. Slang* 116.4, *Hinges creak,* said of an old person. *Ibid* 121.21, *Elbows. . .* hinges. **1950** *WELS (Joking names for the knees)* 2 infs, **WI,** Hinges. **1966** *DARE* (Qu. X36; total Infs questioned, 75) Inf **FL**15, Hinges. **1970** Major *Dict. Afro-Amer. Slang* 66, *Hinges:* (1930's–40's) one's elbows. *Ibid, Hinges creaking:* (1930's–40's) old age.

hinge clam n
Perh **=soft-shell clam.**
1966 *DARE* Tape **ME**17, There's quahogs, and there's hinge clams.

hinge flower n
A **false dragonhead 1** (here: *Physostegia virginiana*).
1940 Clute *Amer. Plant Names* 228, *Physostegia Virginiana. . .* hinge-flower.

‡hinge-jaw n *joc*
1968 *DARE* (Qu. X9, *Joking or uncomplimentary words for a person's mouth . . "I wish he'd shut his ________.")* Inf **MD**9, Hinge-jaw; (Qu. HH7a, *Someone who talks too much, or too loud: "He's an awful ________.")* Inf **MD**9, Hinge-jaw.

hinge mud turtle See **hinge turtle**

hinges of hell n pl Cf **hobs of hell**
The furthest reaches of hell—usu in phrr *hot* (or *black*) *as the hinges of hell* and varr; see quots.
1839 (1863) Kemble *Jrl. Georgian* 255, She (to use a most extraordinary comparison I heard of a negro girl making with regard to her mother) is as black as "de hinges of hell." **1912** *DN* 3.571 **wIN,** *Black as the hinges of hell. . .* Very black. **1912** London *Smoke Bellew* 73 *(DA),* It's colder than the hinges of hell. **1922** *DN* 5.156 **IN,** *Black as the hinges of hell. . .* Very black. **1944** Barbour *Vanishing Eden* 117, In summer in this part of Florida it is hotter than the hinges of Gehenna. **1954** *WELS Suppl.* ceWI, Hotter than the hinges of Hell. **1957** *Sat. Eve. Post Letters* **MA,** *Hot as the hinges of Tophet*—very warm. **1967–70** *DARE* (Qu. B3, *If a day is very hot, you say it's . .* ________) Infs **CA**211, **OH**44, **TX**11, **VA**47, Hotter than (*or* hot as) the hinges of hell; **MI**122, As hot as the hinges—Inf: "of hell" is understood [FW: Inf says this is a southern expression]; **NC**52, Hot as the hinges; (Qu. CC9, *Other words or expressions for hell: "That man is headed straight for ________.")* Infs **NC**72, **IL**47A, The hinges of hell (*or* hades). **1968** *DARE* FW Addit **nwLA,** *Hotter'n the hinges of hades;* very hot.

hinge turtle n Also *hinge mud turtle* [From the plastral hinge]
=box turtle.
1851 *De Bow's Rev.* 11.53 **LA,** Cooter, *Hinge Mud Turtle,* or *Emys Clausa,* is also found here. They never exceed six inches in length (i.e. the shell) and close up like the *testudo clausa,* though not quite so com-

pletely. **1969** *DARE* (Qu. P24, *What kinds of turtles are found around here?*) Inf **IN**69, Hinge turtle.

hinie See **hiney** n[2]

hinker n [Perh var of **hunker** n[1]]
1967 *DARE* (Qu. O5, *The posts standing in the water which . . [landing piers] rest on*) Inf **CO**20, Hinkers.

hinkey See **hickey** n[2]

hinkie See **hickey** n[1] **2a**

hinkty adj See **hincty** adj

hinkty n See **hincty** n

hinky adj[1] [Perh var of *dinky*] Cf **hicky** adj[2]
1968–70 *DARE* (Qu. LL2, . . *Too small to be worth much: "I don't want that little ______ potato."*) Infs **WV**3, 16, Hinky.

hinky adj[2] See **hincty adj 2**

hinky dinky n, also attrib [Redup of **dinky** n[1] **1**]
See quot 1968.
1968 *DARE* (Qu. N37, . . *Names for a branch railroad that is not very important or gives poor service*) Inf **OH**45, Hinky dinky. **1970** *DARE* Tape **IL**114, I could go from Charleston over to Kansas and then there'd be a little hinky-dinky [rail]road down to Westfield.

hinny n [Perh < **hinder** n] *arch*
1895 *DN* 1.397 **NYC,** *Hinny* [hɪnɪ]: the game of leap-frog.

hinsach See **huisache**

hinster n [Cf **hinder** n, Ger *hinderst* hindmost]
The buttocks.
1935 Smiley *Gloss. New Paltz* **seNY,** Does not like to be up to his "hinster" in snow.

‡hi-open-bopen n
1923 *DN* 5.235 **swWI,** *Hi-open-bopens. . .* (1) plu. Fourth-of July mummers. "Here come the hi-open-bopens!" (2) sing. Hence, a man fantastically or badly dressed. "He's a regular hi-open-bopen."

hiou muckamuck See **high-muck-a-muck 1**

hip n[1]
1 in phr *have something on one's hip:* See quots.
1914 *DN* 4.74 **nNH, ME,** *Hip, to have suthin' on yer. . .* To have a bottle of liquor. "Hain't got nawthin' on yer hip, hev ye?" **1919** *NY Eve. Jrl.* (NY) 30 Sept 30 *(Zwilling Coll.),* [Cartoon:] Lamping a late comer at the show as he strolls down the aisle with a something "on his hip." **1923** in 1963 Lardner *Ring Lardner Reader* 470, We will pretend like you have just been introduced to a man named Harley. Don't say to him "Glad to meet you, Mr. Harley. Do you and your wife get along all right?" . . But do say if you feel like it, "Pleased to meet you Mr. Harley. Got anything on the hip?" **1923** *DN* 5.210 **swMO,** *Hip, to have on the. . .* To carry liquor or a concealed weapon. "Bill's got suthin' on 'is hip that drinks right well." "I'd 'a' busted 'im one but I was afeerd he mought have suthin' on 'is hip."
2 in phrr *get one's hips up (on one's shoulders):* To become angry or offended.
1942 *Amer. Mercury* 55.223.89 **Harlem NYC** [Black], You [are] trying to get your hips up on your shoulders 'cause I said you was with a beat broad [=an unprepossessing girl]. **1972** Cooper *NC Mt. Folkl.* 92, *Got his (her) hips up*—became offended.

hip v[1], hence vbl n *hipping*
1 To carry on the hip.
1818 in 1824 Knight *Letters* 93 **KY,** Some mothers here *hip* their infants; as do the Sumatrans. **1843** (1916) Hall *New Purchase* 162 **IN,** Still oftener each [log] is hipped. And hipping is done by one man who has some strength and more dexterity; who adroitly whips up the log on his hip, and trots off with it. **1969** *DARE* (Qu. Y30a, *To take something up and move it from one place to another*) Inf **GA**77, Hip—old-fashioned, = "hippin the baby."
2 To change the diaper of. Cf **hippen**
1967 *DARE* FW Addit **swAR,** *To hip a baby*—to change a diaper.

hip v[2] [Perh from Scots, nEngl dial *hip* to hop, skip] Cf **hyper**
To hurry along.
1871 (1882) Stowe *Fireside Stories* 67, They hadn't more than got in the door before they see old Tom a hippin' along, as highsteppin' as ever. **1950** *WELS (To move about hurriedly)* 1 Inf, **cwWI,** Hipping.

hip n[2] See **hypo**

‡hip and thigh adj phr [Reinterpretation of the biblical phrase; cf Judges 15:8]
1967 *DARE* (Qu. II3, *Expressions to say that people are very friendly toward each other: "They're ______."*) Inf **IL**5, Hip and thigh.

hip barn See **hip-roofed barn**

hip, break one's v phr [By analogy with *break one's neck* to strive to the utmost]
1966 *DARE* (Qu. A22, . . *'To start working hard': "She had only ten minutes to clean the room, but she ______ [and had it done in no time]."*) Inf **MT**5, Broke her hip.

hip deep to a tall Indian adj phr [Cf *knee-high to a grasshopper* very short]
Very deep; see quot.
1958 McCulloch *Woods Words* 86 **Pacific NW,** *Hip deep to a tall Indian*—A measure of snowfall, or mud. **1988** *DARE* File **WI** (as of 1970s), How deep? About hip deep to a tall Indian.

hiper See **hyper**

hiphazard adv [Var of *haphazard,* perh by folk-etym]
1969 *DARE* (Qu. Y38, *Mixed together, confused: "The things in the drawer are all ______."*) Inf **NY**209, Hiphazard.

hip-hoed See **hypo 1**

hip-hop v Also *hippy-hop* Cf **hop** v[1] **1**
To limp.
1966–70 *DARE* (Qu. BB1, *When a person has been injured so that when he walks he steps more heavily on one foot than the other: "He ______."*) Infs **DC**13, **OH**50, Hip(py)-hops.

hipin See **hippen**

hipp See **hypo**

hipped adj[1] [Cf *OED hipped* a.[1] 3 1565–1799; *EDD hipped* ppl. adj.[1] 1 "Injured in the hip"] Cf **hipshot**
See quots.
1899 (1912) Green *VA Folk-Speech* 225, *Hipped. . .* Having the hip sprained or dislocated. **1926** *DN* 5.400 **Ozarks,** *Hipped. . .* Disabled or seriously injured. **1954** *Harder Coll.* **cwTN,** *Hipped.*

hipped adj[2] [Cf *OED hipped* a.[2] "colloq."; 1710–1887; *EDD hipped* ppl adj[2] 1] Cf **hypo 1**
See quots.
1821 (1930) Sewall *Diary* 76 **MD,** Today I am completely *hipped.* Very low spirited. **1899** (1912) Green *VA Folk-Speech* 225, *Hipped. . .* Rendered melancholy; melancholy; mopish. **1966–68** *DARE* (Qu. BB5, *A general feeling of discomfort or illness*) Inf **NC**36, He's hipped; (Qu. BB28, . . *Imaginary diseases*) Inf **TN**12, He's just hipped.

hippen n Also *hip(p)in, hipping* [*OED hipping* "Sc. and north. dial."] **chiefly Sth, S Midl** Cf **hip** v[1] **2, hippie, hippings**
A baby's diaper; rarely v *hippen* to change a diaper.
1870 *Nation* 28 July 56/2 **cs,sePA,** "Hippen" (hipband?) was the polite term for portions of the drapery of young children. **1917** *DN* 4.413 **wNC, IL,** *Hippin'. . .* A diaper; breech clout. **1926** Roberts *Time of Man* 326 **KY,** She . . "stepped clean plumb outen her hippens and walked off." . . If Hen lost his hippens in the pasture why he didn't have no kind brother to pick it up for him. **c1940** Eliason *Word Lists FL* 9, *Hippin'* [hɪpɪn]: Diaper. Rare. **1953** Randolph–Wilson *Down in Holler* 252 **Ozarks,** *Hippin's. . .* Diapers. . . it is used as a verb also, as in this sentence: "Somebody better go hippin' that there baby!" **1965–70** *DARE* (Qu. W19, . . *The folded cloth worn by a baby in place of pants*) 28 Infs, **chiefly Sth, S Midl,** Hippin(s) [15 of 28 Infs comm type 5; 13 of 28 Infs gs educ]; **AR**52, **GA**6, **NC**86, Hipping(s). **1968** Haun *Hawk's Done Gone* 276 **eTN,** He tied the navel cord . . and washed Annie Lee and put her hipin and her nightgown on her. **1976** Garber *Mountain-ese* 41 **Appalachians,** *Hippens* . . diapers—She spends a lot uv time washin' the hippens fer her new baby. **1978** *AP Letters* **neGA** (as of c1900), There are some [words] that are still used by old-timers, such as: . . Hipping—from the Scotch for diaper. **1986** Pederson *LAGS Concordance,* 1 inf, **nwAR,** Hipping—used to call baby's diaper.

hip-petticoat See **hip-slip**

hippety-hop n [*hippety-hop* with a hopping motion or gait]
The children's game hopscotch.
[1920 *Cornhill Mag.* Sept. 332 (*OEDS* at *hippety*), A row of children

playing hippety-hop across a broad lawn.] **1968** *DARE* (Qu. EE19, *The game in which children mark a 'court' on the ground or sidewalk, throw a flat stone in one section, then go on one foot and try to kick it or carry it out*) Infs **IN**23, **LA**20, **VA**27, Hippety-hop.

hippie n
=hippen.
1958 *Hench Coll.* **cVA,** *Hippies*—a baby's diapers. **c1960** *Wilson Coll.* **csKY,** *Hippies*. . . diapers. Rare. **1968** *DARE* (Qu. W19, . . *The folded cloth worn by a baby in place of pants*) Inf **LA**40, Hippies. **1972** *Atlanta Letters* **nwGA,** "Hippies"—Baby Diapers.

hippin See **hippen**

hipping n See **hippen**

hipping vbl n See **hip** v[1]

hippings n pl
See quots.
1927 *AmSp* 2.389 [Vagabond argot], *Hippings*. . anything placed under one when *flopping* (sleeping), to make it easier on the hip-bones. **1942** Berrey–Van den Bark *Amer. Slang* 915.19, [Ranch equipment:] Hippin's, underbedding.

hipple adj [Cf Scots, Ir, nEngl dial *hipple* to limp]
1916 *DN* 4.338 **PA,** *Hipple*. . . Lame. "You can't make that hipple horse run." Perhaps, a contamination of *hipped* and *cripple*.

hippo n[1], v See **hypo**

hippo n[2] [*EDD*]
Ipecac.
1909 *S. Atl. Qrly.* 8.39 **sSC coast** [Gullah], *Ipecac, syrup of ipecac,* or *of ipecachuana* . . : *hippo, hippo syrup* it is and has been since cockney English mariners fetched it home from the Brazils. . . It still remains the vulgar use . . of the tide-water South Carolinian [Footnote: White and black]: " 'Ipecac!' " said my old colored nurse . . "Dat wut [=that's what] dese new-fangle' niggah calls 'hippo' sense dey all gone fool!" [=since they all got foolish]. **1930** Woofter *Black Yeomanry* 54 **seSC** [Gullah], *Hippo:* ipecac. **1950** *PADS* 14.37 **seSC,** *Hippo syrup*. . . Syrup of ipecacuanha. A medical term familiar fifty years ago, but surviving only among the old or sequestered. The cockney English mariners who first reported the native remedy pronounced it *hippecac,* whence *hippo syrup.*

‡hippocanarious adj *joc* Cf **flippercanorious, hypo**
1949 *PADS* 11.22 **CO,** *Hippocanarious*. . . Unmanageable, high-spirited. "Hippocanarious children."

hippoed adj See **hypo 1**

hippoed adv See **hypo 2**

hippy-hop See **hip-hop**

hip-roofed barn n Also *hip-roof barn;* for addit varr see quots **chiefly N Cent, NEast** See Map Cf **gambrel roof**
A barn having either a gambrel or a hip roof. Note: In std usage a *hip roof* has ends which slope in the same way as the sides, while a **gambrel roof** has sides with two separate slopes, the lower steeper than the upper. While in many quots it is impossible to determine which type is meant, gambrel roofs are much more commonly found on barns than hip roofs.

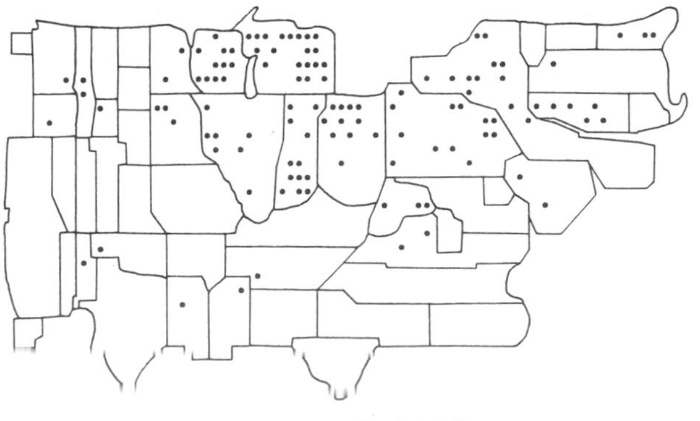

•hip-roofed barn + varr (Qu. M1)

1950 *WELS* [*(Shapes of roofs on barns)* 48 Infs, **WI,** Hip roof; 1 Inf, Hexagonal hip roof]; *(Names for barns according to the way they are built)* 12 Infs, **WI,** Hip-roof barn; 1 Inf, Hip barn. **1965–70** *DARE* (Qu. M1, . . *Kinds of barns*) 116 Infs, **chiefly N Cent, NEast,** Hip-roof(ed) barn; **IN**77, **MI**19, Hip barn; **MS**58, Hip-rooftop barn. **1967** Sloane *Age of Barns* 39, In New England, there are still some stone barns with hip roofs, but few of the frame hip-roofed barns remain in America. [Illustrations show barns with std hip roofs.] **1970** *DARE* Tape **IL**114, [FW:] Do you have a hip-roof barn? [Inf:] Yea, a lot. Now if you ever saw, they were built mostly, hip barns were built, you see, out this way an' they come up then across. That was for hay, whole lot o' hay. Put 'em in there on tracks. . . Oh, you could get in [a] big barn like that, maybe a hunderd ton o' hay. **1976** Wells *Barns U.S.A.* np **ceIA,** It was the first hip-roofed barn in the area when all the others were conventional gable-roof barns. [Photograph shows a barn with a curb or gambrel roof.] [**1984** *MJLF* 10.151 **ME, WI,** *Hip roof.* A rural term for a gambrel roof.]

hipscot(ch) See **hopscotch**

hipsheltered See **hipskeltered**

hipshot adj Also *hipshotten* Cf **hipped** adj[1]
Having a hip out of place; lame, disabled.
a1883 (1911) Bagby *VA Gentleman* 13, Some good-natured old hip-shot fool of a family ghost, who was everlastingly "projicking" around at night, after the girls had quit their talk, making the floors crack. **1899** (1912) Green *VA Folk-Speech* 225, *Hip-shot*. . . Having the hip dislocated or shot out of place; lame; awkward. Hipshotten. **1903** *DN* 2.316 **seMO,** *Hipshotten*. . . having the hip dislocated. **1926** *DN* 5.400 **Ozarks,** *Hipped*. . . Disabled or seriously injured. The form *hip-shot* is also common.

hipshot adv
With one hip higher than the other.
1949 Webber *Backwoods Teacher* 127 **Ozarks** *(Hench Coll.),* He flicked a gadfly off one of his little black mules which stood hipshot, switching its tail. **1968** Stegner *Edge* 22 **CA,** Hip-shot, tennis shoes crossed, chin on hand, he leans on the rail for a bit.

hipshotten See **hipshot** adj

hipsided adj [Var of *lopsided*] Cf **hipskeltered**
1967 *DARE* (Qu. KK70, *Something that has got out of proper shape: "That house is all ______."*) Inf **LA**6, Hipsided.

hipskeltered adj Also *hipsheltered* [Perh blend of **hipshot** + *helter-skelter*] Cf **hipsided**
Askew, lopsided, out of line.
1930 *VA Qrly. Rev.* 6.249 **S Midl,** He may affirm candidly and black-actually that . . the line of his barn roof is hip-skeltered, antegogglin', catawampus or waupajawed. **1984** Wilder *You All Spoken Here* 163 **Sth,** Out of plumb; cattercornered; cattywampused; hipsheltered.

hip-slip n Also *hip-petticoat* **esp Sth** *esp freq among Black speakers*
1965–70 *DARE* (Qu. W16b, *The garment worn by a woman under her dress—if it only goes from the waist down*) Infs **FL**51, **GA**42, **LA**6, **MS**60, Hip-slip; **MS**63, Hip-petticoat. [4 of 5 Infs Black]

hip-swinn(e)y n [*swinn(e)y* varr of *sweeny* muscular atrophy in a horse]
See quot 1953.
1936 *AmSp* 11.315 **Ozarks,** *Hip-swinny*. . . Lumbago. A woman said 'I caint dance, on account I got th' hip-swinny.' **1953** Randolph–Wilson *Down in Holler* 253 **Ozarks,** *Hip-swinney*. . . A weakness of the back, similar to lumbago. Usually refers to horses. . . A man told me that his wallet suffered from *hip-swinney,* meaning that he had no money. **1954** *Harder Coll.* **cwTN,** *Hip-swinney*. . . "Mules has hip-swinney."

‡hip toe n
1968 *DARE* (Qu. K28, *What are the chief diseases that cows have around here?*) Inf **PA**166, Hip toe—comes from bad water.

Hiram n Usu |'Haɪrəm|; also |hɑrm|, |harm|
A Forms.
1891 *DN* 1.156 **cNY,** [hɑrm] . . Hiram. **1968** *DARE* (Qu. II10b, . . *When you don't know his name—what you'd say to a man: "Say, ______, how far is it to the next town?"*) Inf **DE**1, Hiram [harm]—This lets a man know you are a Mason and that you know he is one.

B Sense.

A rustic—also used as a contemptuous term of address. Cf *DS* HH1

1930 Irwin *Amer. Tramp* 99, *Hiram.*—Many of the old-time yeggs [=tramp thieves] preyed upon the country post offices in the districts populated by farmers or, traditionally, "Hirams." **1932** Faulkner *Light in August* 172 **MS,** You better go back to the farm, Hiram. **1942** Berrey–Van den Bark *Amer. Slang* 391.3, *Rustic; Bumpkin. . .* Hiram.

hire v Usu |haɪr, haɪə|; also **esp S Midl** |hɑr| For addit varr see quots See Pronc Intro 3.I.1.g. Pronc-spp *hahr, hoir;* for *hired,* pronc-spp *hard, hi'ed, hord*

A Forms.

1899 Chesnutt *Conjure Woman* 16 **csNC** [Black], Mars Dugal' had hi'ed her. **1911** *DN* 3.550 **WY,** *Hard,* hired. "He is a hard man," he is a hired man. **1924** (1946) Greer–Petrie *Angeline Gits an Eyeful* 3 **csKY,** They actually hord (hired) . . little boys to . . fetch them things fur 'em. **1928** *AmSp* 3.403 **Ozarks,** Such words as *fire, . . hire* have a vowel much like the *a* in *far.* **1936** *AmSp* 11.33 **eTX,** [In addition to being pronounced [haɪɚ],] *Hire, hired . .* are also often pronounced with [a:] [ɑ:], [ɒ:], or in illiterate speech even [ɔ:]. **1940** *AmSp* 15.214 **TX,** Frequently I hear some Southerners, generally those of the lower social brackets, pronouncing . . *hire . .* as if [it] . . were spelled . . *hoir.* **1941** *AmSp* 16.7 **eTX** [Black], The three sounds, [a:], [ɑ:], and [ɒ:] are usual for . . *hire, hired . .* but these words occur with [aɪə] . . and also with a slight off-glide following [a:], [ɑ:], and [ɒ:]. **1941** in 1944 *ADD* **cnWV,** 'He [hɑrjid] some more reapers yesterday.' 'Nobody would [hɑri] him.' Also [haɪrid]. Rural. Almost invariable. Reported. **1949** Webber *Backwoods Teacher* 88 **Ozarks,** "What she don't seem to realize is that us voters hahr her an' pay her wages. **1954** *Harder Coll.* **cwTN,** *Hire*—[hɑr]. **1956** Ker *Vocab. W. TX* 187, *Hired* (sometimes pronounced "hard" by older informants) *hand.* **1960** Criswell *Resp. to PADS 20* **Ozarks,** *Hired . .* [hɑrd]. Still very common. **1976** Garber *Mountain-ese* 38 **Appalachians,** *Hard-hands . .* hired men.

B Senses.

1 To borrow (money) usu at interest. **esp NEng**

1782 in 1884 Essex Inst. *Coll.* 21.282 **neMA,** Voted the Parish Committe full Power to borrow or hire hard Money Enought to Pay of the . . Demand upon the Parish. **1841** Buckingham *America* 3.527 **seMA,** [Near New Bedford, Mass.] to "hire money" is used for to borrow. **1902** McFaul *Ike Glidden* 186 *(DAE),* She can hire the money, and I know she will pay you. **1925** Glasgow *Barren Ground* 339 **VA,** She had borrowed money again, "hiring money" they called it at Pedlar's Mill. **1929** *AmSp* 5.125 **ME,** Folk often spoke of someone who was "all mortgaged up," "had hired money" or had "trusted out his money." Coolidge's remark when urged to a cancellation of the Allies' debts is typical of New England. "They hired the money, didn't they?" **1931–33** *LANE Worksheets* **ceMA,** *Hire . .* to borrow money from a bank [FW sugg]. *Ibid* **neMA,** *Hired . .* If interest is paid the money is hired. *Ibid* **nwCT,** *Hire. . .* If we have to pay interest we hire the money. Borrow and lend are used only of transactions without interest or charge. **1983** *DARE* File **swME,** Warrant of 1983 Town of Baldwin, ME, meeting: . . Article 17. To see if the town will instruct or authorize the selectmen to hire sums of money as are necessary to pay the current expenses of the town for the ensuing year.

2a also with *out,* rarely with *in:* To take a job, find employment.

1800 (1907) Thornton *Diary* 10.173 **PA,** Three young negro women came—I engaged one of them to come on Monday—they came from Marlbro'—to hire here. **1860** (1936) Hawley *Diary* 19.339 **WI,** Hamilton . . hired out at Denver as a blacksmith. **1871** in 1983 *PADS* 70.38 **ce,sePA,** A boy came to hire eat supper here—But we do not want him. **1943** Chase *Jack Tales* 147 **wNC,** "Do you want to hire to do my cookin' and washin' for me?" "Yes," she says, "I'll hire." **1958** McCulloch *Woods Words* 86 **Pacific NW,** *Hire out*—To go to work for a certain camp. **1963** Owens *Look to River* 11 **TX,** I hired out lots o' times down there, but couldn't make enough to get a grounding. **1966** *Wall St. Jrl.* (NY NY) 30 Dec 1/6 *(Hench Coll.),* I went to Bell Helicopter right away and hired in there.

b with *to* or *(out) with:* To accept a job with.

a1756 in 1774 Woolman *Works* 10 **NJ,** A man . . asked me, if I would hire with him to tend shop and keep books. **1920** Hunter *Trail Drivers TX* 100, In the spring of 1890 I hired to Paul Handy of Colorado to drive a herd to that state. *Ibid* 120 (as of 1870), [He] asked me to go along as he had hired to them. **1970** *Current Slang* 5.1.8 [Jargon of railroad employees], *Hire out . .* To start to work for:—I hired out with Southern Pacific in 1965.

3 in phr *hire (something) done* and varr: To pay to have (something) done.

1940 Faulkner *Hamlet* 76 **MS,** Flem Snopes built a new blacksmith shop. . . He hired it done, to be sure. **1943** Chase *Jack Tales* 176 **wNC,** He had plenty of money, so he hired most of the heavy work done and lived right on there. **1946** White *Autobiog.* 35 **KS,** My father, being in his fifties, had to hire all his share of the farm work done. **1963** Edwards *Gravel* 79 **eTN** (as of 1920s), He usually had to hire his plowing and hoeing done. **1970** *DARE* FW Addit **NY,** I hired it sawed—I paid to have it sawed. **1975** Newell *If Nothin' Don't Happen* 15 **nwFL,** We hadn't heard the last of the Yankee who hired the fence built. **1984** Hancock *Choestoe* 23 **neGA,** He kept abreast of agricultural improvements; however, he hired most of the plowing and harvesting done. **1988** *DARE* File **csWI,** Commonly said: I don't have the time to repair the roof so I'll hire it done; **IA, MN, ME,** He had to hire it done; **WI,** I'll hire the painting done. **1989** *NADS* Letters **SD,** My dad was an electrical contractor, so I heard the term [=hire it done] every day, and . . continue to use it today.

hired man n Also *hire man, hired farm man* **widespread, but more freq Nth, N Midl** See Map

A farmhand, laborer; a manservant.

1694 in 1886 NC *Colonial Rec.* 1.395 **NC,** John Mason has proved his rights being Morgan Thomas and his wife and two children and a highred man named John Haws. **1819** in 1822 Flint *Letters* 135 **seIN,** Last night a gentleman from Carolina lodged in the tavern here [at Jeffersonville, Ind]. After a hired man had given him slippers . . he exclaimed, . . "I would not live in a free state, where one white man cleans the boots of another." **1900** Dix *Deacon Bradbury* 23 **VT,** They also invariably had a "hired man," who equally lightened the labors of the farm. **1926** *AmSp* 2.79 **ME,** Servants in Maine are all "hired help." . . The manservant is a "hired man." **1950** *WELS* 51 Infs, **WI,** Hired man; 1 Inf, Hired farm man. **1960** Bailey *Resp. to PADS 20* **KS,** Hired man's house. **1965–70** *DARE* (Qu. L1, *A man who is employed to help with work on a farm*) 287 Infs, **widespread, but more freq Nth, N Midl,** Hired man; **PA**37, Hire man; (Qu. L2, . . *Where a hired man and his family live*) 25 Infs, **chiefly Nth, N Midl,** Hired man's house (*or* home, quarters, tenant house); **MO**16, House for the hired man; **OR**7, Hire man's house; (Qu. HH42, *Names and nicknames for a common laborer;* total Infs questioned, 75) Inf **FL**7, Hired man. **1971** Bright *Word Geog. CA & NV* 193, *Hand* (on a farm or ranch)—*hired man* 31% [of 300 informants].

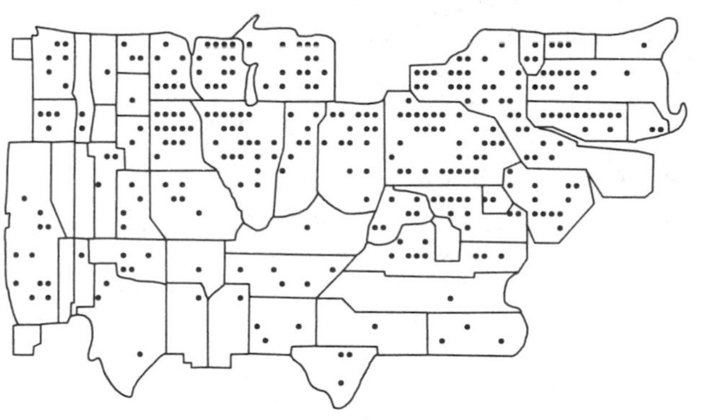

•hired man + varr (Qq. L1, L2, HH42)

hire in See **hire B2a**

hireland n [Literally "one who *hires* (rents) land"; the meaning in quot 1940 is prob due to confusion with *hireling*]

See quots.

1889 *Jrl. Amer. Folkl.* 2.229 **KY, TN,** *Hireland.*—A renter or cropper. **1940** Yoder *Rosanna* 232 **PA,** I'd rather farm another farm than go out and work as a hireland (hireling).

hire man See **hired man**

hire out (with) See **hire B2**

hire (something) done See **hire B3**

hire with, hire to See **hire B2b**

hiricane See **hurricane**

hirm-skirm adj [Pronc-sp for *harum-scarum*]

1936 in 1944 *ADD* **neKY,** We couldn't get along with that hirm-skirm piece of a man.

his adj Pronc-spp *he's, hees*

A Forms. [Cf *EDD hees, he's* (at *his* pos. pron. I. (6), (7)); *SND he's* (at *his* poss. pron.)]

1887 (1967) Harris *Free Joe* 221 **cGA** [Black], I dunner [=don't know] who my young marster would 'a' got ter do he's cookin' en he's washin'. *Ibid* 222, En he uz one er dese yer kinder folks w'at want he's coffee hot. **1919** *DN* 5.38 **OK** [Cherokee], *Hees. . .* His.

B Senses.

1 Its. [Cf *OED his* "*poss. pron., 3rd sing . . neut.* [obs];" *SND his* poss. pron. "freq. of inanimate objects = its."]

1944 *PADS* 2.44 **wNC,** *His. . .* Its. "Each state had his burying plot [at Gettysburg]." **1982** Heat Moon *Blue Highways* 70 **SC** [Black], I says, 'How that water gone get up to me?' He say with a lectric pump. I says, 'We drinks water what come up of his own mind.'

2 Her. [Cf *EDD his* poss. pron. II. 3 "her"]

1928 Peterkin *Scarlet Sister Mary* 343 **seSC** [Black], Si May-e has been a turrible sinner. . . His [=Mary's] soul might be clean but his body ought to be baptized again. **1966** *DARE* (Qu. GG11, *To be quite anxious about something*) Inf **SC**26, Running 'round like a hen with his neck cut off.

hise See **hoist**

hisen See **hisn**

hishy-hash(y) n [By redup from *hash;* cf Intro "Language Changes" I.3; cf *SND hish-hash* "A muddle, confusion, untidy mess"]

A kind of stew; see quots.

1888 Kieffer *Recoll. Drummer Boy* 224 **PA,** When, as was generally the case on a march, our hard-tack had been broken into small pieces in our haversacks, we soaked these in water and fried them in pork fat, stirring well and seasoning with salt and sutler's pepper, thus making what was commonly known as "Hishy-hashy, or a hot-fired stew." **1979** *NC Folkl. Jrl.* 27.3.88 **cPA,** "Make some hishy-hash." That's everything thrown in. An' she up and grabbed a handful of his hair and said, "I'll give ya yer goddamn hishy-hash."

hisn pron Also *hisnts* Also sp *his(s)en, hiss(i)n, hiz(z)en* [c,sEngl dial; prob *his/hisn* by analogy with *my/mine*] **chiefly Sth, S Midl, NEng** Cf **hern** pron

His.

1795 Dearborn *Columbian Grammar* 136, *List of Improprieties,* commonly called *Vulgarisms,* which should never be used in *Speaking, Reading, or Writing. . .* Hizzen for His. **1843** (1916) Hall *New Purchase* 119 **IN,** A stray critter of hissin. **c1885** in 1981 Woodward *Mary Chesnut's Civil War* 249 **SC** (as of 1861) [Black], Negroes say: "Mars Jeems, he don't care for niggers. He'll get rid of the trouble of 'em soon as they are *hisen.*" **1899** (1912) Green *VA Folk-Speech* 226, *Hisn. . .* Same as *his.* His own. **1907** *DN* 3.245 **eME,** *Hisn.* **1908** *DN* 3.320 **eAL, wGA,** *Hisn.* **1909** *DN* 3.412 **nME,** *Hisn.* **1910** Mulford *Hopalong* 153, Taking the button and looking it over. "Yep, it's hissn, all right." **1913** *DN* 4.2 **csME,** *Hisnts. . .* His. . . "That book is hisnts." **1922** (1926) Cady *Rhymes VT* 48, He didn't have no wish to cling / To goods that wasn't hizen. **1926** *DN* 5.383 **NEng,** *His'n.* **1931** Randolph *Ozarks* 68, Whilst thet 'ar pore susy hippoed woman o' hisn was a-pickin' boogers out'n her yeller tags. **1938** Rawlings *Yearling* 173 **nFL,** It's hissen. **1940** (1968) Haun *Hawk's Done Gone* 10 **eTN,** Joe reached over and took it out of her hand and give her hisn. **1959** *VT Hist.* new ser 27.142, *His'n.* **1968** *DARE* FW Addit **MD**20, It's no more your fault than it is hisn. **1969** *DARE* Tape **MO**1, Hisn isn't really a trailer court. **1983** *MJLF* 9.1.43 **ceKY,** *Hisn.*

hi-spier See **hy-spier**

hi spry See **hy spy** n

hi spy See **hy spy** n

hiss v

1 also with *on:* To signal (a dog) to move forward or attack; see quot 1939. [*SND, EDD* (at *hish*)]

1939 *Hall Coll.* **eTN, wNC,** *Hiss (a dog)* . . To whistle, at the same time motioning with the hand, so as to put a dog on the track of an animal. This signal is said to be followed by some words like "Git 'im!". . . "We went in there and that old dog was just a-standin' there. . . We hissed 'im." . . "it was one of the bear hounds . . and he was . . bloody all over. Well, I hissed him, and he went back up the tree." **1954** *True* June 66/3 **TX,** So we took off with four dogs, working half the pack at a time, and I hissed the dogs on after wild cattle. **1967** *DARE* (QR, near Qu. J8) Inf **TN**23, To hiss a dog means to sic a dog. **1970** *Foxfire* Spring–Summer 81 **nGA,** He kep' lookin' on where th'bear had been, an' said directly he stuck his fingers down an' hissed his dog an' said, "Get 'im boy!"

2 with *on;* Transf: see quot.

1970 *DARE* (Qu. Y5, *Words meaning to urge somebody to do something he shouldn't: "Johnny wouldn't have tried that if the other boys hadn't ——.*") Infs **MS**86, **VA**42, Hissed him on.

3 also *hiss 'em* (or *'im*): Sic 'em—used as a command to a dog. [Cf *SND hiss* int.[1] II "a sharp hissing call . . to incite a dog to attack"]

1969–70 *DARE* (Qu. J8, *To tell a dog to attack an animal or a person, you'd say, "——.*") Infs **KY**27, **PA**191, 245, Hiss; **KY**9, Hiss 'im. **1983** *MJLF* 9.1.43 **ceKY** (as of 1956), *Hiss 'em* . . sic 'em.

4 See quot.

1966 *DARE* (Qu. BB11, . . *A deep cough that you can't seem to get rid of: "Listen to him ——.*") Infs **SD**2, Hiss.

5 See quot.

1966 *DARE* (Qu. KK13, *Other words for arguing: "They stood there for an hour ——.*") Inf **FL**4, Hissing.

hiss cat n

1969 *DARE* (Qu. P31, . . *Names or nicknames . . for the . . panther*) Inf **PA**214, Hiss cat.

hisself pron Pronc-spp *(h)isse'f* [Engl dial; cf *OED* (at *himself* pron. IV); *EDD*] **chiefly Sth, S Midl** See Map Cf **heself**

Himself.

1843 (1916) Hall *New Purchase* 172 **IN,** The great apostul hisself. **1851** Hooper *Widow Rugby's Husband* 51 **AL,** He was ugly some, hisself. **1899** (1967) Chesnutt *Wife of Youth* 145, W'en 'e gits so 'e kin he'p 'isse'f we'll put 'im up in de lof' an' hide 'im till de Yankees come. **1899** (1912) Green *VA Folk-Speech* 226, *Hisself. . .* Himself. **1903** *DN* 2.316 **seMO,** *Hisself. . .* 'He has hurt hisself mighty bad.' **1904** *DN* 2.418 **nwAR,** *Hisself. . .* "He sees hisself in the glass." **1908** *DN* 3.320 **eAL, wGA,** *Hisself.* **1923** *DN* 5.210 **swMO,** *Hisse'f.* **1931** *PMLA* 46.1304 **sAppalachians,** Samp's Bob got hisself cracked on the noggin (head) in the fray yestiddy. **1940** Faulkner *Hamlet* 33 **MS,** That fellow that called his self Major Grumby. **1943** *LANE* Map 618 **NH, ME, MA,** *Hisself* is described as common by . . [2 infs]; as rare by . . [1 inf]; and as older though still in use by . . [9 infs]. **1965** Wolfe *Kandy-Kolored Baby* 144 **NC,** Lord, he better know how to do an *about-face* hissef if he comes down here! **1965–70** *DARE* (Qu. BB57, *If someone committed suicide, you'd say he ——*) 58 Infs, **chiefly Sth, S Midl,** Killed (*or* done away with, shot, etc) hisself [35 of 58 Infs comm type 5, 36 of 58 Infs gs educ or less]; (Qu. GG19a) 11 Infs, **chiefly Sth, S Midl,** Stuck on (*or* proud of, etc) hisself. [Further exx throughout *DS;* all exx are mapped.] **1968** *DARE* Tape **VA**9, I was aimin' for him to take 'em hisself. **1976** Warner *Beautiful Swimmers* 172 **MD,** Somebody got hisself a good meal.

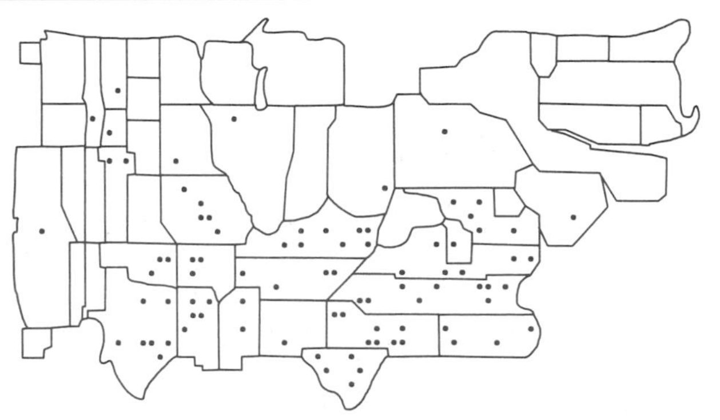

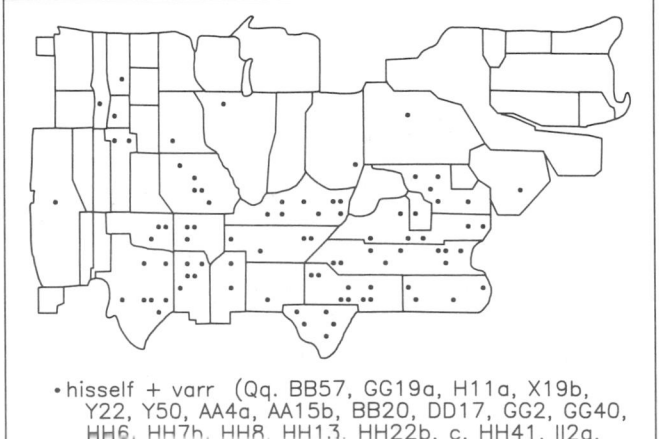

• hisself + varr (Qq. BB57, GG19a, H11a, X19b, Y22, Y50, AA4a, AA15b, BB20, DD17, GG2, GG40, HH6, HH7b, HH8, HH13, HH22b, c, HH41, II2a, II16, II20b, JJ15a, JJ41, JJ45, LL4, OO2a, OO8b)

hiss 'em See **hiss 3**

hissen See **hisn**

hisser n [Cf *hiss*] **chiefly PA** See Map

1965–70 *DARE* (Qu. FF15, *When a firecracker doesn't go off, and you break it in the middle and light the powder, you call it a* ______) 17 Infs, **chiefly PA,** Hisser; (Qu. FF14, . . *Kinds of firecrackers*) Inf **PA**148, Hissers.

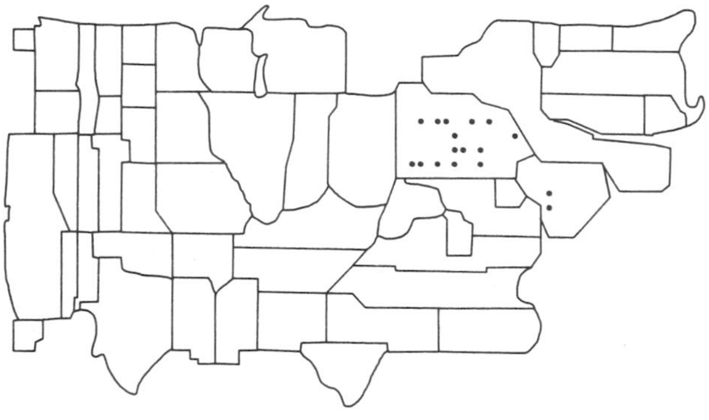

•hisser (Qq. FF15, FF14)

hissie See **hissy**

hiss 'im See **hiss 3**

hissin See **hisn**

hissing snake n Also *hissing sand snake, hissing adder* [See quot 1958]

A **hognose snake,** usu *Heterodon platyrhinos.*

1778 Carver *Travels N. Amer.* 167, The most remarkable of the different species that infest this lake [=Lake Erie], is the hissing-snake, which is of the small speckled kind, and about eighteen inches long. . . Its spots, which are of various dyes, become visibly brighter through rage. **1789** Morse *Amer. Geog.* 39, The hissing snake is most remarkable. It is about eighteen inches long, small and speckled. When you approach it, it flattens itself in a moment, and its spots, which are of various colours, become visibly brighter through rage; at the same time it blows from its mouth, with great force, a subtile wind, said to be of a nauscous smell; and if drawn in with the breath of the unwary traveller, will infallibly bring on a decline, that in a few months must prove mortal. **1807** (1935) Janson *Stranger in Amer.* 76, Mr. Carver's account of the *hissing snake* is supposed to be fabulous. **1949** *Scientific Mth.* 68.57/2, No gallery of American mythical snakes would be complete without mention of the celebrated blow snake, sometimes known as the "hissing snake," "blowing viper," "spreading adder," or "puff adder." This is none other than the common hog-nosed snake *(Heterodon contortrix).* **1952** Ditmars *N. Amer. Snakes* 178, *Hissing "Adder"*. . . When the snake is angry, the head and neck are excessively flattened, producing sinister aspect. **1958** Conant *Reptiles & Amphibians* 138, Hognose Snakes: Genus *Heterodon*. . . *Serpents* of extraordinary behavior. These . . flatten their heads and necks, hiss loudly, and inflate their bodies with air, producing a show of hostility that has earned them . . such dangerous-sounding names as "hissing adder," . . "hissing sand snake." **1970** *DARE* (Qu. P25, . . *Kinds of snakes . . around here*) Inf **KY**84, Hissing adder—solid gray, sometimes black.

hissn See **hisn**

hiss on See **hiss 1, 2**

hissy n, also attrib Also *haw hissy, hissy fit, hussy, huzzy* Also sp *hissie* [Perh hypocoristic form of *hysterical,* or perh from echoic *hiss*] **chiefly Sth, S Midl** Cf **jesse**

An outburst of anger; a temper tantrum; a state of agitation.

1934 *AmSp* 9.71 **TX,** *Hissy* is probably provincial slang. I have heard it for eight or ten years. *He threw a hissy* or *He had a hissy* means that the person in question was very disturbed and very angry. **1949** *PADS* 11.7 **wTX** (as of c1920), *Hissy*. . . A tantrum; a fit of hysteria. "She had a hissy when I told her she couldn't go." **1949** in 1986 *DARE* File **KY,** *Haw hissy*—short form of haw hysterical. **1950** *WELS Suppl.* **WI,** *Huzzy, hussy*—A temper tantrum. "Don't have a ______." Said to a child who couldn't have something. **1960** Criswell *Resp. to PADS 20* **Ozarks** (as of c1920), *Hissy*—A fit of anger. Frequent use. . . "She had a hissy when she tore that new dress on that table." **1965–70** *DARE* (Qu. A21, *When someone is in too much of a hurry you might say, "Now just slow down! Don't* ______.") Infs **AL**43, **OK**9, Get in a hissy; (Qu. GG11, *To be quite anxious about something—for example, waiting for a letter*) Inf **LA**28, All up in a hissy; (Qu. GG15, . . *A person who became over-excited and lost control, "At that point he really* ______.") Inf **AR**51, Throwed a hissy; **VA**21, Had a hissy; (Qu. KK11, *To make great objections or a big fuss about something: "When we asked him to do that, he* ______.") Infs **AL**50, **SC**54, Had a hissy; **TX**33, Pitched a hissy-fit. **1976** Garber *Mountain-ese* 39 **Appalachians,** *Have-a-hissie* . . throw a fit. My wifemate will have a hissie iffen I don't git home in time fer supper. **1982** *DARE* File **NC,** She was about to have a hissy (impatient to do something).

hist See **hoist**

histance See **hoistance**

histe See **hoist**

histing See **hoist C1d**

‡historicuss adj

1922 Gonzales *Black Border* 306 **sSC, GA coasts** [Gullah glossary], *Historicuss*—historic, historical.

‡histronize v

To tell about.

1937 in 1972 *Amer. Slave* 2.87 **SC,** I can histronize de poor white folks' wives and chilluns enduring de time of de Civil War fer you.

hit v

1 Of food plants, esp fruit trees: to produce or bear well; hence n *hit* an abundant or successful crop or yield. [Engl dial; cf *OED hit* v. II. 13 "to 'hit the mark'. . . To come to the desired end; to succeed. . . *Obs.* or *dial.*"; *EDD hit* v. and sb.[1] II. 7, 13] **chiefly Sth, S Midl**

1895 *DN* 1.372 **eTN, seKY, wNC,** *Hit:* set fruit. "The peach trees didn't hit this year"—a late frost destroying the fruit. **1899** (1912) Green *VA Folk-Speech* 226, *Hit*. . . Succeed. "If peaches hit this year it will be the first time in three years." **1903** *DN* 2.316 **seMO,** *Hit*. . . Applied to crops, fruits, etc., as 'Our peaches did not hit this year,' meaning that no peaches grew. This expression may be derived from the fact that unless the pollen falls properly, or hits, no fruit will mature. **1906** *DN* 3.140 **nwAR,** *Hit*. . . To have blossoms that mature into fruit. "Our run-down orchard hit." **1908** *DN* 3.320 **eAL, wGA,** *Hit*. . . "My corn didn't hit this year." **1923** *DN* 5.210 **swMO,** *Hit*. . . To produce fruit, to yield. "The apples didn't hit this year." **1944** *PADS* 2.44 **NC, VA,** *Hit: n.* and *vb.* A successful bearing of a vegetable or fruit crop; to bear vegetables or fruit. "My peach trees didn't hit this year." **1954** *Harder Coll.* **cwTN,** *Hit*. . . Of fruit trees: bear a good crop. Successful bearing of a crop. **1981** *High Coll.* **ceKY** (as of c1930), *Hit* . . for fruit to set, to have a large fine crop. This term is used commonly . . throughout Appalachia. . . "The peaches hit this year, but they didn't last time."

2 also with *it:* To head, start out, or rush away in a particular direction; to go; see quots.

1905 (1909) Beach *Pardners* 20, We hit for camp on the run. *Ibid* 48, So me and 'Kink' Martin . . hit West. **1908** *DN* 3.320 **eAL, wGA,** I must hit it for home. **1934** Carmer *Stars Fell on AL* 39, 'She jest stitched her last quilt,' he says and I hit out. **1935** Davis *Honey* 34 **OR,** The Indian boy untied the pack-horses and hit for the station. **1939** *Hall Coll.* **wNC, eTN,** *Hit (down, in, out)*. . . To go (down, in, out, etc.) with some notion of speed or eagerness. . . "We hit out down what we called the Anthony Ridge." . . "We hit in the Devil's Courthouse after it and wandered around them roughs." . . "He hit . . down the hill, jumped the fence . . and run on to the house." **1954** *Harder Coll.* **cwTN,** *Hit for the bushes*. . . To rush away suddenly, especially when one has diarrhea. **1966** *DARE* (Qu. Y24, . . *To walk, to go on foot: "I can't get a ride, so I'll just have to* ______.") Inf **OK**51, Hit it out afoot. **1968** *DARE* Tape **OH**87, When they . . let 'em out, first thing they hit for is our barns. **1980** Banks *First-Person America* 19 **MT** (as of c1938), By that time, there was a regular stampede, everybody hitting for the stairs.

3 In marble play: to strike an opponent's marble; see quots; hence n *hit* such an act. Cf **hits**

1955 *PADS* 23.20 **cwAL,** *Hit*. . . To strike one marble with another when shooting. . . The act of striking one marble with another. **c1970** Wiersma *Marbles Terms, Hit*. . . To strike with one's marble another's marble and thereby capture it. . . Such an act. *Ibid, Hit*—This occurs when a player knocks a marble out of the ring on a shot. *Ibid, Hit*. . . Knocking a marble out of the circle. *Ibid* **swMI** (as of c1960), *Hit* . . to contact a marble in the playing area with the shooter. . . The contacting of a marble in the playing area with the shooter. **1973** Ferretti *Marble Book* 46, *Hit*. When a marble is knocked out of a ring.

hit n See **hit** v **1, 3**

hit pron See **it** pron

hit a bull in the ass, not to be able to v phr For addit varr see quots

To be a poor marksman; to be clumsy or inept.

1950 *WELS (A very poor marksman: "He couldn't ______.")* 2 Infs, **WI,** Hit a bull (with a handful of peas); 2 Infs, Hit a bull in the ass with a shovel (*or* a handful of tapioca); 1 Inf, Hit a bull in the hind end with a bass fiddle. **1960** Criswell *Resp. to PADS 20* **Ozarks,** Used in the negative to characterize a poor shot with a gun, or sometimes with a stone or other similar weapon. . . frequent but not used in polite gatherings . . *to hit a bull in the ass.* **1984** Wilder *You All Spoken Here* 5 **Sth,** He couldn't hit a bull in the ass with a bass fiddle; he couldn't hit the ground if he fell; clumsy; inept.

hit a knot v phr Also *hit the knots;* for addit varr see quots [From the sound of a power saw hitting a knot in lumber] *joc*

To snore; to sleep.

1925 *AmSp* 1.139 [Logger talk], When the logger . . snores, he "hits the knots." **1950** *WELS (Snoring)* 3 Infs, **WI,** Hit(ting) a knot; 1 Inf, Struck a knot. **1967–70** *DARE* (Qu. X45, . . *Joking expressions . . about snoring*) Infs **CA**4, 196, **CO**20, **MI**67, Hit a knot; **MN**34, Cutting trees and hit a knot; **CA**4, Hit a snag. **1969** Sorden *Lumberjack Lingo* 56 **NEng, Gt Lakes,** *Hit the knots*—To snore.

hit a lick v phr

1 also *hit a lick of work, hit a lick at a snake, hit a tap, hit it a lick (and a promise)* and varr: To lift a finger, make an effort—usu in neg constrs. **chiefly Sth, S Midl, TX** See Map

1924 (1946) Greer–Petrie *Angeline Gits an Eyeful* 2 **csKY,** They never *hit a tap* whilst they wuz thar. **1942** Hurston *Dust Tracks* 24 **FL** [Black], He had never allowed his wife to go out and hit a lick of work for anybody a day in her life. **1960** Criswell *Resp. to PADS 20* **Ozarks,** Hit a tap, lift a finger, lift a hand. **1965–70** *DARE* (Qu. LL18, *To do no work at all, not even make any effort: "She hasn't ______ all day."*) 64 Infs, **chiefly Sth, S Midl, TX,** Hit a lick; **AL**56, **AR**56, **MS**88, **SC**21, 39, 40, Hit a lick at a snake (*or* and a snake); **MS**49, **MO**7, **OK**20, **SC**40, Hit a tap; **SC**44, 59, Hit a lick of work; **SC**34, Hit at a snake; (Qu. KK49, *When you don't have the time or ambition to do something thoroughly: "I'm not going to give the place a real cleaning, I'll just ______."*) Infs **AR**3, 18, 36, **GA**13, 23, 31, 36, **SC**69, Hit it a lick (and a promise, *or* and a miss, *or* here and there and let it go); **GA**7, Hit it lick and promise. **1967** *DARE* FW Addit **GA**19, I wouldn't hit a lick at a snake. **1979** *DARE* File **cGA** [Black], He wouldn't hit a lick at a snake—said about a lazy person. **1984** Wilder *You All Spoken Here* 170 **Sth,** Never turned a tap; never hit a lick: Never lifted a finger.

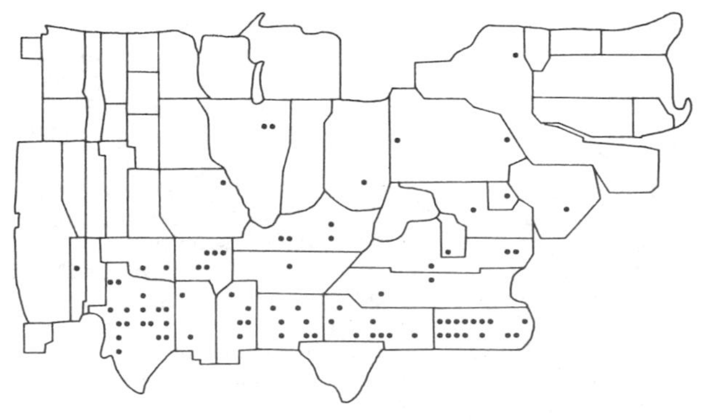

•hit a lick 1 + varr (Qq. LL18, KK49)

2 in phr *hit a straight lick with a crooked stick:* To get justice by indirect means.

1935 Hurston *Mules & Men* 270 **LA** [Black], We needs help. Somebody that can hit a straight lick with a crooked stick.

hit a lick at a snake, hit a lick of work See **hit a lick 1**

hit and a promise n [Var of *lick and a promise,* perh infl by *hit or miss*]

1969 *DARE* (Qu. KK63, *To do a clumsy or hurried job of repairing something: "It will never last—he just ______."*) Inf **MI**92, Gave it a hit and a promise.

hit-and-miss carpet See **hit-or-miss carpet**

hit-and-run n

1969 *DARE* (Qu. EE11, *Bat-and-ball games for just a few players*) Inf **GA**72, Hit-and-run.

hit a snag See **hit a knot**

hit a straight lick with a crooked stick See **hit a lick 2**

hit a tap See **hit a lick 1**

hit-back n

A retort.

1960 Williams *Walk Egypt* 95 **GA,** The squatting one retorted, "I can if I want, but I won't." She paused and sought a hit-back. "My ma says your uncle ain't got nothing in his pockets but his hands."

hit-bat n

1968 *DARE* (Qu. EE11, *Bat-and-ball games for just a few players*) Inf **NC**53, Hit-bat.

hitch v

1 often with adv: To slide or inch oneself along (or up); to move over in order to make room. [Cf *EDD hitch* v.[1] 1 "To move about . . by a series of jerks; to make room"] **chiefly Nth** Cf **ooch**

1856 in 1862 Colt *Went to KS* 51 **NY,** Hear that others are coming from the tents to quarter here—and if they do, why then, I suppose, we must "hitch" along and make room for them. **1909** *DN* 3.420 **Cape Cod MA** (as of a1857), *Hitch along*. . . To move along on a seat without rising. **1931–33** *LANE Worksheets* **swCT,** *Hitch*. . . Some [babies] don't never creep, just hitch and then walk. They can go like the Old Harry too. *Ibid* **csMA,** *Hitch along*. . . To slide on one hip pushing with the other foot. *Ibid* **seRI,** *Hitched along* . . in a sitting position. **1933** Williamson *Woods Colt* 72 **Ozarks,** The car stops, and Morgan hitches out backwards. **1943** *LANE* Map 582 **scattered NEng, exc ME,** *Hitch*. . . A baby is said to hitch or to hitch along when it sits on the floor and moves forward by repeatedly drawing up its knees [17 infs]. **1950** *WELS* 1 Inf, **seWI,** Hitch over. **1967–70** *DARE* (Qu. Y34b, *What babies do before they walk*) Inf **NY**105, Hitch—on their bottom; (Qu. Y52, *To move over—for example on a long bench: "We have to make room for one more. Can you ______ [a little]?"*) Infs **IN**32, **MI**116, **NY**23, 93, 209, 233, Hitch (over *or* along); (Qu. EE36, *To climb the trunk of a tree by holding on with your legs while you pull yourself up with your hands*) Inf **MA**73, You hitch yourself up; **OR**4, Hitching up.

2 with *off* or *out:* See quots. [Cf *EDD hitch* v.[2] 8 "With *off* or *out:* To unharness"]

1928 *Ruppenthal Coll.* **KS,** *Hitch off*—to unhitch; to make loose from a hitch; the opposite of to hitch on. "You may hitch off the wagon and hitch on the plow." **1954** *PADS* 21.30 **SC,** *Hitch out*. . . To unhitch, as a horse from the plow, buggy, etc. The opposite of hitch up.

3 also with *up* or *on;* also *hitch horses* (or *critters*): To agree; to be on friendly terms, get along well. [Cf *EDD hitch* v.[2] 11 "To agree"] **chiefly Nth** See Map *old-fash*

1830 *MA Spy & Worcester Co. Advt.* (Worcester MA) 28 July [4/1] **Sth,** Your notions and mine don't agree; we can never *hitch horses.* **1842** Kirkland *Forest Life* 1.116 **seMI,** I come on to drive a spell for this here old feller . . but I guess we sha'n't hitch long. **1858** Hammett *Piney Woods Tavern* 64, He and I allers hitched our critters together mighty fine, and the old coon never cuts any of his rusties [=does anything disagreeable] about me. **1902** (1904) Rowe *Maid of Bar Harbor* 54 **ME,** He ain't fussy either about what he eats—the only thing we don't hitch hosses on is napkins. **1907** *DN* 3.190 **seNH,** *Hitch horses*. . . To agree well. "They don't hitch horses worth a cent." **1910** Hart *Vigilante Girl* 376 **nCA,** And as for me, I'll just keep away; me and him, we don't always hitch. **1929** *AmSp* 5.129 **ME,** Sometimes a man and his wife "didn't hitch." **1950** *WELS* 23 Infs, **WI,** Hitch (very well). **1965–70** *DARE* (Qu. II11a, *If two people don't get along well together . . "They don't ______."*) 95 Infs, **chiefly Nth,** Hitch; **MI**44, **NY**52, **OK**18, Hitch very well (*or* at all); **IN**73, Hitch up; (Qu. II2a, *When two people begin to be friendly: "He has just recently ______ with John."*) Infs **PA**135, **VA**71, Hitched on (*or* up). [Of all Infs responding to Qu. II11a, 30% were comm type 5, 64% old, 12% young; of those giving these responses, 42% were comm type 5, 82% old, none young.]

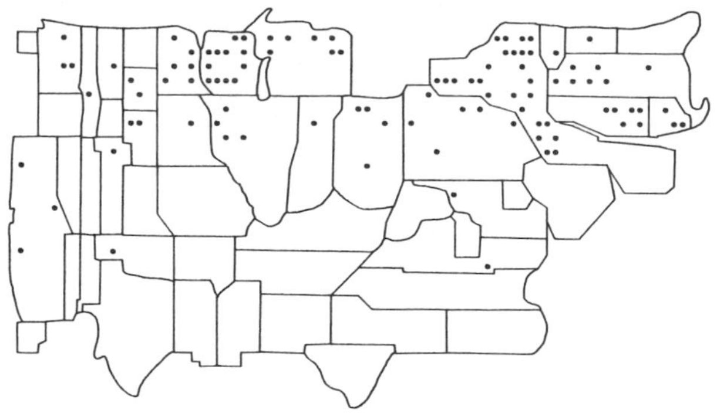

•hitch v 3 + varr (Qq. II11a, II2a)

4 See quot 1893. [From *hitch* to become entangled]

1893 Shands *MS Speech* 36, *Hitch. . .* Used by negroes and illiterate whites to mean *to come together in a fight.* They say: "If you don't stop your projickin [=projecting, i.e., playing tricks, making (unwelcome) overtures], me and you will hitch." [**1926** *AmSp* 1.414 **Okefenokee GA,** I see two ol' buck hitch an' fight one time.]

5 with *up:* To prepare (a meal). [Prob with ref to getting horses ready for work]

1971 *Today Show Letters* **neOR,** I had a woman say "I hitched up my meal" . . [meaning] just to put a meal together; and the longer I visited with her—I knew how typically *pioneerish,* etc. she grew up.

hitch n[1]

1 A vehicle with its horse or team; a team (of horses, oxen, etc). **esp NEast**

1876 VT State Bd. Ag. *Rept. for 1875–76* 3.143, If he can go best in one kind of a hitch, and, in that hitch, make the best time ever made by any horse. **1898** *Christian Herald* (N.Y.) 2 Mar. 167/2 *(OEDS),* Several hitches are a mule and steer together. **1914** *DN* 4.152 **ME,** *Hitch. . .* A horse and carriage. The expressions single *hitch* and double *hitch* are used. **1967–69** *DARE* (Qu. K26, . . *Six oxen . . hitched together two and two*) Infs **CT**25, **MA**37, **NY**200, (Six-ox *or* three-span) hitch; (QR, near Qu. L50) Inf **DC**2, A four-horse hitch. **1969** *DARE* Tape **CA**111, Jack London . . came over the mountains . . with his wife, a butler, and a beautiful four-horse hitch.

2 pronc-sp *hetch:* A crick or pain; see quots.

1934 (1943) *W2, Hitch . . Dial.* A crick; as, he had a hitch in his back. **1949** *PADS* 11.22 **CO,** Hitch. . . A crick. *Ibid* 21, I've got a hitch in my git-along. **1950** *WELS (A sudden muscular pain: in the back)* 2 Infs, **WI,** Hitch. **1954** *Harder Coll.* **cwTN,** *Hitch . .* a crick. **1965–70** *DARE* (Qu. BB3b, *A sudden pain that strikes you in the back*) 13 Infs, **scattered west of the Appalachians,** Hitch (in your get-away); (Qu. BB1, *When a person has been injured so that when he walks he steps more heavily on one foot than the other: "He ——."*) Infs **CA**59, **CT**27, **NE**11, Has a hitch in his get-along (*or* gait); (Qu. BB3a, . . *A pain that strikes you suddenly in the neck*) Inf **KS**7, Hitch; (Qu. BB3c, *A sudden pain that comes in the side*) Infs **CA**53, **LA**15, **SC**67, **UT**4, **WA**13, **WY**5, Hitch (in the side); **AL**4, Hetch; [**CA**106, Hetch-hetchy [*DARE* Ed: Perh a pun on the famous Hetch-Hetchy Dam near Yosemite]]; (Qu. BB4, . . *A pain—for example, in the arm: "He's had a —— in his arm for a week."*) Inf **OH**56, Hitch; (Qu. BB28, *Joking names . . for imaginary diseases*) Inf **TX**79, Hitch in the get-along. **1987** [see **get-along**].

3 An effort, attempt. [Cf *OED hitch* sb. 1. b "*colloq.* A little lift or push up; 'temporary assistance; help through a difficulty'."]

1916 Macy–Hussey *Nantucket Scrap Basket* 135, The next hitch, meaning the next attempt. **1927** *Ruppenthal Coll.* **KS,** *To take another hitch at*—to make a further effort. We will take another hitch at that car and see if we can move it. **c1960** *Wilson Coll.* **csKY,** *Hitch. . .* An effort or period of trying, like a hitch at rafting on the river.

4 See quot.

1968 *DARE* (Qu. Y31, *If a child asked his father to carry him on his back, he might say, "Give me a ——."*) Inf **NY**109, Hitch.

hitch n[2]

A cyprinid fish *(Lavinia exilicauda)* native to California.

1896 U.S. Natl. Museum *Bulletin* 47.209, *Lavinia exilicauda. . . Hitch; Chi or Chigh. . .* Streams of the Coast Range about San Francisco and Monterey, locally common as far north as Clear Lake. **1935** Pratt *Manual Vertebrate Animals* 65, Hitch. . . Color dark, speckled, with silvery sides. **1960** Amer. Fisheries Soc. *List Fishes* 14, Hitch. F[resh-water].

‡hitchamoney n

1982 *Barrick Coll.* **csPA,** *Hitchamōney*—large, clumsy person.

hitch and a haul n

Perh a stalemate, deadlock.

1915 (1916) Johnson *Highways New Engl.* 75, The advantages gained would be almost wholly for those who lived close by. The other parts of the state don't see any gain for them, and they're inclined to fight being taxed for such a purchase. So there's a hitch and a haul and we don't get nowhere.

Hitchcock-berry n

A **raspberry** (here: *Rubus rosifolius*).

1929 Pope *Plants HI* 83, *Rubus rosaefolius. . .* In different localities it is known by different common names, as Olaa-berry, Hitchcock-berry and Thimbleberry.

hitch critters See **hitch** v **3**

hitched, stand v phr Also *stay hitched* [In ref to hitching horses]

To keep quiet, keep a secret; to be trustworthy; see quot.

1968–69 *DARE* (Qu. V2a, . . *A deceiving person, or somebody that you can't trust*) Inf **GA**89, He won't stand hitched—said about a person you can't trust; old-fashioned; (Qu. JJ44, . . *Someone who can be trusted to keep a secret: "Don't worry about him, he'll ——."*) Inf **LA**16, Stay hitched.

hitchhiker n [See quot 1979]

=beggar ticks 1.

1970 *DARE* (Qu. S14, *Other prickly seeds, small and flat, with two prongs at one end, that cling to clothing*) Inf **KY**93, Hitchhikers; (Qu. S15, . . *Other weed seeds that cling*) Inf **KY**93, Hitchhikers. **1979** *DARE* File **Madison WI,** They're called hitchhikers because they hitch onto your pants and then hike along with you. **1980** *DARE* File **csWI** (as of c1950), I grew up on the east side of Madison, and we always called those weed seeds 'hitchhikers.'

hitch horses v phr

1 See **hitch** v **3.**

2 also *hitch teams:* To marry.

1855 *Weekly Oregonian* (Portland OR) 10 Mar 1/3, "Betsy and me have concluded to hitch teams, and we want you to do it." "You wish to be married?" ["]Yes, I believe that's what they call it." **1861** *Atlantic Mth.* 8.157/2, Ef you're a-goin' to stay here, I don't see why you don't hitch hosses with Miss Lucindy. **1942** Berrey–Van den Bark *Amer. Slang* 359.4, *Marry; be married. . .* hitch horses. **1960** Criswell *Resp. to PADS 20* **Ozarks,** *To hitch horses*—to marry, colloq.

hitching weight n Also *hitching ball, ~ block, ~ iron, hitch-weight*

See quot 1965.

1885 Howells *Rise Lapham* 336 **OH,** He got the hitching-weight from under the buggy-seat and made it fast to the mare's bit. **1965** *DARE* File **seNY,** Our Blacksmith here . . , at our Museum Village in Orange County, calls it [=a metal weight fastened by a rope to a horse's halter and placed on the ground beside the horse] a hitching block. . . The Blacksmith is in his 70's and seems to know just what it was called. **1967** *DARE* File **neAL,** A junk trader-swapper tried to sell me a *teel* for $7.50. He first called it a *hitchin' ball. . .* [It] was a small ball of iron weighing about twenty-five pounds with a ring through which the reins were drawn and tied. **1968** *DARE* FW Addit **VA**12, *Hitching block*—Weighed up to 18 lbs. Attached to the bridle by chain. Used only in towns and cities. Not used by horseback riders. "Block your horse [=Set out the hitching block on the ground to keep the horse from moving away]." Also called hitching iron and hootenanny. **1970** Green *Ely* 90, I would hold the horse and put the hitch weight back in her buggy for her.

hitch off See **hitch** v **2**

hitch on v phr See **hitch** v **3**

hitch-on n

1905 *DN* 3.83 **nwAR,** *Hitch-on. . .* Addition. 'He built a hitch-on to his barn.' Not common.

hitch out See **hitch** v **2**

hitchrack n Also *hitchrail* **esp West, S Midl**

A stationary bar to which a horse or team can be fastened to prevent straying.

1903 (1931) Adams *Log Cowboy* 335, Tying our horses in a group to a hitch-rack in the rear of a saloon. **1906** *DN* 3.141 **nwAR,** *Hitch-rack*. . . A bar or frame of wood to which horses are hitched. "There has been considerable said during the past year concerning the need of hitch racks." **1906** H. D. Pittman *Belle of Blue Grass C.* xiii.187 (*DA* at *hitch* v), A slim-legged yellow girl . . swinging by her arms from a hitch rail. **1908** *DN* 3.320 **eAL, wGA,** *Hitch-post, -rack, -rein*. . . Hitching-post, -rack, -rein. **1935** Sandoz *Jules* 70 **wNE** (as of 1880–1930), He hobbled out toward the hitch-racks. **1948** Baumann *Old Man Crow's Boy* 25 **csID,** They started walking toward the hitch rack and their horses. **c1960** *Wilson Coll.* **csKY,** *Hitch rack*. . . A place where horses were tied up, as at the public square in town. **1967** Green *Horse Tradin'* 145 **TX,** I put her bridle on her (it was tied on her saddle horn) and hitched her to the hitch rack. **1968** *DARE* Tape **IN**9, They had an old . . cobble street around the courthouse. . . and they had a hitchrack around that, plumb around, where they hitch the horses—wagons, too.

hitchrein n **esp Sth, S Midl**

A hitching strap.

1899 Ade *Doc' Horne* 7 **Chicago,** I jumped off my horse and threw him one end of my hitch-rein and pulled him out. **1908** [see **hitchrack**]. **1940** Faulkner *Hamlet* 345 **MS,** The teams springing and lunging too, snapping hitch-reins and tongues. **c1960** *Wilson Coll.* **csKY,** *Hitch rein*. . . Bridle rein or rope by which a horse was tied to a post, tree, or rack. **1968** *DARE* (Qu. L51) Inf **IN**32, Hitch-reins. **1976** Brown *Gloss. Faulkner* 103, *Hitch-rein*. . . Hitching strap, a strap that was used for hitching a horse to a post, tree, etc., but was not a part of the regular harness.

hitchrope n

A rope used to keep a horse from straying; a hitching rope.

1896 *DN* 1.418 **cNY,** *Hitch-rope:* a halter. **1953** Morrison *Stones* 265, When he tried to get up, he got his foot caught over the hitchrope and commenced to thrash.

hitch teams See **hitch horses 2**

hitch up See **hitch** v **3, 5**

hitch-up n [Cf *hitch up* to marry] *old-fash*

A marriage; a married couple.

1898 Westcott *Harum* 298 **cNY,** What a nice hitch up they'd make. *Ibid* 336, I putty much made up my mind to try another hitch-up. **1960** Criswell *Resp. to PADS 20* **Ozarks,** Ma gives *hitch up*. . . meaning marriage. I have not heard this. **1960** Wentworth–Flexner *Slang* 260, *Hitch-up*. . . A marriage. c1890; *archaic*.

hitch-up-Matilda n

See quots.

1942 Peattie *Friendly Mts.* 246 **neNY,** The bottom of the former [=Avalanche Pass] is occupied in part by deep, narrow Avalanche Lake, with great gray cliffs and ledges crowding it so closely that in places the trail must be carried on log bridges, locally known as "Hitch-up-Matildas." **1988** *NADS Letters* **neNY** (as of 1978), "Hitch-up-Matilda" . . referred to the old floating bridges. . . When women walked on them, they would either have to hitch up their skirts or the men would have to hitch them up on their backs so their skirts would not get wet.

hitch-weight See **hitching weight**

hith See **height**

hit her v phr See **hit her up**

hite(d) See **hurt**

hither adv, adj Pronc-spp *hether, hyether*

Std senses, var forms.

1837 Sherwood *Gaz. GA* 70, *Provincialisms*. . . *Hyether,* for hither. **1887** [see **hither and yon**]. **1949** [see **hither horse**]. **1967** [see **hither horse**].

‡hither n [Prob var of *dither,* perh infl by *hissy*]

A tizzy, dither.

1969 *DARE* (Qu. GG7, . . *Annoyed or upset: "Though we were only ten minutes late, she was all ______."*) Inf **NY**141, In a hither.

hither and thither adv phr Also *hither-scather, hither-skither, hither-thither;* for addit varr see quots **chiefly Nth, N Midl**

In all directions, helter-skelter.

1950 *WELS* 1 Inf, **cWI,** Hither-skither. **1965–70** *DARE* (Qu. MM12a, . . *'In all directions' . . "He shot into a flock of birds and they went ______."*) Infs **CA**99, **MA**4, **NJ**4, **NY**1, 211, **OH**18, Hither and thither; **IL**4, **NY**143, **SC**11, Hither-thither; **RI**13, Hither-scather; (Qu. MM12b, . . *'In all directions' . . "When she was out on the dance floor, she broke her beads and they went ______."*) Infs **IL**44, 70, **WA**16, Hither and thither; **KS**16, Hither and there; **MA**61, Hither, thither, and yon.

hither and yon adv phr Also *hither and yonder* [*OED hither* adv. 5 "*hither and yon . . dial.* and *U.S.*"] **chiefly Nth, N Midl**

In all directions, helter-skelter; here and there.

1848 Bartlett *Americanisms* 176, *Hither and yon.* This expression is often used in the country towns of New England for *here and there.* **1887** (1967) Harris *Free Joe* 111 **GA** (as of 1876), Looks like folks has mighty bad luck when they go a-rippitin' hether an' yan on the mounting. **1950** *WELS* 3 Infs, **WI,** Hither and yon. **1965–70** *DARE* (Qu. MM12a, . . *'In all directions' . . "He shot into a flock of birds and they went ______."*) 14 Infs, **chiefly Nth, N Midl,** Hither and yon; **MA**46, **NC**9, Hither and yonder; (Qu. MM12b, . . *'In all directions' . . "When she was out on the dance floor, she broke her beads and they went ______."*) Infs **IL**26, **IN**38, **IA**34, **ME**12, **PA**4, 167, Hither and yon. [12 of 15 Infs old] **1969** *DARE* Tape **CT**20, Finally, by writing hither and yon I found out where it was.

hither horse n Also *huther horse* [*hither* nearer; *EDD hither* adv. 2 "To the left"]

=near horse.

1949 Kurath *Word Geog.* 66, *Near-horse*. . . *huther-horse (hither-horse)* [occasional] on the Eastern Shore of Maryland and in southern Delaware. **1967** Faries *Word Geog. MO* 96, *Near horse.* To distinguish the left from the right horse in a team. . . one informant [knew] . . *huther horse.*

hither-scather, hither-skither, hither-thither See **hither and thither**

hit her up v phr Also *hit her* [Cf **hit the ball 1**]

To hurry up, accelerate, proceed at a rapid pace; to cause an engine to accelerate.

1903 Fox *Little Shepherd* 67, Hit her up thar now. **1912** Mulford–Clay *Buck Peters* 63 **TX,** Hit her up or you'll be late. **1925** in 1953 Botkin–Harlow *Treas. Railroad Folkl.* 228, The limited was hittin' her up fifty miles an hour anyway. **1945** Hubbard *Railroad Ave.* 347, *Hit 'er*—Work an engine harder. (Probably a variation of "hit the ball," which means "Get busy—no more fooling!")

hither-which adv

1966 Barnes–Jensen *Dict. UT Slang* 24, *Hither-which* . . henceforth —therefore.

hit it v phr

1 also with *up:* To get along, be on friendly terms, agree. [Cf *OED hit it* 1634–1844 "Now usually *to hit it off*"; *EDD hit* "with *it* . . to agree"] **scattered, but esp PA, MD, DE**

1950 *WELS (If two people don't get along well together: "They don't ______.")* 1 Inf, **cWI,** Hit it up. **1954** *AmSp* 29.228 **cwNJ,** Two people who could not get along, 'They don't hit it.' **1965–70** *DARE* (Qu. II11a, . . *"They don't ______."*) 12 Infs, **scattered, but esp PA, MD, DE,** Hit it (together, too well, very good, *or* very well); **MA**53, **NJ**55, **NY**69, **RI**13, Hit it up (very well); (Qu. II2a, *When two people begin to be friendly: "He has just recently ______ with John."*) Infs **IL**53, **SC**69, Hit it (up); (Qu. KK67, *When people think alike about something: "On that particular thing, we ______."*) Inf **PA**240, Hit it the same; (Qu. KK68, *When people don't think alike about something*) Inf **PA**240, Just don't hit it.

2 See **hit** v **2.**

hit it a lick (and a promise) See **hit a lick 1**

hit it on the ball See **hit the ball 3**

hit it up See **hit it 1**

hit log n

A **bittern** (here: *Botaurus lentiginosus*).

1951 *AmSp* 26.93, Many names for this species [=bittern] . . are in imitation of its queer vocalization; compare such terms as *hit-log* and *slug-toot* used elsewhere.

hit miss of v phr [Cf *OED miss of* (at *miss* v.[1] 23)]

To fail to hit or strike.

1932 Smiley *Gloss. New Paltz* **NY,** "Hit miss of it" is used for saying that it was missed. "I hit miss of it." The expression probably came from striking jumper drill [=a drill that is jumped up and down in the hole being bored], in Father's opinion.

hit-off-the-step n Cf **stoopball**

1967 *DARE* (Qu. EE33, . . *Outdoor games . . that children play*) Inf **MA**33, Hit-off-the-step—you throw a pimple ball off the nosing or the aisle on a step; single, double, etc, determined by distance.

hit on all cylinders v phr For varr see quots [With ref to an internal-combustion engine]

Fig: to be in good form; to function properly; hence v phr *hit on one cylinder* to function poorly.

1912 Mathewson *Pitching* 269, So the best infielder takes time to fit into the infield of a Big League club and have it hit on all four cylinders again. **1920** *NY Eve. Jrl.* (NY) 11 Feb 20 *(Zwilling Coll.)*, [In cartoon:] Judge I didn't steal the coat—I forgot. . . My brain only hits on one cylinder. **1928** *Sat. Eve. Post* 10 Mar 127/1, [Advt:] Modern science offers you a *natural* means to keep you "hitting on all six"—every minute of the day. **1966–69** *DARE* (Qu. GG29, *To be in a good or pleasant mood*) Inf **SD**8, Hitting on all four; (Qu. KK18, *If something is in good running order: "This sewing machine is ______."*; total Infs questioned, 75) Inf **GA**13, Hitting on all six; (Qu. KK29, *To start working very hard: "He was slow at first but now he's really ______."*) Infs **IL**97, **MN**26, **NY**78, Hitting on all cylinders.

hit-or-miss carpet n Also *hit-and-miss carpet* [*hit-or-miss* at random]

See quot 1848.

1848 in 1935 *AmSp* 10.40 **Nantucket MA,** *Hit-or-miss-carpet.* A carpet woven from strips of old cloth sewed together. **1897** Barton *Hero in Homespun* 377 **KY,** They ripped up the new hit-an'-miss carpet for horse blankets. [**1932** Randolph *Ozark Mt. Folks* 109, Some carpets are woven "hit-or-miss" throughout, using the rags just as they come without regard to color.]

hits n Cf **hit** v **3**

In marble play: see quot 1957.

1950 *WELS (Kinds of marble games)* 1 Inf, **ceWI,** Hits—played in a ring. **1957** *Sat. Eve. Post Letters* **WI,** *Hits.* . . A marble game in which marbles must be hit out of a ring.

hit-stick See **hit-the-stick**

hitter n

1 In marble play: see quot. Cf **hit** v **3**

1966 *DARE* (Qu. EE6a, . . *Marbles—the big one that's used to knock others out of the ring*) Inf **NC**7, Big hitter.

2 =**header 3.**

1969 *DARE* (Qu. Y1, . . *A person suddenly falling down: "He slipped on the steps and took quite a ______."*) Inf **IL**39, Hitter.

3 See quot. [Cf *hit the books* to study intensely]

1967 *DARE* (Qu. JJ9, *Somebody who studies too hard or all the time*) Inf **IA**3, Hitter—one who hits the books too hard.

hitter and skitter adv phr [Prob var of **hilter-skilter;** infl by *skitter* to skip along a surface]

1970 *DARE* (Qu. MM12b, . . *'In all directions' . . "When she was out on the dance floor, she broke her beads and they went ______."*) Inf **TN**46, Hitter and skitter.

hitter-titter adv [Perh var of *hither and thither;* cf *SND hither* "Also *hidder*" and Pronc Intro 3.I.17]

1966 *DARE* (Qu. MM12b, . . *"She broke her beads and they went ______."*) Inf **NM**7, Hitter-titter.

hit the ball v phr [Cf **highball n 1a;** cf also quot 1944 at **1** below]

1 In railroading: to speed. Cf **highball** v **2**

1942 Berrey–Van den Bark *Amer. Slang* 781.10 [Railroad lingo], *Speed.* Ball the jack, . . highball, hit the ball. **1943** Farrington *Railroading* 161, These grand trains . . hit the ball at 50 miles an hour. **1944** *AmSp* 19.35 (as of c1915), 'Hit the ball' is the expression describing speed which I remember with certainty. [Footnote to *hit the ball:*] Whether or not this expression is related to 'highball' or derives from the fact that the top of the rail is called the 'ball,' . . I do not know. **1977** Adams *Lang. Railroader* 79, *Hit the ball:* To get speed.

2 By ext: to hurry, go fast, depart quickly.

1930 Irwin *Amer. Tramp* 99 [Hobo lingo], *Hit the ball* . . to travel swiftly. From railroad parlance, where once the "high ball" has been given the train moves. **1942** Berrey–Van den Bark *Amer. Slang* 53.8, *Go fast; hurry.* . . Hit the ball. **1966–69** *DARE* (Qu. Y18, *To leave in a hurry*) Infs **KY**68, **WA**3, Hit the ball.

3 also *hit it on the ball:* To work hard, be energetic or diligent. **scattered, but esp West** See Map *somewhat old-fash*

1926 *AmSp* 1.651 [Hobo lingo], *Hit the ball*—[be] forced to "hustle" for a job. **1927** *Ruppenthal Coll.* **KS,** *Hit the ball*—To be active, diligent, vigilant. "September is the month to hit the ball in lodge work." **1930** Irwin *Amer. Tramp* 99 [Hobo lingo], *Hit the ball.*—To work hard. **1939** FWP *Guide NC* 300, It keeps a man hustling on his toes to make a go of it. You've sure got to hit the ball. **1950** *WELS* 3 Infs, **WI,** Hit the ball. **c1960** *Wilson Coll.* **csKY,** *Hit the ball.* . . Work well, at a good pace. **1965–70** *DARE* (Qu. KK29, *To start working very hard: "He was slow at first but now he's really ______."*) 19 Infs, **scattered, but esp West,** Hit(ting) the ball; **IA**41, Hitting it on the ball; (Qu. A22) Infs **AK**7, **CA**210, **ID**1, **TX**84, Hit the ball; (Qu. Y18) Inf **KY**68, Hit the ball; **WA**3, Hit the ball—to get busy, or on it; (Qu. JJ26, *If somebody has been doing poor work or not enough, the boss might say, "If he wants to keep his job he'd better ______."*) Infs **MS**71, **OK**48, **TX**81, Hit the ball. [21 of 28 Infs old; 6 of 28 Infs mid-aged]

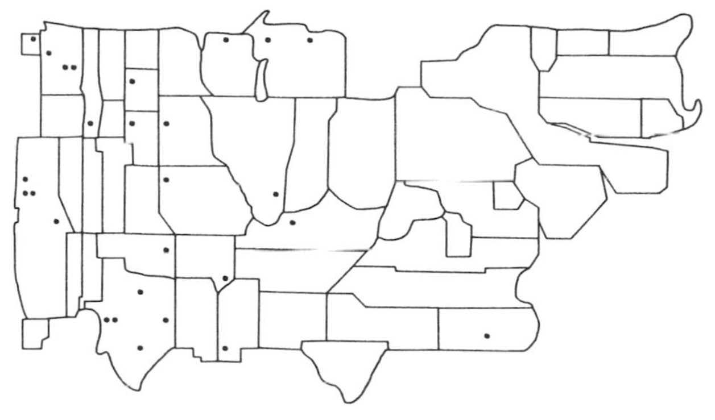

•hit the ball 3 + varr (Qq. KK29, A22, Y18, JJ26)

hit-the-bat n

A bat-and-ball game; see quot 1967.

1957 *Sat. Eve. Post Letters* **cwNY** (as of c1947), Games that our neighborhood children played . . Hit the bat. *Ibid* **WA, CA** (as of c1910), The following activities . . were popular . . Hit the bat. **1967** *DARE* (Qu. EE11, *Bat-and-ball games for just a few players*) Inf **CA**32, Hit-the-bat—the batter hits the ball; it's caught; then the bat is laid down and the ball rolled toward it. If the batter catches the ball after it hits the bat, he's still up; but if he misses, the roller is up.

hit-the-bottle n

In marble play: see quot.

1969 *DARE* (Qu. EE7, . . *Kinds of marble games*) Inf **NY**190, Hit-the-bottle.

hit the breeze v phr Cf **fan the dust**

To depart, start out, travel; to run fast.

1910 Porter *Whirligigs* 163, We got to be hittin' the breeze. **1915** *DN* 4.244 **MT,** *Hit the breeze.* . . = *hit the road,* to set off on the road, usually walking. **1960** Criswell *Resp. to PADS 20* **Ozarks,** *(To run fast)* Hit the breeze.

hit-the-can n Also *hit-the-tin-can*

=**duck on a rock.**

1967–70 *DARE* (Qu. EE18, *Games in which the players set up a stone, a tin can, or something similar, and then try to knock it down*) Infs **IL**47, 51, **IN**73, **MA**38, **MO**21, **NY**23, **OH**77, 80, **PA**94, **RI**11, **VA**109, Hit-the-can; **DC**11, Hit-the-tin-can.

hit the crow's nest v phr [Var of *hit the hay* or ~ *sack*] Cf **hit the tick**

1950 *WELS (Other ways you might say "I'm going to bed.")* 1 Inf, **ceWI,** Hit the crow's nest.

hit the floor with one's hat See **hit the ground with one's hat**

hit the grit v phr

1 To go or depart, esp with speed. **chiefly Sth, S Midl**

1888 *Enquirer* (Troy AL) 28 July (*AmSp* 37.76) **AL,** *Hit the grit.* Get going; get out of here. **1898** Lloyd *Country Life* 16 **AL,** The most easiest and quickest way to git there, is to hit the grit and pull out and go. **1905** *DN* 3.83 **nwAR,** *Hit the grit. . .* To leave; to walk away. 'I guess I'll hit the grit, sein's I've got fired.' **1908** *DN* 3.320 **eAL, wGA.** **1912** *DN* 3.578 **wIN.** **1914** *DN* 4.108 **cKS.** **1915** Hall *Claib Jones* 28 **KY,** He tried to bluff me, and I told him to hit the grit or there would be a dead coon left. **1921** *DN* 5.111 **CA,** *To hit the grit. . .* To set off upon a journey. Cattlemen. **1953** Goodwin *It's Good* 24 **sIL** [Black], "Hit the grit!" she ordered. "And don't stop to talk." **1956** McAtee *Some Dialect NC* 22. **1960** Criswell *Resp. to PADS 20* **Ozarks,** *Hit the grit:* To take to the road, to start out. Common. **1960** Williams *Walk Egypt* 117 **GA,** You'll be all right in a week-two. . . You can hit the grit then.

2 also *hit the gravel;* In railroading: to fall, step, or be thrown off a train; hence vbl n *hitting the grit.*

1908 Johnson *Highways Pacific Coast* 217 **nCA,** Occasionally the train men would push a hobo off while the train was going, and in the hobo's phraseology he then "hit the grit." **1927** *DN* 5.450 [Underworld jargon], *Hit the grit. . .* To be thrown off a train. **1930** *RR Man's Mag.* 470, *Hitting the grit*—Falling off a car. **1932** *RR Mag.* Oct 368, *Hitting the grit or gravel*—Falling off or getting kicked off a car. **1940** Cottrell *Railroader* 129, *Hit the grit*—To step from a moving train.

3 To die.

1986 Pederson *LAGS Concordance,* 1 inf, **cwTN,** Till I hit the grit—till I die.

hit the ground with one's hat v phr Also *hit the (said) floor with one's hat* Cf **bell a buzzard**

To do the simplest thing—usu in neg constrs.

1966–68 *DARE* (Qu. DD15, *A person who is thoroughly drunk*) Infs **MS**16, **SD**5, 8, Couldn't (*or* can't) hit the ground with his hat; (Qu. JJ15a, . . *A person who seems . . very stupid: "He hasn't sense enough to ———.")* Inf **PA**74, Hit the floor with his hat. **1967** *DARE* FW Addit **LA**11, Couser would come back later tipsy and couldn't hit the said floor with his hat. **1989** *DARE* File **TX,** In a recent issue of the newsletter of the Wisconsin chapter of the ACLU there was an interview with the Texas humorist John Henry Faulk in which he said of Ronald Reagan that he "couldn't hit the ground with his hat" unless Nancy showed him how.

‡hit the hacking v phr

1927 *AmSp* 2.357 **WV,** *Hit the hacking . .* to start on a journey, or to work. "It is time to hit the hacking, boys."

hit the high lonesome See **high lonesome 2**

hit the hike v phr Also *hit the hikes* Cf **hit the grit**

To depart, set out.

1914 *DN* 4.108 **cKS,** *Hit the hikes. . .* hit the pike. Also, *hit the grit, trail, turf,* etc. *Ibid* 244 **cMT,** *Hit the breeze, hike, trail. . .* hit the road, to set off on the road, usually walking. "About ten I hit the hike." **1923** *DN* 5.210 **swMO,** *Hit the hike. . .* To depart.

‡hit the jack v phr [Perh blend of **hit the ball 3 + ball the jack 1**]

1950 *WELS (Someone doing poor work or none at all: "If he wants to keep his job, he'll have to ———.")* 1 Inf, **seWI,** Hit the jack.

hit the knots See **hit a knot**

hit the pike v phr *somewhat old-fash* Cf **hit the hike**

To leave, depart hastily, start out on a journey; to quit one's job.

1904 *Hartford Courant* 25 June 6 *(OEDS),* The . . convention, whose delegates were so summarily ordered to hit the pike by the national committee-men. **1905** *DN* 3.62 **NE,** *Hit the . . pike. . .* Go, move on. **1906** *DN* 3.141 **nwAR,** *Hit the pike. . .* To take French leave. "He didn't want to get put on the chain-gang; so he just hit the pike and that was the last we saw of him." **1912** *DN* 3.578 **wIN,** *Hit the pike. . .* To go away hastily. "When they began talking money, I hit the pike." **1914** *DN* 4.108 **cKS,** *Hit the pike.* **1931–33** *LANE Worksheets* **csMA,** *Hitting the pike . .* starting off on a journey. **1956** Sorden–Ebert *Logger's Words* 23, What a lumber-jack tells the timekeeper when he wants his pay check. A statement made indicating he is quitting. . . hit the pike. **1958** McCulloch *Woods Words* 86 **Pacific NW,** *Hit the pike*—To head for town. **1960** Criswell *Resp. to PADS 20* **Ozarks,** *Hit the pike. . .* To start out (on a journey), to leave. A very frequent term from long ago.

hit the said floor with one's hat See **hit the ground with one's hat**

hit the shucks v phr, hence vbl n *hitting the shucks* Also *hit the shocks* [Varr of *hit the hay* or ~ *sack*] Cf **hit the tick**

1968–70 *DARE* (Qu. X40, . . *Ways . . of saying "I'm going to bed")* Infs **MS**86, **VA**13, Hit the shucks; **GA**72, Hit the shucks—a bed made of corn husks. **1973** *DARE* File **Ozarks** (as of c1910), Going to bed was hitting the hay or shucks. . . Mattresses were filled with hay or shucks.

hit the steel See **hit the ties**

hit-the-stick n Also *hit-stick* Cf **cat n 3a**

Any of var outdoor games played with sticks; see quots.

1891 *Jrl. Amer. Folkl.* 4.231 **Brooklyn NYC,** *Hit the stick.* Equal sides are chosen, and bases are determined upon. . . The players of one side arrange themselves around the bases, with one boy near the "home plate." One player from the opposite side also takes his position at the home plate, where he balances a stick . . across the inner end of another stick . . which is laid so as to extend . . beyond the edge of the curb. He then strikes the projecting end a sharp blow with another stick . . so that the smallest stick is tossed into the air. The batsman at once runs to the first base, and so to home, which constitutes one run. The boys on the opposite side try to catch the flying stick, however, and if they are successful . . the batsman is put out. **1957** *Sat. Eve. Post Letters* **swMA** (as of c1920), *Hit the stick*—Played in the street with two sticks. One small stick was leaned against the curb stone and was struck or lifted with a larger stick. The batter ran bases while the fielder tried to retrieve the stick and bring it back to home base before the runner got there, in order to get him out. There were four or more players to a side. **1967–69** *DARE* (Qu. EE10, *A game in which a short stick lying on the ground is flipped into the air and then hit with a longer stick, that's ———*) Infs **IL**69, 84, **TN**32, Hit-stick; **IL**77, **MA**3, **PA**94, Hit-the-stick.

hit the tick v phr, hence vbl n *hitting the tick* [Var of *hit the hay* or ~ *sack*] Cf **hit the shucks**

1927 *AmSp* 2.357 **WV,** *Hit the tick . .* to retire. "I am going to hit the tick now." **c1950** *Hall Coll.* **eTN,** *Hit the tick. . .* To go to bed. Rarely heard now. **1967** *DARE* (Qu. X40, . . *Ways . . of saying "I'm going to bed")* Inf **TN**13, Hit the tick. **1982** *Smithsonian Letters* **WV** (as of c1910), *Hitting the tick* = going to bed.

hit the ties v phr Also *hit the steel* Cf **hit the pike**

See quots.

1907 London *Road* 130, It was up to me to hit the ties to Wadsworth. **1927** *DN* 5.450 [Underworld jargon], *Hit the ties. . .* To walk along the railway. **1958** McCulloch *Woods Words* 86 **Pacific NW,** *Hit the steel*—In the days of railroad logging, to walk the track away from camp, either because fired, or quitting the job. **1977** Adams *Lang. Railroader* 79, *Hit the steel. . .* To hike down the railroad track toward town.

hit-the-tin-can See **hit-the-can**

hit the wicket (or wickie) See **kick the wicket**

hitting the shucks See **hit the shucks**

hitting the tick See **hit the tick**

hit-up n Cf **work-up**

1967 *DARE* (Qu. EE11, *Bat-and-ball games for just a few players*) Inf **PA**54, Hit-up.

hit with a sour apple ppl adj phr

1973 *DARE* File **Ozarks** (as of c1910), Hit with a sour apple. . . Intoxicated.

hit-your-back n Cf **sore-back**

See quot 1970.

[**1937** Shankle *Nicknames* 555, The nickname *Sorebacks,* applied to Virginians. . . the Virginians are so hospitable that they slap one another on the backs until their backs become sore.] **1970** *DARE* FW Addit **VA**41, *Hit-your-back*—nickname for Virginia. Old-fashioned.

hity-tity See **highty-tighty**

hiu muckamuck See **high-muck-a-muck 1**

hive See **heave v A1**

hived up See **hive up**

hiven See **heaven**

hivernant n Also *hiveranno, hiverant, hiverman, hivernan, hivernaut* [Fr *hivernant* winter visitor] **esp West** *hist*

One who spends a winter in the outdoors; see quots.

1928 Vestal *Kit Carson* 60 **Rocky Mts,** He was enjoying the prestige also which belonged to the man who was a genuine hiverman or winterer. **1938** *AmSp* 13.88 **West** (as of c1830) [Trapper talk], The old voyageurs were usually skilled boatmen; those who had passed several winters in the Indian country were called *hiverannos* or *winterers.* **1947** Guthrie *Big Sky* 194 **West** (as of 1837), They were good boys . . brave and willing and wise to mountain ways. They were hivernans—winterers—who could smell an Indian as far as anybody and keep calm and shoot plumb center when the time came. **1966** Giles *Great Adventure* 306 **Rocky Mts** (as of c1833), All the brigades were in, all the winterers, the hivernants, the Rocky Mountain boys, American Fur Company hunters. **1968** Adams *Western Words* 149, *Hiveranno*. . . Also called *hiverant.* **1980** *Reader's Digest* Dec 166 **Gt Lakes,** The black storms racing across the frozen waters still leave modern *hivernauts* as helpless as their ancestors.

hives n pl [Var of *heaves;* cf **heave v A1]**

1968 *DARE* (Qu. K48, *When a horse is short of breath, you say it's* ______) Inf **LA**18, Got the heaves—or hives.

hive up v phr, hence ppl adj *hived up*

To shut oneself up, hole up, take refuge.

1774 (1900) Fithian *Jrl.* 233, Come, Fithian, what do you mean by keeping hived up sweating in your Room. **1856** Holmes *Lena Rivers* 218 **NEng,** There's no kind of use why you should stay hived up with me. I'd as lief be left alone as not. **1884** Baldwin *Yankee School-Teacher* 190 **VA** [Black], Tain't jes' nat'ral f'r young folks ter hive up in de chimbley corner same's you've tooken t' doin'. **1971** Adams *Cowman* 79, The West was also a grazing ground for gunmen and desperadoes. These fellows hived up in town, not on the range.

hive vine n

1 **=partridgeberry.** [See quot 1975]

1876 Hobbs *Bot. Hdbk.* 53, Hive vine, Squaw vine, Mitchella repens. **1889** *Century Dict.* 2845, *Hive-vine*. . . The partridge-berry or squaw-vine, *Mitchella repens.* **1911** Henkel *Amer. Med. Leaves* 34, Hive vine. . . The leaves have no odor and are somewhat astringent and bitter. **1971** Krochmal *Appalachia Med. Plants* 176, Hive vine. . . The bright, orange-red berry and dark green leaves are very attractive. **1975** Hamel–Chiltoskey *Cherokee Plants* 47, Partridge berry, hive vine. . . Tea for hives.

2 A **tick trefoil** (here: *Desmodium rotundifolium*).

1893 *Jrl. Amer. Folkl.* 6.140 **WV,** *Desmodium rotundifolium,* hive vine.

3 The crown vetch *(Coronilla varia).*

1940 Clute *Amer. Plant Names* 18, *C[oronilla] varia*. . . Hive-vine.

hiveweed n Cf **bee weed 1**

An aster.

1927 Harper *Mammals Okefinokee* 213 **GA,** *Aster squarrosus* 'Hive-weed'.

hivvely adj [PaGer *hiwwel, hivvel* hill; *hiwwlich, hivlich* hilly]

1914 *DN* 4.158 **PA,** *Hivvely*. . . Rough. "A hivvely rutschi [**=sliding pond**]."

hi-ya exclam Also *hiah, hi-ye, hi-yi, hi-yuh* [Reduced from *How are you?*]

Used as an informal greeting; see quots.

1914 *DN* 4.159 **cVA,** *Hiah*. . . Hello! (How-are-you?) **1933** Rawlings *South Moon* 23 **nFL,** The men . . waved wide black felt hats and called lustily. "Hi-yuh! How's the work a'comin'?" **1936** Reese *Worleys* 35 **MD** (as of 1865) [Black], Hi-yi, Unc Job! **1940** Chandler *Farewell* 196, Hiya, babe. Long time no see. **1950** *WELS* 4 Infs, **WI,** Hi-ya. **1950** *WELS Suppl.* 4 Infs, **WI,** Hi-ya. **1956** Ker *Vocab. W. TX* 342, 2 infs, Hi-ya; 1 inf, hi-ye. **c1960** *Wilson Coll.* **csKY,** Hi-ya—intimate, pert greeting; recent. **1965–70** *DARE* (Qu. NN10a, *Expressions . . used when you meet somebody you know quite well*) 38 Infs, **scattered, but more freq Nth,** Hi-ya(, kid); (Qu. II10b, *Asking directions of somebody on the street when you don't know his name . . a man*) Inf **NY**69, Hi-ya.

hi-yi exclam[1] See **hi-ya**

hi-yi exclam[2] Also sp *high-yi*

Go! Get going!—used as a call or command to horses.

1872 Twain *Roughing It* 31 **West,** The cracking of the driver's whip, and his "Hi-yi! g'lang!" were music. **1924** *DN* 5.270, *High-yi* (call).

hi-yi exclam[3] [Cf *DJE aye*]

See quot.

1950 *PADS* 14.73 **SC** [Gullah], *Hi-yi*. . . An exclamation of disgust, disapproval.

hi-yoop exclam

Used to express jubilation or excitement; see quot.

1931 Randolph *Ozarks* 48, Hi-yoop! I'm saved! Praise Gawd!

hiyu adj [Chinook Jargon *hiu* plenty] **esp AK, NW** Cf **high-muck-a-muck 1**

See quots.

1938 (1939) Holbrook *Holy Mackinaw* 265, *Hiyu.* Plenty, large, enough, many . . *hiyu muckamuck,* plenty to eat. **1939** FWP *Guide AK* xl, *Hi yu*. . . (C[hinook]) plenty. **1942** *AmSp* 17.225 **NW** [Logger talk], The Northwest loggers have been hospitable to a good many words from the Chinook jargon. Loggers' favorites are *hiyu,* meaning 'plenty, large, enough, many,' as in 'hiyu muckamuck,' plenty to eat. **1958** McCulloch *Woods Words* 86 **Pacific NW,** *Hiyu*—Much (from the Indian). **1977** Jones *OR Folkl.* 101/2, *Hiyu:* Chinook for plenty, large, many.

hi-yuh See **hi-ya**

hiyu muckamuck See **high-muck-a-muck 1**

hiz(z)en See **hisn**

hnyah-hnyah adj

=antigodlin 1.

1954 *PADS* 21.39 **SC,** Out of plumb, said of a door or window frame, house, or other construction when warped or careened out of the rectangular shape or vertical position. . . several other synonymous expressions are used: *whonkum, sigodlin, antigodlin, hnyah-hnyah,* the last with strong nasalization.

ho v

Any of var commands, usu to an animal, spec:

a also *hoa(-ie);* also in var combs: Stop! Slow up! **chiefly Nth, West** See Map

1828 Webster *Amer. Dict., Ho*. . . A word used by teamsters, to stop their teams. . . This word is pronounced also *whō* or *hwo.* **1908** *DN* 3.320 **eAL, wGA,** *Ho*. . . Whoa. **1917** *DN* 4.403 **neOH,** *Ho*. . . Command to horses. **1940** Faulkner *Hamlet* 200 **MS,** Speaking to the horse to slow it. . . "Whoa. Whoa. Ho now. Ho now." **1941** *LANE* Map 221, 6 infs, **chiefly sNEng,** The following calls are used to stop the oxen . . [ho . . hoᵊ . . hoʊ . . ˈho˄ˈho˄ . . ho˄·u . . hou bjɛk]. *Ibid* Map 224, 14 infs, **s,wNEng,** This map presents the calls used in stopping the horses. . . [ho˄ . . hoə . . hoᵁ . . hou· . . ho ˈbæk] etc. **1949** Kurath *Word Geog.* 66, *Calls to Stop a Horse. . . hoa!,* is fairly common in western Connecticut and in Greater New York City, and in the Southern coastal area from Chesapeake Bay to the Neuse. **1950** *WELS (What do you say to make the horses stop?)* 12 Infs, **WI,** Ho; 9 Infs, Ho or whoa; 3 Infs, Ho or wo; 2 Infs, Ho back. **1960** Criswell *Resp. to PADS 20* **Ozarks** *(Making horses stop), Ho* . . and *Ho, boy,* particularly when a horse was scared. **1965–70** *DARE* (Qu. K34, *What do you say to make the horses stop?*) 99 Infs, **chiefly Nth, West,** Ho; **MS**1, **PA**71, Ho boy; **NY**23, Ho back; (Qu. EE20, *When two boys are fighting, and the one who is losing wants to stop, he calls out "______."*) Inf **IL**4, Ho. **1967** *DARE* Tape **TX**49, He started running after Tom . . and I knew Tom would hit him with that fist and if he did it might kill him. I hollered and called 'ho there!' And then he jumped on me. **1967** Faries *Word Geog. MO* 95,

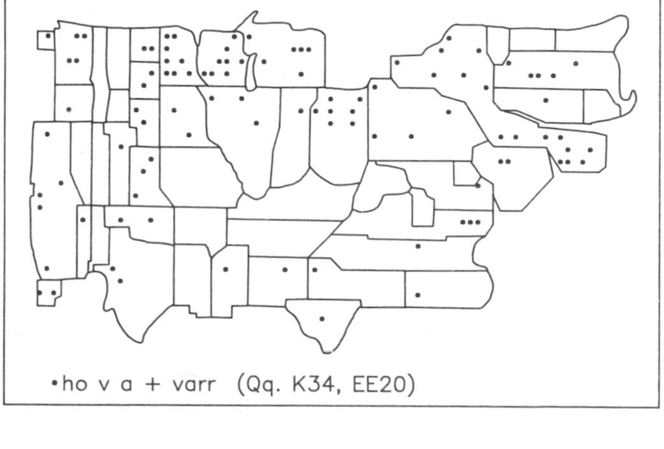

•ho v a + varr (Qq. K34, EE20)

Calls to stop a horse. . . [331] Missouri informants employ the . . call *hoa!* to stop a horse. *Ibid* 178, [33 infs employ *hoa-ie!*] **1986** Pederson *LAGS Concordance* **Gulf Region** *(Whoa! To stop horses)* 30 infs, Ho; 1 inf, Ho—these niggers say; 1 inf, Ho, now, ho, whoa; 1 inf, Ho haw; 1 inf, Ho, whoa—just make a loud noise.

b also *ho boss(y), ~ bessie:* Stand still!—used to a cow during milking. Cf **boss** n[1] **2**

1941 *LANE* Map 220 *(Calls to cows while milking)* 1 inf, **swCT,** [ho^U bɑs]; 1 inf, **nwCT,** [ho tini]. **1965–70** *DARE* (Qu. K81, *To make a cow stand still . . you say "_______."*) 48 Infs, **scattered, but less freq Mid, S Atl,** Ho (boss *or* bessie). **1973** Allen *LAUM* 1.259 (as of c1950), To quiet cows during milking. . . *ho,* also sometimes followed by *boss* or *bossy* . . has scattered occurrences in Minnesota, with a few instances in the eastern parts of the Dakotas and Nebraska. Its seven occurrences in Wisconsin as well might suggest a Northern orientation. **1986** Pederson *LAGS Concordance* **Gulf Region** *(Calls to cows)* 5 infs, Ho—to make (a cow) stand still; 1 inf, Take it easy, ho.

c often *ho back:* Back up! Turn!—used to a horse or mule; see quots. [*EDD ho-back* (at *ho* int. 1 (1))] Cf **back** v **7, haw** v, *hoof back* (at **hoof C**)

1965–70 *DARE* (Qu. K36b, . . *To make a horse go backwards*) 38 Infs, **scattered, but esp Sth, Midl, West,** Ho back; **KS**15, **MO**38, **NC**68, **PA**116, Ho; **NY**189, Ho, steady; **NC**13, Ho, back up; [**KY**49, Wo ho [wo 'ho] back]. **1986** Pederson *LAGS Concordance* **Gulf Region** *(Calls to mules or horses to make them turn left and right in plowing)* 1 inf, Ho—left; 1 inf, Ho—right; 1 inf, Haw or ho [FW: Inf doesn't know what these terms mean.]; 1 inf, Hee and ho; *(To back [a horse])* 1 inf, Ho back; 1 inf, Ho back—[FW: pulled back on reins when he said that].

d also *hoa-ie, ho-ee, ho-wuh:* Come!—see quots. Cf **co** v, **co-ee**

1949 Kurath *Word Geog.* 65, *(Calls to Pigs)*. . . Calls [which] occur in parts of the North Midland . . *hoo-ie!, hoa-ie!, woo-ie!* in northern Delaware and on the lower Susquehanna. . . also in common use in a well-defined area centering on Wheeling, West Virginia, presumably derived from the Delaware Valley. **1965–70** *DARE* (Qu. K80, . . *To get the cows in from the pasture*) Infs **CA**195, **CO**38, **MD**48, Ho (cow); **MD**15, Ho-ee; (Qu. K82, . . *To get horses in from the pasture*) Infs **PA**169, 204, Ho; **SC**57, Ho-ee; (Qu. K83, . . *To call a calf*) Inf **MD**48, Ho; **MD**15, Ho-ee; (Qu. K84, . . *To get the pigs in at feeding time*) Inf **LA**44, Ho! Ho! **1966** Dakin *Dial. Vocab. Ohio R. Valley* 2.276, *(Calls to horses (in pasture))*. . . *Ho!* plus name . . are used in Clark and Marion Counties, Indiana. **1986** Pederson *LAGS Concordance* **Gulf Region** *(Calls to cows)* 1 inf, Ho; 1 inf, Ho—to get their attention; 1 inf, Ho cow—two times, to bring them in; *(Calls to calves)* 1 inf, Ho; 1 inf, Calf, ho, sook; 1 inf, Ho-wuh; *(Calls to pigs . . when feeding them)* 1 inf, Pig, ho; 1 inf, Pig, ho hoey—four times.

e also *hoa, ho boss, ~ up:* Get up! Move!—see quots. Cf **boss** n[1] **2**

1950 *PADS* 14.76 **FL,** *Hoa*. . . A cattleman's call to push the herd along. The precise meaning is often conveyed by the tone. **1965–70** *DARE* (Qu. NN22d, . . *To drive away animals*) Infs **LA**28, 35, **MD**22, Ho (boss). **1986** Pederson *LAGS Concordance (To start horses; to urge horses on)* 1 inf, **csTN,** Ho up—to start.

ho n Also sp *hoe* [Back-formation from *hose* understood as pl; *OED* 1715 →]

A stocking.

1893 Shands *MS Speech* 37, *Ho*. . . Sometimes used by clerks in dry-goods stores to mean *one of a pair of hose, one stocking*. . . Not very general. **1927** *AmSp* 3.10 **Ozarks,** The Ozarker does use *hoe* as a singular of *hose—a good slick hoe shore does purty up a gal's laig!*

hoa See **ho v a, e**

hoagie n, also attrib Also sp *hoagy, hogie* [Etym uncert; cf *AmSp* 42.283-4] **chiefly PA, NJ, but becoming more widely recognized** See Map and Map Section Cf **Cuban sandwich, grinder 3, hero, poor boy, torpedo**

A **submarine sandwich.**

1965–70 *DARE* (Qu. H42, *The kind [of sandwich] in a . . large . . long . . bun, that's a meal in itself*) 83 Infs, **chiefly PA, NJ,** Hoagie; **PA**163, Hoagie [FW: Inf says it's the same as a submarine, although a local restaurant makes a "steak hoagie," which is ground round steak on a hoagie bun.]; **PA**221, Hoagie bun. **1967** *AmSp* 42.283, [The term] *hoagie* . . is used primarily in the Pennsylvania and New Jersey area with a small representation in other regions of the country. **1972** *NYT Article Letters* **ceMO,** Different names for the same sandwich: Philadelphia—Hoagie or Hogie . . St. Louis—Heroes. **1976** *Badger Herald* (Madison WI) 1 July 8, The Philadelphia Food Factory has opened its doors . . and brought a new alien food to . . [Madison]; to wit, the mighty Hoagie, otherwise known as the Grinder, the Sub and Hero. **1977–78** Foster *Lexical Variation* 34 **NJ,** The most important lexical set for . . understanding . . the relative influence of Philadelphia and New York City is the sandwich terms *hero, hoagie,* and *sub(marine). Ibid* 118, [Footnote:] *Sub shops* are found in Philadelphia, but they sell *hoagies* . . [In] one New York City deli, *the Hoagy Hero,* like the *Submarine Hero* . . designate[s] sandwiches with specific ingredients. **1982** McCool *Sam McCool's Pittsburghese* 16 **PA,** *Hoagie:* a submarine sandwich, heated and spicy. **1986** Pederson *LAGS Concordance* **Gulf Region** (*Hero sandwich;* this question was asked chiefly in urban areas) 17 infs, Hoagie (sandwich); 2 infs, Hoagie—heard; 1 inf, Hoagie—heard in cafeteria, packaged at food store; 1 inf, Hoagie—I don't know where I picked that up; 1 inf, Hoagie—northern; 2 infs, Hoagie—submarine sandwich (or super sub); 1 inf, Hoagie—shorter than submarines [with] bologna, ham, etc. **1988** *DARE* File **Madison WI,** At *Cellar Subs* the counter person said "We have only one hoagie, called 'Hoagie Heaven.' It's all fresh ingredients—two kinds of cheese, tomatoes, cucumbers, sprouts, mayonnaise, lettuce, and sliced turkey." *Ibid* **Philadelphia PA** (as of 1950s), Hoagie is a common word . . in Philly. **1989** *Ibid* **Philadelphia PA** (as of 1937), When my mother was dating, a common thing to do was to go to one of the neighborhood groceries on the south side, in the Italian area, and get a hoagie. The grocery owner would make the sandwich on a large Italian bread roll. My mother's hairdresser's mother, an Italian-American, thinks that originally the roll itself was called a hoagie. My mother thinks that the way hoagies spread throughout the city was that the cops would go down there to get these sandwiches and then drive around eating their hoagies.

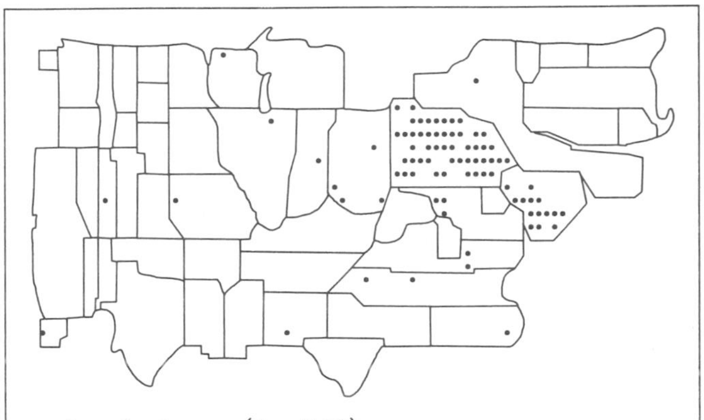

•hoagie + var (Qu. H42)

hoag iron n [Prob var of *hog*] Cf **dog iron 1**

=**andiron.**

1968 *DARE* (Qu. D32, *The metal stands in a fireplace that the logs are laid on*) Inf **MO**17, ['hoᴜg ˌɑˑɪɚnz]—don't ask me what 'hoag' refers to.

hoagy See **hoagie**

hoa-ie See **ho v a, d**

hoaney See **honey**

hoar bumps n pl Cf **cold bumps**

=**gooseflesh.**

1967 *DARE* (Qu. X58, *When you are cold, and little points of skin begin to come on your arms and legs, you have ______*) Inf **CO**33, Hoar bumps.

hoarse up v phr, hence ppl adj phr *hoarsed up*

To make hoarse.

1890 *DN* 1.19 **seNH,** *Hoarsed-up:* 'I'm all hoarsed-up.' 'This cold has hoarsed me up.' Generally used. **1931–33** *LANE Worksheets* **nwVT,** All hoarsed [horst] up—[from hoarse].

hoarwort n

=**cotton rose 2.**

1940 Clute *Amer. Plant Names* 83, *Herba impia*. . . Hoarwort. **1959** Carleton *Index Herb. Plants* 61, *Hoar-wort:* Gifola germanica (Filago).

hoary grass n

A **whitetop** (here: *Scolochloa festucacea*).

1968 *Mackay Miner* (ID) 25 Jan 4/3, The Board of County Commissioners of Custer County, Idaho, does hereby formulate and declare: that weeds known as Canadian Thistle, Wild Morning Glory, Russian Knapweed, White Top or Hoary Grass, Perennial Milk Weed, Leafy Spurge and Cocklebur are noxious weeds.

hoary pea n

=**goat's rue.**

1848 Gray *Manual of Botany* 104, *Tephrosia... Hoary Pea...* Silky-hoary perennial herbs.. with white or purplish racemed flowers. **1876** Hobbs *Bot. Hdbk.* 31, Devil's shoestring, Hoary pea, Tephrosia Virginiana. **1891** Coulter *Botany W. TX* 80, *Tephrosia... Hoary Pea...* Pod densely soft pubescent. **1910** Graves *Flowering Plants* 251, Hoary Pea... The roots are sometimes used medicinally. **1940** Steyermark *Flora MO* 301, Goat's Rue, Hoary Pea, Catgut *(Tephrosia).* **1971** Krochmal *Appalachia Med. Plants* 248, *Tephrosia Virginiana..* Common Names: Virginia tephrosia,.. hoary pea.

hoax n

A cheat; a deceiver.

1869 Stowe *Oldtown Folks* 292 **MA,** Lady Widgery had always been rushed for and contended for by the other sex; and one husband had hardly time to be cold in his grave before the air was filled with the rivalry of candidates to her hand; and after all the beautiful little hoax had nothing for it but her attractive soul-case. **1899** (1912) Green *VA Folk-Speech* 227, *Hoax...* One who misleads or deceives. **1915** *DN* 4.199, *Hoax,* fraud. "He's nothing but a hoax. You can never depend on him." **1968** *DARE* (Qu. V7, *A person who sets out to cheat others while pretending to be honest*) Inf **IA**17, A hoax.

hob n[1] Cf **hobs of hell**

1930 Shoemaker *1300 Words* 31 **cPA Mts** (as of c1900), *Hob*—An alcove in fire-place for keeping contents of utensils warm.

hob n[2] [Perh var of **hod 1,** but perh from *hob-grate* a grate used to support coal inside a stove]

1966 *DARE* (Qu. F44,.. *A container for coal to use in a stove*) Inf **NM**12, Hob [hɒb].

hoba See **hobber**

ho back See **ho** v **a, c**

hobber n Also *hoba* [Pronc-spp for *harbor;* cf *OED harbour* sb.[1] 2. c "The covert or place of retreat of wild animals"]

See quots.

1954 *DE Folkl. Bulletin* 1.16/1, Hobbers (winter quarters for rabbits, groundhogs, snakes, etc.) **1976** Ryland *Richmond Co. VA* 372, *Hoba*—hiding place; "A brush-pile is just a hoba for snakes."

hobble n[1] [Engl dial; *OED hobble* sb. 2 1775] *old-fash*

A difficult or perplexing situation.

1799 in 1893 Washington *Writings* 14.193, I think you Wise men of the East, have got yourselves in a hobble, relatively to France, Great Britain, Russia and the Porte... All cannot be pleased! whom will you offend? **1806** (1970) Webster *Compendious Dict.* 144, *Hobble..* a scrape. **1865** Crockett *Life* 159, At last we quit trying to land... I was down in the cabin of one of the boats.. thinking on what a hobble we had got into; and how much better bear-hunting was on hard land, than floating along on the water. **1899** (1912) Green *VA Folk-Speech* 227, *Hobble...* Difficulty; perplexity; scrape. "I'm in a regular hobble."

hobble n[2], v, hence vbl n *hobbling* [Engl dial *hobbil* n, v; cf *EDD*]

A haycock; to cock hay.

1940–41 Cassidy *WI Atlas* **csWI,** Hobbles [hɑblz] n pl; hobbling [hɑbl̩ɨn] vbl n.

hobble n[3] [Perh var of **hovel n 1a,** or transf from Engl dial *hobble* pigsty; see *EDD hobble* sb.[3]]

A building for housing domestic animals.

1924 *DN* 5.295 **csNH,** *Hobble...* A lean-to, place where cows are kept. **1957** Beck *Folkl. ME* 228, The hobble, commonly known to urbanites as "stable," was built like the bunkhouse, except that it had the added luxury of a pole floor and stalls instead of beds.

hobble n[4]

1966 *DARE* FW Addit **ME**10, Hobbles—short legs, three of 'em, on a skillet.

hobblebush n **esp NEast**

A **viburnum** (here: *Viburnum alnifolium*). Also called **buckrush, devil's shoestring 2, dogberry g, dog hobble 2, dogwood 4, heath apple, mooseberry, moosebush, moosewood, tangle-legs, triptoe, trip-tree, wayfaring tree, wild hydrangea, witch-hobble**

1822 Eaton *Botany* 510 **NEast,** *Viburnum... lantanoides..* hobble-bush, tangle-legs... Stem very flexible and crooked. **1832** MA Hist. Soc. *Coll.* 2d ser 9.157 **cwVT,** [Viburnum] lantanoides, *(Michaux.)*—Hobble bush. **1845** Judd *Margaret* 286 **NJ,** I can get you the leaves, maples, beeches, cherries, hobble-bush and all. These leaves will keep their color a long time. **1848** in 1850 Cooper *Rural Hours* 344 **cNY,** The large leaves of the hobble-bush especially are quite showy now... The long branches will sometimes root themselves anew from the ends, thus making a tangled thicket about them; this habit, indeed, has given to the shrub the name of "hobble-bush." **1961** Douglas *My Wilderness* 214 **NH,** The aspen (which is known locally as popple),.. and hobblebush leave an open effect. **1976** Bruce *How to Grow Wildflowers* 129, One of the most beautiful of all in flower is the Hobble-bush, *V. alnifolium...* Its vernacular name refers to its arching branches, the lower of which tend to strike root where they touch the humus-rich ground of their native woodlands and thus trip unwary walkers.

hobbled ppl adj[1] [Cf *EDD hobble* v.[1] 4 "*Fig.* To hamper, embarrass"]

Handicapped.

1940 Weygandt *Down Jersey* 8 **sNJ,** Certain family names are held everywhere as taboo, every one of that name being considered "poor white trash.".. "We think nothing of the Blanks about here, and hold any man hobbled has anything to do with them."

hobbled ppl adj[2] [*DSL hobbil, hobbel* "To cobble; to mend in a clumsy manner"]

1967 *DARE* (Qu. W29,.. *Expressions.. for things that are sewn carelessly: "They're ______.'*) Inf **MA**72, Hobbled.

hobblefoot n [Prob *hobble* to limp, but cf *EDD* sb. *hobbing-foot* (at *hob* v.[1] 20) "a very big foot"]

1967 *DARE* (Qu. X38, *Joking names for unusually big or clumsy feet*) Inf **IN**13, Hobblefoot ['hɒbl̩,fʊt].

hobbling vbl n

1 See quot. [Cf *EDD hob* v.[3] "To cut down or mow the thistles, coarse grass, &c., left by cattle"]

1967 *DARE* (Qu. L36, *What do you call it.. when you dig out roots and underbrush to make a new field?*) Inf **AL**14, Hobbling.

2 See **hobble** n[2], v.

hobbly See **hubbly**

hobby v Cf **hobbyhorse 3**

To ride up and down on a **seesaw.**

1940 in 1944 *ADD* 626 **swPA, nWV,** *Teeter... hobby..* 'They are hobbyin'.'

hobby adj See **hubby**

hobby n

1 also *hobby bread:* A **corn dodger 1. chiefly eKY, seOH, sWV** Cf **dodger** n[1] **1**

1949 Kurath *Word Geog.* 36 **sWV,** *Hobbies..* small hand shaped corn cakes. *Ibid* 68, In West Virginia south of the Kanawha the.. term [corresponding to *corn dodger*] is *hobby.* **1966** Dakin *Dial. Vocab. Ohio R. Valley* 2.315 **eKY, seOH,** Several speakers in the [Allegheny] Mountains appear to say *hobby bread* = *pone* or *pone bread* although *hobby* usually and commonly means a type of corn griddle cake. *Ibid* 318, *Corn dodger..* = *corn stick* = *hobby* (most often)—stiffer dough, hand-shaped in various shapes, baked several at a time—usually on top of [the] stove or in ashes in a skillet 'n lid, etc. **1967** Faries *Word Geog. MO* 100 **cMO,** *Corn griddle cake...* A single instance of the South Midland *hobby* is recorded, in Benton County. **1967** *DARE* (Qu. H14, *Bread that's made with cornmeal*) Inf **KY**34, Corn hobbies—little round cakes. **1983** *MJLF* 9.1.44 **ceKY,** *Hobbies...* corn dodgers [3 infs].

2 By ext: see quot.

1952 Brown *NC Folkl.* 1.551, *Hobby of bread...* A piece of bread.

hobbyboard n Cf **hobbyhorse 3,** *DS* EE31

=**seesaw.**

1940 in 1944 *ADD* 626 **swPA, nWV,** *Teeter-totter...* hobby-board.

hobby bread See **hobby** n **1**

hobbyhorse n

1 See quot. [Cf *OED hobby-horse* sb. 3. a "A . . buffoon"; →a1616; but perh var of *stalking-horse*]

1966-67 *DARE* (Qu. II34, *If you think somebody is trying to use you to his advantage: "I'm not going to be his ______."*) Infs **GA**9, **TX**35, Hobbyhorse.

2 A **sawbuck.**

1968 *DARE* (Qu. L59, *An implement with an X frame to hold firewood for sawing*) Inf **MD**42, Some people say hobbyhorse.

3 By ext: a homemade **seesaw.** Cf **hobby** v, **hobbyboard**

1970 *DARE* (Qu. EE31) Inf **NC**84, Homemade—called a hobbyhorse—a board over a sawhorse.

4 A clotheshorse; see quot. Cf **Astor's pet horse 1**

1968 *DARE* (Qu. W40, *What do people say about a woman who overdresses or who spends too much on clothes?*) Inf **PA**90, Getting yourself up like a hobbyhorse.

5 **=praying mantis.** Cf **wooden horse**

1968 *DARE* (Qu. R9b) Infs **MD**9, **NC**81, Hobbyhorse.

‡Hobeanin n [Prob var, by metath, of *Bohemian*]

1967 *DARE* (Qu. HH28, . . *People of foreign background: Bohemian*) Inf **CO**7, Hobeanins.

ho bessie See **ho** v **b**

hobgoblin pie n

1967 *DARE* (Qu. NN12b, *Things that people say to put off a child when he asks, "What are you making?"*) Inf **NE**11, Hobgoblin pie.

hobnob adj [Cf *OED hob-nob* adv. 2 "=*Hab nab*. . . hit or miss . . at random"]

1915 *DN* 4.216 [Terms of disparagement], [Adjectives:] *Hob-nob,* at random. "Your books and clothes are always hob-nob."

hobnob v Also *hob or nob* [Cf *OED hob-nob* v. 1 "To drink to each other, drink together" and *hob-nob* phrase 1 "*Hob, nob:* have or have not"]

See quots.

1899 (1912) Green *VA Folk-Speech* 227, *Hobnob*. . . A familiar invitation to drink—to take or not to take. **1942** Berrey-Van den Bark *Amer. Slang* 104.2, *Invitations to drink*. . . hob or nob?

hobnob n^{1} See **hobnobber**

hobnob n^{2} Also *hobnob boot* [Var of *hobnail*]

1967-69 *DARE* (Qu. W42b, . . *Nicknames for men's square-toed shoes*) Inf **NY**214, Hobnobs; (QR, near Qu. W12a) Inf **IA**8, Hobnob boots.

hobnob n^{3}

1967 *DARE* (Qu. X3, *When a woman puts her hair up on her head in a bunch, you call this a ______*) Inf **NY**7, Hobnob.

hobnobber n Also *hobnob* [*hobnob* v to be on familiar terms with someone, esp of a higher social class]

1965-70 *DARE* (Qu. II23, *People who are, or think they are, the best society of a community*) Infs **OH**22, **WI**57, Hobnobbers; **PA**185, Hobnobs.

hobnobble v [*hobnob* + *-le;* nEngl dial, cf *EDD*]

1966 *DARE* (Qu. II2a, *When two people begin to be friendly: "He has just recently ______ with John."*) Inf **AR**41, Started hobnoblin'.

hobnob boot See **hobnob** n^{2}

‡hob-nosh n

1970 *DARE* (Qu. II36a, *Somebody who talks back or gives rude answers: "Did you ever see such a ______?"*) Inf **IL**115, Hob nosh ['hɑbˌnɑš].

hobo egg n Cf **Rocky Mountain egg**

=Alabama egg.

1980 *DARE* File **csWI**, A hobo egg is something you fix on a camping trip. You cut a hole in a piece of toast that's on a griddle; then you put the egg in the hole and fry it.

Hoboken n [*Hoboken* small New Jersey city across the Hudson R from New York City]

1 An out-of-the-way or insignificant place; an imaginary place; *joc or derog*

1925 Krapp *Engl. Lang.* 1.176, The humorous connotation of certain Indian names has always been felt, and names like . . *Hoboken,* . . names of real places, have acquired more than logical significance, as though they were grotesque creations of fancy. **1936** (1947) Mencken *Amer. Lang.* 553, For many years *Hoboken* was the joke-town of New York. **1942** Berrey-Van den Bark *Amer. Slang* 45.4, *Imaginary "hick" town*. . . Hoboken.

2 Hell.

1942 Berrey-Van den Bark *Amer. Slang* 322, *Hell*. . . Hoboken. **1966-67** *DARE* (Qu. CC9, . . *Expressions for hell: "That man is headed straight for ______."*) Inf **NY**10, Hoboken; (Qu. NN26a, *Weakened substitutes for 'hell': "Oh ______!"*) Inf **MA**6, Hell, heaven, or Hoboken.

hob or nob See **hobnob** v

ho boss See **ho** v **b, e**

ho bossy See **ho** v **b**

Hob's Knob n Cf **hobnobber, Nob Hill**

An exclusive residential district.

1965-70 *DARE* (Qu. II24, . . *The part of a town where the well-off people live*) Infs **AZ**15, **MS**1, **NC**72, **NY**156, **PA**185, Hob's Knob.

hobs of hell n pl Also *hubs of Hades, ~ hell, ~ heck, hugs of hell* [**hob** n^{1}]

The hottest part of hell—used fig, in compar phrr.

1939 (1962) Thompson *Body & Britches* 495 **Upstate NY,** Hotter'n the hobs of hell. **1944** *NY Times* (NY) 10 Mar 14/7 **NYC,** What the unnamed Senator no doubt said was that "the hardtack was hard as the hobs of hell," not "hubs," as printed. This simile, to my own personal knowledge, is at least half a century old and was frequently used by the volunteers of '98 to describe the hard-tack issued to the Army during the Spanish-American War. **1967-70** *DARE* (Qu. B3, *If a day is very hot, you say it's . . ______*) Infs **IL**117, **NE**7, **WI**36, Hot as (*or* hotter than) the hubs of hell; **IA**8, Hotter than the hugs of hell; (Qu. HH22b, . . *A very mean person . . "He's meaner than ______."*) Inf **CA**61, The hubs of heck. **1969** *DARE* FW Addit **swMO,** By God it was hotter than the hubs of Hades. **1984** Weaver *TX Crude* 100, Texas hot—*"It's hotter than the hubs of hell."*

hock v^{1} See **hawk** v^{2}

hock v^{2} [Perh transf from *hock* to pawn]

See quots.

1965-70 *DARE* (Qu. V4, . . *Stealing something valuable . . "Yesterday somebody ______ my watch."*) 19 Infs, **esp NEast, N Cent, Upper MW,** Hocked; (Qu. V5a, *To take something of small value that doesn't belong to you . . "Who's been ______ the cookies?"*) Inf **GA**9, Hocking. **1965** *DARE* FW Addit **cnIA,** [hɑk]—steal. "Who hocked my billfold?" **1968** *Sat. Eve. Post* 18 May 26/1 **NY,** A high-school girl in an affluent Westchester County, N.Y., suburb says, "Sometimes girls can brag that half of their wardrobes are made up of 'hocked' [*Sat. Eve. Post* Ed: shoplifted] clothes in the new fashions. I can only think of one or two of my friends who don't 'hock.'" **1971** *Current Slang* 5.4.14 **VT,** *Hock*. . . To steal.

hock cockle n

=buckhorn plantain.

1898 *Bot. Gaz.* 26.251, *Plantago lanceolata* . . hock cockle, Southold, L.I.

hocker n [Prob *hock* to pawn]

c1970 Wiersma *Marbles Terms* **swMI,** *Hocker*—A marble one is willing to trade or which one received in trade.

hockey n^{1} Cf **shinny**

1 also *street hockey, tin can ~:* The game of hockey as informally played, usu with a stick and ball or similar object.

1883 Newell *Games & Songs* 182, *Hockey.* This sport is also called *Shinny.* The ball is struck on the ground with a bent stick. . . The game is much played on the ice, as has been the case from the oldest times in the North. **1899** Champlin-Bostwick *Young Folks' Games* 411, *Hockey, or Shinney,* a game played by any number of persons, each of whom has a stick with a curved end, called a hockey, or shinney, with which he tries to drive a small ball past a line. . . The ball is commonly of rubber, . . but a small block of wood called a nun . . is often used instead. . . Hockey . . rules differ somewhat in different places. **1965-70** *DARE* (Qu. EE10, *A game in which a short stick lying on the ground is flipped into the air and then hit with a longer stick, that's ______*) Infs **CA**73,

IL5, **MO**25, **OH**38, 70, Hockey; (Qu. EE18, *Games in which the players set up a stone, a tin can, or something similar, and then try to knock it down*) Infs **CA**202, **IL**5, 70, Hockey; **IL**29, **WA**1, Tin can hockey; (Qu. EE33, . . *Outdoor games*) Inf **CA**107, Street hockey—hit a rock with a crooked stick; before you hit it you say, "shinny shinny on your own side"; **CO**21, Hockey—hit a tin can with a stick; **KY**66, Hockey—with balls from hedge oranges; **MO**7, Hockey; **MO**15, Hockey game—a tin can was hit or kicked around; **MO**25, Hockey—played on pavement or dirt with a tin can. [*DARE* Ed: It is possible that Infs responding to Qq. EE10, 18 are referring to different games; cf **cat n 3a** and **duck on a rock.** 13 of 14 total Infs old] **1975** Ferretti *Gt. Amer. Book Sidewalk Games* 214 **NYC,** What is as rough as any street game, but which has its origins in organized sport, is Hockey, city-gutter style. . . hockey sticks are made by taping the cut-off corner of an orange-crate to the end of a broomstick, and rolls of black electricians' tape become pucks.

2 also sp *hawk(e)y:* A hockey stick. *old-fash*

1839 Abbott *Caleb in Town* 38 **Boston MA,** Now, a hawky is a small, round stick, about as long as a man's cane, with a crook in the lower end, so that a boy can hit balls and little stones with it, when lying upon the ground. A good hawky is a great prize to a Boston boy. **1854** Shillaber *Life Partington* 178 **NEng,** I've swapped my jackknife, and got a bran-new hawkey that I cut myself in the bushes. **1899** [see **1** above]. **1906** Lovett *Old Boston Boys* 22, Hockeys, too, were a homemade article, few being found for sale in the shops. The sticks, usually hickory, were cut in the suburbs, steamed or soaked in boiling water until the end was pliable, and then bent to the required curve and tied with stout cord until perfectly dry. Some were then wound with copper wire at the point of contact with the ground, and no better hockey has ever been made since.

3 By ext: see quot. [Cf *OED hockey* sb.[2] 1 quot 1842]

1896 *DN* 1.418 **cNY,** *Hockey* . . for *polo.*

hockey n[2], v Also sp *hawky, hockie, hocky* [Etym unknown] **chiefly S Midl** *esp freq among children; sometimes taboo* Cf **cacky** v, n

Fcces; to defecate; also fig.

1886 Amer. Philol. Assoc. *Trans.* 17.37 **eTN,** *Hockie* is used in East Tennessee among little children, which may be connected with the original word "cacky," as also the exclamation of disgust used by an older person to a child that has befouled itself. **1902** *DN* 2.236 **sIL,** *Hawky,* or *hockey*. . . Child's word for go to stool. **1923** *DN* 5.210 **swMO,** *Hockey*. . . Dung. . . To evacuate the bowels, applicable chiefly to that action on the part of a child. **1928** *DN* 6.63 **Ozarks,** A casual mention of the game called *hockey* will paralyze any Ozark audience, for *hockey* means nothing but dung in the hill country. **1947** Willingham *End as Man* 80 **Sth,** 'Don't you try and hand *me* any of that hocky about being a white man!' . . after a while the nigger agreed he was a nigger. **1969** *DARE* File **sIL** (as of c1920), *Hockey* n. and v. *Shit* was a word ladies and children weren't allowed to use, but this was permissible. **1970** *Ibid* **neTX,** Hockey—bowel movement. **1989** *Ibid* **cWI,** I once heard an acquaintance express disbelief about something by saying "That's a bunch of horse hockey."

hockey adj Also sp *hawky* [**hockey** n[2], v] Cf **backsie, cacky** adj

See quots.

1902 *DN* 2.236 **sIL,** *Hawky,* or *hockey*. . . Filthy; defiling to the touch. **1907** *DN* 3.223 **nwAR,** *Hawky*. . . Filthy.

‡**hockidish** n [Perh Du *hagedis* lizard]

Prob a **spring peeper.**

1968 *DARE* (Qu. P21, *Small frogs that sing or chirp loudly in spring*) Inf NY48, Hockidishes—Dutch word, in Dutch community.

hockie n [*hock* the lower part of the leg of a quadruped + *-ie* dimin suff]

1896 *DN* 1.418 **nNY,** *Hockies* . . boiled pig's feet and legs. **1968** *DARE* (QR, near Qu. HH3) Inf **NY**70, Pickled hockies—up further than pig feet.

hockie See **hockey** n[2], v

hockset See **hogshead**

hocky See **hockey** n[2], v

hod n

1 freq *coal hod;* also *coke ~, hod-bucket, hod-pail:* A coal scuttle. **widespread, but esp freq NEng** See Map *somewhat old-fash*

1848 Bartlett *Americanisms* 87, *Coal-hod.* A kettle for carrying coals to the fire. More frequently called, as in England, a *coal-scuttle.* **1870** Alcott *Old-Fashioned Girl* 31 **MA,** Tom, resenting the insult, had forcibly seated her in the coal-hod. **1895** *DN* 1.396 **NY,** In the stove and hardware trade *coal hod* is universal, and this form is more common in cities; in the usage of country families in central N.Y. *coal scuttle* seems to predominate. **1905** *DN* 3.6 **cCT,** *Coal-hod*. . . A kettle for carrying coal to the fire, usually not called coal scuttle. **1949** Kurath *Word Geog.* 59, *Coal hod* is the regular expression in New England and has survived to some extent in parts of the New England settlement area (on the upper Susquehanna, in the Western Reserve). It is common in all of Maryland and is not unknown between the Potomac and the Rappahannock and on the lower Shenandoah. Furthermore, it occurs in the New England settlements around Marietta and in the adjoining part of West Virginia. **1960** *PADS* 34.57 **CO,** *Coal hod.* [*Ibid* 58, Typical of older folk speech . . but . . not necessarily obsolete.] **1965–70** *DARE* (Qu. F44, . . *A container for coal*) 143 Infs, **widespread, but esp freq NEng,** Coal hod; 104 Infs, **scattered, but esp freq NEast,** Hod; **AR**19, **KS**19, Hod-bucket; **KS**19, Hod-pail; **OR**4, Coke hod. [Of all Infs responding to the question, 72% were old; of those giving the responses *coal hod* and *hod,* 87% and 83% respectively were old.] **1973** Allen *LAUM* 1.224 (as of c1950), *(Coal) hod* . . was carried west . . and appears as the second most common U[pper] M[idwest] term . . being the most common in Iowa. It is absent, however, from most of northern Minnesota and from southern Nebraska. . . [In the] mail survey. . . 14% reported [the] older [term] *hod.*

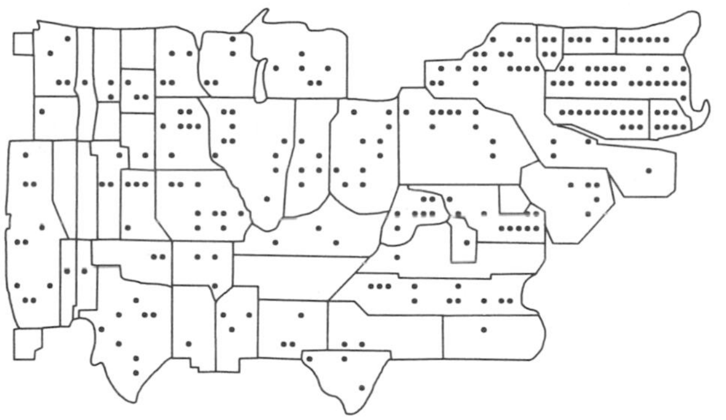

•hod n 1 + varr (Qu. F44)

2 Transf: see quots.

1914 *DN* 4.163 **CO,** *Hod*. . . Pipe. . . "Light your hod and take five." **1940** *AmSp* 15.335 **NE** [Smokers' slang], A pipe is a *hod.* **1950** *WELS* *(Nicknames for a tobacco pipe)* 3 Infs, **WI,** Hod. **1960** Criswell *Resp. to PADS 20* **Ozarks,** *(Tobacco pipe)* Hod—occasional. **1960** Bailey *Resp. to PADS 20* **KS,** *(Tobacco pipe)* Hod.

ho-dad with a shufflin' rod n Cf **doodad 1**

A fictitious item; see quot.

1966 *DARE* (Qu. NN12b, *Things that people say to put off a child when he asks, "What are you making?"*) Inf **NM**11, Ho-dad with a shufflin' rod.

hodag n[1] Also sp *hoedag* [Etym uncert; perh *hoe* + *OED dag* sb.[3] 3. b "A mining tool; an axe"]

See quots.

1958 McCulloch *Woods Words* 86 **Pacific NW,** *Hodag*. . . A grub hoe, planting hoe, fire hoe, or similar tool for grubbing. **1960** Wentworth–Flexner *Slang* 261, *Hoedag*. . . A hoe. *Obs.* **1969** Sorden *Lumberjack Lingo* 56 **NEng, Gt Lakes,** *Hodag*. . . A grub hoe or mattock.

hodag n[2] [Perh transf from **hodag** n[1]; cf quot 1910] **chiefly WI, MI, MN**

A fictitious animal credited with great size and ferocity; see quots.

1910 Cox *Fearsome Creatures* 29, The *hodag* . . has been variously described by woodsmen from Wisconsin and Minnesota. . . Size, about that of a rhinoceros . . slow . . intelligent. Its hairless body is mottled, striped, and checked. . . On the hodag's nose . . is a large spade-shaped bony growth . . so that he can see only straight up. . . The porcupine is its natural food. Upon sighting one . . in . . a spruce the hodag . . spade[s] around the tree, cutting all the roots . . and with a rush rams his shovel nose under the roots and over goes the tree. **1939** Tryon *Fearsome Critters* 25, *The Hodag. . .* A distressingly ugly animal . . fully aware of his upsetting appearance, and is given to frequent fits of bitter weeping. . . This fellow can't endure being laughed at. When angry, he is fierce and dangerously aggressive. **1950** *WELS (Imaginary wild animals)* 8 Infs, **WI,** Hodag. **1958** McCulloch *Woods Words* 86 **Pacific NW,** *Hodag.* **1968–70** *DARE* (Qu. CC17, *Imaginary animals or monsters that people around here tell tales about—especially to tease greenhorns*) Inf **MI**118, Hodag—heard stories of it in northern Wisconsin; **WI**18, Hodag—bear-ox combination; horned animal, huge; heard of in popular version on TV, supposedly a local legendary animal; **WI**19, Hodag. **1975** *WI Then & Now* Aug 6, There are still folks in Rhinelander [WI] who talk about his [=Gene Shepard's] pranks. . . His greatest achievement-cum-hoax . . [was] the monstrous, prehistoric forest animal . . the Hodag. . . Gene . . came across the Hodag . . in 1896. . . It had a head and body rather like an ox but a tail like a lizard or alligator. Along the back were twelve sharply pointed spines; a pair of wicked horns crowned the head and fangs curved down from the sides of the mouth; its cloven hooves ended in thick, pointed claws. The eyes were an eerie green color and the nostrils gave off a red glow. *Ibid* 3, At county fairs until 1906 and once at the state fair, hundreds paid to enter a dimly lighted tent to be . . scared by the monster. . . Most were convinced that the cleverly carved beast covered with ox hide and embellished with bull horns, bear claws, and steel rods was real. **1983** *Hodag Shopper* (Rhinelander WI) [title].

hod-bucket See **hod n 1**

hoddy-doddy n Also *hoddy* [*OED hoddy-doddy* sb. 3 "a noodle; a simpleton. *Obs.*" 1598–1656] *archaic*

A bumpkin; an ignoramus; a person of no importance.

1860 Hundley *Social Relations S. States* 114 **Sth,** [The hoi polloi are] the bluff, straightforward farmers, the independent yeomanry, the drawling and gawky hoddy-doddies from the "hill country". **a1861** (1880) Eastman *Poems* 57 **VT,** That poor hoddy—/ That nobody!—/ Have you ever seen him noticed by the first society? **1951** *New Yorker* 8 Dec 81 **cwNY** (as of c1840s), "What did he look like?". . . "Sam Patch? A meagre, wizened, inconsiderable little hoddy-doddy."

hodgepodge n, adj, adv Also *hodge-pock, hodpodge*

A Forms.

1968 *DARE* (Qu. E22, *If a house is untidy and everything is upset, you might say, "It's a _____!" or "It looks like _____."*) Inf **CA**36, Hodpodge; (Qu. Y38, *Mixed together, confused: "The things in the drawer are all _____."*) Inf **MN**15, Hodge-pock.

B As noun.

Cornmeal mush.

1950 *PADS* 14.37 **cSC,** *Hodgepodge. . .* Mush, made of corn meal.

C As adv.

See quot.

1968 *DARE* (Qu. KK48, *When you work something out as you go, without having a plan or pattern to follow: "I didn't have anything to go by, so I just did it _____."*) Infs **CA**53, **VA**15, Hodgepodge.

hod-pail See **hod n 1**

hodpodge See **hodgepodge**

hoe n[1]

1 See **hoe hand.**

2 also *hoe handle:* A griddle or frying pan. [See quot 1893] **Sth, S Midl** Cf **bread hoe, hoecake, spider**

1893 Shands *MS Speech* 37, *Hoe. . .* A culinary utensil, a kind of skillet without sides. In this are baked *hoe-cakes.* Bartlett says that these cakes are so called because they are baked on hoes . . in some of the interior parts of the country where cooking-vessels are scarce. If this be true, I suppose that *hoe,* the skillet, is derived through *hoe-cake* from *hoe,* the agricultural tool, as the cakes baked on the cooking-vessels are of the same kind as those . . baked on the tools. **1947** *McDavid Coll.* **neGA,** *Hoe*—a griddle for breadmaking. Shallow, may be round or square. **1958** *PADS* 29.11 **cTN,** *Hoe. . .* A frying pan. . . A *spider* (sometimes called *hoe*) is not the same, as it [=a hoe] has no sides—or practically none. It is a griddle for broiling, or for baking top-of-stove breads. **1968** *DARE* (Qu. F1, *A heavy metal pan that's used to fry foods*) Inf **NC**50, Hoe handle—same as spider.

3 in phr *mad as a hoe:* See quot. Cf **hoe handle**

1941 *LANE* Map 473, When a person is very angry he is said to be *as mad as* (or sometimes *madder than*) *. . a wet hen, . . a hoe* [2 infs, **sNEng**], *a hatchet, a meat ax.*

hoe n[2] See **ho n**

hoecake n Also *hoecake (corn-)bread* [See quots 1779, 1860] **chiefly Sth, S Midl** See Map Cf **hoe n[1] 2, hot cake 1, nocake**

Orig a simple corn cake baked on a makeshift griddle; later any of var cakes made from cornmeal or biscuit dough; see quots.

1745 in 1912 *PA Mag. Hist. & Biog.* 36.12 **seNC,** Breakfasted on Tea & Hoe Cake Bread, which we have done in common. **1779** in 1789 Anburey *Travels* 2.335 **cVA,** Hoe-cake is Indian corn ground into meal, kneaded into a dough, and baked before a fire, but as the negroes bake theirs on the hoes that they work with, they have the appellation of hoe-cakes. **1847** (1979) Rutledge *Carolina Housewife* 27 **SC,** *Hoe cake.* Three spoonfuls of hommony, two of rice flour, a little butter, and milk sufficient to make it soft. Bake on a griddle. **1860** Hundley *Social Relations S. States* 87 **Sth,** I have an unextinguishable longing for hoe-cake—real hoe-cake. . . It was originally baked upon a hoe. An old hoe, which had been worn bright, was placed upon live coals of fire, with the eye down, and on it the cake was baked. Now, hoe-cake is baked upon a griddle, or was before cooking-stoves came into use. **1883** (1971) Harris *Nights with Remus* 108 **eGA,** He continued, scraping the burnt crust from his hoe-cake with an old case-knife. **1899** (1912) Green *VA Folk-Speech* 227, *Hoe-cake. . .* Bread made of corn meal, water and salt, baked on the bottom of the blade of an old weeding-hoe. **1903** *DN* 2.316 **seMO,** *Hoe-cake. . .* A kind of corn-bread baked on a board or in an open vessel before a fire. **1907** *DN* 3.232 **nwAR, seMO. 1908** *DN* 3.320 **eAL, wGA. 1937** *Hall Coll.* **ceTN,** *Hoe-cake baker.* An 'oven' or cast iron pan set in the coals for baking hoe cake (corn bread). **1939** *Ibid* **ceTN,** *Hoe cake.* [We would make our] bread out of corn. Put the dough on birch bark, lay bread on the bark on the sap side. Let one side get brown and let it bake on the other side. **1946** *PADS* 5.25 **VA. 1949** Kurath *Word Geog.* 68, Another common Southern expression for a corn griddle cake is *hoe cake.* It is in general use in the Carolinas and in all except the west-central part of Virginia, at least in folk speech or as an old-fashioned term. It does not occur east of Chesapeake Bay, and is rare even in southern Maryland and uncommon in the *johnnikin* area on the coast of North Carolina. **1950** *PADS* 14.37 **SC. 1958** *PADS* 29.11 **TN. 1965–70** *DARE* (Qu. H14, *Bread that's made with cornmeal*) 79 Infs, **chiefly Sth, S Midl,** Hoecake(s); **SC**43, Corn hoecake; **TN**66, Hot-water hoecake; (Qu. H25, *. . Fried cornmeal*) 15 Infs, **Sth, S Midl,** Hoecake; **NC**3, Hoecake bread; (Qu. H18, *. . Special kinds of bread*) Infs **FL**18, 37, **MO**38, **NC**38, 41, **OK**21, **VA**39, Hoecake(s); **AR**2, Hoecake—cornbread without seasoning except salt; **MS**34, Hoecake—cooked in a skillet—like cornbread; **NC**3, Hoecake bread; **NC**48, Hoecake—made in an iron skillet; (Qu. H20b, *. . Other names . . for pancakes*) 10 Infs, **Sth, Midl,** Hoecakes; (Qu. H15, *Bread made with wheat flour*) Infs **FL**11, **NC**51, **SC**7, 26, 32, (Flour) hoecake(s); (Qu. H19, *. . Biscuit*) Inf **GA**81, Hoecake—the rest of the biscuit dough that was left over after biscuits were cut out was baked as a little loaf—old-fashioned; **SC**3, Hoecake—same ingredients as biscuit but fried in grease as one large cake in a frying pan; (Qu. H29) Inf **NC**84, When biscuit dough is kept in one whole mass, or made into a pone, it's called hoecake; hoecake can be baked in oven or on top of stove; (Qu. H30, *An oblong cake cooked in deep fat*) Inf **NC**52, Hoecake—apples or jams inside and fried. **1966–67** *DARE* Tape **AL**1, We didn't have hoecake cornbread, we had biscuit; **AL**20, You know what a hoecake is? . . Why, it's just like you go to bake biscuits only you just pat it out and cook it on top of the stove on one side and then turn it over. . . You don't fry it, you just have your pan hot and let it bake like bread; **FL**41, Hoecake or cornbread is cooked on

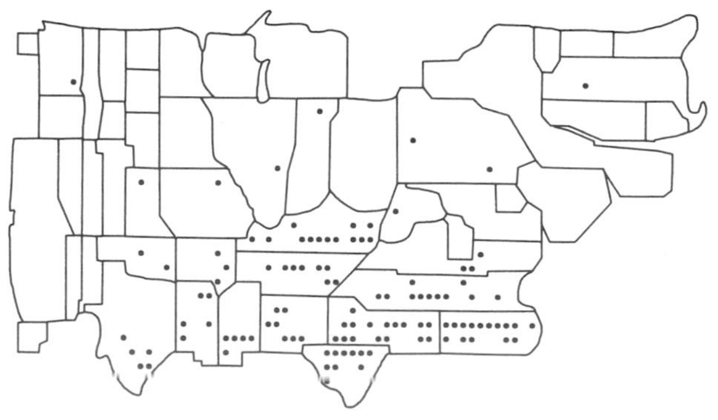

•hoecake + varr (Qq. H14, H25, H18, H20b, H15, H19, H29, H30)

top of the stove. **1972** *Atlanta Letters* **cGA,** *Hoe-cake*. . . Usually a cake of corn meal made with water and no salt; the batter is thin. . . fried on a griddle. . . well oiled or greased. It can be made of wheat flour.

hoecake turner n [**hoecake**] **esp KY** Cf **hot-cake turner**
=**cake turner.**

1969 *DARE* (Qu. F3, *When you're frying things . . you turn them over with a* ———) Infs **KY**37, 69, Hoecake turner. **1981** *Broaddus Coll.* 10 **ceKY** (as of 1958), *Hoe cake turner*—a cooking spatula.

hoe corn v phr
Fig: see quot.

1923 *DN* 5.238 **swWI,** *Hoe corn*. . . To do hard work. "You had better get down to business and hoe corn."

hoe crop See **hoed crop**

hoedag See **hodag** n[1]

hoed crop n Also *hoe crop*
See quot 1952.

1879 *Scribner's Mth.* 19.239/2 **seNY,** The fortunate owner has only to . . give it a year of ordinary cultivation taking from it . . some profitable hoed crop. **1952** Brown *NC Folkl.* 1.551, *Hoe crop*. . . A crop cultivated only with a hoe, no plow being used.—General.

ho-ee See **ho v d**

hoeg See **hog**

hoe grass n [See quot 1937]
A **muhly grass** (here: *Muhlenbergia porteri*).

1937 U.S. Forest Serv. *Range Plant Hdbk.* G82, Bush muhly . . has a variety of other local names. . . Still another name is hoe grass, arising from the fact that when it was plentiful early pioneers hoed it for horse feed. **1941** *Torreya* 41.46, *Muhlenbergia porteri*. . . Hoe grass.

hoe hand n Also rarely *hoe;* pl *hoe people* **Sth, S Midl** Cf **hoe man**
A farm laborer.

1788 (1925) Washington *Diaries* 3.406 **neVA,** Land was also sowed with Buck Wheat. . . the Hoe people were weeding. **1829** in 1910 Commons *Doc. Hist. Amer. Industrial Soc.* 1.231 **MS,** Hoe hands finished rolling logs & burning brush. **1855** Davis *Farm Bk.* 160 *(DA)* **AL,** The Hoes worked in the crab apple cut. [*DARE* Ed: from a plantation diary] **1855** in 1927 Jones *FL Plantation Rec.* 137, The hohands [sic] was able to go over 40 acors [sic] today. **1859** in 1956 Eliason *Tarheel Talk* 277 **NC,** I . . put sam and the hoe hands to hoe. **1904** in 1961 Pringle *Woman Rice Planter* 135 **SC,** [Diary:] He was a fine ploughman and his wife a good hoe hand. **1986** Pederson *LAGS Concordance* **MS,** 2 infs, Hoe hands—chop cotton; 1 inf, Hoe hands—of geese, keep weeds from cotton.

hoe handle n

1 in phrr indicating that a worker is lazy: See quots.

1923 *DN* 5.239 **swWI,** To idle, to loaf, and to talk, while supposed to be at work. "There is he, lettin' the hoe handle suck!" **1985** Ladwig *How to Talk Dirty* 23 **Ozarks,** He's always sucklin' a hoe handle . . lazy hired man.

2 See **hoe** n[1] **2.**

3 See quot. Cf **henfire**

1967 *DARE* (Qu. NN26c, *Weakened substitutes for 'hell': "What the* ———*!"*) Inf **OH**18, Hoe handle.

hoe man n Cf **hoe hand**
A farmer.

1935 Sandoz *Jules* 136 **wNE** (as of 1880–1930), A half-drunken cowboy with his palm on his gun joked of the fool hoe men that ought to be run out of the country. **1936** Adams *Cowboy Lingo* 197, The farmer, of whom the earlier cowboy had so little use, was. . . apt to be referred to by such contemptuous titles as 'churn-twister,' 'plow-chaser,' or 'fool hoeman'.

hoe one's own row See **row**

hoe out v phr **NEast** Cf **wash down**
To clean out or straighten up (a place); to do a cleaning job.

1907 *DN* 3.245 **csME,** *Hoe out*. . . Sweep out. "I'll have to hoe that room out now." Facetious. **1941** *LANE* Map 336 *(Cleans up),* 2 infs, **CT, RI,** Hoe out. **1967–69** *DARE* (Qu. E21, *Talking about a room that needs to be put in order, you might say, "I'm just going to* ——— *this room."*) Infs **NY**23, 92, Hoe it out; **CT**29, Hoe out. **1969** *DARE* Tape **MA**38, I hoed out upstairs and I got rid of quite a lot of stuff.

hoe people See **hoe hand**

hoe pone n Cf **hoecake, pone**

1967 *DARE* (Qu. H19) Inf **TN**13, Hoe pone—biscuit dough not rolled out into biscuits, just place in pan.

‡hoewood n
See quot.

1965 Gould *You Should Start* 79 **ME,** Every year we put some roses on the hoewood table, for thus Aunt Eunice came to know Aunt Helen.

hoffler n [Cf *EDD huffler* sb. 2] Cf **choker 1**
=**hooker** n[1] **2a.**

1956 Sorden–Ebert *Logger's Words* 18 **Gt Lakes,** Hoffler, In pine country a man who fastens a hook during loading operations.

hog n, v Usu |hɔg, hɒg, hɑg|; also |hag, hog|; for addit varr see quots Pronc-spp *hawg, hoeg*

A Forms.

1887 Kirkland *Zury* 57, Thin hawgs is wuth more 'n fat hawgs every time. **1890** *DN* 1.24 **cSC,** [hɔəg]. *Ibid* 72 **LA,** *Hog* . . (with the vowel [ɔ]). **1891** (1900) French *Otto* 179 **AR,** Tacklin' that hoeg. **1903** *DN* 2.292 **Cape Cod MA** (as of a1857), Before final *d, g, o* was long [ɔ] in . . *hog. Ibid* 316 **seMO,** *Hog*. . . Universally pronounced hawg [hɔg]. **1907** *DN* 3.232 **nwAR,** *Hog*. . . Universally pronounced hawg [hɔg]. **1939** *LANE* Map 110, [71 infs, **widespread, but esp eNEng,** [hɒg]; 37 infs, **scattered, but esp seNEng** [hɔg]; 30 infs, **chiefly wNEng** [hɑg]; 1 inf, **swCT** [hag].] **1942** Hall *Smoky Mt. Speech* 31 **eTN, wNC,** [Often also . . [ɔ] is diphthongized into something like [ɔo] . . beginning with the lips slightly spread and ending with extreme rounding.] *Ibid* 32, Examples: . . Before [g], [k]: August ['ɔogəst], . . hog. . . [Occasionally there are] . . [ɒ] and [ɑ] in . . *hog. Hog-wild* was once distinctly [ˌhɑg'wa·ɪld]. **1962** *PADS* 38.21 **IL,** There is one instance of /o/ in [hogs] . . recorded in Woodford County. This seems to be a Southern pronunciation. **1966** *DARE* Tape **AR**42, [FW, from **nwAL:**] You said that you all raised some *h-o-g-s*. And how did you pronounce this? [Inf:] I pronounce it [hɒəgz]. . . [FW:] Where I'd pronounce it [hɔgz]; **IL**80, They would ship the [hoʊ˜gz] out. **1976** Allen *LAUM* 3.264 **Upper MW** (as of c1950), [The majority of infs have a rounded vowel [ɔ] or [ɒ] in *hog,* but a sizeable minority show the unrounded [ɑ]. Of those infs responding [hɑg], the highest concentration is in Minnesota.] **1985** *DARE* File **NC,** With the word *hog*—as with *dog* and perhaps to a lesser extent *log*—there was in the South and South Midland, in the early decades of the 20th century, some belief that the pronunciation [hɑg] was either 'correct' or at least more refined than [hɔg]. Sometime around 1920–22 the official *Critic* of a debating society at U.N.C. criticized the pronunciation [hɔg] of a speaker who replied "It's [hɔgz] in the mountains." To this the Critic responded, "I remind the gentleman that he is in Chapel Hill."

B As noun.

1a A swine of any age, but esp an adult. Note: The sense illustrated here represents a continuation of earlier usage, according to which *hog* is the generic term for a swine, esp one raised for slaughter, and *pig* refers to the immature animal (see *OED hog* sb.[1], *pig* sb.[1]). For the majority of *DARE* Infs *pig* seems to have replaced *hog* as the generic term. **widespread, but least freq Pacific, NEast** Cf **pig**

1630 Higginson *Nevv Englands Plantation* 4, It is scarce to be beleeued how our . . Horses and Hogges doe thriue. **1765** Timberlake *Memoirs* 47 **NC,** The Indians have now a numerous breed of horses, as also hogs. **1872** Schele de Vere *Americanisms* 488, *Hog* takes almost exclusively the place of the English *swine,* which is rarely heard. **1903** *DN* 2.316 **seMO,** *Hog* . . all swine except pigs are so called. 'Pig' is only applied to sucklings, while in the North it is generic. **1907** *DN* 3.232 **nwAR,** *Hog*. . . All swine except pigs are so called. **1939** *LANE* Map 110 **NEng,** [151 responses, Hog (pen, shed, etc); this contrasts with 355 responses, pig (pen, shed, etc).] *Ibid* Map 204, The generic meaning of *hogs* [to include all members of the swine family regardless of age] is indicated as the usual one by twenty-four informants. **1941** *Ibid* Map 301, 1 inf, **ceCT** [Pig pork is] from a young animal; [hog pork is] from an old one. **1965–70** *DARE* (Qu. K60, . . *To give the pigs food*) 363 Infs, **widespread,** Slop (*or* feed, swill, etc) the hog(s); (Qu. K52, *A male pig kept for breeding*) 123 Infs, **widespread exc NEng, Pacific,** Male (*or* stock, boar, etc) hog; (Qu. K58, *A castrated pig*) 13 Infs, **esp Sth, S Midl,** Meat (*or* male, etc) hog; (Qq. M1, 13, 15, 22) 277 Infs, **widespread, but less freq**

NEast, Pacific, Hog pen (*or* lot, house, etc). [Further exx throughout *DS*] **1973** Allen *LAUM* 1.187 **Upper MW** (as of c1950), *Pig* and *hog,* reveal a clear though not sharp Northern-Midland contrast, *pig* being favored in Northern speech territory and *hog* in Midland. **1986** Pederson *LAGS Concordance* **Gulf Region,** [50 infs respond that a hog is "grown" or "full grown" or "adult"; 3 infs say that it is "older," one that it is "nine to twelve months old"; 10 infs say that it is "bigger than a pig" or "large," "larger," or "largest"; 6 infs specify that it is larger than one hundred pounds; 1 inf remarks that "they come to a hog" [=they grow up to be hogs].]

b A boar. *often euphem* Cf **top hog**

1939 *LANE* Map 206 *(Boar),* Veiled terms reported as used chiefly or exclusively by women are [*hog,* 2 infs, **cMA**]. . . The five informants [**scattered eNEng**] who offer *hog* either as their only term for the adult male . . or as a regular, noneuphemistic equivalent of *boar* . . are probably unfamiliar with hog-raising. **c1960** *Wilson Coll.* **csKY,** *Hog.* . . One of the numerous euphemisms for boar. **1965–70** *DARE* (Qu. K52, *A male pig kept for breeding*) 10 Infs, 5 **NYC,** Hog. [*DARE* Ed: 8 of 10 Infs comm type 1; none has any farm experience; it is likely that these Infs are using *hog* in the generic sense.] **1973** Allen *LAUM* 1.249 **Upper MW** (as of c1950), Nearly all the synonyms for *boar* seem to have originated as euphemisms. Several infs. frankly admitted that *boar* implies male sexuality more strongly than is desirable in conversation with women. . . hog [is used by 6 infs]. **1986** Pederson *LAGS Concordance,* 1 inf, **neMS,** Hog—euphemism; 1 inf, **cnLA,** Hog—[inf] prefers to "boar."

c A castrated male or a female swine.

1939 *LANE* Map 204 *(Hogs),* [2 infs, **cCT, seNH,** use the term *hog*] only of castrated males and of females, not of boars. **1965–70** *DARE* (Qu. K58, *A castrated pig*) Infs **CA**36, 111, **CT**22, **IA**31, **NJ**16, **PA**132, **WY**4, Hog; **IA**32, All male pigs are hogs to me; **MI**64, Just hogs. [*DARE* Ed: It is possible that these Infs are using *hog* in the generic sense.] **1986** Pederson *LAGS Concordance* **Gulf Region,** 1 inf, Hog—castrated; 1 inf, Hog—altered; 1 inf, After you castrate him he's a plain hog; 1 inf, Castrated boar—just a plain hog; 1 inf, Hog—his [=the inf's] term; 1 inf, A hog has been "worked on"; 1 inf, A hog = barrow; 1 inf, A hog—cut hog; 1 inf, Hog = sow; 1 inf, Hog—male or large female.

2 in var adj phrr referring to proverbial characteristics of hogs: See quots. Cf **hog clean, hog drunk, hog-tight** adj

1923 Cummins *Sky-high Corral* 21 **nCA,** There was feed enough—they're hog fat. **1929** Howe *Plain People* 190 **KS,** Later it [=a buffalo] became hog fat, and was finally sold to a committee preparing a barbecue. **1941** Percy *Lanterns* 29 **nwMS,** The nice boy, who had never run away and got hog-smelly, had a right to be upset. **1951** Porter *Ragged Roads* 55 **OK,** She was not hog fat; she could see her toes. *Ibid* 117, Another day came three stout ladies and two corpulent gentlemen. In plain old corn-bread language we would just call them "hog fat." **1967–68** *DARE* (Qu. X50, . . *A person who is very fat*) Infs **IL**12, **NJ**16, (Is) hog fat; (Qu. Z14b, *If a child expects to have its own way or have too much attention, you might say, "That child is ______."*) Inf **MI**68, Hog spoiled. **c1970** *Halpert Coll.* **wKY, wTN,** Hog-mean.

3a Pork—usu in phr *hog and hominy* pork and hulled corn or cornbread; also fig; see quots. **Sth, S Midl** Cf **hog meat**

1776 in 1901 Murray *Letters Murray Loyalist* 239 **Baltimore MD,** That I might enjoy in my own Cabin, eat my Hogg & Hominee without anything to make me afraid. **1816** *Thomas' MA Spy or Worcester Gaz.* (MA) 10 Jan 4/4 **VA,** If [a man] . . can be content with hog and hommony, he can live easier in Ohio. **1843** (1916) Hall *New Purchase* 397 **IN,** This was real American, United States' learning!—useful, practical stuff!—such as would enable a fellow to get his own bread and butter; or in New Purchase terms, his hog and hominy. **1856** in 1862 Colt *Went to KS* 34 **NY,** "Hog and hominy," they say, "is western fare." **1903** *DN* 2.316 **seMO,** *Hog and hominy.* . . Corn-bread and pork. (Facetious.) **1907** *DN* 3.232 **nwAR, seMO.** **1908** *DN* 3.320 **eAL, wGA,** *Hog and hominy.* . . Meat (pork) and bread. **1912** *DN* 3.578 **wIN,** *Hog and hominy.* . . Poor rations of any kind. **c1960** *Wilson Coll.* **csKY,** *Hog and hominy.* . . Food and plenty of it; originally probably literally hog-meat and hominy and nothing else. **1982** Ginns *Snowbird Gravy* 16 **nwNC** (as of c1930), We kept a hog, and she fried the meat . . we called it "hog" all the time. Anymore, they call it "pork." **1986** Pederson *LAGS Concordance* 1 inf, **neFL,** Hog and dumplings, hog and rice—old folks said; they didn't say pork.

b also *hog bacon,* Spec. bacon. Cf **hog belly, hogbook 1**

1966–70 *DARE* (Qu. H38, . . *Words for bacon*) Inf **IL**12, Hog bacon; **MO**22, Hog; **SD**5, The hog; **TX**26, Fried hog; [**CO**5, Long hog].

4 A miser, moneygrubber. **scattered, but chiefly Sth, S Midl** See Map Cf **hoggish**

1899 (1912) Green *VA Folk-Speech* 227, *Hog.* . . A mean, stingy, grasping, gluttonous, or filthy person. **1941** *LANE* Map 484 *(Miser, tightwad)* 3 infs, **csMA, nwRI,** Hog. **1954** *Harder Coll.* **cwTN,** *Hog.* . . A person who is greedy: "He's jist a plumb old hog. Grab it all." **1957** Battaglia *Resp. to PADS 20* **eMD,** *(Expressions about greedy people)* He's an awful *hog* or *greedy gut.* **1965–70** *DARE* (Qu. U36a, . . *A person who saves in a mean way or is greedy in money matters: "He's an awful ______."*) 56 Infs, **scattered, but chiefly Sth, S S Midl,** Hog; **AR**36, **FL**31, **MS**15, 31, 72, Hog (about, for, *or* over) money; (Qu. U33, *Names or nicknames for a stingy person*) Infs **IN**13, **KY**50, **VA**31, Hog; (Qu. U36b, . . *A person who saves in a mean way or is greedy in money matters: "She certainly is ______."*) Infs **CA**203, **MA**58, A hog.

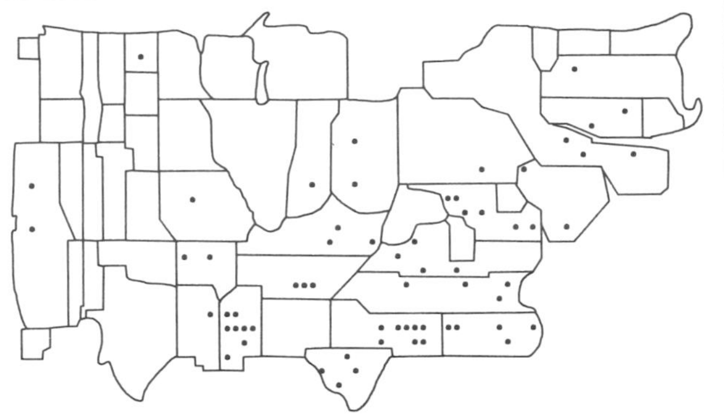

•hog B4 + varr (Qq. U36a, U33, U36b)

5 in phr *another hog off the corn:* See quot.

1927 *AmSp* 2.357 **cwWV,** *Hog off the corn, another* . . one less person to provide for. "When uncle leaves, that will be another hog off the corn."

6 also attrib: A traction engine or railway locomotive, esp a very large or powerful one. Cf **hoghead**

1888 *Walla Walla Union* (WA) 24 Nov 3/4, A gigantic "hog" engine, for use on the Starbuck hill, was taken up the road Wednesday. In the way of an iron horse it was an equine monster, with eight legs or wheels and a body about the size of an ordinary engine. The "hog" will haul nine loaded cars up the heavy Alto grade, while the ordinary road engine had a hard tussel to haul four or five. **1903** *Scientific Amer.* 88.392/2 **PA,** In anthracite drifts steam locomotives of a small and peculiar type known as "hogs" haul the trains. **1916** *DN* 4.356 [Railroad terms], *Hog.* . . A consol [=consolidation] type engine. **1927** *DN* 5.450 [Underworld jargon], *Hog engine.* . . A large, heavy freight locomotive. **1967** *DARE* Tape **ID**6, Locomotives, even before I went to work [on the railroad], they were referred to as hogs. [Inf old] **1977** Adams *Lang. Railroader* 80, *Hog:* A locomotive with an extralarge boiler. Any engine.

7 In the lumber industry: a machine that grinds waste wood into small pieces; see quots. Cf **hog fuel**

1898 *Lumber Trade Jrnl.* 1 Jan. 31 (Advt.) *(OEDS),* The big slab grinding hog for grinding up slabs, edgings and mill refuse into fuel. **1904** *DN* 2.398, *Hog.* . . A machine for grinding logs. **1920** *DN* 5.82 **NW,** *Hog.* The machine used for making "hogged Fuel." Sawmill term. **1930** *DN* 6.88 **cWV,** *Hog.* **1941** Writers' Program *Guide AL* 366, The raucous "hog" (chipper) roared as it ground knotty slabs into fuel for furnaces. **1949** Peattie *Cascades* 164 **NW,** There are leftovers in the sawmill . . ground up by a mechanical monster called the hog and mixed with sawdust for fuel uses or used as fuel alone. **1969** Sorden *Lumberjack Lingo* 56 **NEng, Gt Lakes.**

8 attrib; In facetious place names: see quots.

1906 *DN* 3.141 **nwAR,** *Hog-eye.* . . Facetious name of a hamlet or a small, remote village. [*Ibid, Hog-waller* land. . . Land containing numerous depressions or "hog wallers."] **1935** *AmSp* 10.80 **seMO,** With its hills, hollows, and swamps, southeast Missouri is well adapted to propagation of the *Podunk* idea. . . Since . . surface [lead] mining left the ground pitted with small holes which fill with water, the name *Hog Heaven* is . . used. . . In a county where no stock law exists, *Hog Wallow,* or *Hog-Eye* may be applied. **1965–70** *DARE* (Qu. C34, *Nicknames for nearby settlements*) Inf **AR**39, Hog Eye; **FL**21, **MA**23,

Hog Holler (*or* Hollow); **FL**35, Hog Island; **NC**49, Hog Town; **SC**32, Hog Waller for Walhalla; **TN**44, Hogjaw Holler; (Qu. C35, *Nicknames for the different parts of your town or city*) Inf **IL**81, Hog Ward—raised pigs on west side of town; **PA**215, Hogpen Alley—down on South Street, people used to keep hogs there; (Qu. II25) Inf **IL**80, Hog Ward—the last ward to vote out the hogs. **1982** Heat Moon *Blue Highways* 259 **ID,** I spent the night in Hog Heaven, as early settlers called Moscow, Idaho, after they saw the gustatorial excitement pigs got into snorting up camas roots.

9 A dollar. Cf **hog dollar**

1957 Battaglia *Resp. to PADS 20* **eMD,** *(Words for "dollars": "It cost a hundred ______.")* Hogs. **1960** Wentworth-Flexner *Slang* 261, *Hog*. . . A dollar; the sum of one dollar.

10 In moonshining:

a A **deadman still;** see quot. Cf **groundhog** n **6, stump still**

1969 *DARE* Tape **GA**72, The modern distiller . . he uses different things, but most usually he works in . . what we call a hog or dead man. . . That still, the beer is worked in it and also run in it and he [=the distiller] can't use corn meal or anything that is ground very fine and that kind of whiskey is sump'm that I've never made in my life and . . if I was young again and strong and able to make it I still wouldn't make it. It is made out of the siftin's of wheat. . . they cook that in this box. . . These darn things . . are made with a metal bottom, . . they're made anywhere from 5 feet to 8 feet long.

b See **groundhog** n **6.**

11 **=woodchuck.**

1967–70 *DARE* (Qu. P31, . . *Nicknames . . for the groundhog*) Infs **KY**34, **VA**79, Hog. **1968** *DARE* FW Addit **PA**163, "Groundhog"—used around here, also called "woodchuck" or "hog."

C As verb.

1 freq with *down* or *off;* also with *out:* To harvest or glean (a crop or field) and put it to immediate use by turning in animals to feed; to feed on (a crop or stubble); also vbl nouns *hogging* (*down* or *off*), ppl adj *hogged-down.* **orig Midl, now also Sth**

1859 Beecher *Plain & Pleasant Talk* 122 **cIN,** Some of the best farmers in this region *hog* their corn lands. *Hogging,* is turning the hogs in upon the ripe corn, and letting them harvest it in their own way. . . When the fatting hogs have eaten off the field . . they are turned into another, and the stock-hogs for another year, are let in to glean and root for the waste and trampled corn. **1879** U.S. Dept. Ag. *Special Rept.* 12.215 **cIN,** A farmer here recently rented an out-field to hog down. **1925** *Book of Rural Life* 9.5401, *Hogging down a cornfield*—Where hogs and corn are raised on the same farm, it is often the most economical plan to let the growing and fattening pigs harvest the corn when it matures, thereby turning it directly and without extra labor into a marketable product. **1935** Sandoz *Jules* 367 **wNE** (as of c1920), Mrs. Beckler shot a cow every time she found the gate thrown back and her neighbor's cattle hogging her corn [without her permission]. **1937** Sandoz *Slogum* 294 **NE** (as of 1900–20), When she reached the field there was no tall, green corn, only a ruin of hogged-down stalks, and to her left the hillside was dark with lazy, corn-stuffed steers. **1950** *WELS (When you turn the pigs into some corn to finish it off, you ______.)* 25 Infs, **WI,** Hog (it) down; 10 Infs, Hog it off. **c1960** *Wilson Coll.* **csKY,** *Hog down corn*. . . Allow hogs to eat the corn in the fields rather than gather it. **1965** *DARE* FW Addit **nwFL,** They used to grow peanuts just for hogging off. **1965–66** *DARE* (Qu. L27, *When you turn the pigs into a cornfield to finish it off;* total Infs questioned, 75) 14 Infs, Hog(ging) it off; 7 Infs, Hog(ging) it down; **AR**18, Hog it; **MS**58, Hog it out. **1968** *DARE* Tape **TN**26, One man . . operates a hunnert 'n' fifty acres. . . He's got it in pasture and he cultivates a lot of it . . maybe hogs off a lot of it. . . Just hog it . . you know, plant him a crop of corn, beans, somethin' like that, takes care of his hogs. When it gets time for 'em to eat, just turn 'em in, let 'em go. . . Therefore he saves the cost of gatherin' it . . and then feedin' it to 'em. He's savin' time.

2 with *in:* See quots. [Perh by ext from **hog C1**]

1914 *DN* 4.108 **KS,** *Hog*. . . To sow (grain) without plowing. "I just hogged my wheat into the stubble field." **1920** *Kansas Stockman* 1 Dec *(Ruppenthal Coll.),* Most farmers are hogging their wheat in, that is, drilling it into the stubble without even disking the ground first.

3 In the lumber industry:

a See quot.

1930 Shoemaker *1300 Words* 29 **cPA Mts** (as of c1900), *Hog*—To cut timber in a wasteful and destructive manner.

b vbl n *hogging:* See quot.

1941 Writers' Program *Guide MI* 307, Upstream mill owners, seeing the valuable timber floating unattended past their mills, often stole the logs and cut them into lumber. This practice, known as 'hogging,' precipitated fierce brawls along the Flat, Rogue, Grand, and other rivers.

4 with *around:* See quot.

1958 McCulloch *Woods Words* 86 **Pacific NW,** *Hog around*—Said of a machine which is slipping around on snow or soft ground.

5 To catch fish with the hands; hence vbl n *hogging.* Cf **handfish**

1970 *DARE* (Qu. P13, . . *Ways of fishing*) Infs **KY**86, 88, Hogging—catching by hand; **IL**144, Hogging—reach inside hollow log for hiding fish; [**IL**115, To catch flatheads and hogfish, dive down to nests in hollow logs, grasp fish and pull it out.] **1989** *DARE* File **nwAR,** *Hogging*—hoggin' catfish. You crawl along the bank (of the Buffalo River) and feel in the holes along the bank until you feel a catfish. You poke your finger in their mouth and grab them. Another fella, also from Arkansas, says he'd wear gloves; otherwise you might get finned—grab them in the wrong place and get cut with a fin.

hog age n [Cf Scots-Gael *òg* a young man] *prob arch* Cf **gosling age**

Male adolescence.

1848 in 1935 *AmSp* 10.40/2 **Nantucket MA,** *Hog age.* Between Boyhood & Manhood. **1893** Farmer-Henley *Slang* 3.328, *Hog-age*. . . (American).—The period between boyhood and manhood. **1904** *DN* 2.426 **Cape Cod MA** (as of a1857), *Hog-age*. . . The awkward, ill-mannered age of a boy. **1959** *VT Hist.* new ser 27.142, *Hog age*. . . Adolescent [sic]. . . Rare. Franklin.

hogan n [Navaho "lodge"]

Among loggers:

a See quot.

1958 McCulloch *Woods Words* 86 **Pacific NW,** *Hogan*—A bunk-house.

b in comb *hogan boys:* See quot.

1969 Sorden *Lumberjack Lingo* 56 **NEng, Gt Lakes,** *Hogan boys*—The snakes; D.T. (delerium [sic] tremens) caused by drinking barrel whisky and not eating.

hog and hominy See **hog B3a**

hog-and-panther v

See quot 1977.

1934 (1970) Wilson *Backwoods Amer.* 22 **Ozarks,** Newt said he couldn't rightfully bear to set and listen to preachin's, but one time his wife got come over with holiness and she hawg-an'-pantered [sic] him till he had to take her an' the young 'uns to meetin'. **1977** Jones *OR Folkl.* 101/2 (as of 1946), *Hog-and-panther:* to cajole or henpeck.

Hogan's alley n

1 Among loggers: see quot. Cf **hogan a**

1958 McCulloch *Woods Words* 86 **Pacific NW,** *Hogan's alley*—A wooden walkway between bunkhouses and the wash house.

2 See quot. [Prob from the name of R.F. Outcault's cartoon panels of Manhattan slum life, better known as *The Yellow Kid* (c1895–1901)]

1968–69 *DARE* (Qu. E22, *If a house is untidy and everything is upset, you might say, . . "It looks like ______."*) Infs **NJ**25, **NY**223, Hogan's alley.

Hogan's goat n Cf **Hogan's alley 2**

See quots.

1955 Funk *Heavens to Betsy* 98, When one says that a given TV show, movie, book, or whatever is "like Hogan's goat," he is with reasonable politeness saying that "it stinks terrifically." **1969** *DARE* (Qu. JJ42, *To make an error in judgment and get something quite wrong*) Inf **CA**120, It was fouled up like Hogan's goat.

hogany n

=sweet birch.

1951 *PADS* 15.10, *Betula lenta* L.—Mahogany, hogany, Mitchell County, N.C.

hog apple n

1 **=mayapple.**

1843 Torrey *Flora NY* 1.35, *Podophyllum peltatum.* May-apple. Mandrake. Hog-apple. . . Moist open woods and meadows, in rich soil. **1910** Graves *Flowering Plants* 194 **CT,** *Podophyllum peltatum*. . . Mandrake. . . Hog Apple. **1931** Clute *Common Plants* 98, The hog-apple *(Podophyllum peltatum)* a fruit which is little esteemed. **1966–69** *DARE* (Qu. S4, . . *Mayapple*) Infs **NC**6, 67, Hog apple. **1971** Krochmal *Appalachia Med. Plants* 198, *Podophyllum peltatum*—Common Names: Common mayapple, . . hog apple, . . yellowberry. **1973** Kluger *Wild Flavor* 244 **VT,** The mayapple fruit, sometimes called wild lemon, hog-apple, or "mandrake," is the only part of the mayapple plant that is edible.

2 A **hawthorn,** usu *Crataegus crus-galli.*

1933 Small *Manual SE Flora* 637, *Crataegus*. . . Hog-apples. **1939** Harris *Purslane* 103 **cNC,** She sat opposite and made him eat hacks and hog-apples from the branches she had broken. *Ibid* 89, With a few thorns from the hog-apple bush she pinned together the leaves and fashioned a colorful fall bonnet. **1968** *DARE* FW Addit **cAR,** Hog apples—a name for red haws. **1970** *DARE* (Qu. I46) Inf **TX**89, Hog apples. **1979** Little *Checklist U.S. Trees* 111, *Crataegus crus-galli*. . . *Other common names*—hog-apple, cockspur-thorn.

hog around See **hog C4**

hogas v Cf **boners, hosey**

1895 *DN* 1.389, *Hogas:* = *bonas.* [*Ibid* 384 **eMA,** *bonas*. . . "I bonas it" = "I claim it," or "I take possession of it."]

hogback n, also attrib

1 also *hog side:* Bacon. Cf **hog B3b, hog belly**

1950 *WELS (Other words for bacon)* 2 Infs, **WI,** Hogback. **1968–69** *DARE* (Qu. H38) Infs **CA**91, **PA**213, Hogback; **CA**91, Hog side.

2 Something shaped like the back of a hog; spec:

a An arched back on a horse; a horse with such a back. [Cf *OED hog-backed* a. 1, 1675] Cf **roached back**

1936 Adams *Cowboy Lingo* 87, 'Hog-backed' was a roached back, or the opposite of 'sway-backed.' **1951** Grant *Cowboy Encycl.* 73, *Hog-back*. . . a term for a horse with a roached back. **1964** Jackman–Long *OR Desert* 394 [Horse buyers' jargon], *Hogback*—opposite of sway-back.

b also *hogsback:* A sharply rising hill or ridge of land; an esker. Cf **horseback, whaleback**

1800 in 1921 VT Hist. Soc. *Proc.* 168 **cnVT,** Whats call'd the hogs back is a ridge of mountains on the north side. **1872** Tice *Over Plains* 106 **cnCO,** The "hog backs" . . never have a length of more than five or six times their width. **1889** *Century Dict.* 2851, *Hogback*. . . A low, sharply crested ridge rising upon the adjacent region. . . At the eastern base of the Rocky Mountains the conspicuously projecting upturned edges of the rocky strata are called "hogbacks," and the region where these outcrops are common the "hogback country." **1896** *Advance* 32.433/3 **NE,** The dry knobs, or hog-backs, where the prairie breaks down to the streams. **1937** [see **horseback**]. **1943** Peattie *Great Smokies* 41, A hogback vividly if inelegantly describes a type of mountain so characteristic [of the Appalachian range] that it might almost be called an appalachian. **1956** Gipson *Old Yeller* 19 **TX,** I mounted Jumper . . and rode him . . across a rocky hog-back ridge. **1968** *DARE* FW Addit **cNY,** The hogback is a rise of ground near Windsor. **1969** Sorden *Lumberjack Lingo* 56 **NEng, Gt Lakes,** *Hogsback*—A very sharp rise or ridge. **1988** *DARE* File **NEng** (as of 1960s–80), Having grown up in New England, the word *hogback* for *esker* is very familiar to me. It is the common term used.

c also *hog bristle:* A type of **stake-and-rail** fence; see quot.

1939 *LANE* Map 117 *(Rail Fence),* A *stake-and-rail* fence . . the rails rest in crotches formed by crossed stakes driven into the ground. The rails may slant from these crotches to the ground or may be placed horizontally. . . 1 inf, **nNH,** Hog-back; 1 inf, **nNH,** Hog-bristle.

d See quot. Cf **hog-rib road**

1970 *DARE* (Qu. N27b, *When unpaved roads get very rough, you call them* ______) Inf **TX**81, Hogback.

3 One who votes or runs for political office as an independent; one who has bolted from a political party; also v *hogback* to desert a political party. **eKY**

1911 *DN* 3.538 **eKY,** *Hog-back*. . . An independent voter, a bolter. Political slang, arising in Breathitt County about 1905. *Ibid, Hog-back*. . . To abandon . . "He hog-backed his party." **1940** (1978) Still *River of Earth* 162 **eKY,** "I get a vote any way can be got, buy or swap, hog-back or straddle-pole." **1978** *New Yorker* 21 Aug 79/2 **seKY,** Then, in the general election . . of 1977 [with no Democrat candidate running], when Muncy faced a challenge from an independent candidate—a "hogback" challenge, in local idiom—Muncy received three thousand nine hundred and forty-six votes. . . The hogback got two thousand two hundred and twenty-three votes.

hog bacon See **hog B3b**

hog bass n

=**smallmouth bass.**

1820 Rafinesque *Ohio R. Fishes* 36, *Etheostoma calliura*. . . It is called Minny-bass, Little-bass, Hog-bass, &c. **1935** Caine *Game Fish* 7, *Micropterus dolomieu*. . . Hog Bass . . Trout Perch.

hog bear n [See quots 1926, 1981] **chiefly S Atl**

The black bear *(Ursus americanus).*

1868 *Amer. Naturalist* 1.657 **ME,** I had at one time two tamed [black bears, *Ursus americanus*]. . . One was what is called the "Ranger" Bear. . . The other was what is called a "Hog Bear," and was shorter-legged and blacker. So I am sure the Hog Bear and Ranger are of one species. **1926** (1949) McQueen–Mizell *Hist. Okefenokee* 117 **seGA,** The small black bear, known colloquially as the "Hog Bear," . . is native to the Swamp. . . The common hog bear will catch and devour the first hog it comes in contact with, whether he has ever seen a hog before or not. **1939** FWP *Guide FL* 488 **nwFL,** Swamp lands north of Carrabelle remain one of the few habitats of the Florida black or hog bear. **1951** Teale *North with Spring* 132 **GA,** To the Georgia swampmen the bittern is the "sun-gazer"—just as the Cooper's hawk is the "striker," the black bear is "the hog bear," and cat briers are "bamboo vines." **1967–70** *DARE* (Qu. P32, . . *Wild animals*) Infs **GA**34, 91, **MS**89, Hog bear; **SC**40, Hog bear—small; black bear larger. **1975** Newell *If Nothin' Don't Happen* 96 **nwFL,** Some people call the bears we have here in Florida hog bears, but they ain't nothing really but just ordinary black bears. **1981** Harper–Presley *Okefinokee* 149, The majority opinion among the best-informed local authorities is that two species of bears live in the Okefinokee: a small brown "hog bear," and a large black "cassen-yie bear". . . On the other hand Allen Chesser and John M. Hopkins (both experienced men of the swamp) claim that only the hog bear inhabits the Okefinokee. It is true that the black bear *(Ursus americanus)* varies through two color phases—from black to nearly brown—but in both phases, white patches can be seen on the chest. The diet of the Okefinokee bear is varied: eggs from turtles and alligators, . . and an occasional hog—as the swampers who raise this domestic animal will testify.

hog-bed n

1 A depression in a pile of leaves, pine needles, etc, in which a hog sleeps out-of-doors.

1799 Smith *Acct. Travels* 36 **nOH,** I took my tomahawk and cut down all the dry rotten wood I could get, and beat it small. With it I made a bed like a goose-nest or hog-bed. **1913** Johnson *Highways St. Lawrence to VA* 238 **DE,** We'd strip off our shoes and go for the woods and crawl in the hog beds in the pine shats.

2 also *hog's bed:* A **club moss,** usu *Lycopodium clavatum* or *L. complanatum.*

1830 Rafinesque *Med. Flora* 2.240, *Lycopodium*. . . *Ground pine, Hog bed.* Many sp. *L. clavatum* and *selago* chiefly used. **1889** *Century Dict.* 2851, *Hog-bed*. . . The ground-pine, *Lycopodium complanatum.* **1892** (1974) Millspaugh *Amer. Med. Plants* 180, *Lycopodium clavatum*. . . *Com[mon] names*. . . Common club moss, ground pine, hog's bed. **1900** Lyons *Plant Names* 233, *L[ycopodium] complanatum*. . . Hogbed. **1974** (1977) Coon *Useful Plants* 181, *Lycopodium clavatum*—Club moss, . . plus such other interesting names as . . hog's bed.

3 See quots.

1981 *Broaddus Coll.* 11 **ceKY,** *Hog bed*—a building for hogs.

hog belly n Also *hog bosom* Cf **hogback 2, sow belly**

=**hog B3b.**

1905 (1909) Beach *Pardners* 55 **AK,** 'Bout to-morrer evening we'll be eating hog-bosom on Uncle Sam. **1967–68** *DARE* (Qu. H38, . . *Words for bacon*) Infs **MD**28, **MA**72, Hog belly.

hog berry n

1 A **hackberry** (here: *Celtis occidentalis*).

1908 Britton *N. Amer. Trees* 354, It [=*Celtis occidentalis*] is also known as . . Hog-berry.

2 A **blueberry 1.** Cf **hog cranberry, pigberry**

1953 Randolph–Wilson *Down in Holler* 247 **Ozarks,** The names *buck berry, hog berry,* . . and *he-huckleberry* are applied rather loosely to several species of *Vaccinium.*

hog-bill (nose) See **hognose 3**

hogbit See **-bit**

hog bite n

=**gum succory.**

1894 *Jrl. Amer. Folkl.* 7.91, *Chondrilla juncea* . . hog bite, . . West Va. **1900** Lyons *Plant Names* 97. **1959** Carleton *Index Herb. Plants* 61, *Hog bite:* Chondrilla juncea.

hog boist See **boist**

hog bone n Cf **hambone 1**

1986 Pederson *LAGS Concordance* 1 inf, **Dallas TX,** Hog bone—the knee.

hog bosom See **hog belly**

hog brake n Also *hog-pasture brake*

A **brake** n[1] (here: *Pteridium aquilinum*).

1769 in 1909 Earle *Child Life* 8 **CT,** Give it several times a Day ye following Syrup made of Comfry, Hartshorn, Red Roses, Hog-brake roots, knot-grass, petty-moral roots, sweeten ye Syrup with Melosses. **1891** *Jrl. Amer. Folkl.* 4.149 **NH,** *Pteris aquilina* was Hog Brake, probably because of the mucilaginous roots which the hogs eagerly sought for. **1974** *WI Acad. Rev.* Summer 20, Bracken fern *(Pteridium aquilinum)* . . hog brake. **1976** Bailey–Bailey *Hortus Third* 924, *Pteridium aquilinum* . . Hog-pasture Brake.

hog bristle See **hogback 2c**

hog cane n **LA**

A **cordgrass** (here: *Spartina alterniflora* or *S. cynosuroides*).

1933 *Torreya* 33.82 **LA,** *Spartina glabra* . . Hog cane. **1942** *Ibid* 42.158 **LA,** *Spartina cynosuroides* . . hog cane. **1947** *Jrl. Wildlife Management* 11.52/1 **LA,** The marshes from Cheniere au Tigre to Rollover Bayou harbored the greatest numbers [of blue and snow geese] during the winter of 1941–42, with the result that big cordgrass (*Spartina cynosuroides;* locally known as "hog-cane") . . of that region were literally laid waste. **1951** *PADS* 15.8 **LA,** *Spartina cynosuroides* . . Hog cane.

hog cheese See **hog's head cheese**

hogchoker n Also *hogchoke* [See quots 1855, 1976] **esp C and Mid Atl**

The American sole *(Trinectes maculatus).* Also called **calico B3a, coverclip, doormat, floormat 3**

1855 Smithsonian Inst. *Annual Rept. for 1854* 350 **NJ, Long Is. NY,** *The New York* Sole. . . is familiarly known at Beesley's point under the name of hog-choker, as when seized by the hogs it doubles itself up, and, filling the œsophagus, obstinately resists by the scabrous nature of its scales all effort on the part of the animal to swallow it. **1857** *Harper's New Mth. Mag.* 14.442 **NC,** The refuse fish commonly taken are sturgeon, . . hog-choke or flounder, lampreys, and common eels. **1884** Goode *Fisheries U.S.* 1.177, The nearest relative of the Sole is often called the American Sole, *Achirus lineatus,* and is known on the coast of New Jersey as the Hog-choker, Cover-clip, or Cover. **1885** Kingsley *Std. Nat. Hist.* 3.280, The nearest American relative of the sole . . *Achirus lineatus.* It is a worthless animal, as one of its popular names—hog-choker—suggests. **1954** *PADS* 21.31 **seSC,** *Hog choker.* Small fish are caught with a seine and fed to the hogs, and this tough fish chokes them. **1969** *DARE* FW Addit **ceNC,** *Hogchoker*—a type of fish. **1976** Warner *Beautiful Swimmers* 35 **eMD,** [In winter] the smaller and rough-scaled hog choker takes over as the reigning bottom flatfish. *Ibid* 223, Here was a tiny bottom flatfish with a blunt head and almost completely encircling dorsal and ventral fins. A hog choker, most likely. If there was any doubt you could try pushing him backward along the washboard. . . If the underside scales dug firmly into the grain of the wood and you couldn't budge him, you knew he was a hog choker and that's how he got his name. **1984** [see **doormat**].

hog claim n Also *hog rights* **esp S Midl**

Authorization to hunt wild hogs on a specified tract of land; entitlement to a portion of the meat from such hogs.

1859 Taliaferro *Fisher's R.* 52 **nwNC** (as of 1820s), I had a hog claim over beyant Moor's Fork. **1932** Randolph *Ozark Mt. Folks* 86, A hawg-claim was jest a piece o' paper made out like a deed, givin' th' bearer th' right t' kill so many hawgs, an' signed by th' feller whut sold th' claim. **1959** Lomax *Rainbow Sign* 124 **LA** (as of 1886) [Black], My papa had bought Mister Goody's hog claim—there were wild hogs in the bottoms there in Louisiana, and we paid three hundred dollars for Mister Goody's claim to the hogs in the bottoms joinin our place. **1966** *DARE* Tape **GA**11, We let this man that comes down here lease some of the ground—the hog rights—and he comes in and hunts hogs. . . just for sport. **1975** McDonough *Garden Sass* 67 **AR,** Each settlement had what they called "hog claims." The hogs run wild and eat acorns and roots and bugs and stuff. For two dollars you could buy into this hog claim bunch there, and that gave you the right to the meat whenever they had a hog killing.

hog clean adj phr Cf **hog C1**

Of a field: see quot.

1986 Pederson *LAGS Concordance* 1 inf, **cwLA,** Hog-clean—completely cleared of grass.

hog, close to the adj phr Cf **high on the hog**

1986 Pederson *LAGS Concordance (A tightwad)* 1 inf, **cnLA,** Live close to [the] hog—not "high on the hog."

hog corn n

A field var of **Indian corn.**

1751 (1899) MacSparran *Letter Book* 58 **sRI,** We have but 51 Bushels of good, and 5 Ditto, of Hog Corn. **1787** (1925) Washington *Diaries* 3.276 **nVA,** The other hands had just finished husking and measuring Corn— . . 30 Barrls. sound and 11 Hog Corn—7 Rotten. **1800** (1826) Maude *Niagara* 34 **nNY,** Has produced, per acre, ninety bushels of marketable shelled Corn, (maize) exclusive of inferior or Hog-Corn. **1965–70** *DARE* (Qu. I34, *If you don't have sweet corn, you can always eat young* ______) Infs **AR**17, **GA**16, **IL**94, **MD**44, **NC**79, **NJ**3, 9, **OH**80, **UT**6, **VA**9, 48, Hog corn.

hog cranberry n

1 A **crowberry 1** (here: *Empetrum nigrum*).

1894 *Jrl. Amer. Folkl.* 7.99, *Empetrum nigrum.* . . hog cranberry. Islands of Penobscot Bay, Me. **1915** (1916) Johnson *Highways New Engl.* 188 **Cape Cod MA,** I called his attention to some low vines that overran the ground, whose leafage was brightened with the sparkle of many little red berries. "Those are hog cranberries," he said. **1931** Clute *Common Plants* 98, The hog cranberry (Empetrum nigrum) [is] an inedible fruit.

2 =**bearberry 2.**

1894 *Jrl. Amer. Folkl.* 7.93, *Arctostaphylos Uva-ursi,* . . hog-cranberry, Provincetown, Mass. **1950** Gray–Fernald *Manual of Botany* 1126, *A. Uva-ursi* . . Common Bearberry. . . Hog-Cranberry. **1963** Craighead *Rocky Mt. Wildflowers* 139, *Kinnikinnick Arctostaphylos uva-ursi.* . . Hog Cranberry. **1974** (1977) Coon *Useful Plants* 133, *Arctostaphylos uva-ursi*—Bearberry . . hog-cranberry . . bear's bilberry, etc.

3 A cranberry (here: *Vaccinium oxycoccos*).

1916 *Torreya* 16.239, *Vaccinium oxycoccos* . . Hog cranberry, Matinicus Id., Me.

hog crawl n [**crawl** n[2]] **SC, GA** *obs* Cf *DJE pig crawl*

An enclosure for raising hogs—now preserved only in place names.

1733 *SC Gaz.* (Charleston) 4 Aug 3/2, 200 Acres of Land at *English Santee,* on the north side of the River, joining a large Savannah, very commodious for a Cow-pen or Hog-Crawl. **1936** Smith–Sass *Carolina Rice* 68 **SC coast** (as of c1850), The cow-minder resided at the "hog crawl," which lay just outside of the fence that surrounded the cornfields or provision-land. Its further edge sloped to a small swamp or pond which was included in its area. . . The word [=*crawl*] was in very general use in the first days of Carolina, almost interchanging with "cattle-pen." **1954** *GA Mineral News Letter* 7.38, The dividing line between Dooly and Macon counties Georgia is . . Hog Crawl Creek.

hogcut past pple, ppl adj Cf **-bit, horsethrowed**

1956 Gipson *Old Yeller* 107 **TX,** I remember bumping into the back of one old bar' hog. . . A slashing tusk caught me in the calf of my right leg. . . [Old Yeller] tried to lick my hog-cut leg. *Ibid* 110, That hog-cut leg was sure acting up. . . [Mama said,] "I've seen hog cuts before." *Ibid* 124, We didn't know you'd been hog cut.

hog dog n **esp LA** Cf **Catahoula hog dog**

A dog trained to hunt or herd wild hogs or cattle.

1929 *Sat. Eve. Post* 17 Aug 139/2 **LA,** Hog dogs are descendants of ordinary curs. **1934** Vines *Green Thicket* 65 **cnAL,** Lat's hog dog Jack was the greatest dog that ever bayed a wild hog. **1952** *Argosy* (NY) June 27 **LA,** Unable to drive the boars through heavy woods and dense underbrush, the dogs work them up to white-hot fury by snapping at their snouts and ears, then retreating quickly out of range of the slashing tusks. While one dog draws the leader toward the catch pen, the other rides herd on the stragglers. Hog dogs work the same system to lead wild cattle to the pens. **1962** *Catahoula Hog Dog* 1 **LA,** "Old Lep's" clan was, in all probability, dubbed "Hog Dog" because his was the only breed that ever mastered the fine art of rounding up the semi-domesticated hogs. **1966** *DARE* Tape **GA**3, If you've got good hog dogs. . . Most any kind of dog, if he's trained, will catch a hog. I don't say he'll hold 'im, but he'll catch 'im. . . It's best to have two or more dogs when catching wild hogs. **1967** *DARE* (Qu. J2, . . *Joking or uncomplimentary words . . for dogs*) Inf **LA**10, Hog dog.

hog dollar n **chiefly nCA** Cf **hog B9**

A silver dollar.

1966–69 *DARE* (Qu. U27, *Names for a silver dollar*) Infs **CA**136, 137, 156, 163, 169, **NC**30, Hog dollar. **1978** *NADS Letters* **San Francisco CA,** Colloquially, in 1932, I . . [heard] *hog dollar,* and made a note—Hog dollar, a silver dollar. That is, a large dollar as opposed to two halves or small change.

hog down See **hog C1**

hog-dress v phr, hence ppl adj *hog-dressed*

See quots.

1983 Becker *Fishes WI* 230, Because of their small size, most shovelnose sturgeon are smoked, although a number are "hog dressed" (entrails removed but skin left intact). **1988** *DARE* File **csWI,** A hog-dressed fish is one that's dressed. It's been eviscerated and the head left on.

hog drunk adj phr Cf **dog drunk, hog B2**

Thoroughly drunk.

1966–68 *DARE* (Qu. DD15) Infs **IN**40, **LA**28, **SC**3, Hog drunk; [**GA**72, Drunk as a hog].

hog-Dutch adj [See quot]

1930 Shoemaker *1300 Words* 29 **cPA Mts** (as of c1900), *Hog-Dutch*—"Hoch-Deutsch", of high German origin, one not of Pa. Dutch stock.

hog-ear leaf n

A **plantain** (here: *Plantago rugelii*).

1968 *DARE* (Qu. S21, . . *Weeds . . that are a trouble in gardens and fields*) Inf **OH**82, Hog-ear leaves . . or broadleaf plantain.

hog eye See **hoghead 2**

hog-eyed adj

Of a person: see quots.

1912 *DN* 3.578 **wIN,** *Hog-eyed*. . . Small-eyed. **1923** *DN* 5.210 **swMO,** *Hog eyed*. . . The facial expression resulting from looking upward and sidewise without turning the head. **1970** *DARE* (Qu. X21b, . . *Eyes . . very sharp or piercing*) Inf **NC**88, Hog-eyed—refers to a character trait—someone who can see everything because they say a hog can see the wind.

hog-eye gravy n Cf **frog-eye gravy**

=red-eye gravy.

1969 *DARE* Tape **GA**74, With those biscuits for breakfast we would eat homemade cured ham and the hog-eye gravy. Now that hog-eye gravy . . it's known so well over the South. . . The grease, the cookings from the ham after the ham is removed from the skillet, you pour water into that hot grease and that brings about the hog eye. . . Part of it's black or very dark rich red and part of it's light color and we'd sop that with the biscuits. **1986** Pederson *LAGS Concordance,* 1 inf, **eTN,** Hog-eye gravy.

hog fat See **hog B2**

hog feed n Also *hog food* *often joc* or *derog*

Vegetables or other food considered unappetizing or unfit for human consumption.

1855 Willis *Out-doors at Idlewild* 199 **NY,** This might not be hog-feed *altogether*—possibly not *all* cider-apples and colic—better have a look, at least, before turning hungry away. **1954** *Harder Coll.* **cwTN,** *Hog food*. . . Turnips. **1966–70** *DARE* (Qu. I4, . . *Vegetables . . less commonly grown*) Inf **MS**72, Hog food—collards; (Qu. I8, *When root vegetables get old and tough and are not good to eat, you say they're ______*) Inf **MI**113, Hog feed; (Qu. I25, *Names . . for cucumbers*) Inf **AL**27, Hog food [FW: Inf doesn't like them.]; **GA**3, Hog feed.

hog fence n **scattered, but less freq NEast**

A fence prob made of **hog wire;** see quots.

1965–70 *DARE* (Qu. L63, *Kinds of fences made with wire*) 66 Infs, **scattered, but less freq NEast,** Hog fence; **MS**87, Hog fence—also called net wire fence by some; **NC**87, Hog fence—closely woven at the bottom (for baby pigs), bigger mesh as you go up; 39 inches; **ND**2, Hog fence—sturdier than chicken fence, two lower wires had barbs on them. **1986** Pederson *LAGS Concordance* **Gulf Region,** 3 infs, Hog fence; 2 infs, Hog fence—different from barbwire; 1 inf, Hog fence—woven at bottom, large openings at top; 1 inf, Hog fence—very small mesh.

hog fencing See **hog wire**

hog fennel n

1 also *hog's fennel:* **=dog fennel 1.**

1900 Lyons *Plant Names* 37, *A[nthemis] Cotula*. . . Hog-fennel. **1931** Clute *Common Plants* 98, The hog-fennel is another name for the familiar dogfennel *(Anthemis cotula).* **1931** Harned *Wild Flowers Alleghanies* 591, *Dog's Camomile (Anthemis Cotula . .)*—Various appellations have been generously assigned to this common plant, such as "Dog Daisy," "Pig-sty-daisy," "Hog's Fennel," etc. **1935** (1943) Muenscher *Weeds* 451, *Anthemis Cotula*. . . Hogs fennel. **1959** Carleton *Index Herb. Plants* 61, Hog-Fennel: Anthemis cotula; Peucedanum ostruthium.

2 **=biscuit root 1.**

1925 Jepson *Manual Plants CA* 719, *Lomatium*. . . Hog-Fennel. **1937** U.S. Forest Serv. *Range Plant Hdbk.* W55, The plants [*=Lomatium* spp., *Peucedanum* spp.] are also known locally as hogfennel, . . wild-parsley, and by the generic name, *Cogswellia*. **1942** Hylander *Plant Life* 412, Hog Fennel *(Lomatium),* known as Whisk Broom Parsley in the central states, is a genus with twenty-one species native to the Pacific Coast region; they are plants with white, yellow or purple flowers, common to dry plains and hillsides. **1961** Thomas *Flora Santa Cruz* 260 **cwCA,** *Lomatium*. . . Hog Fennel.

3 A plant of the genus *Peucedanum.*

1900 Lyons *Plant Names* 283, *Peucedanum*. . . Hog-Fennel. . . *P. palustre*. . . Hog-fennel. **1937** [see **2** above]. **1959** [see **1** above].

4 **=cowbane 2.**

1950 Gray–Fernald *Manual of Botany* 1102, *Oxypolis*. . . Hog-fennel. **1970** Correll *Plants TX* 1160, *Oxypolis*. . . Hog-fennel.

hogfish n

Any of numerous fish, as:

a Any of var wrasses, but esp *Lachnolaimus maximus.* [See quot 1902]

1772 in 1924 Phillips *Notes B. Romans* 123 **wFL,** It Abounds here in fish of all kinds, . . the Hog Fish, the Croaker, the Glen Fish, not unlike the Trout in Europe, and of the same Outward Appearance and so Called here. **1882** U.S. Natl. Museum *Bulletin* 16.600, *Lachnolaemus* . . Hog-fishes . . *L. falcatus* . . Hog-fish. **1898** *Ibid* 47.1579, *Lachnolaimus maximus* . . Hogfish. **1902** Jordan–Evermann *Amer. Fishes* 434, This genus contains a single species, *L[achnolaimus] maximus,* the hogfish, capitan, or perro perro, a large, showy species. . . The name "hogfish" refers to the swine-like appearance of the head, jaws and teeth. **1939** Natl. Geogr. Soc. *Fishes* 164, The hogfish [*=Lachnolaimus maximus*] . . , sometimes called capitaine, is beautifully colored and of excellent flavor. **1946** LaMonte *N. Amer. Game Fishes* 92, *Hogfish*—*Lachnolaimus maximus* . . Names: Capitan. **1960** Amer. Fisheries Soc. *List Fishes* 33, Spotfin hogfish . . *Bodianus pulchellus* . . Spanish hogfish . . *Bodianus rufus* . . Red hogfish . . *Decodon puellaris* . . Hogfish . . *Lachnolaimus maximus.*

b A **logperch,** usu *Percina caprodes.* [See quot 1898] **scattered, but esp S Midl**

1820 Rafinesque *Ohio R. Fishes* 38, *Etheostoma caprodes* . . called almost every where Hog-fish. **1839** in 1840 *Boston Jrl. Nat. Hist.* 3.346, *Etheostoma*. . . The most common species found in the Ohio, . . called almost everywhere, Hog-Fish. **1882** U.S. Natl. Museum *Bulletin* 16.499, *P[ercina] caprodes* . . Hog-fish. **1898** *Ibid* 47.1579, From this pig-like snout has come the scientific name *caprodes.* This is a translation of the older name of "hogfish," which Rafinesque heard applied to it [*=Percina caprodes*] in his time and which is still used in the same regions. **1908** Fox *Lonesome Pine* 45 **KY,** Minnows were playing about him. A hog-fish flew for shelter under a rock, and below the ripples a two-pound bass shot like an arrow into deep water. **1965–70** *DARE* (Qu. P1, . . *Freshwater fish . . that are good to eat*) Inf **VA**43, Hogfish; (Qu. P3, *Freshwater fish that are not good to eat*) Infs **IN**58, **KY**11, 68, 93, **NC**49, **VA**1, Hogfish; (Qu. P13, . . *Ways of fishing*) Inf **IL**115, To catch flatheads and hogfish, dive down to nests in hollow logs, grasp fish and pull it out. **1983** Becker *Fishes WI* 907, *Logperch—Percina caprodes*. . . Other common names: zebra fish, . . hogfish.

c A **filefish** (here: *Alutera schoepfi*). *obs*

1873 in 1878 Smithsonian Inst. *Misc. Coll.* 14.2.15, *Ceratacanthus aurantiacus* . . hog-fish.

d A **pigfish** (here: *Orthropristis chrysopterus*). [See quot 1933] **esp Mid Atl**

1878 U.S. Natl. Museum *Proc.* 1.379 **NC,** *Orthopristis fulvomaculatus.* (Mitch.) Gill.—*Hog-fish.* Extremely common everywhere in the harbor. **1882** U.S. Natl. Museum *Bulletin* 16.551, *P[omadasys] fulvomaculatus* . . *Hog-fish*. . . Atlantic coast, from New York southward. **a1883** (1911) Bagby *VA Gentleman* 131, Another name for the nigger-knocker is hogfish, and it is by far the ugliest tenant of the Virginia waters. **1898** U.S. Natl. Museum *Bulletin* 47.1579, *Orthopristis chrysopterus* . . Hogfish. **1899** (1912) Green *VA Folk-Speech* 227, *Hog-fish*. . . A fish found to perfection in the waters of Chesapeake Bay. **1933** LA Dept. of Conserv. *Fishes* 70, *The Pigfish or Hogfish—Orthopristis chrysopterus* . . is appropriately a member of the Grunt family. . . Its "grunt" can often be heard before the fish that has been hooked is landed. **1946** LaMonte *N. Amer. Game Fishes* 66, *Pigfish—Orthopristis chrysopterus* . . Names: Piggie, . . Hogfish. **1965–70** *DARE* (Qu. P2, . . *Kinds of saltwater fish* . . *good to eat*) Infs **NC**12, 27, 78, **VA**55, Hogfish; (Qu. P4, *Saltwater fish that are not good to eat*) Inf **SC**69, Hogfish. **1969** *DARE* FW Addit **ceNC,** *Hogfish*—makes a grunting noise when caught. **1984** *DARE* File **Chesapeake Bay** [Watermen's vocab], Hogfish.

e =lookdown.

1882 U.S. Natl. Museum *Proc.* 5.595, *Selene vomer*. . . Hog-fish. **1911** U.S. Bur. Census *Fisheries 1908* 308, *Blunt-nosed shiner (Selene vomer).*—A familiar food fish found along the Atlantic coast from Florida to Cape Cod and in the Gulf of Mexico. It is known in various places as "hogfish;" . . It is from 8 to 12 inches long.

f =Irish pompano.

1882 U.S. Natl. Museum *Proc.* 5.423 **FL,** Mr. R. E. Earll . . obtained at Indian River six specimens . . of a new species of *Gerres.* They are known as the "Irish pompano" and "hog-fish."

g =pinfish.

1935 Caine *Game Fish* 55, *Salt-water Bream* . . *Lagodon rhomboides* . . Hogfish. **1946** LaMonte *N. Amer. Game Fishes* 71, *Lagodon rhomboides*. . . Names: Salt-water Bream, Pinfish, . . Hogfish.

h A **kingfish.**

1935 Caine *Game Fish* 148, *Whiting—Menticirrhus americanus*. . . Hogfish.

i The common carp *(Cyprinus carpio).*

1949 Caine *N. Amer. Sport Fish* 154, Carp. . . *Colloquial Names*. . . Hogfish.

hog flour n

1966 *DARE* FW Addit **SC,** *Hog flour*—the husks off rice, the separated chaff. They're beat up [*DARE* Ed: =pounded fine?]. Old-fashioned. Rice isn't planted here now.

hog fly n

Perh a tabanid.

1966 *DARE* (Qu. R12, . . *Kinds of flies*) Inf **AR**41, Hog fly.

hog food See **hog feed**

hog-foot oil n Cf **hog-hoof tea**

1970 *DARE* (Qu. BB50b, *Remedies for chest colds*) Inf **NC**83, Hog-foot oil; (Qu. BB50c, *Remedies for infections*) Inf **VA**69, Hog-foot oil—drippings from cooking hog feet. [Both Infs Black]

hog fuel n Also *hogged fuel, hog wood*

Wood that has been put through or is suitable for use in a **hog B7.**

1920 *DN* 5.82 **NW,** *Hogged Fuel*. . . The wood waste from sawmills chopped fine and mixed with sawdust. **1958** McCulloch *Woods Words* 86 **Pacific NW,** *Hog wood*—Pulpwood logs, to be chipped in a hog. **1968** Adams *Western Words* 150, *Hog fuel*—A logger's term for leftover pieces of wood on the ground.

hog-gallows See **gallows n 1c**

hogged-down See **hog C1**

hogged fuel See **hog fuel**

hoggee See **hoggy n**

hogger n

1 Perh a **hogfish.**

1966 *DARE* Tape **ME**22, We get most anything. Starfish, I guess we've even caught hoggers, small hoggers in the traps.

2 See **hoghead 2.**

3 See quot.

1970 *DARE* (Qu. K44, *A bony or poor-looking horse*) Inf **KY**84, Hogger—killed 'em and fed 'em to hogs—old-fashioned word.

4 See quot. Cf **bush hog n**

1970 *DARE* (Qu. L37, *A . . tool used for cutting weeds and grass*) Inf **TX**99, Hogger—attached to a tractor.

hoggie See **hoggy n 1**

hoggineer See **hoghead 2**

hogging See **hog C1, 3b, 5**

hogging down, hogging off See **hog C1**

hogging rope n Also *hogging string*

A length of rope used to hog-tie animals; a **pigging string.**

1942 Berrey–Van den Bark *Amer. Slang* 915.8, Hoggin' rope . . *a piece of rope used to tie an animal's legs together.* **1945** Thorp *Pardner* 162 **SW,** Marsh asked if she would like to run her horse against the winner for some real money. After some talk, she agreed, confident that she could win by five jumps and a hoggin' string. **1958** Latham *Meskin Hound* 62 **cTX,** "I've got her [=a wild sow], Sugar," he said. "Bring a hogging string." Sugar . . helped Jim pull one of the hog's forefeet back and tie it to the hind ones. "Can you tie a hog-knot that'll hold?" he asked. **1961** Adams *Old-Time Cowhand* 127, The short piece of cotton rope used for hogtyin' he calls a "hoggin' rope," or "piggin' string." **1980** *AZ Highways* Feb 2, [Caption:] Note the hogging rope . . under the belt of the cowboy. . . This rope is used to tie-down steers for branding or inoculation.

hoggish adj

1 also *hoggy:* Greedy; avaricious, stingy. [Cf **hog B4**] **scattered, but esp Sth, S Midl** See Map Cf **doggish 2**

1914 *DN* 4.74 **ME, nNH,** *Hoggy*. . . Hoggish. **1954** *Harder Coll.* **cwTN,** *Hoggish*. . . Greedy. "He's hoggish as they come. Don't make 'em no hoggisher." **1965–70** *DARE* (Qu. U36b, *Words and expressions used to describe a person who saves in a mean way or is greedy in money matters: "She certainly is _______."*) 46 Infs, **scattered, but esp freq Sth, S Midl,** Hoggish; **LA**8, Hoggish after money; **OK**31, Hoggy; (Qu. U36a) Infs **AR**18, **LA**28, **NY**249, **VA**1, Hoggish; **NC**85, Hoggy; (Qu. U33, . . *Nicknames for a stingy person*) Inf **OH**53, Hoggish; (Qu. U35, *Words meaning thrifty but not in a complimentary way: "She's not a bad housekeeper, but very _______."*) Inf **OH**41, Hoggish.

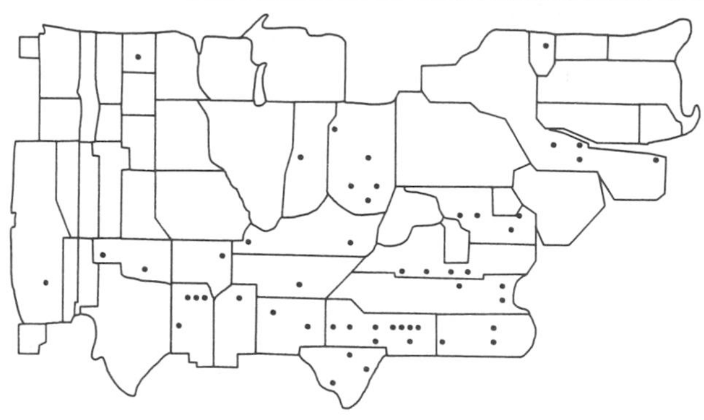

•hoggish 1 + varr (Qq. U36a, b, U33, U35)

2 Stupid.

1986 Pederson *LAGS Concordance (A person who keeps on doing things that don't make any sense)* 1 inf, **ceAR,** Hoggish—stupid; 1 inf, **cGA,** I never was hoggish.

‡hog-goblin n [Perh folk-etym for *hobgoblin*]

1968 *DARE* (Qu. EE41, *A hobgoblin that is used to threaten children and make them behave*) Inf **NY**70, Hog-goblin ['hɑg:ˌɑblən].

hog gum n [*OED* 1756 →; *DJE* a1726 →; see also quot 1908]

=poisonwood (here: *Metopium toxiferum*) or its exudate.

1876 Hobbs *Bot. Hdbk.* 50, Gum, hog . . Rhus metopium. **1900** Lyons *Plant Names* 320, *R[hus] Metopium. . . Gummy exudate,* hog gum. **1908** Rogers *Tree Book* 358, *Hog Gum. . .* The bitter, poisonous juice exudes as a gum from cracks in the thin, orange-brown bark. . . There is an old account that says: "Wild Hogs, when wounded, by natural instinct come to this tree, where by rubbing its balsam on their wounds, they are cured." **1908** Britton *N. Amer. Trees* 611, Poisonwood, . . or Hog-gum, is a monotype. . . Its sap is dangerously poisonous to the touch. **1922** Sargent *Manual Trees* 659, *Metopium toxiferum. . . Hog Gum. . .* The resinous gum obtained from incisions made in the bark is emetic, purgative, and diuretic. . . Florida, . . on the Everglade Keys, . . and on the southern keys.

‡hoggut n Cf **catgut 3, ratgut, rawgut**

Rotgut.

1967 *DARE* (Qu. DD21b, . . *Bad liquor*) Inf **MO**2, Hoggut.

hoggy n

1 also sp *hoggee, hoggie:* A boat laborer on the Erie Canal. **Upstate NY** *hist*

1939 (1962) Thompson *Body & Britches* 236 **NY,** Some of the old-timers tell you that fighting stopped after the Civil War; others say that it started then with the "hoggies", floating laborers. **1940** *Sat. Eve. Post* 10 Feb 11/1 **cNY** (as of 1836), Mott, lacking a stable hand, had hired him at regular hoggie's wages. **1955** Adams *Grandfather* 45 **Upstate NY** (as of 1830s), The hurry-up boat came foaming through the water, the hoggee whaling his tandem with an ox-quirt borrowed for the occasion.

2 See **hog huckleberry.**

hoggy adj

1 See **hoggish 1.**

‡**2** See quot. [Perh from Engl dial *hog* an animal of less than a year] Cf **hog B1a, hog age**

1986 Pederson *LAGS Concordance (Hogs—young)* 1 inf, **cnAL,** Hoggy hog ['hɔ˞ɔgɨ ˌhɔɔg]!

hoggy exclam [Cf *EDD hog* sb.[1] 4 "A young sheep of about a year old"]

1986 Pederson *LAGS Concordance (Calls to sheep)* 1 inf, **cwAR,** Hoggy hoggy hoggy.

hog ham See **hog sausage 2**

hog handle n

1920 *Thompson Coll.* **AL,** Hog handle—a pig's tail.

hog hangers n Cf *hog-gallows* (at **gallows 1c**)

1976 *PA Folklife* Spring 30, *Hog hangers,* a three-legged scaffold, often made of three fence-rails bolted together at one end, used to support carcasses during butchering.

hog haw n Also *hog's haw* [See quot 1884]

A **hawthorn** (here: *Crataegus brachyacantha*).

1884 Sargent *Forests of N. Amer.* 75 **LA, TX,** *Crataegus brachyacantha. . .* Hogs' Haw. . . A tree 9 to 12 meters in height . . borders of streams in low, very rich soil. . . The large blue-black fruit greedily eaten by hogs and other animals. **1908** Rogers *Tree Book* 317, Hog's Haw . . *(C[rataegus] brachyacantha).* **1967–68** *DARE* (Qu. I46, . . *Fruits that grow wild*) Inf **IN**30, Hog haws; (Qu. T16, *What kinds of trees are 'special' around here?*) Inf **AR**52, Hog haw.

hoghead n

1 also *hogger, hogshead;* for addit varr see quots 1945, 1977: A locomotive engineer; the driver of a **hog B6.** Cf **grunt n 2**

1907 *Sunset* 18.290/2 **West,** The motor car [running on railway tracks] proved a surprise . . the anxious gaze of the hoghead . . would see the little car revealed in the blaze of his headlight. **1914** *DN* 4.163 **NW,** *Hogshead. . .* An engineer of a locomotive. **1916** *DN* 4.356, *Hoghead. . .* A locomotive engineer. Far West. **1927** *AmSp* 2.389 [Vagabond argot], A railroader is a *rail;* an engine, a *hog;* an engineer, a *hoghead* or *hogger.* **1932** *RR Mag.* Oct 368, *Hogger, hoghead*—Locomotive engineer. **1943** Writers' Program NC *Bundle of Troubles* 139, He had three years as fireman and thirty-seven as a hoghead on passenger. **1945** Hubbard *Railroad Ave.* 347, An engineer may be called a . . *hogger, hoghead, hogmaster, hoggineer, hog jockey, hog eye, grunt, pigmauler,* etc. Some few engineers object to such designations as disrespectful, which they rarely are. . . *Hoghead* is said to have originated on the Denver & Rio Grande in 1887, being used to label a brakeman's caricature of an engineer. **1956** *AmSp* 31.151 **nwCA,** *Hogger. . .* The engineer of a logging locomotive. **1966–67** *DARE* Tape **ID**6, [FW:] You said you were a hoghead? [Inf:] Yeah. Locomotives, even before I went to work, they were referred to as hogs. . . That was just a slang term, the hogs. Naturally, the man running the hog was the head of it, so he was the hoghead. There was one saying: It took five heads to make up the train crew, engine crew. You had the hoghead, the bakehead, the swellhead, and two pinheads. The hoghead [was] . . the engine man, the bakehead was the fireman—his head down front of the fire shoveling coal. The swellhead was the conductor, who always thought he was the head man, and the two pinheads were the brakemen, who weren't supposed to know anything; **SD**5, [FW:] What did you call the engineer? [Inf:] He was the hogger. **1977** Adams *Lang. Railroader* 80, *Hog eye:* An engineer; also called . . *hog jerker. . . Hogmaster:* An engineer; also called *hog mauler.*

2 Perh a **hog sucker.**

1965 *DARE* (Qu. P1, . . *Freshwater fish . . that are good to eat*) Inf **OK**11, Hoghead.

hog-head cheese See **hog's head cheese**

hoghead chow, hoghead fry See **hog's head cheese**

hog-head hash n Also *hog-head mush* **esp SE** Cf **hash n 1**

=**headcheese 1.**

1966 *DARE* (Qu. H43, *Foods made from parts of the head and inner organs of an animal*) Infs **GA**4, **SC**11, Hog-head hash. **1986** Pederson *LAGS Concordance (Headcheese)* 2 infs, **cTN, seAL,** Hoghead hash; 3 infs, **cnGA, neMS,** Hoghead mush.

hog-head pudding n Also *hog pudding, hog's head pudding* Cf **cripple** n[2]

=**headcheese 1** or **scrapple.**

1965–70 *DARE* (Qu. H43, *Foods made from parts of the head and inner organs of an animal*) Inf **KY**71, Hog's head pudding—from the liquid and cornmeal; **MO**8, Hog's head pudding, they call it hog's head cheese now; **VA**1, Hog's head puddin'; **KY**84, Hog-head pudding; **SC**19, Hog pudding. [All Infs gs educ or less] **1966** [see **hog-head souse**]. **1986** Pederson *LAGS Concordance* 1 inf, **neTN,** Hog pudding—scrapple or cornmeal cooked in juice from headcheese.

hog-head sausage n Cf **hog's head cheese**

See quots.

1966 *DARE* (Qu. H43, *Foods made from parts of the head and inner organs of an animal*) Inf **NC**44, Hog-head sausage. **1986** Pederson *LAGS Concordance (Headcheese)* 1 inf, **cTX,** Hoghead sausage.

hog-head souse n Also *hog's head sauce, ~ souse, hog souse* **Sth, S Midl, esp Lower Missip Valley** Cf **souse**

=**headcheese 1.**

1965–70 *DARE* (Qu. H43, *Foods made from parts of the head and inner organs of an animal*) Infs **AL**15, **GA**4, **KY**84, **LA**2, **MS**79, **TX**12, Hog-head souse; **KY**41, **MO**22, Hog's head souse; **AR**17, Hog's head sauce. [8 of 9 Infs old] **1966** Dakin *Dial. Vocab. Ohio R. Valley* 2.339, A number of miscellaneous terms, none of which seems to have much currency, appear scattered throughout the [Ohio] Valley. Among them are: . . *hog's head souse, hog cheese, hoghead cheese, (hog's) head pudding.* **1971** [see **hog's head cheese**]. **1990** Pederson *LAGS Regional Matrix* 124 **Gulf Region,** [The matrix shows the term *hoghead souse* to be especially common in **AR, wLA, sMS;** it does not occur in **TN** or **nGA**].

Hog Heaven See **hog B8**

hog herd n *joc*

Personal acquaintances.

1942 Perry *Texas* 157, I rustled around among my hog herd and raised about seven hundred dollars.

hoghet See **hogshead**

hog hole n Cf **hog-tight** adj

A hole in a fence through which a hog may pass; also fig.

1897 *KS Univ. Qrly.* (ser B) 6.54, *Hog-hole. . .* a means of evasion, or escape. **1929** *Sat. Eve. Post* 17 Aug 139/3 **LA,** The pens to which the hogs are led are . . strong enough to hold the hogs. . . There is in them a hog hole through which they enter, and which is equipped with a drop trap that can be closed behind them. **1942** Whipple *Joshua* 221 **UT,** Brother Brigham had said they would stop up hog holes in the fences with those who 'had a golden god in their hearts.'

hog-hoof tea n Also *hog's hoof tea* Cf **hog-foot oil**

A remedy; see quots.

[**1945** Saxon *Gumbo Ya-Ya* 247 **LA,** Hoghoof, parched and ground into dust, dissolved in water, moved pain.] **1970** *DARE* (Qu. BB50a, . . *Favorite remedies . . for a cough*) Inf **FL**49, Hog-hoof tea with whiskey; **KY**81, Hog's hoof tea. **1970** Anderson *TX Folk Med.* 21, *Coughs.* . . Take a syrup made of hog hoof tea and sugar. *Brazos [County].* **1986** Pederson *LAGS Concordance* **Gulf Region,** 5 infs, Hog-hoof tea.

hoghopper n

A **grasshopper 1.**

1966 *DARE* (Qu. R6, . . *Grasshoppers*) Inf **MS**16, Hoghopper.

hoghorn sumac n

=**staghorn sumac.**

1970 *NC Folkl.* 18.27, A poultice made from crushed berries of "drupe" or hoghorn sumac *(Rhus typhina)* and stewel [sic] was good for cleaning out poisons.

hog house n

1a A type of shelter, usu within an enclosure, for swine; see quots. **chiefly Upper MW, N Cent; also S Midl** See Map Cf **hog lot, pig parlor**

1638 in 1862 Essex Inst. *Coll.* 4.185/1 **MA,** Granted to John Abby 5 acres nere to mr Throgmortons hoghowse. **1792** Society Useful Arts *Trans.* 1.60 **NY,** Your hog-pen is made without a floor, contiguous to a hog-house or shed, where your hogs may be dry whenever they please. **1857** IL Dept. Ag. *Trans. for 1856–57* 183, No part of a hog house should be left uncovered. **1917** *DN* 4.394 **neOH,** *Hog-house.* . . A building for housing hogs, usually larger and more permanent than a *hog-pen.* **1939** *LANE* Map 110 **widespread throughout NEng,** *Hog house* . . denoting the shelter, i.e. a shed or larger building in the enclosure. **1950** *WELS (Building where pigs are kept)* 30 Infs, **WI,** Hog house. **1964** *PADS* 42.21 **KY,** All [pigs] may live in a *pigpen* or a *hogpen,* but they sleep only in a *hoghouse.* **1965–70** *DARE* (Qu. M15, *The place outdoors where pigs are kept*) 34 Infs, **esp N Cent, Upper MW; also S Midl,** Hog house; (Qu. M22, . . *Buildings . . on farms*) 25 Infs, **esp N Cent, Upper MW; also S Midl,** Hog house; **IN**30, **MO**18, Portable hog house; (Qu. M1, . . *Special kinds of barns*) Infs **IA**26, **IN**42, **MN**4, **MO**2, **MA**16, **SD**3, Hog house.

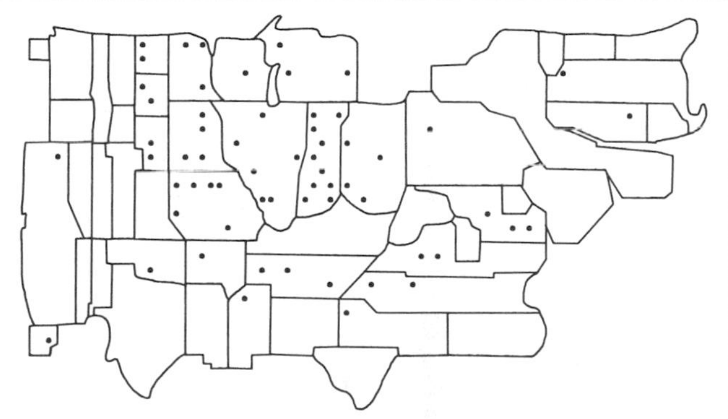

•hog house 1a + var (Qq. M15, M22, M1)

b Spec: =**farrowing house.**

1960 Criswell *Resp. to PADS 20* **Ozarks,** *Hog house*—for sows expecting to farrow. It was usually inside a hog pen or at least a hog lot.

2 See quot. Cf **hog pen 2, pig house**

1966 *DARE* (Qu. V11, . . *Joking names . . for a county or city jail*) Inf **GA**7, Hog house.

hoghset See **hogshead**

hog huckleberry n Also *hoggy* [See quot 1930] Cf **pigberry**

A **huckleberry;** see quots.

1899 *Plant World* 2.199 **PA,** *Hog Huckleberries, Hoggies* for *Gaylussacia resinosa* T. & G. **1930** Shoemaker *1300 Words* 31 **cPA Mts** (as of c1900), *Hog huckleberry*—A large green berry eaten by hogs and bears. **1948** *AmSp* 23.133 **sePA,** *Hog huckleberries.* . . Most of these nouns consist of two elements, either one of which may be English. **1968** McPhee *Pine Barrens* 43 **NJ,** Fred explained . . that "hog huckleberries" are huckleberries and "sugar huckleberries" are blueberries. **1982** *Barrick Coll.* **csPA,** *Hog huckleberry*—less attractive species of wild blueberry.

hogie See **hoagie**

hog in See **hog C2**

hog is out the pen phr Cf **horse B14**

1970 *DARE* (Qu. W24c, *Sayings to warn a man that his trouser-fly is open*) Inf **SC**70, Hog's out the pen.

hog jaw n Also *hog's jaw* [Var of *hog jowl* (at **jowl**)] **chiefly TN, KY, AR**

1950 *WELS (Other words for bacon)* 1 Inf, **WI,** Hog jaw. [FW: Inf's parents are from Kentucky.] **1954** *Harder Coll.* **cwTN,** *Hog jaw* . . a popular dish, often with blackeye peas. **c1970** *Halpert Coll.* **wKY, wTN,** Hog jaw. **1970** *DARE* (Qu. H38, *Other words for bacon*) Inf **KY**84, Hog jaws, same as jowl bacon. **1986** Pederson *LAGS Concordance (Salt pork)* 9 infs, 7 **TN,** 2 **AR,** Hog jaw(s); 2 infs, **TN, AR,** Hog's jaw; *(Bacon)* 1 inf, **TN,** Hog's jaw; *(Cuts of pork)* 1 inf, **AL,** Hog jaw; *(Happy New Year)* 1 inf, **TN,** [Eat] hog jaw and black-eyed peas [on New Year's Day].

hog-jawed adj

1965–70 *DARE* (Qu. X6, *If a person's lower jaw sticks out prominently, you say he's* ______) Infs **KS**18, **KY**94, **MO**39, **SC**55, **TX**26, Hog-jawed. [3 of 5 Infs Black]

hog jerker, hog jockey See **hoghead 2**

hog-killing n **chiefly Sth, S Midl**

1a freq attrib: The annual event of hog butchering; a party held specifically in conjunction with the butchering. Cf **fodder-pulling**

1817 in 1830 Royall *Letters AL* 36, It was hog-killing day at Wells'. **1879** *Harper's New Mth. Mag.* 59.812/1 **MD** [Black], I was vindicated, of course, and was as big as a dog at hog-killing. **a1883** (1911) Bagby *VA Gentleman* 96, They are the fixtures used at hog-killing time. **1939** FWP *Guide NJ* 651 **cwNJ,** Fried scrapple. . . Made from odd scraps of pork at winter "hog killings" and mixed with water-ground corn meal. **1942** Hurston *Dust Tracks* 36 **FL** [Black], Most people were either butchering for themselves, or off helping other folks do their butchering. . . A big pot of hasslits cooking with plenty of seasoning, lean slabs of fresh-killed pork frying for the helpers to refresh themselves after the work is done. Over and above being neighborly and giving aid, there is the food, the drinks and the fun of getting together. . . she was gone to Woodbridge . . to eat at a hog-killing. **1968** *DARE* (Qu. FF2, *What kinds of parties do people favor around here?*) Inf **NJ**18, Hog-killing party used to be held; [**SC**39, Hog-butchering—neighbors would help].

b See quot. Cf **fresh n 4**

1950 *PADS* 14.37 **cSC,** *Hog killin'.* . . Freshly butchered pork meat, including souse, sausage, brains, cracklings, etc.

2 usu *hog-killing time* (or *season, weather*); Transf: the time of year cold enough for butchering hogs, spec late fall or early winter.

1837 Wetmore *Gaz. MO* 70 **ceMO,** The acorns that fall in the timbered tracts feed and fatten the hogs in autumn, at the precise time when the "hog-killing" season is approaching. **1908** *DN* 3.321 **eAL, wGA,** *Hog-killing time* . . a term for early winter (December). The first 'cold snap' (called *hog-killing weather*) is usually taken advantage of to kill and salt down the pork. **1915** *DN* 4.184 **swVA,** *Hog killin' time.* . . A cold snap. **1937** in 1977 *Amer. Slave Suppl. 1* 1.90 **AL,** At hog killing time plenty chittlin's, an' hoglights, as well, as back bone. **1942** Hurston *Dust Tracks* 36 **FL** [Black], It was hog-killing time. . . being January and a bit cool. **1950** *PADS* 14.37 **SC,** *Hog killin'.* . . Hog killing time is a season of severe and lasting cold weather, required for the preserving of meat. **1954** *Harder Coll.* **cwTN,** *Hog killin'.* . . Time to butcher hogs. **1960** Criswell *Resp. to PADS 20* **Ozarks,** *Hog-killing time*—Ma gives this in the regular sense of the time when people normally kill hogs, when the weather is right for it. **1986** Pederson *LAGS Concordance (Frost . . freeze)* 1 inf, **nwMS,** Hog-killing time—frost signals. . . when the weather is cold.

3 usu *hog-killing time:* A lively or boisterous celebration or party.

1903 *DN* 2.316 **seMO,** *Hog-killing time.* . . A lively time; a jollification. From the old-fashioned custom of having a party in connection with the butchering of hogs. **1905** *DN* 3.83 **nwAR,** *Hog-killin' time.* . . An enjoyable time. 'We just had a hog-killin' time.' **1915** *DN* 4.184 **swVA,** *Hog-killin' time.* **1930** *Herald-Advt.* (Huntington WV) 30 Nov sec 3 6/6 **KY, WV,** A "hog-killin' time" is such a time as when the fighting is general and a merry time is being had by all. **1954** *Harder Coll.* **cwTN,** *Hog-killin'.* . . A celebration. **1960** Criswell *Resp. to PADS*

20 **Ozarks,** *Hog-killing time*—very frequent in the . . sense of a big time, a hilarious occasion. Still used. "They shore had a hog-killin' time over there last night at that shindig." **1966** *DARE* (Qu. FF17, . . *A very good or enjoyable time: "We all had a ______ last night."*) Inf **GA**3, Hog-killing time. **1969** *Hall Coll.* **eTN,** *Hog-killin' time*—Used of a party or hoedown with a lot of fun. Everybody would get together and have music and dance. Sometimes merely *hog killin'.* "That was a real hog killin', " said of a boisterous, rollickin' hoedown.

hog-killing season See **hog-killing 2**

hog-killing time See **hog-killing 2, 3**

hog-killing weather See **hog-killing 2**

hog Latin n Cf **dog Latin, pig Latin**

1 Spurious Latin; incomprehensible speech.

1810 (1912) Bell *Journey to OH* 53 **NEast,** The rattlebrain'd fellow . . pass'd us on the road, singing & screaming, advising us to go back & learn hog latin—alias German—or dutch. **1833** in 1834 Davis *Letters Downing* 19 **NY,** "You don't know nothing about Latin; the Gineral can't stomack any thing now without its got Latin in it, ever since they made a Doctor on him down there to Cambridge t'other day; but howsever," says I, "you shall give the address after all, only just let Seth stick a little Hog-latin into it here and there." **1928** Ritchie *Forty-Niners* 248 **CA,** Membership in the "Clampers"—convenient foreshortening of the hog-Latin name [=the Society of **E Clampus Vitus**]—became a patent of nobility in the chivalry of the mines.

2 A jargon produced by systematic alteration of syllables; see quots.

1866 *Galaxy* 1.638, The Fourth of July orator . . adds as many new letters as the boys in their "hog latin," which is made use of to mystify eavesdroppers. A boy asking a friend to go with him says, "Wig-ge you-ge go-ge wig-ge me-ge?" The other, replying in the negative way says, "No-ge, Ige woge." **1883** Newell *Games & Songs* 24, The most common of these [mutated forms of English] . . goes in New England by the name of "Hog Latin." It consists simply in the addition of the syllable *ery,* preceded by the sound of hard *g*. . . "Wiggery youggery goggery wiggery miggery" means only "Will you go with me!" Children sometimes use this device so perpetually that parents fear lest they may never recover the command of their native English. When it ceases to give pleasure, new dialects are devised. **1959** *VT Hist.* new ser 27.142, Hog Latin. . . A term applied to a mispronunciation of a word intended to mislead a third person. Rare. Windham.

hogleg n Also *hog's leg* [From the shape] **esp West**

A large handgun; see quots.

1920 Hunter *Trail Drivers TX* 232 (as of 1886), A "hog-leg," . . better known as a six-shooter gun. **1929** Dobie *Vaquero* 128 **swTX,** Joe plunged in, spurs, leggings, 'hog-legs,' and all. **1936** Adams *Cowboy Lingo* 166 **West,** In 1870 the most famous of all 'six-guns' made its appearance; the Colt 'Single-Action Army,' variously nicknamed 'Peacemaker,' and 'Hog-leg,' the latter term being transferred to any pistol of the frontier type. **1939** FWP *Guide MT* 414, *Hog leg*—Six-shooter in a holster (from its form). **1958** Randolph *Sticks* 57 **Ozarks,** Britt Halliday . . had the biggest hogleg in the Territory. It was a fifty-six caliber with a barrel twelve inches long, and self-cocking besides. **1968** *DARE* (Qu. P37b, *Nicknames for a shotgun*) Inf **MD**5, Hog's leg—sawed-off shotgun. **1975** Newell *If Nothin' Don't Happen* 76 **nwFL,** "Your daddy," she told us, "used to say God made guns and knives to make all men the same size, and I reckon that's true and applies to women as well as men. I know I ain't scared of nobody with that old hog-leg handy."

hog lily n

A **spatterdock** (here: *Nuphar luteum*).

1836 in 1957 Old Farmer's Almanac *Sampler* 98 **NEng,** A nosegay of buttercup, hog lily, and john's-wort. **1893** *Jrl. Amer. Folkl.* 6.136 **MA,** *Nuphar advena*. . . hog lily. Concord. **1910** Graves *Flowering Plants* 183 **CT,** *Nymphaea advena* . . *Nuphar advena* . . Yellow Pond Lily. Spatter-dock. . . Hog Lily.

hog lot n [lot] **chiefly Midl, Sth** Cf **hog house 1a, horse lot 1, 2**

An enclosure, often with a shelter, for swine.

1835 (1841) Cooper *Monikins* 2.145, It was the dirtiest, worst paved, meanest, vilest street he had ever seen, . . instead of using it as a street at all, they would fence it up at each end, and turn it into a hog-lot. **1937** *Hall Coll.* **ceTN,** *Hog lot*. . . A floored pen for fattening hogs. **1950** *WELS (The place outdoors where pigs are kept)* 4 Infs, **WI,** Hog lot. **1960** Criswell *Resp. to PADS 20* **Ozarks** *(Outdoor places for pigs) Hog lot.* Larger, fenced-in place was a hog lot; if large enough, it was a *hog-pasture.* **c1960** *Wilson Coll.* **csKY,** *Hoglot*. . . An inclosure for hogs, bigger than a hogpen (or pigpen). **1965–70** *DARE* (Qu. M15, *The place outdoors where pigs are kept*) 74 Infs, **chiefly Sth, Midl,** Hog lot; (Qu. L65) Inf **KY**43, Hog-lot fence; (Qu. M13) Infs **IL**142, **KY**49, Hog lot. **1973** Allen *LAUM* 1.188 **Upper MW** (as of c1950), Shelter and enclosure for hogs and pigs. . . hog lot [10 infs]. *Ibid* 189, Enclosure only. . . hog lot [6 infs].

hogmaster See **hoghead 2**

hog maul See **hog maw**

hog mauler See **hoghead 2**

hog maw n Also *hog maul, hog's maw* **[maw]**

The stomach of a hog prepared as food; see quots.

1935 *AmSp* 10.172 **sePA,** *Hog's maw* . . may possibly be from the German *Magen* rather than the English *maw.* **1948** *Sat. Eve. Post* 14 Aug 94/4 **sePA,** They see nothing wrong with calling something "head cheese" or "hog maw," and any outlander who can overcome a slight shuddering repugnance to taste them will wonder why he never even heard of such dishes before. **1966–70** *DARE* (Qu. H43, *Foods made from parts of the head and inner organs of an animal*) Inf **DC**12, Hog maul; **GA**13, Hog maw—stomach fried in batter; **PA**239, [hɔg mɔw] [FW: Inf's husband is from SC.]; **SC**38, Hog maw—stomach; **SC**43, Hog maw; **SC**56, Hog maw, same as chitterlings; (Qu. H45, *Dishes made with meat*) Infs **PA**143, 242, Hog maw; (Qu. H48, *Baked dishes made of potatoes cut up with meat or cheese*) Inf **PA**136, Hog maul—sausage, potatoes, pepper, celery. **1967** *DARE* FW Addit **cSC** [Black], Hog maw—cooked stomach of a hog—equivalent of tripe. **1970** *DARE* Tape **PA**242, A traditional Lancaster County Pennsylvania Dutch dish. . . we called it hog maw . . which is the stomach of a pig which is cleaned and then filled with sausage meat. Now, sausage meat is ground pork. . . Take the ground pork and take diced potatoes and maybe a little celery and a little onion. Stuff the well-cleaned stomach with this filling. Sew it up with a string. Put it in the oven and bake it.

hog mean See **hog B2**

hog meat n **Sth, S Midl** Cf **hog B3a**

Pork.

1770 in 1918 *MD Hist. Mag.* 13.74, The sooner you agree the Better, for Hogg meat I Believe will be very dear. **1834** Brackenridge *Recollections* 236 **MO,** He gave us some hogmeat and coarse hominy for supper. **1903** *DN* 2.316 **seMO,** *Hog-meat*. . . Pork. The word 'pork' is seldom used in the South. **1907** *DN* 3.232 **nwAR, seMO,** *Hog-meat*. . . Pork. **1908** *DN* 3.321 **eAL, wGA. 1916** in 1933 Fox–Strangways–Karpeles *Cecil Sharp* 150 **NC,** The only meat they ever eat—and it is very little—is pig, or hog-meat as they call it. **1937** in 1972 *Amer. Slave* 2.39 **SC** [Black], De chillun were fed at de kitchen out-house. . . they got peas, hog meat, corn bread, 'lasses, and buttermilk on Sunday. **1945** FWP *Lay My Burden Down* 129 **LA** (as of 1860s) [Black], Marse come out with great big wagons piled full of mess-poke for us to eat. That what us call hog meat. **1960** Criswell *Resp. to PADS 20* **Ozarks,** *Hog meat*—for *pork,* a more common designation earlier. Less so now. **c1960** *Wilson Coll.* **csKY,** *Hog-meat*. . . Pork rather than all other kinds of meat from hogs. **1966** *DARE* (Qu. BB34b, *What is a poultice made with?* total Infs questioned, 75) Inf **GA**1, Fat hog meat. **1968** *DARE* FW Addit **TN**17, Hog meat is condemned in the Bible. **1986** Pederson *LAGS Concordance* **Gulf Region** *(Salt pork)* 4 infs, (Piece of) hog meat; *(Smoked meat)* 1 inf, Cured hog meat.

hog millet n [See quot 1937]

Millet *(Panicum miliaceum).*

1911 in 1912 NM Ag. Exper. Sta. *Bulletin* 81.48, *Panicum millaceum*. . . *Hog Millet.* Sparingly cultivated at different places in the State and occasionally escaped. **1937** U.S. Forest Serv. *Range Plant Hdbk.* G89, Hog millet . . is an excellent soiling crop, yields fair forage, and the grain is good poultry and hog feed. **1950** Hitchcock–Chase *Manual Grasses* 691, Occasionally the seed is used for feed for hogs, hence it is sometimes known as hog millet. **1976** Bailey–Bailey *Hortus Third* 816, *Hog m[illet]*. . . Used for forage, or the seed for hog feed.

hog molly n

1 =**hog sucker. chiefly Ozarks, Missip Valley**

1877 NY Acad. Sci. *Annals Lyceum Nat. Hist.* 10.346 **GA,** *[Hypentelium nigricans]* Water basin of the Etowah and Oostanaula. . . Known as Hog-molly (Mullet), Crawl-a-bottom, and Hog Sucker. **1882** U.S. Natl. Museum *Bulletin* 16.130, *C[atostomus] nigricans* . . Hog Sucker; . . Hog Molly. **1889** *Century Dict.* 2852, *Hog-molly*. . . The hog-mullet or hog-sucker, *Hypentelium nigricans.* [*Century* Ed: Local, U.S.] **1908** Forbes-Richardson *Fishes of IL* 86, *Catostomus nigricans*. . . Hogsucker; Hogmolly; Stone-roller. **1923** *DN* 5.210 **swMO,** *Hog molly*. . . A species of fish, a kind of sucker. **1928** *Outdoor Life* 35/2 **OK,** I made a leisurely, light-hearted cast with a big "hogmolly"—I never knew where the Choctaws got the name. He was a sucker-mouthed individual with a pied or mottled skin. . . I figured he was just about what should run a big lineside bass crazy. **1933** *AmSp* 8.1.49 **Ozarks,** *Hogmolly*. . . A fish of the sucker family. The term is in common use among the Choctaws in Oklahoma. **1939** *Hall Coll.* **ceTN,** The creek was full of fish—bass, white suckers, silversides, red-horses, hog mollies. **1954** *Milwaukee Jrl.* (WI) 14 Mar sec 4 4/7 **swMO,** Jim Owen, float trip outfitter on Ozark streams for 20 years, has sent many customers a dictionary of hillbilly outdoors terms, as follows: . . Hogmolly, a sucker. **1983** Becker *Fishes WI* 678, *Northern Hog Sucker—Hypentelium nigricans* . . Other common names: hogmolly, . . pugamoo. *Ibid* 907, Logperch—*Percina caprodes* . . Other common names: zebra fish, . . hogmolly.

2 A **logperch** (here: *Percina caprodes*).

1877 NY Acad. Sci. *Annals Lyceum Nat. Hist.* 10.312 **GA,** *Percina caprodes*. . . Abundant in all the tributaries of the Etowah, Oostanaula, and Coosa Rivers. . . This is known to the fishermen as . . *Hog-molly.* The latter appellation is more usually applied to *Catostomus nigricans* [=*Hypentelium nigricans*], and is apparently a corruption of "Hog-mullet." **1882** U.S. Natl. Museum *Bulletin* 16.499, *P[ercina] caprodes*. . . Hog-molly. **1883** U.S. Natl. Museum *Bulletin* 27.466, *Percina caprodes*. . . *Hog Molly; Hog-fish.* Great Lake region; Mississippi Valley southward to Texas; Eastern United States south at least to Potomac River. **1940** *AmSp* 15.52 **sAppalachians, Ozarks,** I *disgust* hawg-mollies an' mounting [=mountain] oysters. **1967-70** *DARE* (Qu. P1, . . *Freshwater fish . . that are good to eat*) Inf **KY**34, Hog mollies; (Qu. P3, *Freshwater fish that are not good to eat*) Infs **MO**37, **KY**39, 82, Hog molly. **1983** [see **hog molly 1**].

3 See quot. Cf **fry 4**

c1960 *Wilson Coll.* **csKY,** *Lamb fries*. . . Testicles of castrated animals served as food. Also called *hog mollies.*

hogmouths n

=**butter-and-eggs 1.**

1896 *DN* 1.418 **ceNY,** *Hogmouths:* toad-flax, butter and eggs *(linaria vulgaris).*

hog mullet n

=**hog sucker.**

1889 *Century Dict.* 2852, *Hog-mullet*. . . The hog-sucker, *Hypentelium nigricans.* **1983** Becker *Fishes WI* 678, *Northern Hog Sucker—Hypentelium nigricans*. . . Other common names: . . hog mullet, . . pugamoo.

hognose n, hence adj *hog-nosed*

1 See **hognose snake.**

2 See **hognose skunk.**

3 as *hog nose;* also *hog-bill (nose), hog rooter:* A human nose seen as porcine; see quots. Cf **bill** n^1 **2, rooter**

1942 Hurston *Dust Tracks* 143 **FL** [Black], An average Southern child, white or black, is raised on simile and invective. They know how to call names. It is an everyday affair to hear somebody called a mullet-headed, mule-eared, wall-eyed, hog-nosed . . so-and-so! **1954** *Harder Coll.* **cwTN,** *Hog bill*. . . Nose. **1966-70** *DARE* (Qu. X14, *Joking words for the nose*) Inf **VA**2, Hog bill; (Qu. X15, . . *Different kinds of noses, according to shape or size*) Infs **CA**184, **TX**26, Hog nose; **NC**41, Hog-bill nose; **SC**3, (Hog) rooter—an especially long nose.

hognose bat n Also *hog-nosed bat*

The long-tongued bat *(Choeronycteris mexicana).*

1952 Burt *Field Guide Mammals* 14, *Hognose Bat*. . . This bat has a *long, slender nose* with a triangular *flap* of skin projecting upward from the tip. **1957** Blair et al. *Vertebrates U.S.* 643, Hog-nosed bat. . . Color dark brown. . . southern edge of Arizona and California. Occurring in buildings.

hog-nosed See **hognose**

hog-nosed adder n Cf **adder** n **1**

=**hognose snake.**

1897 *Oölogist* 14.vi, *Eggs*. . . Can furnish sets of starred species. . . Crocodile. . . Hog-nosed Adder. . . Emeu. **1966-70** *DARE* (Qu. P25, . . *Kinds of snakes*) Infs **IL**132, **ND**5, Hog-nosed adder.

hog-nosed bat See **hognose bat**

hog-nosed skunk See **hognose skunk**

hog-nosed snake See **hognose snake**

hog-nosed water dog n

A **water dog** (here: *Necturus beyeri*).

1955 Carr-Goin *Guide Reptiles* 160 **FL,** *Necturus beyeri*. . . Hog-nosed Waterdog. . . A large, brownish salamander. . . Head widest in front of the gills, tapering gently to the angle of the jaws, then more rapidly to the truncate snout. . . The eastern Gulf coastal region. . . Sand-bottomed streams.

hognose skunk n Also *hognose, hog-nosed skunk* [See quot 1960]

A **skunk** (*Conepatus mesoleucus* or *C. leuconotus*) with a single broad white band on the back and a long snout, native to the southwestern US. Also called **rooter skunk, white-backed skunk**

1918 Nelson *Wild Animals N. Amer.* 584 *(DA),* The persistence with which the Hog-nosed Skunks hunt insects renders them a valuable aid to farmers. **1935** Pratt *Manual Vertebrate Animals* 283, Hog-nose skunk. . . Central and southern Texas to Arizona. **1947** Cahalane *Mammals* 217, Naturalists still have much to learn about the hog-nose, but many of its habits seem to be like those of its striped cousin. **1949** *Pacific Discovery* Jan-Feb 11/2, Hog-nosed skunks, in their search for grubs, plowed up the riverbottoms every night. **1960** Natl. Geogr. Soc. *Wild Animals N. Amer.* 204 **SW,** Hog-nosed skunk. . . has a long flexible muzzle similar to the snout of a hog. It uses this to root for insects, hence the name "rooter skunk." . . long, heavy front claws make this squat and sluggish creature an expert digger—hence another label "badger skunk." **1980** Whitaker *Audubon Field Guide Mammals* 588, Although primarily nocturnal like other skunks, in winter the Hog-nosed Skunk may forage by day. . . The Eastern Hog-nosed Skunk *(Conepatus leuconotus)* found in extreme southern Texas is closely related and . . is sometimes considered a subspecies.

hognose snake n Also *hognose, hog-nosed snake*

A thick-bodied snake (*Heterodon* spp) with a turned-up snout. For other names see **adder** n **1, black adder, black viper, blowing adder, blowing viper, blow snake, buckwheat-nose, deaf adder 1, death adder, flatheaded adder, hissing snake, hog-nosed adder, hog snake, poison viper, puff adder, sand viper, spreadhead, spreading adder, spreading viper, viper**

1743 (1754) Catesby *Nat. Hist. Carolina* 2.56 **NC, SC,** *Anguis Capite Viperino.* The Hog-nose Snake . . [has] the Nose turning up like that of a Hog, his whole Visage being very ugly. **1842** DeKay *Zool. NY* 3.51, *The Hog-Nosed Snake. Heterodon platyrhinos*. . . This well known species has a venomous aspect. . . It is also called . . *Hog-nose*. . . It is rather common in the southern parts of this State. **1888** *Pop. Sci. Mth.* 33.660 **IL,** The blow-snake of Illinois is variously known in other localities as hog-nose, flat-head, viper and puff-adder. **1930** *Copeia* 2.30, *Heterodon contortrix*. . . Hog-nose. . . *Heterodon nasicus*. . . Hog-nose. **1949** *Scientific Mth.* 68.57/2, Since the hog-nosed snake is fairly common in sandy locations, where it preys upon toads, it is not a difficult matter to check on its bad reputation. **1965-70** *DARE* (Qu. P25, . . *Kinds of snakes*) Infs **IA**45, **NE**1, **OH**103, **TN**11, 22, 65, **TX**14, 52, Hognose snake; **LA**34, **VA**47, Hog-nosed snake. **1969** *DARE* FW Addit **ceNC,** Hognose snake. Type of snake common on Hatteras Island. Collected while on walk on the nature trail.

hognose sucker n

=**hog sucker.**

1983 Becker *Fishes WI* 678, *Northern Hog Sucker—Hypentelium nigricans*. . . Other common names: . . hognose sucker, . . pugamoo.

hognut n

1 also *hognut hickory:* A **pignut** (*Carya* spp), esp *Carya glabra.*

1810 Michaux *Histoire des Arbres* 1.21, J[uglans] porcina. . . *Pig nut hickery* . . , dénomination la plus générale dans tous les États-Unis. *Hog nut hickery* . . , plus usitée dans quelques cantons de la Pensylvanie. [=*Juglans porcina*. . . *Pig nut hickery* . . , the most common term in all of the United States. *Hog nut hickery* . . , used more in some counties of Pennsylvania.] **1814** Bigelow *Florula Bostoniensis* 229 **MA,** *Juglans glabra. Muhl.* Pig nut. Hog nut. **1832** Browne *Sylva* 182 **PA,** This tree is generally known in the United States by the name of *Pignut* or *Hognut Hickory.* **1941** *LANE* Map 277, Hicoria glabra (Carya porcina). . . 1 inf, **neMA,** [hɔ·gnʌt]. **1968** *DARE* (Qu. I43, *What kinds of nuts grow* *wild around here?*) Inf **LA**33, Hognuts—these are like pecan nuts; **PA**150, Hognuts. **1979** Little *Checklist U.S. Trees* 76, *Carya tomentosa. . . Mockernut hickory. . . Other common names* . . hognut. **1984** in 1986 *Barrick Coll.* **csPA,** *Hog nuts*—small hickory nuts from smooth-bark tree; see *pig nuts.*

2 =hog peanut 1.

1843 Torrey *Flora NY* 1.164, *Amphicarpæa monica. . .* Common Hog-nut. . . Woods and thickets; common. August–September. In places where this plant abounds, the hogs often root up the ground to obtain the subterraneous nuts.

3 =peanut.

1972 *Atlanta Letters* **GA,** The peanut—Goobers, ground peas, hog nuts.

hognut hickory See **hognut 1**

hogo n[1] Also *hogoo* [Engl, IrEngl dial < Fr *haut goût* [ˌo'gu] a strong aroma or taste] Cf **fogo**

See quots.

1806 (1970) Webster *Compendious Dict.* 144, *Hogo* or *hogoo. . .* A mess of high relish; a stink. **1895** *DN* 1.389 **NH,** *Hogo* . . a strong scent of any kind. **1927** *AmSp* 3.137 **ME coast,** "What is this awful hogo?" would be asked when a bad smell was detected.

hogo n[2] [*EDD ho-go* sb.] Cf **hull-gull**

See quots.

1955 *PADS* 23.20 **cwTN,** *Hogo. . .* A marble game; prob. var. of *holly-golly.* **1973** Ferretti *Marble Book* 114, In *ho-go,* a player holds up a hand, presumably with marbles inside, and asks "Ho-Go?" The other player has to guess how many—if any—this player has. If he guesses correctly, he gets what is in the hand. If he fails, he pays the difference between his guess and the amount held. Also called *handy-dandy.*

hog off See **hog C1**

hog oil n

The rendered fat of hogs; see quots.

1968 *DARE* Tape **GA**22, They'd fatten their hogs on them peanuts and they'd cook out the lard, cook out the fat at least; it wouldn't be lard, it'd be just a little heavier than this cookin' oil that you buy. . . They didn't call it lard, they called it hog oil. **1968** *DARE* FW Addit **GA**22, The Lee family of Billy's Island [in Okefenokee Swamp] always called lard "hog oil." Old-fashioned. **1986** Pederson *LAGS Concordance (Oil)* 1 inf, **seAR,** Hog oil.

hog onion n

1 A **blue dicks** (here: *Brodiaea pulchella*). [From the edible bulbs]

1894 *Jrl. Amer. Folkl.* 7.101 **CA,** *Brodiæa capitata* . . hog onion, Spanish lily. Santa Barbara Co. **1897** Parsons *Wild Flowers CA* 262, *Brodiæa capitata. . .* "Cluster lily," "wild hyacinth," and "hog-onion." **1915** (1926) Armstrong–Thornber *Western Wild Flowers* 16, *Blue Dicks. . .* There are several other names, such as Cluster Lily and Hog-onion.

2 =royal fern.

1959 Carleton *Index Herb. Plants* 61, *Hog-onion:* Osmunda regalis.

hogoo See **hogo** n[1]

hog out See **hog C1**

hog parsley n [Prob var of **pursley**] Cf **pigweed**

A **purslane** such as *Portulaca oleracea,* or similar plant.

1966–69 *DARE* (Qu. S21, . . *Weeds . . that are a trouble in gardens and fields*) Infs **AR**24, **MO**19, **PA**136, Hog parsley. **1982** *Barrick Coll.* **csPA,** *Hog parsley*—purslane? **1989** *DARE* File **PA,** Purslane *(Portulaca oleracea)* is commonly called *hog parsley* in Cumberland and Perry counties.

hog-pasture brake See **hog brake**

hog path n Cf **horse road**

A path worn by hogs; by ext, any small or unimportant road.

1881 Buel *Border Outlaws* 203 **MN,** [He] then declared his knowledge of every road and hog path. **1911** Saunders *Col. Todhunter* 272 **MO,** How far is it from town before you come to that hog-path, Abe? **1966–70** *DARE* (Qu. N29, . . *A less important road running back from a main road*) Inf **TN**53, Hog path; (Qu. N31, *A place in a road where animals regularly go across*) Inf **GA**28, Hog path.

hog peanut n

1 A low perennial plant *(Amphicarpaea bracteata)* of the pea family. [See quot 1961] Also called **goober** n[1] **2, hognut 2, licorice, milk peanut, peavine, wild peanut**

1848 Gray *Manual of Botany* 96, *Amphicarpæa. . .* Hog Pea-nut. **1885** *Outing* 7.180/1 **MA,** A beautifully slender twining vine, bearing the euphonious title of hog-peanut. **1901** Mohr *Plant Life AL* 578, *Falcata comosa. . .* Hog peanut. **1917** Kephart *Camping & Woodcraft* 2.379, *Peanut, Hog.* Wild peanut. *Falcata comosa (Glycine comosa).* New Brunsw. to Fla., west to Lake Superior, Neb., La. **1941** Walker *Lookout* 58 **TN,** The hog or wild peanut . . produces two kinds of fruit,—a pod on the vine holding three or four freckled faced beans while on runner-like stems at the ground are produced very tasty nuts greatly enjoyed by hogs as well as by human beings. **1961** Smith *MI Wildflowers* 209, *Hog-peanut. . .* The underground seeds are said to be good to eat and to have a flavor somewhat like that of raw peanuts. They are . . easily found by hogs—hence the name. **1976** Bailey–Bailey *Hortus Third* 70, *Amphicarpaea. . .* Hog peanut.

2 =peanut.

1968 *DARE* (Qu. I42, . . *Peanuts*) Inf **NJ**46, Some people call some kinds hog peanuts—they don't have 'em around here.

3 A **groundnut B1** (here: *Apios americana*).

1972 Brown *Wildflowers LA* 73, *Hog Peanut. Apios americana. . .* A perennial plant with tuberous rhizomes. . . Fruit a flat, linear pod 2 to 5 inches long.

hogpen n

1 A dirty or disorderly place. [Transf from *hogpen* an enclosure for swine] **chiefly Sth, S Midl** *esp freq among Black speakers* Cf **hog's nest**

[**1942** Hurston *Dust Tracks* 130 **FL** [Black], Dat gal don't do a living thing round dis house. . . Den I has to scuffle up dem stairs and do round, cause effen I didn't, dis here place would be like a hawg-pen.] **c1960** *Wilson Coll.* **csKY,** *Hogpen*—said of a very dirty room or premises. **1965–70** *DARE* (Qu. E22, *If a house is untidy and everything is upset, you might say, "It's a ______!"*) 31 Infs, **chiefly Sth, S Midl,** Hogpen. [9 of 31 Infs Black]

2 See quot. [Prob infl by *pen* abbr for *penitentiary*] Cf **hog house 2, pigpen**

1970 *DARE* (Qu. V11, . . *Joking names . . for a county or city jail*) Inf **NC**85, Hogpen.

Hogpen Alley See **hog B8**

hogpen chamber n Cf **barn chamber, chamber B2**

1949 *McDavid Coll.* **cnNY,** Hog pen chamber ['tʃæmbɚ] = loft.

‡hogpen up v phr

?To stack or to secure in a stack; see quot.

1967 *DARE* Tape **TX**37, When the pulpwood first started here you cut it with . . a crosscut saw . . cut in five-foot lengths. And back then you busted it up . . like bustin' rails an' ricked it up an' hogpenned it up for it to dry 'fore they hauled it.

hog perch n

A **logperch** (here: *Percina caprodes*).

1905 U.S. Bur. Fisheries *Rept. for 1904* 600 **MI,** I captured . . a small perch *(Perca flavescens),* [and] a related form sometimes known as log-perch or hog-perch *(Percina caprodes).* **1911** *Century Dict. Suppl., Hog-perch. . . Percina caprodes,* a percoid fresh-water fish found in the Great Lakes and southward.

hog physic n Also *hog's physic* [See quot 1873]

=cardinal flower.

c1873 in 1976 Miller *Shaker Herbs* 147, *Lobelia cardinalis.* Hog Physic. . . Said to be useful in removing worms from the bowels. **1894** Amer. Folkl. Soc. *Memoirs* 7.93 **MA,** *Lobelia cardinalis,* L., hog physic, Plymouth Co. **1940** Clute *Amer. Plant Names* 106, *L. cardinalis. Cardinal Flower. . .* Hog's physic. **1959** Carleton *Index Herb. Plants* 61, *Hog's physic:* Lobelia cardinalis.

hog pig n [*EDD* (at *hog* sb.[1] (13))] Cf **hog B1b**

1930 Shoemaker *1300 Words* 27 **cPA Mts** (as of c1900), *Hog pig*—A barrow hog

hog pine n

Perh a **loblolly pine.**

1967 *DARE* (Qu. T17, . . *Kinds of pine trees*) Inf **SC**43, Hog pine—sweet smelling—same as sweet pine—not good for lumber.

hog plum n

1 A shrub or tree *(Ximenia americana)* or its fruit, native to Florida. Also called **false sandalwood, pig plum, tallownut, tallowwood, wild lime, wild olive**

1877 Bartlett *Americanisms* 289 **sFL,** *Hog-Plum*. . . A tall shrub of South Florida. It bears a drupe the size of a plum, which is yellow and pleasant to the taste. **1889** (1971) Farmer *Americanisms* 300, *Hog Plum (Ximenia americana).*—A tall growing bush found in South Florida, the fruit of which is in size and shape like a plum, and pleasant to the palate. **1908** Britton *N. Amer. Trees* 377, Hog plum. . . The fruit is edible, and is a favorite food of many birds. **1933** Rawlings *South Moon* 140 **nFL,** The grapes grew singly, as big as hog plums. **1970** *DARE* (Qu. I46) Inf **FL**49, Hog plums. **1979** Little *Checklist U.S. Trees* 295, Hog-plum. . . *Range*—N. to s. Fla. incl. Fla. Keys, mostly near shores.

2 Any of several **wild plums** (*Prunus* spp); see quots.

1884 Sargent *Forests of N. Amer.* 66, *Prunus angustifolia*. . . Chickasaw Plum. Hog Plum. **1893** *Jrl. Amer. Folkl.* 6.140 **TX,** *Prunus Americana,* hog plum. **1896** *Ibid* 9.187 **swMO,** *Prunus hortulana,* . . hog plum. **1897** Sudworth *Arborescent Flora* 237, *Prunus americana*. . . Hog Plum (Colo., Mo.) . . *Prunus angustifolia*. . . Hog Plum (Miss., Tex.) *Ibid* 238, *Prunus umbellata*. . . Hog Plum (Fla.) **1907** Porter *Heart of West* 54 **ID,** I was on my way over to take her a basket of wild hog-plums. **1951** *PADS* 15.33 **TX,** *Prunus minutiflora*. . . Hog . . plum. **1953** Greene–Blomquist *Flowers South* 52, *Hog-Plum . . (Prunus umbellata)*. . . Its reddish to purple fruits are a favorite food for birds. **1966–68** *DARE* (Qu. I46, . . *Fruits that grow wild*) Infs **GA**6, 12, **NC**36, **SC**7, Hog plum(s). **1973** Stephens *Woody Plants* 298, *Prunus rivularis*. . . Hog plum, creek plum. . . *Range:* Kansas, Oklahoma, Texas.

3 =**poisonwood** (here: *Metopium toxiferum*).

1884 Sargent *Forests of N. Amer.* 54 **FL,** *Rhus Metopium*. . . Poison Wood. . . Bum Wood. Hog Plum. **1889** *Century Dict.* 2852, *Hog-plum* . . the poison-wood or coral-sumac of tropical Florida. **1897** Sudworth *Arborescent Flora* 274, *Rhus metopium*. . . *Common Names*. . . Hog Plum.

4 A **ground cherry** (here: *Physalis virginiana*).

1937 *Torreya* 37.100, *Physalis virginiana*. . . Hog plum . . Niagara Falls, N.Y. **1940** Clute *Amer. Plant Names* 266, *Physalis Virginiana.* Hog plum.

5 A **nakedwood** (here: *Colubrina texensis*).

1938 Van Dersal *Native Woody Plants* 106, *Colubrina texensis*. . . *Hog-plum*. . . Fruit: Drupelike capsule, available in June. **1949** *Chi. Tribune* 20 Feb. 30/3 *(DA),* Cedar and mesquite alone are costing Texas ranchers 115 million dollars a year. Add the sage and cactus, . . catclaw, hog plum . . and prickly pear and the toll is terrific. **1960** Vines *Trees SW* 695, *Texas Colubrina*. . . A vernacular name is Hog-plum. The dark-brown or black drupes are persistent. **1967** *DARE* (Qu. I46) Inf **TX**40, Hog plum.

hog potato n

1 also *hog's-potato:* A **death camas:** usu *Zigadenus venenosus,* but also *Z. fremontii.*

1897 Parsons *Wild Flowers CA* 8, It [=*Zigadenus fremontii*] is fatal to horses, but hogs eat it with impunity, from which it is also known as "hogs' potato." **1900** Lyons *Plant Names* 404, *Z[igadenus] venenosus* . . Hog Potato. **1911** Jepson *Flora CA* 106, *Z[igadenus] venenosus* . . Death Camas. . . Very poisonous, especially to sheep. Hogs seem immune, whence "Hog's Potato." **1915** (1926) Armstrong–Thornber *Western Wild Flowers* 8. **1934** Haskin *Wild Flowers Pacific Coast* 35, As a stock poisoning plant death camas [=*Zigadenus venenosus*] is one of the worst. . . Hogs, on the other hand, are not affected by the poison of the plant, and even appear to relish and thrive on it, which has given it among its common names that of "hog potato."

2 =**man-of-the-earth.** Cf **Indian potato**

1900 Lyons *Plant Names* 203, *I[pomaea] pandurata*. . . Man-of-the-earth, Hog Potato. . . *Tubers* feebly cathartic.

3 =**feather bells.**

1940 Clute *Amer. Plant Names* 14, *S[tenanthium] gramineum*. . . Hog-potato. **1959** Carleton *Index Herb. Plants* 61, *Hog-potato:* Stenanthium gramineum.

4 A rush-pea (here: *Hoffmannseggia glauca*).

1970 Kirk *Wild Edible Plants W. U.S.* 255, *Hoffmannseggia densiflora*. . . *Camote-de-Raton, Hog Potato, Rushpea*. . . The tuberous enlargements of the roots may be eaten after roasting or boiling. . . Hog Potato is found in open ground from Kansas to Arizona, Colorado, and southern California.

hog pudding n

1 See **hog-head pudding.**

2 See quot. [Cf *EDD hog's pudding* (at *hog* sb.[1] (15))]

1986 Pederson *LAGS Concordance (Liver pudding)* 1 inf, **neTN,** Hog pudding—liver sausage, cooked, sliced and fried; 1 inf, **swMS,** Hog pudding—liver sausage; 1 inf, **cTN,** Hog pudding or blood pudding—made from hog blood.

hog ranch n **West**

A brothel.

1885 *Santa Fe Weekly New Mexican & Live Stock Jrl.* (NM) 27 Aug 2/4, The Priest girls, who live at what is known as "the hog ranch" in the southwest part of the city, were robbed and otherwise badly treated Saturday night. **1937** Sandoz *Slogum* 57 **NE** (as of 1900–20), When she found the girl in bed with Hab she sent her packing, and made the rounds of the old hog ranches hanging like ticks to the army posts and the Indian Agencies. *Ibid* 115, The place was getting to be just like any other damned dirty hog ranch, with the bunks full o' pants rabbits. **1961** Adams *Old-Time Cowhand* 330, There were many places in the old Northwest, too, called "hog ranches." Them were places of loose women, but they sold whisky too. **1965** Bancroft *Racy Madams* 24 **Denver CO** (as of 1890s), An older established madam . . had operated a house at 1715 Market Street for nine years and then for five years in the mid '90s was involved in a "hog ranch" out of town. **1967** *DARE* (Qu. DD30) Inf **CO**32, Hog ranch. **1978** *NADS Letters* **Denver CO** (as of 1854–60), In the West, in early days, a whorehouse was called a hog ranch. **1984** Smith *SW Vocab.* 126, *Hog Ranch:* A bordello. A shack or log structure on the edge of an army post where a soldier could buy a drink of rot-gut whiskey or a turn with one of the tough females whose loose morals and slatternly appearance gave the place its name.

hog-rassle See **hog-wrestle**

hogreeve n **chiefly NEng** *old-fash* Cf **fence viewer, field driver**

A town official orig responsible for impounding stray hogs but now having largely titular responsibilities.

1636 in 1881 Boston Registry Dept. *Records* 2.13 **MA,** At this meeting Richard Fairebanck is chosen for our Hog Reeve. **1839** *Daily Picayune* (New Orleans LA) 5 Apr 2/4 **New Orleans LA,** It is with no slight satisfaction we announce the important intelligence that Eben Carpenter has allowed himself to be put in nomination for *Hog-Reeve.* **1888** Bryce *Amer. Commonwealth* 2.228 **NEng,** [There are] divers minor officers, such as hog reeves (now usually called field drivers). **1907** *DN* 3.190 **seNH,** *Hog-reeve*. . . An official (usually the most recently married man) chosen at the annual town meeting, whose duty is to impound stray hogs. "It's a great many years since a hog-reeve has had to put a hog in the pound." **1921** in 1969 Frost *Poetry* 207 **NH,** They set a lot (now don't they?) by a record / Of Arthur Amy's having once been up / For Hog Reeve in March Meeting here in Warren. **1944** Holton *Yankees Were Like This* 34 **eMA** (as of 1880s), He had been elected hog-reeve by a large majority, or perhaps it was fence-viewer. **1988** *DARE* File **cwMA,** *Hog reeve* is still an elected office in some New England country towns. Where it survives, the title is now merely nominal and is sometimes awarded jokingly.

hog-rib road n Cf **hogback 2d**

1969 *DARE* (Qu. N27b, *When unpaved roads get very rough, you call them* ______) Inf **GA**77, Hog-rib road.

hog rifle n

1 also *hog rifle gun:* A long-barreled cap-and-ball hunting rifle. **sAppalachians** *old-fash*

1917 *DN* 4.413 **wNC,** *Hog rifle.* A squirrel rifle. The stress falls on *rifle.* **1937** *Hall Coll.* **ceTN,** *Hog rifle,* a cap and ball gun. [My] grandfather used to make them on Roarin' Fork. *Ibid* **ceTN,** Fightin' Creek sold from the mouth to the head for a hog rifle gun—away back before I was born. **1939** *Ibid* **cwNC,** And we was in a laurel thicket and Jack he had a gun—he had one of these here hog rifles. Hit was a good 'un too. **1939** FWP *Guide TN* 132 **eTN,** A unique sport . . is the "turkey shoots" of the mountain people, stemming from the rifle contest of pioneer times. Scorning modern breech loaders, the contestants use long-barreled cap and ball "hog" rifles, patterned after the famous guns of the frontiersmen. **1940** Stuart *Trees of Heaven* 33 **KY,** He ought to be shot at sunset between the eyes with a hog rifle. *Ibid* 86, Tarvin has his long hog rifle, bright and shiny, and a box of long cartridges. **1959** Roberts *Up Cutshin* 27 **seKY,** Looked over the old hog rifle and saw I had just fourteen caps and some powder. So I took my bullet molds and molded me fourteen bullets. **1967–69** *DARE* (Qu. P37a, *Nicknames for a rifle*) Inf **TN**14,

Hog rifle—muzzle-loadin', old-fashioned; (Qu. P38, *What do you put into a rifle to shoot?*) Inf **KY**43, Hog rifle—powder, patching, and a cap. [Both Infs old]

2 See quot.

1949 *AmSp* 24.110 **cnGA,** *Hog rifle*. . . A rifle with a comparatively short barrel, used for killing hogs.

hog rifle gun See **hog rifle 1**

hog rights See **hog claim**

hog rooter See **hognose 3**

hog run See **run** n

hogs ate my brother up, since the adv phr For varr see quots **esp Sth, S Midl**

For a long time; since long ago.

1923 *DN* 5.221 **swMO,** *Since the hogs et up m' brother*. . . A very long time. **1944** *PADS* 2.9 **AL, SC,** *Since the hog et grandma (my little brother):* Expressive of great amusement. "I haven't laughed so much since the hog et grandma." . . Low popular. **1960** *VT Hist.* new ser 28.134, Ain't had so much fun since the pigs et up my little brother. **1966** *DARE* (Qu. A16, *A very long period of time: "I haven't seen him ———."*) Inf **OK**42, Since the hogs eat my little brother up. **1980** *DARE* File **Ozarks** (as of c1920), Ain't had so much fun since the hogs ate my little brother up. **1985** Kidder *House* 296 **MA,** Jim gives a boogieman's laugh, spits out a Bronx cheer, and sings a snatch of "The Tennessee Waltz." He says, "I haven't had so much fun around here since the hogs ate little sister."

hog sausage n [**hog B3a**]

1 A type of pork sausage. Cf **hog meat**

1965–66 *DARE* (Qu. H39, *Kinds of sausage;* total Infs questioned, 75) Infs **GA**1, 4, **MS**55, **OK**21, Hog sausage. **1986** Pederson *LAGS Concordance (Sausage links on a chain)* 1 inf, **swMS,** Hog sausage.

‡2 also *hog ham:* See quot.

1967 *DARE* FW Addit **LA**11, Hog sausage [or] hog ham—pork chops.

hogsback See **hogback 2b**

hog's back son-of-a-bitch n [Cf **hogback 1**] Cf **county attorney, son-of-a-bitch stew**

1924 *DN* 5.286 **Cape Cod MA,** Who would ever guess that 'hog's back son of a bitch' was a delectable dish common in most New England households under a more dignified name? It is nothing more than boiled salt codfish, over which scraps of pork are placed. . . It is commonly designated as such on shipboard, and several times I have heard the name used in what are considered good respectable households.

hog's bed See **hog-bed 2**

hog's cheese See **hog's head cheese**

hogset See **hogshead**

hog's fennel See **hog fennel 1**

hog's hair n

An unidentified turtle; see quot.

1967 *DARE* (Qu. P24, . . *Kinds of turtles*) Inf **MO**7, Hog's hair ['hɒgz ˌhɛr].

hog's haw See **hog haw**

hogshead n Pronc-spp *hockset, hogh(s)et, hogset, hogsit, hogzit, hoxhead* [*OED* 1390 →]

A Forms.

1637 in 1855 New Plymouth Colony *Records* 1.62 **MA,** The p[ar]tie so delinquent shall forfait ten shillings for the said p[ar]cell of hearings, be it firkin, barrell or hodgshead [sic], or any other vessell. **1806** (1904) Roe *Diary* 36 **Long Is. NY,** Fil'd 2 Hogsits. *Ibid* 37, Fil'd a hoghet. *Ibid* 43, We taped [=tapped] a hoghset. **1807** *Ibid* 54, Drawed of[f] a hogset of Sider. **1891** *DN* 1.166 **cNY,** [hɔgzɪt]. **1899** (1912) Green *VA Folk-Speech* 227, *Hockset*. . . Hogshead. . . Hoxhead. **1903** *DN* 2.292 **Cape Cod MA** (as of a1857), *Hogshead* was *hogset*. **1907** *DN* 3.190 **seNH,** *Hogset*. . . Pronunciation of hogshead (a large cask). **1908** *DN* 3.321 **eAL, wGA,** *Hogzit*. . . Hogshead. **1922** (1926) Cady *Rhymes VT* 137, Our smokehouse was a hogsit half. **1931–33** *LANE Worksheets* **RI,** [hɒgzhɪt]—A big barrel. **1965–70** *DARE* (Qu. F14, *A large wooden container for vinegar or cider;* total Infs questioned, 75) Inf **GA**13, ['hagzəd]; **MS**1, ['haˌzɪt]; **MS**22, ['hagzˌhɪd]; (Qu. X50, . . *Nicknames for a person who is very fat*) Inf **DE**3, Big as a ['hagzɪd]. **1967** Key *Tobacco Vocab.* 123 **MD, NC,** ['hɔgzəd]. **1976** Allen *LAUM* 3.329 **ND** (as of c1950), One inf. . . has a voiceless variant for *hogshead,* which for him has medial /ks/ rather than the usual /gz/.

B Sense.

See **hoghead 2.**

hog's head cheese n Also *head-hog cheese, hog-head cheese, hog('s) cheese;* for addit varr see quots **chiefly Sth, S Midl, NEast, esp S Atl, Gulf States** See Map and Map Section

=**headcheese 1;** see quots.

1838 (1852) Gilman *S. Matron* 25 **S Atl,** Her hog's cheese (the English brawn) was delicacy itself. **1847** (1979) Rutledge *Carolina Housewife* 218 **SC,** *Hog's head cheese.* Take the faces of the hogs and boil them. . . season the faces well, as you would do sausages; put it (the meat) upon the skins. . . then tie it up as for a dumpling, not too tight; put it into a press or under a heavy weight for two days, when it will be fit for use. **1941** *LANE* Map 305 *(Head Cheese; Souse)* **chiefly eNEng,** *Hogshead cheese* has level stress, while in *hog's head cheese* the main stress is on *head.* **1946** *PADS* 5.26 **VA,** *Hog's head cheese*. . . A sausage of pig's entrails; fairly common. **1950** *PADS* 14.37 **SC,** *Hog head cheese*. . . Same as *souse.* The word *headcheese* is seldom heard alone. **1965–70** *DARE* (Qu. H43, *Foods made from parts of the head and inner organs of an animal*) 77 Infs, **chiefly Sth,** Hog-head cheese; 40 Infs, **esp Sth, C Atl, eNEng,** Hog's head cheese; **AL**6, **FL**33, **MI**88, **NY**233, Hog cheese; **MS**17, Hog-heads cheese; **NH**11, Head-hog cheese; [**MO**36, Hog's head; **NH**16, Hog's head—without cornmeal; **OK**9, Hog's head—they use brains and everything compressed into a cake; **GA**10, Hog head;] (Qu. H61, . . *Kinds of homemade cheese;* total Infs questioned, 75) Inf **MS**17, Hog-head cheese. **1966** *DARE* Tape **FL**6, You cook your hog's head and feet real tender. . . Well, you get all the bones out and then you grind it up in a mill. . . Then you season it like you want it. . . My mother . . [would] put a plate on it and she'd put her smoothing irons . . in the middle of that plate. . . The next morning . . this grease had been pressed out. . . [She would] wrap . . [the cheese] in clean cloths. . . if you were not going to use it all you could pickle it. . . Pickled hog-head cheese; **FL**36, You can't ever put too much vinegar in hog-head cheese; **FL**41, How you make the hog-head cheese? . . Well, you wash your head good and put it in a pot and boil it. **1971** *AmSp* 46.182 **Chicago IL,** Words with Midland and Southern designations brought to Chicago by recent migrants, especially blacks: *hog souse, hog(s)head cheese.* **1973** Allen *LAUM* 1.288 **Upper MW** (as of c1950), *Hog's head cheese* [reported by only one of 1,038 mail respondents and] not reported in the field in the U[pper] M[idwest]. **1986** Pederson *LAGS Concordance* **Gulf Region,** [The terms *hoghead* and *hog's head (cheese)* for headcheese or souse are widespread throughout the region; among other terms also in use are *hoghead chow, ~ fry,* and *hog's head meat.*]

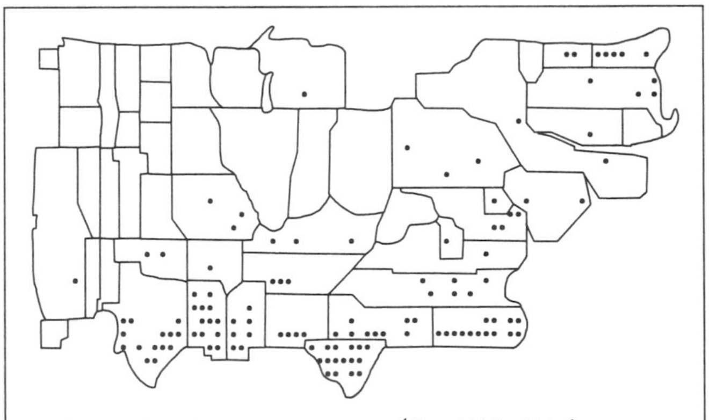

•hog's head cheese + varr (Qq. H43, H61)

hog's head meat See **hog's head cheese**

hog's head pudding See **hog-head pudding**

hog's head sauce (or souse) See **hog-head souse**

hog's hoof tea See **hog-hoof tea**

hog side See **hogback 1**

hogsit See **hogshead**

hog's jaw See **hog jaw**

hog's leg See **hogleg**

hog's maw See **hog maw**

hog smelly See **hog B2**

hog snake n

=**hognose snake.**

1965–70 *DARE* (Qu. P25, . . *Kinds of snakes*) Infs **AL**22, **KS**1, 20, **MD**31, **MA**80, **NM**13, **OK**18, **TN**65, Hog snake.

hog snapper n Cf **hogfish a**

A **wrasse** (here: *Lachnolaimus maximus*).

1960 Amer. Fisheries Soc. *List Fishes* 71, Hog snapper—see hogfish. **1966** *DARE* (Qu. P2, . . *Kinds of saltwater fish . . good to eat*) Inf **FL**24, Hog snappers.

hog's nest n Cf **hogpen 1, hurrah's nest 1**

=**boar's nest 2.**

1895 Brown *Meadow-Grass* 131 **NH,** This room's a real hog's nest, an' I left it as neat as wax!

hog souse See **hog-head souse**

hog's physic See **hog physic**

hog spoiled See **hog B2**

hog's-potato See **hog potato 1**

hog stable See **stable**

hog still See **groundhog n 6**

hog-stitched ppl adj Cf *cat-stitched* (at **cat-clawed**), **hog-swabbled**

1967 *DARE* (Qu. W29, . . *Things that are sewn carelessly*) Inf **NJ**1, Hog-stitched.

hog-stomp n Cf **hog-wrestle**

Fig: see quot.

1968 *DARE* (Qu. FF4, . . *Different kinds of dancing parties*) Inf **KS**15, Hog-stomp.

hog sucker n

A **sucker** (here: *Hypentelium nigricans*). Also called **black horse, black sucker 4, crawl-a-bottom, cream pitcher, hammerhead sucker, hog molly 1, hog mullet, hognose sucker, mud sucker, pugamoo, riffle sucker, stone roller, toter**

1877 NY Acad. Sci. *Annals Lyceum Nat. Hist.* 10.346 **GA,** *[Hypentelium nigricans]* Water basin of the Etowah and Oostanaula. . . Known as Hog-molly (Mullet), Crawl-a-botttom, and Hog Sucker. **1882** U.S. Natl. Museum *Bulletin* 16.130, *C[atostomus] nigricans*. . . Hog Sucker. **1883** *Ibid* 27.478, *Catostomus nigricans. . . Hog Sucker.* . . United States from New York to Florida and westward to Alabama and Kansas; Great Lake region. **1908** Forbes–Richardson *Fishes of IL* 86, *Catostomus Nigricans*. . . Hogsucker. **1941** Writers' Program *Guide WI* 17, The hog sucker is found occasionally in some rivers. **1954** *Harder Coll.* **cwTN,** *Hog sucker*. . . A type of edible fish. **1959** *IN Mag. Hist.* 55.3.212 (as of c1920), And like yellowish-olive, dark-blotched exclamation points on a slate, *Hypentelium nigricans*, the common hog sucker, lay without pattern beneath the unflawed ice. . . Hog suckers, unlike other suckers, were practically boneless and considered excellent at table. **1966** WI Acad. *Trans.* 55.98 **swWI,** Northern hog sucker—*Hypentelium nigricans*. . . This species is abundant locally in medium to large streams, especially in swift water. It is uncommon on the Mississippi River. **1966–68** *DARE* (Qu. P3, *Freshwater fish that are not good to eat*) Infs **NC**36, 53, **VA**27, Hog sucker. **1976** Garber *Mountain-ese* 42 **Appalachians,** *Hog-sucker* . . creek fish —Sol is down at the crick tryin' to grab-hook hog suckers.

hog-swabbled ppl adj Cf **hog-stitched**

1959 *VT Hist.* new ser 27.142 **cwVT,** *Hog-swabbled*. . . Messy; inexpert. Rare.

hog taper n [Prob var of *hagtaper*]

=**mullein.**

1900 Lyons *Plant Names* 390, *Verbascum Thapsus*. . . Hog-taper.

hog thistle n

Prob =**sow thistle.**

1968 *DARE* (Qu. S21, . . *Weeds . . that are a trouble in gardens and fields*) Inf **OH**82, Hog thistles.

hog-tight adj Cf **bull-strong, horse-high, pig-tight**

Of a fence: constructed so as to restrain a hog.

1859 (1968) Bartlett *Americanisms* 198 **MD,** *Hog-tight and Horse-high.* Always used together, of fences that are sufficient to restrain trespassing stock. **1880** Tourgée *Fool's Errand* 194 **Sth,** The split-board paling . . was "horse-high, hog-tight, and bull-strong." **1885** U.S. Bur. Indian Affairs *Report* 110 **KS,** All of these tracts are inclosed with hog-tight fences. **1910** Johnson *Highways Rocky Mts.* 33 **KS,** The field in which the ploughman was at work was fenced with a thorny osage hedge, which he had trimmed and adjusted during the winter so that it was "hog tight." **1954** *Harder Coll.* **cwTN,** *Hog-tight fence*. . . A wire fence stretched so tightly that hogs cannot go under it. **1967–70** *DARE* (Qu. L63, . . *Fences made with wire*) Infs **IL**4, 56, **MN**12, Hog-tight fence; (Qu. L65) Inf **CA**211, Hog-tight fence.

hog-tight v [**hog-tight** adj]

To make (a fence) **hog-tight** adj.

1913 Cather *O Pioneers* 140 **NE,** Why don't you go over there some afternoon and hog-tight her fences?

hog wallered, I'll be exclam [**hog wallow 1**]

1912 *DN* 3.579 **wIN,** *I'll be hog-wallered!* An exclamation of surprise or of scepticism.

hog wallow n

1 A wet and muddy area where swine wallow; see quot 1899.

1829 Dow *Omnifarious Law Exemplified* 51 (Th.S.) *(DA)*, It becomes a trespass to make a dam for a hog wallow. **1888** *Washington* (La.) *Argus* 21 June 2/2, Cesspools, hog wallows and duck ponds in close proximity to wells are liable to defile the water. **1894** *Congressional Record* 18 Jan 1036/1 **PA,** At the back of the barn there was a pool which in the summer was a hog-wallow. **1899** (1912) Green *VA Folk-Speech* 228, *Hog-wallow*. . . A wet, muddy hole where hogs wallow to cool themselves. **1973** Allen *LAUM* 1.188 **MN** (as of c1950), Shelter and enclosure for hogs and pigs. . . [hog] wallow. [1 inf] *Ibid* 189 **NE,** Enclosure only [hog] wallow. [1 inf] **1986** Pederson *LAGS Concordance* **Gulf Region,** 3 infs, Hog wallow; 1 inf, **seAL,** Hog wallow—in hogpen where they lie around; 1 inf, **neLA,** Hog wallow or a mudhole for them to lay in [or] flop around.

2a often attrib: A natural depression in land, often characterized by heavy, clayey soil with poor drainage; such soil itself. **chiefly TX** Cf **black wax, buffalo wallow**

1840 *Amer. Jrl. Science* 39.212 **TX,** From difference of surface, soil, and exposure, there arises a great diversity in the size, depth, and general appearance of the *hog-wallows.* **1857** *TX Almanac* 8, There is a great deal of prairie known as "hog wallow"—rich and waxy. **1858** *Ibid* 126, He found that the hog-wallow prairie and the rank, coarse sedge grass, common in that part of the State, did not suit sheep. **1883** Smith *Rept. for 1881 & 1882* 494 **ceAL,** Local patches of a tenacious clayey soil, called "hog-wallow prairie," are here and there met with in Cowikee lands. **1906** *DN* 3.141 **nwAR,** *Hog-waller land*. . . Land containing numerous depressions or "hog wallers." **1929** Dobie *Vaquero* 38 **cTX,** The very word "hog-wallow" has produced no end of argument among people of the soil. . . not a few citizens have held that the hog-wallows came as a result of "the seven years' drouth back in the time of the Spaniards." During that awful drouth, they argue, cracks cleft the ground so wide and deep that . . numerous sinks—improperly called hog-wallows—marked where they had been. **1967** *DARE* (Qu. C7, . . *Land that usually has some standing water with trees or bushes growing in it*) Inf **TX**11, Hog wallow; (Qu. C31, . . *Heavy, sticky soil*) Inf **TX**11, Hog wallow—has no drainage, holds water; **TX**22, Hog wallow —waxy, black soil. **1986** Pederson *LAGS Concordance*, 1 inf, **ceAL,** Hog wallow—swampy land. **1987** *Nature Conserv. News* 37.2.28 **TX,** Hogwallows (gilgai) dotting site host imperiled gammagrass/switchgrass community.

b Transf: a low mound; land characterized by numerous low mounds.

1853 Hammett *Stray Yankee in TX* 95, The ground we were riding over, of the description known as "hog-wallow," being a succession of small mounds and corresponding hollows. **1898** U.S. Geol. Surv. *Water-Supply Papers* 18.36 **CA,** Its surface is very generally besprinkled with the low mounds usually known in the West as hog-wallows. **1948** *Scientific Mth.* 66.356/1 **CA,** The local term, "hog wallows," is . . very misleading. In thinking of wallows one visualizes circular depressions in flat or gently rolling country. . . Hog-wallow land is the reverse of this: it is composed of mounds, not depressions, sprinkled over fairly flat or gently rolling areas.

c A depression in a cultivated field; see quot 1954.

1905 *DN* 3.83 **nwAR,** *Hog-wallow*. . . Depression in the ground, miry hole. 'That field is so full of hog-wallows I couldn't mow it with a machine.' Common. **1954** *Harder Coll.* **cwTN,** *Hog waller. . .* A hole left in the field when the plowing was not done properly. During the rainy weather it fills with water and resembles mud holes in which hogs lie. "He's a bad plower, he's got hog wallers all over that patch."

d A depression or hole in a road.

1954 *Harder Coll.* **cwTN,** *Full of hog wallers,* of a road: having a rough surface with many holes. **1965–70** *DARE* (Qu. N27b, *When unpaved roads get very rough, you call them ______*) Infs **MS**59, **TN**53, (Full of) hog wallers.

e See **hog B8.**

hog walnut n Cf **pig walnut**

A **pignut** (here: *Carya glabra*).

1941 *LANE* Map 277 **NEng,** The walnut proper . . is not native to New England. The term *walnut* is most commonly used here to denote a hickory nut . . Hicoria glabra (Carya porcina). . . 1 inf, **csCT,** [hɔg wɔlnət], with 'a big shuck and little meat'; . . 1 inf, **seRI,** [hɑg wɒnət], 'no good'; . . 1 inf, **ceRI,** [hɒg wɔlnət], bitter.

hog wampee n

An **arrow arum** (here: *Peltandra virginica*).

1913 *Torreya* 13.228 **SC,** *Peltandra virginica* (L.) . . Hog wampee. . . Hogs are very fond of the roots and leaves of this plant.

hogwash n Cf **horse piss**

Fig: liquor, esp a weak or inferior kind.

[**1883** Harte *In Carquinez Woods* 155, Dunn growled a dissent to Brace's proposition. . . He had "had enough of that hog-wash ladled out to him for genuine liquor."] **1942** Berrey–Van den Bark *Amer. Slang* 99.4, *Weak, inferior liquor. . .* hogwash. **1966–70** *DARE* (Qu. DD21a, . . *Any kind of liquor*) Inf **NY**142, Hogwash; (Qu. DD21b, . . *Bad liquor*) Inf **NY**142, Hogwash; (Qu. DD25, . . *Nicknames . . for beer*) Infs **FL**20, **NC**41, 61, **NY**131, 219, **VA**61, Hogwash; (Qu. DD27, . . *Nicknames . . for wine*) Inf **NC**61, Hogwash.

hogweed n

1 Any of var **amaranths.** Cf **pigweed**

1784 in 1785 Amer. Acad. Arts & Sci. *Memoirs* 1.489 **PA,** *Amaranthus. . .* Hog-Weed. White Amaranthus. Amongst rubbish. August. **1891** Jesup *Plants Hanover NH* 34, *Amarantus* [sic] . . *retroflexus* . . (Hogweed. Pigweed.) **1902** (1974) Chestnut *Plants Indians* 346 **nwCA,** No Indian name was learned for this plant [=*Amaranthus retroflexus*], which is well known as hogweed throughout the district. **1965–70** *DARE* (Qu. S21, . . *Weeds . . that are a trouble in gardens and fields*) 97 Infs, **chiefly Midl,** Hogweed(s); (Qu. I28b, *Kinds of greens that are cooked*) Inf **NH**12, Hogweed—right name is redroot; (Qu. BB51a, . . *Cures for corns or warts*) Inf **VA**46, Hogweed juice. [*DARE* Ed: Some of these Infs may refer instead to other senses of **hogweed.**]

2 Any of var plants of the family Asteraceae, as:

a =ragweed.

1822 Eaton *Botany* 170 **NEast,** *Ambrosia. . . elatior. . .* hogweed. **1832** MA Hist. Soc. *Coll.* 2d ser 9.146 **cwVT,** Ambrosia elatior. . . Hogweed. **1895** U.S. Dept. Ag. *Farmers' Bulletin* 28.25, Hogweed. *Ambrosia trifida.* **1896** *Jrl. Amer. Folkl.* 9.190, *Ambrosia Artemisiaefolia* [sic] . . hogweed, West. **1906** Rydberg *Flora CO* 328, *Ambrosia. . .* Hog-weed. **1943** Weslager *DE Forgotten Folk* 163, Hog Weed (Ragweed)[,] *Ambrosia artemisiifolia. . .* Root makes a strong laxative tea. **1950** Gray–Fernald *Manual of Botany* 1469, *A[mbrosia] artemisiifolia. . .* Hog-weed.

b =horseweed 1.

1900 Lyons *Plant Names* 221, *Leptilon Canadense. . .* Hogweed. **1930** Sievers *Amer. Med. Plants* 37, *Leptilon canadense . .* hogweed. **1931** Harned *Wild Flowers Alleghanies* 562, A very coarse, unattractive weed [=*Erigeron canadensis*] familiarly known to the farmer under the names, Horseweed, . . and Hogweed. **1944** AL Geol. Surv. *Bulletin* 53.227, *L[eptilon] Canadense* [=*Erigeron canadensis*]. . . Horse-weed, or hog-weed. **1950** Gray–Fernald *Manual of Botany* 1447, *Erigeron canadensis. . .* Horse-weed, Hog-weed. **1974** (1977) Coon *Useful Plants* 108, *Erigeron canadensis*—Canadian fleabane, . . hog-weed.

c =boneset 1 (here: *Eupatorium capillifolium*).

1900 Lyons *Plant Names* 155, *Eupatorium capillifolium. . .* Hog-weed.

d =robin's plantain.

1968 *DARE* FW Addit **VA**13, *Hogweed*—common, was once fed to hogs by old mountain people if their hogs were kept in a lot. Book name—*Robin's Plantain.*

3 =lamb's quarters. *hist*

1824 Bigelow *Florula Bostoniensis* 107, *Chenopodium album. . .* Hog-weed. **1847** Wood *Class-Book* 469 **Nth,** C[henopodium] album. . . *White Goose-foot. Hogweed.*

4 =cow parsnip 1.

1900 Lyons *Plant Names* 187, *H[eracleum] sphondylium. . .* Hogweed. **1950** Gray–Fernald *Manual of Botany* 1104, *H[eracleum] sphondylium. . .* Hogweed. **1959** Carleton *Index Herb. Plants* 62, Hogweed. . . *Heracleum sphondylium.* **1974** (1977) Coon *Useful Plants* 259, *Heracleum lanatum*—Cow parsnip, . . hogweed.

5 An unidentified mint (family Lamiaceae).

1969 *DARE* FW Addit **KY**40, *Hogweed*—a mint one to three feet high.

hog wire n, also attrib Also *hog fencing* **scattered, but esp S Atl, Gulf States, Cent** See Map Cf **hog fence**

Orig a heavy barbed wire with four-pointed barbs; later a stout wire mesh; see quots.

1894 (1977) Montgomery Ward *Catalogue* 379/3, Sheep and Hog Fencing. . . Made of No. 16 Galvanized Steel Wire; three-strand selvedge, 3x6 inch mesh. **1927** (1930) *WNID* 1024, *Hog wire.* Barbed wire with four-pointed barbs and weighing about 400 lbs. per mile. *U.S.* **1945** *Hardin Tribune–Herald* (MT) 15 Feb 7/5, [Auction notice:] *Miscellaneous*—6 rolls of hog wire / 2 hog feeders / 1 hog house. **1960** Criswell *Resp. to PADS 20* **Ozarks,** *Hog wire*—Usually two smooth wires twisted over each other with short barbs every six to twelve inches. When woven wire started coming in, people called it hog wire. **1965–70** *DARE* (Qu. L63, *Kinds of fences made with wire*) 70 Infs, **scattered, but esp S Atl, Gulf States, Cent,** Hog wire (fence); **FL**37, American hog-wire fence; **GA**9, Hog wire—coarse woven wire; **LA**8, Hog-wire fence—with 4½- or 5-inch mesh; **LA**12, Hog wire—same as net wire fence; **NM**6, Hog-wire fence—might be called sheep wire by some; **SC**3, Hog wire—rectangles all same size; **MO**25, **NY**23, Hog fencing; (Qu. L65) Infs **IL**69, **OH**45, **WI**30, Hog-wire fence; (Qu. M15) Inf **CO**3, Hog pastures enclosed with hog wire. **1967** *DARE* Tape **IA**10, [FW:] What kind of fences do you have around your farm? [Inf:] Some of it's hog wire on the bottom . . then about 3 or 4 wires on top. . . [FW:] What's the hog wire? [Inf:] It goes down on the ground. . . Some of 'em puts a barb wire right down next to the ground so . . it'll cut their nose if they try to get out. **1986** Pederson *LAGS Concordance* **Gulf Region,** [*Hog wire, hog fencing,* and *hog-wire fencing* are widespread throughout the region and are described variously as having "little squares," "4 inch to 6 inch squares," or being "used also in chicken house."]

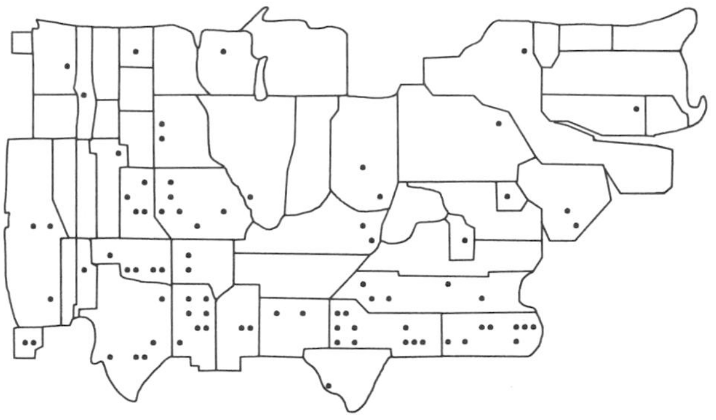

•hog wire + varr (Qq. L63, L65, M15)

hog wood See **hog fuel**

hogwort n

The woolly croton *(Croton capitatus).*

1889 *Century Dict.* 2853, Hogwort. . . An annual euphorbiaceous plant, *Croton capitatus. . .* It occurs from New Jersey to Iowa and southward to Georgia and Texas. **1914** Georgia *Manual Weeds* 261, *Hogwort. . .* A very common and troublesome weed in the southern part of our area, particularly in the Gulf States. **1933** Small *Manual SE Flora* 783, *Hogwort. . .* Waste places, various provinces. **1950** Gray–Fernald *Manual of Botany* 960. **1970** Correll *Plants TX* 935, *Hogwort. . .* Sandy soil in the e[astern] half of the state, in summer through fall.

hog-wrestle n Pronc-spp *hog-rassle, ~-wrastle* **esp Nth** *somewhat old-fash* Cf **hog-stomp**

Fig: a boisterous dance or dancing party; see quots.

1915 *DN* 4.233 **neOH** [Student slang], *Hog-wrastle*. . . A modern dance. **1926** *DN* 5.387 **ME,** *Hog wrestle* (—rassle). . . Contemptuous term for a cheap or vulgar dance. "The dance last night was a regular hog wrestle." Common. **1950** *WELS (A party where the main entertainment is dancing)* 1 Inf, **WI,** Hog-rassle; *(Names and joking names for . . dancing parties)* 1 Inf, **WI,** Hog-rassle. **1965–70** *DARE* (Qu. FF4, . . *Dancing parties*) Infs **DE**7, **MA**45, **NY**66, 84, Hog-wrestle; NY234, Hog rassle. [All Infs old] **1973** Allen *LAUM* 1.377 **ND** (as of c1950), A *dance*. . . hog wrestle. [1 inf, born 1902]

hog yard n **chiefly Nth, N Midl** See Map Cf **cow yard** =**hog lot.**

1639 in 1881 Boston Registry Dept. *Records* 6.23, A fresh marsh without the hogg yard on the left hand lying in the last diuision. **1939** *LANE* Map 110 *(Pig pen; hog house)* 4 infs, **MA, RI,** Hog yard. **1950** *WELS (The place outdoors where pigs are kept)* 9 Infs, **WI,** Hog yard. **1965–70** *DARE* (Qu. M15, *The place outdoors where pigs are kept*) 18 Infs, **chiefly Nth, N Midl,** Hog yard; (Qu. M13) Inf **IA**1, Hog yard. **1966** Dakin *Dial. Vocab. Ohio R. Valley* 2.84, *Hog yard* appears once in the greater Cincinnati area and once in the Pennyroyal [of western Kentucky]. **1973** Allen *LAUM* 1.188 **Upper MW** (as of c1950), Shelter and enclosure for hogs and pigs. . . hog yard. [9 infs] *Ibid* 189, Enclosure only. . . hog yard. [2 infs]

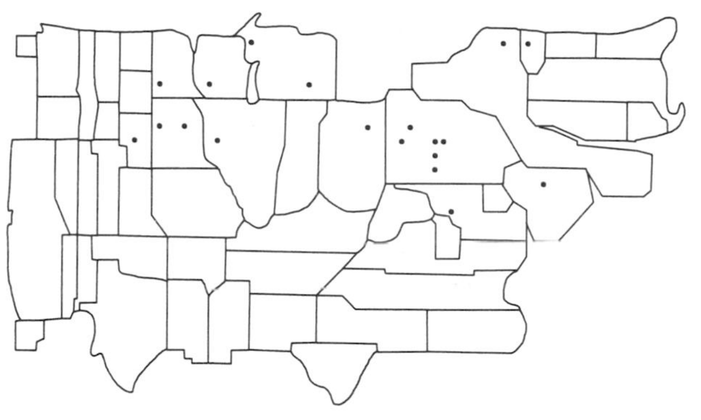
•hog yard (Qq. M15, M13)

hogzit See **hogshead**

ho-hum adj

Easygoing, relaxed.

1968 *DARE* (Qu. KK46, . . *Taking things as they come and not worrying: "The whole family was sort of______."*) Inf **LA**32, Ho-hum ['hoʊ 'hʌm]. [**1969** *Daily Colonist* (Victoria, B.C.) 27 Sept. 2/3 *(OEDS)* **Canada,** People are pretty ho-hum on most parts of the [Vancouver] Island right now . . but if anything does happen, they will be the first to cry for damages.]

hoi See **high** adj

hoick v [Cf *EDD hoick* v. "To hoist, lift up"; *W3 hoick* vt 1 "*chiefly dial:* to yank or pull with a jerk"]

To hoist or snatch up; to hook.

1957 Faulkner *Town* 293 **MS,** She chose one of them out of a cotton field . . hoicked him from between his plow-handles and ordered him to go home and bathe. **1959** Faulkner *Mansion* 393 **MS,** A little kinless tieless frail alien animal . . like a krait or a fer-de-lance . . flung, hoicked on a pitchfork . . into a city street. **1976** Brown *Gloss. Faulkner* 104, *Hoick*. . . Faulkner regularly uses *hoick* to mean "to grab, snatch."

hoigh See **high** adj

hoi polloi n [Orig Gk "masses, rabble"; but here perh infl by *high falutin* or **hoity-toity**]

High society; one who is, or pretends to be, a person of sophistication or high social status; also adj *hoi polloi:* sophisticated, snobbish.

1953 *W3* File **cNJ,** *Hoi-polloi;* Local usage . . applies the term to upper-moneyed classes in depreciatory way. If I used the term I would be referring to an arrogant, phony, affected sophisticate, i.e. "She is a member of the hoi-polloi." **1954** *Ibid* **neOH,** To a number of people apparently the phrase *hoi-polloi* means 'the upper crust of society', and is so used in their conversation. **1965–70** *DARE* (Qu. II23, *People who are, or think they are, the best society of a community*) 10 Infs, **scattered,** Hoi polloi; **HI**6, Hoi pollois; (Qu. II24, . . *Where the well-off people live*) Inf **WA**3, Where the hoi polloi hang out [7 of 12 infs college educ]; [(Qu. GG19a, *When you can see from the way a person acts that he's feeling important or independent: "He surely is ______ these days."*) Inf **MN**35, Hoi falloi ['hoɪ ˌfɑloɪ]; (Qu. HH9, *A very silly or light-headed person*) Inf **MN**35, Pip-squeak, hoi falloi.] **1988** *New Yorker* 19 Sept 51/3 **NYC,** Don't be ridiculous. How can a night-club comedian go on Broadway? My accent would automatically make it lowbrow. They'd write me off as a borscht-belt comedian. If I were a black man with an English accent, they'd think it was profound. But I'm a street-corner character, and Broadway audiences have a hoi-polloi attitude.

hoir See **hire**

hoist n, v Usu |hɔɪst|; also |haɪst| See Pronc Intro 3.I.11 Proncspp *haist, heist, hice, hise, hist(e), hyste* Note: The early pronc of *-oi-* in words like *hoist* was very close to the mod Std E /ɔɪ/. By the 17th cent, however, /aɪ/ had become an accepted pronc and was brought to Amer from Engl. Later, partially under the influence of spelling, /ɔɪ/ was restored in Std E. *Hoist* is itself a var of the earlier *hoise,* with final *t* coming from the past tense/past pple. Some of the varr without final *t* illustrated below may be explained as loss of the final consonant (e.g. quots 1922, 1930), while others may perhaps be survivals of *hoise.*

A Pronc varr.

1829 Kirkham *Engl. Grammar* 194 **NEast,** The following words being often erroneously pronounced by polite people, their correction . . it is presumed, will be useful to many: . . *improper* histe *pronounced* hoist. **1851** Hooper *Widow Rugby's Husband* 49 **AL,** The grinder histed it up agin. **1856** Whitcher *Bedott Papers* 25 **cNY,** A mess o' men in a double team . . hysted us out. **1890** *DN* 1.61 **swOH,** *Heist* [haɪst]: a common pronunciation for *hoist.* **1893** Shands *MS Speech* 11, The negroes and illiterate whites give [oɪ] the sound of [aɪ] in a large number of words . . [haɪst] for *hoist.* **1903** *DN* 2.291 **Cape Cod MA** (as of a1857), *Haist* for *hoist.* **1908** *DN* 3.320 **eAL, wGA,** *Hist* [haɪst]. . . in the preterit . . *histed.* **1915** *DN* 4.184 **swVA,** *Histe.* Variant of *hoist.* **1922** Gonzales *Black Border* 231 **sSC, GA coasts** [Gullah], I graff'um by 'e lef' han' foot en' hice'um up close to one big gum tree. **1930** [see **C1e** below]. **1936** *AmSp* 11.35 **eTX,** Another group of words are still occasionally heard with [aɪ] in more illiterate speech and in jocular usage . . : *hoist.* **1954** *Harder Coll.* **cwTN,** *Hise, hist* [haɪs]: hoist. **c1960** *Wilson Coll.* **csKY,** *Hoist* /haɪst/, older people; otherwise humorous. The word itself has been displaced largely by raise or lift. **1966–68** *DARE* Tape **AK**10, They heist [haɪst] it [=gold ore] up; **ME**17, You heist [haɪst] 'em aboard; **ME**18, You'd see that tree heist [haɪst] a little mite; **ME**22, We heist [haɪst] 'em up; **MI**21, We'd always heist [haɪst] the sail. **1976** Allen *LAUM* 3.268 **MN** (as of c1950), Said to a cow at milking time . . *hoist,* which regularly is pronounced with /ai/. Only one instance turns up in the . . [Upper Midwest], from a southern Minnesota . . inf. . . But in conversation another Minnesotan . . has the same pronunciation with /ai/ as the name of a machine for lifting hay.

B Gram forms.

1908 *DN* 3.320 **eAL, wGA,** *Hist* [haɪst]. . . To hoist. This form is used also in the preterit, but *histed* is the commoner form. **1922** Gonzales *Black Border* 306 **sSC, GA coasts** [Gullah glossary], *Hice*—hoist, hoists, hoisted, hoisting.

C As verb.

1 In var spec applications of std senses: see below.

a Move your leg! Lift your foot!—used as a command to a cow during milking. [Cf *EDD hist* int., v. 2. a] **chiefly Nth, N Midl**

1828 Webster *Amer. Dict., Hoist*. . . To lift and move the leg backwards; a word of command used by milkmaids to cows, when they wish them to lift and set back the right leg. **1894** *DN* 1.341 **wCT,** *Hist* . . used to a cow, as an order to take her hind leg out of the way of the milker. **1912** *DN* 3.567 **cNY,** *Hīst*. . . Raise. Said to a cow. **1923** *DN* 5.210 **swMO,** *H'ist* . . a word of command to a milch cow directing her to step back slightly so her udder may be reached more conveniently. **1939** *LANE* Map 220 *(Calls to cows while milking)* 7 infs, 6 **coastal NEng, Long Is. NY,** Heist (*or* hoist); [1 inf, **swME,** Heist your foot]. **1940–41** Cassidy *WI Atlas (Calls to cows . . during milking)* 1 inf, **csWI,** Heist [means] 'put foot back'—so you could get at udder; 1 inf, **csWI,** Heist—to make them [move a leg]. **1942** McAtee *Dial. Grant Co. IN* 33 (as of 1890s). **1948** Davis *Word Atlas Gt. Lakes* 76, [In the fieldwork records:] *Histe!* . . (rare relic). [1 inf] *Ibid* App 66, [In the checklists:]

Histe! [8 infs] **1961** *AmSp* 36.270 **CO,** *Heist!* . . (a cow call). . . slightly more prominent in younger speech, in both eastern and western Colorado. **1967–68** *DARE* (Qu. K81) Infs **MA**5, **NY**117, **OH**72, Heist. **1973** Allen *LAUM* 1.259 **Upper MW** (as of c1950), *Hoist* . . 61 [checklist] respondents [predominantly from Iowa, Nebraska, and South Dakota]. . . This Midland weighting could reflect origination in southern New Jersey rather than in New England.

‡b See quot. Cf **cotton 4**

1968 *DARE* (Qu. W24a, . . *Expressions . . to warn a woman slyly that her slip is showing*) Inf **NJ**36, Heist it!

c See quots.

1916 Macy–Hussey *Nantucket Scrap Basket* 135, "Hoist"—Most old Nantucketers prefer this word to either lift or raise. They "h'ist" . . even the food to the mouth. **1967** *DARE* (QR, near Qu. E13) Inf **LA**9, When you want sun in you hoist them [=shades]. **1968** *DARE* FW Addit **TN**27, "Heist a window"—old-fashioned for "raise a window."

d In marble play: to raise the hand from the ground when shooting; hence vbl nouns *histing, hysting.* Cf **fen** exclam, **hunch** v **2a**

1843 (1916) Hall *New Purchase* 42 **sePA,** Colonel Wilmar proposed [playing] marbles. . . And at it we went with the zest of boyhood. . . Echo . . called back . . the words in our game. . . Clearings!—'fen!—knuckle-down!— . . histings!—comins about! **1890** *DN* 1.61 **swOH,** "Fen heist" [haɪst]: don't hoist or raise your hand while shooting. *Ibid* 76 **NYC,** "Fen histing" means that it is not permitted to raise the knuckles from the ground in "shooting." **1955** *PADS* 23.20 **cwTN,** *Hoist*. . . To raise the hand from the ground when shooting. **c1970** Wiersma *Marbles Terms* **swMI,** Forbidden: *Histing*—raising the hand from the ground. *Ibid* **NJ,** Hysting—Lifting the knuckle off the ground before the shooter has left the hand. A violation. **1973** Ferretti *Marble Book* 46, *Heist.* To rest one's shooting hand atop the other hand. **1984** *WI State Jrl.* (Madison) 8 Apr sec 9 1/4, Shots known as "histing" (raising the hand from the ground) . . are prohibited.

e also with *up:* To raise (a part of one's body); see quots.

1867 Twain *Jumping Frog* 17, Dan'l give a heave, and hysted up his shoulders. **1872** Twain *Roughing It* 328, Without another word he'd hyste his nose 'n' shove for home. **1930** Woofter *Black Yeomanry* 48 **seSC** [Black], Buh [=Brother] Rahbit hice 'e yehs [=his ears] an' listen. **1960** Criswell *Resp. to PADS 20* **Ozarks,** Common uses [for *hoist*] are found in "hoist her tail"—often used of a cow. **1965** *Dict. Queen's English* 7 **NC,** *Hist*. . . Raise. The squirrel histed his tail and ran across the ground.

f also with *up:* To get up; to stand.

1887 (1967) Harris *Free Joe* 178 **cGA,** Tell me what makes me h'ist up an' walk away. **1892** *DN* 1.210 **csNH,** *H'ist* . . to get up. "Won't you please to h'ist?" **1945** Colcord *Sea Language* 102 **ME, Cape Cod, Long Island,** *Hoist*. . . Alongshore, the word is sometimes used intransitively: "Please h'ist, Deacon Porter, so's I can get this chair past ye."

g refl: To leave quickly; to hurry. Cf **hoist D3**

1960 Criswell *Resp. to PADS 20* **Ozarks,** Common uses [for *hoist*] are found in . . "hoist yourself out of here before I hit you" (in the sense of *run* or *hurry*).

h also with *over:* To move (oneself) along. Cf **hunch** v **3**

1967–70 *DARE* (Qu. Y52, *To move over—for example on a long bench: "We have to make room for one more. Can you ______ [a little]?"*) Infs **MA**5, **MI**116, **NY**144, Heist (over).

i(1) To lead, **line out,** or **raise** (a hymn); to sing or recite (a **call** n[1] **1**); hence noun *hoister* one who leads (a song). **Gulf States, SC** Cf **base D1, deacon** v **1**

1857 *Harper's New Mth. Mag.* 15.572/1, As they have no choir in the congregation, any one who considers himself qualified has authority to *hist* the hymns. **1922** Gonzales *Black Border* 56 **sSC, GA coasts** [Gullah], The last inspiring "sperritual," of African suggestiveness, remained to be sung. Who should raise the tune? Simon Jenkins . . called to his brother-in-law, John Chisolm, "hice'um, Chizzum! You hice de chune." John's resonant voice rolled out—"Jedus, hol' de lion jaw. . . " *"Hol'um, Jedus!"* . . came the responses in bass and treble. **1934** Carmer *Stars Fell on AL* 52, [At a Sacred Harp singing:] "Trebles on the left. Basses on the right. Tenors in the center." . . That's Perfesser Hinton histin' the rhyme." *Ibid* 62, "Only them that been baptized all over and born of the spirit, is invited to take part in this footwashin'. . . Brother John Muckle, will you begin histin' the rhyme?" A raucous barytone lifted a plaintive questioning: "How long, O Savior, O how long." **1942** in 1959 Lomax *Rainbow Sign* 187 **nMS** [Black], He hysts, or lines out, one of the old Dr. Watts hymns. **1959** *Ibid* 60 **AL** [Black], He was a big deacon in the Shiloh Baptist Church, sittin in the amen corner, hystin all the hymns. **1984** Wilder *You All Spoken Here* 180 **Sth,** *Hymn h'ister:* Song leader. *H'ist the tune;* raise the tune: The song leader pitches the tune of the song to be sung.

(2) By ext: to make up words for (a song).

1963 Owens *Look to River* 109 **TX,** "I don't know how to put it in a song, but I'll have me a whang at it." . . He hummed the tune through once, and then again. . . He stopped singing. . . "It ain't no use, Cap'n. I cain't git me no feeling outa something like that [=a boy found running, as if from the scene of a misdeed]—not when we got a tent full o' crap shooters, wife beaters, moonshiners—nigh about anything you'd want to h'ist a tune on."

j with *down:* To move (something) lower. [*OED hoist* v. 2 1794]

1838 Neal *Charcoal Sketches* 75 **Philadelphia PA,** Hyst . . is [also] a . . figurative mode of expression, . . for people sometimes say, "lower him up, and hyst him down." **1975** Gould *ME Lingo* 134, *Hoist* . . used all along the Maine coast for exactly the opposite [of moving up]: a man will stand on a float and call to someone up on the pier, "Hoist down them bait tubs!"

k with *down;* Perh by ext: see quot.

1954 *Harder Coll.* **cwTN,** *Hist down*—back out.

2 ppl adj *heisted:* Pregnant.

1941 *LANE* Map 392 *(Pregnant)* 1 inf, **cwNH,** [hɑɪstɪd], vulgar.

D As noun.

1 A jolt, fall. **chiefly NEast**

1838 Neal *Charcoal Sketches* 74 **Philadelphia PA,** "Hysts"—the popular pronunciation, in these parts, of the word *hoist,* which is used . . to convey the idea of the most complete tumble which man can experience. *Ibid* 75, A hyst is a rapid, forcible performance, which may be done . . either backward or forward, but of necessity with such violence as to knock the breath out of the body, or it is unworthy of the noble appellation of hyst. **1859** Elwyn *Glossary* 59, We use it [=*hoist* or *hist*] as the substantive, and say, "he got a deuce of a hoist," meaning a fall. **1916** Macy–Hussey *Nantucket Scrap Basket* 135 **seMA,** *Hoist*. . . meaning a fall, as "the staging gave way, and he got a bad h'ist." **1945** Colcord *Sea Language* 102 **ME, Cape Cod, Long Island,** My feet went out from under me, and I got an awful h'ist. **1966–67** *DARE* (Qu. Y1, . . *A person suddenly falling down: "He slipped on the steps and took quite a ______."*) Infs **ME**13, **NY**20, Heist; **ME**22, Hoist.

2 In marble play: permission to raise one's hand from the ground; the act of raising one's hand—also used as an exclam to request permission to do so. **[hoist C1d;** cf *EDD heights, heist*] Cf **hunch** n **2a**

1890 *DN* 1.61 **swOH,** In marbles, "I have heist" = I may raise my hand from the ground. **1922** *DN* 5.187 **MA,** *Hice*. . . A call in the ring games given by a boy who wishes to raise his hand for a shot. **1955** *PADS* 23.20 **cwTN,** *Heist.* The act of raising the hand from the ground to shoot. . . *no heists.* **1973** Ferretti *Marble Book* 46, *Heist*. . . Before shooting, a call of "Heist!" is necessary. A call of "No Heist!" by another player means one is out of luck.

3 See quot. **[hoist C1g]**

1960 Criswell *Resp. to PADS 20* **Ozarks,** *Hoist*—a hurry. Very, very frequent, even up to this day. "Get a hoist on you before I take a switch to you."

4 See quot. [*EDD hoist* sb. 3]

1968 *DARE* (Qu. II5b, *When you don't want to have anything to do with a certain person because you don't like him, you might say, "I'd certainly like to give him the ______."*) Inf **NY**43, Heist.

hoistance exclam Pronc-sp *histance* **[hoist C1d]** Cf **clearance(s), hand-roomance**

In marble play: see quot.

1912 Green *VA Folk-Speech* 226, *Histance*. . . Hoistance. In a game of marbles, a player had the right to cry "histance," and put his adversary's taw on a small heap of dirt for a better shot.

hoist down See **hoist C1j, k**

hoister See **hoist C1i(1)**

hoist over See **hoist C1h**

hoist the (green) sail n, exclam Also *hoist the green flag;* for addit varr see quots **esp eMA** Cf **oyster sale, run sheep run**

A children's hiding game played in teams; also used as a call to signal the whereabouts of a team; see quots 1947, 1957.

[**1905** Duncan *Dr. Grenfell's Parish* 136 *(DNE)* **Newfoundland,** When spring came, with the ice still clinging to the coast . . the lads played at 'h'ist-your-sails-an'-run' among the boulders of the hillside.] **1947** Botkin *Treas. New Engl. Folkl.* 755 **eMA** (as of c1910), *Hoist the Green Sail*—They chose captains and sides, and one captain led off his side and hid them somewhere, agreeing on a set of signals, for which they used the names of fruits. . . Immediately they [=the other side] would start . . the first captain following . . crying . . "Ba-na-a-nas!" or "Aw-w-r-un-jes!" The pursuers would try to confuse him and those in hiding by adding their voices to his. . . A wary player should discern whether a certain word meant "stay back" or "come in". . . Sometimes the searchers would discover their quarry, and run . . to claim the victory; sometimes . . they would hear the disappointing cry of the others at the goal, "Hoist the green sail!" **1954** Forbes *Rainbow* 197 **NH,** When the day was ending and it was getting on, too dark for ball games, we played Hoist the Green Flag, . . —running games, running through the dusk, and all over the campus. **1957** *Sat. Eve. Post Letters* **seMA** (as of c1900), We played Hoist the Sails which I thought for many years was Oyster Sales. *Ibid* **ceMA,** Hoist-a-Green-Sail had interesting nuances. The captain of the team in hiding set up field headquarters in the enemy camp, then by means of shouted signals, directed strategic withdrawals of his concealed forces as the hunt ranged dangerously close to the hiding place. *Ibid* **csNJ** (as of 1925), "H'ist the sail, sheepy." This was usually slurred into one long word "H'isasailsheepy." **1965** *DARE* File **Boston MA,** The decade of my active boyhood ran from about 1895 to 1905. . . [We used to play] Hoist the Green Sail. **1967** *DARE* (Qu. EE33, . . *Outdoor games . . that children play*) Inf **MA52,** Hoist the sail. [**1969** Opie–Opie *Children's Games* 182 **England,** *Hoist the green flag*—This curious game . . has been reported only from Scotland and overseas [=Canada and the US]. . . [The] leader is allowed to communicate with his own side . . in a prearranged colour code, thus 'Green' may mean 'danger, stay quiet'. . . The crisis in the game occurs when the seeking side catches sight of the hiders. . . The seekers must either try to catch the hiders or reach the den first, where . . 'the captain of the side which is back first lifts something up above his head and the whole side call "Hoist the green flag" '. . . [Other] Names: . . 'Hoist the Sails' (Toronto), . . 'Run, Sheep, Run' (. . commonly in the United States).]

hoist up See **hoist C1e, f**

hoit See **hurt**

hoity-toity adj, also used absol [Redup] Cf Intro "Language Changes" I.3 **esp Nth, N Midl, CA** See Map Cf **highty-tighty**
Haughty, snobbish, proud.

1872 [see **highty-tighty**]. **1905** [see **highty-tighty**]. **1915** *Sat. Eve. Post* 9 Jan 32/3 **NYC,** Hoity-toity, ain't you? Hoity-toity and white-faced and late, all at once. **1965–70** *DARE* (Qu. HH35, *A woman who puts on a lot of airs: "She's too ______ for me."*) 36 Infs, **esp Nth, N Midl, CA,** Hoity-toity; (Qu. GG19a, . . *Feeling important or independent: "He surely is ______ these days."*) Inf **NY38,** Hoity-toity; (Qu. II23, *Joking names for the people who are, or think they are, the best society . . The ______*) Infs **CA213, NY213,** Hoity-toity. [21 of 39 Infs coll educ] **1967** *DARE* Tape **LA14,** My mother's oldest sister was a very hoity-toity woman, very cultivated and very well-educated, of the old plantation-family type. . . She heard [her brother, who was running for reelection] . . say something, so she assailed him. . . "You know better than to say, 'I was . . born and done raised.' " Uncle Bill . . answered her, "Sister . . you know a man couldn't be elected and reelected . . if he were 'reared.' " **1967** *DARE* FW Addit **LA14,** *Hoity-toity*—said of someone who puts on airs and tries to live up to them. Common.

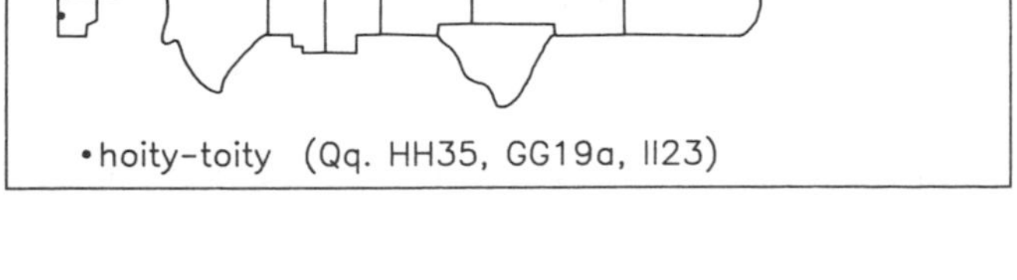

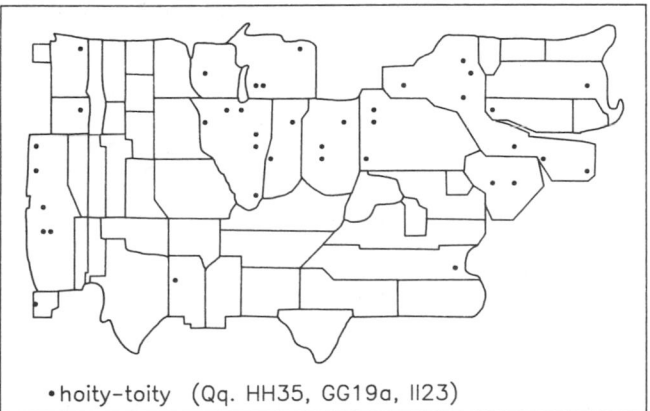

•hoity-toity (Qq. HH35, GG19a, II23)

hojack n

1 =hellgrammite 1.

1889 in 1901 Howard *Insect Book* 212, The names in use in Rhode Island alone for this insect [=*Corydalus cornutus*] . . are: Dobsons, . . hell devils, . . Ho Jack.

‡**2** See quots.

1967 *DARE* (Qu. N37, *Joking names for a branch railroad that is not very important*) Inf **NY5,** Hojack ['ho'jæk] road. **1967** *DARE* FW Addit **cnNY,** *Hojack* ['hoǰæk]—a Toonerville trolley.

hojase n Also *hojasen* [Perh rel to Span *hoja* leaf, *hojoso, -a* leafy]
A **tar bush** (here: *Flourensia cernua*).

1945 Benson–Darrow *Manual SW Trees* 349, *Flourensia cernua. . . Hojase. . .* occurs in isolated areas in southeastern Arizona. **1960** Vines *Trees SW* 994, American Tar-bush . . is also known under the vernacular names of Varnish-bush, Hojasen, and Hojase. **1981** Benson–Darrow *Trees SW Deserts* 295, Hojase. . . Shrubs usually less than 1 m. high. . . Mesas and slopes, often on limestone soils.

hokey, by exclam [Perh abbr of *hocus-pocus*] Also *by hoky-poky, good hokey;* for addit varr see quots *somewhat old-fash*
Used as a mild oath, esp in phrr indicating surprise, annoyance, or anger.

1838 Kettell *Yankee Notions* 124, "By the hokey!" said Josh, . . "I've an all-fired mind to try it though!" [**1840** *Spirit of Times* 25 Jan 561/2 **NY,** Him is done up—used up catawampous—kicked up into eberlasting hoki!] **1844** Stephens *High Life in NY* 1.71 **CT,** By the living hokey, I never see anything like it! **1856** Simms *Eutaw* 161 **SC,** "If you lay a hand in anger upon that young woman, you shall not receive one copper from us." "Does you say so . . ," cried old Rhodes, now thoroughly furious, "then, by the etarnal hokies, I drives you back to your captivation. Turn about, nigger." *Ibid* 219, So good night, ole lady. I'm obliged to you, by the hokies! **1874** (1895) Eggleston *Circuit Rider* 71 **sOH** (as of early 1800s), You're mighty clever, by hokey. **1906** *DN* 3.141 **nwAR,** *Hoky-poky. . .* In the mild oath, "by hoky-poky." **1909** *DN* 3.409 **cnME,** *By hokey. . .* A mild oath. **1912** *DN* 3.572 **wIN,** *By hokey. . .* An exclamation of surprise. **1984** *DARE* File **swWI** (as of 1920s), Cornish miners and their families in Linden, Wisconsin, used to say "Good hokey!" instead of "Good grief!"

hokey-dokey adj, adv Also *hokey-doh* [Varr of *okeydokey*] Cf Intro "Language Changes" I.3 Cf **hunky-dory, okeydoke**
Fine, all right; yes.

1954 Roberts *I Bought Dog* 11 **sAppalachians,** He said, "Hokey doh." Said, "I'll trade you the mill." **1966–70** *DARE* (Qu. KK4, *When things turn out just right, you might say, "Everything is ______ now."*) Infs **KY5, SC32, VA99,** Hokey-dokey.

hokey-dory adj Also *okey-dory* [Varr of *okeydokey* infl by **hunky-dory**]

1966–69 *DARE* (Qu. KK4, *When things turn out just right, you might say, "Everything is ______ now."*) Infs **OK31, VA5,** Hokey-dory; **GA77,** Okey-dory.

hokey-pokey n[1] Also sp *hoky-poky* [*OED hokey-pokey* sb. 2 1884 →] **scattered, but esp PA** *old-fash*
An inexpensive confection, esp flavored ice or ice cream.

1897 *KS Univ. Qrly.* (ser B) 6.88 **MO,** *Hokey pokey:* Candy. **1940** Writers' Program *Guide OH* 90, Here [at the county fair] . . the children rode the ferris wheel and ate "hokey-pokey". **1941** *AN&Q* 1.138/1 **PA,** In my childhood in Pennsylvania in the 1890's, the hoky-poky man came around every summer in his little wagon, ringing his bell. His sign read "Hoky-poky, 1¢." For a cent he laid a little mound of shaved ice on a piece of paper . . then poured over it one's choice of syrups of various flavors. **1941** *New Yorker* 17.30.24/1 **sePA** (as of 1898), Though she had no laws to back her up, she managed to get the Philadelphia peddlers of hokeypokey—ice cream sold from pushcarts, mostly to children—to concoct their wares under more sanitary conditions. **1960** Wentworth–Flexner *Slang* 262, *Hokey-pokey* [also] *hoky-poky* . . Cheap ice cream, candy, confections, primarily made to be attractive to children. . . "In Pittsburgh around 1900 we boys bought from the itinerant 'hokey-pokey ice-cream man' a . . confection called a snowball." . . ["]candy bars on the hokey-pokey counter." **1970** *DARE* FW Addit **eMA,** *Hokey-pokey* *man:* Man who sold ice cream; old-fashioned. **1970** *DARE* File **sIN,** At county fairs 50 years ago, hokey-pokey was a [small square] . . of frozen milk and water (skim milk?), sweetened and flavored, wrapped in wax paper, and frozen hard. **1989** *DARE* File **nePA** (as of c1910), I remember a cold treat. The hokey-pokey man would come around on a hot day and call "Hokey-pokey, penny a lump. The more you eat, the more you want." It wasn't ice cream, wasn't water ice—but a combination. It was served in a small paper cup. In Philadelphia a similar treat was called "yum-yum."

‡hokey-pokey n^{2} [Cf *DSL hoakie*] Cf **hokey, by**

1966 Dakin *Dial. Vocab. Ohio R. Valley* 2.520 **seIL,** [Names for the devil:] Other terms seem to be local or individual. . . In Gallatin County, Illinois, an aged speaker says *hokey-pokey.*

hokey-pokey n^{3} [Redup var of **pokey** jail, perh infl by other senses of *hokey-pokey;* cf Intro "Language Changes" I.3]

See quots.

1968–70 *DARE* (Qu. V11, . . *A county or city jail*) Infs **NY**37, **OK**57, Hokey-pokey. **1989** *DARE* File **Philadelphia PA,** [Letter:] "Hokey-pokey"—We use it when a guy is put into the "slammer." We would say "the vagrant was placed in the 'Hokey-Pokey' until they could determine a satisfactory place for him." It means "jail" or "pokey."

hokie n Cf **bogie** n^{2}

A large marble; see quot.

1970 *DARE* (Qu. EE6a, . . *Marbles—the big one that's used to knock others out of the ring*) Infs **MO**23, **TX**104, Hokie ['hoki]; **TN**46, Big hokie ['hoki].

hokum snivvy n Cf **hookem-snivey**

1968 *DARE* File **RI,** [Newspaper:] Our hokum snivvy was some sort of a stew or boiled dinner effect, we are not sure which (although we ate many of them as a youngster), and as we remember pork or salt pork and onions were an important part. It was . . a good meal for a cold winter's day.

hoky-poky See **hokey-pokey** n^{1}

hoky-poky, by See **hokey, by**

hol See **hold** v **A1b, 2d**

hold v

A Forms.

1 pres: usu *hold;* also:

a *holt. somewhat old-fash*

1837 Sherwood *Gaz. GA* 70, *Holt,* for hold. **1861** Holmes *Venner* 2.186 **wMA,** They say, holt on t' anything for ten year 'n' there'll be some kin' o' use for 't. **1936** *AmSp* 11.315 **Ozarks,** Jest holt your 'tater. **1939** *Sat. Eve. Post* 25 Nov 6/1 **FL,** You ever tried to holt a hawk? **1942** Warnick *Garrett Co. MD* 1 **nwMD** (as of 1900–18), *Holt* (hold).

b *hol(e).* **Sth, S Midl** *esp freq among Black speakers* Cf Pronc Intro 3.I.22

1884 *Anglia* 7.252 **Sth, S Midl** [Black], *Pres.* hole (hold). *Ibid* 271, Hole yo' breff'n wait. **c1885** in 1981 Woodward *Mary Chesnut's Civil War* 249 **SC** (as of 1861) [Black], He'll get rid of the trouble of 'em. . . Not a bit like Ole Marster. He hole 'em tight. **1899** (1967) Chesnutt *Wife of Youth* 65 **NC,** Square Kyahtah's [=Squire Carter is] too sick ter hol' co'te this evenin'. **1922** [see **A2d** below]. **1950** *PADS* 14.79 **FL,** *Hol'* 'em up; hol' 'em close . . hol' 'em tight. Instructions to cowboys to hold the cattle close in, or to hold them still. **1970** *DARE* (Qu. U16) Inf **VA**41, Let me hold it ['lɛmi ˌhoʊlɨt]. [Inf Black]

2 past: usu *held;* also:

a *healt, hel(t).* **Sth, S Midl**

1827 (1939) Sherwood *Gaz. GA* 70, *Helt,* for held. **1884** *Anglia* 7.252 **Sth, S Midl** [Black], *Past* . . helt. **1892** [see **A2c** below]. **1893** [see **A2c** below]. **1899** (1912) Green *VA Folk-Speech* 222, *Helt.* . . Healt. Held. "He healt the horse by the bridle." **1903** *DN* 2.316 **seMO,** *Helt.* . . Held. **1906** *DN* 3.119 **sIL,** *Helt,* pt. and pp. of hold. "I helt the horse an hour." *Ibid* 140 **nwAR,** He helt on like fury. **1908** [see **A2c** below]. **1941** *AmSp* 16.13 **eTX** [Black], In *held* . . the final consonant is frequently [t]. It is also omitted: [hɛəlt], [hɛl]. **1960** Criswell *Resp. to PADS 20* **Ozarks,** *Helt,* pa.—much commoner now than *held.* **1962** *Mt. Life* Spring 16 **sAppalachians,** *Past*—helt . . *Past Participle*—helt. **1967** *DARE* FW Addit **seAR,** Helt [hɛlt] out. **1975** Newell *If Nothin' Don't Happen* 15 **nwFL,** Preacher Elliott helt the funeral for Daddy.

b *hild. arch*

1815 Humphreys *Yankey in England* 105, *Hild,* held. **1893** *DN* 1.277 **wCT,** *Hold* . . Hild. **1899** (1912) Green *VA Folk-Speech* 225, *Hild.*

c *hilt.* **Sth, S Midl**

1851 Hooper *Widow Rugby's Husband* 49 **AL,** The grinder hilt it [=a monkey] to his bosom. **1884** *Anglia* 7.252 **Sth, S Midl** [Black], *Past* . . hilt. **1892** *DN* 1.233 **KY,** *Hilt* or *helt:* for *held.* "He hilt 'im fast." **1893** Shands *MS Speech* 36, *Hilt.* . . Negroes and illiterate whites frequently use this . . for *held.* They also say *helt.* **1902** *DN* 2.236 **sIL,** *Hilt* or *helt.* Preterit of hold. **1908** *DN* 3.319 **eAL, wGA,** *Helt* . . *hilt* . . pret. and pp. of *hold.* **1952** Brown *NC Folkl.* 1.550, *Hilt.* . . Past . . and past participle of *hold.* **1972** *Atlanta Letters* **GA,** Hilt him twel he hollered.

d *hol(d), holt.*

1884 *Anglia* 7.252 **Sth, S Midl** [Black], *Past.* holt . . holed [sic]. **1922** Gonzales *Black Border* 307 **sSC, GA coasts** [Gullah glossary], *Hol'* . . hold, holds, held, holding.

3 past pple: usu *held;* also:

a *helt, hilt.* **Sth, S Midl**

1891 Johnston *Primes & Neighbors* 129 **GA,** They don't want to be al'ays hilt betwix' hawk and buzzard in this kind o' style. **1899** (1967) Chesnutt *Wife of Youth* 67 **NC,** A co'te-martial has be'n hilt an' jestice done. **1906** [see **A2a** above]. **1908** [see **A2c** above]. **1952** [see **A2c** above]. **1962** [see **A2a** above].

b arch *holden*—appar now restricted to formal contexts. Cf **holden** adj

1631 in 1853 MA (Colony) *Rec. of Gov.* 1.86, A Genrall Court, holden att Boston, the 18th day of May, 1631. **1690** (1892) Hammond *Diary* 152 **ceMA,** Court . . holden in Charlestown by adjournmt. **1776** (1906) U.S. Continental Congress *Jrls.* 4.57 **CT,** At a general Assembly . . holden at New Haven. **1856** Cartwright *Autobiog.* 141 **TN,** A camp-meeting holden this year, in the edge of Tennessee. **1932** Randolph *Ozark Mt. Folks* 123, [Notice of public sale:] Sale to be begun and holden on Wednesday, Sept. 7, at 10 o'clock sharp A.M. **1975** Gould *ME Lingo* 134, *Holden*—An ancient past participle heard in formal contexts: Regular stated meeting of Ladies Aid was holden.

B Senses.

1 in var applications of std sense "be in possession of": See below. **esp Sth**

a See quot.

1952 Brown *NC Folkl.* 1.551, *Hold.* . . To examine, to look at. "Let me hold your program."—Rare.

b To lay claim to. Cf **hosey**

1966–70 *DARE* (Qu. V5b, *If you take something that nobody else seems to own, you might say, "Before anybody else gets it, I'm going to* ——— *this."*) Infs **LA**45, **MS**23, **VA**73, Hold.

c To borrow; to lend; see quot. [Cf *EDD hold* v. 17 "to owe, be indebted to"] Cf **borrow** v **B1**

1966 *DARE* (Qu. U16, *If somebody was caught short of money and went to a friend to get some, he might say, "I need five dollars before Saturday, will you* ——— *it to me?"*) Inf **SC**21, Hold; **VA**41, Let me hold it.

2 also with *out:* To take place, be held. Cf **keep**

1894 Riley *Armazindy* 54 **IN,** He wuzn't keerin' whether school helt out er not. **1965** *DARE* Tape **KY**2, Ourn [=church services] don't hold every Sunday.

3 with *to:* To adhere to; to share beliefs or practices with.

1944 Howard *Walkin' Preacher* 214 **Ozarks,** Everyone in Owsley and adjoining communities speculated upon which church his family "held to."

C Phrases.

1 in var phrr meaning to be patient, wait, not be hasty: See below. [By analogy with *hold one's horses*]

a *hold one's potato* and varr: See quots. **Sth, S Midl**

1892 *Congressional Record* 27 Jan 23.1.600/1 **GA,** Now, let me beg of the gentleman to hold his potato. **1936** *AmSp* 11.315 **Ozarks,** *Hold your potato.* . . To be patient. "Jest holt your 'tater, now—I'm a-comin' quick as I kin!" **1946** *PADS* 6.38 **eNC** (as of 1900–10), Hold your taters. (Don't become excited.) **1953** Randolph–Wilson *Down in Holler* 254 **Ozarks,** *Hold your potato.* . . *Hold your corn* is heard occasionally, with the same meaning. **1965–70** *DARE* (Qu. A21, *When someone is in too much of a hurry*) Inf **KY**28, Hold your potater; **NM**11, Hold your tater; (Qu. GG23c, . . *To tell someone to be patient*) Infs **IL**96, **SC**3, Hold your tater; **MS**45, Hold your potato till it gets cool; **NC**41, Hold your potato. **1985** *DARE* File **Appalachians,** Hold your tater—

be patient. **1986** Pederson *LAGS Concordance,* 3 infs, **eTN, cwGA,** Hold your (po)tato.

b *hold one's water* and varr: See quots. **chiefly NEast, Mid Atl** See Map Cf **water**

1912 *DN* 3.578 **wIN,** *Hold one's water. . .* To be patient. Vulgar. "Now, Willie, you just hold your water till the rest of us are ready to go." **1965–70** *DARE* (Qu. GG23b, *If you speak sharply to somebody to make him be patient, you might say, "Hold ______!"*) 16 Infs, **chiefly Nth, esp NEast; also Mid Atl,** Your water; **OH**2, Your dog water; (Qu. GG23c) Infs **MA**41, 71, **NH**10, **NY**92, **WA**6, **WI**20, Hold your water; **PA**227, Hold water; (Qu. A21, *When someone is in too much of a hurry*) Infs **NY**93, 118, Hold your water.

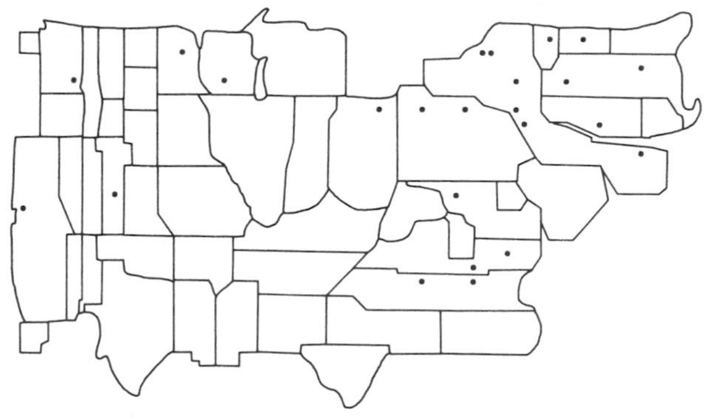

•hold v C1b + varr (Qq. GG23b, c, A21)

c *hold one's head:* See quot.

1970 *DARE* (Qu. GG23b, *If you speak sharply to somebody to make him be patient, you might say, "Hold ______!"*) Infs **TN**53, **VA**46, 69, Your head. [All Infs Black]

d in var other phrr: See quot. *somewhat old-fash*

1965–70 *DARE* (Qu. A21, *When someone is in too much of a hurry you might say*) Inf **MD**14, Hold your pants on; (Qu. GG23c, . . *Expressions [to tell someone to be patient]*) Inf **CA**9, Hold your dispy—disposition; **AL**30, Hold your galluses; **KY**65, Hold your kitties; **MO**21, Hold that mule. [All Infs old] **1986** Pederson *LAGS Concordance,* 1 inf, **cMS,** Just hold your shirt—to an angry man. [Inf old]

2 in phrr indicating unfavorable comparison of one person with another: See below. [By analogy with *hold a candle to*]

a *hold a light to* and varr: See quots. **chiefly Sth, S Midl, esp Gulf States, AR** See Map

1891 Johnston *Primes & Neighbors* 102 **GA,** He never much as hilt a light to the foot I slung in a quintillion [=cotillion] when my dander were up. **1965–70** *DARE* (Qu. LL32, *Expressions meaning that one man's ability is not nearly as great as another man's: "John can't [or doesn't . .] ______ Bill."*) 44 Infs, **chiefly Sth, S Midl, esp Gulf States, AR,** Hold (a) light to; **MS**30, Don't hold a light to; **MD**13, **NC**33, Hold (a) light for; **FL**31, **SC**40, Hold him a candlelight (to).

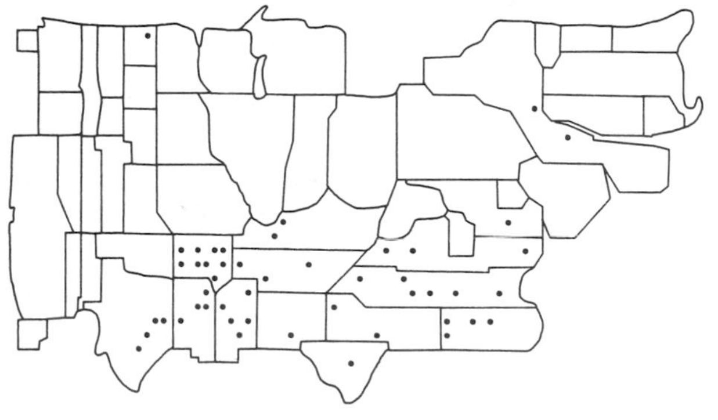

•hold v C2a + varr (Qu. LL32)

b *hold a match* (or *torch*) *to:* See quots. [Prob a blend of *hold a candle to* and *be a match for* where *match* has shifted meaning from "an equal" to "a match stick"] **esp N Cent** Cf **match**

1965–70 *DARE* (Qu. LL32, *Expressions meaning that one man's ability is not nearly as great as another man's: "John can't [or doesn't . .] ______ Bill."*) Infs **IL**97, **IN**80, **MI**44, Hold a match to; **IL**126, Hold a torch to.

c *hold a patch* (or *patching*) *to:* See quots. [Prob a blend of *hold a candle to* and *be a patch on*] Cf **patch**

1939 *AmSp* 14.266 **swIN,** Mary can't hold a patchin' to Susan. **1968–69** *DARE* (Qu. LL32, *Expressions meaning that one man's ability is not nearly as great as another man's: "John can't [or doesn't . .] ______ Bill."*) Infs **CA**136, **IN**38, Hold a patch to.

3 *hold one's mouth, hold the blow:* To stop talking, be silent. [By analogy with *hold one's tongue*] Cf *hush one's mouth* (at **hush B2**)

1935 Sandoz *Jules* 280 **wNE** (as of c1880s), "Hold your mouth." But Mary was in good spirits. "Now you can tell me to hold my mouth, but that don't change things. You still talk like a crazy man." **1968** *DARE* (Qu. X10b, *To tell a person to stop talking—not very politely*) Inf **AK**1, Hold the blow.

hold n Cf **ahold, ahold of, holt**

A Forms.

1 *holt.* [Engl dial; cf *OED holt* sb.[2] c1375 →] **chiefly NEng, Sth, S Midl**

1825 Neal *Brother Jonathan* 2.60 **NEast,** [He cried] "lay holt here; lay holt, every one o' you!"—throwing the reins behind him, into the carriage. **1884** *Anglia* 7.261 **Sth, S Midl** [Black], To git ur holt = to catch hold of. **1892** *DN* 1.239 **cwMO,** *Holt. . .* In Michigan [holt]. . . In New England [hɵlt]. **1893** Shands *MS Speech* 37, *Holt* [holt] . . heard among all classes. **1894** (1934) Robinson *Danvis Folks* 125 **VT,** "Lemme see," said Uncle Lisha, stimulating his brain with the point of an awl. "Oh, yes, I've got a holt on 't." **1908** *DN* 3.321 **eAL, wGA,** *Holt. . .* Ketch holt. Common. **1914** *DN* 4.74 **nNH, ME. 1923** *DN* 5.211 **swMO. 1927** Adams *Congaree* 42 **cSC** [Black], Hold your holt! **1941** Stuart *Men of Mts.* 301 **eKY,** I'd just grab her with loving holts. **1943** *LANE* Map 567 *(Pitch in),* [In the phrase *take (a) hold* the pronunciation *holt* occurs **throughout NEng** but is found less frequently in southern New England.] **1958** McCulloch *Woods Words* 87 **Pacific NW,** *Holt* . . a piece of rigging tied down to a stump or other anchor. **1960** Criswell *Resp. to PADS 20* **Ozarks,** *Holt*—once the usual expression. Still widely used. **c1960** *Wilson Coll.* **csKY,** Hold [holt] or [ə'holt]. **1966** *DARE* Tape **GA**1, The dogs would get a holt to her; **OK**24, My daddy kinda had a holt [hoəˀ] in this country.

2 *helt, hilt.* [Cf **hold** v **A2a, c**]

1952 Brown *NC Folkl.* 1.550, *Hilt. . .* Hold. "I got a hilt of that coon by the hind leg." . . Illiterate. **1954** *Harder Coll.* **cwTN,** *Helt*—A hold.

B Senses.

1 in phrr *best hold, main ~;* usu as *holt:* A special talent, favorite activity. [Cf *OED holt* sb.[2]1 "Hold . . support, sustenance. *dial.*" and *EDD hold* sb. 12 "A hobby, favourite pursuit"]

1884 Twain *Huck. Finn* 183 **MO,** I've done considerble [sic] in the doctoring way in my time. Layin' on o' hands is my best holt. **1906** Peck *Peck's Bad Boy with Circus* 133 **WI,** Pa said driving ten horses was his best hold, and he got up on the driver's seat. **1907** Lincoln *Cape Cod* 92 **MA,** We knew Peter'd have some plan thought out by that time. We'd left a note . . saying that we trusted to him to explain matters. . . We knew that explaining was Peter's main holt. **1932** Randolph *Ozark Mt. Folks* 50, Spellin' was allus our main holt, an' thar was some of 'em got so dang good at it they spelt down th' hull school purty nigh ever' day. **1933** Williamson *Woods Colt* 6 **Ozarks,** You see how he [=a catfish] fries . . an' I'll see how he chaws. Fried cat is my main holt. *Ibid* 124, Windy is a good feller, but dog fights is shore his main holt.

2 as *holt:* A bat-and-ball game; see quot. [Perh a different word]

1940 *Hench Coll.* **VA,** He knew as a boy a ballgame called "holt." In it there were two sets of catchers and batter. Fielders were here and there around. The catcher at one end threw the ball to be hit by the batter at the other end. You put a man out by "chewing," i.e., hitting him with the ball.

hold a light to See **hold** v **C2a**

hold a match to See **hold** v **C2b**

hold a patch(ing) to See **hold** v **C2c**

hold a torch to See **hold** v **C2b**

holdback n, also attrib **Pacific NW**

In logging: see quots.

1958 McCulloch *Woods Words* 87 **Pacific NW,** *Holdback*—Another name for the haulback line particularly when it was held under tension in order to keep the turn [=a unit of logs being yarded] partly off the ground in yarding [=getting logs from the stump to the landing]. *Ibid, Holdback block*—A stout chunk of log slotted into the bottom of a chute . . placed ahead of a turn of logs and held back by a cable . . thus acting as a brake on the logs going down the chute. *Ibid, Holdback line*—A haulback used as a brake on a downhill haul in the O'Gorman system of cable logging. **1967** *DARE* Tape **WA**24, You have a block down below. And that's where you had your holdback line on, and you top that down with chokers on it, and then choke the logs and then you hold your haulback and pick up the main line and you'd pick the logs up and here you come with them. [Inf old, worked as a logger]

hold down v phr [Prob abbr for *hold it down* be quiet] Cf **hold** v **C1, 3**

To be quiet; to remain calm.

1970 *DARE* (Qu. NN19, *When you want people to stop talking for a moment so that you can listen for something, you say*) Inf **TN**46, Hold down. **1986** Pederson *LAGS Concordance (Keep calm)* 2 infs, **cnTN, cMS,** Hold down.

holden past pple See **hold** v **A3b**

holden adj [From past pple of **hold** v (at **A3**); *OED hold* v. 10 "*Obs.* or *arch.*"]

=**beholden,** indebted, obligated.

1794 Williams *Nat. & Civil Hist. VT* 253 **VT,** They could not view themselves as holden . . to submit. **1841** (1969) Emerson *Essays* 170 **MA,** We are holden to men by every sort of tie, by blood, by pride, . . by every circumstance and badge and trifle. **1848** (1940) Arnold *Diaries* 181 **VT,** He was wishing to raise $75,000. But, if 25,000 are subscribed, the subscribers are holden. **1954** *Harder Coll.* **cwTN,** *Holden*—in debt.

holdfast n [From the propensity of the infection to become chronic] Cf **lump jaw, wolf**

A lesion resulting from actinomycosis, a chronic disease esp of the bony tissue of the head.

1894 *DN* 1.331 **NJ,** *Holdfast:* a sore, eating to the bone, which may come from various causes. **1924** *DN* 5.295 **csNH,** *Holdfast*. . . Same as wolf [=a swelling on the neck of cattle], a swelling.

hold fast what I give you n For varr see quots

The children's game **button B2;** also used as a phrase in the game.

1883 Newell *Games & Songs* 150 **GA,** *Hold fast my gold ring.* The children sit in a circle, with hands closed; one takes the ring, and goes around with it, tapping the closed fists of the players as if inserting the ring, and saying: Biddy, biddy, hold fast my gold ring, . . Each child, in turn, is then required to guess who has the ring. [**1899** Champlin–Bostwick *Young Folks' Games* 122, *Button, Button,* a drawing-room game. . . The leader goes to each in turn, saying, "Hold fast what I give you," . . and gives the button . . to any one of the players he chooses.] **1967–68** *DARE* (Qu. EE1, . . *Games . . children play . . in which they form a ring*) Inf **MD**26, Hold tight to what I give you—"it" passed around the circle, cupped hands over each child's cupped hands, dropped an object unseen into one child's hands; some guessing process ensued, where somebody had to guess who had the object; (Qu. EE3, *Games in which you hide an object*) Inf **CA**20, Hold fast all I give you [FW: same as *button, button*].

hold herd v phr

To keep a herd of cattle together.

1941 Writers' Program *Guide WY* 462, *Hold herd*—To keep the herd from drifting. **1966** *DARE* Tape **MT**5, He wanted me to take this horse and help hold herd fer 'im, while he was brandin'. . . 'n' this old cow made that run outa that herd. . . Why, I turned this old pony around to head 'er off.

hold high windows See **high windows**

hold on by one's eyelids See **eyelids, hang by one's 2**

hold one's corn See **hold** v **C1a**

hold one's dog water See **hold** v **C1b**

hold one's hands v phr Cf *twiddle one's thumbs*

To idle away time.

1899 (1912) Green *VA Folk-Speech* 228, *Holding her hands*. . . Idle, unemployed. "There she stands holding her hands." **1966** Barnes–Jensen *Dict. UT Slang* 24, *Hold hands* . . to idle. . . "I'm standing here waiting—just holding my hands." **1966–70** *DARE* (Qu. A10, . . *Doing little unimportant things*) Inf **FL**26, Sitting around holding your hands; (Qu. KK60, *Having nothing in particular to do*) Inf **NC**84, Holding my hands. [**1976** Ryland *Richmond Co. VA* 372, *Holding one's hands*—idle.]

hold one's head See **hold** v **C1c**

hold one's mouth See **hold** v **C3**

hold one's potato See **hold** v **C1a**

hold one's water See **hold** v **C1b**

hold out See **hold** v **B2**

holdover n

1 Food remaining from a previous meal; a leftover. Cf **coldover**

1904 *Los Angeles Express* (CA) 11 Aug 12/2 **Los Angeles CA,** Los Angeles was waiting for the staff of life and doing the best it could on crackers and cheese and holdovers. **1969** *DARE* (Qu. H67, *Food that was not finished at one meal but saved for another*) Inf **NY**66, Holdovers.

2 A layover, stopover.

1966–70 *DARE* (Qu. N38, *On a trip when you have to change trains and wait a while between them, you might say, "I have a two-hour ——— in Chicago."*) 10 Infs, **scattered,** Holdover.

hold-still n

A **fringed orchid** (here: either *Habenaria blephariglottis* or *H. ciliaris*).

1966 *DARE* Wildfl QR Plates 37B, 38 Inf **NC**28, Hold-stills.

hold the blow See **hold** v **C3**

hold them in the road v phr

Have a safe journey!—used as an expression of farewell (orig to the driver of a team of animals).

1966–68 *DARE* (Qu. NN11, *Informal ways of saying 'good-bye' to people you know quite well*) Infs **GA**13, **NC**52, Hold 'em in the road.

hold tight to what I give you See **hold fast what I give you**

hold to See **hold** v **B3**

hole n

1 Any of var bodies of water—often used in place names; see below.

a A pond or sinkhole. **esp S Atl** Cf **alligator hole, wash hole**

1743 (1754) Catesby *Nat. Hist. Carolina* 2.72 **S Atl,** By the continual running of the Water, a small Pond or Hole is usually made before the Mouth of the Spring. **1791** Bartram *Travels* 238 **FL,** A very curious place, called the Alligator-Hole, which was lately formed by an extraordinary eruption or jet of water; it is one of those vast circular sinks. . . the water is transparent, cool . . and well stored with fish; a very large alligator at present is lord or chief. **1970** *DARE* FW Addit **VA**47, Some holes are fresh water. They can get brackish through the occasional addition of tidal water through a gut, but these are spring-fed and can keep themselves fresh, e.g., Turkle Hole on Assateague where deer and ponies drink. **1986** Pederson *LAGS Concordance,* 1 inf, **cMS,** Running water blows out a hole.

b A small bay or harbor; a strait; a channel—usu found in place names. **chiefly MA, VA** Cf **guzzle hole, swash**

1639 in *Va. Hist. Mag.* III.31 *(DA),* Yf the shipps be p'mitted to goe at pleasure and ride in every hole as is desired by them. **1651** in 1889 Plymouth MA *Records* 1.22 **MA,** Nathaniell Morton Requested . . a smale moyetie of land lying betwixt the hieway . . and the water side or Creeke commonly called and known by the name of hobshole. **a1782** (1788) Jefferson *Notes VA* 4, *Rappahanock* affords 4 fathom water to Hobb's hole, and 2 fathom from thence to Fredricksburg. **1801** in 1889 MA Hist. Soc. *Coll.* 4.127, The most frequented though rocky and narrow navigation lies between the North East point of Nonimasit and the South Westerly parts of Falmouth, and is called Wood's hole. A second between Nashant and Pesk is called Robinson's hole. A third, between Pesk and Nashawinna, Quick's hole. **1905** Wasson *Green Shay* 16 **NEng coast,** Afore another pore devil stubs his toe a-tryin' to find a hole in the beach [Footnote: To make a harbor]. **1954** *AmSp* 29.252 **eVA,** *Hole* denotes a narrow way in a channel. This meaning of *hole* is clearly demonstrated in the name of Flood's Hole, which is a narrow, winding channel in the marshes north of Grand View. **1976** *Yankee* Oct 56 **seMA,** I know from 20 years' living in Woods Hole that "The Hole" refers to the channel between the mainland and Nonamessett

Island. . . Narrow straits are known as holes, or guts. . . Quicks Hole and Robinsons Hole . . are narrow straits between the Elizabeth Islands. . . It [=a hole] is not an indication of safe anchorage.

c A deep place in a larger body of water; a pool of still water in a running stream; a water-filled pocket that extends under the bank. **chiefly Sth, S Midl** Cf **cathole**

1792 in 1940 *AmSp* 15.274 **VA,** To the bank of the Creek at a place known by the Twin hole. **1810** *Ibid,* To a hickory & maple in narrows above a deep hole in the creek. **1902** *DN* 2.236 **sIL,** *Hole. . .* A pool, formed by the widening and deepening of a stream in its course, as "feeshin hole," "swimmin hole." **1906** *DN* 3.119 **cwIN,** *Hole. . .* A pool of water in a stream. **1907** *DN* 3.223 **nwAR, sIL. 1941** Perry *Hold Autumn* 44 **TX,** Sam stopped at the old buffalo hole. A buffalo hole is any particularly deep and still pool where people dribble corn kernels to attract the big sucking fish. **1946** Attwood *Length ME* 14, *Hole*—A place where the water is comparatively deep. Devils Hole. **1960** Criswell *Resp. to PADS 20* **Ozarks** *(A wide place in a river)* Holes are usually stretches of deep water from three hundred feet in length to an eighth of a mile. They usually have local names since they are excellent places to catch catfish: the Long Hole, the Round Hole, Huyck's Hole, the Carlock Hole. **1965–70** *DARE* (Qu. P16, *When fishermen throw bits of bait in the water to attract fish*) Infs **AR**51, **ID**3, **MO**15, **TN**26, **TX**33, 35, 37, Baiting the (*or* a) hole; **IA**8, Baiting the hole—don't do that; **OK**11, Baiting the hole—use corn in a sack, bran, anything that will sour; **KS**10, Feeding the hole; **WY**5, Seeding the hole—illegal; (Qu. C4a, . . *A fairly large body of fresh water*) Inf **GA**89, Hole—a wide place in a creek; **KY**11, Hole; **SC**32, Hole—a pool in a creek or branch, 3–4 feet to 10 feet deep; **LA**20, Hole of water. **1986** Pederson *LAGS Concordance,* 1 inf, **csGA,** Gator holes—open places to fish in. **1989** *DARE* File **neMO,** A hole is a spot under the bank of the river. . . It cuts back in under the bank; it's horizontal, not vertical. A good fishin' hole is up to about an arm's length deep and right under the bank.

2 A valley, esp one protected or hidden by steep mountains—freq used in place-names. **NW, CO** Cf **park**

1714 in 1917 Topsfield Hist. Soc. *Town Rec.* 1.185 **neMA,** A Tree marked Standing by ye side of a round Hole or valley. **1787** in 1940 *AmSp* 15.274 **VA,** To ash and Hickory near a valley or hole. **1832** *Eve. and Morning Star* (Independence MO) Oct 7/1 **wWY,** The company was attacked in Piers Hole, on the 12th of July last, by the Black feet Indians. **1845** Frémont *Rept. Rocky Mts.* 279 **neUT,** We descended to *"Brown's hole."* This is a place well known to trappers in the country, where the cañons through which the Colorado runs expand into a narrow but pretty valley. **1850** Hines *Voyage Round World* 323 **OR,** The southern part of this third region . . is distinguished by its steep and rugged mountains, deep and dismal valleys, called *holes,* by mountaineers. **1915** *DN* 4.244 **MT,** *Hole. . .* Valley. **1949** *PADS* 11.22 **CO,** *Hole. . .* A small secluded and isolated park or open space surrounded by mountains. Used with names of people: "Pat's Hole." The holes in Colorado were probably originally hideouts. **1950** *AmSp* 25.163 **CO,** In northwestern Colorado . . *hole* is used instead of *park. . .* The holes are small parks well hidden in high mountains. . . Many of the holes are named after individuals: Pat's Hole, Brown's Hole, etc. **1958** *AmSp* 33.101 **WY,** In Wyoming a word for . . mountain valley is *hole,* as in Jackson Hole. **1970** Stewart *Amer. Place-Names* 208 **MT,** *Big Hole River. . .* flows through a big hole, i.e. isolated valley.

3 often *potato hole:* An excavation in the ground for storing root crops, vegetables and, less freq, dairy products; the quantity of foodstuffs stored in such a place. **chiefly S Midl** See Map Cf **cave n 1, hole v 1**

c1770 in 1832 Boucher *Glossary* 1 **MD,** All the *'moodies* [=sweet potatoes] I / For *Mollsey,* in my *'tatoe-hole,* put by. **1839** *Knickerbocker* 13.305 **ME,** Under a part of the floor, was a small excavation in the earth, which the host called his potato-hole, since, being near the fire, it served in winter to keep his potatoes from freezing. **1843** (1916) Hall *New Purchase* 95 **IN,** Under the parlour, was the Potato Hole! And that held about twenty bushels. The descent into this spacious vault, was accomplished by raising a puncheon and vaulting down on the vegetables. **1846** (1939) Loehr *MN Farmers' Diaries* 70 **Upper Missip Valley,** We took up a hole of Turnips & put them in the Stable. **1940** Wright-Corbett *Pioneer Life* 248, Potato Hole—A hole dug several feet deep in the ground in which potatoes or turnips were kept during the winter. **1954** *McDavid Coll.* **seKY,** Potato hole—root cellar. **1966–70** *DARE* (Qu. M19, *A place for keeping carrots, turnips, potatoes, and so on over the winter*) Infs **AR**4, **KY**28, **NC**35, **OH**50, 77, Hole (in ground); **KY**23, Hole—obsolete practice [Inf old]; **TN**42, Hole—straw; **OH**58, Bury them in a hole; **GA**72, **KY**35, **NC**36, **TN**1, Potato (*or* carrot, turnip, vegetable) hole. **1986** Pederson *LAGS Concordance (A place for storing produce in the winter)* 1 inf, **csGA,** Hole—where potatoes are stored; 3 infs, **eTN,** Potato hole; *(Dairy—storage)* 1 inf, **cwTN,** A milk hole—dug in ground for milk and butter.

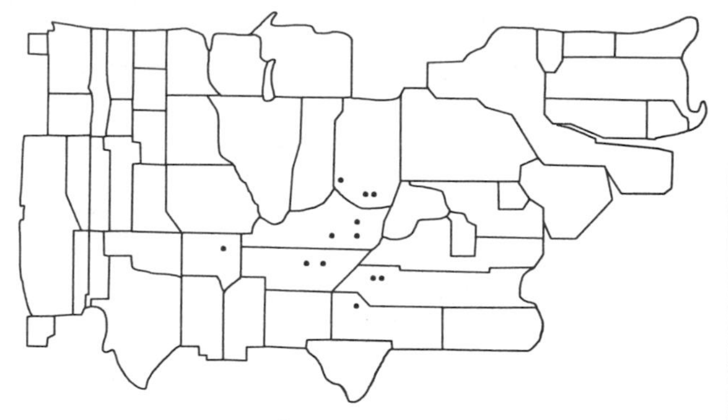

•hole n 3 + varr (Qu. M19)

4 also pl, often in combs: Any of several marble games which involve shooting into a hole; see quots. Cf **bunny-in-the-hole, holey n 1, rolly-holey**

1899 Champlin-Bostwick *Young Folks' Games* 485, *Three Holes. . .* three little holes are made in a row. . . The players in turn shoot . . at the first hole. . . When the second hole is made, the third hole is shot at . . he who first gets his marble into it wins. **1906** Lovett *Old Boston Boys* 43 **MA,** Then there was "ring taw" and "three holes," and lots of other names which have been forgotten. These games were good fun, and kept boys out of doors as well as out of mischief. **1965–70** *DARE* (Qu. EE7, . . *Marble games*) Infs **CA**14, **TX**1, 18, Hole; **CA**190, Holes; **GA**42, Holes—three holes in ground; **FL**48, Hole game; **NV**3, Hole marbles; **HI**9, One-hole—go into hole before can hit other fellow's marble; **NC**22, Three-holes—try to get them in the holes; **TX**37, Four-holes—go progressively from one hole to the other [FW illustr: Three are in a line, with the fourth at a right angle to the third.]; [play with] partners; **GA**13, Four-hole marbles; **HI**6, Five-holes—similar to croquet [=golf]; set thumb in hole and span; go from hole to hole; **HI**9A, Five-holes; [**CA**15, Shooting for holes; **LA**8, Shootin' in the hole;] **RI**3, Hole-in-the-ground—threw marbles, had to scoop them in with fingers; girls played " 'something' in the hole"—can't remember what; also, make hole in ground, put agate in it and you poon [sic] the marbles and try to hit the agate. **1966–70** *DARE* Tape **CA**190, Holes is played with four holes; **GA**13, We played two types of marble games. One of 'em was known as hole marble games, the other one was known as the ring marble game. **c1970** Wiersma *Marbles Terms* **swMI,** *Hole in the ground;* a . . game where the object is to propel one's marble nearer the cavity than one's opponent does. **1973** Ferretti *Marble Book* 46, *Hole games.* Games in which the object is to get marbles in a hole, out of a hole, a certain distance from a hole—always a hole. [*Ibid, Hole.* Also called pot. Holes in marbles games can vary in depth—from the size of a twelve-year-old's heel to something dug out with a garden spade. Shallow holes are called saucers.] **1986** Pederson *LAGS Concordance,* 1 inf, **Miami FL,** Hole—marble game, six or seven holes.

5 Among railroaders:

a A siding, sidetrack—often used in phr *in the hole;* see quots.

1930 *RR Man's Mag.* June 470, *Hole*—Term applied to passing track where one train pulls in to meet another. **1938** Beebe *High Iron* 222, *Hole:* Side track for passing trains on a single track line. **1943** *Sat. Eve. Post* 26 June 75/1 **CA,** A single-track line, the freighters had to spend much time "in the hole"—on sidings—while the priority trains passed. **1968** *AmSp* 43.287 [Railroad vocab], *Hole.* A reserve track. The wreck train, for example, is placed "in the hole" when not in service. The term also designates a "passing track," where, for example, a *drag* might be delayed so that a higher priority train could pass it. **1969** *AmSp* 44.251 **IL,** Freight trains must periodically go *in the hole,* or head into a siding in order to let another train pass on the main line.

b See quot.

1945 Hubbard *Railroad Ave.* 348, *In the hole. . .* in the lower berth of a Pullman [=a sleeping car], as contrasted with *on the top,* in the upper berth.

6 also in combs *hole-fried bread, hole-in-one:* See quot. Cf **doughnut hole, fried hole**

1963 Marsh *Good Housekeeping Cookbook* 490, *Doughnuts. . . "Holes":* Use centers cut out from doughnuts; or using small biscuit cutter, cut all dough into "holes." Fry, sugar. Nice with fruit. **1967–70** *DARE* (Qu. H27, . . *Joking names for doughnuts*) Infs **MA**125, **PA**131, Holes; **AZ**12, Hole-in-one; **LA**9, Hole-fried bread.

7 in var combs referring to an outhouse: See quots. Cf **-holer**

1962 Carrell *Autobiog.* 44 **ceMA** (as of 1880s), The kerosene lantern . . was always kept handy in winter in case you had to make the trip to the two hole house. **1966–68** *DARE* (Qu. M21b, *Joking names for an outside toilet building*) Inf **MN**33, Stinky-hole. **1986** Pederson *LAGS Concordance (Outhouse)* 1 inf, **seAL,** Double hole; 1 inf, **nwFL,** Dump hole.

8 with *the;* Fig: Hell.

1970 *DARE* (Qu. CC9, . . *Expressions for hell: "That man is headed straight for ______."*) Inf **NY**241, The hole.

9 in var combs: See below.

a *hole-in-the-wall* (or *-door*): A place that sells liquor, usu illegally. **esp NEast** See Map Cf **blind tiger 1**

1856 *Iroquois Republican* (Watseka IL) 25 Dec 2/3, The social and moral ulcer, which we deem the retailing . . of ardent spirits to be. . . it is a monstrous, damning crime. . . a "grocery"—a "doggery"—a "hole-in-the-wall"—is an "odious damned spot" in any community. **1887** MN Laws *Genl. Statutes* 2.248, Whoever shall attempt to evade or violate any of the laws of this state . . by means of the artifice or contrivance known as the "Blind Pig," or "Hole in the Wall" . . shall . . be punished. **1965–70** *DARE* (Qu. DD30, . . *A place where liquor is [or was] sold and consumed illegally*) 14 Infs, **chiefly NEast,** Hole-in-the-wall; **MI**107, Hole-in-the-door. [14 of 15 Infs male]

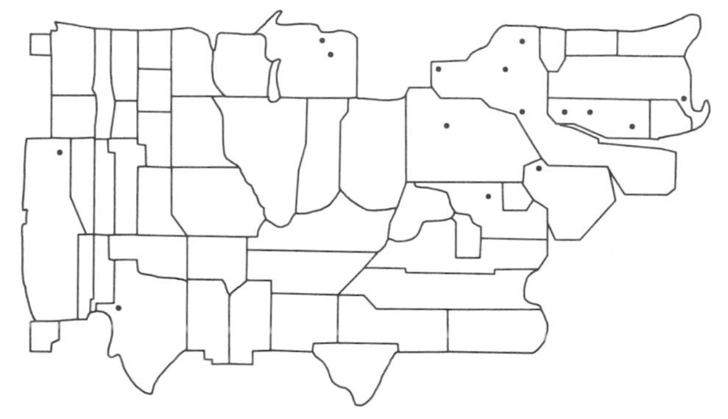

•hole n 9a + varr (Qu. DD30)

b *hole-in-the-wall* (or *-road*) and varr: A small or insignificant place.

1906 *DN* 3.141 **nwAR,** *Hole in the road. . .* A hamlet. "After driving several miles we came to a hole in the road." **1965–70** *DARE* (Qu. C33, . . *An out-of-the-way place, or a very unimportant place*) 16 Infs, **scattered,** (Little) hole-in-the-wall; **DE**1, **FL**37, **MS**2, 45, **MO**2, **NC**10, 25, **TX**17, (Deep *or* wide) hole-in-the-road; **IL**5, Hole-in-the-woods; **MS**55, Hole-in-the-ground. **1986** Pederson *LAGS Concordance,* 2 infs, **csGA, Houston TX,** A (little) hole in the road [is] a very small town; 1 inf, **neFL,** Palatka used to be a hole in the road.

10 in var phrr: See below.

a *crawl into one's hole* and varr: To back down or retreat; see quots.

1889 *Century Dict.* 2856, *To crawl into one's hole,* to retire defeated: used especially of an aggressor who is worsted. **1950** *WELS (To show someone you're the boss: "He thought he could run everything, but I made him ______.")* 1 Inf, **WI,** Crawl in his hole; 1 Inf, Hunt his hole. **1968** *DARE* (Qu. II22, . . *To tell somebody to keep to himself and mind his own business*) Inf **WI**34, Go back in your own hole.

b *down to the last hole* and varr: Completely, perfectly.

1872 Burnham *Memoirs U.S. Secret Service* 348, He wanted to get some U.S. Revenue stamps for his barrels, in trade, if he could get them cheap. This suited Grover, "to a hole." **1966–67** *DARE* (Qu. KK50, *When something is planned out carefully down to the last detail: "He had it all worked out ______."*) Infs **MI**27, **MO**7, Down to the last (nail) hole.

c *in a hole:* Marred by a hole.

1942 Warnick *Garrett Co. MD* 9 **nwMD** (as of 1900–18), *In a hole . .* has a hole worn in it. "His sock is in a hole".

d *not to know one from a hole in the ground* (or *wall*) and varr: Not to recognize a person. **scattered, but esp NEast, N Cent** See Map Cf **Adam's off-ox 1**

1950 *WELS ("I wouldn't know him from ______.")* 13 Infs, **WI,** A hole in the ground; 3 Infs, A hole in the wall; 1 Inf, A hole in the tree. **1958** *VT Hist.* new ser 26.275, Don't know him from a hole in the wall. **1965–70** *DARE* (Qu. II26, . . *Ways of saying that you would not know . . somebody . . "I wouldn't know him from ______."*) 53 Infs, **scattered, but esp NEast, N Cent,** A hole in the ground; 23 Infs, **scattered, but esp NEast,** A hole in the wall; **CT**3, **NY**105, A hole in the fence; **NY**119, A hole in my ass. **1985–87** *DARE* File *(Ways of saying that you would not know . . somebody . . "I wouldn't know him from ______.")* 5 infs, **NJ, seNY, VA,** A hole in the wall; 1 inf, **Los Angeles CA,** A hole in the ground.

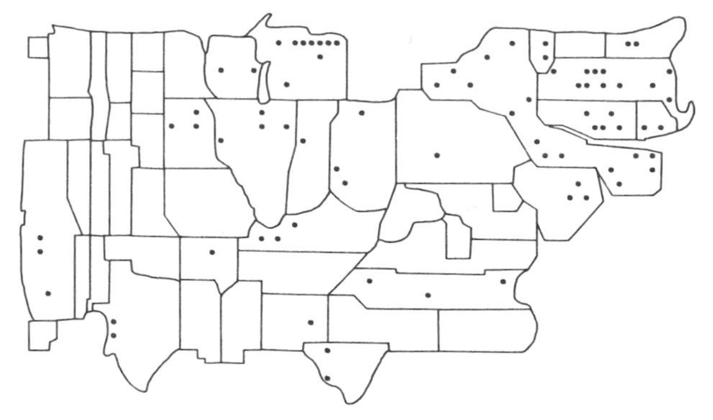

•hole n 10d + varr (Qu. II26)

e *not to know one's ass from a hole in the ground* (or *wall*) and varr: **=ass from one's elbow, not to know one's.**

1960 Bailey *Resp. to PADS 20* **KS** *(Sayings about somebody who seems . . to be very stupid: "He hasn't sense enough to ______.")* [Know his] ass from a hole in the ground. **1965–70** *DARE* (Qu. JJ15b, . . *A person who seems . . very stupid: "He doesn't know ______."*) 82 Infs, **scattered,** His ass (*or* beans, head, etc) from a hole in the ground (*or* hole in the wall).

‡f *the hole is deep enough:* See quot.

1968 *DARE* (Qu. BB56, *Joking expressions for dying*) Inf **CA**59, The hole is deep enough—a mining term.

hole v[1]

1 usu with *up:* To store (potatoes or other vegetables or fruits) in a **hole** n **3;** hence vbl n *holing.* **esp sAppalachians**

1924 Raine *Land of Saddle-Bags* 212 **Appalachians,** A family . . will not starve. If further provender can be laid up, so much the better. They may "hole up" in the garden a pyramid of potatoes, another of cabbage, and another of turnips, and dig them out when the larder runs low. **1927** *DN* 5.469 **Appalachians,** *Hole up. . .* To store *away;* as, to hole up potatoes for the winter. **1967–69** *DARE* (Qu. M19, *A place for keeping carrots, turnips, potatoes . . over the winter*) Infs **KY**9, 28, **TN**19, Hole 'em (up); **OH**50, Mounds covered with straw or leaves, then with earth; called holing. **1968** *DARE* Tape **IN**51, We raised the potaters. We holed 'em up and buried 'em in the ground. [Tossed] around straw like this, put our taters on top of that, then we put straw on top of that, then we covered 'em up wi' dirt. . . [Didn't] care how hard it froze, anytime you wanted some taters, go out and dig you a little hole in that. . . Turnips the same way, apples the same way, we took care of cabbage the same way. **1986** Pederson *LAGS Concordance (Storing produce in the winter)* 3 infs, **TN,** Hole them [=potatoes] up (in the ground); 1 inf, **neTN,** Hole them up in a garden—like a grave; 1 inf, **neTN,** Hole them up in a potato hole; 1 inf, **cnAR,** They used to hole up turnips in winter.

2 To drive (prey) into a hiding place.

1862 *Harper's New Mth. Mag.* 25.8/1 **CA,** We've got him [=a man] holed, any how! It won't take long to root him out [of an adobe building]. **1929** Summers *Annals* 1320 **swVA,** Each claiming that his dog "holed" her [=a wolf]. **1950** Stuart *Hie Hunters* 30 **KY,** If Shootin'

Star [=a hunting dog] puts one in a hole, we'll have to dig it out. If he holes one in a hollow log, we can use the ax part of the mattock to chop him out.

hole v² See **hold v A1b**

hole cover See **cover B2**

hole-fried bread See **hole n 6**

hole-gone adj

Worthless because of having holes.

1940 *Sat. Eve. Post* 22 June 87/1 **swOR,** The boys' wool socks I'd made, and then, when they were hole-gone, had raveled down for the rug.

hole-in-one See **hole n 6**

hole-in-the-door See **hole n 9a**

hole-in-the-ground See **hole n 4**

hole-in-the-ground fieldstone n

1957 *Seattle Daily Times* (WA) 14 Apr 6/1 *(Perrin Coll.),* Oregon basalt stone and Spokane "hole in the ground" fieldstone.

hole-in-the-road See **hole n 9b**

hole-in-the-sand plant n

A low-growing composite desert plant *(Nicolletia occidentalis).*

1941 Jaeger *Wildflowers* 299 **Desert SW,** *Hole-in-the-sand plant. . .* A striking feature of this *Nicolletia* is its habit of always growing in the bottom of shallow depressions which are about the size of hoof-prints and an inch or more deep.

hole in the snow See **pisshole in the snow**

hole-in-the-wall See **hole n 9a, b**

-holer n Cf **hole n 7**

As the last element in var combs: An outhouse having a specified number of seats.

1962 Atwood *Vocab. TX* 53, *Outdoor toilet* . . a number of local, individualistic, and imaginative terms occur occasionally. [Footnote:] For example, . . *one-* (or more) *holer.* **1963** Burroughs *Head-First* 66 **wCO** (as of c1910), The only toilet facility consisted of a one-holer on the alley. **1965–70** *DARE* (Qu. M21b, *Joking names for an outside toilet building*) 61 Infs, **scattered, but less freq Sth, S Midl,** One- (*or* two-, three-, four-)holer; [**PA**3, Shit-holer;] (Qu. M21a, *An outside toilet building*) 11 Infs, **esp Nth,** One- (*or* two-, three-, four-)holer. **1968** *DARE* FW Addit **CA**105, Outside toilet facilities—two-holer, four-holer. **1973** Allen *LAUM* 1.181 (as of c1950), 1 inf, **cwNE,** One holer . . two-holer; 1 inf, **seIA,** Three-holer. **1976** Garber *Mountain-ese* 63 **Appalachians,** *One-holer* . . single service john. **1986** Pederson *LAGS Concordance* **widespread throughout Gulf Region,** [Responses include *one* (or *two, three, four, five*) *-holer;* 1 inf, **Miami FL,** The john was a one-holer with a drop door; 1 inf, **seLA,** Two-holer—considered pretty rich if had one; 1 inf, **ceAR,** Three-holer—small, medium, and large.]

hole up See **hole v¹ 1**

holey adj **esp S Midl, C Atl** See Map Cf **chuckhole 1**

Of a road: bumpy, rough, full of holes.

1965–70 *DARE* (Qu. N27b, *When unpaved roads get very rough, you call them* ______) 16 Infs, **esp S Midl, C Atl,** Holey (roads); **MS**73, Get holey.

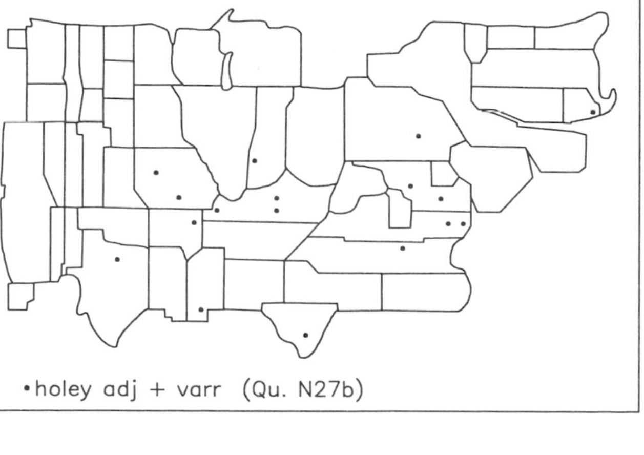

•holey adj + varr (Qu. N27b)

holey n [*holey* prob dimin of **hole n 4** (and folk-etym or punning sp *holy*)]

1 also *holey-bang* (or *-boley, -holey*): Any of several marble games involving one or more shallow holes in the ground; see quots. [Cf *EDD holie*] Cf **bunny-in-the-hole, hole n 4, rolly-holey**

[**1894** (1964) Gomme *Traditional Games* 1.51, *Bun-hole. . .* Sometimes, when several holes are made, the game is called "Holy." *Ibid* 1.218, *Holy Bang*—A game with marbles, which consists in placing a marble in a hole and making it act as a target for the rest. The marble which can hit it three times in succession, and finally be shot into the hole, is the winning ball, and its owner gets all the other marbles which have missed before he played.] **1966** *DARE* File **swIN,** Holey-holey—A children's game played with marbles tossed in a hole and progressing through a series of holes. Can also be played with washers. **1968** *DARE* (Qu. EE7, . . *Marble games*) Inf **TX**54, Holey; **UT**4, Holey—you'd make a little hole in the ground and try to roll your marble into it. The one who got his marble in the hole won all the rest of them. **1970** *DARE* Tape **VA**38, [We] called . . [this game] . . holey-boley. . . The children mostly shot holey-boley. Cut little holes in the ground . . three yards [apart] . . about three holes. . . You'd get down on the ground, or on your knee, and you'd shoot for to go in that [first] hole . . the one [who won] the first hole [would] . . get first shot from then on out as long as he can roll every hole. . . Whoever went up to the far end and come back and get in this [last] hole . . was out . . but if you catch up with him and thump . . his marble, he'd be dead. He was out the game. . . Called it holey-boley. **1973** Ferretti *Marble Book* 69, *Holy bang*—Place a marble in a dug out hole as a target. The first player able to get his marble into the hole and so hit the target marble three times is the winner and collects all of the missed marbles tossed in the game.

2 in combs *holey-boley, holy roller:* A large marble, sometimes glass.

1963 *KY Folkl. Rec.* 9.3.58, *Large marbles* . . holy roller. **1970** *DARE* Tape **VA**38, Then the glass marbles come about [=were produced]. We used to call them holey-boleys.

holey-bang See **holey n 1**

holey-boley See **holey n 1, 2**

holey-holey See **holey n 1**

holey-rolly See **rolly-holey**

holia n

=**humpback salmon.**

1882 U.S. Natl. Museum *Bulletin* 16.305, *O[ncorhynchus] gorbuscha. . . Holia. . .* Pacific coast and rivers . . from Oregon northward. **1887** Goode *Amer. Fishes* 480, The Gorbuscha . . is known as "Holia." **1902** Jordan–Evermann *Amer. Fishes* 150, Among other names applied to this species are . . holia [etc]. **1949** Caine *N. Amer. Sport Fish* 54, *Humpback salmon. . .* This species is also known as . . Holia.

holibut See **halibut**

holiday n [*OED holiday* sb. 3 "*colloq. Naut.* A spot carelessly left uncoated in tarring or painting"; *EDD holiday* sb. 4 "Parts left untouched in dusting, sweeping, painting, & c."]

1 A place overlooked or untouched in a piece of work, esp in painting; see quots.

1916 *DN* 4.266 **Cape Cod MA,** The tiny bare spots remaining after a painter has drawn his brush hastily over a surface are "holidays," spaces in which the painter did no work. **1948** Peattie *Berkshires* 326 **MA,** When he cut hay, he never left "holidays"; he never skimped on the edges; he never failed to scythe around boulders or bits of ledge; and he never allowed hedgerows to encroach on the hayfields. **1960** Wentworth–Flexner *Slang* 263 (as of c1935), *Holiday. . .* A task that has been forgotten or neglected; an unfinished or unsatisfactory job. **1975** Gould *ME Lingo* 135, *Holiday*—A skip in painting, a spot missed by the brush.

2 See quot.

1968 Adams *Western Words* 151, *Holiday*—What the logger calls an open area in the timber.

holiday Christian n Also *holiday Jew* Cf **Christmas and Easter Christian, hickory n B4b, huckleberry 7**

1966–69 *DARE* (Qu. CC7, *Words for a person who goes to church very seldom or not at all*) Inf **NC**61, Holiday Christian; **IL**50, Holiday Jew.

holiness adj, also used absol, usu cap **chiefly Sth, Midl, Cent** See Map

Pertaining or belonging to var fundamentalist Christian sects which emphasize spiritual perfection and sanctification.

1888 *California State Gaz.* 623/2 *(OEDS),* Pasadena . . contains Methodist, Baptist, . . Friends, and Holiness churches. **1928** *Amer. Mercury* Oct 15.185/1, This . . was first preached by the Straight Holiness sects in Kansas in the 1890's. **1938** FWP *Guide MS* 24 **nwMS** [Black], She is "moved by the spirit" she cries, and slowly, rigidly, she begins "the shout," or if it is a Holiness meeting, the "Holy Dance." **c1938** in 1970 Hyatt *Hoodoo* 1.325 **seNC,** My mothaw is a *Holiness* woman. **1954** *Harder Coll.* **cwTN,** *Religion.* . . Methodists; Holiness; usually prefaced with "old." *Holy-Rollers*—Nickname for members of Holiness religion. **1957** Yinger *Religion* 282, Any description of religious trends in the United States that did not refer to the strength of the "holiness" sects . . would be incomplete. . . A strong emphasis on other-worldliness, fundamentalism in doctrine, and a pattern of revivalism are by no means new. **1965–70** *DARE* (Qu. CC3, . . *Religions that have come in recently . . or are a bit different*) 40 Infs, **chiefly Sth, S Midl,** Holiness Church; **IL**135, 143, **IN**22, 69, **MI**9, **NJ**15, **OH**71, Pilgrim Holiness; **KS**2, **NC**9, **OK**28, Pentecostal Holiness; **NY**92, Holiness Mission; **IN**73, Holiness Pilgrim; **KS**15, Pilgrim of Holiness; (Qu. CC2, . . *Predominant religious denominations*) 31 Infs, **chiefly Sth, S Midl, Cent,** Holiness (Church); **IL**135, **NY**94, **OH**61, Pilgrim Holiness; **OK**7, 9, Pentecostal Holiness; **SC**32, Fire-Baptized Holiness; **NC**49, Free-Will Holiness; **SC**32, Lutheran Holiness; **GA**8, Holiness Baptist; (Qu. CC4) Infs **FL**18, **PA**66, **SC**19, Holiness; **KY**84, Holy Rollers [or] Roly Hollers—Pentecostal or Holiness. **1986** Pederson *LAGS Concordance (Names of churches)* 1 inf, **nwFL,** Holiness Church; 1 inf, **nwFL,** Holiness, Pentecostal; 1 inf, **cwAL,** Holiness people—members of Holiness Church; 1 inf, **nwMS,** A Holiness preacher—of the Holiness Church; 1 inf, **cnGA,** She was Holiness faith.

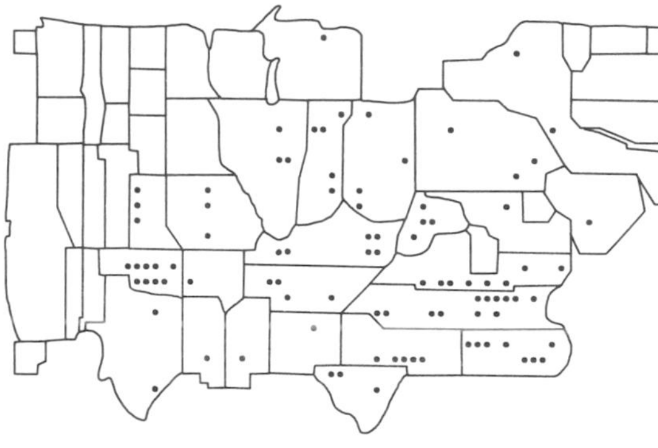

•holiness adj + varr (Qq. CC3, CC2, CC4)

holiness n

A member of a **holiness** church.

1970 *Thompson Coll.* **cnAL** (as of 1930s), *Holiness*—A holy roller. He's a holiness, an they don't bleeve in dancin or smokin. They must be holiness, the way they acted.

holing See **hole** v[1] **1**

holishkes n pl Also *halishkes, holishka(s)* [Yiddish] *among speakers of Jewish or Eastern European background* Cf **golumpki B, prakes**

Stuffed cabbage leaves.

1949 (1986) Leonard *Jewish Cookery* 5, *Jewish Holidays . . Sukkoth.* . . East European Jews include at least one meal of *holishkes* (chopped meat wrapped in cabbage leaves). This dish is called *galuptze* in Russia. *Ibid* 199, *Holishkes* (Meat filled cabbage leaves, also called *Praakes* and *Galuptzi,* depending on locale). **1958** Golden *For 2¢ Plain* 83, I had noodle soup with kreplach . . then I ordered a beautiful piece of boiled beef with a side platter of delightful stuffed cabbage—holishkas—which I worked on with a fork in one hand and a slab of rye bread in the other. **1970** Feinsilver *Yiddish* 186, *Halishkes*—See *Prakes.* *Ibid* 197, *Prakes*—Rolled cabbage leaves stuffed with chopmeat (often with added rice) and cooked in tomato sauce, seasoned sour or sweet-and-sour. Rumanian and Hungarian Jews call them *halishkes.* Also a favored dish of non-Jewish Ukranian Americans, these are available in varying quality in jars and cans, as "stuffed cabbage." **1987** *DARE* File **csWI,** Holishkas are little things you eat, little appetizers. Kreplach, little stuffed cabbage things, all kinds of things like that. You say it "ho" not "ha".

holla See **hollow** n[1], adj

Hollacky n Cf **hunyak, Polack**

1969 *DARE* (Qu. HH28, . . *People of foreign background . . Hollanders*) Inf **MI**103, Hollacky ['hɑləki].

Holland adj Cf **Holland Dutch**

1949 in 1986 *DARE* File, *Holland*—this word used by Western Michiganders in speaking of nationality. "I am Holland" (means I am Dutch).

Holland Dutch n [To distinguish Hollanders from Germans, who were generally called "Dutch"] **esp NY**

A person of Dutch ancestry.

1935 Frederick *PA Dutch* 28, But when they landed finally in New York their troubles just began, for the Holland Dutch in New York who had brought them over now bound them out as virtual slaves, to work out their passage price. **1967–68** *DARE* (Qu. HH28, *Names . . for people of foreign background . . Hollanders*) Infs **IL**26, **NY**68, 96, 102, Holland Dutch. [All Infs old] **1968** *DARE* FW Addit **NYC,** Holland Dutch—refers to people of Dutch ancestry.

hollar See **hollow**

holler v, n[1] Usu |'hɑlə(r)| Pronc-spp *hallow, hollo(o), holloa, hollow, holleh, holluh;* for addit proncs and spp varr see quots [Cf *EDD hollo* v. "Also . . *hollow . . holler*"; cf Intro "Language Changes" IV.1.b]

A Forms.

1699 in 1875 VA *Calendar State Papers* 1.67 **seVA,** We gott to the River side oppisett to the ffort, & theire hollerd & Immediately they answered. **1831** (1940) Motte *Charleston to Harvard* 75 **SC,** Hear the band play and the boys hollour. **1843** (1916) Hall *New Purchase* 78 **IN,** [She told] us we had not "larn'd to holler;" . . [she] had hollored naterally [sic]. *Ibid* 149, [I] hallows like the ole Harry. **1859** (1968) Bartlett *Americanisms* 199, *To Holloo.* (Pron. *holler.*) **1872** Schele de Vere *Americanisms* 489, *Hollow,* to, a verb . . occurs in America . . most commonly as *holler.* **1884** Lanier *Poems* 178 **GA** [Black], Don't you hyar / Somebody holl'in' *"Hoo, Jim, hoo?"* **1892** *DN* 1.239 **swMO,** In Kansas City almost always [hɑlɚ]. . . [So in Michigan.] **1894** *DN* 1.341 **wCT, MA,** *Holler:* to shout. . . *Hollow* (as verb) is substituted by some when talking "afore folks." **1922** Gonzales *Black Border* 307 **sSC, GA coasts** [Gullah glossary], *Holluh.* **1926** Smith *Gullah* 23 **sSC, GA coasts,** "You hailed them then?" "Me duh holleh." **1936** Reese *Worleys* 45 **MD** (as of 1865) [Black], "An' hollow," she told her sullen spouse, "ole niggah, hollow as loud as yo' kin." **1939** *LANE* Map 195, 1 inf, **eCT,** ['hɒlə]; 1 inf, **seRI,** ['hɔlərɪŋ]; 1 inf, **nRI,** ['hɔlə]; 1 inf, **eCT,** 'A calf ['hɒləz], calling for his mother. **1949** Turner *Africanisms* 268, [Dɪ ʌtkwek? . . yu yerɪ dɪ pipl hɒlərɪn ɒl rɒʊŋ an hɒlə so monfəl.] *Ibid* 269, [Translation:] The earthquake? . . You hear the people holloing [sic] all around and hollo so mournful. **1952** [see **C3** below].

B As verb. Cf **shout** v

1 Of an animal: to utter a call or cry; to cry out; hence n *holler* the call or cry of an animal. [Cf *EDD hollo* v. 1 "Of animals: to make a loud noise, to neigh, low, bark, &c"] **chiefly Sth, S Midl** Cf **bellow**

1902 *DN* 2.236 **swIL** [Pioneer dialect], *Holler.* . . To sing, whistle, chirp, or croak, as a bird, insect, or toad-frog. . . 'Spring's come, the brown thrasher's a-hollerin!' 'Lissn [sic] at the toad-frogs a-hollerin!' **1903** *DN* 2.317 **seMO,** *Holler.* . . Of the note of a frog, the chirp of an insect, etc. . . 'The katydids are a hollerin.' **1939** *LANE* Map 195, [Verbs used to designate the cry of a calf:] 3 infs, **sNEng,** Holler; 1 inf, **eCT,** 'A calf hollers, calling for his mother'. **1939** in 1978 Hall *Yarns Gt. Smokies* 31 **wNC,** Johnny . . thought hit was a bear a-comin'. So he . . run a little piece an' he hollered like a dog, barked like a dog, to try to scare the bear away. . . Johnny he hollered loud. *Ibid* 46, Newt Owenby, Wears Valley, said he heard panthers "squall" ("they don't holler.") **1941** *Sat. Eve. Post* 10 May 114/3, Sounds like old rain bird hollering. **1956** in 1978 Hall *Yarns Gt. Smokies* 69, An old hoot owl . . up in a tree hollerin', "Whoo-oo whoo-oo!" **1966–70** *DARE* (Qu. K19, *Noise made by a calf that's taken away from its mother*) Inf **MS**46, Holler; **LA**22, Holler ['hɑlə]; **LA**8, He's gonna holler; **FL**48, It holler all the time, baa baa; **VA**40, Holler baa baa; **MS**21, **RI**2, **SC**9, Hollerin(g); **LA**20, He's hollering ['hɑlən]; (Qu. K21, *The noise a cow makes calling for her calf*) Inf **MD**20, Holler [FW: used by Inf in conv in ref to any noise made by any animal]; **MA**31, She's hollering moo; **RI**2, Hollerin'; (Qu. K40) Inf **LA**20, They say he holler. [6 of 10 Infs Black]

2 To surrender, give up. Cf **calf-rope, holler**

1843 (1973) Porter *Big Bear AR* 41, Who hollered? Which gave up?

1859 (1968) Bartlett *Americanisms* 199, I once heard a Western man say he had "hollered on drinking," meaning that he had quit the practice. **1926** Black *You Can't Win* 43, Holler before you're hurt; that's my motto.

3 in phrr *holler one up* (or *in, out, over*): To summon or call to someone.

1942 *AmSp* 17.130 **IN,** *Holler out* (to call someone out). 'I'll holler him out for you.' **1953** Randolph-Wilson *Down in Holler* 43 **Ozarks,** The verb *holler* is often used in the transitive sense of call or summon. . . "Jim told me to *holler him up* at five o'clock". . . the boy might have *hollered him out* of the house. If a man were riding along the road, people . . could *holler him in. . . holler him over,* that is, call him from his own cabin to ours. **1959** Lomax *Rainbow Sign* 39 **AL** [Black], They hadn't come back yet, so I *hol*lered um up.

4 To complain or grumble; to protest. [By ext from *holler* v to make a loud noise]

1904 Number 1500 *Life in Sing Sing* 249, *Holler.* To complain. **1934** (1943) *W2, Holler,* [Orig. illit. var. of *hollo.*] To cry out, esp. in pain or complaint; protest. . . *Slang, U.S.* **1942** McAtee *Dial. Grant Co. IN* 34 (as of 1890s), *Holler* . . complain. Slang. "What are you hollerin' about?" **c1960** *Wilson Coll.* **csKY,** *Holler. . .* To complain, not necessarily loudly or noisily. **1967** *Boston Globe* 30 Mar. 14/1 *(OEDS),* Everyone hollers about the damage to the children if the schools are shut one day because of a teacher-school committee disagreement.

5 To laugh, guffaw. **scattered, but chiefly Sth, S Midl** See Map

[**1950** *WELS Suppl.* **WI,** Hollered and laughed.] **1965-70** *DARE* (Qu. GG30, *To suddenly break out laughing: "When he told her that, she just ______."*) 36 Infs, **scattered, but chiefly Sth, S Midl,** Hollered; **TN**30, 66, Hollered out; **WV**5, Hollered out loud; **TX**95, Hooped and hollered; **WV**3, Hollered a-laughing; **SC**26, **WV**4, Hollered and laughed; (Qu. GG31) Inf **SC**40, Holler out loud.

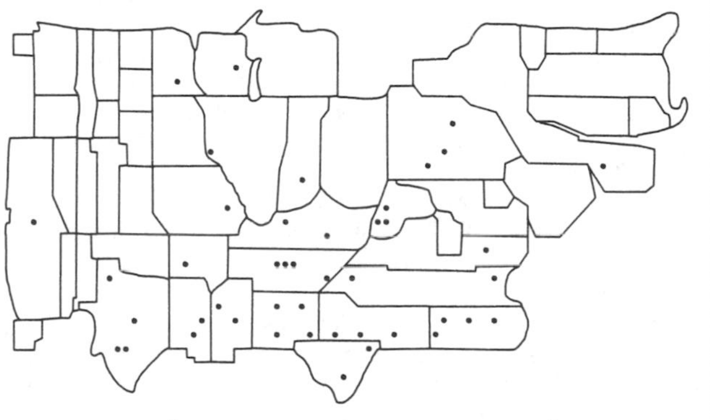

•holler v, n[1] B5 + varr (Qq. GG30, GG31)

6 To preach; to testify or shout concerning one's religious beliefs; hence vbl n, ppl adj *hollering.*

1917 Grant *2 Sides* 77, Robert had taken to the profession of "hollering for the Lord," as they sometimes call Evangelism in that land of sweet expression [=the US]. **1949** Webber *Backwoods Teacher* 142 **sAppalachians** *(Hench Coll.),* The prevailing brand of religion . . "old-time Hollerin' Methodist" and the present-day shouting religions. **1966** *DARE* Tape **AL**13, We got one church there that you go in an' they holler and shout so and they fall down on the floor and you say "Holy Ghost People." **1977** Dillard *Lexicon* 54 [Black], A friend encouraging a preacher may exhort him to "make them holler tonight." *Ibid* 55, The preacher motivates . . increased involvement less by the message he preaches than by his *straining voice;* . . one . . preacher . . "could holler like somebody cryin'."

7 To sing; to yodel; hence vbl n *hollering.*

1934 *Natl. Geogr. Mag.* 65.624 **seGA,** "Hollerin'." . . is yodeling at its best. . . It *is* the grand opera of the Okefinokee . . a common possession of man, woman, and child. . . It is an expression of exuberant spirits . . [or] a hunter's signal . . he was bound for homeward. It is frequently given from a distance of several miles, for the measured cadences of alternating head . . and chest tones have a remarkable carrying power. . . To listen to this melodious sound reverberating through piney woods and cypress bays is even more soul-filling than to hear a hermit thrush's ethereal strains. **1936** Lomax-Lomax *Negro Folk Songs* 113, He [=the American Negro] has hollered and moaned his troubles and his observations on the ways of the world. **1981** Harper-Presley *Okefinokee* 26 **seGA,** Hollerin' . . has been revived at annual "hollering conventions" . . [in] North Carolina. "Hollerin' " has been heard in the rural districts of most southern states, but the swampers' art was special.

8 in phr *holler down the rain barrel:* To announce a pregnancy.

1950 Bracke *Wheat Country* 211 **KS,** When one of the small-town papers reports that a husband "is hollering down the rain barrel," only a rank outsider to the region will fail to know that his wife is pregnant.

C As noun. Cf **shout** n

1 See **B1** above.

2 also *cornfield holler:* A spontaneous musical call; an improvised song; a way of calling, often using a yodeling technique; see quot 1936. **Sth, S Midl** Cf **coon shout, whoop** n

1936 Lomax-Lomax *Negro Folk Songs* 113, The holler is a way of singing—free, gliding from a sustained high note down to the lowest register the singer can reach, often ending there in a grunt. **1945** FWP *Lay My Burden Down* 92 **AL** [Black], One old man he sing: [""]Saturday night and Sunday too / Young gals on my mind./ Monday morning 'way 'fore day / Old Master got me gwine./ Peggy, does you love me now?[""] Then he whoops a sort of nigger holler, what nobody can do just like them old-time darkies. **1956** Longstreet *Real Jazz* 25, "The work-holler, the river-holler and the fisherman-holler are all different. And the cornfield-holler called *Arwhollie* is still heard, as *Don't Mind de Weather.* Full of long, sliding tones, you find hollers in many of Lead Belly's recordings and songs." Huddie Ledbetter . . was a ghost from the past, the last of the real holler-song singers. **1975** Gainer *Witches* 11 **sAppalachians,** *Holler* also means a combination of tones set to words or nonsense syllables, which a young man uses to identify himself, especially when he is approaching the home of his girl after dark. "There comes Jim, I know him by his holler." **1978** Wolfe *I'm On My Journey Home* 1/2, [Hollering, one of the purest and most basic forms of vocal response, was very much a part of the daily life of rural America.] *Ibid* 1/3, Hollering . . had more specific functions. . . distress hollers . . could bring neighbors as readily as an alarm bell. . . Different types of farm animals were routinely summoned by vaguely imitative hollers. . . Some neighbors kept track of each other's well-being by hollering to each other in the morning; if a neighbor didn't answer a holler, he was checked on. **1982** Shaw *Dict. Amer. Pop/Rock* 16, *Arhoolie*—A cornfield holler. An inchoate, unformed, improvised bit of song, chanted either as a bit of musing by a field hand or as communication with another laborer. Arhoolies and other types of hollers anticipated the rise of the Blues. **1987** *NY Times* (NY) 29 July 20/5, [Marianne] Faithfull [=a white British singer] . . [has a] new album[,] . . a collection of mostly vintage songs that range from the urbane . . to a traditional Afro-American field holler first recorded by Leadbelly.

3 also in var phrr: A short or indefinite distance. Cf **hollering distance, whoop** n

1919 *DN* 5.36 **seKY,** *Whoops and a holler, two. . .* A short distance. **1939** in 1944 *ADD* **nWV,** *Whoop and a holler. . .* 'Two whoops and a hollow' = a short distance. **1947** Guthrie *Big Sky* 15 **West,** Name's Deakins. . . Live just several hollers from here. **1952** Brown *NC Folkl.* 1.552, *Hoop and holloa, a. . .* general term expressing a short distance. "He lives just a hoop and a holloa from here." *Ibid* 607, *Whoop and a hollo, a. . .* A short distance; a short time. "He lives a whoop and a hollo from my house." **1965-70** *DARE* (Qu. MM24, . . *Expressions meaning 'a short distance': "The river is just a ______ from the house."*) 17 Infs, **scattered,** A hoop and (a) holler; **GA**31, Scant whoop and a holler; **SC**40, Two hoops and a holler; **IN**35, **NY**22, **RI**6, **TX**1, **VA**21, **WA**28, Hoot and (a) holler; **SC**45, Hop and a holler; **WA**33, Skip and a holler; (Qu. C33, . . *Joking names . . an out-of-the-way place, or a very unimportant place*) Inf **CA**90, Hoop and a holler away; (Qu. MM4) Inf **GA**31, So many whoops and a holler; (Qu. MM6) Inf **VA**2, A holler away [FW: holler means "yell"]. **1978** *UpCountry* Nov 4 **wMA,** Mount Holyoke, sited in South Hadley, Mass., a whoop and a holler up from the Connecticut River, has one of the handsomest campuses in New England.

4 A ruckus, fuss; a complaint—often in phrr *make* (or *put up*) *a holler.* Cf **hurrah B1**

1896 (1898) Ade *Artie* 147 **Chicago IL,** I put up a holler right at the jump. **1901** Willard *World of Graft* 133, Some gamblers were particularly loud in making their "hollers," and threatened to bring about an investigation. **1927** *DN* 5.450 [Underworld jargon], *Holler. . .* The complaint of one who has been injured by a tramp. **c1960** *Wilson Coll.* **csKY,** *Holler*—A complaint. "You ain't got no holler comin' if she gives you back that ring." **1967–68** *DARE* (Qu. KK11, *To make great objections or a big fuss about something: "When we asked him to do that, he ______."*) Inf **MD**24, Put up a great holler; **NY**9, Put up a holler; **VT**10, Made a big holler. [All Infs old]

holler n², adj See **hollow** n¹, adj

holler down the rain barrel See **holler** v **B8**

holler, holler, dogs you foller n, exclam Also *yoller, holler, we shan't foller* [From the refrain of the hunting team] Cf **fox and hounds 1, hare and hound(s)**

A game of chase played in teams; also used as the directional call during the chase.

[**1894** (1964) Gomme *Traditional Games* 1.191, *Hare and Hounds.* . . The Hare . . goes across country. . . The Hounds follow . . and try to catch him before he gets home. . . [The following calls are given by the hound leader if the team needs a clue] "Whoop, whoop, and hollow!/ Good dogs won't follow." . . "Sound your holler,/ Or my little dog shan't foller."] **1966–67** *DARE* (QR, near Qu. EE12) Inf **MI**8, Holler, holler, dogs you foller; **MI**49, Yoller, holler, we shan't foller—if the seeking side was stymied, they'd give that cry; if the other side thought it was safe to do so, they'd yell a little to give a clue.

hollering See **holler** v **B6, 7**

hollering distance n [**holler** n¹ **C3**]

The distance within which a shout can be heard; a short or indefinite distance.

1918 *DN* 5.20 **NC,** *Hollerin' distance,* calling distance. **1935** in 1944 *ADD* **nAL,** *Holler*. . . in hollerin' distance. **1968–69** *DARE* (Qu. MM6, . . *'Very close' or 'only a short distance away': "The house is ______ the park."*) Inf **IN**31, Hollering distance from; (Qu. MM24) Inf **KY**59, Hollering distance [FW: in conv, Inf heard this from country store operator]. **1968** *DARE* FW Addit **VA,** Just *a hollering distance* down the road. Could be a long ways by road, but that's what they said. **c1970** *Halpert Coll.* **wKY,** *Hollering distance*—They live within hollerin' distance.

holler New York See **New York, holler**

holler one in (or out, over, up) See **holler** v **B3a**

hollo, holloa, holloo See **holler** v, n¹

hollow n¹, adj Usu |'hɑlo|; also |'hɑlə, 'hɔ-|; **chiefly Sth, S Midl, esp sAppalachians, Ozarks** |'hɑlər|; **chiefly NEng** |'hɒlə|; for addit varr see **A** below Pronc-spp *hallow, holla(r), holler, holluh* [*EDD hollow* sb., adj. "Also written *hollah* . . *holler* . . *hollo*"] Cf Intro "Language Changes" IV.1.c Cf **-er 1**

A Forms.

1716 in 1895 Providence RI Rec. Comm. *Early Rec.* 9.16, A highway from the south End of the greate Pond to the Greate meadow hallow. **1748** in 1940 *AmSp* 15.274 **VA,** Near the head of a Hallow. **1796** in 1967 *PADS* 48.40 **NC,** *Hollar*—'hollow'. **1891** *DN* 1.117 **cNY,** ['hɑlə, 'hɑlɚ] . . 'hollow'. **1922** Gonzales *Black Border* 307 **sSC, GA coasts** [Gullah glossary], *Holluh*. . . hollow, hollows. **1923** *DN* 5.210 **swMO,** *Holler*. . . A hollow, a narrow valley. . . Hollow [adj]. **1939** *LANE* Map 36, [['hɒ⁽ᵊ⁾lə] predominates **throughout NEng;** 16 infs, **scattered throughout NEng,** ['hɒlo, -loʊ, -lʊ]; 5 infs, **CT, nMA,** ['hɑlə]; 4 infs, **CT,** ['hɑlo, -lʊ]; 4 infs, ['hɔlə, -lo]; 1 inf, **CT,** ['hɑlr]; 1 inf, **sMA,** ['hɒlr].] **1954** *Harder Coll.* **cwTN,** *Hollow* ['hɔlɚ, 'hɑlɚ]. **1965–70** *DARE* (Qu. C19, *What do you call low land running between hills?*) 55 Infs, **scattered,** Hollow; 35 Infs, **Sth, Midl,** Holler; **AL**52, Holler, long holler. **1985** *WI Alumnus Letters* **NY,** There are many ravines in the Bershire [sic] Hills and if one lived there, they lived "up in the holla." I assume they meant hollow or . . holler.

B As noun.

1a A stream which runs in a valley; a branch or tributary of a larger body of water. **esp sAppalachians, Ozarks** Cf **drain** n¹ **C2**

1754 in 1940 *AmSp* 15.274 **VA,** To two white oaks by a drain call'd the white oak hollow. **1859** *Ibid* **VA,** Including part of the old house Branch or hollow and including part of the first branch or hollow below sd . . house. **1916** *Ibid* **VA,** Jawbone Hollow, a tributary of Bull Run. **1927** *DN* 5.475 **Ozarks,** *Holler*. . . Hollow. This word is often used to designate, not the hollow or gorge itself, but the stream of water which flows through the hollow. In many cases the stream has no other name; one does not fish in Mill *creek* or Mill *branch,* but in Mill *holler.* **1969** *DARE* (Qu. C14, *A stretch of still water going off to the side from a river or lake*) Inf **KY**18, Holler.

b See quot.

1960 Bailey *Resp. to PADS 20* **KS,** Wet land with weeds: *Hollow, sink hole.* Kansas was too dry to have many wet places.

2 A mountain pass. Cf **gap** n¹ **1**

1722 in 1899 McClure *Diary* 38, We passed through McCallister's gap. . . It was a hollow through the mountain. **1819** in 1940 *AmSp* 15.274 **VA,** Crossing the said Hollow or gap between Sd. knobs. **1967–69** *DARE* (Qu. C15, *A place in mountains or high hills where you can get through without climbing over the top*) Infs **IL**93, **KY**21, **TN**23, Holler(s); **MA**47, **MO**37, **PA**167, Hollow.

3 An area typically inhabited by poor people or those of foreign background—used in place names. Cf **bottom n 2, burg, flat** n¹ **1e**

1965–70 *DARE* (Qu. C34, *Nicknames for nearby . . villages, or districts*) 30 Infs, **chiefly Nth, Midl, esp NEast,** Skunk (*or* Possum, Sleepy, Dead Man's, Irish, Pratt, Punkin, etc) Hollow; 20 Infs, **chiefly Sth, S Midl,** Frog (*or* Happy, Possum, Scratch-ankle, etc) Holler; **NY**95, They used to call places Somebody's Hollow [or] Holler; (Qu. C35, *Nicknames for the different parts of . . town*) 24 Infs, **chiefly Nth, Midl, esp NEast,** Skunk (*or* Frog, Pious, Smoky, etc) Hollow; **CT**42, **NY**28, The Hollow; **FL**48, **NC**41, Smoky Holler; **NC**30, **VA**2, Sawmill Holler; **GA**17, Goose Holler; **GA**80, Buttermilk Holler; **GA**17, Goose Holler; **GA**80, Buttermilk Holler; **VA**2, Artesian Well Holler, Linden Holler; (Qu. II25, . . *The part of a town where the poorer . . foreign groups live*) Infs **CA**17, **FL**48, **MD**17, **NY**38, **PA**165, **SD**3, Hungry (*or* Piggy, Scum, Sleepy, Smoke, Soapsud) Hollow; **MI**44, **MO**7, (Down in) the Hollow; **NC**36, Possum Holler; (Qu. C33, . . *Names . . for an out-of-the-way . . or a very unimportant place*) Inf **IA**11, Squirrel Hollow; **MA**6, Frog Hollow; **RI**16, Poverty Hollow; [**VA**2, Hoot and holler;] (Qu. HH18) Inf **OK**20, Snuff Hollow people; (Qu. II24, . . *The part of a town where the well-off people live*) Inf **AL**5, Mortgage Hollow.

4 usu *holler:* The abdominal cavity. **sAppalachians**

1895 *DN* 1.372 **eTN,** *Holler:* hollow, inside cavity. "I 'low it struck the holler." (Of a deep cut.) **1917** *DN* 4.413 **wNC,** *Holler*. . . The visceral cavity. "I got wet to the holler." **1939** *Hall Coll.* **sAppalachians,** He run up and stabbed his knife into it [=a bear] and cut a big long gash plumb to the holler of the bear.

5 The part of the foot under the arch.

1904 *DN* 2.420 **nwAR,** The holler of her foot would kill a pis-ant.

C As adj.

See quot.

1894 *Century Illustr. Mag.* 48.873 **NEng,** Some of our Northern farmers . . attach quite another sense to "hollow" when they note the condition of the atmosphere in which sound is easily carried. "The air is so hollow that I can hear a train ten miles off," one will say.

hollow v, n² See **holler** v, n¹

hollow-billed coot n [See quot 1889]

Either of two **scoters:** *Melanitta nigra* or *M. perspicillata.*

1888 Trumbull *Names of Birds* 104, We read . . of its [=*Melanitta perspicillata's*] being known "to some" in New England as *hollow-billed coot. Ibid* 107, It [=*Melanitta nigra*] is called the *hollow-billed coot* on "the Atlantic side of Long Island." **1889** *Century Dict.* 2858, *Hollow-billed*. . . Having a bill appearing inflated and as if hollowed out: used specifically in the phrase *hollow-billed coot,* a local name in the United States of the surf scoter . . and of the black scoter. **1917** (1923) *Birds Amer.* 1.148, *Oidemia americana*. . . Hollow-billed Coot. *Ibid* 1.151, *Oidemia perspicillata*. . . Hollow-billed Coot. **1955** MA Audubon Soc. *Bulletin* 39.377 **NEng,** *Surf Scoter*. . . Hollow-billed Coot (. . The bill is swollen basally.) . . *American Scoter*. . . Hollow-billed Coot.

hollow-butt n Cf **churn-butted**

Of a log or tree stump: see quot 1956.

1956 Sorden–Ebert *Logger's Words* 18 **Gt Lakes,** *Hollow-butt,* 1. A hollow log with questionable floating ability because of defects such as knots and rot. 2. A log with an open center due to rot. [**1965–70** *DARE* (Qu. KK7, *When wood—for example, a tree stump—is starting to decay inside, you'd say, "It's ______ inside."*) Inf **VA**15, Holler at the butt.]

hollow head n

1 Prob =**hollow horn 1.**

c1960 *Wilson Coll.* **csKY,** *Hollow head. . .* A disease of cattle, the same as *hollow horn.* **1966–69** *DARE* (Qu. K28, . . *Chief diseases that cows have*) Infs **KY**46, **NC**37, Holler head.

2 =black-bellied plover.

1888 Trumbull *Names of Birds* 191, *Black-Bellied Plover* . . In New Jersey at Pleasantville (Atlantic Co.), and Atlantic City, *Hollow-Head.* **1917** (1923) *Birds Amer.* 1.256, *Black-Bellied Plover—Squatarola squatarola* . . Hollow-head. **1923** U.S. Dept. Ag. *Misc. Circular* 13.68, *Black-bellied Plover (Squatarola squatarola . .) . .* hollow-head (N.J.) **1970** *DARE* (Qu. Q10, *Other water . . and marsh birds*) Inf **VA**47, Hollow head (black-bellied plover).

hollow horn n Cf **hollow tail**

1 A debilitating disease of cattle mistakenly thought to be caused by hollowness in the horns. **chiefly Sth** See Map

1805 Parkinson *Tour* 87, There were a few half-starved cattle . . and many more complaining of what they call the hollow-horn. This arises from matter in the horn, which kills numbers. **1888** Cody *Story Wild West* 704, Though sick as a cow with hollow-horn myself. **1899** (1912) Green *VA Folk-Speech* 228, *Hollow-horn. . .* A fancied disease of cattle. **1915** *DN* 4.184 **swVA,** *Holler-horn.* **1919** *DN* 5.34 **seKY,** *Holler-horn. . .* A mythical disease in cattle, which is supposed to make their horns hollow. A hole is bored in the horn with a gimlet. This custom gave rise to the epithet applied to people who have acted foolishly: "He ought to be bored for the holler horn." **1948** Wolfe *Farm Gloss.* 163, *Hollow Horn*—This and hollow tail are names given in certain sections to a condition in cattle which causes them to be off feed or just plain sick. There are no such diseases and the condition is usually the symptom of some sickness. **1950** *PADS* 14.38 **SC,** *Hollow-horn* . . and *hollow-tail. . .* Correspondents say there are still many who are convinced of the reality of these two diseases. **1953** Randolph–Wilson *Down in Holler* 253 **Ozarks,** *Holler-horn. . .* A disease of cattle, in which the horns or the bones of the tail are said to disintegrate. **c1960** *Wilson Coll.* **csKY,** *Hollow horn. . .* A [sic] imaginary disease of cattle that are eating feed deficient in vitamins. . . [One] remedy was to bore a hole into the horn and rub in salt and pepper. **1965–70** *DARE* (Qu. K28, *What are the chief diseases that cows have around here?*) 27 Infs, **Sth,** Hollow horn; **GA**3, **KY**86, **TX**105, Holler horn; **VA**38, Holler horn and canker.

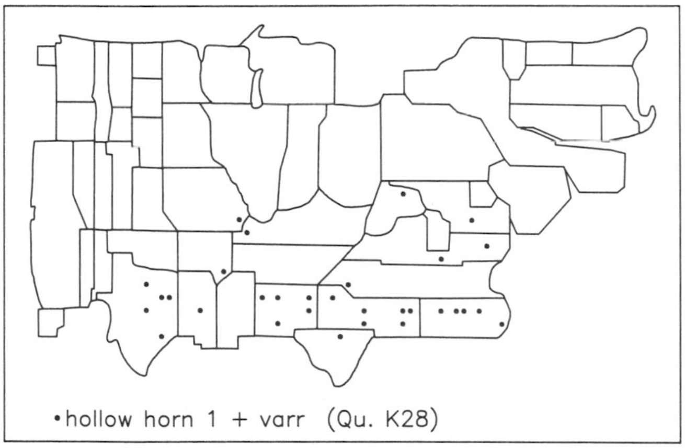

2 =hollow tail.

1923 *DN* 5.210 **swMO,** *Holler horn. . .* A supposed disease of cattle wherein portions of the bone in the tail are said to rot away. The customary treatment is to split the skin of the tail just above the bush and to fill the incision with salt and pepper and turpentine and then bandage the wound tightly. **1931** Randolph *Ozarks* 121, A cow with "holler-horn" is relieved by splitting her tail open and applying a mixture of salt and vinegar. **1953** [see **1** above].

3 Transf: see quot.

[**1919** see **1** above.] **1942** Perry *Texas* 136, A foolish person we sometimes call "a hollow horn."

hollow jack n [Var of **high-low-jack**]

1932 *Hanley Disks* **neMA,** *Hollow jack*—A type of card game. We used to play whist and the hollow jack, double pedro, and poker.

hollow stalk n

A plant disease which causes the pith to decay and dry out.

1966 *PADS* 45.15 **cnKY,** *Hollow stalk. . .* A stalk disease starting at a place on the [tobacco] plant where it has been bruised or damaged. The pith dries out, and the leaves drop off. . . "We haven't had much hollow stalk around here."

hollowstem n

A **whitetop** (here: *Scolochloa festucacea*).

1950 Stevens *ND Plants* 58, *Fluminea festucacea. . .* The local name "hollowstem" refers to the unusually large opening in the stem.

hollow tail n **chiefly Sth, S Midl** See Map Also called **wolf tail** Cf **hollow horn**

A debilitating disease of cattle mistakenly thought to be caused by hollowness in the tail.

1849 in *Soc. Calif. Pion. Quart.* II. (1925) 121 *(DA),* Some (cattle teams) have the hollow horn. . . They have another disease called the hollow tail; for that they split the tail where it is hollow. **1949** Webber *Backwoods Teacher* 205 **Ozarks,** Treatment for "holler tail," . . was to split the skin at the root of the tail. **c1960** *Wilson Coll.* **csKY,** *Hollow tail. . .* A disease of cattle, really a vitamin deficiency. Doctored, formerly, by splitting the end of the tail and rubbing [with] salt and pepper. **1965–70** *DARE* (Qu. K28, *What are the chief diseases that cows have around here?*) 55 Infs, **chiefly Sth, S Midl,** Hollow tail; **GA**3, **KY**86, **NC**53, **TX**105, Holler tail. **1967** *DARE* File **MI,** Hollow tail: A superstitious bovine disease; the cure is to make an incision in a cow or horse's [sic] tail between vertebrae for the salt and sugar. **1968** *DARE* FW Addit **VA**15, Hollow tail—disease of cattle. Field yarrow . . was used to "cure" hollow tail.

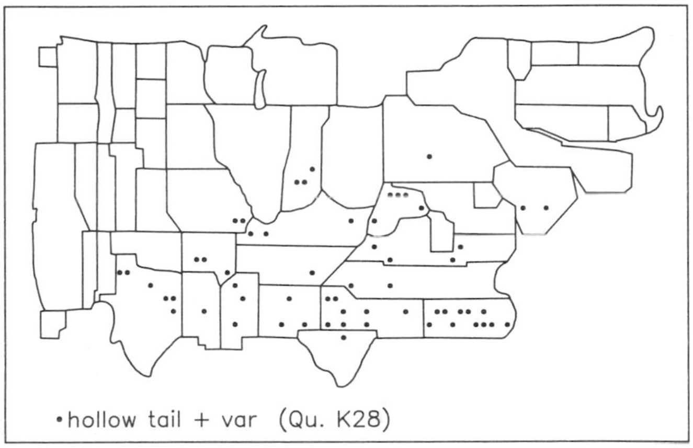

holluh v, n[1] See **holler** v, n[1]

holluh n[2], adj See **hollow** n[1], adj

holly n[1]

1 Std: a plant of the genus *Ilex.* For other names of var spp see **Christmasberry 2, Christmas holly 1, deerberry d, gallberry, Georgia holly, holly hock tree, inkberry, mountain holly, myrtle holly, possumhaw, sarvis holly, white holly, winterberry, yaupon, Yule holly**

2 =islay. [From the holly-like leaves]

1897 Sudworth *Arborescent Flora* 247 **CA,** *Prunus ilicifolia. . .* Holly.

holly n[2] [Heb *challah*]

A braided egg bread eaten on the Sabbath and other Jewish holidays; see quots.

1954 *PADS* 21.30 **SC,** *Holly loaf. . .* An oblong loaf of bread formed by plaiting together strands of dough, used by Jewish families on the eve of the Seventh Day, symbolizing the Divine Presence. **1968** Rosten *Yiddish* 69, *Challa* a Jewish . . bread to rank with the most exquisite productions of the baker's art. . . a Sabbath and holiday delicacy. . . Some American Jews pronounce *challa* "holly," the younger ones not being able to manage the uvular *kh,* the rest thinking "holly" more genteel, because more Americanized. **1970** Feinsilver *Yiddish* 181, *Challe*—Sabbath and holiday bread. . . It's usually spelled "Challa" or "Halla," from which has come the mongrel "Holly." *Ibid* 363, "Holly" for *challe* . . This popular term for Sabbath bread . . has been picked up by many a Gentile—food clerk, gourmet, and others. The term is printed on the labels of some commercial bakeries' product, one company even using the redundant "Holly Bread." **1987** *DARE* File **cIA,** My grandmother, who will be one hundred years old in September and has lived her whole life in Des Moines, Iowa, has called what I know as *challah* "holly" and "holly loaf" as long as I've known her. A devout social atheist Jew, she loves to go to Temple dinners and point out that the holly loaf is probably store-bought.

holly bay n

1 also *bay holly:* =**loblolly bay.**

1833 Eaton *Botany* 161, *Gordonia. . . lasianthus* . . holly-bay. . . Charleston, S.C. **1859** (1968) Bartlett *Americanisms* 250, *Loblolly Bay.* . . An elegant ornamental tree of the maritime parts of the Southern States, called also Holly Bay. **1900** Lyons *Plant Names* 176, *G[ordonia] Lasianthus.* . . Holly Bay, Bay Holly. . . *Bark* astringent, used for tanning. **1940** Clute *Amer. Plant Names* 132, Holly bay. **1979** Little *Checklist U.S. Trees* 140, *Loblolly-bay. . . Other common names* . . bay, holly-bay.

2 A **sweet bay** (here: *Magnolia virginiana*).

1900 Lyons *Plant Names* 236, *M[agnolia] Virginiana.* . . Holly Bay. **1927** (1930) *WNID, Holly bay. a* The loblolly bay. *b* The laurel magnolia.

holly cherry See **hollyleaf cherry**

Holly Eve n [Folk-etym]

Halloween; hence *Holly Eve-er* one who goes out on Halloween.

1936 *AmSp* 11.315 **nwAR, swMO,** *Holly eve.* . . Hallowe'en. **1941** in 1944 *ADD* **nWV,** *Holly Eve.* **c1950** in 1983 *Barrick Coll.* **csPA,** *Holly-eve-ers*—Halloweeners. Frequent in the 1940s and early 1950s.

holly fern n

A **sword fern** (*Polystichum* spp).

1900 Lyons *Plant Names* 141, *D[ryopteris] acrostichoides* . . Holly Fern. **1923** in 1925 Jepson *Manual Plants CA* 35, *P[olystichum] lonchitis.* . . Holly Fern. **1953** Nelson *Plants Rocky Mt. Park* 34, *Holly fern* or *mountain hollyfern, Polystichum lonchitis.* **1973** Hitchcock–Cronquist *Flora Pacific NW* 53, *Polystichum.* . . Holly-fern.

hollygrape n **West**

Any of several spp of **barberry,** but esp **Oregon grape,** which have holly-like leaves and grape-like blue berries.

1937 U.S. Forest Serv. *Range Plant Hdbk.* B99, About a dozen species of hollygrape are commonly found on the western ranges. **1941** Jaeger *Wildflowers* 67 **Desert SW,** *Hollygrape.* . . A Mohave D[esert] shrub, particularly abundant in the New York Mts. **1961** Douglas *My Wilderness* 17 **CO,** In the zone between 8000 feet and 10,000 feet the creeping holly grape, with its holly-like leaves and soft yellow flowers, is reminiscent of Oregon grape. Its berries make excellent jellies; and its leaves that turn brilliant red brighten the forest floor in September. **1963** Craighead *Rocky Mt. Wildflowers* 64, *Holly-grape. Mahonia repens.* . . is a poor forage plant, utilized sparingly by deer and elk. **1967** Dodge *Roadside Wildflowers* 10, *Hollygrape.* . . Also called Fremont mahonia, this attractive bush covers itself . . with . . fragrant yellow flowers.

hollyhock n Pronc-spp *hollyhawk, hollyhork* Cf **wild hollyhock**

Std sense, var forms.

1859 Taliaferro *Fisher's R.* 117 **nwNC** (as of 1820s), I made a 'skuse to Sally to go wim me inter the garden to show me the hollyhawks and all the purty flowers. **1899** (1912) Green *VA Folk-Speech* 228, *Hollyhork.* . . A plant; the hollyhock.

holly hock tree n Cf **hack** n[5] **1, hardhack 3**

A **holly** n[1] **1.**

1930 (1972) Cate *Our Todays* 115 (as of early 1800s), The principal islands of G.A. [perh = "Georgia Atlantica"] are Skidaway, Warsaw, Ossabaw, St. Catherines, Sapelo . . &c. (Blackbeard belongs to the U.S.) . . Trees: live oak, cypress, . . Magnolia, cassina, holly or holly hock tree. **1965** *DARE* (Qu. T5, . . *Kinds of evergreens*) Inf **MS**60, Holly hock tree.

hollyhork See **hollyhock**

hollyleaf cherry n Also *holly(-leaved) cherry* [See quot 1908]

=**islay.**

1897 Sudworth *Arborescent Flora* 247 **CA,** *Hollyleaf Cherry. . . Common Names.* . . Holly-leaved Cherry . . Holly Cherry. **1908** Sudworth *Forest Trees Pacific* 359, Hollyleaf cherry is the most distinct of Pacific cherries on account of its evergreen holly-like foliage. **1916** Parsons *Wild Flowers CA* 63, The holly-leaved cherry is a very ornamental shrub, with its shining, prickly evergreen leaves. **1925** Jepson *Manual Plants CA* 506, *Islay.* . . Also called . . Holly-leaf Cherry. **1942** Hylander *Plant Life* 308, The Hollyleaf Cherry, an evergreen with white flowers and dark purple fruit in small clusters, grows along stream margins and in wet sandy soil on the California coast ranges. **1961** Thomas *Flora Santa Cruz* 200 **cwCA,** Holly-leaved Cherry. . . Common in chaparral, on open hills, and often in relatively pure stands in ravines and gullies. **1970** Kirk *Wild Edible Plants W. U.S.* 246, Holly-leaved Cherry. . . The tough, leathery, roundish leaves bear stiff spiny teeth around the edges.

holly-leaved oak See **holly oak 2**

holly oak n

1 =**bear oak.**

1900 Lyons *Plant Names* 314, *Quercus nana,* . . Bear Oak, . . Holly Oak, Dwarf Black Oak.

2 also *holly-leaved oak:* A **live oak** (here: *Quercus agrifolia*). [See quot 1908]

1908 Sudworth *Forest Trees Pacific* 303, California live oak is one of the commonest, best known of southern California oaks, as well as one of the first to attract the attention of early explorers, who called it "holly-leaved oak," from the resemblance of its leaves to the large American or European evergreen holly. **1910** Jepson *Silva CA* 228, It [=*Quercus agrifolia*] is sometimes called Holly-leaved Oak or Holly Oak, a rather happy common name.

3 A **scrub oak** (here: *Quercus pungens*).

1938 Van Dersal *Native Woody Plants* 222, *Quercus undulata . . pungens* . . , the holly oak. **1967** *DARE* (Qu. T10) Inf **CA**20, Holly oak.

holly rose n

A **rock rose** (here: *Helianthemum canadense*).

1974 (1977) Coon *Useful Plants* 97, *Helianthemum canadense* . . holly rose. . . It grows widely in dry areas in the eastern United States.

holo v Also redup *holoholo;* also in phr *go holoholo* [Haw] **HI**

To walk or move about; to go out (for recreation); hence n *holoholo* the act of running, walking, or going out (for pleasure).

1954–60 Hance et al. *Hawaiian Sugar, Holo*—To run, to walk. *Ibid, Holoholo*—Act of running, walking, going. **1967** Reinecke–Tsuzaki *Hawaiian Loanwords* 96, *Holo.* . . To walk; to run. . . V[ery] S[eldom]. *Ibid, Holoholo.* . . 1. To walk about. . . 3. To walk about taking one's pleasure; to go about amusing oneself; esp., in the phrase "go holoholo." 4. To play. . . V[ery] F[requent]: [children and adults]. [**1967** *DARE* (Qu. OO28a, *Talking about running: "John was so scared he ________.")* Inf **HI**4, Makau holo—scared + run.] **1972** Carr *Da Kine Talk* 114 **HI,** *Holoholo Slippers.* . . 'Slippers to go holoholo in', and, since *holoholo* means 'to go out for pleasure', these are 'slippers for a good time', 'party slippers'. **1981** *Pidgin To Da Max* np **HI,** *Holoholo.* . . to go out. "You like to go holoholo tonight?"

holocan See **hooligan**

holoholo See **holo**

holoku n [Haw] **HI** Cf **muu muu**

A long gown with a train; see quot 1967.

c1833 in 1934 Frear *Lowell & Abigail* 83 **HI,** To our surprise and disgust the man went about dressed in a shirt only and his wife in the *holoku* worn by the common native women. **1873** in 1966 Bishop *Sandwich Is.* 42 **HI,** Every verandah appears a gathering place, and the bright *holokus* of the women, the gay shirts and bandanas of the men . . make me feel that I am in a new world. **1965** Krauss–Alexander *Grove Farm* xv **HI,** [Glossary:] *Holokus*—fitted Mother Hubbards with trains. **1967** Reinecke–Tsuzaki *Hawaiian Loanwords* 96, *Holoku.* . . A gown with a train, introduced by the early missionaries and formerly much worn by native Hawaiian women; still often worn at dress balls and on similar occasions, as well as by the older native Hawaiian women. (A political speech has been described as a "holoku speech—it covers everything and touches on nothing.") V[ery] F[requent]. **1967** *DARE* (Qu. W16a, *The full-length garment that a woman wears under her dress*) Inf **HI**6, Holoku—muu muu used to be for inside slip and the outside one was a holoku slip; (Qu. W22, . . *A loose, full housedress that ties at the waist*) Inf **HI**1, Holoku—does not tie at waist, worn anyplace (in or outdoors) with a train, most elegant. **1987** *DARE* File **HI,** A holoku is a long dress, fitted, with a train. It's somewhat elegant.

holomuu n Also sp *holomu* [Blend of **holoku** + **muu muu**] **HI**

A long gown, not fitted; see quots.

1967 Reinecke–Tsuzaki *Hawaiian Loanwords* 96, *Holomuu, holomu.* . . A gown similar to the *holoku,* but lacking the train. **1967** *DARE* (Qu. W22, . . *A loose, full housedress that ties at the waist*) Inf

HI1, Holomuu—does not tie at waist, worn anyplace (in or outdoors), a fitted muu muu; HI6, Holomuu—with flowing train and tight bodice. **1987** *DARE* File **HI,** A holomuu is a long dress, fitted, but it doesn't have a train. Otherwise, it's similar to a holoku.

holp(e), holp(e)d, holpen, holpt See **help** v

holstein cow n Cf **hurry-up wagon**

1968 *DARE* (Qu. N3, *The car or wagon that takes arrested people to the police station or to jail*) Inf **CA**62, Holstein cow—A name used for them here because they're black and white.

‡holster n

1968 *DARE* (Qu. D32, *The metal stands in a fireplace that the logs are laid on*) Inf **MD**20, Holster.

holt n See **hold** n **A1, B1, 2**

holt v See **hold** v **A1a, 2d**

holupcha, holupka, holupki, holupsi See **golumpki**

holy See **holey** n **1**

holy all-ee all in free exclam Cf **all-ee all-ee (all) in free**

In **hide-and-seek A:** see quot.

1969 *DARE* (Qu. EE15, *When he has caught the first of those that were hiding what does the player who is 'it' call out to the others?*) Inf **NY**213, Holy (*or* all-ee) all-ee all in free [holi (*or* ɔli) ɔli ɔl ɪn fri].

holy bang See **holey 1**

holy bone n Cf **bone** n **8**

1983 *DARE* File **Boston MA,** A professor of Gaelic. . . during a visit to the dock area of Boston, heard an old aphorism from Ireland that was in fairly general use among dock hands. It was "a touch of the holy bone" to describe sexual intercourse, both licit and extra-marital. It also applied to pregnancy, i.e., "She's had a touch of the holy bone".

‡holy cat n

=**cat** n **3c.**

1967 *DARE* (Qu. EE11, *Bat-and-ball games for just a few players*) Inf **MN**2, Holy cat.

holy Christopher See **Christopher**

holycross cholla n

A **prickly pear** (here: *Opuntia ramosissima*).

1942 Amer. Joint Comm. Horticult. Nomenclature *Std. Plant Names* 76/2, *[Opuntia] ramosissima.* Holycross C[holla]. **1985** Dodge *Flowers SW Deserts* 65, Holycross Cholla. . . *Opuntia ramosissima.*

holy dance n Also *holy dancing* [Cf *EDD holy dance* (at *holy* adj.) "A name given to the proceedings of certain religious sects, owing to the excitement and extravagances shown"] Cf **exercise B, holiness adj, holler v B6, shout**

The footwork and other movements executed in a state of religious fervor; see quots 1938, 1954.

1938 FWP *Guide MS* 24 [Black], Soon a woman leaps out into the aisle. She is "moved by the spirit" she cries, and slowly, rigidly, she begins "the shout" or if it is a Holiness meeting, the "Holy Dance." It is shuffling, intricate; her heels thud on the floor. . . The ring . . moves faster and faster, yet the feet keep the step; the rhythm is not broken. **1948** Dick *Dixie Frontier* 198 **Sth** (as of a1850), The "holy dance" was probably a variation of "the jerks" and was ungovernable until it ran its course. *Ibid* 199, The "holy dance" and other ecstasies appeared among both white and black worshippers in Alabama and Mississippi as late as 1835. **1954** *PADS* 21.25 **SC,** Holy dancing, in religious services, is a sort of lively rhythmic shuffle with many worshipers taking part. It is an expression of religious emotion, in which the feet are never crossed. The participants are those who have had the experience of conversion, and the dance is an expression of happiness over the event. **1977** Dillard *Lexicon* 52 [Black], There are some variants [of the religious dance "shouting"], like the term *Holy Dance* among the Holiness sects.

Holy Ghost Dove n Cf **death owl**

1982 Ginns *Snowbird Gravy* 200 **nwNC,** What they call the Holy Ghost Dove, from God, was when somebody was going to get killed or pass away like my grandfather. . . Now, it's the Spirit of God descending in a dove shape. A white dove, whiter than anything you've ever seed on earth. And it comes three days before that person's breath leaves 'em. They'll go quicker than that, but they won't live no longer than that. I've just seed two in my life. *Ibid* 202, One of us, or some of our people, is gonna be dead in three days. . . That was a Holy Ghost Dove.

holy grass n

Std: a grass of the genus *Hierochloe.* Also called **sweet grass, vanilla grass.** For other names of the common sp *H. odorata* see **Indian grass, quack grass, Seneca grass**

holy hay n

A **scurfpea** (here: *Psoralea onobrychis*).

1959 Carleton *Index Herb. Plants* 62, *Holy hay:* Psoralea onobrychis.

Holy Hopper See **Holy Jumper**

Holy Iden n Also *Holy Idam, ~ Idy* [Perh from Efik *Idem* a superhuman being and object of prayer]

In **hoodoo** n **1a:** a special name or prayer used to command favorable circumstances; see quot.

c1938 in 1970 Hyatt *Hoodoo* 1.694 **Memphis TN,** If a *hustlin' womans* [=a prostitute] want tuh git out on de streets an' be lucky, make money. . . I gon'a tell you whut prayer she supposed to wear. She supposed tuh wear de prayer in her purse—*Holy Idy*—de *Holy Name Idy. Ibid,* An' if yo' . . goin' to a . . strange city . . an' want tuh be successful, yo' should walk out in a vacant field . . turn yore face . . south an' use that word *Holy Adam . . Holy Idam*—Hebrew lang'rige. . . [Hyatt:] (Do you know how to spell it?) [Inf:] Not Adam but *Iden—I-D-E-N.* . . [Hyatt:] (It isn't the Garden of Eden?) [Inf:] No suh—*Iden.* Yo' use dis when yore *hustlin'* . . or . . want tuh be successful. Yo' kin jis' walk up to someone an' use dat inward *Iden*—inward—an' ask them fo' a favor—they'll come very near doin' it.

Holy Jumper n Also *Holy Hopper old-fash* Cf **holiness** adj

A member of a Pentecostal or Evangelical religious sect.

1931–33 *LANE Worksheets* **Boston MA,** I got a half brother belongs to these Holy Jumpers. His wife can't talk nothing but religion. **1942** Berrey–Van den Bark *Amer. Slang* 325.2, Holy Hoppers *or* Rollers, *a sect whose members exhibit frenzied religious excitement.* **1950** *WELS* 7 Infs, **WI,** Holy Jumpers; 1 Inf, Holy Jumpers—Church of Christ. **1966–69** *DARE* (Qu. CC3, . . *Religions that have come in recently . . or are a bit different from the common ones*) Inf **MA**55, Used to have Holy Jumpers here; **NC**79, Used to have Holy Jumpers—shout and jump; (Qu. CC4, . . *Nicknames . . for various religions*) Inf **AR**39, Holy Jumper—Holiness [Church]; **MA**40, Holy Jumpers—some religious groups whose services involved jumping around; **MA**59, Holy Jumpers—Jehovah's Witnesses; **MA**72, Holy Jumpers—but I don't know which one it was; **MI**44, Holy Hoppers—I don't know which they are; **MN**19, Holy Jumpers—a sect that was here many years ago; **NC**61, Holy Jumpers; **NC**82, Holy Jumpers—Assembly of God. [9 of 10 Infs old]

holy laugh n **chiefly Sth, S Midl** Cf **holy dance, shout** n

See quots 1942, 1950.

1829 *Western Mth. Rev.* 2.477, Dr. Roberts is very pointed in his testimeny [sic] against the '*abominable* practice of *jumping, pointing, dancing, boreing*'. . . Might he not have added the *'holy laugh?'* **1833** (1918) *MD Hist. Mag.* 13.328, The preacher in the midst of a fervent prayer, will all of a sudden burst out into a loud boisterous laugh. . . The most godly of his brethren join with him. This is called the "Holy Laugh." **1942** (1965) Parrish *Slave Songs* 36 **seGA,** Where the "holy laugh" came from I am unable to say. . . I had read about it, but heard it employed on several occasions before I recognized the mirthless staccato "ha-ha" for what it was. It is unobtrusively introduced to carry on a rhythmical phrase. **1950** *PADS* 14.38 **SC,** *Holy laugh.* . . A mirthless laugh uttered by anyone during a religious meeting.

holy poke n Cf **Baptist cake, huffjuff**

A ball of bread dough fried in deep fat.

1939 Wolcott *Yankee Cook Book* 138 **CT,** *Holy Pokes*—Form bread dough . . into balls the size of large marbles. . . Slip . . into a kettle of [hot] fat . . and fry until golden brown. . . Holy Pokes are a Connecticut favorite. **1952** Tracy *Coast Cookery* 102 **CT,** *Baptist Bread*—Bread fried in deep fat. . . In Connecticut it is known as Holy Pokes.

holy roller See **holey** n **2**

Holy Trinity flower n [Prob from the (usu) three prominent pistils] Cf **passion flower**

=**maypop.**

1951 *PADS* 15.36 **TX,** *Passiflora incarnata* . . Holy Trinity flower.

Holy Trinity lily n

A **spatterdock** (here: *Nuphar luteum*).

1951 *PADS* 15.32 **TX,** *Nymphaea advena* . . Holy Trinity lily.

hom See **home**

homade See **homemade**

homblest See **homely**

hombre n Usu |ˈɔmbre(ɪ)|; also |ˈɑmbreɪ|; for addit varr see quots Pronc-spp *hombrey, ombray, umber, umbry* [Span] **chiefly West, esp SW** *occas derog*

A Forms.

1921 Thorp *Songs Cowboys* 74 **CO,** Come, hombrey, and jest tuck a bowl of chile 'neath your belt! **1932** Bentley *Spanish Terms* 145, *Hombre . . Spanish,* [ˈo:mbre:]; *English,* [ˈo:mbre, ˈo:mbri; ˈha:mbr]. **1933** *AmSp* 8.3.28 [Prison vocabulary], *Hombre* (pronounced omˈbray). **1939** FWP *Guide MT* 414, *Hombre*—Man . . pronounced "umber" in Montana. **1942** Perry *Texas* 137, We, like the Mexicans, refer to men as *"hombres,"* only we call it "umbry". **1987** *DARE* File **csID,** When I was in college in Idaho in the 60's, students would label someone, facetiously, as a "bad hombre" [ˈbæ:d ˈɑ›mˌbreɪ].

B Senses.

1 A man of Mexican or Spanish background. *somewhat old-fash*

[**1846** (1962) Magoffin *Down Santa Fé* 93 **NM,** Not only the children, but *mujeres* [women] and *hombres* [men] swarmed around me like bees.] **1894** *DN* 1.324 **TX** [Spanish and Mexican vocabulary], *Hômbre:* man. Often used to call Mexican *tamale* men or candy peddlers on the street. **1962** Atwood *Vocab. TX* 73, *Person of Mexican origin. . .* of less frequency . . *Hombre. . .* tend[s] to be less popular in the younger groups. **1970** Tarpley *Blinky* **neTX** Map 107, *Nicknames for Mexican people*—[Among infreq resps:] hombres.

2 By ext: any male. *occas joc*

1854 (1932) Bell *Log TX-CA Trail* 212, Came up . . and found an hombre skinning 3 rattlesnakes. **1932** Bentley *Spanish Terms* 145, *Hombre . .* A man; a person. *Hombre* is most commonly used in conjunction with . . "bad," "tough," "good," "mean," "great," and is heard in all parts of the United States although with varying pronunciations. . . [In] the Southwest . . its use is more natural as well as more common. **1933** *AmSp* 8.3.28 [Prison vocabulary], *Hombre. . .* Man, fellow. *Slick hombre* means slippery sharper. **1940** *AmSp* 15.220 **swTX,** Cowboys living a rough and hardy existence occasionally develop into 'tough hombres.' **1967** *DARE* Tape **TX**24, You get up in them canyons, there was some damned rough hombres up there yet. **1987** [see **A** above].

hombug n See **humbug** n **8**

hombug v See **humbug** v **2**

home n, exclam, v, adv Usu |ho(ʊ)m; **esp NEng** |hɵm, hɔm|; **esp eVA** |hʊm|; for addit varr see quots Pronc-sp **esp NEng** *hum;* arch sp *hom* [*EDD home* sb.[1], adv., adj., and v. "Also in forms . . *hom . . hum*"]

A Forms.

1697 in 1901 Derby CT *Town Rec.* 301, My . . hom lot. **1795** Dearborn *Columbian Grammar* 136, *List of Improprieties. . .* Hum for Home. **1815** Humphreys *Yankey in England* 105, *Hum,* home. **1848** Lowell *Biglow* 144 **'Upcountry MA',** Hum, *home.* **1859** (1968) Bartlett *Americanisms* 207, *Hum.* A vulgar pronunciation of *home;* as "My old man ain't to hum," . . New England. . . "When is charity like a top? When it begins to hum." **1891** *DN* 1.156 **cNY,** *hɵm,* 'home.' **1903** *DN* 2.298 **Cape Cod MA** (as of a1857), *Home. . .* Pronounced hum [hʌm]. **1907** *DN* 3.190 **seNH,** *Home. . .* Pronounced with the New England short o, [hɵm]. *Ibid* 213 **nwAR, cCT,** *Hum. . .* Home. Rather infrequent in Arkansas. It does occur, especially with facetious intent. **1941** *LANE* Map 402, [In the phrase "May I escort you home," the forms [hom] and [hoʊm] (and varr) predominate throughout **NEng;** [hɔm] (and varr) are **scattered.**] *Ibid* Map 403, [In the phrr "at home" and "to home," the forms [hom] and [hoʊm] are **widespread NEng;** [hɔ˞m] is **scattered;** [hɵm], 10 infs, **scattered;** [hʌʊm or hʌom], 6 infs, **CT;** [howm], 2 infs, **sNH,** 1 inf **eVT.**] **1942** Hall *Smoky Mt. Speech* 34 **eTN, wNC,** This vowel [=[oʊ]], which, as in most American speech, is usually diphthongized . . is heard in . . home. . . The pure vowel [=[o]] no doubt appears only in rapid speech or in undrawled polysyllables. *Ibid* 35, Apart from rhythmic considerations, the diphthong is usually very audible (sometimes becoming disyllabic) . . before nasals, as in *home* [ho:ʊm] ([ho·u·m] [from one informant]). . . [From one informant] the vowel of *home* begins with a marked central sound [hɜom]. **1951** VA Univ. *Univ. Studies* 5.119 **eVA,** *Home* with the vowel of *foot*—[hʊm]. **1954** *Harder Coll.* **cwTN,** *Home* [hʌm]. **1960** *VT Hist* new ser 27.143, *Home* [hʊm]. . . Occasional. Rural areas. **1961** Kurath–McDavid *Pronc. Engl.* 157, *Home. . .* Besides the usual free vowel /o/ of *know,* two other vowels occur . . in *home* as recorded in . . *not at home:* checked /ɵ/ in New England, and checked /ʊ/ in Virginia. Checked /ɵ/ . . is common in northeastern New England and not infrequent in eastern Massachusetts, Rhode Island, and Connecticut. Though recessive, it is still used by some cultured speakers. . . [It is also found in] New England settlements of Upstate New York . . along the shore of Lake Ontario. *Home* with . . /ʊ/ of *book* has rather wide currency in large parts of eastern Virginia. . . It is common among the folk, less so among the middle class, rare among the cultured. Scattered instances occur in Delaware and in the Carolinas. . . [It] is an isolated relic in Virginia speech. . . In addition . . scattered instances of the /ʌ/ of *sun* and the /u/ of *two* occur in *at home . .* recorded sporadically in the Southern area.

B As noun.

1 The starting place, or place where "it" begins the count in children's games of chase, tag, or hide-and-seek; also the place to which a player returns in such a game. Cf **base B2, goal B, hunk** n[2]

1943 *LANE* Map 585 *(Goal). . .* The base in hide-and-seek . . and other children's games . . 2 infs, **CT,** 2 infs, **RI,** *Home.* **1951** Johnson *Resp. to PADS 20* **DE,** The place where "it" has to wait and count while the others hide, and where the players who hid must return: *home.* **1965–70** *DARE* (Qu. EE14, . . *The place where the player who is 'it' has to wait and count while the others hide*) 255 Infs, **widespread, but slightly more freq Nth, N Midl,** Home. **1966** Dakin *Dial. Vocab. Ohio R. Valley* 2.537, *Goal* [terms used in children's games]. . . *home* and the blend *home-base* compete [with *base*] with considerable currency over a fairly large area. . . *Home* is scattered throughout Kentucky east of the Green River and . . in Ohio and Indiana (at least east of the hills). . . *Home* is more frequently used by relatively younger speakers . . commonly used in the Mountains. **1973** Allen *LAUM* 1.396 **Upper MW** (as of c1950), *Goal* in children's games. . . Two generally equivalent terms . . occur, *base* and *home. . . Home* [10 infs].

2 also *home line:* **=taw line.** Cf **base B3**

1967–70 *DARE* (Qu. EE8, *The line toward which the players roll their marbles before beginning a game, to determine the order of shooting*) Inf **MO**30, Home; **AR**51, Home line.

3 See quot. Cf **homey 1**

1970 Major *Dict. Afro-Amer. Slang* 66, *Home:* (rare) a term of address used by two black people either from the same Southern state or simply from the South (Southern use).

4 in phr *to home:*

a At home; also fig. **chiefly Nth** *somewhat old-fash* Cf **to**

1795 Dearborn *Columbian Grammar* 139, [A list of Improprieties, commonly called Vulgarisms:] To home for At home. **1833** Neal *Down-Easters* 1.62 **ME,** [He] ought to go by the name of old say-nothin' away from our part o' the country, but when he's to home . . he's a match for gab with anybody't ever you come across. **1873** 'S. Coolidge' *What Katy Did* xii *(OEDS),* 'Tain't every girl would know how to take care of a fat old woman, and make her feel to home. **1903** *DN* 2.298 **Cape Cod MA** (as of a1857), *Home. . .* in expression 'to hum,' for at home. **1941** *LANE* Map 403 *(At home),* [The adverbial expression *to home* is found throughout **NEng.**] *To home* is described as more natural or more common by [10 infs, **scattered throughout NEng**]; as incorrect or improper but natural by [4 infs, **wNEng,** 1 inf **eMA**]; and as older or old-fashioned though still in use by [22 infs, **nNEng**]. **1950** *WELS Suppl.* **csWI,** To home—less frequent, less sophisticated—"Keep your dog to home!" *Ibid* **csWI,** In our youth . . we studiously avoided the use of "to home", believing it to be a literal translation of "zu hause". *Ibid* **csWI,** My father, born in 1867, always said "to home" [; however] at school you were taught that "to home" was incorrect. *Ibid* **cwWI,** When I was a boy, the use of "to home" was very common—"He stayed to home" or "He is not to home". *Ibid* **seWI,** "To home"—not well educated, old-fashioned. *Ibid* **seWI,** This county shows a wide usage of "at home", "to home" and "home"—with "to home" more commonly used among people of German language background, and more frequently by older folk; since "to home" annoys me dreadfully, I always hear it. **1955** Roberts *S. from Hell-fer-Sartin* 5 **seKY,** "Get right up here to the fire, Bill, you fellers, and make yourselves to home." **1966** Dakin *Dial. Vocab. Ohio R. Valley* 2.217, Some more old-fashioned rural speakers say *to home.* The use of the old Northern expression *to home . .* is more frequent in Ohio and Indiana. **1968–69** *DARE* (Qu. X32, . . *"Those are mine. You keep your ———."*) Inf **MN**34, Meat-hooks to home; (Qu. II22) Inf **VT**16, Keep your nose to home; (Qu. MM11) Inf **NY**68, To home.

b Toward home.

1935 Hurston *Mules & Men* 192 **FL** [Black], I said, "Come on, Big Sweet, we got to go to home."

5 attrib:

a Associated with the principal dwelling place of a family.

1697 in 1901 Derby CT *Town Rec.* 301, My dwelling house barn orchard and hom lot containing two acres more or les. **1786** (1925) Washington *Diaries* 3.4 **neVA,** Took an Acct. of the Tools about the home house. **1866** Andrews *South* 98 **SC** [Black], De home-house might come to me [=I might inherit the home-house]. **1899** (1912) Green *VA Folk-Speech* 229, *Home-field*. . . The piece of land adjoining the homestead. **1925** Glasgow *Barren Ground* 298 **VA,** The solitary cow . . lived on the lawn or what was called "the home field". **1967** *DARE* Tape **MA**102, The home bog on the back of the property I think is about a sixteenth of an acre. . . They use that almost like a kitchen garden. **1988** Lincoln *Avenue* 237 **wNC** (as of c1940) [Black], The body was at Ferdy Frost's Funeral Home but would soon be brought to the home house on Crockett Street for the wake. The funeral would be tomorrow.

b In ranching: indicating the original, most familiar, or principal place for livestock or ranch hands. **West** Cf **homeplace**

1880 *News & Press* (Cimarron NM) 22 Jan 3/3 **neNM,** All that piece or parcel of land known as the "Home Ranche," containing 1,000 acres . . [was] a portion of the land formerly known as the Beaubien and Miranda Grant. **1897** Lummis *King of Broncos* 37 **NM,** This particular spot was a few miles west from the Toltec Cattle Company's "home ranch"—headquarters of the score of cowboys who "rode the range" of a hundred thousand acres. **1907** White *AZ Nights* 258, Three days ago I had a bunch of cattle stolen right here from the home-ranch corrals. **1939** Rollins *Gone Haywire* 62 **ceMT** (as of 1886), Th' ol' man's bin steadily enlargin' his home range till now it includes mos' all th' headwaters o' Elk Prairie Crick. **1961** Adams *Old-Time Cowhand* 160, Cattle were inclined to remain in a territory with which they were acquainted. That became their "home range." **1966** Barnes-Jensen *Dict. UT Slang* 24, *Home corral*. . . the place where a herd of sheep or cattle comes to be counted or divided.

C As exclam.

Time out!—used to claim a brief break in the game of tag. Cf **free** exclam **2**

1967 *DARE* (Qu. EE17, *In a game of tag, if a player wants to rest, what does he call out so that he can't be tagged?*) Inf **PA**11, Home.

D As verb.

To go or come home. [Cf *OED home* adv. 1. d "With ellipsis of *go*"]

1843 (1847) Field *Drama Pokerville* 141 **MO,** Well, I'd now got to hum to my wife, and what on airth was I to do for my har! **1911** (1916) Porter *Harvester* 41 **IN,** Every night when he left the woods from one to a dozen cocoons . . were stuck in his hat band. . . "Those of you that home with me have no price on your wings." **1932** Faulkner *Light in August* 135 **MS,** The buggy jolted on, the stout, wellkept team eagering, homing, barning.

E As adverb.

In phrr *go* (or *get*) *home;* Fig: to die, to get to heaven. [Cf *OED To go home* (at *home* adv. 1. c) "to die (common dialectally)"; also *EDD go home* (at *home* sb.[1] 2. (7) (b)) "to die . . perish", and *home* v. 8 "*fig.* to die"] Cf **called home, be; long home**

1859 in 1971 *Original Sacred Harp* 343, [Lyrics:] O yes, My Saviour I will trust,/ Oh, what a happy time, when the Christians all get home. **1939** Coffin *Capt. Abby* 94 **ME** (as of 1860s), On October 17, a good sailor went home. "At 12 AM . . Fred Oman . . fell from the boom end and was lost." **1942** Berrey-Van den Bark *Amer. Slang* 117.11, *Die*. . . go home, go home feet first. **1943** *LANE* Map 521 *(Kicked the bucket)* 2 infs, **MA,** Gone home. **1966** *DARE* (Qu. BB55, . . *Expressions . . to say that a person died;* total Infs questioned, 75) Inf **AR**27, Gone home; (Qu. BB57, . . *Suicide*) Inf **AL**4, Got home safe. [Both Infs old] **1978** Wolfe *I'm On My Journey Home* [Phono disc] 6/2, [Lyrics:] Oh, who will come and go with me?/ I am on my journey home./ I'm bound for Canaan's land to see,/ I am on my journey home.

home base n

1 also *home plate;* for addit varr see quots: =**home B1. widespread, but somewhat less freq Nth** See Map Cf **base B2, goal B**

1954 *Harder Coll.* **cwTN,** *Home*—In children's games: home base, same as *base*. **c1960** *Wilson Coll.* **csKY,** *Home base* (or just *home*)—Where *It* counts while the others hide. **1965–70** *DARE* (Qu. EE14, . . *The place where the player who is 'it' has to wait and count while the others hide*) 234 Infs, **widespread, but somewhat less freq Nth,** Home base; **GA**77, **MS**21, **NY**145, **SC**32, 54, Home plate; **GA**77, Home port; **KY**41, Home post; **MI**24, Home ground; **NJ**4, Home goal; **NY**209, Home tree; (Qu. EE13b, *In games in which all the others hide, the one who must try to find them, he's* ______) Inf **MS**21, Home plate man. **1966** Dakin *Dial. Vocab. Ohio R. Valley* 2.537, *Goal* [terms used in children's games]. . . *Home* and the blend *home-base* compete with considerable currency over a fairly large area. . . A number of younger speakers scattered throughout the same sections [as those where *home* is used] use the blend *home-base,* a term which is apparently very common in central Indiana. *Home-base* also appears in the American Bottom [of southwestern Illinois]. **1969** *DARE* Tape **IN**83, [In the game] fox and geese. . . Just make . . like a big wagon wheel in the snow . . with footprints and the home base is the center.

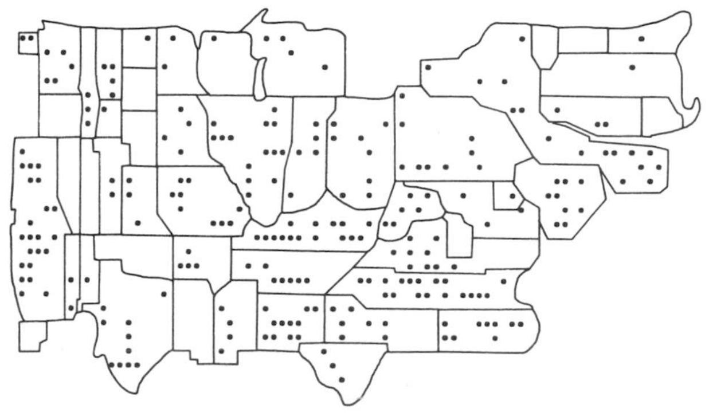

•home base 1 + varr (Qq. EE14, EE13b)

2 See **base** n **B3.**

home boy n Also *home girl* [Cf *W3 boy* n 2a "One native to or orig. belonging to a given place"; *Ibid* 2b "A member of a group, gang, or any kind of association of equals"]

1 also pl *home people:* A person from one's hometown or neighborhood; a person local to a particular area; transf, a friend or close associate; a person with whom one shares a cultural background. *now esp freq among Black and other minority speakers; affectionate* or *derog* Cf **down-homer, pinto**

1930s in 1977 Randolph *Pissing in the Snow* 140 **Ozarks,** One time there was a fellow from Oklahoma a-telling jokes down at the store [in southwestern Missouri]. . . The home boys all laughed like hell when they heard that [joke about incest in Arkansas families], but there was a big farmer from Arkansas come in the store just then, and he got mad. **1934** Wilder *Heaven's My Destination* 53, Snappiest little home-girl in Oklahoma. **1954** Armstrong *Satchmo* 235 **New Orleans** (as of 1922) [Black], Filo . . was a good-looking . . Creole gal. . . "Is this my home boy?" she asked [about me]. . . Filo and we sat around and talked ourselves silly about New Orleans. **1967** *AmSp* 42.238 [Black college slang], *Home boy* and . . *home girl* and *home people,* denote individuals who come from the same hometown as the speaker. *Ibid* 239, The possessive is almost always used with this expression—"my home boy" or "their home girl"—even when the person referred to is only a casual acquaintance or is not even known personally. **1977** Dillard *Lexicon* xiii, [Andrews and Owen in *Black Language*] point out how *home boy* refers either to someone from Harlem, Watts, or some other equally Black community or to one's best friend. **1978** Moore *Homeboys* [Title]. *Ibid* 3, Chicanos who serve sentences in California prisons tend to come from territorially-based youth gang backgrounds. . . they are the homeboys. *Ibid* 99, Prisoners routinely watch the bus bringing new prisoners and immediately identify a barrio carnal (homeboy). . . They offer him help and . . necessities of life . . in turn they get the latest neighborhood gossip. **1980** Folb *Runnin' Down* 45 **Los Angeles CA** [Black], Like you tell 'im [=them] get some joints somewhere—way over dere [=they can obtain some marijuana cigarettes in a distant part of town]. Den dey go way over dere, homeboy ain't dealin' [=the local supplier of that neighborhood isn't selling]. **[1982** Holm-Shilling *Dict. Bahamian Engl.* 105, *Home-boy*. . . term of address or reference to someone from one's own settlement or island.]

2 Transf: someone naive about urban life; a rustic; an unpretentious person. *orig among Black speakers, now more widespread* Cf **hoosier B2a**

1942 *Amer. Mercury* 55.223.89 **Harlem NYC** [Black], Youse just a home-boy, Jelly. Don't try to follow me [=don't try to imitate what I do]. **1970** *DARE* (Qu. HH1, . . *A rustic or countrified person*) Inf **DC**11, Home boy. [Inf Black] **1975** *AmSp* 50.61 **AR** (as of c1970), *Home boy* . . Unpretentious, earthy person (white use, uncommon). **1980** Folb *Runnin' Down* 77 **Los Angeles CA** [Black], The expressions homeboy or homegirl, when used in a pejorative sense, often refer to someone who sticks close to home (close to his or her mother) and has little feel for life on the streets—someone who is "unschooled." **1987** *DARE* File **csWI,** The man I worked with called me "home boy" because we were from the same home town—which was small. But he said it to belittle me, too. He thought I didn't have any street smarts, so he called me "homeboy." He thought I was too "country," you know, a hick. [*DARE* Ed: Speaker and speaker's co-worker both white.] **1987** *Capital Times* (Madison WI) 13 Aug 20, [*Doonesbury* comic strip:] Yo! Home boy! Hear you like to fight! **1989** *DARE* File **Los Angeles CA,** The sixteen-year-old White boy said that he doesn't go around with the White kids in his school; his friends are the home boys. Home boys and home girls are the Chicanos and the Black kids—the non-Whites. They're not gang members. Styles that go with being a home boy are red high-top sneakers and certain types of music. *Ibid,* The Chicano star of a hit TV show, talking to boys convicted of crimes, told them he was a home boy; like them, he grew up in east L.A.

homebreaker n Also *homewrecker* **chiefly S Midl, esp KY**
See quots.

1950 *WELS (Nicknames for Local Clubs)* 2 Infs, **WI,** Homebreakers. **1965–70** *DARE* (Qu. FF23, . . *Joking names . . for . . clubs or lodges*) Infs **KY**11, 41, 84, 89, **MD**23, 39, **NY**35, **NC**40, **OH**60, **WI**47, 66, Homebreaker(s); **KY**70, 75, 84, Homewrecker(s). [9 of 13 Infs comm type 5; 10 of 13 female]

homebringen n [Ger *Heimbringen;* also cf *EDD homebringing* (at *home* sb.[1] 1)] Cf **infare**
See quots.

1895 *DN* 1.382 **NJ,** *Homebringen:* first coming of newly married to the house of the groom's parents, where a feast was prepared and guests were invited. "Volunteers" (uninvited but not always unwelcome guests) often came. There was music and dancing and rather free hospitality, but no drunkenness. [**1987** *DARE* File **WI,** As a young person I knew this, the bringing of the bride to her new home for the first time. The word is "Heimbringen," [pronounced [hem]] in my dialect which is the German [of Wisconsin]. Of course that all died out after 1914.]

home bureau n **NY** Cf **home demonstration club**
=extension club.

1925 *Book of Rural Life* 5.2603, The Home Bureaus are to the home makers what clubs are to girls and boys. . . Anyone can join a Home Bureau and thus go into partnership with Uncle Sam in his effort to carry to the home makers, from the Federal Department of Agriculture, . . all the help that art and science have to offer regarding the making of better homes. *Ibid,* The organized home makers in Illinois, North Carolina, New Jersey and New York are known as *Home Bureaus;* in Iowa, Ohio, California and Tennessee they are called the *Home Department,* or *Home Economics Department,* of the Farm Bureaus; . . in certain other states they are known as *Home Demonstration Clubs.* **1968–69** *DARE* (Qu. FF22a, . . *Clubs and societies . . for women*) Infs **NY**69, 94, 109, 121, 123, 190, 220, Home bureau. [All Infs comm type 4 or 5; 6 of 7 Infs female]

home church n [*home* original]

1966 *DARE* Tape **SC**9, [FW, from **ceSC:**] You call Saint James . . your home church? [Inf:] Yes sir, that's my home church. [FW:] The first church you're raised up in, you call that your home church. [Inf:] That's right, home church. . . Saint James, that's my home church. This here's my second one; **SC**26, [FW, from **ceSC:**] The church you come up in, that's called your . . home church. [Inf:] Yeah, that's my home church. [FW:] Now how you mean your home church? [Inf:] Because I was raised up in that church. . . I might go to other churches but my home church, my foundation, everything I do is in that church. [FW:] Home church. [Inf:] Home church. What you would call it.

home cooking n
Fig: something that pleases or satisfies one.

[**1960** Wentworth–Flexner *Slang* 264, *Home cooking*—satisfying; pleasing.] **1963** Wright *Lawd Today* 93 [Black], Immediately in front marched a young girl twirling a long, brass baton; she was big-limbed, fleshy; she had thick red lips and deep, dark eyes. . . Her uniform fitted her snugly, and her body jerked in answer to every twist of the music. . . The men in the crowd went wild, smiting their thighs and striking one another in the back. . . "Now, ain't that something!" "The hottest stuff in town!" "This is homecooking!" **1970** Major *Dict. Afro–Amer. Slang* 66 [Black], *Home-cooking:* (1940's) anything fine, not especially food. **1988** *WI State Jrl.* (Madison) 31 March 15/3, The hallways were jammed with fans pumped up to cheer their Main Man [=Jesse Jackson]. . . "Run, Jesse, run. . . Win, Jesse, win," a blue-jeaned group chanted as Jackson's caravan of limos and Secret Service vans rolled up. This was a night on which Jesse Jackson badly needed that kind of home cooking.

home demonstration n, freq attrib Cf **extension club** **chiefly Sth, S Midl** See Map *esp in rural areas*
A demonstration in some branch of home economics given or sponsored by an agent of a government extension service—often in comb *home demonstration club.*

1925 *Book of Rural Life* 5.2613, A home demonstration is a piece of work carried out in the home over a period of time for the purpose of collecting evidence to indicate the value of some practice . . which . . [is] being advocated and taught by the extension agent. *Ibid,* [Caption:] Teaching the latest methods of food preservation is a large part of the work of every home demonstration agent. **1925** [see **home bureau**]. **1928** *Dly. Ardmoreite* (Ardmore, Okla.) 4 March 15/1 *(DA),* Miss Maude Andrews, home demonstration agent, took an active part in the show. **1948** *Durant Daily Democrat* (OK) 1 July 5/1, A new home demonstration club has been formed in the county. . . the 46th such club. **1954** *Harder Coll.* **cwTN,** *Home Demonstration*—A club that is supposed to raise the standard of living in the hill homes. **1965–70** *DARE* (Qu. FF22a, . . *Clubs . . for women*) 57 Infs, **chiefly Sth, S Midl,** Home demonstration clubs; **KS**15, Home demonstration units; **MT**4, Chief Cliff home demonstration club; **NC**79, Home demonstration meetings; **OH**60, Home demonstration group; [**GA**86, **IN**30, Demonstration clubs;] (Qu. W32, . . *Names . . for a group of women that meet to sew together*) Infs **OK**7, 47, Home demonstration club; **VA**42, Home demonstration group; [**OH**60, Demonstration group]. [59 of 63 Infs comm type 4 or 5] **1967** *DARE* FW Addit **SC**34, Home demonstration club—formerly, [for] social contacts.

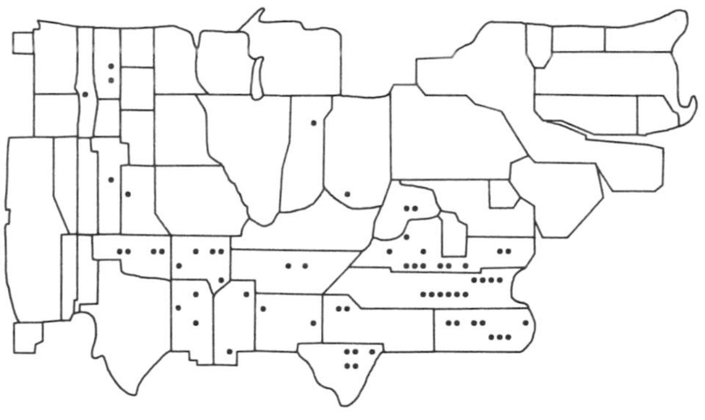

•home demonstration + varr (Qq. FF22a, W32)

home economic(s) club n Also *home ec club* **esp IN** *rural* Cf **home demonstration**
=extension club.

[**1925** see **home bureau.**] **1966–69** *DARE* (Qu. FF22a, . . *Clubs . . for women*) Infs **IN**35, 45A, 76, **MO**5, 19, Home economic(s) club; **IN**5, 16, 28, 49, 61, **WA**1, Home ec club; (Qu. FF1) Inf **WA**1, Home ec club. [All Infs comm type 4 or 5] **1969** *DARE* Tape **IN**76, Any woman who pays her dues of fifty cents a year can join Home Economic Club. . . We give baskets to shut-ins at Christmas time. . . Then we donate to the Red Cross, and part time to the community club. . . [We] learn how to . . keep a good home going, and handcraft.

home evening n Also *family home evening* *among Mormons*
See quots.

1966 *DARE* Tape **NM**8, Now we have what we call home evening. . . A certain night, all the family in that home will gather together. **1987** *DARE* File **csWI,** The home evening originated as a suggestion by the [Mormon] Church that the family meet once a week to learn more about

Church theology. A passage from the scriptures is chosen—perhaps if we're going to plan the budget for the week, the passage will be something about being thrifty. . . We discuss that, and then use that to plan the week. We've had this for the last twenty some years, since the early sixties probably. *Ibid* **DC,** Family home evening is an evening set aside at least once a week for the family to be together and increase their love and understanding of one another. Our family had two family home evenings each week, one for spiritual discussion and study of scripture, and one as a time to do something fun together.

home extension club (or council, society) See **extension club**

home farm n

1 A subsistence farm. Cf **truck garden**

1966 *DARE* Tape **NM6,** Water was run that way for the small home farms. [*Ibid,* [FW:] When farming is done then it's generally just home farming? [Inf:] It's usually just small home farming, just for their own home consumption.]

2 **=infirmary.** [*home* an institution serving as a residence]

1931–33 *LANE Worksheets* **cMA,** *Home farm*—Infirmary. Same as town farm.

home folks n pl Also *home folk* **chiefly Sth, S Midl** Cf **folk**

1 Members of one's immediate or extended family. [Cf *SND hame-folk* at *hame* III Combs.: "family, relatives"]

1887 (1967) Harris *Free Joe* 209 **GA,** Helen and her aunt . . had been sent for, in furtherance of an invitation they had accepted . . "Ole Miss would 'a' come," said Uncle Prince [=a Black servant of the Waverly plantation] . . "but she . . tuck'n sont atter you, ma'am, des like you wuz home folks." **1894** Riley *Armazindy* 19 **IN,** [Title:] *Writin' Back to the Home-folks.* **1909** *DN* 3.398 **nwAR,** *Homefolks.* . . Immediate family. "He's gone to see his homefolks." "He's visiting homefolks." **1941** *LANE* Map 388 *(Relatives),* 1 inf, **sNH,** Home folks; 2 infs, **seNH,** Home folks—rare; 1 inf, **sCT,** Home folks—'That term is going out fast'; 1 inf, **eVT,** Home folk(s)—used as a collective term, thought to be Scotch. **1970** Johnson *White House Diary* 33 **ceTX,** I greeted L. F. McCollum of Continental Oil of Houston as homefolks. **1973** Allen *LAUM* 1.345 **Upper MW** (as of c1950), [10 infs, **scattered,** Home folks.] **1976** Garber *Mountain-ese* 42 **Appalachians,** *Home-folks* . . relatives—John makes hisself ter home, jist like he wuz homefolks.

2 also *home people:* Members of one's neighborhood or community. Cf **home boy 1**

1910 Hart *Vigilante Girl* 384 **nCA,** But this is Tower's home county, and I know his home people better than you do. **1934** (1970) Wilson *Backwoods Amer.* 120 **Ozarks,** The crossroads store revels in its chance for directness, intimacy of merchant and customer, close understanding of regular and seasonal needs of a given farm community. Proprietors are apt to be home folks, bred to the ways and views of their communities. **1941** Percy *Lanterns* 259 **Lower Missip Valley,** Home-folk outside the flooded area . . went into tantrums of homesickness. **1943** in 1944 *ADD* **KY,** *Home-folk.* . . And among home folks who have known me from childhood. Radio. **1951** Johnson *Resp. to PADS 20* **DE,** Somebody who belongs in your home-town or neighborhood: *home folks.*

home free exclam Also *come home free, home free all;* for addit varr see quots [**home** n **B1 + free** exclam **1**] **chiefly east of Missip R, esp NY** See Map Cf **all home (free), all (in) free, all's out('s) (come) in free, free home**

In var hiding and chasing games: used by the player who is "it" to tell the others that one of them has been caught and the others are now "safe"; the phrase called out by a player who has reached base safely; hence adj *home free* safe from being caught by "it."

1895 *DN* 1.397 **s,c,eNY,** *Home free:* in hi-spy and similar games a player is said to be home free when he "touches the gool" before it is touched by the person who is "it"; if the one who is "it" finds a player and calls him by another player's name, both those players are home free. **1965–70** *DARE* (Qu. EE15, *When he has caught the first of those that were hiding what does the player who is 'it' call out to the others?*) 35 Infs, **chiefly east of Missip R,** Home free; **NY**7, 36, 60, 64, 78, 89, Home free all (*or* home); **KY**11, **MI**55, **OH**61, All (others) home free; **MO**2, 4, **OH**20, **TX**33, (All's out) come home free; **IL**130, One-two-three home free; **IN**81, All come in home free; **NY**51, Home safe; **NY**145, Allie allie home free; **PA**224, Everybody home free; (Qu. EE14) Inf **GA**77, Home free—one of the hiders would hollow [=holler] when he reached home port. **1967** *DARE* File **NYC,** *Home free all*—a call for all other players after one has been caught. **c1978** *DARE* File **nNJ** (as of c1955), I would have said "Home free home." **1987** *DARE* File **cIA** (as of 1950s), When somebody ran in to the base safely in hide-and-go-seek or hope-to-see-a-ghost-tonight, that person would yell "home free, home free." When that round of the game was over, "It" would yell "allee allee oxen free."

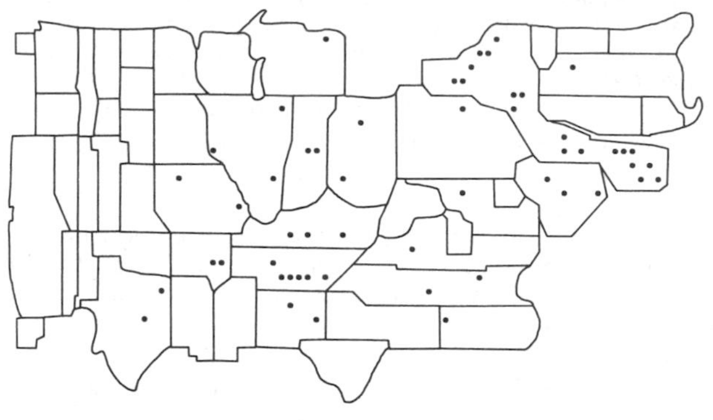

•home free + varr (Qq. EE15, EE14)

home fried potatoes n pl Also *home fries, ~ fry, ~ style potatoes* **chiefly NEast, OH** See Map and Map Section Cf **American fried potatoes 1, hash brown potatoes**

Boiled potatoes, chopped or sliced and then fried in hot grease until brown.

1965–70 *DARE* (Qu. H47, . . *Fried potatoes*) 79 Infs, **chiefly NEast, OH, but less freq NEng,** Home fries; 61 Infs, **chiefly NEast, OH, but less freq NEng,** Home fried; **PA**126, Home fry; **NY**41, 49, Home style. **1968** *DARE* FW Addit **MD,** Home fries—offered by restaurants all over state; sliced in any way and fried. **1968** *NJ Herald* (Newton) 23 June 14/3, Sussex Firemen's Breakfast. . . Menu: Juice—Melon—Coffee—Home Fries. **1977** *Yankee* March 99, *Diner Home fries*—basic formula (the sky's the limit!) Chop . . boiled potatoes. (Add a little diced onions. . .) Place in . . frying pan with hot bacon (or half fat, half butter) and season. . . when the potatoes are brown, serve 'em up. **1978** *Sat. Review* 22 July 51/1 **NYC,** You've got the home fries and you've got the shoestring fries. **1989** *Yankee* 53.2.126 **NEng,** I'm a couple of miles away in a small doughnut joint, . . a platter of fried eggs, pancakes, home fries, and English muffins in front of me.

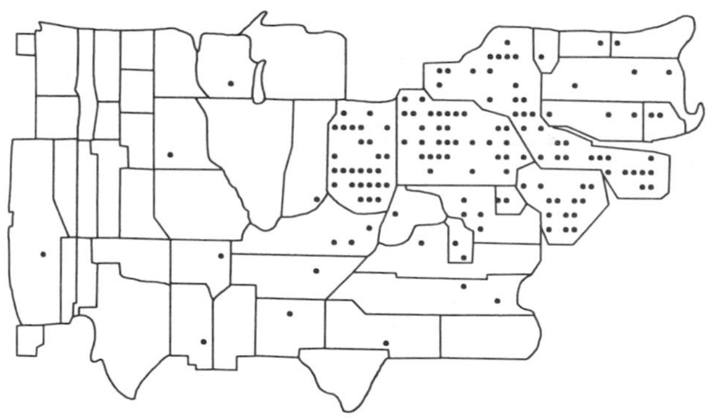

•home fried potatoes + varr (Qu. H47)

home girl See **home boy**

home guard n, sometimes collective Cf **boomer** n[2]

One who is content to stay in the same place for a long time; esp an employee who stays in the same company.

1930 Irwin *Amer. Tramp* 101, *Home Guard.*—A citizen, especially one who has travelled but little; a steady worker, one not easily upset or driven to strike. The term was originated by the old-time yegg and tramp for the simple countryman who grew up in one village or town, and had but little experience with the world and its wiles. . . Looked upon as inferior by their flightier companions, the home guard plugged along at their work during the slack season, and were glad to have the capable boomer's assistance when busy times arrived. **1932** *RR Mag.* Oct 368, *Home Guard*—Employee who stays with one railroad, as contrasted with boomer. **1932** *Santa Fe Employes' Mag.* 26.2.34/2 [Railway lingo], An employe who remains on a division only a short time is a *boomer;* one who stays a long time is a *home guard.* **1941** *AmSp* 16.233 [Logger's talk], *Homeguard.* One who permanently lives in the vicinity. **1949** in 1953 Botkin–Harlow *Treas. Railroad Folkl.* 165, *Boomers. . .* itinerant railroader[s] who . . hit the bottle too much, or carelessly let a boxcar roll off the dock, or perhaps caused a wreck by failing to deliver a train order, and flew the coop, leaving the "home guards" (company men) to face the music. **1956** *Western Folkl.* 15.202 **West** [Among loggers], A home guard is a steady employee.

homekeeper n [Blend of *homemaker* + *housekeeper*] Cf **homework**

A homemaker.

1898 *Advance* 20 Jan 75/1, They suggest a loving home-keeper's thoughtful care and provision for the aged grandfather. **1967** *DARE* Tape **MI**51, After I was married, I was like all other homekeepers. I kept my house and did things like that.

home-kill grease n

1986 Pederson *LAGS Concordance,* 1 inf, **cAR,** Home-kill grease—i.e. lard.

homeland n

1972 Claerbaut *Black Jargon* 68, *Homeland. . .* The black section of the city.

homeless hobo n [*homeless* because it lays its eggs in the nests of other birds]

=cowbird 1.

1950 *WELS (Birds found in your region . . give any other names you have for them)* 1 Inf, **ceWI,** Homeless hobo [for cowbird].

home line See **home B2**

homely adj Usu |'homli|; also **esp NEast** *old-fash* |'hɒm(b)lɪ, 'hɵm-|; for addit varr see quots Cf Intro "Language Changes" I.8 Pronc-spp *hum'ly, humbly;* superlative *homblest* Similarly, n *humbliness* [Cf *EDD homely* adj. "Also in form . . *humly*"]

A Forms.

1815 Humphreys *Yankey in England* 105, *Humbly,* homely. **1857** (1930) DeLong *Jrls.* 9.141 **NY,** All in all the girl's [sic] were the homblest I ever saw anywhere. **1887** Kirkland *Zury* 537 **IL,** *Humbly. . .* Homely. **1891** *DN* 1.142 **cNY,** Short close *o,* so common in New England, is not found in many words of Ith[aca] D[ialect]. . . [hɵmli, hɵmbli (hɒmli, hɒmblist)]. *Ibid* 156, Examples of [vowel] shortening. . . [hɵmli], 'homely'. . . [hɒmlist], 'homeliest'. **1914** *DN* 4.76 **ME, nNH** [Rural locutions], She was mortal hum'ly. **1921** Haswell *Daughter Ozarks* 47 (as of 1880s), His owner's description of him as the "humbliest hoss" was eminently correct. **1933** *AmSp* 8.2.44 **neNY,** [There is] the general use of [ɤ] for [o] in . . *homely* [hɤmlɪ].

B Senses.

1 Reminiscent of the home; home-loving; homey, unpretentious. **esp S Midl**

1901 Harben *Westerfelt* 73 **nGA,** The veranda of the hotel was crowded with loungers, homely men in jeans, slouched hats, and coarse brogans. **1908** *DN* 3.321 **eAL, wGA,** *Homely. . .* Homelike. **1925** Hunter *Trail Drivers TX* 559, Our fare may have been homely, and the menu which we set before them might not have consisted of twelve or fifteen courses, but . . it was very wholesome and appetizing. **1931** Hannum *Thursday April* 46 **wNC,** The sweet smell of the burning wood was homely, and she relaxed a little. **1932** Stong *State Fair* 254 **IA,** Margy looked at the house, which had been open to air all day, stout and spreading and homely. Had she ever left here? **1944** *PADS* 2.44 **wNC, VA,** *Homely. . .* Fond of the home; applying on[e]self to matters about the house. **c1960** *Wilson Coll.* **csKY,** *Homely*—often, as of old . . home-loving.

2 Friendly; familiar, common. [Cf *EDD homely* adj. 1 "Friendly, familiar . . free; regarded as one of the house"]

c1885 in 1981 Woodward *Mary Chesnut's Civil War* 55 **SC** (as of 1861), What a kind welcome these old gentlemen gave me. One, more affectionate and homely than the other, slapped me on the back. **1944** *PADS* 2.44 **wNC, VA,** *Homely. . .* Friendly, familiar. **1950** Wells *Ballad Tree* 267, In the Appalachians, where suspicion of the stranger is oddly mingled with a warm hospitality, he was everywhere welcomed. "We like you," people said, "you're so common and homely." **1951** *PADS* 15.55 **neIN** (as of 1899), *Homely. . .* Familiar about the home. . . in 1899, undoubtedly following local, or at least family, practice, I entitled a school essay, "A Few of Our Homely Birds and Their Relation to Man." **1953** *AmSp* 28.294 **csPA,** *Homely. . .* Congenial, friendly, not standoffish. Popular speech.

homemade adj Pronc-sp *homade*

Homegrown.

1954 *Harder Coll.* **cwTN** (as of 1940), *Home-made tobacco*—Tobacco grown and not bought. [Letter:] He went over to Troy Outland's [place] to buy some home-made tobacco. *Ibid, Homade*—of anything made or sometimes grown at home. "Jest homade backer." **1969** *DARE* Tape **GA**74, The flowers were placed on the great mound of clay, always homemade flowers, never from a nursery. They were homegrown.

homemade cheese n **esp S Midl** Cf **clabber cheese**

Cottage cheese; see quots.

1946 *PADS* 5.26 **wVA,** *Home-made cheese . .* Cheese made of the drained curd of sour milk . . uncommon. **1949** Kurath *Word Geog.* 71 **sAppalachians,** *Home-made cheese . .* has considerable currency in western North Carolina and parts of the Appalachians. **c1950** *LANCS Checklists* **swWI,** *Homemade cheese*—cottage cheese. **1954** *Harder Coll.* **cwTN,** *Homemade cheese. . .* "We don't make no ho-made cheese." **1961** Folk *Word Atlas N. LA* map 1011, [9 infs, Homemade cheese.] **1966** Dakin *Dial. Vocab. Ohio R. Valley* 2.343, *Curds, curd cheese,* and *home-made cheese . .* compete with *clabber cheese* in the northeast and are more common in southern Kentucky from the Mountains to the Mississippi. *Ibid* 344, *Curds* and *home-made cheese* are rarely used along the upper Ohio. **1973** Gawthrop *Dial. Calumet* 72 **nwIN,** [19 infs, Homemade cheese.]

homemade foreigner n [Cf *DAE Homemade Yankee* "A name contemptuously applied during the Civil War to Southerners who remained loyal to the Federal government"]

A US-born Spanish-speaking Black person; see quot.

1942 Kennedy *Palmetto Country* 109 **FL, GA, AL,** Negroes—who constitute a third of the region's population—include influential groups from . . Cuba whose national cultural characteristics linger for several generations. The Spanish-speaking offspring of the Cuban Negroes are called "homemade foreigners" by the native blacks.

home people n

1 See **home folks 2.**

2 See **home boy 1.**

homeplace n **esp Sth, S Midl** Cf **home B5a**

1 The home, outbuildings and immediate land of a family, or simply the home itself, as contrasted with other land or buildings the family might own. Cf **houseseat**

1736 in 1914 NH (Colony) Probate Court *Records* 2.625, I . . bequeath . . My Dwelling house & homeplace where My House Stands. **1816** U. Brown *Journal* I.283 *(DAE),* I was introduced to Jacob Beeson . . as well as his wife & daughter Jane (which was all the family now on the home place.) **1911** Quick *Yellowstone Nights* 97 **SD,** One [section of land] f'r each o' them, you understand, an' the home place f'r mother if anything happened. **1928** Chapman *Happy Mt.* 23 **seTN,** Me 'n' Bess will have been married a great while, an'll have us a home-place all swarved up [=swarming] with childrens. **1931** *AmSp* 7.93 **eKY,** *Homeplace,* the part of a farm on which the house and out-buildings are located. "Everybody expected Mattie's mother to leave her the home-place." **1941** Percy *Lanterns* 9 **nwMS,** She . . managed the thousand-acre home place. **1968** MacDonald *Pale Gray* 71, I've got maybe seventeen, eighteen hundred acres left, scattered around the east county, and except for this hundred right here, my home place, I imagine it would all be for sale if the price was right.

2 often in phr *old homeplace;* Spec: the place where one grew up; see quots.

1944 *PADS* 2.57 **swMO, nSC, cTN,** *Home-place. . .* The farm on which one grew up as distinguished from the "place" on which one lives after marriage. "I'm going to help Pa cut wheat over on the home-place this evenin'." **1946** Foreman *Last Trek* 91, They continued in their attachment to the old home place. **1960** Criswell *Resp. to PADS 20* **Ozarks,** Place where one lives or was born and reared. I call my small rental house "the old home place." I grew up there. **1969** *DARE* Tape **CA**157, Down on the old homeplace . . we used to have a lot of fun; **CA**159, There were four in my family. We were all born there, at the old homeplace . . without a doctor. **1969** *DARE* File **IL,** I have heard here an expression . . —used by old folks (over 70 years old)—speaking of the family farm where they were raised. They call it the homeplace. For example, "When I was down to the homeplace the other day." **1973**

Amer. Folklore Newslet. Spring 2/2 *(OEDS),* I enjoy going back to the old home place, now deserted, and the double-log cabin falling into decay.

home plate See **home base 1**

homeseat n Cf **home B5a, houseseat**

=**homeplace 1.**

1940 (1978) Still *River of Earth* 206 **KY,** "I hear Coonie Todd's a good woman, and sets honor by her dead husband," she said. "Got a homeseat her pure own. That's more'n most folks can brag about."

homespun n [Prob by ext from *homespun* of thread: spun at home; perh infl by obs *spun* of tobacco: twisted into a tight roll; cf *DA spun* a. 1]

See quots.

1950 *WELS (Home-cured tobacco)* 5 Infs, **WI,** Homespun. **1960** Criswell *Resp. to PADS 20* **Ozarks,** *Homegrown tobacco*—Homespun. **1960** Heimann *Tobacco* 146 **VA, NC** (as of c1812), The Virginians and North Carolinians living in what was called the "Virginia District" or the "Tobacco Sack" . . began making "homespun" twist for chewing in much the same way as the New England farmers evolved the homemade cigar. Tobacco growers did not find it difficult to form dry leaf into a coarse, sometimes sweetened twist for their own use. **1966** *PADS* 45.16 **cnKY,** *Homespun. . . long green. . .* "Homespun can cause mosaic [=disease] if the tobacco is exposed to it." **1967** Key *Tobacco Vocab.* 146, *Long green. . .* Cured, but unprocessed tob[acco]. . . (Also *home spun*). *Ibid* **KY,** *Home spun*—"They twist it up into a twist." *Ibid* **MO,** Long green [=] home spun. **c1970** *Halpert Coll.* 11 **wKY,** Have a chew of homespun [is a] hospitable invitation.

homestead v [Transf from *homestead* v to improve a piece of land and build a family residence on it] Cf **boomer** n^2, **home guard**

In phr *homestead the joint:* To remain in one place for a long time; hence *homesteader* one who works in one place over a period of time; one who marries and settles down.

1945 Hubbard *Railroad Ave.* 347, *Homesteader*—A boomer who gets married and settles down. **1958** McCulloch *Woods Words* 87 **Pacific NW,** *Homesteader*—A logger who stays in one camp a long time; not a family man. *Ibid, Homestead the joint*—To stay a long time in one place.

homestead lily n

A **daylily** (here: *Hemerocallis fulva*).

1940 Clute *Amer. Plant Names* 224, *Hemerocallis fulva.* Homestead lily.

homestead the joint See **homestead**

home style potatoes See **home fried potatoes**

home tree n Cf **spar tree, tail tree**

In **high-lead** logging: see quot.

1958 McCulloch *Woods Words* 87 **Pacific NW,** *Home tree*—A spar tree at the landing, as opposed to the tail tree. [*Ibid* 175, *Spar tree*—The key to cable logging. . . the center of operations for each side. . . Location of each spar tree is very important to the success of the logging.]

homework n

Housework.

1968 *DARE* Tape **IN**14, I done a lot of homework when my grandmother was away. . . I helped to cook and keep house for my grandfather.

homewrecker See **homebreaker**

homey n

1 Someone from the same place or social group as oneself—also used as a term of address. Cf **home boy 1**

1946 (1972) Mezzrow-Wolfe *Really Blues* 334, *Homey:* form of greeting between people from the same place. **1978** Moore *Homeboys* 47 **Los Angeles CA** [Chicano], The girls' gangs . . [are] "ambivalent" about their relationship to the boys' gangs of the same neighborhoods . . [although they have some] of the same features . . [as] the boys' gangs . . fighting, and loyalty to one's homies. *Ibid* 77, The "blood brother" bond . . ties affinity groups together. Thus carnal refers not only to one's barrio homies but also, by extension, to all Chicanos. **1988** *AmSp* 63.134 **TN** [Prison talk], *Homey* . . Inmate from the same geographical area as oneself.

2 An unsophisticated person; a rural southern immigrant to the urban north. [Cf *homey* familiar, unpretentious] Cf **home boy 2**

1967-70 *DARE* (Qu. HH1, . . *A rustic or countrified person*) Inf **CA**110, A homey; **MA**8, Homies—a colored person from the rural South; **SC**69, Homey—from down home; [**TX**32, Homely [sic]]. **1970** Major *Dict. Afro-Amer. Slang* 66 [Black], *Homey:* (1930's-40's) a newly arrived Southerner in a Northern city.

hominy n Pronc-spp *homily, hommony, hom'ny* [Prob from or rel to Algonquian *minneash* fruit, berry]

A Forms.

1829 *VA Lit. Museum* 30 Dec 458, *Hominy* or *hommony.* **1922** Gonzales *Black Border* 307 **sSC, GA coasts** [Gullah glossary], *Hom'ny* —hominy. **1986** Pederson *LAGS Concordance* **Gulf Region** *(Hominy)* 31 infs, Homily (grits); 7 infs, Corn (or lye) homily. [*DARE* Ed: 26 of 33 total infs Black]

B Senses.

1 Whole or ground kernels of corn separated from the hull and germ and usu prepared by boiling; now applied esp to whole kernels. **formerly widespread, now chiefly Atlantic, esp S Atl** See Map *somewhat old-fash* Cf **big hominy, grits 1b, hulled corn, little hominy, lye hominy**

1630 Smith *True Travels* 43, Their servants commonly feed upon Milke Homini, which is bruized Indian corne pounded, and boiled thicke, and milke for sauce. **1672** Josselyn *New-Englands Rarities* 53 **MA,** They beat it [=Indian Wheat] in a Morter, and sift the flower out of it; the remainer they call *Homminey,* which they put into a Pot of two or three Gallons, with Water, and boyl it upon a gentle Fire till it be like a Hasty Pudden. **1737** in 1842 *GA Hist. Soc. Coll.* 2.44, Hominy is a sort of a meal much resembling our oat meal in England, made of their Indian corn. **1784** Smyth *Tour U.S.A.* 1.48 **VA,** Homminy is an American dish, made of Indian corn, freed from the husks, boiled whole, . . until it becomes almost a pulp. **1847** (1852) Crowen *Amer. Cookery* 399 **NY,** Opposite the tray . . , let the steak, or fry, . . be placed . . , and dishes of hominy or boiled rice. **1887** Parloa *Miss Parloa's Kitchen Companion* 96 **NEast,** Grits is the name given to fine hominy in some sections of the South, "hominy" there meaning the coarse hominy. **1903** *DN* 2.317 **seMO,** *Hominy. . .* Hulled corn. **1908** *DN* 3.321 **eAL, wGA,** *Hominy. . .* Cracked Indian corn. **1939** [see **hulled corn**]. **1942** [see **grits 2**]. **1950** *PADS* 14.38 **SC,** *Hominy. . .* Coarseground maize prepared for table use; grits; *hominy* grits. **1963** Mencken-McDavid *Amer. Lang.* 699, In South Carolina I was taught that hominy designated what the less fortunate called grits. **1965-70** *DARE* (Qu. H23, . . *Hot cooked breakfast cereal*) 12 Infs, **esp SC,** Hominy; **RI**1, Hulled corn—soaked in lye, then cooked; hominy is like this; **SC**43, Hominy—cooked; grits when raw—old-fashioned; (Qu. H24, . . *Boiled cornmeal*) Inf **FL**49, Hominy and mush made same way, but hominy is harder; **GA**36, Hominy—whole; **PA**63, Hominy; (Qu. H25, . . *Fried cornmeal*) Infs **MA**38, 72, Hominy; (Qu. H50, *Dishes made with beans, peas, or corn*) Infs **MI**104, **NY**20, **WA**14, Hominy; (Qu. P13, . . *Special kinds of bait*) Inf **NC**37, Hominy. **1968** *DARE* Tape **IN**32, I have not forgotten the art of hominy making. . . That again has to be white corn and soda can be used in place of the lye, but we prefer the lye that is made by running rainwater through the wood ashes and soaking the kernels in that until the shells are ready to slip. . . once having removed all the hearts and the shells, why, then we cook it. . . we can either fry it or fix it with sugar and cream or butter

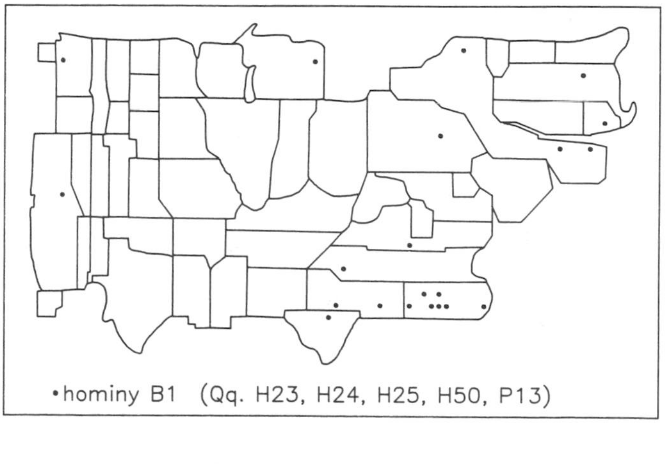

•hominy B1 (Qq. H23, H24, H25, H50, P13)

alone or make a casserole out of it. **1968** *DARE* FW Addit **GA**33, *Hominy grits* [are] big grain hominy. The breakfast cereal variety is just called grits. **1986** Pederson *LAGS Concordance,* 615 infs, **Gulf Region,** Hominy. [Approximately a third of these infs made such comments as "whole grain," "big," "not ground"; 5 infs said that hominy could be either whole or ground.]

2 in phr *all hominy and no ham* and var: See quot 1981.

1981 Hardeman *Shucks* 210, To the southerner, *all hominy and no ham* was a way of saying *all work and no play.* **1984** Wilder *You All Spoken Here* 146 **Sth,** *No ham and all hominy:* All work and no play.

hominy beater n

A **click beetle** or similar insect; see quots.

1816 in 1824 Knight *Letters* 71 **VA,** They never fail of having hominy, which is broken corn and beans mixed . . and the dish is so popular in Virginia, that they have a river named Chicka*hominy;* and also an insect called the hominy-beater. **1872** Schele de Vere *Americanisms* 42, From some fancied resemblance to a kernel thus hulled, a snapping-beetle, or Elater, of Pennsylvania, is called the *"Hominy-beater."* **1968** *DARE* (Qu. R30) Inf **DE**3, Hominy beater: a little beetle—you put your finger on his back and his head would hit down; they are greyish black.

hominy bird n

1 also *homminy-bird:* **=ruby-throated hummingbird.**

1859 Taliaferro *Fisher's R.* 102 **nwNC** (as of 1820s), I gits right inter it, like a homminny-bird (humming-bird) inter a tech-me-not flower. **1934** Vines *Green Thicket* 60 **cnAL,** He had feathers from a few birds he did not know the name of, though he usually called any bird something. He had even killed . . a hominybird (hummingbird) . . for the mighty bed [=the bed to be used after his marriage].

2 A **nuthatch.**

1967 *DARE* (Qu. Q23) Inf **AL**32; Hominy bird.

3 Prob a **goldfinch.**

1969 *DARE* File **KY,** Hominy bird—a yellow bird that sucks flower buds.

hominy grits See **grits 1b**

hominy snow n [See quot 1954] **chiefly S Midl** Cf **corn snow, flour-sifter snow**

Usu an icy and granular snow, but see quots.

1857 in 1934 *KS Hist. Qrly.* 3.162 **neSC,** It then snowed a coarse hominy snow till the ground was white. **1946** *PADS* 6.17 **eNC,** *Hominy snow. . .* Tiny pieces of winter ice or hail. . . Common. **1954** *PADS* 21.30 **SC,** *Hominy snow. . .* Snow in fine grains like hominy grits, as opposed to the large flakes. Not obsolete in South Carolina. **c1960** *Wilson Coll.* **csKY,** *Hominy snow. . .* Small pellets of ice snow or hail. **1966–70** *DARE* (Qu. B39) Infs **AR**52, **GA**73, Hominy snow; **GA**80, Hominy snow—a light, grainy snow; **KY**86, Hominy snow—large, dry flakes; **NC**25, Hominy snow—it never lays [sic]. **1970** *DARE* FW Addit **KY**75, Hominy snow—coarse, grainy snow or lumpy snow that's heavy; **KY**84, Hominy snow—heavy, beady snow that is a mixture of snow and freezing rain.

hommer See **hammer**

hommie n Also *ami, hommy, hummi, hummy, ummie* [Varr of **hommilie**] **PaGer area**

A calf or hornless cow; rarely a lamb—also used to call these animals.

1890 *DN* 1.74 **ePA,** *Hommie:* a young calf. (To children). **1896** *DN* 1.418 **cnMD,** *Hommy:* a calf. **1907** *German Amer. Annals* 6.380 **cs,sePA,** *Hummy*—Little calf. **1935** *AmSp* 10.169 **sePA,** *Hummy* is equivalent to English 'calf'; college students who have used the word have been surprised to learn that it is not perfectly good English. **1946** *PADS* 5.26 **VA,** *(Have a) hommy, (find a) hommy . .* [To c]alve; in the northern Blue Ridge, rare. **1949** Kurath *Word Geog.* 35, *Hommie! . .* a call to calves, also an affectionate term for a calf or a lamb (Pa. Ger. *hammi*), which is current from the Lehigh to the Juniata and southward to the Shenandoah Valley. **1957** Schönfelder *Deutsches Lehngut* 208, Das Wort erscheint in der Schreibung *hommie, hommy, hommilie, hummi* und *hummy.* Es wird angenommen, daß es sich um ein pennsylvaniadeutsches Wort ‚hommi' oder ‚hammi' handelt, das wiederum auf das deutsche Wort ‚Hummel' zurückgeht. In verschiedenen deutschen Dialekten wird ‚Hummel' als Rufnamen für eine Kuh oder als Bezeichnung für eine hörnerloses Tier verwendet. [=The word appears in the spellings *hommie, hommy, hommilie, hummi* and *hummy.* It is assumed that we are dealing with a Pennsylvania German word "hommi" or "hammi", which in turn is derived from the German word "Hummel". In various German dialects "Hummel" is used as a name for a cow or as a designation for a hornless animal.] **1967–68** *DARE* (Qu. K20, *A calf that is sold for meat*) Inf **PA**153, Hummy ['hʌmi], a little calf; (Qq. K80, 83) Infs **PA**137, **VA**32, Hommie; **PA**141, Hummy; **PA**211, Come hommie ['hɑmi]; **MD**26, 29, Ami ['ami] ami ami; **PA**141, Ummie ['ʌmɪ] umi umi. **1967–68** *DARE* FW Addit **sePA,** A hummy ['hʌmi] is a baby cow or a calf; **VA**31, *Hommie* is a small calf; when it's repeated, it is used to call calves or cows; it's old-fashioned [FW: Background of the community is 90% Pennsylvania German]. **1968** *Helen Adolf Festschrift* 36, *Hammi*—This noun, derived from Pennsylvania German *Hammli,* is used by most speakers in the area for 'a little calf,' and it was not until I went to college that I discovered that not everyone in the United States was familiar with this term.

hommilie n Also *humli, ommalie;* for addit varr see quots [PaGer *hamm(e)li;* Swiss Ger *ammeli*] **PaGer area** Cf **hommie**

A calf or dehorned cow—also used to call a calf.

[**1872** Haldeman *PA Dutch* 17, 'Kalb' (calf. .) [in German] is named by children 'hamǝli' when a suckling.] **1896** *DN* 1.418 **PA,** A calf. . . (The word *homily* (!) is used about Tannersville, Pa.) **1914** *DN* 4.158 **ce,c,sePA,** *Humli. . .* A calf. **1949** Kurath *Word Geog.* 64, *Call to calves. . .* The Pennsylvania German call . . *hommilie!* is still current . . from the Lehigh to the Shenandoah and westward to the Alleghenies. **1957** [see **hommie**]. **1969** *DARE* (Qu. K83, . . *Call a calf . . at feeding time*) Inf **IN**67, Ommalie [ɑməli] repeated. [FW: Inf speaks fluent Swiss German; everyone in community over 45 speaks Swiss German.]

homminick n [Cf **hommilie**]

1973 Allen *LAUM* 1.260 **nSD** (as of c1950), [Call to calves:] *Homminick,* a likely phonetic shift from the Pennsylvania German *hommilie,* is locally known but not used by a northern South Dakota inf. living near the Missouri River.

homminny-bird See **hominy bird 1**

hommock See **hummock**

hommony See **hominy**

hommy See **hommie**

hom'ny See **hominy**

homony peg n [Prob var of **mumblety-peg**] Cf **baseball**

1968 *DARE* (Qu. EE5, *Games where you try to make a jackknife stick in the ground*) Inf **PA**148, Homony-peg.

honda n Usu |'hɑndə, 'hɔn-, -do|; also |ˌhɑn'du, hɔn-| Freq *hondo;* also *hindu, hondoo, hond(o)u* [Prob < Span *hondón* an eyelet, perh infl by *honda* a sling] **chiefly West**

1 The leather or metal eye on one end of a rope or strap through which the other end is looped; the piece of rope or strap with the eye on it.

1887 *Scribner's Mag.* 2.508 **West,** *Hondou . .* the slip-knot of the lariat. **1894** *DN* 1.324 **TX** [Mex and Span vocab], *Hondoo, hondou:* the slip-knot of a *reata.* **1932** Bentley *Spanish Terms* 146, *Honda* English modifications *hondoo, hondo* (*Spanish,* ['o:n da:]; *English* ['hɔn do:]; [hɔn 'du:]) From *honda,* a sling for throwing stones. The small loop in one end of a lariat or lasso rope of any kind through which the other end of the rope is threaded, chiefly for lassoing purposes. The *honda* on a good lariat is usually reinforced with leather or metal to eliminate the cutting and burning caused by the swift friction of the rope surfaces when the noose is tightening. This leather piece is sometimes called *honda.* **1935** Davis *Honey* 115 **OR,** The girl, on a long-legged black gelding, followed the herd of led horses and made them keep up by whipping them with the hondo-end of a rawhide rope. **1958** McCulloch *Woods Words* 87 **Pacific NW,** *Hondu*—Same as hindu, a short strap or cable with an eye on one end. . . the word is used by southwestern cattlemen to mean a spliced eye at the end of a rope. **1967** *Platte Co. Views* (Weston MO) 7 Sept 4/7, [Advt:] Stock Wards Farmers Store. . . Lariat rope, 30 ft. quick release honda. . . $1.88. **1967** *DARE* Tape **TX**25, [FW:] What's a hondo? [Inf:] That's a piece of leather that's woven like a button. And it's put over the end of the rope to make a loop to fit around the saddle horn to hold the rope stationary. . . It's like a button hole. . . The honda itself ['hɔndɨtself] is plaited more or less. **1967** *DARE* FW Addit **ND**5, [A] hondu [ˌhɑn'du] [is] the knotted loop on a rope which allows the throwing loop to slip. **1981** *KS Qrly.* 13.2.68 *Hondu. . .* small handmade rawhide loop anchored to the end of a riata so that "loops" can be "built".

2 See quot.

1894 *DN* 1.324 **TX** [Mex and Span vocab], *Hondoo, hondou. . .* A parbuckle used on shipboard to ship and unship casks, spars, and other heavy objects.

hondo(o), hond(o)u See **honda**

hone v Often with *for* [*EDD hone* v.^{2} 2 "To repine for want of; to long or pine for"]

1 also with *after:* To desire strongly; to pine or yearn for; hence n *honing* a yearning or hankering. **chiefly Sth, S Midl**

c1770 in 1833 Boucher *Glossary* 50 **MD,** In vain I thrive,—in vain the world looks gay,/ Still, still I hone for bliss, while Mollsey is away. **1851** Hooper *Widow Rugby's Husband* 20 **AL,** It's strange what a honin' I have for the cussed thing. **1883** (1971) Harris *Nights with Remus* 47 **GA** [Black], He des [=just] nat'ally hone fer ter be los' in de woods some mo'. [Footnote to *hone:*] To pine or long for anything. This is a good old English word, which has been retained in the plantation vocabulary. **1884** in 1933 *DN* 6.348 **TN,** *Hone. . .* "I'm just honin' after food," is another example of the Tennessee patois. **1893** Shands *MS Speech* 37, *Hone. . .* Used by negroes and illiterate whites to mean *to desire strongly, to yearn for.* This word is marked obsolete in Webster, but is very frequently heard among the lower classes of Mississippi, and even educated people sometimes use it. An old preacher of Copiah County . . [said] in a sermon: "If a penitent gets religion, he must hone for it." **1908** *DN* 3.321 **eAL, wGA,** *Hone. . .* To pine, long. "I was honin for a dram." **1915** *DN* 4.226 **wTX,** *Hone. . .* To long for. **1917** *DN* 4.413 **wNC, KY, KS,** *Hone. . .* To desire with craving. "He jes' hones atter it." **1934** (1970) Wilson *Backwoods Amer.* 104 **Ozarks,** They's [=there is] a couple or three red foxes. . . that live a ways up Bresh Creek. . . any [dogs] . . that is honin' to run, you'all had ought to organize to handle them. **1966–69** *DARE* (Qu. GG17, *Other words for longing . . "She had been so lonely—she was really ______ [to see him].*") Inf **CT**23, Honing—old-fashioned [FW sugg]; **GA**67, Honing [FW: Inf has heard it infrequently in Georgia, but often in Kentucky]; **SC**10, Honing [FW sugg]; **WA**6, Honing. [All Infs old] **1976** Garber *Mountain-ese* 42 **Appalachians,** *Hone* . . yearn, long for—I hone fer the day when I can git some more uv Ma's country cookin'.

2 By ext: to look for, seek.

1940 (1942) Clark *Ox-Bow* 143 **NV,** "I thought you liked excitement," I said. "I thought you'd be honing for something to do." **1942** *Time* 16 Mar 17/1 **MS,** They wander . . up & down the . . empty streets of Mississippi towns, honing for something to do. **1944** Wellman *Bowl* 103 **KS,** I reckon Bedestown is a-honin' fo' trouble. . . They're goin' to fight the railroad bond scheme.

hone after See **hone v 1**

hone down v phr [*hone* v to sharpen as if with a *hone* n]

To bear down; see quot.

1951 Giles *Harbin's Ridge* 120 **eKY,** Seemed like we all got creepy and jumpy, . . Papa trying to keep up the work, and Faleecy John honing down trying to do his part.

hone for See **hone v**

hone off v phr

To have sexual intercourse with.

1927 in 1977 Randolph *Pissing in the Snow* 93 **Ozarks,** "But if you will lay down and let me hone you off, you can have the rabbit." So he laid her down and he honed her off. *Ibid* 94, He unhitched the old jenny [=female donkey] from the cart, and the king honed her off.

honest adv Cf Intro "Language Changes" II.8

Honestly; naturally.

1923 *DN* 5.204 **swMO,** Bill comes by his laziness honest. **1942** in 1944 *ADD* **IN,** *Honest. . .* He come by it honest. **1986** Pederson *LAGS Concordance,* 1 inf, **neMS,** Got it honest—behavior; 1 inf, **csTX,** Comes by it honest—behavior.

honest n [Var, perh by folk-etym, of *earnest*]

1963 Wright *Lawd Today* 152 **Chicago IL** [Black], If somebody ever started in on these white folks in honest, you could run 'em square into the ocean.

honest kine adv phr [*honest* + *kine* kind of, like, -ly] **HI** Cf **da kine**

1981 *Pidgin To Da Max* **HI,** *Honest kine* . . Fo' real? You mean it?

honesty n

Std: a plant of the genus *Lunaria,* often grown for the coin-like silicles. Also called **money plant.** For other names of *L. annua* see **gold-and-silver plant, grandpa's specs, matrimony vine, money, money-in-both-pockets, money-seed, moneywort, penny-bank, poor man's shilling, silver dollar, silverleaf, silver shillings, spectacles plant**

honesty-weed n

A **wild indigo** (here: *Baptisia tinctoria*).

1933 Small *Manual SE Flora* 676, *B[aptisia] tinctoria. . .* Honesty-weed.

honewort n

An umbelliferous plant *(Cryptotaenia canadensis).* Also called **honeywort, hornwort 2, wild chervil**

1832 MA Hist. Soc. *Coll.* 2d ser 9.156 **cwVT,** Sison Candense [sic], Hone-wort. **1837** Darlington *Flora Cestrica* 189, *Cryptotaenia canadensis. . .* Hone-wort. . . Woodlands, and shaded places: frequent. **1857** Gray *Manual of Botany* 157, *Honewort. . .* Rich woods, common. . . Plant 2° high. **1891** Jesup *Plants Hanover NH* 17, Honewort. C[ryptotaenia] Canadensis. **1936** IL Nat. Hist. Surv. *Wildflowers* 220, The Honewort is a common woods plant from New Brunswick to Georgia and west to western Ontario, South Dakota and Texas. **1949** Moldenke *Amer. Wild Flowers* 149, Somewhat similar to the sweetcicelies in growth . . is the *honewort, Cryptotaenia canadensis.* **1970** Correll *Plants TX* 1153.

honey n

1 See **honey tree.**

2 See **honey mushroom.**

3 Syrup or sauce.

1896 *DN* 1.418 **CT,** *Honey:* pudding sauce. **1934** *Hanley Disks* **neVT,** Ten quarts [of sap] . . make a pound of honey [=maple syrup].

4 in phr *get* (or *dip*) *in honey;* Fig: to meddle; to get in trouble; see quot.

1940 *Hench Coll.* **VA,** "I told you so! Dipping in honey." "That is what you get for getting in honey." "He's going to get in honey and then, watch out."

5 Used as a term of address to a male friend; see quots.

1938 FWP *Guide DE* 105 **sDE,** A young male visitor in certain parts of the county may be flabbergasted to hear himself addressed by an older man as "Honey." **1967** Fetterman *Stinking Creek* 90 **sAppalachians,** "Honey" is a word of friendship, like the western cowboy's "podner" or the soldier's "buddy." Big, powerful men, men who haul down logs and can fell a mule with a fist, use the word. . . it is a term whose origin nobody seems to know. As visit after visit goes by, the word is used more and more. "Come to the hoss trade if you care to, honey."

6 A person who is difficult to work with; one who overestimates him- or herself; also in phr *she's a honey but the bees don't know it*—used ironically.

1892 *KS Univ. Qrly.* 1.97 **KS,** *Honey:* a fine fellow, generally ironically. **1934** in 1972 Hellman *Coll. Plays* 19, "Has she always been like this?" . . "She's always been a honey. Aunt Amelia's spoiling hasn't helped any, either." **1946** *PADS* 6.38 **eNC,** She's a honey, but the bees don't know it. (Said by boys about some well-dressed silly girl out for a "killing." Disapprovingly.) **1956** McAtee *Some Dialect NC* 23, *Honey.* "She's a honey, but the bees don't know it." Said of a girl who overestimates her charm. **1960** Wentworth–Flexner *Slang* 265, *Honey,* a person who is difficult to please.

7a also *honeydew:* Excrement, dung, garbage.

1942 Berrey–Van den Bark *Amer. Slang* 124.2, *Dung. . .* honey. *Ibid* 239.2, *Rubbish, refuse. . .* honey, garbage. **1950** *AN&Q* 8.172 **seVA** (as of a1863), Slaves . . referred to human feces as "honey." **1965–70** *DARE* (Qu. L17, . . *Names . . for manure used in the fields*) 15 Infs, **scattered, but chiefly Nth, N Midl,** Honey; **IL**116, **NY**99, Honeydew; **NJ**65, Cow honey.

b freq in combs:

(1) *honey dip, ~ house:* A toilet or outdoor privy.

1915 *DN* 4.233 **neOH,** *Honey-house. . .* water-closet. **1968** *DARE* FW Addit **PA**81A, *Honey dip*—a place, the privy.

(2) *honey-dip:* To empty or clean a latrine or outhouse; hence n *honey-dipper,* also *honey-digger;* vbl n *honey-dipping;* ppl adj *honey-dipped.*

1950 *AN&Q* 8.151 **PA,** *Honey-digger* (expression found in Pennsylvania coal country): one who cleans out latrines. *Ibid* 172 **VA,** Before the days of improved plumbing in Petersburg (Va.), the squad that cleaned privies at night was known to boys as the "honey-diggers". **1967** Cerello *Dakota Co. MN* 62, No one ever really volunteered when it came to the chore of honey-dipping the toilet. . . There used to be men that earned a living by travelling the countryside offering to honey-dip for the farmers. . . The honey-dipped wastes were most generally deposited on the patches of land set aside for future garden spots. **1968** *DARE* FW Addit **PA**81A, *Honey-dipper*—one who cleans out outhouses. A honey-dipper worked around here up to the last ten years. **1973** *DARE* File **swPA** (as of 1920s), Once a year . . men came in a huge wagon made of thick boards . . to clean out the big box under the outhouse. They had huge long-handled dippers and they would dip it out and load it into the wagon. . . These men were called honey-dippers. **1987** *DARE* File **neOH** (as of c1968), At Boy Scout Summer Camp, Scouts were told that latrines were periodically emptied by honey-dippers. . . we never saw these honey-dippers at work.

(3) *honey bucket, ~ pot:* A pail or container for excrement or manure.

1959 Carrighar *Moonlight at Midday* 275 (Tabbert *Alaskan Engl.*) **AK,** Other waste is disposed of through what is called the facility, or the honey bucket. This is a chemical toilet, a pail . . enclosed in a large metal box. The box extends through the wall in such a way that the bucket can be removed from the outside by the "sanitary man," who empties and steam-cleans it. **1968** *DARE* (QR, near Qu. L17) Inf **NH**14, Some would use a honey pot—a pail full of manure and water, they would dip out the water and pour it around plants. **1976** *Fairbanks Daily News-Miner* (AK) 14 Jan (Tabbert *Alaskan Engl.*), Residents who use the sanitary service have been asked to dispose of their own honeybuckets contents at the city Dump or they can allow the contents to freeze. . . honeybuckets can be thawed by torch once the dump truck is again back in service. **1985** *DARE* File **Nome AK,** [Letter:] Part of the town is still on honeybuckets. In the political campaign just past one candidate said he was "worried about the 50 people who are still sitting on honeybuckets" and promised to do something about it.

(4) *honey wagon:* Any of var vehicles or moveable structures related to containing or moving excrement, manure, or garbage, as:

(a) A portable toilet.

1942 Berrey–Van den Bark *Amer. Slang* 871.8 [Military usage], *Latrine* . . Honey wagon . . a rolling toilet in a mine. **1983** *9000 Words* 95, *Honey wagon* . . a portable outdoor toilet.

(b) also *honey cart, ~ pot:* A vehicle which empties or carries (away) human waste; see quots.

1926 Willoughby *Trail Eater* 103 (Tabbert *Alaskan Engl.*) **AK,** Only that morning he had passed the Doctor's house and bumped into Luigi, driver of what Nome facetiously termed the "Honey Wagon." **1948** *AmSp* 23.222 [Kriegie [=prisoner-of-war] talk], [There were] repeated references to the tank wagon used to evacuate the latrines as the *honey wagon.* **1950** *AN&Q* 8.172 **seVA,** Before the days of improved plumbing . . the night wagon was [known as] the "honey-wagon." **1957** *Sat. Eve. Post Letters* **NH** (as of 1880s), There were men who cleaned out cesspools and we called their small tank wagons "honey carts." **1960** *AmSp* 35.118, Oxdrawn carts hauled loads of fertilizer [in Korea], the most common kind being human night soil. These conveyances were known [to the American soldiers] as *honey-carts, honey-wagons,* or *honey-pots.* **1967** *DARE* Tape **IA**8, We've had some crappin' cans up here . . that damn thing . . [was] so full, I don't know how the hell they got the last pile up there. But, you know, there wasn't a sewer available and the city had to pay to have one of these honey wagons come clean it out. **1977** *DARE* File **csWI,** We had plumbing problems and had to call the honey wagon many times that year.

(c) A vehicle which carries or spreads manure in a field.

1942 Berrey–Van den Bark *Amer. Slang* 81.25, *Honey wagon,* a manure cart. **1967** *DARE* (QR, near Qu. L17) Inf **IA**1, Honey wagon—a manure wagon [with] a large barrel on it; **PA**33, Honey wagon—liquid without straw mixed in, put in [the] wagon, a new term here. **c1968** *DARE* File **csWI,** *Honey wagon*—manure spreader.

(d) also *honey boat;* By ext: a garbage truck or barge; a garbage can. [Orig military usage]

1942 Berrey–Van den Bark *Amer. Slang* 791.11, *Honey wagon,* a garbage can or bum. **1947** Berrey–Van den Bark *Amer. Slang Suppl.* 13.2 [Military slang], *Honey wagon,* a garbage truck. *Ibid* 46.3, *Honey boat,* a garbage barge. **1987** *DARE* File **csWI** (as of c1973), I worked for awhile on a garbage truck. We called it a honey wagon.

(5) *honey man:* See quot.

1986 Pederson *LAGS Concordance,* 1 inf, **seFL,** Honey man—cleaned outhouses, government employee.

honey v[1] Cf **honeyfuggle**

1 intr; also with *around:* To flatter, wheedle; to display affection.

1806 (1970) Webster *Compendious Dict.* 145, *Honey*. . . to talk kindly. **1872** Schele de Vere *Americanisms* 205 **AL,** Persons indebted to the Tuscaloosa bookstore are respectfully solicited to pay their last year's account forthwith. It is of no use to honey; payments must be made at least once a year. **1887** (1967) Harris *Free Joe* 12 **cGA,** "In my day an' time it wuz allers took to be a bad sign when niggers got to honeyin' 'roun' an' gwine on." "Yessum," said Free Joe. . . "but me an' my ole 'oman, we 'uz raise tergeer [=together], en dey aint bin many days w'en we 'uz 'way fum one 'n'er [=one another] like we is now." **1899** (1912) Green *VA Folk-Speech* 229, *Honey* . . coax; flatter. **1908** [see **2** below]. **1942** Berrey–Van den Bark *Amer. Slang* 354.4, Honey . . *to exchange endearments.* **1967** *DARE* (QR, near Qu. II20a) Inf **CO**7, Honeyed around.

2 tr; also with *up (to), around,* also in phr *honey it up to:* To flatter, sweet-talk, fawn on (someone).

1834 Caruthers *Kentuckian* 1.189 **KY,** He doesn't honey it up to 'em, and mince his words. **1899** (1912) Green *VA Folk-Speech* 229, *Honey*. . . To talk sweetly to. **1908** *DN* 3.321 **eAL, wGA,** *Honey*. . . To seek to display obsequious or fondling actions. "Don't come honeyin around me." Also . . with *up.* "She honeyed him up till she got what she wanted." **1950** *WELS* 1 Inf, **WI,** He's always honeying up to the boss. **1957** Battaglia *Resp. to PADS 20* **eMD,** [To try] too hard to gain somebody else's favor: "He's always trying to honey around the boss." **1966–69** *DARE* (Qu. II20b, . . *Tries too hard to gain somebody else's favor: "He's always trying to ______ the boss."*) Inf **OH**70, Honey; **IL**20, **WA**1, Honey around; **IL**64, Honey up; **MD**30, Honey up to; (QR, near Qu. II20b) Inf **MN**40, Honey him up; (Qu. JJ3a, . . *A special effort to 'get in good' . . "He's trying to ______ again."*) Infs **MN**12, **VA**26, Honey up the teacher; **MD**34, Honey the teacher up; **IA**13, Honey around the teacher.

honey v[2] Pronc-sp *hoaney* [Cf **hone 1**]

=hosey.

1927 *AmSp* 3.169 **NYC,** Children still stand before toyshop windows and call out, "I hozey the drum," or sometimes, "I honey the drum," meaning, "I choose for mine." **1942** *AN&Q* 2.153/2, Children use . . [hosey] and "honey" (pronounced "hoaney") interchangeably. There are many other expressions of the "I stake my claim" idea . . since no word familiar to children seems to express the idea adequately.

honey around See **honey** v[1] **1, 2**

honeyball n

1 freq *honeyballs:* **=buttonbush 1.** [See quot 1936]

1900 Lyons *Plant Names* 90, *C[ephalanthus] occidentalis* . . Honey-ball. **1901** Lounsberry *S. Wild Flowers* 475, Honey-balls. *Cephalanthus occidentalis.* **1936** IL Nat. Hist. Surv. *Wildflowers* 319, The Buttonbush [=*Cephalanthus occidentalis*] is a shrub 3–12 feet high, or sometimes a tree up to 20 feet. It is an excellent honey plant, often called Honey Balls because its fragrant nectar-producing flowers are borne in dense spherical heads. **1940** Clute *Amer. Plant Names* 52, *C[ephalanthus] occidentalis* . . honey-balls. **1973** Stephens *Woody Plants* 458, *Cephalanthus occidentalis* . . honeyball.

2 =huisache.

1960 Vines *Trees SW* 497, *Sweet Acacia*—*Acacia farnesiana*. . . Vernacular names in the United States . . are Acacia-catclaw, Honey-ball.

honeyballs See **honeyball 1**

honeybean n

The fruit of the **honey locust 1.**

1867 De Voe *Market Asst.* 378, *Honey bean* or *sweet locust-fruit*. . . The fruit or pod is flat, crooked, and long, of a reddish brown color, and full of hard seeds, enveloped in a sweet pulpy substance, much like honey.

honey-bean mesquite See **honey mesquite**

honeyberry n

The fruit of a hackberry (here: *Celtis laevigata*).

1976 Yepson *Trees* 279, *Sugarberry* (honey berry . .). The edible purple fruit sweetens as the weather turns cold; the white kernel within tastes something like a date.

honeybloom n [See quot 1828]
=spreading dogbane.
1828 Rafinesque *Med. Flora* 49, *Apocynum androsemifolium.* . . Vulgar Names—Milk-weed, . . Honey-bloom. . . All have a bitter milky juice, and yet the flowers smell of honey, and produce that sweet substance. **c1873** in 1976 Miller *Shaker Herbs* 137, *Bitterroot—Apocynum androsaemifolium*—Honey Bloom. **1940** Clute *Amer. Plant Names* 89, *A[pocynum] androsaemifolium.* Spreading Dogbane. Honeybloom. **1971** Krochmal *Appalachia Med. Plants* 50, *Apocynum androsaemifolium.* . . Common Names: . . honey bloom, . . wild ipecac. **1974** (1977) Coon *Useful Plants* 61, *Apocynum androsaemifolium*—Spreading dogbane, . . honey bloom.

honey boat See **honey** n **7b(4)(d)**

honey bucket See **honey** n **7b(3)**

honey bun n **esp Sth, S Midl**
Any of several types of pastry; see quot.
1966–70 *DARE* (Qu. H30, *An oblong cake, cooked in deep fat*) Infs **GA**4, 92, Honey bun; (Qu. H32, . . *Fancy rolls and pastries*) Infs **KY**48, 84, **NC**72, **TX**85, **VA**78, Honey buns; **KY**74, Honey buns—small and round; **NY**94, Honey buns or sticky buns—brown sugar and nuts, real sticky. **1986** Pederson *LAGS Concordance (Doughnut)* **Gulf Region,** 1 inf, I eat honey bun; 1 inf, Honey bun—long, not twisted; *(What . . do you buy at a bakery . . sweet roll . . long john)* 5 infs, Honey bun(s).

honey cart See **honey** n **7b(4)(b)**

honeycat n *joc*
A **skunk.**
1969 *DARE* (Qu. P26) Inf **IL**81, Honeycat.

honey clover n Also *honey lotus*
=white sweet clover.
1896 *Jrl. Amer. Folkl.* 9.186, *Melilotus alba,* . . honey clover, Greene County, Mo. **1900** Lyons *Plant Names* 243, *Melilotus alba.* . . Honey Lotus. **1937** U.S. Forest Serv. *Range Plant Hdbk.* W123, White sweetclover, known also as bee-clover, honeyclover, . . and white melilot, is a robust biennial herb belonging to the pea family *(Leguminosae).* **1940** Clute *Amer. Plant Names* 20, *Melilotus . . alba* . . honey-clover, honey lotus.

honeycomb n
1 Any of var large fungi; see quot. Cf **honeycomb mushroom**
1967 *DARE* (Qu. S18, *A kind of mushroom that grows like a globe . . sometimes gets as big as a man's head*) Inf **MO**3, Honeycomb: never gets as big as a man's head; (Qu. S19, *Mushrooms that grow out like brackets from the sides of trees*) Inf **MI**15, Honeycomb.
2 See quot; hence adj *honeycombed.*
1968–69 *DARE* (Qu. B35, *Ice that will bend when you step on it, but not break*) Inf **KS**16, Honeycomb; **MN**23, Honeycombed; **NY**206, Honeycombed ice—full of cracks.

honeycomb morel See **honeycomb mushroom**

honeycomb moth n
A bee moth *(Galleria mellonella).*
1854 Emmons *Agriculture NY* 5.253, *Tinea cerella.* . . *Honeycomb Moth.* . . its larva feeds upon the honeycomb, or *beeswax.* **1889** *Century Dict.* 2872, *Honeycomb moth,* a tineid moth of the genus *Galeria* [sic], which infests beehives, depositing its eggs in the comb, where the larvae are developed and undergo their transformations.

honeycomb mushroom n Also *honeycomb morel* [From the cell-like apertures]
A **morel,** esp *Morchella esculenta.*
1902 McIlvaine–Macadam *1000 Amer. Fungi* xxiii, There are several varieties of the Morell in the United States. They are known among the country people who cook and pickle them, as Honey-comb mushrooms. **1924** *Torreya* 24.18 **NY,** The spring mushroom *(Morchella esculenta)* or "honeycomb" mushroom as it is sometimes called makes its appearance in this section almost exclusively in the month of May, although it may come in April a little further south. **1981** Lincoff *Audubon Field Guide Mushrooms* 327, *Yellow morel—Morchella esculenta.* . . Also called the "Honeycomb Morel."

honeycomb rockfish n [See quot 1953]
A **rockfish** (here: *Sebastodes umbrosus*).
1953 Roedel *Common Fishes CA* 131, *Honeycomb Rockfish.* . . Southern California. . . A fine hexagonal network of dark borders about the scale pockets. **1960** Amer. Fisheries Soc. *List Fishes* 38, Honeycomb rockfish. . . *Sebastodes umbrosus.*

honey cone See **cone 2**

honey creek See **honey pond and flitter tree**

honeycup n
1 A **sensitive pea** such as *Cassia robusta.*
1933 Small *Manual SE Flora* 662, *Chamaecrista.* . . Honey-cups. **1949** Moldenke *Amer. Wild Flowers* 126, The *Gulf sensitivepea* or *honeycup, C[assia] robusta,* grows to over 5 feet in height and puts forth a profusion of equally large yellow or white blossoms all through the summer months.
2 An ericaceous shrub *(Zenobia pulverulenta)* native chiefly to the Coastal Plain. [See quots] Also called **mealybush**
1953 Greene–Blomquist *Flowers South* 91, *Honey-Cup (Zenobia pulverulenta)* A . . shrub . . with cup- or bell-shaped white flowers some . . of which are so fragrant that they may be detected by scent at considerable distances. **1964** Batson *Wild Flowers SC* 86, *Honey-cup.* . . Deciduous shrub up to 8 ft. high. . . Flowers white, fragrant, cup-shaped and ¼ in. long.

honey daisy n
=huisache daisy.
1936 Whitehouse *TX Flowers* 182, *Amblyolepis setigera* . . is also called honey . . daisy. . . It has the strong scent common to the bitterweed, but is fragrant in drying.

honeydew n
1 also *honeydew tobacco:* See quot 1911. [Perh once a trademark] *hist*
1844 Lumsden *Amer. Memoranda* 14, My next communication will probably contain full details of the methods adopted by the Virginian planters in the manufacturing of the nigger-head, ladies'-twist, cavendish, plug, pigtail, honey-dew, and other varieties of the stimulating and soothing herb. **1848** (1855) Ruxton *Life Far West* 53 **Rocky Mts,** So well did they like each other's company, so sweet was the "honey-dew" tobacco of which the strange hunter had good store, . . the three had come to the resolution to join company. **1851** Cist *Sketches Cincinnati* 244, Fine cut chewing, of best honeydew and sweet fine cut cavendish. **1854** Greatrex *Whittlings* 52 **CT,** He patronised a quiet bit of "honeydew" occasionally, however, for I saw him take out his box, and push a portion of its contents surreptitiously into his cheek. **1889** *Century Dict.* 2873, *Honeydew.* . . A kind of chewing-tobacco prepared with molasses.
2 Maple sap.
1968 *DARE* (Qu. T4) Inf **MD**20, Honeydew, the sap of these [maple] trees.
3 A gall.
1969 *DARE* File **KY**44, Honeydew: insect-formed bumps on a maple leaf.
4 also *honey dip:* Liquor.
1942 Berrey–Van den Bark *Amer. Slang* 99.1, *Liquor.* . . honey dip. **1968** Adams *Western Words* 152, *Honeydew*—A logger's name for whisky.
5 See **honey** n **7a.**

honeydew squash n Cf **honey-melon squash**
A butternut squash.
1967 *DARE* (Qu. I23) Inf **IL**4, Honeydew squash—shaped like a bell; . . butternut—another name for honeydew.

honeydew tobacco See **honeydew 1**

honey-digger See **honey** n **7b(2)**

honey-dip v See **honey** n **7b(2)**

honey dip n
1 See **honey** n **7b(1).**
2 See **honeydew 4.**

honey-dipped, honey-dipper, honey-dipping See **honey** n **7b(2)**

honey dish n Also *honey stand*
See quots.
1960 Criswell *Resp. to PADS 20* **Ozarks,** *Common dishes:* a fruit or honey dish—tall, with a dome lid on it, now called a compote. **1966–68** *DARE* (Qu. G6, . . *Dishes that you might have on the table for a big dinner or special occasion*) Inf **AR**20, Honey stand—on a stem

with honey in it; IN30, Honey dish; **MO5**, Honey dish—they have one a hundred years old. [All Infs old, comm type 5]

honey-dubber n Cf **brownnose** n, **honey** v[1], **honeyfuggle 2**

1969 *DARE* (Qu. JJ3b, . . *A school child makes a special effort to 'get in good' with the teacher . . "She's an awful ______.")* Inf **NC61**, Honey-dubber.

honeyfackle, honeyfogle See **honeyfuggle**

honeyfoogler See **honeyfuggle 2**

honey frog See **horned frog**

honeyfuddle See **honeyfuggle 4**

honeyfuggle v Also *honeyfackle, honeyfugle, honeyfogle* [Perh var of Engl dial *connyfogle* v. "To hoodwink, entice by flattery" infl by *honey* n; cf also *EDD gallyfuggle* v. "To deceive, take in" and **honey** v[1]] *somewhat old-fash*

1 To swindle or dupe; to intend to cheat or trick; hence vbl n *honeyfuggling.* Cf **bamfoozle 1**

1829 *Va. Lit. Museum* 30 Dec. 458 *(DAE)* **KY,** *Honeyfuggle,* to quiz, to cozen. **1848** Bartlett *Americanisms* 179, *Honey-fogle,* to swindle; to cheat; to lay plans to deceive. **1852** *Knickerbocker* 40.548 **FL,** A neighbor . . *honey-fackled* him in the matter of a *heap* of logs. **1858** *Harper's New Mth. Mag.* 17.270/1, "It's all honey-fuggling". . . "What's honey-fuggling?" "It's cutting it too fat over the left." **1931** *Hench Coll.* **cVA,** Alderman was no judge of men. He never could tell whether a man was a gentleman or a bounder. Anybody could honeyfogle him.

2 To flatter, sweet-talk; to wheedle; to ballyhoo; hence n *honey-foogler* a flatterer.

1856 *Knickerbocker* 48.286 *(OEDS),* They go cavorting out, honey-fuggling their consciences. **1856** U.S. Congress *Congressional Globe* 34th Cong 1st Sess 22 July app 965/1 **NE,** Pardon me for using the word; but Sharp *"honey-fuggled"* around me. **1899** (1912) Green *VA Folk-Speech* 229, *Honeyfuggle.* . . To cajole; wheedle. **1906** *DN* 3.141 **nwAR,** *Honey-fuggle.* . . To cajole, flatter. "He can't honey-fuggle him." **1912** *NY Eve. Jrl.* 8th ed 25 Mar 12 *(Zwilling Coll.),* [Cartoon:] The colonel was up on the platform honey fugling the small town boys to beat the band. He was just starting to tell how he knocked an elephant dead with one punch when—*Crash.* **1912** *DN* 3.578 **wIN,** *Honey fuggle.* . . To win with sweet promises. Sometimes pronounced *fugle.* **1930** Shoemaker *1300 Words* 28 **cPA Mts** (as of c1900), *Honeyfoogler* —One who gets into another's graces by flattery. **1960** Wentworth–Flexner *Slang* 265, *Honeyfuggle[,] honeyfogle.* . . To flatter or cajole; esp. to flatter or cajole one's sweetheart . . or an attractive woman, esp. to do so to gain sexual favor or make her forget anger or displeasure. . . *Archaic.*

3 with *with:* To consort with, "snuggle up to."

1887 *Courier–Jrl.* (Louisville KY) 7 May 4/4, The modern practices in politics of . . temporizing with cranks, demagogues and tricksters instead of sending them to the rear; and of honey-fuggling with rascals instead of hitting them a death-blow between the eyes. **1898** Harte *Stories in Light* 191, Honeyfogling with a horse-thief, eh?

4 To lure, entice.

1888 *Century Illustr. Mag.* 36.81/2 **IL,** He acts like a man that 's got a deadfall all sot, un is a-tryin' to honey-fugle the varmint to git 'im to come underneath. **1894** *DN* 1.331 **NJ,** *Honey-fogle:* to allure by traps. **1902** Harben *Abner Daniel* 157 *(DAE),* He's been tryin' to honeyfuggle the old man into a trade, but I don't think he made a deal with 'im.

5 also *honeyfuddle:* To show affection in public.

1969–70 *DARE* (Qu. AA8, *When people make too much of a show of affection in a public place . . "There they were at the church supper ______ [with each other].")* Inf **GA77**, Honeyfugglin'—old-fashioned; **WV16**, Honeyfuddling.

honeyfuggling See **honeyfuggle 1**

honeyfugle See **honeyfuggle**

honeyfunk v [Perh var of **honeyfuggle,** but cf **honey** v[1] **2**]

1950 *PADS* 14.38 **SC,** *Honeyfunk.* . . To deceive by flattery; to curry favor, especially of a student with a professor or with the authorities. Expresses great contempt. . . *Honeyfunk* is a variant of *honeyfogle, honeyfugle.*

honey grass n

=**melic grass.**

1901 Mohr *Plant Life AL* 382, *Melica mutica. . . Honey Grass.* . . Rich open woods and copses. **1933** Small *Manual SE Flora* 126, *Melica. . . Melic-grasses.* Honey-grasses.

Honey Hill n [Perh **honey** n 7]

1966–68 *DARE* (Qu. C34, *Nicknames for nearby settlements, villages, or districts)* Inf **NC23**, Honey Hill; (Qu. C35, *Nicknames for the different parts of . . town)* Inf **MD26**, Honey Hill—an area where bums hang around; (Qu. II25, . . *The part of a town where the poor . . live)* Inf **MD26**, Honey Hill.

honey hole n

1 An opening put in a log to attract a raccoon; see quot.

1970 Green *Ely* 106, I had drilled many honey holes for coons at the waterfall. . . I drilled a honey hole in the log on the end out of the water. . . After I scanned round . . I looked back to see the tail of a coon hanging down at the end of the log.

‡**2** An especially good fishing spot.

1988 *DARE* File **cnWI** (as of 1986), My friend, who grew up in northwestern Pennsylvania and hunted and fished his whole life, had been a fishing guide for many years in northern Wisconsin. He always called his most productive (and secret) fishing spots his honey holes.

honey honey bee ball n

A children's hiding game; also used in the rhyme to start the game; see quots.

1970 *DARE* (Qu. EE16, *Hiding games that start with a special, elaborate method of sending the players out to hide)* Inf **KY94**, Honey honey bee ball. **1970** *DARE* FW Addit **KY80**, The rhyme said by "it" before beginning to find the others in hide-and-go-seek: Honey honey bee ball / I can't see y'all / All ain't hid / Better holler I. [FW: old-fashioned] **1986** Pederson *LAGS Concordance (Hiding games)* **Little Rock AR,** 1 inf, Honey honey bee ball; 1 inf, Honey honey bee ball—like hide-and-seek, chant. [Both infs Black, female]

honey honey big gum n [Perh orig *honey honey bee gum;* cf **honey honey bee ball**]

=**hide-and-seek B1.**

1970 *DARE* (Qu. EE3, *Games in which you hide an object and then look for it)* Inf **TN55**, Honey honey big gum—similar to "I Spy."

honey horns n *obs* [From the sweetness that may be sucked from the spur of each petal]

A **wild columbine.**

1784 in 1785 Amer. Acad. Arts & Sci. *Memoirs* 1.457 **neMA,** *Aquilegia.* . . Columbine. Honey Horns.

honey house See **honey** n **7b(1)**

honey-in-the-dale n

Prob a **pasqueflower.**

1968 *DARE* (Qu. S23) Inf **NY87**, Honey-in-the-dale.

honey it up to See **honey** v[1] **2**

honey locust n

1 A tree of the genus *Gleditsia,* esp *G. triacanthos* which is also called **black locust, Confederate pintree, honeypod 2, honey shucks, honey sucker 3, honey tree, locust, squeak bean, sweet bean, sweet locust, thorn locust, thorn tree, yellow locust.** See also **water locust**

1739 (1946) Gronovius *Flora Virginica* 193, *Gleditsia.* . . Acacia triacanthos. . . *Honey-locust.* **1784** (1929) Filson *Kentucke* 23, The honey-locust is curiously surrounded with large thorny spikes, bearing broad and long pods in form of peas, has a sweet taste, and makes excellent beer. **1808** (1892) Summer *Tour OH* 1.65 **VA,** The growth chiefly beech, interspersed with grape-vine thickets; a considerable quantity of sycamore, ash, . . honey-locust &c. **1818** in 1824 Knight *Letters* 87 **KY,** As you range the woods, the eye is delighted with the novelty of strange trees; . . the honey-locust, with its long sharp interlocking spines, exemplifying the curse of Eden. **1854** (1932) Bell *Log TX-CA Trail* 35.220, The tast [sic] [of the mesquite bean] resembles that of the Honey Locust. **1872** Tice *Over Plains* 25, Two species of the honey locust *(Gleditchia triacanthos,* and *G. monosperma)* . . occurred occasionally [between Leavenworth and Fairmont]. **1884** Sargent *Forests of N. Amer.* 59, *Gleditsia triacanthos.* . . Honey Locust. *Ibid* 61, *Prosopis juliflora,* De Candolle. . . Honey Locust. **1897** Sudworth *Arborescent Flora* 252, *Prosopis juliflora* (Swartz) de C. . . *Common Names.* . . Honey Locust (Tex., N. Mex.) *Ibid* 253, *Gleditsia triacanthos.* . . Honey Locust. *Ibid* 258, *Robinia pseudacacia* [sic]. . . *Com-*

mon Names. . . Honey Locust (Minn.) *Ibid* 262, *Robinia viscosa*. . . *Common Names*. . . Honey Locust (N.Y., N.J.) **1928** Rosendahl–Butters *Trees MN* 234, *Honey Locust*. . . Pods 15–45 cm. long, bent or twisted, pulp sweetish, edible. **1963** Evers *IL* 24, Other trees of this swamp are overcup oak, . . swamp honey locust, and water elm. *Ibid* 32, Locust, honey—*Gleditsia triacanthos*. . . Locust, swamp honey—*Gleditsia aquatica*. **1965–70** *DARE* (Qu. T16) 9 Infs, **chiefly Gt Lakes,** Honey locust; (Qu. T9) Infs **KS**5, **MO**3, **NH**5, Honey locust; (Qu. T12) Inf **MO**21, Honey locust; (Qu. T15) Inf **IL**47, Honey locust. [*DARE* Ed: Some of these Infs may refer instead to **honey locust 2.**]

2 Any of three **locusts:** usu *Robinia pseudoacacia,* but also *R. hispida* or *R. viscosa.*

1893 *Jrl. Amer. Folkl.* 6.140, *Robinia hispida,* honey locust. N.Y. **1897** [see **1** above]. **1940** Clute *Amer. Plant Names* 21, *R[obinia] hispida*. . . Honey locust. . . *R. viscosa*. . . Honey locust. *Ibid* 270, *Robinia pseudo-acacia*. . . Honey-locust. **1950** Peattie *Nat. Hist. Trees* 416, But country people today, almost everywhere in the northern states, call this tree [=*Robinia pseudoacacia*] Honey Locust because of the sweet breath of the blossoms. Yet the botanical and horticultural works all try to confine the name Honey Locust to . . *Gleditsia triacanthos.* **1960** Vines *Trees SW* 566, Other vernacular names are . . Honey Locust . . and False-acacia Locust. **1968** *DARE* (Qu. T16) Inf **CA**87, Honey locust.

3 A **mesquite** (here: *Prosopis glandulosa* or *P. juliflora*).

1884 [see **1** above]. **1889** *Century Dict.* 2873, *Honey-locust*. . . The name is sometimes given to the mesquit, *Prosopis juliflora,* a native of the southwestern United States. **1897** [see **1** above]. **1900** Lyons *Plant Names* 305, *P. juliflora* (Swz.) DC. . . Honey Locust. **1976** Yepson *Trees* 254, *Mesquite, honey* . . honey locust. . . Honeybees flock to the flowers, and cattle will feed on the pods.

honey locust comb n

1954 *Harder Coll.* **cwTN,** *Honey locust comb*. . . The fruit of a honey locust tree.

honey lotus See **honey clover**

honey man See **honey** n **7b(5)**

honey mangrove n

=black mangrove.

1946 Kopman *Wild Acres* 22 **LA,** The seaside sparrow nests principally in bushes of honey-mangrove, or Avicennia, known locally as "mangle," sometimes as "mangrove," of which the former term is a corruption. **1972** Brown *Wildflowers LA* 154, *Black-mangrove, Honey-mangrove—Avicennia germinans* . . A large evergreen shrub, occasionally a small tree.

honey maple n Cf **honey** n **3**

Prob a **sugar maple.**

1968 *DARE* (Qu. T3) Inf **MD**20, Honey maple; (Qu. T14) Inf **CT**15, Honey maple.

honey melon n Cf **honey-sweet melon**

1968 *DARE* (Qu. I26, . . *Kinds of melons*) Inf **LA**43, A baby watermelon is called a honey melon. [FW: By *baby watermelon* Inf means a small, mature melon.]

honey-melon squash n Cf **honeydew squash**

Prob a butternut squash.

1968 *DARE* (Qu. I23) Inf **IA**43, Honey-melon [squash]—yellow; oblong-shaped.

honey mesquite n Also *honey-bean mesquite* [See quot 1911]

A **mesquite** (here: *Prosopis glandulosa* or *P. juliflora*).

1890 *Century Dict.* 3727, Mesquit. . . Also called *honey-mesquit, honey-locust, honey pod,* and *July-flower.* **1896** *Bot. Gaz.* 22.480, Honey mesquite. **1911** CA Ag. Exper. Sta. Berkeley *Bulletin* 217.1000, *Prosopis juliflora* D.C. . . Honey Mesquite. . . It is reported a good honey plant in the Imperial country, and sometimes furnishes the last crop of honey in that section. **1931** U.S. Dept. Ag. *Misc. Pub.* 101.74, Honey mesquite (*Prosopis glandulosa,* syn. *P. juliflora glandulosa*). *Ibid* 76, The most valuable forage feature of this species is the pod or bean, . . sweet and pulpy within, . . and exceptionally palatable and nutritious. . . The species is a famous honey plant. **1957** Jaeger *N. Amer. Deserts* 63, The deep-rooted honey-bean mesquite (*Prosopis juliflora* . .) is widespread over this desert and sometimes occurs in dense orchard-like thickets or bosques. **1973** Stephens *Woody Plants* 308, Honey mesquite . . has often been destroyed by the rancher for fear it would take over the pastures.

honeymoon fly n Cf **love bug**

An **assassin bug.**

1972 *Milwaukee Jrl.* (WI) 24 Sept sec 1, The biological name for the bug [=love bug] is plecia meanctica [sic]. Along the Texas, Louisiana and Mississippi Gulf Coast, where the insect apparently originates, they are known as honeymoon flies, telephone bugs and double headed bugs.

honey mushroom n Also *honey* [From the yellow, sticky cap]

A mushroom (*Armillariella mellea*). Also called **oak fungus, shoestring fungus**

1938 Boyce *Forest Pathology* 99, *Armillaria mellea* . . , known as the "honey mushroom," causes this disease. **1981** Lincoff *Audubon Field Guide Mushrooms* 736, *Honey Mushroom—Armillariella mellea*. . . Description: *Yellow-brown, sticky cap*. . . Also known as *Armillaria mellea*. . . The Honey produces stringlike runners, or rhizomorphs, . . from which additional fruiting bodies grow. **1987** McKnight–McKnight *Mushrooms* 136, *Honey Mushroom. Armillaria mellea*. . . An excellent edible species when well cooked, for those who can tolerate it.

honey nest n

1969 *DARE* (Qu. R19b, . . *The place where wild bees live and store their honey*) Inf **NJ**59, Honey nest.

honey plant n

=lemon balm.

1900 Lyons *Plant Names* 243, *M[elissa] officinalis* . . Honey-plant. **1930** Sievers *Amer. Med. Plants* 8, *Balm—Melissa officinalis* . . honey plant. **1940** Clute *Amer. Plant Names* 25, *Melissa.* Balm. *M. officinalis*. . . honey-plant. **1974** (1977) Coon *Useful Plants* 160, *Melissa officinalis*—Garden or lemon balm, honey plant, dropsy plant, . . citronele. . . it has long been known for its sweetness and possible medicinal values.

honeypod n

1 A **mesquite** (here: *Prosopis glandulosa* or *P. juliflora*). [See quot 1937]

1884 Sargent *Forests of N. Amer.* 62, *Prosopis juliflora,* De Candolle. . . *Honey Pod*. . . pods rich in grape sugar, edible, and furnishing valuable and important fodder. **1889** *Century Dict.* 2873, *Honey-mesquit*. . . *Prosopis juliflora*. . . Also called *honey-pod.* **1897** Sudworth *Arborescent Flora* 252, *Prosopis juliflora* (Swartz) de C. . . Honey Pod (Tex.) **1937** U.S. Forest Serv. *Range Plant Hdbk.* B112, Honey mesquite is known also as honeypod. . . Its seedpods . . are sweet, rich in protein, and very nutritious. **1976** Yepson *Trees* 254, *Mesquite, honey* . . honeypod. . . The sweet pulp within the pods was once eaten by the Indians, and . . was an ingredient in their bread.

2 A **honey locust 1** (here: *Gleditsia triacanthos*). **esp VA**

1899 (1912) Green *VA Folk-Speech* 229, *Honey-pod*. . . Same as honey-locust. **1941** *Torreya* 41.48, *Gleditsia triacanthos*. . . Honeypod. **1970** *DARE* (Qu. T9) Inf **VA**110, Honeypod; (Qu. T12) Inf **NC**84, Honeypod tree; (Qu. T16) Inf **VA**57, Honeypod.

honey pond and flitter tree n For addit varr see quots **chiefly S Midl**

Fig: used to represent a life of ease and abundance.

1903 *DN* 2.317 **seMO,** *Honey-spring and flitter tree*. . . An expression denoting the abundance of good things. 'He is going to Texas and expects to find the honey-spring and flitter tree.' Equivalent to 'a land flowing with milk and honey.' [**1943** Chase *Jack Tales* 159 **sAppalachians,** Sure as I'm a-livin' it was honey runnin' down the creek bed in the place of water. . . we went on up that honey creek. Well, sir, ever' tree in that holler was a bee-tree. . . the honey was a-drippin' and oozin' out ever'where. . . Jack . . leaned back on a little tree . . something started floppin' down on the ground around us. . . I smelled of it . . then I tasted of it, then I says to Jack, "Fritter!" . . don't you know there we stood in a little grove of fritter-trees. . . We shook down a mess of 'em and dipped 'em in that honey creek and eat fritters and honey till we was nearly foundered.] **1956** in 1978 Hall *Yarns Gt. Smokies* 18 **wNC,** "My father was lookin' for the honey pond in [sic] the flitter tree, my mother always said." (That is, looking for an easier way of life than in the hills of North Carolina.) [**1958** Randolph *Sticks* 96 **Ozarks,** "I like it right here in Stone county [Arkansas]," says he, "where the flitter-tree stands close to the honey-pond."] **1960** Korson *Black Rock* 354 **PA,** When a railroad boomer "pulled the pin" (quit his job) he would tell his friends that he was going to the Indian Valley Line . . where a good job under ideal working conditions could always be found. Western coal miners meant the same thing when they said they were "hunting the honey pond and flitter tree." **1978** *AP Letters* **neGA** (as of c1900), Expressions . . of the pioneers . . from . . mountain and rural areas . . "You'll never find a honey pond and a fritter tree."

honey pot n

1 A quagmire; a muck-filled pocket in soft ground or sand; see quot 1836. **esp ME**

1836 (1838) Haliburton *Clockmaker* (1st ser) 66 **NEng,** Most of them are [=there] dyke marshes have what they call *'honey pots'* in 'em; that is a deep hole all full of squash, where you can't find no bottom. Well, every now and then, when a feller goes to look for his horse, he sees his tail a stickin' right out an eend, from one of these honey pots, and wavin' like a head of broom corn; and sometimes you see two or three trapped there . . half swimmin', half wadin', like rats in a molasses cask. **1909** *DN* 3.412 **nME,** *Honeypot*. . . A place where mud oozes from the ground. **1966** *DARE* FW Addit **sME coast,** *Honey pot*—A small clayey place under the sand on a beach into which one sinks when walking; **cME coast,** Honey pot—A small mucky place in wet ground, where a person's leg might sink into mud up to the knee. **1975** Gould *ME Lingo* 135, *Honeypot*—Seems to be a Maine-ism for a quagmire; a spring mudhole in the highway.

2 pl: A children's game; see quots. [*EDD honey pots* (at *honey* sb. 1. (22) (c)) "A child's game"]

1899 (1909) Earle *Child Life* 345, Honey pots still is played by American children. Halliwell says the "honey pot" was a boy rolled up in a certain stiff position. I have seen it played by two girls carrying a third in a "chair" made by crossing hands. In a popular little book of the last century called *Juvenile Pastimes, or Sports for Four Seasons,* the illustration shows girls playing it. The explanatory verse reads:—"Carry your Honey pot safe and sound / Or it will fall upon the Ground." **1899** Champlin-Bostwick *Young Folks' Games* 412, *Honey-pots,* a game for very small children . . [who] represent honey-pots, while older persons take the part of honey merchant and customers. The honey pots sit . . with hands clasped under their bent knees. . . [The customer and merchant] weigh. . . [the pot by] swinging . . [the child] backward and forward till he is compelled to unclasp his hands. . . The pot . . weigh[s] as many pounds as it has had swings.

3 See **honey** n **7b(3).**

4 See **honey** n **7b(4)(b).**

honey rock melon n Also *honey rock (muskmelon)* **esp Gt Lakes**

A muskmelon; see quot 1974.

1966-70 *DARE* (Qu. I26) Infs **MI**110, 116, **OH**87, Honey rock melons; **MI**63, Honey rock muskmelons; **GA**11, **OH**22, Honey rock(s); **MI**68, Honey rock melon—small muskmelon, very sweet; **OH**3, Honey rock melon—big, bumpy on outside; 7″ in diameter, rough skin. **1974** *Burpee Seeds* 103, *Honey Rock . . (Salmon Flesh)* Deliciously sweet. . . Heavily netted. **1976** Olds Seed Co. *Seeds* 17 **csWI,** Olds' Muskmelons . . *Honey* or *Sugar Rock*. . . This melon has a deep orange flesh and a flavor different from other sorts.

honey shucks n Also *honey shuck* [See quot 1927] **chiefly Sth, esp VA**

A **honey locust 1** (here: *Gleditsia triacanthos*).

1884 Sargent *Forests of N. Amer.* 59, *Gleditschia* [sic] *triacanthos. . . Honey Shucks*. . . Beer is sometimes made domestically by fermenting the sweet, unripe fruit. **1899** (1912) Green *VA Folk-Speech* 229, *Honey-pod*. . . Same as honey-locust. Honey-shuck. **1901** Lounsberry *S. Wild Flowers* 263, Honey locust, or honey shucks, the latter a more familiar appellation to the natives who gather its pods and eat the sweet, pulpy substance between the seeds, is a large, graceful tree. **1927** Keeler *Our Native Trees* 112, *Honey Shucks. Ibid* 114, *Fruit.*—Legumes, . . contain quantity of sweet pulp between the seeds. **1950** Peattie *Nat. Hist. Trees* 404, Honeyshucks is the name used in some parts of Virginia, and very appropriate it is on account of the sweet pods eagerly eaten by cattle and sometimes by nibbling country boys. **1970** *DARE* (Qu. T16) Inf **VA**43, Honey shuck.

honey spring See **honey pond and flitter tree**

honey stand See **honey dish**

honeysuck See **honeysuckle 1**

honeysucker n

1 A honey eater (*Meliphagidae* spp); see quot 1967.

1933 Bryan *Hawaiian Nature* 245, *Honey Suckers*—The *Meliphagidae,* or honey eaters. **1967** *DARE* (Qu. Q23, *The insect-eating bird that goes headfirst down a tree trunk*) Inf **HI**2, Honeysucker—an indigenous group.

2 =**ruby-throated hummingbird.**

1968 *DARE* (QR, near Qu. Q14) Inf **LA**44, Hummingbird is called honeysucker as well.

3 A **honey locust 1** (here: *Gleditsia triacanthos*).

1967-70 *DARE* (Qu. T9) Inf **MO**8, Honeysuckers; (Qu. T12) Inf **DC**13, Honeysucker.

4 A **wild columbine** (here: *Aquilegia canadensis*).

1970 *DARE* (Qu. S26c) Inf **MA**78, Honeysuckers = red columbine.

honeysucker melon n

An unidentified melon.

1967 *DARE* (Qu. I26) Inf **MO**8, Honeysucker melons.

honeysuckle n

1 also *honeysuck, honeysuckle clover:* A clover, usu **red clover** or **white Dutch clover,** or its flower. [*OED* c1265 →; "*Obs.* exc. *dial.*"] **esp NEng**

1790 Deane *New Engl. Farmer* 60/2, The white clover, vulgarly called honey-suckle, is an excellent grass, and seems very natural to this country: But when sown by itself, it does not grow tall enough for mowing. It is good for feeding in pastures, during the fore part of summer. **1814** Bigelow *Florula Bostoniensis* 169 **ceMA,** *Trifolium pratense.* L. *Red clover. Honeysuckle*. . . In its wild state it grows every where, and flowers from May to September. **1858** (1867) Flint *Milch Cows* 184 **NEng,** *White Clover . . ,* often called Honeysuckle, is . . widely diffused over this country. **1872** VT State Bd. Ag. *Report* 1.154, The honeysuckle (white clover) makes the very best butter. **1884** Johnston *Old Mark* 41 **GA,** Honeysuckles, bubby-blossoms, yellow jasmines, haw, . . loaded the air with sweetness. **1896** *Jrl. Amer. Folkl.* 9.186, *Trifolium repens,* . . honeysuckle, honeysuckle clover, Oxford County, M[ain]e. **1898** *Ibid* 11.226, *Trifolium repens,* . . honeysuckle, South Berwick, M[ain]e. **1912** Green *VA Folk-Speech* 229, *Honeysuck*. . . The red clover blossoms are sucked for the honey. *Honeysuckle.* **1940** Clute *Amer. Plant Names* 22, *T. pratense. Red Clover*. . . Honey-suckle clover. . . *T. repens. White Clover*. . . Honeysuckle clover.

2 A plant of the genus *Lonicera.* [*OED* 1548 →] Also called **wild honeysuckle, woodbine.** For other names of var spp see **bearberry honeysuckle, bittersweet, breath of spring, buckbrush 3m, first breath of spring, fly honeysuckle, grape honeysuckle, madreselva, moronel, sweetberry honeysuckle, timber honeysuckle, trumpet honeysuckle, twin honeysuckle, twin sisters**

1637 (1972) Morton *New Engl. Canaan* 67, Hunnisuckles, balme, and divers other good herbes are there. **1784** in 1785 Amer. Acad. Arts & Sci. *Memoirs* 1.418 **neMA,** *Lonicera*. . . *Honeysuckle. Bastard Cherry.* Blossoms yellow, tinged with red. Among bushes in loamy land. June. **1792** Imlay *Western Terr.* 207 **KY,** Every part of the country abounds in a variety of natural flowers. . . honey-suckles, rock honey-suckles, tuberose. **a1817** (1821) Dwight *Travels* 1.46 **NEng,** The *Honeysuckle* . . is a totally different shrub from that, which is known by this name in Great Britain. . . This is a bush. **1874** Aldrich *Prudence Palfrey* 15 **NEng,** The house stood . . covered by a network of vines, honeysuckle and Virginia creeper. **1904** (1932) Rice *Sandy* 176 **KY,** It was a quaint old house, all over honeysuckles and bow-windows and verandas. **1908** Fox *Lonesome Pine* 78 **KY,** The portly old woman . . came out on the porch and welcomed them heartily under the honeysuckle vines. **1954** *Harder Coll.* **cwTN.** **1965-70** *DARE* (Qu. S26c) 371 Infs, **widespread, but less freq West,** Honeysuckle; **NC**18, Bunch honeysuckle; **NJ**67, Honeysuckle rose; **NJ**29, Red honeysuckle; **SC**63, Woods honeysuckle; (Qu. S26a) 17 Infs, **chiefly S Atl, S Midl,** Honeysuckle; **SC**63, Woods honeysuckle; (Qu. S26b) 10 Infs, **chiefly S Midl,** Honeysuckle; (Qu. S26e) 9 Infs, **Atlantic,** Honeysuckle; (Qu. C28) Inf **LA**20, Honeysuckle vines; **MD**20, Honeysuckle swamp; (Qu. I44) Inf **MA**25, Honeysuckle berries; (Qu. K14) Inf **MS**58, Honeysuckle milk; (Qu. S2) Inf **AL**11, Honeysuckle; (Qu. S8) Inf **WV**4, Honeysuckle—vine rather than grass; very hard to get rid of; (Qu. S10) Infs **FL**9, **MS**47, Honeysuckle; (Qu. S21) Infs **NC**14, 47, **SC**63, Honeysuckle; (Qu. S22) Inf **IL**95, Honeysuckle; (Qu. S26d) Infs **CA**70, **IA**27, **VA**11, 40, Honeysuckle; (Qu. T16) Inf **NC**76, Honeysuckle. [Note: Some of these Infs may refer instead to other senses of **honeysuckle.**] **1967** *DARE* Wildfl QR Pl 19.4 Inf **CA**24, Honeysuckle. **1974** Morton *Folk Remedies* 94 **SC,** Honeysuckle is grazed by deer and by cattle.

3 =**rhododendron. scattered, but esp S Midl, Sth**

1731 (1754) Catesby *Nat. Hist. Carolina* 1.57, *Cistus Virginiana, flore & odore Periclymeni.* D. Banister. The *Upright Honysuckle*. . . At the

Ends of the Stalks are produced Bunches of Flowers, resembling our common Honysuckle. **1784** in 1785 Amer. Acad. Arts & Sci. *Memoirs* 1.416 **neMA,** *Azalea... American Honeysuckle. Swamp Pink...* Common in low, swampy land. June. **1822** Eaton *Botany* 199, *Azalea... lapponica* (mountain honeysuckle.) . . *[A.] nudiflora* (early honeysuckle.) . . *[A.] viscosa* (white honeysuckle.) . . *[A.] glauca* . . (fragrant honeysuckle.) **1866** *Land We Love* 1.80/1 **NC,** *Smooth Honeysuckle, (Azalea arborescens.)* This is the most fragrant of our honeysuckles. The flowers are white and roseate. *Ibid, Purple Honeysuckle, (A. nudiflora.) Ibid, Yellow Honeysuckle, (A. calendulacea.)* . . The color varies much, but is generally some shade of yellow. **1883** Hale *Woods NC* 158, *Smooth Honeysuckle*—(Azalea arborescens . .). The most powerfully fragrant of our Honeysuckles. *Ibid* 159, Clammy Honeysuckle *(A. viscosa . .).* Purple Honeysuckle *(A. nudiflora . .).* Yellow Honeysuckle *(A. calendulacea.)* **1892** *Jrl. Amer. Folkl.* 5.100, *Rhododendron nudiflorum...* Honeysuckle. Md. **1907** *DN* 3.190 **NH,** *Honeysuckle...* False honeysuckle; American azalea. "Get a lot of big branches of honeysuckle; you can have the apples on them, if you find any." **1916** Parsons *Wild Flowers CA* 88, *Rhododendron occidentale...* In Oregon it is commonly known as "honeysuckle." **1964** Batson *Wild Flowers SC* 83, *Pink Honeysuckle* . . is a hardy wild flower. . . Vermont to South Carolina. **1966–68** *DARE* (Qu. S26a) Inf **AR**2, Honeysuckle = wild azalea; (Qu. S26c) Inf **SC**63, Woods honeysuckle = wild azalea; (Qu. S26d) Inf **VA**11, Honeysuckle = azalea in woods; (Qu. S26e) Inf **FL**20, Honeysuckle = wild azalea; (Qu. T16) Inf **DC**2, Honeysuckle bush—wild azalea—blossom pink, spidery in shape, come out before leaves. **1968** *Co. Rec.* (Denton MD) 8 May sec 2 3/2, I headed up Mt. Pleasure through wild azaleas in full bloom (down here we call them honeysuckle!) **1970** Correll *Plants TX* 1178, *Rhododendron prinophyllum...* Honeysuckle, early-azalea. **1976** Bruce *How to Grow Wildflowers* 99, But botanically they are now *Rhododendron.* American natives are usually colloquially called "honeysuckle," especially in the South. **1984** Ehle *Last One Home* 199 **NC** (as of c1900), The up-and-down lots have an azalea bush. You see it? Well, not all honeysuckle bushes bloom when transplanted, but that one looks the prettiest you ever saw.

4 A **wild columbine** (here: *Aquilegia canadensis*). **chiefly Nth**

1891 *Jrl. Amer. Folkl.* 4.197 **NH,** Aquilegia we always called *Honeysuckle.* **1892** *Ibid* 5.91, *Aquilegia Canadensis,* honeysuckle. N. E.; Peoria, Ill. **1896** *Ibid* 9.179, *Aquilegia Canadensis,* . . honeysuckle, Madison, Wis. **1907** *DN* 3.190 **NH,** *Honeysuckle...* Wild columbine. Aquilegia canadensis. "Pick me a bunch of honeysuckles, won't you?" **1916** Keeler *Early Wildflowers* 66, *Wild Columbine. Honeysuckle...* Something of a cliff-dweller. **1940** Clute *Amer. Plant Names* 2, *A[quilegia] Canadensis...* Honeysuckle. **1950** *WELS Suppl.* 3 Infs, **WI,** Honeysuckle. **1966–68** *DARE* Wildfl QR Pl.65 Infs **IA**25, **MN**37, **WA**10, 15, Honeysuckle. **1967** *DARE* (Qu. S26e) Inf **NY**21, Honeysuckle = wild columbine. **1976** Bailey–Bailey *Hortus Third* 93, *[Aquilegia] canadensis...* Honeysuckle.

5 Any of numerous other plants, as:

a =**red baneberry.**

1804 (1904) Clark *Orig. Jrls. Lewis & Clark Exped.* 1.96 **swIA,** Two Kind of honeysuckle one which grows to a kind of a Srub Common about Harrodsburgh in Kentucky the other are not so large or tall and bears a flour in clusters short and of a light Pink colour . . the Lieves are destinct & does not surround the stalk.

b A **snowberry** (here: *Symphoricarpos albus*).

1805 (1905) Lewis *Orig. Jrls. Lewis & Clark Exped.* 3.77 **nID,** A kind of honeysuckle which bears a white bury and rises about 4 feet high not common but to the western side of the rockey mountains.

c =**calico bush 1.**

1833 Fergusson *Practical Notes* 216, The *Kalmia latifolia* (Mountain Laurel), here [=Mt. Vernon VA] called Honeysuckle, in a luxuriance and beauty which baffle description.

d An **Indian paintbrush** (here: *Castilleja sessiliflora*).

1897 *Jrl. Amer. Folkl.* 10.52, *Castilleja sessiliflora* . . honeysuckle, Burnside, S. Dak.

e also *honeysuckle penstemon:* A **beardtongue** (here: either *Penstemon centranthifolius* or *P. cordifolius*).

1897 Parsons *Wild Flowers CA* 358, *Scarlet bugler. Penstemon centranthifolius...* The individual flowers bear quite a likeness to those of the honeysuckle, . . and by those who encounter the plant for the first time, it is usually spoken of as "honeysuckle." **1915** (1926) Armstrong–Thornber *Western Wild Flowers* 480, *Honeysuckle Penstemon...* A handsome shrub, with much the general appearance of a Honeysuckle.

f =**chuparosa 2.**

1931 U.S. Dept. Ag. *Misc. Pub.* 101.144, *Thurber anisacanth (Anisacanthus thurberi . .),* known locally as . . honeysuckle . . grows 1½ to 5 feet high, with . . attractive, maroon-red flowers.

g =**he-huckleberry 1.**

1933 *Torreya* 33.84, *Cyrilla racemiflora...* Honeysuckle, Okefinokee Swamp, Ga. **1940** Clute *Amer. Plant Names* 257, *Cyrilla racemiflora...* Honeysuckle.

h A **butterfly weed 2** (here: *Gaura coccinea*).

1950 Stevens *ND Plants* 216, *Gaura coccinea...* Locally it is often honeysuckle, which the flowers do resemble.

i =**scarlet gilia.**

1956 St. John *Flora SE WA* 324, *Gilia aggregata... Fox fire, Honeysuckle...* Corolla scarlet, varying through pink to white.

j =**chuparosa 1.**

1976 Bailey–Bailey *Hortus Third* 618, *[Justicia] californica... Chuparosa, honeysuckle...* Corolla red, straight. Desert regions, s. Calif., Ariz., Baja Calif.

honeysuckle apple n [**honeysuckle 3** + *apple* (see quot 1907)] **esp NEng**

=**swamp apple.**

1878 (1977) Stowe *Poganuc People* 209 **nwCT,** The woods . . were full of the pink and white azalea, and she gathered . . stores of what were called "honeysuckle apples" that grew upon them—fleshy exudations not particularly nice in flavor, but crisp, cool, and much valued among children. **1899** *Jrl. Amer. Folkl.* 12.120 **neMA,** The fungus common on *Rhododendron nudiflorum* is called honeysuckle apples, and is eaten by children and thought to be a fruit. **1907** *DN* 3.190 **NH,** *Honeysuckle-apple...* A fungus growing on the branches of the false honeysuckle (Azalea). "In texture, juiciness, and acidity it is like an apple."

honeysuckle azalea n [**honeysuckle 3**]

A **rhododendron** (here: either *Rhododendron canescens* or *R. prinophyllum*).

1960 Vines *Trees SW* 829, *Rhododendron canescens...* Vernacular names are Honeysuckle Azalea, . . Pinxter Flower [etc]. **1966** Grimm *Recognizing Native Shrubs* 219, *Rhododendron roseum... Flowers* usually bright pink, . . fragrant. . . Also called . . Honeysuckle Azalea.

honeysuckle berry n

=**fragrant sumac.**

1967 *DARE* Wildfl QR (Craighead) Pl.13.10 Inf **CO**15, Honeysuckle berries.

honeysuckle clover See **honeysuckle 1**

honeysuckle penstemon See **honeysuckle 5e**

honeysweet n

1 A **meadowsweet** (here: *Filipendula ulmaria*).

1910 Graves *Flowering Plants* 235 **CT,** *Filipendula Ulmaria...* Honey-sweet. **1940** Clute *Amer. Plant Names* 6, *F[ilipendula] ulmaria* . . honey-sweet. **1949** Moldenke *Amer. Wild Flowers* 119, The *honeysweet* [=*Filipendula ulmaria*], is found as an escape from gardens from Quebec to Massachusetts.

2 A plant *(Tidestromia oblongifolia)* of the amaranth family.

1941 Jaeger *Wildflowers* 55 **Desert SW,** *Honey-Sweet. Tidestromia oblongifolia...* Its name, "honey-sweet," alludes to the sweet-scented, yellow flowers, which often occur in such profusion as to make the plant pronouncedly decorative.

honey-sweet melon n Cf **honey melon**

Prob a **muskmelon.**

1970 *DARE* (Qu. I26) Inf **MI**116, Honey-sweet melon.

honey tree n Also *honey*

=**honey locust 1.**

1705 Beverley *Hist. VA* 2.21, The Honey and Sugar-Trees are likewise spontaneous, near the Heads of the Rivers. The Honey-Tree bears a thick swelling Pod, full of Honey. **1737** (1911) Brickell *Nat. Hist. NC* 71, The *Honey* Tree is so like the *Locust,* that there is scarce any Difference between them, only the *Honey* Tree is more prickley than the former; and are a *Species* of the *Locust.* **1897** Sudworth *Arborescent Flora* 254, *Gleditsia triacanthos... Common Names...* Honey (R.I., N.J., Iowa). **1900** Lyons *Plant Names* 174, Honey. **1940** Clute *Amer. Plant Names* 260, *G[leditsia] triacanthos...* Honey tree.

honey up (to) See **honey** v^1 **2**

honey vine n
=**sand vine.**
1897 *Jrl. Amer. Folkl.* 10.50 **TX,** *Enslenia albida. . .* Honey-vine. **1950** Gray-Fernald *Manual of Botany* 1175, *Ampelamus . .* Sand-vine. . . *A. albidus. . .* Honeyvine.

honey wagon See **honey** n **7b(4)**

honeyweed n
A **woolly-white** (here: *Hymenopappus artemisiaefolius*).
1967 *DARE* Wildfl QR (Wills-Irwin) Pl.60b Inf **TX**44, Honeyweed.

honeywood n Cf **bee tree**
A **linden.**
1967 *DARE* (Qu. T13) Inf **IA**13, Honeywood, because it is used for making beehives—tasteless.

honey worm n
Prob the larva of a wax moth.
1970 *DARE* (Qu. R27) Inf **VA**79, Honey worm, gets in hives.

honeywort n **Plains States**
=**honewort.**
1932 Rydberg *Flora Prairies* 591, Honeywort. . . *C[ryptotaenia] canadensis.* **1940** Gates *Flora KS* 226, Honeywort, Honewort. Rocky woods. **1968** Barkley *Plants KS* 259.

hong(g)ry See **hungry**

honijoker See **hunyak**

honing See **hone** v **1**

honk See **hunk** n[2]

honker n[1]
1 pronc-spp *hawnker, hunker;* also *honker goose:* =**Canada goose.**
1842 Hawes *Sporting Scenes* 1.178 **NY,** We have killed wild geese . . and we know what it is to bring down a glorious gaggle of honkers to our stool. **1879** Williams *Pacific Tourist* 275/2 *(DA),* Three varieties are common, the white and speckled breasted brant, and the hawnker. **1917** (1923) *Birds Amer.* 1.158, *Canada Goose. . . Other Names. . .* Honker. **1923** U.S. Dept. Ag. *Misc. Circular* 35, *Branta canadensis canadensis. . . Vernacular Names. In general use.* Honker, varied to honker goose, big honker, Canada honker, and old honker and corrupted to hunker and hunter. **1948** *Time* 11 Oct 21/2, Honkers were winging south in high Vs and deer were beginning their migration from high country. **1950** *WELS Suppl.* 1 Inf, **WI,** They weren't snow geese—just honkers. **1960** Criswell *Resp. to PADS 20* **Ozarks,** Canada goose. . . *Honkers,* common. **1965-70** *DARE* (Qu. Q6) 52 Infs, **chiefly Nth, Cent, Pacific,** Honkers; **MN**34, 42, Lesser honkers; **MN**42, Greater honkers; **IL**67, Native honkers.
2 A **bullfrog 1.**
1969 *DARE* (Qu. P22) Infs **MA**26, **NY**207, Honker.
3 A nose. *joc*
1942 Berrey-Van den Bark *Amer. Slang* 121.69, *Nose. . .* honker. **1967-69** *DARE* (Qu. X14, *Joking words for the nose*) Infs **MD**15, **MA**3, **OH**84, **PA**162, 199, 231, Honker; (Qu. X15) Inf **MO**27, Honker.

honker n[2] See **hunker** n[1]

honker goose See **honker** n[1]

honkey See **honky 1**

honkey-dooley See **hunky-dory**

honkie See **honky 1**

honking crane n
Appar a **bittern.**
1969 *DARE* (Qu. Q8, *A water bird that makes a booming sound before rain*) Inf **CA**130, Honking crane.

honko holler n Cf **hare and hound(s); holler, holler, dogs you foller**
1968 *DARE* (Qu. EE12, *Games in which one captain hides his team and the other team tries to find it*) Inf **WI**56, Honko holler.

honkry See **hungry**

honky n
1 also *honkey, honkie, hunky:* A White person (but see also quot 1980). [Prob varr of *Hunky* (at **Hunk** n[3] **1**); originally both *hunky* and *honky* were prevalent, but as of the late 1960s *honky* began to predominate] *chiefly among Black speakers; usu derog*
1964 *PADS* 42.31 **Chicago IL** [Black], Negro terms for Caucasian . . *hunky.* **1967** *Daily Progress* (Charlottesville VA) 8 July 22 [Black], H. Rap Brown called on Negroes to arm themselves against a "hunky (white) conspiracy of genocide." **1967** *Newsweek* 24 Apr 16/1 **SC** [Black], Stokely Carmichael . . exhorted: "You have to go for the honkies . . who are keeping you in the ghettos." **1967** *International Herald-Tribune* 8 Sept 14/1 *(Hench Coll.),* We're living a lie in this house. . . We're nothing but honkies and we might as well start facing up to it. **1968-70** *DARE* (Qu. V9, . . *Nicknames . . for a policeman*) Inf **DC**11, Honkies ['haŋkɪz]—when a White cop is involved; (QR, near Qu. HH28) Inf **CA**81, Honky—Negroes call Whites; **PA**236, Honky—English; (QR, near Qu. II10b) Inf **FL**48, Black college students, when going out with Whites, call them Hunky, even to their faces; (Qu. II25, . . *The part of a town where the poorer . . groups live*) Inf **CA**107, Honky Town—West Oakland. **1970** Major *Dict. Afro-Amer. Slang* 67, *Honkey:* a white person; (Southern use, originally). **1970** *Times* (London) 10 Mar 10/3, Mr. Lehman Brightman, a militant South Dakota Sioux who is now president of the United Native Americans . . comments angrily: "Even the name Indian is not ours—it was given us by some dumb honky (white) who got lost and thought he'd landed in India." **1970** *Peace News* 17 Apr 8/4, It is the pacifist who must declare . . that there are neither Panthers [=militant Blacks] nor Pigs [=police], neither Niggers nor Honkies but only human beings. **1971** *Black Scholar* Sept. 35/1 **Chicago IL** *(OEDS),* You screamed on me 'bout that honky gunsel upstairs. **1972** Kochman *Rappin'* 143 [Black], *Honky.* Not exactly a black word because it was originally used by whites to refer to immigrants from Eastern Europe. It is a shortened version of "Bohunk." It became a black word when it was first used by Stokely Carmichael to refer to all whites. Also, the particular pronunciation of the word is black: h*o*nky instead of h*u*nky. The pronunciation change indicates the intensity of the hate black people have for white people. **1980** Folb *Runnin' Down* 54 **Los Angeles CA** [Black], Many [black teenagers] made no distinction between Chicanos and whites and often characterized them in terms usually identified with white people— . . *honky. Ibid* 60, Even more graphic and derogatory labels . . *honky beast* . . while characterizing whites as animal-like, brutal, or evil, do not "picture" whites very extensively.
2 See **Hunk** n[3] **1.**

honky-dori See **hunky-dory**

honky-tonk n [Transf from std sense]
A place or thing that is small or insignificant.
1942 Berrey-Van den Bark *Amer. Slang* 45.2, *Small town. . .* honky-tonk. **1968-70** *DARE* (Qu. C33, . . *Joking names . . for an out-of-the-way . . or . . very unimportant place*) Inf **OK**53, Honky-tonk; (Qu. N37, . . *A branch railroad that is not very important or gives poor service*) Inf **OH**77, Honky-tonk.

honohono n **HI**
1 Basket grass *(Oplismenus hirtellus).*
1888 Hillebrand *Flora Hawaiian Is.* 503, *O. compositus. . .* Common in the outskirts and open glades of forests. Nat. name: "Honohono." [**1965** Neal *Gardens HI* 73, Basket grass, Honohono-maoli, Honohono-kukui. *Oplismenus hirtellus.*] **1968** *Jrl. Engl. Ling.* 2.80 **HI,** *Honohono. . .* Basket grass *(Oplismenus hirtellus),* a creeping weed (often found under the *kukui* or candlenut tree) sometimes used as animal feed. [**1971** Pukui-Elbert *Hawaiian Dict., Honohono.* Short for *honohono-kukui.*]
2 also *false honohono, honohono grass:* A **dayflower** (here: *Commelina diffusa*).
1929 Neal *Honolulu Gardens* 61, *Wandering Jew, honohono (Commelina nudiflora). . .* Commonly in Hawaii, the wandering Jew is known as a low, creeping weed that . . sends up from the axils of broad grasslike leaves small, irregular-shaped, bright-blue flowers. **1929** Pope *Plants HI* 43, Honohono [=*Commelina nudiflora*], or "False Honohono" as it is called by some, is a detestable weed in many respects, while in others it is considered a most valuable forage plant. . . This naturalized plant has in recent years acquired the name honohono, which is quite generally applied to it. . . Honohono grows in considerable amounts among other edible grasses and produces good pasturage for practically all kinds of livestock. **1930** Degener *Ferns of HI* 118, It [=*Vrydagzynea sandwicensis*] therefore might be easily mistaken for a *Commelina* or dayflower, a plant which is incorrectly called *honohono* grass in the Hawaiian Islands. **1954-60** Hance et al. *Hawaiian Sugar* 2 **HI,**

Honohono—Wandering Jew, *Commelina diffusa*. **1967** *DARE* (Qu. S8) Inf **HI4**, Honohono [ˌhonoˈhono]: fed to pigs; wide leaves; grows in water; shiny inside; liquid used to dose cats (dries on skin).

Honolulu vine n

=coral vine 3.

1982 Perry-Hay *Field Guide Plants* 80, *Antigonon leptopus*. . . Honolulu vine. . . The tubers are edible.

honyak, honyock(er) See **hunyak**

hoo v [Cf *SND hooch* II. v. 2 [hux] "To breathe forcibly upon an object to warm it"] Cf **huh**

1986 *DARE* File **cMI,** To hoo [hu] hot coffee or tea is to blow on it in order to cool it off.

hooby n

1982 *Smithsonian Letters* **ceMA,** *Hooby.* It is used to denote a large stone or rock, too heavy to be lifted or carried easily. . . I overheard another airman use it. . . he was a native of Dorchester . . as was I. . . [I found] that it was used mostly by people of Irish descent, generally in the area around South Boston, Dorchester, and Quincy, but not known in other parts of the city.

hooch v Also with *along* [Cf *EDD hootch* v. "Also written *hooch*. . . To crouch, sit huddled up"] Cf **hitch** v **3, hunch** v **3, ooch, scrooch**

To huddle or crowd together; to move over.

c1960 *Wilson Coll.* **csKY,** *Hooch*—To crowd: "We hooched up close together on the truck to keep warm." **1967-68** *DARE* (Qu. Y32, *To squeeze yourself into a small space: "If you're going to fit in there you'll have to ______."*) Inf **MD21,** Hooch [hʊč]; (Qu. Y52, *To move over—for example on a long bench . . "Can you ______?"*) Inf **CA9,** Hooch along.

hooch n[1]

1 also sp *hootch:* Orig **=hoochinoo;** later any alcoholic beverage, esp one that is homemade, of poor quality, or illegal. **widespread, but less freq Sth, S Midl** See Map

[**1897** Hayne *Pioneers Klondyke* 91, The manufacture of "hooch," which is undertaken by the saloon-keepers themselves, is weirdly horrible.] **1904** [see **hoochinoo**]. **1921** *Chicago Herald & Examiner* (IL) 31 Nov 2.4 *(Zwilling Coll.),* [In cartoon "Always Show Papa The Toys":] Some party. Some home made hooch. **1933** *Sun* (Baltimore MD) 4 July 6/7 *(Hench Coll.),* When I lived in Kentucky, four-year old hootch was regarded as a beverage that only the well-to-do could buy. **c1940** Eliason *Word Lists FL* 9 **wFL,** *Hooch:* Any bad liquor made from corn, potatoes, meal, cane-skimmings, or any source or substance that will ferment. **1950** *WELS* 7 Infs, **WI,** Hooch. **1959** Hart *McKay's AK* 31, *Hootch:* Any hard liquor but specifically that which is homemade. **1960** Bailey *Resp. to PADS 20* **KS,** *Snakebite remedy:* hooch. **1965-70** *DARE* (Qu. DD21a, *General words . . for any kind of liquor*) 109 Infs, **chiefly Nth, Midl, West,** Hooch; (Qu. DD21b, . . *Bad liquor*) 17 Infs, **scattered,** Hooch; **CA1,** Bootleg hooch; (Qu. DD21c, *Nicknames for whiskey, especially illegally made*) 44 Infs, **chiefly Nth, N Midl,** Hooch; (Qu. DD25, . . *Nicknames . . for beer*) Infs **IA36, WA18, WI26,** Hooch; (Qu. DD28b, . . *Fermented drinks . . made at home*) Infs **IA3, MA68, NY88,** Hooch; (Qu. DD34, *A party at which there is considerable drinking*) Infs **AK8, MN15, NY213,** Hooch party; (Qu. DD12, . . *A person who drinks steadily or a great deal*) Inf **TN50,** Hooch-head; (Qu. DD31, . . *Homemade hard liquor;* total Infs questioned, 75) Inf **NM6,** Hooch; (Qu. DD32, *A person who sells illegal liquor*) Inf **NY205,** Hooch peddler; (Qu. X53a, . . *An oversize stomach*) Inf **MO17,** A hooch belly. **1974** Dabney *Mountain Spirits* 24 **sAppalachians,** "Hooch" was a frontier term that came from the Indians who called it "hoochino." Hooch later signified white whiskey in Alaska, and also Prohibition-era moonshine.

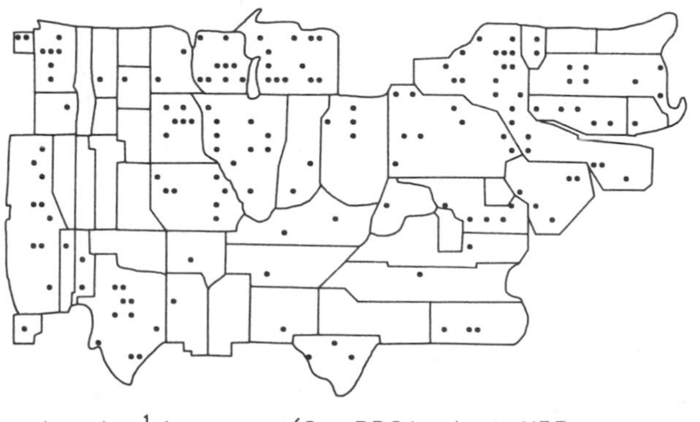

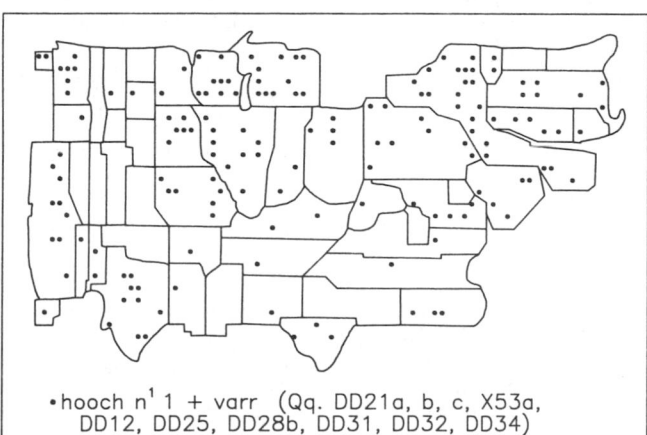

•hooch n[1] 1 + varr (Qq. DD21a, b, c, X53a, DD12, DD25, DD28b, DD31, DD32, DD34)

2 Transf: see quot. [Perh infl by *hooey*]

1970 *DARE* (Qu. NN13, *When you think that the thing somebody has just said is silly or untrue: "Oh, that's a lot of ______."*) Inf **SC69,** Hooch.

‡hooch n[2] [Perh var of **hoosegow**]

1968 *DARE* (Qu. V11, . . *Joking names . . for a county or city jail*) Inf **IN30,** The hooch.

hooch along See **hooch** v

hoochie-coochie n attrib Also sp *hoochy-coochy* Cf **conjure** n **1, goof doctor**

Involved in the practice of **hoodoo** n **1a;** see quots.

1953 in 1973 *McKinley Morganfield a.k.a. Muddy Waters* (Phonodisc), [In the song "(I'm Your) Hoochie Coochie Man":] I got a black cat bone / I got a mojo too / I got the John the Conqueror Root / I'm gonna mess with you / I'm gonna make you girls / Lead me by my hand / Then the world'll know / The hoochie coochie man. **1970** Major *Dict. Afro-Amer. Slang* 67 [Black], *Hoochy-coochy (man or woman):* one who practices voodoo.

hoochinoo n Also *hoochnihoo, hootchenoo, hootchino(o), kootznehoo* [*Hoo(t)chinoo* a Tlingit tribe of Alaska] **chiefly AK** *old-fash* Cf **hooch** n[1] **1**

An alcoholic beverage made by Alaskan natives; a homemade or inferior alcoholic beverage.

1877 *Puget Sound Argus* (Pt. Townsend, Wash.) 23 Nov. *(OEDS),* I have frequently seen soldiers go to the Indian ranch for their morning drink of kootznehoo. **1899** *Boston Morning Jrl.* (MA) 11 Jan 4/5 **AK,** The name of fire-water in Alaska is "hoochinoo," and recently the House gave its official sanction to the word by enacting that no whisky, beer or "hoochinoo" shall be sold in Alaska. . . When the United States laws established prohibition for Alaska the natives of that land began furnishing a mixture of rum and molasses, which has gradually taken the name of "hoochinoo." This is the first legal recognition of the word and Congress is ahead of the dictionary-makers. **1904** (1969) Robins *Magnetic North* 161 **AK,** A portion of its cargo consisted of . . two bottles of hootchino, the maddening drink concocted by the natives out of fermented dough and sugar. Apart from the question of drinking raised again by the 'hootch,[*] it is perhaps possible that . . they were ready to eat. **1940** White *Wild Geese* 214 **AK** (as of 1890s), You wouldn't want to drink hoochnihoo! . . It's made out of molasses or beans or rice or flour or anything that'll ferment. I call it squirrel whisky, because two drinks of it makes you want to climb a tree. **1959** Hart *McKay's AK* 31, *Hootch*. . . Hootchenoo. **1968** *DARE* Tape **AK11** (as of c1910), So much molasses . . packages of hops . . and yeast cakes. That was the hoochinoo and hot cakes. . . That was a very potent drink. *Ibid,* The old [Indian] chief would stand up on a platform and they would shriek in their language and of course they were all pretty well hopped up with their hoochinoo.

hoochy-coochy See **hoochie-coochie**

hood n[1]

1967 *DARE* (QR, near Qu. D27) Inf **LA6A,** The eaves of the house are called the hood.

hood n[2] |hʊd| [Prob infl by **hod 1**]

1968 *DARE* (Qu. F44, . . *A container for coal to use in a stove*) Inf **MN17,** Hood [hʊd]. [Inf's parents both from Sweden]

hooded merganser n Also *hooded head, hooded sheldrake, hooder, hood merganser*

A **merganser** (here: *Lophodytes cucullatus*). Also called **bastard teal, bec scie, Chicago mallard, cock-robin duck, didapper 3, dipper 1, diver, fan-crested duck, fish duck 1, French pheasant, frog duck, fuzzhead, fuzzy-head, garbill, hairy crown, hairy head, hell-diver 4, hootamaganzy, Indian, Irish canvasback, kokus sheldrake, little spikebill, mophead, morning glory, mosshead, mud sheldrake, oyster duck, peaked-bill, pheasant, pickax sheldrake, pied sheldrake, plongeon, pond duck, pond**

fisher, pond sawbill, pond sheldrake, rocket, sawbill, sawbill diver, shagpoll, sharpy sheldrake, shelduck, smew, snowl, spike, spikebill, spiky, strawbill, summer duck, summer sheldrake, swamp sheldrake, tadpole duck, topknot, towhead, tree duck, tuffleheaded duck, water-pheasant, water-witch, whistler, wirecrown, wood duck, wood sawbill, wood sheldrake, zin-zin

1785 Latham *Gen. Syn. Birds* III.II.426 *(OEDS),* Hooded M[erganser] . . size nearly that of a Wigeon. **1823** James *Acct. of Exped.* 1.375, *Mergus cucullatus*—Hooded merganser. **1844** DeKay *Zool. NY* 2.320, *The Hooded Sheldrake.*—Mergus cucullatus. **1923** U.S. Dept. Ag. *Misc. Circular* 13.7, *Hooded Merganser (Lophodytes cucullatus.) . . In local use. . .* hooder. **1938** Oberholser *Bird Life LA* 142, This bird [=hooded merganser], sometimes called the 'hooded shelldrake' or 'sawbill diver', is one of our handsomest ducks. **1944** MA Audubon Soc. *Bulletin* 28.260, The Hooded Mergansers which appeared again this year at Leverett Pond in late October have been attracting the usual amount of attention. **1966–69** *DARE* (Qu. Q5) Infs **GA**25, **IL**32, **MI**2, **PA**155, **VA**47, Hooded merganser; **NY**6, Hood merganser; **PA**155, Hooded head. **1982** Elman *Hunter's Field Guide* 228, *Hooded Merganser* (*Mergus cucullatus,* also classified as *Lophodytes cucullatus*)—Common & Regional Names: fish duck, . . hooder . . wirecrown.

hooded oriole n

A slender oriole *(Icterus cucullatus)* of the southwestern US. Also called **palm-leaf oriole**

1869 (1870) *Amer. Naturalist* 3.186 **CA,** The most peculiar birds not yet mentioned are . . the Little Vireo *(Vireo pusillus)* and Hooded Oriole *(Icterus cucullatus),* also migratory. **1917** (1923) *Birds Amer.* 2.255, Sennett's Oriole, *Icterus cucullatus sennetti,* . . [also called] Sennett's Hooded Oriole. **1961** Ligon *NM Birds* 262, The Hooded Oriole, named from its yellow "hood," or forespot, is a handsome streamlined bird with distinctive song and coloration.

hooded sheldrake See **hooded merganser**

hooden n Cf **hogan a**

1920 Hunter *Trail Drivers TX* 299, The cabin where the bachelor cowboys sometimes sleep in very bad weather is called a "hooden."

hooder See **hooded merganser**

hood flower n

A **jack-in-the-pulpit.**

1966 *DARE* Wildfl QR Pl.3 Inf **OH**82, Hood flower. **1968** *DARE* (Qu. S1) Inf **OH**82, Hood flower.

hoodger See **hoosier**

hoodidoo n [Var of **hoodoo** n]

1966 *DARE* (Qu. CC14, *Words or expressions used here, where one person supposedly casts a spell over another*) Inf **SC**10, Hoodidoo ['hudɨdu]; (Qu. EE41, *A hobgoblin that is used to threaten children and make them behave*) Inf **SC**10, Hoodidoo [hudɨ'du]; (Qu. II36b, *Of somebody who talks back or gives rude answers*) Inf **SC**10, He is a hoodidoo fellow. [Inf Black, Gullah speaker]

hoodle n[1]

Usu an object marble; see quots.

1937 (1947) Bancroft *Games* 161, Object marbles . . variously known as *mibs, miggs, commies, hoodles, ducks.* **1968** *DARE* (Qu. EE6a, . . *Marbles—the big one . . used to knock others out of the ring*) Inf **MD**31, Hoodle ['hudl̩]. **1968** *DARE* FW Addit **cMD,** Cheap marbles—hoodles ['hudl̩]. **c1970** Wiersma *Marbles Terms* **swMI,** *Hoodles*—Marbles inside the circle being shot at. *Ibid, Hoodles*—marbles in the ring. *Ibid* **Chicago IL,** *Hoodles*—An object marble, as distinct from a shooter. **1973** Ferretti *Marble Book* 46, *Hoodles.* Object marbles, to be shot at.

hoodle n[2]

1968 *DARE* (Qu. DD16, *To have a drinking bout . . is to go on a* ———) Inf **MD**42, Hoodle ['hudl̩].

hoodle v, hence ppl adjs *hoodled (up), ufgehoodled* [PaGer < Ger *hudeln* to do something ineptly; to botch] Cf **ferhoodle**

To cobble; to jumble.

1967–68 *DARE* (Qu. KK63, *To do a clumsy or hurried job of repairing something: "It will never last—he just* ———*."*) Inf **MD**26, Hoodled ['hʊdl̩d] it; (Qu. E22, *If a house is untidy and everything is upset*) Inf **PA**22, ['hʊdəld] means messed up or untidy; (Qu. Y38 . . *"The things in the drawer are all* ———*."*) Inf **PA**24, ['hʊdəld]; **PA**18, ['hudəld] up—Dutch; **PA**3, Ufgehoodled ['ufgəˌhʌdəld].

hoodlebug n esp OH Cf **doodlebug 6b, hoodledasher**

A small railroad; see quot.

1967–70 *DARE* (Qu. N37, . . *A branch railroad that is not very important or gives poor service*) Inf **NY**231, Hoodlebug—one-car job, generally; **OH**3, Hoodlebug—the old Chagrin Falls Southern; **OH**22, 66, Hoodlebug. [All Infs old]

hoodled See **hoodle** v

hoodledasher n

See quot 1962.

1939 (1962) Thompson *Body & Britches* 236 **ceNY,** Captain Ed Scouten . . a Civil War veteran . . knew the canal intimately for half a century, and . . lived to command one of the modern "hoodledashers", powered boats which surge along with a barge in front and a couple behind. **1962** Wyld *Low Bridge* 23 **cNY** (as of 19th cent), *Squeezer* and *hoodledasher,* two of the more colorful terms in canalese, have in common the idea of boats in tandem. . . [T]he *hoodledasher* was a hookup where two or more cargoless boats were tied to a full-cargo boat, so one span of mules or horses could draw them all. . . [Hoodledasher] in more recent times refers to powered boats which push one barge and tow one or two others behind.

hoodled up See **hoodle** v

hoodle parlor n [**hoodle** v]

1968 *DARE* (Qu. D7, *A small space . . in a house where you can hide things or get them out of the way*) Inf **OH**81, Hoodle ['hudəl] parlor. [*DARE* Ed: Inf fluent in PaGer]

hoodle potatoes n [Prob **hoodle** v]

1968 *DARE* (Qu. H47, . . *Fried potatoes*) Inf **MD**33, Hoodle ['hudl̩] potatoes—sliced thin, simmered in skillet with water and small amount of shortening.

hoodle tale n

1940 Writers' Program *Guide VA* 143, Stories of the Uncle Remus type were a source of entertainment, especially brief 'hoodle-tales,' such as 'Why the Frog Lives in the Water,' . . Slightly humorous, the tales frequently contained a moral and were directed at both animals and human beings.

hoodling vbl n Cf **eephing, holler** n[1] **C2**

Making percussive effects with the mouth or a simple musical instrument; see quots.

1971 in 1978 Wolfe *I'm On My Journey Home* (Phonodisc) **wTN,** [My maternal uncle] called it hoodlin'; they call it eephin' now. He [=the uncle] got it from somebody at a dance up at Dyersburg, Tennessee. **1975** McDonough *Garden Sass* 231 **AR,** Playing the quills is sometimes called "hoodling" or "reed-blowing" and is an ancient form of making music. *Ibid* 233, More complicated to make than the picking bow or hoodling stick is the fiddle. **1978** Wolfe *I'm On My Journey Home,* [Liner notes:] Eephing (or hoodling) is one of a number of vocal-percussive effects still found in the mid-South. . . Dick Burnett, a blind minstrel from southern Kentucky . . in 1912, featured . . an imitation of a jew's harp, a sound he created by tickling his throat and altering his mouth cavity. . . [G]ospel singers from Missouri . . have also . . [made the sound of a] jew's harp as well as songs created by tapping the cheeks and changing the mouth cavity.

hoodlum n

1 =**English sparrow.** [From *hoodlum* a young street rowdy (which term came into use in San Francisco about 1870), prob in ref to the bird's aggressive habits]

1895 (1907) Wright *Birdcraft* 136, *English Sparrow: Passer domesticus. . .* Hoodlum. **1903** Dawson *Birds OH* 40, *English Sparrow. . . Passer domesticus . .* Hoodlum. **1917** (1923) *Birds Amer.* 3.17, Hoodlum. **1944** Hausman *Amer. Birds* 517, Hoodlum—see Sparrow, English.

2 =**California quail 1.**

1956 *AmSp* 31.186, Hoodlum. California quail. Calif. It 'runs wild' before dogs.

hoodlum wagon n

1 also *hoodlum:* A wagon carrying bedding and miscellaneous supplies on a trail drive or roundup. **West**

1909 *Sat. Eve. Post* 20 Mar 9/2 **NM,** The outfit was engaged in packing the chuck-wagon and the hoodlum. **1919** Wilson *Ma Pettengill* 79 **UT,** The skinners and the mules would get back to camp that night— . . and the hoodlum wagon going back next morning to see what could be salvaged. **1920** Hunter *Trail Drivers TX* 299, In addition to the "chuck wagon," a second wagon for carrying the extra beds and bringing wood and water into camp sometimes goes along. This equipage is called the hoodlum wagon. **1933** *AmSp* 8.1.29 **nTX.** **1944** Adams *Western Words* 78, *Hoodlum wagon*—A slang name for the bed-wagon. **1966** *DARE* Tape **NM**13, In the hoodlum wagon they'd have wood and maybe an extry water and a portion of the beds, grain for the horses, . . horseshoes and so forth.

2 A police van. [Perh infl by *hoodlum* a ruffian] **esp TX, OK, AR**

1949 (1961) Partridge *Underworld Dict.* 341, *Hoodlum wagon,* 'a police-patrol van' (rare and journalistic). **1965–67** *DARE* (Qu. N3, *The . . wagon that takes . . people to the police station*) Infs **AR**22, **OR**5, **TX**23, 35, Hoodlum wagon; **OK**11, They had one here [=Okmulgee] they called a hoodlum wagon; **TX**26, Hoodlum wagon—old-fashioned. [All Infs old, male]

hood merganser See **hooded merganser**

hoodoo n, freq attrib [W Afr, prob from more than one lang]

1 Any of var aspects of conjuration or sympathetic magic; see below. **scattered, but chiefly Sth, esp LA, MS** See Map *esp freq among Black speakers* Cf **voodoo**

a The body of knowledge, system, or practice of magic or conjuration; a medium of luck. Cf **conjure n 1**

1881 *Harper's New Mth. Mag.* 737/1 **seLA** [Black], "De Hoodoo meetin' is my drink," said Dulcie . . "an' somethin' pulls an' pushes me till I git dar." . . Maum Dulcie had made strong resolutions of abstinence as to Hoodoo enticements. **1888** in 1960 *AmSp* 35.268, *Hoo-doo.* A bringer of good luck. **1890** *Jrl. Amer. Folkl.* 3.241, The special use of Voodoo or Hoodoo in the United States as meaning that which brings good luck. **1893** *KS Univ. Qrly.* 1.140, *Hoodoo:* a bringer of bad luck. **1935** Hurston *Mules & Men* 229 **New Orleans LA** [Black], The way we tell it, hoodoo started way back there before everything. Six days of magic spells and mighty words and the world with its elements above and below was made. *Ibid* 231, Nobody knows for sure how many thousands in America are warmed by the fire of hoodoo, because the worship is bound in secrecy. It is not the accepted theology of the Nation and so believers conceal their faith. **1941** Writers' Program SC *Folk Tales* 97 [Black], Conjure is another name for hoodoo, voodoo, coocoo, and goofering, all of which may be found in South Carolina. **1958** Hughes–Bontemps *Negro Folkl.* 191, Frequently graveyard dust is required in the practice of hoodoo, goofer dust as it is often called. *Ibid* 193, *Hoodoo Prescriptions.* *Ibid* 198, 'I don't believe in no hoodoo at all,' declared Bongy Jackson. **1965–70** *DARE* (Qu. CC14, *Words or expressions . . where one person supposedly casts a spell over another*) 58 Infs, **scattered, but chiefly Sth, esp MS,** Hoodoo; **CA**101, **NJ**11, **SC**7, **TX**98, Hoodoo [FW sugg]; **CA**137, Hoodoo [FW sugg]—that's more Negro speech; **FL**18, Hoodoo—Negroes; **KY**6, Hoodoo—Nigger families; **LA**6, Hoodoo—not around here but some folks from Baton Rouge said something about that; **LA**11, Hoodoo—colored people especially believe in that; **LA**14, Hoodoo, hex—there's nothing serious around here, these are joking; **LA**25, Hoodoo [or] voodoo—[FW: Inf uncertain which pronunciation]; hoodoo [FW: used by Inf in conv]; **SC**24, Uses the hoodoo.

b also *hoodoo doctor* (or *man, woman* etc): A practitioner of **hoodoo n 1a.** Cf **goof doctor**

1875 *Cincinnati Commercial* (OH) 12 Dec 1/4 [Black], Supposing you fall in love with a girl and can't get her, and that you go to one of these hoodoos, he will do something awful to her with charms. *Ibid,* She would die . . unless she could get some other hoodoo doctor to take the charm away by a counter charm. **1881** *Harper's New Mth. Mag.* 62.736/1 **seLA** [Black], Who seed yo' las' moon-risin' w'en Hoodoos met a-dancin', an' a-chargin', an' a-rarin', an' a-foamin' at de lips like ze cotton-mouth snake? **1931** Hurston in *Jrl. Amer. Folkl.* 44.320 **Sth,** A man or woman becomes a hoodoo doctor in one of three ways: by heredity, by serving an apprenticeship under an established practitioner, or by the "call." . . All of the hoodoo doctors have non-conjure cases. They prescribe folk medicine, "roots", and are for this reason called "two headed doctors." **c1938** in 1970 Hyatt *Hoodoo* 1.776 **New Orleans LA,** [Hyatt:] Who are these people from Algiers who have altars and candles in the room? [Inf:] Well, those are what you call *hoodoo spirituals.* They are supposed to do whatever you want them to do with prayers. *Ibid* 2.1790 **New Orleans LA,** Yessuh, ev'rybody thinks dat ev'ry *hoodoo person* do dere work wit altars an' things lak dat, but dey doesn't mean anything. **1946** Tallant *Voodoo* 160 **New Orleans LA** [Black], Madame Cazaunoux woke with a grunt. "Me, I was the best damn hoodoo queen what ever lived!" *Ibid* 199, In most Negro neighborhoods there is a "hoodoo woman" or "conjure man," who enjoys to the utmost his superior position and the fear he inspires. **1958** Hughes–Bontemps *Negro Folkl.* 184, *Hoodoo. . .* Moses never would have stood before the Burning Bush, if he had not married Jethro's daughter. Jethro was a great hoodoo man. **1967–70** *DARE* (Qu. BB53b, . . *A doctor who is not very capable or doesn't have a very good reputation*) Inf **MO**8, Hoodoo doctor; (Qu. CC14) Inf **MS**88, Hoodoo doctors. [Both Infs Black] **1977** Dillard *Lexicon* 80 [Black], [Blues lyrics:] Well the hoodoo told me he would give me back my man if he can. . . Well the hoodoo sell something for you but your man said his last goodbye.

c A jinx, charm, spell, or magic force.

1889 *New York Sun* 20 March *(Cent D),* The prospect of pleasing his party and at the same time escaping a *hoodoo* must be irresistibly attractive. **1893** *Chicago Tribune* (IL) 2 July 15/3, Even Charley's hopefulness was shaken by this hoodoo, as he knew there was no cure for it. You could kill the hoodoo of the cross-eyed man or woman by burning the stage properties. **1905** *Out West Mag.* Sept 265 **cAZ,** He had been a mule-skinner in early days, that is, until he found he had a hoodoo on the ivory ball; then he took his nick-name and turned gambler. **1927** Kennedy *Gritny* 148 **sLA** [Black], "Sho soun' like it mus' be some kin to hoodoo." . . "No it 'tain'. . . Unc' Bendigo don' play wid no hoo-doo. It des a natchal n'intment." **1967** Will *Dredgeman* 130, Eventually we were out of Nine Mile Lake, a hoodoo of the first magnitude.

d Bad luck. Cf **bugaboo 2a**

1902 in 1953 Botkin–Harlow *Treas. Railroad Folkl.* 396, Everything that happens to an engine with the hoodoo number [=No. 9] is noticed and remembered. **1912** Mathewson *Pitching* 234, Time and again Ames has pitched brilliantly, to be finally beaten by a small score, because . . the team could not give him any runs by which to win. No wonder the newspapers began to speak of Ames as the "hoodoo" pitcher and the man "who could n't win." **1927** *DN* 5.451 [Underworld jargon], *Hoodoo town. . .* Tramps are exceedingly superstitious. If one happens to have a disastrous experience twice in the same town he immediately regards it as an unlucky, a hoodoo town. **1948** Manfred *Chokecherry* 48 **nwIA,** This spot on the Big Sioux was hoodoo for him. First the bluff cave-in and then this [=a case of blood poisoning]. **1955** Day *HI People* 260, The hulk of the U.S.S. *Bennington,* a "hoodoo ship," was towed across her bow; and this evil omen was recalled when the *F-4* promptly sank. **c1960** *Wilson Coll.* **csKY,** *Hoodoo*—Bad luck is a meaning. **1967** *DARE* (Qu. EE38b, *If the game of tick-tack-toe . . comes out so that neither X nor O wins, you call that* ______) Inf **IA**3, Hoodoo got us.

e A person or thing that is frightening and perh supernatural; see quots. [Cf *DJE hootiah* sb dial "Hootiah, one who lives in the bushes"; also *huodyas* adj dial "a fearful thing; terrible things"] Cf **bugaboo 1**

1929 Sale *Tree Named John* 4 **MS** [Black], Tales of "ha'nts en hoodoos en witches." **1967** LeCompte *Word Atlas* 273 **seLA,** *"Things" that sometimes stay or live in old deserted houses*—hoodoos. [1 of 21 infs]

f See quot. [Perh transf from **hoodoo n 1b**]

1968 *DARE* (Qu. GG39, *Somebody who seems to be looking for reasons to be angry: "He's a* ______*."*) Inf **AK**8, Hoodoo; (Qu. II21, *When somebody behaves unpleasantly or without manners: "The way he behaves, you'd think he was* ______*."*) Inf **AK**8, A hoodoo.

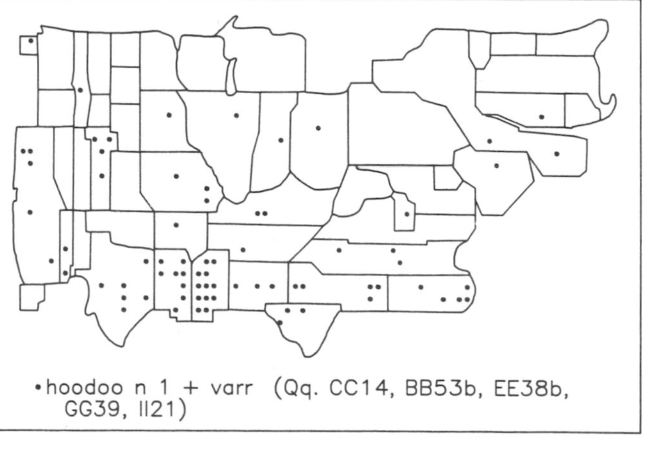

•hoodoo n 1 + varr (Qq. CC14, BB53b, EE38b, GG39, II21)

2 A rock column or pinnacle formed into a fantastic shape by erosion. **[hoodoo 1] West**

1879 (1882–83) Whitman *Specimen Days* 148, I had wanted to go to the Yellowstone river region—wanted specially to see . . the "hoodoo" or goblin land of that country. **1884** H. Butterworth *Zigzag Journeys West. States* 54 *(DAE),* A region . . full of lofty stone monuments, the remnants of erosion, called hoodoos. **1945** Atwood *Rocky Mts.* 76, Erosion has worn away the softer rocks, leaving certain resistant layers stabbing at the sky in fantastic shapes. Sharp pinnacles, spires . . balanced rocks, and distorted, goblinlike forms—so grotesque in shape that they are spoken of as "hoodoos" in our Southwest—have resulted from erosion's chiseling. **1968** Abbey *Desert Solitaire* 2 **UT,** To watch for the first time in my life the sun come up over the hoodoo stone of Arches National Monument. *Ibid,* Turning my back on the . . ramada, the lone juniper and all the hoodoo rocks.

3 See quot.

1951 Grant *Cowboy Encycl.* 132, Rustlers were also called "sticky loopers," "long ropers," and "hoodoos."

4 See quot. [Prob infl by *hoot*]

1967 *DARE* (Qu. GG21b, *If you don't care what a person does, you might say, "Go ahead—I don't give a ______."*) Inf **SC**34, Hoodoo [hu'du].

hoodoo v

1 To practice **hoodoo n 1a;** to charm; to cast a spell on or bring bad luck to; hence vbl n *hoodooing.* Cf **conjure** v, **goofer** v

1908 *DN* 3.321 **eAL, wGA,** *Hoo-doo.* . . To conjure, bewitch, put under a hypnotic spell, etc., bring bad luck to. *Voodoo* is not familiar to me. **1915** (1916) Johnson *Highways New Engl.* 167, One man is known to have hoodooed three schooners. **1926** in 1983 Taft *Blues Lyric Poetry* 125/1 [Black], I believe to my soul: sweet mama going to hoodoo me. **1928** White *Amer. Negro Folk-Songs* 206 (as of 1915–19) **AL, NC,** I'm bound for to [=I must, I intend to] hoodoo this child. **c1938** in 1970 Hyatt *Hoodoo* 1.12 **swAL,** No need a-send me a doctor 'cause ah been *hoodooed* and you have to send a *hoodoo doctor.* **1950** *WELS (Casting a "spell")* 2 Infs, **WI,** Hoodooed. **1967–70** *DARE* (Qu. BB51b, . . *'Magical' cures for corns or warts*) Inf **IL**29, Hoodoo them off; (Qu. CC12b, . . *If a person has a lot of bad luck you might say, "He's been ______."*) Infs **CA**15, **CO**26, **CT**16, **NY**166, **TX**104, Hoodooed; (Qu. CC12a, . . *Bad luck*) Inf **CA**112, Been hoodooed. **1977** Dillard *Lexicon* 127 [Black], *Goofering* . . a general term for conjure itself, like *hoodooing.*

2 To cheat; to bamboozle; to take advantage of.

1897 *KS Univ. Qrly.* (ser B) 6.54 **KS,** *Hoodoo* . . to deceive or cheat in a blustering manner; to deceive by witchcraft, or unusual means. **1908** *DN* 3.321 **eAL, wGA,** *Hoodoo.* . . To cheat one in a trade, defraud. "He hoo-dooed me out of all I had." **c1960** *Wilson Coll.* **csKY,** *Hoodoo*—To cheat. There seems to be no connection with voodoo. [These] people know very little Negro lore. **1966–67** *DARE* (Qu. GG3, *To tease: "See those big boys trying to ______ [that little one]."*) Inf **TX**32, Hoodoo; (Qu. II33, *To get an advantage over somebody by tricky means: "I don't trust him, he's always trying to ______."*) Inf **MS**21, Hoodoo somebody; (Qu. KK36, . . *A person who is easily fooled: "It's easy to ______."*) Inf **OH**8, Hoodoo. **1976** Garber *Mountain-ese* 43 **Appalachians,** *Hoo-doo* . . cheat—Don't let that shyster hoo-doo you out uv your backer [=tobacco] crop.

3 with *up:* To brag.

1967 *DARE* FW Addit **TN**15, *To hoodoo* [hudu] *up*—explained as "to brag on."

4 ppl adj *hoodooed:* Agitated.

1967 *DARE* FW Addit **TN**15, 22, Hoodooed [hudud] is an expression meaning "upset" or "agitated." [FW: used by Inf in conv]

hoodoo bag n Also *hoodoo ball* **[hoodoo n 1]**

=conjure bag.

c1938 in 1970 Hyatt *Hoodoo* 1.227 **seMD,** The way I have heard it, that a *hoodoo bag* is a bag that one carries and it contains a dust called *goofer dust,* and whatever they put it on they can conquer. **1967** *DARE* (Qu. CC14, . . *Expressions used . . where one person supposedly casts a spell over another*) Inf **LA**11, Hoodoo ball—buried at the step, consisted of hair and gum stuck together. [Inf old, coll educ]

hoodoodle v [Perh blend of **hoodoo v 2** + *doodle* to cheat]

1912 *DN* 3.578 **wIN,** *Hoodoodle.* . . To defraud. "A lightning rod agent hoodoodled him out of four hundred dollars."

hoodoo doctor See **hoodoo n 1b**

hoodooed See **hoodoo v 4**

hoodooing See **hoodoo v 1**

hoodoo iron See **hoodoo stick**

hoodoo man See **hoodoo n 1b**

hoodoo stick n Also *hoodoo iron* **[hoodoo n 1]** Cf **doodlebug 5**

A divining rod used in finding ore.

1905 *Out West Mag.* Sept 209 **cAZ,** A paisano of his down in Guadalajara had a pair of hoodoo irons stolen out of the Mission where the priests had them prospecting for buried treasure. . . In Tonto Basin . . [t]here was a man could locate silver nuggets with the hoodoo-stick, every time. **1936** McKenna *Black Range* 111 **swNM** (as of 1880s), My hoodoo stick twirled like a top up there on the summit of Old Kentuck.

hoodoo up See **hoodoo v 3**

hoodoo woman See **hoodoo n 1b**

hoodsie n [Trademark] **MA**

See quot 1971.

1971 *Today Show Letters* **MA,** Hoodsie—a small paper cup of ice cream; it is the trade name of H. P. Hood and Sons, Boston and used as far west as Westfield, Mass. Also used for similar products of other dairy companies. *Ibid* **ceMA,** My father . . one of the early advertising men . . (purportedly) coined the word *Hoodsie.* . . *Hoodsies* are very much on the market. . . They are indeed dixie cups filled with Hood's ice cream. *Ibid* **seMA** (as of c1920s), [In an article about a child's birthday party] there was mention of how many "Hoodsie's" were consumed. *Ibid* **neMA,** In the [19]40s and 50s, our teenagers and their CYO club dances were . . referred to as Hoodsies—the child, the dance . . the ice cream were referred to as Hoodsies—refreshments were Hoodsies. **1980** *DARE* File **Boston MA,** I think Hoodsies are still sold. I couldn't understand what my sister's grandchild was asking for in the early 70s and it turned out to be a Hoodsie. Hood is a big dairy outfit in the Boston area. **1988** *Ibid* **neMA** (as of c1945), Sure, we had hoodsies. They were a little cup of ice cream. We would go by the plant in North Andover on the way to visit my grandmother; **neMA,** Hoodsies used to be common for small containers of ice cream for large groups. I think we have rec[eived] them at Sr. Cit. lunches.

hoodus n

An object without a name; a whatchamacallit. Cf **doohickey 1, dingus** n[1] **1, hootenanny 1**

1931 in 1944 *ADD,* [Newspaper column:] Hoodus. **1942** Berrey–Van den Bark *Amer. Slang* 75.4, *Indefinite object; "gadget"*. . . hoodus.

hoodwort n

A **skullcap** (here: *Scutellaria laterifolia*).

1785 Amer. Acad. Arts & Sci. *Memoirs* 1.463, *Scutellaria. . . Hoodwort.* Blossoms blue. By fences in *Sandwich.* Aug. **1822** Eaton *Botany* 455, *Scutellaria . . lateriflora . .* hoodwort. **1897** *Jrl. Amer. Folkl.* 10.53, *Scutellaria laterifolia . .* hoodwort, West. **1974** (1977) Coon *Useful Plants* 163, *Scutellaria lateriflora . .* hoodwort.

hoody adj Cf *hootsle* (at **hutzel** adj)

1958 *Sat. Eve. Post Letters* **sIN** (as of 1910–20), That hoody little thing ("oo" pronounced as in "food"; meaning small, insignificant; used derisively.)

hoody n |'hudi| [Cf *SND huidin* (at *huid* n. I. 4) "A point of juncture. . . (3) a knot used to join two parts of a fishing line"]

A hook used in fishing for mackerel.

1965 *DARE* (Qu. P13, . . *Ways of fishing . . besides the ordinary hook and line*) Inf **FL**21, A hoody ['hudi]—a hook you troll with for catching mackerel; it has ravelling around it; crochet thread is used.

hooey n

1968 Adams *Western Words* 152 **West,** *Hooey*—The half hitch that completes the tie of a calf's legs by the calf roper. The tie usually consists of two wraps around three legs and the hooey around two of them to hold it secure.

hooey v See **hurry v 1**

hoof n, exclam Usu |huf, hʊf|; also *old-fash* |hʌf, hɒf| Pronc-spp *huf(f)*

A Forms.

1795 Dearborn *Columbian Grammar* 130, *List of Improprieties. . . Huff* for Hoof. **1848** Lowell *Biglow* 144 **'Upcountry' MA,** *Huf,* hoof. **1887** (1967) Harris *Free Joe* 35 **nwGA** [Black], Is dese yer bobolitionists got horns en huffs? . . dey ain't got needer horns ner huffs. **1893** Shands *MS Speech* 38, *Huff* [hɒf]. Negro and illiterate white for *hoof.* **1899** (1912) Green *VA Folk-Speech* 234, *Huffs . . pl.* The huffs of an animal . . also . . in derision . . the feet of people. **1903** *DN* 2.317 **seMO,** *Hoof.* . . Pronounced huff [hʌf]. **1907** *DN* 3.232 **nwAR, seMO,** *Hoof* [hʌf]. *Ibid* 245 **eME,** *Huf.* . . Hoof. Pronunciation of the older generation. *Huf it.* . . To walk. **1961** Kurath–McDavid *Pronc. Engl.* 155, The vowel /ʌ/ of *brush,* rare in *roof,* has rather extensive currency in *hoofs* in the folk speech of the Carolinas, parts of West Virginia, and Delmarva. **1970** *DARE* (Qu. BB50a) Inf **FL**49, Hog-hoof tea [hɒg hʌf ti]. [Inf old, rural, Black]

B As noun.

1 A hoofed animal, esp a cow—often used as a unit of enumeration. [By synecdoche] Cf **head** n **B3**

a1799 in 1828 Webster *Amer. Dict., Hoof.* . . He had not a single *hoof* of any kind to slaughter. *Washington.* **1820** in 1853 Webster *Works* 3.16 **NH,** Small freeholders parted with their last hoof, and the last measure of corn from their granaries, to supply provisions for the troops. **1891** O'Beirne *Leaders Indian Terr.* 116/2, Mr. Muncrief has had much experience with the wild Indians . . and lost many a hoof through the agency of these midnight marauders. **1903** *DN* 2.317 **seMO,** *Hoof.* . head of cattle. 'He has forty huff of cattle.' **1907** *DN* 3.232 **nwAR, seMO,** *Hoof.* . . Head of cattle. **1950** *WELS Suppl.* **WI,** *Hoof*—"He hasn't got a hoof on the place" [means] no livestock of any kind. **1967** *Hall Coll.* **eTN,** [FW:] "Do you have some cows?" [Inf:] "No I ain't got a hoof."

2 in var n and adv phrr indicating entirety: See quots. Cf **hide and tallow**

1927 *AmSp* 3.136 **ME coast,** A badly cheated . . [person] had lost "hide, hoofs and taller." **1940** Brown *Amer. Cooks* 723 **nePA,** In the Wilkes-Barre coal regions a roast of whole goat or kid is enjoyed under the name of "Hoofs, Horns, and Tail." **1966–70** *DARE* (Qu. LL25, . . *Entirely, completely: "He sold out the whole place, _______."*) Inf **FL**36, Hair, hide, nor hoof; (Qu. LL29, *Any sign or trace: "He left last week, and nobody's seen _______ of him since."*) Inf **VA**42, Head, hoof, and hide [laughter]. [Both Infs old, rural]

C As exclam.

Also *hoof back:* Back up! **PaGer area**

[**1924** Lambert *PA Ger. Dict.* 84, *Huf.* . hoof. G Huf. *Ibid, Hufe* . . to back up (of horses), cause to back; huf! back up!] **1968–70** *DARE* (Qu. K36b, *What do you say to make a horse go backwards?*) Inf **PA**153, Hoof [hʊf] back; **PA**158, Hoof [huf] back; **PA**242, Hoof. [All Infs old]

hoof ail n Cf **hoof rot**

1968 *DARE* (Qu. K28, . . *Chief diseases that cows have around here*) Inf **CT**2, Hoof ail.

hoofany n

=**half-over.**

1942 McAtee *Dial. Grant Co. IN* 34 (as of 1890s), *Hoofany* . . a complicated game of leapfrog; described under the name "half-over".

hoof back See **hoof C**

hoof brand n, v

A brand made with a hot iron applied to an animal's hoof; to make such a brand.

1968 Moody *Horse* 44 **nwKS** (as of c1918), Each man could buy his own half of the feeder stock and hoof brand it. **1970** Wolfenstine *Manual of Brands* 53, Hoof brands . . have the disadvantage of having to be renewed at certain intervals. *Ibid* 181, Under the provisions of Kansas law, horn and hoof brands are not considered brands by definition, and consequently cannot be recorded.

hoof fly n

Prob =**heel fly;** see quot.

1967 *DARE* (Qu. R12, . . *Other kinds of flies . . for example, those that fly around animals*) Inf **TX**12, Hoof fly.

hoof rot n

A disease in livestock; see quot.

1965–70 *DARE* (Qu. K28, . . *Chief diseases that cows have around here*) 14 Infs, **scattered,** Hoof rot; (Qu. K47, *What diseases do horses or mules commonly get around here?*) Infs **GA**72, **KS**17, **MS**19, **NY**155, 176, 189, **WA**5, Hoof rot.

hooftie n [Etym unknown] Cf **hoopy** n[1]

See quot 1989.

1979 *NY Times* (NY) 15 Apr sec 1 26/4 **csPA,** [The] Middletown . . Chief of Police . . scoffed at the necessity for issuing such a directive in the first place. "There was no need for issuing that order [that looters would be shot on sight], all the hoofties left town right after the first announcement of radiation dangers," the chief said. Asked for his definition of "hooftie," the Chief answered, "You know, hooftie." **1989** *NADS Letters* **csPA,** *Hooftie*—the term is used in Carlisle, PA, mostly by attorneys around the county courthouse to refer to those types with whom attorneys often deal. The word is synonymous with "redneck" or "townie." Hoofties drive pickup trucks with oversized tires and gun racks and plastic bug screens on the hood . . , drink beer and throw the cans out the windows, get arrested for drunk and disorderly.

hoof worm n Cf **heel fly**

1967 *DARE* (Qu. K28, . . *Chief diseases that cows have around here*) Inf **AL**20, Hoof worm.

hoog exclam Also *hoogie* Pronc-spp *hooig, whoig* [Varr of *hog*]

Used as a call to pigs.

1966 Dakin *Dial. Vocab. Ohio R. Valley* 2.281 fig 96 **eKY,** *Calls to pigs.* . . hoog-ie! [2 of approx 200 infs]. *Ibid* 284, Some eastern Bluegrass residents say *hoogie!* **1966–67** *DARE* (Qu. K84, *The call used around here to get the pigs in at feeding time*) Inf **NC**15, Hoog ['hug]; **IA**6, Whoig [hwoɪg]—repeated. **1973** Allen *LAUM* 1.265 **IA, SD,** (as of c1950), Calls to pigs at feeding time. . . hooig. [2 infs]

hooger, hoogie n See **hoosier**

hoogie exclam See **hoog**

hoo hoo intj [Var of *yoo hoo*] Cf **hui** v

Used as a call to attract someone's attention.

1951 *Milwaukee Jrl.* (WI) 26 Aug sec 5 2/6, [Article "Such Talk You Hear by Milwaukee":] Woman calling to neighbor: Hoo-hoo! What you never heard yet. On scrubbing this morning I lost my teeth. And what is so bad, it should happen right in front of my vacation. **1969** *DARE* (Qu. II15, *When somebody is passing by and you want him or her to stop and talk a while, you might say, "_______."*) Inf **MA**73, Hoo hoo [hu hu]. **1970** *DARE* File **cMA,** Hoo hoo—This was what you called to someone on the street whose attention you wanted to get. If you walked into someone's house and saw no one around you might call "Hoo hoo, anybody home?"

hoo-hoo-owl See **hoo-owl**

hooick exclam [*OED hoicks, hoick* int. "A call used in hunting to incite the hounds" 1607 →]

Used as a call to urge a dog to attack.

1895 Remington *Pony Tracks* 250 **nwNM,** Dan sat on his pony and blew his old cow's horn, and yelled [to his dog]: "Hooick! hooick! get down on him [=a bear], Rocks; hooick! hooick!"

hooig See **hoog**

hoojee, hoojer, hoojie See **hoosier**

hoojin n [Perh var of **hoosier**] Cf **amarugian**

1940 *AmSp* 15.83 **swPA, cnWV,** Vocabulary items from [the isolated mountain communities]. . . *hoojin,* a country 'jake.'

hoojy See **hoosier**

hook n

1 In railroading: a wrecker; see quot 1966.

1930 *RR Mag.* June 470, *Hook*—Wrecking crane or auxiliary. **1938** Beebe *High Iron* 222 [Railroad terms], *Hook:* Wrecking train. **1966** *DARE* Tape **SD**5, [After the train wreck] they had to send for the hooks. . . That's the derrick, wrecker. . . It'll pick up one of them cars just like you and I can pick up this tape recorder. They anchor it to the rail. Got a big boom sticking out of there, cables. Always carry a wrecking crew with them. [Inf was a railroad worker.]

2 A hunch; see quot.

1915 *DN* 4.244 **MT,** *Have a hook.* . . "I had a hook you wouldn't make it."

3 in phr *off the hook:* See quot. [Cf *EDD to be off the hooks* (at *hook* sb.[1] 2. (5)) "to be out of health; to be in a bad temper, unsettled"]

1967 *DARE* (Qu. BB41, *Not seriously ill, but sick enough to be in bed: "He's been _______ for a week."*) Inf **NY**27, Off the hook.

4 rarely *hooker;* usu in combs, esp *stove hook:* The utensil used to lift the lid from a wood-burning stove. Cf **damper 1, eye** n[1] **1, key**

1950 *WELS Suppl.* 1 inf, **cwWI,** *Stove handle*—same as *lid-lifter, stove-hook.* Tool to lift lids of a coal or wood stove. **1965–70** *DARE* (Qu. F11, *The thing . . to remove the lids . . from a wood-burning stove when it is hot*) 42 Infs, **scattered, but less freq Gulf States, S Atl,** Stove hook; **NC**1, Damper hook; **FL**9, **TN**1, 13, Eye hook; **CA**182, **IN**54, 82, **WI**69, Hook; **WA**11, Lid hook; **ME**5, **NJ**9, Stove hooker.

5 A barrel hoop. [Perh folk-etym; cf [hʊp], pronc of *hoop*] Cf Intro "Language Changes" IV.4 *esp freq among Black speakers*

1981 Pederson *LAGS Basic Materials* **Gulf Region,** [11 infs have proncs of the type [hʊk] for *hoop;* 1 inf, [hʉ˘ʉks]; 10 of 12 infs are Black.]

6 in adv phr *right off the hook:* See quot. [Cf *OED off the hooks* (at *hook* sb. 15. d) "Straight off, at once, summarily"] *somewhat old-fash*

1965–68 *DARE* (Qu. A23, *To do something at the very first try*) Infs **AL**11, **MS**63, **PA**141, **WV**13, Right off the hook; **IN**11, **SC**6, Right off the hook [FW sugg]. [All Infs old]

7 See **hooknose.**

hook v

1 Of a cow, bull, or goat: to attack or catch with the horns; hence ppl adj *hooking,* n *hooker,* adj *hooky.* **esp Sth, S Midl** Cf **book** v[2]

1866 *Harper's New Mth. Mag.* 32.816/1 **KY,** He . . asked "why that pipe [=a hookah] was like a cow?" having in mind the obvious answer that it was a *hooker.* **1902** (1903) Lorimer *Letters* 84 *(DAE),* You want to . . distinguish between a cow that's a kicker, but whose intentions are good . . and a hooker, who is vicious on general principles. **1917** in 1949 Handy *Treas. Blues* 113, [Song:] Out in Texas with the hooking cows /. . . For the Hooking cow Blues,/ Oh those Texas cow Blues / Ring in my ear / I seem to hear and see them dancing, prancing out on the ranch./ Oh those Hooking cow Blues. **1937** Sandoz *Slogum* 361 **NE,** Do what any good cowman does with a hooky old heifer that horns all the rest from the feed she can't eat herself. He saws her horns off. **1950** *WELS* 1 Inf, **WI,** Hooker. **1954** Roberts *I Bought Dog* 27 **KY,** [The old woman] limped on then to the horse. . . The horse kicked her brains out. [The old woman] . . made it on to the cow. . . The old cow hooked her guts out. **1966–69** *DARE* (Qu. K16, *A cow with a bad temper*) Infs **FL**7, **LA**15, **SD**8, Hooker; **TX**4, Hooking cow; **SC**43, A bookin' cow—['bʊkɨn] equals hooking [in] Negro use; **LA**12, Mean hooking cow; (Qu. K68, . . *A goat that habitually strikes people with its horns*) Inf **NV**1, Hooking goat; **GA**77, Hooking goat—he's horning you. **1968** Adams *Western Words* 152, *Hooker*—In rodeo, a bull that uses his horns, throwing his head back and around to rid himself of his rider.

2 in phr *hook it on;* By ext: see quot.

1970 *DARE* (Qu. EE21b, *When boys were fighting very actively, you might say, "For a while those fellows really ______.*") Inf **TX**88, Hooked it on. [Inf young]

3 also with *off, also in phr hook out of school:* **=hook school.** [Cf *OED hook* v. "Now *slang* or *dial.* To make off. Also *hook it*"; also *EDD hook* v.[2] 1 "To run away, make off"] Cf **hook Jack**

1892 *DN* 1.210 **NEng,** *Hookin' off:* playing truant. **1900** *DN* 2.41 [College slang], *Hook. . .* To absent one's self from class. **1967–68** *DARE* (Qu. JJ6, *To stay away from school without an excuse*) Inf **PA**66, 247, Hooking. [Infs young] **1972** *PADS* 58.23 **cwAL,** *Played truant. . .* hooked out of school.

4 in phr *hook a ride:*

a To solicit a ride, hitchhike.

1989 *DARE* File **NC** (as of c1930), *Hook rides. . .* This was popular with school boys . . with the meaning, "To solicit and obtain free rides from motorists." The petitioner "hung out" at filling stations and similar establishments and made his plea during the motorist's re-fill. If one succeeded, one had "hooked a ride."

b =hooky bob.

1967 *DARE* (Qu. EE26, . . *Games . . children play in the snow*) Inf **MA**71, Hooking rides. **1967** *DARE* FW Addit **CO**7, *Hooking rides*—grabbing hold of a moving vehicle from a sled, etc., so that the sled is pulled along. **1970** *DARE* Tape **CA**174, In the wintertime, when the snows came . . each one had a sled. . . we could hook rides on the back of the coal trucks and . . let them pull us around.

5 See quot.

1959 *VT Hist.* new ser 27.143 **c,ceVT,** *Hook. . .* To plod. Occasional.

6 in ppl adj phr *hooked to the road:* See quot.

1967 *DARE* Tape **ID**6, Of course during the Great Depression the freight trains were loaded. People . . came from Arkansas—there was nothing there. They were just hooked to the road, which meant they were beating their way on the railroad, looking for something.

7 with *up:* See quot.

1967 *DARE* (Qu. JJ36, *To work out a plan, especially a secret plan: "Mary knows more about that, you and she can ______ together."*) Inf **AZ**1, Hook it up.

8 See quot.

1968 *DARE* (Qu. II11a, *If two people don't get along well together, you'd say, "They don't ______."*) Inf **VT**10, Hook; **NY**92, Hook too well.

hook and bendum n

1914 *DN* 4.74 **nNH, ME,** *Hook an' bendum, a little. . .* Any small, gripping tool.

hook-and-eye adj, often cap [See quots] **Ger settlement areas** Cf **black-bumper, hooker** n[1] **1**

Belonging to a conservative Amish or Mennonite sect—esp in comb *hook-and-eye Dutch;* hence n *hook-and-eye(r)* a member of such a sect.

1903 *N.Y. Times* 9 Sep. *(DA),* He was a member of the Amish sect, commonly known as the Hook and Eye Dutch, for the reason that they wear hooks and eyes in preference to buttons on their clothes. **1938** FWP *Ocean Highway* 170 **NC,** Here is an Amish-Mennonite colony, whose members are sometimes called the "hook-and-eye" Mennonites, because they wear no buttons on their clothing. **1938** FWP *Guide IA* 360, *Littleton, . .* a small settlement of "Hook and Eye Dutch." They are a religious sect . . similar to the Mennonites and Amish, fundamentalists in their doctrine, and strict. **1947** *AmSp* 22.72 **PA,** Two . . pupils . . who came from a conservative Mennonite family, wore 'barn-door britches' and 'crock hair-cuts' and used hooks and eyes instead of buttons. Consequently these 'hook and eye Dutch' were often the butt of fun-making by . . their own more 'progressive' Mennonite brethren and children of 'English' families alike. **1950** Bracke *Wheat Country* 85 **KS,** To know the full story of the American Mennonites, those hard-working, plainly dressed people ("the hook-and-eye Dutch," as they used to be called) clustered around Newton, Kansas, one must go back . . to the Germany and Russia of the nineteenth century. **1966–67** *DARE* (Qu. C36, *Nicknames for special communities or groups;* total Infs questioned, 75) Inf **OK**18, Hook-and-Eyes—the Mennonites; (Qu. CC3, . . *Religions . . a bit different from the common ones*) Inf **NY**7, The Hook-and- Eye—don't believe in buttons and zippers; (Qu. CC4, . . *Nicknames . . for various . . religious groups*) Inf **IA**3, Hook-and-Eyers—for Old Order Amish—because they never used buttons. **1968–88** *DARE* File, A woman called the Amish of Iowa "hook and eye ditties"; **wOR,** The hook-and-eye Dutch would strip chrome from their cars or paint it to cover up its "shininess"; **nWI** (as of c1940), "Hook and eye men" was the term used of Mennonites. The speaker explained that they didn't use buttons because buttons (bone or ivory) came from animals and that was against their religion.

hook a ride See **hook** v **4**

hookaroon n [Blend of *hook* + *pickaroon*]

In logging: a pole with a hook at one end used for maneuvering timber; a peavey.

1956 Sorden–Ebert *Logger's Words* 25, *Pickaroon,* A tool used in pulling small timbers out of the water or in loading ties on cars. Broken axes were sometimes made into pickaroons. Same as hookaroon. **1958** McCulloch *Woods Words* 88 **Pacific NW,** *Hookaroon*—A light, sharp, one-tanged tool for horsing timbers when loading or unloading; also used around bridge or other construction. Same as pickaroon.

hook ax n

1966 *DARE* (Qu. L35, *Hand tools used for cutting underbrush and digging out roots*) Inf **DC**8, Hook ax—6-foot handle, it will cut a small tree down.

hook, bait, and sinker adv phr [Var of *hook, line, and sinker*] Cf **fish pole, line, and sinker**

Completely, entirely.

[**1942** ME Univ. *Studies* 56.64, Over greedy fish would take hook, bait, and sinker. [Footnote:] Fig. Be gullible.] **1968** *DARE* (Qu. KK36, . . *A person who is easily fooled*) Inf **GA**19, He swallows it hook, bait, and sinker.

hookbill n

1 also *hawkbill:* **=largemouth bass.**

1897 U.S. Bur. Fisheries *Report* 185, The conspicuous development of the under jaw in the males led to the local names of 'hawk-bill' and 'hook-bill'; the silvery sides of the fish in summer gave rise to that of 'white trout.'

2 =coho salmon.

1975 Evanoff *Catch More Fish* 78, The coho salmon *(Oncorhynchus kisutch)* is also known as the Pacific salmon, silver salmon, hookbill, and silversides.

hook-billed hawk n Also *hook-bill hawk* [See quot 1955] **=everglade kite.**

1925 Bailey *Birds FL* 67, Hook-billed hawk. **1932** Howell *FL Bird Life* 168, *Everglade Kite: Rostrhamus sociabilis*. . . Other Names: Snail Hawk; Hook-billed Hawk. **1946** Hausman *Eastern Birds* 182, *Everglade Kite Rostrhamus sociabilis*. . . Hook-bill Hawk. **1955** Forbush–May *Birds* 98, *Everglade Kite—Rostrhamus sociabilis* . . Hook-bill Hawk. . . Bill long and slender, strongly hooked. Wings much broader than in other kites, resembling those of Buteos.

hook-billed salmon n Also *hawk-nosed salmon* Cf **hookbill 2, hooknose 2**

=chum salmon.

1857 Swan *NW Coast* 140, There are several varieties of fall salmon, the most plentiful of which is the hawk-nosed, or hook-billed, or dog-tooth salmon (for it has all those names).

hook-bill hawk See **hook-billed hawk**

hook bone n Cf **hug-me-tight 3, pully bone**

1966 *DARE* (Qu. K74, *A bone from the breast of a chicken, shaped like a horseshoe*) Inf **SC26**, Hook bone.

hooked in adj phr Cf **hook-hand**

1916 Macy–Hussey *Nantucket Scrap Basket* 135, *Hooked In*—Walking arm in arm. In the old days an unmarried couple seen on the street "hooked in" were supposed to be engaged, and the gossips would say "oh, they must be engaged, for I saw them on Main street hooked in."

hooked to the road See **hook v 6**

hookem-snivey adj Also sp *hookum-snivy* [*OEDS hookum-snivey* "*dial.* and *slang*. . . deceitful, tricky"] *old-fash*

Petty; deceitful, sneaky.

1938 *Atlantic Mth.* 161.632/2, I asked a Dutchman . . whether their jobholders ever cut up any such hookem-snivey capers with public money as ours do. He replied no, . . if a jobholder tried to get away with any pawky bookkeeping, he would be likely to hear about it. **1939** *AmSp* 14.22 (as of 1890s), [Letter:] Are you acquainted with the extraordinary word *hookumsnivy,* signifying "mean" or "small"? My Quaker grandmother, born in Maryland in 1823, used it in my hearing when she was about seventy years old. She said that it was a barbarism in use among common people and that we must forget it.

hooker n[1]

1 also attrib: A member of a **hook-and-eye** sect. [See quots] **Ger settlement areas**

1880 *Lib. Universal Knowledge* 9.700, The *Amish* Mennonites . . are sometimes called Hookers, because they substitute hooks for buttons on their clothes. **1880** *Harper's New Mth. Mag.* 60.810/1 **neND,** The stricter Mennonites regarded them [=buttons] as a worldly innovation, and, adhering to the use of hooks and eyes, were called "Hookers," in distinction from the more lax brethren, who were called "Buttoners". **1913** PA Ger. Soc. *Proc.* 22.2.82 **PA,** The inn was the first public house west of Philadelphia, kept by a "Hooker" Mennonite. **1951** Carter–Ragusin *Gulf Coast* 219 **swAL,** In 1910 the Amish from Kansas, called the Hooker Mennonites because they used hooks and eyes instead of buttons on their clothes, moved to Baldwin County from Kansas.

2 often *hook tender;* In logging: see below. **chiefly Pacific NW**

a also *hooker on:* The person who attaches the cable hooks to the logs. Cf **choker n 1**

1908 Johnson *Highways Pacific Coast* 273 **WA,** Perhaps the best paid wilderness worker is the hook tender who attaches the donkey engine cable to the logs. His is a dangerous task. **1919** *DN* 5.56 **NW,** *Hook-tender*. . . One who tends to the hooks which grapple the logs. **1947** Jones *Evergreen Land* 248 **WA,** Between the bulls and the log the skid-greaser would be daubing the skid-road with grease, and the hook-tender would be plodding along to make up the turn and watch out for hang-ups. **1950** *Western Folkl.* 9.381 **neCA** [Lumberjack language], *Hooker.* A man who works on the landing and aids in loading logs on the trucks. **1958** McCulloch *Woods Words* 88 **Pacific NW,** *Hooker*. . . A hook-tender, the foreman of a yarding crew. In the early days he tended the grab hooks used in hooking logs together for a pull to the landing; or he told other men what logs to hook. **1969** Sorden *Lumberjack Lingo* 57, *Hooker on*—The man on the ground crew who hooked the chain or tongs onto the log for loading. Same as . . hooker, sender.

b The foreman or straw boss of a yarding crew. Cf **bull of the woods 1**

1905 U.S. Forest Serv. *Bulletin* 61.40 **Pacific** [Logging terms], *Hook tender.* The foreman of a yarding crew; specifically, one who directs the attaching of the cable to a turn of logs. **1938** (1939) Holbrook *Holy Mackinaw* 261, *Hooker.* Short for *hook-tender.* The boss of one yarding crew in high-lead country. **1950** *Western Folkl.* 9.118 **nwOR** [Logger speech], *Hook tender.* Foreman of the rigging crew. **1958** McCulloch *Woods Words* 88 **Pacific NW,** *Hooker*. . . The head man of the choker crew on a skidder. *Ibid, Hooktender*—A foreman in charge of the crew on a logging side. In early days he was the man in charge of skidding, and either hooked on the logs or told the teamsters what logs to hook on. Because he tended hook sometimes, the name has stuck. **1966** *DARE* Tape **MT4**, A hook tender, he was, in a way . . a foreman. . . The rigging slinger was really the foreman. He'd supervise the work in the woods. **1982** *Smithsonian Letters* **swWA, nwOR** (as of early 1900s), I was raised in the lower Columbia river logging country. . . The crew in the woods [was] the hooktender (who was the head of the crew) and the choker setters . . and the whistle punk who signaled the donkey puncher [=engine operator].

3 A drink; a measure of liquor. [*EDD hooker* sb.[1] 3]

1905 (1906) Green *At the Actors' Boarding House* 62 **NYC,** A stiff hooker of whiskey, and then another had the expected effect. **1927** (1943) Hammett *$106000* 67, It took a stiff hooker of whiskey . . to thaw her. **1939** Morley *Kitty Foyle* 268, She gave me such a hooker of brandy I went right to sleep. **1942** *Sat. Review* 25.4 14/2, Take a small glass, pour in a hooker of rye whisky, drop in a piece of ice. **1942** Berrey–Van den Bark *Amer. Slang* 102.2, *A drink of liquor* . . hooker *(esp. a large one)*. *Ibid* 110.5, *Liquor glass or mug* . . hooker, *esp. a large glass or drink.* **1950** *AmSp* 25.34 **New Orleans LA** [Slang in the 1880s], *Hooker.* A drink of whisky . . 1887 . . 'where juice of the corn is retailed at so much a hooker.' **1950** *WELS* 3 Infs, **WI**, Hooker. **1965–70** *DARE* (Qu. DD18, *A drink of liquor, or the amount of liquor taken in one swallow: "He took a good ______ ."*) 19 Infs, **chiefly Nth**, Hooker. [16 of 19 Infs male] **1975** Gould *ME Lingo* 135, *Hooker*. . . A stiff slug of something good for what ails you.

4 See quot. [*hook* v to veer off-course, to curve]

c1970 Wiersma *Marbles Terms, Hooker*—Eastern states. An old, chipped marble that is no longer used because the chips no longer allow the marble to roll straight. Often it's a marble that has been kept by the owner for a long time, and has won many other marbles.

5 See **hook v 1.**

6 See quot.

1966 *DARE* (Qu. R5, *A big brown beetle that comes out in large numbers in spring and early summer, and flies with a buzzing sound*) Inf **FL6**, Hookers.

7 See **hook n 4.**

hooker n[2]

A work boat, esp one used for fishing; an old or clumsy boat. [Du *hoekboot, hoeker,* < *hoek* fishhook] **esp NEng** *somewhat old-fash*

1830 Ames *Mariner's Sketches* 5 **MA,** My *debut* as a blue jacket took place in 1815, on board an "old barn of a hooker," that was built during the war, down east, where every one knows that they build ships by the mile and saw them off in length to accommodate purchasers. **1910** Hart *Vigilante Girl* 117 **nCA,** "He wrote me that he came up the river on a brig." "Yes, I commanded the old hooker." **1918** *DN* 5.16 **Martha's Vineyard MA** [Fishing village inhabitants], *Hooker*. . . A boat, especially of an inferior sort. "It was pretty rugged out there for his old hooker." **1942** *Sun* (Baltimore MD) 8 Mar 17/5 *(Hench Coll.)*, Killdeer is one of the finest yachts afloat. . . Barrelle [is] a plump hooker on which they lived . . while earning their lives [sic] by running trotlines for crabs. **1969** *DARE* Tape **WI76**, They had two . . they always called them hookers, boats. . . They'd load the day's fish and then go that night [from Washington Island] to Green Bay. [Inf old] **1974** *AmSp* 49.62 **ME** (as of c1900), *Hooker*. . . Lumber schooner. **1975** Gould *ME Lingo* 135, *Hooker*—Originally a Dutch fishing boat with sturdy lines; hence any good workboat.

‡hooker boy sandwich n Cf **poor boy**

1966 *DARE* (Qu. H42, . . *[A sandwich] in a . . larger, longer bun, that's a meal in itself*) Inf **MS**46, Hooker boy sandwich.

hooker on See **hooker** n[1] **2a**

hookey exclam Also *hookie, ookey* [*hoo* exclam + *key* perh var of Scots, Engl dial *kye* cows] Cf **co-ee, wookey**

Used as a call to cows; see quots.

1949 Kurath *Word Geog.* 63, *Calls to cows in the pasture. . . wookie!, (whookie!, hookie!)* in the Pennsylvania German settlements on the Lower Susquehanna and from there southward to the head of the Shenandoah, as well as in northern West Virginia . . with scattered instances in the Ohio Valley. **1968** *DARE* (Qu. K80, *The call that's used . . to get the cows in from the pasture*) Inf **VA**27, Hookey ['hʊki]—repeated; **DC**8, Ookey ['u::'ki::]; **MD**18, Ookey ['u:ki].

hookey bob See **hooky bob**

hook-eye orchid n [Prob for *Hooker's orchid*]

A **fringed orchid** (here: *Habenaria orbiculata*).

1966 *DARE* Wildfl QR Pl.35 Inf **NH**4, Hook-eye orchid.

hookface See **hooknose**

hook-hand adv Cf **hooked in**

1909 *S. Atl. Qrly.* 8.46 **sSC coast** [Gullah], To walk arm-in-arm is fuh gone [=to go] hook-han'.

hookie exclam See **hookey**

hookie n [Cf *EDD hookie* (at *hokey* int., sb.) "A meaningless exclamation or mild expletive"]

1968 *DARE* (Qu. GG21b, *If you don't care what a person does, you might say, "Go ahead—I don't give a ______.")* Inf **MD**20, Hookie ['hukiˇ].

hooking vbl n

1932 *Hanley Disks* **seMA,** *Hooking*—Fishing with hooks. The first [season] I went, I went hooking, what they call hooking lines, and the other three years I went seining.

hooking ppl adj See **hook** v **1**

hook it on See **hook** v **2**

hook Jack v phr **NEng, esp MA**

=**hook school.**

1877 Bartlett *Americanisms* 294, *Hook Jack.* To play truant. New England. **1892** *DN* 1.212 **NEng,** I was familiar in my boyhood with the expressions *to play hookey* and *hook Jack.* *Ibid* 216 **Boston MA** (as of 1840–50), I was born and brought up on Fort Hill, Boston . . and in all the period from 1840–1850 the current phrase among the boys was *to hook Jack.* **1913** *Boston Herald* (MA) 20 May 10/5 **ceMA** (as of 1860s), *"Playing Hookey," Etc.* . . When I was a boy in Chelsea in the late sixties, we used to say, "Hook Jack," but before that in Eastport, Me., we used to say, "Sky Jack." **1949** Kurath *Word Geog.* 23, The Plymouth–Cape Cod area has preserved rather few unique expressions, among them . . *hooked Jack* . . for 'played hookey'. *Ibid* fig 158 *(Played Truant)* 6 infs, **Boston and eMA,** *Hooked Jack.* **1967–68** *DARE* (Qu. JJ6, *To stay away from school without an excuse*) Inf **MA**33, Hook Jack; my kids say "skip school".

‡hookle berry n

1959 Roberts *Up Cutshin* 96 **seKY,** Another thing was hookle berries—not huckleberries you know in the hills. This grows up like a sunflower and have a head on 'em. I ain't seen any in a long time. They'd grow in the gyarden.

hookneck squash n

A crookneck squash *(Cucurbita moschata).*

1966–69 *DARE* (Qu. I23) Infs **NJ**16, 55, **NY**65, **PA**196, Hookneck squash.

hooknose n

1 also *hook(face):* A Jew, or someone perceived to be Jewish; see quot 1980. [By ext from *hook* a nose with a prominent bend or curve, usu assoc with a Jewish or Semitic appearance] *derog* Cf **Ikey**

1960 Wentworth–Flexner *Slang* 268, *Hook-nose.* . . A Jew. **1968–69** *DARE* (Qu. HH28, . . *Nicknames . . for people of foreign background*) Infs **CT**6, **IN**80, **MN**25, Hooknose—Jewish. **1980** Folb *Runnin' Down* 61 **Los Angeles CA** [Black], A number of vernacular terms singled out Jews . . none of them were particularly flattering. . . Jews are associated with certain stereotypic facial features . . such as large noses. So there are a number of vernacular terms that characterize apparent Jews as *hook, hookface, hooknose.* . . [A] variety of non-Jewish people, such as Italians, Armenians, and Greeks . . [were] called by these terms because they showed stereotypic Jewish features. **1986** Pederson *LAGS Concordance (Jews)* 1 inf, **Shreveport LA,** Hooknose. [Inf young]

2 =**coho salmon.** Cf **hook-billed salmon**

1972 Sparano *Outdoors Encycl.* 354, *Coho Salmon*—Common Names: . . silver salmon, hooknose.

hooknose squash n

A hubbard squash *(Cucurbita maxima).*

1966 *DARE* (Qu. I23) Inf **OK**27, Hooknose squash: same as hubbard—nine inches long, one and one-half inches in diameter; tapers, and small end has a hook on it.

hook off, hook out of school See **hook** v **3**

hook, play v phr [Var of *play hooky*]

=**hook school.**

1890 *DN* 1.78, *Hookey.* . . "To play hook" in the same sense [as "to play hookey"] is reported from western Pennsylvania. **1968** *DARE* (Qu. JJ6, *To stay away from school without an excuse*) Inf **PA**163, Play hook.

hooks n Also *hooks-and-eyes* [See quot 1948]

An inflammation of the nictitating membrane in the eye of a horse.

1846 U.S. Congress *Congressional Globe* 1 June 15.894/2 **MO,** The operation [of cutting for the "simples"] . . comes from horse surgery—cutting a horse's eye for the hooks. The horse is subject to a disease of the eye, something like cataract, which blinds him; and, when emolient remedies fail, the knife is applied, the diseased part cut away, and then the animal sees clear. **1948** Wolfe *Farm Gloss.* 164, *Hooks in the Eye*—The cartilagenous [sic] structure, called haw, in the eye of lower animals, to assist in removing foreign bodies from the front of the eyeball, sometimes becomes inflamed and the uninformed declares the animal has "hooks in the eye" and often cruelly cuts them out. **1952** Brown *NC Folkl.* 1.552, *Hooks:* . . A disease of the eyes of horses, believed to be caused by the natural "wiper" just above the eyeball. Sometimes a person will cut off this wiper in the belief that this operation will cure the disease. **1966** *DARE* (Qu. K47, *What diseases do horses or mules commonly get around here?*) Inf **GA**3, Hooks-and-eyes (eye disease). **a1975** Lunsford *It Used to Be* 159 **sAppalachians,** Hooks [sic] is the natural wiper that's in the eye of the horse, that the horse uses to brush out some foreign matter that might get in the eye. When it comes up it has a kind of hook and they cut out the hook so that the horse will get well of the disease of the "hooks."

hook school v phr [*hook* v to run off] **esp MD, PA, VA** Cf **hook** v **3, hook Jack; hook, play; hook, shoot a**

To be truant; to skip class.

1949 Kurath *Word Geog.* fig 158, *[Played Truant]—Hooked School.* [2 infs **nPA,** 8 infs **MD,** 2 infs **eVA**] **1967–68** *DARE* (Qu. JJ6, *To stay away from school without an excuse*) Inf **MD**12, Hooked school; **MD**49, Hook school. **1986** Pederson *LAGS Concordance (Skipped school)* 1 inf, **nwLA,** Hooked school.

hook, shoot a v phr Also *shoot the hook, do a hook, throw* ~ **Gulf States**

=**hook school;** by ext, to be absent from one's expected place.

1986 Pederson *LAGS Concordance (Skipped school)* 2 infs, **neFL, csTX,** Do (*or* threw) a hook; 1 inf, **seFL,** Shoot the hook; 2 infs, **ceAL, csTX,** Shot a (*or* the) hook; 1 inf, **csTX,** Shooting a hook—any absence, not just school—"He shot a hook yesterday." [5 of 6 infs Black]

hook snake n

Perh a **horn snake 1.**

1965 *DARE* (Qu. P25) Inf **MS**58, Hook snake.

hook tender See **hooker** n[1] **2**

hookumpake n Also *hookumpate* [Echoic]

=**woodcock** (here: *Philohela minor*).

1898 (1900) Davie *Nests N. Amer. Birds* 134, Although known to the majority of people by its name of Woodcock, it nevertheless has many aliases in different parts of the country which it visits, and is called Big Mud, Big-headed, Blind and Wood and Whistling Snipe; . . Bog Bird, . . Hookum Pake, . . and probably many others. **1899** (1912)

Green *VA Folk-Speech* 230, *Hookumpate*. . . The American woodcock. Imitating the cry. **1917** (1923) *Birds Amer.* 1.225, *Woodcock—Philohela minor*. . Big Mud Snipe; Blind Snipe; . . Hookum Pake; . . Big-eyes. **1923** U.S. Dept. Ag. *Misc. Circular* 13.49, *American Woodcock* . . *In local use*. . . bog-bird (Pa.); bog-sucker (N.B., N.J., Pa.); . . hookumpake (Md.)

hookum-snivy See **hookem-snivey**

hook under n Cf **jumpsies**

In marble play: see quot.

c1970 Wiersma *Marbles Terms* **swMI,** *Hook under*—method of snapping the shooter low to produce a jump shot.

hook up See **hook** v 7

hookworm n

1 Appar a worm used as bait in fishing.

1970 *DARE* (Qu. P6) Inf **TX**88, Hookworm; (Qu. R27) Inf **SC**69, Hookworm—a worm, not a caterpillar.

2 in phr *have the hookworm:* See quot. [*hookworm* a parasitic nematode]

1928 *Ruppenthal Coll.* **KS,** *To have the hook worm*—to be lazy; to have spring fever; to be born tired; to be constitutionally opposed to work.

hooky adj See **hook** v 1

hooky v [Prob from *play hooky;* but perh from **hook** v 3]

=**hook school.**

1968 *DARE* (Qu. JJ6, *To stay away from school without an excuse*) Inf **MD**8, [He's] hookying.

hooky bob v phr, hence freq vbl n *hooky bobbing,* also *hooky bobbins* Also sp *hookey bob* **chiefly NW** Cf **bum-riding**

To hold onto a moving vehicle so as to be towed along over snow or ice.

1965 Bowen *Alaskan Dict.* (Tabbert *Alaskan Engl.*) 18, *Hookey Bob*. . . To hook rides on the back of moving vehicles and slither along the ice road on the soles of one's boots. **1967** *DARE* (Qu. EE24b, *When children go down hill on a sled*) Inf **OR**10, Hooky bobbin'—when you attach sled to car; (Qu. EE26, . . *Games* . . *children play in the snow*) Inf **MA**71, Hooking rides; **WA**22, Hooky bobbing—hold on to fender of car, slide, squatting with shoes sliding. **1968–87** *DARE* File **ID,** *Hooky bobbing*—after a snow when the streets still had snow on them, we used to hook on bumpers of cars or trucks and squat down for a ride. The trick of this was to stay on for a block or so without being caught. It was more exciting when the car swerved; *Ibid,* Hanging on the back of a vehicle and being pulled along on the surface of ice or snow; *Ibid* (as of 1964), My college roommate, an Idaho native, told of "hooky bobbing" in Twin Falls, Idaho. Kids would grab on to the bumper of a car and be pulled along on the snow on their feet; *Ibid* **cnUT, sID,** Hooky bobbing—hanging on the back bumper of a car and skiing on one's shoes on slippery pavement; *Ibid* **seWA,** Growing up in Pullman [WA] . . we referred to hanging on to back bumpers of cars moving on snow/ice as "hooky bobbing". **1974** in 1981 Tabbert *Alaskan Engl.,* [Newspaper article:] "Hooky bobbing," which occurs when a child grabs hold of the rear bumper of a car to slide along behind it, is very dangerous. **1983** *DARE* File **ID** (. . *Games children play in the snow*) Hooky bobbins.

hooky, cut v phr [Blend of *cut school* + *play hooky*]

=**hook school.**

1966 *DARE* (Qu. JJ6, *To stay away from school without an excuse*) Infs **SC**10, 21, Cut hooky.

hooley n Also *huly* [Cf *SND to play huilly wi'* (at *huilie* adv) "to upset, to throw into disorder"; also *hoolachan* n "A Highland reel"; also *EDD hoolybus* sb. "A noise, tumult, uproar"] Cf **hullabaloo**

An uproar; a loud party.

a1877 in 1950 *AmSp* 25.175 **NEng,** *Huly.* A noise, uproar. To raise huly. **1960** *News-Call Bulletin* (San Francisco) 4 Jan. 16/1 *(OEDS),* She can be seen at all the best hoolies in town.

hooley-ann n Also *hoolian, hoolihan* **West**

A type of loop thrown esp in roping horses; see quots.

1927 Sandburg *Amer. Songbag* 12, [Lyrics to "I Ride An Old Paint":] I ride an old Paint, I lead an old Dan,/ I'm goin' to Montan' for to throw the hoolian. **1933** *AmSp* 8.1.29 **nTX,** *Hoolian* (accent on the last syllable). A whirl or twist of a rope that makes the loop stand almost perpendicular. **1935** *Cattleman* 22.1.16/1 **TX,** In roping horses from the remuda . . [the cowboy] uses a loop known throughout the Southwest as a "hooleyann," which is thrown by putting the loop on the ground to the left and as far back as possible. . . [The cowboy] brings the loop as far forward as possible, then back over his right shoulder and throws with an overhand motion much as a pitcher snaps an overhand ball. . . Using the hooleyann, half a dozen men can rope mounts at the same time without exciting the horses. *Ibid* 26.12.23/1 **OK,** Hoolian. . . hooleyann, or hoolihan. . . [T]he hooleyann is the name of a loop that is as handy as the pocket on a shirt. It can be thrown from the ground or from horseback. . . It is a fast loop and . . useful in catching horses in a corral. It is thrown with a rather small loop and has the additional virtue of landing with the honda sliding down the rope, taking up the slack as it goes.

hooligan n Also *holocan, hoolican, hoolikan, ooligan* [Folk-etyms for *eulachon*] **AK**

=**eulachon.**

1914 Everman *Alaska Fisheries and Fur Industries in 1913* 137 (Tabbert *Alaskan Engl.*), The eulachon, candle-fish, or "hooligan" as it is variously termed in Alaska, is a very toothsome member of the smelt family. **1937** Hutchison *Stepping Stones From Alaska to Asia* 29 (Tabbert *Alaskan Engl.*), I passed his mate . . sitting placidly . . watching his supper of "ooligan" cooking. **1940** White *Wild Geese* 414 **AK, CA** (as of 1890s), "And what is hoolican?" "Well," said Harry, taking his time, "you take coal-oil cans and fill them with a very fat, greasy little fish that comes in later in the season, and you stand them out in the sun, and when they've reached the proper state of decomposition—" **1955** U.S. Arctic Info. Center *Gloss., Hoolican, hooligan*. . . Alternate name for the eulachon. **1956** *Seattle Daily Times* (WA) 2 Dec mag sec 7/1 **wWA** (as of 1847), Heath . . received a keg of salted "hoolikans" (eulachon or candlefish, a type of smelt) and some smoked ones as gifts. **1968** *DARE* (Qu. P3) Inf **AK**9, Hooligan—come in from saltwater; (Qu. P4) Inf **AK**1, Eulachon ['juləkən]—also called "hooligan"—prime source of oil or grease among Indians; valued in interior; = "candlefish"—can be burned like a candle. **1979** *Fairbanks Daily News-Miner* (AK) 27 June 27 (Tabbert *Alaskan Engl.*), After fish people dip melted holocans [sic] and smelts. **1981** Tabbert *Alaskan Engl.* 237, The name *hooligan* for this member of the smelt family is one of many variants of *eulachon*. . . According to most sources the word comes to English through Chinook Jargon. . . Although versions beginning with an /h-/ are reported from Canadian usage . . , the form *hooligan* seems to be Alaskan.

hooligan wagon n [Prob var of **hoodlum wagon 1**]

See quots.

1939 Rollins *Gone Haywire* 187 **MT** (as of 1886), In the old-time West, an outfit might have several vehicles in addition to its chuck wagon . . the hooligan wagon (for firewood and water), the calf wagon, and so forth. **1944** Adams *Western Words* 79, *Hooligan wagon*—A wagon used on short drives to carry fuel and water in a country where these commodities are scarce.

hoolihan v, hence vbl n *hoolihaning* **West**

1 To bring down (a steer) by throwing one's weight on its horns; see quots.

1933 (1950) Allen *Cowboy Lore* 11, *Hoolihaning,* the act of leaping forward and alighting on the horns of a steer in bull-dogging in a manner to knock the steer down without having to resort to twisting the animal down with a wrestling hold. Hoolihaning is barred at practically all recognized contests. **1936** McCarthy *Lang. Mosshorn* np **West** [Rodeo term], *Hoolihanng* [sic]. The old-time practice of bulldogging. When this style was permitted, the cowboy would grab the steer by the horns, force its head earthward and soon turn the animal forward on its back. **1940** *Cattleman* 26.12.23/1 **OK,** The dogger who "hoolihans" a steer by throwing his weight on his head and causing him to flop rather than twisting him down ought to find another word to describe his deed.

2 See quot. Cf **hoolihan** n 2

1944 Adams *Western Words* 79, *Hoolihaning* [sic]. . . To throw a big time in town—to paint the town red.

hoolihan n

1 See **hooley-ann.**

2 A ruckus; see quot. Cf **hoolihan** v 2

1984 Smith *SW Vocab.* 105, *Hoolihan:* Generally preceded by . . "throw," the word means to have a high old time, to paint the town, to raise hell. Ordinarily associated with partying, debauchery, and shooting up the town.

3 See quot.

1968 Adams *Western Words* 153, *Hoolihan*—A cowboy's term meaning foul or dirty play.

hoolihaning See **hoolihan** v

hoolikan See **hooligan**

hoomalimali v, n [Haw] **HI**

See quot 1967.

1955 Day *HI People* 310 [Glossary], *Hoomalimali:* flattery, "apple sauce". **1967** Reinecke-Tsuzaki *Hawaiian Loanwords* 96, *Hoomalimali;* /ho'omalimali/. . . [*Ho'o* [=causative prefix to verbs] and redup. of *mali,* to flatter.] 1. To win, or attempt to win, favor by flattery and complaisance; to "softsoap." 2. Flattery; "softsoap"; "hooey"—a word often heard about election time. F[requent]:A[dult]. **1972** Carr *Da Kine Talk* 87 **HI,** *Hawaiian Words Commonly Heard in Hawaii's English. . . Ho'omalimali.* To flatter, flattery.

hoonuh See **una**

hoo-owl n Also *boo-hoo-owl, hoo-hoo-owl* [Echoic] **Sth, S Midl** See Map

A **hoot owl** n **1.**

1902 *DN* 2.236 **sIL,** *Hoo-owl.* . . The word owl not used alone. **1940** in 1944 *ADD* **swPA, nWV,** Boo-hoo owl |bu'hu'|-. Old illit. speaker. **1954** *Harder Coll.* **cwTN,** *Hoo owl:* hoot owl. **1963** TN Folk Lore Soc. *Bulletin* 29.81, *Hoot Owls*—The larger owls—Barred and Great Horned—were *hoot* or *hoo owls.* **1966–69** *DARE* (Qu. Q2, *Other kinds of owls*) 11 Infs, **Sth, S Midl,** Hoo-owl; **AL**31, 32, **SC**7, 40, 57, **TX**62, Hoo-hoo-owl; (Qu. Q1, . . *Owl that makes a shrill, trembling cry*) Infs **DC**4, **GA**16, 25, Hoo-owl; **FL**35, Hoo-hoo-owl.

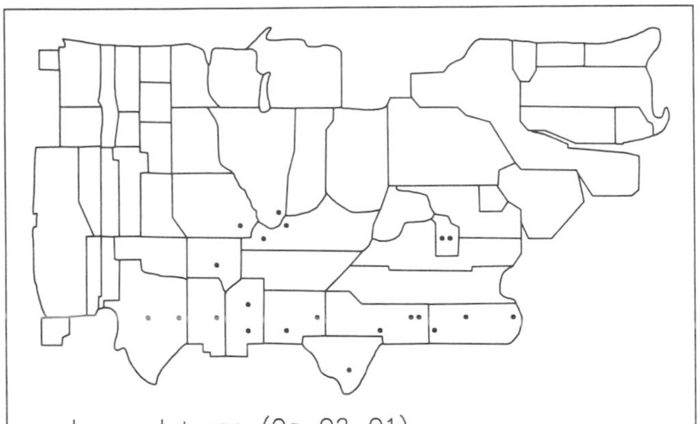

•hoo-owl + var (Qq. Q2, Q1)

hoop exclam See **whoop** exclam

hoop n

1 pl; also *hoop-stick, ~-toss:* The game of quoits; see quot.

1968–70 *DARE* (Qu. EE37, *The game where you try to throw metal rings or something similar over a stake in the ground*) Infs **GA**86, **MI**114, **WI**50, Hoops; **MN**16, Hoops—tossed hoops over [the stake]; **NC**88, **SC**69, Hoop-toss; **MI**89, Hoop-stick.

2 also *hoop roll:* A cartwheel.

1968–70 *DARE* (Qu. EE9c, . . *[When] children spread their arms and turn over sideways*) Inf **MD**29, Hoop [hʊp] roll; **VA**46, Hoop [hwʊp], [hʊp]; [(QR, near Qu. EE9c) Inf **GA**72A, Rolling like a hoop].

hoopapoop n

=hootenanny 1.

1966 *DARE* Tape **OK**24, I think that hoopapoop here on top burnt out. . . [I mean the] thing in there to keep from burnin' the motor up on a pump . . burnt out.

hoop ash n

1 =black ash 1. [See quot 1958]

1763 in 1893 Filson Club *Pub.* 8.132 **KY,** Bounded as follows, to wit: Beginning at a hoop-ash and buckeye, the lower corner of Major Edward Ward's land. **1897** Sudworth *Arborescent Flora* 325, *Fraxinus nigra* . . . Black Ash. . . *Common Names:* . . Hoop Ash (Vt., N.Y., Del., Ohio, Ill., Ind.) **1910** Graves *Flowering Plants* 318 **CT,** *Fraxinus nigra*. . . Hoop Ash. . . The wood is much used for . . barrel hoops. **1916** Seton *Woodcraft Manual Girls* 295, Black Ash, Hoop Ash, or Water Ash *(Fraxinus nigra).* **1930** U.S. Dept. Ag. *Misc. Pub.* 77.60, The black ash. . . is. . . hoop ash. **1958** Petrides *Trees & Shrubs* 34, Black Ash. . . Known also as Hoop . . Ash. Short logs or planks when hammered repeatedly on the ends split along the annual growth rings into thin sheets that can be cut into strips for . . barrel hoops. **1967** Borland *Hill Country* 161 **nwCT,** Sometimes it is called hoop ash, however, which comes from its one-time use in making barrel hoops. It was also used to make barrel staves. But nowadays it is seldom called anything but black ash. **1979** Little *Checklist U.S. Trees* 136, *Fraxinus nigra. . . Other common names* . . hoop ash.

2 =blue ash 1.

1960 Vines *Trees SW* 868, *Fraxinus quadrangulata.* . . is also known under the name of Hoop Ash. . . The tree has been in cultivation since 1823.

3 also *hoop elm:* **hackberry** (here: *Celtis occidentalis*). [See quot 1921]

1787 Amer. Acad. Arts & Sci. *Memoirs* 2.1.157, Hoop Ash, of three, and three and a half feet diameter. **1810** Michaux *Histoire des Arbres* 1.36, Celtis crassifolia. . . *Hoop ash* . . , sur les bords de l'Ohio, en Pensylvanie et en Virginie. [=*Celtis crassifolia. . . Hoop ash* . . , along the Ohio, in Pennsylvania and in Virginia.] **1832** Browne *Sylva* 133, On the Ohio it is called *Hoop Ash,* and in Kentucky, *Hack Berry.* . . As it is elastic and easily divided, it is used for the bottom of common chairs, and by the Indians for baskets. **1877** Bartlett *Americanisms* 36, The Hoop-ash *(Celtis occidentalis),* or Hackberry, is also called Beaver-wood. **1897** Sudworth *Arborescent Flora* 185, *Celtis occidentalis.* . . Hoop Ash (Vt.) **1921** Deam *Trees IN* 148, *Celtis occidentalis.* . . The wood . . before seasoning very much resembles ash. . . and is now much sought after for hoops. It was formerly often known as hoop ash. **1940** Clute *Amer. Plant Names* 164, *C. occidentalis.* . . Hoop ash. *Ibid* 255, *Celtis occidentalis.* Hoop elm. **1960** Vines *Trees SW* 206, Hoop ash.

hoop ball n Cf **spaldeen** n

See quot 1968 *DARE* Tape.

1968 *DARE* (Qu. EE33, . . *Outdoor games*) Inf **NY**118A, Hoop ball. **1968** *DARE* Tape **NY**118, We used to play this game called hoop ball. You take a spalding and [there] would be two fire-escapes that came down from the second floor, and you'd play between them just regular. It was a basketball [game] except you'd play with a spalding instead of a regular basketball.

hoop cheese n [Cf *cheese hoop* a wooden cylinder in which curds are pressed] **chiefly Sth, S Midl**

See quots.

1961 Folk *Word Atlas N. LA* map 1011, *Homemade cheese made out of milk curd*—hoop cheese. [This together with six other terms comprises 11% of the responses given by 275 infs.] **1965** *DARE* (Qu. H61, . . *Kinds of homemade cheese*) Inf **MS**55, Hoop cheese. **1971** *Today Show Letters* **sw,csMS,** Hoop cheese—cheddar cheese in round wooden boxes. **1988** *Atlanta Constitution* (GA) 4 Apr 16/2 **neGA** (as of c1924), As often as not, the train derailed, and I'd just get me some hoop cheese and crackers from the barrel until the train ran again. **1988** *NADS Letters* **MS,** I asked five other native Mississippians "Why is hoop cheese called hoop cheese?" Every one of them responded . . "Because it's made in a hoop." One . . has also heard . . "cheese on the hoop." . . According to a professor in Dairy Science, hoop cheese is usually cheddar cheese that is put into a form called a hoop at a certain point in the process of making it. *Ibid* **nwSC,** *Hoop cheese*—a large round (approximately 15–20 lbs.) of cheddar cheese . . found in the local grocery store and sliced off in the weight of the customer's choosing. *Ibid,* In northeastern Arkansas, where I spent my boyhood, round cheeses were, and still are, called *hoop cheese* because of their shape.

hooped salmon See **hoopid salmon**

hoopee n

A **wolfberry** (here: *Lycium andersonii*).

1903 (1950) Austin *Land of Little Rain* 47 **neCA,** By the south corner, where the campoodie stood, is a single shrub of "hoopee" (Lycium Andersonii), maintaining itself hardly among alien shrubs.

hoopel See **hoople**

hoop elm See **hoop ash 3**

hoopendaddy n Also *hoop-nanny*

=hootenanny 1

1911 *DN* 3.544 **NE,** *Hoopendaddy.* . . Indefinite expression, like *thingumbob,* etc; usually refers to food. "Pass me some of that hoopendaddy." **1942** Berrey–Van den Bark *Amer. Slang* 75.3, *Knicknacks. . .* hoopendaddies . . hoop-nannies. *Ibid* 75.4, *Contrivance; indefinite object. . .* hoop-nanny.

hoopensocker n Cf **hooker** n[1] **3**

1950 *WELS (A big drink)* 1 Inf, **csWI,** Hoopensocker.

hooper n

1 =whistling swan. *hist*

1709 (1967) Lawson *New Voyage* 150 **NC,** The sort of Swans call'd Hoopers, are the least. They abide more in the Salt-Water, and are equally valuable, for Food. **1834** Nuttall *Manual Ornith.* 2.367, Whistling swans. . . are called *Hoopers,* and mostly frequent the sea coast. **1923** U.S. Dept. Ag. *Misc. Circular* 13.38, *Whistling Swan. . . Vernacular Names. . . In local use. . .* Hoopers (N.C.)

2 See **whooper.**

hoopid salmon n Also *hoopid* Also folk-etym sp *hooped salmon* [Appar from the Makah name] **chiefly Pacific NW**

=coho salmon.

1880 *Forest & Stream* 15.130/1, The "hooped" salmon . . is probably, but not certainly, the *Salmo tsuppitch* of Richardson, and its proper specific name is uncertain. **1883** U.S. Natl. Museum *Bulletin* 27.474, *Oncorhynchus kisutch . .* Hoopid salmon. . . Pacific coast of North America from San Francisco northward to Bering Strait. **1884** Goode *Fisheries U.S.* 1.477, On Frazer River it is known by the Musquam name of "Coho"; . . about Cape Flattery [Washington] by the Makah name of "Hoopid." **1896** U.S. Natl. Museum *Bulletin* 47.480, *Oncorhynchus kisutch . .* (. . Hoopid Salmon . .). **1904** *Salmon & Trout* 164, The silver salmon *(Oncorhynchus kisutch)* is also known as . . hoopid and coho salmon. **1946** LaMonte *N. Amer. Game Fishes* 107, *Silver Salmon—Oncorhynchus kisutch. . .* Hoopid, . . White Salmon, . . Arctic Trout.

hoopie See **hoopy**

hooping crane See **whooping crane**

hooping owl n Also *hoop owl* Cf **hoo-owl, hoot owl n 1**

Prob = **screech owl.**

1940–41 Cassidy *WI Atlas* **swWI,** Hoop owl—a small owl. **1969–70** *DARE* (Qu. Q2) Inf **NC**64, Hooping owl ['hupɪŋ] owl; **NC**85, Hoopin' owl; **VA**73, Hooping owl—same as tree owl.

hoople n [Du *hoepel*] *old-fash*

1 also *hoople wheel;* also sp *hoopel:* A hoop rolled by children.

1848 Bartlett *Americanisms* 180, *Hoople. . .* The boys in the city of New York still retain the Dutch name *hoople* for a hoop. **1872** Schele de Vere *Americanisms* 86, Boys . . were . . ignorant of . . [the] meaning . . of the word *hoople,* by which they called their trundling hoops, and which they little suspected they owed to the *hoeple* [sic] of Dutch ancestors. **1907** *St. Nicholas* 34.676/1, [Caption to a picture showing a boy with a large hoop and a stick:] Master Aldrich in his "hoople" days. **1911** *DN* 3.544 **NE,** *Hoopel. . .* Occasional variant of *hoop.* **1957** *Sat. Eve. Post Letters,* A hoop of iron prodded on with a stick [is called] "hoople wheels" in Iowa.

2 See quot. Cf **hoop net**

1978 *Smithsonian* May 79 **NYC,** If the mumbler [=pigeon fancier] had recognized any unfamiliar birds among those settling on his roof, he would have edged over, grain in one hand and a long-handled net called a "hoople" in the other.

hoople wheel See **hoople 1**

hoop-me-koff n [Var of *whooping cough*]

1892 U.S. Bur. Amer. Ethnology *Annual Rept. for 1887–88* 459, While the "hoop-me-koff" was raging among the Mohave the fathers of families afflicted with it were forbidden to touch coffee or salt, and were directed to bathe themselves in the current of the Colorado.

hoop-nanny See **hoopendaddy**

hoop net n **chiefly Missip Valley** Cf **fish basket**

A net used for river fishing; a **fyke.**

1938 Burman *Blow for a Landing* 96 **Lower Missip Valley,** Others of more cheerful visage worked in merry groups on long flatboats, and struggled to pull from the water the great hoop nets so characteristic of the valley. **1943** Weslager *DE Forgotten Folk* 185, The fisherman from Cheswold also makes fykes or "hoop nets" of the typical conical shape, and anchors them in the water near the shore. Two rectangular nets are arranged on either side of the opening into the fyke. The fish enter the fyke and pass through a series of small tapering nets until they reach the smallest . . from which they cannot exit. **1952** Henderson *Home is Upriver* 161 **Lower Missip Valley,** [He] traded his woman to Hereford Albutter for six cans of beans, a hoop net, and a gasboat. **1967–70** *DARE* (Qu. P13, . . *Fishing [with] . . special kinds . . nets*) Infs **LA**10, 20, 26, **MI**108, Hoop nets; **IL**14, Hoop nets—round nets; **IA**22, Hoop nets—big, round hoops; wing nets—hoop nets with wings or projections; **KY**86, Hoop nets—same as barrel nets. **1967–69** *DARE* Tape **LA**5, We caught them in hoop nets. . . Around here we would usually fish anywhere from three and a half foot fronts, seven-hoop nets, some nine-hoop nets, up to about four and a half foot front. [The front is] the first hoop. *Ibid* **WI**75, There's many different kinds of trap nets . . there are . . hoop nets and trammel nets. . . A hoop net is . . held open by great big hoops and . . has this funnel mouth with the device. All fishing is just like the devil's work. . . It's based on deception. They're generally wooden hoops. They lay right on the bottom. . . It looks almost like a long sock. . . They fish suckers with that type of net.

hoop owl See **hooping owl**

hoop pole n Cf **hoop ash, hoopwood**

A length of sapling cut to be made into barrel hoops; occas a sapling suitable for this purpose.

1645 in 1892 Dedham MA *Early Rec.* 3.112, Samll Miles hath libtie to cut 400 lengthes of hoope poles on the common. **1835** Bird *Hawks* 1.76 **PA,** There was a bundle of green hoop-poles, at a cooper's shop. **1843** (1916) Hall *New Purchase* 307 **IN,** On one side the area . . were large heaps of hoop-poles, on another, of barrel staves. **1899** (1912) Green *VA Folk-Speech* 230, *Hoop-pole. . .* A small sapling of green wood, for making hoops for casks. **1940–41** Cassidy *WI Atlas,Hoop*—In the old days, these were made of split hoop poles. *Ibid, Hoops*—made of hoop poles. **1955** McAtee *Dial. Grant Co. IN Suppl. 6* [2], *Hoop pole. . .* hoopwood, the natural growth, also might be called . . hoop poles. Normally . . a hoop pole was so known only from the time of cutting to that of riving, when the halves tapered and notched, were hoops, whether bent or not. **c1960** [see **hoopwood 1**]. **1968** [see **hoopy** n[1] *DARE* Tape].

hoop roll See **hoop 2**

hoops and jingles n pl

1969 *DARE* (Qu. BB13, *Other words . . for chills and fever*) Inf **CA**107, Hoops and jingles.

hoopsisaw intj, n [Cf Ger *hopsassa!* intj "upsy-daisy"]

A As intj.

See quot.

1987 *DARE* File **WI,** I know *hoopsisaw,* with the stress on the first syllable, as an interjection expressing joyfulness. It's not standard German; it's from the south German dialects but also including Frankfurt, the Palatinate, etc.

B As noun.

See quot.

1872 Haldeman *PA Dutch* 59, *Hoopsisaw. . .* A rustic or low dance, and a lively tune adapted to it. Inferior lively music is sometimes called 'hoopsisaw music,' 'a hoopsisaw tune'.

hoop snake n

A snake popularly supposed to take its tail in its mouth and roll like a hoop, and often also thought to have a poisonous spike on its tail; a snake of the southern US sometimes supposed to have these characteristics, as the **horn snake 1,** the **rainbow snake,** or a **racer** (here: *Coluber constrictor*).

1784 Smyth *Tour U.S.A.* 1.265 **cnNC,** From the above circumstance, peculiar to themselves, they have also derived the appellation of hoop snakes. **1840** *S. Lit. Messenger* 6.380/2 **IN,** I never believed in the existence of hoop-snakes neither, until I went out into the western country. **1890** Howells *Boy's Town* 200 **sOH,** Nobody had ever seen a blacksnake do it, and nobody had ever seen a hoopsnake, but the boys believed there was such a snake, and that he would take his tail in his mouth, when he got after a person, and roll himself along swifter than the fastest racehorse could run. **1909** Biol. Soc. DC *Proc.* 22.134 **NC,** *Abastor erythrogramus. Hoop Snake. . .* Vernacular name. **1925** TX Folkl. Soc. *Pub.* 4.47, In some localities in the South, the hoop snake is identified with *Farancia abacura . .* which has a small spine at the end of its tail. **1929** Sale *Tree Named John* 55 **MS,** En a hoop snake—Lawd, Honey, ef you sees one uv dem comin', you jes leave dar, 'ca'se he rolls lak a hoop, en he's got a stinger in 'is tail, en ef he pop dat in you, dar ain no he'p fer you. **1935** Pratt *Manual Vertebrate Animals* 206, *C[oluber]* *constrictor*. . . Blacksnake; blue racer; hoop snake. **1937** Pope *Snakes Alive* 123, Although two . . snakes . . are identified as the hoop snake, neither of them rolls like a hoop nor has a sting in its tail. . . One of these "hoop snakes" is more accurately known as the rainbow snake, the other as the horn snake. **1952** Ditmars *N. Amer. Snakes* 123, It [=*Farancia abacura*] is also called the "Hoop" Snake, being alleged to take tail in its mouth and roll like the rim of a wagon wheel. This allegation may come about from a circular posture sometimes assumed by this snake when resting in inundated grass. **c1960** *Wilson Coll.* **csKY.** **1963** Watkins–Watkins *Yesterday Hills* 155 **cnGA,** "A hoop snake," he says, "is a snake with a horn on it like a rooster's spur. The horn is on its tail, I've seed one. They claim that a hoop snake can stick that spur in a pretty good-sized sapling and it will wilt in twenty-four hours. They are real poison. Folks claim they will git in a circle and roll, but I never seed one do that." **1964** *PADS* 42.19 **KY.** **1966–70** *DARE* (Qu. P25) 10 Infs, **scattered,** Hoop snake. **1970** *DARE* Tape **TX**87, Hoop snake—snake that rolls like a hoop and will actually chase you. This I have really seen.

hoop stick See **hoop 1**

hoop-toss See **hoop 1**

hoopwood n

1 Wood, as of pliable saplings, suitable for making barrel hoops. Cf **hoop pole**

1940–41 Cassidy *WI Atlas,* Hoop-pole trees were planted especially to furnish hoopwood. **1942** McAtee *Dial. Grant Co. IN* 34 (as of 1890s), *Hoopwood* . . small saplings suitable for splitting into hoops. **c1960** *Wilson Coll.* **csKY,** *Hoop-poles* (or *hoopwood*). . . Small trees or poles, usually hickory suitable for making barrel hoops.

2 Spec:

a also *hoopwood tree:* **=hoop ash.**

1770 (1925) Washington *Diaries* 1.428, I markd two Maples, an Elm, and Hoopwood Tree as a Cornr. of the Soldiers Ld. [=land]. **1821** (1898) Fowler *Jrl.* 21 **cKS,** We Set out at our ushal time at ten miles pased a point of Rocks and a Hoop wood tree on them. **1854** Bancroft *Hist. U.S.* VI.379 *(DAE),* He would . . set his mark on a maple, or elm, a hoop-wood, or ash, as the corner of a solder's survey. **1937** *Torreya* 37.96, *Celtis occidentalis*. . . Hoopwood, Kentucky and Virginia. **1940** Clute *Amer. Plant Names* 255, Celtis occidentalis. . . Hoop-wood.

b A **winterberry** (here: *Ilex laevigata*).

1900 Lyons *Plant Names* 199, *I[lex] laevigata*. . . Maine to Virginia. . . Hoop-wood. **1908** Britton *N. Amer. Trees* 622, *Winterberry —Ilex laevigata*. . . is also called the Smooth winterberry and Hoop-wood. **1933** Small *Manual SE Flora* 815, *I. laevigata*. . . Hoopwood. **1940** Clute *Amer. Plant Names* 127, *Smooth Winterberry.* Hoop-wood.

3 A **sea grape** (here: *Coccoloba uvifera*).

1908 Britton *N. Amer. Trees* 379, It [=sea grape] is also called . . Hoop-wood.

hoopwood tree See **hoopwood 2a**

hoopy exclam See **whoopy** exclam

hoopy n[1] Also *hoopie* [See quot 1968 *DARE* Tape]

=hoosier B1a.

1940 in 1944 *ADD* **nWV, eOH,** *Hoopie*. . . A hillbilly. . . ['hupi]. **1968** *DARE* (Qu. HH1, . . *Nicknames for a rustic or countrified person*) Inf **OH**71, Hoopy. **1968** *DARE* Tape **OH**71, A hoopy was a fella who lived down the river west of New Cumberland. . . They would come up on the boats and the potters would order so many hoop poles for the cooper's shop which they employed. . . These fellas would come off the boats lugging these things. . . They were hoopies because they had these hoop poles. **1968** *DARE* FW Addit **OH**71, *Hoopy*—A hillbilly from West Virginia. [The word is] supposedly from "barrel hoop." Men came out of the hills to work in factories making hoops for staves. [Now] a generalized pejorative.

hoopy n[2] **esp TX** See Map

A dilapidated car or other vehicle.

1966–70 *DARE* (Qu. N5, *Nicknames for an automobile, especially an old or broken-down car*) Infs **OR**3, **SD**5, **TX**5, 32, 35, 36, 37, 102; **LA**2, Hoopy—common; **WA**12, Hoopy—especially an old pick up; [**IL**48, Hupmobile—laughter]. [10 of 11 Infs comm types 4 and 5] **1988** Fulghum *All I Really Need* 178 **TX,** Ever come out after work to find your . . battery's dead but you're parked on a hill and you let your old hoopy roll and it fires the first time you pop the clutch?

hoorah See **hurrah**

hooraw, hooray See **hurrah**

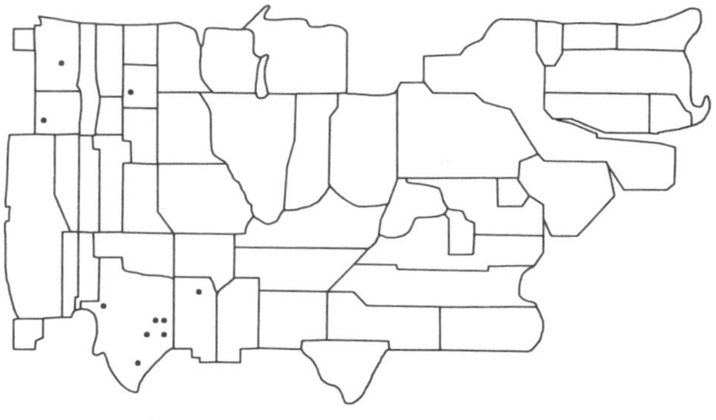

•hoopy n^2 + var (Qu N5)

hooroosh See **huroosh**

hoose See **house**

hoosegow n Also *hoosegaw, hoosgow* Pronc-spp *hoosecow, hoozegow, housgow, housegau* [Span *juzgado* tribunal, court of justice]

1 also *hoosegarden;* abbr *hoose:* A jail or prison; a court house. **orig SW; now widespread** Cf **calaboose**

1909 *NY Eve. Jrl.* (NY) 27 Aug 10 *(Zwilling Coll.),* [In cartoon:] I sentence you to 10 years in the hoozegow breaking rock. **1921** *DN* 5.113 **CA,** *Hoosegaw,* or *hoosegow*. . . A jail, or a prison. Slang. 'They chucked him in the hoosegow.' . . Spanish American, then army usage, then general. **1925** *AmSp* 1.151 [Westernisms], Of interest . . are the words . . originating either in the underworld or in that between-land where the lives of the buffetted seasonal laborer and of the hi-jack meet and mingle. . . men are "vagged" (arrested for vagrancy) by the "harness-bull" . . who . . take[s] them off to the "hoosgow" (jail). **1927** *DN* 5.451 [Underworld jargon], *Hoosgow*. . . A country jail. **1928** French *Ranchman NM* 180 (as of 1888), The latter . . told us that M. had been arrested for perjury and taken to the Housegau. . . He came down with us to the Housegau, an adobe building with a very high wall enclosing a sort of corral at the back. **1932** Bentley *Spanish Terms* 152, *Juzgado* English modification *jusgado, hoosegow* . . *English,* ['huz: ga:u] *or* [hu:z 'ga:u] The past participle of *juzgar* "to judge." A court of justice; a jail; a prison. **1950** *WELS* (*Nicknames for a . . jail*) 26 Infs, **WI,** Hoos(e)gow; 1 Inf, Housgow; 2 Infs, Hoosecow. **1962** Atwood *Vocab. TX* 71, *Local prison*. . . The most prevalent [response] is *calaboose* . . followed by *hoosegow*. . . *Hoosegow* . . is most frequent in Southwest and South Central Texas; it is rare outside the borders of the state. **1965–70** *DARE* (Qu. V11, . . *Joking names . . for a county or city jail*) 265 Infs, **widespread,** Hoosegow; **KS**5, Hoosegarden; **SC**29, Hoose [hus]—county [FW: Inf unsure], calaboose—city. **1981** *KS Qrly.* 13.2.68, *Hoosegow* . . in Paradise Valley, the county jail in Winnemucca [Nevada].

2 An outhouse or restroom. Cf **courthouse 2**

1931 *AmSp* 7.22 **wMT, wWY,** *Hoosegow*—comfort station. **1968** *DARE* (Qu. M21b, *Joking names for an outside toilet building*) Inf **CA**87, Hoosecow ['huzkaʊ].

hoosh exclam [Cf *EDD hoosh int.* 1 "A cry used to scare or drive away fowls, pigs, &c."; *Ger husch* shoo] Cf **hurry** v **1**

Used to drive away var animals; see quot.

1967–70 *DARE* (Qu. NN22a, *Expressions . . to drive away . . flies*) Inf **OH**24, Hoosh; (Qu. NN22d, *Expressions . . to drive away animals other than dogs*) Inf **MA**58, Hoosh (for a hog).

Hoosher bait See **Hoosier cake**

hoosier n, v Usu |'huʒə(r)|; also freq |'huǰə(r)|; for addit varr see **A** below Also *hoogie, hoojy;* pronc-spp *hoo(d)ger, hoojer, hooshier, hooshur;* for addit varr see quots

A Forms.

1831 in 1919 Dunn *Indiana* 2.1154 **IN,** May be called a 'Hoosher.' **1840** *Crockett Almanac* II/I *(DAE),* Luke had got married to one of them cornfed Conneticut Hooshur gals, that you'll see sot a-straddled on every fence in Ohio. **1846** Farnham *Life in Prairie Land* 19 **IN,** We don't know how these Hooshiers will receive any civilities to which they are not accustomed. **1927** *AmSp* 3.111 **ME** [illegible], A "hoojee." **1941** in 1944 *ADD* **VA, WV,** *Mountain hoojy*. . . ['hudʒi]. . . by whites and Negroes. **1941** *Hall Coll.* **neTN,** Hoosiers . . ['hudʒɚz]. . . in town, they speak of "country hoodgers" or "mountain hoodgers". **1967–70** *DARE* (Qu. HH1) Infs **GA**77, **SC**32, 39, ['hujǝ˞]; **SC**31, Hoosier ['hužjǝ˞]; **SC**34, ['hujǝ]; **VA**42, ['hujjǝ]; **LA**25, ['hužɨ]. **c1970** Pederson *Dial. Surv. Rural GA,* 1 inf, **seGA,** ['hʊudʒɜz]. [Inf Black] **1980** *AmSp* 55.202 **csTN,** Cumberland mountaineers were called /hužǝrz/, not /hujǝrz/, by the Middle Tennessee valley people. **1980** *Bluegrass Unlimited* 15.2.50/3 **wNC,** An old country hooger.

B As noun.

1a occas cap; also attrib; also in var combs, esp *country hoosier, mountain ~:* A hillbilly or rustic; an unmannerly or objectionable person. **chiefly Sth, S Midl** *often derog* Cf **cracker 2, farmer 1**

1840 [see A above]. **1846** (1941) Gregg *Diary* 1.212 **MO,** Old King is one of the most perfect samples of a Hoosier Texan I have met with. Fat, chubby, ignorant, and loquacious as Sancho Panza. . . we could believe nothing he said. **1857** in 1907 Godkin *Life* 1.157, A captain . . has great skill . . in distinguishing . . the man who is "some pumpkins" from the mere "cracker" or "hoosier," as the poor [southern] whites are termed. **1927** *AmSp* 3.141 **ME coast,** Why is a tramp who is dirty or terrifying a "hoojee" (surely not from Huguenot)? **1941** in 1944 *ADD* **VA, WV,** *Mountain hoojy.* A hillbilly. . . Reported used in V[irgini]a . . by whites and Negroes. **1941** *Hall Coll.* **neTN,** Hoosiers—people speak of goddamn ['hudʒǝ˞z], a damn feller . . who don't know nothin' except what they've [sic] learned in the mountains. In town, they speak of "country hoodgers" or "mountain hoodgers". . . in North Carolina they speak of "Tennessee Hoosiers"; in Tennessee they speak of "North Carolina Hoosiers". **1942** Berrey–Van den Bark *Amer. Slang* 45.3, *Small country town; "hick" town.* . . hoosier town. **1948** Sandburg *Remembrance* 765 **IL** (as of c1850), Zadock was what the people . . who had come from the Eastern states . . called a "Hoosier," meaning they had come up from Kentucky and Tennessee. **1948** Dick *Dixie Frontier* 24, The first homemakers . . [were] the squatters. . . The name "Hoosier" was often applied to these backwoodsmen even as far south as northern Louisiana and southern Arkansas. *Ibid* 310, The language . . came from the uplanders and. . . was brought into southern Ohio, Indiana, and Illinois and known there as Hoosier dialect. **1966–70** *DARE* (Qu. HH1, . . *Nicknames for a rustic or countrified person*) 23 Infs, **scattered, but esp Missip Valley,** Hoosier; **LA**46, Hoosier—somebody who wears high boots with his pants rolled above them [FW: Inf says this is not a definition, but an example of . . a rustic, countrified person]; **IN**39, Hoosier means hillbilly; **IN**60, Hoosier [FW: Inf protests use of this term]; **MO**6, 9, Hoosier [FW sugg]; **MO**15, Hoosier [FW: Inf has heard occas]; **MO**10, We use "hillbilly" more than "hoosier"; **SC**32, Hoosier—not frequent; **LA**25, ['hužɨ]; **IL**50, Backwoods person, hoosier—from Indiana, boob; **GA**77, Mountain ['hujǝ˞]; **NC**55, Mountain hoosier; **SC**31, Mountain hoosier ['hužjǝ˞]—not insulting; **SC**32, Mountain ['hujǝ˞]—not complimentary; **SC**34, Mountain ['hujǝ]—unkempt, raised back up in the mountains and stays there mostly; **SC**39, Mountain ['hujǝ˞]; **TN**30, Mountain hoosier [FW: this is applied to people from Georgia, Alabama, Mississippi, West Tennessee, etc]; **VA**42, Mountain ['hujjǝ] [FW: Inf used in conv]; **LA**40, **MS**6, 71, **MO**4, (Old) country hoosier; **MO**9, Arkansas hoosier; **IN**68, Dumb hoosier. **1980** *AmSp* 55.199 **Gulf States,** A *rustic.* . . Arkansas hoosier (2 [infs]) . . backwoods hoosier . . Carolina hoosier . . country hoosier (32 [infs]) . . hoogie (3 [infs]) . . hoosier (73 [infs]) . . mountain hoosier (28 [infs]) . . nasty hoosier . . old country hoosier. **1980** *Bluegrass Unlimited* 15.2.50/3 **wNC,** I thought if you got out of North Carolina or Virginia that you were out of the world. Being an old country hooger, I never got to know the modern generation.

b Spec: a White person considered to be objectionable, esp because of racial prejudice. **Sth, S Midl** *among Black speakers; derog* Cf **honky 1**

c1970 Pederson *Dial. Surv. Rural GA (Suppose you [=a Black person] were angry with . . [a White person] and wanted to call the person something insulting, what could you say?)* 1 inf, **seGA,** ['hʊudʒɜz]. [Inf Black] **1974** *NYT Book Rev.* 22 Sept 18/1, Colorful white Southerners that Paul Hemphill eulogizes as the Good Old Boys are likely to be nobody but the same old all too familiar hateful-eyed, razor-backed, lynch-mob-prone, willfully backward, hysterically insecure but undeniably gritty peckerwoods . . crackers . . hoojers and swamp folks once thought to be the primary antagonists of Civil Rights. **1986** Pederson *LAGS Concordance* **AL, GA, MS, TN,** [*Hoosier* is described by two infs as a pejorative for Whites, and defined variously as referring to "honkies . . a sorry white man . . a nasty white person." All infs who use the term *hoosier* explicitly in reference to a White person are Black.] **1988** Lincoln *Avenue* 176 **wNC** (as of c1940) [Black], All them rednecks an' hoogies what come into town . . well, they wasn't 'bout to go home 'til some po' nigger had been made to suffer for their inconvenience and disappointment. . . some nigger or other was bound to pay for their comin' out of the woods an' off them clay patches. *Ibid,* Vernon [=a Black man]. . . didn't set 'round on his tail . . waitin' for them hoogies to come an' lynch him on no tree or pour gas on him an' set him afire. [**1988** *AmSp* 63.134 **TN** [Prison talk], *Hoojie* . . White inmate (used by black inmates).]

2 Among those skilled in a particular field, esp logging: an inexperienced or incompetent person. Cf **buckeye** n **4, farmer 2**

1874 Long *Amer. Wild-Fowl* 144, "Greenhorns" and "hoosiers," as the regular hunters call such fellows. **1927** *DN* 5.451 [Underworld jargon], *Hoosier.* . . An incompetent workman or tramp. **1930** Williams *Logger-Talk* 25 **Pacific NW,** *Hoosier:* Another fighting word with the same connotation as *farmer.* **1937** *Amer. Forests* 43.242 **swWA,** [From] the back counties of Indiana . . presently there came to Cosmopolis a horde of Hoosier farm hands, few of whom had ever seen a sawmill. . . And their efforts to engage in a strange industry were such as to bring the term *hoosier* into use to designate a man who doesn't know his job. **1942** Berrey–Van den Bark *Amer. Slang* 509.19, Hoosier fiend . . *an inexperienced addict.* *Ibid* 786.3, *Inexperienced seaman.* . . hoosier. **1958** McCulloch *Woods Words* 89 **Pacific NW,** *Hoosier.* . . A green man in the woods. **1968** Adams *Western Words* 153, *Hoosier*—A logger's term for a greenhorn. . . *Hoosier* meant first a logger who did not know his trade, then one who could never master the necessary skills, and finally one who regularly slights his job.

3 See **Hoosier cabinet.**

4 =**flathead catfish 1.**

1933 LA Dept. of Conserv. *Fishes* 424, Popularly termed in the northern part of its range the Hoosier, the Yellow Cat is commonly caught on a wide variety of baits. **1983** Becker *Fishes WI* 728, *Flathead Catfish.* . . Other common names: . . Hoosier.

C As verb.

1 with *it:* See quot. **[hoosier B1]**

1942 Berrey–Van den Bark *Amer. Slang* 147.4, Hoosier it, *to be a farmer.*

2 usu with *up;* Of a worker, esp a logger: to work incompetently; to slow down or shirk on a job, usu on purpose; see quots. **[hoosier B2]**

1926 *Amer. Mercury* 7.25.64, When a crew of workmen purposely *hoosier up* on the company, it means . . a "conscious withdrawal of efficiency." **1941** *AmSp* 16.233 [Loggers' talk], *Hoosier up.* To frame up [a] plot for slowing down work. **1956** Sorden–Ebert *Logger's Words* 19 **Gt Lakes,** *Hoosier up.* . . To slow work purposely or botch up a job. **1958** McCulloch *Woods Words* 89 **Pacific NW,** *Hoosier.* . . To louse up the job.

3 with *up:* To play tricks or take sides (against someone or something); to **badmouth.**

1941 *AmSp* 16.233 [Loggers' talk], *Hoosier up.* . . To gang up on someone or against something. **1958** McCulloch *Woods Words* 89 **Pacific NW,** *Hoosier up*—To play jokes on a green logger. **1968** Adams *Western Words* 153, *Hoosier up.* . . To malign.

Hoosier bait See **Hoosier cake**

Hoosier banana See **banana B1**

Hoosier cabinet n Also *Hoosier (kitchen cabinet)* [See quot 1905] *old-fash* Cf **Hoover** n **3**

A type of kitchen cabinet; see quot 1988.

[**1905** U.S. Patent Office *Official Gaz.* 117.242/1, *Kitchen-Cabinets.* The Hoosier Manufacturing Company, New Castle, Ind.] **1910** in 1983 Swedberg-Swedberg *Country Pine Furniture* 56 **IN,** [Newspaper advt:] Wife needs a helper with the work; you can't get a good girl; you've tried it; listen, here's a secret: it's just like play with a / *Hoosier Kitchen Cabinet / You don't* have to feed it, or house it, or teach it, or wage it or beau it. The Hoosier is it. **1967** *DARE* (Qu. D9, *To prevent bread and cake from drying, you put them in a* ______) Inf **CA**19, Hoosier cabinet—bottom space lined with zinc. [FW: a kitchen cupboard, not built in, with the flour sifter, a work surface, etc.] **1986** Pederson *LAGS Concordance,* 1 inf, **ceTX,** Hoosier cabinet. **1988** *DARE* File **csWI,** The Hoosier cabinet was popular back in the 1920s and 30s. It was a kitchen work cupboard usually made of oak, but some were all metal. It had a pullout work surface, a built-in flour bin, and drawers above for baking soda and your spices. It was called a "Hoosier cabinet" because the original manufacturer was the Hoosier company—it was a tradename.

But other companies made Hoosier cabinets, one was The Sterling Company. **1989** *DARE* File **ceWI,** When we moved from West Bend to Plymouth in 1922, my mother took her Hoosier cabinet along. It was a tall cabinet for the kitchen, with bins and drawers and storage. Ours also had a zinc-topped, pull-out 'shelf' which could be used for rolling out pie crust. My mother had her Hoosier cabinet until about 1950.

Hoosier cake n Also *Hoosier bait;* pronc-sp *Hoosher bait* [*Hoosier* one from Indiana] *arch* Cf **horse cake**

A kind of gingerbread; see quots.

1833 in 1919 Dunn *Indiana* 2.1127, My pockets are so shrunk of late / I can not nibble "Hoosher bait." **1859** (1968) Bartlett *Americanisms* 202, *Hoosier Cake.* A Western name for a sort of coarse gingerbread, which, say the Kentuckians, is the best bait to catch a hoosier with, the biped being fond of it. **1919** Dunn *Indiana* 2.1141 **OH** (as of 1830), The man said, 'I guess you want hoosier-bait,' and when he produced it I found that he had the right idea. . . The gingerbread referred to was cooked in square pans—about fifteen inches across.

Hoosier frog n

1 =**mink frog.** Note: The frog is not found in Indiana.

1883 *Amer. Naturalist* 17.945, *The Mink or Hoosier Frog. . .* This frog *(Rana septentrionalis)* seems comparatively unknown, and is found in localities far apart. . . Why it was termed "hoosier frog" I do not know.

2 A subsp of the **gopher frog** (here: *Rana areolata circulosa*).

1892 IN Dept. Geol. & Nat. Resources *Rept. for 1891* 476, *Rana areolata circulosa. . . Hoosier Frog. . .* The striking thing about these frogs is their coloration. The spots . . have . . become so expanded that they cover nearly the whole area. . . Found in northern portions of Indiana and Illinois.

hoosier it See **hoosier C1**

Hoosier kitchen cabinet See **Hoosier cabinet**

Hoosier salamander n

A cave **salamander** (here: *Eurycea lucifuga*).

1892 IN Dept. Geol. & Nat. Resources *Rept. for 1891* 447, *Hoosier Salamander. . .* They are extremely active, and when pursued, escape with great rapidity.

hoosier up See **hoosier C2, 3**

hoot v

1 See quot.

1954 *Harder Coll.* **cwTN,** *Hoot*—to talk too much, or obnoxiously. "He went'n hooted all 'bout the trouble he's been a-havin'."

2 with *on:* To incite.

1970 *DARE* (Qu. Y5, . . *To urge somebody to do something he shouldn't: "Johnny wouldn't have tried that if the other boys hadn't ________.*") Inf **MS**86, Hooted him on.

3 To cough; see quot.

1967–70 *DARE* (Qu. BB11, *Speaking of a deep cough that you can't seem to get rid of: "Listen to him ________.*") Infs **MS**80, **MO**12, **NY**80, **WV**18, Hoot; **NC**61, Hoot [FW sugg].

4 vbl n *hooting:* A type of musical call or way of calling; see quot. Cf **holler** v **B1**

1978 Wolfe *I'm On My Journey Home* 1/4, [Liner notes:] Hollering should . . be distinguished from hooting, a related falsetto style in which the mouth cavity is more strictly controlled and tunes can more readily be executed.

hoot n[1]

1 also *hooter:* A drink or measure of liquor. [Cf *EDD hooter* sb.[2] "A cone-shaped tin vessel used for heating beer"] Cf **hoozle**

1899 (1912) Green *VA Folk-Speech* 230, *Hooter. . .* A dram; a drink; from a tin cup from which the drink was taken. **1938** Stuart *Dark Hills* 247, I'll faze him. You give me two hoots of corn licker. **1968** *DARE* (Qu. DD18, *A drink of liquor, or the amount of liquor taken in one swallow: "He took a good ________.*") Inf **PA**104, Hoot [Inf queries].

2 See quot. [Perh infl by *coot* a codger]

1954 *Harder Coll.* **cwTN,** *Hoot*—uncomplimentary for an old man, usually prefaced with *old.*

3 See quot.

1897 *KS Univ. Qrly.* (ser B) 6.54, *Hoot. . .* a peep; as, I have taken a hoot at Harper's Weekly.

4 also *hooter:* An indefinite distance—often in phr *hoot and a holler* and varr. [*hoot* a sound; a very small amount] Cf **holler** n[1] **C3, hollering distance**

1903 *DN* 2.351, *Hoot. . .* In expression 'two hoots and a look,' for a long distance. Cf. two hoots and a holler. **1942** Berrey–Van den Bark *Amer. Slang* 40.3, *Short distance. . .* hoot, hooter. **1967–69** *DARE* (Qu. MM24, . . *Expressions meaning 'a short distance': "The river is just a ________ from the house."*) Infs **IN**35, **NY**22, **RI**6, **TX**1, **VA**21, **WA**28, Hoot and (a) holler. **1985** Ladwig *How to Talk Dirty* 39 **Ozarks,** The general store is just a hoot and a holler away.

Hoot n[2] [Jakob *Hutter* or *Huter* founder of an Anabaptist sect]

1978 Doig *This House* 195 **MT** (as of c1955), "These fellows are Hoots," he grinned. "They're our neighbors." . . To the south . . lay a ranch colony of a hundred such Hutterites, a shy tranced people who gabbled among themselves in a German dialect and lived barracks-style according to their signals from God. *Ibid* 197, Hoot youngsters were flocking in to gawk at. . . television.

hootamaganzy n [Joc var of **hooded merganser**]

1923 U.S. Dept. Ag. *Misc. Circular* 13.7 **OH,** *Hooded Merganser (Lophodytes cucullatus.) . . In local use. . .* hootamaganzy.

hoot and a holler, hoot and a look See **hoot** n[1] **4**

hoot-and-holler n

1 See quot. Cf **holiness** n

1969 *DARE* (Qu. CC4, . . *Nicknames . . for various religions or religious groups*) Inf **KY**11, Hoot-and-hollers—Holy Rollers.

2 See quot.

1968 *DARE* (Qu. C33, . . *Joking names . . for an out-of-the-way place, or a very unimportant place*) Inf **VA**2, Hoot-and-holler; (Qu. C34) Inf **VA**2, Hoot-and-holler.

hootch n[1] See **hooch** n[1] **1**

hootch n[2] Also *hootchy, hootchelly, hutchy, hutsch(l)i* [PaGer *hutsch, hutschli*] **PaGer area** Cf **hommie, hommilie**

A foal, colt; a pony.

1907 *German Amer. Annals* 9.379 **sePA,** *Hootch* or *hootchy.* Colt. "There's the old mare and the hootchy." . . fr. Pa. Ger. *hutschli,* an imitative word. **1939** Aurand *Quaint Idioms* 16 [PaGer], The neighbor has a nice new *hootchelly* (colt); he has such skinny legs and jumps funny. **1940–41** Cassidy *WI Atlas,* ['huči]—Ohio word for colt. **1942** Warnick *Garrett Co. MD* **nwMD** (as of 1900–1918), *Hutchy. . .* a colt (from Pennsylvania Dutch hutsch). **1968** *Helen Adolf Festschrift* 36, *Hutschi* (or *hutschli*)—This word, used mostly by children in the area [=Pennsylvania German area] for 'a little horse' or 'pony,' is a direct borrowing from the Pennsylvania German dialect word for a foal or colt. **1968** *DARE* FW Addit **VA**31, *Hutchy*—a new-born colt. **1987** *Jrl. Engl. Ling.* 20.2.170 **ePA,** The three informants who responded with the term [=*hutsch(l)i*] are all Mennonites and speakers of Pennsylvania German. When confronted with the word, five other informants said that they have heard it, but these individuals are, with one exception, over 65. The exception was a 20-year-old female who recalled her great-grandmother's using the expression.

hootchelly See **hootch** n[2]

hootchenoo, hootchino(o) See **hoochinoo**

hootchy n[1] See **hootch** n[2]

hootchy n[2] Cf **hoodle** n[1]

1967 *DARE* (Qu. EE6b, *Small marbles or marbles in general*) Inf **MO**5, Hootchies.

hootenanny n Also *hoot(e)naddy, hooznannie* Also sp *hoot(e)nannie, hootnanny*

1 A **dingus** n[1] **1;** an imaginary object.

1930s in 1944 *ADD* **eWV,** *Hootenanny. . . hootnaddy . .* a dingus. Common. Also *hootenaddy.* **1931** *AmSp* 6.258 [Indefinite names], *Hootenannie, hootnannie, hooznannie.* **1941** in 1944 *ADD* **WV,** Hootenanny = dingus. **1949** *PADS* 11.7 **wTX** (as of c1920), *Hootenanny. . .* A word used to designate an article for which no name is known. Occasional. **1950** *WELS (Things people say to put a child off)* 1 Inf, **WI,** Hootenanny for a sky wampus. **1967–70** *DARE* (Qu. NN12b) Infs **CA**105, **KS**5, A hootenanny; **CA**211, A hootenanny on a shindig; **PA**136, A hickey for a hootenanny. [All Infs old] **1969** Sorden *Lumberjack Lingo* 57, *Hoot nanny. . .* A nickname for almost any implement or gadget whose name you do not know. Also called canepas, canepus, kniepus.

2 Any of various tools, appliances, or contrivances, as:

a A device making it possible to saw from under a log.

1938 (1939) Holbrook *Holy Mackinaw* 262, *Hoot-nanny.* A small device used to hold a crosscut saw while sawing a log from underneath. **1958** McCulloch *Woods Words* 89 **Pacific NW,** *Hoot-nanny*—An undercutter, a kind of bracket to support the back side of the saw while cutting a log from the under side.

b A jig for sharpening shears to the correct angle.

1964 Jackman-Long *OR Desert* 145, A good [sheep] shearer... had a frame to hold shears at exactly the right angle when sharpening them on a grindstone. It was called a "hootnanny."

c =hitching weight.

1968 *DARE* FW Addit **swVA,** *Hootenanny*—attached to the bridle [of a horse] by a chain. Weighed up to 18 pounds; used only in towns and cities. Also called hitching iron and hitching block.

d A kind of sleigh.

1968 *DARE* (Qu. N40c, .. *Sleighs for carrying other things*) Inf **MI**76, Hootenanny—loggers.

3 Fig: used as a disparaging epithet; see quots.

1939 *Sat. Eve. Post* 25 Nov 64/3 **Sth,** I be nothing but a big old fat hootnanny. **1941** in 1944 *ADD,* [Radio:] *Hootenanny...* That horse-faced old hootenanny. **1960** Williams *Walk Egypt* 178 **GA,** Wick found you some niggers. He says come-see if they suit you... [The woman is an] ole black hootnanny... Looks like she could wrestle your ma past Monday.

4 Something insignificant; a damn; nonsense. [*hoot* n a very small amount]

1960 Wentworth-Flexner *Slang* 269, *Hootenanny...* Fig., a shout, a hoot, a damn. *Usu. in "I don't give a hootnanny" = I don't give a damn, I don't care.* **1968-69** *DARE* (Qu. GG21b, *If you don't care what a person does, you might say, "Go ahead—I don't give a ______."*) Infs **TX**51, **UT**8, Hootenanny; **AZ**15, Hootenanny what you do; (Qu. NN13, *When you think that the thing somebody has just said is silly or untrue: "Oh, that's a lot of ______."*) Inf **DE**1, Hootenanny.

5 also *hootin' Annie:* See quot. Cf *DS* N37

1950 *WELS (A train that stops at every station)* 2 Infs, **WI,** Hootnanny; 1 Inf, Hootin' Annie.

hootenkack v [Cf **hoot v 2, cack** v^2]

1949 *PADS* 11.23 **CO,** *Hootenkack...* To talk someone into something he doesn't want to do. "Don't hootenkack me. I'm not taking you for a walk."

hootentrankis n

=hootenanny 1.

1944 *PADS* 2.29 **eKY,** *Hootentrankis...* A queer little fixture of some kind. "What's this little hootentrankis down on the steering wheel for?"... Rare.

hooter n

1 =dusky grouse. [See quot 1940] **Pacific** Cf **blue hooter**

1909 Denny *Blazing the Way* 301 **cwWA** (as of 1860s), Late one May evening he came into the old kitchen, laden with charming spoils from the forest, .. a bag of fat "hooters" for the stew or pie so much relished by the settlers. **1923** Dawson *Birds CA* 1592. **1940** Gabrielson *Birds OR* 210, The Sooty Grouse, or "Hooter"... is still a fairly common resident of the wooded areas... The low-pitched *hoot-hoot-hoot,* repeated from four to six times .. [is] audible for amazing distances. **1953** Jewett *Birds WA* 196, The Oregon blue grouse, or hooter, is one of the best-known game birds in the state. **1958** McCulloch *Woods Words* 89 **Pacific NW,** *Hooter*—A male grouse.

2 See **hoot owl n 1.**

3 A tourist.

1941 *LANE* Map 449 **ceVT,** Hooter, usual term for a tourist .. [1 inf].

4 See quot.

1966 *DARE* (Qu. O14b, .. *Different kinds of buoys*) Inf **FL**35, Hooter—whistle buoy.

5 See quot.

1967 *DARE* (Qu. M21b, *Joking names for an outside toilet building*) Inf **WA**23, Hooter—in Idaho.

6 See **hoot** n^1 **1.**

7 See **hoot** n^1 **4.**

hooterville (trolley) n Cf **hootenanny 5, Toonerville trolley**

1968-69 *DARE* (Qu. N37, *Joking names for a branch railroad that is not very important or gives poor service*) Inf **KY**6, Hooterville—a passenger car, a freight car, and a baggage car, engine and caboose; **NY**109, Hooterville trolley.

hootin' Annie See **hootenanny 5**

hooting See **hoot v 4**

hooting owl See **hoot owl n 1**

hootnaddy, hootnannie, hootnanny See **hootenanny**

hoot on See **hoot v 2**

hoot owl n

1 also *hooter, hooting owl, hooty* ~: Any of var owls, such as the barred owl or the **great horned owl.**

1881 *Harper's New Mth. Mag.* 63.693/1, **neNY,** A hoot-owl, sitting unseen above our heads, startles us with a derisive Hu-hu-hu-whoo-oo-oo! **1898** (1900) Davie *Nests N. Amer. Birds* 241, *Great Horned Owl...* It is known as the Hoot or Cat Owl, or "Hooter." **1899** Howe-Sturtevant *Birds RI* 61, Barred Owl. Hoot Owl. **1906** *DN* 3.119 **sIN,** *Hoot-owl...* The screech owl. **1909** *DN* 3.398 **nwAR,** *Hoot-owl...* Screech owl. **1950** *PADS* 14.38 **SC,** *Hoot owl...* The great horned owl; the Florida barred owl. **1960** *PADS* 34.62 **CO,** Hoot owl. **1962** Imhof *AL Birds* 303, *Barn Owl. Tyto alba... Other Names:* Monkey-faced Owl, White Owl, Hoot Owl. **1964** *PADS* 42.19 **KY,** *Hoot owl.* Any large owl. **1965-70** *DARE* (Qu. Q2) 578 Infs, **widespread,** Hoot (owl); **IL**9, **NY**233, **VA**75, Hooter; 29 Infs, **Sth, S Midl,** Hootin' owl; **OK**13, **SC**4, **VA**70, Hooting owl; **CT**13, **IL**17, **IN**45, **MA**78, **MS**16, **WY**1, Hooty owl; (Qu. Q1) 184 Infs, **widespread,** Hoot owl; **MI**67, Little hoot owl; **ND**3, Hooting owl.

2 A late night or early morning working period—usu in phr *hoot owl shift;* one who works such a shift.

1958 McCulloch *Woods Words* 89 **Pacific NW,** *Hoot owl shift*—Any early morning job. **1967** *DARE* File **cnOK,** *Hoot owl*—a night shift, or a person who works a night shift. "He's working hoot owl this week." "He's on hoot owl this week." "What shift are you on? Hoot owl." Used by skilled and unskilled laborers and families. **1977** Jones *OR Folkl.* 101/2, *Hoot owl shift:* shift or period before dawn, lumbering (1947).

hoot owl v phr [**hoot owl n 2**]

1958 McCulloch *Woods Words* 89 **Pacific NW,** *Hoot owl*—To begin work early in the morning, as near daylight as possible, in order to get in a day's work before having to close down for low humidity during the heat of the day.

hoot owl shift See **hoot owl n 2**

hootsle n See **hutzel n**

hootsle adj See **hutzel adj**

hootycackle for a ramshackle to make a sham go round n Cf **hootenanny 1**

=cat's fur to make kitten britches.

1968 *DARE* (Qu. NN12a, *Things that people say to put a child off when he asks too many questions: "What's that for?"*) Inf **PA**165, A hootycackle for a ramshackle to make a sham go round.

hooty owl See **hoot owl n 1**

Hoover n [Herbert *Hoover* US President 1929-33 during the Great Depression]

1 attrib: Associated with the Great Depression or hard times generally; cheap, makeshift; spec:

a *Hoover buggy, ~ cart, ~ wagon:* A horse-drawn vehicle made with parts from an old car; see quots.

1938 FWP *Guide MS* 18, At ten o'clock we are still arriving, in cars, in school busses, in wagons, and a few in "Hoover carts"—an ingeniously contrived two-wheel, automobile-tired lolly brought into prominence by the depression. *Ibid* 490, Between Waynesboro and Lucedale economic and social development has been slower, perhaps, than in any other part of the State... Ox teams, hoover-carts, wooden wash troughs, and bare feet are often seen. **1965-70** *DARE* (Qu. L13, *The kind of wagon used for carrying hay*) Inf **ID**3, Hoover wagon—made from running gears [sic] of an old car; **MS**58, Hoover wagons—steel-tired wagon; (Qu. L57, *A low wooden platform used for bringing stones or heavy things out of the fields*) Inf **AL**2, A Hoover wagon is an old car frame with everything but wheels and couplings made into a horse-drawn vehicle; **MS**66, Hoover wagon; (Qu. N41a, .. *Horse-drawn vehicles .. to carry people*) Inf **GA**40, ['hubə] buggy; **GA**63, Hoover wagon; **NC**6, Hoover buggies; **NC**16, Hoover carts; (Qu. N41c, *Horse-drawn vehicles to carry light* *loads*) Inf **AL**17, Hoover (cut-off) wagon—two wheeled cart from Fords, no gas, took wheels and made a cart; **SC**31, Hoover buggy—put shafts to two front wheels of a T-model; **SC**32, Hoover buggy; **SC**40, Hoover buggy—two wheels, rear end from a car with a body built on it pulled by one mule. **1967** *DARE* FW Addit **SC,** Hoover buggy—a two wheeled cart made from a car, the back end of T-model. Put shafts to it and a seat. **1968** *Sat. Eve. Post* 15 June 63/1 **AL** (as of 1930s), We would break yearling calves . . and then hitch them up to what we called a Hoover cart, something we made out of Model-T rims with a kind of oxen yoke that we made out of poplar trees and pipes.

b *Hoover dust:* A cheap grade of tobacco; hence *Hoover* a cigarette. Cf **dust** n[1] **3**

1939 *AmSp* 14.91 **eTN,** *Hoover dust.* Cheap sacked tobacco. 'He's smoking Hoover dust.' **1952** Callahan *Smoky Mt.* 170 **eTN, wNC,** Symbolic of the Depression days was a cheap smoking tobacco used in the region and known as "Hoover Dust." Its quality was not the highest but it was the best a lot of the boys could afford, and they rolled their cigarettes from it whereas formerly they had reveled in "ready rolls." **1966** *DARE* (Qu. DD6b, *Nicknames for cigarettes*) Inf **MS**6, Hoover. **1967** *DARE* File **SC** (as of 1930s), Hoover dust—same as Bull Durham cigarette tobacco. **1970** *Thompson Coll.* **cnAL** (as of 1930s), Hoover dust—A cheap granulated tobacco, especially Golden Grain brand. Used mostly for smoking in "roll-yer-owns", also chewed. **1984** Wilder *You All Spoken Here* 194 **Sth,** Hoover dust: Smoking tobacco for roll-your-owns produced by the simple procedure of crushing cured leaves of scrap tobacco in one's hands. The name came from President Herbert Clark Hoover, then in office.

c also *Hoover's;* in var combs referring to food: See quots.

1940 *AmSp* 15.447 **eTN,** *Hoover hog.* Rabbit. 'We had Hoover hog for breakfast.' **1940** Brown *Amer. Cooks* 798 **TX,** During the depression, food got so scarce in some places along the Mex-Tex border that the unemployed took to eating that flavorsome little hard-shelled pig, the armadillo. . . With typical Texan frankness, they dubbed the delicacy "Hoover hog." **1945** Mathews *Talking Moon* 6 **KS,** He might resort to eating "Hoover hogs," which was the name given to rabbits by the valley farmers. **1947** *McDavid Coll.* **cnSC,** *Hoover's ham*—salt pork. **1953** Randolph-Wilson *Down in Holler* 254 **Ozarks,** Hoover pork. . . Rabbit meat. . . many families could get no meat except rabbits. **1954** *Harder Coll.* **cwTN,** Hoover gravy . . made with fat, flour, and milk. Everything bad in my part of Tennessee during the early 1930s was ol' Hoover this and ol' Hoover that. *Ibid* **cwTN,** *Hoover pork.* . . Sowbelly. **1961** *McDavid Coll.* **swOK,** *Hoover beans*—pintos & blackeyed peas. **1966-70** *DARE* (Qu. H37, . . *Gravy*) Inf **AL**15, Hoover gravy—thick. During Hoover days, not much else to eat; **AR**17, Hoover gravy—thickened gravy; (Qu. P1, . . *Kinds of freshwater fish . . that are good to eat*) Inf **VA**38, Hoover cat—same as catfish; (Qu. P30, *Wild rabbits*) Inf **AL**2, Hoover hog. **1968** *DARE* FW Addit **LA,** An armadillo came to be called a Hoover hog in East Texas during the Depression. **1972** *DARE* File **nwFL,** Land turtle—Back in hard times, farmers called 'em Hoover steaks. **1982** Heat Moon *Blue Highways* 143 **TX,** In spite of both the belief that armadillos feed on corpses and the animal's susceptibility to leprosy, poor whites ate them with greens and cornbread during the Depression and called them "Hoover hogs" or "Texas turkeys" (on the Christmas table).

d Made by cheap or exploited labor.

1943 Korson *Coal Dust* 183, In non-union areas, however, especially in the South before 1933, operators insisted upon miners giving their loaded [coal] cars a "hump." This extra weight might have amounted to a ton or more for which the miner received no compensation. . . During the depression these extra loads were called "Hoover humps" by the miners. **1958** McCulloch *Woods Words* 89 **Pacific NW,** *Hoover holes*—Choker holes dug by hand during the depression when labor was cheaper than powder.

2 also *Hoover apron, ~ coat, ~ dress:* A coverall, uniform, or housedress with an overlapping, reversible front. [In ref to its popularity when *Hoover* served as food administrator during and after World War I] **chiefly Nth, N Midl** See Map

1946 Ward *Snake Pit* 5 **Nth,** I assume the hoover apron is always fresh and that you would not lap the clean side over the soiled side and attempt in that way to maintain a false front. **1950** *WELS (A loose, full house dress that ties at the waist)* 3 Infs, **WI,** Hoover apron; 1 Inf, Hoover apron—something like a uniform, white, starched; 1 Inf, Hoover apron—has alternate fronts, right on left, left on right; 1 Inf, Hoover apron—usually white; 1 Inf, Hoover coat; 1 Inf, Hoover dress. **1951** Johnson *Resp. to PADS 20* **DE** *(A loose, full house dress that ties at the waist)* Hoover apron. **1965-70** *DARE* (Qu. W22, . . *A loose, full housedress that ties at the waist*) Infs **CT**19, **MA**4, **NJ**33, **NY**45, **PA**134, **VT**3, **WV**16, Hoover apron; **IN**3, **KS**7, Hoover apron [FW: sugg]; **IL**43, Hoover apron—I used to wear one; **MN**33, Hoover apron—old-fashioned; **MA**5, Hoover apron—two fronts cut on slant; **WI**21, Hoover apron—open in front, lapped over in front; **NY**35, Hoover apron [FW: Inf has heard]; **NY**83, Hoover apron [corr to] wrapper; **MI**51, Hoover—the kind of dress a waitress would wear, belted around the middle, usually of plain cloth, whereas a Mother Hubbard was a print more often than it was plain; **WI**21, Hoover—not worn any more.

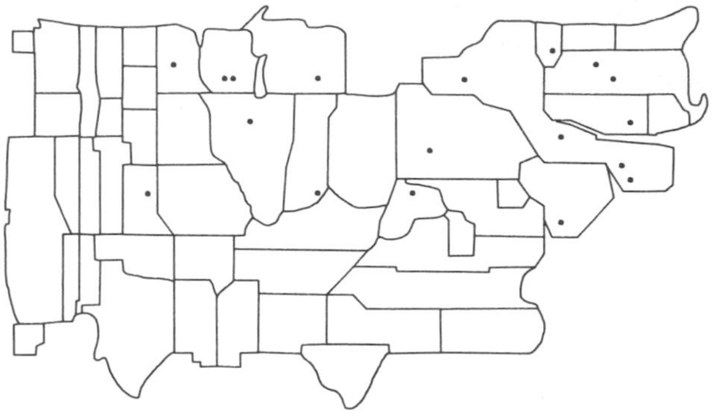

•Hoover n 2 + var (Qu. W22)

3 as *Hoover (kitchen) cabinet:* See quot 1988. [Prob for **Hoosier cabinet**]

1954 Jordan *Hell's Canyon* 42 **ID** (as of 1930s), The top drawer of our Hoover cabinet had to be sacrificed to the sink, which came flush against it, as compact as in any modern kitchen. **1988** *DARE* File **sIN** (as of c1915-40), A Hoover kitchen cabinet was a tall freestanding cabinet, usually white enameled metal, that had drawers below, a metal waist-high work surface, and shelves with doors above.

4 An outhouse. Cf **F.D.R.**

1968 *DARE* (Qu. M21b, *Joking names for an outside toilet building*) Inf UT9, Hoover [laughter]—When Hoover was president, built some on W.P.A.'s [sic].

5 See quot.

1968 *DARE* (QR, near Qu. EE41) Inf **CT**11, A Hoover—when a woman stands up and her skirt is caught up in the back.

Hoover v [Herbert *Hoover*]

1984 Doig *English Creek* 4 **nMT,** During the worst years the Forest Service did lay off some people—Hoovered them, the saying went.

Hoover apron See **Hoover n 2**

Hoover buggy See **Hoover n 1a**

Hoover cabinet See **Hoover n 3**

Hoover cart See **Hoover n 1a**

Hoover coat, Hoover dress See **Hoover n 2**

Hoover dust See **Hoover n 1b**

Hoover kitchen cabinet See **Hoover n 3**

Hoover's ham See **Hoover n 1c**

Hoover wagon See **Hoover n 1a**

hoozegow See **hoosegow**

hoozle n [Cf *OED housel* "Forms . . *husel . . hoo . . houzle.* . . 2. The consecrated elements at the Communion; the . . Eucharist"] Cf **hoot** n[1] **1**
See quot.

1919 *DN* 5.34 **seKY,** *Hoozle.* . . A drink or "swig" of liquor.

hooznannie See **hootenanny**

hop v[1]

1 To limp. [*OED hop* v[1] 3 "To limp"; 1700 →1814] **chiefly Sth, S Midl** See Map *rural* Cf **crowhop v 5**

1965-70 *DARE* (Qu. BB1, *When a person . . steps more heavily on one foot than the other*) 38 Infs, **chiefly Sth, S Midl,** Hops; (Qu. BB2) Inf TN27, Hops on. [33 of 38 Infs comm type 4 or 5]

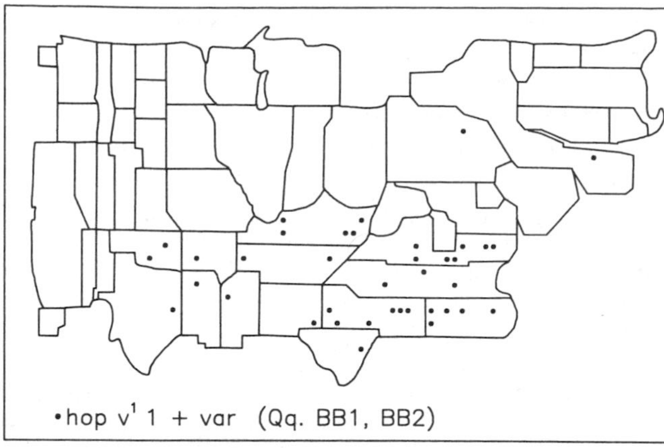
•hop v[1] 1 + var (Qq. BB1, BB2)

2 with *down:* See quot.

1931–33 *LANE Worksheets* **nwRI,** *Hop down*—crouch down.

hop v[2] See **help** v **A2a, A3a**

hop and (a) jump n [Var of *hop, step, and jump*] **esp Sth, S Midl** See Map Cf **holler** n[1] **C3**

A short distance.

1965 Carmony *Speech Terre Haute* 30 **cwIN,** *A little way(s). . . a hop and a jump* [1 of 16 infs]. **1965–70** *DARE* (Qu. MM24, . . *Expressions meaning 'a short distance': "The river is just a _____ from the house."*) 14 Infs, **esp Sth, S Midl,** Hop and a jump; **MO**37A, **VA** 75, Hop and jump; (Qu. MM4) Inf **NC**9, Hop and a jump; (Qu. MM6) Inf **GA**72, Hop and jump. [16 of 19 Infs comm type 4 or 5]

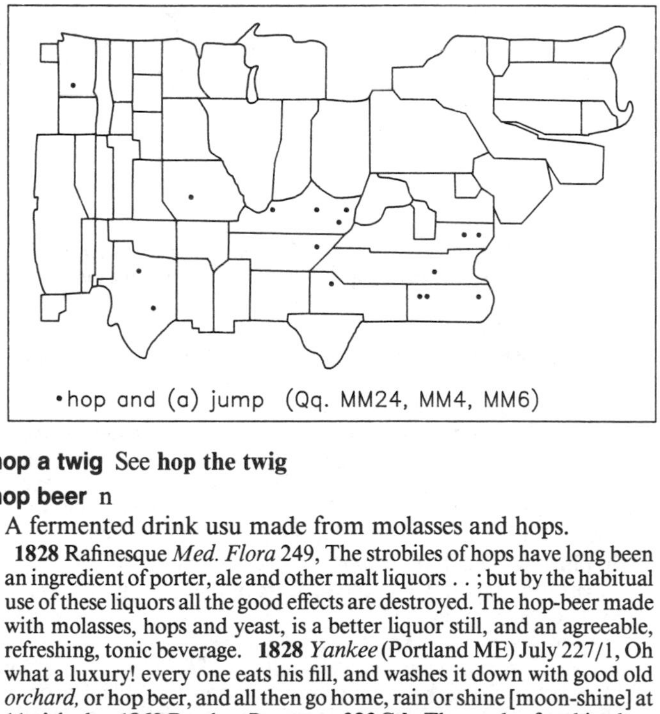
•hop and (a) jump (Qq. MM24, MM4, MM6)

hop a twig See **hop the twig**

hop beer n

A fermented drink usu made from molasses and hops.

1828 Rafinesque *Med. Flora* 249, The strobiles of hops have long been an ingredient of porter, ale and other malt liquors . . ; but by the habitual use of these liquors all the good effects are destroyed. The hop-beer made with molasses, hops and yeast, is a better liquor still, and an agreeable, refreshing, tonic beverage. **1828** *Yankee* (Portland ME) July 227/1, Oh what a luxury! every one eats his fill, and washes it down with good old *orchard,* or hop beer, and all then go home, rain or shine [moon-shine] at 11 o'clock. **1869** Porcher *Resources* 323 **Sth,** The mode of making hop Beer is as follows: For a half barrel of beer, take half a pound of hops, and half a gallon of molasses. . . Boil the hops, adding to them a teacupful of powdered ginger. . . When sufficiently brewed, put it up warm into the cask. . . Then fill it up with water quite up to the bung, which must be left open, to allow it to work. **1931–33** *LANE Worksheets* **csCT,** *Hop beer*—beer with alcohol as opposed to root beer. "We drank ginger ale and hop beer." **1965** Needham-Mussey *Country Things* 139 **sVT,** He also made hop beer. Then his male hop plant died, and so they was all pulled up.

hop bitter beer n [Cf *OED hop bitters* (at *hop* sb.[1] 4. b) "a kind of unfermented liquor flavoured with hops"]

A nonalcoholic drink flavored with hops.

1965 *DARE* (Qu. DD28b, . . *Fermented drinks . . made at home*) Inf **UT**3, Hop bitter beer—not fermented. **1987** *DARE* File **csWI,** During the boil, the hops are put in. After boiling, the liquid is referred to as "fresh wort" or "hop bitter beer." This fresh wort or hop bitter beer is very bitter, but some people do drink it. The liquid at this point in the process is not fermented.

hop bush See **hop tree**

hop cars v phr Cf **hooky bobbing**

1987 *DARE* File, In Holland, Michigan, in the 1950s and 1960s, we would "hop cars" [=hold on to the bumper of a car while it was moving on snow or ice]. Teachers and parents universally forbade "hopping cars."

hop clover n

1 Either of two clovers (here: *Trifolium agrarium* or *T. procumbens*). [Appar from the yellow flowers' resemblance to hops]

1787 (1925) Washington *Diaries* 3.261 **VA,** Sowed . . on the most Westerly square . . 20 lbs of Hop clover. **1822** Eaton *Botany* 491, *Trifolium . . procumbens . .* (hop clover). **1938** [see **2** below]. **1961** Smith *MI Wildflowers* 198, Hop Clover—*Trifolium agrarium.* **1967–69** *DARE* (Qu. S26d) Inf **TN**33, Hop clover; (Qu. S26e) Inf **MA**5, Hop clover. [*DARE* Ed: These Infs may refer instead to **2** below.] **1974** Munz *Flora S. CA* 475, *Trifolium procumbens. . .* Hop Clover.

2 also *hop medic:* Black medic.

1822 Eaton *Botany* 349, *Medicago . . lupulina* (hop medick [sic]). **1936** Winter *Plants NE* 96, *M[edicago] lupulina . .* Hop Clover. **1938** Madison *Wild Flowers OH* 70, Hop Medic. *Medicago lupulina. . .* Yellow Hop Clover. *Trifolium agrarium. . .* Low Hop Clover. *Trifolium procumbens.* **1976** Bailey-Bailey *Hortus Third* 721, *Medicago . . lupulina . .* Black Medic, Hop Clover.

hopd See **help** v **A2b, A3b**

hop down See **hop** v[1] **2**

hope v[1] **Sth, S Midl**

To wish, wish for.

1936 *AmSp* 11.63 **seWV** [Idioms], I hope you good luck (I wish you good luck). **1944** *PADS* 2.34 **NC,** *Hope, to hope luck out of* (a venture). . . "I hope you luck out of [=from] it." **1951** *PADS* 15.70 **nLA,** *Hoped I had. . .* For "I wish I had." **1952** *Hench Coll.* **VA,** [Personal reminiscence:] Heard a farmer say "Well, I hope good weather". . . I've heard this use of "hope" at other times. **1967** *Pike Co. Courier* (Murfreesboro AR) 13 Jan, Miss Virginia Shaw is on the sick list this week and we are hoping her a speedy recovery. **1968** *DARE* (Qu. NN7, . . *"They're getting married next week? Well, _____."*) Inf **GA**28, Hope 'em good luck. **1968** *DARE* FW Addit **LA,** *Hope*—occasionally transitive in the set phrase "I hope you luck".

hope v[2] See **help** v **A1a, A2a, A3a, B2**

Hope n [Cf *SND hope* n.[2] "A small bay or haven. . . Now current in place-names"; *EDD hope* sb.[2] 1 "A small bay; a haven"; 2 "A place of anchorage for ships"] **VA** *arch*

Used in place names; see quots.

1624 in 1940 *AmSp* 15.275 **VA,** Fower hundred acres of land. . . in the precincts of Arthurs Hope in the Corporation of James Citty. **1676** *Ibid,* The people of Charles City County (neer Merchants Hope). **1899** (1912) Green *VA Folk-Speech* 230, *Hope. . .* An inlet; a small bay; a haven. "Archer's Hope," on James River.

hoped See **help** v **A2b, A3b**

hoped up See **help** v **B1**

hopeful n [Cf *OED hopeful* 2. b "as *sb. (colloq.)* A 'hopeful' boy or girl: chiefly ironical"] *old-fash*

1899 (1912) Green *VA Folk-Speech* 230, *Hopeful. . .* A more or less willfull, troublesome, or incorrigible boy or girl, regarded ironically as the rising hope of the family.

hope how soon See **how** conj

hope my die See **hope to my die, I**

hope-to-die adj [*I hope to die* I swear!]

Sworn, true, loyal.

1980 Folb *Runnin' Down* 19 **Los Angeles CA** [Black], Dere all kin' a names fo' d' brothers and sisters. Like you got yo' hope-to-die partner—yo' ace coon, yo' main man, yo' tight—blood and you cain't *git* no closer. *Ibid* 25, You really don' know who you friends are until you git into a bind. Den you know who comes to your rescue. . . Now Beverly, she a righteous hope-to-die partner! *Ibid* 77, You have . . yo' so-called gangs. . . Den you got yo' righteous [=actual] hope-to-die gangs.

hope to my die, I exclam Also *hope my die* [Prob blend of *I hope to die* + *I hope I may die*] **WV, KY** Cf **hope to tell you, I**

Used to make a strong assertion.

1923 (1946) Greer-Petrie *Angeline Doin' Society* 11 **csKY,** Hit looked like a great big red crawfeesh, and I hope to my die, if the thing didn't have laigs with *claws* on 'em. *Ibid* 13, I know you'll think I'm a l'ar, but I hope to my dic, if 'tain't the truth. **1928** in 1944 *ADD* **WV,** 'Hope my die!' = I hope I may die. **1936** *WV Review* Aug. 347, There is hardly an old man or woman that does not drop an expletive or two into almost every conversation. . . Here are some of their favorites . . Hope my die (Hope I may die).

hope to tell you, I exclam

You can believe it!—used with an assertion; see quots.

1956 McAtee *Some Dialect NC* 23, *Hope to tell you, I* . . saying, of emphatic asservation. "I hope to tell you, it's cold." **1966** Barnes-Jensen *Dict. UT Slang* 24, I hope to tell you, she's pretty. **1967** *DARE* (Qu. NN2, *Exclamations of very strong agreement: Somebody says, "I think Smith is absolutely right," and you reply, "________."*) Inf **TX**45, I hope to tell you.

hope up See **help** v **B1**

hopgrasser n [By metath from *grasshopper*] Cf **hoppergrass**

1950 *WELS* 1 Inf, **WI,** Hopgrasser. **1967-69** *DARE* (Qu. R6) Infs **CO**37, **MI**108, Hopgrasser.

hop hornbeam n

1 Std: a tree of the genus *Ostrya* distinguished by the hopslike fruit clusters. Also called **ironwood, leverwood.** For other names of var spp see **deerwood, hardhack 3, hornbeam 3, Indian cedar, wolf hophornbeam**

2 =hornbeam 1.

1952 Taylor *Plants Colonial Days* 49, Hornbeam—*Carpinus caroliniana.* . . Also called . . hop hornbeam—is a slow-growing tree with very slender, shiny, dark brown twigs.

hop-in-John See **hopping John 1**

hop it v phr Cf **hop the twig**

1967 *DARE* (Qu. DD10, *When somebody gives up smoking: "He isn't smoking anymore—a month ago he ________."*) Inf **IA**8, Hopped it.

hopity See **hoppity**

hop-jack n

1942 McAtee *Dial. Grant Co. IN* 80 (as of 1890s), *Hop-jack.* . . plow with a square shovel for covering planted corn.

hop, jump, and skip See **hop, skip, and jump a**

hop master n Cf **hop merchant**

The chrysalis of the **question mark** butterfly.

c1930 Brown *Amer. Folkl. Insect Lore* 4, When the chrysalis of the question-mark butterfly, the "Hop Master," had large golden spots on its back the old-time hop-growers knew that the hop harvest and profits would be large.

hop medic See **hop clover 2**

hop merchant n [See quots 1905, 1940] Cf **hop master**

The comma butterfly *(Polygonia comma);* also its larva and its chrysalis.

1892 IN Dept. Geol. & Nat. Resources *Rept. for 1891* 382, The Comma Butterfly. The Hop Merchant. . . Food plants—hop, elm, and nettles. **1905** Kellogg *Amer. Insects* 453, The pale wood-brown chrysalids with metallic golden or silver spots are commonly known as hop-merchants. If the spots are golden, hops are to bring high prices; if silvery, low prices! **1922** *DN* 5.183 **wNY,** *Hop merchant.* Large green worm, commonly known as the tomato worm, which feeds on the vines of the hop as well as on those of the tomato. **1940** Writers' Program *Guide NY* 643 **cNY,** The growers still search the vines for the bright-colored larvae called 'hop-merchants,' which they examine for the gold or silver spots by which they prognosticate the price they will get for the crop. **1969** *WI Conserv. Bulletin* Mar/Apr 31, The four species of angle wings found in Wisconsin are very similar in habits and in appearance, resembling the hop merchant (Polygonia comma). **1981** Pyle *Audubon Field Guide Butterflies* 610, "Hop Merchant" *(Polygonia comma).* . . Hops . . and nettles . . are preferred host plants.

hop off v phr [Perh var of **fly off 1**] Cf *DS* GG15

1968 *DARE* (Qu. GG15, . . *A person who became over-excited and lost control, "At that point he really ________."*) Inf **CT**6, Hopped off.

hoppagrasse See **hoppergrass 1**

hoppedscotch See **hopscotch**

hopper n

1 =grasshopper 1. [Abbr] **chiefly West, N Cent** See Map Cf **hoppergrass 1**

a1870 Chipman *Notes on Bartlett* 202 *(DAE), Hopper.* . . a grasshopper, especially the ravaging locust called grasshopper at the West. **1885** *Century Illustr. Mag.* 31.29/1 **ID,** I should think he had enough of 'em . . to last him till the 'hoppers come again. **1913** *Pacific Coast Avifauna* 9.47 **CA,** Soon I saw a Sparrow Hawk leave . . an oak tree, and, deftly seizing a flying hopper, it perched by a hole under a dead branch. **a1918** in 1925 Stuart *40 Yrs.* 1.65 **CA,** On frosty mornings the hoppers would be stiff with cold and easily caught. **1949** in 1986 *DARE* File, [Radio:] The plague of hoppers in Wyoming is getting increasingly worse. **1951** Johnson *Resp. to PADS 20* **DE** *(Other names for the grasshopper)* Hopper. **1965-70** *DARE* (Qu. R6) 49 Infs, **chiefly West, N Cent,** Hopper(s).

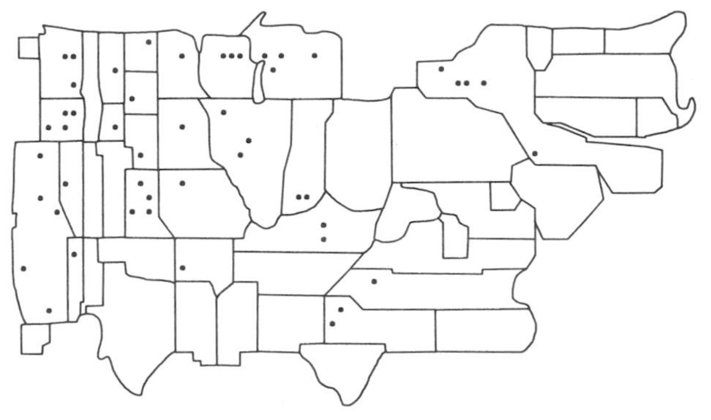

•hopper 1 (Qu. R6)

2 also *coal hopper:* **=hod 1.** Cf **bucket 2d**

1966-70 *DARE* (Qu. F44, . . *A container for coal to use in a stove*) Inf **VA**63, Hopper; **NC**1, Coal hopper; **MO**15, Some of 'em calls 'em coal hoppers.

3 =ashpan. Cf **ash hopper 2**

1967-70 *DARE* (Qu. F12, *The flat metal piece below a wood-burning stove, to catch the ashes*) Infs **AL**27, **KY**77, Hopper.

4 A toilet. **esp NEast** Cf **closet 2**

1965 *DARE* File **ceMA** (as of 1957), The maid on our floor [at college], complaining about the strict new housekeeper [said], "She won't even let us use the word 'hopper' anymore. We're supposed to say 'closet bowl'." **1967-69** *DARE* (Qu. F37, . . *An indoor toilet*) Infs **IN**35, **MA**9, **NJ**2, 17, 54, **PA**26, 150, Hopper. [4 of 7 Infs coll educ]

5 in phr *have one in the hopper:* To be pregnant. [Cf *W3 in the hopper* (at *hopper* n 2. d) "the process of realization or preparation"] Cf **basket 6a**

1968-70 *DARE* (Qu. AA28, . . *Joking or sly expressions . . to say that . . [a woman] is going to have a baby. . . "She[’s] ________."*) Infs **CA**169, **IL**118, **PA**76, **VT**16, Got one in the hopper; **CA**106, Has one in the hopper. **1987** *DARE* File **WI,** If she's got one in the hopper it means, well, it means, come on, you know. All right, I think it means she's pregnant. [Inf male] *Ibid* **WI,** When a woman's got one in the hopper she's pregnant. *Ibid* **MN,** To have one in the hopper means to be pregnant, but I know the phrase "a bun in the oven" better. You'd use "in the hopper" if the woman isn't married. *Ibid* **NYC,** If you "got one in the hopper" you're pregnant. *Ibid* **IA,** I know "have one in the hopper" means to be pregnant.

hoppergrass n [Metath for *grasshopper*]

1 also *hoppagrasse, hoppergrasser:* **=grasshopper 1. chiefly Sth, S Midl** See Map

1829 *Virginia Lit. Museum* I.458 *(DAE), Hoppergrass.* This word is often used in the south for grasshopper. **1884** *Anglia* 7.243 **Sth, S Midl** [Black], *Hoppagrasse.* **1888** Johnston *Mr. Absalom Billingslea* 290 **GA,** I see him hop over a ditch in his cornfield yistiday same's a hoppergrass. **1899** Chesnutt *Conjure Woman* 101 **csNC** [Black], I wa'n't mo' d'n [=more than] knee-high ter a hopper-grass. **1899** (1912) Green *VA Folk-Speech* 230, Hoppergrass. **1903** *DN* 2.317 **seMO,** *Hoppergrass.* **1908** *DN* 3.321 **eAL, wGA,** *Hoppergrass.*.. Grasshopper. Both forms are in use. **1911** *DN* 3.544 **NE,** *Hoppergrass.* **1915** *DN* 4.226 **wTX,** *Hopper-grass.* **1929** Sale *Tree Named John* 65 **MS,** I had t' work hard t' ketch 'ese hoppergrasses. **1940** Stong *Hawkeyes* 276 **IA,** Hey, Mr. Hoppergrass, ain't you got no shoes? **1946** *PADS* 5.26 **VA,** *Hoppergrass.* **1950** *WELS* 2 Infs, **WI,** Hoppergrass. **1965–70** *DARE* (Qu. R6) 87 Infs, **chiefly Sth, S Midl,** Hoppergrass; **FL**29, **GA**54, Hoppergrasser(s).

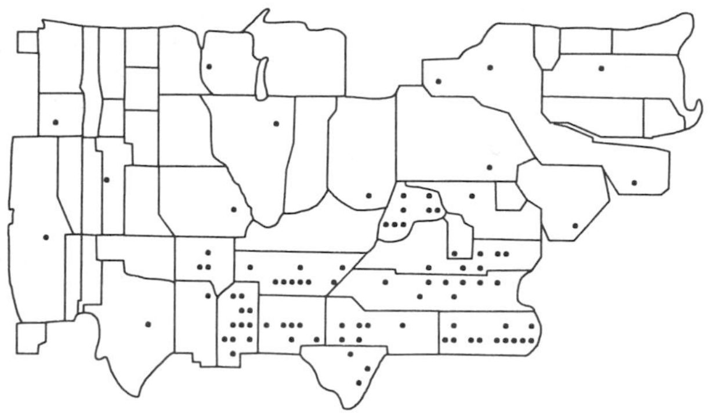

•hoppergrass 1 + var (Qu. R6)

2 Transf: see quot.

1903 *DN* 2.298 **Cape Cod MA** (as of a1857), *Hopper grass.*.. A troublesome woman or child.

hoppergrasser See **hoppergrass 1**

hopper-tailed adj [Cf *EDD hopper-arsed* (at *hopper* sb.[1] 3. (1) (b)) "with protuberant buttocks"; also *SND happer-arsed* (at *happer* n. 1 (1)) and *happer-hippit* (at *happer* n. 1 (3)) "with bony protruding hips"]

Having large buttocks.

1933 *AmSp* 8.1.49 **Ozarks,** *Hopper-tailed.*.. Having broad or prominent buttocks. *What does he look like? Wal, he's a kinder fat, hopper-tailed feller.*

hoppertoad See **hoptoad 1**

hop pillow n *old-fash*

A pillow filled with hops.

1879 *Pub. Ledger (for 1880)* 56 **Philadelphia PA,** A hop pillow, made up on the moment, sprinkled with vinegar and heated in the stove, was an institution to be remembered when the toothache or the earache went to sleep on it. **1884** *Harper's New Mth. Mag.* 69.791/1 **eMA,** There was a hop pillow in a little linen case.

hopping-bug n

A cricket.

1884 Smith *Bill Arp's Scrap Book* 52 **nwGA,** The doors creaked welcome on their hinges, the hoppin-bug chirruped on the hearth.

hopping John n

1 also *happy Jack, happy John, hop-in-John:* A dish usu composed of **black-eyed peas,** rice, and side meat, eaten esp on New Year's Day for good luck; see quots. **chiefly S Atl, esp SC, GA** See Map

1838 (1852) Gilman *S. Matron* 124 **seSC,** Before me .. was an immense field of *hopping John* [Footnote: Bacon and rice]; a good dish, to be sure. **1885** in 1976 Rose *Doc. Hist. Slavery* 397 **SC,** Among the many desirable things our parents brought us, the most delightful was cow pease, rice, and a piece of bacon, cooked together; the mixture was called by the slaves, "Hopping John." **1938** FWP *Ocean Highway* xxviii **SC,** *Hop-In-John:* cow peas, rice, and bacon boiled together. **1950** *PADS* 14.38 **SC,** [Footnote:] Hoppin' John is probably on most tables in S.C. on New Year's Day. This with collard greens is supposed to bring the family plenty of greenbacks and loose change throughout the year. It is believed that one is tempting fate if one fails to have hoppin' John on the table New Year's Day. **1962** *Hench Coll.* **VA,** [Letter:] The conversation we had over the "hoppinjohn" New Year's Day is still remembered. **1965–70** *DARE* (Qu. H50, *Dishes made with .. peas*) 14 Infs, **chiefly S Atl,** Hoppin(g) John—(black-eyed) peas and rice; **DC**12, **GA**24, **MA**122, **SC**9, Hopping John; **GA**67, Hopping John—old-fashioned; **GA**55, Hopping John—rice with peas; country term, old-fashioned; **NJ**67, Hopping John—rice and peas, from West Indies; **SC**22, Hopping John—rice and field peas or cow peas; **FL**19, Hopping John—peas cooked with rice and salt pork; **GA**12, Hopping John—field peas and side meat; **GA**79, Hopping John—black-eyed peas, rice, bacon; **SC**62, Hopping John—(red) peas and rice cooked together with small bits of meat; **SC**4, 11, 21, 46, 70, Hopping John—(peas and rice)—always eaten on New Year's Day (for luck); **GA**3, Hopping Johns [sic]—black-eyed peas; **NC**51, Hopping John—on the South Carolina border more than here; **SC**32, Hopping John—corn, peas, rice [FW sugg]; **TX**65, Hopping John—southern Texas word, grits and black-eyed peas eaten together; **GA**70, Hoppin' John—mix peas with dried fruits; **SC**19, Hoppin' John—cow peas cooked with rice—it's more softer than more harder; **TX**29, Hoppin' John—rice and black-eyed peas, for New Year's Day; **SC**7, Happy Jack—peas and rice; Happy John—peas and grits; (Qu. H45, *Dishes made with meat*) Inf **GA**15, Hopping John—peas, rice and fat meat (pork). **1988** Lincoln *Avenue* 196 **wNC** (as of c1940) [Black], I'd heap rather have a bellyful of .. cornpone an' hoppin' John.

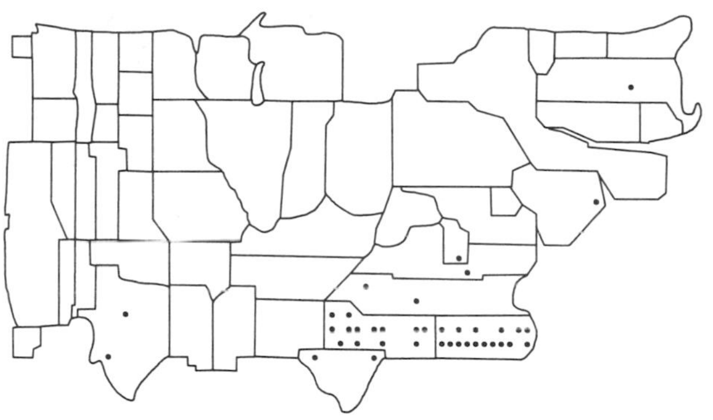

•hopping John 1 + varr (Qq. H50, H45)

2 Transf: a **cowpea.**

1966 *DARE* (Qu. I20, .. *Kinds of beans*) Inf **SC**21, Cowpeas—brownish looking—the pea itself is called hopping John.

3 A **grasshopper 1.**

1970 *DARE* (Qu. R6, .. *Names .. for grasshoppers*) Inf **PA**247, Hopping Johns.

hopping spider n

A jumping spider (family Salticidae).

1970 *DARE* (Qu. R28, .. *Kinds of spiders*) Inf **KY**94, Hopping spiders.

hoppins n pl

1946 in 1953 Botkin–Harlow *Treas. Railroad Folkl.* 235, *Mulligan* [stew]... consists of *hoppins* (any and all vegetables that can be bought, begged, borrowed, or stolen), together with meat acquired the same way. *Ibid* 236, If you want to eat, you'll have to hustle some hoppins.

hoppity n Also *hopity* [Because the pieces are made to *hop* over each other]

See quot 1967.

1895 (1969) Ward *Catalogue* 235/1, The Game of "Hopity" .. is a game of skill... The particular feature of the game is the popular jumping move, pieces being allowed to jump over friend and foe alike to reach the opposite side of the board. **1899** Champlin–Bostwick *Young Folks' Games* 162, *Halma* or *Hoppity,* a kind of *pyramid* played on a checker-board .. by two or four persons with men shaped like the Pawns in *chess.*.. The player's object, as in Pyramid, is to move his own men into the places of their opponents, but either friends or enemies can be jumped, and in any of the possible eight directions, which increases the interest. **1967** Cerello *Dakota Co. MN* 14, *Hoppity*—A game played on a checkerboard of 256 squares. Played by two players with 19 men each, or four with 13 men each. Not many people play hoppity today. I guess it's too hard to learn. Halma is another name for .. hoppity. When you play hoppity you move or leap over any man in an adjacent square.

hoppityscop See **hopscotch**

hoppityscotch See **hopscotch**

hopple v, hence vbl n *hoppling* [*OED hopple* v. 1586 →, sb. a1825] *old-fash*

To hobble a grazing animal; also fig; also n *hopple* a hobble.

1844 Gregg *Commerce* 1.63 **West,** Prior to the date of our trip it had been customary to secure the horses by hoppling them. The 'fore-hopple' (a leathern strap or rope manacle upon the fore legs) . . [is] most convenient. **1858** Hammett *Piney Woods Tavern* 33, If they . . only half trusted him, and sorter tried to hopple him, they'd a plaguy sight best let him alone. **a1889** (1931) Webb *Advent. Santa Fé* 60 (as of 1844), When you want to dismount if near a tree, tie her to the tree before dismounting, then put on the side-hopples and turn her loose. **1899** (1912) Green *VA Folk-Speech* 231, *Hopple*. . . To tie the feet together so as only to walk with short steps. Generally applied to *hopples* for horses. **1906** Casey *Parson's Boys* 135 **sIL** (as of c1860), When we'd reached the cabin, hoppled our horses an' cut grass fer beds, Buck Poundstone was app'inted cook the fust turn. *Ibid* 137, We wartered the horses an' put the hopples on 'em so they could graze. **1913** Johnson *Highways St. Lawrence to VA* 191 **NJ–PA border,** I saw her . . watching her cows that she'd got hoppled and was letting feed along the road.

hoppy frog n Cf *hoppy toad* (at **hoptoad 1**), **rain frog**

Perh a **tree frog.**

c1938 in 1970 Hyatt *Hoodoo* 1.444 **New Orleans LA,** You take you a frog—one of them old hoppy frogs, rainy frogs, you know, be's hopping after de rain in the country.

hoppy John See **hopping John**

hoppyscop, hoppyscotch, hoppyskip See **hopscotch**

hoppytoad See **hoptoad 1**

hop rabbit n

A cottontail.

1968 *DARE* (Qu. P30, . . *Wild rabbits*) Inf **NY**123, Hop rabbit, same as cottontail.

hops n

A **self-heal** (here: *Prunella vulgaris*).

1966 *DARE* Wildfl QR Pl.187 Inf **OH**82, Hops.

hopsage n

1 A shrub of the genus *Grayia* native to the Southwest. [Perh from the similarity of the fruit to that of hops] Also called **horsebrush 3, saltbrush**

1915 (1926) Armstrong–Thornber *Western Wild Flowers* 98, Hop Sage—*Grayia spinosa.* **1923** in 1925 Jepson *Manual Plants CA* 329, *G(rayia) spinosa* . . Hop Sage. **1931** U.S. Dept. Ag. *Misc. Pub.* 101.33, Hop-sages (*Grayia* spp.) **1981** Benson–Darrow *Trees SW Deserts* 171, *Grayia* Hop Sage—Small shrubs similar to the saltbushes but readily distinguished by the practically complete union of the pair of bracts surrounding the fruit.

2 A **saltbush** (here: *Atriplex confertifolia*).

1960 Vines *Trees SW* 237, *Atriplex confertifolia*. . . Also known under the vernacular names of . . Hop-sage, and Sheep Fat.

hop school v phr [Cf *OED, OEDS hop the wag* (at *hop* $v.^1$ 6. a)] Cf **hook Jack**

1969 *DARE* (Qu. JJ6, *To stay away from school without an excuse*) Inf **GA**77, Hop school.

hopscotch n For varr see quots

Std sense, var forms.

1897 (1952) McGill *Narrative* 33, In the game "Hop Scott" the boys and girls played together. **1901** *DN* 2.142 **wNC,** *Hop skot*. . . the same as hop scotch. **1930** in 1975 Albertson *Bessie Smith* 90, [Title:] *New Orleans Hop Scop Blues.* *Ibid* 92, [Song:] You glide, slide, prance, dance. The Hop Scop Blues will make you do a lovely shake. . . dancin' those Hop Scop Blues. **1965–70** *DARE* (Qu. EE19, *The game in which children mark a 'court' on the ground . . throw a flat stone . . then go on one foot*) 34 Infs, **chiefly Sth,** Hopscot; **LA**6, Hopscot—old-fashioned; **AL**3, **NJ**69, Hopscop; **OK**58, Hoppedscotch; **NY**228, Hotscotch; **IN**69, Hotchscotch; **DC**12, Hopskit I think; **MO**1, Hopskit [or] skitch [skɪč]; **NY**69, 75, Hopskip [Infs query]; **NC**43, Hopskip; **NY**1[illegible], H[illegible]; **TN**[illegible], Hipscotch [FW: corr to] hopscotch; **LA**6, Hoppyscop—new-fangled; **KY**74A, Hoppyscotch; **LA**12, Hoppyskip; **GA**1, Hoppityscop; **LA**8, Hoptyscop; **CO**28, Hoppityscotch. **1966–68** *DARE* Tape **AL**3, How's that game, hopscot; **MD**1, Hipscot. . . They still play that in the schools and they mark the schoolyards for that, when we had to do our own marking. . . If they could catch you while you were skippin' you missed out, and if they couldn't catch you while you were skippin' you could play 5 or 6 or 7 or 8 all together. If you could stay on longest, you were the one that was the best at it.

hopsies See **hopsy**

hop, skip, and jump n

Any of var children's games as:

a also *hop, jump, and skip;* for addit varr see quot: The game of hopscotch. *somewhat old-fash*

1965–70 *DARE* (Qu. EE19, *The game in which children mark a 'court' . . throw a flat stone . . then go on one foot*) Infs **CA**137, **MA**29, **NJ**53, Hop, skip, and (a) jump; **IA**21, Hop, skip, and jump—old-fashioned; **MN**12, Hop, skip, jump; **CA**99, **PA**245, Hop, skip, and jump [corr to] hopscotch; **AR**47, Hop and skip [corr to] hop, skip, and jump; **NY**82, Hop and a jump; **CA**22, Hop, jump, and skip—hop once, jump once, skip once; [**MD**34, Hop and skip—involved hopping on a court, but no stone involved]. [All Infs old]

b The game of **fruit basket.**

1969 *DARE* (Qu. EE2, *Games that have one extra player—when a signal is given, the players change places, and the extra one tries to get a place*) Inf **NC**60, Hop, skip, and jump.

c See quot.

1967 *DARE* (Qu. EE1, . . *Games . . children play . . in which they form a ring, and either sing or recite a rhyme*) Inf **AR**47, Hop, skip, and jump.

hopskit(ch), hop skot See **hopscotch**

hopster n

A **grasshopper 1.**

1915 *Lit. Digest* 51.1175/1 **seMI,** But he informed me that it was all right, that they had a grasshopper and were trying to wish good luck on him supposedly by squeezing molasses out of the poor hopster. **1916** *DN* 4.276 **NE,** *Hopster*. . . Grasshopper. See "The Golfer's Evil Eye," by J. G. Anderson in the *New York Sun,* quoted in *The Literary Digest,* Nov. 20, 1915.

hopsy n Also *hopsies*

In marble play: see quot.

c1970 Wiersma *Marbles Terms, Hopsies*—marble hops over another. *Ibid* **Detroit MI** (as of c1960), *Hopsy*—The name of a bouncing shot.

hopt See **help** v **A2b**

hop the lady n

A throw in **mumblety-peg.**

1957 *Sat. Eve. Post Letters* **GA** (as of 1904), The throws [in playing mumble peg] became more complicated, many of them made with two hands. The next was "six times pigeon", then,"hop the lady", "pip the baby" and "break the chicken's neck".

hop the twig v phr Also *hop a twig, jump a twig* [Cf *OED hop the twig* (at *hop* $v.^1$ 6. a) "to depart, go off, or be dismissed suddenly; (also simply *hop, hop off*) to die"; cf also *EDD to hop the twig* (at *hop* $v.^2$ 2. (1)) "to elude one's creditors"]

To die.

1942 Berrey–Van den Bark *Amer. Slang* 117.11, *Die*. . . hop a twig. **1943** *LANE* Map 521 *(Kicked the bucket)* **CT, MA,** 1 inf, Hopped the twig; 1 inf, Jumped a twig; 1 inf, Hopped a twig. **1950** *WELS (Ways . . for saying someone died)* 1 Inf, **WI,** Hopped the twig; [*(Joking ways for saying people got married)* 1 Inf, **WI,** Hopped the twig [*DARE* Ed: Inf perh being ironic, as var of "jumped the broomstick"]]. **1960** Wentworth–Flexner *Slang* 270, *Hop the twig*—To die. **1968** *DARE* (Qu. BB56, *Joking expressions for dying: "He ______."*) Inf **NY**42A, Hopped the twig. **1970** Major *Dict. Afro-Amer. Slang* 67, *Hop a twig:* (1940's) to die.

hoptoad n

1 also *hoppertoad, hoptoady, hoppytoad:* A toad. **scattered, but chiefly NEast** See Map

1827 *Mass. Spy* 28 Nov. (Th.) *(DAE),* An inhabitant of the Middle States talks of 'hop-toads,'—as if all toads were not hoppers. **1830** *MA Spy & Worcester Co. Advt.* (Worcester MA) 28 July 4/1, Don't you know what *hop-toads* are? They're little creatures *what* hop *like a frog does,* and catch a fly in less than no time. **1884** Jewett *Country Dr.* 346 **ME,** When I think how he used to creep about there, side of the road, like a hopper-toad, it does seem amazin'! **1899** Bergen *Animal Lore* 62,

Hop-toad, and hop-toady, *Bufo lentiginosus.* **1902** *DN* 2.236 **sIL,** *Hoptoad,* . . The common toad. **1906** *DN* 3.119 **sIN,** *Hop-toad.* **1907** *DN* 3.223 **sIL, nwAR,** *Hoptoad.* **1911** *DN* 3.544 **NE,** *Hop-toad.* **1938** Damon *Grandma* 139 **CT,** And scratched with adoring straw the warty backs of hoptoads, who seemed to me to have found out some secret of life I didn't know. **1942** Rawlings *Cross Creek* 81 **nFL,** "Look at the little ol' hoppy-toad," he said. "He's got big eyes jus' like our baby." *Ibid* 147, Although the Negro and the backwoodsman call the toad a hoppy-toad and the frog a toady-frog, they make the common distinction between a frog and a toad. **1949** *PADS* 11.23 **CO,** *Hop toad.* **1950** *WELS* 2 Infs, **WI,** Hoptoad. **1965–70** *DARE* (Qu. P23, . . *The animal similar to the frog that lives away from water*) 62 Infs, **chiefly NEast,** Hoptoad; 14 Infs, **chiefly NEast,** Hoppytoad; **CT**23, Hoppertoad; (Qu. B26, *When it's raining very heavily, you say, "It's raining ______.")* Inf **IN**49, Hoptoads; **TX**33, Hoppytoads.

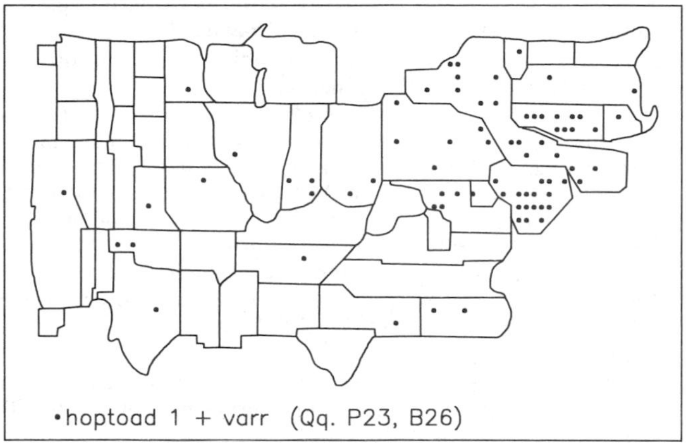

2 In railroading: the device used to derail a car; see quots. [From its shape and its use in making cars "hop" the rails] Cf **rabbit**

1932 *Santa Fe Employes' Mag.* Jan 34, A derail is a *hop toad* or a *rabbit.* **1938** Beebe *High Iron* 222 [Railroad terms], *Hoptoad:* A derail iron. **1958** McCulloch *Woods Words* 89 **Pacific NW,** *Hop toad*—A derailer on a railroad switch to prevent cars from running out on the main track.

hoptoad-stool n

A toadstool.

1969 *DARE* (Qu. I38, . . *Small plants shaped like an umbrella . . not safe to eat*) Inf **MA**55, Hoptoad-stool.

hoptoady See **hoptoad 1**

hop tree n Also *hop bush* [See quots 1857, 1974]

A shrub or tree of the genus *Ptelea.* Also called **shrubby trefoil.** For other names of *P. trifoliata* see **ague bark, dwarf ash 2, penny-tree, pickaway-anise, pistol-cap tree, polecat tree, potato-chip tree, prairie-grub, quinine tree, rattlesnake tree, sang-tree, skunk bush, stinking ash, stinking prairie-bush, swamp dogwood, three-leaved hop tree, wafer ash, wahoo, water ash, wingseed**

1857 Gray *Manual of Botany* 75, *Ptelea. . . Shrubby Trefoil. Hop-tree. . .* Fruit bitter, used as a substitute for hops. **1877** Bartlett *Americanisms* 296, *Hop-tree. (Ptelia trifoliata.)* A tall shrub found in the Eastern States. The fruit, a wafer-like seed, grows in clusters, is a bitter tonic, and has been used as a substitute for hops. **1911** (1916) Porter *Harvester* 387 **IN,** The hop tree has its castanets all green and gold. **1941** Walker *Lookout* 61 **TN,** The hop-tree is occasionally found at . . Lookout. **1951** *PADS* 15.35, *Ptelea trifoliata* . . hop bush. **1974** (1977) Coon *Useful Plants* 238, *Ptelea baldwinii*—Hoptree. . . As in the East, the fruits of this plant have been used as a substitute for hops in brewing. . . *Ptelea trifoliata* . . hoptree. . . The little "wafers" or seeds are the "hops substitute."

Horace n *euphem* Cf **country cousin, grandma** n **B4**

1967 *DARE* (Qu. AA27, . . *Menstruation*) Inf **CO**15, Horace has come. [Inf old]

hord See **hire**

horehound n

1 Std: a plant *(Marrubium vulgare)* of the mint family known for its antitussive qualities. Also called **candyweed 2, coughweed 2, croupweed, marvel, water horehound, white horehound 2 =bugleweed.**

1911 Henkel *Amer. Med. Leaves* 27, Virginia horehound. . . is a native herb. . . It has sedative, tonic, and astringent properties. **1930** Sievers *Amer. Med. Plants* 17, *Bugleweed. . . Other common names* . . Virginia hoarhound [sic]. **1971** Krochmal *Appalachia Med. Plants* 166, *Lycopus virginicus. . . Common Names* . . Horehound.

3 A **boneset 1** (here: *Eupatorium hyssopifolium*).

1974 Morton *Folk Remedies* 59, *"Horehound"* [Not the true *horehound, Marrubium vulgare,* which is native to Europe and cultivated and naturalized in parts of the U.S.] . . *Eupatorium hyssopifolium. . . South Carolina (Current use). . .* "Horehound" decoction is taken every morning as a remedy for diabetes.

horn n

1 A drink of liquor; a measure of liquid. [By ext from *horn* a drinking vessel] Cf **dram** n **1**

1830 Ames *Mariner's Sketches* 91 **MA,** This new Gargantua, declaring that he had made 'quite a decent breakfast, considering the country he was in,' took a good stout horn of gin, and decamped. **1864** Hillard *Last Men* 36 **Mid Atl** (as of c1770), One of 'em handed me his canteen; 'Lem,' said he, 'take a good horn—we're going to march all night['] . . . I took a full drink. **1899** (1912) Green *VA Folk-Speech* 231, *Horn. . .* A draught of strong liquor: as, to take a horn. Probably because early drinking vessels were made of horn. **1911** *DN* 3.538 **eKY,** *Horn. . .* A dram of whiskey. **1940** (1978) Still *River of Earth* 193 **KY,** "I hain't been well lately," he said. "A horn o' Indian Doctor tonic I'm taking after every meal." **1954** *Harder Coll.* **cwTN,** *Horn*—A measure of liquid. "Pa said that." **1969–70** *DARE* (Qu. DD18, *A drink of liquor, or the amount of liquor taken in one swallow: "He took a good ______."*) Infs **IL**115, **NY**209, Horn; **KY**84, Horn, big horn; **WI**77, Horn—"give us another horn."

2 also *horn spoon;* In mining: a scoop, orig of horn, used to determine the presence of gold in washings. **West** *old-fash* Cf **horn** v **2**

1855 *Golden Era* (S.F.) 6 May 2/7 *(DA),* They appear to have prospected pretty well in this way, though with very inferior tools—horn spoon, wooden bowl, and quicksilver. **1875** Bourke *Diary* 15 June **swSD,** The quartz ledges, they have not thoroughly examined, not having any mercury, but have crushed the rock with mortar and pestle and found "color" in horn-spoon. **1877** Wright *Big Bonanza* 111 **swNV,** To test the ores for the precious metals . . pulverized ore was . . placed in a "horn," a little canoe-shaped vessel made of the split horn of an ox, when it was carefully washed out. . . The gold . . was found lying in a yellow streak in the bottom of the horn; generally small particles of gold dust. **1896** (1901) Shinn *Story of Mine* 78 **cwNV,** The prospector then took it in his horn spoon, a flat vessel made from half of an ox horn. . . The quartz prospector prefers the horn, because he only pans out a few ounces of powdered rock, and the flakes are so much finer that a more manageable tool is required than in the case of the placer prospector. **1949** Wynn *Desert Bonanza* 258 **csCA** (as of 1890s), When cow horns were no longer used and horn spoons became a thing of the past, the old timers still frequently called this process of washing small amounts of gravel or mortared rock, "horning." They now use the small frying pans so familiar to the mining country. **1969** *DARE* FW Addit **CA**114, *Horn*—a cow's horn, cut off, heated or soaked to make it flexible, then split open, used as a small gold pan. Later a half of a frying pan was also used and the name carried over. Also called a gold horn.

3 also *cream horn:* A rich pastry; usu called **butter horn.** [From the shape]

1896 (c1973) Farmer *Orig. Cook Book* 397, *Cream Horns.* Roll puff paste in a long rectangular piece. . . Bake in a hot oven until well puffed and slightly browned. . . When cold, fill with Cream Filling or whipped cream sweetened and flavored. **1950** *WELS (Fancy home-baked rolls)* 1 Inf, **ceWI,** Horns. **1967–68** *DARE* (Qu. H28, *Different shapes or types of doughnuts*) Inf **OH**28, Horn, or half moon; **MO**34, Cream horn—contains whipped cream.

4 also *snot horn:* The nose. [From the sound made when blowing the nose or snoring; cf *EDD horn* sb. 10]

1843 (1847) Field *Drama Pokerville* 94, What with the blowing of noses, and a characteristic *bronchitis,* there was the most awful clearing of throats, *hawking,* and horn-blowing that ever Judge Frill had listened to! **1912** *NY Eve. Jrl.* (NY) 24 Jan 14 *(Zwilling Coll.),* [In cartoon "Daffydils":] Donning his raglan he pointed his horn towards the door. **1950** *WELS (Words for the nose)* 3 Infs, **WI,** Horn. **1965–70** *DARE* (Qu. X14, *Joking words for the nose*) Infs **MD**6, **MI**47, **NY**84, Horn; **MA**15, Snot horn; (Qu. X15) Inf **MD**9, Horn; [**MO**8, **NY**66, (Sharp) horn nose;] [(Qu. X45, . . *Joking expressions . . snoring*) Inf **LA**40, Blowing your horn; **NY**2, Tooting his horn]. [All Infs old]

5 The penis. [From the shape when erect; *OEDS* 1785 →]

1953 in 1977 Randolph *Pissing in the Snow* 156 **AR** (as of c1900), Just lay me down easy. . . Now stick the horn in me. **1954** McAtee *Dial. Grant Co. IN Suppl. 4* [1], *Horn. . .* (penis.) ["]The older the buck the stiffer the horn". **1967** *AmSp* 42.228 **CT** [College terms], *Cock movie . . horn movie. . .* An erotic "dirty" moving picture. Formerly shown in some dormitories, these movies are now shown only in fraternity houses, since the latter can compel privacy.

6 See quot. Cf **pump knot**

1968–69 *DARE* (Qu. X60, . . *A lump . . on your head when you get a sharp blow or knock*) Infs **IL**51, **WI**66, Horn; **WI**76, Horn on his head—skin was just broken.

7 See quot.

1968 *DARE* (Qu. O8, *The devices on the sides of a boat that hold the oars in place*) Inf **MN**21, Horns—the forked piece—and sockets—the bracket; same as oarlocks.

8 in var phrr: See below.

a *in a horn:* Used quasi-adverbially or as exclam to express skepticism of another's statement, or denial of one's own. [Sense of *horn* here is uncert; cf *EDD in a horn* (at *horn* sb. 2. (6)) "an expression of incredulity, used in reference to an event which is never likely to happen"] *old-fash* Cf **pig's eye**

1840 in 1965 *AmSp* 40.181 [Horse-racing phrases], *In a horn. . .* "Duane was sold after the first heat to Mr. William N. Friend, of the Camden Course, for $12,000—('in a horn!')." **1840** *Picayune* 10 Sept. 2/5 **sLA** *(DAE),* A Horn Story.—The Baltimore Clipper tells the following story 'in a horn.' **1859** (1968) Bartlett *Americanisms* 203, *In a horn.* A low phrase, now common, used to qualify a falsehood. . . A boy will say, "I saw a man jump over the house," and add *sotto voce, "In a horn;"* meaning thereby directly the reverse. **1897** *Voice* 15 July 3/1 *(DAE),* To give alms with 'a trumpet' and to pray to 'the house' are equally worship 'in a horn.' **1899** (1912) Green *VA Folk-Speech* 231, *Horn. . .* "In a horn." Spoken of as a thing never likely to happen. **1923** *DN* 5.239 **swWI,** *In a horn. . .* Never. "Yes, I'll do it—in a horn!" **1988** *DARE* File **cWI,** "In a horn" is a skeptical response to something somebody says but which you don't believe, or a promise, or a boast that you can't accept. "I'll pay you next week"—"In a horn!" Nobody seems to know the origin. It's much the same as "In a pig's eye!"

b *come out (of) the little end of the horn* and varr: See quots. [Perh in allusion to the cornucopia; see quot 1889] **sAppalachians**

1836 (1838) Haliburton *Clockmaker* (1st ser) 68 **NEng,** Can you wonder that people who keep such an unprofitable stock, come out of the small eend of the horn in the long run? **1846** (1973) Porter *Quarter Race* 24 **cKY,** You *prehaps* never saw such a run of luck; everywhere I touched was *pizen,* and I came out of the *leetle* end of the horn. **1889** (1971) Farmer *Americanisms* 305, *The little end of the horn. . .* The mountain bringing forth a mouse is the prototype of those who come out at *the little end of the horn;* who make much ado about nothing, and whose vast endeavors end in failure. The allusion is to the "Horn of Plenty," one end of which tapers to a point. **1931** *PMLA* 46.1307 **sAppalachians,** He come out o' the leetle eend o' the horn. (Unsuccessful in a trade.) **1944** *PADS* 2.23 **sAppalachians,** He come outn the leetle eend o' the horn. (He was unsuccessful in a deal or trade.) *Ibid* 57 **swMO, VA, NC, SC,** *Horn, to come out at the big end of the. . .* To be successful [*PADS* Ed: Cf. the opposite: *to come out at the little end of the horn*]. **1954** *Harder Coll.* **cwTN,** *Horn*—"He came out the leetle eend o' the horn."

c in phr *put the horns on one:* See quot. [Perh in ref to the devil as having *horns;* cf **horny man**]

1968 *DARE* (Qu. CC14, . . *Expressions used . . where one person supposedly casts a spell over another*) Inf **NY**36, Put the horns on him.

horn v

1 Fig: see below. [*horn* to gore or push with the horns]

a with *off* or *out:* To drive away; to push aside or ward off. *somewhat old-fash*

1850 in 1929 *CA Hist. Soc. Qrly.* 8.3.268, Sutter is wanting to horn out some squatters off what he calls his property. **1851** Hooper *Widow Rugby's Husband* 69 **AL,** You horned me off to get a chance to get gaming witnesses out of the way. **1881** in 1912 Thornton *Amer. Gloss.* 451, Mac Veagh is trying his best to horn Blaine out of the Cabinet herd, just as young buffalo bulls horn out the old ones from the herd when they get superannuated. **c1960** *Wilson Coll.* **csKY,** *Horn off*—Keep someone from getting what he wants, defend oneself.

b See quot.

1911 *DN* 3.544 **NE,** *Horn. . .* Annoy. "You'll horn me to death, if you don't keep quiet."

2 In gold mining: to use a **horn** n **2;** hence vbl n *horning* the process of assaying with such a tool. **West** *hist*

1867 *Terr. Enterprise* (Virginia, Nev.) 1 Jan. 1/4 *(DA),* I found lots of quartz, and pounded and horned and panned, and panned and horned and pounded it till ready to curse all creation. **1896** (1901) Shinn *Story of Mine* 79 **cwNV,** This process [of washing] is called "horning a prospect," or "assaying with a spoon." **1949** [see **horn** n **2**].

3 To serenade (a newly-married couple) with a **horning** n **1;** hence n *horner.* **VT, RI** Cf **bell** v²

1931–33 *LANE Worksheets,* 1 inf, **VT,** They horn them. **1941** *LANE* Map 409, 1 inf, **cwRI,** Once in a while they horn 'em before they get married; 1 inf, **swVT,** If they didn't get a treat, the horners broke into the house and became violent. **1968** *DARE* (QR, near Qu. AA18) Inf **VT**8, Horning—if they [=the newly married couple] didn't treat them, they [=the other people] would horn them at night.

4 To dehorn; hence ppl adj *horned* dehorned.

1967–68 *DARE* (Qu. K13, *A cow that has had her horns cut off*) Infs **MO**26, **OH**47, 87, Horned; **GA**52, She's been horned.

5 vbl n *horning:* See quot.

1950 *PADS* 14.39 **SC,** *Horning. . .* Blowing snuff through a paper cone into the nostril of a woman in labor to hasten delivery of the child. The verb, *to horn,* is not reported so far.

horn-ail n Also *horn distemper* **esp NEng**

=hollow horn 1.

1822 (1972) Deane *New Engl. Farmer* 204, *Horn Distemper,* a disease of neat cattle. . . To effect the cure, the horn should be perforated with a nail gimblet. **1831** *Boston Eve. Transcript* (MA) 22 June 2/4, Our cow died of the "Horn-ail" on Wednesday morning last, after a few days suffering. **1843** *Knickerbocker* 21.254, Hence it is as important to keep the bee-moth out of hives as the horn-distemper out of cattle. **1902** Richards *Mrs. Tree* 165 **NEng,** Wasn't he the man that tried to cure Peckham's cow of the horn ail, bored a hole in her horn and put in salt and pepper,—or was it oil and vinegar? **1911** Shute *Plupy* 245 **NH,** He would buy cows that promptly developed garget, horn-ail, or sevenfold indigestion in every one of their stomachs at once.

hornback n, v, hence vbl n *hornbacking* **FL, GA**

The heavily scaled back of an alligator; also a whole alligator hide with the feet; to skin (an alligator) so as to leave the feet with the hide.

1941 Faherty *Big Old Sun* 124 **FL,** She watched Horace work on the alligator with a long-bladed jackknife. He cut into the skin at the base of the head, near the hornback ridge, and moved along the length of the carcass. He slit the skin from head to tail on each side, below the hornback, along the white borderline of the belly. **1969** *DARE* Tape **GA**48, We didn't keep the feet on for years. I was a grown man before I ever seen it, before we ever had any, hornbacks we call it. Call those hides "hornback" and we keep the feet on, we kept the whole hide on generally. We got to hornbacking them, skinning the whole hide off of them small ones. . . I don't think we ever hornbacked anything much more than five foot long.

hornbeam n

1 pronc-sp *hornbin:* A small, often crooked tree *(Carpinus caroliniana)* noted for its hard strong wood. Also called **black beech, blue beech, hop hornbeam 2, ironwood, lean-wood, lechillo, musclewood, swamp beech, water beech**

1671 in 1893 Providence RI Rec. Comm. *Early Rec.* 3.107, Boundeth on . . the norwesterne Corner with a horne beame, or peckled Tree marked on too [sic] sides. **1766** (1942) Bartram *Diary of a Journey* 47/2 **eFL,** A hammock of oak, hiccory, magnolia, and hornbeam. **1819** Dana *Geog. Sketches* 171 **MS,** The soil is . . thickly covered with timber; such as various species of . . hornbeam, chincapin, wildberry. **1899** (1912) Green *VA Folk-Speech* 231, *Hornbeam. . .* A small tree like a beech, of very hard wood. "Hornbin." **1927** Keeler *Our Native Trees* 319, *Hornbeam.* . . Common along the borders of streams and swamps, loves a deep moist soil. **1966** *DARE* File **ME,** Hornbeam or ironwood—a very tough wood—tree looks like an ash, but leaves are like birch. No grain to wood. **1966–70** *DARE* (Qu. T15) Inf **VA**38, Hornbeam; (Qu. T16) Inf **ME**5, Hornbeam—very tough; **VA**24, Hornbeam. **1967** Borland *Hill Country* 161 **nwCT,** Ironwood must have been so named because the wood is "hard as iron." But another name for it, hornbeam, is obscure unless one remembers that the main part of a deer's antler is called the beam. Hornbeam is as tough as the beam of a deer's horn. **1969** Sorden *Lumberjack Lingo* 57 **NEng, Gt Lakes,** *Horn beam lever*—A piece of wood made from an ironwood sapling. When dry, it was very strong and durable. In early logging days, it was used considerably before the cant hook was perfected.

2 also *swamp hornbeam:* Either of two **tupelos:** usu *Nyssa sylvatica,* but also *N. aquatica.*

1824 Bigelow *Florula Bostoniensis* 380, *Nyssa villosa. . . Swamp Hornbeam.* . . In Massachusetts it is generally called *Hornbeam,* a name properly belonging to the genus Carpinus. **1850** Emerson *Rept. Trees & Shrubs* 313, Often in every part [of Massachusetts], it [=*Nyssa sylvatica*] is called Hornbeam, from the extreme toughness of the wood. **1900** Lyons *Plant Names* 262, *N[yssa] sylvatica.* . . Swamp Hornbeam. **1934** *Hanley Disks* **ME,** Hornbeam is what they call black gum. **1960** Vines *Trees SW* 801, *Nyssa aquatica.* . . Vernacular names are Tupelo Gum . . and Hornbeam. *Ibid* 802, *Nyssa sylvatica.* . . Vernacular names are Swamp-hornbeam, . . Hornbeam, . . and Sour Gum.

3 A **hop hornbeam 1:** usu *Ostrya virginiana,* but also *O. knowltonii.*

1897 Sudworth *Arborescent Flora* 147, *Ostrya virginiana. . . Common Names.* . . Hornbeam (R.I., N.Y., Fla., S.C., La.) **1931** Otis *MI Trees* 113, Hornbeam. Ironwood. *Ostrya virginiana.* **1960** Vines *Trees SW* 145, *Ostrya knowltonii.* . . Some vernacular names are Western Hornbeam and Ironwood. **1979** Little *Checklist U.S. Trees* 181, *Ostrya virginiana. . . Other common names* . . hornbeam.

4 =**planer tree.**

[**1860** Curtis *Cat. Plants NC* 81, *Planer Tree.* . . may very easily be mistaken, at a little distance, for the *Hornbeam.*] **1933** Small *Manual SE Flora* 441, *P[lanera] aquatica.* . . Water-elm. Hornbeam.

5 A **hackberry.**

1968 *DARE* (Qu. T13) Infs **PA**89, **WV**2, Hornbeam.

6 An unidentified plant.

1969 *DARE* (Qu. T16) Inf **MA**55, Hornbeam—['hɔnbim] has a thorn on it—longer than a rose thorn.

horn beetle n Also *horned beetle* [From the horn(s) on the head or pronotum] Cf **horn bug 1**

1 =**betsy bug.**

1910 W.S. Blatchley *Coleoptera* 908 *(DA)* **IN,** This well-known species, commonly known as the 'horn' or 'bess-beetle,' occurs abundantly throughout the state. **1926** Essig *Insects N. Amer.* 439, Front of head with a short bent horn pointing forward. . . Horned Beetles. **1949** Swain *Insect Guide* 145, Bessybugs (Horned Beetles) *Family Passalidae.* **1967–68** *DARE* (Qu. R30) Inf **NJ**21, Horned beetle; **SC**63, Horned beetle—horn on nose, black. [*DARE* Ed: Either Inf may refer instead to **2** below.]

2 A scarab beetle of the subfamily Dynastinae. See also **rhinoceros beetle, unicorn beetle**

1792 Belknap *Hist. NH* 3.180, Horned Beetle, *Scarabæus simson.* **1889** *Century Dict.* 504, *Beetle. . . Horned beetle,* a lamellicorn beetle of the genus *Megalosoma* and some related genera. **1911** *Century Dict. Suppl.,* Horn-beetle. . . Spotted horn-beetle, *Dynastes tityus.*

hornbill cat n

Perh a **horned pout.**

1906 *DN* 3.141 **nwAR,** *Hornbill cat.* . . A kind of catfish.

hornbin See **hornbeam 1**

hornbine n Also *hornpine, hornpipe*

A **black gum 1** (here: *Nyssa sylvatica*).

1793 in 1810 MA Hist. Soc. *Coll.* 1st ser 3.167 **seMA,** The timber here growing is . . spruce, beech, buttonwood, hornbine, and sassafras. **1850** Emerson *Rept. Trees & Shrubs* 313, In Bristol County, and the other south-eastern counties, this [=Nyssa sylvatica] is called . . sometimes Horn Pine. **1894** *Jrl. Amer. Folkl.* 7.90, *Nyssa sylvatica,* . . horn-bine, horn-pine. Southern States. **1900** Lyons *Plant Names* 262, *N[yssa] sylvatica.* . . Hornbine, Hornpine, Hornpipe. **1960** Vines *Trees SW* 802, *Nyssa sylvatica.* . . Vernacular names are . . Hornpipe, Hornpine, Hornbine. **1976** Yepson *Trees* 239, *Gum, black* . . horn pine.

horn-blower n

A **sphinx moth** (here: *Manduca sexta*).

1850 U.S. Patent Office *Annual Rept. for 1849: Ag.* 320 **cwMD,** The greater portion of the first *glut* reappear the same year as *Horn-blowers* and breed myriads. **1874** U.S. Dept. Ag. *Rept. of Secy. for 1873* 157, The tobacco hawk-moth or "horn-blower" of Maryland, *Macrosila (Sphinx) carolina,* Linn., is a large moth, the caterpillar of which, commonly known as the tobacco-worm . . in the Middle States, is very destructive to the leaf of the tobacco-plant. **1911** *Century Dict. Suppl., Horn-blower.* . . A southern United States tobacco-growers' name for the tobacco sphinx-moth, *Phlegethontius carolina,* the parent of the horn-worm of tobacco.

horn, blow one's v phr

1967–68 *DARE* (Qu. X55b, *Words for breaking wind from the bowels*) Inf **CO**22, Blow the horn; **NY**70, Blow your horn.

hornbrush n [See quot 1937]

A **buckbrush 3c** such as *Ceanothus greggii,* or its pod.

1931 U.S. Dept. Ag. *Misc. Pub.* 101.111, *Gregg hornbrush (C. greggii).* . . is a stout, intricately branched shrub. **1937** U.S. Forest Serv. *Range Plant Hdbk.* B39, *Ceanothuses.* . . Hornbrush refers to the typically hard-leaved (horny) species . . and, more especially to the horned pods of that group, which somewhat resemble the head of a viper.

horn bug n Cf **horn beetle 1**

1 =**betsy bug.** [From the horn on the head]

1782 Trumbull *McFingal* 39 **CT,** Thinks hornbugs bullets, or thro' fears / Muskitoes takes for musketeers. **1789** Morse *Amer. Geog.* 62, Of the astonishing variety of Insects found in America, we will mention, . . Horn Bug[,] Flea[,] Gnat [etc]. **1878** (1977) Stowe *Poganuc People* 110 **cwCT,** That Bill is saassy [sic] enough to physic a hornbug.

2 also *horned bug:* A **stag beetle.** [Appar from the sometimes antlerlike mandibles]

1778 Carver *Travels N. Amer.* 493, The *Horned Bug,* or as it is sometimes termed the *Stag Beetle,* is of a dusky brown colour. **1850** Emerson *Rept. Trees & Shrubs* 254 **MA,** The grubs of the hornbug . . live in the trunks and roots of old willows, as well as in those of apple trees and oaks.

3 =**June beetle.**

1899 Bergen *Animal Lore* 63, Horn-bugs, May-bees, May-flies, June-bugs *Lachnosterna. Bernardston, Mass.* **1969** *DARE* (Qu. R5) Inf **MA**68, Horn bug.

horn buoy n [From its intermittently blowing a horn]

1966–68 *DARE* (Qu. O14b, . . *Kinds of buoys*) Inf **GA**28, Horn buoy—off-shore; **SC**9, Horn buoy; **SC**21, Horn buoy—formerly.

horncaster n

Appar a **hornworm.**

1966 *DARE* Tape **DC**5, The worm will get big . . and then it turn to what we call horncaster . . and then he'll be just big like a butterfly. . . he's the one that gonna fly on the 'bacca leaves and put the eggs on the 'bacca leaves.

horn chub See **horned chub**

horn colic n [**horn** n **5**]

See quots.

1912 Green *VA Folk-Speech* 231, *Horn-colic.* . . Pain caused by priapism. **1930** Shoemaker *1300 Words* 30 **cPA Mts** (as of 1900), *Horn colic*—Pain said to be caused by suppressed sexual desire. **1954** in 1977 Randolph *Pissing in the Snow* 235 **Ozarks** (as of early 1900s), She never done no screwing unless they paid her first. A fellow . . come down with the horn colic one night, but he didn't have the two dollars.

horn dace See **horned dace 2**

horn distemper See **horn-ail**

horn-eared sunfish n Also *horned-eared sunfish*

=**red-breasted sunfish.**

1935 Caine *Game Fish* 26, *Red-Breasted Sunfish—Lepomis auritus.* . . Horned-eared Sunfish. **1946** LaMonte *N. Amer. Game Fishes* 139, *Yellowbreast Sunfish.* . . Horn-eared Sunfish.

horned See **horn** v **4**

horned beetle See **horn beetle**

horned bovolopus n

An imaginary animal; see quots.

1934 *Sun* (Baltimore MD) 27 Dec *(Hench Coll.),* In the haunted hollow behind the little wood they say the laughing popperina laughed all the day and the horned bovolopus cavorted on his long toes like a gazelle. **1946** *Ibid* 7 Mar 14/3 *(Hench Coll.),* He sent his model to the researchers of the State Department, who reported 'No such creature'—any more, I suppose, than the deep-hole snallygaster of Western Maryland or the horned bovolopus of Anne Arundel.

horned bug See **horn bug 2**

horned caterpillar See **hornworm**

horned chub n Also *horn(y) chub* [See quot 1884]

=**hornyhead a.**

1878 U.S. Natl. Museum *Bulletin* 12.26 **NC,** The common Horned Chub is very abundant in all the tributaries of the Saluda. **1884** *Ibid* 27.485, *Ceratichthys biguttatus. . .* The horn chub takes its name from the tubercles extensively developed on the head of the adults in the breeding season; it reaches a length of 9 inches, and is used for food. **1968** *DARE* (Qu. P7, *Small fish used as bait for bigger fish*) Inf **PA**168, Horn chubs; **WV**7, Horny chubs. **1983** Becker *Fishes WI* 485, *Nocomis biguttatus. . .* Other common names . . horned chub.

horned dace n

1 also *horned sucker:* A **chubsucker 1** (here: *Erimyzon oblongus*).

1842 DeKay *Zool. NY* 4.199, *The Horned Sucker. Catostomus tuberculatus* [=*Erimyzon oblongus*]. . . Between the eyes and the snout, on each side, . . three . . tubercles. . . The Horned Sucker is common in most of the fresh-water streams of this State, and . . also found in New-Hampshire, Massachusetts, Connecticut, New-Jersey and Pennsylvania. . . It is known under the various popular names of *Barbel, Dace,* and *Horned Dace. . .* The uses of the tubercles are not apparent.

2 also *horn dace:* Either of two related fishes: usu the creek chub *(Semotilus atromaculatus),* but also a **fallfish** (here: *S. corporalis*). [See quot 1884]

1882 U.S. Natl. Museum *Bulletin* 16.221, *S[emotilus] corporalis. . . Chub; Horned Dace. . .* Males with the snout coarsely tuberculate in spring. **1884** Goode *Fisheries U.S.* 1.617, *The Horned Dace—Semotilus corporalis. . .* The "horns" in this and other Minnows and Chubs are dermal excresnces [sic] developed on the males in breeding season. **1896** U.S. Natl. Museum *Bulletin* 47.222, *Semotilus atromaculatus. . .* Horned-dace. **1933** John G. Shedd Aquarium *Guide* 48, *Semotilus atromaculatus—Horned Dace; Fall Fish. . .* It is called Horned Dace because of the prominent tubercles on the head and body of the breeding males. **1967–69** *DARE* (Qu. P3, *Freshwater fish that are not good to eat*) Inf **NY**23, Horned dace—red fins, 4 or 5 inches long; **NY**71, 97, Horned dace; **NY**6, Horn dace—species of minnow; (Qu. P7, *Small fish used as bait for bigger fish*) Inf **PA**180, Horned dace—actually a big chub with horns. **1983** Becker *Fishes WI* 437, *Creek Chub—Semotilus atromaculatus. . .* Other common names: horned dace, northern horned dace.

horned-eared sunfish See **horn-eared sunfish**

horned frog n Also *honey frog, horn(y) frog, hornet frog* **chiefly West, esp TX**

=**horned toad 1.**

1804 *Frederick-Town Herald* (MD) 14 July 3/4 **KY,** They carry with them to the President one of the curious *horned* frogs, which a late ingenious discoverer describes as living in association with ground squirrels and snakes. **1810** Pike *Expeditions* 156, I have seen . . the horn frog, of which the prairie abounds. **1844** Gregg *Commerce* 2.231, The *horned frog* . . or horned lizard, as those of earlier times more rationally called it, is the most famed and curious reptile of the plains. **1854** (1932) Bell *Log TX-CA Trail* 35.221, Seen more Horned Frogs today than before. **1962** Atwood *Vocab. TX* 59, The small flat lizard with horns on its head and back is known in Texas as a . . *horn, horned,* or *horny frog. . .* North Texas prefers the forms with *frog. . .* The form *horned* occasionally appears as *hornet.* **1967** *Refugio Timely Remarks* (TX) 30 Mar 1/1, We're in the market for horned frogs again this year. A prevailing price of five cents each is being established for toads six inches and under in length. **1967–70** *DARE* (Qu. P23) Infs **TX**40, 104, Horny frog. **1970** Tarpley *Blinky* 152 **neTX,** Dry land animal that hops and is supposed to cause warts . . horny-frog . . horned frog. **1986** Pederson *LAGS Concordance* **Gulf Region,** [12 infs, 8 in **TX,** offered the terms *honey, horned, horn,* or *horny frog.*]

horned grebe n Also *horn grebe*

A **grebe** (here: *Colymbus auritus*). Also called **devil-diver 1, dipper 3b, diver, hell-diver, little diver, plongeur, sea didapper, tinker loon, water witch**

1823 James *Acct. of Exped.* 1.374, *Colymbus* (*Podiceps.* Lath.) *cornutus*—Horned grebe. **1917** *DN* 4.426 **LA,** *Horned grebe* (Colymbus auritus). **1917** (1923) *Birds Amer.* 1.8, Horned Grebe—*Colymbus auritus.* **1969** *DARE* (Qu. Q10) Inf **CA**155, Horn grebe.

horned hickory devil See **hickory horned devil**

horned jackrabbit n *joc* Cf **horned rabbit**

See quot.

1961 Adams *Old-Time Cowhand* 155, Because of their [=longhorn cattle's] long horns and speed they were often referred to as "horned jackrabbits."

horned lark n

A small lark (*Eremophila alpestris* and subspp). **chiefly Nth, N Midl** See Map Also called **life bird, prairie bird, prairie lark, road trotter, shore lark, skylark, snow bird, snow lark, spring bird, wheat bird, winter lark**

1839 Audubon *Synopsis Birds* 96, Alauda alpestris, . . Horned Lark. —Male with two erectile pointed tufts of feathers on the anterior lateral parts of the head. **1844** Giraud *Birds Long Is.* 95, *Alauda Alpestris* . . Horned Lark. **1898** (1900) Davie *Nests N. Amer. Birds* 315, Horned Lark. *Otocoris alpestris* . . The common name is derived from the tufts of black feathers over each ear, which at will the bird has the power of erecting like the so-called "horns" of some owls. **1966–70** *DARE* (Qu. Q15) 35 Infs, **chiefly Nth, N Midl,** Horned lark; (Qu. Q7) Inf **RI**17, Horned lark.

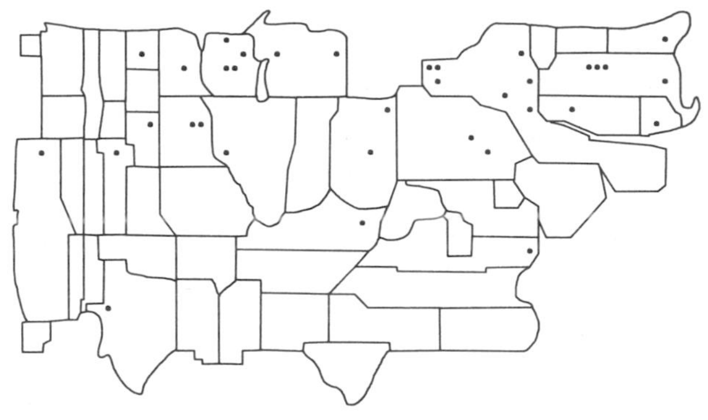

•horned lark (Qq. Q15, Q7)

horned man See **horny man**

horned owl n Also *horn-faced owl, horn(ing) owl, horn-rimmed owl, horny owl;* pronc-sp *hawn'owl* Cf **cat owl**

Any of several owls with prominent ear tufts, such as the **great horned owl,** the **long-eared owl,** or the **screech owl.**

1837 (1962) Williams *Territory FL* 73, There are many birds in Florida. . . Marsh Hawk. . . Horned Owl. . . Whooping Owl [etc]. **1843** (1969) Lewis *Odd Leaves* 151, Suddenly one of those small screech, or horned owls, so common in the South and West, gave forth his discordant cry. **1917** (1923) *Birds Amer.* 2.100, *Long-eared Owl. . .* Lesser Horned Owl. . . Ear-tufts conspicuous. *Ibid* 112, *Bubo virginianus virginianus. . .* Virginia Horned Owl. . . Ear-tufts very conspicuous, about 2 inches in length. **1922** Gonzales *Black Border* 306 **sSC, GA coasts** [Gullah glossary], *Hawn'owl*—the great horned owl. **1940–41** Cassidy *WI Atlas* **swWI,** Horn owl, horned owl—big, with feathers like horns. **1965–70** *DARE* (Qu. Q2) 135 Infs, **widespread,** Horned owl; **IL**32, **NY**73, **PA**6, Big horned owl; **CA**78, Pacific horned owl; 24 Infs, **chiefly Sth, S Midl,** Horn owl; **MI**64, **NY**200, Big horn owl; **MS**16, Horny owl; **OR**1, Horn-rimmed owl; **VT**10, Horn-faced owl; (Qu. Q1) Inf **AR**5, Horned owl; **GA**3, Horning owl.

horned poppy See **horn poppy**

horned pout n

1 also *hornpout (bullhead):* =**brown bullhead 1. chiefly NEng** See Map

1798 *Gazette of the U.S.* Phila., Aug. 3 (1912 Thornton *Amer. Gloss.*) The company concluded to go, for the sake of seeing a horn pout—when at last I drew one up—and behold! what was it, but a cat fish! **1837** in 1874 Hawthorne *Passages Amer. Note-Books* 55, The fish caught were . . three horned pouts. **1882** U.S. Natl. Museum *Bulletin* 16.104, *Amiurus* [sic] *catus*. . . Bull-head; Horned Pout; . . Sacramento Cat. **1907** *DN* 3.190 **NH,** *Hornpout*. . . Common small catfish. "We got a tub full of hornpouts." In Bristol, Ct., *bullhead.* **1911** U.S. Bur. Census *Fisheries 1908* 311, *Horned pout (Ameiurus nebulosus).*—A catfish found in the fresh waters of the Eastern, Northern, and Southern states, and in California. It is also called "bull-head," "bull-pout," "minister," etc. **1931–33** *LANE Worksheets* 3 infs, **CT, RI,** *Hornpout*. . . Bull-head. **1933** LA Dept. of Conserv. *Fishes* 426, *The Horned Pout* . . Ameiurus nebulosus. **1965** Teale *Wandering Through Winter* 178, The most widespread of the American catfish, the bullhead or horned pout, will sometimes move along the bottom of a pond. **1965–70** *DARE* (Qu. P1) 12 Infs, **NEng,** Hornpout; **RI**4, Hornpout bullheads; 7 Infs, **NEng,** Horned pout; (Qu. P3) Infs **MA**13, 50, Hornpout.

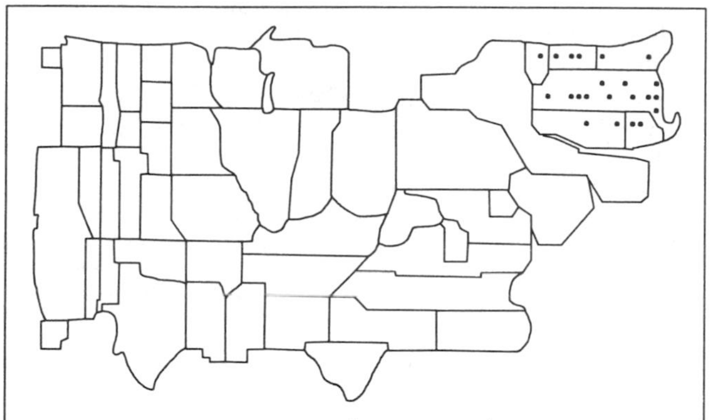
•horned pout 1 + varr (Qq. P1, P3)

2 A black bullhead (here: *Ictalurus melas*).

1908 Forbes–Richardson *Fishes of IL* 188, It is the common bullhead or horned pout of New England and New York, but in this state these names are much more likely to be applied to the more abundant black bullhead *(A. melas),* the commonest of its kind in the smaller creeks. **1956** Harlan–Speaker *IA Fish* 111, *Black Bullhead—Ictalurus melas* . . Other Names—Bullhead, . . horned pout. **1972** Sparano *Outdoors Encycl.* 365, *Black Bullhead*—Common Names: Black bullhead, horned pout. **1983** Becker *Fishes WI* 697, *Black Bullhead* . . Other common names: . . horned pout, . . river snapper.

3 =**white catfish.**

1946 LaMonte *N. Amer. Game Fishes* 163, *White Catfish—Ictalurus catus*. . . Horned Pout.

horned rabbit n *joc* **Cf horned jackrabbit**

1969 *DARE* (Qu. P32, . . *Kinds of wild animals*) Inf **CT**29, Horned rabbits—same as deer.

horned rattlesnake n Also *horned rattler, ~ snake* [See quot 1974]

=**sidewinder.**

1870 CA Acad. Sci. *Proc.* 4.67, The following do not occur west of this region [=the desert region west of the Colorado Valley]. . . *Crotalus cerastes* . . , Horned Rattlesnake [etc]. **1893** in 1900 U.S. Natl. Museum *Annual Rept. for 1898* 1198, The horned rattlesnake, or "sidewinder," as it is known locally throughout the region it inhabits, is the characteristic snake of the Lower Sonoran deserts. **1903** (1950) Austin *Land of Little Rain* 7 **ce,seCA,** It is a question whether it is not better to be bitten by the little horned snake of the desert that goes sidewise and strikes without coiling, than by the tradition of a lost mine. **1947** Pickwell *Amphibians* 204, Outer edge of each supraocular extending out above the eye into a raised and flexible hornlike process distinctly pointed at the tip. . . Horned Rattlesnake. **1974** Shaw–Campbell *Snakes West* 224, The sidewinder is known too from its "horns," the supraoculars that stick out like devil's horns over its eyes, giving it in some areas the name "horned rattler."

horned rush n [Prob from the tufted stems]

Either of two beak rushes: *Rhynchospora macrostachya* or *R. corniculata,* which is also called **pollywog, spade grass, spear grass, spile-market.**

1933 Small *Manual SE Flora* 178, *R[ynchospora]* [sic] *corniculata* . . Horned-rush. . . *R. macrostachya* . . Horned-rush. **1940** Clute *Amer. Plant Names* 157, *Rynchospora* [sic] *corniculata.* Horned Rush. **1946** Tatnall *Flora DE* 57, *R[hynchospora] corniculata* . . Horned Rush. . . *R. macrostachya* . . Horned Rush. **1970** Correll *Plants TX* 308, *Rhynchospora macrostachya* . . Horned-rush. . . *Rhynchospora corniculata* . . Horned-rush.

horned snake n

1 See **horn snake 1.**

2 See **horned rattlesnake.**

horned sucker See **horned dace 1**

horned toad n Also *horn toad, horny toad, hornet toad*

1 A horned lizard (*Phrynosoma* spp) of the southwestern US. Also called **horned frog**

1806 *MA Spy* 16 July (1912 Thornton *Amer. Gloss.*), A venerable Philosopher . . surrounded by piles of . . stuffed squirrel skins, and horned toads. **1885** *Weekly New Mexican Rev.* 18 June 4/6 *(DAE),* In the hills about Santa Fe, and even in its streets, may be found . . [the] little lizard called the horned toad. **1909** (1922) Norris *Third Circle* 105 **seCA,** The tarantulas and horned toads that you buy alive in glass jars. **1921** *DN* 5.114 **CA,** *Hornet toad*. . . Popular etymology from horned toad. *Horny toad.* **1930** OK Univ. Biol. Surv. *Pub.* 227, *Phrynosoma cornutum*. . . Horned Lizard; Horned Toad. **1953** Schmidt *N. Amer. Amphibians* 133, The misnomer "horned toad" is so genuinely popular and well known as the vernacular name for the lizards of the genus *Phrynosoma* that it seems best to adopt it rather than to attempt to force the use of the book name "horned lizard." **1962** Atwood *Vocab. TX* 59, The small flat lizard with horns on its head and back is known in Texas as a *horn, horned,* or *horny toad*. . . the Trans-Pecos leans strongly to *toad* [rather than *frog*]. . . The form *horned* occasionally appears as *hornet.* **1964** Wallace *Frontier Life* 50 **OK** (as of 1893–1906), We laughed at the freakish-looking "horny-toad" with his round, horny back, short legs, tiny pointed tail, prehistoric face, and two prominent horns on the sides of his head. **1967–68** *DARE* (Qu. P23) 10 Infs, **CA,** Horny toad; **CA**12, 105, 109, 120, **MA**1, **WA**1, Horn toad; **CA**17, 65, Horned toad; (Qu. P32) Infs **CA**3, **NM**3, **OK**32, Horny toad; **TX**13, Horned toad. **1967** *DARE* FW Addit **TX,** Horny toad: a horned lizard—covered with horns. Very friendly little fellas. **1979** Behler–King *Audubon Field Guide Reptiles* 514, This lizard [=*Phrynosoma cornutum*] is the common "horned toad" of the pet trade.

2 See quot.

1967 *DARE* (Qu. CC8, *Other names for the devil*) Inf **IL**26, Horned toad.

horned-toad buckwheat n

A **spine-flower** (here: *Chorizanthe rigida*).

1936 *Jrl. Economic Entomology* 29.682 **AZ,** The only food plant of any importance . . was the horned toad buckwheat, *Chorizanthe rigida.* **1941** *Torreya* 41.47, *Chorizanthe rigida*. . . Horned-toad buckwheat, Arizona.

horned worm See **hornworm**

horner See **horn** v **3**

horness See **harness**

hornet n [SwissGer *Hornuss* hornet, from the sound of the disk buzzing through the air] **csWI,** *Swiss German settlement areas*

An outdoor game; see quots; also the disk used in the game.

1941 Writers' Program *Guide WI* 539, One game, played now for more than forty years by Mt. Horeb and Monroe farmers, is *Le Hornuss* (Swiss, Hornet), named for the whizzing sound made by a hard rubber disc which the players whack from one end to the other of a 300-yard field. A sort of long distance ping-pong, *Le Hornuss* is fought with willow sticks called "switches," with shieldlike weapons, called "shingles," and with the hornet itself. . . On crisp Sunday autumn afternoons the Hornet field is abuzz. **1950** *WELS Suppl.* **csWI,** *Hornet*—the name of a game played by people of Swiss background near Mt Vernon. The players had a mallet on the end of a long flexible sapling. The mallet was used to strike a disk. Other players tried to block the motion of the disk by holding up large boards with numbers for scoring on them. The one with the mallet tried to drive the disk up the side of the valley. Much shouting and excitement. [*Ibid, Hornussen*—The Swiss ball game played in the New Glarus region. Ball is thrown and three players try to stop it with big wooden paddles bearing numbers, by which game is scored.]

hornet bee n Cf Intro "Language Changes" I.4

Appar a hornet.

1966 *DARE* (Qu. R21, *Are there any other kinds of stinging insects around here?*) Inf **SC**9, Hornet bee.

hornet clearwing See **hornet moth**

hornet fly n [From its resemblance to a hornet]

=**robber fly.**

1889 *Century Dict.* 2886, *Hornet-fly*. . . A dipterous insect of the family *Asilidæ;* a robber-fly.

hornet frog See **horned frog**

hornet moth n Also *hornet clearwing* [See quot 1926]

A clearwing moth *(Aegeria apiformis).*

1889 *Century Dict.* 2886, *Hornet-clearwing*. . . A hornet-moth, as *Sesia apiformis* or *S. bembeciformis. Ibid, Hornet-moth*. . . A moth of the family *Sesiidæ* and genus Sesia or Ægeria. **1926** Essig *Insects N. Amer.* 720, The hornet moth, *Alcathae apiformis . . (Aegeria)* . . The moths resemble in size and color the European giant hornet, *Vespa crabro.* **1965** Blickenstaff *Insects* 294, Hornet moth . . *Aegeria apiformis.*

hornet's nest n Cf **hurrah's nest 1**

A dangerous tangle; something in a confused or messy condition.

1958 McCulloch *Woods Words* 89 **Pacific NW,** *Hornet's nest*. . . Logs so badly bunched up as to make a tough and dangerous job of setting chokers. . . A ball of stranded cable on a line. **1970** *DARE* (Qu. E22, *If a house is untidy and everything is upset, you might say, "It's a ______!" or "It looks like ______."*) Inf **MA**124, Hornet's nest.

hornet toad See **horned toad**

horneyhead See **hornyhead a**

horn-faced owl See **horned owl**

hornfish n

1 Appar a fish of the genus *Lepisosteus.* Cf **gar n 1**

1821 in 1843 MA Hist. Soc. *Coll.* 2d ser 10.35 **seMA,** In the southerly part of this pond are . . roaches, chubs, horn fish. **1843** Marryat *Travels Snake Indians* 3.290 **eTX,** The horn fish is four feet long, with a bony substance on his upper jaw, strong, curved, and one foot long, which he employs to attack horses, oxen, and even alligators, when pressed by hunger.

2 Either of two related fish:

a =**walleye.**

1877 U.S. Natl. Museum *Bulletin* 10.46, *Stizostethium vitreum*. . . Wall-eyed Pike. . . Horn Fish. **1983** Becker *Fishes WI* 871, Walleye —*Stizostedion vitreum*. . . Other common names: yellow walleye, . . hornfish, blowfish.

b =**sauger.**

1882 U.S. Natl. Museum *Bulletin* 16.526, *S[tizostedium] canadense* . . Sauger; . . horn-fish.

horn fly n [See quot 1913]

A fly *(Haematobia irritans)* that attacks the base of the horns of cattle.

1889 U.S. Dept. Ag. *Rept. of Secy. for 1889* 17, The horn fly, a pest to horned cattle newly imported from Europe. This insect was first noticed in this country rather more than two years ago in the vicinity of Philadelphia, and has since greatly increased and spread to the southward along the Atlantic States until it has now reached southern Virginia. **1905** Kellogg *Amer. Insects* 342, The horn-fly, *Haematobia serrata* . . gets its popular name from the habit of clustering, when not feeding, on the bases of the horns of cattle. **1913** (1979) Barnes *Western Grazing* 320, There are three varieties of flies which bother range animals throughout the West. First in the list is the little black horn fly (Hoematobia serrata) so-called because of its habit of settling in great masses on an animal's head about the base of the horns. The top of the withers is also a favorite camping-place for them. They are so persistent in their blood-sucking attacks that often the base of the horn will be all raw and sore. **1950** *WELS (Kinds of flies)* 1 Inf, **csWI,** Horn fly. **1954** Borror-DeLong *Intro. Insects* 640, The horn fly, *Siphona irritans* . . is a serious pest of cattle. **1966–70** *DARE* (Qu. R12) 79 Infs, **chiefly Sth, S Midl,** Horn fly; (Qu. R10) Infs **AL**2, **FL**16, **TX**37, 59, Horn flies. **1967** *Hooker Co. Tribune* (Mullen NE) 28 Sept 4/4, [Advt:] *Bricon* is deadly to Hornflies and Faceflies, lice and ticks. **1967** *San Augustine Rambler* (TX) 27 July sec 1 4/7, Control horn flies, ticks and lice through regular spray program using recommended insecticides.

horn frog See **horned frog**

horn, go around the v phr [Prob in ref to the long voyage around *Cape Horn*] Cf **elbow, go (all) around one's**

1967–69 *DARE* (Qu. KK52, *To do something in an indirect and complicated way: "I don't know why he had to go ______ to do that."*) Infs **CA**1, **CT**29, **MO**27, **NC**76, Around the horn.

horn grebe See **horned grebe**

hornie n Cf **aggie**

1954 *Sun* (Baltimore MD) 25 Nov 14/7 *(Hench Coll.),* A man . . was holding forth . . on types of marbles he had played with as a boy. He remembers "hornies" (horn agate), "moonies" . . glass agates and so on.

hornie hornie cow's horn See **horns**

horn-in n [*horn in* v phr to intrude]

1967–68 *DARE* (Qu. II18, *Someone who joins . . without being asked*) Infs **AL**25, **NY**100, **NY**105, **PA**25, Horn-in.

horning n, also attrib

1 also *tin horning:* A noisy celebration following a wedding; a **shivaree. chiefly NEast, esp Upstate NY, nPA** See Map Cf **belling** vbl n[2], **horn v 3**

1889 *AN&Q* 4.81, The neighbor [when shot] was engaged in giving . . [the newly married couple] what is called in the despatches a 'charivari,' but is more idiomatically known in some of the rural parts of our country as a 'horning,' and in others as a 'callithumpian serenade.' . . it is distinguished by the extreme atrocity of the noises produced, and by the vigor and persistency with which they are maintained. . . On the score of taste and decency, horning is brutal. **1893** *KS Univ. Qrly.* 1.139 **KS,** *Horning:* a 'chivaree.' **1932** *Hanley Disks* **nwMA,** *Horning*—a serenade; **nwCT,** *Horning*—a noisy celebration after a wedding; they had cornstalk fiddles, hell bells, shotguns—most anything to make a disagreeable noise at a horning. **1941** *LANE* Map 409 *(Serenade)* 35 infs, **widespread, exc eMA, NH, ME,** Horning; 1 inf, **RI,** At a horning the boys go out with horns and make [the] night hideous; 1 inf, **RI,** *Horning,* also called tin horning; 1 inf, **nwMA,** The horning was formerly given by the groom's enemies, now by his friends. It ends with a dance inside the house; 1 inf, **swVT,** The whole town takes part in a *horning bee.* Formerly it was frowned on as 'rowdy'; now it is accepted as an established custom. **1948** Davis *Word Atlas Gt. Lakes* 255 **sMI, OH,** [7 of 270 infs used the term *horning.*] **1950** *WELS* 1 Inf, **WI,** Horning. [Inf old] **1965–70** *DARE* (Qu. AA18, . . *A noisy neighborhood celebration after a wedding, where the married couple is expected to give a treat*) 20 Infs, **chiefly Upstate NY, nPA,** Horning; 9 Infs, **chiefly Upstate NY, nPA,** Horning bee; **MI**49, **NY**75, 221, 223, 232, Horning—old-fashioned; **PA**130, Horning bee—bygone thing; **MA**42, Horning—out in York State they call it; **VT**8, Horning—if they [=the newly married couple] didn't treat them, they [=the other people] would horn them at night; **OH**16A, Shivaree—sometimes called it a horning; **NY**200, Horning party. [35 of 39 Infs comm type 4 or 5] **1968** *DARE* FW Addit **PA**81A, 84, 86, *Horning*—same as skimmelton, shivaree or serenade. Common. **1983** Glimm *Flatlanders* 88 **cnPA,** Now, the horning bee

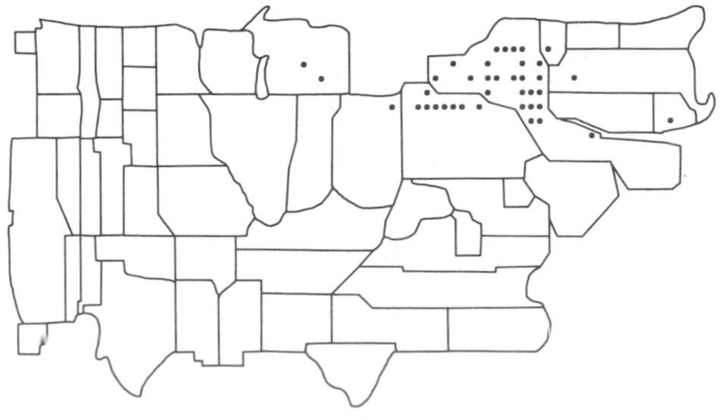

•horning n 1 + varr (Qu. AA18)

was a custom surrounding marriage back in the old days, and it is still practised by some.

2 Transf: hazing, harassment.

1894 Frederic *Marsena* 24 **nNY,** Here were all their resolves . . about scowling at the . . Southern sympathizer in the street, about a "horning" party outside his house at night, about, perhaps, actually riding him on a rail. **1896** *Chi. Record* 12 Feb. 2/4 *(DA),* 'Horning' is peculiar to Dartmouth, and is much in the line of hazing. . . The sophomore class howled beneath the windows of Prof. Foster's study and hurled snowballs and coal at them, breaking the glass.

horning vbl n See **horn** v **2, 5**

horning bush n [*horn* an antler]

1970 *Foxfire* Spring-Summer 71 **nGA,** The hunter would look for tracks, a trail, droppings, and for "horning bushes" that they'd used to rub the velvet from their horns.

horning owl See **horned owl**

horn mullet n

=**hog sucker.**

1889 *Century Dict.* 2886 **Chesapeake Bay,** *Horn-mullet.* . . The stone-roller or black sucker, *Hypentelium* or *Catostomus nigricans.*

horn mushroom n

Perh **horn of plenty 2,** but cf **moose antlers.**

1968 *DARE* (Qu. S18, *A kind of mushroom that grows like a globe . . sometimes gets as big as a man's head)* Inf **WI**37, Horn mushroom, moose mushroom, sponge mushroom [are all the same].

horn off See **horn** v **1a**

horn of plenty n

1 =**cornucopia.**

1929 Neal *Honolulu Gardens* 279, From the Tropics of the Eastern Hemisphere comes a datura popularly known as "cornucopia" or "horn of plenty." Its flowers seem to consist of two or three nested trumpets.

2 A mushroom of the genus *Craterellus.* For other names of var spp see **fairy's loving cup, fairy trumpet, trumpet of death**

1972 Miller *Mushrooms* 152, *Craterellus cornucopioides.* . . "Horn of Plenty". . . Cap trumpet-shaped, dark gray-brown. **1980** Smith-Weber *Mushroom Hunter* 82, *Craterellus fallax.* . . *Horn of Plenty.* . . Edible and choice in spite of its appearance—it is as black when cooked as it is when fresh. **1987** McKnight-McKnight *Mushrooms* 375, Horn of Plenty mushrooms *(Craterellus).*

horn out See **horn** v **1a**

horn owl See **horned owl**

hornpine, hornpipe See **hornbine**

horn poppy n Also *horned poppy* [See quot 1890]

A coastal poppy of the genus *Glaucium.* Also called **sea poppy**

1890 *Century Dict.* 4622, *Horn-poppy,* or *horned poppy,* a small seaside plant of the poppy family, *Glaucium luteum,* with clasping leaves and solitary yellow flowers: so named from the long curved horn-like seed-pods. **1900** Lyons *Plant Names* 173, *G[laucium] Glaucium.* . . Horn Poppy. **1946** Tatnall *Flora DE* 127, *G[laucium] flavum* . . Horn Poppy. **1950** Gray-Fernald *Manual of Botany* 680, *Glaucium.* . . Horn-Poppy. **1976** Bailey-Bailey *Hortus Third* 512, *Glaucium* . . Horned Poppy.

hornpout n

1 See **horned pout 1.**

2 Perh an **eelpout 1.**

1969 *DARE* (Qu. P4, *Saltwater fish . . not good to eat)* Inf **RI**15, Hornpout.

hornpout bullhead See **horned pout**

horn-rimmed owl See **horned owl**

horns n Also *all the horns in the wood, hornie hornie cow's horn* [Cf *DSL Suppl.* 1841] Cf **feathers, feathers, [animal's] feathers**

A children's game; see quot 1909.

1903 *DN* 2.298 **seMA,** *Hornie! hornie! cow's horn.* . . A children's game. **1909** (1923) Bancroft *Games* 223, *Horns.* . . This game is played very much like "Simon says." . . played with all of the players seated, their forefingers placed . . in front of them. One who is leader says:—"All horns up!" [or] "Cat's horns up!" or "Cow's horns up!" whereupon he lifts his own forefingers, pointing upward. Should he name an animal that has horns, all of the players lift their fingers in similar manner, but should he name an animal such as a cat, that has no horns, any player that lifts his fingers in imitation of the leader is out of the game. **1952** Brown *NC Folkl.* 1.63 (as of 1927), *Horns.* [*Ibid* 64, The players put their forefingers down on a flat surface, and the leader says: "Horns, horns, horns, cow's horns" (or goat's, deer's, &c.). As he names the animal, the players raise their hands and point their fingers from the sides of their heads like horns. The play proceeds rapidly. Suddenly the leader says: "Horns, horns, horns, horse's horns" (or bird's, cat's &c.). If a player raises his hands to his head when the animal mentioned has no horns, he must pay a forfeit.] *Ibid* 59, The game [=How Many Fingers] has become merely an ending to the game of 'Horns'. . . If he guesses incorrectly, he is . . pounded [on the back]. **1953** Brewster *Amer. Nonsinging Games* 24, *Feathers.* . . This is known also as Horns . . All the Horns in the Wood. **1966** *DARE* File **IN,** *Horns*—A type of children's game, a finger game.

hornscriggle See **hornswoggle**

horn shark n [Prob from the spine before each dorsal fin]

A small California shark *(Heterodontus francisci).*

1953 Roedel *Common Fishes CA* 12, California Horn Shark—*Heterodontus francisci.* . . This family includes fewer than 10 living species, all referred to a single genus. **1960** Amer. Fisheries Soc. *List Fishes* 6, Horn shark . . *Heterodontus francisci.*

horn snake n

1 also *horned snake, horn-tail snake:* A large, harmless snake *(Farancia abacura)* with a spine-tipped tail, native chiefly to the southern US. Also called **hoop snake, ice pick, mud snake, stinging snake**

1688 in 1695 Royal Soc. London *Philos. Trans. for 1694* 18.134 **VA,** The *Horn-Snake* is, as they [=Virginians] say, another sort of deadly Snake. **1764** in 1925 Fries *Rec. Moravians* 2.581 **NC,** It is said that when the Horn Snake gets angry it will drive its sting into a tree, and the tree will die within twenty-four hours. **1851** Woods *16 Months* 134 **cCA,** I don't know his name, but he has a flat head, looks very brassy, and has a sharp horn at the tail. It answers the description of the horned snake. It is said that, taking the end of its tail in its mouth, it will form a perfect hoop with its body, rolling rapidly over till it reaches the object at which it aims. **1859** Taliaferro *Fisher's R.* 58 **nwNC** (as of 1820s), Now folks may talk as they please 'bout there bein' no sich things as horn-snakes, but what I've seen I've seen. **1909** Biol. Soc. DC *Proc.* 22.134 **NC,** *Farancia abacura.* Red-bellied Horn Snake. **1925** TX Folkl. Soc. *Pub.* 4.47, Stories of a snake that stings . . have been in circulation throughout the Southern states for the past hundred years or more. These stories are usually based on the horn or mud snake, . . which has a short spine at the end of its last caudal vertebra. **1948** *AN&Q* 8.152 **KY,** *Horn-Tail Snake Superstition.* A rural Negro of Ballard County, Kentucky, tells me that the common red-bellied snake has a deadly horn on the end of its tail, and that it strikes with this weapon. However, he himself has never seen a snake to fit this description, but learned of it from a relative in Tennessess [sic]. **1952** Ditmars *N. Amer. Snakes* 122, *Horn Snake.* . . *Farancia abacura abacura.* . . The tail is provided with a spine much sharper than with other snakes. **1966-68** *DARE* (Qu. P25) Inf **GA**7, Horn snake; **LA**34, Ice snake—a water snake with a real pointed tail and it's hard, hard, hard—book name is horn snake.

2 =**glass snake.**

1938 Matschat *Suwannee R.* 263 **nFL,** [And all those stories . . about it sticking its tail in trees and poisoning them . . are false.] *Ibid* 264, "But they do lose their tails, an' get new ones". . . "And the new tail is shorter, and stubby, and generally of a different color, so that it does look like a horn. That's why Cella called it a horn snake." **1958** Conant *Reptiles & Amphibians* 105, Glass Lizards: Genus *Ophisaurus.* . . Their tails are . . fragile. Hence full-tailed specimens are not common. The regenerated tip, sharply pointed and of a different color from the remaining part of the original tail, earns them the name of "horn snake" among country folk.

hornsnoggle See **hornswoggle**

horn spider n

An unidentified spider.

1969 *DARE* (Qu. R28, . . *Kinds of spiders)* Inf **CA**156, Horn spiders—big, yellowish.

horn spoon n

1 See **horn** n **2.**

2 Used as an oath—usu in phr *by the great horn spoon* and varr; see quots. [Etym unknown] *old-fash*

1842 McCarty *Songs* 1.222, He vow'd by the great horn spoon . . / He'd give them a licking, and that pretty soon. **1848** (1894) Lowell *Biglow* 66 **'Upcountry' MA,** "I should like to shoot / The holl gang, by the gret horn spoon!" sez he. **1853** *Knickerbocker* 41.115, 'By the horn spoons!' repeated the skipper suddenly. **1856** Underhill–Thomson *Elephant Club* 72 **NYC,** You do solemnly swear, by the sacred horn spoons. **1914** *DN* 4.74 **nNH, ME,** *Horn-spoon! by the gret.* Exclamation of surprise. **1943** in 1944 *AmSp* 19.117, He says to a professor . . "Do this or get out!" and by the *Great Horned Spoon,* he doeth it or getteth out. **1966–69** *DARE* (Qu. NN29a, *Exclamations beginning with 'great': "Great ______!"*) Inf **CA**136, By the great horn spoon!—my grandmother used to say; **MA**14, Horn spoon; **NM**6, Horned spoon; **OH**66, Horny spoons.

hornswoggle v Also *harnswaggle, hornscriggle, hornsnoggle, hornswaggle, hornswargle*

1 To embarrass, disconcert, confuse; hence ppl adjs *hornswoggled, onswoggled.*

1829 *VA Lit. Museum* 30 Dec 458 **KY,** *Hornswoggle.* . . To embarrass irretrievably. **1840** Haliburton *Clockmaker* (3d ser) 95 **NEng,** I always feel kinder onswoggled like, at dead bodies. **1892** *KS Univ. Qrly.* 1.97 **KS,** *Hornswoggle:* to discomfit. **1933** *Scribner's Mag.* 94.193/1 **nFL,** She's like a cow has tried to jump a high fence and has got hung up on it—she's hornswoggled. **1965–70** *DARE* (Qu. GG2, . . *'Confused, mixed up'*) Infs **MI**63, **WA**3, Hornswoggled.

2 To cheat or trick; to swindle; hence ppl adj *hornswoggled* cheated; n *hornswoggler* a cheater. Cf **bumswiggle, honeyfuggle 1**

1860 *Oregon Argus* 12 May (1912 Thornton *Amer. Gloss.*), P. F. is going to hornswoggle the Douglas Democrats. **1908** *DN* 3.321 **eAL, wGA,** *Horn-snoggle.* . . To cheat, get the better of in a trade. "He horn-snoggled me outen my watch." **1912** *DN* 3.578 **wIN,** *Horn-swaggle.* . . To cheat. Very common. "Don't let him horn-swaggle you." **1916** *DN* 4.276 **NE, MA, IL, LA, KS,** *Hornswoggle.* . . To swindle, cheat, or trick. "Business was business with him, and you had to watch out or he'd hornswoggle you every time." **1917** *DN* 4.437 **NY,** *Hornswoggle.* **1933** *AmSp* 8.50 **Ozarks,** *Hornscriggle.* . . To cheat, to take advantage of. *Them town fellers done hornscriggled ol' man Barton out'n his farm!* **1949** *PADS* 11.23 **CO,** *Hornswoggle, hornswargle.* . . To trick, to fool. "He hornswoggled me into buying his horse." **1950** *WELS (To deceive somebody)* 1 Inf, **WI,** Hornswoggle. **c1960** *Wilson Coll.* **csKY,** *Hornswaggle* (or *harn-*)—Deceive. **1965–70** *DARE* (Qu. II33, *To get an advantage over somebody by tricky means*) 20 Infs, **scattered, but less freq Sth, S Midl,** Hornswoggle; (Qu. V7, *A person who sets out to cheat others while pretending to be honest*) Inf **IA**8, Hornswoggler; (Qu. II32) **MI**4, Hornswoggle; (Qu. KK36, *Talking about a person who is easily fooled: "It's easy to ______."*) Infs **IL**96, **IA**9, **NY**86, **PA**59, 150, Hornswoggle him; (Qu. LL23, *Cheated, treated dishonestly*) Infs **NY**94, **PA**150, **TX**81, Hornswoggled.

3 in phr *I'll be hornswoggled* and varr: Used as an expression of surprise, amazement, disgust.

1834 Caruthers *Kentuckian* 1.61, I wish I may be horn swoggled, if ever I thought to live to see the day when I should *'sculp'* a Christian man. **1866** Smith *Bill Arp* 133, I'll be horn swaggled if the talkin and the writin and the slanderin has got to be done on one side any longer. **1895** *DN* 1.397, *Horn swaggled* ['swɑgəld] or *swuggled* ['swʌgəld]: equivalent to *dingswizzled.* [*Ibid* 396, Expression of surprise, consternation, etc. . . "I'll be dingswizzled."] **1911** *DN* 3.550 **WY,** *Hornswoggled,* exclamation expressing wonder, disgust, etc. "I'll be hornswoggled." **1950** *WELS (Exclamations of surprise)* 1 Inf, **WI,** Hornswoggled; *(Substitutes for "damn" . . "Well I'll be ______ !")* 1 Inf, **WI,** Hornswoggled. **1960** Criswell *Resp. to PADS 20* **Ozarks,** Exclamations of surprise—*Well, I'll be hornswoggled.* **1965–70** *DARE* (Qu. NN25b, *Weakened substitutes for 'damn' or 'damned': "Well, I'll be ______!"*) 21 Infs, **scattered, but less freq S Midl, Mid Atl,** Hornswoggled; (Qu. NN7, *Exclamations of surprise . . "Well, ______."*) Infs **MN**2, **PA**15, 175, **WV**3, (I'll be) hornswoggled; (Qu. NN32, *Exclamations like 'I swear' or 'I vow'*) Inf **TX**11, [I'll] be hornswoggled. **1975** Gould *ME Lingo* 135, *Hornswoggle.* . . Mainers use it . . to indicate amazement. Usually, a happy surprise. When a good friend you haven't seen in years walks into your yard, you may . . exclaim, "Well, I'll be hornswoggled—look who's here!"

hornswoggler See **hornswoggle 2**

horn-tail snake See **horn snake**

horn toad See **horned toad**

hornweed n [*OED* 1884 →]

A **hornwort 1,** esp *Ceratophyllum demersum.*

1900 Lyons *Plant Names* 91, *C[eratophyllum] demersum.* . . Hornweed. **1930** OK Univ. Biol. Surv. *Pub.* 2.61, *Ceratophyllum demersum.* . . Hornweed. Hornwort. **1936** Winter *Plants NE* 180, Hornweed. . . In ponds and streams. . . Found throughout the state.

hornworm n Also *horned worm, horned caterpillar, horny ~* [From the hornlike projection at the end of the abdomen]

A larva of any of several **sphinx moths,** esp those of the genus *Manduca.* For other names see **potato worm, tobacco worm, tomato worm**

1676 Royal Soc. London *Philos. Trans.* 11.635, When the [tobacco] plant is well grown they suffer damage by a Worm that devours the leaf, called a *Horn-worm* (an *Eruca* or Caterpillar). **1800** in 1969 Herndon *Wm. Tatham Tobacco* 21 **VA,** That which is most destructive . . is the *horn* worm, or large green tobacco worm . . or the great horned caterpillar. **1863** U.S. Dept. Ag. *Rept. of Secy. for 1862* 125, The larva [of the Carolina sphinx moth] . . is sometimes called the horn worm. **1924** U.S. Dept. Ag. *Farmers' Bulletin* 1371.38, *Tomato worms, or hornworms.* Certain large green caterpillars are also called tobacco hornworms or tobacco worms, as they feed on both tomato and tobacco plants. . . In spite of the wicked-looking horn on the tail, they are entirely harmless to persons. A single hornworm, when large, can strip a tomato plant in two or three nights, leaving only the stems. **1944** *PADS* 2.67 **NC, VA,** *Horn-worm.* . . Same as *tobacco-worm.* **1966–70** *DARE* (Qu. R27, . . *Kinds of caterpillars or similar worms*) Infs **CT**13, **GA**20, 84, **KY**65, 68, 80, **LA**2, Hornworm; **AL**17, Horned caterpillar; **SC**19, Horny caterpillar; **SC**57, Horned worm; (Qu. R30, . . *Other kinds of beetles*) Inf **PA**6, Hornworm. **1967** *Times–Crescent–Charles Co. Leaf* (La Plata MD) 27 July sec B 5/1, It's a hornworm contest—possibly the only one of its kind if [sic] the world—and you can enter! If you've got worms in your tobacco field or on tomato plants, bring them to the Field Day. . . Mr. Bissell isn't revealing his method of measuring the green worms with diagonal white bars and red or black horns at the tail ends.

hornworm fly n [**hornworm**]

A **sphinx moth** (here: *Manduca quinquemaculata* or *M. sexta*).

1966 *PADS* 45.16 **cnKY,** *Hornworm fly.* . . The moth stage of the tobacco hornworm. It lays its eggs on the leaves of the tobacco plant. **1967** Key *Tobacco Vocab.* **CT, PA,** Hornworm fly.

hornwort n

1 Std: a submerged aquatic plant of the genus *Ceratophyllum.* Also called **cedar moss, coontail 1, fish blankets, hornweed.** For other names of *C. demersum* see **duck sparrowgrass, June grass, nigger wool, water cedar**

2 =**honewort.**

1901 Mohr *Plant Life AL* 647, *Deringa canadensis.* . . Hornwort.

horny caterpillar See **hornworm**

horny chub See **horned chub**

horny cony n

A **filefish** (here: *Monacanthus hispidus*).

1898 U.S. Natl. Museum *Bulletin* 47.1715, *Monacanthus hispidus.* . . Horny Cony.

horny frog See **horned frog**

hornyhead n [From the tubercles on the head]

Any of several cyprinid fishes; see below.

a also *horneyhead:* The creek chub *(Semotilus atromaculatus).* **esp S Atl**

1838 *S. Lit. Messenger* 4.405/2 **GA,** I dont 'spect to cetch any thing vut a few horny-heads no how, vut I'll fish on a while longer. **1845** Thompson *Pineville* 162 **GA,** Sam's wife . . took him to account for spending so many broken days . . in the woods, without bringing home so much as a cut-squirrel or horney-head. **1883** (1971) Harris *Nights with Remus* 104 **GA** [Black], Brer Wolf 'low he gwine ter fish fer horneyheads. **1908** *DN* 3.321 **eAL, wGA,** *Horny-head.* . . A fish with several pairs of hornlike protuberances on the head, the fresh-water chub. **1930** *Copeia* 4.152, *Semotilus atromaculatus thoreauianus.* . . Southern horned dace. . . Locally called 'hornyheads.' **1953** Randolph–Wilson *Down in Holler* 254 **Ozarks,** *Horny-head.* . . A small chub-like fish *(Semotilus atromaculatus).* The male has short, horny protuberances on the scales about the head in the spring. **1960** Criswell *Resp. to PADS 20* **Ozarks,** Finest early spring minnow was the hornyhead.

b A **stone roller** (here: *Campostoma anomalum*).

1854 Wailes *Rept. on Ag. & Geol. MS* 336, Small fish found in the clear creeks of our State, and familiarly known as *horny-heads,* or *Stone-toters,* were obtained during the past summer. **1965** McClane *McClane's Std. Fishing Encycl.* 891/2, Stoneroller. *Campostoma anomalum.* Also known as hornyhead and knottyhead, it is a brownish-olive minnow with a brassy luster.

c A chub *(Nocomis biguttatus)* now found primarily in the Great Lakes states, Mississippi-Ohio valleys, and the Upper Midwest. [See quots 1908, 1983] Also called **horned chub, hornyhead chub, Indian chub, jerker, red-spotted chub, redtail chub, river chub, shiner, stony head**

1859 Taliaferro *Fisher's R.* 109 **nwNC** (as of 1820s), Close under the Blue Ridge we had nothing but chubs, hornyheads, pikes, . . and a few other small varieties of the finny tribes. **1878** U.S. Natl. Museum *Bulletin* 12.33 **nwSC,** *Ceratichthys biguttatus. . .* The "Horny Head" is abundant in all the small streams falling into the Tugaloo. *Ibid* 72, *Fishes of Nashville* [TN], *as given by a Fisherman. . .* "Minnow Tribe." . . Horny Head. **1882** U.S. Natl. Museum *Bulletin* 16.212, *C[eratichthys] biguttatus. . .* Horny Head; River Chub; Jerker. **1908** Forbes-Richardson *Fishes of IL* 167, According to our 137 collections of the horny-head, it is almost wholly a species of the creeks and smaller rivers. **1911** U.S. Bur. Fisheries *Rept. for 1908* 311, *Horney-head.*—A small dace *(Hybopsis kentuckiensis),* found abundantly in rivers from New York to . . the West. **1967** Cross *Hdbk. Fishes KS* 87, The hornyhead is confined to clear, permanent, rocky creeks in Kansas. . . The range and abundance of *H[ybopsis] biguttata* have decreased in the past century. **1983** Becker *Fishes WI* 485, *Hornyhead Chub. . . Nocomis biguttatus. . .* Other common names: hornyhead. . . Breeding males with approximately 60-100 conspicuous tubercles on upper part of head, some tubercles with heavy "spines" pointing anteriorly.

d A **shiner** (here: *Notropis cornutus*).

1983 Becker *Fishes WI* 518, *Common Shiner. Notropis cornutus. . .* Other common names . . hornyhead. . . Breeding males. . . Large tubercules on top of head and on snout, a single row along edge of lower jaw. Scales of back from nape to dorsal fin with small tubercules.

hornyhead chub n [See quot 1983] **chiefly Upper Missip Valley**

=**hornyhead c.**

1943 Eddy-Surber *N. Fishes* 131 **MN,** *Nocomis biguttatus. . .* The hornyhead chub . . is a large species, sometimes reaching a length of 10 inches. . . It builds its nest in fine gravel. **1947** Hubbs-Lagler *Fishes Gt. Lakes* 63, *Hornyhead chub—Nocomis biguttatus. . .* Chiefly in clear, gravelly creeks of moderate size; the younger fish commonly in weed beds. **1956** Harlan-Speaker *IA Fish* 90, The hornyhead chub is one of the most sought for baits for bass and catfish and is used extensively for walleye fishing. **1957** Trautman *Fishes* 292 **OH,** *Hornyhead Chub. . .* Heads of *breeding males* and upper part of the body suffused with pinks, rose and blues, the tubercles a pallid white. **1965** IL Nat. Hist. Surv. *Biol. Notes* 54.7, Hornyhead chub. Generally distributed in the northern half of the state [=IL]. **1972** WI Acad. *Trans.* 40.315, Hornyhead chub—*Nocomis biguttatus.* **1983** [see **hornyhead c**].

hornyhead turbot n [See quot 1953]

A **righteye flounder** (here: *Pleuronichthys verticalis*). Also called **sharpside turbot**

1953 Roedel *Common Fishes CA* 69, *Hornyhead Turbot—Pleuronichthys verticalis. . .* a high, narrow, bony ridge between eyes with sharp, prominent spines at either end. **1960** Amer. Fisheries Soc. *List Fishes* 47, Hornyhead turbot. . . *Pleuronichthys verticalis.* **1973** Knight *Cook's Fish Guide* 393, Hornyhead Turbot.

horny man n Also *horned man* [Cf *EDD Hoorniman* (at *hornie* sb. 1)]

The devil.

1966 Dakin *Dial. Vocab. Ohio R. Valley* 2.520 **KY,** *The devil . . the horny man* [in] Allen County. **1969** *DARE* (Qu. CC8, . . *Names for the devil*) Inf **ME**9, Horned man. **1974** Maurer-Pearl *KY Moonshine* 119, *Horny-man* . . a euphemism for devil.

horny owl See **horned owl**

horny toad n

1 See **horned toad 1.**

2 A toadfish (*Opsanus* spp).

1969 *DARE* File **NC,** *Horny toad:* Toadfish, type of fish, horny on underside, which can be eaten but must first be skinned.

horribles n pl, usu cap [Cf *OED horrible* sb. B "A horrible person or thing"] **MA** Cf **antiques and horribles, fantastic**

See quot 1965.

1884 Barber *Diary* 4 July **MA,** Went to see horribles at 9 & heard speech at 10. **1940** *AmSp* 15.330 **Boston MA,** *'Horribles'*—I doubt if the origin of the Fourth-of-July parade of 'horribles' is as well known as the institution is. . . [O]n such occasions of state as called for a parade of the . . 'Ancients and Honorables' . . it was customary in country villages to burlesque it by a Fourth-of-July parade of 'Antique Horribles' or 'Antiques and Horribles'. . . Nowadays 'Antique' is omitted from the title; but it is still customary that part of the costumes try to look as antiquated as possible while others try to look as frowzy as possible. **1948** Coatsworth *South Shore* 65 **MA,** Independence Day, with its parades and bonfires in the evening . . has a feature new to me, in the "Hingham Horribles," when young people appear as grotesquely disguised as possible. **1965** *DARE* File **MA** (as of 1910), *Horribles*—persons in hideous, ugly garb, usually in the July 4th parade. **1989** *Yankee* July 20 **eMA,** On the Fourth of July . . the "Horribles" parade. In . . eastern Massachusetts towns children dress in full colonial regalia, scary vampire suits, and outlandish gypsy getups and traipse down the main street. . . By the 1850s the uniforms of the militia companies (foremost . . was the Ancient and Honorable Artillery Company . .) had gotten embellished to the point of absurdity. . . What better subject for parody . . ? . . Companies of mounted men gaudily dressed . . mocked the solemnity . . by styling themselves Antique and Horrible, or Antic and Intolerable and parading in high spirits.

horrors n pl Often with *the*

1 An extreme state of apprehension or depression; infreq, a nightmare. *somewhat old-fash*

1780 in 1875 J. & A. Adams *Familiar Letters* 382 **eMA,** London is in the horrors. Governor Hutchinson fell down dead at the first appearance of mobs. **1859** (1968) Bartlett *Americanisms* 203, *Horrors.* "To have the horrors" is to be in low spirits, to have a fit of the blues. **1899** (1912) Green *VA Folk-Speech* 231, *Horrors. . .* Extreme depression; the blues. **1902** *DN* 2.236 **sIL** [Pioneer dialect], *Horrors. . .* Nightmare. **1968** *DARE* (Qu. GG34a, *To feel depressed or in a gloomy mood: "He has the ______ today."*) Inf **MD**31, Horrors.

2 Tremors, esp delirium tremens.

1848 (1855) Ruxton *Life Far West* 67, Paying the penalty in a fit of "horrors"—as *delirium tremens* is most aptly termed by sailors and the unprofessional. **1859** (1968) Bartlett *Americanisms* 203, *Horrors.* "To have the horrors" . . also means to have delirium tremens. . . "[T]his poison . . acts with terrible results on the nerves . . stirring up mania, convulsions, and the horrors. . . "—*Philad. Evening Bulletin,* 1857. **1899** (1912) Green *VA Folk-Speech* 231, *Horrors. . .* Delirium tremens. **1902** *DN* 2.236 **sIL** [Pioneer dialect], *Horrors. . .* Delirium tremens. **1905** *DN* 3.11 **CT,** *Horrors. . .* Delirium tremens. **1937** *Lit. Digest* 123.15.12 [Hobo jargon], John Hollow-legs—a bum with the "hunger horrors." **1946** *PADS* 6.12 **eNC,** *Drunken horrors. . .* Delirium tremens. . . Occasional. **1966-70** *DARE* (Qu. DD22, . . *Delirium tremens*) Infs **LA**14, **ME**1, 9, **NC**13, The horrors; **MA**55, Horrors; **MD**43, **NC**61, 82, **SC**58, Drunken horror(s); **ME**15, Rum horrors.

horry See **harrow**

horse n, v Usu |hɔrs, hɔ(ə)s|; also **chiefly Atlantic** |hɒ(r)s| Pronc-spp *hawse, hawss, hoss, orse;* for addit pronc and sp varr see quots Cf Pronc Intro 3.I.1.e [Cf *EDD horse* "Also . . in forms *harse, herse, hos, hoss*"] Cf **forty** adj, n **A**

A Forms.

1815 Humphreys *Yankey in England* 105, *Hoss,* horse. **1843** (1916) Hall *New Purchase* 116, I now "gathered hossis." **1891** *DN* 1.163 **cNY,** [hɔs] < *horse.* **1892** *DN* 1.212 **ceME,** I pronounce . . *hoarse* [hɔəs] and *horse* [hɔs], with an inclination towards [hos]. **1905** *DN* 3.11 **cCT,** *Horse. . .* Pronounced hoss. **1908** *DN* 3.322 **eAL, wGA,** *Hoss* [hɔs]. . . Horse. **1914** *DN* 4.159 **cVA,** *Horse* [hɔs]. *Ibid,* Hawse. **1914** Brininstool *Trail Dust* 110, When it comes to saddle hawsses there's a difference in steeds. *Ibid,* There is but one breed o' critters that I ever come across / That will allus stand the racket—'tis the / Ol' / Cow / Hawss! **1922** Gonzales *Black Border* 263 **sSC, GA coasts,** Ef my juntlemun kin git uh hawss. *Ibid* 306 [Gullah glossary], *Hawss*—horse, horses. **1926** in 1944 *ADD* **sFL,** *Horse* . . orse. **1939** *LANE* Map 196 *(Horse),* [Generally, in **NEng** the vowel in *horse* is either [ɔ] or [ɒ]. Also, 1 inf, **nwCT,** [hɔ˙s]; 1 inf, **seMA,** 'Horsetraders say [ha·s]'; 1 inf, **seMA,**

[hɔ˞rs], 'affected pron; I'll put an R in it if I can'; 1 inf, **cnMA,** ['ɔ˞əsɨ˅z]; 1 inf, **nwVT,** [hors]; 1 inf, **seNH,** [hɑ˃s], fully back with or without lip-rounding.] **1940** *Sat. Eve. Post* July 20 55/3 **GA** [Black], You can lead a hawse to water. **1961** Kurath–McDavid *Pronc. Engl.* 121 **Atlantic,** The vowels in . . *horse.* . . Except for Pennsylvania and adjoining parts of New Jersey and Maryland, all areas have the /ɔ ~ ɒ/ phoneme of *law, loss* in . . *horse.* . . In areas that lack /r/ after vowels, *horse* /hɔs ~ hɒs/ rimes with *loss.* . . In areas that preserve postvocalic /r/, the /ɔ/ vowel . . is usually shorter than in other positions. . . In Upstate New York and Western New England the /ɔ/ . . [ranges] from [ɒ˄ ~ ɔ] to [ɔ˄ ~ o˅] . . some speakers seem to merge the vowel . . with the /o/ of . . *hoarse.* In Pennsylvania, Maryland, and New Jersey the /ɔ/ . . must . . be regarded as an allophone of /o/. . . On Delmarva the /ɔ/ . . is a weakly rounded [ɒ˅] sound. **1967** *DARE* FW Addit **swNC,** *Hoss* [hɔs]—horse; **sAR, LA,** *Hoss* [hɔs]. **1973** Allen *LAUM* 3.31 **Upper MW** (as of c1950), In . . *[horse]* exists a vocalic range from a lowered [ɔ˅] to [ɒ] and even an occasional unrounded [ɑ]. . . In the U[pper] M[idwest] some northern speakers and many Midland speakers have so coalesced /o/ and /ɔ/ before /r/ that they are unable to distinguish in their own speech such pairs as *hoarse* and *horse.* **1988** *DARE* File **seID, UT,** In rural areas [one hears] "A *harse* is *barn* in a *born,*" [with [ɑr] where other speakers have [ɔr]].

B As noun; also attrib.

1 A male horse in contrast with a mare; a stallion; a gelding; also fig. See **2** below

1777 in 1875 J. & A. Adams *Familiar Letters* 235 **ceMA,** My horse. . . clambers over mountains that my old mare would have stumbled on. **1914** *DN* 4.159 **cVA,** *Horse.* . . Gelded horse. "A horse and a mare." **1931–33** *LANE Worksheets* **CT,** *Horse*—stallion. I've got a pair of horses, one's a mare and one's a horse. **1936** (1951) Faulkner *Absalom* 286 **MS,** He came in and stood over the pallet where the girl and the baby were. . . [H]e . . said, 'Well? . . horse or mare?' . . "[W]ait. You mean that he had got the son at last that he wanted". . . "It wasn't a son. It was a girl." **1939** *LANE* Map 196 *(Horse; gelding), Horse* is used in . . different applications, though not many [people] . . distinguish them consistently in practice. . . *Horse* may refer to male animals only, excluding mares. This meaning is very common . . 'A horse is generally *he* to me' . . 'It's wrong to call a mare a horse'. . . It appears . . in collocations like . . *Is that a horse or a mare.* . . Finally *horse* may refer to geldings only; but definitions of this kind are often qualified by words like 'usually' or 'primarily' . . 'only in the singular.' **1942** *AmSp* 17.238, It [=the word *horse*] . . appears reserved for the male which has been castrated . . a gelding. Thus after maturity horses are differentiated as stallions, mares, and horses. **1965–70** *DARE* (Qu. K30, *A castrated horse;* total Infs questioned, 75) 13 Infs, Horse; (Qu. K31, *A horse that's only partly castrated;* total Infs questioned, 75) Inf **NC**15, Horse; (Qu. K29, *A male horse kept for breeding;* total Infs questioned, 75) Inf **OK**18, Horse.

2 attrib: Of animals; male, spec:

a *horse colt:* A male colt. [*OED horse-colt* 1382 →] Cf Intro "Language Changes" I.4

1848 Bartlett *Americanisms* 181, *Horse-colt.* "We frequently see in advertisements these terms, *horse-colt, mare-colt, &c.* A *horse*-colt is simply a *colt;* a *mare*-colt, merely a *filly.*" **1899** (1912) Green *VA Folk-Speech* 231, *Horse-colt.* . . A young male horse. **1931–33** *LANE Worksheets* **CT,** A horse colt or a mare colt. **1939** *LANE* Map 196 *(Horse; gelding)* 2 infs, **eMA, eCT,** *Horse colt;* 1 inf, **wCT,** *Horse colt,* 'a young stallion'. **1942** *AmSp* 17.238, Among animal breeders the word . . [horse is] used to designate young males. . . A breeder of horses speaks of a new-born colt as a *horse colt* (a male). **1986** Pederson *LAGS Concordance (Male horse)* 1 inf, **ceAR,** Horse colt.

b *horse mule:* A male mule.

1860 (1937) Lewis *Diary Pike's Peak* 14.204 **PA,** Smith & Co. offered . . 2 horse mules $230. **1954** *Harder Coll.* **cwTN,** *Horse mule*—a male mule. **1968** *DARE* Tape **MO**16, [FW:] What sex is the mule, or is it sexless? [Inf:] They got a mare mule an' a . . horse mule. **1984** Burns *Cold Sassy* 62 **nGA** (as of 1906), Said he would lead the charge bareback on old Jack, his mouse-colored horse-mule. **1986** Pederson *LAGS Concordance,* 1 inf, **csAL,** Horse mule—he mule; 1 inf, **swGA,** Horse mule—young mule, apparently male; 1 inf, **cnTN,** Horse mule—male.

3 often *hoss:* Fig: a person, usu a man, showing some notable quality (whether admirable or objectionable)—often used as a term of address. [From any of the qualities attributed to a horse]

1840 (1841) Dana *2 Yrs.* 221, He was "a man, every inch of him," . . though "a bit of a horse," and "a hard customer," yet he was generally liked by the crew. **1843** (1847) Field *Drama Pokerville* **MO,** "Put it into him, hoss!" "Look out old coon!" **1859** (1968) Bartlett *Americanisms* 204, *Hoss.* . . A man remarkable for his strength, courage, etc. A vulgarism peculiar to the West. Even of a prominent lady a Western eulogist will say, "She's a hoss," that is, a sort of Pandora or nonsuch. **1871** Eggleston *Hoosier Schoolmaster* 48 **IN,** In this one art of spelling he was . . to use the usual Flat Creek locution . . "a hoss." . . Jim could "spell like thunder and lightning[”]. **1877** Wright *Big Bonanza* 30 **wUT,** The enthusiastic Johntowners went forth in the dance with ardor and filled the air with splinters from the puncheon floor. When a Johntown "hoss" balanced in front of the "Princess" he made no effort to economise shoe-leather. **1940** *AmSp* 15.216 **wFL,** Varmint might be applied to a contemptible person . . but in Florida *hound* or *hoss* would as likely be used. **c1960** *Wilson Coll.* **csKY,** *Hoss*—Used humorously to designate . . some pompous self-important fellow. **1967–69** *DARE* (Qu. HH27a, *A very able and energetic person who gets things done)* Inf **PA**94, Horse; (Qu. HH40, *Uncomplimentary words for an old man)* Infs **CA**66, **CT**35, Old horse; (Qu. II1, . . *A close friend . . "He's my ______."*) Inf **GA**61, Best horse; **LA**32, Friends—boys—call each other hoss, . . stud; (Qu. KK37, . . *A very sly person: "He's ______."*) Inf **MD**47, A slick hoss [hɔs]. **1967** *DARE* FW Addit **LA,** *Hoss*—form of address for an adolescent boy. "Were you next, Hoss?" *Ibid* **sAR,** *Hoss*—used sometimes among boys with their peers. It seems to imply that the person addressed is "one of the boys," strong and worthy, not "Sunday-schoolish" but no "hood." It may be used when the boy's name is not recalled, or otherwise merely as a friendly gesture. **1970** *DARE* Tape **TN**48, There are more white horses voting than black horses. And the black vote is frequently split. . . Politically Lobe is a segregationist, but at heart, he's not. He knows there are more white horses than black horses, so he decides to ride—he's a politician—decides to ride the white horses.

4 See quots. Cf **dog** n[1] **B3**

1970 *DARE* (Qu. D32, *The metal stands in a fireplace that the logs are laid on)* Infs **MO**16, **SC**42, **VA**69, Horse(s). **c1970** *DARE* File **seGA,** *(Andirons)*—Horse. **1986** Pederson *LAGS Concordance (Andirons)* 2 infs, **seLA, cTX,** Horses.

5 Any of var creatures thought to resemble a horse; see quots.

1930 Shoemaker *1300 Words* 29 **cPA Mts** (as of c1900), *Horse*—A pioneer name for Elk. "Horse hunting", Elk hunting. "Horse Valley", i.e., Elk Valley. **1967–68** *DARE* (Qu. R6, *What other names do people have around here for grasshoppers?)* Infs **LA**26, **TX**32, Horses; (Qu. R9b, *An insect that holds up its front feet as if saying a prayer)* Inf **SC**43, Horse.

6 See **horse mackerel 1.**

7 See quot. **chiefly Atlantic, N Cent** *esp freq among Black speakers*

1965–70 *DARE* (Qu. FF5b, . . *Recent dance steps)* 10 Infs, **chiefly Atlantic, N Cent,** Horse; (Qu. FF5a) Inf **KY**87, Horse. [7 of 11 Infs Black; 6 Infs coll educ]

8 See quot. Cf **pony, saddle**

1968–70 *DARE* (Qu. AA27, . . *Expressions . . for . . menstruation)* Inf **MI**78, Riding a cotton horse; **WV**20, White horse.

9 A joke or laugh at someone's expense—usu in phr *that's a horse on one* and varr.

1896 *DN* 1.418 **c,wNY,** *Horse:* "That's a horse on him," the laugh is on him. **1909** *DN* 3.398 **nwAR,** *Horse.* . . Joke. "That's a horse on you." **1911** *NY Eve. Jrl.* (NY) 27 Jan 16 *(Zwilling Coll.),* Morris is probably . . 90 per cent white man, but he counts as an Indian under tribal law. . . Some horse on the "white man's hope" enthusiasts. **1960** Criswell *Resp. to PADS 20* **Ozarks,** *Horse on you*—used to an opponent in a game when you get an advantage over him—such as an extra fall in wrestling.

10 In weaving: see quot. [*EDD horse* sb. 14 "A fault in warping . . when a pin is missed."]

1937 (1963) Hyatt *Kiverlid* 19 **KY,** I'm agoin' to make has'e all I can with the warpin' and you watch the bars keerful and see that I don't skip a peg and make a 'horse' that would be a sight troublesome.

11 also *horse(back) fight, horse-and-rider, horses:* Any of several games played on land or in water in which a player takes the role of a horse; see quots.

1890 Howells *Boy's Town* 84, With the races came the other plays which involved running, like horse. **1923** Acker *400 Games* 222, *Mount Ball* (Horse and Rider; Pony and Rider)—Basket ball. . . [The players] are equally divided, half being "horses," . . half "riders." The riders, on the backs . . of the horses, pass a basket ball among themselves. When one misses . . all must dismount and run. The horses run to get the ball and the one getting it cries "Halt!" . . [and] must throw it . . to hit a rider. . . If a rider is hit, all of the horses and riders exchange places. **1946** TN Folk Lore Soc. *Bulletin* 12.1.17, Horses were driven and seldom ridden in the game of "Horse." A driver might have only one horse and he might have six or eight or more. Run-aways were common. That was the horse's privilege. **1957** *Sat. Eve. Post Letters* **MA,** *Horse Fights*—two contestants would carry pickaback a rider who would try to unseat opponent by tugging or pushing. Any horse or rider to touch knee to ground was loser. **1967–70** *DARE* (Qu. EE28, *Games played in the water*) Inf **VA**54, Horse—ride on each other's shoulders and try to knock each other off; **IN**39, Horses—get on each other's shoulders, then joust; **TX**33, Horses—hold someone on shoulders and try to unseat other teams; **TX**54, Horses—ride on each other's shoulders and try to topple the other team; **VA**99, Horse-and-rider—[same as] knights-and-horses; **TN**66, Horseback fights—on one another's shoulders; (Qu. EE33, . . *Outdoor games*) Infs **IL**100, **NY**113, Horse.

12 also *horse and horse, ~ on you, ~ race, ~ racing, horses:* A dice game; see quot 1988. Cf **horse apiece**

1934 (1943) *W2, Horse and horse,* a form of gaming, esp. dice throwing, in which the winner has to win a majority of rounds. **1966** *DARE* FW Addit **WA,** *Horses*—dice game played across bar counters. **1968** *DARE* (Qu. EE40, . . *Table games . . using dice*) Inf **MN**42, Horses—player one gets three shakes at most, player two must beat player one's score in same number of shakes; **NC**52, Horse racing; **SC**65, Horse race; **WA**22, Horse; **WA**30, Horse on you. **1985** Keillor *Lake Wobegon* 144, The big booths in back are full of hefty guys jammed in tight—they roll horse with dice out of leather cups and turn and holler at guys lumbering in the front door. **1988** *DARE* File **seWI** (as of 1966), The dice game "horse" is played with five dice and a cup. The game is played by at least two players, and the object is to get the greatest number of high-numbered dice in the smallest number of shakes. The first player has up to three shakes of the dice. The other players get the same number of shakes as the first player. There are three turns per game. After each turn, those who lose the round are said to have a horse on them ("that's a horse on you"). . . Players who lose two turns lose the game.

13 in phrr *draw in one's horse, pull in one's horses:* See quots.

1958 McCulloch *Woods Words* 53 **Pacific NW,** *Drawed in his horns*—Backed down on a deal. Also sometimes said drawed in his horse. **1966** *DARE* (Qu. II31, *In an argument between two people, when one of them claims too much and the other shows him up: "He saw that he was wrong, so he started to ______."*) Inf **NC**14, Pull in his horses.

14 in var phrr indicating that a man's trouser fly is open: See quot. Cf **barn door 2b**

1965–70 *DARE* (Qu. W24c, *Sayings to warn a man that his trouser-fly is open*) Infs **CO**20, **GA**19, **NJ**24, **NY**200, **OH**49, **PA**170, **TX**43, 54, (Your) horse is going to (*or* gonna) get out (*or* away); **NJ**67, **OR**13, **VT**12, Barn door open, (the) horse might get (*or* will come) out; **IL**26, **MN**38, **NJ**20, **WA**24, Horse (is) coming (*or* getting) out (of the barn); **FL**19, **GA**77, **SC**55, Your horse is about (*or* bound) to get out (of the barn); **MN**15, **NJ**1, **OH**48, (Your) horse will get out; **NY**109, **WI**64, Lock the barn door before the horse gets out (*or* away); **NJ**53, **VA**9, Your horse will be (*or* get) out of the stable (if you don't watch it); **CA**132, **TX**26, **WA**33, Horse is (*or* has come, might get) out (of the barn); **OH**97 Close your barn door before the horse gets out; **SC**68, Horse 'bout to come out the stable; **MI**19, Horse barn's open; **AL**17, Horse fixin' to get out; **AZ**1, King's horses, king's horses; **PA**130, You'll lose your horse; **MI**97, Your cows and horses'll get out; **NC**50, Your horse is a-gonna jump outa the stable; **GA**6, Your horses are jumping out. [15 of 37 Infs gs educ or less]

15 attrib; Of size or quantity: large, full; see quots.

1953 Randolph–Wilson *Down in Holler* 254 **Ozarks,** *Horse dose*. . . A very large dose of medicine. "Old Doc Holton give me a horse dose of calomel, an' it damn' near killed me." A *horse quart* means a full quart, as distinguished from a *short quart* or "fifth." The phrase *horse measure* is sometimes heard in this connection. **1954** *Harder Coll.* **cwTN,** *Horse dose*—A very large dose of medicine. **c1960** *Wilson Coll.* **csKY,** *Horse dose*—A big dose of medicine. **1988** *DARE* File **csWI,** The huge vitamin pills prescribed for pregnant women are often called *horse pills* because of their size.

C As verb.

1 with *along:* See quot. [Cf *OED horse* v. 2 "To . . go on horseback"] Cf **buggy** v

1954 *PADS* 21.30 **MO,** *Horse along* . . to go on horseback.

2a Of a mare: to be in heat; hence ppl adj *horsing.* Cf **bull** v

1899 (1912) Green *VA Folk-Speech* 232, A mare in heat. Horseing. **1937** *AmSp* 12.103 **eNE,** A mare in a state of sexual excitement is said to be *horsin'.* **1949** *PADS* 11.7 **wTX,** *Horsing*. . . In heat (of a mare). Common among men. **1954** *Harder Coll.* **cwTN,** *Horsing*—Of a mare: in heat. **1968** *DARE* FW Addit **seNJ,** *Horsin'*—meaning a horse is in heat. "You have to watch the mare when she's horsin'." Heard in conversation.

b also with *around;* Transf; of a person: to act like a sexually aroused mare or stallion; also fig; hence ppl adj *horsing* sexually aroused; eager (to marry); vbl n *horsing* acting in such a way.

1932 (1974) Caldwell *Tobacco Road* 27 **GA,** Ellie May's horsing. *Ibid* 30, Ellie May's acting like she was Lov's woman. . . Look at that horsing Ellie May's doing! . . That's horsing from way back yonder! **1960** Wentworth–Flexner *Slang* 270, *Horse*. . . [taboo] To . . indulge in sexual horseplay. **1962** Faulkner *Reivers* 255 **nMS,** Didn't he have to watch it too . . that man horsing and studding at that gal, and her trying to get away from him. **1965–70** *DARE* (Qu. AA4a, . . *Expressions . . about a man who is very eager to get married . . "He's ______."*) Infs **IN**19, **NY**221, **OR**10, **VA**69, Horsing; **KY**85, **NE**10, Horsing around; **KS**18, **KY**85, **MS**60, **NC**31, **SC**19, 32, **TN**27, Horsing to get married; (Qu. AA4b, . . *Expressions about a woman who is very eager to get married . . "She's ______."*) Infs **IN**8, 19, 26, **MS**1, **NY**205, **VA**69, Horsing; **GA**77, **MS**60, **SC**32, Horsing to get married; (Qu. AA6a, . . *A man who is fond of being with women and tries to attract their attention—if he's nice about it*) Inf **VA**42, He horsed a little bit; **NY**213, Horsin' around; (Qu. AA8, *When people make too much of a show of affection in a public place—for example, "There they were at the church supper ______ [with each other]."*) Infs **MD**5, **WI**7, Horsing around. [21 of 23 Infs comm types 4 or 5]

c also with *for;* By ext: to desire, long for.

1893 Shands *MS Speech* 38, *Horse for*. . . Used by the lower orders of society to mean *to long for, to earnestly desire.* It is evidently derived from a mare's desiring the stallion. . . the expression *to horse for* now has as wide application as the word *desire;* in the parlance of negroes and illiterate whites, a man, woman, or child may horse for anything. **1967** *DARE* (Qu. KK28, *Feeling ambitious and eager to work*) Inf **PA**29, Horsing—if a woman. **1976** Garber *Mountain-ese* 43 **sAppalachians,** Clem is a horsin' to go deer huntin' even afore the season opens.

3 Esp in logging: to haul or raise—usu in phr *horse logs.*

1905 U.S. Forest Serv. *Bulletin* 61.40 [Logging terms], *Horse logs, to.* In river driving, to drag stranded logs back to the stream by the use of peaveys. **1969** Sorden *Lumberjack Lingo* 58 **NEng, Gt Lakes,** *Horse logs*—Used in river driving to drag or roll stranded logs back to the stream by the use of a peavey. Generally done by two men with cant hook or peavy on each side of a log to lift and pull it where it would float. **1971** *Foxfire* Spring–Summer 99 **nGA,** If they was goin' t'build a new barn, th'neighbor men got in and put up th'barn. . . And they didn't have any pulleys'r'anything t'horse those logs up. Three'r'four men'ud get on each end of a log and they'd just come up with it.

4 See quots; hence vbl n *horsing.* [*OED horse* v. 4. b "To elevate on a man's back, in order to be flogged"] *old-fash* Cf **horse-shedding**

1871 (1892) Johnston *Dukesborough Tales* 23 **GA,** "Come out here and go to horsin'." The two nags [=boys taking the part of horses] came out. Master Pate inclined himself forward. . . Master Boatright leaped . . upon his back. The former, gathering the latter's legs under his arms, and drawing as tightly as possible his pants across his middle, began galloping. . . Mr. Meadows . . began to apply . . [a hickory switch] . . to that part of Master Boatright's little body which in his present attitude was most exposed. . . Master Pate must frisk and prance and otherwise imitate a horse. **1899** (1912) Green *VA Folk-Speech* 231, *Horse*. . . To be mounted on another's back to be flogged.

5 See quot. Cf **horse B3**

1952 Brown *NC Folkl.* 1.553, *Hoss*. . . To annoy, blackguard. "Don't hoss me, big boy."—General. Negroes.

6 See quot. [**horse B8**]

1954 *Harder Coll.* **cwTN,** *Hossing*—menstruating.

7 with *over;* In railroading: see quots. [*horse* v to haul or push by force]

1937 *Writer's Digest* 11.41 [Railroad lingo], *Horse her over*—Reverse. **1940** Cottrell *Railroader* 129, *Horse her over*—To put an engine into reverse. On the early, manually operated, reversing equipment it took considerable jockeying to reverse an engine while it was in motion. **1958** McCulloch *Woods Words* 89 **Pacific NW,** *Horse 'er over*—To reverse an engine; on a steam locie, to throw the Johnson bar to the opposite side of the arc for this purpose.

8 ppl adj phr *horsed up:* See quots. Cf **Astor's pet horse 1**

1950 *WELS (When a woman puts on her good clothes and tries to look her best)* 1 Inf, **WI,** [She's] horsed up. **1968–69** *DARE* (Qu. W37, *When a woman puts on her good clothes . . you say she's ______*) Inf **NY**161, All horsed up; (Qu. W38, *When a man dresses himself up in his best clothes, you say he's ______*) Inf **MO**25, Really horsed up. **1988** *DARE* File **ceWI,** We're going someplace informal, so we won't have to get horsed up.

horse ail n

1975 Gould *ME Lingo* 136, *Horse-ail* is an indisposition peculiar to horses, and the word survives for a minor and undiagnosed affliction for humans: "Guess I've got the horse-ail. I been snifflin' and sneezin' all mornin'!" *Spanish mildew* . . suggests malingering; *horse-ail* is likely to be a mild but real disturbance.

horse along See **horse C1**

horse-and-buggy adj Cf **hook-and-eye**

Of Mennonites: eschewing modern conveniences such as automobiles.

1967 *DARE* (Qu. CC2, . . *Predominant religious denominations*) Inf **PA**22, Mennonite Churches—some horse-and-buggy.

horse and horse n See **horse B12**

horse and horse adj, adv phr [See quot 1859] Cf **horse apiece**

Even; equally matched; "neck and neck."

1846 (1973) Porter *Quarter Race* 91 **KY,** "Hoss and hoss!" "Yes; 'hoss and hoss,' and my deal!" **1859** (1968) Bartlett *Americanisms* 204, *Horse and horse.* Even. Originally applied to horses which in running a race come in side by side, or, as the phrase is, "neck and neck;" and then transferred to gamesters. . . "Why . . I sot down to old sledge along with Jake Stebbins. It was horse and horse, and his deal. . . "—*Bunkum's Recollections.* **1906** (1908) Lorimer *Jack Spurlock* 3, It was horse and horse between the professors. **1922** *DN* 5.167 **CT,** *Hoss and hoss.* Means the same as neck and neck or six to a half a dozen. Even. **1927** *AmSp* 2.357 **cwWV,** *Hoss and hoss* . . evenly matched. "The candidates for sheriff are running hoss and hoss." **1942** Berrey–Van den Bark *Amer. Slang* 28.4, *Equal; on terms of equality.* . . horse and horse, hoss and hoss. [*Ibid* 28.5, *Unequal.* Hoss and mule.] *Ibid* 648.10, *Tied.* . . horse and horse. *Ibid* 745.15, [In cardplaying:] Horse and horse . . *on even terms, both sides vulnerable, each with a game to his credit when playing best two out of three.*

horse and log n

1926 *AmSp* 1.416 **Okefenokee GA,** I got up on a horse an' log (that's whut they call 'em). An' I got up on there ter see the Deer a-comin'. [Footnote to *horse an' log:*] This curious expression is applied to the crossed trunks of two fallen trees.

horse and pepper See **hasenpfeffer**

horse-and-rider See **horse B11**

horse-and-rider cloud n Cf **horsetail 1**

1938 Burman *Blow for a Landing* 189 **Lower Missip Valley,** The brilliant blue sky was studded with thin zig zag streaks of cloud, as though a giant with a flaky piece of chalk were scrawling enormous letter S's. . . Willow Joe studied the sky in anxiety. 'Don't like the looks of them horse-and-rider clouds,' he murmured. 'There's a plenty of wind and water when you see them thataway.'

horse and the buggy n

A game; see quot.

1972 Jones–Hawes *Step it Down* 174 **eGA** [Black], *Horse and the Buggy.* . . [O]ne type of play [is categorized] as "the pursuit of vertigo"; "Horse and the Buggy" certainly fits that description. To play it, two children take hands, their arms either crossed or straight, and wheel around, pulling back from each other so that their momentum increases. . . At this galloping pace, the call-and-response pattern for the singing is an essential. [Call and response:] Horse and the buggy,/ Sail away / Sail away, horsey,/ Sail away,/ . . Mabel . . remarked, "When you play it with the boys and they let go your hands, you *would* go sailing."

horse ant n Also *horse piss ant* Cf **saddle-horse ant**

A red ant (*Formica* spp, esp *F. rufa*); see quots.

1889 *Century Dict.* 2890, *Horse-ant.* . . The common red ant, *Formica rufa.* **1967–70** *DARE* (Qu. R17, . . *The big black ants that sting*) Inf **KY**80, Horse ant; **LA**6, Horse ants: red, but have a black mark—big, solitary ants; **DE**3, Horse piss ant: these are great big fuzzy [ants] with some red on them.

horse apiece n Cf **horse B12, horse and horse** adj, adv phr

A draw; see quots.

1980 *DARE* File **cwWI,** [After saying he didn't like either Presidential candidate, one local resident remarked:] "I think it's a horse apiece." **1982** *Ibid* **cwWI,** "It's a horse apiece" means two things are equal and it's difficult to choose one or the other. **1988** *Ibid* **seWI** (as of 1966), The phrase "horse apiece" is used in the dice game "horse" and means "dead even." When two players have each lost one turn, they are said to have "a horse apiece." **1990** *Ibid* **swWI,** If two farmers are discussing the merits of a Ford and a Chevy truck, and the prices are comparable and the dealers give the same service, they might say "It's a horse apiece." That just means "It's six of one and half a dozen of the other," or they are about equal.

horse apple n

1 A cultivated apple used both for cooking and for eating. **chiefly S Midl**

1844 Thompson *Major Jones's Courtship* 102 **GA,** He got snapt on egnog when he heard of my ingagement, and he's ben as meller as hos-apple ever sense. **1852** Fleischmann *Wegweiser* 187, Für die Breitengrade von Mississippi eignet sich besonders der *Limber-Twig* und *Horse-apple.* [=For the stretches along the Mississippi the *Limber-Twig* and *Horse-apple* are especially appropriate.] **1940** (1978) Still *River of Earth* 94 **KY,** There was a baked horse apple in my bucket, oozing sugar from the top, and cushaw blooms, fried in meal batter, tasting like fish. **1949** Arnow *Hunter's Horn* 310 **KY,** Wild-strawberry-picking time in June was hardly finished before . . the first of the white horse apples were falling, begging to be canned or dried or made into vinegar. **1954** *Harder Coll.* **cwTN.** **1956** McAtee *Some Dialect NC* 23, *Horse-apple* . . a large, yellow apple, probably a pippin. **c1960** *Wilson Coll.* **csKY,** Horse apple. . . A well-known old-fashioned apple with a tart and queer flavor; maybe a type of pippin. **1966–69** *DARE* (Qu. I53) Inf **AL**1, Horse apple—big, red, sour; **KY**42, Horse apple—sour, old-fashioned. **1971** *Today Show Letters* **cnAL** (as of a1940), She referred . . to a pie being made of horse apples . . so I asked her what she meant and she said "Well, you know apples usually fed to animals just like horse corn is not used for cornmeal, but is fed to horses."

2 **=Osage orange** or its fruit.

1915 *DN* 4.226 **wTX,** *Horse-apple.* . . The Bois d'arc apple. **1960** Vines *Trees SW* 220, Vernacular names [for trees of the genus *Maclura*] are Hedge-apple, Horse-apple, Mock-orange, and Yellow-wood. **1966** *DARE* (Qu. T13) Inf **OK**52, Fruit of this tree [=Osage orange] called . . horse apple; (Qu. T16) Inf **OK**42, There is a bodark tree. . . It is also called a "horse apple" or "hedge tree." The "oranges" are called "horse apples." **1979** Little *Checklist U.S. Trees* 165. **1985** *DARE* File **sIN,** Horse apple—fruit of the Osage orange.

3 also *horse biscuit, ~ doughnut, ~ dumpling:* A piece of horse manure; by ext, nonsense, a bit of absurdity—also used as exclam. [From the shape] Cf **alley apple 2**

1940 Mencken *Happy Days* 90 **Baltimore MD,** The same wicked boy . . invented the game of dropping horse apples and other such waggish missiles upon the brakemen who rode on top of the box-cars. **1950** *WELS (Barnyard fertilizer . . joking)* 3 Infs, **WI,** Horse apple; 1 Inf, Horse biscuit. [All Infs rural] **1954** *Harder Coll.* **cwTN,** *Horse dumpling*—a piece of horse manure. Euph[emistic] and fac[etious]. **1955** Warren *Angels* 152 **KY,** Maybe now that I got him free of the horse-apple of a lie he had lived with all that time, maybe there wasn't anything to live for now. **1958** *VT Hist.* new ser 26.288, As high as the steam from a heap of warm horse doughnuts on a frosty morning. **1971** Jennings *Cowboys* 99 **West,** "It's kind of pretty." "Horse apples." **1984** Burns *Cold Sassy* 66 **nGA** (as of 1906), He and I had us a great manure war then, throwing dried cow cushions and sheep pills and horse biscuits at each other and dying laughing.

horse around See **horse C2b**

horseback n [From the shape] **NEng**

=hogback 2b

1884 Hurd *Hist. Norfolk Co. MA* 561/2 **ceMA,** In various parts of [Weymouth] . . are unusually fine examples of the sharp, linear hills, called horse-backs or kames and glacial plains, both formed by the ice as it melted or retreated towards the pole. **1889** *Century Dict.* 2851,

Hogback. . . in New England more commonly called *horseback*. **1937** FWP *Guide ME* 4, Spread over the land surface is a remarkable system of *eskers* or *kames*, known variously as 'horse-backs' or 'hog-backs.' These are long ridges of gravel deposited by the receding glacier of the Ice Age, extending from one mile to a hundred and fifty miles in length. **1942** Cannon *Look to the Mt.* 38 **NH,** He'd gone a little out of his way up onto a horseback. It was steep climbing the side of the horseback. **1946** Attwood *Length ME* 14 [Geographical terms], *Horseback*—A long ridge, narrow and with comparatively slight elevation above surrounding land. An esker. A whaleback, hogback . . windrow . . back furrow . . Indian road, Indian railroad.

horseback conversation n

1940 *Hench Coll.* **VA,** "What were you talking about?" "Oh, it was only a horseback conversation." [That means] we didn't talk about anything important.

horsebacker n [*horseback* adv] Cf **bullwhacker**

One who rides a horse, esp as an escort or guard.

1914 *DN* 4.108 **KS,** *Horsebacker*. . . One riding on horseback. **1923** *DN* 5.211 **swMO,** *Horse backer*. . . One who travels on horse. **1942** Berrey–Van den Bark *Amer. Slang* 426.11, *Horseman*. . . horse-backer, hoss-backer. **1955** Sandoz *Miss Morissa* 3 **NE,** Horsebackers had met the coach a mile out to make a flying wedge for it . . to the stage station. . . The galloping escort split the packed crowd, afoot and horseback, turning each side back upon itself. *Ibid,* Most of the horsebackers seemed to be cowboys, with big hats . . guns hanging over their leather chaps, gleaming spurs. *Ibid* 50, The news had been brought in by horsebackers who . . hurried back to cry the alarm. . . "The Black Hills are busted!" they shouted. "The gold's played out!" *Ibid* 70, Half a dozen horsebackers rose up . . to the left, moving parallel to the coach, little more than their heads showing . . not Indians, unless they were disguised.

horseback estimate See **horseback opinion**

horseback fight See **horse B11**

horseback opinion n Also *horseback estimate, ~ guess, ~ impression*

A casual, offhand judgment; an appraisal made without thorough consideration.

1879 *Congressional Record* 23 Apr 9.1.728/1 **FL,** I am not here as a judicial authority or oracle. I can only give a horseback opinion about it. **1903** (1965) Adams *Log Cowboy* 72 **West,** My sister gives it as a horseback opinion that she'd been engaged to this fellow nearly eight months. **1933** *Sun* (Baltimore MD) 30 Aug 10/3 *(Hench Coll.),* The courts were setting up horse-back opinions against the carefully reasoned products of . . observation. **1937** *Ibid* 10 Sept 1/5 *(Hench Coll.),* The chairman made it clear that more money would be provided if the situation demanded. He said $150,000,000 was a "horseback guess" as to the amount that would be required. **1944** *AmSp* 19.153 **wVA,** My horse-back impression . . is that by the average speaker the word is omitted. **1965** *DARE* File **csWI,** (as of 1940s), *Horseback estimate*—a rough estimate (such as might be made of an area of land by a man without getting off his horse).

horseback ride n Also *horsie, horsieback (ride);* for addit varr see quots Cf **backie-horse**

Either a piggyback ride or a ride in which a child straddles the back of one who is on hands and knees; see quot 1988.

1965–70 *DARE* (Qu. Y31, *If a child asked his father to carry him on his back, he might say, "Give me a ______."*) 76 Infs, **scattered,** Horseback (ride); 27 Infs, **scattered,** Horsieback (ride); **AL**3, **LA**20, **MS**45, **MO**17, **OR**1, **PA**142, Horse ride; **FL**2, **PA**167, **SC**3, **TN**4, **WV**18, Horsie (ride); **NC**30, Ridy horsie; [**IL**114, **NC**40, **OK**12, **TX**86, Packhorse (*or* peckhorse) ride; **TX**35, 103, Ride on your (*or* riding the) horse]. **1966** *DARE* Tape **SC**26, Little babies . . want a ride. . . give 'em a ride piggyback. I usually say . . let me ride you on my back, give you a horse ride. **1988** *DARE* File **NYC,** Horsie was when the person got down on all fours and you rode. A piggyback ride meant you were carried on the back of an upright person with your legs hooked under the person's arms; **NYC** (as of 1950s), When I asked for a horsie ride, one of my parents would go down on all fours; a piggyback ride was when they stood up; **cIL** (as of c1975), I used to ask for "horsieback rides" when I was small—that was when my father carried me on his back while he was standing upright; we never said "piggyback"; **seWI,** My parents, my aunt and uncle, they'd get down on their hands and knees and give us kids horseback or horsieback rides.

horse ball tree n Cf **daddynut**

A linden.

1970 *DARE* (Qu. T13) Inf **KY**72, Horse ball tree.

horse balm n

An aromatic plant of the genus *Collinsonia.* Also called **horseweed 2.** For other names of *C. canadensis* see **citronalis, gravelroot 2, hardhack 2, hardock 2, heal-all 4, knobgrass, knotroot, knotweed, mountain balm, ox balm, rattlesnake root, richweed, stoneroot**

1787 *Columbian Mag.* Dec 807/1 **seNY,** *Horse balm,* or *Ox-weed,* smells like balm, but more mild, grows in moist, rich, new grounds and woods, to the height of two feet or more. **1822** Eaton *Botany* 244, *Collinsonia . . canadensis* . . horse balm, rich weed. . . Strong-scented, not unpleasant. Woods. **1832** MA Hist. Soc. *Coll.* 2d ser 9.148 **cwVT,** Collinsonia canadensis. . . Horse balm. **1894** *Harper's New Mth. Mag.* 88.562/2, I passed a luxuriant clump of the plant known as "horse-balm." **1938** Madison *Wild Flowers OH* 136, *Horse Balm*. . . Strongly lemon scented. **1974** (1977) Coon *Useful Plants* 156, Horse . . balm . . extends in most [of] the United States east of the Rockies.

horse barn n **widespread, but less freq Sth, S Midl** See Map Cf **horse lot, horse stable**

A separate building for horses; a section inside a barn specifically for horses.

1854 (1923) Holmes *Tempest & Sunshine* 190 **KY,** I'd as soon be married in the horse barn as there. *Ibid* 207, If it don't suit Lady Tempest, she can go to the hoss barn. **1885** U.S. Bur. Indian Affairs *Report* 130 **MT,** The horse-barn, carpenter-shop, ware-house, and some small buildings. **1907** *DN* 3.191 **seNH,** *Horse-barn*. . . Horse-stable. **1910** *DN* 3.443 **cwNY,** *Horse-barn*. . . Horse-stable. **1917** *DN* 4.394 **neOH, NY, NEng, IL, KS,** *Horse-barn*. . . A farm barn containing a horse-stable; usually in distinction from a *hay-* or *grain-barn.* "He's down at the horse-barn." **1939** *LANE* Map 109 **NEng,** *Horse barn* usually denotes a separate building [for 48 infs]; 1 inf, **swMA,** *Horse barn,* in the main barn. **1950** *WELS (Part of the barn where horses are kept)* 31 Infs, **WI,** Horse barn. **1965–70** *DARE* (Qu. M9, *The part of a barn where horses are kept*) 231 Infs, **chiefly Nth, N Midl, West,** Horse barn; (Qu. M1, . . *Barns . . according to their use*) 164 Infs, **widespread but less freq Sth, S Midl,** Horse barn; **MO**10, Horse and cow barn; (Qu. M22, . . *Other kinds of buildings*) Infs **NY**113, **VA**32, Horse barn; **NY**96, Outside horse barn; **CA**105, Horse and cow barn; (Qu. Q22) Inf **MA**78, Horse-barn bird; (QR, near Qu. W24c) Inf **MI**19, Horse barn's open.

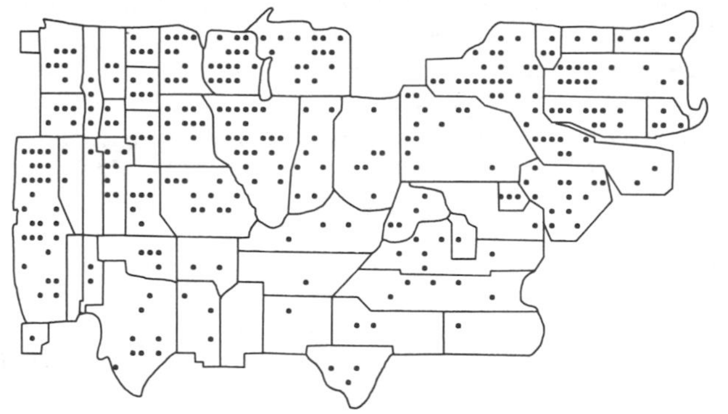

horse-barn bird n Cf **barn sparrow**

=**English sparrow.**

1970 *DARE* (Qu. Q22) Inf **MA**78, Horse-barn bird [hɔsbənbɚd].

horsebean n

1 =**broad bean 1.** [See quot 1889]

1684 (1977) Mather *Essay Providences* 306 **eMA,** The Stone weiged but seven Grains, being much of the shape of our ordinary Horse-beans. **1720** *Amer. Weekly Mercury* 26 May 2/1, Thunder and Lightning . . was followed by Hail as bigg as horse Beans. **1876** Hobbs *Bot. Hdbk.* 55, Horse bean, Vicia faba. **1889** *Century Dict.* 2890, *Horse-bean*. . . A sort of bean so called from being fed to horses, or from its large size. **1913** London *Valley of Moon* 311 **cCA,** You see outside the fence there, clear to the wheel-tracks in the road—horse-beans. **1931–33** *LANE Worksheets* **nwCT,** A horse bean is a large coarse bean. **1976** Bailey–Bailey *Hortus Third* 1155.

2 =Jerusalem thorn. [See quot 1911]

1900 Lyons *Plant Names* 275, *Parkinsonia,* . . Horse-Bean . . *P. aculeata* . . Horse-bean. **1911** *Century Dict. Suppl., Horse-bean.* . . In the southwestern United States . . *Parkinsonia aculeata* . . the twigs of which are eaten by horses. **1959** Munz–Keck *CA Flora* 800, *P[arkinsonia] aculeata* . . Horse-bean.

3 Any of var beans: see quots.

1931–33 *LANE Worksheets* **nwCT,** Horse bean—thick lima bean. **c1955** Reed–Person *Ling. Atlas Pacific NW (Butter beans / large, flat, yellow; not in pods)* 1 inf, Horse beans. **1965–70** *DARE* (Qu. I20, *Other kinds of beans*) Infs **CA**105, 107, **CO**27, **LA**20, 24, **WA**1, Horsebeans; (Qu. I16, *The large flat beans* . . *not eaten in the pod*) Infs **CA**105, 167, 170, 212, **MA**5, Horsebeans; (Qu. I17, *Beans [not pods] that are dark red when they are dry*) Infs **NJ**5, **WA**18, Horsebeans; (Qu. I14, *Kinds of beans that you eat in the pod before they're dry*) Inf **CA**132, Horsebeans.

4 A **jackbean** (here: *Canavalia ensiformis* or *C. gladiata*). [*DJE* 1696 →] **Sth**

1933 Small *Manual SE Flora* 727, *C[anavalia] gladiata.* . . *Horse-bean.* . . The stem and branches climb. **1953** Greene–Blomquist *Flowers South* 61 **FL,** The . . horse-bean *(C[anavalia] gladiata)* has a white or purple corolla sometimes tinged with yellow and a much larger pod. Naturalized from the W[est] I[ndies], it occupies waste places and cultivated ground. **1970** Correll *Plants TX* 883, In addition to the species below [=*Canavalia maritima*], the horse bean, *C. ensiformis* . . , has been cultivated in Texas. **1976** Bailey–Bailey *Hortus Third* 217, *[Canavalia] ensiformis.* . . *Horse bean.* . . Fresh immature seeds are considered to be poisonous.

horse beast n Also *horse critter* [Redund; cf *EDD horse-beast* (at *horse* sb. 1. (9))] Cf Intro "Language Changes" I.4. Cf **cow critter**

A horse.

1834 in 1956 Eliason *Tarheel Talk* 257 **NC,** I give . . unto my son Rezin . . his own choice of horse beast. **1843** (1916) Hall *New Purchase* 101 **IN,** Dick, my nonpareil of "hoss beasts," . . When this remarkable quadruped was foaled is uncertain. **1878** *Appletons' Jrl.* 5.413 **PA,** In Pennsylvania they . . ride to town . . with a *horse-beast* drawing the machine [=a carriage]. **1952** Brown *NC Folkl.* 1.552, *Horse-beast.* . . Horse. *Ibid, Horse-critter.* . . Horse.

horse bird n

=cowbird 1.

c1960 *Wilson Coll.* **csKY,** *Cowbird.* . . A few call it a Horse Bird, from its being seen in the pasture among the stock.

horse biscuit See **horse apple 3**

horse bite n Cf **monkey bite**

1967 *DARE* (Qu. X39, *A mark on the skin where somebody has sucked it hard and brought the blood to the surface*) Inf **MA**1, Monkey bite—perfectly innocent; a hard grab, e.g. just above the knee; no bruise; horse bite [FW: Inf has heard].

horse blanket n

1 See **blanket 3.**

2 A dollar bill. [*horse* + **blanket 4**] *old-fash*

1968 *DARE* (Qu. U26, . . *Nicknames* . . *for a paper dollar*) Infs **DE**1, **MN**12, Horse blanket—for the old-fashioned large size bill. [Both Infs old]

horsebone n

1930 Shoemaker *1300 Words* 31 **cPA Mts** (as of c1900), *Horse-bone*—The neck bone.

horse brier n

A **greenbrier:** usu *Smilax rotundifolia,* but also *S. auriculata.*

1839 in 1856 MI State Ag. Soc. *Trans.* 7.419, Smilax rotundifolia, Linn. Horse brier. Green brier. **1894** *Jrl. Amer. Folkl.* 7.102 **MA,** *Smilax rotundifolia.* . . Horse-brier. **1897** *Ibid* 10.145 **MA,** *Smilax rotundifolia* . . horse brier. **1910** Graves *Flowering Plants* 125 **CT,** *Smilax rotundifolia.* . . Horse Brier. Common. **1949** *Amer. Photography* Apr 245/2, The one best known to anyone who has ever tramped the woods is the catbrier, greenbrier, or horsebrier *(Smilax rotundifolia).* **1960** Vines *Trees SW* 75, *Smilax rotundifolia.* . . Vernacular names for the plant are . . Horse-brier and Sow-brier. *Ibid* 77, *Smilax auriculata.* . . Vernacular names are . . Horse-brier, and Arrow-leaf Smilax. **1962** Carrell *Autobiog.* [2] **ceMA** (as of 1880s), We . . ate the leaves of the horse briar. . . called it Bread and butter.

horse broom n

1966–70 *DARE* (Qu. F36, . . *Brooms*) Inf **IL**122, Horse broom; **CA**182, Horse broom—made of horsehair, used for brushing clothes; **SC**3, Horse broom—homemade, made of straw.

horsebrush n

1 A rangeland shrub of the genus *Tetradymia.* Also called **fartweed 2, felt-thorn.** For another name of *T. glabrata* see **greasewood 2i**

1931 U.S. Dept. Ag. *Misc. Pub.* 101.176, Under normal grazing conditions the palatability of horsebrushes is usually nil or else very low. **1945** Benson–Darrow *Manual SW Trees* 344, *Tetradymia.* Horse Brush. **1973** Hitchcock–Cronquist *Flora Pacific NW* 554, Horse-brush. . . Low shrubs . . occurring in dry, open places in the foothills and plains. **1981** Benson–Darrow *Trees SW Deserts* 353, *Horse Brush* . . usually woolly but in some species the wool falling away early.

2 A marsh elder (here: *Iva frutescens*).

1913 *Torreya* 13.234, *Iva frutescens.* . . Horse brush, St. Vincent I[slan]d, Fla.

3 A **hopsage 1** (here: *Grayia spinosa*).

1931 U.S. Dept. Ag. *Misc. Pub.* 101.33, *Grayia spinosa* . . is a small, bushy shrub, 1 to 3 feet high, variously known also as . . spiny sage, horsebrush, and saltbrush. . . It is eaten . . by all classes of livestock and is considered good for both sheep and cattle.

4 A **guayule** (here: *Parthenium incanum*).

1931 U.S. Dept. Ag. *Misc. Pub.* 101.165, *Mariola* . . , known also as horsebrush, . . is a shrubby plant, growing . . from extreme western Texas to southern Arizona and south into Mexico. Despite its peculiar taste and its rubber content the tender new shoots and the flower heads are sometimes nibbled by goats, cattle, and sheep.

horse bug n Cf **devil's horse 4, fodder horse**

=walkingstick.

1968 *DARE* (Qu. R9a, *An insect from two to four inches long that lives in bushes and looks like a dead twig*) Inf **NY**37, Horse bug.

horse cake n Also *horse gunja*

A horse-shaped piece of **gunja.**

1859 (1968) Bartlett *Americanisms* 204, *Horse-cake.* Gingerbread rudely fashioned into the shape of a horse. **a1883** (1911) Bagby *VA Gentleman* 49, Split his thumb open slicing "hoss-cakes" with a dog-knife. **1930** Stoney–Shelby *Black Genesis* 170 **seSC** [Gullah], Ebe fill a hankcher full o' nicky-nyack an' horse-gunjur (ginger-bread horses) an' t'ing. **1950** *PADS* 14.39 **SC,** *Horse cake.* . . A sweet cake, cut in the shape of a horse and baked. *Horse gunjer.* . . A gingercake in the shape of a horse.

horse cane n

=giant ragweed.

1900 Lyons *Plant Names* 27, *A[mbrosia] trifida.* . . Horse-cane. **1933** Small *Manual SE Flora* 1300, *A[mbrosia] trifida.* . . Horse-cane. **1959** Carleton *Index Herb. Plants* 63. **1974** (1977) Coon *Useful Plants* 101, *Ambrosia trifida*—Great ragweed, horse-cane.

horse chester tree n

=horse chestnut 1.

1968 *DARE* (Qu. T16, *What kinds of trees are 'special' around here?*) Inf **MD**13, Chester tree, horse chester tree.

horse chestnut n

1 Std: a widely cultivated tree *(Aesculus hippocastanum).*

2 =buckeye n 1.

1743 (1754) Catesby *Nat. Hist. Carolina* 2 [app] xxiii, There are in *Carolina* these following . . *Pavia.* Scarlet flowering Horse Chesnut. **1785** (1925) Washington *Diaries* 2.360 **neVA,** Received from Colo. Henry Lee of Westmoreland, 12 Horse Chesnut Trees. **1812** Stoddard *Sketches LA* 123 **FL,** Intermixed with the pines on the more elevated grounds, are the horse chesnut, and several kinds of oak. **1886** Brown *2 College Girls* 156 **NY,** Here stood by the roadside the old dying horse-chestnut. **1912** Sullivan *Heart of Us* 260 **Boston MA,** Dorothy found joy . . in the more limited view . . through the horse-chestnut branches. **1936** Winter *Plants NE* 91, *A[esculus] glabra.* . . American Horse-Chestnut. Nebr. is on the western limit of its range. **1966–70**

DARE (Qu. I43, . . *Kinds of nuts*) Infs **ID**4, **MN**12, **NY**9, 69, 181, **PA**2, 100, Horse chestnuts; (Qu. T16) Inf **PA**234, Horse chestnut. **1979** Little *Checklist U.S. Trees* 44.

horse clam n

A **gaper 1** (here: *Tresus capax*) up to ten inches in length, native on the Pacific coast from Alaska to California. Also called **coho clam**

1920 *DN* 5.82 **wWA,** *Horse clam.* A large, coarse clam. "Now that the festive horse clam has become the 'Washington white clam' of commerce." *Mason County Journal,* Shelton, Washington. **1940** Smith *Puyallup-Nisqually* 187 **nwWA,** Children were allowed all sorts of tidbits such as the necks of dried horse clams, nuts and acorns. **1967** *DARE* (Qu. P18) Inf **WA**20, Horse clam. **1981** Rehder *Audubon Field Guide Seashells* 756, The related Alaskan Gaper or Horse Clam . . is more broadly oval.

horse cobbler n [*EDD cobbler* sb.[1] 3 "The fruit of the horse-chestnut tree"]

1957 *Sat. Eve. Post Letters* **MA,** *Horse cobbler*—the nut from a horse chestnut tree.

horse collar n [From the shape]

1967 *DARE* (Qu. H32, . . *Fancy . . pastries*) Inf **OR**4, Horse collar [FW illustr: round twisted pastry with hole in center].

horse colt See **horse B2a**

horse conch n

A large marine snail *(Pleuroploca gigantea).*

1869 *Amer. Naturalist* 3.464 **FL,** At low tide can be collected . . the Horse Conch *(Fasciolaria gigantea),* of which it is supposed the Indians made their war-trumpets. **1881** Ingersoll *Oyster-Industry* 245, *Horse-conch*—The largest species of Triton. (Florida reefs.) **1974** Abbott *Seashells* 228, Florida Horse Conch. North Carolina to Florida; Texas and Yucatan. **1981** Meinkoth *Audubon Field Guide Seashore* 507, *Florida Horse Conch. . .* This is the largest snail on the Atlantic Coast of the United States, and one of the biggest in the world.

horse coot n

=**white-winged scoter.**

1955 *AmSp* 30.177, And the white-winged scoter is termed *horse coot* in New Jersey.

horse corn n [See quot 1975]

A field var of **Indian corn.**

1964 Wallace *Frontier Life* 71 **swOK** (as of 1893–1906), In the winter, especially on cold, snowy days, the family ate parched "horse corn," the term we used to distinguish it from popcorn. **1966** *Wilson Coll.* **csKY,** Horse corn—the kind grown in the field, as contrasted with sweet corn or garden corn. **1968** *Rockport Democrat* (IN) Sept [nd, np], It is actually made, she said, "by boiling regular horse corn cobs in water with sugar and pectin (Jelly)." **1975** Gould *ME Lingo* 136, *Horse corn*—The standard Maine term for yellow corn, as distinguished from sweet corn. The tendency to suppose this derives from feeding it to horses is probably unjustified; *horse* also means coarse, rough, vulgar.

horse crab See **horsefoot**

horse cracker n Also *horse firecracker*

1966 *DARE* (Qu. FF14, . . *Firecrackers*) Infs **SC**10, 19, Horse crackers; **SC**26, Horse firecracker.

horse crevalle n

A **crevalle a** (here: *Caranx crysos* and *C. hippos*).

1873 in 1878 Smithsonian Inst. *Misc. Coll.* 14.2.25, *Carangus hippos* . . Horse-crevalle . . Cape Cod to Florida. **1887** Goode *Amer. Fishes* 226, *Caranx hippos* . . the "Horse Crevalle" of South Carolina. *Ibid* 228, *Caranx pisquetus,* known about Pensacola as . . "Hard-tail"; . . in South Carolina as the "Horse Crevalle". **1935** Caine *Game Fish* 48, *Caranx crysos* . . Synonyms: . . Hardtail . . Horse Crevalle. **1972** Sparano *Outdoors Encycl.* 377, *Jack Crevalle*—Common Names: . . horse crevalle, toro. Scientific Name: *Caranx hippos.*

horse crippler n Cf **mule crippler cactus**

A **barrel cactus** (here: *Echinocactus texensis*).

1970 Correll *Plants TX* 1104, *Echinocactus texensis. . . Horse crippler. . .* Central spine 1 per areole, curving rigidly downward and exceeding the radials.

horse critter See **horse beast**

horse daisy n

1 An **oxeye** (here: *Chrysanthemum leucanthemum*).

1900 [see **2** below]. **1940** Clute *Amer. Plant Names* 79, *C[hrysanthemum] leucanthemum.* Ox-eye Daisy. . . horse-daisy. **1959** Carleton *Index Herb. Plants* 63, *Horse-daisy:* Chrysanthemum leucanthemum.

2 =**dog fennel 1.**

1900 Lyons *Plant Names* 37, *A[nthemis] Cotula* . . Horse Daisy. *Ibid* 99, *C[hrysanthemum] Leucanthemum* . . Horse-Daisy.

3 =**black-eyed Susan 2.**

1968 *DARE* (Qu. S7, . . *A kind of daisy*) Inf **PA**163, Horse daisy [black-eyed Susan].

horse dam n

In logging: see quot.

1905 U.S. Forest Serv. *Bulletin* 61.40 **Nth,** *Horse dam.* A temporary dam made by placing large logs across a stream, in order to raise the water behind it, so as to float the rear.

horse devil n

A **wild indigo.**

1869 Fuller *Uncle John* 261, The whole plant forms a globular mass, which, when dry, breaks away from the soil and rolls about in the wind, . . greatly to the discomfiture of horses; for which reason it has acquired the bad name of *Horse-devil.*

horse dock n Cf **horse sorrel**

A **dock** n[1]: either **curled dock** or *Rumex orbiculatus.*

1910 Graves *Flowering Plants* 158 **CT,** *Rumex britannica. . .* Great Water Dock. Horse Dock. Occasional. Swamps, fresh and brackish marshes and shallow water along streams. **1956** McAtee *Some Dialect NC* 23, *Horse-dock. . .* Common dock *(Rumex crispus).*

horse doctor n Cf **horsefly 2, horse stinger, snake doctor**

A **dragonfly.**

1954 *Harder Coll.* **cwTN,** *Horse doctor. . .* A fly, same as devil's dragon. **1965** *DARE* File **AR,** My uncle once said that he had heard it was bad luck for "horse doctors" to fly around near the fish pole, but he said he thought the fish bit just as good anyway. **1970** Tarpley *Blinky* 172 **neTX,** *Insect with a double set of transparent wings, seen flying over water. . .* Horse doctor.

horse doughnut See **horse apple 3**

horse duck n

1 =**canvasback duck. esp Gulf States**

1911 *Forest & Stream* 77.173, (Canvasback) *Marila valisineria. . .* Horse Duck, Chef Menteur, La. **1923** U.S. Dept. Ag. *Misc. Circular* 13.18, *Canvasback (Aristonetta valisineria). . . In local use* . . horse-duck (La.) **1955** *AmSp* 30.177, The canvasback is a *horse duck* . . in Louisiana and Texas. **1962** Imhof *AL Birds* 147, *Canvasback—Aythya valisineria* . . Other Name: Horse Duck. **1982** Elman *Hunter's Field Guide* 195, *Canvasback (Aythya valisineria)* Common & Regional Names: can, canny, . . horse-duck.

2 =**scoter.** Cf **horse coot**

1955 *AmSp* 30.177, All of the scoters are known as *horse ducks* on the Delaware River.

horse dumpling See **horse apple 3**

horsed up See **horse C8**

horse-eye bonito n

An **amberjack 2** (here: *Seriola dumerili*).

1972 Sparano *Outdoors Encycl.* 377, *Amberjack. Common Names* . . horse-eye bonito. *Scientific Name: Seriola dumerili.*

horse-eye jack n Also *horse-eyed jack* Cf **horse crevalle**

A **crevalle a** (here: *Caranx latus*).

1887 Goode *Amer. Fishes* 228, *Caranx crumenophthalmus. . .* Its large, protruding eyes are very noticeable features. . . Stearns speaks of a fish, common at Key West, which is known as the "Horse-eyed Jack," and this may prove to be the same species. **1896** U.S. Natl. Museum *Bulletin* 47.921, *Caranx Latus* . . Horse-eye Jack. **1960** Amer. Fisheries Soc. *List Fishes* 29, Horse-eye jack . . *Caranx latus.* **1973** Knight *Cook's Fish Guide* 383/1, Jack . . Horse-eye (not eaten).

horse fiddle n [Cf *SND horse fiddle* (at *horse* n. 2. (12)) "A horse fiddle is an empty box, with a rough edged board drawn forcibly across it, usually for the purposes of disturbing somebody's slumbers about midnight"] Cf **devil's fiddle 1**

Any of var noisemakers used esp at a **shivaree;** hence v *horse-fiddle* to serenade with such a device.

1807 in 1932 IN Hist. Soc. *Pub.* 10.164, The French . . convened around the house of the new couple . . playing on horse fiddles. **1863** Davis *Young Parson* 98, The last time [I went on a spree] was when Strapiron got married; then a parcel of us fellers did horse-fiddle him, not that we had anything agin him, but it did seem funny to see him turn butterfly. **1872** Eggleston *End of the World* 294, Bill Day had a gigantic watchman's rattle, a hickory spring on a cog-wheel. It is called in the West a horse-fiddle, because it is so unlike either a horse or a fiddle. *Ibid* 296, That serenade! Such a . . rattle of horse-fiddle, such a bellowing of dumb-bull. **1905** *DN* 3.83 **nwAR,** *Horse-fiddle.* . . A tin can with a resin-smeared thread passed through a hole punctured at the bottom. Pulling the string produces ear-splitting noises. **1908** *DN* 3.321 **eAL, wGA,** *Horse-fiddle.* . . A string roughened with resin and tied to some object that will rattle when the string is vibrated. **1933** *AmSp* 8.2.25 **NEng,** The instruments of the callathumpian band include . . the horse fiddle (two rails grating on each other), the devil's fiddle. **1940–41** Cassidy *WI Atlas* **csWI,** *Horse fiddle*—a noise-making device used at shivarees, consisting of a wooden frame with a series of clappers on a wheel inside it which was turned by a crank. When this device was placed against a frame house and cranked, the noise was as if the house were being pounded by sledges. **1941** *LANE* Map 409 *(Serenade),* 1 inf, **swVT,** *Horse fiddle,* a long two-by-four plank sawed across the top of a large wooden box. **1942** McAtee *Dial. Grant Co. IN* 35 **ceIN** (as of 1890s), *Horse-fiddle.* . . the term was applied to a crank-operated bird-scarer. . . but this was a rattle, not a fiddle. **1945** *AN&Q* 5.119/2, Horse Fiddle: an instrument used for driving squirrels out of a corn field.

horse fight See **horse B11**

horse firecracker See **horse cracker**

horsefish n

1 =**moonfish.**

1873 in 1878 Smithsonian Inst. *Misc. Coll.* 14.2.24, *Vomer setipinnis.* . . Horse-fish. . . Maine to Florida. **1884** Goode *Fisheries U.S.* 1.322, This fish [=*Selene setipinnis,* is] known on some parts of the coast as the 'Horse-fish.' **1887** Goode *Amer. Fishes* 232, The Horse-fish, *Selene setipinnis,* [is] known in North Carolina as the "Moonfish" or "Sunfish." **1889** *Century Dict.* 2891, *Horse-fish.* . . A fish of the family *Carangidae, Vomer setipinnis.* **1896** U.S. Natl. Museum *Bulletin* 47.934, *Vomer setipinnis* . . Horsefish. **1966** *DARE* (Qu. P2, . . *Kinds of saltwater fish*) Inf **NC**15, Horsefish.

2 also *horse sucker:* A **redhorse** (here: *Moxostoma* spp).

1820 Rafinesque in *Western Rev.* 2.305, Red-tail Sucker. *Catostomus erythrurus* . . Vulgar names Red-horse, Red-tail, Horse-fish, Horse Sucker, &c. **1902** Jordan–Evermann *Amer. Fishes* 63, *Sucking Mullet. Moxostoma crassilabre.* . . Among the vernacular names applied to it are redhorse, horse-fish. **1969** *DARE* (Qu. P1, *Kinds of freshwater fish*) Inf **KY**28, Horsefish.

3 =**sauger.**

1884 Goode *Fisheries U.S.* 424, The "Sauger" [is] known also as the . . "Horse-fish." **1927** Weed *Pike* 45, *Stizostedion.* . . Horse-Fish; Great Lakes region. **1946** LaMonte *N. Amer. Game Fishes* 131, *Sand Pike—Stizostedion canadense* . . Names: Sauger, . . Horsefish, Eastern Sauger. **1949** Caine *N. Amer. Sport Fish* 117, Frequently confused with the walleye it [=the sauger] is also known as Eastern Sauger, . . Horse-fish, . . and Sand Pike.

4 See **horse mackerel 2.**

horseflea weed See **horsefly weed**

horsefly n

1 Std: a stout fly of the family Tabanidae, esp of the genus *Tabanus.* For other names see **bulldog fly, cow fly 1, deer fly 1, gallinipper 1b, greenhead 3**

2 A **dragonfly.** Cf **horse stinger**

1967–70 *DARE* (Qu. R2, . . *Other names . . for the dragonfly*) Infs **MA**16, 40, **MI**96, **MO**3, 39, **TX**62, 96, Horsefly; **KS**8, **MO**12, **NY**198, **UT**13, Horsefly [FW: Infs question the response].

3 See **horsefly weed.**

horsefly weed n Also *horsefly, horseflea weed* [See quot 1859]

A **wild indigo** (here: *Baptisia tinctoria*).

1828 Rafinesque *Med. Flora* 1.79, *Baptisia tinctoria.* . . Horsefly weed. [*Ibid* 80, It is often used to keep the flies from horses, as these insects appear to avoid it.] **1859** (1880) Darlington *Amer. Weeds* 108, Horse-fly Weed . . is often used to drive flies away from horses, being attached to their harness, hence one of the common names. **1889** *Century Dict.* 2891, *Horsefly-weed.* . . A leguminous plant, *Baptisia tinctoria,* the wild indigo or rattlebush. Also *horseflea-weed.* **1901** Lounsberry *S. Wild Flowers* 266, Horse-fly-weed . . is . . much seen in the Alleghany and Cumberland mountains where it is used about the bridles of horses to keep off annoying flies. **1931** Clute *Common Plants* 102, The horse-fly weed *(Baptisia tinctoria)* receives its name from the belief that the fresh branches attached to the harness will keep the flies away from the horses. **1940** Clute *Amer. Plant Names* 17, *B. tinctoria.* . . Horse-flea weed. **1964** Batson *Wild Flowers SC* 62, *Horsefly-weed.* **1976** Bailey–Bailey *Hortus Third* 138, *Horsefly, horsefly weed.* . . A dye plant.

horsefoot n Also *horse(foot) crab* [From its shape]

A **king crab** (here: *Limulus polyphemus*).

1672 Josselyn *New-Englands Rarities* 13, They feed . . upon a shell-fish called a *Horse-foot.* **1806** (1904) Roe *Diary* 31 **NY,** Austin & Colman Sat out this Morning Very Arley to go to the Beech after Clams & Horsfeet. **1870** (1871) *Amer. Naturalist* 4.257, This crustacean . . bears also the popular names Horse Foot Crab, Horseshoe, and King Crab. **1889** *Century Dict.* 2893, *Horseshoe-crab.* . . A merostome of the family *Limulidae,* as *Limulus polyphemus* or *L. moluccanus:* so called from its shape. Also called *horseshoe, horsefoot, horsecrab, horsefoot-crab,* and *king-crab.* **1918** Lincoln *Shavings* 159 **seMA,** They walked along the beach, picked up shells, inspected "horse-foot" crabs, jelly fish and "sand collars [sic for *dollars*]." **1940** Weygandt *Down Jersey* 183 **seNJ,** The insides of horsefeet, or horseshoe crabs . . were the best bait for eels.

horsefoot marlin n [**horsefoot**]

1 =**hudsonian curlew.**

1888 Trumbull *Names of Birds* 200, At Atlantic City, *Horse-foot marlin [Numenius hudsonicus],* because of its fondness for the spawn of that big crustacean known as "horse-foot," "horseshoe," "king-crab," etc. *Ibid* 207, At Somers Point, N.J., *Horse-foot marlin [Limosa fedoa].* **1890** *Century Dict.* 3635 **NJ,** The Hudsonian curlew, *Numenius hudsonicus:* . . *horsefoot marlin.*

2 =**marbled godwit.**

1888 [see **1** above]. **1923** U.S. Dept. Ag. *Misc. Circular* 13.58, *Marbled Godwit (Limosa fedoa).* . . In local use . . horse-foot marlin (N.J.)

horsefoot snipe n [**horsefoot**]

1 =**ruddy turnstone.**

1813 (1824) Wilson *Amer. Ornith.* 7.32, On the coast of Cape May and Egg-Harbor this bird [=the turnstone] is well known by the name of the *Horse-foot Snipe,* from its living, during the months of May and June, almost wholly on the eggs or spawn of the great King Crab, called here by the common people the *Horse-foot.* **1844** DeKay *Zool. NY* 2.216, It [=the turnstone *(Arenaria interpres)*] is known among our *gunners* (a class of men who earn a livelihood by shooting birds) under the names of *Brant-bird, . . Horsefoot Snipe,* and *Beach-bird.* **1927** Forbush *Birds MA* 1.478, *Arenaria interpres. . . Ruddy Turnstone.*—Other names: chicken-bird; . . horse-foot snipe; sea-quail. **1955** MA Audubon Soc. *Bulletin* 39.446, *Ruddy Turnstone.* . . Horsefoot Snipe (Mass., R.I. From the bird's feeding on the eggs of the horsefoot, or king crab.)

2 =**knot.**

1888 Trumbull *Names of Birds* 179, *Tringa canutus.* . . at Pleasantville above mentioned, *Horse-foot snipe.* **1917** (1923) *Birds Amer.* 1.231, *Knot.* . . Other names. Red Sandpiper; . . Horsefoot Snipe. **1923** U.S. Dept. Ag. *Misc. Circular* 13.53, *Knot (Calidris canutus)* . . In local use . . horse-foot snipe (N.J.) **1946** Hausman *Eastern Birds* 276, *Knot —Calidris canutus* . . Other Names—Some twenty-five or more local names, among which are: . . Horse-foot Snipe, . . Whiting.

horse for See **horse C2c**

horse gannet n

=**great blue heron.**

1955 *AmSp* 30.177, A misnomer as to the noun, but a fit as to the adjective, is *horse gannet* for the great blue heron in South Carolina.

horse gentian n

A plant of the genus *Triosteum.* Also called **feverroot 1, feverwort 1.** For other names of *T. perfoliatum* see **Doctor Tinker's weed, genson, ginseng B3, horse ginseng, sweet bitter, tinker's weed, white gentian, white ginseng, wild coffee, wild ipecac, wood ipecac**

1837 Darlington *Flora Cestrica* 159, *T[riosteum] perfoliatum. . . Vulgo* . . Horse Gentian. . . The root of this plant is reputed to be medicinal, as an emetic and cathartic. **1843** Torrey *Flora NY* 1.301, *Horse Gentian* . . has long been a popular medicine. **1876** Hobbs *Bot. Hdbk.* 55, Horse gentian, Fever root, Triosteum perfoliatum. **1914** Georgia *Manual Weeds* 401, *Horse Gentian*. . . A plant formerly in high esteem for its medicinal qualities, but now merely a weed. **1931** Harned *Wild Flowers Alleghanies* 470, *Horse Gentian*. . . A pubescent, coarse perennial . . common on rich, wooded hillsides of the mountains. **1976** Bailey–Bailey *Hortus Third* 1126, *Triosteum* L. Horse gentian, feverwort.

horse ginseng n [See quot 1948]

A **horse gentian** (here: *Triosteum perfoliatum*).

1822 Eaton *Botany* 493, *Triosteum. . . perfoliatum* . . fever root, horse-ginseng. . . Very valuable as a mild cathartic and emetic. **1892** (1974) Millspaugh *Amer. Med. Plants* 74, *Horse-gentian*. . . This coarse, leafy, perennial herb, grows to a height of from 1 to 4 feet. **1948** Stevens *KS Wild Flowers* 357, Various vernacular names have been given to this species . . horse ginseng [etc.] and . . all of them can be rationalized . . the corruption of gentian—ginseng, genson, because Triosteum has sometimes been used in this country as a tonic, substituting for the officinal, European yellow gentian.

horse-gold n

A **buttercup 1** (here: either *Ranunculus acris* or *R. arvensis*).

1900 Lyons *Plant Names* 316, *R[anunculus] arvensis*. . . Horse-gold. . . *R. acris*. . . Horse-gold. **1911** *Century Dict. Suppl., Goldweed*. . . The corn crowfoot, *Ranunculus arvensis*. Also called *horse-gold*. **1959** Carleton *Index Herb. Plants* 63, *Horse Gold:* Ranunculus acris.

horse grass n Cf **horseshoe grass**

Prob a **grama grass.**

1968 *DARE* (Qu. S9, *Other kinds of grass that are hard to get rid of*) Inf NC80, Horse grass—tall, pulls up easy.

horse guard n Also *guard (fly)* [See quot 1954] **chiefly SE**

A **sand wasp** (here: *Bembix carolina*).

1796 in 1916 Hawkins *Letters* 46 **AL,** A large flie called the horse guard come at the same season. **1836** *Knickerbocker* 8.689 **neFL,** I have frequently seen horses come running from the barrens, like furies, . . to seek the spots frequented by the 'guards'—a species of hornet, which catches the flies and protects beasts of all kinds from pain, and doubtless even from death. **1837** (1962) Williams *Territory FL* 71, Horse Guard, a species of large Hornet that burrows in the sand; destroys the flies. **1838** Flagg *Far West* 2.108 **sIL,** A yellow insect . . has made its appearance . . and, from its sweeping destruction of the annoying fly, has been called the "horse-guard." **1954** Borror–DeLong *Intro. Insects* 747, *Bembix carolina* (Fabricius), an insect about an inch long and black with yellow markings, is fairly common in the South; it often hunts for flies near horses, and is called the "horse guard." Other sand wasps are black with yellow, white, or pale-green markings. **1966–68** *DARE* (Qu. R12, . . *Kinds of flies . . common around here—for example, those that fly around animals*) Inf **GA**7, Horse guard—white, chases horseflies; **SC**19, Horse guard—flies around horses and preys on flies; **SC**40, Guard fly—around a cow, but never lights or stings; reputed to drive away horse fly; **SC**43, Horse guard—preys on flies around a horse [or] cow; (Qu. R21, . . *Other kinds of stinging insects*) Inf **NC**49, Hornet—looks like a horse guard; horse guard. **1966** *DARE* Tape **SC**19, Keep them flies off them horses and cattle—he's called a horse guard.

horse gunja See **horse cake**

horsehair fungus n Also *horsehair mushroom*

Either of two mushrooms: *Marasmius androsaceus* or *M. rotula*.

1972 Miller *Mushrooms* 82, *Marasmius rotula*. . . "Horsehair Fungus". . . Very common in eastern North America especially in New England on west to the Lake States. **1987** McKnight–McKnight *Mushrooms* 165, *Horsehair Mushroom*. . . *Marasmius androsaceus*. . . Odor and taste not distinctive; taste rarely slightly bitter.

horsehair grass n Cf **hairgrass**

A grass grown for hay, perh a **fescue.**

1987 *DARE* File **cMN,** The most common hay grown is alfalfa, and some others are rye, timothy, horsehair grass, and slough-hay, which is grown in damp areas.

horsehair mushroom See **horsehair fungus**

horsehair snake n Also *horsehair worm*

A "snake" popularly supposed to develop in water from a horsehair; spec, a gordioid worm. Also called **hair snake**

1897 *Outing* 30.434/2, The creature referred to as a mystery is what is termed the 'horsehair snake,' in reality, a hairworm. **[1899** Bergen *Animal Lore* 94, Horsehairs are popularly believed to "turn into snakes" when placed in water. *General in the United States*. . . A horsehair put into running water, under a stone, for thirty days, will turn into a "snake." *Winn, Me*. . . In order to have horsehairs turn into snakes in water, rainwater must be used. *Cambridge, Mass*. . . A horsehair, to turn into a snake, must have the root left on, to make the head of the snake, into which the hair will turn in nine days. *Eastern Massachusetts*.**]** **1949** *Scientific Amer.* Jan 56/2, Another mythical serpent, confined to the rural scene, is the horsehair snake . . the worm *Paragordius varius*. **1956** McAtee *Some Dialect NC* 23, *Horse-hair snake* . . a thread-worm *(Gordius);* believed to be the transformed hair from a horse's tail or mane. **c1960** *Wilson Coll.* **csKY,** *Horse-hair snake*. . . A thread worm (Gordius, Sp) found in watering troughs and shallow tubs. John Moore has seen lots of them, has even put the horsehairs into a trough and watched them develop into snakes, he says. **1964** *PADS* 42.19, *Horse-hair snake*. Actually a long, slender worm (*Gordius*, sp.), which spends one portion of its life in the body of a large insect and the other in shallow water, as in a watering trough. Thus arose the folk belief that these worms were originally horsehairs. **1968–70** *DARE* (Qu. CC17) Inf **IL**135, Horsehair snake—leave a horsehair in water and it turns into a snake; (Qu. P25) Inf **PA**104, Horsehair snake, about as big as a horsehair; (Qu. R14) Inf **PA**246, Horsehair worms—found in horse troughs.

horsehead n

1 Either of two similar fishes:

a =lookdown.

1882 U.S. Natl. Museum *Bulletin* 16.439, *S[elene] vomer*. . . Horse-head. **1887** Goode *Amer. Fishes* 232, *Selene argentea*. . . In the Chesapeake this fish is often called by the names "Horse-head," and "Look-down." **1933** John G. Shedd Aquarium *Guide* 82, *Argereiosus vomer* . . *Horsehead*. . . Common names all refer to . . grotesque shape.

b A **moonfish** (here: *Vomer setipinnis*).

1889 *Century Dict.* 2891, *Horsehead*. . . A fish of the genus *Selene* or the genus *Vomer;* a moonfish or dollar-fish, as *Selene vomer* or *Vomer setipinnis*. **1973** Knight *Cook's Fish Guide* 383, Horsehead—Moonfish.

2 also *horsehead coot:* **=surf scoter.** [See quot 1955]

1888 Trumbull *Names of Birds* 103, *Surf Scoter*. . . In Maine at Eastport, Millbridge, Bois Bupert Island, Frenchman's Bay, and Portland, *Horse-head Coot,* or *Horse-head*. **1917** (1923) *Birds Amer.* 1.151, *Oidemia perspicillata*. . . Horse-head; Horse-head Coot. **1955** MA Audubon Soc. *Bulletin* 39.377, *Surf scoter*. . . Horse-head; Horse-head Coot (Maine. Means big head.) **1982** Elman *Hunter's Field Guide* 240, *Melanitta perspicillata*. . . *Regional names:* . . horsehead.

3 An unidentified plant, perh of the family Lamiaceae.

1967 *DARE* (Qu. S26e, *Other wildflowers not yet mentioned*) Inf **WY**3, Horsehead—short, purple, two inches high.

horsehead coot See **horsehead 2**

horse-high adj Cf **bull-strong, hog-tight** adj

Of a fence: too high for a horse to jump—usu in phr *horse-high, bull-strong, and pig-tight* and varr; also fig.

1873 Beadle *Undeveloped West* 40 **IA,** A 'lawful fence' required five [strands of wire], which, the local courts consider, will make it "horse-high, bull-strong, and pig-tight." **1942** McAtee *Dial. Grant Co. IN* 35 (as of 1890s), *Horse-high*. . . high enough so that a horse could not readily jump over. *Ibid* 66, A perfect fence would be horse-high, bull-strong, and pig-tight. **1972** *Christian Science Monitor* (Boston MA) 28 Sept. 16/4 *(OEDS),* The pioneers . . tipped the stumps up with their roots in the air, and lined them along so they were, as the saying went, 'horse-high, hog-tight, and bull-strong'. **1975** Gould *ME Lingo* 136, *Horse high*—One of the three primary requisites of a good Maine pasture fence: *Horse high,* bull strong, and hog tight. **1984** Wilder *You All Spoken Here* 117 **Sth,** *Horse-high, bull-strong, pig-tight, and goose-proof*. . . The term applied originally to fences and now pertains to political financial schemes.

horse hole n [Cf *EDD horse wash* (at *horse* sb. 1. (121)) "a roadside pond where horses are watered and their feet washed"] Cf **hole** n **1c**

Appar a place in water deep enough to wash a horse—also used as a place name.

1947 *Sun* (Baltimore MD) 9 June 8/1 *(Hench Coll.),* Fifteen fishing smacks, police boats and a private plane . . [searched] for the body of . . [a] schoolboy, feared drowned in a "horsehole." . . [The boy] had apparently drowned in one of the Shoal Creek "horseholes," where gravel had been scooped from the bottom. **1967** *DARE* (Qu. C35, *Nicknames for the different parts of your town*) Inf **PA**29, Horse Hole; **SC**62, Horse Hole—a section of Beaufort [County]. **1967** *DARE* FW Addit **PA**29, They got a place called the "horse hole" where the Amish wash their horses' shoulders after work or [after] a ride to . . [keep] the shoulders from getting sore.

horse-in n Cf **Boston 2**

1953 Randolph–Wilson *Down in Holler* 254 **Ozarks,** *Horse-in. . .* A marble game still popular in the Ozarks. Played in one big ring, it is similar to the game known as *Boston* in some sections of the Middle West.

horse jockey See **jockey**

horse kick n

See quot.

1974 Morton *Folk Remedies* 127 **SC,** Sour fruits are sucked to relieve the stomach-ache ("horse kick") that precedes diarrhea.

horse knobs n Also *horse knops*

A **star-thistle** (here: usu *Centaurea nigra,* but also *C. jacea*).

1900 Lyons *Plant Names* 89, *C[entaurea] nigra. . .* Horse-knobs. **1903** Porter *Flora PA* 342, *Centaurea nigra. . .* Horse knops. **1914** Georgia *Manual Weeds* 521, *Black Knapweed—Centaurea nigra. . .* Horse-knobs. **1935** (1943) Muenscher *Weeds* 467, *Centaurea jacea . .* Star-thistle, . . Horse-knobs. **1973** Hitchcock–Cronquist *Flora Pacific NW* 499, Horse-knops. . . *C[entaurea] nigra.*

horse-laurel n

A **rosebay** (here: *Rhododendron maximum*).

1894 *Jrl. Amer. Folkl.* 7.93, *Rhododendron maximum . .* horse-laurel, White Haven, P[ennsylvani]a. **1940** Clute *Amer. Plant Names* 43, *R. Maximum. . .* Horse-laurel.

horseleek n

=**houseleek 1.**

1889 *Century Dict.* 2892, *Horseleek . .* A plant, the bullock's-eye [=*Sempervivum tectorum*].

horse-lily n

A **spatterdock** (here: *Nuphar luteum*).

1896 *Jrl. Amer. Folkl.* 9.181, *Nuphar advena. . .* horse-lily, Hartford, Me. **1900** Lyons *Plant Names* 262, Horse Lily. **1910** Graves *Flowering Plants* 183 **CT,** Horse Lily.

horse logs See **horse C3**

horse lot n

1 An outdoor enclosure for livestock, esp horses; a pasture. **chiefly SE, Lower Missip Valley, TX** See Map Cf **corral 1, cow lot, horse pen**

1850 U.S. Patent Office *Annual Rept. for 1849: Ag.* 144 **GA,** The man . . has . . no time to make manure, or to haul out and spread the little that is dropped in his horse-lot. **1892** Harris *Uncle Remus & Friends* 7 **GA** [Black], Dis make Brer Rooster laugh twel you mought er heerd 'im squall all over de hoss lot. **1905** *DN* 3.83 **nwAR,** *Horse-lot. . .* Horse-pasture. 'Cow-lot' and 'barn-lot' are also used. **1910** *DN* 3.443 **cwNY,** *Horse-lot. . .* Horse pasture. **1912** *DN* 3.579 **wIN,** *Horse-lot. . .* A small horse-pasture. **1962** Atwood *Vocab. TX* 49, *Place to enclose horses.* The usual word for a horse enclosure is . . *horse lot. . .* This seems to be retreating to the eastward as *corral . .* gains ground. **1965–70** *DARE* (Qu. M13, *The space near the barn with a fence around it where you keep the livestock*) 24 Infs, **chiefly Sth, Midl,** Horse lot; (Qu. M14, *The open area around or next to the barn*) Infs **FL**15, **MO**10, Horse lot. **1986** Pederson *LAGS Concordance (Barnyard or cow lot)* 53 infs, **Gulf Region,** Horse lot; 2 infs, **wLA, nTX,** Horse lot—next to (*or* around) the barn; 2 infs, **cTN, AR,** Horse lot—for horses and mules; 2 infs, **eTN, nMS,** Horse lot—also called cow lot (*or* barn lot, the lot); 1 inf, **eTN,** Horse lot—where cows were milked; 1 inf, **wFL,** Horse lot—for horses or cows; 1 inf, **nTX,** Horse lot—for horses at night, for feeding.

2 =**horse barn.**

1967–68 *DARE* (Qu. M1, . . *Barns . . according to their use*) Inf **GA**33, Horse lot; (Qu. M22, . . *Buildings . . on farms*) Inf **AL**20, Horse lot. [Both Infs old]

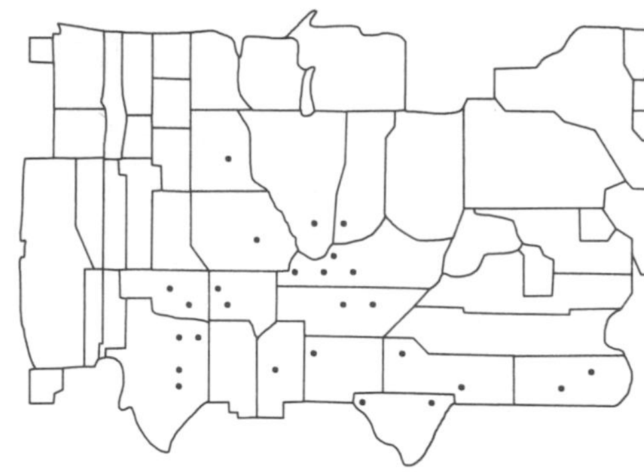

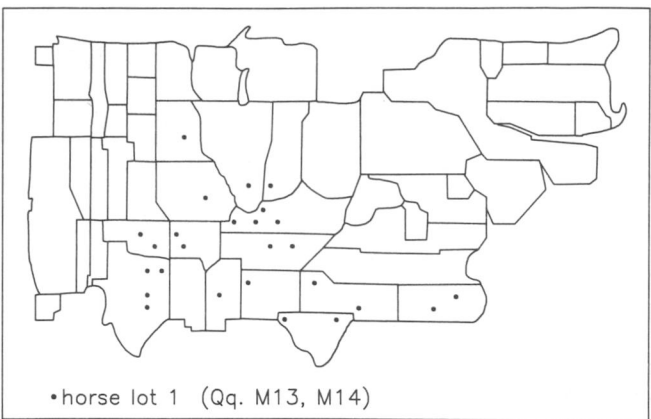

•horse lot 1 (Qq. M13, M14)

horse mackerel n

1 also *horse:* =**bluefish 1. NEast**

1672 Josselyn *New-Englands Rarities* 96, *Blew Fish,* or *Horse . .* are as big usually as the *Salmon,* and better Meat by far. **1814** in 1815 Lit. & Philos. Soc. NY *Trans.* 424, *Horse Mackerel. (Scomber plumbeus). . .* Colour of the head and body such that they often call him *blue-fish.* **1848** in 1935 *DN* 6.453 **RI,** *Horse Mackaral* [sic]. A fish found in the waters of Narragansett bay. **1859** (1968) Bartlett *Americanisms* 37, *Blue-Fish. . .* On the Jersey coast. . . called Horse-Mackerel. **1884** Goode *Fisheries U.S.* 1.433, This fish [=*Pomatomus saltatrix*], which on the coast of New England and the Middle States is called the Bluefish, is also known in Rhode Island as the "Horse Mackerel". **1906** NJ State Museum *Annual Rept. for 1905* 265, *Pomatomus saltatrix. . .* Horse Mackerel. . . A large fish, reaching 3 feet in length, and extremely destructive to other fishes, especially the mackerel. **1935** Caine *Game Fish* 46, *Bluefish. . . Synonyms . .* Horse Mackerel [etc].

2 also *horsefish:* =**bluefin 2.** [See quot 1975] **NEng**

1802 MA Hist. Soc. *Coll.* 1st ser 8.199 **Cape Cod,** The other fishes in the harbour, and on the coast, are the sturgeon, . . horse-mackerel, dog-fish, and several more. **1856** *Porter's Spirit of Times* 29 Nov 205/1, The tail of the one [=blue-fish shark] caught by us was shaped precisely like that of a horse-mackerel. **1947** Coffin *Yankee Coast* 48, Tuna?—Maybe to you. But he is plain horse-fish, horse-mackerel, to the Maine coast man. **1960** Amer. Fisheries Soc. *List Fishes* 62, Horse mackerel—see mackerel, jack; tuna, bluefin. **1975** Gould *ME Lingo* 136, *Horse Mackerel.* Also horsefish, the bluefin tuna. The *horse* in this instance means large or coarse, as in horseplay, horseradish, horse-laughter, etc. Genteel efforts to persuade Maine fishermen to stop saying horsefish because it downgrades the sporty tuna which attracts summer trade have not perceptibly prevailed.

3 =**jack mackerel. CA**

1882 U.S. Natl. Museum *Bulletin* 16.432, *T[rachurus] symmetricus. . . Horse Mackerl* [sic]. . . Coast of California, from San Francisco southward; very abundant in summer. **1896** U.S. Natl. Museum *Bulletin* 47.909, *Trachurus Picturatus. . .* Horse-mackerel. **1946** La-Monte *N. Amer. Game Fishes* 40, *California Horse Mackerel. . . Trachurus symmetricus. . .* Spanish Mackerel, Saurel. **1960** Amer. Fisheries Soc. *List Fishes* 62, Horse mackerel—see mackerel, jack [=*Trachurus symmetricus*].

4 A **crevalle a** (here: *Caranx crysos* and *C. hippos*).

1884 Goode *Fisheries U.S.* 1.324 **NC,** *Caranx pisquetus,* known about Pensacola as the "Jurel," . . and "Hard-tail" . . at Fort Macon as the "Horse Mackerel". **1911** U.S. Bur. Census *Fisheries 1908* 311/2, *Horse-mackerel (Thynnus thynnus). . .* The name is also applied to the bluefish *(Pomatomus saltatrix)* in Rhode Island; to the jurel *(Caranx chrysos)* at Fort Macon; to the crevallé *(Caranx hippos);* to the California hake *(Merluccius productus)* on the Pacific coast; and to several Pacific coast species of little importance. **1935** Caine *Game Fish* 48, *Caranx crysos. . . Synonyms . .* Horse Mackerel [etc]. *Ibid* 59, *Caranx hippos. . . Synonyms . .* Horse Mackerel [etc].

5 =**hake 1b.**

1884 Goode *Fisheries U.S.* 1.243, The name of Horse-mackerel . . is used on our coasts with the greatest carelessness, being applied to *Elops saurus, Anoplapoma fimbria,* and *Merluccius productus.* **1911** [see **4** above].

6 A **sablefish** (here: *Anoplapoma fimbria*).

1884 [see **5** above].

7 A **ten-pounder** (here: *Elops saurus*).

1884 [see **5** above].

8 The Atka **mackerel** *(Pleurogrammus monopterygius)*.

1886 Turner *Contribs. AK* 96 **swAK,** When I arrived at Unalashka in 1878 I heard much talk about the "Mackerel." . . Several persons referred to these fish as . . "Horse Mackerel."

9 =**bonito 1.**

1946 LaMonte *N. Amer. Game Fishes* 20, *Common Bonito Sarda sarda* . . Names: Bonito, . . Horse Mackerel, . . Bloater.

10 An **amberfish. Pacific**

1948 *Sun* (Baltimore MD) 4 Nov 8/4 *(Hench Coll.),* On the Pacific side of the United States the amber fish goes under the name of horse mackerel—it goes most everywhere but in the fish markets. Only a brave few have discovered that it is as tasty as bass.

horseman n

An unidentified flower.

1969 *DARE* (Qu. S26a, . . *Roadside flowers*) Inf **MO**32, Horsemen.

horse-mane oat n *obs*

Side oats *(Avena orientalis)*.

1838 MA Ag. Surv. *Rept. for 1837* 1.33 **neMA,** The Tartarian, or as some call it, the Horse-Mane Oat, from the grain hanging together on one side of the panicle, is sometimes cultivated. **1861** in 1865 IL State Ag. Soc. *Trans. for 1861–64* 5.196, He sows four bushels of seed to the acre, of black Tartarian, or, as sometimes called, horse mane or side oats.

horse marsh n

=**smartweed.**

1913 *Torreya* 13.230, *Polygonum lapathifolium*. . . Horse marsh, Santee Club, S.C.

horsemint n Cf **sweet horsemint**

1 A plant of the genus *Monarda*. Also called **balm B1b, bee-balm 1, bergamot, lemon mint, sweet Mary, wild bergamot.** For other names of var spp see **basil balm b, false balm, Oswego tea, pagoda plant, rignum, sandyland sage**

1784 in 1785 Amer. Acad. Arts & Sci. *Memoirs* 1.460 **neMA,** *Horse mint.* Blossoms blue. By brooks, and in wet meadows. **1858** *Atlantic Mth.* 2.8.11/1 **ceMA,** Horehound, horsemint, and the sensitive fern grew close to the edge. **1876** Hobbs *Bot. Hdbk.* 55, Horse mint. . . Monarda punctata. **1901** Lounsberry *S. Wild Flowers* 455, All in fact of the monardas, or horse-mints, are more than usually pleasing plants, and from early summer stretch out their bloom until late in the autumn. **1943** Peattie *Great Smokies* 196, There was a lilac fleck here and there from the downy horsemint. **1965–70** *DARE* (Qu. S21, . . *Other weeds . . that are a trouble in gardens and fields*) Infs **TX**11, 13, Horsemint; (Qu. S26a, . . *Roadside flowers*) Inf **KY**5, Horsemint—small purple flowers; (Qu. S26b, *Wildflowers that grow in water or wet places*) Inf **MD**18, Horsemint—same as bergamot; bushy, one foot high, long slim leaves, large red flowers; **VA**11, Horsemint—orchid-colored; (Qu. S26e, *Other wildflowers*) Inf **VT**10, Horsemint—tall pink blossoms, grows on the sidehills. **1971** GA Dept. Ag. *Farmers Market Bulletin* 6 Oct 8, Bergamot, also known as Bee-balm and Horse-mint, has always been widely cultivated. . . Monarda fistulosa, otherwise known as Lavender Bergamot and Horse-mint, makes lovely drifts of lavender along country roads in midsummer. 1982 *Barrick Coll.* **csPA,** Horse mint—Monarda.

2 =**mountain mint** (here: *Pycnanthemum* spp). **esp Sth**

1900 Lyons *Plant Names* 210, *K[oellia] incana*. . . Hoary Mountain Mint, . . locally known as Horsemint. **1933** Small *Manual SE Flora* 1171, *Koellia*. . . Mountain-mints. Horse-mints. Basils. **1967** *DARE* Wildfl QR Pl.183A Inf **TX**34, Horsemint. **1975** Duncan–Foote *Wildflowers SE* 162, *White Horse-mint. Pycnanthemum incanum*. . . A perennial to 2 m tall.

3 =**giant hyssop. West**

1937 U.S. Forest Serv. *Range Plant Hdbk.* W9, Nettleleaf horsemint, a tall, coarse, fragrant herb, up to 5 feet high, perennial from rootstocks, is the most important western forage species in the mint family. **1963** Craighead *Rocky Mt. Wildflowers* 161, *Giant-hyssop. . . Other names:* Horsemint. **1967** *DARE* Wildfl QR (Craighead) Pl.20.2 Inf **CO**15, Horsemint. **1973** Hitchcock–Cronquist *Flora Pacific NW* 400, *Agastache*. . . Giant-hyssop; Horse-mint.

4 A calamint (here: *Calamintha nepeta*).

1937 *Torreya* 37.100, *Clinopodium Nepeta*. . . Horse-mint, Monticello, V[irgini]a.

5 Any of var **sages** of the genus *Salvia;* see quot.

1951 *PADS* 15.40 **TX,** *Salvia* spp.—Horse mints and wild salvias are the usual folk names for the taller and more conspicuously flowered mints. If the flower whorls are surrounded by floral bracts, it is some kind of horse mint; flowers running up and down the stems are salvias; also sometimes known as sages.

horse mosquito n

A **mosquito** (here: *Psorophora ciliata*).

1938 Brimley *Insects NC* 322, *P[sorophora] ciliata*. . . Horse Mosquito. Charlotte to Raleigh and east. May to October. **1969–70** *DARE* (Qu. R15b, . . *An extra-big mosquito*) Inf **IL**89, Horse mosquitoes; **TN**52, Horse (or cow) mosquitoes—found around swamps, bite real hard; **CO**31, Horse skeeter.

horse mule See **horse B2b**

horse mullein n

A **mullein** (here: *Verbascum phlomoides*).

1969 *DARE* (Qu. S20, *A common weed that grows on open hillsides: It has velvety green leaves close to the ground, and a tall stalk with small yellow flowers on a spike at the top*) Inf **RI**17, Horse mullein—the taller one, so called because it grew in horse fields.

horse mushroom n

A **field mushroom** (here: *Agaricus arvensis*). Also called **meadow mushroom**

1889 *Century Dict.* 2769, *Hedge-mushroom* . . An edible mushroom, *Agaricus arvensis* . . Also called *horse-mushroom.* **1908** Hard *Mushroom Edible* 310, *Agaricus arvensis*. . . The field or horse mushroom. Edible. **1967** *DARE* (Qu. I37) Inf **MI**63, Horse mushrooms—grow in horse pastures. **1967** *DARE* FW Addit **neOR,** Horse mushroom—grows in manure piles. **1981** Lincoff *Audubon Field Guide Mushrooms* 501, Horse Mushroom—*Agaricus arvensis.* **1987** McKnight–McKnight *Mushrooms* 254, *Horse Mushroom. Agaricus arvensis. . . Odor of anise* usually present. *Ibid* 255, Confusion is rampant on identification of . . Horse Mushroom. Different mushrooms are called by this name in different areas both in Europe and in N. America, and the problem is not likely to be resolved soon.

horse-necked jonquil n

A daffodil.

1954 *PADS* 21.30 **SC,** *Horse-necked jonquil*. . . The daffodil, so called because of the way the flower arches its stem. Obsolescent. Also called *yellow trumpeter.* Charleston.

horse nettle n

1 Either of two weeds of the nightshade family: sometimes *Solanum dimidiatum,* but esp *S. carolinense* which is also called **apple of Sodom, ball nettle, bull nettle 2, Irish plum, radical (weed), sand brier, sand bur, sodom berry, thistle, thornapple, tread soft(ly), wild tomato.**

1822 Eaton *Botany* 463, *Solanum carolinense* . . horse-nettle. **1861** Wood *Class-Book* 578, *S[olanum] carolinense*. . . Horse Nettle. **1903** Porter *Flora PA* 275, *Solanum Carolinense*. . . Horse-nettle. **1967–70** *DARE* (Qu. S17, . . *Other kinds of plants . . that will cause itching and swelling*) Infs **CA**7, 65, 189, **IN**32, **PA**169, **SC**70, **TX**96, Horse nettle(s); (Qu. S21, . . *Other weeds . . around here*) Infs **GA**84, **NJ**45, **PA**132, Horse nettles. **1969** *SC Market Bulletin* 11 Sept 1/1, Noxious weeds 9 per lbs. of horsenettle [in 50 lb bag of tall fescue seed]. **1982** *Barrick Coll.* **csPA,** *Horse nettle*—Solanum carolinense.

2 A **vervain** (here: *Verbena hastata*).

1975 Logan *Land Remembers* 194 **swWI** (as of c1920), We raced ahead of them, . . dodging the ball thistles and the bright clumps of blue vervain we called horse nettle.

3 =**false nettle.**

1966 *DARE* Wildfl QR Pl.45 Inf **OH**14, Horse nettle [=*Boehmeria cylindrica*].

horse onion n

A wild onion.

1966 *DARE* (Qu. I5, *The kind of onions that keep coming up without replanting year after year*) Inf **NC**44, Wild or horse onions.

horse on you See **horse B12**

horse over See **horse C7**

horse pee See **horse piss**

horse pen n Cf **horse lot 1**

An outdoor enclosure for livestock, esp horses.

1738 in 1912 Augusta Co. VA *Chronicles* 2.376 **cVA,** One of ye corners of Col. Carter's Horsepen. **1773** in 1929 Summers *Annals* 592 **swVA,** Ordered that John Crockett and John Adams . . view the nighest and best way from the horse pen to . . the Cove. **1843** (1940) Ferris *Rocky Mts.* 33 **NY,** On the day he left us we reached a fine grove of cotton wood trees of which we made a horse pen . . as a necessary protection for our cattle [=horses and mules]. **1884** *Harper's New Mth. Mag.* 70.107/2 **eVA,** The logs for the horse-pen had been provided. **1962** Atwood *Vocab. TX* 49, *Place to enclose horses. . . (Horse) pen* (7 [% of possible occurrences]) is not a usual term. **1967** *DARE* (Qu. M13, *The space near the barn with a fence around it where you keep the livestock*) Inf **TX**13, Horse pen. **1970** Tarpley *Blinky* 130 **neTX,** *Small enclosure outside where horses are kept. . .* 5.5% [of 200 infs] horse pen.

horse piss n Also *horse pee, ~ urine* **chiefly Sth, S Midl** See Map

Fig: see quots.

1957 Battaglia *Resp. to PADS 20* **eMD,** *Very weak coffee*—horse pee. **1965–70** *DARE* (Qu. DD25, . . *Nicknames . . for beer*) 13 Infs, **chiefly Sth, S Midl,** Horse piss; **MD**15, **VA**69, Horse pee; **GA**72, Horse urine; (Qu. H74a, . . *Coffee according to how it's made—very strong*) Infs **GA**3, **TX**4, Horse piss (with the foam floated off); [**IL**9, **TX**1, Strong as (Kentucky stud) horse piss;] (Qu. H74b, . . *Coffee . . very weak*) Inf **CO**47, Horse piss; (Qu. DD21a, . . *Liquor*) Inf **FL**52, Horse piss.

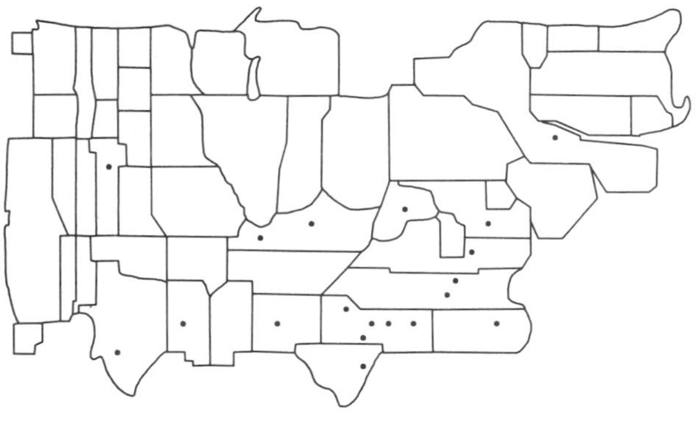

•horse piss + varr (Qq. DD25, H74a, b, DD21a)

horse piss ant See **horse ant**

horsepital See **horspital**

horse plant See **horseweed 9**

horse plum n

A plum, esp *Prunus americana.*

1790 Deane *New Engl. Farmer* 222/2, The horse-plum, a very pleasant tasted juicy fruit, of a large size. **1884** Sargent *Forests of N. Amer.* 65, *Prunus Americana. . .* Horse plum. **1897** Sudworth *Arborescent Flora* 236, *Prunus nigra* . . Horse Plum (Me., Vt.) . . *Prunus americana* . . Horse Plum (Miss., Ark., Colo.) **1900** Lyons *Plant Names* 306, *P[runus] Americana* . . Horse Plum. . . *P. domestica* . . Horse Plum. . . *P. nigra* . . Horse Plum. **1960** Vines *Trees SW* 404, *American Plum—Prunus americana. . .* Other vernacular names are Horse Plum, . . Thorn Plum. **1979** Little *Checklist U.S. Trees* 214, *Prunus nigra* . . *Canada plum* . . Other common names—horse plum . . wild plum.

horse pulling n, also attrib Also *horse pull* **esp N Cent, NEast**

A contest to see which horse or team can pull the heaviest load.

1939 *Sun* (Baltimore MD) 21 Aug 4/8 **cnMD** *(Hench Coll.),* The annual Carroll County Fair opened today. . . The horse-pulling contest will be held Tuesday, followed by more cattle judging. On the less serious side will be six whippet races. **1960** *Washington Post & Times Herald* (DC) 24 Sep *(Hench Coll.),* A Frederick County [Maryland] team won the horse-pulling championship of the Anne Arundel County Fair. **1965** *Bee* (Phillips WI) 19 Aug 1/1, Winners in the horse pulling contest were as follows. **1966–70** *DARE* (Qu. FF16, . . *Local contests*) Infs **IN**26, 32, **MI**25, **MO**18, **NY**123, **WI**20, 68, Horse-pulling contest (*or* fair); **NY**75, Horse pulling—contest where they put weights on a stoneboat; **VT**3, Horse pulling; **KY**73, Horse pulls; **NY**68, Horse pulls—put weights on a stoneboat and see how much a horse or pony can pull; [**IA**11, Horse-and-tractor pulling contest]. **1968** *Rev.-Times* (Oxford NY) 4 July sec A 3/1, Friday's busy day opens with a fine horsepull.

horse race See **horse B12**

horse racer n

1 also *horse runner:* **=ringneck snake.** See **racer** in Map Section

1834 (1879) Brooks *Zóphiël* 252, The ring-necked serpent is still sometimes seen in North America. . . From the extreme swiftness of its movement, it received from the English settlers the name of horse-racer. **1968** *DARE* (Qu. P25, . . *Kinds of snakes . . around here*) Inf **MD**31, Horse runner—black, white ring around neck, non-poisonous.

2 =praying mantis. Cf **horse bug**

1966 *DARE* (Qu. R9b, *An insect that holds up its front feet as if saying a prayer*) Inf **NC**27, Horse racers. **1969** *DARE* FW Addit **eNC,** Horse racer—a long skinny insect sort of like a grasshopper.

horse racing See **horse B12**

horseradish n

1 Std: a perennial plant *(Amoracia rusticana)* grown for its edible roots.

2 =oswego tea.

1968 *DARE* FW Addit **VA**15, Horseradish: oswego tea *(Monarda didyma)* in meadows; old-fashioned.

horse rake n **chiefly Nth** *old-fash*

A horse-drawn hay rake; see quot 1969.

1817 in 1912 IL State Hist. Soc. *Trans. for 1910* 147 **nwVT,** The ground has to be clea[red of] the Cornstock . . by cutting them down and drawing them togethe[r] with a horse Rake. **1818** in 1822 Flint *Letters* 17 **seNY,** A horse rake has been recently invented. **1887** Randall *Lady's Ranche Life* 95 **csMT,** We have been busy haymaking. . . It is cut, and raked up into rows, cocked (with the horse-rake) and carried all in the same day. **1906** in 1913 U.S. Congress *Serial Set* 6166 Doc 719 204, The net proceeds . . shall be expended . . in the purchase of stock cattle, horse teams . . horserakes . . for issue to said Indians [in Idaho]. **1966–69** *DARE* (Qu. L16, *Machines used . . in handling hay*) Infs **MA**5, 25, 42, **MI**67, **NC**54, **RI**12, **WA**31, Horse rake; [**NY**96, Horse-drawn wheel rake]. [7 of 8 Infs old] **1969** *DARE* Tape **CT**29, The horse rake is basically a series of curved teeth hung on an axle between two wheels with a pair of shaves for the horse and a seat for the rider. . . The teeth drag along behind the horse until they've collected a sufficient quantity of hay, then the rider by means of a trip pedal . . release[s] the hay and start[s] over again.

horse road n

An unpaved or unimportant road.

1966 *DARE* (Qu. N27a, . . *Unpaved roads*) Inf **ME**9, Horse road; (Qu. N29, . . *A less important road*) Inf **ME**9, Horse road. **1968** *DARE* Tape **CA**100, It was just a one-way gravel road, you know—a horse road—besides a little old railroad train.

horse runner See **horse racer 1**

horses See **horse B11, 12**

horse sage(brush) n

=bud sagebrush.

1931 U.S. Dept. Ag. *Misc. Pub.* 101.172, *Bud sagebrush* . . is . . known as . . horse sage(brush). . . It has been noted in the Challis National Forest region of Idaho . . and is there reported to be . . a fairly good or good horse browse.

horse salt n *old-fash*

c1938 in 1970 Hyatt *Hoodoo* 1.642, After finely granulated salt was introduced . . this smaller salt was sometimes called *table salt.* In horse-and-buggy days, persons living in towns sometimes called it *horse salt.*

horse's ass n

A sea anemone (Anthozoa).

1945 McAtee *Nomina Abitera* 18 **ME,** Sea anemone (Anthozoa)—Horse's ass.

horse savin n

A **juniper** (here: *Juniperus communis*).

1900 Lyons *Plant Names* 208, *J(uniperus) communis. . .* Horse Savin. **1930** Sievers *Amer. Med. Plants* 25, Common Juniper—*Juniperus communis. . .* Other common names.—Fairy circle, . . horse savin. **1960** Vines *Trees SW* 37, Common Juniper—*Juniperus communis.*

. . Vernacular names are Horse Savin, . . Gin Juniper. **1971** Krochmal *Appalachia Med. Plants* 152, *Juniperus communis*. . . Common Names: Common juniper, . . horse savin.

horsesaw n [By metath from *sawhorse;* cf Intro "Language Changes" I.1] Cf **bucksaw**

1965–70 *DARE* (Qu. L58, *An implement with an A-shaped frame . . that you put boards on to saw them*) Infs **FL**22, **TN**53, Horsesaw.

horse scoop n

=**fresno 2.**

1978–79 *Midw. Lang. & Folklore Newsl.* 1–2.20 **ME,** In Maine the "fresno" is called a "horse scoop," in Indiana a "slip shovel," and in Wisconsin a "slusher."

horse-shed v, hence vbl n *horse-shedding*

1 To try to influence another's opinion, electioneer; to coach; to bribe; hence n *horse-shedder* one who tries to influence opinion. *somewhat old-fash*

1846 Cooper *Redskins* 1.229 **cNY,** The private discussions that were held between pairs, under what is called the "horse-shedding" process. *Ibid,* Your regular "horse-shedder" is employed to frequent taverns where jurors stay, and drop hints before them touching the merits of causes known to be on the calendars. **1856** Hall *College Words* 258 **VT,** *Horse-shedding.* At the University of Vermont, among secret and literary societies, this term is used to express the idea conveyed by the word *electioneering.* **1887** Kirkland *Zury* 537 **IL,** *Horse-shed*. . . To propagate views or advance interest by private or quasi public talk. **1893** *KS Univ. Qrly.* 1.140 **KS,** *Horse-shed:* to try to win over by personal appeal or bribery, as, 'I concluded to horse-shed the judge and try to get a pointer on his decision.' **1901** *Congressional Record* 4 Feb 34.2.1918/1 **MI,** The witnesses were right there. There was no opportunity, as Mr. Lincoln used to say, to "horse-shed" them before they were brought in—before their counsel or attorneys had had any opportunity to change their minds. **1914** *DN* 4.108 **KS,** *Horseshed*. . . To coach. "We don't expect to horseshed any witnesses." **1950** *Perrin Coll.* **NH** (as of early 1900s), The Sanbornton Town Hall was beside the Congregational Church, which was plentifully supplied with horsesheds. At election and town meeting day as a boy I frequently saw the good Republican town fathers strolling to the horsesheds with a farmer or two in tow. Sometimes, it was reported, a dollar changed hands, but more often a swig from a bottle was the form of argument. This was regularly referred to as horseshedding.

2 By ext: see quot.

1888 Bittinger *Hist. Haverhill NH* 361 **cwNH,** Sometimes a little business was initiated [between services on Sunday], incipient steps taken toward purchases or trades. . . The hour was a sort of exchange time, when seller and buyer . . would talk, saying, "If it was to-morrow, what and so." This was generally done in a quiet way and was known as "horse-shedding."

horse-shedder See **horse-shed 1**

horse-shedding vbl n See **horse-shed**

horse-shedding n [Cf *woodshed* a place for administering corporal punishment] Cf **horse C4**

A whipping.

1970 *DARE* FW Addit **Philadelphia PA,** [Newspaper article:] "What they need," Judge Carroll said, "is God's fresh air and a good horse shedding." Asked to define the meaning of "horse shedding," he said: "Discipline, discipline, discipline." The jurist thrrew [sic] his support to the efforts of Specter and Rizzo to stop the city's teenage warfare.

horseshoe n

1 See **horseshoe crab.**

2 =**frogbit.**

1926 *Torreya* 26.4, *Limnobium spongia*. . . Horse-shoe, Florence, La. **1940** Clute *Amer. Plant Names* 263, *Limnobium spongia.* Horse-shoes.

3 A metal plate fastened to the heel or sole of a boot or shoe.

1966–69 *DARE* (Qu. W12a, *Heavy pieces of metal fastened under the soles of boots to keep them from slipping*) Inf **MI**2, Horseshoes—a horseshoe-shaped piece strapped to the heel; (Qu. W12b, *Metal pieces under the tips of shoes to prevent wear*) Inf **PA**230, Horseshoes; **WI**47, Horseshoes—small horseshoe-shaped metal [pieces] in the shoe heel [or] one large metal strip running around the bottom of the heel.

horseshoe crab Also *horseshoe* [From the shape]

A **king crab** (here: *Limulus polyphemus*).

1775 (1962) Romans *Nat. Hist. FL* 302, It was no other than a crab of the kind called . . to the northward a horse-shoe. **1792** Belknap *Hist. NH* 3.183, King Crab, or Horse Shoe. **1850** (1852) Hawthorne *Scarlet Letter* 207 **eMA,** She seized a live horse-shoe by the tail. **1948** *Time* 14 June 1, The underside of this strange sea dweller is shaped like a horseshoe—hence the name horseshoe crab. **1969** *DARE* FW Addit **eNC,** [From a display in the museum at Cape Hatteras:] Horseshoe crab. **1970** *DARE* (Qu. P18, *What kinds of shellfish are common around here?*) Inf **CT**42, Horseshoe crabs. **1978** Whipple *Vintage Nantucket* 248 **MA,** It [=*Limulus polyphemus*] is not a crab but a relative of the spider. It has survived only on the eastern coast of the U.S.; a different species [=*P. moluccanus*], indistinguishable to me, can be found in Asian waters. It is sometimes called the king crab. But its more popular name, horseshoe crab, is obvious from its outline.

horseshoe grass n Cf **horse-mane oat**

A **grama grass 1** (here: *Bouteloua curtipendula*).

1911 *Century Dict. Suppl., Side-oats*. . . A grama-grass, *Atheropogon curtipendulus*. . . Also called *tall grama, jointed grama,* and *prairie-oats,* in Tennessee *horseshoe-grass,* and in the southwestern United States *mesquite* or *mesquite-grass.*

horseshoe violet n Also *horse violet* **NEng, esp MA**

=**bird's-foot violet 1.**

1892 *Jrl. Amer. Folkl.* 5.92, *Viola pedata,* horseshoe violet. Concord, Mass. . . Horse violet. New England. **1893** *Ibid* 6.138, *Viola pedata*. . . Horse-shoe violet. Swansea, Mass.; Boston, Mass. **1936** Eaton *Wild Gardens New Engl.* 17 **MA,** We children called it [=the bird-foot violet] the horseshoe violet, I have no idea why; I have never heard it so called save by people from that Middlesex region. **1940** Clute *Amer. Plant Names* 135, *V[iola] pedata*. . . Horse-violet.

horse smelt n

A **silversides** (here: *Atherinopsis californiensis*).

1953 Roedel *Common Fishes CA* 76, *Atherinopsis californiensis*. . . *Unauthorized Names:* smelt, horse smelt, blue smelt.

horse sorrel n

1 A **sheep sorrel** (here: *Rumex acetosella*).

1843 (1916) Hall *New Purchase* 375 **IN,** Fried ham, cold chicken fixins and horse sorrel pies! **1900** Lyons *Plant Names* 327, *R[umex] Acetosella*. . . Horse Sorrel. **1933** Small *Manual SE Flora* 446, *A[cetosella] Acetosella* [=*Rumex a.*]. . . Horse-Sorrel. **1966–69** *DARE* (Qu. S21, . . *Other weeds*) Inf **VA**15, Horse sorrel; (Qu. S26d, *Wildflowers that grow in meadows*) Inf **PA**192, Horse sorrel. **1973** Hitchcock-Cronquist *Flora Pacific NW* 91, Horse sorrel. . . *R[umex] acetosella.*

2 =**wood sorrel.**

1968 *DARE* FW Addit **VA**15, Horse sorrel—*Oxalis.*

horse sparrow n

Prob =**English sparrow.**

1966–67 *DARE* (Qu. Q21, *Different kinds of sparrows around here*) Inf **NC**3, Horse sparrows; [**SC**43, Horse-shit eater—a kind that stayed around stables—not often seen now [FW: perh a joking name for common sparrow]].

horse spider n

An unidentified spider.

1966 *DARE* (Qu. R28, . . *Different kinds of spiders . . around here*) Inf **SC**24, Horse spider.

horse stable n **chiefly NEast, C Atl, eGt Lakes** See Map on p. 1120 Cf **cow stable, horse barn**

A barn, or section of a barn, spec for horses.

1803 in 1888 Cutler *Life* 2.125 **eCT,** Keep your horse-stable free from dung. **1939** *LANE* Map 109, 62 infs, **NEng,** Horse stable. **1950** *WELS* 8 Infs, **WI,** Horse stable. **1951** Johnson *Resp. to PADS 20* **DE** *(Part of the barn where horses are kept)* Horse stable. **1965–70** *DARE* (Qu. M9, *The part of a barn where horses are kept*) 79 Infs, **chiefly NEast, C Atl, eGt Lakes,** Horse stable(s); (Qu. M1, . . *Kinds of barns . . according to their use*) Infs **CA**207, **DE**5, **MI**71, Horse stable; (Qu. M22) Inf **DE**1, Horse stable. [66 of 81 Infs old] **1986** Pederson *LAGS Concordance,* **Gulf Region,** 16 infs, Horse stable. **1989** Mosher *Stranger* 45 **nVT** (as of 1952), Beyond the woodshed were Mom's chicken house, a tool and machinery shed, a horse stable, a grain room, the milking parlor, and the milkhouse.

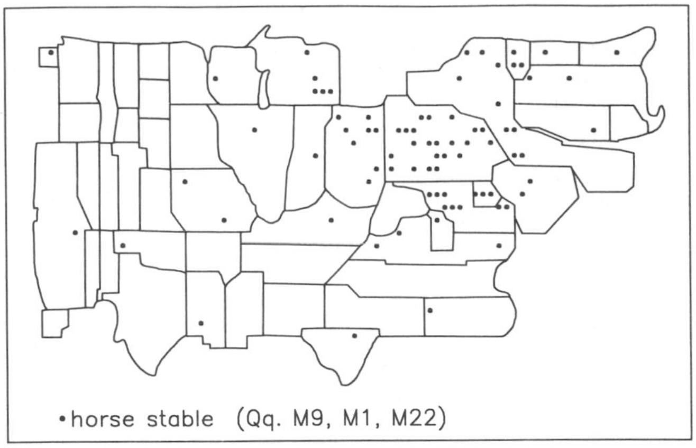

horse's tail See **horsetail 4**

horses' tails See **horsetail 3**

horse stinger n

A **dragonfly.**

1905 Kellogg *Amer. Insects* 76, Dragon-flies? Folks call 'em devil's-darnin'-needles in our parts, . . and other meaningless names are given them, such as . . 'horse-stingers,' . . but in spite of all these silly names and the silly superstitions they represent, dragon-flies are entirely harmless to man. **c1930** Brown *Amer. Folkl. Insect Lore* 7, Dragon-flies. . . Some people called them "Horse-stingers," because of a belief that they stung horses. **1967** Borland *Hill Country* 187 **NE,** And now and then someone spoke of them as "horse stingers" and said they sucked the blood of horses and were a pest that way.

horse stock n

1923 *DN* 5.211 **swMO,** *Horse stock*. . . Horses and mules of any age or sex.

horse sucker See **horsefish 2**

horse sugar n esp Sth

=**sweetleaf.**

1830 Rafinesque *Med. Flora* 2.229, *Hopea tinctoria*. . . *Sweet leaf, Horse sugar*. . . Leaves sweet, eaten with avidity by horses and cattle, their decoction dyes wool and silk of a bright yellow. **1859** (1880) Darlington *Amer. Weeds* 218, The 'Horse Sugar' of the South. . . [is] a favorite food of cattle. **1884** Sargent *Forests of N. Amer.* 105, *Horse sugar*. . . A small tree, 6 to 10 meters in height, . . or often a low shrub. **1901** Lounsberry *S. Wild Flowers* 415, *Horse-sugar*. . . As the English name implies, they [=leaves] are rather sweet to the taste, like sugar. Horses and cows eat them most greedily. **1913** Morley *Carolina Mts.* 47, "Horse sugar," the only North American member of its family, . . is another early blossoming shrub whose flower clusters of little close-set balls of yellow fringe are fragrant and whose bark is aromatic. Its sweetish leaves, which the people say horses like to eat, have given it its popular name, but the botany . . christens it *Symplocos tinctoria*. **1966** Grimm *Recognizing Native Shrubs* 252, *Symplocos tinctoria*. . . Also called Horse-sugar, both horses and cattle relishing the sweetish-tasting leaves. **1974** Morton *Folk Remedies* 151, *Horse-sugar*. . . *South Carolina (Current use):* Root is boiled for "tea" which is drunk, with sugar added, as a beverage during meals.

horsetail n

1 Std: a plant of the genus *Equisetum*. Also called **bottle-brush 2, cattail 2b, fishpole, goose grass 1g, old man's beard, scouring rush, toad pipe.** For other names of var spp see **bull pipes, devil's-guts 2, Dutch rush, foxtail 4, foxtail asparagus, foxtail rush, gunbright, horsetail rush, mare's tail, meadow pine, pewterwort, pine grass, pinetop, polishing rush, scouring brush, scrub grass, shave brush, shave-grass, snake grass, snake rush, snakeweed, winter rush**

2 A **horseweed 1** (here: *Conyza canadensis*).

1876 Hobbs *Bot. Hdbk.* 55, Horse tail, Canada fleabane, Erigeron Canadense. **1930** OK Univ. Biol. Surv. *Pub.* 2.84, *Erigeron canadensis* [sic] . . . Horse-tail, Horse-weed.

3 usu pl; also *horses' tails:* A type of cloud; see quots. Cf **mare's tail**

1911 *Century Dict. Suppl.*, Horsetail. . . In *meteor.*, a form of cirrus cloud. **1950** *WELS (Kinds of clouds)* 1 Inf, **WI,** Horsetails—windswept upwards. **1950** *WELS Suppl.*, I saw the horsetail last year in Iowa, southwest of Strawberry Point. It was the only description I could give for that cloud. Horsetails—fleecy and delicate. Usually precedes rain. **1966–69** *DARE* (Qu. B10, . . *The long trailing clouds high in the sky*) 43 Infs, **scattered,** Horsetails; **NC**53, **OH**17, Horses' tails; **KY**10, **MS**24, Horses' tails, mares' tails; **WI**23, Horses' tails—more used by grandparents before they had weather prophets.

4 as *horse's tail;* Fig: see quot.

1966 *DARE* (Qu. Y9, *Somebody who always follows along behind others: "His little brother is an awful ______.")* Inf **WA**3, Horse's tail—old-fashioned; [**ME**5, He's like a horse's tail, always behind]. [Both Infs old]

horsetail agaric n Also *horsetail mushroom*

=**shaggymane.**

1911 *Century Dict. Suppl.*, *Horsetail agaric,* an edible mushroom, *Coprinus comatus,* having a shaggy pileus. **1943** Fernald–Kinsey *Edible Wild Plants E. N. Amer.* 382, *Horsetail-Mushroom, Coprinus comatus*. . . is one of the most easily recognized of mushrooms.

horsetail beefwood See **horsetail tree**

horsetail fern, horsetail grass See **horsetail rush**

horsetail milkweed n

A **milkweed** (here: *Asclepias subverticillata*).

1937 U.S. Forest Serv. *Range Plant Hdbk.* W29, Horsetail milkweed, . . a poisonous perennial herb, ranks among those plants most deadly to range livestock. . . The . . name, horsetail milkweed, recalls the vegetative resemblance of the plant to some horsetail *(Equisetum)* and to the characteristic milky sap which exudes from the wounds when the plant is injured.

horsetail mushroom See **horsetail agaric**

horsetail rush n Also *horsetail fern, ~ grass*

A **horsetail 1** (here: *Equisetum arvense*).

1876 Hobbs *Bot. Hdbk.* 172, Equisetum arvense, Horsetail rush. **1935** (1943) Muenscher *Weeds* 129, *Equisetum arvense*. . . Field horsetail, Horsetail fern [etc]. **1969** *DARE* (Qu. S26c, *Wildflowers that grow in woods*) Inf **MA**49, Horsetail rushes. **1975** Hamel–Chiltoskey *Cherokee Plants* 39, Horsetail grass. *Equisetum arvense. E. hyemale*. Tea for kidneys; strong tea for constipation.

horsetail tree n Also *horsetail beefwood* [See quot 1889]

A casuarina (here: *Casuarina equisetifolia*).

1889 *Century Dict.* 2893, Horsetail-tree. . . A name of trees or shrubs . . of the genus *Casuarina* . . so called from the leafless, wiry branches, which much resemble the stems of *Equisetum*. **1933** Small *Manual SE Flora* 402, *C[asuarina] equisetifolia*. . . Horsetail-tree. **1960** Vines *Trees SW* 122, *Horsetail Beefwood—Casuarina equisetaefolia*. . . Also known under the vernacular names of Australian-pine, Horsetail-tree. **1976** Bailey–Bailey *Hortus Third* 232, *C[asuarina] equisetifolia*. . . Horsetail tree. **1982** Perry–Hay *Field Guide Plants* 18, *Casuarina equisetifolia* . . horsetail tree.

horse terrapin n

An unidentified turtle.

1926 (1949) McQueen–Mizell *Hist. Okefenokee* 122, There are four kinds of turtles which come out to high land to lay their eggs—the soft-shell turtle, the logger-head turtle, the hard-shell turtle and the horse terrapin.

horse thistle n

1 =**Canada thistle.**

1876 Hobbs *Bot. Hdbk.* 119, Thistle, Horse, Cirsium arvense.

2 =**prickly lettuce.**

1935 (1943) Muenscher *Weeds* 508, *Lactuca Scariola* L. var. *integrata*. . . Horse thistle. . . Widespread and locally abundant throughout the northern United States and southeastern Canada. **1959** Carleton *Index Herb. Plants* 63, *Horse-thistle*. . . Lactuca scariola.

horsethrowed past ppl, ppl adj Also *horsethrew;* pronc-sp *horsethowed* [Cf **throw**] **sAppalachians, Ozarks** Cf **-bit; cow-kicked, I'll be**

Thrown by or from a horse.

1913 Kephart *Highlanders* 225 **sAppalachians,** Ike Morgan Pringle's a-been horse-throwed down the clift, and he's in a manner stone dead.

[*Ibid* 284, In many cases a weak preterite supplants the proper strong one . . knowed, throwed.] **1917** *DN* 4.413 **wNC,** *Horse-throwed.* . . "Ever since I was horse-throwed." **1927** *AmSp* 3.9 **Ozarks,** Compound adjectives are very frequently heard; a horse-throwed neighbor of mine rolled down the mountain and died in a tangle of wind-blowed trees. **1954** *Harder Coll.* **cwTN,** *Horse-th(r)owed*—thrown off a horse. **1967** *DARE* FW Addit **GA**20A, I got horsethrew. **1968** *DARE* (Qu. OO30a, *Talking about a horse throwing the rider: "John got a bad horse and was ______.")* Infs **GA**28, 39, Horsethrew; **GA**19, Got horsethrew.

horsetile See **horstile**

horsetooth corn n [See quot 1911] Cf **dent corn**

An **Indian corn** (here: *Zea mays* var *indentata*).

1868 G. Brackett *Farm Talk* 100 *(DA),* 'Southern corn, I s'pose?' 'Yes; or rather western—the large "horsetooth" variety. **1872** VT State Bd. Ag. *Report* 1.53, We cannot grow the Baldwin . . with more success than we could grow the dent, or the horse-tooth corn of the south and west. **1892** *Jrl. Amer. Folkl.* 5.105 **cIL,** *Zea mays,* . . horse-tooth corn. **1894** (1934) Robinson *Danvis Folks* 37 **VT,** I druther hev a peck o' Dutton corn, yis, er Tucket, than a bushel o' their hoss-tooth corn. **1911** *Century Dict. Suppl., Corn. . . Horse-tooth corn,* a group of varieties of dent corn which have long, flat kernels.

horse-to-water n

In **mumblety-peg:** see quot.

1957 *Sat. Eve. Post Letters* **GA,** *Horse-to-water*—complicated throw in mumble-peg.

horse trap See **trap** n

horse tree n

1 =**whiffletree.** [Cf *SND* (at *horse* n. 2. (49))] Cf **doubletree**

[**1970** *AmSp* 45.64, It is of . . note that other English designations of the swingle tree documented in the *S[urvey of] E[nglish] D[ialects]* have left no trace in American English, as the . . *horse-tree* of Norfolk . . but gave way to *whipple-tree* or *swingle-tree.*] **1976** *PA Folklife* Spring 30, *Horse tree,* a whiffle-tree.

2 See quot. [*EDD* (at *horse* sb. 8) "a clothes-horse"]

1966 *DARE* (Qu. E1, *A piece of furniture that stands against the wall, and you hang clothes . . on it)* Inf **ND**2, Horse tree—moveable.

horse-turd coot n Also *horse-turd dipper*

=**ruddy duck.**

1888 Trumbull *Names of Birds* 110, *Ruddy Duck. . .* At Kennebunk, M[ain]e, *Horse-turd dipper* (the birds being so termed, I am told, from their habit, when alarmed, of huddling together in a mass); . . in Mass[achusetts], . . at North Scituate . . *Horse-turd coot.* **1945** McAtee *Nomina Abitera* 32.

horse-turd doughnut n [From the shape and color]

1969 *DARE* (Qu. H28, . . *Types of doughnuts)* Inf **MA**57, Horse-turd doughnut—made out of biscuit dough, cut in squares, cooked in hot lard, dropped into a kettle of hot molasses—also called Joe Froggers.

horse urine See **horse piss**

horse violet See **horseshoe violet**

horse watertail n

=**musk grass.**

1939 *AmSp* 14.255, A plant belonging to the family *Characeae;* also called *featherbeds, stonewort,* and *horse watertail.*

horseweed n

1 A **fleabane** of the genus *Conyza:* usu *C. canadensis* which is also called **bitterweed, blood staunch, butterweed 1, cocash 1, colt's tail, cow's tail 1, fireweed g, hogweed 2b, horsetail 2, mare's tail, prideweed, scabious, skevish, squaw-weed.**

1830 Rafinesque *Med. Flora* 2.218, *E[rigeron] canadense* is called *Horseweed* in Kentucky, and used for the strangury of horses. **1848** Gray *Manual of Botany* 205, *Horse-weed. . .* Stem erect, wand-like. . . A common weed everywhere. **1876** Hobbs *Bot. Hdbk.* 55, Horse weed, . . Ambrosia trifida. . . Collinsonia Canadensis. . . Spiraea tomentosa. . . Erigeron Canadense. **1911** (1913) Johnson *Highways Gt. Lakes* 324, But here, to my dismay, I was confronted by battalions of horseweeds, growing as thick as they could stand and spindling up to a height of eight or ten feet. **1935** Sandoz *Jules* 27 **wNE,** Children raced through the camp with bows and horseweed lances. **1949** (1958) Stuart *Thread* 70 **KY,** I scythed the small yard and raked the horseweeds from the lot. **1965** Teale *Wandering Through Winter* 244 **KY,** Here in the rich soil the horseweed . . *Leptilon canadense* . . had attained its maximum growth. **1967–69** *DARE* (Qu. S20) Inf **MO**13, Horseweed; (Qu. S21) Infs **MO**11, 32, 37, Horseweeds.

2 A **horse balm:** usu *Collinsonia canadensis.*

1790 L. Castiglioni *Viaggio negli Stati Uniti* II.333 *(OEDS), Collinsonia canadensis,* Lin. Horse-weed. **1791** in 1793 Amer. Philos. Soc. *Trans.* 3.114, Collinsonia canadensis *(Horse-weed, Knot-root),* Hydrophyllum canadense (Scaly-root). **1824** Bigelow *Florula Bostoniensis* 10, *Collinsonia Canadensis. Horse weed. . .* Plant three or four feet high. . . Leaves opposite, very large. **1876** [see **1** above]. **1900** Lyons *Plant Names* 27, *A[mbrosia] trifida. . .* Horse-weed. *Ibid* 111, *C[ollinsonia] Canadensis. . .* Horse-weed. *Ibid* 212, *L[actuca] Canadensis.* . . Horseweed. *Ibid* 221, *L[eptilon] Canadense. . .* Horseweed. *Ibid* 355, *S[piraea] tomentosa. . .* Horse-weed. **1930** Sievers *Amer. Med. Plants* 23, *Citronella Horsebalm. . . Other common names. . .* Horseweed. **1969** *DARE* (Qu. S21) Inf **KY**63, Horseweed—tall big, flat green leaf. **1976** Bailey–Bailey *Hortus Third* 296, *Collinsonia* L. *Horse balm, horseweed. . .* Five spp. of strongly aromatic per[ennial] herbs of e. N. Amer.

3 =**giant ragweed.**

1830 Rafinesque *Med. Flora* 2.190, *A[mbrosia] trifida* is called Horseweed and Wild Hemp, . . sometimes 10 feet high. **1861** Wood *Class-Book* 443, *Horse-weed. . . A. trifida. . .* It is greedily eaten by horses. **1876** [see **1** above]. **1896** *Jrl. Amer. Folkl.* 9.191, *Ambrosia trifida,* . . horseweed, Sulphur Grove, Ohio. **1898** *Ibid* 11.229 **KS,** *Ambrosia trifida. . .* Horseweed. **1900** [see **2** above]. **1912** Blatchley *IN Weed Book* 149, Horse-weed. . . Horses are very fond of this . . , often forsaking other food for its juicy leaves and branches. **1968** *DARE* (Qu. S21) Inf **IA**29, Horseweed—grows 12′ high, raggedy-looking, hard on hay fever.

4 A **hardhack 1** (here: *Spiraea tomentosa*).

1876 [see **1** above]. **1900** [see **2** above].

5 A **wild lettuce:** usu *Lactuca canadensis,* but also *L. serriola.*

1894 *Jrl. Amer. Folkl.* 7.92 **WV,** *Lactuca Canadensis* . . Horse-weed. **1898** *Ibid* 11.230 **KS,** *Lactuca Canadensis* . . horse weed. **1900** [see **2** above]. **1914** Georgia *Manual Weeds* 542. **1936** IL Nat. Hist. Surv. *Wildflowers* 389, The Wild Lettuce or Horseweed . . grows 3–10 feet high. **1971** GA Dept. Ag. *Farmers Market Bulletin* 28 July 8, A delectable and vitamin-teeming relative of domestic varieties, wild lettuce or horseweed, L[actuca] canadensis, grows abundantly in Georgia. **1974** *WI Acad. Rev.* Summer 22, Wild lettuce(s) (*Lactuca scariola*[,] also *L. canadensis*) . . horseweed.

6 =**snakeweed.**

1924 *Amer. Botanist* 30.33, *Gutierrezia. . .* Sometimes it is called "horseweed" because nothing but horses will eat it. **1940** Clute *Amer. Plant Names* 260, *Gutierrezia sarothrae. . .* Horse-weed.

7 A **marsh elder** (here: *Iva xanthifolia*).

1932 Rydberg *Flora Prairies* 763, Horseweed. . . *C[yclachaena] xanthifolia.* **1945** Wodehouse *Hayfever Plants* 135, Prairie ragweed . . also known as horseweed . . , is a tall coarse annual reaching a height of six feet or more. **1947** *Atlantic Mth.* June 61/1 **cTN,** Mr. Henry he pushed down through the hoss weeds thar by the river bank; them weeds higher than a man's head thar in that rich river-bottom land. **1953** Nelson *Plants Rocky Mt. Park* 179, The following composite plants . . have been identified in the park . . *horseweed* or *sumpweed, Iva xanthifolia;* . . and *golden curlybeard.*

8 =**chicory 1.**

1951 *PADS* 15.21, *Cichorium intybus. . .* Horse weed, Keyser, W. Va.

9 also *horse plant:* =**elecampane.**

1968 *DARE* (Qu. S26b) Inf **PA**70, Elecampane or horse plant. **1968** *DARE* Wildfl QR Pl.250 Inf **OH**37, Horseweed.

10 A **mullein.** Cf **horse mullein**

1967 *DARE* (Qu. S20, *A common weed that grows on open hillsides: It has velvety green leaves close to the ground, and a tall stalk with small yellow flowers on a spike at the top*) Inf **MO**13, Horseweed.

horse whipper n

=**coachwhip snake.**

1970 *DARE* (Qu. P25) Inf **NC**85, Black snake also called horse whipper; **VA**46, Horse whipper—very large black snake.

horse witch n Cf **hag** n **1**

1946 Driscoll *Country Jake* 66 **KS,** Knight [=a Black man from Alabama] stoutly maintained that the horse witches rode some of our horses through the sky at night, thus wearing out the poor animals. . . "That-there bay filly, she sho do suffah fum the hoss witches. . . You kin always tell when the hoss witches been ridin' the fillies, 'cause they braids the manes whilst they's a-ridin' 'em.

horsey adj

1 Of a mare: in heat; also transf. Cf **horse C2a, b**

1899 (1912) Green *VA Folk-Speech* 232, *Horsey*. . . Applied to a mare in heat. **1935** *AmSp* 10.95 [Coarse, obscene words], *Horsey*. **1942** McAtee *Dial. Grant Co. IN Suppl. 1* 6 (as of 1890s), *Horsey*. . . applied to a mare in heat.

2 also sp *horsy:* See quots.

1942 Berrey–Van den Bark *Amer. Slang* 235.6, Horsy, horsey, *given to "horseplay"*. **1966–67** *DARE* (Qu. GG19a, . . *A person acts . . important or independent: "He surely is ——— these days."*) Inf **LA**14, Horsey; (Qu. GG23c, . . *Be patient*) Inf **SC**21, Don't get so horsey; (Qu. II36b, *Of somebody who talks back or gives rude answers . . "She certainly is ———!"*) Inf **MS**69, Horsey.

horse yellowleg(s) n [See quot 1955]

=**yellowlegs.**

1925 (1928) Forbush *Birds MA* 1.435, *Totanus melanoleucus*. . . *Greater Yellow-legs*. Other names: . . winter turkey-back . . horse yellow-leg. **1946** Hausman *Eastern Birds* 274, *Greater Yellowlegs—Totanus melanoleucus*. . . Other Names. . . Horse Yellowlegs . . Yelper. **1955** *AmSp* 30.177, *Horse yellowleg* refers to the relatively larger size of the greater yellowlegs in Connecticut. **1956** MA Audubon Soc. *Bulletin* 40.18, *Greater Yellow-legs*. . . Horse Yellow-leg (Conn. Horse, in this connection, means big.)

‡horsey-eyes n

1968 *DARE* (Qu. X26b, *If a person's eyes look in different directions, looking outward, he's ———*) Inf **MI**96, Horsey-eyes—nickname.

horsie See **horseback ride**

horsieback (ride) See **horseback ride**

horsing ppl adj See **horse C2a,b**

horsing vbl n See **horse C2b,4**

horsler n [Var of *hostler*] Cf Intro "Language Changes" I.8 Cf **horstile**

In marble play: see quot.

1893 Shands *MS Speech* 72, *Horsler* [hɔslə]. In the game of ring-men, as it is played in Mississippi, it is the duty of the last man "killed" to put the marbles in the ring for the next game, and this person is called the *horsler*.

horspital n Also sp *horsepital* [Pronc-spp for *hospital*] Cf Intro "Language Changes" I.8 Cf **horstile**

1917 *DN* 4.394 **neOH, KS, KY,** *Horspital* [hɔrspɪtl]. . . More or less jocular form of *hospital*. Reported [also] . . as a serious use. **1917** in 1944 *ADD* **cwWV,** Horspital. **1940** *Ibid* **swPA, nWV border,** ['hɔrspɪtl]. Old illit[erate] speaker. Not jocular. **1942** Hall *Smoky Mt. Speech* 28 **eTN, wNC,** *Hospital* . . ['hɔɚspɪtl] was reported. **c1960** *Wilson Coll.* **csKY,** *Hospital* . . sometimes there is an excrescent /-r/. **1976** Garber *Mountain-ese* 43 **Appalachians,** Horsepital . . hospital.

horstile adj Also sp *horsetile* [Pronc-spp for *hostile*] Cf Intro "Language Changes" I.8 Cf **horspital**

1900 Willard *Tramping* 394 [Glossary], *Horstile:* angry, unfriendly, hostile. **1907** in 1953 Botkin–Harlow *Treas. Railroad Folkl.* 221, "The Northern Pacific's a bad road [=railroad] now. . . the 'bulls' [=railroad agents who police the employees] is 'horstile.' " **1919** *DN* 5.34 **seKY,** *Horstile*. . . Hostile. **1927** *DN* 5.451 [Underworld jargon], *Hostile*. . . Pronounced *horse-tile*.

horsy See **horsey 2**

horticultural bean n Also *hort(icultural), horticulture (bean)* Cf **cranberry bean**

Any of var beans (*Phaseolus* spp) with deep red markings.

1965–70 *DARE* (Qu. I20, *Other kinds of beans that are grown around here*) Infs **MA**6, 68, 74, **NH**5, **PA**2, Horticultural beans; **IN**3, **PA**206, **VA**13, Horticulture beans; (Qu. I17, *Beans [not pods] that are dark red when they are dry*) Infs **MA**98, **VA**26, Horticultural beans; **TN**13, Horticultures; (Qu. I15, *Some of the beans that you eat in the pod have yellow pods; you call these ———*) Inf **TN**13, Horticultures. **1976** *Wanigan Catalog* 7, Horticultural, or shell beans are a class having full pods streaked with red, and seed similarly marked with buff and red. *Ibid,* Davis' Horticultural—Many generations in Maine have been growing this fat, size 5 red hort. *Ibid* 8, Dwarf Horticultural—Syns: Ruby Horticultural, Dwarf Wren's Egg, Speckled Cranberry Bush—One of the many buff horts which came to me with this name. *Ibid* 11, Horticultural. . . I've had this one growing for years, and it always sends out runners. Seed has a dusty pink base color with maroon streaks. Dries early. **1990** *Seed Savers Yearbook* 38, [The Seed Savers Exchange lists four varieties of American heirloom horticultural beans including one] with maroon streaks . . yellow tinge . . from 95 yr.-old neighbor who got it from his father in 30's.

hosebird n [*EDD hosebird* sb. 2 "a rascal; a lazy, clumsy person"]

1949 *McDavid Coll.* **swNY,** Hosebird [or] devilish hosebird—A poor white; older use.

hosen n pl [Engl dial; *hose* + **-en** suff[2]] *arch* Cf **ho**

Stockings.

1891 Amer. Hist. Assoc. *Papers* 5.475 **eNC,** They [=the Croatans] regularly use . . *hosen* for hose; *housen* for houses. **1931** *N. Amer. Rev.* 231.433 **neNJ, seNY** (as of c1880), Within forty miles of New York City . . a race of mountaineers live in the hinterland of the Ramapos. They are known as the Jackson Whites. . . Several of the older Jackson Whites . . used *housen* as plural for *house* and *hosen* for *hose*.

hosepipe n

1986 *DARE* File **cNC,** *Hosepipe*—refers to a garden hose. This term seems to be used by people who grew up west of Charlotte, especially Gaston County.

hosey v, n |'ho(ʊ)zɪ| Also sp *hoz(e)y* [Etym uncert; perh < *holds* + hypocoristic **-ie,** but cf quot 1941] **MA, ME** Cf **boney**

To stake a claim or reserve a right to (something); to choose; the claim so made.

1927 *AmSp* 3.169 **NYC,** Children still stand before toyshop windows and call out, "I hozey the drum," . . meaning, "I choose for mine." **1941** *AN&Q* 2.120/2 **eMA,** The child's word "hosey" ("hozey" or "hozy") . . has persisted in some parts of the country for more than fifty years, transmitted orally, without "literary" recognition. It is used in the sense of "demand," "claim," "choose"—as in "I hosey such-and-such an object." The child who gets the phrase out first claims and receives the thing in question. . . It was in use in and around Boston half a century ago, and is still current in New England. *Ibid* 153/2, Children use . . ["hosey"] . . [for expressions] of the "I stake my claim" idea . . since no word familiar to children seems to express the idea adequately. **1950** *WELS Suppl.* **Boston MA,** *Hozy* ['hoʊzɪ]. "I hozy all these"—said with a gesture of both arms including the things referred to. This is an expression used by a child when claiming the right to an imaginary possession, as of things seen in a shop window, along the road, etc. **1967** *DARE* (Qu. V5b, *If you take something that nobody seems to own, you might say, "Before anybody else gets it, I'm going to ——— this."*) Inf **MA**2, I hosey ['hozi] it. **1971** *Today Show Letters* **ceMA,** Another Bostonianism which I have had to put up with over the years is the expression "I hosey (pronounced 'hoe-zee') that" chair or what have you. This means "I've reserved that," "I've got first shot at that," "that's mine." **1975** Gould *ME Lingo* 136, *Hosey*—To claim something up for grabs. When Father starts to carve the turkey, one child may cry, "I hosey the wishbone!" Mainers generally recognize that the first to cry *hoseys* has established a claim. **1986** *DARE* File **Boston MA,** "I hosey that seat" [means] lay a claim to. Common especially in eastern Massachusetts, but elsewhere in the state too. **1988** *DARE* File **Boston MA** (as of c1920), "I hosey the nibby [=the heel of a loaf of bread]" was very often heard. . . *[Hosey]* applied to other situations as in "I hosey last pick—first extra" when it seemed likely that extra desserts might appear!

hosing (down) vbl n

1966–68 *DARE* (Qu. II27, *If somebody gives you a very sharp scolding, you might say, "I certainly got a ——— for that."*) Inf **MI**4, Hosing; **PA**167, Hosing down.

hospital barn n

1970 *DARE* (Qu. M22, . . *Kinds of buildings . . on farms*) Inf **NJ**65, Hospital barn—for cows calving or for sick animals.

‡hospitality of the house n

1970 *DARE* (Qu. F37, *Names for an indoor toilet*) Inf **MA**98, Hospitality of the house.

hoss See **horse**

hoss and peffer See **hasenpfeffer**

hossname n [Perh blend of *hoss* (see **horse B3**) a person + *named*]

1946 Driscoll *Country Jake* 66 **KS,** "That-there hossname Johnnie . . he ain't long for this world". . . "Hossname" was usually prefixed to anybody's name, except in direct address. It was a vulgarization of "what's-his-name," but was used without any meaning at all by Knight [=a Black man from Alabama]. . . [""]No, hossname Cholly an' hossname Fonce [=two boys] . . they ain't got that sad look. . . but hossname Johnnie, the Lawd do' got his eye on him."

hoss(y) See **hasenpfeffer**

host n

1 A large number or multitude. [*OED* 1613 →] **scattered, but chiefly Sth, S Midl** See Map

1965–70 *DARE* (Qu. LL8b, . . *A large number—for example, of cousins: "She has a whole ______ of cousins."*) 38 Infs, **scattered, but chiefly Sth, S Midl,** Host. **1986** Pederson *LAGS Concordance (If he had seven boys and seven girls, you might say he had a ______ of children)* 5 infs, **Gulf Region,** Host.

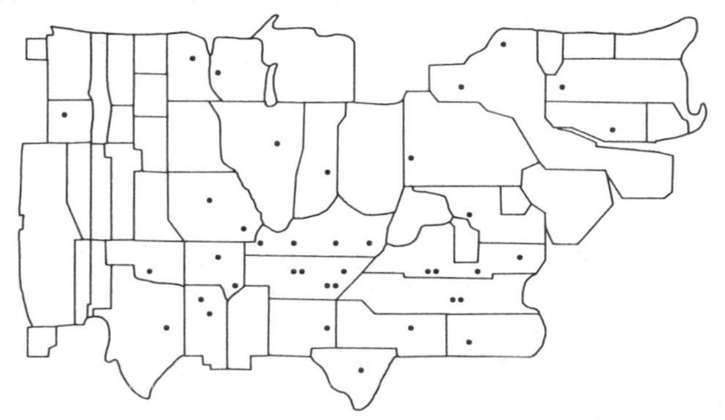

•host 1 (Qu. LL8b)

2 Of mass nouns: a large amount.

1901 *DN* 2.142 **ceNY,** *Host.* . . A good deal. "A host of work." **1935** Smiley *Gloss. New Paltz* **seNY,** *Host*—a large quantity. "A host of stuff."

hosted ppl adj

Tired from entertaining; see quot.

1926 *DN* 5.400 **Ozarks,** *Host.* . . To entertain guests. "We-all ben a'havin' too dam' much comp'ny—th' ol' woman's jes' hosted plum t' death."

Hosteen n [Navaho *hastqi'n*] **NM, AZ**

Mister, old man—used as a respectful term of address.

[**1910** *Ethnologic Dict. Navaho Lang.* 118, *Hastqín,* a man, a husband. *Ibid* 121, The word hastqín which is often prefixed corresponds to our "Mister." . . hastqín tso, Mr. Large, or the large man.] **1938** *Southwestern Lore* Sep. 37 *(DA),* Hosteen Nez smoked store tobacco while Hosteen Yazzie used Zilth-Nut-To—mountain tobacco. **1949** *Desert Mag.* April 23/2 [sic *DA*—quot not found], Hosteen Many Horses was buried in the Country of Standing Rocks. **1984** (1985) Hillerman *Ghostway* 1 **NM,** Hosteen Joseph Joe remembered it like this. . . The driver looked like a Navajo, but yelling at him like that was not a Navajo thing to do because Joseph Joe was eighty-one years old, and the people around Shiprock and up in the Chuska Mountains called him Hosteen, which means "old man" and is a term of great respect.

hot adj

1 also in compar phrr: Intoxicated; see quots. **esp NEng** *somewhat old-fash*

1851 Hall *College Words* 302, Some stage of inebriation: Over the bay, half seas over, hot. **1899** (1912) Green *VA Folk-Speech* 232, *Hot.* . . Half drunk. **1914** *DN* 4.74 **ME, nNH** [Rural locutions], *Hot.* . . Drunk. *Hotter'n a skunk, hotter'n love in hayin'-time.* . . Extremely intoxicated. *Ibid* 78, *Red wagon, hot's a.* . . Very drunk. **1941** *LANE* Map 472, 1 inf, **nwVT,** *Hot,* may . . mean 'drunk'. **1966** *DARE* (Qu. DD13, *When a drinker is just beginning to show the effects of the liquor, you say he's ______*) Inf **ME**6, Hot; (Qu. DD14, *When a person is partly drunk, "He's ______."*) Inf **ME**6, Hot. [Inf old]

2 See quot.

1903 *DN* 2.317 **seMO,** *Hot, while my head is* . . As long as I live. 'I 'low to stay on this place as long as my head's hot.'

3 Of coffee: strong.

1969 *DARE* (Qu. H74a, . . *Coffee . . very strong*) Inf **MO**39, Piping [or] steaming hot. [Inf old] **1988** *DARE* File **cIA,** From the time we began going to restaurants together, my grandmother—who was one hundred this year—would smoothly ignore my irritation and tell the waitress "I want coffee and I want it good and hot now." One day my control snapped and I said "Grandma, they don't leave the coffee pot standing around on the counter." Grandma said in her lofty tone, "I despise weak coffee."

‡**4** Of a road: see quot.

1969 *DARE* (Qu. N27b, *When unpaved roads get very rough, you call them ______*) Inf **NY**156, Hot—meaning rough.

5 Pregnant. Cf **oven**

1968 *DARE* (Qu. AA28, *What joking or sly expressions do women use to say that another is going to have a baby? "She['s] ______."*) Inf **IA**32, Hot. [Inf young]

6 used absol: A meal; food that is served hot; see quots.

1897 *KS Univ. Qrly.* (ser B) 6.88, *Hots:* cry of the street vender [sic] of hot tomales [sic], tenderloins, wienerwursts, etc.—General in cities. **1902** *Bulletin* (San Francisco CA) 11 Oct 6 *(Zwilling Coll.),* [Cartoon of a man calling out a restaurant order:] How's them hots comin. **1942** *Amer. Mercury* 55.223.85 **Harlem NYC** [Black], You got to get out on the beat and collar yourself a hot. *Ibid,* If Jelly really had had some money, he might have staked him . . to a hot. Good Southern cornbread with a piano on a platter [=spareribs]. *Ibid* 91, "S'pose you and me go inside the cafe' here and grab a hot?" **1942** Berrey–Van den Bark *Amer. Slang* 91.14, *Griddle cakes.* . . stack of . . hots. *Ibid* 94.3, A hot, *a hot lunch.* **1984** Wilder *You All Spoken Here* 148 **Sth,** *Three hots and a flop:* Three meals and a bed.

hot v

1 often with *up,* also with *over:* To heat or warm (something); to reheat; hence ppl adj phr *hotted up.* [*OED hot* v. 2 "To heat. (Now *colloq.* or *vulgar*)" 1561 →] **esp Sth, S Midl** Cf **hotten 1**

1913 *DN* 4.1 **wME,** *Hot.* . . To heat. "I will hot the water." **1922** Gonzales *Black Border* 307 **sSC, GA coasts,** [Gullah glossary], *Hot*—heat, heats, heated, heating. **1942** (1971) Campbell *Cloud-Walking* 18 **seKY,** She wanted him to light a fire in the cook room stove and set on pots of water to get hotted up for her to use. **1966** *DARE* (Qu. OO5b, *Talking about heating houses: "Years ago they ______ [the house] with a stove."*) Inf **MS**44, Hot. [Inf Black] **1966** *DARE* Tape **SC**16, Hot your water and put him [=the turtle to be cooked] in dere. [Inf Black] **1973** Allen *LAUM* 1.296 **MN** (as of c1950), *Hot up* . . refer[s] to the act of reheating coffee. [1 inf] **1986** Pederson *LAGS Concordance,* 1 inf, **cTN,** It would just hot the whole house. **1987** Jones-Jackson *When Roots Die* 139 **sSC coast** [Gullah], [Idioms "still very much apparent in daily communication":] Hot the water: bring the water to a boil. **1988** *DARE* File **nwAR,** You hot up leftover food. If my mother saw me taking a leftover from the [re]frigerator . . she'd say "Don't you want to hot that up?" It means heat over.

2 ppl adj phr *hotted up:* See quot.

1969 *DARE* (Qu. AA4b, . . *Expressions about a woman who is very eager to get married? "She's ______."*) Inf **IL**47, All hotted up.

ho't See **hurt**

hot and cold n Also *cold and hot* [From the fig use of the adjs *hot* close and *cold* distant as directional hints in games where one looks for a hidden object; see quots] Cf **hy spy**

A children's seeking game such as hide-the-thimble.

1966–70 *DARE* (Qu. EE3, *Games in which you hide an object and then look for it*) 9 Infs, **scattered,** Hot and cold; **LA**17, Hot and cold—you hide anything, and hint by telling the one looking whether he is "hot" (close) or "cold" (distant); [**NV**7, You're hot and you're cold—an object hidden and seeker directed to it;] **AK**5, Cold and hot.

hot ant n [Prob from the sting]

=**velvet ant.**

1970 *DARE* (Qu. R18, . . *Kinds of ants . . around here*) Inf **SC**69, Hot ant: big, red, fuzzy ants.

hot as Dutch love See **Dutch love, hotter than**

hot ashes, in adj phr

1 Excited; anxious; see quots.

1954 *Harder Coll.* **cwTN,** 'E's jist in hot ashes over gettin' to go to town. **[1969** *DARE* (Qu. GG11, *To be quite anxious about something—for example, waiting for a letter*) Inf **GA**77, Like a worm in hot ashes.]

2 See quot.

1954 *Harder Coll.* **cwTN,** *Hot ashes, in*—In trouble.

hot ass See **hot back**

hot as the hinges of hell See **hinges of hell 2**

hot back n Also *hot ass, ~ bottom* [Cf *OED hot cockles*]

A type of guessing game; see quots.

1968 Adams *Western Words* 155, *Hot back*—A game played by loggers in which a man stooped over blindfolded with his head in a hat and one hand on the small of his back, while the others formed a circle around him. One of the men in the circle would hit the victim's hand, and he would try to guess who had hit him. If he guessed right, he traded places with the striker. *Ibid, Hot bottom*—The same game as *hot back* . . except that the logger gave his victim a resounding whack on the seat of the pants. **1969** Sorden *Lumberjack Lingo* 62 **NEng, Gt Lakes,** *Hot back or hot ass:* A roughhouse game played by lumberjacks in the bunkhouse. Jacks formed a circle; one blindfolded man was in the center of the circle on his hands and knees. Any jack could swat him on the rear end. The blindfolded man had to guess who had swatted him. If he guessed correctly the swatter became the blindfolded jack in the middle of the circle. **1972** *NYT Article Letters* **NYC,** I would like to add the game of "Hot Ass"—in which the boy who was "It", would bend over and any one of the players would "fan" him. It was up to the boy who was "It" to guess the identity of his aggressor. If he guessed wrong he "went down" again until he did. Many of us went home with a "hot ass".

hot ball n

1 also *hot dollar:* A cherry- or cinnamon-flavored candy. **Mid Atl** Cf **red-hot**

1966–70 *DARE* (Qu. H82a, *Cheap candies sold especially for schoolchildren*) Infs **SC**7, 62, Hot balls; **NC**84, Hot balls (or cherry balls); [**AL**15, Hot candy—jawbreaker that is hot;] **MD**8A, Hot dollars—chewy cherry balls; (Qu. H82b, . . *Cheap candy that used to be sold years ago*) Inf **VA**74, Hot balls—cinnamon.

2 also *hot ball stick it to 'em:* Any of several games that involve fighting with (or over) a ball; see quots.

1967 *DARE* (Qu. EE33, . . *Outdoor games*) Inf **TX**26, Hot ball—hit one another with a tennis ball; **AR**55, Hot ball stick it to 'em—make a rag ball and fight with it. **1986** Pederson *LAGS Concordance,* 1 inf, **Houston TX,** Hotball—try to tackle [the] one with the ball.

hot beans n Also *hot beans and butter, hot butter beans;* for addit varr see quots [*EDD hot beans and butter* (at *hot* adj. 2 (4))] **esp MD, NJ, PA** Cf **bread and butter, come to supper; hot belt, hot peas 1**

A hiding game; also the call to signal the start of one of the phases of the game.

1957 *Sat. Eve. Post Letters* **IL,** *Hot beans*—A green or live switch was cut from a . . tree. Whoever started the game hid the switch in the grass by sliding it along the earth at the turf base [while the] others looked the other way. . . When the hider said "ready", all the others rushed to grope on hands and knees in a search for the weapon. The one finding it yelled "hot beans" and had the privilege of swatting anyone in range on the rear end. **1967–70** *DARE* (Qu. EE3, *Games in which you hide an object and then look for it*) Inf **OH**103, Hot beans; **NY**55, Hot beans and butter—hide [a] stick; **PA**167, Hot beans for supper; **MD**2, 8, Hot butter beans; **MD**20, 29, Hot butter beans, come to supper; **NJ**53, "Hot butter blue beans, please come to supper"—you say this after hiding an article, then, all look for it. **1968** *DARE* Tape **MD**19, [In school we played] hot butter beans come to supper. . . Everybody go out but one, had some kind a little old thing you hide and then after you hide it, you say "hot butter beans come to supper" and then they come in and hunt it and when you get close to it they say it's "warm," and if you get closer to it, "hot, hot." Then you look around and find it. . . if you're far away, [they say] "cold, cold cold, you're freezing." **[1969** Opie–Opie *Children's Games* 153, [The name] 'Beans and Butter' (Oxfordshire, 1849), [comes] from the cry to commence the search: Hot boil'd beans and very good butter,/ If you please to come to supper!]

hot belly n Also *hot pepper belly* Cf **pepper belly**

1970 Tarpley *Blinky* 258 **neTX,** *[Nicknames for Mexican People:]* Hot (pepper) belly. *Ibid* 259, [Responses] such as . . *hot belly* are based on a knowledge of the Mexican's fondness for hot, spicy foods.

hot belt n Also *hot belt Charlie* Cf **hot peas 1**

A game in which a belt is concealed; the call used to signal a particular phase of the game; see quot 1986.

[1953 Brewster *Amer. Nonsinging Games* 39 **MO,** *Hide the belt*. . . The . . players hide their eyes [while "It"] . . conceals a belt. . . The finder is allowed to whip anyone he can catch until . . reaching the base. . . When all have reached the base, the finder of the belt becomes "It" and a new game begins.] **1968** *DARE* FW Addit **New Orleans LA,** *Hot belt*—children's game in which a belt is hidden. The one that finds it calls out "stop!" Then that person calls out "hot potato," "hot box," etc, anything irrelevant. When the finder comes to "hot belt," everyone runs to base. The one the finder hits with the belt is "it." [Inf is a ten-year-old girl] **1986** *Wall St. Jrl. Letters, Hot belt Charlie*—one child is chosen to be the leader in the usual "one potato, two potato" method. The child chosen takes a belt or rope if all are wearing suspenders, and hides it somewhere, usually in a neighborhood yard. Meanwhile, the others are waiting on home base, out of sight of the hiding area. When the belt is well concealed, the leader yells out "hot belt Charlie" which is the signal for the others to come and search for the slender treasure. The leader directs the others by letting them know who is "hot" and who is "cold". The one who finds the belt must yell again "hot belt Charlie"—now a signal to the others to run for home base; the finder will chase and swat whomever he or she can until the base is reached. The finder then hides the belt and the game continues.

hot bottom See **hot back**

hot box See **hot place**

hot bread n

1988 *DARE* File **neTX,** In Houston you see "hot bread" on lots of menus, but in Houston "hot bread" means corn bread with chili peppers baked into it. I have an ulcer, so I learned that one real quick.

hot bug See **hot-weather bug**

hot butter beans See **hot beans**

hot cabbage slaw See **hot slaw**

hot cake n

1 A baked or fried cornmeal cake; see quots.

1683 in 1771 Penn *Select Wks.* 610 **sePA,** Their entertainment was . . Twenty Bucks, with hot Cakes of new Corn, both Wheat and Beans, which they make up in a square form, in the leaves of the stem, and bake them in the ashes. **1791** Bartram *Travels* 241, The root of the China brier . . they also mix . . with fine Corn flour, which being fried in fresh bear's oil makes very good hot cakes or fritters. **1951** Johnson *Resp. to PADS 20* **DE** *(Bread made with corn meal)* Hot cakes. **1968** *DARE* (Qu. H25, . . *Fried cornmeal*) Inf **DE**3, Hot cakes.

2 A pancake. **widespread, but less freq NEng** See Map Cf **flapjack 1, griddle cake 1**

[1835 Hoffman *Winter in West* (NY) 1.191 **neIL,** The usual settlers' dinner of fried bacon, venison cutlets, hot cakes, and wild honey . . was soon placed before us.] **1891** Farmer–Henley *Slang* 2.18/2, Buckwheat and other hot cakes form a staple dish at many American tables. **1941** *LANE* Map 289 *(Griddle Cake)* 1 inf, **csNH,** Hot cake. **1946** *PADS* 5.26 **VA,** *Hot-cake* . . A pancake; on the Eastern shore, rare. **1949** Kurath *Word Geog.* 35, *Hot-cakes* . . for griddle cakes made of flour. . . is current only on Delaware Bay, in Philadelphia and its suburbs, and on the Pennsylvania side of the Delaware Valley as far north as Stroudsburg

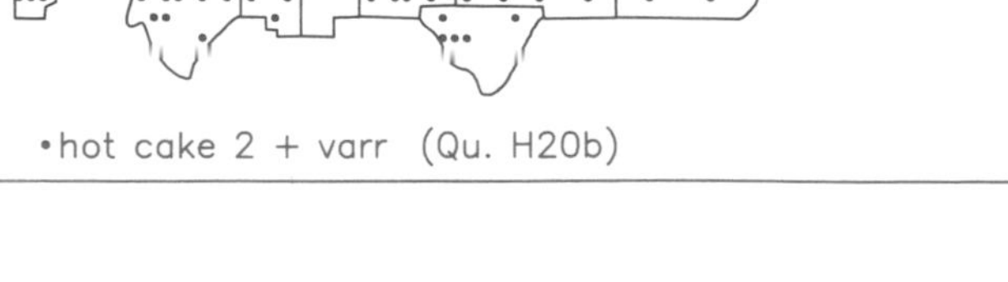

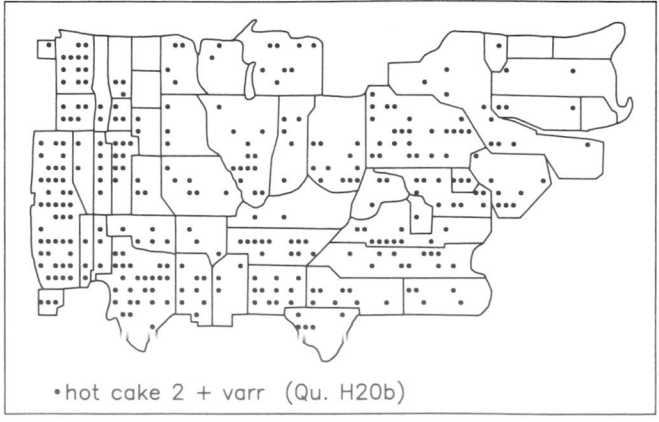

•hot cake 2 + varr (Qu. H20b)

at the Water Gap. It is rare even in Lancaster and Reading, where *flannel cakes,* the regional term of Eastern Pennsylvania, is still in general use. **1965–70** *DARE* (Qu. H20b, . . *Names . . for pancakes*) 320 Infs, **widespread, but less freq NEng,** Hot cakes; **MD**41, Buckwheat hot cakes; **AK**8, Sourdough hot cakes. **1973** Allen *LAUM* 1.283 (as of c1950), *Hot cakes* . . has scattered occurrences in the U[pper] M[idwest], where it is more likely to be found on restaurant menus than in home speech. **1981** *PADS* 67.34 **neMN,** *Pancakes.* . . All of the Iron Range respondents use the general term *pancakes.* . . Other Range responses are single instances of *flapjacks* . . *hot cakes* . . *wheat cakes.*

3 =friedcake 1.

1982 *Greenfield Recorder* (MA) 20 Mar sec A 4/2, A Yankee long ago got off a steam train going West . . to get a little snack to eat. . . He asked the sales clerk for "doughnuts," but she looked bewildered and said, "No, we haven't any doughnuts." The man replied, "Why, of course, you have right there before you." "Oh, you mean hot cakes."

hot-cake griddle See **griddle cake 1**

hot-cake turner n [*hot cake* pancake] **chiefly West** See Map and Map Section

=cake turner.

1951 Johnson *Resp. to PADS 20* **DE** *(When frying foods . . you turn them over with a ______)* Hot-cake turner. **1966–70** *DARE* (Qu. F3, *When you're frying things—for example, eggs—you turn them over with a ______*) 10 Infs, **chiefly West,** Hot-cake turner. [9 of 10 Infs old]

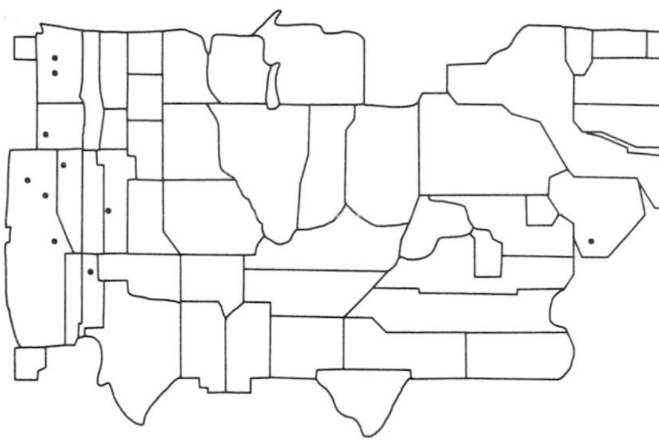

•hot-cake turner (Qu. F3)

hot chicken See **chicken n B7**

hotchscotch See **hopscotch**

hot coals n pl Cf **hot place**

1967 *DARE* (Qu. CC9, . . *Expressions for hell: "That man is headed straight for ______."*) Inf **LA**11, Hot coals.

hot cod n

A jellyfish of the class Scyphozoa.

1956 Rayford *Whistlin' Woman* 135 **AL,** Little jellyfish, called "hot cods," drifted over against us and burned our legs and thighs, a sharp enduring little sting.

hot cold slaw See **hot slaw**

hot coppers n [*OED hot coppers* (at *copper* sb.[1] 8) "a mouth and throat parched through excessive drinking"]

1968 *DARE* (Qu. DD24, . . *Diseases that come from continual drinking*) Inf **LA**45, Hot coppers—when you've got that dry cottony feeling in your throat.

hot country See **hot place**

hot cross bun n Also *hot crossed bun* **esp NEast** See Map

A sweet raised bread roll made with raisins or currants, usu marked with a cross in white frosting.

1896 (c1973) Farmer *Orig. Cook Book* 66, *Hot Cross Buns.* . . milk. . . sugar. . . cinnamon. . . flour. . . yeast cake. . . raisins . . or . . currants. . . when [dough] . . mixed, add raisins, cover, and let rise. . . In morning, shape in forms of large biscuits . . bake . . cool, and with ornamental frosting make a cross on top of each bun. **1939** Wolcott *Yankee Cook Book* 148, *Connecticut Hot Cross Buns.* . . "Goes good at church suppers." **1941** *LANE* Map 283 **CT,** 1 inf, *Bun,* only of the *hot cross bun;* 1 inf, *Bun,* familiar only in *hot cross bun.* **1950** *WELS (Fancy home-baked rolls)* 3 Infs, **WI,** Hot cross buns. **1967–69** *DARE* (Qu. H32, . . *Fancy rolls*) 15 Infs, **esp NEast, eastern N Cent,** Hot cross buns; **VT**16, Hot crossed buns; (Qu. H18, . . *Special kinds of bread*) Inf **NY**70, Hot cross buns. **1986** Pederson *LAGS Concordance* **Gulf Region,** 4 infs, Hot cross bun(s); 1 inf, Hot crossed buns.

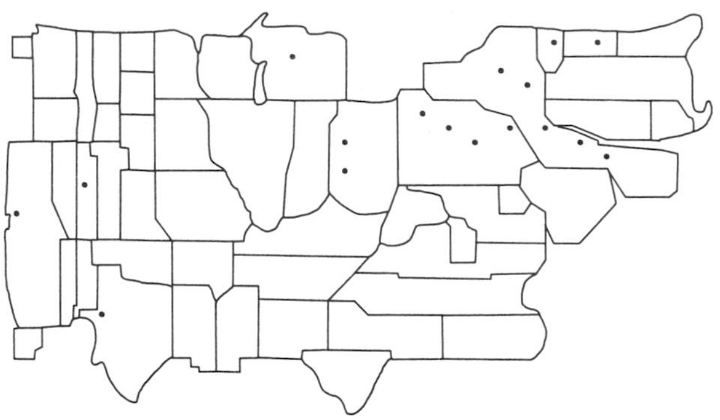

•hot cross bun + var (Qq. H32, H18)

hot deck n Also *hot yard* Cf **cold deck n 3, hot log**

In logging: logs sent directly to the mill, not held in reserve; the landing from which they are sent.

1956 Sorden–Ebert *Logger's Words* 19 **Gt Lakes,** *Hot-deck,* Logs which are to be hauled immediately to the mill, not stored in a pile. **1958** McCulloch *Woods Words* 90 **Pacific NW,** *Hot deck*—A landing at a swing tree from which logs are swung to the head tree as fast as they are yarded, don't get a chance to cool off. Not as widely used as cold deck. **1984** *MJLF* 10.151 **cWI** (as of 1880s), Hot deck. A temporary pile of logs. Maine: Hot yard.

hot dish n

1 A casserole or main dish—sometimes used as a mass noun; see quots. **esp MI, WI, MN, ND** See Map

1950 *WELS (Dishes made with beef)* 3 Infs, **WI,** Hot dish(es). **1950** *WELS Suppl.* **cWI,** *Hot dish*—extremely common local term covering the main dish at a kensington. Usually with a macaroni paste foundation. "Two of us brought hot dish and the others furnished the rest." *Ibid, Hot dish*—A local name for any of the various combinations of wheat pastes with cheese, meat, or fish that one finds at church suppers. A one-dish meal. "The delivery hadn't come by 11:30 so we just had hot dish and salad." **1965–70** *DARE* (Qu. H48, *Baked dishes made of potatoes cut up with meat or cheese*) Infs **MI**9, **MN**1, 11, **ND**3, 10, **WI**5, 41, 53, 76, Hot dish(es); **MN**3, Hot dish—general name for this sort of thing; (Qu. H49, *Dishes made by boiling potatoes with other foods*) Inf **WI**60, Hot dish; (Qu. H45, *Dishes made with meat, fish, or poultry*) Inf **WA**3, Hot dish—what you bring to a picnic for instance; [FW: Inf gave example of tuna, potato chips, and mushroom soup, [or] macaroni and hamburger. She distinguishes "a dish to pass" from a "hot dish." The former is a cold dish, perh a salad.] **1984** Erdrich *Love Medicine* 201 **ND,** [He] had just eaten himself a good-size dinner and she said would he take seconds on the hot dish when he fell over to the floor. **1987** Mohr *How Minnesotan* 13, On your visit to Minnesota, you will sooner or later come face to face with Minnesota's most popular native food, *hotdish.* It

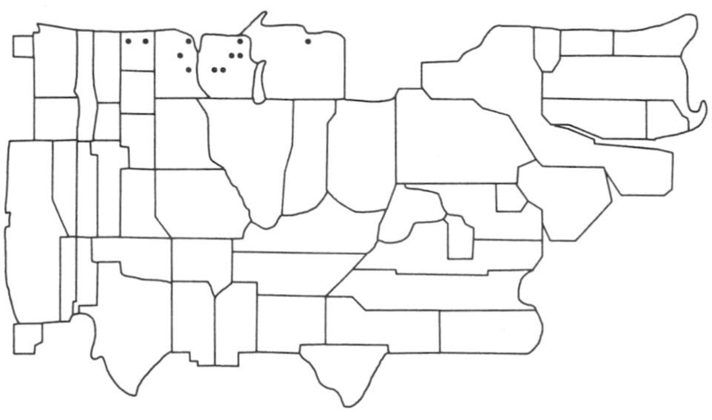

•hot dish 1 (Qq. H48, H45, H49)

can grace any table. A traditional main course, *hotdish* is cooked and served hot in a single baking dish and commonly appears at family reunions and church suppers. *Hotdish* is constructed on a base of canned cream of mushroom soup and canned vegetables. The other ingredients are as varied as the Minnesota landscape. **1988** *DARE* File **ceWI,** People would bring either a hot dish or a salad to a potluck. A hot dish could be a meat dish or macaroni and cheese. Lasagna is a hot dish. *Ibid* **ceWI,** A hot dish is some kind of casserole that you take to a potluck.

2 often attrib in *hot dish meal* (or *dinner, supper*): **=covered-dish meal.** Cf **kensington, hot supper 1**

1950 *WELS (When people bring hot dishes to a meeting place and share them . . you call that a ______)* 2 Infs, **cwWI,** Hot dish (dinner). **1950** *WELS Suppl. Hot dish*—same as "potluck" supper. **1966–69** *DARE* (Qu. H70, *When people bring baked dishes, salads, and so forth to a meeting-place and share them together, that's a ______ meal*) Infs **CA**6, **MD**7, 30, **MA**58, **MT**2, **NH**15, Hot dish (supper); **DC**1, **RI**1, **VT**16, Hot dish [FW sugg]; **NH**15, Hot dish supper if there is a casserole.

hot dog stand is open phr

Fig: see quot.

1966 *DARE* (Qu. W24c, *Sayings to warn a man that his trouser-fly is open*) Inf **SC**26, Hot dog stand is open.

hot dollar See **hot ball 1**

hotel n Usu |ho'tɛl|; **chiefly Sth, S Midl** |'ho,tɛl|; also |'hot,l̩|; for addit varr see quots Cf Intro "Language Changes" IV.2

A Forms.

1891 *DN* 1.143 **cNY,** [hotl̩]. **1895** *DN* 1.375, *Hôtel.* **1910** *DN* 3.443 **cwNY,** *Hotel* ['hotɛl]. . . Strong accent on first syllable. **1915** *DN* 4.226 **wTX,** *Hotel.* Often pronounced *ho-tl.* **1934** Carmer *Stars Fell on AL* 59, He shines shoes at the *ho*tel. **1944** *PADS* 2.15 **SE, LA,** *Hotel* ['hotɛl]: Frequent pronunciation of standard speakers especially in black belt. . . Less common than formerly. **1966–70** *DARE* (Qu. V11) Infs **MD**34, **MI**55, **SC**10, 40, **VA**70, ['hotɛl]; **VA**73, ['hoteəl]. **1966** *DARE* Tape **FL**42, They pavin' to the center . . excluding the corner there at the Exchange Hotel ['hotɛl]. **1968** *DARE* FW Addit **DE**3, *Hotel* ['hoʊ,tɛl]. **1986** Pederson *LAGS Concordance* **Gulf Region,** [50 infs put stress on the first syllable of *hotel.*]

B Senses.

1 also *hotel prime:* A size of soft-shell crab; see quot 1976.

1976 Warner *Beautiful Swimmers* 138 **Chesapeake Bay,** Soft crabs. . . all little crabs, not much more than three inches when shedded out, called "hotels" or "mediums" in the soft crab trade. **1984** *DARE* File **Chesapeake Bay** [Watermen's vocab], Mediums . . hotel primes.

2 also in var combs: A jail. Also called **free hotel**

1942 Berrey–Van den Bark *Amer. Slang* 466.11, *Jail.* . . hotel. **1965–70** *DARE* (Qu. V11, . . *Joking names . . for a county or city jail*) 11 Infs, **scattered,** Crossbar (*or* crowbar, iron-bar) hotel; 11 Infs, **scattered,** County (*or* city) hotel; **CO**20, **MD**19, 34, **MI**105, **SC**40, 69, **TX**94, **VA**70, 73, (Big) hotel; **SC**19, Brick hotel; **DC**4, DC hotel with bars; **SC**10, 40, **TX**26, 106, **VA**42, Free hotel; **MD**42, Hotel detain; **WI**48, Momsen's hotel; **SC**4, 21, 68, **VA**2, Riverside (*or* sea breeze) hotels; **CT**7, Select hotel; **CA**36, **MI**55, **TX**5, Sheriff's hotel; **GA**3, Walled-off hotel.

3 **=fruit basket;** see quot.

1970 *DARE* (Qu. EE2, *Games that have one extra player—when a signal is given, the players change places, and the extra one tries to get a place*) Inf **FL**48, Hotel—just like musical chairs and fruit basket upset; kids are named Atlanta, Miami, etc, (or apple, orange, etc)—Atlanta and Savannah change places at a call from the extra player and he tries to get a chair.

‡hotel pie n [Prob because it is the last thing taken at a hotel meal] Cf **timber sauce**

1967 *DARE* (Qu. G11, . . *A toothpick*) Inf **CO**11, Hotel pie.

hotel prime See **hotel B1**

hotfoot n

A cottontail rabbit.

1982 Elman *Hunter's Field Guide* 369, *Cottontail Rabbit (Sylvilagus)* Common & Regional Names: cooney, . . wood rabbit, hotfoot.

hot-handle iron See **hot iron 1**

hot hant n Also *hot steam* [*hot* adj + *hant* (at **haunt B**)]

A type of ghost; see quots.

1938 Burman *Blow for a Landing* 197 **Lower Missip Valley** [Black], Their hants still goes around in these here woods—hot hants, 'cause they've gone to hell, worst kind of hants there is. You can feel 'em passing, just like somebody was a-blowing hot steam on you. **1960** (1962) Lee *Mockingbird* 41 **sAL,** "What's a Hot Steam?" asked Dill. "Haven't you ever walked along a lonesome road at night and passed by a hot place. . . A Hot Steam's somebody who can't get to heaven, just wallows around on lonesome roads an' if you walk through him, when you die you'll be one too, an' you'll go around at night suckin' people's breath. . . Sometimes they stretch all the way across the road, but if you hafta go through one you say, 'Angel-bright, life-in-death; get off the road, don't suck my breath.' That keeps 'em from wrapping around you—"

hot head n

A type of engine; see quots.

1958 McCulloch *Woods Words* 90 **Pacific NW,** *Hot head*—An old time semi-diesel motor started by heating a plug in the head with a blow torch until red hot. A typical engine of this type was the one cylinder Corliss, a favorite for powering camp machine shops. **1965** Will *Okeechobee Boats* 113 **FL,** The first and maybe the only Diesel engine in any freighter on the lake, was a 15 horsepower horizontal, single cylinder Fairbanks Morse, a "hot head", which meant that you had to light a blow-torch, and heat a metal plug in the cylinder head whenever you had to crank it up. The engine was so hard to start and fuel was so cheap that the engine almost never was shut down.

hot hot adj phr Also *hot hot hot* [See quot 1983] **esp LA**

Extremely hot; also used as an exclam.

1967 *DARE* (Qu. NN20b, *Exclamations caused by sudden pain—a slight burn*) Inf **TX**36, Hot hot. **1968** *DARE* (Qu. B3, *If a day is very hot*) Inf **LA**20, When it's very hot they say it's hot hot; (Qu. B4, *A day when the air is very still, moist, and warm—it's ______*) Inf **LA**33, Hot hot. **1983** *Reinecke Coll.* 6 **LA,** Intensive by triple repetition is very common in La. Fr[ench] and those whose English is influenced by La. French. . . "hot, hot, hot" . . with ascend[ing] pitch. Sometimes only double.

hot house n

1 See **hot place.**

2 A jail.

1970 *DARE* (Qu. V11, *What joking names do you have around here for a county or city jail?*) Inf **TX**89, Hot house. **1970** Tarpley *Blinky* 270 **neTX,** *Names for the jail*—hot house.

hot ice n [Because it appears to be steaming]

Dry ice.

1968 *DARE* Tape **MD**8, [Inf:] She used to make her own homemade ice cream. . . Have you ever seen when you get ice cream in a package and they take this, hot ice. [FW:] Dry ice? [Inf:] Dry ice. Hot ice we used to call it.

hot iron n

1 also *hot-handle iron:* A flatiron. Cf **fire iron 2**

1966–69 *DARE* (Qu. F29, *Different kinds of irons—not electric—used . . for smoothing clothes after they're washed*) 10 Infs, **scattered,** Hot iron; **IN**41, Hot-handle iron. **1967** LeCompte *Word Atlas* 134 **seLA,** *Device . . not electric . . to smooth clothes . .* Hot iron. [1 of 21 infs] **1986** Pederson *LAGS Concordance,* 1 inf, **nwGA,** Hot iron—a smoothing iron.

2 See **hot stick.**

hot link n

See quot 1990.

1986 Pederson *LAGS Concordance,* 4 infs, **wFL, cTX,** Hot links; 1 inf, **neTX,** Hot links—good, cheap lunch. **1990** *DARE* File **TX,** My native Texas students are familiar with the term *hot links.* It means peppery hot sausages linked together in a string, sold in jars of liquid. They are eaten as snacks and are not cooked. You find them in all the convenience stores.

hot log v [Prob back-formation from **hot logging**] Cf **hot deck**

In logging: see quot.

1958 McCulloch *Woods Words* 90 **Pacific NW,** *Hot log*—To log and load out direct from the woods to the mill without logs being stored or cold-decked at any point along the way.

hot logging n Cf **hot deck**

In logging: see quots.

1956 Sorden–Ebert *Logger's Words* 19 **Gt Lakes,** *Hot-logging,* A logging operation in which logs go immediately to the mill. **1968** Adams *Western Words* 156, *Hot logging*—A logging operation in which logs go from the stump to the mill without pause.

hot lunch n Cf **hot supper 1**

1950 *WELS (When people bring hot dishes to a meeting place and share them . . you call that a ______)* 1 Inf, **ceWI,** Hot lunch.

hot-me-tot n Cf **hottentot**

1977 *Yankee* Jan 113 **Isleboro ME,** If you're like some people who are always in a pucker you're liable to get the name of a hot-me-tot, which may have derived from hot-to-trot—or maybe from Hottentot, which is a South African Bushman.

hot mix n Cf **hot pack, hot top** n

A paving mixture of asphalt, bitumen, and gravel applied when the ambient temperature is freezing or above; a road surfaced with such a mixture.

1966 *Russell Rec.* (KS) 11 Aug 7/5, The incident happened Monday morning as both trucks were carrying hot-mix to the road project. **1966–69** *DARE* (Qu. N21, *Roads that are surfaced with smooth black pavement*) Infs **OK**28, **TX**67, **WA**20, Hot mix; (Qu. N23) Inf **MO**37, Hot mix. **1984** Erdrich *Love Medicine* 157 **ND,** All I had to do was adjust the speeds on the belt for sand, rocks, or gravel. . . There was a pyramid for each type of material, which was used to make hot-mix and cement. **1986** Pederson *LAGS Concordance,* **Gulf Region,** 4 infs, Hot mix. **1989** *DARE* File **csWI,** Around here everybody calls the stuff used on the highways 'hot mix,' but when I worked up north a few summers ago with a guy from Massachusetts, he always referred to it as 'hot top.' He said that's what they call it out there.

hot name n

1986 Pederson *LAGS Concordance,* 1 inf, **cnLA,** Hot name—a nickname of abuse. Makes people hot [=angry].

hot needle, sew with a v phr For varr see quots

To sew in a hasty or slipshod manner; to move or act with haste.

1950 *WELS (Expressions about . . sew[ing] . . carelessly)* 4 Infs, **WI,** Sewn (*or* sewed) with a hot needle; 1 Inf, **WI,** Used a hot needle and a burning thread. **1960** Criswell *Resp. to PADS 20* **Ozarks,** One who sews with "a hot needle and a burning thread" is, I believe, one who moves, acts, works with speed. **1966–70** *DARE* (Qu. W29, . . *Expressions . . for things that are sewn carelessly . . "They're ______."*) 10 Infs, **scattered,** Sewn with a hot needle; **CA**137, **SC**2, **TX**40, Sewn with a (red) hot needle and a burning thread; **OR**4, **WI**60, Sewed with (a) hot needle; **PA**130, Made with a hot needle; [hot needled;] **NJ**45, They used a hot needle; (Qu. W28) Inf **NJ**45, Tack it together with a hot needle. **1988** *DARE* File **ceIL** (as of mid 1970s), My mother told me I sewed with a hot needle, meaning I sewed too fast and my stiches were messy. . . She said it was an old saying from where she grew up—"sew with a hot needle and burning thread."

hot-nosed adj Cf **cold nose**

1937 *Hall Coll.* **neTN,** *Hot-nosed*—used of a dog that is better at following a hot trail.

hot oil n

An important person.

1980 *AmSp* 55.202 **swMS** [Black], I ain't scared of nothing, not with no gun. Like I got a dozen people off me one day. . . I say. . . "Now what do you all youngsters think y'all hot oil, ain't you? . . [The informant described] his encounter with the dozen hillbillies, having opened at least one head with brass knuckles and frightening the rest off with a pistol shot over their heads.

hot oven penalty n

In children's games: a kind of gauntlet "run" on hands and knees; see quot.

1967 *DARE* (QR, near Qu. EE33) Inf **MA**52, Go through the hot oven penalty—you go through the others' legs and they would whack you.

hot over See **hot** v **1**

hot pack n Cf **hot mix, hot top** n

1967–69 *DARE* (Qu. N21, *Roads that are surfaced with smooth black pavement*) Inf **MA**1, Hot pack.

hot pants n

1958 McCulloch *Woods Words* 90 **Pacific NW,** *Hot pants*—A wasp, hornet, yellowjacket, or bee.

hot peas n

1 in phr *hot peas and butter:* A type of hiding game; see quots. Cf **hot beans, hot belt**

[**1969** Opie–Opie *Children's Games* 209, *Hot peas*. . . When everybody has gone [to hide] . . the person who was out turns round. . . He shouts 'Hot potatoes', 'Hot soup', 'Hot mackerel', and they must not move; but when he shouts 'Hot peas' they race back to the gate . . and . . people thump . . [the last one] on the back. . . In Cumnock it is [called] 'Hot Peas and Vinegar'.] **1970** *DARE* (Qu. EE3, *Games in which you hide an object and then look for it*) Inf **NY**250, Hot peas and butter [corr to *hot and cold*]—we would hide a belt or anything. **1975** Ferretti *Gt. Amer. Book Sidewalk Games* 114 **NYC,** There is the sadistic version of Hide-and-Seek played on Manhattan's Lower East Side: *Hot Peas and Butter.* "It" does not hide his eyes and count. Instead, all other players hide, and "It" hides his belt. . . ["It"] then summons them back, and as they hunt for the belt, eggs them on. . . Whoever finds the belt is free to chase—and whack—any and all other players before they reach home base. Often, the belt finder conceals his discovery and reveals it only when . . positioned . . between the players and home base.

2 in v phr *catch hot peas:* To get a scolding; see quot. [Perh by ext of penalty given in **1** above]

1966 *DARE* (Qu. II27, *If somebody gives you a very sharp scolding, you might say, "I certainly got a ______ for that."*) Inf **FL**14, I sure caught hot peas for that.

3 also *hot peas with butter;* In jumping rope: =**hot pepper.**

1961 *Western Folkl.* 20.180, *Hot peas*—Same as hot peppers. Children in many sections of the southern United States say hot peas instead of hot peppers. **1974** Skolnik *Jump Rope* 29, *Hot peas:* Fast turning, especially in the Southern United States and in some parts of New York City, where it is sometimes called *hot peas with butter* and occasionally *hot tamales.*

hot peas and butter See **hot peas 1**

hot peas with butter See **hot peas 3**

hot pepper n, occas pl Also *mustard and pepper, pepper(s), red hot pepper* Cf **hot peas 3**

In rope jumping: very fast turning or jumping of the rope; also used as an exclam to signal fast turning.

1946 TN Folk Lore Soc. *Bulletin* 12.1.18, Rope jumping . . offered a chance for the exhibition of individual skill in endurance, speed, and special stunts through . . "Hot Pepper." **1957** *Sat. Eve. Post Letters* **Detroit MI,** *Jump the rope games: pepper*—jumping rope very fast. **1961** *Western Folkl.* 20.180 (as of 1955), *Hot peppers*—A fast rope, applied to anyone who is outjumping her welcome. **1966** *DARE* Tape **AL**6A, [FW:] [In types of jumping rope, there was] hot pepper, you'd go as fast as you could. [Inf:] Hot pepper was real fast. *Ibid* **IN**1, [You] jump . . very fast, what they call peppers or hot peppers. **1967** *DARE* File **NYC** (as of 1950s), *Hot pepper*—turn rope very fast in jump rope games. **1968** *DARE* (Qu. EE33, . . *Outdoor games*) Inf **MD**2, Hot pepper—fast jumping with one rope. **1974** Skolnik *Jump Rope* 29, *Hot Pepper:* The most common American term for a fast-turning rope. Pennsylvania kids often call this *red hot pepper.* **1975** Ferretti *Gt. Amer. Book Sidewalk Games* 218, For the ordinary jumper, the ropes are turned slowly; but for those who are known as terrific jumpers, the Enders [=those who hold the rope ends] deliver "mustard and pepper," a speeded-up turning that tests jumping powers greatly. **1986** Pederson *LAGS Concordance,* 9 infs, **Gulf Region,** Hot pepper; 1 inf, **seFL,** Fire hot-pepper ropes—jumping rope very fast. **1988** *DARE* File **nwMA,** After we were already jumping, we'd yell "hot peppers" and that meant we wanted the rope turners to speed up.

hot pepper belly See **hot belly**

hot pie n

1979 *AmSp* 54.312 **cNY,** As a former Binghamtonian, she also reports another food term from that city: *hot pie* for 'pizza.'

hot place n Freq with *the* Also *hot seat, ~ spot;* for addit varr see quots Cf **hot coals**

Hell.

1839 *Spirit of Times* 21 Dec 498/2 **neAR,** He can out-pull any kivering horse this side of the hot place. **1921** Thorp *Songs Cowboys* 31 **West,** To the hot place with your city,/ Where they herd like frightened rats. **1942** Warnick *Garrett Co. MD* 9 **nwMD** (as of 1900–18), *Hot place*. . . hell. **1950** *WELS (Words for hell)* 16 Infs, **WI,** The hot place; 2 Infs, **WI,** Hot spot. **1960** Bailey *Resp. to PADS 20* **KS** *(Other words for hell)* Hot seat. **1960** Criswell *Resp. to PADS 20* **Ozarks,** *Hot place*—hell. Most frequently used by people who felt qualms about using the word "hell", especially women. **1965–70** *DARE* (Qu. CC9, . . *Expressions for hell:*

"That man is headed straight for ——.") 151 Infs, **widespread, but less freq Sth, S Midl,** [The] hot place; 12 Infs, **scattered, but chiefly Nth, Midl,** (The) hot spot; **CO**14, **IL**29, **MD**40, **MO**20, **NY**213, **PA**237, The hot seat; **MO**35, The hot house; **TX**61, Hot box; **WA**28, Hot country; (Qu. NN26b, *Weakened substitutes for 'hell': "Go to ——!"*) 51 Infs, **scattered, but somewhat less freq Sth, S Midl,** [The] hot place; **CA**196, Hot regions; **GA**72, The hot spot; **WA**28, Hot country; (Qu. HH20c, *Of an idle, worthless person . . "He isn't worth ——."*) Inf **AK**8, Powder to blow him to the hot place; (Qu. NN26a, *Weakened substitutes for 'hell': "Oh ——!"*) Inf **WA**12, Hot place.

hot pond n

In logging: see quot 1956.

1956 Sorden-Ebert *Logger's Words* 19 **Gt Lakes,** *Hot-pond,* Pond at the saw mill kept from freezing by running exhaust steam into it from the engine. Used for holding logs about to be sawed into lumber. **1958** McCulloch *Woods Words* 90 **Pacific NW,** *Hot pond*—A log pond heated in winter so logs can be pulled out to keep the mill going. **1966–67** *DARE* Tape **MI**20, In the winter they'd cut the logs . . haul them to the mill and deck them on the bank of the pond that they had dammed. . . When they couldn't log anymore, then they'd start the mill and break one of those decks and let the logs roll into the pond. . . They didn't use the hot pond. They did in later mills. Artificial hot pond; **MI**56, Pile them [=the logs] all up in decks. Then, by the mill . . there was a hot pond . . it was a good quarter of a mile long. They'd drop them logs into the hot pond, to take the frost out of that log so the saw would [cut it].

hot potato n

Any of var children's games; see quots.

1945 Boyd *Hdbk. Games* 37, *Hot potato*—The players sit or stand in a circle with one in the center, and throw a knotted towel across from one to the other, trying to prevent the center player from touching it. He may touch it at any time, even when it is in the hands of a player or when it falls outside of the circle. . . The one who is at fault in letting the center player touch it exchanges places with him. **1950** *WELS (Games with an extra player)* 1 Inf, **WI,** Hot potato; *(Other outdoor games)* 1 Inf, **WI,** Hot potato. **1968** *DARE* (Qu. EE1, . . *Games . . children play . . in which they form a ring, and either sing or recite a rhyme*) Inf **NY**64, Hot potato; **WI**68, Hot potato—not always with a song.

hot regions See **hot place**

hot rod See **hot stick**

hot roll n **West** Cf **cama**

A cowboy's bedroll and related effects.

1933 *AmSp* 8.1.29 **nTX,** *Hot-roll.* A roll of camp bedding. **1936** McCarthy *Lang. Mosshorn* [np] **West,** *Hot-roll.* . . The cowboy's bedding and belongings. **1940** Writers' Program *Guide NV* 76, The bed carried by the cowboy is known as his *hot roll* or *cama.* **1956** Ker *Vocab. W. TX* 137, *Hot roll*—cowboy's bedroll. *Ibid,* Western and/or cowboy influence appears in the use of . . *hot roll.*

hotscotch See **hopscotch**

hot scramble n

A marble game; see quot.

1975 Ferretti *Gt. Amer. Book Sidewalk Games* 153, *Scrambooch* or *hot scramble* . . all players make up a handful of marbles (mixed bags that include plain glassies, a few prized aggies, perhaps even an aggie shooter, and some valued purees) and then toss them into a patch of dirt. At a given signal—usually, "One, two, three, *shoot!*"—all players race for the area and dive into the pile of marbles, hoping to grab prizes. Definitely not a game of finesse.

hot seat See **hot place**

hot shot n

1 also *hot shots;* In whiskey distilling: see quot 1952. Cf **doublings, first shot, high shots**

1952 Brown *NC Folkl.* 1.553, *Hot-shots.* . . The first distilled liquor that comes from the worm. **1967** *DARE* (Qu. DD21a, . . *Any kind of liquor*) Inf **CA**7, Hot shot. **1969** *DARE* Tape **GA**72, When it [=doublings] comes out condensed at the end of your condenser . . then it is hot shots or high shots.

2 =**hot stick.** **esp West**

1936 McCarthy *Lang. Mosshorn* np **West** [Rodeo terms], *Hot shot.* An electrical charge used to make the tamest horse buck when being ridden by an amateur. The points of the charge are supposed to hit the horse on the shoulders. Hot shots are extensively used in rodeo chutes. **1955** *Sun* (Baltimore MD) 10 Feb 24/3 *(Hench Coll.),* Skilled crewmen no longer use sticks and whips to prod animals into the truck. They use a so-called "hot shot"—a tiny battery-operated instrument which . . encourages the animal to "get aboard" with little urging. **1967–68** *DARE* (Qu. K27, . . *The sharp-pointed stick used to get oxen to move*) Inf **CO**4, Hot shot; **MN**23, Hot shot—a modern one with a battery, gives a shock; **TX**37, Hot shot—today. **1967** *DARE* Tape **TX**25, [FW:] How do they get the animal into [the roping chute]? [Inf:] Just get a hot shot, that's the simpler way. . . That's just a little deal. What it all does is shock them really. It has batteries in it and you stick it to them and it shocks the devil out of them. [You stick it] just anywhere, in the butt or the back, just anyplace that's convenient. **1968** *DARE* File **swNV,** *Hot shot*—electric prod used to move cattle from corral to truck.

hot shots See **hot shot 1**

hot shot wedding n [**hot shot 2**]

A shotgun wedding.

1969 *DARE* (Qu. AA20, *A marriage that takes place because a baby is on the way*) Inf **IL**51, Hotshot wedding.

hot slaw n Also *hot cold slaw, ~ cabbage slaw;* for varr see quots [By analogy with **cold slaw**]

Coleslaw made with a hot vinegar dressing.

a1877 in 1950 *AmSp* 25.175 **cwCT,** *Hot-slaw.* Cabbage minced and heated with vinegar; and thus named to distinguish it from *Kool Slaa* (mistakenly etymologized into *Cold Slaw*). **1895** (1900) Arnold *Century Cook Book* 214, *Hot slaw*—Cut the cabbage . . as for cold slaw. . . Boil. . . Drain . . and pour over it a hot sauce made of . . butter . . salt . . pepper . . cayenne, and . . vinegar. **1905** *N.Y. Ev. Post* 23 Sep. 2 *(DA),* Mince pie, hokey pokey ice cream . . frankfurters with hot slaw—all . . go to stunt the gamin's growth. **1940** Brown *Amer. Cooks* 246 **KS,** *Hot cabbage slaw.* . . Put stewpan over fire with . . bacon grease. Put cabbage in. . . cook . . fill cup with weakened vinegar. Pour over cabbage, cook slowly 1 minute longer. Serve hot. **1950** *WELS (Dishes made with cooked cabbage)* 3 Infs, **WI,** Hot slaw; 1 Inf, Hot slaw—has a vinegar seasoning. **c1965** Randle *Cookbooks* (Ethnic) 18, [Pennsylvania Dutch dishes:] *Hot Cold Slaw.* **1967–70** *DARE* (Qu. H52, *Dishes made with fresh cabbage*) Infs **MD**21, 24, **NJ**21, **OH**76, **PA**60, 115, 203, Hot slaw; **CA**1, Hot cabbage slaw; **NY**105, Hot cole slaw.

hot spit and monkey vomit exclam

1967 *DARE* (Qu. NN8a, *Exclamations of annoyance or disgust: "Oh ——. I've lost my glasses again."*) Inf **TX**33, Hot spit and monkey vomit.

hot spot See **hot place**

hot steam See **hot hant**

hot stick n Also *hot iron, hot rod* **esp SE, Gulf States** Cf **hot shot 2**

A sharp or electrified prod used to make an animal move.

1944 Adams *Western Words* 81, *Hot stick*—A charged rod used in stockyards to prod cattle. **1966–70** *DARE* (Qu. K27, . . *The sharp-pointed stick used to get oxen to move*) Infs **SC**47, **TX**99, Hot stick—electric cattle prod; **TN**53, Hot stick; **FL**6, Hot rods—used in stock pens; **GA**11, 39, Hot rod—electric; **FL**26, Hot iron. [6 of 7 Infs old]

hot supper n

1 See quots 1941, 1954. Cf **hot dish 2**

1941 Writers' Program *Guide SC* 293 **ceSC,** Though fish fries and fish stews are popular community picnics, the favorite way to raise money for church or civic causes is by advertising a 'hot supper.' The public gladly pays for a plate heaped with viands that are samples of the most expert housewives' pet recipes. **1954** *PADS* 21.31 **SC,** *Hot supper.* . . A social gathering with provision of food (usually cold), at which the attendants entertained and amused themselves for hours. Originally the food was evidently served hot, but later, for convenience, it was served cold. Negro usage. Not recently heard. **1967** *DARE* (Qu. F39, *A large pocket knife with blades that fold in and out*) Inf **SC**38, Hot supper knife—with a long blade—carried to suppers by Negroes as weapons.

2 Transf: see quot.

1975 Gould *ME Lingo* 136, *Hot supper*—An exciting occasion, and seldom used for the excellent meal from which it derives. A hot supper is the finest kind; hence, "That was some hot supper of a town meetin'!"

hot tail n

1 A scorpion.

1967 *DARE* (Qu. R21, . . *Stinging insects around here*) Inf **LA**2, Stinging lizard (occasional) or stinging scorpion (most frequent) or hot tail (occasional).

2 See quot. Cf **hot back**

1970 *Thompson Coll.* **AL** (as of 1920s), *Hot tail*—a run-the-gauntlet game in which "it" (one who has violated some ordinance of a group, one being initiated, one disliked) makes his way along between two rows of men or boys who let him have it with their belts (or belt buckles). I have observed the game in Birmingham (high school boys), Guntersville (A National Guard company) and in Tuscaloosa University (college students).

hotted up See **hot** v **1, 2**

hotten v Also with *up* [*hot* adj + **-en** suff[5]]

1 =hot v **1;** to become hot. **Sth, S Midl**

1928 Peterkin *Scarlet Sister Mary* 31 **SC** [Gullah], Come eat a tater first to hotten up you insides so you can move fast. *Ibid* 93, Whyn' you bank de fire last night? . . I got to go borrow [some] . . to hotten me some victuals to eat. *Ibid* 309, Put de kettle up close so de water can hotten. **1929** *AmSp* 5.18 **Ozarks,** *Hotten*. . . To heat. "You-all better take an' hotten up thet 'ar soup." **1935** (1944) Rawlings *Golden Apples* 31 **nFL,** "I'd ruther have coffee, if you got it hot." "There's coals left. I kin hotten it." **1945** *PADS* 3.10 **ceSC,** *Hotten*. . . Not an adjective here but a verb meaning "to make hot." **1975** *DARE* File **eTX, AR,** In east Texas and Arkansas, to hotten (leftover food) is common.

2 See quot. [From *hot* adj pungent, peppery]

1975 *DARE* File **sGA,** *Hotten*—To make more peppery. "Let's hotten up the soup a bit." Not used of heating anything.

‡hottentot n [*Hottentot*] Cf **hoity-toity, hot-me-tot**

1969 *DARE* (Qu. HH35, *A woman who puts on a lot of airs: "She's too ______ for me."*) Inf **NC**61, Hottentot.

hotten up See **hotten**

hot-toothed adj [By analogy with *sweet-toothed*]

Able to tolerate pungent or "peppery" foods.

1887 (1895) Robinson *Uncle Lisha* 133 **wVT,** A 'coon 'ould make a first-rate little bear. . . He's jes' as . . sweet-toothed, an' hot-toothed, tew, fer he'll dig wild turnips an' eat 'em jes' 's a bear will.

hot top n, also attrib **eNEng, TX** Cf **hard-top, hot pack**

=hot mix.

1956 Ker *Vocab. W. TX* 84, *Cement . . paved road* . . hot-top pavement [1 inf]. **1961** (1962) Griffin *Black Like Me* 100 **TX,** Silence above humming tires on the hot-top road. **1965** Gould *You Should Start* 36 **ME,** We used to squat on the schoolyard grass (before hot-top was invented) and play. **1966–68** *DARE* (Qu. N21, *Roads that are surfaced with smooth black pavement*) Infs **ME**5, 10, 15, 22, **MA**27, **NH**14, Hot top (road). **1968** *Yankee* May 68/1 **NH,** Marsh was filled in, buildings went up, sewage systems went down, hot top roads were patted into place, and taxes collected. **1986** Pederson *LAGS Concordance,* 1 inf, **neTX,** Hot top—tar and gravel [road]. **1988** *DARE* File **wMA,** Both my mother and I . . have heard the term hot top used all over New England for what we call a blacktop road; **ME,** A hardtop road is most commonly called a hot top in Maine. **1989** [see **hot mix**].

hot top v phr, hence ppl adj *hot-topped*

To cover an area with **hot top** n.

1966 *Aroostook Republican* (Caribou ME) 8 June 8/6, [Advt:] Now is the time to *Hot Top Your Drive.* **1966** *Ellsworth Amer.* (ME) 29 June 1/1, The attractive building sets back from the highway and in front is a hot-topped parking space with room for 100 cars.

hotty-dotty n [Redup; cf *OED hotter* "*Sc.* and *north. dial.* . . v. 2 To move along with vertical vibration as over a rough surface"; cf also *OED dot and go one* (at *dot* v.[1] 5)]

1969 *DARE* (Qu. N30, . . *A sudden short dip in a road*) Inf **NY**190, Hotty dotty ['hati 'dati].

hot up See **hot** v **1**

hot-water corn bread n Also *hot-water bread, ~ corn cake, ~ hoecake* **chiefly Gulf States, Inland Sth** See Map Cf **corn bread 1, corn pone 1, hoecake**

A type of corn bread; see quots.

1962 Atwood *Vocab. TX* 63, *Hot water (corn) bread* . . apparently the same as *pone.* **1966–70** *DARE* (Qu. H14, *Bread that's made with cornmeal*) Inf **TN**66, Hot-water corn bread; hot-water hoecake; **TN**52, Hot-water corn bread—made it with hot water; **AL**11, Hot-water bread—salt, scald meal, fry it; **LA**12, Hot-water bread—made with boiling salted water so the meal would stick; fried bread—hot-water bread made in a skillet; **TN**57, Hot-water bread—like pone; (Qu. H18, . . *Special kinds of bread*) Infs **KY**37, 94, **MO**29, **TX**33, Hot-water corn bread; (Qu. H24) Inf **TN**49, Hot-water corn bread; (Qu. H25, . . *Fried cornmeal*) Inf **TX**73, Hot-water corn bread. **1986** Pederson *LAGS Concordance (Corn bread)* 31 infs, **Gulf Region,** Hot-water (corn)bread; 4 infs, **wFL, MS, wLA,** Hot-water bread—(fried) corn bread; 3 infs, **neMS, AR, nTX,** Hot-water corn bread—(corn) pones; 3 infs, **nMS, wLA,** Hot-water bread—(corn) pone; 2 infs, **wFL, wLA,** Hot-water bread—baked; 1 inf, **AR,** Hot-water corn bread—ordinary corn bread; 1 inf, **AR,** Old hot-water bread—spoon bread; 1 inf, **nwAR,** Hot-water corn bread—grandparents made; 1 inf, **AR,** Hot-water corn bread—now called hush puppies; 1 inf, **cTN,** Hot-water corn bread—fried mush, with fish; 1 inf, **nTX,** Hot-water corn bread—corn dodger; 1 inf, **nTX,** Hot-water bread—old term for dodger, hush puppy; 1 inf, **wLA,** Hot-water bread—term for dodgers, hoecakes; 1 inf, **nwAR,** Hot-water corn cakes.

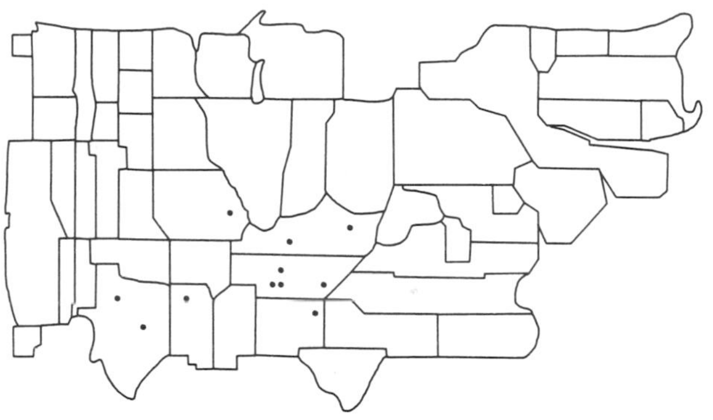

•hot-water corn bread + varr (Qq. H14, H18, H24, H25)

hot-water tea n **Sth, S Midl** Cf **cambric tea, kettle tea**

See quots.

1897 Terhune *Old-Field* 54, "Hot-water-tea" (*i.e.,* milk-and-water sweetened) had not offended her taste yesterday, or ever before. **1899** (1912) Green *VA Folk-Speech* 232, *Hot water tea*. . . A drink made for children of hot water, milk and sugar. **1906** *DN* 3.141 **nwAR,** *Hot water tea*. . . Hot water with an admixture of milk and sugar. **1908** *DN* 3.332 **eAL, wGA,** *Hot-water tea*. . . Same as *kettle-tea.* [*Ibid* 324, *Kettle-tea*. . . Tea made of hot water, milk and sugar.]

hot-weather bug n Also *hot bug, hot-weather bird, ~ fly* **esp NEast, Mid Atl**

A **cicada.**

1967–70 *DARE* (Qu. R7, *Insects that sit in trees or bushes in hot weather and make a sharp, buzzing sound*) Infs **DC**11, **MA**2, 4, **VA**79, Hot-weather bugs; **MA**98, **NY**186, **SC**2, **VA**75, Hot bug; **MI**108, Hot-weather birds; **KY**76, Hot-weather fly; (Qu. R30) Inf **NY**105, Hot bug—same as locust; sings. **1987** *DARE* File **nVA,** We sat talking in her living room on a hot August afternoon. . . "Listen to that hot bug," she suddenly remarked. I recognized the sound as that characteristic of the cicada. . . It is especially audible when the weather is hot.

hot-weed n

A **ragweed** (here: *Ambrosia artemisiifolia*).

1933 Small *Manual SE Flora* 1300, *A[mbrosia] artemisiifolia*. . . Hot-weed.

hot yard See **hot deck**

‡hot yeast n Cf *DS* Z11a, b

1950 *WELS* (*A child whose parents were not married*) 1 Inf, **csWI,** Hot yeast.

hou-hou See **huhu** adj, v

hound See **houndfish 2**

hound and hare See **hare and hound(s)**

hound dog n

1 also attrib; A dog bred or used for hunting. [Redund; cf Intro "Language Changes" I.4] **chiefly Sth, S Midl**

1649 in 1892 Dedham MA *Early Rec.* 3.162, That Care be taken that the young hound doggs be in time taught to hunt. **1768** (1925) Washington *Diaries* 1.293 **VA,** She was shut up with a hound dog. **1840** (1847) Longstreet *GA Scenes* 195 **GA,** Billy's hound-dogs broke up most all my nests. **1911** Saunders *Col. Todhunter* 24 **ceMO,** I'm as hungry as a young hound-dog this very minute. **1913** Kephart *Highlanders* 344 **sAppalachians,** I'd . . shoot enough meat off o' his bones to feed a hound-dog a week. **1942** *Esquire* 17.4.114/2 **neKY,** It was like carryin a full-grown hound-dog pup to carry the fox. **1949** *Hall Coll.* **neTN,** A hound-dog is any huntin' dog. He hunts about anything. **1960** Criswell *Resp. to PADS 20* **Ozarks,** *Hound-dog*—often used for hound. **1968** *DARE* Tape **CA**87, Your grandfather or father saved the hound dog. He didn't want the lion to scratch the life out of the hound dog up there on the mountain. **1974** Fink *Mountain Speech* 12 **wNC, eTN,** *Hound dog* . . hound.

2 A dog of mixed breed; a mongrel—also used as a derog term for a dog in general. **scattered, but esp Lower Missip Valley, TX, S Atl** See Map *usu derog* or *joc*

1950 *WELS (Joking or uncomplimentary words for dogs)* 2 Infs, **WI,** Hound dog. **c1960** *Wilson Coll.* **csKY,** *Hound-dog*. . . Just any worthless dog of mixed breed. **1965–70** *DARE* (Qu. J2, . . *Joking or uncomplimentary words* . . *for dogs*) 25 Infs, **scattered, but esp Lower Missip Valley, TX, S Atl,** (Old) hound dog; (Qu. J1, . . *A dog of mixed breed*) Infs **AR**3, **CO**7, **FL**15, **LA**33, **TX**40, Hound dog. **1968** *McDavid Coll.* **SC,** *Hound dog*—a mongrel. **1986** Pederson *LAGS Concordance (Mongrel* . . *worthless* . . *mixed breed)* 65 infs, **Gulf Region,** Hound dog.

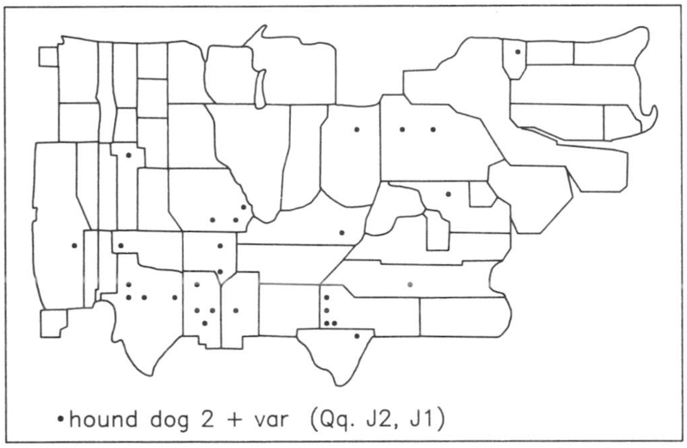
•hound dog 2 + var (Qq. J2, J1)

3 Transf: see quot.

1968 *McDavid Coll.* **SC,** *Hound dog*—A person of racially mixed descent.

4 Fig: see quot.

1968 *DARE* (Qu. II18, *Someone who joins* . . *you and your group without being asked and won't leave*) Inf **VA**25, Hound dog.

5 attrib: See quot. [Perh var of *hangdog* adj ashamed, guilty]

c1960 *Wilson Coll.* **csKY,** *Hound-dog look*—A sneaking, guilty look.

hound-dog mile n

A long distance.

1975 Gould *ME Lingo* 137 **ME,** A *hound-dog* mile, used to measure a walking trail in the woods, is the distance a *hound-dog* chases a rabbit before he (the *hound-dog*) drops dead.

hound ear n

See quot 1968.

1968 Adams *Western Words* 156, *Hound ears and whirlups*—A cow-camp dessert originated by . . a wagon cook of New Mexico. *Hound ears* were made from sour dough which was dropped from a spoon into hot grease and fried brown. The dough usually spread out in the shape of a dog's ears. *Whirlup* . . a sauce . . was poured over the hound ears. **1971** Jennings *Cowboys* 219 **MT, WY** (as of 1877), [He] placidly served up a nice dessert of hound-ears and whirlups. Tonight he added dried fruit to the syrup, and a secret combination of spices to the grease-fried sour-dough. The boys ate as if supper had been last year.

hound-eared sunfish n

=**redbreast sunfish.**

1906 NJ State Museum *Annual Rept. for 1905* 292, *Lepomis auritus*. . . Hound Eared Sun Fish. . . Opercle ending in a long cutaneous flap directed posteriorly and upwards.

houndfish n

1 =**bluefish 1.**

1672 Josselyn *New-Englands Rarities* 24, *Blew Fish* or *Hound Fish,* two kinds, *speckled Hound Fish,* and *Blew Hound Fish* called *Horse Fish.* **1889** *Century Dict.* 2900, *Houndfish*. . . A shark of the genus *Scylliorhinus* and some similar species. . . Also called *hound*. . . The bluefish, *Pomatomus saltatrix,* formerly called *blue houndfish* in Massachusetts. . . The Spanish mackerel, *Scomberomorus maculatus,* formerly called *speckled houndfish* in Massachusetts.

2 also *hound:* Any of var **dogfish 1;** see quots.

1842 DeKay *Zool. NY* 4.355, The American Hound- fish. . . *Mustelus canis.* **1889** [see **1** above]. **1933** John G. Shedd Aquarium *Guide* 20, *Cynias canis* . . Smooth Hound.

3 A **needlefish** (here: *Strongylura acus* or *S. raphidoma*).

1879 U.S. Natl. Museum *Bulletin* 14.54, *Belone Jonesii*. . . Houndfish. **1896** U.S. Natl. Museum *Bulletin* 47.715, *Tylosurus raphidoma*. . . Houndfish. *Ibid* 716, *Tylosurus acus*. . . Houndfish. **1946** LaMonte *N. Amer. Game Fishes* 18, The Needlefishes. . . *Strongylura*. . . Houndfish. **1960** Amer. Fisheries Soc. *List Fishes* 20, Houndfish. . . Strongylura raphidoma.

4 =**Spanish mackerel.**

1884 Goode *Fisheries U.S.* 1.308, The early chronicles of the colonies do not refer to it [=Spanish mackerel] under its present name, but it is possible that this was the "Speckled Hound-fish". . . The "Blew Hound-fish" can be nothing other than the common bluefish of our coast. **1889** [see **1** above]. **1935** Caine *Game Fish* 100, Spanish Mackerel—*Scomberomorus maculalus* [sic]. . . Houndfish.

hounds and deers n Cf **deer and dog(s)**

=**hare and hound(s).**

1901 *DN* 2.142 **wNY,** *Hounds and deers*. . . Another name for hare and hounds.

hound's-tongue n

1 Std: any of var coarse plants of the genus *Cynoglossum,* but esp *C. officinale,* which have tongue-shaped leaves, a "doggy" odor, and burrlike nutlets. [*OED* 1000 →] Also called **beggar's lice 4, boys-and-girls 3, dog burr, forget-me-not 1e, giant forget-me-not, stickseed, wool-mat.** For other names of var spp see **beggar ticks 5, gypsy flower, sheep lice, sticktights, Tory-weed, wild comfrey, wood-mat**

2 A **vanilla leaf,** usu *Carphephorus odoratissima.* **chiefly SE**

1868 (1870) Gray *Field Botany* 191, *L[iatris] odoratissima, Vanilla-plant* of low pine-barrens (also wrongly called *Hound's-tongue*). **1901** Lounsberry *S. Wild Flowers* 502, *T[rilisa] paniculata,* hairy trilisa, differs principally from the hound's tongue . . in having an intensely viscid and pubescent stem. **1933** Small *Manual SE Flora* 1336, *T[rilisa] odoratissima*. . . *Hound's tongue*. . . The leaves contain coumarin and have been used as a flavoring agent. **1964** Batson *Wild Flowers SC* 125, *Hound's Tongue: Trilisa paniculata*. . . Leaves mostly basal, . . rather thick and sometimes slightly toothed.

3 A **bead lily** (here: *Clintonia borealis*).

1897 *Jrl. Amer. Folkl.* 10.145, *Clintonia borealis* . . hound's tongue . . Hartford, M[ain]e.

hound's-tooth violet n

=**dogtooth violet.**

1969 *DARE* (Qu. S11, . . *Other names* . . *for* . . *dog-tooth violet*) Inf **KY**63, Hound's-tooth violet.

ho up See **ho v e**

hour n Usu |aʊr|; also **S Midl, seME, seNY** |æʊ(w)ə|; also **S Midl** |æ:r, ɑ˞r|; also **NY** |ɑʊr|; for addit varr see quots Pronc-spp *aiah, haour* Cf Pronc Intro 3.II.14

Std sense, var forms.

1861 Holmes *Venner* 2.181 **wMA,** An haour after daylight. **1914** *DN* 4.158 **cVA,** *Aiah*. . . Air and hour pronounced alike. "Ah don't mean aiah like a clock; ah mean aiah like this heah." **1930s** in 1944 *ADD* **eWV,** *Hour*. . . ['æʊwr̩]. **1931** *AmSp* 6.400 **seME,** The first element in the diphthong [aʊ] is noticeably tense and fronted. . . [æʊwə] *hour.* **1936** *AmSp* 11.309 **Upstate NY,** [The vowel in] *hour* [has the following forms: 12 infs, [ɑʊ]; 1 inf, [aʊ]; 1 inf, [ɑr]]. **1938** in 1944 *ADD* **wNC,** *Hour. . .* [æʊə]. **1942** Hall *Smoky Mt. Speech* 46 **eTN, wNC,** The second element [of the diphthong [aʊ]] is often reduced. . . hour [æ:ɚ]. . . The loss of the second element is well illustrated by . . ['æjɚz] *hours.* **1942** *AmSp* 17.150 **seNY,** [The vowel in] *hour* [has the following forms: 9 infs, [æʊ]; 3 infs, [aʊ]; 4 infs, [ɑʊ]]. **1944** Kenyon–Knott *Pronc. Dict.* 209, *Hour* [aʊr]; E[astern]S[outhern] [aʊə(r]. **1970** *Thompson Coll.* **AL** (as of 1920s) [Black], Hour ['æwɚ]. **1988** *DARE* File **KY,** My pronunciation of 'hour' is something like [ɑ˄r]—a raised central low vowel and a non-retroflex [r]. For me, 'are' has a lower vowel and a retroflex [r].

hourglass spider n [From the shape of the red mark on the abdomen]

The black widow spider *(Latrodectus mactans).*

1938 Brimley *Insects NC* 473, *L[atrodectus] mactans. . .* Black Widow; Hour-glass Spider. **1967–68** *DARE* (Qu. R28, . . *Kinds of spiders . . around here*) Inf **CA**105, Black widow spider: hourglass ['ɑrɪˌglæs] spider; **MI**65, Hourglass spider—has what looks like an hourglass on his back; anything that gets in his web, he just spins a net around him and rolls him right up; he's long legged.

houri See **haole**

house n, v Usu |haʊs|; also **chiefly Atlantic, esp NEng, Mid and S Atl,** |hɛʊs, hɛos, hæʊs, hæos, hɑʊs, hɐʊs|; also **Delmarva, esp VA,** |həʊs, hus|; also **nND, MN,** |hɐʊs, hɜʊs|; for addit varr see quots Pronc-spp *haouse, hoose, how-ooce* [Cf *EDD house* "Also in forms. . . *hause*"; *SND house* "Also *hoose . . hoos*"]

A Forms.

1861 Holmes *Venner* 1.107 **wMA,** This place was known as . . "the neew haouse," . . [by the] old settlers. *Ibid* 2.185, Stebbins . . requested to see the maän o' the haouse abaout somethin' o' consequence. **1890** *PMLA* 5.198 **nVA,** The sound (au, as in German Haus) is heard among a select few in *house* . . though the usual pronunciation is here [ɛʊ], never [əʊ]. This . . [ɛʊ] is . . short . . in most words; as, *house.* . . the *ou* in . . *house* . . [is] pronounced [hæ-a-əs]. . . [Some people] make a distinction in the time of the two vowels [a, ə], some prolonging the [a] and others the [ə] sound [hæ-aa-əs], [hæ-a-əəs]. **1903** *DN* 2.317 **seMO,** *House. . .* Pronounced hoose [hus]. (Virginia pronunciation.) **1919** in 1944 *ADD* **VA,** *House. . .* how-ooce. **1933** *AmSp* 8.4.59 **Delmarva,** The first element in the diphthong of . . *house* is the tense and fronted [æ] or occasionally a tense [ɛ]. . . In records showing Virginia influence, *house* is [hɐʊs] rather than the coastal [hʌʊs]. **1934–44** in 1944 *ADD* **nWV,** *House. . .* [hæʊs], [hæos]. Distinct [æ]. **1936** *AmSp* 11.34 **eTX,** If a norm may be said to exist for this diphthong . . it is [æʊ], but variations in the first element produce also [aʊ] and [æ˄ʊ]—all of these with various degrees of lengthening and nasalization. Example . . house. **1940** in 1944 *ADD* **AR,** [Radio:] *House. . .* [hæʊs]. **1941** *AmSp* 16.7 **eTX** [Black], In Negro speech . . [[aʊ]] is not often flattened to [æʊ] as in 'hill type' speech, but retains its standard form, with lengthening of the first element. . . *house.* **1942** *AmSp* 17.150 **seNY,** *House* . . [50 infs, [aʊ]; 45 infs, [æʊ]; 35 infs, [ɑʊ]]. **1942** Hall *Smoky Mt. Speech* 45 **wNC, eTN,** The . . word . . [house] almost always . . [has] [æʊ] rather than [aʊ]. . . There are, however, occasional instances of a lower and more retracted vowel . . [ha·ʊs] *house.* **1961** Kurath–McDavid *Pronc. Engl.* 110, In . . Virginia and adjoining parts of Maryland and North Carolina, and . . coastal South Carolina, Georgia, and Florida, the "fast" diphthongs [əʊ, ɐʊ], with centralized beginning, occur regularly before voiceless consonants, as in . . *house.* The extreme variant [əu] is characteristic of the Virginia Piedmont, [ɐu] of its periphery and of the South Carolina coast. **1967** *DARE* FW Addit **KY**31, *House* [haɪs]—old-fashioned, used by older speakers. Typical mountain speech. **1976** Allen *LAUM* 3.26 **Upper MW** (as of c1950), [*House*—16 infs, **NE, eIA,** -[aᵁ, a·ʊ]-; 14 infs, **wNE, sIA,** -[æʊ, a˄ʊ]-; 6 infs, **nND, MN,** -[ɐʊ]-.] *Ibid* 27, In the UM. . . [ɜʊ] is . . a minority feature, recorded particularly in Minnesota and northern North Dakota. . . [In the Upper Midwest] [aᵁ, a·ʊ] seems to be an expanding feature. **1982** *Barrick Coll.* **csPA,** *House*—hɛʊs.

B As noun.

1 A portion or portions of a building used for a dwelling or domestic activity; see below.

a A room; pl *houses* a house of more than one room; see quot 1919. [*EDD house* sb.[1] 6 "A room; a room in any building"] **sAppalachians, esp KY, TN**

1895 *DN* 1.372 **eTN,** *House:* room. This grew up from the custom of having houses of one room, or two connected by a porch, each of which rooms was called a *house.* **1911** *DN* 3.538 **eKY,** *Houses. . .* A dwelling of more than one room. **1919** *DN* 5.32 **seKY,** In a house of two or more rooms, the largest one is . . designated [the big house]. House is synonymous with room, and a dwelling of more than one room is often called "houses." **1937** Eaton *Handicrafts* 48 **sAppalachians,** The most elaborate cabin was that with new rooms or "new houses," as they are called by old inhabitants, built on from time to time. **c1938** *Hall Coll.* **sAppalachians,** *House*—Portion of the old-fashioned mountain house—two separate structures built of logs with an open space between and covered by one roof. "The hall between the houses."

b The main part or general living rooms of a dwelling. [Cf *EDD house* sb.[1] 7; also *OED house* sb.[1] 1. c *dial.*] **Sth, S Midl** Cf **big house 2**

1929 *AmSp* 5.18 **Ozarks,** *House. . .* The possessor of a shanty with several rooms reserves the word *house* for the largest, which is usually in front. "Come inter th' house" means to enter the front room, and may be addressed to a guest who is already in the kitchen or the bedroom. **1947** *McDavid Coll.* **cSC,** *House*—The main part [of the house]. **1958** *PADS* 29.11 **cTN,** *House:* A living room. "Persons refer to the sitting room or living room of their home as the house. . . They might be in another room and request someone to bring the scissors from the lamp table in the house." **1989** Pederson *LAGS Tech. Index* 31 **Gulf Region,** *Sitting room. . .* big house (4 [infs]) . . family house (1) . . house (2).

c See quot. [*OED house* sb.[1] b "The portion of a building . . occupied by one tenant or family. *Sc* and *dial.*" 1529 **→**]

1988 *DARE* File **NYC,** A friend from Manhattan refers to the various apartments in which he has lived as "houses." He always encourages his friends who go to New York to stay with his mother because "there's plenty of room at her house." I was quite surprised the first time I went there. We parked in front of an eighteen-story building, took one of three elevators to the fifth floor, went down a hall lined with doors each of which had a number, and entered what I would have called a three-bedroom apartment. "This," said my friend proudly, "is my mother's house." *Ibid* **NYC,** We all lived in multiple family residences, and we always said "house" for the place someone lived. You'd say "let's go to so-and-so's house." Adults and kids both used "house" in this way.

2 A semisolid mass of vegetation or an islet rising above a water covered grassland or **prairie;** see quot 1938 FWP. **Okefenokee GA** Cf **head** n **B9, hill** n **3, hummock 2**

1926 *AmSp* 1.412 **Okefenokee GA,** The Deer . . went on out ter the edge er the big perairie [=prairie, a water-covered grassland]. An' there they takened up [Footnote: Came to a halt], an' went in [=onto] a house [Footnote: A wooded islet in the watery prairie]. **1938** FWP *U.S. One* 306 **GA,** "Houses," [is] the name given to clumps of bushes and trees growing on more solid areas. . . Swamp "houses" are built . . when gases formed beneath the water . . force masses of vegetation . . from the bottom. . . The surface . . in time is covered with grass, briars, small bushes, and water weeds. When it has accumulated this dèbris, the entire mass either sinks again . . or floats until caught by a clump of trees. During the floating period this earth-raft collects seed from cypress and other trees and in time develops into a "house." Thus "houses" are formed from above and below, many never becoming stable but swaying and trembling under ordinary weight. **1938** Matschat *Suwannee R.* 34 **seGA,** The open flooded marshes . . are dotted with wooded islets, commonly called "houses" because they have enough dry land to furnish camp sites for the hunters of . . animals that live in the swamp. **1968** *DARE* FW Addit **GA**31, A house is a small island; an island is a big island. The name "Cowhouse Island" is redundant. "House" is used only about islands in the Okefenokee; it applies to the east side of the swamp. It's old-fashioned, but survives in place-names. **1968** *DARE* Tape **GA**30, Prairies [are] just a open swamp . . little . . clumps of bushes'll come on, just little places, it's called a house . . ['House' is] just an ol' saying with the old-timers. A place for a bear to hide in or deer . . but it's thick growth. . . Sometimes it [=the house] be small and sometimes it be pretty good little bunch. . . It be solid enough that them bushes would grow; **GA**31, Eventually, those things became islands. In their early stage, we refer to them as a house, an idiomatic expression for a tiny island; **GA**51, These here little thicks all over the Okefenokee Swamp, we call them houses. Just little thicks surrounded by water, there's thousands of them in the swamp, in the prairies. . . They stay in the same place. . . We camp in [=on] it. My daddy learned me to call them that.

3 A toilet room or lounge; see quot. [Cf *OED House of office* (at *house* sb.[1] 14b.) "a privy"]

1981 Mebane *Mary* 163 **cnNC,** [I worked on the line at the tobacco factory and once] in the afternoon I got a ten-minute break in the "house" (toilet). I went there and collapsed into a chair. *Ibid* 165, Word came over the grapevine that the big boss was coming. . . Leaves to the "house" were canceled.

4 One's family; see quot.

1986 Pederson *LAGS Concordance,* 1 inf, **cwMS,** [She] takes after that side of the house.

5 See quot 1967. [Abbr for *houseful*]

1928 Peterkin *Scarlet Sister Mary* 301 **SC coast** [Gullah], I ain' able to cook for no house o chillen. **1967** *DARE* (Qu. LL8b, . . *A large number—for example, of cousins: "She has a whole ______ of cousins."*) Inf **WA**24, House.

6 in phr *give one no house* and var: See quots. Cf *give one no quarter*

1944 in 1988 *DARE* File **swTN,** Give one no house means not to accept someone, usually because of the person's actions. **1960** Wentworth–Flexner *Slang* 275, *House. . .* Personal attention to and interest in another person; encouragement. *Freq. in "give a person a lot of house."* 1951: "[President] Truman told a news conference, 'Wrongdoers have no house *[sic]* with me no matter who they are.' "

C As verb.

Also with *in, up:* To confine indoors.

1967–69 *DARE* (Qu. BB41, *Not seriously ill, but sick enough to be in bed: "He's been ______ for a week."*) Infs **NY**48, **PA**45, Housed; **IL**39, Housed in. **1974** *AmSp* 49.62 **swME** (as of c1900), *House. . .* Keep indoors—"They housed the boy when he took sick." **1986** Pederson *LAGS Concordance,* 1 inf, **neTX,** He can't stand to be housed up—in the office, etc.

house adder See **house snake 1**

House Amish n

A branch of the Amish religious community that holds worship services in a house or barn rather than in a church; a member of this group.

1938 Hark *Hex* 228 **sePA,** Church buildings . . were looked on as a tendency toward worldliness. That's why the particular branch of Amish to which they belonged worshipped in barns and houses. That's why, too, they were called "House Amish," as distinguished from "Church Amish." **1940** *Sat. Eve. Post* 30 Mar 38/2 **sePA,** The Amish are the strictest of all the sects [of Plain People], and, of these, the "house-Amish" are the most invulnerable in their resistance to change. *Ibid* 40/2, The house-Amish will ride in automobiles, provided they have been invited and are not asked to share in the cost. *Ibid* 40/3, Again, we run into the difference between the most conservative, the house-Amish, and the less conservative, the church-Amish. **1950** Klees *PA Dutch* 37, In the Lancaster Plain near Intercourse and Bird in Hand live the House Amish, who, objecting to churches as worldly, worship in houses or barns. . . Church Amish . . have simple meetinghouses like the Quakers. **1967** *DARE* (Qu. CC3, . . *Religions that have come in recently . . or are a bit different*) Inf **PA**27, Old Order Amish—House Amish—buying all the farms. **1988** *NADS Letters,* Most Old Order Amish are "House Amish" (in contrast to the few "Church Amish"). The House Amish hold their services in the houses (or barns) of their members, and they take turns in this.

house ape n

1966 *DARE* (Qu. Z16, *A small child who is rough, misbehaves, and doesn't obey, you'd call him a ______*) Inf **IN**1, House ape [laughter]; **OK**52, House ape.

house blessing n [Calque of Ger *Haussegen* wall text]

See quots.

1967 *DARE* FW Addit **sePA** [PaGer], *House blessing*—a stone set in the house as a type of corner stone but different from a dated corner stone. Sometimes over the mantel, sometimes on the lintel. It has a Bible verse on it. It isn't square, and is made of plaster. The outline is irregular because tulips—considered a religious flower—are drawn in. **1988** *DARE* File, A house blessing is usually a Biblical passage that is painted or in fancy script on the crosspiece over the doorway. Pennsylvania Germans had it. The passage is written in standard German. It's called the haussegen in German. It wasn't just in Pennsylvania, though, because I can remember a few of them in Watertown and Hustisford [Wisconsin].

house-builder n

A **mud dauber** (here: prob *Sceliphron cementarium*).

1898 *Mth. S. Dakotan* 1.97 **SD,** It was in the early morning that a yellow striped hornet commonly known as 'the house-builder' was poising itself in the air and darting every now and then around a full grown tea plant.

housecleaning, have a v phr

1968 *DARE* (Qu. BB18, *To vomit a great deal at once*) Inf **DE**1, Have a housecleaning—occasional.

‡house clothes n pl

Household linens.

1968 *DARE* (QR, near Qu. E1) Inf **SC**4, House clothes—the linens. [Inf old]

house covering See **cover C1**

house finch n

A small, redheaded bird *(Carpodacus mexicanus)* that often nests about houses. Also called **linnet, redhead**

1869 *Amer. Naturalist* 3.183 **CA,** About the gardens are the House Finch . . , the Black Pewee [etc]. **1917** (1923) *Birds Amer.* 3.7, House Finch—*Carpodacus mexicanus frontalis.* **1964** Phillips *Birds AZ* 185, House Finch . . *Carpodacus mexicanus.* **1966–69** *DARE* (Qu. Q21) Infs **CA**115, **CT**6, **WA**15, House finch.

housefrow See **hausfrau**

house garden n

A garden at or near a house, esp one where vegetables are grown for home consumption.

1893 *Harper's New Mth. Mag.* 86.654/2 **NYC,** A row of house gardens has been built on the roofs of the river-side storehouses. **1939** *LANE* Map 121 *(Vegetable garden)* 1 inf, **neCT,** House garden; 1 inf, **seMA,** House garden. **1965–70** *DARE* (Qu. I1, . . *The garden where you grow . . things, to eat at home*) 17 Infs, **scattered,** House garden; (Qu. L6a, . . *A piece of land under cultivation—less than an acre*) Inf **CA**161, House garden. **1986** Pederson *LAGS Concordance (Vegetable garden)* 1 inf, **cwFL,** House garden.

housegau See **hoosegow**

household match n Also *house match* Cf **barn burner 1, farmer match, parlor match**

1967–70 *DARE* (Qu. F46, . . *Matches you can strike anywhere*) 11 Infs, **scattered, but esp freq Nth, Midl,** Household matches; **AR**56, **CA**64, **KY**34, **NY**5, **OH**65, House matches.

household moss See **house moss**

house in See **house C**

housekeep v [Back-formation from *housekeeping* or *housekeeper*]

To keep house.

1842 in 1968 Hawthorne *N. Hawthorne* 1.251 **ceMA,** I housekeep, paint, sew, study German, read. **1886** Amer. Philol. Assoc. *Trans.* 17.46 **Sth,** List of common Southern expressions—many of them vulgarisms. . . To *house-keep* (for *keep house*). **1946** Gould *Yankee Storekeeper* 30 **ME,** My wife, who was just beginning to housekeep . . , was afraid she couldn't roast him right. **1986** Pederson *LAGS Concordance,* 1 inf, **cnGA,** I housekept [FW: kept house].

house kingsnake See **house snake 2**

house kitty n *joc*

A **skunk.**

1968 *DARE* (Qu. P26, *Names and nicknames around here for a skunk*) Inf **LA**15, House kitty—joking.

houselady See **houseman**

houseleek n

1 Std: a succulent plant *(Sempervivum tectorum).* Also called **Aaron's rod 2, bag plant 2, hen and chickens 1a(1), horseleek, live-forever, old-man-and-woman**

2 =**orpine.**

1891 *Jrl. Amer. Folkl.* 4.148, My home was in the small town of Gilsum, New Hampshire, in the southwest part of the State, adjoining Keene. . . Sedum telephium we knew correctly as *Houseleek;* but in other places in New Hampshire I have found it called *Blow-leaf,* and *Aaron's Rod,* both for obvious reasons.

housell adj Also sp *hous'le* [Pronc-sp for *household;* cf *EDD housel* adj. 3] *arch* Cf **housen** n[1] **2, hustlement**

1888 Johnston *Mr. Absalom Billingslea* 196 **GA,** Havin' of a sister to take keer o' his housell affairs. **1891** Johnston *Primes & Neighbors* 106 **GA,** I am thankful that not a dollar nor a cent do I owe for this plantation and niggers, hous'le and kitchen funichurs, stock ner utenchul.

house log n

A log cut specifically for building a house; see quot 1902.

1824 (1928) Kennerly *Diary* 54 **cwVA,** About this time got a party detailed to cut House logs to build a house for Sutler. **1871** *Harper's New Mth. Mag.* 44.46/1 **swOH,** Barely sixteen years of age, according to the tenth row of notches cut upon one of the house-logs. **1902** *DN* 2.237 **sIL** [Pioneer language], *House-log*. . . A log for use in building. The word timber not used in this sense. Also called saw-log. **1925** Stuart *40 Yrs.* 1.263 **swMT** (as of 1863), The nearby mountains furnished an abundance of house logs . . and soon log houses made their appearance. **1941** Stuart *Men of Mts.* 171 **neKY,** When we cut the logs to build our new house, we had a house-raising. . . The men . . lifted a big house log, upon the skids. . . the corner of the long house log was pulled upon the frame of logs. . . Wilburn took his ax and started notching the log.

houseman n Also *houselady*

The host of a **house party.**

1967 *DARE* (QR, near Qu. FF2) Inf **MA**8, House parties . . houseman or houselady provides food and beverages and the guests pay for them.

house martin n [See quot 1956]

=**purple martin.**

1913 Bailey *Birds VA* 253, House Martin. . . The nests are generally placed in some box or house made for them. . . I do not know of a case in this section of their resorting to their old habit of building inside a hollow tree. **1917** *Wilson Bulletin* 29.2.84, *Progne subis*. . . House . . martin, Hickman, K[entuck]y. **1956** MA Audubon Soc. *Bulletin* 40.84, *Purple Martin*. . . House Martin (Mass. From nesting in houses put up for it by man.) **1968–70** *DARE* (Qu. Q14) Infs **GA**65, **MA**78, House martin. **1969** Longstreet *Birds FL* 102, *Purple Martin. Other names:* . . House Martin.

house match See **household match**

house moss n Also *household moss* Cf **dust bunny, floor moss**

Dust that collects under furniture.

1931 *Hench Coll.* **cVA** [Black], Our negro cook used the name "house moss" for the dust balls that collect under beds and elsewhere. **1950** *PADS* 14.39 **SC,** *House moss*. . . Collection of dusty, downy fibers found under furniture where one does not often sweep. Same as "kitties". **1950** *WELS (Soft rolls of dust that collect on the floor under beds or other furniture)* 1 Inf, **WI,** House moss. **1950** *WELS Suppl.,* 1 Inf, **WI,** House moss—fuzzy rolls under furniture; 2 Infs, **WI,** House moss—rolls of dust. **1965–70** *DARE* (Qu. E20) 11 Infs, **scattered, but esp Sth, S Midl, SW,** House moss; **PA**128, Household moss. **1968** *DARE* File **neAL,** House moss [speaker old]. **1982** *Greenfield Recorder* (MA) 27 Nov 6 **csNH,** What do you call the dust fluff that collects under the bed? I had always heard "pussycats," but a friend from Laconia, N.H., always said "house moss."

house mouse n

A rodent *(Peromyscus gossypinus).*

1927 Boston Soc. Nat. Hist. *Proc.* 38.7.343 **Okefenokee GA,** *Peromyscus gossypinus gossypinus*. . . Cotton Mouse. . . Many of the residents of the region do not seem to have bestowed any particular specific name upon this mouse. On Chesser's Island, however, it is known as 'House Mouse.'

housen n^1

1 also sp *houzen;* pronc-sp *housing;* as pl: Houses. [Engl dial; *house* + **-en** $suff^2$] **chiefly N Atl** *old-fash*

1716 Church *Entertaining Passages* 91 **RI,** He . . went to *Nasket* point; where . . coming there found several Housing and small Fields of Corn. **1789** Webster *Dissertations Engl. Lang.* 385 **NEng,** The old plural *housen* is still used for houses. **1795** Dearborn *Columbian Grammar* 136, *List of Improprieties,* commonly called *Vulgarisms,* which should never be used in *Speaking, Reading, or Writing*. . . Housen for Houses. **1823** Cooper *Pioneers* 2.108 **cNY,** Farms and housen. **1829** Kirkham *Engl. Grammar* 192, *Vulgarisms.* Common in New-England. Houzen. **1899** (1912) Green *VA Folk-Speech* 232, *Housen*. . . For houses. **1903** *DN* 2.317 **seMO,** *Housen*. . . Houses. Occasionally heard among old-fashioned people, especially North Carolinians. **1917** *DN* 4.385 **ceNY** (as of 1879), *Housen,* pl. **1918** *DN* 5.16 **Martha's Vineyard MA,** There are two or three housen over on the hill. **1924** *DN* 5.286 **seMA,** 'Housen', the plural for 'house'. **1931–33** [see **2** below]. **1938** FWP *Guide DE* 105 **swDE,** Local variants of English pronunciation may be heard . . "housen" for houses. *Ibid* 500, Teachers fondly despair of making children say . . "houses" for *housen.* **1968** *DARE* FW Addit **NJ**43, *Housen* as the plural of *house* was used by a Black woman from Appalachia.

2 sg; also attrib: A house, household. *arch* Cf **housell**

1818 Fessenden *Ladies Monitor* 172 **VT,** Provincial words and phrases, which ought to be avoided by all who aspire to speak or write the English language correctly. . . *housen* for household. **1862** (1864) Browne *Artemus Ward Book* 201, She slept as secoorly as in her own housen. **1884** Baldwin *Yankee School-Teacher* 19 **NY,** Of "housen stuff" she had but little, but she made that little do. *Ibid* 137 **VA** [Black], "De drefful war done come t' clean out our housen stuff," as mammy phrased it. **1894** *DN* 1.334 **NJ,** The housens need tittavating. *Ibid* 341 **cwCT,** *Housens* as a plural of *house* is heard, though rare. **1931–33** *LANE Worksheets* **seMA,** *Housen*. . . Houses. "That's my housen." Both singular and plural.

housen n^2 See **housing** n^3

house party n **chiefly east of Missip R** *esp freq among Black speakers* Cf **house-rent party**

A social gathering at one's home, usu with dancing and refreshments, for which there may be a fee.

1956 (1957) Stearns *Story of Jazz* 145 **NYC** [Black], Its [=ragtime's] ancestry was long obscured by labels such as "house-party," "rent-party," "parlor social," or simply "Harlem" piano style. **1965–70** *DARE* (Qu. FF2, . . *Kinds of parties*) 23 Infs, **chiefly east of Missip R,** House parties; **FL**48, **SC**69, House parties—dancing and liquor (*or* drinking); **LA**32, House party—go to each other's houses; **MA**8, House parties, pay parties—houseman or houselady provides food and beverages and the guests pay for them; [also] dancing, card playing; **MA**28, House party—drinking—host provides food and guests bring your own bottle; **MA**45, House party—host provides all refreshments and liquor; **VA**71, House party—meet at someone's house and dance; (Qu. DD34, *A party at which there is considerable drinking*) Infs **CA**154, **GA**92, House parties; (QR, near Qu. FF1) Inf **FL**51, Sociable—no different from a house party; (Qu. FF4, . . *Dancing parties*) Inf **CA**154, We mostly dance at house parties; **IL**11, House parties—old-fashioned; **WV**21, House party; (Qu. FF9, *A Christmas gathering . . at someone's home, where there are songs and presents*) Inf **NJ**46, House party. [22 of 36 Infs Black; 15 Infs young] **1966–70** *DARE* Tape **ND**9, When we got a little older . . we had house parties. We'd go to houses where they had pianos and organs and . . some of the women would play and the kids would dance. . . We had fun . . eat at all the parties. Didn't cost much money them days. *Ibid* **MI**120, [Aux Inf:] We felt like havin' a dance, we'd go someplace. One would sing, the other one would play on the comb, the other one with the broom, and then the organ or piano and one would chord an' we'd dance like mad, singing and having a glorious time. [Inf:] We had a lot of house parties at that time—a lot of these farmers around here used to put up something like a corn-husking bee. *Ibid* **PA**113, We have house parties during Christmas. . . Each neighbor entertain[s]. But last year we did it wrong. We made it all on one night, which was just too bad. . . When you got to the second house you didn't feel like eating, the third house you couldn't eat, the fourth house you'd had enough to drink. **1968** *Blues Unlimited* 57.11 **St. Louis MO** (as of 1920s) [Black], He was around here in town then playing houseparties. **1986** Pederson *LAGS Concordance,* 12 infs, **chiefly coastal Gulf Region,** House parties (*or* party). [6 of 12 infs Black] **1989** *Capital Times* (Madison WI) 3 Nov 12/3 **ceWI,** They are said to be . . for-profit house parties. You buy a plastic cup for $2 or $3 and drink all the beer you want.

house pattern n **sAppalachians**

A plan or blueprint, or the cut lumber, intended for the construction of a building; see quots 1934, c1960.

1924 Raine *Land of Saddle-Bags* 104 **sAppalachians,** We speak of a dress-pattern or a trousers-pattern, meaning not the shape, but the material out of which it is to be made. So we need not be surprised at—"He sawed him a house-pattern out of beech." **1931** *AmSp* 7.93 **eKY,** *House-pattern,* the lumber needed in building a house. "Clevie got a house-pattern o' Jeems while the saw-mill was at his place." **1941** *Sat. Eve. Post* 213.45.111/2 **seKY,** I had a house pattern in head. **c1960** *Wilson Coll.* **csKY,** *House pattern*—Pattern or plan or blueprint of a house.

house pewee n

=**phoebe.**

1956 MA Audubon Soc. *Bulletin* 40.83, *Eastern Phoebe. . .* House Pewee (Maine. From its nesting on porch beams or in other crannies of houses.)

house plunder See **plunder**

house-raising n, also attrib **scattered, but esp freq Sth, S Midl** Also *cabin raising* *somewhat old-fash* Cf **barn raising 1**

A community or social gathering for the purpose of building or erecting a home.

1704 in 1866 Essex Inst. *Coll.* 8.223 **neMA,** I was at my L[and]-Lords house raising. **1832** *Polit. Examiner* (Shelbyville, Ky.) 2 June 3/2 *(DA),* Meet as men do at musters, log-rollings, house-raisings . . [and] try the relative strength of these worthy candidates. **1843** (1916) Hall *New Purchase* 202 **IN,** In lieu of such [=political gatherings], every militia muster, cabin-raising, scow-launching . . and so forth, was virtually a political assembly. **1908** *DN* 3.322 **eAL, wGA,** *House-raisin(g). . .* A gathering of neighbors to erect a log house for one of them. **1941** [see **house log**]. **1959** *Hall Coll.* **swNC,** *House raisin'*—A cooperative endeavor to build a house. "We had log rollin's, house raisin's, [and] barn raisin's." **1966–70** *DARE* (Qu. FF2, . . *Kinds of parties*) Inf **CA**136, Used to have barn- or house-raising parties; **SC**69, House-raisings—out on the island—very rural; **WA**1, House-raising; [**MA**69, Raisings of barns, raisings of houses;] (Qu. FF1, . . *A . . group meeting called a 'social' or 'sociable'*) Inf **TX**33, House-raising; **NC**36, Sill-setting—[at a] house-raising, dance after first floor [is] up. **1979** *Foxfire 5* 100 **nGA,** We had a house raisin' t' raise this house, and we had a barn raisin' t' raise th' barn.

house-rent party n Also *house-rent shake, ~ stomp, ~ strut* *chiefly among Black speakers; urban* Cf **house party, rent party**

A social gathering, usu with music, for the purpose of raising money for rent; see quots 1926, 1966.

1925 *Inter-State Tattler* 27 Feb 8/2 **NYC** [Black], I am a tamer of wild women and bitterly against house-rent parties. **1926** (1974) Whiteman-McBride *Jazz* 177, Big sessions of blues were held in the South among the colored people, the biggest of all at 'house rent stomps' when a negro found himself unable to pay his rent. **1932** in 1975 Albertson *Bessie Smith* 54 [Black], [In song "Safety Mama":] Give your house rent shake on Saturday night./ Monday morning you'll hold collectors good and tight. **1938** *N. Y. Amsterdam News* 12 Mar. 17 *(OEDS)* **NYC** [Black], Almost primal emotions, hangover from the old 'down home house rent strut' days. **1955** Shapiro *Hear Me Talkin'* 210 **swOH** (as of 1920) [Black], Joe . . would bash [=play music] at numerous functions and house-rent stomps along Carlisle and John Streets in Cincinnati's black bottom. **1956** (1957) Stearns *Story of Jazz* 168 **Chicago IL** (as of 1920s) [Black], A house-rent party, an unstable social phenomenon that was stimulated by Prohibition and made necessary by the Depression. The object of such a party is to raise the rent, and anybody who can pay a quarter admission is cordially invited. **1966** *DARE* (Qu. DD34, *A party at which there is considerable drinking*) Inf **FL**1, House-rent party—once a month to raise house rent. [Inf Black]

houseroom n Cf **hell room**

Accommodation or space in a house; also fig.

1912 Green *VA Folk-Speech* 223, *House-room. . .* Accomodation [sic] in a house. "They have hardly house-room for themselves in their small house." **1943** Benchley *Benchley Beside Himself* 32, Just how successful these savage strivings were, and just what degree of skill was mastered by these tribal artists, is something which each connoisseur must decide for himself. Personally, I wouldn't give them houseroom. **1951** Johnson *Resp. to PADS 20* **DE,** *("Worthless . . It's not worth ______.")* House room. **1960** Williams *Walk Egypt* 169 **GA,** "They all saying it's your fault, taking him [=the thief] in." . . "I know they saying, 'Toy Crawford give houseroom to the thief. Maybe she was gonna get some of the money.' "

houseseat n Cf **homeplace 1, homeseat**

See quots.

1931 *AmSp* 7.93 **eKY,** *House-seat,* site for a house. "That's a pretty house-seat. I'd like to give it to the oldest boy fer him 'n' Cindy." **1959** Roberts *Up Cutshin* 47 **seKY,** Jim pointed out the old big log house in a bend of the Clover Fork. We stopped and went toward the rustic houseseat, with its rived board roof, puncheoned floor, and beamed and raftered interior.

house shoe n **chiefly Sth, S Midl** See Map Cf **bedroom shoe**

See quots.

1957 Battaglia *Resp. to PADS 20* **eMD** *(Soft shoes, worn only inside the house) House shoes*—old-fashioned. **1965–70** *DARE* (Qu. W21, *Soft shoes that people wear only inside the house*) 209 Infs, **chiefly Sth, S Midl,** House shoes. **1968** *DARE* FW Addit **nwLA,** *House shoes*—soft shoes to wear in the house—common. **c1970** *Halpert Coll.* **wKY,** Fetch me my house shoes now. **1975** *DARE* File **wNC,** My roommate called her bedroom slippers "house shoes."

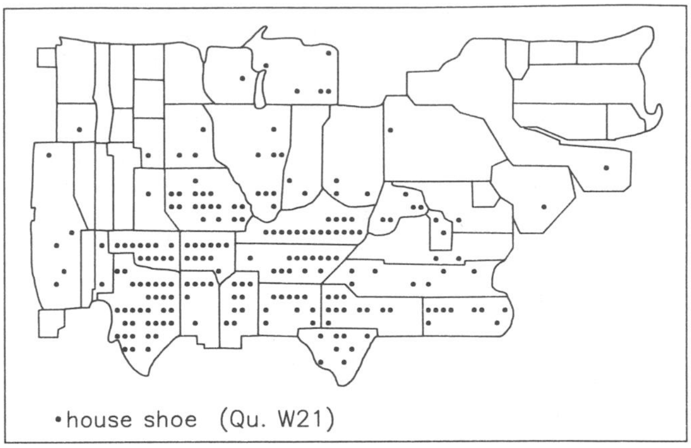

house snake n

1 also *house adder:* A **milk snake** (here: *Lampropeltis triangulum*).

1807 in 1846 MA Hist. Soc. *Coll.* 2d ser 3.54, The milk or house snake, speckled like a rattlesnake. **1842** DeKay *Zool. NY* 3.39, In this State, . . it is called . . *House Snake,* and *Chequered Adder. . .* It is not unfrequently found in outhouses, and in dairies or cellars. **1884** Twain *Huck. Finn* 396 **MO,** [We] grabbed a couple of dozen garters and house-snakes. **1891** in 1895 IL State Lab. Nat. Hist. Urbana *Bulletin* 3.295, *House Snake.* [*Ibid* 296, Farmers frequently find this species in their cellars, where it is supposed to be attracted by the milk.] **1946** Stuart *Tales Plum Grove* 58 **seKY,** We found a house snake on the wall plate. Pa killed it with a corn knife. **1958** Conant *Reptiles & Amphibians* 171, Sometimes called "house snake," but "barn snake" would be more descriptive, for it would reflect the frequency with which farm buildings are entered in search of rodents. **1966–69** *DARE* (Qu. P25) Infs **NH**10, **RI**4, House adder.

2 also *house kingsnake;* Either of two **rat snakes:** the **corn snake** or *Elaphe obsoleta quadrivittata.*

1894 U.S. Natl. Museum *Proc.* 17.326 **FL,** *Callopeltis guttatus* . . is known by different names in different places; for instance, . . "house king-snake" at Oakland, etc. **1952** Ditmars *N. Amer. Snakes* 79, Corn Snake, Red Rat Snake, House Snake, *Elaphe guttata. Ibid* 97, Chicken Snake, . . Striped House Snake, *Elaphe quadrivittata quadrivittata.*

house sorrel n

A **sheep sorrel** (here: *Rumex acetosella*).

1910 Graves *Flowering Plants* 159 **CT,** *Rumex Acetosella* . . House sorrel.

house sparrow n

A sparrow: usu the **English sparrow,** but also the **chipping sparrow.**

1791 Bartram *Travels* 289, Passer domesticus, the little house sparrow or chipping bird. **1855** *Knickerbocker* 46.22, The small house-sparrow, or, as he is generally known, the 'chippin'-bird,' comes to our very doors. **1877** *Harper's New Mth. Mag.* 54.658/2, Even the little house sparrow *(Spizella socialis)* cunningly wove it [=moss] into the foundation of its dwelling. **1910** KY Hist. Soc. *Register* 8.24, *Spizella socialis. . .* Chipping Sparrow. "House Sparrow." **1917** (1923) *Birds Amer.* 3.41. **1962** Imhof *AL Birds* 495, *House Sparrow. Passer domesticus. Ibid* 496, It occurs invariably around houses or other buildings and seems to prosper well in city, small town, or farm.

house swallow n Cf **martin-house swallow**

1 =**chimney swift.**

1956 MA Audubon Soc. *Bulletin* 40.81, *Chimney Swift. . .* House Swallow (Vt. From its frequenting chimneys; it is, however, no swallow.) **1967–69** *DARE* (Qu. Q20) Infs **NY**198, **PA**23, House swallow.

2 =**tree swallow.**

1956 MA Audubon Soc. *Bulletin* 40.84, *Tree Swallow*. . . House Swallow (Mass. As nesting in birdhouses put up for it by man.)

house up See **house C**

housewife n Also *hussif* [*OED housewife* sb. 3 "Usually ['hʌzɪf]. . . In this sense still often spelt *huswife, hussive*"; 1749 → (but see quot 1744 below). This word is generally assumed to be the same as std *housewife,* but is perh rather a hypercorrect form of **hussy** n[1] **B1.**] *old-fash* Cf **comfort bag**

A case or book for needles, thread, etc.

[**1744** in 1967 *AmSp* 42.217 [Scottish traveler in US], He showed me a drawer full of trophies of the fair, which he called his cabinet of curiosities. They consisted of torn fans, fragments of gloves, . . pin-cushions, hussifs, and a deal of other such trumpery.] **1828** Webster *Amer. Dict., Housewife*. . . A little case or bag for articles of female work. **1870** Macrae *Americans* 1.79 **sePA** (as of 1862), The children . . made tens of thousands of little housewives—'comfort bags,' as the soldiers called them—with buttons, needle and thread. **1886** Bates *Old Salem* 28 **MA,** Both had . . odd little housewives of green leather, which hung from their apron-bindings by green ribbons. **1895** *DN* 1.389 **NYC,** *Hussif (housewife):* a flannel book for needles. **1913** (1980) Hardy *OH Schoolmistress* 221 (as of 1863), Men . . gathered up each his comforter bed, his tin cup, plate, . . his little "house-wife" bag of buttons and thread. **1934** (1943) *W2, Housewife*. . . (*pron. usually* ['hʊzɪf]. . .) A little case or bag for needles, thread, scissors, pins, cloth for patching. . . Sometimes spelled *huswife.* **1936** Mitchell *Gone* 269 **GA** (as of 1860s), She had a Christmas present for Ashley. . . a small "housewife," made of flannel, containing the whole precious pack of needles . . three of her linen handkerchiefs, . . two spools of thread and a small pair of scissors. **1939** Montgomery *Days of Old* 62 (as of 1865), [Civil War recollections:] Some of the General's Staff had taken from the prisoner his "housewife" (thread and needle case). **1944** Kenyon-Knott *Pronc. Dict.* 209, Housewife *'sewing-kit'* 'hʌzɪf, 'haʊsˌwaɪf. **1975** Gainer *Witches* 12 **sAppalachians,** *Hussif* . . a rectangular-shaped piece of cloth . . with pockets sewed on it in which to keep needles, thread, and thimbles. "Aunt Sarry kept her hussif hangin' at the left of the fireplace."

house wool n

=**house moss.**

1968 *DARE* (Qu. E20, *Soft rolls of dust that collect on the floor under . . furniture*) Inf **WI**50, House wool.

house wren n

1 A common wren *(Troglodytes aedon).* Also called **Jenny wren, short-tailed wren, stump wren, wood wren**

1808 Wilson *Amer. Ornith.* 1.129, House Wren. . . *Motacilla domestica. Ibid* 1.132, The House Wren inhabits the whole of the United States, in all of which it is migratory. **1895** Minot *Land-Birds New Engl.* 75, The term 'House' Wren, usually applied to this bird, is decidedly a misnomer, since it frequents the fields, the thickets, and even the forest, as much as the vicinity of houses. **1954** *Harder Coll.* **cwTN,** House wren. **1954** Sprunt *FL Bird Life* 330, The House Wren is so called because of its predilection for human habitation and its use of birdhouses erected not only for it, but other birds as well, for it is an aggressive little creature with a temper far in excess of its size. **1956** MA Audubon Soc. *Bulletin* 40.127, House Wren. That name has some folk use, the extent of which, however, is not clear. It alludes to the birds living in nest boxes provided by man. **1968** *DARE* (Qu. Q23) Inf **WI**50, House wren, known as Jenny wren.

2 Either of two other wrens with similar habits: Bewick's wren or Carolina wren.

1955 *Oriole* 20.11 **GA,** *Carolina Wren.—House wren* (from frequenting the vicinity of houses). **1962** Imhof *AL Birds* 385, The Carolina Wren, and sometimes Bewick's Wren, are frequently called House Wren because, like the true House Wren, they live close to houses and often use nest boxes.

housgow See **hoosegow**

housing n[1] [Cf *OED housing* sb.[1] 2. b "dial. sometimes confused with *housen,* pl. of *house*"] Cf **housen** n[1] **1**

See quot.

1899 (1912) Green *VA Folk-Speech* 233, *Housing*. . . A collection of houses; all that appertains to the house or homestead, its outbuildings, etc.

housing n[2] See **housen** n[1] **1**

housing n[3] Also *housen* [Cf *OED housing* sb.[2] 2. b, c] **PA**

See quots.

1930 Shoemaker *1300 Words* 31 **cPA Mts** (as of c1900), *Housings*—The girths and trappings of horse harness. **1976** *PA Folklife* Spring 26 (as of 1925), Public Sale. . . Farming Implements. . . Harness. . . 1 set double harness, 2 housens, tongue straps, lead reins, sleigh bells. *Ibid* 31, Salebills often contain . . evidence of regional phonetics. . . housings are *housens.* **1982** *Barrick Coll.* **csPA,** *Housens—housing[s];* large pieces of leather on side of hames.

houska (twist) n |'hoškə| [Czech *houska* bun, roll]

A braided raised sweet bread; see quots.

1952 Tracy *Coast Cookery* 68 **IL,** *Houska Twist* . . Bohemian sweet bread. . . milk . . yeast . . sugar . . butter . . egg yolks . . white raisins . . blanched almonds . . flour . . Confectioners' sugar. . . Knead [the dough]. . . allow it to rise. . . Divide . . into nine pieces. . . Roll them into ropelike strands, braid the four large pieces, and place on a . . sheet. Braid the three medium pieces and place on top, then . . the two small strands. . . Bake. **1961** Sackett-Koch *KS Folkl.* 207 **cKS** (as of 1959), Wedding Customs. . . They'd feed people by the dozens. . . then they'd make of course their kolaches and rolls and maybe a houska or two several days before. . . Most of the Bohemians have the houska at Christmas time, but they did have it at weddings as well. **1990** *DARE* File **seNE,** *Houska* ['hoškə] is what is also known as Bohemian Christmas bread. We don't save it for Christmas, but serve it at Easter and other special occasions as well. It's a long loaf, with three strands braided together; the dough is sweetened, and has almonds and raisins. Everyone here knows it.

hous'le See **housell**

hout v [Cf *SND hoot* v. Also *hout* "To . . treat . . with contempt"; also cf *OED hout* (at *hoot* v.)]

1914 *DN* 4.74 **ME, nNH,** *Hout*. . . To nag, annoy, vex, worry.

houzen See **housen** n[1] **1**

hove v[1] See **heave** v **A2**

hove v[2] [*EDD, OED "Obs."*]

1986 Pederson *LAGS Concordance,* 1 inf, **cMS,** Couldn't hove it—couldn't wait, stay.

hoved See **heave** v **A2**

hove down See **heave** v **B3**

hovel n

1a A separate shed or section of a barn used as shelter, esp for chickens or cows; see quots. [*OED hovel* sb.[1] 1; *EDD hovel* sb.[1] 1] **esp NEng, sAppalachians** Cf **hobble** n[3], **hover n**

1806 (1970) Webster *Compendious Dict.* 146/1, *Hovel* . . a shed . . shelter. **a1862** (1864) Thoreau *ME Woods* 254, There was a deserted log camp here . . with its "hovel" or barn for cattle. **1899** (1912) Green *VA Folk-Speech* 233, *Hovel*. . . A small house for housing fowls on the ground. **1907** *DN* 3.191 **seNH,** *Hovel*. . . A cow-stable. "Isn't the cow in the hovel?" **1939** *LANE* Map 108 *(Cow stable)* 1 inf, **swCT,** *Hovel,* a crude shelter, thatched with coarse hay or corn stalks and open on two or three sides; 2 infs, **cCT,** *Hovel,* a . . shed (in the pasture or the cow lot); 5 infs, **sNH,** *Hovel,* in the barn; 1 inf, **sNH,** *Hovel,* separate [from the barn]; 1 inf, **ceNH,** *Hovel,* tumble-down shed; 1 inf, **ceNH,** *Hovel,* common; 2 infs, **nME,** *Hovel;* 2 infs, **ME,** *Hovel,* a ramshackle shelter (*or* building); 3 infs, **neVT, ME,** *Hovel,* a (separate) shelter in the woods (*or* pasture *or* on the farm). *Ibid* Map 110 *(Pig pen; hog house)* 1 inf, **sVT,** *Hovel.* **1949** Kurath *Word Geog.* 41, *Hovel* . . [is a] distinctive Piedmont word . . for the chicken house or roost. . . [This] term . . [has] found . . [its] way into the Tidewater area north of the James and into southern Maryland. **1969-70** *DARE* (Qu. M16, *The small shelter for a hen that can be moved about from place to place*) Infs **KY**49, 84, **VA**105, (Chicken) hovel; **VA**57, Hovel—old-fashioned; **VA**77, Hovel—some say. [All Infs comm type 5] **1986** Pederson *LAGS Concordance,* 1 inf, **seTN,** Hovel [refers to chicken coop].

b Esp in logging: a stable for horses or oxen. **chiefly NEng, esp nNH, ME**

1905 U.S. Forest Serv. *Bulletin* 61.40 **nMI, nWI, neMN** [Logging terms], *Hovel*. . . A stable for logging teams. **1907** *DN* 3.245 **eME,** *Hovel*. . . Horse-stable in a logging camp. **1914** *DN* 4.74 **ME, nNH,** *Hovel*. . . Stable, in lumber-camp. **1958** McCulloch *Woods Words* 90 **Pacific NW,** *Hovel*—An ox barn and feed storage shanty. **1966** *DARE* Tape **ME**26, I seen one stable there, one hovel. . . I counted room for twenty-six pair [of horses] in that hovel. . . If it ain't too many horses they just build one hovel. **1968** *DARE* (Qu. M9, *The part of a barn where horses are kept*) Inf **NH**14, Hovel. **1969** Sorden *Lumberjack Lingo* 59 **NEng, Gt Lakes,** *Hovel*—A stable for logging horses or oxen.

2 See quot. Cf **hovel v 2**

1969 Sorden *Lumberjack Lingo* 59 **NEng, Gt Lakes,** *Hovel*. . . A group of camp buildings.

hovel v

1 See quot. [**hovel n 1a**] Cf **hover v**

1899 (1912) Green *VA Folk-Speech* 233, *Hovel*. . . To cover chickens as a hen. "That hen has more chickens than she can hovel."

2 See quot. [**hovel n 2**]

1969 Sorden *Lumberjack Lingo* 59 **NEng, Gt Lakes,** *Hovelled* [sic]—To bunk with another lumberjack.

hover v [*OED hover* v.[1] 5 "To brood over; to cover (the young) with wings and body"] Cf **hovel v 1a**

See quot.

1872 Eggleston *End of the World* 37 **IN,** His sweet-faced mother . . moving about among her throng of children like a hen with more chickens than she can hover. [Footnote to *hover:*] Not until my attention was called to this word . . did I know that in this sense, it is a provincialism. It is so used, at least in half the country, and yet neither of our American dictionaries has it.

hover n [*EDD hover* sb. 13 "A cover, shelter"] **chiefly sMD, nVA, KY, TN** Cf **hovel n 1a**

A shelter or brooder for chickens; a device for holding heat in a brooder; see quots.

1907 *Elementary School Teacher* 7.410 **swWI,** A hover which was made of felt was hung in the brooder. **1949** Kurath *Word Geog.* 41, *Hover* . . [is a] distinctive Piedmont word . . for the chicken house or roost. . . [This] term . . [has] found . . [its] way into the Tidewater area north of the James and into southern Maryland. **c1960** *Wilson Coll.* **csKY,** *Hover*—A small house for a hen and her brood—a hovel. **1966** Dakin *Dial. Vocab. Ohio R. Valley* 2.259, In Kentucky the term *(chicken) hover* . . seems to be used primarily as an equivalent for *coop* . . and perhaps as a synonym for *brooder house* in some cases. It appears occasionally in the Bluegrass . . but is more common in western and southern Kentucky—where *brooder house* is not used. This term . . is not used in the Mountains and is unknown north of the Ohio. **1968–70** *DARE* (Qu. M16, *The small shelter for a hen that can be moved about from place to place*) Infs **KY**90, **VA**24, 43, Hover; **VA**57, Hover—one chicken, old-fashioned; **KY**86, **VA**38, 40, Chicken hover; **TN**26, Chicken hover—this is where they go in at night and stay. **1970** *DARE* FW Addit **csVA,** *Hover*—A portable hen shelter. **1986** Pederson *LAGS Concordance,* 1 inf, **swAL,** Chicken hovers—a smaller shelter for chicks; 1 inf, **nwTN,** Hover—chicken coop.

hover fly n

See quot 1911.

1911 *Century Dict. Suppl., Hover-fly*. . . Any one of very many flies of the families *Syrphidæ* and *Bombyliidæ* which hover over flowers, rapidly vibrating their wings while searching for honey. **1926** Essig *Insects N. Amer.* 566, *Syrphidae.* Syrphid Flies. . . Hover Flies. **1950** *WELS (Small flies)* 1 Inf, **ceWI,** This might be the fly called hover fly that we hear occasionally. **1986** Pederson *LAGS Concordance (Things that make noises in ponds at night)* 1 inf, **neFL,** Hover fly.

how adv

1 What?—used as an interrogative to indicate that something has not been heard or understood. **scattered, but chiefly Nth, N Midl** Cf *do how* (at **do what**)

1815 in 1947 *AmSp* 22.283, *How?* An interrogative very often used in Kentucky & North Carolina when a person does not distinctly hear or understand what is said to him, for *'what do you say.'* **1839** Marryat *Diary* 1.196, The English *what?* implying that you did not hear what was said to you, is changed in America to the word *how?* **1859** (1968) Bartlett *Americanisms* 206, *How?* Used chiefly in New England, like the French *comment?* in asking for the repetition of something not understood. . . "Don't—let me beg you—don't say *'How?'* for 'What?' "—*O. W. Holmes, Poems.* **1907** *DN* 3.213 **cCT, nwAR,** *How*. . . What? **1943** *LANE* Map 394 *(What did you say?)* 47 infs, scattered throughout NEng, Long Is, NY, How. **1965–70** *DARE* (Qu. X18, . . *When one person doesn't quite hear what another person said, what does he say?*) 16 Infs, **chiefly Nth, N Midl,** How? [13 of 16 Infs old] **1973** Allen *LAUM* 1.304 **Upper MW, esp MN** (as of c1950), (*What's that?* . . when failing to hear an utterance). . . *How?* . . [has] Northern distribution mostly in Minnesota. [15 infs total]

2 In ref to naming: What, by what name. Cf **call one's name**

1905 *DN* 3.83, **nwAR,** *How do you call your name?* . . 'What is your name?' **1919** *DN* 5.33 **seKY,** In inquiring after one's name . . "How did ye say ye called yer name?" **1986** Pederson *LAGS Concordance,* 1 inf, **cLA,** How you call that place?

how conj **sAppalachians**

That—used in phr *hope how soon;* see quots.

1923 (1946) Greer-Petrie *Angeline Doin' Society* 2 **csKY,** Lum was mad—speshully at that gal Desdimony, and he hoped *how soon* Othello would choke the life out'n her. **1931** Hannum *Thursday April* 16 **wNC,** I hope how soon hit comes. **1936** *AmSp* 11.63 **WV,** I hope how soon I'll see you (I hope I'll see you soon). **1946** *AmSp* 21.271 **neKY,** *Hope how soon (it happens)*. . . Hope it may happen soon. Common. **1952** Brown *NC Folkl.* 1.553, *How soon*. . . Soon, quickly. "I hope how soon your mother will come back."

how exclam [Cf *EDD how* int. 3] Cf **huh-ee**

1969 *DARE* (Qu. K80, *The call that's used* . . *to get the cows in from the pasture*) Inf **KY**43A, How.

howbeever adv Also *howbesomevuh* Pronc-spp *howbe(e)vuh* [Prob blend of *how be it* + *however;* cf *EDD how it be* (at *how* adv. II. 1. (13)) and quot 1936; cf also *EDD howmiver* (at *howsomever*)]

=**howsomever 1.**

1890 Johnston *Widow Guthrie* 220 **GA** (as of 1830s), Howbeever, it's never worth anybody's while to ast sich questions. [**1936** *N&Q* 170.134 **Somerset England,** *How-be-ever,* however.] **1944** in 1958 Brewer *Dog Ghosts* 60 **TX** [Black], Howbevuh, de nex' comin' Sunday, de cowboy puts on his gamblin' stripe pants . . an' goes to chu'ch up to Edna, Texas. **1957** *Ibid* 7, Hit ver' disencouragin', 'caze evuhbody he 'proach wid dis questshun, dey tell 'im dat dey don' hab de knowledge to know. Fin'ly one day, howbesomevuh, he meets a ole slave. **1953** Brewer *Word Brazos* 16 **eTX** [Black], Howbeevuh, de nex' day attuh de circus was work day on de ole Lee farm, so li'l' Bill . . don' relish goin' to work.

how be you exclam [Var of *how are you;* cf **be B1a(1)**] **chiefly NEng** *old-fash, sometimes joc* Cf **how you be**

Hello—used as a casual greeting.

1938 *Atlantic Mth.* Oct 552/2 **seMO** (as of c1900), Half-awake, I would listen to the slow ceremony of hillbilly greetings. . . 'Howdy, howdy. How be ye?' **1941** *LANE* Map 424 *(How are you?)* [Used as a casual greeting to intimate friends] 91 infs, **throughout NEng,** How be you; 1 inf, **cnCT,** *How are you,* more formal than *how be you;* 1 inf, **ceMA,** *How be you,* usually; 1 inf, **cwMA,** *How be you,* common but always jocular; 1 inf, **neMA,** *How be you,* now only jocular; 1 inf, **nwMA,** *How be you,* jocular when used by persons under forty; 1 inf, **ceVT,** *Are* is exceptional here . . [I] regularly use . . *be;* 1 inf, **seME,** *How be you,* only 'in fun'; 1 inf, **ceME,** *How be you,* jocular; 1 inf, **cwME,** *How be you,* a genuine inquiry after someone's health. **1951** *PADS* 15.66 **NH,** *How be ye?: Greeting.* "How are you?" **1966** *DARE* (Qu. NN10a, *Expressions [such as 'hello'] used when you meet somebody you know quite well*) Infs **MA**68, **NY**94, How be you?—old-fashioned; **WA**11, How be you? **1969** *DARE* FW Addit **ceCT,** *How be you?*—How are you? Joking. **1986** Pederson *LAGS Concordance,* 1 inf, **nwAL,** How be you?—people used to say; 1 inf, **neMS,** How be you?—some folks say; 1 inf, **neTN,** How be you?—expression used by grandmother.

how-come-you-so adj Also *how-came-you-so*

1 Intoxicated. [Cf *EDD how came you so* (at *how* adv. II. 1. (6)) "slightly intoxicated"] *old-fash*

1827 Cooper *Red Rover* 1.280 **cNY,** It is quite in reason to believe your husband was . . a little of what I call how-come-ye-so. **1843** *Knickerbocker* 22.366, We were never 'groggy,' 'intoxicated,' . . 'how-came-ye-so' . . or 'tight,' but *once.* **1911** (1912) Lincoln *Cap'n Warren* 223 **ceMA,** One evenin' Labe was comin' home pretty how-come-you-so, and he fell into Jandab Wixon's well. **1968** *DARE* Tape **MI**96, They used to say they [=river drivers] come up to paint the town red. . . When they got pretty well how-come-you-so, why, they didn't always know just exactly what they were doing.

2 See quot.

1923 *DN* 5.240 **swWI,** *How-came-you-so*. . . Pregnant. "She's how-came-you-so."

how do See **how you do**

how-do-piece n [From *how do you do*]

The part of a cap one touches in greeting.

1946 *PADS* 6.18 **eNC,** *How-do-piece. . .* The visor of a cap. . . Common.

how-do-you-do n

1 pronc-sp *howdy-do:* See quot. Cf **thank-you-ma'am**

1969 *DARE* (Qu. N30, . . *A sudden short dip in a road*) Inf **IL**62A, How-do-you-do; **IN**74, A howdy-do.

2 See quot. [Perh from *how-do-you-do* a predicament]

1969 *DARE* (Qu. V11, . . *Joking names . . for a . . jail*) Inf **GA**72, [ˌhaʊdɪ'du]—from "how-do-you-do."

howdy v [*how do you do*]

1 also with *around;* also *howdy-do:* To say "hello" or exchange casual greetings; to greet; hence vbl n *howdying.* **chiefly Sth, S Midl**

1864 Nichols *40 Yrs.* 387, The Southerner is mighty glad to see you. . . When people salute each other at meeting, he says they are howdyin' and civilizin' each other. **1884** Harris *Mingo* 138 **cGA,** I'm a-huntin' airter you, an' the business I come on hain't got much howdyin' in it. **1887** *Harper's New Mth. Mag.* Mar 545/1, [I] howdyed to him as he sot in his peazzer [=piazza]. **1893** Shands *MS Speech* 72, *Howdy. . .* This word is extensively used by the illiterate classes of Mississippi as a regular verb; as, "We just met and howdied, and then passed on." **1908** *DN* 3.322 **eAL, wGA,** *Howdy. . .* To greet. "I saw them howdyin' one another." **1946** TN Folk Lore Soc. *Bulletin* 12.4.4 **eTN,** He's a-howdyin' whoever 'tis; hit hain't no outlander. **1950** *WELS (If you met somebody on the street and spoke only a few words . . you might say, "We just ______.")* 1 Inf, **WI,** Howdied. **c1960** *Wilson Coll.* **csKY,** *Howdy*—to speak to. "He howdied me." **1967–70** *DARE* (Qu. II12, *Talking about meeting somebody on the street and speaking only a few words . . "We just ______."*) Infs **NY**18, **VA**43, Howdied; **IN**61, I just howdied him; **TX**35, Howdy-doed. **1983** *NY Times* (NY) 18 May **NC,** I like to go and howdy around a bit.

2 in phr *howdy and shake* and varr: To greet and shake hands; to greet and expressly meet; to greet and be introduced to.

1960 *VT Hist.* new ser 28.140, *Howdy.* We howdy but we don't shake. **1968** *DARE* File **eKY,** We've howdy'd but not shook. **c1968** *DARE* File **ID,** The cowboy's response to "Have you two met?" was supposed to have been "We've howdied, but I ain't shook him yet." **1970** *DARE* (Qu. II12, *Talking about meeting somebody on the street and speaking only a few words . . "We just ______."*) Inf **TN**43, Howdied ['hæʊdid] and shook. **1980** *Houston Chron.* (TX) 11 Nov sec 3 np, When two men are discussing a third fellow who is a friend of one, but a mere acquaintance of the other, the second man is apt to explain "We've 'howdyed' but we haven't 'shook' yet."

howdy around See **howdy 1**

howdy-do n See **how-do-you-do 1**

howdy-do v, **howdying** See **howdy 1**

howdy owl n [Perh from its habit of bobbing up and down]

=**burrowing owl.**

1954 Sprunt *FL Bird Life* 252, *Florida Burrowing Owl. . . Local Names:* Ground Owl; Howdy Owl.

how is she intj [Echoic] Cf **catch him**

1966 *DARE* (Qu. NN18, *When somebody sneezes, what do people say to him?*) Inf **NH**5, How is she—pronounced to sound like a sneeze.

how is that for high See **high** adj **B7**

howling Methodist n Also *Methodist howler*

=**shouting Methodist.**

1950 *WELS (Nicknames for different religions)* 2 Infs, **WI,** Howling Methodist. **1966–69** *DARE* (Qu. CC4, . . *Nicknames . . for various . . religious groups*) Infs **ID**4, **IL**11, **WA**6, Howling Methodists; **MA**68, Methodist Howler—obsolete now.

how-much n

See quots.

1942 McAtee *Dial. Grant Co. IN* 35 (as of 1890s), *How-much. . .* Substitute for a name not understood, or unknown, or that one did not desire to mention. "This here Grover how-much, do you know him?" **1990** *DARE* File **csWI,** I introduced a friend to my mother by saying, "Mom, this is John." "John how-much?" inquired Mom, baffling my friend (who didn't realize he was being asked what his last name was).

how-ooce See **house**

how-rie See **haole**

how say adv phr [Perh abbr for *how say you*] Cf *do how* (at **do what**)

=**how** adv **1.**

1951 *PADS* 15.67 **NH,** *Say?, How:* question. "What did you say?"

howse-er, howsever See **howsoever**

how's for adv phr [Var of *how about*]

1930 Williams *Logger-Talk* 24 **Pacific NW,** *How's for:* A phrase which precedes a request, as *How's for a match.*

how's it exclam Also sp *howzit* **HI**

See quot 1981.

1967 *DARE* (Qu. NN10a, *Expressions [such as 'hello'] used when you meet somebody you know quite well*) Infs **HI**8A, 13, How's it? **1981** *Pidgin To Da Max* np **HI,** *Howzit*—Pidgin for "aloha". [Cartoon:] [Hawaiians, greeting each other at a party, say] "Howzit?" "Howzit?" "Howzit?" [Haole, irritated, exclaims] "How's what?!?"

howsoever adv Also *howsever, howse-er* [Cf *EDD howsoever* adv "Also in form . . *[how]sever*"] *arch*

=**howsomever 1.**

1833 in 1834 Davis *Letters Downing* 19 **NY,** You don't know nothing about Latin . . but howsever . . you shall give the address after all, only just let Seth stick a little Hog-latin into it. **1841** (1952) Cooper *Deerslayer* 446, Howsever, turn it [=the earth] does. **1843** (1916) Hall *New Purchase* 79 **IN,** Howsoever keep rite strate along the bottim till you come to the bio—(bayou). *Ibid* 228, Howsever the Doctor's nevy [=nephew] was good pluck. *Ibid* 457, Howse-er, I'll set you over the river afore sun-up. **1851** Burke *Polly Peablossom* 70 **MS,** Howsever, that ain't tellin' you how the sarpint kinder chawed up my darter Sal. *Ibid* 71, I was 'stonished what to make uv that whoppin big lump on behind. Howsever, it was 'simmon time, an' she'd bin eatin er [=a] powerful sight uv um, an' I 'sposed she was gittin fat. **1851** Hooper *Widow Rugby's Husband* 49 **AL,** Howsoever, at last I got close up. **1862** (1864) Browne *Artemus Ward Book* 114 **ME,** He liked his tods too well, howsever, & they floored him.

howsomever adv

1 also *howsomebeever, howsom(e)dever, howsum(d)ever,* and varr: However, nevertheless; notwithstanding that. [*EDD howsomever* adv. "Also in forms . . *-somedever . . -sumdever*"] **scattered, but chiefly S and C Atl, S Midl** Cf **howsoever**

1795 Dearborn *Columbian Grammar* 136, *List of Improprieties,* commonly called *Vulgarisms,* which should never be used in *Speaking, Reading, or Writing. . . Howsomever* for *however.* **1836** (1955) *Crockett Almanacks* 55 **wTN,** Howsomever there was no more praying or preaching that day. **1843** (1916) Hall *New Purchase* 148 **IN,** I dissarned [=discerned] . . a likelihood for a snow storm. Howsomever, this did'nt [sic] *faze* me. *Ibid* 227, Ashford and Bill . . pretends they was a follerin him—howsom'er they couldn't a ketch'd up no how. *Ibid* 395, 'Twas near as good as desperut to try a black crow that distance with a shot-gun. . . Howsomdever, I wanted the load out. **1844** Thompson *Major Jones's Courtship* 13 **GA,** I seed how the game was gwine—but howsumever, I kep talkin to her like a cotton gin in packin time. **1845** Thompson *Pineville* 178 **GA,** Howsomedever, what can't be cured must be indured. **1871** Eggleston *Hoosier Schoolmaster* 110 **sIN,** Howsumdever he'd said he was a-goin' to help, and help he would. **1879** *Scribner's Mth.* 18.257/1 **cGA,** Howsomebeever. . . Neelus have a mightly power of words. **1884** *Anglia* 7.256 **SE** [Black], Howuver . . howsumuver . . *howsumuvver.* **1899** Chesnutt *Conjure Woman* 140 **csNC** [Black], I is made it a rule in my bizness not ter take no notes fum nobody. Howsomeber, suh, ef you is kinder sho't er fun's, mos' lackly we kin make some kin' er bahg'in. **1905** Chesnutt *Col.'s Dream* 150 **csNC** [Black], He jes' flew away! Befo' he got ter de do', howsomevuh, he 'membered he had locked it, so he . . went straight out'n a winder. **1907** *DN* 3.206 **nwAR, Cape Cod MA,** *Howsomever. . .* Howsoever. **1908** *DN* 3.322 **eAL, wGA,** *Howsomever. . .* However. **1968** *DARE* FW Addit **PA**91, *Howsomever*—however [FW: old-fashioned, used by Inf's grandmother]. **1984** Burns *Cold Sassy* 153 **nGA** (as of 1906), Howsome-ever, Miss Love needs something to take her mind off of Mr. Texas.

2 See quot. [*OED howsomever* adv. 1 "*Obs.*"]

1899 (1912) Green *VA Folk-Speech* 233, *Howsomever. . .* In what manner or what degree soever.

howsomevuh, howsum(d)ever, howsumuv(v)er See **howsomever 1**

ho-wuh See **ho v d**

how you be exclam Also *how you was* [Perh varr of **how be you,** or perh abbr for earlier *how do you be*] Cf **be B1a(1), how (you) do**

=**how be you.**

1966–69 *DARE* (Qu. NN10a, *Expressions . . used when you meet somebody you know quite well*) Inf **MS**35, How you be? **AR**55, How you was?—joking [FW: used by Inf in conv]; **TX**1, How you was? **1986** Pederson *LAGS Concordance (Hello)* 1 inf, **swTN,** How you be?

how you do exclam Also *how do* [Abbr for *how do you do*] **esp Sth, S Midl** See Map

Hello—used as a greeting.

1899 (1977) Norris *McTeague* 12 **San Francisco CA,** He said: "How do, Maria?" Maria nodded to him over her shoulder. **1965–70** *DARE* (Qu. NN10b, *Greetings used when you meet somebody you do not know well*) 14 Infs, **esp Sth, S Midl,** How (you *or* y'all) do; (Qu. NN10a, *Expressions . . used when you meet somebody you know quite well*) Infs **GA**73, **NC**1, **SC**34, How (you) do; **SC**32, How ya do. **1973** Allen *LAUM* 1.388 **MN** (as of c1950), (*How do you do?* to a stranger). . . How do. [3 infs] **1986** Pederson *LAGS Concordance* **Gulf Region** *(Hello)* 51 infs, How (you) do.

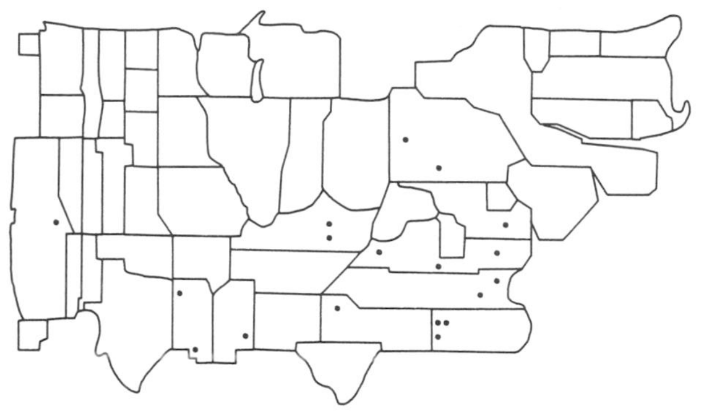

•how you do + varr (Qq. NN10a, b)

how you was See **how you be**

howzit See **how's it**

hoxhead See **hogshead**

hoy exclam Cf **hie**

1 also *hoya:* Used as a command to drive or turn a cow or ox. Cf **haw** v

1950 *WELS Suppl.* **cWI,** A man of Welsh background raised near Wild Rose says "Hoy" or "Hoy boss" when he drives cows; **cwWI,** A woman of Norwegian background says "hoy" to drive cows. **1988** *Lutz Coll.* **neNJ,** The command to an ox to go to the left is "Hoy" or "Hoya."

2 Used to drive away animals.

1969 *DARE* (Qu. NN22d, *Expressions used to drive away animals other than dogs*) Inf **KY**49, [hʌɔɪ].

hoy adj See **high** adj

‡hoya n [Prob var of *hooey* nonsense]

1968 *DARE* FW Addit **New Orleans LA,** *Hoya*—"Oh that's a lot of hoya." Occasional.

hoya exclam See **hoy 1**

hoz(e)y See **hosey**

H snake n

A **rat snake** (here: *Elaphe subocularis*).

1974 Shaw–Campbell *Snakes West* 102, More popularly this snake [=*Elaphe subocularis*] is called the H snake because running along either side of the center of its back are twenty-eight parallel black or dark brown markings that are frequently joined or nearly joined to form an H.

huac n Cf **quawk**

=**black-crowned night heron.**

1917 *Wilson Bulletin* 29.2.78, *Nycticorax nycticorax naevius. . .* huac, Marksville, La.

huajillo n Also *huajilla, guajillo, guajilla* [MexSpan]

1 A **cat's-claw** (here: *Pithecellobium pallens*). Also called **mimosa-bush**

1886 Havard *Flora W. & S. TX for 1885* 500, *Pithecolobium* [sic] *brevifolium. . .* Huajillo. . . Shrub on the lower Rio Grande, with permanent foliage readily eaten by sheep and goats in winter. **1891** Coulter *Botany W. TX* 101, *P. brevifolium . . Huajillo. . .* Shrub, with puberulent branchlets. . . Along the lower Rio Grande. **1892** *DN* 1.190, *Huajíllo:* a shrub of Southwestern Texas (*Pithecolobium* [sic] *brevifolium*). *Ibid* 248, **TX,** *Huajíllo. . .* A diminutive of *huáge* or *guáge.* **1903** Small *Flora SE U.S.* 576, *Huajillo. . .* An evergreen shrub or small tree, sometimes 10 m. high, armed with short spines. **1922** Sargent *Manual Trees* 587, *Huajillo. . . Wood* dark-colored, hard, and heavy. **1960** Vines *Trees SW* 515, *Pithecellobium pallens. . .* Vernacular names are Huajillo, . . Guajilla. **1979** Little *Checklist U.S. Trees* 201, *Pithecellobium pallens . . huajillo. . . Range*—S. Tex. and ne. Mex.

2 Any of several acacias, but usu *Acacia berlandieri,* a well-known honey plant. **chiefly TX**

1937 Parks *Plants TX* 57, *Pithecolobium* [sic] *brevifolium* Benth. Gulf Coast Guajillo . . must not be confused with the prairie Guajillo. *Ibid* 45, *Acacia Berlandieri* Benth. Guajillo. The most famous honey plant of Texas. **1939** Tharp *Vegetation TX* 57, *Acacia . .* [includes] Huajillo. **1951** *PADS* 15.33 **TX,** *Acaciella hirta . .* and *A. berlandieri. . .* These are two of the huajillas from which bees gather specially fine honey. **1960** Vines *Trees SW* 492, *Acacia angustissima* var *hirta. . .* Vernacular names are . . Huajilla, Guajillo. . . The legumes are sometimes eaten by cattle. *Ibid* 498, *Acacia berlandieri. . .* Vernacular names are . . Guajillo, Huajilla. . . The species is a very famous honey plant, producing a clear, white, excellent flavored honey. *Ibid* 499, *Acacia greggii. . .* Vernacular names are Devil Claws, . . Huajilla [etc]. **1967** *DARE* (Qu. T16, *What kinds of trees are 'special' around here?*) Inf **TX**3, Huajilla. **1970** Correll *Plants TX* 773, *Acacia Berlandieri. . . Guajillo. . .* Exceedingly abundant on limestone ridges and caliche cuestas in the Rio Grande Plains. **1979** Little *Checklist U.S. Trees* 37, *Guajillo. . . Other common name*—Berlandier acacia.

3 =**fairy duster.**

1932 AZ Ag. Exp. Sta. *Bulletin* 141.24, The more valuable of these are . . blue and green canutillo or Mormon tea, . . catsclaw, and huajilla or fairy duster. **1945** Benson–Darrow *Manual SW Trees* 156, *Calliandra eriophylla. . . Fairy duster; huajillo; false mesquite.* A low bushy shrub about 1 foot or rarely up to 3 feet high. **1960** Vines *Trees SW* 502, The plant is also known under the vernacular names of Fairy Duster, . . Huajillo [etc]. **1981** Benson–Darrow *Trees SW Deserts* 230, *Huajillo. . .* Common on the slopes and mesas of the . . deserts.

hub n

1 The stake used as a target in games such as quoits or horseshoes; hence *hubber* a quoit which scores by landing against the hub. [Engl dial *hob, hub;* see *OED hub* sb.[1] 2. b, *hob* sb.[2] 2; *EDD hob, hobber* (at *hob* sb.[2] 3)]

1889 *Century Dict.* 2908, *Hub.* A mark at which quoits, etc., are cast. **1899** Champlin–Bostwick *Young Folks' Games* 566, *Quoits,* a game generally played on level sward, by two or more persons, with flat iron rings or disks, which are pitched at a goal or hub. *Ibid* 567, In England the hub or pin was formerly called the "hob." **1940–41** Cassidy *WI Atlas* **cwWI,** Play a game of quoits, . . played with flat, thin stone; circular. Couldn't make no ringers, but you could make hubbers [hʌbɚz].

2 See quot.

1965 Needham–Mussey *Country Things* 17 **sVT,** A rail fence goes in zigzags, as if it was a snake wiggling. . . For a foundation he would put down two round stones, one on top of the other, which he called the hub. If you just put one stone under a fence or a wooden foundation, the moisture creeps up the stone, and rots the wood. With two stones the moisture doesn't crawl up the second stone.

hub v

1 To touch or graze with the hub of a wheel, sometimes purposely; hence vbl n *hubbing.*

1906 *DN* 3.141 **nwAR,** *Hub. . .* To cause the hub of a vehicle to collide with the hub of a passing vehicle. "Look out, brother, don't hub me." **1916** *DN* 4.338 **PA,** *Hub. . .* To graze with the hub of a wheel. **1927**

AmSp 2.357 **WV,** He hubbed my wagon and pushed me into the ditch. **1946** McAtee *Dial. Grant Co. IN Suppl. 3* 6 (as of 1890s), *Hub* . . to hit with the hub of a vehicle; "He hubbed us into the ditch." **1954** *Harder Coll.* **cwTN,** He hubbed me. **1966** *PADS* 46.26 **AR,** *Hub*. . . To catch the hub (of a wagon, etc.) against (so that the vehicle won't move).—"He hubbed the barn with the wagon." **1968** Adams *Western Words* 156, *Hubbing*—Driving a wagon so that the hubs strike gateposts or other objects.

2 Fig; in phrr *hub trouble,* ~ *it:* To experience difficulty.

1936 *AmSp* 11.368 **nLA,** *Hub it.* To get into difficulty; to have a hard time; as, 'With the rain falling and the car miring deeper, we certainly did hub it.' **1939** in 1984 Lambert–Franks *Voices* 12 **OK,** Then the Depression came along, and I hubbed trouble sure enough. Cable-tool jobs was mighty scarce since nearly all the drillin' was done with rotaries. **1967** *DARE* (Qu. CC12a, *Expressions used about bad luck* . . *"Poor Joe. He's really* . . ______.") Inf **AR**51, Been a-hubbin' it; (Qu. CC12b, . . *"He's been* ______.") Inf **AR**51, A-hubbin' it.

hubbard squash n **chiefly Nth, N Midl, West** See Map Cf **blue hubbard squash, mother hubbard squash**

A well-known cultivar of a common squash *(Cucurbita maxima).*

1868 MI State Bd. Ag. *Annual Rept.* 7.349, Thos. Smith, Hamtramck, [exhibited] 8 Hubbard squashes. **1918** Lincoln *Shavings* 259 **seMA,** They probably wouldn't [bother] anybody with a head instead of a Hubbard squash on his shoulders. **1950** *WELS (Kinds of squash)* 46 Infs, Hubbard squash. **1960** Bailey *Resp. to PADS 20* **KS,** Hubbard—large as a small watermelon. **1965–70** *DARE* (Qu. I23, . . *Kinds of squash)* 376 Infs **chiefly Nth, N Midl, West,** Hubbard squash; 10 Infs, **Nth,** Green hubbard squash; **ME**16, **MI**116, **MA**68, 83, **VT**2, Yellow hubbard squash; **MA**6, **NY**68, Golden hubbard squash; **ME**16, **MA**6, Gray hubbard squash; **MA**68, Sage hubbard squash.

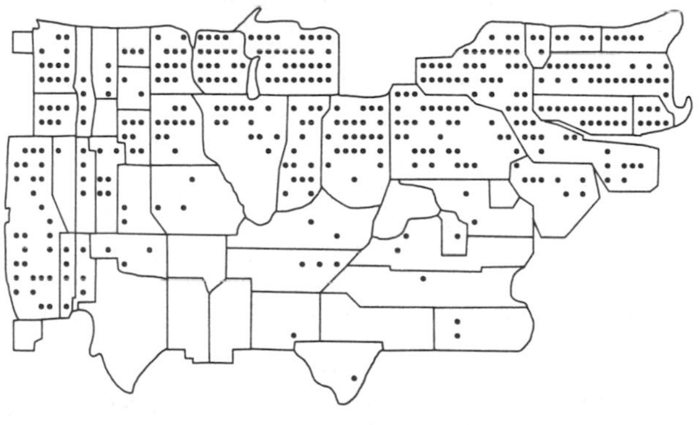

•hubbard squash + varr (Qu. I23)

hubber See **hub n 1**

hubbing See **hub v 1**

hubble n [Var of *EDD hobble* sb.^{1} 8] Cf **hubbly**

A rough place, bump, esp one caused by the freezing of a rutted muddy road.

1818 Fessenden *Ladies Monitor* 172 **VT,** Provincial words and phrases, which ought to be avoided by all who aspire to speak or write the English language correctly. . . *hubble* a rough projection or knoll. **1899** Garland *Boy Life* 52 **nwIA,** They clattered away over the frozen hubbles, to the nearest pond [to go skating]. **1978** *DARE* File **cnMA** (as of c1915), *Hubble* is a word I haven't heard for some years. We used to speak of a road being full of hubbles. It was hard to pull a sled when you were coasting—*sliding* we usually said—if there were too many hubbles in the road. We also spoke of a bumpy road as hubbly.

hubbly adj Also *hobbly* [Engl dial; cf *EDD hobbly* (at *hobble* sb.^{1} 8)] **chiefly NEast** Cf **hubble, hubby**

Of a road, the surface of the sea, etc: rough, bumpy, choppy.

a1870 Chipman *Notes on Bartlett* 206 *(DA), Hubbly.* Said of the surface of ice on roads and streams. . . N[ew] E[ngland]. **1896** *N.Y. Wkly. Witness* 23 Dec. 4/1 *(DA)* **NYC,** Where the snow had been swept off the ice by the wind, some places were hubbly. **1903** *Springfield Republican* (MA) 16 Oct 8/4, Stumbling as over a hubbly field. **1904** *DN* 2.426 **Cape Cod MA** (as of a1857), *Hubbly*. . . Rough. 'It had thawed and frozen and the road and the pond were all hubbly.' **1905** Wasson *Green Shay* 79 **NEng coast,** Don't you know how ungodly chowy and hubbly [Footnote: Rough] it gits down there with the flood tide settin' in ag'in an easterly breeze o' wind? **1930** Shoemaker *1300 Words* 30 **cPA Mts** (as of c1900), *Hobbly*—Rough, uneven. **1949** *Consumer Repts.* Jan 8/1 **NY,** Pick out a hubbly surface or a "washboard" gravel road . . and keep your eye on that nifty plastic hood ornament. **1966** *DARE* (Qu. N27b, *When unpaved roads get very rough, you call them* ______) Inf **ME**10, Hobbly ['hɔblɪ]. **1974** *AmSp* 49.62 **swME** (as of c1900), *Hubbly*. . . Rough, uneven (of the sea and the weather). **1978** [see **hubble**].

hubby adj Also *hobby* [Engl dial; cf *EDD hobby* and *hubbed* (at *hob* v.^{1} 9)]

=**hubbly.**

1848 Bartlett *Americanisms* 183, *Hubby.* Applied to rough roads, particularly when frozen; as, the road is hubby. **1858** in 1884 Weed *Life* 1.18 **OH** (as of 1808), The dozen journeys I made barefooted over the frozen and "hubby" road in December. **1889** *Oregonian* (Portland OR) 16 Dec 5/1, The ground was too rough or "hobby" to make driving pleasant, and out in the country the mud was not frozen hard enough to bear a horse or wagon. **1917** *DN* 4.394 **IA, neOH,** *Hubby*. . . applied exclusively to frozen roads. "The roads are pretty hubby this morning."

‡hub-do n [Cf **hubdub, do n^{1} 2**]

1966 *DARE* (Qu. KK12, *A meeting where there's a lot of talking: "They got together yesterday and had a real* ______.") Inf **OK**31, Hub-do [hʌbdu].

hubdub n [Cf *hubbub*]

A great noise or commotion.

1951 Johnson *Resp. to PADS 20* **DE,** *(A lot of noise or disturbance: "They were making a big* ______ *about something.")* Hubdub.

hub it See **hub v 3**

hubs of Hades (or heck, hell) See **hobs of hell**

hub tree n

1958 McCulloch *Woods Words* 90 **Pacific NW,** *Hub tree*—Another name for the head tree at the landing. The hub of logging activity.

hub trouble See **hub v 3**

hub up to prep phr

In close proximity with.

1954 Tolbert *Bigamy Jones* 41 **wTX** (as of 1870s), My grandfather said he'd rather live hub up to the Comanches than to stay in the settled part of Texas.

huck n^{1} Cf **huck v esp ME**

A foot; a shoe.

1900 Day *Up in ME* 123, They make ye peel your hucks in the street / And walk to the bar in your stocking-feet. **1902** Day *Pine Tree Ballads* 73 **ME,** Pluck, pluck, Pluck, pluck!/ Stubbin' acrost the clam-flat muck!/ Ev'ry time I lift my huck,/—Hearin' the heel of my old boot suck. **1914** *DN* 4.74 **ME, nNH,** *Hucks*. . . Feet. **1929** *AmSp* 5.125 **ME,** "Huck" meant feet.

huck n^{2}

1 A **huckleberry 1** or **2.**

1896 *DN* 1.418, *Hucks:* for *huckleberries.* N[ew] Y[ork] c[ity].

2 See **huckleberry 8.**

huck v Cf **huck n^{1}**

To walk or run.

1900 Day *Up in ME* 56, Some chaps fell down and some they [=some chaps] ducked [to avoid being struck by a flying mallet] / And them fur off, by gosh, they hucked. **1914** *DN* 4.74 **ME, nNH,** *Huck it*. . . To walk.

huckabuck n [Var of *huckaback*] Also *huckabuck towel*

=**huck towel.**

1911 Wharton *Ethan Frome* 151 **MA,** I know there's a huckabuck towel missing. **1939** *LANE* Map 142 *(Bath towel),* 1 inf, **ceMA,** Huckabuck [hʌkəbʌk].

hucka bucka beanstalk See **huckle buckle beanstalk**

huckabuck towel See **huckabuck**

huckberry n

=**hackberry.**

1889 *Century Dict.* 2908, *Huckberry*. . . Same as *hackberry.*

huck chuck n Cf **hill dill, hull-gull**

A game of tag.

1965 *DARE* File **FL** (as of 1900s), *Huck Chuck.* Similar to *Hill Dill.* One boy, "it," would stand in the middle of the street and call "huck chuck". The others, all standing on one side, would run across. The first boy tagged would be "it" for the next game, the second would be "its" helper. Everyone would run back and forth until all were tagged.

huckel barrel n

A barrel used in the game **huckel-de-buck.**

1936 [see **huckel-de-buck**].

huckel-de-buck n

1936 *Jrl. Amer. Folkl.* 49.202 **Ozarks,** "Huckel-de-buck" is a gambling game. . . Several kegs are placed . . inside a[n] . . enclosure, and the player bets his ability to throw a . . ball into a certain keg designated . . the "huckel bar'l."

huckie n [Dimin of *huck* haunch; cf *OED huckle* sb. "A dim. of *huck*. . . 1. The haunch."]

1937 Gardner *Folkl. Schoharie* 15 **ceNY,** They made their way to the home of the Methodist minister and squatted on their "huckies" outside while a guide who accompanied them went inside to interview the minister.

huckleberry n [Prob var of *hurtleberry*]

1 A plant of the genus *Gaylussacia;* also the fruit of such a plant. Also called **blue huckleberry 2.** For other names of var spp see **bangleberry, bearberry 3, bear huckleberry 1, black snap, box huckleberry, buckberry 1, dangleberry 1, dwarf huckleberry 1, gopherberry, grouseberry 2, highbush huckleberry 1, winter huckleberry** **chiefly east of Missip R**

1670 (1937) Denton *Brief Descr.* 4 **Long Island NY,** The Fruits natural to the Island, are *Mulberries, Posimons, Grapes* great and small, *Huckelberries.* **1774** (1957) Fithian *Jrl. & Letters* 128, We supt on Artichoks, & Huckleberries & Milk. **1859** Taliaferro *Fisher's R.* 155 **NC,** I . . took through the huckleberry swamp like a 'coon. **1894** *Harper's New Mth. Mag.* 88.524/2, He would move round the campfire like a cub bear around a huckleberry bush. **1907** *DN* 3.181 **seNH,** *Blueberry. . .* Vaccinium. . . Blueberries have short stems and tiny seeds. The opposite is true of huckleberries. **1948** *Country Gentleman* May 175/2 **KY,** He brought us dewberries, huckleberries and wild gooseberries. **1965–70** *DARE* (Qu. I44, *What kinds of berries grow wild around here?*) 354 Infs, **chiefly east of Missip R,** Huckleberry; **GA**72, Branch huckleberry; **ME**5, Tall huckleberry. [*DARE* Ed: Some of these Infs may refer instead to **2** below.] **1968** [see **2** below]. **1976** Bailey–Bailey *Hortus Third* 498, *Gaylussacia. . . Huckleberry. . .* Distinguished from *Vaccinium* in having ovary 10-celled. . . Huckleberries should have a shady location in peaty or sandy soils.

2 =blueberry 1.

1830 Rafinesque *Med. Flora* 2.272, *Vaccinium. . . Huckle berries. . . V. distichum,* Raf. of Oregon, fine flavor, baked into bread. **1897** Parsons *Wild Flowers CA* 200, *Vaccinium ovatum. . .* The huckleberry is at its best upon the high ridges of the Coast Ranges. . . There its abundant berries become juicy and delicious, and are much sought for preserving and pie-making. **1916** Thoburn *Std. Hist. OK* 1.5, Of wild fruits there are a number of species, including plums, . . huckleberries, currants [etc]. **1926** (1949) McQueen–Mizell *Hist. Okefenokee* 124, There are several kinds of huckleberry in the Okefenokee. There is . . the highland huckleberry, and two kinds of it—the low-bush blue huckleberry and the high-bush. . . Then there is the small blue swamp huckleberry. . . Then there are two kinds of huckleberry which grow in the bushes or jungle of the Okefenokee—a black berry and a blue berry. . . There is also one more kind of huckleberry, which is smooth and not quite as large. **1947** Coffin *Yankee Coast* 6 **ME,** The huckleberry bushes were in full scarlet cry of the ending year. **1960** *Seattle Daily Times* (WA) 23 Oct mag sec 3, Strange about the huckleberries which grow so profusely every summer in many parts of the Cascade Mountains. . . They really are mountain blueberries, not huckleberries. Botany books point out that huckleberries are not to be found west of the Mississippi. The real huckleberry belongs to the Gaylussacia genus. The delicious, deep-purple berries sought in the Cascades every August and September belong to the Vaccinium genus. Vaccinium is Latin for blueberry. But try to tell that to the Yakima Indians. They, and the rest of us, will continue to know the crop as huckleberries. **1965–70** *DARE* (Qu. I44, *What kinds of berries grow wild around here?*) 38 Infs, **West,** Huckleberry; **CA**105, Red huckleberry; (Qu. I53, *Other fruits grown around here: any special varieties?*) Inf **NC**44, Tame huckleberry; (Qu. S26b, *Wildflowers that grow in water or wet places*) Inf **GA**5, Huckleberry; (Qu. S26e, *Other wildflowers not yet mentioned*) Inf **CA**105, Huckleberry; (Qu. T15, *What kinds of swamp trees do you have?*) Inf **MI**65, Huckleberry bushes; (Qu. T16, *What kinds of trees are 'special' around here?*) Infs **CO**22, Huckleberry bush; **MI**96, **TX**106, Huckleberry. **1966** *DARE* Tape **MI**9, I went picking huckleberries; **OK**31, There's bushes is [sic] huckleberries . . grew wild. . . The berries would be in just little clusters. . . When they'd get ripe, they were red. . . They were real sour. **1968** McPhee *Pine Barrens* 43 **NJ,** In the vernacular of the pines, huckleberries are blueberries, wild or cultivated. Huckleberries are also huckleberries, and this confuses outsiders but not pineys. **1982** *Barrick Coll.* **csPA,** Huckleberry—blueberry, esp. wild varieties.

3 =hackberry. Cf **huckberry**

1965–69 *DARE* (Qu. T13, *What other names do you have around here for these trees: . . hackberry?*) Infs **AL**30, **IL**50, **NH**16, Huckleberry; **MS**60, Huckleberry tree.

4 A **cocklebur 1.** Cf **huckleburr**

1957 Battaglia *Resp. to PADS 20* **eMD,** A large round weed seed that clings to your clothing: huckleberry.

5 A person; the desired or suitable person.

1892 *KS Univ. Qrly.* 1.97, *Huckleberry:* the right person, as in, You're my huckleberry. **1906** (1908) Lorimer *Jack Spurlock* 72 **NYC,** If she were looking for a kind, considerate, thoughtful husband . . you were her huckleberry. **1928** *Ruppenthal Coll.* **KS,** He never pays his honest debts, that's the kind of huckleberry he is. I don't get mad easily, but when I do I'm mad all over, for that's the kind of huckleberry I am. **1951** *PADS* 15.56 **IN,** *Huckleberry. . .* Aid, partner, sweetheart. "I'll be your huckleberry."

6 also attrib: A small amount or distance; a negligible thing or person. *old-fash*

1832 Paulding *Westward Ho* 1.182, I . . once [got] within a huckleberry of being smothered to death. **1844** (1855) Lewis *New Hope* 227 **WV,** Why, this thing laying here ain't a circumstance—hardly a huckleberry to him. **1858** Hammett *Piney Woods Tavern* 158 **TX,** Cussin' . . I recon's about a huckleberry above swearin's persimmon. **1865** Sedley *Marian Rooke* 132 **Ohio Valley,** All ye've got in that there cake-basket is no more to what Ike kin show ye than a minner to a whale, nor a huckleberry to a pumkin! **1889** Twain *CT Yankee* 340, The Saracen . . is no huckleberry himself. **1920** Bok *Americanization* 165 **NYC,** He always kept "a huckleberry or two" ahead of his readers.

7 attrib: Indifferent, without zeal. Cf **hickory n B4b**

1892 *KS Univ. Qrly.* 1.97, *Huckleberry:* indifferent, in, a huckleberry Christian.

8 also *huck:* Used as a nickname for a Black person. Cf **persimmon**

1931–33 *LANE Worksheets* **ceCT,** *Huckleberry. . .* Nickname for negro. **1937** *Writer* 50.239 **neOH** [Black], *Huck*—a Negro's name for Negro.

9 in phr *risk a huckleberry to a persimmon:* To bet even a negligible amount of money. Cf **6** above

1832 Paulding *Westward Ho* 1.80, If the horn gets broadside to the current, I wouldn't risk a huckleberry to a persimmon that we don't . . get treed, and sink to the bottom. **1960** Williams *Walk Egypt* 49 **GA,** You can invite them if you want, but I wouldn't risk a huckleberry to a persimmon but we don't see trouble 'fore the evening's out.

10 in phr *huckleberry above one's persimmon* and varr: See below. **Sth, S Midl** *somewhat old-fash*

a Something beyond one's ability. Cf **above one's bend**

1834 Crockett *Narrative* 70, I could just barely write my own name; but to do this, and write the warrants too, was at least a huckleberry over my persimmon. **1846** Thorpe *Mysteries* 166, The way said lion and his companions used to destroy the beasts of the forest, . . was "huckleberry above the persimmon" of any native in the country. **1858** Hammett *Piney Woods Tavern* 45 **TX,** "When I got to the river I jest went in for a big drink, swallered hafe a mile of water, and came over dry shod." "Stranger," says I, [“]ye'r just one huckle-berry above my persimmon.[”] **1872** Schele de Vere *Americanisms* 50 **Sth,** Huckleberry above the persimmons . . is used mainly in the South to express that something apparently simple and easy is far above the ability of the person who made the attempt. **1899** (1912) Green *VA Folk-Speech* 40 **VA,** That is a huckleberry above my persimmon. **1984** Wilder *You All Spoken Here* 151 **Sth,** *Huckleberry over my persimmons* . . that's more than I can take; it's beyond one's knowledge, comprehension.

b Something one degree superior to what it is compared with.

1839 (1840) Simms *Border Beagles* 2.96 **MS,** The literal manner in which Horsey had chosen to accept the coarse figurative language which the urchin had employed was, in western parlance, "a huckleberry above his persimmon". **1859** Taliaferro *Fisher's R.* 47 **nwNC** (as of 1820s), I'll show him I'm a huckleberry over his 'simmon, sartin. **1885** Porter *Incidents* 204, "I am the fleet-surgeon of the Mississippi squadron!" "O thunder!" exclaimed the other . . "I'm a huckleberry above that persimmon, 'cause I'm the chief cook." **1942** in 1946 *PADS* 6.38 **cwVA,** A *huckleberry* above someone. (Wiser or more sophisticated than someone.) **1984** Wilder *You All Spoken Here* 151 **Sth,** *Huckleberry over my persimmons:* You've got a horse on me; you're one up.

11 in phr *the only huckleberry on the bush:* Something unique or special. Cf **5** above

1984 Wilder *You All Spoken Here* 12 **Sth,** She turns the corners square: she thinks she's the *only huckleberry on the bush.*

12 See **huckleberry train.**

huckleberry above one's persimmon See **huckleberry 10**

huckleberry ant n

A large black ant.

1969 *DARE* (Qu. R17, . . *Big black ants that sting*) Inf **GA**77, Huckleberry ant.

huckleberry apple n Cf **oak apple, swamp apple**

A gall.

a1862 (1865) Thoreau *Cape Cod* 119, That kind of gall called Huckleberry-apple.

huckleberry beanstalk n See **huckle buckle beanstalk**

huckleberry bird n

A bird of the genus *Spizella.*

1929 Forbush *Birds MA* 3.82, *Spizella pusilla pusilla* . . *Field Sparrow. Other names:* Bush Sparrow; Huckleberry Bird.

huckleberry bug n

Appar a **stink bug.**

1968 *DARE* (Qu. R30, *What other kinds of beetles are known around here—for example, because of their odor or color or something else?*) Inf **NJ**52, Huckleberry bug—stinks like hell.

huckleberry fence n [Perh in ref to *Huckleberry* Finn's helping to whitewash a fence in Twain's *Adventures of Tom Sawyer*]

1967 *DARE* (Qu. L64, *A wooden fence near the house or garden*) Inf **MI**67, Huckleberry fence—one that had to be painted.

huckleberry lily n

A **wood lily** (here: *Lilium philadelphicum*).

1900 Lyons *Plant Names* 224, *L[ilium] Philadelphicum.* . . Huckleberry Lily. **1940** Clute *Amer. Plant Names* 12, *L. Philadelphicum.* . . Huckleberry-lily. **1949** Moldenke *Amer. Wild Flowers* 323, This lily, also known as . . huckleberry lily, lives in dry woods and thickets.

huckleberry line See **huckleberry train**

huckleberry oak n [See quots 1908, 1937]

A low, shrubby oak, *Quercus vaccinifolia* (also known as *Q. chrysolepis* var *vaccinifolia*), native in California and southern Oregon.

1908 Sudworth *Forest Trees Pacific* 295, Another distinct variety is *Quercus chrysolepis vaccinifolia* . . , a low-massed shrub of very high altitudes, commonly called "huckleberry oak," from the resemblance of its small (three-fourths of an inch to 1 inch long), sparingly or indistinctly toothed, usually smooth leaves. **1921** Hall *Hdbk. Yosemite* 128, At about the 6000-foot contour . . the golden oak becomes replaced by the dwarf huckleberry oak. **1937** U.S. Forest Serv. *Range Plant Hdbk.* B120, Huckleberry oak is a shrubby species of the higher mountains, commonly 2 to 6 feet high and, as the name implies, has small, entire leaves which resemble those of "huckleberry" (*Vaccinium* spp.) **1947** Peattie *Sierra Nevada* 142, Sometimes dwarf forms of such trees as huckleberry oak, buckeye, and California laurel take over completely. **1979** Little *Checklist U.S. Trees* 228, Huckleberry oak . . is a low shrub formerly included in this species [=*Quercus chrysolepis*].

huckleberry-pie adj Cf **apple-pie**

Excellent; highly satisfactory.

1933 Williamson *Woods Colt* 104 **Ozarks** (as of c1920), It's goin' to be huckleberry pie, nothin' to bother 'em an' nothin' to worry 'em.

huckleberry train n Also *huckleberry, ~ line humorous*

A slow rural train which makes frequent stops.

1901 Merwin-Webster *Calumet "K"* 296 **MN,** You'd have thought he was running a huckleberry train from the time he took. **1968-69** *DARE* (Qu. N37, *Joking names for a branch railroad*) Inf **PA**63, Huckleberry train; **VA**20, Huckleberry line; **VA**8, The huckleberry.

huckleberry two-step n

=green-apple quickstep.

1969 *DARE* (Qu. BB19, *Joking names for looseness of the bowels*) Inf **RI**15, Huckleberry two-step.

hucklebuck n

c1960 *Wilson Coll.* **csKY,** *Hucklebuck.* . . A case of nerves, heebie-jeebies.

huckle buckle beanstalk n Also *hucka bucka beanstalk, huckleberry ~* Cf **hide-and-seek B1, I spy** n

A children's game; see quot 1937.

1937 (1947) Bancroft *Games* 132, *Huckle, Buckle, Beanstalk* . . is a form of Hide the Thimble. . . One . . places the object in plain sight but where it would not be likely to be seen. . . The players . . begin to look for it. When one spies it, he does not at once disclose this . . but . . takes his seat . . and says "Huckle, buckle, beanstalk!" **1945** Boyd *Hdbk. Games* 81, The hiders . . hide the object. . . Whenever a player discovers the object, he pretends to continue hunting . . to deceive the other hunters, then takes a seat and says, "Huckle buckle beanstalk." **1950** *WELS (Games in which you hide an object and look for it)* 1 Inf, **WI,** Huckle buckle beanstalk; 1 Inf, Huckle buckle beanstalk—Pack children in hall except It, and It hides an object well in view; then children come and look for it; as each one sees the object she or he sits down and says "Huckle buckle beanstalk"; The first to find the object becomes the next It—after everyone has seen the object; 1 Inf, Hucka bucka beanstalk. **1967-69** *DARE* (Qu. EE3) Infs **IA**46, **IL**116, **NY**123, **PA**181, Huckle buckle beanstalk; **PA**126, Hucka bucka beanstalk; **IL**107, **NC**47, Huckleberry beanstalk.

huckleburr n

Prob a **cockleburr 1.** Cf **huckleberry 4**

1968 *DARE* (Qu. S13, . . *A common wild bush with bunches of round, prickly seeds* . . *dry they stick to your clothing*) Inf **NJ**17, Huckleburr; (Qu. S15, . . *Any other weed seeds that cling to clothing*) Inf **MD**20, Huckleburr (round, brown—size of fingernails—grow near creek [krɪk]).

huckle jee bread n

A children's singing game; see quot.

1914 *DN* 4.108 **KS,** *Huckle jee bread.* Children sitting with hands clasped over the knees rock forward and backward at the *huckles,* or hips, saying in sing-song: "My father and mother / Are sick in bed,/ And I must learn how / To make huckle jee bread,/ Then up with your feet / And down with your head,/ And that is the way / To make huckle jee bread."

hucklemybutt n [Cf *EDD huckle-my-buff* "A beverage composed of beer, eggs, and brandy"]

1950 *Western Folkl.* 9.382 **NM,** *Popular Cures for the Morning After.* . . Drink a hucklemybutt which is bourbon and milk poured over chopped ice.

hucks See **husk** n

huckster n Also *huckster man, husker* **scattered, but chiefly N Midl, C Atl, NEast exc nNEng** See Map Cf **arab** n **B3, truck gardener, vendor**

A peddler.

1682 *Boston Rec.* 154 *(DAE),* Others did as Hucksters . . buy vp the provisions . . & the[n] sell the same againe at extraordinary deare rates. **1798** *Phila. Ordinances* (1812) 157 *(DAE),* No person who follows the business of a huckster, or of selling . . at second hand, shall . . sell . . within the limits of the market. **1843** (1916) Hall *New Purchase* 501 **IN,** Will not he who feasts like Homer's heroes despise the meannesses of a huckster's life? **1899** (1912) Green *VA Folk-Speech* 234, *Huckster.* . . A retailer of small articles; a small dealer in agricultural produce. **1923** Watts *Luther Nichols* 19 **OH,** The hucksters they got to have a license because they drive round an' wear out th' roads. **1950** *WELS Suppl.* **PA,** *Huckster*—peddler of green vegetables and fruit—used in Pennsylvania. Not common in Wisconsin. **1965-70** *DARE* (Qu. U6, *Someone who sells* . . *going from house to house*) 200 Infs, **scattered, but**

chiefly N Midl, C Atl, NEast exc nNEng, Huckster; IL114, 126, OK1, Huckster man; DE5, MO19, VA6, Husker; (Qu. U7, *A man who goes from town to town selling things*) 20 Infs, **esp IN, OH, Upstate NY, PA,** Huckster; (Qu. U5, *Someone who sells . . on a street corner*) 13 Infs, **scattered,** Huckster; **NJ**69, Husker. **1967** Jacobs *Rejoicing* 86 **cIN** (as of c1930), Those of us who had pennies crowded around the door of the huckster wagon calling out what we wanted; the others just stood near, trying to look inside the wonderful machine which carried so many interesting and tasty items. "Take it easy, kids. Take it easy," the huckster man said. . . "Mrs. Brawner would like to do her trading." **1982** *Barrick Coll.* **csPA,** *Huckster*—seller of refreshments, esp. at public sales. **1986** *DARE* File **nOH** (as of c1920), Huckster, a peddler of fruits and vegetables with horse and light wagon going from house to house in the city.

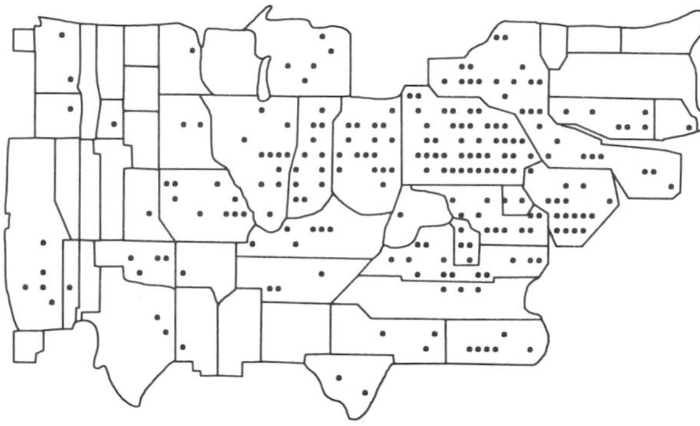

•huckster + varr (Qq. U6, U5, U7)

huck towel n [See quot 1899]

A towel made of cotton, linen, or a cotton-linen blend; also *huck toweling* the fabric used to make such towels.

1889 *Century Dict.* 2908/3, *Huck*. . . A commercial contraction of *huckaback:* as *huck* towels or toweling. [*Ibid, Huckaback*. . . A coarse and . . durable cloth of linen, or linen and cotton, woven . . to have a rough face.] **1915** Sears *Catalogue* 38, *Linen Filled Huck Towels*. . . For those who desire something more durable and more absorbent than cotton huck towels, and still do not feel like paying the price necessary for all linen towels. *Ibid, Embroidery Huck Toweling*. . . "Flower of the Flax" Quality Irish Fancy Huck Toweling . . for guest towels, bureau or sideboard scarfs. *Ibid,* Huck towelings are much in demand for embroidery purposes. **1939** *LANE* Map 142, 1 inf, **neCT,** Huck towel. **1954** (1955) Grau *Black Prince* 164 **LA,** Colored cooks work with huck towels tied around their necks. **1965–70** *DARE* (Qu. G17, *Other kinds of towels*) 40 Infs, **scattered, but less freq S and Mid Atl, West,** Huck towel. **1986** *DARE* File **wMA,** The huck towels I make [on a hand loom] . . will be all linen; used for guest towels or dish towels.

huck wagon n [*huck* abbr for **huckster**]

The vehicle used by a door-to-door peddler.

[**1845** in 1927 *IN Mag. Hist.* 23.180 **seIN,** I have myself seen as many as fourteen huckster wagons at one camp meeting.] **1969** *DARE* (QR, near Qu. U6) Inf **MO**37, Huck wagon.

hucky dummy n

A biscuit with raisins; see quots.

1929 in 1932 *Hench Coll.,* "Hucky dummy" [is] made of sourdough and raisins. **1968** Adams *Western Words* 156, *Huckydummy*—A cowboy's name for baking-powder biscuits with raisins.

hud n [Engl dial; cf *EDD hud* sb. 1]

A shell, pod, hull; a calyx.

1967 Cerello *Dakota Co. MN* 64, I didn't mind picking the berries, but removing the hud was too much. . . The hud of the butternut is very hard to crack. . . We used to dry milkweed huds. . . Peanut huds were always so messy. [Cerello: fairly common.]

hudder n Also *hurter, hutter* [Cf *EDD hooder* sb. 1 "A sheaf of corn placed on a 'stook' to keep off the rain"] **esp Appalachians** See Map *old-fash* Cf **cap** n[1] **1**

The sheaf (or sheaves) placed at the top of a shock of grain; see quot 1953.

1907 *German Amer. Annals* 5.379 **sePA** [PaGer], *Hudder*. (Rare.)—Cap sheaf. That shock of wheat will get wet unless it has a hudder on it. **1953** Randolph-Wilson *Down in Holler* 254 **Ozarks,** *Hudder*. . . The cap on a stack of wheat; it usually consists of two bundles put on crosswise. **1965–70** *DARE* (Qu. L31, *The top bundle of a shock*) Infs **PA**163, 191, 198, **WV**7, Hudder; **PA**13, **VA**24, 26, ['hʌdɚ]; **OH**35, Hudder—sometimes header—it's a cap; **OH**53, Hudder—used two bundles for it; **PA**135, Hutter ['hʌtɚ]; **PA**75, Hutter—two of them; one is placed facing the storm side; **SC**30, Hurter—forms a roof over the cocks; use three bundles for this. [11 of 12 Infs old] **1981** Pederson *LAGS Basic Materials,* 1 inf, **neTN,** ['hʌ˂ddɚ]—cap bundles; 1 inf, **neTN,** ['hʌddɚz]—two bundles on top to shed water; [1 inf, **neTN,** ['hʌ˂dl̩]—a cap bundle].

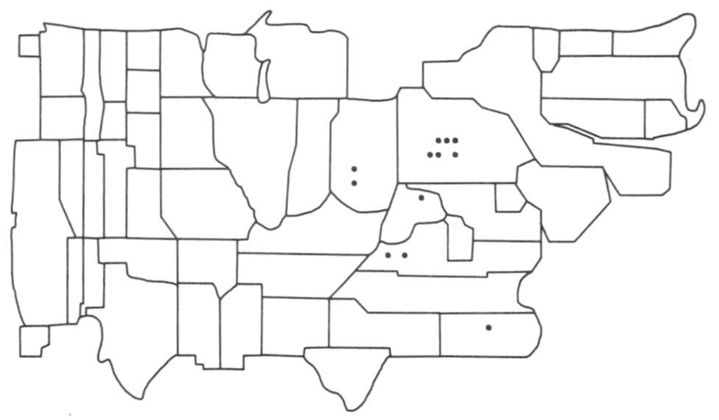

•hudder + varr (Qu. L31)

huddle n [Cf *OED huddle* v. 5 "To hug. Now *dial.*" and v. 6 "To gather or flock in a congested mass"]

1916 Macy-Hussey *Nantucket Scrap Basket* **seMA,** *Huddle*—An old-time name for a dance or ball. All the old-timers will recall "Handy's huddles."

huddle v, hence vbl n *huddling,* n *huddler*

1958 Babcock *I Don't Want* 24 **SC,** I own a "huddler." This was a species of dog, . . who would circle or huddle a covey and put it up in a compact and unmissable clump. *Ibid* 25, I will guarantee that habitual "huddling" will cause more ulcers than anything else that can happen in the field.

huddlement See **-ment** suff

huddler, huddling See **huddle** v

huddup See **hurrup**

huddy v [Per var of *howdy*]

1897 (1952) McGill *Narrative* 31 **ceSC** (as of 1830s), When all are ready along the line [t]he game begins by offering to shake hands or "huddy" across the line, by which banter the stronger expected to pull the weaker over to his side.

hudge v, hence vbl n *hudging* [Var of *EDD hodge* v. 2 "To advance the hand unfairly when discharging a marble"] Cf **fudge** v, **hunch** v **2a**

In marble play: to move the hand ahead of the legal shooting line.

1963 *KY Folkl. Rec.* 9.3.65 **ceKY,** *Attempt to get a more forceful shot by pushing the shooting hand forward when shooting:* . . hudge. **1967** *DARE* FW Addit **nIL,** *Hudging*—moving up closer to the marbles than the drawn line allows.

Hudson Bay tea n Cf **Alaska tea**

A **Labrador tea** (here: *Ledum palustre*).

1962 Salisbury *Quoth the Raven* 48 **AK** (as of c1920), The men pointed out a little plant which they said is called "Hudson Bay tea" and which is used by the natives as we use tea, when they are in the woods, but that was all the good it did. **1972** Viereck-Little *AK Trees* 206, *Ledum decumbens* . . Hudson-Bay-tea. . . Evergreen shrub 1–2 ft . . tall. . . A common shrub in arctic and alpine tundra in sedge tussocks and wet depressions.

Hudsonian curlew n Also *Hudson curlew*

Std: a **curlew 1** (here: *Numenius hudsonicus*). Also called **es-**

kimo curlew, foolish curlew, horsefoot marlin 1, jack, jack curlew, marlin, sicklebill

Hudsonian godwit n

Std: a godwit (here: *Limosa haemastica*). Also called **brantbird 3, curlew 1, doughbird 2, field marlin, goose bird 1, humility 1, ring-tailed marlin, spotrump, straight-billed curlew, whiterump**

huero n |'wero| Also *guero* [MexSpan]

A person with fair skin or light-colored hair.

[**1847** (1973) Ruxton *Advent. Rocky Mts.* 43, In Mexico, people with fair hair and complexions are called guëro, guëra; and, from the caprice of human nature, the guëro is always a favourite of the fair sex.] **1929** Dobie *Vaquero* 50 **swTX,** In person he was a *huero,* or red-complexioned man. **1932** Bentley *Spanish Terms* 147, *Huero* English modification *guero* (. . *English,* gwér o: and wér o:) A person of fair or "sandy" complexion and light or red hair. Americans referring to Mexicans of this type . . call them . . *guero* or *huero.* . . an American seldom refers to a fellow American as a *huero.* A Mexican . . referring to an American blond designates him as *un huero.*

huf(f) n See **hoof**

huff v See **heave v A2**

huff-and-puff n

1968 *DARE* (Qu. N37, *Joking names for a branch railroad*) Inf **CA**36, Huff-and-puff.

huffjuff n Also *huffle juffle* [Perh *huff* to swell (cf *EDD huff* v.[1] 2 "To swell, puff up; to rise in baking" and sb.[3] 10 "Light pastry or pie-crust") + *juff* redup; but also cf *SND juff* "To puff"] Cf **Baptist cake**

A piece of raised bread dough fried in deep fat; see quot 1939.

1939 Wolcott *Yankee Cook Book* 138 **eME,** Form bread dough . . into balls the size of large marbles. . . Slip . . balls into a kettle of fat . . and fry until a golden brown. . . On the Maine Coast they are called Huffjuffs. **1941** *LANE* Map 284 1 inf, **seCT,** Pieces of raised bread dough fried in deep fat. . . Huffle juffles [hʌfl dʒʌflz]. **1952** Tracy *Coast Cookery* 102 **ME,** *Baptist Bread*—Bread fried in deep fat (immersed). In Connecticut it is known as Holy Pokes, in Maine as Huffjuffs.

huffy adj Cf **huffjuff**

Puffy; see quot 1934.

1927 *AmSp* 3.140 **coastal ME,** A "huffy cake" is one which rises much in baking. **1934** (1943) *W2, Huffy.* . . Puffy; . . airy; as *huffy* bread. *Obs.*

huffy n [Cf *huffy* adj, *huff* n]

A huff; a fit of anger or annoyance.

1895 *DN* 1.397, *Huffy.* . . As a noun. "He was all in a huffy." **1901** *DN* 2.142 **c, neAR, IL, NY, TN,** *Huffy,* n.

hug v

1 To shinny up; hence vbl n *hugging;* also *hug-climbing.* **chiefly S Midl** Cf **bear-hug**

1967–69 *DARE* (Qu. EE36, *To climb the trunk of a tree by holding on with your legs while you pull yourself up with your hands*) Infs **DE**3, **KY**40, 75, 85, **NY**200, **TN**55, **VA**42, Hugging; **MO**37, Hug a tree; **LA**8, Hug-climbing.

2 with *around:* See quot.

1937 *Hall Coll.* **wNC, eTN,** To grasp; to cling to by clutching. . . "The bear hugged around a big pine tree."

hug n

1 pl: Clutches; see quot.

1937 *Hall Coll.* **wNC, eTN,** I tried to tote the (dead) bear. I was in its hugs.

2 See quot.

1944 *PADS* 2.44 **NC, cTN, SC, VA,** *Hug.* . . The enclosure made by the arms or the legs or both. "The dog was so scared he set back in my hug and whined."

3 See quot. [Cf *EDD hug* v. 4 "To kiss"]

1968 *DARE* (Qu. AA9, . . *A loud or vigorous kiss*) Inf **MO**9, Hug.

hugag See **hewgag**

hug around See **hug v 2**

hug-climbing See **hug v 1**

huge adj Usu |hjuǰ|; also **esp NYC, Long Island** |juǰ| See Pronc Intro 3.I.19 Cf **humor**

Std sense, var forms.

1942 *AmSp* 17.156 **NYC, Long Island,** Omission of initial [h] before [ju]. . . huge . . 194 [infs] [hj], 23 [infs] [j]. . . This is a somewhat greater loss of [h] than in upstate speech. **1944** *ADD* 308 **cNY** (as of 1920s), [hjudʒ]. **1944** Kenyon–Knott *Pronc. Dict.* 209, *Huge* [hjudʒ, hɪudʒ, judʒ]. **1987** *DARE* File **ceNY,** [Speaking of a football player:] His arms and legs were [juǰ].

hugging See **hug v 1**

hugging old Susan vbl n

1938 FWP *Guide DE* 384 **csDE,** Nevertheless, prisoners sentenced to be whipped frequently dread the public whipping—called "hugging old Susan"—more than the jail sentence.

huggle-de-buck v [Cf **huck** v + *-le* frequentative] Cf **huckel-de-buck**

1968 *DARE* (Qu. A19, . . *Ways of saying "I'll have to hurry": "I'm late, I'll have to ———.")* Inf **TX**54, Huggle-de-buck ['hʌgəl dɨ 'bʌk].

Hughie n [Cf *OEDS Hughie "Austral.* and *N.Z. slang.* . . The 'god' of weather"]

1958 McCulloch *Woods Words* 90 **Pacific NW,** *Hughie*—A name for God. A gnarled old logger away back in the Cascades mountain country said: "It's a good timber country all right enough, but it's so all-fired rough I wisht Hughie had run His harrows over it afore He was finished a-makin' it."

hug-me-close See **hug-me-tight 3**

hug-me-tight n

1 also *hug-me-tight buggy:* A one-horse, two-wheeled vehicle with a seat barely wide enough for two people; see quot c1960. **chiefly Sth, S Midl** *old-fash*

1901 Harben *Westerfelt* 6 **nGA,** Westerfelt certainly is settin' square up to Ab's daughter. I seed 'em takin' a ride in his new hug-me-tight buggy yesterday. **1932** Stribling *Store* 9 **AL,** Take, for example, his own action in rebuking the youth in the little hug-me-tight buggy. **1935** *Hench Coll.* **KY,** In phrase *to ride on the hug-me-tight* = to ride in a buggy at a terrific rate of speed. **1946** *Esquire* Sept 57/1 **eKY,** We didn't have automobiles in our county, nice spring wagons and hug-me-tight buggies. *Ibid,* I watched the buggies, hug-me-tights and the fancy express wagons. **1948** *Jrl. Amer. Folkl.* 61.212 **OH** (as of c1880), Those roads were so bad . . that they kept making the buggies narrower and narrower. . . Some of them got so narrow they used to call them 'Hug-Me-Tights.' **c1960** *Wilson Coll.* **csKY,** *Hug-me-tight.* . . A very narrow-seated buggy. . . "Big enough for just one, but two sat in it." **1966–67** *DARE* FW Addit **SC,** *Hug-me-tight* (a gig), a one-horsed two-wheeled buggy, refers to the whole conveyance, not just the seat. *Ibid, Hug-me-tight*—a buggy with a narrow seat—old-fashioned. **1970** *DARE* (Qu. N41a, . . *Kinds of horse-drawn vehicles*) Inf **VA**51, Hug-me-tight—a small, narrow, one-seated buggy.

2 Transf: see quot.

1950 *WELS (A piece of upholstered furniture that seats two people)* 1 Inf, **cwWI,** Hug-me-tight.

3 also *hug-me-close:* The wishbone or furcula of a fowl; see quots. [Cf *EDD hug-me-close* (at *hug* v. 1) "The merry-thought or clavicle of a fowl"; *SND hug-me-close* "The sidebone of a fowl, regarded as a luck bringer"]

1899 (1912) Green *VA Folk-Speech* 234 **VA,** *Hug-me-close.* . . A fowl's merry-thought; wish bone, or clavicle. **1950** *PADS* 14.39 **SC,** *Hug-me-tight.* . . The scapula of a chicken or turkey and the portion of the meat thereon. Sometimes applied to the wishbone.

hug-me-tight buggy See **hug-me-tight 1**

hugs of hell See **hobs of hell**

huh pron See **her**

huh v [Cf *SND hooch* II. v. 2 "To breathe forcibly upon an object . . before polishing it"; or perh *SND hauch* II. n. 2 "The breathing strongly on a surface to moisten it before polishing. . . Onomat. in origin"] Cf **hoo v**

1947 *AmSp* 22.238 **neOH,** Little Martha describes the act of holding eye-glasses between parted lips while blowing moist breath on them before wiping them clean, by the simple expression, "Huh-ing your glasses."

huh-ee exclam Also *huh-ay, huh-wee* Cf **hurry v 1**

Used as a call to drive animals.

1954 *Harder Coll.* **cwTN,** [hʌ-ɪ]—word used to drive cattle. **1968** *DARE* (Qu. NN22d, *Expressions . . to drive away animals*) Inf **SC**32, Huh-ee ['hʌ-ɪ]; **VA**11, Huh-ay ['hʌ-eɪ]; **KY**84, Huh-wee ['hʌwi].

huh-guh See **hull-gull**

huh not interrog exclam [Prob *huh?* interrog exclam + **not**?] Cf **ainna**

Isn't that so?—used as a tag question.

1965 *DARE* File **swPA,** *Huh not?* ['hʌ nat]. From McKees Rocks, Pennsylvania, in a lower-class slum area, with a mixed population of Polish, Hungarian, Slovak, and some German. It is used at the end of a question, as in "______, right?" or "Isn't that so?"

huhu n See **huhu owl**

huhu adj, v Also *hou-hou* [Haw] **HI**

Angry; to become angry.

1873 in 1966 Bishop *Sandwich Is.* 71 **HI,** *Hou-hou,* meaning "in a huff," I hear on all sides. **1951** *AmSp* 26.21 **HI,** Common localisms in Hawaii, used for convenience or more colorful expression [include] *huhu,* (angry). **1967** Reinecke-Tsuzaki *Hawaiian Loanwords* 96 **HI,** /huhū/. . . 1. To become angry; to be angry with; to scold. 2. Angry; "wild." . . V[ery] F[requently used]. **1967** *DARE* (Qu. K16, *A cow with a bad temper*) Inf **HI**2, Huhu; (Qu. GG4, *Stirred up, angry: " . . he got ______.*") Infs **HI**1, 4, Huhu. **1969** *DARE* FW Addit **HI,** Huhu, ['huhu]. Mad, angry. **1972** Carr *Da Kine Talk* 112 **HI,** Others [=hybrid compounds] have an English word first, followed by a foreign term. . . Several are full predications in the request form: . . *No huhū* 'Don't be angry.' *Ibid* 115, *No huhū!* (English + Hawaiian). . . "No Huhu" is the name of a popular song. . . This phrase has . . appeared on road repair signs . . as an informal Hawaiian way of saying "Pardon the inconvenience." **1981** *Pidgin To Da Max* **HI,** *Huhu.* . . To be upset. Haole: "Relax. Don't get upset." Pidgin: "No huhu, brah." **1984** Sunset *HI Guide* 85, *Huhu*—angry.

huhu owl n Also *huhu* [See quot 1949]

A **hoot owl n 1.**

1949 Turner *Africanisms* 194 **SC, GA coasts** [Gullah], ['Hu'hu] 'owl'—V[ai]. **1951** *AmSp* 26.15 **seSC** [Gullah], *Huhu owl,* 'hoot owl, large owl,' is found occasionally in the South Carolina coastal plain.

huh-wee See **huh-ee**

hui n [Haw] **HI**

A club or association.

[**1898** M.H. Krout *Hawaii* 18 *(OEDS),* Those present, with forty members of a royalist society called *Hui Kalaiaina,* marched to the palace.] **1954** *Ellery Queen's Mystery Mag.* 4.37 **HI,** My father's a good mechanic but he doesn't like living in the city. And now our fishing *hui's* beginning to pay, so he can go home. **1967** Reinecke-Tsuzaki *Hawaiian Loanwords* 97 **HI,** *Hui.* . . 1. Usually, an association for a common purpose, such as planting, fishing, and the administration of land. The Hawaiian land *huis* are legal entities, cotenancies. . . resulting from the purchase by groups of individuals of tracts of land from the government. . . 2. Any sort of association or club. . . V[ery] F[requently used]. **1967** *DARE* (Qq. FF22a, b, *Names of clubs and societies . . for women . . for men*) Inf **HI**1, Hui. A group banded together for a commercial venture, usually a condominium. . . Or [it] may oppose [something]. [It's] beginning to have unfavorable connotations. [It's] not necessarily secret. **1969** *DARE* FW Addit **HI,** *Hui* ['hui]. A society, organization. The name of the library club at the University of Hawaii is *Hui Dui*—see you later in life. Dewey liked to spell his name phonetically. **1972** Carr *Da Kine Talk* 87 **HI,** *Hawaiian Words Commonly Heard in Hawaii's English. . . Hui.* Club, association, corporation. *Ibid* 100, *Hui* . . means a group formed for a purpose, sometimes a syndicate. . . The word is useful and popular in the Islands. During World War II, driving *huis* were formed because of gasoline rationing. . . All kinds of temporary *huis* have been formed for the mutual interests of the participants. **1984** Sunset *HI Guide* 85, *Hui*—club, association.

hui v, intj [Perh Haw *hui* to meet; cf *OED, OEDS cooee*] **HI**

Come here! Hallo!—used to call a person or animal

1967 *DARE* (Qu. II15, *When somebody is passing by and you want . . to . . talk a while, you might say "______."*) Inf **HI**4, Hui ['hu:i]—shout to someone at a distance to attract attention. [**1971** Pukui-Elbert *Hawaiian Dict.* 363, *Hūi.* Halloo. *Modern.*] **1986** *DARE* File **HI,** Everyone calls out "hui" [hui] when they want someone to come to them—people or animals. You hear it all the time; it's Pidgin English.

huisache n Also *guisache, hinsach* [MexSpan] **chiefly TX** Cf **huisachillo**

An acacia: usu *Acacia farnesiana,* but also *A. constricta.* For other names of *A. farnesiana* see **honeyball 2, mesquite, opopanax, popinac, sponge tree, sweet acacia**

1838 Texian *Mexico vs. Texas* 231 *(DA),* The rose-geranium shook its elegant perfume, and the yellow-bloomed *guisache* embalmed the air with odours equal to those of the blossoms of the grapevine. **1892** *DN* 1.190 **TX,** *Huisáche* . . a small tree or shrub with very sweet smelling yellow flowers (*Acacia Farnesiana,* Willd.) From Mexican *huaxin.* **1898** Canfield *Maid of Frontier* 204 *(DAE),* The huisache bore yellow blossoms faintly sweet. **1936** Whitehouse *TX Flowers* 44, *Huisache* (Pronounced *wee satch*). Usually trees or shrubs. . . In southern Texas it is highly valued as a honey crop. **1949** *Boston Daily Globe* (MA) 1 May (fiction mag) 3/2 **swTX,** He discovered another rider sitting his horse in a clump of huisache north of the trail. **1960** Vines *Trees SW* 494, *Acacia constricta.* . . Vernacular names are . . Huisache [etc]. *Ibid* 497, *Acacia farnesiana.* . . Vernacular names in the United States . . are Acacia-catclaw, . . Hinsach, . . Huisache, . . Guisache [etc]. **1967** *DARE* (Qu. T5, *What kinds of evergreens, other than pine, do you have around here?*) Infs **TX**22, 29, Huisache; (Qu. T16, *What kinds of trees are 'special' around here?*) Infs **TX**18, 26, 29, 31, Huisache. **1979** Little *Checklist U.S. Trees* 37, *Acacia farnesiana.* . . Huisache.

huisache daisy n [See quot 1936]

A composite plant *(Amblyolepis setigera)* with yellow flower heads, native to Texas. Also called **honey daisy**

1936 Whitehouse *TX Flowers* 182, Huisache Daisy *(Amblyolepis setigera)* is so called because it often forms a carpet of gold under huisache (pronounced *wee satch*), mesquite, or other chaparral bushes in Southwest-central Texas from March to June. **1970** Correll *Plants TX* 1674, *Huisache-daisy.* Slenderly taprooted annual with a pleasant odor like new-mown (*Medicago* or *Melilotus*) hay.

huisachillo n [Dim of **huisache**] Cf **huajillo 2**

An acacia (here: *Acacia tortuosa*). Also called **cat's-claw**

1960 Vines *Trees SW* 495, *Acacia schaffneri* (S. Wats.) Hermann. . . Also known under the vernacular names of . . Huisachillo. Schaffner Acacia resembles Sweet Acacia, *A. farnesiana,* somewhat, but the legume of the former is much narrower and elongate. **1970** Correll *Plants TX* 771, *Acacia tortuosa. . . Huisachillo.* Usually low rounded shrubs . . , leaves very similar to those of huisache. **1979** Little *Checklist U.S. Trees* 38, *Acacia tortuosa. . . Huisachillo. . . Other common names*—catclaw, twisted acacia, Rio Grande acacia.

hukilau n [Haw] **HI**

1 A fish drive using a net; see quots.

1954 *Ellery Queen's Mystery Mag.* 4.44 **HI,** "We're about ready for the *hukilau.* Come along to the water." He led us seaward, explaining to Bill that *huki* means pull and *lau* means leaf, from the *ti* leaves which are used to frighten fish into the nets. **1967** Reinecke-Tsuzaki *Hawaiian Loanwords* 97 **HI,** *Hukilau.* . . A number of persons drive the fish into a net by enclosing them with ropes hung with leaves, usually of the *ti (cordyline terminalis)* plant, this apparatus being the *lau.* Sometimes loosely used for any type of large fish drive with nets. V[ery] F[requently used]. **1972** *New Yorker* 8 Apr 84/1 **HI,** [Advertisement:] Come to a hukilau. That's a sort of Polynesian fish-in.

2 See quot.

1972 Carr *Da Kine Talk* 87 **HI,** *Hawaiian Words Commonly Heard in Hawaii's English . . Hukilau.* A seine.

hukilau v [Haw] **HI**

To drive fish into a net.

1967 *DARE* (Qu. P13, . . *Ways of fishing . . besides the ordinary hook and line*) Inf **HI**2, Hukilau—'Pull in leaves'. A circular net is paid out from boats; it has floats at the upper edge, sinkers at the lower. It is drawn around a school of fish and pulled toward the shore. Leaves fastened to the upper edge frighten the fish. They swim in and don't try to jump over. It's a community project and all share in the catch. **1967** *DARE* Tape **HI**9, Hukilau—[At the] end of the rope they have a net. . . They surround that certain place, then . . drag the net. . . Some [nets] have . . floaters, . . some . . lay . . on the botton. . . They drag the net in. . . *lau* is leaf. . . The leaves . . are on top . . of the rope. . . When they pull, the fish are . . not [going] to jump over the rope. . . They will go to the net. . . A pocket [is] on the . . bottom of the net. . . On the shore they have about forty, fifty guys, they pull that rope up. . . About six or seven guys . . are swimming around the net and watching how the fish going. **1972** Carr *Da Kine Talk* 87 **HI,** *Hawaiian Words Commonly Heard in Hawaii's English . . Hukilau.* To fish with the seine. **1984** Sunset *HI Guide* 85, *Hukilau*—to fish with a seine.

hukkery n
1930 Shoemaker *1300 Words* 31 **cPA Mts** (as of c1900), *Hukkery*—Cheating, especially in love.

hula blues n Cf **hullabaloo 2**
1954 Piper–Piper *175 Folk Dances* 23 **TX,** *Hula Blues,* Circle of c[ou]ples, each c[ou]ple facing another c[ou]ple. . . [Circles go in opposite directions in] grapevine [movement].

hula palm n [See quot 1929] **HI**
=**fan palm.**
1929 Neal *Honolulu Gardens* 42, *Washingtonia filifera*. . . A large, stately palm . . has a smooth trunk, much of which is covered with a mass of dead leaves, the accumulation of years. In Honolulu they have given rise to the name "hulapalm." *Ibid* 43, *Hula palm . . (Washingtonia robusta . .)* **1965** Neal *Gardens HI* 99, Only two species of *Washingtonia* are known. Both are cultivated in Hawaii, where they are commonly called hula palms or California fan palms.

huldy n
A chicken.
1911 *DN* 3.538 **eKY,** *Huldy,* . . Chicken; Negro term.

hul-gul See **hull-gull**

huli v [Haw] **HI**
To turn or flip over; hence n *hulihuli chicken* chicken cooked by turning on a spit.
1967 Reinecke–Tsuzaki *Hawaiian Loanwords* 97, *Huli*. . . To face about; to turn about; to turn upside down. *Ibid, Hulihuli*. . . To turn over frequently. **1972** Carr *Da Kine Talk* 87 **HI,** *Hawaiian Words Commonly Heard in Hawaii's English*. . . *Huli.* To turn; to change, as an opinion or manner of living. *Ibid* 114, *Hulihuli chicken* (Hawaiian + English). Chicken roasted on a spit or rotisserie and hence, turned. *Hulihuli* is the reduplicated form of *huli* 'to turn'. Organizations often earn money by making and selling hulihuli chicken. **1981** *Pidgin To Da Max* **HI,** *Huli*. . . To turn over; to flip. "Wow, da cah was goeen so fas', da buggah wen huli!" **1986** *DARE* File **HI,** *Hulihuli chicken* is a kind of barbecued chicken, cooked on a spit. It has a smoky flavor from the wood. You wouldn't make hulihuli chicken at home. In Hawaii, it's very common for organizations to raise money by making and selling hulihuli chicken. You don't eat it there; you go buy it and bring it home. Lately, though, there are commercial places selling hulihuli chicken. To make hulihuli chicken, you would make a marinade of soy sauce, sugar and ginger, and use it to baste a half-fryer [=chicken]. Then, continue to baste the chicken while it cooks on the spit.

hull n Usu |hʌl|; also occas |hɔl|; for addit varr see quots
A Forms.
1941 *LANE* Map 275, [**throughout NEng,** [hʌl]; 6 infs, **scattered,** [hɐl]; 5 infs, **eCT, RI,** [hɤl]; 3 infs, **wNEng,** [hɔɫ]; 1 inf, **ceMA,** [hɑl].] **1965** Carmony *Speech Terre Haute* 59 **cwIN,** Before /l/, [ʌ] . . may . . be replaced by /ɔ/, as in hull [hɔ·ɫ]; so that *hall* and *hull* . . are homonymous in some speech. **1967** *DARE* (Qu. P38) Inf **TN**11, [hɜl].
B Senses.

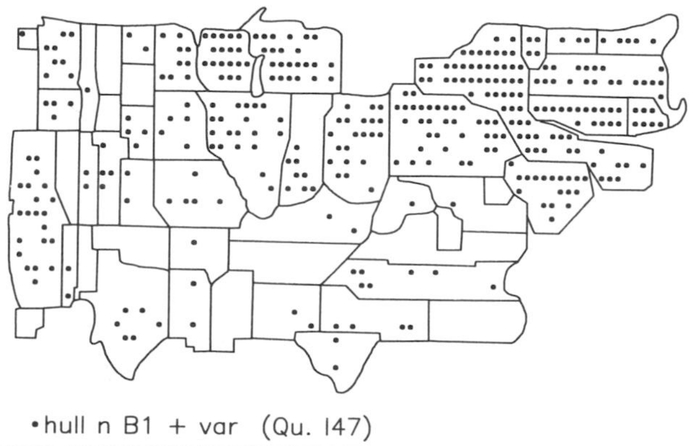
•hull n B1 + var (Qu. 147)

1 The green leaves at the top of a fruit, usu a strawberry. **chiefly Nth, N Midl, Pacific** See Map Cf **cap** n[1] **5**
1889 [see **hull** v 2]. **1907** *DN* 3.223 **nwAR, sIL,** *Hull*. . . Pod or calyx, when persistent on fruit. **1941** *LANE* Map 275 **NEng,** *Hull*. . . The top of a strawberry which must be removed . . consisting of the small green stalk and the calyx of small green leaves. . . Some . . use terms referring separately to the stalk (stem) and to the calyx (hull, cap). [*DARE* Ed: *Hull* predominates throughout New England.] **1950** *WELS* 37 Infs, **WI,** Hull. **1951** Johnson *Resp. to PADS 20* **DE,** *(The green top that pulls off with the stem of a ripe strawberry)* Hull. **1965–70** *DARE* (Qu. I47, . . *The green part that comes off with the stem [of a strawberry]*) 359 Infs, **chiefly Nth, N Midl, Pacific,** Hull.

2 An outer covering, as:
a A removable covering of something edible, spec:
(1) The fleshy outer layer surrounding a nut, esp a walnut or hickory nut. **widespread, but less freq Nth, Rocky Mts** See Map and Map Section Cf **husk** n **B2**
1899 (1912) Green *VA Folk-Speech* 235, *Hull*. . . An outer covering, particularly of a nut or grain. Walnut-hulls. Pea-hulls. **1905** *DN* 3.83 **nwAR,** *Hull*. . . Shell. 'Hulls on nuts are thicker than usual this year.' Universal. **1923** *DN* 5.211 **swMO,** *Hull*. . . The shell or outer husk of a nut. **1948** Davis *Word Atlas Gt. Lakes* 145, Hull—green outer cover of a walnut or hickory nut [is common in central and southern Illinois, Indiana and Ohio.] **1954** *Harder Coll.* **cwTN,** *Hull.* **c1960** *Wilson Coll.* **csKY,** *Hull.* **1960** Criswell *Resp. to PADS 20* **Ozarks,** *Hull,* for the first outside covering. *Shell,* for the inside hard woody covering [of a walnut]. **1965–70** *DARE* (Qu. I39, . . *The thick outside covering of a walnut*) 503 Infs, **widespread, but less freq Nth, Rocky Mts,** Hull; **MO**11, **OK**1, Outer hull; **LA**6, **MO**19, Outside hull; **OK**1, Green hull; (Qu. P13, . . *Ways of fishing*) Inf **GA**89, Poison fish with green walnut hulls. **1966** Dakin *Dial. Vocab. Ohio R. Valley* 2.363, The use of *shell* = ["]hard inner cover" in contrast to *hull* = "soft outer cover" . . is clearly a later and not yet complete development, but the distribution at present suggests that another generation may see the *hull/shell* distinction completely established. *Ibid* 364, The soft, green outer covering of a walnut is regularly called the *hull* by virtually every speaker in the Ohio Valley. Among those who also say *hull* for the hard inner covering of the kernel it [=the soft outer covering] is sometimes called *soft hull, green ~,* or *outside ~.* **1971** Wood *Vocab. Change* 42 **Sth,** *Hull* is the preferred name for the green outer cover of a walnut. *Ibid* 309, 725 [total occurrences]. **1973** Allen *LAUM* 1.307 (as of c1950), *Hull* (the green outer covering of a walnut or hickory nut). *Hull . .* appears . . as the majority term in the U[pper] M[idwest], where its primary concentration in southern Iowa and Nebraska is that of Midland features. **1986** *DARE* File **sIN,** (as of 1920), Walnuts have hulls. The outside green covering is a hull. The inside black covering is the shell.

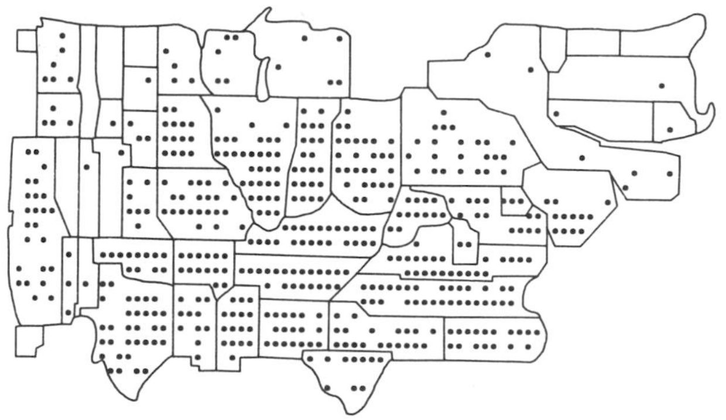
•hull n B2a(1) + varr (Qq. I39, P13)

(2) The hard inner shell of a nut, esp a walnut or hickory nut. **chiefly Sth, S Midl** See Map
1954 *Harder Coll.* **cwTN,** *Hull*. . . Inner . . cover of a walnut. **c1960** *Wilson Coll.* **csKY,** *Hull*. . . The hard covering of a walnut or hickory nut. **1965–70** *DARE* (Qu. I40, *The hard part inside the husk . . of a walnut that you have to break*) 73 Infs, **chiefly Sth, S Midl,** Hull; **GA**9, **TX**26, Inner hull; **MS**63, Hard hull; **NC**50, Inside hull. **1966** Dakin *Dial. Vocab. Ohio R. Valley* 2.363, The hard inner cover surrounding the kernel of a walnut is regularly called the *shell* by the relatively younger speakers everywhere north of the Ohio and throughout most of Ken-

tucky. Many of the oldest generation above the river and in north-central Kentucky say *hull* (sometimes *hard hull* or *inside hull*) and this term is common to speakers of all ages in the Mountains and the Purchase. **1971** Wood *Vocab. Change* 42 **Sth,** The hard inner cover of a walnut is a *shell* in over one-third of the choices. In descending order are *hull, husk,* and *shuck. Ibid* 308, 368 [total occurrences]. **1973** Allen *LAUM* 1.307 (as of c1950), *Hull* is a widespread minor equivalent [of *shell*], especially in Nebraska.

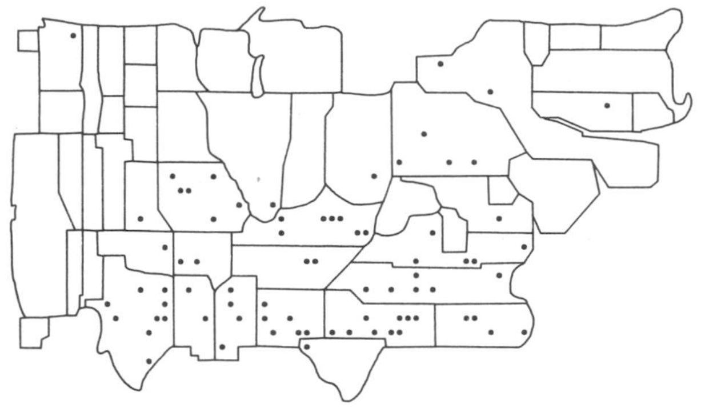

•hull n B2a(2) + varr (Qu. I40)

(3) The pod of a bean or pea; the shell of a peanut. **chiefly Sth, Midl** See Map

1859 (1968) Bartlett *Americanisms* 207, *Hulls.* The husks of peas, etc. **1923** *DN* 5.211 **swMO,** *Hull. . .* The pod of a bean or pea. **1951** Johnson *Resp. to PADS 20* **DE,** *Hulls*—after peas are shelled out. *Hulls*—outside covering of dry beans. **1954** *Harder Coll.* **cwTN,** *Hull. . .* The covering of peas, beans. **1965–70** *DARE* (Qu. I12, *The outside covering of dry beans*) 328 Infs, **chiefly Sth, Midl,** Hull; **NC**81, When green, it's a hull; (Qu. I10, . . *Green peas*) 281 Infs, **chiefly Sth, Midl,** Hull; **AR**51, Pea hull; (Qu. I20) Infs **AR**55, **FL**18, **GA**17, **LA**3, 15, 32, **TX**33, 105, Purple hull beans (*or* peas); **AL**15, **NC**81, Iron (*or* knuckle) hull peas; **GA**9, Purple hull crowder peas; **KY**40, Coffee bean—a brown bean with a red hull; **TX**51, 102, Purple hulls; **TX**62, Blue hull beans; (Qu. I13, *When you take dry beans out of the cover you are*) Inf **LA**33, Taking the hull off; (Qu. I15) Infs, **KY**8, 40, 69, **TN**20, Golden (*or* white, yellow) hull beans; **KY**44, **NC**55, 68, Yellow hulls; (Qu. I17) Inf **GA**6, Red hull peas; (Qu. I19) Infs **AR**17, **MS**1, Purple hull peas; (Qu. BB51a, . . *Cures for corns or warts*) Inf **VA**74, Butterbean hull juice; (Qu. II3, . . *People are very friendly toward each other: "They're ______."*) Infs **SC**10, 26, Like two peas in a hull; **SC**11, Thick as peas in a hull; (Qu. JJ15a, . . *A person who seems . . very stupid: "He hasn't sense enough to ______."*) Inf **AL**25, Fill a peanut hull; (Qu. KK65, . . *'The same sort': "If you like Bob, . . you'll like his brother—they're ______."*) Inf **GA**77, Two peas in the same hull. **1982** *Barrick Coll.* **csPA,** *Hull . . shell,* esp. peas or beans. **1986** *DARE* File **sIN** (as of 1920), Lima beans and green beans have hulls.

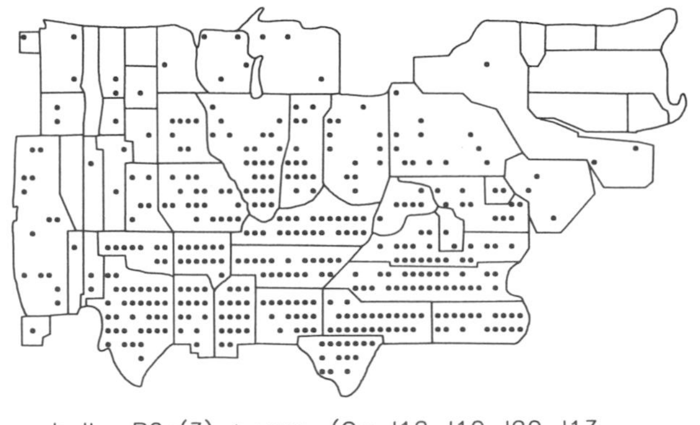

•hull n B2a(3) + varr (Qq. I12, I10, I20, I13, I15, I17, I19, BB51a, II3, JJ15a, KK65)

(4) The hard outer layer of a kernel of corn, esp of a variety such as **flint corn.** Cf **hulled corn**

1877 Bartlett *Americanisms* 302, *Hulled Corn.* Indian corn scalded or boiled in lye, until the hulls come off. **1939** Wolcott *Yankee Cook Book* 106 **NEng,** *Hulled Corn—New Method*—Pick over 1 quart dried yellow corn. Cover with . . water . . [and] soda. . . Boil . . until the hulls are loosened. . . rub off the hulls between hands. **1967** *DARE* Tape **MA**117, Hull corn was processed. . . You take the hull kernel and you cook it in . . water with . . wood ashes . . until the hull'd come off. **1977** *Yankee* Nov 254 **NEng,** *Hulled Corn. . .* Broad, hard, and plump kernels were chosen as they yielded the largest pieces of corn when the hulls were removed.

(5) The outer layer or cuticle of grain, used for livestock feed; hence *hull house* a building for storing feed.

1940 Faulkner *Hamlet* 208 **MS,** He has eaten feed before—hulls and meal, and oats and raw corn and silage and pig-swill. **1966** *DARE* (Qu. M12, *What do you keep food for the cattle in over the winter?*) Inf **AR**15, Hull house. **1976** Brown *Gloss. Faulkner* 107, *Hulls and meal . . : Cottonseed-hulls . .* regularly used as cattle-feed.

(6) The skin of some fruits; see quots.

1954 *Harder Coll.* **cwTN,** *Hull. . .* Outer cover of a tomato, as in *tomato hull.* **1986** *DARE* File **sIN** (as of 1920), Grapes have hulls. "I spit out the hulls when I eat grapes." (This applies to Concord grapes, not the green seedless kind in the markets today—which were not available in southern Indiana in the early 1900's.) . . Tomatoes do not have hulls.

(7) The shell of an egg. **chiefly S Atl, esp GA**

1965 *McDavid Coll.* **SC,** Hull = eggshell. **1966–68** *DARE* (Qu. H34, . . *Parts of an egg*) Infs **AR**55, **FL**36, **GA**8, 10, 19, 46, Hull; (Qu. BB50c, *Remedies for infections*) Inf **GA**17, The skim [sic] inside the hull of an egg and okra blossoms. **1968–69** *DARE* Tape **GA**30, If there's a lot of sand in this nest, when they start hatchin', them eggs don't crack out good. But when they [=alligators] start gruntin' and comin' out a' them hulls, if they's too long at it that old mother alligator will crawl up to that nest and hunt him out and take him right down in the water and hold him light in her mouth and just wash him and rench [=rinse] him in the water back and to, til he comes out o' the hull. **1972** *McDavid Coll.* **GA,** Hull = eggshell *(Black speaker).*

b The protective covering or frame of an animal, as:

(1) See quots. **Sth, S Midl**

1859 (1968) Bartlett *Americanisms* 207, *Hulls. . .* At the South, applied . . to the shells of oysters. **1923** *DN* 5.211 **swMO,** *Hull. . .* The shell of a turtle. **1966–69** *DARE* Tape **GA**48, That turtle now, he has a . . rolled together body. . . We call it hull. That's his . . home. [He] carries with him [for] protection; **GA**51, They're soft-shell turtles. . . They're a whole lot bigger than the gopher [=a tortoise] that stays on the hill . . and the edge of their hull all the way around is limber—you can bend it . . and the gopher's is as hard as a stick; **KY**13, There's two kind o' weevils. One's . . got an awful hard hull on; **LA**5, He [=the turtle] hasn't got just the complete round hull like the streaky-head's got; **SC**15, Some make out what we call hard shrimp, fix 'em up in, y' know, different stuff. . . strip his head off, and his tail off, and the hull.

(2) The hide or carcass of an animal; also fig.

1825 (1930) Sewall *Diary* 102/1 **VA,** Killed my beef which I purchased of Mr. Seaton some weeks ago. . . Rough tallow and hull—$1.00. **1966–67** *DARE* (Qu. K15, *A . . bony, or poor-looking cow*) Infs **AR**21, **TN**1, (Old) hull.

(3) Fig: of a person; see quot. Cf **husk n B7a**

1975 Thomas *Hear the Lambs* 125 **nwAL** (as of 1930s) [Black], He done it [=paid a dollar a day] for a while, but he got so he say de p'visions and house rents is took it up. Lately he been claimin' I was owin' him. Dat man's all hull.

c An ammunition shell, usu an empty one; see quots. **chiefly S Midl**

1913 Kephart *Highlanders* 101 **sAppalachians,** I went to shoot up at him, but my new hulls [Kephart: cartridges] fit loose in this old chamber. **1952** Brown *NC Folkl.* 1.553 **wNC,** *Hull. . .* A cartridge for a rifle, gun, etc. **1953** Randolph–Wilson *Down in Holler* 254 **Ozarks,** *Hull. . .* A shotgun shell, sometimes a rifle or pistol cartridge. Of a pump gun with a broken ejector, a hillman said, "This here weepon don't shuck the hulls no more." A *hull-sponger* is a hunter who mooches ammunition from his fellows. **1957** *AmSp* 32.193 **swMA, sNH,** *Hulls. . .* Empty metallic cartridge cases. Rarely used for .22 brass. **1959** Faulkner *Mansion* 429 **MS,** It didn't even look like a pistol. . . It had two shells in it, the hull and another live one. The cap of the hull was punched all right, only it and the live one both had a little nick jest outside the cap. **1960** Criswell *Resp. to PADS 20* **Ozarks,** *Hull. . .* Common word for a cartridge or for the empty shell. **1966–70**

DARE (Qu. P38, *What do you put into a rifle to shoot?*) Inf **FL4**, Hull—[FW: heard, not used]; **LA7**, Hull—after it's fired; **TN11**, Hull [hɜl]—old-fashioned; (Qu. P38b, *What do you put into a shotgun?* total Infs questioned, 75) Inf **FL4**, Hull—[FW: heard, not used]; **LA7**, Hull—after it's fired it's a hull; **MS66**, Hull. **1986** *DARE* File **ceNY,** A hull is an empty shotgun shell. *Hull* is never used for a rifle casing. I've heard *hull* used with this meaning in New England, Upstate New York, and by Wisconsin people.

d The casing or frame of a mechanical device; see quots.

1947 *McDavid Coll.* **cnGA,** (A radio) *hull* = the chassis (outside) of a receiving set. **1966-67** *DARE* (Qu. JJ10b, *Parts of an ink pen*) Infs **KY33**, Hull (—parts of a fountain pen); **MT5**, Hull.

3 A saddle. **esp West** Cf **cack** n²

1920 Hunter *Trail Drivers TX* 96 (as of c1871), The boys set up a big laugh, but I . . threw my "hull" on [the pony] and galloped around the herd. **1937** *DN* 6.618 **swTX,** Other words for saddle besides *ellum* include *hull* and *cack.* **1940** Writers' Program *Guide NV* 75, A buckaroo's paraphernalia includes the following: the saddle, which the cow-country calls . . *hull.* **1950** *PADS* 14.76 **FL,** *Hull.* . . A saddle. Cowboy speech. **1958** *AmSp* 33.270 **eWA,** *Hull.* A saddle.

hull v

1 also with *out:* To remove the shells of (beans or peas); hence vbl n *hulling.* **[hull n B2a(3)] chiefly Midl** See Map Cf **bean hulling**

1859 (1968) Bartlett *Americanisms* 207, *To Hull.* To free from the husks: accordingly, to *hull* peas, is to shell them. . . Southern. **1923** *DN* 5.211 **swMO,** *Hull.* . . To remove [the pod of a bean or pea]. **1948** Davis *Word Atlas Gt. Lakes* 147 **c,sIL, c,sIN, c,sOH,** Hull—to remove pods from beans. **1949** Kurath *Word Geog.* 29 **Midl,** *To hull beans* . . instead of *to shell beans* is a Midland expression that has lost much ground. It is still common on the lower Susquehanna and in the Ohio Valley, less so in the Alleghenies, in West Virginia, and in the Blue Ridge (as far south as North Carolina). It is rather well established in the greater part of Maryland. **1950** *WELS Suppl.* **sIN,** Hull out beans. **1954** *Harder Coll.* **cwTN,** *Hull.* . . To remove leaves or kernels from bean covers. . . Sometimes *shelling* is heard in place of *hulling.* **1965** Carmony *Speech Terre Haute* 35 **cwIN,** The operation of removing beans from their pods is called *shelling* by half of the informants . . under fifty years of age . . ; those over fifty use the Midland *hulling.* **1965-70** *DARE* (Qu. I13, *When you take dry beans out of the cover you are* ——— *them*) 150 Infs, **chiefly Midl, scattered Sth,** Hulling; (Qu. I11, . . *"She's* ——— *peas."*) 99 Infs, **chiefly Midl,** Hulling; (Qu. FF2, . . *Kinds of parties*) Inf **KY5**, Pea hullings; **MD18**, Bean hulling. **1966** Dakin *Dial. Vocab. Ohio R. Valley* 2.368, Throughout the entire Ohio Valley speakers say that the act of removing beans from the dry pods is *hulling* or *shelling. Hulling* is still the most commonly used term, but is giving way to *shelling.* . . Among speakers in larger towns and cities *shelling* is more common, as it is generally (but far from exclusively) among the relatively younger. **1966** *DARE* Tape **MI28**, I don't bother with peas because. . . they're a nuisance for what you get out of it. I don't think it's worthwhile, because to hull your peas and everything, take care of 'em, it is a job. **1967** Faries *Word Geog. MO* 107, Of the two expressions used . . to describe the removal of beans from their pods, the Midland term *to hull* . . is nearly twice as prevalent as the general term *to shell.* **1973** Allen *LAUM* 1.309 (as of c1950), *Hull* . . survives in the U[pper] M[idwest], where greater frequency in Iowa, Nebraska, and South Dakota attest [sic] its Midland source. . . Most of the 1,028 respondents use *shell* . . the most frequent minor variant is Midland *hull.* **1986** *DARE* File **sIN** (as of 1920), Hull a mess of green beans for dinner. The butter beans are big enough to hull-out.

2 To remove the calyx and stem from the top of (a strawberry). **[hull n B1]**

1889 *Century Dict.* 2912, *Hull.* . . 1. To strip off the hull . . of: as, . . to *hull* strawberries. **1931-33** *LANE Worksheets* **swCT,** *Hulling* ['hʌlɪn]—Removing the stem of; hulling strawberries. **1941** *LANE* Map 275, 11 infs, chiefly **sNEng,** Hull.

3 To wander; to go about idly. [Cf *OED hull* v.² 1 "*Naut.* Of a ship: To float or be driven by the force of the wind or current on the hull alone . . *Obs.*"]

1895 *DN* 1.383 **NJ,** *Hull.* . . To gad about, wander, roam. "He went a-hullen all over the country." **1934** (1943) *W2, Hull.* . . 2. b *Obs. exc. Dial., U.S.* . . to loaf about.

4 with *out:* To pay out, shell out.

1960 Criswell *Resp. to PADS 20* **Ozarks,** *Hull out*—used of money, to pay. "He had to hull out ten dollars for it." Common.

hull adj See **whole**

hullabaloo n Also *halaboo, hallabaloo, hellabal(l)oo, hell-of-a-baloo, hullabal(l)oo, hullamalloo;* for addit varr see quots [Forms beginning in *hall-, holl-* and *hull-* are recorded from nEngl and Scotl from early 1800s; those beginning in *hell-* appear only in the US and are perh infl by *hell.*]

1 A great noise or commotion. **scattered, but less freq Sth, S Midl** See Map

1843 (1916) Hall *New Purchase* xxix **IN,** In a hell-a-blow! *Ibid* 272, From every house, alley, grove, orchard, resounded forth curious groans, outcries, yells, and other hell-a-beloo's of *private prayer! Ibid* 333, Then commenced a hell-a-below. **1844** Thompson *Major Jones's Courtship* 48 **GA,** Sich another hellabeloo as they all made! **1848** Bartlett *Americanisms* 175, *Hellabaloo.* Riotous noise; confusion. Provincial in England. **1851** (1969) Burke *Polly Peablossom* 68 **MS,** I see the preacher tell 'bout Aaron's walkin' stick what turned itself into er sarpent, . . —an' all that kinder hellerbelloo, but that's all moonshine. **1859** Elwyn *Glossary* 55, *Halla-baloo.* **1872** Burnham *Memoirs U.S. Secret Service* 98, "An' I made for the 'crossdrum' lively, you can bet. It *was* a 'big thing,' and a hellabulloo followed, next morning." **1908** *DN* 3.322 **eAL, wGA,** *Hullabaloo.* . . Commotion, ado. "He raised a big hullabaloo." Rarely *hellabaloo.* **1917** *DN* 4.413 **wNC, KS, KY,** *Hellaballoo.* . . Variant of hullaballoo. **1927** *AmSp* 3.139 **ME,** Hullamalloo. **1933** Williamson *Woods Colt* 150 **Ozarks,** The crowd makes more noise . . blowin' horns an' poundin' things an' yellin' insults . . the Gawd-awfullest hullabaloo you ever heerd this side o' Little Rock. **1934** (1943) *W2,* Hallabaloo. **1940** *AmSp* 15.83 **swPA, nWV border,** *Hellabaloo* (a blending of 'hell' and 'hullabaloo'), an angry protest or tirade. **1942** in 1944 *ADD* **WV,** Very common *hell-. Hullabaloo* is a book wd. . . hall-|hɔ'l|—. Common. **1950** *WELS (A lot of noise)* 13 Infs, **WI,** Hullabaloo; 1 Inf, Hallabaloo; 1 Inf, Hellabaloo; 1 Inf, Hulubuloo; 1 Inf, Halaboo. **1960** Criswell *Resp. to PADS 20* **Ozarks,** *Hullaboo,* racket, to-do. **1965-70** *DARE* (Qu. KK16, *A great noise or disturbance*) 39 Infs, **scattered but less freq Sth, S Midl,** Hullabaloo; **CA160**, Hellabaloo; **VT16**, ['hɛləbə,lu], ['hæl-]; **WI70**, Hallabaloo [-æ-]; **ME16**, Hullaboo; (Qu. KK11) Infs **CT4**, **ID2**, **OK9**, **SC2**, **TX81**, Made a big hullabaloo;

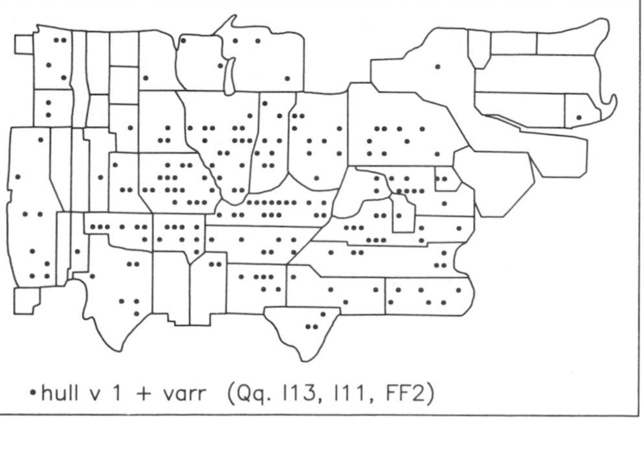

•hull v 1 + varr (Qq. I13, I11, FF2)

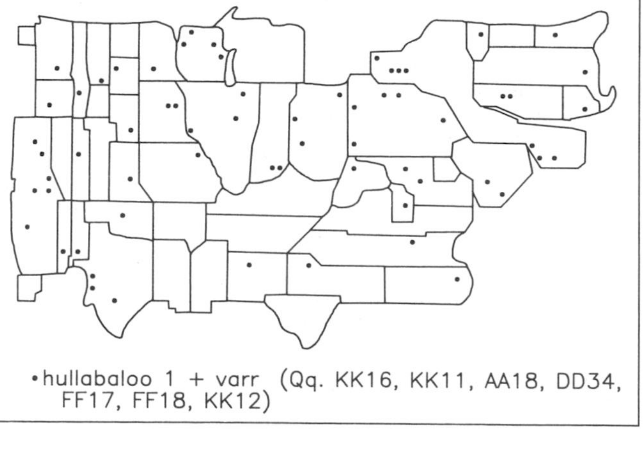

•hullabaloo 1 + varr (Qq. KK16, KK11, AA18, DD34, FF17, FF18, KK12)

PA104, 215, Made a hullabaloo (about it); **CA**127, 209, **IA**21, Raised a (big) hullabaloo; **SD**8, Raised an awful hullabaloo; **NY**163, **VT**16, Made a (big) hellabaloo; (Qu. AA18, . . *A noisy neighborhood celebration*) Inf **NC**14, Hullabaloo; (Qu. DD34) Inf **GA**72, Hullabaloo; (Qu. FF17, . . *"We all had a ——— last night."*) Infs **MA**106, **OH**15, Hullabaloo; **IA**3, Hell-of-a-baloo ['hɛləvəbəlu]; (Qu. FF18) Infs **AL**28, **AZ**11, **MD**28, **OH**63, **TX**11, Had (*or* raised) a hullabaloo; (Qu. KK12) Infs **IN**35, **TX**70, Hullabaloo. **1968** *DARE* Tape **CT**7, Now, if you wanted to put the jail on the best corner in Litchfield now . . there'd be a hell of a hullabaloo ['hɑllɑbɑlu] . . and they'd be up in arms against it.

2 =looby loo.

1949 (1967) Chase *Singing Games* 6, *Hullabaloo. . . Formation:* A single ring for any number. . . Or . . [a]ll the boys in one ring, and all the girls in a ring outside. . . several concentric rings may be formed. . . *Step:* A . . walk, brisk enough to be lively. . . [Then] galop [sic] sideways, or skip. . . [Chorus:] Hullabalooby looby,/ hullabalooby light./ Hullabalooby looby / on a summer night. [Verse:] Put your right hand in,/ put your right hand out./ Shake it a little, a little, a little,/ and turn yourself about. *Whoo!*

hull corn n

1 An **Indian corn.**

1969 *DARE* (Qu. I34, *If you don't have sweet corn, you can always eat young* ———) Inf **CT**39, Hull corn—boiled with cookin' soda.

2 See **hulled corn.**

hull down adv phr [*hull down* of a ship: so distant that its hull is below the horizon]

Completely.

1905 Lincoln *Partners* 264 **seMA,** "I know where we can buy a complete fit-out second-hand . . for three hundred and fifty dollars". . . "You've got me beat, hull down. . . Dirt, dog cheap!"

hulled corn n Also *hull corn* **NEng** Cf **flint corn, hominy B1, hull n B2a(4)**

Dried flint corn with the hulls removed, usually boiled until soft enough to eat.

1788 in 1908 MI Hist. Comm. *MI Hist. Coll.* 11.556, Q. What did he pay for these Goods. A. Two thousand Wampum, two & a half bushels of huld corn. **1877** Bartlett *Americanisms* 302, *Hulled Corn.* Indian corn scalded or boiled in lye, until the hulls come off. It is then rinsed and boiled, making a most palatable dish. **1906** *Pocumtuc Housewife* 36 **sMA,** *Hulled Corn*—Put . . old corn in a kettle of water. Tie a handful of ashes in a cloth and put in. Keep the pot warm . . for two or three days. Then pour off the lye and wash the corn thoroughly. **1922** (1926) Cady *Rhymes VT* 40, The hull-corn man will come next week. **1939** Wolcott *Yankee Cook Book* 106 **NEng,** *Hulled Corn—New Method* . . Dried, yellow corn. Cover with . . water . . [and] soda. Soak overnight. Boil . . until the hulls are loosened, about 3 hours. . . rub off the hulls between hands. . . boil . . until corn is tender. . . Hulled corn is a favorite old New England dish. It is made from yellow corn. . . Hulled corn . . may be purchased . . in two forms—hulled and ready to cook . . or in tins, all cooked, ready to heat and serve. . . Many New Englanders recall peddlers who used to sell hulled corn. **1966–67** *DARE* Tapes **NH**6, We had hulled corn. We didn't make it, we bought it. But I kin remember, even here in Lebanon, when the hull corn man would come around, like a peddler, with his container of hull corn and you would buy it; **MA**117, Hull corn. . . it's awfully good. You take the hull kernel and you cook it in . . water with wood ashes . . until the hull'd come off. . . You'd eat it . . in milk or . . in old-fashioned molasses. **1969** *DARE* (Qu. H23, . . *Hot cooked breakfast cereal*) Inf **RI**1, Hulled corn—soaked in lye, then cooked. Hominy is like this; (Qu. I34, *If you don't have sweet corn, you can always eat young* ———) Inf **CT**39, Hull corn—boiled with cookin' soda. **1977** *Yankee* Nov 254 **NEng,** *Hulled Corn, Hominy and Samp*—Whatever its local name, in certain parts of New England . . dried corn has been a staple of winter diets since the 17th century. . . Hulled corn . . is known as "hominy" throughout the south. . . Some authorities claim that the term "hulled corn" was used to refer to white corn and "samp" was used only for yellow . . , and other authorities claim just the opposite. . . Broad, hard, and plump kernels were chosen as they yielded the largest pieces of corn when the hulls were removed. A hard flint corn has always been the preferred type as it retained its firmness during the hulling process. **1986** *DARE* File **cnMA** (as of c1915), There was a hull(ed)-corn man in our town (Athol) too. He came on foot carrying a closed wooden bucket with handles, and dished the hulled corn out with a measure into a bowl provided by the purchaser. Hulled corn is like hominy now available in cans.

hull-gull n Also sp *hul(l)-gul;* also *huh-guh, hulligull, hully-gull(y)* [Cf *EDD hull* v.[2] 1 "To conceal" and *Gull-stones* (at *gull* sb.[6] 1) "a game played by boys, with rough stones for marbles"; cf also **hogo** n[2]] **S Midl, esp sAppalachians, Ozarks**

A children's guessing game; see quots.

1833 Greene *Life Dr. Dodimus* 1.30 **NEng,** The old people considerately retiring, there was no obstruction to the pleasant games of blind-man's-buff, hunt-the-slipper, break-the-Pope's-neck, change-partners, hull-gull, forfeits, and the like. **1897** (1952) McGill *Narrative* 32 **ceSC** (as of c1830), "Hull gull. Hand full. How many?" was played with chinquepins, being very abundant at that time. **1903** (1963) Newell *Games & Songs* 147, *Hul Gul.* This game is played by three . . or more, who stand in a circle. . . The dialogue is: "Hul Gul."/ "Hands full."/ "Parcel how many?" The second player then guesses the number. . . and so on until all the counters have been gained by one player. . . The counters are beans, grains of corn, marbles, nuts, and, in the South, *chinquapins.* **1915** *DN* 4.184 **swVA,** *Hull-gul.* . . A kind of guessing game. **1936** *Jrl. Amer. Folkl.* 49.199, The game known as "Hully-gully" is very popular in some sections of the Ozarks, and is usually played with grains of parched corn, chinquapins or hazelnuts, but we have seen grown men playing hully-gully with "store-boughten" marbles. It is really a gambling game, and is always "for keeps." **1963** *Mt. Life* 39.2.51 **sAppalachians,** The middle-aged mountain man is likely to be harsh in his evaluation of the youth just rising to maturity. . . "Look at 'im! . . so bowleggedy I'd be willin' . . to bet ye a double handful o' hullgull ches'nits he couldn't hem a blind pig in a fence cyorner." **1968** *DARE* Tape **VA**9, Poppy used to play some chinquapin games. . . He played "huh-guh handful how many." Well I'd say so many, y' know, and sometimes he'd have about fifteen in his hands and I'd get [=win] the game. I'd say "well about fifteen." **1968** *DARE* FW Addit **csOK,** *Hulligull,* Hulligull, How many: Fill hands with marbles, pennies or such; shake hand repeating "hulligull;" other guesses how many; if correct he gets the marbles. Used occasionally; old-fashioned. **1969** *DARE* (Qu. EE3, *Games in which you hide an object*) Inf **IL**92, Hully-gull ['hʌlɨ gʌl]—player picks handful of beans, nuts, popcorn, etc. Others guess how many are hidden. **1980** *Foxfire 6* 292 **nGA,** *Hull Gull*—We would have some chestnuts in our hand and the first person would say, "Hull gull." The second person would ask, "How many?" Then the first person would say, "A handful." Then the second person was supposed to guess how many you had. For each one they missed the guesser had to give the holder however many it was. If they guessed it exactly, the holder had to give them all to the guesser. The object was to try to get all of the hulls.

hull house See **hull n B2a(5)**

hulligull See **hull-gull**

hulling See **hull v 1**

hull out See **hull v 1, 4**

hull over v phr [Prob < *overhaul*]

See quots.

1967 *DARE* FW Addit **neCO,** *Hulled over*—"After these batteries have been hulled over a few times we throw them away." **1987** *NADS Letters* **neIL,** *Hull over* = overhaul. Everybody knowed that!

Hull's Victory n [After naval victory of Isaac *Hull* over British in 1812] **NEast**

A country-dance.

1891 Welch *Recoll. Buffalo* 376 (as of 1830s), At the balls and parties the popular figures in dancing, were the "Contra Dances," viz: . . "Hull's Victory." **1908** Lincoln *Cy Whittaker* 86 **seMA,** So, while the rest of his boy friends sought partners for the "Portland Fancy" and "Hull's Victory" he sat forlorn in a corner. **1938** FWP *Guide NH* 118, The morning star, Virginia reel, quadrille, Hull's Victory . . and money musk are still danced. **1968** *DARE* (Qu. FF5a, *Names for . . steps . . in dancing—in past years*) Inf **MA**73, Hull's Victory.

hully adj [**hull n B2a**]

Full of hulls; by ext, inferior.

1806 (1970) Webster *Compendious Dict.* 147, *Hully.* . . Having hulls or pods . . foul. **1954** *Harder Coll.* **cwTN,** *Hully.* . . Composed of hulls; of mediocre or poor quality.

hully n Cf *DS* X50

1980 Folb *Runnin' Down* 144 **Los Angeles CA** [Black], There is a subjective point at which the voluptuous becomes the obese *(hully).* *Ibid* 243, *Hully*—Obese person.

hully-gull(y) See **hull-gull**

hulubuloo See **hullabaloo**

huly See **hooley**

hum n[1] [echoic]

The gentle sound made by a cow.

1949 Kurath *Word Geog.* 46, *Hum* for 'moo'. *Ibid* 62, *Moo. . .* From Albemarle Sound to the Peedee Valley in South Carolina the expression *hum* is current beside *low.* **1966** Dakin *Dial. Vocab. Ohio R. Valley* 2.251, *Low. . .* In the southern Mountains a few speakers say *hum* (also used on the Carolina coast in contrast to *low* = *bellow*) or *moan* for a softer sound. *Hum* does not appear outside the Mountains. **1971** Wood *Vocab. Change* 46 **Gulf States, GA, AR, OK, TN,** The gentle sound a cow makes at feeding time is *moo. . .* Less often the variants *loo* and *mew, bawl, beller* or *bellow,* and *hum* occur. **1973** Gawthrop *Dial. Calumet* 71 **nwIN,** *Name for gentle sound made by cow at feeding time . .* hum 2 [infs out of 66 infs].

hum n[2] *euphem*

Hell.

1940 *AmSp* 15.221 **TX,** 'What the hum do you mean, you hunkabo' (bohunk)? **1982** *Barrick Coll.* **csPA,** *Hum*—euphemism for *hell.* To give someone hum. To catch hum.

hum n[3] See **home**

human n Usu |'hjumən|; also **esp NYC, Long Island** |'jumən| (see Pronc Intro 3.I.19, cf **humor**); rarely |'hjumɪŋ| (cf **-ing**)

A Forms.

1789 Webster *Dissertations Engl. Lang.* 122, One or two [British] authors affect to pronounce *human,* and about twenty other words beginning with *h,* as tho they were spelt *yuman. . .* I am surprised that . . [this] pronunciation has found so many advocates in this country, as there is none more erroneous. **1920s** in 1944 *ADD* **cNY,** [hjumən]. **1942** *AmSp* 17.156 **seNY,** Omission of initial [h] before [ju]. . . human . . 45 [infs] [hj], 8 [infs] [j]. **1943** in 1944 *ADD* **AR,** ['hjumɪŋz] [pl.]

B Senses.

1 A human being. [Cf *EDD*]

1859 (1968) Bartlett *Americanisms* 207, *Human,* for human being. Western. . . "I had no idee that he was around, and am quite sartin he didn't expect to meet a human in such a place." **1891** Maitland *Amer. Slang Dict.* 146, *Human. . .* for human being; a man. A term much used in the United States. **1893** Shands *MS Speech* 38, *Human* ('hjumən). Illiterate white for *human being.* This class goes so far as to give the word a plural—*humans.* **1899** (1912) Green *VA Folk-Speech* 235, *Human. . .* A human being; a member of the family of mankind. "I didn't see a human." **1903** *DN* 2.317 **seMO,** *Human. . .* Human being. 'I never met a human all the way from my house to town.' **1905** *DN* 3.83 **nwAR,** *Human. . .* Human being. 'They are unanimous in pronouncing him (President Roosevelt) the ugliest human on earth.' **1908** *DN* 3.322 **eAL, wGA,** *Human. . .* Human being. **1950** *WELS (Other words meaning "a person"; "What's ——— to do in a case like that?")* 1 Inf, **WI,** A human. **1966** *DARE* (Qu. HH32) Inf **AR**39, A human. **1969** *Amer. Heritage Dict.* 640, *Human* (noun) is acceptable on all levels . . according to 72 per cent of the Usage Panel. In somewhat earlier usage, *human being* was often recommended as the better choice on a formal level, though *human* has a long history as a noun.

‡**2** attrib: See quots.

1896 *DN* 1.416 **nwTX,** *Human* (saddle): without "horns" . . the "human" saddle is much lighter than the "cowboy" or "Mexican" saddle. **1922** Rollins *Cowboy* 120, The flat English saddle the cowboy termed a "human saddle," "kidney pad," or "postage stamp."

hum and haw v phr Also *hum-haw* [Var of *hem and haw*] Cf **hem-haw chiefly Sth, S Midl**

To make hesitating sounds; to hesitate, to be indecisive; hence n *hum and hah* sounds of hesitation.

1848 Bartlett *Americanisms* 184, *Hums and hahs.* A familiar expression applied to one who hesitates in speaking. 'None of your *hums and hahs!*' that is, be decisive, do not hesitate. **1899** (1912) Green *VA Folk-Speech* 218, To speak with hesitation and the interruption of drawling and unmeaning sounds: as, "To hum and haw." **1909** *DN* 3.398 **nwAR,** *Hum and haw. . .* To hesitate. "He *hummed and hawed* but finally went and done it." **1928** French *Ranchman NM* 282, He hummed and hawed and tried to kid me that I myself was responsible on account of the good character I had given him. **1933** Miller *Lamb in His Bosom* 154 **GA,** Lonzo hummed and hawed. **1966–69** *DARE* (Qu. A11, *When somebody takes too long about coming to a decision, you might say, "I wish he'd quit ———.")* Inf **AR**19, Humming and hawing; (Qu. JJ45) Infs **KY**36, **VA**25, Humming and hawing; **GA**9, Humming ['hʌmɪn] and hawing; **SC**34, Hummin' and a-hawin'; **IN**30, Hum-hawing. [All Infs old]

human ear n Cf **elephant's ear 6, pig ear**

Prob the tree ear *(Auricularia auricula).*

1966 *DARE* (Qu. S19, *Mushrooms that grow out like brackets from the sides of trees)* Inf **MS**16, Human ears.

humanly adj

Appropriate for a human being.

1942 (1971) Campbell *Cloud-Walking* 62 **seKY,** It was a fair and humanly thing for mountain folks to favor their old time pattern of living.

‡**humanus** n [Var of *humus*]

1967 *DARE* (Qu. C30, . . *Loose, dark soil)* Inf **MO**26, Humanus ['hju˘umənɨs].

humbird n [See quots 1946, 1956] **esp NEng**

=**hummingbird 1.**

1634 Wood *New Engl. Prospect* 28, The Humbird is one of the wonders of the Countrey, being no bigger than a Hornet. **1872** Schele de Vere *Americanisms* 377, *Hum-bird.* **1891** Cooke *Huckleberries* 167 **NEng,** I never see a humbird fuller o' buzz. **1946** Hausman *Eastern Birds* 374, *Ruby-throated hummingbird. . . Other names . .* Humbird. . . Their wings [are] . . visible only as a blur and [produce] . . a loud hum. **1956** MA Audubon Soc. *Bulletin* 40.82, *Ruby-throated hummingbird. . .* Humbird (Mass. From the sound made by its buzzing wings.)

humble adj, v Usu |'hʌmbəl|; also **chiefly Sth, S Midl** |'ʌmbəl| Pronc-sp *umble;* arch sp *ombel* [*OED humble* "The pronunciation ['ʌmbl̩] has prevailed down to the 19th c."]

A Std senses, var forms.

1884 in 1973 *AmSp* 48.97 **nwGA,** *Umble*—Humble . . "I enjoy my umble food and my repose." **1893** Shands *MS Speech* 65, *Umble* ['ʌmbl̩]. Used for *humble* by all classes. Not one man in a thousand, in Mississippi, pronounces *humble* correctly, but nearly all make the *h* silent. **1899** (1912) Green *VA Folk-Speech* 211, The initial *h* is always sounded, except, probably, in the words *umble, Umphrey,* and a few others. **1927** Shewmake *Engl. Pronc. VA* 31, *Humble . .* the great majority of speakers seem still to omit the *h . .* though there are of course careful speakers who follow the modern tendency to insert the *h* sound. **1934** (1943) *W2* 1212, *Humble . .* formerly, and still occas. ['ʌmbl̩]. **1942** Hall *Smoky Mt. Speech* 86 **eTN, wNC,** *Humble . .* occur[s] without [h]: . . ['ʌmbəl]. **1956** Eliason *Tarheel Talk* 204 **NC,** In . . *humble . .* the old *h*-less pronunciation is often retained in the South. . . An *h*-less pronunciation is reflected . . by the use of *an* instead of *a* before *humble. Ibid* 312, *Humble* [spelled] ombel [in] 1784 . . umble [in] 1885. **1986** *DARE* File **wNC** (as of 1910–30), *Umble* was the pronunciation for *humble* current at that time.

B As verb.

To behave submissively.

c1938 in 1970 Hyatt *Hoodoo* 2.1185 **seGA,** Dey [=the spirits who are directing you] won't want chew to humble to nobody, 'cause dey ain't goin' humble to nobody.

humblest one in the northeast corner, the n

1928 *Ruppenthal Coll.* **KS,** *The humblest one in the northeast corner*—the most humble of all, with the implication that the northeast corner of the room is the most humble station.

humble-talk v

To speak in a modest or self-effacing manner.

1974 (1975) Shaw *All God's Dangers* 51 **AL** [Black], I humble-talked him just to get his goods about how he felt toward me.

humbliness, humbly See **homely**

humblyfied ppl adj Cf **-ified**

Humbled.

1883 (1971) Harris *Nights with Remus* 203 **GA** [Black], Brer Rabbit had so many 'p'intments fer ter keep out de way er de t'er [=others] creeturs dat he 'gun ter feel monst'us [=monstrously] humblyfied.

humbo n [Etym uncert]

1895 *Sun* (NY NY) 30 July 9/2, Humbo, a name in New Hampshire for maple syrup, cited by the Boston *Commonwealth* as an Indian word. **1907** Hodge *Hdbk. Amer. Indians* 1.578, *Humbo.* A New Hampshire word for maple syrup. . . Horatio Hale sought to bring it into relation with *ombigamisige* in Chippewa and closely related Algonquian dialects, a term signifying 'he makes the maple syrup boil,' or 'boiled sugar drink,' the chief element being the radical *omb,* 'to boil.'

humboldt undercut n Also *humboldt* [*Humboldt* County California]

1956 *AmSp* 31.151 **nwCA,** *Humboldt.* . . A wedge-shaped piece of wood which when cut or sawn out of a tree leaves an *undercut.* **1958** McCulloch *Woods Words* 90 **Pacific NW,** *Humboldt undercut*—An undercut chunk taken out of the stump side of the cut in power saw falling.

humbug n

1 also *(Old) English humbug:* Taffy usu flavored with peppermint; see quot 1969. [*OED humbug* sb. 5 "A kind of sweetmeat. *dial.*"; *EDD* sb. *humbug* "A particular kind of sweetmeat, varying in different localities"]

1838 Kettell *Yankee Notions* 163 **Boston MA,** Their appetites are voratious [sic], and they are extravagantly fond of a certain food called *hhummbugg* [sic], which they swallow in crude lumps, and suffer strange fits of madness while under its effects. **1969** *DARE* Tape **PA**186, Humbugs is what I make usually. . . I use brown sugar and a little orleans molasses, water, boil it until when you drop it a little in real cold water, it snaps apart. . . I flavor that with a little bit of oil of peppermint. Then I pull that until it's . . a good light color. . . draw it out into strips and score it into bites. . . Then when it's cold, break it on the underside. **1986** Atwood *Handmaid's Tale* 139 **Boston MA,** The counters [in a Scrabble game] are like candies, made of peppermint, cool like that. Humbugs, those were called. I would like to put them into my mouth. **1986** *DARE* File **neMA,** Her father loved "humbugs". . . molasses candy. Priscilla's store folks called them "Old English Humbugs", but their cookbook only labeled it "English Humbugs".

2 A piece of raised bread dough fried in deep fat; see quot. Cf **Baptist cake, huffjuff**

1986 *DARE* File **swIN** (as of 1900s), A humbug is a square of lightbread dough cooked in deep fat until puffed up, then dusted with cinnamon and sugar.

3 A device used to lead a bull by the nose; see quot 1872. [*OED humbug* sb. 6 1850 →]

1872 (1876) Knight *Amer. Mech. Dict.* 2.1142, *Humbug.* . . A nippers for grasping the cartilage of the nose. Used with bulls and other refractory bovines. **1966** *DARE* (QR near Qu. K18) Inf **MI**2, Humbug is a ring clamped into a bull's nose so you lead him. [FW: That is different from a ring put permanently in a bull's nose by piercing. Apparently the latter wouldn't be called a "humbug."]

4 A nuisance; also adj *humbug* annoying, troublesome. [Cf *OED humbug* sb. 1 "An imposition *Obs.*" Cf also *SND humbug* n. *DBE humbug* n. "A bother"] **esp HI**

1951 *AmSp* 26.26 **HI,** Some pidgin words have an archaic English flavor: *humbug.* **1972** Carr *Da Kine Talk* 133 **HI,** *Humbug* vs. *troublesome* (adj.), *nuisance* (n.) . . "I was a real rascal, humbug boy." **1981** *Pidgin To Da Max* **HI,** *Humbug* . . Bother, hassle. "Real humbug fo' do all dees ovah, you know!"

5 Trouble; a fight.

1927 Kennedy *Gritny* 97 **sLA** [Black], Don' try an' raise no humbug late in de night like dis. **1969** [see **humbug v 2**]. **1971** Roberts *Third Ear* np [Black], *Humbug* . . a fight.

6 A mistake.

1965 Will *Okeechobee Boats* 141 **FL,** He had his choice of land. . . This happened to be in a dry period when high land was dried out. . . so naturally he chose low ground, and that's where he made a humbug. It started to rain.

7 See quot.

1970 Major *Dict. Afro–Amer. Slang* 68, *Humbug:* anything perplexing or complicated or both.

8 also *hombug:* Something false or deceptive; see below.

a A wild-goose chase. [Prob by ext from *humbug* hoax, deceit] Cf **bug n[1] 4a**

1980 Folb *Runnin' Down* 45 **Los Angeles CA** [Black], Ways of one-upping your antagonist . . *send somebody on a hombug*—on a wild goose chase. *Ibid* 98, Terms like to *send someone on a . . hombug* . . are all movement-related in tone and, in fact, may literally imply sending someone a very long distance. "You send d' sucker on a big ol' goose-chase. . . Dude go . . a long ways. . . Now da's a righteous humbug!" **1986** *DARE* File **cIN** [Black], My grandmother, who was originally from Greensburg, Kentucky, would send me on a humbug to get me out of her hair. She would send me outside to look for something that didn't exist.

b A false arrest.

1980 Folb *Runnin' Down* 242 [Black], *Hombug, humbug.* . . False arrest.

9 A deadbeat; see quot.

1969 *DARE* (Qu. U17, . . *A person who doesn't pay his bills*) Inf **NJ**56, Humbug.

humbug v

1 with *about:* To flounder at sea; to wallow.

1840 (1841) Dana *2 Yrs.* 433 **NEng,** For several days we lay 'humbugging about' in the Horse latitudes, with all sorts of winds and weather. **1908** Wasson *Home from Sea* 189 **NEng** *(OEDS),* We pitch-poled and humbugged about in them latitudes till the Cap'n . . was sick and tired of the whole business.

2 also *hombug:* To fight, to be or act tough; hence vbl n *humbugging;* n *humbugger.* *among Black speakers* [Cf *DBE humbug* v. "To annoy"]

1969 Keiser *Vice Lords* 16 **Chicago IL** [Black], Every once in a while we used to fight with the Vice Ladies. They was boss [=very good] humbuggers. . . one night we had a fight with them and they got us. *Ibid* 19, When he got close, he going to grab the gun. I didn't want to kill him so I shot him in his arm. . . [Then] I went home. . . the rest of our fellows [in the gang] they stayed around the pool hall. There was a boss humbug. *Ibid* 44, Humbugging is actual fighting. Not all situations of enmity end in humbugging. **1971** Roberts *Third Ear* np [Black], *Humbugging* . . being or acting tough; fighting, especially in a group. **1972** Claerbaut *Black Jargon* 69, *Humbuggin'.* . . fighting; brawling: *The cats got to humbuggin', man.* **1980** Folb *Runnin' Down* 242 **Los Angeles CA** [Black], *Hombug, humbug* v. . . Fight. **1986** *DARE* File **NYC** (as of 1966) [Black], Humbug means fight. "We're going to go humbug."

humbug adj See **humbug n 4**

humbug about See **humbug v 1**

humbugger, humbugging See **humbug v 2**

hum-bum n, v

1957 *Sat. Eve. Post Letters* **TX,** "Hum-bum" was our favorite night time sport. One group would be given a head start and the second group would yell "Hum-bum" and start chasing them. Every time the chasers would yell "Hum-bum" the chasees were duty bound to reply. We hum-bummed up streets and alleys for hours. The game usually ended by the harassed cops running us home.

humdurgan n **ME**

See quot 1975.

1905 Wasson *Green Shay* 39 **ME,** He come in. . . let go his little old humdurgan, or killick, or anchor, or whatever it is he clubs her with. *Ibid,* [A humdurgan is an] [a]nchor made from a stone lashed in a forked limb of a tree. **1975** Gould *ME Lingo* 138, *Humdurgan*—A stone lashed to a crotch of a tree limb and used for a rough anchor. The difference between *killick* and *humdurgan* is academic. Some think *killick* was originally a stone placed ashore with a line out to hold a boat in, and a *humdurgan* had the refinement of the crotched stick to make it serviceable in deeper water. In general Maine usage today, the terms are interchangeable.

humgumptious adj [Cf *EDD humgumption* sb. "*Obs.* . . Self-importance; nonsense."] Cf **gumptious 4**

1913 *DN* 4.16 **NE,** *Humgumptious.* Splendid, excellent, pretentious. . . "That is a humgumptious book I am reading." "They are humgumptious people."

hum-haw See **hum and haw**

humid n [Perh folk-etym for *humus*] Cf **humanus**

1968 *DARE* (Qu. C30, . . *Loose, dark soil*) Inf **NY**70, Black humid.

humility n [Explanations vary; see quots 1781, 1917, 1956] **chiefly NEng**

1 Any of several birds of the family Scolopacidae, but esp the willet; see quots.

1634 Wood *New Engl. Prospect* 31, The Humilities or Simplicities (as I may rather call them) bee of two sorts, the biggest being as big as a greene

Plover, the other as big as birds we call knots in *England.* **1781** Peters *Genl. Hist. CT* 256, The Humility is so called, because it speaks the word *humility,* and seldom mounts high in the air. **1832** Williamson *Hist. ME* 1.149, The *Humility* [Footnote: *Tringa Interpres*] has long yellow legs, long neck, is gray spotted . . and is nearly as large as a pigeon. **1839** Audubon *Synopsis Birds* 244, Totanus vociferus. . . Greater Yellow-shanks. Humility. **1870** *Amer. Naturalist* 3.638, *Black-necked stilt* . . is well known to the gunners of Ipswich, who occasionally meet with it, and by whom it is ironically named "Humility." **1876** *Forest & Stream* 7.149/1 **Long Is. NY,** Grass plover [=*Bartramia longicauda*] to which the local appellation generally applied here is humilities, feed in the fields and uplands, always singly, never in flocks, and are very shy, wary birds. **1880** *Ibid* 15.4/2, Great marbled godwit *(Limosa fedoa)*. . . Occasionally called the humility or humilt, which name has also been given to the upland plover. **1881** *Ibid* 17.226/2 **NEng,** The willet or humility *(Symphemia semipalmata . .)* arrives often paired, towards the end of May. **1887** *Ibid* 28.84/2 **eMA,** In Nantucket. . . the Hudsonian godwit *(Limosa hudsonica)* is known as the humility. **1888** Trumbull *Names of Birds* 164, In Massachusetts at Rowley, Ipswich, Salem, Boston markets, North Scituate, Provincetown, North Plymouth, West Barnstable, Chatham, and New Bedford, *Humility* [=*Catophorus semipalmatus.*] . . On the Massachusetts coast this bird is sometimes confused with the Hudsonian Godwit . . ; I have heard, for example, the Godwit called "Humility." *Ibid* 167, *Greater Yellowlegs.* . . Audubon speaks of its being known in Maine as the *Humility* . . , adding that "this is an appellation that ill accords with its vociferous habits." . . Very seldom, or never heard now. *Ibid* 173, On Long Island at Shinnecock Bay and Moriches, *Humility* [=*Bartramia longicauda*]. **1917** (1923) *Birds Amer.* 1.247, Here is a noisy, self-assertive bird, if there ever was one. . . And yet this forward creature [=willet] has been nicknamed "Humility," because it probes for worms in the humble mud in the intervals between the periods when it lifts up the voice on high. **1956** MA Audubon Soc. *Bulletin* 40.18, *Willet.* . . Humility (Maine, Mass. This name was suggested by the bird's bowing movements.). *Greater yellow-legs.* . . Humility (Maine.) *Ibid* 19, *Least sandpiper.* Humility (Mass. From its bowing habits, its small size, or both.) *Ibid* 20, *Hudsonian godwit.* Humility (Mass. From its bowing movements.) *Ibid* 21, *Black-necked stilt.* Humility (Mass. From its bowing movements.)

2 =black-necked stilt.

1870 *Amer. Naturalist* 3.638, *Black-necked Stilt* . . is well known to the gunners of Ipswich [MA], who occasionally meet with it, and by whom it is ironically named "Humility." **1956** [see **1** above].

humli See **hommilie**

hum'ly See **homely**

hummer n

1 =hummingbird 1. [See quot 1917]

1872 Schele de Vere *Americanisms* 377, The tiny *Mango* Humming-bird *(Trochilus colubris)* . . [is] known familiarly . . as *Hum-bird* or *Hummer* simply. [*DARE* Ed: The scientific name identifies the bird as the Ruby-throated Hummingbird, not the Mango Hummingbird which does not occur in the U.S.] **1898** (1900) Davie *Nests N. Amer. Birds* 296, The flowers of the honeysuckle attract great numbers of Hummers. **1914** [see **hummingbird's dinner horn**]. **1917** (1923) *Birds Amer.* 2.181, The distinctive fact about this Hummer [=*Eugenes fulgens*] is that it doesn't hum, at least not in the way which makes that term more or less accurate in describing the sound made by the wings of other members of the family. **1948** *Pacific Discovery* Mar-Apr 14/2 **cwCA,** Both species of hummer have been known to nest and rear their families in the court or nearby. **1964** Phillips *Birds AZ* 62, This hummer [=*Archilochus costae*], and certain swallows, are the first land-birds to return to Arizona in "spring" migration.

2 Something or someone remarkable; a humdinger.

1893 Shands *MS Speech* 38, *Hummer.* . . Used by all classes to mean something that possesses a great degree of excellence; as "That horse is a hummer"; i.e. an extremely good one. **1907** Mulford *Bar-20* 345 **West,** She's a hummer—stands two hands under him an' is a whole lot prettier than that picture Cowan has got over his bar. **1913** *DN* 4.16 **NE,** *Hummer.* Anything of magnitude or note; especially a man or woman of notable parts; a high stepper, a good goer. . . "The play last night was a hummer." **1951** Morgan *Skid Road* 129 **WA,** Little Egypt proved a hummer and she was greeted with tremendous applause in an extremely interesting dance. **1968** *DARE* (Qu. LL5, *Something impressively big*) Inf **PA**104, Hummer. [Inf old]

3 An insignificant or undesirable person; see quots.

1971 Roberts *Third Ear* np [Black], *Hummer* . . a nothing person. **1986** Hendrickson *Amer. Talk* 50, There are many . . others [=New England expressions], including a *hummer* for any bad guy with some saving grace, such as a sense of humor.

4 in phr *on the hummer:*

a Of a machine: out of order.

1950 *WELS Suppl.* 4 Infs, **sWI,** On the hummer. **1960** Bailey *Resp. to PADS 20* **KS,** On the hummer.

b Of a living thing: not feeling well.

1950 *WELS Suppl.* 1 Inf, **csWI,** On the hummer [=under the weather].

c See quot.

1912 *DN* 3.584 **wIN,** *On the hummer.* . . At a disadvantage. "I've got him on the hummer and he knows it."

hummi See **hommie**

hummingbird n

1 Std: a bird of the family Trochilidae. [From the sound of the rapid wing vibration] Also called **humbird, hummer 1.** For other names see **ruby-throated hummingbird, sponge hummer**

2 A noisemaking device; see quot. Cf **bull-roarer**

1912 Green *VA Folk-Speech* 235, *Humming-bird.* . . A thin piece of wood with a string at one end whirled around making a humming noise.

hummingbird brush n

A **bee brush** (here: *Aloysia lycioides*).

1951 *PADS* 15.39 **TX,** *Aloysia ligustrina.* . . Bee, or hummingbird, brush. . . Beloved of bees and hummingbirds.

hummingbird moth n [See quots 1954, 1980]

=sphinx moth.

1848 in 1850 Cooper *Rural Hours* 202, The whole tribe of hawk-moths are now sometimes called humming-bird moths, from these same insects. **1899** Bergen *Animal Lore* 63, Humming-bird moth, any large sphinx moth, family *Sphingidae. General in the United States.* **1936** AZ Univ. *Genl. Bulletin* 3.118, The striped humming bird moth with its oblique red and white bars on its wings may be seen any evening flitting over the petunias. **1954** Borror-DeLong *Intro. Insects* 504, Most of them feed much like hummingbirds, hovering in front of a flower and extending their proboscis into it; these moths are sometimes called hummingbird moths, and in many species the body is about the size of a hummingbird. **1980** Milne-Milne *Audubon Field Guide Insects* 778, *Hummingbird Moth* . . *(Hemaris thysbe)*. . . This moth hovers over flowers in full sunlight, producing a buzz with its wings similar to but softer than that of a hummingbird similarly engaged.

hummingbird sage n [See quots 1911, 1947]

A **sage** (here: *Salvia spathacea*) native to California.

1911 CA Ag. Exper. Sta. Berkeley *Bulletin* 217.1021, *Salvia spathaceae* Greene. Humming Bird Sage. Crimson Sage. . . The humming bird appears to be the only visitor of this bloom. **1925** Jepson *Manual Plants CA* 869, *Crimson sage.* . . Coarse herb with erect simple stems. . . Also called Humming-bird Sage. **1946** Peattie *Pacific Coast* 55 **sCA,** Here is the place to look for a small but attractive flora of herbaceous perennials like the hummingbird sage with its superb scarlet flowers. **1947** *So. Sierran* May 4/2 *(DA),* I had been especially impressed by the Humming-bird Sage, deep crimson in hue.

hummingbird's dinner horn n

A **beardtongue** (here: *Penstemon centranthifolius* or *P. torreyi*).

1914 Saunders *With Flowers in CA* 117, *Penstemon centranthifolius.* . . The bees have no monopoly of its sweets, for upon it the hummers levy special tribute—a fact that gives rise to another pretty name, humming-bird's dinner-horn. **1947** (1976) Curtin *Healing Herbs* 194, Pentstemon [sic] torreyi. . . *Humming-bird's dinner horn.* . . Vivid scarlet blossoms . . trumpet invitations to the humming-birds to become constant attendants.

hummingbird's trumpet n Also *hummingbird trumpet*

A California fuchsia (here: *Zauschneria californica*). Also called **Mexican balsamea, wild fuchsia**

1888 Lindley-Widney *CA of South* 332 **sCA,** A type of faithfulness, a tiny shrub, blooms through every month in the year, *Zeuschneria* [sic], the "humming-bird's trumpet." **1897** Parsons *Wild Flowers CA* 366, *Humming-bird's trumpet.* . . *Zauschneria Californica.* . . It has been cultivated for some time, and is highly prized in Eastern gardens, where it has earned for itself the pretty title of "humming-bird's trumpet." **1959**

Carleton *Index Herb. Plants* 63, *Humming-bird-trumpet:* Zauschneria californica.

hummingbird trumpet See **hummingbird's trumpet**

hummingbird weed n

A **turtlehead** (here: *Chelone glabra*).

1940 Clute *Amer. Plant Names* 255, *Chelone glabra.* Humming-bird weed.

hummock n Also *hammock, hommock;* for addit varr see quots [*OED* 1556 →; ult orig unknown]

1 A small hill, knoll; an elevated clump (of trees or bushes).

1635 *Boston Rec.* 9 *(DA)* **MA,** There stands 3 homocks, with pyne trees upon the south side of the marsh neare the water. **1663** in 1940 *AmSp* 15.270 **eVA,** A homack of five remarkable pines. . . a small hamock of bushes near the bank of Chesapiake Bay. **1716** in 1886 *Narragansett Hist. Reg.* 4.168 **RI,** For the hummock by the watering place, To John Briggs. **1870** Keim *Sheridan's Troopers* 133 **sePA,** At one stage of the journey we struck a remarkably peculiar section, the plain being covered with a number of hummocks of red earth and gravel. **1903** *DN* 2.315 **seMO,** *Hammock*. . . A low hill. **1904** *DN* 2.426 **Cape Cod MA** (as of a1857), *Hummock*. . . A little round knoll. **1919** (1920) Cody-Cooper *Memories Buffalo Bill* 325 **Rocky Mts,** Below can be seen . . the hills of Colorado and the hummocks of Wyoming. **1965-70** *DARE* (Qu. C17, . . *A small, rounded hill*) Infs **CA**90, **DC**2, **MA**10, **NY**34, **OH**12, Hummock; **MI**40, Hummock—slightly larger than a knoll, not a sharp rise, just a gradual slope of the land; **NM**11, Hummock—half an acre to twenty across, on lower ground, generally covered with vegetation; **NY**123, Hummock—just a little one; **RI**12, Hummock—under 50″ [sic] high; **VT**16, Hummock—bigger than a house. **1969** *DARE* Tape **CA**145, There was a jut-up in the middle of this cirque [in Alaska], a hummock or a ridge, and those rams . . would . . get up on that hump in the middle.

2 now usu *hammock:* See below. **chiefly S Atl, esp FL** See Map Note: Some of the following senses are not easily distinguishable.

a An islet of densely clustered, usu hardwood trees, rising above a swampy area or occurring in the midst of pine barrens; the trees themselves.

1773 in 1953 McMullen *Topog. Terms FL* 122, The next Species of high Land differs very little in Soil from the midling Pine Land, and produces live and red Oak Hickery Nut, and wild Mulberry Trees; but this kind of Land is only met with in Groves (:by the Americans called Hammoks:) not exceeding one hundred Acres of Land. **1791** Bartram *Travels 117* **neFL,** Twenty miles of these green fields, interspersed with hommocks or islets of evergreen trees. **1855** Simms *Forayers* 12 **SC,** Let us penetrate at once to the recess, . . emerging suddenly from the thicket and swamp, upon a hammock, an islet of the swamp, covered with mighty trees, pine and beech, a sandy spot, high, dry, and sheltered. **1926** *AmSp* 1.408 **Okefenokee GA,** [He] was in the habit of footing it along the path through the hammock. [Footnote:] A certain type of woods, composed mostly of trees other than pines, such as live-oak and magnolia. **1962** *AmSp* 37.174 **eNC,** A grove of trees is generally called a hammock ['hæmək], and two hills on the island which support some vegetation are called 'First Hammock Hill' and 'Second Hammock Hill'. **1966-70** *DARE* (QR, near Qu. C7) Inf **NC**76, Hammock, the pieces of land in it; (Qu. C13, . . Land that sticks out noticeably into a body of water) Inf **GA**65, Hammock, hummock—over in the swamp, high land, hardwoods grow on it; (Qu. C17, . . *A small, rounded hill*) Inf **FL**21, Hammock—high ridge with oak trees growing on it; (Qu. C28, *A place where underbrush . . and small trees grow together so that it's nearly impossible to get through*) Inf **FL**34, Hammock—if big trees in with it; **FL**48, Hammock—can't penetrate unless you cut your way through; **SC**19, Hammock; (Qu. T1, . . *A bunch of trees growing together in open country, especially on a hill*) Infs **FL**23, 29, 34, **NC**76, Hammock; **FL**4, A hammock or island—in saw grass; **FL**35, Hammocks—especially in wet country; **GA**38, Hammock—hardwood trees growing together; **NC**81, Hammock—in the rush marsh; (Qu. T2a, . . *A piece of land covered with trees . . only a few acres*) Infs **FL**35, **MS**73, Hammock; **FL**32, Hammock—a large area; **FL**39, Hammock—if very thick; **GA**25, Hammock—a high piece of ground with trees on it. **1967** Williams *Greenbones* 124 **GA** (as of c1910), It was a camp meeting in a live-oak hammock. **1968** *DARE* Tape **GA**31, When they get bigger . . when they're not standing very high out of water, they're known as a hammock, where water maybe washes over them during flood periods . . good-sized trees begin to grow. **1971** Craighead *Trees S. FL* 153, The term tropical hardwood hammock is applied to the tree islands that occur on the higher rock land, in the pinelands, and on rock mesas in the glades that rise 1 to 3 feet above the adjacent glade surface. . . Probably over 500 tropical hardwood hammocks formerly dotted the pineland of Dade County. They ranged in size from one-fourth acre to over 100 acres.

b A swampy area, usu with some trees or shrubs.

1823 Vignoles *Observations Floridas* 38 **neFL,** The grounds planted by Mr. Hernandez, are the northern point of a long narrow hammock called Graham's swamp. **1953** McMullen *Topog. Terms FL* 45, Though *hammock* is sometimes used synonymously with *swamp,* the former is distinguished from the latter by being more elevated and drier, having a shrubby undergrowth. **1966-68** *DARE* (Qu. C7, . . *Land that usually has some standing water with trees or bushes*) Inf **FL**6, Hammock ['hæmək]; **GA**31, Hammock. **1966** *DARE* Tape **FL**39, [A hammock is] a low grassy area, lot o' saw grass and some trees. . . There are a lot of different types of hammocks and growth 'cordin' to the location where they are, but they have trees.

c also *hammock land, ~ soil;* often with a qualifier: Earth or soil of the sort found in a **hummock 2a.**

1775 (1962) Romans *Nat. Hist. FL* 17, The hammock land so called from its appearing in tufts among the lofty pines . . the large parcels of it often divide swamps, creeks, or rivers from the pine land, . . its soil is various, in some places a sand of divers colours, and in East Florida, often a white sand; but the true hammock soil is a mixture of clay and blackish sand, and in some spots a kind of ochre, in East Florida some of this is also sometimes found rocky. **1831** in 1956 Eliason *Tarheel Talk* 276 **FL,** There are three qualities of land. Grey Hammock, which is exhaustible and produces 50 to 60 Bush. Corn per acre. . . Blue or black & yellow Hammock 35 to 45 Bush. corn. **1869** *Overland Mth.* 3.130/2 **ceTX,** There is the "chocolate" prairie, . . and the "hummock," (yielding principally small honey-locusts) and the "wire-grass." **1893** *Harper's New Mth. Mag.* Mar 509/1 **FL,** Halifax and Indian river fruit, for instance, usually grown on high shell hammock land or heavy marl hammock land, is quoted regularly at a dollar above the market. **1953** McMullen *Topog. Terms FL* 46, There are various types of hammock lands, such as *high hammock,* the "light" (*i.e.,* high, sandy and light in color), as opposed to the "heavy," or low and dark gray, and *shell hammock.* **1968** *DARE* (Qu. C30, . . *Loose, dark soil*) Inf **LA**27, Hammock land.

d See quots. Cf **intervale**

1819 in 1824 Knight *Letters* 110 **LA,** The intervales between pine tracts and the savannahs, are called *hammocks.* **1869** Brinton *Guide-Book* 42 **nFL,** The northern portion of the Peninsula is composed of "scrubs" . . , pine lands and hammocks (not hummocks—the latter is a New England word with different signification). The hammocks are rich river bottoms, densely timbered. . . They cannot be surpassed for fertility.

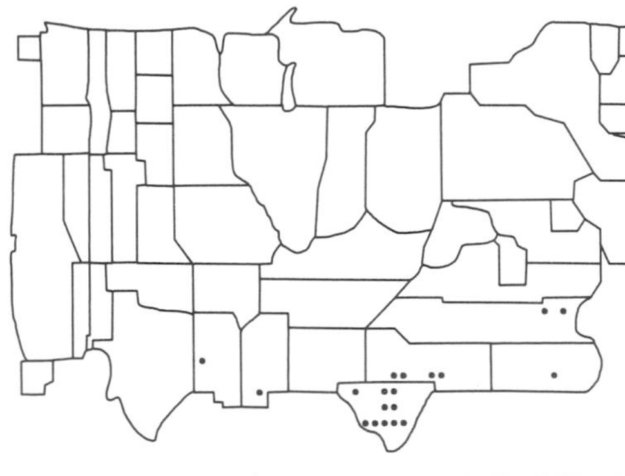

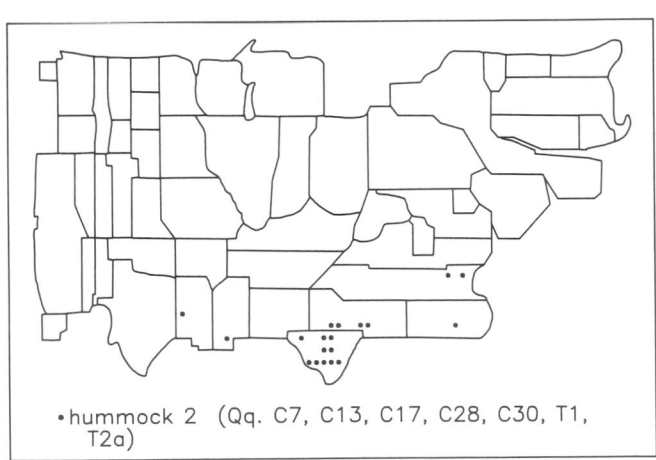

•hummock 2 (Qq. C7, C13, C17, C28, C30, T1, T2a)

3 An island or bank in a river or bay. **C Atl**

c1830 Martin *VA & DC* 181, It was formerly navigable for batteaux for two or three miles to a manufacturing mill, but its bed has now become so obstructed by hammocks, as to impede their progress. **a1883** (1911) Bagby *VA Gentleman* 232, Between the two the boat bravely surmounts every obstacle, be it rocks, rapids, quicksands, hammocks, what not. **1921** in 1940 *AmSp* 15.270 **VA,** There ahead, hummocks and stumps occupied about all there was left of Kittewan Creek. **1923** Earle *Chesapeake Bay Country* 44, Out in the bay, Tangier Island and kindred hummocks form harbors and create the Tangier and Pocomoke sounds. **1976** Warner *Beautiful Swimmers* 8 **Chesapeake Bay,** The larger islands are called hammocks; often they support whole fishing villages or a considerable growth of pine and hardwoods.

4 A small hump or tussock in a field or swamp.

1930 *AmSp* 5.419 **NH,** *Hummock:* a small mound of turf and grass, often formed over a stone in a pasture. *Ibid* 6.151, We find that the following colloquialisms . . are part of the speech of the Middle West and of the South as well as of New Hampshire: . . *hummock.* **1939** *LANE* Map 30 *(Swamp; bog)* 1 inf, **cCT,** Hummock land; 1 inf, **swCT,** Bog swamps have little hummocks. *Ibid* Map 38, The word *hummock,* denoting a small hump in a meadow, pasture, swamp or field, was offered by thirty-eight informants [scattered throughout NEng]. **1966–69** *DARE* (Qu. C17, . . *A small, rounded hill*) Inf **IL**53, Hummock—very small, find them in pastures, could walk over it easily; **MI**67, Hummock—maybe a rise in a field, 3 or 4 feet across, couple feet high; **MA**5, Hummock—not as big as a house. **1971** Craighead *Trees S. FL* 30, Alligator nests are constructed of plant materials heaped up 2 to 3 feet high and 6 to 8 feet wide. . . They form innumerable small hummocks in the saw grass marshes.

hummy See **hommie**

humor n Usu |hjumɚ, -ə|; also **esp Atl** |jumɚ, -ə| See Pronc Intro 3.I.19 Also sp *humour*

A Forms.

1789 Webster *Dissertations Engl. Lang.* 122, In the American pronunciation, *h* is silent in the following . . *humor.* **1927** Shewmake *Engl. Pronc. VA* 31, *Humor[:]* . . the great majority of speakers [in Virginia] seem still to omit the *h* . . though there are of course careful speakers who follow the modern tendency to insert the *h* sounds. **1934** (1943) *W2, Humor.* . . The *h,* formerly silent, is now generally pronounced . . although many good speakers omit it, esp. in the senses relating to mental states, and in the verb. **1941** *LANE* Map 469, [In *humor* [hju], [hʉu] and [ju] (and other variants) are common in **wNEng;** in **cNEng** [ju] becomes increasingly common; in **ME** [ju] predominates.] **1942** Hall *Smoky Mt. Speech* 86 **eTN, wNC,** *Humor* occur[s] without [h]: . . ['jumɚ]. **c1955** Reed–Person *Ling. Atlas Pacific NW,* [27 infs pronounce *humor* with initial /h/; 8 infs use initial /j/.] **1960** Criswell *Resp. to PADS 20* **Ozarks,** Humor (jumɚ)—Invariable older pronunciation. Still current. **1961** Kurath–McDavid *Pronc. Engl.* 178 **Atl,** *Humor*—The prevalent pronunciation of *humor* is |jumз ~ jumə|. With few exceptions, initial |h| occurs only in New England and Upstate New York. It is most common in the Connecticut Valley. **1973** *PADS* 60.60 **seNC,** Seven [infs] used initial /h/ [in *humor*], and only three initial /j/. It is not possible to say whether this results from the encroachment of a spelling pronunciation, or if it is a survival of an older form imported by ancestors who first settled in the North and then moved to North Carolina. **1986** *DARE* File **nePA,** The humor ['jumɚ] of the thing depended on knowing Chaplin.

B Senses.

1 Fluid matter associated with and sometimes thought to cause a rash or swelling; the rash itself. [*EDD humour* sb. 1 "Matter or pus from a wound or sore"; also *SND humour* n. 1]

1899 (1912) Green *VA Folk-Speech* 235, *Humour.* . . Watery matter in some skin breakings-out. **1933** Rawlings *South Moon* 117 **FL,** "Lant [=a man] needs medicine, too," she said. "He's got a humour in his blood and he'll eetch and eetch until he'll scratch his back agin a post like ary hog." **1941** *Hench Coll.* **VA,** *Humors* is still used of animals' diseases. "That cow has humors in her leg."

2 See quot. [*EDD humour* sb. 2 "A sore, boil, or gathering"; *SND humour* n. 1 "A skin eruption"]

1966 *DARE* (Qu. BB24, . . *A rash that comes out suddenly*) Inf **SC**27, A humor ['hjumə]—occasional to common; [used by] both races.

humour See **humor**

hump n

1 In railroading: an artificial hill or incline where gravity is used to switch cars onto different tracks; see quot 1932; hence n *master, hump rat* one who controls cars on such a hill.

1906 Droege *Yards & Terminals* 104, It is now a common proceeding to throw up humps on a level prairie or river bottom and make a gravity yard. **1916** *DN* 4.356, *Hump yard.* . . A train yard where the gravity system of shifting is used. **1932** *RR Mag.* Oct 368, *Hump*—Artificial knoll at end of classification yard over which cars are pushed and allowed to roll to separate tracks on their own momentum. **1967–69** *DARE* Tape **IL**7, I was working on the sections out here by the big humps. There's two large humps out there where they separate the freight trains; **ID**9, A gravity retarder yard [is] very commonly known in railroad language as a hump—because it looks like a hump. . . A locomotive will get ahold of this string of cars and push it up over this hump on signal, . . very slow. . . As it [=the car] goes over the top of this hump, it's inspected by carmen. . . [The cars] will roll down this gravity retarder yard into various tracks; **NC**75, The most important industry [in Galesburg, Illinois] is the railroad. . . They have the largest humps in the world, which is where they make up trains. **1968** *AmSp* 43.287, *Hump rat.* A yard brakeman who controls the speed of cars as they are switched off the "hump". **1969** *AmSp* 44.257, *Hump master*—Employee who controls automatic switches in a hump yard[;] *Hump yard*—Modern yard with an incline that uses gravity to switch cars.

2 A tumble; see quot. [Cf *bump, lump, thump;* cf also **hump knot**]

1966 *DARE* (Qu. Y1, . . *Suddenly falling down: "He slipped . . and took quite a ______.*") Inf **SC**11, Hump.

3 See quot. *euphem*

1967 *DARE* (Qu. GG21a, *If you don't care what a person does, you might tell him, " . . go ahead and do it ______.*") Inf **WA**20, I don't give a hump.

4 See quot.

1966–70 *DARE* (Qu. N30, . . *A sudden short dip in the road*) 9 Infs, **scattered,** Hump.

5 in phrr *get a hump on (oneself), get a hump:* To hurry, exert oneself. **scattered, but esp S Midl, Sth** Cf **hump** v 1

1892 *Harper's New Mth. Mag.* 84.487/2, We do seem to be gittin' a leetle less hump on oursel's than we did then. **1906** *DN* 3.137 **nwAR,** *Get a hump on (one's self).* . . To hurry; to show energy. **1914** *DN* 4.107 **KS,** *Get a [hump] on.* . . To hurry. **1950** *WELS* 1 Inf, **ceWI,** Get a hump on himself. **c1960** *Wilson Coll.* **csKY,** *Get a hump on* . . try harder, exert oneself. **1960** Criswell *Resp. to PADS 20* **Ozarks,** "Get a hump on you"—very common. **1965–70** *DARE* (Qu. A19, . . *"I'm late, I'll have to ______.*") Infs **AR**55, **IA**16, **MD**36, **NC**60, Get a hump (on); **DC**3, Get a hump on me; (Qu. A20) Infs **DC**3, **IL**37, **NJ**17, **SC**62, **WV**8, Get a hump on; **AR**55, **NC**60, Get a hump on you (boy); **MD**14, Get a little hump on you; (Qu. A22) Infs **IA**16, **MD**36, Got a hump on (her); (Qu. Y18) Inf **SC**46, Get a hump on us; (Qu. JJ26) Inf **WA**18, Get a hump on. [11 of 12 Infs old]

6 in phr *on the hump:* Out of order. Cf *on the hummer* (at **hummer 4a**)

1966 *DARE* (Qu. KK19, . . *Temporarily out of order*) Inf **MS**6, On the hump.

hump v

1 often refl or with *it:* To exert oneself; to hurry.

1843 (1973) Porter *Big Bear AR* 126 **MS,** He was breathin' sorter hard, his eye set on the Governor, humpin' himself on politics. **1848** (1855) Ruxton *Life Far West* 178 **Rocky Mts,** Winter was coming on; they would have to 'streak' it night and day, and sleep when their journey was over, which would not be until Pike's Peak was left behind them. It was now October, and the way they'd have to hump it back to the mountains would take the gristle off a painter's tail. **1885** Twain *Huck. Finn* 259 **MO,** I never hunted for no back streets, but humped it straight through the main one. **1905** *DN* 3.62 **NE,** *Hump yourself.* **1913** *DN* 4.11 **MN,** *Hump.* . . "Come on, let us hump along." **1929** in 1931 McCorrison *Letters Fraternity* 194 **csME,** G______ still has the same hunch of the shoulder, that he had when he used to swat the ball, and "hump" for first base. **1947** Guthrie *Big Sky* 139 **West** (as of c1830s), Jourdonnais for once seemed to have lost his hurry. Boone wished he would hump it. **1950** *WELS* 1 Inf, **ceWI,** Hump myself *(or)* yourself. **1960** Criswell *Resp. to PADS 20* **Ozarks,** Hump yourself. **1967** *DARE* (Qu. A19, . . *"I'm late, I'll have to ______.*") Infs **AL**43, 46, **MI**22, **NJ**17, **WV**16, Hump; **ID**5, Hump along; (Qu. A20) Inf **MA**5, Hump yourself—familiar; (Qu. JJ25, *To show somebody that you're the boss: "He thought he could take the place over, but I made him ______.*") Inf **FL**15, Hump; (Qu. Y24, . . *To walk, to go on foot*) Inf **SC**34, Hump it; (Qu. KK29, . . Working very hard) Inf **IN**5, Humping. **1975** Gould *ME Lingo* 138, *Hump*—To move right along: "Now, let's get humpin' here!" Children are told to *hump* right along, not to dilly-dally.

2 To balk; hence adj *humpy.* [Cf *EDD hump* v. 7 "To be dissatisfied with; to sulk. . . Hence *humping*"]

1904 *DN* 2.398 **cNY,** *Hump.* . . To balk, hang back. "I don't know why he should hump on that." *Ibid, Humpy.* . . Balky, reluctant. "You needn't be so humpy over that."

3 To idle, loaf around.

1966 *DARE* (Qu. KK31, *To go about aimlessly looking for distraction: ". . he's just ——— around."*) Inf **SC**10, Humping.

4 usu with *up,* also with *over:* To make oneself smaller; to draw oneself in. [Cf *OED hump* v. 1 "To hunch. (Also with *up*)"]

1967–70 *DARE* (Qu. Y32, *. . Squeeze yourself into a small space*) Infs **KY**21, 42, **MD**17, **MO**8, 37, 39, **NY**233, Hump up; **KY**33, **OH**50, Hump over; **IN**26, Hump.

5 in phr *hump like a dog eating paste:* See quot.

1927 *Ruppenthal Coll.* **KS,** *To hump like a dog eating paste*—To be round-shouldered, stooped, bowed; also, to bend over in laborious effort.

6 To handle freight, esp on a dock; hence vbl n *humping,* n *humper.*

1968 Adams *Western Words* 157, *Humping freight*—In steamboating, loading and unloading freight from a steamboat. **1969** *AmSp* 44.205 [Truckers' talk], *Humper*—See *digger.* [*Ibid* 203, *Digger*—Worker who handles freight on the dock or who loads and unloads vehicles.]

humpback n

1 also *humpback(ed) whale:* A whalebone whale of the genus *Megaptera.* [See quots 1928, 1957]

1725 Royal Soc. London *Philos. Trans.* 33.258 **NEng coast,** Both the Finbacks and Humpbacks are shaped in Reeves longitudinal from Head to Tail on their Bellies and their Sides. **1816** *Niles' Weekly Reg.* 10.199/1, On the 26th of March, two hump-backed whales were killed and caught by the crew of two boats, near Edgartown, Mass. **1844** Lee–Frost *10 Yrs. OR* 92, In the month of January following, two large hump-back whales were driven ashore in the same vicinity. **1867** *Amer. Naturalist* 1.224, Among the Humpbacks, the females exceed the males in size. **1928** Anthony *N. Amer. Mammals* 562, *Humpback Whale. . .* Maximum length of about 50 feet; dorsal fin present as a low "hump". **1946** Dufresne *AK's Animals* 185, The thick-set body of the Humpback Whale and its extremely long barnacle-covered flippers and large flukes serve to identify it. . . The Humpback is blackish in color, variously mottled and with white underparts sometimes extending well up along the sides. **1957** Blair et al. *Vertebrates U.S.* 742, *Genus Megaptera* Gray. Humpback whale. . . Dorsal fin low, humplike.

2 **=black sea bass 1.**

1946 LaMonte *N. Amer. Game Fishes* 48, *Centropristis striatus. . . Names:* Blackfish, Black Sea Bass, . . Humpback.

3 Any of var other fishes: see **humpback buffalo, humpbacked carp, humpback salmon, humpback sucker.**

4 See **humpbacked skeeter.**

5 In logging:

a See quot.

1958 McCulloch *Woods Words* 91 **Pacific NW,** *Humpback. . .* A logging truck returning to the woods with its trailer on its back.

b A person who saws timber; see quot.

1968 Adams *Western Words* 156, *Humpback*—A logger's name for a sawyer.

6 In railroading: see quot.

1977 Adams *Lang. Railroader* 83, *Humpback:* A piece of metal spiked to the ties, used to guide the wheels of a derailed car back onto the track.

7 See **hump nose.**

humpback buffalo n Also *humpback* [See quot 1983]

=smallmouth buffalo.

1933 LA Dept. of Conserv. *Fishes* 442, The Smallmouth Buffalo has . . received a confusion of popular names. Included are . . Humpback Buffalo [etc]. **1967** *DARE* Tape **LA**5, You got two different kinds of buffalo. . . What they call raised-back buffalo is the humpback. **1983** Becker *Fishes WI* 625, *Ictiobus bubalus. . .* Other common names: razorback buffalo, . . humpback buffalo. . . Back highly arched and ridgelike.

humpback cat n

=blue catfish 1.

1968 *DARE* (Qu. P1, *What kinds of freshwater fish are caught around here that are good to eat?*) Inf **GA**25, Humpback cat.

humpbacked butterfish n

A **moonfish** (here: *Vomer setipinnis*).

1884 Goode *Fisheries U.S.* 1.323, The Horse-fish, *Selene setipinnis,* is a frequent summer visitor all along the coast as far north as Wood's Hole, Massachusetts, where it has a peculiar name, the people there calling it the "Hump-backed Butterfish."

humpbacked carp n Also *humpback*

A carpsucker (here: *Carpiodes velifer*).

1957 Trautman *Fishes* 243 **OH,** Commercial fishermen recognized the large adults as a distinct species, called them the "Hump-backed Carp." . . Likewise these men said that until 1920 the "Hump-back" was numerous in the Ohio River from Washington County upstream to the Pennsylvania state line. **1983** Becker *Fishes WI* 638, *Carpiodes velifer. . .* Other common names . . humpbacked carp.

humpbacked salmon See **humpback salmon**

humpbacked skeeter n Also *humpback*

1950 *WELS (Other names or nicknames for a mosquito; any name for an extra big mosquito)* 1 Inf, **ceWI,** Humpbacked skeeter, humpback.

humpbacked sucker See **humpback sucker**

humpbacked whale See **Humpback 1**

humpback grunt n

A **grunt** n **1** (here: *Haemulon sciurus*).

1935 Caine *Game Fish* 88, *Yellow Grunt—Haemulon sciurus . . Synonyms:* Blue-striped Grunt. Boar Grunt. . . Humpback Grunt. **1946** LaMonte *N. Amer. Game Fishes* 66, *Yellow Grunt—Haemulon sciurus . .* Humpback Grunt.

humpback job n

See quots.

1932 *RR Mag.* Oct 368, *Humpback job*—One on a peddler freight. **1940** Cottrell *Railroader* 129, *Humpback job*—Assignment on a local way-freight train.

humpback pickerel n Also *humpbacked pike*

=grass pickerel 1.

1887 Goode *Amer. Fishes* 278, It [=*Esox americanus vermiculatus*] has been called the "Hump-back Pickerel," and is of little value for food. **1911** *Century Dict.* 4484, Hump-backed pike, *Esox vermiculatus.* **1927** Weed *Pike* 42, *Esox americanus. . .* Humpbacked Pickerel; Waterford, Oakland County, Michigan.

humpback salmon n Also *humpback, humpbacked salmon, humpie (salmon), humpy* [See quots 1884, 1904]

A small **salmon** (Here: *Oncorhynchus gorbuscha*) native to the Pacific coast. Also called **dog salmon, haddo, holia, lost salmon, pink salmon**

1807 tr. Garytschev *Voyages* 28 *(DA),* We managed . . to lay in a stock for ourselves of the hump-backed salmon, and other such fish. **1881** *Amer. Naturalist* 15.186, The fact that the hump-back salmon runs only on alternate years in Puget sound . . is well attested. **1884** Goode *Fisheries U.S.* 1.476, This species is known to the Russians still . . by the name of "Gorbuscha," *gorb* meaning hump. The English-speaking people call it generally the "Hump-back Salmon," and often the "Dog Salmon." **1904** *Salmon & Trout* 163, The humpback usually ascends small streams for the purpose of spawning. . . When it first comes in from the ocean, it resembles the quinnat salmon in form and color, but as the spawning season advances it develops a large hump on the back, whence the common name. **1919** *DN* 5.56 **Puget Sound WA,** *Humpie. . .* Humpbacked salmon. The run of *humpie* salmon at all points on the Sound continued unabated. The Sedro-Woolley Courier. **1940** White *Wild Geese* 493 **AK** (as of c1896), At the end of two days a belated small school of humpies bumped their noses against the obstruction and fell back into the pool to think it over. **1962** Salisbury *Quoth the Raven* 121 **seAK,** The commercial species used by the canneries, the sockeye, humpback, dog and coho, enter the Alaskan streams usually in the order named and then is when the really hard work of the natives occurs. **1968** *DARE* (Qu. P1, *What kinds of freshwater fish are caught around here that are good to eat?*) Inf **AK**1, Humpies. **1975** *AK Mag.* Feb 20/3, The *pink* salmon *(Oncorhyncus gorbuscha),* also called the humpy, or humpbacked salmon, is the smallest of the Pacific salmon at maturity. . . It is found from the Columbia River north to Kotzebue Sound, Alaska. **1980** *Fairbanks Daily News–Miner* (AK) 11 Sept 2/4, There were a lot of humpys [sic] this year, and we are thankful about them.

humpback sucker n Also *humpback, humpbacked sucker, humpie* [See quot 1963]

A large sucker *(Xyrauchen texanus)* found throughout most of the Colorado River drainage. Also called **razorback sucker**

1896 U.S. Natl. Museum *Bulletin* 47.184, *Xyrauchen cypho. . .* (Hump-backed Sucker.) **1944** (1967) McNichols *Crazy Weather* 52 **AZ,** It was a native humpback sucker, soft of flesh and full of bones, weighing seven or eight pounds. **1963** Sigler–Miller *Fishes UT* 106, The humpback sucker . . is easily identified, except when young, by the sharp-edged hump on its back, from which it receives its common name. **1965** McClane *McClane's Std. Fishing Encycl.* 411/1, The humpback prefers the slow-moving parts of larger streams. **1966** *DARE* (Qu. P1, *What kinds of freshwater fish are caught around here that are good to eat?*) Inf **NM**10, Humpback or humpie—similar to a sucker.

humpback whale See **humpback 1**

humpback whitefish n

Either of two related fish:

a A **whitefish** (here: *Coregonus pidshian*) native to Alaska.

[**1883** U.S. Natl. Museum *Bulletin* 27.391, The humpback white-fish of the Yukon resembles *Coregonus syrok* C. & V., but appears to be an undescribed species.] **1896** *Ibid* 47.466, *Coregonus nelsonii. . . Hump-back Whitefish. . .* Allied to *Coregonus clupeiformis* [sic], but distinguished by its arched and compressed back. . . A bony species of inferior flavor. **1902** Jordan–Evermann *Amer. Fishes* 123, *Common Whitefish. Coregonus clupeiformis* [sic]. . . is known also as humpback, bowback, and highback whitefish (Lake Superior). *Ibid* 130, *Humpback Whitefish. Coregonus nelsonii . .* occurs in Alaska from Bristol Bay northward. **1960** Amer. Fisheries Soc. *List Fishes* 11, Humpback whitefish . . *Coregonus pidshian.* **1978** *AK Fishing Guide* 83, *The humpback whitefish . .* is the most widely distributed of any whitefish in Alaska.

b also *highback whitefish:* A **whitefish** (here: *Coregonus clupeaformis*) native to the Great Lakes.

1902 [see **a** above]. **1911** U.S. Bur. Census *Fisheries 1908* 318, The common whitefish . . is found in the Great Lakes region and is known as "humpback," "bowback," and "highback" whitefish.

hump day n Also *hump night*

Wednesday, the middle of the week.

1955 *AmSp* 30.226 **swCA,** *Hump night. . .* Wednesday night, which is over the hump of the week. **c1965** *DARE* File **OR,** *Hump day* was used by counselors at summer camp to mean Wednesday. **c1970** *DARE* File **csWI,** Hump day is Wednesday, the middle of the working week. "We're over the hump now." **1986** *Isthmus* (Madison WI) 6 Feb 33, [Advt:] *Wednesday* / Enjoy Hump Day—Hit Bogies [=a bar and restaurant]. **1989** *DARE* File **csMA,** Hump Day—Wednesday.

humped nose See **hump nose**

humper n[1] Also *humper (lake) trout*

See quots.

1965 McClane *McClane's Std. Fishing Encycl.* 461, Presently identified as a race resembling the siscowet in its external appearance is the humper lake trout, which is known to the commercial fishermen as the "paperbelly" or "bank trout." The humper lake trout inhabits isolated offshore reefs (banks) surrounded by deep water. **1983** Becker *Fishes WI* 330, Commercial fishermen and buyers recognize . . at least four variants: *lean trout . . , fat trout . . , half-breeds,* and *humpers. Ibid* 331, The humper as described by Khan and Qadri (1970) . . is more like the siscowet than the lake trout in many characters. . . Rahrer (1965) called attention to the external resemblance of the humper to the siscowet. However, he noted that the humper's thin ventral body wall ("paper-belly") and the limited amount of fat on its viscera would distinguish it from the siscowet. . . The taxonomic status of the humper trout is not yet clear.

humper n[2] See **hump v 6**

humper (lake) trout See **humper** n[1]

humpie n

1 See **humpback salmon.**

2 See **humpback sucker.**

3 A **mooneye** (here: *Hiodon tergisus*).

1976 *DARE* File **Isle Royale MI,** Mooneyes are also called humpies at Rock Harbor.

humpie salmon See **humpback salmon**

humping See **hump v 6**

hump it See **hump v 1**

‡**humpkin** n [Var of *bumpkin*]

1966 *DARE* (Qu. HH1, . . *A rustic or countrified person*) Inf **AR**3, Humpkin.

humpknot n [Redund; from the shape of the contusion] Cf **bumpknot, pumpknot**

1968–69 *DARE* (Qu. X60, . . *A lump . . on your head when you get a sharp blow*) Infs **MO**9, 19, Humpknot.

hump like a dog eating paste See **hump v 8**

‡**humpluggins** n pl [Cf *OED humdudgeon*]

1968 *DARE* (Qu. BB28, . . *Imaginary diseases*) Inf **MD**37, Humpluggins [ˌhəmˈplʌgɨnz].

hump master See **hump n 1**

hump nose n Also *humpback, humped nose*

1966–69 *DARE* (Qu. X15, . . *Different kinds of noses, according to shape*) Infs **MO**17, 37, **MT**2, **PA**18, Hump nose; **NC**37, Humped nose; **TX**32, Humpback.

hump over See **hump v 4**

hump puss n [Chinook *humm opoots* stinking tail]

A **skunk** (here: *Mephitis mephitis*).

1967 *DARE* (Qu. P26, . . *A skunk*) Inf **WA**20, Hump puss (Indian name).

hump rat See **hump n 1**

humps n pl Cf **collywobbles, heaves**

An unspecified disease; see quots.

1884 Smith *Bill Arp's Scrap Book* 54 **nwGA,** I talked with 'em all, and thar was nary one but what had the dyspepsy . . or the rumatics . . or the heaves, or the humps, or somethin. **1989** *DARE* File **nOH** (as of 1930s), The humps—a fit of ill nature.

humptoad n [Prob var of **hoptoad**]

1968 *DARE* (Qu. B26, *When it's raining very heavily, you say, "It's raining ________."*) Inf **MD**19, Humptoads.

hump up See **hump v 4**

humpy adj See **hump v 2**

humpy n

1 A California **sheepshead.**

1946 LaMonte *N. Amer. Game Fishes* 92, *California Sheepshead—Pimelometopon pulcher . .* Names: . . Fathead, Humpy. **1953** Roedel *Common Fishes CA* 117, *Sheep-Head—Pimelometopon pulchrum . .* Unauthorized Names: Redfish, . . humpy.

2 See **humpback salmon.**

hum up v phr [Perh var of **come up 1**]

Move!—used to urge a mule or horse to go forward.

1929 (1954) Faulkner *Sound & Fury* 10 **nMS,** "Go on T.P. Drive that surrey like Roskus told you, now." "Yessum. . . Hum up, Queenie [=a horse]." **1941** O'Donnell *Great Big Doorstep* 55 **seLA,** The mule would not jump the ditch. Juarrelle jerked at the reins. 'Hum up, mule,' she cried. **1942** Faulkner *Go Down* 229 **nMS,** "Hum up here mules!" he said, jerking the reins so that the mules leaped forward. **1942** *Sat. Eve. Post* 16 May 81/1 **eTN,** Wyatt slapped the mules with the slack of the lines. "Hum up, there, Bess! Get along, Tobe!" **1944** *ADD* 309, *Hum up.* = giddap.

‡**humus** n attrib [Perh by analogy with *cumulus*]

1967 *DARE* (Qu. B11, . . *Kinds of clouds*) Inf **IA**7, Humus [ˈhjuməs], clouds—Grampa used to talk about them.

hun n [Abbr for *Hungarian*]

1 =**Hungarian partridge. chiefly Inland Nth**

1950 *WELS* (. . *Kinds of game birds*) 1 Inf, **seWI,** Hun. **1953** Jewett *Birds WA* 218, *Gray Partridge. Perdix perdix . .* Other names: . . Hun; . . Copper Tail. **1956** *AmSp* 31.180, *Hun* (general) . . for the gray or Hungarian partridge. **1957** *AmSp* 32.184, Hun. Gray partridge. General. **1966–68** *DARE* (Qu. Q7, *Names and nicknames for other kinds of game birds around here*) Infs **ID**5, **MN**18, **WA**2, 3, Huns; **MN**33, Huns—partridge; **MT**3, Huns—Hungarian pheasants. **1967** [see **Hungarian partridge 1**]. **1968** *WI Conserv. Bulletin* Sept–Oct 20, Huns [=Hungarian partridges] are most abundant on the open agricultural range of east-central Wisconsin. **1982** [see **Hungarian partridge 1**]. *Ibid,* [Caption:] Small Hun covey, whirring away low over field.

2 usu cap: A person of foreign background, esp German or Hungarian. **scattered, but chiefly Nth, N Midl**

1928 *Ruppenthal Coll.* **KS,** *Hun*—a German; epithet in [the first] World War. **1957** Battaglia *Resp. to PADS 20* **eMD,** *Hun*—Hungarian. **1964** *PADS* 42.39 **Chicago IL,** The most popular terms for Germans have been carried over from World War I, viz., *hun.* **1965–70** *DARE* (Qu. HH28, *Names . . for people of foreign background*) 29 Infs, **scattered, but chiefly Nth, N Midl,** Hun(s)—German(s); 10 Infs, **scattered,** Hun—Hungarian; **MI**110, **NY**12, 206, 232, **WA**9, Hun—German (or) Hungarian; **PA**245, Hun—Hungarian (or) Czechoslovakian. [13 of 16 Infs using *Hun* for "Hungarian" were old.]

hunard See **hundred A4**

hunch v, hence vbl n *hunching*

1a also with *on:* To push or shove; also fig. [*EDD hunch* v. 2 "To push, *gen.* with the shoulder or elbow"]

1806 (1970) Webster *Compendious Dict.* 147, *Hunch. . .* to push with the elbow, strike. **1911** White *Advent. Bobby Orde* 258, Bending to his task the pusher at the rear dug his toes in, while the others hunched. **1935** Hurston *Mules & Men* 107 **FL** [Black], Ole Massa made me so mad. . . Man, Ah laid one cussin' on 'im! Ah'm a man lak dis, Ah won't stan' no hunchin'. Ah betcha he won't bother *me* no mo'. **1967** *DARE* (Qu. Y6, . . *To put pressure on somebody to do something*) Inf **MO**18, Hunch him on. **1967** *DARE* FW Addit **LA**7, Hunch the fire—to stir the fire to make it burn faster, or to add wood to make it burn faster.

b Spec: To nudge, usu to call attention quietly to something.

1856 Whitcher *Bedott Papers* 207 **cNY,** While the elder was a talkin', she kept a hunchin Miss Coon, and grinnin'. **1872** Twain *Roughing It* 385 **West,** *She* never could tell when it [=her glass eye] hopped out, being blind on that side, you see. So somebody would have to hunch her and say, "Your game eye has fetched loose, Miss Wagner dear." **1885** Twain *Huck. Finn* 211 **MO,** Then the king he hunched the duke, private. **1904** *DN* 2.419 **nwAR,** *Hunch. . .* To nudge. "One of the big gals hunched the old man in the ribs with her elbow." **1917** Garland *Son Middle Border* 184 **WI,** Joe Belford hunched his brother. 'Go after him now,' he said. **1928** *Ruppenthal Coll.* **KS,** *Hunch*—to hint, esp. with a physical manifestation as with a shove or tap. **1946** *PADS* 6.18 **eNC,** *Hunch. . .* To nudge (with the elbow). **1960** Criswell *Resp. to PADS 20* **Ozarks,** *Hunch*—To push or nudge (a person), usually to call surreptitious attention to something.

c Of an animal: to push or butt with the head or horns. [*EDD hunch* v. 2 "To . . butt with the horns"; *OED hunch* v. 1 *"Obs."*]

1899 (1912) Green *VA Folk-Speech* 236, *Hunch. . .* To push or jog with the fist or elbow. Or with the head. "The lambs hunched the ewe's bags." **1908** *DN* 3.322 **eAL, wGA,** *Hunch. . .* Of a calf, to butt its mother's udder when sucking. This is supposed to make the cow give down her milk.

2 To cheat, spec:

a In marble play: to move the hand forward while shooting; hence vbl n *hunching.* Cf **fudge** v, **hudge** v

1896 *DN* 1.419 **cNY,** *Hunchin's. . .* "No hunchin's," same as *no fudgins.* **1915** in 1944 *ADD* **cNY,** Used esp. by boys playing marbles. . . 'No fin hunchin'!' **1950** *WELS (Calls used in marbles to stop another player from doing something)* 4 Infs, **WI,** No (or) stop hunching; 1 Inf, Hunching. **1955** *PADS* 23.20 **cwAL,** *Hunch. . .* Same as *fudge.* **1957** *Sat. Eve. Post Letters* **cnGA,** "Hunching" or "fudging" was usually taboo in a strict game. This consisted of a forward motion of the shooting fist simultaneous with the shooting motion of the thumb. **c1970** Wiersma *Marbles Terms* **csMI, NJ,** *Hunch*—propelling the marble with the thumb while the hand is moving forward at the same time. This is an illegal procedure, and leads to the call: "No hunchin'." *Ibid, Hunching*—moving the hand across the ring line when shooting, . . or moving the hand across the spot where the shooter came to rest when shooting inside the ring. *Ibid, Hunching*—forbidden. *Ibid* **Chicago IL** (as of 1960), *Hunchin'*—cheating by moving closer to the circle. "Quit hunchin'." **1973** Ferretti *Marble Book* 47, *Hunching.* Moving the hand forward while shooting. This is cheating too. **1983** *MJLF* 9.1.44 **ceKY,** *Hunch* . . to move the shooting hand toward the object marbles as one shoots. **1984** *WI State Jrl.* (Madison) 8 Apr sec 9 1/4, Shots known as . . "hunching" (moving the hand forward) are prohibited.

b See quot.

1950 *WELS (Cheating at an examination)* 1 Inf, **cnWI,** Hunching.

3 intr: To move, spec:

a =**coon** v **1.**

1913 Porter *Laddie* 153, When she came to the creek, she sat astride the foot log, and hunched along with her hands.

b =**coon** v **2.**

1933 Rawlings *South Moon* 104 **FL,** He hunched up the rough tree trunk, agile as an old 'possum.

c with *over:* To scoot over, slide sideways.

1966–68 *DARE* (Qu. Y52, *To move over—for example on a long bench: "We have to make room for one more. Can you ——— [a little]?"*) Infs **ME**13, 22, **PA**130, Hunch over; **NY**69, Hunch over—old-fashioned; **CT**27, Hunch over—because you start to stand up and don't really stand up—just a little up and a little down.

4 See quot.

1968 *DARE* (Qu. Y27, *To go about aimlessly, with nothing to do: "He's always ——— around."*) Inf **PA**130, Hunching; (Qu. KK31, *To go about aimlessly looking for distraction*) Inf **PA**130, Hunching.

hunch n

1 A hint; a suggestion. [**hunch** v **1b**]

1899 (1900) Ade *Fables in Slang* 123 **IN,** She didn't know how to make a Showing, and there was nobody in Town qualified to give her a quiet Hunch. **1904** Day *Kin o' Ktaadn* 181 **ME,** That was sartinly givin' Thanksgivin' comp'ny a good hard hunch, but some Injuns need it. **1922** Z. Grey *To Last Man* ii.36 *(OEDS),* All shootin' arms an' such are at a premium in the Tonto. . . An' I was givin' you a hunch to come loaded. **1951** *AmSp* 26.183 **NC** (as of 1849), *Hunch. . .* Hint, suggestion. 'Another piece [of writing] gave a few hunches to the inexperienced freshmen.'

2 In marble play:

a pl: See quots. [**hunch** v **2a**]

1963 *KY Folkl. Rec.* 9.3.64, *The act of lifting the shooter to a shooting position above the ground:* . . hunches. **c1970** Wiersma *Marbles Terms* **neIL** (as of 1950s), Hunches—a call used to claim the right to rest your shooting hand upon your free hand, thus gaining the advantage of extra height, therefore extra speed and distance, and perhaps even better accuracy. "Hunches!" "I get hunches."

b See quot.

1970 *DARE* (Qu. EE7, . . *Marble games*) Inf **VA**99, Hunch.

hunching See **hunch** v

hunchmens n pl [Double plural var of *henchmen*]

1980 Folb *Runnin' Down* 124 [Black], I stood between *three* guns—two in the back o' me, one in the front . . and have an Avenue he tell me he gon' blow *me* away. His two hunchmens in the back of me they gonna shoot me with a gun!

hunch on See **hunch** v **1a**

hunch over See **hunch** v **3c**

hund n |hʊnt| [Ger]

1968 *DARE* (Qu. J2, . . *Joking or uncomplimentary words . . for dogs*) Infs **OH**79, **PA**150, **WI**47, Hunt [hʊnt]; (Qu. J1 . . *A dog of mixed breed*) Inf **PA**161, Hund [hʊnt]—an older term—not ever just the Dutch.

hunder See **hundred A3**

hunderd See **hundred A1**

hunde(r)t See **hundred A2**

hundred n, adj Usu |'hʌndrəd|; very freq |'hʌndərd|; for addit varr see **A** below

A Forms.

1 |'hʌndə(r)d|; pronc-spp *hunderd, hundu(r)d;* for addit pronc and sp varr see quots. [By metath] **chiefly Atlantic, Sth, S Midl**

1861 Holmes *Venner* 1.152 **NEng,** It's lasted a hundud year. **1890** *DN* 1.7 **wNY,** There is metathesis in hunderd. **1903** *DN* 2.290 **Cape Cod MA** (as of 1857), *Hunderd . .* for . . *hundred.* **1905** *DN* 3.58 **eNE,** *Hunderd.* **1908** *DN* 3.322 **eAL, wGA,** *Hunderd. . .* Hundred. Universal. **1914** *DN* 4.71 **ME, nNH,** The ole sow dressed off hundurd an' a half. **1922** Gonzales *Black Border* 307 **sSC, GA coasts** [Gullah glossary], *Hund'ud*—hundred, hundreds. **1934** (1943) *W2* 1214, [Footnote:] *Hun'der, hun'derd, hun'dert,* Scot & Dial. vars. of *Hundred.* **1936** *AmSp* 11.165 **eTX,** Hundred is universally ['hʌ̃ndɚd], ['hʌ̃ndəd]. **1939** *LANE* Map 61 *(Hundred)* **NEng,** [Slow forms have [r] plus a vowel in the second syllable, as ['hʌndər̩d]. Quick forms have syllabic [r, ɹ], as ['hʌndrd, -dɹd] or a vowel only, as ['hʌndəd, -ded, -dɨd].] **1942** Hall

Smoky Mt. Speech 87 **eTN, wNC,** Usually ['hʌndɚd]. **1944** Kenyon-Knott *Pronc. Dict.* 210, *Hundred*. . . E[ast and] S[outh] . . -dəd. **1968** *DARE* Tape **GA**30, He had knowed 'em [=alligators] to tote water fer a hunderd yards.

2 |'hʌndə(r)t|; pronc-spp *hunde(r)t.* [By metath and devoicing of final consonant]

1934 [see **A1** above]. **1942** in 1944 *ADD* 309 **cNY,** [hʌndrts]. Hunderts of years old. **1969** *DARE* FW Addit **MA**26, Hundet ['hʌndət].

3 |'hʌndər|; pronc-sp *hunder.* [*SND hunder* II. (2), (4); *EDD hunder.*]

1843 (1916) Hall *New Purchase* 372, Go ridin about the Purchis [=Purchase] on hunder-dollar hossis. **1858** Hammett *Piney Woods Tavern* 111, As long as the hunder and nineteenth psalm besides. **1897** *KS Univ. Qrly.* (ser B) 6.88, *Hunder* . . hundred. **1934** [see **A1** above].

4 |'hʌnə(r)d|; pronc-spp *hunne(r)d, hun'r'd;* arch sp *hunard;* for var see quot 1936. [By metath and assim] **chiefly Sth, S Midl**

1936 *AmSp* 11.234 **eTX,** ['hʌ̃nɚ / əd] . . for . . *hundred* . . in illiterate speech. **1940** in 1944 *ADD* 309 **MS,** 4-hun'r'd-pound sacks. **1941** *AmSp* 16.12 **eTX** [Black], Medial loss. . . *Hundred* . . [is] reduced to ['hʌnəd]. **1942** Hall *Smoky Mt. Speech* 87 **eTN, wNC,** Medial loss of consonants. . . [d] after [n] is in most cases not sounded . . as in . . hundred ['hʌnɚd]. **1956** Eliason *Tarheel Talk* 312 **NC,** *Hundred* . . hunard [in] 1837. **1970** *DARE* (Qu. GG29, *To be in a good . . mood: ". . he seems to be feeling ______.*") Inf **OH**95, Hunned ['hʌnəd] percent. **1978** Doig *This House* 164 **MT** (as of c1955), The sheep are squirting through, just near enough that McGrath can hear me echo his tally, know that it is marked . . *Hunnerd!* . . Again my jack-knife—*a hundred!*—snicks softly.

5 |'hʌnə(r)t|; pronc-spp *hunert, hunnet, hunnit* [By metath, assim and devoicing of final consonant]

1931 *AmSp* 7.46 **NYC,** [Walter Winchell's] phonetic transcriptions are vulgar for the most part, and yet accurate . . *hunnit* for hundred. **1938** Matschat *Suwannee R.* 162 **nFL, sGA,** Most b'ars they kilt weighted upwards of four hunert pounds. **1969** *DARE* FW Addit **MA**26, Hunnet ['hʌnət]. **1976** Garber *Mountain-ese* 44 **Appalachians,** *Hunert* . . hundred—I paid a hunert dollars fer that calf. **1986** *DARE* File **nwAR,** I know just a hunert ways to do that.

B As noun.

1a An administrative division of a county, originally of Virginia, Maryland, Delaware, Pennsylvania, and Maine, but now only in Delaware. [*OED hundred* sb. 5 "In England . . A subdivision of a county or shire, having its own court"]

1621 *Ordin. Virginia* 24 July in Stith *Hist. Virginia* App. iv.33 *(OED),* The other council . . shall consist for the present, of the said council of state, and of two burgesses out of every town, hundred, or other particular plantation. [**1682** in 1852 PA Prov. Council *Minutes* 1.21, Power to Divide the said Countrey, and Islands, into Townes, Hundreds and Counties.] **1723** *Amer. Weekly Mercury* 7 Nov 4/2 **DE,** Run away the 5th of this Instant November, from William Hugh of White-Clay Creek Hundred, in the County of New-Castle, a Servant Man. **1885** Wilhelm *Local Institutions MD* 40, The hundreds of Maryland were in origin a geographical division. . . the oldest civil division in the province was the hundred. *Ibid* 62, An Act of Assembly . . 1824 gave the death blow to the hundreds of Maryland as a civil division. **1885** Ingle *Local Institutions VA* 3.43, Equally involved in obscurity is the beginning of the hundred in Virginia, and the history of its various phases is rather curious, not only because it was the first English local division instituted in America, but besides having both a territorial and personal signification, it assumed different relations to the general government of the colony at different periods. **1938** FWP *Guide DE* 67, The counties are subdivided into hundreds. This quaint political anachronism is still shown on all maps of Delaware, although for purposes of government the hundred is no longer of great importance. **1946** Attwood *Length ME* 14, The province of Maine was divided by Sir Ferdinando Gorges into eight bailiwicks or counties. . . Each of the eight counties was divided into 16 several hundreds. Each hundred was divided into parishes and tithings.

b By ext: see quot.

1950 *PADS* 14.39 **ceSC,** *Hundred*. . . District, neighborhood. "How are things in your hundred?"

2 Any of var games, as:

a pl: A marble game. [*EDD hundred* sb. II. 6]

1973 Ferretti *Marble Book* 70, *Hundreds*—[A] one-hole English game for two players. . . A player getting his shooter or *boss* in the hole receives 10 points, and has the option of either going back to the line for another shot at the hole or shooting at his opponent. A hit . . counts 10 points. A person hitting another gains 10, but the one hit also loses 10, thus achieving 100 points can be a difficult and lengthy venture.

b in combs *one hundred, old ~:* A bat and ball game; see quot 1940. Cf **five hundred 2**

1940 *Hench Coll.* **ceNC,** *Old hundred*—a boy's ball game. A type of baseball: sides are chosen, and a player is put out by being hit by the ball, or by another player with the ball in his hand crossing the forward path of the runner. **1966-68** *DARE* (Qu. EE11, *Bat-and-ball games for just a few players*) Inf **KS**15, One hundred; **NC**4, Old hundred.

3 Any of var kinds of marbles; see quot.

1968 *DARE* (Qu. EE6b, . . *Marbles*) Inf **LA**25, Hundreds—most expensive, crystals; (Qu. EE6d) Inf **IA**29, Hundred tick—a glass marble.

4 in phr *get one's hundreds:* To return safely to base in a children's hiding game; hence vbl n *getting one's hundred* a children's hiding game.

1959 Lomax *Rainbow Sign* 40 **AL** [Black], *It* start out from the base, not far, though, because all us watchin him to see if we could beat him back to the base to get our hundreds. . . Well, here come Sukie round the side of the house, *flyin,* tryin to get her hundreds. **1967** *DARE* (Qu. EE13a, *Games in which every player hides except one*) Inf **LA**8, Counting—also called hiding. The one that be at the base, he counts. They also call it "gettin' your hundred". [Inf Black]

5 in phr *hundred-and-sixty:* A homestead of one hundred and sixty acres.

1945 James *Cherokee Strip* 3 **OK,** His whole hundred-and-sixty was under fence, and a good half of it broken and in crops. **1968** Adams *Western Words* 157, *Hundred-and-sixty*—A westerner's name for a homestead, commonly 160 acres.

hundred holes n [See quot 1950]

A **St. John's wort** (here: *Hypericum perforatum*).

[**1950** Gray-Fernald *Manual of Botany* 1010, *H[ypericum] perforatum*. . . *Leaves* elliptic- to linear-oblong, with pellucid dots.] **1974** (1977) Coon *Useful Plants* 148, *Hypericum perforatum*—St. John's wort . . hundred holes.

hundred steps n

A children's hiding game.

1967 *DARE* (Qu. EE16, *Hiding games that start with a special, elaborate method*) Inf **IA**3, Hundred steps.

hundred ways for Sunday See **Sunday, forty ways till**

hundu(r)d See **hundred A1**

hunert See **hundred A5**

hung See **hang** v **B1**

Hungarian goulash n **esp Nth, N Midl**

A meat stew, usu made with beef, onions, and paprika.

1950 in 1957 Showalter *Mennonite Cookbook* 132 **csPA,** Hungarian Goulash. . . Brown onions, meat and green pepper in hot fat. Cook spaghetti . . and drain. Mix all ingredients. . . Add cheese several minutes before serving. **1951** Johnson *Resp. to PADS 20* **DE** *(Things nicknamed for particular nationalities)* Hungarian goulash. **1965-70** *DARE* (Qu. H45, *Dishes made with meat . . that everyone around here would know, but that people in other places might not*) Infs **NY**86, **OH**18, Hungarian goulash; (Qu. H49) Inf **WA**30, Hungarian goulash; (Qu. H65) Infs **MO**25, **NJ**5, **NY**28, **OH**65, Hungarian goulash; (Qu. HH30) Infs **CO**17, **CT**16, **MN**2, **MO**14, **NY**59, **NY**66, 84, **WA**11, Hungarian goulash.

Hungarian grass n Also *Hungarian millet*

A **bristlegrass 1** (here: *Setaria italica*).

1859 *Guide Illinois Central Railroad Lands* 34 *(OEDS), Hungarian grass.* This cereal, first introduced by the Hungarian exiles, is becoming a favorite with the farmers. **1859** (1942) Patterson *Travel Diary* 80 **IA,** We succeeded in getting two hundred pounds of hungarian [sic] grass for our cattle. **1901** Mohr *Plant Life AL* 135, Hungarian grass and the so-called Johnson grass . . furnish green forage and hay crops throughout the summer. **1950** Hitchcock-Chase *Manual Grasses* 725, *Setaria italica* . . Foxtail millet. . . The smaller forms are known as Hungarian grass. **1968-69** *DARE* (Qu. L9a, *What kinds of grass are grown for hay around here?*) Inf **MA**37, Hungarian millet; **NH**14, Hungarian (three feet high—used to cut out witch grass).

Hungarian partridge n Also *Hungarian grouse, ~ pheasant*

1 A European partridge *(Perdix perdix)* naturalized in the US. Also called **English partridge, gray partridge 1, hun 1,** *Hunky (partridge)* (at **Hunk** n^3 **4)**

1913 *Conn. State Geol. & Nat. Hist. Survey* Bul. 20, 184 *(DA),* As the majority brought to the United States came from Hungary, this bird has become commonly known as the Hungarian Partridge. **1947** *Collier's* 29 Mar 92/2, The true European partridge does exist in this country; but it is known as the Hungarian partridge. **1950** *WELS (Kinds of game birds)* 5 Infs, **WI,** Hungarian partridge. **1951** Kumlien-Hollister *Birds WI* 48, *Perdix perdix . . Hungarian Partridge.* This bird was introduced in 1908. **1955** MA Audubon Soc. *Bulletin* 39.443, *European Partridge. . .* Hungarian Partridge (Conn. Some of the stock was imported from that country.) **1965-70** *DARE* (Qu. Q7, . . *Kinds of game birds)* 10 Infs, **chiefly Upper MW,** Hungarian partridge; **MN**16, Hungarian; **WA**28, Hungarian grouse; **MN**29, Hungarian pheasant and Chinese pheasant or Hungarian partridge; **MT**5, Hungarian pheasant; **MT**3, Huns—Hungarian pheasants. **1967** *DARE* FW Addit **swWA,** A *Hungarian pheasant* or *Hungarian grouse* or *hun* is about nine inches high, and grey—like a grouse. **1982** Elman *Hunter's Field Guide* 44, Since most of America's early importations came from the plains of Hungary, the species *[Perdix perdix]* acquired the name Hungarian partridge, or "Hun," on this continent.

2 =ruffed grouse.

1963 Gromme *Birds WI* 216.

Hungarian pheasant See **Hungarian partridge**

hung by the eyelids See **eyelids, hang by one's 1**

hunger cactus n Also *starvation cactus*

A **prickly pear** (here: *Opuntia polyacantha*).

1968 Barkley *Plants KS* 246, Opuntia polyacantha. . . Hunger Cactus. . . Plains and prairies. **1973** Hitchcock-Cronquist *Flora Pacific NW* 301, Starvation c[actus]. . . *O. polyacantha.*

hunger root See **hungry vine**

‡hunger stick n

1970 *DARE* (Qu. G11, . . *A toothpick)* Inf **TX**97, Hunger stick—when you use it to pretend you are full [but] you aren't.

Hunger Street See **Hungry Hill**

hungry adj, n Usu |'hʌŋgri|; also |'hʌŋri, 'hɔŋ(g)ri|; for addit varr see **A** below Pronc-sp **esp Sth, S Midl** *hongry;* also *hahngry, hawngry, honkry, honggry, hungrey* [Cf *EDD hungry* "Also in form *hongry*"; *OED hungry* "Forms [include] . . *houngrie . . hongry, hongarye*"]

A Forms. [Cf *DBE*] Cf *hunky* at **honky 1**

1883 (1971) Harris *Nights with Remus* 213 **GA** [Black], Dey er all monst'us hongry, en Brer Wolf hongry hisse'f. *Ibid* 256, 'E git honkry fer da pickaninny. **1888** Jones *Negro Myths* 11 **GA coast** [Gullah], Eh tell um eh so hongry eh rady fuh drap. **1889** Edwards *Runaways* 84 **GA,** I come honggry all the way back. **1893** Shands *MS Speech* 37, *Hongry* [hoŋri]. Negro for *hungry.* **1902** *DN* 2.240 **sIL** [Pioneer dialect], *ng.* Usually pronounced *ŋ* not *ŋg* before a consonant. Thus . . hungry . . [is] [hʌŋri.] **1905** *DN* 3.103 **nwAR,** Abnormal vowels. . . [hɔŋri]. **1908** *DN* 3.321 **eAL, wGA,** *Hongry. . .* Hungry. **1914** *DN* 4.160 **cVA,** Ah'm r[ight] s[mart] hahngry. **1953** Randolph-Wilson *Down in Holler* 19 **Ozarks,** Hungry is often pronounced *hongry* or *hawngry.* **1967-70** *DARE* (Qu. H12) Inf **NC**79, ['hʌŋrɨ]. **1968** *DARE* FW Addit **GA**51, Hungry ['hɔŋgrɪ] [FW: said regularly by Inf; also by others]. **1972** Kochman *Rappin'* 143 [Black], The pronunciation of the first syllable [of *hunky*] has been changed to conform to the pronunciation given to the word "hungry" when one is intensely hungry—h*u*ngry is to be just hungry; h*o*ngry is to be famished. [**1982** Holm-Shilling *Dict. Bahamian Engl.* 108, *Hungry* ['hʌŋgri, 'hɔŋgri].]

B As noun.

Appetite; hunger. [Cf *DJE, DBE*] **Sth** *among Black speakers*

1899 Dunbar *Lyrics Hearthside* 131 [Black], D'othah night I's out a walkin' / An I passed a 'simmon tree / Now I's whettin' up my hongry,/ An I's laffin' fit to kill. **1922** Gonzales *Black Border* 307 **sSC, GA coasts** [Gullah glossary], *Hongry*—hungry, hunger. **1937** (1977) Hurston *Their Eyes* 15 **FL** [Black], Ah knowed you'd be hongry. . . Mah mulatto rice ain't so good dis time. . . but Ah reckon it'll kill hongry. **1971** Cunningham *Syntactic Analysis Gullah* 116, *Hungry* 'hunger'.

‡hungry club n

1969 *DARE* (Qu. L32a, *In the early days, how was the grain separated from the straw?*) Inf **MA**15, Hungry club—same thing as a frail—two sticks held together by an eelskin.

Hungry Hill n Also *Hungry Gulch, ~ Hollow, ~ Ridge, ~ Street, Hungry-go-naked Place, Hunger Street*

An area inhabited by poor people; see quot.

1966-70 *DARE* (Qu. C33, . . *Names . . for an out-of-the-way place, or a very unimportant place)* Inf **MD**34, Hungry-go-naked Place; (Qu. C34, *Nicknames for nearby . . villages or districts)* Inf **CA**211, Hungry Gulch; **IA**14, Hungry Ridge—this isn't a town, just an area; (Qu. C35, *Nicknames for the different parts of your town)* Inf **MD**17, Hungry Hollow—a section of Oakland [MD]—poor people, not a good class of people, live there; **MO**13, Hungry Hill—very poor colored people live in this section; **SD**2, Hunger Street; (Qu. II25, . . *The part of a town where the poorer . . or foreign groups live)* Inf **MD**17, Hungry Hollow—a poor section on the outskirts of Oakland [MD]; **MO**13, Hungry Hill—a Negro section; **SD**2, Hungry Street. **1989** *DARE* File **csMA** (as of c1950 and before), The Liberty Street area of Springfield was formerly called "Hungry Hill." It was the site of the big Irish settlement of "potato famine days," the mid 1800s.

hungryroot n

A **spikenard** (here: *Aralia racemosa*).

1910 Graves *Flowering Plants* 296 **CT,** *Aralia racemosa. . .* Hungry-root. . . The root is medicinal and is much used both in professional and domestic practice. **1933** Small *Manual SE Flora* 960, *A. racemosa. . .* Spikenard. Hungry-root. **1940** Clute *Amer. Plant Names* 218, *Aralia racemosa.* Hungry-root.

Hungry Street See **Hungry Hill**

hungryvine n Also *hunger root*

A **greenbrier** (here: *Smilax rotundifolia*).

1900 Lyons *Plant Names* 348, *S[milax] rotundifolia. . .* Hungry-vine. **1940** Clute *Amer. Plant Names* 15, *S[milax] rotundifolia. . .* Hungry-vine, . . hunger-root. **1960** Vines *Trees SW* 75, Vernacular names for the plant are Biscuit-leaves, . . Hungry-vine, . . and Sow-brier.

hung wort n [Perh for **lungwort**]

A **mullein** (here: *Verbascum thapsus*).

1947 (1976) Curtin *Healing Herbs* 166, Verbascum thapsus . . Hung wort.

Hungy See **Hunk** n^3 **1**

hunk n^1

1 See **hunks.**

2 also *hunks:* A hick, country bumpkin. **esp KY, TN**

1890 *DN* 1.65 **KY,** *Hunk. . .* A country fellow; as, "He is a country hunk." **1924** (1946) Greer-Petrie *Angeline Gits an Eyeful* 21 **csKY,** If hit wuz the fashion fur *rich* wimmen to smoke seeg'rets, shorely and undoubtedly hit wuz all right fur us country *hunks* to . . smoke our cob pipes, or chaw. **1970** *DARE* (Qu. HH1, . . *Nicknames for a rustic or countrified person)* Infs **KY**94, **TX**91, Country hunk; **KY**91, Country hunks. **1986** Pederson *LAGS Concordance (A rustic)* 3 infs, **TN,** Country hunk(s).

hunk n^2 Also *honk* [Du *honk* home, goal, base] **NY** *old-fash* Cf **home** n **B1**

In children's games: home base.

1848 Bartlett *Americanisms* 185, *Hunk. . .* A goal or place of refuge. A word much used by New York boys in their play. **1889** *Century Dict.* 2921, *Hunk. . .* In *tag* and other games, the goal; home: as, to reach hunk. *Ibid,* On hunk; at the goal. [*Century:* Local, New York.] **1891** *Jrl. Amer. Folkl.* 4.222 **NYC,** The game [=tag] is sometimes rendered more complicated by certain places which are called "hunks" or "homes" being agreed upon, where the players may find refuge when closely pursued. **1968** *DARE* (Qu. EE14, . . *The place where the player who is 'it' has to wait and count)* Inf **NY**48, Honk. [FW: Inf is descendant of original Dutch settlers.]

Hunk n^3 Usu *Hunky* [Prob var of *Hungarian*]

1 also *Honky, Hungy, Hunkey, Hunkie:* A person of central European origin; a recent immigrant with such a background, esp an uneducated or unskilled laborer. **scattered, but chiefly Nth, N Midl** See Map Cf **bohunk 1, hunyak 1**

1896 *NY Herald* (NY) 13 Jan 3/4, The average Pennsylvanian contemptuously refers to these immigrants as "Hikes" and "Hunks"... "Hunks" is a corruption for Huns, but under this title the Pennsylvanian includes Hungarians, Lithuanians, Slavs, Poles, Magyars and Tyroleans. **1914** *DN* 4.150 **PA,** *Hungy*... Hungarian. **1923** Watts *Luther Nichols* 28 **OH,** He had next him .. a set of recent importations from the old country known along the Pike as "them Hunkies"; they were swarthy, gypsy-looking men and women, undersized but strongly built, jabbering uncouth sounds among themselves. **1929** *AmSp* 4.372 **swPA** [Miners' talk], *Hunkey*—Same as *Bohunk.* **1946** (1972) Mezzrow-Wolfe *Really Blues* 187, Hey there Poppa Mezz, is you anywhere?/ .. Man I'm down with it, stickin' like a honky. *Ibid* 316, Translation... Hello Mezz, have you got any marihuana?/ .. Plenty, old man, my pockets are full as a factory hand's on payday. *Ibid* 334, *Honky:* factory hand. **1948** *Sat. Review* 31 July 5/3, There are chapters on Bayou French, Ozark hillbillies, Navajo Indians, Milwaukee Hunkies, and Minnesota lumberjacks. **1950** *WELS (People of foreign background)* 9 Infs, **WI,** Hungarian: *Hunky;* 1 Inf, Bohemian: *Hunky.* **1957** Battaglia *Resp. to PADS 20* **eMD** *(Nicknames for people of foreign background)* Polish: *Hunky.* **1963** Mencken-McDavid *Amer. Lang.* 371, *Hunk* and *hunkie* (or *hunky* or *hunkey*) are proper [sic] applicable to Hungarians only, but they have been extended to include all Europeans coming from the region east of the German lands and west of Russia, save only the Greeks. **1963** Wright *Lawd Today* 31 **Chicago IL** [Black], That's what's wrong with this country, too many Jews, Dagos, Hunkies, and Mexicans. **1965–70** *DARE* (Qu. HH28, .. *Nicknames .. for people of foreign background*) 133 Infs, **scattered, but chiefly Nth, N Midl east of Missip R,** Hunky; 18 Infs, **scattered, but chiefly Nth, N Midl,** Hunk; **VA**25, Honky ['hɔŋki]—for Hungarian or Italian [133 of 149 Infs referred to Hungarians; others referred to Poles, Italians, Czechoslovakians, and people of other nationalities.]; (Qu. I22a) Inf **IN**30, Hunky peppers; (Qu. I22b, .. *Different kinds of peppers—large hot*) Inf **IN**27, Hunky peppers. **1969** Sorden *Lumberjack Lingo* 59 **NEng, Gt Lakes,** *Hunks*—Foreign-born laborers, usually unskilled, especially Hungarians or southern Slavs. **1986** Pederson *LAGS Concordance,* 1 inf, **Atlanta GA,** Hunkies—Low Germans, like blacks being called niggers; 1 inf, **Dallas TX,** Hunky—Hungarian. [This question was asked chiefly in urban areas.]

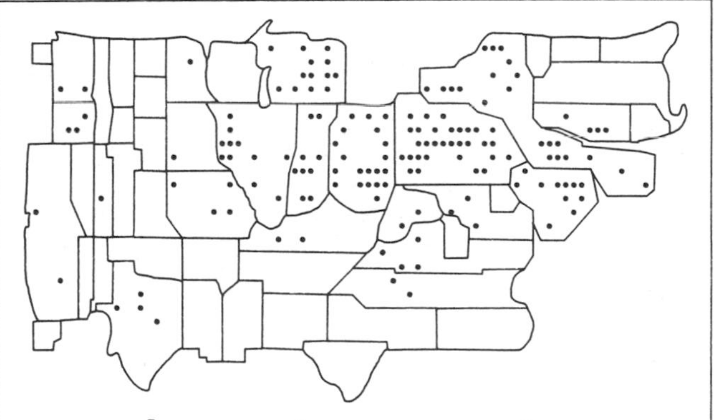

•Hunk n³ 1 + varr (Qq. HH28, I22a, b)

2 By ext: see quot.

1968 *DARE* (Qu. HH3, *A dull and stupid person*) Inf **NJ**33, Hunky.

3 attrib; In unofficial place names: used to designate an area inhabited by people of foreign origin.

1967–70 *DARE* (Qu. C33, .. *Names .. for an out-of-the-way place or a very unimportant place*) Inf **PA**245, Hunky Town—a foreign settlement outside or in town—a "Hunk" is a foreigner; (Qu. C34) Inf **PA**167, Hunky Town; (Qu. C35, *Nicknames for the different parts of your town*) Infs **MI**67, **PA**245, Hunky Town; (Qu. II25, .. *The part of a town where the poorer .. or foreign groups live*) Inf **PA**167, Hunky Town; **NJ**4, Hunky Row—a row of houses built for mill hands most of which were Hungarians.

4 as *Hunky (partridge):* =**Hungarian partridge 1.**

1956 *AmSp* 31.180, *Hunky* (N.Y., Ohio, Mich., N. Dak...) for the gray or Hungarian partridge. **1957** *AmSp* 32.184, Hunky[,] Gray partridge[,] N.Y., Ohio, Mich., N. Dak... Hunky partridge[,] Gray partridge[,] Ohio. **1967** *DARE* (Qu. Q7, *Names .. for .. game birds*) Inf **OH**23, Hunkies.

5 See **honky 1.**

hunk adj Also *hunk(e)y, ahunky* [Perh **hunk** n²] Cf **hunky-dory**

1 Excellent; satisfactory; fortunate. *somewhat old-fash*

1843 (1847) Field *Drama Pokerville* 50, I allow you're just *hunk,* this time, then. **1859** (1968) Bartlett *Americanisms* 208, Hunk... "To be hunk," or "all hunk," is to have reached the goal or place of meeting without being intercepted by one of the opposite party, to be all safe... "Mr. L— had .. made this ground in the waters of the East River without authority; and now he felt himself all hunk, and wanted to get this enormous sum out of the city." **1862** (1864) Browne *Artemus Ward Book* 237, I held her in my arms. I felt her breath upon my cheek! It was Hunkey. **1876** in 1969 *PADS* 52.53 **neIL,** Feel all Hunk. **1900** Day *Up in ME* 23, Balarnced, I sh'd suttin say, a minit—all ahunky. **1906** *DN* 3.124 **nwAR,** *All-hunky (dory)*... Entirely satisfactory. **1908** *DN* 3.286 **eAL, wGA,** *All-hunky (my dory).* **1914** *DN* 4.68 **ME, nNH,** *All a-hunky*... All right. **1942** Berrey-Van den Bark *Amer. Slang* 29.4, *Excellent; first rate*... all-a-hunky... hunk, hunky. *Ibid* 128.3, *In good health*... all-a-hunky .. hunk, hunky. *Ibid* 169.10, *Right; correct.* All-a-hunky .. hunky. *Ibid* 279.6, *Satisfactory*... All-a-hunky .. hunk. **1963** Carson *Social Hist. Bourbon* 118 **DC** (as of 1870s), [Telegram:] Everything looks well. Send on report. Feel hunkey.

2 Even; equal—usu in phrr *get hunk(y).*

1845 *Spirit of Times* (Wilkes) 24 May 146 *(OEDS),* Those who lost their money on Fashion had two or three chances to 'get hunk', especially on the last day. **1903** Lewis *Boss* 93 **NYC,** I don't blame Sheeny Joe... Still, while I don't blame him, it's up to us to get hunk an' even on th' play. **1910** *Sat. Eve. Post* 16 July 15/3 **DC,** I want to get hunky with the Sanitary boss. **1942** Berrey-Van den Bark *Amer. Slang* 28.4, *Equal; on terms of equality.* All-a-hunky .. hunky.

hunkabo n [By metath from **bohunk**] Cf **Hunk** n³ **1**

1940 *AmSp* 15.221 **TX,** What the hum do you mean, you hunkabo?

hunker n¹ Also *honker* [*EDD hunkers* sb. pl.] **chiefly Midl, Sth**

The haunch or buttock; the knee; rarely, the calf.

1859 Taliaferro *Fisher's R.* 152 **nwNC** (as of 1820s), He was ever busy, .. sitting on his "hunkers" cutting out mill-stones in the lonely mountains. **1896** *DN* 1.419 **nwMD, cePA,** *Hunkers:* calves of the legs. "I had to sit on my hunkers." **1902** *DN* 2.237 **sIL,** 'Get down on your hunkers,' *i.e.* kneel down. **1909** *DN* 3.398 **nwAR,** *Hunkers*... Knees. (Usually of animals.) Down on your hunkers! "We thought the cyclone was going to hit us shure, and the old woman went down on her hunkers and commenced praying." **1914** *DN* 4.108 **KS,** *Hunkers*... In the phrase *to sit on one's hunkers.* **1942** McAtee *Dial. Grant Co. IN* 35 (as of 1890s), *Hunkers*... knees; "Get down on your hunkers", i.e. in the attitude of prayer, not in a squat. **1958** Blasingame *Dakota Cowboy* 22 **SD,** Bull .. would sit down on his hunkers like a dog, refusing to get up or to work. **1962** Atwood *Vocab. TX* 70, The most common single term [to designate "what you squat down on"] is *hunkers.* **1965** *DARE* File **swPA** (as of 1920s), *Hunkers*—Buttocks. Getting down on your hunkers meant to stoop. **1966–68** *DARE* (Qu. GG9, .. *Suddenly embarrass somebody and throw him off balance*) Inf **MS**1, Knock him off his hunkers; **NJ**20, Knock him off his hunkers [FW sugg]; (Qu. Y6, .. *Put pressure on somebody to do something*) Inf **TN**23, Get on his hunker; (Qu. X36, *Joking names for the knees;* total Infs questioned, 75) Inf **GA**1, Honkers ['haŋkəz]. **c1970** Pederson *Dial. Surv. Rural GA (What do you call the back part of a man's legs when he is squatting down? .. "He got down on his ______.")* 8 infs, **seGA,** Hunkers; 5 infs, **seGA,** Honkers.

hunker n² See **hunks**

hunker n³ See **honker** n¹ 1

hunker v [Prob **hunker** n]

1 To assume or be in a crouching position, spec: see below; hence ppl adj *hunkered.*

a usu with *down;* also with *back;* To squat; to sit in a squatting position; rarely, to kneel. **scattered, but esp S Midl**

1902 *DN* 2.237 **sIL,** *Hunker down*... To crouch in sitting... To kneel. **1907** *DN* 3.232 **nwAR, seMO,** *Hunker* (down)... To squat down. **1914** *DN* 4.108 **cKS,** *To sit on one's hunkers,* to squat, to hunker. **1923** *DN* 5.211 **swMO,** *Hunker down*... To squat on the heels. Also Hunker up. **1940** Stuart *Trees of Heaven* 60 **neKY,** Fronnie gets up from her hunkered position by the cane-mill burrs. **1941** Faulkner *Men Working* 165 **MS,** Two little girls hunkered back on their knees. **1950** *WELS (Go down on your heels)* 2 Infs, **WI,** Hunker. **1958** *PADS* 29.12 **TN,** Hunker down. **1963** Owens *Look to River* 138 **TX,** He looked dirty and old and hunkered down from so much sitting. **1967** *DARE* FW Addit **sAL, nwGA,** Hunker ['hʌ̃ŋkɚ]—to squat down and rest one's weight on one's heels and lower leg. Sometimes one knee is lower than the other. This position usually implies conversation. While squatting in this position, a person is said to be "hunkering"; **cwWA,** Hunkered down—squatted down.

b usu with *down* or *up;* also with *over:* To hunch one's body or pull one's limbs together out of fear or discomfort, or in an effort to hide or squeeze into a small space; to be in such a position; also fig, to draw in one's horns.

a1930 in 1944 *ADD* **cNY,** '[He] lay hunkered in the corner.' **1944** *PADS* 2.44 **wNC,** *Hunker (up)*. . . To be humped up or bent over awkwardly. "It was so cold he hunkered up in the wagon." **1954** *Harder Coll.* **cwTN,** *Hunker over*—stoop over in order to conceal oneself or to go through a narrow space. "He had to hunker over to git in 'at air cave." "We hunkered over so's they couldn't see us." **1967–70** *DARE* (Qu. Y32, *To squeeze yourself into a small space: "If you're going to fit in there you'll have to ———."*) Infs **KS**12, **KY**63, **MI**108, **MO**11, **OH**38, **OR**1, Hunker down; **IL**116, Hunker down or up; **IL**17, Hunker up. **1967** *DARE* FW Addit **cOR,** Hunker up—to squeeze up, scroonch up. **1979** *Wall St. Jrl.* (NY NY) 10 Aug 1/6 **IN,** Some workers, recently laid off, are packing up and going where jobs are available instead of sticking around. . . And merchants like Mr. Gores are hunkering down for what they fear could be hard times ahead. **1984** *Annals Internal Med.* 100.6.900 **cwAL,** Those with emphysema *hunker down to breathe,* squat down and bend forward to better empty the lungs.

c usu with *down;* Fig: see quots.

1903 *DN* 2.317 **seMO,** *Hunker* or *hunker down*. . . To get down to work. **1986** *DARE* File **neGA,** *Hunker down* . . dig in, buckle down, get down to the job, get serious, apply oneself assiduously, give one's full attention to . . be intent about. . . The metaphorical sense is the commoner one [than the literal sense] around here, being particularly frequent in the catchphrase "Hunker down, you hairy Dogs!" ("hairy Dogs" being the University football team, the Bulldogs). However, I [=John Algeo] believe the metaphor is more than just an Athensism and sportstalk. I think it is widespread Southern, deriving from the custom of literally hunkering down to bargain or carry on serious negotiations. **1986** *DARE* File **ceWI,** I stayed home Friday night to do my taxes. I just hunkered down to it, and it wasn't so bad.

2 with *up:* See quot 1958.

1954 *Harder Coll.* **cwTN,** *Hunker up*—to display sexual desires: "Bet she'd like to hunker up in bed."

3 also with *along:* See quot. Cf **ankle, huck** v

1954 *PADS* 21.31 **SC,** *Hunker*. . . To go, walk. Often with the adv. *along,* as in "I've got to hunker along."

hunker along See **hunker** v **3**

hunker back See **hunker** v **1a**

hunker down See **hunker** v **1a, b, c**

hunkerdown n [From **hunker** v **1a**]

An informal gathering for conversation.

1979 *NY Times* (NY) 2 Dec 47/2 **csWV,** If the weather's chilly, they go inside the garage and hunker down inside [sic] the wood-burning stove. These gatherings occur any time of the year, and people in Pickaway have come to call them "hunkerdowns." *Ibid,* I never watch television because these hunkerdowns are better than TV. No commercials.

hunkered See **hunker** v **1**

hunker over See **hunker** v **1b**

hunkersliding vbl n [*SND* (at *hunker* n. 3. [4] [b]) "dishonorable or shifty conduct"] *arch*

See quots.

1872 (1973) Thompson *Major Jones's Courtship* 229 **GA,** "Now, gentlemen," ses he, "ther aint to be no hunkerslidin nor jockeyin in this business. It's to be a fair race." [**1895** *DN* 1.379 **New Brunswick Canada,** *Hunkersliding:* acting unfairly (especially with negative, "no hunkersliding here").]

hunker up See **hunker** v **1b, 2**

Hunkey n See **Hunk** n[3] **1**

hunkey adj See **hunk** adj

hunkey, by See **hunky, by**

hunkey-dora, hunkidori See **hunky-dory**

Hunkie See **Hunk** n[3] **1**

hunkle n [Var of **hunker** n[1]]

1913 *DN* 4.58 **TN,** *Hunkle*. . . Haunch. *Ibid,* Skrutched on his hunkles (haunches). **1946** *PADS* 5.26 **VA,** *Hunkers (hunkles):* Haunches; fairly common.

hunkle down v phr [Var of **hunker** v **1b**]

1967 *DARE* (Qu. Y32, *To squeeze yourself into a small space: "If you're going to fit in there you'll have to ———."*) Inf **OR**1, Hunkle down.

hunk over v phr

1954 *PADS* 21.31 **cnSC,** *Hunk over*. . . To hand over, with the connotation of misgiving, unwillingness; to fork over.

hunks n

1 also *hunk, hunker:* A worthless person, a good-for-nothing; a surly person. *somewhat old-fash; occas affectionate* [*OED hunks* 1602 →] Cf **Hunk** n[3] **2**

[**1806** (1970) Webster *Compendious Dict.* 147, *Hunks*. . . a sordid mean wretch, miser, niggard.] **1838** Kettell *Yankee Notions 236* **ceMA,** Your miserly hunks with his measureless sums,/ And the twopenny trader that picks up his crumbs,/ All sigh for contentment and quiet. **1899** *OED* **ceNY,** *Hunker*. . . Remembered by Mr. W.J. Stillman as familiarly used *c* 1840 at Shenectady [sic] N.Y., 'to designate a surly, crusty, or stingy old fellow, a curmudgeon.' **1906** *DN* 3.119 **sIN,** *Hunk*. . . A worthless person. "He's an *ornry* hunk." **1909** *DN* 3.412 **cnME,** *Hunks*. . . A general term of reproach. "Old lazy hunks! get out of this." *Hunker*. . . similar to *hunks.* **1919** Kyne *Capt. Scraggs* 204 **CA,** Captain Scraggs was so touched at this delicate little tribute that he turned away and burst into tears. "Aw, shut up, Scraggsy, old hunks. . . You ain't got nothin' to cry about." **1966** *PADS* 46.26 **cnAR** (as of 1952), *Hunk*. . . A worthless scoundrel.—"They thought that old hunk had stole it." **1969** *DARE* (Qu. HH40, *Uncomplimentary words for an old man*) Inf **MA**68, Hunks [hʌŋks].

2 See **hunk** n[1] **2.**

hunks exclam Cf **dubs** exclam **2**

1981 *AmSp* 56.27 **neNJ** (as of 1940s–50s), A child . . could claim a share of anything by shouting *hunks!* The possessor would have to yield part of the loot unless he or she had already shouted *fen hunks!*

hunkt See **hang A2**

hunkum-bunkum adj Cf **bunkum, hunky-dory,** Intro "Language Changes" I.3

See quot 1942.

1908 *DN* 3.322 **eAL, wGA,** *Hunkum-bunkum*. . . Very fine, excellent, good, etc. "That's all hunkum-bunkum." **1913** *DN* 4.24 **eNE,** *Hunkum-bunkum.* Fine, excellent, splendid. . . "What hunkum-bunkum bread you have to-day!" **1942** Berrey–Van den Bark *Amer. Slang* 29.4, *Excellent; first-rate*. . . hunkum-bunkum. *Ibid* 279.6, *Satisfactory.* . . hunkum-bunkum.

hunkus n Cf **bohunkus 1**

1968 *DARE* (Qu. X35, *Joking words for the part of the body that you sit on*) Inf **TX**51, Hunkus ['hʌ̃ŋkəs].

Hunky n[1] See **Hunk** n[3]

hunky n[2] See **honky 1**

hunky adj See **hunk** adj

hunky-adory See **hunky-dory**

hunky, by intj Also *by hunkey*

Used as mild oath.

1901 Harben *Westerfelt* 171 **nGA,** "By hunkey! they're white 'uns [=goose feathers]", he grunted, as he took out a handful. "I 'lowed they was mixed." *Ibid* 180, [On finding a 44 caliber revolver in a man's saddle-bag:] By hunky! it 'u'd dig a tunnel through a rock mountain.

hunky-dory adj Also *honkey-dooley, hunky-doodle, hunky-dunky, hunky-dokey;* for addit varr see quots [Cf **hunk adj**] Cf **hinky-dinky, hunkum-bunkum**

Std sense, var forms.

1876 in 1969 *PADS* 52.53 **neIL,** *Hunky dora*. . . "Feel all hunky dora. **1866** *Galaxy* 2.273, I cannot conceive on any theory of etymology . . why anything that is "hunkey dorey" . . should be so admirable. **1894** Clark *On Cloud Mt.* 137 *(DAE),* 'Oh *we're* hunkidori in a box!' declared the bridegroom. **1905** *DN* 3.62 **NE,** *Hunky doodle*. . . All right. As it should be. **1908** *DN* 3.286 **eAL, wGA,** *All-hunky (my* *dory)*. . . Perfectly satisfactory, quite snug. **1937** in 1944 *ADD* 310 **neKY,** God a uniform in 1917—W'y it was the hunkey-dora thing. **1942** Berrey–Van den Bark *Amer. Slang* 29.4, *Excellent; first-rate*. . . honkey-dooley, honky-dori . . hunky-dorum. **1950** *WELS (To be in a good mood)* 1 Inf, **WI,** Hunky-adory. **1966–70** *DARE* (Qu. KK4, *When things turn out just right . . "Everything is ______ now."*) Infs **NC**51, **OH**56, Hunky-dunky; **NY**75, Hunky-donky; **IL**115, Hunky-dooly; **NC**31, Hunkry-dory ['hʌŋkri 'douri]; (Qu. BB47) Inf **CO**14, Hunky-dokey.

Hunky partridge See **Hunk** n³ **4**

Hunky Row (or Town) See **Hunk** n³ **3**

hunne(r)d See **hundred A4**

hunnet, hunnit See **hundred A5**

hunnuh See **una**

hun'r'd See **hundred A4**

hunt v

‡1 See quot.

1966 *DARE* FW Addit **NM**13, If a horse can't see well, he may "hunt"—meaning that the horse will look for boogers or spooks.

‡2 To be hard to find.

1924 (1946) Greer–Petrie *Angeline Gits an Eyeful* 20 **csKY,** Mis' Clark 'low'd now that . . she had made no mistake in her pet charity. . . and she wuz aimin' to build a big *school'ouse*. . . and *indow* hit. . . That thar wuz shore good news to me, fur I know'd the *money wan't to hunt.*

hunt n See **haunt**

hunt-and-go-seek n Cf **hide-and-seek B1**

1968 *DARE* (Qu. EE3, *Games in which you hide an object and then look for it*) Inf **MN**38, Hunt-and-go-seek—hide any object.

hunter n

1 =**Canada goose.**

1923 U.S. Dept. Ag. *Misc. Circular* 35, *Branta canadensis canadensis*. . . *Vernacular Names. In general use.* Honker . . corrupted to . . hunter.

2 also *huntress:* A cat that is adept at catching rodents. **scattered, but chiefly Nth, CA** See Map Cf **mouse cat**

1950 *WELS* 3 Infs, **WI,** Good hunter; 2 Infs, Hunter. **1965–70** *DARE* (Qu. J6, *A cat that catches lots of rats and mice*) 73 Infs, **scattered Nth, CA,** Hunter; **NY**1, 9, 209, Good hunter; **LA**37, Rat hunter; **WI**30, Huntress. **1967** *DARE* FW Addit **CO**5, Hunter, a good hunter [FW: of a cat].

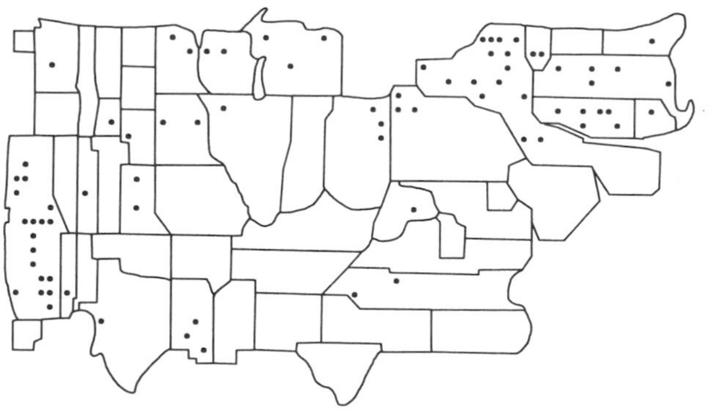

•hunter 2 + varr (Qu. J6)

3 See **hunting spider.**

hunter-and-the-deer n Also *deer-and-hunter, hunter-and-the-dog*

1967–70 *DARE* (Qu. EE33, . . *Outdoor games . . that children play*) Infs **AZ**1, **GA**93, Hunter-and-the-deer; **CA**105, Hunter-and-the-deer [FW sugg]; **PA**206, Hunter-and-the-dog; (Qu. EE13a) Inf **CA**105, Deer-and-hunter—can be played on ground or trees, like "Squirrel" which is played in the hills and trees—actually climbed from tree to tree.

hunter-hunter-hare-o n

A children's hiding game.

1966 *DARE* (Qu. EE12, *Games in which one captain hides his team and the other team tries to find it*) Inf **GA**15, Hunter-hunter-hare-o ['hɛɚo]. **1981** Pederson *LAGS Basic Materials (Hiding games)* 1 inf, **Savannah GA,** ['hʌnə 'hʌnə 'hɛəroʉ]—running and hiding.

hunter's cup See **huntsman's cup**

hunter's fever n Also *hunting fever* Cf **buck fever 1**

1966–68 *DARE* (Qu. P36, *When a hunter sees a[n] . . animal and gets so excited he can't shoot, he has ______*) Infs **CA**75, **NC**3, Hunter's fever; **OR**15, Hunting fever.

hunter's horn See **huntsman's horn**

hunter spider n Cf **hunting spider**

A tarantula.

1867 *Amer. Naturalist* 1.409, This very large hunter-spider makes its appearance in Texas some years as early as the twenty-fifth of May.

hunter's stew n Cf **booya, shepherd's pie**

See quot 1949 Trahey.

1949 Brown *Amer. Cooks* 414, Hunters in the Michigan woods practically live on a kind of hunter's stew which is called variously, "boulyaw," "boyou" or "booyaw." **1949** Trahey *Taste TX* 9, *Hunter's Stew*—1 to 5 pounds of stew meat[;] 1 can each of corn, tomatoes, hominy, okra[;] . . bacon . . Irish potatoes . . onions. . . For meat, . . use . . anything available, from antelope or venison to bear steaks, even cabrito (kid). **1950** *WELS* 1 Inf, **WI,** Hunter's stew. **1968** *DARE* (Qu. H49, *Dishes made by boiling potatoes with other foods*) Inf **PA**146, Hunter's stew.

hunting fever See **hunter's fever**

hunting owl n Cf **day owl 2**

Prob =**short-eared owl.**

1969 *DARE* (Qu. Q2, *Other kinds of owls found around here*) Inf **GA**80, Hunting owl—is after poultry.

hunting spider n Also *hunter* Cf **hunter spider**

See quot 1889.

1889 *Century Dict.* 2922, *Hunter*. . . A spider which hunts for its prey instead of lying in wait for it, as a lycosid or wolf-spider. Also called *hunting-spider*. **1968** *DARE* (Qu. R28, *What different kinds of spiders do you have around here?*) Inf **GA**25, Hunting spider.

hunting the gawk (or gowk) See **gawk** n **4**

huntin'in' See **-ing B**

hunt leaf n

An unidentified plant.

1970 *NC Folkl.* 18.23, Hunt leaf is good for the weak heart.

hunt one's hole See **hole** n **10a**

huntress See **hunter** n **2**

huntsman's cup n Also *hunter's cup* [From the shape of the leaf]

A **pitcher plant** (here: *Sarracenia purpurea*).

1848 Gray *Manual of Botany* 25, *S[arracenia] purpurea*. . . *(Sidesaddle-flower. Huntsman's Cup.)* Leaves pitcher-shaped. **1876** Hobbs *Bot. Hdbk.* 55, Huntsman's cup, Side saddle plant, Sarracenia purpurea. **1893** *Jrl. Amer. Folkl.* 6.137, *Sarracenia purpurea* . . huntsman's cup . . New England. **1910** Graves *Flowering Plants* 213 **CT,** Huntsman's . . Cup. . . The root and leaves are medicinal. **1936** IL Nat. Hist. Surv. *Wildflowers* 137, *Huntman's Cup* . . produces a rosette of pitcher-shaped leaves which may be entirely green but more often are streaked with red or purple. **1964** Batson *Wild Flowers SC* 51, *Hunter's Cup* . . produces horizontal pitcher-shaped leaves in which it is fancied the wing forms the handle. **1968** *DARE* (Qu. S26b, *Wildflowers that grow in water or wet places*) Inf **NJ**31, Hunter's cup.

huntsman's horn n Also *hunter's horn* [From the shape of the leaf]

Either of two **pitcher plants:** usu *Sarracenia flava,* but also *S. purpurea.*

1864 Paige *Catalogue Flowering Plants* 7 **ceNY,** *Sarracenia*. . . *Side-saddle Flower. Huntsman's Horn.* purpurea. . . Swamps; frequent. May-June. **1900** Lyons *Plant Names* 334, *S[arracenia] flava*. . . South-eastern U.S., . . Huntsman's-horn, Biscuits, Dumb watches. **1933** Small *Manual SE Flora* 582, *S. flava*. . . Leaves (summer) . . trumpet-shaped. . . *Huntsman's-horn.* **1954** C. J. Hylander *Macmillan Wild*

Flower Bk. 149 *(OEDS),* Trumpets. *Sarracenia flava.* The tubular insect-catching leaves of this species are longer and more slender, looking more like horns than pitchers. (In fact, another common name is Huntsman's Horn.) **1959** Carleton *Index Herb. Plants* 64, *Huntsman's Horn:* Sarracenia purpurea. **1964** Batson *Wild Flowers SC* 51, *Hunter's Horn: Sarracenia flava. . .* Wet clearings and savannas over the eastern half of state. Summer. Virginia to Florida.

hunt-the-bunny n Cf **bull-in-the-ring 1**

A circle game of escape; see quot.

1969 *DARE* (Qu. EE33, . . *Outdoor games*) Inf **PA**177, Hunt-the-bunny—one kid tries to break out of a circle formed by others.

hunt-the-button n

1 See **button B2.**

2 See quot.

1906 *DN* 3.142 **nwAR,** *Hunt the button. . .* A trick game. Somebody is told to hide a button on his person. After he has done this, he is asked whether he has the button in his mouth, which he is requested to open. Pepper, salt, or flour is then thrown in.

hunt-the-(gray-)fox n

=**fox chase.**

1957 *Sat. Eve. Post Letters* **cIL,** Games: Hunt-the-grey-fox. **1966** *DARE* (Qu. EE33, . . *Outdoor games*) Inf **ME**11, Hunt-the-fox.

hunt-the-hay n

1968 *DARE* (Qu. EE12, *Games in which one captain hides his team and the other team tries to find it*) Inf **LA**23, Hunt-the-hay.

hunt-the-whistle n

1905 *DN* 3.83 **nwAR,** *Hunt the whistle. . .* The name of a game.

hunty gray n [Cf *EDD hunty* sb. "Sc. A boy's game"; also perh *SND* "*hunty* [hunt the] *goorie*" (at *hunt* v. II. 1. (4))]

1940–41 Cassidy *WI Atlas, Hunty gray*—a sort of hide-and-seek, a children's game.

hunyak n, sometimes cap Also *honijoker, honyak, honyock(er), hunyacker, hunyocker* [Perh blend of *Hun* or *Hunk* Hungarian + *Polack*] *derog* Cf **bohunk 1, Hunk** n[3] **1**

1 A person of non-western, usu central or eastern, European background; a recent immigrant, esp an unskilled or uneducated laborer with such a background.

1911 U.S. Immigration Comm. *Dict. Races* 92, *Magyar* . . Hungarian Hun or Hunyak in popular language. **1938** Dannay–Lee *Four of Hearts* 11, Tossing away the stockholders' dough like a hunyak on Saturday night. **1949** *PADS* 11.23 **CO,** *Hunyack . . hunyacker. . .* A foreign workman, one of non-English descent, usually Italian or other Southern European. **1950** *WELS* 3 Infs, **WI,** Hunyak; 1 Inf, **WI,** Hunyocker—any Slav. **1957** Frank *Seven Days* 201, She cooked a Hungarian goulash better than any he had ever tasted at a hunyak table in West Virginia. **1958** [see **2** below]. **1966–67** *DARE* (Qu. HH28, . . *Nicknames . . for people of foreign background*) Inf **IA**9, Hunyaks ['hʌnjɑks]; **MI**4, ['hʌnjæks]—for Poles, Finns, Germans.

2 usu *honyock(er):* A farmer or homesteader, usu one of central European background; one who fenced open range. **MT, ND, SD, WY** *somewhat old-fash; often derog*

1919 Lewis *Free Air* 106 **SD, MT,** I could buy out half these Honyockers! **1939** FWP *Guide MT* 60, For some years the ranchers affected to despise the "honyak," and resisted his advance by cutting fences and pasturing cattle in his fields. **1942** Henry *High Border* 256 **nRocky Mts,** They became known variously not only as drylanders, but also as homesteaders, benchland grangers, woodbillies, woodticks, squatters, and Honijokers, especially if they lived in eastern Montana and the Dakotas. **1958** *AmSp* 33.263, Most common of these [pejorative] terms [for farmers] is *honyocker,* still a fighting word in the western Dakotas. . . This word almost invariably occurs with the *-er* suffix, and is rarely to be confused in form and never in meaning with the similar *honyock. Honyock,* in the sense 'an uncouth countryman, especially of German or Bohemian origin,' is principally found in eastern Nebraska, where many of the early settlers were of German or of Czech birth. Though surely of the same etymology, these terms must be differentiated. **1966** *DARE* (Qu. C34) Inf **SD**5, Honyockers—people who moved in and took up land north of Deadwood; (Qu. HH1, . . *Nicknames for a rustic or countrified person*) Inf **MT**5, Honyockers—called early homesteaders this.

3 also *hawnyock;* By ext: an inexperienced or ignorant person; a hick; a low-class person. Cf **hunk** n[1] **2, Hunk** n[3] **2**

1943 (1945) Smith *Life Putty Knife* 185, Speaking as a pure-bred honyock out of the Middle West. **1952** *AmSp* 27.290 **cIL** (as of c1900), 'He is a hawnyock' (i.e., haw knocker), or 'He has his pockets full of haws' indicated a 'hayseed,' 'yokel.' **1966** *DARE* (Qu. HH18, *Very insignificant or low-grade people*) Inf **MI**4, Hunyaks ['hʌnjæks]; **MI**10, Honyak ['hɑnjɑk]. **1966** *DARE* File **cwIA,** *Hunyak*—"He's always doing such stupid things. He's a real hunyak." **1971** Jennings *Cowboys* 232 **MT, WY** (as of 1877), *Honyock* . . came to mean a green youngster—male; I don't remember anyone ever referring to a girl as a honyock; sometimes spelled "hon yocker."

hup v [*EDD hup(p)* int. and v. 2 "A call to a horse or cow to go on"; 4 "To cry 'hup' to a horse"; *hie* int. and v.[1] 3 (3) *-up* "a call to cows"; *SND hup* [hʌp] int., v. "A call to a horse . . to increase speed, gee-up!"]

Used for var commands to var animals, spec:

a Giddap!—used to make a horse go faster. Cf **come up 1**

1967–68 *DARE* (Qu. K36a, . . *Make a horse go faster*) Inf **IN**40, Hup; **MN**4A, Hup hup ['hʌp 'hʌp].

b Come!—used to call cows.

1968 *DARE* (Qu. K80, *The call that's used . . to get the cows in from the pasture*) Inf **CA**90, Hup [hʌp] bossie.

c Shoo!—used to drive animals away.

1940 Faulkner *Hamlet* 310 **MS,** The nearest animal rose on its hind legs . . and struck twice with its forefeet at Varner's face. . . "Hup, you broom-tailed hay-burning sidewinders," the same voice said. . . and turned to herd them back. **1968** *DARE* (Qu. NN22d, *Expressions used to drive away animals*) Inf **MD**20, Hup [hʌp]—for a cow; **MD**22, Hup [hʊp]—for a cow.

d also *hurp:* Stop!—used as a command to a horse. Cf **hurrup**

1908 *DN* 3.322 **eAL, wGA,** *Hu(r)p. . .* Whoa.

e also *whup:* Stay!—used to tell a dog to stand still.

1969–70 *DARE* (Qu. J9b, . . *Tell a dog to stand without moving*) Inf **KY**35, Hup [hʊp], hold on [FW: repeated]; **KY**86, Whup [hwʌp].

hupple v [Cf *EDD hipple* v.[1] "To heap up hay into small cocks for drying"]

1948 Manfred *Chokecherry* 247 **nwIA,** I kin quick hupple the last couple loads a hay into the barn.

‡hurang n [Perh blend of *hue* and *harangue*] Cf **hurrah B1**

1946 *PADS* 6.18 **eNC** (as of 1900), *Hurang* ['hju'ræŋ]. . . A household rumpus among children. "It's a continual hurang around here."

hurd See **hear** v **A2**

hurdy-gurdy n [Perh because of the circular motion or droning or strident sound]

1 See quot.

1967 *DARE* (Qu. EE32, *A homemade merry-go-round*) Inf **MO**7, Hurdy-gurdy ['hɝdi 'gɝdi].

2 A police wagon.

1969 *DARE* (Qu. N3, *The car or wagon that takes . . people to the police station*) Inf **IN**74, Hurdy gurdy.

hurge grass See **herd's-grass 1**

hurl n [Perh var of *harl* a combed fiber of flax or hemp]

1967 *DARE* FW Addit **ceNY,** *Hurl*—coarse-grade broomcorn.

Huron n

=**largemouth bass.**

1935 Caine *Game Fish* 3 **Sth,** *Large-mouthed Black Bass. . . Synonyms* . . Huron.

huroosh n Also *hooroosh* [Cf *SND huroosh* (at *hurroo* n.) 1. "An excited . . disorderly gathering, a tumult"]

See quot 1912.

1835 in 1970 *DARE* File **nNY,** [Unpublished memorandum:] Mary . . had just landed [from Quebec]. . . Such a harrouche [sic] never was heard. **1836** *Knickerbocker* 8.208, When they were all free, they began to sky-lark, and kick up a hooroosh in all quarters. **1851** (1976) Melville *Moby-Dick* 498, The wind rises. . . Loftiest trucks were made for wildest winds. . . Oh, none but cowards send down their brain trucks in tempest time. What a hooroosh aloft there! I would e'en take it for sublime. **1912** Green *VA Folk-Speech* 236, *Huroosh. . .* Noise; rush; with rapid movement. "The children all came in with a grand huroosh."

hurp See **hup d**

hurra See **hurrah**

hurracane See **hurricane**

hurrah n, v, exclam Usu |hə'rɑ|; freq |'hurɑ|; also |'hurɔ, hu'rɔ, 'hure, hu're, 'hʊrɑ|; for addit varr see quots Pronc-spp *hoorah, hooraw, hooray, hurra(w), hurroo*

A Forms.

1893 Shands *MS Speech* 38, *Hurrah* [hər'ɔ]. **1905** *DN* 3.83 **nwAR,** *Hoorah* ['hurɔ]. **1916** *DN* 4.324 **KS,** *Hurra, hurrah.* **1931–33** *LANE Worksheets* **csMA,** *Hurrah* ['hʊrɑ]. **1953** [see **B1** and **C1** below]. **1966–69** *DARE* (Qu. A20) Inf **GA**7, Hooray [hu're]; (Qu. E22) Inf NC38, Hooraw; (Qq. FF17, 18) Inf **MO**39, Hoorah; (Qu. GG21b) NC9, Hoorah ['hurɑ]; (Qu. HH20c) Inf **MD**41, Hoorah ['hurɑ]; (Qu. KK11) Inf **MD**30, Hurraw [hu'rɔ]; **MS**15, Hoorah; **NC**4, Hooray ['hureɪ]; (Qq. KK15, 16) Inf **CA**114, Hoorah ['hurɑ]; **LA**32, Hooraw ['hurɔ].

B As noun.

1 A ruckus. [Cf *EDD hoo-roo* sb. 1. "A hubbub, noise, tumult"] Cf **hurrah's nest 2**

1848 (1855) Ruxton *Life Far West* 21, Thar' was a hurroo when we rode in with the scalps at the end of our guns. 'Injuns! Injuns!' was the cry from the green horns. **1883** Sweet–Knox *Mexican Mustang* 257 **wTX,** [A railroad station frequented by roughnecks] is what is called, in the classic vernacular of the country, "a hoorah place." **1901** *Munsey's Mag.* 204/1 **CA,** San Francisco was a "hurrah town," the laws were only forming, and altogether unenforced... Robbery .. became almost a regular industry. *Ibid* 209/2, At Somersville, in 1851, a Mexican girl was hanged by Vigilantes for stabbing a big miner, who in the hurrah of a spree kicked in her door. **1923** *DN* 5.211 **swMO,** *Hoorah...* Excited confusion. "Whut's all the hoorah about?" **1940** *Sat. Eve. Post* 3 Feb 15/1 **sMS,** Talbot had raised a hooray at the cabin because Bud wouldn't trade him a jug. **1953** Randolph–Wilson *Down in Holler* 254 **Ozarks,** *Hoorah,* with the accent on the first syllable, .. means a loud noise, a great outcry. "Molly raised a turrible hoorah when she seen Joe in the jailhouse." **1968** *DARE* (Qu. KK11, .. *Make .. a big fuss about something*) Inf **MD**30, Raised a great hurraw [hu'rɔ]; **MS**15, Raised a big hoorah; **NC**4, Made a hooray ['hureɪ] about it; (Qq. KK15, 16, *A disagreement or quarrel* [or *disturbance*]) Inf **CA**114, Hoorah ['hurɑ]; **LA**32, (A big) hooraw ['hurɔ].

2 By ext: an uproarious, enjoyable event. [Cf *EDD hoo-roo* sb. 2 "A fête, public rejoicings of any kind"; also *SND hurroo* n. 1 "High-spirited disorderly gathering"]

[**1931–33** *LANE Worksheets* **csMA,** *Hurrah* ['hʊrɑ]—very fine. "A hurrah of a time."] **1954** *Harder Coll.* **cwTN,** *Hoorah...* A boisterous party. **1969** *DARE* (Qu. FF17, .. *A very good or enjoyable time*) Inf **MO**39, Hoorah; (Qu. FF18, .. *A noisy or boisterous .. party: "They certainly ______ last night."*) Inf **MO**39, Had a hoorah.

3 in neg constrs: The most insignificant thing; a damn. Cf **huckleberry 6**

1908 *DN* 3.321 **eAL, wGA,** *Hoorah in hell...* In the expression 'not worth a hoorah in hell,' i.e., 'absolutely worthless.' **1966–68** *DARE* (Qu. GG21b, *If you don't care what a person does, you might say, ".. I don't give a ______."*) Inf **NC**9, Hoorah ['hurɑ]; (Qu. HH20c, .. *An idle, worthless person... "He isn't worth ______."*) Inf **MD**41, A hoorah ['hurɑ].

4 An imaginary bird. Cf **hurrah's nest 1**

1967 *DARE* (Qu. E22, *If a house is untidy and everything is upset*) Inf NC38, A hooraw'd had a fit.

5 Stuff; a conglomeration of things. Cf **collateral, hurrah's nest 1**

1969 Calhoun *Ball of String* 19, Yessir, all that hoorah was spread out there on tables at the bottom of the hill. Didies and doilies and fancy-made pincushions and all the geegaws that women fix up to sell, plus buckets of ice cream and tubs of strawberries.

6 Teasing. **[hurrah D2]**

1986 Pederson *LAGS Concordance (Touchy)* 1 inf, **ceTX,** He can't take hurrah.

7 See **hurrah bush.**

C As exclam.

1 Used to urge one to hurry.

1853 (1928) Knight *Diary* 44 **IA,** It is all hurry and bustle to get things in order. It's children milk the cows, all hands help yoke these cattle... Hurrah boys. Who tied these horses? **1893** Shands *MS Speech* 38, *Hurrah* [hər'ɔ]. I once knew an old negro cook who always said hurrah for hurry or hurry up... "Hurrah now and less git thoo." **1916** *DN* 4.324 **KS,** *Hurra, hurrah.* Used as an imperative for *hurry,* hasten. "Hurrah, hurra! Get a move on you. We must be getting this job done." **1923** *DN* 5.211 **swMO,** *Hoorah...* Hurry! shouted encouragement to hunting dogs. **1953** Randolph–Wilson *Down in Holler* 254 **Ozarks,** *Hoorah...* To make haste, to hurry. "Hoorah now, an' git them dishes done." The accent is on the second syllable. **1967** *DARE* (Qu. A20, *Joking ways of telling somebody to hurry*) Inf **GA**7, Hooray [hu're].

2 In the game of **hide-and-seek A:** see quot.

1970 *DARE* (Qu. EE15, *When he has caught the first of those that were hiding what does .. 'it' call out?*) Inf **NC**84, Hooray for 'Jack' or 'Mary' and so on as "It" finds kids one by one.

D As verb.

1 To cry "hurrah!"; to prod or drive; hence vbl n *hurrahing.*

1853 (1928) Knight *Diary* 39 **MA,** We crossed the river this morning on a large steam boat .. after a great deal of Hurrahing and trouble to get the cattle all aboard. *Ibid* 48, By driving and hurrahing to the cattle they will almost always follow the horses. **1903** (1965) Adams *Log Cowboy* 274 **West,** "We were determined to get you out of there"... and the latter attempted to hurrah us off to camp.

2 To tease, harass; hence vbl n *hurrahing.*

1905 *DN* 3.83 **nwAR,** *Hoorah* ['hurɔ]... To tease. 'Don't you let 'em hoorah you.' **1908** *DN* 3.321 **eAL, wGA,** *Hoorah...* To guy, joke. "You want to be careful how you hoorah me." **1920** Hunter *Trail Drivers TX* 488 (as of c1880), That little old yearling was a comic sight with those great long horns on its head, and caused lots of fun for the boys. When Governor Bush was looking over the herd he espied this "long-horned" yearling, and began to hurrah Captain Lytle about the animal. **1952** Goyen *Ghost* 24 **TX,** Lucille's husband .. had begun to hurrah her some two or three years back... He had said, "Lucille one thing I cannot stand and that is a fat woman." **1958** Latham *Meskin Hound* 121 **cTX,** Lord A'mighty! I must a-been a sight to bulge an eyeball!.. Lordy, if that Myrtle won't give me a hoorawing! **1967** Green *Horse Tradin'* 165 **cTX,** I had taken so much hurrahing about my little mules, and about them being sold to me for colts, that it was almost unpleasant to live over on the north side of Fort Worth. **1968** *Dallas Morning News* (TX) 10 Aug sec D, I shouldn't tell this on myself. I'll get hoo-rawed. Folks may even think I'm nuts renting a room for an armadillo. **1986** Pederson *LAGS Concordance,* 3 infs **AR, TX,** Hurrahing—joking (with); 1 inf, **csTX,** Hurrahing—name-calling starts it, ends with a fight; 1 inf, **cTX,** I used to hurrah the young folks—badger them; 1 inf **ceTX,** Kind of hurrahing him—teasing him.

3 To raise a ruckus; to create a commotion in (a town). Cf **B1** above

1940 (1946) Raine *Guns* 186 **West,** A turbulent fellow, John had an arm filled with slugs as he 'hurrahed' a town, and it was later amputated. **1957** Burgess *Pillar* 249, If anybody heard it [=a shot], he'd take it for Indians hurrahing around, or hunters. **1986** Pederson *LAGS Concordance,* 1 inf, **neAR,** Hurrahing—raising hell.

hurrah bush n Also *hurrah* **S Atl, esp GA**

A **staggerbush** (here: *Lyonia lucida*).

1853 Simms *Sword & Distaff* 88 **SC,** We're in a pretty close thick .. of Gall and 'Hurrah-bushes.' *Ibid* 89, The wild, matted, tangled, tough and altogether indescribable shrub, which the woodman described as the "Hurrah-bush," and for which we have no better name, constitutes, in poor soil, and on the edges of swamps and drowned lands, one of the most formidable and impenetrable of forest walls. **1926** *AmSp* 1.408 **Okefenokee GA,** His favorite walking-stick of 'hoorah-bush' in hand. [Footnote to *hoorah-bush:*] An evergreen shrub of the heath family, *Pieris nitida.* **1938** Matschat *Suwannee R.* 56 **seGA,** On the other side of the pool was a dense thicket of gallberry and hurrah bushes. **1938** FWP *U.S. One* 252 **FL,** Here mistletoe is found clinging to the black gum, and palmettos grow in profusion. Prickly ash, elbow, and hurrah bushes are common. **1940** (1941) Bell *Swamp Water* 33 **Okefenokee GA,** On the right side of the lake was a jungle wall of many colors .. scarlet ivy trumpets and pink hurrah blossoms. **c1945** Hopkins *Okefenokee* 16 *(DA)* **seGA,** We wrapped stout twine around the bottoms of trouser legs making the trousers a more difficult target for thorny vines and 'hurrah bush' stubble. **1968** *DARE* Tape **GA**30, [Inf:] We got plenty o' that ['huː,rɔː] in here [=Okefenokee Swamp]. [FW:] What is it? [Inf:] It's a bush that grows here in the swamp. It grows thick in some places you have to cut your way through it. The real name for it, I think, is a fetterbush, but we call it the hurrah bush... Won't no insect suck the bloom on it. It has a beautiful bloom .. no kind of insect, nothing don't light on that bloom... A gentleman .. from the government come down here to tag these bushes. . . When he come to that he put *titi* on it . . when he came to that hurrah bush. **1968** *DARE* (Qu. T5, . . *Kinds of evergreens, other than pine*) Inf **GA**25, Hurrah ['hu,rɔ] bush—same as fetterbush.

hurrah grass n

Any of var grasses as:

a =bullgrass 1.

1939 Tharp *Vegetation TX* 45, Hurrah grass (*Paspalum* spp.); in general tends to flourish in low, moist situations. **1966** *DARE* (Qu. S9) Inf **AL**2, Hurrah grass.

b A **panic grass** (here: *Panicum fasciculatum*).

1951 *PADS* 15.8, *Panicum fasciculatum*. . . Hurrah grass, central Texas.

c A **crabgrass 1** (here: *Digitaria sanguinalis*).

1951 *PADS* 15.8, *Digitaria sanguinalis*. . . Hurrah grass, western Texas.

hurrahing See **hurrah D1, 2**

hurrah's nest n

1 A jumbled mess, esp tousled hair or an untidy room. [*hurrah* imaginary bird thought of as noisy and untidy] **now esp S Atl**

1829 in 1886 Longfellow *Life of H.W. Longfellow* 164 **NEng,** A queer-looking Dutchman, with a head like a "hurra's nest" and a great wooden pipe. **1840** (1841) Dana *2 Yrs.* 10, The steerage in which I lived was filled with coils of rigging, spare sails, old junk and ship stores, which had not been stowed away. . . There was a complete "hurrah's nest," as the sailors say, "everything on top and nothing at hand." **1895** Brown *Meadow-Grass* 134 **NH,** I'll clear up this kitchen; it's a real hurrah's nest. **1942** Hurston *Dust Tracks* 103 **FL** [Black], My head looked like a hoo-raw's nest. Why didn't I go comb it? **1945** Colcord *Sea Language* 104 **ME, Cape Cod, Long Island,** *Hôoraw's nest.* The tangle of ropes on deck when a heavy sea has washed the coils from the pins. Alongshore, it characterizes a condition of extreme disorder: "This room looks as if it would ride out—it's a regular hóoraw's nest." **1950** *WELS (If a house is untidy and everything is upset, you say it's a* ______*)* 1 Inf, **WI,** Hooraw's nest. **1965–70** *DARE* (Qu. E22, *If a house is untidy and everything is upset, you might say, "It's a* ______*!" or "It looks like* ______*.")* Inf **DC**1, ['hu,rɔz] nest; **FL**15, [hu'rɔ·z] nest; **GA**36, 46, ['hu,rɔz] nest; **MD**30, [hʊ'rɔz] nest; **NC**38, [hurauz] nest; **NJ**32, Hurrah's nest. [Of 7 Infs, 6 old, 6 college educated, 5 female] **1967** *DARE* FW Addit **sPA,** If a man's or woman's hair is messed up, it looks like a *hurrah's* ['hurɔz] *nest.* **1975** Gould *ME Lingo* 176, "Hooraw's-nest." Any wild jumble of unrelated things; a mess of *culch.*

2 A commotion; racket. Cf **hurrah B1, 2**

1848 Thompson *Major Jones's Travel* 98 **GA,** Sich another *hurra's nest* [as the orchestra at the opera] I never did hear before. **1869** Stowe *Oldtown Folks* 31 **NEng,** You've got our clock all to pieces, and have been keeping up a perfect hurrah's nest in our kitchen. **c1960** *Wilson Coll.* **csKY,** *Hurrah's nest*. . . A lot of commotion or noise for nothing; said of some neighborhood scandal or gossip or political excitement. Also *hooraw's nest.*

3 A mass of dead grass, leaves, twigs etc trapped in the branches of a bush or by some other obstacle.

1889 *Century Illustr. Mag.* 38.503/1 **cnPA,** The old lumberman pointed quietly to a "hurrah's nest" half-way up the slope—on it was coiled a large rattlesnake. [Footnote:] A mass of leaves left by a freshet in the crotch of the divergent branches of a bush. **1916** Kephart *Camping & Woodcraft* 1.213, Observe the more or less continuous line of dead grass, leaves, twigs, mud, and other flotsam or hurrah's-nests left in bushes along the water-front. **1935** Davis *Honey* 88 **OR,** The place was inhumanly well hidden, being simply two big cedar logs thatched over with fallen rubbish to look like an accidental hurrah's nest.

4 See quot.

1916 *Torreya* 16.235 **ME,** [Footnote:] I might add that on this island [=Matinicus Island] I heard the fungoid malformation of trees, known as witches' broom, called hoorah's-nest.

hurraw See **hurrah**

hurr-burr n

=burdock 1.

1876 Hobbs *Bot. Hdbk.* 55, Hurr burr, Burdock, Arctium lappa. **1900** Lyons *Plant Names* 43, *A[rctium lappa]*. . Hurr-bur. **1930** Sievers *Amer. Med. Plants* 17, *Burdock—Arctium minus* . . hurr-burr. **1951** Teale *North with Spring* 218 **NC,** Or he may return with juglans, Kinnikinnic, hackmatack, missey-moosey, daffydowndilly, hurr-burr or robin-runs-away. **1959** Carleton *Index Herb. Plants* 64, Hurr Bur: Arctium lappa.

hurricane n, also attrib Usu |'hɝə,ken|; for varr see **A** below Pronc-spp *haracan, har(r)icane, harrycane, harrykin, herricane, hiricane, hurracane, hurrycane;* for addit varr see quots

A Forms. Cf Pronc Intro 3.I.2.c, 3.II.26 Note: Words for which there are spellings only have been placed with the most likely transcription.

1a |'hʌr(ɪ),ken, -i-, -ɑɪ-|; for addit varr see quot 1965–70. **scattered, but chiefly Nth, esp NEast**

1713 (1901) Hempstead *Diary* 27 *(DAE)* **CT,** A Storm or Hurrycane. **1965–70** *DARE* (Qu. B17, *A destructive wind that blows straight*) 59 Infs, **scattered, but chiefly Nth, esp NEast,** ['hʌrɪken] (*or* [-ɨ-, -ə-, -keɪn, -kɛɪn]); **NJ**8, ['hʌriken]; **NY**137, 227, ['hʌr(r)ɑɪken]; **CA**147, ['hʌrken]; **SC**4, ['hʌrɨkeən]; **FL**21, ['hʌ-əkeɪn]; (Qu. B16) Infs **CT**6, **WA**24, ['hʌrɪken]; (Qu. O19) Infs **MA**45, 62, **NJ**55, ['hʌrɪken]. **1987** *DARE* File **nPA,** ['hʌriken]; **sePA** ['hʌrɪken].

b |'hʌrɪ,kɪn, -i-, -kən, -kn̩|; for addit varr see quot 1965–70. **scattered, but chiefly Sth, S Midl**

1936 *AmSp* 11.161 **eTX,** In less literate speech. . . *Hurricane* is ['hʌrɪkɪn]. **1965–70** *DARE* (Qu. B17) 11 Infs, **scattered, but chiefly Sth, S Midl,** ['hʌrɪkən] (*or* [-ə-]); **GA**17, 27, 31, 36, 66, 67, **NC**46, ['hʌrɪkɪn]; **IL**75, **TN**41, ['hʌrikən]; **NJ**55, ['hʌ-ɪkən]; **AR**6, 19, **FL**3, 7, 11, 15, 19, 26, 27, 37, **MS**11, 17, 24, 55, 72, 73, **TN**30, ['hʌrɪkn̩] (*or* [-ə-]); (Qu. O19) Inf **NY**47, ['hʌrɪkən].

2a |'hɝə,ken, -kən|; for addit varr see quot 1967–70.

1920s in 1944 *ADD* **cNY,** *Hurricane*. . . ['hɚəken] hurracane. **1967–70** *DARE* (Qu. B17) Infs **DC**11, **MO**22, **PA**239, **TN**47, 52, **TX**26, 28, ['hɝəken] (*or* [-ɪ-, -keɪn, -kein]); **PA**248, ['hɝrɪkæn]; **TX**29, 31, ['hɝɪkən]; (Qu. B16) Inf **DC**12, ['hɝəken]. [8 of 11 Infs Black]

b |'hɝɪkn̩, -i-|; for addit varr see quot. **chiefly Appalachians, Mid and S Atl** *somewhat old-fash*

1965–70 *DARE* (Qu. B17) 40 Infs, **chiefly Appalachians, Mid and S Atl,** ['hɝɪkn̩] (*or* [-ɨ-, -ə-]); **FL**33, ['hɝikn̩]; **FL**48, ['hɜ-ɪkn̩]; (Qu. B16) Inf **CO**2, ['hɝɪkn̩]. [36 of 43 Infs old]

3 |'hɛr(ɪ),ken, -i-, -kən, -kn̩|; for addit varr see quots.

1893 Shands *MS Speech* 72, *Hurricane.* This word is pronounced by negroes and illiterate whites . . [hɛriken]. **1899** (1912) Green *VA Folk-Speech* 223, *Herricane*. . . A hurricane. **1965–70** *DARE* (Qu. B17) 20 Infs, **scattered,** ['hɛrɪken] (*or* [hɛr-, -ɨ-, -ə-, -keɪn]); **KY**41, **MI**47, **NY**179, ['hɛr(r)iken]; **IN**3, **KY**84, **NC**39, 83, **SC**19, **VA**55, ['hɛrɪkɪn] (*or* [hɛr-, -ɨ-, -kɨn, -kən]); **IN**7, **KY**83, ['hɛrikɨn]; **SC**26, **TX**102, ['hɛrəkən]; **TX**16, ['hɛrəkan]; 9 Infs **Mid and S Atl, WV,** ['hɛrɪkn̩] (*or* ['hɛr-, -ɨ-, -ə-]); **SC**22 ['hɛrɨkn̩]—Black speakers say this; **FL**35, ['hɛrikn̩]; **MS**2, ['hɛrkn̩]; (Qu. B16) Infs **OR**2, **UT**4, ['hɛrɪken]. **1968** *DARE* FW Addit **nwMO,** ['hɛrɨkən].

4 |'hurɪken, -kɪn|; for addit varr see quot.

1966–68 *DARE* (Qu. B17) Infs **PA**110, 136, ['hurɪken]; **AL**14, ['hurɨkɪn]; **MS**45, ['hurɪkn̩]; **AL**25, ['hu-əkɨn]; **NY**123, ['hjuɚɪken]. [All Infs female]

5 |'hær(ɪ),ken, -i-, -kɪn, -kn̩|; for addit varr see quots. **scattered, but chiefly Sth, S Midl**

1825 Neal *Brother Jonathan* 1.105 **NEng** (as of 1774), Marsy *on* us, *what* a gobble! flock o' wile geese—*in* a harrycane. **1892** *DN* 1.233 **KY,** *Hurricane* ['hæriken]. **1893** Shands *MS Speech* 72, *Hurricane.* This word is pronounced by negroes and illiterate whites . . [hæriken]. **1922** Gonzales *Black Border* 306 **sSC, GA coasts** [Gullah glossary], Harricane—hurricane, hurricanes. **1923** *DN* 5.209 **swMO,** *Harrycane*. . . Hurricane. **1950** Faulkner *Stories* 697 **MS,** Its name was Hurricane Creek . . [but] people called it Harrykin Creek. **1954** *Harder Coll.* **cwTN,** ['hærikeɪn]. **1965–69** *DARE* (Qu. B17, *A destructive wind that blows straight*) Infs **MA**34, **NJ**69, **NY**61, **SC**9, ['hærɪken] (*or* [-ə-]); **AK**7, ['hærken]; **AL**11, **AR**56, **TX**40, ['hærɪkɪn] (*or* [-ə-]); **TX**4, ['hærɪkɨn]—old-fashioned; **AR**52, **DE**1, ['hærɨkən] (*or* [-ə-]); **MS**63, **SC**3, ['hærɪkn̩] (*or* [-ɨ-]); (Qu. B16) Inf **GA**45, ['hærɪkɪn]; (Qu. C34) Inf **NC**5, ['hærikn̩]; (Qu. E22) Inf **TX**52, ['hærɨkən]; (Qu. II14) Inf **OK**27, ['hærɪken]. **1967** *DARE* FW Addit **cAR,** Hurricane Creek is pronounced ['hærɨkən 'krik]. Hurricane's deck is ['hærɨkənz 'dɛk].

6 |'hari,ken, -ɨkən, -ɪkɪn|.

1793 in 1940 *AmSp* 15.275/2 **VA,** Haracan. **1843** (1916) Hall *New Purchase* 313 **IN,** Haricane. **1966–68** *DARE* (Qu. B17, *A destructive wind that blows straight*) Infs **CT**39, **NY**39, 61A, ['harɪken]; **TX**36, 37, ['harɨkɪn]; **AL**6, ['harɨkən]. **1967** *DARE* Tape **TX**8, ['harɪkɪn]

7 |'hɪrɪˌkən, 'hjɪrɪˌken, 'hirɪˌken|.

[**1670** in 1850 Dorchester Antiq. & Hist. Soc. *Coll.* 3.70 **MA,** There arose a fearful Storm (which the *Americans* are wont to call an *Hiracano.*)] **1835** (1927) Evans *Exped. Rocky Mts.* 204 **IN,** The wind came blowing almost to a hiricane which filled the air with sand. **1968** *DARE* (Qu. B17, *A destructive wind that blows straight*) Inf **IN**15, ['hɨrɪkən]; **IN**35, ['hjɨrɪken]; **NY**230, ['hirɪken].

B Senses.

1 Any of various natural phenomena which have been affected by the passage of a wind storm, as:

a also *hurricane ground:* An area or path of land where trees have been blown down or marked by strong winds. **esp Sth, S Midl** *old-fash*

1735 (1901) Hempstead *Diary* 291 **CT,** The Stack . . was made in the Hurrycane this Side the Swamp. **1775** (1962) Romans *Nat. Hist. FL* 307, We . . travelled chiefly through pine land, and some hurricane ground. [Footnote:] Tracts of wood formerly destroyed by hurricanes are so called. **1791** in 1940 *AmSp* 15.275/2 **VA,** To a Sugar tree & Maple near a Harricane. **1793** *Ibid,* Beginning at two white Oaks On the side of a ridge in a haracan. **1903** *DN* 2.316 **seMO,** *Harricane* (hurricane). . . The path of a tornado as shown by fallen timber. 'His farm lays just beyond the harricane.' **1968** Adams *Western Words* 158, *Hurricane*—A logger's term for a path of fallen timber made by a hurricane.

b also *hurricane tree:* A tree scarred or blown down by strong winds.

1775 Adair *Amer. Indians* 337, They had passed over a boggy place . . upon an old hurricane-tree. **1922** Gonzales *Black Border* 306 **sSC, GA coasts** [Gullah glossary], *Harricane tree* . . one thrown down by storm. **1950** *PADS* 14.36 **SC,** *Harricane.* . . A tree uprooted by the wind.

c also *hurricane thick(et):* A dense growth of scrub trees, or cane, in an area where strong winds have blown down the larger trees.

1855 Simms *Forayers* 255 **SC** (as of 1780s), I was in a *'harricane thick,'* on the butt-eend of an almighty big tree. **1891** Sloan *Fogy Days* 176 *(DA),* Now back to the mill pond, where he tries to loose them in the hurricane thicket. **1896** *DN* 1.418 **sKY,** *Harricane* . . thicket where trees have been blown down. **1916** Hall *New Purchase* 467 **IN,** There was a place about eight miles east of Bloomington which was known for many years as the "Hurricane," a region of considerable size, consisting of wild undergrowth and second growth where the great trees of the primitive forests had been leveled with the wind. **1919** *DN* 5.34 **seKY,** *Harricane.* . . A thicket of cane, or other underbrush. **1982** Heat Moon *Blue Highways* 324 **VT,** Then the railroad started carrying in people looking for spruce hurricanes.

d A clump of earth at the base of an uprooted tree; see quot.

1897 (1952) McGill *Narrative* 10 **SC,** The storm logs, with their upturned roots, once everywhere, are yet spoken of, and in Sam's hunting rabbit times he felt sure of his rabbit when his dog treed in a harricane, as those old red and yellow banks of earth at the root of logs were known by that name, the effect taking the name of the cause tho' in a corrupt form.

2 A tornado; see quot 1968.

1865 Crockett *Life* 121, We concluded to go on with the boat to where a great *harricane* had crossed the river, and blowed all the timber down into it. **1968** *DARE* File **swAR** (as of 1953), [Newspaper article:] The evidence of a recent tornado, or as one would say locally "hurricane," gives rise to one or more Hurricane Creeks.

hurricane bird n

=**man-o'-war bird.**

1911 *Century Dict. Suppl., Hurricane-bird.* . . The frigate-bird: so named from a popular belief that when it flies near the water a hurricane will follow. [Rare.] **1917** (1923) *Birds Amer.* 1.107, *Man-O'-War Bird—Fregata aquila* . . Hurricane Bird. **1925** (1928) Forbush *Birds MA* 1.171, *Fregata aquila* . . *Man-o'-war-bird.* . . Hurricane Bird. **1946** Hausman *Eastern Birds* 95, Man-O'-War Bird *Fregata magnificens* . . Hurricane Bird.

hurricane deck n

1 The saddle on a horse. [By transf from *hurricane deck* the promenade or uppermost deck on a steamship where a person is most at risk from sudden motion] **West**

1876 *Silver City* (Ida.) *Avalanche* 7 March 2/2 *(DA),* Leaving Salubria on the hurricane deck of a cayuse, your correspondent wended his doleful way across the snow to the Little Weiser. **1887** *Outing* 10.253/2 **wMT,** It [=the river] may also be . . fished from the hurricane-deck of a cayuse. **1903** (1965) Adams *Log Cowboy* 380 **West,** McCann was transferred to the hurricane deck of a cow horse, which he sat with ease and grace, having served an apprenticeship in the saddle in other days. **1936** McCarthy *Lang. Mosshorn* np **West** [Rodeo term], *Hurricane Deck.* The saddle seat on a horse.

‡**2** in phr *all over hurricane's deck:* See quot.

1967 *DARE* FW Addit **cAR,** "All over hurricane's deck" means in all directions, all around. "They scattered all over hurricane's deck."

hurricane ground (or hill) See **hurricane B1a**

hurricane's deck, all over See **hurricane deck 2**

hurricane thick(et) See **hurricane B1c**

hurricane tree See **hurricane B1b**

hurroo See **hurrah**

hurrup v Also *huddup* [Perh by syncope < *hurry up*] **esp NEng** Cf **hup**

Used as a command to a horse or a cow to come, move, or go faster.

1858 (1892) Holmes *One Hoss Shay* 25 **eMA,** Here comes the wonderful one-hoss-shay,/ Drawn by a rat-tailed, ewe-necked bay./ "Huddup!" said the parson.—Off went they. **1891** Cooke *Huckleberries* 329 **NEng,** Just then the deacon drove up to the gate. . . "Huddup, Whitey! We don't want to be late." **1907** *DN* 3.245 **csME,** *Hurrup.* . . Used in driving a cow. From "hurry up!" Accent on the last syllable. **1907** *DN* 3.191 **seNH,** *Hurrup.* . . Hurry up! Addressed to a cow or a horse. **1968** *DARE* (Qu. K80, *The call . . used . . to get the cows in from the pasture*) Inf **DE**5, Hurrup ['hɝ'ə:p 'hɝ:p].

hurrus See **hearse**

hurry v

1 also *hurry up;* pronc-sp *hooey:* Go away!—used to drive off a cow or another animal.

1893 Shands *MS Speech* 37, *Hooey* ['hu-ɨ]. The sound used to drive cows out of one's way. It is probably a corruption of *hurry.* **1965–69** *DARE* (Qu. NN22d, *Expressions used to drive away animals other than dogs:*) Infs **KY**36, **MS**64, Hurry (for a cow); **MO**8, Hurry (for a cow or cat); **VA**24, Hurry up (for a cow); **MD**20, Hurry ['hɝ-ɨ], (for a cow); **AR**52, Hurry ['hʌ-ɪ],—[FW: Inf's sp is "hurry"].

2 as vbl n: See quot. [Cf *EDD harry* v[2]]

1930 Shoemaker *1300 Words* 29 **cPA Mts** (as of c1900), *Hurrying*—Cattle or horse stealing.

3 To rush and bring.

1970 *DARE* File **csIL,** Hurry me a pack of cigarettes means quickly run and get me a pack.

hurry adv

Quickly.

1892 (1969) Christensen *Afro-Amer. Folk Lore* 24 **sSC coast,** As 'e was pass de locus' tree in a great hurry, de Bear was on de tree. So de Bear call to him, say, "Br'er Rabbit, whar you gwine so hurry wid de rope?"

hurry n [Cf *OED hurry* sb. 2 "Mental agitation or disturbance; perturbation. . . *Obs.*"]

1887 (1967) Harris *Free Joe* 127 **GA,** Peevy rubbed his hands nervously together. . . His agitation was manifest. . . "Well . . I reckon I better be gwine." "Wait till your hurry's over," said Babe, in a gentler tone.

hurry-buggy See **hurry-up wagon**

hurrycane See **hurricane**

hurry-hence n

1966 *DARE* (Qu. GG42, *A reckless person, one who takes foolish chances*) Inf **SC**10, Hurry-hence.

hurrying See **hurry v 2**

hurryment n [*hurry* + **-ment** suffix; also cf *EDD hurrysome* adj. 1 "Confused."]

Confusion; excitement.

1845 Thompson *Pineville* 66 **GA,** What upon yeath [=earth] can they be gwine in sich a hurryment? *Ibid* 174, Somehow in my hurryment I drapt [=dropped] my pan. **1872** (1973) Thompson *Major Jones's Courtship* 52, The big dog he was callin knocked him off the log in his hurryment to git at the coon. *Ibid* 178, I was skeered as bad as she was, and put my trowses on wrong side before in my hurryment.

hurry up See **hurry** v **1**

hurry-up n

1 =accommodation b.

1913 *DN* 4.56 **Cape Cod MA,** *Hurry-up*. . . A jocose name for the "accommodation."

2 also *hurry-up affair, ~ marriage, ~ one, ~ wedding:* See quot 1966–70. **chiefly Nth, Midl**

1935 Sandoz *Jules* 263 **wNE** (as of 1880s), All the next day and night there were dancing and music. . . There will be more hurry-up weddings after this. **1966–70** *DARE* (Qu. AA20, *A marriage that takes place because a baby is on the way*) Infs **CA**79, **NY**234, **OH**28, (A) hurry-up; **IA**25, **MA**12, 69, **ND**3, **UT**9, **VA**34, Hurry-up wedding (*or* marriage); **NY**126, **OH**64, Hurry-up affair (*or* one). [9 of 11 Infs female]

hurry-up cart See **hurry-up wagon**

hurry-up marriage (or one) See **hurry-up** n **2**

hurry-up wagon n Also *hurry-buggy, ~-up cart, hurry-wagon* Cf **hoodlum wagon 2**

A police van.

1893 (1896) Post *Harvard Stories* 118 **Boston MA,** The cop was utterly useless. . . The manager . . told him to send for a hurry-up wagon, and run us all in. We showed the law great respect, though, after the shindy was over. **1904** Day *Kin o' Ktaadn* 113 **ME,** I stepped onto the tavern floor down to town an' a policeman yanked me out and threw me into a hurry-up cart . . an' the judge fined me ten dollars. **1927** *DN* 5.451 [Underworld jargon], *Hurry buggy*. . . The police patrol wagon. **1948** *Sun* (Baltimore MD) 18 Oct 12/6, They [=cops] showed up in a dense swarm, commanded by half a dozen inspectors and with their hurry-wagons backed into every nearly [sic] alley. **1967–69** *DARE* (Qu. N3, *The . . wagon that takes arrested people to the police station or to jail*) Infs **CO**33, **MA**55, 68, Hurry-up wagon.

hurry-up wedding See **hurry-up** n **2**

hurry-wagon See **hurry-up wagon**

hursh See **hush** v

hurst See **hearse**

hurt v Usu |hɝt, hɜt|; also |hʌt, hɜɪt| (cf Pronc Intro 3.II.12) Pronc-spp *hite, hoit, ho't, hut* [Cf *EDD hurt* v. I *Present, Preterite* and *Pp.: "Hot"*; but cf also *DJE hat*[1] "The expected dial form of *hurt* would be */hot/ or */hort/."]

A Pronc varr.

1848 Lowell *Biglow* 144 **'Upcountry' MA,** *Hut,* hurt. **1922** Gonzales *Black Border* 307 **sSC, GA coasts** [Gullah glossary], *Hu't, ho't*. . . hurt, hurts, hurting. **1934** in 1944 *ADD* **OK,** [mɑ heɪd hʌts]. **1944** *ADD* 311 **NYC,** *Hurt*. . . 1930s . . [hɔɪt] hoit. Common rendering of the pron[unciation]. **1947** Ballowe *The Lawd* 179 **LA,** A Duppy [=spirit of a dead person] done *hite* me.

B Gram forms.

Past, past pple, ppl adj: Usu *hurt;* also *hurted;* pronc-spp *hited, hurtid.* [Cf *EDD hurt* v. 2 *"Preterite: . . Horted . . Hotted . . Hurted. . .* 3 *Pp.: . . Horted . . Hurted . . Hurtid"*; also *SND hurt* v. "pa.t. and pa.p. *hurtit, . . -ed . . -id.*"] **chiefly Sth, S Midl, esp S Atl** Cf **-ed 1**

1837 Sherwood *Gaz. GA* 70, [In a list of "provincialisms" to be avoided:] *Hurted,* for hurt. **1884** *Anglia* 7.270 **SE,** To git hurtid = to get hurt. **1893** Shands *MS Speech* 38, *Hurted*. . . Used by illiterate whites for the past tense of *to hurt;* as, "I hurted myself." **1907** Wright *Shepherd* 226 **Ozarks,** He ain't never hurted me. **1922** (1926) Kephart *Highlanders* 358 **sAppalachians,** Hurted. **1927** Adams *Congaree* 73 **cSC** [Black], He make a noise like a hurted beast, but it ain' do no good. **1947** Ballowe *The Lawd* 172 **LA,** We po', an' we black, but we got feelin's, an' they been hited. Quality done wronged us.

C Senses.

1 To care; to be anxious.

1895 *DN* 1.389 **cnMS,** *Hurt* . . "I don't hurt for it," or "I ain't a-hurtin' for it" = "I don't care much for it." **1906** *DN* 3.142 **nwAR,** *Hurt*. . . To be anxious. "No one is hurting to know."

2 often with *for:* To need; to be in need of (something) usu used in progressive.

1956 McAtee *Some Dialect NC* 56, *Hurt:* . . deteriorate. Said of cattle on diminished pasture. "They aint hurtin' any." **1967–69** *DARE* (Qu. U37, . . *Somebody who has plenty of money*) Inf **MN**33, Not hurting; **SC**55, Not hurting any; (Qu. U40) Inf **IN**75, Hurting fer bread, cash; **MN**33, Hurting; (Qu. 41a) **IL**28, Hurting. **1970** Major *Dict. Afro-Amer. Slang* 68 [Black], *Hurting:* to be in extreme need or misfortune. **1974** Fink *Mountain Speech* 13 **wNC, eTN,** *Hurt fer* . . need. "The house is hurting fer a coat of paint." **1976** Garber *Mountain-ese* 45 **Appalachians,** *Hurt* . . need, require—We won't hurt fer any soybean seeds this year cause we raised plenty. *Ibid, Hurting-fur* . . in need—I shore hope it rains, the corn crop is really hurtin' fur water.

3 To harm by means of **hoodoo** n **1a.**

c1938 in 1970 Hyatt *Hoodoo* 1.172 **seNC** [Black], I had a aunt, she got *hurt,* and it started up in her head and it jes' keep on worryin' her head. And so she went to a [hoodoo] *doctor* and found out that somebody had put somepin down for her [=done something involving magic against her]. It somepin wrahpped up in a little bondle and they had it over the door. It was some kinda powder and some sharp instruments in there, look kinda like pins. *Ibid* 177, I've been *hurted* with this here *witch-crafter* twicet in my life. *Ibid* 282, She say, "You know, I got a pain down in this toe." It looked like it would come in spells, you know. . . An' she got bad off, real sick, an' they called de doctor an' tried ev'rything they could an' didn't seem to do her no good. An' one woman come there, she say, "You know one thing, I believe you's *hurt*." She said, "You reckon?" She said, "Yeh, I believe you's *hurt*." . . She had to pay [the root man] fifty-five dollah. *Ibid* 750 **DC,** [Hyatt:] If a person thinks he's *hurt* or anything of that sort, could you give him help in any way? . . [Inf:] Yes, if they was *hurt* and the spirit would show it tuh me, and I would see it and tell them about it. . . [Hyatt:] Would you prescribe any remedy for them? [Inf:] Well, depends upon how they were *hurt*. . . Lots of people comes to me and say that they are *hurt* and they are not.

hurted See **hurt B**

hurter See **hudder**

hurt for See **hurt C2**

hurth See **hearth A1**

hurtid See **hurt B**

hurting n

1 An ache or pain. **chiefly Sth, S Midl** See Map

1902 *DN* 2.237 **sIL** [Pioneer dialect], *Hurtn* [sic]. . . A pain. **1917** *DN* 4.413 **wNC,** *Hurtin'*. . . A pain. **1950** *WELS* 1 Inf, **WI,** Hurting. **c1960** *Wilson Coll.* **csKY,** *Hurting*. . . A sort of indefinite ache or pain, like a hurting in the chest. **1965–70** *DARE* (Qu. BB4, *Other words for a pain . . "He's had a ____ in his arm for a week."*) 77 Infs, **scattered, but chiefly Sth, S Midl,** Hurting; **GA**67, Hurting—[used by] Negroes; (Qu. BB3b) Infs **FL**26, **NH**16, **OH**44, **TN**30, Hurting; (Qu. BB3c) Inf **IN**28, Hurting; **TN**16, Hurtin'. **1965** *DARE* Tape **MS**61, I had t' go t' the doctor for a hurtin' across my breast. . . When I go t' stoop over, why this hurtin' cumulates across here. **1976** Garber *Mountain-ese* 45 **Appalachians,** *Hurtin'* . . pain, soreness. I jist kain't do my work no more since I got this hurtin' in my back.

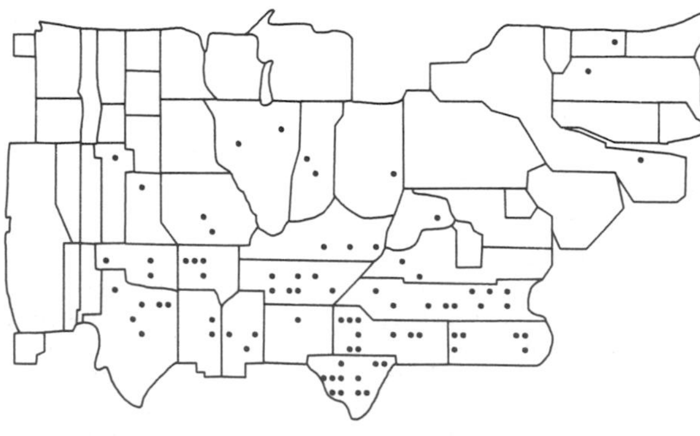

•hurting 1 + var (Qq. BB4, BB3b, c)

2 in phr *put a hurting on:* To cause a physical mark or pain; see quot.

1970 *DARE* (Qu. Y11, *Other words for a very hard blow: "You should have seen Bill go down. Joe really hit him a ____."*) Inf **NY**249, Put a hurting on the cat; (QR near Qu. Y35) Inf **NY**249, Put a hurting on the coffee pot; (QR near Qu. AA9) Inf **NY**241, She put a hurtin' on him—in a good sense. [Both Infs Black, male]

hurtingest ppl adj Cf **-est 1b**

1934 (1943) *W2, Hurtingest*. . . Most painful. *Dial.* **1967** *DARE* (Qu. BB3b, *A sudden pain that strikes you in the back*) Inf **CO**10, It is some kind of hurtingest thing you ever had.

hurtsickle n [See quot 1931]

=**cornflower 1.**

1900 Lyons *Plant Names* 89, *C[entaurea] Cyanus* . . Hurtsickle. **1914** Georgia *Manual Weeds* 521, *Black Knapweed—Centaurea nigra* . . Hurtsickle. **1931** Harned *Wild Flowers Alleghanies* 613, As the plant [=*Centaurea cyanus*] grows older its texture becomes hard and woody, whence its name Hurtsickle, a name applied to it by the farmer who has experienced great annoyance on account of the injury to his sickle while cutting grass or grain in his fields.

hus See **husk** n

husband-high adj **esp Appalachians, Ozarks**

Of a young woman: grown up enough to marry.

1933 Williamson *Woods Colt* 185 **Ozarks,** Nance is growin' up. She's dang near husband high, right now. **1951** Craig *Singing Hills* 120 **swVA nwNC,** When she was husband-high she saw one man shoot at another. **1968** *DARE* File **VA,** *Husband-high:* a girl is husband-high if she is old enough to get married—old-fashioned.

hush n See **husk** n

hush v Usu |hʌš|; also **chiefly Sth, S Midl** |heš, haıš, hʌıš, hɝrš|; for addit varr see quots Cf Pronc Intro 3.I.5.d and 3.I.23 Pronc-spp *hesh, heish, heush, hursh;* for addit varr see quots Cf Intro "Language Changes" I.8

A Forms.

1867 Lowell *Biglow* lxxi **'Upcountry' MA,** *U* changes . . to *e,* always in . . *hush, rush, blush.* **1899** (1912) Green *VA Folk-Speech* 222, *Heish*. . . Hush! The *hei* like in *height.* **1902** *DN* 2.234 **sIL,** *eu.* Diphthong occurring in . . Heush = hush. Pronounced with short e + u as in but, but without drawl. *Ibid* 237, *Heush* [hɛʊš]. **1903** *DN* 2.317 **seMO,** *Hush*. . . Pronounced hesh [hɛš]. **1903** in 1944 *ADD* [Black], Hesh. **1906** *DN* 3.140 **nwAR,** [hɜš]. **1934** *AmSp* 9.212 **Sth,** Standard [ʌ] before [ʃ] . . sometimes becomes [ʌɪ]. . . *hush* (also [hɛʃ], [haɪʃ]). **1937** *AmSp* 12.286 **wVA,** The [r] is normally pronounced, often excrescently. . . [hɜrʃ] . . heard for . . *hush.* **1942** Hall *Smoky Mt. Speech* 39 **wNC, eTN,** There is a sound with a slight [ʊ] flavor which appears in words like . . *hush.* Although suggestive of [ʊ], upon analysis it seems essentially to be [ʌ]. **1956** McAtee *Some Dialect NC* 24, *Hursh:* pronunciation, hush. **1961** Folk *Word Atlas N. LA* 52, An intrusive *r* . . is heard in South Midland [speech] in . . *hush.* **1984** Burns *Cold Sassy* 4 **nGA** (as of 1906), Hesh up, Loma. I ain't finished.

B Senses.

1 also with *up:* Used interjectionally to express astonishment or admiration, sometimes with implied request for more information. **chiefly Sth, S Midl, esp Appalachians**

1846 (1847) Porter *Quarter Race* 88 **KY,** Oh hush! It makes my mouth water now to think what a beautiful row we had. **1898** Dunbar *Folks from Dixie* 62 **Sth** [Black], "Then you can sell chickens and eggs, and we'll go halves on the profits." "Hush, man!" cried 'Lias, in delight. **1909** *DN* 3.347 **eAL, wGA,** *Look a-here hush*. . . 'I am greatly surprised at what you say.' **1910** *DN* 3.458 **Kansas City MO,** An equivalent of the N.E. "I want to know,"—"I want you to hush!" **1912** *DN* 3.579 **wIN,** *Hush up*. . . An expression equivalent to "I can scarcely believe what you say." "Why Martha hush up! He didn't run away from home, did he?" **1935** in 1944 *ADD* **NC,** When I named the price, she cried, 'I wish you'd hush!' This was clearly an invitation to extol the merits of the article still further. **1970** *DARE* (Qu. NN7, *Exclamations of surprise: "They're getting married next week? Well, ______."*) Inf **GA**67A, I want you to hush [laughter]. **1980** *DARE* File **cAR,** We grew up somewhat confused about the word "hush." At school it meant one thing. But when Miss Ina . . said "hush" it did not mean shut your mouth. It meant, "Say that again." [For example] "Miss Ina, did you know your hat's on sideways?" "Hush!" "Yes, ma'am. . . " Miss Ina said hush again and fell back to make adjustments.

2 in phr *hush one's mouth:* To stop talking; also fig, used to express agreement, enjoyment or surprise. **Sth, S Midl** *freq among Black speakers*

1859 Taliaferro *Fisher's R.* 191 **NC** (as of 1820s) [Black], Hush yer mouf! **1903** *DN* 2.317 **seMO,** *Hush*. . . 'Hesh your mouth,' . . stop talking. **1906** *DN* 3.140 **nwAR,** Hesh your mouth. **1926** Van Vechten *Nigger Heaven* 13 [Black], Put ashes in sweet papa's bed so as he can' slip out, moaned Licey in the Creeper's ear. . . Licey chuckled. Hush ma mouf ef Ah doan! **1927** Adams *Congaree* 37 **cSC** [Black], How come you say dat. You better hush your mout'. **1932** (1974) Caldwell *Tobacco Road* 49 **GA,** "Brother Jeeter, you hush your mouth!" she giggled. **c1937** in 1972 *Amer. Slave* 2.250 **SC,** Give them bread to eat and fire to warm by, then, hush your mouth; they is sho' safe then! **1966–70** *DARE* (Qu. X10b, *To tell a person to stop talking—not very politely*) Infs **DE**2, **FL**48, **MI**72, **MO**23, **NY**35, **SC**7, Hush your mouth; **KY**8, Hush your mouth—colored woman says; **TN**63, Hush your mouth—would never use this but have heard it; (Qu. NN7, *Exclamations of surprise*) Inf **VA**69, Hush your mouth; **TN**46, Hush yo' mouf. [8 of 10 Infs female; 5 of 10 Infs Black]

hush cloth n Cf **husher**

See quot 1979.

1934 (1943) *W2, Hush cloth*. . . A silence cloth. **1979** *DARE* File **cnMA** (as of c1915), My mother and her mother always referred to the silence cloth (the soft, heavy cloth under the tablecloth) as the hush cloth.

husher n *somewhat old-fash*

A cover for a chamber-pot lid; see quot 1970.

1937 Sandoz *Slogum* 85 **NE** (as of 1900–20), He said he had summer complaint. . . [but] Old Tit-Ear was scared into the trots by the Bullard business, filling his pants like a damned tenderfoot. . . Gulla fetched a pot with a husher. **1963** Haywood *Yankee Dict.* 87 **NEng,** *Husher*—This was the finely worked crochet piece . . fitted over the cover of an earthernware chamber pot. **1967** Schilla *Prairies* 187 **ND,** She mentioned her mother making "hushers" for chamber-pot covers. These were decorated to match each bedroom. **1970** *DARE* file **csWI,** *Husher*—A crocheted or knitted cover for a china or pottery chamber pot-lid. Purpose: to cut down on breakage and eliminate rattle or clinking. **1980** *DARE* File **cVT** (as of c1900), *Husher*—knit or crocheted cover for a chamber-pot lid.

hush haw exclam [**haw** v]

1959 *VT Hist.* new ser 27.143, *Hush haw!* . . The term used in driving oxen to the left, just as "Gee" turns them to the right. Sometimes used without the *hush.* Common.

hush-hush n [Cf *hush-hush* secret, confidential]

1965 Little *Autobiog. Malcolm X* 90 [Black], And then she started hearing older girls in grade school whispering the hush-hush that "niggers" were such sexual giants and athletes.

hushmagundi n [Perh *hush* var of *hash,* infl by **salmagundi**]

A stew.

1911 Kolb *Jrl.* 11 Oct **PA,** We found a marble cave about 35 ft above the [Colorado] river. . . We were tired but I made several flap jacks and a big pot of hushmagundi.

hush man n

1977 Dillard *Lexicon* 57 [Black], This conference contained, along with fifteen preachers . . one *hush man* (a person used by a preacher to "quell arguments or anything that will cause the preacher embarrassment").

hush-mouth n Cf **hush** v **B2**

1 also attrib: A person who is quiet or retiring; see quots.

1942 Hurston *Dust Tracks* 176 **FL** (as of c1940) [Black], This move . . was his work, and only his hush-mouth nature has caused it to be attributed to many others. **1966–68** *DARE* (Qu. HH24, *Somebody who doesn't talk very much, who keeps his thoughts to himself*) Infs **SC**7, 10, Hush-mouth; (Qu. HH25) Inf **MD**40, He's a hush-mouth. [1 Inf Black]

2 also *hush-mouth dog:* A type of hunting dog; see quots. Cf **hush puppy 6**

1970 Green *Ely* 115 [Black], I trained the two hushmouth dogs to be my bodyguards. **1987** *DARE* File **csWI** [Hunter's lingo], *Hush-mouth*—they're called that because they won't open up [their mouths to bark] on the trail.

3 Something given or taken to keep a person silent.

1949 Turner *Africanisms* 232 [Gullah], A drink of whiskey . . 'hush mouth'. **1984** Wilder *You All Spoken Here* 154 **Sth,** *Hush mouth:* Hush money.

hush-mouth dog See **hush-mouth 2**

hush one's mouth See **hush** v **B2**

hush puppy n [*hush* to quiet + *puppy*]

1 A dollop of cornmeal batter, sometimes seasoned, fried in deep fat; occas a cornmeal dumpling or piece of cornbread.

chiefly Sth, S Midl See Map Cf **ashdog, dogbread, fried puppy 2, hoecake, red horse bread**

1918 *DN* 5.18 **NC,** *Hushpuppy,* a sort of bread prepared very quickly and without salt. **1940** *AmSp* 15.215 **wFL,** In the speech of West Florida crackers. . . I never heard ham gravy spoken of as hushpuppy. . . Our hush-puppy was cornbread crust soaked in bean or pea or greens soup. **1942** Rawlings *Cross Creek Cookery* 28 **nFL,** *Hush-puppies* are. . . a concomitant . . of the fishing trip. Fresh-caught fried fish without hush puppies are as man without woman. . . They derived their name from old fishing and hunting expeditions, when . . folks ate to repletion. . . [and] tossed the remaining cornmeal patties to the dogs, calling, "Hush, puppies!"—and the dogs, devouring them, could ask no more of life, and hushed. **1949** *Times-Picayune* (New Orleans LA) 15 May mag sec 10/2 **cnMS,** Fishing parties, dances, hush-puppy suppers and fish fries kept the MGMers almost too pleasantly busy to proceed with the filming. **1965-70** *DARE* (Qu. H25, . . *Fried cornmeal*) 129 Infs, **chiefly Sth, S Midl, esp SE,** Hush puppies; (Qu. H14, *Bread that's made with cornmeal*) 67 Infs, **chiefly Sth, S Midl,** Hush puppies (*or* puppy); **GA**85, Hush puppy—put onions in and eat with fish; **IL**91, Hush puppy—fried with fish; **IL**131, Hush puppy—seasoned, not the same as corn bread; **KY**8, Hush puppy—with onions; **NC**88, Hush puppy—baking powder, salt, onion, milk, and eggs—either fry in deep fat or bake it; **TX**26, Hush puppy—pure meal (corn bread—little flour added); **TX**51, Hush puppy—fried, has onion in it, good with fish; **TX**91, Hush puppy—shaped by hand in hot water; (Qu. H18, . . *Special kinds of bread*) Infs **FL**11, 18, **GA**62, **NC**36, 41, 48, Hush puppies; (Qu. H24, . . *Boiled cornmeal*) Inf **TX**91, Hush puppies; (Qu. H31, . . *Dough . . cooked in deep fat;* total Infs questioned, 75) Inf **FL**6, Hush puppies; (Qu.H45) Inf **IL**131, Fiddler cats [=catfish] and hush puppies. **1969** *DARE* Tape **GA**86, Hush puppies . . that's like ham an' eggs. Eggs go with ham, hush puppies go with fish. **1970** *DARE* FW Addit **sIL,** *Hush puppies*—a local specialty from the menu of the Mark Twain Inn. **1983** *DARE* File **GA** (as of 1978), *Hush puppies* seems to be the Georgia equivalent of the South Carolina red horse bread.

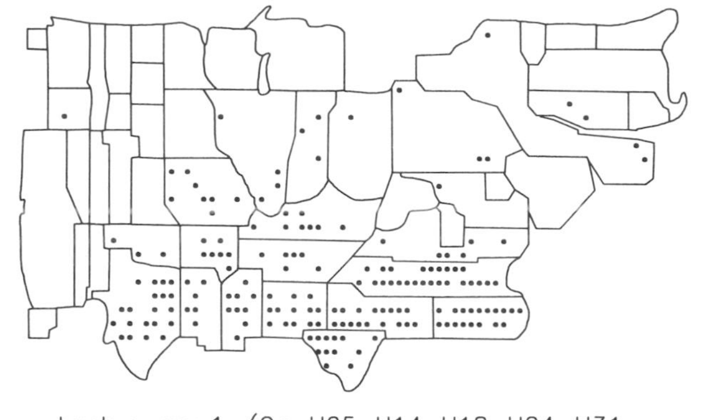

•hush puppy 1 (Qq. H25, H14, H18, H24, H31, H45)

2 See quot. Cf **red horse**

1953 Randolph-Wilson *Down in Holler* 254 **Ozarks,** *Hush-puppy.* . . A patty made of hash, with cornmeal in it.

3 also *hush-puppy gravy:* A type of gravy; see quots. **esp S Midl**

1939 *AmSp* 14.91 **TN Mts,** *Hush-puppy.* Ham gravy. "I sop my bread with hush-puppy." **1941** *Qrly. Jrl. Speech* 27.357, Any [white sauce or cream gravy] left over was given to the dogs which were responsible no doubt for the name "Hush puppy gravy" used to distinguish it from "calico gravy" served with fried ham. **1942** *AmSp* 17.171 **sIL,** Frog-eye gravy. . . the gravy left in the skillet after frying ham. . . something similar . . to . . "hush-puppy" in Tennessee. **1953** Randolph-Wilson *Down in Holler* 254 **Ozarks,** "White sauce or cream gravy" was called *hush-puppy gravy* in pioneer days.

4 A relish; see quot.

1934 *AmSp* 9.71 **TX,** *Hush-puppy* is a relish served with barbeque. It is made of tomatoes, onions, chili, vinegar, etc., and it does not appeal to puppies.

5 See quots. **[hush puppy 1]** Cf **corn dog**

1942 Berrey-Van den Bark *Amer. Slang* 91.68, Hush-puppy, smothered dog, *a frankfurter sandwich with lettuce, onions and a variety of relishes.* **1968** *DARE* (QR, near Qu. H14) Inf **PA**66, Hush puppy, also pig-in-a-blanket, a hot dog wrapped in dough.

6 A mongrel hunting dog. Cf **hush-mouth 2, potlicker**

1947 *Democrat* 30 Oct. 4/3 (*DA* at *pot licker*) **AL,** A [hunting] hound is a hound, regardless of whether he is July, Red Bone, Walker, potlicker or just plain hush-puppy.

hush-puppy gravy See **hush puppy 3**

‡hush the lilac n

A hiding game played in teams; see quot.

1950 *WELS (Games in which one captain hides his team and the other team tries to find it)* 1 Inf, **WI,** Hush the lilac.

hush up See **hush** v **B1**

husk n Usu |hʌsk|; also |hʌs|; rarely |hʌst| Pronc-spp *hus(s), hush, hucks* Note: With some of these forms it is impossible to tell whether a pl or a sg collective is intended.

A Forms. Cf **tusk**

1820-35 in 1956 Eliason *Tarheel Talk* 278 **NC,** Hush collars should have small plats. . . sell for 25 cents. **1892** [see **B4b, c** below]. **1894** [see **B4b, c** below]. **1899** (1912) Green *VA Folk-Speech* 237, *Huss. . .* Husk. . . *n. pl. Husses.* **1941** *LANE* Map 263 *(Husks),* Pronunciations of the type of [hʌsk] . . represent the singular (collective), pronunciations of the type of [hʌsks, hʌss, hʌs] . . the plural. However, the forms [hʌs, hʌ˅s] [in two cases] are designated as either singular or plural. Seven informants state that the word *husk* is not used in the plural . . , i.e. it is used only in the collective sense. [All of the pronc types mentioned are found throughout **NEng;** 7 infs in **wCT, eMA,** give proncs of the type [hʌst(s)].] **1966** [see **B4b** below]. **1984** [see **B6** below].

B Senses. Cf **hull** n **B, shuck** n

1 =**hull** n **B1.** Cf **cap** n[1] **5**

1941 *LANE* Map 275 *(Hull—of a strawberry)* 3 infs, **sNEng,** Husk. **1965-70** *DARE* (Qu. I47, *When you pull the stem out of a strawberry, what do you call the green part that comes off with the stem?*) 15 Infs, Husk. **1968** *DARE* Tape **GA**69, If all the petals an' all the husk are still around the little peach, why, it is protected. **1983** *DARE* File **WY,** [The green part of a strawberry that comes off with the stem is called a] husk.

2 The covering of a nut, as:

a =**hull** n **B2a(1). chiefly Nth, N Midl, West** See Map and Map Section Cf **burr** n[1] **2a**

[**1806** (1970) Webster *Compendious Dict.* 147, *Husk. . .* The covering of some fruits, &c. refuse.] **1941** *LANE* Map 277 **sNEng,** Terms for the green outer covering of the walnut . . were incidentally offered. . . Husk [6 infs]. **1950** *WELS* 21 Infs, **WI,** Husk. **1965-70** *DARE* (Qu. I39, *What do you call the thick outside covering of a walnut?*) 120 Infs, **scattered, but chiefly Nth, N Midl, West,** Husk. **1971** Wood *Vocab. Change* 42 **Sth,** *Husk* [for the green outer cover of a walnut does not] . . exceed . . one-third of the preferences. **1973** Allen *LAUM* 1.307 (as of c1950), *Husk* . . is proportionately much more frequent in the U[pper] M[idwest] [than in New England], where its orientation is clearly Northern. *Ibid, Husk:* Used for hazelnuts. . . for butternuts [in Minnesota]. **1987** *DARE* File **sWI,** *Husk* is the soft green outside cover that rots off, of a hickory nut or a butternut.

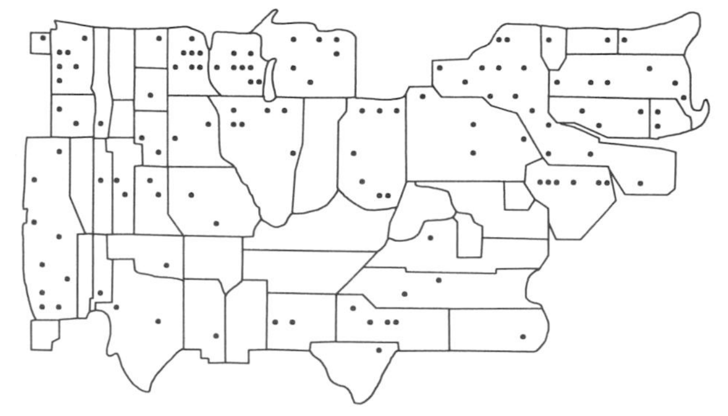

•husk n B2a (Qu. I39)

b =**hull** n **B2a(2).**

1950 *WELS* 1 Inf, **WI,** Husk. **1969** *DARE* (Qu. I40, *The hard part inside . . a walnut that you have to break*) Inf **NY**128, Husk. **1971** Wood *Vocab. Change* 42 **Sth,** The hard inner cover of a walnut is. . . In descending order [after *shell* which predominates] *hull, husk,* and *shuck.* **1973** Allen *LAUM* 1.307 **Upper MW** (as of c1950), *Shell* dominates the 1,021 mail replies. . . Confusion with the next item [=the green outer cover] may have led 39 respondents to mark *husk* as their term.

3 The pod of a bean or pea. Cf **hull n B2a(3)**

1950 *WELS* 6 Infs, **WI,** Husk. **1965–70** *DARE* (Qu. I12, *The outside covering of dry beans*) 51 Infs, **scattered,** Husk; (Qu. I10, *The outside covering of green peas*) 10 Infs, **scattered,** Husk.

4 Any of var parts of an ear of corn, as:

a also used attrib: The cover or outer leaves. **chiefly Nth, Midl** Cf **cap n[1] 8, shuck n**

1679 Royal Soc. London *Philos. Trans.* 12.1067 **CT,** The Husks about the Ear are good Fodder, given for change sometimes after Hay. **1816** in 1824 Knight *Letters* 82 **VA,** What in New England is called the husk of corn, in Virginia is called the *shuck;* and what we [=New Englanders] call cob, they call husk. **1862** in 1919 Hale *Letters* 13, One thing I shall rejoice at,—my own bed,—for this husk thing we sleep on is a beast;—and only the exhaustion produced by our active lives could make it tolerable. **1917** *DN* 4.394 **nOH, NEng, NY, KS,** *Husk*. . . The outer covering of ears of corn. **1932** *AmSp* 7.169 **NE** [Pioneer dial], [Mattresses] . . were filled with corn husks . . and were called "husk ticks". **1941** *LANE* Map 263 **NEng,** *Husks* [predominates over *shucks*]. **1948** Davis *Word Atlas Gt. Lakes* Map 212, *Green leafy cover of ear of corn*—husk [predominates over shuck]. **1949** Kurath *Word Geog.* 47, The North and the Midland have . . *corn husks* . . against Southern *corn shucks.* **1969** *DARE* Tape **GA**77, The husk shuck generally stayed on the [corn] stalk and then the slip shuck would come out of the husk. [*DARE* Ed: The slip shuck was used as a wrapper for sausage.] **1971** Wood *Vocab. Change* 42 **Sth,** *Husk* [the green, leafy cover of an ear of corn] is chosen less than one-fifth of the time except in Oklahoma where it almost reaches one-third. **1973** Allen *LAUM* 1.311 (as of c1950), *Husks*. . . dominates the entire U[pper] M[idwest].

b The bran of a kernel of corn. *somewhat old-fash* Cf **hull n B2a(4), (5)**

1824 Singleton *Letters* 81 *(DA)* **VA,** Husk . . the external envelope of the kernel, which cannot be reduced to meal, and which makes the bran. **1892** Eggleston *Hoosier Schoolmaster* 55 **IN,** [Footnote:] *Husk,* in the Middle States, and in some parts of the South and West, means the bran of the cornmeal, as notably in Davy Crockett's verse: "She sifted the meal, she gimme the hus';/ She baked the bread, she gimme the crus'." **1894** Eggleston in *Century Illustr. Mag.* 47.851, Husk is applied in the middle belt and in the South to the bran of corn-meal. . . In this sense the word has largely lost its final letter. . . Only in Charleston, South Carolina, have I ever heard the corn-bran called "husk" with a *k.* **1899** (1912) Green *VA Folk-Speech* 237, *Huss*. . . Husk. The bran that is sifted out of corn-meal. "Meal-huss." **1958** Hughes–Bontemps *Negro Folkl.* 87, *Slave Song*. . . We bake de bread / Dey gib us de crust / We sif de meal / Dey gib us huss. **1966** *DARE* Tape **AL**1, Boil it until the husk come off this corn; **SC**16, The meal leave here, you put that to one side for your hog—I mean the hucks—and the flour go in there.

c The cob of the ear of corn. **VA** *arch*

1816 [see **B4a** above]. **1892** Eggleston *Hoosier Schoolmaster* 55 **IN,** [Footnote:] In parts of Virginia, before the war, the word *husk* or *hus'* meant the cob or spike of the corn. "I smack you over wid a cawn-hus' " is a threat I have often heard. **1894** Eggleston in *Century Illustr. Mag.* 47.851, I stated in a newspaper article printed about 1869 . . that in one part, at least, of eastern Virginia, "hus" (always, so far as I know, without a trace of *k*) was used for the cob of Indian corn. . . This use of the word has, I believe, become obsolete since the civil war. **1899** (1912) Green *VA Folk-Speech* 237, *Huss*. . . Husk. The spike on which the grains of corn grow.

5 The shell of an oyster. Cf **hull n B2b(1)**

1881 Ingersoll *Oyster-Industry* 245, *Husks.*—Oyster shells.

6 A crust (of bread).

1984 Joyner *Down by Riverside* 149 **sSC coast** [Gullah], "Conjur?" asked ex-slave Sabe Rutledge. "Wouldn't burn a hucks [Joyner: crust of] bread for 'em."

7 Fig:

a Someone who appears to be strong and tough; a thug. [Prob back formation from *husky* adj robust, powerful; cf also *W3 husky* n] Cf **hull n B2b(3)**

1925 in 1953 Botkin–Harlow *Treas. Railroad Folkl.* 227, I got greased for bustin' the foreman. Big husk, but yella as a duck's foot. **1931** Mutschmann *Gloss. Americanisms* 32/1, *Husk*. . . Burly fellow.

b See quot.

1967 *DARE* (Qu. HH40, *Uncomplimentary words for an old man*) Inf **OR**1, Husk [laughter].

husk v Usu |hʌsk|; also |hʌs| **[husk n]**

A Form.

1941 *LANE* Map 263 *(Husks)* 4 infs, **scattered NEng,** [hʌs].

B Senses.

1 To remove the outer covering of var plants, as:

a To strip off the leaves or envelope of an ear of corn; hence vbl n *husking* the act of stripping off the leaves. **chiefly Nth, N Midl** Cf **husking 2, shuck v**

c1622 John Smith in 1964 Lefroy *Hist. Bermudaes* 281, Many of the inhabitants . . hastely cast it [the corn crop] into out houses . . altogether vn-husked, as it came from the feild . . all the good husbands through out the whole Ilands, who had diligently and painefully husked and hung up all their crop, began euery wher to complaine. **1825** Neal *Brother Jonathan* 1.53 **CT,** The *Husking* . . prevails throughout New England only. . . He will permit all the "fellers" and "gals" to tumble and roll about . . eat his pumpkin pies; drink his cider, and waste his apples; under pretence of husking corn. **1875** in 1938 *AmSp* 13.20 **NE,** There's many a reader . . who will. . . [have] husked corn . . and for every ear that he husked whispered many words of love, not forgetting to take a sly kiss between times. **1899** Garland *Boy Life* 220 **nwIA** (as of 1870s), In big fields . . it was the custom to husk in the field, and from the standing stalk. No one but a stubborn Vermonter . . thought of cutting it up to husk from the shock. **1909** in 1944 *ADD* 554, Husk. . . [A Virginia] woman . . told me she was 'husking sweet corn,' when I would have sworn she was 'shucking roastin' ears.' **1917** *DN* 4.394 **NEng, NY, KS,** *Husk.* **1962** *AmSp* 37.172 **seNC,** *Husks* is not recorded in a single instance in central or eastern North Carolina in the *Atlas* records, but it appears in . . Ocracoke . . seven out of seventeen times. . . *husks* seems as current among younger as among older Ocracokers. **1966–70** *DARE* Tape **IN**30, They would bend . . or kneel down around these bunches of corn. They would shuck this corn or husk it by hand and break it off; **MI**120, At night . . a whole bunch of us kids'd get together and get in the barn and we'd husk corn, shuck it; **NH**5, The neighbors would come an' help us with the husking. But that's all done. We don't raise corn to husk around now . . It all goes into the silo.

b =**hull v 1.**

1950 *WELS* 1 Inf, **WI,** Husking. **1955** Potter *Dial. NW OH* 120, *To husk* [beans. Not common; 5 out of 55 infs]. **1965–70** *DARE* (Qu. I13, *When you take dry beans out of the cover you are ______ them*) 23 Infs, **scattered,** Husking; (Qu. I11, *When somebody takes peas out of the covering*) Infs **GA**72, **MI**69, 106, **MO**26, **RI**16, Husking. **1973** Allen *LAUM* 1.309 (as of c1950), To *shell* beans or peas. . . *husk* occur[s] once or twice.

2 with *out;* Of corn: to yield when husked.

1934 *Sun* (Baltimore MD) 10 Nov 17/5 *(Hench Coll.),* 1924 and 1930 . . the only years since 1901 when the corn crop has husked out less than 2,000,000 bushels of grain.

3 See quot.

1881 Ingersoll *Oyster-Industry* 245 **GA,** *Husk.*—To remove the shells from an oyster, or "open" it.

4 Fig: see quot.

1910 Mulford *Hopalong* 129, He determined to husk Meeker's body from its immortal soul.

husker See **huckster**

husking vbl n

1 See **husk v B1a.**

2 also *corn husking;* freq attrib: An event involving the stripping of the covers from ears of corn, as: See below. **[husk v B1a]**

a A social gathering to help husk corn at harvest time, often including music and dancing. **esp NEng, N Cent** See Map Cf **bee n[2], corn shucking 1**

1692 (1862) Mather *Wonders Invisible* 142 **Boston,** This Deponent was desired by the Prisoner, to come unto an Husking of Corn. **1750** in 1867 *Hours at Home* 5.419/2 **cwMA,** Our rural society. . . may be seen in its rudest shape at our military trainings, house-raisings and husking-bees. **1779** in 1915 *New Engl. Hist. & Geneal. Reg.* 69.216 **cnMA,** My wife & Egertons wife & Jonases wife went to Groton a husking bee stayed all night. **1807** (1935) Janson *Stranger in Amer.* 406, In some provinces of the United States, the farmers, on getting in the corn harvest, give a rural fete, in imitation of the ancient English custom of harvest home. This they call a *husking frolic.* **1819** (1821) Nuttall *Jrl.* 29, We took up our lodging where there happened to be a corn-husking, and were kept awake with idle merriment and riot. **1875** in 1938 *AmSp* 13.20 **NE,** Old fashioned husking parties are in vogue in the southwestern part of this county. There's many a reader . . who will remember . . husking bees. **1909** *DN* 3.408 **nME,** *Bee. . .* A neighborhood gathering for special work. Various kinds of bees . . husking bee. **1965–70** *DARE* (Qu. FF2, *What kinds of parties do people favor around here?*) 22 Infs, **esp NEng, N Cent,** (Corn) husking bees; **IN**41, **KY**5, 66, **MA**42, Corn huskings; **CA**137, Husking parties; (Qu. FF1) Inf **IN**32, Corn husking; **NJ**1, Husking bees. **1965–70** *DARE* Tape **IN**30, They would have the husking bees and this . . was just more of a fun thing. . . They'd bring it [=corn] in . . and all the neighbor boys and men . . would come in and . . husk it by hand; **MI**120, These farmers . . used to put up somethin' like a corn-husking bee. That'd be at night. . . A whole bunch of us kids'd get together and get in the barn and . . husk corn; **NH**5, We used to have huskin' bees. . . The neighbors would come an' help us with the husking. But that's all done [=in the past]; **OK**48, They call them a husking bee. The men would go and shuck corn and the women would all go in and . . tack carpet rags.

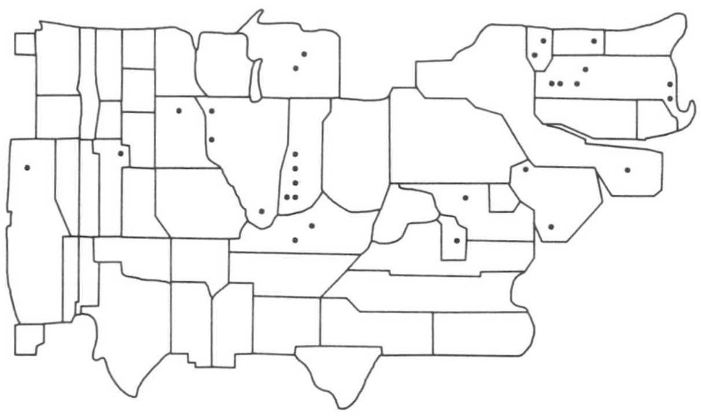

•husking 2a + varr (Qq. FF2, FF1)

b A competition in which contestants vie to husk the most corn in a given period of time. *somewhat old-fash*

1853 Thomas *John Randolph* 97 **MD,** After this, we got to the husking-match safe. **1936** *Time* 14 Dec, [Letter to the editor:] There was a heart-rending mistake in your issue of Nov. 23. In describing the corn-husking contest you called it a "bang-board." **c1938** *Meredith Coll.* **cIA,** [Newspaper headline:] Select site for husking. **1939** *Ibid,* [Unidentified magazine article:] If I were going to define the Middle West, I should say it is the place where a corn-husking contest draws a bigger crowd than an intercollegiate football game. I attended the 1938 Kansas State Corn-Husking Contest and saw thirty thousand people milling about in the prairie dust . . to see . . thirty steel-muscled farmers. **1967–68** *DARE* (Qu. FF16, . . *Local contests or celebrations*) Infs **IA**11, **WI**20, Corn-husking contests; **CT**6, Athletic contests, corn-husking bees—old days; **NJ**33, Memorial parade, corn-husking bee. [All Infs old]

3 Fig: childbirth.

1931–33 *LANE Worksheets* **cwCT,** *Husking.* "They're going to have a husking over at so and so's" means "They're going to have a baby." *Ibid* **nwCT,** *Husking*—Childbirth. "I've been to a husking."

husking pin n Also *husking peg,* ~ *hook*

A hand-held implement used to help remove the shuck from field corn.

1870 U.S. Dept. Ag. *Rept. of Secy. for 1869* 329, *Husking pin. . .* It is a matter of doubt whether with the aid of any one of them [hand-huskers] a man could husk more corn per hour than with the old-fashioned husking pin. **1872** (1876) Knight *Amer. Mech. Dict.* 1143/2, *Husking-peg.* A pin or claw worn upon the hand and used to assist in tearing open the shuck when husking ear corn. **1948** Jacobs *We Chose Country* 136 **WI,** A jab with the husking pin at the silk end of the cob, tearing back the husk, then a half-twist of the ear to break it from the stalk, and a long toss to the basket. **1965** *DARE* File **IA** (as of 1931), [Newspaper:] Armed with husking hooks or pegs, [corn-husking] champions are expected from eight states. *Ibid,* With a husking hook on his bare right hand, Welch bobbed his way thru the acre corn patch. *Ibid* **NE** (as of 1878), An old man wounded a young man with a husking peg. **1970** *DARE* Tape **MI**125, [FW:] When would you husk it [=harvested corn]? [Inf:] Well, you'd start when it dried out. . . [FW:] What did you call that little knife you had in your hand? [Inf:] That was a huskin' hook or a huskin' pin. [Aux Inf:] Oh, you mean to husk the corn with? . . A husking peg, usually. We got some yet. **1989** *DARE* File **csWI** (as of 1940s), A husking pin is a wooden pin, carved with a pointed end and strapped around the wrist. It's worn in the palm of the hand and used like an extension of the third finger. It's used on dry and ripe field corn, not sweet corn.

husk out See **husk** v **B2**

huskroot See **huskwort**

husk-tomato n [See quot 1941]

=ground cherry.

1895 Gray–Bailey *Field Botany* 314, *Physalis,* ground cherry, husk or strawberry tomato. . . *fruiting calyx loosely inflated, 5-angled, much larger than the edible berry.* **1925** Jepson *Manual Plants CA* 894, *P[hysalis] pubescens. . .* Husk tomato. **1929** *Torreya* 29.159 **ME,** Physalis (probably heterophylla), *"Husk tomato."* **1941** Wilder *Little Town on Prairie* 128 *(DA),* The husk-tomatoes were covered with a smooth dull-brown husk. When this was opened there lay the round, bright-purple tomato. **1954** *Harder Coll.* **cwTN,** Tomatoes . . various names: . . husk ("opens like the poison that poisons flies"). **1966** *DARE* (Qu. I46, *Other kinds of fruits that grow wild around here*) Inf **SD**1, Husk-tomato. **1975** Duncan–Foote *Wildflowers SE* 164, *Ground-cherry; Husk-tomato. . .* The fruit is enclosed in a considerably larger papery sac with only a small opening at the tip.

huskwort n Also *huskroot, huskwood*

=colicroot 2.

1900 Lyons *Plant Names* 21, *A[letris] farinosa. . .* Huskwort. **1930** Sievers *Amer. Med. Plants* 4, *Aletris farinosa. . . Other common names. . .* Huskwort. **1940** Clute *Amer. Plant Names* 217, *Aletris farinosa. . .* Huskwort. **1949** Moldenke *Amer. Wild Flowers* 318, *A[letris] farinosa. . .* is often called . . *huskroot.* **1971** Krochmal *Appalachia Med. Plants* 40, Huskwood. . . In Appalachia a mixture of roots and brandy or whisky is drunk as a treatment for rheumatism.

huss exclam [PaGer]

1968 *DARE* (Qu. NN22d, *Expressions used to drive away animals other than dogs*) Inf **MD**30, Huss [hʊs]—for a hog.

huss n See **husk** n

hussian See **hessian**

hussick See **hassock**

hussie See **hussy** n^{1}

hussif See **housewife**

hussy n^{1} Usu |ˈhʌzi, -si|; also |ˈhʊzɨ| Also sp *hussie, huzzy* [Reduced forms of *housewife;* but see etym at **B1** below]

A Forms.

c1940 Eliason *Word Lists FL* 9, *Hussie.* **1966–67** *DARE* (Qu. K16) Inf **TX**6, [ˈhʌzi]; (Qu. AA22) Inf **SC**11, [ˈhʊzɨ]. **1976** *DARE* File **nwOR** (as of c1920), *Hussy or huzzy lounge.*

B Senses.

1 =housewife. [*OED hussy, huzzy* sb. 4 1741 →; *"Obs."* It is possible that this is of independent origin and is cognate with Old Icelandic *húsi* a case]

1806 (1970) Webster *Compendious Dict.* 147, *Hussy* . . kind of bag. **1899** (1912) Green *VA Folk-Speech* 237, *Hussy. . .* Huzzy. A case for scissors, needles, thread, etc. **1934** (1943) *W2, Housewife. . .* A little case or bag for needles, thread, scissors, pins, cloth for patching, etc;—called also *hussy.* **1947** Croy *Corn Country* 280 **Plains States,** *Hussy:* Every family had one. It was a little bag for needles, thread, thimbles, and odds and ends of clothing for patching.

2 Any of var female animals; see quots. [Cf *EDD huss(e)y "Fig.* Applied to horses: a mare, a 'jade' "]

c1940 Eliason *Word Lists FL* 9, *Hussie:* A term applied to a female dog, especially when she is suckling young pups. **1967–69** *DARE* (Qu. K16, *A cow with a bad temper*) Inf **GA**80, Hussy; **TX**6, Fightin' hussy.

hussy n^{2} See **hissy**

hussy lounge n Also *huzzy lounge*

1976 *DARE* File **nwOR** (as of c1920), A daybed [like a chaise lounge] was called a hussy or huzzy lounge.

hustlement n [*OED* c1347 →; "*Obs.* exc. *dial.*"] *relic*

1899 (1912) Green *VA Folk-Speech* 237, *Huslement*. . . *Hustlement*. Furniture. Odds and ends. "Lumber and hustlement about the house."

hustle wagon n [*hustle* v to convey forcibly + *wagon*] Cf **hoodlum wagon 2**

1968 *DARE* (Qu. N3, *The . . wagon that takes arrested people to . . jail*) Inf **OH**87, Hustle wagon.

hut n

In railroading: a caboose or other small car or structure used for shelter by an employee; see quots. Cf **caboose n¹ 2**

1932 *RR Mag.* Oct 368, *Hut*—Caboose; sometimes cab of a locomotive. **1938** Beebe *High Iron* 222 [Railroad terms], *Hut:* Caboose. **1945** Hubbard *Railroad Ave.* 348, *Hut*—Brakeman's shelter just back of the coal bunkers on the tender tank of engines operating through Moffat Tunnel. May also refer to caboose, locomotive cab, switchman's shanty, or crossing watchman's shelter.

hut v See **hurt**

hutch n¹ [*OED hutch* sb. 1 "A chest or coffer"; 1303 →; *EDD hutch* sb. 2 "A cupboard, esp. in a wall"]

1 A chest of drawers. **PA**

1930 Shoemaker *1300 Words* 31 **cPA Mts** (as of c1900), *Hutch*—A chest of drawers. **1935** *AmSp* 10.172 **sePA,** *Hutch* . . a chest of drawers.

2 also *hutch cupboard:* A cupboard or buffet, usu one with cabinet doors below and open shelves above; a set of open shelves set on or forming the upper part of a piece of furniture. Note: This sense, now widespread, was appar popularized by furniture manufacturers early in this century.

1947 *Bakelite Review* Apr 17 (*W3* File), The *hutch* is a unit separate from the (buffet) case and is a two-shelf item which can be set on top, to provide a convenient and decorative support for Chinaware and bric-a-brac. **1949** Williams–Williams *How to Furnish* 124, Some manufacturers of reproduction furniture list what they call hutch cupboards. These are something like a small Welsh dresser—shelves above, cupboards below. . . The name hutch cupboard for this piece of furniture is a misnomer. **1954** *NYT Mag.* 18 Apr 70/4, [Advt:] Hutchcupboard—knotty pine hand made reproduction—46½″ x 70″. [Illustr: Cabinet with two doors and two drawers, two open shelves above] **1956** *NY Times* (NY) 15 Jan 69, [Advt:] 62″ Buffet with Hutch top. [Illustr: The "hutch" has two open shelves in the middle, enclosed shelves at each side] **1967** *DARE* File **scWI,** *Hutch*—sideboard or buffet. **1969** *DARE* (Qu. E5, *A piece of furniture with a flat top for keeping tablecloths, dishes, and such*) Inf **IL**31, Sideboard—old term; built-in hutch—present term. **1987–89** *DARE* File **Chicago IL,** A hutch is a cupboard that fits in the corner. I've always called it a corner hutch. *Ibid* **csWI,** *Hutch* (or china hutch)—A buffet or credenza. Doors below and open glass shelves above. The shelves might have glass doors. You display your china on these shelves. *Ibid* **ceWI** (as of c1920), A hutch was a piece of furniture with a closed cabinet on the bottom and open shelves on top. Prized dishes and knick-knacks were displayed on the shelves, and other dishes and table linens stored below.

3 Transf: see quot.

1969 *DARE* (Qu. E1, *A piece of furniture that stands against the wall, and you hang clothes in/on it*) Inf **MO**20, Hutch—older type with cabinets and hooks.

hutch n² See **hutch goose**

hutch cupboard See **hutch n¹ 2**

hutcherly n Cf **hutzel n 1**

1949 *AmSp* 24.110 **SC,** *Hutcherly*. . . A baked, spiced clingstone peach split several ways while still attached to the stone.

hutch goose n Also *hutch*

=**Hutchins's goose.**

1943 Musgrove–Musgrove *Waterfowl IA* 10, *Hutchins's Goose*. . . Other names . . hutch, hutch goose. . . Marked exactly as the Canada goose, but approximately the size of a large mallard.

Hutchins's goose n

Std: a subsp of the **Canada goose** *(Branta canadensis hutchinsi)*. Also called **brant 1, flight goose, goose brant, gray brant 3, gray goose 1, honker n¹ 1, hutch goose, little goose, marsh goose, mountain goose, mud goose, prairie goose, short-necked goose, southern goose, wild goose, winter goose**

hutchy See **hootch n²**

huther horse See **hither horse**

huthering n [Cf *SND hutherin* (at *hudder* v. 1) "slovenly, slatternly"; *hudder* v. 3 "To heap together in disorder"; n. 2 "A confused . . heap"]

1931 *AmSp* 7.19 **swPA,** *Huthering*. A muss, disorder. "This room is in a huthering."

hutsch(l)i See **hootch n²**

hutspot n [Du] **MI** Cf *hotchpot*

A dish of potatoes and other vegetables, usu simmered with meat.

1940 *AmSp* 15.83 **swMI** [Dutch survivals], *Hutspot* ['hʊtspɔt]. . . A combination of potatoes and cabbage; potatoes and carrots; potatoes and kale, or other vegetable boiled together and crushed. **1969–70** *DARE* (Qu. H45, *Dishes made with meat*) Inf **MI**102, Hutspot ['hʌtspət]—carrots, potatoes, onions, cooked in beef broth and mashed, served with short ribs; [(Qu. H49, *Dishes made by boiling potatoes with other foods*) Inf **IL**51, Mother made a stew of boiled pig knuckles, carrots, potatoes—translation [of] the Holland name is hot pot; we ate it with catsup on it;] (Qu. H50) Inf **MI**122, ['hʊtspolt]—Dutch name, with potatoes and carrot and possibly bacon. [All Infs of Dutch background] [**1972** *Complete World Cookery* 138 **Holland,** *Hutspot* (Boiled beef and vegetables).]

hutter See **hudder**

hutzel n Also sp *hootsle* [Ger]

1 A dried or dried-up fruit.

1950 *PADS* 14.40 **SC,** *Hutzel*. . . Clingstone peach dried on the kernel by cutting through the pulp and exposing it to the sun. Peaches are kept thus for cooking purposes in the winter. **1968** *DARE* (Qu. H18, . . *Special kinds of bread*) Inf **MN**37, Hutzel brot—made with dried pears and nuts; (QR, near Qu. LL3a) Inf **MD**30, Like a hutzel ['hʊtsl̩]—an apple that dries up while still on the tree.

2 Transf: see quot.

1903 *DN* 2.351 **sePA,** *Hootsle* ['hʊtsəl, 'hʊtzəl]. . . Anything small or wizened, or an undersized person.

hutzel adj Also sp *hootsle* [**hutzel n**]

1903 *DN* 2.351 **sePA,** *Hootsle* ['hʊtsəl]. . . Small, contracted; metaphorically of living, as 'they lived in a miserable, hootsle way.'

huxy adj

1906 *DN* 3.142 **nwAR,** *Huxy*. . . Excellent, up-to-date.

huz See **her pron**

huzzy n¹ See **hussy n¹**

huzzy n² See **hissy**

huzzy lounge See **hussy lounge**

huzzy-pocket n

1952 Brown *NC Folkl.* 1.553, *Huzzy-pocket*. . . A pocket which is hung on the wall to put little things in.

hwa See **who**

hy See **i prep**

hyacinth n

1 as *California hyacinth, hyacinth brodiaea:* =**brodiaea. Pacific**

1900 Lyons *Plant Names* 69, *Brodiaea* . . California Hyacinth. **1961** Peck *Manual OR* 214, *B[rodiaea] hyacinthina* . . Hyacinth Brodiaea. **1966** *DARE* (Qu. S26a, . . *Roadside flowers*) Inf **CA**2, Hyacinth brodiaea. **1973** Hitchcock–Cronquist *Flora Pacific NW* 685, Hyacinth brodiaea . . *[Brodiaea hyacinthina]*.

2 Prob a **camas 1** (here: *Camassia scilloides*).

1966–70 *DARE* (Qu. S26a, . . *Roadside flowers*) Infs **MO**7, **SC**27, Hyacinth; (Qu. S26b, *Wildflowers that grow in water or wet places*) Inf **KY**47, Hyacinth; (Qu. S26e, *Other wildflowers not yet mentioned*) Inf **KY**83, Hyacinths.

3 =**water hyacinth. FL**

1966 *DARE* (Qu. S24, *A wild flower that grows in swamps and marshes and looks like a small blue iris: [Sometimes other colors]*) Infs **FL**11, 29, 35, Hyacinth(s); (Qu. S22) Inf **FL**4, Purple hyacinths.

hyacinth bean n
A fabaceous ornamental plant *(Dolichos lablab)* originally Old World, now naturalized and widespread in the US. Also called **black bean 1, Egyptian bean, Jack bean**
1876 Hobbs *Bot. Hdbk.* 55, Hyacinth bean, . . Dolichos lablab. **1900** Lyons *Plant Names* 212, *L[ablab] lablab* . . Hyacinth Bean. **1933** Small *Manual SE Flora* 726, *D[olichos] lablab* . . Hyacinth Bean. **1940** Clute *Amer. Plant Names* 18. **1976** Bailey–Bailey *Hortus Third* 394.

hyacinth brodiaea See **hyacinth 1**

hyah n[1] See **hair** n

hyah n[2] See **hare**

hyah adv See **here A2**

hyah-hyahing vbl n Cf **hurrah B1**
1952 Brown *NC Folkl.* 1.553, *Hyah-hyahing* [hjɑ-hjɑ:ɪŋ]. . . A ruckus, a disturbance.

hyander See **yonder**

hya'r n[1] See **hair** n

hyar n[2] See **hare**

hyar v See **hear** v **A1a**

hyar adv See **here A2**

hyare See **here A2**

hybolic adj [Perh by syncope < *hyperbolic;* but perh blend of *hyper-* or *high(ly)-* + *symbolic*] **HI** Cf **hifalute**
Of speech or writing: pompous, high-flown.
1934 *AmSp* 9.55 **HI,** One of the most distinctive of Hawaiian coinages is *hybolic,* meaning "hifalutin," "difficult of comprehension" (of a word or expression). **1972** Carr *Da Kine Talk* 134, *Hybolic* vs. *pompous, bombastic*—An adjective developed in Hawaii, used to describe a pompous style of speaking or writing. . . "Don't use that kind of hybolic words here!" "Why do you use such hybolic language?" "Sally is hybolic when she meets new people." Possible sources . . high + symbolic . . highfalutin . . hyperbolic. **1981** *Pidgin To Da Max, Hybolic.* To talk like one intellectual-kine haole.

hybred See **high-bred**

hydrangea n
1 Std: a plant of the genus *Hydrangea.* Also called **graybeard 2, high geranium, hills-of-snow, ninebark, old man's beard, seven-bark, silverleaf, swamp snowball, wild hydrangea**
2 as *climbing hydrangea:* A woody vine *(Decumaria barbara)* with flowers somewhat similar to those of **hydrangea 1.** Also called **wood-vamp**
1933 Small *Manual SE Flora* 599, *D[ecumaria] barbara* . . Wood-vamp. Cowitch-vine. Climbing-hydrangea. **1950** Gray–Fernald *Manual of Botany* 747, *Decumaria* . . Climbing Hydrangea. **1972** Brown *Wildflowers LA* 64, Climbing Hydrangea, Wood-vamp—*Decumaria barbara.*

hydrant n
1 A faucet or tap for domestic water, spec:
a An outdoor faucet; a faucet on the side of a house. **scattered, but less freq Nth, Atlantic** See Map Cf **faucet B1**
1833 in 1920 *Catholic Hist. Rev.* 5.241 **MD,** Thousands of Dollars had been expended on buildings which are ill-constructed & inconvenient . . hydrants left insecure against external injury. **1941** Faulkner *Men Working* 202 **MS,** She crossed to the neighbor's yard-hydrant and filled the bucket. **1950** *WELS* 1 Inf, **WI,** Hydrant. **1962** Atwood *Vocab. TX* 103, There is a . . trend toward confining *hydrant* to the device outside the house, *faucet* to its indoor equivalent. **1965–70** *DARE* (Qu. F27b, *What you turn on and off outside the house to get running water*) 185 Infs, **scattered, but less freq Nth, Atlantic,** Hydrant; **IN**35, Outside hydrant. **1966** Dakin *Dial. Vocab. Ohio R. Valley* 2.130, [A few speakers in Ohio, Kentucky, Illinois say] *Hydrant* . . only for a faucet outside the house or in the barnyard. . . in the Greater Cincinnati area and in the Bluegrass to the south some speakers say *hydrant* for either a faucet on the water pipe in the kitchen or for one outside. **1968** *DARE* Tape **LA**22, You have to take and put him [=a crawfish] through some fresh water . . like water you draw at the hydrant, and wash him all off good. **1972** *PADS* 58.15 **cwAL,** The terms for the device in the house are *spicket* (15 [of 27 infs]), *faucet* (10), and *hydrant* (2); the last two are more frequent in educated usage. The terms for the device in the yard are *spicket* (21), *faucet* (4), and *hydrant* (1). The terms for the device on a barrel are *faucet* (10), *spicket* (7), *hydrant, tap, bunhole,* and *peg.* **1986** Pederson *LAGS Concordance* **Gulf Region,** [Approx 250 infs indicate that a hydrant is outside, sometimes specifically on the side of the house, usually simply "in the yard."]

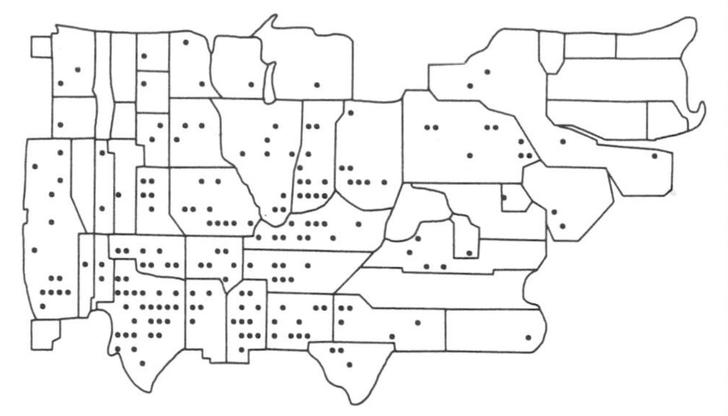
•hydrant 1a + var (Qu. F27b)

b An indoor faucet. **esp SW, Gulf States** See Map
1846 Cooper *Redskins* 2.107 **NY,** I knew that a hydrant stood in the kitchen itself, which gave a full stream of water. **1871** (1975) Levy *Jewish Cookery* 148, *Cabbage.*—Wash it well under the hydrant. . . *Spinach.*—Wash it well after it is picked . . let the hydrant [water] run over it, as that clears off the sand better. **1905** *DN* 3.83 **nwAR,** *Hydrant.* . . Faucet. "You can get a drink at the hydrant in the hall." Common. *Ibid, Hydrant water.* . . "City water," water drawn from a faucet and derived from a general water-works system. "No hydrant water for me." Common. **1941** Faulkner *Men Working* 57 **MS,** Hit'll be mighty convenient in [town]. . . Ever' house has got a hydrant to it. All you got to do fer water is turn a tap. **1965–70** *DARE* (Qu. F27a, *What you turn on and off inside the house to get running water*) 21 Infs, **esp SW, Gulf States,** Hydrant. [17 of 21 Infs old] **1970** Tarpley *Blinky* 96 **neTX,** *Device to turn water on in the house.* . . hydrant [8 infs]. **1972** [see **1a** above]. **1986** Pederson *LAGS Concordance* **Gulf Region,** [Approx 50 infs indicate that a hydrant is (or can be) inside the house, usu specifying that it is "at the sink."]

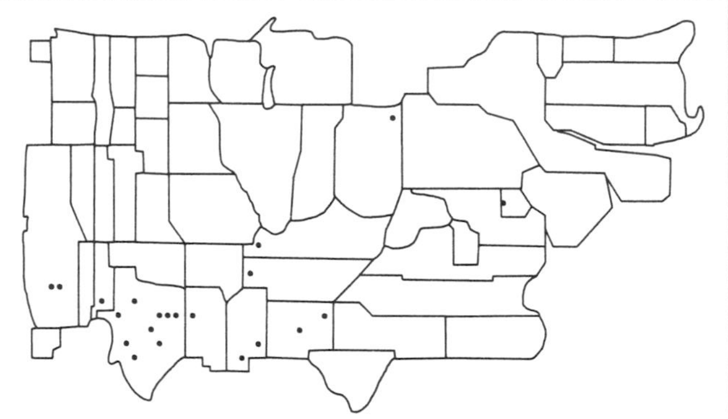
•hydrant 1b (Qu. F27a)

c A drinking fountain.
1957 Battaglia *Resp. to PADS 20* **eMD,** *Drinking fountain:* hydrant.
2 By ext: A tap on a barrel or similar container.
1972 [see **1a** above]. **1986** Pederson *LAGS Concordance* **Gulf Region,** [11 infs indicate that a hydrant can be on a barrel, a keg, or a water cooler.]

hydrophobia n Pronc-sp *hydrophoby* Cf Intro "Language Changes" IV.1.b
Std senses, var form.
1940 Guthrie *Way West* 7, It's like the hydrophoby. You get bit and you're gone. **1965** *DARE* (Qu. K47, *What diseases do horses or mules commonly get around here?*) Inf **OK**8, Hydrophoby. **1970** *DARE* Tape

KY84, This mad wolf got into their chickens . . and the man ran out . . an' the wolf attacked him and at that time there wasn't much treatment for hydrophoby ['ha·ɪdrəˌfobiˇ], so he finally went mad. . . he said this [=hydrophoby] was affecting him to the extent that the water looked green and he felt strong enough to pull trees up by the roots.

hydrophobia skunk n Also *hydrophobia (pole)cat, phoby cat* **chiefly SW**

=spotted skunk.

1917 Anthony *Mammals Amer.* 135, Some species of the Spotted Skunk have been called Hydrophobia Skunk, from the widely prevalent idea that their bite produced madness. **1928** Anthony *N. Amer. Mammals* 125, *Spilogale* has the reputation of giving hydrophobia when it bites man, and one of the names for the Spotted Skunk in the Southwest is "Hydrophobia Skunk" or "Phoby-cat." **1937** Grinnell et al. *Fur-Bearing Mammals CA* 298, *San Diego Spotted Skunk. . . Other Names. . .* Hydrophobia Skunk. *Ibid* 305, Hydrophobia cat is a name for the species [=*Spilogale putorius*] that is widely used in some sections of the southern United States, and it has also been employed in California, especially in the southern part of the State. **1958** Latham *Meskin Hound* 12 **cTX,** I'll shoot him down the way I would a hydrophobia polecat. **1966–67** *DARE* (Qu. P26, *Names and nicknames . . for a skunk*) Infs **NM**13, **TX**11, 19, Hydrophobia cat; **NM**10, Hydrophobia skunk.

hydrophoby See **hydrophobia**

hydropippin n [Perh *hydro-* water + *pippin* a small greenish apple] Cf **green-apple quickstep**

1968 *DARE* (Qu. BB19, *Joking names for looseness of the bowels*) Inf NJ35, Hydropippin.

hyeah v See **hear A1a**

hyeah adv See **here A2**

hyeahd See **hear A2c**

hyear See **hear A1a**

hyear(e)d See **hear A2c**

hyearn See **hear A2b**

hyearth See **hearth A1**

hyeh See **here A2**

hyena n Usu |ˌhaɪ'inə|; also |ˌhaɪ'inɚ, ˌhɑ-| Pronc-sp *hyeny* Cf Intro "Language Changes" I.8., IV.1.b

A Forms.

1892 Garland *Prairie Folks* 105 **IA,** You're a reg'lar ol' hyeny. **1893** Garland *L. Burns* **IA** *(ADD), Hyeny.* **1967** *DARE* (Qu. Z16) Inf **AL**34, Hyena [ˌhaɪ'inɚ]; **SC**29, Little hyena [ˌhɑ'inɚ].

B Sense.

Fig: an unruly animal or child; see quot. **Sth, S Midl**

1967 *DARE* (Qu. K16, *A cow with a bad temper*) Inf **TX**32, Hyena; (Qu. Z16, *A small child who is rough, misbehaves, and doesn't obey*) Inf **AL**34, Hyena [ˌhaɪ'inɚ]; **SC**29, Little hyena [ˌhɑ'inɚ]; **SC**46, Regular hyena. [All Infs female]

hyenous See **heinous**

hyeny See **hyena**

hyer See **here A2**

hyere See **here A1a, A2**

hyether See **hither** adv, adj

hyfer See **hyper**

hygeranium See **high geranium**

hyla n Also *hyla frog* **esp NEng** Cf **peeper**

A tree frog (*Hyla* spp).

1839 MA Zool. & Bot. Surv. *Fishes Reptiles* 242, *H[yla] squirella. . .* The little peeping Hyla. **1887** (1895) Robinson *Uncle Lisha* 158 **wVT,** By that light, when the hylas were beginning to ring their shrill curfew. **1922** Brown *Old Crow* 468 **NEng,** When the dusk came down and the hylas peeped . . she would lose courage. **1923** in 1969 Frost *Poetry* 119 **NEng,** [Title:] *Hyla Brook*—By June our brook's run out of song and speed./ . . And taken with it all the Hyla breed / That shouted in the mist a month ago. **1931–33** *LANE Worksheets* **cnVT,** Hyla frog—smallest kind of frog; same as peeper. **1938** Damon *Grandma* 117 **CT** (as of late 1800s), In the dusk thawing hylas shrilled like sleighbells. **1954** Forbes *Rainbow* 49 **CT** (as of early 1800s), You could almost see the maples redden, and the catkins tumble out. Now the bittern would begin to boom for us, morning and evening, and roughly one million hylas tune up. **1968** *DARE* (Qu. P21, *Small frogs that sing or chirp loudly in the spring*) Inf **NY**123, Hylas.

hyme See **hymn**

hymie n [Perh by confusion of **heinie 1** with *hymie,* a derog term for a Jew]

Used as a nickname for a German or one of German ancestry.

1968 *DARE* (Qu. HH28, . . *Nicknames . . for people of foreign background: German*) Inf **NY**40, Hymie. **1987** *DARE* File **csWI,** I think "hymie" probably refers to Jews, but for me it means Germans. *Ibid* **neOH** (as of 1928), My roommate at Oberlin College was born in Cleveland of German gentile immigrant family and was nicknamed (not derogatorily) Hymie. His actual given name was Russell.

hymn n Usu |hɪm|; also |haɪm| Pronc-spp *hime, hyme*

A Forms. [Cf *SND hime* "Also *hymn.* Sc. variant of Eng. *hymn*"] **Sth, S Midl**

1818 in 1824 Knight *Letters* 107 **KY,** Some words are [pronounced] . . by the lower classes in society . . very uncouthly, as . . hȳmn. **1837** Sherwood *Gaz. GA* 70, *Hime,* for Hymn. **1890** *DN* 1.68 **KY,** *Hyme* [haɪm]. Formerly used for *hymn.* **1893** Shands *MS Speech* 36, *Hime* [haɪm]. This pronunciation of hymn is frequently used in Mississippi by the illiterate whites. **1908** *DN* 3.322 **eAL, wGA,** *Hymn. . .* Sometimes pronounced [haɪm]. **1950** *PADS* 14.37 **SC,** *Hime hister* ['haɪm 'haɪstə]. . . Song leader who "hists" the hymns, "raises the tunes."

B Sense.

See quot.

1939 Rollins *Gone Haywire* 170, From the vicinity of the trail herd. . . was the drone of men "singing to the cattle." The night herders, as they circled around the bedded beasts . . crooned songs or chants, which . . were entitled "hymns." *Ibid* 171, Musically, the hymns . . were sacred airs which, from their simple melodies, were easy to remember. But the words were often far from churchly. Accounts of horse races, unflattering opinions of the cattle, strings of profanity, texts on . . cans, or mere humming, often supplanted the phrases with which prelates were familiar.

hymn sing n

A gathering for the purpose of singing religious songs.

1968 *Budget* (Sugarcreek OH) 25 July 14/3 **VA** [Mennonite community], An outdoor hymn sing was held. **1982** *Greenfield Recorder* (MA) 3 Mar sec A 6/3 (as of c1900), In many families it was a custom for the whole family to gather on Sunday evening around the pump organ and have a good "hymn sing." **1987** *DARE* File **IN,** All Mennonites have beautiful voices and love to sing. My sister who is completely disaffected from Mennonite theology, loves to sing hymns, and my mother says that as long as she goes to hymn sings there's still some hope.

hyo See **here A2**

hypa See **hyper**

hyped up adj phr [Perh var of *hiked up* raised up, worked upward out of place; but cf *EDD hike* v. 4 "With *up:* to pucker in sewing"]

1927 *AmSp* 2.357 **cwWV,** *Hyped up* . . a coat that does not fit well between the shoulders. "That Jew tried to sell me a coat that was all hyped up."

hyper v Also sp *hiper;* pronc-spp *hyfer, hypa* [Etym uncert] **chiefly NEng** Cf **hike** v **1a**

To move quickly; to hurry.

1867 Lowell *Biglow* lviii **'Upcountry' MA,** *Hyper:* to bustle: "I mus' hyper about an' git tea." **1899** Garland *Boy Life* 148 **IA,** The Marshal released Ben. . . "You better put out for home. . . Now, hyper." **1913** *DN* 4.1 **ME, CT,** *Hyfer. . .* To hurry. . . "I shall have to hyfer because it is cold." *Ibid* 4.2 **swME,** *Hypa. . .* To hurry. . . "I used to hypa across the lot." **1914** *DN* 4.74 **ME, nNH** [Rural locutions], *Hyper . . (hiper). . .* To go quickly, to run. "Hyper out-a thar, now!" **1940** in 1944 *ADD* **WV,** *Hyper. . .* I guess I'll be hypering along. **1955** in 1957 Old Farmer's Almanac *Sampler* 241, The blizzard was raging. It was really hypering down. The young traveling salesman's car finally just couldn't get through the next snowdrift. **1965** *DARE* File **WI,** *Hyper* ['haɪpɚ] means "get along"—said to children. **1971** *Ibid* **VT,** [Letter:] *Hyper,* as in "hurry up!" "Get going!" "Run like a whitehead!" . . used in my family. **1975** Gould *ME Lingo* 139, *Hyper*—This . . is used in Maine as a self-sufficient verb: "He was hypering along like a gale o' wind!" To move with great speed.

hypmotize v Similarly, *hypmotism, hypmotist* [Varr of *hypnotize, -tism, -tist* by substitution of homorganic nasal] Cf Lang. Changes IV.4

1967–69 *DARE* (Qu. CC14) Inf **CA**148, Hypmotize [FW: sic]; **IL**43, Hypmotism; **MI**47, Hypmotized ['hɪpmətaɪzd]; **MO**20, Hypmotist.

hypo n Also *hip(p), hippo, hyppo* [Abbrs for *hypochondria: OED hypo* sb.[1] 1711 →; *hyp* sb. c1705 →; *hip* sb.[3] 1710 →; *hip* v.[3] 1842 →]

1 also pl; often with *the:* A state of depression or vague unwellness; an imagined or pretended illness; hence adj *hippoed,* folk-etym *hip-hoed* suffering from depression or an imaginary illness; v *hipp(o)* to afflict with depression; to malinger. **chiefly S Midl** See Map *somewhat old-fash* Cf **hipped** adj[2], **hypochondriac**

1774 (1957) Fithian *Jrl. & Letters* 105 **eVA,** Mrs Green is better, but Miss *Beatty* says she has the *Hipp.* **1836** in 1941 *AmSp* 16.235 **VA,** I am *homesick*. . . I have had the *hyppo,* and all sorts of *Blues.* **1851** (1969) Burke *Polly Peablossom* 163 **GA,** He would give up to the *"hyppo,"* and when in one of his ways, he'd keep his bed for weeks at a time. **1851** (1976) Melville *Moby-Dick* 3 **NY,** Whenever my hypos get such an upper hand on me. **1895** *Jrl. Amer. Folkl.* 8.84 **MA,** To be low spirited was to have the "hypos." **1899** (1912) Green *VA Folk-Speech* 225, *Hipped*. . . Rendered melancholy; melancholy; mopish. **1926** *DN* 5.400 **Ozarks,** *Hippoed*. . . Subject to some imaginary ailment. "Pore Elly's plum hippoed sense she got t' readin' them fool doctor-books." . . hypochrondria was "vulgarly called the hypo" in England as early as 1711. **1956** Settle *Beulah Land* 136 **WV** (as of 1754–74), Ma's headaches is not coming so frequent. I would have wrote before, but she has had the Hip so bad I have not set down for a Moment. **1966–70** *DARE* (Qu. BB5, *A general feeling of discomfort or illness that isn't any one place in particular*) Inf **MD**30, The hippo—used by farmers for this condition; (Qu. BB7, *A feeling that lasts for a short while, with difficult breathing and heart beating fast*) Inf **MD**17, Hippo; (Qu. BB27, *When somebody pretends to be sick . . you'd say he's* ______) Infs **KY**40, 41, 44, 77, **MD**17, **MO**10, **NC**55, Hippoed; **GA**74, Hippoed—he's got a case of hippoes; **KY**6, Hippoing; (Qu. BB28, *Joking names . . for imaginary diseases: "He must have the* ______*."*) Infs **KY**6, 24, 90, Hippo; **VA**30, Hippo; **VA**11, ['hɪp,o]; **TN**38, Hippo—short for hypochondriac; **AR**39, He's hippoed; **TN**14, He's hip-hoed. [12 of 14 Infs old] **1969** *DARE* Tape **MO**15, [The word] was *hippoed*. . . I guess that means they think they can't walk, you see, bein' the hips in it you know? It's a person that just thinks they're sick and they can't get up or do anything and it's called hippoed.

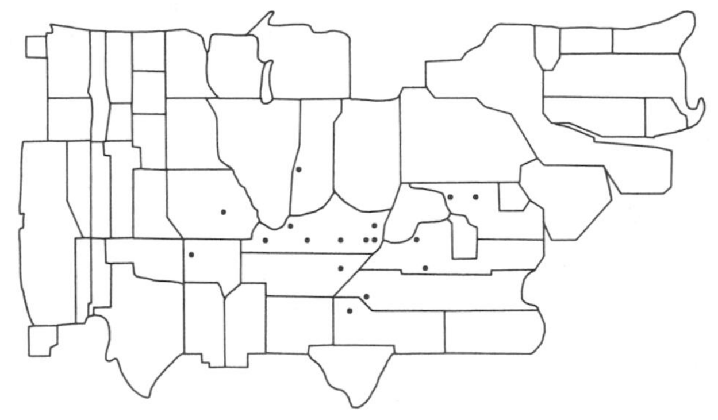

•hypo 1 + varr (Qq. BB27, BB5, BB7, BB28)

2 A pain in the back or leg; hence adv *hippoed* with a limp. [Prob infl by **hipped** adj[1]]

1968–69 *DARE* (Qu. BB1, *When a person has been injured so that . . he steps more heavily on one foot than the other*) Inf **KY**19, Walks hippoed; (Qu. BB3b, *A sudden pain that strikes you in the back*) Inf **VA**11, ['hɪp,o]—back or hip.

hypochitis n [Pseudo-medical; cf **-itis**]

1952 Brown *NC Folkl.* 1.553, *Hypochitis*. . . A disease.

hypochondriac n

1965–70 *DARE* (Qu. BB27, *When somebody pretends to be sick [often to get out of doing something] you'd say he's* ______) 11 Infs, **scattered, but chiefly Nth, N Midl, CA,** Hypochondriac; **CA**154, 170, **MA**122, Hypochondriac. [11 of 14 Infs female; 10 of 14 Infs coll educ]

hypocrite n

1 also *hypocrite-plant:* A plant of the genus *Euphorbia* (here: *E. cyathophora* or *E. heterophylla*).

1940 Clute *Amer. Plant Names* 223, *Euphorbia heterophylla.* Hypocrite-plant. **1967** *DARE* (Qu. S26c, *Wildflowers that grow in woods*) Inf **AL**20, Wild poinsettia—hypocrite, I call it; [it] imitates our Christmas poinsettia; **AL**30, Wild poinsettia (euphorbia): other name—hypocrite.

2 An agnostic or atheist; a person who won't go to church.

c1960 *Wilson Coll.* **csKY,** *Hypocrite*—An agnostic, though this word [=agnostic] was not known. Often a person who will not take any part in church affairs and is thus regarded as an unbeliever or worse. **1965–70** *DARE* (Qu. CC7, *Words for a person who goes to church very seldom or not at all*) 39 Infs, **scattered, but chiefly Sth, Midl,** Hypocrite. [15 of 39 Infs mid-aged, 5 Infs young; 14 of 39 Infs gs educ] **1965** *DARE* FW Addit **OK**7, A hypocrite completely rejects to believe [sic] in religion or Christ at all.

hypocrite-plant See **hypocrite 1**

hyppo See **hypo**

hy-spier n Also *hi-spier* [**hy spy n**]

The player who is "it" in the game **hide-and-seek A.**

1906 Casey *Parson's Boys* 197 **sIL** (as of c1860), When the moon rose all four of them began to play "hi-spy," choosing the one who should act as hunter by repeating the old doggerel stanza: "Eery ory, ickery Ann,/ Filison fallison, Ni'klas John;/ Queevy quavy, English navy,/ Stinklum stanklum *buck*!" With each word the reciter would point his finger at one of the four players, himself included; the one reached when the word "buck" came round was proclaimed "Hi-spier."

hy spy n Also *high spy, hi(e) spy, hi spry* [*OED hy-spy* 1777–1830; *SND hy-spy* (at *hi-spy,* n.); *EDD hy-spy* "Also written *hi-spy*" (at *hie-spy,* sb. and int.)] Cf **I spy** n

1 =**hide-and-seek A.**

1875 (1876) Twain *Tom Sawyer* 217 **neMO,** They had an exhausting good time playing "hi-spy" and "gully-keeper" with a crowd of their schoolmates. **1883** Newell *Games & Songs* 160, *I spy.* [Footnote: Pronounced *Hie* Spy.] **1892** *DN* 1.236 **cwMO,** *Hi-spy.* This is the name given by little girls to out-door hide-and-go-seek. I cannot remember having heard the word used of the in-door game. [*DN* Ed: In New England the game (not confined to girls!) is variously called *I spy, hi spy, hi-spry* (Cape Cod), *hide and (go) seek, hide and whoop.*] **1899** Garland *Boy Life* 28 **nwIA,** Small boys had little recreation beyond occasional games of "hi spy" or "dare gool." **1906** [see **hi-spier**]. **1917** *DN* 4.394 **neOH,** *High spy* in Ashtabula Co. [OH] meant "hide and seek." **1966–70** *DARE* (Qu. EE13a, *Games in which every player hides except one, and that one must try to find the others*) Infs **AL**3, **MD**8, 12, 23, 29, **MA**14, **MS**71, **NY**68, 73, 232, **PA**237, **VA**5, Hy spy. [11 of 12 Infs old] **1968** *DARE* Tape **MD**12, [FW:] How'd you play hy spy? [Inf:] Well, one of the girls or boys would usually get to a tree and cover their face and they'd count t'a hundred. And then they'd say, "Hy, all around my base is caught." So you'd have to be away from the tree . . or wherever he was. And then we'd all have to run. Then he'd go out and try to find the others. And whoever . . was the last one gettin' to the tree or didn't get there would have to be the one to count the next time. **1970** *AmSp* 45.207, As late as the middle of the nineteenth century . . the name *hide-and-seek* was used for a game in which a hidden object was sought by the players. In the third and fourth quarters of the century it also became applied to the now familiar game in which players hide from a seeker or a team of seekers. . . Other names for this game included *I-spy, hi-spy, I-spy-hi, whoop- or hoop-and-hide,* and *hide-and-coop.*

2 =**I spy** n. **scattered east of Missip R, esp OH** See Map Cf **hide-and-seek B1**

1917 *DN* 4.394 **neOH,** *High spy* [haɪ 'spaɪ, 'haɪ spaɪ]. . . The game of "hide the thimble." I did not know the meaning "hide and seek." . . I remember that as children we interpreted [hɑɪ] as = *high,* from the frequent position of the thimble. . . in Ashtabula Co. [OH] . . the . . game was *high spy the thimble.* **1965–70** *DARE* (Qu. EE3, *Games in which you hide an object and then look for it*) 16 Infs, **scattered east of Missip R, esp OH,** Hy spy. [13 of 16 Infs old] **1970** [see **1** above].

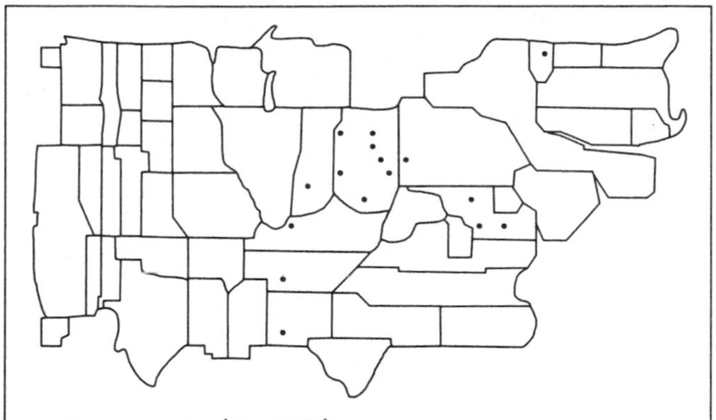
•hy spy n 2 (Qu. EE3)

3 The game **run sheep run.** Cf **hide-and-seek B2**

1970 *DARE* (Qu. EE12, *Games in which one captain hides his team and the other team tries to find it*) Inf **PA**237, Hy spy.

hy spy exclam [**hy spy n**]

=**I spy** exclam.

1968 *DARE* (Qu. EE15, *When he has caught the first of those that were hiding what does the player who is 'it' call out to the others?*) Inf **MD**31, Hy spy, everything's over; **NY**68, Hy spy on so-and-so.

hyssop n *obs* Cf **giant hyssop**

A **sage** (here: *Artemisia* spp).

1805 (1808) Gass *Jrl.* 112 **ND,** There is a great quantity of hyssop in the valleys. **1811** (1817) Bradbury *Travels* 116 **SD,** A species of *Artemisia,* common on the prairies, and known to the hunters by the name of *Hyssop.* **1814** Brackenridge *Views of LA* 29 **sCent,** There are other places . . producing nothing but hyssop and prickly pears. **1911** *Century Dict. Suppl., Hyssop. . .* In the western United States, sage-brush, *Artemisia. . .* Only in old writings.

hyssop skullcap n [Appar from the helmet-shaped appendage on upper lip of calyx of some spp]

A **skullcap** (here: *Scutellaria integrifolia*).

1900 Lyons *Plant Names* 339, *S[cutellaria] integrifolia . .* Hyssop Skullcap. **1901** Lounsberry *S. Wild Flowers* 452, *S[cutellaria] integrifolia,* hyssop skullcap with its linear, oblong entire leaves and blue flowers having white undersides, is another very attractive individual. **1911** NJ State Museum *Annual Rept. for 1910* 665, *Scutellaria integrifolia . .* Hyssop Scullcap. **1931** Harned *Wild Flowers Alleghanies* 422, Hyssop Skullcap *(S[cutellaria] integrifolia) . .* One of the handsomest of the Skullcap group.

hyste See **hoist**

hysteric n Also with *the* [Cf *OED hysteric* sb. B. 3 "In sing.: A convulsive fit of laughter or weeping"]

1966–69 *DARE* (Qu. BB27, *When somebody pretends to be sick [often to get out of doing something] you'd say he's* ______) Inf **TX**71, Got the hysteric; (Qu. BB28, . . *Imaginary diseases: "He must have the* ______*."*) Inf **TX**71, Hysteric; (Qu. GG26, *A feeling of weakness from fear*) Inf **NM**7, Hysteric.

hystericky adj Pronc-sp *highstericky;* aphet form *'stericky* Cf Intro "Language Changes" I.6, 7 *old-fash* Cf **highstrikes**

Hysterical.

1824 Cooper *Pilot* 2.239 *(OEDS),* In order that the women need not be 'stericky in squalls. **1856** Holmes *Lena Rivers* 60 **NEng,** "Do you take anything for your sickness?" A groan was Mrs. Livingstone's only answer. "Little hystericky, I guess." **1894** Wilkins in *Harper's Mag* Sept. 605/2 *(DAE),* You'd better go to bed, Sophy Anne; you're gittin' highstericky. **1906** Johnson *Highways Missip. Valley* 141 **Ozarks,** The people will laugh and cry and scream and holler, and it's as good as a circus. They walk around and are hystericky as can be.

hysterikes See **highstrikes**

hystics n pl [Prob by syncope from *hysterics*] Cf **highstrikes, hysteric**

Hysteria.

1940 Mencken *Happy Days* 115 **Baltimore MD,** The whiskey made her dizzy and set her to weeping, and in a little while she had a full-fledged and alarming attack of what were then called hystics.

hysting See **hoist C1d**

hytry over See **high-over**

hyuh See **here A2**